The National Hockey League

Official Guide & Record Book

2016

D1435744

THE NATIONAL HOCKEY LEAGUE
Official Guide & Record Book/2016

Compiled by the NHL Public Relations Department and the 30 NHL Club Public Relations Directors.

Printed in the United States of America. All rights reserved under the Pan-American and International Copyright Conventions.

**Trade edition published in the United States
and distributed in Canada by**: Triumph Books, 814 N. Franklin Street, Chicago, Illinois 60610
ISBN 978-1-62937-146-7

NHL and media edition published by: Dan Diamond and Associates, Inc., 194 Dovercourt Road, Toronto, Ontario M6J 3C8 Canada
ISBN 978-1-894801-30-0

Staff

For the NHL: Dave McCarthy; Supervising Editor: Greg Inglis; Statistician: Benny Ercolani;
Editorial Staff: Dave Baker, John Dellapina, David Keon, Jennifer Moad, Kelley Rosset, Susan Snow, Julie Young.

Senior Managing Editor: Ralph Dinger   **Associate Managing Editor:** Paul Bontje
Production Editors: John Pasternak, Alex Dubiel, Becky Gowing   **Photo Editor:** Eric Zweig
Publisher: Dan Diamond

Data Management and Typesetting: Caledon Data Management, Eden, Ontario

Printing Consultant: Sunrise Consulting Inc., Toronto, Ontario

Printed in the United States of America by Ripon Printers, Ripon, Wisconsin

Production Management: Dan Diamond and Associates, Inc., Toronto, Ontario

Contributors and Photo Credits: see page 671

For information on **international distrtibution** opportunities, contact Dan Diamond at dda.nhl@sympatico.ca

The National Hockey League
1185 Avenue of the Americas, 14th Floor, New York, New York 10036
1800 McGill College Ave., Suite 2600, Montreal, Quebec H3A 3J6
50 Bay Street, 11th Floor, Toronto, Ontario M5J 2X8

www.nhlofficialguide.com

Table of Contents

Table of Contents *continued*

Introduction

WELCOME TO THE **84**TH EDITION OF *THE NATIONAL HOCKEY LEAGUE OFFICIAL GUIDE & RECORD BOOK*. The 2014-15 season was the second played under the League's new alignment that features two seven-team divisions – the Central and Pacific – in the Western Conference and two eight-team divisions – the Atlantic and Metropolitan – in the Eastern Conference. Sixteen teams qualified for the Stanley Cup Playoffs including the top three in each Division and two wild card teams in each Conference. For the second consecutive season, the Western Conference wild card teams, Minnesota and Winnipeg, both came from the Central Division. *(See the inside front cover for a list of teams in each division and information on the makeup of the regular-season schedule. Also see page 135 for the 2014-15 Final Standings and page 251 for a complete history of the League's playoff formats.)*

Twelve teams finished the season with 100 points or more, topped by the four division winners. The New York Rangers recorded 113 points, Montreal 110 and both St. Louis and Anaheim had 109, but none of these teams earned a berth in the Stanley Cup Final where the third-place team from the Central Division (Chicago, 100 points) defeated the second-place team from the Atlantic Division (Tampa Bay, 108 points) in six close games. Four games in the Final were decided by one goal and three by a 2-1 score. This was the Blackhawks' third championship since 2010 and sixth in franchise history. Over 83 years the franchise won its first three Cup titles. Only six additional campaigns were needed to double that . In the modern NHL where salary cap constraints force clubs to constantly revamp their rosters, Chicago's recent success is a tribute to its strong core group of players led by captain Jonathan Toews and to the management and coaching team assembled by general manager Stan Bowman. Seven players – Toews, Niklas Hjalmarsson, Marian Hossa, Patrick Kane, Duncan Keith, Brent Seabrook and Patrick Sharp – played on all three Cup champions. *(Playoff scores are found on page 239. A list of every playoff overtime game since 1918 begins on page 267 with 2015's games on page 270. The names of the champions as they are engraved on the barrel of the Stanley Cup are on page 243. Year-by-year Cup winners are listed on page 242.)*

NHL regular-season overtime will have a new look for 2015-16 when teams will play three skaters a side for five minutes before going to a shootout if a goal has not been scored. A five-minute sudden-death overtime period became part of regular-season play beginning in 1983-84. This extra period was played five-on-five until 1999-2000 when four-on-four overtime was introduced along with an extra point in the standings for an overtime loss. The number of overtime games in which a goal was scored jumped from 27% in 1998-99 to 43.8% in 1999-2000. The shootout was added in 2005-06, but the number of games decided in overtime remained largely unchanged, ranging from 39.7% to 44.4% over the last four seasons. A version of three-on-three overtime proved very popular in the AHL in 2014-15 resulting in wide-open play and fewer shootouts so in 2015-16, NHL fans will be treated to the game's best players using lots of open ice to try to pop the winner and give their team an extra point in the standings. *(A history of the NHL's Major Rule Changes is found on page 10. Twenty years of team-by-team Regular-Season Overtime Results are found on page 140. A Shootout Summary begins on page 143. Individual Overtime Scoring records are on page 169.)*

Format changes in this edition of the *NHL Guide & Record Book* are found in the NHL Record Book, Draft and Clubs sections. The list of Year-by-Year Individual Regular-Season Leaders *(page 192)* and the all-time NHL Draft Summary *(page 212)* have been inverted so that the most recent seasons are at the top of the table rather than the bottom. Also for previous NHL Drafts, players selected who have not played in the NHL are *listed in italics*. This serves to provide an indicator of the strength of each Draft's top picks. Only five NHL Drafts – 2003, 1983, 1978, 1977 and 1973 – saw every player drafted in the first round reach the NHL. *(Draft coverage begins on page 212. The complete 2015 NHL Draft begins on page 218. Top picks from 2014 to 1969 are on pages 218 to 226.)*

Clubs *(beginning with Anaheim on page 15)* again present 30 mini team guides. Each club's four-page section contains key off-season signings, 2015-16 schedule and personnel, 2014-15 results and individual scoring, year-by-year record, club record book, retired numbers, coach and general manager's biographies, coach/captain/g.m. histories, all-time record vs. other clubs, the last 15 years of draft selections and a front office directory. New this year is additional information for the Dallas Stars *(page 51)* that details the franchise's unique backstory. The Dallas franchise played 26 seasons as the Minnesota North Stars before relocating to Texas in 1993. At the same time Minnesota entered the NHL, another club began play in Oakland, California, as the Seals. This club transferred to Cleveland for the 1976-77 season before merging with Minnesota prior to 1978-79. Oakland/California/Cleveland's results, records and coach/captain/g.m. histories have been added to the Dallas pages.

At the heart of this and every edition of the *NHL Official Guide & Record Book* is data on every one of the more than 7,000 players who have appeared in an NHL game, plus more than 1,000 prospects who have yet to do so. See the Prospect Register *(page 275)*, Active Player Register *(344)*, Goaltender Register *(587)*, Retired Player Index *(612)*, Retired Goaltender Index *(657)*, regular-season and playoff Record Books *(158 and 240)*, Award Winners *(204)*, All-Star Teams *(228)* or Hockey Hall of Fame sections *(235)*. A register of 2015's NHL free agent signings is found on page 666, a trade register on page 668 and late additions on page 663.

A key to the abbreviations and symbols used in individual player and goaltender data panels, along with useful information on how to use the Registers, is found on page 274. Each NHL club's minor-pro affiliates are found on page 12. A list of league abbreviations used in the Prospect, Player and Goaltender Registers is found on page 670.

Thanks to readers, correspondents, members of the media and hockey communications professionals throughout the game who make good use of what we produce.

Best wishes,

Dan Diamond
Publisher

ACCURACY REMAINS THE *GUIDE & RECORD BOOK*'S TOP PRIORITY.

We appreciate comments and clarification from our readers. Please direct these to:

- Ralph Dinger — Senior Managing Editor, 194 Dovercourt Road, Toronto, Ontario M6J 3C8. e-mail: ralph.dda@sympatico.ca.
- Greg Inglis — 1185 Avenue of the Americas, New York, New York 10036 . . . or . . .
- David Keon — 50 Bay Street, 11th Floor, Toronto, Ontario, M5J 2X8

Your involvement makes a better book.

NATIONAL HOCKEY LEAGUE

New York
1185 Avenue of the Americas,
New York, NY 10036,
212/789-2000, Fax: 212/789-2020

Montréal
1800 McGill College Avenue,
Suite 2600,
Montréal, Québec, H3A 3J6
514/841-9220, Fax: 514/841-1040

Toronto
50 Bay Street,
11th Floor,
Toronto, Ontario, M5J 2X8
416/359-7900, Fax: 416/981-2779

League and Club websites: www.nhl.com • Twitter: @NHL

Executive

Commissioner ....Gary B. Bettman
Deputy Commissioner ....William Daly
Chief Operating Officer..John Collins
Senior Executive Vice President of Hockey Operations ....Colin Campbell

---

Commissioner and League Presidents

Gary B. Bettman

Gary B. Bettman took office as the NHL's first Commissioner on February 1, 1993. Since the League was formed in 1917, there have been five League Presidents.

NHL President	Years in Office
Frank Calder	1917-1943
Mervyn "Red" Dutton	1943-1946
Clarence Campbell	1946-1977
John A. Ziegler, Jr.	1977-1992
Gil Stein	1992-1993

Hockey Hall of Fame

Hockey Hall of Fame
Brookfield Place
30 Yonge Street, Toronto, Ontario M5E 1X8
Phone: 416/360-7735 • Executive Fax: 416/360-1501

Lanny McDonald – Chairman of the Board
Jeff Denomme – President and CEO
Craig Baines – Vice-President, Development & Building Operations
Peter Jagla – Vice-President, Marketing & Attraction Services
Ron Ellis - Program Director, HHOF Development Association
Kelly Masse – Director, Corporate & Media Relations
Craig Beckim – Manager, Merchandising & Retail Operations
Darren Boyko – Manager, Special Projects & International Business
Jackie Schwartz – Manager, Marketing & Promotions

D.K. (Doc) Seaman Resource Centre and Archives
400 Kipling Avenue, Toronto, Ontario M8V 3L1
Phone: 416/360-7735 • Fax: 416/251-5770
www.hhof.com, www.imagesonice.net

Phil Pritchard – Vice President, Resource Centre and Curator
Craig Campbell – Manager, Resource Centre and Archives
Izak Westgate – Manager, Outreach and Asst. Curator
Steve Poirier – Coordinator, HHOF Images and Archival Services
Miragh Bitove – Archivist & Collections Registrar

National Hockey League Players' Association

20 Bay Street, Suite 1700, Toronto, Ontario M5J 2N8
Phone: 416/313-2300 • Fax: 416/313-2301
www.nhlpa.com

Tyler Currie	Director, International Affairs
Alex Dagg	Director, Operations
Robert DeGregory	Associate Counsel, Labour
Maria Dennis	Associate Counsel, Labour
Donald Fehr	Executive Director
Stephen Frank	Director, Technology & Security
Adam Larry	Director, Licensing & Associate Counsel
Roland Lee	Director, Salary Cap & Marketplace and Senior Counsel
Jasmine Lew	Director, Business Ops & Associate Counsel
Sandra Monteiro	Chief of Global Business Strategies
Kim Murdoch	Director, Player Insurance & Pensions
Mike Ouellet	Senior Business & Association Counsel
Joe Reekie	Divisional Player Representative
Mathieu Schneider	Special Assistant to the Exec. Director
Richard Smit	Director, Finance and HRR
Devin Smith	Director, Mktg. & Community Relations
Roman Stoykewych	Senior Counsel, Labour
Jonathan Weatherdon	Director, Communications
Steve Webb	Divisional Player Representative
Rob Zamuner	Divisional Player Representative
Don Zavelo	General Counsel

BOARD OF GOVERNORS
CHAIRMAN OF THE BOARD – JEREMY M. JACOBS

NHL On-Ice Officials

*Age at start of 2015-16 season.

Total NHL Games and 2014-15 Games columns count regular-season games only.

Referees

#	Name	Birthplace	*Age	First NHL Game	Total NHL Games	2014-15 Games
42	Jacob Brenk	Detroit Lakes, MI	26			
6	Francis Charron	Ottawa, ON	32	Apr. 5/10	217	76
43	Tom Chmielewski	Colorado Springs, CO	28	Aug. 4/14	20	19
19	Gord Dwyer	Halifax, NS	38	Nov. 19/05	645	75
27	Eric Furlatt	Trois-Rivieres, QC	44	Oct. 8/01	876	76
47	Trevor Hanson	Richmond, BC	31	Oct. 24/13	27	19
2	Mike Hasenfratz	Regina, SK	48	Oct. 21/00	705	0
22	Ghislain Hebert	Bathurst, NB	34	Mar. 2/09	292	74
15	Jean Hebert	Moncton, NB	35	Mar. 30/11	174	76
8	Dave Jackson	Montreal, QC	50	Dec. 22/90	1406	75
25	Marc Joannette	Verdun, QC	46	Oct. 1/99	1002	76
18	Greg Kimmerly	Toronto, ON	51	Nov. 30/96	1082	75
32	Tom Kowal	Vernon, BC	47	Oct. 29/99	885	76
40	Steve Kozari	Penticton, BC	42	Oct. 15/05	613	76
14	Dennis LaRue	Savannah, GA	56	Mar. 26/91	1222	23
17	Frederick L'Ecuyer	Trois-Rivieres, QC	38	Oct. 11/07	404	76
28	Chris Lee	Saint John, N.B.	45	Apr. 2/00	861	75
3	Mike Leggo	North Bay, ON	50	Mar. 3/98	1073	75
41	Mark Lemelin	Albuquerque, NM	34	Jan. 21/13	45	17
46	Dave Lewis	Pickering, ON	32	Oct. 19/15	24	17
21	Thomas John Luxmore	Timmins, ON	30	Nov. 19/13	23	21
26	Rob Martell	Winnipeg, MB	51	Mar. 14/84	[1]964	78
4	Wes McCauley	Georgetown, ON	43	Jan. 20/03	736	76
45	Jon McIsaac	Truro, NS	31	Nov. 21/13	7	4
34	Brad Meier	Dayton, OH	48	Oct. 23/99	1001	75
36	Dean Morton	Peterborough, ON	47	Nov. 11/00	529	54
44	Kendrick Nicholson	Stratford, ON	33	Jan. 17/15	5	5
13	Dan O'Halloran	Essex, ON	51	Oct. 1/95	1153	75
9	Dan O'Rourke	Calgary, AB	43	Oct. 2/99	[2]732	76
20	Tim Peel	Toronto, ON	49	Oct. 21/99	1005	72
16	Brian Pochmara	Detroit, MI	38	Dec. 23/05	543	76
33	Kevin Pollock	Kincardine, ON	45	Mar. 28/00	1006	76
48	Garrett Rank	Kitchener, ON	28	Jan. 15/15	8	8
37	Kyle Rehman	Stettler, AB	37	Jan. 22/08	384	77
39	Evgeny Romasko	Tver, Russia	33	Mar. 9/15	5	5
5	Chris Rooney	Boston, MA	40	Nov. 22/00	901	75
24	Graham Skilliter	La Ronge, SK	31	Jan. 28/13	105	77
38	Francois St. Laurent	Greenfield Park, QC	38	Nov. 10/05	482	75
12	Justin St. Pierre	Dolbeau, QC	43	Nov. 9/05	643	77
11	Kelly Sutherland	Richmond, BC	44	Dec. 19/00	932	70
29	Ian Walsh	Philadelphia, PA	43	Oct. 14/00	846	76
23	Brad Watson	Regina, SK	54	Mar. 7/96	1104	75

[1] plus 3 games as a linesman.   [2] plus 120 games as a linesman.

Linesmen

#	Name	Birthplace	*Age	First NHL Game	Total NHL Games	2014-15 Games
52	Shandor Alphonso	Orangeville, ON	31	Oct. 17/14	46	46
75	Derek Amell	Port Colborne, ON	47	Oct. 11/97	1148	77
59	Steve Barton	Vankleek Hill, ON	43	Nov. 1/00	922	76
87	Devin Berg	Kitchener, ON	33			
96	David Brisebois	Sudbury, ON	39	Oct. 11/99	886	77
74	Lonnie Cameron	Victoria, BC	51	Oct. 5/96	1261	77
50	Scott Cherrey	Drayton, ON	39	Oct. 6/07	544	77
76	Michel Cormier	Trois-Rivieres, QC	41	Oct. 10/03	786	77
88	Mike Cvik	Calgary, AB	53	Oct. 8/87	1832	77
54	Greg Devorski	Guelph, ON	46	Oct. 9/93	1427	77
68	Scott Driscoll	Seaforth, ON	47	Oct. 10/92	1482	60
82	Ryan Galloway	Winnipeg, MB	43	Oct. 17/02	811	77
64	Brandon Gawryletz	Trail, BC	32			
58	Ryan Gibbons	Vancouver, BC	30			
66	Darren Gibbs	Edmonton, AB	49	Oct. 1/97	1111	77
98	John Grandt	Denver, CO	30	22/01/13	117	46
91	Don Henderson	Calgary, AB	47	Mar. 11/95	1249	77
55	Shane Heyer	Summerland, BC	51	Oct. 6/88	[3]1411	77
63	Trent Knorr	Powell River, BC	29	26/02/14	[4]64	50
71	Brad Kovachik	Woodstock, ON	44	Oct. 10/96	1221	77
86	Brad Lazarowich	Vancouver, BC	53	Oct. 9/86	1944	80
78	Brian Mach	Little Falls, MN	41	Oct. 7/00	990	77
83	Matt MacPherson	Antigonish, NS	32	Oct. 11/11	248	76
90	Andy McElman	Chicago Heights, IL	54	Oct. 3/93	1419	86
89	Steve Miller	Stratford, ON	43	Oct. 11/00	979	77
79	Kiel Murchison	Cloverdale, BC	30	21/01/13	180	78
93	Brian Murphy	Dover, NH	50	Oct. 7/88	[5]1625	75
95	Jonny Murray	Beauport, QC	41	Oct. 7/00	914	0
70	Derek Nansen	Ottawa, ON	43	Oct. 11/02	839	77
80	Thor Nelson	Westminister, CA	47	Feb. 16/95	1007	0
77	Tim Nowak	Buffalo, NY	48	Oct. 8/93	1433	77
94	Bryan Pancich	Great Falls, MT	33	Oct. 3/09	398	78
65	Pierre Racicot	Verdun, QC	48	Oct. 12/93	1462	77
73	Vaughan Rody	Winnipeg, MB	46	Oct. 8/00	872	25
84	Anthony Sericolo	Troy, NY	47	Oct. 21/98	1084	77
57	Jay Sharrers	New Westminster, BC	48	Oct. 6/90	[6]1345	77
92	Mark Shewchyk	Waterdown, ON	48	Oct. 9/03	782	78
56	Mark Wheler	North Battleford, SK	50	Oct. 10/92	1522	77

[3] plus 386 games as a referee.   [4] plus 2 games as a referee.   [5] plus 88 games as a referee.   [6] plus 136 games as a referee.

Referees (from top) Mike Leggo, Tim Peel, Marc Joannette, Kevin Pollock and Brad Meier worked their 1,000th NHL regular-season games in 2014-15. Leggo began his NHL career in 1998; Joannette, Meier and Peel in 1999, Pollock in 2000.

NHL History

1917 — National Hockey League organized November 26 in Montreal following suspension of operations by the National Hockey Association of Canada Limited (NHA). Montreal Canadiens, Montreal Wanderers, Ottawa Senators and Quebec Bulldogs attended founding meeting. Delegates decided to use NHA rules.

Toronto Arenas were later admitted as fifth team; Quebec decided not to operate during the first season. Quebec players allocated to remaining four teams.

Frank Calder elected president and secretary-treasurer.

First NHL games played December 19, with Toronto only arena with artificial ice. Clubs played 22-game split schedule.

1918 — Emergency meeting held January 3 due to destruction by fire of Montreal Arena which was home ice for both Canadiens and Wanderers.

Wanderers withdrew, reducing the NHL to three teams; Canadiens played remaining home games at 3,250-seat Jubilee rink.

Quebec franchise sold to P.J. Quinn of Toronto on October 18 on the condition that the team operate in Quebec City for 1918-19 season. Quinn did not attend the November League meeting and Quebec did not play in 1918-19.

1919-20 — NHL reactivated Quebec Bulldogs franchise. Former Quebec players returned to the club. New Mount Royal Arena became home of Canadiens. Toronto Arenas changed name to St. Patricks. Clubs played 24-game split schedule.

1920-21 — H.P. Thompson of Hamilton, Ontario made application for the purchase of an NHL franchise. Quebec franchise shifted to Hamilton with other NHL teams providing players to strengthen the club.

1921-22 — Split schedule abandoned. First and second place teams at the end of full schedule to play for championship.

1922-23 — Clubs agreed that players could not be sold or traded to clubs in any other league without first being offered to all other clubs in the NHL. Norman Albert made the first broadcast of a hockey game on February 8, 1923. The first NHL game was broadcast on February 14, 1923. Foster Hewitt called his first game on February 16, 1923. All games were broadcast on Toronto radio station CFCA.

1923-24 — Ottawa's new 10,000-seat arena opened. First U.S. franchise granted to Boston for following season.

Dr. Cecil Hart Trophy donated to NHL to be awarded to the player judged most useful to his team.

1924-25 — New franchises granted to Boston and Montreal (later named Maroons). NHL now six team league with two clubs in Montreal. Inaugural game in new Montreal Forum played November 29, 1924 as Canadiens defeated Toronto 7-1. Hamilton finished first in the standings, receiving a bye into the finals. But Hamilton players, demanding $200 each for additional games in the playoffs, went on strike. The NHL suspended all players, fining them $200 each. Stanley Cup finalist to be the winner of NHL semi-final between Toronto and Canadiens.

Lady Byng Trophy donated to NHL.
Clubs played 30-game schedule.

1925-26 — Hamilton club dropped from NHL. Players signed by new New York Americans franchise. Pittsburgh Pirates granted franchise. Prince of Wales Trophy donated to NHL.
Clubs played 36-game schedule.

1926-27 — New York Rangers granted franchise May 15, 1926. Chicago Black Hawks and Detroit Cougars granted franchises September 25, 1926. NHL now ten-team league with an American and a Canadian Division.

Stanley Cup came under the control of NHL. In previous seasons, winners of the now-defunct Western or Pacific Coast leagues would play NHL champion in Cup finals.

Toronto franchise sold to a new company controlled by Hugh Aird and Conn Smythe. Name changed from St. Patricks to Maple Leafs.
Clubs played 44-game schedule.

The Montreal Canadiens donated the Vezina Trophy to be awarded to the team allowing the fewest goals-against in regular season play. The winning team would, in turn, present the trophy to the goaltender playing in the greatest number of games during the season.

1930-31 — Detroit franchise changed name from Cougars to Falcons. Pittsburgh transferred to Philadelphia for one season. Pirates changed name to Philadelphia Quakers. Trading deadline for teams set at February 15 of each year. NHL approved operation of farm teams by Rangers, Americans, Falcons and Bruins. Four-sided electric arena clock first demonstrated.

1931-32 — Philadelphia dropped out. Ottawa withdrew for one season. New Maple Leaf Gardens completed. Clubs played 48-game schedule.

1932-33 — Detroit franchise changed name from Falcons to Red Wings. Franchise application received from St. Louis but refused because of additional travel costs. Ottawa team resumed play.

1933-34 — First All-Star Game played as a benefit for injured player Ace Bailey. Leafs defeated All-Stars 7-3 in Toronto.

1934-35 — Ottawa franchise transferred to St. Louis. Team called St. Louis Eagles and consisted largely of Ottawa's players.

1935-36 — Ottawa-St. Louis franchise terminated. Montreal Canadiens finished season with very poor record. To strengthen the club, NHL gave Canadiens first call on the services of all French-Canadian players for three seasons.

1937-38 — Second benefit All-Star game staged November 2 in Montreal in aid of the family of the late Canadiens star Howie Morenz.

Montreal Maroons withdrew from the NHL on June 22, 1938, leaving seven clubs in the League.

1938-39 — Expenses for each club regulated at $5 per man per day for meals and $2.50 per man per day for accommodation.

1939-40 — Benefit All-Star Game played October 29, 1939 in Montreal for the children of the late Albert (Babe) Siebert.

1940-41 — Ross-Tyer puck adopted as the official puck of the NHL. Early in the season it was apparent that this puck was too soft. The Spalding puck was adopted in its place.

On May 16, 1941, Arthur Ross, NHL governor from Boston, donated a perpetual trophy to be awarded annually to the player voted outstanding in the league. Due to wartime restrictions, the trophy was never awarded.

1941-42 — New York Americans changed name to Brooklyn Americans.

1942-43 — Brooklyn Americans withdrew from NHL, leaving six teams: Boston, Chicago, Detroit, Montreal, New York and Toronto. Playoff format saw first-place team play third-place team and second play fourth.
Clubs played 50-game schedule.

Frank Calder, president of the NHL since its inception, died in Montreal. Meryn "Red" Dutton, former manager of the New York Americans, became president. The NHL commissioned the Calder Memorial Trophy to be awarded to the League's outstanding rookie each year.

1945-46 — Philadelphia, Los Angeles and San Francisco applied for NHL franchises.

The Philadelphia Arena Company of the American Hockey League applied for an injunction to prevent the possible operation of an NHL franchise in that city.

1946-47 — Mervyn Dutton retired as president of the NHL prior to the start of the season. He was succeeded by Clarence S. Campbell.

Individual trophy winners and all-star team members to receive $1,000 awards.

Playoff guarantees for players introduced.
Clubs played 60-game schedule.

1947-48 — The first annual All-Star Game for the benefit of the players' pension fund was played when the All-Stars defeated the Stanley Cup Champion Toronto Maple Leafs 4-3 in Toronto on October 13, 1947.

Criteria for awarding Art Ross Trophy changed. Now awarded to top scorer. Elmer Lach was its first winner.

Philadelphia and Los Angeles franchise applications refused.

National Hockey League Pension Society formed.

1949-50 — Clubs played 70-game schedule.
First intra-league draft held April 30, 1950. Clubs allowed to protect 30 players. Remaining players available for $25,000 each.

1951-52 — Referees included in the League's pension plan.

1952-53 — In May of 1952, City of Cleveland applied for NHL franchise. Application denied. In March of 1953, the Cleveland Barons of the AHL challenged the NHL champions for the Stanley Cup. The NHL governors did not accept this challenge.

1953-54 — The James Norris Memorial Trophy presented to the NHL for annual presentation to the League's best defenseman.

Intra-league draft rules amended to allow teams to protect 18 skaters and two goaltenders, claiming price reduced to $15,000.

1954-55 — Each arena to operate an "out-of-town" scoreboard.

1956-57 — Referees and linesmen to wear shirts of black and white vertical stripes. Standardized signals for referees and linesmen introduced.

1960-61 — Canadian National Exhibition, City of Toronto and NHL reach agreement for the construction of a Hockey Hall of Fame on the CNE grounds. Hall opens on August 26, 1961.

1963-64 — Player development league established with clubs operated by NHL franchises located in Minneapolis, St. Paul, Indianapolis, Omaha and, beginning in 1964-65, Tulsa. First universal amateur draft took place. All players of qualifying age (17) unaffected by sponsorship of junior teams available to be drafted.

1964-65 — Conn Smythe Trophy presented to the NHL to be awarded annually to the outstanding player in the Stanley Cup playoffs.

Minimum age of players subject to amateur draft changed to 18.

1965-66 — NHL announced expansion plans for a second six-team division to begin play in 1967-68.

1966-67 — Fourteen applications for NHL franchises received.

Lester Patrick Trophy presented to the NHL to be awarded annually for outstanding service to hockey in the United States.

NHL sponsorship of junior teams ceased, making all players of qualifying age not already on NHL-sponsored lists eligible for the amateur draft.

1967-68 — Six new teams added: California Seals, Los Angeles Kings, Minnesota North Stars, Philadelphia Flyers, Pittsburgh Penguins, St. Louis Blues. New teams to play in West Division. Remaining six teams to play in East Division.

Minimum age of players subject to amateur draft changed to 20.

Clubs played 74-game schedule.

Clarence S. Campbell Trophy awarded to team finishing the regular season in first place in West Division.

California Seals change name to Oakland Seals on December 8, 1967.

1968-69 — Clubs played 76-game schedule.
Amateur draft expanded to cover any amateur player of qualifying age throughout the world.

1970-71 — Two new teams added: Buffalo Sabres and Vancouver Canucks. These teams joined East Division: Chicago switched to West Division. Oakland Seals change name to California Golden Seals prior to season.

Clubs played 78-game schedule.

1971-72 — Playoff format amended. In each division, first to play fourth; second to play third.

1972-73 — Soviet Nationals and Canadian NHL stars play eight pre-season games. Canadians win 4-3-1.

Two new teams added. Atlanta Flames join West Division; New York Islanders join East Division.

1974-75 — Two new teams added: Kansas City Scouts and Washington Capitals. Teams realigned into two nine-team conferences, the Prince of Wales made up of the Norris and Adams Divisions, and the Clarence Campbell made up of the Smythe and Patrick Divisions.

Clubs played 80-game schedule.

1976-77 — California franchise transferred to Cleveland. Team named Cleveland Barons. Kansas City franchise transferred to Denver. Team named Colorado Rockies.

1977-78 — Clarence S. Campbell retires as NHL president. Succeeded by John A. Ziegler, Jr.

1978-79 — Cleveland and Minnesota franchises merge, leaving NHL with 17 teams. Merged team placed in Adams Division, playing home games in Minnesota.

Minimum age of players subject to amateur draft changed to 19.

1979-80 — Four new teams added: Edmonton Oilers, Hartford Whalers, Quebec Nordiques and Winnipeg Jets.

Minimum age of players subject to entry draft changed to 18.

1980-81 — Atlanta franchise shifted to Calgary, retaining "Flames" name.

1981-82 — Teams realigned within existing divisions. New groupings based on geographical areas. Unbalanced schedule adopted.

1982-83 — Colorado Rockies franchise shifted to East Rutherford, New Jersey. Team named New Jersey Devils. Franchise moved to Patrick Division from Smythe; Winnipeg moved to Smythe from Norris.

1991-92 — San Jose Sharks added, making the NHL a 22-team league. NHL celebrates 75th Anniversary Season. The 1991-92 regular season suspended due to a players' strike on April 1, 1992. Play resumed April 12, 1992.

1992-93 — Gil Stein named NHL president (October, 1992). Gary Bettman named first NHL Commissioner (February, 1993). Ottawa Senators and Tampa Bay Lightning added, making the NHL a 24-team league. NHL celebrates Stanley Cup Centennial. Clubs played 84-game schedule.

NHL History — *continued*

1993-94 — Mighty Ducks of Anaheim and Florida Panthers added, making the NHL a 26-team league. Minnesota franchise shifted to Dallas, team named Dallas Stars. Prince of Wales and Clarence Campbell Conferences renamed Eastern and Western. Adams, Patrick, Norris and Smythe Divisions renamed Northeast, Atlantic, Central and Pacific. Winnipeg moved to Central Division from Pacific; Tampa Bay moved to Atlantic Division from Central; Pittsburgh moved to Northeast Division from Atlantic.

1994-95 — A lockout resulted in the cancellation of 468 games from October 1, 1994 to January 19, 1995. Clubs played a 48-game schedule that began January 20, 1995 and ended May 3, 1995. No inter-conference games were played.

1995-96 — Quebec franchise transferred to Denver. Team named Colorado Avalanche and placed in Pacific Division of Western Conference. Clubs to play 82-game schedule.

1996-97 — Winnipeg franchise transferred to Phoenix. Team named Phoenix Coyotes and placed in Central Division of Western Conference.

1997-98 — Hartford franchise transferred to Raleigh. Team named Carolina Hurricanes and remains in Northeast Division of Eastern Conference.

1998-99 — The addition of the Nashville Predators made the NHL a 27-team league and brought about the creation of two new divisions and a League-wide realignment in preparation for further expansion to 30 teams by 2000-2001. Nashville was added to the Central Division of the Western Conference, while Toronto moved into the Northeast Division of the Eastern Conference. Pittsburgh was shifted from Northeast to the Atlantic, while Carolina left the Northeast for the newly created Southeast Division of the Eastern Conference. Florida, Tampa Bay and Washington also joined the Southeast. In the Western Conference, Calgary, Colorado, Edmonton and Vancouver make up the new Northwest Division. Dallas and Phoenix moved from the Central to the Pacific Division.

The NHL retired uniform number 99 in honor of all-time scoring leader Wayne Gretzky who retired at the end of the season.

1999-2000 — Atlanta Thrashers added, making the NHL a 28-team league.

2000-01 — Columbus Blue Jackets and Minnesota Wild added, making the NHL a 30-team league.

2003-04 — First outdoor NHL game. 57,167 attend Heritage Classic at Edmonton's Commonwealth Stadium. Montreal defeated Edmonton 4-3, November 22, 2003.

2004-05 — A lockout resulted in the cancellation of the season.

2007-08 — NHL-record crowd of 71,217 fills Buffalo's Ralph Wilson Stadium on New Year's Day for the 2008 Winter Classic, the first NHL outdoor game in the United States. Sidney Crosby's shootout goal gives the Pittsburgh Penguins a 2-1 win over the Buffalo Sabres.

2011-12 — Atlanta franchise transferred to Winnipeg. Team named Winnipeg Jets.

2012-13 — A lockout resulted in the cancellation of 510 games from October 11, 2012 to January 18, 2013. Clubs played a 48-game schedule that began January 19, 2013 and ended April 27, 2013. No inter-conference games were played.

2013-14 — The NHL's clubs are re-aligned into two conferences each consisting of two divisions. The new alignment places several clubs in more geographically appropriate groupings. The Eastern Conference is made up of the Atlantic and Metropolitan divisions, each with eight teams. The Western Conference is made up of the Central and Pacific divisions, each with seven teams. All 30 teams play in all 30 arenas at least once a season.

2014-15 — Phoenix franchise renamed Arizona Coyotes.

Major Rule Changes

1910-11 — Game changed from two 30-minute periods to three 20-minute periods.

1911-12 — National Hockey Association (forerunner of the NHL) originated six-man hockey, replacing seven-man game.

1917-18 — Goalies permitted to fall to the ice to make saves. Previously a goaltender was penalized for dropping to the ice.

1918-19 — Penalty rules amended. For minor fouls, substitutes not allowed until penalized player had served three minutes. For major fouls, no substitutes for five minutes. For match fouls, no substitutes allowed for the remainder of the game.

With the addition of two lines painted on the ice twenty feet from center, three playing zones were created, producing a forty-foot neutral center ice area in which forward passing was permitted. Kicking the puck was permitted in this neutral zone.

Tabulation of assists began.

1921-22 — Goaltenders allowed to pass the puck forward up to their own blue line.

Overtime limited to twenty minutes.

Minor penalties changed from three minutes to two minutes.

1923-24 — Match foul defined as actions deliberately injuring or disabling an opponent. For such actions, a player was fined not less than $50 and ruled off the ice for the balance of the game. A player assessed a match penalty may be replaced by a substitute at the end of 20 minutes. Match penalty recipients must meet with the League president who can assess additional punishment.

1925-26 — Delayed penalty rules introduced. Each team must have a minimum of four players on the ice at all times.

Two rules were amended to encourage offense: No more than two defensemen permitted to remain inside a team's own blue line when the puck has left the defensive zone. A faceoff to be called for ragging the puck unless shorthanded.

Team captains only players allowed to talk to referees.

Goaltender's leg pads limited to 12-inch width.

Timekeeper's gong to mark end of periods rather than referee's whistle. Teams to dress a maximum of 12 players for each game from a roster of no more than 14 players.

1926-27 — Blue lines repositioned to sixty feet from each goal-line, thereby enlarging the neutral zone and standardizing distance from blue line to goal.

Uniform goal nets adopted throughout NHL with goal posts securely fastened to the ice.

1927-28 — To further encourage offense, forward passes allowed in defending and neutral zones and goaltender's pads reduced in width from 12 to 10 inches.

Game standardized at three twenty-minute periods of stop-time separated by ten-minute intermissions.

Teams to change ends after each period.

Ten minutes of sudden-death overtime to be played if the score is tied after regulation time.

Minor penalty to be assessed to any player other than a goaltender for deliberately picking up the puck while it is in play. Minor penalty to be assessed for deliberately shooting the puck out of play.

The Art Ross goal net adopted as the official net of the NHL.

Maximum length of hockey sticks limited to 53 inches measured from heel of blade to end of handle. No minimum length stipulated.

Home teams given choice of end to defend at start of game.

1928-29 — Forward passing permitted in defensive and neutral zones and into attacking zone if pass receiver is in neutral zone when pass is made. No forward passing allowed inside attacking zone.

Minor penalty to be assessed to any player who delays the game by passing the puck back into his defensive zone.

Ten-minute overtime without sudden-death provision to be played in games tied after regulation time. Games tied after this overtime period declared a draw.

Exclusive of goaltenders, team to dress at least 8 and no more than 12 skaters.

NHL Attendance

Season	Games	Regular Season Attendance	Games	Playoffs Attendance	Total Attendance
1975-76	720	9,103,761	48	726,279	9,830,040
1976-77	720	8,563,890	44	646,279	9,210,169
1977-78	720	8,526,564	45	686,634	9,213,198
1978-79	680	7,758,053	45	694,521	8,452,574
1979-80	840	10,533,623	67	976,699	11,510,322
1980-81	840	10,726,198	68	966,390	11,692,588
1981-82	840	10,710,894	71	1,058,948	11,769,842
1982-83	840	11,020,610	66	1,088,222	12,028,832
1983-84	840	11,359,386	70	1,107,400	12,466,786
1984-85	840	11,633,730	70	1,107,500	12,741,230
1985-86	840	11,621,000	72	1,152,503	12,773,503
1986-87	840	11,855,880	87	1,383,967	13,239,847
1987-88	840	12,117,512	83	1,336,901	13,454,413
1988-89	840	12,417,969	82	1,327,214	13,745,183
1989-90	840	12,579,651	85	1,355,593	13,935,244
1990-91	840	12,343,897	92	1,442,203	13,786,100
1991-92	880	12,769,676	86	1,327,920	14,097,596
1992-93	1,008	14,158,177 [1]	83	1,346,034	15,504,211
1993-94	1,092	16,105,604 [2]	90	1,440,095	17,545,699
1994-95	624 [3]	9,233,884	81	1,329,130	10,563,014
1995-96	1,066	17,041,614	86	1,540,140	18,581,754
1996-97	1,066	17,640,529	82	1,494,878	19,135,407
1997-98	1,066	17,264,678	82	1,507,416	18,772,094
1998-99	1,107	18,001,741	86	1,509,411	19,511,152
1999-2000	1,148	18,800,139	83	1,524,629	20,324,768
2000-01	1,230	20,373,379	86	1,584,011	21,957,390
2001-02	1,230	20,614,613	90	1,691,174	22,305,787
2002-03	1,230	20,408,704	89	1,636,120	22,044,824
2003-04	1,230	20,356,199	89	1,708,691	22,064,890
2004-05	....	....	....	....	....
2005-06	1,230	20,854,169	83	1,530,405	22,384,574
2006-07	1,230	20,861,787	81	1,496,501	22,358,288
2007-08	1,230	21,236,255	85	1,587,054	22,823,309
2008-09	1,230	21,475,223	87	1,639,602	23,114,825
2009-10	1,230	20,996,455	90	1,702,371	22,698,826
2010-11	1,230	21,112,139	89	1,667,624	22,779,763
2011-12	1,230 [4]	21,468,121	86	1,591,856	23,059,977
2012-13	720 [4]	12,792,707	86	1,631,683	14,424,390
2013-14	1,230	21,758,902	93	1,775,557	23,534,459
2014-15	1,230	21,533,419	89	1,701,336	23,234,755

NHL Expansion: the NHL operated as a six-team league from 1942-43 to 1966-67. Six teams were added in 1967-68: California (later to move to Cleveland), Los Angeles, Minnesota (later to move to Dallas), Philadelphia, Pittsburgh and St. Louis. In 1970-71: Buffalo and Vancouver. In 1972-73: Atlanta (later to move to Calgary) and NY Islanders. In 1974-75: Kansas City (later to move to Colorado and then to New Jersey) and Washington. In 1979-80, Hartford (later to move to Carolina), Edmonton, Quebec (later to move to Colorado) and Winnipeg (later to move to Phoenix). In 1991-92, San Jose. In 1992-93, Ottawa and Tampa Bay. In 1993-94, Anaheim and Florida. In 1998-99, Nashville. In 1999-2000, Atlanta (later to move to Winnipeg). In 2000-01, Columbus and Minnesota.

[1] Includes 24 neutral site games • [2] Includes 26 neutral site games
[3] Lockout resulted in the cancellation of 468 games. • [4] Lockout resulted in the cancellation of 510 games.

Major Rule Changes — *continued*

1929-30 — Forward passing permitted inside all three zones but not permitted across either blue line.

Kicking the puck allowed, but a goal cannot be scored by kicking the puck in.

No more than three players including the goaltender may remain in their defensive zone when the puck has gone up ice. Minor penalties to be assessed for the first two violations of this rule in a game; major penalties thereafter.

Goaltenders forbidden to hold the puck. Pucks caught must be cleared immediately. For infringement of this rule, a faceoff to be taken ten feet in front of the goal with no player except the goaltender standing between the faceoff spot and the goal-line.

Highsticking penalties introduced.

Maximum number of players in uniform increased from 12 to 15.

December 21, 1929 — Forward passing rules instituted at the beginning of the 1929-30 season more than doubled number of goals scored. Partway through the season, these rules were further amended to read, "No attacking player allowed to precede the play when entering the opposing defensive zone." This is similar to modern offside rule.

1930-31 — A player without a complete stick ruled out of play and forbidden from taking part in further action until a new stick is obtained. A player who has broken his stick must obtain a replacement at his bench.

A further refinement of the offside rule stated that the puck must first be propelled into the attacking zone before any player of the attacking side can enter that zone; for infringement of this rule a faceoff to take place at the spot where the infraction took place.

1931-32 — Though there is no record of a team attempting to play with two goaltenders on the ice, a rule was instituted which stated that each team was allowed only one goaltender on the ice at one time.

Attacking players forbidden to impede the movement or obstruct the vision of opposing goaltenders.

Defending players with the exception of the goaltender forbidden from falling on the puck within 10 feet of the net.

1932-33 — Each team to have captain on the ice at all times. Maximum number of players in uniform reduced to 14 from 15.

If the goaltender is removed from the ice to serve a penalty, the manager of the club to appoint a substitute.

Match penalty with substitution after five minutes instituted for kicking another player.

1933-34 — Number of players permitted to stand in defensive zone restricted to three including goaltender.

Visible time clocks required in each rink.

Two referees replace one referee and one linesman.

1934-35 — Penalty shot awarded when a player is tripped and thus prevented from having a clear shot on goal, having no player to pass to other than the offending player. Shot taken from inside a 10-foot circle located 38 feet from the goal. The goaltender must not advance more than one foot from his goal-line when the shot is taken.

1937-38 — Rules introduced governing icing the puck.

Penalty shot awarded when a player other than a goaltender falls on the puck within 10 feet of the goal.

1938-39 — Penalty shot modified to allow puck carrier to skate in before shooting.

One referee and one linesman replace two referee system.

Blue line widened to 12 inches.

Maximum number of players in uniform increased from 14 to 15.

1939-40 — A substitute replacing a goaltender removed from ice to serve a penalty may use a goaltender's stick and gloves but no other goaltending equipment.

1940-41 — Flooding ice surface between periods made obligatory.

1941-42 — Penalty shots classified as minor and major. Minor shot to be taken from a line 28 feet from the goal. Major shot, awarded when a player is tripped with only the goaltender to beat, permits the player taking the penalty shot to skate right into the goalkeeper and shoot from point-blank range.

One referee and two linesmen employed to officiate games.

For playoffs, standby minor league goaltenders employed by NHL as emergency substitutes.

1942-43 — Because of wartime restrictions on train scheduling, regular-season overtime was discontinued on November 21, 1942.

Player limit reduced from 15 to 14. Minimum of 12 men in uniform abolished.

1943-44 — Red line at center ice introduced to speed up the game and reduce offside calls. This rule is considered to mark the beginning of the modern era in the NHL.

1945-46 — Goal indicator lights synchronized with official time clock required at all rinks.

1946-47 — System of signals by officials to indicate infractions introduced.

Linesmen from neutral cities employed for all games.

1947-48 — Goal awarded when a player with the puck has an open net to shoot at and a thrown stick prevents the shot on goal. Major penalty to any player who throws his stick in any zone other than defending zone. If a stick is thrown by a player in his defending zone but the thrown stick is not considered to have prevented a goal, a penalty shot is awarded.

All playoff games played until a winner determined, with 20-minute sudden-death overtime periods separated by 10-minute intermissions.

1949-50 — Ice surface painted white.

Clubs allowed to dress 17 players exclusive of goaltenders.

Major penalties incurred by goaltenders served by a member of the goaltender's team instead of resulting in a penalty shot.

1950-51 — Each team required to provide an emergency goaltender in attendance with full equipment at each game for use by either team in the event of illness or injury to a regular goaltender.

1951-52 — Home teams to wear basic white uniforms; visiting teams basic colored uniforms.

Goal crease enlarged from 3 × 7 feet to 4 × 8 feet.

Number of players in uniform reduced to 15 plus goaltenders.

Faceoff circles enlarged from 10-foot to 15-foot radius.

1952-53 — Teams permitted to dress 15 skaters on the road and 16 at home.

1953-54 — Number of players in uniform set at 16 plus goaltenders.

1954-55 — Number of players in uniform set at 18 plus goaltenders up to December 1 and 16 plus goaltenders thereafter. Teams agree to wear colored uniforms at home and white uniforms on the road.

1956-57 — Player serving a minor penalty allowed to return to ice when a goal is scored by opposing team.

1959-60 — Players prevented from leaving their benches to enter into an altercation. Substitutions permitted providing substitutes do not enter into altercation.

1960-61 — Number of players in uniform set at 16 plus goaltenders.

1961-62 — Penalty shots to be taken by the player against whom the foul was committed. In the event of a penalty shot called in a situation where a particular player hasn't been fouled, the penalty shot to be taken by any player on the ice when the foul was committed.

1964-65 — No body contact on faceoffs.

In playoff games, each team to have its substitute goaltender dressed in his regular uniform except for leg pads and body protector. All previous rules governing standby goaltenders terminated.

1965-66 — Teams required to dress two goaltenders for each regular-season game. Maximum stick length increased to 55 inches.

1966-67 — Substitution allowed on coincidental major penalties.

Between-periods intermissions fixed at 15 minutes.

1967-68 — If a penalty incurred by a goaltender is a co-incident major, the penalty to be served by a player of the goaltender's team on the ice at the time the penalty was called. Limit of curvature of hockey stick blade set at 1½ inches.

1969-70 — Limit of curvature of hockey stick blade set at 1 inch.

1970-71 — Home teams to wear basic white uniforms; visiting teams to wear basic colored uniforms.

Limit of curvature of hockey stick blade set at ½ inch.

Minor penalty for deliberately shooting the puck out of the playing area.

1971-72 — Number of players in uniform set at 17 plus 2 goaltenders.

Third man to enter an altercation assessed an automatic game misconduct penalty.

1972-73 — Minimum width of stick blade reduced to 2 inches from 2½ inches.

1974-75 — Bench minor penalty imposed if a penalized player does not proceed directly and immediately to the penalty box.

1976-77 — Rule dealing with fighting amended to provide a major and game misconduct penalty for any player who is clearly the instigator of a fight.

1977-78 — Teams requesting a stick measurement to be assessed a minor penalty in the event that the measured stick does not violate the rules.

1979-80 — Wearing of helmets made mandatory for players entering the NHL.

1980-81 — Maximum stick length increased to 58 inches.

1981-82 — If both of a team's listed goaltenders are incapacitated, the team can dress and play any eligible goaltender who is available.

1982-83 — Number of players in uniform set at 18 plus 2 goaltenders.

1983-84 — Five-minute sudden-death overtime to be played in regular-season games that are tied at the end of regulation time.

1985-86 — Substitutions allowed in the event of co-incidental minor penalties. Maximum stick length increased to 60 inches.

1986-87 — Delayed off-side is no longer in effect once the players of the offending team have cleared the opponents' defensive zone.

1990-91 — The goal lines, blue lines, defensive zone face-off circles and markings all moved one foot out from the end boards, creating 11 feet of room behind the nets and shrinking the neutral zone from 60 to 58 feet.

1991-92 — Video replays employed to assist referees in goal/no goal situations. Size of goal crease increased. Crease changed to semi-circular configuration. Time clock to record tenths of a second in last minute of each period and overtime. Major and game misconduct penalty for checking from behind into boards. Penalties added for crease infringement and unnecessary contact with goaltender. Goal disallowed if puck enters net while a player of the attacking team is standing on the goal crease line, is in the goal crease or places his stick in the goal crease.

1992-93 — No substitutions allowed in the event of coincidental minor penalties called when both teams are at full strength. Minor penalty for attempting to draw a penalty ("diving"). Major and game misconduct penalty for checking from behind into goal frame. Game misconduct penalty for instigating a fight. High sticking redefined to include any use of the stick above waist-height. Previous rule stipulated shoulder-height.

1993-94 — High sticking redefined to allow goals scored with a high stick below the height of the crossbar of the goal frame.

1996-97 — Maximum stick length increased to 63 inches. All players must be clear of the attacking zone prior to the puck being shot into that zone. The opportunity to "tag-up" and return into the zone has been removed.

1998-99 — The league instituted a two-referee system with each team to play 20 regular-season games with two referees and a pair of linesmen. Goal line moved to 13 feet from end boards. Goal crease altered to extend one foot beyond each goal post (eight feet across in total. Sides of crease squared off, extending 4'6". Only the top of the crease remains rounded. Only the top of the crease remains rounded.

1999-2000 — Each team to play 25 home and 25 road games using the two-referee system. Crease rule revised to implement a "no harm, no foul, no video review" standard. Teams to play with four skaters and a goaltender in regular-season overtime. If a goal is scored in regular-season overtime, the winner is awarded two points and the loser one point. In no goal is scored in overtime, both teams are awarded one point.

2000-01 — All games to be played using the two-referee system.

2002-03 — "Hurry-up" faceoff and line-change rules implemented.

2003-04 — Home teams to wear basic colored uniforms; visiting teams to wear basic white uniforms. Maximum length of goaltender's pads set at 38 inches.

2005-06 — The NHL adopted a comprehensive package of rule changes that included the following:

Goal line moved to 11 feet from end boards; blue lines moved to 75 feet from end boards, reducing neutral zone from 54 feet to 50 feet. Center red line eliminated for two-line passes. "Tag-up" off-side rule reinstituted. Goaltender not permitted to play the puck outside a designated trapezoid-shaped area behind the net. A team that ices the puck is not permitted to make any player substitutions prior to the ensuing faceoff. A player who instigates a fight in the final five minutes of regulation time or at any time of overtime to receive a minor, a major, a misconduct and an automatic one-game suspension. The size of goaltender equipment reduced. If a game remains tied after five minutes of overtime, winner determined by shootout.

2011-12 — Rules and penalties modified to address contact with the head.

2015-16 — Teams to play with three skaters and a goaltender in regular-season overtime. Coaches may request video review of off-sides or goaltender interference when a goal is scored.

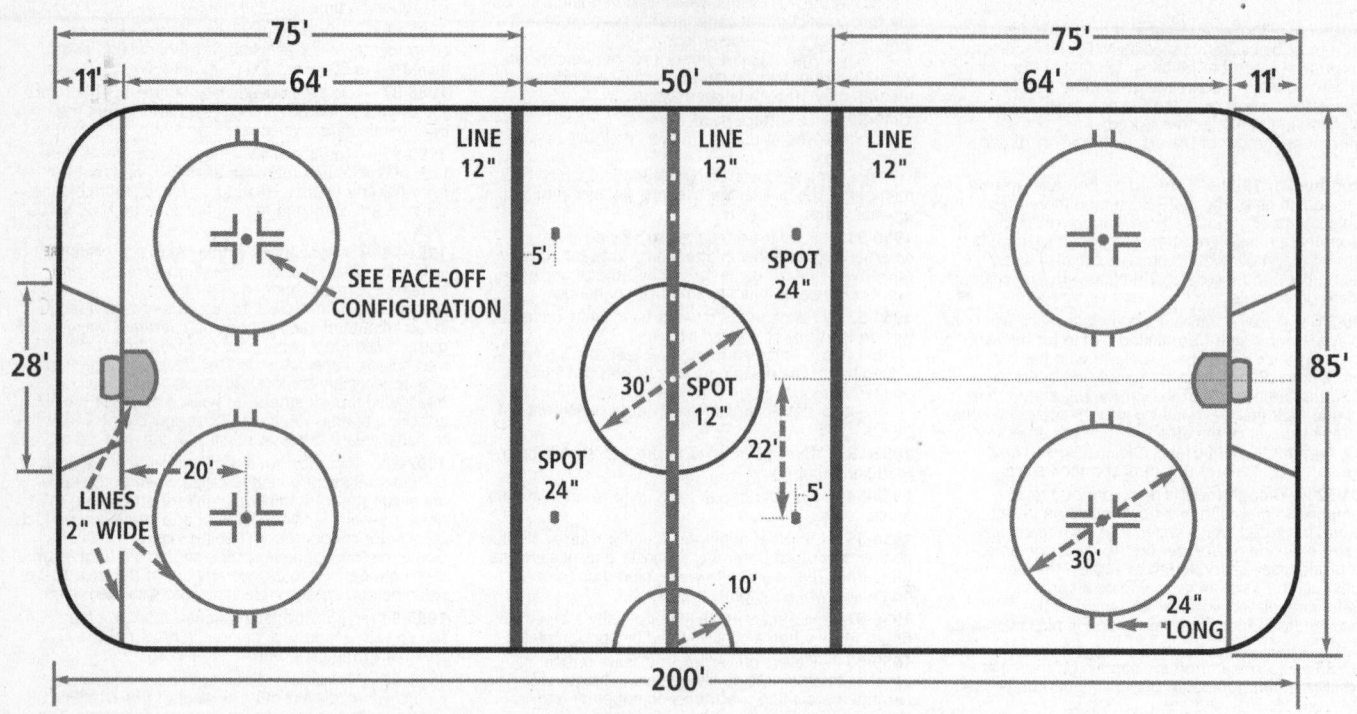

NHL RINK DIMENSIONS

FACEOFF CONFIGURATION

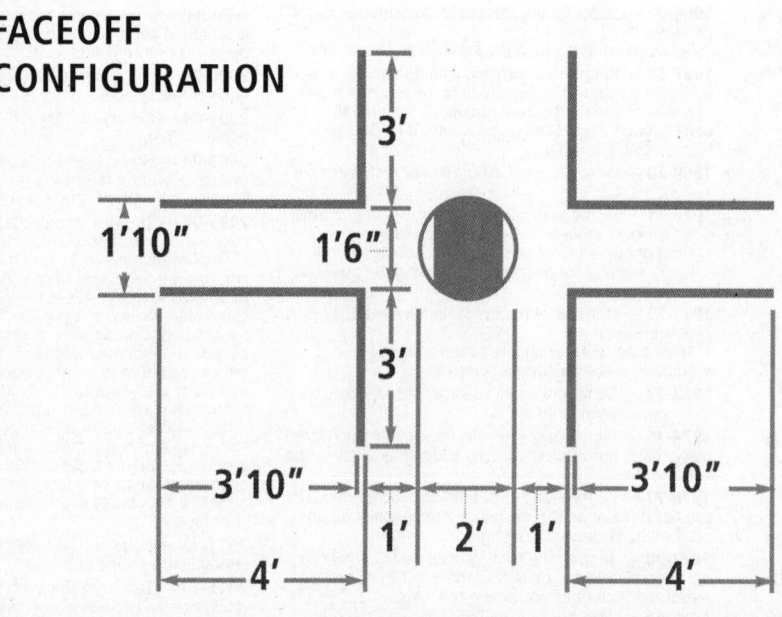

ALL LINES 2" IN WIDTH

Regular-Season NHL Outdoor Games

Date	Location	Venue	Attendance	Final Score				Game-Winning Goal	Time of GWG	Temperature
Nov. 22, 2003¶	Edmonton, Alberta	Commonwealth Stadium	57,167	Montreal	4	Edmonton	3	Richard Zednik	14:18 (3rd)	0°F/–18°C
Jan. 1, 2008*	Buffalo, New York	Ralph Wilson Stadium	71,217	Pittsburgh	2	Buffalo	1	Sidney Crosby	Shootout	33°F/+1°C
Jan. 1, 2009*	Chicago, Illinois	Wrigley Field	40,818	Detroit	6	Chicago	4	Brian Rafalski	3:07 (3rd)	32°F/0°C
Jan. 1, 2010*	Boston, Massachusetts	Fenway Park	38,112	Boston	2	Philadelphia	1	Marco Sturm	1:57 (OT)	35°F/+2°C
Jan. 1, 2011*	Pittsburgh, Pennsylvania	Heinz Field	68,111	Washington	3	Pittsburgh	1	Eric Fehr	11:59 (3rd)	50°F/+10°C
Feb. 20, 2011¶	Calgary, Alberta	McMahon Stadium	41,022	Calgary	4	Montreal	0	Rene Bourque	8:09 (1st)	18°F/–8°C
Jan. 2, 2012*	Philadelphia, Pennsylvania	Citizens Bank Park	46,967	NY Rangers	3	Philadelphia	2	Brad Richards	5:21 (3rd)	41°F/+5°C
Jan. 1, 2014*	Ann Arbor, Michigan	Michigan Stadium	105,491	Toronto	3	Detroit	2	Tyler Bozak	Shootout	13°F/–11°C
Jan. 25, 2014§	Los Angeles, California	Dodger Stadium	54,099	Anaheim	3	Los Angeles	0	Corey Perry	2:45 (1st)	62°F/+17°C
Jan. 26, 2014§	New York, New York	Yankee Stadium	50,105	NY Rangers	7	New Jersey	3	Mats Zuccarello	12:44 (2nd)	25°F/–4°C
Jan. 29, 2014§	New York, New York	Yankee Stadium	50,027	NY Rangers	2	NY Islanders	1	Daniel Carcillo	4:36 (3rd)	22°F/–6°C
Mar. 1, 2014§	Chicago, Illinois	Soldier Field	62,921	Pittsburgh	1	Chicago	5	Jonathan Toews	10:47 (2nd)	17°F/–8°C
Mar. 2, 2014¶	Vancouver, B.C.	BC Place●	54,194	Ottawa	4	Vancouver	2	Cody Ceci	10:11 (2nd)	37°F/+3°C
Jan. 1, 2015*	Washington, D.C.	Nationals Park	43,832	Chicago	2	Washington	3	Troy Brouwer	19:48 (3rd)	37°F/+3°C
Feb. 21, 2015§	Santa Clara, California	Levi's Stadium	70,205	Los Angeles	2	San Jose	1	Marian Gaborik	4:04 (3rd)	57°F/+14°C
Jan. 1, 2016*	Foxborough, Mass.	Gillette Stadium	**68,756	Montreal		Boston				
Feb. 21, 2016§	Minneapolis, Minnesota	TCF Bank Stadium	**52,525	Chicago		Minnesota				
Feb. 27, 2016§	Denver, Colorado	Coors Field	**50,445	Detroit		Colorado				

* - Winter Classic ¶ - Heritage Classic § - Coors Light NHL Stadium Series ● - retractable roof closed ** - seating capacity

Regular-Season NHL Games Played Outside North America

Date	Location	Venue	Attendance	Final Score				Game-Winning Goal	Time of GWG
Oct. 3, 1997	Tokyo, Japan	Yoyogi Arena	10,500	Vancouver	3	Anaheim	2	Pavel Bure	14:41 (2nd)
Oct. 4, 1997	Tokyo, Japan	Yoyogi Arena	10,500	Anaheim	3	Vancouver	2	J.J. Daigneault	13:38 (3rd)
Oct. 9, 1998	Tokyo, Japan	Yoyogi Arena	10,000	San Jose	3	Calgary	3	…	…
Oct. 10, 1998	Tokyo, Japan	Yoyogi Arena	10,000	Calgary	5	San Jose	3	Dave Roche	11:41 (2nd)
Oct. 7, 2000	Saitama, Japan	Saitama Super Arena	13,849	Nashville	3	Pittsburgh	1	Vitali Yachmanev	8:01 (2nd)
Oct. 8, 2000	Saitama, Japan	Saitama Super Arena	13,426	Pittsburgh	3	Nashville	1	Martin Straka	16:16 (3rd)
Sept. 29, 2007	London, England	O2 Arena	17,551	Los Angeles	4	Anaheim	1	Rob Blake	10:15 (2nd)
Sept. 30, 2007	London, England	O2 Arena	17,300	Anaheim	4	Los Angeles	1	Chris Kunitz	15:19 (1st)
Oct. 4, 2008	Prague, Czech Republic	O2 Arena	17,085	NY Rangers	2	Tampa Bay	1	Brandon Dubinsky	14:16 (3rd)
Oct. 4, 2008	Stockholm, Sweden	Ericsson Globe Arena	13,699	Pittsburgh	4	Ottawa	3	Tyler Kennedy	4:35 (OT)
Oct. 5, 2008	Prague, Czech Republic	O2 Arena	17,085	NY Rangers	2	Tampa Bay	1	Scott Gomez	12:12 (2nd)
Oct. 5, 2008	Stockholm, Sweden	Ericsson Globe Arena	13,699	Ottawa	3	Pittsburgh	1	Dany Heatley	12:17 (3rd)
Oct. 2, 2009	Helsinki, Finland	Hartwell Arena	12,056	Florida	4	Chicago	3	Ville Koistinen	Shootout
Oct. 2, 2009	Stockholm, Sweden	Ericsson Globe Arena	13,850	St. Louis	4	Detroit	3	Paul Kariya	17:36 (2nd)
Oct. 3, 2009	Helsinki, Finland	Hartwell Arena	11,526	Chicago	4	Florida	0	Brian Campbell	3:05 (1st)
Oct. 3, 2009	Stockholm, Sweden	Ericsson Globe Arena	13,850	St. Louis	5	Detroit	3	Patrick Berglund	13:37 (2nd)
Oct. 7, 2010	Helsinki, Finland	Hartwell Arena	12,355	Carolina	4	Minnesota	3	Brandon Sutter	18:03 (2nd)
Oct. 8, 2010	Helsinki, Finland	Hartwell Arena	13,465	Carolina	2	Minnesota	1	Jeff Skinner	Shootout
Oct. 8, 2010	Stockholm, Sweden	Ericsson Globe Arena	11,324	San Jose	3	Columbus	2	Logan Couture	10:15 (3rd)
Oct. 9, 2010	Stockholm, Sweden	Ericsson Globe Arena	11,324	Columbus	3	San Jose	2	Ethan Moreau	1:56 (OT)
Oct. 9, 2010	Prague, Czech Republic	O2 Arena	15,299	Phoenix	5	Boston	2	Scottie Upshall	15:02 (2nd)
Oct. 10, 2010	Prague, Czech Republic	O2 Arena	12,990	Boston	3	Phoenix	0	Milan Lucic	12:11 (2nd)
Oct. 7, 2011	Helsinki, Finland	Hartwell Arena	13,349	Buffalo	4	Anaheim	2	Ville Leino	8:30 (1st)
Oct. 7, 2011	Stockholm, Sweden	Ericsson Globe Arena	13,800	Los Angeles	3	NY Rangers	2	Jack Johnson	4:08 (OT)
Oct. 8, 2011	Stockholm, Sweden	Ericsson Globe Arena	13,800	Anaheim	2	NY Rangers	1	Bobby Ryan	Shootout
Oct. 8, 2011	Berlin, Germany	O2 World	14,300	Buffalo	4	Los Angeles	2	Paul Gaustad	13:19 (2nd)

NHL Clubs' Minor-League Affiliations, 2015-16

NHL CLUB	MINOR-LEAGUE AFFILIATES
Anaheim	San Diego Gulls (AHL)
	Utah Grizzlies (ECHL)
Arizona	Springfield Falcons (AHL)
	Rapid City Rush (ECHL)
Boston	Providence Bruins (AHL)
	Gwinnett Gladiators (ECHL)
Buffalo	Rochester Americans (AHL)
	Elmira Jackals (ECHL)
Calgary	Stockton Heat (AHL)
	Adirondack Thunder (ECHL)
Carolina	Charlotte Checkers (AHL)
	Florida Everblades (ECHL)
Chicago	Rockford IceHogs (AHL)
	Indy Fuel (ECHL)
Colorado	San Antonio Rampage (AHL)
	Fort Wayne Komets (ECHL)
Columbus	Lake Erie Monsters (AHL)
	Kalamazoo Wings (ECHL)
Dallas	Texas Stars (AHL)
	Idaho Steelheads (ECHL)
Detroit	Grand Rapids Griffins (AHL)
	Toledo Walleye (ECHL)
Edmonton	Bakersfield Condors (AHL)
	Norfolk Admirals (ECHL)
Florida	Portland Pirates (AHL)
Los Angeles	Ontario Reign (AHL)
	Manchester Monarchs (ECHL)
Minnesota	Iowa Wild (AHL)
	Quad City Mallards (ECHL)

NHL CLUB	MINOR-LEAGUE AFFILIATES
Montreal	St. John's IceCaps (AHL)
	Brampton Beast (ECHL)
Nashville	Milwaukee Admirals (AHL)
	Cincinnati Cyclones (ECHL)
New Jersey	Albany Devils (AHL)
NY Islanders	Bridgeport Sound Tigers (AHL)
	Missouri Mavericks (ECHL)
NY Rangers	Hartford Wolf Pack (AHL)
	Greenville Road Warriors (ECHL)
Ottawa	Binghamton Senators (AHL)
	Evansville IceMen (ECHL)
Philadelphia	Lehigh Valley Phantoms (AHL)
	Reading Royals (ECHL)
Pittsburgh	Wilkes-Barre/Scranton Penguins (AHL)
	Wheeling Nailers (ECHL)
St. Louis	Chicago Wolves (AHL)
	Alaska Aces (ECHL)
San Jose	San Jose Barracuda (AHL)
	Allen Americans (ECHL)
Tampa Bay	Syracuse Crunch (AHL)
	Florida Everblades (ECHL)
Toronto	Toronto Marlies (AHL)
	Orlando Solar Bears (ECHL)
Vancouver	Utica Comets (AHL)
	Kalamazoo Wings (ECHL)
Washington	Hershey Bears (AHL)
	South Carolina Stingrays (ECHL)
Winnipeg	Manitoba Moose (AHL)
	Tulsa Oilers (ECHL)

Anaheim Ducks

Key Off-Season Signings/Acquisitions

2015
June 25 • Re-signed LW **Max Friberg**.
27 • Acquired LW **Carl Hagelin**, a 2nd-round choice in the 2015 NHL Draft and a 6th-round choice in 2015 from NY Rangers for RW **Emerson Etem** and a 2nd-round choice in 2015.
27 • Acquired G **Anton Khudobin** from Carolina for D **James Wisniewski**.
30 • Acquired D **Kevin Bieksa** from Vancouver for a 2nd-round choice in the 2016 NHL Draft.
30 • Named **Paul MacLean** assistant coach.
July 1 • Signed G **Matt Hackett**, C **Chris Mueller** and D **Joe Piskula**.
2 • Re-signed D **Korbinian Holzer**.
3 • Signed C **Shawn Horcoff** and LW **Harry Zolnierczyk**.
10 • Signed RW **Brian McGrattan**.
11 • Signed RW **Chris Stewart**.
15 • Re-signed C **Ryan Kesler**.
16 • Signed D **Shane O'Brien**.
16 • Re-signed C **Chris Wagner** and C **Michael Sgarbossa**.
22 • Re-signed D **Josh Manson**.
Aug. 7 • Re-signed RW **Jakob Silfverberg**.

2014-15 Results: 51w-24L-2oTL-5soL 109pts
1st, Pacific Division • 1st, Western Conference

Year-by-Year Record

Season	GP	Home W	L	T	OL	Road W	L	T	OL	Overall W	L	T	OL	GF	GA	Pts.	Div. Fin.	Conf. Fin.	Playoff Result
2014-15	82	26	12	....	3	25	12	....	4	51	24	....	7	236	226	109	1st, Pac.	1st, West	Lost Conf. Final
2013-14	82	29	8	....	4	25	12	....	4	54	20	....	8	266	209	116	1st, Pac.	1st, West	Lost Second Round
2012-13	48	16	7	....	1	14	5	....	5	30	12	....	6	140	118	66	1st, Pac.	2nd, West	Lost Conf. Quarter-Final
2011-12	82	21	18	....	2	13	18	....	10	34	36	....	12	204	231	80	5th, Pac.	13th, West	Out of Playoffs
2010-11	82	26	13	....	2	21	17	....	3	47	30	....	5	239	235	99	2nd, Pac.	4th, West	Lost Conf. Quarter-Final
2009-10	82	25	11	....	5	14	21	....	6	39	32	....	11	238	251	89	4th, Pac.	11th, West	Out of Playoffs
2008-09	82	20	18	....	3	22	15	....	4	42	33	....	7	245	238	91	2nd, Pac.	8th, West	Lost Conf. Semi-Final
2007-08	82	28	9	....	4	19	18	....	4	47	27	....	8	205	191	102	2nd, Pac.	4th, West	Lost Conf. Quarter-Final
2006-07	**82**	**26**	**6**	....	**9**	**22**	**14**	....	**5**	**48**	**20**	....	**14**	**258**	**208**	**110**	**1st, Pac.**	**2nd, West**	**Won Stanley Cup**
2005-06*	82	26	10	....	5	17	17	....	7	43	27	....	12	254	229	98	3rd, Pac.	6th, West	Lost Conf. Final
2004-05*	....																		
2003-04*	82	19	11	7	4	10	24	3	4	29	35	10	8	184	213	76	4th, Pac.	12th, West	Out of Playoffs
2002-03*	82	22	10	7	2	18	17	2	4	40	27	9	6	203	193	95	2nd, Pac.	7th, West	Lost Final
2001-02*	82	15	19	5	2	14	23	3	1	29	42	8	3	175	198	69	5th, Pac.	13th, West	Out of Playoffs
2000-01*	82	15	20	4	2	10	21	7	3	25	41	11	5	188	245	66	5th, Pac.	15th, West	Out of Playoffs
1999-2000*	82	19	13	7	2	15	20	5	1	34	33	12	3	217	227	83	5th, Pac.	9th, West	Out of Playoffs
1998-99*	82	21	14	6	....	14	20	7	....	35	34	13	....	215	206	83	3rd, Pac.	6th, West	Lost Conf. Quarter-Final
1997-98*	82	12	23	6	....	14	20	7	....	26	43	13	....	205	261	65	6th, Pac.	12th, West	Out of Playoffs
1996-97*	82	23	12	6	....	13	21	7	....	36	33	13	....	245	233	85	2nd, Pac.	4th, West	Lost Conf. Semi-Final
1995-96*	82	22	15	4	....	13	24	4	....	35	39	8	....	234	247	78	4th, Pac.	9th, West	Out of Playoffs
1994-95*	48	11	9	4	....	5	18	1	....	16	27	5	....	125	164	37	6th, Pac.	12th, West	Out of Playoffs
1993-94*	84	14	26	2	....	19	20	3	....	33	46	5	....	229	251	71	4th, Pac.	9th, West	Out of Playoffs

* Mighty Ducks of Anaheim

2015-16 Schedule

Oct.	Sat.	10	at San Jose
	Mon.	12	Vancouver
	Wed.	14	Arizona
	Fri.	16	Colorado
	Sun.	18	Minnesota*
	Thu.	22	at Nashville
	Sat.	24	at Minnesota*
	Mon.	26	at Chicago
	Tue.	27	at Dallas
	Thu.	29	at St. Louis
Nov.	Sun.	1	Nashville*
	Wed.	4	Florida
	Fri.	6	Columbus
	Sat.	7	at San Jose
	Mon.	9	Arizona
	Wed.	11	Edmonton
	Fri.	13	NY Islanders
	Mon.	16	at Carolina
	Tue.	17	at Nashville
	Thu.	19	at Florida
	Sat.	21	at Tampa Bay
	Tue.	24	Calgary
	Wed.	25	at Arizona
	Fri.	27	Chicago*
	Mon.	30	Vancouver
Dec.	Wed.	2	Tampa Bay
	Fri.	4	San Jose
	Sun.	6	Pittsburgh*
	Fri.	11	Carolina
	Thu.	17	at Buffalo
	Sat.	19	at New Jersey
	Mon.	21	at NY Islanders
	Tue.	22	at NY Rangers
	Sun.	27	Philadelphia*
	Tue.	29	at Calgary
	Thu.	31	at Edmonton
Jan.	Fri.	1	at Vancouver
	Sun.	3	Winnipeg
	Wed.	6	Toronto
	Fri.	8	St. Louis
	Sun.	10	Detroit*

	Wed.	13	Ottawa
	Fri.	15	Dallas
	Sun.	17	Los Angeles
	Wed.	20	Minnesota
	Fri.	22	at Washington
	Sat.	23	at Detroit
	Tue.	26	at Boston
Feb.	Tue.	2	San Jose
	Thu.	4	at Los Angeles
	Fri.	5	Arizona
	Mon.	8	at Pittsburgh
	Tue.	9	at Philadelphia
	Thu.	11	at Columbus
	Sat.	13	at Chicago
	Mon.	15	at Calgary*
	Tue.	16	at Edmonton
	Thu.	18	at Vancouver
	Sun.	21	Calgary*
	Wed.	24	Buffalo
	Fri.	26	Edmonton
	Sun.	28	Los Angeles
Mar.	Wed.	2	Montreal
	Thu.	3	at Arizona
	Sat.	5	at Los Angeles*
	Mon.	7	Washington
	Wed.	9	at Colorado
	Fri.	11	at St. Louis
	Mon.	14	New Jersey
	Wed.	16	NY Rangers
	Fri.	18	Boston
	Sun.	20	at Winnipeg*
	Tue.	22	at Montreal
	Thu.	24	at Toronto
	Sat.	26	at Ottawa
	Mon.	28	at Edmonton
	Wed.	30	Calgary
Apr.	Fri.	1	Vancouver
	Sun.	3	Dallas
	Tue.	5	Winnipeg
	Thu.	7	at Los Angeles
	Sat.	9	at Colorado*

* Denotes afternoon game.

Retired Numbers
8 Teemu Selanne 1996-2001, 2005-14

**PACIFIC DIVISION
23rd NHL Season**

Franchise date: June 15, 1993

Hampus Lindholm had a solid season on the Anaheim defense, leading the team's blueliners with 27 assists and topping the club in plus-minus at +25.

2015-16 Player Personnel

FORWARDS	HT	WT	*Age	Place of Birth	S	2014-15 Club
BAILEY, Matt	6-1	197	24	Winnipeg, MB	L	Norfolk
COGLIANO, Andrew	5-10	181	28	Toronto, ON	L	Anaheim
CRAMAROSSA, Joseph	6-0	190	22	Toronto, ON	L	Norfolk
FRIBERG, Max	5-11	200	22	Skovde, Sweden	R	Anaheim-Norfolk
GETZLAF, Ryan	6-4	221	30	Regina, SK	R	Anaheim
HAGELIN, Carl	5-11	186	27	Sodertalje, Sweden	L	NY Rangers
HORCOFF, Shawn	6-1	210	37	Trail, BC	L	Dallas
JACKMAN, Tim	6-2	225	33	Minot, ND	R	Anaheim
KASE, Ondrej	6-0	165	19	Kadan, Czech Republic	L	Chomutov Jr.-Chomutov
KERDILES, Nicolas	6-2	201	21	Lewisville, TX	L	Norfolk
KESLER, Ryan	6-2	202	31	Livonia, MI	R	Anaheim
MAROON, Patrick	6-3	230	27	St Louis, MO	L	Anaheim
McGRATTAN, Brian	6-4	235	34	Hamilton, ON	R	Calgary-Adirondack
MUELLER, Chris	5-11	210	29	West Seneca, NY	R	NY Rangers-Hartford
NATTINEN, Julius	6-2	191	18	Jyvaskyla, Finland	L	JYP-Akatemia
NOESEN, Stefan	6-2	205	22	Plano, TX	R	Anaheim-Norfolk
PERRY, Corey	6-3	212	30	Peterborough, ON	R	Anaheim
RAKELL, Rickard	6-1	192	22	Sundbyberg, Sweden	R	Anaheim-Norfolk
RITCHIE, Nick	6-2	226	19	Orangeville, ON	L	Peterborough-S.S. Marie
SARAULT, Charles	5-11	184	23	Ottawa, ON	L	Norfolk
SEKAC, Jiri	6-2	182	23	Kladno, Czech.	L	Montreal-Anaheim
SGARBOSSA, Michael	5-11	180	23	Campbellville, ON	L	Col-Lake Erie-Norfolk
SILFVERBERG, Jakob	6-1	200	24	Gavle, Sweden	R	Anaheim
SORENSEN, Nick	6-1	182	20	Holback, Denmark	R	Skelleftea
STEWART, Chris	6-2	231	27	Toronto, ON	R	Buffalo-Minnesota
THOMPSON, Nate	6-0	212	31	Anchorage, AK	L	Anaheim
WAGNER, Chris	5-11	201	24	Wellesley, MA	R	Anaheim-Norfolk
ZOLNIERCZYK, Harry	6-0	185	28	Toronto, ON	L	NY Islanders-Bridgeport
DEFENSEMEN						
BIEKSA, Kevin	6-1	198	34	Grimsby, ON	R	Vancouver
DESPRES, Simon	6-4	214	24	Laval, QC	L	Pittsburgh-Anaheim
FOWLER, Cam	6-1	207	23	Windsor, ON	L	Anaheim
GAGNE, Kevin	5-8	176	23	Edmundston, NB	L	Norfolk
HELGESEN, Kenton	6-3	197	21	Grand Prarie, AB	L	Calgary (WHL)
HOLZER, Korbinian	6-3	205	27	Munich, West Germany	R	Toronto-Toronto (AHL)
LINDHOLM, Hampus	6-3	197	21	Helsingborg, Sweden	L	Anaheim
MANSON, Josh	6-3	217	24	Prince Albert, SK	R	Anaheim-Norfolk
MEGNA, Jaycob	6-5	218	22	Plantation, FL	L	Norfolk
MONTOUR, Brandon	6-0	172	21	Brantford, ON	R	Massachusetts-Norfolk
O'BRIEN, Andrew	6-4	205	22	Hamilton, ON	L	Norfolk
O'BRIEN, Shane	6-3	230	32	Port Hope, ON	L	Florida-San Antonio
PISKULA, Joe	6-3	212	31	Antigo, WI	L	Nashville-Milwaukee
STONER, Clayton	6-4	216	30	Port McNeill, BC	L	Anaheim
THEODORE, Shea	6-2	182	20	Langley, BC	L	Seattle-Norfolk
VATANEN, Sami	5-10	183	24	Jyvaskyla, Finland	R	Anaheim
GOALTENDERS	**HT**	**WT**	***Age**	**Place of Birth**	**C**	**2014-15 Club**
ANDERSEN, Frederik	6-4	230	26	Herning, Denmark	L	Anaheim
GIBSON, John	6-3	210	22	Pittsburgh, PA	L	Anaheim-Norfolk
HACKETT, Matt	6-2	171	25	London, ON	L	Buffalo-Rochester
KHUDOBIN, Anton	5-11	203	29	Ust-Kamenogorsk, USSR	L	Carolina

* – Age at start of 2015-16 season

Bob Murray

Executive Vice President and General Manager

Born: Kingston, ON, November 26, 1954.

Bob Murray was named executive vice president and general manager of the Anaheim Ducks on November 12, 2008 after 3 1/2 years as senior vice president of hockey operations. He was named to that original position on July 14, 2005. Murray's astute judgment of hockey talent and player evaluation were instrumental in several trades and acquisitions the Ducks made over his tenure, highlighted by a Stanley Cup championship in 2007. Anaheim has won division titles under Murray in 2012-13, 2013-14 and 2014-15. He was named NHL General Manager of the Year in 2014 and finished third in the voting in 2015.

Murray's responsibilities include overseeing all aspects of player development, playing a key role in the club's professional scouting efforts, contract negotiations and all matters relating to the National Hockey League. He has been instrumental in the organization's success at both the NHL and AHL level. Both the Ducks and American Hockey League's Portland Pirates made Conference Final appearances in 2006, making Anaheim the only organization to have both their NHL and AHL teams advance to their league's respective Conference Finals.

Prior to joining the Ducks, Murray worked as a professional scout with the Vancouver Canucks from 1999 to 2005 under general manager Brian Burke (1998 to 2004). Before his stint in Vancouver, he served as a scouting consultant for Anaheim during the 1998-99 season.

Murray was a member of the Chicago Blackhawks organization for 25 years, serving as general manager from 1997 to 1999. He was promoted to the post after serving as assistant general manager under Bob Pulford for two seasons. Before joining upper management, Murray was named the director of player personnel in 1991 and was largely responsible for the club's draft selections over eight seasons.

Drafted by the Blackhawks in 1974, Murray spent his entire 1,008-game, 15-year career in a Chicago uniform. He became just the fourth player in Blackhawks history to reach the 1,000-game plateau. In addition, he became the first defenseman in club history to appear in 100 postseason contests, reaching the mark during the 1990 Stanley Cup playoffs. In all, Murray had 132 goals and 382 assists for 514 points, and currently ranks second in all-time points among Blackhawk defensemen. He was named to both the 1981 and 1983 NHL All-Star Games. Murray retired at the conclusion of the 1989-90 season. Known for his work ethic, intelligence and determination as a player, Murray remained with the organization as a professional scout following his retirement in 1990.

2014-15 Scoring

* – rookie

Regular Season

Pos	#	Player	Team	GP	G	A	Pts	TOI	+/–	PIM	PP	SH	GW	S	S%
C	15	Ryan Getzlaf	ANA	77	25	45	70	20:05	15	62	3	0	6	191	13.1
R	10	Corey Perry	ANA	67	33	22	55	18:06	13	67	4	0	3	193	17.1
C	17	Ryan Kesler	ANA	81	20	27	47	19:30	–5	75	5	1	4	205	9.8
R	33	Jakob Silfverberg	ANA	81	13	26	39	15:39	15	24	2	1	2	189	6.9
D	45	Sami Vatanen	ANA	67	12	25	37	21:27	5	36	7	1	1	122	9.8
L	19	Patrick Maroon	ANA	71	9	25	34	14:16	–5	82	1	0	1	120	7.5
D	20	James Wisniewski	CBJ	56	8	21	29	21:24	–10	34	7	0	2	127	6.3
			ANA	13	0	5	5	20:13	–3	10	0	0	0	20	0.0
			Total	69	8	26	34	21:11	–13	44	7	0	2	147	5.4
D	47	Hampus Lindholm	ANA	78	7	27	34	21:45	25	32	0	0	1	107	6.5
D	4	Cam Fowler	ANA	80	7	27	34	21:08	4	14	1	1	2	87	8.0
L	39	Matt Beleskey	ANA	65	22	10	32	14:28	13	39	4	0	8	145	15.2
R	67	* Rickard Rakell	ANA	71	9	22	31	12:34	6	10	2	0	1	105	8.6
C	7	Andrew Cogliano	ANA	82	15	14	29	14:36	5	14	0	3	2	134	11.2
C	21	Kyle Palmieri	ANA	57	14	15	29	14:05	–2	37	5	0	4	112	12.5
L	14	Tomas Fleischmann	FLA	52	7	14	21	14:50	12	8	0	0	1	107	6.5
			ANA	14	1	5	6	14:10	0	4	0	0	0	24	4.2
			Total	66	8	19	27	14:42	12	12	0	0	1	131	6.1
D	23	Francois Beauchemin	ANA	64	11	12	23	22:44	17	48	2	0	1	110	10.0
L	46	* Jiri Sekac	MTL	50	7	9	16	13:48	–2	18	2	0	0	56	12.5
			ANA	19	2	5	7	12:56	2	4	0	0	0	29	6.9
			Total	69	9	14	23	13:34	0	22	2	0	0	85	10.6
D	24	Simon Despres	PIT	59	2	15	17	16:22	9	64	0	0	1	76	2.6
			ANA	16	1	5	6	18:39	2	22	0	0	0	27	3.7
			Total	75	3	20	23	16:51	11	86	0	0	1	103	2.9
C	44	Nate Thompson	ANA	80	5	13	18	13:19	0	39	0	1	3	87	5.7
R	16	Emerson Etem	ANA	45	5	5	10	12:14	–6	4	0	0	0	77	6.5
D	3	Clayton Stoner	ANA	69	1	7	8	17:38	–2	68	0	0	1	68	1.5
R	18	Tim Jackman	ANA	55	5	2	7	8:22	–4	86	0	0	1	55	9.1
D	42	* Josh Manson	ANA	28	0	3	3	18:26	1	31	0	0	0	26	0.0
D	37	* Mat Clark	ANA	7	0	1	1	12:46	2	6	0	0	0	2	0.0
D	48	Colby Robak	FLA	7	0	0	0	12:57	–1	2	0	0	0	6	0.0
			ANA	5	0	1	1	15:15	3	0	0	0	0	2	0.0
			Total	12	0	1	1	13:55	2	2	0	0	0	8	0.0
D	77	* Jesse Blacker	ANA	1	0	0	0	6:03	–2	0	0	0	0	0	0.0
L	43	* Max Friberg	ANA	1	0	0	0	8:47	0	0	0	0	0	0	0.0
R	64	* Stefan Noesen	ANA	1	0	0	0	6:54	0	0	0	0	0	0	0.0
L	51	Dany Heatley	ANA	6	0	0	0	12:07	–3	0	0	0	0	8	0.0
D	28	Mark Fistric	ANA	9	0	0	0	14:47	–3	4	0	0	0	1	0.0
R	62	* Chris Wagner	ANA	9	0	0	0	8:47	–2	2	0	0	0	7	0.0

Goaltending

No.	Goaltender	GPI	Mins	Avg	W	L	OT	EN	SO	GA	SA	Sv%	G	A	PIM
31	Frederik Andersen	54	3106	2.38	35	12	5	3	3	123	1436	.914	0	3	4
36	* John Gibson	23	1340	2.60	13	8	0	3	1	58	674	.914	0	0	0
30	Jason LaBarbera	5	207	2.61	2	0	1	1	0	9	99	.909	0	0	0
80	Ilya Bryzgalov	8	329	4.19	1	4	1	1	0	23	150	.847	0	2	0
	Totals	**82**	**5003**	**2.65**	**51**	**24**	**7**	**8**	**4**	**221**	**2367**	**.907**			

Playoffs

Pos	#	Player	Team	GP	G	A	Pts	TOI	+/–	PIM	PP	SH	GW	OT	S	S%
C	15	Ryan Getzlaf	ANA	16	2	18	20	22:25	6	6	2	0	0	0	48	4.2
R	10	Corey Perry	ANA	16	10	8	18	19:54	6	14	2	0	2	1	64	15.6
R	33	Jakob Silfverberg	ANA	16	4	14	18	19:01	6	16	1	0	1	0	41	9.8
C	17	Ryan Kesler	ANA	16	7	6	13	20:28	2	24	1	0	1	0	33	21.2
L	19	Patrick Maroon	ANA	16	7	4	11	17:55	4	6	3	0	1	0	42	16.7
D	45	Sami Vatanen	ANA	16	3	8	11	21:13	5	8	0	0	0	0	35	8.6
D	4	Cam Fowler	ANA	16	2	8	10	23:07	5	2	0	0	0	0	28	7.1
D	47	Hampus Lindholm	ANA	16	2	8	10	23:15	2	10	0	0	0	0	21	9.5
L	39	Matt Beleskey	ANA	16	8	1	9	15:59	–4	2	3	0	3	1	45	17.8
C	7	Andrew Cogliano	ANA	16	3	6	9	16:15	9	4	0	0	0	0	47	6.4
D	23	Francois Beauchemin	ANA	16	0	9	9	25:24	4	2	0	0	0	0	25	0.0
D	24	Simon Despres	ANA	16	1	6	7	20:46	4	6	0	0	1	0	17	5.9
C	44	Nate Thompson	ANA	12	2	4	6	15:28	5	6	0	0	0	0	13	15.4
C	21	Kyle Palmieri	ANA	16	1	3	4	13:11	1	4	0	0	1	0	35	2.9
R	16	Emerson Etem	ANA	12	3	0	3	11:42	1	0	0	0	0	0	23	13.0
D	3	Clayton Stoner	ANA	16	1	0	1	18:13	4	10	0	0	0	0	17	5.9
R	67	* Rickard Rakell	ANA	16	1	0	1	11:32	–2	2	0	0	1	1	20	5.0
L	14	Tomas Fleischmann	ANA	6	0	1	1	10:38	0	0	0	0	0	0	6	0.0
R	62	* Chris Wagner	ANA	2	0	0	0	5:32	0	0	0	0	0	0	0	0.0
L	46	* Jiri Sekac	ANA	7	0	0	0	11:23	0	2	0	0	0	0	6	0.0
R	18	Tim Jackman	ANA	9	0	0	0	6:32	–1	12	0	0	0	0	3	0.0

Goaltending

No.	Goaltender	GPI	Mins	Avg	W	L	EN	SO	GA	SA	Sv%	G	A	PIM
31	Frederik Andersen	16	1050	2.34	11	5	1	1	41	472	.913	0	0	0
	Totals	**16**	**1055**	**2.39**	**11**	**5**	**1**	**1**	**42**	**473**	**.911**			

Club Records

Team

(Figures in brackets for season records are games played; records for fewest points, wins, ties, losses, goals, goals against are for 70 or more games)

Most Points **116** 2013-14 (82)
Most Wins **54** 2013-14 (82)
Most Ties **13** 1996-97 (82), 1997-98 (82), 1998-99 (82)
Most Losses **46** 1993-94 (84)
Most Goals **266** 2013-14 (82)
Most Goals Against **261** 1997-98 (82)
Fewest Points **65** 1997-98 (82)
Fewest Wins **25** 2000-01 (82)
Fewest Ties **5** 1993-94 (84)
Fewest Losses **20** 2006-07 (82), 2013-14 (82)
Fewest Goals **175** 2001-02 (82)
Fewest Goals Against **191** 2007-08 (82)
Longest Winning Streak
Overall .... **13** Dec. 6-18/13
Home .... **13** Jan. 26-Mar. 20/13
Away .... **7** Nov. 28-Dec. 13/06
Longest Undefeated Streak
Overall .... **12** Feb. 22-Mar. 19/97 (7W, 5T)
Home .... **14** Feb. 12-Apr. 9/97 (10W, 4T)
Away .... **7** Nov. 28-Dec. 13/06 (7W)
Longest Losing Streak
Overall .... **8** Oct. 12-30/96, Nov. 3-20/05
Home .... **8** Jan. 10-Feb. 9/01
Away .... **13** Oct. 29-Dec. 22/11
Longest Winless Streak
Overall .... **9** Three times
Home .... **11** Jan. 5-Feb. 14/01 (8L, 3T/OL)
Away .... **13** Nov. 1-Dec. 27/03 (11L, 2T/OL)
Most Shutouts, Season **9** 2002-03 (82)
Most PIM, Season **1,843** 1997-98 (82)
Most Goals, Game .... **8** Jan. 21/98 (Fla. 3 at Ana. 8), Mar. 21/04 (Det. 6 at Ana. 8)

Individual

Most Seasons .... **15** Teemu Selanne
Most Games .... **966** Teemu Selanne
Most Goals, Career .... **457** Teemu Selanne
Most Assists, Career .... **531** Teemu Selanne
Most Points, Career .... **988** Teemu Selanne (457G, 531A)
Most PIM, Career .... **812** George Parros
Most Shutouts, Career .... **32** Jean-Sebastien Giguere
Longest Consecutive Games Streak .... **276** Andy McDonald (Oct. 17/03-Dec. 12/07)
Most Goals, Season .... **52** Teemu Selanne (1997-98)
Most Assists, Season .... **66** Ryan Getzlaf (2008-09)
Most Points, Season .... **109** Teemu Selanne (1996-97; 51G, 58A)
Most PIM, Season .... **285** Todd Ewen (1995-96)
Most Points, Defenseman, Season .... **69** Scott Niedermayer (2006-07; 15G, 54A)
Most Points, Center, Season .... **91** Ryan Getzlaf (2008-09; 25G, 66A)
Most Points, Right Wing, Season .... **109** Teemu Selanne (1996-97; 51G, 58A)
Most Points, Left Wing, Season .... **108** Paul Kariya (1995-96; 50G, 58A)
Most Points, Rookie, Season .... **57** Bobby Ryan (2008-09; 31G, 26A)
Most Shutouts, Season .... **8** Jean-Sebastien Giguere (2002-03)
Most Goals, Game .... **3** Thirty-seven times
Most Assists, Game .... **5** Dmitri Mironov (Dec. 12/97), Teemu Selanne (Nov. 19/06), Ryan Getzlaf (Oct. 29/08)
Most Points, Game .... **5** Fifteen times

General Managers' History

Jack Ferreira, 1993-94 to 1997-98; Pierre Gauthier, 1998-99 to 2001-02; Bryan Murray, 2002-03, 2003-04; Al Coates, 2004-05; Brian Burke, 2005-06 to 2007-08; Brian Burke and Bob Murray, 2008-09; Bob Murray, 2009-10 to date.

Captains' History

Troy Loney, 1993-94; Randy Ladouceur, 1994-95, 1995-96; Paul Kariya, 1996-97; Paul Kariya and Teemu Selanne, 1997-98; Paul Kariya, 1998-99 to 2002-03; Steve Rucchin, 2003-04; Scott Niedermayer, 2005-06, 2006-07; Chris Pronger, 2007-08; Scott Niedermayer, 2008-09, 2009-10; Ryan Getzlaf, 2010-11 to date.

All-time Record vs. Other Clubs

Regular Season

	Total								At Home								On Road							
	GP	W	L	T	OL	GF	GA	PTS	GP	W	L	T	OL	GF	GA	PTS	GP	W	L	T	OL	GF	GA	PTS
Arizona	115	65	32	5	13	345	304	148	58	36	15	3	4	179	143	79	57	29	17	2	9	166	161	69
Boston	28	13	9	2	4	75	74	32	14	6	4	2	2	34	35	16	14	7	5	0	2	41	39	16
Buffalo	30	12	14	3	1	76	85	28	15	7	8	0	0	37	42	14	15	5	6	3	1	39	43	14
Calgary	91	47	35	7	2	265	251	103	45	31	8	6	0	153	109	68	46	16	27	1	2	112	142	35
Carolina	30	15	12	2	1	82	84	33	15	9	5	1	0	48	46	19	15	6	7	1	1	34	38	14
Chicago	83	44	30	5	4	211	199	97	40	23	13	3	1	108	88	50	43	21	17	2	3	103	111	47
Colorado	79	36	31	7	5	217	214	84	40	20	15	3	2	109	104	45	39	16	16	4	3	108	110	39
Columbus	51	25	19	1	6	144	138	57	26	13	8	1	4	81	70	31	25	12	11	0	2	63	68	26
Dallas	113	41	61	5	6	258	332	93	56	25	27	3	1	143	156	54	57	16	34	2	5	115	176	39
Detroit	79	24	43	7	5	185	241	60	40	18	18	4	0	100	105	40	39	6	25	3	5	85	136	20
Edmonton	91	49	35	2	5	247	218	105	46	27	16	2	1	134	115	57	45	22	19	0	4	113	103	48
Florida	27	11	12	3	1	73	80	26	14	6	7	1	0	42	44	13	13	5	5	2	1	31	36	13
Los Angeles	122	57	41	11	13	356	339	138	61	33	13	7	8	205	164	81	61	24	28	4	5	151	175	57
Minnesota	53	27	17	2	7	127	130	63	27	16	8	0	3	71	64	35	26	11	9	2	4	56	66	28
Montreal	26	12	10	2	2	78	77	28	13	6	5	0	2	41	38	14	13	6	5	2	0	37	39	14
Nashville	61	35	19	2	5	170	141	77	31	22	6	0	3	96	65	47	30	13	13	2	2	74	76	30
New Jersey	28	11	13	1	3	67	79	26	15	7	6	1	1	43	38	16	13	4	7	0	2	24	41	10
NY Islanders	28	12	10	4	2	76	74	30	15	6	4	3	2	39	40	17	13	6	6	1	0	37	34	13
NY Rangers	29	16	8	1	4	87	80	37	14	9	3	0	2	50	39	20	15	7	5	1	2	37	41	17
Ottawa	27	14	9	3	1	66	66	32	14	7	4	2	1	33	28	17	13	7	5	1	0	33	38	15
Philadelphia	28	13	8	5	2	86	87	33	15	7	4	2	2	56	53	18	13	6	4	3	0	30	34	15
Pittsburgh	28	10	15	2	1	83	92	23	13	7	5	0	1	42	40	15	15	3	10	2	0	41	52	8
St. Louis	81	38	33	5	5	228	242	86	40	23	15	2	0	119	107	48	41	15	18	3	5	109	135	38
San Jose	123	55	58	4	6	325	356	120	62	28	29	2	3	166	177	61	61	27	29	2	3	159	179	59
Tampa Bay	28	15	12	1	0	75	69	31	14	8	5	1	0	40	35	17	14	7	7	0	0	35	34	14
Toronto	36	10	21	5	0	90	112	25	16	7	8	1	0	49	42	15	20	3	13	4	0	41	70	10
Vancouver	92	40	36	9	7	260	273	96	45	18	15	7	5	129	132	48	47	22	21	2	2	131	141	48
Washington	29	14	11	1	3	86	79	32	14	6	6	1	1	46	46	14	15	8	5	0	2	40	33	18
Winnipeg	20	12	7	0	1	67	58	25	10	5	4	0	1	34	34	11	10	7	3	0	0	33	24	14
Totals	**1656**	**773**	**661**	**107**	**115**	**4505**	**4574**	**1768**	**828**	**436**	**284**	**58**	**50**	**2427**	**2199**	**980**	**828**	**337**	**377**	**49**	**65**	**2078**	**2375**	**788**

Playoffs

	Series	W	L	GP	W	L	T	GF	GA	Last Mtg.	Rnd.	Result
Arizona	1	1	0	7	4	3	0	17	17	1997	CQF	W 4-3
Calgary	2	2	0	12	8	4	0	36	25	2015	SR	W 4-1
Chicago	1	0	1	7	3	4	0	22	24	2015	CF	L 3-4
Colorado	1	1	0	4	4	0	0	16	4	2006	CSF	W 4-0
Dallas	3	2	1	18	10	8	0	47	52	2014	FR	W 4-2
Detroit	6	2	4	32	14	18	0	78	93	2013	CQF	L 3-4
Edmonton	1	0	1	5	1	4	0	13	16	2006	CF	L 1-4
Los Angeles	1	0	1	7	3	4	0	15	19	2014	SR	L 3-4
Minnesota	2	2	0	9	8	1	0	21	10	2007	CQF	W 4-1
Nashville	1	0	1	6	2	4	0	20	22	2011	CQF	L 2-4
New Jersey	1	0	1	7	3	4	0	12	19	2003	F	L 3-4
Ottawa	1	1	0	5	4	1	0	16	11	2007	F	W 4-1
San Jose	1	1	0	6	4	2	0	18	10	2009	CQF	W 4-2
Vancouver	1	1	0	5	4	1	0	14	8	2007	CSF	W 4-1
Winnipeg	1	1	0	4	4	0	0	16	9	2015	FR	W 4-0
Totals	**24**	**14**	**10**	**134**	**76**	**58**	**0**	**361**	**339**			

Playoff Results 2015-2011

Year	Round	Opponent	Result	GF	GA
2015	CF	Chicago	L 3-4	22	24
	SR	Calgary	W 4-1	19	9
	FR	Winnipeg	W 4-0	16	9
2014	SR	Los Angeles	L 3-4	15	19
	FR	Dallas	W 4-2	20	18
2013	CQF	Detroit	L 3-4	21	18
2011	CQF	Nashville	L 2-4	20	22

Abbreviations: Round: F – Final; **CF** – conference final; **CSF** – conference semi-final; **SR** – second round; **CQF** – conference quarter-final; **FR** – first round.

Carolina totals include Hartford, 1993-94 to 1996-97.
Phoenix totals include Winnipeg, 1993-94 to 1995-96.
Colorado totals include Quebec, 1993-94 to 1994-95.
Winnipeg totals include Atlanta Thrashers, 1999-2000 to 2010-11.

2014-15 Results

Oct.	9	at Pittsburgh	4-6
	11	at Detroit	3-2
	13	at Buffalo	5-1
	14	at Philadelphia	4-3†
	17	Minnesota	2-1
	19	St. Louis	3-0
	22	Buffalo	4-1
	24	Columbus	4-1
	26	San Jose	1-4
	28	at Chicago	1-0
	30	at St. Louis	0-2
	31	at Dallas	2-1*
Nov.	2	at Colorado	3-2
	5	NY Islanders	2-3*
	7	Arizona	2-3†
	9	Vancouver	1-2†
	12	Los Angeles	6-5†
	15	at Los Angeles	2-3*
	16	Florida	2-6
	18	at Calgary	3-4†
	20	at Vancouver	4-3†
	23	Arizona	2-1
	25	Calgary	3-2
	28	Chicago	1-4
	29	at San Jose	4-6
Dec.	1	Boston	3-2
	3	Philadelphia	5-4†
	5	at Minnesota	5-4
	7	at Winnipeg	4-3*
	10	Edmonton	2-1
	12	at Edmonton	4-2
	13	at Winnipeg	4-1
	16	at Toronto	2-6
	18	at Montreal	2-1
	19	at Ottawa	2-6
	22	San Jose	3-2*
	27	at Arizona	1-2†
	28	Vancouver	2-1*
	31	San Jose	0-3
Jan.	2	St. Louis	4-3
	4	Nashville	4-3†
	7	NY Rangers	1-4
	11	Winnipeg	5-4†
	14	Toronto	4-0
	16	New Jersey	5-1
	17	at Los Angeles	3-2†
	21	Calgary	6-3
	27	at Vancouver	4-0
	29	at San Jose	3-6
	30	Chicago	1-4
Feb.	3	Carolina	5-4*
	5	at Nashville	5-2
	6	at Washington	2-3†
	8	at Tampa Bay	3-5
	10	at Florida	2-6
	12	at Carolina	2-1
	15	Washington	3-5
	18	Tampa Bay	1-4
	20	at Calgary	6-3
	21	at Edmonton	2-1
	23	Detroit	4-3†
	25	Ottawa	0-3
	27	Los Angeles	4-2
Mar.	1	at Dallas	3-1
	3	at Arizona	4-1
	4	Montreal	3-1
	6	Pittsburgh	2-5
	9	at Vancouver	1-2
	11	at Calgary	3-6
	13	at Minnesota	2-1
	15	Nashville	4-2
	18	Los Angeles	3-2*
	20	Colorado	3-2*
	22	at NY Rangers	2-7
	24	at Columbus	3-5
	26	at Boston	3-2*
	28	at NY Islanders	3-2
	29	at New Jersey	2-1
Apr.	1	Edmonton	5-1
	3	Colorado	2-4
	8	Dallas	0-4
	11	at Arizona	2-1

* – Overtime † – Shootout

NHL Draft Selections 2015-2001

Name in bold denotes played in NHL.

2015
Pick
- 27 Jacob Larsson
- 59 Julius Nattinen
- 80 Brent Gates
- 84 Deven Sideroff
- 148 Troy Terry
- 178 Steven Ruggiero
- 179 Garrett Metcalf

2014
Pick
- 10 Nick Ritchie
- 38 Marcus Pettersson
- 55 Brandon Montour
- 123 Matthew Berkovitz
- 205 Ondrej Kase

2013
Pick
- 26 Shea Theodore
- 45 Nick Sorensen
- 87 Keaton Thompson
- 147 Grant Besse
- 177 Miro Aaltonen

2012
Pick
- 6 **Hampus Lindholm**
- 36 Nicolas Kerdiles
- 87 **Frederik Andersen**
- 97 Kevin Roy
- 108 Andrew O'Brien
- 127 Brian Cooper
- 187 Kenton Helgesen
- 210 Jaycob Megna

2011
Pick
- 30 **Rickard Rakell**
- 39 **John Gibson**
- 53 **William Karlsson**
- 65 Joseph Cramarossa
- 83 Andy Welinski
- 143 **Max Friberg**
- 160 **Josh Manson**

2010
Pick
- 12 **Cam Fowler**
- 29 **Emerson Etem**
- 42 **Devante Smith-Pelly**
- 122 **Chris Wagner**
- 132 Tim Heed
- 161 Andreas Dahlstrom
- 177 Kevin Lind
- 192 Brett Perlini

2009
Pick
- 15 **Peter Holland**
- 26 **Kyle Palmieri**
- 37 **Mat Clark**
- 76 Igor Bobkov
- 106 **Sami Vatanen**
- 136 Radoslav Illo
- 166 Scott Valentine

2008
Pick
- 17 **Jake Gardiner**
- 35 **Nicolas Deschamps**
- 39 **Eric O'Dell**
- 43 **Justin Schultz**
- 71 Josh Brittain
- 83 Marco Cousineau
- 85 **Brandon McMillan**
- 113 Ryan Hegarty
- 143 Stefan Warg
- 208 Nick Pryor

2007
Pick
- 19 Logan MacMillan
- 42 **Eric Tangradi**
- 63 **Maxime Macenauer**
- 92 Justin Vaive
- 93 **Steven Kampfer**
- 98 Sebastian Stefaniszin
- 121 Mattias Modig
- 151 Brett Morrison

2006
Pick
- 19 Mark Mitera
- 38 Bryce Swan
- 83 John de Gray
- 112 **Matt Beleskey**
- 172 **Petteri Wirtanen**

2005
Pick
- 2 **Bobby Ryan**
- 31 **Brendan Mikkelson**
- 63 Jason Bailey
- 127 Bobby Bolt
- 141 **Brian Salcido**
- 197 Jean-Philippe Levasseur

2004
Pick
- 9 **Ladislav Smid**
- 39 Jordan Smith
- 74 Kyle Klubertanz
- 75 **Tim Brent**
- 172 Matt Auffrey
- 203 Gabriel Bouthillette
- 236 Matt Christie
- 269 **Janne Pesonen**

2003
Pick
- 19 **Ryan Getzlaf**
- 28 **Corey Perry**
- 86 Shane Hynes
- 90 Juha Alen
- 119 Nathan Saunders
- 186 **Drew Miller**
- 218 Dirk Southern
- 250 **Shane O'Brien**
- 280 Ville Mantymaa

2002
Pick
- 7 **Joffrey Lupul**
- 37 **Tim Brent**
- 71 Brian Lee
- 103 Joonas Vihko
- 140 George Davis
- 173 Luke Fritshaw
- 261 Francois Caron
- 267 Chris Petrow

2001
Pick
- 5 **Stanislav Chistov**
- 35 **Mark Popovic**
- 69 Joel Stepp
- 102 **Timo Parssinen**
- 105 Vladimir Korsunov
- 118 Brandon Rogers
- 137 **Joel Perrault**
- 170 Jan Tabacek
- 224 **Tony Martensson**
- 232 **Martin Gerber**
- 264 **Pierre-Alexandre Parenteau**

Coaching History

Ron Wilson, 1993-94 to 1996-97; Pierre Page, 1997-98; Craig Hartsburg, 1998-99, 1999-2000; Craig Hartsburg and Guy Charron, 2000-01; Bryan Murray, 2001-02; Mike Babcock, 2002-03 to 2004-05; Randy Carlyle, 2005-06 to 2010-11; Randy Carlyle and Bruce Boudreau, 2011-12; Bruce Boudreau, 2012-13 to date.

Bruce Boudreau

Head Coach

Born: Toronto, ON, January 9, 1955.

Bruce Boudreau was named head coach in Anaheim on November 30, 2011. In his first three full seasons with the team he has led the Ducks to a division title each year.

As head coach of the Washington Capitals between 2007 and 2011, Boudreau won the 2007-08 Jack Adams Award (NHL Coach of the Year) and led his club to the 2009-10 Presidents' Trophy as the NHL's top club in the regular season with a franchise record 54 wins and 121 points.

Before joining the Capitals, Boudreau spent nine seasons as an AHL head coach, including a Calder Cup championship with the Hershey Bears in 2006. He also coached in the Colonial Hockey League, the IHL and the ECHL, winning the Kelly Cup with the Mississippi Sea Wolves of the ECHL in 1999.

Boudreau played parts of eight NHL seasons with the Toronto Maple Leafs and Chicago Blackhawks between 1976 and 1986, recording 28 goals and 42 assists for 70 points in 141 career games. In junior with the Toronto Marlboros, he scored 68 goals and added 97 assists for 165 points in 1974-75, a Canadian Hockey League record until Bobby Smith and Wayne Gretzky surpassed the mark during the 1977-78 season. He also was a top-scoring player in the AHL in the 1980s.

Coaching Record

			Regular Season				Playoffs			
Season	Team	League	GC	W	L	O/T	GC	W	L	T
1992-93	Muskegon	CoHL	60	28	27	5	7	3	4	....
1993-94	Fort Wayne	IHL	81	41	29	11	18	10	8	....
1994-95	Fort Wayne	IHL	39	15	21	3	....	....	....	....
1996-97	Mississippi	ECHL	70	34	26	10	3	0	3	....
1997-98	Mississippi	ECHL	70	34	27	9	....	....	....	....
1998-99	Mississippi	ECHL	70	41	22	7	18	14	4	....
99-2000	Lowell	AHL	80	33	36	11	7	3	4	....
2000-01	Lowell	AHL	80	35	35	10	4	1	3	....
2001-02	Manchester	AHL	80	38	28	14	5	2	3	....
2002-03	Manchester	AHL	80	40	23	17	3	0	3	....
2003-04	Manchester	AHL	80	40	28	12	6	2	4	....
2004-05	Manchester	AHL	80	51	21	8	6	2	4	....
2005-06	Hershey	AHL	80	44	21	15	21	16	5	....
2006-07	Hershey	AHL	80	51	17	12	19	13	6	....
2007-08	Hershey	AHL	15	8	7	0	....	....	....	....
2007-08	**Washington**	**NHL**	**61**	**37**	**17**	**7**	**7**	**3**	**4**	....
2008-09	**Washington**	**NHL**	**82**	**50**	**24**	**8**	**14**	**7**	**7**	....
2009-10	**Washington**	**NHL**	**82**	**54**	**15**	**13**	**7**	**3**	**4**	....
2010-11	**Washington**	**NHL**	**82**	**48**	**23**	**11**	**9**	**4**	**5**	....
2011-12	**Washington**	**NHL**	**22**	**12**	**9**	**1**	....	....	....	....
2011-12	**Anaheim**	**NHL**	**58**	**27**	**23**	**8**	....	....	....	....
2012-13	**Anaheim**	**NHL**	**48**	**30**	**12**	**6**	**7**	**3**	**4**	....
2013-14	**Anaheim**	**NHL**	**82**	**54**	**20**	**8**	**13**	**7**	**6**	....
2014-15	**Anaheim**	**NHL**	**82**	**51**	**24**	**7**	**16**	**11**	**5**	....
	NHL Totals		**599**	**363**	**167**	**69**	**73**	**38**	**35**	....

Jack Adams Award (2008)

Club Directory

Honda Center

Anaheim Ducks
Honda Center
2695 E. Katella Ave.
Anaheim, CA 92806
Phone **714/940-2900**
FAX 714/940-2953
Ticket Information 877/WILDWING
www.anaheimducks.com
Capacity: 17,174

Executive Management

Owners	Henry and Susan Samueli
Chief Executive Officer	Michael Schulman
Executive Vice President/General Manager	Bob Murray
Executive Vice President/Chief Operating Officer	Tim Ryan
Senior Vice President, Hockey Operations	David McNab
Chief Financial Officer/Vice President of Finance	Doug Heller
Vice President, Human Resources	Jay Scott
Vice President/COO, Anaheim Arena	Kevin Starkey
Vice President, Chief Marketing Officer	Aaron Teats
Vice President Sales/Chief Revenue Officer	John Viola
Vice President of Finance, Anaheim Arena	Angela Wergechik
Administrative Services Manager/Executive Assistant	Cheryl Gorman
Executive Assistant	Janet Conley

Coaching Staff

Head Coach	Bruce Boudreau
Assistant Coaches	Trent Yawney, Paul MacLean, Scott Niedermayer
Goaltending Consultant / Video Coordinator	Dwayne Roloson / Joe Piscotty

Hockey Operations

Director of Player Personnel	Rick Paterson
Assistant to the General Manager	Dave Baseggio
Director of Scouting, Amateur / Pro	Martin Madden
Director of Player Development	Todd Marchant
Scouting Staff	Glen Cochrane, Jeff Crisp, Jan-Åke Danielson, Steve Lyons, Martin Madden, Sr., Kevin Murray, Jim Pappin, Stephane Pilotte, Jim Sandlak, Mike Stapleton
Special Assignment Scout & Consultant	Dave Nonis
Hockey Ops, Sr. Mgr. / Coordinator / Exec. Asst.	Ryan Lichtenfels / Chase Flanigan / Colleen McKinnon
Strength & Conditioning Coach	Mark Fitzgerald
Athletic Trainers, Head / Assistant	Joe Huff / Mike Hannegan
Massage Therapist / Physical Therapist	James Partida / Kevin Taylor
Equipment Manager / Asst. Mgr. / Assistant	Doug Shearer / Chris Aldrich / Jeff Tyni
Team Physicians / Oral Surgeon	Orr Limpisvasti / Bao-Thy Grant

Legal

General Counsel / Asst. General Counsel	Bernard Schneider / Katie Rodin

Broadcasting

TV: FSN Prime Ticket (Cable)	John Ahlers, Brian Hayward
Radio: KLAA AM 830 & Ducks Radio Network	Steve Carroll, Dan Wood
Host-Producer / Postgame Radio Host	Kent French / Josh Brewster
Broadcasting Associate	Tiffany Spiritosanto

Communications

Director of Media & Communications	Alex Gilchrist
Media & Communications Manager / Publicist	Steve Hoem / Keren Lynch
Game Night Communications Staff	Steven Brown, Chelsea Gonye, Lisa Parris, Larry Woodard

Community Relations

Director of Community Relations	Wendy Arciero
Community Relations Managers / Coordinator	Jesse Bryson, Laura McNary / Ashley Forbes

Corporate Partnerships

Directors	Graham Siderius / Jason Weiss
Senior Manager	Derek Ohta

Corporate Partnership Activation

Corp. Partnership Activation Sr. Mgr. / Mgr.	Sarah Morales / Terri Awde
Media Services Associate / Activation Coordinators	Randy Bernabe / Adam Blue, Christian Young

Entertainment

Director of Production & Entertainment	Rich Cooley
Entertainment Manager / Associate	Davin Maske / Sarah Moews
Producer / Associate Producer	Peter Uvalle / Gabe Suarez, Josh Guereque
Digital Content Associate	Paul Janicki

Finance

Controller / Financial Analyst / Payroll	Melody Martin / Rosanna Sitzman / Regina Terrana
Accounting Asst. / Accounts Payable	Rob Dumlao / Lou Rae Campbell

Human Resources

H.R. Director / Managers	Gina Galasso / Wendy Mulhall, Donna Vass
Safety & Health Compliance Manager	Jeffery Trout
Human Resources Specialist / Associate	Esther Shimizu / Lisa Monson

Marketing/Brand Management

Director of Marketing & Brand Management	Matt Savant
Sr. Manager, Fan Development Marketing	Joseph Hwang
Fan Development Marketing Manager / Coords.	Champ Baginski / Jason Cooper, Ryan Herrman
Senior Media & Marketing Manager	Adam Mendelsohn
Marketing Manager / Associate	Trent Nielsen / Cindy Iwami
The Rinks, Marketing Manager / Coordinator	Jesse Chatfield / Craig Appleby
Marketing/Promotions Coordinators	G.M. Ciallella/Ryan Johnson
Graphic Designers, Senior / Juniors	Mariana Koontz / Jeff Ipjian, Ruben Segura

Merchandise, Team Store

Director of Merchandising	Jill Bauer
Retail Store Operations / Warehouse Mgr.	Matthew Kato / Andre Moyce

Publications and New Media

Publications & New Media Director / Associate	Adam Brady / Kyle Shohara
Social Media Producer	Anthony Manderichio

Premium Sales and Service

Director of Premium Sales & Service	Jim Panetta
Premium Account Executives	Casey Haakinson, Geoff Matthews, Timothy Thompson
Premium Services Manager / Coordinator	Jana Cannavo / Andrea Berryman

Signature Programs & Events

Senior Manager / Manager / Coordinator	Kris Loomis / Jamie Minkler / David Schenker

Ticket Sales and Customer Service

Director of Ticket Sales and Service	Lisa Johnson
Business Development & Retention Manager	Chris Kenyon
Group & Inside Sales Manager	Matt Payne

Ticketing

Senior Manager of Ticket Operations	James Bakken
Assistant Mgrs., Ticketing / Premium Ticketing	Jonas Calicdan / Gina Bulgheroni

Arizona Coyotes

Key Off-Season Signings/Acquisitions

2015

June 27 • Acquired D **Nicklas Grossmann** and the contract of D **Chris Pronger** from Philadelphia for C **Sam Gagner** and a conditional choice in the 2016 NHL Draft or a 3rd-round choice in 2017.

30 • Acquired C **Boyd Gordon** from Edmonton for LW **Lauri Korpikoski**.

July 1 • Signed C **Antoine Vermette**, RW Brad Richardson, D **Zbynek Michalek**, G **Anders Lindback**, RW **Steve Downie** and C **Dustin Jeffrey**.
1 • Re-signed D **Dylan Reese**.
2 • Signed D **Alex Grant**.
3 • Signed LW **Eric Selleck** and D **Derek Smith**.
7 • Re-signed LW **Mikkel Boedker**.
8 • Named John Slaney assistant coach.
10 • Signed LW **John Scott**.
15 • Re-signed D **Philip Samuelsson** and C **Brendan Shinnimin**.
20 • Re-signed D **Klas Dahlbeck** and LW **Jordan Martinook**.
Aug. 6 • Re-signed D **Brandon Gormley**.

2015-16 Schedule

Oct.					
Fri.	9	at Los Angeles	Tue.	12	Edmonton
Sat.	10	Pittsburgh	Thu.	14	Detroit
Wed.	14	at Anaheim	Sat.	16	New Jersey
Thu.	15	Minnesota	Mon.	18	Buffalo
Sat.	17	Boston	Thu.	21	San Jose
Tue.	20	at New Jersey	Sat.	23	Los Angeles
Thu.	22	at NY Rangers	Mon.	25	at Minnesota
Sat.	24	at Ottawa	Tue.	26	at Winnipeg
Mon.	26	at Toronto	**Feb.** Tue.	2	Los Angeles
Tue.	27	at Boston	Thu.	4	Chicago
Fri.	30	Vancouver	Fri.	5	at Anaheim
Nov. Thu.	5	Colorado	Wed.	10	Vancouver
Sat.	7	NY Rangers	Fri.	12	Calgary
Mon.	9	at Anaheim	Sat.	13	at San Jose
Tue.	10	at Los Angeles	Mon.	15	Montreal
Thu.	12	Edmonton	Thu.	18	Dallas
Sat.	14	at Columbus	Sat.	20	St. Louis
Mon.	16	at NY Islanders	Mon.	22	at Washington
Thu.	19	at Montreal	Tue.	23	at Tampa Bay
Sat.	21	at Winnipeg	Thu.	25	at Florida
Wed.	25	Anaheim	Sat.	27	at Philadelphia*
Fri.	27	Calgary	Mon.	29	at Pittsburgh
Sat.	28	Ottawa	**Mar.** Thu.	3	Anaheim
Dec. Tue.	1	at Nashville	Sat.	5	Florida
Thu.	3	at Detroit	Mon.	7	at Colorado
Fri.	4	at Buffalo	Wed.	9	at Vancouver
Sun.	6	at Carolina*	Fri.	11	at Calgary
Tue.	8	at St. Louis	Sat.	12	at Edmonton
Fri.	11	Minnesota	Thu.	17	San Jose
Sat.	12	Carolina	Sat.	19	Tampa Bay
Thu.	17	Columbus	Sun.	20	at San Jose
Sat.	19	NY Islanders	Tue.	22	Edmonton
Tue.	22	Toronto	Thu.	24	Dallas
Sat.	26	Los Angeles	Sat.	26	Philadelphia
Sun.	27	at Colorado	Mon.	28	Calgary
Tue.	29	Chicago	Thu.	31	at Dallas
Thu.	31	Winnipeg	**Apr.** Sat.	2	Washington
Jan. Sat.	2	at Edmonton*	Mon.	4	at St. Louis
Mon.	4	at Vancouver	Tue.	5	at Chicago
Thu.	7	at Calgary	Thu.	7	at Nashville
Sat.	9	Nashville	Sat.	9	at San Jose

* Denotes afternoon game.

Retired Numbers

7	Keith Tkachuk	1991-2001
9	Bobby Hull*	1972-1980
10	Dale Hawerchuk*	1981-1990
25	Thomas Steen*	1981-1995
27	Teppo Numminen*	1988-2003
97	Jeremy Roenick	1996-2001

* Winnipeg Jets

**PACIFIC DIVISION
37th NHL Season**

Franchise date: June 22, 1979

Transferred from Winnipeg to Phoenix, July 1, 1996.
Team name changed from Phoenix to Arizona, June 27, 2014.

2014-15 Results: 24w-50L-3OTL-5SOL 56PTS
4TH, Pacific Division • 14TH, Western Conference

Year-by-Year Record

		Home				Road				Overall							
Season	GP	W	L	OL		W	L	T	OL	W	L	T	OL	GF	GA	Pts.	Div. Fin.	Conf. Fin.	Playoff Result
2014-15	82	11	25		5	13	25		3	24	50		8	170	272	56	4th, Pac.	14th, West	Out of Playoffs
2013-14	82	22	14		5	15	16		10	37	30		15	216	231	89	4th, Pac.	9th, West	Out of Playoffs
2012-13	48	14	8		2	7	10		7	21	18		9	125	131	51	4th, Pac.	10th, West	Out of Playoffs
2011-12	82	22	13		6	20	14		7	42	27		13	216	204	97	1st, Pac.	3rd, West	Lost Conf. Final
2010-11	82	21	13		7	22	13		6	43	26		13	231	226	99	3rd, Pac.	6th, West	Lost Conf. Quarter-Final
2009-10	82	29	10		2	21	15		5	50	25		7	225	202	107	2nd, Pac.	4th, West	Lost Conf. Quarter-Final
2008-09	82	23	15		3	13	24		4	36	39		7	208	252	79	4th, Pac.	13th, West	Out of Playoffs
2007-08	82	17	20		4	21	17		3	38	37		7	214	231	83	4th, Pac.	@out of Playoffs	
2006-07	82	18	20		3	13	26		2	31	46		5	216	284	67	5th, Pac.	12th, West	Out of Playoffs
2005-06	82	19	18		4	19	21		1	38	39		5	246	271	81	5th, Pac.	12th, West	Out of Playoffs
2004-05	....	....				....				....				....	....	....			
2003-04	82	11	19	7	4	11	17	11	2	22	36	18	6	188	245	68	5th, Pac.	13th, West	Out of Playoffs
2002-03	82	17	16	6	2	14	19	5	3	31	35	11	5	204	230	78	4th, Pac.	11th, West	Out of Playoffs
2001-02	82	27	8	3	3	13	19	6	3	40	27	9	6	228	210	95	2nd, Pac.	6th, West	Lost Conf. Quarter-Final
2000-01	82	21	11	7	2	14	16	10	1	35	27	17	3	214	212	90	4th, Pac.	9th, West	Out of Playoffs
1999-2000	82	22	16	2	1	17	15	6	3	39	31	8	4	232	228	90	3rd, Pac.	6th, West	Lost Conf. Quarter-Final
1998-99	82	23	13	5	....	16	18	7	....	39	31	12	....	205	197	90	4th, Pac.	6th, West	Lost Conf. Quarter-Final
1997-98	82	19	16	6	....	16	19	6	....	35	35	12	....	224	227	82	4th, Cen.	6th, West	Lost Conf. Quarter-Final
1996-97	82	15	19	7	....	23	18	0	....	38	37	7	....	240	243	83	3rd, Cen.	4th, West	Lost Conf. Quarter-Final
1995-96*	82	22	16	3	....	14	24	3	....	36	40	6	....	275	291	78	5th, Cen.	8th, West	Lost Conf. Quarter-Final
1994-95*	48	10	10	4	....	6	15	3	....	16	25	7	....	157	177	39	6th, Cen.	10th, West	Out of Playoffs
1993-94*	84	15	23	4	....	9	28	5	....	24	51	9	....	245	344	57	6th, Cen.	12th, West	Out of Playoffs
1992-93*	84	23	16	3	....	17	21	4	....	40	37	7	....	322	320	87	4th, Smythe		Lost Div. Semi-Final
1991-92*	80	20	14	6	....	13	18	9	....	33	32	15	....	251	244	81	4th, Smythe		Lost Div. Semi-Final
1990-91*	80	17	18	5	....	9	25	6	....	26	43	11	....	260	288	63	5th, Smythe		Out of Playoffs
1989-90*	80	22	13	5	....	15	19	6	....	37	32	11	....	298	290	85	3rd, Smythe		Lost Div. Semi-Final
1988-89*	80	17	18	5	....	9	24	7	....	26	42	12	....	300	355	64	5th, Smythe		Out of Playoffs
1987-88*	80	20	14	6	....	13	22	5	....	33	36	11	....	292	310	77	3rd, Smythe		Lost Div. Semi-Final
1986-87*	80	25	12	3	....	15	20	5	....	40	32	8	....	279	271	88	3rd, Smythe		Lost Div. Final
1985-86*	80	18	19	3	....	8	28	4	....	26	47	7	....	295	372	59	3rd, Smythe		Lost Div. Semi-Final
1984-85*	80	21	13	6	....	22	14	4	....	43	27	10	....	358	332	96	2nd, Smythe		Lost Div. Final
1983-84*	80	17	15	8	....	14	23	3	....	31	38	11	....	340	374	73	4th, Smythe		Lost Div. Semi-Final
1982-83*	80	22	16	2	....	11	23	6	....	33	39	8	....	311	333	74	4th, Smythe		Lost Div. Semi-Final
1981-82*	80	18	13	9	....	15	20	5	....	33	33	14	....	319	332	80	2nd, Norris		Lost Div. Semi-Final
1980-81*	80	7	25	8	....	2	32	6	....	9	57	14	....	246	400	32	6th, Smythe		Out of Playoffs
1979-80*	80	13	19	8	....	7	30	3	....	20	49	11	....	214	314	51	5th, Smythe		Out of Playoffs

* Winnipeg Jets

Oliver Ekman-Larsson led all NHL defensemen with 23 goals in 2014-15 and led the Coyotes in scoring with 43 points.

2015-16 Player Personnel

FORWARDS	HT	WT	*Age	Place of Birth	S	2014-15 Club
BOEDKER, Mikkel	6-0	211	25	Brondby, Denmark	L	Arizona
CHIPCHURA, Kyle	6-2	203	29	Westlock, AB	L	Arizona
CUNNINGHAM, Craig	5-10	184	25	Trail, BC	R	Bos-Prov (AHL)-Ari
DOAN, Shane	6-1	223	38	Halkirk, AB	R	Arizona
DOMI, Max	5-10	198	20	Winnipeg, MB	L	London
DOWNIE, Steve	5-11	191	28	Newmarket, ON	R	Pittsburgh
DUCLAIR, Anthony	5-11	185	20	Pointe-Claire, QC	L	NY Rangers-Quebec (QMJHL)
GAUDET, Tyler	6-3	205	22	Hamilton, ON	L	Arizona-Portland (AHL)
GORDON, Boyd	6-0	202	31	Unity, SK	R	Edmonton
HANZAL, Martin	6-6	230	28	Pisek, Czech.	L	Arizona
LESSIO, Lucas	6-1	212	22	Maple, ON	L	Arizona-Portland (AHL)
RICHARDSON, Brad	6-0	197	30	Belleville, ON	L	Vancouver
RIEDER, Tobias	5-11	190	22	Landshut, Germany	L	Arizona-Portland (AHL)
SAMUELSSON, Henrik	6-3	219	21	Pittsburgh, PA	R	Arizona-Portland (AHL)
SCOTT, John	6-8	259	33	St. Catharines, ON	L	San Jose
SZWARZ, Jordan	5-11	196	24	Burlington, ON	R	Arizona-Portland (AHL)
VERMETTE, Antoine	6-1	198	33	St-Agapit, QC	L	Arizona-Chicago
VITALE, Joe	5-11	205	30	St. Louis, MO	R	Arizona

DEFENSEMEN	HT	WT	*Age	Place of Birth	S	2014-15 Club
DAHLBECK, Klas	6-2	207	24	Katrineholm, Sweden	L	Chi-Rockford-Ari-Port (AHL)
EKMAN-LARSSON, Oliver	6-2	190	24	Karlskrona, Sweden	L	Arizona
GORMLEY, Brandon	6-2	196	23	Murray River, PE	L	Arizona-Portland (AHL)
GROSSMANN, Nicklas	6-4	230	30	Stockholm, Sweden	L	Philadelphia
MICHALEK, Zbynek	6-2	210	32	Jindrichuv Hradec, Czech.	R	Arizona-St. Louis
MURPHY, Connor	6-3	205	22	Dublin, OH	R	Arizona
STONE, Michael	6-3	210	25	Winnipeg, MB	R	Arizona

GOALTENDERS	HT	WT	*Age	Place of Birth	C	2014-15 Club
LINDBACK, Anders	6-6	210	27	Gavle, Sweden	L	Dallas-Texas-Buffalo
SMITH, Mike	6-4	215	33	Kingston, ON	L	Arizona

* – Age at start of 2015-16 season

Captain of the team since 2003-04, Shane Doan is the franchise's all-time leader in games played and enters 2015-16 just 12 goals, 24 assists, and 32 points from taking over top spot in those categories as well.

2014-15 Scoring
* – rookie

Regular Season

Pos	#	Player	Team	GP	G	A	Pts	TOI	+/-	PIM	PP	SH	GW	S	S%
D	23	Oliver Ekman-Larsson	ARI	82	23	20	43	25:12	-18	40	10	1	7	264	8.7
C	9	Sam Gagner	ARI	81	15	26	41	17:14	-28	28	6	0	1	183	8.2
R	19	Shane Doan	ARI	79	14	22	36	18:52	-29	65	5	0	0	189	7.4
R	10	Martin Erat	ARI	79	9	23	32	15:51	-16	48	3	0	1	91	9.9
R	36	Mark Arcobello	EDM	36	7	5	12	15:22	-7	12	0	0	0	54	13.0
			NSH	4	1	0	1	10:35	0	0	0	0	0	3	33.3
			PIT	10	0	2	2	12:05	1	2	0	0	0	13	0.0
			ARI	27	9	7	16	15:40	-4	6	1	0	2	59	15.3
			Total	77	17	14	31	14:48	-10	20	1	0	2	129	13.2
L	89	Mikkel Boedker	ARI	45	14	14	28	17:29	-10	6	3	0	2	79	17.7
C	11	Martin Hanzal	ARI	37	8	16	24	17:44	-1	31	1	0	3	85	9.4
C	8 *	Tobias Rieder	ARI	72	13	8	21	16:53	-19	14	0	3	1	189	6.9
C	28	Lauri Korpikoski	ARI	69	6	15	21	15:14	-27	12	5	0	1	82	7.3
D	26	Michael Stone	ARI	81	3	15	18	20:52	-24	60	0	0	0	144	2.1
C	24	Kyle Chipchura	ARI	70	4	10	14	13:23	-23	82	1	0	0	81	4.9
R	18	David Moss	ARI	60	4	8	12	12:54	-18	24	1	0	0	96	4.2
D	17	John Moore	NYR	38	1	5	6	15:06	7	19	0	0	0	56	1.8
			ARI	19	1	4	5	18:43	-11	11	0	0	0	21	4.8
			Total	57	2	9	11	16:18	-4	30	0	0	0	77	2.6
C	14	Joe Vitale	ARI	70	3	6	9	11:13	-11	36	0	0	0	55	5.5
D	5	Connor Murphy	ARI	73	4	3	7	16:48	-27	42	0	0	0	72	5.6
L	22 *	Craig Cunningham	BOS	32	2	1	3	10:06	-4	2	0	1	0	31	6.5
			ARI	19	1	3	4	11:05	-3	2	0	0	0	23	4.3
			Total	51	3	4	7	10:28	-7	4	0	1	0	54	5.6
L	20	Tye McGinn	S.J.	33	1	4	5	10:20	1	11	0	0	0	35	2.9
			ARI	18	1	1	2	9:39	-1	10	0	0	0	25	4.0
			Total	51	2	5	7	10:06	0	21	0	0	0	60	3.3
R	44	B.J. Crombeen	ARI	58	3	3	6	8:05	-6	79	0	0	0	43	7.0
L	38 *	Lucas Lessio	ARI	26	2	3	5	12:45	-10	4	0	0	0	44	4.5
D	33 *	Brandon Gormley	ARI	27	2	2	4	15:19	-7	10	1	0	0	39	5.1
D	34 *	Klas Dahlbeck	CHI	4	1	0	1	10:23	-1	0	0	0	0	4	25.0
			ARI	19	0	3	3	19:11	-7	6	0	0	0	16	0.0
			Total	23	1	3	4	17:39	-8	8	0	0	0	20	5.0
C	12	Justin Hodgman	ARI	5	1	0	1	11:23	-2	2	1	0	0	3	33.3
R	21	Jordan Szwarz	ARI	9	1	0	1	13:28	-2	2	0	0	0	8	12.5
L	48 *	Jordan Martinook	ARI	8	0	1	1	11:41	-3	0	0	0	0	8	0.0
C	39 *	Brendan Shinnimin	ARI	12	0	1	1	11:02	-1	4	0	0	0	10	0.0
D	45	Andrew Campbell	ARI	33	0	1	1	17:32	-13	10	0	0	0	28	0.0
D	46	Dylan Reese	ARI	1	0	0	0	19:58	-1	0	0	0	0	1	0.0
C	32 *	Tyler Gaudet	ARI	2	0	0	0	9:34	-1	0	0	0	0	1	0.0
C	49	Alexandre Bolduc	ARI	3	0	0	0	10:39	-1	2	0	0	0	3	0.0
C	15 *	Henrik Samuelsson	ARI	3	0	0	0	13:16	-2	2	0	0	0	4	0.0
D	25 *	Philip Samuelsson	ARI	4	0	0	0	16:53	-3	0	0	0	0	4	0.0

Goaltending

No.	Goaltender	GPI	Mins	Avg	W	L	OT	EN	SO	GA	SA	Sv%	G	A	PIM
40	Devan Dubnyk	19	1035	2.72	9	5	2	0	1	47	561	.916	0	0	0
35	* Louis Domingue	7	308	2.73	1	2	1	1	0	14	158	.911	0	0	0
41	Mike Smith	62	3556	3.16	14	42	5	13	0	187	1955	.904	0	1	10
43	Mike McKenna	1	60	5.00	0	1	0	0	0	5	34	.853	0	0	0
	Totals	82	4995	3.21	24	50	8	14	1	267	2722	.902			

Don Maloney
General Manager
Born: Lindsay, ON, September 5, 1958.

Don Maloney was signed as the general manager of the Arizona Coyotes on May 30, 2007. In eight seasons as general manager, Maloney has guided the team to a 291-252-79 record and three postseason appearances. He ranks first all-time in franchise history in wins and points (661) by a general manager.

In 2009-10, Maloney led the Coyotes to the most successful regular season in team history by setting club records with 50 wins and 107 points. He was honored as the inaugural winner of the NHL General Manager of the Year Award in 2010. In 2011-12, the Coyotes won their first division title in franchise history and made their first appearance in the Western Conference Final.

Maloney joined the Coyotes from the New York Rangers for whom he served as vice president of player personnel and assistant general manager. He assisted Rangers' vice president and GM Glen Sather in all player transactions and contract negotiations and was involved with the team's professional and amateur scouting operations. Maloney spent 10 seasons in the Rangers' front office. He played a key role in the Rangers' development of several prospects into productive NHL players, including Henrik Lundqvist. Maloney also served as assistant general manager for Team Canada squads that won gold medals at the 2003 and 2004 World Championships.

Maloney's first front office position in the NHL was as assistant general manager of the New York Islanders following his retirement as a player with the club on January 17, 1991. Maloney later served as Islanders' general manager from August 17, 1992 to December 2, 1995. Among the players drafted during Maloney's tenure with the club were Todd Bertuzzi, Bryan McCabe, Ziggy Palffy, Tommy Salo and Darius Kasparaitis. Maloney then served as Eastern professional scout for the San Jose Sharks during the 1996-97 season prior to joining the Rangers' front office.

As a player, Maloney registered 214 goals, 350 assists and 564 points as well as 815 penalty minutes in 765 regular- season games over 13 NHL campaigns with the Rangers, Hartford Whalers and Islanders. He also collected 22 goals, 35 assists and 57 points in 94 career playoff games. Maloney spent 11 seasons with the Rangers after being selected by the club in the second round (26th overall) of the 1978 NHL Draft. He helped lead the Rangers to the 1979 Stanley Cup Final by posting 20 points (7 goals, 13 assists) that postseason, a playoff record for rookies at the time. Maloney played in the NHL All-Star Game in 1983 and 1984. He was named MVP of the 1984 game.

General Managers' History

John Ferguson, 1979-80 to 1987-88; John Ferguson and Mike Smith, 1988-89; Mike Smith, 1989-90 to 1992-93; Mike Smith and John Paddock, 1993-94; John Paddock, 1994-95, 1995-96; John Paddock and Bobby Smith, 1996-97; Bobby Smith, 1997-98 to 1999-2000; Bobby Smith and Cliff Fletcher, 2000-01; Michael Barnett, 2001-02 to 2006-07; Don Maloney, 2007-08 to date.

Captains' History

Lars-Erik Sjoberg, 1979-80; Morris Lukowich and Scott Campbell, 1980-81; Dave Christian and Barry Long, 1981-82; Dave Christian and Lucien DeBlois, 1982-83; Lucien DeBlois, 1983-84; Dale Hawerchuk, 1984-85 to 1988-89; Randy Carlyle, Dale Hawerchuk and Thomas Steen (tri-captains), 1989-90; Randy Carlyle and Thomas Steen (co-captains), 1990-91; Troy Murray, 1991-92; Troy Murray and Dean Kennedy, 1992-93; Dean Kennedy and Keith Tkachuk, 1993-94; Keith Tkachuk, 1994-95; Kris King, 1995-96; Keith Tkachuk, 1996-97 to 2000-01; Teppo Numminen, 2001-02, 2002-03; Shane Doan, 2003-04 to date.

Coaching History

Tom McVie and Bill Sutherland, 1979-80; Tom McVie, Bill Sutherland and Mike Smith, 1980-81; Tom Watt, 1981-82, 1982-83; Tom Watt and Barry Long, 1983-84; Barry Long, 1984-85; Barry Long and John Ferguson, 1985-86; Dan Maloney, 1986-87, 1987-88; Dan Maloney and Rick Bowness, 1988-89; Bob Murdoch, 1989-90, 1990-91; John Paddock, 1991-92 to 1993-94; John Paddock and Terry Simpson, 1994-95; Terry Simpson, 1995-96; Don Hay, 1996-97; Jim Schoenfeld, 1997-98, 1998-99; Bob Francis, 1999-2000 to 2002-03; Bob Francis and Rick Bowness, 2003-04; Rick Bowness, 2004-05; Wayne Gretzky, 2005-06 to 2008-09; Dave Tippett, 2009-10 to date.

Club Records

Team

(Figures in brackets for season records are games played; records for fewest points, wins, ties, losses, goals, goals against are for 70 or more games)

Most Points	**107**	2009-10 (82)
Most Wins	**50**	2009-10 (82)
Most Ties	**18**	2003-04 (82)
Most Losses	**57**	1980-81 (80)
Most Goals	**358**	1984-85 (80)
Most Goals Against	**400**	1980-81 (80)
Fewest Points	**32**	1980-81 (80)
Fewest Wins	**9**	1980-81 (80)
Fewest Ties	**6**	1995-96 (82)
Fewest Losses	**25**	2009-10 (82)
Fewest Goals	**165**	2014-15 (82)
Fewest Goals Against	**197**	1998-99 (82)
Longest Winning Streak		
Overall	**13**	Dec. 6-28/13
Home	**10**	Nov. 21-Dec. 29/09
Away	**8**	Feb. 25-Apr. 6/85
Longest Undefeated Streak		
Overall	**14**	Oct. 25-Nov. 28/98 (12W, 2T)
Home	**11**	Dec. 23/83-Feb. 5/84 (6W, 5T), Oct. 15-Dec. 20/98 (10W, 1T)
Away	**9**	Feb. 25-Apr. 7/85 (8W, 1T), Dec. 7/03-Jan. 9/04 (5W, 4T/OL)
Longest Losing Streak		
Overall	**10**	Nov. 30-Dec. 20/80, Feb. 6-25/94, Feb. 10-Mar. 3/15
Home	**6**	Oct. 6-Nov. 3/07, Jan. 27-Feb. 16/09, Mar. 12-30/15
Away	**13**	Jan. 26-Apr. 14/94
Longest Winless Streak		
Overall	***30**	Oct. 19-Dec. 20/80 (23L, 7T)
Home	**14**	Oct. 19-Dec. 14/80 (9L, 5T)
Away	**18**	Oct. 10-Dec. 20/80 (16L, 2T)
Most Shutouts, Season	**9**	1998-99 (82), 2010-11 (82)
Most PIM, Season	**2,278**	1987-88 (80)
Most Goals, Game	**12**	Feb. 25/85 (Wpg. 12 at NYR 5)

Individual

Most Seasons	**19**	Shane Doan
Most Games	**1,394**	Shane Doan
Most Goals, Career	**379**	Dale Hawerchuk
Most Assists, Career	**553**	Thomas Steen
Most Points, Career	**929**	Dale Hawerchuk (379G, 550A)
Most PIM, Career	**1,508**	Keith Tkachuk
Most Shutouts, Career	**21**	Nikolai Khabibulin, Ilya Bryzgalov
Longest Consecutive Games Streak	**475**	Dale Hawerchuk (Dec. 19/82-Dec. 10/88)
Most Goals, Season	**76**	Teemu Selanne (1992-93)
Most Assists, Season	**79**	Phil Housley (1992-93)
Most Points, Season	**132**	Teemu Selanne (1992-93; 76G, 56A)
Most PIM, Season	**347**	Tie Domi (1993-94)
Most Points, Defenseman, Season	**97**	Phil Housley (1992-93; 18G, 79A)
Most Points, Center, Season	**130**	Dale Hawerchuk (1984-85; 53G, 77A)
Most Points, Right Wing, Season	**132**	Teemu Selanne (1992-93; 76G, 56A)
Most Points, Left Wing, Season	**98**	Keith Tkachuk (1995-96; 50G, 48A)
Most Points, Rookie, Season	***132**	Teemu Selanne (1992-93; 76G, 56A)
Most Shutouts, Season	**8**	Nikolai Khabibulin (1998-99), Ilya Bryzgalov (2009-10), Mike Smith (2011-12)
Most Goals, Game	**5**	Willy Lindstrom (Mar. 2/82), Alexei Zhamnov (Apr. 1/95)
Most Assists, Game	**5**	Dale Hawerchuk (Mar. 6/84), (Mar. 18/89), (Mar. 4/90), Phil Housley (Jan. 18/93), Keith Tkachuk (Feb. 23/01)
Most Points, Game	**6**	Willy Lindstrom (Mar. 2/82; 5G, 1A), Dale Hawerchuk (Dec. 14/83; 3G, 3A), (Mar. 5/88; 2G, 4A), (Mar. 18/89; 1G, 5A), Thomas Steen (Oct. 24/84; 2G, 4A), Ed Olczyk (Dec. 21/91; 2G, 4A)

* NHL Record.
Records include Winnipeg Jets, 1979-80 through 1995-96.

All-time Record vs. Other Clubs

Regular Season

	Total								At Home								On Road							
	GP	W	L	T	OL	GF	GA	PTS	GP	W	L	T	OL	GF	GA	PTS	GP	W	L	T	OL	GF	GA	PTS
Anaheim	115	45	55	5	10	304	345	105	57	26	24	2	5	161	166	59	58	19	31	3	5	143	179	46
Boston	71	21	42	7	1	214	266	50	36	14	18	3	1	111	120	32	35	7	24	4	0	103	146	18
Buffalo	72	23	40	7	2	192	254	55	35	14	18	2	1	99	112	31	37	9	22	5	1	93	142	24
Calgary	182	75	85	20	2	597	657	172	90	45	34	11	0	319	293	101	92	30	51	9	2	278	364	71
Carolina	72	29	31	8	4	231	249	70	36	15	16	2	3	125	132	35	36	14	15	6	1	106	117	35
Chicago	135	56	59	15	5	379	451	132	69	35	27	5	2	212	215	77	66	21	32	10	3	167	236	55
Colorado	118	49	49	12	8	394	393	118	59	25	22	7	5	204	196	62	59	24	27	5	3	190	197	56
Columbus	51	28	17	4	2	144	119	62	26	16	7	3	0	80	56	35	25	12	10	1	2	64	63	27
Dallas	167	69	76	13	9	480	534	160	83	37	38	4	4	246	257	82	84	32	38	9	5	234	277	78
Detroit	135	47	60	22	6	414	474	122	67	23	27	14	3	195	214	63	68	24	33	8	3	219	260	59
Edmonton	184	74	92	11	7	653	747	166	91	41	41	5	4	353	368	91	93	33	51	6	3	300	379	75
Florida	28	15	8	3	2	73	74	35	15	7	3	3	2	40	39	19	13	8	5	0	0	33	35	16
Los Angeles	212	104	76	25	7	761	711	240	107	60	34	11	2	404	331	133	105	44	42	14	5	357	380	107
Minnesota	53	23	23	3	4	126	136	53	27	12	12	1	2	66	67	27	26	11	11	2	2	60	69	26
Montreal	68	14	43	9	2	180	286	39	34	10	16	7	1	105	127	28	34	4	27	2	1	75	159	11
Nashville	61	28	22	2	9	161	179	67	30	17	9	0	4	87	90	38	31	11	13	2	5	74	89	29
New Jersey	70	38	23	9	0	226	203	85	36	25	8	3	0	130	94	53	34	13	15	6	0	96	109	32
NY Islanders	71	25	33	12	1	223	255	63	36	15	16	4	1	122	122	35	35	10	17	8	0	101	133	28
NY Rangers	72	25	36	6	5	240	271	61	36	15	16	4	1	120	119	35	36	10	20	2	4	120	152	26
Ottawa	31	13	15	2	1	93	112	29	15	6	7	1	1	46	55	14	16	7	8	1	0	47	57	15
Philadelphia	73	27	42	2	2	213	267	58	36	16	18	2	0	115	118	34	37	11	24	0	2	98	149	24
Pittsburgh	72	28	39	3	2	226	259	61	36	16	15	3	2	129	123	37	36	12	24	0	0	97	136	24
St. Louis	138	56	62	18	2	390	446	132	69	33	29	7	0	209	224	73	69	23	33	11	2	181	222	59
San Jose	129	57	56	7	9	360	391	130	66	32	26	3	5	191	186	72	63	25	30	4	4	169	205	58
Tampa Bay	33	15	18	0	0	92	106	30	18	8	10	0	0	44	49	16	15	7	8	0	0	48	57	14
Toronto	92	49	34	8	1	360	321	107	44	24	14	6	0	182	153	54	48	25	20	2	1	178	168	53
Vancouver	182	70	87	20	5	548	631	165	89	44	33	10	2	300	295	100	93	26	54	10	3	248	336	65
Washington	71	28	29	12	2	224	256	70	35	18	9	7	1	123	119	44	36	10	20	5	1	101	137	26
Winnipeg	22	14	4	1	3	66	50	32	12	9	1	1	1	40	25	20	10	5	3	0	2	26	25	12
Totals	**2780**	**1145**	**1256**	**266**	**113**	**8564**	**9443**	**2669**	**1390**	**658**	**548**	**131**	**53**	**4558**	**4465**	**1500**	**1390**	**487**	**708**	**135**	**60**	**4006**	**4978**	**1169**

Playoffs

	Series	W	L	GP	W	L	T	GF	GA	Last Mtg.	Rnd.	Result
Anaheim	1	0	1	7	3	4	0	17	17	1997	CQF	L 3-4
Calgary	3	2	1	13	7	6	0	45	43	1987	DSF	W 4-2
Chicago	1	1	0	6	4	2	0	17	12	2012	CQF	W 4-2
Colorado	1	0	1	5	1	4	0	10	17	2000	CQF	L 1-4
Detroit	4	0	4	23	7	16	0	56	88	2011	CQF	L 0-4
Edmonton	6	0	6	26	4	22	0	75	120	1990	DSF	L 3-4
Los Angeles	1	0	1	5	1	4	0	8	14	2012	CF	L 1-4
Nashville	1	1	0	5	4	1	0	12	9	2012	CSF	W 4-1
St. Louis	2	0	2	11	4	7	0	29	39	1999	CQF	L 3-4
San Jose	1	0	1	5	1	4	0	7	13	2002	CQF	L 1-4
Vancouver	2	0	2	13	5	8	0	34	50	1993	DSF	L 2-4
Totals	**23**	**4**	**19**	**119**	**41**	**78**	**0**	**310**	**422**			

Playoff Results 2015-2011

Year	Round	Opponent	Result	GF	GA
2012	CF	Los Angeles	L 1-4	8	14
	CSF	Nashville	W 4-1	12	9
	CQF	Chicago	W 4-2	17	12
2011	CQF	Detroit	L 0-4	10	18

Abbreviations: Round: CF – conference final; **CSF** – conference semi-final; **CQF** – conference quarter-final; **DSF** – division semi-final.

Calgary totals include Atlanta Flames, 1979-80.
Colorado totals include Quebec, 1979-80 to 1994-95.
New Jersey totals include Colorado Rockies, 1979-80 to 1981-82.
Carolina totals include Hartford, 1979-80 to 1996-97.
Dallas totals include Minnesota North Stars, 1979-80 to 1992-93.
Winnipeg totals include Atlanta Thrashers, 1999-2000 to 2010-11.

2014-15 Results

Oct.	9	Winnipeg	2-6		13	San Jose	2-3
	11	Los Angeles	3-2*		15	Calgary	1-4
	15	Edmonton	7-4		17	at Minnesota	1-3
	18	St. Louis	1-6		18	at Winnipeg	3-4†
	21	at Nashville	3-4†		20	at Chicago	1-6
	23	at Minnesota	0-2		27	at Philadelphia	3-4†
	25	Florida	2-1*		29	at Toronto	3-1
	28	at Tampa Bay	3-7		31	at Ottawa	2-7
	30	at Florida	1-2	**Feb.**	1	at Montreal	3-2
Nov.	1	at Carolina	0-3		3	at Columbus	4-1
	2	at Washington	6-5		5	Carolina	1-2†
	4	Toronto	3-2		7	Detroit	1-3
	7	at Anaheim	3-2†		9	at Chicago	3-2†
	8	NY Islanders	0-1		10	at St. Louis	1-2
	11	Dallas	3-4		13	San Jose	2-4
	13	at Calgary	3-5		14	NY Rangers	1-5
	14	at Vancouver	5-0		16	at Colorado	2-5
	16	at Edmonton	2-1		21	Tampa Bay	2-4
	18	Washington	1-2*		23	at New Jersey	0-3
	20	at Dallas	1-3		24	at NY Islanders	1-5
	22	at San Jose	4-3†		26	at NY Rangers	3-4
	23	at Anaheim	1-2		28	at Boston	1-4
	25	Colorado	3-4*	**Mar.**	3	Anaheim	1-4
	29	Calgary	0-3		5	Vancouver	3-2†
Dec.	1	at Edmonton	5-2		7	Montreal	0-2
	2	at Calgary	2-5		9	Nashville	1-2*
	4	Los Angeles	0-4		12	Chicago	1-2
	6	Boston	2-5		14	New Jersey	1-4
	11	Nashville	1-5		16	at Los Angeles	0-1
	13	Minnesota	3-4†		19	Colorado	2-5
	16	Edmonton	2-1*		21	Pittsburgh	1-3
	20	at Los Angeles	2-4		22	Vancouver	1-3
	22	at Vancouver	1-7		24	at Detroit	5-4*
	23	at Edmonton	5-1		26	at Buffalo	4-3*
	27	Anaheim	2-1†		28	at Pittsburgh	2-3
	29	Philadelphia	4-2		30	Buffalo	1-4
	31	at Dallas	0-6	**Apr.**	3	at San Jose	1-3
Jan.	3	Columbus	6-3		4	San Jose	5-3
	6	St. Louis	0-6		7	at Calgary	2-3
	8	Winnipeg	4-1		9	at Vancouver	0-5
	10	Ottawa	1-5		11	Anaheim	1-2

* – Overtime † – Shootout

NHL Draft Selections 2015-2001

Name in bold denotes played in NHL.

2015
Pick
- 3 Dylan Strome
- 30 Nicholas Merkley
- 32 Christian Fischer
- 63 Kyle Capobianco
- 76 Adin Hill
- 81 Brendan Warren
- 83 Jens Looke
- 123 Conor Garland
- 183 Erik Kallgren

2014
Pick
- 12 Brendan Perlini
- 43 Ryan MacInnis
- 58 Christian Dvorak
- 87 Anton Karlsson
- 117 Michael Bunting
- 133 Dysin Mayo
- 163 David Westlund
- 191 Jared Fiegl
- 193 Edgars Kulda

2013
Pick
- 12 Max Domi
- 39 Laurent Dauphin
- 62 Pavel Laplante
- 133 Connor Clifton
- 163 Brendan Burke
- 193 Jedd Soleway

2012
Pick
- 27 **Henrik Samuelsson**
- 58 **Jordan Martinook**
- 88 James Melindy
- 102 Rhett Holland
- 148 Niklas Tikkinen
- 178 Hunter Fejes
- 184 Marek Langhamer
- 208 Justin Hache

2011
Pick
- 20 **Connor Murphy**
- 51 Alexander Ruuttu
- 56 **Lucas Lessio**
- 84 Harrison Ruopp
- 111 Kale Kessy
- 141 Darian Dziurzynski
- 155 Andrew Fritsch
- 196 Zac Larraza

2010
Pick
- 13 **Brandon Gormley**
- 27 **Mark Visentin**
- 52 Phil Lane
- 57 **Oscar Lindberg**
- 138 **Louis Domingue**

2009
Pick
- 6 **Oliver Ekman-Larsson**
- 36 **Chris Brown**
- 91 Mike Lee
- 97 **Jordan Szwarz**
- 105 Justin Weller
- 157 Evan Bloodoff

2008
Pick
- 8 **Mikkel Boedker**
- 28 **Viktor Tikhonov**
- 49 **Jared Staal**
- 69 **Michael Stone**
- 76 Mathieu Brodeur
- 99 Colin Long
- 159 Brett Hextall
- 189 Tim Billingsley

2007
Pick
- 3 **Kyle Turris**
- 30 Nick Ross
- 32 **Brett Maclean**
- 36 Joel Gistedt
- 103 Vladimir Ruzicka
- 123 Maxim Goncharov
- 153 **Scott Darling**

2006
Pick
- 8 **Peter Mueller**
- 29 **Chris Summers**
- 88 Jonas Ahnelov
- 130 Brett Bennett
- 131 Martin Latal
- 152 Jordan Bendfeld
- 188 Chris Frank
- 196 **Benn Ferriero**

2005
Pick
- 17 **Martin Hanzal**
- 59 Pier-Olivier Pelletier
- 105 **Keith Yandle**
- 148 Anton Krysanov
- 212 Pat Brosnihan

2004
Pick
- 5 **Blake Wheeler**
- 35 Logan Stephenson
- 50 **Enver Lisin**
- 103 Roman Tomanek
- 119 **Kevin Porter**
- 168 Kevin Cormier
- 199 **Chad Kolarik**
- 240 **Aaron Gagnon**
- 261 Will Engasser
- 265 **Daniel Winnik**

2003
Pick
- 77 Tyler Redenbach
- 80 Dmitri Pestunov
- 115 Liam Lindstrom
- 178 Ryan Gibbons
- 208 Randall Gelech
- 242 Eduard Lewandowski
- 272 Sean Sullivan
- 290 Loic Burkhalter

2002
Pick
- 19 Jakub Koreis
- 23 **Ben Eager**
- 46 **David LeNeveu**
- 70 **Joe Callahan**
- 80 **Matt Jones**
- 97 Lance Monych
- 132 **John Zeiler**
- 186 Jeff Pietrasiak
- 216 Ladislav Kouba
- 249 Marcus Smith
- 280 Russell Spence

2001
Pick
- 11 **Fredrik Sjostrom**
- 31 **Matthew Spiller**
- 45 Martin Podlesak
- 78 Beat Forster
- 148 David Klema
- 180 Scott Polaski
- 210 Steve Belanger
- 243 Frantisek Lukes
- 273 Severin Blindenbacher

Dave Tippett
Head Coach
Born: Moosomin, SK, August 25, 1961.

Dave Tippett was named the 17th head coach in Coyotes franchise history on September 24, 2009. In his six seasons as the Coyotes head coach, he has compiled a 217-176-65 record (499 points) and three postseason appearances. Tippett is the all-time winningest coach in franchise history while his .545 points percentage is the highest of any head coach in team history.

In 2011-12, Tippett led the Coyotes to a 42-27-13 record (97 points) and the franchise's first division title. The Coyotes also won their first postseason series since arriving in Arizona (1996) and advanced to the Western Conference Final for the first time in franchise history. In his first season with the team in 2009-10, Tippett guided the Coyotes to a club-record 50 wins and 107 points and the team's first playoff appearance since 2001-02. Tippett was rewarded with the Jack Adams Award as coach of the year.

Prior to Arizona, Tippett spent seven seasons as the head coach of the Dallas Stars from 2002-03 to 2008-09. Under Tippett's leadership, the Stars won two Pacific Division titles (2002-03 and 2005-06), made the playoffs in five out of six years and reached the Western conference final in 2008. His 271 career regular season coaching victories rank him second all-time in Stars history.

Tippett joined the Stars organization on May 16, 2002 after serving as an assistant coach with the Los Angeles Kings for three seasons. Prior to becoming a coach, Tippett played 11 years as a forward in the National Hockey League with the Hartford Whalers, Washington Capitals, Pittsburgh Penguins and Philadelphia Flyers. He played 721 career NHL games collecting 93 goals and 169 assists for 262 points and 317 penalty minutes. He ended his playing career in 1995 as a player-assistant coach with the Houston Aeros (IHL).

Internationally, Tippett captained the 1984 Canadian Olympic team in Sarajevo, Yugoslavia, and he earned a silver medal as a member of the Canadian Olympic team in Albertville, France, in 1992. He was a member of the 1982 NCAA Division I championship squad at the University of North Dakota. Tippett became the head coach of the Houston Aeros in 1995-96. In 1999, he led the team to the Turner Cup championship and was named the IHL coach of the year.

Coaching Record

			Regular Season				Playoffs			
Season	Team	League	GC	W	L	O/T	GC	W	L	T
1995-96	Houston	IHL	42	17	18	7	....	....	....	....
1996-97	Houston	IHL	82	44	30	8	13	8	5	....
1997-98	Houston	IHL	82	50	22	10	4	1	3	....
1998-99	Houston	IHL	82	54	15	13	19	11	8	....
2002-03	**Dallas**	**NHL**	**82**	**46**	**17**	**19**	**12**	**6**	**6**	....
2003-04	**Dallas**	**NHL**	**82**	**41**	**26**	**15**	**5**	**1**	**4**	....
2004-05	**Dallas**				SEASON CANCELLED					
2005-06	**Dallas**	**NHL**	**82**	**53**	**23**	**6**	**5**	**1**	**4**	....
2006-07	**Dallas**	**NHL**	**82**	**50**	**25**	**7**	**7**	**3**	**4**	....
2007-08	**Dallas**	**NHL**	**82**	**45**	**30**	**7**	**18**	**10**	**8**	....
2008-09	**Dallas**	**NHL**	**82**	**36**	**35**	**11**	....	....	....	....
2009-10	**Phoenix**	**NHL**	**82**	**50**	**25**	**7**	**7**	**3**	**4**	....
2010-11	**Phoenix**	**NHL**	**82**	**43**	**26**	**13**	**4**	**0**	**4**	....
2011-12	**Phoenix**	**NHL**	**82**	**42**	**27**	**13**	**16**	**9**	**7**	....
2012-13	**Phoenix**	**NHL**	**48**	**21**	**18**	**9**	....	....	....	....
2013-14	**Phoenix**	**NHL**	**82**	**37**	**30**	**15**	....	....	....	....
2014-15	**Arizona**	**NHL**	**82**	**24**	**50**	**8**	....	....	....	....
	NHL Totals		**950**	**488**	**332**	**130**	**74**	**33**	**41**	....

Jack Adams Award (2010)

Posted a 2-1-2 record as replacement coach when Andy Murray was sidelined following a car accident, February 26 to March 6, 2002, All games are credited to Murray's coaching record.

Club Directory

Gila River Arena

Arizona Coyotes
Gila River Arena
9400 W. Maryland Avenue
Glendale, AZ 85305
Phone **623/772-3200**
FAX 623/772-3201
Tickets 480/563-PUCK
www.ArizonaCoyotes.com
Capacity: 17,125

Club Officers and Executives

Governor	Andrew Barroway
President, CEO & Alt. Governor	Anthony LeBlanc
Executive Vice President, G.M. & Alt. Governor	Don Maloney
Executive Vice President, Corporate & Suite Sales	Mike Humes
Executive Vice President, Ticket Sales & Strategy	Jeff Morander
Senior Vice President & Assistant G.M.	Darcy Regier
Assistant G.M.s, Hockey Ops / Analytics	Chris O'Hearn / John Chayka
Chief Financial Officer	Gregg Olson
Chief Marketing Officer	John Pierce
Vice President of Communications	Rich Nairn
Exec. Asst. to the President & CEO	Karen Gilbert
Exec. Asst. to the Governor & Board of Directors	Moki Salazar

Hockey Operations

Head Coach	Dave Tippett
Coaches, Associate / Assistants	Jim Playfair / Newell Brown, John Slaney
Goaltending Coaches	Jon Elkin, Corey Schwab
Development Coach / Sr. Advisor	Steve Sullivan / Dave King
Video Coach / Strength & Conditioning Coach	Steve Peters / JP Major
Director of Hockey Operations & Analytics	Bob Teofilo
Executive Assistant, Hockey Ops	Ashley James
Head Athletic Trainer / Assistant Trainer	Jason Serbus / Mike Ermatinger
Manual Therapist	Mike Griebel
Equipment: Head Mgr. / Mgr. / Asst. Mgr.	Stan Wilson / Tony Silva / Jason Rudee
Manager of Team Services	Rick Braunstein
Team Services Coordinator & Security	Jim O'Neal
Scouting Directors, Amateur / Pro	Tim Bernhardt / Frank Effinger
Asst. Director of Amateur Scouting	Jeff Twohey
Professional Scouts	David MacLean, Doug Soetaert, Jim Roque
European Scouts	Thomas Carlsson, Max Kolu, Robert Neuhauser
Amateur Scouts	Trevor Hanson, Rob Pulford, Mike Sands, Victor Posa, Bobby Vermette, Glen Zacharias
Team Internist / Orthopedic Surgeons	Drs. Robert Luberto / Brian Shafer, Gary Waslewski
Team Dentist / Opthalmologists	Drs. Byron J. Larsen / George Reiss, Jeffery Edelstein
Springfield (AHL) Coaches, Head / Assistants	Ron Rolston / Mike Bavis, Doug Janik
Springfield (AHL) Athletic Trainer	Mike Booi

Broadcasting

Director of Broadcasting	Doug Cannon
TV Play-by-Play / Color / Host	Matt McConnell / Tyson Nash / Todd Walsh
Radio Play-by-Play Announcer / Color / Host	Bob Heethuis / Nick Boynton / Luke Lapinski

Communications

Sr. Director of News Content	Dave Vest
Media Relations Director / Coordinator	Chris Wojcik / Greg Dillard

Community Relations

Exec. Dir. of Arizona Coyotes Foundation / Manager	Liz Kaplan / Ali Smith
Community Relations Director / Mgr. / Coord.	Olivia Campos / Rachel Korchin / Natalia Protopopoff

Corporate Partnerships & Service

Sr. Director of Corporate Partnerships	Leo Edwards
Sr. Advisor, Business Dev. & Alumni Relations	Cale Hulse
Corporate Partnerships Managers	Mike Akers, Marshall Spalding, Jamie Quint
Corporate Partnerships Service Mgr. / Coords.	Lindsay Foletta, Taylor Popish, Matt Carnot

Finance & Accounting

Controller	David Montgomery
Administrators, Accounts Payable / Payroll	Jessica Fuentes / Lollie Gonzales
Financial Analyst / Staff Accountant	Mark Musallam / Tracy Pyrak, Chris Shelley

Game Presentation

Director of Game Presentation / Coordinator	TBD / Casey Rusnak

Human Resources

Human Resources Manager	Patty Frankenfield
Receptionist	Jessica Glass

Marketing

Sr. Director Marketing	Amy Dimond
Sr. Manager, Creative & Web Services	Scott Jenner
Manager, Content Development/In-Game Host	Lindsey Smith
Managers, Social Media Strategy / CRM	Marissa O'Connor / Stephanie Richter
Manager, Fan Development & Youth Hockey	Matt Shott
Coordinators, Marketing / Mascot	Rebekah Schieck / Jeph Harris

Premium & Suite Sales

Sr. Director of Premium & Suite Sales	Grant Buckborough
Premium Seating Sr. Mgr. / Mgrs.	Mike Briody / Mike Ostrowski, James Whitener
Premium Seating Mgrs. / Service Mgr.	Matt McClelland, Dave Paris / Katrina Hinsberg

Production

Director of Production	Rachel Regnier
Video Graphic Coordinator	Robert Clark
Shooter/Editor	Jon Kingston, Jesse Aranda, Tim Page

Technology

Director of IT	Monty Low
IT Infrastructure Tech / IT Support	Justin Ferguson / Michael Wenzel

Ticket Operations

Sr. Director of Ticket Operations	Doug Vanderheyden
Ticket Operations Manager	Jakub Jaroszewicz
Ticket Operations Associate / Coordinator	Piriya Timratana / CJ Scherrer

Ticket Sales & Service

Vice President of Ticket Sales & Service	Bill Makris
Sr. Director Client Services & Guest Experience	Lindsay Kray
Director Business Development	Sam Bays

Team Information

Regional Sports Network / Radio Station	FOX Sports Arizona / Arizona Sports 98.7 FM
Team Photographer	Norm Hall

Boston Bruins

2014-15 Results: 41W-27L-4OTL-10SOL 96PTS
5TH, Atlantic Division • 9TH, Eastern Conference

Key Off-Season Signings/Acquisitions

2015

- **May 20** • Named **Don Sweeney** general manager.
- **June 26** • Acquired G **Martin Jones**, D **Colin Miller** and a 1st-round choice in the 2015 NHL Draft from Los Angeles for LW **Milan Lucic**.
- **29** • Acquired C **Zac Rinaldo** from Philadelphia for a 3rd-round choice in the 2017 NHL Draft.
- **30** • Re-signed D **Adam McQuaid**.
- **30** • Acquired C **Sean Kuraly** and a 1st-round choice in the 2016 NHL Draft from San Jose for G **Martin Jones**.
- **July 1** • Signed LW **Matt Beleskey**.
- **1** • Acquired RW **Jimmy Hayes** from Florida for RW **Reilly Smith** and the contract of C **Marc Savard**.
- **1** • Re-signed C **Ryan Spooner** and G **Jeremy Smith**.
- **2** • Re-signed D **Chris Breen**.
- **6** • Signed LW **Brandon Defazio**.
- **6** • Re-signed RW **Brett Connolly**.
- **10** • Signed D **Matt Irwin**.

2015-16 Schedule

Oct.	Thu.	8	Winnipeg		Wed.	13	at Philadelphia
	Sat.	10	Montreal		Fri.	15	at Buffalo
	Mon.	12	Tampa Bay*		Sat.	16	Toronto
	Wed.	14	at Colorado		Tue.	19	at Montreal
	Sat.	17	at Arizona		Thu.	21	Vancouver
	Wed.	21	Philadelphia		Sat.	23	Columbus
	Fri.	23	at NY Islanders		Mon.	25	at Philadelphia
	Tue.	27	Arizona		Tue.	26	Anaheim
	Fri.	30	at Florida	Feb.	Tue.	2	Toronto
	Sat.	31	at Tampa Bay		Thu.	4	at Buffalo
Nov.	Tue.	3	Dallas		Sat.	6	Buffalo
	Thu.	5	at Washington		Tue.	9	Los Angeles
	Sat.	7	at Montreal		Thu.	11	at Winnipeg
	Sun.	8	at NY Islanders*		Sat.	13	at Minnesota*
	Thu.	12	Colorado		Sun.	14	at Detroit*
	Sat.	14	Detroit		Tue.	16	at Columbus
	Tue.	17	San Jose		Thu.	18	at Nashville
	Thu.	19	Minnesota		Sat.	20	at Dallas
	Sat.	21	Toronto		Mon.	22	Columbus
	Mon.	23	at Toronto		Wed.	24	Pittsburgh
	Wed.	25	at Detroit		Fri.	26	at Carolina
	Fri.	27	NY Rangers*		Sun.	28	Tampa Bay
Dec.	Wed.	2	at Edmonton	Mar.	Tue.	1	Calgary
	Fri.	4	at Calgary		Thu.	3	Chicago
	Sat.	5	at Vancouver		Sat.	5	Washington
	Mon.	7	Nashville		Mon.	7	at Florida
	Wed.	9	at Montreal		Tue.	8	at Tampa Bay
	Sat.	12	Florida*		Thu.	10	Carolina
	Mon.	14	Edmonton		Sat.	12	NY Islanders*
	Wed.	16	Pittsburgh		Tue.	15	at San Jose
	Fri.	18	at Pittsburgh		Fri.	18	at Anaheim
	Sun.	20	New Jersey*		Sat.	19	at Los Angeles
	Tue.	22	St. Louis		Wed.	23	at NY Rangers
	Sat.	26	Buffalo		Thu.	24	Florida
	Sun.	27	at Ottawa*		Sat.	26	at Toronto
	Tue.	29	Ottawa		Tue.	29	at New Jersey
Jan.	Fri.	1	Montreal*	Apr.	Fri.	1	at St. Louis
	Tue.	5	Washington		Sun.	3	at Chicago*
	Fri.	8	at New Jersey		Tue.	5	Carolina
	Sat.	9	at Ottawa		Thu.	7	Detroit
	Mon.	11	at NY Rangers		Sat.	9	Ottawa*

* Denotes afternoon game.

Retired Numbers

2	Eddie Shore	1926-1940
3	Lionel Hitchman	1925-1934
4	Bobby Orr	1966-1976
5	Dit Clapper	1927-1947
7	Phil Esposito	1967-1975
8	Cam Neely	1986-1996
9	John Bucyk	1957-1978
15	Milt Schmidt	1936-1955
24	Terry O'Reilly	1971-1985
77	Raymond Bourque	1979-2000

ATLANTIC DIVISION
92nd NHL Season

Franchise date: November 1, 1924

Year-by-Year Record

		Home				Road				Overall									
Season	GP	W	L	T	OL	W	L	T	OL	W	L	T	OL	GF	GA	Pts.	Div. Fin.	Conf. Fin.	Playoff Result
2014-15	82	24	10	....	7	17	17	....	7	41	27	....	14	213	211	96	5th, Atl.	9th, East	Out of Playoffs
2013-14	82	31	7	....	3	23	12	....	6	54	19	....	9	261	177	117	1st, Atl.	1st, East	Lost Second Round
2012-13	48	16	5	....	3	12	9	....	3	28	14	....	6	131	109	62	2nd, NE	4th, East	Lost Final
2011-12	82	24	14	....	3	25	15	....	1	49	29	....	4	269	202	102	1st, NE	2nd, East	Lost Conf. Quarter-Final
2010-11	**82**	**22**	**13**	....	**6**	**24**	**12**	....	**5**	**46**	**25**	....	**11**	**246**	**195**	**103**	**1st, NE**	**3rd, East**	**Won Stanley Cup**
2009-10	82	18	17	....	6	21	13	....	7	39	30	....	13	206	200	91	3rd, NE	6th, East	Lost Conf. Semi-Final
2008-09	82	29	6	....	6	24	13	....	4	53	19	....	10	274	196	116	1st, NE	1st, East	Lost Conf. Semi-Final
2007-08	82	21	16	....	4	20	13	....	8	41	29	....	12	212	222	94	3rd, NE	8th, East	Lost Conf. Quarter-Final
2006-07	82	18	19	....	4	17	22	....	2	35	41	....	6	219	289	76	5th, NE	13th, East	Out of Playoffs
2005-06	82	16	15	....	10	13	22	....	6	29	37	....	16	230	266	74	5th, NE	13th, East	Out of Playoffs
2004-05	....	....	....	....	....	....	....	....	....	....	....	....	....	....	....	....			
2003-04	82	18	12	9	2	23	7	6	5	41	19	15	7	209	188	104	1st, NE	2nd, East	Lost Conf. Quarter-Final
2002-03	82	23	11	5	2	13	20	6	2	36	31	11	4	245	237	87	3rd, NE	7th, East	Lost Conf. Quarter-Final
2001-02	82	23	11	2	5	20	13	4	4	43	24	6	9	236	201	101	1st, NE	1st, East	Lost Conf. Quarter-Final
2000-01	82	21	12	5	3	15	18	3	5	36	30	8	8	227	249	88	4th, NE	9th, East	Out of Playoffs
1999-2000	82	12	17	11	1	12	16	8	5	24	33	19	6	210	248	73	5th, NE	12th, East	Out of Playoffs
1998-99	82	22	10	9	....	17	20	4	....	39	30	13	....	214	181	91	3rd, NE	6th, East	Lost Conf. Semi-Final
1997-98	82	19	16	6	....	20	14	7	....	39	30	13	....	221	194	91	2nd, NE	5th, East	Lost Conf. Quarter-Final
1996-97	82	14	20	7	....	12	27	2	....	26	47	9	....	234	300	61	6th, NE	13th, East	Out of Playoffs
1995-96	82	22	14	5	....	18	17	6	....	40	31	11	....	282	269	91	2nd, NE	5th, East	Lost Conf. Quarter-Final
1994-95	48	15	7	2	....	12	11	1	....	27	18	3	....	150	127	57	3rd, NE	4th, East	Lost Conf. Quarter-Final
1993-94	84	20	14	8	....	22	15	5	....	42	29	13	....	289	252	97	2nd, NE	4th, East	Lost Conf. Semi-Final
1992-93	84	29	10	3	....	22	16	4	....	51	26	7	....	332	268	109	1st, Adams		Lost Div. Semi-Final
1991-92	80	23	11	6	....	13	21	6	....	36	32	12	....	270	275	84	2nd, Adams		Lost Conf. Final
1990-91	80	26	9	5	....	18	15	7	....	44	24	12	....	299	264	100	1st, Adams		Lost Conf. Final
1989-90	80	23	13	4	....	23	12	5	....	46	25	9	....	289	232	101	1st, Adams		Lost Final
1988-89	80	17	15	8	....	20	14	6	....	37	29	14	....	289	256	88	2nd, Adams		Lost Div. Final
1987-88	80	24	13	3	....	20	17	3	....	44	30	6	....	300	251	94	2nd, Adams		Lost Final
1986-87	80	25	11	4	....	14	23	3	....	39	34	7	....	301	276	85	3rd, Adams		Lost Div. Semi-Final
1985-86	80	24	9	7	....	13	22	5	....	37	31	12	....	311	288	86	3rd, Adams		Lost Div. Semi-Final
1984-85	80	21	15	4	....	15	19	6	....	36	34	10	....	303	287	82	4th, Adams		Lost Div. Semi-Final
1983-84	80	25	12	3	....	24	13	3	....	49	25	6	....	336	261	104	1st, Adams		Lost Div. Semi-Final
1982-83	80	28	6	6	....	22	14	4	....	50	20	10	....	327	228	110	1st, Adams		Lost Conf. Final
1981-82	80	24	12	4	....	19	15	6	....	43	27	10	....	323	285	96	2nd, Adams		Lost Div. Final
1980-81	80	26	10	4	....	11	20	9	....	37	30	13	....	316	272	87	2nd, Adams		Lost Prelim. Round
1979-80	80	27	9	4	....	19	12	9	....	46	21	13	....	310	234	105	2nd, Adams		Lost Quarter-Final
1978-79	80	25	10	5	....	18	13	9	....	43	23	14	....	316	270	100	1st, Adams		Lost Semi-Final
1977-78	80	29	6	5	....	22	12	6	....	51	18	11	....	333	218	113	1st, Adams		Lost Final
1976-77	80	27	7	6	....	22	16	2	....	49	23	8	....	312	240	106	1st, Adams		Lost Final
1975-76	80	27	5	8	....	21	10	9	....	48	15	17	....	313	237	113	1st, Adams		Lost Semi-Final
1974-75	80	29	5	6	....	11	21	8	....	40	26	14	....	345	245	94	2nd, Adams		Lost Prelim. Round
1973-74	78	33	4	2	....	19	13	7	....	52	17	9	....	349	221	113	1st, East		Lost Final
1972-73	78	27	10	2	....	24	12	3	....	51	22	5	....	330	235	107	2nd, East		Lost Quarter-Final
1971-72	**78**	**28**	**4**	**7**	....	**26**	**9**	**4**	....	**54**	**13**	**11**	....	**330**	**204**	**119**	**1st, East**		**Won Stanley Cup**
1970-71	78	33	4	2	....	24	10	5	....	57	14	7	....	399	207	121	1st; East		Lost Quarter-Final
1969-70	**76**	**27**	**3**	**8**	....	**13**	**14**	**11**	....	**40**	**17**	**19**	....	**277**	**216**	**99**	**2nd, East**		**Won Stanley Cup**
1968-69	76	29	3	6	....	13	15	10	....	42	18	16	....	303	221	100	2nd, East		Lost Semi-Final
1967-68	74	22	9	6	....	15	18	4	....	37	27	10	....	259	216	84	3rd, East		Lost Quarter-Final
1966-67	70	10	21	4	....	7	22	6	....	17	43	10	....	182	253	44	6th		Out of Playoffs
1965-66	70	15	17	3	....	6	26	3	....	21	43	6	....	174	275	48	5th		Out of Playoffs
1964-65	70	12	17	6	....	9	26	0	....	21	43	6	....	166	253	48	6th		Out of Playoffs
1963-64	70	13	15	7	....	5	25	5	....	18	40	12	....	170	212	48	6th		Out of Playoffs
1962-63	70	7	18	10	....	7	21	7	....	14	39	17	....	198	281	45	6th		Out of Playoffs
1961-62	70	9	22	4	....	6	25	4	....	15	47	8	....	177	306	38	6th		Out of Playoffs
1960-61	70	13	17	5	....	2	25	8	....	15	42	13	....	176	254	43	6th		Out of Playoffs
1959-60	70	21	11	3	....	7	23	5	....	28	34	8	....	220	241	64	5th		Out of Playoffs
1958-59	70	21	11	3	....	11	18	6	....	32	29	9	....	205	215	73	2nd		Lost Semi-Final
1957-58	70	15	14	6	....	12	14	9	....	27	28	15	....	199	194	69	4th		Lost Final
1956-57	70	20	9	6	....	14	15	6	....	34	24	12	....	195	174	80	3rd		Lost Final
1955-56	70	14	14	7	....	9	20	6	....	23	34	13	....	147	185	59	5th		Out of Playoffs
1954-55	70	16	10	9	....	7	16	12	....	23	26	21	....	169	188	67	4th		Lost Semi-Final
1953-54	70	22	8	5	....	10	20	5	....	32	28	10	....	177	181	74	4th		Lost Semi-Final
1952-53	70	19	10	6	....	9	19	7	....	28	29	13	....	152	172	69	3rd		Lost Final
1951-52	70	15	12	8	....	10	17	8	....	25	29	16	....	162	176	66	4th		Lost Semi-Final
1950-51	70	13	12	10	....	9	18	8	....	22	30	18	....	178	197	62	4th		Lost Semi-Final
1949-50	70	15	12	8	....	7	20	8	....	22	32	16	....	198	228	60	5th		Out of Playoffs
1948-49	60	18	10	2	....	11	13	6	....	29	23	8	....	178	163	66	2nd		Lost Semi-Final
1947-48	60	12	8	10	....	11	16	3	....	23	24	13	....	167	168	59	3rd		Lost Semi-Final
1946-47	60	18	7	5	....	8	16	6	....	26	23	11	....	190	175	63	3rd		Lost Semi-Final
1945-46	50	11	5	4	....	13	13	4	....	24	18	8	....	167	156	56	2nd		Lost Final
1944-45	50	11	12	2	....	5	18	2	....	16	30	4	....	179	219	36	4th		Lost Semi-Final
1943-44	50	15	8	2	....	4	18	3	....	19	26	5	....	223	268	43	5th		Out of Playoffs
1942-43	50	17	3	5	....	7	14	4	....	24	17	9	....	195	176	57	2nd		Lost Final
1941-42	48	17	4	3	....	8	13	3	....	25	17	6	....	160	118	56	3rd		Lost Semi-Final
1940-41	**48**	**15**	**4**	**5**	....	**12**	**4**	**8**	....	**27**	**8**	**13**	....	**168**	**102**	**67**	**1st**		**Won Stanley Cup**
1939-40	48	20	3	1	....	11	9	4	....	31	12	5	....	170	98	67	1st		Lost Semi-Final
1938-39	**48**	**20**	**2**	**2**	....	**16**	**8**	**0**	....	**36**	**10**	**2**	....	**156**	**76**	**74**	**1st**		**Won Stanley Cup**
1937-38	48	18	3	3	....	12	8	4	....	30	11	7	....	142	89	67	1st, Amn.		Lost Semi-Final
1936-37	48	9	11	4	....	14	7	3	....	23	18	7	....	120	110	53	2nd, Amn.		Lost Quarter-Final
1935-36	48	15	8	1	....	7	12	5	....	22	20	6	....	92	83	50	2nd, Amn.		Lost Quarter-Final
1934-35	48	17	7	0	....	9	9	6	....	26	16	6	....	129	112	58	1st, Amn.		Lost Semi-Final
1933-34	48	11	11	2	....	7	14	3	....	18	25	5	....	111	130	41	4th, Amn.		Out of Playoffs
1932-33	48	19	2	3	....	6	13	5	....	25	15	8	....	124	88	58	1st, Amn.		Lost Semi-Final
1931-32	48	11	10	3	....	4	11	9	....	15	21	12	....	122	117	42	4th, Amn.		Out of Playoffs
1930-31	44	16	1	5	....	12	9	1	....	28	10	6	....	143	90	62	1st, Amn.		Lost Semi-Final
1929-30	44	21	1	0	....	17	4	1	....	38	5	1	....	179	98	77	1st, Amn.		Lost Final
1928-29	**44**	**15**	**6**	**1**	....	**11**	**7**	**4**	....	**26**	**13**	**5**	....	**89**	**52**	**57**	**1st, Amn.**		**Won Stanley Cup**
1927-28	44	13	4	5	....	7	9	6	....	20	13	11	....	77	70	51	1st, Amn.		Lost Semi-Final
1926-27	44	15	7	0	....	6	13	3	....	21	20	3	....	97	89	45	2nd, Amn.		Lost Final
1925-26	36	10	7	1	....	7	8	3	....	17	15	4	....	92	85	38	4th		Out of Playoffs
1924-25	30	3	12	0	....	3	12	0	....	6	24	0	....	49	119	12	6th		Out of Playoffs

2015-16 Player Personnel

FORWARDS	HT	WT	*Age	Place of Birth	S	2014-15 Club
ACCIARI, Noel	5-10	208	23	Johnston, RI	R	Providence College
BELESKEY, Matt	6-0	200	27	Windsor, ON	L	Anaheim
BERGERON, Patrice	6-2	194	30	Ancienne-Lorette, QC	R	Boston
BLIDH, Anton	6-0	200	20	Molnlycke, Sweden	L	Frolunda Jr.-Frolunda
CAMARA, Anthony	6-0	192	22	Toronto, ON	L	Providence (AHL)
CAVE, Colby	6-1	199	20	Battleford, SK	L	Swift Current-Prov (AHL)
CONNOLLY, Brett	6-2	200	23	Prince George, BC	R	Tampa Bay-Boston
DeFAZIO, Brandon	6-2	204	27	Etobicoke, ON	L	Vancouver-Utica
ERIKSSON, Loui	6-2	196	30	Goteborg, Sweden	L	Boston
FERLIN, Brian	6-2	209	23	Jacksonville, FL	R	Boston-Providence (AHL)
GRIFFITH, Seth	5-9	192	22	Wallaceburg, ON	R	Boston-Providence (AHL)
HAYES, Jimmy	6-6	221	25	Boston, MA	R	Florida
KELLY, Chris	6-0	198	34	Toronto, ON	L	Boston
KEMPPAINEN, Joonas	6-3	223	27	Kajaani, Finland	L	Karpat
KHOKHLACHEV, Alex	5-11	184	22	Moscow, Russia	L	Boston-Providence (AHL)
KREJCI, David	6-0	188	29	Sternberk, Czech.	R	Boston
MARCHAND, Brad	5-9	183	27	Halifax, NS	L	Boston
PASTRNAK, David	6-0	167	19	Havirov, Czech Republic	R	Boston-Providence (AHL)
RANDELL, Tyler	6-1	197	24	Scarborough, ON	R	Providence (AHL)
RINALDO, Zac	5-11	169	25	Mississauga, ON	L	Philadelphia
SEXTON, Ben	5-11	182	24	Ottawa, ON	R	Providence (AHL)
SPOONER, Ryan	5-11	181	23	Ottawa, ON	L	Boston-Providence (AHL)
TALBOT, Max	5-11	190	31	Lemoyne, QC	L	Colorado-Boston
DEFENSEMEN						
BREEN, Chris	6-7	224	26	Uxbridge, ON	L	Providence (AHL)
CASTO, Chris	6-1	200	23	St. Paul, MN	R	Providence (AHL)
CHARA, Zdeno	6-9	255	38	Trencin, Czechoslovakia	L	Boston
CROSS, Tommy	6-3	206	26	Hartford, CT	L	Providence (AHL)
IRWIN, Matt	6-2	210	27	Brentwood Bay, BC	L	San Jose
KRUG, Torey	5-9	181	24	Livonia, MI	L	Boston
McQUAID, Adam	6-5	209	28	Charlottetown, PE	R	Boston
MILLER, Colin	6-1	201	22	Sault Ste. Marie, ON	R	Manchester
MILLER, Kevan	6-2	210	27	Los Angeles, CA	R	Boston
MORROW, Joe	6-1	204	22	Edmonton, AB	L	Boston-Providence (AHL)
SEIDENBERG, Dennis	6-1	210	34	Schwenningen, W. Germany	L	Boston
TROTMAN, Zach	6-3	219	25	Novi, MI	R	Boston-Providence (AHL)

GOALTENDERS	HT	WT	*Age	Place of Birth	C	2014-15 Club
McINTYRE, Zane	6-2	205	23	Grand Forks, ND	L	North Dakota
RASK, Tuukka	6-2	185	28	Savonlinna, Finland	L	Boston
SMITH, Jeremy	6-0	176	26	Dearborn, MI	L	Providence (AHL)
SUBBAN, Malcolm	6-2	200	21	Toronto, ON	L	Boston-Providence (AHL)

* – Age at start of 2015-16 season

2014-15 Scoring

* – rookie

Regular Season

Pos	#	Player	Team	GP	G	A	Pts	TOI	+/–	PIM	PP	SH	GW	S	S%
C	37	Patrice Bergeron	BOS	81	23	32	55	18:07	2	44	4	1	4	234	9.8
L	21	Loui Eriksson	BOS	81	22	25	47	18:28	1	14	6	0	4	169	13.0
L	17	Milan Lucic	BOS	81	18	26	44	16:21	13	81	2	0	4	141	12.8
C	34	Carl Soderberg	BOS	82	13	31	44	16:48	10	26	5	0	3	163	8.0
C	63	Brad Marchand	BOS	77	24	18	42	16:54	5	95	2	2	5	180	13.3
D	27	Dougie Hamilton	BOS	72	10	32	42	21:20	–3	41	5	0	2	188	5.3
R	18	Reilly Smith	BOS	81	13	27	40	15:24	7	20	1	0	0	143	9.1
D	47	Torey Krug	BOS	78	12	27	39	19:35	13	20	2	0	0	205	5.9
C	46	David Krejci	BOS	47	7	24	31	18:10	7	22	1	1	1	70	10.0
C	23	Chris Kelly	BOS	80	7	21	28	15:08	6	48	0	1	2	112	6.3
R	88 *	David Pastrnak	BOS	46	10	17	27	13:58	12	8	2	0	3	93	10.8
D	33	Zdeno Chara	BOS	63	8	12	20	23:20	0	42	4	0	0	138	5.8
C	51 *	Ryan Spooner	BOS	29	8	10	18	14:32	2	2	3	0	1	73	11.0
C	25	Maxime Talbot	COL	63	5	10	15	14:00	2	27	0	0	1	73	6.8
			BOS	18	0	3	3	12:13	–3	2	0	0	0	24	0.0
			Total	81	5	13	18	13:36	–1	29	0	0	1	97	5.2
R	14	Brett Connolly	T.B.	50	12	3	15	11:55	4	38	2	0	2	74	16.2
			BOS	5	0	2	2	14:21	–1	10	0	0	0	9	0.0
			Total	55	12	5	17	12:09	3	48	2	0	2	83	14.5
D	44	Dennis Seidenberg	BOS	82	3	11	14	22:06	–1	34	0	0	0	103	2.9
L	20	Daniel Paille	BOS	71	6	7	13	11:30	–9	12	0	1	1	66	9.1
C	11	Gregory Campbell	BOS	70	6	6	12	12:08	1	45	0	1	2	64	9.4
C	53 *	Seth Griffith	BOS	30	6	4	10	13:26	–2	6	1	0	1	33	18.2
D	86	Kevan Miller	BOS	41	2	5	7	18:02	20	15	0	0	1	37	5.4
D	54	Adam McQuaid	BOS	63	1	6	7	18:26	–2	85	0	0	0	60	1.7
D	62 *	Zach Trotman	BOS	27	1	4	5	16:24	–2	0	0	0	1	46	2.2
L	12	Simon Gagne	BOS	23	3	1	4	11:18	0	4	0	0	1	27	11.1
D	43	Matt Bartkowski	BOS	47	0	4	4	16:56	–6	37	0	0	0	67	0.0
D	45 *	Joe Morrow	BOS	15	1	0	1	16:41	3	4	0	0	0	20	5.0
D	79 *	David Warsofsky	BOS	4	0	1	1	17:45	1	0	0	0	0	7	0.0
R	68 *	Brian Ferlin	BOS	7	0	1	1	8:47	0	0	0	0	0	6	0.0
C	52 *	Matt Lindblad	BOS	2	0	0	0	7:45	0	0	0	0	0	3	0.0
C	64	Bobby Robins	BOS	3	0	0	0	7:35	0	14	0	0	0	0	0.0
C	76 *	Alex Khokhlachev	BOS	3	0	0	0	8:12	–2	0	0	0	0	1	0.0

Goaltending

No.	Goaltender	GPI	Mins	Avg	W	L	OT	EN	SO	GA	SA	Sv%	G	A	PIM
40	Tuukka Rask	70	4063	2.30	34	21	13	5	3	156	2011	.922	0	0	8
72	* Niklas Svedberg	18	900	2.33	7	5	1	2	2	35	425	.918	0	0	0
70	* Malcolm Subban	1	31	5.81	0	1	0	0	0	3	6	.500	0	0	0
	Totals	**82**	**5025**	**2.40**	**41**	**27**	**14**	**7**	**5**	**201**	**2449**	**.918**			

Coaching History

Art Ross, 1924-25 to 1933-34; Frank Patrick, 1934-35, 1935-36; Art Ross, 1936-37 to 1938-39; Cooney Weiland, 1939-40, 1940-41; Art Ross, 1941-42 to 1944-45; Dit Clapper, 1945-46 to 1948-49; George Boucher, 1949-50; Lynn Patrick, 1950-51 to 1953-54; Lynn Patrick and Milt Schmidt, 1954-55; Milt Schmidt, 1955-56 to 1960-61; Phil Watson, 1961-62; Phil Watson and Milt Schmidt, 1962-63; Milt Schmidt, 1963-64 to 1965-66; Harry Sinden, 1966-67 to 1969-70; Tom Johnson, 1970-71, 1971-72; Tom Johnson and Bep Guidolin, 1972-73; Bep Guidolin, 1973-74; Don Cherry, 1974-75 to 1978-79; Fred Creighton and Harry Sinden, 1979-80; Gerry Cheevers, 1980-81 to 1983-84; Gerry Cheevers and Harry Sinden, 1984-85; Butch Goring, 1985-86; Butch Goring and Terry O'Reilly, 1986-87; Terry O'Reilly, 1987-88, 1988-89; Mike Milbury, 1989-90, 1990-91; Rick Bowness, 1991-92; Brian Sutter, 1992-93 to 1994-95; Steve Kasper, 1995-96, 1996-97; Pat Burns, 1997-98 to 1999-2000; Pat Burns and Mike Keenan, 2000-01; Robbie Ftorek, 2001-02; Robbie Ftorek and Mike O'Connell, 2002-03; Mike Sullivan, 2003-04 to 2005-06; Dave Lewis, 2006-07; Claude Julien, 2007-08 to date.

Claude Julien

Head Coach

Born: Orleans, ON, April 23, 1960.

The Boston Bruins named Claude Julien the 28th head coach in club history on June 21, 2007. In his first season behind the bench in 2007-08, he guided the Bruins back to the playoffs for the first time since 2003-04. In 2008-09, the Bruins posted the best record in the Eastern Conference and were second overall in the NHL, earning Julien the Jack Adams Award for coach of the year. In 2010-11, he guided the team to a Stanley Cup victory for the first time since 1972. Boston reached the Stanley Cup final again in 2012-13 and won the Presidents' Trophy with the best record in the NHL during the regular season in 2013-14.

Julien joined the Bruins with four years of NHL head coaching experience. In his lone season with New Jersey, he held a record of 47-24-8 before being replaced on April 2, 2007 with three games remaining in the 2006-07 regular season. At the time he was replaced by the Devils, Julien's club was in first place in the Atlantic Division. Prior to being named head coach of the Devils, Julien spent three seasons as the head coach of the Montreal Canadiens, serving from January 2003 until January of 2006. During his tenure with Montreal, Julien led the Canadiens to a record of 72-62-25 in 159 games.

Before joining the NHL coaching ranks, Julien spent four seasons with Hull of the Quebec Major Junior Hockey League and three campaigns with Hamilton of the American Hockey League. While with Hamilton, Julien was co-awarded the Louis A. R. Pieri Award as the league's outstanding coach during the 2002-03 season. Julien has also coached at the international level, having served as an assistant coach to Team Canada at the 2006 World Championship after he led Team Canada to a bronze medal as a head coach at the 2000 World Junior Championship. He will be an associate coach for Canada at the 2014 Sochi Winter Olympics.

A defenseman, Julien's professional playing career spanned 12 seasons from 1981 to 1992, highlighted by stints with the Quebec Nordiques between 1984 and 1986.

Coaching Record

			Regular Season				Playoffs			
Season	Team	League	GC	W	L	O/T	GC	W	L	T
1996-97	Hull	QMJHL	70	48	19	3	14	12	2	....
1996-97	Hull	M-Cup	....	....	....	....	5	3	2	....
1997-98	Hull	QMJHL	70	32	37	1	11	6	5	....
1998-99	Hull	QMJHL	70	23	38	9	23	15	8	....
99-2000	Hull	QMJHL	72	42	24	6	15	9	6	....
2000-01	Hamilton	AHL	80	28	41	11	....	....	....	....
2001-02	Hamilton	AHL	80	37	30	13	15	10	5	....
2002-03	Hamilton	AHL	45	33	9	3	....	....	....	....
2002-03	**Montreal**	**NHL**	**36**	**12**	**16**	**8**	....	....	....	....
2003-04	**Montreal**	**NHL**	**82**	**41**	**30**	**11**	**11**	**4**	**7**	....
2004-05	**Montreal**				SEASON CANCELLED					
2005-06	**Montreal**	**NHL**	**41**	**19**	**16**	**6**	....	....	....	....
2006-07	**New Jersey**	**NHL**	**79**	**47**	**24**	**8**	....	....	....	....
2007-08	**Boston**	**NHL**	**82**	**41**	**29**	**12**	**7**	**3**	**4**	....
2008-09	**Boston**	**NHL**	**82**	**53**	**19**	**19**	**11**	**7**	**4**	....
2009-10	**Boston**	**NHL**	**82**	**39**	**30**	**13**	**13**	**7**	**6**	....
2010-11♦	**Boston**	**NHL**	**82**	**46**	**25**	**11**	**25**	**16**	**9**	....
2011-12	**Boston**	**NHL**	**82**	**49**	**29**	**4**	**7**	**3**	**4**	....
2012-13	**Boston**	**NHL**	**48**	**28**	**14**	**6**	**22**	**14**	**8**	....
2013-14	**Boston**	**NHL**	**82**	**54**	**19**	**9**	**12**	**7**	**5**	....
2014-15	**Boston**	**NHL**	**82**	**41**	**27**	**14**	....	....	....	....
	NHL Totals		**860**	**470**	**278**	**121**	**108**	**61**	**47**	....

♦ Stanley Cup win.
Jack Adams Award (2009)

Club Records

Team

(Figures in brackets for season records are games played; records for fewest points, wins, ties, losses, goals, goals against are for 70 or more games)

Most Points **121** 1970-71 (78)
Most Wins **57** 1970-71 (78)
Most Ties **21** 1954-55 (70)
Most Losses **47** 1961-62 (70), 1996-97 (82)
Most Goals **399** 1970-71 (78)
Most Goals Against **306** 1961-62 (70)
Fewest Points **38** 1961-62 (70)
Fewest Wins **14** 1962-63 (70)
Fewest Ties **5** 1972-73 (78)
Fewest Losses **13** 1971-72 (78)
Fewest Goals **147** 1955-56 (70)
Fewest Goals Against **172** 1952-53 (70)
Longest Winning Streak
Overall .... **14** Dec. 3/29-Jan. 9/30
Home .... **20** Dec. 3/29-Mar. 18/30
Away .... **9** Mar. 2-30/14
Longest Undefeated Streak
Overall .... **23** Dec. 22/40-Feb. 23/41 (15W, 8T)
Home .... **27** Nov. 22/70-Mar. 20/71 (26W, 1T)
Away .... **15** Dec. 22/40-Mar. 16/41 (9W, 6T)
Longest Losing Streak
Overall .... **11** Dec. 3/24-Jan. 5/25
Home .... **11** Dec. 8/24-Feb. 17/25
Away .... **14** Dec. 27/64-Feb. 21/65
Longest Winless Streak
Overall .... **20** Jan. 28-Mar. 11/62 (16L, 4T)
Home .... **11** Dec. 8/24-Feb. 17/25 (11L)
Away .... **14** Three times
Most Shutouts, Season **15** 1927-28 (44)
Most PIM, Season **2,443** 1987-88 (80)
Most Goals, Game .... **14** Jan. 21/45 (NYR 3 at Bos. 14)

Individual

Most Seasons .... **21** John Bucyk, Raymond Bourque
Most Games .... **1,518** Raymond Bourque
Most Goals, Career .... **545** John Bucyk
Most Assists, Career .... **1,111** Raymond Bourque
Most Points, Career .... **1,506** Raymond Bourque (395G, 1,111A)
Most PIM, Career .... **2,095** Terry O'Reilly
Most Shutouts, Career ...... **74** Tiny Thompson
Longest Consecutive Games Streak ... **418** John Bucyk (Jan. 23/69-Mar. 2/75)
Most Goals, Season .... **76** Phil Esposito (1970-71)
Most Assists, Season .... **102** Bobby Orr (1970-71)
Most Points, Season .... **152** Phil Esposito (1970-71; 76G, 76A)
Most PIM, Season .... **302** Jay Miller (1987-88)
Most Points, Defenseman, Season ... ***139** Bobby Orr (1970-71; 37G, 102A)
Most Points, Center, Season ... **152** Phil Esposito (1970-71; 76G, 76A)
Most Points, Right Wing, Season ... **105** Ken Hodge (1970-71; 43G, 62A), (1973-74; 50G, 55A); Rick Middleton (1983-84; 47G, 58A)
Most Points, Left Wing, Season ... **116** John Bucyk (1970-71; 51G, 65A)
Most Points, Rookie, Season ... **102** Joe Juneau (1992-93; 32G, 70A)
Most Shutouts, Season .... **15** Hal Winkler (1927-28)
Most Goals, Game .... **4** Twenty one times
Most Assists, Game .... **6** Ken Hodge (Feb. 9/71); Bobby Orr (Jan. 1/73)
Most Points, Game .... **7** Bobby Orr (Nov. 15/73; 3G, 4A); Phil Esposito (Dec. 19/74; 3G, 4A); Barry Pederson (Apr. 4/82; 3G, 4A); Cam Neely (Oct. 16/88; 3G, 4A)

* NHL Record.

All-time Record vs. Other Clubs

Regular Season

	Total								At Home								On Road							
	GP	W	L	T	OL	GF	GA	PTS	GP	W	L	T	OL	GF	GA	PTS	GP	W	L	T	OL	GF	GA	PTS
Anaheim	28	13	12	2	1	74	75	29	14	7	6	0	1	39	41	15	14	6	6	2	0	35	34	14
Arizona	71	43	20	7	1	266	214	94	35	24	6	4	1	146	103	53	36	19	14	3	0	120	111	41
Buffalo	277	128	109	29	11	894	888	296	137	76	43	14	4	491	400	170	140	52	66	15	7	403	488	126
Calgary	101	56	32	10	3	351	308	125	52	32	12	6	2	187	136	72	49	24	20	4	1	164	172	53
Carolina	191	102	70	16	3	650	556	223	96	56	32	7	1	330	250	120	95	46	38	9	2	320	306	103
Chicago	582	263	236	79	4	1830	1762	609	290	165	91	34	0	1041	820	364	292	98	145	45	4	789	942	245
Colorado	138	70	51	15	2	531	450	157	67	31	26	9	1	244	203	72	71	39	25	6	1	287	247	85
Columbus	18	11	5	0	2	56	42	24	8	5	3	0	0	21	17	10	10	6	2	0	2	35	25	14
Dallas	131	76	29	23	3	508	346	178	65	43	10	10	2	275	160	98	66	33	19	13	1	233	186	80
Detroit	588	240	250	95	3	1769	1759	578	295	158	92	43	2	1031	783	361	293	82	158	52	1	738	976	217
Edmonton	69	45	17	6	1	259	195	97	35	26	6	3	0	146	85	55	34	19	11	3	1	113	110	42
Florida	83	43	29	6	5	237	208	97	43	21	15	4	3	121	94	49	40	22	14	2	2	116	114	48
Los Angeles	135	82	36	13	4	544	418	181	68	47	12	6	3	303	188	103	67	35	24	7	1	241	230	78
Minnesota	16	4	11	0	1	29	46	9	8	1	7	0	0	13	24	2	8	3	4	0	1	16	22	7
Montreal	729	271	346	103	9	1922	2210	654	365	165	138	56	6	1067	991	392	364	106	208	47	3	855	1219	262
Nashville	21	12	4	1	4	61	50	29	10	7	2	1	0	32	20	15	11	5	2	0	4	29	30	14
New Jersey	146	78	39	19	10	493	394	185	75	42	19	8	6	272	216	98	71	36	20	11	4	221	178	87
NY Islanders	157	80	52	21	4	539	462	185	78	43	22	11	2	280	213	99	79	37	30	10	2	259	249	86
NY Rangers	637	290	241	97	9	2005	1850	686	317	169	100	42	6	1113	875	386	320	121	141	55	3	892	975	300
Ottawa	126	73	36	8	9	404	314	163	65	39	18	5	3	219	164	86	61	34	18	3	6	185	150	77
Philadelphia	186	100	59	21	6	614	544	227	94	55	24	11	4	330	256	125	92	45	35	10	2	284	288	102
Pittsburgh	195	107	61	21	6	743	600	241	96	64	22	6	4	398	269	138	99	43	39	15	2	345	331	103
St. Louis	129	62	40	18	9	474	381	151	64	36	15	9	4	257	175	85	65	26	25	9	5	217	206	66
San Jose	32	17	10	5	0	100	88	39	16	9	4	3	0	52	47	21	16	8	6	2	0	48	41	18
Tampa Bay	85	54	21	9	1	288	218	118	43	33	4	6	0	162	93	72	42	21	17	3	1	126	125	46
Toronto	657	291	258	98	10	1943	1952	690	328	181	96	47	4	1075	869	413	329	110	162	51	6	868	1083	277
Vancouver	113	69	28	15	1	447	317	154	57	40	9	7	1	228	134	88	56	29	19	8	0	219	183	66
Washington	148	76	43	21	8	490	407	181	74	42	20	9	3	253	194	96	74	34	23	12	5	237	213	85
Winnipeg	55	32	16	2	5	172	156	71	27	19	4	2	2	98	76	42	28	13	12	0	3	74	80	29
Defunct Clubs	328	191	106	31	0	1021	746	413	164	112	39	13	0	525	306	237	164	79	67	18	0	496	440	176
Totals	**6172**	**2979**	**2267**	**791**	**135**	**19714**	**17956**	**6884**	**3086**	**1748**	**897**	**376**	**65**	**10749**	**8202**	**3937**	**3086**	**1231**	**1370**	**415**	**70**	**8965**	**9754**	**2947**

Playoffs

	Series	W	L	GP	W	L	T	GF	GA	Last Mtg.	Rnd.	Result
Buffalo	8	6	2	45	25	20	0	155	145	2010	CQF	W 4-2
Carolina	4	3	1	26	15	11	0	80	64	2009	CSF	L 3-4
Chicago	7	5	2	28	18	9	1	112	80	2013	F	L 2-4
Colorado	2	1	1	11	6	5	0	37	36	1983	DSF	W 3-1
Dallas	1	0	1	3	0	3	0	13	20	1981	PR	L 0-3
Detroit	8	5	3	38	23	15	0	110	104	2014	FR	W 4-1
Edmonton	2	0	2	9	1	8	0	20	41	1990	F	L 1-4
Florida	1	0	1	5	1	4	0	16	22	1996	CQF	L 1-4
Los Angeles	2	2	0	13	8	5	0	56	38	1977	QF	W 4-2
Montreal	34	9	25	177	71	106	0	436	531	2014	SR	L 3-4
New Jersey	4	1	3	23	8	15	0	60	68	2003	CQF	L 1-4
NY Islanders	2	0	2	11	3	8	0	35	49	1983	CF	L 2-4
NY Rangers	10	7	3	47	26	19	2	130	114	2013	CSF	W 4-1
Philadelphia	6	3	3	31	18	13	0	100	86	2011	CSF	W 4-0
Pittsburgh	5	3	2	23	13	10	0	74	69	2013	CF	W 4-0
St. Louis	2	2	0	8	8	0	0	48	15	1972	SF	W 4-0
Tampa Bay	1	1	0	7	4	3	0	21	21	2011	CF	W 4-3
Toronto	14	6	8	69	34	34	1	175	168	2013	CQF	W 4-3
Vancouver	1	1	0	7	4	3	0	23	8	2011	F	W 4-3
Washington	3	1	2	17	9	8	0	43	37	2012	CQF	L 3-4
Defunct Clubs	3	1	2	11	4	5	2	20	20			
Totals	**120**	**57**	**63**	**609**	**299**	**304**	**6**	**1764**	**1736**			

Playoff Results 2015-2011

Year	Round	Opponent	Result	GF	GA
2014	SR	Montreal	L 3-4	16	20
	FR	Detroit	W 4-1	14	6
2013	F	Chicago	L 2-4	15	17
	CF	Pittsburgh	W 4-0	12	2
	CSF	NY Rangers	W 4-1	16	10
	CQF	Toronto	W 4-3	22	18
2012	CQF	Washington	L 3-4	15	16
2011	**F**	**Vancouver**	**W 4-3**	**23**	**8**
	CF	Tampa Bay	W 4-3	21	21
	CSF	Philadelphia	W 4-0	20	7
	CQF	Montreal	W 4-3	17	17

Abbreviations: Round: F – Final; **CF** – conference final; **CSF** – conference semi-final; **SR** – second round; **CQF** – conference quarter-final; **FR** – first round; **DSF** – division semi-final; **SF** – semi-final; **QF** – quarter-final; **PR** – preliminary round.

Calgary totals include Atlanta Flames, 1972-73 to 1979-80.
Colorado totals include Quebec, 1979-80 to 1994-95.
New Jersey totals include Kansas City, 1974-75, 1975-76, and Colorado Rockies, 1976-77 to 1981-82.
Phoenix totals include Winnipeg, 1979-80 to 1995-96.
Carolina totals include Hartford, 1979-80 to 1996-97.
Dallas totals include Minnesota North Stars, 1967-68 to 1992-93.
Winnipeg totals include Atlanta Thrashers, 1999-2000 to 2010-11.

2014-15 Results

Month	Day	Opponent	Score
Oct.	8	Philadelphia	2-1
	9	at Detroit	1-2
	11	Washington	0-4
	13	Colorado	1-2
	15	at Detroit	3-2†
	16	at Montreal	4-6
	18	at Buffalo	4-0
	21	San Jose	5-3
	23	NY Islanders	2-3
	25	at Toronto	4-1
	28	Minnesota	3-4
	30	at Buffalo	3-2*
Nov.	1	Ottawa	4-2
	4	Florida	2-1*
	6	Edmonton	5-2
	10	New Jersey	4-2
	12	at Toronto	1-6
	13	at Montreal	1-5
	15	Carolina	2-1
	18	St. Louis	2-0
	21	at Columbus	4-3†
	22	Montreal	0-2
	24	Pittsburgh	2-3*
	28	Winnipeg	2-1*
Dec.	1	at Anaheim	2-3
	2	at Los Angeles	0-2
	4	at San Jose	4-7
	6	at Arizona	5-2
	11	Chicago	2-3
	13	Ottawa	2-3†
	16	at Nashville	2-3†
	17	at Minnesota	3-2*
	19	at Winnipeg	1-2
	21	Buffalo	4-3*
	23	Nashville	5-3
	27	at Columbus	2-6
	29	Detroit	5-2
	31	Toronto	3-4†
Jan.	3	Ottawa	2-3*
	4	at Carolina	1-2†
	7	at Pittsburgh	3-2*
	8	New Jersey	3-0
	10	at Philadelphia	3-1
	13	Tampa Bay	4-3
	15	NY Rangers	3-0
	17	Columbus	1-3
	20	at Dallas	3-1
	21	at Colorado	2-3†
	29	at NY Islanders	5-2
	31	Los Angeles	3-1
Feb.	4	at NY Rangers	2-3
	7	NY Islanders	2-1
	8	Montreal	1-3
	10	Dallas	3-5
	13	at Vancouver	2-5
	16	at Calgary	3-4*
	18	at Edmonton	3-4†
	20	at St. Louis	1-5
	22	at Chicago	6-2
	24	Vancouver	1-2
	27	at New Jersey	3-2*
	28	Arizona	4-1
Mar.	5	Calgary	3-4†
	7	Philadelphia	3-2*
	8	Detroit	5-3
	10	at Ottawa	3-1
	12	Tampa Bay	3-2†
	14	at Pittsburgh	2-0
	15	at Washington	0-2
	17	Buffalo	1-2†
	19	at Ottawa	4-6
	21	at Florida	1-2†
	22	at Tampa Bay	3-5
	26	Anaheim	2-3*
	28	NY Rangers	4-2
	29	at Carolina	2-1*
	31	Florida	3-2
Apr.	2	at Detroit	3-2
	4	Toronto	2-1†
	8	at Washington	0-3
	9	at Florida	2-4
	11	at Tampa Bay	2-3†

* – Overtime † – Shootout

NHL Draft Selections 2015-2001

Name in bold denotes played in NHL.

2015
Pick
13 Jakub Zboril
14 Jake Debrusk
15 Zach Senyshyn
37 Brandon Carlo
45 Jakob Forsbacka-Karlsson
52 Jeremy Lauzon
75 Dan Vladar
105 Jesse Gabrielle
165 Cameron Hughes
195 Jack Becker

2014
Pick
25 **David Pastrnak**
56 Ryan Donato
116 Danton Heinen
146 Anders Bjork
206 Emil Johansson

2013
Pick
60 Linus Arnesson
90 Peter Cehlarik
120 Ryan Fitzgerald
150 Wiley Sherman
180 Anton Blidh
210 Mitchell Dempsey

2012
Pick
24 **Malcolm Subban**
85 Matthew Grzelcyk
131 **Seth Griffith**
145 Cody Payne
175 Matthew Benning
205 Colton Hargrove

2011
Pick
9 **Dougie Hamilton**
40 **Alex Khokhlachev**
81 Anthony Camara
121 **Brian Ferlin**
151 Rob O'Gara
181 Lars Volden

2010
Pick
2 **Tyler Seguin**
32 Jared Knight
45 **Ryan Spooner**
97 **Craig Cunningham**
135 **Justin Florek**
165 Zane McIntyre
195 Maxim Chudinov
210 **Zach Trotman**

2009
Pick
25 **Jordan Caron**
86 Ryan Button
112 **Lane MacDermid**
176 Tyler Randell
206 Ben Sexton

2008
Pick
16 **Joe Colborne**
47 **Max Sauve**
77 **Michael Hutchinson**
97 **Jamie Arniel**
173 Nick Tremblay
197 Mark Goggin

2007
Pick
8 **Zach Hamill**
35 Tommy Cross
130 Denis Reul
159 Alain Goulet
169 Radim Ostrcil
189 Jordan Knackstedt

2006
Pick
5 **Phil Kessel**
37 Yury Alexandrov
50 **Milan Lucic**
71 **Brad Marchand**
128 **Andrew Bodnarchuk**
158 Levi Nelson

2005
Pick
22 **Matt Lashoff**
39 **Petr Kalus**
83 **Mikko Lehtonen**
100 **Jonathan Sigalet**
106 **Vladimir Sobotka**
154 Wacey Rabbit
172 Lukas Vantuch
217 Brock Bradford

2004
Pick
63 **David Krejci**
64 **Martins Karsums**
108 Ashton Rome
134 **Kris Versteeg**
160 **Ben Walter**
224 **Matt Hunwick**
255 Anton Hedman

2003
Pick
21 **Mark Stuart**
45 **Patrice Bergeron**
66 **Masi Marjamaki**
107 **Byron Bitz**
118 Frank Rediker
129 Patrik Valcak
153 Mike Brown
183 **Nate Thompson**
247 Benoit Mondou
277 Kevin Regan

2002
Pick
29 **Hannu Toivonen**
56 Vladislav Yevseyev
130 Jan Kubista
153 Peter Hamerlik
228 Dmitri Utkin
259 **Yan Stastny**
290 Pavel Frolov

2001
Pick
19 **Shaone Morrisonn**
77 Darren McLachlan
111 Matti Kaltiainen
147 Jiri Jakes
179 **Andrew Alberts**
209 **Jordan Sigalet**
241 **Milan Jurcina**
282 Marcel Rodman

Captains' History

No captain, 1924-25; Sprague Cleghorn, 1925-26, 1926-27; Lionel Hitchman, 1927-28 to 1930-31; George Owen, 1931-32; Dit Clapper, 1932-33 to 1937-38; Cooney Weiland, 1938-39; Dit Clapper, 1939-40 to 1945-46; Dit Clapper and John Crawford, 1946-47; John Crawford 1947-48 to 1949-50; Milt Schmidt, 1950-51 to 1953-54; Milt Schmidt, Ed Sanford, 1954-55; Fern Flaman, 1955-56 to 1960-61; Don McKenney, 1961-62, 1962-63; Leo Boivin, 1963-64 to 1965-66; John Bucyk, 1966-67; no captain, 1967-68 to 1972-73; John Bucyk, 1973-74 to 1976-77; Wayne Cashman, 1977-78 to 1982-83; Terry O'Reilly, 1983-84, 1984-85; Raymond Bourque, Rick Middleton (co-captains) 1985-86 to 1987-88; Raymond Bourque, 1988-89 to 1999-2000; Jason Allison, 2000-01; no captain, 2001-02; Joe Thornton, 2002-03 to 2004-05; Joe Thornton and no captain, 2005-06; Zdeno Chara, 2006-07 to date.

General Managers' History

Art Ross, 1924-25 to 1953-54; Lynn Patrick, 1954-55 to 1964-65; Hap Emms, 1965-66, 1966-67; Milt Schmidt, 1967-68 to 1971-72; Harry Sinden, 1972-73 to 1999-2000; Harry Sinden and Mike O'Connell, 2000-01; Mike O'Connell, 2001-02 to 2004-05; Mike O'Connell and Jeff Gorton, 2005-06; Peter Chiarelli, 2006-07 to 2014-15; Don Sweeney, 2015-16.

Don Sweeney

General Manager

Born: St. Stevens, NB, August 17, 1966.

Don Sweeney was named general manager of the Boston Bruins on May 20, 2015. He is the eighth man to hold the position, is the fourth who also played for the team (joining Hap Emms, Milt Schmidt and Mike O'Connell) and is the first former Boston draft pick to rise to the post. He oversees all aspects of the team's hockey operations and he also serves the club as an alternate governor on the NHL's Board of Governors.

Sweeney's ascension to the head of the club's hockey operations continues his long legacy with the club, beginning as the team's eighth pick, 166th overall, in the 1984 NHL Draft. He moved through the organization as a player for 15 seasons and in various front office capacities for the previous nine years. In his six seasons as the team's assistant general manager beginning in 2009, he oversaw the development of the team's drafted prospects at the AHL, junior hockey, college and European levels in addition to having a supervisory role in the day-to-day operations of the hockey department. He also oversaw all hockey operations matters for Boston's AHL affiliate in Providence. Sweeney began his front office career in June, 2006, when he was named the team's director of player development.

After being drafted by the Bruins as their eighth pick, Sweeney went on to play four seasons at Harvard University. He earned both NCAA East All-American and ECAC First Team All-Star honors with the Crimson and played in the 1986 NCAA Finals before graduating with a degree in Economics.

The defenseman played 16 seasons in the National Hockey League, including 15 in a Bruins uniform. He is one of just two defensemen and four players in team history to play over 1,000 games in a Boston sweater and he still ranks third on the team's all-time games played list. He also ranks in the top ten of the club's all-time list in career assists by a defenseman. He played his final NHL season with the Dallas Stars in 2003-04.

Club Directory

TD Garden

Boston Bruins
TD Garden
100 Legends Way
Boston, MA 02114
Phone **617/624-BEAR (2327)**
FAX 617/523-7184
www.bostonbruins.com
Capacity: 17,565

Ownership

Owner & Governor, Boston Bruins; Chairman, NHL Board of Governors	Jeremy M. Jacobs
Chief Executive Officer, Boston Bruins	Charlie Jacobs
Alternate Governors	Charlie Jacobs, Jeremy Jacobs, Jr., Louis Jacobs, Harry Sinden, Cam Neely, Don Sweeney
Senior Advisor to the Owner	Harry Sinden

Executive

President	Cam Neely
Sr. Vice President, Sales	Glen Thornborough
Vice President, Finance	Jim Bednarek
Vice President, Marketing	Jen Compton
Vice President, Communications & Content	Matthew Chmura
Vice President, Corporate Partnerships	Chris Johnson
Vice President, Premium Sales & Service	Leah Leahy
Director of Administration	Dale Hamilton-Powers
Executive / Administrative Assistants	Rita Brandano, Maria Poirier / Karen Ondo

Hockey Operations

General Manager	Don Sweeney
Assistant General Manager	Scott Bradley
Executive Director of Player Personnel	John Ferguson
Director of Amateur Scouting	Keith Gretzky
Assistant Director of Amateur Scouting	Scott Fitzgerald
Scouting Staff	P.J. Axelsson, Adam Creighton, Dean Malkoc, Mike McGraw, Tom McVie, Keith Sullivan, Svenake Svensson
Director of Hockey Operations/Analytics	Ryan Nadeau
Assistant to Hockey Administration	Whitney Delorey
Team Road Services Coordinator	John Bucyk

Coaching

Head Coach	Claude Julien
Assistant Coaches	Doug Houda, Doug Jarvis, Joe Sacco
Goaltending Coach	Bob Essensa
Video Analyst	Jeremy Rogalski

Medical, Training and Equipment

Strength & Conditioning Coach	John Whitesides
Athletic Trainer	Don DelNegro
Physical Therapist	Scott Waugh
Assistant Athletic Trainer & Massage Therapist	Derek Repucci
Equipment Manager	Keith Robinson
Assistant Equipment Managers	Jim 'Beets' Johnson, Matt Falconer
Head Team Physician/Orthopedist	Dr. Peter Asnis
Team Internist	Dr. David Judge

Communications

Director of Communications & Content	Eric Tosi
Director of Publications & Information	Heidi Holland
Specialists, Communications / Digital Content	Erika Wentzell / Caryn Switaj
Content Specialist / Administrator	Brandon McNelis / Jessica Isner
Web Video Producer / Graduate Assistant	Mike Penhollow / Alexandra Morey

Marketing and Community Relations

Director of Marketing	Chris DiPierro
Director of Community Relations	Kerry Collins
Director of Digital and Creative	Jenna Carmann
Digital Content Producer	Michael Berger
Marketing Managers, Strategic / Activation / Creative	Yelena Cvek / Lindsay Sparling / Brandon Anthony
Youth Hockey Development Manager	Mike Dargin
Coordinators, Marketing / Marketing Activation	Renee Riva / Jack McGraw
Graphic Designer	Jason Petrie
Associate Graphic Designer	Carley Johnson
Digital Designer	Matt Tranzillo

Boston Bruins Foundation and Alumni Office

Executive Director, Bruins Foundation	Bob Sweeney
Foundation Manager / Coordinator	Shannon Murphy / Zack Fitzgerald
Boston Bruins Alumni Coordinator	Karen Wonoski

Sales, Fan Relations and Retail

Client Services Manager, The Premium Club	Tamala Levin
Director of Ticket Sales	Mark Rodrigues
Retail Manager / Buyer / Coordinator	Mark Maimone / Lauma Cerlins / Liz Dhooge
Fan Relations Manager	John Cadigan
Season Sales Account Executives	Matt Gulley, Kevin Stone, Tina Zettel
Group Sales Account Executives	Rachel Hansen, Alexandra Bottone
Fan Relations Representatives	Keith Ricci, Greg Sbardella, Richard Yutkins, Greg Stoll, Tamara Tierney, Danielle Wiedmeier

Finance, Legal, Human Resources and Box Office

Controller	Rick McGlinchey
Staff Accountant	Linda Bartlett
Accounting Manager / Coordinator	Sean Sullivan / Rick McGlinchey, Jr.
Payroll & Benefits Manager	Botin Bou-James
Assistant General Counsel	Matt Reece
Human Resources Director	Shauna K. Gilhooly
Human Resources Manager/Generalist	Kate Green / Sarah Dahlstedt
Box Office Director / Assistant Manager	Ricky Casady / Courtney McNeice
Assistant Director of Ticket Operations	Jim Foley
Ticket Office Receptionist	Jo-Ann Connolly-White

Broadcasting

TV Rightsholder	New England Sports Network (NESN)
Radio play-by-play / analyst	Jack Edwards / Andy Brickley
Radio Rightsholder	98.5 The Sports Hub (CBS Radio Boston)
Radio play-by-play / analyst	Dave Goucher / Bob Beers

Key Off-Season Signings/Acquisitions

2015
- **May** 28 • Named **Dan Bylsma** head coach.
- **June** 18 • Named **Terry Murray** and **Dave Barr** assistant coaches.
  - 26 • Acquired G **Robin Lehner** and C **David Legwand** from Ottawa for a 1st-round choice in the 2015 NHL Draft.
  - 26 • Acquired C **Ryan O'Reilly** and LW **Jamie McGinn** from Colorado for D **Nikita Zadorov**, C **Mikhail Grigorenko**, LW **J.T. Compher** and a 2nd-round choice in the 2015 NHL Draft.
- **July** 1 • Signed RW **Jason Akeson** and D **Matt Donovan**.
  - 2 • Signed D **Bobby Sanguinetti**.
  - 3 • Signed D **Carlo Colaiacovo** and C **Cal O'Reilly**.
  - 6 • Named **Dan Lambert** assistant coach.
  - 13 • Re-signed C **Philip Varone**.
  - 14 • Re-signed D **Mark Pysyk**.
  - 21 • Re-signed LW **Johan Larsson**.
  - 23 • Re-signed RW **Jerry D'Amigo**.

Buffalo Sabres

2014-15 Results: 23W-51L-3OTL-5SOL 54PTS
8TH, Atlantic Division • 16TH, Eastern Conference

2015-16 Schedule

Oct.	Thu.	8	Ottawa
	Sat.	10	Tampa Bay*
	Mon.	12	Columbus*
	Thu.	15	at Florida
	Sat.	17	at Tampa Bay
	Wed.	21	Toronto
	Fri.	23	Montreal
	Sat.	24	New Jersey
	Tue.	27	at Philadelphia
	Thu.	29	at Pittsburgh
	Fri.	30	Philadelphia
Nov.	Sun.	1	at NY Islanders
	Thu.	5	Tampa Bay
	Sat.	7	Vancouver*
	Tue.	10	at Tampa Bay
	Thu.	12	at Florida
	Sat.	14	San Jose
	Tue.	17	Dallas
	Thu.	19	at St. Louis
	Sat.	21	at Dallas
	Mon.	23	St. Louis
	Wed.	25	Nashville
	Fri.	27	Carolina
	Sat.	28	at Nashville
Dec.	Tue.	1	at Detroit
	Fri.	4	Arizona
	Sun.	6	at Edmonton
	Mon.	7	at Vancouver
	Thu.	10	at Calgary
	Sat.	12	Los Angeles
	Mon.	14	at Detroit
	Tue.	15	New Jersey
	Thu.	17	Anaheim
	Sat.	19	Chicago*
	Sat.	26	at Boston
	Mon.	28	Washington
	Wed.	30	at Washington
	Thu.	31	NY Islanders
Jan.	Sat.	2	Detroit*
	Tue.	5	Florida
	Fri.	8	at Chicago

	Sun.	10	at Winnipeg*
	Tue.	12	at Minnesota
	Fri.	15	Boston
	Sat.	16	Washington
	Mon.	18	at Arizona
	Wed.	20	at Colorado
	Fri.	22	Detroit
	Mon.	25	at NY Rangers
	Tue.	26	at Ottawa
Feb.	Wed.	3	at Montreal
	Thu.	4	Boston
	Sat.	6	at Boston
	Tue.	9	Florida
	Thu.	11	at Philadelphia
	Fri.	12	Montreal
	Sun.	14	Colorado*
	Tue.	16	at Ottawa
	Fri.	19	at Columbus
	Sun.	21	Pittsburgh*
	Wed.	24	at Anaheim
	Fri.	26	at San Jose
	Sat.	27	at Los Angeles
Mar.	Tue.	1	Edmonton
	Thu.	3	Calgary
	Sat.	5	Minnesota*
	Mon.	7	at Toronto
	Tue.	8	NY Rangers
	Thu.	10	at Montreal
	Sat.	12	Carolina*
	Wed.	16	Montreal
	Fri.	18	Ottawa
	Sat.	19	at Toronto
	Tue.	22	at Carolina
	Sat.	26	Winnipeg*
	Mon.	28	at Detroit
	Tue.	29	at Pittsburgh
	Thu.	31	Toronto
Apr.	Sat.	2	at NY Rangers
	Tue.	5	at New Jersey
	Fri.	8	Columbus
	Sat.	9	at NY Islanders

* Denotes afternoon game.

Selected by Buffalo in the first round, 26th overall, in the 2008 Entry Draft, Tyler Ennis stands just 5'9" but he's a big talent. Ennis led the Sabres with 20 goals and 46 points in 2014-15.

Year-by-Year Record

Season	GP	Home W	L	T	OTL	Road W	L	T	OTL	Overall W	L	T	OTL	GF	GA	Pts.	Div. Fin.	Conf. Fin.	Playoff Result
2014-15	82	14	22	....	5	9	29	....	3	23	51	....	8	161	274	54	8th, Atl.	16th, East	Out of Playoffs
2013-14	82	13	21	....	7	8	30	....	3	21	51	....	10	157	248	52	8th, Atl.	16th, East	Out of Playoffs
2012-13	48	11	10	....	3	10	11	....	3	21	21	....	6	125	143	48	5th, NE	12th, East	Out of Playoffs
2011-12	82	21	12	....	8	18	20	....	3	39	32	....	11	218	230	89	3rd, NE	9th, East	Out of Playoffs
2010-11	82	21	16	....	4	22	13	....	6	43	29	....	10	245	229	96	3rd, NE	7th, East	Lost Conf. Quarter-Final
2009-10	82	25	10	....	6	20	17	....	4	45	27	....	10	235	207	100	1st, NE	3rd, East	Lost Conf. Quarter-Final
2008-09	82	23	15	....	3	18	17	....	6	41	32	....	9	250	234	91	3rd, NE	10th, East	Out of Playoffs
2007-08	82	20	15	....	6	19	16	....	6	39	31	....	12	255	242	90	4th, NE	10th, East	Out of Playoffs
2006-07	82	28	10	....	3	25	12	....	4	53	22	....	7	308	242	113	1st, NE	1st, East	Lost Conf. Final
2005-06	82	27	11	....	3	25	13	....	3	52	24	....	6	281	239	110	2nd, NE	4th, East	Lost Conf. Final
2004-05	....																		
2003-04	82	21	13	4	3	16	21	3	1	37	34	7	4	220	221	85	5th, NE	9th, East	Out of Playoffs
2002-03	82	18	16	5	2	9	21	5	6	27	37	10	8	190	219	72	5th, NE	12th, East	Out of Playoffs
2001-02	82	20	16	5	0	15	19	6	1	35	35	11	1	213	200	82	5th, NE	10th, East	Out of Playoffs
2000-01	82	26	12	3	0	20	18	2	1	46	30	5	1	218	184	98	2nd, NE	5th, East	Lost Conf. Semi-Final
1999-2000	82	21	14	5	1	14	18	6	3	35	32	11	4	213	204	85	3rd, NE	8th, East	Lost Conf. Quarter-Final
1998-99	82	23	12	6	....	14	16	11	....	37	28	17	....	207	175	91	4th, NE	7th, East	Lost Final
1997-98	82	20	13	8	....	16	16	9	....	36	29	17	....	211	187	89	3rd, NE	6th, East	Lost Conf. Final
1996-97	82	24	11	6	....	16	19	6	....	40	30	12	....	237	208	92	1st, NE	3rd, East	Lost Conf. Semi-Final
1995-96	82	19	17	5	....	14	25	2	....	33	42	7	....	247	262	73	5th, NE	11th, East	Out of Playoffs
1994-95	48	15	8	1	....	7	11	6	....	22	19	7	....	130	119	51	4th, NE	7th, East	Lost Conf. Quarter-Final
1993-94	84	22	17	3	....	21	15	6	....	43	32	9	....	282	218	95	4th, NE	6th, East	Lost Conf. Quarter-Final
1992-93	84	25	15	2	....	13	21	8	....	38	36	10	....	335	297	86	4th, Adams		Lost Div. Final
1991-92	80	22	13	5	....	9	24	7	....	31	37	12	....	289	299	74	3rd, Adams		Lost Div. Semi-Final
1990-91	80	15	13	12	....	16	17	7	....	31	30	19	....	292	278	81	3rd, Adams		Lost Div. Semi-Final
1989-90	80	27	11	2	....	18	16	6	....	45	27	8	....	286	248	98	2nd, Adams		Lost Div. Semi-Final
1988-89	80	25	12	3	....	13	23	4	....	38	35	7	....	291	299	83	3rd, Adams		Lost Div. Semi-Final
1987-88	80	19	14	7	....	18	18	4	....	37	32	11	....	283	305	85	3rd, Adams		Lost Div. Semi-Final
1986-87	80	18	18	4	....	10	26	4	....	28	44	8	....	280	308	64	5th, Adams		Out of Playoffs
1985-86	80	23	16	1	....	14	21	5	....	37	37	6	....	296	291	80	5th, Adams		Out of Playoffs
1984-85	80	23	10	7	....	15	18	7	....	38	28	14	....	290	237	90	3rd, Adams		Lost Div. Semi-Final
1983-84	80	25	9	6	....	23	16	1	....	48	25	7	....	315	257	103	2nd, Adams		Lost Div. Semi-Final
1982-83	80	25	7	8	....	13	22	5	....	38	29	13	....	318	285	89	3rd, Adams		Lost Div. Final
1981-82	80	23	8	9	....	16	18	6	....	39	26	15	....	307	273	93	3rd, Adams		Lost Div. Semi-Final
1980-81	80	27	7	12	....	18	13	9	....	39	20	21	....	327	250	99	1st, Adams		Lost Quarter-Final
1979-80	80	27	5	8	....	20	12	8	....	47	17	16	....	318	201	110	1st, Adams		Lost Semi-Final
1978-79	80	19	13	8	....	17	15	8	....	36	28	16	....	280	263	88	2nd, Adams		Lost Prelim. Round
1977-78	80	25	7	8	....	19	12	9	....	44	19	17	....	288	215	105	2nd, Adams		Lost Quarter-Final
1976-77	80	27	8	5	....	21	16	3	....	48	24	8	....	301	220	104	2nd, Adams		Lost Quarter-Final
1975-76	80	27	8	5	....	18	14	8	....	46	21	13	....	339	240	105	2nd, Adams		Lost Quarter-Final
1974-75	80	28	6	6	....	21	10	9	....	49	16	15	....	354	240	113	1st, Adams		Lost Final
1973-74	78	23	10	6	....	9	24	6	....	32	34	12	....	242	250	76	5th, East		Out of Playoffs
1972-73	78	30	6	3	....	7	21	11	....	37	27	14	....	257	219	88	4th, East		Lost Quarter-Final
1971-72	78	11	19	9	....	5	24	10	....	16	43	19	....	203	289	51	6th, East		Out of Playoffs
1970-71	78	16	13	10	....	8	26	5	....	24	39	15	....	217	291	63	5th, East		Out of Playoffs

Retired Numbers

2	Tim Horton	1972-1974
7	Rick Martin	1971-1981
11	Gilbert Perreault	1970-1987
14	Rene Robert	1971-1979
16	Pat LaFontaine	1991-1996
18	Danny Gare	1974-1981

ATLANTIC DIVISION
46th NHL Season

Franchise date: May 22, 1970

2015-16 Player Personnel

FORWARDS

	HT	WT	*Age	Place of Birth	S	2014-15 Club
AKESON, Jason	5-10	190	25	Orleans, ON	R	Philadelphia-Lehigh Valley
D'AMIGO, Jerry	5-11	213	24	Binghamton, NY	L	Sprfld-Buf-Roch
DESLAURIERS, Nicolas	6-1	209	24	LaSalle, QC	L	Buffalo
EICHEL, Jack	6-2	199	18	North Chelmsford, MA	R	Boston University
ENNIS, Tyler	5-9	169	26	Edmonton, AB	L	Buffalo
FOLIGNO, Marcus	6-3	223	24	Buffalo, NY	L	Buffalo
GIONTA, Brian	5-7	176	36	Rochester, NY	R	Buffalo
GIRGENSONS, Zemgus	6-1	200	21	Riga, Latvia	L	Buffalo
KANE, Evander	6-2	195	24	Vancouver, BC	L	Winnipeg
LARSSON, Johan	5-11	206	23	Lau, Sweden	L	Buffalo-Rochester
LEGWAND, David	6-2	205	35	Detroit, MI	L	Ottawa
McCORMICK, Cody	6-2	224	32	London, ON	R	Buffalo
McGINN, Jamie	6-1	210	27	Fergus, ON	L	Colorado
MOULSON, Matt	6-1	200	31	North York, ON	L	Buffalo
O'REILLY, Cal	6-0	188	29	Toronto, ON	L	Utica
O'REILLY, Ryan	6-0	200	24	Clinton, ON	L	Colorado
REINHART, Sam	6-1	187	19	North Vancouver, BC	R	Buf-Kootenay-Roch
SCHALLER, Tim	6-2	206	24	Merrimack, NH	L	Buffalo-Rochester
VARONE, Phil	5-10	185	24	Vaughan, ON	L	Buffalo-Rochester

DEFENSEMEN

BOGOSIAN, Zach	6-3	215	25	Massena, NY	R	Winnipeg-Buffalo
COLAIACOVO, Carlo	6-1	200	32	Toronto, ON	L	Philadelphia
DONOVAN, Matt	6-0	195	25	Edmond, OK	L	NY Islanders
GORGES, Josh	6-1	201	31	Kelowna, BC	L	Buffalo
McCABE, Jake	6-0	215	21	Eau Claire, WI	L	Buffalo-Rochester
PYSYK, Mark	6-1	192	23	Edmonton, AB	R	Buffalo-Rochester
RISTOLAINEN, Rasmus	6-4	207	20	Turku, Finland	R	Buffalo
RUHWEDEL, Chad	5-11	181	25	San Diego, CA	R	Buffalo-Rochester
SANGUINETTI, Bobby	6-3	190	27	Trenton, NJ	R	Utica
WEBER, Mike	6-2	212	27	Pittsburgh, PA	L	Buffalo

GOALTENDERS

	HT	WT	*Age	Place of Birth	C	2014-15 Club
JOHNSON, Chad	6-3	205	29	Calgary, AB	L	NY Islanders
LEHNER, Robin	6-5	225	24	Goteborg, Sweden	L	Ottawa

* – Age at start of 2015-16 season

2014-15 Scoring

* - rookie

Regular Season

Pos	#	Player	Team	GP	G	A	Pts	TOI	+/-	PIM	PP	SH	GW	S	S%
C	63	Tyler Ennis	BUF	78	20	26	46	19:06	-19	37	6	1	2	185	10.8
L	26	Matt Moulson	BUF	77	13	28	41	17:41	-11	4	3	0	2	156	8.3
R	12	Brian Gionta	BUF	69	13	22	35	18:03	-13	18	3	1	2	153	8.5
C	28	Zemgus Girgensons	BUF	61	15	15	30	19:04	-16	25	1	3	1	115	13.0
L	82	Marcus Foligno	BUF	57	8	12	20	16:13	-5	50	0	0	0	66	12.1
D	55	Rasmus Ristolainen	BUF	57	8	12	20	20:36	-32	26	4	0	0	121	6.6
D	47	Zach Bogosian	WPG	41	3	10	13	22:10	1	40	0	0	0	74	4.1
			BUF	21	0	7	7	26:34	-7	38	0	0	0	51	0.0
			Total	62	3	17	20	23:39	-6	78	0	0	0	125	2.4
L	22	Johan Larsson	BUF	39	6	10	16	14:30	1	12	1	0	0	50	12.0
L	44	* Nicolas Deslauriers	BUF	82	5	10	15	11:52	-24	71	0	0	1	76	6.6
D	51	* Nikita Zadorov	BUF	60	3	12	15	17:42	-10	51	2	0	1	52	5.8
D	41	Andrej Meszaros	BUF	60	7	7	14	17:54	-13	36	1	0	1	67	10.4
C	19	Cody Hodgson	BUF	78	6	7	13	12:50	-28	12	0	0	0	127	4.7
D	61	Andre Benoit	BUF	59	1	8	9	18:08	-19	20	0	1	0	45	2.2
D	6	Mike Weber	BUF	64	1	6	7	18:44	-22	68	0	0	0	41	2.4
C	25	Mikhail Grigorenko	BUF	25	3	3	6	15:10	-10	2	1	0	0	35	8.6
D	4	Josh Gorges	BUF	46	0	6	6	22:21	-28	16	0	0	0	28	0.0
C	84	* Philip Varone	BUF	28	3	2	5	13:26	-14	10	0	0	0	28	10.7
D	24	Tyson Strachan	BUF	46	0	5	5	18:59	-30	44	0	0	0	38	0.0
C	8	Cody McCormick	BUF	33	1	3	4	11:42	-9	40	0	1	0	31	3.2
D	3	Mark Pysyk	BUF	7	2	1	3	18:10	4	2	0	0	1	4	50.0
C	20	Zac Dalpe	BUF	21	1	2	3	9:16	-11	4	0	0	0	29	3.4
R	36	Patrick Kaleta	BUF	42	0	3	3	8:52	-11	36	0	0	0	25	0.0
C	59	* Tim Schaller	BUF	18	1	1	2	11:20	-5	2	0	0	0	19	5.3
L	37	Matt Ellis	BUF	39	1	1	2	8:19	-12	4	0	0	1	29	3.4
D	5	Chad Ruhwedel	BUF	4	0	1	1	12:27	3	0	0	0	0	3	0.0
C	23	* Sam Reinhart	BUF	9	0	1	1	10:21	-1	2	0	0	0	6	0.0
R	33	* Joel Armia	BUF	1	0	0	0	14:47	0	0	0	0	0	3	0.0
D	29	* Jake McCabe	BUF	2	0	0	0	11:07	0	0	0	0	0	2	0.0
R	49	* Jerry D'Amigo	BUF	9	0	0	0	9:43	-4	2	0	0	0	7	0.0

Goaltending

No.	Goaltender	GPI	Mins	Avg	W	L	OT	EN	SO	GA	SA	Sv%	G	A	PIM
35	Anders Lindback	16	891	2.76	4	8	2	2	0	41	542	.924	0	0	4
30	Michal Neuvirth	27	1544	2.99	6	17	3	2	0	77	941	.918	0	0	0
1	* Andrey Makarov	1	60	3.00	0	1	0	0	0	3	36	.917	0	0	0
1	Jhonas Enroth	37	2204	3.27	13	21	2	5	1	120	1237	.903	0	0	0
31	Matt Hackett	5	250	4.32	0	4	1	1	0	18	155	.884	0	0	0
	Totals	**82**	**4990**	**3.23**	**23**	**51**	**8**	**10**	**1**	**269**	**2921**	**.908**			

Dan Bylsma

Head Coach

Born: Grand Haven, MI, September 19, 1970.

The Buffalo Sabres announced on May 28, 2015, that Dan Bylsma had been hired as the 17th head coach in franchise history. With 479 total games coached during six previous NHL seasons, Bylsma becomes the most experienced head coach to join the Sabres since the team hired Scotty Bowman in 1979.

Bylsma comes to the Sabres after spending six seasons as the head coach of the Pittsburgh Penguins, where he led the team to a 252-117-32 overall regular-season record, becoming the winningest head coach in Penguins history. In 2008-09, his first year as an NHL head coach, Bylsma took over a Pittsburgh team that ranked 10th in the Eastern Conference with just 25 games remaining in the regular season and led them to the franchise's first Stanley Cup title in 16 years. Bylsma won the Jack Adams Award in 2011 as the NHL's coach of the year as the Penguins went 49-25-8 and won the Atlantic Division despite ranking near the top of the league with 350 man games lost due to injury, including Sidney Crosby (41), Jordan Staal (39) and Evgeni Malkin (39). Pittsburgh qualified for the playoffs in all six seasons under Bylsma's leadership, winning two division titles (2012-13, 2013-14) and posting the best record in the Eastern Conference in 2012-13. He became the fastest coach in NHL history to reach 250 wins, a feat he accomplished in just 396 regular-season games. Bylsma led the Penguins to at least 100 points in every full season he spent with the team.

Bylsma has also found success in international competition. He made his international debut as head coach of Team USA at the 2014 Winter Olympics in Sochi, Russia, where the United States went undefeated in group play before finishing fourth in the tournament. Bylsma also served as assistant coach at the 2015 World Championship, where the United States again won their group and went on to earn a bronze medal.

At the time of his hiring by the Penguins in February 2009, Bylsma was in the midst of his first season as head coach of Pittsburgh's AHL affiliate, the Wilkes-Barre/Scranton Penguins, a post he took up after four seasons as assistant coach with the New York Islanders, Wilkes-Barre/Scranton and the Cincinnati Mighty Ducks (AHL). Before his first coaching job as assistant coach in Cincinnati in 2004-05, Bylsma played in parts of nine NHL seasons as a forward for the Los Angeles Kings and the Mighty Ducks of Anaheim, tallying 62 points (19 goals, 43 assists) in 429 regular-season NHL games. He was a member of the 2002-03 Mighty Ducks team that won the first Western Conference Championship in franchise history and eventually fell just one win short of lifting the Stanley Cup.

Coaching Record

			Regular Season				Playoffs			
Season	Team	League	GC	W	L	O/T	GC	W	L	T
2008-09	Wilkes-Barre	AHL	55	36	16	3	....	....	....	.....
2008-09♦	Pittsburgh	NHL	25	18	3	4	24	16	8	.....
2009-10	Pittsburgh	NHL	82	47	28	7	13	7	6	.....
2010-11	Pittsburgh	NHL	82	49	25	8	7	3	4	.....
2011-12	Pittsburgh	NHL	82	51	25	6	6	2	4	.....
2012-13	Pittsburgh	NHL	48	36	12	0	15	8	7	.....
2013-14	Pittsburgh	NHL	82	51	24	7	13	7	6	.....
	NHL Totals		**401**	**252**	**117**	**32**	♦	**78**	**43**	**35**	.....

♦ Stanley Cup win.
Jack Adams Award (2011)

The Sabres named Brian Gionta captain of the team two days prior to their 2014-15 season opener.

Captains' History

Floyd Smith, 1970-71; Gerry Meehan, 1971-72 to 1973-74; Gerry Meehan and Jim Schoenfeld, 1974-75; Jim Schoenfeld, 1975-76, 1976-77; Danny Gare, 1977-78 to 1980-81; Danny Gare and Gilbert Perreault, 1981-82; Gilbert Perreault, 1982-83 to 1985-86; Gilbert Perreault and Lindy Ruff, 1986-87; Lindy Ruff, 1987-88; Lindy Ruff and Mike Foligno, 1988-89; Mike Foligno, 1989-90; Mike Foligno and Mike Ramsey, 1990-91; Mike Ramsey, 1991-92; Mike Ramsey and Pat LaFontaine, 1992-93; Pat LaFontaine and Alexander Mogilny, 1993-94; Pat LaFontaine, 1994-95 to 1996-97; Donald Audette and Michael Peca, 1997-98; Michael Peca, 1998-99, 1999-2000; no captain, 2000-01; Stu Barnes. 2001-02, 2002-03; Miroslav Satan, Chris Drury, James Patrick, J.P. Dumont, Daniel Briere, 2003-04; Daniel Briere and Chris Drury, 2005-06, 2006-07; Jochen Hecht, Toni Lydman, Brian Campbell, Jaroslav Spacek, Jason Pominville, 2007-08; Craig Rivet, 2008-09 to 2010-11; Jason Pominville, 2011-12, 2012-13; no captain, 2013-14; Brian Gionta, 2014-15 to date.

Coaching History

Punch Imlach, 1970-71; Punch Imlach, Floyd Smith and Joe Crozier, 1971-72; Joe Crozier, 1972-73, 1973-74; Floyd Smith, 1974-75 to 1976-77; Marcel Pronovost, 1977-78; Marcel Pronovost and Billy Inglis, 1978-79; Scotty Bowman, 1979-80; Roger Neilson, 1980-81; Jim Roberts and Scotty Bowman, 1981-82; Scotty Bowman 1982-83 to 1984-85; Jim Schoenfeld and Scotty Bowman, 1985-86; Scotty Bowman, Craig Ramsay and Ted Sator, 1986-87; Ted Sator, 1987-88, 1988-89; Rick Dudley, 1989-90, 1990-91; Rick Dudley and John Muckler, 1991-92; John Muckler, 1992-93 to 1994-95; Ted Nolan, 1995-96, 1996-97; Lindy Ruff, 1997-98 to 2011-12; Lindy Ruff and Ron Rolston, 2012-13; Ron Rolston and Ted Nolan, 2013-14; Ted Nolan, 2014-15; Dan Bylsma, 2015-16.

Club Records

Team

(Figures in brackets for season records are games played; records for fewest points, wins, ties, losses, goals, goals against are for 70 or more games)

Most Points 113 1974-75 (80), 2006-07 (82)
Most Wins 53 2006-07 (82)
Most Ties 21 1980-81 (80)
Most Losses 44 1986-87 (80)
Most Goals 354 1974-75 (80)
Most Goals Against 308 1986-87 (80)
Fewest Points 51 1971-72 (78)
Fewest Wins 16 1971-72 (78)
Fewest Ties 5 2000-01 (82)
Fewest Losses 16 1974-75 (80)
Fewest Goals 153 2014-15 (82)
Fewest Goals Against 175 1998-99 (82)

Longest Winning Streak
- **Overall** .... 10 Jan. 4-23/84, Oct. 4-26/06
- **Home** .... 12 Nov. 12/72-Jan. 7/73, Oct. 13-Dec. 10/89
- **Away** .... 10 Dec. 10/83-Jan. 23/84, Oct. 4-Nov. 13/06

Longest Undefeated Streak
- **Overall** .... 14 Mar. 6-Apr. 6/80 (8W, 6T)
- **Home** .... 21 Oct. 8/72-Jan. 7/73 (18W, 3T)
- **Away** .... 10 Dec. 10/83-Jan. 23/84 (10W), Oct. 4-Nov. 13/06 (10W)

Longest Losing Streak
- **Overall** .... 14 Dec. 29/14-Jan. 30/15
- **Home** .... 9 Oct. 4-Nov. 2/13
- **Away** .... 12 Dec. 17/11-Jan. 21/12

Longest Winless Streak
- **Overall** .... 12 Nov. 23-Dec. 20/91 (8L, 4T), Oct. 25-Nov. 19/02 (10L, 2T/OL)
- **Home** .... 12 Jan. 27-Mar. 10/91 (7L, 5T)
- **Away** .... 23 Oct. 30/71-Feb. 19/72 (15L, 8T)

Most Shutouts, Season 13 1997-98 (82)
Most PIM, Season *2,713 1991-92 (80)
Most Goals, Game .... 14 Jan. 21/75 (Wsh. 2 at Buf. 14), Mar. 19/81 (Tor. 4 at Buf. 14)

Individual

Most Seasons .... 17 Gilbert Perreault
Most Games .... 1,191 Gilbert Perreault
Most Goals, Career .... 512 Gilbert Perreault
Most Assists, Career .... 814 Gilbert Perreault
Most Points, Career .... 1,326 Gilbert Perreault (512G, 814A)
Most PIM, Career .... 3,189 Rob Ray
Most Shutouts, Career .... 55 Dominik Hasek
Longest Consecutive Games Streak .... 776 Craig Ramsay (Mar. 27/73-Feb. 10/83)
Most Goals, Season .... 76 Alexander Mogilny (1992-93)
Most Assists, Season .... 95 Pat LaFontaine (1992-93)
Most Points, Season .... 148 Pat LaFontaine (1992-93; 53G, 95A)
Most PIM, Season .... 354 Rob Ray (1991-92)
Most Points, Defenseman, Season .... 81 Phil Housley (1989-90; 21G, 60A)
Most Points, Center, Season .... 148 Pat LaFontaine (1992-93; 53G, 95A)
Most Points, Right Wing, Season .... 127 Alexander Mogilny (1992-93; 76G, 51A)
Most Points, Left Wing, Season .... 95 Rick Martin (1974-75; 52G, 43A)
Most Points, Rookie, Season .... 74 Rick Martin (1971-72; 44G, 30A)
Most Shutouts, Season .... 13 Dominik Hasek (1997-98)
Most Goals, Game .... 5 Dave Andreychuk (Feb. 6/86)
Most Assists, Game .... 5 Gilbert Perreault (Feb. 1/76), (Mar. 9/80), (Jan. 4/84); Dale Hawerchuk (Jan. 15/92); Pat LaFontaine (Mar. 19/92), (Dec. 31/92), (Feb. 10/93)
Most Points, Game .... 7 Gilbert Perreault (Feb. 1/76; 2G, 5A)

* NHL Record.

All-time Record vs. Other Clubs

Regular Season

	Total								At Home								On Road							
	GP	W	L	T	OL	GF	GA	PTS	GP	W	L	T	OL	GF	GA	PTS	GP	W	L	T	OL	GF	GA	PTS
Anaheim	30	15	12	3	0	85	76	33	15	7	5	3	0	43	39	17	15	8	7	0	0	42	37	16
Arizona	72	42	21	7	2	254	192	93	37	23	7	5	2	142	93	53	35	19	14	2	0	112	99	40
Boston	277	120	115	29	13	888	894	282	140	73	45	15	7	488	403	168	137	47	70	14	6	400	491	114
Calgary	101	49	35	16	1	354	313	115	50	31	13	5	1	201	140	68	51	18	22	11	0	153	173	47
Carolina	192	99	69	18	6	657	560	222	95	56	31	7	1	370	273	120	97	43	38	11	5	287	287	102
Chicago	115	53	49	13	0	361	337	119	58	34	17	7	0	211	150	75	57	19	32	6	0	150	187	44
Colorado	137	59	54	20	4	470	474	142	68	36	21	9	2	259	225	83	69	23	33	11	2	211	249	59
Columbus	20	7	11	1	1	51	60	16	11	4	6	0	1	28	31	9	9	3	5	1	0	23	29	7
Dallas	116	55	44	17	0	374	342	127	57	32	14	11	0	206	153	75	59	23	30	6	0	168	189	52
Detroit	124	54	54	13	3	420	415	124	61	35	17	8	1	245	182	79	63	19	37	5	2	175	233	45
Edmonton	69	22	37	10	0	218	252	54	35	13	15	7	0	122	123	33	34	9	22	3	0	96	129	21
Florida	84	45	32	4	3	237	203	97	43	25	14	3	1	122	92	54	41	20	18	1	2	115	111	43
Los Angeles	117	57	41	18	1	436	365	133	58	33	16	9	0	240	162	75	59	24	25	9	1	196	203	58
Minnesota	16	7	9	0	0	35	47	14	8	2	6	0	0	14	26	4	8	5	3	0	0	21	21	10
Montreal	266	122	106	31	7	781	809	282	132	70	37	19	6	400	344	165	134	52	69	12	1	381	465	117
Nashville	19	7	9	1	2	43	55	17	9	1	5	1	2	22	32	5	10	6	4	0	0	21	23	12
New Jersey	145	73	47	17	8	472	414	171	73	40	23	8	2	256	213	90	72	33	24	9	6	216	201	81
NY Islanders	159	77	59	18	5	481	451	177	80	43	25	9	3	264	225	98	79	34	34	9	2	217	226	79
NY Rangers	171	78	60	25	8	547	528	189	87	47	27	10	3	326	265	107	84	31	33	15	5	221	263	82
Ottawa	124	59	48	10	7	345	325	135	61	33	21	3	4	185	150	73	63	26	27	7	3	160	175	62
Philadelphia	167	64	80	20	3	490	532	151	82	40	32	8	2	270	236	90	85	24	48	12	1	220	296	61
Pittsburgh	179	64	74	35	6	582	582	169	89	40	27	17	5	317	249	102	90	24	47	18	1	265	333	67
St. Louis	112	45	52	13	2	344	379	105	57	30	21	6	0	208	181	66	55	15	31	7	2	136	198	39
San Jose	33	22	6	4	1	128	91	49	17	16	1	0	0	75	44	32	16	6	5	4	1	53	47	17
Tampa Bay	86	51	28	5	2	265	219	109	42	24	14	2	2	132	116	52	44	27	14	3	0	133	103	57
Toronto	197	108	63	18	8	711	550	242	99	66	25	6	2	391	259	140	98	42	38	12	6	320	291	102
Vancouver	114	47	48	19	0	379	378	113	57	30	19	8	0	205	166	68	57	17	29	11	0	174	212	45
Washington	149	86	44	15	4	531	393	191	74	45	20	6	3	281	193	99	75	41	24	9	1	250	200	92
Winnipeg	55	22	22	1	10	181	165	55	28	15	9	0	4	112	75	34	27	7	13	1	6	69	90	21
Defunct Clubs	46	25	13	8	0	191	139	58	23	13	5	5	0	94	63	31	23	12	8	3	0	97	76	27
Totals	**3492**	**1634**	**1342**	**409**	**107**	**11311**	**10540**	**3784**	**1746**	**957**	**538**	**197**	**54**	**6229**	**4903**	**2165**	**1746**	**677**	**804**	**212**	**53**	**5082**	**5637**	**1619**

Playoffs

	Series	W	L	GP	W	L	T	GF	GA	Last Mtg.	Rnd.	Result
Boston	8	2	6	45	20	25	0	145	155	2010	CQF	L 2-4
Carolina	1	0	1	7	3	4	0	17	22	2006	CF	L 3-4
Chicago	2	2	0	9	8	1	0	36	17	1980	QF	W 4-0
Colorado	2	0	2	8	2	6	0	27	35	1985	DSF	L 2-3
Dallas	3	1	2	13	5	8	0	37	39	1999	F	L 2-4
Montreal	7	3	4	35	17	18	0	111	124	1998	CSF	W 4-0
New Jersey	1	0	1	7	3	4	0	14	14	1994	CQF	L 3-4
NY Islanders	4	1	3	21	8	13	0	62	70	2007	CQF	W 4-1
NY Rangers	2	2	0	9	6	3	0	28	19	2007	CSF	W 4-2
Ottawa	4	3	1	21	13	8	0	52	47	2007	CF	L 1-4
Philadelphia	9	3	6	50	21	29	0	141	146	2011	CQF	L 3-4
Pittsburgh	2	0	2	10	4	6	0	26	26	2001	CSF	L 3-4
St. Louis	1	1	0	3	2	1	0	7	8	1976	PR	W 2-1
Toronto	1	1	0	5	4	1	0	21	16	1999	CF	W 4-1
Vancouver	2	2	0	7	6	1	0	28	14	1981	PR	W 3-0
Washington	1	0	1	6	2	4	0	11	13	1998	CF	L 2-4
Totals	**50**	**21**	**29**	**256**	**124**	**132**	**0**	**763**	**765**			

Playoff Results 2015-2011

Year	Round	Opponent	Result	GF	GA
2011	CQF	Philadelphia	L 3-4	18	22

Abbreviations: Round: F – Final; **CF** – conference final; **CSF** – conference semi-final; **CQF** – conference quarter-final; **DSF** – division semi-final; **QF** – quarter-final; **PR** – preliminary round.

Calgary totals include Atlanta Flames, 1972-73 to 1979-80.
Carolina totals include Hartford, 1979-80 to 1996-97.
Colorado totals include Quebec, 1979-80 to 1994-95.
Dallas totals include Minnesota North Stars, 1970-71 to 1992-93.
New Jersey totals include Kansas City, 1974-75, 1975-76, and Colorado Rockies, 1976-77 to 1981-82.
Phoenix totals include Winnipeg, 1979-80 to 1995-96.
Winnipeg totals include Atlanta Thrashers, 1999-2000 to 2010-11.

2014-15 Results

Oct.	9	Columbus	1-3		8	at Carolina	2-5
	11	at Chicago	2-6		9	at Tampa Bay	1-2
	13	Anaheim	1-5		13	Detroit	1-3
	14	at Carolina	4-3†		15	Minnesota	0-7
	17	Florida	0-1		17	Philadelphia	3-4
	18	Boston	0-4		18	at Detroit	4-6
	22	at Anaheim	1-4		27	at Calgary	1-4
	23	at Los Angeles	0-2		29	at Edmonton	2-3
	25	at San Jose	2-1		30	at Vancouver	2-5
	28	at Toronto	0-4	Feb.	3	at Montreal	3-2
	30	Boston	2-3*		5	St. Louis	0-3
Nov.	1	at Pittsburgh	0-5		7	Dallas	3-2
	2	Detroit	3-2†		8	NY Islanders	2-3
	5	Montreal	1-2†		10	Ottawa	1-2
	7	Edmonton	2-3		15	Philadelphia	1-2
	8	Pittsburgh	1-6		17	at New Jersey	1-2†
	11	at St. Louis	1-6		19	at Philadelphia	3-2†
	13	at Minnesota	3-6		20	NY Rangers	1-3
	15	Toronto	6-2		22	Nashville	1-2†
	18	San Jose	4-1		24	at Columbus	4-2
	22	at Washington	2-1		26	Vancouver	6-3
	26	Winnipeg	1-2		28	at Florida	3-5
	28	Montreal	2-1	Mar.	3	at Tampa Bay	0-3
	29	at Montreal	4-3†		6	at Ottawa	2-3
Dec.	2	Tampa Bay	2-1†		7	at Washington	1-6
	4	at Tampa Bay	0-5		11	at Toronto	3-4†
	6	at Florida	2-3		14	NY Rangers	0-2
	9	Los Angeles	1-0		16	Washington	3-4†
	11	Calgary	4-3		17	at Boston	2-1†
	13	Florida	4-3*		20	New Jersey	1-3
	15	Ottawa	5-4†		21	at Nashville	0-3
	16	at Winnipeg	1-5		23	at Dallas	3-4
	20	Colorado	1-5		26	Arizona	3-4*
	21	at Boston	3-4*		28	at Colorado	3-5
	23	at Detroit	3-6		30	at Arizona	4-1
	27	NY Islanders	4-3†	Apr.	1	Toronto	4-3
	29	at Ottawa	2-5		3	Chicago	3-4
	31	Tampa Bay	1-5		4	at NY Islanders	0-3
Jan.	2	Florida	0-2		6	Carolina	4-3
	3	at NY Rangers	1-6		10	at Columbus	2-4
	6	at New Jersey	1-4		11	Pittsburgh	0-2

* – Overtime † – Shootout

NHL Draft Selections 2015-2001

Name in bold denotes played in NHL.

2015 Pick		2011 Pick		2007 Pick		2003 Pick	
2	Jack Eichel	16	Joel Armia	31	T.J. Brennan	5	**Thomas Vanek**
51	Brendan Guhle	77	Daniel Catenacci	59	Drew Schiestel	65	Branislav Fabry
92	William Borgen	107	Colin Jacobs	89	**Corey Tropp**	74	**Clarke MacArthur**
122	Devante Stephens	137	Alex Lepkowski	139	Brad Eidsness	106	**Jan Hejda**
152	Giorgio Estephan	167	**Nathan Lieuwen**	147	Jean-Simon Allard	114	Denis Ezhov
182	Ivan Chukarov	197	Brad Navin	179	**Paul Byron**	150	Thomas Morrow
				187	Nick Eno	172	Pavel Voroshnin
				209	Drew Mackenzie	202	**Nathan Paetsch**
2014		**2010**				235	Jeff Weber
Pick		Pick		**2006**		266	Louis-Philippe Martin
2	Sam Reinhart	23	**Mark Pysyk**	Pick			
31	Brendan Lemieux	68	Jerome Leduc	24	Dennis Persson	**2002**	
44	Eric Cornel	75	Kevin Sundher	46	**Jhonas Enroth**	Pick	
49	Vaclav Karabacek	83	Matt MacKenzie	57	**Mike Weber**	11	**Keith Ballard**
61	Jonas Johansson	98	Steven Shipley	117	Felix Schutz	20	**Daniel Paille**
74	Brycen Martin	143	Gregg Sutch	147	**Alex Biega**	76	Michael Tessier
121	Max Willman	173	Cedrick Henley	207	Benjamin Breault	82	John Adams
151	Christopher Brown	203	Christian Isackson			108	Jakub Hulva
181	Victor Olofsson	208	Riley Boychuk	**2005**		121	Marty Magers
				Pick		178	Maxim Scheviev
2013		**2009**		13	Marek Zagrapan	208	**Radoslav Hecl**
Pick		Pick		48	Philip Gogulla	241	**Dennis Wideman**
8	**Rasmus Ristolainen**	13	**Zack Kassian**	87	**Marc-Andre Gragnani**	271	Martin Cizek
16	**Nikita Zadorov**	66	**Brayden McNabb**	96	**Chris Butler**		
35	J.T. Compher	104	**Marcus Foligno**	142	**Nathan Gerbe**	**2001**	
38	Connor Hurley	134	Mark Adams	182	Adam Dennis	Pick	
52	Justin Bailey	164	**Connor Knapp**	191	Vyacheslav Buravchikov	22	**Jiri Novotny**
69	Nicholas Baptiste	194	Maxime Legault	208	Matt Generous	32	**Derek Roy**
129	Cal Petersen			227	Andrew Orpik	50	**Chris Thorburn**
130	Gustav Possler	**2008**				55	**Jason Pominville**
143	Anthony Florentino	Pick		**2004**		155	Michal Vondrka
159	Sean Malone	12	**Tyler Myers**	Pick		234	Calle Aslund
189	Eric Locke	26	**Tyler Ennis**	13	**Drew Stafford**	247	Marek Dubec
		44	**Luke Adam**	43	**Michael Funk**	279	Ryan Jorde
2012		81	Corey Fienhage	71	**Andrej Sekera**		
Pick		101	Justin Jokinen	145	Michal Valent		
12	**Mikhail Grigorenko**	104	Jordon Southorn	176	**Patrick Kaleta**		
14	**Zemgus Girgensons**	134	Jacob Lagace	207	**Mark Mancari**		
44	**Jake McCabe**	164	Nick Crawford	241	**Mike Card**		
73	Justin Kea			273	Dylan Hunter		
133	Logan Nelson						
163	Linus Ullmark						
193	Brady Austin						
204	Judd Peterson						

General Managers' History

Punch Imlach, 1970-71 to 1977-78; Punch Imlach and John Anderson, 1978-79; Scotty Bowman, 1979-80 to 1985-86; Scotty Bowman and Gerry Meehan, 1986-87; Gerry Meehan, 1987-88 to 1992-93; John Muckler, 1993-94 to 1996-97; Darcy Regier, 1997-98 to 2012-13; Darcy Regier and Tim Murray, 2013-14; Tim Murray, 2014-15 to date.

Tim Murray
General Manager
Born: Shawville, QC, October 31, 1963.

Tim Murray had spent 20 years working in the National Hockey League for five different teams when he was named the seventh general manager in Buffalo Sabres history on January 9, 2014.

Murray came to the Sabres after serving as the assistant general manager of the Ottawa Senators for seven years under his uncle, Bryan Murray. Part of his duties as assistant general manager included serving as general manager of Ottawa's American Hockey League affiliate, the 2011 Calder-Cup champion Binghamton Senators. Murray is renowned to have been a strong voice at the draft table during his time in Ottawa and Anaheim, playing a part in selecting current superstars Corey Perry, Ryan Getzlaf and Erik Karlsson.

Prior to being named the Senators' assistant general manager in 2007, Murray spent three years (2002 to 2005) as the director of player personnel for the Anaheim Ducks, where he was responsible for overseeing the amateur draft and college free agents. He also served as the assistant director of player personnel for the New York Rangers for two years (2005 to 2007), where he evaluated potential free agents and also worked as an amateur scout. Murray began his NHL career in 1993-94, when he was hired as an amateur scout for the Detroit Red Wings. He then moved on to the Florida Panthers, where he served as a scout from 1994 to 2002.

Club Directory

First Niagara Center

Buffalo Sabres
First Niagara Center
One Seymour H. Knox III Plaza
Buffalo, NY 14203
Phone **716/855-4100**
Fax 716/855-4110
Tickets, U.S.: 888/GO-SABRES
Canada: 888/669-GOAL
www.sabres.com
Capacity: 19,070

Executive
Owner . . . . Terrence M. Pegula
President . . . . Russ Brandon
Chief Development Officer . . . . Clifford Benson

Hockey Department
General Manager . . . . Tim Murray
Assistant General Manager . . . . Mark Jakubowski
Director of Player Personnel . . . . Kevin Devine
Directors, Scouting / Amateur Scouting . . . Rob Murphy / Greg Royce
Pro Scouts . . . . Jon Christiano, Jim Kovachik, John Van Boxmeer
Head Amateur Scout . . . . Dave Torrie
Amateur Scouts. . . . . Fredrik Andersson, Anders Forsberg, Jerry Forton, Keith Hendrickson, Brandon Jay, Jussi-Kari Koskinen, Iouri Khmylev, Seamus Kotyk, Paul Merritt, Teemu Numminen, Victor Nybladh, Toby O'Brien, Norm Poisson, Kevin Prendergast, Eric Weissman
Scouting Coordinators, Pro/Amateur . . . . . Graham Beamish / Austin Dunne
Hockey Data Analyst / Video Assistant . . . . Jason Nightingale / Neil McKenney
Manager of Travel and Immigration . . . . . . Michael Bermingham
Director of Hockey Technologies . . . . Kyle Kiebzak
Hockey Ops Asst. / Hockey Relations Coord. Brett Ruff / Jessica Kindron

Coaching Staff
Head Coach . . . . Dan Bylsma
Assistant Coaches . . . . Terry Murray, Dave Barr, Dan Lambert
Goaltending Coach / Video Coach . . . . Andrew Allen / Corey Smith
Strength & Conditioning Coach / Asst. S&C Coach . Doug McKenney / J.T. Allaire
Nutritionist . . . . Allyson Odachowski
Athletic Trainer / Assistant Trainer . . . . Tim Macre / Bob Mowry
Massage Therapist / Physical Therapist . . . Chuck Garlow / Michael Adesso
Equipment Managers . . . . Dave Williams / Rip Simonick
Assistant Equipment Manager / Equipment Assistant . George Babcock / Keith Hayes

Player Development
Coordinator of Player Development . . . . Jason Long
Player Development Coach . . . . Randy Cunneyworth, Adam Mair, Krys Barch

Medical
Medical Director . . . . Les Bisson, M.D.
Team Physician / Orthopedist . . . . William Hartrich, M.D. / Mark Fineberg, M.D.
Team Dentist / Doctor Emeritus. . . . . David Croglio / DDS John L. Butsch, M.D.

Legal, Finance and Administration
E.V.P., Finance & Business Operations . . . . Chuck LaMattina
V.P.s, Legal & Administrative Affairs / Human Resources . Dave Zygaj / Christie Joseph
Paralegal . . . . Kim Szymanoski
Human Resources Generalists / Coordinators . Holly Weiskerger, Erin Fierle / Terri O'Brien, Tera DiLeo
Corporate Controller / Accounting Managers . Kristin Zirnheld / Lynn Slanovich, Eric McGuire
Special Project Accountant . . . . Christine Ivansitz
Payroll Manager / Coordinator . . . . Birgid Haensel / Bianca Rodriguez
Accounts Payable Coordinator / Accounting Clerks . Kim Binkley / John Kolkowski, Maggie Stewart
Executive Assistants . . . . Nadine Leone, Lauren Yurko
IT Systems Consultants . . . . Joshua Malthaner, Nate Brozyna

Broadcast and Game Presentation
V.P., Broadcasting. . . . . Chrisanne Bellas
Game Presentation Director . . . . Kelsey Schneider
TV Producer / TV Director . . . . Joe Pinter / Eric Grossman
Production Coordinator / Videoboard Director . Jason Wiese / Jeff Hill
Broadcast Team . . . . Rick Jeanneret (Play-by-Play), Rob Ray (Color), Dan Dunleavy (Play-by-Play/Reporter), Brian Duff (Studio Host), Brad May (Studio Analyst)
Radio Host, Sabres Hockey Hotline . . . . . . Kevin Sylvester

Merchandise
Director, Merchandise. . . . . Mike Kaminska
Merchandise Mgrs., Inventory / Event Sales . . . Glenn Barker, Jeff Smith
Store Manager / Asst. Store Manager . . . . . Theresa Cerabone / Katie Mumbach-Kay

Marketing
E.V.P., Marketing & Brand Strategy . . . . . . Brent Rossi
Directors, Marketing / Business Solutions . . . John Durbin / Scott Miner
Database Marketing Manager. . . . . Tom Matheny
Managers, Social Media / Marketing . . . . . . Craig Kanalley / Cara Foligno
Digital Content Manager . . . . Chris Ryndak

Creative Services
E.V.P., Creative Services . . . . Frank Cravotta
Graphic Designers . . . . Vicki Sitek, Melissa Gebhardt, Lindsey Caber
Traffic Manager . . . . Kim Geis

Public and Community Relations
V.P., Public & Community Relations . . . . Michael Gilbert
Director, Media Relations . . . . Chris Bandura
Manager / Coordinator, Public Relations . . . Ian Ott / Chris Dierken
Community Relations Director / Manager / Assistant . Rich Jureller / Teresa Belbas / Nick Fearby
Youth Hockey Manager / Team Photographer . Ed Grudzinski / Bill Wippert
President, Alumni Relations / Director . . . . . Rob Ray / Larry Playfair

Sales and Business Development
Directors, Corporate Sales / Business Development . Joe Foy / Pete Petrella
Sr. Acct. Exec. / Acct. Exec. . . . . Rob Nugent / Jon Latke
Sr. Partnership Services Mgr. / Partnership Services Mgr. . Katy Ryan / Kristy Wilensky
Television Traffic Coordinator . . . . Dan Peters

Ticket Sales and Operations
V.P., Tickets & Service. . . . . John Sinclair
Director of Ticket Ops. / Box Office Mgr. / Coord. . Marty Maloney / Paul Barker / Gretchen Knott
Ticket Administrator / Receptionist . . . . Melissa Rugg / Saralynn Ruhland
Coordinator, Suite Services / Special Consultant . Michelle Mitchell / Joe Crozier

First Niagara Center Staff
V.P.s, Arena Operations / Arena Events . . . . Stan Makowski, Jr. / Jennifer Van Rysdam
Director, Arena Operations. . . . . Beth Giuliani Gatto
Managers, Marketing / Events . . . . Tracy Mancini / Charlie Cannan, Robert Neumann, Dave Kutter
Managers, Technical Communications . . . . . Mike Queeno, Trevor Ecklund
Chief Engineer / Dir., Bldg. Services / Security Mgr. . Bruce Johnson / Dennis Hooper / Marc Brenner

Calgary Flames

2014-15 Results: 45w-30L-4OTL-3SOL 97PTS
3RD, Pacific Division • 8TH, Western Conference

Key Off-Season Signings/Acquisitions

2015

June 20 • Re-signed C **Mikael Backlund**.
26 • Acquired D **Dougie Hamilton** from Boston for a 1st-round choice in the 2015 NHL Draft and two 2nd-round choices in 2015.

July 1 • Signed RW **Michael Frolik**.
1 • Re-signed G **Karri Ramo**.
23 • Re-signed C **Lance Bouma**.
24 • Re-signed C **Josh Jooris**.
26 • Re-signed C **Paul Byron**.

2015-16 Schedule

Oct.	Wed.	7	Vancouver		Wed.	13	Florida
	Sat.	10	at Vancouver		Sat.	16	at Edmonton
	Tue.	13	St. Louis		Tue.	19	at New Jersey
	Fri.	16	at Winnipeg		Thu.	21	at Columbus
	Sat.	17	Edmonton		Sun.	24	at Carolina
	Tue.	20	Washington		Mon.	25	at Dallas
	Fri.	23	Detroit		Wed.	27	Nashville
	Sun.	25	at NY Rangers	Feb.	Wed.	3	Carolina
	Mon.	26	at NY Islanders		Fri.	5	Columbus
	Wed.	28	at Ottawa		Sat.	6	at Vancouver
	Fri.	30	Montreal		Tue.	9	Toronto
	Sat.	31	at Edmonton		Thu.	11	at San Jose
Nov.	Tue.	3	at Colorado		Fri.	12	at Arizona
	Thu.	5	Philadelphia		Mon.	15	Anaheim*
	Sat.	7	Pittsburgh		Wed.	17	Minnesota
	Tue.	10	at Florida		Fri.	19	Vancouver
	Thu.	12	at Tampa Bay		Sun.	21	at Anaheim*
	Fri.	13	at Washington		Tue.	23	at Los Angeles
	Sun.	15	at Chicago		Thu.	25	NY Islanders
	Tue.	17	New Jersey		Sat.	27	Ottawa
	Fri.	20	Chicago		Mon.	29	at Philadelphia
	Tue.	24	at Anaheim	Mar.	Tue.	1	at Boston
	Fri.	27	at Arizona		Thu.	3	at Buffalo
	Sat.	28	at San Jose		Sat.	5	at Pittsburgh*
Dec.	Tue.	1	Dallas		Mon.	7	San Jose
	Fri.	4	Boston		Wed.	9	Nashville
	Tue.	8	San Jose		Fri.	11	Arizona
	Thu.	10	Buffalo		Mon.	14	St. Louis
	Sat.	12	NY Rangers		Wed.	16	Winnipeg
	Tue.	15	at Nashville		Fri.	18	Colorado
	Thu.	17	at Dallas		Sun.	20	at Montreal
	Sat.	19	at St. Louis*		Mon.	21	at Toronto
	Sun.	20	at Detroit		Thu.	24	at Minnesota
	Tue.	22	Winnipeg		Sat.	26	Chicago
	Sun.	27	Edmonton		Mon.	28	at Arizona
	Tue.	29	Anaheim		Wed.	30	at Anaheim
	Thu.	31	Los Angeles		Thu.	31	at Los Angeles
Jan.	Sat.	2	at Colorado	Apr.	Sat.	2	at Edmonton
	Tue.	5	Tampa Bay		Tue.	5	Los Angeles
	Thu.	7	Arizona		Thu.	7	Vancouver
	Mon.	11	San Jose		Sat.	9	at Minnesota

Denotes afternoon game.

Retired Numbers

9	Lanny McDonald	1981-1989
30	Mike Vernon	1982-1994; 2000-2002

Honored Numbers

2	Al MacInnis	1981-1994

PACIFIC DIVISION
44th NHL Season

Franchise date: June 6, 1972
Transferred from Atlanta to Calgary, June 24, 1980.

Jiri Hudler led the offense during a breakthrough season for the Flames in 2014-15. He established career highs in goals (31), assists (45), points (76) and plus-minus (+17) while recording only 14 penalty minutes to earn the Lady Byng Trophy.

Year-by-Year Record

Season	GP	Home W	L	T	OL	Road W	L	T	OL	Overall W	L	T	OL	GF	GA	Pts.	Div. Fin.	Conf. Fin.	Playoff Result
2014-15	82	23	13	....	5	22	17	....	2	45	30	....	7	241	216	97	3rd, Pac.	8th, West	Lost Second Round
2013-14	82	19	19	....	3	16	21	....	4	35	40	....	7	209	241	77	6th, Pac.	13th, West	Out of Playoffs
2012-13	48	13	9	....	2	6	16	....	2	19	25	....	4	128	160	42	4th, NW	13th, West	Out of Playoffs
2011-12	82	23	12	....	6	14	17	....	10	37	29	....	16	202	226	90	2nd, NW	9th, West	Out of Playoffs
2010-11	82	23	13	....	5	18	16	....	7	41	29	....	12	250	237	94	2nd, NW	10th, West	Out of Playoffs
2009-10	82	20	17	....	4	20	15	....	6	40	32	....	10	204	210	90	2nd, NW	10th, West	Out of Playoffs
2008-09	82	27	10	....	4	19	20	....	2	46	30	....	6	254	248	98	2nd, NW	5th, West	Lost Conf. Quarter-Final
2007-08	82	25	11	....	9	17	19	....	1	42	30	....	10	229	227	94	3rd, NW	7th, West	Lost Conf. Quarter-Final
2006-07	82	32	9	....	2	11	20	....	8	43	29	....	10	258	226	96	3rd, NW	8th, West	Lost Conf. Quarter-Final
2005-06	82	30	7	....	4	16	18	....	7	46	25	....	11	218	200	103	1st, NW	3rd, West	Lost Conf. Quarter-Final
2004-05																			
2003-04	82	21	14	5	1	21	16	2	2	42	30	7	3	200	176	94	3rd, NW	6th, West	Lost Final
2002-03	82	14	16	10	1	15	20	3	3	29	36	13	4	186	228	75	5th, NW	12th, West	Out of Playoffs
2001-02	82	20	14	5	2	12	21	7	1	32	35	12	3	201	220	79	4th, NW	11th, West	Out of Playoffs
2000-01	82	12	18	9	2	15	18	6	2	27	36	15	4	197	236	73	4th, NW	11th, West	Out of Playoffs
1999-2000	82	20	14	6	1	11	22	4	4	31	36	10	5	211	256	77	4th, NW	9th, West	Out of Playoffs
1998-99	82	15	20	6	....	15	20	6	....	30	40	12	....	211	234	72	3rd, NW	9th, West	Out of Playoffs
1997-98	82	18	17	6	....	8	24	9	....	26	41	15	....	217	252	67	5th, Pac.	11th, West	Out of Playoffs
1996-97	82	21	18	2	....	11	23	7	....	32	41	9	....	214	239	73	5th, Pac.	10th, West	Out of Playoffs
1995-96	82	18	18	5	....	16	19	6	....	34	37	11	....	241	240	79	2nd, Pac.	6th, West	Lost Conf. Quarter-Final
1994-95	48	15	7	2	....	9	10	5	....	24	17	7	....	163	135	55	1st, Pac.	3rd, West	Lost Conf. Quarter-Final
1993-94	84	25	12	5	....	17	17	8	....	42	29	13	....	302	256	97	1st, Pac.	3rd, West	Lost Conf. Quarter-Final
1992-93	84	23	14	5	....	20	16	6	....	43	30	11	....	322	282	97	2nd, Smythe		Lost Div. Semi-Final
1991-92	80	19	14	7	....	12	23	5	....	31	37	12	....	296	305	74	5th, Smythe		Out of Playoffs
1990-91	80	29	8	3	....	17	18	5	....	46	26	8	....	344	263	100	2nd, Smythe		Lost Div. Semi-Final
1989-90	80	28	7	5	....	14	16	10	....	42	23	15	....	348	265	99	1st, Smythe		Lost Div. Semi-Final
1988-89	**80**	**32**	**4**	**4**	....	**22**	**13**	**5**	....	**54**	**17**	**9**	....	**354**	**226**	**117**	**1st, Smythe**		**Won Stanley Cup**
1987-88	80	26	11	3	....	22	12	6	....	48	23	9	....	397	305	105	1st, Smythe		Lost Div. Final
1986-87	80	25	13	2	....	21	18	1	....	46	31	3	....	318	289	95	2nd, Smythe		Lost Div. Semi-Final
1985-86	80	23	11	6	....	17	20	3	....	40	31	9	....	354	315	89	2nd, Smythe		Lost Final
1984-85	80	23	11	6	....	18	16	6	....	41	27	12	....	363	302	94	3rd, Smythe		Lost Div. Semi-Final
1983-84	80	22	11	7	....	12	21	7	....	34	32	14	....	311	314	82	2nd, Smythe		Lost Div. Final
1982-83	80	21	12	7	....	11	22	7	....	32	34	14	....	321	317	78	2nd, Smythe		Lost Div. Semi-Final
1981-82	80	20	11	9	....	9	23	8	....	29	34	17	....	334	345	75	3rd, Smythe		Lost Div. Semi-Final
1980-81	80	25	5	10	....	14	22	4	....	39	27	14	....	329	298	92	3rd, Patrick		Lost Semi-Final
1979-80*	80	18	15	7	....	17	17	6	....	35	32	13	....	282	269	83	4th, Patrick		Lost Prelim. Round
1978-79*	80	25	11	4	....	16	20	4	....	41	31	8	....	327	280	90	4th, Patrick		Lost Prelim. Round
1977-78*	80	20	13	7	....	14	14	12	....	34	27	19	....	274	252	87	3rd, Patrick		Lost Prelim. Round
1976-77*	80	22	11	7	....	12	23	5	....	34	34	12	....	264	265	80	3rd, Patrick		Lost Prelim. Round
1975-76*	80	19	14	7	....	16	19	5	....	35	33	12	....	262	237	82	3rd, Patrick		Lost Prelim. Round
1974-75*	80	24	9	7	....	10	22	8	....	34	31	15	....	243	233	83	4th, Patrick		Out of Playoffs
1973-74*	78	17	13	9	....	13	17	9	....	30	34	14	....	214	238	74	4th, West		Lost Quarter-Final
1972-73*	78	16	16	7	....	9	22	8	....	25	38	15	....	191	239	65	7th, West		Out of Playoffs

*Atlanta Flames

2015-16 Player Personnel

FORWARDS	HT	WT	*Age	Place of Birth	S	2014-15 Club
BACKLUND, Mikael	6-0	198	26	Vasteras, Sweden	L	Calgary
BENNETT, Sam	6-1	185	19	Holland Landing, ON	L	Kingston-Calgary
BOLLIG, Brandon	6-2	223	28	St. Charles, MO	L	Calgary
BOUMA, Lance	6-1	210	25	Provost, AB	L	Calgary
BYRON, Paul	5-7	153	26	Ottawa, ON	L	Calgary
COLBORNE, Joe	6-5	213	25	Calgary, AB	L	Calgary
FERLAND, Micheal	6-2	215	23	Swan River, MB	L	Calgary-Adirondack
FROLIK, Michael	6-1	198	27	Kladno, Czech.	L	Winnipeg
GAUDREAU, Johnny	5-9	150	22	Salem, NJ	L	Calgary
GRANLUND, Markus	5-11	185	22	Oulu, Finland	L	Calgary-Adirondack
HUDLER, Jiri	5-10	186	31	Olomouc, Czech.	L	Calgary
JONES, David	6-2	210	31	Guelph, ON	R	Calgary
JOORIS, Josh	6-1	190	25	Burlington, ON	R	Calgary-Adirondack
MONAHAN, Sean	6-2	185	20	Brampton, ON	L	Calgary
RAYMOND, Mason	6-0	185	30	Cochrane, AB	L	Calgary
SHORE, Drew	6-3	205	24	Denver, CO	R	San Antonio-Cgy-Adi
STAJAN, Matt	6-1	192	31	Mississauga, ON	L	Calgary
DEFENSEMEN						
BRODIE, T.J.	6-1	182	25	Chatham, ON	L	Calgary
ENGELLAND, Deryk	6-2	215	33	Edmonton, AB	R	Calgary
GIORDANO, Mark	6-0	200	32	Toronto, ON	L	Calgary
HAMILTON, Dougie	6-5	220	22	Toronto, ON	R	Boston
RUSSELL, Kris	5-10	173	28	Caroline, AB	L	Calgary
SMID, Ladislav	6-3	209	29	Frydlant V Cechach, Czech.	L	Calgary
WIDEMAN, Dennis	6-0	200	32	Kitchener, ON	R	Calgary

GOALTENDERS	HT	WT	*Age	Place of Birth	C	2014-15 Club
HILLER, Jonas	6-2	192	33	Felben Wellhausen, Switz.	R	Calgary
ORTIO, Joni	6-1	185	24	Turku, Finland	L	Calgary-Adirondack
RAMO, Karri	6-2	206	29	Asikkala, Finland	L	Calgary

* – Age at start of 2015-16 season

Bob Hartley

Head Coach

Born: Hawkesbury, ON, September 9, 1960.

The Calgary Flames announced the hiring of Bob Hartley as head coach on May 31, 2012. Hartley joined the Flames following a championship season with the ZSC Lions of Switzerland's National League A in 2011-12. Hartley brings a wealth of experience and winning to the Flames, having coached the Colorado Avalanche for five seasons, during which they won the 2001 Stanley Cup, and coaching the Atlanta Thrashers for parts of five seasons. He also led the Hershey Bears to the 1997 Calder Cup and has Junior A and Major Junior championship rings among his accomplishments. In 2014-15, he led the Flames to the playoffs for the first time since 2008-09 and won the Jack Adams Award as coach of the year.

Hartley began his coaching career with the Junior A team in his hometown of Hawkesbury, Ontario. He was named head coach of the QMJHL's Laval Titan in 1991. After an appearance in the 1993 Memorial Cup, he was hired as an assistant coach by the Quebec Nordiques AHL?affiliate, the Cornwall Aces. He took over as head coach in 1994 and led the Aces to two division titles.

When the Nordiques relocated to Colorado, Hartley became the head coach of their AHL affiliate, the Hershey Bears. He guided the team to four consecutive playoff appearances and a Calder Cup title in 1997. A season later, Hartley was hired as the Colorado Avalanche bench boss. During his five seasons, the Avalanche won four division titles and made four appearances in the Conference Finals and won the Stanley Cup in 2001. When his tenure with the Avalanche franchise ended in December of 2002, he had a franchise record 193 wins.

One month later, Hartley was appointed head coach of the Atlanta Thrashers. He guided the young Thrashers through four seasons of steady improvements including the 2006-07 campaign in which they won their first Southeast Division title and first playoff berth. A slow start for the Thrashers in 2007-08 season resulted in Hartley and the club parting ways.

Hartley went on to work as a televison hockey analyst, but in the summer of 2011, he signed as head coach for the ZSC Lions in Zurich, Switzerland.

Coaching Record

			Regular Season				Playoffs			
Season	Team	League	GC	W	L	O/T	GC	W	L	T
1987-88	Hawkesbury	CJHL	56	9	47	0	....	....	....	....
1988-89	Hawkesbury	CJHL	56	35	19	2	....	....	....	....
1989-90	Hawkesbury	CJHL	56	40	14	2	....	....	....	....
1990-91	Hawkesbury	CJHL	56	42	7	7	....	....	....	....
1991-92	Laval	QMJHL	67	37	25	5	10	4	6	....
1992-93	Laval	QMJHL	70	43	25	2	13	12	1	....
1992-93	Laval	M-Cup	....	....	....	....	5	2	3	....
1994-95	Cornwall	AHL	80	38	33	9	15	8	7	....
1995-96	Cornwall	AHL	80	34	39	7	8	3	5	....
1996-97	Hershey	AHL	80	43	27	10	23	15	8	....
1997-98	Hershey	AHL	80	36	37	7	7	3	4	....
1998-99	**Colorado**	**NHL**	**82**	**44**	**28**	**10**	**19**	**11**	**8**	....
99-2000	**Colorado**	**NHL**	**82**	**42**	**28**	**12**	**17**	**11**	**6**	....
2000-01♦	**Colorado**	**NHL**	**82**	**52**	**16**	**14**	**23**	**16**	**7**	....
2001-02	**Colorado**	**NHL**	**82**	**45**	**28**	**9**	**21**	**11**	**10**	....
2002-03	**Colorado**	**NHL**	**31**	**10**	**8**	**13**	....	....	....	....
2002-03	**Atlanta**	**NHL**	**39**	**19**	**14**	**6**	....	....	....	....
2003-04	**Atlanta**	**NHL**	**82**	**33**	**37**	**12**	....	....	....	....
2004-05	**Atlanta**				SEASON CANCELLED					
2005-06	**Atlanta**	**NHL**	**82**	**41**	**33**	**8**	....	....	....	....
2006-07	**Atlanta**	**NHL**	**82**	**43**	**28**	**11**	**4**	**0**	**4**	....
2007-08	**Atlanta**	**NHL**	**6**	**0**	**6**	**0**	....	....	....	....
2011-12	ZSC Lions Zurich	Swiss	50	27	33	....	15	12	3	....
2012-13	**Calgary**	**NHL**	**48**	**19**	**25**	**4**	....	....	....	....
2013-14	**Calgary**	**NHL**	**82**	**35**	**40**	**7**	....	....	....	....
2014-15	**Calgary**	**NHL**	**82**	**45**	**30**	**7**	**11**	**5**	**6**	....
	NHL Totals		**862**	**428**	**321**	**113**	**95**	**54**	**41**	....

♦ Stanley Cup win.
Jack Adams Award (2015)

2014-15 Scoring

* – rookie

Regular Season

Pos	#	Player	Team	GP	G	A	Pts	TOI	+/–	PIM	PP	SH	GW	S	S%
R	24	Jiri Hudler	CGY	78	31	45	76	18:00	17	14	6	0	5	158	19.6
L	13 *	Johnny Gaudreau	CGY	80	24	40	64	17:43	11	14	8	0	4	167	14.4
C	23	Sean Monahan	CGY	81	31	31	62	19:37	8	12	10	1	8	191	16.2
D	6	Dennis Wideman	CGY	80	15	41	56	24:38	6	34	6	0	2	173	8.7
D	5	Mark Giordano	CGY	61	11	37	48	25:10	13	37	2	1	2	157	7.0
D	7	T.J. Brodie	CGY	81	11	30	41	25:12	15	30	3	1	3	133	8.3
L	17	Lance Bouma	CGY	78	16	18	34	14:00	10	54	0	0	4	104	15.4
D	4	Kris Russell	CGY	79	4	30	34	23:56	18	17	1	0	0	111	3.6
R	19	David Jones	CGY	67	14	16	30	14:20	–3	18	2	0	1	114	12.3
C	8	Joe Colborne	CGY	64	8	20	28	15:25	7	43	1	1	1	67	11.9
C	11	Mikael Backlund	CGY	52	10	17	27	17:44	4	14	0	2	2	103	9.7
R	86 *	Josh Jooris	CGY	60	12	12	24	14:29	1	16	4	0	4	89	13.5
L	21	Mason Raymond	CGY	57	12	11	23	14:48	–8	8	0	0	1	123	9.8
L	32	Paul Byron	CGY	57	6	13	19	14:28	–2	8	1	0	0	62	9.7
C	60 *	Markus Granlund	CGY	48	8	10	18	13:22	–4	16	1	0	1	65	12.3
C	18	Matt Stajan	CGY	59	7	10	17	11:59	7	28	0	0	0	46	15.2
D	29	Deryk Engelland	CGY	76	2	9	11	14:23	–16	53	0	0	0	51	3.9
L	79 *	Michael Ferland	CGY	26	2	3	5	10:31	1	16	0	0	1	34	5.9
L	25	Brandon Bollig	CGY	62	1	4	5	8:35	–9	88	0	0	0	67	1.5
D	33	Raphael Diaz	CGY	56	2	2	4	12:01	–3	10	1	0	1	52	3.8
D	3	David Schlemko	ARI	20	1	3	4	18:06	–5	4	0	0	0	24	4.2
			DAL	5	0	0	0	14:24	0	0	0	0	0	6	0.0
			CGY	19	0	0	0	12:38	6	8	0	0	0	15	0.0
			Total	44	1	3	4	15:19	1	12	0	0	0	45	2.2
C	22	Drew Shore	CGY	11	1	2	3	10:39	–5	0	0	0	0	13	7.7
C	63 *	Sam Bennett	CGY	1	0	1	1	16:00	–1	0	0	0	0	1	0.0
R	57 *	Emile Poirier	CGY	6	0	1	1	7:59	1	0	0	0	0	2	0.0
D	15	Ladislav Smid	CGY	31	0	1	1	13:58	–12	13	0	0	0	21	0.0
D	55 *	John Ramage	CGY	1	0	0	0	18:10	–1	0	0	0	0	4	0.0
D	26 *	Tyler Wotherspoon	CGY	1	0	0	0	20:19	–3	0	0	0	0	1	0.0
D	61 *	Brett Kulak	CGY	1	0	0	0	19:31	0	2	0	0	0	0	0.0
C	10 *	Corban Knight	CGY	2	0	0	0	6:24	0	0	0	0	0	2	0.0
L	45 *	David Wolf	CGY	3	0	0	0	9:23	0	2	0	0	0	1	0.0
C	59	Max Reinhart	CGY	4	0	0	0	8:05	–3	0	0	0	0	3	0.0
D	28	Corey Potter	CGY	6	0	0	0	9:39	–1	0	0	0	0	2	0.0
R	16	Brian McGrattan	CGY	8	0	0	0	6:38	–2	4	0	0	0	10	0.0
R	22	Devin Setoguchi	CGY	12	0	0	0	12:08	–7	4	0	0	0	12	0.0

Goaltending

No.	Goaltender	GPI	Mins	Avg	W	L	OT	EN	SO	GA	SA	Sv%	G	A	PIM
1	Jonas Hiller	52	2871	2.36	26	19	4	10	1	113	1376	.918	0	0	0
37	* Joni Ortio	6	333	2.52	4	2	0	0	1	14	153	.908	0	0	0
31	Karri Ramo	34	1732	2.60	15	9	3	1	2	75	852	.912	0	0	0
	Totals	**82**	**4991**	**2.56**	**45**	**30**	**7**	**11**	**5**	**213**	**2392**	**.911**			

Karri Ramo and Jonas Hiller shared a shutout vs EDM on Apr 4, 2015

Playoffs

Pos	#	Player	Team	GP	G	A	Pts	TOI	+/–	PIM	PP	SH	GW	OT	S	S%
L	13 *	Johnny Gaudreau	CGY	11	4	5	9	19:10	–2	6	2	0	0	0	24	16.7
R	24	Jiri Hudler	CGY	11	4	4	8	16:21	–2	2	3	0	1	0	15	26.7
D	4	Kris Russell	CGY	11	2	5	7	26:44	–9	7	1	0	1	0	13	15.4
D	6	Dennis Wideman	CGY	11	0	7	7	26:28	–2	12	0	0	0	0	18	0.0
C	23	Sean Monahan	CGY	11	3	3	6	19:47	–3	2	1	0	0	0	24	12.5
L	79 *	Micheal Ferland	CGY	9	3	2	5	12:33	3	23	0	0	0	0	12	25.0
R	19	David Jones	CGY	11	2	3	5	14:01	1	2	0	0	0	0	22	9.1
D	7	T.J. Brodie	CGY	11	1	4	5	27:07	3	0	0	0	0	0	14	7.1
C	63 *	Sam Bennett	CGY	11	3	1	4	14:01	–3	8	0	0	1	0	20	15.0
C	18	Matt Stajan	CGY	11	1	3	4	16:07	0	21	0	0	1	0	11	9.1
C	8	Joe Colborne	CGY	11	1	2	3	17:13	–3	20	0	1	0	0	7	14.3
L	25	Brandon Bollig	CGY	11	2	0	2	6:53	–1	38	0	0	0	0	15	13.3
C	11	Mikael Backlund	CGY	11	1	1	2	18:52	–1	8	0	0	1	1	30	3.3
L	21	Mason Raymond	CGY	8	0	2	2	9:40	–4	0	0	0	0	0	9	0.0
C	60 *	Markus Granlund	CGY	3	0	1	1	7:44	1	0	0	0	0	0	2	0.0
D	29	Deryk Engelland	CGY	11	0	1	1	20:03	–1	50	0	0	0	0	11	0.0
D	3	David Schlemko	CGY	11	0	1	1	14:05	1	2	0	0	0	0	15	0.0
C	22	Drew Shore	CGY	1	0	0	0	14:17	–1	2	0	0	0	0	2	0.0
L	45 *	David Wolf	CGY	1	0	0	0	10:25	0	0	0	0	0	0	0	0.0
D	28	Corey Potter	CGY	2	0	0	0	4:45	–1	0	0	0	0	0	1	0.0
L	17	Lance Bouma	CGY	2	0	0	0	14:16	0	2	0	0	0	0	2	0.0
D	33	Raphael Diaz	CGY	3	0	0	0	7:53	1	0	0	0	0	0	1	0.0
D	26 *	Tyler Wotherspoon	CGY	6	0	0	0	6:38	0	0	0	0	0	0	2	0.0
R	86 *	Josh Jooris	CGY	9	0	0	0	11:20	0	4	0	0	0	0	8	0.0

Goaltending

No.	Goaltender	GPI	Mins	Avg	W	L	EN	SO	GA	SA	Sv%	G	A	PIM
1	Jonas Hiller	7	322	2.61	3	3	0	0	14	173	.919	0	0	0
31	Karri Ramo	7	336	2.86	2	3	3	0	16	171	.906	0	0	0
	Totals	**11**	**667**	**2.97**	**5**	**6**	**3**	**0**	**33**	**347**	**.905**			

Captains' History

Keith McCreary, 1972-73 to 1974-75; Pat Quinn, 1975-76, 1976-77; Tom Lysiak, 1977-78, 1978-79; Jean Pronovost, 1979-80; Brad Marsh, 1980-81; Phil Russell, 1981-82, 1982-83; Lanny McDonald, Doug Risebrough, 1983-84; Lanny McDonald, Doug Risebrough, Jim Peplinski, 1984-85 to 1986-87; Lanny McDonald, Jim Peplinski, 1987-88; Lanny McDonald, Jim Peplinski, Tim Hunter, 1988-89; Brad McCrimmon, 1989-90; alternating captains, 1990-91; Joe Nieuwendyk, 1991-92 to 1994-95; Theoren Fleury, 1995-96, 1996-97; Todd Simpson, 1997-98, 1998-99; Steve Smith, 1999-2000; Steve Smith and Dave Lowry, 2000-01; Dave Lowry; Bob Boughner and Craig Conroy, 2001-02; Bob Boughner and Craig Conroy, 2002-03; Jarome Iginla, 2003-04 to 2012-13; Mark Giordano, 2013-14 to date.

Club Records

Team

(Figures in brackets for season records are games played; records for fewest points, wins, ties, losses, goals, goals against are for 70 or more games)

Most Points **117** 1988-89 (80)
Most Wins **54** 1988-89 (80)
Most Ties **19** 1977-78 (80)
Most Losses **41** 1996-97 (82), 1997-98 (82), 1999-2000 (82)
Most Goals **397** 1987-88 (80)
Most Goals Against **345** 1981-82 (80)
Fewest Points **65** 1972-73 (78)
Fewest Wins **25** 1972-73 (78)
Fewest Ties **3** 1986-87 (80)
Fewest Losses **17** 1988-89 (80)
Fewest Goals **186** 2002-03 (82)
Fewest Goals Against **176** 2003-04 (82)
Longest Winning Streak
Overall .... **10** Oct. 14-Nov. 3/78
Home .... **10** Nov. 7-Dec. 12/06
Away .... **7** Nov. 10-Dec. 4/88
Longest Undefeated Streak
Overall .... **13** Nov. 10-Dec. 8/88 (12W, 1T)
Home .... **18** Dec. 29/90-Mar. 14/91 (17W, 1T)
Away .... **9** Feb. 20-Mar. 21/88 (6W, 3T), Nov. 11-Dec. 16/90 (6W, 3T)
Longest Losing Streak
Overall .... **11** Dec. 14/85-Jan. 7/86
Home .... **9** Dec. 27/13-Jan. 16/14
Away .... **13** Feb. 18-Apr. 6/13
Longest Winless Streak
Overall .... **11** Dec. 14/85-Jan. 7/86 (11L), Jan. 5-26/93 (9L, 2T)
Home .... **10** Oct. 21-Dec. 4/00 (6L, 4T/OL)
Away .... **13** Feb. 3-Mar. 29/73 (10L, 3T), Feb. 18-Apr. 6/13 (12L, 1OL/SOL)
Most Shutouts, Season **11** 2003-04 (82)
Most PIM, Season **2,643** 1991-92 (80)
Most Goals, Game .... **13** Feb. 10/93 (S.J. 1 at Cgy. 13)

Individual

Most Seasons .... **16** Jarome Iginla
Most Games .... **1,219** Jarome Iginla
Most Goals, Career .... **525** Jarome Iginla
Most Assists, Career .... **609** Al MacInnis
Most Points, Career .... **1,095** Jarome Iginla (525G, 570A)
Most PIM, Career .... **2,405** Tim Hunter
Most Shutouts, Career .... **41** Miikka Kiprusoff
Longest Consecutive Games Streak .... **441** Jarome Iginla (Oct. 4/07-Mar. 26/13)
Most Goals, Season .... **66** Lanny McDonald (1982-83)
Most Assists, Season .... **82** Kent Nilsson (1980-81)
Most Points, Season .... **131** Kent Nilsson (1980-81; 49G, 82A)
Most PIM, Season .... **375** Tim Hunter (1988-89)
Most Points, Defenseman, Season .... **103** Al MacInnis (1990-91; 28G, 75A)
Most Points, Center, Season .... **131** Kent Nilsson (1980-81; 49G, 82A)
Most Points, Right Wing, Season .... **110** Joe Mullen (1988-89; 51G, 59A)
Most Points, Left Wing, Season .... **90** Gary Roberts (1991-92; 53G, 37A)
Most Points, Rookie, Season .... **92** Joe Nieuwendyk (1987-88; 51G, 41A)
Most Shutouts, Season .... **10** Miikka Kiprusoff (2005-06)
Most Goals, Game .... **5** Joe Nieuwendyk (Jan. 11/89)
Most Assists, Game .... **6** Guy Chouinard (Feb. 25/81), Gary Suter (Apr. 4/86)
Most Points, Game .... **7** Sergei Makarov (Feb. 25/90; 2G, 5A)

Records include Atlanta Flames, 1972-73 through 1979-80.

All-time Record vs. Other Clubs

Regular Season

	Total								At Home								On Road							
	GP	W	L	T	OL	GF	GA	PTS	GP	W	L	T	OL	GF	GA	PTS	GP	W	L	T	OL	GF	GA	PTS
Anaheim	91	37	39	7	8	251	265	89	46	29	15	1	1	142	112	60	45	8	24	6	7	109	153	29
Arizona	182	87	69	20	6	657	597	200	92	53	28	9	2	364	278	117	90	34	41	11	4	293	319	83
Boston	101	35	56	10	0	308	351	80	49	21	24	4	0	172	164	46	52	14	32	6	0	136	187	34
Buffalo	101	36	46	16	3	313	354	91	51	22	18	11	0	173	153	55	50	14	28	5	3	140	201	36
Carolina	67	41	18	7	1	277	210	90	34	26	6	2	0	161	100	54	33	15	12	5	1	116	110	36
Chicago	161	64	66	26	5	472	502	159	81	36	29	13	3	250	242	88	80	28	37	13	2	222	260	71
Colorado	152	69	56	20	7	499	477	165	76	38	25	9	4	260	222	89	76	31	31	11	3	239	255	76
Columbus	51	23	21	0	7	130	139	53	25	14	5	0	6	74	61	34	26	9	16	0	1	56	78	19
Dallas	161	71	58	25	7	504	493	174	80	41	21	14	4	259	208	100	81	30	37	11	3	245	285	74
Detroit	154	67	66	16	5	502	498	155	78	42	28	6	2	271	224	92	76	25	38	10	3	231	274	63
Edmonton	224	114	88	19	3	785	726	250	112	65	37	9	1	427	349	140	112	49	51	10	2	358	377	110
Florida	27	14	8	3	2	73	70	33	13	6	5	1	1	37	39	14	14	8	3	2	1	36	31	19
Los Angeles	226	116	85	21	4	838	745	257	114	68	33	12	1	470	355	149	112	48	52	9	3	368	390	108
Minnesota	80	42	24	4	10	182	185	98	40	24	8	3	5	95	83	56	40	18	16	1	5	87	102	42
Montreal	109	37	55	15	2	304	361	91	56	22	26	7	1	172	179	52	53	15	29	8	1	132	182	39
Nashville	62	29	27	4	2	173	175	64	30	16	9	3	2	91	75	37	32	13	18	1	0	82	100	27
New Jersey	97	62	22	11	2	376	259	137	47	32	6	8	1	203	124	73	50	30	16	3	1	173	135	64
NY Islanders	110	44	45	20	1	341	366	109	54	26	16	11	1	188	162	64	56	18	29	9	0	153	204	45
NY Rangers	111	54	37	15	5	424	352	128	54	30	12	10	2	231	163	72	57	24	25	5	3	193	189	56
Ottawa	35	17	12	4	2	108	87	40	18	12	5	1	0	62	37	25	17	5	7	3	2	46	50	15
Philadelphia	113	44	55	12	2	368	395	102	57	26	21	9	1	219	188	62	56	18	34	3	1	149	207	40
Pittsburgh	100	38	43	18	1	352	339	95	51	27	15	8	1	211	157	63	49	11	28	10	0	141	182	32
St. Louis	163	74	71	14	4	496	502	166	81	41	32	5	3	249	223	90	82	33	39	9	1	247	279	76
San Jose	107	56	39	8	4	327	302	124	53	30	17	4	2	174	135	66	54	26	22	4	2	153	167	58
Tampa Bay	30	13	12	1	4	97	91	31	15	7	6	0	2	45	41	16	15	6	6	1	2	52	50	15
Toronto	128	60	55	12	1	476	437	133	68	40	23	5	0	265	209	85	60	20	32	7	1	211	228	48
Vancouver	259	125	88	33	13	872	823	296	128	70	38	15	5	470	376	160	131	55	50	18	8	402	447	136
Washington	89	42	33	13	1	324	280	98	43	26	10	7	0	169	110	59	46	16	23	6	1	155	170	39
Winnipeg	19	10	8	1	0	61	54	21	9	7	2	0	0	36	23	14	10	3	6	1	0	25	31	7
Defunct Clubs	26	15	7	4	0	94	67	34	13	8	4	1	0	51	34	17	13	7	3	3	0	43	33	17
Totals	**3336**	**1536**	**1309**	**379**	**112**	**10984**	**10502**	**3563**	**1668**	**905**	**524**	**188**	**51**	**5991**	**4826**	**2049**	**1668**	**631**	**785**	**191**	**61**	**4993**	**5676**	**1514**

Playoffs

	Series	W	L	GP	W	L	T	GF	GA	Last Mtg.	Rnd.	Result
Anaheim	2	0	2	12	4	8	0	25	36	2015	SR	L 1-4
Arizona	3	1	2	13	6	7	0	43	45	1987	DSF	L 2-4
Chicago	4	2	2	18	9	9	0	53	54	2009	CQF	L 2-4
Dallas	1	0	1	6	2	4	0	18	25	1981	SF	L 2-4
Detroit	3	1	2	14	6	8	0	26	38	2007	CQF	L 2-4
Edmonton	5	1	4	30	11	19	0	96	132	1991	DSF	L 3-4
Los Angeles	6	2	4	26	13	13	0	112	105	1993	DSF	L 2-4
Montreal	2	1	1	11	5	6	0	32	31	1989	F	W 4-2
NY Rangers	1	0	1	4	1	3	0	8	14	1980	PR	L 1-3
Philadelphia	2	1	1	11	4	7	0	28	43	1981	QF	W 4-3
St. Louis	1	1	0	7	4	3	0	28	22	1986	CF	W 4-3
San Jose	3	1	2	20	10	10	0	68	57	2008	CQF	L 3-4
Tampa Bay	1	0	1	7	3	4	0	14	13	2004	F	L 3-4
Toronto	1	0	1	2	0	2	0	5	9	1979	PR	L 0-2
Vancouver	7	5	2	38	21	17	0	119	110	2015	FR	W 4-2
Totals	**42**	**16**	**26**	**219**	**99**	**120**	**0**	**675**	**734**			

Playoff Results 2015-2011

Year	Round	Opponent	Result	GF	GA
2015	SR	Anaheim	L 1-4	9	19
	FR	Vancouver	W 4-2	18	14

Abbreviations: Round: F – Final; **CF** – conference final; **SR** – second round; **CQF** – conference quarter-final; **FR** – first round; **DSF** – division semi-final; **SF** – semi-final; **QF** – quarter-final; **PR** – preliminary round.

Carolina totals include Hartford, 1979-80 to 1996-97.
Colorado totals include Quebec, 1979-80 to 1994-95.
Dallas totals include Minnesota North Stars, 1972-73 to 1992-93.
New Jersey totals include Kansas City, 1974-75, 1975-76, and Colorado Rockies, 1976-77 to 1981-82.
Phoenix totals include Winnipeg, 1979-80 to 1995-96.
Winnipeg totals include Atlanta Thrashers, 1999-2000 to 2010-11.

2014-15 Results

Oct.	8	Vancouver	2-4
	9	at Edmonton	5-2
	11	at St. Louis	1-4
	14	at Nashville	3-2†
	15	at Chicago	2-1*
	17	at Columbus	2-3
	19	at Winnipeg	4-1
	21	Tampa Bay	1-2*
	23	Carolina	5-0
	25	Washington	1-3
	28	Montreal	1-2†
	31	Nashville	4-3
Nov.	2	at Montreal	6-2
	4	at Washington	4-3*
	6	at Tampa Bay	2-5
	8	at Florida	6-4
	10	at Carolina	1-4
	13	Arizona	5-3
	15	Ottawa	4-2
	18	Anaheim	4-3†
	20	Chicago	3-4
	22	New Jersey	5-4†
	25	at Anaheim	2-3
	26	at San Jose	2-0
	29	at Arizona	3-0
Dec.	2	Arizona	5-2
	4	Colorado	4-3*
	6	San Jose	2-3
	9	at Toronto	1-4
	11	at Buffalo	3-4
	12	at Pittsburgh	1-3
	14	at Chicago	1-2
	16	NY Rangers	2-5
	19	Dallas	1-2
	20	at Vancouver	2-3*
	22	at Los Angeles	4-3*
	27	Edmonton	4-1
	29	Los Angeles	2-1
	31	Edmonton	4-3*
Jan.	2	NY Islanders	1-2
	7	Detroit	2-3
	9	Florida	5-6
	10	at Vancouver	1-0
	15	at Arizona	4-1
	17	at San Jose	4-3*
	19	at Los Angeles	2-1*
	21	at Anaheim	3-6
	27	Buffalo	4-1
	29	Minnesota	0-1
	31	Edmonton	4-2
Feb.	2	Winnipeg	5-2
	4	San Jose	3-1
	6	Pittsburgh	0-4
	9	at San Jose	4-1
	12	at Los Angeles	3-5
	14	Vancouver	3-2
	16	Boston	4-3*
	18	Minnesota	2-3*
	20	Anaheim	3-6
	24	at NY Rangers	0-1
	25	at New Jersey	3-1
	27	at NY Islanders	1-2
Mar.	3	at Philadelphia	3-2*
	5	at Boston	4-3†
	6	at Detroit	5-2
	8	at Ottawa	4-5†
	11	Anaheim	6-3
	13	Toronto	6-3
	14	at Colorado	2-3
	17	St. Louis	0-4
	19	Philadelphia	4-1
	21	Columbus	2-3*
	23	Colorado	3-2
	25	Dallas	3-4†
	27	at Minnesota	2-4
	29	at Nashville	5-2
	30	at Dallas	5-3
Apr.	2	at St. Louis	1-4
	4	at Edmonton	4-0
	7	Arizona	3-2
	9	Los Angeles	3-1
	11	at Winnipeg	1-5

* – Overtime † – Shootout

NHL Draft Selections 2015-2001

Name in bold denotes played in NHL.

2015 Pick		2011 Pick		2007 Pick		2003 Pick	
53	Rasmus Andersson	13	**Sven Baertschi**	24	**Mikael Backlund**	9	**Dion Phaneuf**
60	Oliver Kylington	45	**Markus Granlund**	70	**John Negrin**	39	**Tim Ramholt**
136	Pavel Karnaukhov	57	**Tyler Wotherspoon**	116	**Keith Aulie**	97	Ryan Donally
166	Andrew Mangiapane	104	**Johnny Gaudreau**	143	Mickey Renaud	112	**Jamie Tardif**
196	Riley Bruce	164	**Laurent Brossoit**	186	C.J. Severyn	143	**Greg Moore**
						173	Tyler Johnson
2014 Pick		**2010 Pick**		**2006 Pick**		206	Thomas Bellemare
4	**Sam Bennett**	64	**Max Reinhart**	26	**Leland Irving**	240	Cam Cunning
34	Mason McDonald	73	Joey Leach	87	John Armstrong	270	Kevin Harvey
54	Hunter Smith	103	**John Ramage**	89	Aaron Marvin		
84	Brandon Hickey	108	**Bill Arnold**	118	Hugo Carpentier	**2002 Pick**	
175	Adam Ollas Mattsson	133	**Michael Ferland**	149	Juuso Puustinen	10	**Eric Nystrom**
184	Austin Carroll	193	**Patrick Holland**	179	Jordan Fulton	39	Brian McConnell
				187	Devin Didiomete	90	**Matthew Lombardi**
2013 Pick		**2009 Pick**		209	Per Jonsson	112	Yuri Artemenkov
6	**Sean Monahan**	23	**Tim Erixon**			141	Jiri Cetkovsky
22	**Emile Poirier**	74	Ryan Howse	**2005 Pick**		142	Emanuel Peter
28	Morgan Klimchuk	111	Henrik Bjorklund	26	**Matt Pelech**	146	Viktor Bobrov
67	Keegan Kanzig	141	Spencer Bennett	69	Gord Baldwin	159	Kristofer Persson
135	Eric Roy	171	**Joni Ortio**	74	Dan Ryder	176	**Curtis McElhinney**
157	Tim Harrison	201	Gaelan Patterson	111	J.D. Watt	206	**David Van Der Gulik**
187	Rushan Rafikov			128	Kevin Lalande	207	Pierre Johnsson
198	John Gilmour	**2008 Pick**		158	**Matt Keetley**	238	Jyri Marttinen
		25	**Greg Nemisz**	179	**Brett Sutter**		
2012 Pick		48	Mitch Wahl	221	Myles Rumsey	**2001 Pick**	
21	Mark Jankowski	78	**Lance Bouma**			14	**Chuck Kobasew**
42	Patrick Sieloff	108	Nicholas Larson	**2004 Pick**		41	Andrei Taratukhin
75	Jon Gillies	114	**T.J. Brodie**	24	**Kris Chucko**	56	Andrei Medvedev
105	**Brett Kulak**	168	Ryley Grantham	70	**Brandon Prust**	108	**Tomi Maki**
124	Ryan Culkin	198	Alexander Deilert	98	**Dustin Boyd**	124	Yegor Shastin
165	Coda Gordon			118	Aki Seitsonen	145	James Hakewill
186	Matthew Deblouw			121	Kris Hogg	164	Yuri Trubachev
				173	**Adam Pardy**	207	Garrett Bembridge
				182	Fred Wikner	220	**Dave Moss**
				200	Matt Schneider	233	Joe Campbell
				213	James Spratt	251	Ville Hamalainen
				279	**Adam Cracknell**		

Coaching History

Bernie Geoffrion, 1972-73, 1973-74; Bernie Geoffrion and Fred Creighton, 1974-75; Fred Creighton, 1975-76 to 1978-79; Al MacNeil, 1979-80 to 1981-82; Bob Johnson, 1982-83 to 1986-87; Terry Crisp, 1987-88 to 1989-90; Doug Risebrough, 1990-91; Doug Risebrough and Guy Charron, 1991-92; Dave King, 1992-93 to 1994-95; Pierre Page, 1995-96, 1996-97; Brian Sutter, 1997-98 to 1999-2000; Don Hay and Greg Gilbert, 2000-01; Greg Gilbert, 2001-02; Greg Gilbert, Al MacNeil and Darryl Sutter, 2002-03; Darryl Sutter, 2003-04 to 2005-06; Jim Playfair, 2006-07; Mike Keenan, 2007-08, 2008-09; Brent Sutter, 2009-10 to 2011-12; Bob Hartley, 2012-13 to date.

General Managers' History

Cliff Fletcher, 1972-73 to 1990-91; Doug Risebrough, 1991-92 to 1994-95; Doug Risebrough and Al Coates, 1995-96; Al Coates, 1996-97 to 1999-2000; Craig Button, 2000-01 to 2002-03; Darryl Sutter, 2003-04 to 2009-10; Darryl Sutter and Jay Feaster, 2010-11; Jay Feaster, 2011-12 to 2013-14; Brad Treliving, 2014-15 to date.

Brad Treliving

Executive Vice President and General Manager

Born: Penticton, BC, August 18, 1969.

Brad Treliving joined the Calgary Flames organization as general manager on April 28, 2014. In his first season with the Flames in 2014-15, Calgary reached the playoffs for the first time since 2008-09. Treliving reports directly to president of hockey operations Brian Burke. He is responsible for all team personnel decisions, both players and staff; managing the amateur and pro scouting staffs; as well as other administrative duties. He is also responsible for all player personnel assignments with Flames' minor league affiliates.

Treliving served as the vice president of hockey operations and assistant general manager with the Phoenix Coyotes for seven seasons prior to coming to Calgary. With Phoenix, Treliving worked closely with general manager Don Maloney on the day-to-day administration of the Coyotes' hockey operations. Treliving also served as general manager of the club's American Hockey League affiliate, the Portland Pirates.

Prior to his role with the Coyotes, Treliving served as the president of the Central Hockey League (CHL) for seven years. During his tenure, he guided the CHL to remarkable growth and development including the establishment of numerous successful expansion franchises. In 1996 Treliving co-founded the Western Professional Hockey League (WPHL) and served as the league's vice president and director of hockey operations for five seasons. He played an integral role in the merger of the WPHL and the CHL in May 2001 upon which he began his tenure as president of the league.

Prior to his front office career, Treliving played five seasons of professional hockey from 1990-91 to 1994-95 in the IHL, the AHL and the ECHL. A defenseman, Treliving registered 17 goals and 85 assists for 102 points and 811 penalty minutes in 243 games in the ECHL. As a junior, the native of Penticton, British Columbia, played in the BCJHL and two years in the WHL.

Club Directory

Scotiabank Saddledome

Calgary Flames
Scotiabank Saddledome
P.O. Box 1540 Station M
Calgary, Alberta T2P 3B9
Phone **403/777-2177**
FAX 403/777-2195
www.calgaryflames.com
Capacity: 19,289

Owners . . . . N. Murray Edwards (Chairman), Alvin G. Libin, Allan P. Markin, Jeff McCaig, Clayton H. Riddell

Executive Management
President & Chief Executive Officer . . . . Ken King
Chief Operating Officer. John Bean
President, Hockey Operations . . . . Brian Burke
General Manager . . . . Brad Treliving
Chief Financial Officer. Cam Olson
V.P., Building Operations . . . . Libby Raines
V.P., Finance and Administration. . . . . Ken Zaba
V.P., Advertising, Sponsorship & Marketing. . . . . . . Jim Bagshaw
V.P., Sales, Ticketing & Customer Service . . . . . . Rollie Cyr
V.P., Communications . . . . Peter Hanlon
V.P., Business Development . . . . Jim Peplinski
V.P., Food and Beverage . . . . Doug Collier
Directors, Business Analytics / Retail . . . . Deniece Kennedy / Brent Gibbs
Directors, Human Resources / Building Ops. . . . Betty Mah / Trent Anderson

Hockey Club Personnel
President, Hockey Operations . . . . Brian Burke
General Manager . . . . Brad Treliving
Assistant General Manager. . . . . Craig Conroy
Assistant General Manager. . . . . Brad Pascall
Director, Hockey Administration . . . . Mike Burke
Directors, Player Development. . . . . Ron Sutter, Troy Crowder
Director, Amateur Scouting. . . . . Tod Button
Director, Video and Statistical Analysis . . . . . . Chris Snow
Head Coach . . . . Bob Hartley
Associate Coach . . . . Jacques Cloutier
Assistant Coach . . . . Martin Gelinas
Assistant Coach, Video . . . . Jamie Pringle
Goaltending Coach. . . . . Jordan Sigalet
Team Services Manager . . . . Sean O'Brien
Exec. Asst. to President, Hockey Ops and G.M. . . . . Brenda Koyich
Exec. Asst. to Sr. V.P. Hockey Ops and AGM . . . . Anita Cranston
Pro Scouts . . . . Michael Goulet, Steve Leach, Derek MacKinnon, Steve Pleau, Todd Woodcroft
Scouts . . . . Frank Anzalone, Jim Cummins, Terry Doran, Ari Haanpaa, Bobbie Hagelin, Bob MacMillan, Bob McEwen, Fred Parker, Rob Sumner, Eric Soltys, Ritchie Thibeau, Corey Karkover

Medical/Training Staff
Strength & Conditioning Coach . . . . Ryan van Asten
Athletic Therapist / Asst. Athletic Therapist . . . . . . Kent Kobelka / Mike Gudmundson
Equipment Manager / Asst. Equipment Manager . . Mark DePasquale / Corey Osmak
Massage / Rehab Therapist . . . . Domenic Manchisi / Kevin Wagner
Dressing Room Attendant. . . . . Ben Dumaine
Head Physician . . . . Dr. Ian Auld
Team Physicians . . . . Dr. Jim Thorne, Dr. David Manning
Team Orthopedic Surgeons . . . . Dr. Richard Boorman, Dr. Stephen French
Team Dentists . . . . Dr. Bill Blair, Dr. Kristin Yont

Stockton Heat
Head Coach . . . . Ryan Huska
Assistant Coach . . . . Todd Gill
Assistant Coach . . . . Domenic Pittis
Goaltending Development Coach . . . . Scott Gouthro
Strength and Conditioning Coach . . . . Michael Thompson
Equipment Manager . . . . Peter Bureaux
Athletic Therapist . . . . Marc Paquet
Team Services Manager . . . . Adam Berger

Communications
Vice-President, Communications . . . . Peter Hanlon
Director, Communications & Media Relations . . . Sean Kelso
Coordinator, Public Relations . . . . Greger Buer

Flames Foundation for Life
Executive Director. . . . . Candice Goudie
Coordinators, Community / Alumni Relations . . . . Blake Heynen / Tonya Young

Administration
Chief Operating Officer. . . . . John Bean
Exec. Asst. to President/CEO . . . . Judy O'Brien
Directors, Business Analytics / Human Resources . . . Deniece Kennedy / Betty Mah
Exec. Asst to COO . . . . Coralie Baun

Marketing/Ticketing
V.P. Advertising, Sponsorship & Marketing . . . . Jim Bagshaw
V.P. Business Development . . . . Jim Peplinski
Senior Director / Director, Sponsorship & Sales . . . . Pat Halls / Mark Stiles
Senior Director, Game Presentation & Events. . . . Geordie Macleod
Directors, Corporate Sponsorship / Sponsorship Sales . . Kevin Gross / Mike Mungiello
Director, Marketing & Creative Services . . . . Jillian Frechette
Digital Content Manager . . . . Jason Johnson
Director, Broadcast & Production . . . . Carlo Petrini
Supervisor, Game Presentation . . . . PJ Aucoin
Executive Assistant Marketing . . . . Suzanna Chapman
V.P. Sales, Ticketing & Customer Service . . . . Rollie Cyr
Executive Assistant to V.P. of
    Sales, Ticketing & Customer Service. . . . . Tracy Wood
Director, Sales and Luxury Suites . . . . Mike Franco
Director, Customer Service . . . . Marc Leost
Director, Retail . . . . Brent Gibbs

Miscellaneous
Radio Affiliate . . . . The FAN 960 (960 AM)
TV Affiliate . . . . Rogers Sportsnet, CBC-TV, TSN

Key Off-Season Signings/Acquisitions

2015

June 18 • Re-signed D **Michal Jordan**.

25 • Re-signed LW **Chris Terry**.

27 • Acquired D **James Wisniewski** from Anaheim for G **Anton Khudobin**.

27 • Acquired G **Eddie Lack** from Vancouver for a 3rd-round choice in the 2015 NHL Draft and a 7th-round choice in 2016.

29 • Re-signed C **Andrej Nestrasil**.

July 1 • Re-signed C **Riley Nash** and D **Rasmus Rissanen**.

1 • Signed C **T.J. Hensick**.

7 • Re-signed LW **Zach Boychuk**.

12 • Re-signed RW **Justin Shugg**.

15 • Re-signed C **Brody Sutter**.

Carolina Hurricanes

2014-15 Results: 30w-41L-4OTL-7SOL 71PTS
8TH, Metropolitan Division • 14TH, Eastern Conference

2015-16 Schedule

Oct.	Thu.	8	at Nashville
	Sat.	10	Detroit
	Tue.	13	Florida
	Fri.	16	at Detroit
	Sat.	17	at Washington
	Wed.	21	at Colorado
	Fri.	23	at Los Angeles
	Sat.	24	at San Jose
	Tue.	27	at Detroit
	Thu.	29	at NY Islanders
	Fri.	30	Colorado
Nov.	Sun.	1	Tampa Bay*
	Fri.	6	Dallas
	Sat.	7	Ottawa
	Tue.	10	at NY Rangers
	Thu.	12	Minnesota
	Sat.	14	Philadelphia
	Mon.	16	Anaheim
	Fri.	20	Toronto
	Sun.	22	Los Angeles*
	Mon.	23	at Philadelphia
	Wed.	25	Edmonton
	Fri.	27	at Buffalo
	Mon.	30	at NY Rangers
Dec.	Thu.	3	New Jersey
	Sat.	5	Montreal
	Sun.	6	Arizona*
	Tue.	8	at Dallas
	Fri.	11	at Anaheim
	Sat.	12	at Arizona
	Tue.	15	at Philadelphia
	Fri.	18	Florida
	Sat.	19	at Pittsburgh
	Mon.	21	Washington
	Sat.	26	New Jersey
	Sun.	27	at Chicago
	Tue.	29	at New Jersey
	Thu.	31	Washington
Jan.	Sat.	2	Nashville
	Mon.	4	at Edmonton
	Wed.	6	at Vancouver

	Fri.	8	Columbus
	Sat.	9	at Columbus
	Tue.	12	Pittsburgh
	Thu.	14	at St. Louis
	Fri.	15	Vancouver
	Sun.	17	at Pittsburgh*
	Thu.	21	at Toronto
	Fri.	22	NY Rangers
	Sun.	24	Calgary
	Tue.	26	Chicago
Feb.	Wed.	3	at Calgary
	Fri.	5	at Winnipeg
	Sun.	7	at Montreal*
	Fri.	12	Pittsburgh
	Sat.	13	NY Islanders
	Tue.	16	Winnipeg
	Thu.	18	at Ottawa
	Fri.	19	San Jose
	Sun.	21	Tampa Bay
	Tue.	23	Philadelphia
	Thu.	25	at Toronto
	Fri.	26	Boston
	Sun.	28	St. Louis*
Mar.	Tue.	1	at New Jersey
	Sat.	5	at Tampa Bay
	Tue.	8	Ottawa
	Thu.	10	at Boston
	Sat.	12	at Buffalo*
	Tue.	15	at Washington
	Thu.	17	at Pittsburgh
	Sat.	19	at Minnesota*
	Tue.	22	Buffalo
	Thu.	24	at Columbus
	Sat.	26	NY Islanders
	Sun.	27	New Jersey*
	Tue.	29	at NY Islanders
	Thu.	31	NY Rangers
Apr.	Sat.	2	Columbus
	Tue.	5	at Boston
	Thu.	7	Montreal
	Sat.	9	at Florida

Denotes afternoon game.

Retired Numbers

2	Glen Wesley	1994-2008
10	Ron Francis	1981-1991; 1998-2004
17	Rod Brind'Amour	2000-2010

**METROPOLITAN DIVISION
37th NHL Season**

Franchise date: June 22, 1979

Transferred from Hartford to Carolina, June 25, 1997.

Justin Faulk played all 82 games for Carolina in 2014-15 and was one of just 12 NHL defensemen to log more than 2,000 minutes of total ice time. His 15 goals, 34 assists and 49 points were all career highs.

Year-by-Year Record

Season	GP	Home W	L	T	OL	Road W	L	T	OL	Overall W	L	T	OL	GF	GA	Pts.	Div. Fin.	Conf. Fin.	Playoff Result
2014-15	82	18	16	....	7	12	25	....	4	30	41	....	11	188	226	71	8th, Met.	14th, East	Out of Playoffs
2013-14	82	18	17	....	6	18	18	....	5	36	35	....	11	207	230	83	7th, Met.	13th, East	Out of Playoffs
2012-13	48	9	14	....	1	10	11	....	3	19	25	....	4	128	160	42	3rd, SE	13th, East	Out of Playoffs
2011-12	82	20	14	....	7	13	19	....	9	33	33	....	16	213	243	82	5th, SE	12th, East	Out of Playoffs
2010-11	82	22	14	....	5	18	17	....	6	40	31	....	11	236	239	91	3rd, SE	9th, East	Out of Playoffs
2009-10	82	21	17	....	3	14	20	....	7	35	37	....	10	230	256	80	3rd, SE	11th, East	Out of Playoffs
2008-09	82	26	14	....	1	19	16	....	6	45	30	....	7	239	226	97	2nd, SE	6th, East	Lost Conf. Final
2007-08	82	24	13	....	4	19	20	....	2	43	33	....	6	252	249	92	2nd, SE	9th, East	Out of Playoffs
2006-07	82	21	16	....	4	19	18	....	4	40	34	....	8	241	253	88	3rd, SE	11th, East	Out of Playoffs
2005-06	**82**	**31**	**8**	....	**2**	**21**	**14**	....	**6**	**52**	**22**	....	**8**	**294**	**260**	**112**	**1st, SE**	**2nd, East**	**Won Stanley Cup**
2004-05																			
2003-04	82	13	18	8	2	15	16	6	4	28	34	14	6	172	209	76	3rd, SE	11th, East	Out of Playoffs
2002-03	82	12	17	9	3	10	26	2	3	22	43	11	6	171	240	61	5th, SE	15th, East	Out of Playoffs
2001-02	82	15	13	11	2	20	13	5	3	35	26	16	5	217	217	91	1st, SE	3rd, East	Lost Final
2000-01	82	23	15	3	0	15	17	6	3	38	32	9	3	212	225	88	2nd, SE	8th, East	Lost Conf. Quarter-Final
1999-2000	82	16	16	5	0	17	19	5	0	37	35	10	0	217	216	84	3rd, SE	9th, East	Out of Playoffs
1998-99	82	20	12	9		14	18	9		34	30	18	....	210	202	86	1st, SE	3rd, East	Lost Conf. Quarter-Final
1997-98	82	16	18	7		17	23	1		33	41	8		200	219	74	6th, NE	9th, East	Out of Playoffs
1996-97*	82	23	15	3		9	24	8		32	39	11		226	256	75	5th, NE	10th, East	Out of Playoffs
1995-96*	82	22	15	4		12	24	5		34	39	9		237	259	77	4th, NE	10th, East	Out of Playoffs
1994-95*	48	12	10	2		7	14	3		19	24	5		127	141	43	5th, NE	11th, East	Out of Playoffs
1993-94*	84	14	22	6		13	26	3		27	48	9		227	288	63	6th, NE	13th, East	Out of Playoffs
1992-93*	84	12	25	5		4	24	1		26	52	6		284	369	58	5th, Adams		Out of Playoffs
1991-92*	80	13	17	10		13	24	3		26	41	13		247	283	65	4th, Adams		Lost Div. Semi-Final
1990-91*	80	18	16	6		13	22	5		31	38	11		238	276	73	4th, Adams		Lost Div. Semi-Final
1989-90*	80	17	18	5		21	15	4		38	33	9		275	268	85	4th, Adams		Lost Div. Semi-Final
1988-89*	80	21	17	2		16	21	3		37	38	5		299	299	79	4th, Adams		Lost Div. Semi-Final
1987-88*	80	21	14	5		14	24	2		35	38	7		249	267	77	4th, Adams		Lost Div. Semi-Final
1986-87*	80	26	9	5		17	21	2		43	30	7		287	270	93	1st, Adams		Lost Div. Semi-Final
1985-86*	80	21	17	2		19	19	2		40	36	4		332	302	84	4th, Adams		Lost Div. Final
1984-85*	80	17	18	5		13	23	4		30	41	9		268	318	69	5th, Adams		Out of Playoffs
1983-84*	80	19	16	5		9	26	5		28	42	10		288	320	66	5th, Adams		Out of Playoffs
1982-83*	80	13	22	5		6	32	2		19	54	7		261	403	45	5th, Adams		Out of Playoffs
1981-82*	80	13	17	10		8	24	8		21	41	18		264	351	60	5th, Adams		Out of Playoffs
1980-81*	80	14	17	9		7	24	9		21	41	18		292	372	60	4th, Norris		Out of Playoffs
1979-80*	80	22	12	6		5	22	13		27	34	19		303	312	73	4th, Norris		Lost Prelim. Round

*Hartford Whalers

2015-16 Player Personnel

FORWARDS	HT	WT	*Age	Place of Birth	S	2014-15 Club
BOYCHUK, Zach	5-10	185	26	Airdrie, AB	L	Carolina-Charlotte
BROWN, Patrick	6-1	210	23	Bloomfield Hills, MI	R	Carolina-Charlotte
Di GIUSEPPE, Phillip	6-0	200	21	Toronto, ON	L	Charlotte
GERBE, Nathan	5-5	178	28	Oxford, MI	L	Carolina
HENSICK, T.J.	5-9	170	29	Howell, MI	R	Hamilton
LINDHOLM, Elias	6-1	192	20	Boden , Sweden	L	Carolina
MALONE, Brad	6-2	207	26	Miramichi, NB	L	Carolina
McCLEMENT, Jay	6-1	205	32	Kingston, ON	L	Carolina
McGINN, Brock	6-0	185	21	Fergus, ON	L	Charlotte
NASH, Riley	6-1	200	26	Consort, AB	R	Carolina
NESTRASIL, Andrej	6-2	210	24	Prague, Czech.	L	Det-Car-Charlotte
RASK, Victor	6-2	200	22	Leksand, Sweden	L	Carolina
RYAN, Derek	5-10	170	28	Spokane, WA	R	Orebro
SKINNER, Jeff	5-11	200	23	Markham, ON	L	Carolina
STAAL, Eric	6-4	205	30	Thunder Bay, ON	L	Carolina
STAAL, Jordan	6-4	220	27	Thunder Bay, ON	L	Carolina
SUTTER, Brody	6-5	203	24	Viking, AB	R	Carolina-Charlotte
TERRY, Chris	5-10	195	26	Brampton, ON	L	Carolina-Charlotte
WOODS, Brendan	6-4	210	23	Humboldt, SK	L	Carolina-Charlotte

DEFENSEMEN						
BIEGA, Danny	6-0	205	24	Montreal, QC	R	Carolina-Charlotte
FAULK, Justin	6-0	215	23	South St. Paul, MN	R	Carolina
FLEURY, Haydn	6-3	207	19	Carlyle, SK	L	Red Deer-Charlotte
HAINSEY, Ron	6-3	210	34	Bolton, CT	L	Carolina
HANIFIN, Noah	6-3	206	18	Boston, MA	L	Boston College
JORDAN, Michal	6-1	195	25	Zlin, Czech.	L	Carolina-Charlotte
LILES, John-Michael	5-10	185	34	Indianapolis, IN	L	Carolina
MURPHY, Ryan	5-11	185	22	Aurora, ON	R	Carolina-Charlotte
PESCE, Brett	6-3	200	20	Tarrytown, NY	R	New Hampshire-Charlotte
RISSANEN, Rasmus	6-3	217	24	Kuopio, Finland	L	Carolina-Charlotte
SLAVIN, Jaccob	6-2	205	21	Denver, CO	L	Colorado College
WISNIEWSKI, James	5-11	203	31	Canton, MI	R	Columbus-Anaheim

GOALTENDERS	HT	WT	*Age	Place of Birth	C	2014-15 Club
LACK, Eddie	6-4	187	27	Norrtalje, Sweden	L	Vancouver
MacINTYRE, Drew	6-1	190	32	Charlottetown, PE	L	Charlotte
WARD, Cam	6-1	185		Saskatoon, SK	L	Carolina

* – Age at start of 2015-16 season

2014-15 Scoring
* – rookie

Regular Season

Pos	#	Player	Team	GP	G	A	Pts	TOI	+/-	PIM	PP	SH	GW	S	S%
C	12	Eric Staal	CAR	77	23	31	54	18:50	-13	41	7	0	4	244	9.4
D	27	Justin Faulk	CAR	82	15	34	49	24:25	-19	30	7	2	4	238	6.3
C	16	Elias Lindholm	CAR	81	17	22	39	16:25	-23	14	4	0	4	170	10.0
C	49 *	Victor Rask	CAR	80	11	22	33	16:20	-14	16	2	0	2	172	6.4
C	53	Jeff Skinner	CAR	77	18	13	31	16:02	-24	18	4	0	2	235	7.7
C	14	Nathan Gerbe	CAR	78	10	18	28	16:26	-14	34	2	0	2	235	4.3
C	20	Riley Nash	CAR	68	8	17	25	16:18	-10	12	1	0	0	94	8.5
C	11	Jordan Staal	CAR	46	6	18	24	18:33	-6	14	1	0	1	92	6.5
D	26	John-Michael Liles	CAR	57	2	20	22	19:08	-9	14	0	0	0	90	2.2
C	18	Jay McClement	CAR	82	7	14	21	13:34	-7	17	0	0	2	68	10.3
L	25 *	Chris Terry	CAR	57	11	9	20	12:43	-4	14	3	0	0	71	15.5
C	15 *	Andrej Nestrasil	DET	13	0	2	2	11:03	-3	4	0	0	0	16	0.0
			CAR	41	7	11	18	14:04	2	4	0	0	0	66	10.6
			Total	54	7	13	20	13:21	-1	8	2	0	0	82	8.5
R	28	Alexander Semin	CAR	57	6	13	19	15:55	-10	32	0	0	0	93	6.5
R	24	Brad Malone	CAR	65	7	8	15	10:09	-8	74	0	0	2	65	10.8
D	7	Ryan Murphy	CAR	37	4	9	13	18:17	-11	8	3	0	1	61	6.6
R	39	Patrick Dwyer	CAR	71	5	7	12	12:46	-12	10	0	0	0	77	6.5
D	73	Brett Bellemore	CAR	49	2	8	10	16:22	1	27	0	0	1	26	7.7
D	65	Ron Hainsey	CAR	81	2	8	10	21:05	-14	16	0	0	0	83	2.4
L	22	Zach Boychuk	CAR	31	3	3	6	10:37	0	4	0	0	0	35	8.6
D	47 *	Michal Jordan	CAR	38	2	4	6	15:56	-7	4	2	0	0	44	4.5
D	38	Jack Hillen	WSH	35	0	5	5	12:22	1	10	0	0	0	20	0.0
			CAR	3	0	0	0	18:35	-2	0	0	0	0	4	0.0
			Total	38	0	5	5	12:51	-1	10	0	0	0	24	0.0
D	41 *	Danny Biega	CAR	10	0	2	2	16:08	-5	0	0	0	0	7	0.0
D	45 *	Keegan Lowe	CAR	2	0	0	0	13:50	-2	10	0	0	0	0	0.0
L	56 *	Brendan Woods	CAR	3	0	0	0	6:02	-0	0	0	0	0	3	0.0
L	52 *	Justin Shugg	CAR	3	0	0	0	5:41	0	2	0	0	0	3	0.0
C	48 *	Brody Sutter	CAR	4	0	0	0	7:26	-2	0	0	0	0	4	0.0
C	62 *	Rasmus Rissanen	CAR	6	0	0	0	14:58	-5	4	0	0	0	0	0.0
C	36 *	Patrick Brown	CAR	7	0	0	0	8:52	-4	0	0	0	0	4	0.0

Goaltending

No.	Goaltender	GPI	Mins	Avg	W	L	OT	EN	SO	GA	SA	Sv%	G	A	PIM
30	Cam Ward	51	3026	2.40	22	24	5	5	1	121	1351	.910	0	0	4
31	Anton Khudobin	34	1920	2.72	8	17	6	6	1	87	874	.900	0	0	0
	Totals	82	4999	2.63	30	41	11	11	2	219	2236	.902			

Victor Rask led all Hurricanes rookies with 80 games played, 22 assists and 33 points in 2014-15. He also ranked second to Bo Horvat among all NHL rookies by winning 51 percent of his faceoffs.

Captains' History

Rick Ley, 1979-80; Rick Ley and Mike Rogers, 1980-81; Dave Keon, 1981-82; Russ Anderson, 1982-83; Mark Johnson, 1983-84; Mark Johnson and Ron Francis, 1984-85; Ron Francis, 1985-86 to 1990-91; Randy Ladouceur, 1991-92; Pat Verbeek, 1992-93 to 1994-95; Brendan Shanahan, 1995-96; Keith Primeau, 1996-97, 1997-98; Keith Primeau, 1998-99; Keith Primeau and Ron Francis, 1999-2000; Ron Francis, 2000-01 to 2003-04; Rod Brind'Amour, 2005-06 to 2008-09; Rod Brind'Amour and Eric Staal, 2009-10; Eric Staal, 2010-11 to date.

Coaching History

Don Blackburn, 1979-80; Don Blackburn and Larry Pleau, 1980-81; Larry Pleau, 1981-82; Larry Kish, Larry Pleau and John Cuniff, 1982- 83; Jack Evans, 1983-84 to 1986-87; Jack Evans and Larry Pleau, 1987-88; Larry Pleau, 1988-89; Rick Ley, 1989-90, 1990-91; Jim Roberts, 1991-92; Paul Holmgren, 1992-93; Paul Holmgren and Pierre Maguire, 1993-94; Paul Holmgren, 1994-95; Paul Holmgren and Paul Maurice, 1995-96; Paul Maurice, 1996-97 to 2002-03; Paul Maurice and Peter Laviolette, 2003-04; Peter Laviolette, 2004-05 to 2007-08; Peter Laviolette and Paul Maurice, 2008-09; Paul Maurice, 2009-10, 2010-11; Paul Maurice and Kirk Muller, 2011-12; Kirk Muller, 2012-13, 2013-14; Bill Peters, 2014-15 to date.

Bill Peters
Head Coach

Born: Three Hills, AB, January 13, 1965.

Bill Peters began his tenure as head coach of the Carolina Hurricanes on June 19, 2014. He is the 13th person to serve as head coach in franchise history, and the fourth since the team's arrival in North Carolina in 1997.

This marks Peters' first head coaching position in the NHL. Prior to joining the Hurricanes, Peters served as assistant coach for the Detroit Red Wings for three seasons, working primarily with Detroit's defensemen and penalty kill units. Before joining Detroit's staff, Peters served as head coach of Rockford of the American Hockey League, guiding the Ice Hogs to consecutive 40-win seasons and Calder Cup playoff appearances in 2008-09 and 2009-10. In his final season with Rockford in 2010-11, Peters directed the second-youngest team in the AHL. He helped 28 Rockford players reach the NHL during his three seasons with the club. Eight players who played under Peters for Rockford went on to win the Stanley Cup with Chicago in 2010 or 2013 – Niklas Hjalmarsson, Jordan Henry, Antti Niemi, Corey Crawford, Bryan Bickell, Nick Leddy, Brandon Bollig and Ben Smith.

Before beginning his AHL coaching career, Peters spent three seasons with Spokane of the Western Hockey League, leading the Chiefs to the Memorial Cup title in 2008. Spokane established franchise records with 50 wins and 107 points that season before winning 16 of 21 WHL playoff games to capture the Ed Chynoweth Cup as WHL champions. Peters then guided the Chiefs to four consecutive victories at the Memorial Cup, topping the host Kitchener Rangers 4-1 in the championship game.

Peters got his first experience as a head coach at the University of Lethbridge, serving as the Proghorns' head coach for three seasons from 2002 to 2005. Prior to that, he served as assistant coach for Spokane for four seasons, helping the Chiefs to a 47-win, 100-point campaign and the WHL Western Conference championship in 1999-2000 under current Red Wings' head coach Mike Babcock.

Peters also has gained international head coaching experience for Canada, capturing the gold medal at the 2008 Under-18 Junior World Cup.

Coaching Record

Season	Team	League	Regular Season				Playoffs			
			GC	W	L	O/T	GC	W	L	T
2002-03	U of Lethbridge	CWUAA	28	10	16	2	3	1	2	0
2003-04	U of Lethbridge	CWUAA	28	4	20	4	....			
2004-05	U of Lethbridge	CWUAA	28	3	23	2	....			
2005-06	Spokane	WHL	72	25	39	8	....			
2006-07	Spokane	WHL	72	36	28	8	6	2	4	0
2007-08	Spokane	WHL	72	50	15	7	21	16	5	0
2007-08	Spokane	M-Cup	....				4	4	0	0
2008-09	Rockford	AHL	80	40	34	6	4	0	4	0
2009-10	Rockford	AHL	80	44	30	6	4	0	4	0
2010-11	Rockford	AHL	80	38	33	9	....			
2014-15	**Carolina**	**NHL**	**82**	**30**	**41**	**11**	**....**			
	NHL Totals		82	30	41	11	....			

Club Records

Team

(Figures in brackets for season records are games played; records for fewest points, wins, ties, losses, goals, goals against are for 70 or more games)

Most Points	112	2005-06 (82)
Most Wins	52	2005-06 (82)
Most Ties	19	1979-80 (80)
Most Losses	54	1982-83 (80)
Most Goals	332	1985-86 (80)
Most Goals Against	403	1982-83 (80)
Fewest Points	45	1982-83 (80)
Fewest Wins	19	1982-83 (80)
Fewest Ties	4	1985-86 (80)
Fewest Losses	22	2005-06 (82)
Fewest Goals	171	2002-03 (82)
Fewest Goals Against	202	1998-99 (82)

Longest Winning Streak
Overall...9 Oct. 22-Nov. 11/05, Dec. 31/05-Jan. 19/06, Mar. 18-Apr. 07/09
Home...12 Feb. 20-Apr. 7/09
Away...6 Nov. 10-Dec. 7/90

Longest Undefeated Streak
Overall...10 Jan. 20-Feb. 10/82 (6W, 4T)
Home...12 Feb. 20-Apr. 7/09 (12W)
Away...8 Nov. 11-Dec. 5/96 (4W, 4T)

Longest Losing Streak
Overall...14 Oct. 10-Nov. 13/09
Home...8 Mar. 14-Apr. 9/13
Away...13 Dec. 18/82-Feb. 5/83, Oct. 3-Nov. 28/09

Longest Winless Streak
Overall...14 Jan. 4-Feb. 9/92 (8L, 6T), Oct. 10-Nov. 13/09 (10L, 4OL/SOL)
Home...13 Jan. 15-Mar. 10/85 (11L, 2T)
Away...15 Nov. 11/79-Jan. 9/80 (11L, 4T), Jan. 7-Mar. 2/03 (13L, 2T/OL)

Most Shutouts, Season...8 1998-99 (82)
Most PIM, Season...2,354 1992-93 (84)
Most Goals, Game...11 Feb. 12/84 (Edm. 0 at Hfd. 11), Oct. 19/85 (Mtl. 6 at Hfd. 11), Jan. 17/86 (Que. 6 at Hfd. 11), Mar. 15/86 (Chi. 4 at Hfd. 11)

Individual

Most Seasons...16 Ron Francis
Most Games...1,186 Ron Francis
Most Goals, Career...382 Ron Francis
Most Assists, Career...793 Ron Francis
Most Points, Career...1,175 Ron Francis (382G, 793A)
Most PIM, Career...1,439 Kevin Dineen
Most Shutouts, Career...21 Cam Ward
Longest Consecutive Games Streak...419 Dave Tippett (Mar. 3/84-Oct. 7/89)
Most Goals, Season...56 Blaine Stoughton (1979-80)
Most Assists, Season...69 Ron Francis (1989-90)
Most Points, Season...105 Mike Rogers (1979-80; 44G, 61A), (1980-81; 40G, 65A)
Most PIM, Season...358 Torrie Robertson (1985-86)

Most Points, Defenseman, Season...69 Dave Babych (1985-86; 14G, 55A)
Most Points, Center, Season...105 Mike Rogers (1979-80; 44G, 61A), (1980-81; 40G, 65A)
Most Points, Right Wing, Season...100 Blaine Stoughton (1979-80; 56G, 44A)
Most Points, Left Wing, Season...89 Geoff Sanderson (1992-93; 46G, 43A)
Most Points, Rookie, Season...72 Sylvain Turgeon (1983-84; 40G, 32A)
Most Shutouts, Season...6 Arturs Irbe (1998-99), (2000-01) Kevin Weekes (2003-04) Cam Ward (2008-09)
Most Goals, Game...4 Jordy Douglas (Feb. 3/80) Ron Francis (Feb. 12/84) Eric Staal (Mar. 7/09)
Most Assists, Game...6 Ron Francis (Mar. 5/87)
Most Points, Game...6 Paul Lawless (Jan. 4/87; 2G, 4A) Ron Francis (Mar. 5/87; 6A), (Oct. 8/89; 3G, 3A) Eric Staal (Mar. 7/09; 4G, 2A)

Records include Hartford Whalers, 1979-80 through 1996-97.

All-time Record vs. Other Clubs

Regular Season

	Total							At Home							On Road						
	GP	W	L	T	OL	GF	GA	PTS	GP	W	L	T	OL	GF	GA	PTS	GP	W	L	T	OL	GF	GA	PTS
Anaheim	30	13	12	2	3	84	82	31	15	8	5	1	1	38	34	18	15	5	7	1	2	46	48	13
Arizona	72	35	29	8	0	249	231	78	36	16	14	6	0	117	106	38	36	19	15	2	0	132	125	40
Boston	191	73	98	16	4	556	650	166	95	40	43	9	3	306	320	92	96	33	55	7	1	250	330	74
Buffalo	192	75	94	18	5	560	657	173	97	43	40	11	3	287	287	100	95	32	54	7	2	273	370	73
Calgary	67	19	40	7	1	210	277	46	33	13	15	5	0	110	116	31	34	6	25	2	1	100	161	15
Chicago	69	28	32	7	2	206	237	65	35	17	13	4	1	112	104	39	34	11	19	3	1	94	133	26
Colorado	138	46	69	21	2	426	522	115	68	29	26	12	1	221	226	71	70	17	43	9	1	205	296	44
Columbus	22	11	9	0	2	55	61	24	12	6	4	0	2	32	35	14	10	5	5	0	0	23	26	10
Dallas	73	27	37	6	3	221	267	63	38	16	18	4	0	121	132	36	35	11	19	2	3	100	135	27
Detroit	73	27	36	8	2	214	239	64	36	19	15	1	1	114	99	40	37	8	21	7	1	100	140	24
Edmonton	70	22	35	12	1	242	252	57	34	14	13	7	0	135	110	35	36	8	22	5	1	107	142	22
Florida	109	54	39	11	5	296	302	124	54	35	14	3	2	170	132	75	55	19	25	8	3	126	170	49
Los Angeles	71	29	32	8	2	249	271	68	36	18	12	5	1	124	126	42	35	11	20	3	1	125	145	26
Minnesota	18	8	6	2	2	49	48	20	7	5	1	0	1	16	13	11	11	3	5	2	1	33	35	9
Montreal	190	65	100	20	5	541	688	155	96	38	43	13	2	279	325	91	94	27	57	7	3	262	363	64
Nashville	21	8	10	1	2	50	58	19	11	6	2	1	2	30	29	15	10	2	8	0	0	20	29	4
New Jersey	128	49	63	12	4	372	406	114	64	27	28	8	1	186	191	63	64	22	35	4	3	186	215	51
NY Islanders	128	65	47	9	7	417	390	146	64	32	24	5	3	222	204	72	64	33	23	4	4	195	186	74
NY Rangers	128	51	61	7	9	348	417	118	63	32	24	3	4	197	190	71	65	19	37	4	5	151	227	47
Ottawa	93	49	32	8	4	259	242	110	45	28	11	4	2	134	105	62	48	21	21	4	2	125	137	48
Philadelphia	127	38	65	14	10	351	457	100	64	21	30	9	4	189	223	55	63	17	35	5	6	162	234	45
Pittsburgh	133	58	58	11	6	464	477	133	68	33	28	5	2	241	231	73	65	25	30	6	4	223	246	60
St. Louis	74	27	38	5	4	212	242	63	37	16	18	2	1	107	109	35	37	11	20	3	3	105	133	28
San Jose	32	17	15	0	0	100	104	34	16	9	7	0	0	49	39	18	16	8	8	0	0	51	65	16
Tampa Bay	112	50	44	10	8	321	335	118	57	30	17	7	3	170	167	70	55	20	27	3	5	151	168	48
Toronto	110	60	36	11	3	397	342	134	55	31	17	6	1	209	171	69	55	29	19	5	2	188	171	65
Vancouver	69	25	31	11	2	197	237	63	34	15	14	5	0	108	113	35	35	10	17	6	2	89	124	28
Washington	158	58	78	14	8	427	490	138	79	30	37	10	2	220	234	72	79	28	41	4	6	207	256	66
Winnipeg	82	47	25	4	6	258	234	104	41	20	16	1	4	119	127	45	41	27	9	3	2	139	107	59
Totals	**2780**	**1134**	**1271**	**263**	**112**	**8331**	**9215**	**2643**	**1390**	**647**	**549**	**147**	**47**	**4363**	**4298**	**1488**	**1390**	**487**	**722**	**116**	**65**	**3968**	**4917**	**1155**

Playoffs

	Series	W	L	GP	W	L	T	GF	GA	Last Mtg.	Rnd.	Result
Boston	4	1	3	26	11	15	0	64	80	2009	CSF	W 4-3
Buffalo	1	1	0	7	4	3	0	22	17	2006	CF	W 4-3
Colorado	2	1	1	9	5	4	0	35	34	1987	DSF	L 2-4
Detroit	1	0	1	5	1	4	0	7	14	2002	F	L 1-4
Edmonton	1	1	0	7	4	3	0	19	16	2006	F	W 4-3
Montreal	7	2	5	39	16	23	0	106	125	2006	CQF	W 4-2
New Jersey	4	3	1	24	14	10	0	51	56	2009	CQF	W 4-3
Pittsburgh	1	0	1	4	0	4	0	9	20	2009	CF	L 0-4
Toronto	1	1	0	6	4	2	0	10	6	2002	CF	W 4-2
Totals	**22**	**10**	**12**	**127**	**59**	**68**	**0**	**323**	**368**			

Playoff Results 2015-2011

(Last playoff appearance: 2009)

Abbreviations: Round: F – Final; **CF** – conference final; **CSF** – conference semi-final; **CQF** – conference quarter-final; **DSF** – division semi-final.

Calgary totals include Atlanta Flames, 1979-80.
Dallas totals include Minnesota North Stars, 1979-80 to 1992-93.
Phoenix totals include Winnipeg, 1979-80 to 1995-96.
Colorado totals include Quebec, 1979-80 to 1994-95.
New Jersey totals include Colorado Rockies, 1979-80 to 1981-82.
Winnipeg totals include Atlanta Thrashers, 1999-2000 to 2010-11.

2014-15 Results

Oct.	10	NY Islanders	3-5	10	at St. Louis	4-5†
	11	at NY Islanders	3-4	13	Colorado	3-2†
	14	Buffalo	3-4†	16	Vancouver	0-3
	16	at NY Rangers	1-2†	17	Ottawa	3-2
	21	at Winnipeg	1-3	19	at Toronto	4-1
	23	at Calgary	0-5	27	Tampa Bay	4-2
	24	at Edmonton	3-6	30	St. Louis	2-3†
	28	at Vancouver	1-4	31	at NY Rangers	1-4
Nov.	1	Arizona	3-0	Feb. 3	at Anaheim	4-5*
	2	Los Angeles	3-2	5	at Arizona	2-1†
	4	at Columbus	4-2	7	at San Jose	5-4
	7	Columbus	3-2*	12	Anaheim	1-2
	8	at Washington	3-4*	14	at Minnesota	3-6
	10	Calgary	4-1	16	at Ottawa	6-3
	13	Winnipeg	1-3	17	NY Islanders	1-4
	15	at Boston	1-2	20	Toronto	2-1
	16	San Jose	0-2	21	at New Jersey	1-3
	18	at Dallas	6-4	24	Philadelphia	4-1
	20	at Los Angeles	2-3	27	Washington	3-0
	22	at Colorado	3-4	28	at NY Islanders	5-3
	26	at Florida	0-1	Mar. 2	at Chicago	2-5
	28	at Pittsburgh	4-2	6	Minnesota	1-3
	29	Pittsburgh	2-3	8	Edmonton	7-4
Dec.	2	Nashville	2-1	10	Columbus	3-4†
	4	Washington	1-2	12	Dallas	3-5
	7	Detroit	1-3	14	Florida	0-2
	8	New Jersey	1-2	15	at Columbus	3-2
	11	at Tampa Bay	1-2	17	Ottawa	1-2*
	13	at Philadelphia	1-5	19	at Montreal	0-4
	16	at Montreal	1-4	21	NY Rangers	2-3†
	18	Toronto	1-2	23	Chicago	1-3
	20	NY Rangers	2-3†	26	Pittsburgh	5-2
	21	at NY Rangers	0-1	28	New Jersey	3-1
	23	at New Jersey	2-1†	29	Boston	1-2*
	27	at Tampa Bay	1-2	31	at Washington	2-4
	29	Montreal	1-3	Apr. 2	at Florida	1-6
	31	at Pittsburgh	1-2	4	at Philadelphia	3-2†
Jan.	2	Philadelphia	2-1	6	at Buffalo	3-4
	4	Boston	2-1†	7	at Detroit	2-3
	6	at Nashville	2-3	9	at Philadelphia	3-1
	8	Buffalo	5-2	11	Detroit	0-2

* – Overtime   † – Shootout

NHL Draft Selections 2015-2001

Name in bold denotes played in NHL.

2015 Pick		2011 Pick		2007 Pick		2003 Pick	
5	Noah Hanifin	12	**Ryan Murphy**	11	**Brandon Sutter**	2	**Eric Staal**
35	Sebastian Aho	42	**Victor Rask**	72	**Drayson Bowman**	31	**Danny Richmond**
93	Callum Booth	73	**Keegan Lowe**	102	Justin McCrae	102	Aaron Dawson
96	Nicolas Roy	103	Gregory Hofmann	132	**Chris Terry**	126	Kevin Nastiuk
126	Luke Stevens	163	Matt Mahalak	162	**Brett Bellemore**	130	Matej Trojovsky
138	Spencer Smallman	193	**Brody Sutter**			137	Tyson Strachan
156	Jake Massie			**2006 Pick**		198	Shay Stephenson
169	David Cotton	**2010 Pick**		63	**Jamie McBain**	230	Jamie Hoffmann
186	Steven Lorentz	7	**Jeff Skinner**	93	Harrison Reed	262	Ryan Rorabeck
		37	**Justin Faulk**	123	Bobby Hughes		
2014 Pick		53	**Mark Alt**	153	Stefan Chaput	**2002 Pick**	
7	Haydn Fleury	67	**Danny Biega**	183	Nick Dodge	25	**Cam Ward**
37	Alex Nedeljkovic	85	Austin Levi	213	Justin Krueger	91	Jesse Lane
67	Warren Foegele	105	**Justin Shugg**			160	Daniel Manzato
96	Josh Wesley	167	Tyler Stahl	**2005 Pick**		224	Adam Taylor
97	Lucas Wallmark	187	**Frederik Andersen**	3	**Jack Johnson**		
127	Clark Bishop			58	Nate Hagemo	**2001 Pick**	
187	Kyle Jenkins	**2009 Pick**		64	Joe Barnes	15	Igor Knyazev
		27	**Philippe Paradis**	94	Jakub Vojta	46	**Mike Zigomanis**
2013 Pick		51	**Brian Dumoulin**	123	Ondrej Otcenas	91	Kevin Estrada
5	**Elias Lindholm**	88	Mattias Lindstrom	145	Tim Kunes	110	**Rob Zepp**
66	Brett Pesce	131	Matt Kennedy	159	Risto Korhonen	181	Daniel Boisclair
126	Brent Pedersen	178	**Rasmus Rissanen**	192	**Nicolas Blanchard**	211	Sean Curry
156	Tyler Ganly	208	Tommi Kivisto	198	Kyle Lawson	244	Carter Trevisani
						274	Peter Reynolds
2012 Pick		**2008 Pick**		**2004 Pick**			
38	Phillip Di Giuseppe	14	**Zach Boychuk**	4	**Andrew Ladd**		
47	**Brock McGinn**	45	**Zac Dalpe**	38	**Justin Peters**		
69	Daniel Altshuller	105	**Michal Jordan**	69	**Casey Borer**		
99	Erik Karlsson	165	**Mike Murphy**	109	**Brett Carson**		
115	Trevor Carrick	195	Samuel Morneau	137	Magnus Akerlund		
120	**Jaccob Slavin**			202	Ryan Pottruff		
129	**Brendan Woods**			235	Jonas Fiedler		
159	Collin Olson			268	Martin Vagner		
189	Brendan Collier						

General Managers' History

Jack Kelley, 1979-80; Jack Kelley and Larry Pleau, 1980-81; Larry Pleau, 1981-82, 1982-83; Emile Francis, 1983-84 to 1988-89; Eddie Johnston, 1989-90 to 1991-92; Brian Burke, 1992-93; Paul Holmgren, 1993-94; Jim Rutherford, 1994-95 to 2013-14; Ron Francis, 2014-15 to date.

Ron Francis
Executive Vice President and General Manager

Born: Sault Ste. Marie, ON, March 1, 1963.

Ron Francis was named the eighth general manager in franchise history, and just the second since the team has been located on Carolina, on April 28, 2014. He is the second person to serve as general manager after also playing for the team. Francis spent the previous eight seasons in management with Carolina, most recently serving as vice president of hockey operations. Francis is responsible for all of the team's hockey decisions and also serves as one of the teams' alternate governors.

Following a career in which he established himself as the greatest player in Hurricanes franchise history, Francis re-joined the organization in November 2006 as the team's director of player development. He was promoted to assistant general manager on October 4, 2007, but returned to the team's locker room on December 3, 2008, when he joined new head coach Paul Maurice behind the bench as associate head coach. While serving as a coach, Francis maintained a voice in the Hurricanes' front office decision-making, serving as the team's director of player personnel. He returned to the front office full-time in June 2011, accepting the role of director of hockey operations.

Francis announced his retirement as a player on September 14, 2005, following a 23-year NHL career with Hartford, Pittsburgh, Carolina and Toronto. In 1,731 NHL regular-season games, Francis scored 549 goals and earned 1,249 assists (1,798 points), to rank him fourth all-time on the league's points list behind Wayne Gretzky, Mark Messier and Gordie Howe. Francis' 1,249 assists rank second only to Gretzky (1,963), and he ranks third on the games-played list behind Howe (1,767) and Messier (1,756). The Hartford Whalers drafted Francis in the first round, fourth overall, in the 1981 NHL Draft. He played with the Whalers for 10 seasons before joining Pittsburgh at the trading deadline of the 1990-91 season, helping them win the Stanley Cup in 1991 and 1992. He spent seven full seasons with the Penguins before rejoining the organization that drafted him, when the relocated Carolina Hurricanes signed him as a free agent on July 13, 1998. In 16 seasons with the Hartford/Carolina franchise, Francis played in 1,186 games, scoring 382 goals and earning 793 assists for 1,175 points – all of which are franchise records. The Hurricanes officially retired his number 10 jersey to the arena's rafters on January 28, 2006, and on November 12, 2007, Francis was inducted into the Hockey Hall of Fame. The impact Francis had for the sport of hockey in North Carolina was further recognized on May 2, 2013, when he became the first hockey player inducted into the North Carolina Sports Hall of Fame.

Club Directory

PNC Arena

Carolina Hurricanes
1400 Edwards Mill Rd.
Raleigh, NC 27607
Phone **919/467-7825**
FAX 919/462-0123
Tickets 1.866.NHL.CANES
www.carolinahurricanes.com
Capacity: 18,680

Executive Management

Chief Executive Officer/Owner/Governor	Peter Karmanos, Jr.
President	Don Waddell
Chief Financial Officer	Dennis Moore
Executive Vice President/General Manager	Ron Francis
Executive Vice President/General Manager, PNC Arena	Davin Olsen

Hockey Operations

Assistant GM / Dir of Hockey Ops	Mike Vellucci
Assistant General Managers	Ricky Olczyk, Brian Tatum
Head Coach	Bill Peters
Assistant Coaches	Rod Brind'Amour, Steve Smith
Goaltending Coach / Video Coach	David Marcoux / Chris Huffine
Development Directors, Defensemen / Forwards	Glen Wesley / Cory Stillman
Head Athletic Trainer/Strength Conditioning Coach	Peter Friesen
Assistant Athletic Trainer	Doug Bennett
Equipment Managers	Skip Cunningham, Bob Gorman, Jorge Alves
Asst to the GM/Video Scout	Darren Yorke
Hockey Analyst / Ops Coordinator	Eric Tulsky / Beth Carter
Scouting Directors, Amateur / Pro	Tony MacDonald / Marshall Johnston
Amateur Scouts	Sheldon Ferguson, Robert Kron, Bob Luccini, Bert Marshall
Pro Scouts	Jeff Daniels, Dave Hunter
Charlotte Checkers Head Coach / Asst Coach	Mark Morris / Geordie Kinnear
Charlotte Checkers Head Athletic Trainer	Brian Maddox
Charlotte Checkers Equipment Managers	Steve Latin, Donny White
Charlotte Checkers Goaltending/Video Assistant	Derek Wilkinson

Arena Operations

Vice President, Guest Relations, PNC Arena	Larry Perkins
Director, Arena Marketing	Crystal Pace
Admin Asst / Customer Care Coord	Sarah Saba
Director, Safety and Security	Clinton Peterson
Director, Parking and Traffic	Jared Wright
Director, Event and Guest Services	Steve Congress
Senior Director, Premium Services and Sales	Jack Brockman
Premium Services Director / Sr. Coord / Coord	Jonathan Kramer / Alan Foushee / Allyson Buckmeier
Director, Production	Rob Douglas
Marketing Coordinator	Lindsey Hall
Production Manager / Supervisor	Barry Steiman / Kim Chandler
Senior Director, Operations and Facilities	Alan Wobbleton
Director / Manager, Operations	Craig Stover, Melvin Terrell
Supervisor, Facilities / Operations	Alan Sykes, Sean Sollace
Ticket Operations Vice President / Asst. Manager	Bill Nowicki / Chris Jovino
Arena Box Office Director / Manager	Joe Sousa / Erin Latore
Ice Technician / Receptionist	Jared Dupre / Janet Davis

Broadcasters

Television Play-by-Play / Analyst	John Forslund / Tripp Tracy
Radio Play-by-Play	Chuck Kaiton
TV/Web Host	Michelle McMahon

Communications

VP, Communications and Team Services	Mike Sundheim
Sr. Dir, Communications and Team Services	Kyle Hanlin
Team Photographer	Gregg Forwerck

Finance/Information Technology

Senior Vice President/General Counsel	William Traurig
Accounting Manager / Staff Accountant	Shaun Nicholson / Lee Miller
Accounts Payable / Receivable	Michael Arrington / Patty Hilliard, Temika Smith-Harris
Payroll / Human Resources	Crystal DeDitius, Keitha Stanley
Assistant to the CFO	April Williams
Vice President, Information Technology	Glenn Johnson
Director, IT Services / Client/Server Technologist	Myatt Williams / Larry Kelly

Food and Beverage

Senior Director, VAB Catering	Chris Diamond
Director, Concessions / Director, Catering	Rick Rhodes / Frankie McGee
Manager / Asst. Mgr., Suites Food and Beverage	Hollie Hawkins / Todd Nichols
Manager, F&B Financials and Club Seats	Lori Holtz
Managers, Commissary / Catering	Gary Berry / Melissa Fulkerson
Chefs	Michael Flood, Dennis Atkinson, Kevin Heintz, Lecan Huynh, Pete Aiello
Concessions Manager / Asst. Manager	Jim O'Brien / Barbara Couch

Marketing

Vice President, Marketing/ Exec. Dir., Kids 'n Community Foundation	Doug Warf
Director, Marketing	Mike Forman
Dir., Canesvision and In-Game Marketing	Chris Greenley
Dir., Community Relations and Promotions	Jon Chase
Web Producer / Social Media Specialist	Michael Smith / Coop Elias
Marketing Coordinator	Colleen Hamilton
Manager, Creative Services	Lauren Baxter
Graphic Designer	Kyle Fowlkes
Coordinators, Youth & Amateur Hockey / Mascot	Shane Willis / George Brown
Promotions/Fan Development Coordinator	Ryan O'Quinn
Community Relations Coord/ Kids 'n Community Foundation Grant Specialist	Gabby Pinto
Community Relations Coordinator	Laura Fazzina

Gale Force Media, CanesVision and Wolfpack TV

Producers	Logan McDonald, Christine Williams
Graphics Producer	Rachel Cannon

Merchandise

Director, Merchandise / Assistant, Merchandise	James Blitch / Maria Kimball

Sales

Vice President, Corporate Sponsorships	Jim Ballweg
Senior Corporate Sales Executives	Johnny Gill
Corporate Sales Executive	Justin Buck, Doug Dickman, Maria Madonis; Ryan Martin
Manager – Client Services	Marie Bobalik
Vice President, Ticket Sales / Assistant	Sara Daniel / Karen Prince
Director, Ticket Sales / Group Sales	Peterson Avetta / Tamara Mires
Manager Client Relations / Inside Sales	Ryan Erdman / Dennis Fryer
Account Executives/Business Development	Tim Campbell, Katelin Decker, Greg Perna
CR Database Manager / Coordinator	Jeffery Schum / Jenna Jones
Client Relations Representative	Brian Friedhaber, Joe Welch
Group Sales Managers, Hurricanes / PNC Arena	Brian Kapusta / Brian Slais
Seniro Group Sales Representative	Rich Davis
Group Sales Representatives	Christina Monterosso / Greg Bauman

Chicago Blackhawks

Key Off-Season Signings/Acquisitions

2015

June 29 • Re-signed D **David Rundblad**.
30 • Re-signed G **Michael Leighton**.
30 • Acquired C **Artem Anisimov**, RW **Marko Dano**, RW **Jeremy Morin**, RW **Corey Tropp** and a 4th-round choice in the 2016 NHL Draft from Columbus for LW **Brandon Saad**, C **Alex Broadhurst** and D **Michael Paliotta**.
July 1 • Signed C **Viktor Tikhonov**.
2 • Signed D **Cameron Schilling**.
3 • Re-signed LW **Andrew Desjardins**.
7 • Re-signed D **Trevor van Riemsdyk**.
10 • Acquired D **Trevor Daley** and LW **Ryan Garbutt** from Dallas for LW **Patrick Sharp** and D **Stephen Johns**.

2015-16 Schedule

Oct.	Wed.	7	NY Rangers
	Fri.	9	at NY Islanders
	Sat.	10	NY Islanders
	Wed.	14	at Philadelphia
	Thu.	15	at Washington
	Sat.	17	Columbus
	Thu.	22	Florida
	Sat.	24	Tampa Bay
	Mon.	26	Anaheim
	Thu.	29	at Winnipeg
	Fri.	30	at Minnesota
Nov.	Mon.	2	Los Angeles
	Wed.	4	St. Louis
	Fri.	6	at New Jersey
	Sun.	8	Edmonton
	Thu.	12	New Jersey
	Sat.	14	at St. Louis
	Sun.	15	Calgary
	Wed.	18	at Edmonton
	Fri.	20	at Calgary
	Sat.	21	at Vancouver
	Wed.	25	at San Jose
	Fri.	27	at Anaheim*
	Sat.	28	at Los Angeles
Dec.	Tue.	1	Minnesota
	Thu.	3	at Ottawa
	Sun.	6	Winnipeg*
	Tue.	8	Nashville
	Thu.	10	at Nashville
	Fri.	11	Winnipeg
	Sun.	13	Vancouver
	Tue.	15	Colorado
	Thu.	17	Edmonton
	Sat.	19	at Buffalo*
	Sun.	20	San Jose
	Tue.	22	at Dallas
	Sun.	27	Carolina
	Tue.	29	at Arizona
	Thu.	31	at Colorado
Jan.	Sun.	3	Ottawa
	Tue.	5	at Pittsburgh
	Wed.	6	Pittsburgh
	Fri.	8	Buffalo
	Sun.	10	Colorado
	Tue.	12	Nashville
	Thu.	14	at Montreal
	Fri.	15	at Toronto
	Sun.	17	Montreal
	Tue.	19	at Nashville
	Thu.	21	at Tampa Bay
	Fri.	22	at Florida
	Sun.	24	St. Louis
	Tue.	26	at Carolina
Feb.	Tue.	2	at Colorado
	Thu.	4	at Arizona
	Sat.	6	at Dallas
	Tue.	9	San Jose
	Thu.	11	Dallas
	Sat.	13	Anaheim
	Mon.	15	Toronto
	Wed.	17	at NY Rangers
	Sun.	21	at Minnesota*
	Thu.	25	Nashville
	Sun.	28	Washington*
Mar.	Wed.	2	at Detroit
	Thu.	3	at Boston
	Sun.	6	Detroit*
	Wed.	9	at St. Louis
	Fri.	11	at Dallas
	Mon.	14	Los Angeles
	Wed.	16	Philadelphia
	Fri.	18	at Winnipeg
	Sun.	20	Minnesota
	Tue.	22	Dallas
	Sat.	26	at Calgary
	Sun.	27	at Vancouver*
	Tue.	29	at Minnesota
Apr.	Fri.	1	at Winnipeg
	Sun.	3	Boston*
	Tue.	5	Arizona
	Thu.	7	St. Louis
	Sat.	9	at Columbus

* Denotes afternoon game.

Retired Numbers

1	Glenn Hall	1957-1967
3	Pierre Pilote	1955-1968
	Keith Magnuson	1969-1980
9	Bobby Hull	1957-1972
18	Denis Savard	1980-1990, 1995-1997
21	Stan Mikita	1958-1980
35	Tony Esposito	1969-1984

CENTRAL DIVISION
90th NHL Season

Franchise date: September 25, 1926

2014-15 Results: 48W-28L-3OTL-3SOL 102PTS
3RD, Central Division • 4TH, Western Conference

Year-by-Year Record

		Home				Road				Overall									
Season	GP	W	L	T	OL	W	L	T	OL	W	L	T	OL	GF	GA	Pts.	Div. Fin.	Conf. Fin.	Playoff Result
2014-15	**82**	**24**	**12**	....	**5**	**24**	**16**	....	**1**	**48**	**28**	....	**6**	**229**	**189**	**102**	**3rd, Cen.**	**4th, West**	**Won Stanley Cup**
2013-14	82	27	7	....	7	19	14	....	8	46	21	....	15	267	220	107	3rd, Cen.	5th, West	Lost Conf. Final
2012-13	**48**	**18**	**3**	....	**3**	**18**	**4**	....	**2**	**36**	**7**	....	**5**	**155**	**102**	**77**	**1st, Cen.**	**1st, West**	**Won Stanley Cup**
2011-12	82	27	8	....	6	18	18	....	5	45	26	....	11	248	238	101	4th, Cen.	6th, West	Lost Conf. Quarter-Final
2010-11	82	24	17	....	0	20	12	....	9	44	29	....	9	258	225	97	3rd, Cen.	8th, West	Lost Conf. Quarter-Final
2009-10	**82**	**29**	**8**	....	**4**	**23**	**14**	....	**4**	**52**	**22**	....	**8**	**271**	**209**	**112**	**1st, Cen.**	**2nd, West**	**Won Stanley Cup**
2008-09	82	24	9	....	8	22	15	....	4	46	24	....	12	264	216	104	2nd, Cen.	4th, West	Lost Conf. Final
2007-08	82	23	16	....	2	17	18	....	6	40	34	....	8	239	235	88	3rd, Cen.	10th, West	Out of Playoffs
2006-07	82	17	20	....	4	14	22	....	5	31	42	....	9	201	258	71	5th, Cen.	13th, West	Out of Playoffs
2005-06	82	16	19	....	6	10	24	....	7	26	43	....	13	211	285	65	4th, Cen.	14th, West	Out of Playoffs
2004-05	....	....	....	....	....	....	....	....	....	....	....	....	....	....	....	....			
2003-04	82	13	17	6	5	7	26	5	3	20	43	11	8	188	259	59	5th, Cen.	15th, West	Out of Playoffs
2002-03	82	17	15	7	2	13	18	6	4	30	33	13	6	207	226	79	3rd, Cen.	9th, West	Out of Playoffs
2001-02	82	28	7	5	1	13	20	8	0	41	27	13	1	216	207	96	3rd, Cen.	5th, West	Lost Conf. Quarter-Final
2000-01	82	14	21	4	2	15	19	4	3	29	40	8	5	210	246	71	4th, Cen.	12th, West	Out of Playoffs
1999-2000	82	16	19	5	1	17	18	5	1	33	37	10	2	242	245	78	3rd, Cen.	11th, West	Out of Playoffs
1998-99	82	20	17	4	....	9	24	8	....	29	41	12	....	202	248	70	3rd, Cen.	10th, West	Out of Playoffs
1997-98	82	14	19	8	....	16	20	5	....	30	39	13	....	192	199	73	5th, Cen.	9th, West	Out of Playoffs
1996-97	82	16	21	4	....	18	14	9	....	34	35	13	....	223	210	81	5th, Cen.	8th, West	Lost Conf. Quarter-Final
1995-96	82	22	13	6	....	18	15	8	....	40	28	14	....	273	220	94	2nd, Cen.	3rd, West	Lost Conf. Semi-Final
1994-95	48	11	10	3	....	13	9	2	....	24	19	5	....	156	115	53	3rd, Cen.	4th, West	Lost Conf. Final
1993-94	84	21	16	5	....	18	20	4	....	39	36	9	....	254	240	87	5th, Cen.	6th, West	Lost Conf. Quarter-Final
1992-93	84	25	11	6	....	22	14	6	....	47	25	12	....	279	230	106	1st, Norris		Lost Div. Semi-Final
1991-92	80	23	9	8	....	13	20	7	....	36	29	15	....	257	236	87	2nd, Norris		Lost Final
1990-91	80	28	8	4	....	21	15	4	....	49	23	8	....	284	211	106	1st, Norris		Lost Div. Semi-Final
1989-90	80	25	13	2	....	16	20	4	....	41	33	6	....	316	294	88	1st, Norris		Lost Conf. Final
1988-89	80	16	14	10	....	11	27	2	....	27	41	12	....	297	335	66	4th, Norris		Lost Conf. Final
1987-88	80	21	17	2	....	9	24	7	....	30	41	9	....	284	328	69	3rd, Norris		Lost Div. Semi-Final
1986-87	80	18	13	9	....	11	24	5	....	29	37	14	....	290	310	72	3rd, Norris		Lost Div. Semi-Final
1985-86	80	23	12	5	....	16	21	3	....	39	33	8	....	351	349	86	1st, Norris		Lost Div. Semi-Final
1984-85	80	22	16	2	....	16	19	5	....	38	35	7	....	309	299	83	2nd, Norris		Lost Conf. Final
1983-84	80	25	13	2	....	5	29	6	....	30	42	8	....	277	311	68	4th, Norris		Lost Div. Semi-Final
1982-83	80	29	8	3	....	18	15	7	....	47	23	10	....	338	268	104	1st, Norris		Lost Conf. Final
1981-82	80	20	13	7	....	10	25	5	....	30	38	12	....	332	363	72	4th, Norris		Lost Conf. Final
1980-81	80	21	11	8	....	10	22	8	....	31	33	16	....	304	315	78	2nd, Smythe		Lost Prelim. Round
1979-80	80	21	12	7	....	13	15	12	....	34	27	19	....	241	250	87	1st, Smythe		Lost Quarter-Final
1978-79	80	18	12	10	....	11	24	5	....	29	36	15	....	244	277	73	1st, Smythe		Lost Quarter-Final
1977-78	80	20	9	11	....	12	20	8	....	32	29	19	....	230	220	83	1st, Smythe		Lost Quarter-Final
1976-77	80	19	16	5	....	7	27	6	....	26	43	11	....	240	298	63	3rd, Smythe		Lost Prelim. Round
1975-76	80	17	15	8	....	15	15	10	....	32	30	18	....	254	261	82	1st, Smythe		Lost Quarter-Final
1974-75	80	24	12	4	....	13	23	4	....	37	35	8	....	268	241	82	3rd, Smythe		Lost Quarter-Final
1973-74	78	20	6	13	....	21	8	10	....	41	14	23	....	272	164	105	2nd, West		Lost Semi-Final
1972-73	78	26	9	4	....	16	18	5	....	42	27	9	....	284	225	93	1st, West		Lost Final
1971-72	78	28	3	8	....	18	14	7	....	46	17	15	....	256	166	107	1st, West		Lost Semi-Final
1970-71	78	30	6	3	....	19	14	6	....	49	20	9	....	277	184	107	1st, West		Lost Final
1969-70	76	26	7	5	....	19	15	4	....	45	22	9	....	250	170	99	1st, East		Lost Semi-Final
1968-69	76	20	14	4	....	14	19	5	....	34	33	9	....	280	246	77	6th, East		Out of Playoffs
1967-68	74	20	13	4	....	12	13	12	....	32	26	16	....	212	222	80	4th, East		Lost Semi-Final
1966-67	70	24	5	6	....	17	12	6	....	41	17	12	....	264	170	94	1st		Lost Semi-Final
1965-66	70	21	8	6	....	16	17	2	....	37	25	8	....	240	187	82	2nd		Lost Semi-Final
1964-65	70	20	13	2	....	14	15	6	....	34	28	8	....	224	176	76	3rd		Lost Final
1963-64	70	26	4	5	....	10	18	7	....	36	22	12	....	218	169	84	2nd		Lost Semi-Final
1962-63	70	17	9	9	....	15	12	8	....	32	21	17	....	194	178	81	2nd		Lost Semi-Final
1961-62	70	20	10	5	....	11	16	8	....	31	26	13	....	217	186	75	3rd		Lost Final
1960-61	**70**	**20**	**6**	**9**	....	**9**	**18**	**8**	....	**29**	**24**	**17**	....	**198**	**180**	**75**	**3rd**		**Won Stanley Cup**
1959-60	70	18	11	6	....	10	18	7	....	28	29	13	....	191	180	69	3rd		Lost Semi-Final
1958-59	70	14	12	9	....	14	17	4	....	28	29	13	....	197	208	69	3rd		Lost Semi-Final
1957-58	70	15	17	3	....	9	22	4	....	24	39	7	....	163	202	55	5th		Out of Playoffs
1956-57	70	12	15	8	....	4	24	7	....	16	39	15	....	169	225	47	6th		Out of Playoffs
1955-56	70	9	19	7	....	10	20	5	....	19	39	12	....	155	216	50	6th		Out of Playoffs
1954-55	70	6	21	8	....	7	19	9	....	13	40	17	....	161	235	43	6th		Out of Playoffs
1953-54	70	8	21	6	....	4	30	1	....	12	51	7	....	133	242	31	6th		Out of Playoffs
1952-53	70	14	11	10	....	13	17	5	....	27	28	15	....	169	175	69	4th		Lost Semi-Final
1951-52	70	9	19	7	....	8	25	2	....	17	44	9	....	158	241	43	6th		Out of Playoffs
1950-51	70	8	22	5	....	5	25	5	....	13	47	10	....	171	280	36	6th		Out of Playoffs
1949-50	70	13	18	4	....	9	20	6	....	22	38	10	....	203	244	54	6th		Out of Playoffs
1948-49	60	13	12	5	....	8	19	3	....	21	31	8	....	173	211	50	5th		Out of Playoffs
1947-48	60	10	17	3	....	10	17	3	....	20	34	6	....	195	225	46	6th		Out of Playoffs
1946-47	60	10	17	3	....	9	20	1	....	19	37	4	....	193	274	42	6th		Out of Playoffs
1945-46	50	15	5	5	....	8	15	2	....	23	20	7	....	200	178	53	3rd		Lost Semi-Final
1944-45	50	9	14	2	....	4	16	5	....	13	30	7	....	141	194	33	5th		Out of Playoffs
1943-44	50	15	6	4	....	7	17	1	....	22	23	5	....	178	187	49	4th		Lost Final
1942-43	50	14	3	8	....	3	15	7	....	17	18	15	....	179	180	49	5th		Out of Playoffs
1941-42	48	15	8	1	....	7	15	2	....	22	23	3	....	145	155	47	4th		Lost Quarter-Final
1940-41	48	11	10	3	....	5	15	4	....	16	25	7	....	112	139	39	5th		Lost Semi-Final
1939-40	48	15	7	2	....	8	12	4	....	23	19	6	....	112	120	52	4th		Lost Quarter-Final
1938-39	48	5	13	6	....	7	15	2	....	12	28	8	....	91	132	32	7th		Out of Playoffs
1937-38	**48**	**10**	**10**	**4**	....	**4**	**15**	**5**	....	**14**	**25**	**9**	....	**97**	**139**	**37**	**3rd, Amn.**		**Won Stanley Cup**
1936-37	48	8	13	3	....	6	14	4	....	14	27	7	....	99	131	35	4th, Amn.		Out of Playoffs
1935-36	48	15	7	2	....	6	12	6	....	21	19	8	....	93	92	50	3rd, Amn.		Lost Quarter-Final
1934-35	48	12	9	3	....	14	8	2	....	26	17	5	....	118	88	57	2nd, Amn.		Lost Quarter-Final
1933-34	**48**	**13**	**4**	**7**	....	**7**	**13**	**4**	....	**20**	**17**	**11**	....	**88**	**83**	**51**	**2nd, Amn.**		**Won Stanley Cup**
1932-33	48	12	7	5	....	4	13	7	....	16	20	12	....	88	101	44	4th, Amn.		Out of Playoffs
1931-32	48	13	5	6	....	5	14	5	....	18	19	11	....	86	101	47	2nd, Amn.		Lost Quarter-Final
1930-31	44	13	8	1	....	11	9	2	....	24	17	3	....	108	78	51	2nd, Amn.		Lost Final
1929-30	44	12	9	1	....	9	9	4	....	21	18	5	....	117	111	47	2nd, Amn.		Lost Quarter-Final
1928-29	44	3	13	6	....	4	16	2	....	7	29	8	....	33	85	22	5th, Amn.		Out of Playoffs
1927-28	44	2	18	2	....	5	16	1	....	7	34	3	....	68	134	17	5th, Amn.		Out of Playoffs
1926-27	44	12	8	2	....	7	14	1	....	19	22	3	....	115	116	41	3rd, Amn.		Lost Quarter-Final

2015-16 Player Personnel

FORWARDS	HT	WT	*Age	Place of Birth	S	2014-15 Club
ANISIMOV, Artem	6-4	200	27	Yaroslavl, USSR	L	Columbus
BICKELL, Bryan	6-4	223	29	Bowmanville, ON	L	Chicago
DANO, Marko	5-11	183	20	Eisenstadt , Austria	L	Columbus-Springfield
DESJARDINS, Andrew	6-1	195	29	Lively, ON	R	San Jose-Chicago
GARBUTT, Ryan	6-0	195	30	Winnipeg, MB	L	Dallas
HOSSA, Marian	6-1	207	36	Stara Lubovna, Czech.	L	Chicago
KANE, Patrick	5-11	177	26	Buffalo, NY	L	Chicago
KRUGER, Marcus	6-0	186	25	Stockholm, Sweden	L	Chicago
MORIN, Jeremy	6-1	189	24	Auburn, NY	R	Chi-Rockford-CBJ
NORDSTROM, Joakim	6-1	189	23	Tyreso, Sweden	L	Chicago-Rockford
PANARIN, Artemi	5-11	170	23	Korkino, USSR	R	St. Petersburg
SHAW, Andrew	5-11	179	24	Belleville, ON	R	Chicago
TERAVAINEN, Teuvo	5-11	178	21	Helsinki, Finland	L	Chicago-Rockford
TIKHONOV, Viktor	6-2	189	27	Riga, Latvia	R	St. Petersburg
TOEWS, Jonathan	6-2	201	27	Winnipeg, MB	L	Chicago
TROPP, Corey	6-0	185	26	Grosse Pointe, MI	R	Columbus
VERSTEEG, Kris	5-11	176	29	Lethbridge, AB	R	Chicago
DEFENSEMEN						
DALEY, Trevor	5-11	195	31	Toronto, ON	L	Dallas
HJALMARSSON, Niklas	6-3	197	28	Eksjo, Sweden	L	Chicago
KEITH, Duncan	6-1	192	32	Winnipeg, MB	L	Chicago
RUNDBLAD, David	6-2	187	24	Lycksele, Sweden	R	Chicago
SEABROOK, Brent	6-3	220	30	Richmond, BC	R	Chicago
van RIEMSDYK, Trevor	6-2	188	24	Middletown, NJ	R	Chicago-Rockford

GOALTENDERS	HT	WT	*Age	Place of Birth	C	2014-15 Club
CRAWFORD, Corey	6-2	216	30	Montreal, QC	L	Chicago
DARLING, Scott	6-6	232	26	Lemont, IL	L	Chicago-Rockford

* – Age at start of 2015-16 season

Joel Quenneville

Head Coach

Born: Windsor, ON, September 15, 1958.

Joel Quenneville was named the 37th head coach in Chicago Blackhawks history on October 16, 2008 and in 2009-10 he guided the team to its first Stanley Cup championship since 1961. He led Chicago to Stanley Cup titles again in 2013 and 2015. On March 19, 2014, Quenneville joined Scotty Bowman and Al Arbour as just the third coach in NHL history to reach the 700-win plateau. He originally joined the Blackhawks as a pro scout in September 2008. Quenneville has been a proven winner throughout his career as a head coach in the NHL, including seven seasons with the St. Louis Blues (1996 to 2004) and three with the Colorado Avalanche (2005 to 2008). In his first season behind the bench in Chicago, he led the Blackhawks to the Western Conference Final in just their second playoff appearance since the 1996-97 season.

One of only two men in the history of the NHL (along with Jacques Lemaire) to have played in 800 or more games and coached 1,000 or more, Quenneville is the winningest coach in Blues history, having compiled a 307-191-95 record. He won the 2000 Jack Adams Award as the league's top coach. Quenneville was drafted by the Toronto Maple Leafs in the first round (21st overall) of the 1978 NHL Draft. He spent 13 seasons as an NHL defenseman, netting 54 goals, 136 assists, 190 points and 705 penalty minutes in 803 career games with the Toronto Maple Leafs, Colorado Rockies, New Jersey Devils, Hartford Whalers and Washington Capitals.

Quenneville retired as an active player after the 1991-92 season, when he served as a player-coach for the American Hockey League's St. John's Maple Leafs. Quenneville broke into coaching with the AHL's Springfield Indians before serving as an assistant coach for the Quebec Nordiques/Colorado Avalanche organization for two and a half seasons. He helped Colorado capture the 1996 Stanley Cup in that position before accepting his first NHL head coaching job with St. Louis for the 1996-97 campaign.

Coaching Record

			Regular Season				Playoffs			
Season	Team	League	GC	W	L	O/T	GC	W	L	T
1993-94	Springfield	AHL	80	29	38	13	6	2	4	....
1996-97	**St. Louis**	**NHL**	**40**	**18**	**15**	**7**	**6**	**2**	**4**	....
1997-98	**St. Louis**	**NHL**	**82**	**45**	**29**	**8**	**10**	**6**	**4**	....
1998-99	**St. Louis**	**NHL**	**82**	**37**	**32**	**13**	**13**	**6**	**7**	....
99-2000	**St. Louis**	**NHL**	**82**	**51**	**19**	**12**	**7**	**3**	**4**	....
2000-01	**St. Louis**	**NHL**	**82**	**43**	**22**	**17**	**15**	**9**	**6**	....
2001-02	**St. Louis**	**NHL**	**82**	**43**	**27**	**12**	**10**	**5**	**5**	....
2002-03	**St. Louis**	**NHL**	**82**	**41**	**24**	**17**	**7**	**3**	**4**	....
2003-04	**St. Louis**	**NHL**	**61**	**29**	**23**	**9**	....	....	....	....
2004-05	**Colorado**				SEASON CANCELLED					
2005-06	**Colorado**	**NHL**	**82**	**43**	**30**	**9**	**9**	**4**	**5**	....
2006-07	**Colorado**	**NHL**	**82**	**44**	**31**	**7**	....	....	....	....
2007-08	**Colorado**	**NHL**	**82**	**44**	**31**	**7**	**10**	**4**	**6**	....
2008-09	**Chicago**	**NHL**	**78**	**45**	**22**	**11**	**17**	**9**	**8**	....
2009-10♦	**Chicago**	**NHL**	**82**	**52**	**22**	**8**	**22**	**16**	**6**	....
2010-11	**Chicago**	**NHL**	**82**	**44**	**29**	**9**	**7**	**3**	**4**	....
2011-12	**Chicago**	**NHL**	**82**	**45**	**26**	**11**	**6**	**2**	**4**	....
2012-13♦	**Chicago**	**NHL**	**48**	**36**	**7**	**5**	**23**	**16**	**7**	....
2013-14	**Chicago**	**NHL**	**82**	**46**	**21**	**15**	**19**	**11**	**8**	....
2014-15♦	**Chicago**	**NHL**	**82**	**48**	**28**	**6**	**23**	**16**	**7**	....
	NHL Totals		**1375**	**754**	**438**	**183**	**204**	**115**	**89**	....

♦ Stanley Cup win.
Jack Adams Award (2000)
Assistant coach Mike Haviland posted a 3-1-0 record as replacement coach when Joel Quenneville was sidelined with an ulcer, February 16 to 23, 2011. All games are credited to Quenneville's coaching record.

2014-15 Scoring

* – rookie

Regular Season

Pos	#	Player	Team	GP	G	A	Pts	TOI	+/–	PIM	PP	SH	GW	S	S%
C	19	Jonathan Toews	CHI	81	28	38	66	19:33	30	36	6	2	7	192	14.6
R	88	Patrick Kane	CHI	61	27	37	64	19:51	10	10	6	0	5	186	14.5
R	81	Marian Hossa	CHI	82	22	39	61	18:33	17	32	6	1	2	247	8.9
L	20	Brandon Saad	CHI	82	23	29	52	17:15	7	12	2	0	6	203	11.3
D	2	Duncan Keith	CHI	80	10	35	45	25:33	12	20	3	0	2	171	5.8
R	10	Patrick Sharp	CHI	68	16	27	43	16:48	–8	33	8	0	2	230	7.0
C	80	Antoine Vermette	ARI	63	13	22	35	18:58	–23	34	6	0	1	85	15.3
			CHI	19	0	3	3	14:03	–2	6	0	0	0	24	0.0
			Total	82	13	25	38	17:50	–25	40	6	0	1	109	11.9
C	91	Brad Richards	CHI	76	12	25	37	14:53	3	12	2	0	3	199	6.0
R	23	Kris Versteeg	CHI	61	14	20	34	15:50	11	35	2	0	1	134	10.4
D	7	Brent Seabrook	CHI	82	8	23	31	22:10	–3	27	4	0	2	181	4.4
L	29	Bryan Bickell	CHI	80	14	14	28	12:04	5	38	1	0	3	113	12.4
C	65	Andrew Shaw	CHI	79	15	11	26	14:56	–8	67	5	0	2	146	10.3
D	4	Niklas Hjalmarsson	CHI	82	3	16	19	21:53	25	44	0	0	1	97	3.1
C	16	Marcus Kruger	CHI	81	7	10	17	13:05	–5	32	0	0	1	126	5.6
D	5	David Rundblad	CHI	49	3	11	14	12:47	17	12	0	0	1	58	5.2
D	32	Michal Rozsival	CHI	65	1	12	13	17:00	0	22	0	0	0	56	1.8
C	11	Andrew Desjardins	S.J.	56	5	3	8	10:26	–2	50	0	0	1	43	11.6
			CHI	13	0	2	2	11:59	1	7	0	0	0	16	0.0
			Total	69	5	5	10	10:44	–1	57	0	0	1	59	8.5
D	27	Johnny Oduya	CHI	76	2	8	10	20:17	5	26	0	0	0	76	2.6
L	86	* Teuvo Teravainen	CHI	34	4	5	9	12:47	4	2	0	0	1	66	6.1
L	13	Daniel Carcillo	CHI	39	4	4	8	8:11	3	54	0	0	0	42	9.5
C	42	* Joakim Nordstrom	CHI	38	0	3	3	10:58	–5	4	0	0	0	42	0.0
D	47	* Michael Paliotta	CHI	1	0	1	1	12:45	0	0	0	0	0	2	0.0
C	12	Peter Regin	CHI	4	0	1	1	8:20	1	0	0	0	0	3	0.0
D	57	* Trevor van Riemsdyk	CHI	18	0	1	1	13:32	0	2	0	0	0	21	0.0
L	24	* Phillip Danault	CHI	2	0	0	0	9:30	0	0	0	0	0	2	0.0
R	39	* Kyle Baun	CHI	3	0	0	0	12:32	–1	0	0	0	0	4	0.0
R	38	* Ryan Hartman	CHI	5	0	0	0	8:17	–1	2	0	0	0	8	0.0
D	26	Kyle Cumiskey	CHI	7	0	0	0	13:17	–1	0	0	0	0	5	0.0
D	44	Kimmo Timonen	CHI	16	0	0	0	11:58	–3	2	0	0	0	10	0.0

Goaltending

No.	Goaltender	GPI	Mins	Avg	W	L	OT	EN	SO	GA	SA	Sv%	G	A	PIM
31	* Antti Raanta	14	792	1.89	7	4	1	3	2	25	389	.936	0	0	0
33	* Scott Darling	14	833	1.94	9	4	0	1	1	27	419	.936	0	0	0
50	Corey Crawford	57	3333	2.27	32	20	5	4	2	126	1661	.924	0	1	8
	Totals	**82**	**4994**	**2.23**	**48**	**28**	**6**	**8**	**5**	**186**	**2477**	**.925**			

Playoffs

Pos	#	Player	Team	GP	G	A	Pts	TOI	+/–	PIM	PP	SH	GW	OT	S	S%
R	88	Patrick Kane	CHI	23	11	12	23	20:23	7	0	2	0	3	0	64	17.2
C	19	Jonathan Toews	CHI	23	10	11	21	20:54	7	8	3	1	0	0	61	16.4
D	2	Duncan Keith	CHI	23	3	18	21	31:06	16	4	0	0	3	1	59	5.1
R	81	Marian Hossa	CHI	23	4	13	17	19:51	7	10	1	1	2	0	69	5.8
R	10	Patrick Sharp	CHI	23	5	10	15	15:34	2	8	1	0	0	0	64	7.8
C	91	Brad Richards	CHI	23	3	11	14	16:43	4	8	1	0	0	0	50	6.0
C	65	Andrew Shaw	CHI	23	5	7	12	15:33	–4	36	2	0	0	0	45	11.1
L	20	Brandon Saad	CHI	23	8	3	11	20:16	5	6	0	1	2	0	59	13.6
D	7	Brent Seabrook	CHI	23	7	4	11	26:17	5	10	1	0	1	1	44	15.9
L	86	* Teuvo Teravainen	CHI	18	4	6	10	13:28	2	0	1	0	1	0	26	15.4
C	80	Antoine Vermette	CHI	20	4	3	7	13:07	5	4	0	0	3	1	16	25.0
D	4	Niklas Hjalmarsson	CHI	23	1	5	6	26:02	6	8	0	0	0	0	24	4.2
L	29	Bryan Bickell	CHI	18	0	5	5	14:33	3	14	0	0	0	0	18	0.0
D	27	Johnny Oduya	CHI	23	0	5	5	24:45	–4	6	0	0	0	0	28	0.0
C	16	Marcus Kruger	CHI	23	2	2	4	15:05	–5	4	0	0	1	1	27	7.4
C	11	Andrew Desjardins	CHI	21	1	3	4	13:55	–4	4	0	0	0	0	28	3.6
R	23	Kris Versteeg	CHI	12	1	1	2	13:21	2	6	0	0	0	0	23	4.3
D	32	Michal Rozsival	CHI	10	0	1	1	17:26	–2	6	0	0	0	0	5	0.0
C	42	* Joakim Nordstrom	CHI	3	0	0	0	13:14	–3	0	0	0	0	0	3	0.0
D	57	* Trevor van Riemsdyk	CHI	4	0	0	0	7:02	–1	0	0	0	0	0	1	0.0
D	5	David Rundblad	CHI	5	0	0	0	7:29	2	0	0	0	0	0	2	0.0
D	26	Kyle Cumiskey	CHI	9	0	0	0	9:28	–3	0	0	0	0	0	1	0.0
D	44	Kimmo Timonen	CHI	18	0	0	0	8:39	1	10	0	0	0	0	6	0.0

Goaltending

No.	Goaltender	GPI	Mins	Avg	W	L	EN	SO	GA	SA	Sv%	G	A	PIM
33	* Scott Darling	5	298	2.21	3	1	1	0	11	171	.936	0	0	0
50	Corey Crawford	20	1223	2.31	13	6	1	2	47	616	.924	0	0	0
	Totals	**23**	**1531**	**2.35**	**16**	**7**	**2**	**2**	**60**	**789**	**.924**			

Coaching History

Pete Muldoon, 1926-27; Barney Stanley and Hugh Lehman, 1927-28; Herb Gardiner and Dick Irvin, 1928-29; Tom Shaughnessy and Bill Tobin, 1929-30; Dick Irvin, 1930-31; Bill Tobin, 1931-32; Emil Iverson, Godfrey Matheson and Tommy Gorman, 1932-33; Tommy Gorman, 1933-34; Clem Loughlin, 1934-35 to 1936-37; Bill Stewart, 1937-38; Bill Stewart and Paul Thompson, 1938-39; Paul Thompson, 1939-40 to 1943-44; Paul Thompson and Johnny Gottselig, 1944-45; Johnny Gottselig, 1945-46, 1946-47; Johnny Gottselig and Charlie Conacher, 1947-48; Charlie Conacher, 1948-49, 1949-50; Ebbie Goodfellow, 1950-51, 1951-52; Sid Abel, 1952-53, 1953-54; Frank Eddolls, 1954-55; Dick Irvin, 1955-56; Tommy Ivan, 1956-57; Tommy Ivan and Rudy Pilous, 1957-58; Rudy Pilous, 1958-59 to 1962-63; Billy Reay, 1963-64 to 1975-76; Billy Reay and Bill White, 1976-77; Bob Pulford, 1977-78, 1978-79; Eddie Johnston, 1979-80; Keith Magnuson, 1980-81; Keith Magnuson and Bob Pulford, 1981-82; Orval Tessier, 1982-83, 1983-84; Orval Tessier and Bob Pulford, 1984-85; Bob Pulford, 1985-86, 1986-87; Bob Murdoch, 1987-88; Mike Keenan, 1988-89 to 1991-92; Darryl Sutter, 1992-93 to 1994-95; Craig Hartsburg, 1995-96 to 1997-98; Dirk Graham and Lorne Molleken, 1998-99; Lorne Molleken and Bob Pulford, 1999-2000; Alpo Suhonen, 2000-01; Brian Sutter, 2001-02 to 2004-05; Trent Yawney, 2005-06; Trent Yawney and Denis Savard, 2006-07; Denis Savard, 2007-08; Denis Savard and Joel Quenneville, 2008-09; Joel Quenneville, 2009-10 to date.

Club Records

Team

(Figures in brackets for season records are games played; records for fewest points, wins, ties, losses, goals, goals against are for 70 or more games)

Most Points	112	2009-10 (82)
Most Wins	52	2009-10 (82)
Most Ties	23	1973-74 (78)
Most Losses	56	2005-06 (82)
Most Goals	351	1985-86 (80)
Most Goals Against	363	1981-82 (80)
Fewest Points	31	1953-54 (70)
Fewest Wins	12	1953-54 (70)
Fewest Ties	6	1989-90 (80)
Fewest Losses	14	1973-74 (78)
Fewest Goals	*133	1953-54 (70)
Fewest Goals Against	164	1973-74 (78)
Longest Winning Streak		
Overall	11	Feb. 15-Mar. 6/13
Home	13	Nov. 11-Dec. 20/70
Away	7	Dec. 9-29/64
Longest Undefeated Streak		
Overall	15	Jan. 14-Feb. 16/67 (12W, 3T), Oct. 29-Dec. 3/75 (6W, 9T)
Home	18	Oct. 11-Dec. 20/70 (16W, 2T)
Away	12	Nov. 2-Dec. 16/67 (6W, 6T)
Longest Losing Streak		
Overall	12	Feb. 25-Mar. 25/51
Home	10	Jan. 29-Mar. 21/28
Away	19	Nov. 10/03-Jan. 29/04
Longest Winless Streak		
Overall	21	Dec. 17/50-Jan. 28/51 (18L, 3T)
Home	15	Dec. 16/28-Feb. 28/29 (11L, 4T)
Away	22	Dec. 19/50-Mar. 25/51 (20L, 2T)
Most Shutouts, Season	15	1969-70 (76)
Most PIM, Season	2,663	1991-92 (80)
Most Goals, Game	12	Jan. 30/69 (Chi. 12 at Phi. 0)

Individual

Most Seasons	22	Stan Mikita
Most Games	1,394	Stan Mikita
Most Goals, Career	604	Bobby Hull
Most Assists, Career	926	Stan Mikita
Most Points, Career	1,467	Stan Mikita (541G, 926A)
Most PIM, Career	1,495	Chris Chelios
Most Shutouts, Career	74	Tony Esposito
Longest Consecutive Games Streak	884	Steve Larmer (Oct. 6/82-Apr. 15/93)
Most Goals, Season	58	Bobby Hull (1968-69)
Most Assists, Season	87	Denis Savard (1981-82, 1987-88)
Most Points, Season	131	Denis Savard (1987-88; 44G, 87A)
Most PIM, Season	408	Mike Peluso (1991-92)
Most Points, Defenseman, Season	85	Doug Wilson (1981-82; 39G, 46A)
Most Points, Center, Season	131	Denis Savard (1987-88; 44G, 87A)
Most Points, Right Wing, Season	101	Steve Larmer (1990-91; 44G, 57A)
Most Points, Left Wing, Season	107	Bobby Hull (1968-69; 58G, 49A)
Most Points, Rookie, Season	90	Steve Larmer (1982-83; 43G, 47A)
Most Shutouts, Season	15	Tony Esposito (1969-70)
Most Goals, Game	5	Grant Mulvey (Feb. 3/82)
Most Assists, Game	6	Pat Stapleton (Mar. 30/69)
Most Points, Game	7	Max Bentley (Jan. 28/43; 4G, 3A) Grant Mulvey (Feb. 3/82; 5G, 2A)

* NHL Record.

General Managers' History

Major Frederic McLaughlin, 1926-27 to 1931-32; Major Frederic McLaughlin and Tommy Gorman, 1932-33; Tommy Gorman, 1933-34; Clem Loughlin, 1934-35, 1935-36; Bill Tobin, 1936-37 to 1953-54; Tommy Ivan, 1954-55 to 1976-77; Bob Pulford, 1977-78 to 1989-90; Mike Keenan, 1990-91, 1991-92; Mike Keenan and Bob Pulford, 1992-93; Bob Pulford, 1993-94 to 1996-97; Bob Murray, 1997-98, 1998-99; Bob Murray and Bob Pulford, 1999-2000; Mike Smith, 2000-01 to 2002-03; Mike Smith and Bob Pulford, 2003-04; Bob Pulford, 2004-05; Dale Tallon, 2005-06 to 2008-09; Stan Bowman, 2009-10 to date.

All-time Record vs. Other Clubs

Regular Season

	Total								At Home								On Road							
	GP	W	L	T	OL	GF	GA	PTS	GP	W	L	T	OL	GF	GA	PTS	GP	W	L	T	OL	GF	GA	PTS
Anaheim	83	34	42	5	2	199	211	75	43	20	19	2	2	111	103	44	40	14	23	3	0	88	108	31
Arizona	135	64	47	15	9	451	379	152	66	35	16	10	5	236	167	85	69	29	31	5	4	215	212	67
Boston	582	240	261	79	2	1762	1830	561	292	149	96	45	2	942	789	345	290	91	165	34	0	820	1041	216
Buffalo	115	49	52	13	1	337	361	112	57	32	18	6	1	187	150	71	58	17	34	7	0	150	211	41
Calgary	161	71	60	26	4	502	472	172	80	39	26	13	2	260	222	93	81	32	34	13	2	242	250	79
Carolina	69	34	27	7	1	237	206	76	34	20	10	3	1	133	94	44	35	14	17	4	0	104	112	32
Colorado	121	52	53	9	7	387	415	120	61	31	22	3	5	199	187	70	60	21	31	6	2	188	228	50
Columbus	77	45	24	2	6	260	213	98	38	23	12	1	2	121	90	49	39	22	12	1	4	139	123	49
Dallas	263	131	98	31	3	892	795	296	130	76	39	15	0	481	350	167	133	55	59	16	3	411	445	129
Detroit	729	279	355	84	11	2005	2267	653	366	167	141	51	7	1094	1032	392	363	112	214	33	4	911	1235	261
Edmonton	126	61	48	12	5	447	429	139	63	33	19	7	4	237	209	77	63	28	29	5	1	210	220	62
Florida	31	19	7	3	2	106	71	43	16	9	4	2	1	54	42	21	15	10	3	1	1	52	29	22
Los Angeles	186	91	74	17	4	616	561	203	94	48	35	9	2	316	258	107	92	43	39	8	2	300	303	96
Minnesota	57	24	24	1	8	149	156	57	28	13	12	1	2	75	78	29	29	11	12	0	6	74	78	28
Montreal	559	153	299	103	4	1412	1849	413	278	98	125	55	0	748	770	251	281	55	174	48	4	664	1079	162
Nashville	95	48	35	4	8	271	275	108	48	28	17	1	2	138	129	59	47	20	18	3	6	133	146	49
New Jersey	105	47	34	21	3	353	301	118	52	28	13	10	1	197	141	67	53	19	21	11	2	156	160	51
NY Islanders	106	45	39	20	2	335	356	112	54	30	18	5	1	182	175	66	52	15	21	15	1	153	181	46
NY Rangers	583	246	237	98	2	1700	1658	592	292	131	116	43	2	882	804	307	291	115	121	55	0	818	854	285
Ottawa	28	18	8	2	0	80	77	38	13	9	2	2	0	35	29	20	15	9	6	0	0	45	48	18
Philadelphia	132	45	56	30	1	395	404	121	65	29	17	19	0	224	182	77	67	16	39	11	1	171	222	44
Pittsburgh	129	68	42	17	2	456	392	155	65	43	11	10	1	254	167	97	64	25	31	7	1	202	225	58
St. Louis	296	142	112	35	7	979	898	326	149	87	41	18	3	539	418	195	147	55	71	17	4	440	480	131
San Jose	88	38	37	5	8	257	261	89	44	23	16	2	3	141	134	51	44	15	21	3	5	116	127	38
Tampa Bay	36	16	10	5	5	106	94	42	19	11	5	2	1	59	43	25	17	5	5	3	4	47	51	17
Toronto	643	261	286	96	0	1828	1931	618	323	161	120	42	0	986	839	364	320	100	166	54	0	842	1092	254
Vancouver	180	83	66	22	9	565	486	197	89	54	23	7	5	311	218	120	91	29	43	15	4	254	268	77
Washington	91	41	37	11	2	310	296	95	45	25	13	6	1	172	133	57	46	16	24	5	1	138	163	38
Winnipeg	21	14	7	0	0	65	55	28	10	5	5	0	0	25	24	10	11	9	2	0	0	40	31	18
Defunct Clubs	279	131	107	41	0	724	614	303	139	79	40	20	0	408	268	178	140	52	67	21	0	316	346	125
Totals	**6106**	**2590**	**2584**	**814**	**118**	**18186**	**18313**	**6112**	**3053**	**1536**	**1051**	**410**	**56**	**9747**	**8245**	**3538**	**3053**	**1054**	**1533**	**404**	**62**	**8439**	**10068**	**2574**

Playoffs

	Series	W	L	GP	W	L	T	GF	GA	Last Mtg.	Rnd.	Result
Anaheim	1	1	0	7	4	3	0	24	22	2015	CF	W 4-3
Arizona	1	0	1	6	2	4	0	12	17	2012	CQF	L 2-4
Boston	7	2	5	28	9	18	1	80	112	2013	F	W 4-2
Buffalo	2	0	2	9	1	8	0	17	36	1980	QF	L 0-4
Calgary	4	2	2	18	9	9	0	54	53	2009	CQF	W 4-2
Colorado	2	0	2	12	4	8	0	28	49	1997	CQF	L 2-4
Dallas	6	4	2	33	19	14	0	120	118	1991	DSF	L 2-4
Detroit	16	9	7	81	43	38	0	236	224	2013	CSF	W 4-3
Edmonton	4	1	3	20	8	12	0	77	102	1992	CF	W 4-0
Los Angeles	3	2	1	17	11	6	0	47	46	2014	CF	L 3-4
Minnesota	3	3	0	15	12	3	0	45	27	2015	SR	W 4-0
Montreal	17	5	12	81	29	50	2	185	261	1976	QF	L 0-4
Nashville	2	2	0	12	8	4	0	36	36	2015	FR	W 4-2
NY Islanders	2	0	2	6	0	6	0	6	21	1979	QF	L 0-4
NY Rangers	5	4	1	24	14	10	0	66	54	1973	SF	W 4-1
Philadelphia	2	2	0	10	8	2	0	45	30	2010	F	W 4-2
Pittsburgh	2	1	1	8	4	4	0	24	23	1992	F	L 0-4
St. Louis	11	8	3	56	32	24	0	191	156	2014	FR	W 4-2
San Jose	1	1	0	4	4	0	0	13	7	2010	CF	W 4-0
Tampa Bay	1	1	0	6	4	2	0	13	10	2015	F	W 4-2
Toronto	9	3	6	38	15	22	1	89	111	1995	CQF	W 4-3
Vancouver	5	3	2	28	16	12	0	92	77	2011	CQF	L 3-4
Defunct Clubs	4	2	2	9	5	3	1	16	15			
Totals	**110**	**56**	**54**	**528**	**261**	**262**	**5**	**1516**	**1607**			

Playoff Results 2015-2011

Year	Round	Opponent	Result	GF	GA
2015	**F**	**Tampa Bay**	**W 4-2**	**13**	**10**
	CF	Anaheim	W 4-3	24	22
	SR	Minnesota	W 4-0	13	7
	FR	Nashville	W 4-2	19	21
2014	CF	Los Angeles	L 3-4	23	28
	SR	Minnesota	W 4-2	15	13
	FR	St. Louis	W 4-2	20	14
2013	**F**	**Boston**	**W 4-2**	**17**	**15**
	CF	Los Angeles	W 4-1	14	11
	CSF	Detroit	W 4-3	16	15
	CQF	Minnesota	W 4-1	17	7
2012	CQF	Phoenix	L 2-4	12	17
2011	CQF	Vancouver	L 3-4	22	16

Abbreviations: Round: F – Final; **CF** – conference final; **CSF** – conference semi-final; **SR** – second round; **CQF** – conference quarter-final; **FR** – first round; **DSF** – division semi-final; **SF** – semi-final; **QF** – quarter-final.

Calgary totals include Atlanta Flames, 1972-73 to 1979-80. Carolina totals include Hartford, 1979-80 to 1996-97.
Colorado totals include Quebec, 1979-80 to 1994-95. Dallas totals include Minnesota North Stars, 1967-68 to 1992-93.
New Jersey totals include Kansas City, 1974-75, 1975-76, and Colorado Rockies, 1976-77 to 1981-82.
Phoenix totals include Winnipeg, 1979-80 to 1995-96. Winnipeg totals include Atlanta Thrashers, 1999-2000 to 2010-11.

2014-15 Results

Oct.	9	at Dallas	3-2†		9	at Edmonton	2-5
	11	Buffalo	6-2		11	Minnesota	4-1
	15	Calgary	1-2*		16	Winnipeg	2-4
	18	Nashville	2-1*		18	Dallas	3-6
	21	Philadelphia	4-0		20	Arizona	6-1
	23	at Nashville	2-3		21	at Pittsburgh	3-2†
	25	at St. Louis	2-3		28	at Los Angeles	3-4
	26	Ottawa	2-1		30	at Anaheim	4-1
	28	Anaheim	0-1		31	at San Jose	0-2
	30	at Ottawa	5-4†	**Feb.**	3	at Minnesota	0-3
Nov.	1	at Toronto	2-3		6	at Winnipeg	2-1*
	2	Winnipeg	0-1		8	at St. Louis	4-2
	4	at Montreal	5-0		9	Arizona	2-3†
	7	Washington	2-3		11	Vancouver	4-5*
	9	San Jose	5-2		13	New Jersey	3-1
	11	Tampa Bay	3-2†		15	Pittsburgh	2-1†
	14	at Detroit	1-4		18	Detroit	2-3†
	16	Dallas	6-2		20	Colorado	1-4
	20	at Calgary	4-3		22	Boston	2-6
	22	at Edmonton	7-1		24	Florida	3-2†
	23	at Vancouver	1-4		26	at Florida	3-0
	26	at Colorado	3-2		27	at Tampa Bay	0-4
	28	at Anaheim	4-1	**Mar.**	2	Carolina	5-2
	29	at Los Angeles	4-1		6	Edmonton	2-1†
Dec.	3	St. Louis	4-1		8	NY Rangers	0-1*
	5	Montreal	4-3		12	at Arizona	2-1
	6	at Nashville	3-1		14	at San Jose	6-2
	9	at New Jersey	3-2†		17	NY Islanders	4-1
	11	at Boston	3-2		18	at NY Rangers	1-0
	13	at NY Islanders	2-3		21	at Dallas	0-4
	14	Calgary	2-1		23	at Carolina	3-1
	16	Minnesota	5-3		25	at Philadelphia	1-4
	20	at Columbus	2-3†		27	Columbus	2-5
	21	Toronto	4-0		29	at Winnipeg	4-3
	23	Winnipeg	1-5		30	Los Angeles	4-1
	27	at Colorado	5-2	**Apr.**	2	Vancouver	3-1
	29	Nashville	5-4†		3	at Buffalo	4-3
Jan.	1	at Washington	2-3		5	St. Louis	1-2
	4	Dallas	5-4*		7	Minnesota	1-2
	6	Colorado	0-2		9	at St. Louis	1-2
	8	at Minnesota	4-2		11	at Colorado	2-3

* – Overtime † – Shootout

NHL Draft Selections 2015-2001

Name in bold denotes played in NHL.

2015
Pick
- 54 Graham Knott
- 91 Dennis Gilbert
- 121 Ryan Shea
- 151 Radovan Bondra
- 164 Roy Radke
- 181 Joni Tuulola
- 211 John Dahlstrom

2014
Pick
- 20 Nick Schmaltz
- 83 Matt Iacopelli
- 88 Beau Starrett
- 98 Fredrik Olofsson
- 141 Luc Snuggerud
- 148 Andreas Soderberg
- 178 Dylan Sikura
- 179 Ivan Nalimov
- 208 Jack Ramsey

2013
Pick
- 30 **Ryan Hartman**
- 51 Carl Dahlstrom
- 74 John Hayden
- 111 Robin Norell
- 121 Tyler Motte
- 134 Luke Johnson
- 181 Anthony Louis
- 211 Robin Press

2012
Pick
- 18 **Teuvo Teravainen**
- 48 Dillon Fournier
- 79 Chris Calnan
- 139 Garret Ross
- 149 Travis Brown
- 169 Vincent Hinostroza
- 191 Brandon Whitney
- 199 Matt Tomkins

2011
Pick
- 18 Mark McNeill
- 26 **Phillip Danault**
- 36 **Adam Clendening**
- 43 **Brandon Saad**
- 70 **Michael Paliotta**
- 79 **Klas Dahlbeck**
- 109 Maxim Shalunov
- 139 **Andrew Shaw**
- 169 Sam Jardine
- 199 Alex Broadhurst
- 211 Johan Mattsson

2010
Pick
- 24 **Kevin Hayes**
- 35 Ludvig Rensfeldt
- 54 Justin Holl
- 58 **Kent Simpson**
- 60 Stephen Johns
- 90 **Joakim Nordstrom**
- 120 Rob Flick
- 151 Mirko Hoefflin
- 180 Nick Mattson
- 191 Mac Carruth

2009
Pick
- 28 **Dylan Olsen**
- 59 **Brandon Pirri**
- 89 Dan Delisle
- 119 Byron Froese
- 149 **Marcus Kruger**
- 177 David Pacan
- 195 Paul Phillips
- 209 David Gilbert

2008
Pick
- 11 Kyle Beach
- 68 **Shawn Lalonde**
- 132 Teigan Zahn
- 162 Jonathan Carlsson
- 169 **Ben Smith**
- 179 Braden Birch
- 192 Joe Gleason

2007
Pick
- 1 **Patrick Kane**
- 38 **Bill Sweatt**
- 56 **Akim Aliu**
- 69 Maxime Tanguay
- 86 Josh Unice
- 126 Joe Lavin
- 156 Richard Greenop

2006
Pick
- 3 **Jonathan Toews**
- 33 Igor Makarov
- 61 Simon Danis-Pepin
- 76 Tony Lagerstrom
- 95 Ben Shutron
- 96 Joe Palmer
- 156 Jan-Mikael Juutilainen
- 169 Chris Auger
- 186 **Peter Leblanc**

2005
Pick
- 7 **Jack Skille**
- 43 **Mike Blunden**
- 54 Dan Bertram
- 68 **Evan Brophey**
- 108 **Niklas Hjalmarsson**
- 113 Nathan Davis
- 117 Denis Istomin
- 134 Brennan Turner
- 167 Joe Fallon
- 188 Joe Charlebois
- 202 David Kuchejda
- 203 Adam Hobson

2004
Pick
- 3 **Cam Barker**
- 32 **Dave Bolland**
- 41 **Bryan Bickell**
- 45 Ryan Garlock
- 54 Jakub Sindel
- 68 **Adam Berti**
- 120 Mitch Maunu
- 123 Karel Hromas
- 131 Trevor Kell
- 140 **Jake Dowell**
- 165 Scott McCulloch
- 196 **Petri Kontiola**
- 214 **Troy Brouwer**
- 223 Jared Walker
- 229 Eric Hunter
- 256 Matthew Ford
- 260 Marko Anttila

2003
Pick
- 14 **Brent Seabrook**
- 52 **Corey Crawford**
- 59 **Michal Barinka**
- 151 **Lasse Kukkonen**
- 156 Alexei Ivanov
- 181 Johan Andersson
- 211 **Mike Brodeur**
- 245 **Dustin Byfuglien**
- 275 Michael Grenzy
- 282 **Chris Porter**

2002
Pick
- 21 **Anton Babchuk**
- 54 **Duncan Keith**
- 93 Alexander Kojevnikov
- 128 **Matt Ellison**
- 156 **James Wisniewski**
- 188 Kevin Kantee
- 219 Tyson Kellerman
- 251 Jason Kostadine
- 282 **Adam Burish**

2001
Pick
- 9 **Tuomo Ruutu**
- 29 **Adam Munro**
- 59 **Matt Keith**
- 73 **Craig Anderson**
- 104 Brent MacLellan
- 115 Vladimir Gusev
- 119 Alexei Zotkin
- 142 Tommi Jaminki
- 174 Alexander Golovin
- 186 Petr Puncochar
- 205 Teemu Jaaskelainen
- 216 Oleg Minakov
- 268 Jeff Miles

Captains' History

Dick Irvin, 1926-27 to 1928-29; Duke Dukowski, 1929-30; Ty Arbour, 1930-31; Cy Wentworth, 1931-32; Helge Bostrom, 1932-33; Charlie Gardiner, 1933-34; no captain, 1934-35; Johnny Gottselig, 1935-36 to 1939-40; Earl Seibert, 1940-41, 1941-42; Doug Bentley, 1942-43, 1943-44; Clint Smith 1944-45; John Mariucci, 1945-46; Red Hamill, 1946-47; John Mariucci, 1947-48; Gaye Stewart, 1948-49; Doug Bentley, 1949-50; Jack Stewart, 1950-51, 1951-52; Bill Gadsby, 1952-53, 1953-54; Gus Mortson, 1954-55 to 1956-57; no captain, 1957-58; Ed Litzenberger, 1958-59 to 1960-61; Pierre Pilote, 1961-62 to 1967-68, no captain, 1968-69; Pat Stapleton, 1969-70; no captain, 1970-71 to 1974-75; Stan Mikita and Pit Martin, 1975-76; Stan Mikita, Pit Martin and Keith Magnuson, 1976-77; Keith Magnuson, 1977-78, 1978-79; Keith Magnuson and Terry Ruskowski, 1979-80; Terry Ruskowski, 1980-81, 1981-82; Darryl Sutter, 1982-83 to 1984-85; Darryl Sutter and Bob Murray, 1985-86; Darryl Sutter, 1986-87; no captain, 1987-88; Denis Savard and Dirk Graham, 1988-89; Dirk Graham, 1989-90 to 1994-95; Chris Chelios, 1995-96 to 1998-99; Doug Gilmour, 1999-2000; Tony Amonte, 2000-01, 2001-02; Alex Zhamnov, 2002-03, 2003-04; Adrian Aucoin and Martin Lapointe, 2005-06, 2006-07; no captain, 2007-08; Jonathan Toews, 2008-09 to date.

Stan Bowman

General Manager

Born: Montreal, QC, June 28, 1973.

Stan Bowman was named general manager of the Chicago Blackhawks on July 14, 2009. In his first season on the job in 2009-10, the Blackhawks won the Stanley Cup for the first time since 1961. They won it again in 2013 and 2015. Prior to being named to the position, Bowman had served for eight years in the Blackhawks operations department.

Bowman originally joined the Blackhawks in 2001, serving for four seasons as special assistant to the G.M. before being promoted to director of hockey operations from 2005 to 2007. As assistant G.M. from 2007 to 2009, Bowman attended to the day-to-day administration of the hockey operations department including contract negotiations, free agency, salary arbitration, player movement and player assignment. He also tracked the progress of the Blackhawks prospects at the club's minor league affiliate in Rockford and assisted with player evaluation, prospect development and scouting.

Bowman graduated from the University of Notre Dame in 1995 with degrees in Finance and Computer Applications. He was born in Montreal where his father, current Blackhawks senior advisor and Hall of Fame member Scotty Bowman, was coaching at the time.

Club Directory

United Center

Chicago Blackhawks
United Center
1901 W. Madison Street
Chicago, IL 60612
Phone **312/455-7000**
FAX 312/455-7042
www.chicagoblackhawks.com
Capacity: 19,717

Chairman	W. Rockwell "Rocky" Wirtz
President & CEO	John F. McDonough
Executive Vice President	Jay Blunk
Vice President/General Manager	Stan Bowman
Vice President, Hockey Operations	Al MacIsaac
Vice President, Ticket Ops and Customer Relations	Chris Werner
Vice President, Finance	T.J. Skattum
Assistant General Manager	Norm Maciver
Coordinator, Special Projects/Sr. Exec. Mgmt.	Jillian Smith
Exec. Assts. to VP/GM and Hockey Ops / Exec. VP	Lauren Peterson / Molly Connelly
Coaching Staff	
Head Coach	Joel Quenneville
Assistant Coaches	Mike Kitchen, Kevin Dineen
Goaltending Coach	Jimmy Waite
Video Coach	Matt Meacham
Strength and Conditioning Coach	Paul Goodman
Skating and Skills Development	Kevin Delaney
Development Coaches	Mark Eaton, Yanic Perreault, Anders Sorensen, Derek Plante
Training/Equipment Staff	
Athletic Trainers, Head / Assistant	Mike Gapski / Jeff Thomas
Massage Therapist	Pawel Prylinski
Equipment Manager / Asst. Manager / Assistants	Troy Parchman / Jim Heintzelman / D.J. Kogut, Jeff Uyeno
Medical	
Head Team Physician, Orthopaedics	Dr. Michael Terry
Team Physicians	Drs. George Chiampas, Angelo Costas, Ari Levy, Bradley Merk
Team Dentists	DDS Russ Baer, Martin Marcus, Michael Marcus
Mental Skills Coaches	James Gary
Nutritionist	Julie Burns
Chiropractors	Brian Allen, Stuart Yoss
Hockey Operations and Scouting	
Senior Advisor, Hockey Operations	Scotty Bowman
Senior Director, Amateur Scouting	Mark Kelley
Director, Player Personnel	Pierre Gauthier
Director, Pro Scouting	Ryan Stewart
Directors, Player Development / Recruitment	Barry Smith / Ron Anderson
Director, Hockey Admin./GM, Minor League Affiliations	Mark Bernard
Chief Amateur Scout	Bruce Franklin
Senior Director, Team Services	Tony Ommen
Manager, Player Development	Ian Gentile
Coordinator, Hockey Administration	Kyle Davidson
Player Recruitment	Rick Comley
Amateur Scouts	Mike Doneghy, Rob Facca, Darrell May, Jim McKellar, Peter Nevin
European Scouting, Director / Head / Scout	Mats Hallin / Niklas Blomgren / Karel Pavlik
Pro Scouts	Matt Bardsley, Derek Booth, Wade Brookbank, Alex Brooks, David Cowan, Gord Donnelly, Michael Grier, Richard Kromm, Don Lever, Mike MacPherson, Michel Mottau, Allan Power, Eduard Zankavets
Scouting Coordinator	Hudson Chodos
Team Security	Brian Higgins
Hockey Analytics/Video Analyst	Andrew Contis
Communications, Public Relations and Community Relations	
Senior Director, Comm. and Community Relations	Brandon Faber
Senior Director, Public Relations	Adam Rogowin
Manager / Assistant, Community Relations	Ashley Hinton / Lauren O'Brien
Manager, Team Photography	Chase Agnello-Dean
Coordinators, Public / Media Relations	Meghan Bower / Kevin Orris
Broadcasters	
Television Play-By-Play / Analyst / Studio Host	Pat Foley / Eddie Olczyk / Steve Konroyd
Radio Play-By-Play / Analyst / Studio Host	John Wiedeman / Troy Murray / Judd Sirott
Marketing and Youth Hockey	
Sr. Exec. Director, Marketing	Pete Hassen
Director, Merchandising	Laura Clawson
Youth Hockey Director / Coordinator	Annie Camins / Spencer Montgomery
Manager, In-Game Presentation and Entertainment	A.J. Dolan
Charitable Partnerships Manager / Assistant	Elizabeth Queen / Anna Warner
Events Marketing Mgr. / Mascot Coordinator	Brian Howe / Joe Doyle
Manager, Events Marketing	Brian Howe
Community Liaison	Jamal Mayers
Marketing Assistant	Amber Hughes
Events Marketing Assistant	Paul Unruh
Finance	
Senior Manager, Accounting	Michael Dorsch
Payroll Manager / Finance Analyst	Patricia Walsh / Andrew LeFevour
Human Resources	
Sr. Exec. Director, Human Resources	Marie Sutera
H.R. Manager / Coordinator, H.R. & Office Admin.	Kyleen Howe / Leanne Mayville
Corporate Sponsorships	
Sr. Exec. Director / Director / Assistant	Steve Waight / Sara Bailey / Anthony Stefani
Sr. Manager, Client Services	Kelly Smith
Client Services, Sr. Coordinator / Associate	Kayla Kindred / Brian Szubrych
Sr. Account Execs.	Greg Zinsmeister, Ryan Gallante, Sean Keefer
New Media and Creative Services	
Sr. Director, New Media and Creative Services	Adam Kempenaar
Director, Creative Services	John Sandberg
Coordinator, Social Media	Leah Hendrickson
Graphic Designer / Coord., New Media & Creative Services	Sean Grady / Emerald Gao
Reporter, New Media / Team Historian	Eric Lear / Bob Verdi
Tickets Ops, Customer Relations, Arena Ops	
Exec. Director, Ticket Operations	Jim Bare
Sr. Director, Ticket Sales and Service	Dan Rozenblat
Director, Service and Retention	Julie Lovins
Director, Group Sales	Steve DiLenardi
Coordinator, Ticket Operations	Allison Ferrara
Manager, Group Sales	Nick Zombolas
Sr. Account Exec. / Account Exec, Ticket Sales	Andrew Roan / Jake Tuton
Account Exec., Youth Hockey	Matt Brooks
Manager / Sr. Execs., Customer Service	T.R. Johnson / Kathie Raimondi, Shilpa Rupani
Customer Service Execs.	Neil Desmond, Lindsay Dresser, Rebecca Goldstein, Kevin LeClair, Shannon Pyrz

Key Off-Season Signings/Acquisitions

2015

June 25 • Acquired C **Carl Soderberg** from Boston for a 6th-round choice in the 2016 NHL Draft.

26 • Acquired D **Nikita Zadorov**, C **Mikhail Grigorenko**, LW **J.T. Compher** and a 2nd-round choice in the 2015 NHL Draft from Buffalo for C **Ryan O'Reilly** and LW **Jamie McGinn**.

July 1 • Signed D **Francois Beauchemin** and LW **Blake Comeau**.

7 • Named **Dave Farrish** assistant coach.

27 • Re-signed C **Joey Hishon**.

Aug. 6 • Re-signed G **Calvin Pickard**.

Colorado Avalanche

2014-15 Results: 39w-31L-8otL-4soL 90pts
7th, Central Division • 11th, Western Conference

Defenseman Tyson Barrie was Colorado's team leader with a plus-minus rating of +5 in 2014-15. His 80 games played, 41 assists and 53 points all established new career highs.

2015-16 Schedule

Oct.				
Thu.	8	Minnesota	Fri. 8	Nashville
Sat.	10	Dallas	Sun. 10	at Chicago
Wed.	14	Boston	Tue. 12	Tampa Bay
Fri.	16	at Anaheim	Thu. 14	New Jersey
Sun.	18	at Los Angeles	Sat. 16	at Columbus
Wed.	21	Carolina	Mon. 18	at Winnipeg
Sat.	24	Columbus	Wed. 20	Buffalo
Tue.	27	at Florida	Fri. 22	St. Louis
Thu.	29	at Tampa Bay	Sat. 23	at Dallas
Fri.	30	at Carolina	Tue. 26	at San Jose

Nov.				
Sun.	1	San Jose*	Wed. 27	at Los Angeles
Tue.	3	Calgary	Feb. Tue. 2	Chicago
Thu.	5	at Arizona	Thu. 4	Dallas
Fri.	6	NY Rangers	Sat. 6	Winnipeg
Tue.	10	at Philadelphia	Tue. 9	Vancouver
Thu.	12	at Boston	Thu. 11	at Ottawa
Sat.	14	at Montreal	Fri. 12	at Detroit
Tue.	17	at Toronto	Sun. 14	at Buffalo*
Thu.	19	at Pittsburgh	Wed. 17	Montreal
Sat.	21	at Washington	Sat. 20	at Edmonton
Mon.	23	at Winnipeg	Sun. 21	at Vancouver
Wed.	25	Ottawa	Wed. 24	San Jose
Sat.	28	Winnipeg	Sat. 27	Detroit
Mon.	30	at NY Islanders	Mar. Tue. 1	at Minnesota

Dec.				
Tue.	1	at New Jersey	Thu. 3	Florida
Thu.	3	at NY Rangers	Sat. 5	Nashville*
Sat.	5	at Minnesota	Mon. 7	Arizona
Mon.	7	Minnesota	Wed. 9	Anaheim
Wed.	9	Pittsburgh	Sat. 12	at Winnipeg
Sat.	12	at Nashville	Wed. 16	at Vancouver
Sun.	13	at St. Louis*	Fri. 18	at Calgary
Tue.	15	at Chicago	Sun. 20	at Edmonton
Thu.	17	NY Islanders	Thu. 24	Philadelphia
Sat.	19	Edmonton	Sat. 26	Minnesota*
Mon.	21	Toronto	Mon. 28	at Nashville
Sun.	27	Arizona	Tue. 29	at St. Louis
Mon.	28	at San Jose	Apr. Fri. 1	Washington
Thu.	31	Chicago	Sun. 3	St. Louis

Jan.				
Sat.	2	Calgary	Tue. 5	at Nashville
Mon.	4	Los Angeles	Thu. 7	at Dallas
Wed.	6	St. Louis	Sat. 9	Anaheim*

* Denotes afternoon game.

Retired Numbers

3	J.C. Tremblay*	1972-1979
8	Marc Tardif*	1979-1983
16	Michel Goulet*	1979-1990
19	Joe Sakic	1988-2009
21	Peter Forsberg	1994-04, 07-08, 2010-11
26	Peter Stastny*	1980-1990
33	Patrick Roy	1995-2003
52	Adam Foote	1991-04, 08-11
77	Raymond Bourque	2000-2001

* Quebec Nordiques

CENTRAL DIVISION
37th NHL Season

Franchise date: June 22, 1979

Transferred from Quebec to Denver, June 21, 1995.

Year-by-Year Record

Season	GP	Home W	L	T	OL	Road W	L	T	OL	Overall W	L	T	OL	GF	GA	Pts.	Div. Fin.	Conf. Fin.	Playoff Result
2014-15	82	23	15		3	16	16		9	39	31		12	219	227	90	7th, Cen.	11th, West	Out of Playoffs
2013-14	82	26	11		4	26	11		4	52	22		8	250	220	112	1st, Cen.	2nd, West	Lost First Round
2012-13	48	12	9		3	4	16		4	16	25		7	116	152	39	5th, NW	15th, West	Out of Playoffs
2011-12	82	22	17		2	19	18		4	41	35		6	208	220	88	3rd, NW	11th, West	Out of Playoffs
2010-11	82	16	21		4	14	23		4	30	44		8	227	288	68	4th, NW	14th, West	Out of Playoffs
2009-10	82	24	14		3	19	16		6	43	30		9	244	233	95	2nd, NW	8th, West	Lost Conf. Quarter-Final
2008-09	82	18	21		2	14	24		3	32	45		5	199	257	69	5th, NW	15th, West	Out of Playoffs
2007-08	82	27	12		2	17	19		5	44	31		7	231	219	95	2nd, NW	6th, West	Lost Conf. Semi-Final
2006-07	82	22	16		3	22	15		4	44	31		7	272	251	95	4th, NW	9th, West	Out of Playoffs
2005-06	82	25	10		6	18	20		3	43	30		9	283	257	95	2nd, NW	7th, West	Lost Conf. Semi-Final
2004-05	....	....				....				....				....	....	....			
2003-04	82	19	14	6	2	21	8	7	5	40	22	13	7	236	198	100	2nd, NW	4th, West	Lost Conf. Semi-Final
2002-03	82	21	9	8	3	21	10	5	5	42	19	13	8	251	194	105	1st, NW	3rd, West	Lost Conf. Quarter-Final
2001-02	82	24	12	4	1	21	16	4	0	45	28	8	1	212	169	99	1st, NW	2nd, West	Lost Conf. Final
2000-01	**82**	**28**	**6**	**5**	**2**	**24**	**10**	**5**	**2**	**52**	**16**	**10**	**4**	**270**	**192**	**118**	**1st, NW**	**1st, West**	**Won Stanley Cup**
1999-2000	82	25	12	4	0	17	16	7	1	42	28	11	1	233	201	96	1st, NW	3rd, West	Lost Conf. Final
1998-99	82	21	14	6		23	14	4	....	44	28	10	....	239	205	98	1st, NW	2nd, West	Lost Conf. Final
1997-98	82	21	10	10		18	16	7	....	39	26	17	....	231	205	95	1st, Pac.	4th, West	Lost Conf. Quarter-Final
1996-97	82	26	10	5		23	14	4	....	49	24	9	....	277	205	107	1st, Pac.	1st, West	Lost Conf. Final
1995-96	**82**	**24**	**10**	**7**		**23**	**15**	**3**	....	**47**	**25**	**10**		**326**	**240**	**104**	**1st, Pac.**	**2nd, West**	**Won Stanley Cup**
1994-95*	48	19	1	4		11	12	1		30	13	5		185	134	65	1st, NE	1st, East	Lost Conf. Quarter-Final
1993-94*	84	19	17	6		15	25	2		34	42	8		277	292	76	5th, NE	11th, East	Out of Playoffs
1992-93*	84	23	17	2		24	10	8		47	27	10		351	300	104	2nd, Adams		Lost Div. Semi-Final
1991-92*	80	18	19	3		2	29	9		20	48	12		255	318	52	5th, Adams		Out of Playoffs
1990-91*	80	9	23	8		7	27	6		16	50	14		236	354	46	5th, Adams		Out of Playoffs
1989-90*	80	8	26	6		4	35	1		12	61	7		240	407	31	5th, Adams		Out of Playoffs
1988-89*	80	16	20	4		11	26	3		27	46	7		269	342	61	5th, Adams		Out of Playoffs
1987-88*	80	15	23	2		17	20	3		32	43	5		271	306	69	5th, Adams		Out of Playoffs
1986-87*	80	20	13	7		11	26	3		31	39	10		267	276	72	4th, Adams		Lost Div. Semi-Final
1985-86*	80	23	13	4		20	18	2		43	31	6		330	289	92	1st, Adams		Lost Conf. Final
1984-85*	80	24	12	4		17	18	5		41	30	9		323	275	91	2nd, Adams		Lost Conf. Final
1983-84*	80	24	11	5		18	17	5		42	28	10		360	278	94	3rd, Adams		Lost Div. Final
1982-83*	80	23	10	7		11	24	5		34	34	12		343	336	80	4th, Adams		Lost Div. Semi-Final
1981-82*	80	24	13	3		9	18	13		33	31	16		356	345	82	4th, Adams		Lost Conf. Final
1980-81*	80	18	11	11		12	21	7		30	32	18		314	318	78	4th, Adams		Lost Prelim. Round
1979-80*	80	17	16	7		8	28	4		25	44	11		248	313	61	5th, Adams		Out of Playoffs

* Quebec Nordiques

2015-16 Player Personnel

FORWARDS	HT	WT	*Age	Place of Birth	S	2014-15 Club
AGOZZINO, Andrew	5-10	187	24	Kleinburg, ON	L	Colorado-Lake Erie
BORDELEAU, Patrick	6-6	225	29	Montreal, QC	L	Colorado
BOURKE, Troy	5-10	170	21	Edmonton, AB	L	Lake Erie
CHEEK, Trevor	6-2	205	22	Beverly Hills, CA	L	Lake Erie
CLICHE, Marc-Andre	6-0	202	28	Rouyn-Noranda, QC	R	Colorado
COMEAU, Blake	6-1	202	29	Meadow Lake, SK	R	Pittsburgh
DUCHENE, Matt	5-11	200	24	Haliburton, ON	L	Colorado
EVERBERG, Dennis	6-4	205	23	Vasteras, Sweden	L	Colorado-Lake Erie
GRIGORENKO, Mikhail	6-3	209	21	Khabarovsk, Russia	L	Buffalo-Rochester
HAMILTON, Freddie	6-1	195	23	Toronto, ON	R	S.J.-Wor-Col-Lake Erie
HENLEY, Samuel	6-4	210	22	Val-d'Or, QC	L	Lake Erie
HISHON, Joey	5-10	170	23	Stratford, ON	L	Colorado-Lake Erie
IGINLA, Jarome	6-1	210	38	Edmonton, AB	R	Colorado
LANDESKOG, Gabriel	6-1	210	22	Stockholm, Sweden	L	Colorado
MacKINNON, Nathan	6-0	195	20	Halifax, NS	R	Colorado
MARTINSEN, Andreas	6-3	220	25	Baerum, Norway	L	Dusseldorf
McLEOD, Cody	6-2	210	31	Binscarth, MB	L	Colorado
MEURS, Garrett	5-11	180	22	Wingham, ON	L	Lake Erie-Fort Wayne
MITCHELL, John	6-1	204	30	Oakville, ON	L	Colorado
RANTANEN, Mikko	6-4	211	18	Nousiainen, Finland	L	TPS-TPS Jr.
RENDULIC, Borna	6-2	200	23	Zagreb, Croatia	R	Colorado-Lake Erie
SMITH, Colin	5-10	175	22	Edmonton, AB	R	Colorado-Lake Erie
SODERBERG, Carl	6-3	216	29	Malmo, Sweden	L	Boston
STREET, Ben	5-11	185	28	Coquitlam, BC	L	Colorado-Lake Erie
TANGUAY, Alex	6-1	194	35	Ste-Justine, QC	L	Colorado
WINCHESTER, Jesse	6-1	205	32	Long Sault, ON	R	Colorado

DEFENSEMEN						
BARRIE, Tyson	5-10	190	24	Victoria, BC	R	Colorado
BEAUCHEMIN, Francois	6-1	208	35	Sorel, QC	L	Anaheim
BEAUPRE, Gabriel	6-2	195	22	Levis, QC	L	Lake Erie-Fort Wayne
BIGRAS, Chris	6-1	190	20	Orillia, ON	L	Owen Sound-Lake Erie
CLARK, Mat	6-3	225	24	Wheat Ridge, CO	R	Ana-Norfolk-Lake Erie
CORBETT, Cody	6-1	204	21	Stillwater, MN	L	Lake Erie
ELLIOTT, Stefan	6-1	190	24	Vancouver, BC	R	Colorado-Lake Erie
GEERTSEN, Mason	6-4	205	20	Drayton Valley, AB	L	Vancouver (WHL)-Lake Erie
GUENIN, Nate	6-3	207	32	Alquippa, PA	R	Colorado
HOLDEN, Nick	6-4	210	28	St. Albert, AB	L	Colorado
JOHNSON, Erik	6-4	232	27	Bloomington, MN	R	Colorado
NOREAU, Maxim	6-0	194	28	Montreal, QC	R	Lake Erie
REDMOND, Zach	6-2	205	27	Traverse City, MI	R	Colorado
SIEMENS, Duncan	6-3	205	22	Edmonton, AB	L	Colorado-Lake Erie
STUART, Brad	6-2	215	35	Rocky Mountain House, AB	L	Colorado
ZADOROV, Nikita	6-5	220	20	Moscow, Russia	L	Buffalo

GOALTENDERS	HT	WT	*Age	Place of Birth	C	2014-15 Club
BERRA, Reto	6-4	210	28	Bulach, Switz.	L	Colorado-Lake Erie
MARTIN, Spencer	6-3	200	20	Oakville, ON	L	Mississauga
PICKARD, Calvin	6-1	200	23	Moncton, NB	L	Colorado-Lake Erie
VARLAMOV, Semyon	6-2	209	27	Kuybyshev, USSR	L	Colorado
WILL, Roman	6-1	195	23	Plzen, Czech.	L	Lake Erie-Fort Wayne

* – Age at start of 2015-16 season

2014-15 Scoring
* – rookie

Regular Season

Pos	#	Player	Team	GP	G	A	Pts	TOI	+/-	PIM	PP	SH	GW	S	S%
R	12	Jarome Iginla	COL	82	29	30	59	18:08	0	42	8	0	2	189	15.3
L	92	Gabriel Landeskog	COL	82	23	36	59	18:30	-2	79	8	0	2	214	10.7
L	40	Alex Tanguay	COL	80	22	33	55	18:09	-10	40	2	1	4	104	21.2
C	9	Matt Duchene	COL	82	21	34	55	18:34	3	16	2	0	4	207	10.1
C	90	Ryan O'Reilly	COL	82	17	38	55	19:43	-5	12	2	1	1	171	9.9
D	4	Tyson Barrie	COL	80	12	41	53	21:21	5	26	2	0	0	139	8.6
C	29	Nathan MacKinnon	COL	64	14	24	38	17:02	-7	34	3	0	2	192	7.3
C	7	John Mitchell	COL	68	11	15	26	15:51	-9	32	3	1	1	105	10.5
D	6	Erik Johnson	COL	47	12	11	23	24:25	2	33	3	0	2	115	10.4
D	22	Zach Redmond	COL	59	5	15	20	17:08	-1	24	1	0	1	93	5.4
D	5	Nate Guenin	COL	76	2	13	15	16:50	-1	32	0	0	0	38	5.3
D	2	Nick Holden	COL	78	5	9	14	19:48	-11	28	2	0	2	94	5.3
D	17	Brad Stuart	COL	65	3	10	13	20:21	-4	16	0	0	0	64	4.7
D	8	Jan Hejda	COL	81	1	12	13	20:39	-12	42	0	0	0	84	1.2
C	48	Daniel Briere	COL	57	8	4	12	12:07	-7	18	0	0	3	69	11.6
L	55	Cody McLeod	COL	82	7	5	12	11:11	-2	191	0	1	2	94	7.4
R	45 *	Dennis Everberg	COL	55	3	9	12	11:48	-7	10	0	0	0	62	4.8
R	24	Marc-Andre Cliche	COL	74	2	5	7	10:36	-2	17	0	0	0	68	2.9
L	11	Jamie McGinn	COL	19	4	2	6	14:46	-9	6	1	0	0	36	11.1
C	71 *	Borna Rendulic	COL	11	1	1	2	9:24	1	6	0	0	0	6	16.7
C	38 *	Joey Hishon	COL	13	1	1	2	10:06	-1	0	0	0	1	19	5.3
C	13 *	Freddie Hamilton	S.J.	1	0	0	0	8:27	-1	0	0	0	0	0	0.0
			COL	17	1	0	1	7:31	-1	0	0	0	1	11	9.1
			Total	18	1	0	1	7:34	-2	0	0	0	1	11	9.1
L	32 *	Andrew Agozzino	COL	1	0	1	1	9:45	1	0	0	0	0	1	0.0
C	43 *	Michael Sgarbossa	COL	3	0	1	1	7:05	0	10	0	0	0	2	0.0
C	81	Tomas Vincour	COL	7	0	1	1	7:10	-1	2	0	0	0	2	0.0
C	28 *	Paul Carey	COL	10	0	1	1	7:52	2	0	0	0	0	5	0.0
L	58	Patrick Bordeleau	COL	1	0	0	0	6:46	0	0	0	0	0	0	0.0
D	16 *	Duncan Siemens	COL	1	0	0	0	14:00	0	0	0	0	0	0	0.0
C	37 *	Colin Smith	COL	1	0	0	0	6:06	0	0	0	0	0	1	0.0
D	44	Ryan Wilson	COL	3	0	0	0	11:12	-3	0	0	0	0	3	0.0
C	10	Ben Street	COL	3	0	0	0	11:35	0	0	0	0	0	4	0.0
D	46	Stefan Elliott	COL	5	0	0	0	13:56	-2	2	0	0	0	10	.0.0
R	27	Jordan Caron	BOS	11	0	0	0	7:55	-1	16	0	0	0	4	0.0
			COL	19	0	0	0	8:05	-1	2	0	0	0	8	0.0
			Total	30	0	0	0	8:02	-2	18	0	0	0	12	0.0

Goaltending

No.	Goaltender	GPI	Mins	Avg	W	L	OT	EN	SO	GA	SA	Sv%	G	A	PIM
31 *	Calvin Pickard	16	895	2.35	6	7	3	4	0	35	511	.932	0	0	0
1	Semyon Varlamov	57	3307	2.56	28	20	8	7	5	141	1791	.921	0	0	4
20	Reto Berra	19	748	2.65	5	4	1	3	1	33	403	.918	0	0	0
	Totals	**82**	**5015**	**2.67**	**39**	**31**	**12**	**14**	**6**	**223**	**2719**	**.918**			

Patrick Roy
Head Coach and Vice President of Hockey Operations
Born: Quebec City, QC, October 5, 1965.

The Colorado Avalanche announced on May 23, 2013 that the organization had reached an agreement in principle with Patrick Roy to become the franchise's head coach and vice president of hockey operations. He was formally introduced at a press conference on May 28. Roy is the sixth head coach in Avalanche history and the 14th in franchise history. In his first season with the team in 2013-14, the Avalanche jumped from 29th to third in the NHL's overall standings and won the Central Division title. In addition to his head coaching duties, Roy works with executive vice president of hockey operations Joe Sakic in all player personnel decisions.

Roy spent the previous eight seasons before joining Colorado as head coach and general manager of the Quebec Remparts of the Quebec Major Junior Hockey League. He guided the Remparts to a 348-159-37 record (.674) in 544 regular-season games behind the bench, which included leading Quebec to the 2006 Memorial Cup title as the Canadian Hockey League champions. He is also a part owner of the QMJHL franchise.

Roy, who was inducted into the Hockey Hall of Fame in 2006, retired with the most regular season wins in NHL history (551), a number that currently ranks second all-time. The four-time Stanley Cup champion is still the winningest goaltender in Stanley Cup playoff history with 151 postseason wins. Roy is the only player in league history to win the Conn Smythe Trophy as playoff MVP three times (1986, 1993, 2001). The Quebec City native backstopped the Montreal Canadiens to two Stanley Cup championships (1986, 1993), the first of which was his rookie campaign. Traded to Colorado on December 6, 1995, Roy led the Avalanche to the Stanley Cup during the club's first season in Denver (1996) and again in 2001. He is the only goaltender in NHL history to win 200 or more games with two different teams. Roy won the Vezina Trophy three times (1989, 1990, 1992) and the William Jennings Trophy five times (1987, 1988, 1989, 1992, 2002). He was selected to the NHL All-Star Team on six occasions, the First Team in 1988-89, 1989-90, 1991-92 and 2001-02 and the Second Team in 1987-88 and 1990-91. He participated in 11 NHL All-Star Games and was named to the NHL All-Rookie Team in 1985-86.

Roy, who is the Avalanche's all-time goaltending leader in nearly every statistical category, had his number 33 retired by the organization on October 28, 2003.

Captains' History

Marc Tardif, 1979-80, 1980-81; Robbie Ftorek and Andre Dupont, 1981-82; Mario Marois, 1982-83 to 1984-85; Mario Marois and Peter Stastny, 1985-86; Peter Stastny, 1986-87 to 1989-90; Joe Sakic and Steven Finn, 1990-91; Mike Hough, 1991-92; Joe Sakic, 1992-93 to 2008-09; Adam Foote, 2009-10, 2010-11; Milan Hejduk, 2011-12; Gabriel Landeskog, 2012-13 to date.

Coaching Record

			Regular Season				Playoffs			
Season	Team	League	GC	W	L	O/T	GC	W	L	T
2005-06	Quebec	QMJHL	65	51	12	2	23	14	9	....
2005-06	Quebec	M-Cup	....	....	....	....	4	3	1	....
2006-07	Quebec	QMJHL	69	36	28	5	5	1	4	....
2007-08	Quebec	QMJHL	70	38	28	4	6	2	4	....
2008-09	Quebec	QMJHL	68	49	16	3	17	9	8	....
2009-10	Quebec	QMJHL	68	41	20	7	9	4	5	....
2010-11	Quebec	QMJHL	68	48	16	4	18	11	7	....
2011-12	Quebec	QMJHL	68	43	18	7	11	7	4	....
2012-13	Quebec	QMJHL	68	42	21	5	11	5	6	....
2013-14	Colorado	NHL	82	52	22	8	7	3	4	
2014-15	Colorado	NHL	82	39	31	12				
	NHL Totals		**164**	**91**	**53**	**20**	**7**	**3**	**4**	....

Jack Adams Award (2014)

Club Records

Team

(Figures in brackets for season records are games played; records for fewest points, wins, ties, losses, goals, goals against are for 70 or more games)

Most Points **118** 2000-01 (82)
Most Wins **52** 2000-01 (82), 2013-14 (82)
Most Ties **18** 1980-81 (80)
Most Losses **61** 1989-90 (80)
Most Goals **360** 1983-84 (80)
Most Goals Against **407** 1989-90 (80)
Fewest Points **31** 1989-90 (80)
Fewest Wins **12** 1989-90 (80)
Fewest Ties **5** 1987-88 (80)
Fewest Losses **16** 2000-01 (82)
Fewest Goals **199** 2008-09 (82)
Fewest Goals Against **169** 2001-02 (82)

Longest Winning Streak
Overall .... **12** Jan. 10-Feb. 7/99
Home .... **10** Nov. 26/83-Jan. 10/84, Mar. 6-Apr. 16/95
Away .... **7** Jan. 10-Feb. 7/99

Longest Undefeated Streak
Overall .... **12** Dec. 23/96-Jan. 20/97 (9W, 3T), Jan. 10-Feb. 7/99 (12W)
Home .... **14** Nov. 19/83-Jan. 21/84 (11W, 3T)
Away .... **10** Jan. 10-Mar. 3/99 (8W, 2T)

Longest Losing Streak
Overall .... **14** Oct. 21-Nov. 19/90
Home .... **8** Oct. 21-Nov. 24/90
Away .... **18** Jan. 18-Apr. 1/90

Longest Winless Streak
Overall .... **17** Oct. 21-Nov. 25/90 (15L, 2T)
Home .... **11** Nov. 14-Dec. 26/89 (7L, 4T)
Away .... **33** Oct. 8/91-Feb. 27/92 (25L, 8T)
Most Shutouts, Season **11** 2001-02 (82)
Most PIM, Season **2,104** 1989-90 (80)
Most Goals, Game .... **12** Feb. 1/83 (Hfd. 3 at Que. 12), Oct. 20/84 (Que. 12 at Tor. 3), Dec. 5/95 (S.J. 2 at Col. 12)

Individual

Most Seasons .... **20** Joe Sakic
Most Games .... **1,378** Joe Sakic
Most Goals, Career .... **625** Joe Sakic
Most Assists, Career ...... **1,016** Joe Sakic
Most Points, Career ...... **1,641** Joe Sakic (625G, 1,016A)
Most PIM, Career .... **1,562** Dale Hunter
Most Shutouts, Career .... **37** Patrick Roy
Longest Consecutive Games Streak .... **312** Dale Hunter (Oct. 9/80-Mar. 13/84)
Most Goals, Season .... **57** Michel Goulet (1982-83)
Most Assists, Season .... **93** Peter Stastny (1981-82)
Most Points, Season .... **139** Peter Stastny (1981-82; 46G, 93A)
Most PIM, Season .... **301** Gord Donnelly (1987-88)
Most Points, Defenseman, Season .... **82** Steve Duchesne (1992-93; 20G, 62A)
Most Points, Center, Season .... **139** Peter Stastny (1981-82; 46G, 93A)
Most Points, Right Wing, Season .... **103** Jacques Richard (1980-81; 52G, 51A)
Most Points, Left Wing, Season .... **121** Michel Goulet (1983-84; 56G, 65A)
Most Points, Rookie, Season .... **109** Peter Stastny (1980-81; 39G, 70A)
Most Shutouts, Season .... **9** Patrick Roy (2001-02)
Most Goals, Game .... **5** Mats Sundin (Mar. 5/92), Mike Ricci (Feb. 17/94)
Most Assists, Game .... **5** Eight times
Most Points, Game .... **8** Peter Stastny (Feb. 22/81; 4G, 4A), Anton Stastny (Feb. 22/81; 3G, 5A)

Records include Quebec Nordiques, 1979-80 through 1994-95.

All-time Record vs. Other Clubs

Regular Season

	Total								At Home								On Road							
	GP	W	L	T	OL	GF	GA	PTS	GP	W	L	T	OL	GF	GA	PTS	GP	W	L	T	OL	GF	GA	PTS
Anaheim	79	36	27	7	9	214	217	88	39	19	15	4	1	110	108	43	40	17	12	3	8	104	109	45
Arizona	118	57	44	12	5	393	394	131	59	30	21	5	3	197	190	68	59	27	23	7	2	196	204	63
Boston	138	53	70	15	0	450	531	121	71	26	39	6	0	247	287	58	67	27	31	9	0	203	244	63
Buffalo	137	58	57	20	2	474	470	138	69	35	22	11	1	249	211	82	68	23	35	9	1	225	259	56
Calgary	152	63	67	20	2	477	499	148	76	34	30	11	1	255	239	80	76	29	37	9	1	222	260	68
Carolina	138	71	44	21	2	522	426	165	70	44	17	9	0	296	205	97	68	27	27	12	2	226	221	68
Chicago	121	60	48	9	4	415	387	133	60	33	19	6	2	228	188	74	61	27	29	3	2	187	199	59
Columbus	51	36	11	1	3	177	102	76	26	19	6	0	1	93	55	39	25	17	5	1	2	84	47	37
Dallas	123	60	44	12	7	396	354	139	62	36	15	7	4	219	149	83	61	24	29	5	3	177	205	56
Detroit	117	48	59	5	5	352	396	106	59	25	26	4	4	186	195	58	58	23	33	1	1	166	201	48
Edmonton	152	71	69	8	4	503	538	154	77	40	32	4	1	267	256	85	75	31	37	4	3	236	282	69
Florida	33	20	7	3	3	113	92	46	16	7	5	3	1	46	42	18	17	13	2	0	2	67	50	28
Los Angeles	122	51	58	8	5	420	435	115	60	30	26	3	1	230	204	64	62	21	32	5	4	190	231	51
Minnesota	84	40	32	3	9	228	216	92	42	21	17	2	2	114	104	46	42	19	15	1	7	114	112	46
Montreal	137	53	69	15	0	447	519	121	68	35	28	5	0	230	234	75	69	18	41	10	0	217	285	46
Nashville	64	28	25	5	6	175	182	67	33	17	12	2	2	84	82	38	31	11	13	3	4	91	100	29
New Jersey	82	39	34	8	1	272	266	87	40	22	14	4	0	139	106	48	42	17	20	4	1	133	160	39
NY Islanders	77	37	34	4	2	262	261	80	40	23	12	3	2	140	110	51	37	14	22	1	0	122	151	29
NY Rangers	80	37	36	7	0	272	296	81	40	22	15	3	0	159	145	47	40	15	21	4	0	113	151	34
Ottawa	43	27	12	4	0	173	123	58	20	16	3	1	0	90	59	33	23	11	9	3	0	83	64	25
Philadelphia	80	29	35	14	2	248	276	74	41	18	10	12	1	145	135	49	39	11	25	2	1	103	141	25
Pittsburgh	80	38	32	7	3	318	299	86	38	20	14	2	2	158	139	44	42	18	18	5	1	160	160	42
St. Louis	121	55	51	11	4	377	366	125	61	34	18	7	2	210	157	77	60	21	33	4	2	167	209	48
San Jose	84	42	31	5	6	265	230	95	41	24	11	4	2	139	96	54	43	18	20	1	4	126	134	41
Tampa Bay	37	20	13	3	1	122	96	44	19	14	3	2	0	73	42	30	18	6	10	1	1	49	54	14
Toronto	74	38	26	9	1	277	235	86	34	19	10	5	0	129	109	43	40	19	16	4	1	148	126	43
Vancouver	152	71	58	15	8	497	460	165	76	37	27	8	4	243	217	86	76	34	31	7	4	254	243	79
Washington	77	31	37	9	0	236	271	71	39	17	17	5	0	117	132	39	38	14	20	4	0	119	139	32
Winnipeg	27	12	9	1	5	74	79	30	14	7	4	0	3	39	38	17	13	5	5	1	2	35	41	13
Totals	**2780**	**1281**	**1139**	**261**	**99**	**9149**	**9016**	**2922**	**1390**	**724**	**488**	**138**	**40**	**4832**	**4234**	**1626**	**1390**	**557**	**651**	**123**	**59**	**4317**	**4782**	**1296**

Playoffs

	Series	W	L	GP	W	L	T	GF	GA	Last Mtg.	Rnd.	Result
Anaheim	1	0	1	4	0	4	0	4	16	2006	CSF	L 0-4
Arizona	1	1	0	5	4	1	0	17	10	2000	CQF	W 4-1
Boston	2	1	1	11	5	6	0	36	37	1983	DSF	L 1-3
Buffalo	2	2	0	8	6	2	0	35	27	1985	DSF	W 3-2
Carolina	2	1	1	9	4	5	0	34	35	1987	DSF	W 4-2
Chicago	2	2	0	12	8	4	0	49	28	1997	CQF	W 4-2
Dallas	4	2	2	24	14	10	0	66	62	2006	CQF	W 4-1
Detroit	6	3	3	34	17	17	0	88	97	2008	CSF	L 0-4
Edmonton	2	1	1	12	7	5	0	35	30	1998	CQF	L 3-4
Florida	1	1	0	4	4	0	0	15	4	1996	F	W 4-0
Los Angeles	2	2	0	14	8	6	0	33	23	2002	CQF	W 4-3
Minnesota	3	1	2	20	10	10	0	54	50	2014	FR	L 3-4
Montreal	5	2	3	31	14	17	0	85	105	1993	DSF	L 2-4
New Jersey	1	1	0	7	4	3	0	19	11	2001	F	W 4-3
NY Islanders	1	0	1	4	0	4	0	9	18	1982	CF	L 0-4
NY Rangers	1	0	1	6	2	4	0	19	25	1995	CQF	L 2-4
Philadelphia	2	0	2	11	4	7	0	29	39	1985	CF	L 2-4
St. Louis	1	1	0	5	4	1	0	17	11	2001	CF	W 4-1
San Jose	4	2	2	25	12	13	0	62	71	2010	CQF	L 2-4
Vancouver	2	2	0	10	8	2	0	40	26	2001	CQF	W 4-0
Totals	**45**	**25**	**20**	**256**	**135**	**121**	**0**	**746**	**725**			

Playoff Results 2015-2011

Year	Round	Opponent	Result	GF	GA
2014	FR	Minnesota	L 3-4	20	22

Abbreviations: Round: F – Final; **CF** – conference final; **CSF** – conference semi-final; **CQF** – conference quarter-final; **FR** – first round; **DSF** – division semi-final.

Calgary totals include Atlanta Flames, 1979-80.
Dallas totals include Minnesota North Stars, 1979-80 to 1992-93.
Phoenix totals include Winnipeg, 1979-80 to 1995-96.
Carolina totals include Hartford, 1979-80 to 1996-97.
New Jersey totals include Colorado Rockies, 1979-80 to 1981-82.
Winnipeg totals include Atlanta Thrashers, 1999-2000 to 2010-11.

2014-15 Results

Oct.	9	at Minnesota	0-5		10	Dallas	4-3
	11	Minnesota	0-3		12	at Washington	1-2
	13	at Boston	2-1		13	at Carolina	2-3†
	14	at Toronto	2-3*		15	at Florida	4-2
	16	at Ottawa	3-5		17	at Tampa Bay	2-3†
	18	at Montreal	2-3		19	at St. Louis	1-3
	21	Florida	3-4*		21	Boston	3-2†
	24	Vancouver	7-3		27	at Nashville	3-4*
	26	at Winnipeg	1-2*		30	Nashville	3-0
	28	San Jose	2-3†	**Feb.**	3	at Dallas	3-2†
	30	NY Islanders	5-0		5	Detroit	0-3
Nov.	1	at St. Louis	2-3†		7	at Minnesota	0-1
	2	Anaheim	2-3		8	at Winnipeg	3-5
	4	Vancouver	2-5		12	NY Rangers	3-6
	6	Toronto	4-3†		14	Dallas	4-1
	8	at Philadelphia	3-4		16	Arizona	5-2
	11	at NY Islanders	0-6		18	Los Angeles	1-4
	13	at NY Rangers	4-3†		20	at Chicago	4-1
	15	at New Jersey	3-2		22	Tampa Bay	5-4
	20	Washington	2-3		24	at Nashville	2-5
	22	Carolina	4-3		27	at Dallas	5-4†
	25	at Arizona	4-3*		28	Minnesota	1-3
	26	Chicago	2-3	**Mar.**	4	Pittsburgh	3-1
	29	Dallas	5-2		7	at Columbus	4-0
Dec.	1	Montreal	3-4		8	at Minnesota	3-2
	4	at Calgary	3-4*		10	Los Angeles	2-5
	5	at Winnipeg	2-6		12	New Jersey	2-1†
	9	Nashville	0-3		14	Calgary	3-2
	11	Winnipeg	4-3†		19	at Arizona	5-2
	13	St. Louis	2-3*		20	at Anaheim	2-3*
	18	at Pittsburgh	0-1*		23	at Calgary	2-3
	20	at Buffalo	5-1		25	at Edmonton	3-4
	21	at Detroit	2-1†		26	at Vancouver	4-1
	23	St. Louis	5-0		28	Buffalo	5-3
	27	Chicago	2-5		30	Edmonton	1-4
	29	at St. Louis	0-3	**Apr.**	1	at San Jose	1-5
	31	Philadelphia	4-3*		3	at Anaheim	4-2
Jan.	2	Edmonton	2-1†		4	at Los Angeles	1-3
	4	Columbus	3-4		7	Nashville	3-2
	6	at Chicago	2-0		9	Winnipeg	1-0†
	8	Ottawa	5-2		11	Chicago	3-2

* – Overtime † – Shootout

NHL Draft Selections 2015-2001

Name in bold denotes played in NHL.

2015 Pick		2010 Pick	
10	Mikko Rantanen	17	**Joey Hishon**
39	A.J. Greer	49	**Calvin Pickard**
40	Nicolas Meloche	71	**Michael Bournival**
71	Jean-Christophe Beaudin	95	Stephen Silas
101	Andrei Mironov	107	**Sami Aittokallio**
161	Sergei Boikov	137	Troy Rutkowski
191	Gustav Olhaver	139	Luke Walker
		197	Luke Moffatt

2014 Pick		2009 Pick	
23	Conner Bleackley	3	**Matt Duchene**
84	Kyle Wood	33	**Ryan O'Reilly**
93	Nick Magyar	49	**Stefan Elliott**
114	Alexis Pepin	64	**Tyson Barrie**
144	Anton Lindholm	124	Kieran Millan
174	Maximilian Pajpach	154	Brandon Maxwell
204	Julien Nantel	184	Gus Young

2013 Pick		2008 Pick	
1	**Nathan MacKinnon**	50	**Cameron Gaunce**
32	Chris Bigras	61	Peter Delmas
63	Spencer Martin	110	Kelsey Tessier
93	Mason Geertsen	140	**Mark Olver**
123	Will Butcher	167	Joel Chouinard
153	Ben Storm	170	**Jonas Holos**
183	Wilhelm Westlund	200	Nate Condon

2012 Pick		2007 Pick	
41	Mitchell Heard	14	**Kevin Shattenkirk**
72	Troy Bourke	45	**Colby Cohen**
132	Michael Clarke	49	Trevor Cann
162	Joseph Blandisi	55	**TJ Galiardi**
192	**Colin Smith**	105	**Brad Malone**
		113	Kent Patterson

2011 Pick			
2	**Gabriel Landeskog**	135	**Paul Carey**
11	**Duncan Siemens**	155	Jens Hellgren
93	Joachim Nermark	195	Johan Alcen
123	Garrett Meurs		
153	Gabriel Beaupre		
183	Dillon Donnelly		

2006 Pick	
18	**Chris Stewart**
51	Nigel Williams
59	Codey Burki
81	Mike Carman
110	Kevin Montgomery
201	Billy Sauer

2005 Pick	
34	**Ryan Stoa**
44	**Paul Stastny**
47	Tom Fritsche
52	Chris Durand
88	**T.J. Hensick**
124	Ray Macias
166	Jason Lynch
168	**Justin Mercier**
222	**Kyle Cumiskey**

2004 Pick	
21	**Wojtek Wolski**
55	**Victor Oreskovich**
72	Denis Parshin
154	Richard Demen-Willaume
184	**Derek Peltier**
215	Ian Keserich
239	**Brandon Yip**
267	J.D. Corbin
281	Steve McClellan

2003 Pick	
63	**David Liffiton**
131	David Svagrovsky
146	Mark McCutcheon
163	**Brad Richardson**
204	Linus Videll
225	Brett Hemingway
257	Darryl Yacboski
288	**David Jones**

2002 Pick	
28	**Jonas Johansson**
61	**Johnny Boychuk**
94	Eric Lundberg
107	**Mikko Kalteva**
129	**Tom Gilbert**
164	**Tyler Weiman**
195	Taylor Christie
227	Ryan Steeves
258	Sergei Shemetov
289	Sean Collins

2001 Pick	
63	**Peter Budaj**
97	**Danny Bois**
130	Colt King
143	Frantisek Skladany
144	**Cody McCormick**
149	Mikko Viitanen
165	Pierre-Luc Emond
184	Scott Horvath
196	**Charlie Stephens**
227	**Marek Svatos**

Coaching History

Jacques Demers, 1979-80; Maurice Filion and Michel Bergeron, 1980-81; Michel Bergeron, 1981-82 to 1986-87; Andre Savard and Ron Lapointe, 1987-88; Ron Lapointe and Jean Perron, 1988-89; Michel Bergeron, 1989-90; Dave Chambers, 1990-91; Dave Chambers and Pierre Page, 1991-92; Pierre Page, 1992-93, 1993-94; Marc Crawford, 1994-95 to 1997-98; Bob Hartley, 1998-99 to 2001-02; Bob Hartley and Tony Granato, 2002-03; Tony Granato, 2003-04; Joel Quenneville, 2004-05 to 2007-08; Tony Granato, 2008-09; Joe Sacco, 2009-10 to 2012-13; Patrick Roy, 2013-14 to date.

General Managers' History

Maurice Filion, 1979-80 to 1987-88; Martin Madden, 1988-89; Martin Madden and Maurice Filion, 1989-90; Pierre Page, 1990-91 to 1993-94; Pierre Lacroix, 1994-95 to 2005-06; Francois Giguere, 2006-07 to 2008-09; Greg Sherman, 2009-10 to 2013-14; Joe Sakic, 2014-15 to date.

Joe Sakic
Executive Vice President/General Manager
Born: Burnaby, BC, July 7, 1969

Former Avalanche captain Joe Sakic was named executive vice president of hockey operations on May 10, 2013 and was given responsibility for overseeing all hockey-related decisions. His first move came on May 23, 2013 when he named Patrick Roy head coach/vice president of hockey operations. A month later, Sakic announced Nathan MacKinnon as the first overall pick at the 2013 NHL Draft. On September 19, 2014, the Avalanche officially announced that Sakic was the club's new general manager.

Sakic announced his retirement from the NHL on July 9, 2009, following a career that spanned 20 seasons and 1,378 games with the same organization. He wore the 'C' as team captain for 16 consecutive seasons (17 seasons overall), making him the second-longest serving captain in NHL history. Sakic led the Avalanche to two Stanley Cup titles (1996, 2001) including the city of Denver's first major professional sports championship in 1996. He captured the franchise's first Hart Trophy as league MVP in 2001, won the Conn Smythe Trophy as playoff MVP in 1996, earned the Lester B. Pearson Award (NHLPA MVP) and Lady Byng Trophy (sportsmanship) in 2001 and was named to the NHL's First All-Star Team on three occasions (2001, 2002 and 2004).

Sakic was elected to the Hockey Hall of Fame in 2012, his first year of eligibility. Selected by the Quebec Nordiques in the first round (15th overall) of the 1987 NHL Draft, he retired as the eighth-highest scorer in NHL history with 1,641 career points. He ranked seventh all-time in both playoff goals (84) and playoff points (188-tied), and still holds the NHL record for postseason overtime goals with eight. The Avalanche retired Sakic's number 19 during a pregame ceremony on October 1, 2009.

Club Directory

Pepsi Center

Colorado Avalanche
Pepsi Center
1000 Chopper Circle
Denver, CO 80204
Phone **303/405-1100**
FAX 303/893-0614
Press Box 303/575-1926
www.coloradoavalanche.com
Capacity: 18,007

Executive
Owner . . . . E. Stanley Kroenke
President & Governor . . . . Josh Kroenke
Exec. Vice President/General Manager/Alt. Governor . . Joe Sakic
Sr. VP of Business & Team Operations/Alt. Governor . . Greg Sherman
Assistant General Managers . . . . Craig Billington, Chris MacFarland
Vice President of Hockey Administration . . . . Charlotte Grahame

Coaching Staff
Head Coach/VP of Hockey Operations . . . . Patrick Roy
Assistant Coaches . . . . Tim Army, Dave Farrish
Goaltending Coach . . . . Francois Allaire
Video Coordinator . . . . Brett Heimlich

Training Staff
Head Athletic Trainer . . . . Matthew Sokolowski
Assistant Athletic Trainer/Physical Therapist . . . . . . Scott Woodward
Head Equipment Manager . . . . Mark Miller
Assistant Equipment Managers . . . . Cliff Halstead, Brad Lewkow
Inventory Manager . . . . Wayne Flemming
Strength & Conditioning Coach . . . . Casey Bond
Massage Therapist . . . . Gregorio Pradera

Pro Scouting Staff
Director of Player Personnel . . . . Brad Smith
Assistant Director of Player Personnel . . . . Garth Joy
Pro Scouts . . . . Dan Laperriere, Terry Martin

Amateur Scouting Staff
Director of Amateur Scouting . . . . Alan Hepple
Scouts . . . . Anders Carlsson, Anton Edlund, Rick Lanz, Joni Lehto, Jerome Mesonero, Don Paarup, Norm Robert, Neil Shea

Player Development Staff
Director of Player Development . . . . David Oliver
Development Consultants . . . . Brett Clark, Adam Foote, Brian Willsie

Communications/Team Services/Website & Social Media Staff
Sr. V.P., Communications & Business Operations . . . Jean Martineau
Exec. Director of Media Services . . . . Brendan McNicholas
Team Services Manager . . . . Erin DeGraff
Website/Media Relations Coordinators . . . . Ryan Boulding, Ron Knabenbauer

San Antonio Rampage (AHL affiliate)
Head Coach . . . . Dean Chynoweth
Assistant Coach . . . . Randy Ladouceur
Goaltending Coach . . . . Jean-Ian Filiatrault
Video Coordinator . . . . Steven Petrovek
Head Athletic Trainer . . . . Brent Woodside
Head Equipment Manager . . . . Steven Passineau

Team Information
Practice Facility . . . . South Suburban Family Sports Center
Television Outlet . . . . Altitude Sports & Entertainment Network
Radio . . . . Altitude Radio Network

Picked second overall in the 2011 Entry Draft, Gabriel Landeskog became the youngest captain in NHL history when he was given the C in 2012-13. He tied for the team lead in scoring with 59 points in 2014-15.

Columbus Blue Jackets

2014-15 Results: 42w-35L-3OTL-2SOL 89PTS
5TH, Metropolitan Division • 11TH, Eastern Conference

Key Off-Season Signings/Acquisitions

2015

May **28** • Re-signed D **Cody Goloubef**.

29 • Re-signed D **Justin Falk**.

June **18** • Named **Kenny McCudden** assistant coach.

24 • Re-signed G **Curtis McElhinney**.

30 • Acquired LW **Brandon Saad**, C **Alex Broadhurst** and D **Michael Paliotta** from Chicago for C **Artem Anisimov**, RW **Marko Dano**, RW **Jeremy Morin**, RW **Corey Tropp** and a 4th-round choice in the 2016 NHL Draft.

July **1** • Signed C **Gregory Campbell**.

9 • Re-signed LW **Matt Calvert**.

23 • Re-signed C **Michael Chaput**.

Year-by-Year Record

		Home				Road				Overall								
Season	GP	W	L	T	OL	W	L	T	OL	W	L	T	OL	GF	GA	Pts.	Div. Fin.	Conf. Fin.	Playoff Result
2014-15	82	19	20	....	2	23	15	....	3	42	35	....	5	236	250	89	5th, Met.	11th, East	Out of Playoffs
2013-14	82	22	15	....	4	21	17	....	3	43	32	....	7	231	216	93	4th, Met.	7th, East	Lost First Round
2012-13	48	14	5	....	5	10	12	....	2	24	17	....	7	120	119	55	4th, Cen.	9th, West	Out of Playoffs
2011-12	82	17	21	....	3	12	25	....	4	29	46	....	7	202	262	65	5th, Cen.	15th, West	Out of Playoffs
2010-11	82	17	19	....	5	17	16	....	8	34	35	....	13	215	258	81	5th, Cen.	13th, West	Out of Playoffs
2009-10	82	20	12	....	9	12	23	....	6	32	35	....	15	216	259	79	5th, Cen.	14th, West	Out of Playoffs
2008-09	82	25	13	....	3	16	18	....	7	41	31	....	10	226	230	92	4th, Cen.	7th, West	Lost Conf. Quarter-Final
2007-08	82	20	14	....	7	14	22	....	5	34	36	....	12	193	218	80	4th, Cen.	13th, West	Out of Playoffs
2006-07	82	18	19	....	4	15	23	....	3	33	42	....	7	201	249	73	4th, Cen.	13th, West	Out of Playoffs
2005-06	82	23	18	....	0	12	25	....	4	35	43	....	4	223	279	74	3rd, Cen.	13th, West	Out of Playoffs
2004-05	....																		
2003-04	82	17	18	4	2	8	27	4	2	25	45	8	4	177	238	62	4th, Cen.	14th, West	Out of Playoffs
2002-03	82	20	14	5	2	9	28	3	1	29	42	8	3	213	263	69	5th, Cen.	15th, West	Out of Playoffs
2001-02	82	14	18	5	4	8	29	3	1	22	47	8	5	164	255	57	5th, Cen.	15th, West	Out of Playoffs
2000-01	82	19	15	4	3	9	24	5	3	28	39	9	6	190	233	71	5th, Cen.	13th, West	Out of Playoffs

---

2015-16 Schedule

Oct.	Fri.	9	NY Rangers	Fri.	8	at Carolina
	Sat.	10	at NY Rangers	Sat.	9	Carolina
	Mon.	12	at Buffalo*	Tue.	12	at NY Islanders
	Wed.	14	Ottawa	Wed.	13	at Toronto
	Fri.	16	Toronto	Sat.	16	Colorado
	Sat.	17	at Chicago	Tue.	19	Washington
	Tue.	20	NY Islanders	Thu.	21	Calgary
	Thu.	22	at Minnesota	Sat.	23	at Boston
	Sat.	24	at Colorado	Mon.	25	Montreal
	Tue.	27	at New Jersey	Tue.	26	at Montreal
	Fri.	30	at Washington	Feb. Tue.	2	at Edmonton
	Sat.	31	Winnipeg	Thu.	4	at Vancouver
Nov.	Tue.	3	at San Jose	Fri.	5	at Calgary
	Thu.	5	at Los Angeles	Tue.	9	NY Islanders
	Fri.	6	at Anaheim	Thu.	11	Anaheim
	Tue.	10	Vancouver	Sat.	13	Ottawa
	Fri.	13	at Pittsburgh	Tue.	16	Boston
	Sat.	14	Arizona	Fri.	19	Buffalo
	Tue.	17	St. Louis	Mon.	22	at Boston
	Thu.	19	at Ottawa	Tue.	23	at Detroit
	Fri.	20	Nashville	Thu.	25	New Jersey
	Sun.	22	San Jose*	Sat.	27	Florida*
	Wed.	25	at New Jersey	Mon.	29	at NY Rangers
	Fri.	27	Pittsburgh	Mar. Fri.	4	Edmonton
	Sat.	28	at St. Louis	Sat.	5	at Philadelphia
Dec.	Tue.	1	at Montreal	Tue.	8	Detroit
	Fri.	4	Florida	Fri.	11	Pittsburgh
	Sat.	5	at Philadelphia	Sun.	13	Tampa Bay*
	Tue.	8	Los Angeles	Thu.	17	Detroit
	Thu.	10	at Winnipeg	Sat.	19	New Jersey
	Sat.	12	NY Islanders	Sun.	20	at New Jersey*
	Mon.	14	Tampa Bay	Tue.	22	Philadelphia
	Tue.	15	at Dallas	Thu.	24	Carolina
	Thu.	17	at Arizona	Sat.	26	at Nashville
	Sat.	19	Philadelphia	Mon.	28	at Washington
	Mon.	21	at Pittsburgh	Thu.	31	at NY Islanders
	Sat.	26	at Tampa Bay	Apr. Sat.	2	at Carolina
	Sun.	27	at Florida	Mon.	4	NY Rangers
	Tue.	29	Dallas	Wed.	6	at Toronto
Jan.	Sat.	2	Washington	Fri.	8	at Buffalo
	Tue.	5	Minnesota	Sat.	9	Chicago

* Denotes afternoon game.

METROPOLITAN DIVISION
16th NHL Season

Franchise date: June 25, 1997

Named captain of the team heading into 2015-16, Nick Foligno led the Blue Jackets with 31 goals, 73 points, and a plus-minus rating of +16 in 2014-15. All established new career highs, as did Foligno's 42 assists.

2015-16 Player Personnel

FORWARDS	HT	WT	*Age	Place of Birth	S	2014-15 Club
ANDERSON, Josh	6-3	212	21	Burlington, ON	R	Columbus-Springfield
ATKINSON, Cam	5-8	174	26	Riverside, CT	R	Columbus
BOLL, Jared	6-3	214	29	Charlotte, NC	R	Columbus
BOURQUE, Rene	6-2	217	33	Lac La Biche, AB	L	Mtl-Hamilton-Ana-CBJ
CALVERT, Matt	5-11	187	25	Brandon, MB	L	Columbus
CAMPBELL, Gregory	6-0	197	31	London, ON	L	Boston
CHAPUT, Michael	6-2	197	23	Ile Bizard, QC	L	Columbus-Springfield
CLARKSON, David	6-1	200	31	Toronto, ON	R	Toronto-Columbus
DUBINSKY, Brandon	6-2	216	29	Anchorage, AK	L	Columbus
FOLIGNO, Nick	6-0	210	27	Buffalo, NY	L	Columbus
HARTNELL, Scott	6-2	210	33	Regina, SK	L	Columbus
JENNER, Boone	6-2	208	22	Dorchester, ON	L	Columbus
JOHANSEN, Ryan	6-3	223	23	Port Moody, BC	R	Columbus
KARLSSON, William	6-1	179	22	Marsta, Sweden	L	Ana-Norfolk-CBJ-Sprfld
RYCHEL, Kerby	6-1	205	21	Torrance, CA	L	Columbus-Springfield
SAAD, Brandon	6-1	202	22	Pittsburgh, PA	L	Chicago
WENNBERG, Alexander	6-1	190	21	Stockholm, Sweden	L	Columbus-Springfield

DEFENSEMEN	HT	WT	*Age	Place of Birth	S	2014-15 Club
CONNAUTON, Kevin	6-2	200	25	Edmonton, AB	L	Dallas-Columbus
FALK, Justin	6-5	215	26	Snowflake, MB	L	Minnesota-Iowa-Columbus
GOLOUBEF, Cody	6-1	190	25	Mississauga, ON	R	Columbus-Springfield
JOHNSON, Jack	6-1	238	28	Indianapolis, IN	L	Columbus
MURRAY, Ryan	6-1	208	22	Regina, SK	L	Columbus
PALIOTTA, Michael	6-3	207	22	Westport, CT	R	U. of Vermont-Chicago
PROUT, Dalton	6-3	222	25	LaSalle, ON	R	Columbus
RAMAGE, John	6-0	200	24	Mississauga, ON	R	Calgary-Adirondack
SAVARD, David	6-2	219	24	St. Hyacinthe, QC	R	Columbus
TYUTIN, Fedor	6-2	212	32	Izhevsk, USSR	L	Columbus

GOALTENDERS	HT	WT	*Age	Place of Birth	C	2014-15 Club
BOBROVSKY, Sergei	6-2	182	27	Novokuznetsk, USSR	L	Columbus
FORSBERG, Anton	6-2	176	22	Harnosand, Sweden	L	Columbus-Springfield
McELHINNEY, Curtis	6-3	205	32	London, ON	L	Columbus

* – Age at start of 2015-16 season

Coaching History

Dave King, 2000-01, 2001-02; Dave King and Doug MacLean, 2002-03; Doug MacLean and Gerard Gallant, 2003-04; Gerard Gallant, 2004-05, 2005-06; Gerard Gallant, Gary Agnew and Ken Hitchcock, 2006-07; Ken Hitchcock, 2007-08, 2008-09; Ken Hitchcock and Claude Noel, 2009-10; Scott Arniel, 2010-11; Scott Arniel and Todd Richards, 2011-12; Todd Richards, 2012-13 to date.

Todd Richards

Head Coach

Born: Robbinsdale, MN, October 20, 1966.

Todd Richards was named head coach of the Columbus Blue Jackets on May 14, 2012. He joined the Blue Jackets as an assistant coach on June 20, 2011 and took over as interim head coach on January 9, 2012. He spent his first full season as Blue Jackets bench boss in 2012-13. In 2013-14, Columbus set club records with 43 wins and 93 points and reached the playoffs.

Before joining the Blue Jackets, Richards was the head coach of the Minnesota Wild from 2009 to 2011 after being named the second head coach in Wild history on June 16, 2009. In 2008-09, he served as an assistant coach with the San Jose Sharks and helped the club capture the Presidents' Trophy with an NHL-best 53-18-11 record. He was responsible for the power play in San Jose and that unit ranked third in the NHL at 24.2 percent in 2008-09. During his stint with the Wild, the club's power play unit converted nearly 19 percent of its man advantage opportunities.

Prior to his stint with the Sharks, Richards spent two seasons as the head coach of the Wilkes-Barre/Scranton Penguins in the American Hockey League from 2006 to 2008, leading the club to the 2008 Calder Cup Final. He also coached the PlanetUSA squad at the 2007 AHL All-Star Classic in Toronto. He began his coaching career as an assistant with the American Hockey League's Milwaukee Admirals from 2002 to 2006, helping the club to a pair of West Division titles, two appearances in the Calder Cup Final and the 2004 Calder Cup championship.

Richards played four seasons at the University of Minnesota from 1985 to 1989. He was a three-time WCHA Second All-Star Team pick, helping the Golden Gophers win Western Collegiate Hockey Association titles in 1988 and 1989 and reach the NCAA title game in 1989. He served as the team's captain and earned Second Team All-America honors as a senior. He is the University of Minnesota's all-time leading scorer among defensemen with 30 goals, 128 assists and 158 points.

Montreal's third pick, 33rd overall, in the 1985 NHL Draft, Richards made his professional debut in 1990 and appeared in eight career NHL games with the Hartford Whalers between 1990 and 1992, collecting four assists and four penalty minutes. His playing career would span 13 seasons, mostly in the AHL and International Hockey League. He helped Springfield win the 1991 Calder Cup championship, was a three-time IHL All-Star and won the 2001 Turner Cup title with the Orlando Solar Bears. He wrapped up his career in 2001-02 with Servette Geneve in Switzerland.

Coaching Record

			Regular Season				Playoffs			
Season	Team	League	GC	W	L	O/T	GC	W	L	T
2006-07	Wilkes-Barre	AHL	80	51	23	6	11	5	6	.....
2007-08	Wilkes-Barre	AHL	80	47	26	6	23	14	9	.....
2009-10	Minnesota	NHL	82	38	36	8	.....	.....	.....	.....
2010-11	Minnesota	NHL	82	39	35	8	.....	.....	.....	.....
2011-12	Columbus	NHL	41	18	21	2	.....	.....	.....	.....
2012-13	Columbus	NHL	48	24	17	7	.....	.....	.....	.....
2013-14	Columbus	NHL	82	43	32	7	6	2	4	.....
2014-15	Columbus	NHL	82	42	35	5	.....	.....	.....	.....
	NHL Totals		417	204	176	37	6	2	4	

2014-15 Scoring

* – rookie

Regular Season

Pos	#	Player	Team	GP	G	A	Pts	TOI	+/-	PIM	PP	SH	GW	S	S%
L	71	Nick Foligno	CBJ	79	31	42	73	18:49	16	50	11	0	3	182	17.0
C	19	Ryan Johansen	CBJ	82	26	45	71	19:30	-6	40	7	2	0	202	12.9
L	43	Scott Hartnell	CBJ	77	28	32	60	17:17	1	100	8	0	2	204	13.7
R	13	Cam Atkinson	CBJ	78	22	18	40	16:59	-2	22	7	1	7	212	10.4
D	7	Jack Johnson	CBJ	79	8	32	40	24:09	-13	44	3	0	1	141	5.7
C	17	Brandon Dubinsky	CBJ	47	13	23	36	18:03	11	43	0	1	1	100	13.0
D	58	David Savard	CBJ	82	11	25	36	22:56	0	71	3	0	3	112	9.8
C	42	Artem Anisimov	CBJ	52	7	20	27	16:22	-6	8	0	2	2	88	8.0
L	11	Matt Calvert	CBJ	56	13	10	23	15:59	1	28	0	0	3	93	14.0
D	4	Kevin Connauton	DAL	8	0	2	2	12:05	4	0	0	0	0	10	0.0
			CBJ	54	9	10	19	16:49	1	29	0	0	4	86	10.5
			Total	62	9	12	21	16:12	5	35	0	0	4	96	9.4
C	56	* Marko Dano	CBJ	35	8	13	21	13:15	12	14	0	0	1	84	9.5
C	41	* Alexander Wennberg	CBJ	68	4	16	20	15:37	-19	22	1	0	1	85	4.7
C	38	Boone Jenner	CBJ	31	9	8	17	18:16	-5	12	2	0	2	83	10.8
R	18	David Clarkson	TOR	58	10	5	15	13:52	-11	92	1	0	1	93	10.8
			CBJ	3	0	0	0	12:18	-1	14	0	0	0	2	0.0
			Total	61	10	5	15	13:47	-12	106	1	0	1	95	10.5
D	51	Fedor Tyutin	CBJ	67	3	12	15	19:55	8	40	0	0	0	56	5.4
R	32	Rene Bourque	MTL	13	0	2	2	12:20	-9	2	0	0	0	18	0.0
			ANA	30	2	6	8	12:07	-4	12	1	0	0	44	4.5
			CBJ	8	4	0	4	14:59	-2	4	1	0	1	23	17.4
			Total	51	6	8	14	12:38	-15	22	2	0	1	85	7.1
C	55	Mark Letestu	CBJ	54	7	6	13	13:20	-9	0	0	1	1	63	11.1
D	29	* Cody Goloubef	CBJ	36	0	9	9	15:33	12	19	0	0	0	23	0.0
R	10	Jack Skille	CBJ	45	6	2	8	12:31	-18	16	0	0	0	95	6.3
R	26	Corey Tropp	CBJ	61	1	7	8	8:45	-14	76	0	0	0	22	4.5
D	47	Dalton Prout	CBJ	63	0	8	8	18:24	-14	85	0	0	0	64	0.0
L	9	Jeremy Morin	CHI	15	0	0	0	7:44	0	15	0	0	0	28	0.0
			CBJ	28	2	4	6	11:31	1	13	0	0	0	45	4.4
			Total	43	2	4	6	10:11	1	28	0	0	0	73	2.7
C	20	* William Karlsson	ANA	18	2	1	3	12:08	1	0	0	0	0	24	8.3
			CBJ	3	1	1	2	12:46	2	0	0	0	0	5	20.0
			Total	21	3	2	5	12:13	3	0	0	0	0	29	10.3
C	39	* Michael Chaput	CBJ	33	1	4	5	10:11	-8	21	0	0	0	23	4.3
R	40	Jared Boll	CBJ	72	1	4	5	7:16	-13	109	0	0	1	28	3.6
R	23	Brian Gibbons	CBJ	25	0	5	5	13:49	2	8	0	0	0	21	0.0
D	27	Ryan Murray	CBJ	12	1	2	3	18:54	1	8	0	0	0	8	12.5
L	52	* Kerby Rychel	CBJ	5	0	3	3	10:41	3	2	0	0	0	4	0.0
D	44	Justin Falk	MIN	13	0	0	0	9:07	-6	7	0	0	0	10	0.0
			CBJ	5	1	1	2	15:13	-3	7	0	0	0	8	12.5
			Total	18	1	1	2	10:49	-9	14	0	0	0	18	5.6
C	37	* Sean Collins	CBJ	8	0	2	2	10:20	0	2	0	0	0	4	0.0
D	28	Frédéric St-Denis	CBJ	4	0	1	1	13:17	-1	0	0	0	0	2	0.0
R	53	* Josh Anderson	CBJ	6	0	1	1	13:27	-1	2	0	0	0	6	0.0
R	32	Adam Cracknell	CBJ	17	0	1	1	9:56	-8	2	0	0	0	17	0.0
C	12	Ryan Craig	CBJ	2	0	0	0	7:16	0	0	0	0	0	2	0.0
C	34	Dana Tyrell	CBJ	3	0	0	0	6:56	-1	0	0	0	0	1	0.0
C	25	Luke Adam	CBJ	3	0	0	0	6:26	0	4	0	0	0	4	0.0

Goaltending

No.	Goaltender	GPI	Mins	Avg	W	L	OT	EN	SO	GA	SA	Sv%	G	A	PIM
72	Sergei Bobrovsky	51	2994	2.69	30	17	3	6	2	134	1632	.918	0	2	4
30	Curtis McElhinney	32	1710	2.88	12	14	2	5	0	82	961	.914	0	0	0
31	* Anton Forsberg	5	256	4.69	0	4	0	1	0	20	149	.866	0	0	0
	Totals	82	4998	2.98	42	35	5	12	2	248	2742	.910			

In his first season in Columbus in 2014-15, Scott Hartnell's 32 assists tied a career high, while his 28 goals and 60 points also ranked among his personal bests.

Club Records

Team

(Figures in brackets for season records are games played.)

Most Points 93 2013-14 (82)
Most Wins 43 2013-14 (82)
Most Ties 9 2000-01 (82)
Most Losses 47 2001-02 (82)
Most Goals 236 2014-15 (82)
Most Goals Against 279 2005-06 (82)
Fewest Points 57 2001-02 (82)
Fewest Wins 22 2001-02 (82)
Fewest Ties 8 2001-02 (82), 2002-03 (82), 2003-04 (82)
Fewest Losses 31 2008-09 (82)
Fewest Goals 164 2001-02 (82)
Fewest Goals Against 216 2013-14 (82)

Longest Winning Streak
 Overall .... 9 Mar. 18-Apr. 4/15
 Home .... 6 Dec. 26/07-Jan. 15/08, Mar. 24-Apr. 10/15
 Away .... 8 Mar. 6-28/15

Longest Undefeated Streak
 Overall .... 9 Mar. 18-Apr. 4/15 (5W, 2SOW, 2OTW)
 Home .... 6 Dec. 26/07-Jan. 15/08 (6W), Mar. 24-Apr. 10/15 (4W, 1SOW, 1OTW)
 Away .... 8 Mar. 6-28/15 (5W, 2SOW, 1OTW)

Longest Losing Streak
 Overall .... 8 Nov. 17-Dec. 3/00, Mar. 3-18/04
 Home .... 6 Oct. 12-Nov. 9/01, Mar. 9-27/11
 Away .... 13 Nov. 21/09-Jan. 5/10

Longest Winless Streak
 Overall .... 9 Dec. 4-23/03 (6L, 3OL), Dec. 10-26/09 (7L, 2SOL), Oct. 24-Nov. 11/14 (8L, 1OL)
 Home .... 8 Oct. 4-Nov. 9/01 (6L, 2T/OL), Dec. 4-31/03 (7L, 1T/OL)
 Away .... 14 Oct. 9-Dec. 23/03 (13L, 1T/OL)

Most Shutouts, Season 11 2007-08 (82), 2008-09 (82)
Most PIM, Season 1,505 2002-03 (82)
Most Goals, Game .... 8 Mar. 7/09 (CBJ 8 at Det. 2), Mar. 25/10 (CBJ 8 at Chi. 3), Nov. 10/10 (CBJ 8 at St.L. 1)

Individual

Most Seasons .... 10 Rostislav Klesla
Most Games .... 674 Rick Nash
Most Goals, Career .... 289 Rick Nash
Most Assists, Career ..... 258 Rick Nash
Most Points, Career ...... 547 Rick Nash (289G, 258A)
Most PIM, Career .... 1,134 Jared Boll
Most Shutouts, Career..... 19 Steve Mason
Longest Consecutive
 Games Streak .... 288 RJ Umberger (Oct. 10/08-Jan. 10/12)
Most Goals, Season .... 41 Rick Nash (2003-04)

Most Assists, Season .... 52 Ray Whitney (2002-03)
Most Points, Season .... 79 Rick Nash (2008-09; 40G, 39A)
Most PIM, Season .... 249 Jody Shelley (2002-03)
Most Points, Defenseman,
 Season .... 51 James Wisniewski (2013-14; 7G, 44A)
Most Points, Center,
 Season .... 71 Ryan Johansen (2014-15; 26G, 45A)
Most Points, Right Wing,
 Season .... 65 David Vyborny (2005-06; 22G, 43A)
Most Points, Left Wing,
 Season .... 79 Rick Nash (2008-09; 40G, 39A)
Most Points, Rookie,
 Season .... 39 Rick Nash (2002-03; 17G, 22A)
Most Shutouts, Season .... 10 Steve Mason (2008-09)
Most Goals, Game .... 4 Geoff Sanderson (Mar. 29/03)
Most Assists, Game .... 5 Espen Knutsen (Mar. 24/01)
Most Points, Game........... 5 Espen Knutsen (Mar. 24/01; 5A), Geoff Sanderson (Mar. 29/03; 4G, 1A), Andrew Cassels (Mar. 29/03; 1G, 4A), David Vyborny (Feb. 28/04; 1G, 4A)

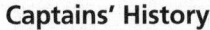

Captains' History

Lyle Odelein, 2000-01, 2001-02; Ray Whitney, 2002-03; Luke Richardson, 2003-04; Luke Richardson and Adam Foote, 2005-06; Adam Foote, 2006-07; Adam Foote and Rick Nash, 2007-08; Rick Nash, 2008-09 to 2011-12; no captain, 2012-13 to 2014-15; Nick Foligno, 2015-16.

All-time Record vs. Other Clubs

Regular Season

	Total								At Home								On Road							
	GP	W	L	T	OL	GF	GA	PTS	GP	W	L	T	OL	GF	GA	PTS	GP	W	L	T	OL	GF	GA	PTS
Anaheim	51	25	22	1	3	138	144	54	25	13	11	0	1	68	63	27	26	12	11	1	2	70	81	27
Arizona	51	19	26	4	2	119	144	44	25	12	11	1	1	63	64	26	26	7	15	3	1	56	80	18
Boston	18	7	7	0	4	42	56	18	10	4	4	0	2	25	35	10	8	3	3	0	2	17	21	8
Buffalo	20	12	7	1	0	60	51	25	9	5	3	1	0	29	23	11	11	7	4	0	0	31	28	14
Calgary	51	28	17	0	6	139	130	62	26	17	5	0	4	78	56	38	25	11	12	0	2	61	74	24
Carolina	22	11	10	0	1	61	55	23	10	5	5	0	0	26	23	10	12	6	5	0	1	35	32	13
Chicago	77	30	37	2	8	213	260	70	39	16	17	1	5	123	139	38	38	14	20	1	3	90	121	32
Colorado	51	14	32	1	4	102	177	33	25	7	15	1	2	47	84	17	26	7	17	0	2	55	93	16
Dallas	51	19	26	0	6	119	148	44	26	9	13	0	4	61	78	22	25	10	13	0	2	58	70	22
Detroit	80	27	41	1	11	182	254	66	41	16	17	1	7	89	121	40	39	11	24	0	4	93	133	26
Edmonton	51	18	27	3	3	132	182	42	26	12	10	3	1	74	86	28	25	6	17	0	2	58	96	14
Florida	18	13	5	0	0	55	41	26	9	7	2	0	0	27	24	14	9	6	3	0	0	28	17	12
Los Angeles	51	21	26	1	3	119	152	46	25	13	10	0	2	68	78	28	26	8	16	1	1	51	74	18
Minnesota	50	26	20	1	3	124	119	56	24	16	7	1	0	66	48	33	26	10	13	0	3	58	71	23
Montreal	17	7	8	1	1	38	43	16	7	2	4	0	1	16	20	5	10	5	4	1	0	22	23	11
Nashville	78	24	43	1	10	171	242	59	38	16	17	0	5	87	108	37	40	8	26	1	5	84	134	22
New Jersey	20	8	10	1	1	46	54	18	11	6	5	0	0	29	29	12	9	2	5	1	1	17	25	6
NY Islanders	22	14	4	1	3	75	62	32	12	9	1	1	1	45	28	20	10	5	3	0	2	30	34	12
NY Rangers	20	9	7	1	3	61	57	22	11	6	5	0	0	33	25	12	9	3	2	1	3	28	32	10
Ottawa	17	6	9	2	0	46	51	14	8	3	4	1	0	23	26	7	9	3	5	1	0	23	25	7
Philadelphia	20	9	8	3	0	57	59	21	10	6	2	2	0	30	21	14	10	3	6	1	0	27	38	7
Pittsburgh	23	8	12	0	3	65	78	19	12	5	4	0	0	38	40	13	11	3	8	0	0	27	38	6
St. Louis	77	28	35	3	11	201	240	70	38	18	13	2	5	107	101	43	39	10	22	1	6	94	139	27
San Jose	51	19	27	0	5	119	145	43	26	14	9	0	3	72	54	31	25	5	18	0	2	47	91	12
Tampa Bay	19	7	9	1	2	39	46	17	9	5	4	1	0	23	21	11	10	2	5	0	2	16	25	6
Toronto	16	7	8	1	0	43	47	15	7	3	4	0	0	21	23	6	9	4	4	1	0	22	24	9
Vancouver	51	17	26	1	7	127	177	43	26	10	11	1	3	61	84	25	25	7	14	0	4	66	93	18
Washington	23	8	9	1	5	69	75	22	13	5	5	0	3	47	42	13	10	3	4	1	2	22	33	9
Winnipeg	18	10	8	0	0	45	40	20	9	5	4	0	0	22	20	10	9	5	4	0	0	23	20	10
Totals	1114	451	525	33	105	2807	3329	1040	557	265	221	18	53	1494	1557	601	557	186	304	15	52	1313	1772	439

Playoffs

	Series	W	L	GP	W	L	T	GF	GA	Last Mtg.	Rnd.	Result
Detroit	1	0	1	4	0	4	0	7	18	2009	CQF	L 0-4
Pittsburgh	1	0	1	6	2	4	0	18	21	2014	FR	L 2-4
Totals	2	0	2	10	2	8	0	25	39			

Winnipeg totals include Atlanta Thrashers, 1999-2000 to 2010-11.

Playoff Results 2015-2011

Year	Round	Opponent	Result	GF	GA
2014	FR	Pittsburgh	L 2-4	18	21

Abbreviations: Round: CQF – conference quarter-final; FR – first round.

2014-15 Results

Oct.	9	at Buffalo	3-1		16	NY Rangers	1-2
	11	NY Rangers	5-2		17	at Boston	3-1
	14	Dallas	2-4		19	at Minnesota	3-1
	17	Calgary	3-2		21	at Winnipeg	0-4
	18	at Ottawa	2-3		27	Washington	4-3
	23	at San Jose	5-4		29	at Florida	2-3
	24	at Anaheim	1-4		31	at Tampa Bay	1-3
	26	at Los Angeles	2-5	Feb.	3	Arizona	1-4
	28	Ottawa	2-5		6	St. Louis	7-1
	31	Toronto	1-4		7	at Ottawa	4-1
Nov.	1	at New Jersey	2-3		9	Los Angeles	3-4
	4	Carolina	2-4		13	Philadelphia	4-3*
	7	at Carolina	2-3*		14	at NY Islanders	3-6
	8	Tampa Bay	4-7		17	at Philadelphia	5-2
	11	at Washington	2-4		19	at Pittsburgh	2-1
	14	at Philadelphia	4-3		21	at Montreal	1-3
	15	San Jose	2-1		22	at NY Rangers	3-4†
	18	Detroit	0-5		24	Buffalo	2-4
	21	Boston	3-4†		26	Montreal	2-5
	22	at Philadelphia	2-4		28	New Jersey	0-2
	25	Winnipeg	2-4	Mar.	1	at Pittsburgh	3-5
	28	Vancouver	0-5		3	Washington	3-5
	29	at Nashville	1-2		6	at New Jersey	3-2
Dec.	1	Florida	2-1		7	Colorado	0-4
	4	at Florida	4-3†		10	at Carolina	4-3†
	6	at Tampa Bay	3-1		12	at Detroit	3-1
	9	Philadelphia	3-2*		13	Edmonton	5-4†
	11	at Washington	3-2*		15	Carolina	2-3
	13	Pittsburgh	4-3†		18	at Edmonton	6-2
	16	at Detroit	1-0†		19	at Vancouver	6-2
	18	Washington	4-5*		21	at Calgary	3-2*
	20	Chicago	3-2†		24	Anaheim	5-3
	22	Nashville	1-5		27	at Chicago	5-3
	27	Boston	6-2		28	at St. Louis	4-2
	31	Minnesota	3-1		31	New Jersey	3-2*
Jan.	3	at Arizona	3-6	Apr.	2	NY Islanders	4-3†
	4	at Colorado	4-3		4	Pittsburgh	5-3
	6	at Dallas	4-2		6	at NY Rangers	3-4*
	9	at Toronto	2-5		8	Toronto	5-0
	10	NY Islanders	2-5		10	Buffalo	4-2
	14	Montreal	2-3		11	at NY Islanders	5-4†

* – Overtime † – Shootout

NHL Draft Selections 2015-2001

Name in bold denotes played in NHL.

2015
Pick
8 Zachary Werenski
29 Gabriel Carlsson
38 Paul Bittner
58 Kevin Stenlund
69 Keegan Kolesar
129 Sam Ruopp
141 Veeti Vainio
159 Vladislav Gavrikov
189 Markus Nutivaara

2014
Pick
16 Sonny Milano
47 Ryan Collins
76 Elvis Merzlikins
77 Blake Siebenaler
107 Julien Pelletier
137 Tyler Bird
197 Olivier LeBlanc

2013
Pick
14 **Alexander Wennberg**
19 **Kerby Rychel**
27 **Marko Dano**
50 Dillon Heatherington
89 Oliver Bjorkstrand
105 Nick Moutrey
165 Markus Soberg
195 Peter Quenneville

2012
Pick
2 **Ryan Murray**
31 Oscar Dansk
62 Joonas Korpisalo
95 **Josh Anderson**
152 Daniel Zaar
182 Gianluca Curcuruto

2011
Pick
37 **Boone Jenner**
66 TJ Tynan
98 Mike Reilly
128 Seth Ambroz
158 Lukas Sedlak
188 **Anton Forsberg**

2010
Pick
4 **Ryan Johansen**
34 Dalton Smith
55 **Petr Straka**
94 Brandon Archibald
102 Mathieu Corbeil
124 Austin Madaisky
154 **Dalton Prout**
184 Martin Ouellette

2009
Pick
21 **John Moore**
56 Kevin Lynch
94 **David Savard**
137 Thomas Larkin
167 Anton Blomqvist
197 Kyle Neuber

2008
Pick
6 **Nikita Filatov**
37 **Cody Goloubef**
107 Steven Delisle
118 Drew Olson
127 **Matt Calvert**
135 **Tomas Kubalik**
137 Brent Regner
157 **Cam Atkinson**
187 **Sean Collins**

2007
Pick
7 **Jakub Voracek**
37 Stefan Legein
53 Will Weber
68 Jake Hansen
94 **Maksim Mayorov**
158 **Allen York**
211 Trent Vogelhuber

2006
Pick
6 **Derick Brassard**
69 **Steve Mason**
85 **Tom Sestito**
113 Ben Wright
129 Robert Nyholm
136 Nick Sucharski
142 Maxime Frechette
159 Jesse Dudas
189 **Derek Dorsett**
194 Matt Marquardt

2005
Pick
6 **Gilbert Brule**
55 **Adam McQuaid**
67 **Kris Russell**
101 **Jared Boll**
131 **Tomas Popperle**
177 Derek Reinhart
189 Kirill Starkov
201 Trevor Hendrikx

2004
Pick
8 **Alexandre Picard**
46 **Adam Pineault**
59 Kyle Wharton
93 **Dan LaCosta**
96 Andrey Plekhanov
133 Petr Pohl
167 Rob Page
190 **Lennart Petrell**
198 Justin Vienneau
231 Brian McGuirk
233 Matt Greer
271 **Grant Clitsome**

2003
Pick
4 **Nikolai Zherdev**
46 **Dan Fritsche**
71 Dmitry Kosmachev
103 Kevin Jarman
104 **Philippe Dupuis**
138 Arsi Piispanen
168 **Marc Methot**
200 Alexander Guskov
233 Mathieu Gravel
283 Trevor Hendrikx

2002
Pick
1 **Rick Nash**
41 **Joakim Lindstrom**
65 **Ole-Kristian Tollefsen**
96 Jeff Genovy
98 Ivan Tkachenko
119 Jekabs Redlihs
133 **Lasse Pirjeta**
168 Tim Konsorada
184 **Jaroslav Balastik**
199 **Greg Mauldin**
225 **Steven Goertzen**
231 Jaroslav Kracik
263 Sergei Mozyakin

2001
Pick
8 **Pascal Leclaire**
38 **Tim Jackman**
53 Kiel McLeod
85 **Aaron Johnson**
87 Per Mars
141 **Cole Jarrett**
173 Justin Aikins
187 Artem Vostrikov
204 Raffaele Sannitz
236 Ryan Bowness
242 **Andrew Murray**

General Managers' History

Doug MacLean, 2000-01 to 2006-07; Scott Howson, 2007-08 to 2011-12; Scott Howson and Jarmo Kekalainen, 2012-13; Jarmo Kekalainen, 2013-14 to date.

Jarmo Kekalainen

General Manager

Born: Tampere, Finland, July 3, 1966.

Jarmo Kekalainen was named the third general manager in Columbus Blue Jackets history on February 13, 2013. In his first full season with the club in 2013-14, the Blue Jackets established new franchise highs with 43 wins and 93 points and reached the playoffs. Kekalainen joined Columbus after serving as the president and general manager of Jokerit in the Finnish Elite League since 2010. He works closely with Blue Jackets president of hockey operations John Davidson on all hockey-related matters involving the club. Kekalainen owns a bachelor's degree in management from Clarkson University and earned a master's in business marketing from the University of Tampere.

Prior to his stint with Jokerit, Kekalainen spent eight seasons with the St. Louis Blues from 2002 to 2010. He joined the Blues as director of amateur scouting and was named assistant general manager as well in 2005. Kekalainen was involved in all facets of hockey operations, including professional scouting efforts and overseeing the club's amateur scouting and draft preparations. During his eight years in St. Louis, the Blues drafted players such as David Backes, Roman Polak, David Perron, T.J. Oshie, Patrik Berglund and Alex Pietrangelo.

Kekalainen was a member of the Ottawa Senators hockey operations department from 1995 to 2002 and served in a variety of roles with the club. He served as Ottawa's director of player personnel for three years and also oversaw the amateur draft and the club's scouting efforts in Europe. Among the players selected by Ottawa during this time were Jason Spezza, Marian Hossa, Martin Havlat, Antoine Vermette and Ray Emery. While working with the Senators, he also served as general manager of HIFK Helsinki in the Finnish Elite League from 1995 to 1999 and led the club to the league championship in 1998.

As a player, Kekalainen appeared in 55 career NHL games with the Senators and Boston Bruins during his career. He also played in the American Hockey League and his native Finland before wrapping up his playing career with Vasteras IK in the Swedish Elite League in 1994-95. Before signing with the Bruins, Kekalainen played two seasons at Clarkson University from 1987 to 1989. He was named to the Eastern Collegiate Athletic Conference First All-Star Team after tallying 19 goals and 25 assists for 44 points in 31 games during the 1988-89 season. He also represented Finland at the 1986 World Junior Championship and the 1991 Canada Cup Tournament.

Club Directory

Nationwide Arena

Columbus Blue Jackets
Nationwide Arena
200 W. Nationwide Blvd.
Columbus, Ohio 43215
Phone **614/246-4625**
FAX 614/246-4007
www.BlueJackets.com
Capacity: 18,144

Ownership/Senior Management

Majority Owner/Governor	John P. McConnell
President/Alternate Governor	Mike Priest
President, Hockey Operations/Alternate Governor	John Davidson

Executive Staff – Business Operations

Executive Vice President, Business Operations	Larry Hoepfner
Senior Vice President/General Counsel	Greg Kirstein
Chief Financial Officer	T.J. LaMendola
Vice President, Communications & Team Services	Todd Sharrock
Vice President, Community Relations/ Exec. Dir. CBJ Foundation	Kathryn Dobbs
Vice President, Corporate Development	A.J. Poole
Vice President, Digital Marketing & Media	Marc Gregory
Vice President, Marketing	J.D. Kershaw
Vice President, Ticket Sales & Service	Joe Andrade

Hockey Operations

General Manager	Jarmo Kekalainen
Assistant General Manager	Bill Zito
Director of Hockey Administration	Josh Flynn
Head Amateur Scout	Ville Siren
Scouting Coordinator	Scott Harris
Amateur Scouts	Mike Antonovich, Josef Boumedienne, Greg Drechsel, Niklas Evertsson, Blake Geoffrion, Derek Ginnell, John Hill, Stephane Leblanc, Chris Morehouse, Rob Riley, Andy Schneider, Milan Tichy
Pro Scouts	Marshall Davidson, Peter Dineen, Bob Halkidis, Doug MacDonald, Sam McMaster
Pro Video Scout	Mike Battaglia
European Video Scout	Simon Barrette
Athletic Trainers, Head / Assistants	Mike Vogt / Nates Goto, Chris Strickland
Equipment Manager / Assistant Mgr. / Assistant	Tim LeRoy / Jamie Healy / Jason Stypinski
Executive Assistant, Hockey Operations	Beth Carlisle

Coaching Staff

Head Coach / Associate Coach	Todd Richards / Craig Hartsburg
Assistant Coaches / Goaltending Coach	Brad Larsen, Kenny McCudden / Ian Clark
Coaches, Strength & Conditioning	Kevin Collins
Development / European Development	Chris Clark / Jarko Ruutu
Video Assistant Coach	Dan Singleton

Corporate Development and Premium Seating

Director of Corporate Development Services	Craig Smith
Director of Corporate Development	Jessica Smith
Corporate Development Account Executives	Erica Bernadas, Ethan Saporito, Charles Tyler, Doug Vinci
Partnership Account Specialists	Samantha Hagan, Amy Ranallo, Molly Taylor, Caitlin Wolcott
Corporate Development Sales Coordinator	Evan Lee
Premium Seating Specialists	Zachary Brown, Danielle Childers

Communications and Team Services

Director of Communications	Karen Davis
Managers, Communications / Team Services	Glenn Odebralski / Julie Gamble

Community Relations

Managers, Mascot Services / CBJ Foundation	Jason Zumpano / Alison Pegg
Manager, Education & Community Partnerships	Maggie Walters
Foundation & Community Relations Coordinator	Katie Green

Game Operations and Event Presentation

Director of Game Operations/Event Presentation	Derek Dawley
Managers, Event Presentation / Sr. Production	Lynn Truitt / Jeff Coltoniak
Senior Editor-Producer / Broadcast Engineer	David Traube / Rick Shepherd

Marketing and Fan Development

Directors, Marketing	Jim Riley
Mgrs., Marketing / Fan Development	Becky Magaw / Joel Siegman
Fan Development/Marketing Coordinator	Mason Fisher
Graphics, Senior Designer / Designer	Jason Duignan / Anthony Zych
Manager, Advertising & Creative Services	Pat Thompson

Digital Marketing & Media

Director, CRM & Analytics	Jeff Eldersveld
Digital Content and Community Manager	Rob Mixer
Coordinators, CRM / Social Media / Digital Marketing	Amy Dunleavy / Andrew Schwepfinger / Adam Carro
Digital Marketing Analyst / CRM & Digital Mktg Fellow	Amy French / Katie Foglia

Human Resources and Legal

Human Resources Director / Assistant	Cheryl Sparks / Ryan Leitenberger
Payroll Manager / Assistant	Christine Parthemore / Karen Albert
Staff Counsel / Paralegal	Pete Olsen / Ken Erney

Finance and Information Technology

Controller / Staff Accountants	Joe Rudolph / Nora Ludwig, Zachary Kramer
Director of IT / Systems Analyst	Jim Connolly / Matthew DeStephen
Accts Payable Coordinator / Receptionist	Heather Benintendi / Erica Pepper

Ticket Sales and Operations

Directors, Ticket Ops / Service & Retention	Mark Metz / Kelly Jones
Directors, New Business Development / Group Sales	Drew Ribarchak / Nick Myers
Managers, Ticket Operations / Inside Sales	Kevin O'Malley, Abby Miller / Justin Dunn
Season Ticket Sales Account Execs.	Maxwell Cohen, Matthew Kill, Tim McDonough, Zoey Osman, Malinda Smith
Group Event Specialists	Leah Cover, Grant Jamieson, James Garland, Matt Menard, Dani Nell, Ashley Smith
Season Ticket Service Coordinators	Brad Bellissimo, Cody Craig, Carmelo Marzullo, Morgan Obendorfer, Courtney Spiegel
Ticket Sales Coordinator	Keeley O'Brien

Broadcasting

Director of Broadcasting	Russ Mollohan
FOX Sports Ohio Play-By-Play / Color	Jeff Rimer / Jody Shelley
Radio Play-By-Play Announcer	Bob McElligott
FOX Sports Ohio Hosts/Reporters	Bill Davidge, Brian Giesenschlag, Dave Maetzold

Dallas Stars

2014-15 Results: 41W-31L-7OTL-3SOL 92PTS
6TH, Central Division • 10TH, Western Conference

Key Off-Season Signings/Acquisitions

2015

April 17 • Re-signed D **John Klingberg**.
June 15 • Re-signed D **Jyrki Jokipakka**.
17 • Re-signed G **Jack Campbell** and D **Patrik Nemeth**.
27 • Acquired G **Antti Niemi** from San Jose for a 7th-round choice in the 2015 NHL Draft.
July 1 • Re-signed RW **Patrick Eaves** and LW **Curtis McKenzie**.
9 • Re-signed D **Jamie Oleksiak**.
10 • Acquired LW **Patrick Sharp** and D **Stephen Johns** from Chicago for D **Trevor Daley** and LW **Ryan Garbutt**.
15 • Signed D **Johnny Oduya**.

2015-16 Schedule

Oct.	Thu.	8	Pittsburgh		Tue.	5	at NY Rangers
	Sat.	10	at Colorado		Thu.	7	Winnipeg
	Tue.	13	Edmonton		Sat.	9	Minnesota
	Thu.	15	at Tampa Bay		Fri.	15	at Anaheim
	Sat.	17	at Florida		Sat.	16	at San Jose
	Tue.	20	at Philadelphia		Tue.	19	at Los Angeles
	Thu.	22	at Pittsburgh		Thu.	21	Edmonton
	Sat.	24	Florida		Sat.	23	Colorado
	Tue.	27	Anaheim		Mon.	25	Calgary
	Thu.	29	Vancouver	**Feb.**	Tue.	2	at Winnipeg
	Sat.	31	San Jose*		Thu.	4	at Colorado
Nov.	Mon.	2	at Toronto		Sat.	6	Chicago
	Tue.	3	at Boston		Tue.	9	at Minnesota
	Fri.	6	at Carolina		Thu.	11	at Chicago
	Sun.	8	at Detroit*		Sat.	13	Washington
	Tue.	10	Toronto		Mon.	15	at Nashville
	Thu.	12	Winnipeg		Tue.	16	at St. Louis
	Sat.	14	Minnesota		Thu.	18	at Arizona
	Tue.	17	at Buffalo		Sat.	20	Boston
	Thu.	19	at Washington		Tue.	23	at Winnipeg
	Sat.	21	Buffalo		Thu.	25	Winnipeg
	Tue.	24	Ottawa		Sat.	27	NY Rangers*
	Fri.	27	Vancouver		Mon.	29	Detroit
	Sat.	28	at Minnesota	**Mar.**	Tue.	1	at Nashville
Dec.	Tue.	1	at Calgary		Fri.	4	New Jersey
	Thu.	3	at Vancouver		Sun.	6	at Ottawa*
	Fri.	4	at Edmonton		Tue.	8	at Montreal
	Tue.	8	Carolina		Fri.	11	Chicago
	Fri.	11	Philadelphia		Sat.	12	St. Louis
	Sat.	12	at St. Louis		Tue.	15	Los Angeles
	Tue.	15	Columbus		Thu.	17	Tampa Bay
	Thu.	17	Calgary		Sat.	19	NY Islanders
	Sat.	19	Montreal		Tue.	22	at Chicago
	Mon.	21	at Minnesota		Thu.	24	at Arizona
	Tue.	22	Chicago		Sat.	26	at San Jose*
	Sat.	26	at St. Louis		Tue.	29	Nashville
	Sun.	27	St. Louis*		Thu.	31	Arizona
	Tue.	29	at Columbus	**Apr.**	Sat.	2	at Los Angeles*
	Thu.	31	Nashville		Sun.	3	at Anaheim
Jan.	Sat.	2	at New Jersey		Thu.	7	Colorado
	Sun.	3	at NY Islanders*		Sat.	9	Nashville

* Denotes afternoon game.

Retired Numbers

7	Neal Broten	1980-1995, 1996-1997
8	Bill Goldsworthy*	1967-1976
19	Bill Masterton*	1967-1968

* Minnesota North Stars

CENTRAL DIVISION
49th NHL Season

Franchise date: June 5, 1967

Transferred from Minnesota to Dallas, June 9, 1993.

Dallas captain Jamie Benn, flanked by Tyler Seguin and his older brother Jordie, collected 10 points (five goals, five assists) in the last three games of the 2014-15 season to finish the year with an NHL-leading 87 points.

Year-by-Year Record

		Home				Road				Overall									
Season	**GP**	**W**	**L**	**T**	**OL**	**W**	**L**	**T**	**OL**	**W**	**L**	**T**	**OL**	**GF**	**GA**	**Pts.**	**Div. Fin.**	**Conf. Fin.**	**Playoff Result**
2014-15	82	17	16	....	8	24	15	....	2	41	31	....	10	261	260	92	6th, Cen.	10th, West	Out of Playoffs
2013-14	82	23	11	....	7	17	20	....	4	40	31	....	11	235	228	91	5th, Cen.	8th, West	Lost First Round
2012-13	48	11	11	....	2	11	11	....	2	22	22	....	4	130	142	48	5th, Pac.	11th, West	Out of Playoffs
2011-12	82	22	16	....	3	20	19	....	2	42	35	....	5	211	222	89	4th, Pac.	10th, West	Out of Playoffs
2010-11	82	22	11	....	8	20	18	....	3	42	29	....	11	227	233	95	5th, Pac.	9th, West	Out of Playoffs
2009-10	82	23	11	....	7	14	20	....	7	37	31	....	14	237	254	88	5th, Pac.	12th, West	Out of Playoffs
2008-09	82	20	16	....	5	16	19	....	6	36	35	....	11	230	257	83	3rd, Pac.	12th, West	Out of Playoffs
2007-08	82	23	16	....	2	22	14	....	5	45	30	....	7	242	207	97	3rd, Pac.	5th, West	Lost Conf. Final
2006-07	82	28	11	....	2	22	14	....	5	50	25	....	7	226	197	107	3rd, Pac.	6th, West	Lost Conf. Quarter-Final
2005-06	82	28	11	....	2	25	12	....	4	53	23	....	6	265	218	112	1st, Pac.	2nd, West	Lost Conf. Quarter-Final
2004-05	....	....	....	....	....	....	....	....	....	....	....	....	....	....	....	....			
2003-04	82	26	7	8	0	15	19	5	2	41	26	13	2	194	175	97	2nd, Pac.	5th, West	Lost Conf. Quarter-Final
2002-03	82	28	5	6	2	18	12	9	2	46	17	15	4	245	169	111	1st, Pac.	1st, West	Lost Conf. Semi-Final
2001-02	82	18	13	6	4	18	15	7	1	36	28	13	5	215	213	90	4th, Pac.	10th, West	Out of Playoffs
2000-01	82	26	10	5	0	22	14	3	2	48	24	8	2	241	187	106	1st, Pac.	3rd, West	Lost Conf. Semi-Final
1999-2000	82	21	11	5	4	22	12	5	2	43	23	10	6	211	184	102	1st, Pac.	2nd, West	Lost Final
1998-99	**82**	**29**	**8**	**4**	....	**22**	**11**	**8**	....	**51**	**19**	**12**	....	**236**	**168**	**114**	**1st, Pac.**	**1st, West**	**Won Stanley Cup**
1997-98	82	26	8	7	....	23	14	4	....	49	22	11	....	242	167	109	1st, Cen.	1st, West	Lost Conf. Final
1996-97	82	25	13	3	....	23	13	5	....	48	26	8	....	252	198	104	1st, Cen.	2nd, West	Lost Conf. Quarter-Final
1995-96	82	14	18	9	....	12	24	5	....	26	42	14	....	227	280	66	6th, Cen.	11th, West	Out of Playoffs
1994-95	48	9	10	5	....	8	13	3	....	17	23	8	....	136	135	42	5th, Cen.	8th, West	Lost Conf. Quarter-Final
1993-94	84	23	12	7	....	19	17	6	....	42	29	13	....	286	265	97	3rd, Cen.	4th, West	Lost Conf. Semi-Final
1992-93*	84	18	17	7	....	18	21	3	....	36	38	10	....	272	293	82	5th, Norris		Out of Playoffs
1991-92*	80	20	16	4	....	12	26	2	....	32	42	6	....	246	278	70	4th, Norris		Lost Div. Semi-Final
1990-91*	80	19	15	6	....	8	24	8	....	27	39	14	....	256	266	68	4th, Norris		Lost Final
1989-90*	80	26	12	2	....	10	28	2	....	36	40	4	....	284	291	76	4th, Norris		Lost Div. Semi-Final
1988-89*	80	17	15	8	....	10	22	8	....	27	37	16	....	258	278	70	3rd, Norris		Lost Div. Semi-Final
1987-88*	80	10	24	6	....	9	24	7	....	19	48	13	....	242	349	51	5th, Norris		Out of Playoffs
1986-87*	80	17	20	3	....	13	20	7	....	30	40	10	....	296	314	70	5th, Norris		Out of Playoffs
1985-86*	80	21	15	4	....	17	18	5	....	38	33	9	....	327	305	85	2nd, Norris		Lost Div. Semi-Final
1984-85*	80	14	19	7	....	11	24	5	....	25	43	12	....	268	321	62	4th, Norris		Lost Div. Final
1983-84*	80	22	14	4	....	17	17	6	....	39	31	10	....	345	344	88	1st, Norris		Lost Conf. Final
1982-83*	80	23	6	11	....	17	18	5	....	40	24	16	....	321	290	96	2nd, Norris		Lost Div. Final
1981-82*	80	21	7	12	....	16	16	8	....	37	23	20	....	346	288	94	1st, Norris		Lost Div. Semi-Final
1980-81*	80	23	10	7	....	12	18	10	....	35	28	17	....	291	263	87	3rd, Adams		Lost Final
1979-80*	80	25	8	7	....	11	20	9	....	36	28	16	....	311	253	88	3rd, Adams		Lost Semi-Final
1978-79*	80	19	15	6	....	9	25	6	....	28	40	12	....	257	289	68	4th, Adams		Out of Playoffs
1977-78*	80	12	24	4	....	6	29	5	....	18	53	9	....	218	325	45	5th, Smythe		Out of Playoffs
1977-78**	80	14	17	9	....	8	28	4	....	22	45	13	....	230	325	57	4th, Adams		Out of Playoffs
1976-77*	80	17	14	9	....	6	25	9	....	23	39	18	....	240	310	64	2nd, Smythe		Lost Prelim. Round
1976-77**	80	14	17	9	....	11	25	4	....	25	42	13		240	292	63	4th, Adams		Out of Playoffs
1975-76*	80	15	22	3	....	5	31	4	....	20	53	7	....	195	303	47	4th, Smythe		Out of Playoffs
1975-76***	80	16	19	5	....	11	23	6	....	27	42	11		250	278	65	4th, Adams		Out of Playoffs
1974-75*	80	17	20	3	....	6	30	4	....	23	50	7	....	221	341	53	4th, Smythe		Out of Playoffs
1974-75***	80	15	15	10	....	4	33	3	....	19	48	13		212	316	51	4th, Adams		Out of Playoffs
1973-74*	78	18	15	6	....	5	23	11	....	23	38	17	....	235	275	63	7th, West		Out of Playoffs
1973-74***	78	11	18	10	....	2	37	0	....	13	55	10		195	342	36	8th, West		Out of Playoffs
1972-73*	78	26	8	5	....	11	22	6	....	37	30	11	....	254	230	85	3rd, West		Lost Quarter-Final
1972-73***	78	11	15	13	....	5	31	3	....	16	46	16		213	323	48	8th, West		Out of Playoffs
1971-72*	78	22	11	6	....	15	18	6	....	37	29	12	....	212	191	86	2nd, West		Lost Quarter-Final
1971-72***	78	14	12	13	....	7	27	5	....	21	39	18		216	288	60	6th, West		Out of Playoffs
1970-71*	78	16	15	8	....	12	19	8	....	28	34	16	....	191	223	72	4th, West		Lost Semi-Final
1970-71***	78	17	21	1	....	3	32	4	....	20	53	5		199	320	45	7th, West		Out of Playoffs
1969-70*	76	11	16	11	....	8	19	11	....	19	35	22	....	224	257	60	3rd, West		Lost Quarter-Final
1969-70†	76	15	16	7	....	7	24	7	....	22	40	14		169	243	58	4th, West		Lost Quarter-Final
1968-69*	76	11	21	6	....	7	22	9	....	18	43	15	....	189	270	51	6th, West		Out of Playoffs
1968-69†	76	17	14	7	....	12	22	4	....	29	36	11		219	251	69	2nd, West		Lost Quarter-Final
1967-68*	74	17	12	8	....	10	20	7	....	27	32	15	....	191	226	69	4th, West		Lost Semi-Final
1967-68††	74	12	16	9	....	3	26	8	....	15	42	17		153	219	47	6th, West		Out of Playoffs

* Minnesota North Stars; ** Cleveland Barons; *** California Golden Seals; † Oakland Seals; †† California/Oakland Seals
California transferred to Cleveland, July 14, 1976. Cleveland and Minnesota merged prior to the 1978-79 season.

2015-16 Player Personnel

FORWARDS	HT	WT	*Age	Place of Birth	S	2014-15 Club
BENN, Jamie	6-2	210	26	Victoria, BC	L	Dallas
EAKIN, Cody	6-0	190	24	Winnipeg, MB	L	Dallas
EAVES, Patrick	6-0	200	31	Calgary, AB	R	Dallas
FIDDLER, Vernon	5-11	205	35	Edmonton, AB	L	Dallas
HEMSKY, Ales	6-0	185	32	Pardubice, Czech.	R	Dallas
McKENZIE, Curtis	6-2	210	24	Golden, BC	L	Dallas-Texas
MOEN, Travis	6-2	210	33	Stewart Valley, SK	L	Montreal-Dallas
NICHUSHKIN, Valeri	6-4	210	20	Chelyabinsk, Russia	L	Dallas-Texas
RITCHIE, Brett	6-3	220	22	Orangeville, ON	R	Dallas-Texas
ROUSSEL, Antoine	6-0	200	25	Roubaix, France	L	Dallas
SCEVIOUR, Colton	6-0	200	26	Red Deer, AB	R	Dallas
SEGUIN, Tyler	6-1	200	23	Brampton, ON	R	Dallas
SHARP, Patrick	6-1	199	33	Winnipeg, MB	R	Chicago
SPEZZA, Jason	6-3	220	32	Mississauga, ON	R	Dallas

DEFENSEMEN	HT	WT	*Age	Place of Birth	S	2014-15 Club
BENN, Jordie	6-2	200	28	Victoria, BC	L	Dallas
DEMERS, Jason	6-1	195	27	Dorval, QC	R	San Jose-Dallas
GOLIGOSKI, Alex	5-11	190	30	Grand Rapids, MN	L	Dallas
JOKIPAKKA, Jyrki	6-3	205	24	Tampere, Finland	L	Dallas-Texas
KLINGBERG, John	6-2	180	23	Lerum, Sweden	R	Dallas-Texas
NEMETH, Patrik	6-3	235	23	Stockholm, Sweden	L	Dallas-Texas
ODUYA, Johnny	6-0	190	34	Stockholm, Sweden	L	Chicago
OLEKSIAK, Jamie	6-7	250	22	Toronto, ON	L	Dallas-Texas

GOALTENDERS	HT	WT	*Age	Place of Birth	C	2014-15 Club
LEHTONEN, Kari	6-4	210	31	Helsinki, Finland	L	Dallas
NIEMI, Antti	6-2	210	32	Vantaa, Finland	L	San Jose

*– Age at start of 2015-16 season

Lindy Ruff
Head Coach
Born: Warburg, AB, February 17, 1960.

Dallas Stars general manager Jim Nill announced on Friday, June 21, 2013, that Lindy Ruff had been hired as the 22nd head coach in franchise history. He is the seventh head coach in Dallas Stars history. In his first season with the Stars in 2013-14 the team returned to the playoffs for the first time since 2008-09. Ruff recorded his 600th career regular-season victory on March 3, 2014.

Ruff is the 8th-winningest head coach in NHL history, one of only 21 to reach the 500-victory plateau, and has the third-most wins of any active NHL coach. Dallas marks his second stint as an NHL head coach after departing the Buffalo Sabres as their all-time franchise leader in wins with a 571-432-162 record. During Ruff's tenure in Buffalo, the team made eight postseason appearances, including four trips to the Eastern Conference Final as well as an appearance in the 1999 Stanley Cup Final. In 2006, he was awarded the Jack Adams Award as the league's top coach for guiding his team to the Conference Final. Ruff was nominated again for the accolade in 2007 for posting consecutive 50-win campaigns and for leading his club to the Presidents' Trophy, which is earned annually by the top team in the regular season.

In Ruff's eight postseason appearances in Buffalo he earned a 57-44 record, which is tied for the 15th-most playoff victories in NHL history. He is also one of only 21 NHL head coaches to guide his team through at least 100 postseason contests.

No stranger to international competition, Ruff coached Canada's national team to a silver medal at the World Championships in 2009, served as an associate coach for the gold medal-winning team at the 2010 Winter Olympic Games in Vancouver, and served as head coach once more at the 2013 World Championships. He will be an associate coach again at the 2014 Olympics.

Prior to his coaching career, the native of Warburg, Alberta, played 691 games in the NHL from 1979 to 1991, posting 300 points (105 goals, 195 assists). He was Buffalo's second-round selection (32nd overall) in 1979.

Coaching Record

Season	Team	League	Regular Season GC	W	L	O/T	Playoffs GC	W	L	T
1997-98	Buffalo	NHL	82	36	29	17	15	10	5	....
1998-99	Buffalo	NHL	82	37	28	17	21	14	7	....
99-2000	Buffalo	NHL	82	35	32	15	5	1	4	....
2000-01	Buffalo	NHL	82	46	30	6	13	7	6	....
2001-02	Buffalo	NHL	82	35	35	12	....			....
2002-03	Buffalo	NHL	82	27	37	18	....			....
2003-04	Buffalo	NHL	82	37	34	11	....			....
2004-05	Buffalo		SEASON CANCELLED							
2005-06	Buffalo	NHL	82	52	24	6	18	11	7	....
2006-07	Buffalo	NHL	82	53	22	7	16	9	7	....
2007-08	Buffalo	NHL	82	39	31	12	....			....
2008-09	Buffalo	NHL	82	41	32	9	....			....
2009-10	Buffalo	NHL	82	45	27	10	6	2	4	....
2010-11	Buffalo	NHL	82	43	29	10	7	3	4	....
2011-12	Buffalo	NHL	82	39	32	11	....			....
2012-13	Buffalo	NHL	17	6	10	1	....			....
2013-14	Dallas	NHL	82	40	31	11	6	2	4	....
2014-15	Dallas	NHL	82	41	31	10	....			....
NHL Totals			**1329**	**652**	**494**	**183**	**107**	**59**	**48**	

Jack Adams Award (2006)
Assistant coaches Brian McCutheon and Scott Arniel posted an 0-1-0 record as replacement coach when Lindy Ruff was sidelined due to a family medical emergency, March 20, 2006. Game is credited to Ruff's coaching record.
Assistant coach James Patrick posted a 2-1-0 record as replacement coach after Lindy Ruff suffered broken ribs on February 6, 2012 and was sidelined from February 8 to 11. Games are credited to Ruff's coaching record.

2014-15 Scoring
*– rookie

Regular Season

Pos	#	Player	Team	GP	G	A	Pts	TOI	+/-	PIM	PP	SH	GW	S	S%
L	14	Jamie Benn	DAL	82	35	52	87	19:56	1	64	10	2	6	253	13.8
C	91	Tyler Seguin	DAL	71	37	40	77	19:33	-1	20	13	0	5	280	13.2
C	90	Jason Spezza	DAL	82	17	45	62	17:13	-7	28	4	0	1	204	8.3
C	20	Cody Eakin	DAL	78	19	21	40	17:11	-1	26	2	2	6	142	13.4
D	3*	John Klingberg	DAL	65	11	29	40	21:50	5	32	2	0	3	98	11.2
D	6	Trevor Daley	DAL	68	16	22	38	22:52	-13	34	6	2	2	113	14.2
D	33	Alex Goligoski	DAL	81	4	32	36	23:48	0	24	0	0	0	122	3.3
R	83	Ales Hemsky	DAL	76	11	21	32	13:38	-8	16	1	0	1	140	7.9
L	38	Vernon Fiddler	DAL	80	13	16	29	13:07	-5	34	3	1	2	132	9.8
C	10	Shawn Horcoff	DAL	76	11	18	29	13:01	9	27	4	0	1	82	13.4
R	18	Patrick Eaves	DAL	47	14	13	27	13:43	12	8	6	0	2	91	15.4
C	22	Colton Sceviour	DAL	71	9	17	26	12:42	1	13	0	0	2	113	8.0
L	21	Antoine Roussel	DAL	80	13	12	25	14:31	-20	148	0	0	1	113	11.5
C	16	Ryan Garbutt	DAL	67	8	17	25	13:33	-9	55	0	1	2	143	5.6
D	4	Jason Demers	S.J.	20	0	3	3	18:11	-6	8	0	0	0	20	0.0
			DAL	61	5	17	22	19:25	3	63	2	0	2	79	6.3
			Total	81	5	20	25	19:07	-3	71	2	0	2	99	5.1
D	24	Jordie Benn	DAL	73	2	14	16	18:03	-5	34	0	0	0	70	2.9
D	2*	Jyrki Jokipakka	DAL	51	0	10	10	16:30	-2	8	0	0	0	40	0.0
R	25*	Brett Ritchie	DAL	31	6	3	9	13:59	-1	12	0	0	1	78	7.7
L	27	Travis Moen	MTL	10	0	0	0	10:29	0	4	0	0	0	9	0.0
			DAL	34	3	6	9	9:03	0	14	0	0	0	25	12.0
			Total	44	3	6	9	9:22	0	18	0	0	0	34	8.8
D	5	Jamie Oleksiak	DAL	36	1	7	8	13:23	0	8	0	0	0	36	2.8
L	11*	Curtis McKenzie	DAL	36	4	1	5	11:32	-4	48	0	0	4	41	9.8
D	37*	Patrik Nemeth	DAL	22	0	3	3	16:12	0	2	0	0	0	16	0.0
R	43	Valeri Nichushkin	DAL	8	0	1	1	13:46	-5	2	0	0	0	6	0.0
L	64*	Brendan Ranford	DAL	1	0	0	0	9:19	0	0	0	0	0	4	0.0
C	39	Travis Morin	DAL	6	0	0	0	12:05	1	0	0	0	0	10	0.0

Goaltending

No.	Goaltender	GPI	Mins	Avg	W	L	OT	EN	SO	GA	SA	Sv%	G	A	PIM
1	Jhonas Enroth	13	630	2.38	5	5	0	6	1	25	267	.906	0	0	0
32	Kari Lehtonen	65	3698	2.94	34	17	10	3	5	181	1875	.903	0	3	2
35	Anders Lindback	10	517	3.71	2	8	0	3	0	32	256	.875	0	1	0
40	Jussi Rynnas	2	92	4.57	0	1	0	0	0	7	44	.841	0	0	0
	Totals	**82**	**4978**	**3.10**	**41**	**31**	**10**	**12**	**6**	**257**	**2454**	**.895**			

Though he played just 65 games in 2014-15, John Klingberg led all first-year defensemen with 29 assists and 40 points. He was named to the NHL's All-Rookie Team.

Coaching History
*– indicates Cal/Oak/Cle

Wren Blair, 1967-68; *Bert Olmstead and Gord Fashoway, 1967-68; Wren Blair and John Muckler, 1968-69; *Fred Glover, 1968-69 to 1970-71; Wren Blair and Charlie Burns, 1969-70; Jack Gordon, 1970-71 to 1972-73; *Fred Glover and Vic Stasiuk, 1971-72; *Garry Young and Fred Glover, 1972-73; Jack Gordon and Parker MacDonald, 1973-74; *Fred Glover and Marshall Johnston, 1973-74; Jack Gordon and Charlie Burns, 1974-75; *Marshall Johnston and Bill McCreary, Sr., 1974-75; Ted Harris,1975-76, 1976-77; *Jack Evans, 1975-76 to 1977-78; Ted Harris, André Beaulieu and Lou Nanne, 1977-78; Harry Howell and Glen Sonmor, 1978-79; Glen Sonmor, 1979-80 to 1981-82; Glen Sonmor and Murray Oliver, 1982-83; Bill Mahoney, 1983-84, 1984-85; Lorne Henning, 1985-86; Lorne Henning and Glen Sonmor, 1986-87; Herb Brooks,1987-88; Pierre Page, 1988-89, 1989-90; Bob Gainey, 1990-91 to 1994-95; Bob Gainey and Ken Hitchcock, 1995-96; Ken Hitchcock, 1996-97 to 2000-01; Ken Hitchcock and Rick Wilson, 2001-02; Dave Tippett, 2002-03 to 2008-09; Marc Crawford, 2009-10, 2010-11; Glen Gulutzan, 2011-12, 2012-13; Lindy Ruff, 2013-14 to date.

Club Records

Team

(Figures in brackets for season records are games played; records for fewest points, wins, ties, losses, goals, goals against are for 70 or more games)

Most Points **114** 1998-99 (82)
Most Wins **53** 2005-06 (82)
Most Ties **22** 1969-70 (76)
Most Losses .... **55** 1973-74 (78) California
.... **53** 1975-76 (80), 1977-78 (80)
Most Goals **346** 1981-82 (80)
Most Goals Against **349** 1987-88 (80)
Fewest Points .... **36** 1973-74 (78) California
.... **45** 1977-78 (80)
Fewest Wins .... **13** 1973-74 (78) California
.... **18** 1968-69 (76), 1977-78 (80)
Fewest Ties **4** 1989-90 (80)
Fewest Losses **19** 1998-99 (82)
Fewest Goals .... **153** 1967-68 (74) Cal./Oakland
.... **189** 1968-69 (76)
Fewest Goals Against **167** 1997-98 (82)
Longest Winning Streak
Overall .... **7** Mar. 16-28/80, Mar. 16-Apr. 2/97, Nov. 22-Dec. 5/97, Jan. 29-Feb. 11/08
Home .... **11** Nov. 4-Dec. 27/72
Away .... **8** Dec. 13/10-Jan. 20/11
Longest Undefeated Streak
Overall .... **15** Dec. 6/98-Jan. 6/99 (12W, 3T)
Home .... **17** Jan. 23-Mar. 20/04 (13W, 4T/OL)
Away .... **10** Jan. 12-Mar. 4/99 (8W, 2T), Dec. 27/02-Feb. 25/03 (7W, 3T/OL)
Longest Losing Streak
Overall .... **10** Feb. 1-20/76
Home .... **6** Jan. 17-Feb. 4/70, Feb. 21-Mar. 8/09
Away .... **10** Dec. 12/09-Jan. 21/10
Longest Winless Streak
Overall .... **20** Jan. 15-Feb. 28/70 (15L, 5T)
Home .... **12** Jan. 17-Feb. 25/70 (8L, 4T)
Away **21** Nov.21/73-Feb. 20/74 (24L)
.... **23** Oct. 25/74-Jan. 28/75 (19L, 4T)
Most Shutouts, Season **11** 2000-01 (82), 2002-03 (82)
Most PIM, Season **2,313** 1987-88 (80)
Most Goals, Game .... **15** Nov. 11/81 (Wpg. 2 at Min. 15)

Individual

Most Seasons .... **21** Mike Modano
Most Games .... **1,459** Mike Modano
Most Goals, Career .... **557** Mike Modano
Most Assists, Career .... **802** Mike Modano
Most Points, Career .... **1,359** Mike Modano (557G, 802A)
Most PIM, Career .... **1,883** Shane Churla
Most Shutouts, Career .... **40** Marty Turco
Longest Consecutive Games Streak .... **442** Danny Grant (Dec. 4/68-Apr. 7/74)
Most Goals, Season .... **55** Dino Ciccarelli (1981-82), Brian Bellows (1989-90)
Most Assists, Season .... **76** Neal Broten (1985-86)
Most Points, Season .... **114** Bobby Smith (1981-82; 43G, 71A)
Most PIM, Season .... **382** Basil McRae (1987-88)
Most Points, Defenseman, Season .... **77** Craig Hartsburg (1981-82; 17G, 60A)
Most Points, Center, Season .... **114** Bobby Smith (1981-82; 43G, 71A)
Most Points, Right Wing, Season .... **106** Dino Ciccarelli (1981-82; 55G, 51A)
Most Points, Left Wing, Season .... **99** Brian Bellows (1989-90; 55G, 44A)
Most Points, Rookie, Season .... **98** Neal Broten (1981-82; 38G, 60A)
Most Shutouts, Season .... **9** Ed Belfour (1997-98), Marty Turco (2003-04)
Most Goals, Game .... **5** Tim Young (Jan. 15/79)
Most Assists, Game .... **5** Murray Oliver (Oct. 24/71), Larry Murphy (Oct. 17/89), Brad Richards (Feb. 28/08)
Most Points, Game .... **7** Bobby Smith (Nov. 11/81; 4G, 3A)

Records include Minnesota North Stars, 1967-68 through 1992-93 and California/Oakland/Cleveland, 1967-68 through 1977-78. Cleveland and Minnesota merged prior to the 1978-79 season.

All-time Record vs. Other Clubs

Regular Season

	Total								At Home								On Road							
	GP	W	L	T	OL	GF	GA	PTS	GP	W	L	T	OL	GF	GA	PTS	GP	W	L	T	OL	GF	GA	PTS
Anaheim	113	67	31	5	10	332	258	149	57	39	12	2	4	176	115	84	56	28	19	3	6	156	143	65
Arizona	167	85	63	13	6	534	480	189	84	43	30	9	2	277	234	97	83	42	33	4	4	257	246	92
Boston	131	32	76	23	0	346	508	87	66	20	33	13	0	186	233	53	65	12	43	10	0	160	275	34
Buffalo	116	44	53	17	2	342	374	107	59	30	22	6	1	189	168	67	57	14	31	11	1	153	206	40
Calgary	161	65	63	25	8	493	504	163	81	40	24	11	6	285	245	97	80	25	39	14	2	208	259	66
Carolina	73	40	27	6	0	267	221	86	35	22	11	2	0	135	100	46	38	18	16	4	0	132	121	40
Chicago	263	101	124	31	7	795	892	240	133	62	51	16	4	445	411	144	130	39	73	15	3	350	481	96
Colorado	123	51	53	12	7	354	396	121	61	32	18	5	6	205	177	75	62	19	35	7	1	149	219	46
Columbus	51	32	14	0	5	148	119	69	25	15	8	0	2	70	58	32	26	17	6	0	3	78	61	37
Detroit	247	103	107	34	3	795	839	243	123	58	44	18	3	413	375	137	124	45	63	16	0	382	464	106
Edmonton	126	66	41	15	4	429	396	151	63	37	17	7	2	224	169	83	63	29	24	8	2	205	227	68
Florida	29	13	10	3	3	84	79	32	14	5	5	2	2	41	47	14	15	8	5	1	1	43	32	18
Los Angeles	225	109	74	32	10	730	659	260	113	66	32	13	2	402	303	147	112	43	42	19	8	328	356	113
Minnesota	56	33	18	1	4	168	143	71	29	22	4	1	2	112	67	47	27	11	14	0	2	56	76	24
Montreal	127	33	73	21	0	326	480	87	64	20	32	12	0	171	216	52	63	13	41	9	0	155	264	35
Nashville	65	36	25	1	3	173	144	76	32	23	8	0	1	97	53	47	33	13	17	1	2	76	91	29
New Jersey	102	52	40	9	1	329	302	114	52	31	14	6	1	185	131	69	50	21	26	3	0	144	171	45
NY Islanders	106	38	50	16	2	310	388	94	52	20	23	8	1	152	187	49	54	18	27	8	1	158	201	45
NY Rangers	134	41	70	22	1	384	462	105	66	22	32	11	1	206	236	56	68	19	38	11	0	178	226	49
Ottawa	30	20	8	0	2	104	77	42	16	11	5	0	0	62	43	22	14	9	3	0	2	42	34	20
Philadelphia	145	40	71	32	2	399	505	114	72	29	25	16	2	234	231	76	73	11	46	16	0	165	274	38
Pittsburgh	138	60	64	12	2	450	484	134	70	40	22	6	2	263	228	88	68	20	42	6	0	187	256	46
St. Louis	273	105	119	43	6	829	876	259	136	64	46	22	4	448	396	154	137	41	73	21	2	381	480	105
San Jose	117	60	44	5	8	320	304	133	58	27	23	4	4	163	156	62	59	33	21	1	4	157	148	71
Tampa Bay	34	20	11	3	0	106	84	43	16	8	7	1	0	52	47	17	18	12	4	2	0	54	37	26
Toronto	208	90	88	28	2	717	690	210	102	53	37	11	1	382	319	118	106	37	51	17	1	335	371	92
Vancouver	179	87	67	22	3	576	562	199	90	49	29	12	0	313	254	110	89	38	38	10	3	263	308	89
Washington	91	46	27	16	2	320	254	110	46	25	11	8	2	170	123	60	45	21	16	8	0	150	131	50
Winnipeg	23	15	6	0	2	72	61	32	11	7	3	0	1	25	20	15	12	8	3	0	1	47	41	17
Defunct Clubs	65	29	24	12	0	207	191	70	33	19	8	6	0	123	86	44	32	10	16	6	0	84	105	26
Totals	**3718**	**1613**	**1541**	**459**	**105**	**11439**	**11732**	**3790**	**1859**	**939**	**636**	**228**	**56**	**6206**	**5428**	**2162**	**1859**	**674**	**905**	**231**	**49**	**5233**	**6304**	**1628**

Cal/Oak/Cle other than those vs. Minnesota North Stars not included. Results vs. North Stars listed under Defunct Clubs.

Playoffs

	Series	W	L	GP	W	L	T	GF	GA	Last Mtg.	Rnd.	Result
Anaheim	3	1	2	18	8	10	0	52	47	2014	FR	L 2-4
Boston	1	1	0	3	3	0	0	20	13	1981	PR	W 3-0
Buffalo	3	2	1	13	8	5	0	39	37	1999	F	W 4-2
Calgary	1	1	0	6	4	2	0	25	18	1981	SF	W 4-2
Chicago	6	2	4	33	14	19	0	118	120	1991	DSF	W 4-2
Colorado	4	2	2	24	10	14	0	62	66	2006	CQF	L 1-4
Detroit	4	0	4	24	8	16	0	50	72	2008	CF	L 2-4
Edmonton	8	6	2	42	27	15	0	118	104	2003	CQF	W 4-2
*Los Angeles	2	1	1	14	7	7	0	51	46	1969	QF	L 3-4
Montreal	2	1	1	13	6	7	0	37	48	1980	QF	W 4-3
New Jersey	1	0	1	6	2	4	0	9	15	2000	F	L 2-4
NY Islanders	1	0	1	5	1	4	0	16	26	1981	F	L 1-4
Philadelphia	2	0	2	11	3	8	0	26	41	1980	SF	L 1-4
*Pittsburgh	2	0	2	10	2	8	0	32	54	1991	F	L 2-4
St. Louis	12	6	6	66	34	32	0	197	187	2001	CSF	L 0-4
San Jose	3	3	0	17	12	5	0	46	30	2008	CSF	W 4-2
Toronto	2	2	0	7	6	1	0	35	26	1983	DSF	W 3-1
Vancouver	2	0	2	12	4	8	0	23	31	2007	CQF	L 3-4
Totals	**59**	**28**	**31**	**324**	**159**	**165**	**0**	**956**	**981**			

* Includes Oakland playoff results.

Calgary totals include Atlanta Flames, 1972-73 to 1979-80. Carolina totals include Hartford, 1979-80 to 1996-97.
Colorado totals include Quebec, 1979-80 to 1994-95.
New Jersey totals include Kansas City, 1974-75, 1975-76, and Colorado Rockies, 1976-77 to 1981-82.
Phoenix totals include Winnipeg, 1979-80 to 1995-96. Winnipeg totals include Atlanta Thrashers, 1999-2000 to 2010-11.

Playoff Results 2015-2011

Year	Round	Opponent	Result	GF	GA
2014	FR	Anaheim	L 2-4	18	20

Abbreviations: Round: F – Final;
CF – conference final; **CSF** – conference semi-final;
CQF – conference quarter-final; **FR** – first round;
DSF – division semi-final; **SF** – semi-final;
QF – quarter-final; **PR** – preliminary round.

2014-15 Results

Oct.	9	Chicago	2-3†		13	Ottawa	5-4
	11	at Nashville	1-4		15	Winnipeg	1-2
	14	at Columbus	4-2		17	Washington	5-4
	16	at Pittsburgh	3-2		18	at Chicago	6-3
	18	Philadelphia	5-6*		20	Boston	1-3
	21	Vancouver	6-3		27	at Montreal	2-3
	24	at New Jersey	3-2†		29	at Ottawa	6-3
	25	at NY Islanders	5-7		31	at Winnipeg	5-2
	28	St. Louis	3-4*	**Feb.**	3	Colorado	2-3†
	31	Anaheim	1-2*		5	Tampa Bay	3-5
Nov.	1	at Minnesota	1-4		7	at Buffalo	2-3
	4	Los Angeles	1-3		8	at NY Rangers	3-2*
	6	Nashville	2-3		10	at Boston	5-3
	8	San Jose	3-5		13	Florida	2-0
	11	at Arizona	4-3		14	at Colorado	1-4
	13	at Los Angeles	2-0		17	at St. Louis	4-1
	15	Minnesota	1-2		19	San Jose	2-5
	16	at Chicago	2-6		21	Detroit	6-7*
	18	Carolina	4-6		22	at Minnesota	2-6
	20	Arizona	3-1		24	at Winnipeg	2-4
	22	Los Angeles	5-4		27	Colorado	4-5†
	25	Edmonton	3-2	**Mar.**	1	Anaheim	1-3
	28	Minnesota	4-5*		3	NY Islanders	3-2*
	29	at Colorado	2-5		5	at Florida	4-3†
Dec.	2	at Toronto	3-5		7	at Tampa Bay	4-5
	4	at Detroit	2-5		10	at Philadelphia	2-1
	6	Montreal	4-1		12	at Carolina	5-3
	9	Winnipeg	2-5		13	at Washington	4-2
	13	New Jersey	4-3		15	St. Louis	0-3
	17	at Vancouver	2-0		19	Pittsburgh	2-1
	19	at Calgary	2-1		21	Chicago	4-0
	21	at Edmonton	6-5†		23	Buffalo	4-3
	23	Toronto	0-4		25	at Calgary	4-3†
	27	at St. Louis	4-3		27	at Edmonton	0-4
	29	NY Rangers	3-2		28	at Vancouver	4-3*
	31	Arizona	6-0		30	Calgary	3-5
Jan.	3	Minnesota	7-1	**Apr.**	3	St. Louis	5-7
	4	at Chicago	4-5*		4	at Nashville	4-3*
	6	Columbus	2-4		6	at San Jose	5-1
	8	at Nashville	2-3*		8	at Anaheim	4-0
	10	at Colorado	3-4		11	Nashville	4-1

* – Overtime † – Shootout

NHL Draft Selections 2015-2001

Name in bold denotes played in NHL.

2015
Pick
12 Denis Gurjanov
49 Roope Hintz
103 Chris Martenet
133 Joseph Cecconi
163 Markus Ruusu

2014
Pick
14 Julius Honka
45 Brett Pollock
75 Alex Peters
105 Michael Prapavessis
115 Brent Moran
135 Miro Karjalainen
154 Aaron Haydon
165 John Nyberg
195 Patrick Sanvido

2013
Pick
10 **Valeri Nichushkin**
29 Jason Dickinson
40 Remi Elie
54 Philippe Desrosiers
68 Niklas Hansson
101 Nicholas Paul
131 Cole Ully
149 Matej Paulovic
182 Aleksi Makela

2012
Pick
13 Radek Faksa
43 Ludwig Bystrom
54 Mike Winther
61 Devin Shore
74 Esa Lindell
104 Gemel Smith
134 Branden Troock
144 Henri Kiviaho
183 Dmitry Sinitsyn

2011
Pick
14 **Jamie Oleksiak**
44 **Brett Ritchie**
105 Emil Molin
135 Troy Vance
165 Matej Stransky
195 **Jyrki Jokipakka**

2010
Pick
11 **Jack Campbell**
41 **Patrik Nemeth**
77 Alexander Guptill
109 Alex Theriau
131 **John Klingberg**

2009
Pick
8 **Scott Glennie**
38 **Alex Chiasson**
69 **Reilly Smith**
129 **Tomas Vincour**
159 **Curtis McKenzie**

2008
Pick
59 Tyler Beskorowany
89 Scott Winkler
149 **Philip Larsen**
176 Matthew Tassone
209 Mike Bergin

2007
Pick
50 Nico Sacchetti
64 Sergei Korostin
112 **Colton Sceviour**
128 Austin Smith
129 **Jamie Benn**
136 Ondrej Roman
149 Michael Neal
172 **Luke Gazdic**

2006
Pick
27 **Ivan Vishnevskiy**
90 Aaron Snow
120 **Richard Bachman**
138 **David McIntyre**
150 Max Warn

2005
Pick
28 **Matt Niskanen**
33 **James Neal**
71 **Rich Clune**
75 **Perttu Lindgren**
146 **Tom Wandell**
160 **Matt Watkins**
223 Pat McGann

2004
Pick
28 **Mark Fistric**
34 Johan Fransson
52 **Raymond Sawada**
56 **Nicklas Grossmann**
86 John Lammers
104 Fredrik Naslund
183 Trevor Ludwig
218 Sergei Kukushkin
248 Lukas Vomela
280 Matt McKnight

2003
Pick
33 **Loui Eriksson**
36 **Vojtech Polak**
54 **B.J. Crombeen**
99 Matt Nickerson
134 Alexander Naurov
144 Eero Kilpelainen
165 Gino Guyer
185 **Francis Wathier**
195 **Drew Bagnall**
196 Elias Granath
259 Niko Vainio

2002
Pick
26 Martin Vagner
32 Janos Vas
34 **Tobias Stephan**
42 Marius Holtet
43 **Trevor Daley**
78 Geoff Waugh
110 Jarkko A. Immonen
147 David Bararuk
180 Kirill Sidorenko
210 Bryan Hamm
243 Tuomas Mikkonen
273 Ned Havern

2001
Pick
26 **Jason Bacashihua**
70 Yared Hagos
92 Anthony Aquino
126 Daniel Volrab
161 **Mike Smith**
167 Michal Blazek
192 **Jussi Jokinen**
255 Marco Rosa
265 Dale Sullivan
285 Marek Tomica

General Managers' History

* – indicates Cal/Oak/Cle

*Rudy Pilous, until June 1967; Wren Blair, 1967-68 to 1973-74; *Bert Olmstead, 1967-68; *Frank Selke Jr. 1968-69, 1969-70; *Frank Selke Jr., Bill Torrey and Fred Glover, 1970-71; *Garry Young, 1971-72; *Garry Young and Fred Glover, 1972-73; *Fred Glover and Garry Young, 1973-74; Jack Gordon, 1974-75 to 1976-77; *Bill McCreary Sr., 1974-75, 1975-76; *Bill McCreary Sr. and Harry Howell, 1976-77; Jack Gordon and Lou Nanne, 1977-78; *Harry Howell, 1977-78; Lou Nanne, 1978-79 to 1986-87; Lou Nanne and Jack Ferreira, 1987-88; Jack Ferreira, 1988-89, 1989-90; Bob Clarke, 1990-91, 1991-92; Bob Gainey, 1992-93 to 2000-01; Bob Gainey and Doug Armstrong, 2001-02; Doug Armstrong, 2002-03 to 2006-07; Doug Armstrong and Brett Hull/Les Jackson, 2007-08; Brett Hull/Les Jackson, 2008-09; Joe Nieuwendyk, 2009-10 to 2012-13; Jim Nill, 2013-14 to date.

Captains' History

* – indicates Cal/Oak/Cle

Bob Woytowich, 1967-68; *Bobby Baun, 1967-68; Moose Vasko, 1968-69; Claude Larose, 1969-70; *Ted Hampson, 1968-69 to 1970-71; Ted Harris, 1970-71 to 1973-74; *Carol Vadnais, 1971-72; *Bert Marshall, 1972-73; *no captain, 1973-74; *Joey Johnston, 1974-75; Bill Goldsworthy, 1974-75, 1975-76; *Jim Neilson and Bob Stewart, 1975-76 to 1977-78 (co-captains); Bill Hogaboam, 1976-77; Nick Beverley, 1977-78; J.P. Parise, 1978-79; Paul Shmyr, 1979-80, 1980-81; Tim Young, 1981-82; Craig Hartsburg, 1982-83; Craig Hartsburg and Brian Bellows, 1983-84; Craig Hartsburg, 1984-85 to 1987-88; Curt Fraser, Bob Rouse and Curt Giles, 1988-89; Curt Giles, 1989-90, 1990-91; Mark Tinordi,1991-92 to 1993-94; Neal Broten and Derian Hatcher, 1994-95; Derian Hatcher,1995-96 to 2002-03; Mike Modano, 2003-04 to 2005-06; Brenden Morrow, 2006-07 to 2012-13; Jamie Benn, 2013-14 to date.

Jim Nill

General Manager

Born: Hanna, AB, April 11, 1958.

Jim Nill was appointed general manager of the Dallas Stars on April 29, 2013. He is the 11th General Manager in franchise history and the sixth since the team moved to Dallas. In his first season with the club in 2013-14, Dallas returned to the playoffs for the first time since 2007-08.

Nill concluded his 15th season as assistant general manager of the Detroit Red Wings, and his 19th season overall as a member of the management team, in 2012-13. His responsibilities with Detroit included directing the amateur scouting department and overseeing all selections at the annual NHL Draft, as well as managing the development of the organization's prospects at both the professional and amateur levels. During Nill's tenure in Detroit, the Red Wings had more wins than any other franchise in the NHL, won the Stanley Cup four times (1997, 1998, 2002 and 2008), the Presidents' Trophy six times (1995, 1996, 2002, 2004, 2006 and 2008), the Central Division title 12 times, and won seven regular season Western Conference titles while never missing the playoffs. He was an integral part of Detroit's drafting of Pavel Datsyuk, Henrik Zetterberg, Niklas Kronwall, Valtteri Filppula, Jimmy Howard and Johan Franzen. Nill was also general manager of Team Canada for the 2004 World Championship, winning a gold medal.

Nill joined the Red Wings' front office in the summer of 1994 following three seasons with the Ottawa Senators. Previously, Nill enjoyed a nine-season NHL career as a right winger with the St. Louis Blues, Vancouver Canucks, Boston Bruins, Winnipeg Jets and Red Wings. He collected 58 goals, 87 assists and 854 penalty minutes in 524 regular season games. Nill later went to Adirondack of the American Hockey League as a player/coach, retiring as a player after the 1990-91 season. A member of the 1979-80 Canadian national and Olympic team, he was a fifth-round pick of the St. Louis Blues (89th overall) in the 1978 draft.

Club Directory

American Airlines Center

Dallas Stars
Office Address:
2601 Avenue of the Stars
Frisco, TX 75034
Phone **214/387-5500**
FAX 214/387-5564
Ticket Information 214/GO STARS
www.dallasstars.com
Capacity: 18,532

Executives

Owner and Governor	R. Thomas Gaglardi
President, CEO and Alternate Governor	James R. Lites
Executive Vice President, Chief Revenue Officer	Brad Alberts
Executive Vice President, Chief Operating Officer	Jason Farris
Executive Assistant to the President	Brittany McMullen

Hockey Operations

General Manager	Jim Nill
Assistant G.M.	Les Jackson
Director of Hockey Operations/Texas Stars G.M.	Scott White
Director of Hockey Administration	Mark Janko
Head Coach	Lindy Ruff
Assistant Coaches	Curt Fraser / James Patrick
Goaltending Coach	Jeff Reese
Coordinators, Video / Player Development	Kelly Forbes / J.J. McQueen
Director, Goaltending Development	Mike Valley
Director, Team Services	Jason Rademan
Directors, Amateur / European Scouting	Joe McDonnell / Kari Takko
Head Pro Scout	Paul McIntosh
Pro Scouts	Danny O'Brien, Doug Overton, Alex Lepore
Amateur Scouts	Bob Gernander, Dennis Holland, Jiri Hrdina, Jimmy Johnston, Mark Leach, Rickard Oquist, Borys Protsenko, Shane Turner, Buddy Powers, Evgueni Tsybouk
Athletic Trainers, Head / Associate	Dave Zeis / Craig Lowry
Equipment Manager / Asst. Mgr / Assistant	Steve Sumner / Dennis Soetaert / Josh Richards
Strength and Conditioning Coach	Brad Jellis
Massage Therapist	Masayasu Takaiwa
Executive Assistant, Hockey Operations	Samantha Hatcher

Production and Entertainment

Vice President, Production and Entertainment	Jason Walsh
Play-By-Play / Analyst / Studio Host	Dave Strader / Daryl Reaugh / Josh Bogorad
Associate Producer / Associate Director	John Sponsler / Doug Foster
Director/Producer	Mark Vittorio
Radio Analysts	Bruce LeVine, Owen Newkirk
Directors, Game Entertainment / Visual Effects	Jason Danby / Jeff Neal
Editors	Hunter Harrington, Kevin Harp
Manager, Productions / Production Assistant	Jerry Miranda / Chandler Smith
Web Producer	Cody Eastwood
Ice Girls Director	Christina Swanson
Production and Entertainment Coordinator	Shae Bryan

Communications

Vice President, Communications	Tom Holy
Media Relations Manager	Ben Fromstein
Corporate Communications Manager	Joe Calvillo

Dallas Stars Foundation

Executive Director, Dallas Stars Foundation	Jessica Dunn
Coordinators, Dallas Stars Foundation	Christa Melia, Katherine Miller
Coordinator, Fitness Stars	Brent Gray

Corporate Partnerships

Vice President, Corporate Partnerships	Grady Raskin
Director, Corporate Partnerships	Christopher Hart
Senior Account Execs / Account Exec.	Christine MacDonald, Jessica Rafizadeh / Shay Butler
Activation Director / Coordinators	Lisa Wile / Julie Johnson, Caroline Morehead, Kimberly Skrepcinski

Business Development / Corporate Development

Vice President, Business Development	Dan Stuchal
Director, Corporate Development	Marty Turco

Finance and Administration

Vice President, Finance and Administration	Toni May
Sr. Director, Finance	Ruth Hill
Payroll Administrator / Accounts Payable	Lauren Radford / Tina Forbes, Joshua Webb
Senior Staff Accountants	David Garcia, Michael Beener
Staff Accountant	Garrett Jensen, Lindsey Lee

Legal and Human Resources

Legal Counsel/Director of Contract Mgmt.	Alana Newhook
Human Resources Director / Generalist	Lindsay Dowdy / Megan Lippe

Corporate Operations

Vice President, Business Operations/CIO	Daniel Doggendorf
VP, Corporate Support and Development	Ed Reusch
Business Operations Assistant	Mackenzie Moore
Technology Engineers	Alex Cheng, Jonathan Geremia, Zacchary Phifer, Jchon Paradise
Front Desk Receptionist	Alexandra Helm

Marketing

Vice President, Marketing	Kelly Calvert
Directors, Marketing / Promotions & Events	Trent Morton / Steve Phillips
Coordinators, Advertising / Promo	Candace Kent / Kevin Hardey
Managers, Social Media / Website	Alex Cerda / Bryan Renahan
Sr. Graphic Designer / Graphic Designer	Chase Hargrove / Anna Kremer

Alumni Association / Youth Hockey Development

Director, Alumni Association	Bob Bassen
Manager, Youth Hockey Development	Kalie Hagood

Ticket Operations

Director, Ticket Operations	Mac Amin
Managers, Ticket Operations	Jason Brayman, Jeff Gogerty, John Schloffman

Ticket Sales

Vice President, Ticket Sales and Service	Matt Bowman
Director, New Business and Premium Sales	Ryan Hoopes
Directors, Customer Service / Group Sales	Daniel Venegas / Megan Morgan

Dr Pepper Arena

General Manager, DPA	Bill Herman
Guest Services Representative	Vic Cox

Dr Pepper StarCenter

Vice President / Asst. V.P. / Director	Damon Boettcher / Aanya Montgomery / David Copland

Detroit Red Wings

Key Off-Season Signings/Acquisitions

2015

June 9 • Named **Jeff Blashill** head coach.
23 • Named **Tony Granato**, **Chris Chelios** and **Pat Ferschweiler** assistant coaches.
30 • Re-signed D **Brendan Smith**.
July 1 • Signed D **Mike Green** and C **Brad Richards**.
1 • Re-signed C **Andy Miele** and G **Tom McCollum**.
8 • Signed LW **Eric Tangradi**.
10 • Re-signed RW **Gustav Nyquist**.
21 • Re-signed RW **Teemu Pulkkinen**.
24 • Re-signed RW **Tomas Jurco**.

2015-16 Schedule

Month	Day	Date	Opponent	Month	Day	Date	Opponent
Oct.	Fri.	9	Toronto		Sun.	10	at Anaheim*
	Sat.	10	at Carolina		Mon.	11	at Los Angeles
	Tue.	13	Tampa Bay		Thu.	14	at Arizona
	Fri.	16	Carolina		Sun.	17	Philadelphia
	Sat.	17	at Montreal		Wed.	20	St. Louis
	Wed.	21	at Edmonton		Fri.	22	at Buffalo
	Fri.	23	at Calgary		Sat.	23	Anaheim
	Sat.	24	at Vancouver		Mon.	25	at NY Islanders
	Tue.	27	Carolina	**Feb.**	Wed.	3	at Tampa Bay
	Fri.	30	Ottawa		Thu.	4	at Florida
	Sat.	31	at Ottawa		Sat.	6	NY Islanders*
Nov.	Tue.	3	Tampa Bay		Mon.	8	Florida
	Fri.	6	at Toronto		Wed.	10	Ottawa
	Sun.	8	Dallas*		Fri.	12	Colorado
	Tue.	10	Washington		Sun.	14	Boston*
	Fri.	13	San Jose		Mon.	15	at NY Islanders*
	Sat.	14	at Boston		Thu.	18	at Pittsburgh
	Mon.	16	at Ottawa		Sat.	20	at Ottawa
	Wed.	18	Washington		Sun.	21	at NY Rangers
	Fri.	20	Los Angeles		Tue.	23	Columbus
	Sat.	21	at St. Louis		Sat.	27	at Colorado
	Wed.	25	Boston		Mon.	29	at Dallas
	Fri.	27	Edmonton	**Mar.**	Wed.	2	Chicago
	Sun.	29	Florida*		Sun.	6	at Chicago*
Dec.	Tue.	1	Buffalo		Tue.	8	at Columbus
	Thu.	3	Arizona		Thu.	10	Winnipeg
	Sat.	5	Nashville		Sat.	12	NY Rangers*
	Tue.	8	at Washington		Sun.	13	Toronto
	Thu.	10	Montreal		Tue.	15	at Philadelphia
	Fri.	11	at New Jersey		Thu.	17	at Columbus
	Mon.	14	Buffalo		Sat.	19	at Florida
	Fri.	18	Vancouver		Tue.	22	at Tampa Bay
	Sun.	20	Calgary		Thu.	24	Montreal
	Tue.	22	New Jersey		Sat.	26	Pittsburgh*
	Sat.	26	at Nashville		Mon.	28	Buffalo
	Mon.	28	at Minnesota		Tue.	29	at Montreal
	Tue.	29	at Winnipeg	**Apr.**	Fri.	1	Minnesota
	Thu.	31	Pittsburgh		Sat.	2	at Toronto
Jan.	Sat.	2	at Buffalo*		Wed.	6	Philadelphia
	Mon.	4	at New Jersey		Thu.	7	at Boston
	Thu.	7	at San Jose		Sat.	9	at NY Rangers*

* Denotes afternoon game.

Retired Numbers

1	Terry Sawchuk	1949-55, 57-64, 1968-69
5	Nicklas Lidstrom	1991-2012
7	Ted Lindsay	1944-57, 64-65
9	Gordie Howe	1946-1971
10	Alex Delvecchio	1951-1973
12	Sid Abel	1938-43, 45-52
19	Steve Yzerman	1983-2006

ATLANTIC DIVISION
90th NHL Season

Franchise date: September 25, 1926

2014-15 Results: 43W-25L-4OTL-10SOL 100PTS
3RD, Atlantic Division • 6TH, Eastern Conference

Year-by-Year Record

		Home				Road				Overall									
Season	GP	W	L	T	OL	W	L	T	OL	W	L	T	OL	GF	GA	Pts.	Div. Fin.	Conf. Fin.	Playoff Result
2014-15	82	22	10	....	9	21	15	....	5	43	25	....	14	235	221	100	3rd, Atl.	6th, East	Lost First Round
2013-14	82	18	13	....	10	21	15	....	5	39	28	....	15	222	230	93	4th, Atl.	8th, East	Lost First Round
2012-13	48	13	7	....	4	11	9	....	4	24	16	....	8	124	115	56	3rd, Cen.	7th, West	Lost Conf. Semi-Final
2011-12	82	31	7	....	3	17	21	....	3	48	28	....	6	248	203	102	3rd, Cen.	5th, West	Lost Conf. Quarter-Final
2010-11	82	21	14	....	6	26	11	....	4	47	25	....	10	261	241	104	1st, Cen.	3rd, West	Lost Conf. Semi-Final
2009-10	82	25	10	....	6	19	14	....	8	44	24	....	14	229	216	102	2nd, Cen.	5th, West	Lost Conf. Semi-Final
2008-09	82	27	9	....	5	24	12	....	5	51	21	....	10	295	244	112	1st, Cen.	2nd, West	Lost Final
2007-08	**82**	**29**	**9**	....	**3**	**25**	**12**	....	**4**	**54**	**21**	....	**7**	**257**	**184**	**115**	**1st, Cen.**	**1st, West**	**Won Stanley Cup**
2006-07	82	29	4	....	8	21	15	....	5	50	19	....	13	254	199	113	1st, Cen.	1st, West	Lost Conf. Final
2005-06	82	27	9	....	5	31	7	....	3	58	16	....	8	305	209	124	1st, Cen.	1st, West	Lost Conf. Quarter-Final
2004-05	....	....	....	....	....	....	....	....	....	....	....	....	....	....	....	....			
2003-04	82	30	7	4	0	18	14	7	2	48	21	11	2	255	189	109	1st, Cen.	1st, West	Lost Conf. Semi-Final
2002-03	82	28	6	5	2	20	14	5	2	48	20	10	4	269	203	110	1st, Cen.	2nd, West	Lost Conf. Quarter-Final
2001-02	**82**	**28**	**7**	**5**	**1**	**23**	**10**	**5**	**3**	**51**	**17**	**10**	**4**	**251**	**187**	**116**	**1st, Cen.**	**1st, West**	**Won Stanley Cup**
2000-01	82	27	9	3	2	22	11	6	2	49	20	9	4	253	202	111	1st, Cen.	2nd, West	Lost Conf. Quarter-Final
1999-2000	82	28	9	3	1	20	13	7	1	48	22	10	2	278	210	108	2nd, Cen.	4th, West	Lost Conf. Semi-Final
1998-99	82	27	12	2	....	16	20	5	....	43	32	7	....	245	202	93	1st, Cen.	3rd, West	Lost Conf. Semi-Final
1997-98	**82**	**25**	**8**	**8**	....	**19**	**15**	**7**	....	**44**	**23**	**15**	....	**250**	**196**	**103**	**2nd, Cen.**	**2nd, West**	**Won Stanley Cup**
1996-97	**82**	**20**	**12**	**9**	....	**18**	**14**	**9**	....	**38**	**26**	**18**	....	**253**	**197**	**94**	**2nd, Cen.**	**3rd, West**	**Won Stanley Cup**
1995-96	82	36	3	2	....	26	10	5	....	62	13	7	....	325	181	131	1st, Cen.	1st, West	Lost Conf. Final
1994-95	48	17	4	3	....	16	7	1	....	33	11	4	....	180	117	70	1st, Cen.	1st, West	Lost Final
1993-94	84	23	13	6	....	23	17	2	....	46	30	8	....	356	275	100	1st, Cen.	1st, West	Lost Conf. Quarter-Final
1992-93	84	25	14	3	....	22	14	6	....	47	28	9	....	369	280	103	2nd, Norris		Lost Div. Semi-Final
1991-92	80	24	12	4	....	19	13	8	....	43	25	12	....	320	256	98	1st, Norris		Lost Div. Final
1990-91	80	26	14	0	....	8	24	8	....	34	38	8	....	273	298	76	3rd, Norris		Lost Div. Semi-Final
1989-90	80	20	14	6	....	8	24	8	....	28	38	14	....	288	323	70	5th, Norris		Out of Playoffs
1988-89	80	20	14	6	....	14	20	6	....	34	34	12	....	313	316	80	1st, Norris		Lost Div. Semi-Final
1987-88	80	24	10	6	....	17	18	5	....	41	28	11	....	322	269	93	1st, Norris		Lost Conf. Final
1986-87	80	20	14	6	....	14	22	4	....	34	36	10	....	260	274	78	2nd, Norris		Lost Conf. Final
1985-86	80	10	26	4	....	7	31	2	....	17	57	6	....	266	415	40	5th, Norris		Out of Playoffs
1984-85	80	19	14	7	....	8	27	5	....	27	41	12	....	313	357	66	3rd, Norris		Lost Div. Semi-Final
1983-84	80	18	20	2	....	13	22	5	....	31	42	7	....	298	323	69	3rd, Norris		Lost Div. Semi-Final
1982-83	80	14	19	7	....	7	25	8	....	21	44	15	....	263	344	57	5th, Norris		Out of Playoffs
1981-82	80	15	19	6	....	6	28	6	....	21	47	12	....	270	351	54	6th, Norris		Out of Playoffs
1980-81	80	16	15	9	....	3	28	9	....	19	43	18	....	252	339	56	5th, Norris		Out of Playoffs
1979-80	80	14	21	5	....	12	22	6	....	26	43	11	....	268	306	63	5th, Norris		Out of Playoffs
1978-79	80	15	17	8	....	8	24	8	....	23	41	16	....	252	295	62	5th, Norris		Out of Playoffs
1977-78	80	22	11	7	....	10	23	7	....	32	34	14	....	252	266	78	2nd, Norris		Lost Quarter-Final
1976-77	80	12	22	6	....	4	33	3	....	16	55	9	....	183	309	41	5th, Norris		Out of Playoffs
1975-76	80	17	15	8	....	9	29	2	....	26	44	10	....	226	300	62	4th, Norris		Out of Playoffs
1974-75	80	17	17	6	....	6	28	6	....	23	45	12	....	259	335	58	4th, Norris		Out of Playoffs
1973-74	78	21	12	6	....	8	27	4	....	29	39	10	....	255	319	68	6th, East		Out of Playoffs
1972-73	78	22	12	5	....	15	17	7	....	37	29	12	....	265	243	86	5th, East		Out of Playoffs
1971-72	78	25	11	3	....	8	24	7	....	33	35	10	....	261	262	76	5th, East		Out of Playoffs
1970-71	78	17	15	7	....	5	30	4	....	22	45	11	....	209	308	55	7th, East		Out of Playoffs
1969-70	76	20	11	7	....	20	10	8	....	40	21	15	....	246	199	95	3rd, East		Lost Quarter-Final
1968-69	76	23	8	7	....	10	23	5	....	33	31	12	....	239	221	78	5th, East		Out of Playoffs
1967-68	74	18	15	4	....	9	20	8	....	27	35	12	....	245	257	66	6th, East		Out of Playoffs
1966-67	70	21	11	3	....	6	28	1	....	27	39	4	....	212	241	58	5th		Out of Playoffs
1965-66	70	20	8	7	....	11	19	5	....	31	27	12	....	221	194	74	4th		Lost Final
1964-65	70	25	7	3	....	15	16	4	....	40	23	7	....	224	175	87	1st		Lost Semi-Final
1963-64	70	23	9	3	....	7	20	8	....	30	29	11	....	191	204	71	4th		Lost Final
1962-63	70	19	10	6	....	13	15	7	....	32	25	13	....	200	194	77	4th		Lost Final
1961-62	70	17	11	7	....	6	22	7	....	23	33	14	....	184	219	60	5th		Out of Playoffs
1960-61	70	15	13	7	....	10	16	9	....	25	29	16	....	195	215	66	4th		Lost Final
1959-60	70	18	14	3	....	8	15	12	....	26	29	15	....	186	197	67	4th		Lost Semi-Final
1958-59	70	13	17	5	....	12	20	3	....	25	37	8	....	167	218	58	6th		Out of Playoffs
1957-58	70	16	11	8	....	13	18	4	....	29	29	12	....	176	207	70	3rd		Lost Semi-Final
1956-57	70	23	7	5	....	15	13	7	....	38	20	12	....	198	157	88	1st		Lost Semi-Final
1955-56	70	21	6	8	....	9	18	8	....	30	24	16	....	183	148	76	2nd		Lost Final
1954-55	**70**	**25**	**5**	**5**	....	**17**	**12**	**6**	....	**42**	**17**	**11**	....	**204**	**134**	**95**	**1st**		**Won Stanley Cup**
1953-54	**70**	**24**	**4**	**7**	....	**13**	**15**	**7**	....	**37**	**19**	**14**	....	**191**	**132**	**88**	**1st**		**Won Stanley Cup**
1952-53	70	20	5	10	....	16	11	8	....	36	16	18	....	222	133	90	1st		Lost Semi-Final
1951-52	**70**	**24**	**7**	**4**	....	**20**	**7**	**8**	....	**44**	**14**	**12**	....	**215**	**133**	**100**	**1st**		**Won Stanley Cup**
1950-51	70	25	3	7	....	19	10	6	....	44	13	13	....	236	139	101	1st		Lost Semi-Final
1949-50	**70**	**19**	**9**	**7**	....	**18**	**10**	**7**	....	**37**	**19**	**14**	....	**229**	**164**	**88**	**1st**		**Won Stanley Cup**
1948-49	60	21	6	3	....	13	13	4	....	34	19	7	....	195	145	75	1st		Lost Final
1947-48	60	16	9	5	....	14	9	7	....	30	18	12	....	187	148	72	2nd		Lost Final
1946-47	60	14	10	6	....	8	17	5	....	22	27	11	....	190	193	55	4th		Lost Semi-Final
1945-46	50	16	5	4	....	4	15	6	....	20	20	10	....	146	159	50	4th		Lost Semi-Final
1944-45	50	19	5	1	....	12	9	4	....	31	14	5	....	218	161	67	2nd		Lost Final
1943-44	50	18	5	2	....	8	13	4	....	26	18	6	....	214	177	58	2nd		Lost Semi-Final
1942-43	**50**	**16**	**4**	**5**	....	**9**	**10**	**6**	....	**25**	**14**	**11**	....	**169**	**124**	**61**	**1st**		**Won Stanley Cup**
1941-42	48	14	7	3	....	5	18	1	....	19	25	4	....	140	147	42	5th		Lost Final
1940-41	48	14	5	5	....	7	11	6	....	21	16	11	....	112	102	53	3rd		Lost Final
1939-40	48	11	10	3	....	5	16	3	....	16	26	6	....	91	126	38	5th		Lost Semi-Final
1938-39	48	14	8	2	....	4	16	4	....	18	24	6	....	107	128	42	5th		Lost Semi-Final
1937-38	48	8	10	6	....	4	15	5	....	12	25	11	....	99	133	35	4th, Amn.		Out of Playoffs
1936-37	**48**	**14**	**5**	**5**	....	**11**	**9**	**4**	....	**25**	**14**	**9**	....	**128**	**102**	**59**	**1st, Amn.**		**Won Stanley Cup**
1935-36	**48**	**14**	**5**	**5**	....	**10**	**11**	**3**	....	**24**	**16**	**8**	....	**124**	**103**	**56**	**1st, Amn.**		**Won Stanley Cup**
1934-35	48	11	8	5	....	8	14	2	....	19	22	7	....	127	114	45	4th, Amn.		Out of Playoffs
1933-34	48	15	5	4	....	9	9	6	....	24	14	10	....	113	98	58	1st, Amn.		Lost Final
1932-33*	48	17	3	4	....	8	12	4	....	25	15	8	....	111	93	58	2nd, Amn.		Lost Semi-Final
1931-32	48	15	3	6	....	3	17	4	....	18	20	10	....	95	108	46	3rd, Amn.		Lost Quarter-Final
1930-31**	44	10	7	5	....	6	14	2	....	16	21	7	....	102	105	39	4th, Amn.		Out of Playoffs
1929-30	44	9	10	3	....	5	14	3	....	14	24	6	....	117	133	34	4th, Amn.		Out of Playoffs
1928-29	44	11	6	5	....	8	10	4	....	19	16	9	....	72	63	47	3rd, Amn.		Lost Quarter-Final
1927-28	44	9	10	3	....	10	9	3	....	19	19	6	....	88	79	44	4th, Amn.		Out of Playoffs
1926-27***	44	5	16	0	....	7	12	4	....	12	28	4	....	76	105	28	5th, Amn.		Out of Playoffs

* Team name changed to Red Wings. ** Team name changed to Falcons. *** Team named Cougars.

2015-16 Player Personnel

FORWARDS	HT	WT	*Age	Place of Birth	S	2014-15 Club
ABDELKADER, Justin	6-2	218	28	Muskegon, MI	L	Detroit
ANDERSSON, Joakim	6-1	211	26	Munkedal, Sweden	L	Detroit
DATSYUK, Pavel	5-11	194	37	Sverdlovsk, USSR	L	Detroit
FERRARO, Landon	6-0	186	24	Trail, BC	R	Detroit-Grand Rapids
FRANZEN, Johan	6-4	232	35	Landsbro, Sweden	L	Detroit
GLENDENING, Luke	5-11	195	26	Grand Rapids, MI	R	Detroit
HELM, Darren	6-0	196	28	Winnipeg, MB	L	Detroit
JURCO, Tomas	6-1	203	22	Kosice, Czech.	L	Detroit
MILLER, Drew	6-2	178	31	Dover, NJ	L	Detroit
NYQUIST, Gustav	5-11	185	26	Halmstad, Sweden	L	Detroit
PULKKINEN, Teemu	5-11	183	23	Vantaa, Finland	R	Detroit-Grand Rapids
RICHARDS, Brad	6-0	196	35	Murray Harbour, PE	L	Chicago
SHEAHAN, Riley	6-3	222	23	St. Catharines, ON	L	Detroit
TATAR, Tomas	5-10	186	24	Ilava, Czech.	L	Detroit
ZETTERBERG, Henrik	6-0	195	34	Njurunda, Sweden	L	Detroit
DEFENSEMEN						
DeKEYSER, Danny	6-3	190	25	Detroit, MI	L	Detroit
ERICSSON, Jonathan	6-4	221	31	Karlskrona, Sweden	L	Detroit
GREEN, Mike	6-1	207	29	Calgary, AB	R	Washington
KINDL, Jakub	6-3	199	28	Sumperk, Czech.	L	Detroit-Grand Rapids
KRONWALL, Niklas	6-0	190	34	Stockholm, Sweden	L	Detroit
QUINCEY, Kyle	6-2	216	30	Kitchener, ON	L	Detroit
SMITH, Brendan	6-2	198	26	Toronto, ON	L	Detroit
GOALTENDERS	**HT**	**WT**	***Age**	**Place of Birth**	**C**	**2014-15 Club**
HOWARD, Jimmy	6-0	218	31	Syracuse, NY	L	Detroit
MRAZEK, Petr	6-2	183	23	Ostrava, Czech.	L	Detroit-Grand Rapids

* – Age at start of 2015-16 season

2014-15 Scoring

* – rookie

Regular Season

Pos	#	Player	Team	GP	G	A	Pts	TOI	+/–	PIM	PP	SH	GW	S	S%
L	40	Henrik Zetterberg	DET	77	17	49	66	19:06	–6	32	4	0	3	227	7.5
C	13	Pavel Datsyuk	DET	63	26	39	65	19:03	12	8	8	0	5	165	15.8
C	21	Tomas Tatar	DET	82	29	27	56	16:13	6	28	9	0	7	211	13.7
C	14	Gustav Nyquist	DET	82	27	27	54	16:39	–11	26	14	0	4	195	13.8
L	8	Justin Abdelkader	DET	71	23	21	44	17:54	3	72	8	0	5	154	14.9
D	55	Niklas Kronwall	DET	80	9	35	44	23:50	–4	40	3	0	1	101	8.9
L	72	Erik Cole	DAL	57	18	15	33	14:31	4	14	2	1	0	98	18.4
			DET	11	3	3	6	14:39	–2	0	1	0	0	24	12.5
			Total	68	21	18	39	14:32	2	14	3	1	0	122	17.2
C	15	Riley Sheahan	DET	79	13	23	36	15:38	–3	16	5	0	0	123	10.6
D	28	Marek Zidlicky	N.J.	63	4	19	23	21:55	–7	42	3	0	0	103	3.9
			DET	21	3	8	11	18:01	–2	14	3	0	1	27	11.1
			Total	84	7	27	34	20:57	–9	56	6	0	1	130	5.4
C	43	Darren Helm	DET	75	15	18	33	15:50	7	12	3	2	1	160	9.4
D	65	Danny Dekeyser	DET	80	2	29	31	20:55	11	42	0	0	1	89	2.2
C	90	Stephen Weiss	DET	52	9	16	25	11:20	–2	16	3	0	1	52	17.3
C	93	Johan Franzen	DET	33	7	15	22	16:03	–12	30	4	0	3	74	9.5
C	41	Luke Glendening	DET	82	12	6	18	14:43	5	34	1	0	2	104	11.5
R	26	Tomas Jurco	DET	63	3	15	18	11:30	6	14	1	0	0	92	3.3
D	27	Kyle Quincey	DET	73	3	15	18	19:28	10	77	0	0	0	90	3.3
D	52	Jonathan Ericsson	DET	82	3	12	15	19:34	–5	70	0	0	0	82	3.7
D	4	Jakub Kindl	DET	35	5	8	13	15:54	2	22	2	0	0	54	9.3
L	20	Drew Miller	DET	82	5	8	13	13:26	–3	25	0	1	0	98	5.1
D	2	Brendan Smith	DET	76	4	9	13	17:53	–2	68	0	0	1	88	4.5
L	56	* Teemu Pulkkinen	DET	31	5	3	8	11:28	5	10	1	0	2	67	7.5
C	18	Joakim Andersson	DET	68	3	5	8	11:37	–4	22	0	0	1	74	4.1
D	61	* Xavier Ouellet	DET	21	2	1	3	16:23	4	2	0	0	0	27	7.4
D	47	* Alexey Marchenko	DET	13	1	1	2	15:25	1	2	0	0	0	7	14.3
R	11	Daniel Cleary	DET	17	1	1	2	9:08	–4	6	0	0	0	17	5.9
D	23	Brian Lashoff	DET	11	0	2	2	13:17	4	6	0	0	0	7	0.0
C	29	* Landon Ferraro	DET	3	1	0	1	11:59	1	0	0	0	1	4	25.0

Goaltending

No.	Goaltender	GPI	Mins	Avg	W	L	OT	EN	SO	GA	SA	Sv%	G	A	PIM
38	* Tom McCollum	2	66	0.91	1	0	0	0	0	1	25	.960	0	0	0
34	* Petr Mrazek	29	1585	2.38	16	9	2	2	3	63	768	.918	0	0	0
35	Jimmy Howard	53	2971	2.44	23	13	11	8	2	121	1350	.910	0	1	2
50	Jonas Gustavsson	7	351	2.56	3	3	1	1	1	15	168	.911	0	0	2
	Totals	**82**	**5018**	**2.52**	**43**	**25**	**14**	**11**	**6**	**211**	**2322**	**.909**			

Playoffs

Pos	#	Player	Team	GP	G	A	Pts	TOI	+/–	PIM	PP	SH	GW	OT	S	S%
C	13	Pavel Datsyuk	DET	7	3	2	5	19:07	–3	2	1	0	1	0	17	17.6
C	21	Tomas Tatar	DET	7	3	1	4	15:45	–3	2	1	0	0	0	18	16.7
D	52	Jonathan Ericsson	DET	7	0	4	4	19:50	0	8	0	0	0	0	5	0.0
C	15	Riley Sheahan	DET	7	2	1	3	14:08	–1	2	2	0	1	0	8	25.0
C	41	Luke Glendening	DET	7	2	1	3	15:31	1	8	0	1	1	0	10	20.0
L	40	Henrik Zetterberg	DET	7	0	3	3	18:02	–4	8	0	0	0	0	18	0.0
D	27	Kyle Quincey	DET	7	0	3	3	19:38	–1	4	0	0	0	0	8	0.0
C	43	Darren Helm	DET	7	0	3	3	19:17	–3	4	0	0	0	0	9	0.0
L	20	Drew Miller	DET	7	1	1	2	16:43	–1	2	0	0	0	0	8	12.5
C	18	Joakim Andersson	DET	7	1	1	2	9:45	1	2	0	0	0	0	6	16.7
C	14	Gustav Nyquist	DET	7	1	1	2	15:39	–2	2	0	0	0	0	15	6.7
R	26	Tomas Jurco	DET	7	1	1	2	8:31	–1	2	1	0	0	0	4	25.0
L	8	Justin Abdelkader	DET	5	0	2	2	16:43	–1	6	0	0	0	0	6	0.0
D	55	Niklas Kronwall	DET	6	0	2	2	23:35	–1	4	0	0	0	0	4	0.0
D	65	Danny Dekeyser	DET	7	1	0	1	21:22	–4	12	0	0	0	0	3	33.3
D	4	Jakub Kindl	DET	1	0	0	0	16:37	–1	0	0	0	0	0	3	0.0
C	90	Stephen Weiss	DET	2	0	0	0	10:28	–1	0	0	0	0	0	1	0.0
D	47	* Alexey Marchenko	DET	3	0	0	0	16:52	–3	0	0	0	0	0	1	0.0
D	2	Brendan Smith	DET	5	0	0	0	16:05	1	6	0	0	0	0	6	0.0
D	28	Marek Zidlicky	DET	6	0	0	0	15:16	0	4	0	0	0	0	8	0.0
C	29	* Landon Ferraro	DET	7	0	0	0	10:08	–2	2	0	0	0	0	10	0.0

Goaltending

No.	Goaltender	GPI	Mins	Avg	W	L	EN	SO	GA	SA	Sv%	G	A	PIM
34	* Petr Mrazek	7	398	2.11	3	4	2	2	14	186	.925	0	0	0
35	Jimmy Howard	1	20	3.00	0	0	0	0	1	12	.917	0	0	0
	Totals	**7**	**422**	**2.42**	**3**	**4**	**2**	**2**	**17**	**200**	**.915**			

Jeff Blashill

Head Coach

Born: Southfield, MI, December 10, 1973.

The Detroit Red Wings announced on June 9, 2015, that Jeff Blashill had been named the 27th head coach in franchise history. Blashill joined the organization in 2011-12, spending one season behind the Red Wings' bench as an assistant coach before being named head coach of the Grand Rapids Griffins, Detroit's American Hockey League affiliate, on June 25, 2012.

With the Griffins, Blashill led the club to three of the most successful campaigns in franchise history, highlighted by a 2012-13 campaign that saw Grand Rapids capture a regular-season Midwest Division title and eventually the first Calder Cup championship in the franchise's 17-year history. In 2014-15, the Griffins won the Midwest Division after reaching 100 points for the first time during Blashill's tenure. The club advanced to the Western Conference Finals for the second time in three seasons before falling to the Utica Comets in six games.

Born in Detroit and raised in Sault Ste. Marie, Michigan, Blashill won the Louis A.R. Pieri Memorial Award as the AHL's most outstanding coach in 2013-14 and was named head coach for the 2014 AHL All-Star Classic. In his three seasons with Grand Rapids, he compiled a 134-71-23 regular-season record and a 29-21 mark in the postseason, winning seven of nine total playoff series. He is the only coach in Griffins history to qualify for the playoffs in three consecutive seasons, leading the team to 92 points or better each year.

Twenty-four players who skated for the Griffins between 2012 and 2015 went on to play at least one NHL game, including Joakim Andersson, Danny DeKeyser, Luke Glendening, Tomas Jurco, Petr Mrazek, Gustav Nyquist, Riley Sheahan and Tomas Tatar, who all moved up to full-time roles with Detroit after winning the Calder Cup with Blashill in 2013. A total of 15 players who appeared for Detroit in 2014-15 spent time in Grand Rapids over the past three years. Additionally, 11 current Red Wings were also regulars in 2011-12, which Blashill spent as an assistant coach in Detroit, helping the team to a 12th consecutive 100-point season.

Blashill joined the Red Wings' organization after one season as the head coach at Western Michigan University in 2010-11, where he doubled the Broncos' win total from the previous season and led the school to its first appearance in the CCHA championship game since 1986. He finished as a finalist for CCHA coach of the year, and was named national coach of the year by College Hockey News, Inside College Hockey and USCHO.com. Blashill made his head coaching debut with the United States Hockey League's Indiana Ice, compiling a 72-43-5 mark as head coach and general manager from 2008 to 2010. The Ice earned a franchise-record 39 wins in 2008-09 and won the Clark Cup as champions of the USHL.

A former goaltender at Ferris State University, Blashill was the Bulldogs' rookie of the year in 1994-95 and earned a spot on the CCHA all-academic team in 1996-97. He began his coaching career with four seasons as an assistant coach for Ferris State from 1998 to 2002, followed by six seasons in the same role with Miami University in which the RedHawks qualified for the NCAA tournament four times. Blashill represented the United States as an assistant coach at international tournaments on three occasions: the 2009 World Junior A Challenge (gold medal), the 2009 World Junior Championship (fifth place) and the 2006 Ivan Hlinka Memorial Tournament (silver medal).

Coaching Record

			Regular Season				Playoffs			
Season	Team	League	GC	W	L	O/T	GC	W	L	T
2008-09	Indiana	USHL	60	39	19	2	13	9	4	0
2009-10	Indiana	USHL	60	33	24	3	9	4	5	0
2010-11	Western Michigan	CCHA	42	19	13	10	....	....	....	....
2012-13	Grand Rapids	AHL	76	42	26	8	24	15	9	0
2013-14	Grand Rapids	AHL	76	46	23	7	10	5	5	0
2014-15	Grand Rapids	AHL	76	46	22	8	16	9	7	0

Club Records

Team

(Figures in brackets for season records are games played; records for fewest points, wins, ties, losses, goals, goals against are for 70 or more games)

Most Points **131** 1995-96 (82)
Most Wins ***62** 1995-96 (82)
Most Ties **18** 1952-53 (70), 1980-81 (80), 1996-97 (82)
Most Losses **57** 1985-86 (80)
Most Goals **369** 1992-93 (84)
Most Goals Against **415** 1985-86 (80)
Fewest Points **40** 1985-86 (80)
Fewest Wins **16** 1976-77 (80)
Fewest Ties **4** 1966-67 (70)
Fewest Losses **13** 1950-51 (70), 1995-96 (82)
Fewest Goals **167** 1958-59 (70)
Fewest Goals Against **132** 1953-54 (70)
Longest Winning Streak
Overall .... **9** Seven times
Home .... ***23** Nov. 5/11-Feb. 19/12
Away .... ***12** Mar. 1-Apr. 15/06
Longest Undefeated Streak
Overall .... **15** Nov. 27-Dec. 28/52 (8W, 7T)
Home .... **19** Dec. 31/00-Apr.7/01 (17W, 2T/OL)
Away .... **15** Oct. 18-Dec. 20/51 (10W, 5T)
Longest Losing Streak
Overall .... **14** Feb. 24-Mar. 25/82
Home .... **7** Feb. 20-Mar. 25/82
Away .... **14** Oct. 19-Dec. 21/66
Longest Winless Streak
Overall .... **19** Feb. 26-Apr. 3/77 (18L, 1T)
Home .... **10** Dec. 11/85-Jan. 18/86 (9L, 1T)
Away .... **26** Dec. 15/76-Apr. 3/77 (23L, 3T)
Most Shutouts, Season **13** 1953-54 (70)
Most. PIM, Season **2,393** 1985-86 (80)
Most Goals, Game .... **15** Jan. 23/44 (NYR 0 at Det. 15)

Individual

Most Seasons .... **25** Gordie Howe
Most Games .... **1,687** Gordie Howe
Most Goals, Career .... **786** Gordie Howe
Most Assists, Career .... **1,063** Steve Yzerman
Most Points, Career .... **1,809** Gordie Howe (786G, 1,023A)
Most PIM, Career .... **2,090** Bob Probert
Most Shutouts, Career .... **85** Terry Sawchuk
Longest Consecutive Games Streak .... **548** Alex Delvecchio (Dec. 13/56-Nov. 11/64)
Most Goals, Season .... **65** Steve Yzerman (1988-89)
Most Assists, Season .... **90** Steve Yzerman (1988-89)
Most Points, Season .... **155** Steve Yzerman (1988-89; 65G, 90A)
Most PIM, Season .... **398** Bob Probert (1987-88)
Most Points, Defenseman, Season .... **80** Nicklas Lidstrom (2005-06; 16G, 64A)
Most Points, Center, Season .... **155** Steve Yzerman (1988-89; 65G, 90A)
Most Points, Right Wing, Season .... **103** Gordie Howe (1968-69; 44G, 59A)
Most Points, Left Wing, Season .... **105** John Ogrodnick (1984-85; 55G, 50A)
Most Points, Rookie, Season .... **87** Steve Yzerman (1983-84; 39G, 48A)
Most Shutouts, Season .... **12** Terry Sawchuk (1951-52), (1953-54), (1954-55) Glenn Hall (1955-56)
Most Goals, Game .... **6** Syd Howe (Feb. 3/44)
Most Assists, Game .... ***7** Billy Taylor (Mar. 16/47)
Most Points, Game .... **7** Carl Liscombe (Nov. 5/42; 3G, 4A), Don Grosso (Feb. 3/44; 1G, 6A), Billy Taylor (Mar. 16/47; 7A)

* NHL Record.

All-time Record vs. Other Clubs

Regular Season

	Total								At Home								On Road							
	GP	W	L	T	OL	GF	GA	PTS	GP	W	L	T	OL	GF	GA	PTS	GP	W	L	T	OL	GF	GA	PTS
Anaheim	79	48	21	7	3	241	185	106	39	30	6	3	0	136	85	63	40	18	15	4	3	105	100	43
Arizona	135	66	43	22	4	474	414	158	68	36	22	8	2	260	219	82	67	30	21	14	2	214	195	76
Boston	588	253	238	95	2	1759	1769	603	293	159	81	52	1	976	738	371	295	94	157	43	1	783	1031	232
Buffalo	124	57	52	13	2	415	420	129	63	39	18	5	1	233	175	84	61	18	34	8	1	182	245	45
Calgary	154	71	66	16	1	498	502	159	76	41	24	10	1	274	231	93	78	30	42	6	0	224	271	66
Carolina	73	38	27	8	0	239	214	84	37	22	8	7	0	140	100	51	36	16	19	1	0	99	114	33
Chicago	729	366	266	84	13	2267	2005	829	363	218	106	33	6	1235	911	475	366	148	160	51	7	1032	1094	354
Colorado	117	64	41	5	7	396	352	140	58	34	17	1	6	201	166	75	59	30	24	4	1	195	186	65
Columbus	80	52	19	1	8	254	182	113	39	28	7	0	4	133	93	60	41	24	12	1	4	121	89	53
Dallas	247	110	97	34	6	839	795	260	124	63	42	16	3	464	382	145	123	47	55	18	3	375	413	115
Edmonton	123	63	36	13	11	449	398	150	62	39	16	3	4	235	180	85	61	24	20	10	7	214	218	65
Florida	32	17	5	5	5	99	79	44	15	6	3	3	3	48	40	18	17	11	2	2	2	51	39	26
Los Angeles	194	85	80	27	2	672	674	199	97	50	34	13	0	372	318	113	97	35	46	14	2	300	356	86
Minnesota	51	33	9	3	6	169	120	75	26	17	4	1	4	100	63	39	25	16	5	2	2	69	57	36
Montreal	576	203	275	96	2	1475	1750	504	287	133	101	53	0	821	734	319	289	70	174	43	2	654	1016	185
Nashville	89	51	26	4	8	280	225	114	45	30	8	2	5	158	101	67	44	21	18	2	3	122	124	47
New Jersey	93	45	36	11	1	313	295	102	47	31	14	2	0	190	142	64	46	14	22	9	1	123	153	38
NY Islanders	103	48	47	6	2	329	337	104	51	27	21	2	1	174	149	57	52	21	26	4	1	155	188	47
NY Rangers	581	263	212	103	3	1772	1596	632	291	169	76	45	1	1023	714	384	290	94	136	58	2	749	882	248
Ottawa	33	20	11	1	1	107	87	42	16	9	6	0	1	52	41	19	17	11	5	1	0	55	46	23
Philadelphia	130	49	60	21	0	416	462	119	66	36	20	10	0	238	203	82	64	13	40	11	0	178	259	37
Pittsburgh	145	65	60	16	4	494	500	150	72	44	14	12	2	279	203	102	73	21	46	4	2	215	297	48
St. Louis	277	121	111	37	8	891	847	287	139	69	49	17	4	494	408	159	138	52	62	20	4	397	439	128
San Jose	86	52	26	4	4	306	234	112	42	30	8	1	3	152	85	64	44	22	18	3	1	154	149	48
Tampa Bay	41	27	9	2	3	152	102	59	20	15	2	1	2	70	37	33	21	12	7	1	1	82	65	26
Toronto	653	280	275	93	5	1853	1877	658	329	172	107	46	4	986	805	394	324	108	168	47	1	867	1072	264
Vancouver	166	87	55	18	6	591	525	198	83	51	20	8	4	330	236	114	83	36	35	10	2	261	289	84
Washington	107	47	42	16	2	348	352	112	54	25	17	11	1	182	156	62	53	22	25	5	1	166	196	50
Winnipeg	18	11	5	0	2	74	56	24	10	6	2	0	2	36	27	14	8	5	3	0	0	38	29	10
Defunct Clubs	282	125	103	54	0	794	682	304	141	76	40	25	0	430	307	177	141	49	63	29	0	364	375	127
Totals	**6106**	**2817**	**2353**	**815**	**121**	**18966**	**18036**	**6570**	**3053**	**1705**	**893**	**390**	**65**	**10422**	**8049**	**3865**	**3053**	**1112**	**1460**	**425**	**56**	**8544**	**9987**	**2705**

2014-15 Results

Oct.	9	Boston	2-1		10	at Washington	1-3
	11	Anaheim	2-3		13	at Buffalo	3-1
	15	Boston	2-3†		15	at St. Louis	3-2*
	17	at Toronto	4-1		17	Nashville	5-2
	18	Toronto	1-0*		18	Buffalo	6-4
	21	at Montreal	1-2*		20	Minnesota	5-4†
	23	Pittsburgh	4-3*		27	at Florida	5-4
	25	at Philadelphia	2-4		29	at Tampa Bay	1-5
	29	at Washington	4-2		31	NY Islanders	4-1
	31	Los Angeles	5-2	**Feb.**	5	at Colorado	3-0
Nov.	2	at Buffalo	2-3†		7	at Arizona	3-1
	4	at Ottawa	1-3		11	at Pittsburgh	1-4
	5	at NY Rangers	3-4*		14	Winnipeg	4-5†
	7	New Jersey	4-2		16	Montreal	0-2
	9	Tampa Bay	3-4†		18	at Chicago	3-2†
	14	Chicago	4-1		21	at Dallas	7-6*
	16	Montreal	1-4		23	at Anaheim	3-4†
	18	at Columbus	5-0		24	at Los Angeles	0-1
	20	at Winnipeg	4-3		26	at San Jose	3-2
	22	at Toronto	1-4		28	at Nashville	4-3
	24	Ottawa	4-3	**Mar.**	4	NY Rangers	2-1*
	26	Philadelphia	5-2		6	Calgary	2-5
	28	at New Jersey	5-4†		8	at Boston	3-5
	30	Vancouver	5-3		9	Edmonton	5-2
Dec.	2	Florida	3-4		12	Columbus	1-3
	4	Dallas	5-2		14	at Philadelphia	2-7
	6	NY Rangers	3-2		15	at Pittsburgh	5-1
	7	at Carolina	3-1		19	at Florida	1-3
	10	Toronto	1-2†		20	at Tampa Bay	1-3
	12	Florida	2-3†		22	St. Louis	2-1*
	13	at Toronto	1-4		24	Arizona	4-5*
	16	Columbus	0-1†		26	San Jose	4-6
	19	NY Islanders	1-2		28	Tampa Bay	4-0
	21	Colorado	1-2†		29	at NY Islanders	4-5
	23	Buffalo	6-3		31	Ottawa	1-2†
	27	at Ottawa	3-2*	**Apr.**	2	Boston	2-3
	29	at Boston	2-5		4	at Minnesota	3-2†
	31	New Jersey	3-1		5	Washington	1-2
Jan.	3	at Vancouver	1-4		7	Carolina	3-2
	6	at Edmonton	4-2		9	at Montreal	3-4*
	7	at Calgary	3-2		11	at Carolina	2-0

* – Overtime † – Shootout

Playoffs

	Series	W	L	GP	W	L	T	GF	GA	Last Mtg.	Rnd.	Result
Anaheim	6	4	2	32	18	14	0	93	78	2013	CQF	W 4-3
Arizona	4	4	0	23	16	7	0	88	56	2011	CQF	W 4-0
Boston	8	3	5	38	15	23	0	104	110	2014	FR	L 1-4
Calgary	3	2	1	14	8	6	0	38	26	2007	CQF	W 4-2
Carolina	1	1	0	5	4	1	0	14	7	2002	F	W 4-1
Chicago	16	7	9	81	38	43	0	224	236	2013	CSF	L 3-4
Colorado	6	3	3	34	17	17	0	97	88	2008	CSF	W 4-0
Columbus	1	1	0	4	4	0	0	18	7	2009	CQF	W 4-0
Dallas	4	4	0	24	16	8	0	72	50	2008	CF	W 4-2
Edmonton	3	0	3	16	4	12	0	43	58	2006	CQF	L 2-4
Los Angeles	2	1	1	10	6	4	0	32	21	2001	CQF	L 2-4
Montreal	12	7	5	62	29	33	0	149	161	1978	QF	L 1-4
Nashville	3	2	1	17	9	8	0	38	34	2012	CQF	L 1-4
New Jersey	1	0	1	4	0	4	0	7	16	1995	F	L 0-4
NY Rangers	5	4	1	23	13	10	0	57	49	1950	F	W 4-3
Philadelphia	1	1	0	4	4	0	0	16	6	1997	F	W 4-0
Pittsburgh	2	1	1	13	7	6	0	34	24	2009	F	L 3-4
St. Louis	7	5	2	40	24	16	0	125	103	2002	CSF	W 4-1
San Jose	5	2	3	29	15	14	0	99	69	2011	CSF	L 3-4
Tampa Bay	1	0	1	7	3	4	0	15	17	2015	FR	L 3-4
Toronto	23	11	12	117	59	58	0	321	311	1993	DSF	L 3-4
Vancouver	1	1	0	6	4	2	0	22	16	2002	CQF	W 4-2
Washington	1	1	0	4	4	0	0	13	7	1998	F	W 4-0
Defunct Clubs	4	3	1	10	7	2	1	21	13			
Totals	**120**	**68**	**52**	**617**	**324**	**292**	**1**	**1740**	**1563**			

Playoff Results 2015-2011

Year	Round	Opponent	Result	GF	GA
2015	FR	Tampa Bay	L 3-4	15	17
2014	FR	Boston	L 1-4	6	14
2013	CSF	Chicago	L 3-4	15	16
	CQF	Anaheim	W 4-3	18	21
2012	CQF	Nashville	L 1-4	9	13
2011	CSF	San Jose	L 3-4	18	18
	CQF	Phoenix	W 4-0	18	10

Abbreviations: Round: F – Final; **CF** – conference final; **CSF** – conference semi-final; **CQF** – conference quarter-final; **FR** – first round; **DSF** – division semi-final; **QF** – quarter-final.

Calgary totals include Atlanta Flames, 1972-73 to 1979-80.
Carolina totals include Hartford, 1979-80 to 1996-97.
Colorado totals include Quebec, 1979-80 to 1994-95.
Dallas totals include Minnesota North Stars, 1967-68 to 1992-93.
New Jersey totals include Kansas City, 1974-75, 1975-76, and Colorado Rockies, 1976-77 to 1981-82.
Phoenix totals include Winnipeg, 1979-80 to 1995-96.
Winnipeg totals include Atlanta Thrashers, 1999-2000 to 2010-11.

NHL Draft Selections 2015-2001

Name in bold denotes played in NHL.

2015
Pick
- 19 Evgeni Svechnikov
- 73 Vili Saarijarvi
- 110 Joren Van Pottelberghe
- 140 Chase Pearson
- 170 Patrick Holway
- 200 Adam Marsh

2014
Pick
- 15 **Dylan Larkin**
- 63 Dominic Turgeon
- 106 Christoffer Ehn
- 136 Chase Perry
- 166 Julius Vahatalo
- 196 Axel Holmstrom
- 201 Alexander Kadeykin

2013
Pick
- 20 Anthony Mantha
- 48 Zach Nastasiuk
- 58 Tyler Bertuzzi
- 79 Mattias Janmark
- 109 David Pope
- 139 Mitchell Wheaton
- 169 Marc McNulty
- 199 Hampus Melen

2012
Pick
- 49 Martin Frk
- 80 Jake Paterson
- 110 Andreas Athanasiou
- 140 Mike McKee
- 170 James De Haas
- 200 Rasmus Bodin

2011
Pick
- 35 **Tomas Jurco**
- 48 **Xavier Ouellet**
- 55 **Ryan Sproul**
- 85 Alan Quine
- 115 Marek Tvrdon
- 145 Philippe Hudon
- 146 Mattias Backman
- 175 Richard Nedomlel
- 205 **Alexey Marchenko**

2010
Pick
- 21 **Riley Sheahan**
- 51 **Calle Jarnkrok**
- 81 Louis-Marc Aubry
- 111 **Teemu Pulkkinen**
- 141 **Petr Mrazek**
- 171 Brooks Macek
- 201 Ben Marshall

2009
Pick
- 32 **Landon Ferraro**
- 60 **Tomas Tatar**
- 75 **Andrej Nestrasil**
- 90 Gleason Fournier
- 150 Nick Jensen
- 180 **Mitch Callahan**
- 210 **Adam Almqvist**

2008
Pick
- 30 **Tom McCollum**
- 91 Max Nicastro
- 121 **Gustav Nyquist**
- 151 Julien Cayer
- 181 Stephen Johnston
- 211 Jesper Samuelsson

2007
Pick
- 27 **Brendan Smith**
- 88 **Joakim Andersson**
- 148 Randy Cameron
- 178 Zack Torquato
- 208 Bryan Rufenach

2006
Pick
- 41 **Cory Emmerton**
- 47 **Shawn Matthias**
- 62 Dick Axelsson
- 92 Daniel Larsson
- 182 **Jan Mursak**
- 191 Nick Oslund
- 212 Logan Pyett

2005
Pick
- 19 **Jakub Kindl**
- 42 **Justin Abdelkader**
- 80 Christofer Lofberg
- 103 **Mattias Ritola**
- 132 **Darren Helm**
- 137 Johan Ryno
- 151 Jeff May
- 175 Juho Mielonen
- 214 Bretton Stamler

2004
Pick
- 97 **Johan Franzen**
- 128 Evan McGrath
- 151 Sergei Kolosov
- 162 Tyler Haskins
- 192 Anton Axelsson
- 226 Steven Covington
- 257 Gennady Stolyarov
- 290 Nils Backstrom

2003
Pick
- 64 **Jimmy Howard**
- 132 **Kyle Quincey**
- 164 Ryan Oulahen
- 170 Andreas Sundin
- 194 Stefan Blom
- 226 Tomas Kollar
- 258 Vladimir Kutny
- 289 Mikael Johansson

2002
Pick
- 58 **Jiri Hudler**
- 63 **Tomas Fleischmann**
- 95 **Valtteri Filppula**
- 131 Johan Berggren
- 166 Logan Koopmans
- 197 Jimmy Cuddihy
- 229 **Derek Meech**
- 260 Pierre-Olivier Beaulieu
- 262 Christian Soderstrom
- 291 **Jonathan Ericsson**

2001
Pick
- 62 Igor Grigorenko
- 121 **Drew MacIntyre**
- 129 Miroslav Blatak
- 157 Andreas Jamtin
- 195 Nick Pannoni
- 258 **Dmitri Bykov**
- 288 Francois Senez

General Managers' History

Art Duncan, 1926-27; Jack Adams, 1927-28 to 1961-62; Sid Abel, 1962-63 to 1969-70; Sid Abel and Ned Harkness, 1970-71; Ned Harkness, 1971-72, 1972-73; Ned Harkness and Jimmy Skinner, 1973-74; Alex Delvecchio, 1974-75, 1975-76; Alex Delvecchio and Ted Lindsay, 1976-77; Ted Lindsay, 1977-78 to 1979-80; Jimmy Skinner, 1980-81, 1981-82; Jim Devellano, 1982-83 to 1989-90; Bryan Murray, 1990-91 to 1993-94; Jim Devellano (Senior Vice President/Hockey), 1994-95 to 1996-97; Ken Holland, 1997-98 to date.

Ken Holland

Executive Vice President and General Manager

Born: Vernon, BC, November 10, 1955.

Ken Holland has served in the Red Wings front office since 1985, and has been the club's general manager since July 18, 1997 after serving three seasons as the club's assistant general manager. He has established himself as one of the most innovative and aggressive GMs in the National Hockey League. Detroit's Stanley Cup victory in 2008 marked the team's third championship under his leadership and he has a gold medal as part of the management group for Team Canada at the 2014 Sochi Winter Olympics. The Red Wings have made the playoffs for 24 consecutive seasons, the longest current streak in pro sports.

Holland oversees all aspects of hockey operations including all matters relating to player personnel, development, contract negotiations and player movements, though he now takes a less prominent role in the NHL draft than he did during his seven years as the club's director of amateur scouting.

At the conclusion of his playing days as a goaltender, spending most of his pro career at the American Hockey League level, Holland began his off-ice career in 1985 as a western Canada scout followed by five years as an amateur scouting director before promotions led to his current position as general manager.

A native of Vernon, British Columbia, Holland played in the junior ranks for Medicine Hat (WHL) in 1974-75. He was Toronto's 13th pick (188th overall) in the 1975 draft but never saw action with the Maple Leafs. Holland twice signed with NHL teams as a free agent — in 1980 with Hartford and 1983 with Detroit. He spent most of his pro career with AHL clubs in Binghamton and Springfield, along with Adirondack, but did appear in four NHL games, making his debut with Hartford in 1980-81 and playing three contests for Detroit in 1983-84.

Club Directory

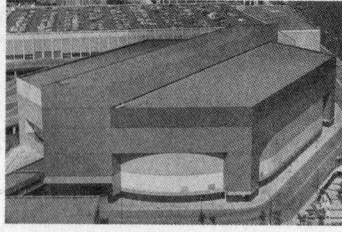

Joe Louis Arena

Detroit Red Wings
Joe Louis Arena
19 Steve Yzerman Drive
Detroit, MI 48226
Phone **313/471-7000**
FAX PR: 313/567-0296
Media Hotline: 313/471-7599
www.detroitredwings.com
Capacity: 20,027

Owner/Governor	Mike Ilitch
Owner/Secretary-Treasurer	Marian Ilitch
President and CEO, Ilitch Holdings/ Alternate Governor Red Wings	Christopher Ilitch
Senior Vice President/Alternate Governor	Jim Devellano
Executive Vice President/General Manager	Ken Holland
Assistant General Manager	Ryan Martin
Special Assistant to the General Manager	Kris Draper
Director of Player Development	Jiri Fischer
President and CEO, Olympia Entertainment/ Alternate Governor Red Wings	Tom Wilson
Vice President Olympia Entertainment/ General Counsel Red Wings	Robert E. Carr
Head Coach	Jeff Blashill
Assistant Coach	Tony Granato
Assistant Coach	Pat Ferschweiler
Assistant Coach	Chris Chelios
Video Coach	Dave Noel-Bernier
Goaltending Coach	Jim Bedard
Director of Pro Scouting	Mark Howe
Pro Scouts	Glenn Merkosky, Bruce Haralson, Kirk Maltby, Archie Henderson
Director of Amateur Scouting	Tyler Wright
Chief Amateur Scout	Jeff Finley
Amateur Scouts	Dave Kolb, Mario Marois, Andrew Dickson, Kelly Harper, Len Quesnelle, Sam Lites, Marty Stein
Director of European Scouting	Hakan Andersson
European Scouts	Vladimir Havluj, Nikolai Vakourov
Vice President of Finance	Paul MacDonald
Executive Assistant	Kim Brodie
General Accountant	Bridget Merritt
Team Travel Coordinator	Julie Dailey
Head Equipment Manager	Paul Boyer
Assistant Equipment Manager	John Remejes
Head Athletic Therapist	Piet Van Zant
Assistant Athletic Therapist	Russ Baumann
Team Masseurs	Sergei Tchekmarev, Ainars Treiguts
Strength and Conditioning Coach	Mike Kadar
Director of Public Relations	Todd Beam
Public Relations Coordinator	Kyle Kujawa
Communications Coordinator	Alex DiFilippo
Community Relations Coordinator	Anne Bowlby
Detroit Red Wings Foundation Coordinator	Kelsey Rentner
Medical Director	Dr. Donald Weaver
Team Physicians	Dr. Anthony Colucci, Dr. Doug Plagens
Team Dentists	Dr. Jeffrey Boogren, Dr. Randy Freij
Team Photographer	Dave Reginek
Radio Announcers, 97.1 The Ticket	Ken Kal, Paul Woods
Television Announcers, FOX Sports Detroit	Ken Daniels, Mickey Redmond

Coaching History

Art Duncan and Duke Keats, 1926-27; Jack Adams, 1927-28 to 1946-47; Tommy Ivan, 1947-48 to 1953-54; Jimmy Skinner, 1954-55 to 1956-57; Jimmy Skinner and Sid Abel, 1957-58; Sid Abel, 1958-59 to 1967-68; Bill Gadsby, 1968-69; Bill Gadsby and Sid Abel, 1969-70; Ned Harkness and Doug Barkley, 1970-71; Doug Barkley and Johnny Wilson, 1971-72; Johnny Wilson, 1972-73; Ted Garvin and Alex Delvecchio, 1973-74; Alex Delvecchio, 1974-75; Doug Barkley and Alex Delvecchio, 1975-76; Alex Delvecchio and Larry Wilson, 1976-77; Bobby Kromm, 1977-78, 1978-79; Bobby Kromm and Ted Lindsay, 1979-80; Ted Lindsay and Wayne Maxner, 1980-81; Wayne Maxner and Billy Dea, 1981-82; Nick Polano, 1982-83 to 1984-85; Harry Neale and Brad Park, 1985-86; Jacques Demers, 1986-87 to 1989-90; Bryan Murray, 1990-91 to 1992-93; Scotty Bowman, 1993-94 to 1997-98; Dave Lewis, Barry Smith (co-coaches) and Scotty Bowman, 1998-99; Scotty Bowman, 1999-2000 to 2001-02; Dave Lewis, 2002-03 to 2004-05; Mike Babcock, 2005-06 to 2014-15; Jeff Blashill, 2015-16.

Captains' History

Art Duncan, 1926-27; Reg Noble, 1927-28 to 1929-30; George Hay, 1930-31; Carson Cooper, 1931-32; Larry Aurie, 1932-33; Herbie Lewis, 1933-34; Ebbie Goodfellow, 1934-35; Doug Young, 1935-36 to 1937-38; Ebbie Goodfellow, 1938-39 to 1940-41; Ebbie Goodfellow and Syd Howe, 1941-42; Sid Abel, 1942-43; Mud Bruneteau, Flash Hollett, 1943-44; Flash Hollett, 1944-45; Flash Hollett and Sid Abel, 1945-46; Sid Abel, 1946-47 to 1951-52; Ted Lindsay, 1952-53 to 1955-56; Red Kelly, 1956-57, 1957-58; Gordie Howe, 1958-59 to 1961-62; Alex Delvecchio, 1962-63 to 1972-73; Alex Delvecchio, Nick Libett, Red Berenson, Gary Bergman, Ted Harris, Mickey Redmond and Larry Johnston, 1973-74; Marcel Dionne, 1974-75; Danny Grant and Terry Harper, 1975-76; Danny Grant and Dennis Polonich, 1976-77; Dan Maloney and Dennis Hextall, 1977-78; Dennis Hextall, Nick Libett and Paul Woods, 1978-79; Dale McCourt, 1979-80; Errol Thompson and Reed Larson, 1980-81; Reed Larson, 1981-82; Danny Gare, 1982-83 to 1985-86; Steve Yzerman, 1986-87 to 2005-06; Nicklas Lidstrom, 2006-07 to 2011-12; Henrik Zetterberg, 2012-13 to date.

Edmonton Oilers

Key Off-Season Signings/Acquisitions

2015

April 13 • Re-signed RW **Nail Yakupov**.
24 • Named **Peter Chiarelli** president of hockey operations and general manager.
May 19 • Named **Todd McLellan** head coach.
June 25 • Named **Jay Woodcroft** and **Jim Johnson** assistant coaches.
26 • Acquired D **Griffin Reinhart** from NY Islanders for a 1st- and 2nd-round choice in the 2015 NHL Draft.
27 • Acquired G **Cam Talbot** and a 7th-round choice in the 2015 NHL Draft from NY Rangers for a 2nd-, 3rd- and 7th-round choice in 2015.
27 • Acquired D **Eric Gryba** from Ottawa for LW **Travis Ewanyk** and a 4th-round choice in the 2015 NHL Draft.
30 • Acquired LW **Lauri Korpikoski** from Arizona for C **Boyd Gordon**.
July 1 • Signed D **Andrej Sekera** and C **Mark Letestu**.
14 • Named **Ian Herbers** assistant coach.
15 • Re-signed D **Justin Schultz**.
16 • Re-signed RW **Tyler Pitlick**.

2014-15 Results: 24w-44L-7OTL-7SOL 62PTS
6TH, Pacific Division • 13TH, Western Conference

2015-16 Schedule

Oct.					
Thu.	8	at St. Louis	Fri.	8	Tampa Bay
Sat.	10	at Nashville	Sun.	10	Florida
Tue.	13	at Dallas	Tue.	13	at Arizona
Thu.	15	St. Louis	Thu.	14	at San Jose
Sat.	17	at Calgary	Sat.	16	Calgary
Sun.	18	at Vancouver	Mon.	18	at Florida
Wed.	21	Detroit	Tue.	19	at Tampa Bay
Fri.	23	Washington	Thu.	21	at Dallas
Sun.	25	Los Angeles	Sat.	23	Nashville
Tue.	27	at Minnesota	**Feb.** Tue.	2	Columbus
Thu.	29	Montreal	Thu.	4	at Ottawa
Sat.	31	Calgary	Sat.	6	at Montreal*
Nov. Tue.	3	Philadelphia	Sun.	7	at NY Islanders*
Fri.	6	Pittsburgh	Tue.	9	at New Jersey
Sun.	8	at Chicago	Thu.	11	Toronto
Wed.	11	at Anaheim	Sat.	13	Winnipeg
Thu.	12	at Arizona	Tue.	16	Anaheim
Sat.	14	at Los Angeles	Thu.	18	Minnesota
Wed.	18	Chicago	Sat.	20	Colorado
Fri.	20	New Jersey	Tue.	23	Ottawa
Mon.	23	at Washington	Thu.	25	at Los Angeles
Wed.	25	at Carolina	Fri.	26	at Anaheim
Fri.	27	at Detroit	Sun.	28	NY Islanders
Sat.	28	at Pittsburgh	**Mar.** Tue.	1	at Buffalo
Mon.	30	at Toronto	Thu.	3	at Philadelphia
Dec. Wed.	2	Boston	Fri.	4	at Columbus
Fri.	4	Dallas	Sun.	6	at Winnipeg
Sun.	6	Buffalo	Tue.	8	San Jose
Wed.	9	San Jose	Thu.	10	at Minnesota
Fri.	11	NY Rangers	Sat.	12	Arizona
Mon.	14	at Boston	Mon.	14	Nashville
Tue.	15	at NY Rangers	Wed.	16	St. Louis
Thu.	17	at Chicago	Fri.	18	Vancouver
Sat.	19	at Colorado	Sun.	20	Colorado
Mon.	21	Winnipeg	Tue.	22	at Arizona
Sat.	26	at Vancouver	Thu.	24	at San Jose
Sun.	27	at Calgary	Sat.	26	at Los Angeles
Tue.	29	Los Angeles	Mon.	28	Anaheim
Thu.	31	Anaheim	**Apr.** Sat.	2	Calgary
Jan. Sat.	2	Arizona*	Wed.	6	Vancouver
Mon.	4	Carolina	Sat.	9	at Vancouver

* Denotes afternoon game.

Retired Numbers

3	Al Hamilton	1972-1980
7	Paul Coffey	1980-1987
9	Glenn Anderson	1980-91, 1996
11	Mark Messier	1980-1991
17	Jari Kurri	1980-1990
31	Grant Fuhr	1981-1991
99	Wayne Gretzky	1979-1988

PACIFIC DIVISION
37th NHL Season
Franchise date: June 22, 1979

Year-by-Year Record

		Home				Road				Overall							Div. Fin.	Conf. Fin.	Playoff Result
Season	GP	W	L	T	OL	W	L	T	OL	W	L	T	OL	GF	GA	Pts.			
2014-15	82	15	23	....	3	9	21	....	11	24	44	....	14	198	283	62	6th, Pac.	13th, West	Out of Playoffs
2013-14	82	16	22	....	3	13	22	....	6	29	44	....	9	203	270	67	7th, Pac.	14th, West	Out of Playoffs
2012-13	48	9	11	....	4	10	11	....	3	19	22	....	7	125	134	45	3rd, NW	12th, West	Out of Playoffs
2011-12	*82	18	17	....	6	14	23	....	4	32	40	....	10	212	239	74	5th, NW	14th, West	Out of Playoffs
2010-11	82	13	22	....	6	12	23	....	6	25	45	....	12	193	269	62	5th, NW	15th, West	Out of Playoffs
2009-10	82	18	19	....	4	9	28	....	8	27	47	....	8	214	284	62	5th, NW	15th, West	Out of Playoffs
2008-09	82	18	17	....	6	20	18	....	3	38	35	....	9	234	248	85	4th, NW	11th, West	Out of Playoffs
2007-08	82	23	17	....	1	18	18	....	5	41	35	....	6	235	251	88	4th, NW	9th, West	Out of Playoffs
2006-07	82	19	19	....	3	13	24	....	4	32	43	....	7	195	248	71	5th, NW	12th, West	Out of Playoffs
2005-06	82	20	15	....	6	21	13	....	7	41	28	....	13	256	251	95	3rd, NW	8th, West	Lost Final
2004-05	....																		
2003-04	82	22	12	4	3	14	17	8	2	36	29	12	5	221	208	89	4th, NW	9th, West	Out of Playoffs
2002-03	82	20	12	5	4	16	20	4	1	36	26	11	9	231	230	92	4th, NW	8th, West	Lost Conf. Quarter-Final
2001-02	82	23	14	4	0	15	14	8	4	38	28	12	4	205	182	92	3rd, NW	9th, West	Out of Playoffs
2000-01	82	23	9	7	2	16	19	5	1	39	28	12	3	243	222	93	2nd, NW	6th, West	Lost Conf. Quarter-Final
1999-2000	82	18	11	9	3	14	15	7	....	32	26	16	8	226	212	88	2nd, NW	8th, West	Lost Conf. Quarter-Final
1998-99	82	17	19	5	....	16	18	7	....	33	37	12	....	230	226	78	3rd, NW	8th, West	Lost Conf. Quarter-Final
1997-98	82	20	16	5	....	15	21	5	....	35	37	10	....	215	224	80	3rd, Pac.	7th, West	Lost Conf. Semi-Final
1996-97	82	21	16	4	....	15	21	5	....	36	37	9	....	252	247	81	3rd, Pac.	7th, West	Lost Conf. Semi-Final
1995-96	82	15	21	5	....	15	23	3	....	30	44	8	....	240	304	68	5th, Pac.	10th, West	Out of Playoffs
1994-95	48	11	12	1	....	6	15	3	....	17	27	4	....	136	183	38	5th, Pac.	11th, West	Out of Playoffs
1993-94	84	17	22	3	....	8	23	11	....	25	45	14	....	261	305	64	6th, Pac.	11th, West	Out of Playoffs
1992-93	84	16	21	5	....	10	29	3	....	26	50	8	....	242	337	60	5th, Smythe		Out of Playoffs
1991-92	80	22	13	5	....	14	21	5	....	36	34	10	....	295	297	82	3rd, Smythe		Lost Conf. Final
1990-91	80	22	15	3	....	15	22	3	....	37	37	6	....	272	272	80	3rd, Smythe		Lost Conf. Final
1989-90	80	**23**	**11**	**6**	....	**15**	**17**	**8**	....	**38**	**28**	**14**	....	**315**	**283**	**90**	**2nd, Smythe**		**Won Stanley Cup**
1988-89	80	21	16	3	....	17	18	5	....	38	34	8	....	325	306	84	3rd, Smythe		Lost Div. Semi-Final
1987-88	80	**28**	**8**	**4**	....	**16**	**17**	**7**	....	**44**	**25**	**11**	....	**363**	**288**	**99**	**2nd, Smythe**		**Won Stanley Cup**
1986-87	80	**29**	**6**	**5**	....	**21**	**18**	**1**	....	**50**	**24**	**6**	....	**372**	**284**	**106**	**1st, Smythe**		**Won Stanley Cup**
1985-86	80	32	6	2	....	24	11	5	....	56	17	7	....	426	310	119	1st, Smythe		Lost Div. Final
1984-85	80	**26**	**7**	**7**	....	**23**	**13**	**4**	....	**49**	**20**	**11**	....	**401**	**298**	**109**	**1st, Smythe**		**Won Stanley Cup**
1983-84	80	**31**	**5**	**4**	....	**26**	**13**	**1**	....	**57**	**18**	**5**	....	**446**	**314**	**119**	**1st, Smythe**		**Won Stanley Cup**
1982-83	80	25	9	6	....	22	12	6	....	47	21	12	....	424	315	106	1st, Smythe		Lost Final
1981-82	80	31	5	4	....	17	12	11	....	48	17	15	....	417	295	111	1st, Smythe		Lost Div. Semi-Final
1980-81	80	17	13	10	....	12	22	6	....	29	35	16	....	328	327	74	4th, Smythe		Lost Quarter-Final
1979-80	80	17	14	9	....	11	25	4	....	28	39	13	....	301	322	69	4th, Smythe		Lost Prelim. Round

Jordan Eberle led Edmonton in scoring for the third time in his five seasons with the club. After the 2014-15 season, he and Oilers teammate Taylor Hall were among the top scorers when Canada won gold at the World Championships.

2015-16 Player Personnel

FORWARDS	HT	WT	*Age	Place of Birth	S	2014-15 Club
DRAISAITL, Leon	6-1	210	19	Cologne, Germany	L	Edmonton-Kelowna
EBERLE, Jordan	5-11	180	25	Regina, SK	R	Edmonton
GAZDIC, Luke	6-3	240	26	Toronto, ON	L	Edmonton-Oklahoma City
HALL, Taylor	6-1	201	23	Calgary, AB	L	Edmonton
HENDRICKS, Matt	6-0	211	34	Blaine, MN	L	Edmonton
KLINKHAMMER, Rob	6-3	220	29	Lethbridge, AB	L	Ari-Pit-Edm
KORPIKOSKI, Lauri	6-1	205	29	Turku, Finland	L	Arizona
LANDER, Anton	6-0	194	24	Sundsvall, Sweden	L	Edmonton-Oklahoma City
LETESTU, Mark	5-10	199	30	Elk Point, AB	R	Columbus
McDAVID, Connor	6-1	195	18	Richmond Hill, ON	L	Erie
NUGENT-HOPKINS, Ryan	6-1	180	22	Burnaby, BC	L	Edmonton
POULIOT, Benoit	6-3	197	29	Alfred, ON	L	Edmonton
PURCELL, Teddy	6-3	203	30	St. Johns, NL	R	Edmonton
YAKUPOV, Nail	5-11	186	22	Nizhnekamsk, Russia	L	Edmonton
DEFENSEMEN						
FAYNE, Mark	6-3	210	28	Nashua, NH	R	Edmonton
FERENCE, Andrew	5-11	187	36	Edmonton, AB	L	Edmonton
GRYBA, Eric	6-4	225	27	Saskatoon, SK	R	Ottawa
KLEFBOM, Oscar	6-3	204	22	Karlstad, Sweden	L	Edmonton-Oklahoma City
NIKITIN, Nikita	6-4	223	29	Omsk, USSR	L	Edmonton
REINHART, Griffin	6-4	202	21	North Vancouver, BC	L	NY Islanders-Bridgeport
SCHULTZ, Justin	6-2	188	25	Kelowna, BC	R	Edmonton
SEKERA, Andrej	6-0	201	29	Bojnice, Czech.	L	Carolina-Los Angeles

GOALTENDERS	HT	WT	*Age	Place of Birth	C	2014-15 Club
SCRIVENS, Ben	6-2	193	29	Spruce Grove, AB	L	Edmonton
TALBOT, Cam	6-3	205	28	Caledonia, ON	L	NY Rangers

* – Age at start of 2015-16 season

Captains' History

Ron Chipperfield, 1979-80; Blair MacDonald and Lee Fogolin, Jr., 1980-81; Lee Fogolin, Jr., 1981-82, 1982-83; Wayne Gretzky, 1983-84 to 1987-88; Mark Messier, 1988-89 to 1990-91; Kevin Lowe, 1991-92; Craig MacTavish, 1992-93, 1993-94; Shayne Corson, 1994-95; Kelly Buchberger, 1995-96 to 1998-99; Doug Weight, 1999-2000, 2000-01; Jason Smith, 2001-02 to 2006-07; Ethan Moreau, 2007-08 to 2009-10; Shawn Horcoff, 2010-11 to 2012-13; Andrew Ference, 2013-14 to date.

Coaching History

Glen Sather, 1979-80; Bryan Watson and Glen Sather, 1980-81; Glen Sather, 1981-82 to 1988-89; John Muckler, 1989-90, 1990-91; Ted Green, 1991-92, 1992-93; Ted Green and Glen Sather, 1993-94; George Burnett and Ron Low, 1994-95; Ron Low, 1995-96 to 1998-99; Kevin Lowe, 1999-2000; Craig MacTavish, 2000-01 to 2008-09; Pat Quinn, 2009-10; Tom Renney, 2010-11, 2011-12; Ralph Krueger, 2012-13; Dallas Eakins, 2013-14; Dallas Eakins, Craig MacTavish and Todd Nelson, 2014-15; Todd McLellan, 2015-16.

Todd McLellan

Head Coach

Born: Melville, SK, October 3, 1967.

The Edmonton Oilers announced on May 19, 2015 that Todd McLellan had been appointed as the club's new head coach. McLellan becomes the 14th head coach in Oilers franchise history. He was hired after serving as the head coach of Team Canada at the 2015 World Hockey Championship, leading Canada to their first gold medal since 2007 with an undefeated record of 10-0.

McLellan spent the previous seven seasons as head coach of the San Jose Sharks, posting a record of 311-163-66 in 540 games. During that span, McLellan led the Sharks to six playoff appearances, four 40-plus win seasons, three 100-point seasons, captured the Presidents' Trophy (2009), three Pacific Division titles and made back-to-back appearances in the Western Conference Final (2010, 2011). No head coach in NHL history has won more games in their first four seasons behind the bench than the 195 collected by Todd McLellan. In, 2010, he became just the third coach in NHL history to record 50-plus wins in his first two seasons as head coach. He was named a finalist for the NHL's Jack Adams Award in 2008-09 and became just the sixth NHL coach (first since 1990) to lead his team to the Presidents' Trophy in his first season as a head coach.

Prior to joining San Jose, McLellan spent three seasons as an assistant coach with the Detroit Red Wings. One of McLellan's key responsibilities was Detroit's power play, which finished first in the NHL in 2005-06 (22.1) and third in 2007-08 (20.7). McLellan won a Stanley Cup in 2008 with the Red Wings, as well as two Presidents' Trophies (2006, 2008). Before entering the NHL coaching ranks, McLellan spent four seasons as a head coach with the American Hockey League's Houston Aeros, capturing the 2003 Calder Cup Championship and being named Minor coach of the year by The Hockey News. He was also selected to coach two AHL All-Star Games during his tenure in Houston. McLellan also spent the 2000-01 season as head coach of the Cleveland Lumberjacks of the International Hockey League.

McLellan spent six seasons in junior hockey as head coach with the Swift Current Broncos of the Western Hockey League, where he also served as the general manager in his final four seasons. He was named the WHL executive of the year in 1997 and WHL coach of the year in 2000. The Broncos also captured division titles in 1996 and 2000 under McLellan. He played his junior hockey in the WHL with the Saskatoon Blades and was drafted by the New York Islanders in the fifth round (106th overall) in the 1986 NHL Draft. He played parts of two seasons with Springfield in the AHL and played in five games with the Islanders in 1987-88, posting two points (one goal, one assist) before a shoulder injury ended his career.

2014-15 Scoring

* – rookie

Regular Season

Pos	#	Player	Team	GP	G	A	Pts	TOI	+/–	PIM	PP	SH	GW	S	S%
C	14	Jordan Eberle	EDM	81	24	39	63	19:02	–16	24	6	0	2	183	13.1
C	93	Ryan Nugent-Hopkins	EDM	76	24	32	56	20:38	–12	25	2	0	2	189	12.7
L	4	Taylor Hall	EDM	53	14	24	38	19:13	–1	40	3	0	0	158	8.9
L	67	Benoit Pouliot	EDM	58	19	15	34	16:37	–1	28	4	1	3	105	18.1
R	16	Teddy Purcell	EDM	82	12	22	34	17:09	–33	24	5	0	0	146	8.2
R	10	Nail Yakupov	EDM	81	14	19	33	15:26	–35	18	5	0	1	191	7.3
C	8	Derek Roy	NSH	26	1	9	10	13:30	0	2	0	0	0	35	2.9
			EDM	46	11	11	22	16:53	–13	22	4	0	2	78	14.1
			Total	72	12	20	32	15:40	–13	24	4	0	2	113	10.6
D	19	Justin Schultz	EDM	81	6	25	31	22:36	–17	12	0	0	1	122	4.9
C	51	Anton Lander	EDM	38	6	14	20	15:00	–12	14	4	0	2	61	9.8
D	84	* Oscar Klefbom	EDM	60	2	18	20	21:59	–21	4	0	0	0	98	2.0
C	23	Matt Hendricks	EDM	71	8	8	16	13:09	–14	76	0	1	0	103	7.8
D	21	Andrew Ference	EDM	70	3	11	14	18:52	–17	39	0	0	0	58	5.2
C	27	Boyd Gordon	EDM	68	6	7	13	13:19	–5	17	1	1	1	65	9.2
R	28	Matt Fraser	BOS	24	3	0	3	10:31	–5	7	0	0	1	29	10.3
			EDM	36	5	4	9	11:40	–11	10	1	0	0	63	7.9
			Total	60	8	4	12	11:13	–16	17	1	0	1	92	8.7
D	86	Nikita Nikitin	EDM	42	4	6	10	19:38	–12	12	2	0	1	80	5.0
C	12	Rob Klinkhammer	ARI	19	3	0	3	11:33	3	4	0	0	0	23	13.0
			PIT	10	1	2	3	11:07	0	0	0	0	0	10	10.0
			EDM	40	1	2	3	11:04	–7	23	0	0	0	31	3.2
			Total	69	5	4	9	11:13	–4	27	0	0	0	64	7.8
C	29	* Leon Draisaitl	EDM	37	2	7	9	12:41	–17	4	1	0	1	49	4.1
D	5	Mark Fayne	EDM	74	2	6	8	17:56	–21	14	0	0	0	78	2.6
C	58	* Andrew Miller	EDM	9	1	5	6	13:45	–2	0	0	0	0	14	7.1
D	85	Martin Marincin	EDM	41	1	4	5	18:38	–4	16	0	0	0	38	2.6
R	13	Steven Pinizzotto	EDM	18	2	2	4	7:55	1	30	0	0	0	15	13.3
L	6	Jesse Joensuu	EDM	20	2	2	4	10:37	–8	14	0	1	0	18	11.1
L	20	Luke Gazdic	EDM	40	2	1	3	7:23	–4	43	0	0	0	26	7.7
D	24	Brad Hunt	EDM	11	1	2	3	19:29	–6	0	1	0	0	20	5.0
R	62	* Iiro Pakarinen	EDM	17	1	2	3	10:08	–4	2	0	0	0	34	2.9
C	15	* Tyler Pitlick	EDM	17	2	0	2	12:26	–3	4	0	0	1	18	11.1
L	48	Ryan Hamilton	EDM	16	1	1	2	13:12	–8	6	1	0	0	12	8.3
D	87	* David Musil	EDM	4	0	2	2	19:48	–2	2	0	0	0	3	0.0
D	88	* Brandon Davidson	EDM	12	1	0	1	15:08	–5	0	0	0	0	7	14.3
D	82	* Jordan Oesterle	EDM	6	0	1	1	14:41	–4	0	0	0	0	7	0.0
D	22	Keith Aulie	EDM	31	0	1	1	14:18	–3	66	0	0	0	25	0.0
L	70	* Curtis Hamilton	EDM	1	0	0	0	8:01	0	5	0	0	0	0	0.0
C	39	* Bogdan Yakimov	EDM	1	0	0	0	11:19	–1	0	0	0	0	1	0.0
D	25	* Darnell Nurse	EDM	2	0	0	0	16:59	–2	0	0	0	0	2	0.0
R	41	Will Acton	EDM	3	0	0	0	10:42	–2	5	0	0	0	2	0.0

Goaltending

No.	Goaltender	GPI	Mins	Avg	W	L	OT	EN	SO	GA	SA	Sv%	G	A	PIM
1	* Laurent Brossoit	1	60	2.00	0	1	0	1	0	2	51	.961	0	0	0
32	Richard Bachman	7	317	2.84	3	2	0	1	1	15	168	.911	0	0	0
30	Ben Scrivens	57	3228	3.16	15	26	11	7	1	170	1542	.890	0	1	4
35	Viktor Fasth	26	1336	3.41	6	15	3	1	0	76	681	.888	0	0	0
34	* Tyler Bunz	1	20	9.00	0	0	0	0	0	3	12	.750	0	0	0
	Totals	**82**	**5004**	**3.31**	**24**	**44**	**14**	**10**	**2**	**276**	**2464**	**.888**			

Coaching Record

			Regular Season				Playoffs			
Season	Team	League	GC	W	L	O/T	GC	W	L	T
1994-95	Swift Current	WHL	72	31	34	7	6	2	4	....
1995-96	Swift Current	WHL	72	36	31	5	6	2	4	....
1996-97	Swift Current	WHL	72	44	23	5	10	4	4	....
1997-98	Swift Current	WHL	72	44	19	9	12	7	5	....
1998-99	Swift Current	WHL	72	34	32	6	6	2	4	....
99-2000	Swift Current	WHL	72	47	18	7	12	6	6	....
2000-01	Cleveland	IHL	82	43	32	7	4	0	4	....
2001-02	Houston	AHL	80	39	26	15	14	8	6	....
2002-03	Houston	AHL	80	47	23	10	23	15	8	....
2003-04	Houston	AHL	80	28	34	18	2	0	2	....
2004-05	Houston	AHL	80	40	28	12	5	1	4	....
2008-09	**San Jose**	**NHL**	**82**	**53**	**18**	**11**	**6**	**2**	**4**	....
2009-10	**San Jose**	**NHL**	**82**	**51**	**20**	**11**	**15**	**8**	**7**	....
2010-11	**San Jose**	**NHL**	**82**	**48**	**25**	**9**	**18**	**9**	**9**	....
2011-12	**San Jose**	**NHL**	**82**	**43**	**29**	**10**	**5**	**1**	**4**	....
2012-13	**San Jose**	**NHL**	**48**	**25**	**16**	**7**	**11**	**7**	**4**	....
2013-14	**San Jose**	**NHL**	**82**	**51**	**22**	**9**	**7**	**3**	**4**	....
2014-15	**San Jose**	**NHL**	**82**	**40**	**33**	**9**	....	....	....	....
	NHL Totals		**540**	**311**	**163**	**66**	**62**	**30**	**32**	....

Assistant coaches Matt Shaw and Jay Woodcrofl posted an 1-2-0 record as replacement coach when Todd McLellan was sidelined due to a concussion suffered February 26, 2012. McLellan returned March 5. Games are credited to McLellan's coaching record.

Club Records

Team

(Figures in brackets for season records are games played; records for fewest points, wins, ties, losses, goals, goals against are for 70 or more games)

Most Points .... 119 — 1983-84 (80), 1985-86 (80)
Most Wins .... 57 — 1983-84 (80)
Most Ties .... 16 — 1980-81 (80), 1999-2000 (82)
Most Losses .... 50 — 1992-93 (84)
Most Goals .... *446 — 1983-84 (80)
Most Goals Against .... 337 — 1992-93 (84)
Fewest Points .... 60 — 1992-93 (84)
Fewest Wins .... 25 — 1993-94 (84)
Fewest Ties .... 5 — 1983-84 (80)
Fewest Losses .... 17 — 1981-82 (80), 1985-86 (80)
Fewest Goals .... 193 — 2014-15 (82)
Fewest Goals Against .... 182 — 2001-02 (82)
Longest Winning Streak
Overall .... 9 — Feb. 20-Mar. 13/01
Home .... 8 — Jan. 19-Feb. 22/85, Feb. 24-Apr. 2/86
Away .... 8 — Dec. 9/86-Jan. 17/87
Longest Undefeated Streak
Overall .... 15 — Oct. 11-Nov. 9/84 (12W, 3T)
Home .... 14 — Nov. 15/89-Jan. 6/90 (11W, 3T)
Away .... 9 — Jan. 17-Mar. 2/82 (6W, 3T), Nov. 23/82-Jan. 18/83 (7W, 2T)
Longest Losing Streak
Overall .... 13 — Dec. 31/09-Jan. 30/10
Home .... 9 — Oct. 16-Nov. 24/93
Away .... 11 — Dec. 23/09-Feb. 10/10
Longest Winless Streak
Overall .... 14 — Oct. 11-Nov. 7/93 (13L, 1T)
Home .... 9 — Oct. 16-Nov. 24/93 (9L)
Away .... 11 — Dec. 18/01-Feb. 8/02 (7L, 4T/OL), Dec. 23/09-Feb. 10/10 (11 loses)
Most Shutouts, Season .... 8 — 1997-98 (82); 2000-01 (82); 2001-02 (82)
Most PIM, Season .... 2,173 — 1987-88 (80)
Most Goals, Game .... 13 — Nov. 19/83 (N.J. 4 at Edm. 13), Nov. 8/85 (Van. 0 at Edm. 13)

Individual

Most Seasons .... 15 — Kevin Lowe
Most Games .... 1,037 — Kevin Lowe
Most Goals, Career .... 583 — Wayne Gretzky
Most Assists, Career .... 1,086 — Wayne Gretzky
Most Points, Career .... 1,669 — Wayne Gretzky (583G, 1,086A)
Most PIM, Career .... 1,747 — Kelly Buchberger
Most Shutouts, Career .... 23 — Tommy Salo
Longest Consecutive Games Streak .... 518 — Craig MacTavish (Oct. 12/86-Jan. 2/93)
Most Goals, Season .... *92 — Wayne Gretzky (1981-82)
Most Assists, Season .... *163 — Wayne Gretzky (1985-86)
Most Points, Season .... *215 — Wayne Gretzky (1985-86; 52G, 163A)
Most PIM, Season .... 286 — Steve Smith (1987-88)
Most Points, Defenseman, Season .... 138 — Paul Coffey (1985-86; 48G, 90A)
Most Points, Center, Season .... *215 — Wayne Gretzky (1985-86; 52G, 163A)
Most Points, Right Wing, Season .... 135 — Jari Kurri (1984-85; 71G, 64A)
Most Points, Left Wing, Season .... 106 — Mark Messier (1982-83; 48G, 58A)
Most Points, Rookie, Season .... 75 — Jari Kurri (1980-81; 32G, 43A)
Most Shutouts, Season .... 8 — Curtis Joseph (1997-98), Tommy Salo (2000-01)
Most Goals, Game .... 5 — Wayne Gretzky (Feb. 18/81), (Dec. 30/81), (Dec. 15/84), (Dec. 6/87); Jari Kurri (Nov. 19/83); Pat Hughes (Feb. 3/84)
Most Assists, Game .... *7 — Wayne Gretzky (Feb. 15/80), (Dec. 11/85), (Feb. 14/86)
Most Points, Game .... 8 — Wayne Gretzky (Nov. 19/83; 3G, 5A), (Jan. 4/84; 4G, 4A); Paul Coffey (Mar. 14/86; 2G, 6A); Sam Gagner (Feb. 2/12; 4G, 4A)

* NHL Record.

All-time Record vs. Other Clubs

Regular Season

	Total								At Home								On Road							
	GP	W	L	T	OL	GF	GA	PTS	GP	W	L	T	OL	GF	GA	PTS	GP	W	L	T	OL	GF	GA	PTS
Anaheim	91	40	45	2	4	218	247	86	45	23	18	0	4	103	113	50	46	17	27	2	0	115	134	36
Arizona	184	99	63	11	11	747	653	220	93	54	29	6	4	379	300	118	91	45	34	5	7	368	353	102
Boston	69	18	42	6	3	195	259	45	34	12	17	3	2	110	113	29	35	6	25	3	1	85	146	16
Buffalo	69	37	21	10	1	252	218	85	34	22	9	3	0	129	96	47	35	15	12	7	1	123	122	38
Calgary	224	91	106	19	8	726	785	209	112	53	43	10	6	377	358	122	112	38	63	9	2	349	427	87
Carolina	70	36	22	12	0	252	242	84	36	23	8	5	0	142	107	51	34	13	14	7	0	110	135	33
Chicago	126	53	59	12	2	429	447	120	63	30	28	5	0	220	210	65	63	23	31	7	2	209	237	55
Colorado	152	73	61	8	10	538	503	164	75	40	26	4	5	282	236	89	77	33	35	4	5	256	267	75
Columbus	51	30	11	3	7	182	132	70	25	19	4	0	2	96	58	40	26	11	7	3	5	86	74	30
Dallas	126	45	57	15	9	396	429	114	63	26	22	8	7	227	205	67	63	19	35	7	2	169	224	47
Detroit	123	47	57	13	6	398	449	113	61	27	22	10	2	218	214	66	62	20	35	3	4	180	235	47
Florida	26	14	9	3	0	77	61	31	12	7	4	1	0	37	26	15	14	7	5	2	0	40	35	16
Los Angeles	194	89	72	30	3	752	696	211	98	47	36	15	0	393	335	109	96	42	36	15	3	359	361	102
Minnesota	79	30	37	4	8	175	213	72	40	16	18	3	3	89	100	38	39	14	19	1	5	86	113	34
Montreal	79	37	35	4	3	262	257	81	42	23	19	0	0	143	130	46	37	14	16	4	3	119	127	35
Nashville	62	26	28	3	5	176	174	60	30	14	13	0	3	82	86	31	32	12	15	3	2	94	88	29
New Jersey	74	34	25	9	6	266	246	83	36	16	12	6	2	145	125	40	38	18	13	3	4	121	121	43
NY Islanders	70	28	27	14	1	242	238	71	34	21	8	5	0	124	94	47	36	7	19	9	1	118	144	24
NY Rangers	68	31	26	9	2	235	236	73	33	14	16	3	0	108	107	31	35	17	10	6	2	127	129	42
Ottawa	35	16	12	4	3	103	96	39	18	8	7	2	1	56	53	19	17	8	5	2	2	47	43	20
Philadelphia	69	29	31	8	1	211	240	67	33	18	8	6	1	114	94	43	36	11	23	2	0	97	146	24
Pittsburgh	70	37	28	4	1	299	248	79	35	24	10	1	0	158	111	49	35	13	18	3	1	141	137	30
St. Louis	125	52	58	11	4	404	422	119	62	29	27	4	2	200	205	64	63	23	31	7	2	204	217	55
San Jose	106	46	43	12	5	310	312	109	54	27	18	7	2	161	136	63	52	19	25	5	3	149	176	46
Tampa Bay	31	18	10	2	1	91	82	39	15	11	4	0	0	44	35	22	16	7	6	2	1	47	47	17
Toronto	94	42	41	8	3	372	342	95	50	25	17	6	2	193	160	58	44	17	24	2	1	179	182	37
Vancouver	226	112	83	19	12	838	749	255	113	64	37	7	5	442	344	140	113	48	46	12	7	396	405	115
Washington	68	29	32	6	1	241	240	65	34	18	12	4	0	132	102	40	34	11	20	2	1	109	138	25
Winnipeg	19	9	5	1	4	65	52	23	10	5	3	1	1	38	30	12	9	4	2	0	3	27	22	11
Totals	**2780**	**1248**	**1146**	**262**	**124**	**9452**	**9268**	**2882**	**1390**	**716**	**495**	**125**	**54**	**4942**	**4283**	**1611**	**1390**	**532**	**651**	**137**	**70**	**4510**	**4985**	**1271**

Playoffs

	Series	W	L	GP	W	L	T	GF	GA	Last Mtg.	Rnd.	Result
Anaheim	1	1	0	5	4	1	0	16	13	2006	CF	W 4-1
Arizona	6	6	0	26	22	4	0	120	75	1990	DSF	W 4-3
Boston	2	2	0	9	8	1	0	41	20	1990	F	W 4-1
Calgary	5	4	1	30	19	11	0	132	96	1991	DSF	W 4-3
Carolina	1	0	1	7	3	4	0	16	19	2006	F	L 3-4
Chicago	4	3	1	20	12	8	0	102	77	1992	CF	L 0-4
Colorado	2	1	1	12	5	7	0	30	35	1998	CQF	W 4-3
Dallas	8	2	6	42	15	27	0	104	118	2003	CQF	L 2-4
Detroit	3	3	0	16	12	4	0	58	43	2006	CQF	W 4-2
Los Angeles	7	5	2	36	24	12	0	154	127	1992	DSF	W 4-2
Montreal	1	1	0	3	3	0	0	15	6	1981	PR	W 3-0
NY Islanders	3	1	2	15	6	9	0	47	58	1984	F	W 4-1
Philadelphia	3	2	1	15	8	7	0	49	44	1987	F	W 4-3
San Jose	1	1	0	6	4	2	0	19	12	2006	CSF	W 4-2
Vancouver	2	2	0	9	7	2	0	35	20	1992	DF	W 4-2
Totals	**49**	**34**	**15**	**251**	**152**	**99**	**0**	**938**	**763**			

Playoff Results 2015-2011

(Last playoff appearance: 2006)

Abbreviations: Round: F – Final;
CF – conference final; **CSF** – conference semi-final;
CQF – conference quarter-final; **DF** – division final;
DSF – division semi-final; **PR** – preliminary round.

Calgary totals include Atlanta Flames, 1979-80.
Colorado totals include Quebec, 1979-80 to 1994-95.
New Jersey totals include Colorado Rockies, 1979-80 to 1981-82.
Winnipeg totals include Atlanta Thrashers, 1999-2000 to 2010-11.
Carolina totals include Hartford, 1979-80 to 1996-97.
Dallas totals include Minnesota North Stars, 1979-80 to 1992-93.
Phoenix totals include Winnipeg, 1979-80 to 1995-96.

2014-15 Results

Oct.	9	Calgary	2-5		9	Chicago	5-2
	11	at Vancouver	4-5†		11	Florida	2-4
	14	at Los Angeles	1-6		13	at St. Louis	2-4
	15	at Arizona	4-7		15	at Tampa Bay	2-3
	17	Vancouver	0-2		17	at Florida	3-2†
	20	Tampa Bay	3-2		20	at Washington	5-4†
	22	Washington	3-2		27	Minnesota	1-2
	24	Carolina	6-3		29	Buffalo	3-2
	27	Montreal	3-0		31	at Calgary	2-4
	29	Nashville	1-4	**Feb.**	2	at San Jose	5-4†
Nov.	1	Vancouver	2-3		4	Pittsburgh	0-2
	4	at Philadelphia	1-4		7	at Toronto	1-5
	6	at Boston	2-5		9	at New Jersey	2-1
	7	at Buffalo	3-2		10	at NY Islanders	2-3
	9	at NY Rangers	3-1		12	at Montreal	4-3*
	11	at Nashville	2-3		14	at Ottawa	2-7
	13	Ottawa	3-4*		16	at Winnipeg	4-5†
	16	Arizona	1-2		18	Boston	4-3†
	19	Vancouver	4-5		20	Minnesota	0-4
	21	New Jersey	0-2		21	Anaheim	1-2
	22	Chicago	1-7		24	at Minnesota	2-1
	25	at Dallas	2-3		28	St. Louis	1-2
	27	at Nashville	0-1*	**Mar.**	3	Los Angeles	2-5
	28	at St. Louis	3-4*		6	at Chicago	1-2†
Dec.	1	Arizona	2-5		8	at Carolina	4-7
	3	at Winnipeg	2-3*		9	at Detroit	2-5
	7	San Jose	2-1		12	at Pittsburgh	4-6
	9	at San Jose	2-5		13	at Columbus	4-5†
	10	at Anaheim	1-2		16	Toronto	4-1
	12	Anaheim	2-4		18	Columbus	3-4†
	14	NY Rangers	0-2		21	Philadelphia	5-4*
	16	at Arizona	1-2*		23	Winnipeg	1-4
	18	at San Jose	3-4		25	Colorado	4-3
	21	Dallas	5-6†		27	Dallas	4-0
	23	Arizona	1-5		30	at Colorado	4-1
	27	at Calgary	1-4	**Apr.**	1	at Anaheim	1-5
	30	Los Angeles	3-2†		2	at Los Angeles	2-8
	31	at Calgary	3-4*		4	Calgary	0-4
Jan.	2	at Colorado	1-2†		7	Los Angeles	4-2
	4	NY Islanders	5-2		9	San Jose	1-3
	6	Detroit	2-4		11	at Vancouver	5-6*

* – Overtime † – Shootout

NHL Draft Selections 2015-2001

Name in bold denotes played in NHL.

2015 Pick		**2011** Pick		**2007** Pick		**2003** Pick	
1	Connor McDavid	1	**Ryan Nugent-Hopkins**	6	**Sam Gagner**	22	**Marc Pouliot**
117	Caleb Jones	19	**Oscar Klefbom**	15	**Alex Plante**	51	**Colin McDonald**
124	Ethan Bear	31	**David Musil**	21	**Riley Nash**	68	**Jean-Francois Jacques**
154	John Marino	62	Samu Perhonen	97	**Linus Omark**	72	Mikhail Zhukov
208	Miroslav Svoboda	74	Travis Ewanyk	127	**Milan Kytnar**	94	**Zack Stortini**
209	Ziyat Paigin	92	Dillon Simpson	157	William Quist	147	Kalle Olsson
		114	**Tobias Rieder**			154	David Rohlfs
2014 Pick		122	Martin Gernat	**2006** Pick		184	Dragan Umicevic
3	**Leon Draisaitl**	182	Frans Tuohimaa	45	**Jeff Petry**	214	**Kyle Brodziak**
91	William Lagesson			75	**Theo Peckham**	215	**Mathieu Roy**
111	Zach Nagelvoort	**2010** Pick		133	Bryan Pitton	248	Josef Hrabal
130	Liam Coughlin	1	**Taylor Hall**	140	Cody Wild	278	**Troy Bodie**
153	Tyler Vesel	31	**Tyler Pitlick**	170	Alexander Bumagin		
183	Keven Bouchard	46	**Martin Marincin**			**2002** Pick	
		48	**Curtis Hamilton**	**2005** Pick		15	Jesse Niinimaki
2013 Pick		61	Ryan Martindale	25	**Andrew Cogliano**	31	**Jeff Deslauriers**
7	**Darnell Nurse**	91	Jeremie Blain	36	**Taylor Chorney**	36	**Jarret Stoll**
56	Marc-Olivier Roy	121	**Tyler Bunz**	81	**Danny Syvret**	44	**Matt Greene**
83	**Bogdan Yakimov**	162	**Brandon Davidson**	86	Robby Dee	79	Brock Radunske
88	Anton Slepyshev	166	Drew Czerwonka	97	**Chris VandeVelde**	106	Ivan Koltsov
94	Jackson Houck	181	Kristians Pelss	120	Viacheslav Trukhno	111	Jonas Almtorp
96	Kyle Platzer	202	Kellen Jones	157	Fredrik Pettersson	123	invalid pick
113	Aidan Muir			220	Matthew Glasser	148	Glenn Fisher
128	Evan Campbell	**2009** Pick				181	Mikko Luoma
158	Ben Betker	10	**Magnus Paajarvi**	**2004** Pick		205	J.F. Dufort
188	Gregory Chase	40	**Anton Lander**	14	**Devan Dubnyk**	211	Patrick Murphy
		71	Troy Hesketh	25	**Rob Schremp**	244	**Dwight Helminen**
2012 Pick		82	Cameron Abney	44	Roman Tesliuk	245	Tomas Micka
1	**Nail Yakupov**	99	Kyle Bigos	57	Geoff Paukovich	274	Fredrik Johansson
32	Mitchell Moroz	101	Toni Rajala	112	**Liam Reddox**		
63	Jujhar Khaira	133	Olivier Roy	146	**Bryan Young**	**2001** Pick	
91	Daniil Zharkov			177	Max Gordichuk	13	**Ales Hemsky**
93	Erik Gustafsson	**2008** Pick		208	Stephane Goulet	43	**Doug Lynch**
123	Joey Laleggia	22	**Jordan Eberle**	242	Tyler Spurgeon	52	Ed Caron
153	John McCarron	103	**Johan Motin**	274	Bjorn Bjurling	84	Kenny Smith
		133	**Philippe Cornet**			133	**Jussi Markkanen**
		163	**Teemu Hartikainen**			154	Jake Brenk
		193	Jordan Bendfeld			185	Mikael Svensk
						215	Dan Baum
						248	**Kari Haakana**
						272	**Ales Pisa**
						278	**Shay Stephenson**

General Managers' History

Larry Gordon, 1979-80; Glen Sather, 1980-81 to 1999-2000; Kevin Lowe, 2000-01 to 2007-08; Steve Tambellini, 2008-09 to 2011-12; Steve Tambellini and Craig MacTavish, 2012-13; Craig MacTavish, 2013-14, 2014-15; Peter Chiarelli, 2015-16.

Peter Chiarelli

President of Hockey Operations and General Manager

Born: Nepean, ON, August 5, 1964.

Peter Chiarelli was appointed president of hockey operations and general manager on April 24, 2015. He reports to CEO Bob Nicholson, and is responsible for all aspects of hockey operations. Chiarelli served as the general manager of the Boston Bruins for the previous eight seasons. He guided the Bruins to the Stanley Cup Final twice during his tenure in Boston, including winning the Stanley Cup in 2011. Chiarelli has also served as a member of the management group for Hockey Canada's national men's team, including the 2014 Winter Olympics and the 2013 Men's World Championships.

Chiarelli graduated from Harvard University with an Economics degree in 1987 and he played for the Harvard men's hockey team from 1983 to 1987. He began his career in hockey after graduating with a law degree from the University of Ottawa and was hired as the director of legal relations for the Ottawa Senators in 2000. In 2004, Chiarelli was promoted to assistant general manager of the Senators and he served in that role until being hired by the Boston Bruins in 2006.

Club Directory

Rexall Place

Edmonton Oilers
11230 – 110 Street
Edmonton, Alberta T5G 3H7
Phone **780/414-GOAL(4625)**
Press Box 780/409-3780
Media Lounge 780/409-3778
FAX 780/409-5890
www.edmontonoilers.com
Capacity: 16,839

Hockey Operations

Owner & Governor	Daryl A. Katz
President and CEO, OEG & Vice Chair OEG	Bob Nicholson
Vice Chair OEG	Kevin Lowe
Chief Commercial Officer	Stew MacDonald
Chief Operating Officer	Darryl Boessenkool
President, Hockey Ops & General Manager	Peter Chiarelli
Sr. Vice Presidents, Hockey Op / Player Personnel	Craig MacTavish / Scott Howson
Director, Player Personnel / Assistant G.M.	Bob Green / Bill Scott
Head Coach	Todd McLellan
Assistant Coaches	Jay Woodcroft, Jim Johnson, Ian Herbers
Goaltending Coaches	Dustin Schwartz, Sylvain Rodrigue
Video Coach / Skating Coach.	Myles Fee / David Pelletier
Player Development, Senior Director	Rick Carriere
Player Development Administrative Asst. / Assistant	Justin Mahe / Ryan Rondeau
Manager, Player Personnel - College Scouting	Kelly Buchberger
Manager, Hockey Admin.	Connie Hadden
Director, Research, Analysis & Software Dev.	Sean Draper
Sr. Coordinators, Video Development / Medical Services.	Brian Ross / Ken Lowe
Family Liaison	Jill Metz
Amateur Scouts	Bob Brown, James Crosson, Joseph Cucci, Bill Dandy, Pelle Eklund, Scott Harlow, Dave Heitz, Frank Musil, Alex Naurov James McGregor
Pro Scouts	Chris Cichocki, Duane Sutter, Matti Virmanen, Paul Messier

Medical and Training Staff

Athletic Therapists, Head / Assistants	T.D. Forss / Chris Davie, Ryan Williams
Equipment Manager / Assistant Managers	Jeff Lang / Brad Harrison, Shane Olmsted
Massage Therapist	Steve Lines
Strength and Conditioning Coach / Assistant	Chad Drummond / Joel Schneider
Team Medical Chief of Staff	Dr. Dhiren Naidu
Team Physicians	Drs. John Clarke, David Reid, Jeff Robinson, Mike Wagner
Team Dentists	Drs. Ben Eastwood, Nathan Kern, Trevor Ushko
Team Optometrist	Dr. Brent Saik
Dressing Room Attendant	Joey Moss

Communications and Broadcast

Sr. Director, Hockey Communications & Media Relations	J.J. Hebert
Manager, Communications & Team Services	Patrick Garland
Coordinator, Communications & Media Relations	Shawn May
Oilers Radio Play-by-Play / Color	Jack Michaels / Bob Stauffer

Marketing

Sr. Vice President, Marketing	Jeff Harrop
Directors, Website & New Media / Social Media	Marc Ciampa / Ryan Frankson
Directors, Brand / Brand Mktg & CRM	Debbie George / Christine McAnally
Managers, Events / Brand Mktg & Database	Jessica Bromley / Avery Hardy
Asst. Manager Events	Kyle Ferguson
Graphic Designers, Senior / Intermediate	Joey Angeles / Cristoval Castillon
Video Production Manager / Producer / Reporter-Host	Jeff Nash / Ryan Hyrcun / Tom Gazzola
Coordinator, Corporate Communications	Kelsey Spohn
Coordinator, New Media / Web Apps/Videographer	Chris Wescott / Heather Weigum / Blaine Sayers
Coordinator, Community & Fan Relations	Derek Fullerton
Director, Game Presentation / Team Photographer	Rich Meyers / Andy Devlin

Operations

Sr. Vice President, Operations	Stu Ballantyne
Senior Advisor, Special Projects	Don Metz
Senior Vice President, Enterprise Security & Risk Mgmt.	Kevin Galvin
Vice President, Facility Operations	Tom Cornwall
Asst. Mgr., Facilities & Ops/Ops Coordinator	Gilbert Da Silva/Macy Beley
Manager, Administration & Operations	Sherry Smith
Transition Directors, Commercial / Shared Services	Steinunn Parsons/Bobbie-Jo Ierino
Vice President, Corp. Communications & Gov't Relations	Tim Shipton
Manager, Corporate Communications	Andrea Rutt
Executive Assistant	Trisha Erb/Jody Craig

Corporate Partnerships

Sr. Director, Partnership Services	Brad Bissonnette
Sr. Directors, Corp. Partnerships	J.F. Amyot, Lisa Munro
Director / Manager, Partnerships	Abe Hajar / Brent Frew
Directr / Coordinator, Exec. Suite Ops	Bob Haromy / Melissa Smart
Partnership Sales Specialists	Hanna Choi, Lonny Erasmus, Shandy Lo, Stephan Tonowski, Jamie Leblanc

Finance and Administration

Chief Financial Officer	Jason Quilley
Chief Project Development Officer	Bob Black
Vice President, Human Resources	Adam Barrie
Senior Director / Coordinator, H.R. & People	Tandy Kustiak / Amber Demharter
Legal	Keely Brown / Imran Hussainaly
Director, Operations & Analysis	Sharon Lyseng
Payroll Managers / Coordinator	Shawna Quigley, Lanette Vermeersch / Nicole Charbonneau
Controller / Assistant Controller	Travis Nielsen, Donna Kuo /Corinne Carey
Director, Finance, Fac & Entertainment	Cody Awid
Accounts Payable Supervisor / Sr. Accountant	Jamie Schenknecht / Eric Motuzas, Rob Mella
Accountant	Brandon Polanski
Coordinators, AR / AP / Acct	Valerie Gauthier / Tanmeet Samra / Erin Barrett
Analysts, Business / Sharepoint Architect	Angela Frecon / Kassam Khahoo / Kelvin Sun
Director, IT / Infrastructure / IT	Kevin Flemming / David Kagan, Ali Smith, Kevin Cheng, Aaron Hammond

Ticket Sales and Customer Relations

Director, Customer Service & Ticket Operations	Jody Young
Director, Ticket Sales / Manager, Ticket Ops	Jared Ginsburg / Gavin Morton
Ticket Operations Coordinator / Assistant	Cheryl Langelier / Sandra Wever
Supervisors, Ticket Services / Client Services	Dianne Kalita, Raelene Dufva / Keenyn Bijou, Brienne Patton
Ticket Account Execs	Derek Perchaluk, Daniel Troiani, Scott Ritchie, Travis Ziegler
Outside Sales/ Insides Sales Reps	Robert Warburton, Jeff Trembley, J.J. White, Zach Snow, Matthew Crossman
Customer Experience Reps	Cindy Barkovic, Kersten Merry, Krista Davie, Louren Sansregret, Samantha Hill, Jun Lee, Sherri Bowles
Client Service Reps	Heather Lefebvre, Randi Rybka, Sabrina Licata, Shandell Barr

Edmonton Oilers Community Foundation

Executive Director, Oilers Community Foundation	Natalie Minckler
Coordinator, Community Partnerships	Emma Brook
Coordinator, Grant and Fund Development	Catherine Williams
ICE School, Program Coordinator	Diane Gurnham
Manager, Charity Auctions	Dwain Tomkow

Florida Panthers

2014-15 Results: 38W-29L-5OTL-10SOL 91PTS
6TH, Atlantic Division • 10TH, Eastern Conference

2015-16 Schedule

Oct.	Sat.	10	Philadelphia	Sun.	10	at Edmonton
	Mon.	12	at Philadelphia	Mon.	11	at Vancouver
	Tue.	13	at Carolina	Wed.	13	at Calgary
	Thu.	15	Buffalo	Sun.	17	at Tampa Bay*
	Sat.	17	Dallas	Mon.	18	Edmonton
	Tue.	20	at Pittsburgh	Fri.	22	Chicago
	Thu.	22	at Chicago	Sat.	23	Tampa Bay
	Sat.	24	at Dallas	Tue.	26	Toronto
	Tue.	27	Colorado	**Feb.** Tue.	2	at Washington
	Fri.	30	Boston	Thu.	4	Detroit
	Sat.	31	Washington	Sat.	6	Pittsburgh
Nov.	Wed.	4	Anaheim	Mon.	8	at Detroit
	Thu.	5	at San Jose	Tue.	9	at Buffalo
	Sat.	7	at Los Angeles*	Fri.	12	St. Louis
	Tue.	10	Calgary	Sat.	13	Nashville
	Thu.	12	Buffalo	Mon.	15	Pittsburgh
	Sat.	14	at Tampa Bay	Thu.	18	San Jose
	Mon.	16	Tampa Bay	Sat.	20	Winnipeg
	Thu.	19	Anaheim	Thu.	25	Arizona
	Sat.	21	NY Rangers	Sat.	27	at Columbus*
	Mon.	23	Los Angeles	Sun.	28	at Minnesota*
	Fri.	27	NY Islanders	**Mar.** Tue.	1	at Winnipeg
	Sun.	29	at Detroit*	Thu.	3	at Colorado
Dec.	Tue.	1	at St. Louis	Sat.	5	at Arizona
	Thu.	3	at Nashville	Mon.	7	Boston
	Fri.	4	at Columbus	Thu.	10	Ottawa
	Sun.	6	at New Jersey	Sat.	12	Philadelphia
	Tue.	8	Ottawa	Mon.	14	at NY Islanders
	Thu.	10	Washington	Tue.	15	at Montreal
	Sat.	12	at Boston*	Thu.	17	at Toronto
	Tue.	15	at NY Islanders	Sat.	19	Detroit
	Thu.	17	at New Jersey	Mon.	21	at NY Rangers
	Fri.	18	at Carolina	Thu.	24	at Boston
	Sun.	20	Vancouver*	Sat.	26	at Tampa Bay
	Tue.	22	Ottawa	Tue.	29	Toronto
	Sun.	27	Columbus	Thu.	31	New Jersey
	Tue.	29	Montreal	**Apr.** Sat.	2	Montreal
Jan.	Sat.	2	NY Rangers	Mon.	4	at Toronto
	Sun.	3	Minnesota	Tue.	5	at Montreal
	Tue.	5	at Buffalo	Thu.	7	at Ottawa
	Thu.	7	at Ottawa	Sat.	9	Carolina

* Denotes afternoon game.

Year-by-Year Record

Season	GP	Home W	L	T	OL	Road W	L	T	OL	Overall W	L	T	OL	GF	GA	Pts.	Div. Fin.	Conf. Fin.	Playoff Result
2014-15	82	21	13	....	7	17	16	....	8	38	29	....	5	206	223	91	6th, Atl.	10th, East	Out of Playoffs
2013-14	82	16	20	....	5	13	25	....	3	29	45	....	8	196	268	66	7th, Atl.	15th, East	Out of Playoffs
2012-13	48	8	11	....	5	7	16	....	1	15	27	....	6	112	171	36	5th, SE	15th, East	Out of Playoffs
2011-12	82	21	9	....	11	17	17	....	7	38	26	....	18	203	227	94	1st, SE	3rd, East	Lost Conf. Quarter-Final
2010-11	82	16	17	....	8	14	23	....	4	30	40	....	12	195	229	72	5th, SE	15th, East	Out of Playoffs
2009-10	82	16	16	....	9	16	21	....	4	32	37	....	13	208	244	77	5th, SE	14th, East	Out of Playoffs
2008-09	82	22	12	....	7	19	18	....	4	41	30	....	11	234	231	93	3rd, SE	9th, East	Out of Playoffs
2007-08	82	18	15	....	8	20	20	....	1	38	35	....	9	216	226	85	3rd, SE	11th, East	Out of Playoffs
2006-07	82	23	12	....	6	12	19	....	10	35	31	....	16	247	257	86	4th, SE	12th, East	Out of Playoffs
2005-06	82	25	11	....	5	12	23	....	6	37	34	....	11	240	257	85	4th, SE	11th, East	Out of Playoffs
2004-05	....																		
2003-04	82	16	15	7	3	12	20	8	1	28	35	15	4	188	221	75	4th, SE	12th, East	Out of Playoffs
2002-03	82	8	21	7	5	16	15	6	4	24	36	13	9	176	237	70	4th, SE	13th, East	Out of Playoffs
2001-02	82	11	23	3	4	11	21	7	2	22	44	10	6	180	250	60	4th, SE	14th, East	Out of Playoffs
2000-01	82	12	18	7	4	10	20	6	5	22	38	13	9	200	246	66	3rd, SE	12th, East	Out of Playoffs
1999-2000	82	26	9	4	2	17	18	2	4	43	27	6	6	244	209	98	2nd, SE	5th, East	Lost Conf. Quarter-Final
1998-99	82	17	17	7	....	13	17	11	....	30	34	18	....	210	228	78	2nd, SE	9th, East	Out of Playoffs
1997-98	82	11	24	6	....	13	19	9	....	24	43	15	....	203	256	63	6th, Atl.	12th, East	Out of Playoffs
1996-97	82	21	12	8	....	14	16	11	....	35	28	19	....	221	201	89	3rd, Atl.	4th, East	Lost Conf. Quarter-Final
1995-96	82	25	12	4	....	16	19	6	....	41	31	10	....	254	234	92	3rd, Atl.	4th, East	Lost Final
1994-95	48	9	12	3	....	11	10	3	....	20	22	6	....	115	127	46	5th, Atl.	9th, East	Out of Playoffs
1993-94	84	15	18	9	....	18	16	8	....	33	34	17	....	233	233	83	5th, Atl.	9th, East	Out of Playoffs

Selected first overall in the 2014 Entry Draft, Aaron Ekblad led all rookie defensemen in games (81) and goals (12) and was second in points (39) and plus-minus (+12) in 2014-15. He was rewarded with the Calder Trophy as rookie of the year.

ATLANTIC DIVISION
23rd NHL Season

Franchise date: June 14, 1993

2015-16 Player Personnel

FORWARDS	HT	WT	*Age	Place of Birth	S	2014-15 Club
BARKOV, Aleksander	6-3	213	20	Tampere, Finland	L	Florida
BJUGSTAD, Nick	6-6	218	23	Minneapolis, MN	R	Florida
BOLLAND, Dave	6-0	184	29	Mimico, ON	R	Florida
CROUSE, Lawson	6-4	215	18	Mt. Brydges, ON	L	Kingston
GRIMALDI, Rocco	5-6	180	22	Anaheim, CA	R	Florida-San Antonio
HOWDEN, Quinton	6-2	189	23	Winnipeg, MB	L	San Antonio
HUBERDEAU, Jonathan	6-1	188	22	Saint-Jerome, QC	L	Florida
JAGR, Jaromir	6-3	230	43	Kladno, Czech.	L	New Jersey-Florida
JOKINEN, Jussi	5-11	198	32	Kalajoki, Finland	L	Florida
MacKENZIE, Derek	5-11	181	34	Sudbury, ON	L	Florida
McKEGG, Greg	6-0	191	23	St.Thomas, ON	L	Toronto-Toronto (AHL)
PIRRI, Brandon	6-0	183	24	Toronto, ON	L	Florida
SMITH, Reilly	6-0	185	24	Toronto, ON	L	Boston
THORNTON, Shawn	6-2	217	38	Oshawa, ON	R	Florida
TROCHECK, Vincent	5-10	182	22	Pittsburgh, PA	R	Florida-San Antonio
WILSON, Garrett	6-2	199	24	Barrie, ON	L	Florida-San Antonio
DEFENSEMEN						
CAMPBELL, Brian	5-10	192	36	Strathroy, ON	L	Florida
EKBLAD, Aaron	6-4	216	19	Windsor, ON	R	Florida
GUDBRANSON, Erik	6-5	216	23	Ottawa, ON	R	Florida
KAMPFER, Steven	5-11	197	27	Ann Arbor, MI	R	Florida-San Antonio
KULIKOV, Dmitry	6-1	204	24	Lipetsk, USSR	L	Florida
MATHESON, Michael	6-2	192	21	Pointe-Claire, QC	L	Boston College-San Antonio
MITCHELL, Willie	6-3	210	38	Port McNeill, BC	L	Florida
OLSEN, Dylan	6-2	223	24	Salt Lake City, UT	L	Florida-San Antonio
PETROVIC, Alex	6-4	206	23	Edmonton, AB	R	Florida-San Antonio

GOALTENDERS	HT	WT	*Age	Place of Birth	C	2014-15 Club
LUONGO, Roberto	6-3	217	36	Montreal, QC	L	Florida
MONTOYA, Al	6-2	203	30	Chicago, IL	L	Florida

*– Age at start of 2015-16 season

2014-15 Scoring
* – rookie

Regular Season

Pos	#	Player	Team	GP	G	A	Pts	TOI	+/-	PIM	PP	SH	GW	S	S%
C	11	Jonathan Huberdeau	FLA	79	15	39	54	16:44	10	38	0	.0	0	169	8.9
R	68	Jaromir Jagr	N.J.	57	11	18	29	17:40	–10	42	2	0	3	119	9.2
			FLA	20	6	12	18	17:15	7	6	2	0	2	50	12.0
			Total	77	17	30	47	17:34	–3	48	4	0	5	169	10.1
L	36	Jussi Jokinen	FLA	81	8	36	44	16:44	–2	34	2	0	0	134	6.0
C	27	Nick Bjugstad	FLA	72	24	19	43	16:34	–7	38	7	0	3	207	11.6
D	5	* Aaron Ekblad	FLA	81	12	27	39	21:48	12	32	6	0	4	170	7.1
R	24	Brad Boyes	FLA	78	14	24	38	15:39	11	20	5	0	4	151	9.3
C	16	Aleksander Barkov	FLA	71	16	20	36	17:29	–4	16	3	0	3	123	13.0
R	12	Jimmy Hayes	FLA	72	19	16	35	15:08	–4	20	2	0	3	166	11.4
D	51	Brian Campbell	FLA	82	3	24	27	23:12	4	22	1	0	0	118	2.5
C	73	Brandon Pirri	FLA	49	22	2	24	14:46	6	14	7	0	4	143	15.4
C	63	Dave Bolland	FLA	53	6	17	23	16:21	4	48	0	1	0	76	7.9
C	21	* Vincent Trocheck	FLA	50	7	15	22	14:00	9	24	1	0	0	89	7.9
D	7	Dmitry Kulikov	FLA	73	3	19	22	21:18	0	48	1	0	0	83	3.6
R	19	Scottie Upshall	FLA	63	8	7	15	12:40	–8	28	0	0	2	93	8.6
D	44	Erik Gudbranson	FLA	76	4	9	13	18:36	–4	58	0	0	1	110	3.6
C	17	Derek MacKenzie	FLA	82	5	6	11	12:27	–17	45	1	0	0	72	6.9
D	33	Willie Mitchell	FLA	66	3	5	8	21:40	1	25	0	0	0	78	3.8
D	4	Dylan Olsen	FLA	44	2	6	8	15:54	–7	20	0	0	0	44	4.5
R	82	Tomas Kopecky	FLA	64	2	6	8	12:54	–19	28	0	0	1	106	1.9
L	22	Shawn Thornton	FLA	46	1	4	5	9:35	–13	50	0	0	0	53	1.9
D	3	Steven Kampfer	FLA	25	2	2	4	17:11	–4	12	0	0	1	28	7.1
D	72	Alex Petrovic	FLA	33	0	3	3	16:15	–4	34	0	0	0	29	0.0
C	23	* Rocco Grimaldi	FLA	7	1	0	1	12:36	1	4	0	0	0	18	5.6
D	74	Shane O'Brien	FLA	9	0	1	1	13:28	–4	5	0	0	0	4	0.0
L	28	Garrett Wilson	FLA	2	0	0	0	8:50	–2	0	0	0	0	5	0.0

Goaltending

No.	Goaltender	GPI	Mins	Avg	W	L	OT	EN	SO	GA	SA	Sv%	G	A	PIM
39	Dan Ellis	8	486	2.35	4	3	1	0	1	19	221	.914	0	0	0
1	Roberto Luongo	61	3528	2.35	28	19	12	6	2	138	1743	.921	0	0	0
35	Al Montoya	20	977	3.01	6	7	2	1	0	49	453	.892	0	0	2
	Totals	**82**	**5023**	**2.54**	**38**	**29**	**15**	**7**	**4**	**213**	**2424**	**.912**			

Roberto Luongo and Al Montoya shared a shutout vs CAR on Nov 26, 2014

Gerard Gallant
Head Coach

Born: Summerside, PEI, September 2, 1963.

Florida Panthers executive vice president and general manager Dale Tallon announced on June 21, 2014 that Gerard Gallant had been named the club's new head coach. Gallant was introduced to the media at a press conference on June 23.

Gallant, who at one time was the head coach of the Columbus Blue Jackets, spent the previous two years (2012 to 2014) serving as an assistant coach with the Montreal Canadiens, helping the team advance to the postseason each year, including the 2014 Eastern Conference Finals. During his two years as an assistant coach, Montreal posted a 75-42-13 mark, including their first 100-point season since 2007-08.

Before coaching in Montreal, Gallant spent three seasons (2009 to 2012) as the head coach of the Saint John Sea Dogs of the Quebec Major Junior Hockey League. During his three seasons with Saint John, he led the Sea Dogs to three first-place finishes, three league final appearances, two QMJHL championships (2011 and 2012) and one Memorial Cup title (2011). Gallant was also named the QMJHL and Canadian Hockey League Coach of the Year in 2010 and 2011. Jonathan Huberdeau of the Panthers played all three years under Gallant and served as team captain of the Sea Dogs during the 2011-2012 season.

Gallant served as head coach of Columbus for parts of three seasons (2003-04, 2005-06, 2006-07) after serving as an assistant with the Blue Jackets (2000 to 2003). He also was an assistant with the New York Islanders (2007 to 2009), the International Hockey League's Fort Wayne Komets (1998-99) and the American Hockey League's Louisville Panthers (1999-2000). Gallant began his coaching career in 1995-96 with the Summerside Capitals of the Maritime Junior Hockey League and led the team to the Royal Bank Cup in 1997.

A native of Summerside, PEI, Gallant was selected by Detroit in the sixth round (107th overall) in the 1981 NHL Draft. He played in 615 NHL games for Detroit (1984 to 1993) and Tampa Bay (1993to 1995) registering 480 points (211 goals, 269 assists) and 1,674 penalty minutes. Gallant recorded four 70-plus point seasons, including his most successful year in 1988-89 when he registered a career high 93 points (39 goals, 54 assists) and was selected as a NHL Second Team All-Star

Coaching Record

			Regular Season				Playoffs			
Season	Team	League	GC	W	L	O/T	GC	W	L	T
1995-96	Summerside	MrJHL	12	6	5	1	....	....	....	....
1996-97	Summerside	MrJHL	55	35	14	6	20	12	8	0
1996-97	Summerside	RB-Cup	....	....	....	....	6	3	2	1
1997-98	Summerside	MrJHL	37	9	22	6	....	....	....	....
2003-04	Columbus	NHL	45	16	24	5	....	....	....	....
2004-05	Columbus		SEASON CANCELLED							
2005-06	Columbus	NHL	82	35	43	4	....	....	....	....
2006-07	Columbus	NHL	15	5	9	1	....	....	....	....
2009-10	Saint John	QMJHL	67	52	15	0	21	14	7	.
2010-11	Saint John	QMJHL	67	57	10	0	19	16	3	.
2010-11	Saint John	M-Cup	....	....	....	....	4	3	1	.
2011-12	Saint John	QMJHL	67	50	17	0	17	16	1	.
2011-12	Saint John	M-Cup	....	....	....	....	4	2	2	.
2014-15	Florida	NHL	82	38	29	15	....	....	....	....
	NHL Totals		224	94	105	25				

Brandon Pirri had 22 goals and two assists for Florida in 2014-15, joining Hockey Hall of Famer Cy Denneny from 1923-24 as the only players in NHL history with 20+ goals and fewer than three assists in a full season.

Coaching History

Roger Neilson, 1993-94, 1994-95; Doug MacLean, 1995-96, 1996-97; Doug MacLean and Bryan Murray, 1997-98; Terry Murray, 1998-99, 1999-2000; Terry Murray and Duane Sutter, 2000-01; Duane Sutter and Mike Keenan, 2001-02; Mike Keenan, 2002-03; Mike Keenan, Rick Dudley and John Torchetti, 2003-04; Jacques Martin, 2004-05 to 2007-08; Peter DeBoer, 2008-09 to 2010-11; Kevin Dineen, 2011-12, 2012-13; Kevin Dineen and Peter Horachek, 2013-14; Gerard Gallant, 2014-15 to date.

Club Records

Team

(Figures in brackets for season records are games played; records for fewest points, wins, ties, losses, goals, goals against are for 70 or more games)

Most Points	98	1999-2000 (82)
Most Wins	43	1999-2000 (82)
Most Ties	19	1996-97 (82)
Most Losses	45	2013-14 (82)
Most Goals	254	1995-96 (82)
Most Goals Against	257	2005-06 (82), 2006-07 (82)
Fewest Points	60	2001-02 (82)
Fewest Wins	22	2000-01 (82), 2001-02 (82)
Fewest Ties	6	1999-2000 (82)
Fewest Losses	26	2011-12 (82)
Fewest Goals	176	2002-03 (82)
Fewest Goals Against	201	1996-97 (82)

Longest Winning Streak

Overall	7	Nov. 2-14/95, Mar. 17-29/06, Mar. 2-16/08
Home	5	Nov. 5-14/95, Mar. 17-Apr. 1/06, Mar. 6-16/08, Jan. 27-Feb. 13/09, Jan. 16-31/10, Mar. 4-17/12
Away	5	Nov. 30-Dec. 12/08

Longest Undefeated Streak

Overall	12	Oct. 5-30/96 (8w, 4т)
Home	8	Nov. 5-26/95 (7w, 1т)
Away	7	Dec. 7-29/93 (5w, 2т), Oct. 5-29/96 (4w, 3т)

Longest Losing Streak

Overall	13	Feb. 7-Mar. 23/98
Home	6	Feb. 25-Mar. 23/98
Away	13	Oct. 27-Dec. 17/05

Longest Winless Streak

Overall	15	Feb. 1-Mar. 23/98 (14L, 1т)
Home	13	Feb. 5-Mar. 24/03 (11L, 2т/OL)
Away	16	Jan. 2-Mar. 21/98 (12L, 4т)

Most Shutouts, Season	9	2008-09 (82)
Most PIM, Season	1,994	2001-02 (82)
Most Goals, Game	10	Nov. 26/97 (Bos. 5 at Fla. 10)

Individual

Most Seasons	11	Stephen Weiss
Most Games	654	Stephen Weiss
Most Goals, Career	188	Olli Jokinen
Most Assists, Career	249	Stephen Weiss
Most Points, Career	419	Olli Jokinen (188G, 231A)
Most PIM, Career	1,702	Paul Laus
Most Shutouts, Career	27	Roberto Luongo

Longest Consecutive

Games Streak	376	Olli Jokinen (Dec. 27/02-Apr. 5/08)
Most Goals, Season	59	Pavel Bure (2000-01)
Most Assists, Season	53	Viktor Kozlov (1999-2000)
Most Points, Season	94	Pavel Bure (1999-2000; 58G, 36A)
Most PIM, Season	354	Peter Worrell (2001-02)

Most Points, Defenseman,

Season	57	Robert Svehla (1995-96; 8G, 49A)

Most Points, Center,

Season	91	Olli Jokinen (2006-07; 39G, 52A)

Most Points, Right Wing,

Season	94	Pavel Bure (1999-2000; 58G, 36A)

Most Points, Left Wing,

Season	71	Ray Whitney (1999-2000; 29G, 42A)

Most Points, Rookie,

Season	50	Jesse Belanger (1993-94; 17G, 33A)

Most Shutouts, Season	7	Roberto Luongo (2003-04) Tomas Vokoun (2009-10)
Most Goals, Game	4	Mark Parrish (Oct. 30/98) Pavel Bure (Jan. 1/00), (Feb. 10/01)
Most Assists, Game	4	Eight times
Most Points, Game	6	Olli Jokinen (Mar. 17/07; 2G, 4A)

Captains' History

Brian Skrudland, 1993-94 to 1996-97; Scott Mellanby, 1997-98 to 2000-01; Pavel Bure, 2001-02; no captain, 2002-03; Olli Jokinen, 2003-04 to 2007-08; no captain, 2008-09; Bryan McCabe, 2009-10, 2010-11; no captain, 2011-12; Ed Jovanovski, 2012-13, 2013-14; Willie Mitchell, 2014-15 to date.

All-time Record vs. Other Clubs

Regular Season

	Total								At Home								On Road							
	GP	W	L	T	OL	GF	GA	PTS	GP	W	L	T	OL	GF	GA	PTS	GP	W	L	T	OL	GF	GA	PTS
Anaheim	27	13	10	3	1	80	73	30	13	6	5	2	0	36	31	14	14	7	5	1	1	44	42	16
Arizona	28	10	12	3	3	74	73	26	13	5	7	0	1	35	33	11	15	5	5	3	2	39	40	15
Boston	83	34	37	6	6	208	237	80	40	16	17	2	5	114	116	39	43	18	20	4	1	94	121	41
Buffalo	84	35	38	4	7	203	237	81	41	20	17	1	3	111	115	44	43	15	21	3	4	92	122	37
Calgary	27	10	10	3	4	70	73	27	14	4	6	2	2	31	36	12	13	6	4	1	2	39	37	15
Carolina	109	44	43	11	11	302	296	110	55	28	11	8	8	170	126	72	54	16	32	3	3	132	170	38
Chicago	31	9	16	3	3	71	106	24	15	4	8	1	2	29	52	11	16	5	8	2	1	42	54	13
Colorado	33	10	17	3	3	92	113	26	17	4	12	0	1	50	67	9	16	6	5	3	2	42	46	17
Columbus	18	5	8	0	5	41	55	15	9	3	2	0	4	24	27	10	9	2	6	0	1	17	28	5
Dallas	29	13	12	3	1	79	84	30	15	6	7	1	1	32	43	14	14	7	5	2	0	47	41	16
Detroit	32	10	14	5	3	79	99	28	17	4	9	2	2	39	51	12	15	6	5	3	1	40	48	16
Edmonton	26	9	9	3	5	61	77	26	14	5	2	2	5	35	40	17	12	4	7	1	0	26	37	9
Los Angeles	28	10	14	3	1	69	78	24	13	6	3	3	1	32	31	16	15	4	11	0	0	37	47	8
Minnesota	17	4	10	1	2	28	50	11	9	3	5	0	1	17	26	7	8	1	5	1	1	11	24	4
Montreal	83	37	30	6	10	201	216	90	43	19	17	3	4	113	115	45	40	18	13	3	6	88	101	45
Nashville	22	8	6	3	5	55	55	24	11	6	1	1	3	34	26	16	11	2	5	2	2	21	29	8
New Jersey	86	28	44	7	7	186	247	70	43	17	18	4	4	102	111	42	43	11	26	3	3	84	136	28
NY Islanders	87	43	28	8	8	256	238	102	43	23	11	6	3	138	123	55	44	20	17	2	5	118	115	47
NY Rangers	86	32	41	6	7	197	253	77	43	18	17	2	6	103	118	44	43	14	24	4	1	94	135	33
Ottawa	83	32	44	3	4	222	261	71	42	16	24	1	1	118	133	34	41	16	20	2	3	104	128	37
Philadelphia	86	32	42	7	5	211	255	76	42	13	24	1	4	101	140	31	44	19	18	6	1	110	115	45
Pittsburgh	82	35	34	4	9	231	234	83	41	22	16	1	2	122	109	47	41	13	18	3	7	109	125	36
St. Louis	29	7	17	3	2	47	76	19	14	4	6	2	2	27	32	12	15	3	11	1	0	20	44	7
San Jose	28	11	10	7	0	70	74	29	14	5	4	5	0	37	38	15	14	6	6	2	0	33	41	14
Tampa Bay	117	58	37	10	12	360	319	138	58	33	12	4	9	188	154	79	59	25	25	6	3	172	165	59
Toronto	71	30	29	7	5	210	204	72	37	16	14	5	2	109	102	39	34	14	15	2	3	101	102	33
Vancouver	27	8	10	6	3	63	79	25	13	3	5	5	0	31	40	13	14	5	5	1	3	32	39	12
Washington	114	45	51	9	9	289	341	108	57	26	27	4	5	155	158	61	57	19	29	5	4	134	183	47
Winnipeg	83	33	33	5	12	226	267	83	42	20	15	1	6	116	120	47	41	13	18	4	6	110	147	36
Totals	**1656**	**655**	**706**	**142**	**153**	**4281**	**4775**	**1605**	**828**	**357**	**317**	**65**	**89**	**2249**	**2313**	**868**	**828**	**298**	**389**	**77**	**64**	**2032**	**2462**	**737**

Playoffs

	Series	W	L	GP	W	L	T	GF	GA	Last Mtg.	Rnd.	Result
Boston	1	1	0	5	4	1	0	22	16	1996	CQF	W 4-1
Colorado	1	0	1	4	0	4	0	4	15	1996	F	L 0-4
New Jersey	2	0	2	11	3	8	0	23	30	2012	CQF	L 3-4
NY Rangers	1	0	1	5	1	4	0	10	13	1997	CQF	L 1-4
Philadelphia	1	1	0	6	4	2	0	15	11	1996	CSF	W 4-2
Pittsburgh	1	1	0	7	4	3	0	20	15	1996	CF	W 4-3
Totals	**7**	**3**	**4**	**38**	**16**	**22**	**0**	**94**	**100**			

Colorado totals include Quebec, 1993-94 to 1994-95.
Phoenix totals include Winnipeg, 1993-94 to 1995-96.

Carolina totals include Hartford, 1993-94 to 1996-97.
Winnipeg totals include Atlanta Thrashers, 1999-2000 to 2010-11.

Playoff Results 2015-2011

Year	Round	Opponent	Result	GF	GA
2012	CQF	New Jersey	L 3-4	17	18

Abbreviations: Round: F – Final;
CF – conference final; **CSF** – conference semi-final;
CQF – conference quarter-final.

2014-15 Results

Oct.	9	at Tampa Bay	2-3*		15	Colorado	2-4
	11	New Jersey	1-5		17	Edmonton	2-3†
	13	Ottawa	0-1		19	Vancouver	1-2
	17	at Buffalo	1-0		27	Detroit	4-5
	18	at Washington	1-2†		29	Columbus	3-2
	21	at Colorado	4-3*		31	at New Jersey	1-3
	25	at Arizona	1-2*	Feb.	2	at NY Rangers	3-6
	30	Arizona	2-1		3	at NY Islanders	4-2
Nov.	1	Philadelphia	2-1		5	Los Angeles	3-2
	4	at Boston	1-2*		8	Nashville	2-3†
	6	at Philadelphia	1-4		10	Anaheim	6-2
	8	Calgary	4-6		12	at Minnesota	1-2
	11	San Jose	4-1		13	at Dallas	0-2
	14	NY Islanders	3-4†		15	St. Louis	1-2†
	16	at Anaheim	6-2		17	at Toronto	3-2
	18	at Los Angeles	2-5		19	at Montreal	2-3†
	20	at San Jose	3-2†		21	at Ottawa	1-4
	22	at Nashville	2-3†		22	at Pittsburgh	1-5
	24	Minnesota	1-4		24	at Chicago	2-3†
	26	Carolina	1-0		26	Chicago	0-3
	28	Ottawa	3-2		28	Buffalo	5-3
Dec.	1	at Columbus	1-2	Mar.	1	Tampa Bay	4-3
	2	at Detroit	4-3		3	Toronto	2-3
	4	Columbus	3-4†		5	Dallas	3-4†
	6	Buffalo	3-2		7	NY Islanders	4-3†
	8	at St. Louis	2-4		12	Winnipeg	4-2
	12	at Detroit	3-2†		14	at Carolina	2-0
	13	at Buffalo	3-4*		15	at NY Rangers	1-2
	16	Washington	2-1†		17	Montreal	2-1
	18	at Philadelphia	2-1†		19	Detroit	3-1
	20	at Pittsburgh	1-3		21	Boston	2-1†
	22	Pittsburgh	4-3†		24	at Tampa Bay	3-4
	28	Toronto	6-4		26	at Toronto	4-1
	30	Montreal	1-2†		28	at Montreal	2-3*
	31	NY Rangers	2-5		29	at Ottawa	4-2
Jan.	2	at Buffalo	2-0		31	at Boston	2-3
	4	at Washington	3-4	Apr.	2	Carolina	6-1
	8	at Vancouver	3-1		4	Tampa Bay	0-4
	9	at Calgary	6-5		5	Montreal	1-4
	11	at Edmonton	4-2		9	Boston	4-2
	13	at Winnipeg	2-8		11	New Jersey	3-2

* – Overtime   † – Shootout

NHL Draft Selections 2015-2001

Name in bold denotes played in NHL.

2015 Pick		2011 Pick		2007 Pick		2003 Pick	
11	Lawson Crouse	3	**Jonathan Huberdeau**	10	**Keaton Ellerby**	3	**Nathan Horton**
77	Sam Montembeault	33	Rocco Grimaldi	40	**Michal Repik**	25	**Anthony Stewart**
88	Thomas Schemitsch	59	Rasmus Bengtsson	71	**Evgeni Dadonov**	38	**Kamil Kreps**
102	Denis Malgin	64	**Vincent Trocheck**	101	Matt Rust	55	**Stefan Meyer**
132	Karch Bachman	76	Logan Shaw	131	John Lee	105	Martin Lojek
162	Chris Wilkie	87	**Jonathan Racine**	181	Corey Syvret	124	James Pemberton
192	Patrick Shea	91	Kyle Rau	191	Ryan Watson	141	Dan Travis
206	Ryan Bednard	124	Yaroslav Kosov	202	Sergei Gayduchenko	162	Martin Tuma
		154	Eddie Wittchow			171	Denis Stasyuk
2014		184	**Iiro Pakarinen**	**2006**		223	Dany Roussin
Pick				Pick		234	Petr Kadlec
1	**Aaron Ekblad**	**2010**		10	**Michael Frolik**	264	John Hecimovic
32	Jayce Hawryluk	Pick		73	Brady Calla	265	**Tanner Glass**
65	Juho Lammikko	3	**Erik Gudbranson**	103	**Michael Caruso**		
92	Joe Wegwerth	19	**Nick Bjugstad**	116	Derrick Lapoint	**2002**	
143	Miguel Fidler	25	**Quinton Howden**	155	Peter Aston	Pick	
182	Hugo Fagerblom	33	John McFarland	193	Marc Cheverie	3	**Jay Bouwmeester**
		36	**Alex Petrovic**			9	**Petr Taticek**
2013		50	Connor Brickley	**2005**		40	**Rob Globke**
Pick		69	Joe Basaraba	Pick		67	**Gregory Campbell**
2	**Aleksander Barkov**	92	Sam Brittain	20	**Kenndal McArdle**	134	Topi Jaakola
31	Ian McCoshen	93	Ben Gallacher	32	Tyler Plante	158	Vince Bellissimo
92	Evan Cowley	99	Joonas Donskoi	90	Dan Collins	169	Jeremy Swanson
97	Michael Downing	123	Zach Hyman	93	Olivier Legault	196	Mikael Vuorio
98	Matt Buckles	153	Corey Durocher	104	Matt Duffy	200	Denis Yachmenev
122	Christopher Clapperton	183	Ronald Boyd	161	**Brian Foster**	232	Peter Hafner
152	Josh Brown			164	Roman Derlyuk		
206	MacKenzie Weegar	**2009**		224	Zach Bearson	**2001**	
		Pick				Pick	
2012		14	**Dmitry Kulikov**	**2004**		4	**Stephen Weiss**
Pick		44	**Drew Shore**	Pick		24	**Lukas Krajicek**
23	Michael Matheson	67	Josh Birkholz	7	**Rostislav Olesz**	34	Greg Watson
84	Steven Hodges	107	**Garrett Wilson**	37	David Shantz	64	**Tomas Malec**
114	Alexander Delnov	135	**Corban Knight**	53	**David Booth**	68	**Grant McNeill**
174	Francis Beauvillier	138	Wade Megan	105	Evan Schafer	117	Mike Woodford
194	Jonatan Nielsen	165	**Scott Timmins**	152	Bret Nasby	136	Billy Thompson
				267	Spencer Dillon	169	Dustin Johner
		2008		283	Luke Beaverson	200	Toni Koivisto
		Pick				231	Kyle Bruce
		31	**Jacob Markstrom**			263	Jan Blanar
		46	**Colby Robak**			267	**Ivan Majesky**
		80	Adam Comrie				
		100	A.J. Jenks				
		190	**Matt Bartkowski**				

General Managers' History

Bob Clarke, 1993-94; Bryan Murray, 1994-95 to 1999-2000; Bryan Murray and Bill Torrey, 2000-01; Bill Torrey and Chuck Fletcher, 2001-02; Rick Dudley, 2002-03, 2003-04; Mike Keenan, 2004-05, 2005-06; Jacques Martin, 2006-07 to 2008-09; Randy Sexton, 2009-10; Dale Tallon, 2010-11 to date.

Dale Tallon

Executive Vice President and General Manager

Born: Noranda, QC, October 19, 1950.

Dale Tallon was named general manager of the Florida Panthers on May 17, 2010. Tallon has been responsible for reshaping the club's hockey operations department, as well as the team's player personnel. Key draft choices during his tenure include Aaron Ekblad (#1 in 2014), Aleksander Barkov (#2 in 2013), Jonathan Huberdeau (#3 in 2011), Erik Gubranson (#3 in 2010) and Nick Bjugstad (#19 in 2010). Both Ekblad and Huberdeau went on to win the Calder Trophy as rookie of the year.

Prior to joining the Panthers, Tallon spent 33 years with the Blackhawks organization as a front office executive, player and broadcast personality. He served as Chicago's general manager from June 2005 to July 2009 after having served as assistant general manager from November 2003 to June 2005. Tallon was responsible for drafting or acquiring many of the players who led the Blackhawks to the Stanley Cup in 2010, including Jonathan Toews, Patrick Kane, Marian Hossa, Patrick Sharp, Kris Versteeg, John Madden and Brian Campbell.

As a player, Tallon was the Vancouver Canucks' first-round selection (second overall) in the 1970 NHL Draft. The Noranda, Quebec native played in 642 NHL contests with Vancouver (1970 to 1973), Chicago (1973 to 1978) and Pittsburgh (1978 to 1980) registering 336 points (98 goals, 238 assists) and 568 penalty minutes. Tallon recorded a career-high 17 goals in 69 games with Vancouver during the 1971-72 season and appeared in the 1971 and 1972 NHL All-Star Games. In 1972, Tallon was picked as an alternate for Team Canada for the Summit Series against the Soviet Union. After retiring following the 1979-80 season, Tallon served as a color analyst for Chicago radio and television broadcasts for 16 seasons.

Prior to joining the Panthers, Tallon spent the 2009-10 season serving as a senior advisor of hockey operations for the Blackhawks. He also served four years (1998 to 2002) as director of player personnel before returning to the radio and television booth prior to the 2002-03 season.

Club Directory

BB&T Center

Florida Panthers
BB&T Center
One Panther Parkway
Sunrise, FL 33323
Phone **954/835-7000**
FAX 954/835-7700
www.floridapanthers.com
Twitter @FlaPanthers
Capacity: 15,720

Ownership
Chairman, Owner & Governor . . . . Vincent J. Viola
Vice Chairman, Partner & Alternate Governor . . . . . Douglas A. Cifu
Executive Chairman . . . . Peter Luukko
Chief Executive Officer, President & Alt. Governor . . Rory A. Babich
Exec. Vice President & G.M., Hockey . . . . Dale Tallon
Special Advisor to the G.M./Alternate Governor . . . William Torrey
Chief Operating Officer . . . . Matthew Caldwell
Executive Vice President . . . . Charlie Turano
Executive Vice President . . . . Richard Adler
Executive Vice President, Sales . . . . Jim Willits
Chief Financial Officer . . . . Amy Perry
Vice President, Corporate Partnerships . . . . Greg Rieber
Vice President, Broadcasting and Panthers Alumni . Randy Moller
Vice President, Event Programming . . . . Kevin Grove
Vice President, General Manager of Panthers IceDen . Jeff Campol
Vice President, Information Technology . . . . John Spade
Vice President, Marketing . . . . Pamela Zager-Maya

Hockey Operations
Vice President, Hockey Operations
  and Special Projects . . . . Travis Viola
General Manager, Portland Pirates . . . . Eric Joyce
Director, Hockey Operations . . . . Mike Dixon
Director of Player Personnel . . . . Scott Luce
Director, Hockey Analytics . . . . Brian MacDonald
Manager, Player Development . . . . Bryan McCabe
Pro Scouts . . . . Peter Mahovlich, Jim McKenzie, Al Tuer
Head Amateur Scout . . . . Erin Ginnell
Assistant Head Amateur Scout . . . . Jason Bukala
Amateur Scouts . . . . Fred Bandel, Craig Demetrick, Paul Gallagher,
  Jari Kekalainen, Kent Nilsson, Billy Ryan
Team Services Manager . . . . Jerome Burke
Video Coordinator . . . . Tommy Cruz

Coaching Staff
Head Coach . . . . Gerard Gallant
Assistant Coaches . . . . Mike Kelly, John Madden
Goaltending Coach . . . . Robb Tallas
Goalie Development/Scout . . . . Pierre Groulx
Strength & Conditioning Coach . . . . Tommy Powers
Skating & Skills Coach . . . . Paul Vincent

Training Staff
Head Athletic Trainer . . . . David Zenobi
Assistant Athletic Trainer . . . . Tommy Alva
Physical Therapist . . . . Steve Dischiavi
Massage Therapist . . . . Steve Squier
Head Equipment Manager . . . . Chris Scoppetto
Equipment Manager . . . . Chris Moody
Assistant Equipment Manager . . . . Dakota King

Public Relations & Communications
Director, Communications . . . . TBA
Director, Digital Media . . . . Adelyn Biedenbach
Digital & Social Media Assistant . . . . Chrissy Parente
Communications Associate . . . . Mike Lewis

Broadcasting
Television / Radio . . . . FOX Sports Florida / 560 WQAM
TV Play-By-Play / Color Analyst . . . . Steve Goldstein / Denis Potvin
Television Analyst . . . . Randy Moller
Radio Play-By-Play . . . . TBA
Panthers Preview/Review Host . . . . Drew Goldfarb

Key Off-Season Signings/Acquisitions

2015

June 26 • Acquired LW **Milan Lucic** from Boston for G **Martin Jones**, D **Colin Miller** and a 1st-round choice in the 2015 NHL Draft.

26 • Re-signed C **Tyler Toffoli**.

July 1 • Signed G **Jhonas Enroth**.

6 • Re-signed D **Jamie McBain**.

15 • Re-signed LW **Andy Andreoff**.

16 • Re-signed C **Nick Shore**.

Los Angeles Kings

2014-15 Results: 40w-27L-7oTL-8soL 95pts
4TH, Pacific Division • 9TH, Western Conference

2015-16 Schedule

Oct.	Wed.	7	San Jose
	Fri.	9	Arizona
	Tue.	13	Vancouver
	Fri.	16	Minnesota
	Sun.	18	Colorado
	Thu.	22	at San Jose
	Fri.	23	Carolina
	Sun.	25	at Edmonton
	Tue.	27	at Winnipeg
	Sat.	31	Nashville*
Nov.	Mon.	2	at Chicago
	Tue.	3	at St. Louis
	Thu.	5	Columbus
	Sat.	7	Florida*
	Tue.	10	Arizona
	Thu.	12	NY Islanders
	Sat.	14	Edmonton
	Tue.	17	at Philadelphia
	Fri.	20	at Detroit
	Sun.	22	at Carolina*
	Mon.	23	at Florida
	Wed.	25	at Tampa Bay
	Sat.	28	Chicago
Dec.	Tue.	1	Vancouver
	Sat.	5	Pittsburgh*
	Sun.	6	Tampa Bay
	Tue.	8	at Columbus
	Fri.	11	at Pittsburgh
	Sat.	12	at Buffalo
	Mon.	14	at Ottawa
	Thu.	17	at Montreal
	Sat.	19	at Toronto
	Tue.	22	San Jose
	Sat.	26	at Arizona
	Mon.	28	at Vancouver
	Tue.	29	at Edmonton
	Thu.	31	at Calgary
Jan.	Sat.	2	Philadelphia*
	Mon.	4	at Colorado
	Thu.	7	Toronto
	Sat.	9	St. Louis
	Mon.	11	Detroit
	Sat.	16	Ottawa*
	Sun.	17	at Anaheim
	Tue.	19	Dallas
	Thu.	21	Minnesota
	Sat.	23	at Arizona
	Sun.	24	at San Jose
	Wed.	27	Colorado
Feb.	Tue.	2	at Arizona
	Thu.	4	Anaheim
	Tue.	9	at Boston
	Thu.	11	at NY Islanders
	Fri.	12	at NY Rangers
	Sun.	14	at New Jersey*
	Tue.	16	at Washington
	Thu.	18	at St. Louis
	Sat.	20	at Nashville
	Tue.	23	Calgary
	Thu.	25	Edmonton
	Sat.	27	Buffalo
	Sun.	28	at Anaheim
Mar.	Thu.	3	Montreal
	Sat.	5	Anaheim*
	*Mon.	7	Vancouver
	Wed.	9	Washington
	Sat.	12	New Jersey
	Mon.	14	at Chicago
	Tue.	15	at Dallas
	Thu.	17	NY Rangers
	Sat.	19	Boston
	Mon.	21	at Nashville
	Tue.	22	at Minnesota
	Thu.	24	at Winnipeg
	Sat.	26	Edmonton
	Mon.	28	at San Jose
	Thu.	31	Calgary
Apr.	Sat.	2	Dallas*
	Mon.	4	at Vancouver
	Tue.	5	at Calgary
	Thu.	7	Anaheim
	Sat.	9	Winnipeg

* Denotes afternoon game.

Retired Numbers

4	Rob Blake	1990-01, 06-08
16	Marcel Dionne	1975-1987
18	Dave Taylor	1977-1994
20	Luc Robitaille	1986-94, 97-01, 2003-2006
30	Rogie Vachon	1971-1978
99	Wayne Gretzky	1988-1996

PACIFIC DIVISION
49th NHL Season

Franchise date: June 5, 1967

Anze Kopitar and Drew Doughty are a big part of the Kings' defense. Kopitar was a finalist for the Selke Trophy and Doughty for the Norris in 2014-15. Doughty led the NHL in total time on ice at 2,377:40.

Year-by-Year Record

Season	GP	Home W	L	T	OL	Road W	L	T	OL	Overall W	L	T	OL	GF	GA	Pts.	Div. Fin.	Conf. Fin.	Playoff Result
2014-15	82	25	9	....	7	15	18	....	8	40	27	..	15	220	205	95	4th, Pac.	9th, West	Out of Playoffs
2013-14	**82**	**23**	**14**	**....**	**4**	**23**	**14**	**....**	**4**	**46**	**28**	**..**	**8**	**206**	**174**	**100**	**3rd, Pac.**	**6th, West**	**Won Stanley Cup**
2012-13	48	19	4	....	1	8	12	....	4	27	16	..	5	133	118	59	2nd, Pac.	5th, West	Lost Conf. Final
2011-12	**82**	**22**	**14**	**....**	**5**	**18**	**13**	**....**	**10**	**40**	**27**	**..**	**15**	**194**	**179**	**95**	**3rd, Pac.**	**8th, West**	**Won Stanley Cup**
2010-11	82	25	13	....	3	21	17	....	3	46	30	..	6	219	198	98	4th, Pac.	7th, West	Lost Conf. Quarter-Final
2009-10	82	22	13	....	6	24	14	....	3	46	27	..	9	241	219	101	3rd, Pac.	6th, West	Lost Conf. Quarter-Final
2008-09	82	18	15	....	8	16	22	....	3	34	37	..	11	207	234	79	5th, Pac.	14th, West	Out of Playoffs
2007-08	82	17	21	....	3	15	22	....	4	32	43	..	7	231	266	71	5th, Pac.	15th, West	Out of Playoffs
2006-07	82	16	16	....	9	11	25	....	5	27	41	..	14	227	283	68	4th, Pac.	14th, West	Out of Playoffs
2005-06	82	26	14	....	1	16	21	....	4	42	35	..	5	249	270	89	4th, Pac.	10th, West	Out of Playoffs
2004-05																			
2003-04	82	15	16	9	1	13	13	7	8	28	29	16	9	205	217	81	3rd, Pac.	11th, West	Out of Playoffs
2002-03	82	19	19	2	1	14	18	4	5	33	37	6	6	203	221	78	3rd, Pac.	8th, West	Out of Playoffs
2001-02	82	22	12	6	1	18	15	5	3	40	27	11	4	214	190	95	3rd, Pac.	7th, West	Lost Conf. Quarter-Final
2000-01	82	20	12	8	1	18	16	5	2	38	28	13	3	252	228	92	3rd, Pac.	6th, West	Lost Conf. Semi-Final
1999-2000	82	21	13	5	2	18	14	7	2	39	27	12	4	245	228	94	2nd, Pac.	5th, West	Lost Conf. Quarter-Final
1998-99	82	18	20	3	....	14	25	2	....	32	45	5	....	189	222	69	5th, Pac.	11th, West	Out of Playoffs
1997-98	82	22	16	3	....	16	17	8	....	38	33	11	....	227	225	87	2nd, Pac.	6th, West	Lost Conf. Quarter-Final
1996-97	82	18	16	7	....	10	27	4	....	28	43	11	....	214	268	67	6th, Pac.	12th, West	Out of Playoffs
1995-96	82	16	16	9	....	8	24	9	....	24	40	18	....	256	302	66	6th, Pac.	12th, West	Out of Playoffs
1994-95	48	7	11	6	....	9	12	3	....	16	23	9	....	142	174	41	4th, Pac.	9th, West	Out of Playoffs
1993-94	84	18	19	5	....	9	26	7	....	27	45	12	....	294	322	66	5th, Pac.	10th, West	Out of Playoffs
1992-93	84	22	15	5		17	20	5		39	35	10		338	340	88	3rd, Smythe		Lost Final
1991-92	80	20	11	9		15	20	5		35	31	14		287	296	84	2nd, Smythe		Lost Div. Semi-Final
1990-91	80	26	9	5		20	15	5		46	24	10		340	254	102	1st, Smythe		Lost Div. Final
1989-90	80	21	16	3		13	23	4		34	39	7		338	337	75	4th, Smythe		Lost Div. Final
1988-89	80	25	12	3		17	19	4		42	31	7		376	335	91	2nd, Smythe		Lost Div. Final
1987-88	80	19	18	3		11	24	5		30	42	8		318	359	68	4th, Smythe		Lost Div. Semi-Final
1986-87	80	20	17	3		11	24	5		31	41	8		318	341	70	4th, Smythe		Lost Div. Semi-Final
1985-86	80	9	27	4		14	22	4		23	49	8		284	389	54	5th, Smythe		Out of Playoffs
1984-85	80	20	14	6		14	18	8		34	32	14		339	326	82	4th, Smythe		Lost Div. Semi-Final
1983-84	80	13	19	8		10	25	5		23	44	13		309	376	59	5th, Smythe		Out of Playoffs
1982-83	80	20	13	7		7	28	5		27	41	12		308	365	66	5th, Smythe		Out of Playoffs
1981-82	80	19	15	6		5	26	9		24	41	15		314	369	63	4th, Smythe		Lost Div. Final
1980-81	80	22	11	7		21	13	6		43	24	13		337	290	99	2nd, Norris		Lost Prelim. Round
1979-80	80	18	13	9		12	23	5		30	36	14		290	313	74	2nd, Norris		Lost Prelim. Round
1978-79	80	20	13	7		14	21	5		34	34	12		292	286	80	3rd, Norris		Lost Prelim. Round
1977-78	80	18	16	6		13	18	9		31	34	15		243	245	77	2nd, Norris		Lost Quarter-Final
1976-77	80	20	13	7		14	18	8		34	31	15		271	241	83	2nd, Norris		Lost Quarter-Final
1975-76	80	22	13	5		16	20	4		38	33	9		263	265	85	2nd, Norris		Lost Prelim. Round
1974-75	80	22	7	11		20	10	10		42	17	21		269	185	105	2nd, Norris		Lost Prelim. Round
1973-74	78	22	13	4		11	20	8		33	33	12		233	231	78	3rd, West		Lost Quarter-Final
1972-73	78	21	11	7		10	25	4		31	36	11		232	245	73	6th, West		Out of Playoffs
1971-72	78	14	20	5		6	29	4		20	49	9		206	305	49	7th, West		Out of Playoffs
1970-71	78	17	14	8		8	26	5		25	40	13		239	303	63	5th, West		Out of Playoffs
1969-70	76	12	22	4		2	30	6		14	52	10		168	290	38	6th, West		Out of Playoffs
1968-69	76	19	14	5		5	28	5		24	42	10		185	260	58	4th, West		Lost Semi-Final
1967-68	74	20	13	4		11	20	6		31	33	10		200	224	72	2nd, West		Lost Quarter-Final

2015-16 Player Personnel

FORWARDS	HT	WT	*Age	Place of Birth	S	2014-15 Club
ANDREOFF, Andy	6-1	206	24	Pickering, ON	L	Los Angeles-Manchester
BROWN, Dustin	6-0	205	30	Ithaca, NY	R	Los Angeles
CARTER, Jeff	6-4	210	30	London, ON	R	Los Angeles
CLIFFORD, Kyle	6-2	208	24	Ayr, ON	L	Los Angeles
GABORIK, Marian	6-1	202	33	Trencin, Czech.	L	Los Angeles
KING, Dwight	6-4	230	26	Meadow Lake, SK	L	Los Angeles
KOPITAR, Anze	6-3	228	28	Jesenice, Yugoslavia	L	Los Angeles
LEWIS, Trevor	6-1	197	28	Salt Lake City, UT	R	Los Angeles
LUCIC, Milan	6-3	228	27	Vancouver, BC	L	Boston
NOLAN, Jordan	6-3	226	26	Garden River First Nation, ON	L	Los Angeles
PEARSON, Tanner	6-1	205	23	Kitchener, ON	L	Los Angeles
SHORE, Nick	6-1	194	23	Denver, CO	R	Los Angeles-Manchester
TOFFOLI, Tyler	6-1	197	23	Scarborough, ON	R	Los Angeles

DEFENSEMEN						
DOUGHTY, Drew	6-1	201	25	London, ON	R	Los Angeles
GREENE, Matt	6-3	233	32	Grand Ledge, MI	R	Los Angeles
MARTINEZ, Alec	6-1	205	28	Rochester Hills, MI	L	Los Angeles
McBAIN, Jamie	6-1	181	27	Edina, MN	R	Los Angeles-Manchester
McNABB, Brayden	6-4	209	24	Davidson, SK	L	Los Angeles
MUZZIN, Jake	6-3	216	26	Woodstock, ON	L	Los Angeles
SCHULTZ, Jeff	6-6	222	29	Calgary, AB	L	Los Angeles-Manchester
VOYNOV, Slava	6-0	201	25	Chelyabinsk, USSR	R	Los Angeles

GOALTENDERS	HT	WT	*Age	Place of Birth	C	2014-15 Club
ENROTH, Jhonas	5-10	166	27	Stockholm, Sweden	L	Buffalo-Dallas
QUICK, Jonathan	6-1	218	29	Milford, CT	L	Los Angeles

* – Age at start of 2015-16 season

2014-15 Scoring

* – rookie

Regular Season

Pos	#	Player	Team	GP	G	A	Pts	TOI	+/–	PIM	PP	SH	GW	S	S%
C	11	Anze Kopitar	L.A.	79	16	48	64	19:23	–2	10	6	0	4	134	11.9
C	77	Jeff Carter	L.A.	82	28	34	62	17:58	7	28	10	1	5	218	12.8
C	73	Tyler Toffoli	L.A.	76	23	26	49	14:35	25	37	3	5	3	200	11.5
R	12	Marian Gaborik	L.A.	69	27	20	47	16:54	7	16	11	0	2	174	15.5
D	8	Drew Doughty	L.A.	82	7	39	46	28:59	3	56	1	0	2	219	3.2
D	14	Justin Williams	L.A.	81	18	23	41	15:49	8	29	4	0	2	174	10.3
D	6	Jake Muzzin	L.A.	76	10	31	41	22:41	–4	22	4	0	3	173	5.8
L	23	Dustin Brown	L.A.	82	11	16	27	16:31	–17	26	1	0	3	189	5.8
L	74	Dwight King	L.A.	81	13	13	26	14:23	–3	21	0	0	1	127	10.2
C	22	Trevor Lewis	L.A.	73	9	16	25	14:06	8	14	0	1	2	143	6.3
D	3	Brayden McNabb	L.A.	71	2	22	24	15:53	11	52	0	0	1	74	2.7
D	7	Andrej Sekera	CAR	57	2	17	19	22:46	–7	8	1	0	0	77	2.6
			L.A.	16	1	3	4	19:12	4	6	0	0	0	23	4.3
			Total	73	3	20	23	21:59	–3	14	1	0	0	100	3.0
D	27	Alec Martinez	L.A.	56	6	16	22	19:55	9	10	1	0	1	103	5.8
C	28	Jarret Stoll	L.A.	73	6	11	17	15:29	3	58	3	0	2	83	7.2
L	70 *	Tanner Pearson	L.A.	42	12	4	16	13:17	14	14	1	0	3	68	17.6
C	10	Mike Richards	L.A.	53	5	11	16	13:21	–10	39	1	0	1	63	7.9
L	13	Kyle Clifford	L.A.	80	6	9	15	10:44	5	87	0	0	1	117	5.1
D	44	Robyn Regehr	L.A.	67	3	10	13	20:19	10	45	0	0	0	63	4.8
C	71	Jordan Nolan	L.A.	60	6	3	9	9:57	–6	54	0	0	1	44	13.6
D	2	Jamie McBain	L.A.	26	3	6	9	12:41	4	4	0	0	0	18	16.7
D	2	Matt Greene	L.A.	82	3	6	9	15:48	1	54	0	0	0	69	4.3
C	37 *	Nick Shore	L.A.	34	1	6	7	11:05	0	10	0	0	0	33	3.0
C	15 *	Andy Andreoff	L.A.	18	2	1	3	8:34	1	18	0	0	1	14	14.3
D	26	Slava Voynov	L.A.	6	0	2	2	23:11	0	2	0	0	0	5	0.0
D	55	Jeff Schultz	L.A.	9	0	1	1	16:44	1	4	0	0	0	7	0.0
L	36	David Van Der Gulik	L.A.	1	0	0	0	5:15	0	0	0	0	0	1	0.0

Goaltending

No.	Goaltender	GPI	Mins	Avg	W	L	OT	EN	SO	GA	SA	Sv%	G	A	PIM
32	Jonathan Quick	72	4184	2.24	36	22	13	8	6	156	1896	.918	0	1	18
31 *	Martin Jones	15	775	2.25	4	5	2	4	3	29	307	.906	0	1	0
	Totals	82	4991	2.37	40	27	15	12	9	197	2215	.911			

Captains' History

Bob Wall, 1967-68, 1968-69; Larry Cahan, 1969-70, 1970-71; Bob Pulford, 1971-72, 1972-73; Terry Harper, 1973-74, 1974-75; Mike Murphy, 1975-76 to 1980-81; Dave Lewis, 1981-82, 1982-83; Terry Ruskowski, 1983-84, 1984-85; Dave Taylor, 1985-86 to 1988-89; Wayne Gretzky, 1989-90 to 1991-92; Wayne Gretzky and Luc Robitaille, 1992-93; Wayne Gretzky, 1993-94, 1994-95; Wayne Gretzky and Rob Blake, 1995-96; Rob Blake, 1996-97 to 2000-01; Mattias Norstrom, 2001-02 to 2006-07; Rob Blake, 2007-08; Dustin Brown, 2008-09 to date.

Coaching History

Red Kelly, 1967-68, 1968-69; Hal Laycoe and Johnny Wilson, 1969-70; Larry Regan, 1970-71; Larry Regan and Fred Glover, 1971-72; Bob Pulford, 1972-73 to 1976-77; Ron Stewart, 1977-78; Bob Berry, 1978-79 to 1980-81; Parker MacDonald and Don Perry, 1981-82; Don Perry, 1982-83; Don Perry, Rogie Vachon and Roger Neilson, 1983-84; Pat Quinn, 1984-85, 1985-86; Pat Quinn and Mike Murphy 1986-87; Mike Murphy, Rogie Vachon and Robbie Ftorek, 1987-88; Robbie Ftorek, 1988-89; Tom Webster, 1989-90 to 1991-92; Barry Melrose, 1992-93, 1993-94; Barry Melrose and Rogie Vachon, 1994-95; Larry Robinson, 1995-96 to 1998-99; Andy Murray, 1999-2000 to 2004-05; Andy Murray and John Torchetti, 2005-06; Marc Crawford, 2006-07, 2007-08; Terry Murray, 2008-09 to 2010-11; Terry Murray and Darryl Sutter, 2011-12; Darryl Sutter, 2012-13 to date.

Coaching Record

			Regular Season				Playoffs			
Season	Team	League	GC	W	L	O/T	GC	W	L	T
1992-93	Chicago	NHL	84	47	25	12	4	0	4	....
1993-94	Chicago	NHL	84	39	36	9	6	2	4	....
1994-95	Chicago	NHL	48	24	19	5	16	9	7	....
1997-98	San Jose	NHL	82	34	38	10	6	2	4	....
1998-99	San Jose	NHL	82	31	33	18	6	2	4	....
99-2000	San Jose	NHL	82	35	30	17	12	5	7	....
2000-01	San Jose	NHL	82	40	27	15	6	2	4	....
2001-02	San Jose	NHL	82	44	27	11	12	7	5	....
2002-03	San Jose	NHL	24	8	12	4	....			
2002-03	Calgary	NHL	46	18	19	9	....			
2003-04	Calgary	NHL	82	42	30	10	26	15	11	....
2004-05	Calgary		SEASON CANCELLED							
2005-06	Calgary	NHL	82	46	25	11	7	3	4	....
2011-12 ◆	Los Angeles	NHL	49	25	13	11	20	16	4	....
2012-13	Los Angeles	NHL	48	27	16	5	18	9	9	....
2013-14 ◆	Los Angeles	NHL	82	46	28	8	26	16	10	....
2014-15	Los Angeles	NHL	82	40	27	15				
	NHL Totals		1121	547	404	170	165	88	77	....

◆ Stanley Cup win.

Darryl Sutter
Head Coach
Born: Viking, AB, August 19, 1958.

Darryl Sutter was named the 24th head coach in Kings history on December 20, 2011. The team had a record of 15-14-4 when Sutter took over and posted a mark of 25-13-11 under him. A strong finish saw them claim the eighth and final playoff spot in the Western Conference and an impressive 16-4 playoff run saw the Kings win the Stanley Cup for the first time in franchise history. It was also Sutter's first Stanley Cup win. The Kings reached the Western Conference final in 2012-13 and won the Stanley Cup for the second time in three years in 2013-14. They also tied a club record with 46 wins in the regular season.

Sutter had a career head coaching record of 409-320-131 in 860 regular season games over 12 seasons when hired by the Kings. His team's had eclipsed the 40-win mark four times, 100 points twice and finished in first place three times. He is also only one of nine head coaches in NHL history to lead three different teams to 100 wins. Only Scotty Bowman and Ron Wilson have coached four different teams to 100 wins. Sutter led the Calgary Flames to Game 7 of the 2004 Stanley Cup Final and Chicago to the 1995 Western Conference Final.

Before coming to Los Angeles, Sutter was the general manager of the Flames from the 2003-04 season until he resigned on December 28, 2010. Sutter also served as Calgary's head coach from 2002-03 through 2005-06. He was the head coach of the San Jose Sharks for parts of six seasons (1997-98 through the start of the 2002-03 season), where he worked under current Kings president/general manager Dean Lombardi, then the GM of the Sharks. As in Calgary, the Sharks increased their point total every season Sutter was the head coach. He led San Jose to a first-place finish in the Pacific Division in 2001-02 with a 44-27-11 record (99 points). Sutter was relieved of his duties with the Sharks on December 1, 2002.

Sutter was the head coach of the Chicago Blackhawks for three seasons (1992-93 through 1994-95) and served as Chicago's assistant coach in 1987-88 and as associate coach in 1990-91 and 1991-92. He led Chicago to a first-place finish in the Norris Division (and the best record in the Campbell Conference) in 1992-93 with a 47-25-12 record and 106 points. Sutter's head coaching experience also includes two seasons in the International Hockey League, where he coached the Saginaw Hawks in 1988-89 and he led the Indianapolis Ice to the Turner Cup Championship in 1989-90.

As a player, Sutter played in 406 career NHL regular season games (all with the Blackhawks), recording 279 points (161 goals, 118 assists) and 288 penalty minutes. He scored 20-plus goals in five of his eight NHL seasons, including a career-high 40 goals in 1980-81. He served as Chicago's captain from 1982 to 1985 and again in 1986-87. Darryl is one of seven Sutter brothers, six of whom played in the NHL. His son Brett currently plays in the Carolina Hurricanes organization.

Club Records

Team

(Figures in brackets for season records are games played; records for fewest points, wins, ties, losses, goals, goals against are for 70 or more games)

Most Points	**105**	1974-75 (80)
Most Wins	**46**	1990-91 (80), 2009-10 (82), 2010-11 (82), 2013-14 (82)
Most Ties	**21**	1974-75 (80)
Most Losses	**52**	1969-70 (76)
Most Goals	**376**	1988-89 (80)
Most Goals Against	**389**	1985-86 (80)
Fewest Points	**38**	1969-70 (76)
Fewest Wins	**14**	1969-70 (76)
Fewest Ties	**5**	1998-99 (82)
Fewest Losses	**17**	1974-75 (80)
Fewest Goals	**168**	1969-70 (76)
Fewest Goals Against	**174**	2013-14 (82)
Longest Winning Streak		
Overall	**9**	Jan. 21-Feb. 6/10
Home	**12**	Oct. 10-Dec. 5/92
Away	**8**	Dec. 18/74-Jan. 16/75, Feb. 26-Mar. 27/14
Longest Undefeated Streak		
Overall	**11**	Feb. 28-Mar. 24/74 (9W, 2T)
Home	**13**	Oct. 10-Dec. 8/92 (12W, 1T)
Away	**11**	Oct. 10-Dec. 11/74 (6W, 5T)
Longest Losing Streak		
Overall	**11**	Mar. 16-Apr. 4/04
Home	**9**	Feb. 8-Mar. 12/86
Away	**11**	Jan. 11-Feb. 15/70
Longest Winless Streak		
Overall	**17**	Jan. 29-Mar. 5/70 (13L, 4T)
Home	**9**	Jan. 29-Mar. 5/70 (8L, 1T), Feb. 8-Mar. 12/86 (9L)
Away	**20**	Jan. 11-Apr. 3/70 (16L, 4T)
Most Shutouts, Season	**13**	2013-14 (82)
Most PIM, Season	**2,247**	1992-93 (84)
Most Goals, Game	**12**	Nov. 29/84 (Van. 1 at L.A. 12)

Individual

Most Seasons	**17**	Dave Taylor
Most Games	**1,111**	Dave Taylor
Most Goals, Career	**557**	Luc Robitaille
Most Assists, Career	**757**	Marcel Dionne
Most Points Career	**1,307**	Marcel Dionne (550G, 757A)
Most PIM, Career	**1,846**	Marty McSorley
Most Shutouts, Career	**37**	Jonathan Quick
Longest Consecutive Games Streak	**330**	Anze Kopitar (Mar. 21/07-Mar. 26/11)
Most Goals, Season	**70**	Bernie Nicholls (1988-89)
Most Assists, Season	**122**	Wayne Gretzky (1990-91)
Most Points, Season	**168**	Wayne Gretzky (1988-89; 54G, 114A)
Most PIM, Season	**399**	Marty McSorley (1992-93)
Most Points, Defenseman, Season	**76**	Larry Murphy (1980-81; 16G, 60A)
Most Points, Center, Season	**168**	Wayne Gretzky (1988-89; 54G, 114A)
Most Points, Right Wing, Season	**112**	Dave Taylor (1980-81; 47G, 65A)
Most Points, Left Wing, Season	***125**	Luc Robitaille (1992-93; 63G, 62A)
Most Points, Rookie, Season	**84**	Luc Robitaille (1986-87; 45G, 39A)
Most Shutouts, Season	**10**	Jonathan Quick (2011-12)
Most Goals, Game	**4**	Seventeen times
Most Assists, Game	**6**	Bernie Nicholls (Dec. 1/88), Tomas Sandstrom (Oct. 9/93)
Most Points, Game	**8**	Bernie Nicholls (Dec. 1/88; 2G, 6A)

* NHL Record.

All-time Record vs. Other Clubs

Regular Season

	Total								At Home								On Road							
	GP	W	L	T	OL	GF	GA	PTS	GP	W	L	T	OL	GF	GA	PTS	GP	W	L	T	OL	GF	GA	PTS
Anaheim	122	54	44	11	13	339	356	132	61	33	17	4	7	175	151	77	61	21	27	7	6	164	205	55
Arizona	212	83	96	25	8	711	761	199	105	47	42	14	2	380	357	110	107	36	54	11	6	331	404	89
Boston	135	40	81	13	1	418	544	94	67	25	34	7	1	230	241	58	68	15	47	6	0	188	303	36
Buffalo	117	42	56	18	1	365	436	103	59	26	24	9	0	203	196	61	58	16	32	9	1	162	240	42
Calgary	226	89	109	21	7	745	838	206	112	55	45	9	3	390	368	122	114	34	64	12	4	355	470	84
Carolina	71	34	27	8	2	271	249	78	35	21	11	3	0	145	125	45	36	13	16	5	2	126	124	33
Chicago	186	78	86	17	5	561	616	178	92	41	40	8	3	303	300	93	94	37	46	9	2	258	316	85
Colorado	122	63	47	8	4	435	420	138	62	36	18	5	3	231	190	80	60	27	29	3	1	204	230	58
Columbus	51	29	18	1	3	152	119	62	26	17	8	1	0	74	51	35	25	12	10	0	3	78	68	27
Dallas	225	84	101	32	8	659	730	208	112	50	40	19	3	356	328	122	113	34	61	13	5	303	402	86
Detroit	194	82	80	27	5	674	672	196	97	48	34	14	1	356	300	111	97	34	46	13	4	318	372	85
Edmonton	194	75	80	30	9	696	752	189	96	39	36	15	6	361	359	99	98	36	44	15	3	335	393	90
Florida	28	15	10	3	0	78	69	33	15	11	4	0	0	47	37	22	13	4	6	3	0	31	32	11
Minnesota	53	24	16	5	8	131	120	61	26	12	8	2	4	67	62	30	27	12	8	3	4	64	58	31
Montreal	139	30	89	20	0	384	577	80	70	21	40	9	0	210	271	51	69	9	49	11	0	174	306	29
Nashville	61	29	24	3	5	173	160	66	31	14	14	0	3	92	91	31	30	15	10	3	2	81	69	35
New Jersey	97	53	30	11	3	375	302	120	48	30	11	6	1	212	148	67	49	23	19	5	2	163	154	53
NY Islanders	101	45	42	12	2	316	318	104	50	25	17	7	1	177	148	58	51	20	25	5	1	139	170	46
NY Rangers	129	46	64	16	3	400	475	111	66	26	28	10	2	214	230	64	63	20	36	6	1	186	245	47
Ottawa	29	19	8	2	0	104	72	40	15	12	2	1	0	62	29	25	14	7	6	1	0	42	43	15
Philadelphia	141	41	83	15	2	372	498	99	72	22	42	8	0	205	242	52	69	19	41	7	2	167	256	47
Pittsburgh	152	71	59	18	4	516	477	164	74	45	18	8	3	276	197	101	78	26	41	10	1	240	280	63
St. Louis	193	73	96	22	2	566	616	170	96	47	36	12	1	323	270	107	97	26	60	10	1	243	346	63
San Jose	136	60	57	7	12	377	399	139	68	38	23	4	3	201	178	83	68	22	34	3	9	176	221	56
Tampa Bay	31	12	16	2	1	69	82	27	16	4	10	2	0	35	47	10	15	8	6	0	1	34	35	17
Toronto	143	62	58	21	2	485	479	147	70	36	24	10	0	246	202	82	73	26	34	11	2	239	277	65
Vancouver	237	103	98	32	4	794	772	242	120	63	39	16	2	449	354	144	117	40	59	16	2	345	418	98
Washington	104	56	33	13	2	394	356	127	53	32	14	6	1	206	154	71	51	24	19	7	1	188	202	56
Winnipeg	20	11	4	0	5	73	63	27	10	7	0	0	3	47	31	17	10	4	4	0	2	26	32	10
Defunct Clubs	69	38	20	11	0	232	185	87	35	27	6	2	0	141	76	56	34	11	14	9	0	91	109	31
Totals	**3718**	**1541**	**1632**	**424**	**121**	**11865**	**12513**	**3627**	**1859**	**910**	**685**	**211**	**53**	**6414**	**5733**	**2084**	**1859**	**631**	**947**	**213**	**68**	**5451**	**6780**	**1543**

Playoffs

	Series	W	L	GP	W	L	T	GF	GA	Last Mtg.	Rnd.	Result
Anaheim	1	1	0	7	4	3	0	19	15	2014	SR	W 4-3
Arizona	1	1	0	5	4	1	0	14	8	2012	CF	W 4-1
Boston	2	0	2	13	5	8	0	38	56	1977	QF	L 2-4
Calgary	6	4	2	26	13	13	0	105	112	1993	DSF	W 4-2
Chicago	3	1	2	17	6	11	0	46	47	2014	CF	W 4-3
Colorado	2	0	2	14	6	8	0	23	33	2002	CQF	L 3-4
*Dallas	2	1	1	14	7	7	0	46	51	1969	QF	W 4-3
Detroit	2	1	1	10	4	6	0	21	32	2001	CQF	W 4-2
Edmonton	7	2	5	36	12	24	0	127	154	1992	DSF	L 2-4
Montreal	1	0	1	5	1	4	0	12	15	1993	F	L 1-4
New Jersey	1	1	0	6	4	2	0	16	8	2012	F	W 4-2
NY Islanders	1	0	1	4	1	3	0	10	21	1980	PR	L 1-3
NY Rangers	3	1	2	11	5	6	0	29	42	2014	F	W 4-1
St. Louis	4	2	2	18	8	10	0	40	48	2013	CQF	W 4-2
San Jose	3	2	1	20	10	10	0	60	52	2014	FR	W 4-3
Toronto	3	1	2	12	5	7	0	31	41	1993	CF	W 4-3
Vancouver	5	3	2	28	15	13	0	96	93	2012	CQF	W 4-1
Totals	**47**	**21**	**26**	**246**	**110**	**136**	**0**	**733**	**828**			

* Includes series with Oakland 1969.

Playoff Results 2015-2011

Year	Round	Opponent	Result	GF	GA
2014	**F**	**NY Rangers**	**W 4-1**	**15**	**10**
	CF	Chicago	W 4-3	28	23
	SR	Anaheim	W 4-3	19	15
	FR	San Jose	W 4-3	26	22
2013	CF	Chicago	L 1-4	11	14
	CSF	San Jose	W 4-3	14	10
	CQF	St. Louis	W 4-2	12	10
2012	**F**	**New Jersey**	**W 4-2**	**16**	**8**
	CF	Phoenix	W 4-1	14	8
	CSF	St. Louis	W 4-0	15	6
	CQF	Vancouver	W 4-1	12	8
2011	CQF	San Jose	L 2-4	20	20

Abbreviations: Round: F – Final; **CF** – conference final; **CSF** – conference semi-final; **SR** – second round; **CQF** – conference quarter-final; **FR** – first round; **DSF** – division semi-final; **QF** – quarter-final; **PR** – preliminary round.

Calgary totals include Atlanta Flames, 1972-73 to 1979-80.
Carolina totals include Hartford, 1979-80 to 1996-97.
Colorado totals include Quebec, 1979-80 to 1994-95.
Dallas totals include Minnesota North Stars, 1967-68 to 1992-93.
New Jersey totals include Kansas City, 1974-75, 1975-76, and Colorado Rockies, 1976-77 to 1981-82.
Phoenix totals include Winnipeg, 1979-80 to 1995-96.
Winnipeg totals include Atlanta Thrashers, 1999-2000 to 2010-11.

2014-15 Results

Oct.	8	San Jose	0-4
	11	at Arizona	2-3*
	12	Winnipeg	4-1
	14	Edmonton	6-1
	16	St. Louis	1-0†
	19	Minnesota	2-1
	23	Buffalo	2-0
	26	Columbus	5-2
	28	at Philadelphia	2-3*
	30	at Pittsburgh	0-3
	31	at Detroit	2-5
Nov.	2	at Carolina	2-3
	4	at Dallas	3-1
	6	NY Islanders	1-2†
	8	Vancouver	5-1
	12	at Anaheim	5-6†
	13	Dallas	0-2
	15	Anaheim	3-2*
	18	Florida	5-2
	20	Carolina	3-2
	22	at Dallas	4-5
	25	at Nashville	3-4†
	26	at Minnesota	4-0
	29	Chicago	1-4
Dec.	2	Boston	2-0
	4	at Arizona	4-0
	6	Philadelphia	1-2
	9	at Buffalo	0-1
	11	at Ottawa	5-3
	12	at Montreal	2-6
	14	at Toronto	3-4†
	16	at St. Louis	2-5
	18	St. Louis	6-4
	20	Arizona	4-2
	22	Calgary	3-4*
	27	San Jose	3-1
	29	at Calgary	1-2
	30	at Edmonton	2-3†
Jan.	1	at Vancouver	3-2
	3	Nashville	6-7*
	8	NY Rangers	3-4
	10	Winnipeg	4-5†
	12	Toronto	2-0
	14	New Jersey	3-5
	17	Anaheim	2-3†
	19	Calgary	1-2*
	21	at San Jose	2-4
	28	Chicago	4-3
	31	at Boston	1-3
Feb.	3	at Washington	0-4
	5	at Florida	2-3
	7	at Tampa Bay	4-2
	9	at Columbus	4-3
	12	Calgary	5-3
	14	Washington	3-1
	16	Tampa Bay	3-2
	18	at Colorado	4-1
	21	at San Jose	2-1
	24	Detroit	1-0
	26	Ottawa	0-1
	27	at Anaheim	2-4
Mar.	1	at Winnipeg	2-5
	3	at Edmonton	5-2
	5	Montreal	4-3†
	7	Pittsburgh	0-1*
	10	at Colorado	5-2
	12	at Vancouver	4-0
	14	Nashville	1-2
	16	Arizona	1-0
	18	at Anaheim	2-3*
	21	Vancouver	1-4
	23	at New Jersey	3-1
	24	at NY Rangers	4-2
	26	at NY Islanders	3-2
	28	at Minnesota	1-4
	30	at Chicago	1-4
Apr.	2	Edmonton	8-2
	4	Colorado	3-1
	6	at Vancouver	1-2†
	7	at Edmonton	2-4
	9	at Calgary	1-3
	11	San Jose	4-1

* – Overtime † – Shootout

NHL Draft Selections 2015-2001

Name in bold denotes played in NHL.

2015 Pick		2011 Pick		2007 Pick		2003 Pick	
43	Erik Cernak	49	Christopher Gibson	4	**Thomas Hickey**	13	**Dustin Brown**
74	Alexander Dergachev	80	**Andy Andreoff**	52	**Oscar Moller**	26	**Brian Boyle**
99	Austin Wagner	82	**Nick Shore**	61	**Wayne Simmonds**	27	**Jeff Tambellini**
134	Matt Schmalz	110	Michael Mersch	82	Bryan Cameron	44	Konstantin Pushkarev
187	Chaz Reddekopp	140	Joel Lowry	95	**Alec Martinez**	82	Ryan Munce
194	Matt Roy	200	Michael Schumacher	109	**Dwight King**	152	**Brady Murray**
				124	Linden Rowat	174	**Esa Pirnes**
2014 Pick		**2010** Pick		137	Joshua Turnbull	231	**Matt Zaba**
29	Adrian Kempe	15	Derek Forbort	184	Josh Kidd	244	Mike Sullivan
50	Roland McKeown	47	**Tyler Toffoli**	188	Matt Fillier	274	Marty Guerin
60	Alex Lintuniemi	70	Jordan Weal				
90	Michael Amadio	148	Kevin Gravel	**2006** Pick		**2002** Pick	
120	Steven Johnson	158	Maxim Kitsyn	11	**Jonathan Bernier**	18	**Denis Grebeshkov**
150	Alec Dillon			17	**Trevor Lewis**	50	Sergei Anshakov
157	Jake Marchment	**2009** Pick		48	Joe Ryan	66	**Petr Kanko**
180	Matthew Mistele	5	**Brayden Schenn**	74	**Jeff Zatkoff**	104	**Aaron Rome**
209	Spencer Watson	35	**Kyle Clifford**	86	Bud Holloway	115	Mark Rooneem
210	Jacob Middleton	84	**Nicolas Deslauriers**	114	Niclas Andersen	152	Greg Hogeboom
		95	Jean-Francois Berube	134	David Meckler	157	Joel Andresen
2013 Pick		96	**Linden Vey**	144	Martin Nolet	185	Ryan Murphy
37	Valentin Zykov	126	David Kolomatis	164	Constantin Braun	215	Mikhail Lyubushin
103	Justin Auger	156	Michael Pelech			248	Tuukka Pulliainen
118	Hudson Fasching	179	**Brandon Kozun**	**2005** Pick		279	**Connor James**
146	Patrik Bartosak	186	**Jordan Nolan**	11	**Anze Kopitar**		
148	Jonny Brodzinski	198	**Nic Dowd**	50	Dany Roussin	**2001** Pick	
178	Zachary Leslie			60	T.J. Fast	18	Jens Karlsson
191	Dominik Kubalik	**2008** Pick		72	**Jonathan Quick**	30	**David Steckel**
		2	**Drew Doughty**	139	Patrik Hersley	49	**Mike Cammalleri**
2012 Pick		13	**Colten Teubert**	184	Ryan McGinnis	51	**Jaroslav Bednar**
30	**Tanner Pearson**	32	**Slava Voynov**	206	Josh Meyers	83	Henrik Juntunen
121	Nikolay Prokhorkin	63	Robert Czarnik	226	John Seymour	116	**Richard Petiot**
151	Colin Miller	74	**Andrew Campbell**			152	Terry Denike
171	Tomas Hyka	88	Geordie Wudrick	**2004** Pick		153	Tuukka Mantyla
181	Paul Ladue	123	**Andrei Loktionov**	11	**Lauri Tukonen**	214	**Cristobal Huet**
211	Nick Ebert	153	Justin Azevedo	95	Paul Baier	237	Mike Gabinet
		183	Garrett Roe	110	Ned Lukacevic	277	Sebastien Laplante
				143	Eric Neilson		
				174	**Scott Parse**		
				205	Mike Curry		
				221	**Daniel Taylor**		
				238	**Yutaka Fukufuji**		
				264	Valtteri Tenkanen		

General Managers' History

Larry Regan, 1967-68 to 1972-73; Larry Regan and Jake Milford, 1973-74; Jake Milford, 1974-75 to 1976-77; George Maguire, 1977-78 to 1982-83; George Maguire and Rogie Vachon, 1983-84; Rogie Vachon, 1984-85 to 1991-92; Nick Beverley, 1992-93, 1993-94; Sam McMaster, 1994-95 to 1996-97; Dave Taylor, 1997-98 to 2005-06; Dean Lombardi, 2006-07 to date.

Dean Lombardi
President and General Manager
Born: Holyoke, MA, March 5, 1958.

The Kings entered into a new executive era when the club hired Dean Lombardi as president and general manager on April 21, 2006. Coming to Los Angeles as a veteran of 20 NHL seasons in the front office as an executive and a pro scout, Lombardi brought a well-earned reputation for being one of hockey's true visionaries while possessing a solid track record of success, building from within, and of development on the ice and infrastructure off the ice. In 2010, the Kings returned to the playoffs for the first time since 2002 and in 2012 they became Stanley Cup champions for the first time in franchise history. Los Angeles reached the Western Conference final in 2012-13 and won the Stanley Cup for the second time in three years in 2013-14..

Lombardi was formerly a member of the San Jose Sharks front office for 13 years, including seven seasons as general manager, followed by three years as a pro scout for the Philadelphia Flyers from 2003 to 2006. As an executive in the San Jose front office beginning in 1990, Lombardi first served as assistant general manager (a post he held the previous two seasons with the Minnesota North Stars) for the expansion Sharks before being elevated to vice president, director of hockey operations in 1992. Four years later, he was promoted to executive vice president and general manager. During his tenure as general manager in San Jose from 1996 to 2003, Lombardi helped build the Sharks into one of the premier teams in the NHL.

Prior to joining the North Stars, Lombardi spent three seasons as a player representative, including the representation of five members of the 1988 United States Olympic team, and at the time he joined Minnesota's front office Lombardi was only the second former player agent to be employed in an NHL front office (Brian Burke/Vancouver Canucks was the other).

Born in Holyoke, Massachusetts, and raised in nearby Ludlow, Lombardi received his undergraduate degree from the University of New Haven where he finished third in his class. On the ice he was the hockey team's captain his final two seasons, and he received a full athletic scholarship and the school's student-athlete of the year award. In 1985, Lombardi earned his Law degree (with honors) from Tulane Law School where he specialized in Labor Law.

Club Directory

STAPLES Center

Los Angeles Kings
STAPLES Center
1111 South Figueroa Street
Los Angeles, CA 90015
Phone **213/742-7100**
GM FAX 310/535-4525
www.lakings.com
Capacity: 18,230

Ownership
Owner . . . . Philip F. Anschutz
Owner . . . . Edward P. Roski, Jr.
Alternate Governor . . . . Dan Beckerman
Executive Assistant to the Alternate Governor . . . . Tanya Brice

Kings Executive
President/General Manager, Alternate Governor . . . . . Dean Lombardi
President, Business Operations, Alt. Governor . . . . . Luc Robitaille
Chief Operating Officer . . . . Kelly Cheeseman
Executive Assistant, President/General Manager . . . . . . Tiffany Frost
Executive Assistant, President, Business Ops . . . . . . Kehly Sloane
Executive Assistant, Chief Operating Officer . . . . Alicia Briones
Office Coordinator . . . . Kiki Oldani

Hockey Operations
Vice President, Assistant General Manager . . . . Rob Blake
VP, Hockey Ops and Director, Player Personnel . . . . Michael Futa
Special Assistant to the General Manager . . . . Jack Ferreira
Sr. Vice President/Hockey Ops and Legal Affairs . . . . . Jeff Solomon
Director of Team Operations . . . . Marshall Dickerson

Coaches
Head Coach . . . . Darryl Sutter
Associate Head Coach / Assistant Coach . . . . John Stevens / Davis Payne
Goaltending Coach . . . . Bill Ranford

Player Development
Director, Player Development . . . . Nelson Emerson
Senior Advisor/Development Coach . . . . Mike O'Connell
Goaltender Development . . . . Dusty Imoo
Development Consultant . . . . Glen Murray

Training Staff – Medical
Head Athletic Trainer . . . . Chris Kingsley
Assistant Athletic Trainer . . . . Myles Hirayama
Strength and Conditioning Coach . . . . Matt Price

Training Staff – Equipment
Head Equipment Manager . . . . Darren Granger
Equipment Assistant Managers / Assistant . . . . Dana Bryson, Joe Alexander / Bobby Halfacre

Medical
Team Physician / Internist . . . . Dr. Ronald Kvitne / Dr. Michael Mellman
Team Dentist / Opthalmologist . . . . Dr. Ken Ochi / Dr. Howard Lazerson

Scouts/Hockey Operations
Scouting Operations Coordinator/Asst. to the G.M. . . . . Lee Callans
Senior Pro Scout / Pro Scout . . . . Rob Laird / Joe Paterson
Scouting Directors, Amateur / Europe . . . . Mark Yannetti / Christian Ruuttu
Amateur Scouts . . . . Niklas Andersson, Chris Byrne, Bob Crocker, Bob Friedlander, Denis Fugere, Tony Gasparini, Clay Leibel, Brent McEwen
Collegiate Scouts . . . . Mike Donnelly, Mark Mullen
Video Technician . . . . Bill Gurney

Broadcasters
TV Station / Play-by-Play / Analyst . . . . FOX Sports West / Bob Miller / Jim Fox
Radio Flagship / Play-by-Play / Analyst . . . . KABC 790 / Nick Nickson / Daryl Evans

Communications and Content
Vice President, Communications and Broadcasting . . . . . Michael Altieri
Senior Director, Communications and Content . . . . Jeff Moeller
Director, Communications and Media Services . . . . Mike Kalinowski
Supervisor, Communications . . . . Eddie Fischermann
Beat Reporter . . . . Jon Rosen

Hockey Development and Community Relations
Senior Director, Hockey Development,
 Community Relations and Alumni Relations . . . . James Cefaly

Finance / Human Resources / IT
Vice President, Finance . . . . Joe Leibfried
Human Resources Manager / Assistant . . . . Eva Bassett / AnnMarie Francis
Lead Technology Engineer . . . . Darshan Parikh
Controller / Staff Accountant / Finance Manager . . . . . Scott Sangrey / Charles Borjon / Yvonne Luong

Game Presentation and Events
Game Presentation Vice President / Director . . . . Danny Zollars / Brooklyn Boyars
Director of Production . . . . Aaron Brenner
Game Presentation Sr. Manager / Manager/ Assistant . . Tim Smith / Janelle Morgan / April Alba
Associate Producer . . . . Rob McPherson
Video Editor & Animator . . . . Jeff Lewis
Coordinator, Production & Content . . . . Kate Archer

Group Sales
Vice President, Group Sales . . . . Matt Rosenfeld

Marketing
Marketing Vice President / Sr. Director . . . . Jonathan Lowe / Heather Bardocz

Marketing Intelligence
Vice President, Digital Strategy and Analytics . . . . Aaron LeValley
Digital Media Director / Sr. Producer / Coordinator . . . . Pat Donahue / Edward Valencia / Alex Kinkopf
Senior Manager, CRM and Analytics . . . . Lisa Rollins
Database Mktg. Mgr. / Membership Programs Supervisor . Gretchen Kiker / Jason Kitkay

Sponsorship Sales and Service
Partnership Activation Vice President / Sr. Director . . . . Russell Silvers / Nam McGrail
Global Partnerships Vice President / Sr. Director . . . . . Josh Veilleux / Kim Cantor
Partnership Activation Manager / Account Executive . . . . Therese Nguyen / Stephanie Nienhuis

Ticket Sales and Service
Senior Directors, Ticket Sales & Service / Ticket Ops . . . Mason Donley / Elizabeth Hauck
Ticket Sales & Service Sr. Manager / Manager / Supervisor . Adam Cheever / Brandon Bittel / Courtney Ports
Ticket Operations Manager / Coordinator . . . . Samantha Lewis / Joseph Carlucci
Season Ticket Service Sr. Executives . . . . Scott Servetnick, Cory Romero
VIP Service Executive . . . . Melina Kent
Ticket Sales and Service Account Executives . . . . Lisa Dolan, TJ Comrie, Ryan Rock, Katie Hazelrigg
Customer Service and Sales Representative . . . . Claire Winderl
Ticket Sales, Service and Ops Assistant . . . . Cheyenne Cantor

Minnesota Wild

2014-15 Results: 46w-28L-5OTL-3SOL 100PTS
4TH, Central Division • 6TH, Western Conference

2015-16 Schedule

Oct.	Thu.	8	at Colorado		Sun.	10	New Jersey
	Sat.	10	St. Louis		Tue.	12	Buffalo
	Thu.	15	at Arizona		Fri.	15	Winnipeg
	Fri.	16	at Los Angeles		Sat.	16	at Nashville
	Sun.	18	at Anaheim*		Wed.	20	at Anaheim
	Thu.	22	Columbus		Thu.	21	at Los Angeles
	Sat.	24	Anaheim*		Sat.	23	at San Jose*
	Sun.	25	at Winnipeg*		Mon.	25	Arizona
	Tue.	27	Edmonton	Feb.	Tue.	2	at NY Islanders
	Fri.	30	Chicago		Thu.	4	at NY Rangers
	Sat.	31	at St. Louis		Sat.	6	at St. Louis
Nov.	Thu.	5	Nashville		Tue.	9	Dallas
	Sat.	7	Tampa Bay		Thu.	11	Washington
	Tue.	10	Winnipeg		Sat.	13	Boston*
	Thu.	12	at Carolina		Mon.	15	at Vancouver
	Sat.	14	at Dallas		Wed.	17	at Calgary
	Tue.	17	at Pittsburgh		Thu.	18	at Edmonton
	Thu.	19	at Boston		Sun.	21	Chicago*
	Sat.	21	Nashville		Tue.	23	NY Islanders
	Wed.	25	Vancouver		Thu.	25	at Philadelphia
	Fri.	27	Winnipeg*		Fri.	26	at Washington
	Sat.	28	Dallas		Sun.	28	Florida*
Dec.	Tue.	1	at Chicago	Mar.	Tue.	1	Colorado
	Thu.	3	Toronto		Thu.	3	at Toronto
	Sat.	5	Colorado		Sat.	5	at Buffalo*
	Mon.	7	at Colorado		Sun.	6	St. Louis
	Fri.	11	at Arizona		Thu.	10	Edmonton
	Sat.	12	at San Jose		Sat.	12	at Montreal
	Tue.	15	Vancouver		Tue.	15	at Ottawa
	Thu.	17	NY Rangers		Thu.	17	at New Jersey
	Sat.	19	at Nashville		Sat.	19	Carolina*
	Mon.	21	Dallas		Sun.	20	at Chicago
	Tue.	22	Montreal		Tue.	22	Los Angeles
	Sat.	26	Pittsburgh		Thu.	24	Calgary
	Mon.	28	Detroit		Sat.	26	at Colorado*
	Thu.	31	at St. Louis		Tue.	29	Chicago
Jan.	Sat.	2	at Tampa Bay		Thu.	31	Ottawa
	Sun.	3	at Florida	Apr.	Fri.	1	at Detroit
	Tue.	5	at Columbus		Sun.	3	at Winnipeg
	Thu.	7	Philadelphia		Tue.	5	San Jose
	Sat.	9	at Dallas		Sat.	9	Calgary

* Denotes afternoon game.

Year-by-Year Record

Season	GP	Home W	L	T	OL	Road W	L	T	OL	Overall W	L	T	OL	GF	GA	Pts.	Div. Fin.	Conf. Fin.	Playoff Result
2014-15	82	22	13	....	6	24	15	....	2	46	28		8	231	201	100	4th, Cen.	6th, West	Lost Second Round
2013-14	82	26	10	....	5	17	17	....	7	43	27		12	207	206	98	4th, Cen.	7th, West	Lost Second Round
2012-13	48	14	8	....	2	12	11	....	1	26	19		3	122	127	55	2nd, NW	8th, West	Lost Conf. Quarter-Final
2011-12	82	20	17	....	4	15	19	....	7	35	36		11	177	226	81	4th, NW	12th, West	Out of Playoffs
2010-11	82	19	17	....	5	20	18	....	3	39	35		8	206	233	86	3rd, NW	12th, West	Out of Playoffs
2009-10	82	25	12	....	4	13	24	....	4	38	36		8	219	246	84	4th, NW	13th, West	Out of Playoffs
2008-09	82	23	11	....	7	17	22	....	2	40	33		9	219	200	89	3rd, NW	9th, West	Out of Playoffs
2007-08	82	25	11	....	5	19	17	....	5	44	28		10	223	218	98	1st, NW	3rd, West	Lost Conf. Quarter-Final
2006-07	82	29	7	....	5	19	19	....	3	48	26		8	235	191	104	2nd, NW	7th, West	Lost Conf. Quarter-Final
2005-06	82	23	16	....	2	15	20	....	6	38	36		8	231	215	84	5th, NW	11th, West	Out of Playoffs
2004-05	...																		
2003-04	82	19	13	7	2	11	16	13	1	30	29	20	3	188	183	83	5th, NW	10th, West	Out of Playoffs
2002-03	82	25	13	3	0	17	16	7	1	42	29	10	1	198	178	95	3rd, NW	6th, West	Lost Conf. Final
2001-02	82	14	14	8	5	12	21	4	4	26	35	12	9	195	238	73	5th, NW	12th, West	Out of Playoffs
2000-01	82	14	13	10	4	11	26	3	1	25	39	13	5	168	210	68	5th, NW	14th, West	Out of Playoffs

The Wild were eight points out of a playoff spot when Devan Dubnyk made his team debut on January 15, 2015. He set a club record with 38 straight starts, going 27-9-2 with a 1.78 goals-against average, to lead Minnesota into the playoffs.

CENTRAL DIVISION
16th NHL Season

Franchise date: June 25, 1997

2015-16 Player Personnel

FORWARDS	HT	WT	*Age	Place of Birth	S	2014-15 Club
CARTER, Ryan	6-1	205	32	White Bear Lake, MN	L	Minnesota
COYLE, Charlie	6-3	221	23	E. Weymouth, MA	R	Minnesota
DALPE, Zac	6-1	195	25	Paris, ON	R	Buffalo-Rochester
FONTAINE, Justin	5-10	177	27	Bonnyville, AB	R	Minnesota
GRANLUND, Mikael	5-10	186	23	Oulu, Finland	L	Minnesota
HAULA, Erik	5-11	192	24	Pori, Finland	L	Minnesota
KOIVU, Mikko	6-3	222	32	Turku, Finland	L	Minnesota
NIEDERREITER, Nino	6-2	209	23	Chur, Switzerland	L	Minnesota
PARISE, Zach	5-11	197	31	Minneapolis, MN	L	Minnesota
POMINVILLE, Jason	6-0	185	32	Repentigny, QC	R	Minnesota
SCHROEDER, Jordan	5-8	175	25	Prior Lake, MN	R	Minnesota-Iowa
SUTTER, Brett	6-0	200	28	Viking, AB	L	Minnesota-Iowa
VANEK, Thomas	6-2	217	31	Vienna, Austria	R	Minnesota
ZUCKER, Jason	5-11	188	23	Newport Beach, CA	L	Minnesota

DEFENSEMEN	HT	WT	*Age	Place of Birth	S	2014-15 Club
BLUM, Jonathon	6-1	188	26	Long Beach, CA	R	Minnesota-Iowa
BRODIN, Jonas	6-1	194	22	Karlstad, Sweden	L	Minnesota
DUMBA, Matt	6-0	187	21	Regina, SK	R	Minnesota-Iowa
FOLIN, Christian	6-3	215	24	Molndal, Sweden	R	Minnesota-Iowa
PROSSER, Nate	6-2	203	29	Elk River, MN	R	Minnesota
REILLY, Mike	6-2	187	22	Chicago, IL	L	U. of Minnesota
SCANDELLA, Marco	6-2	207	25	Montreal, QC	L	Minnesota
SPURGEON, Jared	5-9	176	25	Edmonton, AB	R	Minnesota
STRACHAN, Tyson	6-3	215	30	Melfort, SK	R	Buffalo
SUTER, Ryan	6-1	200	30	Madison, WI	L	Minnesota

GOALTENDERS	HT	WT	*Age	Place of Birth	C	2014-15 Club
BACKSTROM, Niklas	6-2	197	37	Helsinki, Finland	L	Minnesota
DUBNYK, Devan	6-5	210	29	Regina, SK	L	Arizona-Minnesota
KUEMPER, Darcy	6-5	205	25	Saskatoon, SK	L	Minnesota-Iowa

* – Age at start of 2015-16 season

Mike Yeo

Head Coach

Born: North Bay, ON, July 31, 1973.

Mike Yeo was named head coach of the Minnesota Wild on June 17, 2011. The hiring came 366 days after Yeo had been tabbed to lead the Houston Aeros, the Wild's primary developmental affiliate in the American Hockey League. In his one year as a head coach, he led the Aeros to an appearance in the Calder Cup Finals. Yeo joined the Wild franchise with the Aeros after spending the previous five seasons as assistant coach of the NHL's Pittsburgh Penguins. During Yeo's tenure in Pittsburgh he helped lead the Penguins to the 2008-09 Stanley Cup championship. Yeo led the Wild to their first playoff appearance since 2008 in 2013 and the team returned to the playoffs again in 2014 and 2015.

Yeo played five seasons with the Aeros (1994 to 1999) and was the captain of Houston's 1999 Turner Cup Championship team. He joined the Aeros in 1994 after playing the previous four seasons with the Sudbury Wolves (Ontario Hockey Leaue). As a left winger, he accumulated 127 points (55 goals, 72 assists) and 511 penalty minutes over 317 games during his Aeros playing career. Yeo enjoyed career-highs of 20 goals, 21 assists, 41 points and 128 penalty minutes during the 1997-98 season while serving as team captain. The native of North Bay, Ontario posted 18 points (six goals, 12 assists) and 65 penalty minutes in 57 games during the 1998-99 season. He also added four assists and 11 penalty minutes in nine games during the Aeros' run to the Turner Cup. Yeo joined the Wilkes-Barre/Scranton Penguins for the 1999-2000 season and played in 19 games before suffering a career-ending knee injury.

After his injury, Yeo joined the Wilkes-Barre/Scranton coaching staff where he spent six seasons as the assistant coach of Pittsburgh's AHL affiliate. During his tenure in Wilkes-Barre/Scranton, Yeo helped the Penguins to a Western Conference championship in 2001, an Eastern Conference championship in 2005, and two trips to the Calder Cup Finals. He made the jump to the NHL's Pittsburgh Penguins under head coach Michel Therrien in December 2005. During his first full season in 2006-07, Yeo helped the Penguins to a 47-point improvement from the previous season, the fourth-largest turnaround from one season to the next in NHL history. In Yeo's second season, he helped lead the Penguins to the Stanley Cup Final for the first time since the 1992 season. Yeo remained on staff in Pittsburgh during the 2008-09 season after Dan Byslma replaced Therrien on February 15, 2009, and the Penguins went on to win their third Stanley Cup championship in franchise history.

Coaching Record

			Regular Season				Playoffs			
Season	Team	League	GC	W	L	O/T	GC	W	L	T
2010-11	Houston	AHL	80	46	28	6	24	14	10	....
2011-12	**Minnesota**	**NHL**	**82**	**35**	**36**	**11**	....	....	....	....
2012-13	**Minnesota**	**NHL**	**48**	**26**	**19**	**3**	**5**	**1**	**4**	....
2013-14	**Minnesota**	**NHL**	**82**	**43**	**27**	**12**	**13**	**6**	**7**	....
2014-15	**Minnesota**	**NHL**	**82**	**46**	**28**	**8**	**10**	**4**	**6**	....
	NHL Totals		**294**	**150**	**110**	**34**	**28**	**11**	**17**	....

2014-15 Scoring

* – rookie

Regular Season

Pos	#	Player	Team	GP	G	A	Pts	TOI	+/–	PIM	PP	SH	GW	S	S%
L	11	Zach Parise	MIN	74	33	29	62	19:11	21	41	11	0	3	259	12.7
R	29	Jason Pominville	MIN	82	18	36	54	18:17	9	8	3	0	4	252	7.1
L	26	Thomas Vanek	MIN	80	21	31	52	16:12	–6	37	5	0	2	171	12.3
C	9	Mikko Koivu	MIN	80	14	34	48	19:16	2	38	4	0	4	179	7.8
C	64	Mikael Granlund	MIN	68	8	31	39	17:53	17	20	0	0	2	99	8.1
D	20	Ryan Suter	MIN	77	2	36	38	29:03	7	48	1	0	1	150	1.3
R	22	Nino Niederreiter	MIN	80	24	13	37	14:32	2	28	6	1	5	149	16.1
R	44	Chris Stewart	BUF	61	11	14	25	16:00	–30	63	5	0	0	116	9.5
			MIN	20	3	8	11	15:30	4	25	0	0	0	39	7.7
			Total	81	14	22	36	15:52	–26	88	5	0	0	155	9.0
C	3	Charlie Coyle	MIN	82	11	24	35	14:33	13	39	1	0	4	120	9.2
R	14	Justin Fontaine	MIN	71	9	22	31	11:57	13	12	0	0	2	104	8.7
L	16	Jason Zucker	MIN	51	21	5	26	15:03	–9	18	1	1	3	124	16.9
D	46	Jared Spurgeon	MIN	66	9	16	25	22:37	3	6	3	0	2	128	7.0
D	6	Marco Scandella	MIN	64	11	12	23	21:43	8	56	1	0	4	112	9.8
C	21	Kyle Brodziak	MIN	73	9	11	20	13:02	–6	47	0	1	0	86	10.5
L	23	Sean Bergenheim	FLA	39	8	10	18	14:09	2	34	0	0	2	84	9.5
			MIN	17	1	0	1	10:44	–4	6	0	0	0	24	4.2
			Total	56	9	10	19	13:07	–2	40	0	0	2	108	8.3
D	25	Jonas Brodin	MIN	71	3	14	17	24:10	21	8	0	0	1	95	3.2
D	55 *	Matt Dumba	MIN	58	8	8	16	15:00	13	23	2	0	2	86	9.3
L	56	Erik Haula	MIN	72	7	7	14	12:09	–7	32	1	0	1	92	7.6
C	18	Ryan Carter	MIN	53	3	10	13	10:05	3	55	0	1	0	47	6.4
L	24	Matt Cooke	MIN	29	4	6	10	12:36	0	13	0	0	0	24	16.7
D	5 *	Christian Folin	MIN	40	2	8	10	15:12	3	13	0	0	0	39	5.1
C	10	Jordan Schroeder	MIN	25	3	5	8	10:51	9	2	0	0	0	48	6.3
D	39	Nate Prosser	MIN	63	2	5	7	12:47	–1	32	0	0	1	38	5.3
D	33	Jordan Leopold	STL	7	0	0	0	13:04	0	2	0	0	0	1	0.0
			CBJ	18	1	2	3	17:14	–7	9	1	0	0	21	4.8
			MIN	18	0	1	1	13:19	1	8	0	0	0	17	0.0
			Total	43	1	3	4	14:55	–6	19	1	0	0	39	2.6
L	27	Brett Sutter	MIN	6	0	3	3	9:18	1	4	0	0	0	6	0.0
L	19	Stephane Veilleux	MIN	12	1	1	2	7:41	0	10	0	0	1	9	11.1
D	7	Jonathon Blum	MIN	4	0	1	1	9:52	–3	2	0	0	0	3	0.0
D	4	Stu Bickel	MIN	9	0	1	1	5:26	1	46	0	0	0	3	0.0
D	2	Keith Ballard	MIN	14	0	1	1	12:03	–3	26	0	0	0	5	0.0
C	53 *	Tyler Graovac	MIN	3	0	0	0	9:13	0	0	0	0	0	4	0.0

Goaltending

No.	Goaltender	GPI	Mins	Avg	W	L	OT	EN	SO	GA	SA	Sv%	G	A	PIM
40	Devan Dubnyk	39	2293	1.78	27	9	2	0	5	68	1064	.936	0	2	2
35	Darcy Kuemper	31	1569	2.60	14	12	2	4	3	68	718	.905	0	0	0
32	Niklas Backstrom	19	1005	3.04	5	7	3	2	0	51	452	.887	0	0	2
33	John Curry	2	72	4.17	0	0	1	0	0	5	25	.800	0	0	0
	Totals	**82**	**4973**	**2.39**	**46**	**28**	**8**	**6**	**8**	**198**	**2265**	**.913**			

Playoffs

Pos	#	Player	Team	GP	G	A	Pts	TOI	+/–	PIM	PP	SH	GW	OT	S	S%
L	11	Zach Parise	MIN	10	4	6	10	18:53	0	4	1	1	0	0	20	20.0
R	29	Jason Pominville	MIN	10	3	3	6	17:28	–1	0	2	0	1	0	33	9.1
C	64	Mikael Granlund	MIN	10	2	4	6	17:50	2	0	0	0	1	0	18	11.1
R	22	Nino Niederreiter	MIN	10	4	1	5	15:05	–2	10	0	0	1	0	19	21.1
D	55 *	Matt Dumba	MIN	10	2	2	4	16:05	–1	2	2	0	0	0	15	13.3
C	9	Mikko Koivu	MIN	10	1	3	4	18:13	–4	2	1	0	0	0	14	7.1
D	46	Jared Spurgeon	MIN	10	1	3	4	21:19	0	4	1	0	0	0	11	9.1
L	26	Thomas Vanek	MIN	10	0	4	4	14:11	–7	2	0	0	0	0	19	0.0
D	6	Marco Scandella	MIN	10	2	1	3	20:43	4	0	0	0	0	0	17	11.8
L	16	Jason Zucker	MIN	10	2	1	3	14:10	–1	2	0	0	0	0	21	9.5
D	20	Ryan Suter	MIN	10	0	3	3	26:58	–8	0	0	0	0	0	13	0.0
R	14	Justin Fontaine	MIN	6	1	1	2	10:45	0	2	0	0	1	0	4	25.0
C	3	Charlie Coyle	MIN	10	1	1	2	14:22	–3	0	0	0	0	0	14	7.1
L	24	Matt Cooke	MIN	7	0	2	2	11:08	1	4	0	0	0	0	8	0.0
R	44	Chris Stewart	MIN	8	0	2	2	15:58	–3	2	0	0	0	0	9	0.0
L	56	Erik Haula	MIN	2	1	0	1	10:59	1	0	0	0	0	0	4	25.0
C	18	Ryan Carter	MIN	1	0	0	0	6:18	0	0	0	0	0	0	0	0.0
D	39	Nate Prosser	MIN	1	0	0	0	4:02	–1	2	0	0	0	0	0	0.0
L	23	Sean Bergenheim	MIN	3	0	0	0	10:09	–2	0	0	0	0	0	1	0.0
C	10	Jordan Schroeder	MIN	3	0	0	0	11:13	0	0	0	0	0	0	5	0.0
D	33	Jordan Leopold	MIN	9	0	0	0	12:00	–3	0	0	0	0	0	7	0.0
C	21	Kyle Brodziak	MIN	10	0	0	0	12:30	–3	2	0	0	0	0	12	0.0
D	25	Jonas Brodin	MIN	10	0	0	0	21:52	–2	0	0	0	0	0	3	0.0

Goaltending

No.	Goaltender	GPI	Mins	Avg	W	L	EN	SO	GA	SA	Sv%	G	A	PIM
35	Darcy Kuemper	1	23	0.00	0	0	0	0	0	9	1.000	0	0	0
40	Devan Dubnyk	10	570	2.53	4	6	3	1	24	260	.908	0	1	0
	Totals	**10**	**600**	**2.70**	**4**	**6**	**3**	**1**	**27**	**272**	**.901**			

Club Records

Team

(Figures in brackets for season records are games played.)

Record		
Most Points	**104**	2006-07 (82)
Most Wins	**48**	2006-07 (82)
Most Ties	**20**	2003-04 (82)
Most Losses	**39**	2000-01 (82)
Most Goals	**235**	2006-07 (82)
Most Goals Against	**246**	2009-10 (82)
Fewest Points	**68**	2000-01 (82)
Fewest Wins	**25**	2000-01 (82)
Fewest Ties	**10**	2002-03 (82)
Fewest Losses	**26**	2006-07 (82)
Fewest Goals	**168**	2000-01 (82)
Fewest Goals Against	**178**	2002-03 (82)
Longest Winning Streak		
Overall	**9**	Mar. 8-24/07
Home	**8**	Oct. 5-Nov. 2/06, Dec. 5/06-Jan. 2/07
Away	**12**	Feb. 18-Apr. 9/15
Longest Undefeated Streak		
Overall	**9**	Dec. 13-30/03 (4W, 5T/OL) Mar. 8-24/07 (9W)
Home	**9**	Dec. 13/00-Jan. 10/01 (5W, 4T/OL)
Away	**7**	Dec. 6-30/03 (2W, 5T/OL)
Longest Losing Streak		
Overall	**8**	Mar. 10-26/11
Home	**5**	Feb. 28-Mar. 13/12, Apr. 1-21/13
Away	**11**	Nov. 20/06-Jan. 9/07 Dec. 13/11-Jan. 19/12
Longest Winless Streak		
Overall	**12**	Mar. 11-Apr. 4/01 (9L, 3T/OL)
Home	**8**	Feb. 26-Mar. 28/01 (5L, 3T/OL)
Away	**12**	Dec. 18/03-Jan. 31/04 (5L, 7T/OL)
Most Shutouts, Season	**8**	2006-07 (82), 2008-09 (82), 2013-14 (82)
Most PIM, Season	**1,209**	2001-02 (82), 2005-06 (82)
Most Goals, Game	**8**	Mar. 25/04 (Min. 8 at Chi. 2) Apr. 10/09 (Nsh. 2 at Min. 8)

Individual

Record		
Most Seasons	**10**	Nick Schultz, Pierre-Marc Bouchard
Most Games	**743**	Nick Schultz
Most Goals, Career	**219**	Marian Gaborik
Most Assists, Career	**356**	Mikko Koivu
Most Points, Career	**500**	Mikko Koivu (144G, 356A)
Most PIM, Career	**698**	Matt Johnson
Most Shutouts, Career	**28**	Niklas Backstrom
Longest Consecutive Games Streak	**288**	Antti Laaksonen (Oct. 6/00-Dec. 29/03)
Most Goals, Season	**42**	Marian Gaborik (2007-08)
Most Assists, Season	**50**	Pierre-Marc Bouchard (2007-08)
Most Points, Season	**83**	Marian Gaborik (2007-08; 42G, 41A)
Most PIM, Season	**201**	Matt Johnson (2002-03)
Most Points, Defenseman, Season	**46**	Brent Burns (2010-11; 17G, 29A)
Most Points, Center, Season	**71**	Mikko Koivu (2009-10; 22G, 49A)
Most Points, Right Wing, Season	**83**	Marian Gaborik (2007-08; 42G, 41A)
Most Points, Left Wing, Season	**79**	Brian Rolston (2005-06; 34G, 45A)
Most Points, Rookie, Season	**36**	Marian Gaborik (2000-01; 18G, 18A)
Most Shutouts, Season	**8**	Niklas Backstrom (2008-09)
Most Goals, Game	**5**	Marian Gaborik (Dec. 20/07)
Most Assists, Game	**4**	Andrew Brunette (Mar. 10/02) Marian Gaborik (Oct. 26/02) Pascal Dupuis (Mar. 25/04) Eric Belanger (Nov. 15/07) Mikko Koivu (Oct. 16/08, Jan. 2/11)
Most Points, Game	**6**	Marian Gaborik (Oct. 26/02; 2G, 4A), (Dec. 20/07; 5G, 1A)

Captains' History

Sean O'Donnell, Scott Pellerin, Wes Walz, Brad Bombardir, Darby Hendrickson, 2000-01; Jim Dowd, Filip Kuba, Brad Brown, Andrew Brunette, 2001-02; Brad Bombardir, Matt Johnson, Sergei Zholtok, 2002-03; Brad Brown, Andrew Brunette, Richard Park, Brad Bombardir, Jim Dowd, 2003-04; Alex Henry, Filip Kuba, Willie Mitchell, Brian Rolston, Wes Walz, 2005-06; Brian Rolston, Keith Carney, Mark Parrish, 2006-07; Pavol Demitra, Brian Rolston, Mark Parrish, Nick Schultz, Marian Gaborik, 2007-08; Mikko Koivu, Kim Johnsson, Andrew Brunette, 2008-09; Mikko Koivu, 2009-10 to date.

General Managers' History

Doug Risebrough, 2000-01 to 2008-09; Chuck Fletcher, 2009-10 to date.

Coaching History

Jacques Lemaire, 2000-01 to 2008-09; Todd Richards, 2009-10, 2010-11; Mike Yeo, 2011-12 to date.

2014-15 Results

Oct.	9	Colorado	5-0		13	at Pittsburgh	2-7
	11	at Colorado	3-0		15	at Buffalo	7-0
	17	at Anaheim	1-2		17	Arizona	3-1
	19	at Los Angeles	1-2		19	Columbus	1-3
	23	Arizona	2-0		20	at Detroit	4-5†
	25	Tampa Bay	7-2		27	at Edmonton	2-1
	27	at NY Rangers	4-5		29	at Calgary	1-0
	28	at Boston	4-3	**Feb.**	1	at Vancouver	4-2
	30	San Jose	4-3†		3	Chicago	3-0
Nov.	1	Dallas	4-1		7	Colorado	1-0
	4	Pittsburgh	1-4		9	Vancouver	5-3
	6	at Ottawa	0-3		10	at Winnipeg	1-2*
	8	at Montreal	1-4		12	Florida	2-1
	11	at New Jersey	1-3		14	Carolina	6-3
	13	Buffalo	6-3		16	at Vancouver	2-3
	15	at Dallas	2-1		18	at Calgary	3-2*
	16	Winnipeg	4-3*		20	at Edmonton	4-0
	20	at Philadelphia	3-2		22	Dallas	6-2
	22	at Tampa Bay	1-2		24	Edmonton	1-2
	24	at Florida	4-1		26	at Nashville	4-2
	26	Los Angeles	0-4		28	at Colorado	3-1
	28	at Dallas	5-4*	**Mar.**	3	Ottawa	3-2†
	29	St. Louis	2-3†		5	at Washington	2-1
Dec.	3	Montreal	2-1		6	at Carolina	3-1
	5	Anaheim	4-5		8	Colorado	2-3
	9	NY Islanders	5-4		10	New Jersey	6-2
	11	at San Jose	1-2		13	Anaheim	1-2
	13	at Arizona	4-3†		14	at St. Louis	3-1
	16	at Chicago	3-5		17	at Nashville	3-2*
	17	Boston	2-3*		19	Washington	2-3
	20	Nashville	5-6*		21	St. Louis	6-3
	23	Philadelphia	2-5		23	at Toronto	2-1
	27	Winnipeg	3-4*		24	at NY Islanders	2-1†
	29	at Winnipeg	3-2		27	Calgary	4-2
	31	at Columbus	1-3		28	Los Angeles	4-1
Jan.	2	Toronto	3-1	**Apr.**	2	NY Rangers	2-3
	3	at Dallas	1-7		4	Detroit	2-3†
	6	San Jose	3-4*		6	Winnipeg	0-2
	8	Chicago	2-4		7	at Chicago	2-1
	10	Nashville	1-3		9	at Nashville	4-2
	11	at Chicago	1-4		11	at St. Louis	2-4

* – Overtime † – Shootout

All-time Record vs. Other Clubs

Regular Season

	Total								At Home								On Road							
	GP	W	L	T	OL	GF	GA	PTS	GP	W	L	T	OL	GF	GA	PTS	GP	W	L	T	OL	GF	GA	PTS
Anaheim	53	24	24	2	3	130	127	53	26	13	9	2	2	66	56	30	27	11	15	0	1	64	71	23
Arizona	53	27	21	3	2	136	126	59	26	13	10	2	1	69	60	29	27	14	11	1	1	67	66	30
Boston	16	12	2	0	2	46	29	26	8	5	1	0	2	22	16	12	8	7	1	0	0	24	13	14
Buffalo	16	9	5	0	2	47	35	20	8	3	3	0	2	21	21	8	8	6	2	0	0	26	14	12
Calgary	80	34	34	4	8	185	182	80	40	21	12	1	6	102	87	49	40	13	22	3	2	83	95	31
Carolina	18	8	6	2	2	48	49	20	11	6	3	2	0	35	33	14	7	2	3	0	2	13	16	6
Chicago	57	32	22	1	2	156	149	67	29	18	10	0	1	78	74	37	28	14	12	1	1	78	75	30
Colorado	84	41	33	3	7	216	228	92	42	22	15	1	4	112	114	49	42	19	18	2	3	104	114	43
Columbus	50	23	19	1	7	119	124	54	26	16	6	0	4	71	58	36	24	7	13	1	3	48	66	18
Dallas	56	22	26	1	7	143	168	52	27	16	9	0	2	76	56	34	29	6	17	1	5	67	112	18
Detroit	51	15	25	3	8	120	169	41	25	7	9	2	7	57	69	23	26	8	16	1	1	63	100	18
Edmonton	79	45	24	4	6	213	175	100	39	24	12	1	2	113	86	51	40	21	12	3	4	100	89	49
Florida	17	12	2	1	2	50	28	27	8	6	0	1	1	24	11	14	9	6	2	0	1	26	17	13
Los Angeles	53	24	18	5	6	120	131	59	27	12	8	3	4	58	64	31	26	12	10	2	2	62	67	28
Montreal	15	6	6	1	2	38	51	15	7	4	2	0	1	18	22	9	8	2	4	1	1	20	29	6
Nashville	57	26	23	5	3	155	160	60	29	15	10	3	1	92	85	34	28	11	13	2	2	63	75	26
New Jersey	16	5	6	2	3	43	49	15	8	4	2	1	1	27	21	10	8	1	4	1	2	16	28	5
NY Islanders	18	11	6	0	1	56	44	23	9	6	2	0	1	30	26	13	9	5	4	0	0	26	18	10
NY Rangers	18	6	11	0	1	45	55	13	10	4	5	0	1	28	30	9	8	2	6	0	0	17	25	4
Ottawa	15	4	8	1	2	33	50	11	8	2	4	1	1	18	27	6	7	2	4	0	1	15	23	5
Philadelphia	17	6	10	1	0	28	49	13	7	3	3	1	0	13	18	7	10	3	7	0	0	15	31	6
Pittsburgh	17	10	6	1	0	51	40	21	8	4	3	1	0	22	20	9	9	6	3	0	0	29	20	12
St. Louis	56	25	19	5	7	138	135	62	29	16	7	2	4	84	63	38	27	9	12	3	3	54	72	24
San Jose	53	21	25	2	5	121	146	49	26	13	9	1	3	68	66	30	27	8	16	1	2	53	80	19
Tampa Bay	18	11	5	1	1	54	40	24	9	7	2	0	0	32	20	14	9	4	3	1	1	22	20	10
Toronto	14	6	8	0	0	31	36	12	6	4	2	0	0	16	10	8	8	2	6	0	0	15	26	4
Vancouver	79	34	31	5	9	204	209	82	40	21	14	2	3	117	98	47	39	13	17	3	6	87	111	35
Washington	16	9	6	0	1	34	34	19	8	7	1	0	0	22	13	14	8	2	5	0	1	12	21	5
Winnipeg	22	12	5	1	4	59	54	29	11	6	2	1	2	29	24	15	11	6	3	0	2	30	30	14
Totals	**1114**	**520**	**436**	**55**	**103**	**2819**	**2872**	**1198**	**557**	**298**	**175**	**28**	**56**	**1520**	**1348**	**680**	**557**	**222**	**261**	**27**	**47**	**1299**	**1524**	**518**

Playoffs

	Series	W	L	GP	W	L	T	GF	GA	Last Mtg.	Rnd.	Result
Anaheim	2	0	2	9	1	8	0	10	21	2007	CQF	L 1-4
Chicago	3	0	3	15	3	12	0	27	45	2015	SR	L 0-4
Colorado	3	2	1	20	10	10	0	50	54	2014	FR	W 4-3
St. Louis	1	1	0	6	4	2	0	17	14	2015	FR	W 4-2
Vancouver	1	1	0	7	4	3	0	26	17	2003	CSF	W 4-3
Totals	**10**	**4**	**6**	**57**	**22**	**35**	**0**	**130**	**151**			

Winnipeg totals include Atlanta Thrashers, 1999-2000 to 2010-11.

Playoff Results 2015-2011

Year	Round	Opponent	Result	GF	GA
2015	SR	Chicago	L 0-4	7	13
	FR	St. Louis	W 4-2	17	14
2014	SR	Chicago	L 2-4	13	15
	FR	Colorado	W 4-3	22	20
2013	CQF	Chicago	L 1-4	7	17

Abbreviations: Round: CSF – conference semi-final; **SR** – second round; **CQF** – conference quarter-final; **FR** – first round.

NHL Draft Selections 2015-2001

Name in bold denotes played in NHL.

2015
Pick
20 Joel Eriksson Ek
50 Jordan Greenway
111 Ales Stezka
135 Kirill Kaprizov
171 Nicholas Boka
201 Gustav Bouramman
204 Jack Sadek

2014
Pick
18 Alex Tuch
80 Louis Belpedio
109 Kaapo Kahkonen
139 Tanner Faith
160 Pontus Sjalin
167 Chase Lang
169 Reid Duke
199 Pavel Jenys

2013
Pick
46 Gustav Olofsson
81 Kurtis Gabriel
107 Dylan Labbe
137 Carson Soucy
167 Avery Peterson
197 Nolan De Jong
200 Alexandre Belanger

2012
Pick
7   **Matt Dumba**
46 Raphael Bussieres
68 John Draeger
98 Adam Gilmour
128 Daniel Gunnarsson
158 Christoph Bertschy
188 Louis Nanne

2011
Pick
10 **Jonas Brodin**
28 Zack Phillips
60 Mario Lucia
131 Nick Seeler
161 Steve Michalek
191 **Tyler Graovac**

2010
Pick
9   **Mikael Granlund**
39 **Brett Bulmer**
56 **Johan Larsson**
59 **Jason Zucker**
159 Johan Gustafsson
189 Dylen McKinlay

2009
Pick
16 **Nick Leddy**
77 **Matt Hackett**
103 **Kris Foucault**
116 Alex Fallstrom
161 **Darcy Kuemper**
163 Jere Sallinen
182 **Erik Haula**
193 Anthony Hamburg

2008
Pick
23 **Tyler Cuma**
55 **Marco Scandella**
115 Sean Lorenz
145 Eero Elo

2007
Pick
16 **Colton Gillies**
110 **Justin Falk**
140 **Cody Almond**
170 Harri Ilvonen
200 **Carson McMillan**

2006
Pick
9   **James Sheppard**
40 Ondrej Fiala
72 **Cal Clutterbuck**
102 Kyle Medvec
132 Niko Hovinen
162 Julian Walker
192 Chris Hickey

2005
Pick
4   **Benoit Pouliot**
57 **Matt Kassian**
65 Kristofer Westblom
110 Kyle Bailey
122 Morten Madsen
129 Anthony Aiello
199 Riley Emmerson

2004
Pick
12 A.J. Thelen
42 Roman Voloshenko
78 **Peter Olvecky**
79 **Clayton Stoner**
111 **Ryan Jones**
114 **Patrick Bordeleau**
117 Julien Sprunger
161 Jean-Claude Sawyer
175 Aaron Boogaard
195 Jean-Michel Rizk
206 **Anton Khudobin**
272 **Kyle Wilson**

2003
Pick
20 **Brent Burns**
56 **Patrick O'Sullivan**
78 **Danny Irmen**
157 Marcin Kolusz
187 Miroslav Kopriva
207 Georgy Misharin
219 Adam Courchaine
251 Mathieu Melanson
281 Jean-Michel Bolduc

2002
Pick
8   **Pierre-Marc Bouchard**
38 **Josh Harding**
72 Mike Erickson
73 **Barry Brust**
155 Armands Berzins
175 **Matt Foy**
204 Niklas Eckerblom
237 **Christoph Brandner**
268 Mikhail Tyulyapkin
269 Maxim Hannula

2001
Pick
6   **Mikko Koivu**
36 **Kyle Wanvig**
74 Chris Heid
93 **Stephane Veilleux**
103 Tony Virta
202 **Derek Boogaard**
239 Jake Riddle

Chuck Fletcher
General Manager
Born: Montreal, QC, April 29, 1967.

The Minnesota Wild announced the hiring of Chuck Fletcher as the second general manager in club history on May 22, 2009. During the summer of 2012, Fletcher made his mark with the acquisition of Zach Parise and Ryan Suter, two of the biggest names available on the free-agent market, and the Wild made their first playoff appearance since 2008 in the spring of 2013. They returned to the playoffs again in 2014 and 2015.

Fletcher has been to the Stanley Cup Final in management with three different teams (Florida, Anaheim and Pittsburgh). With the Penguins from 2006 to 2009, he worked closely with general manager Ray Shero on all hockey-related matters, including scouting, overseeing the development of young prospects and contract negotiations. Fletcher also managed hockey operations for the club's American Hockey League affiliate, the Wilkes-Barre/Scranton Penguins. Under his leadership, Wilkes-Barre/Scranton reached the AHL's Calder Cup finals in 2007-08, and the division finals in 2008-09.

Fletcher, the son of Hockey Hall of Famer Cliff Fletcher, had extensive NHL management experience before he joined the Penguins in July 2006 – including a four-year stint with the Anaheim Ducks from 2003 to 2006 as director of hockey operations, assistant general manager, and vice president of amateur scouting and player development.

The Montreal native also spent nine years in the front office of the Florida Panthers from 1993 to 2002, working seven seasons as assistant general manager and part of one season (2001-02) as interim general manager. In 1996, the Panthers advanced to the Stanley Cup Final.

Fletcher graduated from Harvard in 1990 and spent one year as the sales and merchandising coordinator for Hockey Canada and two years as a player representative for Newport Sports Management before making the transition to the front office.

Club Directory

Minnesota Wild
317 Washington Street
St. Paul, MN 55102
Phone **651/602-6000**
FAX 651/222-1055
Tickets 651/222-9453
www.wild.com
Capacity: 17,954

Xcel Energy Center

Board Members
Craig Leipold (Owner/Governor), Matt Hulsizer (Minority Owner), Quinn Martin, Mark Pacchini and Jac Sperling

Investors in MSE
Craig Leipold (Owner/Governor), Matt Hulsizer (Minority Owner); Limited Partners: Robert Hubbard, Stanley E. Hubbard, Stanley S. Hubbard, Horace H. Irvine III, Robert Marvin, Robert O. Naegele, Jr., Ford Nicholson, Todd Nicholson, Vance Opperman and Michael Reilly

Owner/Governor	Craig Leipold
Minority Owner	Matt Hulsizer
EVP / General Manager	Chuck Fletcher
Chief Operating Officer	Matt Majka
Executive Vice President, Chief Financial Officer	Jeff Pellegrom
VP, New Business Development / Asst. to Chairman	Jamie Spencer
Vice President Corp. Partnerships and Retail Mgmt.	Carin Anderson
Vice President, Marketing Intelligence	Mitch Helgerson
Vice President, Facility Admin. / G.M., RiverCentre	Jim Ibister
Vice President / G.M., Xcel Energy Center	Jack Larson
Vice President, Brand Content & Communications	John Maher
Vice President and General Counsel	Steve Weinreich
Executive Assistants	Deb Hanson, Stephanie Huseby

Hockey Operations
Assistant General Manager	Brent Flahr
Head Coach	Mike Yeo
Assistant Coaches	Rick Wilson, Darryl Sydor, Darby Hendrickson, Andrew Brunette
Goalie Coach	Bob Mason
Strength and Conditioning Coach	Kirk Olson
Video Coach	Jonas Plumb
Director, Player Personnel/Development	Blair Mackasey/Brad Bombardir
Director, Hockey Administration	Shep Harder
Chief Amateur Scout	Guy Lapointe
Team Operations	Andrew Heydt
Scouting Video Coordinator	Tom Minton
Hockey Ops Coordinator / Administrator	Ben Resnick / Cindy Sweiger
Media Relations Director / Coordinator	Aaron Sickman / Carly Peters / Megan Kogut
Scouts	Marc Chamard, Craig Channell, Paul Charles, Martin Gendron, Brian Fortin, Christopher Hamel, Jamie Hislop, Brian Hunter, Chris Kelleher, Martin Nanne, Frank Neal, Ricard Perrson, Pavel Routa, Ernie Vargas, Darren Yopyk
Head Athletic Trainer / Assistant	Don Fuller / John Worley
Head Equipment Manager / Assistants	Tony DaCosta / Matt Benz, Rick Bronwell
Massage Therapist	Travis Green
Medical Staff	Drs. Sheldon Burns, Joel Boyd, Brad Nelson, Dan Peterson, Chris Larson
Oral Surgeon / Team Dentists	David Hamlar / Kyle Edlund, Mike Pelke

Ticket Sales and Service
Senior Director, Fan Relations	Maria Troje
Director, Ticket Operations	Chris Turns
Senior Manager, New Business Development	Jason Stern

Marketing Intelligence
Director, Marketing Partnerships	Wayne Petersen
Sr. Business Analyst	Bjorn Kadlec
Marketing Manager	Bridget Johnson

Retail Operation
Retail Operations Manager / Buyer	Scott Sarkis / Jen Meyers
Managers, Arena Store / Warehouse	Kyle Gardner / Mitch Krueger
Managers, Maplewood / Southdale Stores	Ryan Geris / Jerry Hudson

Corporate Partnerships and Suite Sales
Senior Account Executive	Bryan Bellows
Account Executive	Jeff Hunsaker
Sr. Mgr. Partnership Activation	Ed Souter
Suite Sales Manager	Mark Fasching

Brand Content and Communications/Broadcasting
Manager, Game Presentation	Paul Loomis
Manager, Production Facilities Operations	Hank Dolan
Manager, Broadcasting and Production	Maggie Kukar
Coordinators, Radio Ops / Production Services	Kevin Falness / Dustin Peterson
Radio Play-By-Play / Analyst	Bob Kurtz / Tom Reid
Television Play-By-Play / Analyst	Anthony LaPanta / Mike Greenlay
Manager, Web and Creative Services	Matt Minnichsoffer
Manager, Digital Content	Ross Hollebon
Lead Graphic Designer / Graphic Designer	Rebecca Finlay / Allison Thompson / Katie Vannelli
Team Curator / Mascot Coordinator	Roger Godin / Robert Hathaway
Social and Digital Media Coordinator	Katlyn Gambill

Community Relations
Executive Director, Wild Foundation	Rachel Schuldt
Coordinator, Community Relations	Bre Tobias

Finance and Accounting
Controller	Trevor Shannon
Sr. Accounting Manager	Tim Kauppi

Human Resources
Director, HR and Organizational Development	Monica Laurent
Human Resources Generalist	Rachel Link

Information Technology
Senior IT Manager / IT Generalist	Mike Vevea / Josh Kielbasa / Richard Jacobson

Miscellaneous
Radio Network Flagship	KFAN 100.3 FM
Television Network	FOX Sports Net North
Team Photographer / Public Address Announcer	Bruce Kluckhohn / Adam Abrams

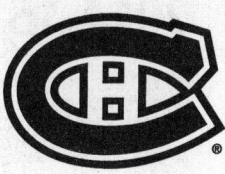

Montreal Canadiens

2014-15 Results: 50W-22L-5OTL-5SOL 110PTS
1ST, Atlantic Division • 2ND, Eastern Conference

Key Off-Season Signings/Acquisitions

2015

June
- 1 • Re-signed C **Gabriel Dumont**.
- 2 • Re-signed D **Jeff Petry**.
- 13 • Re-signed D **Nathan Beaulieu**.
- 15 • Re-signed C **Torrey Mitchell**.
- 30 • Re-signed C **Brian Flynn**.

July
- 1 • Acquired RW **Zack Kassian** and a 5th-round choice in the 2016 NHL Draft from Vancouver for LW **Brandon Prust**.
- 1 • Signed D **Mark Barberio**.
- 1 • Re-signed D **Greg Pateryn**.
- 2 • Re-signed LW **Christian Thomas**.
- 14 • Re-signed LW **Michael Bournival**.
- 15 • Re-signed D **Jarred Tinordi**.
- 24 • Signed RW **Alexander Semin**.
- 30 • Re-signed C **Alex Galchenyuk**.

2015-16 Schedule

Oct.	Wed.	7	at Toronto
	Sat.	10	at Boston
	Sun.	11	at Ottawa
	Tue.	13	at Pittsburgh
	Thu.	15	NY Rangers
	Sat.	17	Detroit
	Tue.	20	St. Louis
	Fri.	23	at Buffalo
	Sat.	24	Toronto
	Tue.	27	at Vancouver
	Thu.	29	at Edmonton
	Fri.	30	at Calgary
Nov.	Sun.	1	Winnipeg
	Tue.	3	Ottawa
	Thu.	5	NY Islanders
	Sat.	7	Boston
	Wed.	11	at Pittsburgh
	Sat.	14	Colorado
	Mon.	16	Vancouver
	Thu.	19	Arizona
	Fri.	20	at NY Islanders
	Sun.	22	NY Islanders
	Wed.	25	at NY Rangers
	Fri.	27	at New Jersey
	Sat.	28	New Jersey
Dec.	Tue.	1	Columbus
	Thu.	3	Washington
	Sat.	5	at Carolina
	Wed.	9	Boston
	Thu.	10	at Detroit
	Sat.	12	Ottawa
	Tue.	15	San Jose
	Thu.	17	Los Angeles
	Sat.	19	at Dallas
	Mon.	21	at Nashville
	Tue.	22	at Minnesota
	Sat.	26	at Washington
	Mon.	28	at Tampa Bay
	Tue.	29	at Florida
Jan.	Fri.	1	at Boston*
	Tue.	5	at Philadelphia
	Wed.	6	New Jersey
	Sat.	9	Pittsburgh
	Thu.	14	Chicago
	Sat.	16	at St. Louis
	Sun.	17	at Chicago
	Tue.	19	Boston
	Sat.	23	at Toronto
	Mon.	25	at Columbus
	Tue.	26	Columbus
Feb.	Tue.	2	at Philadelphia
	Wed.	3	Buffalo
	Sat.	6	Edmonton*
	Sun.	7	Carolina*
	Tue.	9	Tampa Bay
	Fri.	12	at Buffalo
	Mon.	15	at Arizona
	Wed.	17	at Colorado
	Fri.	19	Philadelphia
	Mon.	22	Nashville
	Wed.	24	at Washington
	Sat.	27	Toronto
	Mon.	29	at San Jose
Mar.	Wed.	2	at Anaheim
	Thu.	3	at Los Angeles
	Sat.	5	at Winnipeg
	Tue.	8	Dallas
	Thu.	10	Buffalo
	Sat.	12	Minnesota
	Tue.	15	Florida
	Wed.	16	at Buffalo
	Sat.	19	at Ottawa
	Sun.	20	Calgary
	Tue.	22	Anaheim
	Thu.	24	at Detroit
	Sat.	26	NY Rangers
	Tue.	29	Detroit
	Thu.	31	at Tampa Bay
Apr.	Sat.	2	at Florida
	Tue.	5	Florida
	Thu.	7	at Carolina
	Sat.	9	Tampa Bay

* Denotes afternoon game.

Retired Numbers

1	Jacques Plante	1952-1963
2	Doug Harvey	1947-1961
3	Butch Bouchard	1941-1956
4	Jean Béliveau	1950-1971
5	Bernard Geoffrion	1950-1964
	Guy Lapointe	1968-1982
7	Howie Morenz	1923-1937
9	Maurice Richard	1942-1960
10	Guy Lafleur	1971-1984
12	Dickie Moore	1951-1963
	Yvan Cournoyer	1963-1979
16	Henri Richard	1955-1975
	Elmer Lach	1940-1954
18	Serge Savard	1966-1981
19	Larry Robinson	1972-1989
23	Bob Gainey	1973-1989
29	Ken Dryden	1970-1979
33	Patrick Roy	1984-1996

ATLANTIC DIVISION
99th NHL Season

Franchise date: November 26, 1917

Year-by-Year Record

Season	GP	Home W	L	T	OL	Road W	L	T	OL	Overall W	L	T	OL	GF	GA	Pts.	Div. Fin.	Conf. Fin.	Playoff Result
2014-15	82	26	9	....	6	24	13	....	4	50	22	....	10	221	189	110	1st, Atl.	2nd, East	Lost Second Round
2013-14	82	23	13	....	5	23	15	....	3	46	28	....	8	215	204	100	3rd, Atl.	4th, East	Lost Conf. Final
2012-13	48	14	7	....	3	15	7	....	2	29	14	....	5	149	126	63	1st, NE	2nd, East	Lost Conf. Quarter-Final
2011-12	82	16	15	....	10	15	20	....	6	31	35	....	16	212	226	78	5th, NE	15th, East	Out of Playoffs
2010-11	82	24	11	....	6	20	19	....	2	44	30	....	8	216	209	96	2nd, NE	6th, East	Lost Conf. Quarter-Final
2009-10	82	20	16	....	5	19	17	....	5	39	33	....	10	217	223	88	4th, NE	8th, East	Lost Conf. Final
2008-09	82	24	10	....	7	17	20	....	4	41	30	....	11	249	247	93	2nd, NE	8th, East	Lost Conf. Quarter-Final
2007-08	82	22	13	....	6	25	12	....	4	47	25	....	10	262	222	104	1st, NE	1st, East	Lost Conf. Semi-Final
2006-07	82	26	12	....	3	16	22	....	3	42	34	....	6	245	256	90	4th, NE	10th, East	Out of Playoffs
2005-06	82	24	13	....	4	18	18	....	5	42	31	....	9	243	247	93	3rd, NE	7th, East	Lost Conf. Quarter-Final
2004-05	....	....	....	....	....	....	....	....	....	....	....	....	....	....	....	....			
2003-04	82	23	13	4	1	18	17	3	3	41	30	7	4	208	192	93	4th, NE	7th, East	Lost Conf. Semi-Final
2002-03	82	16	16	5	4	14	19	3	5	30	35	8	9	206	234	77	4th, NE	10th, East	Out of Playoffs
2001-02	82	21	13	6	1	15	18	6	2	36	31	12	3	207	209	87	4th, NE	8th, East	Lost Conf. Semi-Final
2000-01	82	15	20	4	2	13	20	4	4	28	40	8	6	206	232	70	5th, NE	11th, East	Out of Playoffs
1999-2000	82	18	17	5	1	17	17	4	3	35	34	9	4	196	194	83	4th, NE	10th, East	Out of Playoffs
1998-99	82	21	15	5	....	11	24	6	....	32	39	11	....	184	209	75	5th, NE	11th, East	Out of Playoffs
1997-98	82	15	17	9	....	22	15	4	....	37	32	13	....	235	208	87	4th, NE	7th, East	Lost Conf. Semi-Final
1996-97	82	17	17	7	....	14	19	8	....	31	36	15	....	249	276	77	4th, NE	8th, East	Lost Conf. Quarter-Final
1995-96	82	23	12	6	....	17	20	4	....	40	32	10	....	265	248	90	3rd, NE	6th, East	Lost Conf. Quarter-Final
1994-95	48	15	5	4	....	3	18	3	....	18	23	7	....	125	148	43	6th, NE	11th, East	Out of Playoffs
1993-94	84	26	12	4	....	15	17	10	....	41	29	14	....	283	248	96	3rd, NE	5th, East	Lost Conf. Quarter-Final
1992-93	**84**	**27**	**13**	**2**	....	**21**	**17**	**4**	....	**48**	**30**	**6**	....	**326**	**280**	**102**	**3rd, Adams**		**Won Stanley Cup**
1991-92	80	27	8	5	....	14	20	6	....	41	28	11	....	267	207	93	1st, Adams		Lost Div. Final
1990-91	80	23	12	5	....	16	18	6	....	39	30	11	....	273	249	89	2nd, Adams		Lost Div. Final
1989-90	80	26	8	6	....	15	20	5	....	41	28	11	....	288	234	93	3rd, Adams		Lost Div. Final
1988-89	80	30	6	4	....	23	12	5	....	53	18	9	....	315	218	115	1st, Adams		Lost Final
1987-88	80	26	8	6	....	19	14	7	....	45	22	13	....	298	238	103	1st, Adams		Lost Div. Final
1986-87	80	27	9	4	....	14	20	6	....	41	29	10	....	277	241	92	2nd, Adams		Lost Conf. Final
1985-86	**80**	**25**	**11**	**4**	....	**15**	**22**	**3**	....	**40**	**33**	**7**	....	**330**	**280**	**87**	**2nd, Adams**		**Won Stanley Cup**
1984-85	80	24	10	6	....	17	17	6	....	41	27	12	....	309	262	94	1st, Adams		Lost Div. Final
1983-84	80	19	19	2	....	16	21	3	....	35	40	5	....	286	295	75	4th, Adams		Lost Conf. Final
1982-83	80	25	6	9	....	17	18	5	....	42	24	14	....	350	286	98	2nd, Adams		Lost Div. Semi-Final
1981-82	80	25	6	9	....	21	11	8	....	46	17	17	....	360	223	109	1st, Adams		Lost Div. Semi-Final
1980-81	80	31	7	2	....	14	15	11	....	45	22	13	....	332	232	103	1st, Norris		Lost Prelim. Round
1979-80	80	30	7	3	....	17	13	10	....	47	20	13	....	328	240	107	1st, Norris		Lost Quarter-Final
1978-79	**80**	**29**	**6**	**5**	....	**23**	**11**	**6**	....	**52**	**17**	**11**	....	**337**	**204**	**115**	**1st, Norris**		**Won Stanley Cup**
1977-78	**80**	**32**	**4**	**4**	....	**27**	**6**	**7**	....	**59**	**10**	**11**	....	**359**	**183**	**129**	**1st, Norris**		**Won Stanley Cup**
1976-77	**80**	**33**	**1**	**6**	....	**27**	**7**	**6**	....	**60**	**8**	**12**	....	**387**	**171**	**132**	**1st, Norris**		**Won Stanley Cup**
1975-76	**80**	**32**	**3**	**5**	....	**26**	**8**	**6**	....	**58**	**11**	**11**	....	**337**	**174**	**127**	**1st, Norris**		**Won Stanley Cup**
1974-75	80	27	8	5	....	20	6	14	....	47	14	19	....	374	225	113	1st, Norris		Lost Semi-Final
1973-74	78	24	12	3	....	21	12	6	....	45	24	9	....	293	240	99	2nd, East		Lost Quarter-Final
1972-73	**78**	**29**	**4**	**6**	....	**23**	**6**	**10**	....	**52**	**10**	**16**	....	**329**	**184**	**120**	**1st, East**		**Won Stanley Cup**
1971-72	78	29	3	7	....	17	13	9	....	46	16	16	....	307	205	108	3rd, East		Lost Quarter-Final
1970-71	**78**	**29**	**7**	**3**	....	**13**	**16**	**10**	....	**42**	**23**	**13**	....	**291**	**216**	**97**	**3rd, East**		**Won Stanley Cup**
1969-70	76	21	9	8	....	17	13	8	....	38	22	16	....	244	201	92	5th, East		Out of Playoffs
1968-69	**76**	**26**	**7**	**5**	....	**20**	**12**	**6**	....	**46**	**19**	**11**	....	**271**	**202**	**103**	**1st, East**		**Won Stanley Cup**
1967-68	**74**	**26**	**5**	**6**	....	**16**	**17**	**4**	....	**42**	**22**	**10**	....	**236**	**167**	**94**	**1st, East**		**Won Stanley Cup**
1966-67	70	19	9	7	....	13	16	6	....	32	25	13	....	202	188	77	2nd		Lost Final
1965-66	**70**	**23**	**11**	**1**	....	**18**	**10**	**7**	....	**41**	**21**	**8**	....	**239**	**173**	**90**	**1st**		**Won Stanley Cup**
1964-65	**70**	**20**	**8**	**7**	....	**16**	**15**	**4**	....	**36**	**23**	**11**	....	**211**	**185**	**83**	**2nd**		**Won Stanley Cup**
1963-64	70	22	7	6	....	14	14	7	....	36	21	13	....	209	167	85	1st		Lost Semi-Final
1962-63	70	15	10	10	....	13	9	13	....	28	19	23	....	225	183	79	3rd		Lost Semi-Final
1961-62	70	26	2	7	....	16	12	7	....	42	14	14	....	259	166	98	1st		Lost Semi-Final
1960-61	70	24	6	5	....	17	13	5	....	41	19	10	....	254	188	92	1st		Lost Semi-Final
1959-60	**70**	**23**	**4**	**8**	....	**17**	**14**	**4**	....	**40**	**18**	**12**	....	**255**	**178**	**92**	**1st**		**Won Stanley Cup**
1958-59	**70**	**21**	**8**	**6**	....	**18**	**10**	**7**	....	**39**	**18**	**13**	....	**258**	**158**	**91**	**1st**		**Won Stanley Cup**
1957-58	**70**	**23**	**8**	**4**	....	**20**	**9**	**6**	....	**43**	**17**	**10**	....	**250**	**158**	**96**	**1st**		**Won Stanley Cup**
1956-57	**70**	**23**	**6**	**6**	....	**12**	**17**	**6**	....	**35**	**23**	**12**	....	**210**	**155**	**82**	**2nd**		**Won Stanley Cup**
1955-56	**70**	**29**	**5**	**1**	....	**16**	**10**	**9**	....	**45**	**15**	**10**	....	**222**	**131**	**100**	**1st**		**Won Stanley Cup**
1954-55	70	26	5	4	....	15	13	7	....	41	18	11	....	228	157	93	2nd		Lost Final
1953-54	70	27	5	3	....	8	19	8	....	35	24	11	....	195	141	81	2nd		Lost Final
1952-53	**70**	**18**	**12**	**5**	....	**10**	**11**	**14**	....	**28**	**23**	**19**	....	**155**	**148**	**75**	**2nd**		**Won Stanley Cup**
1951-52	70	22	8	5	....	12	18	5	....	34	26	10	....	195	164	78	2nd		Lost Final
1950-51	70	17	10	8	....	8	20	7	....	25	30	15	....	173	184	65	3rd		Lost Final
1949-50	70	17	8	10	....	12	14	9	....	29	22	19	....	172	150	77	2nd		Lost Semi-Final
1948-49	60	19	8	3	....	9	15	6	....	28	23	9	....	152	126	65	3rd		Lost Semi-Final
1947-48	60	13	13	4	....	7	16	7	....	20	29	11	....	147	169	51	5th		Out of Playoffs
1946-47	60	19	6	5	....	15	10	5	....	34	16	10	....	189	138	78	1st		Lost Final
1945-46	**50**	**16**	**6**	**3**	....	**12**	**11**	**2**	....	**28**	**17**	**5**	....	**172**	**134**	**61**	**1st**		**Won Stanley Cup**
1944-45	50	21	2	2	....	17	6	2	....	38	8	4	....	228	121	80	1st		Lost Semi-Final
1943-44	**50**	**22**	**0**	**3**	....	**16**	**5**	**4**	....	**38**	**5**	**7**	....	**234**	**109**	**83**	**1st**		**Won Stanley Cup**
1942-43	50	14	4	7	....	5	15	5	....	19	19	12	....	181	191	50	4th		Lost Semi-Final
1941-42	48	12	10	2	....	6	17	1	....	18	27	3	....	134	173	39	6th		Lost Quarter-Final
1940-41	48	11	9	4	....	5	17	2	....	16	26	6	....	121	147	38	6th		Lost Quarter-Final
1939-40	48	5	14	5	....	5	19	0	....	10	33	5	....	90	168	25	7th		Out of Playoffs
1938-39	48	8	11	5	....	7	13	4	....	15	24	9	....	115	146	39	6th		Lost Quarter-Final
1937-38	48	13	4	7	....	5	13	6	....	18	17	13	....	123	128	49	3rd, Cdn.		Lost Quarter-Final
1936-37	48	16	8	0	....	8	10	6	....	24	18	6	....	115	111	54	1st, Cdn.		Lost Semi-Final
1935-36	48	5	11	8	....	6	15	3	....	11	26	11	....	82	123	33	4th, Cdn.		Out of Playoffs
1934-35	48	11	11	2	....	8	12	4	....	19	23	6	....	110	145	44	3rd, Cdn.		Lost Quarter-Final
1933-34	48	16	6	2	....	6	14	4	....	22	20	6	....	99	101	50	2nd, Cdn.		Lost Quarter-Final
1932-33	48	15	5	4	....	3	20	1	....	18	25	5	....	92	115	41	3rd, Cdn.		Lost Quarter-Final
1931-32	48	18	3	3	....	7	13	4	....	25	16	7	....	128	111	57	1st, Cdn.		Lost Semi-Final
1930-31	**44**	**15**	**3**	**4**	....	**11**	**7**	**4**	....	**26**	**10**	**8**	....	**129**	**89**	**60**	**1st, Cdn.**		**Won Stanley Cup**
1929-30	**44**	**13**	**5**	**4**	....	**8**	**9**	**5**	....	**21**	**14**	**9**	....	**142**	**114**	**51**	**2nd, Cdn.**		**Won Stanley Cup**
1928-29	44	12	4	6	....	10	3	9	....	22	7	15	....	71	43	59	1st, Cdn.		Lost Semi-Final
1927-28	44	12	7	3	....	14	4	4	....	26	11	7	....	116	48	59	1st, Cdn.		Lost Semi-Final
1926-27	44	15	5	2	....	13	9	0	....	28	14	2	....	99	67	58	2nd, Cdn.		Lost Semi-Final
1925-26	36	5	12	1	....	6	12	0	....	11	24	1	....	79	108	23	7th		Out of Playoffs
1924-25	30	10	5	0	....	7	6	2	....	17	11	2	....	93	56	36	3rd		Lost Final
1923-24	**24**	**10**	**2**	**0**	....	**3**	**9**	**0**	....	**13**	**11**	**0**	....	**59**	**48**	**26**	**2nd**		**Won Stanley Cup**
1922-23	24	10	2	0	....	3	7	2	....	13	9	2	....	73	61	28	2nd		Lost NHL Final
1921-22	24	8	3	1	....	4	8	0	....	12	11	1	....	88	94	25	3rd		Out of Playoffs
1920-21	24	9	3	0	....	4	8	0	....	13	11	0	....	112	99	26	3rd and 2nd*		Out of Playoffs
1919-20	24	8	4	0	....	5	7	0	....	13	11	0	....	129	113	26	2nd and 3rd*		Out of Playoffs
1918-19	18	7	2	0	....	3	6	0	....	10	8	0	....	88	78	20	1st and 2nd*		Cup Final/No Decision
1917-18	22	8	3	0	....	5	6	0	....	13	9	0	....	115	84	26	1st and 3rd*		Lost NHL Final

* Season played in two halves with no combined standing at end.
From 1917-18 through 1925-26, NHL champions played against PCHA/WCHL champions for Stanley Cup.

2015-16 Player Personnel

FORWARDS	HT	WT	*Age	Place of Birth	S	2014-15 Club
BOURNIVAL, Michael	5-11	195	23	Shawinigan, QC	L	Montreal-Hamilton
DE LA ROSE, Jacob	6-3	207	20	Arvika, Sweden	L	Montreal-Hamilton
DESHARNAIS, David	5-7	176	29	Laurier-Station, QC	L	Montreal
ELLER, Lars	6-2	209	26	Rodovre, Denmark	L	Montreal
FLYNN, Brian	6-1	180	27	Lynnfield, MA	R	Buffalo-Montreal
GALCHENYUK, Alex	6-1	198	21	Milwaukee, WI	L	Montreal
GALLAGHER, Brendan	5-9	182	23	Edmonton, AB	R	Montreal
KASSIAN, Zack	6-3	214	24	Windsor, ON	R	Vancouver
MITCHELL, Torrey	5-11	189	30	Montreal, QC	R	Buffalo-Montreal
PACIORETTY, Max	6-2	214	26	New Canaan, CT	L	Montreal
PLEKANEC, Tomas	5-11	198	32	Kladno, Czech.	L	Montreal
SEMIN, Alexander	6-2	209	31	Krasnoyarsk, USSR	R	Carolina
SMITH-PELLY, Devante	6-0	220	23	Scarborough, ON	R	Anaheim-Montreal
THOMAS, Christian	5-9	179	23	Toronto, ON	R	Montreal-Hamilton
WEISE, Dale	6-2	205	27	Winnipeg, MB	R	Montreal
DEFENSEMEN						
BARBERIO, Mark	6-1	199	25	Montreal, QC	L	Tampa Bay
BEAULIEU, Nathan	6-2	201	22	Strathroy, ON	L	Montreal-Hamilton
EMELIN, Alexei	6-2	217	29	Togliatti, USSR	L	Montreal
GILBERT, Tom	6-2	204	32	Bloomington, MN	R	Montreal
MARKOV, Andrei	6-0	197	36	Voskresensk, USSR	L	Montreal
PATERYN, Greg	6-2	222	25	Sterling Heights, MI	R	Montreal-Hamilton
PETRY, Jeff	6-3	198	27	Ann Arbor, MI	R	Edmonton-Montreal
SUBBAN, P.K.	6-0	214	26	Toronto, ON	R	Montreal
TINORDI, Jarred	6-6	225	23	Burnsville, MN	L	Montreal-Hamilton

GOALTENDERS	HT	WT	*Age	Place of Birth	C	2014-15 Club
PRICE, Carey	6-3	216	28	Anahim Lake, BC	L	Montreal
TOKARSKI, Dustin	6-0	204	26	Watson, SK	L	Montreal-Hamilton

* – Age at start of 2015-16 season

Michel Therrien

Head Coach

Born: Montreal, QC, November 4, 1963.

The Montreal Canadiens announced the appointment of Michel Therrien as the club's head coach on June 5, 2012. After finishing 15th in the Eastern Conference in 2011-12, Therrien led the Canadiens to a division title in 2012-13. Montreal enjoyed a 100-point season in 2013-14 and reached the Eastern Conference Final. The Canadiens won another division title in 2014-15.

This is Therrien's second stint with the Canadiens, having previously served as a head coach in the organization from 1997 to 2003. The Montreal native joined the franchise in June 1997 taking over behind the bench of the Canadiens' American Hockey League affiliate in Fredericton. In 1999-2000, he became the first head coach of the Quebec Citadelles leading the team to the Atlantic Division Championship in its inaugural season. On November 20, 2000, Therrien became the 25th head coach in Canadiens history. He led the Canadiens to their first playoff appearance in four years in 2001-02.

After Montreal, Therrien spent six years with the Pittsburgh Penguins organization, coaching the club's AHL affiliate in Wilkes-Barre/Scranton from 2003 to 2005, before being promoted to Pittsburgh and leading the Penguins to new heights from 2005 to 2009. Therrien's team was off to a 21-1-3 start in the AHL when he was summoned to Pittsburgh to take over as head coach on December 15, 2005. In 2006-07, his second season behind the Pens' bench, he was a finalist for the Jack Adams Award as NHL coach of the year after leading the Penguins to 105 points and a 47-point improvement over the previous season. It was the fourth-biggest turnaround from one season to the next in NHL history. In 2007-08 under Therrien's guidance, the Penguins kept the same pace and earned 102 regular season points making their way to the Stanley Cup Final, dropping a six-game decision to the Detroit Red Wings. It was the Penguins first division title since 1997-98 and their first berth to the Cup finals since 1991-92.

Before joining the Canadiens, Therrien coached the Laval Titan and the Granby Predateurs in the Quebec Major Junior Hockey League, winning the Memorial Cup with Granby in 1996. In his playing days, he was a solid defenseman who captured the Calder Cup in 1985 as a member of the Sherbrooke Canadiens.

Coaching Record

			Regular Season				Playoffs			
Season	Team	League	GC	W	L	O/T	GC	W	L	T
1990-91	Laval	QMJHL	3	2	1	0	....	....	....	....
1991-92	Laval	QMJHL	3	1	2	....	....	....	....	....
1993-94	Laval	QMJHL	58	41	16	1	21	14	7	....
1993-94	Laval	M-Cup	....	....	....	....	5	2	3	....
1994-95	Laval	QMJHL	63	41	21	1	20	14	6	....
1995-96	Granby	QMJHL	62	49	11	2	20	16	4	....
1995-96	Granby	M-Cup	....	....	....	....	4	3	1	....
1996-97	Granby	QMJHL	67	42	19	6	5	1	4	....
1997-98	Fredericton	AHL	80	33	32	15	4	1	3	....
1998-99	Fredericton	AHL	80	33	36	11	15	9	6	....
99-2000	Quebec	AHL	80	37	34	9	3	0	3	....
2000-01	**Montreal**	**NHL**	**62**	**23**	**27**	**12**	....	....	....	....
2000-01	Quebec	AHL	19	12	6	1	....	....	....	....
2001-02	**Montreal**	**NHL**	**82**	**36**	**31**	**15**	**12**	**6**	**6**	....
2002-03	**Montreal**	**NHL**	**46**	**18**	**19**	**9**	....	....	....	....
2003-04	Wilkes-Barre	AHL	80	34	28	18	24	12	12	....
2004-05	Wilkes-Barre	AHL	80	39	27	14	11	5	6	....
2005-06	**Pittsburgh**	**NHL**	**51**	**14**	**29**	**8**	....	....	....	....
2005-06	Wilkes-Barre	AHL	25	21	1	3	....	....	....	....
2006-07	**Pittsburgh**	**NHL**	**82**	**47**	**24**	**11**	**5**	**1**	**4**	....
2007-08	**Pittsburgh**	**NHL**	**82**	**47**	**27**	**8**	**20**	**14**	**6**	....
2008-09	**Pittsburgh**	**NHL**	**57**	**27**	**25**	**5**	....	....	....	....
2012-13	**Montreal**	**NHL**	**48**	**29**	**14**	**5**	**5**	**1**	**4**	....
2013-14	**Montreal**	**NHL**	**82**	**46**	**28**	**8**	**18**	**11**	**7**	....
2014-15	**Montreal**	**NHL**	**82**	**50**	**22**	**10**	**12**	**6**	**6**	....
	NHL Totals		**674**	**337**	**246**	**91**	**72**	**39**	**33**	....

2014-15 Scoring

* – rookie

Regular Season

Pos	#	Player	Team	GP	G	A	Pts	TOI	+/–	PIM	PP	SH	GW	S	S%
L	67	Max Pacioretty	MTL	80	37	30	67	19:23	38	32	7	3	10	302	12.3
C	14	Tomas Plekanec	MTL	82	26	34	60	19:09	8	46	7	3	5	248	10.5
D	76	P.K. Subban	MTL	82	15	45	60	26:12	21	74	8	0	5	170	8.8
D	79	Andrei Markov	MTL	81	10	40	50	24:54	22	38	4	0	1	135	7.4
C	51	David Desharnais	MTL	82	14	34	48	17:14	22	24	2	0	4	90	15.6
R	11	Brendan Gallagher	MTL	82	24	23	47	16:35	18	31	3	0	6	254	9.4
C	27	Alex Galchenyuk	MTL	80	20	26	46	16:25	8	39	3	0	1	163	12.3
R	22	Dale Weise	MTL	79	10	19	29	12:10	21	34	0	0	1	91	11.0
C	81	Lars Eller	MTL	77	15	12	27	15:29	–6	42	1	0	7	150	10.0
R	15	P.A. Parenteau	MTL	56	8	14	22	14:59	0	30	3	0	1	97	8.2
D	26	Jeff Petry	EDM	59	4	11	15	20:57	–25	32	1	0	1	103	3.9
			MTL	19	3	4	7	22:11	–3	10	0	0	0	23	13.0
			Total	78	7	15	22	21:15	–28	42	1	0	1	126	5.6
R	21	Devante Smith-Pelly	ANA	54	5	12	17	14:38	1	12	0	1	1	76	6.6
			MTL	20	1	2	3	13:17	–2	12	0	0	0	28	3.6
			Total	74	6	14	20	14:16	–1	24	0	1	1	104	5.8
L	8	Brandon Prust	MTL	82	4	14	18	12:57	6	134	0	0	0	78	5.1
C	32	Brian Flynn	BUF	54	5	12	17	15:53	–3	8	0	0	0	73	6.8
			MTL	9	0	0	0	9:04	–2	0	0	0	0	9	0.0
			Total	63	5	12	17	14:54	–5	8	0	0	0	82	6.1
C	17	Torrey Mitchell	BUF	51	6	7	13	15:20	–6	26	0	0	2	45	13.3
			MTL	14	0	1	1	10:03	–2	8	0	0	0	10	0.0
			Total	65	6	8	14	14:11	–8	34	0	0	2	55	10.9
D	74	Alexei Emelin	MTL	68	3	11	14	19:49	5	59	0	0	0	43	7.0
D	55	Sergei Gonchar	DAL	3	0	1	1	13:01	–1	2	0	0	0	1	0.0
			MTL	45	1	12	13	17:59	7	16	0	0	0	45	2.2
			Total	48	1	13	14	17:41	6	18	0	0	0	46	2.2
D	77	Tom Gilbert	MTL	72	4	8	12	19:20	10	30	0	0	0	70	5.7
D	28	Nathan Beaulieu	MTL	64	1	8	9	15:41	6	45	0	0	0	62	1.6
L	25 *	Jacob de La Rose	MTL	33	4	2	6	13:47	–5	12	0	1	0	38	10.5
L	49	Michael Bournival	MTL	29	3	2	5	7:53	3	4	0	0	1	27	11.1
C	20	Manny Malhotra	MTL	58	1	3	4	10:51	–6	12	0	0	1	46	2.2
D	43	Mike Weaver	MTL	31	0	4	4	14:09	0	6	0	0	0	8	0.0
R	58 *	Sven Andrighetto	MTL	12	2	1	3	9:24	0	0	0	0	0	12	16.7
D	6	Bryan Allen	ANA	6	0	1	1	18:12	0	4	0	0	0	4	0.0
			MTL	5	0	1	1	12:44	–2	2	0	0	0	2	0.0
			Total	11	0	2	2	15:43	–2	6	0	0	0	6	0.0
D	24	Jarred Tinordi	MTL	13	0	2	2	12:04	–5	19	0	0	0	5	0.0
L	60 *	Christian Thomas	MTL	18	1	0	1	9:05	–2	7	0	0	0	26	3.8
L	38	Drayson Bowman	MTL	3	0	0	0	6:30	0	0	0	0	0	0	0.0
C	37 *	Gabriel Dumont	MTL	3	0	0	0	9:07	–1	0	0	0	0	4	0.0
L	17	Eric Tangradi	MTL	7	0	0	0	7:43	–3	17	0	0	0	5	0.0
D	64 *	Greg Pateryn	MTL	17	0	0	0	12:39	0	6	0	0	0	10	0.0

Goaltending

No.	Goaltender	GPI	Mins	Avg	W	L	OT	EN	SO	GA	SA	Sv%	G	A	PIM
31	Carey Price	66	3977	1.96	44	16	6	5	9	130	1953	.933	0	1	4
35	* Dustin Tokarski	17	1005	2.75	6	6	4	3	0	46	509	.910	0	1	0
	Totals	**82**	**5007**	**2.20**	**50**	**22**	**10**	**8**	**9**	**184**	**2470**	**.926**			

Playoffs

Pos	#	Player	Team	GP	G	A	Pts	TOI	+/–	PIM	PP	SH	GW	OT	S	S%
D	76	P.K. Subban	MTL	12	1	7	8	26:45	1	31	0	0	0	0	36	2.8
L	67	Max Pacioretty	MTL	11	5	2	7	19:50	2	16	1	1	0	0	46	10.9
R	11	Brendan Gallagher	MTL	12	3	2	5	18:01	5	0	0	0	1	0	42	7.1
D	77	Tom Gilbert	MTL	12	2	3	5	19:34	5	14	0	0	0	0	13	15.4
C	17	Torrey Mitchell	MTL	12	1	4	5	12:30	4	6	0	0	0	0	9	11.1
C	14	Tomas Plekanec	MTL	12	1	3	4	20:23	3	6	0	0	0	0	37	2.7
L	8	Brandon Prust	MTL	12	1	3	4	13:46	1	35	0	0	0	0	20	5.0
C	27	Alex Galchenyuk	MTL	12	1	3	4	16:00	1	10	0	0	1	1	24	4.2
D	26	Jeff Petry	MTL	12	2	1	3	22:16	2	4	1	0	0	0	27	7.4
R	22	Dale Weise	MTL	12	2	1	3	12:30	3	16	0	0	1	1	27	7.4
C	32	Brian Flynn	MTL	6	1	2	3	10:59	–1	0	0	0	1	0	10	10.0
C	51	David Desharnais	MTL	11	1	2	3	16:14	–1	4	0	0	1	0	15	6.7
C	81	Lars Eller	MTL	12	1	2	3	15:59	0	4	0	1	0	0	26	3.8
R	21	Devante Smith-Pelly	MTL	12	1	2	3	12:18	–1	2	0	0	0	0	22	4.5
D	64 *	Greg Pateryn	MTL	7	0	3	3	10:57	2	0	0	0	0	0	6	0.0
R	15	P.A. Parenteau	MTL	8	1	1	2	14:21	0	2	0	0	1	0	15	6.7
D	79	Andrei Markov	MTL	12	1	1	2	24:04	–1	8	0	0	0	0	15	6.7
D	74	Alexei Emelin	MTL	12	0	2	2	21:29	1	10	0	0	0	0	9	0.0
D	28	Nathan Beaulieu	MTL	5	0	1	1	12:55	1	0	0	0	0	0	3	0.0
L	25 *	Jacob de La Rose	MTL	12	0	0	0	12:40	0	4	0	0	0	0	14	0.0

Goaltending

No.	Goaltender	GPI	Mins	Avg	W	L	EN	SO	GA	SA	Sv%	G	A	PIM
31	Carey Price	12	752	2.23	6	6	1	1	28	352	.920	0	0	2
	Totals	**12**	**755**	**2.30**	**6**	**6**	**1**	**1**	**29**	**353**	**.918**			

Coaching History

Jack Laviolette, 1909-10; Adolphe Lecours, 1910-11; Napoleon Dorval, 1911-12, 1912-13; Jimmy Gardner, 1913-14, 1914-15; Newsy Lalonde, 1915-16 to 1920-21; Newsy Lalonde and Léo Dandurand, 1921-22; Léo Dandurand, 1922-23 to 1925-26; Cecil Hart, 1926-27 to 1931-32; Newsy Lalonde, 1932-33, 1933-34; Newsy Lalonde and Léo Dandurand, 1934-35; Sylvio Mantha, 1935-36; Cecil Hart, 1936-37, 1937-38; Cecil Hart and Jules Dugal, 1938-39; Babe Siebert, 1939*; Pit Lepine, 1939-40; Dick Irvin 1940-41 to 1954-55; Toe Blake, 1955-56 to 1967-68; Claude Ruel, 1968-69, 1969-70; Claude Ruel and Al MacNeil, 1970-71; Scotty Bowman, 1971-72 to 1978-79; Bernie Geoffrion and Claude Ruel, 1979-80; Claude Ruel, 1980-81; Bob Berry, 1981-82, 1982-83; Bob Berry and Jacques Lemaire, 1983-84; Jacques Lemaire, 1984-85; Jean Perron, 1985-86 to 1987-88; Pat Burns, 1988-89 to 1991-92; Jacques Demers, 1992-93 to 1994-95; Jacques Demers, Jacques Laperriere, Mario Tremblay, 1995-96; Mario Tremblay, 1996-97; Alain Vigneault, 1997-98 to 1999-2000; Alain Vigneault and Michel Therrien, 2000-01; Michel Therrien, 2001-02; Michel Therrien and Claude Julien, 2002-03; Claude Julien, 2003-04, 2004-05; Claude Julien and Bob Gainey, 2005-06; Guy Carbonneau, 2006-07, 2007-08; Guy Carbonneau and Bob Gainey, 2008-09; Jacques Martin, 2009-10, 2010-11; Jacques Martin and Randy Cunneyworth, 2011-12; Michel Therrien, 2012-13 to date.

* Named coach in summer but died before 1939-40 season began.

Club Records

Team

(Figures in brackets for season records are games played; records for fewest points, wins, ties, losses, goals, goals against are for 70 or more games)

Most Points .... *132 — 1976-77 (80)
Most Wins .... 60 — 1976-77 (80)
Most Ties .... 23 — 1962-63 (70)
Most Losses .... 40 — 1983-84 (80), 2000-01 (82)
Most Goals .... 387 — 1976-77 (80)
Most Goals Against .... 295 — 1983-84 (80)
Fewest Points .... 65 — 1950-51 (70)
Fewest Wins .... 25 — 1950-51 (70)
Fewest Ties .... 5 — 1983-84 (80)
Fewest Losses .... *8 — 1976-77 (80)
Fewest Goals .... 155 — 1952-53 (70)
Fewest Goals Against ...... *131 — 1955-56 (70)

Longest Winning Streak
- **Overall** .... 12 — Jan. 6-Feb. 3/68
- **Home** .... 13 — Nov. 2/43-Jan. 8/44, Jan. 30-Mar. 26/77
- **Away** .... 8 — Dec. 18/77-Jan. 18/78, Jan. 21-Feb. 21/82

Longest Undefeated Streak
- **Overall** .... 28 — Dec. 18/77-Feb. 23/78 (23W, 5T)
- **Home** .... *34 — Nov. 1/76-Apr. 2/77 (28W, 6T)
- **Away** .... *23 — Nov. 27/74-Mar. 12/75 (14W, 9T)

Longest Losing Streak
- **Overall** .... 12 — Feb. 13-Mar. 13/26
- **Home** .... 7 — Dec. 16/39-Jan. 18/40, Oct. 28-Nov. 25/00
- **Away** .... 10 — Jan. 16-Mar. 13/26

Longest Winless Streak
- **Overall** .... 12 — Feb. 13-Mar. 13/26 (12L), Nov. 28-Dec. 29/35 (8L, 4T)
- **Home** .... 15 — Dec. 16/39-Mar. 7/40 (12L, 3T)
- **Away** .... 12 — Nov. 26/33-Jan. 28/34 (8L, 4T), Oct. 20-Dec. 13/51 (8L, 4T)

Most Shutouts, Season ...... *22 — 1928-29 (44)
Most PIM, Season .... 1,847 — 1995-96 (82)
Most Goals, Game .... *16 — Mar. 3/20 (Mtl. 16 at Que. 3)

Individual

Most Seasons .... 20 — Henri Richard, Jean Béliveau
Most Games .... 1,256 — Henri Richard
Most Goals, Career .... 544 — Maurice Richard
Most Assists, Career .... 728 — Guy Lafleur
Most Points, Career .... 1,246 — Guy Lafleur (518G, 728A)
Most PIM, Career .... 2,248 — Chris Nilan
Most Shutouts, Career .... 75 — George Hainsworth
Longest Consecutive Games Streak .... 560 — Doug Jarvis (Oct. 8/75-Apr. 4/82)
Most Goals, Season .... 60 — Steve Shutt (1976-77), Guy Lafleur (1977-78)
Most Assists, Season .... 82 — Pete Mahovlich (1974-75)
Most Points, Season .... 136 — Guy Lafleur (1976-77; 56G, 80A)
Most PIM, Season .... 358 — Chris Nilan (1984-85)
Most Points, Defenseman, Season .... 85 — Larry Robinson (1976-77; 19G, 66A)
Most Points, Center, Season .... 117 — Pete Mahovlich (1974-75; 35G, 82A)
Most Points, Right Wing, Season .... 136 — Guy Lafleur (1976-77; 56G, 80A)
Most Points, Left Wing, Season .... 110 — Mats Naslund (1985-86; 43G, 67A)
Most Points, Rookie, Season .... 71 — Mats Naslund (1982-83; 26G, 45A), Kjell Dahlin (1985-86; 32G, 39A)
Most Shutouts, Season ...... *22 — George Hainsworth (1928-29)
Most Goals, Game .... 6 — Newsy Lalonde (Jan. 10/20)
Most Assists, Game .... 6 — Elmer Lach (Feb. 6/43)
Most Points, Game .... 8 — Maurice Richard (Dec. 28/44; 5G, 3A), Bert Olmstead (Jan. 9/54; 4G, 4A)

* NHL Record.

All-time Record vs. Other Clubs

Regular Season

	Total								At Home								On Road							
	GP	W	L	T	OL	GF	GA	PTS	GP	W	L	T	OL	GF	GA	PTS	GP	W	L	T	OL	GF	GA	PTS
Anaheim	26	12	11	2	1	77	78	27	13	5	5	2	1	39	37	13	13	7	6	0	0	38	41	14
Arizona	68	45	14	9	0	286	180	99	34	28	4	2	0	159	75	58	34	17	10	7	0	127	105	41
Boston	729	355	264	103	7	2210	1922	820	364	211	103	47	3	1219	855	472	365	144	161	56	4	991	1067	348
Buffalo	266	113	107	31	15	809	781	272	134	70	44	12	8	465	381	160	132	43	63	19	7	344	400	112
Calgary	109	57	36	15	1	361	304	130	53	30	15	8	0	182	132	68	56	27	21	7	1	179	172	62
Carolina	190	105	59	20	6	688	541	236	94	60	25	7	2	363	262	129	96	45	34	13	4	325	279	107
Chicago	559	303	152	103	1	1849	1412	710	281	178	55	48	0	1079	664	404	278	125	97	55	1	770	748	306
Colorado	137	69	50	15	3	519	447	156	69	41	16	10	2	285	217	94	68	28	34	5	1	234	230	62
Columbus	17	9	4	1	3	43	38	22	10	4	3	1	2	23	22	11	7	5	1	0	1	20	16	11
Dallas	127	73	33	21	0	480	326	167	63	41	13	9	0	264	155	91	64	32	20	12	0	216	171	76
Detroit	576	277	200	96	3	1750	1475	653	289	176	68	43	2	1016	654	397	287	101	132	53	1	734	821	256
Edmonton	79	38	32	4	5	257	262	85	37	19	11	4	3	127	119	45	42	19	21	0	2	130	143	40
Florida	83	40	33	6	4	216	201	90	40	19	14	3	4	101	88	45	43	21	19	3	0	115	113	45
Los Angeles	139	89	29	20	1	577	384	199	69	49	9	11	0	306	174	109	70	40	20	9	1	271	210	90
Minnesota	15	8	5	1	1	51	38	18	8	5	2	1	0	29	20	11	7	3	3	0	1	22	18	7
Nashville	18	10	5	1	2	46	50	23	9	6	2	0	1	25	22	13	9	4	3	1	1	21	28	10
New Jersey	145	71	60	10	4	456	400	156	72	38	26	6	2	218	184	84	73	33	34	4	2	238	216	72
NY Islanders	157	84	50	15	8	506	444	191	78	47	17	9	5	278	214	108	79	37	33	6	3	228	230	83
NY Rangers	617	330	190	94	3	2073	1596	757	309	204	64	40	1	1189	707	449	308	126	126	54	2	884	889	308
Ottawa	125	61	50	5	9	363	369	136	63	34	22	4	3	189	177	75	62	27	28	1	6	174	192	61
Philadelphia	184	84	68	30	2	585	548	200	93	47	31	14	1	318	273	109	91	37	37	16	1	267	275	91
Pittsburgh	201	118	54	23	6	784	571	265	100	69	18	10	3	437	265	151	101	49	36	13	3	347	306	114
St. Louis	126	73	28	22	3	476	339	171	64	42	12	7	3	267	176	94	62	31	16	15	0	209	163	77
San Jose	32	15	11	4	2	87	81	36	16	11	3	2	0	50	27	24	16	4	8	2	2	37	54	12
Tampa Bay	85	40	34	6	5	226	215	91	42	21	15	1	5	114	103	48	43	19	19	5	0	112	112	43
Toronto	728	347	285	88	8	2227	2019	790	364	214	102	43	5	1260	916	476	364	133	183	45	3	967	1103	314
Vancouver	122	79	27	13	3	483	318	174	60	43	11	5	1	263	148	92	62	36	16	8	2	220	170	82
Washington	156	74	57	17	8	497	402	173	79	42	25	8	4	275	188	96	77	32	32	9	4	222	214	77
Winnipeg	55	35	13	2	5	167	119	77	28	20	5	0	3	97	62	43	27	15	8	2	2	70	57	34
Defunct Clubs	461	246	155	60	0	1365	1075	552	231	148	58	25	0	779	469	321	230	98	97	35	0	586	606	231
Totals	**6332**	**3260**	**2116**	**837**	**119**	**20514**	**16935**	**7476**	**3166**	**1922**	**798**	**382**	**64**	**11416**	**7786**	**4290**	**3166**	**1338**	**1318**	**455**	**55**	**9098**	**9149**	**3186**

Playoffs

	Series	W	L	GP	W	L	T	GF	GA	Last Mtg.	Rnd.	Result
Boston	34	25	9	177	106	71	0	531	436	2014	SR	W 4-3
Buffalo	7	4	3	35	18	17	0	124	111	1998	CSF	L 0-4
Calgary	2	1	1	11	6	5	0	31	32	1989	F	L 2-4
Carolina	7	5	2	39	23	16	0	125	106	2006	CQF	L 2-4
Chicago	17	12	5	81	50	29	2	261	185	1976	QF	W 4-0
Colorado	5	3	2	31	17	14	0	105	85	1993	DSF	W 4-2
Dallas	2	1	1	13	7	6	0	48	37	1980	QF	L 3-4
Detroit	12	5	7	62	33	29	0	161	149	1978	QF	W 4-1
Edmonton	1	0	1	3	0	3	0	6	15	1981	PR	L 0-3
Los Angeles	1	1	0	5	4	1	0	15	12	1993	F	W 4-1
New Jersey	1	0	1	5	1	4	0	11	22	1997	CQF	L 1-4
NY Islanders	4	3	1	22	14	8	0	64	55	1993	CF	W 4-1
NY Rangers	15	7	8	67	36	29	2	203	178	2014	CF	L 2-4
Ottawa	2	1	1	11	5	6	0	21	32	2015	FR	W 4-2
Philadelphia	6	3	3	31	16	15	0	93	89	2010	CF	L 1-4
Pittsburgh	2	2	0	13	8	5	0	37	33	2010	CSF	W 4-3
St. Louis	3	3	0	12	12	0	0	42	14	1977	QF	W 4-0
Tampa Bay	3	1	2	14	6	8	0	34	41	2015	SR	L 2-4
Toronto	15	8	7	71	42	29	0	215	160	1979	QF	W 4-0
Vancouver	1	1	0	5	4	1	0	20	9	1975	QF	W 4-1
Washington	1	1	0	7	4	3	0	20	22	2010	CQF	W 4-3
Defunct Clubs	10*	5	4	28	15	9	4	70	71			
Totals	**151***	**92**	**58**	**743**	**427**	**308**	**8**	**2237**	**1894**			

* 1919 Final incomplete due to influenza epidemic.

Playoff Results 2015-2011

Year	Round	Opponent	Result	GF	GA
2015	SR	Tampa Bay	L 2-4	13	17
	FR	Ottawa	W 4-2	12	12
2014	CF	NY Rangers	L 2-4	15	20
	SR	Boston	W 4-3	20	16
	FR	Tampa Bay	W 4-0	16	10
2013	CQF	Ottawa	L 1-4	9	20
2011	CQF	Boston	L 3-4	17	17

Abbreviations: Round: F – Final; **CF** – conference final; **CSF** – conference semi-final; **SR** – second round; **CQF** – conference quarter-final; **FR** – first round; **DSF** – division semi-final; **QF** – quarter-final; **PR** – preliminary round.

Calgary totals include Atlanta Flames, 1972-73 to 1979-80. Carolina totals include Hartford, 1979-80 to 1996-97.
Colorado totals include Quebec, 1979-80 to 1994-95. Dallas totals include Minnesota North Stars, 1967-68 to 1992-93.
New Jersey totals include Kansas City, 1974-75, 1975-76, and Colorado Rockies, 1976-77 to 1981-82.
Phoenix totals include Winnipeg, 1979-80 to 1995-96. Winnipeg totals include Atlanta Thrashers, 1999-2000 to 2010-11.

2014-15 Results

Oct.	8	at Toronto	4-3
	9	at Washington	2-1†
	11	at Philadelphia	4-3†
	13	at Tampa Bay	1-7
	16	Boston	6-4
	18	Colorado	3-2
	21	Detroit	2-1*
	25	NY Rangers	3-1
	27	at Edmonton	0-3
	28	at Calgary	2-1†
	30	at Vancouver	2-3*
Nov.	2	Calgary	2-6
	4	Chicago	0-5
	5	at Buffalo	2-1†
	8	Minnesota	4-1
	11	Winnipeg	3-0
	13	Boston	5-1
	15	Philadelphia	6-3
	16	at Detroit	4-1
	18	Pittsburgh	0-4
	20	St. Louis	4-1
	22	at Boston	2-0
	23	at NY Rangers	0-5
	28	at Buffalo	1-2
	29	Buffalo	3-4†
Dec.	1	at Colorado	4-3
	3	at Minnesota	1-2
	5	at Chicago	3-4
	6	at Dallas	1-4
	9	Vancouver	3-1
	12	Los Angeles	6-2
	16	Carolina	4-1
	18	Anaheim	1-2
	20	Ottawa	4-1
	23	at NY Islanders	3-1
	29	at Carolina	3-1
	30	at Florida	2-1†
Jan.	2	at New Jersey	4-2
	3	at Pittsburgh	4-1
	6	Tampa Bay	2-4
	10	Pittsburgh	1-2*
	14	at Columbus	3-2
	15	at Ottawa	1-4
	17	NY Islanders	6-4
	20	Nashville	2-1*
	27	Dallas	3-2
	29	at NY Rangers	1-0
	31	Washington	1-0*
Feb.	1	Arizona	2-3
	3	Buffalo	2-3
	7	New Jersey	6-2
	8	at Boston	3-1
	10	Philadelphia	2-1*
	12	Edmonton	3-4*
	14	Toronto	2-1†
	16	at Detroit	2-0
	18	at Ottawa	2-4
	19	Florida	2-3†
	21	Columbus	3-1
	24	at St. Louis	5-2
	26	at Columbus	5-2
	28	Toronto	4-0
Mar.	2	at San Jose	0-4
	4	at Anaheim	1-3
	5	at Los Angeles	3-4†
	7	at Arizona	2-0
	10	Tampa Bay	0-1*
	12	Ottawa	2-5
	14	at NY Islanders	3-1
	16	at Tampa Bay	2-4
	17	at Florida	3-2
	19	Carolina	4-0
	21	San Jose	2-0
	24	at Nashville	2-3*
	26	at Winnipeg	2-5
	28	Florida	3-2*
	30	Tampa Bay	3-5
Apr.	2	Washington	4-5†
	3	at New Jersey	2-3†
	5	at Florida	4-1
	9	Detroit	4-3*
	11	at Toronto	4-3†

* – Overtime † – Shootout

NHL Draft Selections 2015-2001

Name in bold denotes played in NHL.

2015 Pick		2011 Pick		2007 Pick		2003 Pick	
26	Noah Juulsen	17	**Nathan Beaulieu**	12	**Ryan McDonagh**	10	**Andrei Kostitsyn**
87	Lukas Vejdemo	97	Josiah Didier	22	**Max Pacioretty**	40	Cory Urquhart
131	Matthew Bradley	108	Olivier Archambault	43	**P.K. Subban**	61	**Maxim Lapierre**
177	Simon Bourque	113	Magnus Nygren	65	Olivier Fortier	79	**Ryan O'Byrne**
207	Jeremiah Addison	138	Darren Dietz	73	**Yannick Weber**	113	**Corey Locke**
		168	Daniel Pribyl	133	Joe Stejskal	123	Danny Stewart
2014 Pick		198	Colin Sullivan	142	Andrew Conboy	177	Chris Heino-Lindberg
26	Nikita Scherbak			163	Nichlas Torp	188	**Mark Flood**
73	Brett Lernout	**2010** Pick		192	Scott Kishel	217	Oskari Korpikari
125	Nikolas Koberstein	22	**Jarred Tinordi**			241	Jimmy Bonneau
147	Daniel Audette	113	Mark MacMillan	**2006** Pick		271	Jaroslav Halak
177	Hayden Hawkey	117	Morgan Ellis	20	David Fischer		
207	Jake Evans	147	**Brendan Gallagher**	49	**Ben Maxwell**	**2002** Pick	
		207	John Westin	53	**Mathieu Carle**	14	**Chris Higgins**
2013 Pick				66	**Ryan White**	45	Tomas Linhart
25	Michael McCarron	**2009** Pick		139	Pavel Valentenko	99	Michael Lambert
34	**Jacob de La Rose**	18	**Louis Leblanc**	199	Cameron Cepek	182	**Andre Deveaux**
36	Zachary Fucale	65	**Joonas Nattinen**			212	**Jonathan Ferland**
55	Artturi Lehkonen	79	Mac Bennett	**2005** Pick		275	Konstantin Korneev
71	Connor Crisp	109	Alexander Avtsin	5	**Carey Price**		
86	**Sven Andrighetto**	139	**Gabriel Dumont**	45	**Guillaume Latendresse**	**2001** Pick	
116	Martin Reway	169	Dustin Walsh	121	Juraj Mikus	7	**Mike Komisarek**
176	Jeremy Gregoire	199	Michael Cichy	130	Mathieu Aubin	25	**Alexander Perezhogin**
		211	Petteri Simila	190	**Matt D'Agostini**	37	**Duncan Milroy**
2012 Pick				200	**Sergei Kostitsyn**	71	**Tomas Plekanec**
3	**Alex Galchenyuk**	**2008** Pick		229	Philippe Paquet	109	**Martti Jarventie**
33	Sebastian Collberg	56	Danny Kristo			171	Eric Himelfarb
51	Dalton Thrower	86	Steve Quailer	**2004** Pick		203	Andrew Archer
64	Tim Bozon	116	Jason Missiaen	18	**Kyle Chipchura**	266	Viktor Ujcik
94	Brady Vail	138	Maxim Trunev	84	**Alexei Emelin**		
122	Charles Hudon	206	Patrick Johnson	100	**J.T. Wyman**		
154	Erik Nystrom			150	**Mikhail Grabovski**		
				181	Loic Lacasse		
				212	Jon Gleed		
				246	**Greg Stewart**		
				262	**Mark Streit**		
				278	Alex Dulac-Lemelin		

Captains' History

Jack Laviolette, 1909-10; Newsy Lalonde, 1910-11; Jack Laviolette, 1911-12; Newsy Lalonde, 1912-13; Jimmy Gardner, 1913-14, 1914-15; Howard McNamara, 1915-16; Newsy Lalonde, 1916-17 to 1921-22; Sprague Cleghorn, 1922-23 to 1924-25; Bill Coutu, 1925-26; Sylvio Mantha, 1926-27 to 1931-32; George Hainsworth, 1932-33; Sylvio Mantha, 1933-34 to 1935-36; Babe Siebert, 1936-37 to 1938-39; Walt Buswell, 1939-40; Toe Blake, 1940-41 to 1946-47; Toe Blake and Bill Durnan, 1947-48; Butch Bouchard, 1948-49 to 1955-56; Maurice Richard, 1956-57 to 1959-60; Doug Harvey, 1960-61; Jean Béliveau, 1961-62 to 1970-71; Henri Richard, 1971-72 to 1974-75; Yvan Cournoyer, 1975-76 to 1977-78; Yvan Cournoyer and Serge Savard (interim), 1978-79; Serge Savard, 1979-80, 1980-81; Bob Gainey, 1981-82 to 1988-89; Guy Carbonneau and Chris Chelios, 1989-90; Guy Carbonneau, 1990-91 to 1993-94; Kirk Muller and Mike Keane, 1994-95; Mike Keane and Pierre Turgeon, 1995-96; Pierre Turgeon and Vincent Damphousse, 1996-97; Vincent Damphousse, 1997-98, 1998-99; Saku Koivu, 1999-2000 to 2008-09; no captain, 2009-10; Brian Gionta, 2010-11 to 2013-14; no captain, 2014-15.

General Managers' History

Jack Laviolette and Joseph Cattarinich, 1909-10; George Kennedy, 1910-11 to 1920-21; Leo Dandurand, 1921-22 to 1934-35; Ernest Savard, 1935-36; Cecil Hart, 1936-37, 1937-38; Cecil Hart and Jules Dugal, 1938-39; Jules Dugal, 1939-40; Tom P. Gorman, 1940-41 to 1945-46; Frank J. Selke, 1946-47 to 1963-64; Sam Pollock, 1964-65 to 1977-78; Irving Grundman, 1978-79 to 1982-83; Serge Savard, 1983-84 to 1994-95; Serge Savard and Réjean Houle, 1995-96; Réjean Houle, 1996-97 to 1999-2000; Réjean Houle and Andre Savard, 2000-01; Andre Savard, 2001-02, 2002-03; Bob Gainey, 2003-04 to 2008-09; Bob Gainey and Pierre Gauthier, 2009-10; Pierre Gauthier, 2010-11, 2011-12; Marc Bergevin, 2012-13 to date.

Marc Bergevin

Executive Vice President and General Manager

Born: Montreal, QC, August 11, 1965.

The Montreal Canadiens announced the appointment of Marc Bergevin as executive vice president and general manager on May 2, 2012. Bergevin became the 17th general manager in Canadiens history after having spent the previous seven seasons with the Chicago Blackhawks where he was the assistant general manager under Stan Bowman in 2011-12. After finishing 15th in the Eastern Conference in 2011-12, the Canadiens won a division title in 2012-13 and Bergevin finished third in voting as NHL General Manager of the Year. He finished second in voting in 2013-14 after the Canadiens posted a 100-point season and reached the Eastern Conference Final. Montreal won another division title in 2014-15.

Bergevin held various positions within the Blackhawks organization, including director of player personnel for two seasons (2009 to 2011), and won the Stanley Cup in 2009-10. He served as an assistant coach on Joel Quenneville's staff during the 2008-09 campaign and also spent three years on the Blackhawks scouting staff (2005 to 2008), including one season as director of professional scouting (2007-08).

Originally selected by the Blackhawks in the third round (60th overall) in the 1983 NHL Draft, Bergevin enjoyed a 20-season career as a defenseman in the National Hockey League, collecting 181 points (36 goals, 145 assists) in 1,191 regular season games with Chicago, the New York Islanders, Hartford Whalers, Tampa Bay Lightning, Detroit Red Wings, St. Louis Blues, Pittsburgh Penguins and Vancouver Canucks. Bergevin also skated in 80 playoff contests, reaching the Conference Finals in 1996 (Detroit) and in 2001 (Pittsburgh). He played his junior hockey in the Quebec Major Junior Hockey League with the Chicoutimi Sagueneens, from 1982 to 1984.

Club Directory

Bell Centre

Club de hockey Canadien
1909, avenue des
Canadiens-de-Montréal
Montréal, QC H3B 5E8
Phone: **514/932-2582**
Media Hotline: 514/989-2835
www.canadiens.com
Capacity: 21,287

Executive Management

Owner, President and CEO, Club de hockey Canadien, Bell Centre & evenko	Geoff Molson
Executive VP and Chief Operating Officer	Kevin Gilmore
Executive VP Hockey and General Manager, Hockey	Marc Bergevin
Executive VP and Chief Financial Officer	Fred Steer
Executive VP and General Manager, Facilities Ops	Alain Gauthier
Executive Vice President, Corporate Affairs and Chief Legal Officer	France Margaret Bélanger
Senior Vice President, Communications	Donald Beauchamp
President, Effix – Advertising and Sponsorship Sales	François Seigneur
President, Canadiens Alumni	Réjean Houle
Executive VP & General Manager, evenko	Jacques Aubé
Executive Assistant to the Owner, President and CEO	Rolande Bernier
Executive Assistant to the Exec.VP and COO	Carina Houle
Executive Assistant to the Exec. VP, Corporate Affairs and Chief Legal Officer	Maryse Cartwright

Hockey Operations

Executive Assistant to the General Manager	Susan Cryans
Senior VP, Hockey Operations	Rick Dudley
Assistant General Managers	Larry Carrière, Scott Mellanby
VP, Player Personnel & Director, Amateur Scouting	Trevor Timmins
Directors, Legal Affairs / Player Development / Pro Scouting	John Sedgwick / Martin Lapointe / Vaughn Karpan
Player Development Coach	Rob Ramage
Head Coach	Michel Therrien
Assistant Coaches	Clément Jodoin, Jean-Jacques Daigneault, Dan Lacroix
Coaches, Goaltending / Video / Asst. Video	Stéphane Waite / Mario Leblanc / Éric Gravel
Strength & Conditioning Coach	Pierre Allard
Professional Scouts	Doug Gibson, Scott Masters, Mark Mowers
Assistant Director of Amateur Scouting	Frank Jay
Chief Amateur Scout	Shane Churla
Amateur Scouting Staff	Donald Audette, Alvin Backus, Elmer Benning, Bill Berglund, Serge Boisvert, Bobby Kinsella, Michal Krupa, Hannu Laine, Steve Ludzik Jr., Ken Morin, Christer Rockstrom, Artem Telepin, Pat Westrum
Team Services & Hockey Admin. Manager	Claudine Crépin
Coordinators, Team Services / Scouting	Alain Gagnon / Ken Morin

Medical and Training Staff

Chief Surgeon	Dr. David S. Mulder
Head Team Physician / Orthopedic Surgeon	Dr. Vincent J. Lacroix / Dr. Paul A. Martineau
Assistants to the Chief Surgeon	Dr. Tarek Razek, Dr. Kosar Khwaja, Dr. Dan Deckelbaum
Dentist	Dr. Jean-François Desjardins
Consultant, Sports Psychology	Dr. David Scott
Head Athletic Therapist / Athletic Therapist	Graham Rynbend / Nick Addey-Jibb
Asst. Athletic Therapist / Massage Therapist	Vincent Roof-Racine / Claude Thériault
Consultants, Osteopathy / Physiotherapy	Dave Campbell / Donald Balmforth / Steve Villeneuve
Equipment Manager	Pierre Gervais
Assistants to the Equipment Manager	Patrick Langlois, Pierre Ouellette, Richard Généreux

Communications

Executive Director of Media Relations	Dominick Saillant
Executive Assistant to the Sr VP Communications	Sylvie Lambert
Communications Manager	François Marchand
Manager, Research and Translation	Carl Lavigne

Community Relations/Montreal Canadiens Children's Foundation

Director of Community Relations / Exec. Dir., Foundation	Geneviève Paquette
Managers, Development / Fundraising & Partnerships	Patrick Mahoney / Ryan Frank
Coordinators, Foundation / Community Relations	Sylvie Nadeau, Marie-Pier Perron / Sara Pontbriand

Ticketing and Suite Services

Vice President, Sales	Vincent Lucier
Exec. Dir. / Director / Coord. Luxury Suites and Services	Richard Primeau
Coordinators, Sales / Luxury Suite Services	Sarah Jasmin / Marie-Claude Quesnel
Director, Luxury Suites Services	Sabina D'Ascoli

Marketing/Creative Services/Game Operations

Vice President, Marketing	Dino Di Pancrazio
Executive Director, Marketing	Jon Trzcienski
Executive Director, Creative Services and Video	Jean Simard
Director / Manager, Digital Media	Alexandre Harvey / Vincent Cauchy
Group Manager, HabsTV and Editorial	Shauna Denis
Manager, Consumer Products	Maxime St. Laurent
Senior Coordinator, Promotions & Events	Vanessa Harrison
Managers, Media Planning / Creative Services	Jonathan B. Mailhot / David Bayreuther
Manager, Business Development and Events	Dave McGinnis
Coordinator, Sponsor Integration and Branding	Anne-Frédérique Laporte
Manager, Youth Hockey Development	Stéphane Verret
Coordinators, Game Presentation / Video / Photo	Carl Abran / Marie-Claude Brulé / Florence Labelle

Building Operations

Adm. Asst. to the Exe. VP and GM, Facilities Ops	Marie-France Beaulieu
Vice Presidents Operations and Labour Relations	Xavier Luydlin, Alec Beaudry, Caroline Hamel
Vice President / Asst. Director, Ticket Operations	Cathy D'Ascoli / Lucie Masse
Exec. Directors, Hospitality / Building Services	Marco Carrier / Patrick Auger
Assistant Director, Customer Experience Center	Isabelle Naud-Rodrigue

Information Technology

Vice President, Info and Communication Tech.	Pierre-Éric Belzile
Director – Information and Communication Technology	Jacques Farand
Senior IT Analyst, Development	Louis Pennimpede

Human Resources / Finance

Vice President, Human Resources	Maryse Landry
Executive Assistant to the Executive VP and CFO	Christine Ouellette
Controller / Assistant Controller / Payroll Admin	Raymond Lamarche / Bernadette Kajjouni / Teresa Nola

Broadcasting

Play-by-play TV/Radio	Pierre Houde (RDS), John Bartlett (Rogers Sportsnet), Félix Séguin (TVA Sports), Martin McGuire (Cogéco 98.5 FM), Dan Robertson (TSN Radio 690)
Color TV/Radio	Marc Denis (RDS), Jason York (Rogers Sportsnet), Patrick Lalime (TVA Sports), Dany Dubé (Cogéco 98.5 FM), Sergio Momesso (TSN Radio 690)
Radio/television flagships	RDS (Cable), Rogers Sportsnet (Cable), TVA Sports (Cable), Cogéco (98.5 FM), TSN Radio (690 AM)

Nashville Predators

2014-15 Results: 47W-25L-4OTL-6SOL 104PTS
2ND, Central Division • 3RD, Western Conference

Year-by-Year Record

Season	GP	Home W	Home L	Home T	Home OL	Road W	Road L	Road T	Road OL	Overall W	Overall L	Overall T	Overall OL	GF	GA	Pts.	Div. Fin.	Conf. Fin.	Playoff Result
2014-15	82	28	9	....	4	19	16	....	6	47	25	....	10	232	208	104	2nd, Cen.	3rd, West	Lost First Round
2013-14	82	19	17	....	5	19	15	....	7	38	32	....	12	216	242	88	6th, Cen.	10th, West	Out of Playoffs
2012-13	48	11	9	....	4	5	14	....	5	16	23	....	9	111	139	41	5th, Cen.	14th, West	Out of Playoffs
2011-12	82	26	10	....	5	22	16	....	3	48	26	....	8	237	210	104	2nd, Cen.	4th, West	Lost Conf. Semi-Final
2010-11	82	24	9	....	8	20	18	....	3	44	27	....	11	219	194	99	2nd, Cen.	5th, West	Lost Conf. Semi-Final
2009-10	82	24	14	....	3	23	15	....	3	47	29	....	6	225	225	100	3rd, Cen.	7th, West	Lost Conf. Quarter-Final
2008-09	82	24	13	....	4	16	21	....	4	40	34	....	8	213	233	88	5th, Cen.	10th, West	Out of Playoffs
2007-08	82	23	14	....	4	18	18	....	5	41	32	....	9	230	229	91	2nd, Cen.	8th, West	Lost Conf. Quarter-Final
2006-07	82	28	8	....	5	23	15	....	3	51	23	....	8	272	212	110	2nd, Cen.	4th, West	Lost Conf. Quarter-Final
2005-06	82	32	8	....	1	17	17	....	7	49	25	....	8	259	227	106	2nd, Cen.	4th, West	Lost Conf. Quarter-Final
2004-05	....																		
2003-04	82	22	10	7	2	16	19	4	2	38	29	11	4	216	217	91	3rd, Cen.	8th, West	Lost Conf. Quarter-Final
2002-03	82	18	17	5	1	9	18	8	6	27	35	13	7	183	206	74	4th, Cen.	13th, West	Out of Playoffs
2001-02	82	17	16	8	0	11	25	5	0	28	41	13	0	196	230	69	4th, Cen.	14th, West	Out of Playoffs
2000-01	82	16	18	7	0	18	18	2	3	34	36	9	3	186	200	80	3rd, Cen.	10th, West	Out of Playoffs
1999-2000	82	15	21	3	2	13	19	4	5	28	40	7	7	199	240	70	4th, Cen.	13th, West	Out of Playoffs
1998-99	82	15	22	4	....	13	25	3	....	28	47	7	....	190	261	63	4th, Cen.	12th, West	Out of Playoffs

2015-16 Schedule

Oct.	Thu.	8	Carolina	Sat.	9	at Arizona
	Sat.	10	Edmonton	Tue.	12	at Chicago
	Tue.	13	at New Jersey	Thu.	14	at Winnipeg
	Thu.	15	at NY Islanders	Sat.	16	Minnesota
	Sat.	17	at Ottawa	Tue.	19	Chicago
	Tue.	20	Tampa Bay	Thu.	21	at Winnipeg
	Thu.	22	Anaheim	Sat.	23	at Edmonton
	Sat.	24	Pittsburgh	Tue.	26	at Vancouver
	Wed.	28	at San Jose	Wed.	27	at Calgary
	Sat.	31	at Los Angeles*	**Feb.** Tue.	2	St. Louis
Nov.	Sun.	1	at Anaheim*	Thu.	4	Philadelphia
	Thu.	5	at Minnesota	Sat.	6	San Jose
	Sat.	7	St. Louis	Tue.	9	Washington
	Tue.	10	Ottawa	Fri.	12	at Tampa Bay
	Thu.	12	Toronto	Sat.	13	at Florida
	Sat.	14	Winnipeg	Mon.	15	Dallas
	Tue.	17	Anaheim	Thu.	18	Boston
	Fri.	20	at Columbus	Sat.	20	Los Angeles
	Sat.	21	at Minnesota	Mon.	22	at Montreal
	Mon.	23	at NY Rangers	Tue.	23	at Toronto
	Wed.	25	at Buffalo	Thu.	25	at Chicago
	Fri.	27	at Philadelphia*	Sat.	27	St. Louis*
	Sat.	28	Buffalo	**Mar.** Tue.	1	Dallas
Dec.	Tue.	1	Arizona	Thu.	3	New Jersey
	Thu.	3	Florida	Sat.	5	at Colorado*
	Sat.	5	at Detroit	Tue.	8	at Winnipeg
	Mon.	7	at Boston	Wed.	9	at Calgary
	Tue.	8	at Chicago	Sat.	12	at Vancouver
	Thu.	10	Chicago	Mon.	14	at Edmonton
	Sat.	12	Colorado	Thu.	17	NY Islanders
	Tue.	15	Calgary	Fri.	18	at Washington
	Thu.	17	at St. Louis	Mon.	21	Los Angeles
	Sat.	19	Minnesota	Thu.	24	Vancouver
	Mon.	21	Montreal	Sat.	26	Columbus
	Sat.	26	Detroit	Mon.	28	Colorado
	Mon.	28	NY Rangers	Tue.	29	at Dallas
	Tue.	29	at St. Louis	Thu.	31	at Pittsburgh
	Thu.	31	at Dallas	**Apr.** Sat.	2	San Jose
Jan.	Sat.	2	at Carolina	Tue.	5	Colorado
	Tue.	5	Winnipeg	Thu.	7	Arizona
	Fri.	8	at Colorado	Sat.	9	at Dallas

* Denotes afternoon game.

CENTRAL DIVISION
18th NHL Season

Franchise date: June 25, 1997

Pekka Rinne missed 51 games after hip surgery in 2013-14, but returned to go 41-17-6 for Nashville in 2014-15. Rinne tied for second in the NHL in wins and ranked third with a goals-against average of 2.18.

2015-16 Player Personnel

FORWARDS	HT	WT	*Age	Place of Birth	S	2014-15 Club
ARVIDSSON, Viktor	5-9	177	22	Skelleftea, Sweden	R	Nashville-Milwaukee
BASS, Cody	6-0	203	28	Owen Sound, ON	R	Rockford
BOURQUE, Gabriel	5-10	195	25	Rimouski, QC	L	Nashville
FIALA, Kevin	5-10	180	19	St. Gallen, Switzerland	L	HV 71-Nsh-Milwaukee
FISHER, Mike	6-1	215	35	Peterborough, ON	R	Nashville
FORSBERG, Filip	6-1	186	21	Ostervala, Sweden	R	Nashville
GAUSTAD, Paul	6-5	223	33	Fargo, ND	L	Nashville
HODGSON, Cody	6-0	192	25	Toronto, ON	R	Buffalo
JARNKROK, Calle	5-11	156	24	Gavle, Sweden	R	Nashville
MOSES, Steve	5-9	170	26	Leominster, MA	R	Jokerit
NEAL, James	6-2	208	28	Whitby, ON	L	Nashville
NYSTROM, Eric	6-1	195	32	Syosset, NY	L	Nashville
RIBEIRO, Mike	6-0	177	35	Montreal, QC	L	Nashville
SALOMAKI, Miikka	5-11	198	22	Raahe, Finland	L	Nashville-Milwaukee
SISSONS, Colton	6-1	187	21	North Vancouver, BC	R	Milwaukee
SMITH, Craig	6-1	202	26	Madison, WI	R	Nashville
WATSON, Austin	6-4	193	23	Ann Arbor, MI	R	Milwaukee
WILSON, Colin	6-1	216	25	Greenwich, CT	L	Nashville
DEFENSEMEN						
ALLEN, Conor	6-1	210	25	Chicago, IL	L	NY Rangers-Hartford
ALM, Johan	6-3	209	23	Skelleftea, Sweden	L	Milwaukee
BARTLEY, Victor	6-0	203	27	Ottawa, ON	L	Nashville
BITETTO, Anthony	6-1	210	25	Island Park, NY	L	Nashville-Milwaukee
EKHOLM, Mattias	6-4	204	25	Borlange, Sweden	L	Nashville
ELLIS, Ryan	5-10	175	24	Hamilton, ON	R	Nashville
JACKMAN, Barret	6-0	203	34	Trail, BC	L	St. Louis
JONES, Seth	6-4	205	21	Arlington, TX	R	Nashville
JOSI, Roman	6-1	192	25	Bern, Switzerland	L	Nashville
NAKYVA, Kristian	6-0	198	24	Helsinki, Finland	L	Lulea
WEBER, Shea	6-4	233	30	Sicamous, BC	R	Nashville

GOALTENDERS	HT	WT	*Age	Place of Birth	C	2014-15 Club
HUTTON, Carter	6-1	195	29	Thunder Bay, ON	L	Nashville
MAZANEC, Marek	6-4	187	24	Pisek, Czech.	R	Nashville-Milwaukee
RINNE, Pekka	6-5	204	32	Kempele, Finland	L	Nashville

* – Age at start of 2015-16 season

Captains' History

Tom Fitzgerald, 1998-99 to 2001-02; Greg Johnson, 2002-03 to 2005-06; Kimmo Timonen, 2006-07; Jason Arnott, 2007-08 to 2009-10; Shea Weber, 2010-11 to date.

Coaching History

Barry Trotz, 1998-99 to 2013-14; Peter Laviolette, 2014-15 to date.

Peter Laviolette

Head Coach

Born: Norwood, MA, December 7, 1964.

The Nashville Predators hired 2006 Stanley Cup-winning coach Peter Laviolette as the second head coach in team history on May 6, 2014. In his first season with the club in 2014-15, the Predators posted 104 points and returned to the playoffs after a two-year absence. Laviolette finished third in voting for the Jack Adams Award as coach of the year.

Prior to Nashville, Laviolette spent parts of 12 seasons with the New York Islanders (2001 to 2003), Carolina Hurricanes (2003 to 2009) and Philadelphia Flyers (2009 to 2014) and each of the three teams improved exponentially in the first full season after he took the helm. Laviolette won 52 games in his first full season with Carolina in 2005-06 – earning him runner-up honors for the Jack Adams Award in the closest vote in award history – and winning the Stanley Cup. Laviolette's offensive-minded philosophy is evidenced by his teams' often ranking about the NHL's top 10 in goals scored. Multiple young, developing players who have gone on to become dependable NHL players and in some cases superstars were cultivated under Laviolette's watch, including Eric Staal in Carolina and Claude Giroux in Philadelphia.

Second in wins among U.S.-born NHL coaches, Laviolette has led the United States' entry at the World Championships in 2004 (bronze), 2005 and 2014. He has also represented his country in four Olympic Games, first as a player in the 1988 Calgary Games and the 1994 Lillehammer Games, then as a head coach at the 2006 Torino Games, and as an assistant at the 2014 Sochi Games.

After amassing 268 points (78 goals, 190 assists) in 594 minor-league games in the American and International hockey leagues (Indianapolis, Colorado, Denver, Flint, Binghamton, Providence and San Diego) from 1986 to 1997, and appearing in 12 games for the New York Rangers in 1988-89, Laviolette began his coaching career with the ECHL's Wheeling Nailers in 1997. After posting a 37-24-9 record and reaching the conference finals in his rookie coaching season, he was hired as head coach of the AHL's Providence Bruins, and led the team to an AHL-best 56 wins and a Calder Cup in 1998-99, just one season after the team had won just 19 games and finished last in the league. Following the 1999-2000 season, the 1999 AHL Coach of the Year was promoted to assistant coach of the parent Boston Bruins, which he held for a single campaign (2000-01) before starting his NHL head coaching career with the Islanders in 2001-02.

2014-15 Scoring

* – rookie

Regular Season

Pos	#	Player	Team	GP	G	A	Pts	TOI	+/–	PIM	PP	SH	GW	S	S%
L	9 *	Filip Forsberg	NSH	82	26	37	63	17:19	15	24	6	0	6	237	11.0
C	63	Mike Ribeiro	NSH	82	15	47	62	18:44	11	52	1	0	3	96	15.6
D	59	Roman Josi	NSH	81	15	40	55	26:28	15	26	3	0	4	201	7.5
D	6	Shea Weber	NSH	78	15	30	45	26:22	15	72	5	1	2	237	6.3
C	15	Craig Smith	NSH	82	23	21	44	15:44	11	44	6	0	4	252	9.1
C	33	Colin Wilson	NSH	77	20	22	42	16:12	19	22	3	0	5	172	11.6
C	12	Mike Fisher	NSH	59	19	20	39	18:26	4	39	7	1	1	111	17.1
L	18	James Neal	NSH	67	23	14	37	18:05	12	57	3	0	6	221	10.4
D	44	Cody Franson	TOR	55	6	26	32	21:23	–7	26	4	0	0	92	6.5
			NSH	23	1	3	4	15:25	0	2	1	0	0	35	2.9
			Total	78	7	29	36	19:37	–7	28	5	0	0	127	5.5
C	10	Mike Santorelli	TOR	57	11	18	29	14:57	7	8	0	1	1	102	10.8
			NSH	22	1	3	4	12:54	–7	6	0	0	1	43	2.3
			Total	79	12	21	33	14:23	0	14	0	1	2	145	8.3
D	4	Ryan Ellis	NSH	58	9	18	27	18:58	8	27	2	0	0	118	7.6
D	3	Seth Jones	NSH	82	8	19	27	19:52	3	20	2	1	0	123	6.5
C	7	Matt Cullen	NSH	62	7	18	25	13:00	8	16	0	0	1	90	7.8
C	19 *	Calle Jarnkrok	NSH	74	7	11	18	12:50	2	18	0	0	1	95	7.4
D	14	Mattias Ekholm	NSH	80	7	11	18	19:00	12	52	1	0	1	86	8.1
L	41	Taylor Beck	NSH	62	8	8	16	11:55	–4	18	2	0	3	78	10.3
C	28	Paul Gaustad	NSH	73	4	10	14	12:26	7	60	0	0	1	54	7.4
L	57	Gabriel Bourque	NSH	69	3	10	13	12:00	–13	10	0	0	0	76	3.9
L	24	Eric Nystrom	NSH	60	7	5	12	13:11	0	15	0	1	1	60	11.7
L	25	Viktor Stalberg	NSH	25	2	8	10	11:53	0	18	0	0	1	27	7.4
D	64	Victor Bartley	NSH	37	0	10	10	13:26	1	26	0	0	0	28	0.0
D	20	Anton Volchenkov	NSH	46	0	7	7	13:10	4	14	0	0	0	35	0.0
R	67 *	Miikka Salomaki	NSH	1	1	0	1	10:49	1	0	0	0	0	4	25.0
L	16	Rich Clune	NSH	1	0	0	0	5:30	0	0	0	0	0	0	0.0
D	47	Joe Piskula	NSH	1	0	0	0	16:27	–1	2	0	0	0	0	0.0
L	56 *	Kevin Fiala	NSH	1	0	0	0	11:25	–1	0	0	0	0	3	0.0
L	38 *	Viktor Arvidsson	NSH	6	0	0	0	10:15	0	0	0	0	0	9	0.0
D	83 *	Anthony Bitetto	NSH	7	0	0	0	11:46	–1	7	0	0	0	2	0.0

Goaltending

No.	Goaltender	GPI	Mins	Avg	W	L	OT	EN	SO	GA	SA	Sv%	G	A	PIM
35	Pekka Rinne	64	3851	2.18	41	17	6	8	4	140	1807	.923	0	1	8
39	* Marek Mazanec	2	106	2.26	0	1	0	1	0	4	47	.915	0	0	0
30	Carter Hutton	18	1010	2.61	6	7	4	5	1	44	450	.902	0	0	0
	Totals	**82**	**5010**	**2.42**	**47**	**25**	**10**	**14**	**5**	**202**	**2318**	**.913**			

Playoffs

Pos	#	Player	Team	GP	G	A	Pts	TOI	+/–	PIM	PP	SH	GW	OT	S	S%
L	9 *	Filip Forsberg	NSH	6	4	2	6	20:35	1	4	1	0	0	0	22	18.2
C	33	Colin Wilson	NSH	6	5	0	5	19:44	–1	0	4	0	1	0	19	26.3
L	18	James Neal	NSH	6	4	1	5	20:37	0	8	1	0	0	0	25	16.0
C	15	Craig Smith	NSH	6	2	3	5	20:33	2	0	0	0	1	0	33	6.1
C	63	Mike Ribeiro	NSH	6	1	4	5	23:21	2	4	0	0	0	0	11	9.1
D	3	Seth Jones	NSH	6	0	4	4	28:02	–6	6	0	0	0	0	8	0.0
L	25	Viktor Stalberg	NSH	6	1	2	3	14:08	1	0	0	0	0	0	18	5.6
D	4	Ryan Ellis	NSH	6	0	3	3	26:24	4	2	0	0	0	0	13	0.0
C	7	Matt Cullen	NSH	6	1	1	2	17:19	–1	4	0	0	0	0	11	9.1
D	44	Cody Franson	NSH	5	0	2	2	14:36	1	0	0	0	0	0	6	0.0
C	19 *	Calle Jarnkrok	NSH	6	0	2	2	16:28	–2	0	0	0	0	0	8	0.0
C	10	Mike Santorelli	NSH	4	1	0	1	13:20	2	0	0	0	0	0	7	14.3
D	59	Roman Josi	NSH	6	1	0	1	31:36	–5	0	0	0	0	0	21	4.8
D	14	Mattias Ekholm	NSH	6	1	0	1	26:24	4	2	0	0	0	0	6	16.7
D	6	Shea Weber	NSH	2	0	1	1	25:49	0	2	0	0	0	0	2	0.0
C	12	Mike Fisher	NSH	3	0	1	1	11:32	1	0	0	0	0	0	2	0.0
D	20	Anton Volchenkov	NSH	1	0	0	0	13:51	0	2	0	0	0	0	0	0.0
L	56 *	Kevin Fiala	NSH	1	0	0	0	11:05	–1	0	0	0	0	0	2	0.0
D	64	Victor Bartley	NSH	4	0	0	0	11:21	0	2	0	0	0	0	3	0.0
L	41	Taylor Beck	NSH	5	0	0	0	12:55	–2	2	0	0	0	0	6	0.0
L	57	Gabriel Bourque	NSH	5	0	0	0	15:25	–3	2	0	0	0	0	4	0.0
C	28	Paul Gaustad	NSH	6	0	0	0	15:56	–1	22	0	0	0	0	5	0.0

Goaltending

No.	Goaltender	GPI	Mins	Avg	W	L	EN	SO	GA	SA	Sv%	G	A	PIM
35	Pekka Rinne	6	425	2.68	2	4	0	0	19	208	.909	0	1	0
	Totals	**6**	**429**	**2.66**	**2**	**4**	**0**	**0**	**19**	**208**	**.909**			

Coaching Record

			Regular Season				Playoffs			
Season	Team	League	GC	W	L	O/T	GC	W	L	T
1997-98	Wheeling	ECHL	70	37	24	9	15	8	7	....
1998-99	Providence	AHL	80	56	16	8	19	15	4	....
99-2000	Providence	AHL	80	33	38	9	14	10	4	....
2001-02	**NY Islanders**	**NHL**	**82**	**42**	**28**	**12**	**7**	**3**	**4**	....
2002-03	**NY Islanders**	**NHL**	**82**	**35**	**34**	**13**	**5**	**1**	**4**	....
2003-04	**Carolina**	**NHL**	**52**	**20**	**22**	**10**	....	....	....	....
2004-05	**Carolina**			SEASON CANCELLED						
2005-06 ♦	**Carolina**	**NHL**	**82**	**52**	**22**	**8**	**25**	**16**	**9**	....
2006-07	**Carolina**	**NHL**	**82**	**40**	**34**	**8**	....	....	....	....
2007-08	**Carolina**	**NHL**	**82**	**43**	**33**	**6**	....	....	....	....
2008-09	**Carolina**	**NHL**	**25**	**12**	**11**	**2**	....	....	....	....
2009-10	**Philadelphia**	**NHL**	**57**	**28**	**24**	**5**	**23**	**14**	**9**	....
2010-11	**Philadelphia**	**NHL**	**82**	**47**	**23**	**12**	**11**	**4**	**7**	....
2011-12	**Philadelphia**	**NHL**	**82**	**47**	**26**	**9**	**11**	**5**	**6**	....
2012-13	**Philadelphia**	**NHL**	**48**	**23**	**22**	**3**	....	....	....	....
2013-14	**Philadelphia**	**NHL**	**3**	**0**	**3**	**0**	....	....	....	....
2014-15	**Nashville**	**NHL**	**82**	**47**	**25**	**10**	**6**	**2**	**4**	....
	NHL Totals		**841**	**436**	**307**	**98**	**88**	**45**	**43**	....

♦ Stanley Cup win.

Club Records

Team

(Figures in brackets for season records are games played; records for fewest points, wins, ties, losses, goals, goals against are for 70 or more games)

Most Points	110	2006-07 (82)
Most Wins	51	2006-07 (82)
Most Ties	13	2001-02 (82), 2002-03 (82)
Most Losses	47	1998-99 (82)
Most Goals	272	2006-07 (82)
Most Goals Against	261	1998-99 (82)
Fewest Points	63	1998-99 (82)
Fewest Wins	27	2002-03 (82)
Fewest Ties	7	1998-99 (82)
		1999-2000 (82)
Fewest Losses	23	2006-07 (82)
Fewest Goals	183	2002-03 (82)
Fewest Goals Against	194	2010-11 (82)

Longest Winning Streak

Overall	8	Oct. 5-25/05
Home	9	Dec. 16/14-Feb. 3/15
Away	7	Oct. 16-Nov. 4/06

Longest Undefeated Streak

Overall	8	Dec. 18/99-Jan. 1/00 (5W, 3T/OL), Oct. 5-25/05 (8W)
Home	11	Dec. 20/03-Jan. 31/04 (9W, 2T/OL), Nov. 3-Dec. 23/01 (8W, 3T/OL)
Away	7	Oct. 16-Nov. 4/06 (7W)

Longest Losing Streak

Overall	8	Apr. 4-19/13
Home	6	Jan. 21-Feb. 15/99, Feb. 26-Mar. 21/02, Feb. 21-Mar. 20/08, Apr. 4-15/13, Mar. 1-25/14
Away	10	Mar. 14-Apr. 27/13

Longest Winless Streak

Overall	15	Mar. 10-Apr. 6/03 (10L, 5T/OL)
Home	9	Jan. 21-Mar. 2/99 (8L, 1T)
Away	10	Mar. 14-Apr. 27/13 (7L, 3OL/SOL)

Most Shutouts, Season	11	2006-07 (82)
Most PIM, Season	1,533	2005-06 (82)
Most Goals, Game	9	Mar. 4/04 (Nsh. 9 at Pit. 4), Mar. 18/06 (Cgy. 4 at Nsh. 9), Nov. 18/14 (Nsh. 9 at Tor. 2)

Individual

Most Seasons	15	David Legwand
Most Games	956	David Legwand
Most Goals, Career	210	David Legwand
Most Assists, Career	356	David Legwand
Most Points, Career	566	David Legwand (210G, 356A)
Most PIM, Career	725	Jordin Tootoo
Most Shutouts, Career	36	Pekka Rinne
Longest Consecutive Games Streak	269	Karlis Skrastins (Feb. 21/00-Apr. 6/03)
Most Goals, Season	33	Jason Arnott (2008-09)
Most Assists, Season	54	Paul Kariya (2005-06)
Most Points, Season	85	Paul Kariya (2005-06; 31G, 54A)
Most PIM, Season	242	Patrick Cote (1998-99)
Most Points, Defenseman, Season	56	Shea Weber (2013-14; 23G, 33A)
Most Points, Center, Season	72	Jason Arnott (2007-08; 28G, 44A)
Most Points, Right Wing, Season	72	J.P. Dumont (2007-08; 29G, 43A)
Most Points, Left Wing, Season	85	Paul Kariya (2005-06; 31G, 54A)
Most Points, Rookie, Season	63	Filip Forsberg (2014-15; 26G, 37A)
Most Shutouts, Season	7	Pekka Rinne (2008-09),(2009-10)
Most Goals, Game	4	Eric Nystrom (Jan. 24/14)
Most Assists, Game	5	Marek Zidlicky (Feb. 18/04)

All-time Record vs. Other Clubs

Regular Season

			Total							At Home							On Road				
	GP	W	L	T	OL	GF	GA	PTS	GP	W	L	T	OL	GF	GA	PTS	GP	W	L	T	OL	GF	GA	PTS
Anaheim	61	24	27	2	8	141	170	58	30	15	10	2	3	76	74	35	31	9	17	0	5	65	96	23
Arizona	61	31	24	2	4	179	161	68	31	18	10	2	1	89	74	39	30	13	14	0	3	90	87	29
Boston	21	8	10	1	2	50	61	19	11	6	5	0	0	30	29	12	10	2	5	1	2	20	32	7
Buffalo	19	11	6	1	1	55	43	24	10	4	5	0	1	23	21	9	9	7	1	1	0	32	22	15
Calgary	62	29	22	4	7	175	173	69	32	18	10	1	3	100	82	40	30	11	12	3	4	75	91	29
Carolina	21	12	7	1	1	58	50	26	10	8	2	0	0	29	20	16	11	4	5	1	1	29	30	10
Chicago	95	43	40	4	8	275	271	98	47	24	17	3	3	146	133	54	48	19	23	1	5	129	138	44
Colorado	64	31	25	5	3	182	175	70	31	17	10	3	1	100	91	38	33	14	15	2	2	82	84	32
Columbus	78	53	18	1	6	242	171	113	40	31	5	1	3	134	84	66	38	22	13	0	3	108	87	47
Dallas	65	28	33	1	3	144	173	60	33	19	12	1	1	91	76	40	32	9	21	0	2	53	97	20
Detroit	89	34	43	4	8	225	280	80	44	21	18	2	3	124	122	47	45	13	25	2	5	101	158	33
Edmonton	62	33	23	3	3	174	176	72	32	17	12	3	0	88	94	37	30	16	11	0	3	86	82	35
Florida	22	11	7	3	1	55	55	26	11	7	2	2	0	29	21	16	11	4	5	1	1	26	34	10
Los Angeles	61	29	25	3	4	160	173	65	30	12	14	3	1	69	81	28	31	17	11	0	3	91	92	37
Minnesota	57	26	19	5	7	160	155	64	28	15	8	2	3	75	63	35	29	11	11	3	4	85	92	29
Montreal	18	7	5	1	5	50	46	20	9	4	1	1	3	28	21	12	9	3	4	0	2	22	25	8
New Jersey	21	9	9	0	3	48	61	21	11	4	5	0	2	29	29	10	10	5	4	0	1	24	32	11
NY Islanders	19	11	6	0	2	51	48	24	10	7	3	0	0	28	23	14	9	4	3	0	2	23	25	10
NY Rangers	20	9	9	1	1	45	56	20	9	3	5	0	1	20	29	7	11	6	4	1	0	25	27	13
Ottawa	19	8	10	0	1	47	54	17	9	4	4	0	1	19	19	9	10	4	6	0	0	28	35	8
Philadelphia	20	8	7	3	2	44	55	21	9	4	2	2	1	22	19	11	11	4	5	1	1	22	36	10
Pittsburgh	21	10	8	2	1	63	57	23	11	6	4	0	1	35	27	13	10	4	4	2	0	28	30	10
St. Louis	95	45	36	4	10	214	243	104	48	24	15	3	6	109	115	57	47	21	21	1	4	105	128	47
San Jose	61	28	25	2	6	152	157	64	30	17	11	1	1	80	74	36	31	11	14	1	5	72	83	28
Tampa Bay	20	9	8	2	1	54	57	21	11	6	4	0	1	31	29	13	9	3	4	2	0	23	28	8
Toronto	17	10	6	1	0	56	41	21	6	4	2	0	0	18	16	8	11	6	4	1	0	38	25	13
Vancouver	62	23	31	2	6	157	188	54	32	12	13	1	6	86	88	31	30	11	18	1	0	71	100	23
Washington	21	9	7	1	4	57	58	23	11	6	2	1	2	32	27	15	10	3	5	0	2	25	31	8
Winnipeg	26	15	8	1	2	71	65	33	13	9	4	0	0	40	30	18	13	6	4	1	2	31	35	15
Totals	1278	604	504	60	110	3384	3473	1378	639	342	215	34	48	1775	1611	766	639	262	289	26	62	1609	1862	612

Playoffs

	Series	W	L	GP	W	L	T	GF	GA	Last Mtg.	Rnd.	Result
Anaheim	1	1	0	6	4	2	0	22	20	2011	CQF	W 4-2
Arizona	1	0	1	5	1	4	0	9	12	2012	CSF	L 1-4
Chicago	2	0	2	12	4	8	0	36	36	2015	FR	L 2-4
Detroit	3	1	2	17	8	9	0	34	38	2012	CQF	W 4-1
San Jose	2	0	2	10	2	8	0	24	33	2007	CQF	L 1-4
Vancouver	1	0	1	6	2	4	0	11	14	2011	CSF	L 2-4
Totals	10	2	8	56	21	35	0	136	153			

Winnipeg totals include Atlanta Thrashers, 1999-2000 to 2010-11.

Playoff Results 2015-2011

Year	Round	Opponent	Result	GF	GA
2015	FR	Chicago	L 2-4	21	19
2012	CSF	Phoenix	L 1-4	9	12
	CQF	Detroit	W 4-1	13	9
2011	CSF	Vancouver	L 2-4	11	14
	CQF	Anaheim	W 4-2	22	20

Abbreviations: Round: CSF – conference semi-final; **CQF** – conference quarter-final; **FR** – first round.

2014-15 Results

Oct.							
Oct.	9	Ottawa	3-2	13		Vancouver	5-1
	11	Dallas	4-1	16		Washington	4-3
	14	Calgary	2-3†	17	at	Detroit	2-5
	17	at	Winnipeg	2-0	20	at Montreal	1-2*
	18	at Chicago	1-2*	27		Colorado	4-3*
	21		Arizona	4-3†	29	at St. Louis	4-5†
	23		Chicago	3-2	30	at Colorado	0-3
	25		Pittsburgh	0-3	Feb.	1	at Pittsburgh	4-0
	29	at Edmonton	4-1		3		Toronto	4-3
	31	at Calgary	3-4		5		Anaheim	2-5
Nov.	2	at Vancouver	3-1		7		NY Rangers	3-2
	4	at Winnipeg	1-3		8	at Florida	3-2†
	6	at Dallas	3-2		10		Tampa Bay	3-2*
	8	at St. Louis	2-1		12		Winnipeg	3-1
	11		Edmonton	3-2		14		New Jersey	3-1
	13	at St. Louis	3-4		17		San Jose	5-1
	15		Winnipeg	2-1		19	at NY Islanders	2-5
	18	at Toronto	9-2		21	at Philadelphia	2-3†
	20	at Ottawa	2-3		22	at Buffalo	2-1†
	22		Florida	3-2†		24		Colorado	5-2
	25		Los Angeles	4-3†		26		Minnesota	2-4
	27		Edmonton	1-0*		28		Detroit	3-4
	29		Columbus	2-1	Mar.	2	at NY Rangers	1-4
Dec.	2	at Carolina	1-2		3	at New Jersey	1-3
	4		St. Louis	4-3		5		NY Islanders	3-4
	6		Chicago	1-3		7		Winnipeg	1-3
	9	at Colorado	3-0		9	at Arizona	2-1*
	11	at Arizona	5-1		12	at San Jose	0-2
	13	at San Jose	0-2		14	at Los Angeles	2-4
	16		Boston	3-2†		15	at Anaheim	2-4
	20	at Minnesota	6-5*		17		Minnesota	2-3*
	22	at Columbus	5-1		21		Buffalo	3-0
	23	at Boston	3-5		24		Montreal	2-4
	27		Philadelphia	4-1		26	at Tampa Bay	3-2
	29	at Chicago	4-5†		28	at Washington	4-3
	30		St. Louis	3-2		29		Calgary	2-5
Jan.	3	at Los Angeles	7-6*		31		Vancouver	4-5†
	4	at Anaheim	3-4†	Apr.	4		Dallas	3-4*
	6		Carolina	3-2		7	at Colorado	2-3
	8		Dallas	3-2†		9		Minnesota	2-4
	10	at Minnesota	3-1		11	at Dallas	1-4

* – Overtime † – Shootout

NHL Draft Selections 2015-2001

Name in bold denotes played in NHL.

2015
Pick	
55	Yakov Trenin
85	Thomas Novak
100	Anthony Richard
115	Alexandre Carrier
145	Karel Vejmelka
175	Tyler Moy
205	Evan Smith

2014
Pick	
11	**Kevin Fiala**
42	Vladislav Kamenev
51	Jack Dougherty
62	Justin Kirkland
112	**Viktor Arvidsson**
132	Joonas Lyytinen
162	Aaron Irving

2013
Pick	
4	**Seth Jones**
64	Jonathan Diaby
95	Felix Girard
99	Juuse Saros
125	Saku Maenalanen
140	Teemu Kivihalme
155	Emil Pettersson
171	Tommy Veilleux
185	Wade Murphy
203	Janne Juvonen

2012
Pick	
37	Pontus Aberg
50	**Colton Sissons**
66	Jimmy Vesey
89	Brendan Leipsic
112	Zach Stepan
118	Mikko Vainonen
164	Simon Fernholm
172	Max Gortz
179	**Marek Mazanec**

2011
Pick	
38	**Magnus Hellberg**
52	**Miikka Salomaki**
94	Josh Shalla
112	Garrett Noonan
142	Simon Karlsson
170	Chase Balisy
202	Brent Andrews

2010
Pick	
18	**Austin Watson**
78	Taylor Aronson
126	Patrick Cehlin
168	**Anthony Bitetto**
194	David Elsner
198	**Joonas Rask**

2009
Pick	
11	**Ryan Ellis**
41	Zach Budish
42	Charles-Olivier Roussel
70	**Taylor Beck**
72	**Michael Latta**
98	**Craig Smith**
102	**Mattias Ekholm**
110	Nick Oliver
132	**Gabriel Bourque**
192	Cam Reid

2008
Pick	
7	**Colin Wilson**
18	Chet Pickard
38	**Roman Josi**
136	Taylor Stefishen
166	Jeff Foss
201	Jani Lajunen
207	**Anders Lindback**

2007
Pick	
23	**Jonathon Blum**
54	Jeremy Smith
58	**Nick Spaling**
81	**Ryan Thang**
114	Ben Ryan
119	Mark Santorelli
144	**Andreas Thuresson**
174	Robert Dietrich
204	Atte Engren

2006
Pick	
56	**Blake Geoffrion**
105	Niko Snellman
146	**Mark Dekanich**
176	Ryan Flynn
206	Viktor Sjodin

2005
Pick	
18	**Ryan Parent**
78	**Teemu Laakso**
79	**Cody Franson**
150	**Cal O'Reilly**
176	Ryan Maki
213	Scott Todd
230	**Patric Hornqvist**

2004
Pick	
15	**Alexander Radulov**
81	Vaclav Meidl
107	Nick Fugere
139	Kyle Moir
147	**Janne Niskala**
178	**Mike Santorelli**
193	Kevin Schaeffer
209	Stanislav Balan
243	Denis Kulyash
258	**Pekka Rinne**
275	Craig Switzer

2003
Pick	
7	**Ryan Suter**
35	Konstantin Glazachev
37	**Kevin Klein**
49	**Shea Weber**
76	Richard Stehlik
89	Paul Brown
92	**Alexander Sulzer**
98	Grigory Shafigulin
117	Teemu Lassila
133	Rustam Sidikov
210	Andrei Mukhachev
213	Miroslav Hanuljak
268	Lauris Darzins

2002
Pick	
6	**Scottie Upshall**
102	**Brandon Segal**
138	Patrick Jarrett
172	**Mike McKenna**
203	Josh Morrow
235	Kaleb Betts
264	Matt Davis
266	Steven Spencer

2001
Pick	
12	**Dan Hamhuis**
33	**Timofei Shishkanov**
42	Tomas Slovak
75	Denis Platonov
76	Oliver Setzinger
98	**Jordin Tootoo**
178	Anton Lavrentiev
240	Gustav Grasberg
271	**Mikko Lehtonen**

General Managers' History

David Poile, 1998-99 to date.

David Poile

President of Hockey Operations and General Manager

Born: Toronto, ON, February 14, 1949.

Hired as the first general manager in franchise history on July 9, 1997, David Poile has been committed to building the team through the NHL Draft. In 2003-04, Nashville reached the playoffs for the first time in franchise history. During the 2006-07 season, the team was in contention for first overall in the NHL, setting club records with 51 wins and 110 points. Though forced to rebuild the roster for 2007-08, the Predators reached the playoffs for the fourth year in a row. Poile has an impressive reputation as an NHL leader and in 2001 he received the Lester Patrick Trophy for his contributions to hockey in the United States. His father, Norman "Bud" Poile, had won the honor in 1989. He served as Associate G.M. for the 2010 U.S. Olympic Team and U.S. squads for the 2009 and 2010 IIHF World Championships and was the general manager of the 2014 U.S. Olympic team at Sochi. He was a finalist for the NHL's inaugural G.M. of the Year Award in 2010 and was a finalist for the award again in 2011 and 2012.

Prior to joining Nashville, Poile spent 15 seasons as vice president/general manager of the Washington Capitals. During his tenure in Washington, the Capitals made 14 postseason appearances, winning their only Patrick Division title in 1989 and advancing to the Conference Finals in 1990. During Poile's 15 years in Washington, the Capitals compiled a record of 594-454-132, finished second in the Patrick Division seven times and recorded 90-or-more points seven different seasons.

Poile started his professional hockey career as an administrative assistant for the Atlanta Flames in 1972, shortly after graduating from Northeastern University in Boston. At Northeastern, he was hockey team captain, leading scorer and most valuable player for two years. In 1977, he was named assistant general manager of the Atlanta Flames (who moved to Calgary in 1980), serving as the manager and coordinator of the Flames farm club.

Poile was instrumental in the NHL's adoption of the instant replay rule in 1991. He was awarded *Inside Hockey*'s man of the year for his leadership on the issue. He has also been honored three times as *The Sporting News* NHL executive of the year in 1982-83, 1983-84 and 2006-07. Poile served as general manager of the 1998 and 1999 U.S. national teams for the World Championships.

Club Directory

Bridgestone Arena

Nashville Predators
Bridgestone Arena
501 Broadway
Nashville, TN 37203
Phone **615/770-2300**
FAX 615/770-2309
Ticket Information 615/770-PUCK
www.nashvillepredators.com
Capacity: 17,113

Owner	Predators Holdings LLC
Investor Group	Christopher Cigarran, Thomas Cigarran, Joel and Holly Dobberpuhl, David Freeman, Herbert Fritch, DeWitt Thompson V, John Thompson, W. Brett Wilson & Warren Woo
Chairman and Governor	Thomas Cigarran
Pres. of Hockey Ops/G.M./Alt. Gov.	David Poile
Chief Executive Officer/Alt. Gov.	Jeff Cogen
President/COO/Alt. Gov	Sean Henry
Exec. V.P., General Counsel and Chief Financial Officer	Michelle Kennedy
Sr. V.P., Communications and P.R.	Gerry Helper
Sr. V.P., Corporate Development	Chris Junghans

Hockey Operations

Assistant General Manager	Paul Fenton
Director of Hockey Operations	Brian Poile
Hockey Operations Manager / Assistants	Brandon Walker / Paul Cook, Matt Hamann
Head Coach	Peter Laviolette
Assistant Coaches	Phil Housley, Kevin McCarthy
Goaltending Coach	Ben Vanderklok
Strength and Conditioning Coach	David Good
Video Coach / Coordinator / Assistant	Lawrence Feloney / Jeremy Coupal / Mat Myers
Director of Player Development	Scott Nichol
Chief Amateur Scout	Jeff Kealty
Professional Scouts	Nick Beverley, Shawn Dineen, Vaclav Nedomansky
North American Amateur Scouts	J-P Glaude, Tom Nolan, Ryan Rezmierski, Glen Sanders, David Westby
European Scouts	Martin Bakula, Lucas Bergman, Janne Kekalainen
Head Athletic Trainer / Assistant Trainers	Andy Hosler / D.J. Amadio, Jeff Biddle
Equipment Manager / Asst. Manager	Pete Rogers / Jeff Camelio
Equipment Assistant / Locker Room Attendant	Brad Peterson / Craig 'Partner' Baugh

Medical Staff

Team Doctors	Drs. John E. Kuhn, Paul J. Rummo, Charles L. Cox, Alex Diamond, Daniel S. Weikert, Sean Donahue, Chris Ellis, Kent Higdon, Gary Solomon, Joseph L. Fredi, Stephane Braun, Blair Summitt, Wesley Thayer, Jody Jones, Cliff Brown

Communications/Development

Manager of Communications	Kevin Wilson
Interactive Media & Communications Coordinator	Brooks Bratten
Community Relations Sr. Director / Mgr. / Coordinator	Rebecca King / Kristen Finch / Snow Rose
Team Photographer	John Russell

Corporate Partnerships

Sr. Dir. / Dir., Corporate Partnerships	Delmar Smith / Jeremy Burson
Director, Corporate Development	Jack Burk
Account Executives, Corporate Development	Jon Dickerson, Evan Lindsay, Jordan Wright
Sr. Account Service Mgrs., Corporate Partnerships	Jennifer Maxwell, Paige Ciuffo
Account Manager, Corporate Partnerships	Robin Lee
Business Analytics Manager	Lindsay Rutledge

Marketing

Vice President, Marketing	Danny Shaklan
Mgr., Marketing Entertainment / Interactive	Adam DeVault / Thomas Willis
Youth Hockey & Fan Development Director	Andee Boiman
Youth Hockey & Fan Development Coordinator	Elizabeth Wardlow
Marketing Manager / Coordinator	Sandy Weaver / Megan Stock
Manager, Creative Services	Chuck Stephens
Graphic Designers	Jackie Fisher, Brennan Scott

Premium Seats

Vice President of Service and Retention	Britt Kincheloe
Director / Sr. Manager, Premium Seat Sales	Chris Burton / Tim Wilson
Club Services Manager	Courtney Reilly

Finance/Administration/Human Resources

Sr. Vice President, Finance	Beth Snider
Vice President, Human Resources	Allison Simms
Director, Payroll / Accounting Coordinator	Susan Charnley / Brandy Tatum
Controller	Jane Avinger
Director, Financial Reporting	Kyle Clayton
Exec. Assistant / Office Assistant	Beth DeGrandis / Alyssa Visbeen
Human Resources Director / Admin. Asst.	Courtni Mosley / Pier Vaughn
Associate General Counsel	Sean Marshall

Event Technology/Game Presentation

Directors, Tech. Ops. / Event Presentation	Patrick Abell / Brian Campbell
Game Presentation Coordinator	Shane Blinder
Sr. Dir. Information Technology / Manager / Help Desk	Casey Millar / Michael Paul / Tommy Nelson

Broadcast

Broadcast and Entertainment, Sr. Director / Producer	Bob Kohl / David White
Television Play-by-Play Announcer / Color	Willy Daunic / Stu Grimson
Radio Play-by-Play Announcer / Color	Pete Weber / Brent Peterson, Chris Mason
Television Pre and Postgame Hosts	Mark Howard, Terry Crisp
Rinkside Reporter	Lyndsay Rowley
Video Production Manager	Mitch Jordan
Associate Producer	Brett Newkirk

Ticket Operations

Ticket Sales Vice President / Sr. Dir. / Dir.	Nat Harden / Marty Mulford / Brad Gillispie
Director of Business Strategy	Jordan Kolosey
Vice President of Event Operations	David Chadwell
Director, Ticketing	Lonnie Wilkerson
Senior Manager, Ticket Operations	Sara Shear

New Jersey Devils

2014-15 Results: 32w-36L-7OTL-7SOL 78PTS
7TH, Metropolitan Division • 13TH, Eastern Conference

Key Off-Season Signings/Acquisitions

2015
May 4 • Named **Ray Shero** general manager.
9 • Re-signed RW **Jordin Tootoo**.
June 2 • Named **John Hynes** head coach.
17 • Named **Geoff Ward** and **Alain Nasreddine** assistant coaches.
27 • Acquired RW **Kyle Palmieri** from Anaheim for a 2nd-round choice in the 2015 NHL Draft and a 3rd-round choice in 2016.
July 1 • Signed D **John Moore**.
14 • Re-signed D **Eric Gelinas**.
17 • Re-signed LW **Stefan Matteau**.
18 • Re-signed D **Seth Helgeson**.
25 • Re-signed D **Adam Larsson**.

2015-16 Schedule

Oct.	Fri.	9	Winnipeg	Fri.	8	Boston
	Sat.	10	at Washington	Sun.	10	at Minnesota
	Tue.	13	Nashville	Tue.	12	at St. Louis
	Fri.	16	San Jose	Thu.	14	at Colorado
	Sun.	18	at NY Rangers*	Sat.	16	at Arizona
	Tue.	20	Arizona	Tue.	19	Calgary
	Thu.	22	at Ottawa	Thu.	21	Ottawa
	Sat.	24	at Buffalo	Sat.	23	at Winnipeg
	Tue.	27	Columbus	Tue.	26	at Pittsburgh
	Thu.	29	at Philadelphia	Feb. Tue.	2	NY Rangers
	Sat.	31	NY Islanders*	Thu.	4	at Toronto
Nov.	Tue.	3	at NY Islanders	Sat.	6	Washington*
	Fri.	6	Chicago	Mon.	8	at NY Rangers
	Sun.	8	Vancouver*	Tue.	9	Edmonton
	Tue.	10	St. Louis	Sat.	13	at Philadelphia*
	Thu.	12	at Chicago	Sun.	14	Los Angeles*
	Sat.	14	Pittsburgh	Tue.	16	Philadelphia
	Tue.	17	at Calgary	Fri.	19	NY Islanders
	Fri.	20	at Edmonton	Sat.	20	at Washington
	Sun.	22	at Vancouver	Tue.	23	NY Rangers
	Wed.	25	Columbus	Thu.	25	at Columbus
	Fri.	27	Montreal	Fri.	26	Tampa Bay
	Sat.	28	at Montreal	Mar. Tue.	1	Carolina
Dec.	Tue.	1	Colorado	Thu.	3	at Nashville
	Thu.	3	at Carolina	Fri.	4	at Dallas
	Fri.	4	Philadelphia	Sun.	6	Pittsburgh*
	Sun.	6	Florida	Thu.	10	at San Jose
	Tue.	8	at Toronto	Sat.	12	at Los Angeles
	Fri.	11	Detroit	Mon.	14	at Anaheim
	Sun.	13	at NY Islanders*	Thu.	17	Minnesota
	Tue.	15	at Buffalo	Sat.	19	at Columbus
	Thu.	17	Florida	Sun.	20	Columbus*
	Sat.	19	Anaheim	Thu.	24	at Pittsburgh
	Sun.	20	at Boston*	Fri.	25	Washington
	Tue.	22	at Detroit	Sun.	27	at Carolina*
	Sat.	26	at Carolina	Tue.	29	Boston
	Tue.	29	Carolina	Thu.	31	at Florida
	Wed.	30	at Ottawa	Apr. Sat.	2	at Tampa Bay
Jan.	Sat.	2	Dallas	Tue.	5	Buffalo
	Mon.	4	Detroit	Thu.	7	Tampa Bay
	Wed.	6	at Montreal	Sat.	9	Toronto

Denotes afternoon game.

Retired Numbers

3	Ken Daneyko	1982-2003
4	Scott Stevens	1991-2005
27	Scott Niedermayer	1991-2004

METROPOLITAN DIVISION
42nd NHL Season

Franchise date: June 11, 1974

Transferred from Denver to New Jersey, June 30, 1982.
Transferred from Kansas City to Denver, August 25, 1976.

Mike Cammalleri led the Devils with 27 goals during his first season with the team in 2014-15. It was the third-highest total of Cammalleri's NHL career despite the fact he played just 68 games. He will wear sweater #13 in 2015-16.

Year-by-Year Record

Season	GP	Home W	L	T	OL	Road W	L	T	OL	Overall W	L	T	OL	GF	GA	Pts.	Div. Fin.	Conf. Fin.	Playoff Result
2014-15	82	19	14	....	8	13	22	....	6	32	36	....	14	181	216	78	7th, Met.	13th, East	Out of Playoffs
2013-14	82	21	11	....	9	14	18	....	9	35	29	....	18	197	208	88	6th, Met.	10th, East	Out of Playoffs
2012-13	48	13	9	....	2	6	10	....	8	19	19	....	10	112	129	48	5th, Atl.	11th, East	Out of Playoffs
2011-12	82	24	13	....	4	24	15	....	2	48	28	....	6	228	209	102	4th, Atl.	6th, East	Lost Final
2010-11	82	22	16	....	3	16	23	....	2	38	39	....	5	174	209	81	4th, Atl.	11th, East	Out of Playoffs
2009-10	82	27	10	....	4	21	17	....	3	48	27	....	7	222	191	103	1st, Atl.	2nd, East	Lost Conf. Quarter-Final
2008-09	82	28	12	....	1	23	15	....	3	51	27	....	4	244	209	106	1st, Atl.	3rd, East	Lost Conf. Quarter-Final
2007-08	82	25	14	....	2	21	15	....	5	46	29	....	7	206	197	99	2nd, Atl.	4th, East	Lost Conf. Quarter-Final
2006-07	82	25	10	....	6	24	14	....	3	49	24	....	9	216	201	107	1st, Atl.	2nd, East	Lost Conf. Semi-Final
2005-06	82	27	11	....	3	19	16	....	6	46	27	....	9	242	229	101	1st, Atl.	3rd, East	Lost Conf. Semi-Final
2004-05	....																		
2003-04	82	22	13	5	1	21	12	7	1	43	25	12	2	213	164	100	2nd, Atl.	6th, East	Lost Conf. Quarter-Final
2002-03	**82**	**25**	**11**	**3**	**2**	**21**	**9**	**7**	**4**	**46**	**20**	**10**	**6**	**216**	**166**	**108**	**1st, Atl.**	**2nd, East**	**Won Stanley Cup**
2001-02	82	22	13	4	2	19	15	5	2	41	28	9	4	205	187	95	3rd, Atl.	6th, East	Lost Conf. Quarter-Final
2000-01	82	24	11	6	0	24	8	6	3	48	19	12	3	295	195	111	1st, Atl.	1st, East	Lost Final
1999-2000	**82**	**28**	**9**	**3**	**1**	**17**	**15**	**5**	**4**	**45**	**24**	**8**	**5**	**251**	**203**	**103**	**2nd, Atl.**	**4th, East**	**Won Stanley Cup**
1998-99	82	19	14	8	....	28	10	3	....	47	24	11	....	248	196	105	1st, Atl.	1st, East	Lost Conf. Quarter-Final
1997-98	82	29	10	2	....	19	13	9	....	48	23	11	....	225	166	107	1st, Atl.	1st, East	Lost Conf. Quarter-Final
1996-97	82	23	9	9	....	22	14	5	....	45	23	14	....	231	182	104	1st, Atl.	1st, East	Lost Conf. Semi-Final
1995-96	82	22	17	2	....	15	16	10	....	37	33	12	....	215	202	86	6th, Atl.	9th, East	Out of Playoffs
1994-95	**48**	**14**	**4**	**6**	....	**8**	**14**	**2**	....	**22**	**18**	**8**	....	**136**	**121**	**52**	**2nd, Atl.**	**5th, East**	**Won Stanley Cup**
1993-94	84	29	11	2	....	18	14	10	....	47	25	12	....	306	220	106	2nd, Atl.	2nd, East	Lost Conf. Final
1992-93	84	24	14	4	....	16	23	3	....	40	37	7	....	308	299	87	4th, Patrick		Lost Div. Semi-Final
1991-92	80	24	12	4	....	14	19	3	....	38	31	11	....	289	259	87	4th, Patrick		Lost Div. Semi-Final
1990-91	80	23	10	7	....	9	23	8	....	32	33	15	....	272	264	79	4th, Patrick		Lost Div. Semi-Final
1989-90	80	22	15	3	....	15	19	6	....	37	34	9	....	295	288	83	2nd, Patrick		Lost Div. Semi-Final
1988-89	80	17	18	5	....	10	23	7	....	27	41	12	....	281	325	66	5th, Patrick		Out of Playoffs
1987-88	80	23	16	1	....	15	20	5	....	38	36	6	....	295	296	82	4th, Patrick		Lost Conf. Final
1986-87	80	20	17	3	....	9	28	3	....	29	45	6	....	293	368	64	6th, Patrick		Out of Playoffs
1985-86	80	17	21	2	....	11	28	1	....	28	49	3	....	300	374	59	6th, Patrick		Out of Playoffs
1984-85	80	13	21	6	....	9	27	4	....	22	48	10	....	264	346	54	5th, Patrick		Out of Playoffs
1983-84	80	10	28	2	....	7	28	5	....	17	56	7	....	231	350	41	5th, Patrick		Out of Playoffs
1982-83	80	11	20	9	....	6	29	5	....	17	49	14	....	230	338	48	5th, Patrick		Out of Playoffs
1981-82**	80	14	21	5	....	4	28	8	....	18	49	13	....	241	362	49	5th, Smythe		Out of Playoffs
1980-81**	80	15	16	9	....	7	29	4	....	22	45	13	....	258	344	57	5th, Smythe		Out of Playoffs
1979-80**	80	11	20	9	....	8	28	5	....	19	48	13	....	234	308	51	6th, Smythe		Out of Playoffs
1978-79**	80	8	24	8	....	7	29	4	....	15	53	12	....	210	331	42	4th, Smythe		Out of Playoffs
1977-78**	80	17	14	9	....	2	26	12	....	19	40	21	....	257	305	59	2nd, Smythe		Lost Prelim. Round
1976-77**	80	12	20	8	....	8	26	6	....	20	46	14	....	226	307	54	5th, Smythe		Out of Playoffs
1975-76*	80	8	24	8	....	4	32	4	....	12	56	12	....	190	351	36	5th, Smythe		Out of Playoffs
1974-75*	80	12	20	8	....	3	34	3	....	15	54	11	....	184	328	41	5th, Smythe		Out of Playoffs

*Kansas City Scouts. **Colorado Rockies.

2015-16 Player Personnel

FORWARDS	HT	WT	*Age	Place of Birth	S	2014-15 Club
BADDOCK, Brandon	6-4	210	20	Vermilion, AB	L	Edmonton (WHL)
BLACK, Graham	6-0	190	22	Regina, SK	L	Albany
BLANDISI, Joseph	6-0	205	21	Markham, ON	L	Barrie
BOUCHER, Reid	5-10	190	22	Lansing, MI	L	New Jersey-Albany
CAMMALLERI, Mike	5-9	190	33	Toronto, ON	L	New Jersey
CHATHAM, Connor	6-2	225	19	Belleville, IL	R	Plymouth
CLOWE, Ryane	6-3	225	33	St. John's, NL	L	New Jersey
COLEMAN, Blake	5-11	200	23	Plano, TX	L	Miami U.
ELIAS, Patrik	6-1	195	39	Trebic, Czech.	L	New Jersey
GIONTA, Stephen	5-7	185	31	Rochester, NY	R	New Jersey
HENRIQUE, Adam	6-0	195	25	Brantford, ON	L	New Jersey
JOHNSON, Ben	6-0	195	21	Hancock, MI	L	Albany-Orlando
JOSEFSON, Jacob	6-0	190	24	Stockholm, Sweden	L	New Jersey
KALININ, Sergey	6-3	190	24	Omsk, Russia	L	Omsk
KUJAWINSKI, Ryan	6-2	200	20	Kirkland Lake, ON	L	Kingston-North Bay
MATTEAU, Stefan	6-2	220	21	Chicago, IL	L	New Jersey-Albany
O'BRIEN, Jim	6-2	200	26	Maplewood, MN	R	Novokuznetsk-Hershey
PALMIERI, Kyle	5-11	195	24	Smithtown, NY	R	Anaheim-Norfolk
PIETILA, Blake	6-0	195	22	Milford, MI	L	Michigan Tech
QUENNEVILLE, John	6-1	200	19	Edmonton, AB	L	Brandon
RUUTU, Tuomo	6-0	205	32	Vantaa, Finland	L	New Jersey-Albany
SISLO, Mike	5-11	195	27	Superior, WI	R	New Jersey-Albany
SPEERS, Blake	5-11	185	18	Sault Ste. Marie, ON	R	Sault Ste. Marie
THOMPSON, Paul	6-1	205	26	Methuen, MA	R	Albany
THOMSON, Ben	6-4	210	22	Brampton, ON	L	Albany
TOOTOO, Jordin	5-9	195	32	Churchill, MB	R	New Jersey
ZACHA, Pavel	6-3	210	18	Brno, Czech Republic	L	Sarnia
ZAJAC, Travis	6-3	205	30	Winnipeg, MB	R	New Jersey

DEFENSEMEN						
BURLON, Brandon	6-0	190	25	Nobleton, ON	L	Albany
GELINAS, Eric	6-4	215	24	Vanier, ON	L	New Jersey
GRAGNANI, Marc-Andre	6-2	200	28	Montreal, QC	L	Bern
GREENE, Andy	5-11	190	32	Trenton, MI	L	New Jersey
HELGESON, Seth	6-4	215	24	Faribault, MN	L	New Jersey-Albany
HRABARENKA, Raman	6-5	235	23	Mogilev, Belarus	R	New Jersey-Albany
JACOBS, Joshua	6-2	195	19	Shelby Township, MI	R	Michigan State
KELLY, Dan	6-1	210	26	Morrisonville, NY	L	Albany
LARSSON, Adam	6-3	210	22	Skelleftea, Sweden	R	New Jersey-Albany
MERRILL, Jon	6-3	205	23	Oklahoma City, OK	L	New Jersey
MOORE, John	6-3	200	24	Winnetka, IL	L	NY Rangers-Arizona
MOZIK, Vojtech	6-2	195	22	Praha, Czech Rep.	R	Plzen
REHILL, Ryan	6-3	215	19	Edmonton, AB	R	Kamloops
SCARLETT, Reece	6-1	185	22	Edmonton, AB	R	Albany
SEVERSON, Damon	6-2	205	21	Brandon, MB	R	New Jersey
WHITE, Colton	6-1	185	18	London, ON	L	Sault Ste. Marie

GOALTENDERS	HT	WT	*Age	Place of Birth	C	2014-15 Club
BLACKWOOD, Mackenzie	6-4	215	18	Thunder Bay, ON	L	Barrie
DANIS, Yann	6-0	185	34	Lafontaine, QC	L	Norfolk-Hartford
KINKAID, Keith	6-2	195	26	Farmingville, NY	L	New Jersey-Albany
SCHNEIDER, Cory	6-2	205	29	Marblehead, MA	L	New Jersey
WEDGEWOOD, Scott	6-2	190	23	Etobicoke, ON	L	Albany

* – Age at start of 2015-16 season

2014-15 Scoring
* – rookie

Regular Season

Pos	#	Player	Team	GP	G	A	Pts	TOI	+/-	PIM	PP	SH	GW	S	S%
C	14	Adam Henrique	N.J.	75	16	27	43	17:44	-6	34	5	0	3	127	12.6
L	23	Mike Cammalleri	N.J.	68	27	15	42	18:19	2	28	9	2	8	156	17.3
L	26	Patrik Elias	N.J.	69	13	21	34	17:38	-20	12	5	0	1	114	11.4
L	21	Scott Gomez	N.J.	58	7	27	34	16:30	-10	23	0	0	1	70	10.0
R	18	Steve Bernier	N.J.	67	16	16	32	12:56	2	28	4	0	2	107	15.0
C	19	Travis Zajac	N.J.	74	11	14	25	19:03	-3	29	4	2	0	112	9.8
D	5	Adam Larsson	N.J.	64	3	21	24	20:57	2	34	0	0	1	91	3.3
D	6	Andy Greene	N.J.	82	3	19	22	23:32	1	20	0	0	1	83	3.6
R	17	Michael Ryder	N.J.	47	6	13	19	14:28	-1	30	0	0	0	89	6.7
D	22	Eric Gelinas	N.J.	61	6	13	19	16:27	-2	42	3	0	2	112	5.4
D	28 *	Damon Severson	N.J.	51	5	12	17	21:57	-13	22	0	0	0	93	5.4
R	20	Jordin Tootoo	N.J.	68	10	5	15	10:27	1	72	1	0	1	75	13.3
D	9	Martin Havlat	N.J.	40	5	9	14	14:48	-11	10	3	0	1	49	10.2
D	7	Jon Merrill	N.J.	66	2	12	14	20:33	-14	24	2	0	0	47	4.3
R	15	Tuomo Ruutu	N.J.	77	7	6	13	10:51	-3	28	0	0	0	74	9.5
R	11	Stephen Gionta	N.J.	61	5	8	13	13:11	4	12	0	0	1	84	6.0
C	16	Jacob Josefson	N.J.	62	6	5	11	12:25	0	24	0	3	1	61	9.8
C	8	Dainius Zubrus	N.J.	74	4	6	10	14:39	-9	42	0	1	0	72	5.6
C	12	Damien Brunner	N.J.	12	2	5	7	15:08	-1	8	0	0	0	29	6.9
D	10	Peter Harrold	N.J.	43	3	2	5	15:14	-10	4	0	0	0	31	9.7
L	29	Ryane Clowe	N.J.	13	1	3	4	15:40	-1	4	0	0	0	15	6.7
D	32	Mark Fraser	N.J.	34	0	4	4	16:16	2	55	0	0	0	19	0.0
D	24	Bryce Salvador	N.J.	15	0	2	2	18:30	-5	20	0	0	0	13	0.0
C	12	Tim Sestito	N.J.	15	0	2	2	9:53	-1	33	0	0	0	10	0.0
D	33 *	Seth Helgeson	N.J.	22	0	2	2	13:27	4	18	0	0	0	11	0.0
R	33	Joe Whitney	N.J.	4	1	0	1	6:52	-1	0	0	0	1	1	100.0
C	25 *	Stefan Matteau	N.J.	7	1	0	1	11:52	0	4	0	0	0	8	12.5
C	12 *	Reid Boucher	N.J.	11	1	0	1	11:08	-4	0	0	0	0	20	5.0
R	34	Mike Sislo	N.J.	10	0	1	1	12:12	-2	2	0	0	0	13	0.0
D	34 *	Raman Hrabarenka	N.J.	1	0	0	0	11:55	-1	0	0	0	0	0	0.0

Goaltending

No.	Goaltender	GPI	Mins	Avg	W	L	OT	EN	SO	GA	SA	Sv%	G	A	PIM
35	Cory Schneider	69	3924	2.26	26	31	9	12	5	148	1982	.925	0	2	0
1	* Keith Kinkaid	19	925	2.59	6	5	4	1	0	40	469	.915	0	0	0
40	Scott Clemmensen	3	102	4.71	0	0	1	0	0	8	54	.852	0	0	0
	Totals	82	4998	2.51	32	36	14	13	5	209	2518	.917			

Cory Schneider was busy in 2014-15, ranking fourth in the league with 69 games played. He made the third-most saves in the NHL with 1,834 on 1,982 shots for a .925 save percentage that ranked him fifth in the league.

Ray Shero
Executive Vice President/General Manager
Born: St. Paul, MN, July 28, 1962.

Ray Shero was named the fourth general manager in New Jersey Devils history on May 4, 2015.

Shero spent eight seasons, 2006-07 through 2013-14, as executive vice president and general manager of the Pittsburgh Penguins. During that time, the team compiled a 373-193-56 (.645) mark, won the 2009 Stanley Cup championship, two consecutive Eastern Conference titles in 2007-08 and 2008-09 and had three first-place divisional finishes. He was named the 2012-13 recipient of the General Manager of the Year Award, as voted on by the 30 NHL general managers, a panel of NHL executives, as well as print and broadcast media. Previously, Shero spent 14 seasons as an assistant general manager with the Ottawa Senators (1993 to 1998) and Nashville Predators (1998 to 2006). Shero has been actively involved with USA Hockey, is a member of its national team advisory board, and most recently served as associate general manager for the 2014 Winter Olympic Games. He also spent seven seasons as a player agent prior to making the transition to the front office.

A forward in his playing days, Shero was drafted by Los Angeles in the 11th round (216th overall) of the 1982 NHL Draft. He played four seasons collegiately at St. Lawrence University (Canton, New York), and served as the team's captain on two occasions. He led the school in scoring twice, and graduated in 1984 as one of the top-ten scorers in Saints' history. The son of the late Hockey Hall of Fame head coach Fred Shero, Ray and his dad are one of the few father-son tandems to both have their names engraved on the Stanley Cup. Fred Shero served as the Devils' radio commentator in the 1980s.

Captains' History
Simon Nolet, 1974-75 to 1976-77; Wilf Paiement, 1977-78; Gary Croteau, 1978-79; Mike Christie, Rene Robert and Lanny McDonald, 1979-80; Lanny McDonald, 1980-81; Lanny McDonald and Rob Ramage, 1981-82; Don Lever, 1982-83; Don Lever and Mel Bridgman, 1983-84; Mel Bridgman, 1984-85 to 1986-87; Kirk Muller, 1987-88 to 1990-91; Bruce Driver, 1991-92; Scott Stevens, 1992-93 to 2002-03; Scott Stevens and Scott Niedermayer, 2003-04; no captain, 2005-06; Patrik Elias, 2006-07; Patrik Elias and Jamie Langenbrunner, 2007-08; Jamie Langenbrunner, 2008-09 to 2010-11; Zach Parise, 2011-12; Bryce Salvador, 2012-13 to date.

General Managers' History
Sid Abel, 1974-75; Sid Abel and Baz Bastien, 1975-76; Ray Miron, 1976-77 to 1980-81; Bill MacMillan, 1981-82, 1982-83; Bill MacMillan and Max McNab, 1983-84; Max McNab 1984-85 to 1986-87; Lou Lamoriello, 1987-88 to 2014-15; Ray Shero, 2015-16.

Club Records

Team

(Figures in brackets for season records are games played; records for fewest points, wins, ties, losses, goals, goals against are for 70 or more games)

Most Points	111	2000-01 (82)
Most Wins	51	2008-09 (82)
Most Ties	*21	1977-78 (80)
	15	1990-91 (80)
Most Losses	56	1975-76 (80), 1983-84 (80)
Most Goals	308	1992-93 (84)
Most Goals Against	374	1985-86 (80)
Fewest Points	*36	1975-76 (80)
	41	1983-84 (80)
Fewest Wins	*12	1975-76 (80)
	17	1982-83 (80), 1983-84 (80)
Fewest Ties	3	1985-86 (80)
Fewest Losses	19	2000-01 (82)
Fewest Goals	174	2010-11 (82)
Fewest Goals Against	164	2003-04 (82)
Longest Winning Streak		
Overall	13	Feb. 26-Mar. 23/01
Home	11	Feb. 9-Mar. 20/09
Away	10	Feb. 27-Apr. 7/01
Longest Undefeated Streak		
Overall	13	Four times
Home	15	Jan. 8-Mar. 15/97 (9W, 6T)
Away	10	Feb. 27-Apr. 7/01 (10W)
Longest Losing Streak		
Overall	*14	Dec. 30/75-Jan. 29/76
	10	Oct. 14-Nov. 4/83
Home	9	Dec. 22/85-Feb. 6/86
Away	12	Oct. 19-Dec. 1/83
Longest Winless Streak		
Overall	*27	Feb. 12-Apr. 4/76 (21L, 6T)
	18	Oct. 20-Nov. 26/82 (14L 4T)
Home	*14	Feb. 12-Mar. 30/76 (10L, 4T), Feb. 4-Mar. 31/79 (12L, 2T)
	9	Dec. 22/85-Feb. 6/86 (9L)
Away	*32	Nov. 12/77-Mar. 15/78 (22L, 10T)
	14	Dec. 26/82-Mar. 5/83 (13L, 1T)
Most Shutouts, Season	14	2003-04 (82)
Most PIM, Season	2,494	1988-89 (80)
Most Goals, Game	9	Nine times

Individual

Most Seasons	21	Martin Brodeur
Most Games	1,283	Ken Daneyko
Most Goals, Career	406	Patrik Elias
Most Assists, Career	611	Patrik Elias
Most Points, Career	1,017	Patrik Elias (406G, 611A)
Most PIM, Career	2,519	Ken Daneyko
Most Shutouts, Career	124	Martin Brodeur
Longest Consecutive Games Streak	401	Travis Zajac (Oct. 26/06-Apr. 10/11)
Most Goals, Season	48	Brian Gionta (2005-06)
Most Assists, Season	60	Scott Stevens (1993-94)
Most Points, Season	96	Patrik Elias (2000-01; 40G, 56A)
Most PIM, Season	295	Krzysztof Oliwa (1997-98)
Most Points, Defenseman, Season	78	Scott Stevens (1993-94; 18G, 60A)
Most Points, Center, Season	94	Kirk Muller (1987-88; 37G, 57A)
Most Points, Right Wing, Season	89	Brian Gionta (2005-06; 48G, 41A)
Most Points, Left Wing, Season	96	Patrik Elias (2000-01; 40G, 56A)
Most Points, Rookie, Season	70	Scott Gomez (1999-2000; 19G, 51A)
Most Shutouts, Season	12	Martin Brodeur (2006-07)
Most Goals, Game	4	Six times
Most Assists, Game	5	Greg Adams (Oct. 10/85), Kirk Muller (Mar. 25/87), Tom Kurvers (Feb. 13/89), Scott Gomez (Mar. 30/03)
Most Points, Game	6	Kirk Muller (Oct. 29/86; 3G, 3A)

* Records include Kansas City Scouts and Colorado Rockies, 1974-75 through 1981-82.

All-time Record vs. Other Clubs

Regular Season

	Total								At Home								On Road							
	GP	W	L	T	OL	GF	GA	PTS	GP	W	L	T	OL	GF	GA	PTS	GP	W	L	T	OL	GF	GA	PTS
Anaheim	28	16	10	1	1	79	67	34	13	9	3	0	1	41	24	19	15	7	7	1	0	38	43	15
Arizona	70	23	37	9	1	203	226	56	34	15	12	6	1	109	96	37	36	8	25	3	0	94	130	19
Boston	146	49	72	19	6	394	493	123	71	24	34	11	2	178	221	61	75	25	38	8	4	216	272	62
Buffalo	145	55	66	17	7	414	472	134	72	30	31	9	2	201	216	71	73	25	35	8	5	213	256	63
Calgary	97	24	60	11	2	259	376	61	50	17	30	3	0	135	173	37	47	7	30	8	2	124	203	24
Carolina	128	67	46	12	3	406	372	149	64	38	21	4	1	215	186	81	64	29	25	8	2	191	186	68
Chicago	105	37	44	21	3	301	353	98	53	23	17	11	2	160	156	59	52	14	27	10	1	141	197	39
Colorado	82	35	35	8	4	266	272	82	42	21	15	4	2	160	133	48	40	14	20	4	2	106	139	34
Columbus	20	11	5	1	3	54	46	26	9	6	1	1	1	25	17	14	11	5	4	0	2	29	29	12
Dallas	102	41	49	9	3	302	329	94	50	26	19	3	2	171	144	57	52	15	30	6	1	131	185	37
Detroit	93	37	43	11	2	295	313	87	46	23	13	9	1	153	123	56	47	14	30	2	1	142	190	31
Edmonton	74	31	33	9	1	246	266	72	38	17	18	3	0	121	121	37	36	14	15	6	1	125	145	35
Florida	86	51	25	7	3	247	186	112	43	29	10	3	1	136	84	62	43	22	15	4	2	111	102	50
Los Angeles	97	33	51	11	2	302	375	79	49	21	23	5	0	154	163	47	48	12	28	6	2	148	212	32
Minnesota	16	9	5	2	0	49	43	20	8	6	1	1	0	28	16	13	8	3	4	1	0	21	27	7
Montreal	145	64	68	10	3	400	456	141	73	36	32	4	1	216	238	77	72	28	36	6	2	184	218	64
Nashville	21	12	6	0	3	61	48	27	10	5	4	0	1	32	24	11	11	7	2	0	2	29	24	16
NY Islanders	231	85	113	22	11	672	791	203	114	50	47	11	6	358	366	117	117	35	66	11	5	314	425	86
NY Rangers	231	94	102	27	8	686	765	223	117	60	46	7	4	378	361	131	114	34	56	20	4	308	404	92
Ottawa	84	49	25	5	5	216	194	108	42	26	13	2	1	116	95	55	42	23	12	3	4	100	99	53
Philadelphia	229	103	103	18	5	677	754	229	114	65	39	8	2	380	346	140	115	38	64	10	3	297	408	89
Pittsburgh	221	109	91	17	4	717	710	239	112	60	37	13	2	380	331	135	109	49	54	4	2	337	379	104
St. Louis	102	37	49	14	2	315	346	90	51	23	20	7	1	158	138	54	51	14	29	7	1	157	208	36
San Jose	33	18	11	2	2	106	82	40	18	10	6	1	1	62	44	22	15	8	5	1	1	44	38	18
Tampa Bay	88	54	21	7	6	289	200	121	45	31	10	2	2	159	98	66	43	23	11	5	4	130	102	55
Toronto	131	46	57	20	8	389	424	120	64	26	19	15	4	213	198	71	67	20	38	5	4	176	226	49
Vancouver	106	32	53	17	4	300	362	85	54	22	23	6	3	163	171	53	52	10	30	11	1	137	191	32
Washington	198	87	96	13	2	569	648	189	98	51	39	7	1	293	278	110	100	36	57	6	1	276	370	79
Winnipeg	55	31	16	3	5	163	128	70	28	16	8	1	3	80	62	36	27	15	8	2	2	83	66	34
Defunct Clubs	16	6	5	5	0	44	46	17	8	4	2	2	0	25	19	10	8	2	3	3	0	19	27	7
Totals	**3180**	**1346**	**1397**	**328**	**109**	**9421**	**10143**	**3129**	**1590**	**790**	**593**	**159**	**48**	**5000**	**4642**	**1787**	**1590**	**556**	**804**	**169**	**61**	**4421**	**5501**	**1342**

Playoffs

	Series	W	L	GP	W	L	T	GF	GA	Last Mtg.	Rnd.	Result
Anaheim	1	1	0	7	4	3	0	19	12	2003	F	W 4-3
Boston	4	3	1	23	15	8	0	68	60	2003	CQF	W 4-1
Buffalo	1	1	0	7	4	3	0	14	14	1994	CQF	W 4-3
Carolina	4	1	3	24	10	14	0	56	51	2009	CQF	L 3-4
Colorado	1	0	1	7	3	4	0	11	19	2001	F	L 3-4
Dallas	1	1	0	6	4	2	0	15	9	2000	F	W 4-2
Detroit	1	1	0	4	4	0	0	16	7	1995	F	W 4-0
Florida	2	2	0	11	8	3	0	30	23	2012	CQF	W 4-3
Los Angeles	1	0	1	6	2	4	0	8	16	2012	F	L 2-4
Montreal	1	1	0	5	4	1	0	22	11	1997	CQF	W 4-1
NY Islanders	1	1	0	6	4	2	0	23	18	1988	DSF	W 4-2
NY Rangers	6	2	4	34	16	18	0	90	93	2012	CF	W 4-2
Ottawa	3	1	2	18	7	11	0	40	41	2007	CSF	L 1-4
Philadelphia	6	3	3	30	14	16	0	77	75	2012	CSF	W 4-1
Pittsburgh	5	2	3	29	15	14	0	86	80	2001	CF	W 4-1
Tampa Bay	2	2	0	11	8	3	0	33	22	2007	CQF	W 4-2
Toronto	2	2	0	13	8	5	0	37	27	2001	CSF	W 4-3
Washington	2	1	1	13	6	7	0	43	44	1990	DSF	L 2-4
Totals	**44**	**25**	**19**	**254**	**136**	**118**	**0**	**688**	**622**			

Playoff Results 2015-2011

Year	Round	Opponent	Result	GF	GA
2012	F	Los Angeles	L 2-4	8	16
	CF	NY Rangers	W 4-2	15	14
	CSF	Philadelphia	W 4-1	18	11
	CQF	Florida	W 4-3	18	17

Abbreviations: Round: F – Final; **CF** – conference final; **CSF** – conference semi-final; **CQF** – conference quarter-final; **DSF** – division semi-final.

Calgary totals include Atlanta Flames, 1974-75 to 1979-80.
Colorado totals include Quebec, 1979-80 to 1994-95.
Phoenix totals include Winnipeg, 1979-80 to 1995-96.
Carolina totals include Hartford, 1979-80 to 1996-97.
Dallas totals include Minnesota North Stars, 1974-75 to 1992-93.
Winnipeg totals include Atlanta Thrashers, 1999-2000 to 2010-11.

2014-15 Results

Oct.	9	at Philadelphia	6-4
	11	at Florida	5-1
	14	at Tampa Bay	2-1
	16	at Washington	2-6
	18	San Jose	2-4
	21	NY Rangers	3-4*
	24	Dallas	2-3†
	25	at Ottawa	3-2*
	28	at Pittsburgh	3-8
	30	Winnipeg	2-1†
Nov.	1	Columbus	3-2
	4	St. Louis	0-1
	6	at St. Louis	3-4
	7	at Detroit	2-4
	10	at Boston	2-4
	11	Minnesota	3-1
	14	at Washington	1-0
	15	Colorado	2-3
	18	at Winnipeg	1-3
	21	at Edmonton	2-0
	22	at Calgary	4-5†
	25	at Vancouver	0-2
	28	Detroit	4-5†
	29	at NY Islanders	1-3
Dec.	2	at Pittsburgh	0-1
	4	at Toronto	5-3
	6	Washington	1-4
	8	at Carolina	2-1
	9	Chicago	2-3†
	11	at Philadelphia	1-4
	13	at Dallas	3-4
	15	at NY Islanders	2-3†
	17	Ottawa	0-2
	19	Tampa Bay	3-2†
	20	Washington	0-4
	23	Carolina	1-2†
	27	at NY Rangers	1-3
	29	Pittsburgh	3-1
	31	at Detroit	1-3
Jan.	2	Montreal	2-4
	3	Philadelphia	5-2
	6	Buffalo	4-1
	8	at Boston	0-3
	9	NY Islanders	2-3*
	14	at Los Angeles	5-3
	16	at Anaheim	1-5
	19	at San Jose	5-2
	28	Toronto	2-1†
	30	Pittsburgh	1-2*
	31	Florida	3-1
Feb.	3	Ottawa	2-1
	6	Toronto	4-1
	7	at Montreal	2-6
	9	Edmonton	1-2
	13	at Chicago	1-3
	14	at Nashville	1-3
	17	Buffalo	2-1†
	20	Vancouver	4-2
	21	Carolina	3-1
	23	Arizona	3-0
	25	Calgary	1-3
	27	Boston	2-3*
	28	at Columbus	2-0
Mar.	3	Nashville	3-1
	6	Columbus	2-3
	8	Philadelphia	5-2
	10	at Minnesota	2-6
	12	at Colorado	1-2†
	14	at Arizona	4-1
	17	Pittsburgh	2-0
	20	at Buffalo	3-1
	21	NY Islanders	0-3
	23	Los Angeles	1-3
	26	at Washington	2-3*
	28	at Carolina	1-3
	29	Anaheim	1-2
	31	at Columbus	2-3*
Apr.	3	Montreal	3-2†
	4	at NY Rangers	1-6
	7	NY Rangers	2-4
	9	at Tampa Bay	3-4*
	11	at Florida	2-3

* – Overtime † – Shootout

NHL Draft Selections 2015-2001

Name in bold denotes played in NHL.

2015
Pick
6 Pavel Zacha
42 Mackenzie Blackwood
67 Blake Speers
97 Colton White
157 Brett Seney

2014
Pick
30 John Quenneville
41 Joshua Jacobs
71 Connor Chatham
131 Ryan Rehill
152 Joey Dudek
161 Brandon Baddock

2013
Pick
42 Steven Santini
73 Ryan Kujawinski
100 Miles Wood
160 Myles Bell
208 Anthony Brodeur

2012
Pick
29 **Stefan Matteau**
60 **Damon Severson**
90 Ben Johnson
96 Ben Thomson
135 Graham Black
150 Alexander Kerfoot
180 Artur Gavrus

2011
Pick
4 **Adam Larsson**
69 forfeited pick
75 Blake Coleman
99 **Reid Boucher**
129 Blake Pietila
159 Reece Scarlett
189 Patrick Daly

2010
Pick
38 **Jon Merrill**
84 Scott Wedgewood
114 Joe Faust
174 Maxime Clermont
204 Mauro Jorg

2009
Pick
20 **Jacob Josefson**
54 **Eric Gelinas**
73 **Alexander Urbom**
114 **Seth Helgeson**
144 Derek Rodwell
174 Ashton Bernard
204 Curtis Gedig

2008
Pick
24 **Mattias Tedenby**
52 Brandon Burlon
54 **Patrice Cormier**
82 **Adam Henrique**
112 Matt Delahey
142 Kory Nagy
172 David Wohlberg
202 Harry Young
205 Jean-Sebastien Berube

2007
Pick
57 Mike Hoeffel
79 **Nick Palmieri**
87 Corbin McPherson
117 **Matt Halischuk**
177 Vili Sopanen
207 Ryan Molle

2006
Pick
30 **Matthew Corrente**
58 **Alexander Vasyunov**
67 Kirill Tulupov
77 Vladimir Zharkov
107 Tyler Miller
148 **Olivier Magnan**
178 Tony Romano
208 Kyell Henegan

2005
Pick
23 Niclas Bergfors
38 Jeff Frazee
84 **Mark Fraser**
99 **Patrick Davis**
155 **Mark Fayne**
170 Sean Zimmerman
218 Alexander Sundstrom

2004
Pick
20 **Travis Zajac**
155 Alexander Mikhailishin
185 Josh Disher
216 **Pierre-Luc**
    Letourneau-Leblond
217 **Tyler Eckford**
250 Nathan Perkovich
282 Valeri Klimov

2003
Pick
17 **Zach Parise**
42 **Petr Vrana**
93 Ivan Khomutov
167 Zach Tarkir
197 Jason Smith
261 **Joey Tenute**
292 Arseny Bondarev

2002
Pick
51 Anton Kadeykin
53 **Barry Tallackson**
64 Jason Ryznar
84 Marek Chvatal
85 Ahren Nittel
117 **Cam Janssen**
154 Krisjanis Redlihs
187 Eric Johansson
218 **Ilkka Pikkarainen**
250 Dan Glover
281 Bill Kinkel

2001
Pick
28 Adrian Foster
44 Igor Pohanka
48 **Tuomas Pihlman**
60 Victor Uchevatov
67 Robin Leblanc
72 **Brandon Nolan**
128 Andrei Posnov
163 **Andreas Salomonsson**
194 James Massen
229 **Aaron Voros**
257 Yevgeny Gamalei

John Hynes
Head Coach
Born: Warwick, RI, February 10, 1975.

The New Jersey Devils named John Hynes as the 17th head coach in team history. The announcement was made by Devils' general manager Ray Shero on June 2, 2015.

Hynes joins the Devils after spending the previous six seasons with Wilkes-Barre/Scranton (AHL), including the past five years, 2010-11 through 2014-15, as head coach. During that time, he led the Penguins to a 231-126-27 (.637) mark, including five straight 40-plus victory campaigns. Hynes guided Wilkes-Barre/Scranton to five consecutive playoff berths, including consecutive AHL Eastern Conference finals appearances in 2012-13 and 2013-14. His teams allowed the league's fewest goals in four of the five years. In Hynes' first season behind the Pens' bench, he was named the 2010-11 coach of the year after finishing with the AHL's best record. Hynes became the second-fastest coach in AHL history to reach the 100 career wins mark, doing so in just 152 games. In the second round of the 2013 Calder Cup playoffs, the Pens became the first team in league history to overcome a 3-0 deficit by winning games six and seven on the road. Hynes originally joined the organization as an assistant coach in 2009-10.

Hynes spent six seasons from 2003 to 2009 as head coach of USA Hockey's national team development program, posting an overall record of 188-131-26. He led the U.S. under-18 national team to three medals at the World Under-18 Championships, winning the gold in 2006, silver in 2004 and bronze in 2008. Hynes also served as assistant coach on the U.S. squad that won gold at the 2004 World Junior tourney. He worked as an assistant coach at both Wisconsin in 2002-03 and UMass-Lowell in 2000-01. Hynes began his coaching career as a graduate assistant at Boston University under legendary coach Jack Parker. A forward, he spent four seasons at B.U. including four straight NCAA Frozen Fours, and was a member of the Terriers' 1995 NCAA Championship Team.

Coaching Record

Season	Team	League	GC	Regular Season				Playoffs			
				W	L	O/T		GC	W	L	T
2003-04	USNTDP	U18	55	29	19	7		....	....	....	....
2004-05	USNTDP	U17	53	31	18	4		....	....	....	....
2005-06	USNTDP	U18	53	31	19	3		....	....	....	....
2006-07	USNTDP	U17	62	22	36	4		....	....	....	....
2007-08	USNTDP	U18	57	33	22	2		....	....	....	....
2008-09	USNTDP	U17	65	42	17	6		....	....	....	....
2010-11	Wilkes-Barre/Scranton	AHL	80	58	21	1		12	6	6	0
2011-12	Wilkes-Barre/Scranton	AHL	76	44	25	7		12	6	6	0
2012-13	Wilkes-Barre/Scranton	AHL	76	42	30	4		15	8	7	0
2013-14	Wilkes-Barre/Scranton	AHL	76	42	26	8		17	9	8	0
2014-15	Wilkes-Barre/Scranton	AHL	76	45	24	7		8	4	4	0

Club Directory

New Jersey Devils
Prudential Center
25 Lafayette Street
Newark, NJ 07102
Phone **973/757-6100**
FAX 973/757-6399
www.newjerseydevils.com
Capacity: 16,592

Prudential Center

Owner/Chairman/Governor	Joshua Harris
Owner/Vice Chairman/Alternate Governor	David Blitzer
Co-Owners	Alan Fournier, Marc Leder, Michael Rubin
CEO, NJ Devils & Prudential Center/Alt. Governor	Scott O'Neil
President of Business Operations	Hugh Weber
Executive Vice President/General Manager	Ray Shero
Assistant General Manager	Tom Fitzgerald
Sr. Vice President, Hockey Operations/ General Manager, Albany/Scout	Chris Lamoriello
Senior Vice President, Communications	Mike Levine
Vice President, Hockey Operations	Stephen Pellegrini

Club Personnel

Head Coach	John Hynes
Assistant Coaches	Geoff Ward, Alain Nasreddine
Goaltending Coach	Chris Terreri
Special Assignment Coaches	Jacques Caron, Jacques Laperriere
Director, Amateur Scouting	Paul Castron
Assistant Director, Scouting	Claude Carrier
Amateur Scouting Staff	Jeremy Conte, Glen Dirk, Milt Fisher, Steve Kariya, Scott Lachance, Jan Ludvig, Pierre Mondou, Gates Orlando, Lou Reycroft, Steve Smith, Geoff Stevens, Ed Thomlinson
European Scouting Staff	Timo Blomqvist, Dan Labraaten, Vaclav Slansky, Jr.
Pro Scouting Staff	Bob Hoffmeyer, Claude Noel, Andre Savard
Development/Skills Coach	Pertti Hasanen
Goaltending Development Coach	Scott Clemmensen
Hockey Operations Video Coordinator	Taran Singleton
Video Assistants	Matthew DeMado, Sean Andrake
Scouting Staff Assistant	Callie A. Smith
Head Trainer	Richard Stinziano
Assistant Trainer	Kevin Morley
Equipment Manager	Rich Matthews
Assistant Equipment Managers	Jason McGrath, Mike Thibault
Strength/Conditioning Coach	Joe Lorincz
Massage Therapist	Brian Smith
Chief Medical Officer	Dr. Jonathan L. Glashow
Team Orthopedist	Dr. Michael Shindle
Sports Medicine Internist	Dr. Michael Farber
Team Dentists	Dr. H. Hugh Gardy, Dr. Jason Schepis
Video Consultant	Mitch Kaufman
Head Coach, Albany	Rick Kowalsky
Assistant Coach, Albany	Sergei Brylin
Video Coordinator, Albany	Mike Regan
Athletic Trainer, Albany	Scott Stanhibel
Equipment Manager, Albany	Andrew Schmidt
Assistant Equipment Manager, Albany	Corey Wood

Executive Vice President / General Manager's Office

Hockey Ops Exec. Asst. to the Exec. V.P./G.M.	Marie Carnevale
Administrative Assistant	Christine Garcia
Finance Manager	Kristin Farina

Analytics

Director, Analytics	Sunny Mehta
Data Scientist	Sai Okabayashi

Computer Operations

Senior Director, Programming/Computer Ops	Jack Skelley

Communications

Director, Communications/Team Services	Pete Albietz
Director, Website Content	Eric Marin
Assistant Director, Communications	Daniel Beam
Staff Assistant	James Stolfi

Alumni Representatives
Ken Daneyko, Bruce Driver, Grant Marshall, Jim Dowd, Colin White

Television/Radio

Television Outlet	MSG Plus
TV Play-by-Play / Color	Steve Cangialosi / Ken Daneyko
Radio Outlet	Sports Radio 66 AM/101.9 FM WFAN
Radio Play-by-Play / Color	Matt Loughlin / Sherry Ross

Coaching History

Bep Guidolin, 1974-75; Bep Guidolin, Sid Abel and Eddie Bush, 1975-76; Johnny Wilson, 1976-77; Pat Kelly, 1977-78; Pat Kelly and Aldo Guidolin, 1978-79; Don Cherry, 1979-80; Bill MacMillan, 1980-81; Bert Marshall and Marshall Johnston, 1981-82; Bill MacMillan, 1982-83; Bill MacMillan and Tom McVie, 1983-84; Doug Carpenter, 1984-85 to 1986-87; Doug Carpenter and Jim Schoenfeld, 1987-88; Jim Schoenfeld, 1988-89; Jim Schoenfeld and John Cunniff, 1989-90; John Cunniff and Tom McVie, 1990-91; Tom McVie, 1991-92; Herb Brooks, 1992-93; Jacques Lemaire, 1993-94 to 1997-98; Robbie Ftorek, 1998-99; Robbie Ftorek and Larry Robinson, 1999-2000; Larry Robinson, 2000-01; Larry Robinson and Kevin Constantine, 2001-02; Pat Burns, 2002-03 to 2004-05; Larry Robinson and Lou Lamoriello, 2005-06; Claude Julien and Lou Lamoriello, 2006-07; Brent Sutter, 2007-08, 2008-09; Jacques Lemaire, 2009-10; John MacLean and Jacques Lemaire, 2010-11; Peter DeBoer, 2011-12 to 2014-15; John Hynes, 2015-16.

New York Islanders

Key Off-Season Signings/Acquisitions

2015
June 30 • Re-signed C **Anders Lee**.
July 1 • Signed G **Thomas Greiss**.
1 • Re-signed D **Thomas Hickey**.

2014-15 Results: 47w-28L-1OTL-6SOL 101PTS
3RD, Metropolitan Division • 5TH, Eastern Conference

2015-16 Schedule

Oct.	Fri.	9	Chicago
	Sat.	10	at Chicago
	Mon.	12	Winnipeg*
	Thu.	15	Nashville
	Sat.	17	San Jose
	Tue.	20	at Columbus
	Fri.	23	Boston
	Sat.	24	at St. Louis
	Mon.	26	Calgary
	Thu.	29	Carolina
	Sat.	31	at New Jersey*
Nov.	Sun.	1	Buffalo
	Tue.	3	New Jersey
	Thu.	5	at Montreal
	Sun.	8	Boston*
	Tue.	10	at San Jose
	Thu.	12	at Los Angeles
	Fri.	13	at Anaheim
	Mon.	16	Arizona
	Fri.	20	Montreal
	Sun.	22	at Montreal
	Wed.	25	Philadelphia
	Fri.	27	at Florida
	Sat.	28	at Tampa Bay
	Mon.	30	Colorado
Dec.	Wed.	2	NY Rangers
	Fri.	4	St. Louis
	Sat.	5	at Ottawa
	Tue.	8	at Philadelphia
	Sat.	12	at Columbus
	Sun.	13	New Jersey*
	Tue.	15	Florida
	Thu.	17	at Colorado
	Sat.	19	at Arizona
	Mon.	21	Anaheim
	Sun.	27	Toronto
	Tue.	29	at Toronto
	Thu.	31	at Buffalo
Jan.	Sat.	2	at Pittsburgh
	Sun.	3	Dallas*
	Thu.	7	Washington
	Sat.	9	at Philadelphia*
	Tue.	12	Columbus
	Thu.	14	NY Rangers
	Sun.	17	Vancouver*
	Fri.	22	at Ottawa
	Sat.	23	Philadelphia
	Mon.	25	Detroit
Feb.	Tue.	2	Minnesota
	Thu.	4	at Washington
	Sat.	6	at Detroit*
	Sun.	7	Edmonton*
	Tue.	9	at Columbus
	Thu.	11	Los Angeles
	Sat.	13	at Carolina
	Mon.	15	Detroit*
	Thu.	18	Washington
	Fri.	19	at New Jersey
	Tue.	23	at Minnesota
	Thu.	25	at Calgary
	Sun.	28	at Edmonton
Mar.	Tue.	1	at Vancouver
	Thu.	3	at Winnipeg
	Sun.	6	at NY Rangers*
	Tue.	8	Pittsburgh
	Wed.	9	at Toronto
	Sat.	12	at Boston*
	Mon.	14	Florida
	Tue.	15	at Pittsburgh
	Thu.	17	at Nashville
	Sat.	19	at Dallas
	Mon.	21	Philadelphia
	Wed.	23	Ottawa
	Fri.	25	at Tampa Bay
	Sat.	26	at Carolina
	Tue.	29	Carolina
	Thu.	31	Columbus
Apr.	Sat.	2	Pittsburgh*
	Mon.	4	Tampa Bay
	Tue.	5	at Washington
	Thu.	7	at NY Rangers
	Sat.	9	Buffalo

* Denotes afternoon game.

Retired Numbers

5	Denis Potvin	1973-1988
9	Clark Gillies	1974-1986
19	Bryan Trottier	1975-1990
22	Mike Bossy	1977-1987
23	Bob Nystrom	1972-1986
31	Billy Smith	1972-1989

METROPOLITAN DIVISION
44th NHL Season

Franchise date: June 6, 1972

Islanders captain John Tavares bounced back from an injury in 2013-14 to finish second in the NHL with 86 points in 2014-15. Jaroslav Halak, in his first full season with the club, set a new team record with 38 wins.

Year-by-Year Record

Season	GP	Home W	L	T	OL	Road W	L	T	OL	Overall W	L	T	OL	GF	GA	Pts.	Div. Fin.	Conf. Fin.	Playoff Result
2014-15	82	25	14	....	2	22	14	....	5	47	28	....	7	252	230	101	3rd, Met.	5th, East	Lost First Round
2013-14	82	13	19	....	9	21	18	....	2	34	37	....	11	225	267	79	8th, Met.	14th, East	Out of Playoffs
2012-13	48	10	11	....	3	14	6	....	4	24	17	....	7	139	139	55	3rd, Atl.	8th, East	Lost Conf. Quarter-Final
2011-12	82	17	18	....	6	17	19	....	5	34	37	....	11	203	255	79	5th, Atl.	14th, East	Out of Playoffs
2010-11	82	17	18	....	6	13	21	....	7	30	39	....	13	229	264	73	5th, Atl.	14th, East	Out of Playoffs
2009-10	82	23	14	....	4	11	23	....	7	34	37	....	11	222	264	79	5th, Atl.	13th, East	Out of Playoffs
2008-09	82	17	18	....	6	9	29	....	3	26	47	....	9	201	279	61	5th, Atl.	15th, East	Out of Playoffs
2007-08	82	18	18	....	5	17	20	....	4	35	38	....	9	194	243	79	5th, Atl.	13th, East	Out of Playoffs
2006-07	82	22	13	....	6	18	17	....	6	40	30	....	12	248	240	92	4th, Atl.	8th, East	Lost Conf. Quarter-Final
2005-06	82	20	18	....	3	16	22	....	3	36	40	....	6	230	278	78	4th, Atl.	12th, East	Out of Playoffs
2004-05	....																		
2003-04	82	25	11	4	1	13	18	7	3	38	29	11	4	237	210	91	3rd, Atl.	8th, East	Lost Conf. Quarter-Final
2002-03	82	18	15	5	0	17	16	6	2	35	34	11	2	224	231	83	3rd, Atl.	8th, East	Lost Conf. Quarter-Final
2001-02	82	21	13	5	2	21	15	3	2	42	28	8	4	239	220	96	2nd, Atl.	5th, East	Lost Conf. Quarter-Final
2000-01	82	12	27	1	1	9	24	6	2	21	51	7	3	185	268	52	5th, Atl.	13th, East	Out of Playoffs
1999-2000	82	10	25	5	1	14	23	4	0	24	48	9	1	194	275	58	5th, Atl.	13th, East	Out of Playoffs
1998-99	82	11	23	7	....	13	25	3	....	24	48	10	....	194	244	58	5th, Atl.	13th, East	Out of Playoffs
1997-98	82	17	20	4	....	13	23	7	....	30	41	11	....	212	225	71	4th, Atl.	10th, East	Out of Playoffs
1996-97	82	19	18	4	....	10	23	8	....	29	41	12	....	240	250	70	7th, Atl.	12th, East	Out of Playoffs
1995-96	82	14	21	6	....	8	29	4	....	22	50	10	....	229	315	54	7th, Atl.	13th, East	Out of Playoffs
1994-95	48	10	11	3	....	5	17	2	....	15	28	5	....	126	158	35	7th, Atl.	13th, East	Out of Playoffs
1993-94	84	23	15	4	....	13	21	8	....	36	36	12	....	282	264	84	4th, Atl.	8th, East	Lost Conf. Quarter-Final
1992-93	84	20	19	3	....	20	18	4	....	40	37	7	....	335	297	87	3rd, Patrick		Lost Conf. Final
1991-92	80	20	15	5	....	14	20	6	....	34	35	11	....	291	299	79	5th, Patrick		Out of Playoffs
1990-91	80	15	19	6	....	10	26	4	....	25	45	10	....	223	290	60	6th, Patrick		Out of Playoffs
1989-90	80	15	17	8	....	16	21	3	....	31	38	11	....	281	288	73	4th, Patrick		Lost Div. Semi-Final
1988-89	80	19	18	3	....	9	29	2	....	28	47	5	....	265	325	61	6th, Patrick		Out of Playoffs
1987-88	80	24	10	6	....	15	21	4	....	39	31	10	....	308	267	88	1st, Patrick		Lost Div. Semi-Final
1986-87	80	20	15	5	....	15	18	7	....	35	33	12	....	279	281	82	3rd, Patrick		Lost Div. Final
1985-86	80	22	11	7	....	17	18	5	....	39	29	12	....	327	284	90	3rd, Patrick		Lost Div. Semi-Final
1984-85	80	26	11	3	....	14	23	3	....	40	34	6	....	345	312	86	3rd, Patrick		Lost Div. Final
1983-84	80	28	11	1	....	22	15	3	....	50	26	4	....	357	269	104	1st, Patrick		Lost Final
1982-83	**80**	**26**	**11**	**3**	**....**	**16**	**15**	**9**	**....**	**42**	**26**	**12**	**....**	**302**	**226**	**96**	**2nd, Patrick**		**Won Stanley Cup**
1981-82	**80**	**33**	**3**	**4**	**....**	**21**	**13**	**6**	**....**	**54**	**16**	**10**	**....**	**385**	**250**	**118**	**1st, Patrick**		**Won Stanley Cup**
1980-81	**80**	**23**	**6**	**11**	**....**	**25**	**12**	**3**	**....**	**48**	**18**	**14**	**....**	**355**	**260**	**110**	**1st, Patrick**		**Won Stanley Cup**
1979-80	**80**	**26**	**9**	**5**	**....**	**13**	**19**	**8**	**....**	**39**	**28**	**13**	**....**	**281**	**247**	**91**	**2nd, Patrick**		**Won Stanley Cup**
1978-79	80	31	3	6	....	20	12	8	....	51	15	14	....	358	214	116	1st, Patrick		Lost Semi-Final
1977-78	80	29	3	8	....	19	14	7	....	48	17	15	....	334	210	111	1st, Patrick		Lost Quarter-Final
1976-77	80	24	11	5	....	23	10	7	....	47	21	12	....	288	193	106	2nd, Patrick		Lost Semi-Final
1975-76	80	24	8	8	....	18	13	9	....	42	21	17	....	297	190	101	2nd, Patrick		Lost Semi-Final
1974-75	80	22	6	12	....	11	19	10	....	33	25	22	....	264	221	88	3rd, Patrick		Lost Semi-Final
1973-74	78	13	17	9	....	6	24	9	....	19	41	18	....	182	247	56	8th, East		Out of Playoffs
1972-73	78	10	25	4	....	2	35	2	....	12	60	6	....	170	347	30	8th, East		Out of Playoffs

2015-16 Player Personnel

FORWARDS	HT	WT	*Age	Place of Birth	S	2014-15 Club
BAILEY, Josh	6-1	194	26	Bowmanville, ON	L	NY Islanders
CIZIKAS, Casey	5-11	201	24	Toronto, ON	L	NY Islanders
CLUTTERBUCK, Cal	5-11	215	27	Welland, ON	R	NY Islanders
GRABNER, Michael	6-1	202	28	Villach, Austria	L	NY Islanders
GRABOVSKI, Mikhail	5-11	183	31	Potsdam, East Germany	L	NY Islanders
KULEMIN, Nikolay	6-1	226	29	Magnitogorsk, USSR	L	NY Islanders
LEE, Anders	6-2	227	25	Edina, MN	L	NY Islanders-Bridgeport
MARTIN, Matt	6-3	215	26	Windsor, ON	L	NY Islanders
NELSON, Brock	6-3	196	23	Warroad, MN	L	NY Islanders
NIELSEN, Frans	6-1	190	31	Herning, Denmark	L	NY Islanders
OKPOSO, Kyle	6-0	216	27	St. Paul, MN	R	NY Islanders
STROME, Ryan	6-1	196	22	Mississauga, ON	R	NY Islanders
TAVARES, John	6-1	209	25	Mississauga, ON	L	NY Islanders
DEFENSEMEN						
BOYCHUK, Johnny	6-2	225	31	Edmonton, AB	R	NY Islanders
de HAAN, Calvin	6-1	193	24	Carp, ON	L	NY Islanders
HAMONIC, Travis	6-2	217	25	St. Malo, MB	R	NY Islanders
HICKEY, Thomas	6-0	190	26	Calgary, AB	L	NY Islanders
LEDDY, Nick	6-0	191	24	Eden Prairie, MN	L	NY Islanders
MAYFIELD, Scott	6-5	218	22	St. Louis, MO	R	NY Islanders-Bridgeport
PULOCK, Ryan	6-2	212	21	Dauphin, MB	R	Bridgeport
STRAIT, Brian	6-1	209	27	Boston, MA	L	NY Islanders

GOALTENDERS	HT	WT	*Age	Place of Birth	C	2014-15 Club
GREISS, Thomas	6-1	220	29	Fussen, West Germany	L	Pittsburgh
HALAK, Jaroslav	5-11	186	30	Bratislava, Czech.	L	NY Islanders

* – Age at start of 2015-16 season

Jack Capuano

Head Coach

Born: Cranston, RI, July 7, 1966.

Jack Capuano was named the interim head coach of the New York Islanders on November 15, 2010. Islanders general manager Garth Snow announced his decision to remove the "interim" title and officially name Capuano the club's head coach on April 12, 2011. In 2012-13, he guided the Islanders into the playoffs for the first time since 2007. They returned to the postseason again in 2014-15.

Capuano made his debut in the midst of one of the worst winless streaks in team history and was tasked with turning the season around. Right after Capuano took the reigns, the team posted a 1-8-2 record, but that wouldn't last. After their rough start, Capuano led the Islanders to a 25-21-8 record in their last 54 games of the season, making the Islanders one of the best teams in the Eastern Conference after December 15. The coach had a 15-12-6 record after the All-Star Break.

Capuano joined the Islanders organization in the 2005-06 season as an assistant coach with the Islanders. The native of Cranston, Rhode Island, was named head coach of the Bridgeport Sound Tigers on April 30, 2007. In four seasons he had a 133-100-22 mark as head coach of the Sound Tigers. From 1997 to 2005 he served as the general manager of the Pee Dee Pride of the East Coast Hockey League. Capuano also served as the head coach of the 2005 U.S. Under-18 Select Team at the Five Nations Cup in Slovakia.

Capuano began his coaching career in 1995 as an assistant coach with the Tallahassee Tiger Sharks of the ECHL after ending a pro playing career that included stints with Toronto, Vancouver and Boston of the NHL and Newmarket, Springfield and Maine of the American Hockey League. The former First Team AHCA All-American captained the University of Maine to a Hockey East championship and NCAA Frozen Four appearance in 1998.

Coaching Record

			Regular Season				Playoffs			
Season	Team	League	GC	W	L	O/T	GC	W	L	T
1996-97	Knoxville	ECHL	16	7	8	1	....	....	....	....
1997-98	Pee Dee	ECHL	70	34	25	11	8	3	5	....
1998-99	Pee Dee	ECHL	70	51	15	4	13	7	6	....
2000-01	Pee Dee	ECHL	15	9	5	1	....	....	....	....
2007-08	Bridgeport	AHL	80	40	36	4	....	....	....	....
2008-09	Bridgeport	AHL	80	49	23	8	5	1	4	....
2009-10	Bridgeport	AHL	80	38	32	10	5	1	4	....
2010-11	Bridgeport	AHL	15	6	9	0	....	....	....	....
2010-11	**NY Islanders**	**NHL**	**65**	**26**	**29**	**10**	....	....	....	....
2011-12	**NY Islanders**	**NHL**	**82**	**34**	**37**	**11**	....	....	....	....
2012-13	**NY Islanders**	**NHL**	**48**	**24**	**17**	**7**	**6**	**2**	**4**	....
2013-14	**NY Islanders**	**NHL**	**82**	**34**	**37**	**11**	....	....	....	....
2014-15	**NY Islanders**	**NHL**	**82**	**47**	**28**	**7**	**7**	**3**	**4**	....
	NHL Totals		**359**	**165**	**148**	**46**	**13**	**5**	**8**	....

2014-15 Scoring

* – rookie

Regular Season

Pos	#	Player	Team	GP	G	A	Pts	TOI	+/–	PIM	PP	SH	GW	S	S%
C	91	John Tavares	NYI	82	38	48	86	20:40	5	46	13	0	8	278	13.7
R	21	Kyle Okposo	NYI	60	18	33	51	19:33	–8	12	6	0	2	195	9.2
C	18	Ryan Strome	NYI	81	17	33	50	15:23	23	47	1	1	2	179	9.5
C	51	Frans Nielsen	NYI	78	14	29	43	16:34	8	12	4	1	4	157	8.9
C	29	Brock Nelson	NYI	82	20	22	42	15:52	6	24	10	0	3	190	10.5
C	27 *	Anders Lee	NYI	76	25	16	41	14:23	9	33	5	0	6	197	12.7
C	12	Josh Bailey	NYI	70	15	26	41	16:46	3	12	2	0	1	140	10.7
D	2	Nick Leddy	NYI	78	10	27	37	20:21	18	14	1	0	1	120	8.3
D	55	Johnny Boychuk	NYI	72	9	26	35	21:40	15	14	5	0	1	192	4.7
D	3	Travis Hamonic	NYI	71	5	28	33	21:47	15	85	1	0	0	132	3.8
L	86	Nikolay Kulemin	NYI	82	15	16	31	14:52	7	21	0	3	0	115	13.0
D	14	Thomas Hickey	NYI	81	2	20	22	18:55	–12	26	0	0	1	82	2.4
D	11	Lubomir Visnovsky	NYI	53	5	15	20	19:31	–3	8	2	0	1	85	5.9
C	84	Mikhail Grabovski	NYI	51	9	10	19	14:16	3	8	0	0	2	81	11.1
C	53	Casey Cizikas	NYI	70	9	9	18	12:31	–2	24	0	2	2	90	10.0
R	15	Cal Clutterbuck	NYI	76	7	9	16	12:43	1	60	0	2	4	124	5.6
L	17	Matt Martin	NYI	78	8	6	14	11:16	–4	114	0	0	2	90	8.9
C	26	Tyler Kennedy	S.J.	25	4	5	9	11:03	1	8	0	0	2	48	8.3
			NYI	13	2	3	5	11:23	–3	2	0	0	0	31	6.5
			Total	38	6	8	14	11:09	–2	10	0	0	2	79	7.6
R	40	Michael Grabner	NYI	34	8	5	13	12:56	4	4	0	0	0	63	12.7
D	44	Calvin De Haan	NYI	65	1	11	12	19:00	3	24	0	1	0	92	1.1
R	13	Colin McDonald	NYI	18	2	6	8	10:30	–3	0	0	0	0	29	6.9
D	37	Brian Strait	NYI	52	2	5	7	18:22	–1	32	0	0	0	59	3.4
C	89	Cory Conacher	NYI	15	1	2	3	13:28	–3	14	0	0	0	23	4.3
D	46	Matt Donovan	NYI	12	0	3	3	17:34	4	0	0	0	0	12	0.0
L	36	Eric Boulton	NYI	10	2	0	2	7:11	–1	30	0	0	0	9	22.2
L	48	Kael Mouillierat	NYI	6	1	1	2	8:40	–3	8	0	0	0	1	100.0
D	8 *	Griffin Reinhart	NYI	8	0	1	1	14:10	1	6	0	0	0	4	0.0
L	16	Harry Zolnierczyk	NYI	2	0	0	0	11:07	–1	0	0	0	0	1	0.0

Goaltending

No.	Goaltender	GPI	Mins	Avg	W	L	OT	EN	SO	GA	SA	Sv%	G	A	PIM
41	Jaroslav Halak	59	3550	2.43	38	17	4	6	6	144	1673	.914	0	1	2
60	Kevin Poulin	1	65	2.77	0	0	1	0	0	3	26	.885	0	0	0
30	Michal Neuvirth	5	306	2.94	1	3	1	1	0	15	126	.881	0	0	0
33	Chad Johnson	19	1053	3.08	8	8	1	1	0	54	488	.889	0	0	0
	Totals	**82**	**5008**	**2.68**	**47**	**28**	**7**	**8**	**6**	**224**	**2321**	**.903**			

Playoffs

Pos	#	Player	Team	GP	G	A	Pts	TOI	+/–	PIM	PP	SH	GW	OT	S	S%
C	91	John Tavares	NYI	7	2	4	6	19:18	2	2	0	0	1	1	18	11.1
C	12	Josh Bailey	NYI	7	2	3	5	17:25	1	0	0	0	0	0	12	16.7
D	2	Nick Leddy	NYI	7	0	5	5	24:39	0	0	0	0	0	0	15	0.0
C	18	Ryan Strome	NYI	7	2	2	4	17:32	1	2	0	0	1	0	12	16.7
R	21	Kyle Okposo	NYI	7	2	1	3	18:30	1	2	0	0	0	0	16	12.5
R	15	Cal Clutterbuck	NYI	7	2	1	3	12:49	1	26	0	0	0	0	12	16.7
C	29	Brock Nelson	NYI	6	2	0	2	14:20	1	2	0	0	0	0	8	25.0
C	51	Frans Nielsen	NYI	7	1	1	2	16:10	–1	0	0	0	0	0	11	9.1
L	86	Nikolay Kulemin	NYI	7	1	1	2	15:42	0	2	0	0	1	0	5	20.0
D	11	Lubomir Visnovsky	NYI	4	0	2	2	16:19	5	0	0	0	0	0	5	0.0
D	55	Johnny Boychuk	NYI	7	0	2	2	26:00	–1	2	0	0	0	0	20	0.0
C	53	Casey Cizikas	NYI	7	1	0	1	13:41	1	0	0	0	0	0	11	9.1
R	40	Michael Grabner	NYI	2	0	1	1	11:44	1	2	0	0	0	0	0	0.0
D	44	Calvin De Haan	NYI	5	0	1	1	17:20	–2	2	0	0	0	0	3	0.0
C	27 *	Anders Lee	NYI	5	0	1	1	14:45	–2	7	0	0	0	0	8	0.0
D	14	Thomas Hickey	NYI	7	0	1	1	21:25	5	2	0	0	0	0	14	0.0
L	17	Matt Martin	NYI	7	0	1	1	11:54	1	12	0	0	0	0	9	0.0
D	8 *	Griffin Reinhart	NYI	1	0	0	0	12:42	–2	0	0	0	0	0	1	0.0
R	13	Colin McDonald	NYI	2	0	0	0	11:45	1	2	0	0	0	0	1	0.0
D	46	Matt Donovan	NYI	2	0	0	0	11:20	0	10	0	0	0	0	1	0.0
D	42 *	Scott Mayfield	NYI	2	0	0	0	12:25	–1	0	0	0	0	0	1	0.0
C	26	Tyler Kennedy	NYI	3	0	0	0	10:33	–3	2	0	0	0	0	7	0.0
C	84	Mikhail Grabovski	NYI	3	0	0	0	14:26	–1	0	0	0	0	0	5	0.0
D	37	Brian Strait	NYI	7	0	0	0	18:49	–3	4	0	0	0	0	4	0.0

Goaltending

No.	Goaltender	GPI	Mins	Avg	W	L	EN	SO	GA	SA	Sv%	G	A	PIM
30	Michal Neuvirth	1	11	0.00	0	0	0	0	0	6	1.000	0	0	0
41	Jaroslav Halak	7	418	2.30	3	4	0	0	16	215	.926	0	0	2
	Totals	**7**	**431**	**2.23**	**3**	**4**	**0**	**0**	**16**	**221**	**.928**			

Coaching History

Phil Goyette and Earl Ingarfield, 1972-73; Al Arbour, 1973-74 to 1985-86; Terry Simpson, 1986-87, 1987-88; Terry Simpson and Al Arbour, 1988-89; Al Arbour, 1989-90 to 1993-94; Lorne Henning, 1994-95; Mike Milbury, 1995-96; Mike Milbury and Rick Bowness, 1996-97; Rick Bowness and Mike Milbury, 1997-98; Mike Milbury and Bill Stewart, 1998-99; Butch Goring, 1999-2000; Butch Goring and Lorne Henning, 2000-01; Peter Laviolette, 2001-02, 2002-03; Steve Stirling, 2003-04, 2004-05; Steve Stirling and Brad Shaw, 2005-06; Ted Nolan, 2006-07, 2007-08; Scott Gordon, 2008-09, 2009-10; Scott Gordon and Jack Capuano, 2010-11; Jack Capuano, 2011-12 to date.

Club Records

Team

(Figures in brackets for season records are games played; records for fewest points, wins, ties, losses, goals, goals against are for 70 or more games)

Record		
Most Points	**118**	1981-82 (80)
Most Wins	**54**	1981-82 (80)
Most Ties	**22**	1974-75 (80)
Most Losses	**60**	1972-73 (78)
Most Goals	**385**	1981-82 (80)
Most Goals Against	**347**	1972-73 (78)
Fewest Points	**30**	1972-73 (78)
Fewest Wins	**12**	1972-73 (78)
Fewest Ties	**4**	1983-84 (80)
Fewest Losses	**15**	1978-79 (80)
Fewest Goals	**170**	1972-73 (78)
Fewest Goals Against	**190**	1975-76 (80)
Longest Winning Streak		
Overall	**15**	Jan. 21-Feb. 20/82
Home	**14**	Jan. 2-Feb. 25/82
Away	**8**	Feb. 27-Mar. 29/81
Longest Undefeated Streak		
Overall	**15**	Three times
Home	**23**	Oct. 17/78-Jan. 20/79 (19W, 4T), Jan. 2-Apr. 3/82 (21W, 2T)
Away	**8**	Three times
Longest Losing Streak		
Overall	**14**	Oct. 23-Nov. 24/10
Home	**8**	Nov. 27-Dec. 28/13
Away	**15**	Jan. 20-Mar. 31/73
Longest Winless Streak		
Overall	**15**	Nov. 22-Dec. 21/72 (12L, 3T)
Home	**9**	Mar. 2-Apr. 6/99 (7L, 2T)
Away	**20**	Nov. 3/72-Jan. 13/73 (19L, 1T)
Most Shutouts, Season	**10**	1975-76 (80)
Most PIM, Season	**1,857**	1986-87 (80)
Most Goals, Game	**11**	Dec. 20/83 (Pit. 3 at NYI 11), Mar. 3/84 (NYI 11 at Tor. 6)

Individual

Record		
Most Seasons	**17**	Billy Smith
Most Games	**1,123**	Bryan Trottier
Most Goals, Career	**573**	Mike Bossy
Most Assists, Career	**853**	Bryan Trottier
Most Points, Career	**1,353**	Bryan Trottier (500G, 853A)
Most PIM, Career	**1,879**	Mick Vukota
Most Shutouts, Career	**25**	Glenn Resch
Longest Consecutive Games Streak	**576**	Billy Harris (Oct. 7/72-Nov. 30/79)
Most Goals, Season	**69**	Mike Bossy (1978-79)
Most Assists, Season	**87**	Bryan Trottier (1978-79)
Most Points, Season	**147**	Mike Bossy (1981-82; 64G, 83A)
Most PIM, Season	**356**	Brian Curran (1986-87)
Most Points, Defenseman, Season	**101**	Denis Potvin (1978-79; 31G, 70A)
Most Points, Center, Season	**134**	Bryan Trottier (1978-79; 47G, 87A)
Most Points, Right Wing, Season	**147**	Mike Bossy (1981-82; 64G, 83A)
Most Points, Left Wing, Season	**100**	John Tonelli (1984-85; 42G, 58A)
Most Points, Rookie, Season	**95**	Bryan Trottier (1975-76; 32G, 63A)
Most Shutouts, Season	**7**	Glenn Resch (1975-76)
Most Goals, Game	**5**	Bryan Trottier (Dec. 23/78), (Feb. 13/82) John Tonelli (Jan. 6/81)
Most Assists, Game	**6**	Mike Bossy (Jan. 6/81)
Most Points, Game	**8**	Bryan Trottier (Dec. 23/78; 5G, 3A)

Captains' History

Ed Westfall, 1972-73 to 1975-76; Ed Westfall and Clark Gillies, 1976-77; Clark Gillies, 1977-78, 1978-79; Denis Potvin, 1979-80 to 1986-87; Brent Sutter, 1987-88 to 1990-91; Brent Sutter and Pat Flatley, 1991-92; Pat Flatley, 1992-93 to 1995-96; no captain, 1996-97; Bryan McCabe and Trevor Linden, 1997-98; Trevor Linden, 1998-99; Kenny Jonsson, 1999-2000, 2000-01; Michael Peca, 2001-02 to 2003-04; Alexei Yashin, 2005-06, 2006-07; Bill Guerin, 2007-08; Bill Guerin and no captain, 2008-09; Doug Weight, 2009-10, 2010-11; Mark Streit, 2011-12, 2012-13; John Tavares, 2013-14 to date.

All-time Record vs. Other Clubs

Regular Season

	Total								At Home								On Road							
	GP	W	L	T	OL	GF	GA	PTS	GP	W	L	T	OL	GF	GA	PTS	GP	W	L	T	OL	GF	GA	PTS
Anaheim	28	12	11	4	1	74	76	29	13	6	6	1	0	34	37	13	15	6	5	3	1	40	39	16
Arizona	71	34	24	12	1	255	223	81	35	17	9	8	1	133	101	43	36	17	15	4	0	122	122	38
Boston	157	56	77	21	3	462	539	136	79	32	37	10	0	249	259	74	78	24	40	11	3	213	280	62
Buffalo	159	64	70	18	7	451	481	153	79	36	31	9	3	226	217	84	80	28	39	9	4	225	264	69
Calgary	110	46	44	20	0	366	341	112	56	29	18	9	0	204	153	67	54	17	26	11	0	162	188	45
Carolina	128	54	62	9	3	390	417	120	64	27	32	4	1	186	195	59	64	27	30	5	2	204	222	61
Chicago	106	41	43	20	2	356	335	104	52	22	14	15	1	181	153	60	54	19	29	5	1	175	182	44
Colorado	77	36	35	4	2	261	262	78	37	22	14	1	0	151	122	45	40	14	21	3	2	110	140	33
Columbus	22	7	9	1	5	62	75	20	10	5	2	0	3	34	30	13	12	2	7	1	2	28	45	7
Dallas	106	52	35	16	3	388	310	123	54	28	16	8	2	201	158	66	52	24	19	8	1	187	152	57
Detroit	103	49	46	6	2	337	329	106	52	27	19	4	2	188	155	60	51	22	27	2	0	149	174	46
Edmonton	70	28	27	14	1	238	242	71	36	20	7	9	0	144	118	49	34	8	20	5	1	94	124	22
Florida	87	36	40	8	3	238	256	83	44	22	19	2	1	115	118	47	43	14	21	6	2	123	138	36
Los Angeles	101	44	44	12	1	318	316	101	51	26	19	5	1	170	139	58	50	18	25	7	0	148	177	43
Minnesota	18	7	9	0	2	44	56	16	9	4	4	0	1	18	26	9	9	3	5	0	1	26	30	7
Montreal	157	58	82	15	2	444	506	133	79	36	36	6	1	230	228	79	78	22	46	9	1	214	278	54
Nashville	19	8	10	0	1	48	51	17	9	5	3	0	1	25	23	11	10	3	7	0	0	23	28	6
New Jersey	231	124	78	22	7	791	672	277	117	71	32	11	3	425	314	156	114	53	46	11	4	366	358	121
NY Rangers	254	111	118	19	6	816	854	247	127	65	50	8	4	448	400	142	127	46	68	11	2	368	454	105
Ottawa	84	24	46	11	3	226	294	62	43	12	24	6	1	126	159	31	41	12	22	5	2	100	135	31
Philadelphia	253	97	125	26	5	773	834	225	128	59	51	15	3	431	387	136	125	38	74	11	2	342	447	89
Pittsburgh	236	103	99	22	12	832	835	240	116	60	40	8	8	446	386	136	120	43	59	14	4	386	449	104
St. Louis	107	48	35	20	4	368	339	120	55	27	14	11	3	203	150	68	52	21	21	9	1	165	189	52
San Jose	33	14	14	3	2	101	95	33	16	7	6	2	1	53	51	17	17	7	8	1	1	48	44	16
Tampa Bay	88	43	36	3	6	257	237	95	44	25	16	1	2	135	111	53	44	18	20	2	4	122	126	42
Toronto	145	72	60	7	6	512	469	157	71	40	24	3	4	268	211	87	74	32	36	4	2	244	258	70
Vancouver	104	50	38	13	3	354	322	116	52	27	13	10	2	184	151	66	52	23	25	3	1	170	171	50
Washington	201	89	86	13	13	663	635	204	100	51	41	2	6	359	309	110	101	38	45	11	7	304	326	94
Winnipeg	55	30	19	2	4	197	161	66	27	13	14	0	0	91	78	26	28	17	5	2	4	106	83	40
Defunct Clubs	26	15	5	6	0	110	74	36	13	11	0	2	0	75	33	24	13	4	5	4	0	35	41	12
Totals	**3336**	**1452**	**1427**	**347**	**110**	**10732**	**10636**	**3361**	**1668**	**832**	**611**	**170**	**55**	**5733**	**4972**	**1889**	**1668**	**620**	**816**	**177**	**55**	**4999**	**5664**	**1472**

Playoffs

	Series	W	L	GP	W	L	T	GF	GA	Last Mtg.	Rnd.	Result
Boston	2	2	0	11	8	3	0	49	35	1983	CF	W 4-2
Buffalo	4	3	1	21	13	8	0	70	62	2007	CQF	L 1-4
Chicago	2	2	0	6	6	0	0	21	6	1979	QF	W 4-0
Colorado	1	1	0	4	4	0	0	18	9	1982	CF	W 4-0
Dallas	1	1	0	5	4	1	0	26	16	1981	F	W 4-1
Edmonton	3	2	1	15	9	6	0	58	47	1984	F	L 1-4
Los Angeles	1	1	0	4	3	1	0	21	10	1980	PR	W 3-1
Montreal	4	1	3	22	8	14	0	55	64	1993	CF	L 1-4
New Jersey	1	0	1	6	2	4	0	18	23	1988	DSF	L 2-4
NY Rangers	8	5	3	39	20	19	0	129	132	1994	CQF	L 0-4
Ottawa	1	0	1	5	1	4	0	7	13	2003	CQF	L 1-4
Philadelphia	4	1	3	25	11	14	0	69	83	1987	DF	L 3-4
Pittsburgh	4	3	1	25	13	12	0	84	83	2013	CQF	L 2-4
Tampa Bay	1	0	1	5	1	4	0	5	12	2004	CQF	L 1-4
Toronto	3	1	2	17	9	8	0	54	42	2002	CQF	L 3-4
Vancouver	2	2	0	6	6	0	0	26	14	1982	F	W 4-0
Washington	7	5	2	37	21	16	0	114	104	2015	FR	L 3-4
Totals	**49**	**30**	**19**	**253**	**139**	**114**	**0**	**824**	**755**			

Calgary totals include Atlanta Flames, 1972-73 to 1979-80. Carolina totals include Hartford, 1979-80 to 1996-97.
Colorado totals include Quebec, 1979-80 to 1994-95. Dallas totals include Minnesota North Stars, 1972-73 to 1992-93.
New Jersey totals include Kansas City, 1974-75, 1975-76, and Colorado Rockies, 1976-77 to 1981-82.
Phoenix totals include Winnipeg, 1979-80 to 1995-96. Winnipeg totals include Atlanta Thrashers, 1999-2000 to 2010-11.

Playoff Results 2015-2011

Year	Round	Opponent	Result	GF	GA
2015	FR	Washington	L 3-4	15	16
2013	CQF	Pittsburgh	L 2-4	17	25

Abbreviations: Round: F – Final; **CF** – conference final; **CQF** – conference quarter-final; **FR** – first round; **DF** – division final; **DSF** – division semi-final; **QF** – quarter-final; **PR** – preliminary round.

2014-15 Results

Oct.	10	at Carolina	5-3		10	at Columbus	5-2
	11	Carolina	4-3		13	at NY Rangers	3-0
	14	at NY Rangers	6-3		16	Pittsburgh	6-3
	16	San Jose	4-3†		17	at Montreal	4-6
	18	at Pittsburgh	1-3		19	Philadelphia	7-4
	21	Toronto	2-5		27	NY Rangers	4-1
	23	at Boston	3-2		29	Boston	2-5
	25	Dallas	7-5		31	at Detroit	1-4
	28	Winnipeg	3-4	**Feb.**	3	Florida	2-4
	30	at Colorado	0-5		5	at Philadelphia	3-2†
Nov.	1	at San Jose	1-3		7	at Boston	1-2
	5	at Anaheim	3-2*		8	at Buffalo	3-2
	6	at Los Angeles	2-1†		10	Edmonton	3-2
	8	at Arizona	1-0		12	Toronto	3-2
	11	Colorado	6-0		14	Columbus	6-3
	14	at Florida	4-3†		16	NY Rangers	5-6
	15	at Tampa Bay	2-5		17	at Carolina	4-1
	18	Tampa Bay	5-2		19	Nashville	5-2
	21	at Pittsburgh	5-4†		21	at Washington	2-3†
	22	Pittsburgh	4-1		22	Vancouver	0-4
	24	Philadelphia	1-0†		24	Arizona	5-1
	26	Washington	3-2*		27	Calgary	2-1
	28	at Washington	2-5		28	Carolina	3-5
	29	New Jersey	3-1	**Mar.**	3	at Dallas	2-3*
Dec.	2	Ottawa	3-2*		5	at Nashville	4-3
	4	at Ottawa	2-1		7	at Florida	3-4†
	6	St. Louis	4-6		9	at Toronto	4-3*
	9	at Minnesota	4-5		10	NY Rangers	1-2
	11	at St. Louis	3-6		13	Ottawa	1-2
	13	Chicago	3-2		14	Montreal	1-3
	15	New Jersey	3-2†		17	at Chicago	1-4
	19	at Detroit	2-1		21	at New Jersey	3-0
	20	Tampa Bay	3-1		24	Minnesota	1-2†
	23	Montreal	1-3		26	Los Angeles	2-3
	27	at Buffalo	3-4†		28	Anaheim	2-3
	29	Washington	4-3*		29	Detroit	5-4
	31	at Winnipeg	5-2	**Apr.**	2	at Columbus	3-4†
Jan.	2	at Calgary	2-1		4	Buffalo	3-0
	4	at Edmonton	2-5		7	at Philadelphia	4-5
	6	at Vancouver	2-3		10	at Pittsburgh	3-1
	9	at New Jersey	3-2*		11	Columbus	4-5†

* – Overtime † – Shootout

NHL Draft Selections 2015-2001

Name in bold denotes played in NHL.

2015 Pick		2011 Pick		2007 Pick		2004 Pick	
16	Mathew Barzal	5	**Ryan Strome**	62	Mark Katic	16	**Petteri Nokelainen**
28	Anthony Beauvillier	34	**Scott Mayfield**	76	Jason Gregoire	47	**Blake Comeau**
82	Mitchell Vande Sompel	50	**Johan Sundstrom**	106	Maxim Gratchev	82	Sergei Ogorodnikov
112	Parker Wotherspoon	63	Andrey Pedan	166	Blake Kessel	115	**Wes O'Neill**
147	Ryan Pilon	95	Robbie Russo	196	Simon Lacroix	148	**Steve Regier**
172	Andong Song	125	**John Persson**			179	Jaroslav Mrazek
202	Petter Hansson	127	Brenden Kichton	**2006 Pick**		210	Emil Axelsson
		185	Mitchell Theoret	7	**Kyle Okposo**	227	**Chris Campoli**
2014 Pick				60	**Jesse Joensuu**	244	Jason Pitton
5	Michael Dal Colle	**2010 Pick**		70	Robin Figren	276	Sylvain Michaud
28	Joshua Ho-Sang	5	**Nino Niederreiter**	100	**Rhett Rakhshani**		
78	Ilya Sorokin	30	**Brock Nelson**	108	Jase Weslosky	**2003 Pick**	
95	Linus Soderstrom	65	Kirill Kabanov	115	Tomas Marcinko	15	**Robert Nilsson**
108	Devon Toews	82	Jason Clark	119	Doug Rogers	48	Dmitri Chernykh
155	Kyle Schempp	125	Tony Dehart	126	**Shane Sims**	53	Evgeny Tunik
200	Lukas Sutter	185	Cody Rosen	141	Kim Johansson	58	**Jeremy Colliton**
				160	**Andrew MacDonald**	120	Stefan Blaho
2013 Pick		**2009 Pick**		171	Brian Day	182	**Bruno Gervais**
15	**Ryan Pulock**	1	**John Tavares**	173	Stefan Ridderwall	212	Denis Rehak
70	Eamon McAdam	12	**Calvin de Haan**	190	Troy Mattila	238	Cody Blanshan
76	Taylor Cammarata	31	**Mikko Koskinen**			246	Igor Volkov
106	Stephon Williams	62	**Anders Nilsson**	**2005 Pick**			
136	Victor Crus-Rydberg	92	**Casey Cizikas**	15	**Ryan O'Marra**	**2002 Pick**	
166	Alan Quine	122	Anton Klementyev	46	**Dustin Kohn**	22	**Sean Bergenheim**
196	Kyle Burroughs	152	**Anders Lee**	76	Shea Guthrie	87	**Frans Nielsen**
				144	**Masi Marjamaki**	149	Marcus Paulsson
2012 Pick		**2008 Pick**		180	Tyrell Mason	189	Alexei Stonkus
4	**Griffin Reinhart**	9	**Josh Bailey**	196	Nick Tuzzolino	220	Brad Topping
34	Ville Pokka	36	Corey Trivino	210	Luciano Aquino	252	Martin Chabada
65	Adam Pelech	40	**Aaron Ness**			283	Per Braxenholm
103	Loic Leduc	53	**Travis Hamonic**	**2001 Pick**			
125	Doyle Somerby	66	David Toews	101	Cory Stillman		
155	Jesse Graham	72	Jyri Niemi	132	Dusan Salficky		
185	Jake Bischoff	73	Kirill Petrov	166	**Andy Chiodo**		
		96	Matt Donovan	197	Jan Holub		
		102	David Ullstrom	228	Mike Bray		
		126	Kevin Poulin	260	Bryan Perez		
		148	**Matt Martin**	280	Roman Kuhtinov		
		156	**Jared Spurgeon**	287	Juha-Pekka Ketola		
		175	**Justin Dibenedetto**				

General Managers' History

Bill Torrey, 1972-73 to 1991-92; Don Maloney, 1992-93 to 1994-95; Don Maloney, Darcy Regier and Mike Milbury, 1995-96; Mike Milbury, 1996-97 to 2005-06; Neil Smith and Garth Snow, 2006-07; Garth Snow, 2007-08 to date.

Garth Snow
General Manager
Born: Wrentham, MA, June 28, 1969.

Former Islanders' goaltender Garth Snow retired as a player on July 18, 2006 to become the fifth general manager of the New York Islanders. In his first season as general manager, Snow successfully bolstered the lineup with several key additions that helped to propel the Islanders into the postseason for the first time since the 2003–04 season and earned Snow the title of NHL Executive of the Year from *Sports Illustrated*.

Snow spent four seasons with the Islanders and 12 in the NHL. The goaltender was 135-147-44 with a 2.80 goals-against average and .901 save percentage over 368 games with Quebec, Philadelphia, Vancouver, Pittsburgh and the Islanders. Originally selected in the sixth round by Quebec in the 1987 NHL Draft, the native of Wrentham, Massachusetts signed with the Islanders as a free agent on July 1, 2001.

Club Directory

Barclays Center

New York Islanders
Executive Office
1255 Hempstead Turnpike
Uniondale, NY 11553
Phone 516/501-6700
FAX 516/501-6850
www.newyorkislanders.com
Arena
Barclays Center
620 Atlantic Ave.
Brooklyn, NY 11217
Capacity: 15,795

Governor	Charles B. Wang
G.M., President & Alternate Governor	Garth Snow
Alternate Governors	Scott Malkin, Jon Ledecky, Art McCarthy, Roy Reichbach
Sr. Vice President & Alternate Governor	Michael Picker
Sr. Vice President of Marketing and Sales	Paul Lancey
Barclays Center CEO	Brett Yormark
Barclays Center COO	Fred Mangione

Hockey Operations

Manager, Hockey Administration	Joanne Holewa
Assistant G.M. & Assistant Coach	Doug Weight
Director of Pro Scouting	Ken Morrow
Assistant to the General Manager	Kerry Gwydir
Head Coach	Jack Capuano
Assistant Coaches	Greg Cronin, Bob Corkum, Matt Bertani
Goalie Coach	Mike Dunham
Skill Development Coach	Bernie Cassell
Director of Sports Performance	Sean Donellan
Director of Player Development	Eric Cairns
Player Development	Marty Reasoner
Equipment Manager / Asst. Manager / Assistant	Scott Boggs / Richard Krouse / Kevin Putzig
Head Athletic Trainer / Assistant Trainer	Damien Hess / Philip E. Watson
Massage Therapist	Jim Miccio
Strength and Conditioning Coach	Derrek Douglas
Head Amateur Scout	Velli-Pekka Kautonen
Scouts	Mario Saraceno, Tim Maclean, Chris O'Sullivan, David Hymovitz, Jay Saraceno, Jeff Napierala, Don McDuff, Dennis Maxwell, Matti Kautto, Trent Klatt

Administration

Deputy General Counsel	Stacey Sabo
Human Resources Manager / Coordinator	Michele Finkelstein / Megan Lynch
IT Manager	Pawel Tauter
Receptionist / Office Attendant	Bonnie Dreher / Todd Aronovich

Ticket Sales and Operations

Vice President, Ticket Sales	Ralph Sellitti
Senior Director, Sports Ticketing Operations	Paul Kavanaugh
Ticket Manager	Adam Ortiz
Executive Director of Group Sales	Kirk King
Senior Director of Global Partnerships	Chris Lombardo
Director of Ticket Sales	Emmanuel Jacobo
Manager of Group and Inside Sales	Theresa Power
Premium Account Executives, Tickets Sales	Lauren Garan, Andrew Gilberti, Ryan Moore, Sam Berg, Mike Kim, David Koblentz, Chris Baldi, Bryce Mitchell, Brian Frankel
Account Managers, VIP Services	Rachel Lowe, Steen Weiss, Robert Aanonsen, Leah Paplia, Marc Gerstein, Jake Weinstein, Bryan Viggiano, Nick Thompson, Anthony Infante
Coordinators, Group Sales / Ticket Sales	Deena Sena / Lauren Herzlich

Media Relations / Communications

Director of Communications	Kimber Auerbach
Communications Manager / Coordinator	Jesse Eisenberg / Greg Picker

Community Relations, Fan Development, Marketing and Operations

Barclays Center Sr. VP/Chief Marketing Officer	Elisa Padilla
Barclays Center Exec. VP, Global Partnerships	Mike Zabodsky
Community Relations Manager	Ann Rina
Event Operations Coordinator	Ryan McLear
Manager, Amateur Hockey Development	Jocelyne Cummings
Director, Islanders Game Presentation	TJ Roche
Coordinators, Game Operations / Marketing	Mallory Mullane / Joseph Paciullo
Web Content Producer	Cory Wright

Retail and Merchandise Operations

Director of Retail Operations	Terry Goldstein
Pro Shop Manager / Asst. Manager	Tim Murray / Nicolo Valenti
Merchandise Coordinator	Robert Marsala

Finance

Controller / Accounting Manager	Frank Romano / Chris Vardaro
Payroll Manager / A/P Coordinator	Christine Bowler / Janet Nelson
Staff Accountant	Lisa Viera

New York Rangers

Key Off-Season Signings/Acquisitions

2015

June 27 • Acquired RW **Emerson Etem** and a 2nd-round choice in the 2015 NHL Draft from Anaheim for LW **Carl Hagelin**, a 2nd-round choice in 2015 and a 6th-round choice in 2015.

27 • Acquired G **Antti Raanta** from Chicago for RW **Ryan Haggerty**.

July 1 • Named **Jeff Gorton** general manager.

1 • Signed D **Raphael Diaz**, C **Jayson Megna**, LW **Viktor Stalberg**, C **Brian Gibbons** and C **Matt Lindblad**.

3 • Signed C **Luke Adam**.

15 • Re-signed C **J.T. Miller**, RW **Jesper Fast** and D **Dylan McIlrath**.

27 • Re-signed C **Derek Stepan**.

2014-15 Results: 53W-22L-2OTL-5SOL 113PTS

1ST, Metropolitan Division • 1ST, Eastern Conference

2015-16 Schedule

Oct.	Wed.	7	at Chicago		Mon.	11	Boston
	Fri.	9	at Columbus		Thu.	14	at NY Islanders
	Sat.	10	Columbus		Sat.	16	at Philadelphia*
	Tue.	13	Winnipeg		Sun.	17	at Washington*
	Thu.	15	at Montreal		Tue.	19	Vancouver
	Sun.	18	New Jersey*		Fri.	22	at Carolina
	Mon.	19	San Jose		Sun.	24	at Ottawa*
	Thu.	22	Arizona		Mon.	25	Buffalo
	Sat.	24	at Philadelphia	**Feb.**	Tue.	2	at New Jersey
	Sun.	25	Calgary		Thu.	4	Minnesota
	Fri.	30	Toronto		Sat.	6	at Philadelphia*
Nov.	Tue.	3	Washington		Mon.	8	New Jersey
	Fri.	6	at Colorado		Wed.	10	at Pittsburgh
	Sat.	7	at Arizona		Fri.	12	Los Angeles
	Tue.	10	Carolina		Sun.	14	Philadelphia
	Thu.	12	St. Louis		Wed.	17	Chicago
	Sat.	14	at Ottawa*		Thu.	18	at Toronto
	Sun.	15	Toronto		Sun.	21	Detroit
	Thu.	19	at Tampa Bay		Tue.	23	at New Jersey
	Sat.	21	at Florida		Thu.	25	at St. Louis
	Mon.	23	Nashville		Sat.	27	at Dallas*
	Wed.	25	Montreal		Mon.	29	Columbus
	Fri.	27	at Boston*	**Mar.**	Thu.	3	at Pittsburgh
	Sat.	28	Philadelphia*		Fri.	4	at Washington
	Mon.	30	Carolina		Sun.	6	NY Islanders*
Dec.	Wed.	2	at NY Islanders		Tue.	8	at Buffalo
	Thu.	3	Colorado		Sat.	12	at Detroit*
	Sun.	6	Ottawa		Sun.	13	Pittsburgh*
	Wed.	9	at Vancouver		Wed.	16	at Anaheim
	Fri.	11	at Edmonton		Thu.	17	at Los Angeles
	Sat.	12	at Calgary		Sat.	19	at San Jose*
	Tue.	15	Edmonton		Mon.	21	Florida
	Thu.	17	at Minnesota		Wed.	23	Boston
	Fri.	18	at Winnipeg		Sat.	26	at Montreal
	Sun.	20	Washington		Sun.	27	Pittsburgh
	Tue.	22	Anaheim		Thu.	31	at Carolina
	Mon,	28	at Nashville	**Apr.**	Sat.	2	Buffalo
	Wed.	30	at Tampa Bay		Mon.	4	at Columbus
Jan.	Sat.	2	at Florida		Tue.	5	Tampa Bay
	Tue.	5	Dallas		Thu.	7	NY Islanders
	Sat.	9	Washington*		Sat.	9	Detroit*

* Denotes afternoon game.

Retired Numbers

1	Ed Giacomin	1965-1975
2	Brian Leetch	1987-2004
3	Harry Howell	1952-1969
7	Rod Gilbert	1960-1977
9	Andy Bathgate	1952-1964
	Adam Graves	1991-2001
11	Mark Messier	1991-97; 2000-04
35	Mike Richter	1989-2003

METROPOLITAN DIVISION
90th NHL Season

Franchise date: May 15, 1926

Year-by-Year Record

		Home				Road				Overall									
Season	GP	W	L	T	OL	W	L	T	OL	W	L	T	OL	GF	GA	Pts.	Div. Fin.	Conf. Fin.	Playoff Result
2014-15	82	25	11	....	5	28	11	....	2	53	22	....	7	252	192	113	1st, Met.	1st, East	Lost Conf. Final
2013-14	82	20	17	....	4	25	14	....	2	45	31	....	6	218	193	96	2nd, Met.	5th, East	Lost Final
2012-13	48	16	6	....	2	10	12	....	2	26	18	....	4	130	112	56	2nd, Atl.	6th, East	Lost Conf. Semi-Final
2011-12	82	27	12	....	2	24	12	....	5	51	24	....	7	226	187	109	1st, Atl.	1st, East	Lost Conf. Final
2010-11	82	20	17	....	4	24	16	....	1	44	33	....	5	233	198	93	3rd, Atl.	8th, East	Lost Conf. Quarter-Final
2009-10	82	18	17	....	6	20	16	....	5	38	33	....	11	222	218	87	4th, Atl.	9th, East	Out of Playoffs
2008-09	82	26	11	....	4	17	19	....	5	43	30	....	9	210	218	95	4th, Atl.	7th, East	Lost Conf. Quarter-Final
2007-08	82	25	13	....	3	17	14	....	10	42	27	....	13	213	199	97	3rd, Atl.	5th, East	Lost Conf. Semi-Final
2006-07	82	21	15	....	5	21	15	....	5	42	30	....	10	242	216	94	3rd, Atl.	6th, East	Lost Conf. Semi-Final
2005-06	82	25	10	....	6	19	16	....	6	44	26	....	12	257	215	100	3rd, Atl.	6th, East	Lost Conf. Quarter-Final
2004-05	....	....	....	....	....	....	....	....	....	....	....	....	....	....	....	....			
2003-04	82	13	21	3	4	14	19	4	4	27	40	7	8	206	250	69	4th, Atl.	13th, East	Out of Playoffs
2002-03	82	17	18	4	2	15	18	6	2	32	36	10	4	210	231	78	4th, Atl.	9th, East	Out of Playoffs
2001-02	82	19	19	2	1	17	19	2	3	36	38	4	4	227	258	80	4th, Atl.	11th, East	Out of Playoffs
2000-01	82	17	20	3	1	16	23	2	0	33	43	5	1	250	290	72	4th, Atl.	10th, East	Out of Playoffs
1999-2000	82	15	20	5	1	14	18	7	2	29	38	12	3	218	246	73	4th, Atl.	11th, East	Out of Playoffs
1998-99	82	17	19	5	....	16	19	6	....	33	38	11	....	217	227	77	4th, Atl.	10th, East	Out of Playoffs
1997-98	82	14	18	9	....	11	21	9	....	25	39	18	....	197	231	68	5th, Atl.	11th, East	Out of Playoffs
1996-97	82	21	14	6	....	17	20	4	....	38	34	10	....	258	231	86	4th, Atl.	5th, East	Lost Conf. Final
1995-96	82	22	10	9	....	19	17	5	....	41	27	14	....	272	237	96	2nd, Atl.	3rd, East	Lost Conf. Semi-Final
1994-95	48	11	10	3	....	11	13	0	....	22	23	3	....	139	134	47	4th, Atl.	8th, East	Lost Conf. Semi-Final
1993-94	**84**	**28**	**8**	**6**	....	**24**	**16**	**2**	....	**52**	**24**	**8**	....	**299**	**231**	**112**	**1st, Atl.**	**1st, East**	**Won Stanley Cup**
1992-93	84	20	17	5	....	14	22	6	....	34	39	11	....	304	308	79	6th, Patrick		Out of Playoffs
1991-92	80	28	8	4	....	22	17	1	....	50	25	5	....	321	246	105	1st, Patrick		Lost Div. Final
1990-91	80	22	11	7	....	14	20	6	....	36	31	13	....	297	265	85	2nd, Patrick		Lost Div. Semi-Final
1989-90	80	20	11	9	....	16	20	4	....	36	31	13	....	279	267	85	1st, Patrick		Lost Div. Final
1988-89	80	21	17	2	....	16	18	6	....	37	35	8	....	310	307	82	3rd, Patrick		Lost Div. Semi-Final
1987-88	80	22	13	5	....	14	21	5	....	36	34	10	....	300	283	82	5th, Patrick		Out of Playoffs
1986-87	80	18	18	4	....	16	20	4	....	34	38	8	....	307	323	76	4th, Patrick		Lost Div. Semi-Final
1985-86	80	20	18	2	....	16	20	4	....	36	38	6	....	280	276	78	4th, Patrick		Lost Conf. Final
1984-85	80	16	18	6	....	10	26	4	....	26	44	10	....	295	345	62	4th, Patrick		Lost Div. Semi-Final
1983-84	80	27	12	1	....	15	17	8	....	42	29	9	....	314	304	93	4th, Patrick		Lost Div. Semi-Final
1982-83	80	24	13	3	....	11	22	7	....	35	35	10	....	306	287	80	4th, Patrick		Lost Div. Final
1981-82	80	19	15	6	....	20	12	8	....	39	27	14	....	316	306	92	2nd, Patrick		Lost Div. Final
1980-81	80	17	13	10	....	13	23	4	....	30	36	14	....	312	317	74	4th, Patrick		Lost Semi-Final
1979-80	80	22	10	8	....	16	22	2	....	38	32	10	....	308	284	86	3rd, Patrick		Lost Quarter-Final
1978-79	80	19	13	8	....	21	16	3	....	40	29	11	....	316	292	91	3rd, Patrick		Lost Final
1977-78	80	18	15	7	....	12	22	6	....	30	37	13	....	279	280	73	4th, Patrick		Lost Prelim. Round
1976-77	80	17	18	5	....	12	19	9	....	29	37	14	....	272	310	72	4th, Patrick		Out of Playoffs
1975-76	80	16	16	8	....	13	26	1	....	29	42	9	....	262	333	67	4th, Patrick		Out of Playoffs
1974-75	80	21	11	8	....	16	18	6	....	37	29	14	....	319	276	88	2nd, Patrick		Lost Prelim. Round
1973-74	78	26	7	6	....	14	17	8	....	40	24	14	....	300	251	94	3rd, East		Lost Semi-Final
1972-73	78	26	8	5	....	21	15	3	....	47	23	8	....	297	208	102	3rd, East		Lost Semi-Final
1971-72	78	26	6	7	....	22	11	6	....	48	17	13	....	317	192	109	2nd, East		Lost Final
1970-71	78	30	2	7	....	19	16	4	....	49	18	11	....	259	177	109	2nd, East		Lost Semi-Final
1969-70	76	22	8	8	....	16	14	8	....	38	22	16	....	246	189	92	4th, East		Lost Quarter-Final
1968-69	76	27	7	4	....	14	19	5	....	41	26	9	....	231	196	91	3rd, East		Lost Quarter-Final
1967-68	74	22	8	7	....	17	15	5	....	39	23	12	....	226	183	90	2nd, East		Lost Quarter-Final
1966-67	70	18	12	5	....	12	16	7	....	30	28	12	....	188	189	72	4th		Lost Semi-Final
1965-66	70	12	16	7	....	6	25	4	....	18	41	11	....	195	261	47	6th		Out of Playoffs
1964-65	70	8	19	8	....	12	19	4	....	20	38	12	....	179	246	52	5th		Out of Playoffs
1963-64	70	14	13	8	....	8	25	2	....	22	38	10	....	186	242	54	5th		Out of Playoffs
1962-63	70	12	17	6	....	10	19	6	....	22	36	12	....	211	233	56	5th		Out of Playoffs
1961-62	70	16	11	8	....	10	21	4	....	26	32	12	....	195	207	64	4th		Lost Semi-Final
1960-61	70	15	15	5	....	7	23	5	....	22	38	10	....	204	248	54	5th		Out of Playoffs
1959-60	70	10	15	10	....	7	23	5	....	17	38	15	....	187	247	49	6th		Out of Playoffs
1958-59	70	14	16	5	....	12	16	7	....	26	32	12	....	201	217	64	5th		Out of Playoffs
1957-58	70	14	15	6	....	18	10	7	....	32	25	13	....	195	188	77	2nd		Lost Semi-Final
1956-57	70	15	12	8	....	11	18	6	....	26	30	14	....	184	227	66	4th		Lost Semi-Final
1955-56	70	20	7	8	....	12	21	2	....	32	28	10	....	204	203	74	3rd		Lost Semi-Final
1954-55	70	10	12	13	....	7	23	5	....	17	35	18	....	150	210	52	5th		Out of Playoffs
1953-54	70	18	12	5	....	11	19	5	....	29	31	10	....	161	182	68	5th		Out of Playoffs
1952-53	70	11	14	10	....	6	23	6	....	17	37	16	....	152	211	50	6th		Out of Playoffs
1951-52	70	16	13	6	....	7	21	7	....	23	34	13	....	192	219	59	5th		Out of Playoffs
1950-51	70	14	11	10	....	6	18	11	....	20	29	21	....	169	201	61	5th		Out of Playoffs
1949-50	70	19	12	4	....	9	19	7	....	28	31	11	....	170	189	67	4th		Lost Final
1948-49	60	13	12	5	....	5	19	6	....	18	31	11	....	133	172	47	6th		Out of Playoffs
1947-48	60	11	12	7	....	10	14	6	....	21	26	13	....	176	201	55	4th		Lost Semi-Final
1946-47	60	11	14	5	....	11	18	1	....	22	32	6	....	167	186	50	5th		Out of Playoffs
1945-46	50	8	12	5	....	5	16	4	....	13	28	9	....	144	191	35	6th		Out of Playoffs
1944-45	50	7	11	7	....	4	18	3	....	11	29	10	....	154	247	32	6th		Out of Playoffs
1943-44	50	4	17	4	....	2	22	1	....	6	39	5	....	162	310	17	6th		Out of Playoffs
1942-43	50	7	13	5	....	4	18	3	....	11	31	8	....	161	253	30	6th		Out of Playoffs
1941-42	48	15	8	1	....	14	9	1	....	29	17	2	....	177	143	60	1st		Lost Semi-Final
1940-41	48	13	7	4	....	8	12	4	....	21	19	8	....	143	125	50	4th		Lost Quarter-Final
1939-40	**48**	**17**	**4**	**3**	....	**10**	**7**	**7**	....	**27**	**11**	**10**	....	**136**	**77**	**64**	**2nd**		**Won Stanley Cup**
1938-39	48	13	8	3	....	13	8	3	....	26	16	6	....	149	105	58	2nd		Lost Semi-Final
1937-38	48	15	5	4	....	12	10	2	....	27	15	6	....	149	96	60	2nd, Amn.		Lost Quarter-Final
1936-37	48	9	7	8	....	10	13	1	....	19	20	9	....	117	106	47	3rd, Amn.		Lost Final
1935-36	48	11	6	7	....	8	11	5	....	19	17	12	....	91	96	50	4th, Amn.		Out of Playoffs
1934-35	48	11	8	5	....	11	12	1	....	22	20	6	....	137	139	50	3rd, Amn.		Lost Semi-Final
1933-34	48	11	7	6	....	10	12	2	....	21	19	8	....	120	113	50	3rd, Amn.		Lost Quarter-Final
1932-33	**48**	**12**	**7**	**5**	....	**11**	**10**	**3**	....	**23**	**17**	**8**	....	**135**	**107**	**54**	**3rd, Amn.**		**Won Stanley Cup**
1931-32	48	13	7	4	....	10	10	4	....	23	17	8	....	134	112	54	1st, Amn.		Lost Final
1930-31	44	10	9	3	....	9	7	6	....	19	16	9	....	106	87	47	3rd, Amn.		Lost Semi-Final
1929-30	44	11	5	6	....	6	12	4	....	17	17	10	....	136	143	44	3rd, Amn.		Lost Semi-Final
1928-29	44	12	6	4	....	9	7	6	....	21	13	10	....	72	65	52	2nd, Amn.		Lost Final
1927-28	**44**	**10**	**8**	**4**	....	**9**	**8**	**5**	....	**19**	**16**	**9**	....	**94**	**79**	**47**	**2nd, Amn.**		**Won Stanley Cup**
1926-27	44	13	5	4	....	12	8	2	....	25	13	6	....	95	72	56	1st, Amn.		Lost Quarter-Final

2015-16 Player Personnel

FORWARDS	HT	WT	*Age	Place of Birth	S	2014-15 Club
BRASSARD, Derick	6-1	202	28	Hull, QC	L	NY Rangers
ETEM, Emerson	6-1	210	23	Long Beach, CA	L	Anaheim-Norfolk
FAST, Jesper	6-0	185	23	Nassjo, Sweden	R	NY Rangers-Hartford
GLASS, Tanner	6-1	210	31	Regina, SK	L	NY Rangers
HAYES, Kevin	6-5	225	23	Boston, MA	L	NY Rangers
KREIDER, Chris	6-3	226	24	Boxford, MA	L	NY Rangers
MILLER, J.T.	6-1	205	22	East Palestine, OH	L	NY Rangers-Hartford
MOORE, Dominic	6-0	192	35	Sarnia, ON	L	NY Rangers
NASH, Rick	6-4	220	31	Brampton, ON	L	NY Rangers
STALBERG, Viktor	6-3	206	29	Stockholm, Sweden	L	Nashville-Milwaukee
STEPAN, Derek	6-0	196	25	Hastings, MN	R	NY Rangers
STOLL, Jarret	6-1	213	33	Melville, SK	R	Los Angeles
ZUCCARELLO, Mats	5-7	179	28	Oslo, Norway	L	NY Rangers

DEFENSEMEN	HT	WT	*Age	Place of Birth	S	2014-15 Club
BOYLE, Dan	5-11	190	39	Ottawa, ON	R	NY Rangers
DIAZ, Raphael	5-11	197	29	Baar, Switz.	R	Calgary
GIRARDI, Dan	6-1	208	31	Welland, ON	R	NY Rangers
KLEIN, Kevin	6-1	199	30	Kitchener, ON	R	NY Rangers
McDONAGH, Ryan	6-1	216	26	St.Paul, MN	L	NY Rangers
STAAL, Marc	6-4	207	28	Thunder Bay, ON	L	NY Rangers
YANDLE, Keith	6-1	190	29	Boston, MA	L	Arizona-NY Rangers

GOALTENDERS	HT	WT	*Age	Place of Birth	C	2014-15 Club
LUNDQVIST, Henrik	6-1	188	33	Are, Sweden	L	NY Rangers
RAANTA, Antti	6-0	187	26	Rauma, Finland	L	Chicago-Rockford

* – Age at start of 2015-16 season

2014-15 Scoring

* – rookie

Regular Season

Pos	#	Player	Team	GP	G	A	Pts	TOI	+/–	PIM	PP	SH	GW	S	S%
L	61	Rick Nash	NYR	79	42	27	69	17:27	29	36	6	4	8	304	13.8
C	16	Derick Brassard	NYR	80	19	41	60	17:23	9	34	6	0	3	168	11.3
C	21	Derek Stepan	NYR	68	16	39	55	18:10	26	22	3	2	3	155	10.3
R	26	Martin St Louis	NYR	74	21	31	52	17:33	12	20	5	0	1	144	14.6
D	93	Keith Yandle	ARI	63	4	37	41	23:54	–32	32	2	0	0	185	2.2
			NYR	21	2	9	11	19:55	6	8	0	0	2	47	4.3
			Total	84	6	46	52	22:54	–26	40	2	0	2	232	2.6
C	36	Mats Zuccarello	NYR	78	15	34	49	17:15	17	45	0	0	3	154	9.7
C	20	Chris Kreider	NYR	80	21	25	46	15:42	24	88	7	0	5	180	11.7
R	13	* Kevin Hayes	NYR	79	17	28	45	13:02	15	22	1	1	1	111	15.3
L	62	Carl Hagelin	NYR	82	17	18	35	15:13	18	46	1	0	4	185	9.2
D	27	Ryan McDonagh	NYR	71	8	25	33	23:07	23	26	3	0	2	148	5.4
C	28	Dominic Moore	NYR	82	10	17	27	13:48	5	28	0	2	3	116	8.6
D	8	Kevin Klein	NYR	65	9	17	26	18:29	24	25	0	0	4	76	11.8
C	10	J.T. Miller	NYR	58	10	13	23	12:41	5	23	2	0	3	92	10.9
D	22	Dan Boyle	NYR	65	9	11	20	20:14	18	20	3	0	3	116	7.8
D	18	Marc Staal	NYR	80	5	15	20	21:08	18	42	0	0	0	97	5.2
D	5	Dan Girardi	NYR	82	4	16	20	22:41	12	22	1	0	1	111	3.6
C	45	James Sheppard	S.J.	57	5	11	16	13:43	–3	28	0	0	0	68	7.4
			NYR	14	2	0	2	11:21	–1	9	0	0	1	11	18.2
			Total	71	7	11	18	13:15	–4	37	0	0	1	79	8.9
R	19	* Jesper Fast	NYR	58	6	8	14	11:48	–1	8	0	0	0	52	11.5
D	44	Matt Hunwick	NYR	55	2	9	11	15:48	17	16	0	0	1	72	2.8
L	63	* Anthony Duclair	NYR	18	1	6	7	12:09	4	4	0	0	0	18	5.6
L	15	Tanner Glass	NYR	66	1	5	6	10:14	–12	98	0	0	0	53	1.9
D	55	Chris Summers	ARI	17	0	3	3	13:42	–12	8	0	0	0	13	0.0
			NYR	3	0	0	0	17:15	0	0	0	0	0	2	0.0
			Total	20	0	3	3	14:14	–12	8	0	0	0	15	0.0
C	14	Chris Mueller	NYR	7	1	1	2	10:27	–1	0	1	0	0	10	10.0
D	4	Michael Kostka	NYR	7	0	1	1	15:23	1	0	0	0	0	7	0.0
L	25	* Ryan Bourque	NYR	1	0	0	0	11:49	–1	0	0	0	0	1	0.0
C	48	* Oscar Lindberg	NYR	1	0	0	0	8:18	0	0	0	0	0	2	0.0
D	42	* Dylan McIlrath	NYR	1	0	0	0	8:02	0	9	0	0	0	0	0.0
D	37	* Conor Allen	NYR	4	0	0	0	12:12	–1	4	0	0	0	2	0.0
L	24	Ryan Malone	NYR	6	0	0	0	10:01	–4	4	0	0	0	6	0.0

Goaltending

No.	Goaltender	GPI	Mins	Avg	W	L	OT	EN	SO	GA	SA	Sv%	G	A	PIM
70	* Mackenzie Skapski	2	119	0.50	2	0	0	0	1	1	45	.978	0	0	0
33	Cam Talbot	36	2095	2.21	21	9	4	3	5	77	1038	.926	0	0	0
30	Henrik Lundqvist	46	2743	2.25	30	13	3	3	5	103	1329	.922	0	1	0
	Totals	**82**	**4983**	**2.25**	**53**	**22**	**7**	**6**	**11**	**187**	**2418**	**.923**			

Playoffs

Pos	#	Player	Team	GP	G	A	Pts	TOI	+/–	PIM	PP	SH	GW	OT	S	S%
C	16	Derick Brassard	NYR	19	9	7	16	17:48	9	20	2	0	1	0	55	16.4
L	61	Rick Nash	NYR	19	5	9	14	18:30	8	4	2	0	0	0	69	7.2
C	21	Derek Stepan	NYR	19	5	7	12	19:31	–1	10	2	0	1	1	48	10.4
D	93	Keith Yandle	NYR	19	2	9	11	18:00	7	10	0	0	0	0	32	6.3
D	22	Dan Boyle	NYR	19	3	7	10	19:48	–3	2	1	0	1	0	32	9.4
C	20	Chris Kreider	NYR	19	7	2	9	17:14	–1	14	2	0	2	0	38	18.4
D	27	Ryan McDonagh	NYR	19	3	6	9	23:30	2	8	2	0	2	1	33	9.1
C	10	J.T. Miller	NYR	19	1	7	8	14:38	3	2	0	0	0	0	32	3.1
R	13	* Kevin Hayes	NYR	19	2	5	7	14:12	–3	2	1	0	1	1	25	8.0
R	26	Martin St. Louis	NYR	19	1	6	7	16:30	–1	4	1	0	0	0	32	3.1
R	19	* Jesper Fast	NYR	19	3	3	6	14:49	1	2	0	0	0	0	21	14.3
L	62	Carl Hagelin	NYR	19	2	3	5	16:37	–4	6	0	0	1	1	36	5.6
D	8	Kevin Klein	NYR	14	0	4	4	19:05	–1	2	0	0	0	0	21	0.0
D	5	Dan Girardi	NYR	19	0	4	4	21:37	5	4	0	0	0	0	29	0.0
C	28	Dominic Moore	NYR	19	1	2	3	14:49	–7	12	0	0	1	0	33	3.0
C	45	James Sheppard	NYR	13	1	1	2	8:54	2	8	0	0	1	0	12	8.3
C	36	Mats Zuccarello	NYR	5	0	2	2	14:35	1	0	0	0	0	0	13	0.0
L	15	Tanner Glass	NYR	19	0	1	1	9:20	–2	31	0	0	0	0	12	0.0
D	18	Marc Staal	NYR	19	0	1	1	20:40	–8	10	0	0	0	0	12	0.0
D	44	Matt Hunwick	NYR	6	0	0	0	11:47	0	0	0	0	0	0	2	0.0

Goaltending

No.	Goaltender	GPI	Mins	Avg	W	L	EN	SO	GA	SA	Sv%	G	A	PIM
30	Henrik Lundqvist	19	1166	2.11	11	8	0	0	41	570	.928	0	0	0
	Totals	**19**	**1179**	**2.09**	**11**	**8**	**0**	**0**	**41**	**570**	**.928**			

Alain Vigneault

Head Coach

Born: Quebec City, QC, May 14, 1961.

The New York Rangers officially named Alain Vigneault as the club's head coach on June 21, 2013. He is the 35th head coach in franchise history. A three-time Jack Adams Award finalist, and the 2007 winner of the award presented to the NHL's top coach, Vigneault joined the Rangers after spending seven seasons with the Vancouver Canucks. In his first season in New York, Vigneault led the Rangers to the Stanley Cup Final. In 2014-15, the Rangers won the Presidents' Trophy and Vigneault was runner-up for the Jack Adams Award. He previously coached the Canucks to a pair of Presidents' Trophy wins – in 2010-11 and 2011-12 – six Northwest Division titles, five seasons with 100 or more points, and an appearance in the 2011 Stanley Cup Final, where Vancouver lost in seven games to the Boston Bruins. Vigneault is Vancouver's all-time leader in coaching victories with 313.

After being a successful head coach in the Quebec Major Junior Hockey League and as an assistant with the Ottawa Senators, Vigneault earned his first NHL head coaching job with the Canadiens in 1997-98. Vigneault led the Canadiens to the second round of the playoffs that season, before missing out on the postseason the next two years – although he still earned a Jack Adams nomination for his outstanding work in 1999-2000. After being relieved of his duties by Montreal 20 games into the 2000-01 campaign, Vigneault coached once again in the QMJHL and then in the minor leagues for Vancouver before becoming the Canucks head coach prior to the 2006-07 season. His most successful season behind the bench in Vancouver was 2010-11 when the Canucks won 54 games, totaled 117 points, captured the Presidents' Trophy as the top team in the league over the regular season, and then fell just one victory shy of winning the Stanley Cup. A year later Vigneault's Canucks edged the Rangers by just two points, 111 to 109, to win the Presidents' Trophy again.

Coaching Record

			Regular Season				Playoffs			
Season	Team	League	GC	W	L	O/T	GC	W	L	T
1986-87	Trois-Rivieres	QMJHL	70	28	40	2	....	....	....	....
1987-88	Hull	QMJHL	70	43	23	4	19	12	7	....
1987-88	Hull	M-Cup	....	....	....	....	4	1	3	....
1988-89	Hull	QMJHL	70	40	25	5	9	5	4	....
1989-90	Hull	QMJHL	70	36	29	5	11	4	7	....
1990-91	Hull	QMJHL	70	36	27	7	6	2	4	....
1991-92	Hull	QMJHL	70	41	24	5	6	2	4	....
1995-96	Beauport	QMJHL	31	19	7	5	20	13	7	....
1996-97	Beauport	QMJHL	70	24	44	2	4	1	3	....
1997-98	**Montreal**	**NHL**	**82**	**37**	**32**	**13**	**10**	**4**	**6**	....
1998-99	**Montreal**	**NHL**	**82**	**32**	**39**	**11**	....	....	....	....
99-2000	**Montreal**	**NHL**	**82**	**35**	**34**	**13**	....	....	....	....
2000-01	**Montreal**	**NHL**	**20**	**5**	**13**	**2**	....	....	....	....
2003-04	PEI	QMJHL	70	40	19	11	11	6	5	....
2004-05	PEI	QMJHL	70	24	39	7	....	....	....	....
2005-06	Manitoba	AHL	80	44	24	12	13	7	6	....
2006-07	**Vancouver**	**NHL**	**82**	**49**	**26**	**7**	**12**	**5**	**7**	....
2007-08	**Vancouver**	**NHL**	**82**	**39**	**33**	**10**	....	....	....	....
2008-09	**Vancouver**	**NHL**	**82**	**45**	**27**	**10**	**10**	**6**	**4**	....
2009-10	**Vancouver**	**NHL**	**82**	**49**	**28**	**5**	**12**	**6**	**6**	....
2010-11	**Vancouver**	**NHL**	**82**	**54**	**19**	**9**	**25**	**15**	**10**	....
2011-12	**Vancouver**	**NHL**	**82**	**51**	**22**	**9**	**5**	**1**	**4**	....
2012-13	**Vancouver**	**NHL**	**48**	**26**	**15**	**7**	**4**	**0**	**4**	....
2013-14	**NY Rangers**	**NHL**	**82**	**45**	**31**	**6**	**25**	**13**	**12**	....
2014-15	**NY Rangers**	**NHL**	**82**	**53**	**22**	**7**	**19**	**11**	**8**	....
	NHL Totals		**970**	**520**	**341**	**109**	**122**	**61**	**61**	....

Jack Adams Award (2007)

Coaching History

Lester Patrick, 1926-27 to 1938-39; Frank Boucher, 1939-40 to 1947-48; Frank Boucher and Lynn Patrick, 1948-49; Lynn Patrick, 1949-50; Neil Colville, 1950-51; Neil Colville and Bill Cook, 1951-52; Bill Cook, 1952-53; Frank Boucher and Muzz Patrick, 1953-54; Muzz Patrick, 1954-55; Phil Watson, 1955-56 to 1958-59; Phil Watson, Muzz Patrick and Alf Pike, 1959-60; Alf Pike, 1960-61; Doug Harvey, 1961-62; Muzz Patrick and Red Sullivan, 1962-63; Red Sullivan, 1963-64, 1964-65; Red Sullivan and Emile Francis, 1965-66; Emile Francis, 1966-67, 1967-68; Bernie Geoffrion and Emile Francis, 1968-69; Emile Francis, 1969-70 to 1972-73; Larry Popein and Emile Francis, 1973-74; Emile Francis, 1974-75; Ron Stewart and John Ferguson, 1975-76; John Ferguson, 1976-77; Jean-Guy Talbot, 1977-78; Fred Shero, 1978-79, 1979-80; Fred Shero and Craig Patrick, 1980-81; Herb Brooks, 1981-82 to 1983-84; Herb Brooks and Craig Patrick, 1984-85; Ted Sator, 1985-86; Ted Sator, Tom Webster and Phil Esposito, 1986-87; Michel Bergeron, 1987-88; Michel Bergeron and Phil Esposito, 1988-89; Roger Neilson, 1989-90 to 1991-92; Roger Neilson and Ron Smith, 1992-93; Mike Keenan, 1993-94; Colin Campbell, 1994-95 to 1996-97; Colin Campbell and John Muckler, 1997-98; John Muckler, 1998-99; John Muckler and John Tortorella, 1999-2000; Ron Low, 2000-01, 2001-02; Bryan Trottier and Glen Sather, 2002-03; Glen Sather and Tom Renney, 2003-04; Tom Renney, 2004-05 to 2007-08; Tom Renney and John Tortorella, 2008-09; John Tortorella, 2009-10 to 2012-13; Alain Vigneault, 2013-14 to date.

Club Records

Team

(Figures in brackets for season records are games played; records for fewest points, wins, ties, losses, goals, goals against are for 70 or more games)

Most Points	**113**	2014-15 (82)
Most Wins	**53**	2014-15 (82)
Most Ties	**21**	1950-51 (70)
Most Losses	**44**	1984-85 (80)
Most Goals	**321**	1991-92 (80)
Most Goals Against	**345**	1984-85 (80)
Fewest Points	**47**	1965-66 (70)
Fewest Wins	**17**	1952-53 (70), 1954-55 (70), 1959-60 (70)
Fewest Ties	**4**	2001-02 (82)
Fewest Losses	**17**	1971-72 (78)
Fewest Goals	**150**	1954-55 (70)
Fewest Goals Against	**177**	1970-71 (78)
Longest Winning Streak		
Overall	**10**	Dec. 19/39-Jan. 13/40, Jan. 19-Feb. 10/73
Home	**14**	Dec. 19/39-Feb. 25/40
Away	**7**	Jan. 12-Feb. 12/35, Oct. 28-Nov. 29/78
Longest Undefeated Streak		
Overall	**19**	Nov. 23/39-Jan. 13/40 (14W, 5T)
Home	**24**	Oct. 14/70-Jan. 31/71 (18W, 6T), Oct. 24/95-Feb.15/96 (18W, 6T)
Away	**11**	Nov. 5/39-Jan. 13/40 (6W, 5T)
Longest Losing Streak		
Overall	**11**	Oct. 30-Nov. 27/43
Home	**7**	Oct. 20-Nov. 14/76, Mar. 24-Apr. 14/93
Away	**10**	Oct. 30-Dec. 23/43, Feb. 8-Mar. 15/61
Longest Winless Streak		
Overall	**21**	Jan. 23-Mar. 19/44 (17L, 4T)
Home	**10**	Jan. 30-Mar. 19/44 (7L, 3T)
Away	**16**	Oct. 9-Dec. 20/52 (12L, 4T)
Most Shutouts, Season	**13**	1928-29 (44)
Most PIM, Season	**2,018**	1989-90 (80)
Most Goals, Game	**12**	Nov. 21/71 (Cal. 1 at NYR 12)

Individual

Most Seasons	**18**	Rod Gilbert
Most Games	**1,160**	Harry Howell
Most Goals, Career	**406**	Rod Gilbert
Most Assists, Career	**741**	Brian Leetch
Most Points, Career	**1,021**	Rod Gilbert (406G, 615A)
Most PIM, Career	**1,226**	Ron Greschner
Most Shutouts, Career	**55**	Henrik Lundqvist
Longest Consecutive Games Streak	**560**	Andy Hebenton (Oct. 7/55-Mar. 24/63)
Most Goals, Season	**54**	Jaromir Jagr (2005-06)
Most Assists, Season	**80**	Brian Leetch (1991-92)
Most Points, Season	**123**	Jaromir Jagr (2005-06; 54G, 69A)
Most PIM, Season	**305**	Troy Mallette (1989-90)
Most Points, Defenseman, Season	**102**	Brian Leetch (1991-92; 22G, 80A)
Most Points, Center, Season	**109**	Jean Ratelle (1971-72; 46G, 63A)
Most Points, Right Wing, Season	**123**	Jaromir Jagr (2005-06; 54G, 69A)
Most Points, Left Wing, Season	**106**	Vic Hadfield (1971-72; 50G, 56A)
Most Points, Rookie, Season	**76**	Mark Pavelich (1981-82; 33G, 43A)
Most Shutouts, Season	**13**	John Ross Roach (1928-29)
Most Goals, Game	**5**	Don Murdoch (Oct. 12/76) Mark Pavelich (Feb. 23/83)
Most Assists, Game	**5**	Walt Tkaczuk (Feb. 12/72) Rod Gilbert (Mar. 2/75), (Mar. 30/75), (Oct. 8/76) Don Maloney (Jan. 3/87) Brian Leetch (Apr. 18/95) Wayne Gretzky (Feb. 15/99)
Most Points, Game	**7**	Steve Vickers (Feb. 18/76; 3G, 4A)

Captains' History

Bill Cook, 1926-27 to 1936-37; Art Coulter, 1937-38 to 1941-42; Ott Heller; 1942-43 to 1944-45; Neil Colville 1945-46 to 1948-49; Buddy O'Connor, 1949-50; Frank Eddolls, 1950-51; Frank Eddolls and Allan Stanley, 1951-52; Allan Stanley, 1952-53; Allan Stanley and Don Raleigh, 1953-54; Don Raleigh, 1954-55; Harry Howell, 1955-56, 1956-57; Red Sullivan, 1957-58 to 1960-61; Andy Bathgate, 1961-62, 1962-63; Andy Bathgate and Camille Henry, 1963-64; Camille Henry and Bob Nevin, 1964-65; Bob Nevin 1965-66 to 1970-71; Vic Hadfield, 1971-72 to 1973-74; Brad Park, 1974-75; Brad Park and Phil Esposito, 1975-76; Phil Esposito, 1976-77, 1977-78; Dave Maloney, 1978-79, 1979-80; Dave Maloney, Walt Tkaczuk and Barry Beck, 1980-81; Barry Beck, 1981-82 to 1985-86; Ron Greschner, 1986-87; Ron Greschner and Kelly Kisio, 1987-88; Kelly Kisio, 1988-89 to 1990-91; Mark Messier, 1991-92 to 1996-97; Brian Leetch, 1997-98 to 1999-2000; Mark Messier, 2000-01 to 2003-04; no captain, 2005-06; Jaromir Jagr, 2006-07, 2007-08; Chris Drury, 2008-09 to 2010-11; Ryan Callahan, 2011-12, 2012-13; Ryan Callahan and no captain, 2013-14; Ryan McDonagh, 2014-15 to date.

All-time Record vs. Other Clubs

Regular Season

	Total								At Home								On Road							
	GP	W	L	T	OL	GF	GA	PTS	GP	W	L	T	OL	GF	GA	PTS	GP	W	L	T	OL	GF	GA	PTS
Anaheim	29	12	15	1	1	80	87	26	15	7	7	1	0	41	37	15	14	5	8	0	1	39	50	11
Arizona	72	41	25	6	0	271	240	88	36	24	10	2	0	152	120	50	36	17	15	4	0	119	120	38
Boston	637	250	288	97	2	1850	2005	599	320	144	121	55	0	975	892	343	317	106	167	42	2	875	1113	256
Buffalo	171	68	73	25	5	528	547	166	84	38	28	15	3	263	221	94	87	30	45	10	2	265	326	72
Calgary	111	42	54	15	0	352	424	99	57	28	24	5	0	189	193	61	54	14	30	10	0	163	231	38
Carolina	128	70	49	7	2	417	348	149	65	42	17	4	2	227	151	90	63	28	32	3	0	190	197	59
Chicago	583	239	244	98	2	1658	1700	578	291	121	115	55	0	854	818	297	292	118	129	43	2	804	882	281
Colorado	80	36	31	7	6	296	272	85	40	21	12	4	3	151	113	49	40	15	19	3	3	145	159	36
Columbus	20	10	8	1	1	57	61	22	9	5	2	1	1	32	28	12	11	5	6	0	0	25	33	10
Dallas	134	71	39	22	2	462	384	166	68	38	18	11	1	226	178	88	66	33	21	11	1	236	206	78
Detroit	581	215	261	103	2	1596	1772	535	290	138	94	58	0	882	749	334	291	77	167	45	2	714	1023	201
Edmonton	68	28	29	9	2	236	235	67	35	12	16	6	1	129	127	31	33	16	13	3	1	107	108	36
Florida	86	48	28	6	4	253	197	106	43	25	14	4	0	135	94	54	43	23	14	2	4	118	103	52
Los Angeles	129	67	45	16	1	475	400	151	63	37	20	6	0	245	186	80	66	30	25	10	1	230	214	71
Minnesota	18	12	6	0	0	55	45	24	8	6	2	0	0	25	17	12	10	6	4	0	0	30	28	12
Montreal	617	193	326	94	4	1596	2073	484	308	128	125	54	1	889	884	311	309	65	201	40	3	707	1189	173
Nashville	20	10	7	1	2	56	45	23	11	4	5	1	1	27	25	10	9	6	2	0	1	29	20	13
New Jersey	231	110	87	27	7	765	686	254	114	60	31	20	3	404	308	143	117	50	56	7	4	361	378	111
NY Islanders	254	124	104	19	7	854	816	274	127	70	41	11	5	454	368	156	127	54	63	8	2	400	448	118
Ottawa	83	37	39	3	4	226	235	81	41	15	24	0	2	109	122	32	42	22	15	3	2	117	113	49
Philadelphia	280	124	112	37	7	833	827	292	140	66	47	23	4	444	394	159	140	58	65	14	3	389	433	133
Pittsburgh	262	123	105	23	11	932	876	280	132	69	50	9	4	495	428	151	130	54	55	14	7	437	448	129
St. Louis	135	76	42	16	1	473	367	169	65	45	13	6	1	255	157	97	70	31	29	10	0	218	210	72
San Jose	33	22	8	3	0	117	87	47	15	10	4	1	0	55	40	21	18	12	4	2	0	62	47	26
Tampa Bay	89	43	34	5	7	280	267	98	46	24	16	2	4	150	129	54	43	19	18	3	3	130	138	44
Toronto	602	225	275	95	7	1738	1909	552	302	130	112	56	4	937	886	320	300	95	163	39	3	801	1023	232
Vancouver	115	76	30	8	1	469	327	161	59	40	13	5	1	252	155	86	56	36	17	3	0	217	172	75
Washington	205	92	89	18	6	695	698	208	102	50	40	9	3	371	337	112	103	42	49	9	3	324	361	96
Winnipeg	55	26	18	1	10	159	153	63	28	10	11	1	6	74	80	27	27	16	7	0	4	85	73	36
Defunct Clubs	278	169	64	45	0	901	581	383	139	87	30	22	0	460	290	196	139	82	34	23	0	441	291	187
Totals	**6106**	**2659**	**2535**	**808**	**104**	**18680**	**18664**	**6230**	**3053**	**1494**	**1062**	**447**	**50**	**9902**	**8527**	**3485**	**3053**	**1165**	**1473**	**361**	**54**	**8778**	**10137**	**2745**

Playoffs

	Series	W	L	GP	W	L	T	GF	GA	Last Mtg.	Rnd.	Result
Boston	10	3	7	47	19	26	2	114	130	2013	CSF	L 1-4
Buffalo	2	0	2	9	3	6	0	19	28	2007	CSF	L 2-4
Calgary	1	1	0	4	3	1	0	14	8	1980	PR	W 3-1
Chicago	5	1	4	24	10	14	0	54	66	1973	SF	L 1-4
Colorado	1	1	0	6	4	2	0	25	19	1995	CQF	W 4-2
Detroit	5	1	4	23	10	13	0	49	57	1950	F	L 3-4
Florida	1	1	0	5	4	1	0	13	10	1997	CQF	W 4-1
Los Angeles	3	2	1	11	6	5	0	42	29	2014	F	L 1-4
Montreal	15	8	7	67	29	36	2	178	203	2014	CF	W 4-2
New Jersey	6	4	2	34	18	16	0	93	90	2012	CF	L 2-4
NY Islanders	8	3	5	39	19	20	0	132	129	1994	CQF	W 4-0
Ottawa	1	1	0	7	4	3	0	14	13	2012	CQF	W 4-3
Philadelphia	11	5	6	54	24	30	0	172	173	2014	FR	W 4-3
Pittsburgh	6	2	4	32	12	20	0	83	101	2015	FR	W 4-1
St. Louis	1	1	0	6	4	2	0	29	22	1981	QF	W 4-2
Tampa Bay	1	0	1	7	3	4	0	21	21	2015	CF	L 3-4
Toronto	8	5	3	35	19	16	0	86	86	1971	QF	W 4-2
Vancouver	1	1	0	7	4	3	0	21	19	1994	F	W 4-3
Washington	9	5	4	55	27	28	0	134	144	2015	SR	W 4-3
Winnipeg	1	1	0	4	4	0	0	17	6	2007	CQF	W 4-0
Defunct Clubs	9	6	3	22	11	7	4	43	29			
Totals	**105**	**52**	**53**	**498**	**237**	**253**	**8**	**1353**	**1383**			

Playoff Results 2015-2011

Year	Round	Opponent	Result	GF	GA
2015	CF	Tampa Bay	L 3-4	21	21
	SR	Washington	W 4-3	13	12
	FR	Pittsburgh	W 4-1	11	8
2014	F	Los Angeles	L 1-4	10	15
	CF	Montreal	W 4-2	20	15
	SR	Pittsburgh	W 4-3	15	14
	FR	Philadelphia	W 4-3	19	16
2013	CSF	Boston	L 1-4	10	16
	CQF	Washington	W 4-3	16	12
2012	CF	New Jersey	L 2-4	14	15
	CSF	Washington	W 4-3	15	13
	CQF	Ottawa	W 4-3	14	13
2011	CQF	Washington	L 1-4	8	13

Abbreviations: Round: F – Final; **CF** – conference final; **CSF** – conference semi-final; **SR** – second round; **CQF** – conference quarter-final; **FR** – first round; **SF** – semi-final; **QF** – quarter-final; **PR** – preliminary round.

Calgary totals include Atlanta Flames, 1972-73 to 1979-80.
Colorado totals include Quebec, 1979-80 to 1994-95.
New Jersey totals include Kansas City, 1974-75, 1975-76, and Colorado Rockies, 1976-77 to 1981-82.
Phoenix totals include Winnipeg, 1979-80 to 1995-96.
Carolina totals include Hartford, 1979-80 to 1996-97.
Dallas totals include Minnesota North Stars, 1967-68 to 1992-93.
Winnipeg totals include Atlanta Thrashers, 1999-2000 to 2010-11.

2014-15 Results

Month	Day	Opponent	Score
Oct.	9	at St. Louis	3-2
	11	at Columbus	2-5
	12	Toronto	3-6
	14	NY Islanders	3-6
	16	Carolina	2-1†
	19	San Jose	4-0
	21	at New Jersey	4-3*
	25	at Montreal	1-3
	27	Minnesota	5-4
Nov.	1	Winnipeg	0-1†
	3	St. Louis	3-4†
	5	Detroit	4-3*
	8	at Toronto	4-5
	9	Edmonton	1-3
	11	Pittsburgh	5-0
	13	Colorado	3-4†
	15	at Pittsburgh	2-3†
	17	Tampa Bay	1-5
	19	Philadelphia	2-0
	23	Montreal	5-0
	26	at Tampa Bay	3-4
	28	at Philadelphia	3-0
	29	Philadelphia	5-2
Dec.	1	Tampa Bay	3-6
	6	at Detroit	2-3
	8	Pittsburgh	4-3*
	13	at Vancouver	5-1
	14	at Edmonton	2-0
	16	at Calgary	5-2
	20	at Carolina	3-2†
	21	Carolina	1-0
	23	Washington	4-2
	27	New Jersey	3-1
	29	at Dallas	2-3
	31	at Florida	5-2
Jan.	3	Buffalo	6-1
	7	at Anaheim	4-1
	8	at Los Angeles	4-3
	10	at San Jose	3-1
	13	NY Islanders	0-3
	15	at Boston	0-3
	16	at Columbus	2-1
	18	at Pittsburgh	5-2
	20	Ottawa	3-2*
	27	at NY Islanders	1-4
	29	Montreal	0-1
	31	Carolina	4-1
Feb.	2	Florida	6-3
	4	Boston	3-2
	7	at Nashville	2-3
	8	Dallas	2-3*
	10	at Toronto	5-4
	12	at Colorado	6-3
	14	at Arizona	5-1
	16	at NY Islanders	6-5
	19	Vancouver	4-5†
	20	at Buffalo	3-1
	22	Columbus	4-3†
	24	Calgary	1-0
	26	Arizona	4-3
	28	at Philadelphia	2-4
Mar.	2	Nashville	4-1
	4	at Detroit	1-2*
	8	at Chicago	1-0*
	10	at NY Islanders	2-1
	11	at Washington	3-1
	14	at Buffalo	2-0
	15	Florida	2-1
	18	Chicago	0-1
	21	at Carolina	3-2†
	22	Anaheim	7-2
	24	Los Angeles	2-4
	26	at Ottawa	5-1
	28	at Boston	2-4
	29	Washington	2-5
	31	at Winnipeg	3-2
Apr.	2	at Minnesota	3-2
	4	New Jersey	6-1
	6	Columbus	4-3*
	7	at New Jersey	4-2
	9	Ottawa	0-3
	11	at Washington	4-2

* – Overtime † – Shootout

NHL Draft Selections 2015-2001

Name in bold denotes played in NHL.

2015 Pick		2010 Pick		2006 Pick		2003 Pick	
41	Ryan Gropp	10	**Dylan McIlrath**	21	**Bobby Sanguinetti**	12	**Hugh Jessiman**
62	Robin Kovacs	40	**Christian Thomas**	54	**Artem Anisimov**	50	**Ivan Baranka**
79	Sergei Zborovsky	100	Andrew Yogan	84	Ryan Hillier	75	Ken Roche
89	Aleksi Saarela	130	Jason Wilson	104	David Kveton	122	**Corey Potter**
113	Brad Morrison	157	**Jesper Fast**	137	Tomas Zaborsky	149	**Nigel Dawes**
119	Daniel Bernhardt	190	Randy McNaught	174	Eric Hunter	176	Ivan Dornic
184	Adam Huska			204	Lukas Zeliska	179	Philippe Furrer
		2009 Pick				180	**Chris Holt**
2014 Pick		19	**Chris Kreider**	**2005** Pick		209	**Dylan Reese**
59	Brandon Halverson	47	Ethan Werek	12	**Marc Staal**	243	Jan Marek
85	Keegan Iverson	80	**Ryan Bourque**	40	**Michael Sauer**		
104	Ryan Mantha	127	**Roman Horak**	56	**Marc-Andre Cliche**	**2002** Pick	
118	Igor Shesterkin	140	Scott Stajcer	66	**Brodie Dupont**	33	Lee Falardeau
122	Richard Nejezchleb	170	Dan Maggio	77	Dalyn Flatt	81	Marcus Jonasen
140	Daniel Walcott	200	Mikhail Pashnin	107	**Tom Pyatt**	127	Nate Guenin
142	Tyler Nanne			147	Trevor Koverko	143	Mike Walsh
		2008 Pick		178	Greg Beller	177	Jake Taylor
2013 Pick		20	**Michael Del Zotto**	211	**Ryan Russell**	194	Kim Hirschovits
65	Adam Tambellini	51	**Derek Stepan**			226	**Joey Crabb**
75	Pavel Buchnevich	75	**Evgeny Grachev**	**2004** Pick		240	**Petr Prucha**
80	**Anthony Duclair**	90	**Tomas Kundratek**	6	**Al Montoya**	270	Rob Flynn
110	Ryan Graves	111	**Dale Weise**	19	**Lauri Korpikoski**		
170	**Mackenzie Skapski**	141	Chris Doyle	36	Darin Olver	**2001** Pick	
		171	Mitch Gaulton	48	**Dane Byers**	10	**Dan Blackburn**
2012 Pick				51	Bruce Graham	40	**Fedor Tyutin**
28	**Brady Skjei**	**2007** Pick		60	**Brandon Dubinsky**	79	**Garth Murray**
59	Cristoval Nieves	17	Alexei Cherepanov	73	Zdenek Bahensky	113	**Bryce Lampman**
119	Calle Andersson	48	Antoine Lafleur	80	Billy Ryan	139	Shawn Collymore
142	Thomas Spelling	138	Max Campbell	127	**Ryan Callahan**	176	**Marek Zidlicky**
		168	**Carl Hagelin**	135	Roman Psurny	206	Petr Preucil
2011 Pick		193	David Skokan	169	Jordan Foote	226	Pontus Petterstrom
15	**J.T. Miller**	198	Danny Hobbs	247	Jonathan Paiement	230	Leonid Zhvachkin
72	Steven Fogarty			266	**Jakub Petruzalek**	238	**Ryan Hollweg**
106	Michael St. Croix					269	Juris Stals
134	Shane McColgan						
136	Samuel Noreau						
172	Peter Ceresnak						

General Managers' History

Lester Patrick, 1926-27 to 1944-45; Lester Patrick and Frank Boucher, 1945-46; Frank Boucher, 1946-47 to 1954-55; Muzz Patrick, 1955-56 to 1963-64; Muzz Patrick and Emile Francis, 1964-65; Emile Francis, 1965-66 to 1974-75; Emile Francis and John Ferguson, 1975-76; John Ferguson, 1976-77, 1977-78; Fred Shero, 1978-79, 1979-80; Fred Shero and Craig Patrick, 1980-81; Craig Patrick, 1981-82 to 1985-86; Phil Esposito, 1986-87 to 1988-89; Neil Smith, 1989-90 to 1999-2000; Glen Sather, 2000-01 to 2014-15; Jeff Gorton, 2015-16.

Jeff Gorton
General Manager
Born: Melrose, MA, June 6, 1968

New York Rangers president Glen Sather announced on July 1 that Jeff Gorton had been named the 11th general manager in franchise history. Gorton had been a member of the Rangers organization for the previous eight seasons and served as the team's assistant general manager over the last four seasons. He joined the Rangers in 2007 as a professional scout, and served three seasons as assistant director, player personnel before becoming the team's assistant general manager.

During Gorton's tenure with the Rangers, he has played a key role in the selection of current Blueshirts Derek Stepan, Chris Kreider, Jesper Fast, and J.T. Miller in the NHL Draft. Gorton was vital in the Rangers' acquisitions of Ryan McDonagh, Rick Nash, Derick Brassard, and Keith Yandle through trades, as well as the signing of free agents Kevin Hayes and Mats Zuccarello.

Prior to joining the Rangers, Gorton spent 15 seasons with the Boston Bruins organization, serving as the Bruins' assistant general manager during the final seven years of his tenure. In that role, he was involved in contract negotiations, scouting operations and the team's American Hockey League affiliate in Providence. Gorton served as Boston's interim general manager from March 27 to July 8, 2006, directing the Bruins' efforts at the 2006 NHL Draft and negotiating contracts and trades at the start of the 2006 free agency period. At the 2006 NHL Draft, Gorton was instrumental in landing Bruins' star players Brad Marchand and Tuukka Rask (in a trade), as well as former Bruins' stars Phil Kessel and Milan Lucic. He also acquired All-Star free agents Zdeno Chara and Marc Savard.

Gorton originally joined the Bruins organization in their public relations department at the beginning of the 1992-93 season. He became the Bruins' director of scouting information in October 1994, where he created the scouting database which networks the club's scouts via computer, and coordinated video on prospects in preparation of scouting assignments and the annual NHL Draft. Gorton holds a degree in physical education from Bridgewater State College, and a Masters in sports management from Springfield College.

Club Directory

Madison Square Garden

New York Rangers
14th Floor
2 Pennsylvania Plaza
New York, New York 10121
Phone **212/465-6486**
PR FAX 212/465-6494
www.newyorkrangers.com
Capacity: 18,006

Team Executive Management
Exec. Chairman, The Madison Square Garden Company . James L. Dolan
President & Chief Executive Officer,
The Madison Square Garden Company. . . . . Doc O'Connor
President. . . . . Glen Sather
Exec. V.P.,Tickets, Clubs & Corporate Hospitality . . . . . Howard Jacobs
Sr. V.P., Marketing NYR/Sports Properties . . . . Janet Duch
Sr. V.P., Legal & Business Affairs, Sports Ops . . . . John Master
Sr. V.P., Sports Team Operations . . . . Mark Piazza
Sr. V.P., Public Relations & Player Recruitment . . . . John Rosasco
Deputy General Counsel & Sr. V.P.,
Legal & Business Affairs, Team Operations . . . . Marc Schoenfeld
V.P., Finance . . . . Jeanine McGrory

Hockey Club Personnel
General Manager . . . . Jeff Gorton
Sr. V.P., Asst. G.M., & G.M., Hartford Wolf Pack . . . . . Jim Schoenfeld
Head Coach . . . . Alain Vigneault
Associate Coach . . . . Scott Arniel
Assistant Coaches . . . . Ulf Samuelsson, Darryl Williams
Assistant Coach & Goaltending Coach . . . . Benoit Allaire
Video Coach . . . . Jerry Dineen
Director, Player Care & Development/Analytics
and Hockey Technology . . . . Jim Sullivan
Director, Player Personnel . . . . Gordie Clark
Assistant Director, Player Personnel . . . . Steve Greeley
Director of Professional Scouting . . . . Kevin Maxwell
Senior Advisor to the President & General Manager . . . . Mike Barnett
Hockey Consultant . . . . Doug Risebrough
Hockey & Business Operations . . . . Adam Graves
Director of European Scouting . . . . Nickolai Bobrov
European Scouts . . . . Jan Gajdosik, Oto Hascak, Anders Kallur,
Vladimir Lutchenko
Amateur Scouts. . . . . Larry Bernard, Rich Brown, Brendon Clark,
Daniel Dore, Peter Stephan, Tom Thompson
Professional Scouts . . . . Rick Kehoe, Gilles Leger, Justin Sather
Head Athletic Trainer . . . . Jim Ramsay
Equipment Manager / Asst. Manager . . . . Acacio Marques / Billy Southard
Massage Therapist/Assistant Trainer . . . . Bruce Lifrieri
Strength & Conditioning Coach / Assistant Coach . . . . . Reg Grant / Adam Virgile
Strength & Conditioning Consultant, Europe . . . . Daniel Hedin
Director, MSG Training Center Operations . . . . Alex Case

Sports Team Operations
Vice President, Sports Team Ops . . . . Jason Vogel
Director, MSG Sports Travel . . . . Sharon Toledo
Managers, Sports Team Ops . . . . Caroline Giglio, Brian Wendth

Hockey Operations
Managers, Scouting / Hockey Admin . . . . Victor Saljanin / Katie Condon
Executive Administrative Assistant . . . . Barbara Steppe
Director of Operations, MSG Training Center . . . . Miguel Vazquez
Manager, Building Operations, MSG Training Center . . . Steve Kaminski

Medical Staff
Chief Medical Officer & Sr. V.P., Player Care. . . . . Dr. Lisa Callahan
Head Team Physician . . . . Dr. Bryan Kelly
Team Physician . . . . Dr. Kenton Fibel
Medical Consultant . . . . Dr. Ronald Weissman
Team Dentists . . . . Drs. Don Salomon, Joe Esposito

Public Relations
Vice President, Communications, MSG Sports . . . . Ryan Watson
Director, Public Relations . . . . Ryan Nissan
Manager / Coordinator, Public Relations. . . . . Lindsay Hayes / Michael Rappaport

Marketing
Manager, Rangers Marketing . . . . Anthony Zucconi
Coordinator, Marketing. . . . . Greer O'Keefe
Senior Design Director / Art Director . . . . Joanecy Kagalingan / Tarek Awad

Marketing Operations
Vice President, Marketing Ops, MSG Sports . . . . Jeanie Baumgartner
Managers, Marketing Ops, MSG Sports . . . . Christelle Durand, Stephanie Kwok

Event Presentation
Vice President, Event Presentation . . . . Greg Kwizak
Music Director, MSG Sports . . . . Ray Castoldi
Manager / Coordinator, Event Presentation . . . . Justin Casserly / Alexa Segal
Manager, Video Production . . . . Cory Gershon

Community Relations and Fan Development
V.P., Fan Development & Community Relations . . . . Rick Nadeau
Directors, Fan Development / Community Relations . . . . Alexandra Setoodeh, David Martella
Managers, Field Marketing / Community Relations . . . . . Mike Fasulo / Felicia Ganthier
Director, Special Projects &
Community Relations Representative . . . . Rod Gilbert

Merchandise
Vice President, Merchandise . . . . Shirley Short
Director, Merchandising Analytics & Planning . . . . Paula Garcia
Senior Merchandise Buyers . . . . Alexis Michaelides, Justin Poidomani

Digital
Vice President, Digital, MSG Sports . . . . Vicki Shapiro
Rangers Digital Director / Specialist . . . . Adam Skollar / Matt Calamia
Manager, Website Production and Analytics. . . . . Lisa Hayward
Manager, Rangers Content Producer . . . . Jim Cerny

MSG Photo Services
Official Photographer of Madison Square Garden . . . . . . George Kalinsky
Vice President, MSG Photo Services . . . . Rebecca Taylor
Editor/ Manager / Coordinator, MSG Photo Services . . . . Carly Boyle / Kevin McMahon / Emma
Lomax-Cohen

Legal & Business Affairs
V.P.s, Legal & Business Affairs . . . . Jamaal Lesane / Christina Song

Additional Information
Television / Radio Network . . . . MSG Network / MSG Radio

Ottawa Senators

2014-15 Results: 43w-26l-6otl-7sol 99pts
4th, Atlantic Division • 7th, Eastern Conference

Key Off-Season Signings/Acquisitions

2015
May **9** • Signed G **Matt O'Connor**.
20 • Re-signed G **Andrew Hammond**.
June **18** • Re-signed C **Jean-Gabriel Pageau**.
23 • Re-signed C **Mika Zibanejad**.
25 • Re-signed RW **Mark Stone**.
July **1** • Signed C **Eric O'Dell** and D **Michael Kostka**.
2 • Named **Andre Tourigny** assistant coach.
26 • RW **Alex Chiasson** awarded one-year contract in arbitration.
Aug. **3** • LW **Mike Hoffman** awarded one-year contract in arbitration.

2015-16 Schedule

Oct.	Thu.	8	at Buffalo	Sat.	9	Boston
	Sat.	10	at Toronto	Sun.	10	at Washington
	Sun.	11	Montreal	Wed.	13	at Anaheim
	Wed.	14	at Columbus	Sat.	16	at Los Angeles*
	Thu.	15	at Pittsburgh	Mon.	18	at San Jose
	Sat.	17	Nashville	Thu.	21	at New Jersey
	Thu.	22	New Jersey	Fri.	22	NY Islanders
	Sat.	24	Arizona	Sun.	24	NY Rangers*
	Wed.	28	Calgary	Tue.	26	Buffalo
	Fri.	30	at Detroit	Feb. Tue.	2	at Pittsburgh
	Sat.	31	Detroit	Thu.	4	Edmonton
Nov.	Tue.	3	at Montreal	Sat.	6	Toronto
	Thu.	5	Winnipeg	Mon.	8	Tampa Bay
	Sat.	7	at Carolina	Wed.	10	at Detroit
	Tue.	10	at Nashville	Thu.	11	Colorado
	Thu.	12	Vancouver	Sat.	13	at Columbus
	Sat.	14	NY Rangers*	Tue.	16	Buffalo
	Mon.	16	Detroit	Thu.	18	Carolina
	Thu.	19	Columbus	Sat.	20	Detroit
	Sat.	21	Philadelphia	Tue.	23	at Edmonton
	Tue.	24	at Dallas	Thu.	25	at Vancouver
	Wed.	25	at Colorado	Sat.	27	at Calgary
	Sat.	28	at Arizona	Mar. Tue.	1	St. Louis
Dec.	Tue.	1	Philadelphia	Thu.	3	Tampa Bay
	Thu.	3	Chicago	Sat.	5	at Toronto
	Sat.	5	NY Islanders	Sun.	6	Dallas*
	Sun.	6	at NY Rangers	Tue.	8	at Carolina
	Tue.	8	at Florida	Thu.	10	at Florida
	Thu.	10	at Tampa Bay	Sat.	12	Toronto
	Sat.	12	at Montreal	Tue.	15	Minnesota
	Mon.	14	Los Angeles	Fri.	18	at Buffalo
	Wed.	16	at Washington	Sat.	19	Montreal
	Fri.	18	San Jose	Sat.	22	Washington
	Sun.	20	at Tampa Bay*	Wed.	23	at NY Islanders
	Tue.	22	at Florida	Sat.	26	Anaheim
	Sun.	27	Boston*	Wed.	30	at Winnipeg
	Tue.	29	at Boston	Thu.	31	at Minnesota
	Wed.	30	New Jersey	Apr. Sat.	2	at Philadelphia*
Jan.	Sun.	3	at Chicago	Tue.	5	Pittsburgh
	Mon.	4	at St. Louis	Thu.	7	Florida
	Thu.	7	Florida	Sat.	9	at Boston*

* Denotes afternoon game.

Retired Numbers

8 Frank Finnigan 1924-1934

ATLANTIC DIVISION
24th NHL Season

Franchise date: December 16, 1991

Year-by-Year Record

Season	GP	Home W	Home L	Home T	Home OL	Road W	Road L	Road T	Road OL	W	L	T	Overall OL	GF	GA	Pts.	Div. Fin.	Conf. Fin.	Playoff Result
2014-15	82	23	13	....	5	20	13	....	8	43	26	....	13	238	215	99	4th, Atl.	7th, East	Lost First Round
2013-14	82	18	17	....	6	19	14	....	8	37	31	....	14	236	265	88	5th, Atl.	11th, East	Out of Playoffs
2012-13	48	15	6	....	3	10	11	....	3	25	17	....	6	116	104	56	4th, NE	7th, East	Lost Conf. Semi-Final
2011-12	82	20	17	....	4	21	14	....	6	41	31	....	10	249	240	92	5th, NE	8th, East	Lost Conf. Quarter-Final
2010-11	82	16	20	....	5	16	20	....	5	32	40	....	10	192	250	74	5th, NE	13th, East	Out of Playoffs
2009-10	82	26	11	....	4	18	21	....	2	44	32	....	6	225	238	94	2nd, NE	5th, East	Lost Conf. Quarter-Final
2008-09	82	22	12	....	7	14	23	....	4	36	35	....	11	217	237	83	4th, NE	11th, East	Out of Playoffs
2007-08	82	22	15	....	4	21	16	....	4	43	31	....	8	261	247	94	2nd, NE	7th, East	Lost Conf. Quarter-Final
2006-07	82	25	13	....	3	23	12	....	6	48	25	....	9	288	222	105	2nd, NE	4th, East	Lost Final
2005-06	82	29	9	....	3	23	12	....	6	52	21	....	9	314	211	113	1st, NE	1st, East	Lost Conf. Semi-Final
2004-05	....																		
2003-04	82	23	8	5	5	20	15	5	1	43	23	10	6	262	189	102	3rd, NE	5th, East	Lost Conf. Quarter-Final
2002-03	82	28	9	3	1	24	12	5	0	52	21	8	1	263	182	113	1st, NE	1st, East	Lost Conf. Final
2001-02	82	21	13	3	4	18	14	6	3	39	27	9	7	243	208	94	3rd, NE	7th, East	Lost Conf. Semi-Final
2000-01	82	26	7	5	3	22	14	4	1	48	21	9	4	274	205	109	1st, NE	2nd, East	Lost Conf. Quarter-Final
1999-2000	82	24	10	5	2	17	18	6	0	41	28	11	2	244	210	95	2nd, NE	6th, East	Lost Conf. Quarter-Final
1998-99	82	22	11	8		22	12	7		44	23	15		239	179	103	1st, NE	2nd, East	Lost Conf. Quarter-Final
1997-98	82	18	16	7		16	17	8		34	33	15		193	200	83	5th, NE	8th, East	Lost Conf. Semi-Final
1996-97	82	16	17	8		15	19	7		31	36	15		226	234	77	3rd, NE	7th, East	Lost Conf. Quarter-Final
1995-96	82	8	28	5		10	31	0		18	59	5		191	291	41	6th, NE	13th, East	Out of Playoffs
1994-95	48	5	16	3		4	18	2		9	34	5		117	174	23	7th, NE	14th, East	Out of Playoffs
1993-94	84	8	30	4		6	31	5		14	61	9		201	397	37	7th, NE	14th, East	Out of Playoffs
1992-93	84	9	29	4		1	41	0		10	70	4		202	395	24	6th, Adams		Out of Playoffs

Erik Karlsson played all 82 games in 2014-15 and led all defensemen with 66 points. He also ranked third in the NHL in ice time. Sparked by an amazing debut by goalie Andrew Hammond, Ottawa went 23-4-4 down the stretch to make the playoffs.

2015-16 Player Personnel

FORWARDS	HT	WT	*Age	Place of Birth	S	2014-15 Club
CHIASSON, Alex	6-4	209	25	Montreal, QC	R	Ottawa
GREENING, Colin	6-3	215	29	St. John's, NL	L	Ottawa-Binghamton
HOFFMAN, Mike	6-1	183	25	Kitchener, ON	L	Ottawa
LAZAR, Curtis	6-0	210	20	Salmon Arm, BC	R	Ottawa
MacARTHUR, Clarke	6-0	190	30	Lloydminster, AB	L	Ottawa
MICHALEK, Milan	6-2	215	30	Jindrichuv Hradec, Czech.	L	Ottawa
NEIL, Chris	6-1	215	36	Markdale, ON	R	Ottawa
PAGEAU, Jean-Gabriel	5-9	180	22	Ottawa, ON	R	Ottawa-Binghamton
PRINCE, Shane	5-11	185	22	Rochester, NY	L	Ottawa-Binghamton
PUEMPEL, Matt	6-2	209	22	Windsor, ON	L	Ottawa-Binghamton
RYAN, Bobby	6-2	208	28	Cherry Hill, NJ	R	Ottawa
SMITH, Zack	6-2	209	27	Medicine Hat, AB	L	Ottawa-Binghamton
STONE, Mark	6-2	204	23	Winnipeg, MB	R	Ottawa
TURRIS, Kyle	6-1	190	26	New Westminster, BC	R	Ottawa
ZIBANEJAD, Mika	6-2	211	22	Huddinge, Sweden	R	Ottawa

DEFENSEMEN						
BOROWIECKI, Mark	6-2	215	26	Ottawa, ON	L	Ottawa
CECI, Cody	6-3	207	21	Ottawa, ON	L	Ottawa
COWEN, Jared	6-5	235	24	Saskatoon, SK	L	Ottawa
KARLSSON, Erik	6-0	184	25	Landsbro, Sweden	R	Ottawa
METHOT, Marc	6-3	228	30	Ottawa, ON	L	Ottawa-Binghamton
PHILLIPS, Chris	6-3	219	37	Calgary, AB	L	Ottawa
WIDEMAN, Chris	5-10	180	25	St. Louis, MO	R	Binghamton
WIERCIOCH, Patrick	6-5	206	25	Burnaby, BC	L	Ottawa

GOALTENDERS	HT	WT	*Age	Place of Birth	C	2014-15 Club
ANDERSON, Craig	6-2	184	34	Park Ridge, IL	L	Ottawa
HAMMOND, Andrew	6-1	217	27	Surrey, BC	L	Ottawa-Binghamton

* – Age at start of 2015-16 season

Coaching History

Rick Bowness, 1992-93 to 1994-95; Rick Bowness, Dave Allison and Jacques Martin, 1995-96; Jacques Martin, 1996-97 to 2000-01; Jacques Martin and Roger Neilson, 2001-02; Jacques Martin, 2002-03, 2003-04; Bryan Murray, 2004-05 to 2006-07; John Paddock and Bryan Murray, 2007-08; Craig Hartsburg and Cory Clouston, 2008-09; Cory Clouston, 2009-10, 2010-11; Paul MacLean, 2011-12 to 2013-14; Paul MacLean and Dave Cameron, 2014-15; Dave Cameron, 2015-16.

Dave Cameron
Head Coach

Born: Summerside, PE, July 29, 1958.

Dave Cameron took over as head coach of the Ottawa Senators on December 8, 2014. The club was 11-11-5 at the time and went 32-15-8 under Cameron to make the playoffs. He had spent the previous three-plus seasons as assistant coach with the Senators after being appointed to the position on June 23, 2011.

Prior to joining the Senators, Cameron spent four seasons as the head coach and general manager of the Mississauga St. Michael's Majors of the Ontario Hockey League. In his final season with the Majors, he led the club to the OHL's best record and the Memorial Cup and OHL finals. In four years with Mississauga, the Majors posted a 145-87-40 record in 272 regular-season games. Cameron also served as head coach for Canada's national junior team, winning a silver medal at the 2011 World Junior Championship. He was an associate coach for the national junior team in 2010, winning a silver medal after winning a gold medal as an assistant coach in 2009 when the tournament was held in Ottawa. Prior to joining Mississauga, Cameron spent three seasons in the Senators organization as the head coach of the American Hockey League's Binghamton Senators.

Cameron came to Binghamton from the Toronto St. Michael's Majors of the OHL, where he had served as head coach and director of hockey operations. Cameron also served as head coach of Canada's national men's summer under-18 team at the 2004 U-18 Junior World Cup, winning a gold medal. He led the same team to a fourth-place finish at the tournament in 2003. As a player, Cameron appeared in 168 NHL games, recording 53 points (25 goals, 28 assists) with the Colorado Rockies and the New Jersey Devils between 1981 and 1984. He was originally selected by the New York Islanders in the eighth round (135th overall) of the 1978 NHL Draft.

Coaching Record

Season	Team	League	GC	W	L	O/T	GC	W	L	T
				Regular Season				Playoffs		
1995-96	Detroit	CoHL	74	33	32	9	10	5	5	0
1996-97	Port Huron	CoHL	74	38	31	5	5	2	3	0
1997-98	Sault Ste. Marie	OHL	66	20	36	10	....	....	....	....
1998-99	Sault Ste. Marie	OHL	68	31	27	10	5	1	4	0
2000-01	St. Michael's	OHL	68	35	23	10	18	8	10	0
2001-02	St. Michael's	OHL	68	40	19	9	15	8	7	0
2002-03	St. Michael's	OHL	68	32	24	12	19	11	8	0
2003-04	St. Michael's	OHL	68	38	21	9	18	10	8	0
2004-05	Binghamton	AHL	80	47	21	12	6	2	4	0
2005-06	Binghamton	AHL	80	35	37	8	....	....	....	....
2006-07	Binghamton	AHL	80	23	48	9	....	....	....	....
2007-08	St. Michael's	OHL	68	31	32	5	4	0	4	0
2008-09	St. Michael's	OHL	68	39	26	3	11	6	5	0
2009-10	St. Michael's	OHL	68	42	20	6	16	9	7	0
2010-11	St. Michael's	OHL	68	53	13	2	20	15	5	0
2010-11	St. Michael's	M-Cup					5	3	2	0
2014-15	**Ottawa**	**NHL**	**55**	**32**	**15**	**8**	**6**	**2**	**4**	**0**
	NHL Totals		55	32	15	8	6	2	4	0

2014-15 Scoring

* – rookie

Regular Season

Pos	#	Player	Team	GP	G	A	Pts	TOI	+/-	PIM	PP	SH	GW	S	S%
D	65	Erik Karlsson	OTT	82	21	45	66	27:15	7	42	6	0	3	292	7.2
R	61	* Mark Stone	OTT	80	26	38	64	17:01	21	14	5	1	6	157	16.6
C	7	Kyle Turris	OTT	82	24	40	64	19:12	5	36	4	1	6	215	11.2
R	6	Bobby Ryan	OTT	78	18	36	54	17:28	5	24	4	0	5	221	8.1
C	68	* Mike Hoffman	OTT	79	27	21	48	14:33	16	14	1	0	4	199	13.6
C	93	Mika Zibanejad	OTT	80	20	26	46	16:26	0	20	4	0	0	150	13.3
L	16	Clarke MacArthur	OTT	62	16	20	36	17:00	-6	36	6	0	5	140	11.4
L	9	Milan Michalek	OTT	66	13	21	34	16:22	3	33	5	1	1	130	10.0
C	17	David Legwand	OTT	80	9	18	27	13:53	1	32	6	0	0	91	9.9
C	90	Alex Chiasson	OTT	76	11	15	26	13:22	-5	67	3	0	1	105	10.5
R	22	Erik Condra	OTT	68	9	14	23	14:27	13	30	0	1	1	106	8.5
D	5	Cody Ceci	OTT	81	5	16	21	19:17	-4	6	1	0	0	130	3.8
C	44	Jean-Gabriel Pageau	OTT	50	10	9	19	14:11	4	9	0	2	2	97	10.3
C	27	* Curtis Lazar	OTT	67	6	9	15	12:53	1	14	0	0	0	92	6.5
D	46	Patrick Wiercioch	OTT	56	3	10	13	18:03	3	28	1	0	2	79	3.8
D	62	Eric Gryba	OTT	75	0	12	12	15:39	11	97	0	0	0	64	0.0
D	3	Marc Methot	OTT	45	1	10	11	22:40	22	18	0	0	0	49	2.0
D	74	Mark Borowiecki	OTT	63	1	10	11	15:54	15	107	0	0	0	30	3.3
D	2	Jared Cowen	OTT	54	3	6	9	18:09	-11	45	0	0	1	47	6.4
R	25	Chris Neil	OTT	38	4	3	7	9:44	5	78	1	0	0	23	17.4
L	26	* Matt Puempel	OTT	13	2	1	3	8:01	6	8	0	0	0	14	14.3
L	15	Zack Smith	OTT	37	2	1	3	12:02	-8	18	0	0	0	38	5.3
D	4	Chris Phillips	OTT	36	0	3	3	20:53	1	14	0	0	0	29	0.0
C	10	Colin Greening	OTT	26	1	0	1	9:49	-5	29	0	0	0	39	2.6
C	10	* Shane Prince	OTT	2	0	1	1	10:28	1	0	0	0	0	2	0.0

Goaltending

No.	Goaltender	GPI	Mins	Avg	W	L	OT	EN	SO	GA	SA	Sv%	G	A	PIM
32	* Chris Driedger	1	23	0.00	0	0	0	0	0	0	10	1.000	0	0	0
30	Andrew Hammond	24	1411	1.79	20	1	2	0	3	42	707	.941	0	1	0
41	Craig Anderson	35	2093	2.49	14	13	8	2	3	87	1134	.923	0	0	4
40	Robin Lehner	25	1471	3.02	9	12	3	3	0	74	779	.905	0	1	0
	Totals	**82**	**5026**	**2.48**	**43**	**26**	**13**	**5**	**6**	**208**	**2635**	**.921**			

Playoffs

Pos	#	Player	Team	GP	G	A	Pts	TOI	+/-	PIM	PP	SH	GW	OT	S	S%
D	46	Patrick Wiercioch	OTT	6	2	2	4	19:17	0	4	1	0	0	0	12	16.7
D	65	Erik Karlsson	OTT	6	1	3	4	28:58	-2	2	1	0	0	0	17	5.9
C	93	Mika Zibanejad	OTT	6	1	3	4	15:42	0	1	0	0	0	0	14	7.1
R	61	* Mark Stone	OTT	6	0	4	4	19:10	0	2	0	0	0	0	14	0.0
C	68	* Mike Hoffman	OTT	6	1	2	3	13:01	-3	2	0	0	0	0	16	6.3
L	16	Clarke MacArthur	OTT	6	2	0	2	15:58	-2	18	0	0	0	0	15	13.3
R	6	Bobby Ryan	OTT	6	2	0	2	15:17	1	0	0	0	0	0	11	18.2
C	7	Kyle Turris	OTT	6	1	1	2	19:49	-2	18	1	0	0	0	21	4.8
D	5	Cody Ceci	OTT	6	0	2	2	17:59	0	0	0	0	0	0	5	0.0
L	9	Milan Michalek	OTT	6	1	0	1	16:44	-2	4	0	0	0	0	14	7.1
R	22	Erik Condra	OTT	6	1	0	1	17:31	1	0	0	0	0	0	14	7.1
R	25	Chris Neil	OTT	2	0	0	0	7:14	-1	0	0	0	0	0	1	0.0
C	17	David Legwand	OTT	3	0	0	0	9:51	-3	0	0	0	0	0	4	0.0
C	15	Zack Smith	OTT	3	0	0	0	9:53	-1	0	0	0	0	0	3	0.0
R	90	Alex Chiasson	OTT	4	0	0	0	9:14	-3	4	0	0	0	0	5	0.0
D	3	Marc Methot	OTT	6	0	0	0	23:48	-1	6	0	0	0	0	5	0.0
D	62	Eric Gryba	OTT	6	0	0	0	16:06	-2	14	0	0	0	0	5	0.0
D	74	Mark Borowiecki	OTT	6	0	0	0	16:23	-1	6	0	0	0	0	5	0.0
C	44	Jean-Gabriel Pageau	OTT	6	0	0	0	15:33	0	0	0	0	0	0	14	0.0
C	27	* Curtis Lazar	OTT	6	0	0	0	13:51	0	0	0	0	0	0	9	0.0

Goaltending

No.	Goaltender	GPI	Mins	Avg	W	L	EN	SO	GA	SA	Sv%	G	A	PIM
41	Craig Anderson	4	247	0.97	2	1	1	4	142	.972	0	0	0	
30	Andrew Hammond	2	122	3.44	0	2	0	0	7	81	.914	0	0	0
	Totals	**6**	**372**	**1.94**	**2**	**4**	**1**	**1**	**12**	**224**	**.946**			

Mike Hoffman's 27 goals for the Senators was tops on the team in 2014-15 and ranked him first among all NHL rookies.

Club Records

Team

(Figures in brackets for season records are games played; records for fewest points, wins, ties, losses, goals, goals against are for 70 or more games)

Most Points **113** 2002-03 (82), 2005-06 (82)
Most Wins **52** 2002-03 (82), 2005-06 (82)
Most Ties **15** 1996-97 (82), 1997-98 (82), 1998-99 (82)
Most Losses **70** 1992-93 (84)
Most Goals **312** 2005-06 (82)
Most Goals Against **397** 1993-94 (84)
Fewest Points **24** 1992-93 (84)
Fewest Wins **10** 1992-93 (84)
Fewest Ties **4** 1992-93 (84)
Fewest Losses **21** 2000-01 (82), 2002-03 (82), 2005-06 (82)
Fewest Goals **191** 1995-96 (82)
Fewest Goals Against **179** 1998-99 (82)
Longest Winning Streak
  Overall .... **11** Jan. 14-Feb. 4/10
  Home .... **9** Mar. 5-Apr. 7/09
  Away .... **6** Mar. 18-Apr. 5/03, Jan. 14-Feb. 3/10
Longest Undefeated Streak
  Overall .... **11** Four times
  Home .... **12** Dec. 18/03-Jan. 24/04 (10W, 2T/OL)
  Away .... **7** Three times
Longest Losing Streak
  Overall .... **14** Mar. 2-Apr. 7/93
  Home .... **11** Oct. 27-Dec. 8/93
  Away .... ***38** Oct. 10/92-Apr. 3/93**
Longest Winless Streak
  Overall .... **21** Oct. 10-Nov. 23/92 (20L, 1T)
  Home .... ***17** Oct. 28/95-Jan. 27/96 (15L, 2T)
  Away .... ***38** Oct. 10/92-Apr. 3/93 (38L)
Most Shutouts, Season **10** 2001-02 (82)
Most PIM, Season **1,716** 1992-93 (84)
Most Goals, Game .... **11** Nov. 13/01 (Ott. 11 at Wsh. 5)

Individual

Most Seasons .... **17** Daniel Alfredsson, Chris Phillips
Most Games, Career .... **1,179** Chris Phillips
Most Goals, Career .... **426** Daniel Alfredsson
Most Assists, Career .... **682** Daniel Alfredsson
Most Points, Career .... **1,108** Daniel Alfredsson (426G, 682A)
Most PIM, Career .... **2,294** Chris Neil
Most Shutouts, Career .... **30** Patrick Lalime
Longest Consecutive Games Streak .... **292** Alexei Yashin (Dec. 31/95-Apr. 17/99)
Most Goals, Season .... **50** Dany Heatley (2005-06), (2006-07)
Most Assists, Season .... **71** Jason Spezza (2005-06)
Most Points, Season .... **105** Dany Heatley (2006-07; 50G, 55A)
Most PIM, Season .... **318** Mike Peluso (1992-93)
Most Points, Defenseman, Season .... **78** Erik Karlsson (2011-12; 19G, 59A)
Most Points, Center, Season .... **94** Alexei Yashin (1998-99; 44G, 50A)
Most Points, Right Wing, Season .... **103** Daniel Alfredsson (2005-06; 43G, 60A)
Most Points, Left Wing, Season .... **105** Dany Heatley (2006-07; 50G, 55A)
Most Points, Rookie, Season .... **79** Alexei Yashin (1993-94; 30G, 49A)
Most Shutouts, Season .... **8** Patrick Lalime (2002-03)
Most Goals, Game .... **4** Marian Hossa (Jan. 2/03), Dany Heatley (Oct. 29/05), Daniel Alfredsson (Nov. 2/05), Martin Havlat (Nov. 2/05), Alex Kovalev (Jan. 3/10)
Most Assists, Game .... **5** Marian Hossa (Jan. 4/01)
Most Points, Game .... **7** Daniel Alfredsson (Jan. 24/08; 3G, 4A)

* NHL Record.
** NHL records do not include neutral site games.

General Managers' History

Mel Bridgman, 1992-93; Randy Sexton, 1993-94, 1994-95; Randy Sexton and Pierre Gauthier, 1995-96; Pierre Gauthier, 1996-97, 1997-98; Rick Dudley, 1998-99; Marshall Johnston, 1999-2000 to 2001-02; John Muckler, 2002-03 to 2006-07; Bryan Murray, 2007-08 to date.

Captains' History

Laurie Boschman, 1992-93; Brad Shaw, Mark Lamb and Gord Dineen, 1993-94; Randy Cunneyworth, 1994-95 to 1997-98; Alexei Yashin, 1998-99; Daniel Alfredsson, 1999-2000 to 2012-13; Jason Spezza, 2013-14; Erik Karlsson, 2014-15 to date.

All-time Record vs. Other Clubs

Regular Season

	Total								At Home								On Road							
	GP	W	L	T	OL	GF	GA	PTS	GP	W	L	T	OL	GF	GA	PTS	GP	W	L	T	OL	GF	GA	PTS
Anaheim	27	10	12	3	2	66	66	25	13	5	5	1	2	38	33	13	14	5	7	2	0	28	33	12
Arizona	31	16	12	2	1	112	93	35	16	8	6	1	1	57	47	18	15	8	6	1	0	55	46	17
Boston	126	45	67	8	6	314	404	104	61	24	31	3	3	150	185	54	65	21	36	5	3	164	219	50
Buffalo	124	55	45	10	14	325	345	134	63	30	18	7	8	175	160	75	61	25	27	3	6	150	185	59
Calgary	35	14	15	4	2	87	108	34	17	9	4	3	1	50	46	22	18	5	11	1	1	37	62	12
Carolina	93	36	45	8	4	242	259	84	48	23	18	4	3	137	125	53	45	13	27	4	1	105	134	31
Chicago	28	8	13	2	5	77	80	23	15	6	6	0	3	48	45	15	13	2	7	2	2	29	35	8
Colorado	43	12	24	4	3	123	173	31	23	9	11	3	0	64	83	21	20	3	13	1	3	59	90	10
Columbus	17	9	4	2	2	51	46	22	9	5	2	1	1	25	23	12	8	4	2	1	1	26	23	10
Dallas	30	10	19	0	1	77	104	21	14	5	8	0	1	34	42	11	16	5	11	0	0	43	62	10
Detroit	33	12	17	1	3	87	107	28	17	5	9	1	2	46	55	13	16	7	8	0	1	41	52	15
Edmonton	35	15	15	4	1	96	103	35	17	7	7	2	1	43	47	17	18	8	8	2	0	53	56	18
Florida	83	48	29	3	3	261	222	102	41	23	14	2	2	128	104	50	42	25	15	1	1	133	118	52
Los Angeles	29	8	17	2	2	72	104	20	14	6	6	1	1	43	42	14	15	2	11	1	1	29	62	6
Minnesota	15	10	3	1	1	50	33	22	7	5	2	0	0	23	15	10	8	5	1	1	1	27	18	12
Montreal	125	59	54	5	7	369	363	130	62	34	24	1	3	192	174	72	63	25	30	4	4	177	189	58
Nashville	19	11	6	0	2	54	47	24	10	6	2	0	2	35	28	14	9	5	4	0	0	19	19	10
New Jersey	84	30	40	5	9	194	216	74	42	16	19	3	4	99	100	39	42	14	21	2	5	95	116	35
NY Islanders	84	49	18	11	6	294	226	115	41	24	9	5	3	135	100	56	43	25	9	6	3	159	126	59
NY Rangers	83	43	34	3	3	235	226	92	42	17	21	3	1	113	117	38	41	26	13	0	2	122	109	54
Philadelphia	84	36	38	8	2	239	260	82	42	21	15	6	0	128	122	48	42	15	23	2	2	111	138	34
Pittsburgh	91	34	40	9	8	266	299	85	46	18	18	5	5	142	148	46	45	16	22	4	3	124	151	39
St. Louis	29	14	13	2	0	77	89	30	15	7	8	0	0	35	48	14	14	7	5	2	0	42	41	16
San Jose	28	11	12	4	1	74	73	27	14	5	5	4	0	44	41	14	14	6	7	0	1	30	32	13
Tampa Bay	86	52	28	2	4	302	224	110	42	29	13	0	0	152	94	58	44	23	15	2	4	150	130	52
Toronto	104	52	40	3	9	298	298	116	52	29	17	1	5	149	146	64	52	23	23	2	4	149	152	52
Vancouver	35	13	16	2	4	78	106	32	17	7	8	1	1	39	50	16	18	6	8	1	3	39	56	16
Washington	84	40	35	5	4	262	256	89	42	25	15	1	1	147	118	52	42	15	20	4	3	115	138	37
Winnipeg	55	32	14	2	7	209	163	73	28	16	6	1	5	106	71	38	27	16	8	1	2	103	92	35
Totals	**1740**	**784**	**725**	**115**	**116**	**4991**	**5093**	**1799**	**870**	**424**	**327**	**60**	**59**	**2577**	**2409**	**967**	**870**	**360**	**398**	**55**	**57**	**2414**	**2684**	**832**

Playoffs

	Series	W	L	GP	W	L	T	GF	GA	Last Mtg.	Rnd.	Result
Anaheim	1	0	1	5	1	4	0	11	16	2007	F	L 1-4
Buffalo	4	1	3	21	8	13	0	47	52	2007	CF	W 4-1
Montreal	2	1	1	11	6	5	0	32	21	2015	FR	L 2-4
New Jersey	3	2	1	18	11	7	0	41	40	2007	CSF	W 4-1
NY Islanders	1	1	0	5	4	1	0	13	7	2003	CQF	W 4-1
NY Rangers	1	0	1	7	3	4	0	13	14	2012	CQF	L 3-4
Philadelphia	2	2	0	11	8	3	0	28	12	2003	CSF	W 4-2
Pittsburgh	4	1	3	20	7	13	0	53	72	2013	CSF	L 1-4
Tampa Bay	1	1	0	5	4	1	0	23	13	2006	CQF	W 4-1
Toronto	4	0	4	24	8	16	0	42	57	2004	CQF	L 3-4
Washington	1	0	1	5	1	4	0	7	18	1998	CSF	L 1-4
Totals	**24**	**9**	**15**	**132**	**61**	**71**	**0**	**310**	**322**			

Playoff Results 2015-2011

Year	Round	Opponent	Result	GF	GA
2015	FR	Montreal	L 2-4	12	12
2013	CSF	Pittsburgh	L 1-4	11	22
	CQF	Montreal	W 4-1	20	9
2012	CQF	NY Rangers	L 3-4	13	14

Abbreviations: Round: F – Final; **CF** – conference final; **CSF** – conference semi-final; **CQF** – conference quarter-final; **FR** – first round.

Colorado totals include Quebec, 1992-93 to 1994-95.
Dallas totals include Minnesota North Stars, 1992-93.
Winnipeg totals include Atlanta Thrashers, 1999-2000 to 2010-11.
Carolina totals include Hartford, 1992-93 to 1996-97.
Phoenix totals include Winnipeg, 1992-93 to 1995-96.

2014-15 Results

Month	Day	Opponent	Score
Oct.	9	at Nashville	2-3
	11	at Tampa Bay	3-2†
	13	at Florida	1-0
	16	Colorado	5-3
	18	Columbus	3-2
	25	New Jersey	2-3*
	26	at Chicago	1-2
	28	at Columbus	5-2
	30	Chicago	4-5†
Nov.	1	at Boston	2-4
	4	Detroit	3-1
	6	Minnesota	3-0
	8	Winnipeg	1-2†
	9	Toronto	3-5
	11	at Vancouver	3-4*
	13	at Edmonton	4-3*
	15	at Calgary	2-4
	20	Nashville	3-2
	22	St. Louis	2-3
	24	at Detroit	3-4
	25	at St. Louis	3-2†
	28	at Florida	2-3
	29	at Tampa Bay	1-4
Dec.	2	at NY Islanders	2-3*
	4	NY Islanders	1-2
	6	at Pittsburgh	2-3
	7	Vancouver	4-3*
	11	Los Angeles	3-5
	13	at Boston	3-2†
	15	at Buffalo	4-5†
	17	at New Jersey	2-0
	19	Anaheim	6-2
	20	at Montreal	1-4
	22	at Washington	1-2
	27	Detroit	2-3*
	29	Buffalo	5-2
Jan.	3	at Boston	3-2*
	4	Tampa Bay	2-4
	6	at Philadelphia	1-2†
	8	at Colorado	2-5
	10	at Arizona	5-1
	13	at Dallas	4-5
	15	Montreal	4-1
	17	Carolina	2-3
	20	at NY Rangers	2-3*
	21	Toronto	4-3
	29	Dallas	3-6
	31	Arizona	7-2
Feb.	3	at New Jersey	1-2
	5	Washington	1-2
	7	Columbus	1-4
	10	at Buffalo	2-1
	12	Pittsburgh	4-5†
	14	Edmonton	7-2
	16	Carolina	3-6
	18	Montreal	4-2
	21	Florida	4-1
	25	at Anaheim	3-0
	26	at Los Angeles	1-0
	28	at San Jose	4-2
Mar.	3	at Minnesota	2-3†
	4	at Winnipeg	3-1
	6	Buffalo	3-2
	8	Calgary	5-4†
	10	Boston	1-3
	12	at Montreal	5-2
	13	at NY Islanders	2-1
	15	Philadelphia	2-1†
	17	at Carolina	2-1*
	19	Boston	6-4
	21	Toronto	5-3
	23	San Jose	5-2
	26	NY Rangers	1-5
	28	at Toronto	3-4*
	29	Florida	2-4
	31	at Detroit	2-1†
Apr.	2	Tampa Bay	2-1*
	4	Washington	4-3*
	5	at Toronto	2-3†
	7	Pittsburgh	4-3*
	9	at NY Rangers	3-0
	11	at Philadelphia	3-1

* – Overtime † – Shootout

NHL Draft Selections 2015-2001

Name in bold denotes played in NHL.

2015
Pick
18	Thomas Chabot
21	Colin White
36	Gabriel Gagne
48	Filip Chlapik
107	Christian Wolanin
109	Filip Ahl
139	Christian Jaros
199	Joel Daccord

2014
Pick
40	Andreas Englund
70	Miles Gendron
100	Shane Eiserman
189	Kelly Summers
190	Francis Perron

2013
Pick
17	**Curtis Lazar**
78	Marcus Hogberg
102	Tobias Lindberg
108	Ben Harpur
138	Vincent Dunn
161	Chris Leblanc
168	Quentin Shore

2012
Pick
15	**Cody Ceci**
76	**Chris Driedger**
82	Jarrod Maidens
106	Timothy Boyle
136	Robert Baillargeon
166	Francois Brassard
196	Mikael Wikstrand

2011
Pick
6	**Mika Zibanejad**
21	**Stefan Noesen**
24	**Matt Puempel**
61	**Shane Prince**
96	**Jean-Gabriel Pageau**
126	Fredrik Claesson
156	Darren Kramer
171	Max McCormick
186	Jordan Fransoo
204	Ryan Dzingel

2010
Pick
76	Jakub Culek
106	Marcus Sorensen
178	**Mark Stone**
196	Bryce Aneloski

2009
Pick
9	**Jared Cowen**
39	**Jakob Silfverberg**
46	**Robin Lehner**
100	Chris Wideman
130	**Mike Hoffman**
146	Jeff Costello
160	Corey Cowick
190	Brad Peltz
191	Michael Sdao

2008
Pick
15	**Erik Karlsson**
42	**Patrick Wiercioch**
79	**Zack Smith**
109	Andre Petersson
119	**Derek Grant**
139	**Mark Borowiecki**
199	Emil Sandin

2007
Pick
29	**Jim O'Brien**
60	Ruslan Bashkirov
90	Louie Caporusso
120	Ben Blood

2006
Pick
28	**Nick Foligno**
68	**Eric Gryba**
91	**Kaspars Daugavins**
121	Pierre-Luc Lessard
151	Ryan Daniels
181	Kevin Koopman
211	**Erik Condra**

2005
Pick
9	**Brian Lee**
70	Vitali Anikeyenko
95	**Cody Bass**
98	**Ilya Zubov**
115	Janne Kolehmainen
136	Tomas Kudelka
186	Dmitri Megalinsky
204	**Colin Greening**

2004
Pick
23	**Andrej Meszaros**
58	Kirill Lyamin
77	Shawn Weller
87	**Peter Regin**
89	Jeff Glass
122	**Alexander Nikulin**
141	Jim McKenzie
156	**Roman Wick**
219	Joe Cooper
251	Matthew McIlvane
284	John Wikner

2003
Pick
29	**Patrick Eaves**
67	Igor Mirnov
100	Philippe Seydoux
135	Mattias Karlsson
142	Tim Cook
166	Sergei Gimayev
228	Will Colbert
260	Ossi Louhivaara
291	**Brian Elliott**

2002
Pick
16	**Jakub Klepis**
47	**Alexei Kaigorodov**
75	Arttu Luttinen
113	Scott Dobben
125	Johan Bjork
150	Brock Hooton
246	Josef Vavra
276	Vitali Atyushov

2001
Pick
2	**Jason Spezza**
23	**Tim Gleason**
81	Neil Komadoski
99	**Ray Emery**
127	**Christoph Schubert**
162	Stefan Schauer
193	**Brooks Laich**
218	Jan Platil
223	**Brandon Bochenski**
235	Neil Petruic
256	Gregg Johnson
286	**Toni Dahlman**

Bryan Murray

Executive Vice President and General Manager

Born: Shawville, QC, December 5, 1942.

On June 18, 2007, Bryan Murray was appointed as the seventh general manager of the Ottawa Senators. Murray had joined the organization on June 8, 2004, when he was named the club's head coach. Murray resigned as senior vice president and general manager of Anaheim to take the coaching position in Ottawa. As coach in Ottawa in 2006–07, Murray led the Senators to the Stanley Cup Final for the first time in franchise history, only to lose to his former Anaheim team. He also has previous front office experience as vice president and general manager of the Florida Panthers from 1994 to 2001, assembling a team that reached the Stanley Cup Final in just its third year of existence in 1996.

Murray, who was back behind the bench in Ottawa briefly in 2007-08, began his NHL career as head coach of the Washington Capitals in 1981. He has served 16+ years behind the bench, coaching more than 1,300 regular-season and playoff games, including 672 wins. He earned the Jack Adams Award as coach of the year in 1983-84. Murray's regular-season coaching record in Ottawa is 107-55-20 and includes winning the 2007 Prince of Wales Trophy as the NHL's Eastern Conference champions.

Coaching Record

Season	Team	League	GC	W	L	O/T	GC	W	L	T
1981-82	Washington	NHL	66	25	28	13	....			
1982-83	Washington	NHL	80	39	25	16	4	1	3	....
1983-84	Washington	NHL	80	48	27	5	8	4	4	....
1984-85	Washington	NHL	80	46	25	9	5	2	3	....
1985-86	Washington	NHL	80	50	23	7	9	5	4	....
1986-87	Washington	NHL	80	38	32	10	7	3	4	....
1987-88	Washington	NHL	80	38	33	9	14	7	7	....
1988-89	Washington	NHL	80	41	29	10	6	2	4	....
1989-90	Washington	NHL	46	18	24	4	....			
1990-91	Detroit	NHL	80	34	38	8	7	3	4	....
1991-92	Detroit	NHL	80	43	25	12	11	4	7	....
1992-93	Detroit	NHL	84	47	28	9	7	3	4	....
1997-98	Florida	NHL	59	17	31	11	....			
2001-02	Anaheim	NHL	82	29	42	11	....			
2004-05	Ottawa			SEASON CANCELLED						
2005-06	Ottawa	NHL	82	52	21	9	10	5	5	....
2006-07	Ottawa	NHL	82	48	25	9	20	13	7	....
2007-08	Ottawa	NHL	18	7	9	2	4	0	4	....
	NHL Totals		1239	620	465	154	112	52	60	....

Jack Adams Award (1984)

Club Directory

Canadian Tire Centre

Ottawa Senators
Canadian Tire Centre
1000 Palladium Drive
Ottawa, Ontario
K2V 1A5
Phone **613/599-0250**
FAX 613/599-5562
www.ottawasenators.com
Capacity: 18,533

Executive
Owner, Governor and Chairman	Eugene Melnyk
President and Alternate Governor	Cyril Leeder
Chief Financial Officer	Ken Taylor
Chief Marketing Officer and V.P. of Ticketing	Peter O'Leary
Exec. V.P., G.M., President of Hockey Ops. and Alt. Gov.	Bryan Murray
V.P., Strategic Development	Geoff Publow
V.P. and Executive Director, Canadian Tire Centre	Tom Conroy
Exec. Assistant to the President	Kathy Downs

Hockey Operations
Assistant General Manager	Pierre Dorion
Assistant General Manager	Randy Lee
Manager of Hockey Administration	Allison Vaughan
Manager, Team Services	Jordan Silmser
Scouting and Development Consultant	Shean Donovan
Assistant, Hockey Operations	Sean McCauley
Head Coach	Dave Cameron
Assistant Coaches	Jason Smith, André Tourigny
Goaltending Coach	Rick Wamsley
Video Coach	Tim Pattyson
Conditioning Coach	Chris Schwarz
Assistant Conditioning Coach	Rob Mouland
Head Athletic Therapist	Gerry Townend
Assistant Athletic Therapist	Domenic Nicoletta
Equipment Manager	John Forget
Assistant Equipment Manager	Ian Cox
Massage Therapist	Shawn Markwick

Scouts
Chief Amateur Scout	Bob Lowes
Amateur Scouts	Don Boyd, Vaclav Burda, George Fargher, Bob Janecyk, Frank Kollar, Trent Mann, Lew Mongelluzzo, Justin Murray, Mikko Ruutu
Chief Professional Scout	Jim Clark
Pro Scouts	Michael Abbamont, John Perpich, Nick Polano

Communications
Senior Director, Communications	Brian Morris
Manager, Communications	Chris Moore
Coordinator, Communications	Amanda Nigh
Translator	Eric Tremblay

Broadcasting
V.P., Broadcast and Digital Content	Jim Steel
Video Producers	Nick Gilmore, Christopher Skinner
Content Producer	Craig Medaglia

Legal
Senior Legal Council	Richard Stacey

Corporate Partnerships, Premium Client Services and Ticketing
Sr. V.P., Corporate Strategy and Sales	Mark Bonneau
Exec. Ass't. to Sr. V.P., Corporate Strategy and Sales	Brooke Brown
Director, Corporate Partnerships	Bill Courchaine
Sr. Corporate Account Managers	Steve Chestnut, Michael Lummack, Steve Katzman
Director, Business Development	Gina Gianetto
Director, Season-Seat Membership & Group Ticket Sales	Chris Atack
Director, Sales	Geoff Ross
Manager, Ticket Sales Planning and Analytics	Scott MacIntosh
Manager, Group Sales and Service	Devon Hogan
Director, Premium Services	Christine Clancy
Manager, Suite Operations	Tracey Bonner
Manager, Corporate Services	Kristin Wood

Data Management and Analytics
Director, Analytics	Tom Gillis
Business System Analyst/Project Manager	Michael Freeman
Manager, Ticket Sales Strategy and Analytics	Scott MacIntosh

Finance
Senior Director, Finance	Marcello Pecora
Controller, Capital Sports Properties Inc.	Lisa Saumure
Controller, Capital Sports & Entertainment	Andrea Tunks
Exec. Assistant to the CFO	Colette Hiscott

Information Technology
IT Director / Architect	Darren Just / Don Morin

Marketing
Senior Director, Marketing	Michael Wallace
Director, Merchandise Operations	Kevin Lawton
Director, Game Entertainment	Paul Gallant
Director, Fan and Community Development	Aaron Robinson
Director, Digital Sales and Marketing	Lauren Rigato
Manager, Digital Production	Alex Forbes
Art Director	Edtmun Jasvins
Exec. Assistant to the CMO and V.P. of Ticketing	Deborah Wilson

Operations and Events
Assistant to the V.P. and Executive Director	Linda Julian
Director, Engineering and Operations	Ed Healy
Director, Canadian Tire Centre Marketing	Krista Galbraith
Managers, Engineering / Event Production / Operations	Konstantinos Capordelis / Tim Swords / Alex Gagnon

People Department
Director, People Department	Sandi Horner

Sens Foundation
President	Danielle Robinson
Director, Business Dvlpt. and Corp. Partner Relations	Jonathan Bodden
Director, Communications & Community Investments	Brad Weir

Miscellaneous
Radio	TSN 1200 (English), 94,5 FM (French)
Television	TSN and RDS
Team Photographer	Freestyle Photography (Andre Ringuette)
Anthem Singer	Lyndon Slewidge
Mascot	Spartacat

Philadelphia Flyers

2014-15 Results: 33w-31l-7otl-11sol 84pts
6TH, Metropolitan Division • 12TH, Eastern Conference

Key Off-Season Signings/Acquisitions

2015

May 18 • Named **Dave Hakstol** head coach.

June 27 • Acquired C **Sam Gagner** and a conditional choice in the 2016 NHL Draft or a 3rd-round choice in 2017 from Arizona for D **Nicklas Grossmann** and the contract of D **Chris Pronger**.

29 • Re-signed C **Chris VandeVelde**.

30 • Re-signed C **Ryan White**.

July 1 • Signed G **Michal Neuvirth**.

2 • Signed G **Jason LaBarbera**.

3 • Signed RW **Colin McDonald**.

16 • Re-signed D **Michael Del Zotto**.

28 • Re-signed C **Sean Couturier**.

30 • Re-signed RW **Jakub Voracek**.

2015-16 Schedule

Oct.	Thu.	8	at Tampa Bay		Sat.	16	NY Rangers*
	Sat.	10	at Florida		Sun.	17	at Detroit
	Mon.	12	Florida		Tue.	19	Toronto
	Wed.	14	Chicago		Thu.	21	at Pittsburgh
	Tue.	20	Dallas		Sat.	23	at NY Islanders
	Wed.	21	at Boston		Mon.	25	Boston
	Sat.	24	NY Rangers		Wed.	27	at Washington
	Tue.	27	Buffalo	Feb.	Tue.	2	Montreal
	Thu.	29	New Jersey		Thu.	4	at Nashville
	Fri.	30	at Buffalo		Sat.	6	NY Rangers*
Nov.	Mon.	2	at Vancouver		Sun.	7	at Washington*
	Tue.	3	at Edmonton		Tue.	9	Anaheim
	Thu.	5	at Calgary		Thu.	11	Buffalo
	Sat.	7	at Winnipeg		Sat.	13	New Jersey*
	Tue.	10	Colorado		Sun.	14	at NY Rangers
	Thu.	12	Washington		Sun.	14	at New Jersey
	Sat.	14	at Carolina		Fri.	19	at Montreal
	Tue.	17	Los Angeles		Sat.	20	at Toronto
	Thu.	19	San Jose		Tue.	23	at Carolina
	Sat.	21	at Ottawa		Thu.	25	Minnesota
	Mon.	23	Carolina		Sat.	27	Arizona*
	Wed.	25	at NY Islanders		Mon.	29	Calgary
	Fri.	27	Nashville*	Mar.	Thu.	3	Edmonton
	Sat.	28	at NY Rangers*		Sat.	5	Columbus
Dec.	Tue.	1	at Ottawa		Mon.	7	Tampa Bay
	Fri.	4	at New Jersey		Fri.	11	at Tampa Bay
	Sat.	5	Columbus		Sat.	12	at Florida
	Tue.	8	NY Islanders		Tue.	15	Detroit
	Thu.	10	at St. Louis		Wed.	16	at Chicago
	Fri.	11	at Dallas		Sat.	19	Pittsburgh*
	Tue.	15	Carolina		Mon.	21	at NY Islanders
	Thu.	17	Vancouver		Tue.	22	at Columbus
	Sat.	19	at Columbus		Thu.	24	at Colorado
	Mon.	21	St. Louis		Sat.	26	at Arizona
	Sun.	27	at Anaheim*		Mon.	28	Winnipeg
	Wed.	30	at San Jose		Wed.	30	Washington
Jan.	Sat.	2	at Los Angeles*	Apr.	Sat.	2	Ottawa*
	Tue.	5	Montreal		Sun.	3	at Pittsburgh*
	Thu.	7	at Minnesota		Wed.	6	at Detroit
	Sat.	9	NY Islanders*		Thu.	7	Toronto
	Wed.	13	Boston		Sat.	9	Pittsburgh*

* Denotes afternoon game.

Year-by-Year Record

Season	GP	Home W	L	T	OL	Road W	L	T	OL	Overall W	L	T	OL	GF	GA	Pts.	Div. Fin.	Conf. Fin.	Playoff Result
2014-15	82	23	11	....	7	10	20	....	11	33	31	....	18	215	234	84	6th, Met.	12th, East	Out of Playoffs
2013-14	82	24	14	....	3	18	16	....	7	42	30	....	10	236	235	94	3rd, Met.	6th,. East	Lost First Round
2012-13	48	15	7	....	2	8	15	....	1	23	22	....	3	133	141	49	4th, Atl.	10th, East	Out of Playoffs
2011-12	82	22	13	....	6	25	13	....	3	47	26	....	9	264	232	103	3rd, Atl.	5th, East	Lost Conf. Semi-Final
2010-11	82	22	12	....	7	25	11	....	5	47	23	....	12	259	223	106	1st, Atl.	2nd, East	Lost Conf. Semi-Final
2009-10	82	24	14	....	3	17	21	....	3	41	35	....	6	236	225	88	3rd, Atl.	7th, East	Lost Final
2008-09	82	24	13	....	4	20	14	....	7	44	27	....	11	264	238	99	3rd, Atl.	5th, East	Lost Conf. Quarter-Final
2007-08	82	21	14	....	6	21	15	....	5	42	29	....	11	248	233	95	4th, Atl.	6th, East	Lost Conf. Final
2006-07	82	10	24	....	7	12	24	....	5	22	48	....	12	214	303	56	5th, Atl.	15th, East	Out of Playoffs
2005-06	82	22	13	....	6	23	13	....	5	45	26	....	11	267	259	101	2nd, Atl.	5th, East	Lost Conf. Quarter-Final
2004-05	.....																		
2003-04	82	24	11	3	3	16	10	12	3	40	21	15	6	229	186	101	1st, Atl.	3rd, East	Lost Conf. Final
2002-03	82	21	10	8	2	24	10	5	2	45	20	13	4	211	166	107	1st, Atl.	4th, East	Lost Conf. Semi-Final
2001-02	82	20	13	5	3	22	14	5	0	42	27	10	3	234	192	97	1st, Atl.	2nd, East	Lost Conf. Quarter-Final
2000-01	82	26	11	4	0	17	14	7	3	43	25	11	3	240	207	100	2nd, Atl.	4th, East	Lost Conf. Quarter-Final
1999-2000	82	25	6	7	3	20	16	5	0	45	22	12	3	237	179	105	1st, Atl.	1st, East	Lost Conf. Final
1998-99	82	21	9	11	....	16	17	8	....	37	26	19	....	231	196	93	2nd, Atl.	5th, East	Lost Conf. Quarter-Final
1997-98	82	24	11	6	....	18	18	5	....	42	29	11	....	242	193	95	2nd, Atl.	3rd, East	Lost Conf. Quarter-Final
1996-97	82	23	12	6	....	22	12	7	....	45	24	13	....	274	217	103	2nd, Atl.	2nd, East	Lost. Final
1995-96	82	27	9	5	....	18	15	8	....	45	24	13	....	282	208	103	1st, Atl.	1st, East	Lost Conf. Semi-Final
1994-95	48	16	7	1	....	12	9	3	....	28	16	4	....	150	132	60	1st, Atl.	3rd, East	Lost Conf. Final
1993-94	84	19	20	3	....	16	19	7	....	35	39	10	....	294	314	80	6th, Atl.	10th, East	Out of Playoffs
1992-93	84	23	14	5	....	13	23	6	....	36	37	11	....	319	319	83	5th, Patrick		Out of Playoffs
1991-92	80	22	11	7	....	10	26	4	....	32	37	11	....	252	273	75	6th, Patrick		Out of Playoffs
1990-91	80	18	16	6	....	15	21	4	....	33	37	10	....	252	267	76	5th, Patrick		Out of Playoffs
1989-90	80	17	19	4	....	13	20	7	....	30	39	11	....	290	297	71	6th, Patrick		Out of Playoffs
1988-89	80	22	15	3	....	14	21	5	....	36	36	8	....	307	285	80	4th, Patrick		Lost Conf. Final
1987-88	80	20	14	6	....	18	19	3	....	38	33	9	....	292	292	85	3rd, Patrick		Lost Div. Semi-Final
1986-87	80	29	9	2	....	17	17	6	....	46	26	8	....	310	245	100	1st, Patrick		Lost Final
1985-86	80	33	6	1	....	20	17	3	....	53	23	4	....	335	241	110	1st, Patrick		Lost Div. Semi-Final
1984-85	80	32	4	4	....	21	16	3	....	53	20	7	....	348	241	113	1st, Patrick		Lost Final
1983-84	80	25	10	5	....	19	16	5	....	44	26	10	....	350	290	98	3rd, Patrick		Lost Div. Semi-Final
1982-83	80	29	8	3	....	20	15	5	....	49	23	8	....	326	240	106	1st, Patrick		Lost Div. Semi-Final
1981-82	80	25	10	5	....	13	21	6	....	38	31	11	....	325	313	87	3rd, Patrick		Lost Div. Semi-Final
1980-81	80	23	9	8	....	18	15	7	....	41	24	15	....	313	249	97	2nd, Patrick		Lost Quarter-Final
1979-80	80	27	5	8	....	21	7	12	....	48	12	20	....	327	254	116	1st, Patrick		Lost Final
1978-79	80	26	10	4	....	14	15	11	....	40	25	15	....	281	248	95	2nd, Patrick		Lost Quarter-Final
1977-78	80	29	6	5	....	16	14	10	....	45	20	15	....	296	200	105	2nd, Patrick		Lost Semi-Final
1976-77	80	33	6	1	....	15	10	15	....	48	16	16	....	323	213	112	1st, Patrick		Lost Semi-Final
1975-76	80	36	2	2	....	15	11	14	....	51	13	16	....	348	209	118	1st, Patrick		Lost Final
1974-75	**80**	**32**	**6**	**2**	**....**	**19**	**12**	**9**	**....**	**51**	**18**	**11**	**....**	**293**	**181**	**113**	**1st, Patrick**		**Won Stanley Cup**
1973-74	**78**	**28**	**6**	**5**	**....**	**22**	**10**	**7**	**....**	**50**	**16**	**12**	**....**	**273**	**164**	**112**	**1st, West**		**Won Stanley Cup**
1972-73	78	27	8	4	....	10	22	7	....	37	30	11	....	296	256	85	2nd, West		Lost Semi-Final
1971-72	78	19	13	7	....	7	25	7	....	26	38	14	....	200	236	66	5th, West		Out of Playoffs
1970-71	78	20	10	9	....	8	23	8	....	28	33	17	....	207	225	73	3rd, West		Lost Quarter-Final
1969-70	76	11	14	13	....	6	21	11	....	17	35	24	....	197	225	58	5th, West		Out of Playoffs
1968-69	76	14	16	8	....	6	19	13	....	20	35	21	....	174	225	61	3rd, West		Lost Quarter-Final
1967-68	74	17	13	7	....	14	19	4	....	31	32	11	....	173	179	73	1st, West		Lost Quarter-Final

Flyers captain Claude Giroux celebrates with Jakub Voracek and Wayne Simmonds. Voracek was second in the NHL with 59 assists in 2014-15, while Simmonds led the Flyers with 28 goals.

Retired Numbers

1	Bernie Parent	1967-1971, 1973-1979
2	Mark Howe	1982-1992
4	Barry Ashbee	1970-1974
7	Bill Barber	1972-1985
16	Bobby Clarke	1969-1984

METROPOLITAN DIVISION
49th NHL Season

Franchise date: June 5, 1967

2015-16 Player Personnel

FORWARDS

	HT	WT	*Age	Place of Birth	S	2014-15 Club
BELLEMARE, Pierre-Edouard	5-11	198	30	Paris, France	L	Philadelphia
COUTURIER, Sean	6-3	211	22	Phoenix, AZ	L	Philadelphia
GAGNER, Sam	5-11	202	26	London, ON	R	Arizona
GIROUX, Claude	5-11	185	27	Hearst, ON	R	Philadelphia
LECAVALIER, Vincent	6-4	215	35	Ile Bizard, QC	L	Philadelphia
McDONALD, Colin	6-2	214	31	Wethersfield, CT	R	NY Islanders-Bridgeport
PORTER, Chris	6-1	206	31	Toronto, ON	L	St. Louis
RAFFL, Michael	6-0	200	26	Villach, Austria	L	Philadelphia
READ, Matt	5-10	185	29	Ilderton, ON	R	Philadelphia
SCHENN, Brayden	6-1	195	24	Saskatoon, SK	L	Philadelphia
SIMMONDS, Wayne	6-2	185	27	Scarborough, ON	R	Philadelphia
UMBERGER, RJ	6-2	214	33	Pittsburgh, PA	L	Philadelphia
VANDEVELDE, Chris	6-2	190	28	Moorhead, MN	L	Philadelphia-Lehigh Valley
VORACEK, Jakub	6-2	214	26	Kladno, Czech.	R	Philadelphia
WHITE, Ryan	6-0	200	27	Brandon, MB	R	Philadelphia-Lehigh Valley

DEFENSEMEN

DEL ZOTTO, Michael	6-0	195	25	Stouffville, ON	L	Philadelphia
GUDAS, Radko	6-0	204	25	Prague, Czech.	R	Tampa Bay
MacDONALD, Andrew	6-1	204	29	Judique, NS	L	Philadelphia
MANNING, Brandon	6-1	205	25	Prince George, BC	L	Philadelphia-Lehigh Valley
MEDVEDEV, Evgeni	6-3	187	28	Chelyabinsk, Russia	L	Kazan
SCHENN, Luke	6-2	225	25	Saskatoon, SK	R	Philadelphia
SCHULTZ, Nick	6-1	203	33	Strasbourg, SK	L	Philadelphia
STREIT, Mark	5-11	191	37	Bern, Switz.	L	Philadelphia

GOALTENDERS

	HT	WT	*Age	Place of Birth	C	2014-15 Club
MASON, Steve	6-4	210	27	Oakville, ON	R	Philadelphia
NEUVIRTH, Michal	6-0	209	27	Usti nad Labem, Czech.	L	Buffalo-NY Islanders

* – Age at start of 2015-16 season

Coaching History

Keith Allen, 1967-68, 1968-69; Vic Stasiuk, 1969-70, 1970-71; Fred Shero, 1971-72 to 1977-78; Bob McCammon and Pat Quinn, 1978-79; Pat Quinn, 1979-80, 1980-81; Pat Quinn and Bob McCammon, 1981-82; Bob McCammon, 1982-83, 1983-84; Mike Keenan, 1984-85 to 1987-88; Paul Holmgren, 1988-89 to 1990-91; Paul Holmgren and Bill Dineen, 1991-92; Bill Dineen, 1992-93; Terry Simpson, 1993-94; Terry Murray, 1994-95 to 1996-97; Wayne Cashman and Roger Neilson, 1997-98; Roger Neilson, 1998-99, 1999-2000; Craig Ramsay and Bill Barber, 2000-01; Bill Barber, 2001-02; Ken Hitchcock, 2002-03 to 2005-06; Ken Hitchcock and John Stevens, 2006-07; John Stevens, 2007-08, 2008-09; John Stevens and Peter Laviolette, 2009-10; Peter Laviolette, 2010-11 to 2012-13; Peter Laviolette and Craig Berube, 2013-14; Craig Berube, 2014-15; Dave Hakstol, 2015-16.

Dave Hakstol

Head Coach

Born: Warburg, AB, July 30, 1968.

Philadelphia Flyers general manager Ron Hextall announced on May 18, 2015 that Dave Hakstol had been named the 19th head coach in Flyers history. Hakstol joined the Flyers from the University of North Dakota where he spent the previous 11 seasons compiling an overall record of 289-143-43 with a .654 winning percentage in 475 games. In 2014-15, he led North Dakota to a 29-10-3 record with a .726 winning percentage and a berth in the NCAA Frozen Four.

North Dakota made the NCAA tournament in every one of Hakstol's 11 seasons and reached the Frozen Four seven times in that span, which is the most of any program in the country during that period. Hakstol led North Dakota to an overall postseason record of 54-24 for a .692 winning percentage, including a 17-11 record in the NCAA tournament, during his tenure. He joined the school's coaching staff in 2000 as an assistant coach, and took over the head coaching job four years later. Under Hakstol's watch, North Dakota won three regular season conference championships – two in the Western Collegiate Hockey Association (2008-09, 2010-11) and one in the National Collegiate Hockey Conference (2014-15). North Dakota also won WCHA playoff championships in 2005-06, 2009-10, 2010-11 and 2011-12. Hakstol received conference coach of the year honors twice, in the WCHA in 2008-09 and in the NCHC in 2014-15. He was also an eight-time finalist for the Spencer Penrose Award as national coach of the year.

Hakstol's program produced 20 NHL players and a total of 46 that have played professionally at some level. His former players include Jonathan Toews, Matt Greene, T.J. Oshie, Travis Zajac, Drew Stafford and Chris VandeVelde. He has also had seven players named Hobey Baker Award finalists, including Ryan Duncan who won the award in 2007, and 11 players named All-Americans.

Coaching Record

				Regular Season				Playoffs			
Season	Team	League	GC	W	L	O/T		GC	W	L	T
1996-97	Sioux City	USHL	53	8	43	2		....	....	....	....
1997-98	Sioux City	USHL	56	35	18	3		5	1	4	0
1998-99	Sioux City	USHL	56	34	19	3		5	2	3	0
1999-00	Sioux City	USHL	58	27	26	5		5	2	3	0
2004-05	North Dakota	WCHA	45	25	15	5		....	....	....	....
2005-06	North Dakota	WCHA	46	29	16	1		....	....	....	....
2006-07	North Dakota	WCHA	43	24	14	5		....	....	....	....
2007-08	North Dakota	WCHA	43	28	11	4		....	....	....	....
2008-09	North Dakota	WCHA	43	24	15	4		....	....	....	....
2009-10	North Dakota	WCHA	43	25	13	5		....	....	....	....
2010-11	North Dakota	WCHA	44	32	9	3		....	....	....	....
2011-12	North Dakota	WCHA	42	26	13	3		....	....	....	....
2012-13	North Dakota	WCHA	42	22	13	7		....	....	....	....
2013-14	North Dakota	NCHC	42	25	14	3		....	....	....	....
2014-15	North Dakota	NCHC	42	29	10	3		....	....	....	....

2014-15 Scoring

* – rookie

Regular Season

Pos	#	Player	Team	GP	G	A	Pts	TOI	+/–	PIM	PP	SH	GW	S	S%
R	93	Jakub Voracek	PHI	82	22	59	81	18:35	1	78	11	0	3	221	10.0
R	28	Claude Giroux	PHI	81	25	48	73	20:33	-3	36	14	0	4	279	9.0
D	32	Mark Streit	PHI	81	9	43	52	22:22	-8	36	4	0	0	144	6.3
R	17	Wayne Simmonds	PHI	75	28	22	50	16:48	-5	66	14	0	6	188	14.9
C	10	Brayden Schenn	PHI	82	18	29	47	17:04	-5	34	7	0	6	156	11.5
C	14	Sean Couturier	PHI	82	15	22	37	18:23	4	28	1	1	0	148	10.1
D	15	Michael Del Zotto	PHI	64	10	22	32	21:55	-5	34	1	1	4	119	8.4
R	24	Matt Read	PHI	80	8	22	30	17:33	-4	14	2	0	2	142	5.6
C	12	Michael Raffl	PHI	67	21	7	28	14:11	6	34	2	1	2	134	15.7
C	40	Vincent Lecavalier	PHI	57	8	12	20	12:38	-7	36	1	0	0	103	7.8
C	18	R.J. Umberger	PHI	67	9	6	15	13:49	-9	19	2	0	0	96	9.4
C	76	Chris Vandevelde	PHI	72	9	6	15	11:43	-6	28	0	0	0	70	12.9
D	55	Nick Schultz	PHI	80	2	13	15	19:02	1	47	0*	0	1	69	2.9
D	8	Nicklas Grossmann	PHI	68	5	9	14	17:39	8	32	0	0	0	43	11.6
C	22	Luke Schenn	PHI	58	3	11	14	18:04	-2	18	0	0	0	67	4.5
C	25	Ryan White	PHI	34	6	6	12	11:43	4	30	0	1	0	45	13.3
L	78	Pierre-Edouard Belle	PHI	81	6	6	12	12:49	-3	18	0	0	1	113	5.3
D	47	Andrew MacDonald	PHI	58	2	10	12	20:00	-5	41	1	0	0	62	3.2
D	26	Carlo Colaiacovo	PHI	33	2	6	8	16:29	0	10	0	0	0	42	4.8
L	49	Scott Laughton	PHI	31	2	4	6	12:43	-1	17	0	0	0	51	3.9
L	36	Zac Rinaldo	PHI	58	1	5	6	8:55	-9	102	0	0	0	45	2.2
D	43	* Brandon Manning	PHI	11	0	3	3	17:09	3	7	0	0	0	10	0.0
R	51	* Petr Straka	PHI	3	0	2	2	9:27	1	0	0	0	0	2	0.0
R	38	* Oliver Lauridsen	PHI	1	0	0	0	10:26	-1	10	0	0	0	2	0.0
D	39	* Mark Alt	PHI	1	0	0	0	9:25	-1	0	0	0	0	0	0.0
D	53	* Shayne Gostisbehere	PHI	2	0	0	0	12:33	-2	0	0	0	0	2	0.0
C	41	Blair Jones	PHI	4	0	0	0	6:55	-4	2	0	0	0	4	0.0
C	52	* Nick Cousins	PHI	11	0	0	0	8:49	1	2	0	0	0	6	0.0
R	42	* Jason Akeson	PHI	13	0	0	0	8:03	-1	8	0	0	0	9	0.0

Goaltending

No.	Goaltender	GPI	Mins	Avg	W	L	OT	EN	SO	GA	SA	Sv%	G	A	PIM
35	Steve Mason	51	2885	2.25	18	18	11	4	3	108	1490	.928	0	3	2
72	Rob Zepp	10	519	2.89	5	2	0	0	0	25	223	.888	0	0	0
29	Ray Emery	31	1570	3.06	10	11	7	6	0	80	758	.894	0	0	4
	Totals	82	5021	2.66	33	31	18	10	3	223	2481	.910			

Sean Couturier played all 82 games for the second straight season in 2014-15 and established a new career high with 15 goals.

Captains' History

Lou Angotti, 1967-68; Ed Van Impe, 1968-69 to 1971-72; Ed Van Impe and Bobby Clarke, 1972-73; Bobby Clarke, 1973-74 to 1978-79; Mel Bridgman, 1979-80, 1980-81; Bill Barber, 1981-82; Bill Barber and Bobby Clarke, 1982-83; Bobby Clarke, 1983-84; Dave Poulin, 1984-85 to 1988-89; Dave Poulin and Ron Sutter, 1989-90; Ron Sutter, 1990-91; Rick Tocchet, 1991-92; no captain, 1992-93; Kevin Dineen, 1993-94; Eric Lindros, 1994-95 to 1998-99; Eric Lindros and Eric Desjardins, 1999-2000; Eric Desjardins, 2000-01; Eric Desjardins and Keith Primeau, 2001-02; Keith Primeau, 2002-03, 2003-04; Keith Primeau and Derian Hatcher, 2005-06; Peter Forsberg, 2006-07; Jason Smith, 2007-08; Mike Richards, 2008-09 to 2010-11; Chris Pronger, 2011-12; Claude Giroux, 2012-13 to date.

Club Records

Team

(Figures in brackets for season records are games played; records for fewest points, wins, ties, losses, goals, goals against are for 70 or more games)

Most Points	118	1975-76 (80)
Most Wins	53	1984-85 (80), 1985-86 (80)
Most Ties	*24	1969-70 (76)
Most Losses	48	2006-07 (82)
Most Goals	350	1983-84 (80)
Most Goals Against	319	1992-93 (84)
Fewest Points	56	2006-07 (82)
Fewest Wins	17	1969-70 (76)
Fewest Ties	4	1985-86 (80)
Fewest Losses	12	1979-80 (80)
Fewest Goals	173	1967-68 (74)
Fewest Goals Against	164	1973-74 (78)
Longest Winning Streak		
Overall	13	Oct. 19-Nov. 17/85
Home	20	Jan. 4-Apr. 3/76
Away	8	Dec. 22/82-Jan. 16/83
Longest Undefeated Streak		
Overall	*35	Oct. 14/79-Jan. 6/80 (25W, 10T)
Home	26	Oct. 11/79-Feb. 3/80 (19W, 7T)
Away	16	Oct. 20/79-Jan. 6/80 (11W, 5T)
Longest Losing Streak		
Overall	9	Dec. 8-27/06
Home	13	Nov. 29/06-Feb. 8/07
Away	8	Oct. 25-Nov. 26/72, Mar. 3-29/88
Longest Winless Streak		
Overall	12	Feb. 24-Mar. 16/99 (8L, 4T)
Home	13	Nov. 29/06-Feb. 8/07 (13L)
Away	19	Oct. 23/71-Jan. 27/72 (15L, 4T)
Most Shutouts, Season	13	1974-75 (80)
Most PIM, Season	2,621	1980-81 (80)
Most Goals, Game	13	Mar. 22/84 (Pit. 4 at Phi. 13), Oct. 18/84 (Van. 2 at Phi. 13)

Individual

Most Seasons	15	Bobby Clarke
Most Games	1,144	Bobby Clarke
Most Goals, Career	420	Bill Barber
Most Assists, Career	852	Bobby Clarke
Most Points, Career	1,210	Bobby Clarke (358G, 852A)
Most PIM, Career	1,817	Rick Tocchet
Most Shutouts, Career	50	Bernie Parent
Longest Consecutive Game Streak	484	Rod Brind'Amour (Feb. 24/93-Apr. 18/99)
Most Goals, Season	61	Reggie Leach (1975-76)
Most Assists, Season	89	Bobby Clarke (1974-75), (1975-76)
Most Points, Season	123	Mark Recchi (1992-93; 53G, 70A)
Most PIM, Season	*472	Dave Schultz (1974-75)
Most Points, Defenseman, Season	82	Mark Howe (1985-86; 24G, 58A)
Most Points, Center, Season	119	Bobby Clarke (1975-76; 30G, 89A)
Most Points, Right Wing, Season	123	Mark Recchi (1992-93; 53G, 70A)
Most Points, Left Wing, Season	112	Bill Barber (1975-76; 50G, 62A)
Most Points, Rookie, Season	82	Mikael Renberg (1993-94; 38G, 44A)
Most Shutouts, Season	12	Bernie Parent (1973-74), (1974-75)
Most Goals, Game	4	Sixteen times
Most Assists, Game	6	Eric Lindros (Feb. 26/97)
Most Points, Game	8	Tom Bladon (Dec. 11/77; 4G, 4A)

* NHL Record.

All-time Record vs. Other Clubs

Regular Season

	Total								At Home								On Road							
	GP	W	L	T	OL	GF	GA	PTS	GP	W	L	T	OL	GF	GA	PTS	GP	W	L	T	OL	GF	GA	PTS
Anaheim	28	10	9	5	4	87	86	29	13	4	4	3	2	34	30	13	15	6	5	2	2	53	56	16
Arizona	73	44	26	2	1	267	213	91	37	26	10	0	1	149	98	53	36	18	16	2	0	118	115	38
Boston	186	65	90	21	10	544	614	161	92	37	41	10	4	288	284	88	94	28	49	11	6	256	330	73
Buffalo	167	83	58	20	6	532	490	192	85	49	20	12	4	296	220	114	82	34	38	8	2	236	270	78
Calgary	113	57	41	12	3	395	368	129	56	35	15	3	3	207	149	76	57	22	26	9	0	188	219	53
Carolina	127	75	31	14	7	457	351	171	63	41	13	5	4	234	162	91	64	34	18	9	3	223	189	80
Chicago	132	57	45	30	0	404	395	144	67	40	16	11	0	222	171	91	65	17	29	19	0	182	224	53
Colorado	80	37	24	14	5	276	248	93	39	26	9	2	2	141	103	56	41	11	15	12	3	135	145	37
Columbus	20	8	7	3	2	59	57	21	10	6	3	1	0	38	27	13	10	2	4	2	2	21	30	8
Dallas	145	73	40	32	0	505	399	178	73	46	11	16	0	274	165	108	72	27	29	16	0	231	234	70
Detroit	130	60	49	21	0	462	416	141	64	40	13	11	0	259	178	91	66	20	36	10	0	203	238	50
Edmonton	69	32	28	8	1	240	211	73	36	23	11	2	0	146	97	48	33	9	17	6	1	94	114	25
Florida	86	47	28	7	4	255	211	105	44	19	15	6	4	115	110	48	42	28	13	1	0	140	101	57
Los Angeles	141	85	38	15	3	498	372	188	69	43	17	7	2	256	167	95	72	42	21	8	1	242	205	93
Minnesota	17	10	5	1	1	49	28	22	10	7	2	0	1	31	15	15	7	3	3	1	0	18	13	7
Montreal	184	70	78	30	6	548	585	176	91	38	34	16	3	275	267	95	93	32	44	14	3	273	318	81
Nashville	20	9	4	3	4	55	44	25	11	6	2	1	2	36	22	15	9	3	2	2	2	19	22	10
New Jersey	229	108	93	18	10	754	677	244	115	67	33	10	5	408	297	149	114	41	60	8	5	346	380	95
NY Islanders	253	130	88	26	9	834	773	295	125	76	33	11	5	447	342	168	128	54	55	15	4	387	431	127
NY Rangers	280	119	117	37	7	827	833	282	140	68	54	14	4	433	389	154	140	51	63	23	3	394	444	128
Ottawa	84	40	30	8	6	260	239	94	42	25	13	2	2	138	111	54	42	15	17	6	4	122	128	40
Pittsburgh	273	150	85	30	8	988	831	338	136	95	29	8	4	544	356	202	137	55	56	22	4	444	475	136
St. Louis	145	85	40	17	3	504	367	190	72	49	13	10	0	279	163	108	73	36	27	7	3	225	204	82
San Jose	35	14	13	4	4	98	100	36	17	6	6	2	3	53	56	17	18	8	7	2	1	45	44	19
Tampa Bay	88	43	34	8	3	266	251	97	43	21	13	7	2	137	111	51	45	22	21	1	1	129	140	46
Toronto	171	92	54	22	3	593	466	209	85	53	24	8	0	312	203	114	86	39	30	14	3	281	263	95
Vancouver	115	70	32	13	0	466	339	153	59	38	20	1	0	245	178	77	56	32	12	12	0	221	161	76
Washington	203	108	69	19	7	704	610	242	104	65	31	6	2	390	293	138	99	43	38	13	5	314	317	104
Winnipeg	55	36	11	3	5	201	150	80	27	17	5	2	3	106	79	39	28	19	6	1	2	95	71	41
Defunct Clubs	69	37	18	14	0	239	156	88	34	24	4	6	0	137	67	54	35	13	14	8	0	102	89	34
Totals	**3718**	**1854**	**1285**	**457**	**122**	**12367**	**10880**	**4287**	**1859**	**1090**	**514**	**193**	**62**	**6630**	**4910**	**2435**	**1859**	**764**	**771**	**264**	**60**	**5737**	**5970**	**1852**

Playoffs

	Series	W	L	GP	W	L	T	GF	GA	Last Mtg.	Rnd.	Result
Boston	6	3	3	31	13	18	0	86	100	2011	CSF	L 0-4
Buffalo	9	6	3	50	29	21	0	146	141	2011	CQF	W 4-3
Calgary	2	1	1	11	7	4	0	43	28	1981	QF	L 3-4
Chicago	2	0	2	10	2	8	0	30	45	2010	F	L 2-4
Colorado	2	2	0	11	7	4	0	39	29	1985	CF	W 4-2
Dallas	2	2	0	11	8	3	0	41	26	1980	SF	W 4-1
Detroit	1	0	1	4	0	4	0	6	16	1997	F	L 0-4
Edmonton	3	1	2	15	7	8	0	44	49	1987	F	L 3-4
Florida	1	0	1	6	2	4	0	11	15	1996	CSF	L 2-4
Montreal	6	3	3	31	15	16	0	89	93	2010	CF	W 4-1
New Jersey	6	3	3	30	16	14	0	75	77	2012	CSF	L 1-4
NY Islanders	4	3	1	25	14	11	0	83	69	1987	DF	W 4-3
NY Rangers	11	6	5	54	30	24	0	173	172	2014	FR	L 3-4
Ottawa	2	0	2	11	3	8	0	12	28	2003	CSF	L 2-4
Pittsburgh	6	4	2	35	19	16	0	121	115	2012	CQF	W 4-2
St. Louis	2	0	2	11	3	8	0	20	34	1969	QF	L 0-4
Tampa Bay	2	1	1	13	7	6	0	45	34	2004	CF	L 3-4
Toronto	6	5	1	36	22	14	0	119	85	2004	CSF	W 4-2
Vancouver	1	1	0	3	2	1	0	15	9	1979	PR	W 2-1
Washington	4	2	2	23	11	12	0	78	85	2008	CQF	W 4-3
Totals	**78**	**43**	**35**	**421**	**217**	**204**	**0**	**1276**	**1250**			

Calgary totals include Atlanta Flames, 1972-73 to 1979-80. Carolina totals include Hartford, 1979-80 to 1996-97.
Colorado totals include Quebec, 1979-80 to 1994-95. Dallas totals include Minnesota North Stars, 1967-68 to 1992-93.
New Jersey totals include Kansas City, 1974-75, 1975-76, and Colorado Rockies, 1976-77 to 1981-82.
Phoenix totals include Winnipeg, 1979-80 to 1995-96. Winnipeg totals include Atlanta Thrashers, 1999-2000 to 2010-11.

Playoff Results 2015-2011

Year	Round	Opponent	Result	GF	GA
2014	FR	NY Rangers	L 3-4	16	19
2012	CSF	New Jersey	L 1-4	11	18
	CQF	Pittsburgh	W 4-2	30	26
2011	CSF	Boston	L 0-4	7	20
	CQF	Buffalo	W 4-3	22	18

Abbreviations: Round: F – Final; **CF** – conference final; **CSF** – conference semi-final; **CQF** – conference quarter-final; **FR** – first round; **DF** – division final; **SF** – semi-final; **QF** – quarter-final; **PR** – preliminary round.

2014-15 Results

Oct.	8	at Boston	1-2
	9	New Jersey	4-6
	11	Montreal	3-4†
	14	Anaheim	3-4†
	18	at Dallas	6-5*
	21	at Chicago	0-4
	22	at Pittsburgh	5-3
	25	Detroit	4-2
	28	Los Angeles	3-2*
	30	at Tampa Bay	3-4
Nov.	1	at Florida	1-2
	4	Edmonton	4-1
	6	Florida	4-1
	8	Colorado	4-3
	14	Columbus	3-4
	15	at Montreal	3-6
	19	at NY Rangers	0-2
	20	Minnesota	2-3
	22	Columbus	4-2
	24	at NY Islanders	0-1†
	26	at Detroit	2-5
	28	NY Rangers	0-3
	29	at NY Rangers	2-5
Dec.	2	at San Jose	1-2
	3	at Anaheim	4-5†
	6	at Los Angeles	2-1
	9	at Columbus	2-3*
	11	New Jersey	4-1
	13	Carolina	5-1
	16	Tampa Bay	1-3
	18	Florida	1-2†
	20	at Toronto	7-4
	21	at Winnipeg	4-3*
	23	at Minnesota	5-2
	27	at Nashville	1-4
	29	at Arizona	2-4
	31	at Colorado	3-4*
Jan.	2	at Carolina	1-2
	3	at New Jersey	2-5
	6	Ottawa	2-1†
	8	Washington	3-2*
	10	Boston	1-3
	12	Tampa Bay	7-3
	14	at Washington	0-1
	15	Vancouver	0-4
	17	at Buffalo	4-3
	19	at NY Islanders	4-7
	20	Pittsburgh	3-2*
	27	Arizona	4-3†
	29	Winnipeg	5-2
	31	Toronto	1-0
Feb.	5	NY Islanders	2-3†
	8	at Washington	3-1
	10	at Montreal	1-2*
	13	at Columbus	3-4*
	15	at Buffalo	2-1
	17	Columbus	2-5
	19	Buffalo	2-3†
	21	Nashville	3-2†
	22	Washington	3-2
	24	at Carolina	1-4
	26	at Toronto	2-3
	28	NY Rangers	4-2
Mar.	3	Calgary	2-3*
	5	St. Louis	3-1
	7	at Boston	2-3*
	8	at New Jersey	2-5
	10	Dallas	1-2
	12	at St. Louis	0-1†
	14	Detroit	7-2
	15	at Ottawa	1-2†
	17	at Vancouver	1-4
	19	at Calgary	1-4
	21	at Edmonton	4-5*
	25	Chicago	4-1
	28	San Jose	2-3†
Apr.	1	at Pittsburgh	4-1
	4	at Carolina	2-3†
	5	Pittsburgh	4-1
	7	NY Islanders	5-4
	9	Carolina	1-3
	11	Ottawa	1-3

* – Overtime † – Shootout

NHL Draft Selections 2015-2001

Name in bold denotes played in NHL.

2015

Pick	
7	Ivan Provorov
24	Travis Konecny
70	Felix Sandstrom
90	Matej Tomek
98	Samuel Dove-Mcfalls
104	Mikhail Vorobyev
128	David Kase
158	Cooper Marody
188	Ivan Fedotov

2014

Pick	
17	Travis Sanheim
48	Nicolas Aube-Kubel
86	Mark Friedman
138	Oskar Lindblom
168	Radel Fazleev
198	Jesper Pettersson

2013

Pick	
11	Samuel Morin
41	Robert Hagg
72	Tyrell Goulbourne
132	Terrance Amorosa
162	Merrick Madsen
192	David Drake

2012

Pick	
20	**Scott Laughton**
45	Anthony Stolarz
78	**Shayne Gostisbehere**
111	Fredric Larsson
117	Taylor Leier
141	Reece Willcox
201	Valeri Vasiliev

2011

Pick	
8	**Sean Couturier**
68	**Nick Cousins**
116	Colin Suellentrop
118	Marcel Noebels
176	Petr Placek
206	Derek Mathers

2010

Pick	
89	**Michael Chaput**
119	**Tye McGinn**
149	Michael Parks
179	Nick Luukko
206	Ricard Blidstrand
209	**Brendan Ranford**

2009

Pick	
81	Adam Morrison
87	Simon Bertilsson
142	Nic Riopel
153	Dave Labrecque
172	**Eric Wellwood**
196	**Oliver Lauridsen**

2008

Pick	
19	**Luca Sbisa**
67	**Marc-Andre Bourdon**
84	Jacob Deserres
178	**Zac Rinaldo**
196	**Joacim Eriksson**

2007

Pick	
2	**James van Riemsdyk**
41	**Kevin Marshall**
66	Garrett Klotz
122	Mario Kempe
152	**Jon Kalinski**
161	**Patrick Maroon**
182	Brad Phillips

2006

Pick	
22	**Claude Giroux**
39	**Andreas Nodl**
42	Mike Ratchuk
55	Denis Bodrov
79	**Jon Matsumoto**
101	Joonas Lehtivuori
109	Jakub Kovar
145	**Jon Rheault**
175	Michael Dupont
205	Andrei Popov

2005

Pick	
29	**Steve Downie**
91	**Oskars Bartulis**
119	**Jeremy Duchesne**
152	Josh Beaulieu
174	John Flatters
215	Matt Clackson

2004

Pick	
92	Rob Bellamy
101	R.J. Anderson
124	**David Laliberte**
144	Chris Zarb
149	Gino Pisellini
170	Ladislav Scurko
171	Frederik Cabana
232	**Martin Houle**
253	Travis Gawryletz
286	**Triston Grant**
291	John Carter

2003

Pick	
11	**Jeff Carter**
24	**Mike Richards**
69	**Colin Fraser**
81	**Stefan Ruzicka**
85	**Alexandre Picard**
87	**Ryan Potulny**
95	Rick Kozak
108	Kevin Romy
140	David Tremblay
191	Rejean Beauchemin
193	Ville Hostikka

2002

Pick	
4	**Joni Pitkanen**
105	Rosario Ruggeri
126	Konstantin Baranov
161	Dov Grumet-Morris
192	Nikita Korovkin
193	**Joey Mormina**
201	Mathieu Brunelle

2001

Pick	
27	**Jeff Woywitka**
95	**Patrick Sharp**
146	**Jussi Timonen**
150	Bernd Bruckler
158	Roman Malek
172	**Dennis Seidenberg**
177	Andrei Razin
208	Thierry Douville
225	**David Printz**

General Managers' History

Bud Poile, 1967-68, 1968-69; Bud Poile and Keith Allen, 1969-70; Keith Allen, 1970-71 to 1982-83; Bob McCammon, 1983-84; Bob Clarke, 1984-85 to 1989-90; Russ Farwell, 1990-91 to 1993-94; Bob Clarke, 1994-95 to 2005-06; Bob Clarke and Paul Holmgren, 2006-07; Paul Holmgren, 2007-08 to 2013-14; Ron Hextall, 2014-15 to date.

Ron Hextall

General Manager

Born: Brandon, MB, May 3, 1964.

Ron Hextall was named general manager of the Philadelphia Flyers on May 7, 2014 after serving as assistant GM and director of hockey operations during the 2013-14 season. Hextall returned to the Flyers after spending the previous seven seasons with the Los Angeles Kings, where he held the title of vice president and assistant general manager. In Los Angeles, Hextall assisted in all facets of the Kings' hockey operations department while helping the team win the 2012 Stanley Cup championship. He also served as the general manager of the Manchester Monarchs, Los Angeles's primary affiliate in the American Hockey League.

Prior to joining the Kings, Hextall spent seven seasons in the Flyers front office. He became a pro scout in 1999 upon his retirement as a player, and served in that role for three seasons before being promoted to director of pro player personnel in 2002. In his front office positions with the Flyers, Hextall was instrumental in the club's three Atlantic Division titles and two trips to the Eastern Conference Finals while the club averaged nearly 102 points per season.

Hextall played 11 years of his 13-year career with the Flyers, while also playing a year each with Quebec and the New York Islanders. He led the Flyers to the Stanley Cup Final in his rookie season of 1986-87, winning the Vezina Trophy as the NHL's top goaltender and the Conn Smythe Trophy as Most Valuable Player in the 1987 Stanley Cup Final, despite losing to the Edmonton Oilers in seven games. He was also named to both the NHL All-Rookie and NHL First All-Star Teams that season. Hextall played for the Flyers until 1992 and then returned to Philadelphia from 1994 until his retirement in 1999, making another trip to the Stanley Cup Final in 1997. He is the franchise's all-time leader among goaltenders in games played (489) and wins (240), while ranking third in shutouts (18). His NHL career included a total of 608 regular season games, a 296-214-69 record including 23 shutouts, a 2.97 goals-against-average and a .895 save-percentage. On December 8, 1987, he became the first goaltender in the history of the NHL to score a goal by shooting the puck into the net as the Flyers defeated the Boston Bruins by a score of 5-2 at the Spectrum. On April 11, 1989, during a Flyers 8-5 playoff victory against the Washington Capitals at the Capital Centre, he collected his second career goal and became the first goalie to score a goal in an NHL playoff game.

A native of Brandon, Manitoba, Hextall was originally selected by the Flyers in the sixth-round (119th overall) of the 1982 NHL Draft. He is the fourth Hextall to play in the NHL following his father, Bryan Jr., his grandfather, Hall of Famer Bryan, Sr., and his uncle Dennis, who played for the Kings during the 1969-70 season. His son Brett was drafted by the Phoenix Coyotes in the sixth-round of the 2008 NHL Draft.

Club Directory

Wells Fargo Center

Philadelphia Flyers
Wells Fargo Center
3601 South Broad Street
Philadelphia, PA 19148-5290
Phone **215/465-4500**
PR FAX 215/218-7837
www.philadelphiaflyers.com
Capacity: 19,541

Executive Management

Chairman and Governor	Ed Snider
President and COO, Comcast-Spectacor	Dave Scott
President, Philadelphia Flyers	Paul Holmgren
General Manager	Ron Hextall
Senior Vice President	Bob Clarke
Alternate Governors	Paul Holmgren, Shawn Tilger, Phil Weinberg
COO, Business Operations	Shawn Tilger
Executive Assistants	Sharon Allison, Cheri Arnao, Ann Marie Nasuti

Hockey Club Personnel

Assistant General Manager	Barry Hanrahan
Head Coach	Dave Hakstol
Assistant Coaches	Gord Murphy, Joe Mullen, Ian Laperriere
Goaltending Coach / Video Coach	Kim Dillabaugh / /Adam Patterson
Director of Scouting	Chris Pryor
Head Pro Scout	Dave Brown
Pro Scouts	John Chapman, Ross Fitzpatrick, Al Hill, Ilkka Sinisalo
College Scouts	Wade Clarke
Amateur Scouts	Mark Greig, Joakim Grundberg, Todd Hearty, Ken Hoodikoff, Jack McIlhargey, Simon Nolet, Dennis Patterson, Rick Pracey, Nick Pryor, Vaclav Slansky
Scouting Consultant	Bill Barber
Player Development	Kjell Samuelsson, John Riley, Brady Robinson
Director of Team Services	Bryan Hardenbergh
Manager of Hockey Analytics	Ian Anderson
Executive Asst. / Administrative Asst.	Dianna Taylor / Jody Clarke

Medical/Training

Director of Medical Services	Jim McCrossin
Assistant Athletic Trainer	Sal Raffa
Strength & Conditioning Coach	Ryan Podell
Massage Therapist	Jack Kelly
Team Physicians	Peter DeLuca, M.D.; Gary Dorshimer, M.D.; Guy Lanzi, D.M.D.; Frank Brady, D.C.
Head Equipment Manager	Derek Settlemyre
Equipment Managers	Harry Bricker, Anthony Oratorio
Assistant Equipment Trainer	Mike Craytor

Business Development

Vice President, Business Development	Rob Johnson
Digital Media Manager / Specialist	Samantha Wood / Christine Mina
Corporate Partnerships Manager	Steve Coskey

Communications

Senior Director, Communications	Zack Hill
Director, Public Relations	Joe Siville
Manager, Broadcasting & Media Services	Brian Smith

Customer Service

Vice President, Revenue Support	Cindy Stutman
Senior Manager, Customer Service	Courtney Sams
Customer Service Account Managers	Vincent Galasso, Niles McFate, Sean Naylor, Michelle Siporin
Client Communications Manager / Coord.	Shannon Bowes / TBD
Season Ticket Holder Programs/Services Coord.	Amanda Perkins

Finance

Chief Financial Officer	Angelo Cardone
Controller / Senior Accountants	Judy Zdunkiewicz / Ryan Gilles, Chris Boyer
Staff Accountants	Eric Wojciechowski, Candy McKnight
Payroll Accountant / Accounting Clerk	Renee Eiler / Michele Dominic

Marketing

Marketing Senior Director / Manager	Joe Heller / Hung Tran
Game Presentation Senior Director / Manager	Anthony Gioia / Corinne Yamada
Senior Manager, Community Relations	Jason Tempesta
Manager, Youth & Amateur Hockey	Rob Baer
Ambassadors of Hockey	Bob Kelly, Bernie Parent
Fan Relations Assistant	Jerry Callahan
Producer/Director	Artie Halstead
Graphics Designer / Video Editor	Mike Cahill / Chris Shay
Public Address Announcer / Anthem Singer	Lou Nolan / Lauren Hart

Ticket Sales

Vice President, Sales	Bryan Anton
Ticket Sales Director / Coordinator	Ilkka Kortesluoma / Samantha Clapp
Direct Marketing Manager	Justine Pletnick
Managers, Sales / Client Development	Dan Ryan / James Darlington
Account Executives	Josh Wentz, Nick Marchesiello, Ryan Pirrone, Charlie Wanner
Group Sales Account Executive	Steve Luongo
Client Development Executives	Fran Walmsley, Vicki Rees-Jones, Brendan Fuller, Danielle Kuhman, Rick Halverson, Charles O'Donnell
Sales Associates	Chris McLendon, Matt Trichon, Dave Tierno, Gino Catena, Asher Halbert, Matt Lantieri, Cameron Lucas, John Kramer, Mike Miller

Ticketing

Vice President, Ticket Operations	Cecilia Baker
Director, Ticketing	Dan McGinnes
Ticket Office Manager / Asst. Manager	Linda Fleischer / Michael Snyder
Ticket Operations Coordinator	Brian Hawkins

Broadcast

TV Rightsholders	Comcast SportsNet, The Comcast Network (TCN)
TV Play-by-Play / Color	Jim Jackson / Keith Jones, Bill Clement
Rinkside Analyst	Chris Therien
Radio Rightsholder	97.5 The Fanatic
Radio Play-by-Play / Color	Tim Saunders / Steve Coates

Key Off-Season Signings/Acquisitions

2015

June 29 • Re-signed D **Ian Cole**.

July 1 • Acquired RW **Phil Kessel**, RW **Tyler Biggs** and D **Tim Erixon** from Toronto for RW **Kasperi Kapanen**, C **Nick Spaling**, D **Scott Harrington** and a 3rd-round choice in the 2016 NHL Draft.

1 • Signed D **David Warsofsky**, D **Steve Oleksy** and LW **Kael Mouillierat**.

9 • Re-signed D **Brian Dumoulin**.

13 • Re-signed RW **Bobby Farnham**.

15 • Re-signed RW **Beau Bennett**.

17 • Re-signed C **Dominik Uher**.

28 • Acquired C **Nick Bonino**, D **Adam Clendening** and a 2nd-round choice in the 2016 NHL Draft from Vancouver for C **Brandon Sutter** and a 3rd-round choice in 2016.

28 • Signed C **Eric Fehr**.

Aug. 6 • Signed C **Matt Cullen**.

2015-16 Schedule

Oct.	Thu.	8	at Dallas		Tue.	12	at Carolina	
	Sat.	10	at Arizona		Fri.	15	at Tampa Bay	
	Tue.	13	Montreal		Sun.	17	Carolina*	
	Thu.	15	Ottawa		Mon.	18	at St. Louis	
	Sat.	17	Toronto		Thu.	21	Philadelphia	
	Tue.	20	Florida		Sat.	23	Vancouver*	
	Thu.	22	Dallas		Sun.	24	at Washington*	
	Sat.	24	at Nashville		Tue.	26	New Jersey	
	Wed.	28	at Washington	**Feb.**	Tue.	2	Ottawa	
	Thu.	29	Buffalo		Fri.	5	at Tampa Bay	
	Sat.	31	at Toronto		Sat.	6	at Florida	
Nov.	Wed.	4	at Vancouver		Mon.	8	Anaheim	
	Fri.	6	at Edmonton		Wed.	10	NY Rangers	
	Sat.	7	at Calgary		Fri.	12	at Carolina	
	Wed.	11	Montreal		Mon.	15	at Florida	
	Fri.	13	Columbus		Thu.	18	Detroit	
	Sat.	14	at New Jersey		Sat.	20	Tampa Bay*	
	Tue.	17	Minnesota		Sun.	21	at Buffalo*	
	Thu.	19	Colorado		Wed.	24	at Boston	
	Sat.	21	San Jose		Sat.	27	Winnipeg*	
	Wed.	25	St. Louis		Mon.	29	Arizona	
	Fri.	27	at Columbus	**Mar.**	Thu.	3	NY Rangers	
	Sat.	28	Edmonton		Sat.	5	Calgary*	
Dec.	Tue.	1	at San Jose		Sun.	6	at New Jersey*	
	Sat.	5	at Los Angeles*		Tue.	8	at NY Islanders	
	Sun.	6	at Anaheim*		Fri.	11	at Columbus	
	Wed.	9	at Colorado		Sun.	13	at NY Rangers*	
	Fri.	11	Los Angeles		Tue.	15	NY Islanders	
	Mon.	14	Washington		Thu.	17	Carolina	
	Wed.	16	at Boston		Sat.	19	at Philadelphia*	
	Fri.	18	Boston		Sun.	20	Washington	
	Sat.	19	Carolina		Thu.	24	New Jersey	
	Mon.	21	Columbus		Sat.	26	at Detroit*	
	Sat.	26	at Minnesota		Sun.	27	at NY Rangers	
	Sun.	27	at Winnipeg		Tue.	29	Buffalo	
	Wed.	30	Toronto		Thu.	31	Nashville	
	Thu.	31	at Detroit	**Apr.**	Sat.	2	at NY Islanders*	
Jan.	Sat.	2	NY Islanders		Sun.	3	Philadelphia*	
	Tue.	5	Chicago		Tue.	5	at Ottawa	
	Wed.	6	at Chicago		Thu.	7	at Washington	
	Sat.	9	at Montreal		Sat.	9	at Philadelphia*	

Denotes afternoon game.

Retired Numbers

21	Michel Brière	1969-1970
66	Mario Lemieux	1984-2006

METROPOLITAN DIVISION 49th NHL Season

Franchise date: June 5, 1967

Pittsburgh Penguins

2014-15 Results: 43w-27L-6OTL-6SOL 98PTS
4TH, Metropolitan Division • 8TH, Eastern Conference

Sidney Crosby led the NHL with an average of 1.09 points per game in the 77 games he played in 2014-15. Overall, he finished third in the race for the Art Ross Trophy with 84 points on 28 goals and 56 assists.

Year-by-Year Record

Season	GP	Home W	L	T	OL	Road W	L	T	OL	Overall W	L	T	OL	GF	GA	Pts.	Div. Fin.	Conf. Fin.	Playoff Result
2014-15	82	23	14	....	4	20	13	....	8	43	27	....	12	221	210	98	4th, Met.	8th, East	Lost First Round
2013-14	82	28	9	....	4	23	15	....	3	51	24	....	7	249	207	109	1st, Met.	2nd, East	Lost Second Round
2012-13	48	18	6	....	0	18	6	....	0	36	12	....	0	165	119	72	1st, Atl.	1st, East	Lost Conf. Final
2011-12	82	29	10	....	2	22	15	....	4	51	25	....	6	282	221	108	2nd, Atl.	4th, East	Lost Conf. Quarter-Final
2010-11	82	25	14	....	2	24	11	....	6	49	25	....	8	238	199	106	2nd, Atl.	4th, East	Lost Conf. Quarter-Final
2009-10	82	25	12	....	4	22	16	....	3	47	28	....	7	257	237	101	2nd, Atl.	4th, East	Lost Conf. Semi-Final
2008-09	82	25	13	....	3	20	15	....	6	45	28	....	9	264	239	99	2nd, Atl.	4th, East	**Won Stanley Cup**
2007-08	82	26	10	....	5	21	17	....	3	47	27	....	8	247	216	102	1st, Atl.	2nd, East	Lost Final
2006-07	82	26	10	....	5	21	14	....	6	47	24	....	11	277	246	105	2nd, Atl.	5th, East	Lost Conf. Quarter-Final
2005-06	82	12	21	....	8	10	25	....	6	22	46	....	14	244	316	58	5th, Atl.	15th, East	Out of Playoffs
2004-05																			
2003-04	82	13	22	6	0	10	25	2	4	23	47	8	4	190	303	58	5th, Atl.	15th, East	Out of Playoffs
2002-03	82	15	22	2	2	12	22	4	3	27	44	6	5	189	255	65	5th, Atl.	14th, East	Out of Playoffs
2001-02	82	16	20	4	1	12	21	4	4	28	41	8	5	198	249	69	5th, Atl.	12th, East	Out of Playoffs
2000-01	82	24	15	2	0	18	13	7	3	42	28	9	3	281	256	96	3rd, Atl.	6th, East	Lost Conf. Final
1999-2000	82	23	11	7	0	14	20	1	6	37	31	8	6	241	236	88	3rd, Atl.	7th, East	Lost Conf. Semi-Final
1998-99	82	21	10	10	....	17	20	4	....	38	30	14	....	242	225	90	3rd, Atl.	8th, East	Lost Conf. Semi-Final
1997-98	82	25	12	16	....	19	14	8	....	40	24	18	....	228	188	98	1st, NE	2nd, East	Lost Conf. Quarter-Final
1996-97	82	25	11	5	....	13	25	3	....	38	36	8	....	285	280	84	2nd, NE	6th, East	Lost Conf. Quarter-Final
1995-96	82	32	9	0	....	17	20	4	....	49	29	4	....	362	284	102	1st, NE	2nd, East	Lost Conf. Final
1994-95	48	18	5	1	....	11	11	2	....	29	16	3	....	181	158	61	2nd, NE	2nd, East	Lost Conf. Semi-Final
1993-94	84	25	9	8	....	19	18	5	....	44	27	13	....	299	285	101	1st, NE	3rd, East	Lost Conf. Quarter-Final
1992-93	84	32	6	4	....	24	15	3	....	56	21	7	....	367	268	119	1st, Patrick		Lost Div. Final
1991-92	80	21	13	6	....	18	19	3	....	39	32	9	....	343	308	87	3rd, Patrick		**Won Stanley Cup**
1990-91	80	25	12	3	....	16	21	3	....	41	33	6	....	342	305	88	1st, Patrick		**Won Stanley Cup**
1989-90	80	22	15	3	....	10	25	5	....	32	40	8	....	318	359	72	5th, Patrick		Out of Playoffs
1988-89	80	24	13	3	....	16	20	4	....	40	33	7	....	347	349	87	2nd, Patrick		Lost Div. Final
1987-88	80	22	12	6	....	14	23	3	....	36	35	9	....	319	316	81	6th, Patrick		Out of Playoffs
1986-87	80	19	15	6	....	11	23	6	....	30	38	12	....	297	290	72	5th, Patrick		Out of Playoffs
1985-86	80	20	15	5	....	14	23	3	....	34	38	8	....	313	305	76	5th, Patrick		Out of Playoffs
1984-85	80	17	20	3	....	7	31	2	....	24	51	5	....	276	385	53	6th, Patrick		Out of Playoffs
1983-84	80	7	29	4	....	9	29	2	....	16	58	6	....	254	390	38	6th, Patrick		Out of Playoffs
1982-83	80	14	22	4	....	4	31	5	....	18	53	9	....	257	394	45	6th, Patrick		Out of Playoffs
1981-82	80	21	11	8	....	10	25	5	....	31	36	13	....	310	337	75	4th, Patrick		Lost Div. Semi-Final
1980-81	80	21	16	3	....	9	21	10	....	30	37	13	....	302	345	73	3rd, Norris		Lost Prelim. Round
1979-80	80	20	13	7	....	10	24	6	....	30	37	13	....	251	303	73	3rd, Norris		Lost Prelim. Round
1978-79	80	23	12	5	....	13	19	8	....	36	31	13	....	281	279	85	2nd, Norris		Lost Quarter-Final
1977-78	80	16	15	9	....	9	22	9	....	25	37	18	....	254	321	68	4th, Norris		Out of Playoffs
1976-77	80	22	12	6	....	12	21	7	....	34	33	13	....	240	252	81	3rd, Norris		Lost Prelim. Round
1975-76	80	23	11	6	....	12	22	6	....	35	33	12	....	339	303	82	3rd, Norris		Lost Prelim. Round
1974-75	80	25	5	10	....	12	23	5	....	37	28	15	....	326	289	89	3rd, Norris		Lost Quarter-Final
1973-74	78	15	18	6	....	13	23	3	....	28	41	9	....	242	273	65	5th, West		Out of Playoffs
1972-73	78	24	11	4	....	8	26	5	....	32	37	9	....	257	265	73	5th, West		Out of Playoffs
1971-72	78	18	15	6	....	8	23	8	....	26	38	14	....	220	258	66	4th, West		Lost Quarter-Final
1970-71	78	18	12	9	....	3	25	11	....	21	37	20	....	221	240	62	6th, West		Out of Playoffs
1969-70	76	17	13	8	....	9	25	4	....	26	38	12	....	182	238	64	2nd, West		Lost Semi-Final
1968-69	76	12	20	6	....	8	25	5	....	20	45	11	....	189	252	51	5th, West		Out of Playoffs
1967-68	74	15	12	10	....	12	22	3	....	27	34	13	....	195	216	67	5th, West		Out of Playoffs

2015-16 Player Personnel

FORWARDS	HT	WT	*Age	Place of Birth	S	2014-15 Club
ARCHIBALD, Josh	5-10	176	23	Regina, SK	R	Wheeling-Wilkes-Barre
BENNETT, Beau	6-2	195	23	Gardena, CA	R	Pittsburgh-Wilkes-Barre
BIGGS, Tyler	6-2	205	22	Binghamton, NY	R	Orlando-Toronto (AHL)
BONINO, Nick	6-1	196	27	Hartford, CT	L	Vancouver
CROSBY, Sidney	5-11	200	28	Cole Harbour, NS	L	Pittsburgh
CULLEN, Matt	6-1	200	38	Virginia, MN	L	Nashville
DEA, Jean-Sebastien	6-11	175	21	Laval, QC	R	Wheeling-Wilkes-Barre
DUPUIS, Pascal	6-1	205	36	Laval, QC	L	Pittsburgh
FARNHAM, Bobby	5-10	188	26	North Andover, MA	L	Pittsburgh-Wilkes-Barre
FEHR, Eric	6-4	212	30	Winkler, MB	R	Washington
HORNQVIST, Patric	5-11	189	28	Sollentuna, Sweden	R	Pittsburgh
KESSEL, Phil	6-0	202	28	Madison, WI	R	Toronto
KUHNHACKL, Tom	6-2	196	23	Landshut, Germany	L	Wilkes-Barre
KUNITZ, Chris	6-0	195	36	Regina, SK	L	Pittsburgh
MALKIN, Evgeni	6-3	195	29	Magnitogorsk, USSR	L	Pittsburgh
MARCANTUONI, Matia	6-0	200	21	Woodbridge, ON	R	Wheeling-Wilkes-Barre
MOUILLIERAT, Kael	6-0	188	28	Edmonton, AB	L	NY Islanders-Bridgeport
PERRON, David	6-0	198	27	Sherbrooke, QC	R	Edmonton-Pittsburgh
PLOTNIKOV, Sergei	6-2	205	25	Komsomolsk-na-Amur, Russia	L	Yaroslavl
PORTER, Kevin	6-0	190	29	Detroit, MI	L	Grand Rapids
RUST, Bryan	5-11	192	23	Pontiac, MI	R	Pittsburgh-Wilkes-Barre
SHEARY, Conor	5-9	175	23	Melrose, MA	L	Wilkes-Barre
SIMON, Dominik	5-11	176	21	Prague, Czech Rep.	L	Plzen
SUNDQVIST, Oscar	6-3	209	21	Boden, Sweden	R	Skelleftea
UHER, Dominik	6-1	202	22	Ostrava, Czech.	L	Pittsburgh-Wilkes-Barre
WILSON, Scott	5-11	184	23	Oakville, ON	L	Pittsburgh-Wilkes-Barre
ZLOBIN, Anton	5-11	209	22	Moscow, Russia	R	Wilkes-Barre
DEFENSEMEN						
ANDERSEN, Niclas	6-1	207	27	Grums, Sweden	L	Brynas
CLENDENING, Adam	5-11	187	22	Niagara Falls, NY	R	Chi-Rockford-Van-Utica
COLE, Ian	6-1	219	26	Ann Arbour, MI	L	St. Louis-Pittsburgh
DUMOULIN, Brian	6-4	219	24	Biddeford, ME	L	Pittsburgh-Wilkes-Barre
ERIXON, Tim	6-2	190	24	Port Chester, NY	L	Columbus-Chicago-Toronto
LETANG, Kris	6-0	201	28	Montreal, QC	R	Pittsburgh
LOVEJOY, Ben	6-2	205	31	Concord, NH	R	Anaheim-Pittsburgh
MAATTA, Olli	6-2	206	21	Jyvaskyla, Finland	L	Pittsburgh
McNEILL, Reid	6-4	215	23	London, ON	L	Wilkes-Barre
OLEKSY, Steve	6-0	190	29	Chesterfield, MI	R	Washington-Hershey
O'NEILL, Will	6-1	190	27	Boston, MA	L	St. John's
POULIOT, Derrick	5-11	195	21	Estevan, SK	L	Pittsburgh-Wilkes-Barre
RUOPP, Harrison	6-3	192	22	Zehner, SK	R	Wheeling-Wilkes-Barre
SCUDERI, Rob	6-1	212	36	Syosset, NY	L	Pittsburgh
WARSOFSKY, David	5-9	170	25	Marshfield, MA	L	Boston-Providence (AHL)

GOALTENDERS	HT	WT	*Age	Place of Birth	C	2014-15 Club
FLEURY, Marc-Andre	6-2	180	30	Sorel, QC	L	Pittsburgh
JARRY, Tristan	6-2	194	20	Surrey, BC	L	Edmonton
MURRAY, Matt	6-4	178	21	Thunder Bay, ON	L	Wilkes-Barre
ZATKOFF, Jeff	6-2	179	28	Detroit, MI	L	Pittsburgh-Wilkes-Barre

* – Age at start of 2015-16 season

Jim Rutherford

Executive Vice President and General Manager

Born: Beeton, ON, February 17, 1949.

Jim Rutherford was named general manager of the Pittsburgh Penguins on June 6, 2014. Rutherford, one of the most respected executives in hockey, was general manager of the Carolina/Hartford franchise for 20 years and led the Carolina Hurricanes to the Stanley Cup in 2006. He stepped down from that position in April of 2014. He had been expected to continue in an advisory role with the Hurricanes until the Penguins opportunity arose.

Rutherford was named general manager of the NHL's Hartford Whalers on June 28, 1994 and helped transition the club to Carolina in 1997. He also served as team president. He was named the NHL's Executive of the Year by The Hockey News in 2002 and 2006 and by The Sporting News in 2006. Under Rutherford's leadership, the Hurricanes made two trips to the Stanley Cup Final, winning the Eastern Conference championship in 2002 and 2006, reached the conference finals in 2009 and captured three division titles.

Rutherford played 13 seasons in the NHL as a goaltender, including parts of three seasons with the Penguins from 1971 to 1974. He was a first-round draft pick of the Detroit Red Wings in 1969 and played in the NHL from 1970 to 1983 with Detroit, Pittsburgh, Toronto and Los Angeles. He appeared in 115 games with the Penguins, posting a 44-49-14 record and a 3.14 goals-against average.

When his playing career ended, Rutherford joined the Compuware Sports Corporation as director of hockey operations in 1983. He oversaw youth and junior hockey for the Detroit-based company and was named general manager of the Windsor Spitfires of the Ontario Hockey League after Compuware bought the major junior franchise in 1984. He was honored as the OHL's Executive of the Year in 1987 and 1988.

2014-15 Scoring

* – rookie

Regular Season

Pos	#	Player	Team	GP	G	A	Pts	TOI	+/–	PIM	PP	SH	GW	S	S%
C	87	Sidney Crosby	PIT	77	28	56	84	19:58	5	47	10	0	3	237	11.8
C	71	Evgeni Malkin	PIT	69	28	42	70	18:58	–2	60	9	0	4	212	13.2
D	58	Kris Letang	PIT	69	11	43	54	25:29	12	79	2	1	1	197	5.6
R	72	Patric Hornqvist	PIT	64	25	26	51	17:39	12	38	6	0	4	220	11.4
L	39	David Perron	EDM	38	5	14	19	16:59	–17	20	0	0	1	74	6.8
			PIT	43	12	10	22	17:37	–8	42	3	0	1	122	9.8
			Total	81	17	24	41	17:19	–25	62	3	0	2	196	.8.7
L	14	Chris Kunitz	PIT	74	17	23	40	17:53	2	56	9	1	5	170	10.0
C	26	Daniel Winnik	TOR	58	7	18	25	16:50	15	19	0	0	0	70	10.0
			PIT	21	2	7	9	16:06	8	8	0	0	1	27	7.4
			Total	79	9	25	34	16:38	23	27	0	0	1	97	9.3
C	16	Brandon Sutter	PIT	80	21	12	33	17:19	6	14	3	4	4	180	11.7
L	17	Blake Comeau	PIT	61	16	15	31	15:17	6	65	0	0	5	147	10.9
R	23	Steve Downie	PIT	72	14	14	28	12:26	2	238	3	0	2	104	13.5
C	13	Nick Spaling	PIT	82	9	18	27	15:14	–2	26	1	0	0	90	10.0
D	7	Paul Martin	PIT	74	3	17	20	22:47	17	20	0	0	0	61	4.9
D	28	Ian Cole	STL	54	4	5	9	15:03	16	44	0	0	0	52	7.7
			PIT	20	1	7	8	18:29	–2	7	0	0	0	31	3.2
			Total	74	5	12	17	15:58	14	51	0	0	0	83	6.0
D	10	Christian Ehrhoff	PIT	49	3	11	14	21:45	8	26	0	0	3	110	2.7
D	12	Ben Lovejoy	ANA	40	1	10	11	18:33	3	17	0	0	0	50	2.0
			PIT	20	1	2	3	21:13	–7	8	0	0	0	36	2.8
			Total	60	2	12	14	19:26	–4	25	0	0	0	86	2.3
R	19	Beau Bennett	PIT	49	4	8	12	12:29	–1	16	0	0	1	81	4.9
L	9	Pascal Dupuis	PIT	16	6	5	11	16:38	2	4	2	0	1	44	13.6
C	40	Maxim Lapierre	STL	45	2	7	9	10:21	–2	16	0	0	0	43	4.7
			PIT	35	0	2	2	11:10	–13	16	0	0	0	43	0.0
			Total	80	2	9	11	10:42	–15	32	0	0	0	86	2.3
D	4	Rob Scuderi	PIT	82	1	9	10	19:08	9	17	0	0	0	52	1.9
D	3	Olli Maatta	PIT	20	1	8	9	20:42	1	10	0	0	0	27	3.7
D	51 *	Derrick Pouliot	PIT	34	2	5	7	17:32	–11	4	1	0	2	56	3.6
R	27	Craig Adams	PIT	70	1	6	7	9:44	–1	44	0	0	1	51	2.0
C	25	Andrew Ebbett	PIT	24	1	5	6	9:00	1	2	0	0	0	21	4.8
R	36 *	Bryan Rust	PIT	14	1	1	2	12:01	–3	4	0	0	0	34	2.9
D	8 *	Brian Dumoulin	PIT	8	1	0	1	15:40	0	2	0	0	0	4	25.0
C	59	Jayson Megna	PIT	12	0	1	1	11:02	–2	14	0	0	0	13	0.0
C	43 *	Scott Wilson	PIT	1	0	0	0	4:21	0	0	0	0	0	0	0.0
C	46 *	Dominik Uher	PIT	2	0	0	0	6:27	–1	0	0	0	0	0	0.0
D	44	Taylor Chorney	PIT	7	0	0	0	12:10	–1	0	0	0	0	4	0.0
D	6 *	Scott Harrington	PIT	10	0	0	0	15:48	–10	4	0	0	0	9	0.0
R	34 *	Bobby Farnham	PIT	11	0	0	0	7:10	0	24	0	0	0	6	0.0

Goaltending

No.	Goaltender	GPI	Mins	Avg	W	L	OT	EN	SO	GA	SA	Sv%	G	A	PIM
37	Jeff Zatkoff	1	37	1.62	0	1	0	0	0	1	17	.941	0	0	0
29	Marc-Andre Fleury	64	3776	2.32	34	20	9	5	10	146	1831	.920	0	1	6
1	Thomas Greiss	20	1159	2.59	9	6	3	2	0	50	546	.908	0	0	0
	Totals	**82**	**5002**	**2.45**	**43**	**27**	**12**	**7**	**10**	**204**	**2401**	**.915**			

Playoffs

Pos	#	Player	Team	GP	G	A	Pts	TOI	+/–	PIM	PP	SH	GW	OT	S	S%
C	87	Sidney Crosby	PIT	5	2	2	4	20:09	1	0	0	0	0	0	10	20.0
R	72	Patric Hornqvist	PIT	5	2	1	3	18:43	1	2	0	0	0	0	17	11.8
L	14	Chris Kunitz	PIT	5	1	2	3	18:11	2	8	1	0	1	0	6	16.7
C	16	Brandon Sutter	PIT	5	1	1	2	15:57	–1	2	1	0	0	0	12	8.3
C	13	Nick Spaling	PIT	5	1	1	2	13:40	1	4	0	0	0	0	5	20.0
D	7	Paul Martin	PIT	5	0	2	2	24:35	–3	2	0	0	0	0	5	0.0
R	23	Steve Downie	PIT	5	0	2	2	10:39	1	4	0	0	0	0	4	0.0
D	12	Ben Lovejoy	PIT	5	0	2	2	22:55	–3	0	0	0	0	0	10	0.0
D	28	Ian Cole	PIT	5	0	2	2	23:00	0	8	0	0	0	0	9	0.0
L	17	Blake Comeau	PIT	5	1	0	1	14:12	0	8	0	0	0	0	5	20.0
L	39	David Perron	PIT	5	0	1	1	17:17	–1	4	0	0	0	0	12	0.0
R	19	Beau Bennett	PIT	2	0	0	0	8:01	0	0	0	0	0	0	2	0.0
C	43 *	Scott Wilson	PIT	3	0	0	0	6:43	0	0	0	0	0	0	3	0.0
D	4	Rob Scuderi	PIT	5	0	0	0	21:59	0	0	0	0	0	0	2	0.0
C	40	Maxim Lapierre	PIT	5	0	0	0	13:58	–2	0	0	0	0	0	8	0.0
C	71	Evgeni Malkin	PIT	5	0	0	0	19:19	–1	0	0	0	0	0	11	0.0
C	26	Daniel Winnik	PIT	5	0	0	0	13:52	–6	2	0	0	0	0	2	0.0
D	44	Taylor Chorney	PIT	5	0	0	0	16:35	0	2	0	0	0	0	3	0.0
D	8 *	Brian Dumoulin	PIT	5	0	0	0	14:06	1	0	0	0	0	0	6	0.0

Goaltending

No.	Goaltender	GPI	Mins	Avg	W	L	EN	SO	GA	SA	Sv%	G	A	PIM
29	Marc-Andre Fleury	5	312	2.12	1	4	0	0	11	150	.927	0	0	0
	Totals	**5**	**314**	**2.10**	**1**	**4**	**0**	**0**	**11**	**150**	**.927**			

Coaching History

Red Sullivan, 1967-68, 1968-69; Red Kelly, 1969-70 to 1971-72; Red Kelly and Ken Schinkel, 1972-73; Ken Schinkel and Marc Boileau, 1973-74; Marc Boileau, 1974-75; Marc Boileau and Ken Schinkel, 1975-76; Ken Schinkel, 1976-77; Johnny Wilson, 1977-78 to 1979-80; Eddie Johnston, 1980-81 to 1982-83; Lou Angotti, 1983-84; Bob Berry, 1984-85 to 1986-87; Pierre Creamer, 1987-88; Gene Ubriaco, 1988-89; Gene Ubriaco and Craig Patrick, 1989-90; Bob Johnson, 1990-91; Scotty Bowman, 1991-92, 1992-93; Eddie Johnston, 1993-94 to 1995-96; Eddie Johnston and Craig Patrick, 1996-97; Kevin Constantine, 1997-98, 1998-99; Kevin Constantine and Herb Brooks, 1999-2000; Ivan Hlinka, 2000-01; Ivan Hlinka and Rick Kehoe, 2001-02; Rick Kehoe, 2002-03; Ed Olczyk, 2003-04, 2004-05; Ed Olczyk and Michel Therrien, 2005-06; Michel Therrien, 2006-07, 2007-08; Michel Therrien and Dan Bylsma, 2008-09; Dan Bylsma, 2009-10 to 2013-14; Mike Johnston, 2014-15 to date.

Club Records

Team

(Figures in brackets for season records are games played; records for fewest points, wins, ties, losses, goals, goals against are for 70 or more games)

Most Points	**119**	1992-93 (84)
Most Wins	**56**	1992-93 (84)
Most Ties	**20**	1970-71 (78)
Most Losses	**58**	1983-84 (80)
Most Goals	**367**	1992-93 (84)
Most Goals Against	**394**	1982-83 (80)
Fewest Points	**38**	1983-84 (80)
Fewest Wins	**16**	1983-84 (80)
Fewest Ties	**4**	1995-96 (82)
Fewest Losses	**21**	1992-93 (84)
Fewest Goals	**182**	1969-70 (76)
Fewest Goals Against	**188**	1997-98 (82)
Longest Winning Streak		
Overall	*17	Mar. 9-Apr. 10/93
Home	13	Nov. 15/13-Jan. 15/14
Away	7	Mar. 14-Apr. 9/93, Oct. 3-Nov. 3/09, Nov. 6-Dec. 11/10
Longest Undefeated Streak		
Overall	18	Mar. 9-Apr. 14/93 (17W, 1T)
Home	20	Nov. 30/74-Feb. 22/75 (12W, 8T)
Away	8	Mar. 14-Apr. 14/93 (7W, 1T)
Longest Losing Streak		
Overall	18	Jan. 13-Feb. 22/04
Home	*14	Dec. 31/03-Feb. 22/04
Away	18	Dec. 23/82-Mar. 4/83
Longest Winless Streak		
Overall	18	Jan. 2-Feb. 10/83 (17L, 1T), Jan. 13-Feb. 22/04 (18L)
Home	16	Dec. 31/03-Mar. 4/04 (15L, 1T/OL)
Away	18	Oct. 25/70-Jan. 14/71 (11L, 7T), Dec. 23/82-Mar. 4/83 (18L)
Most Shutouts, Season	**9**	1998-99 (82)
Most PIM, Season	**2,670**	1988-89 (80)
Most Goals, Game	**12**	Mar. 15/75 (Wsh. 1 at Pit. 12), Dec. 26/91 (Tor. 1 at Pit. 12)

Individual

Most Seasons	**17**	Mario Lemieux
Most Games	**915**	Mario Lemieux
Most Goals, Career	**690**	Mario Lemieux
Most Assists, Career	**1,033**	Mario Lemieux
Most Points, Career	**1,723**	Mario Lemieux (690G, 1,033A)
Most PIM, Career	**1,048**	Kevin Stevens
Most Shutouts, Career	**38**	Marc-Andre Fleury
Longest Consecutive Games Streak	**313**	Ron Schock (Oct. 24/73-Apr. 3/77)
Most Goals, Season	**85**	Mario Lemieux (1988-89)
Most Assists, Season	**114**	Mario Lemieux (1988-89)
Most Points, Season	**199**	Mario Lemieux (1988-89; 85G, 114A)
Most PIM, Season	**409**	Paul Baxter (1981-82)
Most Points, Defenseman, Season	**113**	Paul Coffey (1988-89; 30G, 83A)
Most Points, Center, Season	**199**	Mario Lemieux (1988-89; 85G, 114A)
Most Points, Right Wing, Season	***149**	Jaromir Jagr (1995-96; 62G, 87A)
Most Points, Left Wing, Season	**123**	Kevin Stevens (1991-92; 54G, 69A)
Most Points, Rookie, Season	**102**	Sidney Crosby (2005-06; 39G, 63A)
Most Shutouts, Season	**10**	Marc-Andre Fleury (2014-15)
Most Goals, Game	**5**	Mario Lemieux (Dec. 31/88), (Apr. 9/93), (Mar. 26/96)
Most Assists, Game	**6**	Ron Stackhouse (Mar. 8/75) Greg Malone (Nov. 28/79) Mario Lemieux (Oct. 15/88), (Dec. 5/92), (Nov. 1/95)
Most Points, Game	**8**	Mario Lemieux (Oct. 15/88; 2G, 6A), (Dec. 31/88; 5G, 3A)

* NHL Record.

General Managers' History

Jack Riley, 1967-68 to 1969-70; Red Kelly, 1970-71; Red Kelly and Jack Riley, 1971-72; Jack Riley, 1972-73; Jack Riley and Jack Button, 1973-74; Jack Button, 1974-75; Wren Blair, 1975-76; Wren Blair and Baz Bastien, 1976-77; Baz Bastien, 1977-78 to 1982-83; Eddie Johnston, 1983-84 to 1987-88; Tony Esposito, 1988-89; Tony Esposito and Craig Patrick, 1989-90; Craig Patrick, 1990-91 to 2005-06; Ray Shero, 2006-07 to 2013-14; Jim Rutherford, 2014-15 to date.

Captains' History

Ab McDonald, 1967-68; Earl Ingarfield and no captain, 1968-69; no captain, 1969-70 to 1972-73; Ron Schock, 1973-74 to 1976-77; Jean Pronovost, 1977-78; Orest Kindrachuk, 1978-79 to 1980-81; Randy Carlyle, 1981-82 to 1983-84; Mike Bullard, 1984-85, 1985-86; Mike Bullard and Terry Ruskowski, 1986-87; Dan Frawley and Mario Lemieux, 1987-88; Mario Lemieux, 1988-89 to 1993-94; Ron Francis, 1994-95; Mario Lemieux, 1995-96, 1996-97; Ron Francis, 1997-98; Jaromir Jagr, 1998-99 to 2000-01; Mario Lemieux, 2001-02 to 2004-05; Mario Lemieux and no captain, 2005-06; no captain, 2006-07; Sidney Crosby, 2007-08 to date.

All-time Record vs. Other Clubs

Regular Season

	Total								At Home								On Road							
	GP	W	L	T	OL	GF	GA	PTS	GP	W	L	T	OL	GF	GA	PTS	GP	W	L	T	OL	GF	GA	PTS
Anaheim	28	16	8	2	2	92	83	36	15	10	3	2	0	52	41	22	13	6	5	0	2	40	42	14
Arizona	72	41	28	3	0	259	226	85	36	24	12	0	0	136	97	48	36	17	16	3	0	123	129	37
Boston	195	67	102	21	5	600	743	160	99	41	40	15	3	331	345	100	96	26	62	6	2	269	398	60
Buffalo	179	80	62	35	2	582	582	197	90	48	23	18	1	333	265	115	89	32	39	17	1	249	317	82
Calgary	100	44	38	18	0	339	352	106	49	28	11	10	0	182	141	66	51	16	27	8	0	157	211	40
Carolina	133	64	53	11	5	477	464	144	65	34	24	6	1	246	223	75	68	30	29	5	4	231	241	69
Chicago	129	44	64	17	4	392	456	109	64	32	23	7	2	225	202	73	65	12	41	10	2	167	254	36
Colorado	80	35	37	7	1	299	318	78	42	19	18	5	0	160	160	43	38	16	19	2	1	139	158	35
Columbus	23	15	6	0	2	78	65	32	11	8	3	0	0	38	27	16	12	7	3	0	2	40	38	16
Dallas	138	66	59	12	1	484	450	145	68	42	20	6	0	256	187	90	70	24	39	6	1	228	263	55
Detroit	145	64	62	16	3	500	494	147	73	48	21	4	0	297	215	100	72	16	41	12	3	203	279	47
Edmonton	70	29	35	4	2	248	299	64	35	19	13	3	0	137	141	41	35	10	22	1	2	111	158	23
Florida	82	43	31	4	4	234	231	94	41	25	12	3	1	125	109	54	41	18	19	1	3	109	122	40
Los Angeles	152	63	70	18	1	477	516	145	78	42	26	10	0	280	240	94	74	21	44	8	1	197	276	51
Minnesota	17	6	9	1	1	40	51	14	9	3	5	0	1	20	29	7	8	3	4	1	0	20	22	7
Montreal	201	60	110	23	8	571	784	151	101	39	46	13	3	306	347	94	100	21	64	10	5	265	437	57
Nashville	21	9	9	2	1	57	63	21	10	4	3	2	1	30	28	11	11	5	6	0	0	27	35	10
New Jersey	221	95	101	17	8	710	717	215	109	56	45	4	4	379	337	120	112	39	56	13	4	331	380	95
NY Islanders	236	111	96	22	7	835	832	251	120	63	40	14	3	449	386	143	116	48	56	8	4	386	446	108
NY Rangers	262	116	113	23	10	876	932	265	130	62	49	14	5	448	437	143	132	54	64	9	5	428	495	122
Ottawa	91	48	30	9	4	299	266	109	45	25	13	4	3	151	124	57	46	23	17	5	1	148	142	52
Philadelphia	273	93	143	30	7	831	988	223	137	60	54	22	1	475	444	143	136	33	89	8	6	356	544	80
St. Louis	139	51	65	18	5	433	462	125	69	33	22	12	2	248	202	80	70	18	43	6	3	185	260	45
San Jose	33	13	13	3	4	118	96	33	14	7	4	1	2	54	41	17	19	6	9	2	2	64	55	16
Tampa Bay	83	45	29	5	4	270	229	99	42	27	9	3	3	160	106	60	41	18	20	2	1	110	123	39
Toronto	173	80	71	17	5	624	613	182	87	47	33	6	1	346	284	101	86	33	38	11	4	278	329	81
Vancouver	110	61	37	11	1	437	384	134	55	35	13	7	0	237	185	77	55	26	24	4	1	200	199	57
Washington	208	101	86	16	5	753	734	223	103	57	37	7	2	382	321	123	105	44	49	9	3	371	413	100
Winnipeg	55	42	10	0	3	211	145	87	27	23	3	0	1	119	71	47	28	19	7	0	2	92	74	40
Defunct Clubs	69	35	16	18	0	256	194	88	35	22	6	7	0	148	93	51	34	13	10	11	0	108	101	37
Totals	**3718**	**1637**	**1593**	**383**	**105**	**12382**	**12769**	**3762**	**1859**	**983**	**631**	**205**	**40**	**6750**	**5828**	**2211**	**1859**	**654**	**962**	**178**	**65**	**5632**	**6941**	**1551**

Playoffs

	Series	W	L	GP	W	L	T	GF	GA	Last Mtg.	Rnd.	Result
Boston	5	2	3	23	10	13	0	69	74	2013	CF	L 0-4
Buffalo	2	2	0	10	6	4	0	26	26	2001	CSF	W 4-3
Carolina	1	1	0	4	4	0	0	20	9	2009	CF	W 4-0
Chicago	2	1	1	8	4	4	0	23	24	1992	F	W 4-0
Columbus	1	1	0	6	4	2	0	21	18	2014	FR	W 4-2
*Dallas	2	2	0	10	8	2	0	54	32	1991	F	W 4-2
Detroit	2	1	1	13	6	7	0	24	34	2009	F	W 4-3
Florida	1	0	1	7	3	4	0	15	20	1996	CF	L 3-4
Montreal	2	0	2	13	5	8	0	33	37	2010	CSF	L 3-4
New Jersey	5	3	2	29	14	15	0	80	86	2001	CF	L 1-4
NY Islanders	4	1	3	25	12	13	0	83	84	2013	CQF	W 4-2
NY Rangers	6	4	2	32	20	12	0	101	83	2015	FR	L 1-4
Ottawa	4	3	1	20	13	7	0	72	53	2013	CSF	W 4-1
Philadelphia	6	2	4	35	16	19	0	115	121	2012	CQF	L 2-4
St. Louis	3	1	2	13	6	7	0	40	45	1981	PR	L 2-3
Tampa Bay	1	0	1	7	3	4	0	14	22	2011	CQF	L 3-4
Toronto	3	0	3	12	4	8	0	27	39	1999	CSF	L 2-4
Washington	8	7	1	49	30	19	0	164	143	2009	CSF	W 4-3
Totals	**58**	**31**	**27**	**316**	**168**	**148**	**0**	**981**	**950**			

* Includes series with Oakland 1980.

Calgary totals include Atlanta Flames, 1972-73 to 1979-80. Carolina totals include Hartford, 1979-80 to 1996-97.
Colorado totals include Quebec, 1979-80 to 1994-95. Dallas totals include Minnesota North Stars, 1967-68 to 1992-93.
New Jersey totals include Kansas City, 1974-75, 1975-76, and Colorado Rockies, 1976-77 to 1981-82.
Phoenix totals include Winnipeg, 1979-80 to 1995-96. Winnipeg totals include Atlanta Thrashers, 1999-2000 to 2010-11.

Playoff Results 2015-2011

Year	Round	Opponent	Result	GF	GA
2015	FR	NY Rangers	L 1-4	8	11
2014	SR	NY Rangers	L 3-4	14	15
	FR	Columbus	W 4-2	21	18
2013	CF	Boston	L 0-4	2	12
	CSF	Ottawa	W 4-1	22	11
	CQF	NY Islanders	W 4-2	25	17
2012	CQF	Philadelphia	L 2-4	26	30
2011	CQF	Tampa Bay	L 3-4	14	22

Abbreviations: Round: F – Final; **CF** – conference final; **CSF** – conference semi-final; **SR** – second round; **CQF** – conference quarter-final; **FR** – first round; **PR** – preliminary round.

2014-15 Results

Oct.	9	Anaheim	6-4
	11	at Toronto	5-2
	16	Dallas	2-3
	18	NY Islanders	3-1
	22	Philadelphia	3-5
	23	at Detroit	3-4*
	25	at Nashville	3-0
	28	New Jersey	8-3
	30	Los Angeles	3-0
Nov.	1	Buffalo	5-0
	4	at Minnesota	4-1
	6	at Winnipeg	4-3†
	8	at Buffalo	6-1
	11	at NY Rangers	0-5
	14	at Toronto	2-1
	15	NY Rangers	3-2†
	18	at Montreal	4-0
	21	NY Islanders	4-5†
	22	at NY Islanders	1-4
	24	at Boston	3-2*
	26	Toronto	4-3*
	28	Carolina	2-4
	29	at Carolina	3-2
Dec.	2	New Jersey	1-0
	4	Vancouver	0-3
	6	Ottawa	3-2
	8	at NY Rangers	3-4*
	12	Calgary	3-1
	13	at Columbus	3-4†
	15	Tampa Bay	4-2
	18	Colorado	1-0*
	20	Florida	3-1
	22	at Florida	3-4†
	23	at Tampa Bay	3-4
	27	Washington	0-3
	29	at New Jersey	1-3
	31	Carolina	2-1
Jan.	2	Tampa Bay	6-3
	3	Montreal	1-4
	7	Boston	2-3*
	10	at Montreal	2-1*
	13	Minnesota	7-2
	16	at NY Islanders	3-6
	18	NY Rangers	2-5
	20	at Philadelphia	2-3*
	21	Chicago	2-3†
	27	Winnipeg	5-3
	28	at Washington	0-4
	30	at New Jersey	2-1*
Feb.	1	Nashville	0-4
	4	at Edmonton	2-0
	6	at Calgary	4-0
	7	at Vancouver	0-5
	11	Detroit	4-1
	12	at Ottawa	5-4†
	15	at Chicago	1-2†
	17	Washington	1-3
	19	Columbus	1-2
	21	at St. Louis	4-2
	22	Florida	5-1
	25	at Washington	4-3
Mar.	1	Columbus	5-3
	4	at Colorado	1-3
	6	at Anaheim	5-2
	7	at Los Angeles	1-0*
	9	at San Jose	1-2†
	12	Edmonton	6-4
	14	Boston	0-2
	15	Detroit	1-5
	17	at New Jersey	0-2
	19	at Dallas	1-2
	21	at Arizona	3-1
	24	St. Louis	2-3*
	26	at Carolina	2-5
	28	Arizona	3-2
	29	San Jose	3-2†
Apr.	1	Philadelphia	1-4
	4	at Columbus	3-5
	5	at Philadelphia	1-4
	7	at Ottawa	3-4*
	10	NY Islanders	1-3
	11	at Buffalo	2-0

* – Overtime † – Shootout

NHL Draft Selections 2015-2001

Name in bold denotes played in NHL.

2015
Pick
46 Daniel Sprong
137 Dominik Simon
167 Frederik Tiffels
197 Nikita Pavlychev

2014
Pick
22 Kasperi Kapanen
113 Sam Lafferty
145 Anthony Angello
173 Jaden Lindo
203 Jeff Taylor

2013
Pick
44 Tristan Jarry
77 Jake Guentzel
119 Ryan Segalla
164 Dane Birks
179 Blaine Byron
209 Troy Josephs

2012
Pick
8 **Derrick Pouliot**
22 **Olli Maatta**
52 Teddy Blueger
81 Oscar Sundqvist
83 Matt Murray
92 Matia Marcantuoni
113 Sean Maguire
143 Clark Seymour
173 Anton Zlobin

2011
Pick
23 **Joe Morrow**
54 **Scott Harrington**
144 **Dominik Uher**
174 Josh Archibald
209 **Scott Wilson**

2010
Pick
20 **Beau Bennett**
80 **Bryan Rust**
110 Tom Kuhnhackl
140 **Kenny Agostino**
152 Joe Rogalski
170 Reid McNeill

2009
Pick
30 **Simon Despres**
61 **Philip Samuelsson**
63 **Ben Hanowski**
121 Nick Petersen
123 Alex Velischek
151 Andy Bathgate
181 Viktor Ekbom

2008
Pick
120 Nathan Moon
150 **Alexander Pechurski**
180 Patrick Killeen
210 Nick D'Agostino

2007
Pick
20 Angelo Esposito
51 Keven Veilleux
78 **Robert Bortuzzo**
80 Casey Pierro-Zabotel
111 **Luca Caputi**
118 **Alex Grant**
141 **Jake Muzzin**
171 **Dustin Jeffrey**

2006
Pick
2 **Jordan Staal**
32 **Carl Sneep**
65 **Brian Strait**
125 **Chad Johnson**
185 Timo Seppanen

2005
Pick
1 **Sidney Crosby**
61 Michael Gergen
62 **Kris Letang**
125 Tommi Leinonen
126 Tim Crowder
194 Jean-Philippe Paquet
195 **Joe Vitale**

2004
Pick
2 **Evgeni Malkin**
31 Johannes Salmonsson
61 **Alex Goligoski**
67 **Nick Johnson**
85 Brian Gifford
99 **Tyler Kennedy**
130 Michal Sersen
164 Moises Gutierrez
194 Chris Peluso
222 Jordan Morrison
228 David Brown
259 Brian Ihnacak

2003
Pick
1 **Marc-Andre Fleury**
32 **Ryan Stone**
70 **Jonathan Filewich**
73 **Daniel Carcillo**
121 **Paul Bissonnette**
161 Evgeni Isakov
169 Lukas Bolf
199 **Andy Chiodo**
229 Stephen Dixon
232 **Joe Jensen**
263 **Matt Moulson**

2002
Pick
5 **Ryan Whitney**
35 Ondrej Nemec
69 **Erik Christensen**
101 Daniel Fernholm
136 Andrew Sertich
137 **Cam Paddock**
171 Robert Goepfert
202 Patrik Baertschi
234 **Max Talbot**
239 Ryan Lannon
265 Dwight Labrosse

2001
Pick
21 **Colby Armstrong**
54 **Noah Welch**
86 **Drew Fata**
96 Alexandre Rouleau
120 **Tomas Surovy**
131 Ben Eaves
156 Andy Schneider
217 Tomas Duba
250 Brandon Crawford-West

Mike Johnston

Head Coach

Born: Dartmouth, NS, February 19, 1957.

Pittsburgh Penguins executive vice president and general manager Jim Rutherford named Mike Johnston the team's head coach on June 25, 2014. Johnston has a long coaching resume that includes eight seasons as an assistant/associate coach in the NHL with the Vancouver Canucks from 1999 to 2006 and the Los Angeles Kings from 2006 to 2008.

For the previous six seasons before taking over in Pittsburgh, Johnson was the head coach and general manager of the Portland Winter Hawks of the Western Hockey League. His teams reached the WHL final in each of his last four seasons. Johnston also worked full-time for Canada's national team for five seasons from 1994 to 1999, serving in varying roles as associate coach, head coach and general manager. He was head coach of Team Canada at the 1999 World Championships and also was an assistant coach for Canada at the Olympics (1998), at the World Championships (six times) and the World Junior Championships (twice). His international accomplishments include five medals at the World Championships (two gold, two silver and one bronze) and two gold medals at the World Junior Championships.

Johnston played collegiate hockey at Acadia University from 1975 to 1978 and at Brandon University from 1978 to 1980. He began his head coaching career at Camrose Lutheran College in 1982, and later worked as an assistant coach at the University of Calgary before landing the head coaching job at the University of New Brunswick in 1989.

Johnston has co-authored two hockey books with former NHL player Ryan Walter: "Simply The Best: Insights and Strategies From Great Hockey Coaches" and "Hockey Plays and Strategies."

Coaching Record

			Regular Season				Playoffs			
Season	**Team**	**League**	**GC**	**W**	**L**	**O/T**	**GC**	**W**	**L**	**T**
1982-83	Camrose	ACAC	24	12	12	0	2	0	2	0
1983-84	Camrose	ACAC	25	15	10	0	2	0	2	0
1984-85	Camrose	ACAC	25	14	11	0	2	0	2	0
1985-86	Camrose	ACAC	25	14	9	2	2	0	2	0
1986-87	Camrose	ACAC	25	13	11	1	3	1	2	0
1986-87	Camrose	CCAA	....	....	....	....	4	2	2	0
1989-90	U of New Brunswick	AUS	21	11	9	1	3	1	2	0
1990-91	U of New Brunswick	AUS	26	12	11	3	3	1	2	0
1991-92	U of New Brunswick	AUS	26	18	7	1	4	2	2	0
1992-93	U of New Brunswick	AUS	26	18	7	1	6	4	2	0
1993-94	U of New Brunswick	AUS	26	16	9	1	7	4	3	0
1998-99	Canada	Exhib	46	21	17	8	9	6	3	0
2008-09	Portland	WHL	56	16	35	5	....	....	....	....
2009-10	Portland	WHL	70	42	25	3	13	6	7	0
2010-11	Portland	WHL	72	50	19	3	21	13	8	0
2011-12	Portland	WHL	71	49	18	4	22	15	7	0
2012-13	Portland	WHL	24	20	4	0	....	....	....	....
2013-14	Portland	WHL	72	54	13	5	21	15	6	0
2014-15	**Pittsburgh**	**NHL**	**82**	**43**	**27**	**12**	**5**	**1**	**4**	....
	NHL Totals		**82**	**43**	**27**	**12**	**5**	**1**	**4**	....

Club Directory

CONSOL Energy Center

Pittsburgh Penguins
CONSOL Energy Center
1001 Fifth Avenue
Pittsburgh, PA 15219
Phone **412/642-1300**
PR FAX 412/255-1988
www.pittsburghpenguins.com
Capacity: 18,387

Executive Management

Co-Owner/Chairman	Mario Lemieux
Co-Owner	Ron Burkle
CEO/President	David Morehouse
COO/General Counsel	Travis Williams

Hockey Operations

Executive V.P./General Manager	Jim Rutherford
Associate General Manager	Jason Botterill
Assistant General Manager	Bill Guerin
Vice President, Hockey Operations	Jason Karmanos
Head Coach	Mike Johnston
Assistant Coaches	Gary Agnew, Rick Tocchet
Goaltending Coach	Mike Bales
Special Assistant to the Head Coach	Jacques Martin
Video Coordinator	Andy Saucier
AHL Head Coach / Assistant Coach	Mike Sullivan / Jay Leach
Strength & Conditioning Coach	TBD
Development Coaches, Player / Goaltender	Mark Recchi / Mike Buckley
Manager, Team Services / Hockley Ops Assistant	Jim Britt / Erik Heasley
Head Athletic Trainer / Asst. Trainers	Chris Stewart / Curtis Bell, Patrick Steidle
Team Physician / Assistant Team Physician	Dr. Dharmesh Vyas / Dr. Melissa McLane
Director, Sport Science	Andy O'Brien
Sports Massage Therapist	Andreas Hüppi
Head Equipment Mgr. / Asst. Mgrs.	Dana Heinze / Teddy Richards, Daniel Kroll, Jon Taglianetti
Physical Therapist	Rick Joreitz
Consultants, Skating / Mental Training	Marianne Watkins / Aimee Kimball

Scouting

Director, Player Personnel	Dan Mackinnon
Director, Amateur Scouting	Randy Sexton
Director, Professional Scouting	Derek Clancey
Professional Scout	Al Santilli
Amateur Scouts	Scott Bell, Luc Gauthier, Jay Heinbuck, Wayne Meier, Ron Pyette, Warren Young, Chris DiPiero, Brian Fitzgerald, Frank Golden
Head European Scout / European Scout	Patrik Allvin / Tommy Westlund
Special Assignment Scout	Gilles Meloche

Administration

Executive Assistant	Susan Heiss
Shipping/Receiving Coordinator / Receptionist	Brett Hart / Kelly Hart

Partnership Sales

Senior Vice President, Sales	Terry Kalna
Executive Director, Partnership Sales	Rich Hixon
Sr. Director, Partnership Sales & Media	Mark Turley
Director / Sr. Managers, Client Services	Lori Wineland / Julie Klausner, Lindsay Mulvihill, Amanda Susko
Manager, Partnership Sales	Robbie Hofmann
Partnership Sales	Andrew Taglianetti
Corporate Sales Liaison	Pierre Larouche
Coordinator	Jim Meyer
Executive Producer	Ray Walker
Radio Play-by-Play / Color	Mike Lange / Phil Bourque

Communications

Vice President, Communications	Tom McMillan
Communications Senior Director / Manager	Jennifer Bullano / Jason Seidling

Marketing

Vice President, Marketing	James Santilli
Sr. Director, Marketing	Ross Miller
Director, Fan Development & Special Events	Jill Shipley
New Media Coordinators	Dave Geier, Drew Hancherick, Andi Perelman
Sr. Director, Creative Services & Publications	Barbara Pilarski
Graphic Designers	Erin Halley, Dave Scheponik
Managers, Amateur Hockey Development	Michael Chaisson
Coordinators, Fan Development / Marketing	Laura Spencer / Christine Ourlicht
Content Director / Manager	Sam Kasan / Michelle Crechiolo

Game Entertainment

Sr. Director, Production and Game Presentation	Rod Murray
Director, Game Presentation	Bill Wareham
Manager, Production Operations	Mike Davenport
Game Entertainment Producers	Mark Cottington, Leo McCafferty, Andrew McIntyre, Meghan McManimon, John Otte
Motion Graphics Designers	Dave Distilli, Padraig Driscoll, Aaron Spiegel
Pens TV Talent/Producer	Celina Pompeani

Finance

Vice President & Controller	Kevin Hart
Director, Finance	Mark Kuczinski
Payroll Manager / Accounts Payable	Andrea Winschel / Tawni Love
Sr. Accountant	Troy Ussack

CONSOL Energy Center Operations

Senior Director, Technology	Erik Watts
Director, Video Production & Technical Ops.	Andrew Warren
Systems Administrators / Jr. Administrator	Dave Meyner, Jason Henry / Justin Mellor
Building Audio/Video Specialist	Aaron Miller

Ticketing

Vice President, Ticket Sales	Chad Slencak
Directors, Customer Service / Ticket Sales / Premium	Kathy Davis / George Murphy / Brian Magness
Database Marketing Director / Manager	Erin Exley / Dana DiCello
Manager, Box Office Operations	Jason Onufer
Box Office Manager / Coordinator	Caroline Coulson / Kelly Gabany
Ticket Sales Account Execs	George Birman, Jeff Blizman, Bonnie Golinski, Nicole Kyslinger-Rudy, Chuck Pukansky
Managers, Group Sales / Premium Seating	Michael Zatchey / Kyle Lux
Premium Services Manager / Representative	Julia Drost / Jonathan Seelnacht
Customer Service Representatives	Holly Bandish, Daniel Gardner

Penguins Foundation

President, Penguins Foundation	David Soltesz
Director, Foundation Programs / Program Coord.	TBD / Emily Boccardi
Director, Community/Alumni Relations	Cindy Himes
Community Relations Coordinator	TBD
Community Relations/Alumni Liaison	Ed Johnston, Jack Reilly

Key Off-Season Signings/Acquisitions

2015

July 1 • Re-signed C **Jori Lehtera** and D **Chris Butler**.

2 • Acquired RW **Troy Brouwer**, G **Pheonix Copley** and a 3rd-round choice in the 2016 NHL Draft from Washington for RW **T.J. Oshie**.

2 • Re-signed D **Robert Bortuzzo**.

3 • Signed C **Kyle Brodziak**, RW **Jordan Caron** and D **Peter Harrold**.

3 • Re-signed G **Jake Allen** and RW **Dmitrij Jaskin**.

6 • Signed D **Andre Benoit**.

7 • Re-signed RW **Vladimir Tarasenko**.

8 • Re-signed RW **Magnus Paajarvi**.

2015-16 Schedule

Oct.	Thu.	8	Edmonton		Mon.	4	Ottawa
	Sat.	10	at Minnesota		Wed.	6	at Colorado
	Tue.	13	at Calgary		Fri.	8	at Anaheim
	Thu.	15	at Edmonton		Sat.	9	at Los Angeles
	Fri.	16	at Vancouver		Tue.	12	New Jersey
	Sun.	18	at Winnipeg*		Thu.	14	Carolina
	Tue.	20	at Montreal		Sat.	16	Montreal
	Sat.	24	NY Islanders		Mon.	18	Pittsburgh
	Tue.	27	Tampa Bay		Wed.	20	at Detroit
	Thu.	29	Anaheim		Fri.	22	at Colorado
	Sat.	31	Minnesota		Sun.	24	at Chicago
Nov.	Tue.	3	Los Angeles	Feb.	Tue.	2	at Nashville
	Wed.	4	at Chicago		Thu.	4	San Jose
	Sat.	7	at Nashville		Sat.	6	Minnesota
	Tue.	10	at New Jersey		Tue.	9	Winnipeg
	Thu.	12	at NY Rangers		Fri.	12	at Florida
	Sat.	14	Chicago		Sun.	14	at Tampa Bay
	Mon.	16	Winnipeg		Tue.	16	Dallas
	Tue.	17	at Columbus		Thu.	18	Los Angeles
	Thu.	19	Buffalo		Sat.	20	at Arizona
	Sat.	21	Detroit		Mon.	22	San Jose
	Mon.	23	at Buffalo		Thu.	25	NY Rangers
	Wed.	25	at Pittsburgh		Sat.	27	at Nashville*
	Sat.	28	Columbus		Sun.	28	at Carolina*
Dec.	Tue.	1	Florida	Mar.	Tue.	1	at Ottawa
	Fri.	4	at NY Islanders		Sun.	6	at Minnesota
	Sat.	5	Toronto		Wed.	9	Chicago
	Tue.	8	Arizona		Fri.	11	Anaheim
	Thu.	10	Philadelphia		Sat.	12	at Dallas
	Sat.	12	Dallas		Mon.	14	at Calgary
	Sun.	13	Colorado*		Wed.	16	at Edmonton
	Tue.	15	at Winnipeg		Sat.	19	at Vancouver
	Thu.	17	Nashville		Tue.	22	at San Jose
	Sat.	19	Calgary*		Fri.	25	Vancouver
	Mon.	21	at Philadelphia		Sat.	26	at Washington
	Tue.	22	at Boston		Tue.	29	Colorado
	Sat.	26	Dallas	Apr.	Fri.	1	Boston
	Sun.	27	at Dallas*		Sun.	3	at Colorado
	Tue.	29	Nashville		Mon.	4	Arizona
	Thu.	31	Minnesota		Thu.	7	at Chicago
Jan.	Sat.	2	at Toronto		Sat.	9	Washington

Denotes afternoon game.

Retired Numbers

2	Al MacInnis	1994-2004
3	Bob Gassoff	1973-1977
8	Barclay Plager	1967-1977
11	Brian Sutter	1976-1988
16	Brett Hull	1987-1998
24	Bernie Federko	1976-1989

CENTRAL DIVISION
49th NHL Season

Franchise date: June 5, 1967

St. Louis Blues

2014-15 Results: 51w-24l-3otl-4sol 109pts
1st, Central Division • 2nd, Western Conference

Vladimir Tarasenko led the Blues with 37 goals and 73 points in 2014-15. The 24-year-old was the youngest St. Louis player to reach the 30-goal plateau since Brendan Shanahan in 1991-92.

Year-by-Year Record

Season	GP	Home W	L	T	OL	Road W	L	T	OL	Overall W	L	T	OL	GF	GA	Pts.	Div. Fin.	Conf. Fin.	Playoff Result
2014-15	82	27	12		2	24	12		5	51	24		7	248	201	109	1st, Cen.	2nd, West	Lost First Round
2013-14	82	28	9		4	24	14		3	52	23		7	248	191	111	2nd, Cen.	3rd, West	Lost First Round
2012-13	48	15	8		1	14	9		1	29	17		2	129	115	60	2nd, Cen.	4th, West	Lost Conf. Quarter-Final
2011-12	82	30	6		5	19	16		6	49	22		11	210	165	109	1st, Cen.	2nd, West	Lost Conf. Semi-Final
2010-11	82	23	13		5	15	20		6	38	33		11	240	234	87	4th, Cen.	11th, West	Out of Playoffs
2009-10	82	18	18		5	22	14		5	40	32		10	225	223	90	4th, Cen.	9th, West	Out of Playoffs
2008-09	82	23	13		5	18	18		5	41	31		10	233	233	92	3rd, Cen.	6th, West	Lost Conf. Quarter-Final
2007-08	82	20	15		6	13	21		7	33	36		13	205	237	79	5th, Cen.	14th, West	Out of Playoffs
2006-07	82	18	19		4	16	16		9	34	35		13	214	254	81	3rd, Cen.	10th, West	Out of Playoffs
2005-06	82	12	23		6	9	23		9	21	46		15	197	292	57	5th, Cen.	15th, West	Out of Playoffs
2004-05	....																		
2003-04	82	23	11	7	0	16	19	4	2	39	30	11	2	191	198	91	2nd, Cen.	7th, West	Lost Conf. Quarter-Final
2002-03	82	23	11	4	3	18	13	7	3	41	24	11	6	253	222	99	2nd, Cen.	5th, West	Lost Conf. Quarter-Final
2001-02	82	27	12	1	1	16	15	7	3	43	27	8	4	227	188	98	2nd, Cen.	4th, West	Lost Conf. Semi-Final
2000-01	82	28	5	5	3	15	17	7	2	43	22	12	5	249	195	103	2nd, Cen.	4th, West	Lost Conf. Final
1999-2000	82	24	9	7	1	27	10	4	0	51	19	11	1	248	165	114	1st, Cen.	1st, West	Lost Conf. Quarter-Final
1998-99	82	18	17	6	....	19	15	7	....	37	32	13	....	237	209	87	2nd, Cen.	5th, West	Lost Conf. Semi-Final
1997-98	82	26	10	5	....	19	19	3	....	45	29	8	....	256	204	98	3rd, Cen.	3rd, West	Lost Conf. Semi-Final
1996-97	82	17	20	4	....	19	15	7	....	36	35	11	....	236	239	83	4th, Cen.	6th, West	Lost Conf. Quarter-Final
1995-96	82	15	17	9	....	17	17	7	....	32	34	16	....	219	248	80	4th, Cen.	5th, West	Lost Conf. Semi-Final
1994-95	48	16	6	2	....	12	9	3	....	28	15	5	....	178	135	61	2nd, Cen.	2nd, West	Lost Conf. Quarter-Final
1993-94	84	23	11	8	....	17	22	3	....	40	33	11	....	270	283	91	4th, Cen.	5th, West	Lost Conf. Quarter-Final
1992-93	84	22	13	7	....	15	23	4	....	37	36	11	....	282	278	85	4th, Norris		Lost Div. Final
1991-92	80	25	12	3	....	11	21	8	....	36	33	11	....	279	266	83	3rd, Norris		Lost Div. Semi-Final
1990-91	80	24	9	7	....	23	13	4	....	47	22	11	....	310	250	105	2nd, Norris		Lost Div. Final
1989-90	80	20	15	5	....	17	19	4	....	37	34	9	....	295	279	83	2nd, Norris		Lost Div. Final
1988-89	80	22	11	7	....	11	24	5	....	33	35	12	....	275	285	78	2nd, Norris		Lost Div. Final
1987-88	80	18	17	5	....	16	21	3	....	34	38	8	....	278	294	76	2nd, Norris		Lost Div. Final
1986-87	80	21	12	7	....	11	21	8	....	32	33	15	....	281	293	79	1st, Norris		Lost Div. Semi-Final
1985-86	80	23	11	6	....	14	23	3	....	37	34	9	....	302	291	83	3rd, Norris		Lost Conf. Final
1984-85	80	21	12	7	....	16	19	5	....	37	31	12	....	299	288	86	1st, Norris		Lost Div. Semi-Final
1983-84	80	23	14	3	....	9	27	4	....	32	41	7	....	293	316	71	2nd, Norris		Lost Div. Final
1982-83	80	16	16	8	....	9	24	7	....	25	40	15	....	285	316	65	4th, Norris		Lost Div. Semi-Final
1981-82	80	22	14	4	....	10	26	4	....	32	40	8	....	315	349	72	3rd Norris		Lost Div. Final
1980-81	80	29	7	4	....	16	11	13	....	45	18	17	....	352	281	107	1st, Smythe		Lost Quarter-Final
1979-80	80	20	13	7	....	14	21	5	....	34	34	12	....	266	278	80	2nd, Smythe		Lost Prelim. Round
1978-79	80	14	20	6	....	4	30	6	....	18	50	12	....	249	348	48	3rd, Smythe		Out of Playoffs
1977-78	80	12	20	8	....	8	27	5	....	20	47	13	....	195	304	53	4th, Smythe		Out of Playoffs
1976-77	80	22	13	5	....	10	26	4	....	32	39	9	....	239	276	73	1st, Smythe		Lost Quarter-Final
1975-76	80	20	12	8	....	9	24	7	....	29	37	14	....	249	290	72	3rd, Smythe		Lost Prelim. Round
1974-75	80	23	13	4	....	12	18	10	....	35	31	14	....	269	267	84	2nd, Smythe		Lost Prelim. Round
1973-74	78	16	16	7	....	10	24	5	....	26	40	12	....	206	248	64	6th, West		Out of Playoffs
1972-73	78	21	11	7	....	11	23	5	....	32	34	12	....	233	251	76	4th, West		Lost Quarter-Final
1971-72	78	17	17	5	....	11	22	6	....	28	39	11	....	208	247	67	3rd, West		Lost Semi-Final
1970-71	78	23	7	9	....	11	18	10	....	34	25	19	....	223	208	87	2nd, West		Lost Quarter-Final
1969-70	76	24	9	5	....	13	18	7	....	37	27	12	....	224	179	86	1st, West		Lost Final
1968-69	76	21	8	9	....	16	17	5	....	37	25	14	....	204	157	88	1st, West		Lost Final
1967-68	74	18	12	7	....	9	19	9	....	27	31	16	....	177	191	70	3rd, West		Lost Final

2015-16 Player Personnel

FORWARDS	HT	WT	*Age	Place of Birth	S	2014-15 Club
BACKES, David	6-3	221	31	Blaine, MN	R	St. Louis
BERGLUND, Patrik	6-3	217	27	Vasteras, Sweden	L	St. Louis
BRODZIAK, Kyle	6-2	208	31	St. Paul, AB	R	Minnesota
BROUWER, Troy	6-3	213	30	Vancouver, BC	R	Washington
CANNONE, Pat	5-11	192	29	Bayport, NY	R	Chicago (AHL)
CARON, Jordan	6-3	204	24	Sayabec, QC	L	Bos-Prov (AHL)-Col
GOC, Marcel	6-1	197	32	Calw, West Germany	L	Pittsburgh-St. Louis
JASKIN, Dmitrij	6-2	196	22	Omsk, Russia	L	St. Louis-Chicago (AHL)
JOKINEN, Olli	6-2	210	36	Kuopio, Finland	L	Nsh-Tor-St.L.
KRISTO, Danny	6-0	195	25	Edina, MN	R	Hartford
LEHTERA, Jori	6-2	191	27	Helsinki, Finland	L	St. Louis
McRAE, Philip	6-2	200	25	Minneapolis, MN	L	Chicago (AHL)
OTT, Steve	6-0	189	33	Summerside, PE	L	St. Louis
PAAJARVI, Magnus	6-3	208	24	Norrkoping, Sweden	L	St. Louis-Chicago (AHL)
REAVES, Ryan	6-1	224	28	Winnipeg, MB	R	St. Louis
SCHWARTZ, Jaden	5-10	190	23	Melfort, SK	L	St. Louis
SOBOTKA, Vladimir	5-10	197	28	Trebic, Czech.	L	Omsk
STASTNY, Paul	6-0	205	29	Quebec City, QC	L	St. Louis
STEEN, Alexander	5-11	212	31	Winnipeg, MB	L	St. Louis
TARASENKO, Vladimir	6-0	219	23	Yaroslavl, USSR	L	St. Louis
WELSH, Jeremy	6-3	210	27	Bayfield, ON	L	Chicago (AHL)
DEFENSEMEN						
ABELTSHAUSER, Konrad	6-5	225	23	Bad Tolz, Germany	L	Worcester-Allen
BORTUZZO, Robert	6-4	215	26	Thunder Bay, ON	R	Pittsburgh-St. Louis
BOUWMEESTER, Jay	6-4	212	32	Edmonton, AB	L	St. Louis
BUTLER, Chris	6-1	196	28	St. Louis, MO	L	St. Louis-Chicago (AHL)
GUNNARSSON, Carl	6-2	196	28	Orebro, Sweden	L	St. Louis
HARROLD, Peter	5-11	180	32	Kirtland Hills, OH	R	New Jersey-Albany
PIETRANGELO, Alex	6-3	201	25	King City, ON	R	St. Louis
SHATTENKIRK, Kevin	5-11	207	26	New Rochelle, NY	R	St. Louis

GOALTENDERS	HT	WT	*Age	Place of Birth	C	2014-15 Club
ALLEN, Jake	6-2	195	25	Fredericton, NB	L	St. Louis
ELLIOTT, Brian	6-2	209	30	Newmarket, ON	L	St. Louis
LUNDSTROM, Niklas	6-1	194	22	Varmdo, Sweden	L	Chicago (AHL)-Alaska

* – Age at start of 2015-16 season

Coaching History

Lynn Patrick and Scotty Bowman, 1967-68; Scotty Bowman, 1968-69, 1969-70; Al Arbour and Scotty Bowman, 1970-71; Sid Abel, Bill McCreary and Al Arbour, 1971-72; Al Arbour and Jean-Guy Talbot, 1972-73; Jean-Guy Talbot and Lou Angotti, 1973-74; Lou Angotti, Lynn Patrick and Garry Young, 1974-75; Garry Young, Lynn Patrick and Leo Boivin, 1975-76; Emile Francis, 1976-77; Leo Boivin and Barclay Plager, 1977-78; Barclay Plager, 1978-79; Barclay Plager and Red Berenson, 1979-80; Red Berenson, 1980-81; Red Berenson and Emile Francis, 1981-82; Emile Francis and Barclay Plager, 1982-83; Jacques Demers, 1983-84 to 1985-86; Jacques Martin, 1986-87, 1987-88; Brian Sutter, 1988-89 to 1991-92; Bob Plager and Bob Berry, 1992-93; Bob Berry, 1993-94; Mike Keenan, 1994-95, 1995-96; Mike Keenan, Jim Roberts and Joel Quenneville, 1996-97; Joel Quenneville, 1997-98 to 2002-03; Joel Quenneville and Mike Kitchen, 2003-04; Mike Kitchen, 2004-05, 2005-06; Mike Kitchen and Andy Murray, 2006-07; Andy Murray, 2007-08, 2008-09; Andy Murray and Davis Payne, 2009-10; Davis Payne, 2010-11; Davis Payne and Ken Hitchcock, 2011-12; Ken Hitchcock, 2012-13 to date.

Ken Hitchcock

Head Coach

Born: Edmonton, AB, December 17, 1951.

Ken Hitchcock was named the 24th head coach in St. Louis Blues history on November 6, 2011. The team was 6-7-0 at the time. Hitchcock led the Blues to a record of 43-15-11 the rest of the way and third place in the overall standings. He was rewarded with the Jack Adams Award as coach of the year. His Blues set a franchise record with 52 wins in 2013-14. St. Louis won the Central Division title in 2014-15 and Hitchcock joined Scotty Bowman, Al Arbour and Joel Quenneville as the only coaches in NHL history to reach 700 wins.

In 14 full seasons behind the bench prior to his arrival in St. Louis, Hitchcock led his teams to nine Stanley Cup playoff appearances and six division titles while recording at least 40 wins nine times and 100 points on eight occasions. He won the Stanley Cup with Dallas in 1999 when the team set club records with 51 wins and 114 points. He also won the Presidents' Trophy twice and was nominated for the Jack Adams Award three times. In Philadelphia from 2002 to 2006, he posted three straight 100-point seasons. While coaching Columbus, Hitchcock became the 13th coach in NHL history to record 500 wins on February 19, 2009.

Hitchcock began his professional coaching career as an assistant coach with the Philadelphia Flyers from 1990 to 1993 before spending two-plus seasons as the head coach of the Kalamazoo Wings/Michigan K-Wings, Dallas' International Hockey League affiliate. Prior to joining the professional ranks, Hitchcock was one of the winningest coaches in the history of the Western Hockey League with the Kamloops Blazers from 1984 to 1990. He was the league's coach of the year in 1986-87 and 1989-90 and was also named the Canadian Major Junior coach of the year in 1989-90 after leading Kamloops to the WHL championship.

Hitchcock has also represented Canada at numerous international competitions, including serving as an associate coach at the Winter Olympics in 2002 (gold), 2006, 2010 (gold), and 2014 (gold). He also helped Team Canada win the World Cup of Hockey Tournament in 2004 as an associate coach and was an assistant on gold medal-winning squads at the 2002 World Championship and the 1987 World Junior Championships.

2014-15 Scoring

* – rookie

Regular Season

Pos	#	Player	Team	GP	G	A	Pts	TOI	+/–	PIM	PP	SH	GW	S	S%
R	91	Vladimir Tarasenko	STL	77	37	36	73	17:37	27	31	8	0	6	264	14.0
L	20	Alexander Steen	STL	74	24	40	64	19:58	8	33	8	0	5	223	10.8
C	17	Jaden Schwartz	STL	75	28	35	63	18:14	13	16	8	0	4	184	15.2
R	42	David Backes	STL	80	26	32	58	18:38	7	104	10	0	3	183	14.2
C	74	T.J. Oshie	STL	72	19	36	55	18:50	17	51	3	0	4	162	11.7
C	26	Paul Stastny	STL	74	16	30	46	17:37	5	40	7	0	7	143	11.2
D	27	Alex Pietrangelo	STL	81	7	39	46	25:24	–2	28	1	0	2	195	3.6
C	12	Jori Lehtera	STL	75	14	30	44	16:12	21	48	2	1	2	103	13.6
D	22	Kevin Shattenkirk	STL	56	8	36	44	22:33	19	52	4	0	1	135	5.9
C	21	Patrik Berglund	STL	77	12	15	27	14:34	–2	26	0	0	0	145	8.3
R	23 *	Dmitrij Jaskin	STL	54	13	5	18	13:28	7	16	3	0	4	108	12.0
D	5	Barret Jackman	STL	80	2	13	15	16:48	3	47	0	0	1	86	2.3
D	19	Jay Bouwmeester	STL	72	2	11	13	22:39	7	24	0	0	0	92	2.2
R	75	Ryan Reaves	STL	81	6	6	12	8:31	–3	116	0	0	1	55	10.9
D	6	Zbynek Michalek	ARI	53	2	6	8	21:05	–6	12	0	0	0	67	3.0
			STL	15	2	2	4	19:36	3	6	0	0	0	19	10.5
			Total	68	4	8	12	20:45	–3	18	0	0	0	86	4.7
C	9	Steve Ott	STL	78	3	9	12	11:38	–8	86	0	0	0	49	6.1
D	4	Carl Gunnarsson	STL	61	2	10	12	18:03	10	2	0	0	0	54	3.7
C	13	Olli Jokinen	NSH	48	3	3	6	13:30	2	26	0	0	0	83	3.6
			TOR	6	0	1	1	14:17	1	2	0	0	0	10	0.0
			STL	8	1	2	3	11:00	3	0	0	0	1	17	5.9
			Total	62	4	6	10	13:15	6	28	0	0	1	110	3.6
D	25	Chris Butler	STL	33	3	6	9	17:11	8	23	0	1	0	54	5.6
C	57	Marcel Goc	PIT	43	2	4	6	12:26	–2	4	0	0	0	43	4.7
			STL	31	1	2	3	10:37	–1	4	0	0	0	34	2.9
			Total	74	3	6	9	11:40	–3	8	0	0	0	77	3.9
D	41	Robert Bortuzzo	PIT	38	2	4	6	15:27	–6	68	0	0	0	37	5.4
			STL	13	1	1	2	14:06	–3	25	0	0	0	19	5.3
			Total	51	3	5	8	15:06	–9	93	0	0	0	56	5.4
D	48 *	Petteri Lindbohm	STL	23	2	1	3	15:34	–1	26	0	0	0	32	6.3
L	32	Chris Porter	STL	24	1	1	2	9:33	–3	6	0	0	1	24	4.2
R	18 *	Ty Rattie	STL	11	0	2	2	9:06	0	2	0	0	0	8	0.0
L	56	Magnus Paajarvi	STL	10	0	1	1	9:47	–2	6	0	0	0	9	0.0
C	29	Colin Fraser	STL	1	0	0	0	4:42	–1	0	0	0	0	1	0.0

Goaltending

No.	Goaltender	GPI	Mins	Avg	W	L	OT	EN	SO	GA	SA	Sv%	G	A	PIM
1	Brian Elliott	46	2546	2.26	26	14	3	4	5	96	1150	.917	0	3	0
34	* Jake Allen	37	2077	2.28	22	7	4	1	4	79	909	.913	0	2	2
30	Martin Brodeur	7	356	2.87	3	3	0	0	1	17	169	.899	0	0	0
	Totals	**82**	**5003**	**2.36**	**51**	**24**	**7**	**5**	**10**	**197**	**2233**	**.912**			

Playoffs

Pos	#	Player	Team	GP	G	A	Pts	TOI	+/–	PIM	PP	SH	GW	OT	S	S%
D	22	Kevin Shattenkirk	STL	6	0	8	8	22:55	2	2	0	0	0	0	13	0.0
R	91	Vladimir Tarasenko	STL	6	6	1	7	17:22	–4	0	2	0	2	0	14	42.9
C	21	Patrik Berglund	STL	6	2	2	4	13:57	4	0	0	0	0	0	11	18.2
L	20	Alexander Steen	STL	6	1	3	4	19:34	–3	2	0	1	0	0	15	6.7
C	17	Jaden Schwartz	STL	6	1	2	3	18:00	–2	0	0	0	0	0	15	6.7
R	42	David Backes	STL	6	1	1	2	19:06	2	2	0	0	0	0	10	10.0
C	74	T.J. Oshie	STL	6	1	1	2	19:07	–3	0	0	0	0	0	16	6.3
C	12	Jori Lehtera	STL	5	0	2	2	14:53	–2	0	0	0	0	0	2	0.0
D	27	Alex Pietrangelo	STL	6	0	2	2	26:47	1	0	0	0	0	0	23	0.0
C	26	Paul Stastny	STL	6	1	0	1	17:28	–3	4	0	0	0	0	8	12.5
R	75	Ryan Reaves	STL	6	1	0	1	8:43	1	0	0	0	0	0	2	50.0
L	32	Chris Porter	STL	3	0	1	1	8:10	1	0	0	0	0	0	2	0.0
R	23 *	Dmitrij Jaskin	STL	6	0	1	1	12:55	1	2	0	0	0	0	6	0.0
C	57	Marcel Goc	STL	4	0	0	0	8:26	–1	0	0	0	0	0	4	0.0
D	5	Barret Jackman	STL	6	0	0	0	12:59	–1	4	0	0	0	0	1	0.0
C	9	Steve Ott	STL	6	0	0	0	11:14	0	26	0	0	0	0	6	0.0
D	6	Zbynek Michalek	STL	6	0	0	0	16:21	–2	4	0	0	0	0	4	0.0
D	19	Jay Bouwmeester	STL	6	0	0	0	20:28	–1	2	0	0	0	0	5	0.0
D	4	Carl Gunnarsson	STL	6	0	0	0	17:50	1	0	0	0	0	0	2	0.0

Goaltending

No.	Goaltender	GPI	Mins	Avg	W	L	EN	SO	GA	SA	Sv%	G	A	PIM
34	* Jake Allen	6	328	2.20	2	4	3	0	12	125	.904	0	0	0
1	Brian Elliott	1	26	2.31	0	0	1	0	1	7	.857	0	0	0
	Totals	**6**	**360**	**2.83**	**2**	**4**	**4**	**0**	**17**	**136**	**.875**			

NHL Coaching Record

			Regular Season				Playoffs			
Season	**Team**	**League**	**GC**	**W**	**L**	**O/T**	**GC**	**W**	**L**	**T**
1995-96	Dallas	NHL	43	15	23	5	....	....	....	....
1996-97	Dallas	NHL	82	48	26	8	7	3	4	....
1997-98	Dallas	NHL	82	49	22	11	17	10	7	....
1998-99♦	Dallas	NHL	82	51	19	12	23	16	7	....
99-2000	Dallas	NHL	82	43	23	16	23	14	9	....
2000-01	Dallas	NHL	82	48	24	10	10	4	6	....
2001-02	Dallas	NHL	50	23	17	10	....	....	....	....
2002-03	Philadelphia	NHL	82	45	20	17	13	6	7	....
2003-04	Philadelphia	NHL	82	40	21	21	18	11	7	....
2004-05	Philadelphia				SEASON CANCELLED					
2005-06	Philadelphia	NHL	82	45	26	11	6	2	4	....
2006-07	Philadelphia	NHL	8	1	6	1	....	....	....	....
2006-07	Columbus	NHL	62	28	29	5	....	....	....	....
2007-08	Columbus	NHL	82	34	36	12	....	....	....	....
2008-09	Columbus	NHL	82	41	31	10	4	0	4	....
2009-10	Columbus	NHL	58	22	27	9	....	....	....	....
2011-12	St. Louis	NHL	69	43	15	11	9	4	5	....
2012-13	St. Louis	NHL	48	29	17	2	6	2	4	....
2013-14	St. Louis	NHL	82	52	23	7	6	2	4	....
2014-15	St. Louis	NHL	82	51	24	7	6	2	4	....
	NHL Totals		1322	708	429	185	148	76	72	....

♦ Stanley Cup win.
Jack Adams Award (2012)

Club Records

Team

(Figures in brackets for season records are games played; records for fewest points, wins, ties, losses, goals, goals against are for 70 or more games)

Most Points 114 1999-2000 (82)
Most Wins 52 2013-14 (82)
Most Ties 19 1970-71 (78)
Most Losses 50 1978-79 (80)
Most Goals 352 1980-81 (80)
Most Goals Against 349 1981-82 (80)
Fewest Points 48 1978-79 (80)
Fewest Wins 18 1978-79 (80)
Fewest Ties 7 1983-84 (80)
Fewest Losses 18 1980-81 (80)
Fewest Goals 177 1967-68 (74)
Fewest Goals Against 157 1968-69 (76)

Longest Winning Streak
Overall ....10 Jan. 3-23/02
Home ....9 Jan. 26-Feb. 26/91
Away ....10 Jan. 21-Mar. 2/00

Longest Undefeated Streak
Overall ....12 Nov. 10-Dec. 8/68
                             (5W, 7T),
                             Nov. 24-Dec. 26/00
                             (11W, 1T/OL)
Home ....11 Four times
Away ....11 Jan. 21-Mar. 4/00
                             (10W, 1T/OL)

Longest Losing Streak
Overall ....13 Mar. 16-Apr. 8/06
Home ....7 Oct. 22-Nov. 26/05,
                             Nov. 25-Dec. 17/06
Away ....10 Jan. 20-Mar. 8/82,
                             Dec. 29/05-Feb. 1/06,
                             Feb. 16-Mar. 15/08

Longest Winless Streak
Overall ....13 Mar. 16-Apr. 8/06
                             (13L)
Home ....7 Dec. 28/82-Jan. 25/83
                             (5L, 2T),
                             Oct. 22-Nov. 26/05
                             (7L)
Away ....17 Jan. 23-Apr. 7/74
                             (14L, 3T)
Most Shutouts, Season 15 2011-12 (82)
Most PIM, Season 2,041 1990-91 (80)
Most Goals, Game ....11 Feb. 26/94
                             (St.L. 11 at Ott. 1)

Individual

Most Seasons ....13 Bernie Federko
Most Games ....927 Bernie Federko
Most Goals, Career ....527 Brett Hull
Most Assists, Career ....721 Bernie Federko
Most Points, Career ....1,073 Bernie Federko
                             (352G, 721A)
Most PIM, Career ....1,786 Brian Sutter
Most Shutouts, Career ....20 Jaroslav Halak
Longest Consecutive
  Games Streak ....662 Garry Unger
                             (Feb. 7/71-Apr. 8/79)
Most Goals, Season ....86 Brett Hull
                             (1990-91)
Most Assists, Season ....90 Adam Oates
                             (1990-91)
Most Points, Season ....131 Brett Hull
                             (1990-91; 86G, 45A)
Most PIM, Season ....306 Bob Gassoff
                             (1975-76)
Most Points, Defenseman,
  Season ....78 Jeff Brown
                             (1992-93; 25G, 53A)

Most Points, Center,
  Season ....115 Adam Oates
                             (1990-91; 25G, 90A)
Most Points, Right Wing,
  Season ....131 Brett Hull
                             (1990-91; 86G, 45A)
Most Points, Left Wing,
  Season ....102 Brendan Shanahan
                             (1993-94; 52G, 50A)
Most Points, Rookie,
  Season ....73 Jorgen Pettersson
                             (1980-81; 37G, 36A)
Most Shutouts, Season ....9 Brian Elliott
                             (2011-12)
Most Goals, Game ....6 Red Berenson
                             (Nov. 7/68)
Most Assists, Game ....5 Brian Sutter
                             (Nov. 22/83)
                             Bernie Federko
                             (Feb. 27/88)
                             Adam Oates
                             (Jan. 26/91)
                             Dallas Drake
                             (Oct. 29/03)
Most Points, Game ....7 Red Berenson
                             (Nov. 7/68; 6G, 1A)
                             Garry Unger
                             (Mar. 13/71; 3G, 4A)

All-time Record vs. Other Clubs
Regular Season

			Total							At Home							On Road			
	GP	W	L	T	OL	GF	GA	PTS	GP	W	L	T	OL	GF	GA	PTS	GP	W	L	T	OL	GF	GA	PTS
Anaheim	81	38	32	5	6	242	228	87	41	23	10	3	5	135	109	54	40	15	22	2	1	107	119	33
Arizona	138	64	51	18	5	446	390	151	69	35	22	11	1	222	181	82	69	29	29	7	4	224	209	69
Boston	129	49	62	18	0	381	474	116	65	30	26	9	0	206	217	69	64	19	36	9	0	175	257	47
Buffalo	112	54	45	13	0	379	344	121	55	33	15	7	0	198	136	73	57	21	30	6	0	181	208	48
Calgary	163	75	68	14	6	502	496	170	82	40	31	9	2	279	247	91	81	35	37	5	4	223	249	79
Carolina	74	42	26	5	1	242	212	90	37	23	10	3	1	133	105	50	37	19	16	2	0	109	107	40
Chicago	296	119	130	35	12	898	979	285	147	75	52	17	3	480	440	170	149	44	78	18	9	418	539	115
Colorado	121	55	51	11	4	366	377	125	60	35	19	4	2	209	167	76	61	20	32	7	2	157	210	49
Columbus	77	46	25	3	3	240	201	98	39	28	9	1	1	139	94	58	38	18	16	2	2	101	107	40
Dallas	273	125	100	43	5	876	829	298	137	75	40	21	1	480	381	172	136	50	60	22	4	396	448	126
Detroit	277	119	113	37	8	847	891	283	138	66	48	20	4	439	397	156	139	53	65	17	4	408	494	127
Edmonton	125	62	46	11	6	422	404	141	63	33	20	7	3	217	204	76	62	29	26	4	3	205	200	65
Florida	29	19	7	3	0	76	47	41	15	11	3	1	0	44	20	23	14	8	4	2	0	32	27	18
Los Angeles	193	98	70	22	3	616	566	221	97	61	25	10	1	346	243	133	96	37	45	12	2	270	323	88
Minnesota	56	26	19	5	6	135	138	63	27	15	6	3	3	72	54	36	29	11	13	2	3	63	84	27
Montreal	126	31	72	22	1	339	476	85	62	16	30	15	1	163	209	48	64	15	42	7	0	176	267	37
Nashville	95	46	32	4	13	243	214	109	47	25	16	1	5	128	105	56	48	21	16	3	8	115	109	53
New Jersey	102	51	36	14	1	346	315	117	51	30	13	7	1	208	157	68	51	21	23	7	0	138	158	49
NY Islanders	107	39	46	20	2	339	368	100	52	22	19	9	2	189	165	55	55	17	27	11	0	150	203	45
NY Rangers	135	43	74	16	2	367	473	104	70	29	30	10	1	210	218	69	65	14	44	6	1	157	255	35
Ottawa	29	13	11	2	3	89	77	31	14	5	5	2	2	41	42	14	15	8	6	0	1	48	35	17
Philadelphia	145	43	81	17	4	367	504	107	73	30	34	7	2	204	225	69	72	13	47	10	2	163	279	38
Pittsburgh	139	70	49	18	2	462	433	160	70	46	17	6	1	260	185	99	69	24	32	12	1	202	248	61
San Jose	89	51	31	2	5	272	229	109	47	25	20	1	1	136	119	52	42	26	11	1	4	136	110	57
Tampa Bay	35	21	9	3	2	124	96	47	16	13	3	0	0	60	38	26	19	8	6	3	2	64	58	21
Toronto	211	95	88	25	3	680	676	218	107	61	30	14	2	364	291	138	104	34	58	11	1	316	385	80
Vancouver	180	90	63	18	9	593	514	207	89	50	25	9	5	316	250	114	91	40	38	9	4	277	264	93
Washington	91	40	38	12	1	311	298	93	46	23	15	8	0	179	142	54	45	17	23	4	1	132	156	39
Winnipeg	25	16	4	1	4	75	57	37	11	8	2	0	1	34	22	17	14	8	2	1	3	41	35	20
Defunct Clubs	65	36	14	15	0	226	155	87	32	25	4	3	0	131	55	53	33	11	10	12	0	95	100	34
Totals	3718	1676	1493	432	117	11501	11461	3901	1859	991	599	218	51	6222	5218	2251	1859	685	894	214	66	5279	6243	1650

Playoffs

	Series	W	L	GP	W	L	T	GF	GA	Last Mtg.	Rnd.	Result
Arizona	2	2	0	11	7	4	0	39	29	1999	CQF	W 4-3
Boston	2	0	2	8	0	8	0	15	48	1972	SF	L 0-4
Buffalo	1	0	1	3	1	2	0	8	7	1976	PR	L 1-2
Calgary	1	0	1	7	3	4	0	22	28	1986	CF	L 3-4
Chicago	11	3	8	56	24	32	0	156	191	2014	FR	L 2-4
Colorado	1	0	1	5	1	4	0	11	17	2001	CF	L 1-4
Dallas	12	6	6	66	32	34	0	187	197	2001	CSF	W 4-0
Detroit	7	2	5	40	16	24	0	103	125	2002	CSF	L 1-4
Los Angeles	4	2	2	18	10	8	0	48	40	2013	CQF	L 2-4
Minnesota	1	0	1	6	2	4	0	14	17	2015	FR	L 2-4
Montreal	3	0	3	12	0	12	0	14	42	1977	QF	L 0-4
NY Rangers	1	0	1	6	2	4	0	22	29	1981	QF	L 2-4
Philadelphia	2	2	0	11	8	3	0	34	20	1969	QF	W 4-0
Pittsburgh	3	2	1	13	7	6	0	45	40	1981	PR	W 3-2
San Jose	4	2	2	23	12	11	0	61	51	2012	CQF	W 4-1
Toronto	5	3	2	31	17	14	0	88	90	1996	CQF	W 4-2
Vancouver	3	0	3	18	6	12	0	55	77	2009	CQF	L 0-4
Totals	63	24	39	334	148	186	0	920	1026			

Playoff Results 2015-2011

Year	Round	Opponent	Result	GF	GA
2015	FR	Minnesota	L 2-4	14	17
2014	FR	Chicago	L 2-4	14	20
2013	CQF	Los Angeles	L 2-4	10	12
2012	CSF	Los Angeles	L 0-4	6	15
	CQF	San Jose	W 4-1	14	8

Abbreviations: Round: CF – conference final; CSF – conference semi-final; CQF – conference quarter-final; FR – first round; SF – semi-final; QF – quarter-final; PR – preliminary round.

Calgary totals include Atlanta Flames, 1972-73 to 1979-80.
Colorado totals include Quebec, 1979-80 to 1994-95.
New Jersey totals include Kansas City, 1974-75, 1975-76, and Colorado Rockies, 1976-77 to 1981-82.
Phoenix totals include Winnipeg, 1979-80 to 1995-96.
Carolina totals include Hartford, 1979-80 to 1996-97.
Dallas totals include Minnesota North Stars, 1967-68 to 1992-93.
Colorado totals include Colorado Rockies, 1976-77 to 1981-82.
Winnipeg totals include Atlanta Thrashers, 1999-2000 to 2010-11.

2014-15 Results

Oct.	9	NY Rangers	2-3		10	Carolina	5-4†
	11	Calgary	4-1		13	Edmonton	4-2
	16	at Los Angeles	0-1†		15	Detroit	2-3*
	18	at Arizona	6-1		17	Toronto	3-0
	19	at Anaheim	0-3		19	Colorado	3-1
	23	Vancouver	1-4		29	Nashville	5-4†
	25	Chicago	3-2		30	at Carolina	3-2†
	28	at Dallas	4-3*	Feb.	1	at Washington	4-3
	30	Anaheim	2-0		3	Tampa Bay	2-1*
Nov.	1	Colorado	3-2†		5	at Buffalo	3-0
	3	at NY Rangers	4-3†		6	at Columbus	1-7
	4	at New Jersey	1-0		8	Chicago	2-4
	6	New Jersey	4-3		10	Arizona	2-4
	8	Nashville	1-2		12	at Tampa Bay	6-3
	11	Buffalo	6-1		15	at Florida	2-1†
	13	Nashville	4-3		17	Dallas	1-4
	15	Washington	4-1		20	Boston	5-1
	18	at Boston	0-2		21	Pittsburgh	2-4
	20	at Montreal	1-4		24	Montreal	2-5
	22	at Ottawa	3-2		26	at Winnipeg	2-1†
	23	at Winnipeg	4-2		28	at Edmonton	2-1
	25	Ottawa	2-3†	Mar.	1	at Vancouver	5-6†
	28	Edmonton	4-3*		5	at Philadelphia	1-3
	29	at Minnesota	3-2†		7	at Toronto	6-1
Dec.	3	at Chicago	1-4		10	Winnipeg	5-4
	4	at Nashville	3-4		12	Philadelphia	1-0†
	6	at NY Islanders	6-4		14	Minnesota	1-3
	8	Florida	4-2		15	at Dallas	3-0
	11	NY Islanders	6-3		17	at Calgary	4-0
	13	at Colorado	3-2*		19	at Winnipeg	3-6
	16	Los Angeles	5-2		21	at Minnesota	3-6
	18	at Los Angeles	4-6		22	at Detroit	1-2*
	20	at San Jose	2-3*		24	at Pittsburgh	3-2*
	23	at Colorado	0-5		28	Columbus	2-4
	27	Dallas	3-4		30	Vancouver	2-4
	29	Colorado	3-0	Apr.	2	Calgary	4-1
	30	at Nashville	2-3		3	at Dallas	7-5
Jan.	2	at Anaheim	3-4		5	at Chicago	2-1
	3	at San Jose	2-3		7	Winnipeg	0-1†
	6	at Arizona	6-0		9	Chicago	2-1
	8	San Jose	7-2		11	Minnesota	4-2

* – Overtime † – Shootout

NHL Draft Selections 2015-2001

Name in bold denotes played in NHL.

2015

Pick	
56	Vince Dunn
94	Adam Musil
116	Glenn Gawdin
127	Niko Mikkola
146	Luke Opilka
176	Liam Dunda

2014

Pick	
21	Robby Fabbri
33	Ivan Barbashev
52	Maxim Letunov
82	Jake Walman
94	Ville Husso
110	Austin Poganski
124	Jaedon Descheneau
172	C.J. Yakimowicz
176	Samuel Blais
202	Dwyer Tschantz

2013

Pick	
47	Thomas Vannelli
57	William Carrier
112	Zach Pochiro
173	Santeri Saari

2012

Pick	
25	Jordan Schmaltz
56	Sam Kurker
67	Mackenzie MacEachern
86	Colton Parayko
116	Nicholas Walters
146	Francois Tremblay
176	**Petteri Lindbohm**
206	Tyrel Seaman

2011

Pick	
32	**Ty Rattie**
41	**Dmitrij Jaskin**
46	Joel Edmundson
88	Jordan Binnington
102	Yannick Veilleux
132	Niklas Lundstrom
162	Ryan Tesink
192	Teemu Eronen

2010

Pick	
14	**Jaden Schwartz**
16	**Vladimir Tarasenko**
44	Sebastian Wannstrom
74	Max Gardiner
104	Jani Hakanpaa
134	Cody Beach
164	Stephen Macaulay

2009

Pick	
17	**David Rundblad**
48	Brett Ponich
78	Sergei Andronov
108	Tyler Shattock
168	David Shields
202	Max Tardy

2008

Pick	
4	**Alex Pietrangelo**
33	**Philip McRae**
34	**Jake Allen**
65	**Jori Lehtera**
70	James Livingston
87	Ian Schultz
95	**David Warsofsky**
125	Kristofer Berglund
155	Anthony Nigro
185	Paul Karpowich

2007

Pick	
13	**Lars Eller**
18	**Ian Cole**
26	**David Perron**
39	Simon Hjalmarsson
44	**Aaron Palushaj**
85	Brett Sonne
96	**Cade Fairchild**
100	Travis Erstad
160	**Anthony Peluso**
190	Trevor Nill

2006

Pick	
1	**Erik Johnson**
25	**Patrik Berglund**
31	**Tomas Kana**
64	**Jonas Junland**
94	Ryan Turek
106	**Reto Berra**
124	Andy Sackrison
154	Matthew McCollem
184	Alexander Hellstrom

2005

Pick	
24	**T.J. Oshie**
37	**Scott Jackson**
85	**Ben Bishop**
156	**Ryan Reaves**
169	Mike Gauthier
171	**Nick Drazenovic**
219	Nikolai Lemtyugov

2004

Pick	
17	**Marek Schwarz**
49	**Carl Soderberg**
83	Viktor Alexandrov
116	Michal Birner
136	**Nikita Nikitin**
180	**Roman Polak**
211	David Fredriksson
277	Jonathan Michel Boutin

2003

Pick	
30	**Shawn Belle**
62	**David Backes**
84	Konstantin Barulin
88	**Zack Fitzgerald**
101	Konstantin Zakharov
127	**Alexandre Bolduc**
148	**Lee Stempniak**
159	**Chris Beckford-Tseu**
189	Jonathan Lehun
221	Evgeny Skachkov
253	Andrei Pervyshin
284	Juhamatti Aaltonen

2002

Pick	
48	Alexei Shkotov
62	Andrei Mikhnov
89	Tomas Troliga
120	Robin Jonsson
165	Justin Maiser
190	**D.J. King**
221	Jonas Johnson
253	**Tom Koivisto**
284	Ryan MacMurchy

2001

Pick	
57	**Jay McClement**
89	Tuomas Nissinen
122	Igor Valeev
159	Dmitri Semin
190	Brett Scheffelmaier
253	**Petr Cajanek**
270	Grant Jacobsen
283	Simon Skoog

General Managers' History

Lynn Patrick, 1967-68; Scotty Bowman, 1968-69 to 1970-71; Lynn Patrick and Sid Abel, 1971-72; Sid Abel, 1972-73; Charles Catto, 1973-74; Gerry Ehman and Dennis Ball, 1974-75; Dennis Ball, 1975-76; Emile Francis, 1976-77 to 1982-83; Ron Caron, 1983-84 to 1993-94; Mike Keenan, 1994-95, 1995-96; Mike Keenan and Ron Caron, 1996-97; Larry Pleau, 1997-98 to 2009-10; Doug Armstrong, 2010-11 to date.

Captains' History

Al Arbour, 1967-68 to 1969-70; Red Berenson and Barclay Plager, 1970-71; Barclay Plager, 1971-72 to 1975-76; no captain, 1976-77; Red Berenson, 1977-78; Barry Gibbs, 1978-79; Brian Sutter, 1979-80 to 1987-88; Bernie Federko, 1988-89; Rick Meagher, 1989-90; Scott Stevens, 1990-91; Garth Butcher, 1991-92; Brett Hull, 1992-93 to 1994-95; Brett Hull, Shayne Corson and Wayne Gretzky, 1995-96; no captain, 1996-97; Chris Pronger, 1997-98 to 2001-02; Al MacInnis, 2002-03, 2003-04; Dallas Drake, 2005-06, 2006-07; Eric Brewer, 2007-08 to 2010-11; David Backes, 2011-12 to date.

Doug Armstrong

Executive Vice President and General Manager

Born: Sarnia, ON, September 24, 1964.

Doug Armstrong was named the Blues' executive vice president and general manager on July 1, 2010 after serving two seasons with the club as vice president of player personnel. In his second season on the job in 2011-12, Armstrong was the NHL G.M. of the Year after his moves (which included hiring Ken Hitchcock as coach) helped the team rebound from a slow start to post the best defensive record in the NHL and a 109-point season. The Blues set a club record with 52 wins in 2013-14 and had 111 points. They won the Central Division title in 2014-15.

Prior to being hired in St. Louis, Armstrong spent 17 years with the Dallas Stars organization and the last six seasons (from January 25, 2002, to 2008) as the club's general manager. He was a part of the Stars' organization since the club moved to Dallas in 1993 and helped lead the franchise to two Presidents' Trophies, two Western Conference titles and the 1999 Stanley Cup championship. Prior to being named the team's seventh general manager, Armstrong served nine years as the assistant general manager under Bob Gainey. As Gainey's assistant, Armstrong worked on contract negotiations and season scheduling, and handled the day-to-day operations of the hockey department.

On the international level, Armstrong was the associate director of player personnel for Team Canada at the 2010 Winter Olympics in Vancouver and was involved with the management team again at Sochi in 2014, helping Canada earn a pair of gold medals. He also served as general manager for Team Canada and won the silver medal at the 2009 World Championship in Switzerland. He was the assistant general manager for Team Canada at the 2002 World Championship and 2008 World Championship (silver medal) and served as a special advisor to Steve Yzerman for the Canadian team that won gold at the 2007 World Championship. Armstrong is the son of former NHL linesman Neil Armstrong who was inducted into the Hockey Hall of Fame in 1991.

Club Directory

Scottrade Center

St. Louis Blues
Scottrade Center
1401 Clark Avenue at Brett Hull Way
St. Louis, MO 63103
Phone **314/622-2500**
FAX 314/622-2582
www.stlouisblues.com
Capacity: 19,150

Ownership

Tom Stillman, Jerald Kent, Donn Lux, James Cooper, Jo Ann Taylor Kindle, Steve Maritz, Edward Potter, Mr. & Mrs. Andrew Taylor, David Steward, James Kavanaugh, John Danforth, Christopher Danforth, Jim Johnson III, Scott McCuaig, John Ross, Jr., Tom Schlafly

Executive

Chairman and Governor	Tom Stillman
President of Hockey Operations/G.M./Alt. Governor	Doug Armstrong
President and CEO, Business Operations	Chris Zimmerman
Group V.P., Ticketing & Guest Experience	Josh Bender
Group V.P., Brand, Community & Partnership Development	Steve Chapman
Group V.P., Sports & Entertainment Operations	Alex Rodrigo
Group V.P., Chief Financial Officer	Phil Siddle
Executive V.P.s	Bruce Affleck, Brett Hull
Sr. V.P., Marketing and Public Relations	Mike Caruso
Sr. V.P., Corporate Sponsorship	Eric Stisser
Vice President, Corporate Sponsorship	Bryan Lucas
Vice President, Hockey Operations	Dave Taylor
Exec. Asst. to the G.M.	Donna Lembke
Exec. Asst. to the Chairman & CEO	Lisa Cwiklowski

Hockey Operations

Assistant General Manager	Martin Brodeur
Assistant General Manager	Kevin McDonald
Senior Advisor to the General Manager	Al MacInnis
Senior Advisor for Amateur Scouting	Larry Pleau
Head Coach	Ken Hitchcock
Associate Coach / Assistant Coaches	Brad Shaw / Ray Bennett, Kirk Muller
Goaltending Coach / Video Coach	Jim Corsi / Sean Ferrell
Strength and Conditioning Coach	Nelson Ayotte
Sr. Director, Media Relations/Team Services	Rich Jankowski
Scouting Directors, Amateur / Pro	Bill Armstrong / Rob DiMaio
Directors, Hockey Administration / Player Development	Ryan Miller / Tim Taylor
Sports Psychologist	Dr. Scot McFadden
Goalie Development Coach	Ty Conklin
Assistant Director, Media Relations	Dan O'Neill
Head of European Scouting	Jan Vopat
Amateur Scouts	Tony Feltrin, Dan Ginnell, J Niemiec, Michel Picard
Part-Time Amateur Scouts	Corey Banika, Vincent Montalbano, Blair Nicholson, Michel Picard

Training

Head Medical Trainer / Asst. Athletic Trainer	Ray Barile / Chris Palmer
Equipment Manager / Asst. Manager / Assistant	Bert Godin / Joel Farnsworth / Chad O'Neil
Massage Therapist	Nate Schmitt

Medical

Orthopedic Surgeons	Drs. Matt Matava, Rick Wright
Internists	Drs. Aaron Birenbaum, William Birenbaum
Neurosurgeon	Dr. Ralph Dacey
General / Plastic Surgeons	Dr. Michael Brunt / Dr. Tom Francel
Dentist / Oral Surgeon	Dr. Ron Sherstoff / Dr. Ken Kram
Ophthalmologist / Optometrist	Dr. Gill Grand / Dr. David Seibel
Chiropractor	Dr. Michael Murphy

Broadcasting

Radio / Television Stations	KMOX 1120 AM / FOX Sports Midwest
Dir., Broadcasting and Radio Play-by-Play	Chris Kerber
Radio Color Analyst, Community Relations	Kelly Chase
Community Relations, KMOX Radio 1120 AM	Bob Plager
Television Play-by-Play / Color	John Kelly / Darren Pang, Bernie Federko
FOX Sports Midwest Analyst / Host	Jim Hayes / Pat Parris / Andy Strickland

Marketing

Sr. Director, Event Presentation	Chris Frome
Sr. Director, Promotions/Digital Strategy	Matt Gardner
Sr. Director, Advertising/Event Marketing	Megan Little
Director, Game Entertainment/Amateur Hockey	Lamont Buford
Director, Digital Media	Chris Pinkert
Director, Branding and Creative	Brenda Wilbur
Director, Alumni Relations	Terry Yake

Event Operations

Public Address Announcer	Tom Calhoun
Organist / Music Coordinator	Jeremy Boyer / Carl Middleman
Video Producer / Editor / In-Game Host	Peter Saguto / Peter Jodlowski / Angella Sharpe

Sponsorship

Director, Community Relations/Blues 14 Fund	Randy Girsch
Director, Corporate Sponsorships	Mary Greener
Director, Sponsorship Services	Jackie Miller

Ticket Sales and Service

Sr. Director, Ticket & Group Sales	Jennifer Nevins
Sr. Director, Premium Seating & Suite Sales	Nick Wierciak
Director, Group and Event Suite Sales	Kari Takmajian
Director, Premium Seating & Suite Service	Melissa Gale
Director, Retention & Guest Experience	Ashley Hoffman

CRM & Analytics

Director, CRM & Analytics / Database Manager	Keira Hertz / Mike VanMassenhove

Ticket Operations

Sr. Director, Ticket Operations	Tere Hubert
Sr. Manager / Managers, Ticket Operations	Greg Rapini / Justin Malmberg, Tiffany Stamper
Ticket Sales	Juanita Hall, Jeff Jovanovic, Brittany Bommarito, Todd Morris, Debbie Nyberg, Peggie O'Connor

Finance

Finance Controller	Stephen Kruse
Managers, Accounting	Kristy Atwater, Craig Bryant, Mike Tonjes
Manager, IT	Larry Womack
Coordinator, Accounts Payable	Mindy Wallace

Retail

Retail Director	George Pavlik
Retail Managers / Store Manager	Amy Dugan, Barry Smith / Matt Tierney

Guest Services

Director, Guest Services & Security	Robert Schnettler
Manager, Guest & Premium Services	Allison Click

Human Resources

Director/ Administrator, Human Resources	Jamie Sackman / Tiffany Stern
Manager / Assistant Manager, Payroll	Pam Di Rie / Crystal Strasburg

Building Operations

Interim Director, Building Operations	Phillip Ransford
Manager, Event Operations	Kevin Casey

San Jose Sharks

2014-15 Results: 40W-33L-3OTL-6SOL 89PTS
5TH, Pacific Division • 12TH, Western Conference

Key Off-Season Signings/Acquisitions

2015
May 28 • Named **Peter DeBoer** head coach.
June 27 • Re-signed C **Melker Karlsson**, D **Karl Stollery** and G **Troy Grosenick**.
30 • Acquired G **Martin Jones** from Boston for C **Sean Kuraly** and a 1st-round choice in the 2016 NHL Draft.
30 • Re-signed D **Brenden Dillon**.
July 1 • Signed D **Paul Martin**.
2 • Named **Bob Boughner** assistant coach.
3 • Signed RW **Joel Ward**.

Year-by-Year Record

Season	GP	Home W	L	T	OL	Road W	L	T	OL	Overall W	L	T	OL	GF	GA	Pts.	Div. Fin.	Conf. Fin.	Playoff Result
2014-15	82	19	17	....	5	21	16	....	4	40	33	....	9	228	232	89	5th, Pac.	12th, West	Out of Playoffs
2013-14	82	29	7	....	5	22	15	....	4	51	22	....	9	249	200	111	2nd, Pac.	4th, West	Lost First Round
2012-13	48	17	2	....	5	8	14	....	2	25	16	....	7	124	116	57	3rd, Pac.	6th, West	Lost Conf. Semi-Final
2011-12	82	26	12	....	3	17	17	....	7	43	29	....	10	228	210	96	2nd, Pac.	7th, West	Lost Conf. Quarter-Final
2010-11	82	25	11	....	5	23	14	....	4	48	25	....	9	248	213	105	1st, Pac.	2nd, West	Lost Conf. Final
2009-10	82	27	6	....	8	24	14	....	3	51	20	....	11	264	215	113	1st, Pac.	1st, West	Lost Conf. Final
2008-09	82	32	5	....	4	21	13	....	7	53	18	....	11	257	204	117	1st, Pac.	1st, West	Lost Conf. Quarter-Final
2007-08	82	22	13	....	6	27	10	....	4	49	23	....	10	222	193	108	1st, Pac.	5th, West	Lost Conf. Semi-Final
2006-07	82	25	12	....	4	26	14	....	1	51	26	....	5	258	199	107	2nd, Pac.	5th, West	Lost Conf. Semi-Final
2005-06	82	25	9	....	7	19	18	....	4	44	27	....	11	266	242	99	2nd, Pac.	5th, West	Lost Conf. Semi-Final
2004-05	....																		
2003-04	82	24	8	7	2	19	13	5	4	43	21	12	6	219	183	104	1st, Pac.	2nd, West	Lost Conf. Final
2002-03	82	17	16	5	3	11	21	4	5	28	37	9	8	214	239	73	5th, Pac.	14th, West	Out of Playoffs
2001-02	82	25	11	3	2	19	16	5	1	44	27	8	3	248	199	99	1st, Pac.	3rd, West	Lost Conf. Semi-Final
2000-01	82	22	14	4	1	18	13	8	2	40	27	12	3	217	192	95	2nd, Pac.	5th, West	Lost Conf. Quarter-Final
1999-2000	82	21	14	3	3	14	16	7	4	35	30	10	7	225	214	87	4th, Pac.	8th, West	Lost Conf. Semi-Final
1998-99	82	17	15	9	....	14	18	9	....	31	33	18	....	196	191	80	4th, Pac.	7th, West	Lost Conf. Quarter-Final
1997-98	82	17	19	5	....	17	19	5	....	34	38	10	....	210	216	78	4th, Pac.	8th, West	Lost Conf. Quarter-Final
1996-97	82	14	23	4	....	13	24	4	....	27	47	8	....	211	278	62	7th, Pac.	13th, West	Out of Playoffs
1995-96	82	12	26	3	....	8	29	4	....	20	55	7	....	252	357	47	7th, Pac.	13th, West	Out of Playoffs
1994-95	48	10	13	1	....	9	12	3	....	19	25	4	....	129	161	42	3rd, Pac.	7th, West	Lost Conf. Semi-Final
1993-94	84	19	13	10	....	14	22	6	....	33	35	16	....	252	265	82	3rd, Pac.	8th, West	Lost Conf. Semi-Final
1992-93	84	8	33	1	....	3	38	1	....	11	71	2	....	218	414	24	6th, Smythe		Out of Playoffs
1991-92	80	14	23	3	....	3	35	2	....	17	58	5	....	219	359	39	6th, Smythe		Out of Playoffs

2015-16 Schedule

Oct. Wed. 7 at Los Angeles
Sat. 10 Anaheim
Tue. 13 at Washington
Fri. 16 at New Jersey
Sat. 17 at NY Islanders
Mon. 19 at NY Rangers
Thu. 22 Los Angeles
Sat. 24 Carolina
Wed. 28 Nashville
Sat. 31 at Dallas*
Nov. Sun. 1 at Colorado*
Tue. 3 Columbus
Thu. 5 Florida
Sat. 7 Anaheim
Tue. 10 NY Islanders
Fri. 13 at Detroit
Sat. 14 at Buffalo
Tue. 17 at Boston
Thu. 19 at Philadelphia
Sat. 21 at Pittsburgh
Sun. 22 at Columbus*
Wed. 25 Chicago
Sat. 28 Calgary
Dec. Tue. 1 Pittsburgh
Fri. 4 at Anaheim
Sat. 5 Tampa Bay
Tue. 8 at Calgary
Wed. 9 at Edmonton
Sat. 12 Minnesota
Tue. 15 at Montreal
Thu. 17 at Toronto
Fri. 18 at Ottawa
Sun. 20 at Chicago
Tue. 22 at Los Angeles
Mon. 28 Colorado
Wed. 30 Philadelphia
Jan. Sat. 2 Winnipeg
Thu. 7 Detroit
Sat. 9 Toronto*
Mon. 11 at Calgary
Tue. 12 at Winnipeg

Thu. 14 Edmonton
Sat. 16 Dallas
Mon. 18 Ottawa
Thu. 21 at Arizona
Sat. 23 Minnesota*
Sun. 24 Los Angeles
Tue. 26 Colorado
Feb. Tue. 2 at Anaheim
Thu. 4 at St. Louis
Sat. 6 at Nashville
Tue. 9 at Chicago
Thu. 11 Calgary
Sat. 13 Arizona
Tue. 16 at Tampa Bay
Thu. 18 at Florida
Fri. 19 at Carolina
Mon. 22 at St. Louis
Wed. 24 at Colorado
Fri. 26 Buffalo
Sun. 28 at Vancouver*
Mon. 29 Montreal
Mar. Thu. 3 at Vancouver
Sat. 5 Vancouver
Mon. 7 at Calgary
Tue. 8 at Edmonton
Thu. 10 New Jersey
Sat. 12 Washington
Tue. 15 Boston
Thu. 17 at Arizona
Sat. 19 NY Rangers*
Sun. 20 Arizona
Tue. 22 St. Louis
Thu. 24 Edmonton
Sat. 26 Dallas*
Mon. 28 Los Angeles
Tue. 29 at Vancouver
Thu. 31 Vancouver
Apr. Sat. 2 at Nashville
Tue. 5 at Minnesota
Thu. 7 Winnipeg
Sat. 9 Arizona

* Denotes afternoon game.

Brent Burns ranked fourth among NHL defensemen with 17 goals in 2014-15. His career-best 43 assists and 60 points also ranked highly among the blue line leaders.

PACIFIC DIVISION
25th NHL Season
Franchise date: May 9, 1990

2015-16 Player Personnel

FORWARDS	HT	WT	*Age	Place of Birth	S	2014-15 Club
BROWN, Mike	5-11	202	30	Chicago, IL	R	San Jose
CARPENTER, Ryan	6-0	190	24	Oviedo, FL	R	Worcester
COUTURE, Logan	6-1	200	26	Guelph, ON	L	San Jose
DONSKOI, Joonas	6-0	195	23	Raahe, Finland	R	Karpat
EMANUELSSON, Petter	6-0	200	24	Kiruna, Sweden	R	Worcester
GOLDOBIN, Nikolay	5-10	185	20	Moscow, Russia	L	HIFK-Worcester
GOODROW, Barclay	6-2	215	22	Aurora, ON	L	San Jose-Worcester
HALEY, Micheal	5-10	205	29	Guelph, ON	L	San Jose-Worcester
HERTL, Tomas	6-2	210	21	Prague, Czech Rep.	L	San Jose
KARLSSON, Melker	6-0	180	25	Lycksele, Sweden	R	San Jose-Worcester
LERG, Bryan	5-10	175	29	Livonia, MI	L	San Jose-Worcester
MARLEAU, Patrick	6-2	220	36	Swift Current, SK	L	San Jose
McCARTHY, John	6-1	195	29	Boston, MA	L	Chicago (AHL)-Worcester
NIETO, Matt	5-11	190	22	Long Beach, CA	L	San Jose
PAVELSKI, Joe	5-11	190	31	Plover, WI	R	San Jose
SMITH, Ben	5-11	200	27	Winston-Salem, NC	R	Chicago-San Jose
THORNTON, Joe	6-4	220	36	London, ON	L	San Jose
TIERNEY, Chris	6-0	195	21	Keswick, ON	L	San Jose-Worcester
TORRES, Raffi	6-0	215	34	Toronto, ON	L	Did Not Play-Injured
WARD, Joel	6-1	226	34	Toronto, ON	R	Washington
WINGELS, Tommy	6-0	200	27	Evanston, IL	R	San Jose

DEFENSEMEN	HT	WT	*Age	Place of Birth	S	2014-15 Club
BERGMAN, Julius	6-1	195	19	Stockholm, Sweden	R	London-Worcester
BRAUN, Justin	6-2	205	28	St. Paul, MN	R	San Jose
BURNS, Brent	6-5	230	30	Ajax, ON	R	San Jose
CUNDARI, Mark	5-9	195	25	Woodbridge, ON	L	Adirondack
DeMELO, Dylan	6-1	195	22	London, ON	R	Worcester
DILLON, Brenden	6-4	225	24	Surrey, BC	L	Dallas-San Jose
MARTIN, Paul	6-1	200	34	Minneapolis, MN	L	Pittsburgh
McNALLY, Patrick	6-2	190	23	Glen Head, NY	L	Harvard
MUELLER, Mirco	6-3	205	20	Winterthur, Switz.	L	San Jose-Worcester
STOLLERY, Karl	5-11	180	27	Camrose, AB	L	Col-Lake Erie-S.J.-Wor
TENNYSON, Matt	6-2	205	25	Pleasanton, CA	R	San Jose-Worcester
VLASIC, Marc-Edouard	6-1	205	28	Montreal, QC	L	San Jose

GOALTENDERS	HT	WT	*Age	Place of Birth	C	2014-15 Club
GROSENICK, Troy	6-1	185	26	Brookfield, WI	L	San Jose-Worcester
JONES, Martin	6-4	190	25	North Vancouver, BC	L	Los Angeles
STALOCK, Alex	6-0	190	28	St. Paul, MN	L	San Jose

* – Age at start of 2015-16 season

2014-15 Scoring

* – rookie

Regular Season

Pos	#	Player	Team	GP	G	A	Pts	TOI	+/-	PIM	PP	SH	GW	S	S%
C	8	Joe Pavelski	S.J.	82	37	33	70	20:07	12	29	19	0	5	261	14.2
C	39	Logan Couture	S.J.	82	27	40	67	19:04	-6	12	6	2	4	263	10.3
C	19	Joe Thornton	S.J.	78	16	49	65	18:25	-4	30	4	0	0	131	12.2
D	88	Brent Burns	S.J.	82	17	43	60	23:57	-9	65	7	0	2	245	6.9
C	12	Patrick Marleau	S.J.	82	19	38	57	19:35	-17	12	7	0	4	233	8.2
C	57	Tommy Wingels	S.J.	75	15	21	36	16:28	-7	40	4	1	1	158	9.5
C	48	Tomas Hertl	S.J.	82	13	18	31	14:33	-5	16	3	0	4	145	9.0
L	83	Matt Nieto	S.J.	72	10	17	27	15:15	-12	20	1	0	1	135	7.4
C	68	* Melker Karlsson	S.J.	53	13	11	24	15:26	-3	20	1	0	2	100	13.0
D	44	Marc-Edouard Vlasic	S.J.	70	9	14	23	22:06	12	23	0	0	3	98	9.2
D	61	Justin Braun	S.J.	70	1	22	23	21:01	8	48	0	0	0	94	1.1
C	50	* Chris Tierney	S.J.	43	6	15	21	12:14	3	6	1	0	1	48	12.5
C	52	Matt Irwin	S.J.	53	8	11	19	17:01	3	18	1	0	1	93	8.6
R	21	Ben Smith	CHI	61	5	4	9	13:35	-1	2	0	0	0	77	6.5
			S.J.	19	2	3	5	11:20	3	0	0	0	1	15	13.3
			Total	80	7	7	14	13:03	2	2	0	0	1	92	7.6
C	89	* Barclay Goodrow	S.J.	60	4	8	12	11:04	-1	35	0	0	2	68	5.9
D	4	Brenden Dillon	DAL	20	0	2	2	20:36	-2	23	0	0	0	16	0.0
			S.J.	60	2	7	9	19:13	-11	54	0	1	1	75	2.7
			Total	80	2	9	11	19:34	-13	77	0	1	1	91	2.2
D	80	* Matt Tennyson	S.J.	27	2	6	8	17:34	0	16	1	0	0	37	5.4
D	27	Scott Hannan	S.J.	58	2	5	7	16:18	0	26	0	0	0	53	3.8
L	20	John Scott	S.J.	38	3	1	4	7:27	0	87	0	0	0	19	15.8
D	41	* Mirco Mueller	S.J.	39	1	3	4	16:57	-8	10	0	0	0	31	3.2
D	43	Taylor Fedun	S.J.	7	0	4	4	16:59	0	4	0	0	0	12	0.0
R	37	Adam Burish	S.J.	20	1	2	3	11:08	-6	33	0	0	0	22	4.5
L	42	Bryan Lerg	S.J.	2	1	0	1	12:36	-1	0	0	0	0	8	12.5
C	71	* Daniil Tarasov	S.J.	5	0	1	1	7:34	2	0	0	0	0	5	0.0
C	38	Micheal Haley	S.J.	4	0	0	0	7:30	-1	11	0	0	0	1	0.0
R	76	Eriah Hayes	S.J.	4	0	0	0	9:58	-2	2	0	0	0	10	0.0
D	3	Karl Stollery	COL	5	0	0	0	11:25	3	2	0	0	0	5	0.0
			S.J.	5	0	0	0	18:02	-4	4	0	0	0	6	0.0
			Total	10	0	0	0	14:43	-1	6	0	0	0	11	0.0
R	18	Mike Brown	S.J.	12	0	0	0	8:12	0	22	0	0	0	11	0.0

Goaltending

No.	Goaltender	GPI	Mins	Avg	W	L	OT	EN	SO	GA	SA	Sv%	G	A	PIM
34	* Troy Grosenick	2	118	1.53	1	1	0	1	1	3	58	.948	0	0	0
31	Antti Niemi	61	3588	2.59	31	23	7	12	5	155	1811	.914	0	3	0
32	Alex Stalock	22	1237	2.62	8	9	2	1	2	54	553	.902	0	0	2
	Totals	82	4982	2.72	40	33	9	14	8	226	2436	.907			

With 37 goals in 2014-15, Joe Pavelski led the Sharks for the second straight season. He finished third overall in the NHL with 41 goals in 2013-14.

Peter DeBoer

Head Coach

Born: Dunnville, ON, June 13, 1968.

San Jose Sharks general manager Doug Wilson announced on May 28, 2015, that Peter DeBoer had been named the eighth head coach in Sharks franchise history. This season will mark DeBoer's 21st consecutive season as a head coach, serving at both the NHL and Canadian Hockey League levels.

DeBoer spent the previous three-plus seasons as head coach of the New Jersey Devils. In 248 games coached with New Jersey, DeBoer posted a 114-93-41 record and ranks as the second-winningest coach in Devils franchise history, behind Jacques Lemaire. In 2011-12, after finishing with 102 points, he led the team to the Stanley Cup final, alongside current Sharks director of player development Larry Robinson, who served as assistant coach on DeBoer's staff. The Devils fell to the Los Angeles Kings in six games. Prior to coaching in New Jersey, DeBoer spent three seasons as head coach of the Florida Panthers. In 2008-09, his first season as an NHL head coach, he coached the Panthers to their then second-best season in franchise history with 93 points. In 246 games coached with Florida, DeBoer posted a 103-107-36 record.

Prior to coaching in the NHL, DeBoer was one of the most distinguished coaches in Ontario Hockey League history. He spent 13 seasons coaching with Detroit, Plymouth and Kitchener in the OHL, won the Memorial Cup in 2003 and the OHL championship in 2003 and 2008 with Kitchener. Winner of the OHL coach of the year award in 1999 and 2000 with Plymouth, he was also named the Canadian Hockey League coach of the year in 2000. During his time in the OHL, he led his team to the league's best overall record four times (1998-99, 1999-2000, 2002-03, 2007-08) and is one of only eight coaches in OHL history to reach the 500+ win mark.

Internationally, DeBoer has frequently been selected to represent his native Canada, including serving as an assistant coach for the Canadian World Championship squad in 2015 (gold medal), 2014 and 2010. Additionally, he was a member of the coaching staff for Canada's World Junior Championship team in 2005 (gold medal) and 1998. He also served on the Team Canada coaching staff for the 2007 Canada-Russia Super Series. DeBoer was selected by the Toronto Maple Leafs in the 1988 NHL Draft (12th round, 237th overall) while playing for the Windsor Spitfires (OHL). He played three seasons (1989 to 1991) professionally with the Milwaukee Admirals of the International Hockey League. DeBoer holds a law degree from the University of Windsor and University of Detroit through the Dual J.D. Program.

Coaching Record

			Regular Season					Playoffs			
Season	Team	League	GC	W	L	O/T		GC	W	L	T
1995-96	Detroit	OHL	66	40	22	4		17	9	8	....
1996-97	Detroit	OHL	66	26	34	6		5	1	4	....
1997-98	Plymouth	OHL	66	37	22	7		15	8	7	....
1998-99	Plymouth	OHL	66	51	11	4		11	7	4	....
99-2000	Plymouth	OHL	68	45	18	5		23	15	8	....
2000-01	Plymouth	OHL	68	43	15	10		19	14	5	....
2001-02	Kitchener	OHL	68	35	22	11		4	0	4	....
2002-03	Kitchener	OHL	68	46	14	8		21	16	5	....
2002-03	Kitchener	M-Cup	....	....	....	....		4	4	0	....
2003-04	Kitchener	OHL	68	34	26	8		5	1	4	....
2004-05	Kitchener	OHL	68	35	20	13		15	9	6	....
2005-06	Kitchener	OHL	68	47	19	2		5	1	4	....
2006-07	Kitchener	OHL	68	47	17	4		9	5	4	....
2007-08	Kitchener	OHL	68	53	11	4		20	16	4	....
2007-08	Kitchener	M-Cup	....	....	....	....		5	2	3	....
2008-09	**Florida**	**NHL**	82	41	30	11		....	....	....	....
2009-10	**Florida**	**NHL**	82	32	37	13		....	....	....	....
2010-11	**Florida**	**NHL**	82	30	40	12		....	....	....	....
2011-12	**New Jersey**	**NHL**	82	48	28	6		24	14	10	....
2012-13	**New Jersey**	**NHL**	48	19	19	10		....	....	....	....
2013-14	**New Jersey**	**NHL**	82	35	29	18		....	....	....	....
2014-15	**New Jersey**	**NHL**	36	12	17	7		....	....	....	....
	NHL Totals		494	217	200	77		24	14	10	

Club Records

Team

(Figures in brackets for season records are games played; records for fewest points, wins, ties, losses, goals, goals against are for 70 or more games)

Most Points .... 117 — 2008-09 (82)
Most Wins .... 53 — 2008-09 (82)
Most Ties .... 18 — 1998-99 (82)
Most Losses .... *71 — 1992-93 (84)
Most Goals .... 266 — 2005-06 (82)
Most Goals Against .... 414 — 1992-93 (84)
Fewest Points .... 24 — 1992-93 (84)
Fewest Wins .... 11 — 1992-93 (84)
Fewest Ties .... *2 — 1992-93 (84)
Fewest Losses .... 18 — 2008-09 (82)
Fewest Goals .... 196 — 1998-99 (82)
Fewest Goals Against .... 183 — 2003-04 (82)
Longest Winning Streak
- **Overall** .... 11 — Feb. 21-Mar. 14/08
- **Home** .... 9 — Oct. 9-Nov. 8/08
- **Away** .... 10 — Nov. 14-Dec. 31/07

Longest Undefeated Streak
- **Overall** .... 10 — Nov. 27-Dec. 19/01 (9W, 1T/OL)
- **Home** .... 11 — Nov. 15-Dec. 29/03 (8W, 3T/OL)
- **Away** .... 10 — Dec. 26/00-Feb. 16/01 (6W, 4T/OL)

Longest Losing Streak
- **Overall** .... *17 — Jan. 4-Feb. 12/93
- **Home** .... 9 — Nov. 19-Dec. 19/92
- **Away** .... 19 — Nov. 27/92-Feb. 12/93

Longest Winless Streak
- **Overall** .... 20 — Dec. 29/92-Feb. 12/93 (19L, 1T)
- **Home** .... 9 — Nov. 19-Dec. 19/92 (9L), Oct. 16-Nov. 18/03 (4L, 5T/OL)
- **Away** .... 19 — Nov. 27/92-Feb. 12/93 (19L)

Most Shutouts, Season .... 11 — 2003-04 (82), 2006-07 (82)
Most PIM, Season .... 2,134 — 1992-93 (84)
Most Goals, Game .... 10 — Jan. 13/96 (S.J. 10 at Pit. 8), Mar. 30/02 (CBJ 2 at S.J. 10)

Individual

Most Seasons .... 17 — Patrick Marleau
Most Games, Career .... 1,329 — Patrick Marleau
Most Goals, Career .... 456 — Patrick Marleau
Most Assists, Career .... 567 — Joe Thornton
Most Points, Career .... 988 — Patrick Marleau (456G, 532A)
Most PIM, Career .... 1,001 — Jeff Odgers
Most Shutouts, Career .... 50 — Evgeni Nabokov
Longest Consecutive Games Streak .... 379 — Joe Thornton (Dec. 1/05-Mar. 27/10)
Most Goals, Season .... 56 — Jonathan Cheechoo (2005-06)
Most Assists, Season .... 92 — Joe Thornton (2006-07)
Most Points, Season .... 114 — Joe Thornton (2006-07; 22G, 92A)
Most PIM, Season .... 326 — Link Gaetz (1991-92)
Most Points, Defenseman, Season .... 64 — Sandis Ozolinsh (1993-94; 26G, 38A)
Most Points, Center, Season .... 114 — Joe Thornton (2006-07; 22G, 92A)
Most Points, Right Wing, Season .... 93 — Jonathan Cheechoo (2005-06; 56G, 37A)
Most Points, Left Wing, Season .... 83 — Patrick Marleau (2009-10; 44G, 39A)
Most Points, Rookie, Season .... 59 — Pat Falloon (1991-92; 25G, 34A)
Most Shutouts, Season .... 9 — Evgeni Nabokov (2003-04)
Most Goals, Game .... 4 — Owen Nolan (Dec. 19/95), Tomas Hertl (Oct. 8/13)
Most Assists, Game .... 4 — Nineteen times
Most Points, Game .... 6 — Owen Nolan (Oct. 4/99; 3G, 3A)

* NHL Record.

Captains' History

Doug Wilson, 1991-92, 1992-93; Bob Errey, 1993-94; Bob Errey and Jeff Odgers, 1994-95; Jeff Odgers, 1995-96; Todd Gill, 1996-97, 1997-98; Owen Nolan, 1998-99 to 2002-03; Mike Ricci, Vincent Damphousse, Alyn McCauley, Patrick Marleau, 2003-04; Patrick Marleau, 2005-06 to 2008-09; Rob Blake, 2009-10; Joe Thornton, 2010-11 to 2013-14; no captain, 2014-15.

Coaching History

George Kingston, 1991-92, 1992-93; Kevin Constantine, 1993-94, 1994-95; Kevin Constantine and Jim Wiley, 1995-96; Al Sims, 1996-97; Darryl Sutter, 1997-98 to 2001-02; Darryl Sutter, Cap Raeder and Ron Wilson, 2002-03; Ron Wilson, 2003-04 to 2007-08; Todd McLellan, 2008-09 to 2014-15; Peter DeBoer, 2015-16.

General Managers' History

Jack Ferreira, 1991-92; Chuck Grillo (V.P. Director of Player Personnel), 1992-93 to 1995-96; Chuck Grillo and Dean Lombardi, 1996-97; Dean Lombardi, 1997-98 to 2002-03; Doug Wilson, 2003-04 to date.

All-time Record vs. Other Clubs

Regular Season

	Total								At Home								On Road							
	GP	W	L	T	OL	GF	GA	PTS	GP	W	L	T	OL	GF	GA	PTS	GP	W	L	T	OL	GF	GA	PTS
Anaheim	123	64	47	4	8	356	325	140	61	32	24	2	3	179	159	69	62	32	23	2	5	177	166	71
Arizona	129	65	47	7	10	391	360	147	63	34	17	4	8	205	169	80	66	31	30	3	2	186	191	67
Boston	32	10	16	5	1	88	100	26	16	6	7	2	1	41	48	15	16	4	9	3	0	47	52	11
Buffalo	33	7	20	4	2	91	128	20	16	6	5	4	1	47	53	17	17	1	15	0	1	44	75	3
Calgary	107	43	50	8	6	302	327	100	54	24	23	4	3	167	153	55	53	19	27	4	3	135	174	45
Carolina	32	15	15	0	2	104	100	32	16	8	6	0	2	65	51	18	16	7	9	0	0	39	49	14
Chicago	88	45	31	5	7	261	257	102	44	26	13	3	2	127	116	57	44	19	18	2	5	134	141	45
Colorado	84	37	37	5	5	230	265	84	43	24	18	1	0	134	126	49	41	13	19	4	5	96	139	35
Columbus	51	32	15	0	4	145	119	68	25	20	3	0	2	91	47	42	26	12	12	0	2	54	72	26
Dallas	117	52	47	5	13	304	320	122	59	25	24	1	9	148	157	60	58	27	23	4	4	156	163	62
Detroit	86	30	47	4	5	234	306	69	44	19	20	3	2	149	154	43	42	11	27	1	3	85	152	26
Edmonton	106	48	38	12	8	312	310	116	52	28	14	5	5	176	149	66	54	20	24	7	3	136	161	50
Florida	28	10	9	7	2	79	70	29	14	6	4	2	2	41	33	16	14	4	5	5	0	38	37	13
Los Angeles	136	69	53	7	7	399	377	152	68	43	20	3	2	221	176	91	68	26	33	4	5	178	201	61
Minnesota	53	30	15	2	6	146	121	68	27	18	6	1	2	80	53	39	26	12	9	1	4	66	68	29
Montreal	32	13	14	4	1	81	87	31	16	10	3	2	1	54	37	23	16	3	11	2	0	27	50	8
Nashville	61	31	22	2	6	157	152	70	31	19	7	1	4	83	72	43	30	12	15	1	2	74	80	27
New Jersey	33	13	16	2	2	82	106	30	15	6	7	1	1	38	44	14	18	7	9	1	1	44	62	16
NY Islanders	33	16	11	3	3	95	101	38	17	9	5	1	2	44	48	21	16	7	6	2	1	51	53	17
NY Rangers	33	8	20	3	2	87	117	21	18	4	11	2	1	47	62	11	15	4	9	1	1	40	55	10
Ottawa	28	13	11	4	0	73	74	30	14	8	6	0	0	32	30	16	14	5	5	4	0	41	44	14
Philadelphia	35	17	14	4	0	100	98	38	18	8	8	2	0	44	45	18	17	9	6	2	0	56	53	20
Pittsburgh	33	17	11	3	2	96	118	39	19	11	6	2	0	55	64	24	14	6	5	1	2	41	54	15
St. Louis	89	36	45	2	6	229	272	80	42	15	22	1	4	110	136	35	47	21	23	1	2	119	136	45
Tampa Bay	34	16	14	2	2	113	98	36	16	8	7	1	0	61	48	17	18	8	7	1	2	52	50	19
Toronto	43	18	20	5	0	116	130	41	20	9	8	3	0	51	51	21	23	9	12	2	0	65	79	20
Vancouver	106	46	46	9	5	305	320	106	55	23	23	5	4	160	158	55	51	23	23	4	1	145	162	51
Washington	35	23	9	1	2	114	92	49	17	11	3	1	2	59	43	25	18	12	6	0	0	55	49	24
Winnipeg	20	13	3	2	2	64	42	30	10	7	2	1	0	33	19	15	10	6	1	1	2	31	23	15
Totals	**1820**	**837**	**743**	**121**	**119**	**5154**	**5292**	**1914**	**910**	**467**	**322**	**58**	**63**	**2742**	**2501**	**1055**	**910**	**370**	**421**	**63**	**56**	**2412**	**2791**	**859**

Playoffs

	Series	W	L	GP	W	L	T	GF	GA	Last Mtg.	Rnd.	Result
Anaheim	1	0	1	6	2	4	0	10	18	2009	CQF	L 2-4
Arizona	1	1	0	5	4	1	0	13	7	2002	CQF	W 4-1
Calgary	3	2	1	20	10	10	0	57	68	2008	CQF	W 4-3
Chicago	1	0	1	4	0	4	0	7	13	2010	CF	L 0-4
Colorado	4	2	2	25	13	12	0	71	62	2010	CQF	W 4-2
Dallas	3	0	3	17	5	12	0	30	46	2008	CSF	L 2-4
Detroit	5	3	2	29	14	15	0	69	99	2011	CSF	W 4-3
Edmonton	1	0	1	6	2	4	0	12	19	2006	CSF	L 2-4
Los Angeles	3	1	2	20	10	10	0	52	60	2014	FR	L 3-4
Nashville	2	2	0	10	8	2	0	33	24	2007	CQF	W 4-1
St. Louis	4	2	2	23	11	12	0	51	61	2012	CQF	L 1-4
Toronto	1	0	1	7	3	4	0	21	26	1994	CSF	L 3-4
Vancouver	2	1	1	9	5	4	0	28	28	2013	CQF	W 4-0
Totals	**31**	**14**	**17**	**181**	**87**	**94**	**0**	**454**	**531**			

Carolina totals include Hartford, 1991-92 to 1996-97.
Dallas totals include Minnesota North Stars, 1991-92 to 1992-93.
Winnipeg totals include Atlanta Thrashers, 1999-2000 to 2010-11.

Playoff Results 2015-2011

Year	Round	Opponent	Result	GF	GA
2014	FR	Los Angeles	L 3-4	22	26
2013	CSF	Los Angeles	L 3-4	10	14
	CQF	Vancouver	W 4-0	15	8
2012	CQF	St. Louis	L 1-4	8	14
2011	CF	Vancouver	L 1-4	13	20
	CSF	Detroit	W 4-3	18	18
	CQF	Los Angeles	W 4-2	20	20

Abbreviations: Round: CF – conference final; **CSF** – conference semi-final; **CQF** – conference quarter-final; **FR** – first round.

Colorado totals include Quebec, 1991-92 to 1994-95.
Phoenix totals include Winnipeg, 1991-92 to 1995-96.

2014-15 Results

Oct.	8	at Los Angeles	4-0
	11	Winnipeg	3-0
	14	at Washington	6-5†
	16	at NY Islanders	3-4†
	18	at New Jersey	4-2
	19	at NY Rangers	0-4
	21	at Boston	3-5
	23	Columbus	4-5
	25	Buffalo	1-2
	26	at Anaheim	4-1
	28	at Colorado	3-2†
	30	at Minnesota	3-4†
Nov.	1	NY Islanders	3-1
	6	Vancouver	2-3
	8	at Dallas	5-3
	9	at Chicago	2-5
	11	at Florida	1-4
	13	at Tampa Bay	2-1
	15	at Columbus	1-2
	16	at Carolina	2-0
	18	at Buffalo	1-4
	20	Florida	2-3†
	22	Arizona	3-4†
	26	Calgary	0-2
	29	Anaheim	6-4
Dec.	2	Philadelphia	2-1
	4	Boston	7-4
	6	at Calgary	3-2
	7	at Edmonton	1-2
	9	Edmonton	5-2
	11	Minnesota	2-1
	13	Nashville	2-0
	18	Edmonton	4-3
	20	St. Louis	3-2*
	22	at Anaheim	2-3*
	27	at Los Angeles	1-3
	30	Vancouver	1-3
	31	at Anaheim	3-0
Jan.	3	St. Louis	2-7
	5	at Winnipeg	3-2
	6	at Minnesota	4-3*
	8	at St. Louis	2-7
	10	NY Rangers	1-3
	13	at Arizona	3-2
	15	Toronto	3-1
	17	Calgary	3-4*
	19	New Jersey	2-5
	21	Los Angeles	4-2
	29	Anaheim	6-3
	31	Chicago	2-0
Feb.	2	Edmonton	4-5†
	4	at Calgary	1-3
	5	at Vancouver	5-1
	7	Carolina	4-5
	9	Calgary	1-4
	11	Washington	4-5*
	13	at Arizona	4-2
	15	Tampa Bay	2-5
	17	at Nashville	1-5
	19	at Dallas	5-2
	21	Los Angeles	1-2
	26	Detroit	2-3
	28	Ottawa	2-4
Mar.	2	Montreal	4-0
	3	at Vancouver	6-2
	7	Vancouver	2-3
	9	Pittsburgh	2-1†
	12	Nashville	2-0
	14	Chicago	2-6
	17	at Winnipeg	2-5
	19	at Toronto	4-1
	21	at Montreal	0-2
	23	at Ottawa	2-5
	26	at Detroit	6-4
	28	at Philadelphia	3-2†
	29	at Pittsburgh	2-3†
Apr.	1	Colorado	5-1
	3	Arizona	3-1
	4	at Arizona	3-5
	6	Dallas	1-5
	9	at Edmonton	3-1
	11	at Los Angeles	1-4

* – Overtime † – Shootout

NHL Draft Selections 2015-2001

Name in bold denotes played in NHL.

2015 Pick		**2011** Pick		**2007** Pick		**2003** Pick	
9	Timo Meier	47	**Matt Nieto**	9	**Logan Couture**	6	**Milan Michalek**
31	Jeremy Roy	89	Justin Sefton	28	**Nicholas Petrecki**	16	**Steve Bernier**
86	Mike Robinson	133	Sean Kuraly	83	**Timo Pielmeier**	43	**Josh Hennessy**
106	Adam Helewka	166	Daniil Sobchenko	91	Tyson Sexsmith	47	**Matt Carle**
130	Karlis Cukste	179	Dylan Demelo	165	Patrik Zackrisson	139	Patrick Ehelechner
142	Rudolfs Balcers	194	Colin Blackwell	173	**Nick Bonino**	201	Jonathan Tremblay
160	Adam Parsells			201	**Justin Braun**	205	**Joe Pavelski**
190	Marcus Vela	**2010** Pick		203	**Frazer McLaren**	216	Kai Hospelt
193	John Kupsky	28	**Charlie Coyle**			236	Alexander Hult
		88	Max Gaede	**2006** Pick		267	Brian O'Hanley
2014 Pick		127	Cody Ferriero	16	**Ty Wishart**	276	Carter Lee
27	Nikolay Goldobin	129	**Freddie Hamilton**	36	**Jamie McGinn**		
46	Julius Bergman	136	Isaac MacLeod	98	James Delory	**2002** Pick	
53	Noah Rod	163	Konrad Abeltshauser	143	Ashton Rome	27	Mike Morris
72	Alex Schoenborn	188	Lee Moffie	202	**John McCarthy**	52	Dan Spang
81	Dylan Sadowy	200	Chris Crane	203	Jay Barriball	86	Jonas Fiedler
102	Alexis Vanier					139	**Kris Newbury**
149	Rourke Chartier	**2009** Pick		**2005** Pick		163	Tom Walsh
171	Kevin Labanc	43	William Wrenn	8	**Devin Setoguchi**	217	**Tim Conboy**
		57	Taylor Doherty	35	**Marc-Edouard Vlasic**	288	Michael Hutchins
2013 Pick		147	**Phil Varone**	112	**Alex Stalock**		
18	Mirco Mueller	189	Marek Viedensky	140	Taylor Dakers	**2001** Pick	
49	Gabryel Boudreau	207	Dominik Bielke	149	**Derek Joslin**	20	**Marcel Goc**
117	Fredrik Bergvik			162	P.J. Fenton	106	**Christian Ehrhoff**
141	Michael Brodzinski	**2008** Pick		183	Will Colbert	107	**Dimitri Patzold**
151	Gage Ausmus	62	Justin Daniels	193	Tony Lucia	140	**Tomas Plihal**
201	Jacob Jackson	92	Samuel Groulx			175	**Ryane Clowe**
207	Emil Galimov	106	Harri Sateri	**2004** Pick		182	**Tom Cavanagh**
		146	Julien Demers	22	**Lukas Kaspar**		
2012 Pick		177	**Tommy Wingels**	94	**Thomas Greiss**		
17	**Tomas Hertl**	186	**Jason Demers**	126	**Torrey Mitchell**		
55	**Chris Tierney**	194	Drew Daniels	129	Jason Churchill		
109	Christophe Lalancette			153	Steven Zalewski		
138	Daniel O'Regan			201	**Mike Vernace**		
168	Clifford Watson			225	David MacDonald		
198	Joakim Ryan			234	Derek MacIntyre		
				288	Brian Mahoney-Wilson		
				289	Christian Jensen		

Doug Wilson
Executive Vice President and General Manager
Born: Ottawa, ON, July 5, 1957.

Since taking charge of the Sharks hockey department on May 13, 2003, Doug Wilson has guided the team to its most successful era since the franchise's inception, capturing the Presidents' Trophy (2009) and five Pacific Division titles (2004, 2008, 2009, 2010, 2011). Under Wilson, the Sharks advanced to the Western Conference Final in 2004, 2010 and 2011.

Wilson has overall authority regarding all hockey-related operations. He oversees player personnel decisions, contract negotiation, scouting, player evaluation and draft day preparation. In his previous role as the team's director of pro development (1997 to 2003), the 16-year NHL veteran's responsibilities included evaluating talent at all professional and minor league levels and continuous assessment of the Sharks roster and reserve list. Working closely with the entire hockey department, Wilson has played a major role in creating a positive atmosphere in the Sharks dressing room.

Wilson draws on a vast amount of hockey knowledge. He was an integral member of the NHL Players' Association for four years (1993 to 1997) and is a past president of the NHLPA and served a consultant to Team Canada, winners of four consecutive World Junior gold medals in the 1990s. His brother Murray was a member of four Stanley Cup championship teams with Montreal in the 1970s. With the Ottawa 67s in junior, Wilson played for Hall of Famer Hec Kilrea, junior hockey's winningest coach.

In 2004, Wilson was named to the NHL's Game Committee, a panel of players, coaches, executives and media responsible for examining all aspects of the game. This committee included Hall of Fame Coach Scotty Bowman, Pittsburgh's Mario Lemieux and St. Louis Blues President of Hockey Operations John Davidson, among others.

A first-round draft choice (sixth overall) by the Blackhawks in 1977 after a stellar junior career, Wilson played 14 seasons in Chicago and still ranks as that club's highest scoring defenseman with 225 goals and 554 assists for 779 points. He led all Blackhawks defensemen in scoring for 10 consecutive seasons (1980-81 through 1990-91) and captured the 1982 James Norris Memorial Trophy, as the League's top defenseman, when he tallied 39 goals and 85 points — still Blackhawks single-season records for goals and points for a defenseman.

Acquired by San Jose from Chicago just before the Sharks inaugural season (1991-92), Wilson brought instant credibility and respect to the young franchise. He played two seasons for the Sharks, serving as the franchise's first team captain (1991 to 1993). He played his 1,000th NHL game on Nov. 21, 1992 and was named San Jose's nominee (1992 and 1993) for the King Clancy Award for leadership and humanitarian contributions both on-and off-the-ice.

Wilson announced his retirement as a member of the Sharks during training camp in 1993-94 after playing 1,024 regular-season and 95 playoff games. He played in seven NHL All-Star Games (six with Chicago and one with San Jose) and earned one First and two Second Team All-Star selections.

Club Directory

SAP Center at San Jose

San Jose Sharks
SAP Center at San Jose
525 West Santa Clara Street
San Jose, CA 95113
Phone **408/287-7070**
FAX 408/999-5797
www.sjsharks.com
Capacity: 17,562

Ownership Group
Hasso Plattner, Gary Valenzuela, Gordon Russell, Rudy Staedler

Sharks Sports and Entertainment Advisory Board
Hasso Plattner, Gary Valenzuela, Scott McNealy, Rouven Westphal

Hockey Operations
General Manager	Doug Wilson
Vice President & Assistant General Manager	Joe Will
Head Coach	Peter DeBoer
Director of Player Development	Larry Robinson
Assistant Coach	Bob Boughner
Assistant Coach/Goaltending Coach	Johan Hedberg
Development Coach / Video Coordinator	Mike Ricci / Dan Darrow
Director, Scouting	Tim Burke
Scouts	Gilles Cote, Pat Funk, Dirk Graham, Rob Grillo, Brian Gross, Shin Larsson, Bryan Marchment, Jason Rowe, Niklas Sundstrom, Mike Yandle
Athletic Trainers, Head / Assistant	Ray Tufts, ATC / Wes Howard, ATC
Strength & Conditioning Coordinator	Mike Potenza
Massage Therapist	Arnulfo Aguirre, CMT, ART
Equipment Manager / Assistant Manager	Mike Aldrich / Vinny Ferraiuolo
Director, Hockey Admin. / Team Services Mgr.	Rosemary Tebaldi / Ryan Stenn
Hockey Operations Analyst	Doug Wilson, Jr.
Equipment Asst. & Transport / Cleaning Specialist	Roy Sneesby, Norma Hernandez
Head Team Physician	Mark Davies MD
Team Physicians	Drs. Scott Crow, Anthony Abene, AJ Uy, Young Yoon, Chris Fowler, David Nix, Harley Goldberg, Katherine Gray
Team Dentist / Chiropractic Consultant	Don Goudy, DDS / Mike McMurray, DC

Business and Building Operations
Chief Operating Officer	John Tortora
Executive V.P., Business and Building Ops.	Jim Goddard
Executive V.P., Chief Sales & Mktg. Officer	Flavil Hampsten
Vice President, SSE Marketing & Digital	Doug Bentz
Vice Presidents, Sales & Service / Finance	John Castro / Ken Caveney
Vice President, Media Relations & Broadcasting	Scott Emmert
Vice President, Sharks Ice & Worcester Sharks	Jon Gustafson
Vice Presidents, People / Business Intelligence	Fiona Ow Giuffre / Neda Tabatabaie
Vice Presidents, Booking & Events / Building Ops	Steve Kirsner / Rich Sotelo
Executive Assistants	Rebeca Gomez, Sarah Sproule, Dori Ortega

Ticket Sales
Director of Ticket Sales	Mike Nieves
Ticket Ops. Sr. Manager / Manager	Scott Fitzsimmons / TBD
Account Sales Managers	Ted Chuba, Mike Hollywood, Adam King, Eric Manuta, Zach Plaza, Brian Lauer, Mark Goodwin, Jess Dudek, Dustin Frediani, Ryan Silva, Sara Dugan

Corporate Partnerships
Senior Sales Manager, Corporate Partnerships	Jennifer Birmingham
Senior Service Manager, Corporate Partnerships	Jen De Carlo
Sales Managers, Corporate Partnerships	Spencer Neft, Stephen Gracio

Suite Sales and Service
Suite Sales & Service Director / Managers	Bruce Ross / Ted Chuba, Julie Kennedy

Event Presentation
Director of Event Presentation	Steve Maroni

Marketing and Digital Media
Managers, Marketing / Digital Media	Courtney Jankovich / Patrick Hooper
Creative Services Manager / Graphic Designer	Brittney Thorp / Caitlynn Steinberg
Digital Media Production Manager / Coord.	Dustin Lamendola / Nathan Hone
Digital Media Content Developer	Sarah Peters
Coordinators, Social Media / CRM Marketing	Nicole Graziol / Stacy McGranor

Media Relations
Media Relations Manager / Coordinator	Ben Guerrero / Nicolas Carrillo

Public Relations and Fan Development / Sharks Foundation
Director of Public Relations & Fan Development	Jim Sparaco
Managers, Mascot Ops / Fan Development	Tim Patnode / Tim Howell
Sharks Foundation Manager / Coordinators	Heather Hooper / Casey Roberts, Jenne Johnson

Broadcasting
Television Play-By-Play / Color Analyst	Randy Hahn / Jamie Baker
Radio Play-By-Play / Color Analysts	Dan Rusanowsky / Bret Hedican, David Maley
Production Associate	Elisabeth Farkas

Building Operations
Director, Booking & Events	James Hamnett
Directors, Building Services / Ticket Operations	Monte Chavez / Patrick Doherty
Facilities Technical Director / Chief Engineer	Greg Carrolan / Eric Gold
Building Services Managers	Bruce Tharaldson, Ray Romero
Technical Services Lead / EMT Manager	Matthew Galvin / David Falco
Receptionist / Administrative Assistant	Starley Lindley / Yvette Rangel

Finance
Controller	Stephanie Reitz

Information Technology
Director of IT / Systems Administrator / Support Specialist	Allison Aiello / Cara Browning / Tony Harrell

Human Resources
Business Partner	Jeannine Turner

Legal
Counsel / Legal Coordinator	Maggie Carlyle / Mary Grace Miller

Miscellaneous
Television Rightsholder	Comcast SportsNet California
Radio Network Flagship	98.5 KFOX (KUFX FM)
Team Photographers	Don Smith, Rocky Widner
P.A. Announcer / Mascot	Danny Miller / S.J. Sharkie

Tampa Bay Lightning

2014-15 Results: 50w-24L-3otl-5sol 108pts
2ND, Atlantic Division • 3RD, Eastern Conference

Key Off-Season Signings/Acquisitions

2015

June	28	• Re-signed C **Jonathan Marchessault**.
	29	• Re-signed RW **Mike Blunden**.
	30	• Re-signed D **Andrej Sustr** and LW **Mike Angelidis**.
July	1	• Signed RW **Erik Condra**.
	17	• Re-signed C **Vladislav Namestnikov** and D **Luke Witkowski**.
	21	• Signed LW **Tye McGinn**.

2015-16 Schedule

Oct.	Thu.	8	Philadelphia		Sat.	9	at Vancouver
	Sat.	10	at Buffalo*		Tue.	12	at Colorado
	Mon.	12	at Boston*		Fri.	15	Pittsburgh
	Tue.	13	at Detroit		Sun.	17	Florida*
	Thu.	15	Dallas		Tue.	19	Edmonton
	Sat.	17	Buffalo		Thu.	21	Chicago
	Tue.	20	at Nashville		Sat.	23	at Florida
	Fri.	23	at Winnipeg		Wed.	27	Toronto
	Sat.	24	at Chicago	**Feb.**	Wed.	3	Detroit
	Tue.	27	at St. Louis		Fri.	5	Pittsburgh
	Thu.	29	Colorado		Mon.	8	at Ottawa
	Sat.	31	Boston		Tue.	9	at Montreal
Nov.	Sun.	1	at Carolina*		Fri.	12	Nashville
	Tue.	3	at Detroit		Sun.	14	St. Louis
	Thu.	5	at Buffalo		Tue.	16	San Jose
	Sat.	7	at Minnesota		Thu.	18	Winnipeg
	Tue.	10	Buffalo		Sat.	20	at Pittsburgh*
	Thu.	12	Calgary		Sun.	21	at Carolina
	Sat.	14	Florida		Tue.	23	Arizona
	Mon.	16	at Florida		Fri.	26	at New Jersey
	Thu.	19	NY Rangers		Sun.	28	at Boston
	Sat.	21	Anaheim		Mon.	29	at Toronto
	Wed.	25	Los Angeles	**Mar.**	Thu.	3	at Ottawa
	Fri.	27	at Washington*		Sat.	5	Carolina
	Sat.	28	NY Islanders		Mon.	7	at Philadelphia
Dec.	Wed.	2	at Anaheim		Tue.	8	Boston
	Sat.	5	at San Jose		Fri.	11	Philadelphia
	Sun.	6	at Los Angeles		Sun.	13	at Columbus*
	Thu.	10	Ottawa		Tue.	15	at Toronto
	Sat.	12	Washington		Thu.	17	at Dallas
	Mon.	14	at Columbus		Sat.	19	at Arizona
	Tue.	15	at Toronto		Tue.	22	Detroit
	Fri.	18	at Washington		Fri.	25	NY Islanders
	Sun.	20	Ottawa*		Sat.	26	Florida
	Tue.	22	Vancouver		Mon.	28	Toronto
	Sat.	26	Columbus		Thu.	31	Montreal
	Mon.	28	Montreal	**Apr.**	Sat.	2	New Jersey
	Wed.	30	NY Rangers		Mon.	4	at NY Islanders
Jan.	Sat.	2	Minnesota		Tue.	5	at NY Rangers
	Tue.	5	at Calgary		Thu.	7	at New Jersey
	Fri.	8	at Edmonton		Sat.	9	at Montreal

* Denotes afternoon game.

Year-by-Year Record

Season	GP	Home W	L	T	OL	Road W	L	T	OL	Overall W	L	T	OL	GF	GA	Pts	Div. Fin.	Conf. Fin.	Playoff Result
2014-15	82	32	8	....	1	18	16	....	7	50	24	....	8	262	211	108	2nd, Atl.	3rd, East	Lost Final
2013-14	82	25	10	....	6	21	17	....	3	46	27	....	9	240	215	101	2nd, Atl.	3rd, East	Lost First Round
2012-13	48	12	10	....	2	6	16	....	2	18	26	....	4	148	150	40	4th, SE	14th, East	Out of Playoffs
2011-12	82	25	14	....	2	13	22	....	6	38	36	....	8	235	281	84	3rd, SE	10th, East	Out of Playoffs
2010-11	82	25	11	....	5	21	14	....	6	46	25	....	11	247	240	103	2nd, SE	5th, East	Lost Conf. Final
2009-10	82	21	14	....	6	13	22	....	6	34	36	....	12	217	260	80	4th, SE	12th, East	Out of Playoffs
2008-09	82	12	18	....	11	12	22	....	7	24	40	....	18	210	279	66	5th, SE	14th, East	Out of Playoffs
2007-08	82	20	18	....	3	11	24	....	4	31	42	....	9	223	267	71	5th, SE	15th, East	Out of Playoffs
2006-07	82	22	18	....	1	22	15	....	4	44	33	....	5	253	261	93	2nd, SE	7th, East	Lost Conf. Quarter-Final
2005-06	82	25	14	....	2	18	19	....	4	43	33	....	6	252	260	92	2nd, SE	8th, East	Lost Conf. Quarter-Final
2004-05					......														
2003-04	**82**	**24**	**10**	**4**	**3**	**22**	**12**	**4**	**3**	**46**	**22**	**8**	**6**	**245**	**192**	**106**	**1st, SE**	**1st, East**	**Won Stanley Cup**
2002-03	82	22	9	7	3	14	16	9	2	36	25	16	5	219	210	93	1st, SE	3rd, East	Lost Conf. Semi-Final
2001-02	82	16	17	5	3	11	23	6	1	27	40	11	4	178	219	69	3rd, SE	13th, East	Out of Playoffs
2000-01	82	17	19	3	2	7	28	3	3	24	47	6	5	201	280	59	5th, SE	14th, East	Out of Playoffs
1999-2000	82	13	20	4	4	6	27	5	3	19	47	9	7	204	310	54	4th, SE	14th, East	Out of Playoffs
1998-99	82	12	25	4	....	7	29	5	....	19	54	9	....	179	292	47	4th, SE	14th, East	Out of Playoffs
1997-98	82	11	23	7	....	6	32	3	....	17	55	10	....	151	269	44	7th, Atl.	13th, East	Out of Playoffs
1996-97	82	15	18	8	....	17	22	2	....	32	40	10	....	217	247	74	4th, Atl.	11th, East	Out of Playoffs
1995-96	82	22	14	5	....	16	18	7	....	38	32	12	....	238	248	88	5th, Atl.	8th, East	Lost Conf. Quarter-Final
1994-95	48	14	10	0	....	7	14	3	....	21	28	3	....	120	144	37	6th, Atl.	12th, East	Out of Playoffs
1993-94	84	14	22	6	....	16	21	5	....	30	43	11	....	224	251	71	7th, Atl.	12th, East	Out of Playoffs
1992-93	84	12	27	3	....	11	27	4	....	23	54	7	....	245	332	53	6th, Norris		Out of Playoffs

Victor Hedman had 10 goals in 59 games during the regular season and proved himself to be among the NHL's best defensemen in the playoffs. He played all 26 postseason games for Tampa Bay and trailed only Chicago's Duncan Keith in total ice time.

ATLANTIC DIVISION
24th NHL Season

Franchise date: December 16, 1991

2015-16 Player Personnel

FORWARDS	HT	WT	*Age	Place of Birth	S	2014-15 Club
BOYLE, Brian	6-7	244	30	Hingham, MA	L	Tampa Bay
BROWN, J.T.	5-11	170	25	High Point, NC	R	Tampa Bay
CALLAHAN, Ryan	5-11	190	30	Rochester, NY	R	Tampa Bay
CONDRA, Erik	6-0	190	29	Trenton, MI	R	Ottawa
DROUIN, Jonathan	5-11	191	20	Ste-Agathe, QC	L	Tampa Bay-Syracuse
FILPPULA, Valtteri	6-0	195	31	Vantaa, Finland	L	Tampa Bay
JOHNSON, Tyler	5-9	182	25	Spokane, WA	R	Tampa Bay
KILLORN, Alex	6-2	205	26	Halifax, NS	L	Tampa Bay
KUCHEROV, Nikita	5-11	171	22	Maikop, Russia	L	Tampa Bay
MARCHESSAULT, Jon	5-9	175	24	Cap-Rouge, QC	R	Tampa Bay-Syracuse
McGINN, Tye	6-2	205	25	Fergus, ON	L	San Jose-Arizona
NAMESTNIKOV, Vladislav	6-0	179	22	Zhukovsky, Russia	L	Tampa Bay-Syracuse
PALAT, Ondrej	6-0	180	24	Frydek-Mistek, Czech.	L	Tampa Bay
PAQUETTE, Cedric	6-1	198	22	Gaspe, QC	L	Tampa Bay-Syracuse
STAMKOS, Steven	6-0	190	25	Markham, ON	R	Tampa Bay

DEFENSEMEN	HT	WT	*Age	Place of Birth	S	2014-15 Club
CARLE, Matt	6-0	205	31	Anchorage, AK	L	Tampa Bay
COBURN, Braydon	6-5	220	30	Calgary, AB	L	Philadelphia-Tampa Bay
GARRISON, Jason	6-2	218	30	White Rock, BC	L	Tampa Bay
HEDMAN, Victor	6-6	233	24	Ornskoldsvik, Sweden	L	Tampa Bay
KOEKKOEK, Slater	6-2	184	21	Winchester, ON	L	Tampa Bay-Syracuse
NESTEROV, Nikita	6-0	191	22	Chelyabinsk, Russia	L	Tampa Bay-Syracuse
STRALMAN, Anton	5-11	190	29	Tibro, Sweden	R	Tampa Bay
SUSTR, Andrej	6-7	220	24	Plzen, Czech.	R	Tampa Bay

GOALTENDERS	HT	WT	*Age	Place of Birth	C	2014-15 Club
BISHOP, Ben	6-7	214	28	Denver, CO	L	Tampa Bay
VASILEVSKIY, Andrei	6-3	204	21	Tyumen, Russia	L	Tampa Bay-Syracuse

* – Age at start of 2015-16 season

Coaching History

Terry Crisp, 1992-93 to 1996-97; Terry Crisp, Rick Paterson and Jacques Demers, 1997-98; Jacques Demers, 1998-99; Steve Ludzik, 1999-2000; Steve Ludzik and John Tortorella, 2000-01; John Tortorella, 2001-02 to 2007-08; Barry Melrose and Rick Tocchet, 2008-09; Rick Tocchet, 2009-10; Guy Boucher, 2010-11, 2011-12; Guy Boucher and Jon Cooper, 2012-13; Jon Cooper, 2013-14 to date.

Jon Cooper

Head Coach

Born: Prince George, BC, August 23, 1967.

The Tampa Bay Lightning named Jon Cooper as the eighth head coach in franchise history on March 25, 2013. In his first full season with the club in 2013-14, Cooper led the Lightning back to the playoffs after a two-year absence. The team tied a club record with 46 wins and he finished third in voting for the Jack Adams Award as coach of the year. In 2014-15, the Lightning set club records with 50 wins and 108 points and reached the Stanley Cup Final.

Cooper joined the Lightning after having spent the previous three seasons behind the bench of Tampa Bay's top minor league affiliate, the Norfolk Admirals, from 2010 to 2012 and the Syracuse Crunch in 2012-13. He compiled a 133-62-26 regular-season record (.661) in 221 games in the American Hockey League.

Cooper was awarded the Louis A.R. Pieri Memorial Award as the AHL's top coach in 2011-12 after guiding the Admirals to a franchise-record 55 wins and 113 points en route to the team's first Calder Cup Championship. Along the way, Cooper and his team set a North American professional hockey record, winning a remarkable 28 consecutive games. Norfolk also earned the Macgregor Kilpatrick Trophy as the AHL's regular-season points champion, while capturing the league's East Division title. Cooper led Norfolk to a 94-44-18 record in the regular season and a 17-7 mark in the playoffs during two seasons behind the bench. In 2012-13, he led the Syracuse Crunch to a 39-18-8 record, the best in the AHL at the time, despite a number of key players being recalled to the Lightning before he himself was summoned to Tampa Bay.

Before joining the AHL ranks, Cooper also found success in the United States Hockey League with the Green Bay Gamblers, posting an 84-27-9 record in two seasons. Under Cooper's guidance the Gamblers posted back-to-back seasons with the best record in the USHL and won the 2010 Clark Cup. In his first season in 2008-09, Green Bay saw a 50-point improvement from the previous year, setting a USHL record for largest single-season improvement. He was rewarded with the 2009 and 2010 USHL General Manager of the Year Awards, as well as being named the 2010 USHL Coach of the Year.

Cooper played high school hockey at Notre Dame in Wilcox, Saskatchewan. He then moved on to Hofstra University in the NCAA, where he played four seasons of Division I lacrosse and spent one season on Hofstra's hockey team. He then went on to earn a law degree from Thomas M. Cooley Law School in Lansing, Michigan, eventually closing his practice in 2003 to pursue a career in coaching.

2014-15 Scoring

* – rookie

Regular Season

Pos	#	Player	Team	GP	G	A	Pts	TOI	+/–	PIM	PP	SH	GW	S	S%
C	91	Steven Stamkos	T.B.	82	43	29	72	19:22	2	49	13	0	6	268	16.0
C	9	Tyler Johnson	T.B.	77	29	43	72	17:14	33	24	8	0	6	203	14.3
R	86	Nikita Kucherov	T.B.	82	29	36	65	14:57	38	37	2	0	2	191	15.2
L	18	Ondrej Palat	T.B.	75	16	47	63	17:25	31	24	3	1	5	139	11.5
R	24	Ryan Callahan	T.B.	77	24	30	54	17:44	9	41	10	0	4	191	12.6
C	51	Valtteri Filppula	T.B.	82	12	36	48	19:01	–14	24	2	0	0	91	13.2
D	6	Anton Stralman	T.B.	82	9	30	39	21:56	22	26	2	0	0	138	6.5
C	17	Alex Killorn	T.B.	71	15	23	38	16:55	8	36	1	1	5	130	11.5
D	77	Victor Hedman	T.B.	59	10	28	38	22:41	12	40	3	0	2	115	8.7
L	27 *	Jonathan Drouin	T.B.	70	4	28	32	13:14	3	34	3	0	0	76	5.3
D	5	Jason Garrison	T.B.	70	4	26	30	20:00	27	19	1	0	3	111	3.6
C	11	Brian Boyle	T.B.	82	15	9	24	12:59	3	54	0	3	5	140	10.7
C	13 *	Cedric Paquette	T.B.	64	12	7	19	13:36	4	51	0	2	3	91	13.2
D	25	Matthew Carle	T.B.	59	4	14	18	20:29	12	26	1	0	0	73	5.5
C	90 *	Vladislav Namestnikov	T.B.	43	9	7	16	11:59	1	13	1	0	3	46	19.6
D	62	Andrej Sustr	T.B.	72	0	13	13	17:42	10	34	0	0	0	55	0.0
D	55	Braydon Coburn	PHI	39	1	8	9	20:14	–1	16	0	0	0	45	2.2
			T.B.	4	0	2	2	17:01	3	9	0	0	0	1	0.0
			Total	43	1	10	11	19:56	2	25	0	0	0	46	2.2
R	23	J.T. Brown	T.B.	52	3	6	9	10:36	–2	30	0	0	0	74	4.1
L	10	Brenden Morrow	T.B.	70	3	5	8	9:19	–1	64	0	0	0	28	10.7
D	89 *	Nikita Nesterov	T.B.	27	2	5	7	16:03	6	16	1	0	0	44	4.5
D	8	Mark Barberio	T.B.	52	1	6	7	16:46	–4	16	0	0	0	53	1.9
D	7	Radko Gudas	T.B.	31	2	3	5	17:00	–5	34	0	0	1	63	3.2
C	42 *	Jon Marchessault	T.B.	2	1	0	1	11:56	1	0	0	0	0	3	33.3
R	46	Mike Blunden	T.B.	2	0	0	0	9:47	–1	2	0	0	0	0	0.0
L	15	Mike Angelidis	T.B.	3	0	0	0	7:20	0	12	0	0	0	0	0.0
D	29 *	Slater Koekkoek	T.B.	3	0	0	0	16:35	0	2	0	0	0	6	0.0
D	53 *	Luke Witkowski	T.B.	16	0	0	0	15:11	0	15	0	0	0	10	0.0

Goaltending

No.	Goaltender	GPI	Mins	Avg	W	L	OT	EN	SO	GA	SA	Sv%	G	A	PIM
30	Ben Bishop	62	3519	2.32	40	13	5	4	4	136	1620	.916	0	4	4
88	* Andrei Vasilevskiy	16	864	2.36	7	5	1	2	1	34	415	.918	0	0	0
20	Evgeni Nabokov	11	553	3.15	3	6	2	1	0	29	245	.882	0	1	2
	Totals	**82**	**4977**	**2.48**	**50**	**24**	**8**	**7**	**5**	**206**	**2287**	**.910**			

Playoffs

Pos	#	Player	Team	GP	G	A	Pts	TOI	+/–	PIM	PP	SH	GW	OT	S	S%
C	9	Tyler Johnson	T.B.	26	13	10	23	18:30	7	24	2	1	4	1	60	21.7
R	86	Nikita Kucherov	T.B.	26	10	12	22	16:59	7	14	3	0	3	2	57	17.5
C	17	Alex Killorn	T.B.	26	9	9	18	20:10	3	12	1	0	2	0	66	13.6
C	91	Steven Stamkos	T.B.	26	7	11	18	18:33	2	20	2	0	1	0	65	10.8
L	18	Ondrej Palat	T.B.	26	8	8	16	19:10	5	12	4	0	0	0	43	18.6
C	51	Valtteri Filppula	T.B.	26	4	10	14	19:13	–6	4	2	0	1	0	31	12.9
D	77	Victor Hedman	T.B.	26	1	13	14	23:57	11	6	1	0	0	0	64	1.6
D	6	Anton Stralman	T.B.	26	1	8	9	22:30	1	8	0	0	0	0	52	1.9
R	24	Ryan Callahan	T.B.	25	2	6	8	16:52	3	14	1	0	0	0	56	3.6
D	5	Jason Garrison	T.B.	23	2	5	7	19:29	–2	8	1	0	1	0	31	6.5
D	89 *	Nikita Nesterov	T.B.	17	1	5	6	10:46	5	8	0	0	0	0	11	9.1
D	55	Braydon Coburn	T.B.	26	1	3	4	16:59	–6	21	0	0	1	0	39	2.6
C	13 *	Cedric Paquette	T.B.	24	3	0	3	12:47	–6	28	0	1	1	0	17	17.6
D	25	Matthew Carle	T.B.	25	0	3	3	16:30	–10	4	0	0	0	0	23	0.0
R	23	J.T. Brown	T.B.	24	1	1	2	12:20	–5	0	0	0	0	0	39	2.6
C	11	Brian Boyle	T.B.	25	1	1	2	13:39	–3	10	0	1	0	0	35	2.9
D	62	Andrej Sustr	T.B.	26	1	1	2	15:14	4	18	0	0	0	0	16	6.3
C	90 *	Vladislav Namestnikov	T.B.	12	0	1	1	7:51	–2	4	0	0	0	0	3	0.0
D	8	Mark Barberio	T.B.	1	0	0	0	8:44	–1	0	0	0	0	0	1	0.0
C	42 *	Jon Marchessault	T.B.	2	0	0	0	11:27	0	0	0	0	0	0	3	0.0
L	27 *	Jonathan Drouin	T.B.	6	0	0	0	10:02	–6	2	0	0	0	0	6	0.0
L	10	Brenden Morrow	T.B.	24	0	0	0	8:40	–2	22	0	0	0	0	13	0.0

Goaltending

No.	Goaltender	GPI	Mins	Avg	W	L	EN	SO	GA	SA	Sv%	G	A	PIM
30	Ben Bishop	25	1459	2.18	13	11	2	3	53	669	.921	0	3	4
88	* Andrei Vasilevskiy	4	113	3.19	1	1	1	0	6	57	.895	0	0	0
	Totals	**26**	**1588**	**2.34**	**14**	**12**	**3**	**3**	**62**	**729**	**.915**			

Coaching Record

			Regular Season				Playoffs			
Season	Team	League	GC	W	L	O/T	GC	W	L	T
2003-04	Texarkana	NAHL	56	30	24	2	4	0	4	0
2004-05	Texarkana	NAHL	56	36	15	5	9	4	5	0
2005-06	Texarkana	NAHL	58	42	12	4	8	3	5	0
2006-07	St. Louis	NAHL	62	43	14	5	12	9	3	0
2007-08	St. Louis	NAHL	58	47	9	2	11	9	1	1
2008-09	Green Bay	USHL	60	39	17	4	7	4	3	....
2009-10	Green Bay	USHL	60	45	10	5	12	9	3	....
2010-11	Norfolk	AHL	80	39	26	15	6	2	4	....
2011-12	Norfolk	AHL	76	55	18	3	18	15	3	....
2012-13	Syracuse	AHL	65	39	18	8	....	....	....	....
2012-13*	**Tampa Bay**	**NHL**	**15**	**4**	**8**	**3**	....	....	....	....
2013-14	**Tampa Bay**	**NHL**	**82**	**46**	**27**	**9**	**4**	**0**	**4**	....
2014-15	**Tampa Bay**	**NHL**	**82**	**50**	**24**	**8**	**26**	**14**	**12**	....
	NHL Totals		**179**	**100**	**59**	**20**	**30**	**14**	**16**	....

* Hired by Tampa Bay on March 25, 2013 but did not appear behind the bench until March 29. Assistant coaches Dan Lacroix, Martin Raymond, and Steve Thomas worked a 3-2 loss at Winnipeg on March 24. Lacroix and Thomas worked a 2-1 win vs. Buffalo on March 26.

Club Records

Team

(Figures in brackets for season records are games played; records for fewest points, wins, ties, losses, goals, goals against are for 70 or more games)

Most Points	**108**	2014-15 (82)
Most Wins	**50**	2014-15 (82)
Most Ties	**16**	2002-03 (82)
Most Losses	**55**	1997-98 (82)
Most Goals	**247**	2010-11 (82)
Most Goals Against	**332**	1992-93 (84)
Fewest Points	**44**	1997-98 (82)
Fewest Wins	**17**	1997-98 (82)
Fewest Ties	**6**	2000-01 (82)
Fewest Losses	**22**	2003-04 (82)
Fewest Goals	**151**	1997-98 (82)
Fewest Goals Against	**192**	2003-04 (82)
Longest Winning Streak		
Overall	**8**	Feb. 23-Mar. 6/04
Home	**10**	Dec. 11/14-Jan. 31/15
Away	**7**	Jan. 7-Feb. 1/07
Longest Undefeated Streak		
Overall	**13**	Mar. 7-Apr. 2/03 (7W, 6T/OL)
Home	**10**	Jan. 29-Mar. 12/04 (9W, 1T/OL)
Away	**7**	Feb. 23-Mar. 10/04 (6W, 1T/OL), Jan. 7-Feb. 1/07 (7W)
Longest Losing Streak		
Overall	**13**	Jan. 3-Feb. 2/98
Home	**10**	Jan. 3-Feb. 26/98
Away	**11**	Oct. 24-Dec. 10/97
Longest Winless Streak		
Overall	**16**	Oct. 10-Nov. 17/97 (15L, 1T), Jan. 2-Feb. 5/98 (14L, 2T)
Home	**11**	Jan. 2-Feb. 26/98 (10L, 1T)
Away	**17**	Dec. 2/99-Feb. 19/00 (14L, 3T/OL)
Most Shutouts, Season	**9**	2001-02 (82)
Most PIM, Season	**1,823**	1997-98 (82)
Most Goals, Game	**9**	Nov. 8/03 (Pit. 0 at T.B. 9)

Individual

Most Seasons	**14**	Vincent Lecavalier
Most Games, Career	**1,037**	Vincent Lecavalier
Most Goals, Career	**383**	Vincent Lecavalier
Most Assists, Career	**588**	Martin St. Louis
Most Points, Career	**953**	Martin St. Louis (365G, 588A)
Most PIM, Career	**828**	Chris Gratton
Most Shutouts, Career	**14**	Nikolai Khabibulin
Longest Consecutive Games Streak	**499**	Martin St. Louis (Nov. 17/05-Dec. 6/11)
Most Goals, Season	**60**	Steven Stamkos (2011-12)
Most Assists, Season	**68**	Brad Richards (2005-06), Martin St. Louis (2010-11)
Most Points, Season	**108**	Vincent Lecavalier (2006-07; 52G, 56A)
Most PIM, Season	**265**	Zenon Konopka (2009-10)
Most Points, Defenseman, Season	**65**	Roman Hamrlik (1995-96; 16G, 49A)
Most Points, Center, Season	**108**	Vincent Lecavalier (2006-07; 52G, 56A)
Most Points, Right Wing, Season	**102**	Martin St. Louis (2006-07; 43G, 59A)
Most Points, Left Wing, Season	**80**	Cory Stillman (2003-04; 25G, 55A) Vinny Prospal (2005-06; 25G, 55A)
Most Points, Rookie, Season	**62**	Brad Richards (2000-01; 21G, 41A)
Most Shutouts, Season	**7**	Nikolai Khabibulin (2001-02)
Most Goals, Game	**4**	Chris Kontos (Oct. 7/92), Martin St. Louis (Jan. 18/14)
Most Assists, Game	**5**	Mark Recchi (Mar. 1/09), Martin St. Louis (Nov. 18/10)
Most Points, Game	**6**	Doug Crossman (Nov. 7/92; 3G, 3A)

Captains' History

No captain, 1992-93 to 1994-95; Paul Ysebaert, 1995-96, 1996-97; Paul Ysebaert and Mikael Renberg, 1997-98; Rob Zamuner, 1998-99; Bill Houlder, Chris Gratton and Vincent Lecavalier, 1999-2000; Vincent Lecavalier, 2000-01; no captain, 2001-02; Dave Andreychuk, 2002-03 to 2004-05; Dave Andreychuk and no captain, 2005-06; Tim Taylor, 2006-07, 2007-08; Vincent Lecavalier, 2008-09 to 2012-13; Martin St. Louis and Steven Stamkos, 2013-14; Steven Stamkos, 2014-15 to date.

All-time Record vs. Other Clubs

Regular Season

	Total								At Home								On Road							
	GP	W	L	T	OL	GF	GA	PTS	GP	W	L	T	OL	GF	GA	PTS	GP	W	L	T	OL	GF	GA	PTS
Anaheim	28	12	11	1	4	69	75	29	14	7	6	0	1	34	35	15	14	5	5	1	3	35	40	14
Arizona	33	18	14	0	1	106	92	37	15	8	6	0	1	57	48	17	18	10	8	0	0	49	44	20
Boston	85	22	47	9	7	218	288	60	42	18	18	3	3	125	126	42	43	4	29	6	4	93	162	18
Buffalo	86	30	44	5	7	219	265	72	44	14	23	3	4	103	133	35	42	16	21	2	3	116	132	37
Calgary	30	16	12	1	1	91	97	34	15	8	6	1	0	50	52	17	15	8	6	0	1	41	45	17
Carolina	112	52	45	10	5	335	321	119	55	32	19	3	1	168	151	68	57	20	26	7	4	167	170	51
Chicago	36	15	14	5	2	94	106	37	17	9	4	3	1	51	47	22	19	6	10	2	1	43	59	15
Colorado	37	14	16	3	4	96	122	35	18	11	4	1	2	54	49	25	19	3	12	2	2	42	73	10
Columbus	19	11	7	1	0	46	39	23	10	8	2	0	0	25	16	16	9	3	5	1	0	21	23	7
Dallas	34	11	18	3	2	84	106	27	18	4	11	2	1	37	54	11	16	7	7	1	1	47	52	16
Detroit	41	12	26	2	1	102	152	27	21	8	11	1	1	65	82	18	20	4	15	1	0	37	70	9
Edmonton	31	11	16	2	2	82	91	26	16	7	6	2	1	47	47	17	15	4	10	0	1	35	44	9
Florida	117	49	47	10	11	319	360	119	59	28	20	6	5	165	172	67	58	21	27	4	6	154	188	52
Los Angeles	31	17	10	2	2	82	69	38	15	7	6	0	2	35	34	16	16	10	4	2	0	47	35	22
Minnesota	18	6	10	1	1	40	54	14	9	4	3	1	1	20	22	10	9	2	7	0	0	20	32	4
Montreal	85	39	33	6	7	215	226	91	43	19	14	5	5	112	112	48	42	20	19	1	2	103	114	43
Nashville	20	9	8	2	1	57	54	21	9	4	3	2	0	28	23	10	11	5	5	0	1	29	31	11
New Jersey	88	27	47	7	7	200	289	68	43	15	20	5	3	102	130	38	45	12	27	2	4	98	159	30
NY Islanders	88	42	37	3	6	237	257	93	44	24	14	2	4	126	122	54	44	18	23	1	2	111	135	39
NY Rangers	89	41	39	5	4	267	280	91	43	21	17	3	2	138	130	47	46	20	22	2	2	129	150	44
Ottawa	86	32	44	2	8	224	302	74	44	19	20	2	3	130	150	43	42	13	24	0	5	94	152	31
Philadelphia	88	37	40	8	3	251	266	85	45	22	20	1	2	140	129	47	43	15	20	7	1	111	137	38
Pittsburgh	83	33	42	5	3	229	270	74	41	21	18	2	0	123	110	44	42	12	24	3	3	106	160	30
St. Louis	35	11	18	3	3	96	124	28	19	8	7	3	1	58	64	20	16	3	11	0	2	38	60	8
San Jose	34	16	16	2	0	98	113	34	18	9	8	1	0	50	52	19	16	7	8	1	0	48	61	15
Toronto	80	29	43	2	6	207	266	66	40	16	21	1	2	99	121	35	40	13	22	1	4	108	145	31
Vancouver	28	10	13	2	3	82	105	25	14	7	5	0	2	50	50	16	14	3	8	2	1	32	55	9
Washington	116	38	64	6	8	304	400	90	58	23	31	2	2	154	183	50	58	15	33	4	6	150	217	40
Winnipeg	82	42	28	4	8	258	229	96	41	26	10	1	4	142	97	57	41	16	18	3	4	116	132	39
Totals	**1740**	**702**	**809**	**112**	**117**	**4708**	**5418**	**1633**	**870**	**407**	**353**	**56**	**54**	**2488**	**2541**	**924**	**870**	**295**	**456**	**56**	**63**	**2220**	**2877**	**709**

Playoffs

	Series	W	L	GP	W	L	T	GF	GA	Last Mtg.	Rnd.	Result
Boston	1	0	1	7	3	4	0	21	21	2011	CF	L 3-4
Calgary	1	1	0	7	4	3	0	13	14	2004	F	W 4-3
Chicago	1	0	1	6	2	4	0	10	13	2015	F	L 2-4
Detroit	1	1	0	7	4	3	0	17	15	2015	FR	W 4-3
Montreal	3	2	1	14	8	6	0	41	34	2015	SR	W 4-2
New Jersey	2	0	2	11	3	8	0	22	33	2007	CQF	L 2-4
NY Islanders	1	1	0	5	4	1	0	12	5	2004	CQF	W 4-1
NY Rangers	1	1	0	7	4	3	0	21	21	2015	CF	W 4-3
Ottawa	1	0	1	5	1	4	0	13	23	2006	CQF	L 1-4
Philadelphia	2	1	1	13	6	7	0	34	45	2004	CF	W 4-3
Pittsburgh	1	1	0	7	4	3	0	22	14	2011	CQF	W 4-3
Washington	2	2	0	10	8	2	0	30	25	2011	CSF	W 4-0
Totals	**17**	**10**	**7**	**99**	**51**	**48**	**0**	**256**	**263**			

Carolina totals include Hartford, 1992-93 to 1996-97.
Dallas totals include Minnesota North Stars, 1992-93.
Winnipeg totals include Atlanta Thrashers, 1999-2000 to 2010-11.
Colorado totals include Quebec, 1992-93 to 1994-95.
Phoenix totals include Winnipeg, 1992-93 to 1995-96.

Playoff Results 2015-2011

Year	Round	Opponent	Result	GF	GA
2015	F	Chicago	L 2-4	10	13
	CF	NY Rangers	W 4-3	21	21
	SR	Montreal	W 4-2	17	13
	FR	Detroit	W 4-3	17	15
2014	FR	Montreal	L 0-4	10	16
2011	CF	Boston	L 3-4	21	21
	CSF	Washington	W 4-0	16	10
	CQF	Pittsburgh	W 4-3	22	14

Abbreviations: Round: F – Final; **CF** – conference final; **CSF** – conference semi-final; **CQF** – conference quarter-final; **FR** – first round.

2014-15 Results

Oct.	9	Florida	3-2*		6	at Montreal	4-2
	11	Ottawa	2-3†		9	Buffalo	2-1
	13	Montreal	7-1		12	at Philadelphia	3-7
	14	New Jersey	1-2		13	at Boston	3-4
	18	at Vancouver	4-2		15	Edmonton	3-2
	20	at Edmonton	2-3		17	Colorado	3-2†
	21	at Calgary	2-1*		20	Vancouver	4-1
	24	at Winnipeg	4-2		27	at Carolina	2-4
	25	at Minnesota	2-7		29	Detroit	5-1
	28	Arizona	7-3		31	Columbus	3-1
	30	Philadelphia	4-3	**Feb.**	3	at St. Louis	1-2*
Nov.	1	Washington	4-3		5	at Dallas	5-3
	6	Calgary	5-2		7	Los Angeles	2-4
	8	at Columbus	7-4		8	Anaheim	5-3
	9	at Detroit	4-3†		10	at Nashville	2-3*
	11	at Chicago	2-3†		12	St. Louis	3-6
	13	San Jose	1-2		15	at San Jose	5-2
	15	NY Islanders	5-2		16	at Los Angeles	2-3
	17	at NY Rangers	5-1		18	at Anaheim	4-1
	18	at NY Islanders	2-5		21	at Arizona	4-2
	20	at Toronto	2-5		22	at Colorado	4-5
	22	Minnesota	2-1		27	Chicago	4-0
	26	NY Rangers	4-3	**Mar.**	1	at Florida	3-4
	29	Ottawa	4-1		3	Buffalo	3-0
Dec.	1	at NY Rangers	6-3		5	Toronto	4-2
	2	at Buffalo	1-2†		7	Dallas	5-4
	4	Buffalo	5-0		10	at Montreal	1-0*
	6	Columbus	1-3		12	at Boston	2-3†
	9	Washington	3-5		14	Winnipeg	1-2
	11	Carolina	2-1		16	Montreal	4-2
	13	at Washington	2-4		20	Detroit	3-1
	15	at Pittsburgh	2-4		22	Boston	5-3
	16	at Philadelphia	3-1		24	Florida	4-3
	19	at New Jersey	2-3†		26	Nashville	2-3
	20	at NY Islanders	1-3		28	at Detroit	0-4
	23	Pittsburgh	4-3		30	at Montreal	5-3
	27	Carolina	2-1		31	at Toronto	1-3
	29	Toronto	3-2	**Apr.**	2	at Ottawa	1-2*
	31	at Buffalo	5-1		4	at Florida	4-0
Jan.	2	at Pittsburgh	3-6		9	New Jersey	4-3*
	4	at Ottawa	4-2		11	Boston	3-2†

* – Overtime † – Shootout

NHL Draft Selections 2015-2001

Name in bold denotes played in NHL.

2015

Pick	
33	Mitchell Stephens
44	Matthew Spencer
64	Dennis Yan
72	Anthony Cirelli
118	Jonne Tammela
120	Mathieu Joseph
150	Ryan Zuhlsdorf
153	Kristian Oldham
180	Boko Imama

2014

Pick	
19	Anthony DeAngelo
35	Dominik Masin
57	Johnathan MacLeod
79	Brayden Point
119	Ben Thomas
170	Cristiano DiGiacinto
185	Cameron Darcy

2013

Pick	
3	**Jonathan Drouin**
33	Adam Erne
124	**Kristers Gudlevskis**
154	Henri Ikonen
184	Saku Salminen
186	Joel Vermin

2012

Pick	
10	**Slater Koekkoek**
19	**Andrei Vasilevskiy**
40	Dylan Blujus
53	Brian Hart
71	Tanner Richard
101	**Cedric Paquette**
161	Jake Dotchin
202	Nikita Gusev

2011

Pick	
27	**Vladislav Namestnikov**
58	**Nikita Kucherov**
148	**Nikita Nesterov**
178	Adam Wilcox
201	Matthew Peca
208	**Ondrej Palat**

2010

Pick	
6	**Brett Connolly**
63	Brock Beukeboom
66	**Radko Gudas**
72	Adam Janosik
96	Geoffrey Schemitsch
118	Jimmy Mullin
156	Brendan O'Donnell
186	Teigan Zahn

2009

Pick	
2	**Victor Hedman**
29	**Carter Ashton**
52	**Richard Panik**
93	Alex Hutchings
148	Michael Zador
162	Jaroslav Janus
183	Kirill Gotovets

2008

Pick	
1	**Steven Stamkos**
117	**James Wright**
122	**Dustin Tokarski**
147	Kyle DeCoste
152	**Mark Barberio**
160	**Luke Witkowski**
182	Matias Sointu
203	David Carle

2007

Pick	
47	**Dana Tyrell**
75	Luca Cunti
77	**Alex Killorn**
107	Mitch Fadden
150	Matt Marshall
167	**Johan Harju**
183	Torrie Jung
197	Michael Ward
210	Justin Courtnall

2006

Pick	
15	**Riku Helenius**
78	**Kevin Quick**
168	Dane Crowley
198	Denis Kazionov

2005

Pick	
30	**Vladimir Mihalik**
73	**Radek Smolenak**
89	Chris Lawrence
92	Marek Bartanus
102	**Blair Jones**
133	Stanislav Lascek
163	Marek Kvapil
165	Kevin Beech
225	John Wessbecker

2004

Pick	
30	Andy Rogers
65	Mark Tobin
102	**Mike Lundin**
158	Brandon Elliott
163	Dusty Collins
188	Jan Zapletal
191	**Karri Ramo**
245	Justin Keller

2003

Pick	
34	Mike Egener
41	**Matt Smaby**
96	Jonathan Boutin
192	**Doug O'Brien**
224	**Gerald Coleman**
227	**Jay Rosehill**
255	Raimonds Danilics
256	Brady Greco
273	Albert Vishnyakov
286	Zbynek Hrdel
287	**Nick Tarnasky**

2002

Pick	
60	Adam Henrich
100	Dmitri Kazionov
135	Joe Pearce
162	Gerard Dicaire
170	P.J. Atherton
174	Karri Akkanen
183	**Paul Ranger**
213	**Fredrik Norrena**
233	Vasily Koshechkin
255	**Ryan Craig**
256	**Darren Reid**
286	Alexei Glukhov
287	John Toffey

2001

Pick	
3	**Alexander Svitov**
47	Alexander Polushin
61	Andreas Holmqvist
94	**Evgeny Artyukhin**
123	Aaron Lobb
138	Paul Lynch
188	Art Femenella
219	Dennis Packard
222	Jeremy Van Hoof
252	J.F. Soucy
259	Dmitri Bezrukov
261	Vitali Smolyaninov
281	Ilja Solarev
289	Henrik Bergfors

General Managers' History

Phil Esposito, 1992-93 to 1997-98; Phil Esposito and Jacques Demers, 1998-99; Rick Dudley, 1999-2000, 2000-01; Rick Dudley and Jay Feaster, 2001-02; Jay Feaster, 2002-03 to 2007-08; Brian Lawton, 2008-09, 2009-10; Steve Yzerman, 2010-11 to date.

Steve Yzerman

Vice President and General Manager

Born: Cranbrook, BC, May 9, 1965.

Steve Yzerman – the iconic Detroit Red Wing player and executive – was named the sixth general manager in Lightning history on May 25, 2010. In his first season with the club in 2010-11 Yzerman was a finalist for the G.M of the Year award as Tampa Bay returned to the playoffs for the first time since 2006-07 and reached the Eastern Conference Final after tying a club record with 46 wins during the regular season. In 2014-15, Tampa Bay set new club records with 50 wins and 108 point en route to reaching the Stanley Cup Final and Yzerman was rewarded as G.M of the year.

Before joining the Lightning Yzerman spent four seasons as vice president with the Red Wings, working closely with general manager Ken Holland, senior vice president Jim Devellano and assistant general manager Jim Nill on evaluating talent at both the professional and amateur levels. He also contributed valuable input on trades, free agent signings and at the NHL Draft each summer. Yzerman served as general manager for Canada at the 2007 and 2008 World Championships, bringing home gold and silver respectively. He then led Canada to an Olympic gold medal victory on home ice in Vancouver at the 2010 Winter Olympics as executive director, and won gold again in that role at the 2014 Sochi Olympics. Yzerman also won an Olympic gold medal as a player with Canada in 2002.

Yzerman is a four-time Stanley Cup champion, winning three as a player (1997, 1998 and 2002) and another as a member of Detroit's management team (2008). Overall he spent 27 seasons with the franchise. He was inducted into the Hockey Hall of Fame in 2009, his first year of eligibility. Recognized as one of the best centers in NHL history, Yzerman retired on July 3, 2006 after a remarkable 22-year NHL career with the Red Wings. He ranks among the NHL's all-time leaders with 1,514 career games, 692 goals, 1,063 assists and 1,755 career points. Even more impressive than his career statistics may be his 20-year run as captain in Detroit, the longest tenure in NHL and major sports history. Yzerman was named captain of the Red Wings prior to the 1986-87 season, making him the youngest captain in franchise history at 21-years-old.

During his illustrious career Yzerman was selected to the NHL All-Star Game on nine occasions. He also won the Bill Masterton Trophy (perseverance, sportsmanship and dedication to hockey) in 2003, the Frank J. Selke Trophy (best defensive forward) in 2000, the Conn Smythe Trophy (playoff MVP) in 1998, the Lester B. Pearson Award (the NHLPA's top player) in 1989 and was also selected to the NHL All-Rookie Team in 1984.

Club Directory

Amalie Arena

Tampa Bay Lightning
Amalie Arena
401 Channelside Drive
Tampa, FL 33602
Phone **813/301-6500**
FAX 813/301-1480
Ticket Info. 813/301-6600
www.tampabaylightning.com
Capacity: 19,204

Executive Staff	
Owner, Governor & Chairman	Jeff Vinik
Chief Executive Officer and Alternate Governor	Steve Griggs
VP, General Manager, and Alternate Governor	Steve Yzerman
VP of Finance	Doug Riefler
EVP of Communications	Bill Wickett
EVP of Sales and Marketing	Jarrod Dillon
EVP and General Counsel	Jim Shimberg
EVP, Corporate Partnerships, Suite Sales & Service	Bill Abercrombie
VP of Corporate Relations	Phil Esposito
VPs, H.R. / Corporate & Community Affairs	Keith Harris / Dave Andreychuk
VPs, Guest Experience / Ticket Ops	Mary Milne / Jim Mannino
VPs, Event Booking / Game Presentation	Elmer Straub / John Franzone
VP, Philanthropy & Community Initiatives	Elizabeth Frazier
Exec. Asst. to Owner and CEO / EVP Finance	Sharon Love
Exec. Asst. to President and General Counsel	Sabrina Odria
Coaching Staff	
Head Coach	Jon Cooper
Associate Coach / Assistant Coaches	Rick Bowness / Steve Thomas
Coaches, Goaltending / Video / Player Development	Frantz Jean / Nigel Kirwan / Stacy Roest
Strength & Conditioning Coach / Manual Therapist	Mark Lambert / Christian Rivas
Hockey Operations	
Asst. G.M., G.M., Syracuse Crunch	Julien BriseBois
Asst. G.M., Director of Player Personnel	Pat Verbeek
Senior Advisor to the General Manager	Tom Kurvers
Amateur Scouting Director / Head Scout	Al Murray / Darryl Plandowski
Director of Team Services	Ryan Belec
Manager of Hockey Admin / Statistical Analyst	Elizabeth Koharski / Michael Peterson
Head Athletic Trainer / Assistant Trainer	Tom Mulligan / Mike Poirier
Equipment Manager / Assistant Managers	Ray Thill / Rob Kennedy, Clay Roffer
Media	
Director of Public Relations	Brian Breseman
Editorial Content Manager	Trevor van Knotsenburg
Beat Writer / Team Photographer	Bryan Burns / Scott Audette
Community Relations and Lightning Foundation	
Senior Director of Community Relations	Kasey Smith
Exec. Director of Community Hockey Development	Jay Feaster
Community Rep. / Hockey Manager / Coordinator	Brian Bradley / Tom Garavaglia / Josh Dreith
Coordinator	Amanda Puccinelli
Finance	
Sr. Director of Business Strategy and Analytics	Chris Kamke
Business Analyst / Finance Director	Matthew Samost / Michelle Davidson
Senior / Staff Accountant	Tim Ennis / Scott Peterson
Managers, Accounts Payable / Receivable	Donna Clark / Angela Edwards
Human Resources	
Associate General Counsel	Danna Haydar
Director of H.R. / Generalist	Nicole Parente / Charlea Jackson
Front Desk Administrator	Audrey Flowers
Information Technology	
Director of IT Services / IT Help Desk	Michael Davidson / Bryan Ririe
Ticket Office	
Ticket Supervisors, Sports / Event	Helen Junker / Bobby Loman
Premium and Staffing Supervisor	Missy Davis
Ticket Coordinators, Sport / Sport / Event	Hayden Buttner / Krisjan Mackus / Christina Guarneri
Client Sales and Services	
Executive Suite Director / Specialists	Matt Hill, Toni Connor, Erin Bailey
Account Membership Executives	Shannon Dixie, Dan Schlindwein, Joe Russano, Madelyn Anthony, Daniel Lozada, Jason Hill
Season Ticket Membership Manager / Asst. Mgr.	Lakisha Sharpe / Thomas Gregory
Coordinators, Member Services / Ticket Services	Rachel Kilman/ Charlene Beverly
Corporate Partnership & Activation	
Partnership Development Sr. Director / Director	Mike Harrison / Chris Potenza
Partnership Activation Director / Reps.	Julia Wyman / Shannon Burrows, Michael Wozney, Emily Williams
Partnership Development Sr. Manager / Manager	Casey Cole / Suzy O'Malley
Partnership Development Coordinator / Executive	Joshua Korlin / Justin Versaggi
Ticket Sales	
Sr. Director of New Business Development	Ryan Bringger
Directors, Inside Sales / Group Sales	Ryan Cook / Ryan Niemeyer
Sr. Director, Season Ticket Membership	Travis Pelleymounter
Corporate Sales Managers	Rich Sadowsky, Adam Lawson, Gary Napert, Brian Specia, Curtis Walker, Jim Van Dam, David Boettinger, Tony Econ, TJ Abone, Tommy Curtis
Suite Sales Director / Managers	Matt Hill / Adam Laws, Katie Valone
Group Sales	Brian Boksen, Chris Duffy, Oisin Crean, Danny Rowen, Kate Kasunic, Tyler Thompson, Kyle Laga
Account Representatives	Nate Black, John Curry, Meghan Iacofano, Mario Sgroi, Nicky Gordon, Dani Ratner, Leslie Redfield, Derek Moore
Database Coordinator	T.J. Aufiero
Marketing	
Digital Media Manager	Andrew DeWitt
Entertainment Manager	Kelli Yeloushan
Sr. Event Marketing Director	Angela Parone
Creative Director / Graphic Designers	Brittany Austin / Carolina Bermudez, Nick Meader
Coordinators	Jenna Baldwin, Justin Savoie, Patrick Gardenier, Gabe Marte
Digital Marketing Manager / Media Buyer	Patrick Abts / Samantha Krone
Hockey Reporter	Michelle Gingras
Arena Management	
EVP & G.M., Amalie Arena / SportService	Darryl Benge / Bruce Ground
Directors, Arena Departments	Rhett Blewett, Daryl Niles
Managers, Arena Departments	Steven Butler, Kevin Alexander, Amy Ford, Michael O'Donnell, April Kelly, Tom Miracle, Stevan Simms, Brendon Hite, Michael Silva, Tom Dacey, Tripp Turbiville, Susan Danielik, Kim Seeley, Ken Ramella
Ice Operations Technician	Patrick Jesso
Security Supervisor	Russ Snyder
Coordinators / Operations Analyst	Samantha Nemeroff, Alayn Hornick, Justin Bechtold / Sam Carr
Broadcast & Game Presentation	
Director of Production Systems	Jorge Rosell
Managers, Radio / A/V / Production Systems	Matt Sammon / JC Kent / Jorge Rosell
Flagship Station, Television	SunSports Network
Radio Stations	WFLA 970 AM, WDCF 1350 AM, WZHR 1400 AM, WSRQ 1220 AM/106.9 FM/98.9 FM, WDBO 580 AM, WKFL 1220 AM, WWJB 1450 AM/103.9 FM/101.1 FM, WKII 1070 AM
TV Play-by-Play / Color / Reporter	Rick Peckham / TBD / Paul Kennedy
Radio Play-by-Play / Analyst	David Mishkin / Phil Esposito
Sr. Coordinator / Coordinators	Brian Fink / Tyler Brewer, Josh Boyd, Kristin Cullina, Jim Wilson

Toronto Maple Leafs

2014-15 Results: 30W-44L-3OTL-5SOL 68PTS
7TH, Atlantic Division • 15TH, Eastern Conference

Key Off-Season Signings/Acquisitions

2015

May 20 • Named **Mike Babcock** head coach.
June 4 • Re-signed D **T.J. Brennan**.
16 • Named **Jim Hiller**, **D.J. Smith** and **Andrew Brewer** assistant coaches.
27 • Acquired D **Martin Marincin** from Edmonton for LW **Brad Ross** and a 4th-round choice in the 2015 NHL Draft.
July 1 • Acquired RW **Kasperi Kapanen**, C **Nick Spaling**, D **Scott Harrington** and a 3rd-round choice in the 2016 NHL Draft from Pittsburgh for RW **Phil Kessel**, RW **Tyler Biggs** and D **Tim Erixon**.
1 • Signed C **Daniel Winnik**, RW **PA Parenteau**, RW **Mark Arcobello** and D **Matt Hunwick**.
1 • Re-signed RW **Richard Panik**.
5 • Re-signed C **Nazem Kadri**.
6 • Signed C **Shawn Matthias**.
12 • Acquired LW **Taylor Beck** from Nashville for LW **Jamie Devane**.
23 • Named **Lou Lamoriello** general manager.
Aug. 2 • Re-signed G **Jonathan Bernier**.

2015-16 Schedule

Month	Day	Date	Opponent
Oct.	Wed.	7	Montreal
	Fri.	9	at Detroit
	Sat.	10	Ottawa
	Fri.	16	at Columbus
	Sat.	17	at Pittsburgh
	Wed.	21	at Buffalo
	Sat.	24	at Montreal
	Mon.	26	Arizona
	Fri.	30	at NY Rangers
	Sat.	31	Pittsburgh
Nov.	Mon.	2	Dallas
	Wed.	4	Winnipeg
	Fri.	6	Detroit
	Sat.	7	at Washington
	Tue.	10	at Dallas
	Thu.	12	at Nashville
	Sat.	14	Vancouver
	Sun.	15	at NY Rangers
	Tue.	17	Colorado
	Fri.	20	at Carolina
	Sat.	21	at Boston
	Mon.	23	Boston
	Sat.	28	Washington
	Mon.	30	Edmonton
Dec.	Wed.	2	at Winnipeg
	Thu.	3	at Minnesota
	Sat.	5	at St. Louis
	Tue.	8	New Jersey
	Tue.	15	Tampa Bay
	Thu.	17	San Jose
	Sat.	19	Los Angeles
	Mon.	21	at Colorado
	Tue.	22	at Arizona
	Sun.	27	at NY Islanders
	Tue.	29	NY Islanders
	Wed.	30	at Pittsburgh
Jan.	Sat.	2	St. Louis
	Wed.	6	at Anaheim
	Thu.	7	at Los Angeles
	Sat.	9	at San Jose*
	Wed.	13	Columbus
	Fri.	15	Chicago
	Sat.	16	at Boston
	Tue.	19	at Philadelphia
	Thu.	21	Carolina
	Sat.	23	Montreal
	Tue.	26	at Florida
	Wed.	27	at Tampa Bay
Feb.	Tue.	2	at Boston
	Thu.	4	New Jersey
	Sat.	6	at Ottawa
	Tue.	9	at Calgary
	Thu.	11	at Edmonton
	Sat.	13	at Vancouver*
	Mon.	15	at Chicago
	Thu.	18	NY Rangers
	Sat.	20	Philadelphia
	Tue.	23	Nashville
	Thu.	25	Carolina
	Sat.	27	at Montreal
	Mon.	29	Tampa Bay
Mar.	Wed.	2	at Washington
	Thu.	3	Minnesota
	Sat.	5	Ottawa
	Mon.	7	Buffalo
	Wed.	9	NY Islanders
	Sat.	12	at Ottawa
	Sun.	13	at Detroit
	Tue.	15	Tampa Bay
	Thu.	17	Florida
	Sat.	19	Buffalo
	Mon.	21	Calgary
	Thu.	24	Anaheim
	Sat.	26	Boston
	Mon.	28	at Tampa Bay
	Tue.	29	at Florida
	Thu.	31	at Buffalo
Apr.	Sat.	2	Detroit
	Mon.	4	Florida
	Wed.	6	Columbus
	Thu.	7	at Philadelphia
	Sat.	9	at New Jersey

* Denotes afternoon game.

Retired Numbers

5	Bill Barilko	1946-1951
6	Ace Bailey	1926-1934

ATLANTIC DIVISION
99th NHL Season

Franchise date: November 26, 1917

Year-by-Year Record

		Home				Road				Overall									
Season	GP	W	L	T	OL	W	L	T	OL	W	L	T	OL	GF	GA	Pts.	Div. Fin.	Conf. Fin.	Playoff Result
2014-15	82	22	17	....	2	8	27	....	6	30	44	....	8	211	262	68	7th, Atl.	15th, East	Out of Playoffs
2013-14	82	24	16	....	1	14	20	....	7	38	36	....	8	231	256	84	6th, Atl.	12th, East	Out of Playoffs
2012-13	48	13	9	....	2	13	8	....	3	26	17	....	5	145	133	57	3rd, NE	5th, East	Lost Conf. Quarter-Final
2011-12	82	18	16	....	7	17	21	....	3	35	37	....	10	231	264	80	4th, NE	13th, East	Out of Playoffs
2010-11	82	18	15	....	8	19	19	....	3	37	34	....	11	218	251	85	4th, NE	10th, East	Out of Playoffs
2009-10	82	18	17	....	6	12	21	....	8	30	38	....	14	214	267	74	5th, NE	15th, East	Out of Playoffs
2008-09	82	16	16	....	9	18	19	....	4	34	35	....	13	250	293	81	5th, NE	12th, East	Out of Playoffs
2007-08	82	18	17	....	6	18	18	....	5	36	35	....	11	231	260	83	5th, NE	12th, East	Out of Playoffs
2006-07	82	21	15	....	5	19	16	....	6	40	31	....	11	258	269	91	3rd, NE	9th, East	Out of Playoffs
2005-06	82	26	12	....	3	15	21	....	5	41	33	....	8	257	270	90	4th, NE	9th, East	Out of Playoffs
2004-05	....	....	....	....	....	....	....	....	....	....	....	....	....	....	....	....			
2003-04	82	22	14	3	2	23	10	7	1	45	24	10	3	242	204	103	2nd, NE	4th, East	Lost Conf. Semi-Final
2002-03	82	24	13	4	0	20	15	3	3	44	28	7	3	236	208	98	2nd, NE	5th, East	Lost Conf. Quarter-Final
2001-02	82	24	11	6	0	19	14	4	4	43	25	10	4	249	207	100	2nd, NE	4th, East	Lost Conf. Final
2000-01	82	19	11	7	4	18	18	4	1	37	29	11	5	232	207	90	3rd, NE	7th, East	Lost Conf. Semi-Final
1999-2000	82	24	12	5	0	21	15	2	3	45	27	7	3	246	222	100	1st, NE	3rd, East	Lost Conf. Semi-Final
1998-99	82	23	13	5	....	22	17	2	....	45	30	7	....	268	231	97	2nd, NE	4th, East	Lost Conf. Final
1997-98	82	16	20	5	....	14	23	4	....	30	43	9	....	194	237	69	6th, Cen.	10th, West	Out of Playoffs
1996-97	82	18	20	3	....	12	24	5	....	30	44	8	....	230	273	68	6th, Cen.	11th, West	Out of Playoffs
1995-96	82	19	15	7	....	15	21	5	....	34	36	12	....	247	252	80	3rd, Cen.	4th, West	Lost Conf. Quarter-Final
1994-95	48	15	7	2	....	6	12	6	....	21	19	8	....	135	146	50	4th, Cen.	5th, West	Lost Conf. Quarter-Final
1993-94	84	23	15	4	....	20	14	8	....	43	29	12	....	280	243	98	2nd, Cen.	2nd, West	Lost Conf. Final
1992-93	84	25	11	6	....	19	18	5	....	44	29	11	....	288	241	99	3rd, Norris		Lost Conf. Final
1991-92	80	21	16	3	....	9	27	4	....	30	43	7	....	234	294	67	5th, Norris		Out of Playoffs
1990-91	80	15	21	4	....	8	25	7	....	23	46	11	....	241	318	57	5th, Norris		Out of Playoffs
1989-90	80	24	14	2	....	14	24	2	....	38	38	4	....	337	358	80	3rd, Norris		Lost Div. Semi-Final
1988-89	80	15	20	5	....	13	26	1	....	28	46	6	....	259	342	62	5th, Norris		Out of Playoffs
1987-88	80	14	20	6	....	7	29	4	....	21	49	10	....	273	345	52	4th, Norris		Lost Div. Semi-Final
1986-87	80	22	14	4	....	10	28	2	....	32	42	6	....	286	319	70	4th, Norris		Lost Div. Final
1985-86	80	16	21	3	....	9	27	4	....	25	48	7	....	311	386	57	4th, Norris		Lost Div. Final
1984-85	80	10	28	2	....	10	24	6	....	20	52	8	....	253	358	48	5th, Norris		Out of Playoffs
1983-84	80	17	16	7	....	9	29	2	....	26	45	9	....	303	387	61	5th, Norris		Out of Playoffs
1982-83	80	20	15	5	....	8	25	7	....	28	40	12	....	293	330	68	3rd, Norris		Lost Div. Semi-Final
1981-82	80	12	20	8	....	8	24	8	....	20	44	16	....	298	380	56	5th, Norris		Out of Playoffs
1980-81	80	14	21	5	....	14	16	10	....	28	37	15	....	322	367	71	5th, Adams		Lost Prelim. Round
1979-80	80	17	19	4	....	18	21	1	....	35	40	5	....	304	327	75	4th, Adams		Lost Prelim. Round
1978-79	80	20	12	8	....	14	21	5	....	34	33	13	....	267	252	81	3rd, Adams		Lost Quarter-Final
1977-78	80	21	13	6	....	20	16	4	....	41	29	10	....	271	237	92	3rd, Adams		Lost Semi-Final
1976-77	80	18	13	9	....	15	19	6	....	33	32	15	....	301	285	81	3rd, Adams		Lost Quarter-Final
1975-76	80	23	12	5	....	11	19	10	....	34	31	15	....	294	276	83	3rd, Adams		Lost Quarter-Final
1974-75	80	19	12	9	....	12	21	7	....	31	33	16	....	280	309	78	3rd, Adams		Lost Quarter-Final
1973-74	78	21	11	7	....	14	16	9	....	35	27	16	....	274	230	86	4th, East		Lost Quarter-Final
1972-73	78	20	12	7	....	7	29	3	....	27	41	10	....	247	279	64	6th, East		Out of Playoffs
1971-72	78	21	11	7	....	12	20	7	....	33	31	14	....	209	208	80	4th, East		Lost Quarter-Final
1970-71	78	24	9	6	....	13	24	2	....	37	33	8	....	248	211	82	4th, East		Lost Quarter-Final
1969-70	76	18	13	7	....	11	21	6	....	29	34	13	....	222	242	71	6th, East		Out of Playoffs
1968-69	76	20	8	10	....	15	18	5	....	35	26	15	....	234	217	85	4th, East		Lost Quarter-Final
1967-68	74	24	9	4	....	9	22	6	....	33	31	10	....	209	176	76	5th, East		Out of Playoffs
1966-67	**70**	**21**	**8**	**6**	....	**11**	**19**	**5**	....	**32**	**27**	**11**	....	**204**	**211**	**75**	**3rd**		**Won Stanley Cup**
1965-66	70	22	9	4	....	12	16	7	....	34	25	11	....	208	187	79	3rd		Lost Semi-Final
1964-65	70	17	15	3	....	13	11	11	....	30	26	14	....	204	173	74	4th		Lost Semi-Final
1963-64	**70**	**22**	**7**	**6**	....	**11**	**18**	**6**	....	**33**	**25**	**12**	....	**192**	**172**	**78**	**3rd**		**Won Stanley Cup**
1962-63	**70**	**21**	**8**	**6**	....	**14**	**15**	**6**	....	**35**	**23**	**12**	....	**221**	**180**	**82**	**1st**		**Won Stanley Cup**
1961-62	**70**	**25**	**5**	**5**	....	**12**	**17**	**6**	....	**37**	**22**	**11**	....	**232**	**180**	**85**	**2nd**		**Won Stanley Cup**
1960-61	70	21	6	8	....	18	13	4	....	39	19	12	....	234	176	90	2nd		Lost Semi-Final
1959-60	70	20	9	6	....	15	17	3	....	35	26	9	....	199	195	79	2nd		Lost Final
1958-59	70	17	13	5	....	10	19	6	....	27	32	11	....	189	201	65	4th		Lost Final
1957-58	70	12	16	7	....	9	22	4	....	21	38	11	....	192	226	53	6th		Out of Playoffs
1956-57	70	12	16	7	....	9	18	8	....	21	34	15	....	174	192	57	5th		Out of Playoffs
1955-56	70	19	10	6	....	5	23	7	....	24	33	13	....	153	181	61	4th		Lost Semi-Final
1954-55	70	14	10	11	....	10	14	11	....	24	24	22	....	147	135	70	3rd		Lost Semi-Final
1953-54	70	22	6	7	....	10	18	7	....	32	24	14	....	152	131	78	3rd		Lost Semi-Final
1952-53	70	17	12	6	....	10	18	7	....	27	30	13	....	156	167	67	5th		Out of Playoffs
1951-52	70	17	10	8	....	12	15	8	....	29	25	16	....	168	157	74	3rd		Lost Semi-Final
1950-51	**70**	**22**	**8**	**5**	....	**19**	**8**	**8**	....	**41**	**16**	**13**	....	**212**	**138**	**95**	**2nd**		**Won Stanley Cup**
1949-50	70	18	9	8	....	13	18	4	....	31	27	12	....	176	173	74	3rd		Lost Semi-Final
1948-49	**60**	**12**	**8**	**10**	....	**10**	**17**	**3**	....	**22**	**25**	**13**	....	**147**	**161**	**57**	**4th**		**Won Stanley Cup**
1947-48	**60**	**22**	**3**	**5**	....	**10**	**12**	**8**	....	**32**	**15**	**13**	....	**182**	**143**	**77**	**1st**		**Won Stanley Cup**
1946-47	**60**	**20**	**8**	**2**	....	**11**	**11**	**8**	....	**31**	**19**	**10**	....	**209**	**172**	**72**	**2nd**		**Won Stanley Cup**
1945-46	50	10	13	2	....	9	11	5	....	19	24	7	....	174	185	45	5th		Out of Playoffs
1944-45	**50**	**13**	**9**	**3**	....	**11**	**13**	**1**	....	**24**	**22**	**4**	....	**183**	**161**	**52**	**3rd**		**Won Stanley Cup**
1943-44	50	13	11	1	....	10	12	3	....	23	23	4	....	214	174	50	3rd		Lost Semi-Final
1942-43	50	17	6	2	....	5	13	7	....	22	19	9	....	198	159	53	3rd		Lost Semi-Final
1941-42	**48**	**18**	**6**	**0**	....	**9**	**12**	**3**	....	**27**	**18**	**3**	....	**158**	**136**	**57**	**2nd**		**Won Stanley Cup**
1940-41	48	16	5	3	....	12	9	3	....	28	14	6	....	145	99	62	2nd		Lost Semi-Final
1939-40	48	15	3	6	....	10	14	0	....	25	17	6	....	134	110	56	3rd		Lost Final
1938-39	48	13	8	3	....	6	12	6	....	19	20	9	....	114	107	47	3rd		Lost Final
1937-38	48	13	6	5	....	11	9	4	....	24	15	9	....	151	127	57	1st, Cdn.		Lost Final
1936-37	48	14	9	1	....	8	12	4	....	22	21	5	....	119	115	49	3rd, Cdn.		Lost Quarter-Final
1935-36	48	15	4	5	....	8	15	1	....	23	19	6	....	126	106	52	2nd, Cdn.		Lost Final
1934-35	48	16	6	2	....	14	8	2	....	30	14	4	....	157	111	64	1st, Cdn.		Lost Final
1933-34	48	19	2	3	....	7	11	6	....	26	13	9	....	174	119	61	1st, Cdn.		Lost Semi-Final
1932-33	48	16	4	4	....	8	14	2	....	24	18	6	....	119	111	54	1st, Cdn.		Lost Final
1931-32	**48**	**17**	**4**	**3**	....	**6**	**14**	**4**	....	**23**	**18**	**7**	....	**155**	**127**	**53**	**2nd, Cdn.**		**Won Stanley Cup**
1930-31	44	15	4	3	....	7	9	6	....	22	13	9	....	118	99	53	2nd, Cdn.		Lost Quarter-Final
1929-30	44	10	8	4	....	7	13	2	....	17	21	6	....	116	124	40	4th, Cdn.		Out of Playoffs
1928-29	44	15	5	2	....	6	13	3	....	21	18	5	....	85	69	47	3rd, Cdn.		Lost Semi-Final
1927-28	44	9	8	5	....	9	10	3	....	18	18	8	....	89	88	44	4th, Cdn.		Out of Playoffs
1926-27*	44	10	10	2	....	5	14	3	....	15	24	5	....	79	94	35	5th, Cdn.		Out of Playoffs
1925-26	36	11	5	2	....	1	16	1	....	12	21	3	....	92	114	27	6th		Out of Playoffs
1924-25	30	10	5	0	....	9	6	0	....	19	11	0	....	90	84	38	2nd		Lost NHL S-Final
1923-24	24	7	5	0	....	3	9	0	....	10	14	0	....	59	85	20	3rd		Out of Playoffs
1922-23	24	10	1	1	....	3	9	0	....	13	10	1	....	82	88	27	3rd		Out of Playoffs
1921-22	**24**	**8**	**4**	**0**	....	**5**	**6**	**1**	....	**13**	**10**	**1**	....	**98**	**97**	**27**	**2nd**		**Won Stanley Cup**
1920-21	24	9	3	0	....	6	6	0	....	15	9	0	....	105	100	30	2nd and 1st***		Lost NHL Final
1919-20**	24	8	4	0	....	4	8	0	....	12	12	0	....	119	106	24	3rd and 2nd***		Out of Playoffs
1918-19	18	5	4	0	....	0	9	0	....	5	13	0	....	64	92	10	3rd and 3rd***		Out of Playoffs
1917-18	**22**	**10**	**1**	**0**	....	**3**	**8**	**0**	....	**13**	**9**	**0**	....	**108**	**109**	**26**	**2nd and 1st*****		**Won Stanley Cup**

* Name changed from St. Patricks to Maple Leafs (February, 1927). ** Name changed from Arenas to St. Patricks.
*** Season played in two halves with no combined standing at end.
From 1917-18 through 1925-26, NHL champions played against PCHA/WCHL champions for Stanley Cup.

2015-16 Player Personnel

FORWARDS	HT	WT	*Age	Place of Birth	S	2014-15 Club
ARCOBELLO, Mark	5-10	185	27	Milford, CT	R	Edm-Nsh-Pit-Ari
BECK, Taylor	6-2	206	24	St. Catharines, ON	R	Nashville
BOZAK, Tyler	6-1	195	29	Regina, SK	R	Toronto
HOLLAND, Peter	6-2	194	24	Toronto, ON	L	Toronto
HORTON, Nathan	6-2	229	30	Welland, ON	R	Did Not Play-Injured
KADRI, Nazem	6-0	188	25	London, ON	L	Toronto
KOMAROV, Leo	5-11	198	28	Narva, USSR	L	Toronto
LUPUL, Joffrey	6-1	206	32	Fort Saskatchewan, AB	R	Toronto
MATTHIAS, Shawn	6-4	223	27	Mississauga, ON	L	Vancouver
PARENTEAU, Pierre-Alexandre	6-0	193	32	Hull, QC	R	Montreal
SPALING, Nick	6-1	201	27	Palmerston, ON	L	Pittsburgh
van RIEMSDYK, James	6-3	200	26	Middletown, NJ	L	Toronto
WINNIK, Daniel	6-2	207	30	Toronto, ON	L	Toronto-Pittsburgh
DEFENSEMEN						
BRENNAN, T.J.	6-1	216	26	Willingboro, NJ	L	Rockford-Tor-Tor (AHL)
GARDINER, Jake	6-2	184	25	Minnetonka, MN	L	Toronto
HUNWICK, Matt	5-11	190	30	Warren, MI	L	NY Rangers
MARINCIN, Martin	6-4	203	23	Kosice, Czech.	L	Edmonton-Oklahoma City
PHANEUF, Dion	6-3	214	30	Edmonton, AB	L	Toronto
POLAK, Roman	6-0	236	29	Ostrava, Czech.	R	Toronto
RIELLY, Morgan	6-1	205	21	Vancouver, BC	L	Toronto
ROBIDAS, Stephane	5-11	190	38	Sherbrooke, QC	R	Toronto

GOALTENDERS	HT	WT	*Age	Place of Birth	C	2014-15 Club
BERNIER, Jonathan	6-0	185	27	Laval, QC	L	Toronto
REIMER, James	6-2	208	27	Morweena, MB	L	Toronto

* – Age at start of 2015-16 season

Coaching History

Dick Carroll, 1917-18, 1918-19; Frank Heffernan and Harry Sproule, 1919-20; Frank Carroll, 1920-21; George O'Donohue, 1921-22; George O'Donohue and Charles Querrie, 1922-23; Charles Querrie, 1923-24; Eddie Powers, 1924-25, 1925-26; Charles Querrie, Mike Rodden and Alex Romeril, 1926-27; Conn Smythe, 1927-28 to 1929-30; Conn Smythe and Art Duncan, 1930-31; Art Duncan, Conn Smythe and Dick Irvin, 1931-32; Dick Irvin, 1932-33 to 1939-40; Hap Day, 1940-41 to 1949-50; Joe Primeau, 1950-51 to 1952-53; King Clancy, 1953-54 to 1955-56; Howie Meeker, 1956-57; Billy Reay, 1957-58; Billy Reay and Punch Imlach, 1958-59; Punch Imlach, 1959-60 to 1968-69; John McLellan, 1969-70 to 1972-73; Red Kelly, 1973-74 to 1976-77; Roger Neilson, 1977-78, 1978-79; Floyd Smith, Dick Duff and Punch Imlach, 1979-80; Joe Crozier and Mike Nykoluk, 1980-81; Mike Nykoluk, 1981-82 to 1983-84; Dan Maloney, 1984-85, 1985-86; John Brophy, 1986-87, 1987-88; John Brophy and George Armstrong, 1988-89; Doug Carpenter, 1989-90; Doug Carpenter and Tom Watt, 1990-91; Tom Watt, 1991-92; Pat Burns, 1992-93 to 1994-95; Pat Burns and Nick Beverley, 1995-96; Mike Murphy, 1996-97, 1997-98; Pat Quinn, 1998-99 to 2005-06; Paul Maurice, 2006-07, 2007-08; Ron Wilson, 2008-09 to 2010-11; Ron Wilson and Randy Carlyle, 2011-12; Randy Carlyle, 2012-13, 2013-14; Randy Carlyle and Peter Horachek, 2014-15; Mike Babcock, 2015-16.

Mike Babcock

Head Coach

Born: Manitouwadge, ON, April 29, 1963.

Brendan Shanahan, president and alternate governor of the Toronto Maple Leafs, announced on May 20, 2015, that Mike Babcock had been named the 30th head coach in the club's history. Babcock joined the Leafs after serving as head coach of the Detroit Red Wings for the previous 10 seasons.

Under his leadership in Detroit, Babcock posted a 458-223-105 regular season record as he became their franchise leader in games coached (786) and wins. In his time with the Red Wings, the club twice captured the Presidents' Trophy as the NHL's regular-season champion (2005-06 and 2007-08) and made the playoffs in each of his 10 seasons. In 2007-08, Babcock led the Red Wings to a Stanley Cup championship in just his third season with the team, securing his first NHL title and the 11th in team history. Babcock was named a finalist for the Jack Adams Award as the NHL's coach of the year in 2008 and 2014.

Prior to joining the Red Wings, Babcock spent two seasons with the Mighty Ducks of Anaheim (2002 to 2004), where in his first season as head coach he led the Ducks to their first appearance in the Stanley Cup final. Throughout his tenure as an NHL head coach, Babcock has led his teams to the Stanley Cup final three times and the Western Conference Finals four times. Before stepping behind the bench in Anaheim, Babcock spent two seasons (2000 to 2002) as head coach of the Cincinnati Mighty Ducks of the American Hockey League. He had moved to Cincinnati following a six-year run at the helm of the Spokane Chiefs of the Western Hockey League (1994-95 through 1999-2000).

In international play, Babcock has represented Canada at several competitions. Most notably, he became the only coach in hockey history to lead Canada to gold medals in consecutive Olympic appearances after guiding Canada in Vancouver (2010) and Sochi, Russia (2014). In 2004, he led Team Canada to a gold medal at the World Championships. In 1997, he took part in his first international coaching experience at the World Junior Championships as Canada also captured gold. Babcock is the only coach in the "Triple Gold Club," an exclusive group of individuals who have captured the three most prestigious championships in hockey (a World Championship, an Olympic gold medal and the Stanley Cup).

2014-15 Scoring

* – rookie

Regular Season

Pos	#	Player	Team	GP	G	A	Pts	TOI	+/–	PIM	PP	SH	GW	S	S%
C	81	Phil Kessel	TOR	82	25	36	61	18:47	–34	30	8	0	4	280	8.9
L	21	James van Riemsdyk	TOR	82	27	29	56	19:05	–33	43	9	1	4	248	10.9
C	42	Tyler Bozak	TOR	82	23	26	49	19:08	–34	44	12	2	3	154	14.9
C	43	Nazem Kadri	TOR	73	18	21	39	17:36	–7	28	3	1	1	176	10.2
D	44	Morgan Rielly	TOR	81	8	21	29	20:20	–16	14	1	0	0	148	5.4
D	3	Dion Phaneuf	TOR	70	3	26	29	23:43	–11	108	2	0	1	138	2.2
C	47	Leo Komarov	TOR	62	8	18	26	14:41	0	18	0	1	1	84	9.5
C	24	Peter Holland	TOR	62	11	14	25	14:31	0	31	1	1	3	93	11.8
D	51	Jake Gardiner	TOR	79	4	20	24	20:58	–23	24	0	0	0	100	4.0
R	19	Joffrey Lupul	TOR	55	10	11	21	15:29	–10	26	2	0	1	97	10.3
R	18	Richard Panik	TOR	76	11	6	17	11:38	–8	49	2	0	1	87	12.6
L	20	David Booth	TOR	59	7	6	13	11:56	–8	25	0	0	2	107	6.5
D	2	Eric Brewer	T.B.	17	0	4	4	17:50	5	18	0	0	0	14	0.0
			ANA	9	1	1	2	17:15	–6	6	0	0	0	7	14.3
			TOR	18	2	3	5	20:11	–4	12	0	0	1	12	16.7
			Total	44	3	8	11	18:41	–5	36	0	0	1	33	9.1
C	15	Joakim Lindstrom	STL	34	3	3	6	11:04	–8	8	2	0	0	41	7.3
			TOR	19	1	3	4	10:30	–7	4	0	0	0	20	5.0
			Total	53	4	6	10	10:52	–15	12	2	0	0	61	6.6
D	46	Roman Polak	TOR	56	5	4	9	21:05	–22	48	0	0	1	61	8.2
D	33	Tim Erixon	CBJ	19	1	5	6	16:57	–3	4	1	0	0	20	5.0
			CHI	8	0	0	0	9:59	1	4	0	0	0	6	0.0
			TOR	15	1	0	1	15:47	–5	6	0	0	0	10	10.0
			Total	42	2	5	7	15:13	–7	14	1	0	0	36	5.6
D	12	Stephane Robidas	TOR	52	1	6	7	17:04	8	34	0	0	0	34	2.9
D	55	Korbinian Holzer	TOR	34	0	6	6	17:06	3	25	0	0	0	32	0.0
C	23	Trevor Smith	TOR	54	2	3	5	11:03	–9	12	0	0	0	46	4.3
R	67 *	Brandon Kozun	TOR	20	2	2	4	7:54	–3	6	0	0	0	8	25.0
C	22	Zach Sill	PIT	42	1	2	3	8:17	–3	60	0	0	0	26	3.8
			TOR	21	0	1	1	8:33	–2	24	0	0	0	17	0.0
			Total	63	1	3	4	8:22	–5	84	0	0	0	43	2.3
D	50 *	Stuart Percy	TOR	9	0	3	3	18:04	–4	2	0	0	0	13	0.0
C	53 *	Sam Carrick	TOR	16	1	1	2	6:29	1	9	0	0	0	17	5.9
D	57 *	Andrew MacWilliam	TOR	12	0	2	2	15:24	–6	12	0	0	0	5	0.0
C	37 *	Casey Bailey	TOR	6	1	0	1	9:02	1	2	0	0	0	9	11.1
L	32 *	Josh Leivo	TOR	9	1	0	1	7:39	–1	4	0	0	0	10	10.0
D	25	Tj Brennan	TOR	6	0	1	1	16:48	–7	9	0	0	0	11	0.0
R	28	Colton Orr	TOR	1	0	0	0	6:06	0	0	0	0	0	0	0.0
C	36 *	Greg McKegg	TOR	3	0	0	0	9:11	0	0	0	0	0	1	0.0
R	40	Troy Bodie	TOR	5	0	0	0	4:37	0	5	0	0	0	1	0.0
R	37	Carter Ashton	TOR	7	0	0	0	6:13	–3	0	0	0	0	4	0.0
D	8 *	Petter Granberg	TOR	7	0	0	0	11:26	1	6	0	0	0	1	0.0
R	39	Matt Frattin	TOR	9	0	0	0	7:03	0	4	0	0	0	6	0.0

Goaltending

No.	Goaltender	GPI	Mins	Avg	W	L	OT	EN	SO	GA	SA	Sv%	G	A	PIM
45	Jonathan Bernier	58	3177	2.87	21	28	7	7	2	152	1735	.912	0	1	0
34	James Reimer	35	1767	3.16	9	16	1	5	0	93	1001	.907	0	0	2
	Totals	**82**	**4990**	**3.09**	**30**	**44**	**8**	**12**	**2**	**257**	**2748**	**.906**			

Coaching Record

			Regular Season				Playoffs			
Season	Team	League	GC	W	L	O/T	GC	W	L	T
1988-89	Red Deer	ACAC	24	18	4	2	6	5	1	....
1988-89	Red Deer	CCAA	....	....	....	....	4	3	1	....
1989-90	Red Deer	ACAC	24	11	12	1	5	2	3	....
1990-91	Red Deer	ACAC	25	19	6	0	3	1	2	....
1991-92	Moose Jaw	WHL	72	33	36	3	4	0	4	....
1992-93	Moose Jaw	WHL	72	27	42	3	....	....	....	....
1993-94	U of Lethbridge	CIAU	28	19	7	2	....	....	....	....
1994-95	Spokane	WHL	72	32	36	4	11	6	5	....
1995-96	Spokane	WHL	72	50	18	4	9	3	6	....
1996-97	Spokane	WHL	72	35	33	4	9	4	5	....
1997-98	Spokane	WHL	72	45	23	4	18	10	8	....
1998-99	Spokane	WHL	72	19	44	9	....	....	....	....
99-2000	Spokane	WHL	72	47	19	6	20	15	5	....
2000-01	Cincinnati	AHL	80	41	26	13	4	1	3	....
2001-02	Cincinnati	AHL	80	33	33	14	3	1	2	....
2002-03	**Anaheim**	**NHL**	**82**	**40**	**27**	**15**	**21**	**15**	**6**	....
2003-04	**Anaheim**	**NHL**	**82**	**29**	**35**	**18**	....	....	....	....
2004-05	**Anaheim**				SEASON CANCELLED					
2005-06	**Detroit**	**NHL**	**82**	**58**	**16**	**8**	**6**	**2**	**4**	....
2006-07	**Detroit**	**NHL**	**82**	**50**	**19**	**13**	**18**	**10**	**8**	....
2007-08 ♦	**Detroit**	**NHL**	**82**	**54**	**21**	**7**	**22**	**16**	**6**	....
2008-09	**Detroit**	**NHL**	**82**	**51**	**21**	**10**	**23**	**15**	**8**	....
2009-10	**Detroit**	**NHL**	**82**	**44**	**24**	**14**	**12**	**5**	**7**	....
2010-11	**Detroit**	**NHL**	**82**	**47**	**25**	**10**	**11**	**7**	**4**	....
2011-12	**Detroit**	**NHL**	**82**	**48**	**28**	**6**	**5**	**1**	**4**	....
2012-13	**Detroit**	**NHL**	**48**	**24**	**16**	**8**	**14**	**7**	**7**	....
2013-14	**Detroit**	**NHL**	**82**	**39**	**28**	**15**	**5**	**1**	**4**	....
2014-15	**Detroit**	**NHL**	**82**	**43**	**25**	**14**	**7**	**3**	**4**	....
	NHL Totals		**950**	**527**	**285**	**138**	**144**	**82**	**62**	....

♦ Stanley Cup win.

Club Records

Team

(Figures in brackets for season records are games played; records for fewest points, wins, ties, losses, goals, goals against are for 70 or more games)

Most Points	**103**	2003-04 (82)
Most Wins	**45**	1998-99 (82), 1999-2000 (82), 2003-04 (82)
Most Ties	**22**	1954-55 (70)
Most Losses	**52**	1984-85 (80)
Most Goals	**337**	1989-90 (80)
Most Goals Against	**387**	1983-84 (80)
Fewest Points	**48**	1984-85 (80)
Fewest Wins	**20**	1981-82 (80), 1984-85 (80)
Fewest Ties	**4**	1989-90 (80)
Fewest Losses	**16**	1950-51 (70)
Fewest Goals	**147**	1954-55 (70)
Fewest Goals Against	***131**	1953-54 (70)
Longest Winning Streak		
Overall	**10**	Oct. 7-28/93
Home	**9**	Nov. 11-Dec. 26/53, Mar. 6-Apr. 7/07
Away	**7**	Nov. 14-Dec. 15/40, Dec. 4/60-Jan. 5/61, Jan. 29-Feb. 22/03
Longest Undefeated Streak		
Overall	**11**	Oct. 15-Nov. 8/50 (8W, 3T), Jan. 6-Feb. 1/94 (7W, 4T)
Home	**18**	Nov. 28/33-Mar. 10/34 (15W, 3T), Oct. 31/53-Jan. 23/54 (16W, 2T)
Away	**9**	Nov. 30/47-Jan. 11/48 (4W, 5T)
Longest Losing Streak		
Overall	**10**	Jan. 15-Feb. 8/67
Home	**7**	Nov. 11-Dec. 5/84
Away	**11**	Feb. 20-Apr. 1/88
Longest Winless Streak		
Overall	**15**	Dec. 26/87-Jan. 25/88 (11L, 4T)
Home	**11**	Dec. 19/87-Jan. 25/88 (7L, 4T), Feb. 11-Mar. 29/12 (9L, 2OL/SOL)
Away	**18**	Oct. 6/82-Jan. 5/83 (13L, 5T)
Most Shutouts, Season	**13**	1953-54 (70)
Most PIM, Season	**2,419**	1989-90 (80)
Most Goals, Game	**14**	Mar. 16/57 (NYR 1 at Tor. 14)

Individual

Most Seasons	**21**	George Armstrong
Most Games	**1,187**	George Armstrong
Most Goals, Career	**420**	Mats Sundin
Most Assists, Career	**620**	Borje Salming
Most Points, Career	**987**	Mats Sundin (420G, 567A)
Most PIM, Career	**2,265**	Tie Domi
Most Shutouts, Career	**62**	Turk Broda
Longest Consecutive Games Streak	**486**	Tim Horton (Feb. 11/61-Feb. 4/68)
Most Goals, Season	**54**	Rick Vaive (1981-82)
Most Assists, Season	**95**	Doug Gilmour (1992-93)
Most Points, Season	**127**	Doug Gilmour (1992-93; 32G, 95A)
Most PIM, Season	**365**	Tie Domi (1997-98)
Most Points, Defenseman, Season	**79**	Ian Turnbull (1976-77; 22G, 57A)
Most Points, Center, Season	**127**	Doug Gilmour (1992-93; 32G, 95A)
Most Points, Right Wing, Season	**97**	Wilf Paiement (1980-81; 40G, 57A)
Most Points, Left Wing, Season	**99**	Dave Andreychuk (1993-94; 53G, 46A)
Most Points, Rookie, Season	**66**	Peter Ihnacak (1982-83; 28G, 38A)
Most Shutouts, Season	**13**	Harry Lumley (1953-54)
Most Goals, Game	**6**	Corb Denneny (Jan. 26/21), Darryl Sittler (Feb. 7/76)
Most Assists, Game	**6**	Babe Pratt (Jan. 8/44), Doug Gilmour (Feb. 13/93)
Most Points, Game	***10**	Darryl Sittler (Feb. 7/76; 6G, 4A)

* NHL Record.

Honored Numbers

1	Turk Broda	1936-43, 1945-52
	Johnny Bower	1958-1970
4	Hap Day	1926-1937
	Red Kelly	1959-1967
7	King Clancy	1930-1937
	Tim Horton	1949-50, 1951-70
9	Charlie Conacher	1929-1938
	Ted Kennedy	1942-55, 1956-57
10	Syl Apps	1936-43, 1945-48
	George Armstrong	1949-50, 1951-71
13	Mats Sundin	1994-2008
17	Wendel Clark	1985-94, 96-98, 2000
21	Borje Salming	1973-1989
27	Frank Mahovlich	1956-1968
	Darryl Sittler	1970-1982
93	Doug Gilmour	1992-97, 2003

All-time Record vs. Other Clubs

Regular Season

	Total								At Home								On Road							
	GP	W	L	T	OL	GF	GA	PTS	GP	W	L	T	OL	GF	GA	PTS	GP	W	L	T	OL	GF	GA	PTS
Anaheim	36	21	9	5	1	112	90	48	20	13	2	4	1	70	41	31	16	8	7	1	0	42	49	17
Arizona	92	35	48	8	1	321	360	79	48	21	24	2	1	168	178	45	44	14	24	6	0	153	182	34
Boston	657	268	282	98	9	1952	1943	643	329	168	108	51	2	1083	868	389	328	100	174	47	7	869	1075	254
Buffalo	197	71	99	18	9	550	711	169	98	44	38	12	4	291	320	104	99	27	61	6	5	259	391	65
Calgary	128	56	56	12	4	437	476	128	60	33	18	7	2	228	211	75	68	23	38	5	2	209	265	53
Carolina	110	39	54	11	6	342	397	95	55	21	28	5	1	171	188	48	55	18	26	6	5	171	209	47
Chicago	643	286	260	96	1	1931	1828	669	320	166	99	54	1	1092	842	387	323	120	161	42	0	839	986	282
Colorado	74	27	36	9	2	235	277	65	40	17	18	4	1	126	148	39	34	10	18	5	1	109	129	26
Columbus	16	8	5	1	2	47	43	19	9	4	3	1	1	24	22	10	7	4	2	0	1	23	21	9
Dallas	208	90	89	28	1	690	717	209	106	52	37	17	0	371	335	121	102	38	52	11	1	319	382	88
Detroit	653	280	278	93	2	1877	1853	655	324	169	107	47	1	1072	867	386	329	111	171	46	1	805	986	269
Edmonton	94	44	41	8	1	342	372	97	44	25	17	2	0	182	179	52	50	19	24	6	1	160	193	45
Florida	71	34	28	7	2	204	210	77	34	18	13	2	1	102	101	39	37	16	15	5	1	102	109	38
Los Angeles	143	60	61	21	1	479	485	142	73	36	25	11	1	277	239	84	70	24	36	10	0	202	246	58
Minnesota	14	8	5	0	1	36	31	17	8	6	2	0	0	26	15	12	6	2	3	0	1	10	16	5
Montreal	728	293	335	88	12	2019	2227	686	364	186	126	45	7	1103	967	424	364	107	209	43	5	916	1260	262
Nashville	17	6	9	1	1	41	56	14	11	4	6	1	0	25	38	9	6	2	3	0	1	16	18	5
New Jersey	131	65	38	20	8	424	389	158	67	42	16	5	4	226	176	93	64	23	22	15	4	198	213	65
NY Islanders	145	66	63	7	9	469	512	148	74	38	28	4	4	258	244	84	71	28	35	3	5	211	268	64
NY Rangers	602	282	217	95	8	1909	1738	667	300	166	92	39	3	1023	801	374	302	116	125	56	5	886	937	293
Ottawa	104	49	44	3	8	298	298	109	52	27	18	2	5	152	149	61	52	22	26	1	3	146	149	48
Philadelphia	171	57	89	22	3	466	593	139	86	33	37	14	2	263	281	82	85	24	52	8	1	203	312	57
Pittsburgh	173	76	73	17	7	613	624	176	86	42	30	11	3	329	278	98	87	34	43	6	4	284	346	78
St. Louis	211	91	92	25	3	676	680	210	104	59	31	11	3	385	316	132	107	32	61	14	0	291	364	78
San Jose	43	20	18	5	0	130	116	45	23	12	9	2	0	79	65	26	20	8	9	3	0	51	51	19
Tampa Bay	80	49	24	2	5	266	207	105	40	26	11	1	2	145	108	55	40	23	13	1	3	121	99	50
Vancouver	138	54	61	22	1	465	476	131	67	30	25	11	1	239	222	72	71	24	36	11	0	226	254	59
Washington	135	59	64	10	2	454	466	130	66	36	23	6	1	266	215	79	69	23	41	4	1	188	251	51
Winnipeg	53	29	16	1	7	187	141	66	26	15	7	1	3	95	75	34	27	14	9	0	4	92	66	32
Defunct Clubs	465	242	173	50	0	1468	1260	534	232	158	53	21	0	861	515	337	233	84	120	29	0	607	745	197
Totals	**6332**	**2765**	**2667**	**783**	**117**	**19440**	**19576**	**6430**	**3166**	**1667**	**1051**	**393**	**55**	**10732**	**9004**	**3782**	**3166**	**1098**	**1616**	**390**	**62**	**8708**	**10572**	**2648**

Playoffs

	Series	W	L	GP	W	L	T	GF	GA	Last Mtg.	Rnd.	Result
Boston	14	8	6	69	34	34	1	168	175	2013	CQF	L 3-4
Buffalo	1	0	1	5	1	4	0	16	21	1999	CF	L 1-4
Calgary	1	1	0	2	2	0	0	9	5	1979	PR	W 2-0
Carolina	1	0	1	6	2	4	0	6	10	2002	CF	L 2-4
Chicago	9	6	3	38	22	15	1	111	89	1995	CQF	L 3-4
Dallas	2	0	2	7	1	6	0	26	35	1983	DSF	L 1-3
Detroit	23	12	11	117	58	59	0	311	321	1993	DSF	W 4-3
Los Angeles	3	2	1	12	7	5	0	41	31	1993	CF	L 3-4
Montreal	15	7	8	71	29	42	0	160	215	1979	QF	L 0-4
New Jersey	2	0	2	13	5	8	0	27	37	2001	CSF	L 3-4
NY Islanders	3	2	1	17	8	9	0	42	54	2002	CQF	W 4-3
NY Rangers	8	3	5	35	16	19	0	86	86	1971	QF	L 2-4
Ottawa	4	4	0	24	16	8	0	57	42	2004	CQF	W 4-3
Philadelphia	6	1	5	36	14	22	0	85	119	2004	CSF	L 2-4
Pittsburgh	3	3	0	12	8	4	0	39	27	1999	CSF	W 4-2
St. Louis	5	2	3	31	14	17	0	90	88	1996	CQF	L 2-4
San Jose	1	1	0	7	4	3	0	26	21	1994	CSF	W 4-3
Vancouver	1	0	1	5	1	4	0	9	16	1994	CF	L 1-4
Defunct Clubs	8	6	2	24	12	10	2	59	57			
Totals	**110**	**58**	**52**	**531**	**254**	**273**	**4**	**1368**	**1449**			

Playoff Results 2015-2011

Year	Round	Opponent	Result	GF	GA
2013	CQF	Boston	L 3-4	18	22

Abbreviations: Round: CF – conference final; **CSF** – conference semi-final; **CQF** – conference quarter-final; **DSF** – division semi-final; **QF** – quarter-final; **PR** – preliminary round.

Calgary totals include Atlanta Flames, 1972-73 to 1979-80.
Colorado totals include Quebec, 1979-80 to 1994-95.
New Jersey totals include Kansas City, 1974-75, 1975-76, and Colorado Rockies, 1976-77 to 1981-82.
Phoenix totals include Winnipeg, 1979-80 to 1995-96.
Carolina totals include Hartford, 1979-80 to 1996-97.
Dallas totals include Minnesota North Stars, 1967-68 to 1992-93.
Winnipeg totals include Atlanta Thrashers, 1999-2000 to 2010-11.

2014-15 Results

Oct.	8	Montreal	3-4
	11	Pittsburgh	2-5
	12	at NY Rangers	6-3
	14	Colorado	3-2*
	17	Detroit	1-4
	18	at Detroit	0-1*
	21	at NY Islanders	5-2
	25	Boston	1-4
	28	Buffalo	4-0
	31	at Columbus	4-1
Nov.	1	Chicago	3-2
	4	at Arizona	2-3
	6	at Colorado	3-4†
	8	NY Rangers	5-4
	9	at Ottawa	5-3
	12	Boston	6-1
	14	Pittsburgh	1-2
	15	at Buffalo	2-6
	18	Nashville	2-9
	20	Tampa Bay	5-2
	22	Detroit	4-1
	26	at Pittsburgh	3-4*
	29	Washington	6-2
Dec.	2	Dallas	5-3
	4	New Jersey	3-5
	6	Vancouver	5-2
	9	Calgary	4-1
	10	at Detroit	2-1†
	13	Detroit	4-1
	14	Los Angeles	4-3†
	16	Anaheim	6-2
	18	at Carolina	1-4
	20	Philadelphia	4-7
	21	at Chicago	0-4
	23	at Dallas	4-0
	28	at Florida	4-6
	29	at Tampa Bay	2-3
	31	at Boston	4-3†
Jan.	2	at Minnesota	1-3
	3	at Winnipeg	1-5
	7	Washington	2-6
	9	Columbus	5-2
	12	at Los Angeles	0-2
	14	at Anaheim	0-4
	15	at San Jose	1-3
	17	at St. Louis	0-3
	19	Carolina	1-4
	21	at Ottawa	3-4
	28	at New Jersey	1-2†
	29	Arizona	1-3
	31	at Philadelphia	0-1
Feb.	3	at Nashville	3-4
	6	at New Jersey	1-4
	7	Edmonton	5-1
	10	NY Rangers	4-5
	12	at NY Islanders	2-3
	14	at Montreal	1-2†
	17	Florida	2-3
	20	at Carolina	1-2
	21	Winnipeg	4-3*
	26	Philadelphia	3-2
	28	at Montreal	0-4
Mar.	1	at Washington	0-4
	3	at Florida	3-2
	5	at Tampa Bay	2-4
	7	St. Louis	1-6
	9	NY Islanders	3-4*
	11	Buffalo	4-3†
	13	at Calgary	3-6
	14	at Vancouver	1-4
	16	at Edmonton	1-4
	19	San Jose	1-4
	21	at Ottawa	3-5
	23	Minnesota	1-2
	26	Florida	1-4
	28	Ottawa	4-3*
	31	Tampa Bay	3-1
Apr.	1	at Buffalo	3-4
	4	at Boston	1-2†
	5	Ottawa	3-2†
	8	at Columbus	0-5
	11	Montreal	3-4†

* – Overtime † – Shootout

NHL Draft Selections 2015-2001

Name in bold denotes played in NHL.

2015
Pick
4	Mitch Marner
34	Travis Dermott
61	Jeremy Bracco
65	Andrew Nielsen
68	Martins Dzierkals
95	Jesper Lindgren
125	Dmytro Timashov
155	Stephen Desrocher
185	Nikita Korostelev

2014
Pick
8	William Nylander
68	Rinat Valiev
103	J.J. Piccinich
128	Dakota Joshua
158	Nolan Vesey
188	Pierre Engvall

2013
Pick
21	Frederik Gauthier
82	Carter Verhaeghe
142	Fabrice Herzog
172	Antoine Bibeau
202	Andreas Johnson

2012
Pick
5	**Morgan Rielly**
35	Matt Finn
126	Dominic Toninato
156	Connor Brown
157	Ryan Rupert
209	Viktor Loov

2011
Pick
22	Tyler Biggs
25	**Stuart Percy**
86	**Josh Leivo**
100	Tom Nilsson
130	Tony Cameranesi
152	**David Broll**
173	Dennis Robertson
190	Garret Sparks
203	Max Everson

2010
Pick
43	Brad Ross
62	**Greg McKegg**
79	Sondre Olden
116	**Petter Granberg**
144	**Sam Carrick**
146	Daniel Brodin
182	Josh Nicholls

2009
Pick
7	**Nazem Kadri**
50	Kenny Ryan
58	Jesse Blacker
68	Jamie Devane
128	Eric Knodel
158	Jerry D'Amigo
188	Barron Smith

2008
Pick
5	**Luke Schenn**
60	**Jimmy Hayes**
98	Mikhail Stefanovich
128	**Greg Pateryn**
129	Joel Champagne
130	Jerome Flaake
158	Grant Rollheiser
188	**Andrew MacWilliam**

2007
Pick
74	Dale Mitchell
99	**Matt Frattin**
104	Ben Winnett
134	Juraj Mikus
164	Chris Didomenico
194	**Carl Gunnarsson**

2006
Pick
13	**Jiri Tlusty**
44	**Nikolai Kulemin**
99	**James Reimer**
111	**Korbinian Holzer**
161	**Viktor Stalberg**
166	Tyler Ruegsegger
180	**Leo Komarov**

2005
Pick
21	**Tuukka Rask**
82	**Phil Oreskovic**
153	Alex Berry
173	Johan Dahlberg
216	**Anton Stralman**
228	**Chad Rau**

2004
Pick
90	**Justin Pogge**
113	Roman Kukumberg
157	Dmitri Vorobiev
187	**Robbie Earl**
220	Maxim Semenov
252	Jan Steber
285	Pierce Norton

2003
Pick
57	John Doherty
91	Martin Sagat
125	Konstantin Volkov
158	**John Mitchell**
220	**Jeremy Williams**
237	Shaun Landolt

2002
Pick
24	**Alexander Steen**
57	**Matt Stajan**
74	Todd Ford
88	Dominic D'Amour
122	David Turon
191	**Ian White**
222	Scott May
254	**Jarkko Immonen**
285	**Staffan Kronwall**

2001
Pick
17	**Carlo Colaiacovo**
39	**Karel Pilar**
65	**Brendan Bell**
82	**Jay Harrison**
88	Nicolas Corbeil
134	**Kyle Wellwood**
168	**Maxim Kondratiev**
183	Jaroslav Sklenar
198	Ivan Kolozvary
213	Jan Chovan
246	**Tomas Mojzis**
276	Mike Knoepfli

General Managers' History

Charles Querrie, 1917-18 to 1926-27; Conn Smythe, 1927-28 to 1953-54; Hap Day, 1954-55 to 1956-57; Howie Meeker, summer 1957; Stafford Smythe 1957-58; Stafford Smythe and Punch Imlach, 1958-59; Punch Imlach, 1959-60 to 1968-69; Jim Gregory, 1969-70 to 1978-79; Punch Imlach, 1979-80, 1980-81; Punch Imlach and Gerry McNamara, 1981-82; Gerry McNamara, 1982-83 to 1986-87; Gerry McNamara and Gord Stellick, 1987-88; Gord Stellick, 1988-89; Floyd Smith, 1989-90, 1990-91; Cliff Fletcher, 1991-92 to 1996-97; Ken Dryden, 1997-98, 1998-99; Pat Quinn, 1999-2000 to 2002-03; John Ferguson Jr., 2003-04 to 2006-07; John Ferguson Jr. and Cliff Fletcher, 2007-08; Cliff Fletcher and Brian Burke, 2008-09; Brian Burke, 2009-10 to 2011-12; Brian Burke and Dave Nonis, 2012-13; Dave Nonis, 2013-14, 2014-15; Lou Lamoriello, 2015-16.

Lou Lamoriello
General Manager

Born: Providence, RI, October 21, 1942.

Brendan Shanahan, president and alternate governor of the Toronto Maple Leafs, announced on July 23, 2015 that Lou Lamoriello had been named the 16th general manager in the club's history. Lamoriello joined the Leafs after spending the previous 28 years in the New Jersey Devils organization.

Lamoriello first joined the Devils as president and general manager in 1987. Under his leadership, New Jersey went to the Stanley Cup playoffs 21 times, won nine division titles, went to the Stanley Cup Final five times and won the Cup on three occasions (1995, 2000 and 2003). The Devils also made 13 consecutive postseason berths from 1997 to 2010 and finished with a winning record every season from 1992-93 through 2009-10.

Lamoriello also served as interim head coach during three different seasons — most recently the 2014-15 season as he served as co-coach alongside Scott Stevens and Adam Oates for the final 46 games of the regular season (20-19-7). On May 4, 2015, Ray Shero was introduced as the Devils' new general manager while Lamoriello remained in his role as president of hockey operations. He finished as the longest serving general manager of any one team in the history of the NHL at 28 years (1987 to 2015).

In 1996, Lamoriello served as general manager for Team USA as they won the World Cup of Hockey. He was also general manager of Team USA at the 1998 Nagano Winter Olympics. His many accomplishments have earned him a number of prestigious awards, including induction into the Hockey Hall of Fame in the Builder category in 2009 and into the U.S. Hockey Hall of Fame in 2012.

Coaching Record

			Regular Season				Playoffs			
Season	Team	League	GC	W	L	O/T	GC	W	L	T
2005-06	New Jersey	NHL	50	32	14	4	9	5	4	....
2006-07	New Jersey	NHL	3	2	0	1	11	5	6	....
	NHL Totals		**53**	**34**	**14**	**5**	**20**	**10**	**10**	....

Posted an 0-1 playoff record as replacement coach when Jim Schoenfeld was suspended, May 10, 1988. Loss is credited to Schoenfeld's coaching record.
Shared a 20-19-7 record with Adam Oates and Scott Stevens while serving as co-head coaches from December 27, 2014 to the end of the 2014-15 season. The games are not officially credited to anyone's coaching record.

Club Directory

Air Canada Centre

Toronto Maple Leafs
Air Canada Centre
40 Bay St.
Toronto, Ontario M5J 2X2
Phone **416/815-5700**
FAX 416/359-9331
mapleleafs.nhl.com
Capacity: 18,819

Board of Directors
Lawrence M. Tanenbaum, George Cope, Dale Lastman, Edward Rogers, Guy Laurence, Mary Ann Turcke, Siim Vanaselja, Tony Staffieri

Maple Leaf Sports & Entertainment
Chairman, NHL Governor	Lawrence M. Tanenbaum
Alternate NHL Governor	Dale Lastman
President & CEO	Tim Leiweke
Chief Financial Officer	Ian Clarke
Chief Project Development Officer	Bob Hunter
Chief Commercial Officer	Dave Hopkinson
Chief Legal & Development Officer	Peter Miller

Hockey Operations
President & Alternate Governor	Brendan Shanahan
General Manager	Lou Lamoriello
Assistant General Manager	Kyle Dubas
Director of Player Personnel	Mark Hunter
Assistant to the General Manager	Brandon Pridham
Senior Advisor	Cliff Fletcher
Head Coach	Mike Babcock
Assistant Coaches	Jim Hiller, D.J. Smith and Andrew Brewer
Goaltending Coach	Steve Briere
Director of Player Development	Scott Pellerin
Director of Player Evaluation	Jim Paliafito
Director, Hockey and Scouting Operations	Reid Mitchell
Director of Team Services, Hockey Operations	Bradley Holland
Video Coordinator	Adam Jancelewicz
Director of Amateur Scouting	Dave Morrison
Special Assignment Scout	Jacques Lemaire
Pro Scouts	Mike Penny, Bryan Stewart, Tom Watt
Amateur Scouts	Wes Clark, Lindsay Hofford, John Lilley, Garth Malarchuk
European Scouts	Thommie Bergman, Nikolai Ladygin
Player Evaluation Consultant	Wes Clark
Player Development Consultant	Darryl Belfry
Skating Development Consultant	Barb Underhill
Skill Development Consultant	Mike Ellis
Community Representatives	Wendel Clark, Darryl Sittler, George Armstrong
Administrative Assistant, Hockey Operations	Leanne Hederson
Exec. Assistant to the President and CEO	Laura Patterson
Exec. Assistant to the GM and Hockey Operations.	Megan Arnoldi

Medical and Training Staff
Director of Sports Science and Performance	Dr. Jeremy Bettle
Strength and Conditioning Coach	Matthew J. Herring
Associate Strength and Conditioning Coach	Peter Renzetti
Head Athletic Therapist	Paul Ayotte
Massage Therapist	Todd Bean
Equipment Manager	Brian Papineau
Assistant Equipment Managers	Tom Blatchford, Bobby Hastings
Medical Director, Maple Leafs and Marlies	Dr. Noah Forman
Orthopedic Consultant	Dr. John Theodoropoulos
Team Dentists	Dr. Marvin Lean, Dr. Charles Goldberg

Communications
Director, Media Relations	Steve Keogh
Senior Manager, Media Relations	Scott McNaughton
Coordinator, Media Relations	Ian Meagher

Broadcasting
Vice President, Content.	Alyson Walker
Talent, Leafs TV	Joe Bowen, Paul Hendrick, Bob McGill
Radio,Play-By-Play / Colour	Joe Bowen / Jim Ralph

Captains' History

Ken Randall, 1917-18, 1918-19; Frank Heffernan, 1919-20; Reg Noble, 1920-21, 1921-22; Reg Noble and Jack Adams, 1922-23; Jack Adams, 1923-24, 1924-25; Babe Day, 1925-26; Bert Corbeau, 1926-27; Hap Day, 1927-28 to 1936-37; Charlie Conacher, 1937-38; Red Horner, 1938-39, 1939-40; Syl Apps, 1940-41 to 1942-43; Bob Davidson, 1943-44, 1944-45; Syl Apps, 1945-46 to 1947-48; Ted Kennedy, 1948-49 to 1954-55; Sid Smith, 1955-56; Jimmy Thomson, Ted Kennedy, 1956-57; George Armstrong, 1957-58 to 1968-69; Dave Keon, 1969-70 to 1974-75; Darryl Sittler, 1975-76 to 1980-81; Rick Vaive, 1981-82 to 1985-86; no captain, 1986-87 to 1988-89; Rob Ramage, 1989-90, 1990-91; Wendel Clark, 1991-92 to 1993-94; Doug Gilmour, 1994-95 to 1996-97; Mats Sundin, 1997-98 to 2007-08; no captain, 2008-09, 2009-10; Dion Phaneuf, 2010-11 to date.

Key Off-Season Signings/Acquisitions

2015

June 29 • Re-signed G **Jacob Markstrom** and RW **Linden Vey**.

     30 • Re-signed D **Alex Biega**.

July   1 • Acquired LW **Brandon Prust** from Montreal for RW **Zack Kassian** and a 5th-round choice in the 2016 NHL Draft.

     1 • Signed D **Matt Bartkowski**, D **Taylor Fedun** and G **Richard Bachman**.

     1 • Re-signed D **Yannick Weber**.

     8 • Re-signed D **Frank Corrado**.

   28 • Acquired C **Brandon Sutter** and a 3rd-round choice in the 2016 NHL Draft from Pittsburgh for C **Nick Bonino**, D **Adam Clendening** and a 2nd-round choice in 2016.

   28 • Re-signed LW **Sven Baertschi**.

2015-16 Schedule

Oct.	Wed.	7	at Calgary
	Sat.	10	Calgary
	Mon.	12	at Anaheim
	Tue.	13	at Los Angeles
	Fri.	16	St. Louis
	Sun.	18	Edmonton
	Thu.	22	Washington
	Sat.	24	Detroit
	Tue.	27	Montreal
	Thu.	29	at Dallas
	Fri.	30	at Arizona
Nov.	Mon.	2	Philadelphia
	Wed.	4	Pittsburgh
	Sat.	7	at Buffalo*
	Sun.	8	at New Jersey*
	Tue.	10	at Columbus
	Thu.	12	at Ottawa
	Sat.	14	at Toronto
	Mon.	16	at Montreal
	Wed.	18	at Winnipeg
	Sat.	21	Chicago
	Sun.	22	New Jersey
	Wed.	25	at Minnesota
	Fri.	27	at Dallas
	Mon.	30	at Anaheim
Dec.	Tue.	1	at Los Angeles
	Thu.	3	Dallas
	Sat.	5	Boston
	Mon.	7	Buffalo
	Wed.	9	NY Rangers
	Sun.	13	at Chicago
	Tue.	15	at Minnesota
	Thu.	17	at Philadelphia
	Fri.	18	at Detroit
	Sun.	20	at Florida*
	Tue.	22	at Tampa Bay
	Sat.	26	Edmonton
	Mon.	28	Los Angeles
Jan.	Fri.	1	Anaheim
	Mon.	4	Arizona
	Wed.	6	Carolina

	Sat.	9	Tampa Bay
	Mon.	11	Florida
	Thu.	14	at Washington
	Fri.	15	at Carolina
	Sun.	17	at NY Islanders*
	Tue.	19	at NY Rangers
	Thu.	21	at Boston
	Sat.	23	at Pittsburgh*
	Tue.	26	Nashville
Feb.	Thu.	4	Columbus
	Sat.	6	Calgary
	Tue.	9	at Colorado
	Wed.	10	at Arizona
	Sat.	13	Toronto*
	Mon.	15	Minnesota
	Thu.	18	Anaheim
	Fri.	19	at Calgary
	Sun.	21	Colorado
	Thu.	25	Ottawa
	Sun.	28	San Jose*
Mar.	Tue.	1	NY Islanders
	Thu.	3	San Jose
	Sat.	5	at San Jose
	Mon.	7	at Los Angeles
	Wed.	9	Arizona
	Sat.	12	Nashville
	Mon.	14	Winnipeg
	Wed.	16	Colorado
	Fri.	18	at Edmonton
	Sat.	19	St. Louis
	Tue.	22	at Winnipeg
	Thu.	24	at Nashville
	Fri.	25	at St. Louis
	Sun.	27	Chicago*
	Tue.	29	San Jose
	Thu.	31	at San Jose
Apr.	Fri.	1	at Anaheim
	Mon.	4	Los Angeles
	Wed.	6	at Edmonton
	Thu.	7	at Calgary
	Sat.	9	Edmonton

Denotes afternoon game.

Retired Numbers

10	Pavel Bure	1991-1998
12	Stan Smyl	1978-1991
16	Trevor Linden	1988-1998; 2001-2008
19	Markus Naslund	1996-2008

PACIFIC DIVISION
46th NHL Season

Franchise date: May 22, 1970

Vancouver Canucks

2014-15 Results: 48w-29L-3OTL-2SOL 101PTS
2ND, Pacific Division • 5TH, Western Conference

In his first season with Vancouver in 2014-15, Radim Vrbata led the team with 31 goals and posted career highs with 32 assists and 63 points.

Year-by-Year Record

Season	GP	Home				Road				Overall							Div. Fin.	Conf. Fin.	Playoff Result
		W	L	T	OL	W	L	T	OL	W	L	T	OL	GF	GA	Pts.			
2014-15	82	24	15	....	2	24	14	....	3	48	29	....	5	242	222	101	2nd, Pac.	5th, West	Lost First Round
2013-14	82	20	15	....	6	16	20	....	5	36	35	....	11	196	223	83	5th, Pac.	12th, West	Out of Playoffs
2012-13	48	15	6	....	3	11	9	....	4	26	15	....	7	127	121	59	1st, NW	3rd, West	Lost Conf. Quarter-Final
2011-12	82	27	10	....	4	24	12	....	5	51	22	....	9	249	198	111	1st, NW	1st, West	Lost Conf. Quarter-Final
2010-11	82	27	9	....	5	27	10	....	4	54	19	....	9	262	185	117	1st, NW	1st, West	Lost Final
2009-10	82	30	8	....	3	19	20	....	2	49	28	....	5	272	222	103	1st, NW	3rd, West	Lost Conf. Semi-Final
2008-09	82	24	12	....	5	21	15	....	5	45	27	....	10	246	220	100	1st, NW	3rd, West	Lost Conf. Semi-Final
2007-08	82	21	15	....	5	18	18	....	5	39	33	....	10	213	215	88	5th, NW	11th, West	Out of Playoffs
2006-07	82	26	11	....	4	23	15	....	3	49	26	....	7	222	201	105	1st, NW	3rd, West	Lost Conf. Semi-Final
2005-06	82	25	10	....	6	17	22	....	2	42	32	....	8	256	255	92	4th, NW	9th, West	Out of Playoffs
2004-05	....	....	....	....	....	....	....	....	....	....	....	....	....	....	....	....			
2003-04	82	21	13	7	0	22	11	5	3	43	24	10	5	235	194	101	1st, NW	3rd, West	Lost Conf. Quarter-Final
2002-03	82	22	13	6	0	23	10	7	1	45	23	13	1	264	208	104	2nd, NW	4th, West	Lost Conf. Semi-Final
2001-02	82	23	11	5	2	19	19	2	1	42	30	7	3	254	211	94	2nd, NW	8th, West	Lost Conf. Quarter-Final
2000-01	82	21	12	5	3	15	16	6	4	36	28	11	7	239	238	90	3rd, NW	8th, West	Lost Conf. Quarter-Final
1999-2000	82	16	14	5	6	14	15	10	2	30	29	15	8	227	237	83	3rd, NW	10th, West	Out of Playoffs
1998-99	82	14	21	6	....	9	26	6	....	23	47	12	....	192	258	58	4th, NW	13th, West	Out of Playoffs
1997-98	82	15	22	4	....	10	21	10	....	25	43	14	....	224	273	64	7th, Pac.	13th, West	Out of Playoffs
1996-97	82	20	17	4	....	15	23	3	....	35	40	7	....	257	273	77	4th, Pac.	9th, West	Out of Playoffs
1995-96	82	15	19	7	....	17	16	8	....	32	35	15	....	278	278	79	3rd, Pac.	7th, West	Lost Conf. Quarter-Final
1994-95	48	10	8	6	....	8	10	6	....	18	18	12	....	153	148	48	2nd, Pac.	6th, West	Lost Conf. Semi-Final
1993-94	84	20	19	3	....	21	21	0	....	41	40	3	....	279	276	85	2nd, Pac.	7th, West	Lost Final
1992-93	84	27	11	4	....	19	18	5	....	46	29	9	....	346	278	101	1st, Smythe		Lost Div. Final
1991-92	80	23	10	7	....	19	16	5	....	42	26	12	....	285	250	96	1st, Smythe		Lost Div. Final
1990-91	80	18	17	5	....	10	26	4	....	28	43	9	....	243	315	65	4th, Smythe		Lost Div. Semi-Final
1989-90	80	13	16	11	....	12	25	3	....	25	41	14	....	245	306	64	5th, Smythe		Out of Playoffs
1988-89	80	19	15	6	....	14	24	2	....	33	39	8	....	251	253	74	4th, Smythe		Lost Div. Semi-Final
1987-88	80	15	20	5	....	10	26	4	....	25	46	9	....	272	320	59	5th, Smythe		Out of Playoffs
1986-87	80	17	19	4	....	12	24	4	....	29	43	8	....	282	314	66	5th, Smythe		Out of Playoffs
1985-86	80	17	18	5	....	6	26	8	....	23	44	13	....	282	333	59	4th, Smythe		Lost Div. Semi-Final
1984-85	80	15	21	4	....	10	25	5	....	25	46	9	....	284	401	59	5th, Smythe		Out of Playoffs
1983-84	80	20	16	4	....	12	23	5	....	32	39	9	....	306	328	73	3rd, Smythe		Lost Div. Semi-Final
1982-83	80	20	12	8	....	10	23	7	....	30	35	15	....	303	309	75	3rd, Smythe		Lost Div. Semi-Final
1981-82	80	20	8	12	....	10	25	5	....	30	33	17	....	290	286	77	2nd, Smythe		Lost Final
1980-81	80	17	12	11	....	11	20	9	....	28	32	20	....	289	301	76	3rd, Smythe		Lost Prelim. Round
1979-80	80	14	17	9	....	13	20	7	....	27	37	16	....	256	281	70	3rd, Smythe		Lost Prelim. Round
1978-79	80	15	18	7	....	10	24	6	....	25	42	13	....	217	291	63	2nd, Smythe		Lost Prelim. Round
1977-78	80	13	15	12	....	7	28	5	....	20	43	17	....	239	320	57	3rd, Smythe		Out of Playoffs
1976-77	80	13	21	6	....	12	21	7	....	25	42	13	....	235	294	63	4th, Smythe		Out of Playoffs
1975-76	80	20	12	8	....	13	20	7	....	33	32	15	....	271	272	81	2nd, Smythe		Lost Prelim. Round
1974-75	80	23	12	5	....	15	20	5	....	38	32	10	....	271	254	86	1st, Smythe		Lost Quarter-Final
1973-74	78	14	18	7	....	10	25	4	....	24	43	11	....	224	296	59	7th, East		Out of Playoffs
1972-73	78	17	18	4	....	5	29	5	....	22	47	9	....	233	339	53	7th, East		Out of Playoffs
1971-72	78	14	20	5	....	6	30	3	....	20	50	8	....	203	297	48	7th, East		Out of Playoffs
1970-71	78	17	18	4	....	7	28	4	....	24	46	8	....	229	296	56	6th, East		Out of Playoffs

2015-16 Player Personnel

FORWARDS	HT	WT	*Age	Place of Birth	S	2014-15 Club
BAERTSCHI, Sven	5-11	187	23	Langenthal, Switzerland	L	Cgy-Adi-Van-Utica
BURROWS, Alexandre	6-1	188	34	Pincourt, QC	L	Vancouver
DORSETT, Derek	6-0	192	28	Kindersley, SK	R	Vancouver
HANSEN, Jannik	6-1	195	29	Herlev, Denmark	R	Vancouver
HIGGINS, Chris	6-0	205	32	Smithtown, NY	L	Vancouver
HORVAT, Bo	6-0	206	20	Rodney, ON	L	Vancouver-Utica
KENINS, Ronalds	6-0	201	24	Riga, Latvia	L	Vancouver-Utica
PRUST, Brandon	6-0	194	31	London, ON	L	Montreal
SEDIN, Daniel	6-1	187	35	Ornskoldsvik, Sweden	L	Vancouver
SEDIN, Henrik	6-2	188	35	Ornskoldsvik, Sweden	L	Vancouver
SUTTER, Brandon	6-3	190	26	Huntington, NY	R	Pittsburgh
VEY, Linden	6-0	183	24	Wakaw, SK	R	Vancouver
VRBATA, Radim	6-1	194	34	Mlada Boleslav, Czech.	R	Vancouver
DEFENSEMEN						
BARTKOWSKI, Matt	6-1	196	27	Pittsburgh, PA	L	Boston
CORRADO, Frank	6-2	191	22	Woodbridge, ON	R	Vancouver-Utica
EDLER, Alexander	6-3	215	29	Ostersund, Sweden	L	Vancouver
HAMHUIS, Dan	6-1	209	32	Smithers, BC	L	Vancouver
SBISA, Luca	6-2	198	25	Ozieri, Italy	L	Vancouver
TANEV, Chris	6-2	185	25	Toronto, ON	R	Vancouver
WEBER, Yannick	5-11	200	27	Morges, Switz.	R	Vancouver

GOALTENDERS	HT	WT	*Age	Place of Birth	C	2014-15 Club
MARKSTROM, Jacob	6-6	196	25	Gavle, Sweden	L	Vancouver-Utica
MILLER, Ryan	6-2	168	35	East Lansing, MI	L	Vancouver

* – Age at start of 2015-16 season

Willie Desjardins

Head Coach

Born: Climax, SK, February 11, 1957.

Vancouver Canucks general manager Jim Benning announced on June 23, 2014 that Willie Desjardins had been named head coach of the Vancouver Canucks. With the appointment, Desjardins became the 18th head coach in club history. In his first season with the club in 2014-15, Desjardins led the Canucks back to the playoffs after missing the postseason in 2013-14.

Desjardins joined the Canucks from the Texas Stars, whom he had led to the 2014 Calder Cup championship six days before. In his first year with the Stars in 2012-13, he led Texas to its first South Division regular season title and the number-one seed in the Western Conference for the 2013 playoffs and was rewarded with the Louis A.R. Pieri Award as the American Hockey League's coach of the year.

Prior to his tenure in the AHL, Desjardins spent two seasons in the NHL as an associate coach with the Dallas Stars from 2010 to 2012. He also served as head coach (2002 to 2010) and general manager (2005 to 2010) of the Western Hockey League's Medicine Hat Tigers, where he led the team to two Memorial Cup tournaments and to the Memorial Cup final in 2007. Desjardins won the Dunc McCallum Memorial Trophy as WHL coach of the year for the 2005-06 season and was also the recipient of the Brian Kilrea coach of the year award as the top coach in the Canadian Hockey League in 2006. His first stint in the WHL was as head coach of the Saskatoon Blades in 1997-98. He previously spent six seasons (1988 to 1994) as head coach at the University of Calgary, leading the Dinos to two Canada West University Athletic Association championships, followed by two seasons coaching in Japan, where he won a championship in 1994-95.

On the international stage, Desjardins has represented Canada as head coach in 2010 (silver medal) and assistant coach in 2009 (gold) at the World Junior Championships. He was an assistant coach for the Canadian national men's team in 1998-99, when the team finished fourth at the 1999 World Championship in Norway.

Desjardins played major junior hockey for the Lethbridge Broncos of the Western Hockey League from 1974 through 1977. He won the 1982-83 Major W.J. "Danny" McLeod Award as the University Cup Tournament MVP, selected by the members of the CIS Men's Hockey Coaches Association.

Coaching Record

			Regular Season				Playoffs			
Season	Team	League	GC	W	L	O/T	GC	W	L	T
1988-89	U of Calgary	CWUAA	28	21	7	0	6	3	3	0
1989-90	U of Calgary	CWUAA	28	21	6	1	4	4	0	0
1989-90	U of Calgary	U-Cup	....	....	....	....	1	0	1	0
1990-91	U of Calgary	CWUAA	28	22	5	1	3	1	2	0
1991-92	U of Calgary	CWUAA	28	15	11	2	3	1	2	0
1992-93	U of Calgary	CWUAA	28	17	8	3	3	1	2	0
1993-94	U of Calgary	CWUAA	28	17	7	4	5	3	2	0
1994-95	Seibu Tokyo	JIHL	30	20	9	1	5	3	2	0
1995-96	Seibu Tokyo	JIHL	40	30	9	1	3	3	0	0
1996-97	Saskatoon	WHL	39	10	23	6	6	2	4	0
2002-03	Medicine Hat	WHL	72	29	34	9	11	7	4	0
2003-04	Medicine Hat	WHL	72	40	20	12	20	16	4	0
2003-04	Medicine Hat	M-Cup	....	....	....	....	4	1	3	0
2004-05	Medicine Hat	WHL	72	45	21	6	13	6	7	0
2005-06	Medicine Hat	WHL	72	47	16	9	13	9	4	0
2006-07	Medicine Hat	WHL	72	52	17	3	23	16	7	0
2006-07	Medicine Hat	M-Cup	....	....	....	....	4	2	2	0
2007-08	Medicine Hat	WHL	72	43	22	7	5	1	4	0
2008-09	Medicine Hat	WHL	72	36	29	7	11	4	7	0
2009-10	Medicine Hat	WHL	72	41	23	8	12	6	6	0
2012-13	Texas	AHL	76	43	22	11	9	4	5	0
2013-14	Texas	AHL	76	48	18	10	21	15	6	0
2014-15	**Vancouver**	**NHL**	**82**	**48**	**29**	**5**	**6**	**2**	**4**	....
	NHL Totals		**82**	**48**	**29**	**5**	**6**	**2**	**4**	....

2014-15 Scoring

* – rookie

Regular Season

Pos	#	Player	Team	GP	G	A	Pts	TOI	+/–	PIM	PP	SH	GW	S	S%
L	22	Daniel Sedin	VAN	82	20	56	76	18:21	5	18	4	0	5	226	8.8
C	33	Henrik Sedin	VAN	82	18	55	73	18:36	11	22	5	0	0	101	17.8
R	17	Radim Vrbata	VAN	79	31	32	63	16:36	6	20	12	0	7	267	11.6
C	13	Nick Bonino	VAN	75	15	24	39	16:55	7	22	1	0	6	149	10.1
L	20	Chris Higgins	VAN	77	12	24	36	15:47	8	16	3	0	1	171	7.0
L	14	Alexandre Burrows	VAN	70	18	15	33	15:28	0	68	4	1	3	145	12.4
R	36	Jannik Hansen	VAN	81	16	17	33	13:58	–6	27	0	1	2	145	11.0
D	23	Alexander Edler	VAN	74	8	23	31	23:58	13	54	5	0	2	175	4.6
C	27	Shawn Matthias	VAN	78	18	9	27	13:06	–3	16	1	0	0	132	13.6
C	53 *	Bo Horvat	VAN	68	13	12	25	12:15	–8	16	0	1	1	93	14.0
R	51	Derek Dorsett	VAN	79	7	18	25	12:02	4	175	0	2	3	89	7.9
R	7 *	Linden Vey	VAN	75	10	14	24	13:10	–3	18	4	0	2	61	16.4
D	2	Dan Hamhuis	VAN	59	1	22	23	21:31	0	44	1	0	0	82	1.2
D	6	Yannick Weber	VAN	65	11	10	21	17:11	4	30	5	0	1	117	9.4
R	15	Brad Richardson	VAN	45	8	13	21	14:28	0	34	0	1	1	66	12.1
D	8	Christopher Tanev	VAN	70	2	18	20	21:04	8	12	0	0	1	53	3.8
R	9	Zack Kassian	VAN	42	10	6	16	12:37	–5	81	1	0	3	55	18.2
D	3	Kevin Bieksa	VAN	60	4	10	14	20:49	0	77	0	0	1	99	4.0
L	41 *	Ronalds Kenins	VAN	30	4	8	12	12:16	–2	8	0	0	0	38	10.5
D	18	Ryan Stanton	VAN	54	3	8	11	16:00	9	35	0	0	0	59	5.1
D	5	Luca Sbisa	VAN	76	3	8	11	18:46	–8	46	0	0	2	79	3.8
L	47	Sven Baertschi	CGY	15	0	4	4	9:12	–3	6	0	0	0	11	0.0
			VAN	3	2	0	2	12:02	0	4	0	0	0	4	50.0
			Total	18	2	4	6	9:40	–3	10	0	0	0	15	13.3
D	44 *	Adam Clendening	CHI	4	1	1	2	13:10	1	2	1	0	0	2	50.0
			VAN	17	0	2	2	17:27	1	8	0	0	0	15	0.0
			Total	21	1	3	4	16:38	2	10	1	0	0	17	5.9
C	21	Brandon McMillan	ARI	50	1	2	3	10:22	–18	16	0	0	0	44	2.3
			VAN	8	0	1	1	11:01	–1	0	0	0	0	7	0.0
			Total	58	1	3	4	10:28	–19	16	0	0	0	51	2.0
D	55	Alex Biega	VAN	7	1	0	1	15:47	–2	0	0	0	1	7	14.3
D	26 *	Frank Corrado	VAN	10	1	0	1	15:40	–7	0	0	0	0	8	12.5
L	29	Tom Sestito	VAN	3	0	1	1	6:14	1	7	0	0	0	1	0.0
L	39	Brandon Defazio	VAN	2	0	0	0	5:56	0	0	0	0	0	2	0.0
L	46 *	Nicklas Jensen	VAN	5	0	0	0	9:33	–1	0	0	0	0	7	0.0

Goaltending

No.	Goaltender	GPI	Mins	Avg	W	L	OT	EN	SO	GA	SA	Sv%	G	A	PIM
31	Eddie Lack	41	2324	2.45	18	13	4	8	2	95	1201	.921	0	0	2
30	Ryan Miller	45	2542	2.53	29	15	1	5	6	107	1198	.911	0	0	0
35	Jacob Markstrom	3	78	3.08	1	1	0	1	0	4	33	.879	0	0	0
	Totals	**82**	**4980**	**2.65**	**48**	**29**	**5**	**14**	**9**	**220**	**2446**	**.910**			

Ryan Miller and Eddie Lack shared a shutout vs NYI on Feb 22, 2015

Playoffs

Pos	#	Player	Team	GP	G	A	Pts	TOI	+/–	PIM	PP	SH	GW	OT	S	S%
L	22	Daniel Sedin	VAN	6	2	2	4	18:21	–1	0	0	0	1	0	22	9.1
R	17	Radim Vrbata	VAN	6	2	2	4	16:09	–2	0	1	0	0	0	21	9.5
R	36	Jannik Hansen	VAN	6	2	2	4	16:27	1	0	0	0	0	0	8	25.0
C	33	Henrik Sedin	VAN	6	1	3	4	18:49	–1	2	1	0	0	0	15	6.7
C	53 *	Bo Horvat	VAN	6	1	3	4	12:40	1	2	0	0	0	0	10	10.0
C	13	Nick Bonino	VAN	6	1	2	3	16:35	–2	4	0	0	0	0	13	7.7
D	23	Alexander Edler	VAN	6	0	3	3	23:40	3	4	0	0	0	0	6	0.0
D	8	Christopher Tanev	VAN	6	0	3	3	22:00	4	0	0	0	0	0	4	0.0
L	41 *	Ronalds Kenins	VAN	5	1	1	2	10:52	2	4	0	0	0	0	5	20.0
L	20	Chris Higgins	VAN	6	1	1	2	16:35	0	2	1	0	1	0	15	6.7
C	27	Shawn Matthias	VAN	6	1	1	2	12:12	–3	10	0	0	0	0	4	25.0
D	5	Luca Sbisa	VAN	6	1	1	2	17:26	–2	7	0	0	0	0	6	16.7
L	14	Alexandre Burrows	VAN	3	0	2	2	14:22	1	21	0	0	0	0	11	0.0
C	21	Brandon McMillan	VAN	2	1	0	1	8:51	1	4	0	0	0	0	3	33.3
D	2	Dan Hamhuis	VAN	6	0	1	1	19:39	–2	16	0	0	0	0	5	0.0
R	7 *	Linden Vey	VAN	1	0	0	0	9:59	0	0	0	0	0	0	2	0.0
L	47	Sven Baertschi	VAN	2	0	0	0	9:39	0	0	0	0	0	0	0	0.0
R	15	Brad Richardson	VAN	5	0	0	0	12:36	–3	15	0	0	0	0	8	0.0
D	3	Kevin Bieksa	VAN	6	0	0	0	18:19	–1	9	0	0	0	0	5	0.0
R	51	Derek Dorsett	VAN	6	0	0	0	12:36	–3	20	0	0	0	0	5	0.0
D	6	Yannick Weber	VAN	6	0	0	0	19:10	–5	12	0	0	0	0	13	0.0

Goaltending

No.	Goaltender	GPI	Mins	Avg	W	L	EN	SO	GA	SA	Sv%	G	A	PIM
30	Ryan Miller	3	156	2.31	1	1	2	0	6	67	.910	0	0	0
31	Eddie Lack	4	198	3.03	1	3	0	0	10	88	.886	0	0	0
	Totals	**6**	**360**	**3.00**	**2**	**4**	**2**	**0**	**18**	**157**	**.885**			

Captains' History

Orland Kurtenbach, 1970-71 to 1973-74; no captain, 1974-75; Andre Boudrias, 1975-76; Chris Oddleifson, 1976-77; Don Lever, 1977-78; Don Lever and Kevin McCarthy, 1978-79; Kevin McCarthy, 1979-80 to 1981-82; Stan Smyl, 1982-83 to 1989-90; Dan Quinn, Doug Lidster and Trevor Linden, 1990-91; Trevor Linden, 1991-92 to 1996-97; Mark Messier, 1997-98 to 1999-2000; Markus Naslund, 2000-01 to 2007-08; Roberto Luongo, 2008-09, 2009-10; Henrik Sedin, 2010-11 to date.

Coaching History

Hal Laycoe, 1970-71, 1971-72; Vic Stasiuk, 1972-73; Bill McCreary and Phil Maloney, 1973-74; Phil Maloney, 1974-75, 1975-76; Phil Maloney and Orland Kurtenbach, 1976-77; Orland Kurtenbach, 1977-78; Harry Neale, 1978-79 to 1980-81; Harry Neale and Roger Neilson, 1981-82; Roger Neilson, 1982-83; Roger Neilson and Harry Neale, 1983-84; Bill Laforge and Harry Neale, 1984-85; Tom Watt, 1985-86, 1986-87; Bob McCammon, 1987-88 to 1989-90; Bob McCammon and Pat Quinn, 1990-91; Pat Quinn, 1991-92 to 1993-94; Rick Ley, 1994-95; Rick Ley and Pat Quinn, 1995-96; Tom Renney, 1996-97; Tom Renney and Mike Keenan, 1997-98; Mike Keenan and Marc Crawford, 1998-99; Marc Crawford, 1999-2000 to 2005-06; Alain Vigneault, 2006-07 to 2012-13; John Tortorella, 2013-14; Willie Desjardins, 2014-15 to date.

Club Records

Team

(Figures in brackets for season records are games played; records for fewest points, wins, ties, losses, goals, goals against are for 70 or more games)

Most Points	**117**	2010-11 (82)
Most Wins	**54**	2010-11 (82)
Most Ties	**20**	1980-81 (80)
Most Losses	**50**	1971-72 (78)
Most Goals	**346**	1992-93 (84)
Most Goals Against	**401**	1984-85 (80)
Fewest Points	**48**	1971-72 (78)
Fewest Wins	**20**	1971-72 (78), 1977-78 (80)
Fewest Ties	**3**	1993-94 (84)
Fewest Losses	**19**	2010-11 (82)
Fewest Goals	**192**	1998-99 (82)
Fewest Goals Against	**185**	2010-11 (82)
Longest Winning Streak		
Overall	**10**	Nov. 9-30/02
Home	**11**	Feb. 3-Mar. 19/09
Away	**9**	Mar. 5-29/11
Longest Undefeated Streak		
Overall	**14**	Jan.26-Feb. 25/03 (10W, 4T/OL)
Home	**18**	Nov. 4/92-Jan. 16/93 (16W, 2T)
Away	**9**	Feb. 4-Mar. 3/03 (6W, 3T/OL), Mar. 5-29/11 (9W)
Longest Losing Streak		
Overall	**10**	Oct. 23-Nov. 11/97
Home	**6**	Dec. 18/70-Jan. 20/71
Away	**12**	Nov. 28/81-Feb. 6/82
Longest Winless Streak		
Overall	**13**	Nov. 9-Dec. 7/73 (10L, 3T)
Home	**11**	Dec. 18/70-Feb. 6/71 (10L, 1T)
Away	**20**	Jan. 2-Apr. 2/86 (14L, 6T)
Most Shutouts, Season	**10**	2008-09 (82)
Most PIM, Season	**2,326**	1992-93 (84)
Most Goals, Game	**11**	Mar. 28/71 (Cal. 5 at Van. 11), Nov. 25/86 (L.A. 5 at Van. 11), Mar. 1/92 (Cgy. 0 at Van. 11)

Individual

Most Seasons	**16**	Trevor Linden
Most Games	**1,140**	Trevor Linden
Most Goals, Career	**346**	Markus Naslund
Most Assists, Career	**704**	Henrik Sedin
Most Points, Career	**915**	Henrik Sedin (211G, 704A)
Most PIM, Career	**2,127**	Gino Odjick
Most Shutouts, Career	**38**	Roberto Luongo
Longest Consecutive Games Streak	**679**	Henrik Sedin (Mar. 21/04-Jan. 18/13)
Most Goals, Season	**60**	Pavel Bure (1992-93), (1993-94)
Most Assists, Season	**83**	Henrik Sedin (2009-10)
Most Points, Season	**112**	Henrik Sedin (2009-10; 29G, 83A)
Most PIM, Season	**372**	Donald Brashear (1997-98)
Most Points, Defenseman, Season	**63**	Doug Lidster (1986-87; 12G, 51A)
Most Points, Center, Season	**112**	Henrik Sedin (2009-10; 29G, 83A)
Most Points, Right Wing, Season	**110**	Pavel Bure (1992-93; 60G, 50A)
Most Points, Left Wing, Season	**104**	Markus Naslund (2002-03; 48G, 56A), Daniel Sedin (2010-11; 41G, 63A)
Most Points, Rookie, Season	**60**	Ivan Hlinka (1981-82; 23G, 37A) Pavel Bure (1991-92; 34G, 26A)
Most Shutouts, Season	**9**	Roberto Luongo (2008-09)
Most Goals, Game	**4**	Twelve times
Most Assists, Game	**6**	Patrik Sundstrom (Feb. 29/84)
Most Points, Game	**7**	Patrik Sundstrom (Feb. 29/84; 1G, 6A)

All-time Record vs. Other Clubs

Regular Season

	Total								At Home								On Road							
	GP	W	L	T	OL	GF	GA	PTS	GP	W	L	T	OL	GF	GA	PTS	GP	W	L	T	OL	GF	GA	PTS
Anaheim	92	43	35	9	5	273	260	100	47	23	20	2	2	141	131	50	45	20	15	7	3	132	129	50
Arizona	182	92	63	20	7	631	548	211	93	57	25	10	1	336	248	125	89	35	38	10	6	295	300	86
Boston	113	29	67	15	2	317	447	75	56	19	28	8	1	183	219	47	57	10	39	7	1	134	228	28
Buffalo	114	48	45	19	2	378	379	117	57	29	17	11	0	212	174	69	57	19	28	8	2	166	205	48
Calgary	259	101	120	33	5	823	872	240	131	58	51	18	4	447	402	138	128	43	69	15	1	376	470	102
Carolina	69	33	25	11	0	237	197	77	35	19	10	6	0	124	89	44	34	14	15	5	0	113	108	33
Chicago	180	75	78	22	5	486	565	177	91	47	29	15	0	268	254	109	89	28	49	7	5	218	311	68
Colorado	152	66	61	15	10	460	497	157	76	35	29	7	5	243	254	82	76	31	32	8	5	217	243	75
Columbus	51	32	11	2	6	177	127	72	25	18	4	0	3	93	66	39	26	14	7	2	3	84	61	33
Dallas	179	70	81	22	6	562	576	168	89	41	35	10	3	308	263	95	90	29	46	12	3	254	313	73
Detroit	166	61	81	18	6	525	591	146	83	37	33	10	3	289	261	87	83	24	48	8	3	236	330	59
Edmonton	226	95	103	19	9	749	838	218	113	53	44	12	4	405	396	122	113	42	59	7	5	344	442	96
Florida	27	13	6	6	2	79	63	34	14	6	2	5	1	39	32	18	13	7	4	1	1	40	31	16
Los Angeles	237	102	96	32	7	772	794	243	117	61	35	16	5	418	345	143	120	41	61	16	2	354	449	100
Minnesota	79	40	26	5	8	209	204	93	39	23	7	3	6	111	87	55	40	17	19	2	2	98	117	38
Montreal	122	30	79	13	0	318	483	73	62	18	36	8	0	170	220	44	60	12	43	5	0	148	263	29
Nashville	62	37	22	2	1	188	157	77	30	18	10	1	1	100	71	38	32	19	12	1	0	88	86	39
New Jersey	106	57	32	17	0	362	300	131	52	31	10	11	0	191	137	73	54	26	22	6	0	171	163	58
NY Islanders	104	41	48	13	2	322	354	97	52	26	23	3	0	171	170	55	52	15	25	10	2	151	184	42
NY Rangers	115	31	76	8	0	327	469	70	56	17	36	3	0	172	217	37	59	14	40	5	0	155	252	33
Ottawa	35	20	12	2	1	106	78	43	18	11	6	1	0	56	39	23	17	9	6	1	1	50	39	20
Philadelphia	115	32	67	13	3	339	466	80	56	12	30	12	2	161	221	38	59	20	37	1	1	178	245	42
Pittsburgh	110	38	57	11	4	384	437	91	55	25	23	4	3	199	200	57	55	13	34	7	1	185	237	34
St. Louis	180	72	88	18	2	514	593	164	91	42	39	9	1	264	277	94	89	30	49	9	1	250	316	70
San Jose	106	51	40	9	6	320	305	117	51	24	18	4	5	162	145	57	55	27	22	5	1	158	160	60
Tampa Bay	28	16	9	2	1	105	82	35	14	9	2	2	1	55	32	21	14	7	7	0	0	50	50	14
Toronto	138	62	52	22	2	476	465	148	71	36	22	11	2	254	226	85	67	26	30	11	0	222	239	63
Washington	89	40	38	9	2	291	283	91	44	23	15	5	1	156	135	52	45	17	23	4	1	135	148	39
Winnipeg	18	12	4	1	1	60	44	26	9	7	1	1	0	30	16	15	9	5	3	0	1	30	28	11
Defunct Clubs	38	24	11	3	0	153	116	51	19	14	3	2	0	82	48	30	19	10	8	1	0	71	68	21
Totals	**3492**	**1463**	**1533**	**391**	**105**	**10943**	**11590**	**3422**	**1746**	**839**	**643**	**210**	**54**	**5840**	**5375**	**1942**	**1746**	**624**	**890**	**181**	**51**	**5103**	**6215**	**1480**

Playoffs

	Series	W	L	GP	W	L	T	GF	GA	Last Mtg.	Rnd.	Result
Anaheim	1	0	1	5	1	4	0	8	14	2007	CSF	L 1-4
Arizona	2	2	0	13	8	5	0	50	34	1993	DSF	W 4-2
Boston	1	0	1	7	3	4	0	8	23	2011	F	L 3-4
Buffalo	2	0	2	7	1	6	0	14	28	1981	PR	L 0-3
Calgary	7	2	5	38	17	21	0	110	119	2015	FR	L 2-4
Chicago	5	2	3	28	12	16	0	77	92	2011	CQF	W 4-3
Colorado	2	0	2	10	2	8	0	26	40	2001	CQF	L 0-4
Dallas	2	2	0	12	8	4	0	31	23	2007	CQF	W 4-3
Detroit	1	0	1	6	2	4	0	16	22	2002	CQF	L 2-4
Edmonton	2	0	2	9	2	7	0	20	35	1992	DF	L 2-4
Los Angeles	5	2	3	28	13	15	0	93	96	2012	CQF	L 1-4
Minnesota	1	0	1	7	3	4	0	17	26	2003	CSF	L 3-4
Montreal	1	0	1	5	1	4	0	9	20	1975	QF	L 1-4
Nashville	1	1	0	6	4	2	0	14	11	2011	CSF	W 4-2
NY Islanders	2	0	2	6	0	6	0	14	26	1982	F	L 0-4
NY Rangers	1	0	1	7	3	4	0	19	21	1994	F	L 3-4
Philadelphia	1	0	1	3	1	2	0	9	15	1979	PR	L 1-2
St. Louis	3	3	0	18	12	6	0	55	53	2009	CQF	W 4-0
San Jose	2	1	1	9	4	5	0	28	28	2013	CQF	L 0-4
Toronto	1	1	0	5	4	1	0	16	9	1994	CF	W 4-1
Totals	**43**	**16**	**27**	**229**	**101**	**128**	**0**	**634**	**735**			

Calgary totals include Atlanta Flames, 1972-73 to 1979-80.
Carolina totals include Hartford, 1979-80 to 1996-97.
Colorado totals include Quebec, 1979-80 to 1994-95.
Dallas totals include Minnesota North Stars, 1970-71 to 1992-93.
New Jersey totals include Kansas City, 1974-75, 1975-76, and Colorado Rockies, 1976-77 to 1981-82.
Phoenix totals include Winnipeg, 1979-80 to 1995-96.
Winnipeg totals include Atlanta Thrashers, 1999-2000 to 2010-11.

Playoff Results 2015-2011

Year	Round	Opponent	Result	GF	GA
2015	FR	Calgary	L 2-4	14	18
2013	CQF	San Jose	L 0-4	8	15
2012	CQF	Los Angeles	L 1-4	8	12
2011	F	Boston	L 3-4	8	23
	CF	San Jose	W 4-1	20	13
	CSF	Nashville	W 4-2	14	11
	CQF	Chicago	W 4-3	16	22

Abbreviations: Round: F – Final; **CF** – conference final; **CSF** – conference semi-final; **SR** – second round; **CQF** – conference quarter-final; **FR** – first round; **DF** – division final; **DSF** – division semi-final; **QF** – quarter-final; **PR** – preliminary round.

2014-15 Results

Oct.	8	at Calgary	4-2		15	at Philadelphia	4-0
	11	Edmonton	5-4†		16	at Carolina	3-0
	17	at Edmonton	2-0		19	at Florida	2-1
	18	Tampa Bay	2-4		20	at Tampa Bay	1-4
	21	at Dallas	3-6		27	Anaheim	0-4
	23	at St. Louis	4-1		30	Buffalo	5-2
	24	at Colorado	3-7	**Feb.**	1	Minnesota	2-4
	26	Washington	4-2		3	Winnipeg	3-2*
	28	Carolina	4-1		5	San Jose	1-5
	30	Montreal	3-2*		7	Pittsburgh	5-0
Nov.	1	at Edmonton	3-2		9	at Minnesota	3-5
	2	Nashville	1-3		11	at Chicago	5-4*
	4	at Colorado	5-2		13	Boston	5-2
	6	at San Jose	3-2		14	at Calgary	2-3
	8	at Los Angeles	1-5		16	Minnesota	3-2
	9	at Anaheim	2-1†		19	at NY Rangers	5-4†
	11	Ottawa	4-3*		20	at New Jersey	2-4
	14	Arizona	0-5		22	at NY Islanders	4-0
	19	at Edmonton	5-4		24	at Boston	2-1
	20	Anaheim	3-4†		26	at Buffalo	3-6
	23	Chicago	4-1	**Mar.**	1	St. Louis	6-5†
	25	New Jersey	2-0		3	San Jose	2-6
	28	at Columbus	5-0		5	at Arizona	2-3†
	30	at Detroit	3-5		7	at San Jose	3-2
Dec.	2	at Washington	4-3		9	Anaheim	2-1
	4	at Pittsburgh	3-0		12	Los Angeles	0-4
	6	at Toronto	2-5		14	Toronto	4-1
	7	at Ottawa	3-4*		17	Philadelphia	4-1
	9	at Montreal	1-3		19	Columbus	2-6
	13	NY Rangers	1-5		21	at Los Angeles	4-1
	17	Dallas	0-2		22	at Arizona	3-1
	20	Calgary	3-2*		24	Winnipeg	5-2
	22	Arizona	7-1		26	Colorado	1-4
	28	at Anaheim	1-2*		28	Dallas	3-4*
	30	at San Jose	3-1		30	at St. Louis	4-1
Jan.	1	Los Angeles	2-3		31	at Nashville	5-4†
	3	Detroit	4-1	**Apr.**	2	at Chicago	1-3
	6	NY Islanders	3-2		4	at Winnipeg	4-5
	8	Florida	1-3		6	Los Angeles	2-1†
	10	Calgary	0-1		9	Arizona	5-0
	13	at Nashville	1-5		11	Edmonton	6-5*

* – Overtime † – Shootout

NHL Draft Selections 2015-2001

Name in bold denotes played in NHL.

2015
Pick
- 23 **Brock Boeser**
- 66 Guillaume Brisebois
- 114 Dmitri Zhukenov
- 144 Carl Neill
- 149 Adam Gaudette
- 174 Lukas Jasek
- 210 Tate Olson

2014
Pick
- 6 **Jake Virtanen**
- 24 Jared McCann
- 36 Thatcher Demko
- 66 Nikita Tryamkin
- 126 Gustav Forsling
- 156 Kyle Pettit
- 186 Mackenze Stewart

2013
Pick
- 9 **Bo Horvat**
- 24 Hunter Shinkaruk
- 85 Cole Cassels
- 115 Jordan Subban
- 145 Anton Cederholm
- 175 Mike Williamson
- 205 Miles Liberati

2012
Pick
- 26 Brendan Gaunce
- 57 Alexandre Mallet
- 147 Ben Hutton
- 177 Wesley Myron
- 207 Matthew Beattie

2011
Pick
- 29 **Nicklas Jensen**
- 71 David Honzik
- 90 Alexandre Grenier
- 101 Joseph Labate
- 120 Ludwig Blomstrand
- 150 **Frank Corrado**
- 180 Pathrik Westerholm
- 210 Henrik Tommernes

2010
Pick
- 115 Patrick McNally
- 145 Adam Polasek
- 172 Alex Friesen
- 175 Jonathan Iilahti
- 205 Sawyer Hannay

2009
Pick
- 22 Jordan Schroeder
- 53 Anton Rodin
- 83 **Kevin Connauton**
- 113 Jeremy Price
- 143 Peter Andersson
- 173 Joe Cannata
- 187 Steven Anthony

2008
Pick
- 10 **Cody Hodgson**
- 41 Yann Sauve
- 131 Prab Rai
- 161 Mats Froshaug
- 191 Morgan Clark

2007
Pick
- 25 Patrick White
- 33 Taylor Ellington
- 145 Charles-Antoine Messier
- 146 Ilja Kablukov
- 176 Taylor Matson
- 206 Dan Gendur

2006
Pick
- 14 **Michael Grabner**
- 82 Daniel Rahimi
- 163 **Sergei Shirokov**
- 167 Juraj Simek
- 197 Evan Fuller

2005
Pick
- 10 **Luc Bourdon**
- 51 **Mason Raymond**
- 114 Alexandre Vincent
- 138 Matt Butcher
- 185 **Kris Fredheim**
- 205 **Mario Bliznak**

2004
Pick
- 26 **Cory Schneider**
- 91 **Alexander Edler**
- 125 Andrew Sarauer
- 159 **Mike Brown**
- 189 Julien Ellis
- 254 David Schulz
- 287 **Jannik Hansen**

2003
Pick
- 23 **Ryan Kesler**
- 60 Marc-Andre Bernier
- 111 **Brandon Nolan**
- 128 Ty Morris
- 160 Nicklas Danielsson
- 190 Chad Brownlee
- 222 Francois-Pierre Guenette
- 252 Sergei Topol
- 254 **Nathan McIver**
- 285 Matthew Hansen

2002
Pick
- 49 Kirill Koltsov
- 55 Denis Grot
- 68 **Brett Skinner**
- 83 Lukas Mensator
- 114 John Laliberte
- 151 **Rob McVicar**
- 214 Marc-Andre Roy
- 223 Ilja Krikunov
- 247 Matt Violin
- 277 Thomas Nussli
- 278 Matt Gens

2001
Pick
- 16 **RJ Umberger**
- 66 **Fedor Fedorov**
- 114 Evgeny Gladskikh
- 151 **Kevin Bieksa**
- 212 **Jason King**
- 245 Konstantin Mikhailov

General Managers' History

Bud Poile, 1970-71, 1971-72; Bud Poile and Hal Laycoe, 1972-73; Hal Laycoe and Phil Maloney, 1973-74; Phil Maloney, 1974-75 to 1976-77; Jake Milford, 1977-78 to 1981-82; Harry Neale, 1982-83 to 1984-85; Jack Gordon, 1985-86, 1986-87; Pat Quinn, 1987-88 to 1996-97; Pat Quinn and Mike Keenan, 1997-98; Brian Burke, 1998-99 to 2003-04; David Nonis, 2004-05 to 2007-08; Mike Gillis, 2008-09 to 2013-14; Jim Benning, 2014-15 to date.

Jim Benning
General Manager
Born: Edmonton, AB, April 29, 1963.

Vancouver Canucks president of hockey operations Trevor Linden confirmed at a Canucks' Town Hall Meeting on May 21, 2014 that Jim Benning had been named general manager of the team. Benning was officially introduced on May 23, 2014. In his first season in the role in 2014-15 the Canucks returned to the playoffs after having missed the postseason the previous year.

Benning is the 11th general manager in club history. He joined Vancouver after serving in the capacity of the Boston Bruins assistant general manager for seven years. In that role he acted as an advisor to general manager Peter Chiarelli on all matters pertaining to player evaluation, trades and free agent signings, in addition to assisting the general manager in overseeing all individuals in their specific duties for the Bruins. Benning initially joined the Bruins as director of player personnel in 2006.

The Edmonton, Alberta native also previously held a 12-year tenure with the Buffalo Sabres. For eight of those seasons, Benning served as the team's director of amateur scouting. In that position, he oversaw the club's scouting staff and led the team at the annual NHL Draft, in addition to scouting prospects at the high school, college and junior hockey levels as well as in Europe.

A former defenceman, Benning was drafted by the Toronto Maple Leafs with their first pick, sixth overall, in the 1981 NHL Draft and played nine seasons in the National Hockey League with the Maple Leafs and Vancouver Canucks. Benning accumulated 243 points (52 goals, 191 assists) and 461 penalty minutes in 605 career games. He played one season in Europe before retiring as a player in 1992 and attended college for one year before joining the Anaheim organization as an amateur scout.

Club Directory

Rogers Arena

Vancouver Canucks
Rogers Arena
800 Griffiths Way
Vancouver, B.C. V6B 6G1
Phone **604/899-4600**
FAX 604/899-4640
www.canucks.com
Capacity: 18,870

Executive Directory – Vancouver Canucks Limited Partnership
Chairman, Canucks L.P. and Governor, NHL . . . . . . Francesco Aquilini
Alternate Governors, NHL . . . . Roberto Aquilini, Paolo Aquilini
President, Hockey Operations and Alt. Governor, NHL . Trevor Linden
Chief Operating Officer and Alt. Governor, NHL . . . Victor de Bonis
General Manager and Alt. Governor, NHL. . . . . Jim Benning
Assistant General Manager . . . . John Weisbrod
Executive Vice President, Sales and Service . . . . . . Trent Carroll
Executive Vice President and Arena General Manager . Michael Doyle
Vice President, Hockey Administration,
    Entertainment and Content. . . . . TC Carling
Vice President and General Counsel, Vancouver Canucks and Canucks Sports & Entertainment
    . . . . Chris Gear
Vice President and CFO. Todd Kobus
Vice President, Communications
    and Community Partnerships. . . . . Chris Brumwell
Vice President, Construction . . . . Harvey Jones
Vice President, Hospitality and Event Operations . . . Jeff Stipec
Vice President, Ticket and Suite Sales and Service . . Michael Cosentino
Executive Office Manager . . . . Cheryl Loveseth

Hockey Operations
President and Alt. Governor, NHL . . . . Trevor Linden
General Manager and Alt. Governor, NHL. . . . . Jim Benning
Assistant General Manager. . . . . John Weisbrod
Sr. Advisor to GM & Director, Player Development . . Stan Smyl
Vice President, Hockey Administration,
    Entertainment and Content. . . . . TC Carling
Vice President and General Counsel, Vancouver Canucks and Canucks Sports & Entertainment
    . . . . Chris Gear
Assistant Director Player Development . . . . Jonathan Wall
Assistant Director Player Development. . . . . Ryan Johnson
Consultants, Goaltending / Power Skating . . . . Dan Cloutier / Ryan Lounsbury
Manager, Team Services . . . . Mike Brown
Executive Assistant . . . . Andrea Lobo / Joan Stobbs

Coaching Staff
Head Coach . . . . Willie Desjardins
Assistant Coaches. . . . . Glen Gulutzan, Doug Lidster, Perry Pearn
Goaltending Coach / Video Coach . . . . Roland Melanson / Ben Cooper
Skill Coach . . . . Glenn Carnegie
Strength & Conditioning Coach / Asst. Coach . . . . . Roger Takahashi / Eric Renaghan

Utica Comets (AHL Affiliate)
Head Coach, Utica Comets. . . . . Travis Green
Assistant Coaches, Utica Comets . . . . Nolan Baumgartner, Paul Jerrard

Communications and Community Partnership
Vice President, Communications
    and Community Partnerships. . . . . Chris Brumwell
Director, Media Relations and Team Operations . . . Ben Brown
Manager, Media Relations and Publications . . . . . . Stephanie Maniago
Coordinator, Media Relations and Publications . . . . Alfred De Vera
Director, Community Partnerships. . . . . Alex Oxenham
Program Managers, Community Partnerships . . . . . Jessica Hoffman, Tara Clarke
Program Manager, Canucks for Kids Fund . . . . Diana Campbell
Manager, Hockey Development and Alumni Liaison . . Rod Brathwaite
Coordinator, Community Partnerships and
    Mascot Liaison . . . . Paul Buckley

Scouting Staff
Director, Amateur Scouting. . . . . Judd Brackett
Chief Amateur Scout . . . . Ron Delorme
Associate Chief Scout . . . . Thomas Gradin
Amateur Scouts . . . . Lucien DeBlois Brian Chapman, Sergei Chibisov, Ted Hampson,
    Inge Hammarstrom, Wyatt Smith, Dan Palango,
    Chris MacDonald, Tim Lenardon, Harold Snepsts, Ken Cook,
    Brandon Benning, Jonathan Bates, Mike Addesa
Professional Scouts . . . . Neil Komadoski, Lars Lindgren, Brett Henning,
    Lou Crawford

Medical and Training Staff
Director, Rehabilitation . . . . Dr. Rick Celebrini
Team Physician & Director, Medical Services . . . . . . Dr. Mike Wilkinson
Head Athletic Therapist. Jon Sanderson
Assistant Athletic Therapist . . . . Dave Zarn
Equipment Manager . . . . Pat O'Neill
Assistant Equipment Manager. . . . . Brian Hamilton
Trainer's Assistant. . . . . Mackenzie Stewart
Game Dressing Room Attendants . . . . John Jukich, Ron Shute, Ferdie De Guzman,
    Trevor Penrose
Team Physician . . . . Dr. Bill Regan
Team Dentist . . . . Dr. Keith Lim
Team Chiropractor . . . . Dr. Glenn Cashman
Team Optometrist. . . . . Dr. Alan R. Boyco

Broadcast
Director, Game Entertainment & Content . . . . Ryan Nicholas
Director, Game Presentation . . . . Mike Hall
Senior Producer, Game & Events. . . . . Art Green
Manager, Game Entertainment & Events . . . . Cam Goudreau
Manager, Content . . . . Briana Griffith
Writer. . . . . Derek Jory
Senior Producer . . . . Jason Steensma
Senior Editor . . . . Gayla Anderson
Coordinator, Game Entertainment & Events . . . . . . Rebecca Grant
Senior Broadcast Technician . . . . Greg Story
Canucks TV Reporter . . . . Joey Kenward
Editor . . . . Lawren Cody
Segment Producers. . . . . Jessica McNeill / Shawn Edstrom
Content Producer . . . . Paul Albi

Washington Capitals

2014-15 Results: 45w-26L-7OTL-4SOL 101PTS
2ND, Metropolitan Division • 4TH, Eastern Conference

It was another big offensive season for Nicklas Backstrom and Alex Ovechkin in Washington in 2014-15. Ovechkin led the NHL with 53 goals and Backstrom topped the circuit with 60 assists.

2015-16 Schedule

Oct.	Sat.	10	New Jersey
	Tue.	13	San Jose
	Thu.	15	Chicago
	Sat.	17	Carolina
	Tue.	20	at Calgary
	Thu.	22	at Vancouver
	Fri.	23	at Edmonton
	Wed.	28	Pittsburgh
	Fri.	30	Columbus
	Sat.	31	at Florida
Nov.	Tue.	3	at NY Rangers
	Thu.	5	Boston
	Sat.	7	Toronto
	Tue.	10	at Detroit
	Thu.	12	at Philadelphia
	Fri.	13	Calgary
	Wed.	18	at Detroit
	Thu.	19	Dallas
	Sat.	21	Colorado
	Mon.	23	Edmonton
	Wed.	25	Winnipeg
	Fri.	27	Tampa Bay*
	Sat.	28	at Toronto
Dec.	Thu.	3	at Montreal
	Sat.	5	at Winnipeg*
	Tue.	8	Detroit
	Thu.	10	at Florida
	Sat.	12	at Tampa Bay
	Mon.	14	at Pittsburgh
	Wed.	16	Ottawa
	Fri.	18	Tampa Bay
	Sun.	20	at NY Rangers
	Mon.	21	at Carolina
	Sat.	26	Montreal
	Mon.	28	at Buffalo
	Wed.	30	Buffalo
	Thu.	31	at Carolina
Jan.	Sat.	2	at Columbus
	Tue.	5	at Boston
	Thu.	7	at NY Islanders
	Sat.	9	at NY Rangers*
	Sun.	10	Ottawa
	Thu.	14	Vancouver
	Sat.	16	at Buffalo
	Sun.	17	NY Rangers*
	Tue.	19	at Columbus
	Fri.	22	Anaheim
	Sun.	24	Pittsburgh*
	Wed.	27	Philadelphia
Feb.	Tue.	2	Florida
	Thu.	4	NY Islanders
	Sat.	6	at New Jersey
	Sun.	7	Philadelphia*
	Tue.	9	at Nashville
	Thu.	11	at Minnesota
	Sat.	13	at Dallas
	Tue.	16	Los Angeles
	Thu.	18	at NY Islanders
	Sat.	20	New Jersey
	Mon.	22	Arizona
	Wed.	24	Montreal
	Fri.	26	Minnesota
	Sun.	28	at Chicago*
Mar.	Wed.	2	Toronto
	Fri.	4	NY Rangers
	Sat.	5	at Boston
	Mon.	7	at Anaheim
	Wed.	9	at Los Angeles
	Sat.	12	at San Jose
	Tue.	15	Carolina
	Fri.	18	Nashville
	Sun.	20	at Pittsburgh
	Tue.	22	at Ottawa
	Fri.	25	at New Jersey
	Sat.	26	St. Louis
	Mon.	28	Columbus
	Wed.	30	at Philadelphia
Apr.	Fri.	1	at Colorado
	Sat.	2	at Arizona
	Tue.	5	NY Islanders
	Thu.	7	Pittsburgh
	Sat.	9	at St. Louis

* Denotes afternoon game.

Retired Numbers

5	Rod Langway	1982-1993
7	Yvon Labre	1974-1981
11	Mike Gartner	1979-1989
32	Dale Hunter	1987-1999

METROPOLITAN DIVISION
42nd NHL Season

Franchise date: June 11, 1974

Year-by-Year Record

Season	GP	Home W	L	T	OL	Road W	L	T	OL	Overall W	L	T	OL	GF	GA	Pts.	Div. Fin.	Conf. Fin.	Playoff Result
2014-15	82	23	13	....	5	22	13	....	6	45	26	....	11	242	203	101	2nd, Met.	4th, East	Lost Second Round
2013-14	82	21	13	....	7	17	17	....	7	38	30	....	14	235	240	90	5th, Met.	9th, East	Out of Playoffs
2012-13	48	15	8	....	1	12	10	....	2	27	18	....	3	149	130	57	1st, SE	3rd, East	Lost Conf. Quarter-Final
2011-12	82	26	11	....	4	16	21	....	4	42	32	....	8	222	230	92	2nd, SE	7th, East	Lost Conf. Semi-Final
2010-11	82	25	8	....	8	23	15	....	3	48	23	....	11	224	197	107	1st, SE	1st, East	Lost Conf. Semi-Final
2009-10	82	30	5	....	6	24	10	....	7	54	15	....	13	318	233	121	1st, SE	1st, East	Lost Conf. Quarter-Final
2008-09	82	29	9	....	3	21	15	....	5	50	24	....	8	272	245	108	1st, SE	2nd, East	Lost Conf. Semi-Final
2007-08	82	23	15	....	3	20	16	....	5	43	31	....	8	242	231	94	1st, SE	3rd, East	Lost Conf. Quarter-Final
2006-07	82	17	17	....	7	11	23	....	7	28	40	....	14	235	286	70	5th, SE	14th, East	Out of Playoffs
2005-06	82	16	18	....	7	13	23	....	5	29	41	....	12	237	306	70	5th, SE	14th, East	Out of Playoffs
2004-05	....																		
2003-04	82	13	20	6	2	10	26	4	1	23	46	10	3	186	253	59	5th, SE	13th, East	Out of Playoffs
2002-03	82	24	13	2	2	15	16	6	4	39	29	8	6	224	220	92	2nd, SE	6th, East	Lost Conf. Quarter-Final
2001-02	82	21	12	6	2	15	21	5	0	36	33	11	2	228	240	85	2nd, SE	9th, East	Out of Playoffs
2000-01	82	24	9	6	2	17	18	4	2	41	27	10	4	233	211	96	1st, SE	3rd, East	Lost Conf. Quarter-Final
1999-2000	82	26	5	8	2	18	19	4	0	44	24	12	2	227	194	102	1st, SE	2nd, East	Lost Conf. Quarter-Final
1998-99	82	16	23	2	....	15	22	4	....	31	45	6	....	200	218	68	3rd, SE	12th, East	Out of Playoffs
1997-98	82	23	12	6	....	17	18	6	....	40	30	12	....	219	202	92	3rd, Atl.	4th, East	Lost Final
1996-97	82	19	17	5	....	14	23	4	....	33	40	9	....	214	231	75	5th, Atl.	7th, East	Out of Playoffs
1995-96	82	21	15	5	....	18	17	6	....	39	32	11	....	234	204	89	4th, Atl.	7th, East	Lost Conf. Quarter-Final
1994-95	48	15	6	3	....	7	12	5	....	22	18	8	....	136	120	52	3rd, Atl.	6th, East	Lost Conf. Quarter-Final
1993-94	84	21	16	9	....	22	19	1	....	39	35	10	....	277	263	88	3rd, Atl.	7th, East	Lost Conf. Semi-Final
1992-93	84	21	15	6	....	22	19	1	....	43	34	7	....	325	286	93	2nd, Patrick		Lost Div. Semi-Final
1991-92	80	25	12	3	....	20	15	5	....	45	27	8	....	330	275	98	2nd, Patrick		Lost Div. Semi-Final
1990-91	80	21	14	5	....	16	22	2	....	37	36	7	....	258	258	81	3rd, Patrick		Lost Div. Final
1989-90	80	19	18	3	....	17	20	3	....	36	38	6	....	284	275	78	3rd, Patrick		Lost Conf. Final
1988-89	80	25	12	3	....	16	17	7	....	41	29	10	....	305	259	92	1st, Patrick		Lost Div. Semi-Final
1987-88	80	22	14	4	....	16	19	5	....	38	33	9	....	281	249	85	2nd, Patrick		Lost Div. Final
1986-87	80	22	15	3	....	16	17	7	....	38	32	10	....	285	278	86	2nd, Patrick		Lost Div. Semi-Final
1985-86	80	30	8	2	....	20	15	5	....	50	23	7	....	315	272	107	2nd, Patrick		Lost Div. Final
1984-85	80	27	11	2	....	19	14	7	....	46	25	9	....	322	240	101	2nd, Patrick		Lost Div. Semi-Final
1983-84	80	26	11	3	....	22	16	2	....	48	27	5	....	308	226	101	2nd, Patrick		Lost Div. Final
1982-83	80	22	12	6	....	17	13	10	....	39	25	16	....	306	283	94	3rd, Patrick		Lost Div. Semi-Final
1981-82	80	16	16	8	....	10	25	5	....	26	41	13	....	319	338	65	5th, Patrick		Out of Playoffs
1980-81	80	16	17	7	....	10	19	11	....	26	36	18	....	286	317	70	5th, Patrick		Out of Playoffs
1979-80	80	20	14	6	....	7	26	7	....	27	40	13	....	261	293	67	5th, Patrick		Out of Playoffs
1978-79	80	15	19	6	....	9	22	9	....	24	41	15	....	273	338	63	4th, Norris		Out of Playoffs
1977-78	80	10	23	7	....	7	26	7	....	17	49	14	....	195	321	48	5th, Norris		Out of Playoffs
1976-77	80	17	15	8	....	7	27	6	....	24	42	14	....	221	307	62	4th, Norris		Out of Playoffs
1975-76	80	6	26	8	....	5	33	2	....	11	59	10	....	224	394	32	5th, Norris		Out of Playoffs
1974-75	80	7	28	5	....	1	39	0	....	8	67	5	....	181	446	21	5th, Norris		Out of Playoffs

2015-16 Player Personnel

FORWARDS	HT	WT	*Age	Place of Birth	S	2014-15 Club
BACKSTROM, Nicklas	6-1	208	27	Gavle, Sweden	L	Washington
BEAGLE, Jay	6-3	215	29	Calgary, AB	R	Washington
BOURQUE, Chris	5-8	174	29	Boston, MA	L	Hartford
BROWN, Chris	6-2	215	24	Flower Mound, TX	R	Washington-Hershey
BURAKOVSKY, Andre	6-2	188	20	Klagenfurt , Austria	L	Washington-Hershey
CAMPER, Carter	5-9	176	27	Rocky River, OH	R	Binghamton
CAREY, Paul	6-0	190	27	Boston, MA	L	Col-Lake Erie-Prov (AHL)
CHIMERA, Jason	6-3	213	36	Edmonton, AB	L	Washington
COLLINS, Sean	6-3	205	26	Saskatoon, SK	L	Columbus-Springfield
GALIEV, Stanislav	6-1	187	23	Moscow, Russia	R	Washington-Hershey
JOHANSSON, Marcus	6-1	205	25	Landskrona, Sweden	L	Washington
KUZNETSOV, Evgeny	6-0	172	23	Chelyabinsk, Russia	L	Washington
LAICH, Brooks	6-2	210	32	Wawota, SK	L	Washington
LATTA, Michael	6-0	209	24	Kitchener, ON	R	Washington
MITCHELL, Garrett	5-11	183	24	Regina, SK	R	Hershey
O'BRIEN, Liam	6-1	205	21	Halifax, NS	L	Washington-Hershey
OSHIE, T.J.	5-11	189	28	Mt. Vernon, WA	R	St. Louis
OVECHKIN, Alex	6-3	230	30	Moscow, USSR	R	Washington
SILL, Zach	6-0	202	27	Truro, NS	L	Pittsburgh-Toronto
WILLIAMS, Justin	6-1	189	34	Cobourg, ON	R	Los Angeles
WILSON, Tom	6-4	210	21	Toronto, ON	R	Washington-Hershey
DEFENSEMEN						
ALZNER, Karl	6-2	217	27	Burnaby, BC	L	Washington
CARLSON, John	6-3	212	25	Natick, MA	R	Washington
CARRICK, Connor	5-11	185	21	Orland Park, IL	R	Hershey
CHORNEY, Taylor	6-1	189	28	Thunder Bay, ON	L	Pittsburgh-Wilkes-Barre
MOORE, Mike	6-1	210	30	Calgary, AB	L	Hershey
NESS, Aaron	5-10	187	25	Roseau, MN	L	Bridgeport
NISKANEN, Matt	6-0	209	28	Virginia, MN	R	Washington
ORLOV, Dmitry	6-0	210	24	Novokuznetsk, USSR	L	Hershey
ORPIK, Brooks	6-2	219	35	San Francisco, CA	L	Washington
SCHMIDT, Nate	6-0	194	24	St. Cloud, MN	L	Washington-Hershey

GOALTENDERS	HT	WT	*Age	Place of Birth	C	2014-15 Club
ELLIS, Dan	6-1	195	35	Saskatoon, SK	L	Florida-San Antonio
GRUBAUER, Philipp	6-1	184	23	Rosenheim, Germany	L	Washington-Hershey
HOLTBY, Braden	6-2	203	26	Lloydminster, SK	L	Washington
PETERS, Justin	6-1	210	29	Blyth, ON	L	Washington-Hershey

* – Age at start of 2015-16 season

Barry Trotz

Head Coach

Born: Winnipeg, MB, July 15, 1962.

Majority owner Ted Leonsis and president Dick Patrick announced on May 26, 2014 that they had named Barry Trotz as the team's head coach. Trotz is the 17th coach in Capitals history and joined Washington after spending 15 seasons as coach of the Nashville Predators. In his first season with the Capitals in 2014-15, the team had 101 points and returned to the playoffs.

Trotz was previously the longest tenured coach in the NHL and only coach in the Predators history. Trotz has put himself among some legendary names, ranking third all-time in both games coached (1,196) and wins (557) with a single franchise. He is one of just six coaches in all four major North American sports leagues to have coached or managed each of a team's first 15 seasons of existence (MLB: Connie Mack - 50, Philadelphia (AL); NFL Curly Lambeau - 29, Green Bay, Tom Landry - 29, Dallas, Hank Stram - 15, Kansas City, Paul Brown - 15, Cleveland). Trotz has also been the finalist for the Jack Adams Award, awarded annually to the NHL's top head coach, twice (2010 and 2011) while finishing in the top five on four other occasions since 2006.

Prior to joining the Predators, Trotz spent five seasons (1992 to 1997) as the coach of the Capitals' primary developmental affiliate in the American Hockey League. He was named coach of the Baltimore Skipjacks in 1992 after one season as an assistant coach. Following the franchise's relocation to Portland, Maine, in 1993, he led the Portland Pirates to two Calder Cup finals appearances during the next four seasons. In 1994-95, Trotz coached Portland to a Calder Cup championship and a league-best 43-27-10 record and captured AHL Coach of the Year honors. In 2006 he was honored with election to the Pirates' Hall of Fame.

Trotz earned the first of his back-to-back Jack Adams nominations in 2009-10 when he was runner-up for the award after leading his club to a 100-point season (47-29-6) despite the NHL's 28th-highest payroll. Trotz was again nominated for the award in 2010-11 after guiding the Predators to the fifth seed in the Western Conference (44-27-11) despite losing 348 man-games due to injury, a number that ranked among the top three in the league, and being the fifth youngest roster down the stretch and the youngest among playoff teams. That success continued in 2011-12 when he finished fifth in Adams voting after steering the team to their third-best record in franchise history and to top 10 rankings in goals for (eighth), goals against (eighth), power-play percentage (first) and penalty-kill percentage (10th). On November 12, 2011, against the Montreal Canadiens, he hit the 1,000-game milestone, and on March 30, 2012, reached the 500-win mark.

2014-15 Scoring

* – rookie

Regular Season

Pos	#	Player	Team	GP	G	A	Pts	TOI	+/–	PIM	PP	SH	GW	S	S%
L	8	Alex Ovechkin	WSH	81	53	28	81	20:19	10	58	25	0	11	395	13.4
C	19	Nicklas Backstrom	WSH	82	18	60	78	20:31	5	40	3	0	3	153	11.8
D	74	John Carlson	WSH	82	12	43	55	23:04	11	28	3	1	3	193	6.2
C	90	Marcus Johansson	WSH	82	20	27	47	16:28	6	10	3	0	1	138	14.5
D	52	Mike Green	WSH	72	10	35	45	19:06	15	34	1	0	2	159	6.3
R	20	Troy Brouwer	WSH	82	21	22	43	17:31	11	53	8	2	3	145	14.5
C	92	* Evgeny Kuznetsov	WSH	80	11	26	37	13:19	10	24	4	0	1	127	8.7
L	22	Curtis Glencross	CGY	53	9	19	28	16:40	3	39	2	0	1	87	10.3
			WSH	18	4	3	7	12:36	–1	6	2	0	0	21	19.0
			Total	71	13	22	35	15:38	2	45	4	0	1	108	12.0
R	42	Joel Ward	WSH	82	19	15	34	16:51	–4	30	6	0	4	138	13.8
R	16	Eric Fehr	WSH	75	19	14	33	14:51	8	20	1	1	4	142	13.4
D	2	Matt Niskanen	WSH	82	4	27	31	22:21	7	47	2	0	0	117	3.4
L	65	* Andre Burakovsky	WSH	53	9	13	22	12:55	12	10	2	0	2	65	13.8
D	27	Karl Alzner	WSH	82	5	16	21	19:25	14	20	0	0	0	72	6.9
C	83	Jay Beagle	WSH	62	10	10	20	12:48	6	20	0	0	2	84	11.9
C	21	Brooks Laich	WSH	66	7	13	20	14:43	–2	24	0	0	2	106	6.6
L	25	Jason Chimera	WSH	77	7	12	19	12:56	–1	51	0	0	2	96	7.3
D	44	Brooks Orpik	WSH	78	0	19	19	21:47	5	66	0	0	0	66	0.0
R	43	Tom Wilson	WSH	67	4	13	17	10:56	–1	172	0	0	0	79	5.1
D	6	Tim Gleason	CAR	55	1	6	7	16:39	–18	44	0	0	0	44	2.3
			WSH	17	0	2	2	15:16	5	11	0	0	0	10	0.0
			Total	72	1	8	9	16:19	–13	55	0	0	0	54	1.9
C	46	* Michael Latta	WSH	53	0	6	6	8:22	4	68	0	0	0	24	0.0
D	88	Nate Schmidt	WSH	39	1	3	4	13:53	–2	10	0	0	0	40	2.5
C	87	* Liam O'Brien	WSH	13	1	1	2	7:32	4	23	0	0	0	16	6.3
R	49	* Stanislav Galiev	WSH	2	1	0	1	9:23	1	0	0	0	0	2	50.0
C	67	* Chris Brown	WSH	5	1	0	1	6:27	1	2	0	0	0	4	25.0
D	61	Steve Oleksy	WSH	1	0	0	0	12:11	–1	0	0	0	0	1	0.0
R	23	Chris Conner	WSH	2	0	0	0	8:49	1	4	0	0	0	3	0.0
L	17	Aaron Volpatti	WSH	2	0	0	0	9:37	0	0	0	0	0	1	0.0
D	45	* Cameron Schilling	WSH	4	0	0	0	11:22	1	4	0	0	0	2	0.0

Goaltending

No.	Goaltender	GPI	Mins	Avg	W	L	OT	EN	SO	GA	SA	Sv%	G	A	PIM
31	* Philipp Grubauer	1	65	1.85	1	0	0	0	0	2	25	.920	0	0	0
70	Braden Holtby	73	4247	2.22	41	20	10	4	9	157	2044	.923	0	2	2
35	Justin Peters	12	647	3.25	3	6	1	1	0	35	294	.881	0	0	0
	Totals	**82**	**5002**	**2.39**	**45**	**26**	**11**	**5**	**9**	**199**	**2368**	**.916**			

Playoffs

Pos	#	Player	Team	GP	G	A	Pts	TOI	+/–	PIM	PP	SH	GW	OT	S	S%
L	8	Alex Ovechkin	WSH	14	5	4	9	19:57	–3	6	1	0	0	0	61	8.2
R	42	Joel Ward	WSH	14	3	6	9	19:02	1	2	0	0	1	0	39	7.7
C	19	Nicklas Backstrom	WSH	14	3	5	8	21:35	–3	2	1	0	1	1	24	12.5
C	92	* Evgeny Kuznetsov	WSH	14	5	2	7	16:36	4	8	0	0	1	0	42	11.9
L	25	Jason Chimera	WSH	14	3	4	7	15:35	4	4	0	0	1	0	35	8.6
D	74	John Carlson	WSH	14	1	5	6	23:57	3	4	1	0	0	0	41	2.4
C	83	Jay Beagle	WSH	14	1	4	5	15:47	0	4	0	0	1	0	24	4.2
D	27	Karl Alzner	WSH	14	2	2	4	20:13	0	6	0	0	1	0	13	15.4
C	90	Marcus Johansson	WSH	14	1	3	4	17:38	2	2	0	0	0	0	18	5.6
D	2	Matt Niskanen	WSH	14	0	4	4	23:47	–2	0	0	0	0	0	22	0.0
L	65	* Andre Burakovsky	WSH	11	2	1	3	12:24	2	0	0	0	1	0	17	11.8
R	20	Troy Brouwer	WSH	14	0	3	3	17:58	–3	10	0	0	0	0	20	0.0
C	21	Brooks Laich	WSH	14	1	1	2	11:56	1	0	0	0	0	0	15	6.7
D	44	Brooks Orpik	WSH	14	0	2	2	22:17	5	8	0	0	0	0	16	0.0
D	52	Mike Green	WSH	14	0	2	2	18:23	–1	14	0	0	0	0	27	0.0
L	22	Curtis Glencross	WSH	10	1	0	1	10:24	–5	2	0	0	0	0	14	7.1
R	43	Tom Wilson	WSH	13	0	1	1	7:43	–2	25	0	0	0	0	7	0.0
D	6	Tim Gleason	WSH	14	0	1	1	13:07	–3	5	0	0	0	0	7	0.0
R	16	Eric Fehr	WSH	4	0	0	0	9:53	–1	2	0	0	0	0	2	0.0
C	46	* Michael Latta	WSH	4	0	0	0	6:55	–1	2	0	0	0	0	0	0.0

Goaltending

No.	Goaltender	GPI	Mins	Avg	W	L	EN	SO	GA	SA	Sv%	G	A	PIM
70	Braden Holtby	13	806	1.71	6	7	2	1	23	412	.944	0	1	0
31	* Philipp Grubauer	1	60	3.00	1	0	0	0	3	21	.857	0	0	0
	Totals	**14**	**872**	**1.93**	**7**	**7**	**2**	**1**	**28**	**435**	**.936**			

Coaching Record

			Regular Season				Playoffs			
Season	Team	League	GC	W	L	O/T	GC	W	L	T
1992-93	Baltimore	AHL	80	28	40	12	7	3	4	....
1993-94	Portland	AHL	80	43	27	10	8	6	2	....
1994-95	Portland	AHL	80	46	22	12	7	3	4	....
1995-96	Portland	AHL	80	32	34	14	24	14	10	....
1996-97	Portland	AHL	80	37	26	17	5	2	3	....
1998-99	**Nashville**	**NHL**	**82**	**28**	**47**	**7**	....	....	....	....
99-2000	**Nashville**	**NHL**	**82**	**28**	**40**	**14**	....	....	....	....
2000-01	**Nashville**	**NHL**	**82**	**34**	**36**	**12**	....	....	....	....
2001-02	**Nashville**	**NHL**	**82**	**28**	**41**	**13**	....	....	....	....
2002-03	**Nashville**	**NHL**	**82**	**27**	**35**	**20**	....	....	....	....
2003-04	**Nashville**	**NHL**	**82**	**38**	**29**	**15**	**6**	**2**	**4**	....
2004-05	**Nashville**				SEASON CANCELLED					
2005-06	**Nashville**	**NHL**	**82**	**49**	**25**	**8**	**5**	**1**	**4**	....
2006-07	**Nashville**	**NHL**	**82**	**51**	**23**	**8**	**5**	**1**	**4**	....
2007-08	**Nashville**	**NHL**	**82**	**41**	**32**	**9**	**6**	**2**	**4**	....
2008-09	**Nashville**	**NHL**	**82**	**40**	**34**	**8**	....	....	....	....
2009-10	**Nashville**	**NHL**	**82**	**47**	**29**	**6**	**6**	**2**	**4**	....
2010-11	**Nashville**	**NHL**	**82**	**44**	**27**	**11**	**12**	**6**	**6**	....
2011-12	**Nashville**	**NHL**	**82**	**48**	**26**	**8**	**10**	**5**	**5**	....
2012-13	**Nashville**	**NHL**	**48**	**16**	**23**	**9**	....	....	....	....
2013-14	**Nashville**	**NHL**	**82**	**38**	**32**	**12**	....	....	....	....
2014-15	**Washington**	**NHL**	**82 ***	**45**	**26**	**11**	**14**	**7**	**7**	....
	NHL Totals		**1278**	**602**	**505**	**171**	**64**	**26**	**38**	....

Club Records

Team

(Figures in brackets for season records are games played; records for fewest points, wins, ties, losses, goals, goals against are for 70 or more games)

Most Points	**121**	2009-10 (82)
Most Wins	**54**	2009-10 (82)
Most Ties	**18**	1980-81 (80)
Most Losses	**67**	1974-75 (80)
Most Goals	**330**	1991-92 (80)
Most Goals Against	***446**	1974-75 (80)
Fewest Points	***21**	1974-75 (80)
Fewest Wins	***8**	1974-75 (80)
Fewest Ties	**5**	1974-75 (80), 1983-84 (80)
Fewest Losses	**15**	2009-10 (82)
Fewest Goals	**181**	1974-75 (80)
Fewest Goals Against	**194**	1999-00 (82)
Longest Winning Streak		
Overall	**14**	Jan. 13-Feb. 7/10
Home	**13**	Jan. 5-Mar. 6/10
Away	**6**	Feb. 26-Apr. 1/84, Feb. 20-Mar. 15/11
Longest Undefeated Streak		
Overall	**14**	Nov. 24-Dec. 23/82 (9W, 5T), Jan. 17-Feb. 18/84 (13W, 1T), Jan. 13-Feb. 7/10 (14W)
Home	**13**	Nov. 25/92-Jan. 31/93 (9W, 4T), Dec. 27/99-Feb. 23/00 (11W, 2T/OL), Jan. 5-Mar. 6/10 (13W)
Away	**10**	Nov. 24/82-Jan. 8/83 (6W, 4T)
Longest Losing Streak		
Overall	***17**	Feb. 18-Mar. 26/75
Home	**11**	Feb. 18-Mar. 30/75
Away	**37**	Oct. 9/74-Mar. 26/75
Longest Winless Streak		
Overall	**25**	Nov. 29/75-Jan. 21/76 (22L, 3T)
Home	**14**	Dec. 3/75-Jan. 21/76 (11L, 3T)
Away	**37**	Oct. 9/74-Mar. 26/75 (37L)
Most Shutouts, Season	**9**	1995-96 (82), 2014-15 (82)
Most PIM, Season	**2,204**	1989-90 (80)
Most Goals, Game	**12**	Feb. 6/90 (Que. 2 at Wsh. 12), Jan. 11/03 (Fla. 2 at Wsh. 12)

Individual

Most Seasons	**16**	Olie Kolzig
Most Games	**983**	Calle Johansson
Most Goals, Career	**475**	Alex Ovechkin
Most Assists, Career	**427**	Nicklas Backstrom
Most Points, Career	**895**	Alex Ovechkin (475G, 420A)
Most PIM, Career	**2,003**	Dale Hunter
Most Shutouts, Career	**35**	Olie Kolzig
Longest Consecutive Games Streak	**422**	Bob Carpenter (Oct. 7/81-Nov. 22/86)
Most Goals, Season	**65**	Alex Ovechkin (2007-08)
Most Assists, Season	**76**	Dennis Maruk (1981-82)
Most Points, Season	**136**	Dennis Maruk (1981-82; 60G, 76A)
Most PIM, Season	**339**	Alan May (1989-90)
Most Points, Defenseman, Season	**81**	Larry Murphy (1986-87; 23G, 58A)
Most Points, Center, Season	**136**	Dennis Maruk (1981-82; 60G, 76A)
Most Points, Right Wing, Season	**102**	Mike Gartner (1984-85; 50G, 52A)
Most Points, Left Wing, Season	**112**	Alex Ovechkin (2007-08; 65G, 47A)
Most Points, Rookie, Season	**106**	Alex Ovechkin (2005-06; 52G, 54A)
Most Shutouts, Season	**9**	Jim Carey (1995-96), Braden Holtby (2014-15)
Most Goals, Game	**5**	Bengt Gustafsson (Jan. 8/84), Peter Bondra (Feb. 5/94)
Most Assists, Game	**6**	Mike Ridley (Jan. 7/89)
Most Points, Game	**7**	Dino Ciccarelli (Mar. 18/89; 4G, 3A), Jaromir Jagr (Jan. 11/03; 3G, 4A)

* NHL Record.

All-time Record vs. Other Clubs

Regular Season

	Total								At Home								On Road							
	GP	W	L	T	OL	GF	GA	PTS	GP	W	L	T	OL	GF	GA	PTS	GP	W	L	T	OL	GF	GA	PTS
Anaheim	29	14	13	1	1	79	86	30	15	7	7	0	1	33	40	15	14	7	6	1	0	46	46	15
Arizona	71	31	26	12	2	256	224	76	36	21	9	5	1	137	101	48	35	10	17	7	1	119	123	28
Boston	148	51	68	21	8	407	490	131	74	28	30	12	4	213	237	72	74	23	38	9	4	194	253	59
Buffalo	149	48	81	15	5	393	531	116	75	25	38	9	3	200	250	62	74	23	43	6	2	193	281	54
Calgary	89	34	41	13	1	280	324	82	46	24	15	6	1	170	155	55	43	10	26	7	0	110	169	27
Carolina	158	86	50	14	8	490	427	194	79	47	24	4	4	256	207	102	79	39	26	10	4	234	220	92
Chicago	91	39	40	11	1	296	310	90	46	25	15	5	1	163	138	56	45	14	25	6	0	133	172	34
Colorado	77	37	30	9	1	271	236	84	38	20	13	4	1	139	119	45	39	17	17	5	0	132	117	39
Columbus	23	14	6	1	2	75	69	31	10	6	1	1	2	33	27	15	13	8	5	0	0	42	42	16
Dallas	91	29	45	16	1	254	320	75	45	16	20	8	1	131	150	41	46	13	25	8	0	123	170	34
Detroit	107	44	44	16	3	352	348	107	53	26	22	5	0	196	166	57	54	18	22	11	3	156	182	50
Edmonton	68	33	28	6	1	240	241	73	34	21	10	2	1	138	109	45	34	12	18	4	0	102	132	28
Florida	114	60	36	9	9	341	289	138	57	33	14	5	5	183	134	76	57	27	22	4	4	158	155	62
Los Angeles	104	35	54	13	2	356	394	85	51	20	23	7	1	202	188	48	53	15	31	6	1	154	206	37
Minnesota	16	7	8	0	1	34	34	15	8	6	2	0	0	21	12	12	8	1	6	0	1	13	22	3
Montreal	156	65	69	17	5	402	497	152	77	36	30	9	2	214	222	83	79	29	39	8	3	188	275	69
Nashville	21	11	8	1	1	58	57	24	10	7	3	0	0	31	25	14	11	4	5	1	1	27	32	10
New Jersey	198	98	74	13	13	648	569	222	100	58	29	6	7	370	276	129	98	40	45	7	6	278	293	93
NY Islanders	201	99	84	13	5	635	663	216	101	52	36	11	2	326	304	117	100	47	48	2	3	309	359	99
NY Rangers	205	95	86	18	6	698	695	214	103	52	38	9	4	361	324	117	102	43	48	9	2	337	371	97
Ottawa	84	39	35	5	5	256	262	88	42	23	13	4	2	138	115	52	42	16	22	1	3	118	147	36
Philadelphia	203	76	101	19	7	610	704	178	99	43	41	13	2	317	314	101	104	33	60	6	5	293	390	77
Pittsburgh	208	91	95	16	6	734	753	204	105	52	40	9	4	413	371	117	103	39	55	7	2	321	382	87
St. Louis	91	39	39	12	1	298	311	91	45	24	17	4	0	156	132	52	46	15	22	8	1	142	179	39
San Jose	35	11	20	1	3	92	114	26	18	6	9	0	3	49	55	15	17	5	11	1	0	43	59	11
Tampa Bay	116	72	31	6	7	400	304	157	58	39	11	4	4	217	150	86	58	33	20	2	3	183	154	71
Toronto	135	66	53	10	6	466	454	148	69	42	21	4	2	251	188	90	66	24	32	6	4	215	266	58
Vancouver	89	40	39	9	1	283	291	90	45	24	17	4	0	148	135	52	44	16	22	5	1	135	156	38
Winnipeg	83	45	26	5	7	271	234	102	41	26	9	3	3	149	117	58	42	19	17	2	4	122	117	44
Defunct Clubs	20	6	13	1	0	58	81	13	10	2	8	0	0	28	42	4	10	4	5	1	0	30	39	9
Totals	**3180**	**1415**	**1343**	**303**	**119**	**10033**	**10312**	**3252**	**1590**	**811**	**565**	**153**	**61**	**5383**	**4803**	**1836**	**1590**	**604**	**778**	**150**	**58**	**4650**	**5509**	**1416**

Playoffs

	Series	W	L	GP	W	L	T	GF	GA	Last Mtg.	Rnd.	Result
Boston	3	2	1	17	8	9	0	37	43	2012	CQF	W 4-3
Buffalo	1	1	0	6	4	2	0	13	11	1998	CF	W 4-2
Detroit	1	0	1	4	0	4	0	7	13	1998	F	L 0-4
Montreal	1	0	1	7	3	4	0	22	20	2010	CQF	L 3-4
New Jersey	2	1	1	13	7	6	0	44	43	1990	DSF	W 4-2
NY Islanders	7	2	5	37	16	21	0	104	114	2015	FR	W 4-3
NY Rangers	9	4	5	55	28	27	0	144	134	2015	SR	L 3-4
Ottawa	1	1	0	5	4	1	0	18	7	1998	CSF	W 4-1
Philadelphia	4	2	2	23	12	11	0	85	78	2008	CQF	L 3-4
Pittsburgh	8	1	7	49	19	30	0	143	164	2009	CSF	L 3-4
Tampa Bay	2	0	2	10	2	8	0	25	30	2011	CSF	L 0-4
Totals	**39**	**14**	**25**	**226**	**103**	**123**	**0**	**642**	**657**			

Playoff Results 2015-2011

Year	Round	Opponent	Result	GF	GA
2015	SR	NY Rangers	L 3-4	12	13
	FR	NY Islanders	W 4-3	16	15
2013	CQF	NY Rangers	L 3-4	12	16
2012	CSF	NY Rangers	L 3-4	13	15
	CQF	Boston	W 4-3	16	15
2011	CSF	Tampa Bay	L 0-4	10	16
	CQF	NY Rangers	W 4-1	13	8

Abbreviations: Round: F – Final; **CF** – conference final; **CSF** – conference semi-final; **SR** – second round; **CQF** – conference quarter-final; **FR** – first round; **DSF** – division semi-final.

Calgary totals include Atlanta Flames, 1974-75 to 1979-80. Carolina totals include Hartford, 1979-80 to 1996-97.
Colorado totals include Quebec, 1979-80 to 1994-95. Dallas totals include Minnesota North Stars, 1974-75 to 1992-93.
New Jersey totals include Kansas City, 1974-75, 1975-76, and Colorado Rockies, 1976-77 to 1981-82.
Phoenix totals include Winnipeg, 1979-80 to 1995-96. Winnipeg totals include Atlanta Thrashers, 1999-2000 to 2010-11.

2014-15 Results

Month	Day	Opponent	Score	Month	Day	Opponent	Score
Oct.	9	Montreal	1-2†		12	Colorado	2-1
	11	at Boston	4-0		14	Philadelphia	1-0
	14	San Jose	5-6†		16	at Nashville	3-4
	16	New Jersey	6-2		17	at Dallas	4-5
	18	Florida	2-1†		20	Edmonton	4-5†
	22	at Edmonton	2-3		27	at Columbus	3-4
	25	at Calgary	3-1		28	Pittsburgh	4-0
	26	at Vancouver	2-4		31	at Montreal	0-1*
	29	Detroit	2-4	**Feb.**	1	St. Louis	3-4
Nov.	1	at Tampa Bay	3-4		3	Los Angeles	4-0
	2	Arizona	5-6		5	at Ottawa	2-1
	4	Calgary	3-4*		6	Anaheim	3-2†
	7	at Chicago	3-2		8	Philadelphia	1-3
	8	Carolina	4-3*		11	at San Jose	5-4*
	11	Columbus	4-2		14	at Los Angeles	1-3
	14	New Jersey	0-1		15	at Anaheim	5-3
	15	at St. Louis	1-4		17	at Pittsburgh	3-1
	18	at Arizona	2-1*		19	Winnipeg	5-1
	20	at Colorado	3-2		21	NY Islanders	3-2†
	22	Buffalo	1-2		22	at Philadelphia	2-3
	26	at NY Islanders	2-3*		25	Pittsburgh	3-4
	28	NY Islanders	5-2		27	at Carolina	0-3
	29	at Toronto	2-6	**Mar.**	1	Toronto	4-0
Dec.	2	Vancouver	3-4		3	at Columbus	5-3
	4	at Carolina	2-1		5	Minnesota	1-2
	6	at New Jersey	4-1		7	Buffalo	6-1
	9	at Tampa Bay	5-3		11	NY Rangers	1-3
	11	Columbus	2-3*		13	Dallas	2-4
	13	Tampa Bay	4-2		15	Boston	2-0
	16	at Florida	1-2†		16	at Buffalo	4-3†
	18	at Columbus	5-4*		19	at Minnesota	3-2
	20	at New Jersey	4-0		21	at Winnipeg	0-3
	22	Ottawa	2-1		26	New Jersey	3-2*
	23	at NY Rangers	2-4		28	Nashville	3-4
	27	at Pittsburgh	3-0		29	at NY Rangers	5-2
	29	at NY Islanders	3-4*		31	Carolina	4-2
Jan.	1	Chicago	3-2	**Apr.**	2	at Montreal	5-4†
	4	Florida	4-3		4	at Ottawa	3-4*
	7	at Toronto	6-2		5	at Detroit	2-1
	8	at Philadelphia	2-3*		8	Boston	3-0
	10	Detroit	3-1		11	NY Rangers	2-4

* – Overtime † – Shootout

NHL Draft Selections 2015-2001

Name in bold denotes played in NHL.

2015
Pick
- 22 Ilya Samsonov
- 57 Jonas Siegenthaler
- 143 Connor Hobbs
- 173 Colby Williams

2014
Pick
- 13 **Jakub Vrana**
- 39 Vitek Vanecek
- 89 Nathan Walker
- 134 Shane Gersich
- 159 Steven Spinner
- 194 Kevin Elgestal

2013
Pick
- 23 **Andre Burakovsky**
- 53 Madison Bowey
- 61 Zachary Sanford
- 144 Blake Heinrich
- 174 Brian Pinho
- 204 Tyler Lewington

2012
Pick
- 11 **Filip Forsberg**
- 16 **Tom Wilson**
- 77 Chandler Stephenson
- 100 Thomas Di Pauli
- 107 Austin Wuthrich
- 137 **Connor Carrick**
- 167 Riley Barber
- 195 Christian Djoos
- 197 Jaynen Rissling
- 203 Sergey Kostenko

2011
Pick
- 117 Steffen Soberg
- 147 Patrick Koudys
- 177 Travis Boyd
- 207 Garrett Haar

2010
Pick
- 26 **Evgeny Kuznetsov**
- 86 Stanislav Galiev
- 112 **Philipp Grubauer**
- 142 Caleb Herbert
- 176 Samuel Carrier

2009
Pick
- 24 **Marcus Johansson**
- 55 **Dmitry Orlov**
- 85 **Cody Eakin**
- 115 **Patrick Wey**
- 145 Brett Flemming
- 175 Garrett Mitchell
- 205 Benjamin Casavant ·

2008
Pick
- 21 Anton Gustafsson
- 27 **John Carlson**
- 57 Eric Mestery
- 58 Dmitry Kugryshev
- 93 **Braden Holtby**
- 144 Joel Broda
- 174 Greg Burke
- 204 Stefan Della Rovere

2007
Pick
- 5 **Karl Alzner**
- 34 Josh Godfrey
- 46 Theo Ruth
- 84 Phil Desimone
- 108 Brett Bruneteau
- 125 Brett Leffler
- 154 Dan Dunn
- 180 Justin Taylor
- 185 Nick Larson
- 199 Andrew Glass

2006
Pick
- 4 **Nicklas Backstrom**
- 23 **Semyon Varlamov**
- 34 **Michal Neuvirth**
- 35 Francois Bouchard
- 52 Keith Seabrook
- 97 **Oskar Osala**
- 122 Luke Lynes
- 127 Maxime Lacroix
- 157 Brent Gwidt
- 177 **Mathieu Perreault**

2005
Pick
- 14 Sasha Pokuluk
- 27 **Joe Finley**
- 109 Andrew Thomas
- 118 Patrick McNeill
- 143 Daren Machesney
- 181 **Tim Kennedy**
- 209 Viktor Dovgan

2004
Pick
- 1 **Alex Ovechkin**
- 27 **Jeff Schultz**
- 29 **Mike Green**
- 33 **Chris Bourque**
- 62 Mikhail Yunkov
- 66 **Sami Lepisto**
- 88 Clayton Barthel
- 132 Oscar Hedman
- 138 Pasi Salonen
- 166 Peter Guggisberg
- 197 **Andrew Gordon**
- 230 Justin Mrazek
- 263 **Travis Morin**

2003
Pick
- 18 **Eric Fehr**
- 83 Steve Werner
- 109 Andreas Valdix
- 155 Josh Robertson
- 249 **Andrew Joudrey**
- 279 Mark Olafson

2002
Pick
- 12 **Steve Eminger**
- 13 **Alexander Semin**
- 17 **Boyd Gordon**
- 59 Maxime Daigneault
- 77 Patrick Wellar
- 92 Derek Krestanovich
- 109 Jevon Desautels
- 118 Petr Dvorak
- 145 Rob Gherson
- 179 Marian Havel
- 209 Joni Lindlof
- 242 Igor Ignatushkin
- 272 Patric Blomdahl

2001
Pick
- 58 **Nathan Paetsch**
- 90 **Owen Fussey**
- 125 Jeff Lucky
- 160 Artem Ternavsky
- 191 Zbynek Novak
- 221 **Johnny Oduya**
- 249 Matt Maglione
- 254 Peter Polcik
- 275 Robert Muller
- 284 Viktor Hubl

General Managers' History

Milt Schmidt, 1974-75; Milt Schmidt and Max McNab, 1975-76; Max McNab, 1976-77 to 1980-81; Max McNab and Roger Crozier, 1981-82; David Poile, 1982-83 to 1996-97; George McPhee, 1997-98 to 2013-14; Brian MacLellan, 2014-15 to date.

Brian MacLellan
Senior Vice President and General Manager
Born: Guelph, ON, October 27, 1958.

Majority owner Ted Leonsis and president Dick Patrick announced on May 26, 2014 that the Washington Capitals had promoted Brian MacLellan to senior vice president and general manager. MacLellan is the sixth general manager in Capitals history after spending the previous 13 seasons with Washington, seven as the team's assistant general manager, player personnel. In his first season as general manager in 2014-15, the team had 101 points and returned to the playoffs.

In his previous role MacLellan oversaw the club's professional scouting staff and worked closely with the team's American Hockey League affiliate, the Hershey Bears, who won the Calder Cup in 2006, 2009 and 2010. MacLellan, who served as a pro scout for the Capitals from 2000 to 2003 and then was promoted to director of player personnel, assisted and advised the general manager in all player-related matters.

MacLellan, who won a Stanley Cup with the Calgary Flames in 1989, had a 10-year NHL career in which he skated for the Los Angeles Kings, New York Rangers, Minnesota North Stars, Calgary Flames and Detroit Red Wings. A forward who played 606 NHL games, MacLellan recorded 172 goals, and 241 assists for 413 points. He also won a silver medal with Team Canada at the 1985 World Championship in Prague.

The Guelph, Ontario, native played hockey at Bowling Green State University from 1978 to 1982, where he graduated with a bachelor of science in business administration. In 1982 he was named an All-America defenseman and First-Team All-CCHA. MacLellan earned his MBA in finance from the University of St. Thomas in 1995 and went on to work for an investment consulting firm in Minneapolis before joining the Capitals as a pro scout.

Club Directory

Verizon Center

Washington Capitals
627 N. Glebe Road, Suite 850
Arlington, VA 22203
Phone **202/266-2200**
PR FAX 202/266-2360
www.washingtoncaps.com
Capacity: 18,506

Ownership . . . . Monumental Sports & Entertainment
Founder, Chairman, Majority Owner and CEO. . . . . Ted Leonsis
Vice Chairman and President, COO. . . . . Dick Patrick
Vice Chairmen . . . . Raul Fernandez, Sheila Johnson
MSE Partners . . . . Scott Brickman, Neil D. Cohen, Jack Davies, Richard Fairbank, Michelle D. Freeman, Richard Kay, Jeong Kim, Mark D. Lerner, Roger Mody, Anthony Nader, Fred Schaufeld, Earl Stafford, George Stamas, Cliff White

Hockey Operations
Senior Vice President and General Manager . . . . . . Brian MacLellan
Assistant General Manager . . . . Ross Mahoney
Assistant General Manager, Dir. of Legal Affairs . . . Don Fishman
Head Coach . . . . Barry Trotz
Assistant Coaches . . . . Lane Lambert, Todd Reirden, Blaine Forsythe
Video Coach . . . . Brett Leonhardt
Goaltending Coach . . . . Mitch Korn
Pro Development Coach . . . . Olaf Kolzig
Associate Goaltending Coach . . . . Scott Murray
Strength and Conditioning Coach . . . . Mark Nemish
Director, Hockey Operations . . . . Kris Wagner
Hockey Operations Assistant . . . . Evan Gold
Manager, Team Services . . . . Rob Tillotson
Hershey Bears, Head Coach / Assistant Coach . . . . Troy Mann, Bryan Helmer

Scouting Staff
Director, Player Development . . . . Steve Richmond
Pro Scout, Dir. Of Minor League Operations . . . . . . Chris Patrick
Pro Scouts . . . . Jason Fitzsimmons, Martin Pouliot, Brian Sutherby
Amateur Scouts . . . . Darrell Baumgartner, Steve Bowman, Alan Haworth, Phil Horner, Ed McColgan, Wil Nichol, Terry Richardson, A.J. Toews
European Scouts . . . . Vojtech Kucera, Petri Skriko, Mats Weiderstal

Medical Staff
Head Athletic Trainer / Assistant Trainer . . . . Greg Smith / Ben Reisz
Massage Therapist . . . . Curtis Millar

Training Staff
Head Equipment Manager . . . . Brock Myles
Assistant Equipment Manager . . . . Craig Leydig
Equipment Assistant . . . . Dave Marin

Business Operations
Vice President, Administration . . . . Michelle Trostle
Senior Director, Information Technology . . . . Brian McPartland
Office Assistant / Receptionist . . . . Valerie Garrett / Chuquita Pettus
Chief Building Engineer . . . . Larry Hollen

Communications
Senior Vice President, Communications and
   CCO, Monumental Sports & Entertainment . . . . . Kurt Kehl
Senior Director, Communications . . . . Sergey Kocharov
Media Relations Manager . . . . Pace Sagester
Communications Coordinator . . . . Megan Eichenberg
Senior Editor and Content Strategist . . . . Mike Vogel
Digital Content Producer . . . . James Heuser

Broadcasting
Radio Rightsholder . . . . WJFK
Radio Play-by-Play / Analyst . . . . John Walton / Ken Sabourin
Television Rightsholder . . . . Comcast SportsNet
Television Play-by-Play / Analyst . . . . Joe Beninati / Craig Laughlin ·
Television Reporters / Studio Analyst . . . . Al Koken, Jill Sorenson / Alan May

Captains' History

Doug Mohns, 1974-75; Bill Clement and Yvon Labre, 1975-76; Yvon Labre, 1976-77, 1977-78; Guy Charron, 1978-79; Ryan Walter, 1979-80 to 1981-82; Rod Langway, 1982-83 to 1991-92; Rod Langway and Kevin Hatcher, 1992-93; Kevin Hatcher, 1993-94; Dale Hunter, 1994-95 to 1998-99; Adam Oates, 1999-2000, 2000-01; Brendan Witt and Steve Konowalchuk, 2001-02; Steve Konowalchuk, 2002-03; Steve Konowalchuk and no captain, 2003-04; Jeff Halpern, 2005-06; Chris Clark, 2006-07 to 2008-09; Chris Clark and Alex Ovechkin, 2009-10; Alex Ovechkin, 2010-11 to date.

Coaching History

Jim Anderson, Red Sullivan and Milt Schmidt, 1974-75; Milt Schmidt and Tom McVie, 1975-76; Tom McVie, 1976-77, 1977-78; Danny Belisle, 1978-79; Danny Belisle and Gary Green, 1979-80; Gary Green, 1980-81; Gary Green, Roger Crozier and Bryan Murray, 1981-82; Bryan Murray, 1982-83 to 1988-89; Bryan Murray and Terry Murray, 1989-90; Terry Murray, 1990-91 to 1992-93; Terry Murray and Jim Schoenfeld, 1993-94; Jim Schoenfeld, 1994-95 to 1996-97; Ron Wilson, 1997-98 to 2001-02; Bruce Cassidy, 2002-03; Bruce Cassidy and Glen Hanlon, 2003-04; Glen Hanlon, 2004-05 to 2006-07; Glen Hanlon and Bruce Boudreau, 2007-08; Bruce Boudreau, 2008-09 to 2010-11; Bruce Boudreau and Dale Hunter, 2011-12; Adam Oates, 2012-13, 2013-14; Barry Trotz, 2014-15 to date.

Key Off-Season Signings/Acquisitions

2015

June 17 • Re-signed RW **Anthony Peluso**.
 18 • Re-signed D **Ben Chiarot**.
 30 • Re-signed RW **Drew Stafford**.
July 1 • Signed C **Alexander Burmistrov**.
 1 • Re-signed D **Adam Pardy** and RW **Matt Halischuk**.
 2 • Signed RW **Matt Fraser**.
 2 • Re-signed C **Patrice Cormier**.
 3 • Signed D **Andrew MacWilliam**.
 10 • Re-signed D **Paul Postma**.

Winnipeg Jets

2014-15 Results: 43w-26L-7OTL-6SOL 99PTS
5TH, Central Division • 7TH, Western Conference

Year-by-Year Record

Season	GP	Home W	L	T	OL	Road W	L	T	OL	Overall W	L	T	OL	GF	GA	Pts.	Div. Fin.	Conf. Fin.	Playoff Result
2014-15	82	23	13	....	5	20	13	....	8	43	26	....	13	230	210	99	5th, Cen.	7th, West	Lost First Round
2013-14	82	18	17	....	6	19	18	....	4	37	35	....	10	227	237	84	7th, Cen.	11th, West	Out of Playoffs
2012-13	48	13	10	....	1	11	11	....	2	24	21	....	3	128	144	51	2nd, SE	9th, East	Out of Playoffs
2011-12	82	23	13	....	5	14	22	....	5	37	35	....	10	225	246	84	4th, SE	11th, East	Out of Playoffs
2010-11*	82	17	17	....	7	17	19	....	5	34	36	....	12	223	269	80	4th, SE	12th, East	Out of Playoffs
2009-10*	82	19	16	....	6	16	18	....	7	35	34	....	13	234	256	83	2nd, SE	8th, East	Out of Playoffs
2008-09*	82	18	21	....	2	17	20	....	4	35	41	....	6	·257	280	76	4th, SE	13th, East	Out of Playoffs
2007-08*	82	19	19	....	3	15	21	....	5	34	40	....	8	216	272	76	4th, SE	14th, East	Out of Playoffs
2006-07*	82	23	12	....	6	20	16	....	5	43	28	....	11	246	245	97	1st, SE	3rd, East	Lost Conf. Quarter-Final
2005-06*	82	24	13	....	4	17	20	....	4	41	33	....	8	281	275	90	3rd, SE	10th, East	Out of Playoffs
2004-05*	....	....				....				....									
2003-04*	82	18	17	4	2	15	20	3	2	33	37	8	4	214	243	78	2nd, SE	10th, East	Out of Playoffs
2002-03*	82	15	19	4	3	16	20	3	2	31	39	7	5	226	284	74	3rd, SE	11th, East	Out of Playoffs
2001-02*	82	11	21	9	0	8	26	2	5	19	47	11	5	187	288	54	5th, SE	15th, East	Out of Playoffs
2000-01*	82	10	23	6	2	13	22	6	0	23	45	12	2	211	289	60	4th, SE	13th, East	Out of Playoffs
1999-2000*	82	9	26	3	3	5	31	4	1	14	57	7	4	170	313	39	5th, SE	15th, East	Out of Playoffs

* Atlanta Thrashers

2015-16 Schedule

Oct.	Thu.	8	at Boston		Sun.	10	Buffalo*
	Fri.	9	at New Jersey		Tue.	12	San Jose
	Mon.	12	at NY Islanders*		Thu.	14	Nashville
	Tue.	13	at NY Rangers		Fri.	15	at Minnesota
	Fri.	16	Calgary		Mon.	18	Colorado
	Sun.	18	St. Louis*		Thu.	21	Nashville
	Fri.	23	Tampa Bay		Sat.	23	New Jersey
	Sun.	25	Minnesota*		Tue.	26	Arizona
	Tue.	27	Los Angeles	Feb.	Tue.	2	Dallas
	Thu.	29	Chicago		Fri.	5	Carolina
	Sat.	31	at Columbus		Sat.	6	at Colorado
Nov.	Sun.	1	at Montreal		Tue.	9	at St. Louis
	Wed.	4	at Toronto		Thu.	11	Boston
	Thu.	5	at Ottawa		Sat.	13	at Edmonton
	Sat.	7	Philadelphia		Tue.	16	at Carolina
	Tue.	10	at Minnesota		Thu.	18	at Tampa Bay
	Thu.	12	at Dallas		Sat.	20	at Florida
	Sat.	14	at Nashville		Tue.	23	Dallas
	Mon.	16	at St. Louis		Thu.	25	at Dallas
	Wed.	18	Vancouver		Sat.	27	at Pittsburgh*
	Sat.	21	Arizona	Mar.	Tue.	1	Florida
	Mon.	23	Colorado		Thu.	3	NY Islanders
	Wed.	25	at Washington		Sat.	5	Montreal
	Fri.	27	at Minnesota*		Sun.	6	Edmonton
	Sat.	28	at Colorado		Tue.	8	Nashville
Dec.	Wed.	2	Toronto		Thu.	10	at Detroit
	Sat.	5	Washington*		Sat.	12	Colorado
	Sun.	6	at Chicago*		Mon.	14	at Vancouver
	Thu.	10	Columbus		Wed.	16	at Calgary
	Fri.	11	at Chicago		Fri.	18	Chicago
	Tue.	15	St. Louis		Sun.	20	Anaheim*
	Fri.	18	NY Rangers		Tue.	22	Vancouver
	Mon.	21	at Edmonton		Thu.	24	Los Angeles
	Tue.	22	at Calgary		Sat.	26	at Buffalo*
	Sun.	27	Pittsburgh		Mon.	28	at Philadelphia
	Tue.	29	Detroit		Wed.	30	Ottawa
	Thu.	31	at Arizona	Apr.	Fri.	1	Chicago
Jan.	Sat.	2	at San Jose		Sun.	3	Minnesota
	Sun.	3	at Anaheim		Tue.	5	at Anaheim
	Tue.	5	at Nashville		Thu.	7	at San Jose
	Thu.	7	at Dallas		Sat.	9	at Los Angeles

* Denotes afternoon game.

Blake Wheeler and Mark Scheifele stand at the Jets bench on April 20, 2015, in front of white-clad fans in the stands prior to the first playoff game in Winnipeg since 1996.

CENTRAL DIVISION
17th NHL Season

Franchise date: June 25, 1997

Transferred from Atlanta to Winnipeg, June 21, 2011.

2015-16 Player Personnel

FORWARDS	HT	WT	*Age	Place of Birth	S	2014-15 Club
BURMISTROV, Alexander	6-1	180	23	Kazan, Russia	L	Kazan
CORMIER, Patrice	6-2	215	25	Moncton, NB	L	Winnipeg-St. John's
FRASER, Matt	6-1	204	25	Red Deer, AB	L	Boston-Edmonton
HALISCHUK, Matt	5-11	187	27	Toronto, ON	R	Winnipeg
LADD, Andrew	6-3	205	29	Maple Ridge, BC	L	Winnipeg
LITTLE, Bryan	5-11	185	27	Edmonton, AB	R	Winnipeg
LOWRY, Adam	6-5	210	22	St. Louis, MO	L	Winnipeg
PELUSO, Anthony	6-3	235	26	North York, ON	R	Winnipeg
PERREAULT, Mathieu	5-10	185	27	Drummondville, QC	L	Winnipeg
SCHEIFELE, Mark	6-2	195	22	Kitchener, ON	R	Winnipeg
STAFFORD, Drew	6-2	214	29	Milwaukee, WI	R	Buffalo-Winnipeg
THORBURN, Chris	6-3	230	32	Sault Ste. Marie, ON	R	Winnipeg
WHEELER, Blake	6-5	225	29	Robbinsdale, MN	R	Winnipeg
DEFENSEMEN						
BYFUGLIEN, Dustin	6-5	265	30	Minneapolis, MN	R	Winnipeg
CHIAROT, Ben	6-3	215	24	Hamilton, ON	L	Winnipeg-St. John's
CLITSOME, Grant	5-11	215	30	Gloucester, ON	L	Winnipeg
ENSTROM, Toby	5-10	180	30	Nordingra, Sweden	L	Winnipeg
HARRISON, Jay	6-4	220	32	Oshawa, ON	L	Carolina-Winnipeg
MYERS, Tyler	6-8	219	25	Houston, TX	R	Buffalo-Winnipeg
PARDY, Adam	6-4	220	31	Bonavista, NL	L	Winnipeg
POSTMA, Paul	6-3	195	26	Red Deer, AB	R	Winnipeg
STUART, Mark	6-2	213	31	Rochester, MN	L	Winnipeg
TROUBA, Jacob	6-2	187	21	Rochester, MI	R	Winnipeg

GOALTENDERS	HT	WT	*Age	Place of Birth	C	2014-15 Club
HUTCHINSON, Michael	6-3	192	25	Barrie, ON	R	Winnipeg
PAVELEC, Ondrej	6-3	220	28	Kladno, Czech.	L	Winnipeg

* – Age at start of 2015-16 season

Paul Maurice

Head Coach

Born: Sault Ste. Marie, ON, January 30, 1967.

The Winnipeg Jets announced on January 12, 2014 that Paul Maurice had been hired as their head coach. He is the second head coach in franchise history since the team's move from Atlanta to Winnipeg in 2011. In his first full season behind the bench in 2014-15, Maurice led the Jets to the playoffs for just the second time in franchise history.

Maurice had a career NHL coaching record of 460-457-167 in 14 seasons with the Carolina Hurricanes/Hartford Whalers and the Toronto Maple Leafs. He won his 400th career NHL game when the Hurricanes defeated the Buffalo Sabres in overtime on February 11, 2010, and on November 28, 2010, he became the 19th coach, and the youngest in history, to coach 1,000 NHL games. In his first head coaching stint with the Hurricanes, Maurice guided Carolina to the 2002 Eastern Conference title and two Southeast Division crowns as well as four consecutive winning seasons from 1998 to 2002. On March 16, 2010, he became just the 10th coach in NHL history to spend more than 800 games behind the bench for one franchise.

Prior to re-joining the Hurricanes, the Sault Ste. Marie, Ontario native collected a record of 76-66-22 during two full seasons as head coach of the Toronto Maple Leafs from 2006 to 2008. Maurice led the Maple Leafs to 40 victories in 2006-07 and recorded his 300th NHL victory on March 6, 2007. Most recently, Maurice spent the 2012-13 season as head coach of Magnitogorsk Metallurg of the KHL.

Prior to moving to the NHL level during the summer of 1995 as an assistant coach with the Hartford Whalers, Maurice spent two seasons as head coach of the Ontario Hockey League's Detroit Jr. Red Wings. While in Detroit, he compiled a regular-season record of 86-38-8 and led the team to the 1995 OHL Championship and an appearance in the Memorial Cup. That season, he finished second in voting to Guelph's Craig Hartsburg for the Matt Leyden Trophy, which is annually awarded to the OHL's Coach of the Year.

Maurice played his junior hockey with the OHL's Windsor Spitfires (1984 to 1988) and was Philadelphia's 12th choice, 252nd overall, in the 1985 NHL Draft. Maurice had his career cut short due to an eye injury, and began coaching as an assistant with the Jr. Red Wings shortly thereafter.

Coaching Record

			Regular Season				Playoffs			
Season	Team	League	GC	W	L	O/T	GC	W	L	T
1993-94	Detroit	OHL	66	42	20	4	17	11	6	....
1994-95	Detroit	OHL	44	18	4	....	21	16	5	....
1994-95	Detroit	M-Cup	....	....	....	....	5	3	2	....
1995-96	**Hartford**	**NHL**	**70**	**29**	**33**	**8**	....	....	....	....
1996-97	**Hartford**	**NHL**	**82**	**32**	**39**	**11**	....	....	....	....
1997-98	**Carolina**	**NHL**	**82**	**33**	**41**	**8**	....	....	....	....
1998-99	**Carolina**	**NHL**	**82**	**34**	**30**	**18**	**6**	**2**	**4**	....
99-2000	**Carolina**	**NHL**	**82**	**37**	**35**	**10**	....	....	....	....
2000-01	**Carolina**	**NHL**	**82**	**38**	**32**	**12**	**6**	**2**	**4**	....
2001-02	**Carolina**	**NHL**	**82**	**35**	**26**	**21**	**23**	**13**	**10**	....
2002-03	**Carolina**	**NHL**	**82**	**22**	**43**	**17**	....	....	....	....
2003-04	**Carolina**	**NHL**	**30**	**8**	**12**	**10**	....	....	....	....
2005-06	Toronto	AHL	80	41	29	10	5	1	4	....
2006-07	**Toronto**	**NHL**	**82**	**40**	**31**	**11**	....	....	....	....
2007-08	**Toronto**	**NHL**	**82**	**36**	**35**	**11**	....	....	....	....
2008-09	**Carolina**	**NHL**	**57**	**33**	**19**	**5**	**18**	**8**	**10**	....
2009-10	**Carolina**	**NHL**	**82**	**35**	**37**	**10**	....	....	....	....
2010-11	**Carolina**	**NHL**	**82**	**40**	**31**	**11**	....	....	....	....
2011-12	**Carolina**	**NHL**	**25**	**8**	**13**	**4**	....	....	....	....
2012-13	Magnitogorsk	KHL	52	27	13	12	7	3	4	....
2013-14	**Winnipeg**	**NHL**	**35**	**18**	**12**	**5**	....	....	....	....
2014-15	**Winnipeg**	**NHL**	**82**	**43**	**26**	**13**	**4**	**0**	**4**	....
	NHL Totals		**1201**	**521**	**495**	**185**	**57**	**25**	**32**	....

2014-15 Scoring

* – rookie

Regular Season

Pos	#	Player	Team	GP	G	A	Pts	TOI	+/–	PIM	PP	SH	GW	S	S%
L	16	Andrew Ladd	WPG	81	24	38	62	20:04	9	72	9	0	6	224	10.7
R	26	Blake Wheeler	WPG	79	26	35	61	19:39	26	73	2	4	6	244	10.7
C	18	Bryan Little	WPG	70	24	28	52	19:55	8	24	9	1	3	148	16.2
C	55	Mark Scheifele	WPG	82	15	34	49	18:35	11	24	3	0	2	170	8.8
D	33	Dustin Byfuglien	WPG	69	18	27	45	22:41	5	124	5	0	3	209	8.6
R	12	Drew Stafford	BUF	50	9	15	24	15:58	–18	39	2	0	1	91	9.9
			WPG	26	9	10	19	17:29	6	8	2	0	0	56	16.1
			Total	76	18	25	43	16:29	–12	47	4	0	1	147	12.2
R	67	Michael Frolik	WPG	82	19	23	42	17:30	4	18	3	3	4	206	9.2
C	85	Mathieu Perreault	WPG	62	18	23	41	16:15	7	38	5	0	2	129	14.0
C	91	Jiri Tlusty	CAR	52	13	10	23	17:12	–17	16	6	0	0	97	13.4
			WPG	20	1	7	8	12:56	–1	4	0	0	0	26	3.8
			Total	72	14	17	31	16:01	–18	20	6	0	0	123	11.4
R	20	Lee Stempniak	NYR	53	9	9	18	12:26	7	18	0	0	1	86	10.5
			WPG	18	6	4	10	13:33	1	2	0	0	2	29	20.7
			Total	71	15	13	28	12:43	8	20	0	0	3	115	13.0
D	57	Tyler Myers	BUF	47	4	9	13	25:03	–15	61	1	0	0	72	5.6
			WPG	24	3	12	15	23:49	9	16	1	0	0	52	5.8
			Total	71	7	21	28	24:38	–6	77	2	0	0	124	5.6
L	17 *	Adam Lowry	WPG	80	11	12	23	13:45	1	46	0	1	2	104	10.6
D	39	Toby Enstrom	WPG	60	4	19	23	23:34	13	36	1	0	0	58	6.9
L	9	Evander Kane	WPG	37	10	12	22	19:18	–1	56	4	1	1	126	7.9
D	8	Jacob Trouba	WPG	65	7	15	22	23:18	2	46	1	0	0	133	5.3
R	22	Chris Thorburn	WPG	81	7	7	14	8:05	–5	76	0	0	2	67	10.4
D	5	Mark Stuart	WPG	70	2	12	14	19:12	5	69	0	0	1	51	3.9
C	19	Jim Slater	WPG	82	5	8	13	9:12	–4	58	0	0	1	51	9.8
D	23	Jay Harrison	CAR	20	1	3	4	16:30	–5	42	0	0	0	23	4.3
			WPG	35	2	3	5	15:36	4	23	1	0	0	27	7.4
			Total	55	3	6	9	15:55	–1	65	1	0	0	50	6.0
D	2	Adam Pardy	WPG	55	0	9	9	15:01	9	40	0	0	0	29	0.0
R	15	Matt Halischuk	WPG	47	3	5	8	9:44	5	6	0	0	1	59	5.1
D	63 *	Ben Chiarot	WPG	40	2	6	8	17:01	5	22	0	0	0	37	5.4
D	4	Paul Postma	WPG	42	2	4	6	14:07	1	16	2	0	0	40	5.0
D	24	Grant Clitsome	WPG	24	0	4	4	16:21	4	8	0	0	0	22	0.0
R	14	Anthony Peluso	WPG	49	1	1	2	5:52	–3	86	0	0	0	23	4.3
L	21	Tj Galiardi	WPG	38	1	0	1	10:27	–8	2	0	0	0	35	2.9
D	7	Keaton Ellerby	WPG	1	0	1	1	16:58	–1	0	0	0	0	0	0.0
C	51 *	Andrew Copp	WPG	1	0	1	1	13:16	2	0	0	0	0	4	0.0
C	58	Eric O'Dell	WPG	11	0	1	1	7:26	0	19	0	0	0	6	0.0
C	28	Patrice Cormier	WPG	1	0	0	0	4:54	0	0	0	0	0	0	0.0
D	49	Julien Brouillette	WPG	1	0	0	0	9:33	0	0	0	0	0	0	0.0
L	48 *	Carl Klingberg	WPG	2	0	0	0	3:18	–1	0	0	0	0	0	0.0

Goaltending

No.	Goaltender	GPI	Mins	Avg	W	L	OT	EN	SO	GA	SA	Sv%	G	A	PIM
31	Ondrej Pavelec	50	2838	2.28	22	16	8	6	5	108	1353	.920	0	0	2
34	* Michael Hutchinso	38	2138	2.39	21	10	5	5	2	85	986	.914	0	0	0
	Totals	**82**	**5010**	**2.44**	**43**	**26**	**13**	**11**	**7**	**204**	**2350**	**.913**			

Playoffs

Pos	#	Player	Team	GP	G	A	Pts	TOI	+/–	PIM	PP	SH	GW	OT	S	S%
C	18	Bryan Little	WPG	4	2	1	3	19:15	–3	0	1	0	0	0	10	20.0
L	17 *	Adam Lowry	WPG	4	1	2	3	14:46	0	2	0	0	0	0	5	20.0
D	5	Mark Stuart	WPG	4	1	1	2	17:45	1	2	0	0	0	0	3	33.3
R	12	Drew Stafford	WPG	4	1	1	2	17:19	–1	0	0	0	0	0	9	11.1
C	85	Mathieu Perreault	WPG	3	0	2	2	17:03	–2	0	0	0	0	0	8	0.0
D	8	Jacob Trouba	WPG	4	0	2	2	19:05	–1	2	0	0	0	0	8	0.0
D	2	Adam Pardy	WPG	2	1	0	1	18:16	–1	2	0	0	0	0	3	33.3
R	20	Lee Stempniak	WPG	4	1	0	1	12:44	2	0	0	0	0	0	8	12.5
R	26	Blake Wheeler	WPG	4	1	0	1	19:14	–3	2	0	0	0	0	11	9.1
D	57	Tyler Myers	WPG	4	1	0	1	24:22	–2	2	1	0	0	0	6	16.7
D	39	Toby Enstrom	WPG	4	0	1	1	20:46	–3	0	0	0	0	0	3	0.0
D	33	Dustin Byfuglien	WPG	4	0	1	1	23:00	–4	4	0	0	0	0	12	0.0
L	16	Andrew Ladd	WPG	4	0	1	1	20:29	–3	4	0	0	0	0	13	0.0
C	55	Mark Scheifele	WPG	4	0	1	1	17:40	–2	4	0	0	0	0	2	0.0
R	15	Matt Halischuk	WPG	1	0	0	0	9:18	–1	0	0	0	0	0	1	0.0
D	63 *	Ben Chiarot	WPG	2	0	0	0	13:42	–2	2	0	0	0	0	2	0.0
R	22	Chris Thorburn	WPG	4	0	0	0	7:29	0	0	0	0	0	0	4	0.0
C	19	Jim Slater	WPG	4	0	0	0	9:33	–1	0	0	0	0	0	2	0.0
C	91	Jiri Tlusty	WPG	4	0	0	0	10:12	–2	0	0	0	0	0	2	0.0
R	67	Michael Frolik	WPG	4	0	0	0	17:22	–2	2	0	0	0	0	6	0.0

Goaltending

No.	Goaltender	GPI	Mins	Avg	W	L	EN	SO	GA	SA	Sv%	G	A	PIM
31	Ondrej Pavelec	4	241	3.73	0	4	1	0	15	137	.891	0	0	0
	Totals	**4**	**245**	**3.92**	**0**	**4**	**1**	**0**	**16**	**138**	**.884**			

Club Records

Team
(Figures in brackets for season records are games played.)

Most Points	99	2014-15 (82)
Most Wins	43	2006-07 (82), 2014-15 (82)
Most Ties	12	2000-01 (82)
Most Losses	57	1999-2000 (82)
Most Goals	281	2005-06 (82)
Most Goals Against	313	1999-2000 (82)
Fewest Points	39	1999-2000 (82)
Fewest Wins	14	1999-2000 (82)
Fewest Ties	7	1999-2000 (82), 2002-03 (82)
Fewest Losses	28	2006-07 (82)
Fewest Goals	170	1999-2000 (82)
Fewest Goals Against	204	2014-15 (82)

Longest Winning Streak
Overall...........6 Mar. 6-16/09, Nov. 19-30/10
Home.............7 Mar. 2-18/07
Away.............4 Jan. 13-Feb. 7/03, Nov. 3-21/07, Feb. 3-16/09, Nov. 12-Dec. 5/09

Longest Undefeated Streak
Overall...........6 Mar. 6-16/09 (6w), Nov. 19-30/10 (6w)
Home.............7 Mar. 2-18/07 (7w)

Away.............7 Oct. 21-Nov. 13/00 (3w, 4T/OL)

Longest Losing Streak
Overall...........12 Jan. 24-Feb. 20/00
Home.............11 Jan. 24-Mar. 16/00
Away.............10 Oct. 6-Nov. 18/01, Feb. 16-Mar. 18/08

Longest Winless Streak
Overall...........16 Jan. 16-Feb. 20/00 (14L, 2T/OL)
Home.............*17 Jan. 19-Mar. 29/00 (15L, 2T/OL)
Away.............10 Oct. 6-Nov. 18/01 (10L)

Most Shutouts, Season.......7 2014-15 (82)
Most PIM, Season.......1,505 2003-04 (82)
Most Goals, Game.........9 Nov. 12/05 (Atl. 9 at Car. 0)

Individual

Most Seasons	8	Ilya Kovalchuk
Most Games	594	Ilya Kovalchuk
Most Goals, Career	328	Ilya Kovalchuk
Most Assists, Career	287	Ilya Kovalchuk
Most Points, Career	615	Ilya Kovalchuk (328G, 287A)
Most PIM, Career	656	Chris Thorburn
Most Shutouts, Career	16	Ondrej Pavelec

Longest Consecutive
Games Streak.........252 Vyacheslav Kozlov (Jan. 9/07-Jan. 21/10)
Most Goals, Season.........52 Ilya Kovalchuk (2005-06), (2007-08)

Most Assists, Season	69	Marc Savard (2005-06)
Most Points, Season	100	Marian Hossa (2006-07; 43G, 57A)
Most PIM, Season	226	Jeff Odgers (2000-01)

Most Points, Defenseman,
Season.................53 Dustin Byfuglien (2010-11; 20G, 33A) (2011-12; 12G, 41A)

Most Points, Center,
Season.................97 Marc Savard (2005-06; 28G, 69A)

Most Points, Right Wing,
Season.................100 Marian Hossa (2006-07; 43G, 57A)

Most Points, Left Wing,
Season.................98 Ilya Kovalchuk (2005-06; 52G, 46A)

Most Points, Rookie,
Season.................67 Dany Heatley (2001-02; 26G, 41A)

Most Shutouts, Season.......5 Ondrej Pavelec (2014-15)

Most Goals, Game.........4 Pascal Rheaume (Jan. 19/02), Ilya Kovalchuk (Nov. 11/05)

Most Assists, Game.........4 Seven times
Most Points, Game.........5 Seven times

* NHL Record.
Records include Atlanta Thrashers, 1999-2000 through 2010-11.

Captains' History
Kelly Buchberger, 1999-2000; Steve Staios, 2000-01; Ray Ferraro, 2001-02; Shawn McEachern, 2002-03, 2003-04; Scott Mellanby, 2005-06, 2006-07; Bobby Holik, 2007-08; no captain and Ilya Kovalchuk, 2008-09; Ilya Kovalchuk, 2009-10; Andrew Ladd, 2010-11 to date.

Coaching History
Curt Fraser, 1999-2000 to 2001-02; Curt Fraser, Don Waddell and Bob Hartley, 2002-03; Bob Hartley, 2003-04 to 2006-07; Bob Hartley and Don Waddell, 2007-08; John Anderson, 2008-09, 2009-10; Craig Ramsay, 2010-11; Claude Noel, 2011-12, 2012-13; Claude Noel and Paul Maurice, 2013-14; Paul Maurice, 2014-15 to date.

General Managers' History
Don Waddell, 1999-2000 to 2009-10; Rick Dudley, 2010-11; Kevin Cheveldayoff, 2011-12 to date.

All-time Record vs. Other Clubs
Regular Season

	Total								At Home								On Road							
	GP	W	L	T	OL	GF	GA	PTS	GP	W	L	T	OL	GF	GA	PTS	GP	W	L	T	OL	GF	GA	PTS
Anaheim	20	8	9	0	3	58	67	19	10	3	6	0	1	24	33	7	10	5	3	0	2	34	34	12
Arizona	22	7	11	1	3	50	66	18	10	5	3	0	2	25	26	12	12	2	8	1	1	25	40	6
Boston	55	21	26	4	6	156	172	50	28	15	12	0	1	80	74	31	27	6	14	2	5	76	98	19
Buffalo	55	32	17	1	5	165	181	70	27	19	4	1	3	90	69	42	28	13	13	0	2	75	112	28
Calgary	19	8	9	1	1	54	61	18	10	6	2	1	1	31	25	14	9	2	7	0	0	23	36	4
Carolina	82	31	38	4	9	234	258	75	41	11	23	3	4	107	139	29	41	20	15	1	5	127	119	46
Chicago	21	7	10	0	4	55	65	18	11	2	6	0	3	31	40	7	10	5	4	0	1	24	25	11
Colorado	27	14	6	1	6	79	74	35	13	7	3	1	2	41	35	17	14	7	3	0	4	38	39	18
Columbus	18	8	9	0	1	40	45	17	9	4	5	0	0	20	23	8	9	4	4	0	1	20	22	9
Dallas	23	8	14	0	1	61	72	17	12	4	7	0	1	41	47	9	11	4	7	0	0	20	25	8
Detroit	18	7	9	0	2	56	74	16	8	3	5	0	0	29	38	6	10	4	4	0	2	27	36	10
Edmonton	19	9	9	1	0	52	65	19	9	5	4	0	0	22	27	10	10	4	5	1	0	30	38	9
Florida	83	45	25	5	8	267	226	103	41	24	9	4	4	147	110	56	42	21	16	1	4	120	116	47
Los Angeles	20	9	11	0	0	63	73	18	10	6	4	0	0	32	26	12	10	3	7	0	0	31	47	6
Minnesota	22	9	10	1	2	54	59	21	11	5	5	0	1	30	30	11	11	4	5	1	1	24	29	10
Montreal	55	18	31	2	4	119	167	42	27	14	13	0	2	57	70	24	28	8	18	0	2	62	97	18
Nashville	26	10	12	1	3	65	71	24	13	6	4	1	2	35	31	15	13	4	8	0	1	30	40	9
New Jersey	55	21	26	3	5	128	163	50	27	10	14	2	1	66	83	23	28	11	12	1	4	62	80	27
NY Islanders	55	23	25	2	5	161	197	53	28	9	13	2	4	83	106	24	27	14	12	0	1	78	91	29
NY Rangers	55	28	23	1	3	153	159	60	27	11	14	0	2	73	85	24	28	17	9	1	1	80	74	36
Ottawa	55	21	32	2	0	163	209	44	27	10	16	1	0	92	103	21	28	11	16	1	0	71	106	23
Philadelphia	55	16	31	3	5	150	201	40	28	8	15	1	4	71	95	21	27	8	16	2	1	79	106	19
Pittsburgh	55	13	36	0	6	145	211	32	28	9	16	0	3	74	92	21	27	4	20	0	3	71	119	11
St. Louis	25	8	12	1	4	57	75	21	14	5	6	1	2	35	41	13	11	3	6	0	2	22	34	8
San Jose	20	5	13	2	0	42	64	12	10	2	6	0	2	23	31	7	10	2	7	1	0	19	33	5
Tampa Bay	82	36	29	4	13	229	258	89	41	22	10	3	6	132	116	53	41	14	19	1	7	97	142	36
Toronto	53	23	24	1	5	141	187	52	27	13	12	0	2	66	92	28	26	10	12	1	3	75	95	24
Vancouver	18	5	10	1	2	44	60	13	9	4	4	0	1	28	30	9	9	1	6	1	1	16	30	4
Washington	83	33	37	5	8	234	271	79	42	21	16	2	3	117	122	47	41	12	21	3	5	117	149	32
Totals	**1196**	**483**	**554**	**45**	**114**	**3275**	**3851**	**1125**	**598**	**260**	**257**	**26**	**55**	**1702**	**1839**	**601**	**598**	**223**	**297**	**19**	**59**	**1573**	**2012**	**524**

Playoffs

	Series	W	L	GP	W	L	T	GF	GA	Last Mtg.	Rnd.	Result
Anaheim	1	0	1	4	0	4	0	9	16	2015	FR	L 0-4
NY Rangers	1	0	1	4	0	4	0	6	17	2007	CQF	L 0-4
Totals	**2**	**0**	**2**	**8**	**0**	**8**	**0**	**15**	**33**			

Playoff Results 2015-2011

Year	Round	Opponent	Result	GF	GA
2015	FR	Anaheim	L 0-4	9	16

Abbreviations: Round: CQF – conference quarter-final; **FR** – first round.

2014-15 Results

Oct.								
9	at Arizona	6-2		10	at Los Angeles	5-4†
11	at San Jose	0-3		11	at Anaheim	4-5†
12	at Los Angeles	1-4		13	Florida	8-2
17	Nashville	0-2		15	at Dallas	2-1
19	Calgary	1-4		16	at Chicago	4-2
21	Carolina	3-1		18	Arizona	4-3†
24	Tampa Bay	1-4		21	Columbus	4-5
26	Colorado	2-1*		27	at Pittsburgh	3-5
28	at NY Islanders	4-3		29	at Philadelphia	2-5
30	at New Jersey	1-2†		31	Dallas	2-5

Nov.				Feb.			
1	at NY Rangers	1-0†		2	at Calgary	2-5
2	at Chicago	1-0		3	at Vancouver	2-3*
4	Nashville	3-1		6	Chicago	1-2*
6	Pittsburgh	3-4†		8	Colorado	5-3
8	at Ottawa	2-1†		10	Minnesota	2-1*
11	at Montreal	0-3		12	at Nashville	1-3
13	at Carolina	3-1		14	at Detroit	5-4†
15	at Nashville	1-2		16	Edmonton	5-4†
16	at Minnesota	3-4*		19	at Washington	1-5
18	New Jersey	3-1		21	at Toronto	3-4*
20	Detroit	3-4		24	Dallas	4-2
23	St. Louis	2-4		26	St. Louis	1-2†
25	at Columbus	4-2	Mar.	1	Los Angeles	5-2
26	at Buffalo	2-1		4	Ottawa	1-3
28	at Boston	1-2*		7	at Nashville	3-1

Dec.							
3	Edmonton	3-2*		10	at St. Louis	4-5
5	Colorado	6-2		12	at Florida	2-4
7	Anaheim	3-4*		14	at Tampa Bay	2-4
9	at Dallas	5-2		17	San Jose	5-2
11	at Colorado	3-4†		19	St. Louis	2-1†
13	Anaheim	1-4		21	Washington	3-0
16	Buffalo	5-1		23	at Edmonton	4-1
19	Boston	2-1		24	at Vancouver	2-5
21	Philadelphia	3-4*		26	Montreal	5-2
23	at Chicago	5-1		29	Chicago	3-4
27	at Minnesota	4-3*		31	NY Rangers	2-3
29	Minnesota	2-3	Apr.	4	at Vancouver	2-4
31	NY Islanders	2-5		6	at Minnesota	2-0

Jan.							
3	Toronto	5-1		7	at St. Louis	1-0
5	San Jose	2-3		9	at Colorado	0-1†
8	at Arizona	1-4		11	Calgary	5-1

* – Overtime † – Shootout

NHL Draft Selections 2015-2001

Name in bold denotes played in NHL.

2015 Pick		2011 Pick		2007 Pick		2003 Pick	
17	Kyle Connor	7	**Mark Scheifele**	67	**Spencer Machacek**	8	**Braydon Coburn**
25	Jack Roslovic	67	**Adam Lowry**	115	Niclas Lucenius	110	Jim Sharrow
47	Jansen Harkins	78	Brennan Serville	175	**John Albert**	116	**Guillaume Desbiens**
78	Erik Foley	119	Zachary Yuen	205	**Paul Postma**	136	Michael Vannelli
108	Michael Spacek	149	Austen Brassard			145	**Brett Sterling**
168	Mason Appleton	157	Jason Kasdorf	**2006 Pick**		175	Mike Hamilton
198	Sami Niku	187	Aaron Harstad	12	**Bryan Little**	203	Denis Loginov
203	Matteo Gennaro			43	Riley Holzapfel	239	**Toby Enstrom**
		2010 Pick		80	Michael Forney	269	Rylan Kaip

2014 Pick				135	Alex Kangas		
9	Nikolaj Ehlers	8	**Alexander**	165	Jonas Enlund	**2002 Pick**	
69	Jack Glover		**Burmistrov**	195	Jesse Martin	2	**Kari Lehtonen**
99	Chase De Leo	87	**Julian Melchiori**	200	**Arturs Kulda**	30	**Jim Slater**
101	Nelson Nogier	101	Ivan Telegin	210	Will O'Neill	116	**Patrick Dwyer**
129	C.J. Franklin	128	Fredrik			124	Lane Manson
164	Pavel Kraskovsky		Pettersson-Wentzel	**2005 Pick**		144	Paul Flache
192	Matt Ustaski	150	Yasin Cisse	16	Alex Bourret	167	Brad Schell
		155	Kendall McFaull	41	**Ondrej Pavelec**	198	**Nathan Oystrick**
2013 Pick		160	Tanner Lane	49	Chad Denny	230	Colton Fretter
13	Josh Morrissey	169	Sebastian Owuya	53	Andrew Kozek	236	Tyler Boldt
43	Nic Petan	199	Peter Stoykewych	116	**Jordan Smotherman**	257	Pauli Levokari
59	Eric Comrie			135	Tomas Pospisil		
84	Jimmy Lodge	**2009 Pick**		187	**Andrei Zubarev**	**2001 Pick**	
91	J.C. Lipon	4	**Evander Kane**	207	Myles Stoesz	1	**Ilya Kovalchuk**
104	**Andrew Copp**	34	**Carl Klingberg**			80	**Michael Garnett**
114	Jan Kostalek	45	**Jeremy Morin**	**2004 Pick**		100	Brian Sipotz
127	Tucker Poolman	117	Eddie Pasquale	10	**Boris Valabik**	112	Milan Gajic
190	Brenden Kichton	120	**Ben Chiarot**	40	**Grant Lewis**	135	**Colin Stuart**
194	Marcus Karlstrom	125	Cody Sol	76	**Scott Lehman**	189	**Pasi Nurminen**
		155	Jimmy Bubnick	106	Chad Painchaud	199	Matt Suderman
2012 Pick		185	Levko Koper	142	Juraj Gracik	201	Colin FitzRandolph
9	**Jacob Trouba**	203	Jordan Samuels-Thomas	186	Dan Turple	262	Mario Cartelli
39	Lukas Sutter			204	Miikka Tuomainen		
70	Scott Kosmachuk	**2008 Pick**		237	Mitch Carefoot		
130	Connor Hellebuyck	3	**Zach Bogosian**	270	Matt Siddall		
160	Ryan Olsen	29	Daultan Leveille				
190	Jamie Phillips	64	Danick Paquette				
		94	Vinny Saponari				
		124	Nicklas Lasu				
		154	Chris Carrozzi				
		184	**Zach Redmond**				

Kevin Cheveldayoff
Executive Vice President and General Manager

Born: Blaine Lake, SK, February 4, 1970.

Kevin Cheveldayoff was given his first assignment as general manager of an NHL hockey club when he was named to the position by the Winnipeg Jets on June 8, 2011. In 2014-15 the team reached the playoffs for the first time.

Prior to joining the Jets, Cheveldayoff had spent two seasons with the Chicago Blackhawks and served as the club's assistant general manager/senior director, hockey operations in 2010-11. During his tenure in Chicago, the Blackhawks won the 2010 Stanley Cup championship, the team's first since 1961.

Before joining the Blackhawks on August 3, 2009, Cheveldayoff spent the previous 12 seasons as the general manager of the Chicago Wolves, guiding the franchise to four league championships, which included the 2002 and 2008 Calder Cup titles in the American Hockey League and the 1998 and 2000 International Hockey League's Turner Cup. Overall, Cheveldayoff was a part of seven league championships during his 15-year management career before being hired in Winnipeg, including two Turner Cup titles in three seasons as the assistant vice president of hockey operations and assistant coach for the Denver and Utah Grizzlies (1994 to 1997).

Cheveldayoff was the architect of 12 Wolves teams that compiled a .615 regular-season winning percentage (544-320-114) and 10 postseason berths from 1997 to 2009. Eight of those clubs reached the 100-point mark during the regular season while earning four division titles and six postseason conference championships.

Cheveldayoff was originally drafted by the New York Islanders with their first pick (16th overall) in the 1988 NHL Draft. He began his career in the AHL with the Capital District Islanders, serving as the alternate captain from 1991 to 1993. He held the same role with the Salt Lake Golden Eagles in 1993-94, earning the team's "Unsung Hero Award" after racking up a career-high 216 penalty minutes in 73 games. Known as a defensive defenseman during his playing days, a knee injury cut his professional career short after five seasons.

Club Directory

MTS Centre

Winnipeg Jets
MTS Centre
345 Graham Avenue
Winnipeg, Manitoba, R3C 5S6
Phone **204/987-7825**
FAX 204/926-5555
www.winnipegjets.com
Twitter @NHLJets
Capacity: 15,294

Senior Management
Executive Chairman & Governor	Mark Chipman
Executive VP & Chief Operating Officer	John Olfert
Executive VP & General Manager	Kevin Cheveldayoff
President, TN Development	Jim Ludlow
Senior VP & Assistant General Manager	Craig Heisinger
Senior VP, Venues & Entertainment	Kevin Donnelly
Senior VP, Sales & Marketing	Norva Riddell
VP, Finance & CFO	Lorna Daniels
VP, Patron & Venue Services	Robert Thorsten
VP, Marketing & Brand Development	Dorian Morphy
VP, Human Resources	Dawn Haus
VP, Corporate Partnerships	Matt Cockell
VP, AHL Operations & General Counsel	Dan Hursh
General Manager, MTS Iceplex	Gavin Johnstone

Hockey Operations
Executive VP & General Manager	Kevin Cheveldayoff
Senior VP & Assistant General Manager	Craig Heisinger
Assistant General Manager	Larry Simmons
Executive Assistant, Hockey Operations	Katie Ferniuk
Head Coach	Paul Maurice
Assistant Coaches	Charlie Huddy, Pascal Vincent
Goaltending Coach	Wade Flaherty
Video Coach	Matt Prefontaine
Head Equipment Manager	Jason McMaster
Assistant Equipment Managers	Mark Grehan, Mike Flaman
Head Athletic Therapist	Rob Milette
Assistant Athletic Therapist	Brad Shaw
Director of Fitness	Dr. Craig Slaunwhite
Massage Therapist	Al Pritchard
Coordinator, Team Travel	Silvana Gosgnach
Director Security, Winnipeg Jets	Ken Shipley
Coordinator, Team Services	Chris Kreviazuk
Scouting & Hockey Video Coordinator	Barrett Leganchuk

Scouting Staff
Director, Pro Scouting	Mark Dobson
Director, Amateur Scouting	Marcel Comeau
Head Scout	Mark Hillier
Pro Scouts	Jack Birch, Bruce Southern, Peter Ratchuk, Carter Sears, Ryan Bowness
Amateur Scouts	Evgeny Bogdanovich, Pat Carmichael, Chris Snell, Scott Scoville, Bob Owen, Yanick Lemay, Ed Friesen, Brian Renfrew, Vladimir Havluj, Scott Robson, Max Giese
Coordinator, Player Development	Jimmy Roy
Player Development Assistant	Mike Keane

Medical Staff
Head Physician	Dr. Peter MacDonald
Assistant Physicians	Dr. Greg Stranges, Dr. Jamie Dubberley
Primary Care	Dr. Mike MacKay, Dr. Swee Teo
Team Dentist	Dr. Gene Solmundson

Marketing & Communications
Senior Director, Game Production & Broadcast Services	Kyle Balharry
Director, Creative & Marketing Services	Josh Dudych
Director, Digital & Marketing Services	Andrew Wilkinson
Senior Director, Corporate Communications	Scott Brown
Manager, Hockey Communications	Keegan Goodrich
Coordinator, Hockey Communications	Zach Peters
Senior Producer, Visual Media	Steve Godkin
Producers, Visual Media	Curtis Robson, Nate Rollo, Braiden Watling
Coordinators, Web Content	Ryan Dittrick, Mitchell Clinton
Coordinator, Digital Media	Fabio Bellisario
Senior Graphic Designer	Jessie Greenwood
Graphic Designers	Allison Ferley, Marc Gomez

Sales
Director, Ticket Administration & CRM	Mitch Brennan
Director, Ticket Sales & Account Service	Linzy Jones

Retail Operations
Director, Retail Operations	Dave Blackmore
Director, Retail Development	Dan Suga

Community Relations
Director, Community Relations	Barrett Paulsen
Marketing & Community Relations Coordinator	Katie Dicks

Finance
VP, Finance & CFO	Lorna Daniels
Controller	Lindsay McLean
Controller	Ashley Paluk

Event Management
Director, Security & Event Management	Kim Boulet
Director, Event Marketing	Alayne Nott
Director, Event Production	Kevin Clifford
Manager, Audio/Video & Broadcast Services	Noah Baird

Information Systems
Director, Information Technology	Dan Gill
Senior Systems Administrator	Darryl Elyk
Network Administrator	Ryan Cullen

Winnipeg Jets True North Foundation
Executive Director, WJTNF	Dwayne Green

Building Operations
Senior Director, Facility Operations	Ed Meichsner
Chief Engineer & Manager, Ice Operations	Derek King

2014-15 Final Standings

Standings

Abbreviations: GP - games played; **W** - wins; **L** - losses; **OT** - overtime and shootout losses; **GF** - goals for; **GA** - goals against; **PTS** - points.

Note: teams receive two points for a Win (W), one point for an Overtime or Shootout Loss (OT)

EASTERN CONFERENCE

Atlantic Division

		GP	W	L	OT	GF	GA	PTS
Montreal	(A1)	82	50	22	10	221	189	110
Tampa Bay	(A2)	82	50	24	8	262	211	108
Detroit	(A3)	82	43	25	14	235	221	100
Ottawa	(W1)	82	43	26	13	238	215	99
Boston		82	41	27	14	213	211	96
Florida		82	38	29	15	206	223	91
Toronto		82	30	44	8	211	262	68
Buffalo		82	23	51	8	161	274	54

Metropolitan Division

		GP	W	L	OT	GF	GA	PTS
NY Rangers	(M1)	82	53	22	7	252	192	113
Washington	(M2)	82	45	26	11	242	203	101
NY Islanders	(M3)	82	47	28	7	252	230	101
Pittsburgh	(W2)	82	43	27	12	221	210	98
Columbus		82	42	35	5	236	250	89
Philadelphia		82	33	31	18	215	234	84
New Jersey		82	32	36	14	181	216	78
Carolina		82	30	41	11	188	226	71

WESTERN CONFERENCE

Central Division

		GP	W	L	OT	GF	GA	PTS
St. Louis	(C1)	82	51	24	7	248	201	109
Nashville	(C2)	82	47	25	10	232	208	104
Chicago	(C3)	82	48	28	6	229	189	102
Minnesota	(W1)	82	46	28	8	231	201	100
Winnipeg	(W2)	82	43	26	13	230	210	99
Dallas		82	41	31	10	261	260	92
Colorado		82	39	31	12	219	227	90

Pacific Division

		GP	W	L	OT	GF	GA	PTS
Anaheim	(P1)	82	51	24	7	236	226	109
Vancouver	(P2)	82	48	29	5	242	222	101
Calgary	(P3)	82	45	30	7	241	216	97
Los Angeles		82	40	27	15	220	205	95
San Jose		82	40	33	9	228	232	89
Edmonton		82	24	44	14	198	283	62
Arizona		82	24	50	8	170	272	56

INDIVIDUAL LEADERS

Goal Scoring

Player	Team	GP	G
Alex Ovechkin	Washington	81	53
Steven Stamkos	Tampa Bay	82	43
Rick Nash	NY Rangers	79	42
John Tavares	NY Islanders	82	38
Tyler Seguin	Dallas	71	37
Vladimir Tarasenko	St. Louis	77	37
Max Pacioretty	Montreal	80	37
Joe Pavelski	San Jose	82	37
Jamie Benn	Dallas	82	35
Corey Perry	Anaheim	67	33
Zach Parise	Minnesota	74	33
Jiri Hudler	Calgary	78	31
Radim Vrbata	Vancouver	79	31
Nick Foligno	Columbus	79	31
Sean Monahan	Calgary	81	31

Assists

Player	Team	GP	A
Nicklas Backstrom	Washington	82	60
Jakub Voracek	Philadelphia	82	59
Sidney Crosby	Pittsburgh	77	56
Daniel Sedin	Vancouver	82	56
Henrik Sedin	Vancouver	82	55
Jamie Benn	Dallas	82	52
Henrik Zetterberg	Detroit	77	49
Joe Thornton	San Jose	78	49
Anze Kopitar	Los Angeles	79	48
Claude Giroux	Philadelphia	81	48
John Tavares	NY Islanders	82	48
Ondrej Palat	Tampa Bay	75	47
Mike Ribeiro	Nashville	82	47
Keith Yandle	Ari.-NYR	84	46

Power-play Goals

Player	Team	GP	PP
Alex Ovechkin	Washington	81	25
Joe Pavelski	San Jose	82	19
Wayne Simmonds	Philadelphia	75	14
Claude Giroux	Philadelphia	81	14
Gustav Nyquist	Detroit	82	14
Tyler Seguin	Dallas	71	13
Steven Stamkos	Tampa Bay	82	13
John Tavares	NY Islanders	82	13

Shorthand Goals

Player	Team	GP	SH
Tyler Toffoli	Los Angeles	76	5
Rick Nash	NY Rangers	79	4
Blake Wheeler	Winnipeg	79	4
Brandon Sutter	Pittsburgh	80	4
9 Players tied with			3

Game-winning Goals

Player	Team	GP	GW
Alex Ovechkin	Washington	81	11
Max Pacioretty	Montreal	80	10
Matt Beleskey	Anaheim	65	8
Mike Cammalleri	New Jersey	68	8
Rick Nash	NY Rangers	79	8
Sean Monahan	Calgary	81	8
John Tavares	NY Islanders	82	8

Shots

Player	Team	GP	S
Alex Ovechkin	Washington	81	395
Rick Nash	NY Rangers	79	304
Max Pacioretty	Montreal	80	302
Erik Karlsson	Ottawa	82	292
Tyler Seguin	Dallas	71	280
Phil Kessel	Toronto	82	280
Claude Giroux	Philadelphia	81	279
John Tavares	NY Islanders	82	278
Steven Stamkos	Tampa Bay	82	268
Radim Vrbata	Vancouver	79	267

Shooting Percentage

(minimum 48 shots)

Player	Team	GP	G	S	S%
Alex Tanguay	Colorado	80	22	104	21.2
Jiri Hudler	Calgary	78	31	158	19.6
Benoit Pouliot	Edmonton	58	19	105	18.1
Henrik Sedin	Vancouver	82	18	101	17.8
Mike Cammalleri	New Jersey	68	27	156	17.3

Plus/Minus

Player	Team	GP	+/-
Max Pacioretty	Montreal	80	38
Nikita Kucherov	Tampa Bay	82	38
Tyler Johnson	Tampa Bay	77	33
Ondrej Palat	Tampa Bay	75	31
Jonathan Toews	Chicago	81	30

* – rookie eligible for Calder Trophy

Alex Ovechkin celebrates his 50th goal of the season at home versus Carolina on March 31, 2015. The Washington superstar led the NHL in goals for the third season in a row in 2014-15 and the fifth time in his career.

Individual Leaders

Abbreviations: GP – games played; **G** – goals; **A** – assists; **Pts** – points; **+/–** – difference between Goals For (**GF**) scored when a player is on the ice with his team at even strength or shorthanded and Goals Against (**GA**) scored when the same player is on the ice with his team at even strength or on a power play; **PIM** – penalties in minutes; **PP** – power play goals; **SH** – shorthanded goals; **GW** – game-winning goals; **S** – shots on goal; **S%** – percentage of shots on goal resulting in goals.

Individual Scoring Leaders for Art Ross Trophy

Player	Team	GP	G	A	Pts	+/–	PIM	PP	SH	GW	S	S%
Jamie Benn	Dallas	82	35	52	87	1	64	10	2	6	253	13.8
John Tavares	NY Islanders	82	38	48	86	5	46	13	0	8	278	13.7
Sidney Crosby	Pittsburgh	77	28	56	84	5	47	10	0	3	237	11.8
Alex Ovechkin	Washington	81	53	28	81	10	58	25	0	11	395	13.4
Jakub Voracek	Philadelphia	82	22	59	81	1	78	11	0	3	221	10.0
Nicklas Backstrom	Washington	82	18	60	78	5	40	3	0	3	153	11.8
Tyler Seguin	Dallas	71	37	40	77	-1	20	13	0	5	280	13.2
Jiri Hudler	Calgary	78	31	45	76	17	14	6	0	5	158	19.6
Daniel Sedin	Vancouver	82	20	56	76	5	18	4	0	5	226	8.8
Vladimir Tarasenko	St. Louis	77	37	36	73	27	31	8	0	6	264	14.0
Nick Foligno	Columbus	79	31	42	73	16	50	11	0	3	182	17.0
Claude Giroux	Philadelphia	81	25	48	73	-3	36	14	0	4	279	9.0
Henrik Sedin	Vancouver	82	18	55	73	11	22	5	0	0	101	17.8
Steven Stamkos	Tampa Bay	82	43	29	72	2	49	13	0	6	268	16.0
Tyler Johnson	Tampa Bay	77	29	43	72	33	24	8	0	6	203	14.3
Ryan Johansen	Columbus	82	26	45	71	-6	40	7	2	0	202	12.9
Joe Pavelski	San Jose	82	37	33	70	12	29	19	0	5	261	14.2
Evgeni Malkin	Pittsburgh	69	28	42	70	-2	60	9	0	4	212	13.2
Ryan Getzlaf	Anaheim	77	25	45	70	15	62	3	0	6	191	13.1
Rick Nash	NY Rangers	79	42	27	69	29	36	6	4	3	304	13.8
Max Pacioretty	Montreal	80	37	30	67	38	32	7	3	10	302	12.3
Logan Couture	San Jose	82	27	40	67	-6	12	6	2	4	263	10.3
Jonathan Toews	Chicago	81	28	38	66	30	36	6	2	7	192	14.6
Erik Karlsson	Ottawa	82	21	45	66	7	42	6	0	3	292	7.2
Henrik Zetterberg	Detroit	77	17	49	66	-6	32	4	0	3	227	7.5

Defensemen Scoring Leaders

Player	Team	GP	G	A	Pts	+/–	PIM	PP	SH	GW	S	S%
Erik Karlsson	Ottawa	82	21	45	66	7	42	6	0	3	292	7.2
Brent Burns	San Jose	82	17	43	60	-9	65	7	0	2	245	6.9
P.K. Subban	Montreal	82	15	45	60	21	74	8	0	5	170	8.8
Dennis Wideman	Calgary	80	15	41	56	6	34	6	0	2	173	8.7
Roman Josi	Nashville	81	15	40	55	15	26	3	0	4	201	7.5
John Carlson	Washington	82	12	43	55	11	28	3	1	3	193	6.2
Kris Letang	Pittsburgh	69	11	43	54	12	79	2	1	1	197	5.6
Tyson Barrie	Colorado	80	12	41	53	5	26	2	0	0	139	8.6
Mark Streit	Philadelphia	81	9	43	52	-8	36	4	0	0	144	6.3
Keith Yandle	Ari.-NYR	84	6	46	52	-26	40	2	0	2	232	2.6
Andrei Markov	Montreal	81	10	40	50	22	38	4	0	1	135	7.4
Justin Faulk	Carolina	82	15	34	49	-19	30	7	2	4	238	6.3
Mark Giordano	Calgary	61	11	37	48	13	37	2	1	2	157	7.0
Alex Pietrangelo	St. Louis	81	7	39	46	-2	28	1	0	2	195	3.6
Drew Doughty	Los Angeles	82	7	39	46	3	56	1	0	2	219	3.2
Dustin Byfuglien	Winnipeg	69	18	27	45	5	124	5	0	3	209	8.6
Shea Weber	Nashville	78	15	30	45	15	72	5	1	2	237	6.3
Mike Green	Washington	72	10	35	45	15	34	1	0	2	159	6.3
Duncan Keith	Chicago	80	10	35	45	12	20	3	0	2	171	5.8
Niklas Kronwall	Detroit	80	9	35	44	-4	40	3	0	1	101	8.9
Kevin Shattenkirk	St. Louis	56	8	36	44	19	52	4	0	1	135	5.9
Oliver Ekman-Larsson	Arizona	82	23	20	43	-18	40	10	1	7	264	8.7
Dougie Hamilton	Boston	72	10	32	42	-3	41	5	0	2	188	5.3
T.J. Brodie	Calgary	81	11	30	41	15	30	3	1	3	133	8.3
Jake Muzzin	Los Angeles	76	10	31	41	-4	22	4	0	3	173	5.8

CONSECUTIVE SCORING STREAKS

Goals

Games	Player	Team	G
6	Max Pacioretty	Montreal	7
6	*Filip Forsberg	Nashville	7
5	Marian Gaborik	Los Angeles	7
5	Ryan Johansen	Columbus	6
5	Alexander Steen	St. Louis	5
5	Alex Ovechkin	Washington	5
5	Jamie Benn	Dallas	5
5	Gabriel Landeskog	Colorado	5
5	*Melker Karlsson	San Jose	5

Assists

Games	Player	Team	A
7	Tyler Johnson	Tampa Bay	11
7	Keith Yandle	Arizona	9
7	Jordan Eberle	Edmonton	9
6	Jason Spezza	Dallas	9
6	Jiri Hudler	Calgary	8
6	Mark Giordano	Calgary	8
6	Derick Brassard	NY Rangers	8
6	Nicklas Backstrom	Washington	8
6	Jaden Schwartz	St. Louis	8
6	Evgeni Malkin	Pittsburgh	7
6	Jamie Benn	Dallas	7
6	Ryan Johansen	Columbus	7
6	Clarke MacArthur	Ottawa	6
6	Nick Foligno	Columbus	6

Points

Games	Player	Team	G	A	PTS
13	Ryan Johansen	Columbus	8	8	16
11	Evgeni Malkin	Pittsburgh	5	11	16
11	Rick Nash	NY Rangers	8	6	14
10	Jakub Voracek	Philadelphia	5	14	19
10	Alexander Steen	St. Louis	7	11	18
10	Ryan Johansen	Columbus	5	8	13
9	David Backes	St. Louis	8	8	16
9	Mark Giordano	Calgary	5	9	14
9	*Mark Stone	Ottawa	8	5	13
9	Ryan Johansen	Columbus	8	4	12
9	Drew Stafford	Buf-Wpg	4	7	11
9	Cody Franson	Toronto	2	9	11
8	Henrik Sedin	Vancouver	6	7	13
8	Ryan Getzlaf	Anaheim	4	9	13
8	Jamie Benn	Dallas	7	6	13
8	Ryan O'Reilly	Colorado	5	8	13
8	Scott Hartnell	Columbus	4	7	11
8	Brandon Dubinsky	Columbus	4	7	11
8	Nick Foligno	Columbus	2	9	11
8	Thomas Vanek	Minnesota	6	4	10
8	Wayne Simmonds	Philadelphia	6	4	10
8	Joe Thornton	San Jose	4	5	9
8	Radim Vrbata	Vancouver	3	6	9
8	Mathieu Perreault	Winnipeg	5	4	9
8	Mikael Backlund	Calgary	3	6	9
8	Michael Frolik	Winnipeg	5	3	8

— rookie eligible for Calder Trophy

Jamie Benn of Dallas poses with four pucks from his four points on the last day of the NHL season. He moved past John Tavares and Sidney Crosby to lead in league in scoring in 2014-15.

Individual Rookie Scoring Leaders

Player	Team	GP	G	A	Pts	+/–	PIM	PP	SH	GW	S	S%
Mark Stone	Ottawa	80	26	38	64	21	14	5	1	6	157	16.6
Johnny Gaudreau	Calgary	80	24	40	64	11	14	8	0	4	167	14.4
Filip Forsberg	Nashville	82	26	37	63	15	24	6	0	6	237	11.0
Mike Hoffman	Ottawa	79	27	21	48	16	14	1	0	4	199	13.6
Kevin Hayes	NY Rangers	79	17	28	45	15	22	1	1	1	111	15.3
Anders Lee	NY Islanders	76	25	16	41	9	33	5	0	6	197	12.7
John Klingberg	Dallas	65	11	29	40	5	32	2	0	3	98	11.2
Aaron Ekblad	Florida	81	12	27	39	12	32	6	0	4	170	7.1
Evgeny Kuznetsov	Washington	80	11	26	37	10	24	4	0	1	127	8.7
Victor Rask	Carolina	80	11	22	33	–14	16	2	0	2	172	6.4
Jonathan Drouin	Tampa Bay	70	4	28	32	3	34	3	0	0	76	5.3
Rickard Rakell	Anaheim	71	9	22	31	6	10	2	0	1	105	8.6
David Pastrnak	Boston	46	10	17	27	12	8	2	0	3	93	10.8
Bo Horvat	Vancouver	68	13	12	25	–8	16	0	1	1	93	14.0
Melker Karlsson	San Jose	53	13	11	24	–3	20	1	0	2	100	13.0
Josh Jooris	Calgary	60	12	12	24	1	16	4	0	4	89	13.5
Linden Vey	Vancouver	75	10	14	24	–3	18	4	0	2	61	16.4
Adam Lowry	Winnipeg	80	11	12	23	1	46	0	1	2	104	10.6
Jiri Sekac	Mtl.-Ana.	69	9	14	23	0	22	2	0	0	85	10.6
Andre Burakovsky	Washington	53	9	13	22	12	10	2	0	2	65	13.8
Vincent Trocheck	Florida	50	7	15	22	9	24	1	0	0	89	7.9
Tobias Rieder	Arizona	72	13	8	21	–19	14	0	3	1	189	6.9
Marko Dano	Columbus	35	8	13	21	12	14	0	0	1	84	9.5
Chris Tierney	San Jose	43	6	15	21	3	6	1	0	1	48	12.5

Goal Scoring

Player	Team	GP	G
Mike Hoffman	Ottawa	79	27
Mark Stone	Ottawa	80	26
Filip Forsberg	Nashville	82	26
Anders Lee	NY Islanders	76	25
Johnny Gaudreau	Calgary	80	24
Kevin Hayes	NY Rangers	79	17
Melker Karlsson	San Jose	53	13
Dmitrij Jaskin	St. Louis	54	13
Bo Horvat	Vancouver	68	13
Tobias Rieder	Arizona	72	13

Assists

Player	Team	GP	A
Johnny Gaudreau	Calgary	80	40
Mark Stone	Ottawa	80	38
Filip Forsberg	Nashville	82	37
John Klingberg	Dallas	65	29
Jonathan Drouin	Tampa Bay	70	28
Kevin Hayes	NY Rangers	79	28
Aaron Ekblad	Florida	81	27
Evgeny Kuznetsov	Washington	80	26
Rickard Rakell	Anaheim	71	22
Victor Rask	Carolina	80	22
Mike Hoffman	Ottawa	79	21

Power-play Goals

Player	Team	GP	PP
Johnny Gaudreau	Calgary	80	8
Aaron Ekblad	Florida	81	6
Filip Forsberg	Nashville	82	6
Anders Lee	NY Islanders	76	5
Mark Stone	Ottawa	80	5
Josh Jooris	Calgary	60	4
Linden Vey	Vancouver	75	4
Evgeny Kuznetsov	Washington	80	4

Shorthand Goals

Player	Team	GP	SH
Tobias Rieder	Arizona	72	3
Cedric Paquette	Tampa Bay	64	2
Jacob De La Rose	Montreal	33	1
Craig Cunningham	Bos.-Ari.	51	1
Bo Horvat	Vancouver	68	1
Kevin Hayes	NY Rangers	79	1
Mark Stone	Ottawa	80	1
Adam Lowry	Winnipeg	80	1

Game-winning Goals

Player	Team	GP	GW
Anders Lee	NY Islanders	76	6
Mark Stone	Ottawa	80	6
Filip Forsberg	Nashville	82	6
Dmitrij Jaskin	St. Louis	54	4
Josh Jooris	Calgary	60	4
Mike Hoffman	Ottawa	79	4
Johnny Gaudreau	Calgary	80	4
Aaron Ekblad	Florida	81	4

Shots

Player	Team	GP	S
Filip Forsberg	Nashville	82	237
Mike Hoffman	Ottawa	79	199
Anders Lee	NY Islanders	76	197
Tobias Rieder	Arizona	72	189
Victor Rask	Carolina	80	172

Shooting Percentage
(minimum 48 shots)

Player	Team	GP	G	S	S%
Mark Stone	Ottawa	80	26	157	16.6
Kevin Hayes	NY Rangers	79	17	111	15.3
Johnny Gaudreau	Calgary	80	24	167	14.4
Bo Horvat	Vancouver	68	13	93	14.0
Mike Hoffman	Ottawa	79	27	199	13.6

Plus/Minus

Player	Team	GP	+/–
Mark Stone	Ottawa	80	21
Mike Hoffman	Ottawa	79	16
Kevin Hayes	NY Rangers	79	15
Filip Forsberg	Nashville	82	15
Tanner Pearson	Los Angeles	42	14

Three-or-More-Goal Games

Player	Team	Date	Final Score	G
Cam Atkinson	Columbus	Mar 27	CBJ 5 Chi. 2	3
David Backes	St. Louis	Jan 6	St.L. 6 Ari. 0	4
Nicklas Backstrom	Washington	Dec 13	T.B. 2 Wsh. 4	3
Jamie Benn	Dallas	Feb 17	Dal. 4 St.L. 1	3
Jamie Benn	Dallas	Apr 11	Nsh. 1 Dal. 4	3
Mikkel Boedker	Arizona	Oct 15	Edm. 4 Ari. 7	3
Tyler Bozak	Toronto	Mar 28	Ott. 3 Tor. 4	3
Blake Comeau	Pittsburgh	Nov 26	Tor. 3 Pit. 4	3
Nick Foligno	Columbus	Apr 4	Pit. 3 CBJ 5	3
Alex Galchenyuk	Montreal	Dec 16	Car. 1 Mtl. 4	3
*Johnny Gaudreau	Calgary	Dec 22	Cgy. 4 L.A. 3	3
Jannik Hansen	Vancouver	Nov 23	Chi. 1 Van. 4	3
Martin Hanzal	Arizona	Nov 14	Ari. 5 Van. 0	3
Scott Hartnell	Columbus	MaR 24	Ana. 3 CBJ 5	3
Jaromir Jagr	New Jersey	Jan 3	Phi. 2 N.J. 5	3
Tyler Johnson	Tampa Bay	Dec 23	Pit. 3 T.B. 4	3
*Josh Jooris	Calgary	Dec 2	Ari. 2 Cgy. 5	3
Nikita Kucherov	Tampa Bay	Oct 28	Ari. 3 T.B. 7	3
Jori Lehtera	St. Louis	Nov 11	Buf. 1 St.L. 6	3
Elias Lindholm	Carolina	Mar 8	Edm. 4 Car. 7	3
Bryan Little	Winnipeg	Dec 5	Col. 4 Wpg.6	3
Nathan MacKinnon	Colorado	Feb 22	T.B. 4 Col. 5	3
Shawn Matthias	Vancouver	Feb 13	Bos. 2 Van. 5	3
Rick Nash	NY Rangers	Dec 23	Wsh. 2 NYR 4	3
James Neal	Nashville	Oct 23	Chi. 2 Nsh. 3	3
Nino Niederreiter	Minnesota	Nov 13	Buf. 3 Min. 6	3
Frans Nielsen	NY Islanders	Oct 25	Dal. 5 NYI 7	3
Ryan Nugent-Hopkins	Edmonton	Mar 8	Edm. 4 Car. 7	3
Kyle Okposo	NY Islanders	Jan 16	Pit. 3 NYI 6	4
T.J. Oshie	St. Louis	Jan 3	St.L. 7 S.J. 2	3
*Cedric Paquette	Tampa Bay	Jan 29	Det. 1 T.B. 5	3
Joe Pavelski	San Jose	Feb 13	S.J. 4 Ari. 2	3
Mathieu Perreault	Winnipeg	Jan 13	Fla. 2 Wpg.8	4
Corey Perry	Anaheim	Oct 9	Ana. 4 Pit. 6	3
Corey Perry	Anaheim	Oct 22	Buf. 1 Ana. 4	3
Corey Perry	Anaheim	Jan 14	Tor. 0 Ana. 4	3
Mason Raymond	Calgary	Oct 9	Cgy. 5 Edm. 2	3
Bobby Ryan	Ottawa	Dec 29	Buf. 2 Ott. 5	3
Jaden Schwartz	St. Louis	Oct 18	St.L. 6 Ari. 1	3
Jaden Schwartz	St. Louis	Apr 3	St.L. 7 Dal. 5	3
Tyler Seguin	Dallas	Oct 14	Dal. 4 CBJ 2	3
Tyler Seguin	Dallas	Nov 8	S.J. 5 Dal. 3	3
Steven Stamkos	Tampa Bay	Oct 13	Mtl. 1 T.B. 7	3
Derek Stepan	NY Rangers	Dec 27	N.J. 1 NYR 3	3
Vladimir Tarasenko	St. Louis	Oct 28	St.L. 4 Dal. 3	3
Vladimir Tarasenko	St. Louis	Dec 16	LA. 2 St.L. 5	3
Jiri Tlusty	Carolina	Oct 11	Car. 7 NYI 4	3
Tyler Toffoli	Los Angeles	Feb 12	Cgy. 3 L.A. 5	3
Henrik Zetterberg	Detroit	Jan 18	Buf. 4 Det. 6	3

* — rookie eligible for Calder Trophy

2014-15 Penalty Shots

(For shootout statistics, see page 145.)

Scored

Ryan Kesler (Ana.) scored against Michal Neuvirth (Buf.) Oct. 13. Final score: Ana. 5 at Buf. 1

Taylor Hall (Edm.) scored against Ben Bishop (T.B.) Oct. 20. Final score: T.B. 2 at Edm. 3

Anze Kopitar (L.A.) scored against Frederik Andersen (Ana.) Nov. 12. Final score: L.A. 5 at Ana. 6

Dale Weise (Mtl.) scored against Niklas Svedberg (Bos.) Nov. 13. Final score: Bos. 1 at Mtl. 5

Boone Jenner (CBJ) scored against Thomas Greiss (Pit.) Dec. 13. Final score: Pit. 3 at CBJ 4

Nino Niederreiter (Min.) scored against Antti Raanta (Chi.) Dec. 16. Final score: Min. 3 at Chi. 5

Joe Thornton (S.J.) scored against Ryan Miller (Van.) Dec. 30. Final score: Van. 3 at S.J. 1

Brad Malone (Car.) scored against Frederik Andersen (Ana.) Feb. 3. Final score: Car. 4 at Ana. 5

Phil Kessel (Tor.) scored against Eddie Lack (Van.) Mar. 14. Final score: Tor. 1 at Van. 4

Andrew Miller (Edm.) scored against Kari Lehtonen (Dal.) Mar. 27. Final score: Dal. 0 at Edm. 4

Brandon Dubinsky (CBJ) scored against Cory Schneider (N.J.) Mar. 31. Final score: N.J. 2 at CBJ 3

Andrew Cogliano (Ana.) scored against Ben Scrivens (Edm.) Apr. 1. Final score: Edm. 1 at Ana. 5

Travis Moen (Dal.) scored against Brian Elliott (St.L.) Apr. 3. Final score: STL 7 at Dal. 5

Cody Eakin (Dal.) scored against Pekka Rinne (Nsh.) Apr. 4. Final score: Dal. 4 at Nsh. 3

Stopped

Marc-Andre Fleury (Pit.) stopped Nate Thompson (Ana.) Oct. 9. Final score: Ana. 4 at Pit. 6

Curtis McElhinney (CBJ) stopped Mike Hoffman (Ott.) Oct. 18. Final score: CBJ 2 at Ott. 3

Cory Schneider (N.J.) stopped Tommy Wingels (S.J.) Oct. 18. Final score: S.J. 4 at N.J. 2

Craig Anderson (Ott.) stopped Andrew Shaw (Chi.) Oct. 26. Final score: Ott. 1 at Chi. 2

Jimmy Howard (Det.) stopped Dustin Brown (L.A.) Oct. 31. Final score: L.A. 2 at Det. 5

Henrik Lundqvist (NYR) stopped Gustav Nyquist (Det.) Nov. 5. Final score: Det. 3 at NYR 4

Anton Forsberg (CBJ) stopped Nikita Kucherov (T.B.) Nov. 8. Final score: T.B. 7 at CBJ 4

Roberto Luongo (Fla.) stopped Patrick Marleau (S.J.) Nov. 20. Final score: Fla. 3 at S.J. 2

Pekka Rinne (Nsh.) stopped Jordan Eberle (Edm.) Nov. 27. Final score: Edm. 0 at Nsh. 1

Ryan Miller (Van.) stopped Martin St. Louis (NYR) Dec. 13. Final score: NYR 5 at Van. 1

Cory Schneider (N.J.) stopped Alex Ovechkin (Wsh.) Dec. 20. Final score: Wsh. 4 at N.J. 0

Ryan Miller (Van.) stopped Joe Pavelski (S.J.) Dec. 30. Final score: Van. 3 at S.J. 1

Tuukka Rask (Bos.) stopped Phil Kessel (Tor.) Dec. 31. Final score: Tor. 4 at Bos. 3

Corey Crawford (Chi.) stopped Jason Zucker (Min.) Jan. 11. Final score: Min. 1 at Chi. 4

Sergei Bobrovsky (CBJ) stopped Zach Parise (Min.) Jan. 19. Final score: CBJ 3 at Min. 1

Roberto Luongo (Fla.) stopped Carl Hagelin (NYR) Feb. 2. Final score: Fla. 3 at NYR 6

Petr Mrazek (Det.) stopped Martin Erat (Ari.) Feb. 7. Final score: Det. 3 at Ari. 1

Thomas Greiss (Pit.) stopped Bobby Ryan (Ott.) Feb. 12. Final score: Pit. 5 at Ott. 4

Cam Talbot (NYR) stopped Tobias Rieder (Ari.) Feb. 14. Final score: NYR 5 at Ari. 1

Michal Neuvirth (Buf.) stopped Adam Henrique (N.J.) Feb. 17. Final score: Buf. 1 at N.J. 2

Scott Darling (Chi.) stopped Derek MacKenzie (Fla.) Feb. 24. Final score: Fla. 2 at Chi. 3

Jaroslav Halak (NYI) stopped Michaal Ferland (Cgy.) Feb. 27. Final score: CGY 1 at NYI 2

Al Montoya (Fla.) stopped Tyler Johnson (T.B.) Mar. 1. Final score: T.B. 3 at Fla. 4

Braden Holtby (Wsh.) stopped Scott Hartnell (CBJ) Mar. 3. Final score: Wsh. 5 at CBJ 3

Anders Lindback (Buf.) stopped Alex Ovechkin (Wsh.) Mar. 7. Final score: Buf. 1 at Wsh. 6

Kari Lehtonen (Dal.) stopped Brandon Saad (Chi.) Mar. 21. Final score: Chi. 0 at Dal. 4

Craig Anderson (Ott.) stopped Joakim Lindstrom (Tor.) Mar. 28. Final score: Ott. 3 at Tor. 4

Total Shots:	41
Total Goals:	14
Total Saves:	27

Cody Eakin of Dallas beat Nashville's Pekka Rinne on a penalty shot in overtime to give the Stars a 4-3 win over the Predators.

Goaltending Leaders

Minimum 25 games

Goals Against Average

Goaltender	Team	GP	MINS	GA	Avg
Carey Price	Montreal	66	3977	130	1.96
Devan Dubnyk	Ari.-Min.	58	3328	115	2.07
Pekka Rinne	Nashville	64	3851	140	2.18
Cam Talbot	NY Rangers	36	2095	77	2.21
Braden Holtby	Washington	73	4247	157	2.22
Jonathan Quick	Los Angeles	72	4184	156	2.24

Save Percentage

Goaltender	Team	GP	MINS	GA	SA	S%	W	L	OT
Carey Price	Montreal	66	3977	130	1953	.933	44	16	6
Devan Dubnyk	Ari.-Min.	58	3328	115	1625	.929	36	14	4
Steve Mason	Philadelphia	51	2885	108	1490	.928	18	18	11
Cam Talbot	NY Rangers	36	2095	77	1038	.926	21	9	4
Cory Schneider	New Jersey	69	3924	148	1982	.925	26	31	9
Corey Crawford	Chicago	57	3333	126	1661	.924	32	20	5

Wins

Goaltender	Team	GP	W	L	OT
Carey Price	Montreal	66	44	16	6
Pekka Rinne	Nashville	64	41	17	6
Braden Holtby	Washington	73	41	20	10
Ben Bishop	Tampa Bay	62	40	13	5
Jaroslav Halak	NY Islanders	59	38	17	4

Shutouts

Goaltender	Team	GP	MINS	SO	W	L	OT
Marc-Andre Fleury	Pittsburgh	64	3776	10	34	20	9
Carey Price	Montreal	66	3977	9	44	16	6
Braden Holtby	Washington	73	4247	9	41	20	10
Ryan Miller	Vancouver	45	2542	6	29	15	1
Devan Dubnyk	Ari.-Min.	58	3328	6	36	14	4
Jaroslav Halak	NY Islanders	59	3550	6	38	17	4
Jonathan Quick	Los Angeles	72	4184	6	36	22	13

Team-by-Team Point Totals

2010-11 to 2014-15

(Ranked by five-year point %)

Team	14-15	13-14	12-13	11-12	10-11	Pts%
Pittsburgh	98	109	72	108	106	.656
Chicago	102	107	77	101	97	.644
Boston	96	117	62	102	103	.638
St. Louis	109	111	60	109	87	.633
Vancouver	101	83	59	111	117	.626
Anaheim	109	116	66	80	99	.625
NY Rangers	113	96	56	109	93	.621
San Jose	89	111	57	96	105	.609
Detroit	100	93	56	102	104	.605
Montreal	110	100	63	78	96	.594
Washington	101	90	57	92	107	.594
Los Angeles	95	100	59	95	98	.594
Tampa Bay	108	101	40	84	103	.580
Nashville	104	88	41	104	99	.580
Philadelphia	84	94	49	103	106	.580
Minnesota	100	98	55	81	86	.559
Dallas	92	91	48	89	95	.552
Ottawa	99	88	56	92	74	.543
Calgary	97	77	42	90	94	.532
Winnipeg	99	84	51	84	80	.529
Colorado	90	112	39	88	68	.528
New Jersey	78	88	48	102	81	.528
Arizona	56	89	51	97	99	.521
NY Islanders	101	79	55	79	73	.515
Columbus	89	93	55	65	81	.509
Toronto	68	84	57	80	85	.497
Carolina	71	83	42	82	91	.491
Florida	91	66	36	94	72	.477
Buffalo	54	52	48	89	96	.451
Edmonton	62	67	45	74	62	.412

Team Record When Scoring First Goal of a Game

Team	FG	W	L	OT
Anaheim	47	36	5	6
Arizona	33	14	16	3
Boston	43	29	9	5
Buffalo	36	19	14	3
Calgary	36	25	8	3
Carolina	36	22	8	6
Chicago	46	35	9	2
Colorado	37	25	10	2
Columbus	37	27	9	1
Dallas	45	29	10	6
Detroit	42	25	8	9
Edmonton	34	16	12	6
Florida	33	23	5	5
Los Angeles	41	27	5	9
Minnesota	45	35	6	4
Montreal	39	32	3	4
Nashville	38	27	5	6
New Jersey	45	24	11	10
NY Islanders	49	29	15	5
NY Rangers	50	41	6	3
Ottawa	46	27	11	8
Philadelphia	32	22	4	6
Pittsburgh	49	33	9	7
San Jose	41	29	9	3
St. Louis	46	36	6	4
Tampa Bay	46	35	7	4
Toronto	31	21	6	4
Vancouver	35	27	6	2
Washington	43	37	2	4
Winnipeg	49	32	10	7

Team Plus/Minus Differential

Team	GF	PPGF	Net GF	GA	PPGA	Net GA	Goal Differential
NY Rangers	252	39	213	192	37	155	+58
Tampa Bay	262	53	209	211	42	169	+40
Montreal	221	40	181	189	42	147	+34
St. Louis	248	56	192	201	42	159	+33
Chicago	229	46	183	189	35	154	+29
Washington	242	60	182	203	50	153	+29
Winnipeg	230	48	182	210	56	154	+28
Nashville	232	42	190	208	45	163	+27
Anaheim	236	37	199	226	52	174	+25
Minnesota	231	39	192	201	32	169	+23
NY Islanders	252	50	202	230	48	182	+20
Ottawa	238	47	191	215	44	171	+20
Calgary	241	48	193	216	36	180	+13
Los Angeles	220	47	173	205	45	160	+13
Vancouver	242	46	196	222	38	184	+12
Boston	213	38	175	211	44	167	+8
Pittsburgh	221	49	172	210	42	168	+4
Detroit	235	70	165	221	55	166	-1
Dallas	261	55	206	260	49	211	-5
Columbus	236	53	183	250	60	190	-7
Florida	206	40	166	223	50	173	-7
Colorado	219	37	182	227	37	190	-8
San Jose	228	55	173	232	48	184	-11
Philadelphia	215	60	155	234	61	173	-18
New Jersey	181	41	140	216	52	164	-24
Toronto	211	45	166	262	52	210	-44
Carolina	188	45	143	226	29	197	-54
Edmonton	198	41	157	283	51	232	-75
Buffalo	161	30	131	274	64	210	-79
Arizona	170	46	124	272	65	207	-83

Team Record When Leading, Trailing, Tied

	Leading after 1 period			Leading after 2 periods			Trailing after 1 period			Trailing after 2 periods			Tied after 1 period			Tied after 2 periods		
Team	W	L	OT	W	L	OT	W	L	OT	W	L	OT	W	L	OT	W	L	OT
Anaheim	26	3	3	30	0	2	7	14	1	12	23	0	18	7	3	9	1	5
Arizona	12	9	2	14	1	2	7	23	1	2	35	2	5	18	5	8	14	4
Boston	23	5	3	27	1	3	2	11	6	6	20	0	16	11	5	8	6	11
Buffalo	9	6	1	11	3	3	4	28	2	3	37	2	10	17	5	9	11	3
Calgary	16	2	0	24	1	1	13	14	3	10	20	4	16	14	4	11	9	2
Carolina	17	2	5	22	3	4	5	28	4	2	34	3	8	11	2	6	4	4
Chicago	26	3	0	25	0	0	7	15	1	6	18	2	15	10	5	17	10	4
Colorado	16	6	1	23	2	2	8	14	6	6	27	3	15	11	5	10	2	7
Columbus	22	4	1	20	2	2	7	21	2	4	28	1	13	10	2	18	5	2
Dallas	21	6	1	29	4	5	7	16	4	7	19	1	13	9	5	5	8	4
Detroit	15	2	0	26	1	4	10	11	2	11	19	3	18	12	12	6	5	7
Edmonton	10	7	6	17	4	6	2	24	5	2	32	3	12	13	3	5	8	5
Florida	15	3	1	21	4	3	3	18	6	3	22	6	20	8	8	14	3	6
Los Angeles	21	3	5	27	3	5	8	16	5	3	20	5	11	8	5	10	4	5
Minnesota	27	3	2	28	2	2	5	14	3	8	21	3	14	11	3	10	5	3
Montreal	15	3	4	32	2	3	11	17	3	6	19	1	24	2	4	12	1	6
Nashville	20	3	4	27	3	5	6	18	2	6	20	2	21	4	4	14	2	3
New Jersey	16	4	7	25	1	6	4	17	3	2	27	4	12	15	4	5	8	4
NY Islanders	20	8	2	25	3	4	8	9	2	5	18	0	19	11	3	17	7	3
NY Rangers	29	2	3	36	0	1	8	7	1	6	14	0	16	13	3	11	7	6
Ottawa	16	5	2	23	2	3	11	6	3	9	17	4	16	15	8	11	7	6
Philadelphia	19	2	5	19	0	3	5	21	6	3	24	7	9	8	7	11	7	8
Pittsburgh	25	5	4	30	2	2	6	15	5	0	18	5	14	6	3	13	7	5
San Jose	22	5	1	28	4	3	8	16	5	5	23	3	10	12	3	7	6	3
St. Louis	21	4	1	32	2	4	8	16	0	7	15	2	22	4	6	12	7	1
Tampa Bay	25	2	3	33	0	2	8	10	1	3	21	2	17	12	4	14	3	4
Toronto	16	3	2	19	3	1	4	33	1	6	39	0	10	8	5	5	2	7
Vancouver	17	4	1	30	1	3	9	16	2	5	23	1	22	9	2	13	5	1
Washington	26	2	2	35	2	3	4	14	5	2	18	3	15	10	4	6	6	4
Winnipeg	23	5	6	30	2	6	5	12	1	1	20	4	15	9	6	9	4	4

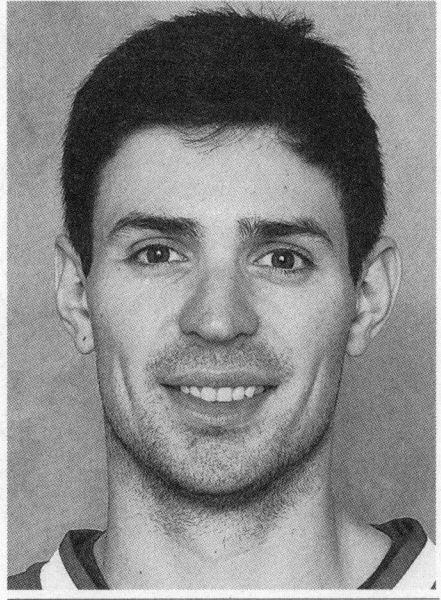

Vezina, Hart and Ted Lindsay award winner Carey Price of the Canadiens led the NHL with 44 wins, a 1.96 goals-against average, and a .933 save percentage as Montreal went 50-22-10 for 110 points in 2014-15.

Team Statistics

TEAMS' HOME AND ROAD RECORD

Eastern Conference

Team	GP	W	L	OT	GF	GA	PTS	GP	W	L	OT	GF	GA	PTS
			Home								Road			
NYR	41	25	11	5	125	99	55	41	28	11	2	127	93	58
MTL	41	26	9	6	122	92	58	41	24	13	4	99	97	52
T.B.	41	32	8	1	141	89	65	41	18	16	7	121	122	43
WSH	41	23	13	5	123	95	51	41	22	13	6	119	108	50
NYI	41	25	14	2	136	112	52	41	22	14	5	116	118	49
DET	41	22	10	9	122	103	53	41	21	15	5	113	118	47
OTT	41	23	13	5	136	119	51	41	20	13	8	102	96	48
PIT	41	23	14	4	118	105	50	41	20	13	8	103	105	48
BOS	41	24	10	7	110	92	55	41	17	17	7	103	119	41
FLA	41	21	13	7	109	110	49	41	17	16	8	97	113	42
CBJ	41	19	20	2	116	133	40	41	23	15	3	120	117	49
PHI	41	23	11	7	121	102	53	41	10	20	11	94	132	31
N.J.	41	19	14	8	91	90	46	41	13	22	6	90	126	32
CAR	41	18	16	7	93	94	43	41	12	25	4	95	132	28
TOR	41	22	17	2	132	128	46	41	8	27	6	79	134	22
BUF	41	14	22	5	83	120	33	41	9	29	3	78	154	21
TOTAL	656	359	215	82	1878	1683	800	656	284	279	93	1656	1884	661

Western Conference

Team	GP	W	L	OT	GF	GA	PTS	GP	W	L	OT	GF	GA	PTS
ANA	41	26	12	3	117	110	55	41	25	12	4	119	116	54
ST.L.	41	27	12	2	126	95	56	41	24	12	5	122	106	53
NSH	41	28	9	4	121	100	60	41	19	16	6	111	108	44
CHI	.41	24	12	5	117	93	53	41	24	16	1	112	96	49
VAN	.41	24	15	2	119	110	50	41	24	14	3	123	112	51
MIN	41	22	13	6	127	104	50	41	24	15	2	104	97	50
WPG	41	23	13	5	128	102	51	41	20	13	8	102	108	48
CGY	41	23	13	5	125	109	51	41	22	17	2	116	107	46
L.A.	41	25	9	7	116	87	57	41	15	18	8	104	118	38
DAL	41	17	16	8	128	132	42	41	24	15	2	133	128	50
COL	41	23	15	3	120	111	49	41	16	16	9	99	116	41
S.J.	41	19	17	5	114	115	43	41	21	16	4	114	117	46
EDM	41	15	23	3	96	125	33	41	9	21	11	102	158	29
ARI	41	11	25	5	78	133	27	41	13	25	3	92	139	29
TOTAL	574	307	204	63	1632	1526	677	574	280	226	68	1553	1626	628
	1230	666	419	145	3510	3209	1477	1230	564	505	161	3209	3510	1289

TEAMS' DIVISIONAL RECORD

Atlantic Division

Team	Total	vs. Atl.	vs. Met.	Total	vs. Cen.	vs. Pac.	Total Pts.
		vs. EAST		vs. WEST			
MTL	37-11-6	18-9-3	19-2-3	13-11-4	8-5-1	5-6-3	110
T.B.	34-15-5	21-5-4	13-10-1	16-9-3	6-5-3	10-4-0	108
DET	24-20-10	10-12-8	14-8-2	19-5-4	12-0-2	7-5-2	100
OTT	27-18-9	17-9-4	10-9-5	16-8-4	5-6-3	11-2-1	99
BOS	30-16-8	15-9-6	15-7-2	11-11-6	6-6-2	5-5-4	96
FLA	27-19-8	16-9-5	11-10-3	11-10-7	2-7-5	9-3-2	91
TOR	20-27-7	13-13-4	7-14-3	10-17-1	5-8-1	5-9-0	68
BUF	16-32-6	10-16-4	6-16-2	7-19-2	1-12-1	6-7-1	54

Metropolitan Division

Team	Total	vs. Atl.	vs. Met.	Total	vs. Cen.	vs. Pac.	Total Pts.
NYR	35-17-2	12-11-1	23-6-1	18-5-5	7-3-4	11-2-1	113
WSH	33-13-8	16-4-4	17-9-4	12-13-3	6-8-0	6-5-3	101
NYI	33-16-5	12-10-2	21-6-3	14-12-2	6-6-2	8-6-0	101
PIT	25-21-8	16-4-4	9-17-4	18-6-4	7-4-3	11-2-1	98
CBJ	26-23-5	11-12-11	5-11-4	16-12-0	8-6-0	8-6-0	89
PHI	21-22-11	9-9-6	12-13-5	12-9-7	8-4-2	4-5-5	84
N.J.	23-21-10	13-8-3	10-13-7	9-15-4	3-8-3	6-7-1	78
CAR	21-25-8	8-13-3	13-12-5	9-16-3	3-9-2	6-7-1	71

Central Division

Team	Total	vs. Atl.	vs. Met.	Total	vs. Cen.	vs. Pac.	Total Pts.
ST.L.	21-8-3	10-3-3	11-5-0	30-16-4	17-11-1	13-5-3	109
NSH	20-10-2	11-4-1	9-6-1	27-15-8	15-9-5	12-6-3	104
CHI	20-9-3	11-4-1	9-5-2	28-19-3	15-14-0	13-5-3	102
MIN	17-12-3	10-3-3	7-9-0	29-16-5	17-8-4	12-8-1	100
WPG	17-10-5	9-5-2	8-5-3	26-16-8	16-8-5	10-8-3	99
DAL	19-11-2	7-8-1	12-3-1	22-20-8	8-14-7	14-6-1	92
COL	17-10-5	9-4-3	8-6-2	22-21-7	14-12-4	8-9-3	90

Pacific Division

Team	Total	vs. Atl.	vs. Met.	Total	vs. Cen.	vs. Pac.	Total Pts.
ANA	17-13-2	9-7-0	8-6-2	34-11-5	16-5-0	18-6-5	109
VAN	21-10-1	8-7-1	13-3-0	27-19-4	10-10-11	7-9-3	101
CGY	14-14-4	8-5-3	6-9-1	31-16-3	9-10-2	22-6-1	97
L.A.	16-12-4	9-6-1	7-6-3	24-15-11	10-8-31	4-7-8	95
S.J.	13-15-4	6-9-1	7-6-3	27-18-5	12-7-1	15-11-4	89
EDM	15-14-3	8-7-1	7-7-2	9-30-1	15-9-7	4-21-4	62
ARI	10-19-3	6-10-0	4-9-3	14-31-5	2-14-5	12-17-0	56

Tampa Bay's Ben Bishop stops Nick Foligno of Columbus as the Lightning ran their home-winning streak to an NHL-best 10 in a row on January 31, 2015.

TEAM STREAKS

Consecutive Wins

Games	Team	From	To
9	Columbus	Mar. 18	Apr. 4
8	Chicago	Nov. 26	Dec. 11
8	NY Rangers	Dec. 8	Dec. 27
8	Los Angeles	Feb. 7	Feb. 24
7	Anaheim	Oct. 11	Oct. 24
7	Pittsburgh	Oct. 25	Nov. 8
7	St. Louis	Oct. 25	Nov. 6
7	Anaheim	Dec. 1	Dec. 13
7	Columbus	Dec. 1	Dec. 16
7	St. Louis	Jan. 17	Feb. 5
7	Ottawa	Mar. 12	Mar. 23

Consecutive Home Wins

Games	Team	From	To
10	Tampa Bay	Dec. 11	Jan. 31
9	Nashville	Dec. 16	Feb. 3
8	Chicago	Nov. 9	Dec. 21
8	San Jose	Nov. 29	Dec. 20
7	Nashville	Nov. 11	Dec. 4
7	NY Islanders	Nov. 11	Dec. 2
7	Washington	Dec. 13	Jan. 14
6	Los Angeles	Oct. 12	Oct. 26
6	Boston	Nov. 1	Nov. 18
6	Buffalo	Nov. 28	Dec. 15
6	Detroit	Dec. 23	Jan. 31
6	Minnesota	Feb. 3	Feb. 22
6	Nashville	Feb. 7	Feb. 24
6	Columbus	Mar. 24	Apr. 10

Consecutive Road Wins

Games	Team	From	To
12	Minnesota	Feb. 18	Apr. 9
8	Columbus	Mar. 6	Mar. 28
6	Chicago	Nov. 26	Dec. 11
6	Montreal	Dec. 23	Jan. 14
6	NY Rangers	Mar. 8	Mar. 26
5	Calgary	Dec. 22	Jan. 19
5	St. Louis	Jan. 3	Feb. 5
5	NY Rangers	Feb. 10	Feb. 20
5	Anaheim	Feb. 12	Mar. 3
5	Vancouver	Mar. 7	Mar. 31

TEAM PENALTIES

Abbreviations: GP – games played; **PEN** – total penalty minutes including bench minutes; **BMI** – total bench minor minutes; **AVG** – average penalty minutes/game calculated by dividing total penalty minutes less bench minor minutes by games played

Team	GP	PEN	BMI	AVG	Team	GP	PEN	BMI	AVG
CAR	82	549	12	6.7	ARI	82	776	10	9.5
CHI	82	596	26	7.3	DAL	82	789	18	9.6
CGY	82	626	18	7.6	T.B.	82	812	18	9.9
EDM	82	677	10	8.3	TOR	82	823	10	10.0
NSH	82	693	10	8.5	MTL	82	833	12	10.2
NYI	82	700	18	8.5	PHI	82	833	24	10.2
NYR	82	712	16	8.7	OTT	82	841	18	10.3
DET	82	724	22	8.8	BUF	82	853	20	10.4
FLA	82	733	18	8.9	WSH	82	857	10	10.5
MIN	82	728	14	8.9	ANA	82	887	10	10.8
L.A.	82	744	10	9.1	VAN	82	892	32	10.9
N.J.	82	760	14	9.3	ST.L.	82	904	14	11.0
S.J.	82	760	10	9.3	CBJ	82	978	12	11.9
COL	82	771	18	9.4	WPG	82	1068	14	13.0
BOS	82	778	14	9.5	PIT	82	1123	24	13.7
					TOT	**1230**	**23820**	**476**	**19.4**

Tyler Toffoli of the Los Angeles Kings led the league with five shorthand goals in 2014-15. Toffoli had 23 goals and 26 assists during his first full season in the NHL.

TEAMS' POWER-PLAY RECORD

Abbreviations: ADV – total advantages; **PPGF** – power-play goals for; **%** – calculated by dividing number of power-play goals by total advantages.

	Home					Road					Overall				
	Team	GP	ADV	PPGF	%	Team	GP	ADV	PPGF	%	Team	GP	ADV	PPGF	%
1	PHI	41	132	37	28.0	ST.L.	41	122	31	25.4	WSH	82	237	60	25.3
2	WSH	41	123	33	26.8	WSH	41	114	27	23.7	DET	82	294	70	23.8
3	DET	41	154	41	26.6	DAL	41	129	30	23.3	PHI	82	256	60	23.4
4	S.J.	41	126	30	23.8	ARI	41	112	26	23.2	ST.L.	82	251	56	22.3
5	T.B.	41	140	32	22.9	N.J.	41	102	22	21.6	S.J.	82	254	55	21.7
6	L.A.	41	136	30	22.1	CBJ	41	121	26	21.5	CBJ	82	244	53	21.7
7	MTL	41	122	27	22.1	DET	41	140	29	20.7	ARI	82	230	46	20.0
8	PIT	41	132	29	22.0	S.J.	41	128	25	19.5	VAN	82	238	46	19.3
9	CBJ	41	123	27	22.0	CHI	41	128	25	19.5	N.J.	82	212	41	19.3
10	CAR	41	116	25	21.6	CGY	41	116	22	19.0	PIT	82	254	49	19.3
11	BOS	41	104	22	21.2	EDM	41	111	21	18.9	L.A.	82	247	47	19.0
12	VAN	41	128	27	21.1	PHI	41	124	23	18.5	DAL	82	290	55	19.0
13	TOR	41	146	30	20.5	OTT	41	132	24	18.2	CGY	82	255	48	18.8
14	NYI	41	138	28	20.3	WPG	41	139	25	18.0	T.B.	82	282	53	18.8
15	MIN	41	138	27	19.6	COL	41	121	21	17.4	CAR	82	240	45	18.8
16	ST.L.	41	129	25	19.4	VAN	41	110	19	17.3	NYI	82	267	50	18.7
17	CGY	41	139	26	18.7	NYR	41	116	20	17.2	BOS	82	213	38	17.8
18	WPG	41	130	23	17.7	NSH	41	134	23	17.2	WPG	82	269	48	17.8
19	N.J.	41	110	19	17.3	NYI	41	129	22	17.1	EDM	82	232	41	17.7
20	ARI	41	118	20	16.9	PIT	41	122	20	16.4	CHI	82	261	46	17.6
21	EDM	41	121	20	16.5	CAR	41	124	20	16.1	NYR	82	232	39	16.8
22	FLA	41	133	22	16.5	FLA	41	113	18	15.9	OTT	82	280	47	16.8
23	NYR	41	116	19	16.4	ANA	41	117	18	15.4	MTL	82	243	40	16.5
24	ANA	41	118	19	16.1	L.A.	41	111	17	15.3	FLA	82	246	40	16.3
25	CHI	41	133	21	15.8	T.B.	41	142	21	14.8	NSH	82	259	42	16.2
26	DAL	41	161	25	15.5	BOS	41	109	16	14.7	TOR	82	283	45	15.9
27	OTT	41	148	23	15.5	BUF	41	107	13	12.1	MIN	82	246	39	15.9
28	NSH	41	125	19	15.2	MIN	41	108	12	11.1	ANA	82	235	37	15.7
29	BUF	41	117	17	14.5	TOR	41	137	15	10.9	COL	82	247	37	15.0
30	COL	41	126	16	12.7	MTL	41	121	13	10.7	BUF	82	224	30	13.4
Totals		**1230**	**3882**	**759**	**19.6**		**1230**	**3639**	**644**	**17.7**		**1230**	**7521**	**1403**	**18.7**

TEAMS' PENALTY KILLING RECORD

Abbreviations: TSH – total times shorthanded; **PPGA** – power-play goals against; **%** – calculated by dividing times short minus power-play goals against by times short.

	Home					Road					Overall				
	Team	GP	TSH	PPGA	%	Team	GP	TSH	PPGA	%	Team	GP	TSH	PPGA	%
1	MIN	41	123	15	87.8	CAR	41	100	13	87.0	MIN	82	234	32	86.3
2	T.B.	41	124	17	86.3	VAN	41	149	20	86.6	VAN	82	266	38	85.7
3	CHI	41	94	13	86.2	PIT	41	137	20	85.4	PIT	82	277	42	84.8
4	COL	41	129	18	86.0	MIN	41	111	17	84.7	CAR	82	190	29	84.7
5	ANA	41	131	20	84.7	NYR	41	122	19	84.4	COL	82	241	37	84.6
6	ST.L.	41	123	19	84.6	OTT	41	136	22	83.8	NYR	82	235	37	84.3
7	VAN	41	117	18	84.6	COL	41	112	19	83.0	MTL	82	257	42	83.7
8	MTL	41	123	19	84.6	MTL	41	134	23	82.8	T.B.	82	257	42	83.7
9	PIT	41	140	22	84.3	ST.L.	41	134	23	82.8	ST.L.	82	257	42	83.7
10	NYR	41	113	18	84.1	BOS	41	135	25	81.5	CHI	82	211	35	83.4
11	WSH	41	130	21	83.8	DAL	41	130	24	81.5	OTT	82	257	44	82.9
12	DET	41	142	23	83.8	CBJ	41	161	30	81.4	BOS	82	244	44	82.0
13	L.A.	41	129	22	82.9	WPG	41	155	29	81.3	WPG	82	308	56	81.8
14	BOS	41	109	19	82.6	CHI	41	117	22	81.2	WSH	82	266	50	81.2
15	WPG	41	153	27	82.4	T.B.	41	133	25	81.2	ANA	82	274	52	81.0
16	N.J.	41	119	21	82.4	TOR	41	131	25	80.9	L.A.	82	236	45	80.9
17	CAR	41	90	16	82.2	CGY	41	99	20	79.8	DET	82	288	55	80.9
18	FLA	41	117	21	82.1	NSH	41	124	25	79.8	NSH	82	234	45	80.8
19	NSH	41	110	20	81.8	NYI	41	107	22	79.4	DAL	82	254	49	80.7
20	OTT	41	121	22	81.8	N.J.	41	149	31	79.2	CGY	82	186	36	80.6
21	PHI	41	131	24	81.7	EDM	41	113	24	78.8	N.J.	82	268	52	80.6
22	CGY	41	87	16	81.6	WSH	41	136	29	78.7	TOR	82	266	52	80.5
23	BUF	41	123	23	81.3	L.A.	41	107	23	78.5	CBJ	82	303	60	80.2
24	TOR	41	135	27	80.0	FLA	41	133	29	78.2	FLA	82	250	50	80.0
25	DAL	41	124	25	79.8	DET	41	146	32	78.1	S.J.	82	223	48	78.5
26	S.J.	41	107	22	79.4	S.J.	41	116	26	77.6	NYI	82	218	48	78.0
27	CBJ	41	142	30	78.9	ANA	41	143	32	77.6	PHI	82	266	61	77.1
28	NYI	41	111	26	76.6	ARI	41	143	32	77.6	EDM	82	219	51	76.7
29	ARI	41	136	33	75.7	PHI	41	135	37	72.6	ARI	82	279	65	76.7
30	EDM	41	106	27	74.5	BUF	41	134	41	69.4	BUF	82	257	64	75.1
Totals		**1230**	**3639**	**644**	**82.3**		**1230**	**3882**	**759**	**80.4**		**1230**	**7521**	**1403**	**81.3**

SHORTHAND GOALS FOR

	Home			Road			Overall		
	Team	GP	SHGF	Team	GP	SHGF	Team	GP	SHGF
1	NYI	41	8	ANA	41	7	WPG	82	10
2	BOS	41	5	WPG	41	7	NYI	82	10
3	NYR	41	5	VAN	41	6	ANA	82	9
4	MTL	41	5	DAL	41	6	NYR	82	9
5	TOR	41	4	BUF	41	5	DAL	82	9
6	OTT	41	4	L.A.	41	5	BOS	82	8
7	CGY	41	3	CBJ	41	4	TOR	82	7
8	PIT	41	3	N.J.	41	4	MTL	82	7
9	T.B.	41	3	NYR	41	4	L.A.	82	7
10	NSH	41	3	EDM	41	4	BUF	82	7
11	DAL	41	3	T.B.	41	4	N.J.	82	7
12	CHI	41	3	BOS	41	3	T.B.	82	7
13	S.J.	41	3	COL	41	3	CGY	82	6
14	WPG	41	3	CGY	41	3	VAN	82	6
15	N.J.	41	3	PIT	41	3	PIT	82	6
16	L.A.	41	2	TOR	41	3	OTT	82	6
17	BUF	41	2	DET	41	3	CBJ	82	5
18	PHI	41	2	ARI	41	3	S.J.	82	4
19	WSH	41	2	MTL	41	2	WSH	82	4
20	MIN	41	2	OTT	41	2	NSH	82	4
21	ANA	41	2	NYI	41	2	MIN	82	4
22	ST.L.	41	1	WSH	41	2	COL	82	4
23	ARI	41	1	MIN	41	2	EDM	82	4
24	CAR	41	1	PHI	41	1	ARI	82	4
25	CBJ	41	1	S.J.	41	1	PHI	82	3
26	COL	41	1	FLA	41	1	DET	82	3
27	DET	41	0	CAR	41	1	CHI	82	3
28	EDM	41	0	ST.L.	41	1	ST.L.	82	2
29	FLA	41	0	NSH	41	1	CAR	82	2
30	VAN	41	0	CHI	41	0	FLA	82	1
		1230	**75**		**1230**	**93**		**1230**	**168**

SHORTHAND GOALS AGAINST

	Home			Road			Overall		
	Team	GP	SHGA	Team	GP	SHGA	Team	GP	SHGA
1	COL	41	0	MTL	41	1	VAN	82	2
2	L.A.	41	1	VAN	41	1	L.A.	82	2
3	MIN	41	1	CBJ	41	1	COL	82	2
4	CAR	41	1	BOS	41	1	BOS	82	3
5	VAN	41	1	CHI	41	1	CGY	82	3
6	ANA	41	1	CGY	41	1	MIN	82	3
7	BOS	41	2	NYI	41	1	NYI	82	3
8	CGY	41	2	L.A.	41	1	MTL	82	4
9	WSH	41	2	ARI	41	1	WSH	82	4
10	DET	41	2	PHI	41	2	CAR	82	4
11	T.B.	41	2	S.J.	41	2	S.J.	82	5
12	NYI	41	2	FLA	41	2	CBJ	82	5
13	WPG	41	2	COL	41	2	ST.L.	82	5
14	ST.L.	41	3	WSH	41	2	NSH	82	5
15	NSH	41	3	MIN	41	2	WPG	82	5
16	S.J.	41	3	EDM	41	2	PHI	82	6
17	NYR	41	3	ST.L.	41	2	ANA	82	6
18	MTL	41	3	NSH	41	2	T.B.	82	6
19	N.J.	41	3	NYR	41	3	FLA	82	6
20	BUF	41	4	OTT	41	3	NYR	82	6
21	PHI	41	4	WPG	41	3	DAL	82	7
22	DAL	41	4	CAR	41	3	CHI	82	7
23	FLA	41	4	DAL	41	3	EDM	82	7
24	CBJ	41	4	PIT	41	4	ARI	82	7
25	EDM	41	5	BUF	41	4	BUF	82	8
26	OTT	41	5	T.B.	41	4	N.J.	82	8
27	ARI	41	6	N.J.	41	5	DET	82	8
28	CHI	41	6	ANA	41	5	OTT	82	8
29	TOR	41	7	TOR	41	5	PIT	82	11
30	PIT	41	7	DET	41	6	TOR	82	12
		1230	**93**		**1230**	**75**		**1230**	**168**

Regular-Season Overtime Results

2014-15 to 1994-95

	2014-15				2013-14				2012-13				2011-12				2010-11			
Team	**GP**	**W**	**L**	**SO**	**GP**	**W**	**L**	**SO**	**GP**	**W**	**L**	**SO**	**GP**	**W**	**L**	**SO**	**GP**	**W**	**L**	**SO**
ANA	23	8	2	13	18	7	2	9	13	1	3	9	17	2	5	10	18	9	3	6
ARI/PHX/WPG	18	5	3	10	24	3	8	13	14	1	3	10	22	3	3	16	20	2	7	11
BOS	27	9	4	14	16	4	3	9	11	1	3	7	15	2	1	12	14	1	5	8
BUF	17	1	3	13	20	3	5	12	14	1	2	11	23	5	4	14	25	10	9	6
CGY	20	9	4	7	21	7	4	10	6	2	1	3	21	2	7	12	23	2	5	16
CAR/HFD	17	1	4	12	17	4	7	6	6	1	3	2	20	3	10	7	22	6	6	10
CHI	18	3	3	12	22	1	7	14	16	5	0	11	22	4	4	14	19	4	4	11
COL/QUE	24	2	8	14	23	10	4	9	12	3	5	4	22	7	4	11	20	6	7	7
CBJ	19	5	3	11	15	3	5	7	17	5	3	9	13	2	2	9	23	5	5	13
DAL/MIN	18	4	7	7	17	2	6	9	8	2	3	3	16	4	1	11	21	5	4	12
DET	25	7	4	14	24	4	6	14	12	2	3	7	18	3	3	12	23	9	6	8
EDM	21	2	7	12	18	5	6	7	11	2	4	5	17	2	3	12	16	2	3	11
FLA	24	1	5	18	16	0	2	14	10	1	5	4	25	1	7	17	22	6	5	11
L.A.	18	1	7	10	20	4	2	14	8	1	1	6	24	3	6	15	17	1	4	12
MIN	16	4	5	7	23	3	4	16	10	3	1	6	24	2	2	20	16	5	3	8
MTL	23	6	5	12	21	7	5	9	10	2	3	5	23	2	4	17	16	5	5	6
NSH	24	8	4	12	17	3	3	11	14	3	3	8	16	3	3	10	19	2	7	10
N.J.	20	1	7	12	27	9	5	13	13	1	3	9	22	4	2	16	15	7	3	5
NYI	20	6	1	13	24	4	5	15	13	2	4	7	21	3	7	11	24	7	7	10
NYR	17	6	2	9	12	2	3	7	12	4	0	8	19	8	2	9	17	3	2	12
OTT	26	7	6	13	24	3	7	14	12	2	2	8	21	5	6	10	14	2	5	7
PHI	26	5	7	14	17	4	2	11	6	2	1	3	19	6	2	11	18	3	5	10
PIT	22	6	6	10	18	4	4	10	5	2	0	3	17	2	3	12	23	5	5	13
ST.L.	21	5	3	13	23	4	2	17	15	0	3	12	22	3	5	14	18	3	5	10
S.J.	15	2	3	10	19	3	4	12	11	4	1	6	18	3	1	14	19	5	4	10
T.B.	15	4	3	8	23	6	3	14	6	1	1	4	21	10	5	6	25	8	5	12
TOR	16	3	3	10	22	5	4	13	7	2	0	5	19	5	5	9	18	2	5	11
VAN	17	6	3	8	22	6	4	12	13	1	1	11	24	7	2	15	17	4	4	9
WSH	21	5	7	9	28	4	3	21	10	4	3	3	19	7	4	8	25	9	5	11
WPG/ATL	24	4	7	13	23	5	4	14	9	4	0	5	20	6	6	8	27	10	5	12
Totals	**306**	**136**		**170**	**307**	**129**		**178**	**162**	**65**		**97**	**300**	**119**		**181**	**297**	**148**		**149**

	2009-10				2008-09				2007-08				2006-07				2005-06			
Team	**GP**	**W**	**L**	**SO**	**GP**	**W**	**L**	**SO**	**GP**	**W**	**L**	**SO**	**GP**	**W**	**L**	**SO**	**GP**	**W**	**L**	**SO**
ANA	19	3	3	13	19	5	4	10	20	4	1	15	23	5	4	14	18	3	5	10
ARI/PHX/WPG	26	5	1	20	11	1	4	6	16	4	1	11	12	2	3	7	15	6	2	7
BOS	27	4	4	19	17	3	4	10	21	3	5	13	19	4	2	13	22	4	8	10
BUF	20	6	4	10	19	2	4	13	21	5	3	13	22	5	3	14	17	6	1	10
CGY	15	2	3	10	12	3	4	5	16	3	7	6	15	2	5	8	15	2	4	9
CAR/HFD	19	5	5	9	17	7	2	8	13	5	3	5	14	6	3	5	20	4	6	10
CHI	23	6	2	15	22	6	5	11	17	4	4	9	18	3	2	13	22	7	7	8
COL/QUE	18	2	4	12	17	3	1	13	18	4	4	10	15	3	3	9	15	3	3	9
CBJ	20	3	5	12	21	5	3	13	17	2	4	11	16	4	2	10	18	6	1	11
DAL/MIN	23	2	4	17	22	5	5	12	15	3	4	8	22	6	3	13	21	3	5	13
DET	25	5	5	15	19	3	6	10	14	2	2	10	18	3	5	10	15	3	5	7
EDM	17	1	2	14	16	1	5	10	25	4	2	19	11	1	4	6	26	6	4	16
FLA	21	2	3	16	18	4	3	11	18	4	3	11	21	3	8	10	23	8	6	9
L.A.	23	4	1	18	19	3	3	13	14	2	4	8	20	2	8	10	15	4	4	7
MIN	18	5	1	12	17	3	6	8	19	6	2	11	25	7	1	17	14	1	5	8
MTL	25	8	5	12	22	4	4	14	20	5	4	11	14	2	1	11	18	7	6	5
NSH	20	6	2	12	20	6	3	11	17	5	4	8	17	3	3	11	17	3	5	9
N.J.	15	2	2	11	19	9	2	8	22	7	3	12	22	3	1	18	22	4	5	13
NYI	25	6	5	14	15	3	4	8	19	5	6	8	22	2	7	13	18	3	3	12
NYR	15	1	7	7	22	3	3	16	25	4	4	17	22	3	5	14	23	4	8	11
OTT	16	5	1	10	18	3	5	10	14	3	3	8	13	2	3	8	13	2	3	8
PHI	12	2	3	7	21	6	5	10	17	3	5	9	16	3	6	7	22	7	5	10
PIT	21	6	5	10	21	6	3	12	16	1	4	11	27	6	5	16	19	4	8	7
ST.L.	20	3	5	12	20	4	4	12	17	1	8	8	23	4	7	12	22	3	7	12
S.J.	19	1	5	13	21	4	6	11	19	3	4	12	8	1	3	4	21	9	4	8
T.B.	21	5	5	11	23	2	8	13	13	2	8	3	20	5	3	12	18	6	2	10
TOR	23	5	10	8	23	4	6	13	19	5	7	7	19	4	4	11	18	7	1	10
VAN	13	4	1	8	18	5	3	10	20	4	1	15	24	12	3	9	16	4	4	8
WSH	24	6	7	11	18	6	3	9	19	7	4	8	19	4	3	12	21	2	6	13
WPG/ATL	19	2	7	10	17	4	5	8	23	6	2	15	25	7	7	11	18	5	3	10
Totals	**301**	**117**		**184**	**282**	**123**		**159**	**272**	**116**		**156**	**281**	**117**		**164**	**281**	**136**		**145**

	2003-04				2002-03				2001-02				2000-01				1999-2000			
Team	**GP**	**W**	**L**	**T**	**GP**	**W**	**L**	**T**	**GP**	**W**	**L**	**T**	**GP**	**W**	**L**	**T**	**GP**	**W**	**L**	**T**
ANA	22	4	8	10	21	6	6	9	14	3	3	8	20	4	5	11	18	3	3	12
ARI/PHX/WPG	29	5	6	18	20	4	5	11	19	4	6	9	23	3	3	17	16	4	4	8
BOS	30	8	7	15	21	6	4	11	24	9	9	6	20	4	8	8	26	1	6	19
BUF	13	2	4	7	21	3	8	10	16	4	1	11	10	4	1	5	20	5	4	11
CGY	13	3	3	7	19	2	6	11	17	2	3	12	22	3	4	15	26	11	5	10
CAR/HFD	25	5	6	14	15	4	3	8	27	6	5	16	18	6	3	9	14	4	0	10
CHI	23	4	8	11	23	6	4	13	17	3	1	13	15	2	5	8	17	5	2	10
COL/QUE	28	8	7	13	23	4	6	13	13	4	1	8	20	6	4	10	17	5	1	11
CBJ	18	6	4	8	28	7	8	13	15	2	5	8	18	3	6	9	...	...	...	...
DAL/MIN	18	3	2	13	24	5	4	15	21	3	5	13	16	6	2	8	19	3	6	10
DET	20	7	2	11	21	7	4	10	24	10	4	10	23	10	4	9	16	4	2	10
EDM	23	6	5	12	27	7	9	11	19	3	4	12	20	5	3	12	27	3	8	16
FLA	24	5	4	15	26	4	9	13	16	0	6	10	24	2	9	13	15	3	6	6
L.A.	27	2	9	16	19	6	7	6	18	3	4	11	19	3	3	13	21	5	4	12
MIN	24	1	3	20	19	8	1	10	21	0	9	12	22	4	5	13	...	...	...	...
MTL	16	5	4	7	19	2	9	8	17	2	3	12	16	2	6	8	17	4	4	9
NSH	22	7	4	11	24	8	6	10	18	5	0	13	17	5	3	9	18	4	7	7
N.J.	21	7	2	12	25	5	7	13	19	6	4	9	20	5	3	12	16	3	5	8
NYI	17	2	4	11	18	5	2	11	18	6	4	8	12	2	3	7	15	5	1	9
NYR	18	3	8	7	20	6	4	10	13	5	4	4	11	5	1	5	21	6	3	12
OTT	19	3	6	10	16	7	1	8	19	3	7	9	16	3	4	9	15	2	2	11
PHI	23	2	6	15	23	6	4	13	16	3	3	10	19	5	3	11	21	6	3	12
PIT	19	7	4	8	14	3	5	6	20	7	5	8	15	3	3	9	17	3	6	8
ST.L.	24	11	2	11	19	2	8	9	18	6	4	8	23	6	5	12	17	5	1	11
S.J.	21	3	6	12	23	6	6	11	13	2	3	8	22	7	3	12	21	4	7	10
T.B.	18	4	6	8	23	2	5	16	19	4	4	11	13	2	5	6	16	0	7	9
TOR	17	4	3	10	17	7	3	7	17	3	4	10	19	3	5	11	17	7	3	7
VAN	26	11	5	10	19	5	1	13	14	4	3	7	23	5	7	11	27	4	8	15
WSH	14	1	3	10	20	6	6	8	19	6	2	11	16	2	4	10	19	5	2	12
WPG/ATL	18	6	4	8	19	7	5	7	19	3	5	11	16	2	2	12	11	0	4	7
Totals	**315**	**145**		**170**	**313**	**156**		**157**	**270**	**121**		**149**	**274**	**122**		**152**	**260**	**114**		**146**

	1998-99				1997-98				1996-97				1995-96				1994-95			
Team	**GP**	**W**	**L**	**T**	**GP**	**W**	**L**	**T**	**GP**	**W**	**L**	**T**	**GP**	**W**	**L**	**T**	**GP**	**W**	**L**	**T**
ANA	17	1	3	13	20	3	4	13	16	3	0	13	16	6	2	8	7	2	0	5
ARI/PHX/WPG	15	2	1	12	14	0	2	12	16	5	4	7	8	2	0	6	9	0	2	7
BOS	17	2	2	13	17	3	1	13	15	3	3	9	19	2	6	11	8	2	3	3
BUF	23	3	3	17	21	3	1	17	21	5	4	12	15	2	6	7	9	1	1	7
CGY	16	3	1	12	22	4	3	15	16	3	4	9	16	2	3	11	9	1	1	7
CAR/HFD	24	1	5	18	12	2	2	8	18	3	4	11	14	2	3	9	9	1	1	7
CHI	15	1	2	12	18	1	4	13	19	1	5	13	19	1	4	14	7	2	0	5
COL/QUE	12	2	0	10	22	2	3	17	15	2	3	10	6	1	0	5	8	0	0	8
CBJ	...	...	...	...	...	...	...	...	...	...	...	...	...	...	...	...	...	...	...	...
DAL/MIN	16	3	1	12	17	5	1	11	15	4	3	8	15	1	0	14	9	0	1	8
DET	10	2	1	7	15	0	0	15	27	7	2	18	11	3	1	7	4	0	0	4
EDM	20	3	5	12	15	3	2	10	16	1	6	9	14	4	2	8	7	1	2	4
FLA	21	1	2	18	20	3	2	15	26	3	4	19	13	0	3	10	9	0	3	6
L.A.	12	5	2	5	16	3	2	11	14	0	3	11	23	3	2	18	9	0	0	9
MIN	...	...	...	...	...	...	...	...	...	...	...	...	...	...	...	...	...	...	...	...
MTL	15	0	4	11	20	3	4	13	21	2	4	15	15	2	3	10	10	1	2	7
NSH	10	1	2	7	...	...	...	...	...	...	...	...	...	...	...	...	...	...	...	...
N.J.	15	3	1	11	16	2	3	11	17	1	2	14	19	7	0	12	11	1	2	8
NYI	17	1	6	10	13	0	2	11	17	3	2	12	17	2	5	10	7	1	1	5
NYR	19	5	3	11	24	2	4	18	13	3	0	10	17	2	1	14	3	0	0	3
OTT	18	1	2	15	17	2	0	15	17	0	2	15	8	0	3	5	7	1	1	5
PHI	24	2	3	19	15	3	1	11	18	3	2	13	20	4	3	13	8	3	1	4
PIT	22	7	1	14	23	3	2	18	13	1	4	8	9	3	2	4	5	1	1	3
ST.L.	15	1	1	13	12	2	2	8	13	1	1	11	18	1	1	16	7	1	1	5
S.J.	21	1	2	18	12	0	2	10	12	3	1	8	9	1	1	7	5	1	0	4
T.B.	12	1	2	9	13	0	3	10	16	4	2	10	18	3	3	12	7	2	2	3
TOR	14	6	1	7	10	1	0	9	10	1	1	8	18	4	2	12	8	0	0	8
VAN	13	0	1	12	17	0	3	14	14	5	2	7	20	1	4	15	13	0	1	12
WSH	11	2	3	6	17	4	1	12	13	2	2	9	16	4	1	11	9	0	1	8
WPG/ATL	...	...	...	...	...	...	...	...	...	...	...	...	...	...	...	...	...	...	...	...
Totals	**222**	**60**		**162**	**219**	**54**		**165**	**214**	**70**		**144**	**201**	**64**		**137**	**101**	**26**		**75**

Abbreviations: GP – games played; **W** – overtime win; **L** – overtime loss;
SO – game tied after overtime. Game decided in shootout. (2005-06 to date); See page **XXX**.
T – game tied after overtime. (Up to and including 2003-04.)

2014-15 Shootout Summary

Team Shootout Statistics

	GP	W	L	W%	G	S	S%	GA	SA	Sv%
Anaheim	13	8	5	.615	19	40	.475	15	41	.634
Arizona	10	5	5	.500	9	31	.290	9	30	.700
Boston	14	4	10	.286	9	60	.150	13	58	.776
Buffalo	13	8	5	.615	14	45	.311	11	44	.750
Calgary	7	4	3	.571	9	29	.310	8	29	.724
Carolina	12	5	7	.417	8	39	.205	9	37	.757
Chicago	12	9	3	.750	17	36	.472	8	39	.795
Colorado	14	10	4	.714	23	52	.442	15	50	.700
Columbus	11	9	2	.818	16	46	.348	8	46	.826
Dallas	7	4	3	.571	10	32	.313	8	32	.750
Detroit	14	4	10	.286	16	52	.308	23	50	.540
Edmonton	12	5	7	.417	10	63	.159	13	64	.797
Florida	18	8	10	.444	22	81	.272	25	84	.702
Los Angeles	10	2	8	.200	5	35	.143	12	33	.636
Minnesota	7	4	3	.571	10	25	.400	10	27	.630
Montreal	12	7	5	.583	15	44	.341	13	45	.711
Nashville	12	6	6	.500	12	42	.286	14	40	.650
New Jersey	12	5	7	.417	11	36	.306	12	34	.647
NY Islanders	13	7	6	.538	15	46	.326	13	43	.698
NY Rangers	9	4	5	.444	9	26	.346	11	28	.607
Ottawa	13	6	7	.462	16	54	.296	17	53	.679
Philadelphia	14	3	11	.214	12	53	.226	21	53	.604
Pittsburgh	10	4	6	.400	12	36	.333	14	38	.632
St. Louis	13	9	4	.692	16	39	.410	11	41	.732
San Jose	10	4	6	.400	11	46	.239	13	47	.723
Tampa Bay	8	3	5	.375	5	21	.238	9	22	.591
Toronto	10	5	5	.500	10	32	.313	13	34	.618
Vancouver	8	6	2	.750	10	20	.500	4	21	.810
Washington	9	5	4	.556	16	47	.340	14	46	.696
Winnipeg	13	7	6	.538	13	46	.283	14	45	.689
Totals	**170**				**380**	**1254**	**.303**			

Team Shootout Leaders

Wins

	W	L	W%
Colorado	10	4	.714
St. Louis	9	4	.692
Chicago	9	3	.750
Columbus	9	2	.818
Anaheim	8	5	.615
Buffalo	8	5	.615
Florida	8	10	.444
Montreal	7	5	.583
NY Islanders	7	6	.539
Winnipeg	7	6	.539

Goals Scored

	G	S	S%
Colorado	23	52	.442
Florida	22	81	.272
Anaheim	19	40	.475
Chicago	17	36	.472
St. Louis	16	39	.410
Columbus	16	46	.348
Washington	16	47	.340
Detroit	16	52	.308
Ottawa	16	54	.296
Montreal	15	44	.341
NY Islanders	15	46	.326

Fewest Goals Against

	GA	SA	Sv%
Vancouver	4	21	.810
Columbus	8	46	.826
Chicago	8	39	.795
Dallas	8	32	.750
Calgary	8	29	.724
Carolina	9	37	.757
Arizona	9	30	.700
Tampa Bay	9	22	.591
Minnesota	10	27	.630

Winning Percentage

	W	L	W%
Columbus	9	2	.818
Chicago	9	3	.750
Vancouver	6	2	.750
Colorado	10	4	.714
St. Louis	9	4	.692
Anaheim	8	5	.615
Buffalo	8	5	.615
Montreal	7	5	.583
Minnesota	4	3	.571
Dallas	4	3	.571
Calgary	4	3	.571

Shootout Games

	GP	W	L
Florida	18	8	10
Colorado	14	10	4
Boston	14	4	10
Detroit	14	4	10
Philadelphia	14	3	11
St. Louis	13	9	4
Anaheim	13	8	5
Buffalo	13	8	5
NY Islanders	13	7	6
Winnipeg	13	7	6
Ottawa	13	6	7

Shootout Abbreviations

G ....Goals Scored
GA ......Goals Against
GDG ...Game Deciding Goal
S ....Shots Taken
SA ......Shots Against
S% ....Goal Scoring %
Sv%....Save %
W%....Win %

Individual Shootout Leaders – Skaters

Shootout Goals Scored

	Team	G	S	S%
Jakob Silfverberg	Ana.	9	13	.692
Gustav Nyquist	Det.	8	14	.571
Nathan MacKinnon	Col.	6	9	.667
Patrick Kane	Chi.	6	10	.600
Ryan Johansen	CBJ	6	11	.546
Jonathan Toews	Chi.	6	12	.500
Vladimir Tarasenko	St.L.	6	12	.500
Matt Duchene	Col.	6	14	.429
9 players tied with		5		

Shootout Shots Taken

	Team	S	G	S%
Gustav Nyquist	Det.	14	8	.571
Matt Duchene	Col.	14	6	.429
Nick Bjugstad	Fla.	14	4	.286
Derek Roy	Nsh.-Edm.	14	3	.214
Jakob Silfverberg	Ana.	13	9	.692
Kyle Turris	Ott.	13	4	.308
Jonathan Huberdeau	Fla.	13	3	.231
11 players tied with		12		

Shootout Scoring Percentage

(min. 5 shots taken)	Team	S%	S	G
Jakob Silfverberg	Ana.	.692	13	9
Nathan MacKinnon	Col.	.667	9	6
Jacob Josefson	N.J.	.625	8	5
Patrick Kane	Chi.	.600	10	6
Chris Higgins	Van.	.600	5	3
Alexander Wennberg	CBJ	.600	5	3
Patrik Elias	N.J.	.600	5	3
Dave Bolland	Fla.	.600	5	3
Gustav Nyquist	Det.	.571	14	8
Mike Santorelli	Tor.-Nsh.	.571	7	4
P-A Parenteau	Mtl.	.571	7	4
Wayne Simmonds	Phi.	.571	7	4

Shootout Game-Deciding Goals

	Team	GDG	S	G
P-A Parenteau	Mtl.	4	7	4
Jonathan Toews	Chi.	4	12	6
Jacob Josefson	N.J.	3	8	5
Antoine Vermette	Ari.-Chi.	3	9	5
Ryan Johansen	CBJ	3	11	6
Kyle Okposo	NYI	3	10	6
David Perron	Edm.-Pit.	3	8	4
Filip Forsberg	Nsh.	3	8	3
Bobby Ryan	Ott.	3	11	4
28 players tied with		2		

Individual Shootout Leaders

Goaltenders

Goaltender Shootout Wins

	Team	W	L
Sergei Bobrovsky	CBJ	7	1
Roberto Luongo	Fla.	7	8
Jhonas Enroth	Buf.-Dal.	6	0
Brian Elliott	St.L.	6	2
Corey Crawford	Chi.	6	2
Semyon Varlamov	Col.	6	3
Frederik Andersen	Ana.	6	4
Jaroslav Halak	NYI	5	3
Carey Price	Mtl.	4	2
Eddie Lack	Van.	4	2
Devan Dubnyk	Ari.-Min.	4	3
Pekka Rinne	Nsh.	4	4
Ondrej Pavelec	Wpg.	4	5

Goaltender Shootout Shots Against

	Team	SA	GA	Sv%
Roberto Luongo	Fla.	75	21	.720
Tuukka Rask	Bos.	49	12	.755
Braden Holtby	Wsh.	39	11	.718
Ben Scrivens	Edm.	38	9	.763
Steve Mason	Phi.	37	15	.595
Sergei Bobrovsky	CBJ	36	4	.889
Antti Niemi	S.J.	35	8	.771
Semyon Varlamov	Col.	33	10	.697
Frederik Andersen	Ana.	32	11	.656
Marc-Andre Fleury	Pit.	32	12	.625
Jimmy Howard	Det.	32	17	.469
Ondrej Pavelec	Wpg.	31	12	.613
Jaroslav Halak	NYI	30	9	.700

Goaltender Shootout Save Percentage

(min. 20 shots faced)	Team	Sv%	SA	GA
Jhonas Enroth	Buf.-Dal.	.958	24	1
Sergei Bobrovsky	CBJ	.889	36	4
Niklas Svedberg	Bos.	.889	9	1
Michael Hutchinson	Wpg.	.857	14	2
Anton Khudobin	Car.	.846	13	2
Viktor Fasth	Edm.	.833	24	4
Dan Ellis	Fla.	.833	6	1
Martin Jones	L.A.	.833	6	1
Karri Ramo	Cgy.	.824	17	3
Carey Price	Mtl.	.818	22	4

Jakob Silfverberg of the Anaheim Ducks led the NHL with nine shootout goals in 13 attempts in 2014-15. He also topped the League with a .692 shootout scoring percentage.

Shootout Register, 2014-15

Skaters

Player	Team	S	G	S%	GDG
Karl Alzner	Wsh.	1	0	.000	0
Artem Anisimov	CBJ	3	0	.000	0
Mark Arcobello	Edm.-Nsh.-Pit.-Ari.	2	0	.000	0
Cam Atkinson	CBJ	7	2	.286	1
Keith Aulie	Edm.	1	0	.000	0
Nicklas Backstrom	Wsh.	10	3	.300	2
Josh Bailey	NYI	3	1	.333	1
Tyson Barrie	Col.	2	0	.000	0
Jamie Benn	Dal.	4	1	.250	0
Beau Bennett	Pit.	1	0	.000	0
Sean Bergenheim	Fla.-Min.	1	1	1.000	0
Patrice Bergeron	Bos.	12	3	.250	2
Bryan Bickell	Chi.	1	0	.000	0
Nick Bjugstad	Fla.	14	4	.286	2
Mikkel Boedker	Ari.	5	1	.200	1
Dave Bolland	Fla.	5	3	.600	2
Nick Bonino	Van.	7	3	.429	2
Reid Boucher	N.J.	1	0	.000	0
Zach Boychuk	Car.	1	0	.000	0
Brad Boyes	Fla.	7	2	.286	0
Tyler Bozak	Tor.	10	3	.300	1
Daniel Briere	Col.	2	1	.500	0
Troy Brouwer	Wsh.	2	1	.500	1
Dustin Brown	L.A.	1	0	.000	0
Andre Burakovsky	Wsh.	1	0	.000	0
Brent Burns	S.J.	5	2	.400	1
Alexandre Burrows	Van.	1	1	1.000	1
Ryan Callahan	T.B.	5	2	.400	2
Matt Calvert	CBJ	3	0	.000	0
Mike Cammalleri	N.J.	4	1	.250	0
Brian Campbell	Fla.	1	0	.000	0
Matthew Carle	T.B.	1	0	.000	0
John Carlson	Wsh.	1	1	1.000	0
Jeff Carter	L.A.	9	2	.222	1
Alex Chiasson	Ott.	2	0	.000	0
Jason Chimera	Wsh.	1	0	.000	0
Cal Clutterbuck	NYI	2	1	.500	1
Joe Colborne	Cgy.	4	1	.250	1
Erik Cole	Dal.-Det.	1	0	.000	0
Nick Cousins	Phi.	1	1	1.000	0
Logan Couture	S.J.	8	3	.375	0
Sean Couturier	Phi.	8	1	.125	0
Charlie Coyle	Min.	2	1	.500	1
Sidney Crosby	Pit.	9	5	.556	1
Pavel Datsyuk	Det.	11	3	.273	1
David Desharnais	Mtl.	12	4	.333	1
Simon Despres	Pit.-Ana.	1	0	.000	0
Shane Doan	Ari.	3	1	.333	1
Drew Doughty	L.A.	1	0	.000	0
Steve Downie	Pit.	1	0	.000	0
Jonathan Drouin	T.B.	2	0	.000	0
Brandon Dubinsky	CBJ	1	0	.000	0
Matt Duchene	Col.	14	6	.429	2
Patrick Eaves	Dal.	1	0	.000	0
Jordan Eberle	Edm.	12	2	.167	0
Aaron Ekblad	Fla.	1	0	.000	0
Patrik Elias	N.J.	5	3	.600	1
Lars Eller	Mtl.	2	0	.000	0
Ryan Ellis	Nsh.	5	1	.200	1
Tyler Ennis	Buf.	12	5	.417	2
Martin Erat	Ari.	1	0	.000	0
Loui Eriksson	Bos.	4	0	.000	0
Eric Fehr	Wsh.	4	1	.250	0
Vernon Fiddler	Dal.	3	1	.333	0
Valtteri Filppula	T.B.	1	0	.000	0
Tomas Fleischmann	Fla.-Ana.	2	0	.000	0
Brian Flynn	Buf.-Mtl.	2	2	1.000	2
Marcus Foligno	Buf.	1	0	.000	0
Nick Foligno	CBJ	4	0	.000	0
Filip Forsberg	Nsh.	8	3	.375	3
Matt Fraser	Bos.-Edm.	2	0	.000	0
Marian Gaborik	L.A.	6	2	.333	0
Sam Gagner	Ari.	8	2	.250	1
Alex Galchenyuk	Mtl.	11	4	.364	1
Brendan Gallagher	Mtl.	4	1	.250	1
Johnny Gaudreau	Cgy.	6	2	.333	0
Nathan Gerbe	Car.	4	1	.250	0
Ryan Getzlaf	Ana.	2	0	.000	0
Brian Gionta	Buf.	7	2	.286	0
Zemgus Girgensons	Buf.	8	2	.250	2
Claude Giroux	Phi.	12	1	.083	0
Scott Gomez	N.J.	6	2	.333	1
Barclay Goodrow	S.J.	2	0	.000	0
Mikael Granlund	Min.	1	0	.000	0
Mike Green	Wsh.	1	0	.000	0
Colin Greening	Ott.	1	0	.000	0
Seth Griffith	Bos.	2	0	.000	0
Erik Gudbranson	Fla.	1	0	.000	0
Taylor Hall	Edm.	2	0	.000	0
Dougie Hamilton	Bos.	1	0	.000	0
Ryan Hamilton	Edm.	1	0	.000	0
Martin Havlat	N.J.	1	0	.000	0
Jimmy Hayes	Fla.	2	0	.000	0
Kevin Hayes	NYR	1	0	.000	0
Dany Heatley	Ana.	1	0	.000	0
Victor Hedman	T.B.	1	1	1.000	1
Darren Helm	Det.	2	1	.500	1
Ales Hemsky	Dal.	3	0	.000	0
Matt Hendricks	Edm.	3	0	.000	0
Tomas Hertl	S.J.	3	0	.000	0
Chris Higgins	Van.	5	3	.600	2
Cody Hodgson	Buf.	2	1	.500	1
Mike Hoffman	Ott.	5	0	.000	0
Peter Holland	Tor.	3	1	.333	1
Shawn Horcoff	Dal.	2	1	.500	1
Patric Hornqvist	Pit.	1	0	.000	0
Jonathan Huberdeau	Fla.	13	3	.231	1
Jiri Hudler	Cgy.	6	2	.333	1
Jarome Iginla	Col.	3	2	.667	2
Jaromir Jagr	N.J.-Fla.	2	0	.000	0
Dmitrij Jaskin	St.L.	1	0	.000	0
Boone Jenner	CBJ	2	1	.500	1
Ryan Johansen	CBJ	11	6	.546	3
Jack Johnson	CBJ	2	1	.500	1
Jussi Jokinen	Fla.	12	2	.167	0
Olli Jokinen	Nsh.-Tor.-St.L.	1	0	.000	0
Josh Jooris	Cgy.	2	1	.500	0
Jacob Josefson	N.J.	8	5	.625	3
Nazem Kadri	Tor.	3	1	.333	1
Evander Kane	Wpg.	5	2	.400	1
Patrick Kane	Chi.	10	6	.600	2
Melker Karlsson	S.J.	4	2	.500	0
William Karlsson	Ana.-CBJ	1	1	1.000	1
Tyler Kennedy	S.J.-NYI	1	0	.000	0
Ryan Kesler	Ana.	10	4	.400	2
Alex Khokhlachev	Bos.	1	1	1.000	1
Dwight King	L.A.	1	0	.000	0
Oscar Klefbom	Edm.	1	0	.000	0
John Klingberg	Dal.	2	0	.000	0
Rob Klinkhammer	Ari.-Pit.-Edm.	1	1	1.000	1
Corban Knight	Cgy.	1	0	.000	0
Mikko Koivu	Min.	6	3	.500	1
Tomas Kopecky	Fla.	1	0	.000	0
Anze Kopitar	L.A.	9	1	.111	1
David Krejci	Bos.	5	1	.200	1
Niklas Kronwall	Det.	2	0	.000	0
Torey Krug	Bos.	6	1	.167	0
Nikita Kucherov	T.B.	5	2	.400	0
Nikolay Kulemin	NYI	1	0	.000	0
Dmitry Kulikov	Fla.	1	0	.000	0
Chris Kunitz	Pit.	2	0	.000	0
Evgeny Kuznetsov	Wsh.	9	5	.556	2
Andrew Ladd	Wpg.	10	2	.200	1
Brooks Laich	Wsh.	1	1	1.000	0
Anton Lander	Edm.	2	0	.000	0
Gabriel Landeskog	Col.	3	1	.333	0
Michael Latta	Wsh.	1	0	.000	0
Scott Laughton	Phi.	1	0	.000	0
Vincent Lecavalier	Phi.	4	0	.000	0
David Legwand	Ott.	1	0	.000	0
Jori Lehtera	St.L.	1	1	1.000	1
Lucas Lessio	Ari.	2	1	.500	0
Kris Letang	Pit.	5	2	.400	0
Mark Letestu	CBJ	6	2	.333	1
Trevor Lewis	L.A.	1	0	.000	0
Elias Lindholm	Car.	5	2	.400	1
Joakim Lindstrom	St.L.-Tor.	3	1	.333	1
Bryan Little	Wpg.	9	2	.222	2
Milan Lucic	Bos.	2	0	.000	0
Joffrey Lupul	Tor.	4	2	.500	1
Clarke MacArthur	Ott.	1	0	.000	0
Derek MacKenzie	Fla.	1	1	1.000	0
Nathan MacKinnon	Col.	9	6	.667	2
Evgeni Malkin	Pit.	6	1	.167	0
Brad Marchand	Bos.	8	2	.250	0
Martin Marincin	Edm.	1	1	1.000	1
Patrick Marleau	S.J.	6	1	.167	0
Jay McClement	Car.	1	0	.000	0
Milan Michalek	Ott.	2	1	.500	0
John Mitchell	Col.	2	0	.000	0
Willie Mitchell	Fla.	1	0	.000	0
Sean Monahan	Cgy.	6	2	.333	1
Dominic Moore	NYR	1	0	.000	0
Jeremy Morin	Chi.-CBJ	1	1	1.000	0
Brenden Morrow	T.B.	1	0	.000	0
Matt Moulson	Buf.	10	2	.200	1
Rick Nash	NYR	5	2	.400	2
Riley Nash	Car.	1	0	.000	0
Brock Nelson	NYI	2	0	.000	0
Andrej Nestrasil	Det.-Car.	1	0	.000	0
Frans Nielsen	NYI	12	5	.417	1
Matt Nieto	S.J.	1	0	.000	0
Matt Niskanen	Wsh.	1	0	.000	0
Ryan Nugent-Hopkins	Edm.	5	1	.200	0
Gustav Nyquist	Det.	14	8	.571	1
Ryan O'Reilly	Col.	6	3	.500	2
Kyle Okposo	NYI	10	5	.500	3
Dylan Olsen	Fla.	1	1	1.000	0
Brooks Orpik	Wsh.	1	1	1.000	0
T.J. Oshie	St.L.	11	4	.364	2
Alex Ovechkin	Wsh.	8	2	.250	0
Max Pacioretty	Mtl.	3	2	.667	0
Iiro Pakarinen	Edm.	1	0	.000	0
Ondrej Palat	T.B.	2	0	.000	0
P-A Parenteau	Mtl.	7	4	.571	4
Zach Parise	Min.	7	2	.286	1
David Pastrnak	Bos.	4	0	.000	0
Joe Pavelski	S.J.	9	2	.222	1
Mathieu Perreault	Wpg.	5	1	.200	1
David Perron	Edm.-Pit.	8	4	.500	3
Corey Perry	Ana.	9	3	.333	2
Jeff Petry	Edm.-Mtl.	1	0	.000	0
Brandon Pirri	Fla.	7	3	.429	1
Tomas Plekanec	Mtl.	3	0	.000	0
Jason Pominville	Min.	4	3	.750	1
Benoit Pouliot	Edm.	2	0	.000	0
Derrick Pouliot	Pit.	1	0	.000	0
Teddy Purcell	Edm.	6	2	.333	1
Rickard Rakell	Ana.	1	1	1.000	0
Victor Rask	Car.	6	1	.167	1
Mason Raymond	Cgy.	1	0	.000	0
Matt Read	Phi.	5	0	.000	0
Zach Redmond	Col.	1	0	.000	0
Brad Richards	Chi.	1	0	.000	0
Antoine Roussel	Dal.	1	1	1.000	0
Derek Roy	Nsh.-Edm.	14	3	.214	1
Tuomo Ruutu	N.J.	1	0	.000	0
Bobby Ryan	Ott.	11	4	.364	3
Michael Ryder	N.J.	1	0	.000	0
Martin St. Louis	NYR	3	1	.333	0
Mike Santorelli	Tor.-Nsh.	7	4	.571	1
Colton Sceviour	Dal.	3	2	.667	1
Mark Scheifele	Wpg.	2	0	.000	0
Brayden Schenn	Phi.	3	0	.000	0
David Schlemko	Ari.-Dal.-Cgy.	2	1	.500	1
Justin Schultz	Edm.	2	0	.000	0
Tyler Seguin	Dal.	4	3	.750	1
Alexander Semin	Car.	3	0	.000	0
Damon Severson	N.J.	1	0	.000	0
Patrick Sharp	Chi.	7	3	.429	2
Kevin Shattenkirk	St.L.	2	2	1.000	2
Andrew Shaw	Chi.	1	1	1.000	0
Riley Sheahan	Det.	2	1	.500	0
James Sheppard	S.J.-NYR	1	0	.000	0
Jakob Silfverberg	Ana.	13	9	.692	2
Wayne Simmonds	Phi.	7	4	.571	2
Jeff Skinner	Car.	6	0	.000	0
Brendan Smith	Det.	1	0	.000	0
Craig Smith	Nsh.	9	2	.222	0
Reilly Smith	Bos.	9	1	.111	0
Carl Soderberg	Bos.	2	0	.000	0
Jason Spezza	Dal.	6	1	.167	1
Ryan Spooner	Bos.	2	0	.000	0
Eric Staal	Car.	3	1	.333	1
Drew Stafford	Buf.-Wpg.	4	2	.500	1
Steven Stamkos	T.B.	3	0	.000	0
Alexander Steen	St.L.	10	2	.200	1
Lee Stempniak	NYR-Wpg.	3	1	.333	0
Derek Stepan	NYR	4	2	.500	1
Chris Stewart	Buf.-Min.	2	0	.000	0
Jarret Stoll	L.A.	1	0	.000	0
Mark Stone	Ott.	3	1	.333	1
Ryan Strome	NYI	4	0	.000	0
P.K. Subban	Mtl.	1	0	.000	0
Brandon Sutter	Pit.	4	1	.250	1
Max Talbot	Col.-Bos.	1	1	1.000	1
Alex Tanguay	Col.	9	3	.333	1
Vladimir Tarasenko	St.L.	12	6	.500	2
Tomas Tatar	Det.	9	3	.333	1
John Tavares	NYI	11	3	.273	1
Matt Tennyson	S.J.	1	0	.000	0
Chris Terry	Car.	7	3	.429	2
Joe Thornton	S.J.	3	0	.000	0
Jiri Tlusty	Car.-Wpg.	1	0	.000	0
Jonathan Toews	Chi.	12	6	.500	4
Tyler Toffoli	L.A.	4	0	.000	0
Vincent Trocheck	Fla.	5	1	.200	1
Kyle Turris	Ott.	13	4	.308	0
Scottie Upshall	Fla.	1	0	.000	0
James van Riemsdyk	Tor.	5	0	.000	0
Thomas Vanek	Min.	1	1	1.000	0
Sami Vatanen	Ana.	1	1	1.000	1
Antoine Vermette	Ari.-Chi.	9	5	.556	3
Kris Versteeg	Chi.	1	0	.000	0
Jakub Voracek	Phi.	12	5	.417	1
Radim Vrbata	Van.	7	3	.429	1
Joel Ward	Wsh.	1	1	1.000	0
Stephen Weiss	Det.	3	0	.000	0
Alexander Wennberg	CBJ	5	3	.600	2
Blake Wheeler	Wpg.	12	4	.333	1
Justin Williams	L.A.	1	0	.000	0
Tom Wilson	Wsh.	1	0	.000	0
Tommy Wingels	S.J.	1	1	1.000	1
Nail Yakupov	Edm.	6	1	.167	1
Travis Zajac	N.J.	2	0	.000	0
Henrik Zetterberg	Det.	4	0	.000	0
Mika Zibanejad	Ott.	11	5	.454	1
Marek Zidlicky	N.J.-Det.	2	0	.000	0
Mats Zuccarello	NYR	7	3	.429	2

Goaltenders

Goaltender	Team	W	L	SA	GA	Sv %
Jake Allen	St.L.	3	2	15	4	.733
Frederik Andersen	Ana.	6	4	32	11	.656
Craig Anderson	Ott.	1	3	20	6	.700
Richard Bachman	Edm.	0	0	2	0	1.000
Niklas Backstrom	Min.	1	1	6	2	.667
Jonathan Bernier	Tor.	3	4	26	11	.577
Reto Berra	Col.	2	0	4	1	.750
Ben Bishop	T.B.	3	3	17	6	.647
Sergei Bobrovsky	CBJ	7	1	36	4	.889
Ilya Bryzgalov	Ana.	0	1	3	2	.333
Scott Clemmensen	N.J.	0	1	4	2	.500
Corey Crawford	Chi.	6	2	29	6	.793
Scott Darling	Chi.	3	0	7	0	1.000
Devan Dubnyk	Ari.-Min.	4	3	29	9	.690
Brian Elliott	St.L.	6	2	26	7	.731
Dan Ellis	Fla.	1	1	6	1	.833
Ray Emery	Phi.	0	4	14	6	.571
Jhonas Enroth	Buf.-Dal.	6	0	24	1	.958
Viktor Fasth	Edm.	3	2	24	4	.833
Marc-Andre Fleury	Pit.	3	5	32	12	.625
John Gibson	Ana.	1	0	3	1	.667
Thomas Greiss	Pit.	1	1	6	2	.667
Philipp Grubauer	Wsh.	1	0	3	1	.667
Jaroslav Halak	NYI	5	3	30	9	.700
Andrew Hammond	Ott.	2	2	19	7	.632
Jonas Hiller	Cgy.	1	2	12	5	.583
Braden Holtby	Wsh.	3	3	39	11	.718
Jimmy Howard	Det.	2	8	32	17	.469
Michael Hutchinson	Wpg.	3	1	14	2	.857
Carter Hutton	Nsh.	2	2	15	7	.533
Chad Johnson	NYI	2	1	8	2	.750
Martin Jones	L.A.	0	1	6	1	.833
Anton Khudobin	Car.	3	2	13	2	.846
Keith Kinkaid	N.J.	2	2	12	4	.667
Darcy Kuemper	Min.	1	1	5	3	.400
Jason LaBarbera	Ana.	1	0	3	1	.667
Eddie Lack	Van.	4	2	16	4	.750
Robin Lehner	Ott.	3	2	14	4	.714
Kari Lehtonen	Dal.	2	3	21	6	.714
Anders Lindback	Dal.-Buf.	2	2	15	4	.733
Henrik Lundqvist	NYR	2	3	17	6	.647
Roberto Luongo	Fla.	7	8	75	21	.720
Steve Mason	Phi.	2	7	37	15	.595
Curtis McElhinney	CBJ	2	1	10	4	.600
Ryan Miller	Van.	2	0	5	0	1.000
Al Montoya	Fla.	0	1	3	3	.000
Petr Mrazek	Det.	2	2	18	6	.667
Evgeni Nabokov	T.B.	0	2	5	3	.400
Michal Neuvirth	Buf.-NYI	2	4	18	9	.500
Antti Niemi	S.J.	3	4	35	8	.771
Ondrej Pavelec	Wpg.	4	5	31	12	.613
Justin Peters	Wsh.	1	1	4	2	.500
Calvin Pickard	Col.	2	1	13	4	.692
Kevin Poulin	NYI	0	1	3	1	.667
Carey Price	Mtl.	4	2	22	4	.818
Jonathan Quick	L.A.	2	7	27	11	.593
Antti Raanta	Chi.	0	1	3	2	.333
Karri Ramo	Cgy.	3	1	17	3	.824
Tuukka Rask	Bos.	3	9	49	12	.755
James Reimer	Tor.	2	1	8	2	.750
Pekka Rinne	Nsh.	4	4	25	7	.720
Cory Schneider	N.J.	3	4	18	6	.667
Ben Scrivens	Edm.	2	5	38	9	.763
Mike Smith	Ari.	3	3	17	5	.706
Alex Stalock	S.J.	1	2	12	5	.583
Niklas Svedberg	Bos.	1	1	9	1	.889
Cam Talbot	NYR	2	2	11	5	.545
Dustin Tokarski	Mtl.	3	3	23	9	.609
Semyon Varlamov	Col.	6	3	33	10	.697
Cam Ward	Car.	2	5	24	7	.708
Rob Zepp	Phi.	1	0	2	0	1.000

NHL Record Book

Year-By-Year Final Standings & Leading Scorers

*Stanley Cup winner

1917-18

First Half

Team	GP	W	L	T	GF	GA	PTS
Montreal	14	10	4	0	81	47	20
Toronto	14	8	6	0	71	75	16
Ottawa	14	5	9	0	67	79	10
**Mtl. Wanderers	6	1	5	0	17	35	2

**Montreal Arena burned down and Wanderers forced to withdraw from League. Montreal Canadiens and Toronto each counted a win for defaulted games with Wanderers.

Second Half

Team	GP	W	L	T	GF	GA	PTS
*Toronto	8	5	3	0	37	34	10
Ottawa	8	4	4	0	35	35	8
Montreal	8	3	5	0	34	37	6

Leading Scorers

Player	Team	GP	G	A	PTS	PIM
Joe Malone	Montreal	20	44	4	48	30
Cy Denneny	Ottawa	20	36	10	46	80
Reg Noble	Toronto	20	30	10	40	35
Newsy Lalonde	Montreal	14	23	7	30	51
Corb Denneny	Toronto	21	20	9	29	14
Harry Cameron	Toronto	21	17	10	27	28
Didier Pitre	Montreal	20	17	6	23	29
Eddie Gerard	Ottawa	20	13	7	20	26
Jack Darragh	Ottawa	18	14	5	19	26
Frank Nighbor	Ottawa	10	11	8	19	6
Harry Meeking	Toronto	21	10	9	19	28

1918-19

First Half

Team	GP	W	L	T	GF	GA	PTS
• Montreal	10	7	3	0	57	50	14
Ottawa	10	5	5	0	39	39	10
Toronto	10	3	7	0	42	49	6

Second Half

Team	GP	W	L	T	GF	GA	PTS
Ottawa	8	7	1	0	32	14	14
Montreal	8	3	5	0	31	28	6
Toronto	8	2	6	0	22	43	4

• NHL Champion. Stanley Cup not awarded due to influenza epidemic.

Leading Scorers

Player	Team	GP	G	A	PTS	PIM
Newsy Lalonde	Montreal	17	22	10	32	40
Odie Cleghorn	Montreal	17	22	6	28	22
Frank Nighbor	Ottawa	18	19	9	28	27
Cy Denneny	Ottawa	18	18	4	22	58
Didier Pitre	Montreal	17	14	5	19	12
Alf Skinner	Toronto	17	12	4	16	26
Harry Cameron	Tor., Ott.	14	11	3	14	35
Jack Darragh	Ottawa	14	11	3	14	33
Ken Randall	Toronto	15	8	6	14	27
Sprague Cleghorn	Ottawa	18	7	6	13	27

1919-20

First Half

Team	GP	W	L	T	GF	GA	PTS
Ottawa	12	9	3	0	59	23	18
Montreal	12	8	4	0	62	51	16
Toronto	12	5	7	0	52	62	10
Quebec	12	2	10	0	44	81	4

Second Half

Team	GP	W	L	T	GF	GA	PTS
*Ottawa	12	10	2	0	62	41	20
Toronto	12	7	5	0	67	44	14
Montreal	12	5	7	0	67	62	10
Quebec	12	2	10	0	47	96	4

Leading Scorers

Player	Team	GP	G	A	PTS	PIM
Joe Malone	Quebec	24	39	10	49	12
Newsy Lalonde	Montreal	23	37	9	46	34
Frank Nighbor	Ottawa	23	26	15	41	18
Corb Denneny	Toronto	24	24	12	36	20
Jack Darragh	Ottawa	23	22	14	36	22
Reg Noble	Toronto	24	24	9	33	52
Amos Arbour	Montreal	22	21	5	26	13
Cully Wilson	Toronto	23	20	6	26	86
Didier Pitre	Montreal	22	14	12	26	6
Punch Broadbent	Ottawa	21	19	6	25	40

1920-21

First Half

Team	GP	W	L	T	GF	GA	PTS
*Ottawa	10	8	2	0	49	23	16
Toronto	10	5	5	0	39	47	10
Montreal	10	4	6	0	37	51	8
Hamilton	10	3	7	0	34	38	6

Second Half

Team	GP	W	L	T	GF	GA	PTS
Toronto	14	10	4	0	66	53	20
Montreal	14	9	5	0	75	48	18
Ottawa	14	6	8	0	48	52	12
Hamilton	14	3	11	0	58	94	6

Leading Scorers

Player	Team	GP	G	A	PTS	PIM
Newsy Lalonde	Montreal	24	33	10	43	36
Babe Dye	Ham., Tor.	24	35	5	40	32
Cy Denneny	Ottawa	24	34	5	39	10
Joe Malone	Hamilton	20	28	9	37	6
Frank Nighbor	Ottawa	24	19	10	29	10
Reg Noble	Toronto	24	19	8	27	54
Harry Cameron	Toronto	24	18	9	27	35
Goldie Prodger	Hamilton	24	18	9	27	8
Corb Denneny	Toronto	20	19	7	26	29
Jack Darragh	Ottawa	24	11	15	26	20

1921-22

Team	GP	W	L	T	GF	GA	PTS
Ottawa	24	14	8	2	106	84	30
*Toronto	24	13	10	1	98	97	27
Montreal	24	12	11	1	88	94	25
Hamilton	24	7	17	0	88	105	14

Leading Scorers

Player	Team	GP	G	A	PTS	PIM
Punch Broadbent	Ottawa	24	32	14	46	28
Cy Denneny	Ottawa	22	27	12	39	20
Babe Dye	Toronto	24	31	7	38	39
Harry Cameron	Toronto	24	18	17	35	22
Joe Malone	Hamilton	24	24	7	31	4
Corb Denneny	Toronto	24	19	9	28	28
Reg Noble	Toronto	24	17	11	28	19
Sprague Cleghorn	Montreal	24	17	9	26	80
George Boucher	Ottawa	23	13	12	25	12
Odie Cleghorn	Montreal	23	21	3	24	26

All-Time Standings of NHL Teams

(ranked by percentage)

Active Teams

Team	Games	Wins	Losses	Ties	OT Losses	SO Losses	Goals For	Goals Against	Points	Pts %	First Season
Montreal	6332	3260	2116	837	68	51	20514	16935	7476	.590	1917-18
Philadelphia	3718	1854	1285	457	60	62	12367	10880	4287	.577	1967-68
Boston	6172	2979	2267	791	73	62	19714	17956	6884	.558	1924-25
Buffalo	3492	1634	1342	409	56	51	11311	10540	3784	.542	1970-71
Nashville	1278	604	504	60	58	52	3384	3473	1378	.539	1998-99
Detroit	6106	2817	2353	815	61	60	18966	18036	6570	.538	1926-27
Minnesota	1114	520	436	55	48	55	2819	2872	1198	.538	2000-01
Calgary	3336	1536	1309	379	63	49	10984	10502	3563	.534	1972-73
Anaheim	1656	773	661	107	57	58	4505	4574	1768	.534	1993-94
San Jose	1820	837	743	121	66	53	5154	5292	1914	.526	1991-92
Colorado	2780	1281	1139	261	64	35	9149	9016	2922	.526	1979-80
St. Louis	3718	1676	1493	432	63	54	11501	11461	3901	.525	1967-68
Edmonton	2780	1248	1146	262	69	55	9452	9268	2882	.518	1979-80
Ottawa	1740	784	725	115	61	55	4991	5093	1799	.517	1992-93
Washington	3180	1415	1343	303	62	57	10033	10312	3252	.511	1974-75
NY Rangers	6106	2659	2535	808	56	48	18680	18664	6230	.510	1926-27
Dallas	3718	1613	1541	459	61	44	11439	11732	3790	.510	1967-68
Toronto	6332	2765	2667	783	63	54	19440	19576	6430	.508	1917-18
Pittsburgh	3718	1637	1593	383	66	39	12382	12769	3762	.506	1967-68
NY Islanders	3336	1452	1427	347	63	47	10732	10636	3361	.504	1972-73
Chicago	6106	2590	2584	814	60	58	18186	18313	6112	.500	1926-27
New Jersey	3180	1346	1397	328	53	56	9421	10143	3129	.492	1974-75
Vancouver	3492	1463	1533	391	50	55	10943	11590	3422	.490	1970-71
Los Angeles	3718	1541	1632	424	66	55	11865	12513	3627	.488	1967-68
Florida	1656	655	706	142	81	72	4281	4775	1605	.485	1993-94
Arizona	2780	1145	1256	266	59	54	8564	9443	2669	.480	1979-80
Carolina	2780	1134	1271	263	69	43	8331	9215	2643	.475	1979-80
Winnipeg	1196	483	554	45	66	48	3275	3851	1125	.470	1999-2000
Tampa Bay	1740	702	809	112	70	47	4708	5418	1633	.469	1992-93
Columbus	1114	451	525	33	51	54	2807	3329	1040	.467	2000-01

Defunct Teams

Team	Games	Wins	Losses	Ties	Goals For	Goals Against	Points	Pts %	First Season	Last Season
Ottawa Senators	542	258	221	63	1458	1333	579	.534	1917-18	1933-34
Montreal Maroons	622	271	260	91	1474	1405	633	.509	1924-25	1937-38
NY/Brooklyn Americans	784	255	402	127	1643	2182	637	.406	1925-26	1941-42
Hamilton Tigers	126	47	78	1	414	475	95	.377	1920-21	1924-25
Cleveland Barons	160	47	87	26	470	617	120	.375	1976-77	1977-78
Pittsburgh Pirates	212	67	122	23	376	519	157	.370	1925-26	1929-30
Calif./Oakland Seals	698	182	401	115	1826	2580	479	.343	1967-68	1975-76
St. Louis Eagles	48	11	31	6	86	144	28	.292	1934-35	1934-35
Quebec Bulldogs	24	4	20	0	91	177	8	.167	1919-20	1919-20
Montreal Wanderers	6	1	5	0	17	35	2	.167	1917-18	1917-18
Philadelphia Quakers	44	4	36	4	76	184	12	.136	1930-31	1930-31

Calgary totals include Atlanta Flames, 1972-73 to 1979-80.
Carolina totals include Hartford, 1979-80 to 1996-97.
Colorado totals include Quebec, 1979-80 to 1994-95.
Dallas totals include Minnesota North Stars, 1967-68 to 1992-93.
Detroit totals include Cougars, 1926-27 to 1929-30, and Falcons, 1930-31 to 1931-32.
New Jersey totals include Kansas City, 1974-75 to 1975-76, and Colorado Rockies, 1976-77 to 1981-82.
Phoenix totals include Winnipeg, 1979-80 to 1995-96.
Toronto totals include Arenas, 1917-18 to 1918-19, and St. Patricks, 1919-20 to 1925-26.
Winnipeg totals include Atlanta Thrashers, 1999-2000 to 2010-11.

1922-23

Team	GP	W	L	T	GF	GA	PTS
*Ottawa	24	14	9	1	77	54	29
Montreal	24	13	9	2	73	61	28
Toronto	24	13	10	1	82	88	27
Hamilton	24	6	18	0	81	110	12

Leading Scorers

Player	Team	GP	G	A	PTS	PIM
Babe Dye	Toronto	22	26	11	37	19
Cy Denneny	Ottawa	24	23	11	34	28
Billy Boucher	Montreal	24	24	7	31	55
Jack Adams	Toronto	23	19	9	28	42
Mickey Roach	Hamilton	24	17	10	27	8
Odie Cleghorn	Montreal	24	19	6	25	18
George Boucher	Ottawa	24	14	9	23	58
Reg Noble	Toronto	24	12	11	23	47
Cully Wilson	Hamilton	23	16	5	21	46
Aurel Joliat	Montreal	24	12	9	21	37

1923-24

Team	GP	W	L	T	GF	GA	PTS
Ottawa	24	16	8	0	74	54	32
*Montreal	24	13	11	0	59	48	26
Toronto	24	10	14	0	59	85	20
Hamilton	24	9	15	0	63	68	18

Leading Scorers

Player	Team	GP	G	A	PTS	PIM
Cy Denneny	Ottawa	22	22	2	24	10
George Boucher	Ottawa	21	13	10	23	38
Billy Boucher	Montreal	23	16	6	22	48
Billy Burch	Hamilton	24	16	6	22	6
Aurel Joliat	Montreal	24	15	5	20	27
Babe Dye	Toronto	19	16	3	19	23
Jack Adams	Toronto	22	14	4	18	51
Reg Noble	Toronto	24	12	5	17	79
Frank Nighbor	Ottawa	20	11	6	17	16
Howie Morenz	Montreal	24	13	3	16	20
King Clancy	Ottawa	24	8	8	16	26

1924-25

Team	GP	W	L	T	GF	GA	PTS
Hamilton	30	19	10	1	90	60	39
Toronto	30	19	11	0	90	84	38
• Montreal	30	17	11	2	93	56	36
Ottawa	30	17	12	1	83	66	35
Mtl. Maroons	30	9	19	2	45	65	20
Boston	30	6	24	0	49	119	12

• NHL Champion (Stanley Cup won by Victoria Cougars, WCHL)

Leading Scorers

Player	Team	GP	G	A	PTS	PIM
Babe Dye	Toronto	29	38	8	46	41
Cy Denneny	Ottawa	29	27	15	42	16
Aurel Joliat	Montreal	25	30	11	41	85
Howie Morenz	Montreal	30	28	11	39	46
Red Green	Hamilton	30	19	15	34	81
Jack Adams	Toronto	27	21	10	31	67
Billy Boucher	Montreal	30	17	13	30	92
Billy Burch	Hamilton	27	20	7	27	10
Jimmy Herberts	Boston	30	17	7	24	55
Hooley Smith	Ottawa	30	10	13	23	81

1925-26

Team	GP	W	L	T	GF	GA	PTS
Ottawa	36	24	8	4	77	42	52
*Mtl. Maroons	36	20	11	5	91	73	45
Pittsburgh	36	19	16	1	82	70	39
Boston	36	17	15	4	92	85	38
NY Americans	36	12	20	4	68	89	28
Toronto	36	12	21	3	92	114	27
Montreal	36	11	24	1	79	108	23

Leading Scorers

Player	Team	GP	G	A	PTS	PIM
Nels Stewart	Mtl. Maroons	36	34	8	42	119
Cy Denneny	Ottawa	36	24	12	36	18
Carson Cooper	Boston	36	28	3	31	10
Jimmy Herberts	Boston	36	26	5	31	47
Howie Morenz	Montreal	31	23	3	26	39
Jack Adams	Toronto	36	21	5	26	52
Aurel Joliat	Montreal	35	17	9	26	52
Billy Burch	NY Americans	36	22	3	25	33
Hooley Smith	Ottawa	28	16	9	25	53
Frank Nighbor	Ottawa	35	12	13	25	40

1926-27

Canadian Division

Team	GP	W	L	T	GF	GA	PTS
*Ottawa	44	30	10	4	86	69	64
Montreal	44	28	14	2	99	67	58
Mtl. Maroons	44	20	20	4	71	68	44
NY Americans	44	17	25	2	82	91	36
Toronto	44	15	24	5	79	94	35

American Division

Team	GP	W	L	T	GF	GA	PTS
NY Rangers	44	25	13	6	95	72	56
Boston	44	21	20	3	97	89	45
Chicago	44	19	22	3	115	116	41
Pittsburgh	44	15	26	3	79	108	33
Detroit	44	12	28	4	76	105	28

Leading Scorers

Player	Team	GP	G	A	PTS	PIM
Bill Cook	NY Rangers	44	33	4	37	58
Dick Irvin	Chicago	43	18	18	36	34
Howie Morenz	Montreal	44	25	7	32	49
Frank Fredrickson	Det., Bos.	41	18	13	31	46
Babe Dye	Chicago	41	25	5	30	14
Ace Bailey	Toronto	42	15	13	28	82
Frank Boucher	NY Rangers	44	13	15	28	17
Billy Burch	NY Americans	43	19	8	27	40
Harry Oliver	Boston	42	18	6	24	17
Duke Keats	Bos., Det.	42	16	8	24	52

1927-28

Canadian Division

Team	GP	W	L	T	GF	GA	PTS
Montreal	44	26	11	7	116	48	59
Mtl. Maroons	44	24	14	6	96	77	54
Ottawa	44	20	14	10	78	57	50
Toronto	44	18	18	8	89	88	44
NY Americans	44	11	27	6	63	128	28

American Division

Team	GP	W	L	T	GF	GA	PTS
Boston	44	20	13	11	77	70	51
*NY Rangers	44	19	16	9	94	79	47
Pittsburgh	44	19	17	8	67	76	46
Detroit	44	19	19	6	88	79	44
Chicago	44	7	34	3	68	134	17

Leading Scorers

Player	Team	GP	G	A	PTS	PIM
Howie Morenz	Montreal	43	33	18	51	66
Aurel Joliat	Montreal	44	28	11	39	105
Frank Boucher	NY Rangers	44	23	12	35	15
George Hay	Detroit	42	22	13	35	20
Nels Stewart	Mtl. Maroons	41	27	7	34	104
Art Gagne	Montreal	44	20	10	30	75
Bun Cook	NY Rangers	44	14	14	28	45
Bill Carson	Toronto	32	20	6	26	36
Frank Finnigan	Ottawa	38	20	5	25	34
Bill Cook	NY Rangers	43	18	6	24	42
Duke Keats	Det., Chi.	38	14	10	24	60

1928-29

Canadian Division

Team	GP	W	L	T	GF	GA	PTS
Montreal	44	22	7	15	71	43	59
NY Americans	44	19	13	12	53	53	50
Toronto	44	21	18	5	85	69	47
Ottawa	44	14	17	13	54	67	41
Mtl. Maroons	44	15	20	9	67	65	39

American Division

Team	GP	W	L	T	GF	GA	PTS
*Boston	44	26	13	5	89	52	57
NY Rangers	44	21	13	10	72	65	52
Detroit	44	19	16	9	72	63	47
Pittsburgh	44	9	27	8	46	80	26
Chicago	44	7	29	8	33	85	22

Leading Scorers

Player	Team	GP	G	A	PTS	PIM
Ace Bailey	Toronto	44	22	10	32	78
Nels Stewart	Mtl. Maroons	44	21	8	29	74
Carson Cooper	Detroit	43	18	9	27	14
Howie Morenz	Montreal	42	17	10	27	47
Andy Blair	Toronto	44	12	15	27	41
Frank Boucher	NY Rangers	44	10	16	26	8
Harry Oliver	Boston	43	17	6	23	24
Bill Cook	NY Rangers	43	15	8	23	41
Jimmy Ward	Mtl. Maroons	43	14	8	22	46

Seven players tied with 19 points

1929-30

Canadian Division

Team	GP	W	L	T	GF	GA	PTS
Mtl. Maroons	44	23	16	5	141	114	51
*Montreal	44	21	14	9	142	114	51
Ottawa	44	21	15	8	138	118	50
Toronto	44	17	21	6	116	124	40
NY Americans	44	14	25	5	113	161	33

American Division

Team	GP	W	L	T	GF	GA	PTS
Boston	44	38	5	1	179	98	77
Chicago	44	21	18	5	117	111	47
NY Rangers	44	17	17	10	136	143	44
Detroit	44	14	24	6	117	133	34
Pittsburgh	44	5	36	3	102	185	13

Leading Scorers

Player	Team	GP	G	A	PTS	PIM
Cooney Weiland	Boston	44	43	30	73	27
Frank Boucher	NY Rangers	42	26	36	62	16
Dit Clapper	Boston	44	41	20	61	48
Bill Cook	NY Rangers	44	29	30	59	56
Hec Kilrea	Ottawa	44	36	22	58	72
Nels Stewart	Mtl. Maroons	44	39	16	55	81
Howie Morenz	Montreal	44	40	10	50	72
Normie Himes	NY Americans	44	28	22	50	15
Joe Lamb	Ottawa	44	29	20	49	119
Dutch Gainor	Boston	42	18	31	49	39

1930-31

Canadian Division

Team	GP	W	L	T	GF	GA	PTS
*Montreal	44	26	10	8	129	89	60
Toronto	44	22	13	9	118	99	53
Mtl. Maroons	44	20	18	6	105	106	46
NY Americans	44	18	16	10	76	74	46
Ottawa	44	10	30	4	91	142	24

American Division

Team	GP	W	L	T	GF	GA	PTS
Boston	44	28	10	6	143	90	62
Chicago	44	24	17	3	108	78	51
NY Rangers	44	19	16	9	106	87	47
Detroit	44	16	21	7	102	105	39
Philadelphia	44	4	36	4	76	184	12

Leading Scorers

Player	Team	GP	G	A	PTS	PIM
Howie Morenz	Montreal	39	28	23	51	49
Ebbie Goodfellow	Detroit	44	25	23	48	32
Charlie Conacher	Toronto	37	31	12	43	78
Bill Cook	NY Rangers	43	30	12	42	39
Ace Bailey	Toronto	40	23	19	42	46
Joe Primeau	Toronto	38	9	32	41	18
Nels Stewart	Mtl. Maroons	42	25	14	39	75
Frank Boucher	NY Rangers	44	12	27	39	20
Cooney Weiland	Boston	44	25	13	38	14
Bun Cook	NY Rangers	44	18	17	35	72
Aurel Joliat	Montreal	43	13	22	35	73

1931-32

Canadian Division

Team	GP	W	L	T	GF	GA	PTS
Montreal	48	25	16	7	128	111	57
*Toronto	48	23	18	7	155	127	53
Mtl. Maroons	48	19	22	7	142	139	45
NY Americans	48	16	24	8	95	142	40

American Division

Team	GP	W	L	T	GF	GA	PTS
NY Rangers	48	23	17	8	134	112	54
Chicago	48	18	19	11	86	101	47
Detroit	48	18	20	10	95	108	46
Boston	48	15	21	12	122	117	42

Leading Scorers

Player	Team	GP	G	A	PTS	PIM
Busher Jackson	Toronto	48	28	25	53	63
Joe Primeau	Toronto	46	13	37	50	25
Howie Morenz	Montreal	48	24	25	49	46
Charlie Conacher	Toronto	44	34	14	48	66
Bill Cook	NY Rangers	48	34	14	48	33
Dave Trottier	Mtl. Maroons	48	26	18	44	94
Hooley Smith	Mtl. Maroons	43	11	33	44	49
Babe Siebert	Mtl. Maroons	48	21	18	39	64
Dit Clapper	Boston	48	17	22	39	21
Aurel Joliat	Montreal	48	15	24	39	46

1932-33

Canadian Division

Team	GP	W	L	T	GF	GA	PTS
Toronto	48	24	18	6	119	111	54
Mtl. Maroons	48	22	20	6	135	119	50
Montreal	48	18	25	5	92	115	41
NY Americans	48	15	22	11	91	118	41
Ottawa	48	11	27	10	88	131	32

American Division

Team	GP	W	L	T	GF	GA	PTS
Boston	48	25	15	8	124	88	58
Detroit	48	25	15	8	111	93	58
*NY Rangers	48	23	17	8	135	107	54
Chicago	48	16	20	12	88	101	44

Leading Scorers

Player	Team	GP	G	A	PTS	PIM
Bill Cook	NY Rangers	48	28	22	50	51
Busher Jackson	Toronto	48	27	17	44	43
Baldy Northcott	Mtl. Maroons	48	22	21	43	30
Hooley Smith	Mtl. Maroons	48	20	21	41	66
Paul Haynes	Mtl. Maroons	48	16	25	41	18
Aurel Joliat	Montreal	48	18	21	39	53
Marty Barry	Boston	48	24	13	37	40
Bun Cook	NY Rangers	48	22	15	37	35
Nels Stewart	Boston	47	18	18	36	62
Howie Morenz	Montreal	46	14	21	35	32
Johnny Gagnon	Montreal	48	12	23	35	64
Eddie Shore	Boston	48	8	27	35	102
Frank Boucher	NY Rangers	46	7	28	35	4

1933-34

Canadian Division

Team	GP	W	L	T	GF	GA	PTS
Toronto	48	26	13	9	174	119	61
Montreal	48	22	20	6	99	101	50
Mtl. Maroons	48	19	18	11	117	122	49
NY Americans	48	15	23	10	104	132	40
Ottawa	48	13	29	6	115	143	32

American Division

Team	GP	W	L	T	GF	GA	PTS
Detroit	48	24	14	10	113	98	58
*Chicago	48	20	17	11	88	83	51
NY Rangers	48	21	19	8	120	113	50
Boston	48	18	25	5	111	130	41

Leading Scorers

Player	Team	GP	G	A	PTS	PIM
Charlie Conacher	Toronto	42	32	20	52	38
Joe Primeau	Toronto	45	14	32	46	8
Frank Boucher	NY Rangers	48	14	30	44	4
Marty Barry	Boston	48	27	12	39	12
Cecil Dillon	NY Rangers	48	13	26	39	10
Nels Stewart	Boston	48	21	17	38	68
Busher Jackson	Toronto	38	20	18	38	38
Aurel Joliat	Montreal	48	22	15	37	27
Hooley Smith	Mtl. Maroons	47	18	19	37	58
Paul Thompson	Chicago	48	20	16	36	17

1934-35

Canadian Division

Team	GP	W	L	T	GF	GA	PTS
Toronto	48	30	14	4	157	111	64
*Mtl. Maroons	48	24	19	5	123	92	53
Montreal	48	19	23	6	110	145	44
NY Americans	48	12	27	9	100	142	33
St. Louis	48	11	31	6	86	144	28

American Division

Team	GP	W	L	T	GF	GA	PTS
Boston	48	26	16	6	129	112	58
Chicago	48	26	17	5	118	88	57
NY Rangers	48	22	20	6	137	139	50
Detroit	48	19	22	7	127	114	45

Leading Scorers

Player	Team	GP	G	A	PTS	PIM
Charlie Conacher	Toronto	47	36	21	57	24
Syd Howe	St.L., Det.	50	22	25	47	34
Larry Aurie	Detroit	48	17	29	46	24
Frank Boucher	NY Rangers	48	13	32	45	2
Busher Jackson	Toronto	42	22	22	44	27
Herbie Lewis	Detroit	47	16	27	43	26
Art Chapman	NY Americans	47	9	34	43	4
Marty Barry	Boston	48	20	20	40	33
Sweeney Schriner	NY Americans	48	18	22	40	6
Nels Stewart	Boston	47	21	18	39	45
Paul Thompson	Chicago	48	16	23	39	20

1935-36

Canadian Division

Team	GP	W	L	T	GF	GA	PTS
Mtl. Maroons	48	22	16	10	114	106	54
Toronto	48	23	19	6	126	106	52
NY Americans	48	16	25	7	109	122	39
Montreal	48	11	26	11	82	123	33

American Division

Team	GP	W	L	T	GF	GA	PTS
*Detroit	48	24	16	8	124	103	56
Boston	48	22	20	6	92	83	50
Chicago	48	21	19	8	93	92	50
NY Rangers	48	19	17	12	91	96	50

Leading Scorers

Player	Team	GP	G	A	PTS	PIM
Sweeney Schriner	NY Americans	48	19	26	45	8
Marty Barry	Detroit	48	21	19	40	16
Paul Thompson	Chicago	45	17	23	40	19
Bill Thoms	Toronto	48	23	15	38	29
Charlie Conacher	Toronto	44	23	15	38	74
Hooley Smith	Mtl. Maroons	47	19	19	38	75
Doc Romnes	Chicago	48	13	25	38	6
Art Chapman	NY Americans	47	10	28	38	14
Herbie Lewis	Detroit	45	14	23	37	25
Baldy Northcott	Mtl. Maroons	48	15	21	36	41

1936-37

Canadian Division

Team	GP	W	L	T	GF	GA	PTS
Montreal	48	24	18	6	115	111	54
Mtl. Maroons	48	22	17	9	126	110	53
Toronto	48	22	21	5	119	115	49
NY Americans	48	15	29	4	122	161	34

American Division

Team	GP	W	L	T	GF	GA	PTS
*Detroit	48	25	14	9	128	102	59
Boston	48	23	18	7	120	110	53
NY Rangers	48	19	20	9	117	106	47
Chicago	48	14	27	7	99	131	35

Leading Scorers

Player	Team	GP	G	A	PTS	PIM
Sweeney Schriner	NY Americans	48	21	25	46	17
Syl Apps	Toronto	48	16	29	45	10
Marty Barry	Detroit	48	17	27	44	6
Larry Aurie	Detroit	45	23	20	43	20
Busher Jackson	Toronto	46	21	19	40	12
Johnny Gagnon	Montreal	48	20	16	36	38
Bob Gracie	Mtl. Maroons	47	11	25	36	18
Nels Stewart	Bos., NYA	43	23	12	35	37
Paul Thompson	Chicago	47	17	18	35	28
Bill Cowley	Boston	46	13	22	35	4

1937-38

Canadian Division

Team	GP	W	L	T	GF	GA	PTS
Toronto	48	24	15	9	151	127	57
NY Americans	48	19	18	11	110	111	49
Montreal	48	18	17	13	123	128	49
Mtl. Maroons	48	12	30	6	101	149	30

American Division

Team	GP	W	L	T	GF	GA	PTS
Boston	48	30	11	7	142	89	67
NY Rangers	48	27	15	6	149	96	60
*Chicago	48	14	25	9	97	139	37
Detroit	48	12	25	11	99	133	35

Leading Scorers

Player	Team	GP	G	A	PTS	PIM
Gordie Drillon	Toronto	48	26	26	52	4
Syl Apps	Toronto	47	21	29	50	9
Paul Thompson	Chicago	48	22	22	44	14
Georges Mantha	Montreal	47	23	19	42	12
Cecil Dillon	NY Rangers	48	21	18	39	6
Bill Cowley	Boston	48	17	22	39	8
Sweeney Schriner	NY Americans	49	21	17	38	22
Bill Thoms	Toronto	48	14	24	38	14
Clint Smith	NY Rangers	48	14	23	37	0
Nels Stewart	NY Americans	48	19	17	36	29
Neil Colville	NY Rangers	45	17	19	36	11

1938-39

Team	GP	W	L	T	GF	GA	PTS
*Boston	48	36	10	2	156	76	74
NY Rangers	48	26	16	6	149	105	58
Toronto	48	19	20	9	114	107	47
NY Americans	48	17	21	10	119	157	44
Detroit	48	18	24	6	107	128	42
Montreal	48	15	24	9	115	146	39
Chicago	48	12	28	8	91	132	32

Leading Scorers

Player	Team	GP	G	A	PTS	PIM
Toe Blake	Montreal	48	24	23	47	10
Sweeney Schriner	NY Americans	48	13	31	44	20
Bill Cowley	Boston	34	8	34	42	2
Clint Smith	NY Rangers	48	21	20	41	2
Marty Barry	Detroit	48	13	28	41	4
Syl Apps	Toronto	44	15	25	40	4
Tom Anderson	NY Americans	48	13	27	40	14
Johnny Gottselig	Chicago	48	16	23	39	15
Paul Haynes	Montreal	47	5	33	38	27
Roy Conacher	Boston	47	26	11	37	12
Lorne Carr	NY Americans	46	19	18	37	16
Neil Colville	NY Rangers	48	18	19	37	12
Phil Watson	NY Rangers	48	15	22	37	42

1939-40

Team	GP	W	L	T	GF	GA	PTS
Boston	48	31	12	5	170	98	67
*NY Rangers	48	27	11	10	136	77	64
Toronto	48	25	17	6	134	110	56
Chicago	48	23	19	6	112	120	52
Detroit	48	16	26	6	91	126	38
NY Americans	48	15	29	4	106	140	34
Montreal	48	10	33	5	90	168	25

Leading Scorers

Player	Team	GP	G	A	PTS	PIM
Milt Schmidt	Boston	48	22	30	52	37
Woody Dumart	Boston	48	22	21	43	16
Bobby Bauer	Boston	48	17	26	43	2
Gordie Drillon	Toronto	43	21	19	40	13
Bill Cowley	Boston	48	13	27	40	24
Bryan Hextall	NY Rangers	48	24	15	39	52
Neil Colville	NY Rangers	48	19	19	38	22
Syd Howe	Detroit	46	14	23	37	17
Toe Blake	Montreal	48	17	19	36	48
Murray Armstrong	NY Americans	48	16	20	36	12

1940-41

Team	GP	W	L	T	GF	GA	PTS
*Boston	48	27	8	13	168	102	67
Toronto	48	28	14	6	145	99	62
Detroit	48	21	16	11	112	102	53
NY Rangers	48	21	19	8	143	125	50
Chicago	48	16	25	7	112	139	39
Montreal	48	16	26	6	121	147	38
NY Americans	48	8	29	11	99	186	27

Leading Scorers

Player	Team	GP	G	A	PTS	PIM
Bill Cowley	Boston	46	17	45	62	16
Bryan Hextall	NY Rangers	48	26	18	44	16
Gordie Drillon	Toronto	42	23	21	44	2
Syl Apps	Toronto	41	20	24	44	6
Lynn Patrick	NY Rangers	48	20	24	44	12
Syd Howe	Detroit	48	20	24	44	8
Neil Colville	NY Rangers	48	14	28	42	28
Eddie Wiseman	Boston	48	16	24	40	10
Bobby Bauer	Boston	48	17	22	39	2
Sweeney Schriner	Toronto	48	24	14	38	6
Roy Conacher	Boston	40	24	14	38	7
Milt Schmidt	Boston	44	13	25	38	23

1941-42

Team	GP	W	L	T	GF	GA	PTS
NY Rangers	48	29	17	2	177	143	60
*Toronto	48	27	18	3	158	136	57
Boston	48	25	17	6	160	118	56
Chicago	48	22	23	3	145	155	47
Detroit	48	19	25	4	140	147	42
Montreal	48	18	27	3	134	173	39
Brooklyn	48	16	29	3	133	175	35

Leading Scorers

Player	Team	GP	G	A	PTS	PIM
Bryan Hextall	NY Rangers	48	24	32	56	30
Lynn Patrick	NY Rangers	47	32	22	54	18
Don Grosso	Detroit	48	23	30	53	13
Phil Watson	NY Rangers	48	15	37	52	48
Sid Abel	Detroit	48	18	31	49	45
Toe Blake	Montreal	47	17	28	45	19
Bill Thoms	Chicago	47	15	30	45	8
Gordie Drillon	Toronto	48	23	18	41	6
Syl Apps	Toronto	38	18	23	41	0
Tom Anderson	Brooklyn	48	12	29	41	54

1942-43

Team	GP	W	L	T	GF	GA	PTS
*Detroit	50	25	14	11	169	124	61
Boston	50	24	17	9	195	176	57
Toronto	50	22	19	9	198	159	53
Montreal	50	19	19	12	181	191	50
Chicago	50	17	18	15	179	180	49
NY Rangers	50	11	31	8	161	253	30

Leading Scorers

Player	Team	GP	G	A	PTS	PIM
Doug Bentley	Chicago	50	33	40	73	18
Bill Cowley	Boston	48	27	45	72	10
Max Bentley	Chicago	47	26	44	70	2
Lynn Patrick	NY Rangers	50	22	39	61	28
Lorne Carr	Toronto	50	27	33	60	15
Billy Taylor	Toronto	50	18	42	60	2
Bryan Hextall	NY Rangers	50	27	32	59	28
Toe Blake	Montreal	48	23	36	59	28
Elmer Lach	Montreal	45	18	40	58	14
Buddy O'Connor	Montreal	50	15	43	58	2

1943-44

Team	GP	W	L	T	GF	GA	PTS
*Montreal	50	38	5	7	234	109	83
Detroit	50	26	18	6	214	177	58
Toronto	50	23	23	4	214	174	50
Chicago	50	22	23	5	178	187	49
Boston	50	19	26	5	223	268	43
NY Rangers	50	6	39	5	162	310	17

Leading Scorers

Player	Team	GP	G	A	PTS	PIM
Herb Cain	Boston	48	36	46	82	4
Doug Bentley	Chicago	50	38	39	77	22
Lorne Carr	Toronto	50	36	38	74	9
Carl Liscombe	Detroit	50	36	37	73	17
Elmer Lach	Montreal	48	24	48	72	23
Clint Smith	Chicago	50	23	49	72	4
Bill Cowley	Boston	36	30	41	71	12
Bill Mosienko	Chicago	50	32	38	70	10
Art Jackson	Boston	49	28	41	69	8
Gus Bodnar	Toronto	50	22	40	62	18

1944-45

Team	GP	W	L	T	GF	GA	PTS
Montreal	50	38	8	4	228	121	80
Detroit	50	31	14	5	218	161	67
*Toronto	50	24	22	4	183	161	52
Boston	50	16	30	4	179	219	36
Chicago	50	13	30	7	141	194	33
NY Rangers	50	11	29	10	154	247	32

Leading Scorers

Player	Team	GP	G	A	PTS	PIM
Elmer Lach	Montreal	50	26	54	80	37
Maurice Richard	Montreal	50	50	23	73	36
Toe Blake	Montreal	49	29	38	67	15
Bill Cowley	Boston	49	25	40	65	2
Ted Kennedy	Toronto	49	29	25	54	14
Bill Mosienko	Chicago	50	28	26	54	0
Joe Carveth	Detroit	50	26	28	54	6
Ab DeMarco	NY Rangers	50	24	30	54	10
Clint Smith	Chicago	50	23	31	54	0
Syd Howe	Detroit	46	17	36	53	6

1945-46

Team	GP	W	L	T	GF	GA	PTS
*Montreal	50	28	17	5	172	134	61
Boston	50	24	18	8	167	156	56
Chicago	50	23	20	7	200	178	53
Detroit	50	20	20	10	146	159	50
Toronto	50	19	24	7	174	185	45
NY Rangers	50	13	28	9	144	191	35

Leading Scorers

Player	Team	GP	G	A	PTS	PIM
Max Bentley	Chicago	47	31	30	61	6
Gaye Stewart	Toronto	50	37	15	52	8
Toe Blake	Montreal	50	29	21	50	2
Clint Smith	Chicago	50	26	24	50	2
Maurice Richard	Montreal	50	27	21	48	50
Bill Mosienko	Chicago	40	18	30	48	12
Ab DeMarco	NY Rangers	50	20	27	47	20
Elmer Lach	Montreal	50	13	34	47	34
Alex Kaleta	Chicago	49	19	27	46	17
Billy Taylor	Toronto	48	23	18	41	14
Pete Horeck	Chicago	50	20	21	41	34

1946-47

Team	GP	W	L	T	GF	GA	PTS
Montreal	60	34	16	10	189	138	78
*Toronto	60	31	19	10	209	172	72
Boston	60	26	23	11	190	175	63
Detroit	60	22	27	11	190	193	55
NY Rangers	60	22	32	6	167	186	50
Chicago	60	19	37	4	193	274	42

Leading Scorers

Player	Team	GP	G	A	PTS	PIM
Max Bentley	Chicago	60	29	43	72	12
Maurice Richard	Montreal	60	45	26	71	69
Billy Taylor	Detroit	60	17	46	63	35
Milt Schmidt	Boston	59	27	35	62	40
Ted Kennedy	Toronto	60	28	32	60	27
Doug Bentley	Chicago	52	21	34	55	18
Bobby Bauer	Boston	58	30	24	54	4
Roy Conacher	Detroit	60	30	24	54	6
Bill Mosienko	Chicago	59	25	27	52	2
Woody Dumart	Boston	60	24	28	52	12

1947-48

Team	GP	W	L	T	GF	GA	PTS
*Toronto	60	32	15	13	182	143	77
Detroit	60	30	18	12	187	148	72
Boston	60	23	24	13	167	168	59
NY Rangers	60	21	26	13	176	201	55
Montreal	60	20	29	11	147	169	51
Chicago	60	20	34	6	195	225	46

Leading Scorers

Player	Team	GP	G	A	PTS	PIM
Elmer Lach	Montreal	60	30	31	61	72
Buddy O'Connor	NY Rangers	60	24	36	60	8
Doug Bentley	Chicago	60	20	37	57	16
Gaye Stewart	Tor., Chi.	61	27	29	56	83
Max Bentley	Chi., Tor.	59	26	28	54	14
Bud Poile	Tor., Chi.	58	25	29	54	17
Maurice Richard	Montreal	53	28	25	53	89
Syl Apps	Toronto	55	26	27	53	12
Ted Lindsay	Detroit	60	33	19	52	95
Roy Conacher	Chicago	52	22	27	49	4

1948-49

Team	GP	W	L	T	GF	GA	PTS
Detroit	60	34	19	7	195	145	75
Boston	60	29	23	8	178	163	66
Montreal	60	28	23	9	152	126	65
*Toronto	60	22	25	13	147	161	57
Chicago	60	21	31	8	173	211	50
NY Rangers	60	18	31	11	133	172	47

Leading Scorers

Player	Team	GP	G	A	PTS	PIM
Roy Conacher	Chicago	60	26	42	68	8
Doug Bentley	Chicago	58	23	43	66	38
Sid Abel	Detroit	60	28	26	54	49
Ted Lindsay	Detroit	50	26	28	54	97
Jim Conacher	Det., Chi.	59	26	23	49	43
Paul Ronty	Boston	60	20	29	49	11
Harry Watson	Toronto	60	26	19	45	0
Billy Reay	Montreal	60	22	23	45	33
Gus Bodnar	Chicago	59	19	26	45	14
Johnny Peirson	Boston	59	22	21	43	45

1949-50

Team	GP	W	L	T	GF	GA	PTS
*Detroit	70	37	19	14	229	164	88
Montreal	70	29	22	19	172	150	77
Toronto	70	31	27	12	176	173	74
NY Rangers	70	28	31	11	170	189	67
Boston	70	22	32	16	198	228	60
Chicago	70	22	38	10	203	244	54

Leading Scorers

Player	Team	GP	G	A	PTS	PIM
Ted Lindsay	Detroit	69	23	55	78	141
Sid Abel	Detroit	69	34	35	69	46
Gordie Howe	Detroit	70	35	33	68	69
Maurice Richard	Montreal	70	43	22	65	114
Paul Ronty	Boston	70	23	36	59	8
Roy Conacher	Chicago	70	25	31	56	16
Doug Bentley	Chicago	64	20	33	53	28
Johnny Peirson	Boston	57	27	25	52	49
Metro Prystai	Chicago	65	29	22	51	31
Bep Guidolin	Chicago	70	17	34	51	42

1950-51

Team	GP	W	L	T	GF	GA	PTS
Detroit	70	44	13	13	236	139	101
*Toronto	70	41	16	13	212	138	95
Montreal	70	25	30	15	173	184	65
Boston	70	22	30	18	178	197	62
NY Rangers	70	20	29	21	169	201	61
Chicago	70	13	47	10	171	280	36

Leading Scorers

Player	Team	GP	G	A	PTS	PIM
Gordie Howe	Detroit	70	43	43	86	74
Maurice Richard	Montreal	65	42	24	66	97
Max Bentley	Toronto	67	21	41	62	34
Sid Abel	Detroit	69	23	38	61	30
Milt Schmidt	Boston	62	22	39	61	33
Ted Kennedy	Toronto	63	18	43	61	32
Ted Lindsay	Detroit	67	24	35	59	110
Tod Sloan	Toronto	70	31	25	56	105
Red Kelly	Detroit	70	17	37	54	24
Sid Smith	Toronto	70	30	21	51	10
Cal Gardner	Toronto	66	23	28	51	42

1951-52

Team	GP	W	L	T	GF	GA	PTS
*Detroit	70	44	14	12	215	133	100
Montreal	70	34	26	10	195	164	78
Toronto	70	29	25	16	168	157	74
Boston	70	25	29	16	162	176	66
NY Rangers	70	23	34	13	192	219	59
Chicago	70	17	44	9	158	241	43

Leading Scorers

Player	Team	GP	G	A	PTS	PIM
Gordie Howe	Detroit	70	47	39	86	78
Ted Lindsay	Detroit	70	30	39	69	123
Elmer Lach	Montreal	70	15	50	65	36
Don Raleigh	NY Rangers	70	19	42	61	14
Sid Smith	Toronto	70	27	30	57	6
Bernie Geoffrion	Montreal	67	30	24	54	66
Bill Mosienko	Chicago	70	31	22	53	10
Sid Abel	Detroit	62	17	36	53	32
Ted Kennedy	Toronto	70	19	33	52	33
Milt Schmidt	Boston	69	21	29	50	57
Johnny Peirson	Boston	68	20	30	50	30

1952-53

Team	GP	W	L	T	GF	GA	PTS
Detroit	70	36	16	18	222	133	90
*Montreal	70	28	23	19	155	148	75
Boston	70	28	29	13	152	172	69
Chicago	70	27	28	15	169	175	69
Toronto	70	27	30	13	156	167	67
NY Rangers	70	17	37	16	152	211	50

Leading Scorers

Player	Team	GP	G	A	PTS	PIM
Gordie Howe	Detroit	70	49	46	95	57
Ted Lindsay	Detroit	70	32	39	71	111
Maurice Richard	Montreal	70	28	33	61	112
Wally Hergesheimer	NY Rangers	70	30	29	59	10
Alex Delvecchio	Detroit	70	16	43	59	28
Paul Ronty	NY Rangers	70	16	38	54	20
Metro Prystai	Detroit	70	16	34	50	12
Red Kelly	Detroit	70	19	27	46	8
Bert Olmstead	Montreal	69	17	28	45	83
Fleming Mackell	Boston	65	27	17	44	63
Jim McFadden	Chicago	70	23	21	44	29

1953-54

Team	GP	W	L	T	GF	GA	PTS
*Detroit	70	37	19	14	191	132	88
Montreal	70	35	24	11	195	141	81
Toronto	70	32	24	14	152	131	78
Boston	70	32	28	10	177	181	74
NY Rangers	70	29	31	10	161	182	68
Chicago	70	12	51	7	133	242	31

Leading Scorers

Player	Team	GP	G	A	PTS	PIM
Gordie Howe	Detroit	70	33	48	81	109
Maurice Richard	Montreal	70	37	30	67	112
Ted Lindsay	Detroit	70	26	36	62	110
Bernie Geoffrion	Montreal	54	29	25	54	87
Bert Olmstead	Montreal	70	15	37	52	85
Red Kelly	Detroit	62	16	33	49	18
Dutch Reibel	Detroit	69	15	33	48	18
Ed Sandford	Boston	70	16	31	47	42
Fleming Mackell	Boston	67	15	32	47	60
Ken Mosdell	Montreal	67	22	24	46	64
Paul Ronty	NY Rangers	70	13	33	46	18

1954-55

Team	GP	W	L	T	GF	GA	PTS
*Detroit	70	42	17	11	204	134	95
Montreal	70	41	18	11	228	157	93
Toronto	70	24	24	22	147	135	70
Boston	70	23	26	21	169	188	67
NY Rangers	70	17	35	18	150	210	52
Chicago	70	13	40	17	161	235	43

Leading Scorers

Player	Team	GP	G	A	PTS	PIM
Bernie Geoffrion	Montreal	70	38	37	75	57
Maurice Richard	Montreal	67	38	36	74	125
Jean Béliveau	Montreal	70	37	36	73	58
Dutch Reibel	Detroit	70	25	41	66	15
Gordie Howe	Detroit	64	29	33	62	68
Red Sullivan	Chicago	69	19	42	61	51
Bert Olmstead	Montreal	70	10	48	58	103
Sid Smith	Toronto	70	33	21	54	14
Ken Mosdell	Montreal	70	22	32	54	82
Danny Lewicki	NY Rangers	70	29	24	53	8

1955-56

Team	GP	W	L	T	GF	GA	PTS
*Montreal	70	45	15	10	222	131	100
Detroit	70	30	24	16	183	148	76
NY Rangers	70	32	28	10	204	203	74
Toronto	70	24	33	13	153	181	61
Boston	70	23	34	13	147	185	59
Chicago	70	19	39	12	155	216	50

Leading Scorers

Player	Team	GP	G	A	PTS	PIM
Jean Béliveau	Montreal	70	47	41	88	143
Gordie Howe	Detroit	70	38	41	79	100
Maurice Richard	Montreal	70	38	33	71	89
Bert Olmstead	Montreal	70	14	56	70	94
Tod Sloan	Toronto	70	37	29	66	100
Andy Bathgate	NY Rangers	70	19	47	66	59
Bernie Geoffrion	Montreal	59	29	33	62	66
Dutch Reibel	Detroit	68	17	39	56	10
Alex Delvecchio	Detroit	70	25	26	51	24
Dave Creighton	NY Rangers	70	20	31	51	43
Bill Gadsby	NY Rangers	70	9	42	51	84

1956-57

Team	GP	W	L	T	GF	GA	PTS
Detroit	70	38	20	12	198	157	88
*Montreal	70	35	23	12	210	155	82
Boston	70	34	24	12	195	174	80
NY Rangers	70	26	30	14	184	227	66
Toronto	70	21	34	15	174	192	57
Chicago	70	16	39	15	169	225	47

Leading Scorers

Player	Team	GP	G	A	PTS	PIM
Gordie Howe	Detroit	70	44	45	89	72
Ted Lindsay	Detroit	70	30	55	85	103
Jean Béliveau	Montreal	69	33	51	84	105
Andy Bathgate	NY Rangers	70	27	50	77	60
Ed Litzenberger	Chicago	70	32	32	64	48
Maurice Richard	Montreal	63	33	29	62	74
Don McKenney	Boston	69	21	39	60	31
Dickie Moore	Montreal	70	29	29	58	56
Henri Richard	Montreal	63	18	36	54	71
Norm Ullman	Detroit	64	16	36	52	47

1957-58

Team	GP	W	L	T	GF	GA	PTS
*Montreal	70	43	17	10	250	158	96
NY Rangers	70	32	25	13	195	188	77
Detroit	70	29	29	12	176	207	70
Boston	70	27	28	15	199	194	69
Chicago	70	24	39	7	163	202	55
Toronto	70	21	38	11	192	226	53

Leading Scorers

Player	Team	GP	G	A	PTS	PIM
Dickie Moore	Montreal	70	36	48	84	65
Henri Richard	Montreal	67	28	52	80	56
Andy Bathgate	NY Rangers	65	30	48	78	42
Gordie Howe	Detroit	64	33	44	77	40
Bronco Horvath	Boston	67	30	36	66	71
Ed Litzenberger	Chicago	70	32	30	62	63
Fleming Mackell	Boston	70	20	40	60	72
Jean Béliveau	Montreal	55	27	32	59	93
Alex Delvecchio	Detroit	70	21	38	59	22
Don McKenney	Boston	70	28	30	58	22

1958-59

Team	GP	W	L	T	GF	GA	PTS
*Montreal	70	39	18	13	258	158	91
Boston	70	32	29	9	205	215	73
Chicago	70	28	29	13	197	208	69
Toronto	70	27	32	11	189	201	65
NY Rangers	70	26	32	12	201	217	64
Detroit	70	25	37	8	167	218	58

Leading Scorers

Player	Team	GP	G	A	PTS	PIM
Dickie Moore	Montreal	70	41	55	96	61
Jean Béliveau	Montreal	64	45	46	91	67
Andy Bathgate	NY Rangers	70	40	48	88	48
Gordie Howe	Detroit	70	32	46	78	57
Ed Litzenberger	Chicago	70	33	44	77	37
Bernie Geoffrion	Montreal	59	22	44	66	30
Red Sullivan	NY Rangers	70	21	42	63	56
Andy Hebenton	NY Rangers	70	33	29	62	8
Don McKenney	Boston	70	32	30	62	20
Tod Sloan	Chicago	59	27	35	62	79

1959-60

Team	GP	W	L	T	GF	GA	PTS
*Montreal	70	40	18	12	255	178	92
Toronto	70	35	26	9	199	195	79
Chicago	70	28	29	13	191	180	69
Detroit	70	26	29	15	186	197	67
Boston	70	28	34	8	220	241	64
NY Rangers	70	17	38	15	187	247	49

Leading Scorers

Player	Team	GP	G	A	PTS	PIM
Bobby Hull	Chicago	70	39	42	81	68
Bronco Horvath	Boston	68	39	41	80	60
Jean Béliveau	Montreal	60	34	40	74	57
Andy Bathgate	NY Rangers	70	26	48	74	28
Henri Richard	Montreal	70	30	43	73	66
Gordie Howe	Detroit	70	28	45	73	46
Bernie Geoffrion	Montreal	59	30	41	71	36
Don McKenney	Boston	70	20	49	69	28
Vic Stasiuk	Boston	69	29	39	68	121
Dean Prentice	NY Rangers	70	32	34	66	43

1960-61

Team	GP	W	L	T	GF	GA	PTS
Montreal	70	41	19	10	254	188	92
Toronto	70	39	19	12	234	176	90
*Chicago	70	29	24	17	198	180	75
Detroit	70	25	29	16	195	215	66
NY Rangers	70	22	38	10	204	248	54
Boston	70	15	42	13	176	254	43

Leading Scorers

Player	Team	GP	G	A	PTS	PIM
Bernie Geoffrion	Montreal	64	50	45	95	29
Jean Béliveau	Montreal	69	32	58	90	57
Frank Mahovlich	Toronto	70	48	36	84	131
Andy Bathgate	NY Rangers	70	29	48	77	22
Gordie Howe	Detroit	64	23	49	72	30
Norm Ullman	Detroit	70	28	42	70	34
Red Kelly	Toronto	64	20	50	70	12
Dickie Moore	Montreal	57	35	34	69	62
Henri Richard	Montreal	70	24	44	68	91
Alex Delvecchio	Detroit	70	27	35	62	26

1961-62

Team	GP	W	L	T	GF	GA	PTS
Montreal	70	42	14	14	259	166	98
*Toronto	70	37	22	11	232	180	85
Chicago	70	31	26	13	217	186	75
NY Rangers	70	26	32	12	195	207	64
Detroit	70	23	33	14	184	219	60
Boston	70	15	47	8	177	306	38

Leading Scorers

Player	Team	GP	G	A	PTS	PIM
Bobby Hull	Chicago	70	50	34	84	35
Andy Bathgate	NY Rangers	70	28	56	84	44
Gordie Howe	Detroit	70	33	44	77	54
Stan Mikita	Chicago	70	25	52	77	97
Frank Mahovlich	Toronto	70	33	38	71	87
Alex Delvecchio	Detroit	70	26	43	69	18
Ralph Backstrom	Montreal	66	27	38	65	29
Norm Ullman	Detroit	70	26	38	64	54
Bill Hay	Chicago	60	11	52	63	34
Claude Provost	Montreal	70	33	29	62	22

1962-63

Team	GP	W	L	T	GF	GA	PTS
*Toronto	70	35	23	12	221	180	82
Chicago	70	32	21	17	194	178	81
Montreal	70	28	19	23	225	183	79
Detroit	70	32	25	13	200	194	77
NY Rangers	70	22	36	12	211	233	56
Boston	70	14	39	17	198	281	45

Leading Scorers

Player	Team	GP	G	A	PTS	PIM
Gordie Howe	Detroit	70	38	48	86	100
Andy Bathgate	NY Rangers	70	35	46	81	54
Stan Mikita	Chicago	65	31	45	76	69
Frank Mahovlich	Toronto	67	36	37	73	56
Henri Richard	Montreal	67	23	50	73	57
Jean Béliveau	Montreal	69	18	49	67	68
John Bucyk	Boston	69	27	39	66	36
Alex Delvecchio	Detroit	70	20	44	64	8
Bobby Hull	Chicago	65	31	31	62	27
Murray Oliver	Boston	65	22	40	62	38

1963-64

Team	GP	W	L	T	GF	GA	PTS
Montreal	70	36	21	13	209	167	85
Chicago	70	36	22	12	218	169	84
*Toronto	70	33	25	12	192	172	78
Detroit	70	30	29	11	191	204	71
NY Rangers	70	22	38	10	186	242	54
Boston	70	18	40	12	170	212	48

Leading Scorers

Player	Team	GP	G	A	PTS	PIM
Stan Mikita	Chicago	70	39	50	89	146
Bobby Hull	Chicago	70	43	44	87	50
Jean Béliveau	Montreal	68	28	50	78	42
Andy Bathgate	NYR, Tor.	71	19	58	77	34
Gordie Howe	Detroit	69	26	47	73	70
Kenny Wharram	Chicago	70	39	32	71	18
Murray Oliver	Boston	70	24	44	68	41
Phil Goyette	NY Rangers	67	24	41	65	15
Rod Gilbert	NY Rangers	70	24	40	64	62
Dave Keon	Toronto	70	23	37	60	6

1964-65

Team	GP	W	L	T	GF	GA	PTS
Detroit	70	40	23	7	224	175	87
*Montreal	70	36	23	11	211	185	83
Chicago	70	34	28	8	224	176	76
Toronto	70	30	26	14	204	173	74
NY Rangers	70	20	38	12	179	246	52
Boston	70	21	43	6	166	253	48

Leading Scorers

Player	Team	GP	G	A	PTS	PIM
Stan Mikita	Chicago	70	28	59	87	154
Norm Ullman	Detroit	70	42	41	83	70
Gordie Howe	Detroit	70	29	47	76	104
Bobby Hull	Chicago	61	39	32	71	32
Alex Delvecchio	Detroit	68	25	42	67	16
Claude Provost	Montreal	70	27	37	64	28
Rod Gilbert	NY Rangers	70	25	36	61	52
Pierre Pilote	Chicago	68	14	45	59	162
John Bucyk	Boston	68	26	29	55	24
Ralph Backstrom	Montreal	70	25	30	55	41
Phil Esposito	Chicago	70	23	32	55	44

1965-66

Team	GP	W	L	T	GF	GA	PTS
*Montreal	70	41	21	8	239	173	90
Chicago	70	37	25	8	240	187	82
Toronto	70	34	25	11	208	187	79
Detroit	70	31	27	12	221	194	74
Boston	70	21	43	6	174	275	48
NY Rangers	70	18	41	11	195	261	47

Leading Scorers

Player	Team	GP	G	A	PTS	PIM
Bobby Hull	Chicago	65	54	43	97	70
Stan Mikita	Chicago	68	30	48	78	58
Bobby Rousseau	Montreal	70	30	48	78	20
Jean Béliveau	Montreal	67	29	48	77	50
Gordie Howe	Detroit	70	29	46	75	83
Norm Ullman	Detroit	70	31	41	72	35
Alex Delvecchio	Detroit	70	31	38	69	16
Bob Nevin	NY Rangers	69	29	33	62	10
Henri Richard	Montreal	62	22	39	61	47
Murray Oliver	Boston	70	18	42	60	30

1966-67

Team	GP	W	L	T	GF	GA	PTS
Chicago	70	41	17	12	264	170	94
Montreal	70	32	25	13	202	188	77
*Toronto	70	32	27	11	204	211	75
NY Rangers	70	30	28	12	188	189	72
Detroit	70	27	39	4	212	241	58
Boston	70	17	43	10	182	253	44

Leading Scorers

Player	Team	GP	G	A	PTS	PIM
Stan Mikita	Chicago	70	35	62	97	12
Bobby Hull	Chicago	66	52	28	80	52
Norm Ullman	Detroit	68	26	44	70	26
Kenny Wharram	Chicago	70	31	34	65	21
Gordie Howe	Detroit	69	25	40	65	53
Bobby Rousseau	Montreal	68	19	44	63	58
Phil Esposito	Chicago	69	21	40	61	40
Phil Goyette	NY Rangers	70	12	49	61	6
Doug Mohns	Chicago	61	25	35	60	58
Henri Richard	Montreal	65	21	34	55	28
Alex Delvecchio	Detroit	70	17	38	55	10

1967-68

East Division

Team	GP	W	L	T	GF	GA	PTS
*Montreal	74	42	22	10	236	167	94
NY Rangers	74	39	23	12	226	183	90
Boston	74	37	27	10	259	216	84
Chicago	74	32	26	16	212	222	80
Toronto	74	33	31	10	209	176	76
Detroit	74	27	35	12	245	257	66

West Division

Team	GP	W	L	T	GF	GA	PTS
Philadelphia	74	31	32	11	173	179	73
Los Angeles	74	31	33	10	200	224	72
St. Louis	74	27	31	16	177	191	70
Minnesota	74	27	32	15	191	226	69
Pittsburgh	74	27	34	13	195	216	67
Oakland	74	15	42	17	153	219	47

Leading Scorers

Player	Team	GP	G	A	PTS	PIM
Stan Mikita	Chicago	72	40	47	87	14
Phil Esposito	Boston	74	35	49	84	21
Gordie Howe	Detroit	74	39	43	82	53
Jean Ratelle	NY Rangers	74	32	46	78	18
Rod Gilbert	NY Rangers	73	29	48	77	12
Bobby Hull	Chicago	71	44	31	75	39
Norm Ullman	Det., Tor.	71	35	37	72	28
Alex Delvecchio	Detroit	74	22	48	70	14
John Bucyk	Boston	72	30	39	69	8
Kenny Wharram	Chicago	74	27	42	69	18

1968-69
East Division

Team	GP	W	L	T	GF	GA	PTS
*Montreal	76	46	19	11	271	202	103
Boston	76	42	18	16	303	221	100
NY Rangers	76	41	26	9	231	196	91
Toronto	76	35	26	15	234	217	85
Detroit	76	33	31	12	239	221	78
Chicago	76	34	33	9	280	246	77

West Division

Team	GP	W	L	T	GF	GA	PTS
St. Louis	76	37	25	14	204	157	88
Oakland	76	29	36	11	219	251	69
Philadelphia	76	20	35	21	174	225	61
Los Angeles	76	24	42	10	185	260	58
Pittsburgh	76	20	45	11	189	252	51
Minnesota	76	18	43	15	189	270	51

Leading Scorers

Player	Team	GP	G	A	PTS	PIM
Phil Esposito	Boston	74	49	77	126	79
Bobby Hull	Chicago	74	58	49	107	48
Gordie Howe	Detroit	76	44	59	103	58
Stan Mikita	Chicago	74	30	67	97	52
Ken Hodge	Boston	75	45	45	90	75
Yvan Cournoyer	Montreal	76	43	44	87	31
Alex Delvecchio	Detroit	72	25	58	83	8
Red Berenson	St. Louis	76	35	47	82	43
Jean Béliveau	Montreal	69	33	49	82	55
Frank Mahovlich	Detroit	76	49	29	78	38
Jean Ratelle	NY Rangers	75	32	46	78	26

1969-70
East Division

Team	GP	W	L	T	GF	GA	PTS
Chicago	76	45	22	9	250	170	99
*Boston	76	40	17	19	277	216	99
Detroit	76	40	21	15	246	199	95
NY Rangers	76	38	22	16	246	189	92
Montreal	76	38	22	16	244	201	92
Toronto	76	29	34	13	222	242	71

West Division

Team	GP	W	L	T	GF	GA	PTS
St. Louis	76	37	27	12	224	179	86
Pittsburgh	76	26	38	12	182	238	64
Minnesota	76	19	35	22	224	257	60
Oakland	76	22	40	14	169	243	58
Philadelphia	76	17	35	24	197	225	58
Los Angeles	76	14	52	10	168	290	38

Leading Scorers

Player	Team	GP	G	A	PTS	PIM
Bobby Orr	Boston	76	33	87	120	125
Phil Esposito	Boston	76	43	56	99	50
Stan Mikita	Chicago	76	39	47	86	50
Phil Goyette	St. Louis	72	29	49	78	16
Walt Tkaczuk	NY Rangers	76	27	50	77	38
Jean Ratelle	NY Rangers	75	32	42	74	28
Red Berenson	St. Louis	67	33	39	72	38
Jean-Paul Parise	Minnesota	74	24	48	72	72
Gordie Howe	Detroit	76	31	40	71	58
Frank Mahovlich	Detroit	74	38	32	70	59
Dave Balon	NY Rangers	76	33	37	70	100
John McKenzie	Boston	72	29	41	70	114

1970-71
East Division

Team	GP	W	L	T	GF	GA	PTS
Boston	78	57	14	7	399	207	121
NY Rangers	78	49	18	11	259	177	109
*Montreal	78	42	23	13	291	216	97
Toronto	78	37	33	8	248	211	82
Buffalo	78	24	39	15	217	291	63
Vancouver	78	24	46	8	229	296	56
Detroit	78	22	45	11	209	308	55

West Division

Team	GP	W	L	T	GF	GA	PTS
Chicago	78	49	20	9	277	184	107
St. Louis	78	34	25	19	223	208	87
Philadelphia	78	28	33	17	207	225	73
Minnesota	78	28	34	16	191	223	72
Los Angeles	78	25	40	13	239	303	63
Pittsburgh	78	21	37	20	221	240	62
California	78	20	53	5	199	320	45

Leading Scorers

Player	Team	GP	G	A	PTS	PIM
Phil Esposito	Boston	78	76	76	152	71
Bobby Orr	Boston	78	37	102	139	91
John Bucyk	Boston	78	51	65	116	8
Ken Hodge	Boston	78	43	62	105	113
Bobby Hull	Chicago	78	44	52	96	32
Norm Ullman	Toronto	73	34	51	85	24
Wayne Cashman	Boston	77	21	58	79	100
John McKenzie	Boston	65	31	46	77	120
Dave Keon	Toronto	76	38	38	76	4
Jean Béliveau	Montreal	70	25	51	76	40
Fred Stanfield	Boston	75	24	52	76	12

1971-72
East Division

Team	GP	W	L	T	GF	GA	PTS
*Boston	78	54	13	11	330	204	119
NY Rangers	78	48	17	13	317	192	109
Montreal	78	46	16	16	307	205	108
Toronto	78	33	31	14	209	208	80
Detroit	78	33	35	10	261	262	76
Buffalo	78	16	43	19	203	289	51
Vancouver	78	20	50	8	203	297	48

West Division

Team	GP	W	L	T	GF	GA	PTS
Chicago	78	46	17	15	256	166	107
Minnesota	78	37	29	12	212	191	86
St. Louis	78	28	39	11	208	247	67
Pittsburgh	78	26	38	14	220	258	66
Philadelphia	78	26	38	14	200	236	66
California	78	21	39	18	216	288	60
Los Angeles	78	20	49	9	206	305	49

Leading Scorers

Player	Team	GP	G	A	PTS	PIM
Phil Esposito	Boston	76	66	67	133	76
Bobby Orr	Boston	76	37	80	117	106
Jean Ratelle	NY Rangers	63	46	63	109	4
Vic Hadfield	NY Rangers	78	50	56	106	142
Rod Gilbert	NY Rangers	73	43	54	97	64
Frank Mahovlich	Montreal	76	43	53	96	36
Bobby Hull	Chicago	78	50	43	93	24
Yvan Cournoyer	Montreal	73	47	36	83	15
John Bucyk	Boston	78	32	51	83	4
Bobby Clarke	Philadelphia	78	35	46	81	87
Jacques Lemaire	Montreal	77	32	49	81	26

1972-73
East Division

Team	GP	W	L	T	GF	GA	PTS
*Montreal	78	52	10	16	329	184	120
Boston	78	51	22	5	330	235	107
NY Rangers	78	47	23	8	297	208	102
Buffalo	78	37	27	14	257	219	88
Detroit	78	37	29	12	265	243	86
Toronto	78	27	41	10	247	279	64
Vancouver	78	22	47	9	233	339	53
NY Islanders	78	12	60	6	170	347	30

West Division

Team	GP	W	L	T	GF	GA	PTS
Chicago	78	42	27	9	284	225	93
Philadelphia	78	37	30	11	296	256	85
Minnesota	78	37	30	11	254	230	85
St. Louis	78	32	34	12	233	251	76
Pittsburgh	78	32	37	9	257	265	73
Los Angeles	78	31	36	11	232	245	73
Atlanta	78	25	38	15	191	239	65
California	78	16	46	16	213	323	48

Leading Scorers

Player	Team	GP	G	A	PTS	PIM
Phil Esposito	Boston	78	55	75	130	87
Bobby Clarke	Philadelphia	78	37	67	104	80
Bobby Orr	Boston	63	29	72	101	99
Rick MacLeish	Philadelphia	78	50	50	100	69
Jacques Lemaire	Montreal	77	44	51	95	16
Jean Ratelle	NY Rangers	78	41	53	94	12
Mickey Redmond	Detroit	76	52	41	93	24
John Bucyk	Boston	78	40	53	93	12
Frank Mahovlich	Montreal	78	38	55	93	51
Jim Pappin	Chicago	76	41	51	92	82

1973-74
East Division

Team	GP	W	L	T	GF	GA	PTS
Boston	78	52	17	9	349	221	113
Montreal	78	45	24	9	293	240	99
NY Rangers	78	40	24	14	300	251	94
Toronto	78	35	27	16	274	230	86
Buffalo	78	32	34	12	242	250	76
Detroit	78	29	39	10	255	319	68
Vancouver	78	24	43	11	224	296	59
NY Islanders	78	19	41	18	182	247	56

West Division

Team	GP	W	L	T	GF	GA	PTS
*Philadelphia	78	50	16	12	273	164	112
Chicago	78	41	14	23	272	164	105
Los Angeles	78	33	33	12	233	231	78
Atlanta	78	30	34	14	214	238	74
Pittsburgh	78	28	41	9	242	273	65
St. Louis	78	26	40	12	206	248	64
Minnesota	78	23	38	17	235	275	63
California	78	13	55	10	195	342	36

Leading Scorers

Player	Team	GP	G	A	PTS	PIM
Phil Esposito	Boston	78	68	77	145	58
Bobby Orr	Boston	74	32	90	122	82
Ken Hodge	Boston	76	50	55	105	43
Wayne Cashman	Boston	78	30	59	89	111
Bobby Clarke	Philadelphia	77	35	52	87	113
Rick Martin	Buffalo	78	52	34	86	38
Syl Apps Jr.	Pittsburgh	75	24	61	85	37
Darryl Sittler	Toronto	78	38	46	84	55
Lowell MacDonald	Pittsburgh	78	43	39	82	14
Brad Park	NY Rangers	78	25	57	82	148
Dennis Hextall	Minnesota	78	20	62	82	138

1974-75
PRINCE OF WALES CONFERENCE
Norris Division

Team	GP	W	L	T	GF	GA	PTS
Montreal	80	47	14	19	374	225	113
Los Angeles	80	42	17	21	269	185	105
Pittsburgh	80	37	28	15	326	289	89
Detroit	80	23	45	12	259	335	58
Washington	80	8	67	5	181	446	21

Adams Division

Team	GP	W	L	T	GF	GA	PTS
Buffalo	80	49	16	15	354	240	113
Boston	80	40	26	14	345	245	94
Toronto	80	31	33	16	280	309	78
California	80	19	48	13	212	316	51

CLARENCE CAMPBELL CONFERENCE
Patrick Division

Team	GP	W	L	T	GF	GA	PTS
*Philadelphia	80	51	18	11	293	181	113
NY Rangers	80	37	29	14	319	276	88
NY Islanders	80	33	25	22	264	221	88
Atlanta	80	34	31	15	243	233	83

Smythe Division

Team	GP	W	L	T	GF	GA	PTS
Vancouver	80	38	32	10	271	254	86
St. Louis	80	35	31	14	269	267	84
Chicago	80	37	35	8	268	241	82
Minnesota	80	23	50	7	221	341	53
Kansas City	80	15	54	11	184	328	41

Leading Scorers

Player	Team	GP	G	A	PTS	PIM
Bobby Orr	Boston	80	46	89	135	101
Phil Esposito	Boston	79	61	66	127	62
Marcel Dionne	Detroit	80	47	74	121	14
Guy Lafleur	Montreal	70	53	66	119	37
Pete Mahovlich	Montreal	80	35	82	117	64
Bobby Clarke	Philadelphia	80	27	89	116	125
Rene Robert	Buffalo	74	40	60	100	75
Rod Gilbert	NY Rangers	76	36	61	97	22
Gilbert Perreault	Buffalo	68	39	57	96	36
Rick Martin	Buffalo	68	52	43	95	72

1975-76
PRINCE OF WALES CONFERENCE
Norris Division

Team	GP	W	L	T	GF	GA	PTS
*Montreal	80	58	11	11	337	174	127
Los Angeles	80	38	33	9	263	265	85
Pittsburgh	80	35	33	12	339	303	82
Detroit	80	26	44	10	226	300	62
Washington	80	11	59	10	224	394	32

Adams Division

Team	GP	W	L	T	GF	GA	PTS
Boston	80	48	15	17	313	237	113
Buffalo	80	46	21	13	339	240	105
Toronto	80	34	31	15	294	276	83
California	80	27	42	11	250	278	65

CLARENCE CAMPBELL CONFERENCE
Patrick Division

Team	GP	W	L	T	GF	GA	PTS
Philadelphia	80	51	13	16	348	209	118
NY Islanders	80	42	21	17	297	190	101
Atlanta	80	35	33	12	262	237	82
NY Rangers	80	29	42	9	262	333	67

Smythe Division

Team	GP	W	L	T	GF	GA	PTS
Chicago	80	32	30	18	254	261	82
Vancouver	80	33	32	15	271	272	81
St. Louis	80	29	37	14	249	290	72
Minnesota	80	20	53	7	195	303	47
Kansas City	80	12	56	12	190	351	36

Leading Scorers

Player	Team	GP	G	A	PTS	PIM
Guy Lafleur	Montreal	80	56	69	125	36
Bobby Clarke	Philadelphia	76	30	89	119	136
Gilbert Perreault	Buffalo	80	44	69	113	36
Bill Barber	Philadelphia	80	50	62	112	104
Pierre Larouche	Pittsburgh	76	53	58	111	33
Jean Ratelle	Bos., NYR	80	36	69	105	18
Pete Mahovlich	Montreal	80	34	71	105	76
Jean Pronovost	Pittsburgh	80	52	52	104	24
Darryl Sittler	Toronto	79	41	59	100	90
Syl Apps Jr.	Pittsburgh	80	32	67	99	24

1976-77
PRINCE OF WALES CONFERENCE
Norris Division

Team	GP	W	L	T	GF	GA	PTS
*Montreal	80	60	8	12	387	171	132
Los Angeles	80	34	31	15	271	241	83
Pittsburgh	80	34	33	13	240	252	81
Washington	80	24	42	14	221	307	62
Detroit	80	16	55	9	183	309	41

Adams Division

Team	GP	W	L	T	GF	GA	PTS
Boston	80	49	23	8	312	240	106
Buffalo	80	48	24	8	301	220	104
Toronto	80	33	32	15	301	285	81
Cleveland	80	25	42	13	240	292	63

CLARENCE CAMPBELL CONFERENCE
Patrick Division

Team	GP	W	L	T	GF	GA	PTS
Philadelphia	80	48	16	16	323	213	112
NY Islanders	80	47	21	12	288	193	106
Atlanta	80	34	34	12	264	265	80
NY Rangers	80	29	37	14	272	310	72

Smythe Division

Team	GP	W	L	T	GF	GA	PTS
St. Louis	80	32	39	9	239	276	73
Minnesota	80	23	39	18	240	310	64
Chicago	80	26	43	11	240	298	63
Vancouver	80	25	42	13	235	294	63
Colorado	80	20	46	14	226	307	54

Leading Scorers

Player	Team	GP	G	A	PTS	PIM
Guy Lafleur	Montreal	80	56	80	136	20
Marcel Dionne	Los Angeles	80	53	69	122	12
Steve Shutt	Montreal	80	60	45	105	28
Rick MacLeish	Philadelphia	79	49	48	97	42
Gilbert Perreault	Buffalo	80	39	56	95	30
Tim Young	Minnesota	80	29	66	95	58
Jean Ratelle	Boston	78	33	61	94	22
Lanny McDonald	Toronto	80	46	44	90	77
Darryl Sittler	Toronto	73	38	52	90	89
Bobby Clarke	Philadelphia	80	27	63	90	71

1977-78
PRINCE OF WALES CONFERENCE
Norris Division

Team	GP	W	L	T	GF	GA	PTS
*Montreal	80	59	10	11	359	183	129
Detroit	80	32	34	14	252	266	78
Los Angeles	80	31	34	15	243	245	77
Pittsburgh	80	25	37	18	254	321	68
Washington	80	17	49	14	195	321	48

Adams Division

Team	GP	W	L	T	GF	GA	PTS
Boston	80	51	18	11	333	218	113
Buffalo	80	44	19	17	288	215	105
Toronto	80	41	29	10	271	237	92
Cleveland	80	22	45	13	230	325	57

CLARENCE CAMPBELL CONFERENCE
Patrick Division

Team	GP	W	L	T	GF	GA	PTS
NY Islanders	80	48	17	15	334	210	111
Philadelphia	80	45	20	15	296	200	105
Atlanta	80	34	27	19	274	252	87
NY Rangers	80	30	37	13	279	280	73

Smythe Division

Team	GP	W	L	T	GF	GA	PTS
Chicago	80	32	29	19	230	220	83
Colorado	80	19	40	21	257	305	59
Vancouver	80	20	43	17	239	320	57
St. Louis	80	20	47	13	195	304	53
Minnesota	80	18	53	9	218	325	45

Leading Scorers

Player	Team	GP	G	A	PTS	PIM
Guy Lafleur	Montreal	78	60	72	132	26
Bryan Trottier	NY Islanders	77	46	77	123	46
Darryl Sittler	Toronto	80	45	72	117	100
Jacques Lemaire	Montreal	76	36	61	97	14
Denis Potvin	NY Islanders	80	30	64	94	81
Mike Bossy	NY Islanders	73	53	38	91	6
Terry O'Reilly	Boston	77	29	61	90	211
Gilbert Perreault	Buffalo	79	41	48	89	20
Bobby Clarke	Philadelphia	71	21	68	89	83
Lanny McDonald	Toronto	74	47	40	87	54
Wilf Paiement	Colorado	80	31	56	87	114

1978-79
PRINCE OF WALES CONFERENCE
Norris Division

Team	GP	W	L	T	GF	GA	PTS
*Montreal	80	52	17	11	337	204	115
Pittsburgh	80	36	31	13	281	279	85
Los Angeles	80	34	34	12	292	286	80
Washington	80	24	41	15	273	338	63
Detroit	80	23	41	16	252	295	62

Adams Division

Team	GP	W	L	T	GF	GA	PTS
Boston	80	43	23	14	316	270	100
Buffalo	80	36	28	16	280	263	88
Toronto	80	34	33	13	267	252	81
Minnesota	80	28	40	12	257	289	68

CLARENCE CAMPBELL CONFERENCE
Patrick Division

Team	GP	W	L	T	GF	GA	PTS
NY Islanders	80	51	15	14	358	214	116
Philadelphia	80	40	25	15	281	248	95
NY Rangers	80	40	29	11	316	292	91
Atlanta	80	41	31	8	327	280	90

Smythe Division

Team	GP	W	L	T	GF	GA	PTS
Chicago	80	29	36	15	244	277	73
Vancouver	80	25	42	13	217	291	63
St. Louis	80	18	50	12	249	348	48
Colorado	80	15	53	12	210	331	42

Leading Scorers

Player	Team	GP	G	A	PTS	PIM
Bryan Trottier	NY Islanders	76	47	87	134	50
Marcel Dionne	Los Angeles	80	59	71	130	30
Guy Lafleur	Montreal	80	52	77	129	28
Mike Bossy	NY Islanders	80	69	57	126	25
Bob MacMillan	Atlanta	79	37	71	108	14
Guy Chouinard	Atlanta	80	50	57	107	14
Denis Potvin	NY Islanders	73	31	70	101	58
Bernie Federko	St. Louis	74	31	64	95	14
Dave Taylor	Los Angeles	78	43	48	91	124
Clark Gillies	NY Islanders	75	35	56	91	68

1979-80
PRINCE OF WALES CONFERENCE
Norris Division

Team	GP	W	L	T	GF	GA	PTS
Montreal	80	47	20	13	328	240	107
Los Angeles	80	30	36	14	290	313	74
Pittsburgh	80	30	37	13	251	303	73
Hartford	80	27	34	19	303	312	73
Detroit	80	26	43	11	268	306	63

Adams Division

Team	GP	W	L	T	GF	GA	PTS
Buffalo	80	47	17	16	318	201	110
Boston	80	46	21	13	310	234	105
Minnesota	80	36	28	16	311	253	88
Toronto	80	35	40	5	304	327	75
Quebec	80	25	44	11	248	313	61

CLARENCE CAMPBELL CONFERENCE
Patrick Division

Team	GP	W	L	T	GF	GA	PTS
Philadelphia	80	48	12	20	327	254	116
*NY Islanders	80	39	28	13	281	247	91
NY Rangers	80	38	32	10	308	284	86
Atlanta	80	35	32	13	282	269	83
Washington	80	27	40	13	261	293	67

Smythe Division

Team	GP	W	L	T	GF	GA	PTS
Chicago	80	34	27	19	241	250	87
St. Louis	80	34	34	12	266	278	80
Vancouver	80	27	37	16	256	281	70
Edmonton	80	28	39	13	301	322	69
Winnipeg	80	20	49	11	214	314	51
Colorado	80	19	48	13	234	308	51

Leading Scorers

Player	Team	GP	G	A	PTS	PIM
Marcel Dionne	Los Angeles	80	53	84	137	32
Wayne Gretzky	Edmonton	79	51	86	137	21
Guy Lafleur	Montreal	74	50	75	125	12
Gilbert Perreault	Buffalo	80	40	66	106	57
Mike Rogers	Hartford	80	44	61	105	10
Bryan Trottier	NY Islanders	78	42	62	104	68
Charlie Simmer	Los Angeles	64	56	45	101	65
Blaine Stoughton	Hartford	80	56	44	100	16
Darryl Sittler	Toronto	73	40	57	97	62
Blair MacDonald	Edmonton	80	46	48	94	6
Bernie Federko	St. Louis	79	38	56	94	24

1980-81
PRINCE OF WALES CONFERENCE
Norris Division

Team	GP	W	L	T	GF	GA	PTS
Montreal	80	45	22	13	332	232	103
Los Angeles	80	43	24	13	337	290	99
Pittsburgh	80	30	37	13	302	345	73
Hartford	80	21	41	18	292	372	60
Detroit	80	19	43	18	252	339	56

Adams Division

Team	GP	W	L	T	GF	GA	PTS
Buffalo	80	39	20	21	327	250	99
Boston	80	37	30	13	316	272	87
Minnesota	80	35	28	17	291	263	87
Quebec	80	30	32	18	314	318	78
Toronto	80	28	37	15	322	367	71

CLARENCE CAMPBELL CONFERENCE
Patrick Division

Team	GP	W	L	T	GF	GA	PTS
*NY Islanders	80	48	18	14	355	260	110
Philadelphia	80	41	24	15	313	249	97
Calgary	80	39	27	14	329	298	92
NY Rangers	80	30	36	14	312	317	74
Washington	80	26	36	18	286	317	70

Smythe Division

Team	GP	W	L	T	GF	GA	PTS
St. Louis	80	45	18	17	352	281	107
Chicago	80	31	33	16	304	315	78
Vancouver	80	28	32	20	289	301	76
Edmonton	80	29	35	16	328	327	74
Colorado	80	22	45	13	258	344	57
Winnipeg	80	9	57	14	246	400	32

Leading Scorers

Player	Team	GP	G	A	PTS	PIM
Wayne Gretzky	Edmonton	80	55	109	164	28
Marcel Dionne	Los Angeles	80	58	77	135	70
Kent Nilsson	Calgary	80	49	82	131	26
Mike Bossy	NY Islanders	79	68	51	119	32
Dave Taylor	Los Angeles	72	47	65	112	130
Peter Stastny	Quebec	77	39	70	109	37
Charlie Simmer	Los Angeles	65	56	49	105	62
Mike Rogers	Hartford	80	40	65	105	32
Bernie Federko	St. Louis	78	31	73	104	47
Jacques Richard	Quebec	78	52	51	103	39
Rick Middleton	Boston	80	44	59	103	16
Bryan Trottier	NY Islanders	73	31	72	103	74

1981-82
CLARENCE CAMPBELL CONFERENCE
Norris Division

Team	GP	W	L	T	GF	GA	PTS
Minnesota	80	37	23	20	346	288	94
Winnipeg	80	33	33	14	319	332	80
St. Louis	80	32	40	8	315	349	72
Chicago	80	30	38	12	332	363	72
Toronto	80	20	44	16	298	380	56
Detroit	80	21	47	12	270	351	54

Smythe Division

Team	GP	W	L	T	GF	GA	PTS
Edmonton	80	48	17	15	417	295	111
Vancouver	80	30	33	17	290	286	77
Calgary	80	29	34	17	334	345	75
Los Angeles	80	24	41	15	314	369	63
Colorado	80	18	49	13	241	362	49

PRINCE OF WALES CONFERENCE
Adams Division

Team	GP	W	L	T	GF	GA	PTS
Montreal	80	46	17	17	360	223	109
Boston	80	43	27	10	323	285	96
Buffalo	80	39	26	15	307	273	93
Quebec	80	33	31	16	356	345	82
Hartford	80	21	41	18	264	351	60

Patrick Division

Team	GP	W	L	T	GF	GA	PTS
*NY Islanders	80	54	16	10	385	250	118
NY Rangers	80	39	27	14	316	306	92
Philadelphia	80	38	31	11	325	313	87
Pittsburgh	80	31	36	13	310	337	75
Washington	80	26	41	13	319	338	65

Leading Scorers

Player	Team	GP	G	A	PTS	PIM
Wayne Gretzky	Edmonton	80	92	120	212	26
Mike Bossy	NY Islanders	80	64	83	147	22
Peter Stastny	Quebec	80	46	93	139	91
Dennis Maruk	Washington	80	60	76	136	128
Bryan Trottier	NY Islanders	80	50	79	129	88
Denis Savard	Chicago	80	32	87	119	82
Marcel Dionne	Los Angeles	78	50	67	117	50
Bobby Smith	Minnesota	80	43	71	114	82
Dino Ciccarelli	Minnesota	76	55	51	106	138
Dave Taylor	Los Angeles	78	39	67	106	130

1982-83
CLARENCE CAMPBELL CONFERENCE
Norris Division

Team	GP	W	L	T	GF	GA	PTS
Chicago	80	47	23	10	338	268	104
Minnesota	80	40	24	16	321	290	96
Toronto	80	28	40	12	293	330	68
St. Louis	80	25	40	15	285	316	65
Detroit	80	21	44	15	263	344	57

Smythe Division

Team	GP	W	L	T	GF	GA	PTS
Edmonton	80	47	21	12	424	315	106
Calgary	80	32	34	14	321	317	78
Vancouver	80	30	35	15	303	309	75
Winnipeg	80	33	39	8	311	333	74
Los Angeles	80	27	41	12	308	365	66

PRINCE OF WALES CONFERENCE
Adams Division

Boston	80	50	20	10	327	228	110
Montreal	80	42	24	14	350	286	98
Buffalo	80	38	29	13	318	285	89
Quebec	80	34	34	12	343	336	80
Hartford	80	19	54	7	261	403	45

Patrick Division

Philadelphia	80	49	23	8	326	240	106
*NY Islanders	80	42	26	12	302	226	96
Washington	80	39	25	16	306	283	94
NY Rangers	80	35	35	10	306	287	80
New Jersey	80	17	49	14	230	338	48
Pittsburgh	80	18	53	9	257	394	45

Leading Scorers

Player	Team	GP	G	A	PTS	PIM
Wayne Gretzky	Edmonton	80	71	125	196	59
Peter Stastny	Quebec	75	47	77	124	78
Denis Savard	Chicago	78	35	86	121	99
Mike Bossy	NY Islanders	79	60	58	118	20
Marcel Dionne	Los Angeles	80	56	51	107	22
Barry Pederson	Boston	77	46	61	107	47
Mark Messier	Edmonton	77	48	58	106	72
Michel Goulet	Quebec	80	57	48	105	51
Glenn Anderson	Edmonton	72	48	56	104	70
Kent Nilsson	Calgary	80	46	58	104	10
Jari Kurri	Edmonton	80	45	59	104	22

1983-84
CLARENCE CAMPBELL CONFERENCE
Norris Division

Team	GP	W	L	T	GF	GA	PTS
Minnesota	80	39	31	10	345	344	88
St. Louis	80	32	41	7	293	316	71
Detroit	80	31	42	7	298	323	69
Chicago	80	30	42	8	277	311	68
Toronto	80	26	45	9	303	387	61

Smythe Division

*Edmonton	80	57	18	5	446	314	119
Calgary	80	34	32	14	311	314	82
Vancouver	80	32	39	9	306	328	73
Winnipeg	80	31	38	11	340	374	73
Los Angeles	80	23	44	13	309	376	59

PRINCE OF WALES CONFERENCE
Adams Division

Boston	80	49	25	6	336	261	104
Buffalo	80	48	25	7	315	257	103
Quebec	80	42	28	10	360	278	94
Montreal	80	35	40	5	286	295	75
Hartford	80	28	42	10	288	320	66

Patrick Division

NY Islanders	80	50	26	4	357	269	104
Washington	80	48	27	5	308	226	101
Philadelphia	80	44	26	10	350	290	98
NY Rangers	80	42	29	9	314	304	93
New Jersey	80	17	56	7	231	350	41
Pittsburgh	80	16	58	6	254	390	38

Leading Scorers

Player	Team	GP	G	A	PTS	PIM
Wayne Gretzky	Edmonton	74	87	118	205	39
Paul Coffey	Edmonton	80	40	86	126	104
Michel Goulet	Quebec	75	56	65	121	76
Peter Stastny	Quebec	80	46	73	119	73
Mike Bossy	NY Islanders	67	51	67	118	8
Barry Pederson	Boston	80	39	77	116	64
Jari Kurri	Edmonton	64	52	61	113	14
Bryan Trottier	NY Islanders	68	40	71	111	59
Bernie Federko	St. Louis	79	41	66	107	43
Rick Middleton	Boston	80	47	58	105	14

1984-85
CLARENCE CAMPBELL CONFERENCE
Norris Division

Team	GP	W	L	T	GF	GA	PTS
St. Louis	80	37	31	12	299	288	86
Chicago	80	38	35	7	309	299	83
Detroit	80	27	41	12	313	357	66
Minnesota	80	25	43	12	268	321	62
Toronto	80	20	52	8	253	358	48

Smythe Division

*Edmonton	80	49	20	11	401	298	109
Winnipeg	80	43	27	10	358	332	96
Calgary	80	41	27	12	363	302	94
Los Angeles	80	34	32	14	339	326	82
Vancouver	80	25	46	9	284	401	59

PRINCE OF WALES CONFERENCE
Adams Division

Montreal	80	41	27	12	309	262	94
Quebec	80	41	30	9	323	275	91
Buffalo	80	38	28	14	290	237	90
Boston	80	36	34	10	303	287	82
Hartford	80	30	41	9	268	318	69

Patrick Division

Philadelphia	80	53	20	7	348	241	113
Washington	80	46	25	9	322	240	101
NY Islanders	80	40	34	6	345	312	86
NY Rangers	80	26	44	10	295	345	62
New Jersey	80	22	48	10	264	346	54
Pittsburgh	80	24	51	5	276	385	53

Leading Scorers

Player	Team	GP	G	A	PTS	PIM
Wayne Gretzky	Edmonton	80	73	135	208	52
Jari Kurri	Edmonton	73	71	64	135	30
Dale Hawerchuk	Winnipeg	80	53	77	130	74
Marcel Dionne	Los Angeles	80	46	80	126	46
Paul Coffey	Edmonton	80	37	84	121	97
Mike Bossy	NY Islanders	76	58	59	117	38
John Ogrodnick	Detroit	79	55	50	105	30
Denis Savard	Chicago	79	38	67	105	56
Bernie Federko	St. Louis	76	30	73	103	27
Mike Gartner	Washington	80	50	52	102	71

1985-86
CLARENCE CAMPBELL CONFERENCE
Norris Division

Team	GP	W	L	T	GF	GA	PTS
Chicago	80	39	33	8	351	349	86
Minnesota	80	38	33	9	327	305	85
St. Louis	80	37	34	9	302	291	83
Toronto	80	25	48	7	311	386	57
Detroit	80	17	57	6	266	415	40

Smythe Division

Edmonton	80	56	17	7	426	310	119
Calgary	80	40	31	9	354	315	89
Winnipeg	80	26	47	7	295	372	59
Vancouver	80	23	44	13	282	333	59
Los Angeles	80	23	49	8	284	389	54

PRINCE OF WALES CONFERENCE
Adams Division

Quebec	80	43	31	6	330	289	92
*Montreal	80	40	33	7	330	280	87
Boston	80	37	31	12	311	288	86
Hartford	80	40	36	4	332	302	84
Buffalo	80	37	37	6	296	291	80

Patrick Division

Philadelphia	80	53	23	4	335	241	110
Washington	80	50	23	7	315	272	107
NY Islanders	80	39	29	12	327	284	90
NY Rangers	80	36	38	6	280	276	78
Pittsburgh	80	34	38	8	313	305	76
New Jersey	80	28	49	3	300	374	59

Leading Scorers

Player	Team	GP	G	A	PTS	PIM
Wayne Gretzky	Edmonton	80	52	163	215	52
Mario Lemieux	Pittsburgh	79	48	93	141	43
Paul Coffey	Edmonton	79	48	90	138	120
Jari Kurri	Edmonton	78	68	63	131	22
Mike Bossy	NY Islanders	80	61	62	123	14
Peter Stastny	Quebec	76	41	81	122	60
Denis Savard	Chicago	80	47	69	116	111
Mats Naslund	Montreal	80	43	67	110	16
Dale Hawerchuk	Winnipeg	80	46	59	105	44
Neal Broten	Minnesota	80	29	76	105	47

When Neal Broten cracked the top 10 with a career-high 105 points in 1985-86 it marked the first time in NHL history that an American-born player reached the 100-point plateau.

1986-87
CLARENCE CAMPBELL CONFERENCE
Norris Division

Team	GP	W	L	T	GF	GA	PTS
St. Louis	80	32	33	15	281	293	79
Detroit	80	34	36	10	260	274	78
Chicago	80	29	37	14	290	310	72
Toronto	80	32	42	6	286	319	70
Minnesota	80	30	40	10	296	314	70

Smythe Division

*Edmonton	80	50	24	6	372	284	106
Calgary	80	46	31	3	318	289	95
Winnipeg	80	40	32	8	279	271	88
Los Angeles	80	31	41	8	318	341	70
Vancouver	80	29	43	8	282	314	66

PRINCE OF WALES CONFERENCE
Adams Division

Hartford	80	43	30	7	287	270	93
Montreal	80	41	29	10	277	241	92
Boston	80	39	34	7	301	276	85
Quebec	80	31	39	10	267	276	72
Buffalo	80	28	44	8	280	308	64

Patrick Division

Philadelphia	80	46	26	8	310	245	100
Washington	80	38	32	10	285	278	86
NY Islanders	80	35	33	12	279	281	82
NY Rangers	80	34	38	8	307	323	76
Pittsburgh	80	30	38	12	297	290	72
New Jersey	80	29	45	6	293	368	64

Leading Scorers

Player	Team	GP	G	A	PTS	PIM
Wayne Gretzky	Edmonton	79	62	121	183	28
Jari Kurri	Edmonton	79	54	54	108	41
Mario Lemieux	Pittsburgh	63	54	53	107	57
Mark Messier	Edmonton	77	37	70	107	73
Doug Gilmour	St. Louis	80	42	63	105	58
Dino Ciccarelli	Minnesota	80	52	51	103	92
Dale Hawerchuk	Winnipeg	80	47	53	100	54
Michel Goulet	Quebec	75	49	47	96	61
Tim Kerr	Philadelphia	75	58	37	95	57
Raymond Bourque	Boston	78	23	72	95	36

1987-88
CLARENCE CAMPBELL CONFERENCE
Norris Division

Team	GP	W	L	T	GF	GA	PTS
Detroit	80	41	28	11	322	269	93
St. Louis	80	34	38	8	278	294	76
Chicago	80	30	41	9	284	328	69
Toronto	80	21	49	10	273	345	52
Minnesota	80	19	48	13	242	349	51

Smythe Division

Calgary	80	48	23	9	397	305	105
*Edmonton	80	44	25	11	363	288	99
Winnipeg	80	33	36	11	292	310	77
Los Angeles	80	30	42	8	318	359	68
Vancouver	80	25	46	9	272	320	59

PRINCE OF WALES CONFERENCE
Adams Division

Montreal	80	45	22	13	298	238	103
Boston	80	44	30	6	300	251	94
Buffalo	80	37	32	11	283	305	85
Hartford	80	35	38	7	249	267	77
Quebec	80	32	43	5	271	306	69

Patrick Division

NY Islanders	80	39	31	10	308	267	88
Washington	80	38	33	9	281	249	85
Philadelphia	80	38	33	9	292	292	85
New Jersey	80	38	36	6	295	296	82
NY Rangers	80	36	34	10	300	283	82
Pittsburgh	80	36	35	9	319	316	81

Leading Scorers

Player	Team	GP	G	A	PTS	PIM
Mario Lemieux	Pittsburgh	77	70	98	168	92
Wayne Gretzky	Edmonton	64	40	109	149	24
Denis Savard	Chicago	80	44	87	131	95
Dale Hawerchuk	Winnipeg	80	44	77	121	59
Luc Robitaille	Los Angeles	80	53	58	111	82
Peter Stastny	Quebec	76	46	65	111	69
Mark Messier	Edmonton	77	37	74	111	103
Jimmy Carson	Los Angeles	80	55	52	107	45
Hakan Loob	Calgary	80	50	56	106	47
Michel Goulet	Quebec	80	48	58	106	56

1988-89

CLARENCE CAMPBELL CONFERENCE

Norris Division

Team	GP	W	L	T	GF	GA	PTS
Detroit	80	34	34	12	313	316	80
St. Louis	80	33	35	12	275	285	78
Minnesota	80	27	37	16	258	278	70
Chicago	80	27	41	12	297	335	66
Toronto	80	28	46	6	259	342	62

Smythe Division

Team	GP	W	L	T	GF	GA	PTS
*Calgary	80	54	17	9	354	226	117
Los Angeles	80	42	31	7	376	335	91
Edmonton	80	38	34	8	325	306	84
Vancouver	80	33	39	8	251	253	74
Winnipeg	80	26	42	12	300	355	64

PRINCE OF WALES CONFERENCE

Adams Division

Team	GP	W	L	T	GF	GA	PTS
Montreal	80	53	18	9	315	218	115
Boston	80	37	29	14	289	256	88
Buffalo	80	38	35	7	291	299	83
Hartford	80	37	38	5	299	290	79
Quebec	80	27	46	7	269	342	61

Patrick Division

Team	GP	W	L	T	GF	GA	PTS
Washington	80	41	29	10	305	259	92
Pittsburgh	80	40	33	7	347	349	87
NY Rangers	80	37	35	8	310	307	82
Philadelphia	80	36	36	8	307	285	80
New Jersey	80	27	41	12	281	325	66
NY Islanders	80	28	47	5	265	325	61

Leading Scorers

Player	Team	GP	G	A	PTS	PIM
Mario Lemieux	Pittsburgh	76	85	114	199	100
Wayne Gretzky	Los Angeles	78	54	114	168	26
Steve Yzerman	Detroit	80	65	90	155	61
Bernie Nicholls	Los Angeles	79	70	80	150	96
Rob Brown	Pittsburgh	68	49	66	115	118
Paul Coffey	Pittsburgh	75	30	83	113	193
Joe Mullen	Calgary	79	51	59	110	16
Jari Kurri	Edmonton	76	44	58	102	69
Jimmy Carson	Edmonton	80	49	51	100	36
Luc Robitaille	Los Angeles	78	46	52	98	65

1989-90

CLARENCE CAMPBELL CONFERENCE

Norris Division

Team	GP	W	L	T	GF	GA	PTS
Chicago	80	41	33	6	316	294	88
St. Louis	80	37	34	9	295	279	83
Toronto	80	38	38	4	337	358	80
Minnesota	80	36	40	4	284	291	76
Detroit	80	28	38	14	288	323	70

Smythe Division

Team	GP	W	L	T	GF	GA	PTS
Calgary	80	42	23	15	348	265	99
*Edmonton	80	38	28	14	315	283	90
Winnipeg	80	37	32	11	298	290	85
Los Angeles	80	34	39	7	338	337	75
Vancouver	80	25	41	14	245	306	64

PRINCE OF WALES CONFERENCE

Adams Division

Team	GP	W	L	T	GF	GA	PTS
Boston	80	46	25	9	289	232	101
Buffalo	80	45	27	8	286	248	98
Montreal	80	41	28	11	288	234	93
Hartford	80	38	33	9	275	268	85
Quebec	80	12	61	7	240	407	31

Patrick Division

Team	GP	W	L	T	GF	GA	PTS
NY Rangers	80	36	31	13	279	267	85
New Jersey	80	37	34	9	295	288	83
Washington	80	36	38	6	284	275	78
NY Islanders	80	31	38	11	281	288	73
Pittsburgh	80	32	40	8	318	359	72
Philadelphia	80	30	39	11	290	297	71

Leading Scorers

Player	Team	GP	G	A	PTS	PIM
Wayne Gretzky	Los Angeles	73	40	102	142	42
Mark Messier	Edmonton	79	45	84	129	79
Steve Yzerman	Detroit	79	62	65	127	79
Mario Lemieux	Pittsburgh	59	45	78	123	78
Brett Hull	St. Louis	80	72	41	113	24
Bernie Nicholls	L.A., NYR	79	39	73	112	86
Pierre Turgeon	Buffalo	80	40	66	106	29
Pat LaFontaine	NY Islanders	74	54	51	105	38
Paul Coffey	Pittsburgh	80	29	74	103	95
Joe Sakic	Quebec	80	39	63	102	27
Adam Oates	St. Louis	80	23	79	102	30

1990-91

CLARENCE CAMPBELL CONFERENCE

Norris Division

Team	GP	W	L	T	GF	GA	PTS
Chicago	80	49	23	8	284	211	106
St. Louis	80	47	22	11	310	250	105
Detroit	80	34	38	8	273	298	76
Minnesota	80	27	39	14	256	266	68
Toronto	80	23	46	11	241	318	57

Smythe Division

Team	GP	W	L	T	GF	GA	PTS
Los Angeles	80	46	24	10	340	254	102
Calgary	80	46	26	8	344	263	100
Edmonton	80	37	37	6	272	272	80
Vancouver	80	28	43	9	243	315	65
Winnipeg	80	26	43	11	260	288	63

PRINCE OF WALES CONFERENCE

Adams Division

Team	GP	W	L	T	GF	GA	PTS
Boston	80	44	24	12	299	264	100
Montreal	80	39	30	11	273	249	89
Buffalo	80	31	30	19	292	278	81
Hartford	80	31	38	11	238	276	73
Quebec	80	16	50	14	236	354	46

Patrick Division

Team	GP	W	L	T	GF	GA	PTS
*Pittsburgh	80	41	33	6	342	305	88
NY Rangers	80	36	31	13	297	265	85
Washington	80	37	36	7	258	258	81
New Jersey	80	32	33	15	272	264	79
Philadelphia	80	33	37	10	252	267	76
NY Islanders	80	25	45	10	223	290	60

Leading Scorers

Player	Team	GP	G	A	PTS	PIM
Wayne Gretzky	Los Angeles	78	41	122	163	16
Brett Hull	St. Louis	78	86	45	131	22
Adam Oates	St. Louis	61	25	90	115	29
Mark Recchi	Pittsburgh	78	40	73	113	48
John Cullen	Pit., Hfd.	78	39	71	110	101
Joe Sakic	Quebec	80	48	61	109	24
Steve Yzerman	Detroit	80	51	57	108	34
Theoren Fleury	Calgary	79	51	53	104	136
Al MacInnis	Calgary	78	28	75	103	90
Steve Larmer	Chicago	80	44	57	101	79

1991-92

CLARENCE CAMPBELL CONFERENCE

Norris Division

Team	GP	W	L	T	GF	GA	PTS
Detroit	80	43	25	12	320	256	98
Chicago	80	36	29	15	257	236	87
St. Louis	80	36	33	11	279	266	83
Minnesota	80	32	42	6	246	278	70
Toronto	80	30	43	7	234	294	67

Smythe Division

Team	GP	W	L	T	GF	GA	PTS
Vancouver	80	42	26	12	285	250	96
Los Angeles	80	35	31	14	287	296	84
Edmonton	80	36	34	10	295	297	82
Winnipeg	80	33	32	15	251	244	81
Calgary	80	31	37	12	296	305	74
San Jose	80	17	58	5	219	359	39

PRINCE OF WALES CONFERENCE

Adams Division

Team	GP	W	L	T	GF	GA	PTS
Montreal	80	41	28	11	267	207	93
Boston	80	36	32	12	270	275	84
Buffalo	80	31	37	12	289	299	74
Hartford	80	26	41	13	247	283	65
Quebec	80	20	48	12	255	318	52

Patrick Division

Team	GP	W	L	T	GF	GA	PTS
NY Rangers	80	50	25	5	321	246	105
Washington	80	45	27	8	330	275	98
*Pittsburgh	80	39	32	9	343	308	87
New Jersey	80	38	31	11	289	259	87
NY Islanders	80	34	35	11	291	299	79
Philadelphia	80	32	37	11	252	273	75

Leading Scorers

Player	Team	GP	G	A	PTS	PIM
Mario Lemieux	Pittsburgh	64	44	87	131	94
Kevin Stevens	Pittsburgh	80	54	69	123	254
Wayne Gretzky	Los Angeles	74	31	90	121	34
Brett Hull	St. Louis	73	70	39	109	48
Luc Robitaille	Los Angeles	80	44	63	107	95
Mark Messier	NY Rangers	79	35	72	107	76
Jeremy Roenick	Chicago	80	53	50	103	23
Steve Yzerman	Detroit	79	45	58	103	64
Brian Leetch	NY Rangers	80	22	80	102	26
Adam Oates	St.L., Bos.	80	20	79	99	22

1992-93

CLARENCE CAMPBELL CONFERENCE

Norris Division

Team	GP	W	L	T	GF	GA	PTS
Chicago	84	47	25	12	279	230	106
Detroit	84	47	28	9	369	280	103
Toronto	84	44	29	11	288	241	99
St. Louis	84	37	36	11	282	278	85
Minnesota	84	36	38	10	272	293	82
Tampa Bay	84	23	54	7	245	332	53

Smythe Division

Team	GP	W	L	T	GF	GA	PTS
Vancouver	84	46	29	9	346	278	101
Calgary	84	43	30	11	322	282	97
Los Angeles	84	39	35	10	338	340	88
Winnipeg	84	40	37	7	322	320	87
Edmonton	84	26	50	8	242	337	60
San Jose	84	11	71	2	218	414	24

PRINCE OF WALES CONFERENCE

Adams Division

Team	GP	W	L	T	GF	GA	PTS
Boston	84	51	26	7	332	268	109
Quebec	84	47	27	10	351	300	104
*Montreal	84	48	30	6	326	280	102
Buffalo	84	38	36	10	335	297	86
Hartford	84	26	52	6	284	369	58
Ottawa	84	10	70	4	202	395	24

Patrick Division

Team	GP	W	L	T	GF	GA	PTS
Pittsburgh	84	56	21	7	367	268	119
Washington	84	43	34	7	325	286	93
NY Islanders	84	40	37	7	335	297	87
New Jersey	84	40	37	7	308	299	87
Philadelphia	84	36	37	11	319	319	83
NY Rangers	84	34	39	11	304	308	79

Leading Scorers

Player	Team	GP	G	A	PTS	PIM
Mario Lemieux	Pittsburgh	60	69	91	160	38
Pat LaFontaine	Buffalo	84	53	95	148	63
Adam Oates	Boston	84	45	97	142	32
Steve Yzerman	Detroit	84	58	79	137	44
Teemu Selanne	Winnipeg	84	76	56	132	45
Pierre Turgeon	NY Islanders	83	58	74	132	26
Alexander Mogilny	Buffalo	77	76	51	127	40
Doug Gilmour	Toronto	83	32	95	127	100
Luc Robitaille	Los Angeles	84	63	62	125	100
Mark Recchi	Philadelphia	84	53	70	123	95

1993-94

EASTERN CONFERENCE

Northeast Division

Team		GP	W	L	T	GF	GA	PTS
Pittsburgh	(2)	84	44	27	13	299	285	101
Boston	(4)	84	42	29	13	289	252	97
Montreal	(5)	84	41	29	14	283	248	96
Buffalo	(6)	84	43	32	9	282	218	95
Quebec		84	34	42	8	277	292	76
Hartford		84	27	48	9	227	288	63
Ottawa		84	14	61	9	201	397	37

Atlantic Division

Team		GP	W	L	T	GF	GA	PTS
*NY Rangers	(1)	84	52	24	8	299	231	112
New Jersey	(3)	84	47	25	12	306	220	106
Washington	(7)	84	39	35	10	277	263	88
NY Islanders	(8)	84	36	36	12	282	264	84
Florida		84	33	34	17	233	233	83
Philadelphia		84	35	39	10	294	314	80
Tampa Bay		84	30	43	11	224	251	71

WESTERN CONFERENCE

Central Division

Team		GP	W	L	T	GF	GA	PTS
Detroit	(1)	84	46	30	8	356	275	100
Toronto	(3)	84	43	29	12	280	243	98
Dallas	(4)	84	42	29	13	286	265	97
St. Louis	(5)	84	40	33	11	270	283	91
Chicago	(6)	84	39	36	9	254	240	87
Winnipeg		84	24	51	9	245	344	57

Pacific Division

Team		GP	W	L	T	GF	GA	PTS
Calgary	(2)	84	42	29	13	302	256	97
Vancouver	(7)	84	41	40	3	279	276	85
San Jose	(8)	84	33	35	16	252	265	82
Anaheim		84	33	46	5	229	251	71
Los Angeles		84	27	45	12	294	322	66
Edmonton		84	25	45	14	261	305	64

Leading Scorers

Player	Team	GP	G	A	PTS	PIM
Wayne Gretzky	Los Angeles	81	38	92	130	20
Sergei Fedorov	Detroit	82	56	64	120	34
Adam Oates	Boston	77	32	80	112	45
Doug Gilmour	Toronto	83	27	84	111	105
Pavel Bure	Vancouver	76	60	47	107	86
Jeremy Roenick	Chicago	84	46	61	107	125
Mark Recchi	Philadelphia	84	40	67	107	46
Brendan Shanahan	St. Louis	81	52	50	102	211
Dave Andreychuk	Toronto	83	53	46	99	98
Jaromir Jagr	Pittsburgh	80	32	67	99	61

1994-95

EASTERN CONFERENCE
Northeast Division

Team		GP	W	L	T	GF	GA	PTS
Quebec	(1)	48	30	13	5	185	134	65
Pittsburgh	(3)	48	29	16	3	181	158	61
Boston	(4)	48	27	18	3	150	127	57
Buffalo	(7)	48	22	19	7	130	119	51
Hartford		48	19	24	5	127	141	43
Montreal		48	18	23	7	125	148	43
Ottawa		48	9	34	5	117	174	23

Atlantic Division

Team		GP	W	L	T	GF	GA	PTS
Philadelphia	(2)	48	28	16	4	150	132	60
*New Jersey	(5)	48	22	18	8	136	121	52
Washington	(6)	48	22	18	8	136	120	52
NY Rangers	(8)	48	22	23	3	139	134	47
Florida		48	20	22	6	115	127	46
Tampa Bay		48	17	28	3	120	144	37
NY Islanders		48	15	28	5	126	158	35

WESTERN CONFERENCE
Central Division

Team		GP	W	L	T	GF	GA	PTS
Detroit	(1)	48	33	11	4	180	117	70
St. Louis	(3)	48	28	15	5	178	135	61
Chicago	(4)	48	24	19	5	156	115	53
Toronto	(5)	48	21	19	8	135	146	50
Dallas	(8)	48	17	23	8	136	135	42
Winnipeg		48	16	25	7	157	177	39

Pacific Division

Team		GP	W	L	T	GF	GA	PTS
Calgary	(2)	48	24	17	7	163	135	55
Vancouver	(6)	48	18	18	12	153	148	48
San Jose	(7)	48	19	25	4	129	161	42
Los Angeles		48	16	23	9	142	174	41
Edmonton		48	17	27	4	136	183	38
Anaheim		48	16	27	5	125	164	37

Leading Scorers

Player	Team	GP	G	A	PTS	PIM
Jaromir Jagr	Pittsburgh	48	32	38	70	37
Eric Lindros	Philadelphia	46	29	41	70	60
Alex Zhamnov	Winnipeg	48	30	35	65	20
Joe Sakic	Quebec	47	19	43	62	30
Ron Francis	Pittsburgh	44	11	48	59	18
Theoren Fleury	Calgary	47	29	29	58	112
Paul Coffey	Detroit	45	14	44	58	72
Mikael Renberg	Philadelphia	47	26	31	57	20
John LeClair	Mtl., Phi.	46	26	28	54	30
Mark Messier	NY Rangers	46	14	39	53	40
Adam Oates	Boston	48	12	41	53	8

1995-96

EASTERN CONFERENCE
Northeast Division

Team		GP	W	L	T	GF	GA	PTS
Pittsburgh	(2)	82	49	29	4	362	284	102
Boston	(5)	82	40	31	11	282	269	91
Montreal	(6)	82	40	32	10	265	248	90
Hartford		82	34	39	9	237	259	77
Buffalo		82	33	42	7	247	262	73
Ottawa		82	18	59	5	191	291	41

Atlantic Division

Team		GP	W	L	T	GF	GA	PTS
Philadelphia	(1)	82	45	24	13	282	208	103
NY Rangers	(3)	82	41	27	14	272	237	96
Florida	(4)	82	41	31	10	254	234	92
Washington	(7)	82	39	32	11	234	204	89
Tampa Bay	(8)	82	38	32	12	238	248	88
New Jersey		82	37	33	12	215	202	86
NY Islanders		82	22	50	10	229	315	54

WESTERN CONFERENCE
Central Division

Team		GP	W	L	T	GF	GA	PTS
Detroit	(1)	82	62	13	7	325	181	131
Chicago	(3)	82	40	28	14	273	220	94
Toronto	(4)	82	34	36	12	247	252	80
St. Louis	(5)	82	32	34	16	219	248	80
Winnipeg	(8)	82	36	40	6	275	291	78
Dallas		82	26	42	14	227	280	66

Pacific Division

Team		GP	W	L	T	GF	GA	PTS
*Colorado	(2)	82	47	25	10	326	240	104
Calgary	(6)	82	34	37	11	241	240	79
Vancouver	(7)	82	32	35	15	278	278	79
Anaheim		82	35	39	8	234	247	78
Edmonton		82	30	44	8	240	304	68
Los Angeles		82	24	40	18	256	302	66
San Jose		82	20	55	7	252	357	47

Leading Scorers

Player	Team	GP	G	A	PTS	PIM
Mario Lemieux	Pittsburgh	70	69	92	161	54
Jaromir Jagr	Pittsburgh	82	62	87	149	96
Joe Sakic	Colorado	82	51	69	120	44
Ron Francis	Pittsburgh	77	27	92	119	56
Peter Forsberg	Colorado	82	30	86	116	47
Eric Lindros	Philadelphia	73	47	68	115	163
Paul Kariya	Anaheim	82	50	58	108	20
Teemu Selanne	Wpg., Ana.	79	40	68	108	22
Alexander Mogilny	Vancouver	79	55	52	107	16
Sergei Fedorov	Detroit	78	39	68	107	48

1996-97

EASTERN CONFERENCE
Northeast Division

Team		GP	W	L	T	GF	GA	PTS
Buffalo	(2)	82	40	30	12	237	208	92
Pittsburgh	(6)	82	38	36	8	285	280	84
Ottawa	(7)	82	31	36	15	226	234	77
Montreal	(8)	82	31	36	15	249	276	77
Hartford		82	32	39	11	226	256	75
Boston		82	26	47	9	234	300	61

Atlantic Division

Team		GP	W	L	T	GF	GA	PTS
New Jersey	(1)	82	45	23	14	231	182	104
Philadelphia	(3)	82	45	24	13	274	217	103
Florida	(4)	82	35	28	19	221	201	89
NY Rangers	(5)	82	38	34	10	258	231	86
Washington		82	33	40	9	214	231	75
Tampa Bay		82	32	40	10	217	247	74
NY Islanders		82	29	41	12	240	250	70

WESTERN CONFERENCE
Central Division

Team		GP	W	L	T	GF	GA	PTS
Dallas	(2)	82	48	26	8	252	198	104
*Detroit	(3)	82	38	26	18	253	197	94
Phoenix	(5)	82	38	37	7	240	243	83
St. Louis	(6)	82	36	35	11	236	239	83
Chicago	(8)	82	34	35	13	223	210	81
Toronto		82	30	44	8	230	273	68

Pacific Division

Team		GP	W	L	T	GF	GA	PTS
Colorado	(1)	82	49	24	9	277	205	107
Anaheim	(4)	82	36	33	13	245	233	85
Edmonton	(7)	82	36	37	9	252	247	81
Vancouver		82	35	40	7	257	273	77
Calgary		82	32	41	9	214	239	73
Los Angeles		82	28	43	11	214	268	67
San Jose		82	27	47	8	211	278	62

Leading Scorers

Player	Team	GP	G	A	PTS	PIM
Mario Lemieux	Pittsburgh	76	50	72	122	65
Teemu Selanne	Anaheim	78	51	58	109	34
Paul Kariya	Anaheim	69	44	55	99	6
John LeClair	Philadelphia	82	50	47	97	58
Wayne Gretzky	NY Rangers	82	25	72	97	28
Jaromir Jagr	Pittsburgh	63	47	48	95	40
Mats Sundin	Toronto	82	41	53	94	59
Ziggy Palffy	NY Islanders	80	48	42	90	43
Ron Francis	Pittsburgh	81	27	63	90	20
Brendan Shanahan	Hfd., Det.	81	47	41	88	131

1997-98

EASTERN CONFERENCE
Northeast Division

Team		GP	W	L	T	GF	GA	PTS
Pittsburgh	(2)	82	40	24	18	228	188	98
Boston	(5)	82	39	30	13	221	194	91
Buffalo	(6)	82	36	29	17	211	187	89
Montreal	(7)	82	37	32	13	235	208	87
Ottawa	(8)	82	34	33	15	193	200	83
Carolina		82	33	41	8	200	219	74

Atlantic Division

Team		GP	W	L	T	GF	GA	PTS
New Jersey	(1)	82	48	23	11	225	166	107
Philadelphia	(3)	82	42	29	11	242	193	95
Washington	(4)	82	40	30	12	219	202	92
NY Islanders		82	30	41	11	212	225	71
NY Rangers		82	25	39	18	197	231	68
Florida		82	24	43	15	203	256	63
Tampa Bay		82	17	55	10	151	269	44

WESTERN CONFERENCE
Central Division

Team		GP	W	L	T	GF	GA	PTS
Dallas	(1)	82	49	22	11	242	167	109
*Detroit	(3)	82	44	23	15	250	196	103
St. Louis	(4)	82	45	29	8	256	204	98
Phoenix	(6)	82	35	35	12	224	227	82
Chicago		82	30	39	13	192	199	73
Toronto		82	30	43	9	194	237	69

Pacific Division

Team		GP	W	L	T	GF	GA	PTS
Colorado	(2)	82	39	26	17	231	205	95
Los Angeles	(5)	82	38	33	11	227	225	87
Edmonton	(7)	82	35	37	10	215	224	80
San Jose	(8)	82	34	38	10	210	216	78
Calgary		82	26	41	15	217	252	67
Anaheim		82	26	43	13	205	261	65
Vancouver		82	25	43	14	224	273	64

Leading Scorers

Player	Team	GP	G	A	PTS	PIM
Jaromir Jagr	Pittsburgh	77	35	67	102	64
Peter Forsberg	Colorado	72	25	66	91	94
Pavel Bure	Vancouver	82	51	39	90	48
Wayne Gretzky	NY Rangers	82	23	67	90	28
John LeClair	Philadelphia	82	51	36	87	32
Ziggy Palffy	NY Islanders	82	45	42	87	34
Ron Francis	Pittsburgh	81	25	62	87	20
Teemu Selanne	Anaheim	73	52	34	86	30
Jason Allison	Boston	81	33	50	83	60
Jozef Stumpel	Los Angeles	77	21	58	79	53

1998-99

EASTERN CONFERENCE
Northeast Division

Team		GP	W	L	T	GF	GA	PTS
Ottawa	(2)	82	44	23	15	239	179	103
Toronto	(4)	82	45	30	7	268	231	97
Boston	(6)	82	39	30	13	214	181	91
Buffalo	(7)	82	37	28	17	207	175	91
Montreal		82	32	39	11	184	209	75

Atlantic Division

Team		GP	W	L	T	GF	GA	PTS
New Jersey	(1)	82	47	24	11	248	196	105
Philadelphia	(5)	82	37	26	19	231	196	93
Pittsburgh	(8)	82	38	30	14	242	225	90
NY Rangers		82	33	38	11	217	227	77
NY Islanders		82	24	48	10	194	244	58

Southeast Division

Team		GP	W	L	T	GF	GA	PTS
Carolina	(3)	82	34	30	18	210	202	86
Florida		82	30	34	18	210	228	78
Washington		82	31	45	6	200	218	68
Tampa Bay		82	19	54	9	179	292	47

WESTERN CONFERENCE
Central Division

Team		GP	W	L	T	GF	GA	PTS
Detroit	(3)	82	43	32	7	245	202	93
St Louis	(5)	82	37	32	13	237	209	87
Chicago		82	29	41	12	202	248	70
Nashville		82	28	47	7	190	261	63

Pacific Division

Team		GP	W	L	T	GF	GA	PTS
*Dallas	(1)	82	51	19	12	236	168	114
Phoenix	(4)	82	39	31	12	205	197	90
Anaheim	(6)	82	35	34	13	215	206	83
San Jose	(7)	82	31	33	18	196	191	80
Los Angeles		82	32	45	5	189	222	69

Northwest Division

Team		GP	W	L	T	GF	GA	PTS
Colorado	(2)	82	44	28	10	239	205	98
Edmonton	(8)	82	33	37	12	230	226	78
Calgary		82	30	40	12	211	234	72
Vancouver		82	23	47	12	192	258	58

Leading Scorers

Player	Team	GP	G	A	PTS	PIM
Jaromir Jagr	Pittsburgh	81	44	83	127	66
Teemu Selanne	Anaheim	75	47	60	107	30
Paul Kariya	Anaheim	82	39	62	101	40
Peter Forsberg	Colorado	78	30	67	97	108
Joe Sakic	Colorado	73	41	55	96	29
Alexei Yashin	Ottawa	82	44	50	94	54
Eric Lindros	Philadelphia	71	40	53	93	120
Theoren Fleury	Cgy., Col.	75	40	53	93	86
John LeClair	Philadelphia	76	43	47	90	30
Pavol Demitra	St Louis	82	37	52	89	16

1999-2000

EASTERN CONFERENCE
Northeast Division

Team		GP	W	L	T	OTL	GF	GA	PTS
Toronto	(3)	82	45	27	7	3	246	222	100
Ottawa	(6)	82	41	28	11	2	244	210	95
Buffalo	(8)	82	35	32	11	4	213	204	85
Montreal		82	35	34	9	4	196	194	83
Boston		82	24	33	19	6	210	248	73

Atlantic Division

Team		GP	W	L	T	OTL	GF	GA	PTS
Philadelphia	(1)	82	45	22	12	3	237	179	105
*New Jersey	(4)	82	45	24	8	5	251	203	103
Pittsburgh	(7)	82	37	31	8	6	241	236	88
NY Rangers		82	29	38	12	3	218	246	73
NY Islanders		82	24	48	9	1	194	275	58

Southeast Division

Team		GP	W	L	T	OTL	GF	GA	PTS
Washington	(2)	82	44	24	12	2	227	194	102
Florida	(5)	82	43	27	6	6	244	209	98
Carolina		82	37	35	10	0	217	216	84
Tampa Bay		82	19	47	9	7	204	310	54
Atlanta		82	14	57	7	4	170	313	39

WESTERN CONFERENCE
Central Division

Team		GP	W	L	T	OTL	GF	GA	PTS
St. Louis	(1)	82	51	19	11	1	248	165	114
Detroit	(4)	82	48	22	10	2	278	210	108
Chicago		82	33	37	10	2	242	245	78
Nashville		82	28	40	7	7	199	240	70

Pacific Division

Team		GP	W	L	T	OTL	GF	GA	PTS
Dallas	(2)	82	43	23	10	6	211	184	102
Los Angeles	(5)	82	39	27	12	4	245	228	94
Phoenix	(6)	82	39	31	8	4	232	228	90
San Jose	(8)	82	35	30	10	7	225	214	87
Anaheim		82	34	33	12	3	217	227	83

Northwest Division

Team		GP	W	L	T	OTL	GF	GA	PTS
Colorado	(3)	82	42	28	11	1	233	201	96
Edmonton	(7)	82	32	26	16	8	226	212	88
Vancouver		82	30	29	15	8	227	237	83
Calgary		82	31	36	10	5	211	256	77

Leading Scorers

Player	Team	GP	G	A	PTS	PIM
Jaromir Jagr	Pittsburgh	63	42	54	96	50
Pavel Bure	Florida	74	58	36	94	16
Mark Recchi	Philadelphia	82	28	63	91	50
Paul Kariya	Anaheim	74	42	44	86	24
Teemu Selanne	Anaheim	79	33	52	85	12
Owen Nolan	San Jose	78	44	40	84	110
Tony Amonte	Chicago	82	43	41	84	48
Mike Modano	Dallas	77	38	43	81	48
Joe Sakic	Colorado	60	28	53	81	28
Steve Yzerman	Detroit	78	35	44	79	34

2000-01

EASTERN CONFERENCE

Northeast Division

Team		GP	W	L	T	OTL	GF	GA	PTS
Ottawa	(2)	82	48	21	9	4	274	205	109
Buffalo	(5)	82	46	30	5	1	218	184	98
Toronto	(7)	82	37	29	11	5	232	207	90
Boston		82	36	30	8	8	227	249	88
Montreal		82	28	40	8	6	206	232	70

Atlantic Division

Team		GP	W	L	T	OTL	GF	GA	PTS
New Jersey	(1)	82	48	19	12	3	295	195	111
Philadelphia	(4)	82	43	25	11	3	240	207	100
Pittsburgh	(6)	82	42	28	9	3	281	256	96
NY Rangers		82	33	43	5	1	250	290	72
NY Islanders		82	21	51	7	3	185	268	52

Southeast Division

Team		GP	W	L	T	OTL	GF	GA	PTS
Washington	(3)	82	41	27	10	4	233	211	96
Carolina	(8)	82	38	32	9	3	212	225	88
Florida		82	22	38	13	9	200	246	66
Atlanta		82	23	45	12	2	211	289	60
Tampa Bay		82	24	47	6	5	201	280	59

WESTERN CONFERENCE

Central Division

Team		GP	W	L	T	OTL	GF	GA	PTS
Detroit	(2)	82	49	20	9	4	253	202	111
St. Louis	(4)	82	43	22	12	5	249	195	103
Nashville		82	34	36	9	3	186	200	80
Chicago		82	29	40	8	5	210	246	71
Columbus		82	28	39	9	6	190	233	71

Pacific Division

Team		GP	W	L	T	OTL	GF	GA	PTS
Dallas	(3)	82	48	24	8	2	241	187	106
San Jose	(5)	82	40	27	12	3	217	192	95
Los Angeles	(7)	82	38	28	13	3	252	228	92
Phoenix		82	35	27	17	3	214	212	90
Anaheim		82	25	41	11	5	188	245	66

Northwest Division

Team		GP	W	L	T	OTL	GF	GA	PTS
*Colorado	(1)	82	52	16	10	4	270	192	118
Edmonton	(6)	82	39	28	12	3	243	222	93
Vancouver	(8)	82	36	28	11	7	239	238	90
Calgary		82	27	36	15	4	197	236	73
Minnesota		82	25	39	13	5	168	210	68

Leading Scorers

Player	Team	GP	G	A	PTS	PIM
Jaromir Jagr	Pittsburgh	81	52	69	121	42
Joe Sakic	Colorado	82	54	64	118	30
Patrik Elias	New Jersey	82	40	56	96	51
Alex Kovalev	Pittsburgh	79	44	51	95	96
Jason Allison	Boston	82	36	59	95	85
Martin Straka	Pittsburgh	82	27	68	95	38
Pavel Bure	Florida	82	59	33	92	58
Doug Weight	Edmonton	82	25	65	90	91
Ziggy Palffy	Los Angeles	73	38	51	89	20
Peter Forsberg	Colorado	73	27	62	89	54

2001-02

EASTERN CONFERENCE

Northeast Division

Team		GP	W	L	T	OTL	GF	GA	PTS
Boston	(1)	82	43	24	6	9	236	201	101
Toronto	(4)	82	43	25	10	4	249	207	100
Ottawa	(7)	82	39	27	9	7	243	208	94
Montreal	(8)	82	36	31	12	3	207	209	87
Buffalo		82	35	35	11	1	213	200	82

Atlantic Division

Team		GP	W	L	T	OTL	GF	GA	PTS
Philadelphia	(2)	82	42	27	10	3	234	192	97
NY Islanders	(5)	82	42	28	8	4	239	220	96
New Jersey	(6)	82	41	28	9	4	205	187	95
NY Rangers		82	36	38	4	4	227	258	80
Pittsburgh		82	28	41	8	5	198	249	69

Southeast Division

Team		GP	W	L	T	OTL	GF	GA	PTS
Carolina	(3)	82	35	26	16	5	217	217	91
Washington		82	36	33	11	2	228	240	85
Tampa Bay		82	27	40	11	4	178	219	69
Florida		82	22	44	10	6	180	250	60
Atlanta		82	19	47	11	5	187	288	54

WESTERN CONFERENCE

Central Division

Team		GP	W	L	T	OTL	GF	GA	PTS
*Detroit	(1)	82	51	17	10	4	251	187	116
St. Louis	(4)	82	43	27	8	4	227	188	98
Chicago	(5)	82	41	27	13	1	216	207	96
Nashville		82	28	41	13	0	196	230	69
Columbus		82	22	47	8	5	164	255	57

Pacific Division

Team		GP	W	L	T	OTL	GF	GA	PTS
San Jose	(3)	82	44	27	8	3	248	199	99
Phoenix	(6)	82	40	27	9	6	228	210	95
Los Angeles	(7)	82	40	27	11	4	214	190	95
Dallas		82	36	28	13	5	215	213	90
Anaheim		82	29	42	8	3	175	198	69

Northwest Division

Team		GP	W	L	T	OTL	GF	GA	PTS
Colorado	(2)	82	45	28	8	1	212	169	99
Vancouver	(8)	82	42	30	7	3	254	211	94
Edmonton		82	38	28	12	4	205	182	92
Calgary		82	32	35	12	3	201	220	79
Minnesota		82	26	35	12	9	195	238	73

Leading Scorers

Player	Team	GP	G	A	PTS	PIM
Jarome Iginla	Calgary	82	52	44	96	77
Markus Naslund	Vancouver	81	40	50	90	50
Todd Bertuzzi	Vancouver	72	36	49	85	110
Mats Sundin	Toronto	82	41	39	80	94
Jaromir Jagr	Washington	69	31	48	79	30
Joe Sakic	Colorado	82	26	53	79	18
Pavol Demitra	St. Louis	82	35	43	78	46
Adam Oates	Wsh., Phi.	80	14	64	78	28
Mike Modano	Dallas	78	34	43	77	38
Ron Francis	Carolina	80	27	50	77	18

2002-03

EASTERN CONFERENCE

Northeast Division

Team		GP	W	L	T	OTL	GF	GA	PTS
Ottawa	(1)	82	52	21	8	1	263	182	113
Toronto	(5)	82	44	28	7	3	236	208	98
Boston	(7)	82	36	31	11	4	245	237	87
Montreal		82	30	35	8	9	206	234	77
Buffalo		82	27	37	10	8	190	219	72

Atlantic Division

Team		GP	W	L	T	OTL	GF	GA	PTS
*New Jersey	(2)	82	46	20	10	6	216	166	108
Philadelphia	(4)	82	45	20	13	4	211	166	107
NY Islanders	(8)	82	35	34	11	2	224	231	83
NY Rangers		82	32	36	10	4	210	231	78
Pittsburgh		82	27	44	6	5	189	255	65

Southeast Division

Team		GP	W	L	T	OTL	GF	GA	PTS
Tampa Bay	(3)	82	36	25	16	5	219	210	93
Washington	(6)	82	39	29	8	6	224	220	92
Atlanta		82	31	39	7	5	226	284	74
Florida		82	24	36	13	9	176	237	70
Carolina		82	22	43	11	6	171	240	61

WESTERN CONFERENCE

Central Division

Team		GP	W	L	T	OTL	GF	GA	PTS
Detroit	(2)	82	48	20	10	4	269	203	110
St. Louis	(5)	82	41	24	11	6	253	222	99
Chicago		82	30	33	13	6	207	226	79
Nashville		82	27	35	13	7	183	206	74
Columbus		82	29	42	8	3	213	263	69

Pacific Division

Team		GP	W	L	T	OTL	GF	GA	PTS
Dallas	(1)	82	46	17	15	4	245	169	111
Anaheim	(7)	82	40	27	9	6	203	193	95
Los Angeles		82	33	37	6	6	203	221	78
Phoenix		82	31	35	11	5	204	230	78
San Jose		82	28	37	9	8	214	239	73

Northwest Division

Team		GP	W	L	T	OTL	GF	GA	PTS
Colorado	(3)	82	42	19	13	8	251	194	105
Vancouver	(4)	82	45	23	13	1	264	208	104
Minnesota	(6)	82	42	29	10	1	198	178	95
Edmonton	(8)	82	36	26	11	9	231	230	92
Calgary		82	29	36	13	4	186	228	75

Leading Scorers

Player	Team	GP	G	A	PTS	PIM
Peter Forsberg	Colorado	75	29	77	106	70
Markus Naslund	Vancouver	82	48	56	104	52
Joe Thornton	Boston	77	36	65	101	109
Milan Hejduk	Colorado	82	50	48	98	52
Todd Bertuzzi	Vancouver	82	46	51	97	144
Pavol Demitra	St. Louis	78	36	57	93	32
Glen Murray	Boston	82	44	48	92	64
Mario Lemieux	Pittsburgh	67	28	63	91	43
Dany Heatley	Atlanta	77	41	48	89	58
Ziggy Palffy	Los Angeles	76	37	48	85	47
Mike Modano	Dallas	79	28	57	85	30

2003-04

EASTERN CONFERENCE

Northeast Division

Team		GP	W	L	T	OTL	GF	GA	PTS
Boston	(2)	82	41	19	15	7	209	188	104
Toronto	(4)	82	45	24	10	3	242	204	103
Ottawa	(5)	82	43	23	10	6	262	189	102
Montreal	(7)	82	41	30	7	4	208	192	93
Buffalo		82	37	34	7	4	220	221	85

Atlantic Division

Team		GP	W	L	T	OTL	GF	GA	PTS
Philadelphia	(3)	82	40	21	15	6	229	186	101
New Jersey	(6)	82	43	25	12	2	213	164	100
NY Islanders	(8)	82	38	29	11	4	237	210	91
NY Rangers		82	27	40	7	8	206	250	69
Pittsburgh		82	23	47	8	4	190	303	58

Southeast Division

Team		GP	W	L	T	OTL	GF	GA	PTS
*Tampa Bay	(1)	82	46	22	8	6	245	192	106
Atlanta		82	33	37	8	4	214	243	78
Carolina		82	28	34	14	6	172	209	76
Florida		82	28	35	15	4	188	221	75
Washington		82	23	46	10	3	186	253	59

WESTERN CONFERENCE

Central Division

Team		GP	W	L	T	OTL	GF	GA	PTS
Detroit	(1)	82	48	21	11	2	255	189	109
St. Louis	(7)	82	39	30	11	2	191	198	91
Nashville	(8)	82	38	29	11	4	216	217	91
Columbus		82	25	45	8	4	177	238	62
Chicago		82	20	43	11	8	188	259	59

Pacific Division

Team		GP	W	L	T	OTL	GF	GA	PTS
San Jose	(2)	82	43	21	12	6	219	183	104
Dallas	(5)	82	41	26	13	2	194	175	97
Los Angeles		82	28	29	16	9	205	217	81
Anaheim		82	29	35	10	8	184	213	76
Phoenix		82	22	36	18	6	188	245	68

Northwest Division

Team		GP	W	L	T	OTL	GF	GA	PTS
Vancouver	(3)	82	43	24	10	5	235	194	101
Colorado	(4)	82	40	22	13	7	236	198	100
Calgary	(6)	82	42	30	7	3	200	176	94
Edmonton		82	36	29	12	5	221	208	89
Minnesota		82	30	29	20	3	188	183	83

Leading Scorers

Player	Team	GP	G	A	PTS	PIM
Martin St. Louis	Tampa Bay	82	38	56	94	24
Ilya Kovalchuk	Atlanta	81	41	46	87	63
Joe Sakic	Colorado	81	33	54	87	42
Markus Naslund	Vancouver	78	35	49	84	58
Marian Hossa	Ottawa	81	36	46	82	46
Patrik Elias	New Jersey	82	38	43	81	44
Daniel Alfredsson	Ottawa	77	32	48	80	24
Cory Stillman	Tampa Bay	81	25	55	80	36
Robert Lang	Wsh., Det.	69	30	49	79	24
Brad Richards	Tampa Bay	82	26	53	79	12
Alex Tanguay	Colorado	69	25	54	79	42

2004-05

SEASON CANCELLED

2005-06

EASTERN CONFERENCE

Northeast Division

Team		GP	W	L	OL	GF	GA	PTS
Ottawa	(1)	82	52	21	9	314	211	113
Buffalo	(4)	82	52	24	6	281	239	110
Montreal	(7)	82	42	31	9	243	247	93
Toronto		82	41	33	8	257	270	90
Boston		82	29	37	16	230	266	74

Atlantic Division

Team		GP	W	L	OL	GF	GA	PTS
New Jersey	(3)	82	46	27	9	242	229	101
Philadelphia	(5)	82	45	26	11	267	259	101
NY Rangers	(6)	82	44	26	12	257	215	100
NY Islanders		82	36	40	6	230	278	78
Pittsburgh		82	22	46	14	244	316	58

Southeast Division

Team		GP	W	L	OL	GF	GA	PTS
*Carolina	(2)	82	52	22	8	294	260	112
Tampa Bay	(8)	82	43	33	6	252	260	92
Atlanta		82	41	33	8	281	275	90
Florida		82	37	34	11	240	257	85
Washington		82	29	41	12	237	306	70

WESTERN CONFERENCE

Central Division

Team		GP	W	L	OL	GF	GA	PTS
Detroit	(1)	82	58	16	8	305	209	124
Nashville	(4)	82	49	25	8	259	227	106
Columbus		82	35	43	4	223	279	74
Chicago		82	26	43	13	211	285	65
St. Louis		82	21	46	15	197	292	57

Pacific Division

Dallas	(2)	82	53	23	6	265	218	112
San Jose	(5)	82	44	27	11	266	242	99
Anaheim	(6)	82	43	27	12	254	229	98
Los Angeles		82	42	35	5	249	270	89
Phoenix		82	38	39	5	246	271	81

Northwest Division

Calgary	(3)	82	46	25	11	218	200	103
Colorado	(7)	82	43	30	9	283	257	95
Edmonton	(8)	82	41	28	13	256	251	95
Vancouver		82	42	32	8	256	255	92
Minnesota		82	38	36	8	231	215	84

Leading Scorers

Player	Team	GP	G	A	PTS	PIM
Joe Thornton	Bos., S.J.	81	29	96	125	61
Jaromir Jagr	NY Rangers	82	54	69	123	72
Alex Ovechkin	Washington	81	52	54	106	52
Dany Heatley	Ottawa	82	50	53	103	86
Daniel Alfredsson	Ottawa	77	43	60	103	50
Sidney Crosby	Pittsburgh	81	39	63	102	110
Eric Staal	Carolina	82	45	55	100	81
Ilya Kovalchuk	Atlanta	78	52	46	98	68
Marc Savard	Atlanta	82	28	69	97	100
Jonathan Cheechoo	San Jose	82	56	37	93	58

2006-07

EASTERN CONFERENCE

Northeast Division

Team		GP	W	L	OL	GF	GA	PTS
Buffalo	(1)	82	53	22	7	308	242	113
Ottawa	(4)	82	48	25	9	288	222	105
Toronto		82	40	31	11	258	269	91
Montreal		82	42	34	6	245	256	90
Boston		82	35	41	6	219	289	76

Atlantic Division

New Jersey	(2)	82	49	24	9	216	201	107
Pittsburgh	(5)	82	47	24	11	277	246	105
NY Rangers	(6)	82	42	30	10	242	216	94
NY Islanders	(8)	82	40	30	12	248	240	92
Philadelphia		82	22	48	12	214	303	56

Southeast Division

Atlanta	(3)	82	43	28	11	246	245	97
Tampa Bay	(7)	82	44	33	5	253	261	93
Carolina		82	40	34	8	241	253	88
Florida		82	35	31	16	247	257	86
Washington		82	28	40	14	235	286	70

WESTERN CONFERENCE

Central Division

Detroit	(1)	82	50	19	13	254	199	113
Nashville	(4)	82	51	23	8	272	212	110
St. Louis		82	34	35	13	214	254	81
Columbus		82	33	42	7	201	249	73
Chicago		82	31	42	9	201	258	71

Pacific Division

*Anaheim	(2)	82	48	20	14	258	208	110
San Jose	(5)	82	51	26	5	258	199	107
Dallas	(6)	82	50	25	7	226	197	107
Los Angeles		82	27	41	14	227	283	68
Phoenix		82	31	46	5	216	284	67

Northwest Division

Vancouver	(3)	82	49	26	7	222	201	105
Minnesota	(7)	82	48	26	8	235	191	104
Calgary	(8)	82	43	29	10	258	226	96
Colorado		82	44	31	7	272	251	95
Edmonton		82	32	43	7	195	248	71

Leading Scorers

Player	Team	GP	G	A	PTS	PIM
Sidney Crosby	Pittsburgh	79	36	84	120	60
Joe Thornton	San Jose	82	22	92	114	44
Vincent Lecavalier	Tampa Bay	82	52	56	108	44
Dany Heatley	Ottawa	82	50	55	105	74
Martin St. Louis	Tampa Bay	82	43	59	102	28
Marian Hossa	Atlanta	82	43	57	100	49
Joe Sakic	Colorado	82	36	64	100	46
Jaromir Jagr	NY Rangers	82	30	66	96	78
Marc Savard	Boston	82	22	74	96	96
Daniel Briere	Buffalo	81	32	63	95	89

2007-08

EASTERN CONFERENCE

Northeast Division

Team		GP	W	L	OL	GF	GA	PTS
Montreal	(1)	82	47	25	10	262	222	104
Ottawa	(7)	82	43	31	8	261	247	94
Boston	(8)	82	41	29	12	212	222	94
Buffalo		82	39	31	12	255	242	90
Toronto		82	36	35	11	231	260	83

Atlantic Division

Pittsburgh	(2)	82	47	27	8	247	216	102
New Jersey	(4)	82	46	29	7	206	197	99
NY Rangers	(5)	82	42	27	13	213	199	97
Philadelphia	(6)	82	42	29	11	248	233	95
NY Islanders		82	35	38	9	194	243	79

Southeast Division

Washington	(3)	82	43	31	8	242	231	94
Carolina		82	43	33	6	252	249	92
Florida		82	38	35	9	216	226	85
Atlanta		82	34	40	8	216	272	76
Tampa Bay		82	31	42	9	223	267	71

WESTERN CONFERENCE

Central Division

*Detroit	(1)	82	54	21	7	257	184	115
Nashville	(8)	82	41	32	9	230	229	91
Chicago		82	40	34	8	239	235	88
Columbus		82	34	36	12	193	218	80
St. Louis		82	33	36	13	205	237	79

Pacific Division

San Jose	(2)	82	49	23	10	222	193	108
Anaheim	(4)	82	47	27	8	205	191	102
Dallas	(5)	82	45	30	7	242	207	97
Phoenix		82	38	37	7	214	231	83
Los Angeles		82	32	43	7	231	266	71

Northwest Division

Minnesota	(3)	82	44	28	10	223	218	98
Colorado	(6)	82	44	31	7	231	219	95
Calgary	(7)	82	42	30	10	229	227	94
Edmonton		82	41	35	6	235	251	88
Vancouver		82	39	33	10	213	215	88

Leading Scorers

Player	Team	GP	G	A	PTS	PIM
Alex Ovechkin	Washington	82	65	47	112	40
Evgeni Malkin	Pittsburgh	82	47	59	106	78
Jarome Iginla	Calgary	82	50	48	98	83
Pavel Datsyuk	Detroit	82	31	66	97	20
Joe Thornton	San Jose	82	29	67	96	59
Henrik Zetterberg	Detroit	75	43	49	92	34
Vincent Lecavalier	Tampa Bay	81	40	52	92	89
Jason Spezza	Ottawa	76	34	58	92	66
Daniel Alfredsson	Ottawa	70	40	49	89	34
Ilya Kovalchuk	Atlanta	79	52	35	87	52

2008-09

EASTERN CONFERENCE

Northeast Division

Team		GP	W	L	OL	GF	GA	PTS
Boston	(1)	82	53	19	10	274	196	116
Montreal	(8)	82	41	30	11	249	247	93
Buffalo		82	41	32	9	250	234	91
Ottawa		82	36	35	11	217	237	83
Toronto		82	34	35	13	250	293	81

Atlantic Division

New Jersey	(3)	82	51	27	4	244	209	106
*Pittsburgh	(4)	82	45	28	9	264	239	99
Philadelphia	(5)	82	44	27	11	264	238	99
NY Rangers	(7)	82	43	30	9	210	218	95
NY Islanders		82	26	47	9	201	279	61

Southeast Division

Washington	(2)	82	50	24	8	272	245	108
Carolina	(6)	82	45	30	7	239	226	97
Florida		82	41	30	11	234	231	93
Atlanta		82	35	41	6	257	280	76
Tampa Bay		82	24	40	18	210	279	66

WESTERN CONFERENCE

Central Division

Detroit	(2)	82	51	21	10	295	244	112
Chicago	(4)	82	46	24	12	264	216	104
St. Louis	(6)	82	41	31	10	233	233	92
Columbus	(7)	82	41	31	10	226	230	92
Nashville		82	40	34	8	213	233	88

Pacific Division

San Jose	(1)	82	53	18	11	257	204	117
Anaheim	(8)	82	42	33	7	245	238	91
Dallas		82	36	35	11	230	257	83
Phoenix		82	36	39	7	208	252	79
Los Angeles		82	34	37	11	207	234	79

Northwest Division

Vancouver	(3)	82	45	27	10	246	220	100
Calgary	(5)	82	46	30	6	254	248	98
Minnesota		82	40	33	9	219	200	89
Edmonton		82	38	35	9	234	248	85
Colorado		82	32	45	5	199	257	69

Leading Scorers

Player	Team	GP	G	A	PTS	PIM
Evgeni Malkin	Pittsburgh	82	35	78	113	80
Alex Ovechkin	Washington	79	56	54	110	72
Sidney Crosby	Pittsburgh	77	33	70	103	76
Pavel Datsyuk	Detroit	81	32	65	97	34
Zach Parise	New Jersey	82	45	49	94	24
Ilya Kovalchuk	Atlanta	79	43	48	91	50
Ryan Getzlaf	Anaheim	81	25	66	91	121
Jarome Iginla	Calgary	82	35	54	89	37
Marc Savard	Boston	82	25	63	88	70
Nicklas Backstrom	Washington	82	22	66	88	46

2009-10

EASTERN CONFERENCE

Northeast Division

Team		GP	W	L	OL	GF	GA	PTS
Buffalo	(3)	82	45	27	10	235	207	100
Ottawa	(5)	82	44	32	6	225	238	94
Boston	(6)	82	39	30	13	206	200	91
Montreal	(8)	82	39	33	10	217	223	88
Toronto		82	30	38	14	214	267	74

Atlantic Division

New Jersey	(2)	82	48	27	7	222	191	103
Pittsburgh	(4)	82	47	28	7	257	237	101
Philadelphia	(7)	82	41	35	6	236	225	88
NY Rangers		82	38	33	11	222	218	87
NY Islanders		82	34	37	11	222	264	79

Southeast Division

Washington	(1)	82	54	15	13	318	233	121
Atlanta		82	35	34	13	234	256	83
Carolina		82	35	37	10	230	256	80
Tampa Bay		82	34	36	12	217	260	80
Florida		82	32	37	13	208	244	77

WESTERN CONFERENCE

Central Division

*Chicago	(2)	82	52	22	8	271	209	112
Detroit	(5)	82	44	24	14	229	216	102
Nashville	(7)	82	47	29	6	225	225	100
St. Louis		82	40	32	10	225	223	90
Columbus		82	32	35	15	216	259	79

Pacific Division

San Jose	(1)	82	51	20	11	264	215	113
Phoenix	(4)	82	50	25	7	225	202	107
Los Angeles	(6)	82	46	27	9	241	219	101
Anaheim		82	39	32	11	238	251	89
Dallas		82	37	31	14	237	254	88

Northwest Division

Vancouver	(3)	82	49	28	5	272	222	103
Colorado	(8)	82	43	30	9	244	233	95
Calgary		82	40	32	10	204	210	90
Minnesota		82	38	36	8	219	246	84
Edmonton		82	27	47	8	214	284	62

Leading Scorers

Player	Team	GP	G	A	PTS	PIM
Henrik Sedin	Vancouver	82	29	83	112	48
Sidney Crosby	Pittsburgh	81	51	58	109	71
Alex Ovechkin	Washington	72	50	59	109	89
Nicklas Backstrom	Washington	82	33	68	101	50
Steven Stamkos	Tampa Bay	82	51	44	95	38
Martin St. Louis	Tampa Bay	82	29	65	94	12
Brad Richards	Dallas	80	24	67	91	14
Joe Thornton	San Jose	79	20	69	89	54
Patrick Kane	Chicago	82	30	58	88	20
Marian Gaborik	NY Rangers	76	42	44	86	37

2010-11

EASTERN CONFERENCE

Northeast Division

Team		GP	W	L	OT	GF	GA	PTS
*Boston	(3)	82	46	25	11	246	195	103
Montreal	(6)	82	44	30	8	216	209	96
Buffalo	(7)	82	43	29	10	245	229	96
Toronto		82	37	34	11	218	251	85
Ottawa		82	32	40	10	192	250	74

Atlantic Division

Philadelphia	(2)	82	47	23	12	259	223	106
Pittsburgh	(4)	82	49	25	8	238	199	106
NY Rangers	(8)	82	44	33	5	233	198	93
New Jersey		82	38	39	5	174	209	81
NY Islanders		82	30	39	13	229	264	73

Southeast Division

Washington	(1)	82	48	23	11	224	197	107
Tampa Bay	(5)	82	46	25	11	247	240	103
Carolina		82	40	31	11	236	239	91
Atlanta		82	34	36	12	223	269	80
Florida		82	30	40	12	195	229	72

WESTERN CONFERENCE

Central Division

Detroit	(3)	82	47	25	10	261	241	104
Nashville	(5)	82	44	27	11	219	194	99
Chicago	(8)	82	44	29	9	258	225	97
St. Louis		82	38	33	11	240	234	87
Columbus		82	34	35	13	215	258	81

Pacific Division

San Jose	(2)	82	48	25	9	248	213	105
Anaheim	(4)	82	47	30	5	239	235	99
Phoenix	(6)	82	43	26	13	231	226	99
Los Angeles	(7)	82	46	30	6	219	198	98
Dallas		82	42	29	11	227	233	95

Northwest Division

Vancouver	(1)	82	54	19	9	262	185	117
Calgary		82	41	29	12	250	237	94
Minnesota		82	39	35	8	206	233	86
Colorado		82	30	44	8	227	288	68
Edmonton		82	25	45	12	193	269	62

Leading Scorers

Player	Team	GP	G	A	PTS	PIM
Daniel Sedin	Vancouver	82	41	63	104	32
Martin St. Louis	Tampa Bay	82	31	68	99	12
Corey Perry	Anaheim	82	50	48	98	104
Henrik Sedin	Vancouver	82	19	75	94	40
Steven Stamkos	Tampa Bay	82	45	46	91	74
Jarome Iginla	Calgary	82	43	43	86	40
Alex Ovechkin	Washington	79	32	53	85	41
Teemu Selanne	Anaheim	73	31	49	80	49
Henrik Zetterberg	Detroit	80	24	56	80	40
Brad Richards	Dallas	72	28	49	77	24

2011-12

EASTERN CONFERENCE

Northeast Division

		GP	W	L	OT	GF	GA	PTS
Boston	(2)	82	49	29	4	269	202	102
Ottawa	(8)	82	41	31	10	249	240	92
Buffalo		82	39	32	11	218	230	89
Toronto		82	35	37	10	231	264	80
Montreal		82	31	35	16	212	226	78

Atlantic Division

NY Rangers	(1)	82	51	24	7	226	187	109
Pittsburgh	(4)	82	51	25	6	282	221	108
Philadelphia	(5)	82	47	26	9	264	232	103
New Jersey	(6)	82	48	28	6	228	209	102
NY Islanders		82	34	37	11	203	255	79

Southeast Division

Florida	(3)	82	38	26	18	203	227	94
Washington	(7)	82	42	32	8	222	230	92
Tampa Bay		82	38	36	8	235	281	84
Winnipeg		82	37	35	10	225	246	84
Carolina		82	33	33	16	213	243	82

WESTERN CONFERENCE

Central Division

St. Louis	(2)	82	49	22	11	210	165	109
Nashville	(4)	82	48	26	8	237	210	104
Detroit	(5)	82	48	28	6	248	203	102
Chicago	(6)	82	45	26	11	248	238	101
Columbus		82	29	46	7	202	262	65

Pacific Division

Phoenix	(3)	82	42	27	13	216	204	97
San Jose	(7)	82	43	29	10	228	210	96
*Los Angeles	(8)	82	40	27	15	194	179	95
Dallas		82	42	35	5	211	222	89
Anaheim		82	34	36	12	204	231	80

Northwest Division

Vancouver	(1)	82	51	22	9	249	198	111
Calgary		82	37	29	16	202	226	90
Colorado		82	41	35	6	208	220	88
Minnesota		82	35	36	11	177	226	81
Edmonton		82	32	40	10	212	239	74

Leading Scorers

Player	Team	GP	G	A	PTS	PIM
Evgeni Malkin	Pittsburgh	75	50	59	109	70
Steven Stamkos	Tampa Bay	82	60	37	97	66
Claude Giroux	Philadelphia	77	28	65	93	29
Jason Spezza	Ottawa	80	34	50	84	36
Ilya Kovalchuk	New Jersey	77	37	46	83	33
Phil Kessel	Toronto	82	37	45	82	20
James Neal	Pittsburgh	80	40	41	81	87
John Tavares	NY Islanders	82	31	50	81	26
Henrik Sedin	Vancouver	82	14	67	81	52
Patrik Elias	New Jersey	81	26	52	78	16

2012-13

EASTERN CONFERENCE

Northeast Division

		GP	W	L	OT	GF	GA	PTS
Montreal	(2)	48	29	14	5	149	126	63
Boston	(4)	48	28	14	6	131	109	62
Toronto	(5)	48	26	17	5	145	133	57
Ottawa	(7)	48	25	17	6	116	104	56
Buffalo		48	21	21	6	125	143	48

Atlantic Division

Pittsburgh	(1)	48	36	12	0	165	119	72
NY Rangers	(6)	48	26	18	4	130	112	56
NY Islanders	(8)	48	24	17	7	139	139	55
Philadelphia		48	23	22	3	133	141	49
New Jersey		48	19	19	10	112	129	48

Southeast Division

Washington	(3)	48	27	18	3	149	130	57
Winnipeg		48	24	21	3	128	144	51
Carolina		48	19	25	4	128	160	42
Tampa Bay		48	18	26	4	148	150	40
Florida		48	15	27	6	112	171	36

WESTERN CONFERENCE

Central Division

*Chicago	(1)	48	36	7	5	155	102	77
St. Louis	(4)	48	29	17	2	129	115	60
Detroit	(7)	48	24	16	8	124	115	56
Columbus		48	24	17	7	120	119	55
Nashville		48	16	23	9	111	139	41

Pacific Division

Anaheim	(2)	48	30	12	6	140	118	66
Los Angeles	(5)	48	27	16	5	133	118	59
San Jose	(6)	48	25	16	7	124	116	57
Phoenix		48	21	18	9	125	131	51
Dallas		48	22	22	4	130	142	48

Northwest Division

Vancouver	(3)	48	26	15	7	127	121	59
Minnesota	(8)	48	26	19	3	122	127	55
Edmonton		48	19	22	7	125	134	45
Calgary		48	19	25	4	128	160	42
Colorado		48	16	25	7	116	152	39

Leading Scorers

Player	Team	GP	G	A	PTS	PIM
Martin St. Louis	Tampa Bay	48	17	43	60	14
Steven Stamkos	Tampa Bay	48	29	28	57	32
Alex Ovechkin	Washington	48	32	24	56	36
Sidney Crosby	Pittsburgh	36	15	41	56	16
Patrick Kane	Chicago	47	23	32	55	8
Eric Staal	Carolina	48	18	35	53	54
Chris Kunitz	Pittsburgh	48	22	30	52	39
Phil Kessel	Toronto	48	20	32	52	18
Taylor Hall	Edmonton	45	16	34	50	33
Ryan Getzlaf	Anaheim	44	15	34	49	41

2013-14

EASTERN CONFERENCE

Atlantic Division

		GP	W	L	OT	GF	GA	PTS
Boston	(A1)	82	54	19	9	261	177	117
Tampa Bay	(A2)	82	46	27	9	240	215	101
Montreal	(A3)	82	46	28	8	215	204	100
Detroit	(W2)	82	39	28	15	222	230	93
Ottawa		82	37	31	14	236	265	88
Toronto		82	38	36	8	231	256	84
Florida		82	29	45	8	196	268	66
Buffalo		82	21	51	10	157	248	52

Metropolitan Division

Pittsburgh	(M1)	82	51	24	7	249	207	109
NY Rangers	(M2)	82	45	31	6	218	193	96
Philadelphia	(M3)	82	42	30	10	236	235	94
Columbus	(W1)	82	43	32	7	231	216	93
Washington		82	38	30	14	235	240	90
New Jersey		82	35	29	18	197	208	88
Carolina		82	36	35	11	207	230	83
NY Islanders		82	34	37	11	225	267	79

WESTERN CONFERENCE

Central Division

		GP	W	L	OT	GF	GA	PTS
Colorado	(C1)	82	52	22	8	250	220	112
St. Louis	(C2)	82	52	23	7	248	191	111
Chicago	(C3)	82	46	21	15	267	220	107
Minnesota	(W1)	82	43	27	12	207	206	98
Dallas	(W2)	82	40	31	11	235	228	91
Nashville		82	38	32	12	216	242	88
Winnipeg		82	37	35	10	227	237	84

Pacific Division

Anaheim	(P1)	82	54	20	8	266	209	116
San Jose	(P2)	82	51	22	9	249	200	111
*Los Angeles	(P3)	82	46	28	8	206	174	100
Phoenix		82	37	30	15	216	231	89
Vancouver		82	36	35	11	196	223	83
Calgary		82	35	40	7	209	241	77
Edmonton		82	29	44	9	203	270	67

Leading Scorers

Player	Team	GP	G	A	PTS	PIM
Sidney Crosby	Pittsburgh	80	36	68	104	46
Ryan Getzlaf	Anaheim	77	31	56	87	31
Claude Giroux	Philadelphia	82	28	58	86	46
Tyler Seguin	Dallas	80	37	47	84	18
Corey Perry	Anaheim	81	43	39	82	65
Phil Kessel	Toronto	82	37	43	80	27
Taylor Hall	Edmonton	75	27	53	80	44
Alex Ovechkin	Washington	78	51	28	79	48
Joe Pavelski	San Jose	82	41	38	79	32
Jamie Benn	Dallas	81	34	45	79	64
Nicklas Backstrom	Washington	82	18	61	79	54

2014-15

EASTERN CONFERENCE

Atlantic Division

		GP	W	L	OT	GF	GA	PTS
Montreal	(A1)	82	50	22	10	221	189	110
Tampa Bay	(A2)	82	50	24	8	262	211	108
Detroit	(A3)	82	43	25	14	235	221	100
Ottawa	(W1)	82	43	26	13	238	215	99
Boston		82	41	27	14	213	211	96
Florida		82	38	29	15	206	223	91
Toronto		82	30	44	8	211	262	68
Buffalo		82	23	51	8	161	274	54

Metropolitan Division

NY Rangers	(M1)	82	53	22	7	252	192	113
Washington	(M2)	82	45	26	11	242	203	101
NY Islanders	(M3)	82	47	28	7	252	230	101
Pittsburgh	(W2)	82	43	27	12	221	210	98
Columbus		82	42	35	5	236	250	89
Philadelphia		82	33	31	18	215	234	84
New Jersey		82	32	36	14	181	216	78
Carolina		82	30	41	11	188	226	71

WESTERN CONFERENCE

Central Division

St. Louis	(C1)	82	51	24	7	248	201	109
Nashville	(C2)	82	47	25	10	232	208	104
*Chicago	(C3)	82	48	28	6	229	189	102
Minnesota	(W1)	82	46	28	8	231	201	100
Winnipeg	(W2)	82	43	26	13	230	210	99
Dallas		82	41	31	10	261	260	92
Colorado		82	39	31	12	219	227	90

Pacific Division

Anaheim	(P1)	82	51	24	7	236	226	109
Vancouver	(P2)	82	48	29	5	242	222	101
Calgary	(P3)	82	45	30	7	241	216	97
Los Angeles		82	40	27	15	220	205	95
San Jose		82	40	33	9	228	232	89
Edmonton		82	24	44	14	198	283	62
Arizona		82	24	50	8	170	272	56

Leading Scorers

Player	Team	GP	G	A	PTS	PIM
Jamie Benn	Dallas	82	35	52	87	64
John Tavares	NY Islanders	82	38	48	86	46
Sidney Crosby	Pittsburgh	77	28	56	84	47
Alex Ovechkin	Washington	81	53	28	81	58
Jakub Voracek	Philadelphia	82	22	59	81	78
Nicklas Backstrom	Washington	82	18	60	78	40
Tyler Seguin	Dallas	71	37	40	77	20
Jiri Hudler	Calgary	78	31	45	76	14
Daniel Sedin	Vancouver	82	20	56	76	18
Vladimir Tarasenko	St. Louis	77	37	36	73	31

Note: Detailed statistics for 2014-15 are listed in the Final Statistics, 2014-15 section of the *NHL Guide & Record Book*. **See page 135.**

Team Records

Regular Season

FINAL STANDINGS

MOST POINTS, ONE SEASON:
- **132 – Montreal Canadiens**, 1976-77. 60w-8L-12T. 80GP
- 131 – Detroit Red Wings, 1995-96. 62w-13L-7T. 82GP
- 129 – Montreal Canadiens, 1977-78. 59w-10L-11T. 80GP

BEST POINTS PERCENTAGE, ONE SEASON:
- **.875 – Boston Bruins**, 1929-30. 38w-5L-1T. 77PTS in 44GP
- .830 – Montreal Canadiens, 1943-44. 38w-5L-7T. 83PTS in 50GP
- .825 – Montreal Canadiens, 1976-77. 60w-8L-12T. 132PTS in 80GP
- .806 – Montreal Canadiens, 1977-78. 59w-10L-11T. 129PTS in 80GP
- .802 – Chicago Blackhawks, 2012-13. 36w-7L-5OTL. 77PTS in 48GP
- .800 – Montreal Canadiens, 1944-45. 38w-8L-4T. 80PTS in 50GP

FEWEST POINTS, ONE SEASON:
- **8 – Quebec Bulldogs**, 1919-20. 4w-20L-0T. 24GP
- 10 – Toronto Arenas, 1918-19. 5w-13L-0T. 18GP
- 12 – Hamilton Tigers, 1920-21. 6w-18L-0T. 24GP
- – Hamilton Tigers, 1922-23. 6w-18L-0T. 24GP
- – Boston Bruins, 1924-25. 6w-24L-0T. 30GP
- – Philadelphia Quakers, 1930-31. 4w-36L-4T. 44GP

FEWEST POINTS, ONE SEASON (MINIMUM 70-GAME SCHEDULE):
- **21 – Washington Capitals**, 1974-75. 8w-67L-5T. 80GP
- 24 – Ottawa Senators, 1992-93. 10w-70L-4T. 84GP
- – San Jose Sharks, 1992-93. 11w-71L-2T. 84GP
- 30 – New York Islanders, 1972-73. 12w-60L-6T. 78GP

WORST POINTS PERCENTAGE, ONE SEASON:
- **.131 – Washington Capitals**, 1974-75. 8w-67L-5T. 21PTS in 80GP
- .136 – Philadelphia Quakers, 1930-31. 4w-36L-4T. 12PTS in 44GP
- .143 – Ottawa Senators, 1992-93. 10w-70L-4T. 24PTS in 84GP
- – San Jose Sharks, 1992-93. 11w-71L-2T. 24PTS in 84GP
- .148 – Pittsburgh Pirates, 1929-30. 5w-36L-3T. 13PTS in 44GP

TEAM WINS

Most Wins

MOST WINS, ONE SEASON:
- **62 – Detroit Red Wings**, 1995-96. 82GP
- 60 – Montreal Canadiens, 1976-77. 80GP
- 59 – Montreal Canadiens, 1977-78. 80GP

MOST HOME WINS, ONE SEASON:
- **36 – Philadelphia Flyers**, 1975-76. 40GP
- **– Detroit Red Wings**, 1995-96. 41GP
- 33 – Boston Bruins, 1970-71. 39GP
- – Boston Bruins, 1973-74. 39GP
- – Montreal Canadiens, 1976-77. 40GP
- – Philadelphia Flyers, 1976-77. 40GP
- – New York Islanders, 1981-82. 40GP
- – Philadelphia Flyers, 1985-86. 40GP

MOST ROAD WINS, ONE SEASON:
- **31 – Detroit Red Wings**, 2005-06. 41GP
- 28 – New Jersey Devils, 1998-99. 41GP
- – New York Rangers, 2014-15. 41GP
- 27 – Montreal Canadiens, 1976-77. 40GP
- – Montreal Canadiens, 1977-78. 40GP
- – St. Louis Blues, 1999-2000. 41GP
- – San Jose Sharks, 2007-08. 41GP
- – Vancouver Canucks, 2010-11. 41GP
- 26 – Boston Bruins, 1971-72. 39GP
- – Montreal Canadiens, 1975-76. 40GP
- – Edmonton Oilers, 1983-84. 40GP
- – Detroit Red Wings, 1995-96. 41GP
- – San Jose Sharks, 2006-07. 41GP
- – Detroit Red Wings, 2010-11. 41GP
- – Colorado Avalanche, 2013-14. 41GP

Fewest Wins

FEWEST WINS, ONE SEASON:
- **4 – Quebec Bulldogs**, 1919-20. 24GP
- **– Philadelphia Quakers**, 1930-31. 44GP
- 5 – Toronto Arenas, 1918-19. 18GP
- Pittsburgh Pirates, 1929-30. 44GP

FEWEST WINS, ONE SEASON (MINIMUM 70-GAME SCHEDULE):
- **8 – Washington Capitals**, 1974-75. 80GP
- 9 – Winnipeg Jets, 1980-81. 80GP
- 10 – Ottawa Senators, 1992-93. 84GP

FEWEST HOME WINS, ONE SEASON:
- **2 – Chicago Blackhawks**, 1927-28. 22GP
- 3 – Boston Bruins, 1924-25. 15GP
- – Chicago Blackhawks, 1928-29. 22GP
- – Philadelphia Quakers, 1930-31. 22GP

FEWEST HOME WINS, ONE SEASON (MINIMUM 70-GAME SCHEDULE):
- **6 – Chicago Blackhawks**, 1954-55. 35GP
- **– Washington Capitals**, 1975-76. 40GP
- 7 – Boston Bruins, 1962-63. 35GP
- – Washington Capitals, 1974-75. 40GP
- – Winnipeg Jets, 1980-81. 40GP
- – Pittsburgh Penguins, 1983-84. 40GP

FEWEST ROAD WINS, ONE SEASON:
- **0 – Toronto Arenas**, 1918-19. 9GP
- **– Quebec Bulldogs**, 1919-20. 12GP
- **– Pittsburgh Pirates**, 1929-30. 22GP
- 1 – Hamilton Tigers, 1921-22. 12GP
- – Toronto St. Patricks, 1925-26. 18GP
- – Philadelphia Quakers, 1930-31. 22GP
- – New York Americans, 1940-41. 24GP
- – Washington Capitals, 1974-75. 40GP
- * – Ottawa Senators, 1992-93. 41GP

FEWEST ROAD WINS, ONE SEASON (MINIMUM 70-GAME SCHEDULE):
- **1 – Washington Capitals**, 1974-75. 40GP
- * **– Ottawa Senators**, 1992-93. 41GP
- 2 – Boston Bruins, 1960-61. 35GP
- – Los Angeles Kings, 1969-70. 38GP
- – New York Islanders, 1972-73. 39GP
- – California Golden Seals, 1973-74. 39GP
- – Colorado Rockies, 1977-78. 40GP
- – Winnipeg Jets, 1980-81. 40GP
- – Quebec Nordiques, 1991-92. 40GP

TEAM LOSSES

Fewest Losses

FEWEST LOSSES, ONE SEASON:
- **5 – Ottawa Senators**, 1919-20. 24GP
- **– Boston Bruins**, 1929-30. 44GP
- **– Montreal Canadiens**, 1943-44. 50GP

FEWEST HOME LOSSES, ONE SEASON:
- **0 – Ottawa Senators**, 1922-23. 12GP
- **– Montreal Canadiens**, 1943-44. 25GP
- 1 – Toronto Arenas, 1917-18. 11GP
- – Ottawa Senators, 1918-19. 9GP
- – Ottawa Senators, 1919-20. 12GP
- – Toronto St. Patricks, 1922-23. 12GP
- – Boston Bruins, 1929-30. 22GP
- – Boston Bruins, 1930-31. 22GP
- – Montreal Canadiens, 1976-77. 40GP
- – Quebec Nordiques, 1994-95. 24GP

FEWEST ROAD WINS, ONE SEASON:
- **3 – Montreal Canadiens**, 1928-29. 22GP
- 4 – Ottawa Senators, 1919-20. 12GP
- – Montreal Canadiens, 1927-28. 22GP
- – Boston Bruins, 1929-30. 20GP
- – Boston Bruins, 1940-41. 24GP
- – Chicago Blackhawks, 2012-13. 24GP

FEWEST LOSSES, ONE SEASON (MINIMUM 70-GAME SCHEDULE):
- **8 – Montreal Canadiens**, 1976-77. 80GP
- 10 – Montreal Canadiens, 1972-73. 78GP
- – Montreal Canadiens, 1977-78. 80GP
- 11 – Montreal Canadiens, 1975-76. 80GP

FEWEST HOME LOSSES, ONE SEASON (MINIMUM 70-GAME SCHEDULE):
- **1 – Montreal Canadiens**, 1976-77. 40GP
- 2 – Montreal Canadiens, 1961-62. 35GP
- – New York Rangers, 1970-71. 39GP
- – Philadelphia Flyers, 1975-76. 40GP

FEWEST ROAD LOSSES, ONE SEASON (MINIMUM 70-GAME SCHEDULE):
- **6 – Montreal Canadiens**, 1972-73. 39GP
- **– Montreal Canadiens**, 1974-75. 40GP
- **– Montreal Canadiens**, 1977-78. 40GP
- 7 – Detroit Red Wings, 1951-52. 35GP
- – Montreal Canadiens, 1976-77. 40GP
- – Philadelphia Flyers, 1979-80. 40GP
- – Boston Bruins, 2003-04. 41GP
- – Detroit Red Wings, 2005-06. 41GP

Most Losses

MOST LOSSES, ONE SEASON:
- **71 – San Jose Sharks**, 1992-93. 84GP
- 70 – Ottawa Senators, 1992-93. 84GP
- 67 – Washington Capitals, 1974-75. 80GP
- 61 – Quebec Nordiques, 1989-90. 80GP
- – Ottawa Senators, 1993-94. 84GP

MOST HOME LOSSES, ONE SEASON:
- *32 – **San Jose Sharks**, 1992-93. 41GP
- 29 – Pittsburgh Penguins, 1983-84. 40GP
- * – Ottawa Senators, 1993-94. 41GP

MOST ROAD LOSSES, ONE SEASON:
- *40 – **Ottawa Senators**, 1992-93. 41GP
- 39 – Washington Capitals, 1974-75. 40GP
- 37 – California Golden Seals, 1973-74. 39GP
- * – San Jose Sharks, 1992-93. 41GP

* – Does not include neutral site games

TEAM TIES
Most Ties

MOST TIES, ONE SEASON:
24 – Philadelphia Flyers, 1969-70. 76GP
23 – Montreal Canadiens, 1962-63. 70GP
– Chicago Blackhawks, 1973-74. 78GP

MOST HOME TIES, ONE SEASON:
13 – New York Rangers, 1954-55. 35GP
– **Philadelphia Flyers**, 1969-70. 38GP
– **California Golden Seals**, 1971-72. 39GP
– **California Golden Seals**, 1972-73. 39GP
– **Chicago Blackhawks**, 1973-74. 39GP

MOST ROAD TIES, ONE SEASON:
15 – Philadelphia Flyers, 1976-77. 40GP
14 – Montreal Canadiens, 1952-53. 35GP
– Montreal Canadiens, 1974-75. 40GP
– Philadelphia Flyers, 1975-76. 40GP

Fewest Ties

FEWEST TIES, ONE SEASON (Since 1926-27):
1 – Boston Bruins, 1929-30. 44GP
2 – Montreal Canadiens, 1926-27. 44GP
– New York Americans, 1926-27. 44GP
– Boston Bruins, 1938-39. 48GP
– New York Rangers, 1941-42. 48GP
– San Jose Sharks, 1992-93. 84GP

FEWEST TIES, ONE SEASON (MINIMUM 70-GAME SCHEDULE):
2 – San Jose Sharks, 1992-93. 84GP
3 – New Jersey Devils, 1985-86. 80GP
– Calgary Flames, 1986-87. 80GP
– Vancouver Canucks, 1993-94. 84GP

WINNING STREAKS
LONGEST WINNING STREAK, ONE SEASON:
17 Games – Pittsburgh Penguins, Mar. 9 – Apr. 10, 1993.
15 Games – New York Islanders, Jan. 21 – Feb. 20, 1982.
– Pittsburgh Penguins, Mar. 2 – 30, 2013.
14 Games – Boston Bruins, Dec. 3, 1929 – Jan. 9, 1930.
– Washington Capitals, Jan.13 – Feb. 7, 2010.

LONGEST HOME WINNING STREAK, ONE SEASON:
23 Games – Detroit Red Wings, Nov. 5, 2011 – Feb. 19, 2012.
20 Games – Boston Bruins, Dec. 3, 1929 – Mar. 18, 1930.
– Philadelphia Flyers, Jan. 4 – Apr. 3, 1976.

LONGEST ROAD WINNING STREAK, ONE SEASON:
12 Games – Detroit Red Wings, Mar. 1 – Apr. 15, 2006.
– **Minnesota Wild**, Feb. 18 – Apr. 9, 2015.
10 Games – Buffalo Sabres, Dec. 10, 1983 – Jan. 23, 1984.
– St. Louis Blues, Jan. 21 – Mar. 2, 2000.
– New Jersey Devils, Feb. 27 – Apr. 7, 2001.
– Buffalo Sabres, Oct. 4 – Nov. 13, 2006.
– San Jose Sharks, Nov. 14 – Dec. 31, 2007.

LONGEST WINNING STREAK FROM START OF SEASON:
10 Games – Toronto Maple Leafs, 1993-94.
– **Buffalo Sabres**, 2006-07.
8 Games – Toronto Maple Leafs, 1934-35.
– Buffalo Sabres, 1975-76.
– Nashville Predators, 2005-06.
7 Games – Edmonton Oilers, 1983-84.
– Quebec Nordiques, 1985-86.
– Pittsburgh Penguins, 1986-87.
– Pittsburgh Penguins, 1994-95.
– Washington Capitals, 2011-12.
– San Jose Sharks, 2012-13.

LONGEST HOME WINNING STREAK FROM START OF SEASON:
11 Games – Chicago Blackhawks, 1963-64.
10 Games – Ottawa Senators, 1925-26.
9 Games – Montreal Canadiens, 1953-54.
– Chicago Blackhawks, 1971-72.
– San Jose Sharks, 2008-09.

LONGEST ROAD WINNING STREAK FROM START OF SEASON:
10 Games – Buffalo Sabres, Oct.4 – Nov. 13, 2006.
9 Games – New Jersey Devils, Oct. 8 – Nov. 12, 2009.
7 Games – Toronto Maple Leafs, Nov. 14 – Dec. 15, 1940.
– Philadelphia Flyers, Oct. 12 – Nov. 16, 1985.
– Detroit Red Wings, Oct. 6 – Nov. 6, 2005.
– Pittsburgh Penguins, Oct. 3 – Nov. 3, 2009.

LONGEST WINNING STREAK, INCLUDING PLAYOFFS:
15 Games – Detroit Red Wings, Feb. 27 – Apr. 5, 1955.
(9 regular-season games, 6 playoff games)
– **New Jersey Devils**, Mar. 28 – Apr. 29, 2006.
(11 regular-season games, 4 playoff games)

LONGEST HOME WINNING STREAK, INCLUDING PLAYOFFS:
24 Games – Philadelphia Flyers, Jan. 4 – Apr. 25, 1976.
(20 regular-season games, 4 playoff games)

LONGEST ROAD WINNING STREAK, INCLUDING PLAYOFFS:
11 Games – New Jersey Devils, Feb. 27 – Apr. 17, 2001.
(10 regular-season games, 1 playoff game)

UNDEFEATED STREAKS
LONGEST UNDEFEATED STREAK, ONE SEASON:
35 Games – Philadelphia Flyers, Oct. 14, 1979 – Jan. 6, 1980. 25w-10T
28 Games – Montreal Canadiens, Dec. 18, 1977 – Feb. 23, 1978. 23w-5T

LONGEST HOME UNDEFEATED STREAK, ONE SEASON:
34 Games – Montreal Canadiens, Nov. 1, 1976 – Apr. 2, 1977. 28w-6T
27 Games – Boston Bruins, Nov. 22, 1970 – Mar. 20, 1971. 26w-1T

LONGEST ROAD UNDEFEATED STREAK, ONE SEASON:
23 Games – Montreal Canadiens, Nov. 27, 1974 – Mar. 12, 1975. 14w-9T
17 Games – Montreal Canadiens, Dec. 18, 1977 – Mar. 1, 1978. 14w-3T

LONGEST UNDEFEATED STREAK FROM START OF SEASON:
15 Games – Edmonton Oilers, 1984-85. 12w-3T
14 Games – Montreal Canadiens, 1943-44. 11w-3T

LONGEST HOME UNDEFEATED STREAK FROM START OF SEASON:
26 Games – Philadelphia Flyers, Oct. 11, 1979 – Feb. 3, 1980. 19w-7T

LONGEST ROAD UNDEFEATED STREAK FROM START OF SEASON:
15 Games – Detroit Red Wings, Oct. 18 – Dec. 20, 1951. 10w-5T

LONGEST UNDEFEATED STREAK, INCLUDING PLAYOFFS:
24 Games – Montreal Canadiens, Feb. 21 – Apr. 11, 1980.
15w-6T in regular season and 3w in playoffs.
21 Games – Philadelphia Flyers, Mar. 9 – May 4, 1975.
13w-1T in regular season and 7w in playoffs.
– Pittsburgh Penguins, Mar. 9 – Apr. 22, 1993.
17w-1T in regular season and 3w in playoffs.

LONGEST HOME UNDEFEATED STREAK, INCLUDING PLAYOFFS:
38 Games – Montreal Canadiens, Nov. 1, 1976 – Apr. 26, 1977.
28w-6T in regular season and 4w in playoffs.

LONGEST ROAD UNDEFEATED STREAK, INCLUDING PLAYOFFS:
13 Games – Philadelphia Flyers, Feb. 26 – Apr. 21, 1977. 6w-4T in regular season and 3w in playoffs.
– **Montreal Canadiens**, Feb. 26 – Apr. 20, 1980. 6w-4T in regular season and 3w in playoffs.
– **New York Islanders**, Mar. 16 – May 1, 1980. 3w-3T in regular season and 7w in playoffs.

TEAM POINT STREAKS
LONGEST TEAM POINT STREAK, ONE SEASON:
35 Games – Philadelphia Flyers, Oct. 14, 1979 – Jan. 6, 1980. 25w-10T
28 Games – Montreal Canadiens, Dec. 18, 1977 – Feb. 23, 1978. 23w-5T
24 Games – Chicago Blackhawks, Jan. 19 – Mar. 6, 2013. 21w-3OL

LONGEST TEAM POINT STREAK FROM START OF SEASON:
24 Games – Chicago Blackhawks, Jan. 19 – Mar. 6, 2013. 21w-3OL
16 Games – Anaheim Ducks, Oct. 6 – Nov. 9, 2006. 12w-4OL
15 Games – Edmonton Oilers, Oct. 11 – Nov. 9, 1984. 12w-3T
14 Games – Montreal Canadiens, Oct. 30 – Dec. 4, 1943. 11w-3T

LOSING STREAKS
LONGEST LOSING STREAK, ONE SEASON:
17 Games – Washington Capitals, Feb. 18 – Mar. 26, 1975.
– **San Jose Sharks**, Jan. 4 – Feb. 12, 1993.
15 Games – Philadelphia Quakers, Nov. 29, 1930 – Jan. 8, 1931.

LONGEST HOME LOSING STREAK, ONE SEASON:
14 Games – Pittsburgh Penguins, Dec. 31, 2003 – Feb. 22, 2004.
11 Games – Boston Bruins, Dec. 8, 1924 – Feb. 17, 1925.
– Washington Capitals, Feb. 18 – Mar. 30, 1975.
– Ottawa Senators, Oct. 27 – Dec. 8, 1993.

LONGEST ROAD LOSING STREAK, ONE SEASON:
***38 Games – Ottawa Senators**, Oct. 10, 1992 – Apr. 3, 1993.
37 Games – Washington Capitals, Oct. 9, 1974 – Mar. 26, 1975.

LONGEST LOSING STREAK FROM START OF SEASON:
11 Games – New York Rangers, 1943-44.
7 Games – Montreal Canadiens, 1938-39.
– Chicago Blackhawks, 1947-48.
– Washington Capitals, 1983-84.
– Chicago Blackhawks, 1997-98.

LONGEST HOME LOSING STREAK FROM START OF SEASON:
8 Games – Los Angeles Kings, Oct. 13 – Nov. 6, 1971.

LONGEST ROAD LOSING STREAK FROM START OF SEASON:
***38 Games – Ottawa Senators**, Oct. 10, 1992 – Apr. 3, 1993.

WINLESS STREAKS
LONGEST WINLESS STREAK, ONE SEASON:
30 Games – Winnipeg Jets, Oct. 19 – Dec. 20, 1980. 23L-7T
27 Games – Kansas City Scouts, Feb. 12 – Apr. 4, 1976. 21L-6T
25 Games – Washington Capitals, Nov. 29, 1975 – Jan. 21, 1976. 22L-3T

LONGEST HOME WINLESS STREAK, ONE SEASON:
17 Games – Ottawa Senators, Oct. 28, 1995 – Jan. 27, 1996. 15L-2T
– **Atlanta Thrashers**, Jan. 19 – Mar. 29, 2000. 15L-2T
16 Games – Pittsburgh Penguins, Dec. 31, 2003 – Mar. 4, 2004. 15L-1T

LONGEST ROAD WINLESS STREAK, ONE SEASON:
***38 Games – Ottawa Senators**, Oct. 10, 1992 – Apr. 3, 1993. 38L
37 Games – Washington Capitals, Oct. 9, 1974 – Mar. 26, 1975. 37L

LONGEST WINLESS STREAK FROM START OF SEASON:
15 Games – New York Rangers, 1943-44. 14L-1T
11 Games – Pittsburgh Pirates, 1927-28. 8L-3T
– Minnesota North Stars, 1973-74. 5L-6T
– San Jose Sharks, 1995-96. 7L-4T

LONGEST HOME WINLESS STREAK FROM START OF SEASON:
11 Games – Pittsburgh Penguins, Oct. 8 – Nov. 19, 1983. 9L-2T

LONGEST ROAD WINLESS STREAK FROM START OF SEASON:
***38 Games – Ottawa Senators**, Oct. 10, 1992 – Apr. 3, 1993. 38L

NON-SHUTOUT STREAKS

LONGEST NON-SHUTOUT STREAK:
264 Games – Calgary Flames, Nov. 12, 1981 – Jan. 9, 1985.
261 Games – Los Angeles Kings, Mar. 15, 1986 – Oct. 22, 1989.
244 Games – Washington Capitals, Oct. 31, 1989 – Nov. 11, 1993.
236 Games – New York Rangers, Dec. 20, 1989 – Dec. 13, 1992.
230 Games – Quebec Nordiques, Feb. 10, 1980 – Jan. 12, 1983.

LONGEST NON-SHUTOUT STREAK, INCLUDING PLAYOFFS:
264 Games – Los Angeles Kings, Mar. 15, 1986 – Apr. 6, 1989.
   (5 playoff games in 1987; 5 in 1988; 2 in 1989).
262 Games – Chicago Blackhawks, Mar. 14, 1970 – Feb. 21, 1973.
   (8 playoff games in 1970; 18 in 1971; 8 in 1972).
251 Games – Quebec Nordiques, Feb. 10, 1980 – Jan. 12, 1983.
   (5 playoff games in 1981; 16 in 1982).
246 Games – Pittsburgh Penguins, Jan. 7, 1989 – Oct. 26, 1991.
   (11 playoff games in 1989; 24 in 1991).

TEAM GOALS

Most Goals

MOST GOALS, ONE SEASON:
446 – Edmonton Oilers, 1983-84. 80GP
426 – Edmonton Oilers, 1985-86. 80GP
424 – Edmonton Oilers, 1982-83. 80GP
417 – Edmonton Oilers, 1981-82. 80GP
401 – Edmonton Oilers, 1984-85. 80GP

MOST GOALS, ONE TEAM, ONE GAME:
16 – Montreal Canadiens, Mar. 3, 1920, at Quebec. Montreal won 16-3.

MOST GOALS, BOTH TEAMS, ONE GAME:
21 – Montreal Canadiens (14), Toronto St. Patricks (7), Jan. 10, 1920, at Montreal.
   – **Edmonton Oilers (12), Chicago Blackhawks (9)**, Dec. 11, 1985, at Chicago.
20 – Edmonton Oilers (12), Minnesota North Stars (8), Jan. 4, 1984, at Edmonton.
   – Toronto Maple Leafs (11), Edmonton Oilers (9), Jan. 8, 1986, at Toronto.
19 – Montreal Wanderers (10), Toronto Arenas (9), Dec. 19, 1917, at Montreal.
   – Montreal Canadiens (16), Quebec Bulldogs (3), Mar. 3, 1920, at Quebec.
   – Montreal Canadiens (13), Hamilton Tigers (6), Feb. 26, 1921, at Montreal.
   – Boston Bruins (10), New York Rangers (9), Mar. 4, 1944, at Boston.
   – Detroit Red Wings (10), Boston Bruins (9), Mar. 16, 1944, at Detroit.
   – Vancouver Canucks (10), Minnesota North Stars (9), Oct. 7, 1983, at Vancouver.

MOST GOALS, ONE TEAM, ONE PERIOD:
9 – Buffalo Sabres, Mar. 19, 1981, at Buffalo, second period during 14-4 win over Toronto.
8 – Detroit Red Wings, Jan. 23, 1944, at Detroit, third period during 15-0 win over NY Rangers.
   – Boston Bruins, Mar. 16, 1969, at Boston, second period during 11-3 win over Toronto.
   – New York Rangers, Nov. 21, 1971, at NY Rangers, third period during 12-1 win over California.
   – Philadelphia Flyers, Mar. 31, 1973, at Philadelphia, second period during 10-2 win over NY Islanders.
   – Buffalo Sabres, Dec. 21, 1975, at Buffalo, third period during 14-2 win over Washington.
   – Minnesota North Stars, Nov. 11, 1981, at Minnesota, second period during 15-2 win over Winnipeg.
   – Pittsburgh Penguins, Dec. 17, 1991, at Pittsburgh, second period during 10-2 win over San Jose.
   – Washington Capitals, Feb. 3, 1999, at Washington, second period during 10-1 win over Tampa Bay.

MOST GOALS, BOTH TEAMS, ONE PERIOD:
12 – Buffalo Sabres (9), Toronto Maple Leafs (3), Mar. 19, 1981, at Buffalo, second period. Buffalo won 14-4.
   – **Edmonton Oilers (6), Chicago Blackhawks (6)**, Dec. 11, 1985, at Chicago, second period. Edmonton won 12-9.
10 – New York Rangers (7), New York Americans (3), Mar. 16, 1939, at NY Americans, third period. NY Rangers won 11-5.
   – Toronto Maple Leafs (6), Detroit Red Wings (4), Mar. 17, 1946, at Detroit, third period. Toronto won 11-7.
   – Buffalo Sabres (6), Vancouver Canucks (4), Jan. 8, 1976, at Buffalo, third period. Buffalo won 8-5.
   – Buffalo Sabres (5), Montreal Canadiens (5), Oct. 26, 1982, at Montreal, first period. Teams tied 7-7.
   – Quebec Nordiques (6), Boston Bruins (4), Dec. 7, 1982, at Quebec, second period. Quebec won 10-5.
   – Vancouver Canucks (6), Calgary Flames (4), Jan. 16, 1987, at Vancouver, first period. Vancouver won 9-5.
   – Detroit Red Wings (7), Winnipeg Jets (3), Nov. 25, 1987, at Detroit, third period. Detroit won 10-8.
   – Chicago Blackhawks (5), St. Louis Blues (5), Mar. 15, 1988, at St. Louis, third period. Teams tied 7-7.

MOST CONSECUTIVE GOALS, ONE TEAM, ONE GAME:
15 – Detroit Red Wings, Jan. 23, 1944, at Detroit during 15-0 win over NY Rangers.

Fewest Goals

FEWEST GOALS, ONE SEASON:
33 – Chicago Blackhawks, 1928-29. 44GP
45 – Montreal Maroons, 1924-25. 30GP
46 – Pittsburgh Pirates, 1928-29. 44GP

FEWEST GOALS, ONE SEASON (MINIMUM 70-GAME SCHEDULE):
133 – Chicago Blackhawks, 1953-54. 70GP
147 – Toronto Maple Leafs, 1954-55. 70GP
   – Boston Bruins, 1955-56. 70GP
150 – New York Rangers, 1954-55. 70GP

TEAM POWER-PLAY GOALS

MOST POWER-PLAY GOALS, ONE SEASON:
119 – Pittsburgh Penguins, 1988-89. 80GP
113 – Detroit Red Wings, 1992-93. 84GP
111 – New York Rangers, 1987-88. 80GP
110 – Pittsburgh Penguins, 1987-88. 80GP
   – Winnipeg Jets, 1987-88. 80GP

TEAM SHORTHAND GOALS

MOST SHORTHAND GOALS, ONE SEASON:
36 – Edmonton Oilers, 1983-84. 80GP
28 – Edmonton Oilers, 1986-87. 80GP
27 – Edmonton Oilers, 1985-86. 80GP
   – Edmonton Oilers, 1988-89. 80GP

TEAM GOALS-PER-GAME

HIGHEST GOALS-PER-GAME AVERAGE, ONE SEASON:
5.58 – Edmonton Oilers, 1983-84. 446G in 80GP.
5.38 – Montreal Canadiens, 1919-20. 129G in 24GP.
5.33 – Edmonton Oilers, 1985-86. 426G in 80GP.
5.30 – Edmonton Oilers, 1982-83. 424G in 80GP.
5.23 – Montreal Canadiens, 1917-18. 115G in 22GP.

LOWEST GOALS-PER-GAME AVERAGE, ONE SEASON:
0.75 – Chicago Blackhawks, 1928-29. 33G in 44GP.
1.05 – Pittsburgh Pirates, 1928-29. 46G in 44GP.
1.20 – New York Americans, 1928-29. 53G in 44GP.

TEAM ASSISTS

MOST ASSISTS, ONE SEASON:
737 – Edmonton Oilers, 1985-86. 80GP
736 – Edmonton Oilers, 1983-84. 80GP
706 – Edmonton Oilers, 1981-82. 80GP

FEWEST ASSISTS, ONE SEASON (Since 1926-27):
45 – New York Rangers, 1926-27. 44GP

FEWEST ASSISTS, ONE SEASON (MINIMUM 70-GAME SCHEDULE):
206 – Chicago Blackhawks, 1953-54. 70GP

TEAM TOTAL POINTS

MOST SCORING POINTS, ONE SEASON:
1,182 – Edmonton Oilers, 1983-84. (446G-736A) 80GP
1,163 – Edmonton Oilers, 1985-86. (426G-737A) 80GP
1,123 – Edmonton Oilers, 1981-82. (417G-706A) 80GP

MOST SCORING POINTS, ONE TEAM, ONE GAME:
40 – Buffalo Sabres, Dec. 21, 1975, at Buffalo. Buffalo defeated Washington 14-2, and had 26A.
39 – Minnesota North Stars, Nov. 11, 1981, at Minnesota. Minnesota defeated Winnipeg 15-2, and had 24A.
37 – Detroit Red Wings, Jan. 23, 1944, at Detroit. Detroit defeated NY Rangers 15-0, and had 22A.
   – Toronto Maple Leafs, Mar. 16, 1957, at Toronto. Toronto defeated NY Rangers 14-1, and had 23A.
   – Buffalo Sabres, Feb. 25, 1978, at Cleveland. Buffalo defeated Cleveland 13-3, and had 24A.
   – Calgary Flames, Feb. 10, 1993, at Calgary. Calgary defeated San Jose 13-1, and had 24A.

MOST SCORING POINTS, BOTH TEAMS, ONE GAME:
62 – Edmonton Oilers, Chicago Blackhawks, Dec. 11, 1985, at Chicago. Edmonton won 12-9. Edmonton had 24A, Chicago, 17A.
53 – Quebec Nordiques, Washington Capitals, Feb. 22, 1981, at Washington. Quebec won 11-7. Quebec had 22A, Washington, 13A.
   – Edmonton Oilers, Minnesota North Stars, Jan. 4, 1984, at Edmonton. Edmonton won 12-8. Edmonton had 20A, Minnesota, 13A.
   – Minnesota North Stars, St. Louis Blues, Jan. 27, 1984, at St. Louis. Minnesota won 10-8. Minnesota had 19A, St. Louis, 16A.
   – Toronto Maple Leafs, Edmonton Oilers, Jan. 8, 1986, at Toronto. Toronto won 11-9. Toronto had 17A, Edmonton, 16A.
52 – Montreal Maroons, New York Americans, Feb. 18, 1936, at NY Americans. Teams tied 8-8. NY Americans had 20A, Montreal, 16A. (3A allowed for each goal.)
   – Vancouver Canucks, Minnesota North Stars, Oct. 7, 1983, at Vancouver. Vancouver won 10-9. Vancouver had 16A, Minnesota, 17A.

MOST SCORING POINTS, ONE TEAM, ONE PERIOD:
23 – New York Rangers, Nov. 21, 1971, at NY Rangers, third period during 12-1 win over California. NY Rangers had 8G, 15A.
   – **Buffalo Sabres**, Dec. 21, 1975, at Buffalo, third period during 14-2 win over Washington. Buffalo had 8G, 15A.
   – **Buffalo Sabres**, Mar. 19, 1981, at Buffalo, second period during 14-4 win over Toronto. Buffalo had 9G, 14A.

22 – Detroit Red Wings, Jan. 23, 1944, at Detroit, third period during 15-0 win over NY Rangers. Detroit had 8G, 14A.
– Boston Bruins, Mar. 16, 1969, at Boston, second period during 11-3 win over Toronto. Boston had 8G, 14A.
– Minnesota North Stars, Nov. 11, 1981, at Minnesota, second period during 15-2 win over Winnipeg. Minnesota had 8G, 14A.
– Pittsburgh Penguins, Dec. 17, 1991, at Pittsburgh, second period during 10-2 win over San Jose. Pittsburgh had 8G, 14A.
– Washington Capitals, Feb. 3, 1999, at Washington, second period during 10-1 win over Tampa Bay. Washington had 8G, 14A.

MOST SCORING POINTS, BOTH TEAMS, ONE PERIOD:
35 – Edmonton, Oilers, Chicago Blackhawks, Dec. 11, 1985, at Chicago, second period. Edmonton won 12-9. Edmonton had 6G, 12A; Chicago, 6G, 11A.
31 – Buffalo Sabres, Toronto Maple Leafs, Mar. 19, 1981, at Buffalo, second period. Buffalo won 14-4. Buffalo had 9G, 14A; Toronto, 3G, 5A.
29 – Winnipeg Jets, Detroit Red Wings, Nov. 25, 1987, at Detroit, third period. Detroit won 10-8. Detroit had 7G, 13A; Winnipeg, 3G, 6A.
– Chicago Blackhawks, St. Louis Blues, Mar. 15, 1988, at St. Louis, third period. Teams tied 7-7. St. Louis had 5G, 10A; Chicago, 5G, 9A.

FASTEST GOALS

FASTEST SIX GOALS, BOTH TEAMS:
3:00 – Quebec Nordiques, Washington Capitals, Feb. 22, 1981, at Washington. Scorers: Peter Stastny, Quebec, 18:51; Pierre Lacroix, Quebec, 19:57 (first period); Anton Stastny, Quebec, 0:34; Jacques Richard, Quebec, 1:07 and 1:37; Rick Green, Washington, 1:51 (second period). Quebec won 11-7.
3:15 – Montreal Canadiens, Toronto Maple Leafs, Jan. 4, 1944, at Montreal, first period. Scorers: Maurice Richard, Montreal, 14:10; Don Webster, Toronto, 15:13; Fern Majeau, Montreal, 15:41; Phil Watson, Montreal, 15:52; Lorne Carr, Toronto, 16:55; Butch Bouchard, Montreal, 17:25. Montreal won 6-3.

FASTEST FIVE GOALS, BOTH TEAMS:
1:24 – Chicago Blackhawks, Toronto Maple Leafs, Oct. 15, 1983, at Toronto, second period. Scorers: Gaston Gingras, Toronto, 16:49; Denis Savard, Chicago, 17:12; Steve Larmer, Chicago, 17:27; Denis Savard, Chicago, 17:42; John Anderson, Toronto, 18:13. Toronto won 10-8.
1:39 – Detroit Red Wings, Toronto Maple Leafs, Nov. 15, 1944, at Toronto, third period. Scorers: Ted Kennedy, Toronto, 10:36 and 10:55; Harold Jackson, Detroit, 11:48; Steve Wojciechowski, Detroit, 12:02; Don Grosso, Detroit, 12:15. Detroit won 8-4.

FASTEST FIVE GOALS, ONE TEAM:
2:07 – Pittsburgh Penguins, Nov. 22, 1972, at Pittsburgh, third period. Scorers: Bryan Hextall, Jr., 12:00; Jean Pronovost, 12:18; Al McDonough, 13:40; Ken Schinkel, 13:49; Ron Schock, 14:07. Pittsburgh defeated St. Louis 10-4.
2:37 – New York Islanders, Jan. 26, 1982, at NY Islanders, first period. Scorers: Duane Sutter, 1:31; John Tonelli, 2:30; Bryan Trottier, 2:46 and 3:31; Duane Sutter, 4:08. NY Islanders defeated Pittsburgh 9-2.
2:55 – Boston Bruins, Dec. 19, 1974, at Boston. Scorers: Bobby Schmautz, 19:13 (first period); Ken Hodge, 0:18; Phil Esposito, 0:43; Don Marcotte, 0:58; John Bucyk, 2:08 (second period). Boston defeated NY Rangers 11-3.

FASTEST FOUR GOALS, BOTH TEAMS:
0:49 – St. Louis Blues, Dallas Stars, Apr. 3, 2015, at Dallas. Scorers: Travis Moen, Dallas, 19:49 (first period); Patrik Berglund, St. Louis, 0:15; Jaden Schwartz, St. Louis, 0:32; Jamie Benn, Dallas, 0:38 (second period). St. Louis won 7-5.
0:53 – Chicago Blackhawks, Toronto Maple Leafs, Oct. 15, 1983, at Toronto, second period. Scorers: Gaston Gingras, Toronto, 16:49; Denis Savard, Chicago, 17:12; Steve Larmer, Chicago, 17:27; Denis Savard, Chicago, 17:42. Toronto won 10-8.
0:57 – Quebec Nordiques, Detroit Red Wings, Jan. 27, 1990, at Quebec, first period. Scorers: Paul Gillis, Quebec, 18:01; Claude Loiselle, Quebec, 18:12; Joe Sakic, Quebec, 18:27; Jimmy Carson, Detroit, 18:58. Detroit won 8-6

FASTEST FOUR GOALS, ONE TEAM:
1:20 – Boston Bruins, Jan. 21, 1945, at Boston, second period. Scorers: Bill Thoms, 6:34; Frank Mario, 7:08 and 7:27; Ken Smith, 7:54. Boston defeated NY Rangers 14-3.

FASTEST THREE GOALS, BOTH TEAMS:
0:15 – Minnesota North Stars, New York Rangers, Feb. 10, 1983, at Minnesota, second period. Scorers: Mark Pavelich, NY Rangers, 19:18; Ron Greschner, NY Rangers, 19:27; Willi Plett, Minnesota, 19:33. Minnesota won 7-5.
0:17 – Minnesota Wild, Buffalo Sabres, Nov. 13, 2014, at Minnesota, first period. Scorers: Ryan Carter, Minnesota, 6:07; Nino Niederreiter, Minnesota, 6:14; Zemgus Girgensons, Buffalo, 6:24. Minnesota won 6-3.

FASTEST THREE GOALS, ONE TEAM:
0:20 – Boston Bruins, Feb. 25, 1971, at Boston, third period. Scorers: John Bucyk, 4:50; Ed Westfall, 5:02; Ted Green, 5:10. Boston defeated Vancouver 8-3.
0:21 – Chicago Blackhawks, Mar. 23, 1952, at NY Rangers, third period. Bill Mosienko scored all three goals, at 6:09, 6:20 and 6:30. Chicago defeated NY Rangers 7-6.
– Washington Capitals, Nov. 23, 1990, at Washington, first period. Scorers: Michal Pivonka, 16:18; Stephen Leach, 16:29 and 16:39. Washington defeated Pittsburgh 7-3.

FASTEST THREE GOALS FROM START OF PERIOD, BOTH TEAMS:
0:38 – St. Louis Blues, Dallas Stars, Apr. 3, 2015, at Dallas, second period. Scorers: Patrik Berglund, St. Louis, 0:15; Jaden Schwartz, St. Louis, 0:32; Jamie Benn, Dallas, 0:38. St. Louis won 7-5.

FASTEST THREE GOALS FROM START OF PERIOD, ONE TEAM:
0:53 – Calgary Flames, Feb. 10, 1993, at Calgary, third period. Scorers: Gary Suter, 0:17; Chris Lindberg, 0:40; Ron Stern, 0:53. Calgary defeated San Jose 13-1.

FASTEST TWO GOALS, BOTH TEAMS:
0:02 – St. Louis Blues, Boston Bruins, Dec. 19, 1987, at Boston, third period. Scorers: Ken Linseman, Boston, 19:50; Doug Gilmour, St. Louis, 19:52. St. Louis won 7-5.
*0:03 – Chicago Blackhawks, Minnesota North Stars, Nov. 5, 1988, at Minnesota, third period. Scorers: Steve Thomas, Chicago, 6:03; Dave Gagner, Minnesota, 6:06. Teams tied 5-5.
* – Newspaper accounts of this game note that the clock was slow to start after the first goal was scored.
– Washington Capitals, Tampa Bay Lightning, Dec. 9, 2014, at Tampa Bay, third period. Scorers: Valtteri Filppula, Tampa Bay, 19:56; Alex Ovechkin, Washington, 19:59. Washington won 5-3.

FASTEST TWO GOALS, ONE TEAM:
0:03 – St. Louis Eagles, Mar. 12, 1935, at St. Louis, third period. Scorers: Frank Jerwa, 14:50; Joe Lamb, 14:53. St. Louis defeated Detroit 3-2.
– Minnesota Wild, Jan. 21, 2004, at Minnesota, third period. Scorers: Jim Dowd, 19:44; Richard Park, 19:47. Minnesota defeated Chicago 4-2.
0:04 – Montreal Maroons, Jan. 3, 1931, at Montreal, third period. Nels Stewart scored both goals, at 8:24 and 8:28. Mtl. Maroons defeated Boston 5-3.
– Buffalo Sabres, Oct. 17, 1974, at Buffalo, third period. Scorers: Lee Fogolin, Jr., 14:55; Don Luce, 14:59. Buffalo defeated California 6-1.
– Toronto Maple Leafs, Dec. 29, 1988, at Quebec, third period. Scorers: Ed Olczyk, 5:24; Gary Leeman, 5:28. Toronto defeated Quebec 6-5.
– Calgary Flames, Oct. 17, 1989, at Quebec, third period. Scorers: Doug Gilmour, 19:45; Paul Ranheim, 19:49. Teams tied 8-8.
– NY Rangers, Oct. 9, 1991, at NY Rangers, third period. Scorers: Kris King, 19:45; James Patrick, 19:49. NY Rangers defeated NY Islanders 5-3.
– Winnipeg Jets, Dec. 15, 1995, at Winnipeg, second period. Deron Quint scored both goals, at 7:51 and 7:55. Winnipeg defeated Edmonton 9-4.
– New York Rangers, Oct. 19, 2014, at NY Rangers, second period. Scorers: Martin St. Louis, 19:16; Rick Nash, 19:20. NY Rangers defeated San Jose 4-0.

FASTEST TWO GOALS FROM START OF GAME, ONE TEAM:
0:24 – Edmonton Oilers, Mar. 28, 1982, at Los Angeles. Scorers: Mark Messier, 0:14; Dave Lumley, 0:24. Edmonton defeated Los Angeles 6-2.
0:27 – Boston Bruins, Feb. 14, 2003, at Florida. Mike Knuble scored both goals, at 0:10 and 0:27. Boston defeated Florida 6-5.
0:29 – Pittsburgh Penguins, Dec. 6, 1980, at Pittsburgh. Scorers: George Ferguson, 0:17; Greg Malone, 0:29. Pittsburgh defeated Chicago 6-4.

FASTEST TWO GOALS FROM START OF PERIOD, BOTH TEAMS:
0:14 – New York Rangers, Quebec Nordiques, Nov. 5, 1983, at Quebec, third period. Scorers: Andre Savard, Quebec, 0:08; Pierre Larouche, NY Rangers, 0:14. Teams tied 4-4.
0:25 – St. Louis Blues, Chicago Blackhawks, Feb. 2, 2006, at St. Louis, second period. Scorers: Peter Cajanek, St. Louis, 0:10; Tyler Arnason, Chicago, 0:25. St. Louis won 6-5.
0:28 – Boston Bruins, Montreal Canadiens, Oct. 11, 1989, at Montreal, third period. Scorers: Jim Wiemer, Boston 0:10; Tom Chorske, Montreal 0:28. Montreal won 4-2.

FASTEST TWO GOALS FROM START OF PERIOD, ONE TEAM:
0:21 – Chicago Blackhawks, Nov. 5, 1983, at Minnesota, second period. Scorers: Ken Yaremchuk, 0:12; Darryl Sutter, 0:21. Minnesota defeated Chicago 10-5.
0:24 – Edmonton Oilers, Mar. 28, 1982, at Los Angeles, first period. Scorers: Mark Messier, 0:14; Dave Lumley, 0:24. Edmonton defeated Los Angeles 6-2.
0:27 – Boston Bruins, Feb. 14, 2003, at Florida. Mike Knuble scored both goals, at 0:10 and 0:27. Boston defeated Florida 6-5.

50, 40, 30, 20-GOAL SCORERS

MOST 50-OR-MORE GOAL SCORERS, ONE SEASON:
3 – Edmonton Oilers, 1983-84. 80GP. Wayne Gretzky, 87; Glenn Anderson, 54; Jari Kurri, 52.
– Edmonton Oilers, 1985-86. 80GP. Jari Kurri, 68; Glenn Anderson, 54; Wayne Gretzky, 52.
2 – Boston Bruins, 1970-71. 78GP. Phil Esposito, 76; John Bucyk, 51.
– Boston Bruins, 1973-74. 78GP. Phil Esposito, 68; Ken Hodge, 50.
– Philadelphia Flyers, 1975-76. 80GP. Reggie Leach, 61; Bill Barber, 50.
– Pittsburgh Penguins, 1975-76. 80GP. Pierre Larouche, 53; Jean Pronovost, 52.
– Montreal Canadiens, 1976-77. 80GP. Steve Shutt, 60; Guy Lafleur, 56.
– Los Angeles Kings, 1979-80. 80GP. Charlie Simmer, 56; Marcel Dionne, 53.
– Montreal Canadiens, 1979-80. 80GP. Pierre Larouche, 50; Guy Lafleur, 50.
– Los Angeles Kings, 1980-81. 80GP. Marcel Dionne, 58; Charlie Simmer, 56.
– Edmonton Oilers, 1981-82. 80GP. Wayne Gretzky, 92; Mark Messier, 50.
– New York Islanders, 1981-82. 80GP. Mike Bossy, 64; Bryan Trottier, 50.
– Edmonton Oilers, 1984-85. 80GP. Wayne Gretzky, 73; Jari Kurri, 71.
– Washington Capitals, 1984-85. 80GP. Bob Carpenter, 53; Mike Gartner, 50.
– Edmonton Oilers, 1986-87. 80GP. Wayne Gretzky, 62; Jari Kurri, 54.
– Calgary Flames, 1987-88. 80GP. Joe Nieuwendyk, 51; Hakan Loob, 50.
– Los Angeles Kings, 1987-88. 80GP. Jimmy Carson, 55; Luc Robitaille, 53.
– Calgary Flames, 1988-89. 80GP. Joe Nieuwendyk, 51; Joe Mullen, 50.
– Los Angeles Kings, 1988-89. 80GP. Bernie Nicholls, 70; Wayne Gretzky, 54.
– Buffalo Sabres, 1992-93. 84GP. Alexander Mogilny, 76; Pat LaFontaine, 53.
– Pittsburgh Penguins, 1992-93. 84GP. Mario Lemieux, 69; Kevin Stevens, 55.
– St. Louis Blues, 1992-93. 84GP. Brett Hull, 54; Brendan Shanahan, 51.
– Detroit Red Wings, 1993-94. 84GP. Sergei Fedorov, 56; Ray Sheppard, 52.
– St. Louis Blues, 1993-94. 84GP. Brett Hull, 57; Brendan Shanahan, 52.
– Pittsburgh Penguins, 1995-96. 82GP. Mario Lemieux, 69; Jaromir Jagr, 62.

MOST 40-OR-MORE GOAL SCORERS, ONE SEASON:

4 – Edmonton Oilers, 1982-83. 80GP. Wayne Gretzky, 71; Glenn Anderson, 48; Mark Messier, 48; Jari Kurri, 45.
– **Edmonton Oilers**, 1983-84. 80GP. Wayne Gretzky, 87; Glenn Anderson, 54; Jari Kurri, 52; Paul Coffey, 40.
– **Edmonton Oilers**, 1984-85. 80GP. Wayne Gretzky, 73; Jari Kurri, 71; Mike Krushelnyski, 43; Glenn Anderson, 42.
– **Edmonton Oilers**, 1985-86. 80GP. Jari Kurri, 68; Glenn Anderson, 54; Wayne Gretzky, 52; Paul Coffey, 48.
– **Calgary Flames**, 1987-88. 80GP. Joe Nieuwendyk, 51; Hakan Loob, 50; Mike Bullard, 48; Joe Mullen, 40.
3 – Boston Bruins, 1970-71. 78GP. Phil Esposito, 76; John Bucyk, 51; Ken Hodge, 43.
– New York Rangers, 1971-72. 78GP. Vic Hadfield, 50; Jean Ratelle, 46; Rod Gilbert, 43.
– Buffalo Sabres, 1975-76. 80GP. Danny Gare, 50; Rick Martin, 49; Gilbert Perreault, 44.
– Montreal Canadiens, 1979-80. 80GP. Guy Lafleur, 50; Pierre Larouche, 50; Steve Shutt, 47.
– Buffalo Sabres, 1979-80. 80GP. Danny Gare, 56; Rick Martin, 45; Gilbert Perreault, 40.
– Los Angeles Kings, 1980-81. 80GP. Marcel Dionne, 58; Charlie Simmer, 56; Dave Taylor, 47.
– Los Angeles Kings, 1984-85. 80GP. Marcel Dionne, 46; Bernie Nicholls, 46; Dave Taylor, 41.
– New York Islanders, 1984-85. 80GP. Mike Bossy, 58; Brent Sutter, 42; John Tonelli, 42.
– Chicago Blackhawks, 1985-86. 80GP. Denis Savard, 47; Troy Murray, 45; Al Secord, 40.
– Chicago Blackhawks, 1987-88. 80GP. Denis Savard, 44; Rick Vaive, 43; Steve Larmer, 41.
– Edmonton Oilers, 1987-88. 80GP. Craig Simpson, 43; Jari Kurri, 43; Wayne Gretzky, 40.
– Los Angeles Kings, 1988-89. 80GP. Bernie Nicholls, 70; Wayne Gretzky, 54; Luc Robitaille, 46.
– Los Angeles Kings, 1990-91. 80GP. Luc Robitaille, 45; Tomas Sandstrom, 45; Wayne Gretzky, 41.
– Pittsburgh Penguins, 1991-92. 80GP. Kevin Stevens, 54; Mario Lemieux, 44; Joe Mullen, 42.
– Pittsburgh Penguins, 1992-93. 84GP. Mario Lemieux, 69; Kevin Stevens, 55; Rick Tocchet, 48.
– Calgary Flames, 1993-94. 84GP. Gary Roberts, 41; Robert Reichel, 40; Theoren Fleury, 40.
– Pittsburgh Penguins, 1995-96. 82GP. Mario Lemieux, 69; Jaromir Jagr, 62; Petr Nedved, 45.

MOST 30-OR-MORE GOAL SCORERS, ONE SEASON:

6 – Buffalo Sabres, 1974-75. 80GP. Rick Martin, 52; Rene Robert, 40; Gilbert Perreault, 39; Don Luce, 33; Rick Dudley, 31; Danny Gare, 31.
– **New York Islanders**, 1977-78. 80GP. Mike Bossy, 53; Bryan Trottier, 46; Clark Gillies, 35; Denis Potvin, 30; Bob Nystrom, 30; Bob Bourne, 30.
– **Winnipeg Jets**, 1984-85. 80GP. Dale Hawerchuk, 53; Paul MacLean, 41; Laurie Boschman, 32; Brian Mullen, 32; Doug Smail, 31; Thomas Steen, 30.
5 – Chicago Blackhawks, 1968-69. 76GP
– Boston Bruins, 1970-71. 78GP
– Montreal Canadiens, 1971-72. 78GP
– Philadelphia Flyers, 1972-73. 78GP
– Boston Bruins, 1973-74. 78GP
– Montreal Canadiens, 1974-75. 80GP
– Montreal Canadiens, 1975-76. 80GP
– Pittsburgh Penguins, 1975-76. 80GP
– New York Islanders, 1978-79. 80GP
– Detroit Red Wings, 1979-80. 80GP
– Philadelphia Flyers, 1979-80. 80GP
– New York Islanders, 1980-81. 80GP
– St. Louis Blues, 1980-81. 80GP
– Chicago Blackhawks, 1981-82. 80GP
– Edmonton Oilers, 1981-82. 80GP
– Montreal Canadiens, 1981-82. 80GP
– Quebec Nordiques, 1981-82. 80GP
– Washington Capitals, 1981-82. 80GP
– Edmonton Oilers, 1982-83. 80GP
– Edmonton Oilers, 1983-84. 80GP
– Edmonton Oilers, 1984-85. 80GP
– Los Angeles Kings, 1984-85. 80GP
– Edmonton Oilers, 1985-86. 80GP
– Edmonton Oilers, 1986-87. 80GP
– Edmonton Oilers, 1987-88. 80GP
– Edmonton Oilers, 1988-89. 80GP
– Detroit Red Wings, 1991-92. 80GP
– New York Rangers, 1991-92. 80GP
– Pittsburgh Penguins, 1991-92. 80GP
– Detroit Red Wings, 1992-93. 84GP
– Pittsburgh Penguins, 1992-93. 84GP

MOST 20-OR-MORE GOAL SCORERS, ONE SEASON:

11 – Boston Bruins, 1977-78. 80GP. Peter McNab, 41; Terry O'Reilly, 29; Bobby Schmautz, 27; Stan Jonathan, 27; Jean Ratelle, 25; Rick Middleton, 25; Wayne Cashman, 24; Gregg Sheppard, 23; Brad Park, 22; Don Marcotte, 20; Bob Miller, 20.
10 – Boston Bruins, 1970-71. 78GP
– Montreal Canadiens, 1974-75. 80GP
– St. Louis Blues, 1980-81. 80GP

100-POINT SCORERS

MOST 100-OR-MORE-POINT SCORERS, ONE SEASON:

4 – Boston Bruins, 1970-71. 78GP. Phil Esposito, 76G-76A-152PTS; Bobby Orr, 37G-102A-139PTS; John Bucyk, 51G-65A-116PTS; Ken Hodge, 43G-62A-105PTS.
– **Edmonton Oilers**, 1982-83. 80GP. Wayne Gretzky, 71G-125A-196PTS; Mark Messier, 48G-58A-106PTS; Glenn Anderson, 48G-56A-104PTS; Jari Kurri, 45G-59A-104PTS.
– **Edmonton Oilers**, 1983-84. 80GP. Wayne Gretzky, 87G-118A-205PTS; Paul Coffey, 40G-86A-126PTS; Jari Kurri, 52G-61A-113PTS; Mark Messier, 37G-64A-101PTS.
– **Edmonton Oilers**, 1985-86. 80GP. Wayne Gretzky, 52G-163A-215PTS; Paul Coffey, 48G-90A-138PTS; Jari Kurri, 68G-63A-131PTS; Glenn Anderson, 54G-48A-102PTS.
– **Pittsburgh Penguins**, 1992-93. 84GP. Mario Lemieux, 69G-91A-160PTS; Kevin Stevens, 55G-56A-111PTS; Rick Tocchet, 48G-61A-109PTS; Ron Francis, 24G-76A-100PTS.
3 – Boston Bruins, 1973-74. 78GP. Phil Esposito, 68G-77A-145PTS; Bobby Orr, 32G-90A-122PTS; Ken Hodge, 50G-55A-105PTS.
– New York Islanders, 1978-79. 80GP. Bryan Trottier, 47G-87A-134PTS; Mike Bossy, 69G-57A-126PTS; Denis Potvin, 31G-70A-101PTS.
– Los Angeles Kings, 1980-81. 80GP. Marcel Dionne, 58G-77A-135PTS; Dave Taylor, 47G-65A-112PTS; Charlie Simmer, 56G-49A-105PTS.
– Edmonton Oilers, 1984-85. 80GP. Wayne Gretzky, 73G-135A-208PTS; Jari Kurri, 71G-64A-135PTS; Paul Coffey, 37G-84A-121PTS.
– New York Islanders, 1984-85. 80GP. Mike Bossy, 58G-59A-117PTS; Brent Sutter, 42G-60A-102PTS; John Tonelli, 42G-58A-100PTS.
– Edmonton Oilers, 1986-87. 80GP. Wayne Gretzky, 62G-121A-183PTS; Jari Kurri, 54G-54A-108PTS; Mark Messier, 37G-70A-107PTS.
– Pittsburgh Penguins, 1988-89. 80GP. Mario Lemieux, 85G-114A-199PTS; Rob Brown, 49G-66A-115PTS; Paul Coffey, 30G-83A-113PTS.
– Pittsburgh Penguins, 1995-96. 82GP. Mario Lemieux, 69G-92A-161PTS; Jaromir Jagr, 62G-87A-149PTS; Ron Francis, 27G-92A-119PTS.

SHOTS ON GOAL

MOST SHOTS, BOTH TEAMS, ONE GAME:

141 – New York Americans, Pittsburgh Pirates, Dec. 26, 1925, at NY Americans. NY Americans won 3-1 with 73 shots; Pittsburgh had 68 shots.

MOST SHOTS, ONE TEAM, ONE GAME:

83 – Boston Bruins, Mar. 4, 1941, at Boston. Boston defeated Chicago 3-2.
82 – Toronto St. Patricks, Jan. 10, 1925 at Toronto. Toronto defeated Hamilton 3-1.
81 – Toronto St. Patricks, Feb. 14, 1925 at Toronto. Toronto defeated Hamilton 3-1.
73 – New York Americans, Dec. 26, 1925, at NY Americans. NY Americans defeated Pittsburgh 3-1.
– Boston Bruins, Mar. 21, 1991, at Boston. Boston tied Quebec 3-3.
72 – Boston Bruins, Dec. 10, 1970, at Boston. Boston defeated Buffalo 8-2.

MOST SHOTS, ONE TEAM, ONE PERIOD:

33 – Boston Bruins, Mar. 4, 1941, at Boston, second period. Boston defeated Chicago 3-2.

TEAM GOALS AGAINST

Fewest Goals Against

FEWEST GOALS AGAINST, ONE SEASON:

42 – Ottawa Senators, 1925-26. 36GP
43 – Montreal Canadiens, 1928-29. 44GP
48 – Montreal Canadiens, 1923-24. 24GP
– Montreal Canadiens, 1927-28. 44GP

FEWEST GOALS AGAINST, ONE SEASON (MINIMUM 70-GAME SCHEDULE):

131 – Toronto Maple Leafs, 1953-54. 70GP
– **Montreal Canadiens**, 1955-56. 70GP
132 – Detroit Red Wings, 1953-54. 70GP
133 – Detroit Red Wings, 1951-52. 70GP
– Detroit Red Wings, 1952-53. 70GP

LOWEST GOALS-AGAINST-PER-GAME AVERAGE, ONE SEASON:

0.98 – Montreal Canadiens, 1928-29. 43GA in 44GP.
1.09 – Montreal Canadiens, 1927-28. 48GA in 44GP.
1.17 – Ottawa Senators, 1925-26. 42GA in 36GP.

Most Goals Against

MOST GOALS AGAINST, ONE SEASON:

446 – Washington Capitals, 1974-75. 80GP
415 – Detroit Red Wings, 1985-86. 80GP
414 – San Jose Sharks, 1992-93. 84GP
407 – Quebec Nordiques, 1989-90. 80GP
403 – Hartford Whalers, 1982-83. 80GP

HIGHEST GOALS-AGAINST-PER-GAME AVERAGE, ONE SEASON:

7.38 – Quebec Bulldogs, 1919-20. 177GA in 24GP.
6.20 – New York Rangers, 1943-44. 310GA in 50GP.
5.58 – Washington Capitals, 1974-75. 446GA in 80GP.

MOST POWER-PLAY GOALS AGAINST, ONE SEASON:

122 – Chicago Blackhawks, 1988-89. 80GP
120 – Pittsburgh Penguins, 1987-88. 80GP
116 – Washington Capitals, 2005-06. 82GP
115 – New Jersey Devils, 1988-89. 80GP
– Ottawa Senators, 1992-93. 84GP
114 – Los Angeles Kings, 1992-93. 84GP

MOST SHORTHAND GOALS AGAINST, ONE SEASON:

22 – Pittsburgh Penguins, 1984-85. 80GP
– **Minnesota North Stars**, 1991-92. 80GP
– **Colorado Avalanche**, 1995-96. 82GP
21 – Calgary Flames, 1984-85. 80GP
– Pittsburgh Penguins, 1989-90. 80GP

TEAM SHOOTOUT RECORDS

MOST SHOOTOUT GAMES, ONE SEASON:
  21 – Washington, 2013-14 (10w, 11L)
  20 – Phoenix, 2009-10 (14w, 6L)
     – Minnesota, 2011-12 (11w, 9L)

MOST SHOOTOUT GAMES, ALL-TIME:
  121 – Florida (49w, 72L)
  118 – Chicago (60w, 58L)
  117 – New Jersey (61w, 56L)

MOST SHOOTOUT WINS, ONE SEASON:
  15 – Edmonton, 2007-08, 19GP
  14 – Phoenix, 2009-10, 20GP
  12 – Dallas, 2005-06, 13GP
     – New Jersey, 2011-12, 16GP

MOST SHOOTOUT WINS, ALL-TIME:
  65 – Pittsburgh, 104GP
     – Buffalo, 116GP
  64 – NY Islanders, 111GP

MOST SHOOTOUT HOME WINS, ONE SEASON:
  8 – Edmonton, 2007-08, 9GP
     – New Jersey, 2011-12, 12GP
  7 – Toronto, 2013-14 8GP
     – NY Rangers, 2008-09, 9GP
     – NY Islanders, 2009-10, 9GP
     – Anaheim, 2007-08, 10GP
     – Minnesota, 2006-07, 11GP

MOST SHOOTOUT HOME WINS, ALL-TIME:
  37 – New Jersey, 65GP
  31 – Buffalo, 58GP
     – Chicago, 58GP

MOST SHOOTOUT ROAD WINS, ONE SEASON:
  8 – Phoenix, 2009-10, 12GP
     – Calgary, 2010-11, 12GP
  7 – NY Rangers, 2011-12, 7GP
     – Dallas, 2005-06, 8GP
     – Dallas, 2006-07, 9GP
     – Edmonton, 2007-08, 10GP
     – Boston, 2009-10, 10GP
     – Pittsburgh, 2010-11, 10GP

MOST SHOOTOUT ROAD WINS, ALL-TIME:
  37 – Pittsburgh, 59GP
  36 – Dallas, 52GP
     – Colorado, 56GP

MOST SHOOTOUT SHOTS TAKEN, ONE SEASON:
  90 – Phoenix, 2009-10, 20GP
  81 – Florida, 2014-15, 18GP
  80 – Washington, 2013-14, 21GP

MOST SHOOTOUT SHOTS TAKEN, ALL-TIME:
  437 – Florida, 121GP
  429 – Buffalo, 116GP
  423 – Los Angeles, 113GP

MOST SHOOTOUT GOALS SCORED, ONE SEASON:
  34 – Phoenix, 2009-10, 20GP, 90s
  28 – New Jersey, 2011-12, 16GP, 49s
  27 – Minnesota, 2006-07, 17GP, 62s
     – Los Angeles, 2009-10, 18GP, 74s
     – Washington, 2013-14, 21GP, 80s

MOST SHOOTOUT GOALS SCORED, ALL-TIME:
  148 – NY Islanders, 111GP (398s)
     – Buffalo, 116GP (429s)
  143 – Los Angeles, 113GP (423s)

BEST SHOOTOUT SCORING PERCENTAGE, ONE SEASON:
  .750 – Pittsburgh, 2012-13, 3GP (6G, 8s)
  .636 – St. Louis, 2012-13, 6GP (14G, 22s)
  .600 – Colorado, 2012-13, 4GP (6G, 10s)
     – Minnesota, 2012-13, 6GP (9G, 15s)

BEST SHOOTOUT SCORING PERCENTAGE, ALL-TIME:
  .393 – Colorado, 98GP (134G, 341s)
  .375 – St. Louis, 111GP (136G, 363s)
  .372 – NY Islanders, 111GP (148G, 398s)

FEWEST SHOOTOUT GOALS AGAINST, ONE SEASON:
  1 – Washington, 2012-13, 3GP (9SA)
  2 – Colorado, 2010-11, 7GP (27SA)
     – Pittsburgh, 2012-13, 3GP (8SA)
     – Carolina, 2012-13, 2GP (5SA)

FEWEST SHOOTOUT GOALS AGAINST, ALL-TIME:
  82 – Carolina, 74GP (229SA)
  93 – Tampa Bay, 93GP (329SA)
  96 – Pittsburgh, 104GP (354SA)

BEST SHOOTOUT WINNING PERCENTAGE, ONE SEASON:
  1.000 – Pittsburgh, 2012-13, 3GP (3w)
     – Washington, 2012-13, 3GP (3w)
  .923 – Dallas, 2005-06, 13GP (12w)

BEST SHOOTOUT WINNING PERCENTAGE, ALL-TIME:
  .643 – Colorado, 98GP (63w)
  .625 – Pittsburgh, 104GP (65w)
  .581 – Dallas, 105GP (61w)

SHUTOUTS

MOST SHUTOUTS, ONE SEASON:
  22 – Montreal Canadiens, 1928-29. All by George Hainsworth. 44GP
  16 – New York Americans, 1928-29. Roy Worters 13, Flat Walsh 3. 44GP
  15 – Ottawa Senators, 1925-26. All by Alec Connell. 36GP
     – Ottawa Senators, 1927-28. All by Alec Connell. 44GP
     – Boston Bruins, 1927-28. All by Hal Winkler. 44GP
     – Chicago Blackhawks, 1969-70. All by Tony Esposito. 76GP
     – St. Louis Blues, 2011-12. Brian Elliott 9, Jaroslav Halak 6. 82GP

MOST CONSECUTIVE SHUTOUTS, ONE SEASON:
  6 – Ottawa Senators, Jan. 31 – Feb. 18, 1928. All by Alec Connell.

MOST CONSECUTIVE SHUTOUTS TO START SEASON:
  5 – Toronto Maple Leafs, Nov. 13 – 22, 1930. Lorne Chabot 3, Benny Grant 2.

MOST GAMES SHUTOUT, ONE SEASON:
  20 – Chicago Blackhawks, 1928-29. 44GP

MOST CONSECUTIVE GAMES SHUTOUT:
  8 – Chicago Blackhawks, Feb. 7 – 28, 1929.

MOST CONSECUTIVE GAMES SHUTOUT TO START SEASON:
  3 – Montreal Maroons, Nov. 11 – 18, 1930.

TEAM PENALTIES

MOST PENALTY MINUTES, ONE SEASON:
  2,713 – Buffalo Sabres, 1991-92. 80GP
  2,670 – Pittsburgh Penguins, 1988-89. 80GP
  2,663 – Chicago Blackhawks, 1991-92. 80GP
  2,643 – Calgary Flames, 1991-92. 80GP
  2,621 – Philadelphia Flyers, 1980-81. 80GP

MOST PENALTIES, BOTH TEAMS, ONE GAME:
  85 – Edmonton Oilers (44), Los Angeles Kings (41), Feb. 28, 1990, at Los Angeles. Edmonton received 26 minors, 7 majors, 6 10-minute misconducts, 4 game misconducts and 1 match penalty; Los Angeles received 26 minors, 9 majors, 3 10-minute misconducts and 3 game misconducts.

MOST PENALTY MINUTES, BOTH TEAMS, ONE GAME:
  419 – Ottawa Senators (206), Philadelphia Flyers (213), Mar. 5, 2004, at Philadelphia. Ottawa received 8 minors, 10 majors, 4 10-minute misconducts and 10 game misconducts. Philadelphia received 9 minors, 11 majors, 4 10-minute misconducts and 10 game misconducts.

MOST PENALTIES, ONE TEAM, ONE GAME:
  44 – Edmonton Oilers, Feb. 28, 1990, at Los Angeles. Edmonton received 26 minors, 7 majors, 6 10-minute misconducts, 4 game misconducts and 1 match penalty.
  42 – Minnesota North Stars, Feb. 26, 1981, at Boston. Minnesota received 18 minors, 13 majors, 4 10-minute misconducts and 7 game misconducts.
     – Boston Bruins, Feb. 26, 1981, at Boston vs. Minnesota. Boston received 20 minors, 13 majors, 3 10-minute misconducts and 6 game misconducts.

MOST PENALTY MINUTES, ONE TEAM, ONE GAME:
  213 – Philadelphia Flyers, Mar. 5, 2004, at Philadelphia. Philadelphia received 9 minors, 11 majors, 4 10-minute misconducts and 10 game misconducts.

MOST PENALTIES, BOTH TEAMS, ONE PERIOD:
  67 – Minnesota North Stars (34), Boston Bruins (33), Feb. 26, 1981, at Boston, first period. Minnesota received 15 minors, 8 majors, 4 10-minute misconducts and 7 game misconducts. Boston had 16 minors, 8 majors, 3 10-minute misconducts and 6 game misconducts.

MOST PENALTY MINUTES, BOTH TEAMS, ONE PERIOD:
  409 – Ottawa Senators (200), Philadelphia Flyers (209), Mar. 5, 2004, at Philadelphia, third period. Ottawa received 5 minors, 10 majors, 4 10-minute misconducts and 10 game misconducts. Philadelphia received 7 minors, 11 majors, 4 10-minute misconducts and 10 game misconducts.

MOST PENALTIES, ONE TEAM, ONE PERIOD:
  34 – Minnesota North Stars, Feb. 26, 1981, at Boston, first period. Minnesota received 15 minors, 8 majors, 4 10-minute misconducts and 7 game misconducts.

MOST PENALTY MINUTES, ONE TEAM, ONE PERIOD:
  209 – Philadelphia Flyers, Mar. 5, 2004, at Philadelphia vs. Ottawa, third period. Philadelphia received 7 minors, 11 majors, 4 10-minute misconducts and 10 game misconducts.
  200 – Ottawa Senators, Mar. 5, 2004, at Philadelphia, third period. Ottawa received 5 minors, 10 majors, 4 10-minute misconducts and 10 game misconducts.

NHL Individual Scoring Records – History

Six individual scoring records stand as benchmarks in the history of the game: most goals, single-season and career; most assists, single-season and career; and most points, single-season and career. The evolution of these six records is traced here, beginning with 1917-18, the NHL's first season. New research has resulted in changes to scoring records in the NHL's first nine seasons.

MOST GOALS, ONE SEASON

44 —Joe Malone, Montreal, 1917-18.
    Scored goal #44 against Toronto's Harry Holmes on March 2, 1918 and finished the season with 44 goals.
50 —Maurice Richard, Montreal, 1944-45.
    Scored goal #45 against Toronto's Frank McCool on February 25, 1945 and finished the season with 50 goals.
50 —Bernie Geoffrion, Montreal, 1960-61.
    Scored goal #50 against Toronto's Cesare Maniago on March 16, 1961 and finished the season with 50 goals.
50 —Bobby Hull, Chicago, 1961-62.
    Scored goal #50 against NY Rangers' Gump Worsley on March 25, 1962 and finished the season with 50 goals.
54 —Bobby Hull, Chicago, 1965-66.
    Scored goal #51 against NY Rangers' Cesare Maniago on March 12, 1966 and finished the season with 54 goals.
58 —Bobby Hull, Chicago, 1968-69.
    Scored goal #55 against Boston's Gerry Cheevers on March 20, 1969 and finished the season with 58 goals.
76 —Phil Esposito, Boston, 1970-71.
    Scored goal #59 against Los Angeles' Denis DeJordy on March 11, 1971 and finished the season with 76 goals.
92 —Wayne Gretzky, Edmonton, 1981-82.
    Scored goal #77 against Buffalo's Don Edwards on February 24, 1982 and finished the season with 92 goals.

MOST ASSISTS, ONE SEASON

10 —Cy Denneny, Ottawa, 1917-18.
    —Reg Noble, Toronto, 1917-18.
    —Harry Cameron, Toronto, 1917-18.
    —Newsy Lalonde, Montreal, 1918-19.
15 —Frank Nighbor, Ottawa, 1919-20.
    —Jack Darragh, Ottawa, 1920-21.
17 —Harry Cameron, Toronto, 1921-22.
18 —Dick Irvin, Chicago, 1926-27.
    —Howie Morenz, Montreal, 1927-28.
36 —Frank Boucher, NY Rangers, 1929-30.
37 —Joe Primeau, Toronto, 1931-32.
45 —Bill Cowley, Boston, 1940-41.
    —Bill Cowley, Boston, 1942-43.
49 —Clint Smith, Chicago, 1943-44.
54 —Elmer Lach, Montreal, 1944-45.
55 —Ted Lindsay, Detroit, 1949-50.
56 —Bert Olmstead, Montreal, 1955-56.
58 —Jean Beliveau, Montreal, 1960-61.
    —Andy Bathgate, NY Rangers/Toronto, 1963-64.
59 —Stan Mikita, Chicago, 1964-65.
62 —Stan Mikita, Chicago, 1966-67.
77 —Phil Esposito, Boston, 1968-69.
87 —Bobby Orr, Boston, 1969-70.
102 —Bobby Orr, Boston, 1970-71.
109 —Wayne Gretzky, Edmonton, 1980-81.
120 —Wayne Gretzky, Edmonton, 1981-82.
125 —Wayne Gretzky, Edmonton, 1982-83.
135 —Wayne Gretzky, Edmonton, 1984-85.
163 —Wayne Gretzky, Edmonton, 1985-86.

MOST POINTS, ONE SEASON

48 —Joe Malone, Montreal, 1917-18.
49 —Joe Malone, Montreal, 1919-20.
51 —Howie Morenz, Montreal, 1927-28.
73 —Cooney Weiland, Boston, 1929-30.
    —Doug Bentley, Chicago, 1942-43.
82 —Herb Cain, Boston, 1943-44.
86 —Gordie Howe, Detroit, 1950-51.
95 —Gordie Howe, Detroit, 1952-53.
96 —Dickie Moore, Montreal, 1958-59.
97 —Bobby Hull, Chicago, 1965-66.
    —Stan Mikita, Chicago, 1966-67.
126 —Phil Esposito, Boston, 1968-69.
152 —Phil Esposito, Boston, 1970-71.
164 —Wayne Gretzky, Edmonton, 1980-81.
212 —Wayne Gretzky, Edmonton, 1981-82.
215 —Wayne Gretzky, Edmonton, 1985-86.

MOST REGULAR-SEASON GOALS, CAREER

44 —Joe Malone, Montreal.
    Malone led the NHL in goals in the league's first season with 44 goals in 20 games in 1917-18.
54 —Cy Denneny, Ottawa.
    Denneny passed Malone during the 1918-19 season, and led the NHL in goals with 54 after two seasons.
143 —Joe Malone, Montreal, Quebec Bulldogs, Hamilton.
    Malone passed Denneny during the 1919-20 season and finished his career with 143 goals.
248 —Cy Denneny, Ottawa, Boston.
    Denneny passed Malone with goal #144 during the 1922-23 season and finished his career with 248 goals.
271 —Howie Morenz, Montreal, Chicago, NY Rangers.
    Morenz passed Denneny with goal #249 during the 1933-34 season and finished his career with 271 goals.
324 —Nels Stewart, Montreal Maroons, Boston, NY Americans.
    Stewart passed Morenz with goal #272 during the 1936-37 season and finished his career with 324 goals.
544 —Maurice Richard, Montreal.
    Richard passed Stewart with goal #325 on Nov. 8, 1952 and finished his career with 544 goals.
801 —Gordie Howe, Detroit, Hartford.
    Howe passed Richard with goal #545 on Nov. 10, 1963 and finished his career with 801 goals.
894 —Wayne Gretzky, Edmonton, Los Angeles, St. Louis, NY Rangers.
    Gretzky passed Howe with goal #802 on March 23, 1994 and finished his career with 894 goals.

Seen here celebrating with some of his former Boston teammates as coach of the Stanley Cup-winning Bruins in 1940-41, Cooney Weiland (bottom center, in suit) shattered the previous single-season record when he scored 73 points in 44 games in 1929-30 after the NHL introduced forward passing in all three zones.

Gordie Howe and Wayne Gretzky admire an autographed commemorative shirt they've both signed after Gretzky surpassed Howe as the NHL's all-time scoring leader with his 1,851st point on October 15, 1989. Gretzky broke the record as a visitor with the Los Angeles Kings at his old home in Edmonton.

MOST REGULAR-SEASON ASSISTS, CAREER

(minimum 100 assists)

100 — Frank Boucher, Ottawa, NY Rangers.
    In 1930-31, Boucher became the first NHL player to reach the 100-assist milestone.

263 — Frank Boucher, Ottawa, NY Rangers.
    Boucher retired as the NHL's career assist leader in 1938 with 253. He returned to the NHL in 1943-44 and remained the NHL's career assist leader until he was overtaken by Bill Cowley in 1943-44. He finished his career with 263 assists.

353 — Bill Cowley, St. Louis Eagles, Boston.
    Cowley passed Boucher with assist #264 in 1943-44. He retired as the NHL's career assist leader in 1947 with 353.

408 — Elmer Lach, Montreal.
    Lach passed Cowley with assist #354 in 1951-52. He retired as the NHL's career assist leader in 1954 with 408.

1,049 — Gordie Howe, Detroit, Hartford.
    Howe passed Lach with assist #409 in 1957-58. He retired as the NHL's career assist leader in 1980 with 1,049.

1,963 — Wayne Gretzky, Edmonton, Los Angeles, St. Louis, NY Rangers.
    Gretzky passed Howe with assist #1,050 in 1987-88. He retired as the NHL's current career assist leader with 1,963.

MOST REGULAR-SEASON POINTS, CAREER

(minimum 100 points)

100 — Joe Malone, Montreal, Quebec Bulldogs, Hamilton.
    In 1919-20, Malone became the first player in NHL history to record 100 points.

200 — Cy Denneny, Ottawa.
    In 1923-24, Denneny became the first player in NHL history to record 200 points.

300 — Cy Denneny, Ottawa.
    In 1926-27, Denneny became the first player in NHL history to record 300 points.

333 — Cy Denneny, Ottawa, Boston.
    Denneny retired as the NHL's career point-scoring leader in 1929 with 333 points.

472 — Howie Morenz, Montreal, Chicago, NY Rangers.
    Morenz passed Cy Denneny with point #334 in 1931-32. At the time his career ended in 1937, he was the NHL's career point-scoring leader with 472 points.

515 — Nels Stewart, Montreal Maroons, Boston, NY Americans.
    Stewart passed Morenz with point #473 in 1938-39. He retired as the NHL's career point-scoring leader in 1940 with 515 points.

528 — Syd Howe, Ottawa, Philadelphia Quakers, Toronto, St. Louis Eagles, Detroit.
    Howe passed Nels Stewart with point #516 on March 8, 1945. He retired as the NHL's career point-scoring leader in 1946 with 528 points.

548 — Bill Cowley, St. Louis Eagles, Boston.
    Cowley passed Syd Howe with point #529 on Feb. 12, 1947. He retired as the NHL's career point-scoring leader in 1947 with 548 points.

610 — Elmer Lach, Montreal.
    Lach passed Bill Cowley with point #549 on Feb. 23, 1952. He remained the NHL's career point-scoring leader until he was overtaken by Maurice Richard in 1953-54. He finished his career with 623 points.

946 — Maurice Richard, Montreal.
    Richard passed teammate Elmer Lach with point #611 on Dec. 12, 1953. He remained the NHL's career point-scoring leader until he was overtaken by Gordie Howe in 1959-60. He finished his career with 965 points.

1,850 — Gordie Howe, Detroit, Hartford.
    Howe passed Richard with point #947 on Jan. 16, 1960. He retired as the NHL's career point-scoring leader in 1980 with 1,850 points.

2,857 — Wayne Gretzky, Edmonton, Los Angeles, St. Louis, NY Rangers.
    Gretzky passed Howe with point #1,851 on Oct. 15, 1989. He retired as the NHL's current career points leader with 2,857.

Individual Records

Regular Season

SEASONS

MOST SEASONS:
- **26 – Gordie Howe**, Detroit, 1946-47 – 1970-71; Hartford, 1979-80.
- **– Chris Chelios**, Montreal, Chicago, Detroit, Atlanta 1983-84 – 2003-04, 2005-06 – 2009-10.
- 25 – Mark Messier, Edmonton, NY Rangers, Vancouver, 1979-80 – 2003-04.
- 24 – Alex Delvecchio, Detroit, 1950-51 – 1973-74.
- – Tim Horton, Toronto, NY Rangers, Pittsburgh, Buffalo, 1949-50, 1951-52 – 1973-74.
- 23 – John Bucyk, Detroit, Boston, 1955-56 – 1977-78.
- – Ron Francis, Hartford, Pittsburgh, Carolina, Toronto, 1981-82 – 2003-04.
- – Al MacInnis, Calgary, St. Louis, 1981-82 – 2003-04.
- – Dave Andreychuk, Buffalo, Toronto, New Jersey, Boston, Colorado, Tampa Bay, 1982-83 – 2003-04, 2005-06.

GAMES

MOST GAMES:
- **1,767 – Gordie Howe**, Detroit, 1946-47 – 1970-71; Hartford, 1979-80.
- 1,756 – Mark Messier, Edmonton, NY Rangers, Vancouver, 1979-80 – 2003-04.
- 1,731 – Ron Francis, Hartford, Pittsburgh, Carolina, Toronto, 1981-82 – 2003-04.
- 1,652 – Mark Recchi, Pittsburgh, Philadelphia, Montreal, Carolina, Tampa Bay, Boston, 1988-89 – 2003-04, 2005-06 – 2010-11.
- 1,651 – Chris Chelios, Montreal, Chicago, Detroit, Atlanta, 1983-84 – 2003-04, 2005-06 – 2009-10.
- 1,639 – Dave Andreychuk, Buffalo, Toronto, New Jersey, Boston, Colorado, Tampa Bay, 1982-83 – 2003-04, 2005-06.
- 1,635 – Scott Stevens, Washington, St. Louis, New Jersey, 1982-83 – 2003-04.

MOST GAMES, INCLUDING PLAYOFFS:
- **1,992 – Mark Messier**, Edmonton, NY Rangers, Vancouver, 1,756 regular-season games, 236 playoff games.
- 1,924 – Gordie Howe, Detroit, Hartford, 1,767 regular-season games, 157 playoff games.
- 1,917 – Chris Chelios, Montreal, Chicago, Detroit, Atlanta, 1,651 regular-season games, 266 playoff games.
- 1,902 – Ron Francis, Hartford, Pittsburgh, Carolina, Toronto, 1,731 regular-season games, 171 playoff games.
- 1,868 – Scott Stevens, Washington, St. Louis, New Jersey, 1,635 regular-season games, 233 playoff games.

MOST CONSECUTIVE GAMES:
- **964 – Doug Jarvis**, Montreal, Washington, Hartford, Oct. 8, 1975 – Oct. 10, 1987.
- 914 – Garry Unger, Toronto, Detroit, St. Louis, Atlanta, Feb. 24, 1968 – Dec. 21, 1979.
- 884 – Steve Larmer, Chicago, Oct. 6, 1982 – Apr. 15, 1993.
- 776 – Craig Ramsay, Buffalo, Mar. 27, 1973 – Feb. 10, 1983.
- 737 – Jay Bouwmeester, Florida, Calgary, St. Louis, Mar. 6, 2004 – Nov. 22, 2014.
- 679 – Henrik Sedin, Vancouver, Mar. 21, 2004 – Jan. 18, 2014.
- 630 – Andy Hebenton, NY Rangers, Boston, Oct. 7, 1955 – Mar. 22, 1964.

GOALS

MOST GOALS:
- **894 – Wayne Gretzky**, Edmonton, Los Angeles, St. Louis, NY Rangers, in 20 seasons. 1,487GP
- 801 – Gordie Howe, Detroit, Hartford, in 26 seasons. 1,767GP
- 741 – Brett Hull, Calgary, St. Louis, Dallas, Detroit, Phoenix, in 19 seasons. 1,269GP
- 731 – Marcel Dionne, Detroit, Los Angeles, NY Rangers, in 18 seasons. 1,348GP
- 722 – Jaromir Jagr, Pittsburgh, Washington, NY Rangers, Philadelphia, Dallas, Boston, New Jersey, Florida, in 21 seasons. 1,550GP
- 717 – Phil Esposito, Chicago, Boston, NY Rangers, in 18 seasons. 1,282GP

MOST GOALS, INCLUDING PLAYOFFS:
- **1,016 – Wayne Gretzky**, Edmonton, Los Angeles, St. Louis, NY Rangers, 894G in 1,487 regular-season games, 122G in 208 playoff games.
- 869 – Gordie Howe, Detroit, Hartford, 801G in 1,767 regular-season games, 68G in 157 playoff games.
- 844 – Brett Hull, Calgary, St. Louis, Dallas, Detroit, Phoenix, 741G in 1,269 regular-season games, 103G in 202 playoff games.
- 803 – Mark Messier, Edmonton, NY Rangers, Vancouver, 694G in 1,756 regular-season games, 109G in 236 playoff games.
- 800 – Jaromir Jagr, Pittsburgh, Washington, NY Rangers, Philadelphia, Dallas, Boston, New Jersey, Florida, 722G in 1,550 regular-season games, 78G in 202 playoff games.
- 778 – Phil Esposito, Chicago, Boston, NY Rangers, 717G in 1,282 regular-season games, 61G in 130 playoff games.

MOST GOALS, ONE SEASON:
- **92 – Wayne Gretzky**, Edmonton, 1981-82. 80GP – 80 game schedule.
- 87 – Wayne Gretzky, Edmonton, 1983-84. 74GP – 80 game schedule.
- 86 – Brett Hull, St. Louis, 1990-91. 78GP – 80 game schedule.
- 85 – Mario Lemieux, Pittsburgh, 1988-89. 76GP – 80 game schedule.
- 76 – Phil Esposito, Boston, 1970-71. 78GP – 78 game schedule.
- – Alexander Mogilny, Buffalo, 1992-93. 77GP – 84 game schedule.
- – Teemu Selanne, Winnipeg, 1992-93. 84GP – 84 game schedule.
- 73 – Wayne Gretzky, Edmonton, 1984-85. 80GP – 80 game schedule.
- 72 – Brett Hull, St. Louis, 1989-90. 80GP – 80 game schedule.
- 71 – Wayne Gretzky, Edmonton, 1982-83. 80GP – 80 game schedule.
- – Jari Kurri, Edmonton, 1984-85. 73GP – 80 game schedule.
- 70 – Mario Lemieux, Pittsburgh, 1987-88. 77GP – 80 game schedule.
- – Bernie Nicholls, Los Angeles, 1988-89. 79GP – 80 game schedule.
- – Brett Hull, St. Louis, 1991-92. 73GP – 80 game schedule.

MOST GOALS, ONE SEASON, INCLUDING PLAYOFFS:
- **100 – Wayne Gretzky**, Edmonton, 1983-84. 87G in 74 regular-season games, 13G in 19 playoff games.
- 97 – Wayne Gretzky, Edmonton, 1981-82, 92G in 80 regular-season games, 5G in 5 playoff games.
- – Mario Lemieux, Pittsburgh, 1988-89, 85G in 76 regular-season games, 12G in 11 playoff games.
- – Brett Hull, St. Louis, 1990-91, 86G in 78 regular-season games, 11G in 13 playoff games.
- 90 – Wayne Gretzky, Edmonton, 1984-85, 73G in 80 regular-season games, 17G in 18 playoff games.
- – Jari Kurri, Edmonton, 1984-85, 71G in 80 regular-season games, 19G in 18 playoff games.
- 85 – Mike Bossy, NY Islanders, 1980-81, 68G in 79 regular-season games, 17G in 18 playoff games.
- – Brett Hull, St. Louis, 1989-90, 72G in 80 regular-season games, 13G in 12 playoff games.
- 83 – Wayne Gretzky, Edmonton, 1982-83, 71G in 73 regular-season games, 12G in 16 playoff games.
- – Alexander Mogilny, Buffalo, 1992-93, 76G in 77 regular-season games, 7G in 7 playoff games.

MOST GOALS, 50 GAMES FROM START OF SEASON:
- **61 – Wayne Gretzky**, Edmonton, 1981-82. Oct. 7, 1981 – Jan. 22, 1982. (80-game schedule)
- – **Wayne Gretzky**, Edmonton, 1983-84. Oct. 5, 1983 – Jan. 25, 1984. (80-game schedule)
- 54 – Mario Lemieux, Pittsburgh, 1988-89. Oct. 7, 1988 – Jan. 31, 1989. (80-game schedule)
- 53 – Wayne Gretzky, Edmonton, 1984-85. Oct. 11, 1984 – Jan. 28, 1985. (80-game schedule)
- 52 – Brett Hull, St. Louis, 1990-91. Oct. 4, 1990 – Jan. 26, 1991. (80-game schedule)
- 50 – Maurice Richard, Montreal, 1944-45. Oct. 28, 1944 – Mar. 18, 1945. (50-game schedule)
- – Mike Bossy, NY Islanders, 1980-81. Oct. 11, 1980 – Jan. 24, 1981. (80-game schedule)
- – Brett Hull, St. Louis, 1991-92. Oct. 5, 1991 – Jan. 28, 1992. (80-game schedule)

MOST GOALS, ONE GAME:
- **7 – Joe Malone**, Quebec, Jan. 31, 1920, at Quebec. Quebec 10, Toronto 6.
- 6 – Newsy Lalonde, Montreal, Jan. 10, 1920, at Montreal. Montreal 14, Toronto 7.
- – Joe Malone, Quebec, Mar. 10, 1920, at Quebec. Quebec 10, Ottawa 4.
- – Corb Denneny, Toronto, Jan. 26, 1921, at Toronto. Toronto 10, Hamilton 3.
- – Cy Denneny, Ottawa, Mar. 7, 1921, at Ottawa. Ottawa 12, Hamilton 5.
- – Syd Howe, Detroit, Feb. 3, 1944, at Detroit. Detroit 12, NY Rangers 2.
- – Red Berenson, St. Louis, Nov. 7, 1968, at Philadelphia. St. Louis 8, Philadelphia 0.
- – Darryl Sittler, Toronto, Feb. 7, 1976, at Toronto. Toronto 11, Boston 4.

Combined, Gordie Howe and Alex Delvecchio played 49 seasons for the Red Wings. Howe spent 25 of his 26 NHL seasons in Detroit, while Delvecchio played his entire 24-year career in the Motor City.

Seen here in action against the Boston Bruins during the 1970s, Red Berenson is the only NHL player to score six goals in a road game. The St. Louis Blues won this game 8-0 in Philadelphia on November 7, 1968.

MOST GOALS, ONE ROAD GAME:

6 – **Red Berenson**, St. Louis, Nov. 7, 1968, at Philadelphia. St. Louis 8, Philadelphia 0.

5 – Joe Malone, Montreal, Dec. 19, 1917, at Ottawa. Montreal 7, Ottawa 4.
 – Red Green, Hamilton, Dec. 5, 1924, at Toronto. Hamilton 10, Toronto 3.
 – Babe Dye, Toronto, Dec. 22, 1924, at Boston. Toronto 10, Boston 1.
 – Punch Broadbent, Mtl. Maroons, Jan. 7, 1925, at Hamilton. Mtl. Maroons 6, Hamilton 2.
 – Don Murdoch, NY Rangers, Oct. 12, 1976, at Minnesota. NY Rangers 10, Minnesota 4.
 – Tim Young, Minnesota, Jan. 15, 1979, at NY Rangers. Minnesota 8, NY Rangers 1.
 – Willy Lindstrom, Winnipeg, Mar. 2, 1982, at Philadelphia. Winnipeg 7, Philadelphia 6.
 – Bengt Gustafsson, Washington, Jan. 8, 1984, at Philadelphia. Washington 7, Philadelphia 1.
 – Wayne Gretzky, Edmonton, Dec. 15, 1984, at St. Louis. Edmonton 8, St. Louis 2.
 – Dave Andreychuk, Buffalo, Feb. 6, 1986, at Boston. Buffalo 8, Boston 6.
 – Mats Sundin, Quebec, Mar. 5, 1992, at Hartford. Quebec 10, Hartford 4.
 – Mario Lemieux, Pittsburgh, Apr. 9, 1993, at NY Rangers. Pittsburgh 10, NY Rangers 4.
 – Mike Ricci, Quebec, Feb. 17, 1994, at San Jose. Quebec 8, San Jose 2.
 – Alex Zhamnov, Winnipeg, Apr. 1, 1995, at Los Angeles. Winnipeg 7, Los Angeles 7.
 – Johan Franzem, Detroit, Feb 2, 2011, at Ottawa. Detroit 7, Ottawa 5.

MOST GOALS, ONE PERIOD:

4 – **Busher Jackson**, Toronto, Nov. 20, 1934, at St. Louis, third period. Toronto 5, St. Louis 2.
 – **Max Bentley**, Chicago, Jan. 28, 1943, at Chicago, third period. Chicago 10, NY Rangers 1.
 – **Clint Smith**, Chicago, Mar. 4, 1945, at Chicago, third period. Chicago 6, Montreal 4.
 – **Red Berenson**, St. Louis, Nov. 7, 1968, at Philadelphia, second period. St. Louis 8, Philadelphia 0.
 – **Wayne Gretzky**, Edmonton, Feb. 18, 1981, at Edmonton, third period. Edmonton 9, St. Louis 2.
 – **Grant Mulvey**, Chicago, Feb. 3, 1982, at Chicago, first period. Chicago 9, St. Louis 5.
 – **Bryan Trottier**, NY Islanders, Feb. 13, 1982, at NY Islanders, second period. NY Islanders 8, Philadelphia 2.
 – **Al Secord**, Chicago, Jan. 7, 1987, at Chicago, second period. Chicago 6, Toronto 4.
 – **Joe Nieuwendyk**, Calgary, Jan. 11, 1989, at Calgary, second period. Calgary 8, Winnipeg 3.
 – **Peter Bondra**, Washington, Feb. 5, 1994, at Washington, first period. Washington 6, Tampa Bay 3.
 – **Mario Lemieux**, Pittsburgh, Jan. 26, 1997, at Montreal, third period. Pittsburgh 5, Montreal 2.

ASSISTS

MOST ASSISTS:

1,963 – Wayne Gretzky, Edmonton, Los Angeles, St. Louis, NY Rangers, in 20 seasons. 1,487GP
1,249 – Ron Francis, Hartford, Pittsburgh, Carolina, Toronto, in 23 seasons. 1,731GP
1,193 – Mark Messier, Edmonton, NY Rangers, Vancouver, in 25 seasons. 1,756GP
1,169 – Raymond Bourque, Boston, Colorado, in 22 seasons. 1,612GP
1,135 – Paul Coffey, Edmonton, Pittsburgh, Los Angeles, Detroit, Hartford, Philadelphia, Chicago, Carolina, Boston, in 21 seasons. 1,409GP

MOST ASSISTS, INCLUDING PLAYOFFS:

2,223 – Wayne Gretzky, Edmonton, Los Angeles, St. Louis, NY Rangers, 1,963A in 1,487 regular-season games, 260A in 208 playoff games.
1,379 – Mark Messier, Edmonton, NY Rangers, Vancouver, 1,193A in 1,756 regular-season games, 186A in 236 playoff games.
1,346 – Ron Francis, Hartford, Pittsburgh, Carolina, Toronto, 1,249A in 1,731 regular-season games, 97A in 171 playoff games.
1,308 – Raymond Bourque, Boston, Colorado, 1,169A in 1,612 regular-season games, 139A in 214 playoff games.
1,272 – Paul Coffey, Edmonton, Pittsburgh, Los Angeles, Detroit, Hartford, Philadelphia, Chicago, Carolina, Boston, 1,135A in 1,409 regular-season games, 137A in 194 playoff games.

MOST ASSISTS, ONE SEASON:

163 – Wayne Gretzky, Edmonton, 1985-86. 80GP – 80 game schedule.
135 – Wayne Gretzky, Edmonton, 1984-85. 80GP – 80 game schedule.
125 – Wayne Gretzky, Edmonton, 1982-83. 80GP – 80 game schedule.
122 – Wayne Gretzky, Los Angeles, 1990-91. 78GP – 80 game schedule.
121 – Wayne Gretzky, Edmonton, 1986-87. 79GP – 80 game schedule.
120 – Wayne Gretzky, Edmonton, 1981-82. 80GP – 80 game schedule.
118 – Wayne Gretzky, Edmonton, 1983-84. 74GP – 80 game schedule.
114 – Mario Lemieux, Pittsburgh, 1988-89. 76GP – 80 game schedule.
 – Wayne Gretzky, Los Angeles, 1988-89. 78GP – 80 game schedule.
109 – Wayne Gretzky, Edmonton, 1980-81. 80GP – 80 game schedule.
 – Wayne Gretzky, Edmonton, 1987-88. 64GP – 80 game schedule.
102 – Bobby Orr, Boston, 1970-71. 78GP – 78 game schedule.
 – Wayne Gretzky, Los Angeles, 1989-90. 73GP – 80 game schedule.

MOST ASSISTS, ONE SEASON, INCLUDING PLAYOFFS:
174 – Wayne Gretzky, Edmonton, 1985-86,
163A in 80 regular-season games, 11A in 10 playoff games.
165 – Wayne Gretzky, Edmonton, 1984-85,
135A in 80 regular-season games, 30A in 18 playoff games.
151 – Wayne Gretzky, Edmonton, 1982-83,
125A in 80 regular-season games, 26A in 16 playoff games.
150 – Wayne Gretzky, Edmonton, 1986-87,
121A in 79 regular-season games, 29A in 21 playoff games.
140 – Wayne Gretzky, Edmonton, 1983-84,
118A in 74 regular-season games, 22A in 19 playoff games.
– Wayne Gretzky, Edmonton, 1987-88,
109A in 64 regular-season games, 31A in 19 playoff games.
133 – Wayne Gretzky, Los Angeles, 1990-91,
122A in 78 regular-season games, 11A in 12 playoff games.
131 – Wayne Gretzky, Los Angeles, 1988-89,
114A in 78 regular-season games, 17A in 11 playoff games.
127 – Wayne Gretzky, Edmonton, 1981-82,
120A in 80 regular-season games, 7A in 5 playoff games.
123 – Wayne Gretzky, Edmonton, 1980-81,
109A in 80 regular-season games, 14A in 9 playoff games.
121 – Mario Lemieux, Pittsburgh, 1988-89,
114A in 76 regular-season games, 7A in 11 playoff games.

MOST ASSISTS, ONE GAME:
7 – Billy Taylor, Detroit, Mar. 16, 1947, at Chicago. Detroit 10, Chicago 6.
– **Wayne Gretzky**, Edmonton, Feb. 15, 1980, at Edmonton.
Edmonton 8, Washington 2.
– **Wayne Gretzky**, Edmonton, Dec. 11, 1985, at Chicago.
Edmonton 12, Chicago 9.
– **Wayne Gretzky**, Edmonton, Feb. 14, 1986, at Edmonton.
Edmonton 8, Quebec 2.
6 – Six assists have been recorded in one game on 24 occasions since
Elmer Lach of Montreal first accomplished the feat vs. Boston on
Feb. 6, 1943. The most recent player is Eric Lindros of Philadelphia
on Feb. 26, 1997 at Ottawa.

MOST ASSISTS, ONE ROAD GAME:
7 – Billy Taylor, Detroit, Mar. 16, 1947, at Chicago. Detroit 10, Chicago 6.
– **Wayne Gretzky**, Edmonton, Dec. 11, 1985, at Chicago.
Edmonton 12, Chicago 9.
6 – Bobby Orr, Boston, Jan. 1, 1973, at Vancouver. Boston 8, Vancouver 2.
– Patrik Sundstrom, Vancouver, Feb. 29, 1984, at Pittsburgh.
Vancouver 9, Pittsburgh 5.
– Mario Lemieux, Pittsburgh, Dec. 5, 1992, at San Jose.
Pittsburgh 9, San Jose 4.
– Eric Lindros, Philadelphia, Feb. 26, 1997, at Ottawa.
Philadelphia 8, Ottawa 5.

MOST ASSISTS, ONE PERIOD:
5 – Dale Hawerchuk, Winnipeg, Mar. 6, 1984, at Los Angeles,
second period. Winnipeg 7, Los Angeles 3.
4 – Four assists have been recorded in one period on 70 occasions since
Mickey Roach of Hamilton first accomplished the feat vs. Toronto
on Feb. 23, 1921. The most recent player is Rostislav Klesla of Phoenix
on Mar. 28, 2013 vs. Nashville.

POINTS

MOST POINTS:
2,857 – Wayne Gretzky, Edmonton, Los Angeles, St. Louis, NY Rangers,
in 20 seasons. 1,487GP (894G–1,963A)
1,887 – Mark Messier, Edmonton, NY Rangers, Vancouver,
in 25 seasons. 1,756GP (694G–1,193A)
1,850 – Gordie Howe, Detroit, Hartford, in 26 seasons. 1,767GP (801G–1,049A)
1,802 – Jaromir Jagr, Pittsburgh, Washington, NY Rangers, Philadelphia, Dallas,
Boston, New Jersey, Florida, in 21 seasons. 1,550GP (722G–1,080A)
1,798 – Ron Francis, Hartford, Pittsburgh, Carolina, Toronto,
in 23 seasons. 1,731GP (549G–1,249A)
1,771 – Marcel Dionne, Detroit, Los Angeles, NY Rangers,
in 18 seasons. 1,348GP (731G–1,040A)

MOST POINTS, INCLUDING PLAYOFFS:
3,239 – Wayne Gretzky, Edmonton, Los Angeles, St. Louis, NY Rangers,
2,857PTS in 1,487 regular-season games, 382PTS in 208 playoff games.
2,182 – Mark Messier, Edmonton, NY Rangers, Vancouver,
1,887PTS in 1,756 regular-season games, 295PTS in 236 playoff games.
2,010 – Gordie Howe, Detroit, Hartford,
1,850PTS in 1,767 regular-season games, 160PTS in 157 playoff games.
2,001 – Jaromir Jagr, Pittsburgh, Washington, NY Rangers, Philadelphia, Dallas,
Boston, New Jersey, Florida, 1,802PTS in 1,550 regular-season games,
199PTS in 202 playoff games.
1,941 – Ron Francis, Hartford, Pittsburgh, Carolina, Toronto,
1,798PTS in 1,731 regular-season games, 143PTS in 171 playoff games.
1,940 – Steve Yzerman, Detroit,
1,755PTS in 1,514 regular-season games, 185PTS in 196 playoff games.

MOST POINTS, ONE SEASON:
215 – Wayne Gretzky, Edmonton, 1985-86. 80GP – 80 game schedule.
212 – Wayne Gretzky, Edmonton, 1981-82. 80GP – 80 game schedule.
208 – Wayne Gretzky, Edmonton, 1984-85. 80GP – 80 game schedule.
205 – Wayne Gretzky, Edmonton, 1983-84. 74GP – 80 game schedule.
199 – Mario Lemieux, Pittsburgh, 1988-89. 76GP – 80 game schedule.
196 – Wayne Gretzky, Edmonton, 1982-83. 80GP – 80 game schedule.
183 – Wayne Gretzky, Edmonton, 1986-87. 79GP – 80 game schedule.
168 – Mario Lemieux, Pittsburgh, 1987-88. 77GP – 80 game schedule.
– Wayne Gretzky, Los Angeles, 1988-89. 78GP – 80 game schedule.
164 – Wayne Gretzky, Edmonton, 1980-81. 80GP – 80 game schedule.
163 – Wayne Gretzky, Los Angeles, 1990-91. 78GP – 80 game schedule.
161 – Mario Lemieux, Pittsburgh, 1995-96. 70GP – 82 game schedule.
160 – Mario Lemieux, Pittsburgh, 1992-93. 60GP – 84 game schedule.

MOST POINTS, ONE SEASON, INCLUDING PLAYOFFS:
255 – Wayne Gretzky, Edmonton, 1984-85,
208PTS in 80 regular-season games, 47PTS in 18 playoff games.
240 – Wayne Gretzky, Edmonton, 1983-84,
205PTS in 74 regular-season games, 35PTS in 19 playoff games.
234 – Wayne Gretzky, Edmonton, 1982-83,
196PTS in 80 regular-season games, 38PTS in 16 playoff games.
– Wayne Gretzky, Edmonton, 1985-86,
215PTS in 80 regular-season games, 19PTS in 10 playoff games.
224 – Wayne Gretzky, Edmonton, 1981-82,
212PTS in 80 regular-season games, 12PTS in 5 playoff games.
218 – Mario Lemieux, Pittsburgh, 1988-89,
199PTS in 76 regular-season games, 19PTS in 11 playoff games.
217 – Wayne Gretzky, Edmonton, 1986-87,
183PTS in 79 regular-season games, 34PTS in 21 playoff games.
192 – Wayne Gretzky, Edmonton, 1987-88,
149PTS in 64 regular-season games, 43PTS in 19 playoff games.
190 – Wayne Gretzky, Los Angeles, 1988-89,
168PTS in 78 regular-season games, 22PTS in 11 playoff games.
188 – Mario Lemieux, Pittsburgh, 1995-96,
161PTS in 70 regular-season games, 27PTS in 18 playoff games.
185 – Wayne Gretzky, Edmonton, 1980-81,
164PTS in 80 regular-season games, 21PTS in 9 playoff games.

MOST POINTS, ONE GAME:
10 – Darryl Sittler, Toronto, Feb. 7, 1976, at Toronto, 6G-4A.
Toronto 11, Boston 4.
8 – Maurice Richard, Montreal, Dec. 28, 1944, at Montreal, 5G-3A.
Montreal 9, Detroit 1.
– Bert Olmstead, Montreal, Jan. 9, 1954, at Montreal, 4G-4A.
Montreal 12, Chicago 1.
– Tom Bladon, Philadelphia, Dec. 11, 1977, at Philadelphia, 4G-4A.
Philadelphia 11, Cleveland 1.
– Bryan Trottier, NY Islanders, Dec. 23, 1978, at NY Islanders, 5G-3A.
NY Islanders 9, NY Rangers 4.
– Peter Stastny, Quebec, Feb. 22, 1981, at Washington, 4G-4A.
Quebec 11, Washington 7.
– Anton Stastny, Quebec, Feb. 22, 1981, at Washington, 3G-5A.
Quebec 11, Washington 7.
– Wayne Gretzky, Edmonton, Nov. 19, 1983, at Edmonton, 3G-5A.
Edmonton 13, New Jersey 4.
– Wayne Gretzky, Edmonton, Jan. 4, 1984, at Edmonton, 4G-4A.
Edmonton 12, Minnesota 8.
– Paul Coffey, Edmonton, Mar. 14, 1986, at Edmonton, 2G-6A.
Edmonton 12, Detroit 3.
– Mario Lemieux, Pittsburgh, Oct. 15, 1988, at Pittsburgh, 2G-6A.
Pittsburgh 9, St. Louis 2.
– Bernie Nicholls, Los Angeles, Dec. 1, 1988, at Los Angeles, 2G-6A.
Los Angeles 9, Toronto 3.
– Mario Lemieux, Pittsburgh, Dec. 31, 1988, at Pittsburgh, 5G-3A.
Pittsburgh 8, New Jersey 6.
– Sam Gagner, Edmonton, Feb. 2, 2012, at Edmonton, 4G-4A.
Edmonton 8, Chicago 4.

MOST POINTS, ONE ROAD GAME:
8 – Peter Stastny, Quebec, Feb. 22, 1981, at Washington. 4G-4A.
Quebec 11, Washington 7.
– **Anton Stastny**, Quebec, Feb. 22, 1981, at Washington. 3G-5A.
Quebec 11, Washington 7.
7 – Red Green, Hamilton, Dec. 5, 1924, at Toronto. 5G-2A.
Hamilton 10, Toronto 3.
– Billy Taylor, Detroit, Mar. 16, 1947, at Chicago. 7A. Detroit 10, Chicago 6.
– Red Berenson, St. Louis, Nov. 7, 1968, at Philadelphia. 6G-1A.
St. Louis 8, Philadelphia 0.
– Gilbert Perreault, Buffalo, Feb. 1, 1976, at California. 2G-5A.
Buffalo 9, California 5.
– Peter Stastny, Quebec, Apr. 1, 1982, at Boston. 3G-4A. Quebec 8, Boston 5.
– Wayne Gretzky, Edmonton, Nov. 6, 1983, at Winnipeg. 4G-3A.
Edmonton 8, Winnipeg 5.
– Patrik Sundstrom, Vancouver, Feb. 29, 1984, at Pittsburgh. 1G-6A.
Vancouver 9, Pittsburgh 5.
– Wayne Gretzky, Edmonton, Dec. 11, 1985, at Chicago. 7A.
Edmonton 12, Chicago 9.
– Cam Neely, Boston, Oct. 16, 1988, at Chicago. 3G-4A.
Boston 10, Chicago 3.
– Mario Lemieux, Pittsburgh, Jan. 21, 1989, at Edmonton. 2G-5A.
Pittsburgh 7, Edmonton 4.
– Dino Ciccarelli, Washington, Mar. 18, 1989, at Hartford. 4G-3A.
Washington 8, Hartford 2.
– Mats Sundin, Quebec, Mar. 5, 1992, at Hartford. 5G-2A.
Quebec 10, Hartford 4.
– Mario Lemieux, Pittsburgh, Dec. 5, 1992, at San Jose. 1G-6A.
Pittsburgh 9, San Jose 4.
– Eric Lindros, Philadelphia, Feb. 26, 1997, at Ottawa. 1G-6A.
Philadelphia 8, Ottawa 5.
– Daniel Alfredsson, Ottawa, Jan. 24, 2008, at Tampa Bay. 3G-4A.
Ottawa 8, Tampa Bay 4.

MOST POINTS, ONE PERIOD:
6 – Bryan Trottier, NY Islanders, Dec. 23, 1978, at NY Islanders, second period. 3G-3A. NY Islanders 9, NY Rangers 4.
5 – Bill Cook, NY Rangers, Mar. 12, 1933, at NY Americans, third period. 3G-2A. NY Rangers 8, NY Americans 2.
– **Les Cunningham**, Chicago, Jan. 28, 1940, at Chicago, third period. 2G-3A. Chicago 8, Montreal 1.
– **Max Bentley**, Chicago, Jan. 28, 1943, at Chicago, third period. 4G-1A. Chicago 10, NY Rangers 1.
– **Leo Labine**, Boston, Nov. 28, 1954, at Boston, second period. 3G-2A. Boston 6, Detroit 2.
– **Darryl Sittler**, Toronto, Feb. 7, 1976, at Toronto, second period. 3G-2A. Toronto 11, Boston 4.
– **Grant Mulvey**, Chicago, Feb. 3, 1982, at Chicago, first period. 4G-1A. Chicago 9, St. Louis 5.
– **Dale Hawerchuk**, Winnipeg, Mar. 6, 1984, at Los Angeles, second period. 5A. Winnipeg 7, Los Angeles 3.
– **Jari Kurri**, Edmonton, Oct. 26, 1984, at Edmonton, second period. 2G-3A. Edmonton 8, Los Angeles 2.
– **Pat Elynuik**, Winnipeg, Jan. 20, 1989, at Winnipeg, second period. 2G-3A. Winnipeg 7, Pittsburgh 3.
– **Ray Ferraro**, Hartford, Dec. 9, 1989, at Hartford, first period. 3G-2A. Hartford 7, New Jersey 3.
– **Stephane Richer**, Montreal, Feb. 14, 1990, at Montreal, first period. 2G-3A. Montreal 10, Vancouver 1.
– **Cliff Ronning**, Vancouver, Apr. 15, 1993, at Los Angeles, third period. 3G-2A. Vancouver 8, Los Angeles 6.
– **Peter Forsberg**, Colorado, Mar. 3, 1999, at Florida, third period. 2G-3A. Colorado 7, Florida 5.
– **Sam Gagner**, Edmonton, Feb. 2, 2012, at Edmonton, third period. 3G-2A. Edmonton 8, Chicago 4.

POWER-PLAY AND SHORTHAND GOALS

MOST POWER-PLAY GOALS, CAREER:
274 – Dave Andreychuk, Buffalo, Toronto, New Jersey, Boston, Colorado, Tampa Bay, in 23 seasons. 1,639GP.
265 – Brett Hull, Calgary, St. Louis, Dallas, Detroit, Phoenix, in 19 seasons. 1,269GP.
255 – Teemu Selanne, Winnipeg, Anaheim, San Jose, Colorado, in 21 seasons. 1,451GP.
249 – Phil Esposito, Chicago, Boston, NY Rangers, in 18 seasons. 1,282GP.

MOST POWER-PLAY GOALS, ONE SEASON:
34 – Tim Kerr, Philadelphia, 1985-86. 76GP – 80 game schedule.
32 – Dave Andreychuk, Buffalo, Toronto, 1992-93. 83GP – 84 game schedule.
31 – Joe Nieuwendyk, Calgary, 1987-88. 75GP – 80 game schedule.
– Mario Lemieux, Pittsburgh, 1988-89. 76GP – 80 game schedule.
– Mario Lemieux, Pittsburgh, 1995-96. 70GP – 82 game schedule.
29 – Michel Goulet, Quebec, 1987-88. 80GP – 80 game schedule.
– Brett Hull, St. Louis, 1990-91. 78GP – 80 game schedule.
– Brett Hull, St. Louis, 1992-93. 80GP – 84 game schedule.

MOST POWER-PLAY GOALS, ONE GAME
4 – Camille Henry, NY Rangers, Mar. 13, 1954, at Detroit. NY Rangers 5, Detroit 2.
– **Bernie Geoffrion**, Montreal, Feb. 19, 1955, at Montreal. Montreal 10, NY Rangers 2.
– **Bryan Trottier**, NY Islanders, Feb. 13, 1982, at NY Islanders. NY Islanders 8, Philadelphia 2.
– **Chris Valentine**, Washington, Feb. 27, 1982, at Washington. Washington 7, Hartford 1.
– **Dave Andreychuk**, Buffalo, Mar. 19, 1992, at Los Angeles. Buffalo 8, Los Angeles 2.
– **Mario Lemieux**, Pittsburgh, Mar. 20, 1993, at Pittsburgh. Pittsburgh 9, Philadelphia 4.
– **Luc Robitaille**, Los Angeles, Nov. 25, 1993, at Quebec. Quebec 8, Los Angeles 6.
– **Scott Mellanby**, St. Louis, Mar. 6, 2003, at St. Louis. St. Louis 6, Phoenix 3.

MOST SHORTHAND GOALS, ONE SEASON:
13 – Mario Lemieux, Pittsburgh, 1988-89. 76GP – 80 game schedule.
12 – Wayne Gretzky, Edmonton, 1983-84. 74GP – 80 game schedule.
11 – Wayne Gretzky, Edmonton, 1984-85. 80GP – 80 game schedule.
10 – Marcel Dionne, Detroit, 1974-75. 80GP – 80 game schedule.
– Mario Lemieux, Pittsburgh, 1987-88. 77GP – 80 game schedule.
– Dirk Graham, Chicago, 1988-89. 80GP – 80 game schedule.

MOST SHORTHAND GOALS, ONE GAME:
3 – Theoren Fleury, Calgary, Mar. 9, 1991, at St. Louis. Calgary 8, St. Louis 4.

OVERTIME SCORING
MOST OVERTIME GOALS, CAREER:
19 – Jaromir Jagr, Pittsburgh, Washington, NY Rangers, Philadelphia, Dallas, New Jersey.
16 – Patrik Elias, New Jersey.
15 – Alex Ovechkin, Washington.
– Mats Sundin, Quebec, Toronto.
– Sergei Fedorov, Detroit, Anaheim, Columbus, Washington.
14 – Ilya Kovalchuk, Atlanta, New Jersey.
13 – Steve Thomas, Toronto, Chicago, NY Islanders, New Jersey, Anaheim.
– Olli Jokinen, Los Angeles, NY Islanders, Florida, NY Rangers.
– Scott Niedermayer, New Jersey, Anaheim.
– Daniel Sedin, Vancouver.

MOST OVERTIME ASSISTS, CAREER:
21 – Nicklas Lidstrom, Detroit.
– **Patrik Elias**, New Jersey.
20 – Henrik Sedin, Vancouver.
18 – Mark Messier, Edmonton, NY Rangers, Vancouver.
– Pavol Demitra, Ottawa, St. Louis, Los Angeles, Minnesota, Vancouver.
– Tomas Kaberle, Toronto.
17 – Adam Oates, Detroit, St. Louis, Boston, Washington, Philadelphia, Anaheim.
– Cory Stillman, Calgary, St. Louis, Tampa Bay, Carolina, Ottawa, Florida.
– Ray Whitney, San Jose, Edmonton, Florida, Columbus, Detroit, Carolina, Phoenix.

MOST OVERTIME POINTS, CAREER:
37 – Patrik Elias, New Jersey. 16G-21A
35 – Jaromir Jagr, Pittsburgh, Washington, NY Rangers, Philadelphia, Dallas. New Jersey, Florida. 19G-16A
31 – Sergei Fedorov, Detroit, Anaheim, Columbus, Washington. 15G-16A
29 – Ilya Kovalchuk, Atlanta, New Jersey. 14G-15A
28 – Mats Sundin, Quebec, Toronto. 15G-13A
27 – Pavol Demitra, Ottawa, St. Louis, Los Angeles, Minnesota, Vancouver. 9G-18A
26 – Daniel Sedin, Vancouver. 13G-13A
– Mark Messier, Edmonton, NY Rangers, Vancouver. 8G-18A
25 – Joe Thornton, Boston, San Jose. 9G-16A
– Tomas Kaberle, Toronto, Boston. 7G-18A
– Nicklas Lidstrom, Detroit. 4G-21A

MOST OVERTIME GOALS, ONE SEASON:
5 – Steven Stamkos, Tampa Bay, 2011-12.
4 – Howie Morenz, Montreal, 1929-30.
– Frank Finnigan, Ottawa, 1929-30.
– Johnny Gagnon, Montreal, 1936-37.
– Mats Sundin, Toronto, 1999-2000.
– Scott Niedermayer, New Jersey, 2001-02.
– Patrik Elias, New Jersey, 2003-04.
– Markus Naslund, Vancouver, 2003-04.
– Olli Jokinen, Florida, 2005-06.
– Daniel Sedin, Vancouver, 2006-07.
– Ilya Kovalchuk, New Jersey, 2010-11.
– John Tavares, NY Islanders, 2014-15.

SHOOTOUT GOALS

MOST SHOOTOUT GOALS, ONE SEASON:
11 – Ilya Kovalchuk, New Jersey, 2011-12, (14s)
10 – Wojtek Wolski, Colorado, 2008-09, (12s)
– Jussi Jokinen, Dallas, 2005-06, (13s)
– Alex Tanguay, Calgary, 2010-11, (16s)

MOST SHOOTOUT GOALS, ALL-TIME:
40 – Jonathan Toews, Chicago, (80s)
39 – Brad Boyes, Boston, St. Louis, Buffalo, NY Islanders, Florida, (87s)
– Zach Parise, New Jersey, Minnesota, (90s)
– Mikko Koivu, Minnesota, (90s)

MOST SHOOTOUT SHOTS TAKEN, ONE SEASON:
18 – Radim Vrbata, Phoenix, 2009-10, (8G)
17 – Lauri Korpikoski, Phoenix, 2009-10, (7G)
– Nicklas Backstrom, Washington, 2013-14, (7G)
– Jack Johnson, Los Angeles, 2009-10, (6G)
– Sam Gagner, Edmonton, 2007-08, (5G)

MOST SHOOTOUT SHOTS TAKEN, ALL-TIME:
92 – Alex Ovechkin, Washington, (27G)
91 – Pavel Datsyuk, Detroit, (38G)
90 – Mikko Koivu, Minnesota, (39G)
– Zach Parise, New Jersey, Minnesota, (39G)

BEST SHOOTOUT SCORING PERCENTAGE, ONE SEASON: (minimum 5 shots)
.900 – Jarret Stoll, Los Angeles, 2010-11, (9G, 10s)
.857 – Petteri Nummelin, Minnesota, 2006-07, (6G, 7s)
– Joffrey Lupul, Toronto, 2013-14, (6G, 7s)
.833 – Wojtek Wolski, Colorado, 2008-09, (10G, 12s)
– Patrik Elias, New Jersey, 2007-08, (5G, 6s)
– Thomas Vanek, Buffalo, 2010-11, (5G, 6s)
– Matt Hendricks, Washington, 2011-12, (5G, 6s)
– Daniel Alfredsson, Ottawa, 2011-12, (5G, 6s)

BEST SHOOTOUT SCORING PERCENTAGE, CAREER: (minimum 10 shots)
.800 – Petteri Nummelin, Minnesota, (8G, 10s)
.609 – Jakob Silfverberg, Ottawa, Anaheim, (14G, 23s)
.587 – Vyacheslav Kozlov, Atlanta 27G, 46s)
.583 – Trevor Linden, Vancouvers, (7G, 12s)

MOST GAME DECIDING SHOOTOUT GOALS, ONE SEASON:
7 – Ilya Kovalchuk, New Jersey, 2011-12, (14s)
6 – Adrian Aucoin, Phoenix, 2009-10, (9s)
5 – Miroslav Satan, NY Islanders, 2005-06, (10s)
– Vyacheslav Kozlov, Atlanta, 2006-07, (11s)
– Viktor Kozlov, New Jersey, 2005-06, (12s)
– T.J. Oshie, St.Louis, 2013-14, (12s)
– Phil Kessel, Boston, 2007-08, (13s)
– Ales Kotalik, Buffalo, Edmonton, 2008-09, (13s)
– Anze Kopitar, Los Angeles, 2013-14, (13s)

MOST GAME DECIDING SHOOTOUT GOALS, CAREER:
16 – T.J. Oshie, St.Louis, (59s)
– **Sidney Crosby**, Pittsburgh, (71s)
– **Frans Nielsen**, NY Islanders, (72s)
– **Patrick Kane**, Chicago, (87s))
– **Mikko Koivu**, Minnesota, (90s)

SCORING BY A CENTER

MOST GOALS BY A CENTER, CAREER:
894 – **Wayne Gretzky**, Edmonton, Los Angeles, St. Louis, NY Rangers, in 20 seasons. 1,487GP
731 – Marcel Dionne, Detroit, Los Angeles, NY Rangers, in 18 seasons. 1,348GP
717 – Phil Esposito, Chicago, Boston, NY Rangers, in 18 seasons. 1,282GP
694 – Mark Messier, Edmonton, NY Rangers, Vancouver, in 25 seasons. 1,756GP
692 – Steve Yzerman, Detroit, in 22 seasons. 1,514GP

MOST GOALS BY A CENTER, ONE SEASON:
92 – **Wayne Gretzky**, Edmonton, 1981-82. 80GP – 80 game schedule.
87 – Wayne Gretzky, Edmonton, 1983-84. 74GP – 80 game schedule.
85 – Mario Lemieux, Pittsburgh, 1988-89. 76GP – 80 game schedule.
76 – Phil Esposito, Boston, 1970-71. 78GP – 78 game schedule.
73 – Wayne Gretzky, Edmonton, 1984-85. 80GP – 80 game schedule.

MOST ASSISTS BY A CENTER, CAREER:
1,963 – **Wayne Gretzky**, Edmonton, Los Angeles, St. Louis, NY Rangers, in 20 seasons. 1,487GP
1,249 – Ron Francis, Hartford, Pittsburgh, Carolina, Toronto, in 23 seasons. 1,731GP
1,193 – Mark Messier, Edmonton, NY Rangers, Vancouver, in 25 seasons. 1,756GP
1,079 – Adam Oates, Detroit, St. Louis, Boston, Washington, Philadelphia, Anaheim, Edmonton, in 19 seasons. 1,337GP
1,063 – Steve Yzerman, Detroit, in 22 seasons. 1,514GP

MOST ASSISTS BY A CENTER, ONE SEASON:
163 – **Wayne Gretzky**, Edmonton, 1985-86. 80GP – 80 game schedule.
135 – Wayne Gretzky, Edmonton, 1984-85. 80GP – 80 game schedule.
125 – Wayne Gretzky, Edmonton, 1982-83. 80GP – 80 game schedule.
122 – Wayne Gretzky, Los Angeles, 1990-91. 78GP – 80 game schedule.
121 – Wayne Gretzky, Edmonton, 1986-87. 79GP – 80 game schedule.

MOST POINTS BY A CENTER, CAREER:
2,857 – **Wayne Gretzky**, Edmonton, Los Angeles, St. Louis, NY Rangers, in 20 seasons. 1,487GP (894G-1,963A)
1,887 – Mark Messier, Edmonton, NY Rangers, Vancouver, in 25 seasons. 1,756GP (694G-1,193A)
1,798 – Ron Francis, Hartford, Pittsburgh, Carolina, Toronto, in 23 seasons. 1,731GP (549G-1,249A)
1,771 – Marcel Dionne, Detroit, Los Angeles, NY Rangers, in 18 seasons. 1,348GP (731G-1,040A)
1,755 – Steve Yzerman, Detroit, in 22 seasons. 1,514GP (692G-1,063A)

MOST POINTS BY A CENTER, ONE SEASON:
215 – **Wayne Gretzky**, Edmonton, 1985-86. 80GP – 80 game schedule.
212 – Wayne Gretzky, Edmonton, 1981-82. 80GP – 80 game schedule.
208 – Wayne Gretzky, Edmonton, 1984-85. 80GP – 80 game schedule.
205 – Wayne Gretzky, Edmonton, 1983-84. 74GP – 80 game schedule.
199 – Mario Lemieux, Pittsburgh, 1988-89. 76GP – 80 game schedule.

SCORING BY A LEFT WING

MOST GOALS BY A LEFT WING, CAREER:
668 – **Luc Robitaille**, Los Angeles, Pittsburgh, NY Rangers, Detroit, in 19 seasons. 1,431GP
656 – Brendan Shanahan, New Jersey, St. Louis, Hartford, Detroit, NY Rangers, in 21 seasons. 1,524GP
640 – Dave Andreychuk, Buffalo, Toronto, New Jersey, Boston, Colorado, Tampa Bay, in 23 seasons. 1,639GP
610 – Bobby Hull, Chicago, Winnipeg, Hartford, in 16 seasons. 1,063GP
556 – John Bucyk, Detroit, Boston, in 23 seasons. 1,540GP

MOST GOALS BY A LEFT WING, ONE SEASON:
65 – **Alex Ovechkin**, Washington, 2007-08. 82GP – 82 game schedule.
63 – Luc Robitaille, Los Angeles, 1992-93. 84GP – 84 game schedule.
60 – Steve Shutt, Montreal, 1976-77. 80GP – 80 game schedule.
58 – Bobby Hull, Chicago, 1968-69. 74GP – 76 game schedule.
57 – Michel Goulet, Quebec, 1982-83. 80GP – 80 game schedule.

MOST ASSISTS BY A LEFT WING, CAREER:
813 – **John Bucyk**, Detroit, Boston, in 23 seasons. 1,540GP
726 – Luc Robitaille, Los Angeles, Pittsburgh, NY Rangers, Detroit, in 19 seasons. 1,431GP
698 – Dave Andreychuk, Buffalo, Toronto, New Jersey, Boston, Colorado, Tampa Bay, in 23 seasons. 1,639GP
   – Brendan Shanahan, New Jersey, St. Louis, Hartford, Detroit, NY Rangers, in 21 seasons. 1,524GP
679 – Ray Whitney, San Jose, Edmonton, Florida, Columbus, Detroit, Carolina, Phoenix, Dallas, in 22 seasons. 1,330GP
604 – Michel Goulet, Quebec, Chicago, in 15 seasons. 1,089GP

MOST ASSISTS BY A LEFT WING, ONE SEASON:
70 – **Joe Juneau**, Boston, 1992-93. 84GP – 84 game schedule.
69 – Kevin Stevens, Pittsburgh, 1991-92. 80GP – 80 game schedule.
67 – Mats Naslund, Montreal, 1985-86. 80GP – 80 game schedule.
65 – John Bucyk, Boston, 1970-71. 78GP – 78 game schedule.
   – Michel Goulet, Quebec, 1983-84. 75GP – 80 game schedule.
64 – Mark Messier, Edmonton, 1983-84. 73GP – 80 game schedule.

MOST POINTS BY A LEFT WING, CAREER:
1,394 – **Luc Robitaille**, Los Angeles, Pittsburgh, NY Rangers, Detroit, in 19 seasons. 1,431GP (668G-726A)
1,369 – John Bucyk, Detroit, Boston, in 23 seasons. 1,540GP (556G-813A)
1,354 – Brendan Shanahan, New Jersey, St. Louis, Hartford, Detroit, NY Rangers, in 21 seasons. 1,524GP (656G-698A)
1,338 – Dave Andreychuk, Buffalo, Toronto, New Jersey, Boston, Colorado, Tampa Bay, in 23 seasons. 1,639GP (640G-698A)
1,170 – Bobby Hull, Chicago, Winnipeg, Hartford, in 16 seasons. 1,063GP (610G-560A)

MOST POINTS BY A LEFT WING, ONE SEASON:
125 – **Luc Robitaille**, Los Angeles, 1992-93. 84GP – 84 game schedule.
123 – Kevin Stevens, Pittsburgh, 1991-92. 80GP – 80 game schedule.
121 – Michel Goulet, Quebec, 1983-84. 75GP – 80 game schedule.
116 – John Bucyk, Boston, 1970-71. 78GP – 78 game schedule.
112 – Bill Barber, Philadelphia, 1975-76. 80GP – 80 game schedule.
   – Alex Ovechkin, Washington, 2007-08. 82GP – 82 game schedule.

SCORING BY A RIGHT WING

MOST GOALS BY A RIGHT WING, CAREER:
801 – **Gordie Howe**, Detroit, Hartford, in 26 seasons. 1,767GP
741 – Brett Hull, Calgary, St. Louis, Dallas, Detroit, Phoenix, in 19 seasons. 1,269GP
722 – Jaromir Jagr, Pittsburgh, Washington, NY Rangers, Philadelphia, Dallas, Boston, New Jersey, Florida, in 21 seasons. 1,733GP
708 – Mike Gartner, Washington, Minnesota, NY Rangers, Toronto, Phoenix, in 19 seasons. 1,432GP
684 – Teemu Selanne, Winnipeg, Anaheim, San Jose, Colorado, in 21 seasons. 1,451GP
608 – Dino Ciccarelli, Minnesota, Washington, Detroit, Tampa Bay, Florida, in 19 seasons. 1,232GP

MOST GOALS BY A RIGHT WING, ONE SEASON:
86 – **Brett Hull**, St. Louis, 1990-91. 78GP – 80 game schedule.
76 – Alexander Mogilny, Buffalo, 1992-93. 77GP – 84 game schedule.
   – Teemu Selanne, Winnipeg, 1992-93. 84GP – 84 game schedule.
72 – Brett Hull, St. Louis, 1989-90. 80GP – 80 game schedule.
71 – Jari Kurri, Edmonton, 1984-85. 73GP – 80 game schedule.
70 – Brett Hull, St. Louis, 1991-92. 73GP – 80 game schedule.

MOST ASSISTS BY A RIGHT WING, CAREER:
1,080 – **Jaromir Jagr**, Pittsburgh, Washington, NY Rangers, Philadelphia, Dallas, Boston, New Jersey, Florida, in 21 seasons. 1,550GP
1,049 – Gordie Howe, Detroit, Hartford, in 26 seasons. 1,767GP
956 – Mark Recchi, Pittsburgh, Philadelphia, Montreal, Carolina, Atlanta, Boston, in 22 seasons. 1,652GP
797 – Jari Kurri, Edmonton, Los Angeles, NY Rangers, Anaheim, Colorado, in 17 seasons. 1,251GP
793 – Guy Lafleur, Montreal, NY Rangers, Quebec, in 17 seasons. 1,126GP

MOST ASSISTS BY A RIGHT WING, ONE SEASON:
87 – **Jaromir Jagr**, Pittsburgh, 1995-96. 82GP – 82 game schedule.
83 – Mike Bossy, NY Islanders, 1981-82. 80GP – 80 game schedule.
   – Jaromir Jagr, Pittsburgh, 1998-99. 81GP – 82 game schedule.
80 – Guy Lafleur, Montreal, 1976-77. 80GP – 80 game schedule.
77 – Guy Lafleur, Montreal, 1978-79. 80GP – 80 game schedule.

Ray Whitney played with eight different teams during his 22 seasons in the NHL and ranks fifth all-time among left wingers with 679 career assists.

MOST POINTS BY A RIGHT WING, CAREER:

1,850 – Gordie Howe, Detroit, Hartford, in 26 seasons. 1,767GP (801G-1,049A)
1,802 – Jaromir Jagr, Pittsburgh, Washington, NY Rangers, Philadelphia, Dallas, Boston, New Jersey, Florida in 21 seasons. 1,550GP (722G-1,080A)
1,533 – Mark Recchi, Pittsburgh, Philadelphia, Montreal, Carolina, Atlanta, Boston, in 22 seasons. 1,652GP (577G-956A)
1,457 – Teemu Selanne, Winnipeg, Anaheim, San Jose, Colorado, in 21 seasons. 1,451GP (684G-773A)
1,398 – Jari Kurri, Edmonton, Los Angeles, NY Rangers, Anaheim, Colorado, in 17 seasons. 1,251GP (601G-797A)
1,391 – Brett Hull, Calgary, St. Louis, Dallas, Detroit, Phoenix, in 19 seasons. 1,269GP (741G-650A)

MOST POINTS BY A RIGHT WING, ONE SEASON:

149 – Jaromir Jagr, Pittsburgh, 1995-96. 82GP – 82 game schedule.
147 – Mike Bossy, NY Islanders, 1981-82. 80GP – 80 game schedule.
136 – Guy Lafleur, Montreal, 1976-77. 80GP – 80 game schedule.
135 – Jari Kurri, Edmonton, 1984-85. 73GP – 80 game schedule.
132 – Guy Lafleur, Montreal, 1977-78. 78GP – 80 game schedule.
– Teemu Selanne, Winnipeg, 1992-93. 84GP – 84 game schedule.

SCORING BY A DEFENSEMAN

MOST GOALS BY A DEFENSEMAN, CAREER:

410 – Raymond Bourque, Boston, Colorado, in 22 seasons. 1,612GP
396 – Paul Coffey, Edmonton, Pittsburgh, Los Angeles, Detroit, Hartford, Philadelphia, Chicago, Carolina, Boston, in 21 seasons. 1,409GP
340 – Al MacInnis, Calgary, St. Louis, in 23 seasons. 1,416GP
338 – Phil Housley, Buffalo, Winnipeg, St. Louis, Calgary, New Jersey, Washington, Chicago, Toronto, in 21 seasons. 1,495GP
310 – Denis Potvin, NY Islanders, in 15 seasons. 1,060GP

MOST GOALS BY A DEFENSEMAN, ONE SEASON:

48 – Paul Coffey, Edmonton, 1985-86. 79GP – 80 game schedule.
46 – Bobby Orr, Boston, 1974-75. 80GP – 80 game schedule.
40 – Paul Coffey, Edmonton, 1983-84. 80GP – 80 game schedule.
39 – Doug Wilson, Chicago, 1981-82. 76GP – 80 game schedule.
37 – Bobby Orr, Boston, 1970-71. 78GP – 78 game schedule.
– Bobby Orr, Boston, 1971-72. 76GP – 78 game schedule.
– Paul Coffey, Edmonton, 1984-85. 80GP – 80 game schedule.

MOST GOALS BY A DEFENSEMAN, ONE GAME:

5 – Ian Turnbull, Toronto, Feb. 2, 1977, at Toronto. Toronto 9, Detroit 1.
4 – Harry Cameron, Toronto, Dec. 26, 1917, at Toronto. Toronto 7, Montreal 5.
– Harry Cameron, Montreal, Mar. 3, 1920, at Quebec. Montreal 16, Quebec 3.
– Sprague Cleghorn, Montreal, Jan. 14, 1922, at Montreal. Montreal 10, Hamilton 6.
– John McKinnon, Pittsburgh, Nov. 19, 1929, at Pittsburgh. Pittsburgh 10, Toronto 5.
– Hap Day, Toronto, Nov. 19, 1929, at Pittsburgh. Pittsburgh 10, Toronto 5.
– Tom Bladon, Philadelphia, Dec. 11, 1977, at Philadelphia. Philadelphia 11, Cleveland 1.
– Ian Turnbull, Los Angeles, Dec. 12, 1981, at Los Angeles. Los Angeles 7, Vancouver 5.
– Paul Coffey, Edmonton, Dec. 26, 1984, at Calgary. Edmonton 6, Calgary 5.

MOST ASSISTS BY A DEFENSEMAN, CAREER:

1,169 – Raymond Bourque, Boston, Colorado, in 22 seasons. 1,612GP
1,135 – Paul Coffey, Edmonton, Pittsburgh, Los Angeles, Detroit, Hartford, Philadelphia, Chicago, Carolina, Boston, in 21 seasons. 1,409GP
934 – Al MacInnis, Calgary, St. Louis, in 23 seasons. 1,416GP
929 – Larry Murphy, Los Angeles, Washington, Minnesota, Pittsburgh, Toronto, Detroit, in 21 seasons. 1,615GP
894 – Phil Housley, Buffalo, Winnipeg, St. Louis, Calgary, New Jersey, Washington, Chicago, Toronto, in 21 seasons. 1,495GP

MOST ASSISTS BY A DEFENSEMAN, ONE SEASON:

102 – Bobby Orr, Boston, 1970-71. 78GP – 78 game schedule.
90 – Bobby Orr, Boston, 1973-74. 74GP – 78 game schedule.
– Paul Coffey, Edmonton, 1985-86. 79GP – 80 game schedule.
89 – Bobby Orr, Boston, 1974-75. 80GP – 80 game schedule.
87 – Bobby Orr, Boston, 1969-70. 76GP – 78 game schedule.

MOST ASSISTS BY A DEFENSEMAN, ONE GAME:

6 – Babe Pratt, Toronto, Jan. 8, 1944, at Toronto. Toronto 12, Boston 3.
– Pat Stapleton, Chicago, Mar. 30, 1969, at Chicago. Chicago 9, Detroit 5.
– Bobby Orr, Boston, Jan. 1, 1973, at Vancouver. Boston 8, Vancouver 2.
– Ron Stackhouse, Pittsburgh, Mar. 8, 1975, at Pittsburgh. Pittsburgh 8, Philadelphia 2.
– Paul Coffey, Edmonton, Mar. 14, 1986, at Edmonton. Edmonton 12, Detroit 3.
– Gary Suter, Calgary, Apr. 4, 1986, at Calgary. Calgary 9, Edmonton 3.

MOST POINTS BY A DEFENSEMAN, CAREER:

1,579 – Raymond Bourque, Boston, Colorado, in 22 seasons. 1,612GP (410G-1,169A)
1,531 – Paul Coffey, Edmonton, Pittsburgh, Los Angeles, Detroit, Hartford, Philadelphia, Chicago, Carolina, Boston, in 21 seasons. 1,409GP (396G-1,135A)
1,274 – Al MacInnis, Calgary, St. Louis, in 23 seasons. 1,416GP (340G-934A)
1,232 – Phil Housley, Buffalo, Winnipeg, St. Louis, Calgary, New Jersey, Washington, Chicago, Toronto, in 21 seasons. 1,495GP (338G-894A)
1,216 – Larry Murphy, Los Angeles, Washington, Minnesota, Pittsburgh, Toronto, Detroit, in 21 seasons. 1,615GP (287G-929A)

MOST POINTS BY A DEFENSEMAN, ONE SEASON:

139 – Bobby Orr, Boston, 1970-71. 78GP – 78 game schedule.
138 – Paul Coffey, Edmonton, 1985-86. 79GP – 80 game schedule.
135 – Bobby Orr, Boston, 1974-75. 80GP – 80 game schedule.
126 – Paul Coffey, Edmonton, 1983-84. 80GP – 80 game schedule.
122 – Bobby Orr, Boston, 1973-74. 74GP – 78 game schedule.

MOST POINTS BY A DEFENSEMAN, ONE GAME:

8 – Tom Bladon, Philadelphia, Dec. 11, 1977, at Philadelphia. 4G-4A. Philadelphia 11, Cleveland 1.
– **Paul Coffey**, Edmonton, Mar. 14, 1986, at Edmonton. 2G-6A. Edmonton 12, Detroit 3.
7 – Bobby Orr, Boston, Nov. 15, 1973, at Boston. 3G-4A. Boston 10, NY Rangers 2.

SCORING BY A GOALTENDER

MOST POINTS BY A GOALTENDER, CAREER:

48 – Tom Barrasso, Buffalo, Pittsburgh, Ottawa, Carolina, Toronto, St. Louis, in 19 seasons. 777GP
47 – Martin Brodeur, New Jersey, St. Louis, in 22 seasons. 1,266GP
46 – Grant Fuhr, Edmonton, Toronto, Buffalo, Los Angeles, St. Louis, Calgary, in 19 seasons. 868GP

MOST POINTS BY A GOALTENDER, ONE SEASON:

14 – Grant Fuhr, Edmonton, 1983-84. 45GP – 80 game schedule.
9 – Curtis Joseph, St. Louis, 1991-92. 60GP – 80 game schedule.
8 – Mike Palmateer, Washington, 1980-81. 49GP – 80 game schedule.
– Grant Fuhr, Edmonton, 1987-88. 75GP – 80 game schedule.
– Ron Hextall, Philadelphia, 1988-89. 64GP – 80 game schedule.
– Tom Barrasso, Pittsburgh, 1992-93. 63GP – 84 game schedule.

MOST POINTS BY A GOALTENDER, ONE GAME:

3 – Jeff Reese, Calgary, Feb. 10, 1993, at Calgary. Calgary 13, San Jose 1.

Defenseman Sprague Cleghorn scored four goals for the Canadiens in a 10-6 win over the Hamilton Tigers on January 14, 1922. His brother Odie Cleghorn, a forward, also had four goals in that game.

SCORING BY A ROOKIE

MOST GOALS BY A ROOKIE, ONE SEASON:
76 – Teemu Selanne, Winnipeg, 1992-93. 84GP – 84 game schedule.
53 – Mike Bossy, NY Islanders, 1977-78. 73GP – 80 game schedule.
52 – Alex Ovechkin, Washington, 2005-06. 81GP – 82 game schedule.
51 – Joe Nieuwendyk, Calgary, 1987-88. 75GP – 80 game schedule.
45 – Dale Hawerchuk, Winnipeg, 1981-82. 80GP – 80 game schedule.
– Luc Robitaille, Los Angeles, 1986-87. 79GP – 80 game schedule.

MOST GOALS BY A PLAYER IN HIS FIRST NHL SEASON, ONE GAME:
5 – Joe Malone, Montreal, Dec. 19, 1917, at Ottawa.
Montreal 7, Ottawa 4.
– Harry Hyland, Mtl. Wanderers, Dec. 19, 1917, at Montreal.
Mtl Wanderers 10, Toronto 9.
– Joe Malone, Montreal, Jan. 12, 1918, at Montreal.
Montreal 9, Ottawa 4.
– Joe Malone, Montreal, Feb. 2, 1918, at Montreal.
Montreal 11, Toronto 2.
– Mickey Roach, Toronto, Mar. 6, 1920, at Toronto. Toronto 11, Quebec 2.
– Howie Meeker, Toronto, Jan. 8, 1947, at Toronto. Toronto 10, Chicago 4.
– Don Murdoch, NY Rangers, Oct. 12, 1976, at Minnesota.
NY Rangers 10, Minnesota 4.

MOST GOALS BY A PLAYER IN HIS FIRST NHL GAME:
5 – Joe Malone, Montreal, Dec. 19, 1917, at Ottawa. Montreal 7, Ottawa 4.
– Harry Hyland, Mtl. Wanderers, Dec. 19, 1917, at Montreal.
Mtl Wanderers 10, Toronto 9.
3 – Alex Smart, Montreal, Jan. 14, 1943, at Montreal. Montreal 5, Chicago 1.
– Real Cloutier, Quebec, Oct. 10, 1979, at Quebec. Atlanta 5, Quebec 3.
– Fabian Brunnstrom, Dallas, Oct. 15, 2008, at Dallas.
Dallas 6, Nashville 4.
– Derek Stepan, NY Rangers, Oct. 9, 2010, at Buffalo.
NY Rangers 6, Buffalo 3.

MOST ASSISTS BY A ROOKIE, ONE SEASON:
70 – Peter Stastny, Quebec, 1980-81. 77GP – 80 game schedule.
– Joe Juneau, Boston, 1992-93. 84GP – 84 game schedule.
63 – Bryan Trottier, NY Islanders, 1975-76. 80GP – 80 game schedule.
– Sidney Crosby, Pittsburgh, 2005-06. 81GP – 82 game schedule.
62 – Sergei Makarov, Calgary, 1989-90. 80GP – 80 game schedule.
60 – Larry Murphy, Los Angeles, 1980-81. 80GP – 80 game schedule.

MOST ASSISTS BY A PLAYER IN HIS FIRST NHL SEASON, ONE GAME:
7 – Wayne Gretzky, Edmonton, Feb. 15, 1980, at Edmonton.
Edmonton 8, Washington 2.
6 – Gary Suter, Calgary, Apr. 4, 1986, at Calgary. Calgary 9, Edmonton 3.

MOST ASSISTS BY A PLAYER IN HIS FIRST NHL GAME:
4 – Dutch Reibel, Detroit, Oct. 8, 1953, at Detroit. Detroit 4, NY Rangers 1.
– Roland Eriksson, Minnesota, Oct. 6, 1976, at NY Rangers.
NY Rangers 6, Minnesota 5.
3 – Al Hill, Philadelphia, Feb. 14, 1977, at Philadelphia. Philadelphia 6,
St. Louis 4.
– Jarno Kultanen, Boston, Oct. 5, 2000, at Boston. Boston 4, Ottawa 4.
– Stanislav Chistov, Anaheim, Oct. 10, 2002, at St. Louis. Anaheim 4,
St. Louis 3.
– Dominic Moore, NY Rangers, Nov. 1, 2003, at Montreal. NY Rangers 5,
Montreal 1.

MOST POINTS BY A ROOKIE, ONE SEASON:
132 – Teemu Selanne, Winnipeg, 1992-93. 84GP – 84 game schedule.
109 – Peter Stastny, Quebec, 1980-81. 77GP – 80 game schedule.
106 – Alex Ovechkin, Washington, 2005-06. 81GP – 82 game schedule.
103 – Dale Hawerchuk, Winnipeg, 1981-82. 80GP – 80 game schedule.
102 – Joe Juneau, Boston, 1992-93. 84GP – 84 game schedule.
– Sidney Crosby, Pittsburgh, 2005-06. 81GP – 82 game schedule.
100 – Mario Lemieux, Pittsburgh, 1984-85. 73GP – 80 game schedule.

MOST POINTS BY A PLAYER IN HIS FIRST NHL SEASON, ONE GAME:
8 – Peter Stastny, Quebec, Feb. 22, 1981, at Washington. 4G-4A.
Quebec 11, Washington 7.
– Anton Stastny, Quebec, Feb. 22, 1981, at Washington. 3G-5A.
Quebec 11, Washington 7.
7 – Wayne Gretzky, Edmonton, Feb. 15, 1980, at Edmonton. 7A.
Edmonton 8, Washington 2.
– Sergei Makarov, Calgary, Feb. 25, 1990, at Calgary. 2G-5A.
Calgary 10, Edmonton 4.
6 – Wayne Gretzky, Edmonton, Mar. 29, 1980, at Toronto. 2G-4A.
Edmonton 8, Toronto 5.
– Gary Suter, Calgary, Apr. 4, 1986, at Calgary. 6A.
Calgary 9, Edmonton 3.

MOST POINTS BY A PLAYER IN HIS FIRST NHL GAME:
5 – Joe Malone, Montreal, Dec. 19, 1917, at Ottawa. 5G*.
Montreal 7, Ottawa 4.
– Harry Hyland, Mtl. Wanderers, Dec. 19, 1917, at Montreal. 5G*.
Mtl Wanderers 10, Toronto 9.
– Al Hill, Philadelphia, Feb. 14, 1977, at Philadelphia. 2G-3A.
Philadelphia 6, St. Louis 4.
4 – Alex Smart, Montreal, Jan. 14, 1943, at Montreal. 3G-1A.
Montreal 5, Chicago 1.
– Dutch Reibel, Detroit, Oct. 8, 1953, at Detroit. 4A.
Detroit 4, NY Rangers 1.
– Roland Eriksson, Minnesota, Oct. 6, 1976, at NY Rangers. 4A.
NY Rangers 6, Minnesota 5.
– Stanislav Chistov, Anaheim, Oct. 10, 2002, at St. Louis. 1G-3A.
Anaheim 4, St. Louis 3.

– Official assists not awarded in 1917-18.

SCORING BY A ROOKIE DEFENSEMAN

MOST GOALS BY A ROOKIE DEFENSEMAN, ONE SEASON:
23 – Brian Leetch, NY Rangers, 1988-89. 68GP – 80 game schedule.
22 – Barry Beck, Colorado Rockies, 1977-78. 75GP – 80 game schedule.
20 – Dion Phaneuf, Calgary, 2005-06. 82GP – 82 game schedule.

MOST ASSISTS BY A ROOKIE DEFENSEMAN, ONE SEASON:
60 – Larry Murphy, Los Angeles, 1980-81. 80GP – 80 game schedule.
55 – Chris Chelios, Montreal, 1984-85. 74GP – 80 game schedule.
50 – Stefan Persson, NY Islanders, 1977-78. 66GP – 80 game schedule.
– Gary Suter, Calgary, 1985-86. 80GP – 80 game schedule.
49 – Nicklas Lidstrom, Detroit, 1991-92. 80GP – 80 game schedule.

MOST POINTS BY A ROOKIE DEFENSEMAN, ONE SEASON:
76 – Larry Murphy, Los Angeles, 1980-81. 80GP – 80 game schedule.
71 – Brian Leetch, NY Rangers, 1988-89. 68GP – 80 game schedule.
68 – Gary Suter, Calgary, 1985-86. 80GP – 80 game schedule.
66 – Phil Housley, Buffalo, 1982-83. 77GP – 80 game schedule.
65 – Raymond Bourque, Boston, 1979-80. 80GP – 80 game schedule.

Joe Juneau (left) tied the NHL record set by Peter Stastny in 1980-81 when he collected 70 assists as a rookie with the Boston Bruins in 1992-93.
Anton Stastny (right) shares the record with his brother Peter for the most points in one game by a player in his rookie season.
Both had eight points for the Quebec Nordiques in a game against the Washington Capitals on February 22, 1981.

PER-GAME SCORING AVERAGES

HIGHEST GOALS-PER-GAME AVERAGE, CAREER
(AMONG PLAYERS WITH 200-OR-MORE GOALS):
.762 – **Mike Bossy**, NY Islanders, 1977-78 – 1986-87, with 573G in 752GP.
.756 – Cy Denneny, Ottawa, Boston, 1917-18 – 1928-29, with 248G in 328GP.
.754 – Mario Lemieux, Pittsburgh, 1984-85 – 1996-97, 2000-01 – 2003-04, 2005-06, with 690G in 915GP.
.742 – Babe Dye, Toronto, Hamilton, Chicago, NY Americans, 1919-20 – 1930-31, with 201G in 271GP.
.625 – Alex Ovechkin, Washington, 2005-06 – 2014-15, with 475G in 760GP.
.623 – Pavel Bure, Vancouver, Florida, NY Rangers, 1991-92 – 2002-03, with 437G in 702GP.

HIGHEST GOALS-PER-GAME AVERAGE, ONE SEASON
(AMONG PLAYERS WITH 20-OR-MORE GOALS):
2.20 – **Joe Malone**, Montreal, 1917-18, with 44G in 20GP.
1.80 – Cy Denneny, Ottawa, 1917-18, with 36G in 20GP.
1.64 – Newsy Lalonde, Montreal, 1917-18, with 23G in 14GP.
1.63 – Joe Malone, Quebec, 1919-20, with 39G in 24GP.
1.61 – Newsy Lalonde, Montreal, 1919-20, with 37G in 23GP.

HIGHEST GOALS-PER-GAME AVERAGE, ONE SEASON
(AMONG PLAYERS WITH 50-OR-MORE GOALS):
1.18 – **Wayne Gretzky**, Edmonton, 1983-84, with 87G in 74GP.
1.15 – Wayne Gretzky, Edmonton, 1981-82, with 92G in 80GP.
– Mario Lemieux, Pittsburgh, 1992-93, with 69G in 60GP.
1.12 – Mario Lemieux, Pittsburgh, 1988-89, with 85G in 76GP.
1.10 – Brett Hull, St. Louis, 1990-91, with 86G in 78GP.
1.02 – Cam Neely, Boston, 1993-94, with 50G in 49GP.
1.00 – Maurice Richard, Montreal, 1944-45, with 50G in 50GP.

HIGHEST ASSISTS-PER-GAME AVERAGE, CAREER
(AMONG PLAYERS WITH 300-OR-MORE ASSISTS):
1.320 – **Wayne Gretzky**, Edmonton, Los Angeles, St. Louis, NY Rangers, 1979-80 – 1998-99, with 1,963A in 1,487GP.
1.129 – Mario Lemieux, Pittsburgh, 1984-85 – 1996-97, 2000-01 – 2003-04, 2005-06, with 1,033A in 915GP.
.982 – Bobby Orr, Boston, Chicago, 1966-67 – 1978-79, with 645A in 657GP.
.898 – Peter Forsberg, Quebec, Colorado, Philadelphia, Nashville, 1994-95 – 2000-01, 2002-03, 2003-04, 2005-06 – 2007-08, 2010-11 with 636A in 708GP.
.879 – Sidney Crosby, Pittsburgh, 2005-06 – 2014-15, with 551A in 627GP.

HIGHEST ASSISTS-PER-GAME AVERAGE, ONE SEASON
(AMONG PLAYERS WITH 35-OR-MORE ASSISTS):
2.04 – **Wayne Gretzky, Edmonton**, 1985-86, with 163A in 80GP.
1.70 – Wayne Gretzky, Edmonton, 1987-88, with 109A in 64GP.
1.69 – Wayne Gretzky, Edmonton, 1984-85, with 135A in 80GP.
1.59 – Wayne Gretzky, Edmonton, 1983-84, with 118A in 74GP.
1.56 – Wayne Gretzky, Edmonton, 1982-83, with 125A in 80GP.
– Wayne Gretzky, Los Angeles, 1990-91, with 122A in 78GP.
1.53 – Wayne Gretzky, Edmonton, 1986-87, with 121A in 79GP.
1.52 – Mario Lemieux, Pittsburgh, 1992-93, with 91A in 60GP.
1.50 – Wayne Gretzky, Edmonton, 1981-82, with 120A in 80GP.
– Mario Lemieux, Pittsburgh, 1988-89, with 114A in 76GP.

HIGHEST POINTS-PER-GAME AVERAGE, CAREER
(AMONG PLAYERS WITH 500-OR-MORE POINTS):
1.921 – **Wayne Gretzky**, Edmonton, Los Angeles, St. Louis, NY Rangers, 1979-80 – 1998-99, with 2,857PTS (894G-1,963A) in 1,487GP.
1.883 – Mario Lemieux, Pittsburgh, 1984-85 – 1996-97, 2000-01 – 2003-04, 2005-06, with 1,723PTS (690G-1,033A) in 915GP.
1.497 – Mike Bossy, NY Islanders, 1977-78 – 1986-87, with 1,126PTS (573G-553A) in 752GP.
1.360 – Sidney Crosby, Pittsburgh, 2005-06 – 2014-15, with 853PTS (302G-551A) in 627GP.
1.393 – Bobby Orr, Boston, Chicago, 1966-67 – 1978-79, with 915PTS (270G-645A) in 657GP.

HIGHEST POINTS-PER-GAME AVERAGE, ONE SEASON
(AMONG PLAYERS WITH 50-OR-MORE POINTS):
2.77 – **Wayne Gretzky**, Edmonton, 1983-84, with 205PTS in 74GP.
2.69 – Wayne Gretzky, Edmonton, 1985-86, with 215PTS in 80GP.
2.67 – Mario Lemieux, Pittsburgh, 1992-93, with 160PTS in 60GP.
2.65 – Wayne Gretzky, Edmonton, 1981-82, with 212PTS in 80GP.
2.62 – Mario Lemieux, Pittsburgh, 1988-89, with 199PTS in 76GP.
2.60 – Wayne Gretzky, Edmonton, 1984-85, with 208PTS in 80GP.
2.45 – Wayne Gretzky, Edmonton, 1982-83, with 196PTS in 80GP.
2.33 – Wayne Gretzky, Edmonton, 1987-88, with 149PTS in 64GP.
2.32 – Wayne Gretzky, Edmonton, 1986-87, with 183PTS in 79GP.
2.30 – Mario Lemieux, Pittsburgh, 1995-96, with 161PTS in 70GP.
2.18 – Mario Lemieux, Pittsburgh, 1987-88, with 168PTS in 77GP.
2.15 – Wayne Gretzky, Los Angeles, 1988-89, with 168PTS in 78GP.
2.09 – Wayne Gretzky, Los Angeles, 1990-91, with 163PTS in 78GP.
2.08 – Mario Lemieux, Pittsburgh, 1989-90, with 123PTS in 59GP.

SCORING PLATEAUS

MOST 20-OR-MORE GOAL SEASONS:
22 – **Gordie Howe**, Detroit, Hartford, in 26 seasons.
20 – Ron Francis, Hartford, Pittsburgh, Carolina, Toronto, in 23 seasons.
19 – Dave Andreychuk, Buffalo, Toronto, New Jersey, Boston, Colorado, Tampa Bay, in 23 seasons.
– Brendan Shanahan, New Jersey, St. Louis, Hartford, Detroit, NY Rangers, in 21 seasons.
18 – Jaromir Jagr, Pittsburgh, Washington, NY Rangers, Philadelphia, Dallas, Boston, New Jersey, Florida, in 21 seasons.
17 – Marcel Dionne, Detroit, Los Angeles, NY Rangers, in 18 seasons.
– Mike Gartner, Washington, Minnesota, NY Rangers, Toronto, Phoenix, in 19 seasons.
– Wayne Gretzky, Edmonton, Los Angeles, St. Louis, NY Rangers, in 20 seasons.
– Mark Messier, Edmonton, NY Rangers, Vancouver, in 25 seasons.
– Brett Hull, Calgary, St. Louis, Dallas, Detroit, Phoenix, in 19 seasons.
– Joe Sakic, Quebec, Colorado, in 20 seasons.
– Mats Sundin, Quebec, Toronto, Vancouver, in 18 seasons.
– Teemu Selanne, Winnipeg, Anaheim, San Jose, Colorado, in 21 seasons.

MOST CONSECUTIVE 20-OR-MORE GOAL SEASONS:
22 – **Gordie Howe**, Detroit, 1949-50 – 1970-71.
19 – Brendan Shanahan, New Jersey, St. Louis, Hartford, Detroit, NY Rangers, 1988-89 – 2007-08.
17 – Marcel Dionne, Detroit, Los Angeles, NY Rangers, 1971-72 – 1987-88.
– Brett Hull, Calgary, St. Louis, Dallas, Detroit, 1987-88 – 2003-04.
– Jaromir Jagr, Pittsburgh, Washington, NY Rangers, 1990-91 – 2007-08.
– Mats Sundin, Quebec, Toronto, 1990-91 – 2007-08.

Mats Sundin scored 20 goals or more during the first 17 of the 18 seasons he played in the NHL. Only Gordie Howe, Ron Francis, Dave Andreychuk, Brendan Shanahan and Jaromir Jagr have recorded more 20-goal seasons, and all played more than 20 years in the NHL.

MOST 30-OR-MORE GOAL SEASONS:
17 – Mike Gartner, Washington, Minnesota, NY Rangers, Toronto, Phoenix, in 19 seasons.
15 – Jaromir Jagr, Pittsburgh, Washington, NY Rangers, Philadelphia, Dallas, Boston, New Jersey, Florida, in 21 seasons.
14 – Gordie Howe, Detroit, Hartford, in 26 seasons.
  – Marcel Dionne, Detroit, Los Angeles, NY Rangers, in 18 seasons.
  – Wayne Gretzky, Edmonton, Los Angeles, St. Louis, NY Rangers, in 20 seasons.
13 – Bobby Hull, Chicago, Winnipeg, Hartford, in 16 seasons.
  – Phil Esposito, Chicago, Boston, NY Rangers, in 18 seasons.
  – Brett Hull, Calgary, St. Louis, Dallas, Detroit, Phoenix, in 19 seasons.
  – Mats Sundin, Quebec, Toronto, Vancouver, in 18 seasons.

MOST CONSECUTIVE 30-OR-MORE GOAL SEASONS:
15 – Mike Gartner, Washington, Minnesota, NY Rangers, Toronto, 1979-80 – 1993-94.
  – Jaromir Jagr, Pittsburgh, Washington, NY Rangers, 1991-92 – 2006-07.
13 – Bobby Hull, Chicago, 1959-60 – 1971-72.
  – Phil Esposito, Boston, 1967-68 – 1979-80.
  – Wayne Gretzky, Edmonton, Los Angeles, 1979-80 – 1991-92.

MOST 40-OR-MORE GOAL SEASONS:
12 – Wayne Gretzky, Edmonton, Los Angeles, St. Louis, NY Rangers, in 20 seasons.
10 – Marcel Dionne, Detroit, Los Angeles, NY Rangers, in 18 seasons.
  – Mario Lemieux, Pittsburgh, in 17 seasons.
9 – Mike Bossy, NY Islanders, in 10 seasons.
  – Mike Gartner, Washington, Minnesota, NY Rangers, Toronto, Phoenix, in 19 seasons.

MOST CONSECUTIVE 40-OR-MORE GOAL SEASONS:
12 – Wayne Gretzky, Edmonton, Los Angeles, 1979-80 – 1990-91.
9 – Mike Bossy, NY Islanders, 1977-78 – 1985-86.
8 – Luc Robitaille, Los Angeles, 1986-87 – 1993-94.
7 – Phil Esposito, Boston, 1968-69 – 1974-75.
  – Michel Goulet, Quebec, 1981-82 – 1987-88.
  – Jari Kurri, Edmonton, 1982-83 – 1988-89.

MOST 50-OR-MORE GOAL SEASONS:
9 – Mike Bossy, NY Islanders, in 10 seasons.
  – Wayne Gretzky, Edmonton, Los Angeles, St. Louis, NY Rangers, in 20 seasons.
6 – Guy Lafleur, Montreal, NY Rangers, Quebec, in 17 seasons.
  – Marcel Dionne, Detroit, Los Angeles, NY Rangers, in 18 seasons.
  – Mario Lemieux, Pittsburgh, in 17 seasons.
  – Alex Ovechkin, Washington, in 10 seasons.
5 – Bobby Hull, Chicago, Winnipeg, Hartford, in 16 seasons.
  – Phil Esposito, Chicago, Boston, NY Rangers, in 18 seasons.
  – Brett Hull, Calgary, St. Louis, Dallas, Detroit, Phoenix, in 19 seasons.
  – Steve Yzerman, Detroit, in 22 seasons.
  – Pavel Bure, Vancouver, Florida, NY Rangers, in 12 seasons.

MOST CONSECUTIVE 50-OR-MORE GOAL SEASONS:
9 – Mike Bossy, NY Islanders, 1977-78 – 1985-86.
8 – Wayne Gretzky, Edmonton, 1979-80 – 1986-87.
6 – Guy Lafleur, Montreal, 1974-75 – 1979-80.
5 – Phil Esposito, Boston, 1970-71 – 1974-75.
  – Marcel Dionne, Los Angeles, 1978-79 – 1982-83.
  – Brett Hull, St. Louis, 1989-90 – 1993-94.

MOST 60-OR-MORE GOAL SEASONS:
5 – Mike Bossy, NY Islanders, in 10 seasons.
  – Wayne Gretzky, Edmonton, Los Angeles, St. Louis, NY Rangers, in 20 seasons.
4 – Phil Esposito, Chicago, Boston, NY Rangers, in 18 seasons.
  – Mario Lemieux, Pittsburgh, in 17 seasons.

MOST CONSECUTIVE 60-OR-MORE GOAL SEASONS:
4 – Wayne Gretzky, Edmonton, 1981-82 – 1984-85.
3 – Mike Bossy, NY Islanders, 1980-81 – 1982-83.
  – Brett Hull, St. Louis, 1989-90 – 1991-92.
2 – Phil Esposito, Boston, 1970-71 – 1971-72, 1973-74 – 1974-75.
  – Jari Kurri, Edmonton, 1984-85 – 1985-86.
  – Mario Lemieux, Pittsburgh, 1987-88 – 1988-89.
  – Steve Yzerman, Detroit, 1988-89 – 1989-90.
  – Pavel Bure, Vancouver, 1992-93 – 1993-94.

MOST 100-OR-MORE POINT SEASONS:
15 – Wayne Gretzky, Edmonton, Los Angeles, St. Louis, NY Rangers, in 20 seasons.
10 – Mario Lemieux, Pittsburgh, in 17 seasons.
8 – Marcel Dionne, Detroit, Los Angeles, NY Rangers, in 18 seasons.
7 – Mike Bossy, NY Islanders, in 10 seasons.
  – Peter Stastny, Quebec, New Jersey, St. Louis, in 15 seasons.

MOST CONSECUTIVE 100-OR-MORE POINT SEASONS:
13 – Wayne Gretzky, Edmonton, Los Angeles, 1979-80 – 1991-92.
6 – Bobby Orr, Boston, 1969-70 – 1974-75.
  – Guy Lafleur, Montreal, 1974-75 – 1979-80.
  – Mike Bossy, NY Islanders, 1980-81 – 1985-86.
  – Peter Stastny, Quebec, 1980-81 – 1985-86.
  – Mario Lemieux, Pittsburgh, 1984-85 – 1989-90.
  – Steve Yzerman, Detroit, 1987-88 – 1992-93.

THREE-OR-MORE-GOAL GAMES

MOST THREE-OR-MORE GOAL GAMES, CAREER:
50 – Wayne Gretzky, Edmonton, Los Angeles, St. Louis, NY Rangers, in 20 seasons, 37 three-goal games, 9 four-goal games, 4 five-goal games.
40 – Mario Lemieux, Pittsburgh, in 17 seasons, 27 three-goal games, 10 four-goal games, 3 five-goal games.
39 – Mike Bossy, NY Islanders, in 10 seasons, 30 three-goal games, 9 four-goal games.
33 – Brett Hull, Calgary, St. Louis, Dallas, Detroit, Phoenix, in 19 seasons, 30 three-goal games, 3 four-goal games.
32 – Phil Esposito, Chicago, Boston, NY Rangers, in 18 seasons, 27 three-goal games, 5 four-goal games.

MOST THREE-OR-MORE GOAL GAMES, ONE SEASON:
10 – Wayne Gretzky, Edmonton, 1981-82. 6 three-goal games, 3 four-goal games, 1 five-goal game.
  – Wayne Gretzky, Edmonton, 1983-84. 6 three-goal games, 4 four-goal games.
9 – Mike Bossy, NY Islanders, 1980-81. 6 three-goal games, 3 four-goal games.
  – Mario Lemieux, Pittsburgh, 1988-89. 7 three-goal games, 1 four-goal game, 1 five-goal game.
8 – Brett Hull, St. Louis, 1991-92. 8 three-goal games.
7 – Joe Malone, Montreal, 1917-18. 2 three-goal games, 2 four-goal games, 3 five-goal games.
  – Phil Esposito, Boston, 1970-71. 7 three-goal games.
  – Rick Martin, Buffalo, 1975-76. 6 three-goal games, 1 four-goal game.
  – Alexander Mogilny, Buffalo, 1992-93. 5 three-goal games, 2 four-goal games.

SCORING STREAKS

LONGEST CONSECUTIVE GOAL-SCORING STREAK:
16 Games – Punch Broadbent, Ottawa, 1921-22. 27G
14 Games – Joe Malone, Montreal, 1917-18. 35G
13 Games – Newsy Lalonde, Montreal, 1920-21. 24G
  – Charlie Simmer, Los Angeles, 1979-80. 17G
12 Games – Cy Denneny, Ottawa, 1917-18. 23G
  – Dave Lumley, Edmonton, 1981-82. 15G
  – Mario Lemieux, Pittsburgh, 1992-93. 18G

LONGEST CONSECUTIVE ASSIST-SCORING STREAK:
23 Games – Wayne Gretzky, Los Angeles, 1990-91. 48A
18 Games – Adam Oates, Boston, 1992-93. 28A
17 Games – Wayne Gretzky, Edmonton, 1983-84. 38A
  – Paul Coffey, Edmonton, 1985-86. 27A
  – Wayne Gretzky, Los Angeles, 1989-90. 35A
16 Games – Jaromir Jagr, Pittsburgh, 2000-01. 24A

LONGEST CONSECUTIVE POINT-SCORING STREAK:
51 Games – Wayne Gretzky, Edmonton, 1983-84. 61G-92A-153PTS
46 Games – Mario Lemieux, Pittsburgh, 1989-90. 39G-64A-103PTS
39 Games – Wayne Gretzky, Edmonton, 1985-86. 33G-75A-108PTS
30 Games – Wayne Gretzky, Edmonton, 1982-83. 24G-52A-76PTS
  – Mats Sundin, Quebec, 1992-93. 21G-25A-46PTS

LONGEST CONSECUTIVE POINT-SCORING STREAK FROM START OF SEASON:
51 Games – Wayne Gretzky, Edmonton, 1983-84. 61G-92A-153PTS. Streak ended by Los Angeles and goaltender Markus Mattsson on Jan. 28, 1984.

LONGEST CONSECUTIVE POINT-SCORING STREAK BY A DEFENSEMAN:
28 Games – Paul Coffey, Edmonton, 1985-86. 16G-39A-55PTS
19 Games – Raymond Bourque, Boston, 1987-88. 6G-21A-27PTS
17 Games – Raymond Bourque, Boston, 1984-85. 4G-24A-28PTS
  – Brian Leetch, NY Rangers, 1991-92. 5G-24A-29PTS
16 Games – Gary Suter, Calgary, 1987-88. 8G-17A-25PTS
15 Games – Bobby Orr, Boston, 1970-71. 10G-23A-33PTS
  – Bobby Orr, Boston, 1973-74. 8G-15A-23PTS
  – Steve Duchesne, Quebec, 1992-93. 4G-17A-21PTS
  – Chris Chelios, Chicago, 1995-96. 4G-16A-20PTS

LONGEST CONSECUTIVE POINT-SCORING STREAK BY A ROOKIE:
20 Games –Paul Stastny, Colorado, 2006-07. 11G-18A-29PTS
17 Games –Teemu Selanne, Winnipeg, 1992-93. 20G-14A-34PTS
16 Games –Peter Stastny, Quebec, 1980-81
15 Games – Jude Drouin, Minnesota North Stars, 1970-71

FASTEST GOALS AND ASSISTS

FASTEST GOAL FROM START OF A GAME:
0:05 – Merlyn Phillips, Montreal Maroons, Dec. 29, 1926, at Chicago. Chicago 5, Mtl. Maroons 4
  – Doug Smail, Winnipeg, Dec. 20, 1981, at Winnipeg. Winnipeg 5, St. Louis 4.
  – Bryan Trottier, NY Islanders, Mar. 22, 1984, at Boston. NY Islanders 3, Boston 3.
  – Alexander Mogilny, Buffalo, Dec. 21, 1991, at Toronto. Buffalo 4, Toronto 1.
0:06 – Henry Boucha, Detroit, Jan. 28, 1973, at Montreal. Detroit 4, Montreal 2.
  – Jean Pronovost, Pittsburgh, Mar. 25, 1976, at St. Louis. St. Louis 5, Pittsburgh 2.
  – Alex Burrows, Vancouver, Mar. 16, 2013, at Vancouver. Detroit 5, Vancouver 2
0:07 – Charlie Conacher, Toronto, Feb. 6, 1932, at Toronto. Toronto 6, Boston 0.
  – Danny Gare, Buffalo, Dec. 17, 1978, at Buffalo. Buffalo 6, Vancouver 3.
  – Tiger Williams, Los Angeles, Feb. 14, 1987, at Los Angeles. Los Angeles 5, Hartford 2.
  – Evgeni Malkin, Pittsburgh, Jan. 5, 2011, at Pittsburgh. Pittsburgh 8, Tampa Bay 1.

FASTEST GOAL FROM START OF A PERIOD:
  0:04 – **Claude Provost**, Montreal, Nov. 9, 1957, at Montreal,
     second period. Montreal 4, Boston 2.
     – **Denis Savard**, Chicago, Jan. 12, 1986, at Chicago,
     third period. Chicago 4, Hartford 2.
     – **James van Riemsdyk**, Toronto, Mar. 28, 2014, at Philadelphia,
     second period. Toronto 4, Philadelphia 2.

FASTEST GOAL BY A PLAYER IN HIS FIRST NHL GAME:
  0:15 – **Gus Bodnar**, Toronto, Oct. 30, 1943, at Toronto.
     Toronto 5, NY Rangers 2.
  0:18 – Danny Gare, Buffalo, Oct. 10, 1974, at Buffalo.
     Buffalo 9, Boston 5.
  0:20 – Alexander Mogilny, Buffalo, Oct. 5, 1989, at Buffalo.
     Buffalo 4, Quebec 3.

FASTEST TWO GOALS FROM START OF A GAME:
  0:27 – **Mike Knuble**, Boston, Feb. 14, 2003, at Florida.
     0:10 and 0:27. Boston 6, Florida 5.

FASTEST TWO GOALS:
  0:04 – **Nels Stewart**, Mtl. Maroons, Jan. 3, 1931, at Mtl. Maroons.
     8:24 and 8:28, third period. Mtl. Maroons 5, Boston 3.
     – **Deron Quint**, Winnipeg, Dec. 15, 1995, at Winnipeg.
     7:51 and 7:55, second period. Winnipeg 9, Edmonton 4.
  0:05 – Pete Mahovlich, Montreal, Feb. 20, 1971, at Montreal.
     12:16 and 12:21, third period. Montreal 7, Chicago 1.
     – Nathan Gerbe, Buffalo, Jan. 21, 2011at Buffalo.
     16:38 and 16:43, third period. NY Islanders 5, Buffalo 2.
  0:06 – Jim Pappin, Chicago, Feb. 16, 1972, at Chicago.
     2:57 and 3:03, third period. Chicago 3, Philadelphia 3.
     – Ralph Backstrom, Los Angeles, Nov. 2, 1972, at Los Angeles.
     8:30 and 8:36, third period. Los Angeles 5, Boston 2.
     – Lanny McDonald, Calgary, Mar. 22, 1984, at Calgary.
     16:23 and 16:29, first period. Detroit 6, Calgary 4.
     – Sylvain Turgeon, Hartford, Mar. 28, 1987, at Hartford.
     13:59 and 14:05, second period. Hartford 5, Pittsburgh 4.

FASTEST THREE GOALS:
  0:21 – **Bill Mosienko**, Chicago, Mar. 23, 1952, at NY Rangers, against
     goaltender Lorne Anderson. Mosienko scored at 6:09, 6:20 and 6:30 of
     third period, all with both teams at full strength. Chicago 7, NY Rangers 6.
  0:44 – Jean Béliveau, Montreal, Nov. 5, 1955, at Montreal, against goaltender
     Terry Sawchuk. Béliveau scored at 0:42, 1:08 and 1:26 of second period,
     all with Montreal holding a 6-4 man advantage. Montreal 4, Boston 2.

FASTEST THREE ASSISTS:
  0:21 – **Gus Bodnar**, Chicago, Mar. 23, 1952, at NY Rangers, Bodnar assisted on
     Bill Mosienko's three goals at 6:09, 6:20 and 6:30 of third period.
     Chicago 7, NY Rangers 6.
  0:44 – Bert Olmstead, Montreal, Nov. 5, 1955, at Montreal, Olmstead assisted on
     Jean Béliveau's three goals at 0:42, 1:08 and 1:26 of second period.
     Montreal 4, Boston 2.

SHOTS ON GOAL

MOST SHOTS ON GOAL, ONE SEASON:
  550 – **Phil Esposito**, Boston, 1970-71. 78GP – 78 game schedule.
  528 – Alex Ovechkin, Washington, 2008-09. 79GP – 82 game schedule.
  446 – Alex Ovechkin, Washington, 2007-08. 82GP – 82 game schedule.
  429 – Paul Kariya, Anaheim, 1998-99. 82GP – 82 game schedule.
  426 – Phil Esposito, Boston, 1971-72. 76GP – 78 game schedule.

*Claude Provost scored just four seconds after the start of the second
period in Montreal's 4-2 win over Boston on November 9, 1957.
Provost took a Marcel Bonin pass from the faceoff and when Bruins
defenseman Doug Mohns fell down, had a clear path to the net.*

PENALTIES

MOST PENALTY MINUTES, CAREER:
  3,966 – **Tiger Williams**, Toronto, Vancouver, Detroit, Los Angeles, Hartford,
     in 14 seasons. 962GP
  3,565 – Dale Hunter, Quebec, Washington, Colorado, in 19 seasons. 1,407GP
  3,515 – Tie Domi, Toronto, NY Rangers, Winnipeg, in 16 seasons. 1,020GP
  3,381 – Marty McSorley, Pittsburgh, Edmonton, Los Angeles, NY Rangers, San Jose,
     Boston, in 17 seasons. 961GP
  3,300 – Bob Probert, Detroit, Chicago, in 17 seasons. 935GP

MOST PENALTY MINUTES, CAREER, INCLUDING PLAYOFFS:
  4,421 – **Tiger Williams**, Toronto, Vancouver, Detroit, Los Angeles, Hartford,
     3,966 in 962 regular-season games; 455 in 83 playoff games.
  4,294 – Dale Hunter, Quebec, Washington, Colorado,
     3,565 in 1,407 regular-season games; 729 in 186 playoff games.
  3,755 – Marty McSorley, Pittsburgh, Edmonton, Los Angeles, NY Rangers, San Jose,
     Boston, 3,381 in 961 regular-season games; 374 in 115 playoff games.
  3,753 – Tie Domi, Toronto, NY Rangers, Winnipeg, 3,515 in 1,020 regular-season
     games; 238 in 98 playoff games.
  3,584 – Chris Nilan, Montreal, NY Rangers, Boston,
     3,043 in 688 regular-season games; 541 in 111 playoff games.

MOST PENALTY MINUTES, ONE SEASON:
  472 – **Dave Schultz**, Philadelphia, 1974-75.
  409 – Paul Baxter, Pittsburgh, 1981-82.
  408 – Mike Peluso, Chicago, 1991-92.
  405 – Dave Schultz, Los Angeles, Pittsburgh, 1977-78.

MOST PENALTIES, ONE GAME:
  10 – **Chris Nilan**, Boston, Mar. 31, 1991, at Boston vs. Hartford. 6 minors,
     2 majors, 1 10-minute misconduct, 1 game misconduct.
  9 – Jim Dorey, Toronto, Oct. 16, 1968, at Toronto vs. Pittsburgh. 4 minors,
     2 majors, 2 10-minute misconducts, 1 game misconduct.
     – Dave Schultz, Pittsburgh, Apr. 6, 1978, at Detroit. 5 minors, 2 majors,
     2 10-minute misconducts.
     – Randy Holt, Los Angeles, Mar. 11, 1979, at Philadelphia. 1 minor,
     3 majors, 2 10-minute misconducts, 3 game misconducts.
     – Russ Anderson, Pittsburgh, Jan. 19, 1980, at Pittsburgh vs. Edmonton.
     3 minors, 3 majors, 3 game misconducts.
     – Kim Clackson, Quebec, Mar. 8, 1981, at Quebec vs. Chicago. 4 minors,
     3 majors, 2 game misconducts.
     – Terry O'Reilly, Boston, Dec. 19, 1984, at Hartford. 5 minors, 3 majors,
     1 game misconduct.
     – Larry Playfair, Los Angeles, Dec. 9, 1986, at NY Islanders. 6 minors,
     2 majors, 1 10-minute misconduct.
     – Marty McSorley, Los Angeles, Apr. 14, 1992, at Vancouver. 5 minors,
     2 majors, 1 10-minute misconduct, 1 game misconduct.
     – Reed Low, St. Louis, Dec. 31, 2002, at Detroit. 4 minors,
     1 major, 1 10-minute misconduct, 3 game misconducts.

MOST PENALTY MINUTES, ONE GAME:
  67 – **Randy Holt**, Los Angeles, Mar. 11, 1979, at Philadelphia.
     1 minor, 3 majors, 2 10-minute misconducts, 3 game misconducts.
  57 – Brad Smith, Toronto, Nov. 15, 1986, at Toronto vs. Detroit.
     1 minor, 3 majors, 2 10-minute misconducts, 2 game misconducts.
     – Reed Low, St. Louis, Feb. 28, 2002, at St. Louis vs. Calgary.
     1 minor, 3 majors, 1 10-minute misconduct, 3 game misconducts.

MOST PENALTIES, ONE PERIOD:
  9 – **Randy Holt**, Los Angeles, Mar. 11, 1979, at Philadelphia, first period.
     1 minor, 3 majors, 2 10-minute misconducts, 3 game misconducts.

MOST PENALTY MINUTES, ONE PERIOD:
  67 – **Randy Holt**, Los Angeles, Mar. 11, 1979, at Philadelphia, first period.
     1 minor, 3 majors, 2 10-minute misconducts, 3 game misconducts.

GOALTENDING

MOST GAMES APPEARED IN BY A GOALTENDER, CAREER:
  1,266 – **Martin Brodeur**, New Jersey, St. Louis, 1991-92 – 2003-04,
     2005-06 – 2014-15.
  1,029 – Patrick Roy, Montreal, Colorado,1984-85 – 2002-03.
  971 – Terry Sawchuk, Detroit, Boston, Toronto, Los Angeles, NY Rangers,
     1949-50 – 1969-70.
  963 – Ed Belfour, Chicago, San Jose, Dallas, Toronto, Florida,
     1988-89 – 2003-04, 2005-06, 2006-07.
  943 – Curtis Joseph, St. Louis, Edmonton, Toronto, Detroit, Phoenix, Calgary,
     1989-90 – 2003-04, 2005-06 – 2008-09.

MOST CONSECUTIVE COMPLETE GAMES BY A GOALTENDER:
  502 – **Glenn Hall**, Detroit, Chicago. Played 502 games from beginning of
     1955-56 season through first 12 games of 1962-63 season. In his 503rd
     straight game, Nov. 7, 1962, at Chicago, Hall was removed from the
     game against Boston with a back injury in the first period.

MOST GAMES APPEARED IN BY A GOALTENDER, ONE SEASON:
  79 – **Grant Fuhr**, St. Louis, 1995-96.
  78 – Martin Brodeur, New Jersey, 2006-07.
  77 – Martin Brodeur, New Jersey, 1995-96.
     – Bill Ranford, Edmonton, Boston, 1995-96.
     – Arturs Irbe, Carolina, 2000-01.
     – Marc Denis, Columbus, 2002-03.
     – Evgeni Nabokov, San Jose, 2007-08.
     – Martin Brodeur, New Jersey, 2007-08.
     – Martin Brodeur, New Jersey, 2009-10.

MOST MINUTES PLAYED BY A GOALTENDER, CAREER:
  74,439 – **Martin Brodeur**, New Jersey, St. Louis, 1991-92 – 2003-04,
     2005-06 – 2014-15.
  60,235 – Patrick Roy, Montreal, Colorado, 1984-85 – 2002-03.
  57,194 – Terry Sawchuk, Detroit, Boston, Toronto, Los Angeles,
     NY Rangers, 1949-50 – 1969-70.

MOST MINUTES PLAYED BY A GOALTENDER, ONE SEASON:
4,697 – Martin Brodeur, New Jersey, 2006-07.
4,635 – Martin Brodeur, New Jersey, 2007-08.
4,561 – Evgeni Nabokov, San Jose, 2007-08.
4,555 – Martin Brodeur, New Jersey, 2003-04.
4,511 – Marc Denis, Columbus, 2002-03.

MOST SHUTOUTS, CAREER:
125 – Martin Brodeur, New Jersey, St. Louis, in 22 seasons.
(1991-92, 1993-94 – 2003-04, 2005-06 – 2014-15)
103 – Terry Sawchuk, Detroit, Boston, Toronto, Los Angeles, NY Rangers,
in 21 seasons. (1949-50 – 1969-70)
94 – George Hainsworth, Montreal, Toronto, in 11 seasons.
(1926-27 – 1936-37)

MOST SHUTOUTS, ONE SEASON:
22 – George Hainsworth, Montreal, 1928-29. 44GP
15 – Alec Connell, Ottawa, 1925-26. 36GP
– Alec Connell, Ottawa, 1927-28. 44GP
– Hal Winkler, Boston, 1927-28. 44GP
– Tony Esposito, Chicago, 1969-70. 63GP
14 – George Hainsworth, Montreal, 1926-27. 44GP

LONGEST SHUTOUT SEQUENCE BY A GOALTENDER:
460:49 – Alec Connell, Ottawa, 1927-28, six consecutive shutouts.
(Forward passing not permitted in attacking zones in 1927-28.)
343:05 – George Hainsworth, Montreal, 1928-29, four consecutive shutouts.
(Forward passing not permitted in attacking zones in 1928-29.)
332:01 – Brian Boucher, Phoenix, 2003-04, five consecutive shutouts.
324:40 – Roy Worters, NY Americans, 1930-31, four consecutive shutouts.
309:21 – Bill Durnan, Montreal, 1948-49, four consecutive shutouts.

MOST WINS BY A GOALTENDER, CAREER:
691 – Martin Brodeur, New Jersey, St. Louis, in 22 seasons. 1,266GP
551 – Patrick Roy, Montreal, Colorado, in 19 seasons. 1,029GP
484 – Ed Belfour, Chicago, San Jose, Dallas, Toronto, Florida,
in 17 seasons. 963GP
454 – Curtis Joseph, St. Louis, Edmonton, Toronto, Detroit, Phoenix, Calgary,
in 19 seasons. 943GP
447 – Terry Sawchuk, Detroit, Boston, Toronto, Los Angeles, NY Rangers,
in 21 seasons. 971GP

MOST WINS BY A GOALTENDER, ONE SEASON:
48 – Martin Brodeur, New Jersey, 2006-07. 78GP
47 – Bernie Parent, Philadelphia, 1973-74. 73GP
– Roberto Luongo, Vancouver, 2006-07. 76GP
46 – Evgeni Nabokov, San Jose, 2007-08. 77GP
45 – Miikka Kiprusoff, Calgary, 2008-09. 76GP
– Martin Brodeur, New Jersey, 2009-10. 77GP

LONGEST WINNING STREAK BY A GOALTENDER, ONE SEASON:
17 – Gilles Gilbert, Boston, 1975-76.
14 – Tiny Thompson, Boston, 1929-30.
– Ross Brooks, Boston, 1973-74.
– Don Beaupre, Minnesota, 1985-86.
– Tom Barrasso, Pittsburgh, 1992-93.
– Jonas Hiller, Anaheim, 2013-14.

LONGEST UNDEFEATED STREAK BY A GOALTENDER, ONE SEASON:
32 Games – Gerry Cheevers, Boston, 1971-72. 24W-8T
31 Games – Pete Peeters, Boston, 1982-83. 26W-5T
27 Games – Pete Peeters, Philadelphia, 1979-80. 22W-5T

LONGEST UNDEFEATED STREAK BY A GOALTENDER IN HIS FIRST NHL SEASON:
23 Games – Grant Fuhr, Edmonton, 1981-82. 15W-8T

LONGEST UNDEFEATED STREAK BY A GOALTENDER FROM START OF CAREER:
16 Games – Patrick Lalime, Pittsburgh, 1996-97. 14W-2T

MOST 30-OR-MORE WIN SEASONS BY A GOALTENDER:
14 – Martin Brodeur, New Jersey, St. Louis, in 22 seasons.
13 – Patrick Roy, Montreal, Colorado, in 19 seasons.
9 – Ed Belfour, Chicago, San Jose, Dallas, Toronto, Florida, in 17 seasons.
– Henrik Lundqvist, NY Rangers, in 10 seasons.
8 – Tony Esposito, Montreal, Chicago, in 16 seasons.
7 – Jacques Plante, Montreal, NY Rangers, St. Louis, Toronto, Boston,
in 18 seasons.
– Ken Dryden, Montreal, in 8 seasons.
– Curtis Joseph, St. Louis, Edmonton, Toronto, Detroit, Phoenix, Calgary,
in 19 seasons.
– Dominik Hasek, Chicago, Buffalo, Detroit, Ottawa, in 16 seasons.
– Miikka Kiprusoff, San Jose, Calgary, in 12 seasons.
– Ryan Miller, Buffalo, St. Louis, Vancouver, in 12 seasons.
– Roberto Luongo, NY Islanders, Florida, Vancouver, in 15 seasons.
– Marc-Andre Fleury, Pittsburgh, in 11 seasons.

MOST CONSECUTIVE 30-OR-MORE WIN SEASONS BY A GOALTENDER:
12 – Martin Brodeur, New Jersey, 1995-96 – 2003-04, 2005-06 – 2007-08.
8 – Patrick Roy, Montreal, Colorado, 1995-96 – 2002-03.
7 – Tony Esposito, Chicago, 1969-70 – 1975-76.
– Miikka Kiprusoff, Calgary, 2005-06 – 2011-12.
– Henrik Lundqvist, NY Rangers, 2005-06 – 2011-12.
– Roberto Luongo, Florida, Vancouver, 2005-06 – 2011-12.
– Ryan Miller, Buffalo, 2005-06 – 2011-12.
6 – Jacques Plante, Montreal, 1954-55 – 1959-60.
– Marty Turco, Dallas, 2002-03, 2003-04, 2005-06 – 2008-09.

MOST 40-OR-MORE WIN SEASONS BY A GOALTENDER:
8 – Martin Brodeur, New Jersey, St. Louis, in 22 seasons.
3 – Terry Sawchuk, Detroit, Boston, Toronto, Los Angeles, NY Rangers,
in 21 seasons.
– Jacques Plante, Montreal, NY Rangers, St. Louis, Toronto, Boston,
in 18 seasons.
– Miikka Kiprusoff, San Jose, Calgary, in 12 seasons.
– Evgeni Nabokov, San Jose, NY Islanders, in 13 seasons.
2 – Bernie Parent, Boston, Philadelphia, Toronto, in 13 seasons.
– Ken Dryden, Montreal, in 8 seasons.
– Ed Belfour, Chicago, San Jose, Dallas, Toronto, Florida, in 17 seasons.
– Ryan Miller, Buffalo, St. Louis, Vancouver, in 12 seasons.
– Roberto Luongo, NY islanders, Florida, Vancouver, in 15 seasons.
– Marc-Andre Fleury, Pittsburgh, in 11 seasons.

MOST CONSECUTIVE 40-OR-MORE WIN SEASONS BY A GOALTENDER:
3 – Martin Brodeur, New Jersey, 2005-06 – 2007-08.
– **Evgeni Nabokov**, San Jose, 2007-08 – 2009-10.
2 – Terry Sawchuk, Detroit, 1950-51, 1951-52.
– Bernie Parent, Philadelphia, 1973-74, 1974-75.
– Ken Dryden, Montreal, 1975-76, 1976-77.
– Martin Brodeur, New Jersey, 1999-2000, 2000-01.
– Miikka Kiprusoff, Calgary, 2005-06, 2006-07.

MOST LOSSES BY A GOALTENDER, CAREER:
397 – Martin Brodeur, New Jersey, St. Louis in 22 seasons. 1,266GP
352 – Gump Worsley, NY Rangers, Montreal, Minnesota, in 21 seasons. 861GP
– Curtis Joseph, St. Louis, Edmonton, Toronto, Detroit, Phoenix, Calgary,
in 19 seasons. 943GP
351 – Gilles Meloche, Chicago, California, Cleveland, Minnesota, Pittsburgh,
in 18 seasons. 788GP
346 – John Vanbiesbrouck, NY Rangers, Florida, Philadelphia, NY Islanders,
New Jersey, in 20 seasons. 882GP
341 – Sean Burke, New Jersey, Hartford, Carolina, Vancouver, Philadelphia,
Florida, Phoenix, Tampa Bay, Los Angeles, in 18 seasons. 820GP

MOST LOSSES BY A GOALTENDER, ONE SEASON:
48 – Gary Smith, California, 1970-71. 71GP
47 – Al Rollins, Chicago, 1953-54. 66GP
46 – Peter Sidorkiewicz, Ottawa, 1992-93. 64GP

GOALTENDER SHOOTOUT RECORDS

MOST SHOOTOUT WINS, ONE SEASON:
10 – Mathieu Garon, Edmonton, 2007-08. 10GP
– **Jonathan Quick**, Los Angelesm 2010-11. 10GP
– **Ryan Miller,** Buffalo, 2006-07. 14GP
– **Martin Brodeur,** New Jersey, 2006-07. 16GP

MOST SHOOTOUT WINS, CAREER:
52 – Ryan Miller, Buffalo, St.Louis, Vancouver. 82GP
50 – Henrik Lundqvist, NY Rangers. 86GP
48 – Marc-Andre Fleury, Pittsburgh. 72GP
42 – Martin Brodeur, New Jersey, St. Louis. 72GP

MOST SHOOTOUT SHOTS AGAINST, ONE SEASON:
75 – Roberto Luongo, Florida, 2014-15. 21GA
62 – Ilya Bryzgalov, Phoenix, 2009-10. 17GA
60 – Martin Brodeur, New Jersey, 2006-07. 20GA
54 – Roberto Luongo, Vancouver, 2007-08. 15GA
– Jimmy Howard, Detroit, 2009-10. 17GA

MOST SHOOTOUT SHOTS AGAINST, CAREER:
340 – Roberto Luongo, Florida, Vancouver. 108GA
327 – Henrik Lundqvist, NY Rangers. 82GA
284 – Ryan Miller, Buffalo, St.Louis, Vancouver. 81GA
244 – Martin Brodeur, New Jersey, St. Louis. 75GA

BEST SHOOTOUT SAVE PERCENTAGE, ONE SEASON: *(minimum 20 shots)*
.958 – Jhonas Enroth, Buffalo, Dallas, 2014-15. 24S-1GA
.938 – Mathieu Garon, Edmonton, 2007-08. 32S-2GA
.917 – Semyon Varlamov, Colorado, 2011-12. 24S-2GA
.900 – Marc Denis, Tampa Bay, 2006-07. 20S-2GA

BEST SHOOTOUT SAVE PERCENTAGE, CAREER: *(minimum 40 shots)*
.854 – Marc Denis, Columbus, Tampa Bay, Montreal. 41S-6GA
.805 – Eddie Lack, Vancouver. 41S-8GA
.764 – Brent Johnson, Washington, Pittsburgh. 55S-13GA
.757 – Jhonas Enroth, Buffalo, Dallas. 70S-17GA

Active NHL Players' Three-or-More-Goal Games

Regular Season

Teams named are the ones the players were with at the time of their multiple-scoring games. Players listed alphabetically.

Player	Team(s)	3-Goals	4-Goals	5-Goals
Abdelkader, Justin	Detroit	1	—	—
Atkinson, Cam	Columbus	2	—	—
Backes, David	St. Louis	2	1	—
Backstrom, Nicklas	Washington	1	—	—
Benn, Jamie	Dallas	2	—	—
Bergenheim, Sean	NY Islanders	1	—	—
Bergeron, Patrice	Boston	1	—	—
Boedker, Mikkel	Arizona	1	—	—
Bonino, Nick	Anaheim	1	—	—
Booth, David	Florida	2	—	—
Boulton, Eric	Atlanta	1	—	—
Bourque, Rene	Calgary	3	—	—
Boyes, Brad	Boston	1	—	—
Boyle, Dan	Tampa Bay	1	—	—
Bozak, Tyler	Toronto	1	—	—
Brouwer, Troy	Washington	1	—	—
Brown, Dustin	Los Angeles	3	—	—
Burns, Brent	San Jose	1	—	—
Burrows, Alexandre	Vancouver	3	—	—
Byfuglien, Dustin	Chicago	1	—	—
Callahan, Ryan	NY Rangers	2	—	—
Calvert, Matt	Columbus	1	—	—
Cammalleri, Mike	Cgy., Mtl.	5	—	—
Carcillo, Daniel	Phoenix	1	—	—
Carter, Jeff	Phi., CBJ, L.A.	5	—	—
Chara, Zdeno	Boston	1	—	—
Cleary, Daniel	Detroit	1	—	—
Clowe, Ryane	San Jose	1	—	—
Cogliano, Andrew	Anaheim	2	—	—
Cole, Erik	Car., Edm., Mtl.	7	—	—
Comeau, Blake	NYI, Pit.	2	—	—
Crombeen, B.J.	St. Louis	1	—	—
Crosby, Sidney	Pittsburgh	8	—	—
Cullen, Matt	Carolina	1	—	—
Doan, Shane	Phoenix	1	—	—
Duchene, Matt	Colorado	1	—	—
Dupuis, Pascal	Pittsburgh	1	—	—
Eaves, Patrick	Detroit	1	—	—
Elias, Patrik	New Jersey	7	1	—
Eller, Lars	Montreal	—	1	—
Erat, Martin	Nashville	2	—	—
Eriksson, Loui	Dallas	2	—	—
Fiddler, Vernon	Phoenix	1	—	—
Fisher, Mike	Ottawa	1	—	—
Fleischmann, Tomas	Colorado	1	—	—
Foligno, Nick	Columbus	1	—	—
Fontaine, Justin	Minnesota	1	—	—
Franzen, Johan	Detroit	2	—	1
Gaborik, Marian	Min., NYR	12	1	1
Gagner, Sam	Edmonton	1	1	—
Galchenyuk, Alex	Montreal	1	—	—
Gaudreau, Johnny	Calgary	1	—	—
Gionta, Brian	New Jersey	1	—	—
Glencross, Curtis	Calgary	3	—	—
Gomez, Scott	New Jersey	2	—	—
Gonchar, Sergei	Washington	1	—	—
Grabner, Michael	Van., NYI	2	—	—
Grabovski, Mikhail	Washington	1	—	—
Hagelin, Carl	NY Rangers	1	—	—
Hall, Taylor	Edmonton	4	—	—
Hansen, Jannik	Vancouver	1	—	—
Hanzal, Martin	Phx., Ari.	2	—	—
Hartnell, Scott	Nsh., Phi., CBJ	8	—	—
Havlat, Martin	Ott., S.J.	4	1	—
Heatley, Dany	Atl., Ott., S.J.	8	1	—
Helm, Darren	Detroit	1	—	—
Hemsky, Ales	Edmonton	1	—	—
Hertl, Tomas	San Jose	—	1	—
Higgins, Chris	Montreal	1	—	—
Horcoff, Shawn	Edmonton	1	—	—
Horton, Nathan	Florida	2	—	—
Hossa, Marian	Ott., Atl.	6	1	—
Iginla, Jarome	Calgary	11	1	—
Jagr, Jaromir	Pit., NYR, N.J.	14	1	—
Johnson, Tyler	Tampa Bay	2	—	—
Jokinen, Jussi	Dal., Pit.	1	1	—
Jokinen, Olli	Fla., Phx., Cgy.	7	—	—
Jooris, Josh	Calgary	1	—	—
Kadri, Nazim	Toronto	2	—	—
Kelly, Chris	Ottawa	1	—	—
Kesler, Ryan	Vancouver	3	—	—
Kessel, Phil	Bos., Tor.	5	—	—
King, Dwight	Los Angeles	1	—	—
Kopecky, Tomas	Florida	1	—	—
Kopitar, Anze	Los Angeles	2	—	—
Kreider, Chris	NY Rangers	1	—	—
Krejci, David	Boston	3	—	—

Player	Team(s)	3-Goals	4-Goals	5-Goals
Kucherov, Nikita	Tampa Bay	1	—	—
Kunitz, Chris	Ana., Pit.	3	1	—
Ladd, Andrew	Chicago	1	—	—
Laich, Brooks	Washington	1	—	—
Lapierre, Maxim	Montreal	1	—	—
Lecavalier, Vincent	T.B., Phi.	7	—	—
Legwand, David	Nashville	2	—	—
Lehtera, Jori	St. Louis	1	—	—
Lindholm, Elias	Carolina	1	—	—
Little, Bryan	Atl., Wpg.	2	—	—
Lombardi, Matthew	Calgary	1	—	—
Lucic, Milan	Boston	2	—	—
Lupul, Joffrey	Phi., Tor.	3	—	—
MacKinnon, Nathan	Colorado	1	—	—
Malkin, Evgeni	Pittsburgh	9	—	—
Malone, Ryan	Pit., T.B.	4	—	—
Marchand, Brad	Boston	1	—	—
Marleau, Patrick	San Jose	4	—	—
Matthias, Shawn	Vancouver	1	—	—
McClement, Jay	St. Louis	1	—	—
Michalek, Milan	Ottawa	2	—	—
Morrow, Brenden	Dallas	1	—	—
Moss, Dave	Calgary	1	—	—
Moulson, Matt	NY Islanders	2	1	—
Mueller, Peter	Phoenix	2	—	—
Nash, Rick	CBJ, NYR	6	—	—
Neal, James	Dal., Pit., Nsh.	5	—	—
Niederreiter, Nino	Minnesota	1	—	—
Nielsen, Frans	NY Islanders	1	—	—
Nugent-Hopkins, Ryan	Edmonton	2	—	—
Nyquist, Gustav	Detroit	1	—	—
Nystrom, Eric	Nashville	—	1	—
Okposo, Kyle	NY Islanders	—	1	—
Oshie, T.J.	St. Louis	2	—	—
Ott, Steve	Dallas	1	—	—
Ovechkin, Alex	Washington	10	3	—
Pacioretty, Max	Montreal	4	—	—
Palmieri, Kyle	Anaheim	1	—	—
Paquette, Cedric	Tampa Bay	1	—	—
Parise, Zach	New Jersey	2	—	—
Pavelski, Joe	San Jose	4	—	—
Perreault, Mathieu	Wsh., Wpg.	1	1	—
Perron, David	St.L., Edm.	2	—	—
Perry, Corey	Anaheim	8	—	—
Petersen, Toby	Pittsburgh	1	—	—
Plekanec, Thomas	Montreal	1	—	—
Pominville, Jason	Buffalo	2	—	—
Purcell, Teddy	Tampa Bay	2	—	—
Raymond, Mason	Van., Cgy.	3	—	—
Read, Matt	Philadelphia	1	—	—
Ribeiro, Mike	Dallas	1	—	—
Richards, Brad	NY Rangers	1	—	—
Richards, Mike	Philadelphia	2	—	—
Richardson, Brad	Los Angeles	1	—	—
Roy, Derek	Buffalo	4	—	—

Player	Team(s)	3-Goals	4-Goals	5-Goals
Rupp, Mike	Pittsburgh	1	—	—
Ruutu, Tuomo	Carolina	1	—	—
Ryan, Bobby	Ana., Ott.	4	—	—
Ryder, Michael	Montreal	2	—	—
Schwartz, Jaden	St. Louis	2	—	—
Sedin, Daniel	Vancouver	4	1	—
Sedin, Henrik	Vancouver	1	—	—
Seguin, Tyler	Bos., Dal.	4	1	—
Semin, Alexander	Washington	7	—	—
Setoguchi, Devin	San Jose	1	—	—
Sharp, Patrick	Chicago	4	—	—
Simmonds, Wayne	Philadelphia	1	—	—
Skinner, Jeff	Carolina	2	—	—
Sobotka, Vladimir	St. Louis	1	—	—
Spezza, Jason	Ottawa	5	—	—
Staal, Eric	Carolina	12	1	—
Staal, Jordan	Pittsburgh	2	—	—
Stafford, Drew	Buffalo	6	—	—
Stalberg, Viktor	Chicago	1	—	—
Stamkos, Steven	Tampa Bay	8	—	—
Stastny, Paul	Colorado	1	—	—
Steen, Alex	Toronto	1	—	—
Stempniak, Lee	Phx., Cgy.	1	—	—
Stepan, Derek	NY Rangers	3	—	—
Stewart, Chris	Col., St.L.	3	—	—
Subban, P.K.	Montreal	1	—	—
Suter, Ryan	Minnesota	1	—	—
Tanguay, Alex	Colorado	2	—	—
Tarasenko, Vladimir	St. Louis	2	—	—
Tavares, John	NY Islanders	5	—	—
Thornton, Joe	Bos., S.J.	4	—	—
Tlusty, Jiri	Carolina	2	—	—
Toews, Jonathan	Chicago	3	—	—
Toffoli, Tyler	Los Angeles	1	—	—
Torres, Raffi	Vancouver	1	—	—
Umberger, RJ	Phi., CBJ	3	—	—
Upshall, Scottie	Phoenix	1	—	—
Vanek, Thomas	Buf., Mtl.	8	1	—
van Riemsdyk, James	Philadelphia	1	—	—
Vermette, Antoine	Ott., Phx.	3	—	—
Versteeg, Kris	Florida	1	—	—
Visnovsky, Lubomir	L.A., Ana.	2	—	—
Voracek, Jakub	Philadelphia	1	—	—
Vrbata, Radim	Col., Car., Phx.	5	—	—
Ward, Joel	Washington	1	—	—
Weiss, Stephen	Florida	2	—	—
Wheeler, Blake	Boston	1	—	—
Williams, Jason	Detroit	1	—	—
Williams, Justin	Carolina	1	—	—
Yakupov, Nail	Edmonton	1	—	—
Zajac, Travis	New Jersey	1	—	—
Zetterberg, Henrik	Detroit	6	—	—
Zubrus, Dainius	Mtl., N.J.	1	1	—

Kyle Okposo of the New York Islanders celebrates his first-star selection after a four-goal game in a 6-3 win over Pittsburgh on January 16, 2015. It was the first hat trick of Okposo's NHL career.

Top 100 All-Time Goal-Scoring Leaders

* active player

	Player	Goals	Games	Goals per game	Seasons
1.	Wayne Gretzky, Edm., L.A., St.L., NYR .	894	1487	.601	20
2.	Gordie Howe, Det., Hfd.	801	1767	.453	26
3.	Brett Hull, Cgy., St.L., Dal., Det., Phx.	741	1269	.584	20
4.	Marcel Dionne, Det., L.A., NYR	731	1348	.542	18
* 5.	Jaromir Jagr, Pit., Wsh., NYR, Phi., Dal., Bos., N.J., Fla.	722	1550	.466	21
6.	Phil Esposito, Chi., Bos., NYR	717	1282	.559	18
7.	Mike Gartner, Wsh., Min., NYR, Tor., Phx.	708	1432	.494	19
8.	Mark Messier, Edm., NYR, Van.	694	1756	.395	25
9.	Steve Yzerman, Det.	692	1514	.457	22
10.	Mario Lemieux, Pit.	690	915	.754	18
11.	Teemu Selanne, Wpg., Ana., S.J., Col. . .	684	1451	.471	21
12.	Luc Robitaille, L.A., Pit., NYR, Det. . . .	668	1431	.467	19
13.	Brendan Shanahan, N.J., St.L., Hfd., Det., NYR	656	1524	.430	21
14.	Dave Andreychuk, Buf., Tor., N.J., Bos., Col., T.B.	640	1639	.390	23
15.	Joe Sakic, Que., Col.	625	1378	.454	20
16.	Bobby Hull, Chi., Wpg., Hfd.	610	1063	.574	16
17.	Dino Ciccarelli, Min., Wsh., Det., T.B., Fla.	608	1232	.494	19
18.	Jari Kurri, Edm., L.A., NYR, Ana., Col. . .	601	1251	.480	17
* 19.	Jarome Iginla, Cgy., Pit., Bos., Col. . . .	589	1392	.423	19
20.	Mark Recchi, Pit., Phi., Mtl., Car., Atl., T.B., Bos.	577	1652	.349	22
21.	Mike Bossy, NYI	573	752	.762	10
22.	Joe Nieuwendyk, Cgy., Dal., N.J., Tor., Fla.	564	1257	.449	20
23.	Mats Sundin, Que., Tor., Van.	564	1346	.419	18
24.	Mike Modano, Min., Dal., Det.	561	1499	.374	22
25.	Guy Lafleur, Mtl., NYR, Que.	560	1126	.497	17
26.	John Bucyk, Det., Bos.	556	1540	.361	23
27.	Ron Francis, Hfd., Pit., Car., Tor.	549	1731	.317	23
28.	Michel Goulet, Que., Chi.	548	1089	.503	15
29.	Maurice Richard, Mtl.	544	978	.556	18
30.	Stan Mikita, Chi.	541	1394	.388	22
31.	Keith Tkachuk, Wpg., Phx., St.L., Atl. . .	538	1201	.448	18
32.	Frank Mahovlich, Tor., Det., Mtl.	533	1181	.451	18
33.	Bryan Trottier, NYI, Pit.	524	1279	.410	18
34.	Pat Verbeek, N.J., Hfd., NYR, Dal., Det.	522	1424	.367	20
35.	Dale Hawerchuk, Wpg., Buf., St.L., Phi.	518	1188	.436	16
36.	Pierre Turgeon, Buf., NYI, Mtl., St.L., Dal., Col.	515	1294	.398	19
37.	Jeremy Roenick, Chi., Phx., Phi., L.A., S.J.	513	1363	.376	20
38.	Gilbert Perreault, Buf.	512	1191	.430	17
39.	Jean Beliveau, Mtl.	507	1125	.451	20
40.	Peter Bondra, Wsh., Ott., Atl., Chi. . . .	503	1081	.465	16
41.	Joe Mullen, St.L., Cgy., Pit., Bos.	502	1062	.473	17
42.	Lanny McDonald, Tor., Col., Cgy.	500	1111	.450	16
43.	Glenn Anderson, Edm., Tor., NYR, St.L.	498	1129	.441	16
44.	Jean Ratelle, NYR, Bos.	491	1281	.383	21
45.	Norm Ullman, Det., Tor.	490	1410	.348	20
* 46.	Marian Hossa, Ott., Atl., Pit., Det., Chi.	486	1172	.415	17
47.	Brian Bellows, Min., Mtl., T.B., Ana., Wsh.	485	1188	.408	17
48.	Darryl Sittler, Tor., Phi., Det.	484	1096	.442	15
49.	Sergei Fedorov, Det., Ana., CBJ, Wsh.	483	1248	.387	18
* 50.	Alex Ovechkin, Wsh.	475	760	.625	10
51.	Bernie Nicholls, L.A., NYR, Edm., N.J., Chi., S.J.	475	1127	.421	18
52.	Alexander Mogilny, Buf., Van., N.J., Tor.	473	990	.478	16
53.	Denis Savard, Chi., Mtl., T.B.	473	1196	.395	17
54.	Pat LaFontaine, NYI, Buf., NYR	468	865	.541	15
* 55.	Patrick Marleau, S.J.	456	1329	.343	17
56.	Alex Delvecchio, Det.	456	1549	.294	24
57.	Theoren Fleury, Cgy., Col., NYR, Chi. . .	455	1084	.420	15
58.	Rod Brind'Amour, St.L., Phi., Car.	452	1484	.305	21
59.	Peter Stastny, Que., N.J., St.L.	450	977	.461	15
60.	Doug Gilmour, St.L., Cgy., Tor., N.J., Chi., Buf., Mtl.	450	1474	.305	20
61.	Rick Middleton, NYR, Bos.	448	1005	.446	14
62.	Daniel Alfredsson, Ott., Det.	444	1246	.356	18
63.	Rick Vaive, Van., Tor., Chi., Buf.	441	876	.503	13
64.	Steve Larmer, Chi., NYR	441	1006	.438	15
65.	Rick Tocchet, Phi., Pit., L.A., Bos., Wsh., Phx.	440	1144	.385	18
66.	Gary Roberts, Cgy., Car., Tor., Fla., Pit., T.B.	438	1224	.358	22
67.	Pavel Bure, Van., Fla., NYR	437	702	.623	12
68.	Vincent Damphousse, Tor., Edm., Mtl., S.J.	432	1378	.313	18
69.	Dave Taylor, L.A.	431	1111	.388	17
70.	Alex Kovalev, NYR, Pit., Mtl., Ott., Fla. .	430	1316	.327	19

Passed by Jaromir Jagr in 2014-15, Phil Esposito now ranks sixth all-time in goals scored. He trailed only Gordie Howe at his retirement in 1981.

	Player	Goals	Games	Goals per game	Seasons
71.	Bill Guerin, N.J., Edm., Bos., Dal., St.L., S.J., NYI, Pit.	429	1263	.340	18
72.	Yvan Cournoyer, Mtl.	428	968	.442	16
73.	Brian Propp, Phi., Bos., Min., Hfd.	425	1016	.418	15
74.	Steve Shutt, Mtl., L.A.	424	930	.456	13
75.	Owen Nolan, Que., Col., S.J., Tor., Phx., Cgy., Min.	422	1200	.352	18
76.	Stephane Richer, Mtl., N.J., T.B., St.L., Pit.	421	1054	.399	17
77.	Steve Thomas, Tor., Chi., NYI, N.J., Ana., Det.	421	1235	.341	20
78.	Bill Barber, Phi.	420	903	.465	12
79.	Ilya Kovalchuk, Atl., N.J.	417	816	.511	11
80.	Jason Arnott, Edm., N.J., Dal., Nsh., Wsh., St.L.	417	1244	.335	18
81.	Tony Amonte, NYR, Chi., Phx., Phi., Cgy.	416	1174	.354	16
82.	Garry Unger, Tor., Det., St.L., Atl., L.A., Edm.	413	1105	.374	16
83.	John MacLean, N.J., S.J., NYR, Dal. . . .	413	1194	.346	18
* 84.	Vincent Lecavalier, T.B., Phi.	411	1163	.353	16
85.	Raymond Bourque, Bos., Col.	410	1612	.254	22
86.	Ray Ferraro, Hfd., NYI, NYR, L.A., Atl., St.L.	408	1258	.324	18
87.	John LeClair, Mtl., Phi., Pit.	406	967	.420	16
88.	Rod Gilbert, NYR	406	1065	.381	18
* 89.	Patrik Elias, N.J.	406	1224	.332	19
90.	John Ogrodnick, Det., Que., NYR	402	928	.433	14
91.	Paul Kariya, Ana., Col., Nsh., St.L. . . .	402	989	.406	15
92.	Dave Keon, Tor., Hfd.	396	1296	.306	18
93.	Paul Coffey, Edm., Pit., L.A., Det., Hfd., Phi., Chi., Car., Bos.	396	1409	.281	21
94.	Cam Neely, Van., Bos.	395	726	.544	13
95.	Pierre Larouche, Pit., Mtl., Hfd., NYR	395	812	.486	14
96.	Markus Naslund, Pit., Van., NYR	395	1117	.354	15
97.	Tomas Sandstrom, NYR, L.A., Pit., Det., Ana.	394	983	.401	15
98.	Bernie Geoffrion, Mtl., NYR	393	883	.445	16
99.	Jean Pronovost, Pit., Atl., Wsh.	391	998	.392	14
100.	Martin St. Louis, Cgy., T.B., NYR	391	1134	.345	16

Top 100 Active Goal-Scoring Leaders

Player	Goals	Games	Goals per game	Seasons
1. **Jaromir Jagr**, Pit., Wsh., NYR, Phi., Dal., Bos., N.J., Fla.	722	1550	.466	21
2. **Jarome Iginla**, Cgy., Pit., Bos., Col.	589	1392	.423	19
3. **Marian Hossa**, Ott., Atl., Pit., Det., Chi.	486	1172	.415	17
4. **Alex Ovechkin**, Wsh.	475	760	.625	10
5. **Patrick Marleau**, S.J.	456	1329	.343	17
6. **Vincent Lecavalier**, T.B., Phi.	411	1163	.353	16
7. **Patrik Elias**, N.J.	406	1224	.332	19
8. **Rick Nash**, CBJ, NYR	378	862	.439	12
9. **Marian Gaborik**, Min., NYR, CBJ, L.A.	374	879	.425	14
10. **Dany Heatley**, Atl., Ott., S.J., Min., Ana.	372	869	.428	13
11. **Shane Doan**, Wpg., Phx., Ari.	368	1394	.264	19
12. **Joe Thornton**, Bos., S.J.	358	1285	.279	17
13. **Daniel Sedin**, Van.	327	1061	.308	14
14. **Olli Jokinen**, L.A., NYI, Fla., Phx., Cgy., NYR, Wpg., Nsh., Tor., St.L.	321	1231	.261	17
15. **Eric Staal**, Car.	312	846	.369	11
16. **Sidney Crosby**, Pit.	302	627	.482	10
17. **Thomas Vanek**, Buf., NYI, Mtl., Min.	298	743	.401	10
18. **Pavel Datsyuk**, Det.	298	887	.336	13
19. **Corey Perry**, Ana.	296	722	.410	10
20. **Henrik Zetterberg**, Det.	296	836	.354	12
21. **Brad Richards**, T.B., Dal., NYR, Chi.	288	1058	.272	14
22. **Jeff Carter**, Phi., CBJ, L.A.	283	718	.394	10
23. **Scott Hartnell**, Nsh., Phi., CBJ	278	1030	.270	14
24. **Steven Stamkos**, T.B.	276	492	.561	7
25. **Alex Tanguay**, Col., Cgy., Mtl., T.B.	275	1018	.270	15
26. **Zach Parise**, N.J., Min.	274	691	.397	10
27. **Evgeni Malkin**, Pit.	268	587	.457	9
28. **Jason Spezza**, Ott., Dal.	268	768	.349	12
29. **Erik Cole**, Car., Edm., Mtl., Dal., Det.	265	892	.297	13
30. **Brenden Morrow**, Dal., Pit., St.L., T.B.	265	991	.267	15
31. **Mike Cammalleri**, L.A., Cgy., Mtl., N.J.	263	737	.357	12
32. **Brian Gionta**, N.J., Mtl., Buf.	262	845	.310	13
33. **Patrick Sharp**, Phi., Chi.	249	745	.334	12
34. **Phil Kessel**, Bos., Tor.	247	668	.370	9
35. **Radim Vrbata**, Col., Car., Chi., Phx., T.B., Van.	246	871	.282	13
36. **Mike Fisher**, Ott., Nsh.	245	946	.259	15
37. **Martin Havlat**, Ott., Chi., Min., S.J., N.J.	241	788	.306	14
38. **Alexander Semin**, Wsh., Car.	238	635	.375	10
39. **Jason Pominville**, Buf., Min.	237	752	.315	11
40. **Michael Ryder**, Mtl., Bos., Dal., N.J.	237	806	.294	11
41. **Joe Pavelski**, S.J.	228	643	.355	9
42. **Justin Williams**, Phi., Car., L.A.	227	918	.247	14
43. **Dainius Zubrus**, Phi., Mtl., Wsh., Buf., N.J.	225	1243	.181	18
44. **Chris Kunitz**, Ana., Atl., Pit.	224	733	.306	11
45. **Jonathan Toews**, Chi.	223	565	.395	8
46. **David Legwand**, Nsh., Det., Ott.	223	1057	.211	16
47. **Sergei Gonchar**, Wsh., Bos., Pit., Ott., Dal., Mtl.	220	1301	.169	20
48. **Matt Cullen**, Ana., Fla., Car., NYR, Ott., Min., Nsh.	219	1212	.181	17
49. **Anze Kopitar**, L.A.	218	683	.319	9
50. **Mike Ribeiro**, Mtl., Dal., Wsh., Phx., Nsh.	217	947	.229	15
51. **Henrik Sedin**, Van.	211	1092	.193	14
52. **Ryan Getzlaf**, Ana.	208	710	.293	10
53. **Dustin Brown**, L.A.	207	802	.258	11
54. **Patrice Bergeron**, Bos.	206	740	.278	11
55. **Patrick Kane**, Chi.	205	576	.356	8
56. **Nathan Horton**, Fla., Bos., CBJ	203	627	.324	10
57. **Brad Boyes**, S.J., Bos., St.L., Buf., NYI, Fla.	203	762	.266	11
58. **Ryan Kesler**, Van., Ana.	202	736	.274	11
59. **Tomas Plekanec**, Mtl.	202	761	.265	11
60. **Milan Michalek**, S.J., Ott.	200	697	.287	11
61. **Joffrey Lupul**, Ana., Edm., Phi., Tor.	194	655	.296	11
62. **Antoine Vermette**, Ott., CBJ, Phx., Ari., Chi.	194	834	.233	11
63. **Derek Roy**, Buf., Dal., Van., St.L., Nsh., Edm.	189	738	.256	11
64. **Bobby Ryan**, Ana., Ott.	188	526	.357	8
65. **Pascal Dupuis**, Min., NYR, Atl., Pit.	188	853	.220	14
66. **Johan Franzen**, Det.	187	600	.312	10
67. **Jochen Hecht**, St.L., Edm., Buf.	186	833	.223	14
68. **David Backes**, St.L.	185	648	.285	9
69. **Andrew Ladd**, Car., Chi., Atl., Wpg.	185	691	.268	10
70. **Michal Handzus**, St.L., Phx., Phi., Chi., L.A., S.J.	185	1009	.183	15
71. **James Neal**, Dal., Pit., Nsh.	184	480	.383	7
72. **Loui Eriksson**, Dal., Bos.	182	643	.283	9
73. **Alexander Steen**, Tor., St.L.	180	679	.265	10
74. **Shawn Horcoff**, Edm., Dal.	180	949	.190	14
75. **Scott Gomez**, N.J., NYR, Mtl., S.J., Fla.	180	1045	.172	15
76. **Ryan Malone**, Pit., T.B., NYR	179	647	.277	11
77. **Mike Richards**, Phi., L.A.	179	710	.252	10

Eric Staal scored the 300th goal of his career on January 6, 2015. He had 23 goals and 31 assists for the Hurricanes in 2014-15.

Player	Goals	Games	Goals per game	Seasons
78. **RJ Umberger**, Phi., CBJ	178	740	.241	10
79. **Paul Stastny**, Col., St.L.	176	612	.288	9
80. **Martin Erat**, Nsh., Wsh., Phx., Ari.	176	881	.200	13
81. **Alexandre Burrows**, Van.	175	688	.254	10
82. **John Tavares**, NYI	174	432	.403	6
83. **Ruslan Fedotenko**, Phi., T.B., NYI, Pit., NYR	173	863	.200	12
84. **Zdeno Chara**, NYI, Ott., Bos.	169	1195	.141	17
85. **Matt Cooke**, Van., Wsh., Pit., Min.	167	1046	.160	16
86. **Lee Stempniak**, St.L., Tor., Phx., Cgy., Pit., NYR, Wpg.	165	708	.233	10
87. **Dan Cleary**, Chi., Edm., Phx., Det.	165	938	.176	17
88. **Ryan Callahan**, NYR, T.B.	162	547	.296	9
89. **Chris Higgins**, Mtl., NYR, Cgy., Fla., Van.	162	678	.239	11
90. **Jussi Jokinen**, Dal., T.B., Car., Pit., Fla.	157	741	.212	10
91. **Ales Hemsky**, Edm., Ott., Dal.	157	748	.210	12
92. **Stephen Weiss**, Fla., Det.	156	732	.213	13
93. **Matt Moulson**, L.A., NYI, Buf., Min.	154	474	.325	8
94. **Drew Stafford**, Buf., Wpg.	154	589	.261	9
95. **Dan Boyle**, Fla., T.B., S.J., NYR	153	1019	.150	16
96. **Jamie Benn**, Dal.	151	426	.354	6
97. **Dustin Penner**, Ana., Edm., L.A., Wsh.	151	589	.256	9
98. **Jordan Staal**, Pit., Car.	151	607	.249	9
99. **Rene Bourque**, Chi., Cgy., Mtl., Ana., CBJ.	148	611	.242	10
100. **Tuomo Ruutu**, Chi., Car., N.J.	148	702	.211	11

Top 100 All-Time Assist Leaders

* active player

Player	Assists	Games	Assists per game	Seasons
1. **Wayne Gretzky**, Edm., L.A., St.L., NYR .	**1963**	1487	1.320	20
2. **Ron Francis**, Hfd., Pit., Car., Tor.	**1249**	1731	.722	23
3. **Mark Messier**, Edm., NYR, Van.	**1193**	1756	.679	25
4. **Raymond Bourque**, Bos., Col.	**1169**	1612	.725	22
5. **Paul Coffey**, Edm., Pit., L.A., Det., Hfd., Phi., Chi., Car., Bos.	**1135**	1409	.806	21
* 6. **Jaromir Jagr**, Pit., Wsh., NYR, Phi., Dal., Bos., N.J., Fla.	**1080**	1550	.697	21
7. **Adam Oates**, Det., St.L., Bos., Wsh., Phi., Ana., Edm.	**1079**	1337	.807	19
8. **Steve Yzerman**, Det.	**1063**	1514	.702	22
9. **Gordie Howe**, Det., Hfd.	**1049**	1767	.594	26
10. **Marcel Dionne**, Det., L.A., NYR	**1040**	1348	.772	18
11. **Mario Lemieux**, Pit.	**1033**	915	1.129	18
12. **Joe Sakic**, Que., Col.	**1016**	1378	.737	20
13. **Doug Gilmour**, St.L., Cgy., Tor., N.J., Chi., Buf., Mtl.	**964**	1474	.654	20
14. **Mark Recchi**, Pit., Phi., Mtl., Car., Atl., T.B., Bos.	**956**	1652	.579	22
15. **Al MacInnis**, Cgy., St.L.	**934**	1416	.660	23
16. **Larry Murphy**, L.A., Wsh., Min., Pit., Tor., Det.	**929**	1615	.575	21
17. **Stan Mikita**, Chi.	**926**	1394	.664	22
18. **Bryan Trottier**, NYI, Pit.	**901**	1279	.704	18
* 19. **Joe Thornton**, Bos., S.J.	**901**	1285	.701	17
20. **Phil Housley**, Buf., Wpg., St.L., Cgy., N.J., Wsh., Chi., Tor.	**894**	1495	.598	21
21. **Dale Hawerchuk**, Wpg., Buf., St.L., Phi.	**891**	1188	.750	16
22. **Nicklas Lidstrom**, Det.	**878**	1564	.561	20
23. **Phil Esposito**, Chi., Bos., NYR	**873**	1282	.681	18
24. **Denis Savard**, Chi., Mtl., T.B.	**865**	1196	.723	17
25. **Bobby Clarke**, Phi.	**852**	1144	.745	15
26. **Alex Delvecchio**, Det.	**825**	1549	.533	24
27. **Gilbert Perreault**, Buf.	**814**	1191	.683	17
28. **Mike Modano**, Min., Dal., Det.	**813**	1499	.542	22
29. **John Bucyk**, Det., Bos.	**813**	1540	.528	23
30. **Pierre Turgeon**, Buf., NYI, Mtl., St.L., Col.	**812**	1294	.628	19
31. **Jari Kurri**, Edm., L.A., NYR, Ana., Col. . .	**797**	1251	.637	17
32. **Guy Lafleur**, Mtl., NYR, Que.	**793**	1126	.704	17
33. **Peter Stastny**, Que., N.J., St.L.	**789**	977	.808	15
34. **Mats Sundin**, Que., Tor., Van.	**785**	1346	.583	18
35. **Brian Leetch**, NYR, Tor., Bos.	**781**	1205	.648	18
36. **Jean Ratelle**, NYR, Bos.	**776**	1281	.606	21
37. **Vincent Damphousse**, Tor., Edm., Mtl., S.J.	**773**	1378	.561	18
38. **Teemu Selanne**, Wpg., Ana., S.J., Col. . .	**773**	1451	.533	21
39. **Chris Chelios**, Mtl., Chi., Det., Atl. . . .	**763**	1651	.462	26
40. **Bernie Federko**, St.L., Det.	**761**	1000	.761	14
41. **Doug Weight**, NYR, Edm., St.L., Car., Ana., NYI	**755**	1238	.610	20
42. **Larry Robinson**, Mtl., L.A.	**750**	1384	.542	20
43. **Denis Potvin**, NYI	**742**	1060	.700	15
44. **Norm Ullman**, Det., Tor.	**739**	1410	.524	20
45. **Bernie Nicholls**, L.A., NYR, Edm., N.J., Chi., S.J.	**734**	1127	.651	18
46. **Rod Brind'Amour**, St.L., Phi., Car.	**732**	1484	.493	21
47. **Luc Robitaille**, L.A., Pit., NYR, Det.	**726**	1431	.507	19
48. **Daniel Alfredsson**, Ott., Det.	**713**	1246	.572	18
49. **Jean Beliveau**, Mtl.	**712**	1125	.633	20
50. **Scott Stevens**, Wsh., St.L., N.J.	**712**	1635	.435	22
* 51. **Henrik Sedin**, Van.	**704**	1092	.645	14
52. **Jeremy Roenick**, Chi., Phx., Phi., L.A., S.J.	**703**	1363	.516	20
53. **Brendan Shanahan**, N.J., St.L., Hfd., Det., NYR	**698**	1524	.458	21
54. **Dave Andreychuk**, Buf., Tor., N.J., Bos., Col., T.B.	**698**	1639	.426	23
55. **Dale Hunter**, Que., Wsh., Col.	**697**	1407	.495	19
56. **Sergei Fedorov**, Det., Ana., CBJ, Wsh. . .	**696**	1248	.558	18
57. **Henri Richard**, Mtl.	**688**	1256	.548	20
58. **Brad Park**, NYR, Bos., Det.	**683**	1113	.614	17
59. **Bobby Smith**, Min., Mtl.	**679**	1077	.630	15
60. **Ray Whitney**, S.J., Edm., Fla., CBJ, Det., Car., Phx., Dal.	**679**	1330	.511	22
61. **Brett Hull**, Cgy., St.L., Dal., Det., Phx. . .	**650**	1269	.512	20
62. **Bobby Orr**, Bos., Chi.	**645**	657	.982	12
63. **Martin St. Louis**, Cgy., T.B., NYR	**642**	1134	.566	16
64. **Gary Suter**, Cgy., Chi., S.J.	**641**	1145	.560	17
65. **Dave Taylor**, L.A.	**638**	1111	.574	17
66. **Darryl Sittler**, Tor., Phi., Det.	**637**	1096	.581	15
67. **Borje Salming**, Tor., Det.	**637**	1148	.555	17
* 68. **Jarome Iginla**, Cgy., Pit., Bos., Col.	**637**	1392	.458	19
69. **Peter Forsberg**, Que., Col., Phi., Nsh. . . .	**636**	708	.898	14
70. **Neal Broten**, Min., Dal., N.J., L.A.	**634**	1099	.577	17
71. **Theoren Fleury**, Cgy., Col., NYR, Chi. . . .	**633**	1084	.584	15

Best known for his booming slap shot, Bobby Hull scored 610 goals in the NHL, but also had 560 assists, ranking him 100th all-time in this category.

Player	Assists	Games	Assists per game	Seasons
72. **Mike Gartner**, Wsh., Min., NYR, Tor., Phx.	**627**	1432	.438	19
73. **Andy Bathgate**, NYR, Tor., Det., Pit. . . .	**624**	1069	.584	17
74. **Sergei Zubov**, NYR, Pit., Dal.	**619**	1068	.580	16
* 75. **Brad Richards**, T.B., Dal., NYR, Chi. . . .	**616**	1058	.582	14
76. **Rod Gilbert**, NYR	**615**	1065	.577	18
* 77. **Patrik Elias**, N.J.	**611**	1224	.499	19
78. **Michel Goulet**, Que., Chi.	**604**	1089	.555	15
79. **Kirk Muller**, N.J., Mtl., NYI, Tor., Fla., Dal.	**602**	1349	.446	19
80. **Glenn Anderson**, Edm., Tor., NYR, St.L. .	**601**	1129	.532	16
81. **Alex Kovalev**, NYR, Pit., Mtl., Ott., Fla. .	**599**	1316	.455	19
82. **Dino Ciccarelli**, Min., Wsh., Det., T.B., Fla.	**592**	1232	.481	19
* 83. **Sergei Gonchar**, Wsh., Bos., Pit., Ott., Dal., Mtl.	**591**	1301	.454	20
84. **Doug Wilson**, Chi., S.J.	**590**	1024	.576	16
85. **Dave Keon**, Tor., Hfd.	**590**	1296	.455	18
86. **Paul Kariya**, Ana., Col., Nsh., St.L.	**587**	989	.594	15
87. **Dave Babych**, Wpg., Hfd., Van., Phi., L.A.	**581**	1195	.486	19
88. **Brian Propp**, Phi., Bos., Min., Hfd.	**579**	1016	.570	15
89. **Saku Koivu**, Mtl., Ana.	**577**	1124	.513	18
* 90. **Pavel Datsyuk**, Det.	**571**	887	.644	13
91. **Steve Larmer**, Chi., NYR.	**571**	1006	.568	15
* 92. **Marian Hossa**, Ott., Atl., Pit., Det., Chi. .	**570**	1172	.486	17
93. **Frank Mahovlich**, Tor., Det., Mtl.	**570**	1181	.483	18
94. **Scott Niedermayer**, N.J., Ana.	**568**	1263	.450	18
* 95. **Scott Gomez**, N.J., NYR, Mtl., S.J., Fla. .	**567**	1045	.543	15
96. **Craig Janney**, Bos., St.L., S.J., Wpg., Phx., T.B., NYI	**563**	760	.741	12
97. **Cliff Ronning**, St.L., Van., Phx., Nsh., L.A., Min., NYI	**563**	1137	.495	18
98. **Joe Nieuwendyk**, Cgy., Dal., N.J., Tor., Fla.	**562**	1257	.447	20
99. **Joe Mullen**, St.L., Cgy., Pit., Bos.	**561**	1062	.528	17
100. **Bobby Hull**, Chi., Wpg., Hfd.	**560**	1063	.527	16

Top 100 Active Assist Leaders

Player	Assists	Games	Assists per game	Seasons
1. Jaromir Jagr, Pit., Wsh., NYR, Phi., Dal., Bos., N.J., Fla.	1080	1550	.697	21
2. Joe Thornton, Bos., S.J.	901	1285	.701	17
3. Henrik Sedin, Van.	704	1092	.645	14
4. Jarome Iginla, Cgy., Pit., Bos., Col.	637	1392	.458	19
5. Brad Richards, T.B., Dal., NYR, Chi.	616	1058	.582	14
6. Patrik Elias, N.J.	611	1224	.499	19
7. Sergei Gonchar, Wsh., Bos., Pit., Ott., Dal., Mtl.	591	1301	.454	20
8. Pavel Datsyuk, Det.	571	887	.644	13
9. Marian Hossa, Ott., Atl., Pit., Det., Chi.	570	1172	.486	17
10. Scott Gomez, N.J., NYR, Mtl., S.J., Fla.	567	1045	.543	15
11. Daniel Sedin, Van.	554	1061	.522	14
12. Alex Tanguay, Col., Cgy., Mtl., T.B.	553	1018	.543	15
13. Sidney Crosby, Pit.	551	627	.879	10
14. Patrick Marleau, S.J.	532	1329	.400	17
15. Shane Doan, Wpg., Phx., Ari.	530	1394	.380	19
16. Vincent Lecavalier, T.B., Phi.	520	1163	.447	16
17. Mike Ribeiro, Mtl., Dal., Wsh., Phx., Nsh.	501	947	.529	15
18. Henrik Zetterberg, Det.	490	836	.586	12
19. Jason Spezza, Ott., Dal.	481	768	.626	12
20. Ryan Getzlaf, Ana.	470	710	.662	10
21. Evgeni Malkin, Pit.	434	587	.739	9
22. Eric Staal, Car.	430	846	.508	11
23. Olli Jokinen, L.A., NYI, Fla., Phx., Cgy., NYR, Wpg., Nsh., Tor., St.L.	429	1231	.348	17
24. Dan Boyle, Fla., T.B., S.J., NYR	428	1019	.420	16
25. Nicklas Backstrom, Wsh.	427	577	.740	8
26. Alex Ovechkin, Wsh.	420	760	.553	10
27. Dany Heatley, Atl., Ott., S.J., Min., Ana.	419	869	.482	13
28. Matt Cullen, Ana., Fla., Car., NYR, Ott., Min., Nsh.	407	1212	.336	17
29. Anze Kopitar, L.A.	392	683	.574	9
30. Andrei Markov, Mtl.	384	846	.454	14
31. David Legwand, Nsh., Det., Ott.	381	1057	.360	16
32. Brian Campbell, Buf., S.J., Chi., Fla.	380	920	.413	15
33. Marian Gaborik, Min., NYR, CBJ, L.A.	377	879	.429	14
34. Ales Hemsky, Edm., Ott., Dal.	369	748	.493	12
35. Martin Erat, Nsh., Wsh., Phx., Ari.	369	881	.419	13
36. Zdeno Chara, NYI, Ott., Bos.	369	1195	.309	17
37. Lubomir Visnovsky, L.A., Edm., Ana., NYI	367	883	.416	14
38. Dainius Zubrus, Phi., Mtl., Wsh., Buf., N.J.	359	1243	.289	18
39. Mikko Koivu, Min.	356	681	.523	10
40. Justin Williams, Phi., Car., L.A.	355	918	.387	14
41. Patrick Kane, Chi.	352	576	.611	8
42. Martin Havlat, Ott., Chi., Min., S.J., N.J.	352	788	.447	14
43. Patrice Bergeron, Bos.	344	740	.465	11
44. Jason Pominville, Buf., Min.	342	752	.455	11
45. Duncan Keith, Chi.	340	766	.444	10
46. Derek Roy, Buf., Dal., Van., St.L., Nsh., Edm.	335	738	.454	11
47. Paul Stastny, Col., St.L.	328	612	.536	9
48. Rick Nash, CBJ, NYR	319	862	.370	12
49. Scott Hartnell, Nsh., Phi., CBJ.	319	1030	.310	14
50. Marek Zidlicky, Nsh., Min., N.J., Det.	316	783	.404	11
51. Shawn Horcoff, Edm., Dal.	316	949	.333	14
52. Thomas Vanek, Buf., NYI, Mtl., Min.	310	743	.417	10
53. Brenden Morrow, Dal., Pit., St.L., T.B.	310	991	.313	15
54. Claude Giroux, Phi.	306	496	.617	8
55. Corey Perry, Ana.	306	722	.424	10
56. Mike Richards, Phi., L.A.	303	710	.427	10
57. Jussi Jokinen, Dal., T.B., Car., Pit., Fla.	301	741	.406	10
58. Mark Streit, Mtl., NYI, Phi.	300	654	.459	9
59. Ryan Suter, Nsh., Min.	299	749	.399	10
60. Michal Handzus, St.L., Phx., Phi., Chi., L.A., S.J.	298	1009	.295	15
61. Tomas Plekanec, Mtl.	297	761	.390	11
62. David Krejci, Bos.	292	551	.530	9
63. Zach Parise, N.J., Min.	292	691	.423	10
64. Chris Kunitz, Ana., Atl., Pit.	287	733	.392	11
65. Jonathan Toews, Chi.	283	565	.501	8
66. Dion Phaneuf, Cgy., Tor.	283	750	.377	10
67. Mike Cammalleri, L.A., Cgy., Mtl., N.J.	281	737	.381	12
68. Radim Vrbata, Col., Car., Chi., Phx., T.B., Van.	281	871	.323	13
69. Jay Bouwmeester, Fla., Cgy., St.L.	279	918	.304	12
70. Brad Boyes, S.J., Bos., St.L., Buf., NYI, Fla.	278	762	.365	11
71. Patrick Sharp, Phi., Chi.	277	745	.372	12
72. Jochen Hecht, St.L., Edm., Buf.	277	833	.333	14
73. Alexander Semin, Wsh., Car.	275	635	.433	10
74. Mike Fisher, Ott., Nsh.	275	946	.291	15
75. Phil Kessel, Bos., Tor.	273	668	.409	9
76. Niklas Kronwall, Det.	268	674	.398	11
77. Stephen Weiss, Fla., Det.	267	732	.365	13
78. Erik Cole, Car., Edm., Mtl., Dal., Det.	267	892	.299	13
79. John-Michael Liles, Col., Tor., Car.	263	719	.366	11
80. Loui Eriksson, Dal., Bos.	259	643	.403	9
81. Dennis Wideman, St.L., Bos., Fla., Wsh., Cgy.	258	707	.365	10
82. Brian Gionta, N.J., Mtl., Buf.	258	845	.305	13
83. Joe Pavelski, S.J.	257	643	.400	9
84. Keith Yandle, Phx., Ari., NYR	255	579	.440	9
85. Christian Ehrhoff, S.J., Van., Buf., Pit.	255	741	.344	11
86. Brad Stuart, S.J., Bos., Cgy., L.A., Det., Col.	255	1050	.243	15
87. Alexander Steen, Tor., St.L.	249	679	.367	10
88. Jakub Voracek, CBJ, Phi.	248	531	.467	7
89. Mike Green, Wsh.	247	575	.430	10
90. Brent Seabrook, Chi.	247	763	.324	10
91. Michael Ryder, Mtl., Bos., Dal., N.J.	247	806	.306	11
92. Pierre-Marc Bouchard, Min., NYI	246	593	.415	11
93. Shea Weber, Nsh.	246	685	.359	10
94. Jeff Carter, Phi., CBJ, L.A.	239	718	.333	11
95. Jarret Stoll, Edm., L.A.	239	792	.302	12
96. Antoine Vermette, Ott., CBJ, Phx., Ari., Chi.	239	834	.287	11
97. Ryan Kesler, Van., Ana.	238	736	.323	11
98. Dan Hamhuis, Nsh., Van.	238	814	.292	11
99. Andrew Ladd, Car., Chi., Atl., Wpg.	235	691	.340	10
100. Dustin Brown, L.A.	235	802	.293	11

With 571 assists in his career, Detroit's Pavel Datsyuk has climbed into the top 10 among active players in the NHL. Datsyuk had 26 goals and 39 assists for 65 points in just 63 games played in 2014-15.

Top 100 All-Time Point Leaders

* active player

Mark Messier poses with the pucks from his 500th-goal game on November 6, 1995. Messier trails only his longtime teammate Wayne Gretzky among the NHL's all-time points leaders.

	Player	Points	Games	Points per game	Goals	Assists	Seasons
1.	**Wayne Gretzky**, Edm., L.A., St.L., NYR	**2857**	1487	1.921	894	1963	20
2.	**Mark Messier**, Edm., NYR, Van.	**1887**	1756	1.075	694	1193	25
3.	**Gordie Howe**, Det., Hfd.	**1850**	1767	1.047	801	1049	26
* 4.	**Jaromir Jagr**, Pit., Wsh., NYR, Phi., Dal., Bos., N.J., Fla.	**1802**	1550	1.163	722	1080	21
5.	**Ron Francis**, Hfd., Pit., Car., Tor.	**1798**	1731	1.039	549	1249	23
6.	**Marcel Dionne**, Det., L.A., NYR	**1771**	1348	1.314	731	1040	18
7.	**Steve Yzerman**, Det.	**1755**	1514	1.159	692	1063	22
8.	**Mario Lemieux**, Pit.	**1723**	915	1.883	690	1033	18
9.	**Joe Sakic**, Que., Col.	**1641**	1378	1.191	625	1016	20
10.	**Phil Esposito**, Chi., Bos., NYR	**1590**	1282	1.240	717	873	18
11.	**Raymond Bourque**, Bos., Col.	**1579**	1612	.980	410	1169	22
12.	**Mark Recchi**, Pit., Phi., Mtl., Car., Atl., T.B., Bos.	**1533**	1652	.928	577	956	22
13.	**Paul Coffey**, Edm., Pit., L.A., Det., Hfd., Phi., Chi., Car., Bos.	**1531**	1409	1.087	396	1135	21
14.	**Stan Mikita**, Chi.	**1467**	1394	1.052	541	926	22
15.	**Teemu Selanne**, Wpg., Ana., S.J., Col.	**1457**	1451	1.004	684	773	21
16.	**Bryan Trottier**, NYI, Pit.	**1425**	1279	1.114	524	901	18
17.	**Adam Oates**, Det., St.L., Bos., Wsh., Phi., Ana., Edm.	**1420**	1337	1.062	341	1079	19
18.	**Doug Gilmour**, St.L., Cgy., Tor., N.J., Chi., Buf., Mtl.	**1414**	1474	.959	450	964	20
19.	**Dale Hawerchuk**, Wpg., Buf., St.L., Phi.	**1409**	1188	1.186	518	891	16
20.	**Jari Kurri**, Edm., L.A., NYR, Ana., Col.	**1398**	1251	1.118	601	797	17
21.	**Luc Robitaille**, L.A., Pit., NYR, Det.	**1394**	1431	.974	668	726	19
22.	**Brett Hull**, Cgy., St.L., Dal., Det., Phx.	**1391**	1269	1.096	741	650	20
23.	**Mike Modano**, Min., Dal., Det.	**1374**	1499	.917	561	813	22
24.	**John Bucyk**, Det., Bos.	**1369**	1540	.889	556	813	23
25.	**Brendan Shanahan**, N.J., St.L., Hfd., Det., NYR	**1354**	1524	.888	656	698	21
26.	**Guy Lafleur**, Mtl., NYR, Que.	**1353**	1126	1.202	560	793	17
27.	**Mats Sundin**, Que., Tor., Van.	**1349**	1346	1.002	564	785	18
28.	**Denis Savard**, Chi., Mtl., T.B.	**1338**	1196	1.119	473	865	17
29.	**Dave Andreychuk**, Buf., Tor., N.J., Bos., Col., T.B.	**1338**	1639	.816	640	698	23
30.	**Mike Gartner**, Wsh., Min., NYR, Tor., Phx.	**1335**	1432	.932	708	627	19
31.	**Pierre Turgeon**, Buf., NYI, Mtl., St.L., Dal., Col.	**1327**	1294	1.026	515	812	19
32.	**Gilbert Perreault**, Buf.	**1326**	1191	1.113	512	814	17
33.	**Alex Delvecchio**, Det.	**1281**	1549	.827	456	825	24
34.	**Al MacInnis**, Cgy., St.L.	**1274**	1416	.900	340	934	23
35.	**Jean Ratelle**, NYR, Bos.	**1267**	1281	.989	491	776	21
* 36.	**Joe Thornton**, Bos., S.J.	**1259**	1285	.980	358	901	17
37.	**Peter Stastny**, Que., N.J., St.L.	**1239**	977	1.268	450	789	15
38.	**Phil Housley**, Buf., Wpg., St.L., Cgy., N.J., Wsh., Chi., Tor.	**1232**	1495	.824	338	894	21
39.	**Norm Ullman**, Det., Tor.	**1229**	1410	.872	490	739	20
* 40.	**Jarome Iginla**, Cgy., Pit., Bos., Col.	**1226**	1392	.881	589	637	19
41.	**Jean Beliveau**, Mtl.	**1219**	1125	1.084	507	712	20
42.	**Jeremy Roenick**, Chi., Phx., Phi., L.A., S.J.	**1216**	1363	.892	513	703	20
43.	**Larry Murphy**, L.A., Wsh., Min., Pit., Tor., Det.	**1216**	1615	.753	287	929	21
44.	**Bobby Clarke**, Phi.	**1210**	1144	1.058	358	852	15
45.	**Bernie Nicholls**, L.A., NYR, Edm., N.J., Chi., S.J.	**1209**	1127	1.073	475	734	18
46.	**Vincent Damphousse**, Tor., Edm., Mtl., S.J.	**1205**	1378	.874	432	773	18
47.	**Dino Ciccarelli**, Min., Wsh., Det., T.B., Fla.	**1200**	1232	.974	608	592	19
48.	**Rod Brind'Amour**, St.L., Phi., Car.	**1184**	1484	.798	452	732	21
49.	**Sergei Fedorov**, Det., Ana., CBJ, Wsh.	**1179**	1248	.945	483	696	18
50.	**Bobby Hull**, Chi., Wpg., Hfd.	**1170**	1063	1.101	610	560	16
51.	**Daniel Alfredsson**, Ott., Det.	**1157**	1246	.929	444	713	18
52.	**Michel Goulet**, Que., Chi.	**1152**	1089	1.058	548	604	15
53.	**Nicklas Lidstrom**, Det.	**1142**	1564	.730	264	878	20
54.	**Bernie Federko**, St.L., Det.	**1130**	1000	1.130	369	761	14
55.	**Mike Bossy**, NYI	**1126**	752	1.497	573	553	10
56.	**Joe Nieuwendyk**, Cgy., Dal., N.J., Tor., Fla.	**1126**	1257	.896	564	562	20
57.	**Darryl Sittler**, Tor., Phi., Det.	**1121**	1096	1.023	484	637	15
58.	**Frank Mahovlich**, Tor., Det., Mtl.	**1103**	1181	.934	533	570	18
59.	**Glenn Anderson**, Edm., Tor., NYR, St.L.	**1099**	1129	.973	498	601	16
60.	**Theoren Fleury**, Cgy., Col., NYR, Chi.	**1088**	1084	1.004	455	633	15
61.	**Dave Taylor**, L.A.	**1069**	1111	.962	431	638	17
62.	**Keith Tkachuk**, Wpg., Phx., St.L., Atl.	**1065**	1201	.887	538	527	18
63.	**Ray Whitney**, S.J., Edm., Fla., CBJ, Det., Car., Phx., Dal.	**1064**	1330	.800	385	679	22
64.	**Joe Mullen**, St.L., Cgy., Pit., Bos.	**1063**	1062	1.001	502	561	17
65.	**Pat Verbeek**, N.J., Hfd., NYR, Dal., Det.	**1063**	1424	.746	522	541	20
* 66.	**Marian Hossa**, Ott., Atl., Pit., Det., Chi.	**1056**	1172	.901	486	570	17
67.	**Denis Potvin**, NYI	**1052**	1060	.992	310	742	15
68.	**Henri Richard**, Mtl.	**1046**	1256	.833	358	688	20
69.	**Bobby Smith**, Min., Mtl.	**1036**	1077	.962	357	679	15
70.	**Martin St. Louis**, Cgy., T.B., NYR	**1033**	1134	.911	391	642	16
71.	**Doug Weight**, NYR, Edm., St.L., Car., Ana., NYI	**1033**	1238	.834	278	755	20
72.	**Alexander Mogilny**, Buf., Van., N.J., Tor.	**1032**	990	1.042	473	559	16
73.	**Alex Kovalev**, NYR, Pit., Mtl., Ott., Fla.	**1029**	1316	.782	430	599	19
74.	**Brian Leetch**, NYR, Tor., Bos.	**1028**	1205	.853	247	781	18
75.	**Brian Bellows**, Min., Mtl., T.B., Ana., Wsh.	**1022**	1188	.860	485	537	17
76.	**Rod Gilbert**, NYR	**1021**	1065	.959	406	615	18
77.	**Dale Hunter**, Que., Wsh., Col.	**1020**	1407	.725	323	697	19
* 78.	**Patrik Elias**, N.J.	**1017**	1224	.831	406	611	19
79.	**Pat LaFontaine**, NYI, Buf., NYR	**1013**	865	1.171	468	545	15
80.	**Steve Larmer**, Chi., NYR	**1012**	1006	1.006	441	571	15
81.	**Lanny McDonald**, Tor., Col., Cgy.	**1006**	1111	.905	500	506	16
82.	**Brian Propp**, Phi., Bos., Min., Hfd.	**1004**	1016	.988	425	579	15
83.	**Paul Kariya**, Ana., Col., Nsh., St.L.	**989**	989	1.000	402	587	15
84.	**Rick Middleton**, NYR, Bos.	**988**	1005	.983	448	540	14
* 85.	**Patrick Marleau**, S.J.	**988**	1329	.743	456	532	17
86.	**Dave Keon**, Tor., Hfd.	**986**	1296	.761	396	590	18
87.	**Andy Bathgate**, NYR, Tor., Det., Pit.	**973**	1069	.910	349	624	17
88.	**Maurice Richard**, Mtl.	**965**	978	.987	544	421	18
89.	**Kirk Muller**, N.J., Mtl., NYI, Tor., Fla., Dal.	**959**	1349	.711	357	602	19
90.	**Larry Robinson**, Mtl., L.A.	**958**	1384	.692	208	750	20
91.	**Rick Tocchet**, Phi., Pit., L.A., Bos., Wsh., Phx.	**952**	1144	.832	440	512	18
92.	**Chris Chelios**, Mtl., Chi., Det., Atl.	**948**	1651	.574	185	763	26
93.	**Jason Arnott**, Edm., N.J., Dal., Nsh., Wsh., St.L.	**938**	1244	.754	417	521	18
94.	**Steve Thomas**, Tor., Chi., NYI, N.J., Ana., Det.	**933**	1235	.755	421	512	20
* 95.	**Vincent Lecavalier**, T.B., Phi.	**931**	1163	.801	411	520	16
96.	**Neal Broten**, Min., Dal., N.J., L.A.	**923**	1099	.840	289	634	17
97.	**Bobby Orr**, Bos., Chi.	**915**	657	1.393	270	645	12
* 98.	**Henrik Sedin**, Van.	**915**	1092	.838	211	704	14
99.	**Gary Roberts**, Cgy., Car., Tor., Fla., Pit., T.B.	**910**	1224	.743	438	472	22
100.	**Scott Stevens**, Wsh., St.L., N.J.	**908**	1635	.555	196	712	22

Top 100 Active Points Leaders

Player	Points	Games	Points per game	Goals	Assists	Seasons
1. Jaromir Jagr, Pit., Wsh., NYR, Phi., Dal., Bos., N.J., Fla. . . .	1802	1550	1.163	722	1080	21
2. Joe Thornton, Bos., S.J.	1259	1285	.980	358	901	17
3. Jarome Iginla, Cgy., Pit., Bos., Col.	1226	1392	.881	589	637	19
4. Marian Hossa, Ott., Atl., Pit., Det., Chi.	1056	1172	.901	486	570	17
5. Patrik Elias, N.J.	1017	1224	.831	406	611	19
6. Patrick Marleau, S.J.	988	1329	.743	456	532	17
7. Vincent Lecavalier, T.B., Phi..	931	1163	.801	411	520	16
8. Henrik Sedin, Van.	915	1092	.838	211	704	14
9. Brad Richards, T.B., Dal., NYR, Chi.	904	1058	.854	288	616	14
10. Shane Doan, Wpg., Phx., Ari.	898	1394	.644	368	530	19
11. Alex Ovechkin, Wsh.	895	760	1.178	475	420	10
12. Daniel Sedin, Van.	881	1061	.830	327	554	14
13. Pavel Datsyuk, Det.	869	887	.980	298	571	13
14. Sidney Crosby, Pit.	853	627	1.360	302	551	10
15. Alex Tanguay, Col., Cgy., Mtl., T.B.	828	1018	.813	275	553	15
16. Sergei Gonchar, Wsh., Bos., Pit., Ott., Dal., Mtl.	811	1301	.623	220	591	20
17. Dany Heatley, Atl., Ott., S.J., Min., Ana.	791	869	.910	372	419	13
18. Henrik Zetterberg, Det.	786	836	.940	296	490	12
19. Marian Gaborik, Min., NYR, CBJ, L.A.	751	879	.854	374	377	14
20. Olli Jokinen, L.A., NYI, Fla., Phx., Cgy., NYR, Wpg., Nsh., Tor., St.L.	750	1231	.609	321	429	17
21. Jason Spezza, Ott., Dal.	749	768	.975	268	481	12
22. Scott Gomez, N.J., NYR, Mtl., S.J., Fla.	747	1045	.715	180	567	15
23. Eric Staal, Car..	742	846	.877	312	430	11
24. Mike Ribeiro, Mtl., Dal., Wsh., Phx., Nsh.	718	947	.758	217	501	15
25. Evgeni Malkin, Pit.	702	587	1.196	268	434	9
26. Rick Nash, CBJ, NYR	697	862	.809	378	319	12
27. Ryan Getzlaf, Ana.	678	710	.955	208	470	10
28. Matt Cullen, Ana., Fla., Car., NYR, Ott., Min., Nsh.	626	1212	.517	219	407	17
29. Anze Kopitar, L.A.	610	683	.893	218	392	9
30. Thomas Vanek, Buf., NYI, Mtl., Min.	608	743	.818	298	310	10
31. David Legwand, Nsh., Det., Ott. . . . . ,	604	1057	.571	223	381	16
32. Corey Perry, Ana.	602	722	.834	296	306	10
33. Scott Hartnell, Nsh., Phi., CBJ	597	1030	.580	278	319	14
34. Martin Havlat, Ott., Chi., Min., S.J., N.J.	593	788	.753	241	352	14
35. Dainius Zubrus, Phi., Mtl., Wsh., Buf., N.J.	584	1243	.470	225	359	18
36. Justin Williams, Phi., Car., L.A.	582	918	.634	227	355	14
37. Dan Boyle, Fla., T.B., S.J., NYR	581	1019	.570	153	428	16
38. Jason Pominville, Buf., Min. .	579	752	.770	237	342	11
39. Brenden Morrow, Dal., Pit., St.L., T.B.	575	991	.580	265	310	15
40. Nicklas Backstrom, Wsh. . . .	572	577	.991	145	427	8
41. Zach Parise, N.J., Min..	566	691	.819	274	292	10
42. Patrick Kane, Chi.	557	576	.967	205	352	8
43. Patrice Bergeron, Bos.	550	740	.743	206	344	11
44. Martin Erat, Nsh., Wsh., Phx., Ari.	545	881	.619	176	369	13
45. Mike Cammalleri, L.A., Cgy., Mtl., N.J.	544	737	.738	263	281	12
46. Zdeno Chara, NYI, Ott., Bos. .	538	1195	.450	169	369	17
47. Erik Cole, Car., Edm., Mtl., Dal., Det.	532	892	.596	265	267	13
48. Radim Vrbata, Col., Car., Chi., Phx., T.B., Van.	527	871	.605	246	281	13
49. Patrick Sharp, Phi., Chi.	526	745	.706	249	277	12
50. Ales Hemsky, Edm., Ott., Dal.	526	748	.703	157	369	12
51. Derek Roy, Buf., Dal., Van., St.L., Nsh., Edm.	524	738	.710	189	335	11
52. Jeff Carter, Phi., CBJ, L.A. . . .	522	718	.727	283	239	10
53. Phil Kessel, Bos., Tor.	520	668	.778	247	273	9
54. Brian Gionta, N.J., Mtl., Buf. .	520	845	.615	262	258	13
55. Mike Fisher, Ott., Nsh.	520	946	.550	245	275	15
56. Alexander Semin, Wsh., Car. .	513	635	.808	238	275	10
57. Chris Kunitz, Ana., Atl., Pit. . .	511	733	.697	224	287	11
58. Jonathan Toews, Chi.	506	565	.896	223	283	8
59. Paul Stastny, Col., St.L.	504	612	.824	176	328	9
60. Mikko Koivu, Min.	500	681	.734	144	356	10
61. Tomas Plekanec, Mtl.	499	761	.656	202	297	11
62. Steven Stamkos, T.B.	498	492	1.012	276	222	7
63. Shawn Horcoff, Edm., Dal. . .	496	949	.523	180	316	14

Brad Richards (now with the Red Wings) collected his 900th point on March 12, 2015, when he scored the game-winning goal at 7:11 of the third period in Chicago's 2-1 win at Arizona.

Player	Points	Games	Points per game	Goals	Assists	Seasons
64. Lubomir Visnovsky, L.A., Edm., Ana., NYI	495	883	.561	128	367	14
65. Andrei Markov, Mtl..	492	846	.582	108	384	14
66. Joe Pavelski, S.J.	485	643	.754	228	257	9
67. Michael Ryder, Mtl., Bos., Dal., N.J.	484	806	.600	237	247	11
68. Michal Handzus, St.L., Phx., Phi., Chi., L.A., S.J.	483	1009	.479	185	298	15
69. Mike Richards, Phi., L.A.	482	710	.679	179	303	10
70. Brad Boyes, S.J., Bos., St.L., Buf., NYI, Fla.	481	762	.631	203	278	11
71. Jochen Hecht, St.L., Edm., Buf.	463	833	.556	186	277	13
72. Jussi Jokinen, Dal., T.B., Car., Pit., Fla.	458	741	.618	157	301	10
73. Brian Campbell, Buf., S.J., Chi., Fla.	456	920	.496	76	380	15
74. Claude Giroux, Phi..	450	496	.907	144	306	8
75. Dustin Brown, L.A.	442	802	.551	207	235	11
76. Loui Eriksson, Dal., Bos.	441	643	.686	182	259	9
77. Ryan Kesler, Van., Ana.	440	736	.598	202	238	11
78. Antoine Vermette, Ott., CBJ, Phx., Ari., Chi.	433	834	.519	194	239	11
79. Alexander Steen, Tor., St.L. . .	429	679	.632	180	249	11
80. Milan Michalek, S.J., Ott. . . .	428	697	.614	200	228	11
81. Stephen Weiss, Fla., Det.	423	732	.578	156	267	13
82. Nathan Horton, Fla., Bos., CBJ.	421	627	.671	203	218	10
83. Andrew Ladd, Car., Chi., Atl., Wpg.	420	691	.608	185	235	10
84. David Backes, St.L.	415	648	.640	185	230	9
85. Duncan Keith, Chi.	415	766	.542	75	340	10
86. David Krejci, Bos.	409	551	.742	117	292	9
87. Joffrey Lupul, Ana., Edm., Phi., Tor.	406	655	.620	194	212	11
88. Pascal Dupuis, Min., NYR, Atl., Pit.	405	853	.475	188	217	14
89. John Tavares, NYI	401	432	.928	174	227	6
90. Marek Zidlicky, Nsh., Min., N.J., Det.	401	783	.512	85	316	11
91. Dion Phaneuf, Cgy., Tor.	400	750	.533	117	283	10
92. Matt Cooke, Van., Wsh., Pit., Min.	398	1046	.380	167	231	16
93. Shea Weber, Nsh.	392	685	.572	146	246	10
94. Bobby Ryan, Ana., Ott.	391	526	.743	188	203	8
95. Dan Cleary, Chi., Edm., Phx., Det.	387	938	.413	165	222	17
96. Mark Streit, Mtl., NYI, Phi. . .	384	654	.587	84	300	9
97. RJ Umberger, Phi., CBJ	381	740	.515	178	203	10
98. Jarret Stoll, Edm., L.A.	379	792	.479	140	239	12
99. Jakub Voracek, CBJ, Phi.	372	531	.701	124	248	7
100. Jiri Hudler, Det., Cgy.	371	604	.614	145	226	10

Top 100 All-Time Games Played Leaders

* active player

Player	Games Played	Seasons
1. **Gordie Howe**, Det., Hfd.	1767	26
2. **Mark Messier**, Edm., NYR, Van.	1756	25
3. **Ron Francis**, Hfd., Pit., Car., Tor.	1731	23
4. **Mark Recchi**, Pit., Phi., Mtl., Car., Atl., T.B., Bos.	1652	22
5. **Chris Chelios**, Mtl., Chi., Det., Atl.	1651	26
6. **Dave Andreychuk**, Buf., Tor., N.J., Bos., Col., T.B.	1639	23
7. **Scott Stevens**, Wsh., St.L., N.J.	1635	22
8. **Larry Murphy**, L.A., Wsh., Min., Pit., Tor., Det.	1615	21
9. **Raymond Bourque**, Bos., Col.	1612	22
10. **Nicklas Lidstrom**, Det.	1564	20
* 11. **Jaromir Jagr**, Pit., Wsh., NYR, Phi., Dal., Bos., N.J., Fla.	1550	21
12. **Alex Delvecchio**, Det.	1549	24
13. **John Bucyk**, Det., Bos.	1540	23
14. **Brendan Shanahan**, N.J., St.L., Hfd., Det., NYR	1524	21
15. **Steve Yzerman**, Det.	1514	22
16. **Mike Modano**, Min., Dal., Det.	1499	22
17. **Phil Housley**, Buf., Wpg., St.L., Cgy., N.J., Wsh., Chi., Tor.	1495	21
18. **Wayne Gretzky**, Edm., L.A., St.L., NYR	1487	20
19. **Rod Brind'Amour**, St.L., Phi., Car.	1484	21
20. **Doug Gilmour**, St.L., Cgy., Tor., N.J., Chi., Buf., Mtl.	1474	20
21. **Glen Wesley**, Bos., Hfd., Car., N.J.	1457	20
22. **Teemu Selanne**, Wpg., Ana., S.J., Col.	1451	21
23. **Tim Horton**, Tor., NYR, Pit., Buf.	1446	24
24. **Mike Gartner**, Wsh., Min., NYR, Tor., Phx.	1432	19
25. **Luc Robitaille**, L.A., Pit., NYR, Det.	1431	19
26. **Scott Mellanby**, Phi., Edm., Fla., St.L., Atl.	1431	21
27. **Pat Verbeek**, N.J., Hfd., NYR, Dal., Det.	1424	20
28. **Luke Richardson**, Tor., Edm., Phi., CBJ, T.B., Ott.	1417	21
29. **Al MacInnis**, Cgy., St.L.	1416	23
30. **Harry Howell**, NYR, Oak., Cal., L.A.	1411	21
31. **Norm Ullman**, Det., Tor.	1410	20
32. **Paul Coffey**, Edm., Pit., L.A., Det., Hfd., Phi., Chi., Car., Bos.	1409	21
33. **Dale Hunter**, Que., Wsh., Col.	1407	19
34. **Roman Hamrlik**, T.B., Edm., NYI, Cgy., Mtl., Wsh., NYR	1395	20
* 35. **Shane Doan**, Wpg., Phx., Ari.	1394	19
36. **Stan Mikita**, Chi.	1394	22
* 37. **Jarome Iginla**, Cgy., Pit., Bos., Col.	1392	19
38. **Doug Mohns**, Bos., Chi., Min., Atl., Wsh.	1390	22
39. **Larry Robinson**, Mtl., L.A.	1384	20
40. **Trevor Linden**, Van., NYI, Mtl., Wsh.	1382	19
41. **Vincent Damphousse**, Tor., Edm., Mtl., S.J.	1378	18
42. **Joe Sakic**, Que., Col.	1378	20
43. **Dean Prentice**, NYR, Bos., Det., Pit., Min.	1378	22
44. **Teppo Numminen**, Wpg., Phx., Dal., Buf.	1372	20
45. **Jeremy Roenick**, Chi., Phx., Phi., L.A., S.J.	1363	20
46. **Ron Stewart**, Tor., Bos., St.L., NYR, Van., NYI	1353	21
47. **Kirk Muller**, N.J., Mtl., NYI, Tor., Fla., Dal.	1349	19
48. **Marcel Dionne**, Det., L.A., NYR	1348	18
49. **Mats Sundin**, Que., Tor., Van.	1346	18
50. **Adam Oates**, Det., St.L., Bos., Wsh., Phi., Ana., Edm.	1337	19
51. **Ray Whitney**, S.J., Edm., Fla., CBJ, Det., Car., Phx., Dal.	1330	22
* 52. **Patrick Marleau**, S.J.	1329	17
53. **Guy Carbonneau**, Mtl., St.L., Dal.	1318	19
54. **Alex Kovalev**, NYR, Pit., Mtl., Ott., Fla.	1316	19
55. **Red Kelly**, Det., Tor.	1316	20
56. **Bobby Holik**, Hfd., N.J., NYR, Atl.	1314	18
* 57. **Sergei Gonchar**, Wsh., Bos., Pit., Ott., Dal., Mtl.	1301	20
58. **Dave Keon**, Tor., Hfd.	1296	18
59. **Pierre Turgeon**, Buf., NYI, Mtl., St.L., Dal., Col.	1294	19
60. **Darryl Sydor**, L.A., Dal., CBJ, T.B., Pit., St.L.	1291	18
61. **Mathieu Schneider**, Mtl., NYI, Tor., NYR, L.A., Det., Ana., Atl., Van., Phx.	1289	21
* 62. **Joe Thornton**, Bos., S.J.	1285	17
63. **Ken Daneyko**, N.J.	1283	20
64. **Phil Esposito**, Chi., Bos., NYR	1282	18
65. **Jean Ratelle**, NYR, Bos.	1281	21
66. **James Patrick**, NYR, Hfd., Cgy., Buf.	1280	21
67. **Bryan Trottier**, NYI, Pit.	1279	18
68. **Martin Gelinas**, Edm., Que., Van., Car., Cgy., Fla., Nsh.	1273	19
69. **Ryan Smyth**, Edm., NYI, Col., L.A.	1270	19
70. **Rob Blake**, L.A., Col., S.J.	1270	20
71. **Brett Hull**, Cgy., St.L., Dal., Det., Phx.	1269	20
72. **Martin Brodeur**, N.J., St.L.	1266	22
73. **Bill Guerin**, N.J., Edm., Bos., Dal., St.L., S.J., NYI, Pit.	1263	18
74. **Scott Niedermayer**, N.J., Ana.	1263	18
75. **Radek Dvorak**, Fla., NYR, Edm., St.L., Atl., Dal., Ana., Car.	1260	18
76. **Ray Ferraro**, Hfd., NYI, NYR, L.A., Atl., St.L.	1258	18
77. **Joe Nieuwendyk**, Cgy., Dal., N.J., Tor., Fla.	1257	20
78. **Brian Rolston**, N.J., Col., Bos., Min., NYI	1256	17
79. **Craig Ludwig**, Mtl., NYI, Min., Dal.	1256	17
80. **Henri Richard**, Mtl.	1256	20

In terms of careers spent in only one city, Chicago's Stan Mikita trails only Detroit stars Nicklas Lidstrom, Alex Delvecchio and Steve Yzerman with 1,394 games played for the Blackhawks.

Player	Games Played	Seasons
81. **Kevin Lowe**, Edm., NYR	1254	19
82. **Jari Kurri**, Edm., L.A., NYR, Ana., Col.	1251	17
83. **Sergei Fedorov**, Det., Ana., CBJ, Wsh.	1248	18
84. **Bill Gadsby**, Chi., NYR, Det.	1248	20
85. **Daniel Alfredsson**, Ott., Det.	1246	18
86. **Jason Arnott**, Edm., N.J., Dal., Nsh., St.L.	1244	18
87. **Allan Stanley**, NYR, Chi., Bos., Tor., Phi.	1244	21
* 88. **Dainius Zubrus**, Phi., Mtl., Wsh., Buf., N.J.	1243	18
89. **Doug Weight**, NYR, Edm., St.L., Car., Ana., NYI	1238	20
90. **Steve Thomas**, Tor., Chi., NYI, N.J., Ana., Det.	1235	20
91. **Dino Ciccarelli**, Min., Wsh., Det., T.B., Fla.	1232	19
* 92. **Olli Jokinen**, L.A., NYI, Fla., Phx., Cgy., NYR, Wpg., Nsh., Tor., St.L.	1231	17
93. **Ed Westfall**, Bos., NYI	1226	18
94. **Sean O'Donnell**, L.A., Min., N.J., Bos., Phx., Ana., Phi., Chi.	1224	17
* 95. **Patrik Elias**, N.J.	1224	19
96. **Gary Roberts**, Cgy., Car., Tor., Fla., Pit., T.B.	1224	22
97. **Brad McCrimmon**, Bos., Phi., Cgy., Det., Hfd., Phx.	1222	18
98. **Eric Nesterenko**, Tor., Chi.	1219	21
99. **Claude Lemieux**, Mtl., N.J., Col., Phx., Dal., S.J.	1215	21
* 100. **Matt Cullen**, Ana., Fla., Car., NYR, Ott., Min., Nsh.	1212	17

Top 100 Active Games Played Leaders

Player	Games Played	Seasons
1. **Jaromir Jagr**, Pit., Wsh., NYR, Phi., Dal., Bos., N.J., Fla.	1550	21
2. **Shane Doan**, Wpg., Phx., Ari.	1394	19
3. **Jarome Iginla**, Cgy., Pit., Bos., Col.	1392	19
4. **Patrick Marleau**, S.J.	1329	17
5. **Sergei Gonchar**, Wsh., Bos., Pit., Ott., Dal., Mtl.	1301	20
6. **Joe Thornton**, Bos., S.J.	1285	17
7. **Dainius Zubrus**, Phi., Mtl., Wsh., Buf., N.J.	1243	18
8. **Olli Jokinen**, L.A., NYI, Fla., Phx., Cgy., NYR, Wpg., Nsh., Tor., St.L.	1231	17
9. **Patrik Elias**, N.J.	1224	19
10. **Matt Cullen**, Ana., Fla., Car., NYR, Ott., Min., Nsh.	1212	17
11. **Zdeno Chara**, NYI, Ott., Bos.	1195	17
12. **Chris Phillips**, Ott.	1179	17
13. **Marian Hossa**, Ott., Atl., Pit., Det., Chi.	1172	17
14. **Vincent Lecavalier**, T.B., Phi.	1163	16
15. **Henrik Sedin**, Van.	1092	14
16. **Daniel Sedin**, Van.	1061	14
17. **Brad Richards**, T.B., Dal., NYR, Chi.	1058	14
18. **David Legwand**, Nsh., Det., Ott.	1057	16
19. **Scott Hannan**, S.J., Col., Wsh., Cgy., Nsh.	1055	16
20. **Brad Stuart**, S.J., Bos., Cgy., L.A., Det., Col.	1050	15
21. **Matt Cooke**, Van., Wsh., Pit., Min.	1046	16
22. **Scott Gomez**, N.J., NYR, Mtl., S.J., Fla.	1045	15
23. **Scott Hartnell**, Nsh., Phi., CBJ	1030	14
24. **Dan Boyle**, Fla., T.B., S.J., NYR	1019	16
25. **Alex Tanguay**, Col., Cgy., Mtl., T.B.	1018	15
26. **Michal Handzus**, St.L., Phx., Phi., Chi., L.A., S.J.	1009	15
27. **Eric Brewer**, NYI, Edm., St.L., T.B., Ana., Tor.	1009	16
28. **Brenden Morrow**, Dal., Pit., St.L., T.B.	991	15
29. **Manny Malhotra**, NYR, Dal., CBJ, S.J., Van., Car., Mtl.	991	16
30. **Nick Schultz**, Min., Edm., CBJ, Phi.	960	13
31. **Craig Adams**, Car., Chi., Pit.	951	14
32. **Shawn Horcoff**, Edm., Dal.	949	14
33. **Mike Ribeiro**, Mtl., Dal., Wsh., Phx., Nsh.	947	15
34. **Mike Fisher**, Ott., Nsh.	946	15
35. **Dan Cleary**, Chi., Edm., Phx., Det.	938	17
36. **Stephane Robidas**, Mtl., Dal., Chi., Ana., Tor.	937	15
37. **Brian Campbell**, Buf., S.J., Chi., Fla.	920	15
38. **Jay Bouwmeester**, Fla., Cgy., St.L.	918	12
39. **Justin Williams**, Phi., Car., L.A.	918	14
40. **Andrew Ference**, Pit., Cgy., Bos., Edm.	901	15
41. **Chris Neil**, Ott.	893	13
42. **Erik Cole**, Car., Edm., Mtl., Dal., Det.	892	13
43. **Michal Rozsival**, Pit., NYR, Phx., Chi.	890	14
44. **Pavel Datsyuk**, Det.	887	13
45. **Lubomir Visnovsky**, L.A., Edm., Ana., NYI	883	14
46. **Martin Erat**, Nsh., Wsh., Phx., Ari.	881	13
47. **Marian Gaborik**, Min., NYR, CBJ, L.A.	879	14
48. **Radim Vrbata**, Col., Car., Chi., Phx., T.B., Van.	871	13
49. **Dany Heatley**, Atl., Ott., S.J., Min., Ana.	869	13
50. **Jason Chimera**, Edm., CBJ, Wsh.	869	14
51. **Roberto Luongo**, NYI, Fla., Van.	864	15
52. **Ruslan Fedotenko**, Phi., T.B., NYI, Pit., NYR	863	12
53. **Rick Nash**, CBJ, NYR	862	12
54. **Willie Mitchell**, N.J., Min., Dal., Van., L.A., Fla.	861	15
55. **Pascal Dupuis**, Min., NYR, Atl., Pit.	853	14
56. **Eric Staal**, Car.	846	11
57. **Andrei Markov**, Mtl.	846	14
58. **Brian Gionta**, N.J., Mtl., Buf.	845	13
59. **Henrik Zetterberg**, Det.	836	12
60. **Antoine Vermette**, Ott., CBJ, Phx., Ari., Chi.	834	11
61. **Jochen Hecht**, St.L., Edm., Buf.	833	14
62. **Dan Hamhuis**, Nsh., Van.	814	11
63. **Michael Ryder**, Mtl., Bos., Dal., N.J.	806	11
64. **Barret Jackman**, St.L.	803	13
65. **Dustin Brown**, L.A.	802	11
66. **Jarret Stoll**, Edm., L.A.	792	12
67. **Martin Havlat**, Ott., Chi., Min., S.J., N.J.	788	14
68. **Bryce Salvador**, St.L., N.J.	786	13
69. **Marek Zidlicky**, Nsh., Min., N.J., Det.	783	11
70. **Brooks Orpik**, Pit., Wsh.	781	12
71. **Steve Ott**, Dal., Buf., St.L.	774	12
72. **Matt Stajan**, Tor., Cgy.	774	12
73. **Jason Spezza**, Ott., Dal.	768	12
74. **Duncan Keith**, Chi.	766	10
75. **Jay McClement**, St.L., Col., Tor., Car.	764	10
76. **Brent Seabrook**, Chi.	763	10
77. **Brad Boyes**, S.J., Bos., St.L., Buf., NYI, Fla.	762	11
78. **Tomas Plekanec**, Mtl.	761	11
79. **Alex Ovechkin**, Wsh.	760	10
80. **Trevor Daley**, Dal.	756	11
81. **Ron Hainsey**, Mtl., CBJ, Atl., Wpg., Car.	754	12
82. **Jason Pominville**, Buf., Min.	752	11
83. **Dion Phaneuf**, Cgy., Tor.	750	10
84. **Ryan Suter**, Nsh., Min.	749	10
85. **Ales Hemsky**, Edm., Ott., Dal.	748	12
86. **Patrick Sharp**, Phi., Chi.	745	12
87. **Thomas Vanek**, Buf., NYI, Mtl., Min.	743	10
88. **Fedor Tyutin**, NYR, CBJ	742	11
89. **Jussi Jokinen**, Dal., T.B., Car., Pit., Fla.	741	10
90. **Christian Ehrhoff**, S.J., Van., Buf., Pit.	741	11
91. **RJ Umberger**, Phi., CBJ	740	10
92. **Patrice Bergeron**, Bos.	740	11
93. **Chris Kelly**, Ott., Bos.	740	11
94. **Derek Roy**, Buf., Dal., Van., St.L., Nsh., Edm.	738	11
95. **Mike Cammalleri**, L.A., Cgy., Mtl., N.J.	737	12
96. **Ryan Kesler**, Van., Ana.	736	11
97. **Vernon Fiddler**, Nsh., Phx., Dal.	736	12
98. **Chris Kunitz**, Ana., Atl., Pit.	733	11
99. **Stephen Weiss**, Fla., Det.	732	13
100. **Tim Gleason**, L.A., Car., Tor., Wsh.	727	11

Despite returning to Europe for three seasons from 2008 through 2011, Jaromir Jagr became the 15th player in NHL history to top 1,500 games played during the 2014-15 season. The Florida Panthers are his eighth team.

Goaltending Records

All-Time Shutout Leaders (Minimum 54 Shutouts)

	Goaltender	Team	Shutouts	Games	Seasons
1.	**Martin Brodeur**	New Jersey	124	1,259	21
	(1991-2015)	St. Louis	1	7	1
		Total	**125**	**1,266**	**22**
2.	**Terry Sawchuk**	Detroit	85	734	14
	(1949-1970)	Boston	11	102	2
		Toronto	4	91	3
		Los Angeles	2	36	1
		NY Rangers	1	8	1
		Total	**103**	**971**	**21**
3.	**George Hainsworth**	Montreal	75	318	7½
	(1926-1937)	Toronto	19	147	3½
		Total	**94**	**465**	**11**
4.	**Glenn Hall**	Detroit	17	148	4
	(1952-1971)	Chicago	51	618	10
		St. Louis	16	140	4
		Total	**84**	**906**	**18**
5.	**Jacques Plante**	Montreal	58	556	11
	(1952-1973)	NY Rangers	5	98	2
		St. Louis	10	69	2
		Toronto	7	106	2¾
		Boston	2	8	¼
		Total	**82**	**837**	**18**
6.	**Alec Connell**	Ottawa	64	293	8
	(1924-1937)	Detroit	6	48	1
		NY Americans	0	1	1
		Mtl. Maroons	11	75	2
		Total	**81**	**417**	**12**
7.	**Tiny Thompson**	Boston	74	468	10¼
	(1928-1940)	Detroit	7	85	1¾
		Total	**81**	**553**	**12**
8.	**Dominik Hasek**	Chicago	1	25	2
	(1990-2008)	Buffalo	55	491	9
		Detroit	20	176	4
		Ottawa	5	43	1
		Total	**81**	**735**	**16**
9.	**Tony Esposito**	Montreal	2	13	1
	(1968-1984)	Chicago	74	873	15
		Total	**76**	**886**	**16**
10.	**Ed Belfour**	Chicago	30	415	7⅔
	(1988-2007)	San Jose	1	13	⅓
		Dallas	27	307	5
		Toronto	17	170	3
		Florida	1	58	1
		Total	**76**	**963**	**17**
11.	**Lorne Chabot**	NY Rangers	21	80	2
	(1926-1937)	Toronto	32	214	5
		Montreal	8	47	1
		Chicago	8	48	1
		Mtl. Maroons	2	16	1
		NY Americans	1	6	1
		Total	**72**	**411**	**11**
12.	**Harry Lumley**	Detroit	26	324	6½
	(1943-1960)	NY Rangers	0	1	½
		Chicago	5	134	2
		Toronto	34	267	4
		Boston	6	78	3
		Total	**71**	**804**	**16**
13.	***Roberto Luongo**	NY Islanders	1	24	1
	(1999-2015)	Florida	29	392	6¼
		Vancouver	38	448	7¾
		Total	**68**	**864**	**15**
14.	**Roy Worters**	Pittsburgh Pirates	22	123	3
	(1925-1937)	NY Americans	45	360	9
		**Montreal	0	1	
		Total	**67**	**484**	**12**
15.	**Patrick Roy**	Montreal	29	551	11½
	(1984-2003)	Colorado	37	478	7½
		Total	**66**	**1,029**	**19**
16.	**Turk Broda**	Toronto	62	629	14
	(1936-1952)				
17.	**Evgeni Nabokov**	San Jose	50	563	10
	(1999-2015)	NY Islanders	9	123	3
		Tampa Bay	0	11	1
		Total	**59**	**697**	**14**
18.	**Clint Benedict**	Ottawa	19	158	7
	(1917-1930)	Mtl. Maroons	39	204	6
		Total	**58**	**362**	**13**
19.	**John Ross Roach**	Toronto	13	222	7
	(1921-1935)	NY Rangers	30	89	4
		Detroit	15	180	3
		Total	**58**	**491**	**14**
20.	***Henrik Lundqvist**	NY Rangers	55	620	10
	(2005-2015)				
21.	**Bernie Parent**	Boston	1	57	2
	(1965-1979)	Philadelphia	50	486	9½
		Toronto	3	65	1½
		Total	**54**	**608**	**13**
22.	**Ed Giacomin**	NY Rangers	49	539	10¼
	(1965-1978)	Detroit	5	71	2¾
		Total	**54**	**610**	**13**

* Active goalie
** Played 1 game for Montreal in 1929-30.

Ten or More Shutouts, One Season

Number of Shutouts	Goaltender	Team	Season	Length of Schedule
22	George Hainsworth	Montreal	1928-29	44
15	Alec Connell	Ottawa	1925-26	36
	Alec Connell	Ottawa	1927-28	44
	Hal Winkler	Boston	1927-28	44
	Tony Esposito	Chicago	1969-70	76
14	George Hainsworth	Montreal	1926-27	44
13	Clint Benedict	Mtl. Maroons	1926-27	44
	Alec Connell	Ottawa	1926-27	44
	George Hainsworth	Montreal	1927-28	44
	John Ross Roach	NY Rangers	1928-29	44
	Roy Worters	NY Americans	1928-29	44
	Harry Lumley	Toronto	1953-54	70
	Dominik Hasek	Buffalo	1997-98	82
12	Tiny Thompson	Boston	1928-29	44
	Charlie Gardiner	Chicago	1930-31	44
	Terry Sawchuk	Detroit	1951-52	70
	Terry Sawchuk	Detroit	1953-54	70
	Terry Sawchuk	Detroit	1954-55	70
	Glenn Hall	Detroit	1955-56	70
	Bernie Parent	Philadelphia	1973-74	78
	Bernie Parent	Philadelphia	1974-75	80
	Martin Brodeur	New Jersey	2006-07	82
11	Lorne Chabot	NY Rangers	1927-28	44
	Hap Holmes	Detroit	1927-28	44
	Roy Worters	Pittsburgh Pirates	1927-28	44
	Clint Benedict	Mtl. Maroons	1928-29	44
	Joe Miller	Pittsburgh Pirates	1928-29	44
	Tiny Thompson	Boston	1932-33	48
	Terry Sawchuk	Detroit	1950-51	70
	Dominik Hasek	Buffalo	2000-01	82
	Martin Brodeur	New Jersey	2003-04	82
	Henrik Lundqvist	NY Rangers	2010-11	82
10	Lorne Chabot	NY Rangers	1926-27	44
	Lorne Chabot	Toronto	1928-29	44
	Dolly Dolson	Detroit	1928-29	44
	John Ross Roach	Detroit	1932-33	48
	Charlie Gardiner	Chicago	1933-34	48
	Tiny Thompson	Boston	1935-36	48
	Frank Brimsek	Boston	1938-39	48
	Bill Durnan	Montreal	1948-49	60
	Harry Lumley	Toronto	1952-53	70
	Gerry McNeil	Montreal	1952-53	70
	Tony Esposito	Chicago	1973-74	78
	Ken Dryden	Montreal	1976-77	80
	Martin Brodeur	New Jersey	1996-97	82
	Martin Brodeur	New Jersey	1997-98	82
	Byron Dafoe	Boston	1998-99	82
	Roman Cechmanek	Philadelphia	2000-01	82
	Ed Belfour	Toronto	2003-04	82
	Miikka Kiprusoff	Calgary	2005-06	82
	Henrik Lundqvist	NY Rangers	2007-08	82
	Steve Mason	Columbus	2008-09	82
	Jonathan Quick	Los Angeles	2011-12	82
	Marc-Andre Fleury	Pittsburgh	**2014-15**	82

All-Time Win Leaders

(Minimum 275 Wins)

	Goaltender	Wins	GP	Dec.	Losses	OT/Ties	Seas.
1.	Martin Brodeur	691	1,266	1,242	397	154	22
2.	Patrick Roy	551	1,029	997	315	131	19
3.	Ed Belfour	484	963	929	320	125	18
4.	Curtis Joseph	454	943	902	352	96	19
5.	Terry Sawchuk	447	971	949	330	172	21
6.	Jacques Plante	437	837	828	246	145	18
7.	Tony Esposito	423	886	880	306	151	16
8.	Glenn Hall	407	906	896	326	163	18
9.	Grant Fuhr	403	868	812	295	114	19
10.	Chris Osgood	401	744	712	216	95	17
11.*	Roberto Luongo	401	864	837	331	105	15
12.	Dominik Hasek	389	735	707	223	95	16
13.	Mike Vernon	385	781	750	273	92	19
14.	John Vanbiesbrouck	374	882	839	346	119	20
15.	Andy Moog	372	713	669	209	88	18
16.	Tom Barrasso	369	777	732	277	86	19
17.	Rogie Vachon	355	795	773	291	127	16
18.	Evgeni Nabokov	353	697	666	227	86	14
19.*	Henrik Lundqvist	339	620	612	208	65	10
20.	Gump Worsley	335	861	837	352	150	21
21.	Nikolai Khabibulin	333	799	764	334	97	18
22.	Harry Lumley	330	803	801	329	142	16
23.	Sean Burke	324	820	775	341	110	18
24.*	Ryan Miller	323	604	591	209	58	12
25.*	Marc-Andre Fleury	322	595	566	189	55	11
26.	Miikka Kiprusoff	319	623	603	213	71	12
27.	Billy Smith	305	680	643	233	105	18
28.	Olaf Kolzig	303	719	687	297	87	17
29.	Turk Broda	302	629	627	224	101	14
30.	Mike Richter	301	666	632	258	73	15
31.	Tomas Vokoun	300	700	666	288	78	15
32.	Ron Hextall	296	608	579	214	69	13
33.	Mike Liut	294	664	639	271	74	13
34.	Ed Giacomin	289	609	594	209	96	13
35.	Jose Theodore	286	648	609	254	69	16
36.	Dan Bouchard	286	655	631	232	113	14
37.	Tiny Thompson	284	553	553	194	75	12
38.	Marty Turco	275	543	508	167	66	11

* active goaltender

Active Win Leaders

(Minimum 200 Wins)

	Goaltender	Teams	Wins	GP	Dec.	Losses	OT/Ties	Seas.
1.	Roberto Luongo	NYI, Fla., Van.	401	864	837	331	105	15
2.	Henrik Lundqvist	NY Rangers	339	620	612	208	65	10
3.	Ryan Miller	Buf., St.L., Van.	323	604	591	209	59	11
4.	Marc-Andre Fleury	Pittsburgh	322	595	566	189	55	11
5.	Kari Lehtonen	Atlanta, Dallas	248	510	487	184	55	11
6.	Cam Ward	Carolina	246	512	495	191	58	10
7.	Carey Price	Montreal	223	435	426	153	50	8
8.	Ilya Bryzgalov	Ana., Phx., Phi., Edm., Min.	221	465	437	162	54	12
9.	Jonathan Quick	Los Angeles	212	407	397	139	46	8
10.	Pekka Rinne	Nashville	204	381	362	115	43	10

Active Shutout Leaders

(Minimum 30 Shutouts)

	Goaltender	Teams	Shutouts	Games	Seasons
1.	Roberto Luongo	NYI, Fla., Van.	68	864	15
2.	Henrik Lundqvist	NY Rangers	55	620	10
3.	Marc-Andre Fleury	Pittsburgh	38	595	11
4.	Jonathan Quick	Los Angeles	37	407	8
5.	Jaroslav Halak	Mtl., St.L., Wsh., NYI	36	331	9
6.	Pekka Rinne	Nashville	36	381	10
7.	Ryan Miller	Buf., St.L., Van.	35	604	12
8.	Carey Price	Montreal	34	435	8
9.	Ilya Bryzgalov	Ana., Phx., Phi., Edm., Min.	34	465	12
10.	Antii Niemi	Chicago, San Jose	32	338	7
11.	Kari Lehtonen	Atlanta, Dallas	32	510	11
12.	Brian Elliott	Ott., Col., St.L.	30	281	8

Goals-Against Average Leaders (Minimum 25 games played)

(Exceptions: Minimum 13 games played, 1994-95, 2012-13; minimum 26 games played, 1992-93, 1993-94; minimum 15 games played, 1917-18 to 1925-26)

Season	Goaltender, Team	GP	Mins.	GA	SO	AVG.	Season	Goaltender, Team	GP	Mins.	GA	SO	AVG.
2014-15	Carey Price, Montreal	66	3,977	130	9	1.96	1964-65	Johnny Bower, Toronto	34	2,040	81	3	2.38
2013-14	Josh Harding, Minnesota	29	1,668	46	3	1.65	1963-64	Johnny Bower, Toronto	51	3,009	106	5	2.11
2012-13	Craig Anderson, Ottawa	24	1,421	40	3	1.69	1962-63	Don Simmons, Toronto	28	1,680	69	1	2.46
2011-12	Brian Elliott, St. Louis	38	2,235	58	9	1.56	1961-62	Jacques Plante, Montreal	70	4,200	166	4	2.37
2010-11	Tim Thomas, Boston	57	3,634	112	9	2.00	1960-61	Charlie Hodge, Montreal	30	1,800	74	4	2.47
2009-10	Tuukka Rask, Boston	45	2,562	84	5	1.97	1959-60	Jacques Plante, Montreal	69	4,140	175	3	2.54
2008-09	Tim Thomas, Boston	54	3,259	114	5	2.10	1958-59	Jacques Plante, Montreal	67	4,000	144	9	2.16
2007-08	Chris Osgood, Detroit	43	2,409	84	4	2.09	1957-58	Jacques Plante, Montreal	57	3,386	119	9	2.11
2006-07	Niklas Backstrom, Minnesota	41	2,227	73	5	1.97	1956-57	Jacques Plante, Montreal	61	3,660	122	9	2.00
2005-06	Miikka Kiprusoff, Calgary	74	4,380	151	10	2.07	1955-56	Jacques Plante, Montreal	64	3,840	119	7	1.86
2003-04	Miikka Kiprusoff, Calgary	38	2,301	65	4	1.69	1954-55	Harry Lumley, Toronto	69	4,140	134	8	1.94
2002-03	Marty Turco, Dallas	55	3,203	92	7	1.72	1953-54	Harry Lumley, Toronto	69	4,140	128	13	1.86
2001-02	Patrick Roy, Colorado	63	3,773	122	9	1.94	1952-53	Terry Sawchuk, Detroit	63	3,780	120	9	1.90
2000-01	Marty Turco, Dallas	26	1,266	40	3	1.90	1951-52	Terry Sawchuk, Detroit	70	4,200	133	12	1.90
99-2000	Brian Boucher, Philadelphia	35	2,038	65	4	1.91	1950-51	Al Rollins, Toronto	40	2,367	70	5	1.77
1998-99	Ron Tugnutt, Ottawa	43	2,508	75	3	1.79	1949-50	Bill Durnan, Montreal	64	3,840	141	8	2.20
1997-98	Ed Belfour, Dallas	61	3,581	112	9	1.88	1948-49	Bill Durnan, Montreal	60	3,600	126	10	2.10
1996-97	Martin Brodeur, New Jersey	67	3,838	120	10	1.88	1947-48	Turk Broda, Toronto	60	3,600	143	5	2.38
1995-96	Ron Hextall, Philadelphia	53	3,102	112	4	2.17	1946-47	Bill Durnan, Montreal	60	3,600	138	4	2.30
1994-95	Dominik Hasek, Buffalo	41	2,416	85	5	2.11	1945-46	Bill Durnan, Montreal	40	2,400	104	4	2.60
1993-94	Dominik Hasek, Buffalo	58	3,358	109	7	1.95	1944-45	Bill Durnan, Montreal	50	3,000	121	1	2.42
1992-93	Felix Potvin, Toronto	48	2,781	116	2	2.50	1943-44	Bill Durnan, Montreal	50	3,000	109	2	2.18
1991-92	Patrick Roy, Montreal	67	3,935	155	5	2.36	1942-43	Johnny Mowers, Detroit	50	3,010	124	6	2.47
1990-91	Ed Belfour, Chicago	74	4,127	170	4	2.47	1941-42	Frank Brimsek, Boston	47	2,930	115	3	2.35
1989-90	Mike Liut, Hartford, Washington	37	2,161	91	4	2.53	1940-41	Turk Broda, Toronto	48	2,970	99	5	2.00
1988-89	Patrick Roy, Montreal	48	2,744	113	4	2.47	1939-40	Dave Kerr, NY Rangers	48	3,000	77	8	1.54
1987-88	Pete Peeters, Washington	35	1,896	88	2	2.78	1938-39	Frank Brimsek, Boston	43	2,610	68	10	1.56
1986-87	Brian Hayward, Montreal	37	2,178	102	1	2.81	1937-38	Tiny Thompson, Boston	48	2,970	89	7	1.80
1985-86	Bob Froese, Philadelphia	51	2,728	116	5	2.55	1936-37	Normie Smith, Detroit	48	2,980	102	6	2.05
1984-85	Tom Barrasso, Buffalo	54	3,248	144	5	2.66	1935-36	Tiny Thompson, Boston	48	2,930	82	10	1.68
1983-84	Pat Riggin, Washington	41	2,299	102	4	2.66	1934-35	Lorne Chabot, Chicago	48	2,940	88	8	1.80
1982-83	Pete Peeters, Philadelphia	62	3,611	142	8	2.36	1933-34	Wilf Cude, Detroit, Montreal	30	1,920	47	5	1.47
1981-82	Denis Herron, Montreal	27	1,547	68	3	2.64	1932-33	Tiny Thompson, Boston	48	3,000	88	11	1.76
1980-81	Richard Sevigny, Montreal	33	1,777	71	2	2.40	1931-32	Charlie Gardiner, Chicago	48	2,989	92	4	1.85
1979-80	Bob Sauve, Buffalo	32	1,880	74	4	2.36	1930-31	Roy Worters, NY Americans	44	2,760	74	8	1.61
1978-79	Ken Dryden, Montreal	47	2,814	108	5	2.30	1929-30	Tiny Thompson, Boston	44	2,680	98	3	2.19
1977-78	Ken Dryden, Montreal	52	3,071	105	5	2.05	1928-29	George Hainsworth, Montreal	44	2,800	43	22	0.92
1976-77	Michel Larocque, Montreal	26	1,525	53	4	2.09	1927-28	George Hainsworth, Montreal	44	2,730	48	13	1.05
1975-76	Ken Dryden, Montreal	62	3,580	121	8	2.03	1926-27	Clint Benedict, Mtl. Maroons	43	2,748	65	13	1.42
1974-75	Bernie Parent, Philadelphia	68	4,041	137	12	2.03	1925-26	Alec Connell, Ottawa	36	2,251	42	15	1.12
1973-74	Bernie Parent, Philadelphia	73	4,314	136	12	1.89	1924-25	Georges Vezina, Montreal	30	1,860	56	5	1.81
1972-73	Ken Dryden, Montreal	54	3,165	119	6	2.26	1923-24	Georges Vezina, Montreal	24	1,459	48	3	1.97
1971-72	Tony Esposito, Chicago	48	2,780	82	9	1.77	1922-23	Clint Benedict, Ottawa	24	1,478	54	4	2.18
1970-71	Jacques Plante, Toronto	40	2,329	73	4	1.88	1921-22	Clint Benedict, Ottawa	24	1,508	84	2	3.34
1969-70	Ernie Wakely, St. Louis	30	1,651	58	4	2.11	1920-21	Clint Benedict, Ottawa	24	1,457	75	2	3.09
1968-69	Jacques Plante, St. Louis	37	2,139	70	5	1.96	1919-20	Clint Benedict, Ottawa	24	1,444	64	5	2.66
1967-68	Gump Worsley, Montreal	40	2,213	73	6	1.98	1918-19	Clint Benedict, Ottawa	18	1,113	53	2	2.86
1966-67	Glenn Hall, Chicago	32	1,664	66	2	2.38	1917-18	Georges Vezina, Montreal	21	1,282	84	1	3.93
1965-66	Johnny Bower, Toronto	35	1,998	75	3	2.25							

All-Time Regular-Season NHL Coaching Register

Regular Season, 1917-2015

Coach	Team	Games Coached	Wins	Losses	O/T	Years	Cup Wins	Career
Abel, Sid	Chicago	140	39	79	22	2		
	Detroit	811	340	339	132	12		
	St. Louis	10	3	6	1	1		
	Kansas City	3	0	3	0	1		
	Totals	964	382	427	155	16		1952-76
Adams, Jack	Detroit	964	413	390	161	20	3	1927-47
Agnew, Gary	Columbus	5	0	4	1	1		2006-07
Allen, Keith	Philadelphia	150	51	67	32	2		1967-69
Allison, Dave	Ottawa	25	2	22	1	1		1995-96
Anderson, Jim	Washington	54	4	45	5	1		1974-75
Anderson, John	Atlanta	164	70	75	19	2		2008-10
Angotti, Lou	St. Louis	32	6	20	6	2		
	Pittsburgh	80	16	58	6	1		
	Totals	112	22	78	12	3		1973-84
Arbour, Al	St. Louis	107	42	40	25	3		
	NY Islanders	1500	740	537	223	20	4	
	Totals	1607	782	577	248	23	4	1970-08
Armstrong, George	Toronto	47	17	26	4	1		1988-89
Arniel, Scott	Columbus	123	45	60	18	2		2010-12
Babcock, Mike	Anaheim	164	69	62	33	3		
	Detroit	786	458	223	105	10	1	
	Totals	950	527	285	138	13	1	2002-15
Barber, Bill	Philadelphia	136	73	40	23	2		2000-02
Barkley, Doug	Detroit	77	20	46	11	3		1970-76
Beaulieu, Andre	Minnesota	32	6	23	3	1		1977-78
Belisle, Danny	Washington	96	28	51	17	2		1978-80
Berenson, Red	St. Louis	204	100	72	32	3		1979-82
Bergeron, Michel	Quebec	634	265	283	86	8		
	NY Rangers	158	73	67	18	2		
	Totals	792	338	350	104	10		1980-90
Berry, Bob	Los Angeles	240	107	94	39	3		
	Montreal	223	116	71	36	3		
	Pittsburgh	240	88	127	25	3		
	St. Louis	157	73	63	21	2		
	Totals	860	384	355	121	11		1978-94
Berube, Craig	Philadelphia	161	75	58	28	2		2013-15
Beverley, Nick	Toronto	17	9	6	2	1		1995-96
Blackburn, Don	Hartford	140	42	63	35	2		1979-81
Blair, Wren	Minnesota	147	48	65	34	3		1967-70
Blake, Toe	Montreal	914	500	255	159	13	8	1955-68
Boileau, Marc	Pittsburgh	151	66	61	24	3		1973-76
Boivin, Leo	St. Louis	97	28	53	16	2		1975-78
Boucher, Frank	NY Rangers	527	181	263	83	11	1	1939-54
Boucher, George	Mtl. Maroons	12	6	5	1	1		
	Ottawa	48	13	29	6	1		
	St. Louis	35	9	20	6	1		
	Boston	70	22	32	16	1		
	Totals	165	50	86	29	4		1930-50
Boucher, Guy	Tampa Bay	195	97	78	20	3		2010-13
Boudreau, Bruce	Washington	329	201	88	40	5		
	Anaheim	270	162	79	29	4		
	Totals	599	363	167	69	8		2007-15
Bowman, Scotty	St. Louis	238	110	83	45	4		
	Montreal	634	419	110	105	8	5	
	Buffalo	404	210	134	60	7		
	Pittsburgh	164	95	53	16	2	1	
	Detroit	701	410	193	98	9	3	
	Totals	2141	1244	573	324	30	9	1967-02
Bowness, Rick	Winnipeg	28	8	17	3	1		
	Boston	80	36	32	12	1		
	Ottawa	235	39	178	18	4		
	NY Islanders	100	38	50	12	2		
	Phoenix	20	2	12	6	2		
	Totals	463	123	289	51	10		1988-05
Brooks, Herb	NY Rangers	285	131	113	41	4		
	Minnesota	80	19	48	13	1		
	New Jersey	84	40	37	7	1		
	Pittsburgh	57	29	21	7	1		
	Totals	506	219	219	68	7		1981-00
Brophy, John	Toronto	193	64	111	18	3		1986-89
Burnett, George	Edmonton	35	12	20	3	1		1994-95
Burns, Charlie	Minnesota	86	22	50	14	2		1969-75
Burns, Pat	Montreal	320	174	104	42	4		
	Toronto	281	133	107	41	4		
	Boston	254	105	97	52	4		
	New Jersey	164	89	45	30	3	1	
	Totals	1019	501	353	165	15	1	1988-05
Bush, Eddie	Kansas City	32	1	23	8	1		1975-76
Bylsma, Dan	Pittsburgh	401	252	117	32	6	1	2008-14
Cameron, Dave	Ottawa	55	32	15	8	1		2014-15
Campbell, Colin	NY Rangers	269	118	108	43	4		1994-98
Capuano, Jack	NY Islanders	359	165	148	46	5		2010-15
Carbonneau, Guy	Montreal	230	124	83	23	3		2006-09
Carlyle, Randy	Anaheim	516	273	182	61	7	1	
	Toronto	188	91	78	19	4		
	Totals	704	364	260	80	10	1	2005-15
Carpenter, Doug	New Jersey	290	100	166	24	4		
	Toronto	91	39	47	5	2		
	Totals	381	139	213	29	6		1984-91
Carroll, Dick	Toronto	40	18	22	0	2	1	1917-19
Carroll, Frank	Toronto	24	15	9	0	1		1920-21
Cashman, Wayne	Philadelphia	61	32	20	9	1		1997-98

Coach	Team	Games Coached	Wins	Losses	O/T	Years	Cup Wins	Career
Cassidy, Bruce	Washington	110	47	47	16	2		2002-04
Chambers, Dave	Quebec	98	19	64	15	2		1990-92
Chapman, Art	NY Americans	48	8	29	11	1		
	Brooklyn	48	16	29	3	1		
	Totals	96	24	58	14	2		1940-42
Charron, Guy	Calgary	16	6	7	3	1		
	Anaheim	49	14	26	9	1		
	Totals	65	20	33	12	2		1991-01
Cheevers, Gerry	Boston	376	204	126	46	5		1980-85
Cherry, Don	Boston	400	231	105	64	5		
	Colorado	80	19	48	13	1		
	Totals	480	250	153	77	6		1974-80
Clancy, King	Mtl. Maroons	18	6	11	1	1		
	Toronto	210	80	81	49	3		
	Totals	228	86	92	50	4		1937-56
Clapper, Dit	Boston	230	102	88	40	4		1945-49
Cleghorn, Odie	Pittsburgh	168	62	86	20	4		1925-29
Cleghorn, Sprague	Mtl. Maroons	48	19	22	7	1		1931-32
Clouston, Cory	Ottawa	198	95	83	20	3		2008-11
Colville, Neil	NY Rangers	93	26	41	26	2		1950-52
Conacher, Charlie	Chicago	162	56	84	22	3		1947-50
Conacher, Lionel	NY Americans	44	14	25	5	1		1929-30
Constantine, Kevin	San Jose	157	55	78	24	3		
	Pittsburgh	189	86	64	39	3		
	New Jersey	31	20	8	3	1		
	Totals	377	161	150	66	7		1993-02
Cook, Bill	NY Rangers	117	34	59	24	2		1951-53
Cooper, Jon	Tampa Bay *	179	100	59	20	3		2012-15

* Hired by Tampa Bay on March 25, 2013 but did not appear behind the bench until March 29. Assistant coaches Dan Lacroix, Martin Raymond, and Steve Thomas worked a 3-2 loss at Winnipeg on March 24. Lacroix and Thomas worked a 2-1 win vs. Buffalo on March 26.

Coach	Team	Games Coached	Wins	Losses	O/T	Years	Cup Wins	Career
Crawford, Marc	Quebec	48	30	13	5	1		
	Colorado	246	135	75	36	3	1	
	Vancouver	529	246	189	94	8		
	Los Angeles	164	59	84	21	2		
	Dallas	164	79	60	25	2		
	Totals	1151	549	421	181	16	1	1994-11
Creamer, Pierre	Pittsburgh	80	36	35	9	1		1987-88
Creighton, Fred	Atlanta	348	156	136	56	5		
	Boston	73	40	20	13	1		
	Totals	421	196	156	69	6		1974-80
Crisp, Terry	Calgary	240	144	63	33	3	1	
	Tampa Bay	391	142	204	45	6		
	Totals	631	286	267	78	9	1	1987-98
Crozier, Joe	Buffalo	192	77	80	35	3		
	Toronto	40	13	22	5	1		
	Totals	232	90	102	40	4		1971-81
Crozier, Roger	Washington	1	0	1	0	1		1981-82
Cunneyworth, Randy	Montreal	50	18	23	9	1		2011-12
Cunniff, John	Hartford	13	3	9	1	1		
	New Jersey	133	59	56	18	2		
	Totals	146	62	65	19	3		1982-91
Curry, Alex	Ottawa	36	24	8	4	1		1925-26
Dandurand, Leo	Montreal	163	78	76	9	6	1	1940-50
Day, Hap	Toronto	546	259	206	81	10	5	
Dea, Billy	Detroit	11	3	8	0	1		1981-82
DeBoer, Peter	Florida	246	103	107	36	3		
	New Jersey	248	114	93	41	4		
	Totals	494	217	200	77	7		2008-15
Delvecchio, Alex	Detroit	245	82	131	32	4		1973-77
Demers, Jacques	Quebec	80	25	44	11	2		
	St. Louis	240	106	106	28	3		
	Detroit	320	137	136	47	4		
	Montreal	220	107	86	27	4	1	
	Tampa Bay	147	34	96	17	2		
	Totals	1007	409	468	130	14	1	1979-99
Denneny, Cy	Ottawa	48	11	27	10	1		1932-33
Desjardins, Willie	Vancouver	82	48	29	5	1		2014-15
Dineen, Bill	Philadelphia	140	60	60	20	2		1991-93
Dineen, Kevin	Florida	146	56	62	28	3		2011-14
Dudley, Rick	Buffalo	188	85	72	31	3		
	Florida	40	13	15	12	1		
	Totals	228	98	87	43	4		1989-04
Duff, Dick	Toronto	2	0	2	0	1		1979-80
Dugal, Jules	Montreal	18	9	6	3	1		1938-39
Duncan, Art	Detroit	33	10	21	2	1		
	Toronto	47	21	16	10	2		
	Totals	80	31	37	12	3		1926-32
Dutton, Red	NY Americans	192	66	97	29	4		1936-40
Eakins, Dallas	Edmonton	113	36	63	14	2		2013-15
Eddolls, Frank	Chicago	70	13	40	17	1		1954-55
Esposito, Phil	NY Rangers	45	24	21	0	2		1986-89
Evans, Jack	California	80	27	42	11	1		
	Cleveland	160	47	87	26	2		
	Hartford	374	163	174	37	5		
	Totals	614	237	303	74	8		1975-88
Ferguson, John	NY Rangers	121	43	59	19	2		
	Winnipeg	14	7	6	1	1		
	Totals	135	50	65	20	3		1975-86
Filion, Maurice	Quebec	6	1	3	2	1		1980-81
Francis, Bob	Phoenix	390	165	144	81	5		1999-04
Francis, Emile	NY Rangers	654	342	209	103	10		
	St. Louis	124	46	64	14	3		
	Totals	778	388	273	117	13		1965-83
Fraser, Curt	Atlanta	279	64	169	46	4		1999-03
Fredrickson, Frank	Pittsburgh	44	5	36	3	1		1929-30

Coach	Team	Games Coached	Wins	Losses	O/T	Years	Cup Wins	Career
Ftorek, Robbie	Los Angeles	132	65	56	11	2		
	New Jersey	156	88	44	24	2		
	Boston	155	76	52	27	2		
	Totals	443	229	152	62	6		1987-03
Gadsby, Bill	Detroit	78	35	31	12	2		1968-70
Gainey, Bob	Minnesota	244	95	119	30	3		
	Dallas	171	70	71	30	3		
	Montreal	57	29	21	7	2		
	Totals	472	194	211	67	8		1990-09
Gallant, Gerard	Columbus	142	56	76	10	4		
	Florida	82	38	29	15	1		
	Totals	224	94	105	25	5		2003-15
Gardiner, Herb	Chicago	32	5	23	4	1		1928-29
Gardner, Jimmy	Hamilton	30	19	10	1	1		1924-25
Garvin, Ted	Detroit	11	2	8	1	1		1973-74
Geoffrion, Bernie	NY Rangers	43	22	18	3	1		
	Atlanta	208	77	92	39	3		
	Montreal	30	15	9	6	1		
	Totals	281	114	119	48	5		1968-80
Gerard, Eddie	Ottawa	22	9	13	0	1		
	Mtl. Maroons	294	129	122	43	7	1	
	NY Americans	92	34	40	18	2		
	St. Louis	13	2	11	0	1		
	Totals	421	174	186	61	11	1	1917-35
Gilbert, Greg	Calgary	121	42	56	23	3		2000-03
Gill, David	Ottawa	132	64	41	27	3	1	1926-29
Glover, Fred	Oakland	152	51	76	25	2		
	California	204	45	131	28	4		
	Los Angeles	68	18	42	8	1		
	Totals	424	114	249	61	6		1968-74
Goodfellow, Ebbie	Chicago	140	30	91	19	2		1950-52
Gordon, Jackie	Minnesota	289	116	123	50	5		1970-75
Gordon, Scott	NY Islanders	181	64	94	23	3		2008-11
Goring, Butch	Boston	93	42	38	13	2		
	NY Islanders	147	41	88	18	2		
	Totals	240	83	126	31	4		1985-01
Gorman, Tommy	NY Americans	80	31	33	16	2		
	Chicago	73	28	28	17	2	1	
	Mtl. Maroons	174	74	71	29	4	1	
	Totals	327	133	132	62	8	2	1925-38
Gottselig, Johnny	Chicago	187	62	105	20	4		1944-48
Goyette, Phil	NY Islanders	50	6	40	4	1		1972-73
Graham, Dirk	Chicago	59	16	35	8	1		1998-99
Granato, Tony	Colorado	215	104	78	33	3		2002-09
Green, Gary	Washington	157	50	78	29	3		1979-82
Green, Pete	Ottawa	150	94	52	4	6	3	1919-25
Green, Shorty	NY Americans	44	11	27	6	1		1927-28
Green, Ted	Edmonton	188	65	102	21	3		1991-94
Gretzky, Wayne	Phoenix	328	143	161	24	4		2005-09
Guidolin, Aldo	Colorado	59	12	39	8	1		1978-79
Guidolin, Bep	Boston	104	72	23	9	2		
	Kansas City	125	26	84	15	2		
	Totals	229	98	107	24	4		1972-76
Gulutzan, Glen	Dallas	130	64	57	9	2		2011-13
Hanlon, Glen	Washington	239	78	122	39	5		2003-08
Harkness, Ned	Detroit	38	12	22	4	1		1970-71
Harris, Ted	Minnesota	179	48	104	27	3		1975-78
Hart, Cecil	Montreal	394	196	125	73	9	2	1926-39
Hartley, Bob	Colorado	359	193	108	58	5	1	
	Atlanta	291	136	118	37	6		
	Calgary	212	99	95	18	3		
	Totals	862	428	321	113	13	1	1998-15
Hartsburg, Craig	Chicago	246	104	102	40	3		
	Anaheim	197	80	82	35	3		
	Ottawa	48	17	24	7	1		
	Totals	491	201	208	82	7		1995-09
Harvey, Doug	NY Rangers	70	26	32	12	1		1961-62
Hay, Don	Phoenix	82	38	37	7	1		
	Calgary	68	23	28	17	1		
	Totals	150	61	65	24	2		1996-01
Heffernan, Frank	Toronto	12	5	7	0	1		1919-20
Helmer, Rosie	NY Americans	48	16	25	7	1		1935-36
Henning, Lorne	Minnesota	158	68	72	18	2		
	NY Islanders	65	19	39	7	2		
	Totals	223	87	111	25	4		1985-01
Hitchcock, Ken	Dallas	503	277	154	72	7	1	
	Philadelphia	254	131	73	50	5		
	Columbus	284	125	123	36	4		
	St. Louis	281	175	79	27	4		
	Totals	1322	708	429	185	19	1	1995-15
Hlinka, Ivan	Pittsburgh	86	42	32	12	2		2000-02
Holmgren, Paul	Philadelphia	264	107	126	31	4		
	Hartford	161	54	93	14	4		
	Totals	425	161	219	45	8		1988-96
Horachek, Peter	Florida	66	26	36	4	1		
	Toronto	42	9	28	5	1		
	Totals	108	35	64	9	2		2013-15
Howell, Harry	Minnesota	11	3	6	2	1		1978-79
Hunter, Dale	Washington	60	30	23	7	1		2011-12
Imlach, Punch	Toronto	770	370	275	125	12	4	
	Buffalo	119	32	62	25	2		
	Totals	889	402	337	150	14	4	1958-80
Ingarfield, Earl	NY Islanders	28	6	20	2	1		1972-73
Inglis, Bill	Buffalo	56	28	18	10	1		1978-79
Irvin, Dick	Chicago	126	45	62	19	3		
	Toronto	426	215	152	59	9	1	
	Montreal	896	431	313	152	15	3	
	Totals	1448	691	527	230	27	4	1928-56
Ivan, Tommy	Detroit	470	262	118	90	7	3	
	Chicago	103	26	56	21	2		
	Totals	573	288	174	111	9	3	1947-58
Iverson, Emil	Chicago	21	8	7	6	1		1932-33
Johnson, Bob	Calgary	400	193	155	52	5		
	Pittsburgh	80	41	33	6	1	1	
	Totals	480	234	188	58	6	1	1982-91
Johnson, Tom	Boston	208	142	43	23	3	1	1970-73
Johnston, Eddie	Chicago	80	34	27	19	1		
	Pittsburgh	516	232	224	60	7		
	Totals	596	266	251	79	8		1979-97
Johnston, Marshall	California	69	13	45	11	2		
	Colorado	56	15	32	9	1		
	Totals	125	28	77	20	3		1973-82
Johnston, Mike	Pittsburgh	82	43	27	12	1		2014-15
Julien, Claude	Montreal	159	72	62	25	4		
	New Jersey	79	47	24	8	1		
	Boston	622	351	192	88	8	1	
	Totals	860	470	278	121	13	1	2002-15
Kasper, Steve	Boston	164	66	78	20	2		1995-97
Keats, Duke	Detroit	11	2	7	2	1		1926-27
Keenan, Mike	Philadelphia	320	190	102	28	4		
	Chicago	320	153	126	41	4		
	NY Rangers	84	52	24	8	1	1	
	St. Louis	163	75	66	22	3		
	Vancouver	108	36	54	18	2		
	Boston	74	33	26	15	1		
	Florida	153	45	73	35	3		
	Calgary	164	88	60	16	2		
	Totals	1386	672	531	183	20	1	1984-09
Kehoe, Rick	Pittsburgh	160	55	81	22	2		2001-03
Kelly, Pat	Colorado	101	22	54	25	2		1977-79
Kelly, Red	Los Angeles	150	55	75	20	2		
	Pittsburgh	274	90	132	52	4		
	Toronto	318	133	123	62	4		
	Totals	742	278	330	134	10		1967-77
King, Dave	Calgary	216	109	76	31	3		
	Columbus	204	64	106	34	3		
	Totals	420	173	182	65	6		1992-03
Kingston, George	San Jose	164	28	129	7	2		1991-93
Kish, Larry	Hartford	49	12	32	5	1		1982-83
Kitchen, Mike	St. Louis	131	38	70	23	4		2003-07
Kromm, Bobby	Detroit	231	79	111	41	3		1977-80
Krueger, Ralph	Edmonton	48	19	22	7	1		2012-13
Kurtenbach, Orland	Vancouver	125	36	62	27	2		1976-78
Laflamme, Jerry	Mtl. Maroons	44	23	16	5	1		1929-30
LaForge, Bill	Vancouver	20	4	14	2	1		1984-85
Lalonde, Newsy	Montreal	207	96	97	14	8		
	NY Americans	44	17	25	2	1		
	Ottawa	88	31	45	12	2		
	Totals	339	144	167	28	11		1917-35
Lamoriello, Lou	New Jersey *	53	34	14	5	2		2005-15

* Shared a record of 20-19-7 with co-coaches Adam Oates and Scott Stevens over the final 46 games of the 2014-15 season. Games are not officially attributed to anyone's coaching record.

Coach	Team	Games Coached	Wins	Losses	O/T	Years	Cup Wins	Career
Laperriere, Jacques	Montreal	1	0	1	0	1		1995-96
Lapointe, Ron	Quebec	89	33	50	6	2		1987-89
Laviolette, Peter	NY Islanders	164	77	62	25	2		
	Carolina	323	167	122	34	6	1	
	Philadelphia	272	145	98	29	5		
	Nashville	82	47	25	10	1		
	Totals	841	436	307	98	14	1	2001-15
Laycoe, Hal	Los Angeles	24	5	18	1	1		
	Vancouver	156	44	96	16	2		
	Totals	180	49	114	17	3		1969-72
Lehman, Hugh	Chicago	21	3	17	1	1		1927-28
Lemaire, Jacques	Montreal	97	48	37	12	2		
	New Jersey	509	276	166	67	7	1	
	Minnesota	656	293	255	108	9		
	Totals	1262	617	458	187	18	1	1983-11
Lepine, Pit	Montreal	48	10	33	5	1		1939-40
LeSueur, Percy	Hamilton	10	3	7	0	1		1923-24
Lewis, Dave	Detroit *	169	100	42	27	4		
	Boston	82	35	41	6	1		
	Totals	251	135	83	33	5		1998-07

* Shared a record of 4-1-0 with co-coach Barry Smith in 1998-99

Coach	Team	Games Coached	Wins	Losses	O/T	Years	Cup Wins	Career
Ley, Rick	Hartford	160	69	71	20	2		
	Vancouver	124	47	50	27	2		
	Totals	284	116	121	47	4		1989-96
Lindsay, Ted	Detroit	29	5	21	3	2		1979-81
Long, Barry	Winnipeg	205	87	93	25	3		1983-86
Loughlin, Clem	Chicago	144	61	63	20	3		1934-37
Low, Ron	Edmonton	341	139	162	40	6		
	NY Rangers	164	69	81	14	2		
	Totals	505	208	243	54	7		1994-02
Lowe, Kevin	Edmonton	82	32	26	24	1		1999-00
Ludzik, Steve	Tampa Bay	121	31	67	23	2		1999-01
MacDonald, Parker	Minnesota	61	20	30	11	1		
	Los Angeles	42	13	24	5	1		
	Totals	103	33	54	16	2		1973-82
MacLean, Doug	Florida	187	83	71	33	3		
	Columbus	79	24	43	12	2		
	Totals	266	107	114	45	5		1995-04
MacLean, John	New Jersey	33	9	22	2	1		2010-11
MacLean, Paul	Ottawa	239	114	90	35	4		2011-15
MacMillan, Bill	Colorado	80	22	45	13	1		
	New Jersey	100	19	67	14	2		
	Totals	180	41	112	27	3		1980-84

Coach	Team	Games Coached	Wins	Losses	O/T	Years	Cup Wins	Career
MacNeil, Al	Montreal	55	31	15	9	1	1	
	Atlanta	80	35	32	13	1		
	Calgary	171	72	66	33	3		
	Totals	306	138	113	55	5	1	1970-03
MacTavish, Craig	Edmonton	661	301	255	105	10		2000-15
Magnuson, Keith	Chicago	132	49	57	26	2		1980-82
Mahoney, Bill	Minnesota	93	42	39	12	2		1983-85
Maloney, Dan	Toronto	160	45	100	15	2		
	Winnipeg	212	91	93	28	3		
	Totals	372	136	193	43	5		1984-89
Maloney, Phil	Vancouver	232	95	105	32	4		1973-77
Mantha, Sylvio	Montreal	48	11	26	11	1		1935-36
Marshall, Bert	Colorado	24	3	17	4	1		1981-82
Martin, Jacques	St. Louis	160	66	71	23	2		
	Ottawa	692	341	235	116	9		
	Florida	246	110	100	36	4		
	Montreal	196	96	75	25	3		
	Totals	1294	613	481	200	18		1986-12
Matheson, Godfrey	Chicago	2	0	2	0	1		1932-33
Maurice, Paul	Hartford	152	61	72	19	2		
	Carolina	768	323	319	126	11		
	Toronto	164	76	66	22	2		
	Winnipeg	117	61	38	18	2		
	Totals	1201	521	495	185	17		1995-15
Maxner, Wayne	Detroit	129	34	68	27	2		1980-82
McCammon, Bob	Philadelphia	218	119	68	31	4		
	Vancouver	294	102	156	36	4		
	Totals	512	221	224	67	8		1978-91
McCreary, Bill	St. Louis	24	6	14	4	1		
	Vancouver	41	9	25	7	1		
	California	32	8	20	4	1		
	Totals	97	23	59	15	3		1971-75
McGuire, Pierre	Hartford	67	23	37	7	1		1993-94
McLellan, John	Toronto	310	126	139	45	4		1969-73
McLellan, Todd	San Jose	540	311	163	66	7		2008-15
McVie, Tom	Washington	204	49	122	33	3		
	Winnipeg	105	20	67	18	2		
	New Jersey	153	57	74	22	3		
	Totals	462	126	263	73	8		1975-92
Meeker, Howie	Toronto	70	21	34	15	1		1956-57
Melrose, Barry	Los Angeles	209	79	101	29	3		
	Tampa Bay	16	5	7	4	1		
	Totals	225	84	108	33	4		1992-09
Milbury, Mike	Boston	160	90	49	21	2		
	NY Islanders	191	56	111	24	4		
	Totals	351	146	160	45	6		1989-99
Molleken, Lorne	Chicago	47	18	19	10	2		1998-00
Muckler, John	Minnesota	35	6	23	6	1		
	Edmonton	160	75	65	20	2	1	
	Buffalo	268	125	109	34	4		
	NY Rangers	185	70	88	27	3		
	Totals	648	276	285	87	10	1	1968-00
Muldoon, Pete	Chicago	44	19	22	3	1		1926-27
Muller, Kirk	Carolina	187	80	80	27	3		2011-14
Munro, Dunc	Mtl. Maroons	32	14	13	5	1		1930-31
Murdoch, Bob	Chicago	80	30	41	9	1		
	Winnipeg	160	63	75	22	2		
	Totals	240	93	116	31	3		1987-91
Murphy, Mike	Los Angeles	65	20	37	8	2		
	Toronto	164	60	87	17	2		
	Totals	229	80	124	25	4		1986-98
Murray, Andy	Los Angeles	480	215	176	89	7		
	St. Louis	258	118	102	38	4		
	Totals	738	333	278	127	11		1999-10
Murray, Bryan	Washington	672	343	246	83	9		
	Detroit	244	124	91	29	3		
	Florida	59	17	31	11	1		
	Anaheim	82	29	42	11	1		
	Ottawa	182	107	55	20	4		
	Totals	1239	620	465	154	18		1981-08
Murray, Terry	Washington	325	163	134	28	5		
	Philadelphia	212	118	64	30	3		
	Florida	200	79	79	42	3		
	Los Angeles	275	139	106	30	4		
	Totals	1012	499	383	130	15		1989-12
Nanne, Lou	Minnesota	29	7	18	4	1		1977-78
Neale, Harry	Vancouver	407	142	189	76	6		
	Detroit	35	8	23	4	1		
	Totals	442	150	212	80	7		1978-86
Neilson, Roger	Toronto	160	75	62	23	2		
	Buffalo	80	39	20	21	1		
	Vancouver	133	51	61	21	3		
	Los Angeles	28	8	17	3	1		
	NY Rangers	280	141	104	35	4		
	Florida	132	53	56	23	2		
	Philadelphia	185	92	57	36	3		
	Ottawa	2	1	1	0	1		
	Totals	1000	460	378	162	16		1977-02
Nelson, Todd	Edmonton	46	17	22	7	1		2014-15
Noel, Claude	Columbus	24	10	8	6	1		
	Winnipeg	177	80	79	18	3		
	Totals	201	90	87	24	4		2009-14
Nolan, Ted	Buffalo	308	113	159	36	4		
	NY Islanders	163	74	68	21	2		
	Totals	471	187	227	57	6		1995-15
Nykoluk, Mike	Toronto	280	89	144	47	4		1980-84
Oates, Adam	Washington	130	65	48	17	2		
	New Jersey *	....	....	....	....	0		
	Totals	130	65	48	17	3		2012-15

* Shared a record of 20-19-7 with co-coaches Lou Lamoriello and Scott Stevens for New Jersey over the final 46 games of the 2014-15 season. Games are not officially attributed to anyone's coaching record.

Coach	Team	Games Coached	Wins	Losses	O/T	Years	Cup Wins	Career
O'Connell, Mike	Boston	9	3	3	3	1		2002-03
O'Donoghue, George	Toronto	29	15	13	1	2	1	1921-23
Olczyk, Ed	Pittsburgh	113	31	64	18	3		2003-06
Oliver, Murray	Minnesota	37	18	12	7	1		1982-83
Olmstead, Bert	Oakland *	74	15	42	17	1		1967-68

* Olmstead, who was also GM, turned over bench duties to assistant coach Gord Fashoway for the last 22 games of the season. Fashoway posted a 5-11-6 record. All games are credited to Olmstead's coaching record.

Coach	Team	Games Coached	Wins	Losses	O/T	Years	Cup Wins	Career
O'Reilly, Terry	Boston	227	115	86	26	3		1986-89
Paddock, John	Winnipeg	281	106	138	37	4		
	Ottawa	64	36	22	6	1		
	Totals	345	142	160	43	5		1991-08
Page, Pierre	Minnesota	160	63	77	20	2		
	Quebec	230	98	103	29	3		
	Calgary	164	66	78	20	2		
	Anaheim	82	26	43	13	1		
	Totals	636	253	301	82	8		1988-98
Park, Brad	Detroit	45	9	34	2	1		1985-86
Paterson, Rick	Tampa Bay	6	0	6	0	1		1997-98
Patrick, Craig	NY Rangers	95	37	45	13	2		
	Pittsburgh	74	29	36	9	2		
	Totals	169	66	81	22	4		1980-97
Patrick, Frank	Boston	96	48	36	12	2		1934-36
Patrick, Lester	NY Rangers	604	281	216	107	13	2	1926-39
Patrick, Lynn	NY Rangers	107	40	51	16	2		
	Boston	310	117	130	63	5		
	St. Louis	26	8	15	3	3		
	Totals	443	165	196	82	10		1948-76
Patrick, Muzz	NY Rangers	136	43	66	27	4		1953-63
Payne, Davis	St. Louis	137	67	55	15	3		2009-12
Perron, Jean	Montreal	240	126	84	30	3	1	
	Quebec	47	16	26	5	1		
	Totals	287	142	110	35	4	1	1985-89
Perry, Don	Los Angeles	168	52	85	31	3		1981-84
Peters, Bill	Carolina	82	30	41	11	1		2014-15
Pike, Alf	NY Rangers	123	36	66	21	2		1959-61
Pilous, Rudy	Chicago	387	162	151	74	6	1	1957-63
Plager, Barclay	St. Louis	178	49	96	33	4		1977-83
Plager, Bob	St. Louis	11	4	6	1	1		1992-93
Playfair, Jim	Calgary	82	43	29	10	1		2006-07
Pleau, Larry	Hartford	224	81	117	26	5		1980-89
Polano, Nick	Detroit	240	79	127	34	3		1982-85
Popein, Larry	NY Rangers	41	18	14	9	1		1973-74
Powers, Eddie	Toronto	66	31	32	3	2		1924-26
Primeau, Joe	Toronto	210	97	71	42	3	1	1950-53
Pronovost, Marcel	Buffalo	104	52	29	23	2		1977-79
Pulford, Bob	Los Angeles	396	178	150	68	5		
	Chicago	433	185	180	68	7		
	Totals	829	363	330	136	12		1972-00
Quenneville, Joel	St. Louis	593	307	191	95	8		
	Colorado	246	131	92	23	4		
	Chicago	536	316	155	65	7	3	
	Totals	1375	754	438	183	19	3	1996-15
Querrie, Charles	Toronto	72	29	38	5	3		1922-27
Quinn, Mike	Quebec	24	4	20	0	1		1919-20
Quinn, Pat	Philadelphia	262	141	73	48	4		
	Los Angeles	202	75	101	26	3		
	Vancouver	280	141	111	28	5		
	Toronto	574	300	196	78	8		
	Edmonton	82	27	47	8	1		
	Totals	1400	684	528	188	21		1978-10
Raeder, Cap	San Jose	1	1	0	0	1		2002-03
Ramsay, Craig	Buffalo	21	4	15	2	1		
	Philadelphia	28	12	12	4	1		
	Atlanta	82	34	36	12	1		
	Totals	131	50	63	18	3		1986-11
Randall, Ken	Hamilton	14	6	8	0	1		1923-24
Reay, Billy	Toronto	90	26	50	14	2		
	Chicago	1012	516	335	161	14		
	Totals	1102	542	385	175	16		1957-77
Regan, Larry	Los Angeles	88	27	47	14	2		1970-72
Renney, Tom	Vancouver	101	39	53	9	2		
	NY Rangers	327	164	117	46	6		
	Edmonton	164	57	85	22	2		
	Totals	592	260	255	77	10		1996-12
Richards, Todd	Minnesota	164	77	71	16	2		
	Columbus	253	127	105	21	4		
	Totals	417	204	176	37	6		2009-15
Risebrough, Doug	Calgary	144	71	56	17	2		1990-92
Roberts, Jim	Buffalo	45	21	16	8	1		
	Hartford	80	26	41	13	1		
	St. Louis	9	3	3	3	1		
	Totals	134	50	60	24	3		1981-97
Robinson, Larry	Los Angeles	328	122	161	45	4		
	New Jersey	173	87	56	30	4	1	
	Totals	501	209	217	75	8	1	1995-06
Rodden, Mike	Toronto	2	0	2	0	1		1926-27
Rolston, Ron	Buffalo	51	19	26	6	2		2012-14
Romeril, Alex	Toronto	13	7	5	1	1		1926-27

Coach	Team	Games Coached	Wins	Losses	O/T	Years	Cup Wins	Career
Ross, Art	Mtl. Wanderers	6	1	5	0	1		
	Hamilton	24	6	18	0	1		
	Boston	772	387	290	95	17	2	
	Totals	802	394	313	95	19	2	1917-45
Roy, Patrick	Colorado	164	91	53	20	2		2013-15
Ruel, Claude	Montreal	305	172	82	51	5	1	1968-81
Ruff, Lindy	Buffalo	1165	571	432	162	16		
	Dallas	164	81	62	21	2		
	Totals	1329	652	494	183	18		1997-15
Sacco, Joe	Colorado	294	130	134	30	4		2009-13
Sather, Glen	Edmonton	842	464	268	110	11	4	
	NY Rangers	90	33	39	18	2		
	Totals	932	497	307	128	13	4	1979-04
Sator, Ted	NY Rangers	99	41	48	10	2		
	Buffalo	207	96	89	22	3		
	Totals	306	137	137	32	4		1985-89
Savard, Andre	Quebec	24	10	13	1	1		1987-88
Savard, Denis	Chicago	147	65	66	16	3		2006-09
Schinkel, Ken	Pittsburgh	203	83	92	28	4		1972-77
Schmidt, Milt	Boston	726	245	360	121	11		
	Washington	44	5	34	5	2		
	Totals	770	250	394	126	13		1954-76
Schoenfeld, Jim	Buffalo	43	19	19	5	1		
	New Jersey	124	50	59	15	3		
	Washington	249	113	102	34	4		
	Phoenix	164	74	66	24	2		
	Totals	580	256	246	78	10		1985-99
Shaughnessy, Tom	Chicago	21	10	8	3	1		1929-30
Shaw, Brad	NY Islanders	40	18	18	4	1		2005-06
Shero, Fred	Philadelphia	554	308	151	95	7	2	
	NY Rangers	180	82	74	24	3		
	Totals	734	390	225	119	10	2	1971-81
Simpson, Joe	NY Americans	144	42	72	30	3		1932-35
Simpson, Terry	NY Islanders	187	81	82	24	3		
	Philadelphia	84	35	39	10	1		
	Winnipeg	97	43	47	7	2		
	Totals	368	159	168	41	6		1986-96
Sims, Al	San Jose	82	27	47	8	1		1996-97
Sinden, Harry	Boston	327	153	116	58	6	1	1966-85
Skinner, Jimmy	Detroit	247	123	78	46	4	1	1954-58
Smeaton, Cooper	Philadelphia	44	4	36	4	1		1930-31
Smith, Alf	Ottawa	18	12	6	0	1		1918-19
Smith, Barry	Detroit *	5	4	1	0	1		1998-99

* Results Shared with co-coach Dave Lewis

Coach	Team	Games Coached	Wins	Losses	O/T	Years	Cup Wins	Career
Smith, Floyd	Buffalo	241	143	62	36	4		
	Toronto	68	30	33	5	1		
	Totals	309	173	95	41	5		1971-80
Smith, Mike	Winnipeg	23	2	17	4	1		1980-81
Smith, Ron	NY Rangers	44	15	22	7	1		1992-93
Smythe, Conn	Toronto	135	58	57	20	5		1927-32
Sonmor, Glen	Minnesota	421	177	161	83	7		1978-87
Sproule, Harvey	Toronto	12	7	5	0	1		1919-20
Stanley, Barney	Chicago	23	4	17	2	1		1927-28
Stasiuk, Vic	Philadelphia	154	45	68	41	2		
	California	75	21	38	16	1		
	Vancouver	78	22	47	9	1		
	Totals	307	88	153	66	4		1969-73
Stevens, John	Philadelphia	263	120	109	34	4		
	Los Angeles	4	2	2	0	1		
	Totals	267	122	111	34	5		2006-12
Stewart, Bill	Chicago	69	22	35	12	2	1	1937-39
Stewart, Bill	NY Islanders	37	11	19	7	1		1998-99
Stewart, Ron	NY Rangers	39	15	20	4	1		
	Los Angeles	80	31	34	15	1		
	Totals	119	46	54	19	2		1975-78
Stirling, Steve	NY Islanders	124	56	51	17	3		2003-06
Suhonen, Alpo	Chicago	82	29	41	12	1		2000-01
Sullivan, Mike	Boston	164	70	56	38	3		2003-06
Sullivan, Red	NY Rangers	196	58	103	35	4		
	Pittsburgh	150	47	79	24	2		
	Washington	18	2	16	0	1		
	Totals	364	107	198	59	7		1962-75
Sutherland, Bill	Winnipeg	32	7	22	3	2		1979-81
Sutter, Brent	New Jersey	164	97	56	11	2		
	Calgary	246	118	90	38	3		
	Totals	410	215	146	49	5		2007-12

Coach	Team	Games Coached	Wins	Losses	O/T	Years	Cup Wins	Career
Sutter, Brian	St. Louis	320	153	124	43	4		
	Boston	216	120	73	23	3		
	Calgary	246	87	117	42	4		
	Chicago	246	91	103	52	4		
	Totals	1028	451	417	160	14		1988-05
Sutter, Darryl	Chicago	216	110	80	26	3		
	San Jose	434	192	167	75	6		
	Calgary	210	107	73	30	4		
	Los Angeles	261	138	84	39	4	2	
	Totals	1121	547	404	170	16	2	1992-15
Sutter, Duane	Florida	72	22	35	15	2		2000-02
Talbot, Jean-Guy	St. Louis	120	52	53	15	2		
	NY Rangers	80	30	37	13	1		
	Totals	200	82	90	28	3		1972-78
Tessier, Orval	Chicago	213	99	93	21	3		1982-85
Therrien, Michel	Montreal	402	202	141	59	6		
	Pittsburgh	272	135	105	32	4		
	Totals	674	337	246	91	10		2000-15
Thompson, Paul	Chicago	272	104	127	41	7		1938-45
Thompson, Percy	Hamilton	48	13	35	0	2		1920-22
Tippett, Dave	Dallas	492	271	156	65	7		
	Phoenix/Arizona	458	217	176	65	6		
	Totals	950	488	332	130	13		2002-15
Tobin, Bill	Chicago	71	29	29	13	2		1929-32
Tocchet, Rick	Tampa Bay	148	53	69	26	2		2008-10
Torchetti, John	Florida	27	10	12	5	1		
	Los Angeles	12	5	7	0	1		
	Totals	39	15	19	5	2		2003-06
Tortorella, John	NY Rangers	319	171	118	30	6		
	Tampa Bay	535	239	222	74	8	1	
	Vancouver	82	36	35	11	1		
	Totals	936	446	375	115	15	1	1999-14
Tremblay, Mario	Montreal	159	71	63	25	2		1995-97
Trottier, Bryan	NY Rangers	54	21	26	7	1		2002-03
Trotz, Barry	Nashville	1196	557	479	160	16		
	Washington	82	45	26	11	1		
	Totals	1278	602	505	171	17		1998-15
Ubriaco, Gene	Pittsburgh	106	50	47	9	2		1988-90
Vachon, Rogie	Los Angeles	10	4	3	3	3		1983-95
Vigneault, Alain	Montreal	266	109	118	39	4		
	Vancouver	540	313	170	57	7		
	NY Rangers	164	98	53	13	2		
	Totals	970	520	341	109	13		1997-15
Waddell, Don	Atlanta	86	38	39	9	2		2002-08
Watson, Bryan	Edmonton	18	4	9	5	1		1980-81
Watson, Phil	NY Rangers	295	119	124	52	5		
	Boston	84	16	55	13	2		
	Totals	379	135	179	65	7		1955-63
Watt, Tom	Winnipeg	181	72	85	24	3		
	Vancouver	160	52	87	21	2		
	Toronto	149	52	80	17	2		
	Totals	490	176	252	62	7		1981-92
Webster, Tom	NY Rangers	18	5	9	4	1		
	Los Angeles	240	115	94	31	3		
	Totals	258	120	103	35	4		1986-92
Weiland, Cooney	Boston	96	58	20	18	2	1	1939-41
White, Bill	Chicago	46	16	24	6	1		1976-77
Wiley, Jim	San Jose	57	17	37	3	1		1995-96
Wilson, Johnny	Los Angeles	52	9	34	9	1		
	Detroit	145	67	56	22	2		
	Colorado	80	20	46	14	1		
	Pittsburgh	240	91	105	44	3		
	Totals	517	187	241	89	7		1969-80
Wilson, Larry	Detroit	36	3	29	4	1		1976-77
Wilson, Rick	Dallas	32	13	11	8	1		2001-02
Wilson, Ron	Anaheim	296	120	145	31	4		
	Washington	410	192	159	59	5		
	San Jose	385	206	122	57	6		
	Toronto	310	130	135	45	4		
	Totals	1401	648	561	192	19		1993-12
Yawney, Trent	Chicago	103	33	55	15	2		2005-07
Yeo, Mike	Minnesota	294	150	110	34	4		2011-15
Young, Garry	California	12	2	7	3	1		
	St. Louis	98	41	41	16	2		
	Totals	110	43	48	19	3		1972-76

Bob Hartley (far left) won the Jack Adams Award as coach of the year in 2014-15. He led the Calgary Flames to a 20-point improvement over the previous season which was the highest jump in the Western Conference and the third highest overall in the NHL. Calgary had a 45-30-7 record for 97 points. Alain Vigneault (center) guided the Rangers to the Presidents' Trophy, setting club records with 53 wins (53-22-7) and 113 points. In his first season in Nashville, Peter Laviolette (right) led the Predators back to the playoffs for the first time since 2012 with 47 wins and 104 points.

Year-by-Year Individual Regular-Season Leaders

Season	Goals	G	Assists	A	Points	Pts.	Penalty Minutes	PIM
2014-15	Alex Ovechkin	53	Nicklas Backstrom	60	Jamie Benn	87	Steve Downie	238
2013-14	Alex Ovechkin	51	Sidney Crosby	68	Sidney Crosby	104	Tom Sestito	213
2012-13	Alex Ovechkin	32	Martin St. Louis	43	Martin St. Louis	60	Colton Orr	155
2011-12	Steven Stamkos	60	Henrik Sedin	67	Evgeni Malkin	109	Derek Dorsett	235
2010-11	Corey Perry	50	Daniel Sedin	75	Daniel Sedin	104	Zenon Konopka	307
2009-10	Sidney Crosby, Steven Stamkos	51	Henrik Sedin	83	Henrik Sedin	112	Zenon Konopka	265
2008-09	Alex Ovechkin	56	Evgeni Malkin	78	Evgeni Malkin	113	Daniel Carcillo	254
2007-08	Alex Ovechkin	65	Joe Thornton	67	Alex Ovechkin	112	Daniel Carcillo	324
2006-07	Vincent Lecavalier	52	Joe Thornton	92	Sidney Crosby	120	Ben Eager	233
2005-06	Jonathan Cheechoo	56	Joe Thornton	96	Joe Thornton	125	Sean Avery	257
2004-05	....	....	....	....	....	....		
2003-04	Rick Nash, Jarome Iginla, Ilya Kovalchuk	41	Scott Gomez, Martin St. Louis	56	Martin St. Louis	94	Sean Avery	261
2002-03	Milan Hejduk	50	Peter Forsberg	77	Peter Forsberg	106	Jody Shelley	249
2001-02	Jarome Iginla	52	Adam Oates	64	Jarome Iginla	96	Peter Worell	354
2000-01	Pavel Bure	59	Jaromir Jagr, Adam Oates	69	Jaromir Jagr	121	Matthew Barnaby	265
99-2000	Pavel Bure	58	Mark Recchi	63	Jaromir Jagr	96	Denny Lambert	219
1998-99	Teemu Selanne	47	Jaromir Jagr	83	Jaromir Jagr	127	Rob Ray	261
1997-98	Teemu Selanne, Peter Bondra	52	Jaromir Jagr, Wayne Gretzky	67	Jaromir Jagr	102	Donald Brashear	372
1996-97	Keith Tkachuk	52	Mario Lemieux, Wayne Gretzky	72	Mario Lemieux	122	Gino Odjick	371
1995-96	Mario Lemieux	69	Mario Lemieux, Ron Francis	92	Mario Lemieux	161	Matthew Barnaby	335
1994-95	Peter Bondra	34	Ron Francis	48	Jaromir Jagr, Eric Lindros	70	Enrico Ciccone	225
1993-94	Pavel Bure	60	Wayne Gretzky	92	Wayne Gretzky	130	Tie Domi	347
1992-93	Teemu Selanne, Alexander Mogilny	76	Adam Oates	97	Mario Lemieux	160	Marty McSorley	399
1991-92	Brett Hull	70	Wayne Gretzky	90	Mario Lemieux	131	Mike Peluso	408
1990-91	Brett Hull	86	Wayne Gretzky	122	Wayne Gretzky	163	Rob Ray	350
1989-90	Brett Hull	72	Wayne Gretzky	102	Wayne Gretzky	142	Basil McRae	351
1988-89	Mario Lemieux	85	Mario Lemieux, Wayne Gretzky	114	Mario Lemieux	199	Tim Hunter	375
1987-88	Mario Lemieux	70	Wayne Gretzky	109	Mario Lemieux	168	Bob Probert	398
1986-87	Wayne Gretzky	62	Wayne Gretzky	121	Wayne Gretzky	183	Tim Hunter	361
1985-86	Jari Kurri	68	Wayne Gretzky	163	Wayne Gretzky	215	Joe Kocur	377
1984-85	Wayne Gretzky	73	Wayne Gretzky	135	Wayne Gretzky	208	Chris Nilan	358
1983-84	Wayne Gretzky	87	Wayne Gretzky	118	Wayne Gretzky	205	Chris Nilan	338
1982-83	Wayne Gretzky	71	Wayne Gretzky	125	Wayne Gretzky	196	Randy Holt	275
1981-82	Wayne Gretzky	92	Wayne Gretzky	120	Wayne Gretzky	212	Paul Baxter	409
1980-81	Mike Bossy	68	Wayne Gretzky	109	Wayne Gretzky	164	Tiger Williams	343
1979-80	Charlie Simmer, Danny Gare, Blaine Stoughton	56	Wayne Gretzky	86	Marcel Dionne, Wayne Gretzky	137	Jimmy Mann	287
1978-79	Mike Bossy *	69	Bryan Trottier	87	Bryan Trottier	134	Tiger Williams	298
1977-78	Guy Lafleur	60	Bryan Trottier	77	Guy Lafleur	132	Dave Schultz	405
1976-77	Steve Shutt	60	Guy Lafleur	80	Guy Lafleur	136	Tiger Williams	338
1975-76	Reggie Leach	61	Bobby Clarke	89	Guy Lafleur	125	Steve Durbano	370
1974-75	Phil Esposito	61	Bobby Orr, Bobby Clarke	89	Bobby Orr	135	Dave Schultz	472
1973-74	Phil Esposito	68	Bobby Orr	90	Phil Esposito	145	Dave Schultz	348
1972-73	Phil Esposito	55	Phil Esposito	75	Phil Esposito	130	Dave Schultz	259
1971-72	Phil Esposito	66	Bobby Orr	80	Phil Esposito	133	Bryan Watson	212
1970-71	Phil Esposito	76	Bobby Orr	102	Phil Esposito	152	Keith Magnuson	291
1969-70	Phil Esposito	43	Bobby Orr	87	Bobby Orr	120	Keith Magnuson	213
1968-69	Bobby Hull	58	Phil Esposito	77	Phil Esposito	126	Forbes Kennedy	219
1967-68	Bobby Hull	44	Phil Esposito	49	Stan Mikita	87	Barclay Plager	153
1966-67	Bobby Hull	52	Stan Mikita	62	Stan Mikita	97	John Ferguson	177
1965-66	Bobby Hull	54	Stan Mikita, Bobby Rousseau, Jean Beliveau	48	Bobby Hull	97	Reggie Fleming	166
1964-65	Norm Ullman	42	Stan Mikita	59	Stan Mikita	87	Carl Brewer	177
1963-64	Bobby Hull	43	Andy Bathgate	58	Stan Mikita	89	Vic Hadfield	151
1962-63	Gordie Howe	38	Henri Richard	50	Gordie Howe	86	Howie Young	273
1961-62	Bobby Hull	50	Andy Bathgate	56	Bobby Hull, Andy Bathgate	84	Lou Fontinato	167
1960-61	Bernie Geoffrion	50	Jean Beliveau	58	Bernie Geoffrion	95	Pierre Pilote	165
1959-60	Bobby Hull, Bronco Horvath	39	Don McKenney	49	Bobby Hull	81	Carl Brewer	150
1958-59	Jean Beliveau	45	Dickie Moore	55	Dickie Moore	96	Ted Lindsay	184
1957-58	Dickie Moore	36	Henri Richard	52	Dickie Moore	84	Lou Fontinato	152
1956-57	Gordie Howe	44	Ted Lindsay	55	Gordie Howe	89	Gus Mortson	147
1955-56	Jean Beliveau	47	Bert Olmstead	56	Jean Beliveau	88	Lou Fontinato	202
1954-55	Maurice Richard, Bernie Geoffrion	38	Bert Olmstead	48	Bernie Geoffrion	75	Fern Flaman	150
1953-54	Maurice Richard	37	Gordie Howe	48	Gordie Howe	81	Gus Mortson	132
1952-53	Gordie Howe	49	Gordie Howe	46	Gordie Howe	95	Maurice Richard	112
1951-52	Gordie Howe	47	Elmer Lach	50	Gordie Howe	86	Gus Kyle	127
1950-51	Gordie Howe	43	Gordie Howe, Ted Kennedy	43	Gordie Howe	86	Gus Mortson	142
1949-50	Maurice Richard	43	Ted Lindsay	55	Ted Lindsay	78	Bill Ezinicki	144
1948-49	Sid Abel	28	Doug Bentley	43	Roy Conacher	68	Bill Ezinicki	145
1947-48	Ted Lindsay	33	Doug Bentley	37	Elmer Lach	61	Bill Barilko	147
1946-47	Maurice Richard	45	Billy Taylor	46	Max Bentley	72	Gus Mortson	133
1945-46	Gaye Stewart	37	Elmer Lach	34	Max Bentley	61	Jack Stewart	73
1944-45	Maurice Richard	50	Elmer Lach	54	Elmer Lach	80	Pat Egan	86
1943-44	Doug Bentley	38	Clint Smith	49	Herb Cain	82	Mike McMahon	98
1942-43	Doug Bentley	33	Bill Cowley	45	Doug Bentley	73	Jimmy Orlando	89 *
1941-42	Lynn Patrick	32	Phil Watson	37	Bryan Hextall	56	Pat Egan	124
1940-41	Bryan Hextall	26	Bill Cowley	45	Bill Cowley	62	Jimmy Orlando	99
1939-40	Bryan Hextall	24	Milt Schmidt	30	Milt Schmidt	52	Red Horner	87
1938-39	Roy Conacher	26	Bill Cowley	34	Toe Blake	47	Red Horner	85
1937-38	Gordie Drillon	26	Syl Apps	29	Gordie Drillon	52	Art Coulter	90
1936-37	Larry Aurie, Nels Stewart	23	Syl Apps	29	Sweeney Schriner	46	Red Horner	124
1935-36	Charlie Conacher, Bill Thoms	23	Art Chapman	28	Sweeney Schriner	45	Red Horner	167
1934-35	Charlie Conacher	36	Art Chapman	34	Charlie Conacher	57	Red Horner	125
1933-34	Charlie Conacher	32	Joe Primeau	32	Charlie Conacher	52	Red Horner	126 *
1932-33	Bill Cook	28	Frank Boucher	28	Bill Cook	50	Red Horner	144
1931-32	Charlie Conacher, Bill Cook	34	Joe Primeau	37	Busher Jackson	53	Red Dutton	107
1930-31	Charlie Conacher	31	Joe Primeau	32	Howie Morenz	51	Harvey Rockburn	118
1929-30	Cooney Weiland	43	Frank Boucher	36	Cooney Weiland	73	Joe Lamb	119
1928-29	Ace Bailey	22	Frank Boucher	16	Ace Bailey	32	Red Dutton	139
1927-28	Howie Morenz	33	Howie Morenz	18	Howie Morenz	51	Eddie Shore	165
1926-27	Bill Cook	33	Dick Irvin	18	Bill Cook	37	Nels Stewart	133
1925-26	Nels Stewart	34	Frank Nighbor	13	Nels Stewart	42	Bert Corbeau	121
1924-25	Babe Dye	38	Cy Denneny, Red Green	15	Babe Dye	46	George Boucher	95
1923-24	Cy Denneny	22	George Boucher	10	Cy Denneny	24	Reg Noble	79
1922-23	Babe Dye	26	Eddie Gerard	13	Babe Dye	37	George Boucher	58
1921-22	Punch Broadbent	32	Harry Cameron	17	Punch Broadbent	46	Sprague Cleghorn	63
1920-21	Babe Dye	35	Jack Darragh	15	Newsy Lalonde	43	Bert Corbeau	86
1919-20	Joe Malone	39	Frank Nighbor	15	Joe Malone	49	Cully Wilson	86
1918-19	Newsy Lalonde, Odie Cleghorn	22	Newsy Lalonde	10	Newsy Lalonde	32	Joe Hall	135
1917-18	Joe Malone	44	Cy Denneny, Reg Noble, Harry Cameron	10	Joe Malone	48	Joe Hall	100

* Match Misconduct penalty not included in total penalty minutes.
1946-47 was the first season that a Match penalty was automatically written into the player's total penalty minutes as 20 minutes.
Beginning in 1947-48 all penalties, Match, Game Misconduct, and Misconduct, are written as 10 minutes.

One Season Scoring Records

Goals-Per-Game Leaders, One Season

(Among players with 20 goals or more in one season)

Player	Team	Season	Games	Goals	Goals per game average
Joe Malone	Montreal	1917-18	20	44	2.20
Cy Denneny	Ottawa	1917-18	20	36	1.80
Newsy Lalonde	Montreal	1917-18	14	23	1.64
Joe Malone	Quebec	1919-20	24	39	1.63
Newsy Lalonde	Montreal	1919-20	23	37	1.61
Reg Noble	Toronto	1917-18	20	30	1.50
Babe Dye	Ham., Tor.	1920-21	24	35	1.46
Cy Denneny	Ottawa	1920-21	24	34	1.42
Joe Malone	Hamilton	1920-21	20	28	1.40
Newsy Lalonde	Montreal	1920-21	24	33	1.38
Punch Broadbent	Ottawa	1921-22	24	32	1.33
Babe Dye	Toronto	1924-25	29	38	1.31
Babe Dye	Toronto	1921-22	24	31	1.29
Newsy Lalonde	Montreal	1918-19	17	22	1.29
Odie Cleghorn	Montreal	1918-19	17	22	1.29
Cy Denneny	Ottawa	1921-22	22	27	1.23
Aurel Joliat	Montreal	1924-25	25	30	1.20
Wayne Gretzky	Edmonton	1983-84	74	87	1.18
Babe Dye	Toronto	1922-23	22	26	1.18
Wayne Gretzky	Edmonton	1981-82	80	92	1.15
Mario Lemieux	Pittsburgh	1992-93	60	69	1.15
Frank Nighbor	Ottawa	1919-20	23	26	1.13
Mario Lemieux	Pittsburgh	1988-89	76	85	1.12
Brett Hull	St. Louis	1990-91	78	86	1.10
Cam Neely	Boston	1993-94	49	50	1.02
Maurice Richard	Montreal	1944-45	50	50	1.00
Reg Noble	Toronto	1919-20	24	24	1.00
Corb Denneny	Toronto	1919-20	24	24	1.00
Joe Malone	Hamilton	1921-22	24	24	1.00
Billy Boucher	Montreal	1922-23	24	24	1.00
Cy Denneny	Ottawa	1923-24	22	22	1.00
Alexander Mogilny	Buffalo	1992-93	77	76	0.99
Mario Lemieux	Pittsburgh	1995-96	70	69	0.99
Cooney Weiland	Boston	1929-30	44	43	0.98
Phil Esposito	Boston	1970-71	78	76	0.97
Jari Kurri	Edmonton	1984-85	73	71	0.97

Brian Leetch became the fifth defenseman in NHL history to top 100 points in 1991-92. He had 22 goals and 80 assists in 80 games. Only defensemen Bobby Orr and Paul Coffey have had more assists in a single season.

Assists-Per-Game Leaders, One Season

(Among players with 35 assists or more in one season)

Player	Team	Season	Games	Assists	Assists per game average
Wayne Gretzky	Edmonton	1985-86	80	163	2.04
Wayne Gretzky	Edmonton	1987-88	64	109	1.70
Wayne Gretzky	Edmonton	1984-85	80	135	1.69
Wayne Gretzky	Edmonton	1983-84	74	118	1.59
Wayne Gretzky	Edmonton	1982-83	80	125	1.56
Wayne Gretzky	Los Angeles	1990-91	78	122	1.56
Wayne Gretzky	Edmonton	1986-87	79	121	1.53
Mario Lemieux	Pittsburgh	1992-93	60	91	1.52
Wayne Gretzky	Edmonton	1981-82	80	120	1.50
Mario Lemieux	Pittsburgh	1988-89	76	114	1.50
Adam Oates	St. Louis	1990-91	61	90	1.48
Wayne Gretzky	Los Angeles	1988-89	78	114	1.46
Wayne Gretzky	Los Angeles	1989-90	73	102	1.40
Wayne Gretzky	Edmonton	1980-81	80	109	1.36
Mario Lemieux	Pittsburgh	1991-92	64	87	1.36
Mario Lemieux	Pittsburgh	1989-90	59	78	1.32
Bobby Orr	Boston	1970-71	78	102	1.31
Mario Lemieux	Pittsburgh	1995-96	70	92	1.31
Mario Lemieux	Pittsburgh	1987-88	77	98	1.27
Bobby Orr	Boston	1973-74	74	90	1.22
Wayne Gretzky	Los Angeles	1991-92	74	90	1.22
Joe Thornton	Bos., S.J.	2005-06	81	96	1.19
Ron Francis	Pittsburgh	1995-96	77	92	1.19
Mario Lemieux	Pittsburgh	1985-86	79	93	1.18
Bobby Clarke	Philadelphia	1975-76	76	89	1.17
Peter Stastny	Quebec	1981-82	80	93	1.16
Adam Oates	Boston	1992-93	84	97	1.15
Doug Gilmour	Toronto	1992-93	83	95	1.14
Wayne Gretzky	Los Angeles	1993-94	81	92	1.14
Paul Coffey	Edmonton	1985-86	79	90	1.14
Bobby Orr	Boston	1969-70	76	87	1.14
Bryan Trottier	NY Islanders	1978-79	76	87	1.14
Bobby Orr	Boston	1972-73	63	72	1.14
Bill Cowley	Boston	1943-44	36	41	1.14
Sidney Crosby	Pittsburgh	2012-13	36	41	1.14
Pat LaFontaine	Buffalo	1992-93	84	95	1.13
Steve Yzerman	Detroit	1988-89	80	90	1.13
Paul Coffey	Pittsburgh	1987-88	46	52	1.13
Joe Thornton	San Jose	2006-07	82	92	1.12
Bobby Orr	Boston	1974-75	80	89	1.11
Bobby Clarke	Philadelphia	1974-75	80	89	1.11
Paul Coffey	Pittsburgh	1988-89	75	83	1.11

Player	Team	Season	Games	Assists	Assists per game average
Wayne Gretzky	Los Angeles	1992-93	45	49	1.11
Denis Savard	Chicago	1982-83	78	86	1.10
Denis Savard	Chicago	1981-82	80	87	1.09
Denis Savard	Chicago	1987-88	80	87	1.09
Wayne Gretzky	Edmonton	1979-80	79	86	1.09
Ron Francis	Pittsburgh	1994-95	44	48	1.09
Paul Coffey	Edmonton	1983-84	80	86	1.08
Elmer Lach	Montreal	1944-45	50	54	1.08
Peter Stastny	Quebec	1985-86	76	81	1.07
Jaromir Jagr	Pittsburgh	1995-96	82	87	1.06
Mark Messier	Edmonton	1989-90	79	84	1.06
Sidney Crosby	Pittsburgh	2006-07	79	84	1.06
Peter Forsberg	Colorado	1995-96	82	86	1.05
Paul Coffey	Edmonton	1984-85	80	84	1.05
Marcel Dionne	Los Angeles	1979-80	80	84	1.05
Bobby Orr	Boston	1971-72	76	80	1.05
Mike Bossy	NY Islanders	1981-82	80	83	1.04
Adam Oates	Boston	1993-94	77	80	1.04
Phil Esposito	Boston	1968-69	74	77	1.04
Bryan Trottier	NY Islanders	1983-84	68	71	1.04
Jason Spezza	Ottawa	2005-06	68	71	1.04
Pete Mahovlich	Montreal	1974-75	80	82	1.03
Kent Nilsson	Calgary	1980-81	80	82	1.03
Peter Stastny	Quebec	1982-83	75	77	1.03
Peter Forsberg	Colorado	2002-03	75	77	1.03
Denis Savard	Chicago	1988-89	58	59	1.02
Jaromir Jagr	Pittsburgh	1998-99	81	83	1.02
Doug Gilmour	Toronto	1993-94	83	84	1.01
Henrik Sedin	Vancouver	2009-10	82	83	1.01
Bernie Nicholls	Los Angeles	1988-89	79	80	1.01
Guy Lafleur	Montreal	1979-80	74	75	1.01
Guy Lafleur	Montreal	1976-77	80	80	1.00
Marcel Dionne	Los Angeles	1984-85	80	80	1.00
Brian Leetch	NY Rangers	1991-92	80	80	1.00
Bryan Trottier	NY Islanders	1977-78	77	77	1.00
Mike Bossy	NY Islanders	1983-84	67	67	1.00
Jean Ratelle	NY Rangers	1971-72	63	63	1.00
Steve Yzerman	Detroit	1993-94	58	58	1.00
Ron Francis	Hartford	1985-86	53	53	1.00
Guy Chouinard	Calgary	1980-81	52	52	1.00
Elmer Lach	Montreal	1943-44	48	48	1.00

Points-Per-Game Leaders, One Season

(Among players with 50 points or more in one season)

Player	Team	Season	Games	Points	Points per game average	Player	Team	Season	Games	Points	Points per game average
Wayne Gretzky	Edmonton	1983-84	74	205	2.77	Denis Savard	Chicago	1987-88	80	131	1.64
Wayne Gretzky	Edmonton	1985-86	80	215	2.69	Wayne Gretzky	Los Angeles	1991-92	74	121	1.64
Mario Lemieux	Pittsburgh	1992-93	60	160	2.67	Steve Yzerman	Detroit	1992-93	84	137	1.63
Wayne Gretzky	Edmonton	1981-82	80	212	2.65	Marcel Dionne	Los Angeles	1978-79	80	130	1.63
Mario Lemieux	Pittsburgh	1988-89	76	199	2.62	Dale Hawerchuk	Winnipeg	1984-85	80	130	1.63
Wayne Gretzky	Edmonton	1984-85	80	208	2.60	Mark Messier	Edmonton	1989-90	79	129	1.63
Wayne Gretzky	Edmonton	1982-83	80	196	2.45	Bryan Trottier	NY Islanders	1983-84	68	111	1.63
Wayne Gretzky	Edmonton	1987-88	64	149	2.33	Pat LaFontaine	Buffalo	1991-92	57	93	1.63
Wayne Gretzky	Edmonton	1986-87	79	183	2.32	Charlie Simmer	Los Angeles	1980-81	65	105	1.62
Mario Lemieux	Pittsburgh	1995-96	70	161	2.30	Guy Lafleur	Montreal	1978-79	80	129	1.61
Mario Lemieux	Pittsburgh	1987-88	77	168	2.18	Bryan Trottier	NY Islanders	1981-82	80	129	1.61
Wayne Gretzky	Los Angeles	1988-89	78	168	2.15	Phil Esposito	Boston	1974-75	79	127	1.61
Wayne Gretzky	Los Angeles	1990-91	78	163	2.09	Steve Yzerman	Detroit	1989-90	79	127	1.61
Mario Lemieux	Pittsburgh	1989-90	59	123	2.08	Peter Stastny	Quebec	1985-86	76	122	1.61
Wayne Gretzky	Edmonton	1980-81	80	164	2.05	Mario Lemieux	Pittsburgh	1996-97	76	122	1.61
Mario Lemieux	Pittsburgh	1991-92	64	131	2.05	Michel Goulet	Quebec	1983-84	75	121	1.61
Bill Cowley	Boston	1943-44	36	71	1.97	Sidney Crosby	Pittsburgh	2010-11	41	66	1.61
Phil Esposito	Boston	1970-71	78	152	1.95	Wayne Gretzky	Los Angeles	1993-94	81	130	1.60
Wayne Gretzky	Los Angeles	1989-90	73	142	1.95	Bryan Trottier	NY Islanders	1977-78	77	123	1.60
Steve Yzerman	Detroit	1988-89	80	155	1.94	Bobby Orr	Boston	1972-73	63	101	1.60
Bernie Nicholls	Los Angeles	1988-89	79	150	1.90	Guy Chouinard	Calgary	1980-81	52	83	1.60
Adam Oates	St. Louis	1990-91	61	115	1.89	Elmer Lach	Montreal	1944-45	50	80	1.60
Phil Esposito	Boston	1973-74	78	145	1.86	Pierre Turgeon	NY Islanders	1992-93	83	132	1.59
Jari Kurri	Edmonton	1984-85	73	135	1.85	Steve Yzerman	Detroit	1987-88	64	102	1.59
Mike Bossy	NY Islanders	1981-82	80	147	1.84	Mike Bossy	NY Islanders	1978-79	80	126	1.58
Jaromir Jagr	Pittsburgh	1995-96	82	149	1.82	Paul Coffey	Edmonton	1983-84	80	126	1.58
Mario Lemieux	Pittsburgh	1985-86	79	141	1.78	Marcel Dionne	Los Angeles	1984-85	80	126	1.58
Bobby Orr	Boston	1970-71	78	139	1.78	Bobby Orr	Boston	1969-70	76	120	1.58
Jari Kurri	Edmonton	1983-84	64	113	1.77	Eric Lindros	Philadelphia	1995-96	73	115	1.58
Mario Lemieux	Pittsburgh	2000-01	43	76	1.77	Charlie Simmer	Los Angeles	1979-80	64	101	1.58
Pat LaFontaine	Buffalo	1992-93	84	148	1.76	Teemu Selanne	Winnipeg	1992-93	84	132	1.57
Bryan Trottier	NY Islanders	1978-79	76	134	1.76	Jaromir Jagr	Pittsburgh	1998-99	81	127	1.57
Mike Bossy	NY Islanders	1983-84	67	118	1.76	Bobby Clarke	Philadelphia	1975-76	76	119	1.57
Paul Coffey	Edmonton	1985-86	79	138	1.75	Guy Lafleur	Montreal	1975-76	80	125	1.56
Phil Esposito	Boston	1971-72	76	133	1.75	Dave Taylor	Los Angeles	1980-81	72	112	1.56
Peter Stastny	Quebec	1981-82	80	139	1.74	Sidney Crosby	Pittsburgh	2012-13	36	56	1.56
Wayne Gretzky	Edmonton	1979-80	79	137	1.73	Denis Savard	Chicago	1982-83	78	121	1.55
Jean Ratelle	NY Rangers	1971-72	63	109	1.73	Ron Francis	Pittsburgh	1995-96	77	119	1.55
Marcel Dionne	Los Angeles	1979-80	80	137	1.71	Joe Thornton	Bos., S.J.	2005-06	81	125	1.54
Herb Cain	Boston	1943-44	48	82	1.71	Mike Bossy	NY Islanders	1985-86	80	123	1.54
Guy Lafleur	Montreal	1976-77	80	136	1.70	Kevin Stevens	Pittsburgh	1991-92	80	123	1.54
Dennis Maruk	Washington	1981-82	80	136	1.70	Bobby Orr	Boston	1971-72	76	117	1.54
Phil Esposito	Boston	1968-69	74	126	1.70	Mike Bossy	NY Islanders	1984-85	76	117	1.54
Guy Lafleur	Montreal	1974-75	70	119	1.70	Kevin Stevens	Pittsburgh	1992-93	72	111	1.54
Mario Lemieux	Pittsburgh	1986-87	63	107	1.70	Doug Bentley	Chicago	1943-44	50	77	1.54
Adam Oates	Boston	1992-93	84	142	1.69	Doug Gilmour	Toronto	1992-93	83	127	1.53
Bobby Orr	Boston	1974-75	80	135	1.69	Marcel Dionne	Los Angeles	1976-77	80	122	1.53
Marcel Dionne	Los Angeles	1980-81	80	135	1.69	Sidney Crosby	Pittsburgh	2006-07	79	120	1.52
Guy Lafleur	Montreal	1977-78	78	132	1.69	Jaromir Jagr	Pittsburgh	99-2000	63	96	1.52
Guy Lafleur	Montreal	1979-80	74	125	1.69	Eric Lindros	Philadelphia	1996-97	52	79	1.52
Rob Brown	Pittsburgh	1988-89	68	115	1.69	Eric Lindros	Philadelphia	1994-95	46	70	1.52
Jari Kurri	Edmonton	1985-86	78	131	1.68	Marcel Dionne	Detroit	1974-75	80	121	1.51
Brett Hull	St. Louis	1990-91	78	131	1.68	Mike Bossy	NY Islanders	1980-81	79	119	1.51
Phil Esposito	Boston	1972-73	78	130	1.67	Paul Coffey	Edmonton	1984-85	80	121	1.51
Cooney Weiland	Boston	1929-30	44	73	1.66	Dale Hawerchuk	Winnipeg	1987-88	80	121	1.51
Alexander Mogilny	Buffalo	1992-93	77	127	1.65	Paul Coffey	Pittsburgh	1988-89	75	113	1.51
Peter Stastny	Quebec	1982-83	75	124	1.65	Alex Ovechkin	Washington	2009-10	72	109	1.51
Bobby Orr	Boston	1973-74	74	122	1.65	Jaromir Jagr	Pittsburgh	1996-97	63	95	1.51
Kent Nilsson	Calgary	1980-81	80	131	1.64	Cam Neely	Boston	1993-94	49	74	1.51

Only Wayne Gretzky and Mario Lemieux have had more points in a single season than the 155 Steve Yzerman scored in 1988-89. With 65 goals and 90 assists in 80 games that year, Yzerman averaged 1.94 points-per-game.

Calgary's Joe Nieuwendyk (left) was just the second rookie in NHL history (behind Mike Bossy) to score 50 goals when he had 51 for the Flames in 1987-88. Johnny Gaudreau (right) didn't set any rookie records, but the Flames freshman led all rookies with 40 assists during the 2014-15 season.

Rookie Scoring Records

All-Time Top 50 Goal-Scoring Rookies

	Rookie	Team	Position	Season	GP	G	A	PTS
1.	* Teemu Selanne	Winnipeg	Right wing	1992-93	84	**76**	56	132
2.	* Mike Bossy	NY Islanders	Right wing	1977-78	73	**53**	38	91
3.	* Alex Ovechkin	Washington	Left wing	2005-06	81	**52**	54	106
4.	* Joe Nieuwendyk	Calgary	Center	1987-88	75	**51**	41	92
5.	* Dale Hawerchuk	Winnipeg	Center	1981-82	80	**45**	58	103
	* Luc Robitaille	Los Angeles	Left wing	1986-87	79	**45**	39	84
7.	Rick Martin	Buffalo	Left wing	1971-72	73	**44**	30	74
	Barry Pederson	Boston	Center	1981-82	80	**44**	48	92
9.	* Steve Larmer	Chicago	Right wing	1982-83	80	**43**	47	90
	* Mario Lemieux	Pittsburgh	Center	1984-85	73	**43**	57	100
11.	Eric Lindros	Philadelphia	Center	1992-93	61	**41**	34	75
12.	Darryl Sutter	Chicago	Left wing	1980-81	76	**40**	22	62
	Sylvain Turgeon	Hartford	Left wing	1983-84	76	**40**	32	72
	Warren Young	Pittsburgh	Left wing	1984-85	80	**40**	32	72
15.	Eric Vail	Atlanta	Left wing	1974-75	72	**39**	21	60
	* Peter Stastny	Quebec	Center	1980-81	77	**39**	70	109
	Anton Stastny	Quebec	Left wing	1980-81	80	**39**	46	85
	Steve Yzerman	Detroit	Center	1983-84	80	**39**	48	87
	Sidney Crosby	Pittsburgh	Center	2005-06	81	**39**	63	102
20.	* Gilbert Perreault	Buffalo	Center	1970-71	78	**38**	34	72
	Neal Broten	Minnesota	Center	1981-82	73	**38**	60	98
	Ray Sheppard	Buffalo	Right wing	1987-88	74	**38**	27	65
	Mikael Renberg	Philadelphia	Left wing	1993-94	83	**38**	44	82
24.	Jorgen Pettersson	St. Louis	Left wing	1980-81	62	**37**	36	73
	Jimmy Carson	Los Angeles	Center	1986-87	80	**37**	42	79
26.	Mike Foligno	Detroit	Right wing	1979-80	80	**36**	35	71
	Paul MacLean	Winnipeg	Right wing	1981-82	74	**36**	25	61
	Mike Bullard	Pittsburgh	Center	1981-82	75	**36**	27	63
	Tony Granato	NY Rangers	Right wing	1988-89	78	**36**	27	63
30.	Marian Stastny	Quebec	Right wing	1981-82	74	**35**	54	89
	Brian Bellows	Minnesota	Right wing	1982-83	78	**35**	30	65
	Tony Amonte	NY Rangers	Right wing	1991-92	79	**35**	34	69
33.	Nels Stewart	Mtl. Maroons	Center	1925-26	36	**34**	8	42
	* Danny Grant	Minnesota	Left wing	1968-69	75	**34**	31	65
	Norm Ferguson	Oakland	Right wing	1968-69	76	**34**	20	54
	Brian Propp	Philadelphia	Left wing	1979-80	80	**34**	41	75
	Wendel Clark	Toronto	Left wing	1985-86	66	**34**	11	45
	* Pavel Bure	Vancouver	Right wing	1991-92	65	**34**	26	60
	Michael Grabner	NY Islanders	Right wing	2010-11	76	**34**	18	52
40.	* Willi Plett	Atlanta	Right wing	1976-77	64	**33**	23	56
	Dale McCourt	Detroit	Center	1977-78	76	**33**	39	72
	Steve Bozek	Los Angeles	Center	1981-82	71	**33**	23	56
	Ron Flockhart	Philadelphia	Center	1981-82	72	**33**	39	72
	Mark Pavelich	NY Rangers	Center	1981-82	79	**33**	43	76
	Jason Arnott	Edmonton	Center	1993-94	78	**33**	35	68
	* Evgeni Malkin	Pittsburgh	Center	2006-07	78	**33**	52	85
47.	Bill Mosienko	Chicago	Right wing	1943-44	50	**32**	38	70
	Michel Bergeron	Detroit	Right wing	1975-76	72	**32**	27	59
	* Bryan Trottier	NY Islanders	Center	1975-76	80	**32**	63	95
	Don Murdoch	NY Rangers	Right wing	1976-77	59	**32**	24	56
	Jari Kurri	Edmonton	Left wing	1980-81	75	**32**	43	75
	Bobby Carpenter	Washington	Center	1981-82	80	**32**	35	67
	Petr Klima	Detroit	Left wing	1985-86	74	**32**	24	56
	Kjell Dahlin	Montreal	Right wing	1985-86	77	**32**	39	71
	Darren Turcotte	NY Rangers	Right wing	1989-90	76	**32**	34	66
	Joe Juneau	Boston	Center	1992-93	84	**32**	70	102
	Marek Svatos	Colorado	Right wing	2005-06	61	**32**	18	50
	Logan Couture	San Jose	Center	2010-11	79	**32**	24	56

* Calder Trophy Winner

All-Time Top 50 Point-Scoring Rookies

	Rookie	Team	Position	Season	GP	G	A	PTS
1.	* Teemu Selanne	Winnipeg	Right wing	1992-93	84	76	56	**132**
2.	* Peter Stastny	Quebec	Center	1980-81	77	39	70	**109**
3.	* Alex Ovechkin	Washington	Left wing	2005-06	81	52	54	**106**
4.	* Dale Hawerchuk	Winnipeg	Center	1981-82	80	45	58	**103**
5.	Joe Juneau	Boston	Center	1992-93	84	32	70	**102**
	Sidney Crosby	Pittsburgh	Center	2005-06	81	39	63	**102**
7.	* Mario Lemieux	Pittsburgh	Center	1984-85	73	43	57	**100**
8.	Neal Broten	Minnesota	Center	1981-82	73	38	60	**98**
9.	* Bryan Trottier	NY Islanders	Center	1975-76	80	32	63	**95**
10.	Barry Pederson	Boston	Center	1981-82	80	44	48	**92**
	* Joe Nieuwendyk	Calgary	Center	1987-88	75	51	41	**92**
12.	* Mike Bossy	NY Islanders	Right wing	1977-78	73	53	38	**91**
13.	* Steve Larmer	Chicago	Right wing	1982-83	80	43	47	**90**
14.	Marian Stastny	Quebec	Right wing	1981-82	74	35	54	**89**
15.	Steve Yzerman	Detroit	Center	1983-84	80	39	48	**87**
16.	* Sergei Makarov	Calgary	Right wing	1989-90	80	24	62	**86**
17.	Anton Stastny	Quebec	Left wing	1980-81	80	39	46	**85**
18.	* Evgeni Malkin	Pittsburgh	Center	2006-07	78	33	52	**85**
19.	* Luc Robitaille	Los Angeles	Left wing	1986-87	79	45	39	**84**
20.	Mikael Renberg	Philadelphia	Left wing	1993-94	83	38	44	**82**
21.	Jimmy Carson	Los Angeles	Center	1986-87	80	37	42	**79**
	Sergei Fedorov	Detroit	Center	1990-91	77	31	48	**79**
	Alexei Yashin	Ottawa	Center	1993-94	83	30	49	**79**
24.	Paul Stastny	Colorado	Center	2006-07	82	28	50	**78**
25.	Marcel Dionne	Detroit	Center	1971-72	78	28	49	**77**
26.	Larry Murphy	Los Angeles	Defense	1980-81	80	16	60	**76**
	Mark Pavelich	NY Rangers	Center	1981-82	79	33	43	**76**
	Dave Poulin	Philadelphia	Center	1983-84	73	31	45	**76**
29.	Brian Propp	Philadelphia	Left wing	1979-80	80	34	41	**75**
	Jari Kurri	Edmonton	Left wing	1980-81	75	32	43	**75**
	Denis Savard	Chicago	Center	1980-81	76	28	47	**75**
	Mike Modano	Minnesota	Center	1989-90	80	29	46	**75**
	Eric Lindros	Philadelphia	Center	1992-93	61	41	34	**75**
34.	Rick Martin	Buffalo	Left wing	1971-72	73	44	30	**74**
	* Bobby Smith	Minnesota	Center	1978-79	80	30	44	**74**
36.	Jorgen Pettersson	St. Louis	Left wing	1980-81	62	37	36	**73**
37.	* Gilbert Perreault	Buffalo	Center	1970-71	78	38	34	**72**
	Dale McCourt	Detroit	Center	1977-78	76	33	39	**72**
	Ron Flockhart	Philadelphia	Center	1981-82	72	33	39	**72**
	Sylvain Turgeon	Hartford	Left wing	1983-84	76	40	32	**72**
	Carey Wilson	Calgary	Center	1984-85	74	24	48	**72**
	Warren Young	Pittsburgh	Left wing	1984-85	80	40	32	**72**
	Alex Zhamnov	Winnipeg	Center	1992-93	68	25	47	**72**
	* Patrick Kane	Chicago	Right wing	2007-08	82	21	51	**72**
45.	Mike Foligno	Detroit	Right wing	1979-80	80	36	35	**71**
	Dave Christian	Winnipeg	Center	1980-81	80	28	43	**71**
	Mats Naslund	Montreal	Left wing	1982-83	74	26	45	**71**
	Kjell Dahlin	Montreal	Right wing	1985-86	77	32	39	**71**
	* Brian Leetch	NY Rangers	Defense	1988-89	68	23	48	**71**
50.	Bill Mosienko	Chicago	Right wing	1943-44	50	32	38	**70**
	* Scott Gomez	New Jersey	Center	99-2000	82	19	51	**70**

* Calder Trophy Winner

50-Goal Seasons

Bernie Geoffrion

Reggie Leach

Lanny McDonald

Player	Team	Date of 50th Goal	Score		Goaltender	Player's Game No.	Team Game No.	Total Goals	Total Games	Age When First 50th Scored (Yrs. & Mos.)
Maurice Richard	Mtl.	Mar. 18/45	Mtl. 4	at Bos. 2	Harvey Bennett	50	50	50	50	23.7
Bernie Geoffrion	Mtl.	Mar. 16/61	Tor. 2	at Mtl. 5	Cesare Maniago	62	68	50	64	30.1
Bobby Hull	Chi.	Mar. 25/62	Chi. 1	at NYR 4	Gump Worsley	70	70	50	70	23.2
Bobby Hull	Chi.	Mar. 2/66	Det. 4	at Chi. 5	Hank Bassen	52	57	54	65	
Bobby Hull	Chi.	Mar. 18/67	Chi. 5	at Tor. 9	Bruce Gamble	63	66	52	66	
Bobby Hull	Chi.	Mar. 5/69	NYR 4	at Chi. 4	Ed Giacomin	64	66	58	74	
Phil Esposito	Bos.	Feb. 20/71	Bos. 4	at L.A. 5	Denis DeJordy	58	58	76	78	29.0
John Bucyk	Bos.	Mar. 16/71	Bos. 11	at Det. 4	Roy Edwards	69	69	51	78	35.10
Phil Esposito	Bos.	Feb. 20/72	Bos. 3	at Chi. 1	Tony Esposito	60	60	66	76	
Bobby Hull	Chi.	Apr. 2/72	Det. 1	at Chi. 6	Andy Brown	78	78	50	78	
Vic Hadfield	NYR	Apr. 2/72	Mtl. 6	at NYR 5	Denis DeJordy	78	78	50	78	31.6
Phil Esposito	Bos.	Mar. 25/73	Buf. 1	at Bos. 6	Roger Crozier	75	75	55	78	
Mickey Redmond	Det.	Mar. 27/73	Det. 8	at Tor. 1	Ron Low	73	75	52	76	25.3
Rick MacLeish	Phi.	Apr. 1/73	Phi. 4	at Pit. 5	Cam Newton	78	78	50	78	23.2
Phil Esposito	Bos.	Feb. 20/74	Bos. 5	at Min. 5	Cesare Maniago	56	56	68	78	
Mickey Redmond	Det.	Mar. 23/74	NYR 3	at Det. 5	Ed Giacomin	69	71	51	76	
Ken Hodge	Bos.	Apr. 6/74	Bos. 2	at Mtl. 6	Michel Larocque	75	77	50	76	29.10
Rick Martin	Buf.	Apr. 7/74	St.L. 2	at Buf. 5	Wayne Stephenson	78	78	52	78	22.9
Phil Esposito	Bos.	Feb. 8/75	Bos. 8	at Det. 5	Jim Rutherford	54	54	61	79	
Guy Lafleur	Mtl.	Mar. 29/75	K.C. 1	at Mtl. 4	Denis Herron	66	76	53	70	23.6
Danny Grant	Det.	Apr. 2/75	Wsh. 3	at Det. 8	John Adams	78	78	50	80	29.2
Rick Martin	Buf.	Apr. 3/75	Bos. 2	at Buf. 4	Ken Broderick	67	79	52	68	
Reggie Leach	Phi.	Mar. 14/76	Atl. 1	at Phi. 6	Dan Bouchard	69	69	61	80	25.11
Jean Pronovost	Pit.	Mar. 24/76	Bos. 5	at Pit. 5	Gilles Gilbert	74	74	52	80	30.3
Guy Lafleur	Mtl.	Mar. 27/76	K.C. 2	at Mtl. 8	Denis Herron	76	76	56	80	
Bill Barber	Phi.	Apr. 3/76	Buf. 2	at Phi. 5	Al Smith	79	79	50	80	23.9
Pierre Larouche	Pit.	Apr. 3/76	Wsh. 5	at Pit. 4	Ron Low	75	79	53	76	20.5
Danny Gare	Buf.	Apr. 4/76	Tor. 2	at Buf. 5	Gord McRae	79	80	50	79	21.11
Steve Shutt	Mtl.	Mar. 1/77	Mtl. 5	at NYI 4	Glenn Resch	65	65	60	80	24.8
Guy Lafleur	Mtl.	Mar. 6/77	Mtl. 1	at Buf. 4	Don Edwards	68	68	56	80	
Marcel Dionne	L.A.	Apr. 2/77	Min. 2	at L.A. 7	Pete LoPresti	79	79	53	80	25.8
Guy Lafleur	Mtl.	Mar. 8/78	Wsh. 3	at Mtl. 4	Jim Bedard	63	65	60	78	
Mike Bossy	NYI	Apr. 1/78	Wsh. 2	at NYI 3	Bernie Wolfe	69	76	53	73	21.2
Mike Bossy	NYI	Feb. 24/79	Det. 1	at NYI 3	Rogie Vachon	58	58	69	80	
Marcel Dionne	L.A.	Mar. 11/79	L.A. 3	at Phi. 6	Wayne Stephenson	68	68	59	80	
Guy Lafleur	Mtl.	Mar. 31/79	Pit. 3	at Mtl. 5	Denis Herron	76	76	52	80	
Guy Chouinard	Atl.	Apr. 6/79	NYR 2	at Atl. 9	John Davidson	79	79	50	80	22.5
Marcel Dionne	L.A.	Mar. 12/80	L.A. 2	at Pit. 4	Nick Ricci	70	70	53	80	
Mike Bossy	NYI	Mar. 16/80	NYI 6	at Chi. 1	Tony Esposito	68	71	51	75	
Charlie Simmer	L.A.	Mar. 19/80	Det. 3	at L.A. 4	Jim Rutherford	57	73	56	64	26.0
Pierre Larouche	Mtl.	Mar. 25/80	Chi. 4	at Mtl. 8	Tony Esposito	72	75	50	73	
Danny Gare	Buf.	Mar. 27/80	Det. 1	at Buf. 10	Jim Rutherford	71	75	56	76	
Blaine Stoughton	Hfd.	Mar. 28/80	Hfd. 4	at Van. 4	Glen Hanlon	75	75	56	80	27.0
Guy Lafleur	Mtl.	Apr. 2/80	Mtl. 7	at Det. 2	Rogie Vachon	72	78	50	74	
Wayne Gretzky	Edm.	Apr. 2/80	Min. 1	at Edm. 1	Gary Edwards	78	79	51	79	19.2
Reggie Leach	Phi.	Apr. 3/80	Wsh. 2	at Phi. 4	empty net	75	79	50	76	
Mike Bossy	NYI	Jan. 24/81	Que. 3	at NYI 7	Ron Grahame	50	50	68	79	
Charlie Simmer	L.A.	Jan. 26/81	L.A. 7	at Que. 5	Michel Dion	51	51	56	65	
Marcel Dionne	L.A.	Mar. 8/81	L.A. 4	at Wpg. 1	Markus Mattsson	68	68	58	80	
Wayne Babych	St.L.	Mar. 12/81	St.L. 3	at Mtl. 4	Richard Sevigny	70	68	54	78	22.9
Wayne Gretzky	Edm.	Mar. 15/81	Edm. 3	at Cgy. 3	Pat Riggin	69	69	55	80	
Rick Kehoe	Pit.	Mar. 16/81	Pit. 7	at Edm. 6	Eddie Mio	70	70	55	80	29.7
Jacques Richard	Que.	Mar. 29/81	Mtl. 0	at Que. 4	Richard Sevigny	76	75	52	78	28.6
Dennis Maruk	Wsh.	Apr. 5/81	Det. 2	at Wsh. 7	Larry Lozinski	80	80	50	80	25.3
Wayne Gretzky	Edm.	Dec. 30/81	Phi. 5	at Edm. 7	empty net	39	39	92	80	
Dennis Maruk	Wsh.	Feb. 21/82	Wpg. 3	at Wsh. 6	Doug Soetaert	61	61	60	80	
Mike Bossy	NYI	Mar. 4/82	Tor. 1	at NYI 10	Michel Larocque	66	66	64	80	
Dino Ciccarelli	Min.	Mar. 8/82	St.L. 1	at Min. 8	Mike Liut	67	68	55	76	22.1
Rick Vaive	Tor.	Mar. 24/82	St.L. 3	at Tor. 4	Mike Liut	72	75	54	77	22.10
Blaine Stoughton	Hfd.	Mar. 28/82	Min. 5	at Hfd. 2	Gilles Meloche	76	76	52	80	
Rick Middleton	Bos.	Mar. 28/82	Bos. 5	at Buf. 9	Paul Harrison	72	77	51	75	28.11
Marcel Dionne	L.A.	Mar. 30/82	Cgy. 7	at L.A. 5	Pat Riggin	75	77	50	78	
Mark Messier	Edm.	Mar. 31/82	L.A. 3	at Edm. 7	Mario Lessard	78	79	50	78	21.3
Bryan Trottier	NYI	Apr. 3/82	Phi. 3	at NYI 6	Pete Peeters	79	79	50	80	25.9
Lanny McDonald	Cgy.	Feb. 18/83	Cgy. 1	at Buf. 5	Bob Sauve	60	60	66	80	30.0
Wayne Gretzky	Edm.	Feb. 19/83	Edm. 10	at Pit. 7	Nick Ricci	60	60	71	80	
Michel Goulet	Que.	Mar. 5/83	Hfd. 3	at Que. 10	Mike Veisor	67	67	57	80	22.11
Mike Bossy	NYI	Mar. 12/83	Wsh. 2	at NYI 6	Al Jensen	70	71	60	79	
Marcel Dionne	L.A.	Mar. 17/83	Que. 3	at L.A. 4	Dan Bouchard	71	71	56	80	
Al Secord	Chi.	Mar. 20/83	Tor. 3	at Chi. 7	Mike Palmateer	73	73	54	80	25.0
Rick Vaive	Tor.	Mar. 30/83	Tor. 4	at Det. 2	Gilles Gilbert	76	78	51	78	
Wayne Gretzky	Edm.	Jan. 7/84	Hfd. 3	at Edm. 5	Greg Millen	42	42	87	74	
Michel Goulet	Que.	Mar. 8/84	Que. 8	at Pit. 6	Denis Herron	63	69	56	75	
Rick Vaive	Tor.	Mar. 14/84	Min. 3	at Tor. 3	Gilles Meloche	69	72	52	76	
Mike Bullard	Pit.	Mar. 14/84	Pit. 6	at L.A. 7	Markus Mattsson	71	72	51	76	23.0
Jari Kurri	Edm.	Mar. 15/84	Edm. 2	at Mtl. 3	Rick Wamsley	57	73	52	64	23.10
Glenn Anderson	Edm.	Mar. 21/84	Hfd. 3	at Edm. 5	Greg Millen	76	76	54	80	23.6
Tim Kerr	Phi.	Mar. 22/84	Pit. 4	at Phi. 13	Denis Herron	74	75	54	79	24.3

Player	Team	Date of 50th Goal	Score		Goaltender	Player's Game No.	Team Game No.	Total Goals	Total Games	Age When First 50th Scored (Yrs. & Mos.)
Mike Bossy	NYI	Mar. 31/84	NYI 3	at Wsh. 1	Pat Riggin	67	79	51	67	
Wayne Gretzky	Edm.	Jan. 26/85	Pit. 3	at Edm. 6	Denis Herron	49	49	73	80	
Jari Kurri	Edm.	Feb. 3/85	Hfd. 3	at Edm. 6	Greg Millen	50	53	71	73	
Mike Bossy	NYI	Mar. 5/85	Phi. 5	at NYI 4	Bob Froese	61	65	58	76	
Michel Goulet	Que.	Mar. 6/85	Buf. 3	at Que. 4	Tom Barrasso	62	73	55	69	
Tim Kerr	Phi.	Mar. 7/85	Wsh. 6	at Phi. 9	Pat Riggin	63	65	54	74	
John Ogrodnick	Det.	Mar. 13/85	Det. 6	at Edm. 7	Grant Fuhr	69	69	55	79	25.9
Bob Carpenter	Wsh.	Mar. 21/85	Wsh. 2	at Mtl. 1	Steve Penney	72	72	53	80	21.9
Dale Hawerchuk	Wpg.	Mar. 29/85	Chi. 5	at Wpg. 5	W. Skorodenski	77	77	53	80	21.11
Mike Gartner	Wsh.	Apr. 7/85	Pit. 3	at Wsh. 7	Brian Ford	80	80	50	80	25.5
Jari Kurri	Edm.	Mar. 4/86	Edm. 6	at Van. 2	Richard Brodeur	63	65	68	78	
Mike Bossy	NYI	Mar. 11/86	Cgy. 4	at NYI 8	Reggie Lemelin	67	67	61	80	
Glenn Anderson	Edm.	Mar. 14/86	Det. 3	at Edm. 12	Greg Stefan	63	71	54	72	
Michel Goulet	Que.	Mar. 17/86	Que. 8	at Mtl. 6	Patrick Roy	67	72	53	75	
Wayne Gretzky	Edm.	Mar. 18/86	Wpg. 2	at Edm. 6	Brian Hayward	72	72	52	80	
Tim Kerr	Phi.	Mar. 20/86	Pit. 1	at Phi. 5	Roberto Romano	68	72	58	76	
Wayne Gretzky	Edm.	Feb. 4/87	Edm. 6	at Min. 5	Don Beaupre	55	55	62	79	
Dino Ciccarelli	Min.	Mar. 7/87	Pit. 7	at Min. 3	Gilles Meloche	66	66	52	80	
Mario Lemieux	Pit.	Mar. 12/87	Que. 3	at Pit. 6	Mario Gosselin	53	70	54	63	21.5
Tim Kerr	Phi.	Mar. 17/87	NYR 1	at Phi. 4	J. Vanbiesbrouck	67	71	58	75	
Jari Kurri	Edm.	Mar. 17/87	N.J. 4	at Edm. 7	Craig Billington	69	70	54	79	
Mario Lemieux	Pit.	Feb. 2/88	Wsh. 2	at Pit. 3	Pete Peeters	51	54	70	77	
Steve Yzerman	Det.	Mar. 1/88	Buf. 0	at Det. 4	Tom Barrasso	64	64	50	64	22.10
Joe Nieuwendyk	Cgy.	Mar. 12/88	Buf. 4	at Cgy. 10	Tom Barrasso	66	70	51	75	21.5
Craig Simpson	Edm.	Mar. 15/88	Buf. 4	at Edm. 6	Jacques Cloutier	71	71	56	80	21.1
Jimmy Carson	L.A.	Mar. 26/88	Chi. 5	at L.A. 9	Darren Pang	77	77	55	88	19.8
Luc Robitaille	L.A.	Apr. 1/88	L.A. 6	at Cgy. 3	Mike Vernon	79	79	53	80	21.10
Hakan Loob	Cgy.	Apr. 3/88	Min. 1	at Cgy. 4	Don Beaupre	80	80	50	80	27.9
Stephane Richer	Mtl.	Apr. 3/88	Mtl. 4	at Buf. 4	Tom Barrasso	72	80	50	72	21.10
Mario Lemieux	Pit.	Jan. 20/89	Pit. 3	at Wpg. 7	Pokey Reddick	44	46	85	76	
Bernie Nicholls	L.A.	Jan. 28/89	Edm. 7	at L.A. 6	Grant Fuhr	51	51	70	79	27.7
Steve Yzerman	Det.	Feb. 5/89	Det. 6	at Wpg. 2	Pokey Reddick	55	55	65	80	
Wayne Gretzky	L.A.	Mar. 4/89	Phi. 2	at L.A. 6	Ron Hextall	66	67	54	78	
Joe Nieuwendyk	Cgy.	Mar. 21/89	NYI 1	at Cgy. 4	Mark Fitzpatrick	72	74	51	77	
Joe Mullen	Cgy.	Mar. 31/89	Wpg. 1	at Cgy. 4	Bob Essensa	78	79	51	79	32.1
Brett Hull	St.L.	Feb. 6/90	Tor. 4	at St.L. 6	Jeff Reese	54	54	72	80	25.6
Steve Yzerman	Det.	Feb. 24/90	Det. 3	at NYI 3	Glenn Healy	63	63	62	79	
Cam Neely	Bos.	Mar. 10/90	Bos. 3	at NYI 3	Mark Fitzpatrick	69	71	55	76	24.9
Brian Bellows	Min.	Mar. 22/90	Min. 5	at Det. 1	Tim Cheveldae	75	75	55	80	25.6
Pat LaFontaine	NYI	Mar. 24/90	NYI 5	at Edm. 5	Bill Ranford	71	77	54	74	25.1
Stephane Richer	Mtl.	Mar. 24/90	Mtl. 4	at Hfd. 7	Peter Sidorkiewicz	75	77	51	75	
Gary Leeman	Tor.	Mar. 28/90	NYI 6	at Tor. 3	Mark Fitzpatrick	78	78	51	80	26.1
Luc Robitaille	L.A.	Mar. 31/90	L.A. 3	at Van. 6	Kirk McLean	79	79	52	80	
Brett Hull	St.L.	Jan. 25/91	St.L. 9	at Det. 4	David Gagnon	49	49	86	78	
Cam Neely	Bos.	Mar. 26/91	Bos. 7	at Que. 4	empty net	67	78	51	69	
Theoren Fleury	Cgy.	Mar. 26/91	Van. 2	at Cgy. 7	Bob Mason	77	77	51	79	22.9
Steve Yzerman	Det.	Mar. 30/91	NYR 5	at Det. 6	Mike Richter	79	79	51	80	
Brett Hull	St.L.	Jan. 28/92	St.L. 3	at L.A. 3	Kelly Hrudey	50	50	70	73	
Jeremy Roenick	Chi.	Mar. 7/92	Chi. 2	at Bos. 1	Daniel Berthiaume	67	67	53	80	22.2
Kevin Stevens	Pit.	Mar. 24/92	Pit. 3	at Det. 4	Tim Cheveldae	74	74	54	80	26.11
Gary Roberts	Cgy.	Mar. 31/92	Edm. 2	at Cgy. 5	Bill Ranford	73	77	53	76	25.10
Alexander Mogilny	Buf.	Feb. 3/93	Hfd. 2	at Buf. 3	Sean Burke	46	53	76	77	23.11
Teemu Selanne	Wpg.	Feb. 28/93	Min. 6	at Wpg. 7	Darcy Wakaluk	63	63	76	84	22.6
Pavel Bure	Van.	Mar. 1/93	Van. 5	at Buf. 2*	Grant Fuhr	63	63	60	83	21.11
Steve Yzerman	Det.	Mar. 10/93	Det. 6	at Edm. 3	Bill Ranford	70	70	58	84	
Luc Robitaille	L.A.	Mar. 15/93	L.A. 4	at Buf. 2	Grant Fuhr	69	69	63	84	
Brett Hull	St.L.	Mar. 20/93	St.L. 2	at L.A. 3	Robb Stauber	73	73	54	80	
Mario Lemieux	Pit.	Mar. 21/93	Pit. 6	at Edm. 4**	Ron Tugnutt	48	72	69	60	
Kevin Stevens	Pit.	Mar. 21/93	Pit. 6	at Edm. 4**	Ron Tugnutt	62	72	55	72	
Dave Andreychuk	Tor.	Mar. 23/93	Tor. 5	at Wpg. 4	Bob Essensa	72	73	54	83	29.6
Pat LaFontaine	Buf.	Mar. 28/93	Ott. 1	at Buf. 3	Peter Sidorkiewicz	75	75	53	84	
Pierre Turgeon	NYI	Apr. 2/93	NYI 3	at NYR 2	Mike Richter	75	76	58	83	23.8
Mark Recchi	Phi.	Apr. 3/93	T.B. 2	at Phi. 6	J-C Bergeron	77	77	53	84	25.2
Brendan Shanahan	St.L.	Apr. 15/93	T.B. 5	at St.L. 6	Pat Jablonski	71	84	51	71	24.3
Jeremy Roenick	Chi.	Apr. 15/93	Tor. 2	at Chi. 3	Felix Potvin	84	84	50	84	
Cam Neely	Bos.	Mar. 7/94	Wsh. 3	at Bos. 6	Don Beaupre	44	66	50	49	
Sergei Fedorov	Det.	Mar. 15/94	Van. 2	at Det. 5	Kirk McLean	67	69	56	82	24.3
Pavel Bure	Van.	Mar. 23/94	Van. 6	at L.A. 3	empty net	65	73	60	76	
Adam Graves	NYR	Mar. 23/94	NYR 5	at Edm. 3	Bill Ranford	74	74	52	84	25.11
Dave Andreychuk	Tor.	Mar. 24/94	S.J. 2	at Tor. 1	Arturs Irbe	73	74	53	83	
Brett Hull	St.L.	Mar. 25/94	Dal. 3	at St.L. 5	Andy Moog	71	74	52	81	
Ray Sheppard	Det.	Mar. 29/94	Hfd. 2	at Det. 6	Sean Burke	74	76	52	82	27.10
Brendan Shanahan	St.L.	Apr. 12/94	St.L. 5	at Dal. 9	Andy Moog	80	83	52	81	
Mike Modano	Dal.	Apr. 12/94	St.L. 5	at Dal. 9	Curtis Joseph	75	83	50	76	23.11
Mario Lemieux	Pit.	Feb. 23/96	Hfd. 4	at Pit. 5	Sean Burke	50	59	69	70	
Jaromir Jagr	Pit.	Feb. 23/96	Hfd. 4	at Pit. 5	Sean Burke	59	59	62	82	24.0
Alexander Mogilny	Van.	Feb. 29/96	St.L. 2	at Van. 2	Grant Fuhr	60	63	55	79	
Peter Bondra	Wsh.	Apr. 3/96	Wsh. 5	at Buf. 1	Andrei Trefilov	62	77	52	67	28.1
Joe Sakic	Col.	Apr. 7/96	Col. 4	at Dal. 1	empty net	79	79	51	82	26.7
John LeClair	Phi.	Apr. 10/96	Phi. 5	at N.J. 1	Corey Schwab	80	80	51	82	26.7
Keith Tkachuk	Wpg.	Apr. 12/96	L.A. 3	at Wpg. 5	empty net	75	81	50	76	24.0
Paul Kariya	Ana.	Apr. 14/96	Wpg. 2	at Ana. 5	N. Khabibulin	82	82	50	82	21.5
Keith Tkachuk	Phx.	Apr. 6/97	Phx. 1	at Col. 2	Patrick Roy	78	79	52	81	
Teemu Selanne	Ana.	Apr. 9/97	L.A. 1	at Ana. 4	empty net	77	81	51	78	
Mario Lemieux	Pit.	Apr. 11/97	Pit. 2	at Fla. 4	J. Vanbiesbrouck	75	81	50	76	

Mike Gartner

Steve Yzerman

Adam Graves

Peter Bondra

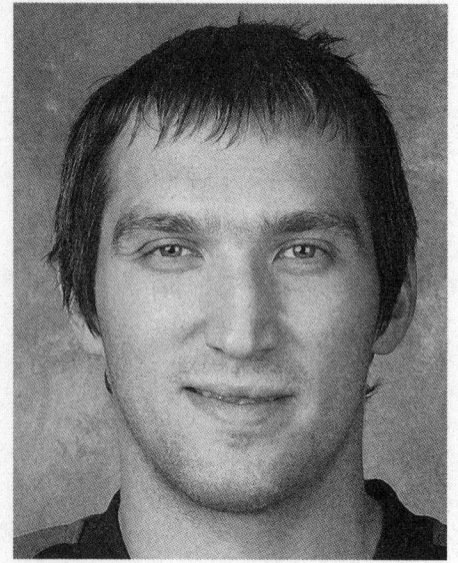
Alex Ovechkin

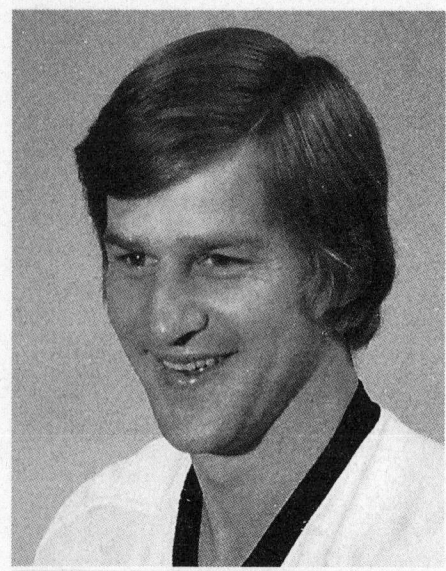
Bobby Orr

Player	Team	Date of 50th Goal	Score			Goaltender	Player's Game No.	Team Game No.	Total Goals	Total Games	Age When First 50th Scored (Yrs. & Mos.)
John LeClair	Phi.	Apr. 13/97	N.J. 4	at	Phi. 5	Mike Dunham	82	82	50	82	
Teemu Selanne	Ana.	Mar. 25/98	Ana. 3	at	Chi. 2	Jeff Hackett	66	71	52	73	
John LeClair	Phi.	Apr. 13/98	Phi. 1	at	Buf. 2	Dominik Hasek	79	79	51	82	
Pavel Bure	Van.	Apr. 17/98	Cgy. 4	at	Van. 2	Dwayne Roloson	81	81	51	82	
Peter Bondra	Wsh.	Apr. 18/98	Wsh. 4	at	Car. 3	Mike Fountain	75	80	52	76	
Pavel Bure	Fla.	Mar. 18/00	Fla. 4	at	NYI 2	empty net	63	71	58	74	
Pavel Bure	Fla.	Mar. 16/01	Pit. 6	at	Fla. 3	Johan Hedberg	72	72	59	82	
Joe Sakic	Col.	Apr. 4/01	Ana. 1	at	Col. 1	J-S Giguere	80	80	54	82	
Jaromir Jagr	Pit.	Apr. 4/01	T.B. 2	at	Pit. 4	Kevin Weekes	80	80	52	81	
Jarome Iginla	Cgy.	Apr. 7/02	Cgy. 2	at	Chi. 3	Jocelyn Thibault	79	79	52	82	24.9
Milan Hejduk	Col.	Apr. 6/03	St.L. 2	at	Col. 5	Brent Johnson	82	82	50	82	27.1
Jaromir Jagr	NYR	Mar. 24/06	NYR 2	at	Fla. 3	Roberto Luongo	70	70	54	82	
Ilya Kovalchuk	Atl.	Apr. 6/06	Atl. 2	at	T.B. 3	Sean Burke	72	76	52	78	22.11
Jonathan Cheechoo	S.J.	Apr. 10/06	S.J. 3	at	Phx. 2	David LeNeveu	78	78	56	82	25.8
Alex Ovechkin	Wsh.	Apr. 13/06	Wsh. 3	at	Atl. 5	Mike Dunham	78	79	52	81	20.6
Dany Heatley	Ott.	Apr. 18/06	Ott. 5	at	NYR 1	Henrik Lundqvist	82	82	50	82	25.2
Vincent Lecavalier	T.B.	Mar. 30/07	T.B. 4	at	Car. 2	Cam Ward	78	78	52	82	26.11
Dany Heatley	Ott.	Apr. 7/07	Ott. 6	at	Bos. 3	Tim Thomas	82	82	50	82	
Alex Ovechkin	Wsh.	Mar. 3/08	Bos. 2	at	Wsh. 10	Tim Thomas	67	67	65	82	
Ilya Kovalchuk	Atl.	Mar. 18/08	Atl. 2	at	Phi. 3	Antero Niittymaki	72	75	52	79	
Jarome Iginla	Cgy.	Apr. 5/08	Cgy. 7	at	Van. 1	Curtis Sanford	82	82	50	82	
Alex Ovechkin	Wsh.	Mar. 19/09	Wsh. 5	at	T.B. 2	Mike McKenna	70	73	56	79	
Alex Ovechkin	Wsh.	Apr. 9/10	Atl. 2	at	Wsh. 5	Ondrej Pavelec	71	81	50	72	
Steven Stamkos	T.B.	Apr. 10/10	Fla. 3	at	T.B. 4	S. Clemmensen	81	81	51	82	20.2
Sidney Crosby	Pit.	Apr. 11/10	Pit. 6	at	NYI 5	Dwayne Roloson	81	82	51	81	22.8
Corey Perry	Ana.	Apr. 6/11	S.J. 2	at	Ana. 6	Antero Niittymaki	80	80	50	82	25.11
Steven Stamkos	T.B.	Mar. 13/12	Bos. 1	at	T.B. 6	Marty Turco	69	69	60	82	
Evgeni Malkin	Pit.	Apr. 7/12	Phi. 2	at	Pit. 4	Sergei Bobrovsky	75	82	50	82	25.8
Alex Ovechkin	Wsh.	Apr. 8/14	Wsh. 4	at	St.L. 1	Ryan Miller	75	79	51	78	
Alex Ovechkin	Wsh.	Mar. 31/15	Car. 2	at	Wsh. 4	Cam Ward	76	77	53	81	

* neutral site game played at Hamilton; ** neutral site game played at Cleveland

100-Point Seasons

Player	Team	Date of 100th Point	G or A	Score			Player's Game No.	Team Game No.	G - A	PTS	Total Games	Age when first 100th point scored (Yrs. & Mos.)
Phil Esposito	Bos.	Mar. 2/69	(G)	Pit. 0	at	Bos. 4	60	62	49-77 —	126	74	27.1
Bobby Hull	Chi.	Mar. 20/69	(G)	Chi. 5	at	Bos. 5	71	71	58-49 —	107	76	30.2
Gordie Howe	Det.	Mar. 30/69	(G)	Det. 5	at	Chi. 9	76	76	44-59 —	103	76	41.0
Bobby Orr	Bos.	Mar. 15/70	(G)	Det. 5	at	Bos. 5	67	67	33-87 —	120	76	22.11
Phil Esposito	Bos.	Feb. 6/71	(A)	Buf. 3	at	Bos. 4	51	51	76-76 —	152	78	
Bobby Orr	Bos.	Feb. 20/71	(A)	Bos. 4	at	L.A. 5	58	58	37-102 —	139	78	
John Bucyk	Bos.	Mar. 13/71	(G)	Bos. 6	at	Van. 3	68	68	51-65 —	116	78	35.10
Ken Hodge	Bos.	Mar. 21/71	(A)	Buf. 7	at	Bos. 5	72	72	43-62 —	105	78	26.9
Jean Ratelle	NYR	Feb. 18/72	(A)	NYR 2	at	Cal. 2	58	58	46-63 —	109	63	31.4
Phil Esposito	Bos.	Feb. 19/72	(A)	Bos. 6	at	Min. 4	59	59	66-67 —	133	76	
Bobby Orr	Bos.	Mar. 2/72	(A)	Van. 3	at	Bos. 7	64	64	37-80 —	117	76	
Vic Hadfield	NYR	Mar. 25/72	(A)	NYR 3	at	Mtl. 3	74	74	50-56 —	106	78	31.5
Phil Esposito	Bos.	Mar. 3/73	(A)	Bos. 1	at	Mtl. 5	64	64	55-75 —	130	78	
Bobby Clarke	Phi.	Mar. 29/73	(G)	Atl. 2	at	Phi. 4	76	76	37-67 —	104	78	23.7
Bobby Orr	Bos.	Mar. 31/73	(G)	Bos. 3	at	Tor. 7	62	77	29-72 —	101	63	
Rick MacLeish	Phi.	Apr. 1/73	(G)	Phi. 4	at	Pit. 5	78	78	50-50 —	100	78	23.3
Phil Esposito	Bos.	Feb. 13/74	(A)	Bos. 9	at	Cal. 6	53	53	68-77 —	145	78	
Bobby Orr	Bos.	Mar. 12/74	(A)	Buf. 0	at	Bos. 4	62	66	32-90 —	122	74	
Ken Hodge	Bos.	Mar. 24/74	(A)	Mtl. 3	at	Bos. 6	72	72	50-55 —	105	76	
Phil Esposito	Bos.	Feb. 8/75	(A)	Bos. 8	at	Det. 5	54	54	61-66 —	127	79	
Bobby Orr	Bos.	Feb. 13/75	(A)	Bos. 1	at	Buf. 3	57	57	46-89 —	135	80	
Guy Lafleur	Mtl.	Mar. 7/75	(G)	Wsh. 4	at	Mtl. 8	56	66	53-66 —	119	70	24.6
Marcel Dionne	Det.	Mar. 9/75	(A)	Det. 5	at	Phi. 8	67	67	47-74 —	121	80	23.7
Pete Mahovlich	Mtl.	Mar. 9/75	(G)	Mtl. 5	at	NYR 3	67	67	35-82 —	117	80	29.5
Bobby Clarke	Phi.	Mar. 22/75	(A)	Min. 0	at	Phi. 4	72	72	27-89 —	116	80	
Rene Robert	Buf.	Apr. 5/75	(A)	Buf. 4	at	Tor. 2	74	80	40-60 —	100	74	26.4
Guy Lafleur	Mtl.	Mar. 10/76	(G)	Mtl. 5	at	Chi. 1	69	69	56-69 —	125	80	
Bobby Clarke	Phi.	Mar. 11/76	(A)	Buf. 1	at	Phi. 6	64	68	30-89 —	119	76	
Bill Barber	Phi.	Mar. 18/76	(A)	Van. 2	at	Phi. 3	71	71	50-62 —	112	80	23.8
Gilbert Perreault	Buf.	Mar. 21/76	(A)	K.C. 1	at	Buf. 3	73	73	44-69 —	113	80	25.4
Pierre Larouche	Pit.	Mar. 24/76	(G)	Bos. 5	at	Pit. 5	70	74	53-58 —	111	76	20.4
Pete Mahovlich	Mtl.	Mar. 28/76	(A)	Mtl. 2	at	Bos. 2	77	77	34-71 —	105	80	
Jean Ratelle	Bos.	Mar. 30/76	(G)	Buf. 4	at	Bos. 4	77	77	36-69 —	105	80	
Jean Pronovost	Pit.	Apr. 2/76	(A)	Wsh. 5	at	Pit. 4	79	79	52-52 —	104	80	30.4
Darryl Sittler	Tor.	Apr. 3/76	(A)	Bos. 4	at	Tor. 2	78	79	41-59 —	100	79	25.7
Guy Lafleur	Mtl.	Feb. 26/77	(A)	Cle. 3	at	Mtl. 5	63	63	56-80 —	136	80	

Player	Team	Date of 100th Point	G or A	Score	Player's Game No.	Team Game No.	G - A — PTS	Total Games	Age when first 100th point scored (Yrs. & Mos.)
Marcel Dionne	L.A.	Mar. 5/77	(G)	Pit. 3 at L.A. 3	67	67	53-69 — 122	80	
Steve Shutt	Mtl.	Mar. 27/77	(A)	Mtl. 6 at Det. 0	77	77	60-45 — 105	80	24.9
Bryan Trottier	NYI	Feb. 25/78	(A)	Chi. 1 at NYI 7	59	60	46-77 — 123	77	21.7
Guy Lafleur	Mtl.	Feb. 28/78	(G)	Det. 3 at Mtl. 9	69	61	60-72 — 132	78	
Darryl Sittler	Tor.	Mar. 12/78	(A)	Tor. 7 at Pit. 1	67	67	45-72 — 117	80	
Guy Lafleur	Mtl.	Feb. 27/79	(A)	Mtl. 3 at NYI 7	61	61	52-77 — 129	80	
Bryan Trottier	NYI	Mar. 6/79	(A)	Buf. 3 at NYI 2	59	63	47-87 — 134	76	
Marcel Dionne	L.A.	Mar. 8/79	(G)	L.A. 4 at Buf. 6	66	66	59-71 — 130	80	
Mike Bossy	NYI	Mar. 11/79	(G)	NYI 4 at Bos. 4	66	66	69-57 — 126	80	22.2
Bob MacMillan	Atl.	Mar. 15/79	(A)	Atl. 4 at Phi. 5	68	69	37-71 — 108	79	26.6
Guy Chouinard	Atl.	Mar. 30/79	(G)	L.A. 3 at Atl. 5	75	75	50-57 — 107	80	22.5
Denis Potvin	NYI	Apr. 8/79	(A)	NYI 5 at NYR 2	73	80	31-70 — 101	73	25.5
Marcel Dionne	L.A.	Feb. 6/80	(A)	L.A. 3 at Hfd. 7	53	53	53-84 — 137	80	
Guy Lafleur	Mtl.	Feb. 10/80	(A)	Mtl. 3 at Bos. 2	55	55	50-75 — 125	74	
Wayne Gretzky	Edm.	Feb. 24/80	(A)	Bos. 4 at Edm. 2	61	62	51-86 — 137	79	19.2
Bryan Trottier	NYI	Mar. 30/80	(A)	NYI 9 at Que. 6	75	77	42-62 — 104	78	
Gilbert Perreault	Buf.	Apr. 1/80	(A)	Buf. 5 at Atl. 2	77	77	40-66 — 106	80	
Mike Rogers	Hfd.	Apr. 4/80	(A)	Que. 2 at Hfd. 9	79	79	44-61 — 105	80	25.5
Charlie Simmer	L.A.	Apr. 5/80	(G)	Van. 5 at L.A. 3	64	80	56-45 — 101	64	26.0
Blaine Stoughton	Hfd.	Apr. 6/80	(A)	Det. 3 at Hfd. 5	80	80	56-44 — 100	80	27.0
Wayne Gretzky	Edm.	Feb. 6/81	(G)	Wpg. 4 at Edm. 10	53	53	55-109 — 164	80	
Marcel Dionne	L.A.	Feb. 12/81	(A)	L.A. 5 at Chi. 5	58	58	58-77 — 135	80	
Charlie Simmer	L.A.	Feb. 14/81	(A)	Bos. 5 at L.A. 4	59	59	56-49 — 105	65	
Kent Nilsson	Cgy.	Feb. 27/81	(G)	Hfd. 1 at Cgy. 5	64	64	49-82 — 131	80	24.6
Mike Bossy	NYI	Mar. 3/81	(G)	Edm. 8 at NYI 8	65	66	68-51 — 119	79	
Dave Taylor	L.A.	Mar. 14/81	(G)	Min. 4 at L.A. 10	63	70	47-65 — 112	72	25.3
Mike Rogers	Hfd.	Mar. 22/81	(G)	Tor. 3 at Hfd. 3	74	74	40-65 — 105	80	
Bernie Federko	St.L.	Mar. 28/81	(A)	Buf. 4 at St.L. 7	74	76	31-73 — 104	78	24.10
Rick Middleton	Bos.	Mar. 28/81	(A)	Chi. 2 at Bos. 5	76	76	44-59 — 103	80	27.4
Bryan Trottier	NYI	Mar. 29/81	(G)	NYI 5 at Wsh. 4	69	76	31-72 — 103	73	
Jacques Richard	Que.	Mar. 29/81	(A)	Mtl. 0 at Que. 4	75	76	52-51 — 103	78	28.6
Peter Stastny	Que.	Mar. 29/81	(A)	Mtl. 0 at Que. 4	73	76	39-70 — 109	77	24.6
Wayne Gretzky	Edm.	Dec. 27/81	(G)	L.A. 3 at Edm. 10	38	38	92-120 — 212	80	
Mike Bossy	NYI	Feb. 13/82	(A)	Phi. 2 at NYI 8	55	55	64-83 — 147	80	
Peter Stastny	Que.	Feb. 16/82	(A)	Wpg. 3 at Que. 7	60	60	46-93 — 139	80	
Dennis Maruk	Wsh.	Feb. 20/82	(G)	Wsh. 3 at Min. 7	60	60	60-76 — 136	80	26.3
Bryan Trottier	NYI	Feb. 23/82	(G)	Chi. 1 at NYI 5	61	61	50-79 — 129	80	
Denis Savard	Chi.	Feb. 27/82	(A)	Chi. 5 at L.A. 3	64	64	32-87 — 119	80	21.1
Bobby Smith	Min.	Mar. 3/82	(A)	Det. 4 at Min. 6	66	66	43-71 — 114	80	24.1
Marcel Dionne	L.A.	Mar. 6/82	(G)	L.A. 6 at Hfd. 7	64	66	50-67 — 117	78	
Dave Taylor	L.A.	Mar. 20/82	(A)	Pit. 5 at L.A. 7	71	72	39-67 — 106	78	
Dale Hawerchuk	Wpg.	Mar. 24/82	(G)	L.A. 3 at Wpg. 5	74	74	45-58 — 103	80	18.11
Dino Ciccarelli	Min.	Mar. 27/82	(A)	Min. 6 at Bos. 5	72	76	55-52 — 107	76	21.8
Glenn Anderson	Edm.	Mar. 28/82	(G)	Edm. 6 at L.A. 2	78	78	38-67 — 105	80	21.7
Mike Rogers	NYR	Apr. 2/82	(G)	Pit. 7 at NYR 5	79	79	38-65 — 103	80	
Wayne Gretzky	Edm.	Jan. 5/83	(A)	Edm. 8 at Wpg. 3	42	42	71-125 — 196	80	
Mike Bossy	NYI	Mar. 3/83	(A)	Tor. 1 at NYI 5	66	67	60-58 — 118	79	
Peter Stastny	Que.	Mar. 5/83	(A)	Hfd. 3 at Que. 10	62	67	47-77 — 124	75	
Denis Savard	Chi.	Mar. 6/83	(A)	Mtl. 4 at Chi. 5	65	67	35-86 — 121	78	
Mark Messier	Edm.	Mar. 23/83	(G)	Edm. 4 at Wpg. 7	73	76	48-58 — 106	77	22.2
Barry Pederson	Bos.	Mar. 26/83	(A)	Hfd. 4 at Bos. 7	73	76	46-61 — 107	77	22.0
Marcel Dionne	L.A.	Mar. 26/83	(A)	Edm. 9 at L.A. 3	75	75	56-51 — 107	80	
Michel Goulet	Que.	Mar. 27/83	(A)	Que. 6 at Buf. 6	77	77	57-48 — 105	80	22.11
Glenn Anderson	Edm.	Mar. 29/83	(A)	Edm. 7 at Van. 4	70	78	48-56 — 104	72	
Jari Kurri	Edm.	Mar. 29/83	(A)	Edm. 7 at Van. 4	78	78	45-59 — 104	80	22.10
Kent Nilsson	Cgy.	Mar. 29/83	(G)	L.A. 3 at Cgy. 5	78	78	46-58 — 104	80	
Wayne Gretzky	Edm.	Dec. 18/83	(G)	Edm. 7 at Wpg. 5	34	34	87-118 — 205	74	
Paul Coffey	Edm.	Mar. 4/84	(A)	Mtl. 1 at Edm. 6	68	68	40-86 — 126	80	22.9
Michel Goulet	Que.	Mar. 4/84	(A)	Que. 1 at Buf. 1	62	67	56-65 — 121	75	
Jari Kurri	Edm.	Mar. 7/84	(G)	Chi. 4 at Edm. 7	53	69	52-61 — 113	64	
Peter Stastny	Que.	Mar. 8/84	(A)	Que. 8 at Pit. 6	69	69	46-73 — 119	80	
Mike Bossy	NYI	Mar. 8/84	(G)	Tor. 5 at NYI 9	56	68	51-67 — 118	67	
Barry Pederson	Bos.	Mar. 14/84	(A)	Bos. 4 at Det. 2	71	71	39-77 — 116	80	
Bryan Trottier	NYI	Mar. 18/84	(G)	NYI 4 at Hfd. 5	62	73	40-71 — 111	68	
Bernie Federko	St.L.	Mar. 20/84	(A)	Wpg. 3 at St.L. 9	75	76	41-66 — 107	79	
Rick Middleton	Bos.	Mar. 27/84	(G)	Bos. 6 at Que. 4	77	77	47-58 — 105	80	
Dale Hawerchuk	Wpg.	Mar. 27/84	(G)	Wpg. 3 at L.A. 3	77	77	37-65 — 102	80	
Mark Messier	Edm.	Mar. 27/84	(G)	Edm. 9 at Cgy. 2	72	79	37-64 — 101	73	
Wayne Gretzky	Edm.	Dec. 29/84	(A)	Det. 3 at Edm. 6	35	35	73-135 — 208	80	
Jari Kurri	Edm.	Jan. 29/85	(G)	Edm. 4 at Cgy. 2	48	51	71-64 — 135	73	
Mike Bossy	NYI	Feb. 23/85	(G)	Bos. 1 at NYI 7	56	60	58-59 — 117	76	
Dale Hawerchuk	Wpg.	Feb. 25/85	(A)	Wpg. 12 at NYR 5	64	64	53-77 — 130	80	
Marcel Dionne	L.A.	Mar. 5/85	(A)	Pit. 0 at L.A. 6	66	66	46-80 — 126	80	
Brent Sutter	NYI	Mar. 12/85	(A)	NYI 6 at St.L. 5	68	68	42-60 — 102	72	22.10
John Ogrodnick	Det.	Mar. 22/85	(A)	NYR 3 at Det. 5	73	73	55-50 — 105	79	25.9
Paul Coffey	Edm.	Mar. 26/85	(G)	Edm. 7 at NYI 5	74	74	37-84 — 121	80	
Denis Savard	Chi.	Mar. 29/85	(A)	Chi. 5 at Wpg. 5	75	76	38-67 — 105	79	
Peter Stastny	Que.	Apr. 2/85	(A)	Bos. 4 at Que. 6	74	77	32-68 — 100	75	
Bernie Federko	St.L.	Apr. 4/85	(A)	NYR 5 at St.L. 4	74	78	30-73 — 103	76	
Paul MacLean	Wpg.	Apr. 6/85	(A)	Wpg. 6 at Edm. 5	78	79	41-60 — 101	79	27.1
Bernie Nicholls	L.A.	Apr. 6/85	(A)	Van. 4 at L.A. 4	80	80	46-54 — 100	80	22.9
John Tonelli	NYI	Apr. 6/85	(A)	N.J. 5 at NYI 7	80	80	42-58 — 100	80	28.1
Mike Gartner	Wsh.	Apr. 7/85	(G)	Pit. 3 at Wsh. 7	80	80	50-52 — 102	80	25.6
Mario Lemieux	Pit.	Apr. 7/85	(G)	Pit. 3 at Wsh. 7	73	80	43-57 — 100	73	19.6

Gilbert Perreault

Dale Hawerchuk

Brent Sutter

Peter Stastny

Rob Brown

Wayne Gretzky

Player	Team	Date of 100th Point	G or A	Score		Player's Game No.	Team Game No.	G - A — PTS	Total Games	Age when first 100th point scored (Yrs. & Mos.)
Wayne Gretzky	Edm.	Jan. 4/86	(A)	Hfd. 3	at Edm. 4	39	39	52-163 — 215	80	
Mario Lemieux	Pit.	Feb. 15/86	(G)	Van. 4	at Pit. 9	55	56	48-93 — 141	79	
Paul Coffey	Edm.	Feb. 19/86	(A)	Tor. 5	at Edm. 9	59	60	48-90 — 138	79	
Peter Stastny	Que.	Mar. 1/86	(A)	Buf. 8	at Que. 4	66	68	41-81 — 122	76	
Jari Kurri	Edm.	Mar. 2/86	(A)	Phi. 1	at Edm. 2	62	64	68-63 — 131	78	
Mike Bossy	NYI	Mar. 8/86	(G)	Wsh. 6	at NYI 2	65	65	61-62 — 123	80	
Denis Savard	Chi.	Mar. 12/86	(A)	Buf. 7	at Chi. 6	69	69	47-69 — 116	80	
Mats Naslund	Mtl.	Mar. 13/86	(A)	Mtl. 2	at Bos. 3	70	70	43-67 — 110	80	26.4
Michel Goulet	Que.	Mar. 24/86	(A)	Que. 1	at Min. 0	70	75	53-50 — 103	75	
Glenn Anderson	Edm.	Mar. 25/86	(G)	Edm. 7	at Det. 2	66	74	54-48 — 102	72	
Neal Broten	Min.	Mar. 26/86	(A)	Min. 6	at Tor. 1	76	76	29-76 — 105	80	26.4
Dale Hawerchuk	Wpg.	Mar. 31/86	(A)	Wpg. 5	at L.A. 2	78	78	46-59 — 105	80	
Bernie Federko	St.L.	Apr. 5/86	(G)	Chi. 5	at St.L. 7	79	79	34-68 — 102	80	
Wayne Gretzky	Edm.	Jan. 11/87	(A)	Cgy. 3	at Edm. 5	42	42	62-121 — 183	79	
Jari Kurri	Edm.	Mar. 14/87	(A)	Buf. 3	at Edm. 5	67	68	54-54 — 108	79	
Mario Lemieux	Pit.	Mar. 18/87	(A)	St.L. 4	at Pit. 5	55	72	54-53 — 107	63	
Mark Messier	Edm.	Mar. 19/87	(A)	Edm. 4	at Cgy. 5	71	71	37-70 — 107	77	
Dino Ciccarelli	Min.	Mar. 30/87	(A)	NYR 6	at Min. 5	78	78	52-51 — 103	80	
Doug Gilmour	St.L.	Apr. 2/87	(A)	Buf. 3	at St.L. 5	78	78	42-63 — 105	80	23.10
Dale Hawerchuk	Wpg.	Apr. 5/87	(A)	Wpg. 3	at Cgy. 1	80	80	47-53 — 100	80	
Mario Lemieux	Pit.	Jan. 20/88	(G)	Pit. 8	at Chi. 3	45	48	70-98 — 168	77	
Wayne Gretzky	Edm.	Feb. 11/88	(A)	Edm. 7	at Van. 2	43	56	40-109 — 149	64	
Denis Savard	Chi.	Feb. 12/88	(A)	St.L. 3	at Chi. 4	57	57	44-87 — 131	80	
Dale Hawerchuk	Wpg.	Feb. 23/88	(G)	Wpg. 4	at Pit. 3	61	61	44-77 — 121	80	
Steve Yzerman	Det.	Feb. 27/88	(A)	Det. 4	at Que. 5	63	63	50-52 — 102	64	22.10
Peter Stastny	Que.	Mar. 8/88	(A)	Hfd. 4	at Que. 6	63	67	46-65 — 111	76	
Mark Messier	Edm.	Mar. 15/88	(A)	Buf. 4	at Edm. 6	68	71	37-74 — 111	77	
Jimmy Carson	L.A.	Mar. 26/88	(A)	Chi. 5	at L.A. 9	77	77	55-52 — 107	80	19.8
Hakan Loob	Cgy.	Mar. 26/88	(A)	Van. 1	at Cgy. 6	76	76	50-56 — 106	80	27.9
Mike Bullard	Cgy.	Mar. 26/88	(A)	Van. 1	at Cgy. 6	76	76	48-55 — 103	79	27.1
Michel Goulet	Que.	Mar. 27/88	(A)	Pit. 6	at Que. 3	76	76	48-58 — 106	80	
Luc Robitaille	L.A.	Mar. 30/88	(G)	Cgy. 7	at L.A. 9	78	78	53-58 — 111	80	22.1
Mario Lemieux	Pit.	Dec. 31/88	(A)	N.J. 6	at Pit. 8	36	38	85-114 — 199	76	
Wayne Gretzky	L.A.	Jan. 21/89	(A)	L.A. 4	at Hfd. 5	47	48	54-114 — 168	78	
Bernie Nicholls	L.A.	Jan. 21/89	(A)	L.A. 4	at Hfd. 5	48	48	70-80 — 150	79	
Steve Yzerman	Det.	Jan. 27/89	(G)	Tor. 1	at Det. 8	50	50	65-90 — 155	80	
Rob Brown	Pit.	Mar. 16/89	(A)	Pit. 2	at N.J. 1	60	72	49-66 — 115	68	20.11
Paul Coffey	Pit.	Mar. 20/89	(A)	Pit. 2	at Min. 7	69	74	30-83 — 113	75	
Joe Mullen	Cgy.	Mar. 23/89	(A)	L.A. 2	at Cgy. 4	74	75	51-59 — 110	79	32.1
Jari Kurri	Edm.	Mar. 29/89	(A)	Edm. 5	at Van. 2	75	79	44-58 — 102	76	
Jimmy Carson	Edm.	Apr. 2/89	(A)	Edm. 2	at Cgy. 4	80	80	49-51 — 100	80	
Mario Lemieux	Pit.	Jan. 28/90	(G)	Pit. 2	at Buf. 7	50	50	45-78 — 123	59	
Wayne Gretzky	L.A.	Jan. 30/90	(A)	N.J. 2	at L.A. 5	51	51	40-102 — 142	73	
Steve Yzerman	Det.	Feb. 19/90	(A)	Mtl. 5	at Det. 5	61	61	62-65 — 127	79	
Mark Messier	Edm.	Feb. 20/90	(A)	Edm. 4	at Van. 2	62	62	45-84 — 129	79	
Brett Hull	St.L.	Mar. 3/90	(A)	NYI 4	at St.L. 5	67	67	72-41 — 113	80	25.7
Bernie Nicholls	NYR	Mar. 12/90	(A)	L.A. 6	at NYR 2	70	71	39-73 — 112	79	
Pierre Turgeon	Buf.	Mar. 25/90	(A)	N.J. 4	at Buf. 3	76	76	40-66 — 106	80	20.7
Paul Coffey	Pit.	Mar. 25/90	(A)	Pit. 2	at Hfd. 4	77	77	29-74 — 103	80	
Pat LaFontaine	NYI	Mar. 27/90	(G)	Cgy. 4	at NYI 2	72	78	54-51 — 105	74	25.1
Adam Oates	St.L.	Mar. 29/90	(A)	Pit. 4	at St.L. 5	79	79	23-79 — 102	80	27.7
Joe Sakic	Que.	Mar. 31/90	(G)	Hfd. 3	at Que. 2	79	79	39-63 — 102	80	20.8
Ron Francis	Hfd.	Mar. 31/90	(A)	Hfd. 3	at Que. 2	79	79	32-69 — 101	80	27.0
Luc Robitaille	L.A.	Apr. 1/90	(A)	L.A. 4	at Cgy. 8	80	80	52-49 — 101	80	
Wayne Gretzky	L.A.	Jan. 30/91	(A)	N.J. 4	at L.A. 2	50	51	41-122 — 163	78	
Brett Hull	St.L.	Feb. 23/91	(G)	Bos. 2	at St.L. 9	60	62	86-45 — 131	78	
Mark Recchi	Pit.	Mar. 5/91	(G)	Van. 1	at Pit. 4	66	67	40-73 — 113	78	23.1
Steve Yzerman	Det.	Mar. 10/91	(G)	Det. 4	at St.L. 1	72	72	51-57 — 108	80	
John Cullen	Hfd.	Mar. 16/91	(A)	N.J. 2	at Hfd. 6	71	71	39-71 — 110	78	26.7
Adam Oates	St.L.	Mar. 17/91	(A)	St.L. 4	at Chi. 6	54	73	25-90 — 115	61	
Joe Sakic	Que.	Mar. 19/91	(A)	Edm. 7	at Que. 6	74	74	48-61 — 109	80	
Steve Larmer	Chi.	Mar. 24/91	(A)	Min. 4	at Chi. 5	76	76	44-57 — 101	80	29.9
Theoren Fleury	Cgy.	Mar. 26/91	(A)	Van. 1	at Cgy. 7	77	77	51-53 — 104	79	22.9
Al MacInnis	Cgy.	Mar. 28/91	(A)	Edm. 4	at Cgy. 4	78	78	28-75 — 103	78	27.8
Brett Hull	St.L.	Mar. 2/92	(G)	St.L. 5	at Van. 3	66	66	70-39 — 109	73	
Wayne Gretzky	L.A.	Mar. 3/92	(A)	Phi. 1	at L.A. 4	60	66	31-90 — 121	74	
Kevin Stevens	Pit.	Mar. 7/92	(A)	Pit. 3	at L.A. 5	66	66	54-69 — 123	80	26.11
Mario Lemieux	Pit.	Mar. 10/92	(A)	Cgy. 2	at Pit. 5	53	67	44-87 — 131	64	
Luc Robitaille	L.A.	Mar. 17/92	(A)	Wpg. 4	at L.A. 5	73	73	44-63 — 107	80	
Mark Messier	NYR	Mar. 22/92	(G)	N.J. 3	at NYR 6	74	75	35-72 — 107	79	
Jeremy Roenick	Chi.	Mar. 29/92	(A)	Tor. 1	at Chi. 5	77	77	53-50 — 103	80	22.2
Steve Yzerman	Det.	Apr. 14/92	(G)	Det. 7	at Min. 4	79	80	45-58 — 103	79	
Brian Leetch	NYR	Apr. 16/92	(G)	Pit. 1	at NYR 7	80	80	22-80 — 102	80	24.1
Mario Lemieux	Pit.	Dec. 31/92	(G)	Tor. 3	at Pit. 3	38	39	69-91 — 160	60	
Pat LaFontaine	Buf.	Feb. 10/93	(A)	Buf. 6	at Wpg. 2	55	55	53-95 — 148	84	
Adam Oates	Bos.	Feb. 14/93	(A)	Bos. 3	at T.B. 3	58	58	45-97 — 142	84	
Steve Yzerman	Det.	Feb. 24/93	(A)	Det. 7	at Buf. 10	64	64	58-79 — 137	84	
Pierre Turgeon	NYI	Feb. 28/93	(A)	NYI 7	at Hfd. 6	62	63	58-74 — 132	83	
Doug Gilmour	Tor.	Mar. 3/93	(A)	Min. 1	at Tor. 3	64	64	32-95 — 127	83	
Alexander Mogilny	Buf.	Mar. 5/93	(A)	Hfd. 4	at Buf. 2	58	65	76-51 — 127	77	24.1
Mark Recchi	Phi.	Mar. 7/93	(G)	Phi. 3	at N.J. 7	66	66	53-70 — 123	84	
Teemu Selanne	Wpg.	Mar. 9/93	(G)	Wpg. 4	at T.B. 2	68	68	76-56 — 132	84	22.7

Player	Team	Date of 100th Point	G or A	Score		Player's Game No.	Team Game No.	G - A PTS	Total Games	Age when first 100th point scored (Yrs. & Mos.)
Luc Robitaille	L.A.	Mar. 15/93	(A)	L.A. 4	at Buf. 2	69	69	63-62 — 125	84	
Kevin Stevens	Pit.	Mar. 23/93	(A)	S.J. 2	at Pit. 7	63	73	55-56 — 111	72	
Mats Sundin	Que.	Mar. 27/93	(G)	Phi. 3	at Que. 8	71	75	47-67 — 114	80	22.1
Pavel Bure	Van.	Apr. 1/93	(G)	Van. 5	at T.B. 3	77	77	60-50 — 110	83	22.0
Jeremy Roenick	Chi.	Apr. 4/93	(G)	St.L. 4	at Chi. 5	79	79	50-57 — 107	84	
Craig Janney	St.L.	Apr. 4/93	(G)	St.L. 4	at Chi. 5	79	79	24-82 — 106	84	25.7
Rick Tocchet	Pit.	Apr. 7/93	(G)	Mtl. 3	at Pit. 4	77	81	48-61 — 109	80	28.11
Joe Sakic	Que.	Apr. 8/93	(A)	Que. 2	at Bos. 6	75	81	48-57 — 105	78	
Ron Francis	Pit.	Apr. 9/93	(A)	Pit. 10	at NYR 4	82	82	24-76 — 100	84	
Brett Hull	St.L.	Apr. 11/93	(G)	Min. 1	at St.L. 5	78	82	54-47 — 101	80	
Theoren Fleury	Cgy.	Apr. 11/93	(G)	Cgy. 3	at Van. 6	82	82	34-66 — 100	83	
Joe Juneau	Bos.	Apr. 14/93	(A)	Bos. 4	at Ott. 2	84	84	32-70 — 102	84	25.3
Wayne Gretzky	L.A.	Feb. 14/94	(A)	Bos. 3	at L.A. 2	56	56	38-92 — 130	81	
Sergei Fedorov	Det.	Mar. 1/94	(A)	Cgy. 2	at Det. 5	63	63	56-64 — 120	82	24.2
Doug Gilmour	Tor.	Mar. 23/94	(G)	Tor. 1	at Fla. 1	74	74	27-84 — 111	83	
Adam Oates	Bos.	Mar. 26/94	(A)	Mtl. 3	at Bos. 6	68	75	32-80 — 112	77	
Mark Recchi	Phi.	Mar. 27/94	(A)	Ana. 3	at Phi. 2	76	76	40-67 — 107	84	
Pavel Bure	Van.	Mar. 28/94	(G)	Tor. 2	at Van. 3	68	76	60-47 — 107	76	
Jeremy Roenick	Chi.	Mar. 31/94	(G)	Chi. 3	at Wsh. 6	78	78	46-61 — 107	84	
Brendan Shanahan	St.L.	Apr. 12/94	(G)	St.L. 5	at Dal. 9	80	83	52-50 — 102	81	25.2
Mario Lemieux	Pit.	Jan. 16/96	(G)	Col. 5	at Pit. 2	38	44	69-92 — 161	70	
Jaromir Jagr	Pit.	Feb. 6/96	(G)	Bos. 5	at Pit. 6	52	52	62-87 — 149	82	23.11
Ron Francis	Pit.	Mar. 9/96	(A)	N.J. 4	at Pit. 3	61	66	27-92 — 119	77	
Peter Forsberg	Col.	Mar. 9/96	(A)	Col. 7	at Van. 5	68	68	30-86 — 116	82	22.7
Joe Sakic	Col.	Mar. 17/96	(A)	Edm. 1	at Col. 8	70	70	51-69 — 120	82	
Eric Lindros	Phi.	Mar. 25/96	(A)	Hfd. 0	at Phi. 3	65	73	47-68 — 115	73	23
Teemu Selanne	Ana.	Mar. 25/96	(A)	Ana. 1	at Det. 5	70	73	40-68 — 108	79	
Alexander Mogilny	Van.	Mar. 25/96	(A)	L.A. 1	at Van. 4	72	75	55-52 — 107	79	
Wayne Gretzky	St.L.	Mar. 28/96	(A)	N.J. 4	at St.L. 4	76	75	23-79 — 102	80	
Doug Weight	Edm.	Mar. 30/96	(G)	Tor. 4	at Edm. 3	76	76	25-79 — 104	82	25.3
Sergei Fedorov	Det.	Apr. 2/96	(A)	Det. 3	at S.J. 6	72	76	39-68 — 107	78	
Paul Kariya	Ana.	Apr. 7/96	(G)	Ana. 5	at S.J. 3	78	78	50-58 — 108	82	21.5
Mario Lemieux	Pit.	Mar. 8/97	(A)	Phi. 2	at Pit. 3	61	65	50-72 — 122	76	
Teemu Selanne	Ana.	Apr. 1/97	(A)	Chi. 3	at Ana. 3	74	78	51-58 — 109	78	
Jaromir Jagr	Pit.	Apr. 15/98	(G)	T.B. 1	at Pit. 5	76	80	35-67 — 102	77	
Jaromir Jagr	Pit.	Mar. 13/99	(G)	Phi. 0	at Pit. 4	65	65	44-83 — 127	81	
Teemu Selanne	Ana.	Apr. 5/99	(A)	Ana. 2	at Det. 3	69	76	47-60 — 107	75	
Paul Kariya	Ana.	Apr. 17/99	(G)	Ana. 3	at S.J. 3	82	82	39-62 — 101	82	
Jaromir Jagr	Pit.	Mar. 10/01	(G)	Cgy. 3	at Pit. 6	68	68	52-69 — 121	81	
Joe Sakic	Col.	Mar. 18/01	(G)	Min. 3	at Col. 4	72	72	54-64 — 118	82	
Markus Naslund	Van.	Mar. 27/03	(A)	Phx. 1	at Van. 5	78	78	48-56 — 104	82	29.8
Peter Forsberg	Col.	Mar. 31/03	(A)	S.J. 1	at Col. 3	72	79	29-77 — 106	79	
Joe Thornton	Bos.	Apr. 4/03	(A)	Buf. 5	at Bos. 8	77	82	36-65 — 101	77	23.9
Jaromir Jagr	NYR	Mar. 18/06	A	Tor. 2	at NYR 5	67	67	54-69 — 123	82	
Joe Thornton	S.J.	Mar. 21/06	A	S.J. 6	at St.L. 0	66	67	29-96 — 125	81	
Alex Ovechkin	Wsh.	Apr. 10/06	G	Wsh. 2	at Bos. 1	77	78	52-54 — 106	81	20.6
Dany Heatley	Ott.	Apr. 13/06	A	Fla. 5	at Ott. 4	80	80	50-53 — 103	82	25.2
Daniel Alfredsson	Ott.	Apr. 15/06	A	Ott. 1	at Tor. 5	76	81	43-60 — 103	77	33.4
Eric Staal	Car.	Apr. 15/06	A	Car. 2	at T.B. 3	81	81	45-55 — 100	82	21.5
Sidney Crosby	Pit.	Apr. 17/06	A	NYI 1	at Pit. 6	80	81	39-63 — 102	81	18.8
Sidney Crosby	Pit.	Mar. 10/07	G	NYR 2	at Pit. 3	65	68	36-84 — 120	79	
Joe Thornton	S.J.	Mar. 22/07	A	S.J. 5	at Atl. 1	75	75	22-92 — 114	82	
Vincent Lecavalier	T.B.	Mar. 24/07	A	Ott. 7	at T.B. 2	76	76	52-56 — 108	82	26.11
Dany Heatley	Ott.	Mar. 31/07	G	Ott. 5	at NYI 2	79	79	50-55 — 105	82	
Martin St. Louis	T.B.	Mar. 31/07	A	Wsh. 2	at T.B. 5	79	79	43-59 — 102	82	31.10
Marian Hossa	Atl.	Apr. 7/07	A	T.B. 2	at Atl. 3	82	82	43-57 — 100	82	28.3
Joe Sakic	Col.	Apr. 8/07	G	Cgy. 3	at Col. 6	82	82	36-64 — 100	82	
Alex Ovechkin	Wsh.	Mar. 18/08	A	Wsh. 4	at Nsh. 2	74	74	65-47 — 112	82	
Evgeni Malkin	Pit.	Mar. 22/08	G	N.J. 1	at Pit. 7	75	75	47-59 — 106	82	21.8
Evgeni Malkin	Pit.	Mar. 17/09	G	Atl. 2	at Pit. 6	72	72	35-78 — 113	82	
Alex Ovechkin	Wsh.	Mar. 27/09	G	T.B. 3	at Wsh. 5	73	76	56-54 — 110	79	
Sidney Crosby	Pit.	Apr. 7/09	G	Pit. 6	at T.B. 4	75	80	33-70 — 103	77	
Henrik Sedin	Van.	Mar. 27/10	A	Van. 2	at S.J. 4	75	75	29-83 — 112	82	29.7
Alex Ovechkin	Wsh.	Mar. 28/10	A	Cgy. 5	at Wsh. 3	65	75	50-59 — 109	72	
Sidney Crosby	Pit.	Apr. 6/10	A	Wsh. 6	at Pit. 3	78	79	51-58 — 109	81	
Nicklas Backstrom	Wsh.	Apr. 9/10	A	Atl. 2	at Wsh. 5	81	81	33-68 — 101	82	22.5
Daniel Sedin	Van.	Mar. 31/11	A	L.A. 1	at Van. 3	78	78	41-63 — 104	82	30.7
Evgeni Malkin	Pit.	Mar. 29/12	G	Pit. 3	at NYI 5	70	77	50-59 — 109	75	
Sidney Crosby	Pit.	Apr. 1/14	A	Car. 4	at Pit. 1	76	76	36-68 — 104	80	

Pavel Bure

Markus Naslund

Daniel Sedin

Five-or-more-Goal Games

Player	Team	Date	Score	Opposing Goaltender(s)
SEVEN GOALS				
Joe Malone	Quebec Bulldogs	Jan. 31/20	Tor. 6 at Que. 10	Ivan Mitchell (4); Howard Lockhart (3)
SIX GOALS				
Newsy Lalonde	Montreal	Jan. 10/20	Tor. 7 at Mtl. 14	Ivan Mitchell (2); Howard Lockhart (4)
Joe Malone	Quebec Bulldogs	Mar. 10/20	Ott. 4 at Que. 10	Clint Benedict
Corb Denneny	Toronto St. Pats	Jan. 26/21	Ham. 3 at Tor. 10	Howard Lockhart
Cy Denneny	Ottawa Senators	Mar. 7/21	Ham. 5 at Ott. 12	Howard Lockhart
Syd Howe	Detroit	Feb. 3/44	NYR 2 at Det. 12	Ken McAuley
Red Berenson	St. Louis	Nov. 7/68	St.L. 8 at Phi. 0	Doug Favell
Darryl Sittler	Toronto	Feb. 7/76	Bos. 4 at Tor. 11	Dave Reece
FIVE GOALS				
Joe Malone	Montreal	Dec. 19/17	Mtl. 7 at Ott. 4	Clint Benedict
Harry Hyland	Mtl. Wanderers	Dec. 19/17	Tor. 9 at Mtl. W. 10	Sammy Hebert (3); Art Brooks (2)
Joe Malone	Montreal	Jan. 12/18	Ott. 4 at Mtl. 9	Clint Benedict
Joe Malone	Montreal	Feb. 2/18	Tor. 2 at Mtl. 11	Hap Holmes
Mickey Roach	Toronto St. Pats	Mar. 6/20	Que. 2 at Tor. 11	Howard Lockhart
Newsy Lalonde	Montreal	Dec. 16/20	Ham. 5 at Mtl. 10	Howard Lockhart
Babe Dye	Toronto St. Pats	Dec. 16/22	Mtl. 2 at Tor. 7	Georges Vezina
Red Green	Hamilton Tigers	Dec. 5/24	Ham. 10 at Tor. 3	John Ross Roach
Babe Dye	Toronto St. Pats	Dec. 22/24	Tor. 10 at Bos. 1	Hec Fowler; George Redding (1)
Punch Broadbent	Mtl. Maroons	Jan. 7/25	Mtl. 6 at Ham. 2	Jake Forbes
Pit Lepine	Montreal	Dec. 14/29	Ott. 4 at Mtl. 5	Alex Connell
Howie Morenz	Montreal	Mar. 18/30	NYA 3 at Mtl. 8	Roy Worters
Charlie Conacher	Toronto	Jan. 19/32	NYA 3 at Tor. 11	Roy Worters (3); Al Shields (2)
Ray Getliffe	Montreal	Feb. 6/43	Bos. 3 at Mtl. 8	Frank Brimsek
Maurice Richard	Montreal	Dec. 28/44	Det. 1 at Mtl. 8	Harry Lumley
Howie Meeker	Toronto	Jan. 8/47	Chi. 4 at Tor. 10	Paul Bibeault
Bernie Geoffrion	Montreal	Feb. 19/55	NYR 2 at Mtl. 10	Gump Worsley
Bobby Rousseau	Montreal	Feb. 1/64	Det. 3 at Mtl. 9	Roger Crozier
Yvan Cournoyer	Montreal	Feb. 15/75	Chi. 3 at Mtl. 12	Mike Veisor
Don Murdoch	NY Rangers	Oct. 12/76	NYR 10 at Min. 4	Gary Smith
Ian Turnbull	Toronto	Feb. 2/77	Det. 1 at Tor. 9	Ed Giacomin (2); Jim Rutherford (3)
Bryan Trottier	NY Islanders	Dec. 23/78	NYR 4 at NYI 9	Wayne Thomas (3); John Davidson (1)
Tim Young	Minnesota	Jan. 15/79	Min. 8 at NYR 1	Doug Soetaert (3); Wayne Thomas (2)
John Tonelli	NY Islanders	Jan. 6/81	Tor. 3 at NYI 6	Jiri Crha (4); empty net (1)
Wayne Gretzky	Edmonton	Feb. 18/81	St.L. 2 at Edm. 9	Mike Liut (3); Ed Staniowski (2)
Wayne Gretzky	Edmonton	Dec. 30/81	Phi. 5 at Edm. 7	Pete Peeters (4); empty net (1)
Grant Mulvey	Chicago	Feb. 3/82	St.L. 5 at Chi. 9	Mike Liut (4); Gary Edwards (1)
Bryan Trottier	NY Islanders	Feb. 13/82	Phi. 2 at NYI 8	Pete Peeters
Willy Lindstrom	Winnipeg	Mar. 2/82	Wpg. 7 at Phi. 6	Pete Peeters
Mark Pavelich	NY Rangers	Feb. 23/83	Hfd. 3 at NYR 11	Greg Millen
Jari Kurri	Edmonton	Nov. 19/83	N.J. 4 at Edm. 13	Glenn Resch (3); Ron Low (2)
Bengt Gustafsson	Washington	Jan. 8/84	Wsh. 7 at Phi. 1	Pelle Lindbergh
Pat Hughes	Edmonton	Feb. 3/84	Cgy. 5 at Edm. 10	Don Edwards (3); Reggie Lemelin (2)
Wayne Gretzky	Edmonton	Dec. 15/84	Edm. 8 at St.L. 2	Rick Wamsley (4); Mike Liut (1)
Dave Andreychuk	Buffalo	Feb. 6/86	Buf. 8 at Bos. 6	Pat Riggin (1); Doug Keans (4)
Wayne Gretzky	Edmonton	Dec. 6/87	Min. 4 at Edm. 8	Don Beaupre (4); Kari Takko (1)
Mario Lemieux	Pittsburgh	Dec. 31/88	N.J. 6 at Pit. 8	Bob Sauve (3); Chris Terreri (1); empty net (1)
Joe Nieuwendyk	Calgary	Jan. 11/89	Wpg. 3 at Cgy. 8	Daniel Berthiaume
Mats Sundin	Quebec	Mar. 5/92	Que. 10 at Hfd. 4	Peter Sidorkiewicz (3); Kay Whitmore (2)
Mario Lemieux	Pittsburgh	Apr. 9/93	Pit. 10 at NYR 4	Corey Hirsch (3); Mike Richter (2)
Peter Bondra	Washington	Feb. 5/94	T.B. 3 at Wsh. 6	Daren Puppa (4); Pat Jablonski (1)
Mike Ricci	Quebec	Feb. 17/94	Que. 8 at S.J. 2	Arturs Irbe (3); Jimmy Waite (2)
Alex Zhamnov	Winnipeg	Apr. 1/95	Wpg. 7 at L.A. 7	Kelly Hrudey (3); Grant Fuhr (2)
Mario Lemieux	Pittsburgh	Mar. 26/96	St.L. 4 at Pit. 8	Grant Fuhr (4); Jon Casey (4)
Sergei Fedorov	Detroit	Dec. 26/96	Wsh. 4 at Det. 5	Jim Carey
Marian Gaborik	Minnesota	Dec. 20/07	NYR 3 at Min. 6	Henrik Lundqvist
Johan Franzen	Detroit	Feb. 2/11	Det. 7 at Ott. 5	Robin Lehner (3); Brian Elliott (2); empty net (1)

Players' 500th Goals

Regular Season

Player	Team	Date	Game No.	Score	Opposing Goaltender	Total Goals	Total Games
Maurice Richard	Montreal	Oct. 19/57	863	Chi. 1 at Mtl. 3	Glenn Hall	544	978
Gordie Howe	Detroit	Mar. 14/62	1,045	Det. 2 at NYR 3	Gump Worsley	801	1,767
Bobby Hull	Chicago	Feb. 21/70	861	NYR. 2 at Chi. 4	Ed Giacomin	610	1,063
Jean Béliveau	Montreal	Feb. 11/71	1,101	Min. 2 at Mtl. 6	Gilles Gilbert	507	1,125
Frank Mahovlich	Montreal	Mar. 21/73	1,105	Van. 2 at Mtl. 3	Dunc Wilson	533	1,181
Phil Esposito	Boston	Dec. 22/74	803	Det. 4 at Bos. 5	Jim Rutherford	717	1,282
John Bucyk	Boston	Oct. 30/75	1,370	St.L. 2 at Bos. 3	Yves Bélanger	556	1,540
Stan Mikita	Chicago	Feb. 27/77	1,221	Van. 4 at Chi. 3	Cesare Maniago	541	1,394
Marcel Dionne	Los Angeles	Dec. 14/82	887	L.A. 2 at Wsh. 7	Al Jensen	731	1,348
Guy Lafleur	Montreal	Dec. 20/83	918	Mtl. 6 at N.J. 0	Glenn Resch	560	1,126
Mike Bossy	NY Islanders	Jan. 2/86	647	Bos. 5 at NYI 7	empty net	573	752
Gilbert Perreault	Buffalo	Mar. 9/86	1,159	N.J. 3 at Buf. 4	Alain Chevrier	512	1,191
Wayne Gretzky	Edmonton	Nov. 22/86	575	Van. 2 at Edm. 5	empty net	894	1,487
Lanny McDonald	Calgary	Mar. 21/89	1,107	NYI 1 at Cgy. 4	Mark Fitzpatrick	500	1,111
Bryan Trottier	NY Islanders	Feb. 13/90	1,104	Cgy. 4 at NYI 2	Rick Wamsley	524	1,279
Mike Gartner	NY Rangers	Oct. 14/91	936	Wsh. 5 at NYR 3	Mike Liut	708	1,432
Michel Goulet	Chicago	Feb. 16/92	951	Cgy. 5 at Chi. 5	Jeff Reese	548	1,089
Jari Kurri	Los Angeles	Oct. 17/92	833	Bos. 6 at L.A. 8	empty net	601	1,251
Dino Ciccarelli	Detroit	Jan. 8/94	946	Det. 6 at L.A. 3	Kelly Hrudey	608	1,232
Mario Lemieux	Pittsburgh	Oct. 26/95	605	Pit. 7 at NYI 5	Tommy Soderstrom	690	915
Mark Messier	NY Rangers	Nov. 6/95	1,141	Cgy. 2 at NYR 4	Rick Tabaracci	694	1,756
Steve Yzerman	Detroit	Jan. 17/96	906	Col. 2 at Det. 3	Patrick Roy	692	1,514
Dale Hawerchuk	St. Louis	Jan. 31/96	1,103	St.L. 4 at Tor. 0	Felix Potvin	518	1,188
Brett Hull	St. Louis	Dec. 22/96	693	L.A. 4 at St.L. 7	Stephane Fiset	741	1,269
Joe Mullen	Pittsburgh	Mar. 14/97	1,052	Pit. 3 at Col. 6	Patrick Roy	502	1,062
Dave Andreychuk	New Jersey	Mar. 15/97	1,070	Wsh. 2 at N.J. 3	Bill Ranford	640	1,639
Luc Robitaille	Los Angeles	Jan. 7/99	928	Buf. 2 at L.A. 4	Dwayne Roloson	668	1,431
Pat Verbeek	Detroit	Mar. 22/00	1,285	Cgy. 2 at Det. 2	Fred Brathwaite	522	1,424
Ron Francis	Carolina	Jan. 2/02	1,533	Bos. 6 at Car. 3	Byron Dafoe	549	1,731
Brendan Shanahan	Detroit	Mar. 23/02	1,100	Det. 2 at Col. 0	Patrick Roy	656	1,524
Joe Sakic	Colorado	Dec. 11/02	1,044	Col. 1 at Van. 3	Dan Cloutier	625	1,378
Joe Nieuwendyk	New Jersey	Jan. 17/03	1,094	N.J. 2 at Car. 1	Kevin Weekes	564	1,257
*Jaromir Jagr	Washington	Feb. 4/03	928	Wsh. 5 at T.B. 1	John Grahame	722	1,550
Pierre Turgeon	Colorado	Nov. 8/05	1,229	S.J. 2 at Col. 5	Vesa Toskala	515	1,294
Mats Sundin	Toronto	Oct. 14/06	1,162	Cgy. 4 at Tor. 5	Miikka Kiprusoff	564	1,346
Teemu Selanne	Anaheim	Nov. 22/06	982	Ana. 2 at Col. 3	Jose Theodore	684	1,451
Peter Bondra	Chicago	Dec. 22/06	1,050	Tor. 1 at Chi. 3	J.S. Aubin	503	1,081
Mark Recchi	Pittsburgh	Jan. 26/07	1,303	Pit. 4 at Dal. 3	Marty Turco	577	1,652
Mike Modano	Dallas	Mar. 13/07	1,225	Phi. 2 at Dal. 3	Antero Niittymaki	561	1,499
Jeremy Roenick	San Jose	Nov. 10/07	1,267	Phx. 1 at S.J. 4	Alex Auld	513	1,363
Keith Tkachuk	St. Louis	Apr. 6/08	1,055	St.L. 4 at CBJ 1	empty net	538	1,201
*Jarome Iginla	Calgary	Jan. 7/12	1,149	Min. 1 at Cgy. 3	Niklas Backstrom	589	1,392

*Active

Jean Béliveau passed away on December 2, 2014 and was commemorated throughout the rest of the season with a number 4 on a patch on the Canadiens' sweaters and on the ice behind the nets at the Bell Centre in Montreal. On February 11, 1971, Béliveau became the fourth player in NHL history to score 500 goals.

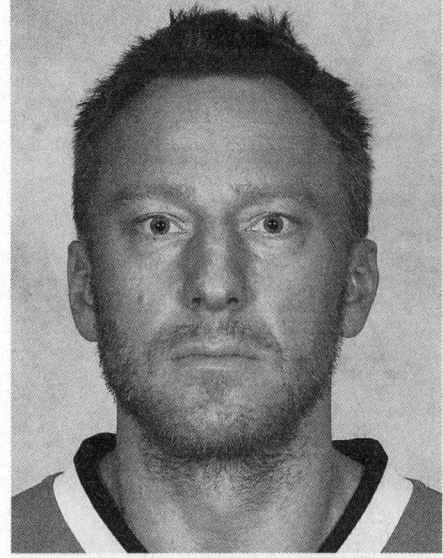

Players' 1,000th Points

Regular Season

Player	Team	Date	Game No.	G or A	Score			Total Points G A PTS			Total Games
Gordie Howe	Detroit	Nov. 27/60	938	(A)	Tor. 0	at	Det. 2	801-1,049-1,850			1,767
Jean Béliveau	Montreal	Mar. 3/68	911	(G)	Mtl. 2	at	Det. 5	507-712-1,219			1,125
Alex Delvecchio	Detroit	Feb. 16/69	1,143	(A)	L.A. 3	at	Det. 6	456-825-1,281			1,549
Bobby Hull	Chicago	Dec. 13/70	909	(A)	Min. 2	at	Chi. 5	610-560-1,170			1,063
Norm Ullman	Toronto	Oct. 16/71	1,113	(A)	NYR 5	at	Tor. 3	490-739-1,229			1,410
Stan Mikita	Chicago	Oct. 15/72	924	(A)	St.L. 3	at	Chi. 1	541-926-1,467			1,394
John Bucyk	Boston	Nov. 9/72	1,144	(G)	Det. 3	at	Bos. 8	556-813-1,369			1,540
Frank Mahovlich	Montreal	Feb. 17/73	1,090	(A)	Phi. 7	at	Mtl. 6	533-570-1,103			1,181
Henri Richard	Montreal	Dec. 20/73	1,194	(A)	Mtl. 2	at	Buf. 2	358-688-1,046			1,256
Phil Esposito	Boston	Feb. 15/74	745	(A)	Bos. 4	at	Van. 2	717-873-1,590			1,282
Rod Gilbert	NY Rangers	Feb. 19/77	1,027	(G)	NYR 2	at	NYI 5	406-615-1,021			1,065
Jean Ratelle	Boston	Apr. 3/77	1,007	(A)	Tor. 4	at	Bos. 7	491-776-1,267			1,281
Marcel Dionne	Los Angeles	Jan. 7/81	740	(G)	L.A. 5	at	Hfd. 3	731-1,040-1,771			1,348
Guy Lafleur	Montreal	Mar. 4/81	720	(G)	Wpg. 3	at	Mtl. 9	560-793-1,353			1,126
Bobby Clarke	Philadelphia	Mar. 19/81	922	(G)	Bos. 3	at	Phi. 5	358-852-1,210			1,144
Gilbert Perreault	Buffalo	Apr. 3/82	871	(A)	Buf. 5	at	Mtl. 4	512-814-1,326			1,191
Darryl Sittler	Philadelphia	Jan. 20/83	927	(A)	Cgy. 2	at	Phi. 5	484-637-1,121			1,096
Wayne Gretzky	Edmonton	Dec. 19/84	424	(A)	L.A. 3	at	Edm. 7	894-1,963-2,875			1,487
Bryan Trottier	NY Islanders	Jan. 29/85	726	(G)	Min. 4	at	NYI 4	524-901-1,425			1,279
Mike Bossy	NY Islanders	Jan. 24/86	656	(A)	NYI 7	at	Wsh. 5	573-553-1,126			752
Denis Potvin	NY Islanders	Apr. 4/87	987	(G)	Buf. 6	at	NYI 6	310-742-1,052			1,060
Bernie Federko	St. Louis	Mar. 19/88	855	(A)	Hfd. 5	at	St.L. 3	369-761-1,130			1,000
Lanny McDonald	Calgary	Mar. 7/89	1,101	(G)	Wpg. 5	at	Cgy. 9	500-506-1,006			1,111
Peter Stastny	Quebec	Oct. 19/89	682	(G)	Que. 5	at	Chi. 3	450-789-1,239			977
Jari Kurri	Edmonton	Jan. 2/90	716	(A)	Edm. 6	at	St.L. 4	601-797-1,398			1,251
Denis Savard	Chicago	Mar. 11/90	727	(A)	St.L. 6	at	Chi. 4	473-865-1,338			1,196
Paul Coffey	Pittsburgh	Dec. 22/90	770	(A)	Pit. 4	at	NYI 3	396-1,135-1,531			1,409
Mark Messier	Edmonton	Jan. 13/91	822	(A)	Edm. 5	at	Phi. 3	694-1,193-1,887			1,756
Dave Taylor	Los Angeles	Feb. 5/91	930	(A)	L.A. 3	at	Phi. 2	431-638-1,069			1,111
Michel Goulet	Chicago	Feb. 23/91	878	(G)	Chi. 3	at	Min. 3	548-604-1,152			1,089
Dale Hawerchuk	Buffalo	Mar. 8/91	781	(G)	Chi. 5	at	Buf. 3	518-891-1,409			1,188
Bobby Smith	Minnesota	Nov. 30/91	986	(A)	Min. 4	at	Tor. 3	357-679-1,036			1,077
Mike Gartner	NY Rangers	Jan. 4/92	971	(G)	NYR 4	at	N.J. 6	708-627-1,335			1,432
Raymond Bourque	Boston	Feb. 29/92	933	(A)	Wsh. 5	at	Bos. 5	410-1,169-1,579			1,612
Mario Lemieux	Pittsburgh	Mar. 24/92	513	(A)	Pit. 3	at	Det. 4	690-1,033-1,723			915
Glenn Anderson	Toronto	Feb. 22/93	954	(G)	Tor. 8	at	Van. 1	498-601-1,099			1,129
Steve Yzerman	Detroit	Feb. 24/93	737	(A)	Det. 7	at	Buf. 10	692-1,063-1,755			1,514
Ron Francis	Pittsburgh	Oct. 28/93	893	(A)	Que. 7	at	Pit. 3	549-1,249-1,798			1,731
Bernie Nicholls	New Jersey	Feb. 13/94	858	(G)	N.J. 3	at	T.B. 3	475-734-1,209			1,127
Dino Ciccarelli	Detroit	Mar. 9/94	957	(G)	Det. 5	at	Cgy. 1	608-592-1,200			1,232
Brian Propp	Hartford	Mar. 19/94	1,008	(A)	Hfd. 5	at	Phi. 3	425-579-1,004			1,016
Joe Mullen	Pittsburgh	Feb. 7/95	935	(A)	Fla. 3	at	Pit. 7	502-561-1,063			1,062
Steve Larmer	NY Rangers	Mar. 8/95	983	(A)	N.J. 4	at	NYR 6	441-571-1,012			1,006
Doug Gilmour	Toronto	Dec. 23/95	935	(A)	Edm. 1	at	Tor. 6	450-964-1,414			1,474
Larry Murphy	Toronto	Mar. 27/96	1,228	(G)	Tor. 6	at	Van. 2	287-929-1,216			1,615
Dave Andreychuk	New Jersey	Apr. 7/96	998	(G)	NYR 2	at	N.J. 4	640-698-1,338			1,639
Adam Oates	Washington	Oct. 8/97	830	(A)	Wsh. 6	at	NYI 3	341-1,079-1,420			1,337
Phil Housley	Washington	Nov. 8/97	1,081	(A)	Edm. 1	at	Wsh. 2	338-894-1,232			1,495
Dale Hunter	Washington	Jan. 9/98	1,308	(A)	Phi. 1	at	Wsh. 4	323-697-1,020			1,407
Pat LaFontaine	NY Rangers	Jan. 22/98	847	(G)	Phi. 4	at	NYR 3	468-545-1,013			865
Luc Robitaille	Los Angeles	Jan. 29/98	882	(A)	Cgy. 3	at	L.A. 5	668-726-1,394			1,431
Al MacInnis	St. Louis	Apr. 7/98	1,056	(A)	St.L. 3	at	Det. 5	340-934-1,274			1,416
Brett Hull	Dallas	Nov. 14/98	815	(A)	Dal. 3	at	Bos. 1	741-650-1,391			1,269
Brian Bellows	Washington	Jan. 2/99	1,147	(A)	Tor. 2	at	Wsh. 5	485-537-1,022			1,188
Pierre Turgeon	St. Louis	Oct. 9/99	881	(G)	St.L. 4	at	Edm. 3	515-812-1,327			1,294
Joe Sakic	Colorado	Dec. 27/99	810	(A)	St.L. 1	at	Col. 5	625-1,016-1,641			1,378
Pat Verbeek	Detroit	Feb. 27/00	1,275	(A)	T.B. 1	at	Det. 3	522-541-1,063			1,424
V. Damphousse	San Jose	Oct. 14/00	1,090	(A)	Bos. 2	at	S.J. 5	432-773-1,205			1,378
*Jaromir Jagr	Pittsburgh	Dec. 30/00	763	(G)	Ott. 3	at	Pit. 5	722-1,080-1,802			1,550
Mark Recchi	Philadelphia	Mar. 13/01	920	(A)	St.L. 2	at	Phi. 5	577-956-1,533			1,652
Theoren Fleury	NY Rangers	Oct. 29/01	960	(A)	Dal. 2	at	NYR 4	455-633-1,088			1,084
B. Shanahan	Detroit	Jan. 12/02	1,073	(A)	Dal. 2	at	Det. 5	656-698-1,354			1,524
Jeremy Roenick	Philadelphia	Jan. 30/02	961	(G)	Phi. 1	at	Ott. 3	513-703-1,216			1,363
Mike Modano	Dallas	Nov. 15/02	965	(A)	Col. 2	at	Dal. 4	561-813-1,374			1,499
Joe Nieuwendyk	New Jersey	Feb. 23/03	1,094	(G)	N.J. 4	at	Pit. 3	564-562-1,126			1,257
Mats Sundin	Toronto	Mar. 10/03	994	(G)	Tor. 3	at	Edm. 2	564-785-1,349			1,346
Sergei Fedorov	Anaheim	Feb. 14/04	965	(A)	Ana. 2	at	Van. 1	483-696-1,179			1,248
Alexander Mogilny	Toronto	Mar. 15/04	946	(G)	Tor. 6	at	Buf. 5	473-559-1,032			990
Brian Leetch	Boston	Oct. 18/05	1,151	(A)	Bos. 3	at	Mtl. 4	247-781-1,028			1,205
Teemu Selanne	Anaheim	Jan. 30/06	928	(G)	L.A. 3	at	Ana. 4	684-773-1,457			1,451
Rod Brind'Amour	Carolina	Nov. 4/06	1,202	(G)	Car. 3	at	Ott. 2	452-732-1,184			1,484
Keith Tkachuk	St. Louis	Nov. 30/08	1,077	(G)	St.L. 4	at	Atl. 2	538-527-1,065			1,201
Doug Weight	NY Islanders	Jan. 2/09	1,167	(A)	NYI 4	at	Phx. 5	278-755-1,033			1,238
Nicklas Lidstrom	Detroit	Oct. 15/09	1,336	(A)	L.A. 2	at	Det. 5	264-878-1,142			1,564
Daniel Alfredsson	Ottawa	Oct. 22/10	1,009	(G)	Ott. 4	at	Buf. 2	444-713-1,157			1,246
Alex Kovalev	Ottawa	Nov. 22/10	1,249	(G)	L.A. 2	at	Ott. 3	430-599-1,029			1,316
*Jarome Iginla	Calgary	Apr. 1/11	1,103	(G)	Cgy. 3	at	St.L. 2	589-637-1,226			1,392
*Joe Thornton	San Jose	Apr. 8/11	994	(G)	S.J. 3	at	Phx. 4	358-901-1,259			1,285
Ray Whitney	Phoenix	Mar. 31/12	1,226	(A)	Ana. 0	at	Phx. 4	385-679-1,064			1,330
*Marian Hossa	Chicago	Oct. 30/14	1,100	(G)	Chi. 5	at	Ott. 1	486-570-1,056			1,172
Martin St. Louis	NY Rangers	Nov. 28/14	1,082	(G)	NYR 3	at	Phi. 0	391-642-1,033			1,134
*Patrik Elias	New Jersey	Jan. 6/15	1,187	(A)	Buf. 1	at	N.J. 4	406-611-1,017			1,224

*Active

Martin St. Louis (top), Marian Hossa (middle) and Patrik Elias (bottom) all each reached the 1,000-point milestone during the 2014-15 season.

Individual Awards

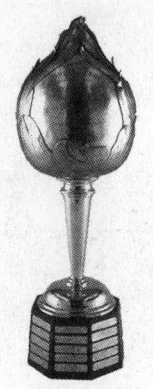
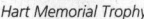

Hart Memorial Trophy

Art Ross Trophy

Calder Memorial Trophy

James Norris Memorial Trophy

HART MEMORIAL TROPHY

An annual award "to the player adjudged to be the most valuable to his team." Winner selected in a poll by the Professional Hockey Writers' Association in the 30 NHL cities at the end of the regular schedule.

History: The Hart Memorial Trophy was presented by the National Hockey League in 1960 after the original Hart Trophy was retired to the Hockey Hall of Fame. The original Hart Trophy was donated to the NHL in 1924 by Dr. David A. Hart, father of Cecil Hart, former manager-coach of the Montreal Canadiens.

2014-15 Winner: **Carey Price, Montreal Canadiens**
Runners-up: **Alex Ovechkin, Washington Capitals**
John Tavares, New York Islanders

Goaltender Carey Price is the winner of the Hart Memorial Trophy for the first time in his career. Price was a runaway winner, receiving 139 first-place votes from the 157 ballots cast. Named on 155 ballots, he received 14 second-place votes and two third-place votes for a total of 1,498 points. Alex Ovechkin of Washington was named on 150 ballots, with eight first-place votes, 75 seconds, 45 thirds, 18 fourths and four fifth-place votes for a total of 888 points. John Tavares was named on 151 ballots, including four first-place votes, and had 739 points to finish in third place. No one else received any first-place votes. Rounding out the top ten in balloting were Sidney Crosby of Pittsburgh (138 points), Ryan Getzlaf of Anaheim (70 points), Pekka Rinne of Nashville (49 points), Erik Karlsson of Ottawa (32 points) and Jonathan Toews of Chicago (31 points).

Price, who also won the Vezina Trophy and shared the William M. Jennings Trophy with Chicago's Corey Crawford, backstopped the Canadiens to their best regular season since 1988-89. He led the NHL in wins (44), goals-against average (1.96) and save percentage (.933), becoming the first goaltender to lead in all three categories since Ed Belfour in 1990-91. In doing so, Price surpassed the franchise record for wins in one season (42), set by Jacques Plante in 1955-56 and equaled by Plante in 1961-62 and Ken Dryden in 1975-76. The first-time Hart Trophy finalist is the first goaltender to capture MVP honors since Montreal's Jose Theodore in 2002.

ART ROSS TROPHY

An annual award "to the player who leads the league in scoring points at the end of the regular season."

History: Arthur Howey Ross, former manager-coach of the Boston Bruins, presented the trophy to the National Hockey League in 1947. If two players finish the schedule with the same number of points, the trophy is awarded in the following manner: 1. Player with most goals. 2. Player with fewer games played. 3. Player scoring first goal of the season.

2014-15 Winner: **Jamie Benn, Dallas Stars**
Runners-up: **John Tavares, New York Islanders**
Sidney Crosby, Pittsburgh Penguins

Left wing Jamie Benn of the Dallas Stars won his first career Art Ross Trophy. Benn entered the final day of the regular season third in the NHL scoring race with 83 points, one behind Pittsburgh Penguins center Sidney Crosby and New York Islanders center John Tavares. Benn moved to the front by tallying four points (three goals, one assist) in a 4-1 win over Nashville, including a goal and an assist in the final 2:05 of the third period. His late surge increased his season total to 87 points (35 goals, 52 assists), one more than Tavares (38 goals, 48 assists, 86 points), who notched a goal and an assist in a 5-4 shootout loss to Columbus, and three more than Crosby (28 goals, 56 assists, 84 points), who did not record a point in his team's 2-0 win at Buffalo that clinched the Penguins a playoff berth. Benn, the first player in Stars history to win the scoring title, notched multiple points in five of his final six games of the season (7 goals, 8 assists, 15 points), including 10 points in his last three contests. The Stars captain established career highs in goals, assists and points, ahead of his previous highs of 34, 45 and 79, respectively, set in 2013-14.

CALDER MEMORIAL TROPHY

An annual award "to the player selected as the most proficient in his first year of competition in the National Hockey League." Winner selected in a poll by the Professional Hockey Writers' Association at the end of the regular schedule.

History: From 1936-37 until his death in 1943, Frank Calder, NHL President, bought a trophy each year to be given permanently to the outstanding rookie. After Calder's death, the NHL presented the Calder Memorial Trophy in his memory and the trophy is to be kept in perpetuity. To be eligible for the award, a player cannot have played more than 25 games in any single preceding season nor in six or more games in each of any two preceding seasons in any major professional league. Beginning in 1990-91, to be eligible for this award a player must not have attained his twenty-sixth birthday by September 15th of the season in which he is eligible.

2014-15 Winner: **Aaron Ekblad, Florida Panthers**
Runners-up: **Mark Stone, Ottawa Senators**
Johnny Gaudreau, Calgary Flames

Florida Panthers defenseman Aaron Ekblad won the Calder Memorial Trophy. Ekblad, who began the season as an 18-year-old (born February 7, 1996), was selected first overall in the 2014 NHL Draft. He is the second Panthers player in the past three years to be voted the league's top rookie, following Jonathan Huberdeau's Calder Trophy win in 2013. Ekblad won the vote in a close three-way race, receiving 71 first-place votes, 39 second-place votes, 24 third-place votes, 12 fourth-place votes and eight fifth-place votes for a total of 1,147 points. Ekblad was named on 154 of the 157 ballots cast. Mark Stone of Ottawa had 47 first-place votes and finished as runner-up with 1,078 points. Calgary's Johnny Gaudreau had 33 first-place votes to finish third with 1,026 points. Filip Forsberg of Nashville received the final six first-place votes and finished fourth with 594 points. John Klingberg of Dallas (127 points), Ottawa's Mike Hoffman (57), Kevin Hayes of the Rangers (15), Michael Hutchinson of Winnipeg (13), Anders Lee of the Islanders (12) and Jake Allen of St. Louis (10) rounded out the top 10.

Ekblad set Panthers club records for goals (12), assists (27) and points (39) by a rookie defenseman. His 39 points were two shy of the NHL record for an 18-year-old defenseman set by Bobby Orr in 1966-67 (13 goals, 28 assists, 41 points). Ekblad led the Panthers in plus-minus (+12) and was on the ice for 88 Florida goals scored, the most of any player on the roster.

JAMES NORRIS MEMORIAL TROPHY

An annual award "to the defense player who demonstrates throughout the season the greatest all-round ability in the position." Winner selected in a poll by the Professional Hockey Writers' Association at the end of the regular schedule.

History: The James Norris Memorial Trophy was presented in 1953 by the four children of the late James Norris in memory of the former owner-president of the Detroit Red Wings.

2014-15 Winner: **Erik Karlsson, Ottawa Senators**
Runners-up: **Drew Doughty, Los Angeles Kings**
P.K. Subban, Montreal Canadiens

Erik Karlsson of the Ottawa Senators won the James Norris Memorial Trophy for the second time in his career. Karlsson, who previously captured the award in 2012, joins Duncan Keith as the NHL's only active defensemen with multiple Norris Trophy wins. Karlsson was named on 146 of 157 ballots, including 44 first-place votes and 42 second-place selections, accumulating 964 points in a tight three-way race. Drew Doughty of Los Angeles received 53 first-place votes but only 889 points overall. P.K. Subban of Montreal was named first on 24 ballots and collected 801 points. Nashville's Shea Weber had 26 first-place votes but finished fourth with 614 points. Roman Josi of Nashville had three first-place votes and 222 points to finish fifth. Mark Giordano of Calgary, Duncan Keith of Chicago, Kris Letang of Pittsburgh, Ryan Suter of Minnesota (two), Dustin Byfuglien of Winnipeg and Niklas Kronwall of Detroit also received first-place votes.

Karlsson led all defensemen in points (66) for the third time in the past four seasons, including a career-high 21 goals. He appeared in all 82 games for the second consecutive campaign, ranking third in the NHL in total time on ice (2,234:55) and average time on ice (27:15) to carry the Senators to a 23-4-4 record down the stretch en route to their 15th playoff berth in franchise history.

Vezina Trophy

Lady Byng Memorial Trophy

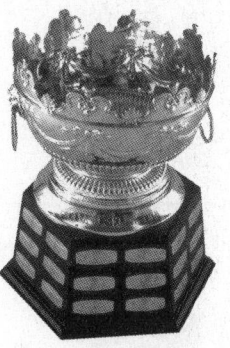

Frank J. Selke Trophy

William M. Jennings Trophy

VEZINA TROPHY

An annual award "to the goalkeeper adjudged to be the best at his position" as voted by the general managers of each of the 30 clubs.

History: Leo Dandurand, Louis Letourneau and Joe Cattarinich, former owners of the Montreal Canadiens, presented the trophy to the National Hockey League in 1926-27 in memory of Georges Vezina, outstanding goalkeeper of the Canadiens who collapsed during an NHL game on November 28, 1925, and died of tuberculosis a few months later. Before the 1981-82 season, the goalkeeper(s) of the team allowing the fewest number of goals during the regular season were awarded the Vezina Trophy.

2014-15 Winner: Carey Price, Montreal Canadiens
Runners-up: Pekka Rinne, Nashville Predators
Devan Dubnyk, Minnesota Wild

Carey Price of the Montreal Canadiens captured the Vezina Trophy for the first time. Twelve other goalies in Canadiens history have had their names engraved on the trophy, more than any other team. Price was a near unanimous choice with 27 of 30 first-place votes from NHL general managers and three second-place votes for 144 points. Pekka Rinne of Nashville had one first-place vote and 60 points. Devan Dubnyk of Minnesota had one first-place vote and finished third in the balloting with 28 points. Braden Holtby of Washington had 26 points to finish in fourth place. Henrik Lundqvist of the Rangers received one first-place vote and one third-place vote to finish fifth with six points. Chicago's Corey Crawford had a second-place vote for three points, while Andrew Hammond of Ottawa, Jonathan Quick of Los Angeles and Cam Talbot of the Rangers all had one third-place vote for a single point.

Price led the NHL in wins (44), goals-against average (1.96) and save percentage (.933), becoming the first to pace the league in all three categories since Ed Belfour with the Blackhawks in 1990-91. Price broke the franchise record of 42 wins in one season set by Jacques Plante in 1955-56 and 1961-62 and equaled by Ken Dryden in 1975-76. Price's save percentage was the third highest since the NHL began tracking the stat in 1976-77. He also tied for second in the NHL with a career high nine shutouts, the most for Montreal since Ken Dryden had 10 in 1976-77.

LADY BYNG MEMORIAL TROPHY

An annual award "to the player adjudged to have exhibited the best type of sportsmanship and gentlemanly conduct combined with a high standard of playing ability." Winner selected in a poll by the Professional Hockey Writers' Association at the end of the regular schedule.

History: Lady Byng, wife of Canada's Governor-General at the time, presented the Lady Byng Trophy in the 1924-25 season. After Frank Boucher of the New York Rangers won the award seven times in eight seasons, he was given the trophy to keep and Lady Byng donated another trophy in 1936. After Lady Byng's death in 1949, the National Hockey League presented a new trophy, changing the name to Lady Byng Memorial Trophy.

2014-15 Winner: Jiri Hudler, Calgary Flames
Runners-up: Pavel Datsyuk, Detroit Red Wings
Anze Kopitar, Los Angeles Kings

Jiri Hudler of the Calgary Flames was the winner of the Lady Byng Memorial Trophy. Hudler polled 700 voting points, including 52 first-place ballots, for a tight win over four-time Lady Byng Trophy winner Pavel Datsyuk of Detroit. Datsyuk had 29 first-place votes and 648 points. Anze Kopitar of Los Angeles finished third with 11 first-place votes and 379 points. Daniel Sedin of Vancouver was fourth with six first-place votes and 267 points. Sean Monahan of Calgary had 13 first-place votes but finished fifth overall with 232 points. Minnesota's Jason Pominville had eight first-place votes and finished sixth overall with 205 points. Matt Moulson of Buffalo (150 points), Logan Couture of San Jose (148), Ryan O'Reilly of Colorado (139) and Chicago's Patrick Kane (130) rounded out the top 10.

Hudler finished eighth in the NHL scoring race and established career highs in goals (31), assists (45) and points (76), helping the Flames qualify for the Stanley Cup playoffs for the first time since 2009. Hudler tallied 23 points in March for the most points by any player in a calendar month in 2014-15 and the most by a Flames player since December, 2006 when Jarome Iginla had 10 goals and 16 assists. Hudler was assessed just 14 penalty minutes all season, fewest among the NHL's top 20 scorers.

FRANK J. SELKE TROPHY

An annual award "to the forward who best excels in the defensive aspects of the game." Winner selected in a poll by the Professional Hockey Writers' Association at the end of the regular schedule.

History: Presented to the National Hockey League in 1977 by the Board of Governors of the NHL in honor of Frank J. Selke, one of the great architects of Montreal and Toronto championship teams.

2014-15 Winner: Patrice Bergeron, Boston Bruins
Runners-up: Jonathan Toews, Chicago Blackhawks
Anze Kopitar, Los Angeles Kings

Center Patrice Bergeron of the Boston Bruins captured the Frank Selke Trophy for the second year in a row and the third time in four seasons. Bergeron garnered 1,083 voting points, including 75 first-place votes, to finish ahead of Jonathan Toews of Chicago in a very tight race. Toews had 51 first-place votes and 1,051 points in a finish that recalled the neck-and-neck race of 2013 when Toews edged Bergeron 1,260-1,250. Anze Kopitar of Los Angeles was third with five first-place votes and 364 points. David Backes of St. Louis garnered seven first-place votes but finished fourth in the balloting with 363 points. Detroit's Pavel Datsyuk was fifth with three first-place votes and 238 points. Max Pacioretty of Montreal had seven first-place votes and 156 points to finish in sixth place.

Bergeron was the NHL's top performer in the face-off circle in 2014-15, leading the league in total face-offs (1,951), wins (1,175) and winning percentage (60.2). He also ranked among the league's top five forwards in a host of statistics that measure team puck possession while on the ice at five-on-five, including SAT (shot attempts differential), SAT Rel% (ratio of player's on-ice SAT vs. off-ice SAT) and SAT Close (SAT in one-goal games in periods one and two, and tie games in period three).

WILLIAM M. JENNINGS TROPHY

An annual award "to the goalkeeper(s) having played a minimum of 25 games (13 games in 2012-13) for the team with the fewest goals scored against it." Winners selected on regular-season play.

History: The Jennings Trophy was presented in 1981-82 by the National Hockey League's Board of Governors to honor the late William M. Jennings, longtime governor and president of the New York Rangers and one of the great builders of hockey in the United States.

2014-15 Winners: Corey Crawford, Chicago Blackhawks
Carey Price, Montreal Canadiens
Runners-up: Henrik Lundqvist/Cam Talbot, New York Rangers

Corey Crawford of the Chicago Blackhawks and Carey Price of the Montreal Canadiens won the William M. Jennings Trophy. The Blackhawks and Canadiens finished the regular season tied with an NHL-low 189 goals allowed, and Crawford and Price saw the most action for their respective teams. This marks the first time that goaltenders on two teams claimed the Jennings Trophy since 2002-03, when New Jersey's Martin Brodeur and Philadelphia's Roman Cechmanek and Robert Esche captured Jennings honors after the Devils and Flyers tied for the league's lowest goals-against total. Crawford captured the Jennings Trophy for the second time in three seasons, posting a 32-20-5 record with a 2.27 goals-against average, .924 save percentage and two shutouts in 57 appearances. Price, who won his first Jennings Trophy, set a franchise record for victories by going 44-16-6, and led the NHL in wins, goals-against average (1.96) and save percentage (.933). He shared second place in shutouts (nine) with Braden Holtby of the Washington Capitals.

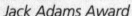

Jack Adams Award

Bill Masterton
Memorial Trophy

Lester Patrick Trophy

Conn Smythe Trophy

JACK ADAMS AWARD

An annual award presented by the National Hockey League Broadcasters' Association to "the NHL coach adjudged to have contributed the most to his team's success." Winner selected by a poll among members of the NHL Broadcasters' Association at the end of the regular season.

History: The award was presented by the NHL Broadcasters' Association in 1974 to commemorate the late Jack Adams, coach and general manager of the Detroit Red Wings, whose lifetime dedication to hockey serves as an inspiration to all who aspire to further the game.

2014-15 Winner: **Bob Hartley, Calgary Flames**
Runners-up: **Alain Vigneault, New York Rangers**
Peter Laviolette, Nashville Predators

Calgary Flames head coach Bob Hartley was the winner of the Jack Adams Award. Hartley was a top-three selection on 63 of the 75 ballots cast, including 37 first-place votes, for 237 voting points. The Jack Adams win is a first for both Hartley and the Flames. Alain Vigneault of the New York Rangers was second with 14 first-place votes and 121 points. Nashville's Peter Laviolette finished third with 81 points, including six first-place votes. Paul Maurice of Winnipeg also received six first-place votes, but was fourth overall with 79 points. Barry Trotz of Washington (two), Ottawa's Dave Cameron (two), Mike Babcock of Detroit (three), Jon Cooper of Tampa Bay (one), Willie Desjardins of Vancouver (one), Jack Capuano of the Islanders (two) and Gerard Gallant of Florida (one) also received first-place votes.

Hartley led the Flames (45-30-7 for 97 points) to a 20-point gain in the standings over 2013-14, the highest jump among Western Conference teams and the third highest in the NHL overall, in capturing their first playoff berth since 2009. Calgary was among the NHL's best late-game teams, tying for first place in overtime wins (nine), ranking second in third-period goal differential (+31), third in wins when trailing after two periods (10) and fifth in points percentage when leading after 40 minutes (.923, 24-1-1). The Flames also recorded 1,557 blocked shots, tops in the NHL and the highest single-season total since the statistic was introduced.

BILL MASTERTON MEMORIAL TROPHY

An annual award under the trusteeship of the Professional Hockey Writers' Association to "the National Hockey League player who best exemplifies the qualities of perseverance, sportsmanship and dedication to hockey." Winner selected by a poll among the 30 chapters of the PHWA at the end of the regular season. A $2,500 grant from the PHWA is awarded annually to the Bill Masterton Scholarship Fund, based in Bloomington, MN, in the name of the Masterton Trophy winner.

History: The trophy was presented by the NHL Writers' Association in 1968 to commemorate the late Bill Masterton, a player with the Minnesota North Stars, who exhibited to a high degree the qualities of perseverance, sportsmanship and dedication to hockey, and who died January 15, 1968.

2014-15 Winner: **Devan Dubnyk, Minnesota Wild**
Runners-up: **Andrew Hammond, Ottawa Senators**
Kris Letang, Pittsburgh Penguins

Minnesota Wild goaltender Devan Dubnyk is the 2014-15 recipient of the Bill Masterton Memorial Trophy. Dubnyk earned his team's Masterton Trophy nomination on the strength of a remarkable second-half run. Eight points outside of a playoff spot when he made his team debut on January 15, 2015, the 29-year-old backstopped the Wild (his fifth NHL organization in the past two seasons) to their third consecutive trip to the Stanley Cup playoffs. Dubnyk set a franchise record with 38 straight starts following his acquisition from Arizona, and went 27-9-2 with a 1.78 goals-against average, a .936 save percentage and five shutouts with the Wild. Overall, he finished the season second in the NHL with a 2.07 goals-against average and .929 save percentage and was voted a finalist for the Vezina Trophy as the league's top goaltender.

LESTER PATRICK TROPHY

An annual award "for outstanding service to hockey in the United States." Eligible recipients are players, officials, coaches, executives and referees. Winners are selected by an award committee consisting of the commissioner of the NHL, an NHL governor, a representative of the New York Rangers, a member of the Hockey Hall of Fame builder's section, a member of the Hockey Hall of Fame player's section, a member of the U.S. Hockey Hall of Fame, a member of the NHL Broadcasters' Association and a member of the Professional Hockey Writers' Association. Each except the League Commissioner is rotated annually. The winner receives a miniature of the trophy.

History: Presented by the New York Rangers in 1966 to honor the late Lester Patrick, longtime general manager and coach of the New York Rangers, whose teams finished out of the playoffs only once in his first 16 years with the club.

2014 Winner: **Bill Daly**   **2015 Winner:**   **Bob Crocker**
Paul Holmgren   **Jeremy Jacobs**

Bill Daly was named deputy commissioner of the NHL on July 22, 2005. He serves as the chief consultant to Commissioner Gary Bettman on all issues that impact the league's operation and overall business. Daly is the point person for the NHL's dealings with USA Hockey, College Hockey Inc., the American Hockey League and United States Hockey League.

Paul Holmgren, president of the Philadelphia Flyers, played 10 seasons for the Flyers and the Minnesota North Stars from 1975 to 1985. He served as assistant coach, head coach, assistant general manager, and general manger of the Flyers before assuming his current position in 2014. Holmgren has been widely involved in furthering the sport throughout his career in various roles for USA Hockey.

Bob Crocker is the dean of New England hockey scouts. A graduate of Boston University, he later coached the team's first-year recruits before becoming head coach at Penn from 1973 to 1976. He then put in 15 years as an assistant general manager with the Hartford Whalers. Since then, he has been a scout for the New York Rangers and Los Angeles Kings, helping to win the Stanley Cup in 1994, 2012 and 2014.

Jeremy Jacobs has owned the Boston Bruins since 1975 and is one of the most respected sports business leaders in the world. He has served as Chairman of the NHL Board of Governors since 2007 and serves on its Executive Committee. Jacobs is frequently cited as one of the most influential people in sports business.

CONN SMYTHE TROPHY

An annual award "to the most valuable player for his team in the playoffs." Winner selected by the Professional Hockey Writers' Association at the conclusion of the final game in the Stanley Cup Final.

History: Presented by Maple Leaf Gardens Limited in 1964 to honor Conn Smythe, the former coach, manager, president and owner-governor of the Toronto Maple Leafs.

2014-15 Winner: **Duncan Keith, Chicago Blackhawks**

Chicago Blackhawks defenseman Duncan Keith is the winner of the Conn Smythe Trophy. He is the first defenseman to be named playoff MVP since Scott Niedermayer of Anaheim in 2007 and the tenth defenseman to win it since the award was first presented in 1965. Keith led all playoff performers with 715:37 of ice time, averaging 31:06 of time on ice per game. His 21 points in the playoffs equaled Chris Chelios's team record for a defenseman set in 1991-92 and were tied for the most by a defenseman in the last 20 years with Chris Pronger in 2006. Defensemen Paul Coffey (25 in 1985), Al MacInnis (24 in 1989), Brian Leetch (23 in 1994) and Bobby Orr (19 in 1972) are the only ones to have more assists in one playoff year than the 18 Keith had in 2015. All three goals he scored stood as game-winning tallies, including his goal to give Chicago a 1-0 lead in their game-six Stanley Cup-clinching victory against Tampa Bay. His plus-minus rating of +16 was the best in the postseason and surpassed his previous playoff high of +10 when Chicago won the Stanley Cup in 2013. Keith was also a member of Chicago's 2010 Cup champions.

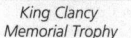

King Clancy
Memorial Trophy

NHL General Manager
of the Year Award

Maurice "Rocket" Richard Trophy

Ted Lindsay Award

Presidents' Trophy

KING CLANCY MEMORIAL TROPHY

An annual award "to the player who best exemplifies leadership qualities on and off the ice and has made a noteworthy humanitarian contribution in his community."

History: The King Clancy Memorial Trophy was presented to the National Hockey League by the Board of Governors in 1988 to honor the late Frank "King" Clancy.

2014-15 Winner: **Henrik Zetterberg**

Detroit Red Wings forward Henrik Zetterberg is the recipient of the King Clancy Memorial Trophy. The Red Wings captain rebounded from an injury-shortened 2013-14 campaign to lead his club in assists (49) and points (66) in 2014-15. Zetterberg capped a productive campaign with four points in the final two games of the regular season, rallying the Red Wings to a berth in the Stanley Cup playoffs for a franchise-record 24th consecutive season - the longest active streak in North American professional sports. Honored in 2013 with the NHL Foundation Player Award for outstanding charitable and community work, Zetterberg and his wife, Emma, give back to the Metro Detroit community through numerous initiatives including Metro Detroit area children's hospitals and mentoring nonprofits at each Red Wings home game during the regular season in the Zetterberg Foundation Suite. Zetterberg also funds a high school hockey scholarship each year and underwrites the Hockey Weekly High School All-Star Banquet. As the team spokesman for the Red Wings' annual Smoke Detector Collection since 2006, Zetterberg personally matches all donations. He and his wife also built the Chige Primary School in Kemba, Ethiopia, in cooperation with Action Aid Ethiopia. Construction of the Belta Telo Middle School began in 2013 and was completed in 2014. In May 2014, the Zetterberg Foundation broke ground on a Water Project in the village of Kemba which will supply 3,000 people of the village with clean, drinkable water for life when it is complete in December of 2015. He also supports microloan programs in Ethiopia and Guatemala to provide women with the opportunity to start their own businesses and work themselves out of poverty. In addition, the Zetterberg Foundation has financed and built six houses for former debt slaves in Nepal.

MAURICE "ROCKET" RICHARD TROPHY

An annual award "presented to the player finishing the regular season as the League's goal-scoring leader."

History: A gift to the NHL from the Montreal Canadiens in 1999, the Maurice "Rocket" Richard Trophy honors one of the game's greatest stars. During his 18-year career with the Canadiens from 1942-43 through 1959-60, Richard was the first player in NHL history to score 50 goals in a season and 500 in his career. He played on eight Stanley Cup champions and led the League in goal scoring five times.

2014-15 Winner: **Alex Ovechkin, Washington Capitals**
Runners-up   **Steven Stamkos, Tampa Bay Lightning**
                  Rick Nash, New York Rangers

Washington Capitals forward Alex Ovechkin claimed his third consecutive and fifth career Maurice "Rocket" Richard Trophy as the NHL's goal-scoring leader, adding to the ones he earned in 2007-08, 2008-09, 2012-13 and 2013-14. Ovechkin became the sixth player in NHL history to record six 50-goal seasons, joining Mike Bossy (9), Wayne Gretzky (9), Marcel Dionne (6), Guy Lafleur (6) and Mario Lemieux (6). He also led the league and set a career high/franchise record with 25 power-play goals, while his 11 game-winning goals paced the NHL and matched a personal best. Ovechkin, who finished 2014-15 ahead of Tampa Bay Lightning center Steven Stamkos (43) and New York Rangers left wing Rick Nash (42), scored 41 of his 53 goals in the final 55 games of season (0.75 GPG). He posted his 473rd and 474th career goals on April 2, 2015 to surpass Peter Bondra (472) as the leading goal-scorer in Capitals history.

NHL GENERAL MANAGER OF THE YEAR AWARD

An annual award presented to recognize the work of the league's general managers, voting for this new award is conducted among the 30 club general managers and a panel of NHL executives, print and broadcast media at the conclusion of the regular season.

History: This award was first presented in 2010.

2014-15 Winner: **Steve Yzerman, Tampa Bay Lightning**
Runners-up: **Glen Sather, New York Rangers**
                  Bob Murray, Anaheim Ducks

Steve Yzerman of the Tampa Bay Lightning is the winner of the NHL General Manager of the Year Award. Yzerman received nine first-place votes, ten second-place votes and five third-place votes for a total of 80 points. Glen Sather of the New York Rangers received seven first-place votes and 49 points. Bob Murray of Anaheim, who won the award in 2013-14, was third in voting this year with three first-place votes and 36 points. Ottawa's Bryan Murray received five first-place votes but finished fourth with 32 points, while Garth Snow of the Islanders had three first-place votes and 28 points. Calgary's Brad Treliving (three), Nashville's David Poile (two), Winnipeg's Kevin Cheveldayoff (two), Minnesota's Chuck Fletcher (one), Chicago's Stan Bowman (one) and Washington's Brian MacLellan (one) all received first-place votes as well.

After leading Tampa Bay to the Conference Finals in 2010-11, his first season in charge, Yzerman oversaw the rebuild to a roster that reached the Stanley Cup Final with just two holdovers from the 2011 squad: cornerstone center Steven Stamkos and defenseman Victor Hedman. Bolstered by key acquisitions at the Entry Draft (Nikita Kucherov, Ondrej Palat), via free agency (Brian Boyle, Valtteri Filppula, Tyler Johnson, Anton Stralman) and trades (Ben Bishop, Ryan Callahan, Braydon Coburn, Jason Garrison), the Lightning set franchise records with 50 wins and 108 points during the 2014-15 season and led the NHL with 262 goals and 32 home wins.

TED LINDSAY AWARD

The Ted Lindsay Award is presented annually to the "most outstanding player" in the NHL as voted by fellow members of the National Hockey League Players' Association. The winner receives $20,000, and the two finalists receive $10,000 each to donate to the grassroots hockey program of their choice, through the NHLPA's Goals & Dreams Fund.

History: On April 29, 2010, the Ted Lindsay Award was introduced to recognize Lindsay's pioneering efforts in the establishment of the NHL Players' Association. Carrying on the tradition established by the Lester B. Pearson Award, it remains the only award voted on by the players themselves. The award was originally created in 1971 in honor of the late Lester B. Pearson, former Prime Minister of Canada.

2014-15 Winner: **Carey Price, Montreal Canadiens**
Runners-up: **Jamie Benn, Dallas Stars**
                  Alex Ovechkin, Washington Capitals

Goaltender Carey Price of the Montreal Canadiens is the winner of the Ted Lindsay Award. Price joins three-time "Most Outstanding Player" winner Guy Lafleur (1976-77, 1977-78, 1978-79) as the only members of the Canadiens to win the award and joins Mike Liut (1980-81) and Dominik Hasek (1996-97, 1997-98) as the only goaltenders to be so honored.

During the 2014-15 regular season, Price played 66 games and helped lead the Canadiens to the second-best record in the NHL with a mark of 50-22-10. Price was 44-16-6, leading the NHL and setting a new Canadiens record in wins, as well as leading the league in goals-against average (1.96) and save percentage (.933), which earned him both the Hart Memorial Trophy and the Vezina Trophy as well.

MARK MESSIER NHL LEADERSHIP AWARD
presented by Bridgestone

An annual award presented "to the player who exemplifies great leadership qualitites to his team, on and off the ice during the regular season." Suggestions for nominees are solicited from fans, clubs and NHL personnel, but the selection of the three finalists and the ultimate winner is made by Mark Messier himself.

History: Presented by Bridgestone in honor of one of hockey's great leaders, this award was first handed out in 2007.

2014-15 Winner: Jonathan Toews, Chicago Blackhawks
Runners-up: Ryan Getzlaf, Anaheim Ducks
Andrew Ladd, Winnipeg Jets

Jonathan Toews of the Chicago Blackhawks is the recipient of the Mark Messier NHL Leadership Award. Chicago's captain since he was just 20-years-old, Toews led the club with 28 goals and 38 assists for 66 points during the 2014-15 regular season to guide the Blackhawks to their seventh consecutive playoff berth. He also built upon his work in the community, where he actively participates in various team endeavors, including Make-A-Wish visits and the Four Feathers Golf Invitational. Independently, Toews served as the honorary chairperson for the Israel Idonije Fundraiser, which helps underserved communities by providing programs focused on social and emotional life skills; supported The Winnipeg Foundation in creating its Nourishing Potential campaign; and continued his role with Misericordia, a Chicago group that offers care for those with mild to profound developmental disabilities.

PRESIDENTS' TROPHY

An annual award to the club finishing the regular-season with the best overall record.

History: Presented to the National Hockey League in 1985-86 by the NHL Board of Governors to recognize the team compiling the top regular-season record.

2014-15 Winner: New York Rangers
Runners-up: Montreal Canadiens
Anaheim Ducks

The New York Rangers captured the Presidents' Trophy for the second time in franchise history in 2014-15, leading the NHL with 113 points on a record of 53-22-7. The Rangers, who won the award previously in 1993-94, broke the franchise records for wins (52) and points (112) that had been set that season. The Rangers were the only team that ranked third or higher in the NHL in both goals per game (third - 3.02) and goals against per game (third - 2.28) and finished a season third or higher in both categories for the first time since 1972-73. The Blueshirts also established franchise records for road wins (28) and road points (58). Their 28 road wins were tied for the most by an Eastern Conference team in one season in NHL history. The Montreal Canadiens won their second division title in the past three seasons, finishing atop the Atlantic Division with a record of 50-22-10 for 110 points, while the Anaheim Ducks won the Pacific Division and finished first in the Western Conference with a record of 51-24-7 and 109 points.

NHL FOUNDATION PLAYER AWARD

An annual award presented to "an NHL player who applies the core values of hockey – commitment, perseverance and teamwork – to enrich the lives of people in his community." In recognition of this dedication, the NHL Foundation annually awards $25,000 to a current player's charity.

History: NHL players have a long-standing tradition of supporting charities and other important causes in their communities. NHL member clubs are constant in their quest to help local schools, hospitals and charitable organizations. Clubs submit nominations for the NHL Foundation Player Award and the finalists are selected by a judging panel. This award was first presented in 1998.

2014-15 Winner: Brent Burns, San Jose Sharks
Runners-up: Mark Giordano, Calgary Flames
Henrik Lundqvist, New York Rangers

San Jose Sharks defenseman Brent Burns is the recipient of the 2014-15 NHL Foundation Player Award. Burns has selected two beneficiaries for the financial award: Defending the Blue Line, affording children of military members the opportunity to participate in the game of hockey by providing hockey equipment, game tickets and unique experiences with professional athletes, and Folds of Honor, which provides educational scholarships for family members of injured and/or deceased military men and women.

Burns is heralded for his passion for giving back to the game and fans. He has established "Burnzie's Buzzcut" – a fundraiser in which he and his teammates shave their heads to raise money and awareness for charities such as the San Francisco Zoo and the Katie Moore Foundation, in support of close friend and former teammate Dominic Moore.

E.J. McGUIRE AWARD OF EXCELLENCE

An annual award presented to the NHL Entry Draft prospect who best exemplifies commitment to excellence through strength of character, competitiveness and athleticism.

History: First presented in 2015, this award commemorates E.J. McGuire, who joined the NHL's Central Scouting Bureau in 2002 and assumed day-to day responsibility for the department in 2005. McGuire was responsible for several advancements in scouting including the implementation of new technology. He also did much to improve the NHL's annual scouting combine. He passed away in 2011.

2014-15 Winner: Travis Konecny, Philadelphia Flyers

Travis Konecny, who was selected 24th overall by the Philadelphia Flyers at the 2015 NHL Entry Draft, is the inaugural winner of the E.J. McGuire Award of Excellence. As captain of the Ottawa 67's (OHL), the 18-year-old Konecny recorded 68 points (29 goals, 39 assists) in 60 games and also was voted Best Skater and ranked second for Best Stickhandler in a poll of the OHL's Eastern Conference coaches for the 2014-15 regular season. Throughout the past season and at various tournaments and events including the NHL Scouting Combine, Konecny displayed the skills, qualities and character that distinguish him as an ideal teammate and role model.

NATIONAL HOCKEY LEAGUE INDIVIDUAL AWARD WINNERS

CONN SMYTHE TROPHY

	Winner	
2015	Duncan Keith	Chicago
2014	Justin Williams	Los Angeles
2013	Patrick Kane	Chicago
2012	Jonathan Quick	Los Angeles
2011	Tim Thomas	Boston
2010	Jonathan Toews	Chicago
2009	Evgeni Malkin	Pittsburgh
2008	Henrik Zetterberg	Detroit
2007	Scott Niedermayer	Anaheim
2006	Cam Ward	Carolina
2005	....	....
2004	Brad Richards	Tampa Bay
2003	Jean-Sebastien Giguere	Anaheim
2002	Nicklas Lidstrom	Detroit
2001	Patrick Roy	Colorado
2000	Scott Stevens	New Jersey
1999	Joe Nieuwendyk	Dallas
1998	Steve Yzerman	Detroit
1997	Mike Vernon	Detroit
1996	Joe Sakic	Colorado
1995	Claude Lemieux	New Jersey
1994	Brian Leetch	NY Rangers
1993	Patrick Roy	Montreal
1992	Mario Lemieux	Pittsburgh
1991	Mario Lemieux	Pittsburgh
1990	Bill Ranford	Edmonton
1989	Al MacInnis	Calgary
1988	Wayne Gretzky	Edmonton
1987	Ron Hextall	Philadelphia
1986	Patrick Roy	Montreal
1985	Wayne Gretzky	Edmonton
1984	Mark Messier	Edmonton
1983	Billy Smith	NY Islanders
1982	Mike Bossy	NY Islanders
1981	Butch Goring	NY Islanders
1980	Bryan Trottier	NY Islanders
1979	Bob Gainey	Montreal
1978	Larry Robinson	Montreal
1977	Guy Lafleur	Montreal
1976	Reggie Leach	Philadelphia
1975	Bernie Parent	Philadelphia
1974	Bernie Parent	Philadelphia
1973	Yvan Cournoyer	Montreal
1972	Bobby Orr	Boston
1971	Ken Dryden	Montreal
1970	Bobby Orr	Boston
1969	Serge Savard	Montreal
1968	Glenn Hall	St. Louis
1967	Dave Keon	Toronto
1966	Roger Crozier	Detroit
1965	Jean Beliveau	Montreal

FRANK J. SELKE TROPHY

	Winner		Runner-up
2015	Patrice Bergeron, Bos.		Jonathan Toews, Chi.
2014	Patrice Bergeron, Bos.		Anze Kopitar, L.A.
2013	Jonathan Toews, Chi.		Patrice Bergeron, Bos.
2012	Patrice Bergeron, Bos.		David Backes, St.L.
2011	Ryan Kesler, Van.		Jonathan Toews, Chi.
2010	Pavel Datsyuk, Det.		Ryan Kesler, Van.
2009	Pavel Datsyuk, Det.		Mike Richards, Phi.
2008	Pavel Datsyuk, Det.		John Madden, N.J.
2007	Rod Brind'Amour, Car.		Samuel Pahlsson, Ana.
2006	Rod Brind'Amour, Car.		Jere Lehtinen, Dal.
2005	....		....
2004	Kris Draper, Det.		John Madden, N.J.
2003	Jere Lehtinen, Dal.		John Madden, N.J.
2002	Michael Peca, NYI		Craig Conroy, Cgy.
2001	John Madden, N.J.		Joe Sakic, Col.
2000	Steve Yzerman, Det.		Michal Handzus, St.L.
1999	Jere Lehtinen, Dal.		Magnus Arvedson, Ott.
1998	Jere Lehtinen, Dal.		Michael Peca, Buf.
1997	Michael Peca, Buf.		Peter Forsberg, Col.
1996	Sergei Fedorov, Det.		Ron Francis, Pit.
1995	Ron Francis, Pit.		Esa Tikkanen, St.L.
1994	Sergei Fedorov, Det.		Doug Gilmour, Tor.
1993	Doug Gilmour, Tor.		Dave Poulin, Bos.
1992	Guy Carbonneau, Mtl.		Sergei Fedorov, Det.
1991	Dirk Graham, Chi.		Esa Tikkanen, Edm.
1990	Rick Meagher, St.L.		Guy Carbonneau, Mtl.
1989	Guy Carbonneau, Mtl.		Esa Tikkanen, Edm.
1988	Guy Carbonneau, Mtl.		Steve Kasper, Bos.
1987	Dave Poulin, Phi.		Guy Carbonneau, Mtl.
1986	Troy Murray, Chi.		Ron Sutter, Phi.
1985	Craig Ramsay, Buf.		Doug Jarvis, Wsh.
1984	Doug Jarvis, Wsh.		Bryan Trottier, NYI
1983	Bobby Clarke, Phi.		Jari Kurri, Edm.
1982	Steve Kasper, Bos.		Bob Gainey, Mtl.
1981	Bob Gainey, Mtl.		Craig Ramsay, Buf.
1980	Bob Gainey, Mtl.		Craig Ramsay, Buf.
1979	Bob Gainey, Mtl.		Don Marcotte, Bos.
1978	Bob Gainey, Mtl.		Craig Ramsay, Buf.

BILL MASTERTON MEMORIAL TROPHY

	Winner	
2015	Devan Dubnyk	Minnesota
2014	Dominic Moore	NY Rangers
2013	Josh Harding	Minnesota
2012	Max Pacioretty	Montreal
2011	Ian Laperriere	Philadelphia
2010	Jose Theodore	Washington
2009	Steve Sullivan	Nashville
2008	Jason Blake	Toronto
2007	Phil Kessel	Boston
2006	Teemu Selanne	Anaheim
2005	....	....
2004	Bryan Berard	Chicago
2003	Steve Yzerman	Detroit
2002	Saku Koivu	Montreal
2001	Adam Graves	NY Rangers
2000	Ken Daneyko	New Jersey
1999	John Cullen	Tampa Bay
1998	Jamie McLennan	St. Louis
1997	Tony Granato	San Jose
1996	Gary Roberts	Calgary
1995	Pat LaFontaine	Buffalo
1994	Cam Neely	Boston
1993	Mario Lemieux	Pittsburgh
1992	Mark Fitzpatrick	NY Islanders
1991	Dave Taylor	Los Angeles
1990	Gord Kluzak	Boston
1989	Tim Kerr	Philadelphia
1988	Bob Bourne	Los Angeles
1987	Doug Jarvis	Hartford
1986	Charlie Simmer	Boston
1985	Anders Hedberg	NY Rangers
1984	Brad Park	Detroit
1983	Lanny McDonald	Calgary
1982	Glenn Resch	Colorado
1981	Blake Dunlop	St. Louis
1980	Al MacAdam	Minnesota
1979	Serge Savard	Montreal
1978	Butch Goring	Los Angeles
1977	Ed Westfall	NY Islanders
1976	Rod Gilbert	NY Rangers
1975	Don Luce	Buffalo
1974	Henri Richard	Montreal
1973	Lowell MacDonald	Pittsburgh
1972	Bobby Clarke	Philadelphia
1971	Jean Ratelle	NY Rangers
1970	Pit Martin	Chicago
1969	Ted Hampson	Oakland
1968	Claude Provost	Montreal

ART ROSS TROPHY

	Winner	Runner-up
2015	Jamie Benn, Dal.	John Tavares, NYI
2014	Sidney Crosby, Pit.	Ryan Getzlaf, Ana.
2013	Martin St. Louis, T.B.	Steven Stamkos, T.B.
2012	Evgeni Malkin, Pit.	Steven Stamkos, T.B.
2011	Daniel Sedin, Van.	Martin St. Louis, T.B.
2010	Henrik Sedin, Van.	Sidney Crosby, Pit.
2009	Evgeni Malkin, Pit.	Alex Ovechkin, Wsh.
2008	Alex Ovechkin, Wsh.	Evgeni Malkin, Pit.
2007	Sidney Crosby, Pit.	Joe Thornton, S.J.
2006	Joe Thornton, Bos., S.J.	Jaromir Jagr, NYR
2005	....	....
2004	Martin St. Louis, T.B.	Ilya Kovalchuk, Atl.
2003	Peter Forsberg, Col.	Markus Naslund, Van.
2002	Jarome Iginla, Cgy.	Markus Naslund, Van.
2001	Jaromir Jagr, Pit.	Joe Sakic, Col.
2000	Jaromir Jagr, Pit.	Pavel Bure, Fla.
1999	Jaromir Jagr, Pit.	Teemu Selanne, Ana.
1998	Jaromir Jagr, Pit.	Peter Forsberg, Col.
1997	Mario Lemieux, Pit.	Teemu Selanne, Ana.
1996	Mario Lemieux, Pit.	Jaromir Jagr, Pit.
1995	Jaromir Jagr, Pit.	Eric Lindros, Phi.
1994	Wayne Gretzky, L.A.	Sergei Fedorov, Det.
1993	Mario Lemieux, Pit.	Pat LaFontaine, Buf.
1992	Mario Lemieux, Pit.	Kevin Stevens, Pit.
1991	Wayne Gretzky, L.A.	Brett Hull, St.L.
1990	Wayne Gretzky, L.A.	Mark Messier, Edm.
1989	Mario Lemieux, Pit.	Wayne Gretzky, L.A.
1988	Mario Lemieux, Pit.	Wayne Gretzky, Edm.
1987	Wayne Gretzky, Edm.	Jari Kurri, Edm.
1986	Wayne Gretzky, Edm.	Mario Lemieux, Pit.
1985	Wayne Gretzky, Edm.	Jari Kurri, Edm.
1984	Wayne Gretzky, Edm.	Paul Coffey, Edm.
1983	Wayne Gretzky, Edm.	Peter Stastny, Que.
1982	Wayne Gretzky, Edm.	Mike Bossy, NYI
1981	Wayne Gretzky, Edm.	Marcel Dionne, L.A.
1980	Marcel Dionne, L.A.	Wayne Gretzky, Edm.
1979	Bryan Trottier, NYI	Marcel Dionne, L.A.
1978	Guy Lafleur, Mtl.	Bryan Trottier, NYI
1977	Guy Lafleur, Mtl.	Marcel Dionne, L.A.
1976	Guy Lafleur, Mtl.	Bobby Clarke, Phi.
1975	Bobby Orr, Bos.	Phil Esposito, Bos.
1974	Phil Esposito, Bos.	Bobby Orr, Bos.
1973	Phil Esposito, Bos.	Bobby Clarke, Phi.
1972	Phil Esposito, Bos.	Bobby Orr, Bos.
1971	Phil Esposito, Bos.	Bobby Orr, Bos.
1970	Bobby Orr, Bos.	Phil Esposito, Bos.
1969	Phil Esposito, Bos.	Bobby Hull, Chi.
1968	Stan Mikita, Chi.	Phil Esposito, Bos.
1967	Stan Mikita, Chi.	Bobby Hull, Chi.
1966	Bobby Hull, Chi.	Stan Mikita, Chi.
1965	Stan Mikita, Chi.	Norm Ullman, Det.
1964	Stan Mikita, Chi.	Bobby Hull, Chi.
1963	Gordie Howe, Det.	Andy Bathgate, NYR
1962	Bobby Hull, Chi.	Andy Bathgate, NYR
1961	Bernie Geoffrion, Mtl.	Jean Beliveau, Mtl.
1960	Bobby Hull, Chi.	Bronco Horvath, Bos.
1959	Dickie Moore, Mtl.	Jean Beliveau, Mtl.
1958	Dickie Moore, Mtl.	Henri Richard, Mtl.
1957	Gordie Howe, Det.	Ted Lindsay, Det.
1956	Jean Beliveau, Mtl.	Gordie Howe, Det.
1955	Bernie Geoffrion, Mtl.	Maurice Richard, Mtl.
1954	Gordie Howe, Det.	Maurice Richard, Mtl.
1953	Gordie Howe, Det.	Ted Lindsay, Det.
1952	Gordie Howe, Det.	Ted Lindsay, Det.
1951	Gordie Howe, Det.	Maurice Richard, Mtl.
1950	Ted Lindsay, Det.	Sid Abel, Det.
1949	Roy Conacher, Chi.	Doug Bentley, Chi.
1948*	Elmer Lach, Mtl.	Buddy O'Connor, NYR
1947	Max Bentley, Chi.	Maurice Richard, Mtl.
1946	Max Bentley, Chi.	Gaye Stewart, Tor.
1945	Elmer Lach, Mtl.	Maurice Richard, Mtl.
1944	Herb Cain, Bos.	Doug Bentley, Chi.
1943	Doug Bentley, Chi.	Bill Cowley, Bos.
1942	Bryan Hextall, NYR	Lynn Patrick, NYR
1941	Bill Cowley, Bos.	Bryan Hextall, NYR
1940	Milt Schmidt, Bos.	Woody Dumart, Bos.
1939	Toe Blake, Mtl.	Sweeney Schriner, NYA
1938	Gordie Drillon, Tor.	Syl Apps, Tor.
1937	Sweeney Schriner, NYA	Syl Apps, Tor.
1936	Sweeney Schriner, NYA	Marty Barry, Det.
1935	Charlie Conacher, Tor.	Syd Howe, St.L., Det.
1934	Charlie Conacher, Tor.	Joe Primeau, Tor
1933	Bill Cook, NYR	Busher Jackson, Tor.
1932	Busher Jackson, Tor.	Joe Primeau, Tor.
1931	Howie Morenz, Mtl.	Ebbie Goodfellow, Det.
1930	Cooney Weiland, Bos.	Frank Boucher, NYR
1929	Ace Bailey, Tor.	Nels Stewart, Mtl.M
1928	Howie Morenz, Mtl.	Aurel Joliat, Mtl.
1927	Bill Cook, NYR	Dick Irvin, Chi.
1926	Nels Stewart, Mtl.M.	Cy Denneny, Ott.
1925	Babe Dye, Tor.	Cy Denneny, Ott.
1924	Cy Denneny, Ott.	Billy Boucher, Mtl.
1923	Babe Dye, Tor.	Cy Denneny, Ott.
1922	Punch Broadbent, Ott.	Cy Denneny, Ott.
1921	Newsy Lalonde, Mtl.	Babe Dye, Ham., Tor.
1920	Joe Malone, Que.	Newsy Lalonde, Mtl.
1919	Newsy Lalonde, Mtl.	Odie Cleghorn, Mtl.
1918	Joe Malone, Mtl.	Cy Denneny, Ott.

* Trophy first awarded in 1948.
Scoring leaders listed from 1918 to 1947.

HART MEMORIAL TROPHY

	Winner	Runner-up
2015	Carey Price, Mtl.	Alex Ovechkin, Wsh.
2014	Sidney Crosby, Pit.	Ryan Getzlaf, Ana.
2013	Alex Ovechkin, Wsh.	Sidney Crosby, Pit.
2012	Evgeni Malkin, Pit.	Steven Stamkos, T.B.
2011	Corey Perry, Ana.	Daniel Sedin, Van.
2010	Henrik Sedin, Van.	Alex Ovechkin, Wsh.
2009	Alex Ovechkin, Wsh.	Evgeni Malkin, Pit.
2008	Alex Ovechkin, Wsh.	Evgeni Malkin, Pit.
2007	Sidney Crosby, Pit.	Roberto Luongo, Van.
2006	Joe Thornton, Bos., S.J.	Jaromir Jagr, NYR
2005	....	....
2004	Martin St. Louis, T.B.	Jarome Iginla, Cgy.
2003	Peter Forsberg, Col.	Markus Naslund, Van.
2002	Jose Theodore, Mtl.	Jarome Iginla, Cgy.
2001	Joe Sakic, Col.	Mario Lemieux, Pit.
2000	Chris Pronger, St.L.	Jaromir Jagr, Pit.
1999	Jaromir Jagr, Pit.	Alexei Yashin, Ott.
1998	Dominik Hasek, Buf.	Jaromir Jagr, Pit.
1997	Dominik Hasek, Buf.	Paul Kariya, Ana.
1996	Mario Lemieux, Pit.	Mark Messier, NYR
1995	Eric Lindros, Phi.	Jaromir Jagr, Pit.
1994	Sergei Fedorov, Det.	Dominik Hasek, Buf.
1993	Mario Lemieux, Pit.	Doug Gilmour, Tor.
1992	Mark Messier, NYR	Patrick Roy, Mtl.
1991	Brett Hull, St.L.	Wayne Gretzky, L.A.
1990	Mark Messier, Edm.	Raymond Bourque, Bos.
1989	Wayne Gretzky, L.A.	Mario Lemieux, Pit.
1988	Mario Lemieux, Pit.	Grant Fuhr, Edm.
1987	Wayne Gretzky, Edm.	Raymond Bourque, Bos.
1986	Wayne Gretzky, Edm.	Mario Lemieux, Pit.
1985	Wayne Gretzky, Edm.	Dale Hawerchuk, Wpg.
1984	Wayne Gretzky, Edm.	Rod Langway, Wsh.
1983	Wayne Gretzky, Edm.	Pete Peeters, Bos.
1982	Wayne Gretzky, Edm.	Bryan Trottier, NYI
1981	Wayne Gretzky, Edm.	Mike Liut, St.L.
1980	Wayne Gretzky, Edm.	Marcel Dionne, L.A.
1979	Bryan Trottier, NYI	Guy Lafleur, Mtl.
1978	Guy Lafleur, Mtl.	Bryan Trottier, NYI
1977	Guy Lafleur, Mtl.	Bobby Clarke, Phi.
1976	Bobby Clarke, Phi.	Denis Potvin, NYI
1975	Bobby Clarke, Phi.	Rogie Vachon, L.A.
1974	Phil Esposito, Bos.	Bernie Parent, Phi.
1973	Bobby Clarke, Phi.	Phil Esposito, Bos.
1972	Bobby Orr, Bos.	Ken Dryden, Mtl.
1971	Bobby Orr, Bos.	Phil Esposito, Bos.
1970	Bobby Orr, Bos.	Tony Esposito, Chi.
1969	Phil Esposito, Bos.	Jean Beliveau, Mtl.
1968	Stan Mikita, Chi.	Jean Beliveau, Mtl.
1967	Stan Mikita, Chi.	Ed Giacomin, NYR
1966	Bobby Hull, Chi.	Jean Beliveau, Mtl.
1965	Bobby Hull, Chi.	Norm Ullman, Det.
1964	Jean Beliveau, Mtl.	Bobby Hull, Chi.
1963	Gordie Howe, Det.	Stan Mikita, Chi.
1962	Jacques Plante, Mtl.	Doug Harvey, NYR
1961	Bernie Geoffrion, Mtl.	Johnny Bower, Tor.
1960	Gordie Howe, Det.	Bobby Hull, Chi.
1959	Andy Bathgate, NYR	Gordie Howe, Det.
1958	Gordie Howe, Det.	Andy Bathgate, NYR
1957	Gordie Howe, Det.	Jean Beliveau, Mtl.
1956	Jean Beliveau, Mtl.	Tod Sloan, Tor.
1955	Ted Kennedy, Tor.	Harry Lumley, Tor.
1954	Al Rollins, Chi.	Red Kelly, Det.
1953	Gordie Howe, Det.	Al Rollins, Chi.
1952	Gordie Howe, Det.	Elmer Lach, Mtl.
1951	Milt Schmidt, Bos.	Maurice Richard, Mtl.
1950	Chuck Rayner, NYR	Ted Kennedy, Tor.
1949	Sid Abel, Det.	Bill Durnan, Mtl.
1948	Buddy O'Connor, NYR	Frank Brimsek, Bos.
1947	Maurice Richard, Mtl.	Milt Schmidt, Bos.
1946	Max Bentley, Chi.	Gaye Stewart, Tor.
1945	Elmer Lach, Mtl.	Maurice Richard, Mtl.
1944	Babe Pratt, Tor.	Bill Cowley, Bos.
1943	Bill Cowley, Bos.	Doug Bentley, Chi.
1942	Tom Anderson, Bro.	Syl Apps, Tor.
1941	Bill Cowley, Bos.	Dit Clapper, Bos.
1940	Ebbie Goodfellow, Det.	Syl Apps, Tor.
1939	Toe Blake, Mtl.	Syl Apps, Tor.
1938	Eddie Shore, Bos.	Paul Thompson, Chi.
1937	Babe Siebert, Mtl.	Lionel Conacher, Mtl.M
1936	Eddie Shore, Bos.	Hooley Smith, Mtl.M
1935	Eddie Shore, Bos.	Charlie Conacher, Tor.
1934	Aurel Joliat, Mtl.	Lionel Conacher, Chi.
1933	Eddie Shore, Bos.	Bill Cook, NYR
1932	Howie Morenz, Mtl.	Ching Johnson, NYR
1931	Howie Morenz, Mtl.	Eddie Shore, Bos.
1930	Nels Stewart, Mtl.M.	Lionel Hitchman, Bos.
1929	Roy Worters, NYA	Ace Bailey, Tor.
1928	Howie Morenz, Mtl.	Roy Worters, Pit.
1927	Herb Gardiner, Mtl.	Bill Cook, NYR
1926	Nels Stewart, Mtl.M.	Sprague Cleghorn, Bos.
1925	Billy Burch, Ham.	Howie Morenz, Mtl.
1924	Frank Nighbor, Ott.	Sprague Cleghorn, Mtl.

MARK MESSIER NHL LEADERSHIP AWARD

	Winner	
2015	Jonathan Toews	Chicago
2014	Dustin Brown	Los Angeles
2013	Daniel Alfredsson	Ottawa
2012	Shane Doan	Phoenix
2011	Zdeno Chara	Boston
2010	Sidney Crosby	Pittsburgh
2009	Jarome Iginla	Calgary
2008	Mats Sundin	Toronto
2007	Chris Chelios	Detroit

WILLIAM M. JENNINGS TROPHY

	Winner	Runner-up
2015	Carey Price, Mtl. (tie)	Henrik Lundqvist, NYR
	Corey Crawford, Chi. (tie)	Cam Talbot, NYR
2014	Jonathan Quick, L.A.	Tuukka Rask, Bos.
		Chad Johnson, Bos.
2013	Corey Crawford, Chi.	Craig Anderson, Ott.
	Ray Emery, Chi.	
2012	Brian Elliott, St.L.	Jonathan Quick, L.A.
	Jaroslav Halak, St.L.	
2011	Roberto Luongo, Van.	Pekka Rinne, Nsh.
	Cory Schneider, Van.	
2010	Martin Brodeur, N.J.	Tim Thomas, Bos.
		Tuukka Rask, Bos.
2009	Tim Thomas, Bos.	Niklas Backstrom, Min.
	Manny Fernandez, Bos.	
2008	Chris Osgood, Det.	Jean-Sebastien Giguere, Ana.
	Dominik Hasek, Det.	
2007	Niklas Backstrom, Min.	Dominik Hasek, Det.
	Manny Fernandez, Min.	
2006	Miikka Kiprusoff, Cgy.	Manny Legace, Det.
		Chris Osgood, Det.
2005	....	....
2004	Martin Brodeur, N.J.	Marty Turco, Dal.
2003	Martin Brodeur, N.J. (tie)	Marty Turco, Dal.
	Roman Cechmanek, Phi.	Ron Tugnutt, Dal.
	Robert Esche, Phi. (tie)	
2002	Patrick Roy, Col.	Tommy Salo, Edm.
2001	Dominik Hasek, Buf.	Ed Belfour, Dal.
		Marty Turco, Dal.
2000	Roman Turek, St.L.	John Vanbiesbrouck, Phi.
		Brian Boucher, Phi.
1999	Ed Belfour, Dal.	Dominik Hasek, Buf.
	Roman Turek, Dal.	
1998	Martin Brodeur, N.J.	Ed Belfour, Dal.
1997	Martin Brodeur, N.J.	Chris Osgood, Det.
	Mike Dunham, N.J.	Mike Vernon, Det.
1996	Chris Osgood, Det.	Martin Brodeur, N.J.
	Mike Vernon, Det.	
1995	Ed Belfour, Chi.	Mike Vernon, Det.
		Chris Osgood, Det.
1994	Dominik Hasek, Buf.	Martin Brodeur, N.J.
	Grant Fuhr, Buf.	Chris Terreri, N.J.
1993	Ed Belfour, Chi.	Felix Potvin, Tor.
		Grant Fuhr, Tor.
1992	Patrick Roy, Mtl.	Ed Belfour, Chi.
1991	Ed Belfour, Chi.	Patrick Roy, Mtl.
1990	Andy Moog, Bos.	Patrick Roy, Mtl.
	Reggie Lemelin, Bos.	Brian Hayward, Mtl.
1989	Patrick Roy, Mtl.	Mike Vernon, Cgy.
	Brian Hayward, Mtl.	Rick Wamsley, Cgy.
1988	Patrick Roy, Mtl.	Clint Malarchuk, Wsh.
	Brian Hayward, Mtl.	Pete Peeters, Wsh.
1987	Patrick Roy, Mtl.	Ron Hextall, Phi.
	Brian Hayward, Mtl.	
1986	Bob Froese, Phi.	Al Jensen, Wsh.
	Darren Jensen, Phi.	Pete Peeters, Wsh.
1985	Tom Barrasso, Buf.	Pat Riggin, Wsh.
	Bob Sauve, Buf.	
1984	Al Jensen, Wsh.	Tom Barrasso, Buf.
	Pat Riggin, Wsh.	Bob Sauve, Buf.
1983	Roland Melanson, NYI	Pete Peeters, Bos.
	Billy Smith, NYI	
1982	Rick Wamsley, Mtl.	Billy Smith, NYI
	Denis Herron, Mtl.	Roland Melanson, NYI

MAURICE "ROCKET" RICHARD TROPHY

	Winner	
2015	Alex Ovechkin	Washington
2014	Alex Ovechkin	Washington
2013	Alex Ovechkin	Washington
2012	Steven Stamkos	Tampa Bay
2011	Corey Perry	Anaheim
2010	Sidney Crosby	Pittsburgh
	Steven Stamkos	Tampa Bay
2009	Alex Ovechkin	Washington
2008	Alex Ovechkin	Washington
2007	Vincent Lecavalier	Tampa Bay
2006	Jonathan Cheechoo	San Jose
2005	....	....
2004	Rick Nash	Columbus
	Jarome Iginla	Calgary
	Ilya Kovalchuk	Atlanta
2003	Milan Hejduk	Colorado
2002	Jarome Iginla	Calgary
2001	Pavel Bure	Florida
2000	Pavel Bure	Florida
1999	Teemu Selanne	Anaheim

NHL GENERAL MANAGER OF THE YEAR AWARD

	Winner	
2015	Steve Yzerman	Tampa Bay
2014	Bob Murray	Anaheim
2013	Ray Shero	Pittsburgh
2012	Doug Armstrong	St. Louis
2011	Mike Gillis	Vancouver
2010	Don Maloney	Phoenix

LADY BYNG MEMORIAL TROPHY

	Winner	Runner-up
2015	Jiri Hudler, Cgy.	Pavel Datsyuk, Det.
2014	Ryan O'Reilly, Col.	Martin St. Louis, T.B., NYR
2013	Martin St. Louis, T.B.	Patrick Kane, Chi
2012	Brian Campbell, Fla.	Jordan Eberle, Edm.
2011	Martin St. Louis, T.B.	Nicklas Lidstrom, Det.
2010	Martin St. Louis, T.B.	Brad Richards, Dal.
2009	Pavel Datsyuk, Det.	Martin St. Louis, T.B.
2008	Pavel Datsyuk, Det.	Martin St. Louis, T.B.
2007	Pavel Datsyuk, Det.	Martin St. Louis, T.B.
2006	Pavel Datsyuk, Det.	Brad Richards, T.B.
2005	....	
2004	Brad Richards, T.B.	Daniel Alfredsson, Ott.
2003	Alexander Mogilny, Tor.	Nicklas Lidstrom, Det.
2002	Ron Francis, Car.	Joe Sakic, Col.
2001	Joe Sakic, Col.	Nicklas Lidstrom, Det.
2000	Pavol Demitra, St.L.	Nicklas Lidstrom, Det.
1999	Wayne Gretzky, NYR	Nicklas Lidstrom, Det.
1998	Ron Francis, Pit.	Teemu Selanne, Ana.
1997	Paul Kariya, Ana.	Teemu Selanne, Ana.
1996	Paul Kariya, Ana.	Adam Oates, Bos.
1995	Ron Francis, Pit.	Adam Oates, Bos.
1994	Wayne Gretzky, L.A.	Adam Oates, Bos.
1993	Pierre Turgeon, NYI	Adam Oates, Bos.
1992	Wayne Gretzky, L.A.	Joe Sakic, Que.
1991	Wayne Gretzky, L.A.	Brett Hull, St.L.
1990	Brett Hull, St.L.	Wayne Gretzky, L.A.
1989	Joe Mullen, Cgy.	Wayne Gretzky, L.A.
1988	Mats Naslund, Mtl.	Wayne Gretzky, Edm.
1987	Joe Mullen, Cgy.	Wayne Gretzky, Edm.
1986	Mike Bossy, NYI	Jari Kurri, Edm.
1985	Jari Kurri, Edm.	Joe Mullen, St.L.
1984	Mike Bossy, NYI	Rick Middleton, Bos.
1983	Mike Bossy, NYI	Rick Middleton, Bos.
1982	Rick Middleton, Bos.	Mike Bossy, NYI
1981	Rick Kehoe, Pit.	Wayne Gretzky, Edm.
1980	Wayne Gretzky, Edm.	Marcel Dionne, L.A.
1979	Bob MacMillan, Atl.	Marcel Dionne, L.A.
1978	Butch Goring, L.A.	Peter McNab, Bos.
1977	Marcel Dionne, L.A.	Jean Ratelle, Bos.
1976	Jean Ratelle, NYR-Bos.	Jean Pronovost, Pit.
1975	Marcel Dionne, Det.	John Bucyk, Bos.
1974	John Bucyk, Bos.	Lowell MacDonald, Pit.
1973	Gilbert Perreault, Buf.	Jean Ratelle, NYR
1972	Jean Ratelle, NYR	John Bucyk, Bos.
1971	John Bucyk, Bos.	Dave Keon, Tor.
1970	Phil Goyette, St.L.	John Bucyk, Bos.
1969	Alex Delvecchio, Det.	Ted Hampson, Oak.
1968	Stan Mikita, Chi.	John Bucyk, Bos.
1967	Stan Mikita, Chi.	Dave Keon, Tor.
1966	Alex Delvecchio, Det.	Bobby Rousseau, Mtl.
1965	Bobby Hull, Chi.	Alex Delvecchio, Det.
1964	Kenny Wharram, Chi.	Dave Keon, Tor.
1963	Dave Keon, Tor.	Camille Henry, NYR
1962	Dave Keon, Tor.	Claude Provost, Mtl.
1961	Red Kelly, Tor.	Norm Ullman, Det.
1960	Don McKenney, Bos.	Andy Hebenton, NYR
1959	Alex Delvecchio, Det.	Andy Hebenton, NYR
1958	Camille Henry, NYR	Don Marshall, Mtl.
1957	Andy Hebenton, NYR	Dutch Reibel, Det.
1956	Dutch Reibel, Det.	Floyd Curry, Mtl.
1955	Sid Smith, Tor.	Danny Lewicki, NYR
1954	Red Kelly, Det.	Don Raleigh, NYR
1953	Red Kelly, Det.	Wally Hergesheimer, NYR
1952	Sid Smith, Tor.	Red Kelly, Det.
1951	Red Kelly, Det.	Woody Dumart, Bos.
1950	Edgar Laprade, NYR	Red Kelly, Det.
1949	Bill Quackenbush, Det.	Harry Watson, Tor.
1948	Buddy O'Connor, NYR	Syl Apps, Tor.
1947	Bobby Bauer, Bos.	Syl Apps, Tor.
1946	Toe Blake, Mtl.	Clint Smith, Chi.
1945	Bill Mosienko, Chi.	Syd Howe, Det.
1944	Clint Smith, Chi.	Herb Cain, Bos.
1943	Max Bentley, Chi.	Buddy O'Connor, Mtl.
1942	Syl Apps, Tor.	Gordie Drillon, Tor.
1941	Bobby Bauer, Bos.	Gordie Drillon, Tor.
1940	Bobby Bauer, Bos.	Clint Smith, NYR
1939	Clint Smith, NYR	Marty Barry, Det.
1938	Gordie Drillon, Tor.	Clint Smith, NYR
1937	Marty Barry, Det.	Gordie Drillon, Tor.
1936	Doc Romnes, Chi.	Sweeney Schriner, NYA
1935	Frank Boucher, NYR	Russ Blinco, Mtl.M
1934	Frank Boucher, NYR	Joe Primeau, Tor.
1933	Frank Boucher, NYR	Joe Primeau, Tor.
1932	Joe Primeau, Tor.	Frank Boucher, NYR
1931	Frank Boucher, NYR	Normie Himes, NYA
1930	Frank Boucher, NYR	Normie Himes, NYA
1929	Frank Boucher, NYR	Harold Darragh, Pit.
1928	Frank Boucher, NYR	George Hay, Det.
1927	Billy Burch, NYA	Dick Irvin, Chi.
1926	Frank Nighbor, Ott.	Billy Burch, NYA
1925	Frank Nighbor, Ott.	none

VEZINA TROPHY

	Winner	Runner-up
2015	Carey Price, Mtl.	Pekka Rinne, Nsh.
2014	Tuukka Rask, Bos.	Semyon Varlamov, Col.
2013	Sergei Bobrovsky, CBJ	Henrik Lundqvist, NYR.
2012	Henrik Lundqvist, NYR	Jonathan Quick, L.A.
2011	Tim Thomas, Bos.	Pekka Rinne, Nsh.
2010	Ryan Miller, Buf.	Ilya Bryzgalov, Phx.
2009	Tim Thomas, Bos.	Steve Mason, CBJ
2008	Martin Brodeur, N.J.	Evgeni Nabokov, S.J.
2007	Martin Brodeur, N.J.	Roberto Luongo, Van.
2006	Miikka Kiprusoff, Cgy.	Martin Brodeur, N.J.
2005	....	
2004	Martin Brodeur, N.J.	Miikka Kiprusoff, Cgy.
2003	Martin Brodeur, N.J.	Marty Turco, Dal.
2002	Jose Theodore, Mtl.	Patrick Roy, Col.
2001	Dominik Hasek, Buf.	Roman Cechmanek, Phi.
2000	Olaf Kolzig, Wsh.	Roman Turek, St.L.
1999	Dominik Hasek, Buf.	Curtis Joseph, Tor.
1998	Dominik Hasek, Buf.	Martin Brodeur, N.J.
1997	Dominik Hasek, Buf.	Martin Brodeur, N.J.
1996	Jim Carey, Wsh.	Chris Osgood, Det.
1995	Dominik Hasek, Buf.	Ed Belfour, Chi.
1994	Dominik Hasek, Buf.	John Vanbiesbrouck, Fla.
1993	Ed Belfour, Chi.	Tom Barrasso, Pit.
1992	Patrick Roy, Mtl.	Kirk McLean, Van.
1991	Ed Belfour, Chi.	Patrick Roy, Mtl.
1990	Patrick Roy, Mtl.	Daren Puppa, Buf.
1989	Patrick Roy, Mtl.	Mike Vernon, Cgy.
1988	Grant Fuhr, Edm.	Tom Barrasso, Buf.
1987	Ron Hextall, Phi.	Mike Liut, Hfd.
1986	John Vanbiesbrouck, NYR	Bob Froese, Phi.
1985	Pelle Lindbergh, Phi.	Tom Barrasso, Buf.
1984	Tom Barrasso, Buf.	Reggie Lemelin, Cgy.
1983	Pete Peeters, Bos.	Roland Melanson, NYI
1982	Billy Smith, NYI	Grant Fuhr, Edm.
1981	Richard Sevigny, Mtl.	Pete Peeters, Phi.
	Denis Herron, Mtl.	Rick St. Croix, Phi.
	Michel Larocque, Mtl.	
1980	Bob Sauve, Buf.	Gerry Cheevers, Bos.
	Don Edwards, Buf.	Gilles Gilbert, Bos.
1979	Ken Dryden, Mtl.	Glenn Resch, NYI
	Michel Larocque, Mtl.	Billy Smith, NYI
1978	Ken Dryden, Mtl.	Bernie Parent, Phi.
	Michel Larocque, Mtl.	Wayne Stephenson, Phi.
1977	Ken Dryden, Mtl.	Glenn Resch, NYI
	Michel Larocque, Mtl.	Billy Smith, NYI
1976	Ken Dryden, Mtl.	Glenn Resch, NYI
		Billy Smith, NYI
1975	Bernie Parent, Phi.	Rogie Vachon, L.A.
		Gary Edwards, L.A.
1974	Bernie Parent, Phi. (tie)	Gilles Gilbert, Bos.
	Tony Esposito, Chi. (tie)	
1973	Ken Dryden, Mtl.	Ed Giacomin, NYR
		Gilles Villemure, NYR
1972	Tony Esposito, Chi.	Cesare Maniago, Min.
	Gary Smith, Chi.	Gump Worsley, Min.
1971	Ed Giacomin, NYR	Tony Esposito, Chi.
	Gilles Villemure, NYR	
1970	Tony Esposito, Chi.	Jacques Plante, St.L.
		Ernie Wakely, St.L.
1969	Jacques Plante, St.L.	Ed Giacomin, NYR
	Glenn Hall, St.L.	
1968	Gump Worsley, Mtl.	Johnny Bower, Tor.
	Rogie Vachon, Mtl.	Bruce Gamble, Tor.
1967	Glenn Hall, Chi.	Charlie Hodge, Mtl.
	Denis DeJordy, Chi.	
1966	Gump Worsley, Mtl.	Glenn Hall, Chi.
	Charlie Hodge, Mtl.	
1965	Terry Sawchuk, Tor.	Roger Crozier, Det.
	Johnny Bower, Tor.	
1964	Charlie Hodge, Mtl.	Glenn Hall, Chi.
1963	Glenn Hall, Chi.	Johnny Bower, Tor.
		Don Simmons, Tor.
1962	Jacques Plante, Mtl.	Johnny Bower, Tor.
1961	Johnny Bower, Tor.	Glenn Hall, Chi.
1960	Jacques Plante, Mtl.	Glenn Hall, Chi.
1959	Jacques Plante, Mtl.	Johnny Bower, Tor.
		Ed Chadwick, Tor.
1958	Jacques Plante, Mtl.	Gump Worsley, NYR
		Marcel Paille, NYR
1957	Jacques Plante, Mtl.	Glenn Hall, Det.
1956	Jacques Plante, Mtl.	Glenn Hall, Det.
1955	Terry Sawchuk, Det.	Harry Lumley, Tor.
1954	Harry Lumley, Tor.	Terry Sawchuk, Det.
1953	Terry Sawchuk, Det.	Gerry McNeil, Mtl.
1952	Terry Sawchuk, Det.	Al Rollins, Tor.
1951	Al Rollins, Tor.	Terry Sawchuk, Det.
1950	Bill Durnan, Mtl.	Harry Lumley, Det.
1949	Bill Durnan, Mtl.	Harry Lumley, Det.
1948	Turk Broda, Tor.	Harry Lumley, Det.
1947	Bill Durnan, Mtl.	Turk Broda, Tor.
1946	Bill Durnan, Mtl.	Frank Brimsek, Bos.
1945	Bill Durnan, Mtl.	Frank McCool, Tor. (tie)
		Harry Lumley, Det. (tie)
1944	Bill Durnan, Mtl.	Paul Bibeault, Tor.
1943	Johnny Mowers, Det.	Turk Broda, Tor.
1942	Frank Brimsek, Bos.	Turk Broda, Tor.
1941	Turk Broda, Tor.	Frank Brimsek, Bos. (tie)
		Johnny Mowers, Det. (tie)
1940	Dave Kerr, NYR	Frank Brimsek, Bos.
1939	Frank Brimsek, Bos.	Dave Kerr, NYR
1938	Tiny Thompson, Bos.	Dave Kerr, NYR
1937	Normie Smith, Det.	Dave Kerr, NYR
1936	Tiny Thompson, Bos.	Mike Karakas, Chi.
1935	Lorne Chabot, Chi.	Alex Connell, Mtl.M
1934	Charlie Gardiner, Chi.	Wilf Cude, Det.
1933	Tiny Thompson, Bos.	John Ross Roach, Det.
1932	Charlie Gardiner, Chi.	Alex Connell, Det.
1931	Roy Worters, NYA	Charlie Gardiner, Chi.
1930	Tiny Thompson, Bos.	Charlie Gardiner, Chi.
1929	George Hainsworth, Mtl.	Tiny Thompson, Bos.
1928	George Hainsworth, Mtl.	Alex Connell, Ott.
1927	George Hainsworth, Mtl.	Clint Benedict, Mtl.M

CALDER MEMORIAL TROPHY

	Winner	Runner-up
2015	Aaron Ekblad, Fla.	Mark Stone, Ott.
2014	Nathan MacKinnon, Col.	Ondrej Palat, T.B.
2013	Jonathan Huberdeau, Fla.	Brendan Gallagher, Mtl.
2012	Gabriel Landeskog, Col.	Ryan Nugent-Hopkins, Edm.
2011	Jeff Skinner, Car.	Logan Couture, S.J.
2010	Tyler Myers, Buf.	Jimmy Howard, Det.
2009	Steve Mason, CBJ	Bobby Ryan, Ana.
2008	Patrick Kane, Chi.	Nicklas Backstrom, Wsh.
2007	Evgeni Malkin, Pit.	Paul Stastny, Col.
2006	Alex Ovechkin, Wsh.	Sidney Crosby, Pit.
2005	....	
2004	Andrew Raycroft, Bos.	Michael Ryder, Mtl.
2003	Barret Jackman, St.L.	Henrik Zetterberg, Det.
2002	Dany Heatley, Atl.	Ilya Kovalchuk, Atl.
2001	Evgeni Nabokov, S.J.	Brad Richards, T.B.
2000	Scott Gomez, N.J.	Brad Stuart, S.J.
1999	Chris Drury, Col.	Marian Hossa, Ott.
1998	Sergei Samsonov, Bos.	Mattias Ohlund, Van.
1997	Bryan Berard, NYI	Jarome Iginla, Cgy.
1996	Daniel Alfredsson, Ott.	Eric Daze, Chi.
1995	Peter Forsberg, Que.	Jim Carey, Wsh.
1994	Martin Brodeur, N.J.	Jason Arnott, Edm.
1993	Teemu Selanne, Wpg.	Joe Juneau, Bos.
1992	Pavel Bure, Van.	Nicklas Lidstrom, Det
1991	Ed Belfour, Chi.	Sergei Fedorov, Det.
1990	Sergei Makarov, Cgy.	Mike Modano, Min.
1989	Brian Leetch, NYR	Trevor Linden, Van.
1988	Joe Nieuwendyk, Cgy.	Ray Sheppard, Buf.
1987	Luc Robitaille, L.A.	Ron Hextall, Phi.
1986	Gary Suter, Cgy.	Wendel Clark, Tor.
1985	Mario Lemieux, Pit.	Chris Chelios, Mtl.
1984	Tom Barrasso, Buf.	Steve Yzerman, Det.
1983	Steve Larmer, Chi.	Phil Housley, Buf.
1982	Dale Hawerchuk, Wpg.	Barry Pederson, Bos.
1981	Peter Stastny, Que.	Larry Murphy, L.A.
1980	Raymond Bourque, Bos.	Mike Foligno, Det.
1979	Bobby Smith, Min	Ryan Walter, Wsh.
1978	Mike Bossy, NYI	Barry Beck, Col.
1977	Willi Plett, Atl.	Don Murdoch, NYR
1976	Bryan Trottier, NYI	Glenn Resch, NYI
1975	Eric Vail, Atl.	Pierre Larouche, Pit.
1974	Denis Potvin, NYI	Tom Lysiak, Atl.
1973	Steve Vickers, NYR	Bill Barber, Phi.
1972	Ken Dryden, Mtl.	Rick Martin, Buf.
1971	Gilbert Perreault, Buf.	Jude Drouin, Min.
1970	Tony Esposito, Chi.	Bill Fairbairn, NYR
1969	Danny Grant, Min.	Norm Ferguson, Oak.
1968	Derek Sanderson, Bos.	Jacques Lemaire, Mtl.
1967	Bobby Orr, Bos.	Ed Van Impe, Chi.
1966	Brit Selby, Tor.	Bert Marshall, Det.
1965	Roger Crozier, Det.	Ron Ellis, Tor.
1964	Jacques Laperriere, Mtl.	John Ferguson, Mtl.
1963	Kent Douglas, Tor.	Doug Barkley, Det.
1962	Bobby Rousseau, Mtl.	Cliff Pennington, Bos.
1961	Dave Keon, Tor.	Bob Nevin, Tor.
1960	Bill Hay, Chi.	Murray Oliver, Det.
1959	Ralph Backstrom, Mtl.	Carl Brewer, Tor.
1958	Frank Mahovlich, Tor.	Bobby Hull, Chi.
1957	Larry Regan, Bos.	Ed Chadwick, Tor.
1956	Glenn Hall, Det.	Andy Hebenton, NYR
1955	Ed Litzenberger, Chi.	Don McKenney, Bos.
1954	Camille Henry, NYR	Dutch Reibel, Det.
1953	Gump Worsley, NYR	Gord Hannigan, Tor.
1952	Bernie Geoffrion, Mtl.	Hy Buller, NYR
1951	Terry Sawchuk, Det.	Al Rollins, Tor.
1950	Jack Gelineau, Bos.	Phil Maloney, Bos.
1949	Pentti Lund, NYR	Allan Stanley, NYR
1948	Jim McFadden, Det.	Pete Babando, Bos.
1947	Howie Meeker, Tor.	Jim Conacher, Det.
1946	Edgar Laprade, NYR	George Gee, Chi.
1945	Frank McCool, Tor.	Ken Smith, Bos.
1944	Gus Bodnar, Tor.	Bill Durnan, Mtl.
1943	Gaye Stewart, Tor.	Glen Harmon, Mtl.
1942	Grant Warwick, NYR	Buddy O'Connor, Mtl.
1941	John Quilty, Mtl.	Johnny Mowers, Det.
1940	Kilby MacDonald, NYR	Wally Stanowski, Tor.
1939	Frank Brimsek, Bos.	Roy Conacher, Bos.
1938	Cully Dahlstrom, Chi.	Murph Chamberlain, Tor.
1937	Syl Apps, Tor.	Gordie Drillon, Tor.
1936	Mike Karakas, Chi.	Bucko McDonald, Det.
1935	Sweeney Schriner, NYA	Bert Connelly, NYR
1934	Russ Blinco, Mtl.M.	none
1933	Carl Voss, Det.	none

E.J. MCGUIRE AWARD OF EXCELLANCE

	Winner
2015	Travis Konecny

NHL LIFETIME ACHIEVEMENT AWARD

	Winner
2015	not awarded
2014	not awarded
2013	not awarded
2012	not awarded
2011	not awarded
2010	not awarded
2009	Jean Beliveau
2008	Gordie Howe

JAMES NORRIS MEMORIAL TROPHY

	Winner	Runner-up
2015	Erik Karlsson, Ott.	Drew Doughty, L.A.
2014	Duncan Keith, Chi.	Zdeno Chara, Bos.
2013	P.K. Subban, Mtl.	Ryan Suter, Min.
2012	Erik Karlsson, Ott.	Shea Weber, Nsh.
2011	Nicklas Lidstrom, Det.	Shea Weber, Nsh.
2010	Duncan Keith, Chi.	Mike Green, Wsh.
2009	Zdeno Chara, Bos.	Mike Green, Wsh.
2008	Nicklas Lidstrom, Det.	Dion Phaneuf, Cgy.
2007	Nicklas Lidstrom, Det.	Scott Niedermayer, Ana.
2006	Nicklas Lidstrom, Det.	Scott Niedermayer, Ana.
2005	....	
2004	Scott Niedermayer, N.J.	Zdeno Chara, Ott.
2003	Nicklas Lidstrom, Det.	Al MacInnis, St.L.
2002	Nicklas Lidstrom, Det.	Chris Chelios, Det.
2001	Nicklas Lidstrom, Det.	Raymond Bourque, Col.
2000	Chris Pronger, St.L.	Nicklas Lidstrom, Det.
1999	Al MacInnis, St.L.	Nicklas Lidstrom, Det.
1998	Rob Blake, L.A.	Nicklas Lidstrom, Det.
1997	Brian Leetch, NYR	V. Konstantinov, Det.
1996	Chris Chelios, Chi.	Raymond Bourque, Bos.
1995	Paul Coffey, Det.	Chris Chelios, Chi.
1994	Raymond Bourque, Bos.	Scott Stevens, N.J.
1993	Chris Chelios, Chi.	Raymond Bourque, Bos.
1992	Brian Leetch, NYR	Raymond Bourque, Bos.
1991	Raymond Bourque, Bos.	Al MacInnis, Cgy.
1990	Raymond Bourque, Bos.	Al MacInnis, Cgy.
1989	Chris Chelios, Mtl	Paul Coffey, Pit.
1988	Raymond Bourque, Bos.	Scott Stevens, Wsh.
1987	Raymond Bourque, Bos.	Mark Howe, Phi.
1986	Paul Coffey, Edm.	Mark Howe, Phi.
1985	Paul Coffey, Edm.	Raymond Bourque, Bos.
1984	Rod Langway, Wsh.	Paul Coffey, Edm.
1983	Rod Langway, Wsh.	Mark Howe, Phi.
1982	Doug Wilson, Chi.	Raymond Bourque, Bos.
1981	Randy Carlyle, Pit.	Denis Potvin, NYI
1980	Larry Robinson, Mtl.	Borje Salming, Tor.
1979	Denis Potvin, NYI	Larry Robinson, Mtl.
1978	Denis Potvin, NYI	Brad Park, Bos.
1977	Larry Robinson, Mtl.	Borje Salming, Tor.
1976	Denis Potvin, NYI	Brad Park, NYR-Bos.
1975	Bobby Orr, Bos.	Denis Potvin, NYI
1974	Bobby Orr, Bos.	Brad Park, NYR
1973	Bobby Orr, Bos.	Guy Lapointe, Mtl.
1972	Bobby Orr, Bos.	Brad Park, NYR
1971	Bobby Orr, Bos.	Brad Park, NYR
1970	Bobby Orr, Bos.	Brad Park, NYR
1969	Bobby Orr, Bos.	Tim Horton, Tor.
1968	Bobby Orr, Bos.	J.C. Tremblay, Mtl
1967	Harry Howell, NYR	Pierre Pilote, Chi.
1966	Jacques Laperriere, Mtl.	Pierre Pilote, Chi.
1965	Pierre Pilote, Chi.	Jacques Laperriere, Mtl.
1964	Pierre Pilote, Chi.	Tim Horton, Tor.
1963	Pierre Pilote, Chi.	Carl Brewer, Tor.
1962	Doug Harvey, NYR	Pierre Pilote, Chi.
1961	Doug Harvey, Mtl.	Marcel Pronovost, Det.
1960	Doug Harvey, Mtl.	Allan Stanley, Tor.
1959	Tom Johnson, Mtl.	Bill Gadsby, NYR
1958	Doug Harvey, Mtl.	Bill Gadsby, NYR
1957	Doug Harvey, Mtl.	Red Kelly, Det.
1956	Doug Harvey, Mtl.	Bill Gadsby, NYR
1955	Doug Harvey, Mtl.	Red Kelly, Det.
1954	Red Kelly, Det.	Doug Harvey, Mtl.

JACK ADAMS AWARD

	Winner	Runner-up
2015	Bob Hartley, Cgy.	Alain Vigneault, NYR
2014	Patrick Roy, Col.	Mike Babcock, Det.
2013	Paul MacLean, Ott.	Joel Quenneville, Chi.
2012	Ken Hitchcock, St.L.	John Tortorella, NYR
2011	Dan Bylsma, Pit.	Alain Vigneault, Van.
2010	Dave Tippett, Phx.	Barry Trotz, Nsh.
2009	Claude Julien, Bos.	Andy Murray, St.L.
2008	Bruce Boudreau, Wsh.	Guy Carbonneau, Mtl.
2007	Alain Vigneault, Van.	Lindy Ruff, Buf.
2006	Lindy Ruff, Buf.	Peter Laviolette, Car.
2005	....	
2004	John Tortorella, T.B.	Ron Wilson, S.J.
2003	Jacques Lemaire, Min.	John Tortorella, T.B.
2002	Bob Francis, Phx.	Brian Sutter, Chi.
2001	Bill Barber, Phi.	Scotty Bowman, Det.
2000	Joel Quenneville, St.L.	Alain Vigneault, Mtl.
1999	Jacques Martin, Ott.	Pat Quinn, Tor.
1998	Pat Burns, Bos.	Larry Robinson, L.A.
1997	Ted Nolan, Buf.	Ken Hitchcock, Dal.
1996	Scotty Bowman, Det.	Doug MacLean, Fla.
1995	Marc Crawford, Que.	Scotty Bowman, Det.
1994	Jacques Lemaire, N.J.	Kevin Constantine, S.J.
1993	Pat Burns, Tor.	Brian Sutter, Bos.
1992	Pat Quinn, Van.	Roger Neilson, NYR
1991	Brian Sutter, St.L.	Tom Webster, L.A.
1990	Bob Murdoch, Wpg.	Mike Milbury, Bos.
1989	Pat Burns, Mtl.	Bob McCammon, Van.
1988	Jacques Demers, Det.	Terry Crisp, Cgy.
1987	Jacques Demers, Det.	Jack Evans, Hfd.
1986	Glen Sather, Edm.	Jacques Demers, St.L.
1985	Mike Keenan, Phi.	Barry Long, Wpg.
1984	Bryan Murray, Wsh.	Scotty Bowman, Buf.
1983	Orval Tessier, Chi.	
1982	Tom Watt, Wpg.	
1981	Red Berenson, St.L.	Bob Berry, L.A.
1980	Pat Quinn, Phi.	
1979	Al Arbour, NYI	Fred Shero, NYR
1978	Bobby Kromm, Det.	Don Cherry, Bos.
1977	Scotty Bowman, Mtl.	Tom McVie, Wsh.
1976	Don Cherry, Bos.	
1975	Bob Pulford, L.A.	
1974	Fred Shero, Phi.	

LESTER PATRICK TROPHY

	Winner	
2015	Bob Crocker	Jeremy Jacobs
2014	Bill Daly	Paul Holmgren
2013	Kevin Allen	
2012	Dick Patrick	Bob Chase-Wallestein
2011	Jeff Sauer	Tony Rossi
	Mark Johnson	Bob Pulford
2010	Jerry York	Jack Parker
	Cam Neely	Dave Andrews
2009	Mark Messier	Jim Devellano
	Mike Richter	
2008	Brian Burke	Phil Housley
	Ted Lindsay	Bob Naegele, Jr.
2007	Brian Leetch	Cammi Granato
	Stan Fischler	John Halligan
2006	Red Berenson	Marcel Dionne
	Reed Larson	Glen Sonmor
	Steve Yzerman	
2005	....	
2004	John Davidson	Mike Emrick
	Ray Miron	
2003	Raymond Bourque	Ron DeGregorio
	Willie O'Ree	
2002	Herb Brooks	Larry Pleau
	1960 U.S. Olympic Team	
2001	Gary Bettman	Scotty Bowman
	David Poile	
2000	Mario Lemieux	Craig Patrick
	Lou Vairo	
1999	Harry Sinden	
	1998 U.S. Olympic Women's Team	
1998	Neal Broten	Peter Karmanos
	John Mayasich	Max McNab
1997	Bill Cleary	* Seymour H. Knox III
	Pat LaFontaine	
1996	George Gund	Ken Morrow
	Milt Schmidt	
1995	Bob Fleming	Brian Mullen
	Joe Mullen	
1994	Wayne Gretzky	Robert Ridder
1993	*Frank Boucher	* Mervyn "Red" Dutton
	Bruce McNall	Gil Stein
1992	Al Arbour	Art Berglund
	Lou Lamoriello	
1991	Rod Gilbert	Mike Ilitch
1990	Len Ceglarski	
1989	Dan Kelly	Lou Nanne
	*Lynn Patrick	Bud Poile
1988	Keith Allen	Fred Cusick
	Bob Johnson	
1987	*Hobey Baker	Frank Mathers
1986	John MacInnes	Jack Riley
1985	Jack Butterfield	Arthur M. Wirtz
1984	*Arthur Howey Ross	John A. Ziegler, Jr.
1983	Bill Torrey	
1982	Emile P. Francis	
1981	Charles M. Schulz	
1980	Bobby Clarke	Frederick A. Shero
	Edward M. Snider	1980 U.S. Olympic Team
1979	Bobby Orr	
1978	Phil Esposito	Tom Fitzgerald
	William T. Tutt	William W. Wirtz
1977	Murray A. Armstrong	John P. Bucyk
	John Mariucci	
1976	George A. Leader	Stanley Mikita
	Bruce A. Norris	
1975	William L. Chadwick	Donald M. Clark
	Thomas N. Ivan	
1974	*Weston W. Adams, Sr.	* Charles L. Crovat
	Alex Delvecchio	Murray Murdoch
1973	Walter L. Bush, Jr.	
1972	Clarence S. Campbell	John A. "Snooks" Kelly
	*James D. Norris	Ralph "Cooney" Weiland
1971	William M. Jennings	* Terrance G. Sawchuk
	*John B. Sollenberger	
1970	*James C. V. Hendy	Edward W. Shore
1969	Robert M. Hull	* Edward J. Jeremiah
1968	*Walter A. Brown	* Gen. John R. Kilpatrick
	Thomas F. Lockhart	
1967	*Charles F. Adams	Gordon Howe
	*James Norris, Sr.	
1966	J.J. "Jack" Adams	
	* awarded posthumously	

NHL FOUNDATION PLAYER AWARD

	Winner	
2015	Brent Burns	San Jose
2014	Patrice Bergeron	Boston
2013	Henrik Zetterberg	Detroit
2012	Mike Fisher	Nashville
2011	Dustin Brown	Los Angeles
2010	Ryan Miller	Buffalo
2009	Rick Nash	Columbus
2008	Trevor Linden	Vancouver
	Vincent Lecavalier	Tampa Bay
2007	Joe Sakic	Colorado
2006	Marty Turco	Dallas
2004	Jarome Iginla	Calgary
2003	Darren McCarty	Detroit
2002	Ron Francis	Carolina
2001	Olaf Kolzig	Washington
2000	Adam Graves	NY Rangers
1999	Rob Ray	Buffalo
1998	Kelly Chase	St. Louis

KING CLANCY MEMORIAL TROPHY

	Winner	
2015	Henrik Zetterberg	Detroit
2014	Andrew Ference	Edmonton
2013	Patrice Bergeron	Boston
2012	Daniel Alfredsson	Ottawa
2011	Doug Weight	NY Islanders
2010	Shane Doan	Phoenix
2009	Ethan Moreau	Edmonton
2008	Vincent Lecavalier	Tampa Bay
2007	Saku Koivu	Montreal
2006	Olaf Kolzig	Washington
2005	....	
2004	Jarome Iginla	Calgary
2003	Brendan Shanahan	Detroit
2002	Ron Francis	Carolina
2001	Shjon Podein	Colorado
2000	Curtis Joseph	Toronto
1999	Rob Ray	Buffalo
1998	Kelly Chase	St. Louis
1997	Trevor Linden	Vancouver
1996	Kris King	Winnipeg
1995	Joe Nieuwendyk	Calgary
1994	Adam Graves	NY Rangers
1993	Dave Poulin	Boston
1992	Raymond Bourque	Boston
1991	Dave Taylor	Los Angeles
1990	Kevin Lowe	Edmonton
1989	Bryan Trottier	NY Islanders
1988	Lanny McDonald	Calgary

PRESIDENTS' TROPHY

	Winner	Runner-up
2015	New York Rangers	Montreal Canadiens
2014	Boston Bruins	Anaheim Ducks
2013	Chicago Blackhawks	Pittsburgh Penguins
2012	Vancouver Canucks	New York Rangers
2011	Vancouver Canucks	Washington Capitals
2010	Washington Capitals	San Jose Sharks
2009	San Jose Sharks	Boston Bruins
2008	Detroit Red Wings	San Jose Sharks
2007	Buffalo Sabres	Detroit Red Wings
2006	Detroit Red Wings	Ottawa Senators
2005	....	
2004	Detroit Red Wings	Tampa Bay Lightning
2003	Ottawa Senators	Dallas Stars
2002	Detroit Red Wings	Boston Bruins
2001	Colorado Avalanche	Detroit Red Wings
2000	St. Louis Blues	Detroit Red Wings
1999	Dallas Stars	New Jersey Devils
1998	Dallas Stars	New Jersey Devils
1997	Colorado Avalanche	Dallas Stars
1996	Detroit Red Wings	Colorado Avalanche
1995	Detroit Red Wings	Quebec Nordiques
1994	New York Rangers	New Jersey Devils
1993	Pittsburgh Penguins	Boston Bruins
1992	New York Rangers	Washington Capitals
1991	Chicago Blackhawks	St. Louis Blues
1990	Boston Bruins	Calgary Flames
1989	Calgary Flames	Montreal Canadiens
1988	Calgary Flames	Montreal Canadiens
1987	Edmonton Oilers	Philadelphia Flyers
1986	Edmonton Oilers	Philadelphia Flyers

TED LINDSAY AWARD

	Winner	
2015	Carey Price	Montreal
2014	Sidney Crosby	Pittsburgh
2013	Sidney Crosby	Pittsburgh
2012	Evgeni Malkin	Pittsburgh
2011	Daniel Sedin	Vancouver
2010	Alex Ovechkin	Washington
2009	Alex Ovechkin	Washington
2008	Alex Ovechkin	Washington
2007	Sidney Crosby	Pittsburgh
2006	Jaromir Jagr	NY Rangers
2005	....	
2004	Martin St. Louis	Tampa Bay
2003	Markus Naslund	Vancouver
2002	Jarome Iginla	Calgary
2001	Joe Sakic	Colorado
2000	Jaromir Jagr	Pittsburgh
1999	Jaromir Jagr	Pittsburgh
1998	Dominik Hasek	Buffalo
1997	Dominik Hasek	Buffalo
1996	Mario Lemieux	Pittsburgh
1995	Eric Lindros	Philadelphia
1994	Sergei Fedorov	Detroit
1993	Mario Lemieux	Pittsburgh
1992	Mark Messier	NY Rangers
1991	Brett Hull	St. Louis
1990	Mark Messier	Edmonton
1989	Steve Yzerman	Detroit
1988	Mario Lemieux	Pittsburgh
1987	Wayne Gretzky	Edmonton
1986	Mario Lemieux	Pittsburgh
1985	Wayne Gretzky	Edmonton
1984	Wayne Gretzky	Edmonton
1983	Wayne Gretzky	Edmonton
1982	Wayne Gretzky	Edmonton
1981	Mike Liut	St. Louis
1980	Marcel Dionne	Los Angeles
1979	Marcel Dionne	Los Angeles
1978	Guy Lafleur	Montreal
1977	Guy Lafleur	Montreal
1976	Guy Lafleur	Montreal
1975	Bobby Orr	Boston
1974	Phil Esposito	Boston
1973	Bobby Clarke	Philadelphia
1972	Jean Ratelle	NY Rangers
1971	Phil Esposito	Boston

NHL Draft

Draft Summary

Following is a summary of the players drafted from the Ontario Hockey League (OHL), Quebec Major Junior Hockey League (QMJHL), Western Hockey League (WHL), United States colleges, United States high schools, European leagues and other North American leagues since 1969. "Other" may include Canadian and U.S. Jr. A and Jr. B, minor professional leagues (AHL, IHL), midget and other teams playing in leagues not listed above.

Year	Total Picks	OHL Picks	%	QMJHL Picks	%	WHL Picks	%	College Picks	%	Hi School Picks	%	Int'l Picks	%	Other Picks	%
Total	10599	2229	21.0	1116	10.5	1931	18.2	1138	10.8	851	8.0	2129	20.1	1205	11.4
2015	211	31	14.7	30	14.2	34	16.1	9	4.3	12	5.7	55	26.0	40	19.0
2014	210	41	19.5	17	8.1	37	17.7	5	2.4	13	6.2	51	24.3	46	21.9
2013	211	37	17.5	31	14.7	33	15.6	6	2.8	15	7.1	46	21.8	43	20.4
2012	211	48	22.7	19	9.0	32	15.2	9	4.3	19	9.0	43	20.4	41	19.4
2011	210	46	21.9	22	10.4	33	15.7	11	5.2	18	8.6	48	22.9	32	15.2
2010	210	42	20.0	22	10.4	43	20.5	9	4.2	22	10.5	39	18.6	33	15.7
2009	210	45	21.4	23	11.0	31	14.8	7	3.3	19	9.0	41	19.5	44	21.0
2008	211	46	21.8	27	12.8	37	17.5	9	4.2	15	7.1	39	18.5	38	18.0
2007	211	35	16.6	25	11.8	37	17.5	8	3.8	14	6.6	36	17.0	56	56.5
2006	213	29	13.6	25	11.7	24	11.2	18	8.4	19	8.9	63	29.5	35	16.4
2005	230	43	18.7	23	10.0	43	18.7	13	5.6	18	7.8	50	21.7	40	17.4
2004	291	42	14.4	27	9.3	44	15.1	28	9.6	18	6.2	88	30.2	44	15.1
2003	292	44	15.1	38	13.0	41	14.0	23	7.9	10	3.4	93	31.8	43	14.7
2002	290	35	12.1	23	7.9	43	14.8	41	14.1	6	2.1	110	37.9	32	11.0
2001	289	41	14.2	26	9.0	45	15.6	24	8.3	8	2.8	119	41.2	26	9.0
2000	293	39	13.3	21	7.2	41	14.0	35	11.9	7	2.4	123	42.0	27	9.2
1999	272	52	19.1	20	7.4	40	14.7	36	13.2	9	3.3	94	34.6	21	7.7
1998	258	50	19.4	41	15.9	44	17.1	27	10.5	7	2.7	75	29.1	14	5.4
1997	246	52	21.1	19	7.7	63	25.6	26	10.6	4	1.6	63	25.6	19	7.7
1996	241	51	21.2	31	12.9	54	22.4	25	10.4	6	2.5	58	24.1	16	6.6
1995	234	54	23.1	35	15.0	55	23.5	5	2.1	2	0.9	69	29.5	14	6.0
1994	286	45	15.7	28	9.8	66	23.1	6	2.1	28	9.8	80	28.0	33	11.5
1993	286	60	21.0	23	8.0	44	15.4	17	5.9	33	11.5	78	27.3	31	10.8
1992	264	57	21.6	22	8.3	45	17.0	9	3.4	25	9.5	84	31.8	22	8.3
1991	264	43	16.3	25	9.5	40	15.2	43	16.3	37	14.0	55	20.8	21	8.0
1990	250	39	15.6	14	5.6	33	13.2	38	15.2	57	22.8	53	21.2	16	6.4
1989	252	39	15.5	16	6.3	44	17.5	48	19.0	47	18.7	38	15.1	20	7.9
1988	252	32	12.7	22	8.7	30	11.9	48	19.0	56	22.2	39	15.5	25	9.9
1987	252	32	12.7	17	6.7	36	14.3	40	15.9	69	27.4	38	15.1	20	7.9
1986	252	66	26.2	22	8.7	32	12.7	22	8.7	40	15.9	28	11.1	42	16.7
1985	252	59	23.4	15	6.0	48	19.0	20	7.9	48	19.0	31	12.3	31	12.3
1984	250	55	22.0	16	6.4	37	14.8	22	8.8	44	17.6	40	16.0	36	14.4
1983	242	57	23.6	24	9.9	41	16.9	14	5.8	35	14.5	34	14.0	37	15.3
1982	252	60	23.8	17	6.7	55	21.8	20	7.9	47	18.7	35	13.9	18	7.1
1981	211	59	28.0	28	13.3	37	17.5	21	10.0	17	8.1	32	15.2	17	8.1
1980	210	73	34.8	24	11.4	41	19.5	42	20.0	7	3.3	13	6.2	10	4.8
1979	126	48	38.1	19	15.1	37	29.4	15	11.9	-	-	6	4.8	1	0.8
1978	234	59	25.2	22	9.4	48	20.5	73	31.2	-	-	16	6.8	16	6.8
1977	185	42	22.7	40	21.6	44	23.8	49	26.5	-	-	5	2.7	5	2.7
1976	135	47	34.8	18	13.3	33	24.4	26	19.3	-	-	8	5.9	3	2.2
1975	217	55	25.3	28	12.9	57	26.3	59	27.2	-	-	6	2.8	12	5.5
1974	247	69	27.9	40	16.2	66	26.7	41	16.6	-	-	6	2.4	25	10.1
1973	168	56	33.3	24	14.3	49	29.2	25	14.9	-	-	-	-	14	8.3
1972	152	46	30.3	30	19.7	44	28.9	21	13.8	-	-	-	-	11	7.2
1971	117	41	35.0	13	11.1	28	23.9	22	18.8	-	-	-	-	13	11.1
1970	115	51	44.3	13	11.3	22	19.1	16	13.9	-	-	-	-	13	11.3
1969	84	36	42.9	11	13.1	20	23.8	7	8.3	-	-	1	1.2	9	10.7

Total Players Drafted (1969-2015): 10,599

Connor McDavid signs autographs at the Top Prospects Clinic as part of the 2015 NHL Draft Weekend at the Panthers Ice Den in Coral Gables, Florida. One day later, the Edmonton Oilers made him the number-one selection.

History

Year	Location	Date	# Drafted
2015	BT&T Center, Florida	June 26-27	211
2014	Wells Fargo Center, Philadelphia	June 27-28	210
2013	Prudential Center, New Jersey	June 30	211
2012	CONSOL Energy Center, Pittsburgh	June 22-23	211
2011	Xcel Energy Center, Minnesota	June 24-25	210
2010	STAPLES Center, Los Angeles	June 25-26	210
2009	Bell Centre, Montreal	June 26-27	210
2008	Scotiabank Place, Ottawa	June 20-21	211
2007	Nationwide Arena, Columbus	June 22-23	211
2006	General Motors Place, Vancouver	June 24	213
2005	Sheraton Hotel and Towers, Ottawa	July 30	230
2004	RBC Center, Carolina	June 26-27	291
2003	Gaylord Entertainment Center, Nashville	June 21-22	292
2002	Air Canada Centre, Toronto	June 22-23	290
2001	National Car Rental Center, Florida	June 23-24	289
2000	Saddledome, Calgary	June 24-25	293
1999	FleetCenter, Boston	June 26	272
1998	Marine Midland Arena, Buffalo	June 27	258
1997	Civic Arena, Pittsburgh	June 21	246
1996	Kiel Center, St. Louis	June 22	241
1995	Edmonton Coliseum	July 8	234
1994	Hartford Civic Center	June 28-29	286
1993	Le Colisée, Quebec	June 26	286
1992	Montreal Forum	June 20	264
1991	Memorial Auditorium, Buffalo	June 22	264
1990	B.C. Place, Vancouver	June 16	250
1989	Met Sports Center, Minnesota	June 17	252
1988	Montreal Forum	June 11	252
1987	Joe Louis Arena, Detroit	June 13	252
1986	Montreal Forum	June 21	252
1985	Toronto Convention Centre	June 15	252
1984	Montreal Forum	June 9	250
1983	Montreal Forum	June 8	242
1982	Montreal Forum	June 9	252
1981	Montreal Forum	June 10	211
1980	Montreal Forum	June 11	210
1979	Queen Elizabeth Hotel, Montreal	August 9	126
1978	Queen Elizabeth Hotel, Montreal	June 15	234
1963–1977	Montreal	—	1542

First Selections

Year	Player	Pos	Team	Drafted From	Age
2015	Connor McDavid	C	Edmonton	Erie Otters	18.5
2014	Aaron Ekblad	D	Florida	Barrie Colts	18.4
2013	Nathan MacKinnon	C	Colorado	Halifax Mooseheads	17.10
2012	Nail Yakupov	RW	Edmonton	Sarnia Sting	18.8
2011	Ryan Nugent-Hopkins	C	Edmonton	Red Deer Rebels	18.2
2010	Taylor Hall	LW	Edmonton	Windsor Spitfires	18.7
2009	John Tavares	C	NY Islanders	London Knights	18.9
2008	Steven Stamkos	C	Tampa Bay	Sarnia Sting	18.4
2007	Patrick Kane	RW	Chicago	London Knights	18.7
2006	Erik Johnson	D	St. Louis	U.S. National U-18	18.3
2005	Sidney Crosby	C	Pittsburgh	Rimouski Oceanic	17.11
2004	Alex Ovechkin	LW	Washington	Dynamo Moscow (Russia)	18.9
2003	Marc-Andre Fleury	G	Pittsburgh	Cape Breton Screaming Eagles	18.0
2002	Rick Nash	LW	Columbus	London Knights	18.0
2001	Ilya Kovalchuk	LW	Atlanta	Spartak (Russia)	18.2
2000	Rick DiPietro	G	NY Islanders	Boston University Terriers	18.9
1999	Patrik Stefan	C	Atlanta	Long Beach Ice Dogs (IHL)	18.9
1998	Vincent Lecavalier	C	Tampa Bay	Rimouski Oceanic	18.2
1997	Joe Thornton	C	Boston	Sault Ste. Marie Greyhounds	17.11
1996	Chris Phillips	D	Ottawa	Prince Albert Raiders	18.3
1995	Bryan Berard	D	Ottawa	Detroit Jr. Red Wings	18.4
1994	Ed Jovanovski	D	Florida	Windsor Spitfires	18.0
1993	Alexandre Daigle	C	Ottawa	Victoriaville Tigres	18.5
1992	Roman Hamrlik	D	Tampa Bay	ZPS Zlin (Czech.)	18.2
1991	Eric Lindros	C	Quebec	Oshawa Generals	18.3
1990	Owen Nolan	RW	Quebec	Cornwall Royals	18.4
1989	Mats Sundin	RW	Quebec	Nacka (Sweden)	18.4
1988	Mike Modano	C	Minnesota	Prince Albert Raiders	18.0
1987	Pierre Turgeon	C	Buffalo	Granby Bisons	17.10
1986	Joe Murphy	C	Detroit	Michigan State Spartans	18.8
1985	Wendel Clark	LW/D	Toronto	Saskatoon Blades	18.7
1984	Mario Lemieux	C	Pittsburgh	Laval Voisins	18.8
1983	Brian Lawton	C	Minnesota	Mount St. Charles HS	18.11
1982	Gord Kluzak	D	Boston	Nanaimo Islanders	18.3
1981	Dale Hawerchuk	C	Winnipeg	Cornwall Royals	18.2
1980	Doug Wickenheiser	C	Montreal	Regina Pats	19.2
1979	Rob Ramage	D	Colorado	London Knights	20.5
1978	Bobby Smith	C	Minnesota	Ottawa 67's	20.4
1977	Dale McCourt	C	Detroit	St. Catharines Fincups	20.4
1976	Rick Green	D	Washington	London Knights	20.3
1975	Mel Bridgman	C	Philadelphia	Victoria Cougars	20.1
1974	Greg Joly	D	Washington	Regina Pats	20.0
1973	Denis Potvin	D	NY Islanders	Ottawa 67's	19.7
1972	Billy Harris	RW	NY Islanders	Toronto Marlboros	20.4
1971	Guy Lafleur	RW	Montreal	Quebec Remparts	19.9
1970	Gilbert Perreault	C	Buffalo	Montreal Jr. Canadiens	19.7
1969	Rejean Houle	LW	Montreal	Montreal Jr. Canadiens	19.8
1968	Michel Plasse	G	Montreal	Drummondville Rangers	20.0
1967	Rick Pagnutti	D	Los Angeles	Garson Native Sons	20.6
1966	Barry Gibbs	D	Boston	Estevan Bruins	17.7
1965	Andre Veilleux	RW	NY Rangers	Montreal Ranger Jr. B	17.5
1964	Claude Gauthier	RW	Detroit	Comite des jeunes (Rosemont)	16.9
1963	Garry Monahan	LW	Montreal	St. Michael's Juveniles	16.7

Ontario Hockey League Draft Selections by Club

Total	Club	'15	'14	'13	'12	'11	'10	'09	'08	'07	'06	'05	'04	'03	'02	'01	'00	'99	'98	'97	'96	'95	'94	'93	'92	'91	'90	'89	'88	'87	'86	'85	'69 to '84
38	Barrie	4	3	–	1	2	2	2	2	–	–	1	1	1	3	6	3	4	2	–	–	–	–	–	–	–	–	–	–	–	–	–	–
74	Belleville	–	1	2	4	1	1	1	3	4	2	2	–	–	2	3	1	5	2	5	–	3	3	–	4	1	2	4	–	2	5	4	–
35	Erie	3	1	1	2	–	2	3	1	5	–	2	2	–	2	2	3	2	1	3	–	–	–	–	–	–	–	–	–	–	–	–	–
88	Guelph	–	1	5	4	2	–	5	3	1	1	2	2	4	1	3	5	1	6	5	7	2	2	–	4	–	2	8	3	6			
109	Kingston	1	3	2	–	2	2	2	–	4	2	–	1	1	2	–	4	1	4	4	3	2	5	3	2	2	–	1	1	4	3	48	
154	Kitchener	–	2	2	3	3	1	1	2	4	–	4	2	1	4	1	1	–	5	3	2	4	2	4	1	1	3	5	7	1	2	3	6 75
165	London	2	2	6	6	2	2	1	3	1	3	1	3	6	4	2	2	1	4	8	1	4	1	1	4	3	1	3	3	6	2	3	1 74
32	Mississauga/St. Mike's	–	–	1	1	3	3	4	4	–	–	–	–	4	5	1	5	1	–														
27	Niagara/Mississauga	2	4	1	1	3	3	–	1	3	1	3	2	–	2	–																	
40	North Bay/Brampton	1	2	1	1	–	–	2	2	3	–	4	4	2	4	3	3	6	2	–													
169	Oshawa	3	2	2	2	5	2	3	2	2	2	–	3	3	3	1	2	3	4	3	1	10	1	4	4	4	2	4	2	3	6	6	75
148	Ottawa	2	2	1	1	2	4	1	2	1	1	3	2	–	3	2	6	2	5	2	1	1	4	6	5	5	–	1	2	3	3	73	
50	Owen Sound	2	1	3	5	3	4	3	1	1	2	1	1	1	–	1	2	3	2	3	4	2	1	1	–								
177	Peterborough	2	2	–	2	3	2	2	2	1	1	2	5	5	1	2	1	4	1	5	4	5	2	4	4	3	4	2	2	5	2	9	88
76	Plymouth	–	5	1	3	4	3	2	2	3	2	3	3	3	3	3	6	2	2	4	3	6	2	7	2	2	–						
83	Saginaw/N. Bay Cents	1	1	3	3	4	1	3	3	–	2	3	1	2	2	3	2	2	–	1	1	2	7	2	5	2	4	1	3	3	3	3	–
42	Sarnia	2	2	–	2	1	1	–	4	1	1	3	–	5	2	1	3	1	3	2	7	1	–										
130	Sault Ste. Marie	4	4	3	3	4	2	1	2	3	–	1	3	1	1	1	1	4	1	4	3	4	3	1	7	5	47						
120	Sudbury	–	2	–	3	1	2	2	1	2	4	–	1	1	2	–	5	5	3	1	2	2	10	2	8	2	1	–	1	3	5	47	
100	Windsor	–	3	1	4	1	4	5	4	2	2	3	2	2	2	2	2	1	5	1	4	3	–	3	–	1	2	5	–	7	3	24	

Clubs no longer operating

Total	Club	'15	'14	'13	'12	'11	'10	'09	'08	'07	'06	'05	'04	'03	'02	'01	'00	'99	'98	'97	'96	'95	'94	'93	'92	'91	'90	'89	'88	'87	'86	'85	'69 to '84
27	Brantford	–	–	–	–	–	–	–	–	–	–	–	–	–	–	–	–	–	–	–	–	–	–	–	–	–	–	–	–	–	–	–	27
37	Cornwall	–	–	–	–	–	–	–	–	–	–	–	–	–	–	–	–	–	–	–	–	5	3	3	2	3	3	2	1	14			
62	Hamilton	–	–	–	–	–	–	–	–	–	–	–	–	–	–	–	–	–	–	–	–	–	–	2	–	4	4	6	3	43			
20	Montreal	–	–	–	–	–	–	–	–	–	–	–	–	–	–	–	–	–	–	–	–	–	–	–	–	–	–	–	–	20			
5	Newmarket	–	–	–	–	–	–	–	–	–	–	–	–	–	–	–	–	–	–	–	–	2	3	–									
72	Niagara Falls	–	–	–	–	–	–	–	–	–	–	–	–	–	–	–	6	2	3	4	4	4	4	–	41								
52	St. Catharines	–	–	–	–	–	–	–	–	–	–	–	–	–	–	–	–	–	–	–	–	–	–	–	–	–	–	52					
97	Toronto	–	–	–	–	–	–	–	–	–	–	–	–	–	–	–	–	–	–	–	–	–	–	2	2	1	4	3	85				

Quebec Major Junior Hockey League Draft Selections by Club

Total	Club	'15	'14	'13	'12	'11	'10	'09	'08	'07	'06	'05	'04	'03	'02	'01	'00	'99	'98	'97	'96	'95	'94	'93	'92	'91	'90	'89	'88	'87	'86	'85	'69 to '84
12	Acadie-Bathurst	1	–	–	1	–	–	–	–	–	–	–	–	2	–	3	2	–	–														
29	Baie-Comeau	1	1	4	1	1	–	1	2	1	3	–	3	2	1	3	2	–	3														
14	Blainville-Boisbriand[1]	1	1	2	1	1	1	1	2	4	–																						
23	Cape Breton	1	3	1	1	1	1	–	1	–	3	2	2	1	1	–	3																
30	Charlottetown[2]	2	1	3	–	1	1	2	2	–	2	8	1	3	1	1	2	–															
58	Chicoutimi	1	–	1	1	1	–	3	–	4	–	1	3	1	1	–	1	2	–	2	3	1	1	–	1	1	2	1	3	11			
60	Drummondville	1	–	–	2	–	3	–	–	2	2	1	1	–	1	1	–	2	2	3	4	1	2	–	4	1	4	2	2	15			
85	Gatineau/Hull	2	2	2	1	1	3	–	1	1	2	–	4	4	5	2	–	4	3	–	3	3	1	3	3	3	3	2	2	3	4	–	18
42	Halifax	1	1	4	1	2	3	–	2	3	1	3	6	–	3	2	–	3	2	3	1	3	–										
26	Moncton	1	1	–	1	–	2	2	1	1	3	1	2	3	2	–	2	2	1	–													
34	Quebec	2	–	3	3	–	1	1	3	2	2	2	1	3	1	3	–	3	4	–													
39	Rimouski	1	–	4	2	–	2	2	3	–	4	–	4	2	2	5	–																
26	Rouyn-Noranda	2	2	2	1	–	1	1	2	1	3	–	2	–	4	1	3	–															
21	Saint John	7	1	–	5	2	2	1	2	1	–																						
90	Shawinigan	2	–	1	2	3	1	6	–	1	1	3	2	2	1	1	3	1	4	2	1	1	3	4	2	3	–	40					
83	Sherbrooke[3]	2	1	–	–	2	1	2	3	2	5	2	1	–	3	–	–	5	1	–	4	2	3	–	44								
33	Val-d'Or	1	2	2	1	3	1	–	2	–	–	2	1	1	–	1	2	2	3	–	2	4	2	1	–								
43	Victoriaville	1	1	2	1	3	–	1	1	1	–	–	3	1	3	2	1	2	3	1	1	6	2	–	1	–	4	–	–				

Former club names: [1] –Montreal / St. John's, [2] –PEI / Montreal Rocket, [3] –Lewiston / Sherbrooke Castors/Beavers.

Clubs no longer operating

Total	Club	'15	'14	'13	'12	'11	'10	'09	'08	'07	'06	'05	'04	'03	'02	'01	'00	'99	'98	'97	'96	'95	'94	'93	'92	'91	'90	'89	'88	'87	'86	'85	'69 to '84
21	Beauport	–	–	–	–	–	–	–	–	–	–	–	–	–	–	–	3	3	7	3	1	3	1	–	–	–	–	–	–				
45	Cornwall	–	–	–	–	–	–	–	–	–	–	–	–	–	–	–	–	–	–	–	–	–	–	–	–	–	–	–	–	–	45		
30	Granby	–	–	–	–	–	–	–	–	–	–	–	–	–	–	1	3	2	5	1	–	2	–	2	–	4	2	2	3				
54	Laval	–	–	–	–	–	–	–	–	–	–	–	3	1	2	4	5	2	1	4	3	3	1	3	5	–	17						
12	Longueuil	–	–	–	–	–	–	–	–	–	–	–	–	–	–	–	–	–	–	3	–	2	1	2	1	2							
32	Montreal Jrs.	–	–	–	–	–	–	–	–	–	–	–	–	–	–	–	–	–	–	–	–	–	–	–	–	–	–	–	32				
47	Quebec pre '85	–	–	–	–	–	–	–	–	–	–	–	–	–	–	–	–	–	–	–	–	–	–	–	–	–	–	3	44				
15	St. Hyacinthe	–	–	–	–	–	–	–	–	–	–	–	4	–	4	1	2	1	3	–													
16	St. Jean	–	–	–	–	–	–	–	–	–	–	–	–	1	1	2	1	3	–	1	3	–	1	1	2								
2	St. Jerome	–	–	–	–	–	–	–	–	–	–	–	–	–	–	–	–	–	–	–	–	–	–	–	–	–	–	2					
28	Sorel	–	–	–	–	–	–	–	–	–	–	–	–	–	–	–	–	–	–	–	–	–	–	–	–	–	–	–	28				
47	Trois Rivieres	–	–	–	–	–	–	–	–	–	–	–	–	–	–	–	–	–	–	–	–	1	2	1	3	3	1	–	3	33			
27	Verdun	–	–	–	–	–	–	–	–	–	–	–	–	–	–	–	–	–	3	–	–	1	3	–	3	–	17						

2015 NHL Draft Order of Selection

The first 14 picks of the 2015 Draft were determined by the NHL's annual Draft Drawing, a weighted lottery system used to determine the order of selection.

The 14 teams that did not qualify for the 2015 Stanley Cup Playoffs, or clubs that acquired those clubs' 2015 first-round draft picks, participated in the drawing.

No club can move down more than one position as a result of the Draft Drawing. For 2015, the Edmonton Oilers won the right to the first overall pick, moving up from third overall.

(Note that transferred draft choices are indicated as "L.A. – Bos." with the team that selected the player listed at right.)

In the first round of the 2015 Draft, the order of selection was as follows:

a) The winner of the Draft Drawing followed by the remaining non-playoff teams, in inverse order of points. (Note that the original holder of each selection is listed followed by the club that acquired and used that selection in the first round of the 2015 Draft.)

1. Edmonton
2. Buffalo
3. Arizona
4. Toronto
5. Carolina
6. New Jersey
7. Philadelphia
8. Columbus
9. San Jose
10. Colorado
11. Florida
12. Dallas
13. L.A. – Bos.
14. Boston

b) Clubs eliminated in the first two rounds of the 2015 Stanley Cup Playoffs, regular-season division winners excluded, in inverse order of points;

15. Cgy. – Bos.
16. Pit. – NYI
17. Winnipeg
18. Ottawa
19. Detroit
20. Minnesota
21. NYI – Ott.
22. Washington

c) Regular-season division winning clubs eliminated in the first two rounds of the 2015 Stanley Cup Playoffs, in inverse order of points;

23. Vancouver
24. Nsh. – Phi.
25. St.L. – Wpg.
26. Montreal

d) Clubs eliminated in the 2015 Conference Finals, in inverse order of points;

27. Anaheim
28. NYR – NYI

e) Loser of Stanley Cup Final

29. T.B. – CBJ

f) Stanley Cup champion

30. Chi. – Ari.

In the second and subsequent rounds Buffalo Sabres – the club with the fewest regular-season points – picked first. Arizona Coyotes – the club with the second fewest regular-season points – picked second.

Chicago selected Andrew Shaw (top) from the Owen Sound Attack of the OHL with their eighth pick in 2011. Shaw was selected 139th overall. Cedric Paquette was taken by Tampa Bay with the 101st pick in 2012 from Blainville-Boisbriand in the QMJHL.

Western Hockey League Draft Selections by Club

Total	Club	'15	'14	'13	'12	'11	'10	'09	'08	'07	'06	'05	'04	'03	'02	'01	'00	'99	'98	'97	'96	'95	'94	'93	'92	'91	'90	'89	'88	'87	'86	'85	'69 to '84
113	Brandon	2	3	2	1	1	2	2	2	1	1	2	–	3	4	2	–	–	4	5	2	6	5	2	1	1	1	–	3	3	1	2	49
50	Calgary	1	5	1	3	–	2	2	2	4	1	2	5	3	2	1	4	6	3	–	3	–	–	–	–	–	–	–	–	–	–	–	–
16	Edmonton	–	5	2	3	4	1	1	–	–	–	–	–	–	–	–	–	–	–	–	–	–	–	–	–	–	–	–	–	–	–	–	–
18	Everett	1	–	2	2	–	3	2	1	3	4	–	–	–	–	–	–	–	–	–	–	–	–	–	–	–	–	–	–	–	–	–	–
116	Kamloops	1	1	2	2	–	2	2	–	1	1	2	5	2	5	2	4	4	1	3	4	5	9	2	3	6	4	5	1	3	4	4	26
49	Kelowna	2	2	4	2	1	1	3	4	2	–	2	4	4	1	1	1	2	2	7	4	–	–	–	–	–	–	–	–	–	–	–	–
30	Kootenay[1]	–	4	1	–	1	3	1	–	1	1	3	2	1	3	2	1	2	–	4	–	–	–	–	–	–	–	–	–	–	–	–	–
95	Lethbridge	2	1	–	–	1	–	1	2	2	1	–	2	2	2	1	3	–	1	5	1	3	3	4	3	7	4	3	3	–	1	5	32
114	Medicine Hat	1	–	2	–	1	2	1	2	–	2	4	2	3	3	2	–	1	4	2	7	2	6	1	3	3	1	4	1	5	2	6	41
69	Moose Jaw	–	1	–	2	1	3	–	3	1	1	3	3	3	3	3	5	1	2	4	4	4	3	2	3	2	1	3	–	3	1	4	–
132	Portland	2	4	4	3	4	8	1	–	2	1	3	2	1	2	–	6	1	3	3	1	2	3	4	4	1	1	4	1	3	4	2	52
89	Prince Albert	2	2	1	1	2	–	1	–	–	–	2	4	2	1	4	2	3	3	5	3	4	3	5	2	6	4	3	3	1	6	6	8
35	Prince George	4	–	2	1	–	1	1	–	1	4	1	2	2	–	4	–	2	4	2	2	2	–	–	–	–	–	–	–	–	–	–	–
56	Red Deer	1	3	1	1	2	1	4	1	1	1	1	1	4	4	6	1	1	5	3	4	2	5	3	–	–	–	–	–	–	–	–	–
122	Regina	5	–	2	1	–	2	1	3	3	1	1	–	2	1	2	2	4	2	3	4	2	3	–	4	–	1	5	–	2	3	4	59
124	Saskatoon	–	2	–	3	4	4	3	3	3	–	4	1	–	–	4	1	4	2	2	2	2	4	2	3	2	2	3	4	4	5	1	50
103	Seattle	4	–	1	1	2	1	–	2	1	1	3	2	5	1	5	4	6	2	8	1	5	5	4	2	3	6	2	4	2	1	3	16
70	Spokane	1	–	1	–	3	–	2	3	3	1	4	1	–	3	3	2	1	1	4	5	4	4	4	7	5	1	2	3	1	–	–	1
76	Swift Current	2	3	1	2	3	–	1	4	2	2	1	2	2	4	1	3	1	2	2	1	4	4	5	1	1	2	2	2	5	–	–	11
59	Tri-City	2	–	1	–	1	2	–	2	–	–	2	4	1	3	2	2	1	4	1	6	6	2	2	5	3	3	4	–	–	–	–	–
24	Vancouver	–	–	2	2	2	2	1	3	4	1	3	2	1	1	–	–	–	–	–	–	–	–	–	–	–	–	–	–	–	–	–	–
11	Victoria[2]	1	1	1	2	–	3	1	–	2	–	–	–	–	–	–	–	–	–	–	–	–	–	–	–	–	–	–	–	–	–	–	–
	Clubs no longer operating																																
13	Billings	–	–	–	–	–	–	–	–	–	–	–	–	–	–	–	–	–	–	–	–	–	–	–	–	–	–	–	–	–	–	–	13
66	Calgary[3]	–	–	–	–	–	–	–	–	–	–	–	–	–	–	–	–	–	–	–	–	–	–	–	–	–	–	–	–	–	2	3	65
34	Edmonton *pre '78*	–	–	–	–	–	–	–	–	–	–	–	–	–	–	–	–	–	–	–	–	–	–	–	–	–	–	–	–	–	–	–	34
12	Estevan	–	–	–	–	–	–	–	–	–	–	–	–	–	–	–	–	–	–	–	–	–	–	–	–	–	–	–	–	–	–	–	12
39	Flin Flon	–	–	–	–	–	–	–	–	–	–	–	–	–	–	–	–	–	–	–	–	–	–	–	–	–	–	–	–	–	–	–	39
11	Kelowna Wings	–	–	–	–	–	–	–	–	–	–	–	–	–	–	–	–	–	–	–	–	–	–	–	–	–	–	–	–	–	–	5	6
6	Nanaimo	–	–	–	–	–	–	–	–	–	–	–	–	–	–	–	–	–	–	–	–	–	–	–	–	–	–	–	–	–	–	–	6
62	New Westm'r	–	–	–	–	–	–	–	–	–	–	–	–	–	–	–	–	–	–	–	–	–	–	–	–	–	–	–	1	2	1	1	57
12	Tacoma	–	–	–	–	–	–	–	–	–	–	–	–	–	–	–	–	–	–	–	–	2	5	2	3	–	–	–	–	–	–	–	–
2	Vancouver Nats	–	–	–	–	–	–	–	–	–	–	–	–	–	–	–	–	–	–	–	–	–	–	–	–	–	–	–	–	–	–	–	2
79	Victoria	–	–	–	–	–	–	–	–	–	–	–	–	–	–	–	–	–	–	–	–	–	2	2	1	–	2	4	4	2	1	2	59
34	Winnipeg	–	–	–	–	–	–	–	–	–	–	–	–	–	–	–	–	–	–	–	–	–	–	–	–	–	–	–	–	–	–	–	34

Former club names: [1]–Edmonton Ice, [2]–Chilliwack; [3]–Centennials '69-'73, Wranglers '77-'87.

U.S. College Hockey Draft Selections by School

Total	Club	'15	'14	'13	'12	'11	'10	'09	'08	'07	'06	'05	'04	'03	'02	'01	'00	'99	'98	'97	'96	'95	'94	'93	'92	'91	'90	'89	'88	'87	'86	'85	'69 to '84	
39	Boston College	1	1	–	–	–	–	–	1	–	1	1	1	1	3	2	3	–	3	3	2	–	–	–	–	–	–	2	–	2	1	–	12	
56	Boston U.	1	–	–	–	3	–	1	1	–	1	–	1	–	3	2	1	3	2	1	1	1	–	1	1	2	2	1	3	2	2	1	20	
28	Bowling Green	–	–	–	–	–	–	–	–	–	1	1	–	–	1	1	–	1	1	1	–	–	–	–	1	3	1	2	3	–	–	–	11	
34	Clarkson	–	–	–	–	–	1	–	–	–	1	–	–	–	–	–	1	1	3	–	–	–	–	1	1	2	3	1	1	1	–	–	17	
33	Colorado	–	–	–	–	–	–	–	–	1	–	1	–	2	1	1	2	1	3	–	–	1	–	–	–	–	2	–	1	–	1	–	16	
36	Cornell	–	–	–	2	–	–	–	–	–	–	1	2	2	1	–	2	2	–	1	–	–	–	–	–	–	2	5	2	1	–	2	11	
46	Denver	–	–	1	1	1	–	–	–	–	–	2	1	–	1	–	–	1	–	3	–	–	–	–	–	–	–	1	1	4	2	1	26	
35	Harvard	1	–	–	–	–	1	–	–	–	–	1	–	–	3	2	2	1	2	1	3	–	1	2	–	–	–	2	1	1	–	2	10	
25	Lake Superior	–	–	–	–	–	1	–	–	–	–	–	–	–	1	–	–	1	–	1	1	–	–	1	–	1	3	2	3	–	3	–	7	
22	Maine	–	–	–	–	–	–	–	–	–	1	–	1	2	–	–	1	4	1	1	1	–	–	1	–	–	1	2	3	–	1	–	2	
24	Miami U.	–	–	–	–	–	–	2	1	1	1	1	2	–	1	1	–	–	1	–	–	–	–	1	1	2	–	2	4	2	–	1	–	
71	Michigan	1	1	1	1	–	1	–	–	1	2	1	3	2	3	2	1	2	3	1	3	–	1	1	2	4	5	3	2	1	–	1	23	
49	Michigan State	–	–	–	–	–	1	–	–	–	1	–	2	1	4	–	2	2	1	1	1	–	1	1	1	4	5	4	4	1	1	–	11	
46	Michigan Tech	1	–	–	–	–	–	–	–	–	–	–	–	–	–	–	1	–	–	–	–	1	–	2	1	–	2	1	2	1	1	2	2	31
69	Minnesota	–	–	–	–	–	–	1	–	1	1	1	–	2	3	–	3	3	1	2	3	2	–	–	–	–	–	1	1	1	2	–	41	
32	New Hampshire	–	–	1	–	–	–	–	–	–	–	–	1	–	1	–	2	1	–	1	–	–	–	–	–	–	–	–	1	–	–	–	24	
40	North Dakota	–	–	–	–	1	–	–	–	–	1	–	1	1	1	–	1	1	–	2	–	–	–	–	–	1	1	2	–	–	–	–	27	
30	Northeastern	–	–	–	–	1	–	–	–	–	–	–	–	–	–	–	–	1	1	–	–	–	–	–	–	–	1	1	–	–	1	1	22	
24	Northern Mich.	–	–	–	–	–	1	–	1	–	–	–	2	2	–	–	1	–	–	–	1	–	–	–	–	1	–	2	1	4	–	–	8	
35	Notre Dame	–	–	–	1	1	1	–	–	1	1	–	2	–	2	1	1	2	–	2	1	–	–	–	–	–	–	–	–	–	–	–	19	
21	Ohio State	–	–	–	–	–	–	–	–	–	–	1	–	1	2	2	–	1	–	1	1	–	–	1	1	1	1	–	2	2	–	–	4	
37	Providence	–	–	1	–	–	–	–	–	–	2	–	–	1	1	–	2	–	2	1	–	–	–	–	–	–	1	–	–	–	1	1	24	
27	RPI	–	–	–	–	1	–	–	1	–	–	–	–	–	–	1	2	2	–	1	–	–	–	–	1	3	–	–	2	2	–	1	10	
23	St. Lawrence	–	–	–	–	–	–	–	–	–	–	–	–	–	1	–	–	1	–	1	1	–	–	1	–	2	1	1	1	1	1	1	10	
20	Vermont	–	–	–	–	–	–	–	–	–	–	1	–	–	–	2	–	–	–	–	1	–	1	–	–	1	–	–	1	–	–	2	11	
26	W. Michigan	1	–	–	–	1	–	1	–	–	1	–	–	–	1	–	–	–	1	1	–	–	–	2	–	4	1	1	1	1	2	–	8	
49	Wisconsin	–	–	–	2	1	1	–	2	–	–	–	2	–	–	–	3	2	–	–	–	–	–	–	–	1	–	1	–	1	–	1	32	
16	Yale	–	–	–	–	–	–	–	–	–	1	–	2	–	3	–	–	–	–	–	–	–	–	1	–	–	–	1	–	2	1	–	5	

Colleges with fewer than 15 players selected: 14 - Brown; 13 - Colgate, Minn.-Duluth; 10 - Dartmouth, Ferris State, Princeton, St.Cloud State; 10 - Merrimack; 7 - Mass.-Lowell, Union College; 6 - Illinois-Chicago, St. Louis; 5 - Nebraska-Omaha, Pennsylvania, Mass.-Amherst, Minnesota State (Mankato); 4 - Alaska-Anchorage; 3 - Babson College, Alaska (Fairbanks); 1 - Air Force, American International College, Army, Bemidji State, Greenway, Hamilton, Quinnipiac, St. Anselm College, St. Thomas, Salem State, San Diego U., Wisconsin-River Falls.

U.S. High and Prep Schools Draft Selections by School (More than 10 players drafted)

Total	School (State)	'15	'14	'13	'12	'11	'10	'09	'08	'07	'06	'05	'04	'03	'02	'01	'00	'99	'98	'97	'96	'95	'94	'93	'92	'91	'90	'89	'88	'87	'86	'80 to '85
15	Avon Old Farms (CT)	–	–	–	–	1	–	1	1	1	–	–	–	–	–	–	–	–	1	1	–	–	–	–	–	–	3	3	–	1	1	1
16	Belmont Hill (MA)	–	–	–	–	–	–	–	–	–	1	–	–	–	–	–	–	–	–	–	–	–	1	–	2	1	2	3	1	1	1	3
11	Canterbury (CT)	–	–	–	–	–	–	–	–	–	–	–	–	1	–	–	–	–	–	–	–	–	–	1	2	–	2	–	3	–	2	–
16	Catholic Memorial (MA)	–	–	–	–	–	–	–	–	–	–	–	2	–	–	–	–	–	1	–	–	–	2	1	2	–	–	3	1	2	–	2
12	Choate-Rosemary (CT)	–	–	–	–	1	–	–	1	–	–	–	–	–	–	–	1	–	–	–	–	–	–	–	1	1	1	–	3	2	–	1
13	Culver Mil. Acad. (IN)	1	–	–	–	–	–	–	–	–	–	–	–	–	–	–	–	–	–	–	–	–	–	2	2	1	2	2	1	2	–	–
24	Cushing Acad. (MA)	2	–	–	–	–	1	–	–	–	1	1	2	–	–	1	–	–	–	1	1	–	2	2	–	1	3	2	3	–	–	1
15	Deerfield (IL)	–	1	–	–	–	–	–	–	1	–	–	1	1	1	–	2	1	–	–	–	–	–	–	–	1	–	2	1	1	–	2
24	Edina (MN)	–	2	1	1	2	–	2	1	–	–	–	–	–	–	–	–	–	–	–	–	–	–	–	1	–	1	2	2	1	–	8
12	Grand Rapids (MI)	–	–	1	1	–	–	–	–	1	–	–	–	–	–	–	–	1	–	–	–	–	–	–	–	1	2	2	1	–	–	2
15	Hill-Murray (MN)	–	–	–	–	–	–	–	–	–	–	–	–	–	–	–	–	–	–	–	–	–	1	–	–	–	3	2	–	3	3	3
15	Hotchkiss (CT)	–	–	1	–	1	–	1	–	–	–	–	1	–	–	1	–	–	–	–	2	1	3	–	–	–	1	–	1	–	1	1
11	Kent School (CT)	–	–	–	1	–	–	–	2	–	–	–	–	–	–	–	–	–	–	–	–	–	2	–	–	–	–	–	–	–	1	5
11	Lawrence Academy (MA)	1	–	–	–	–	–	–	–	–	–	–	–	–	–	–	–	–	–	–	1	–	1	1	–	1	1	–	2	–	–	3
14	Minnetonka (MN)	–	–	–	–	–	2	1	1	–	–	–	–	–	–	–	–	–	–	–	–	–	–	–	–	1	–	2	–	3	–	4
13	Mount St. Charles (RI)	–	–	–	–	–	–	–	–	–	–	–	–	–	–	–	–	–	–	–	–	–	–	–	–	–	1	1	3	1	2	5
11	Nobles (MA)	1	–	1	3	–	1	1	–	2	–	1	–	–	–	–	–	1	–	–	–	–	–	–	–	–	–	–	–	–	–	1
19	Northwood (NY)	–	–	–	–	–	–	–	1	–	–	–	1	–	–	–	1	–	–	–	–	–	1	1	–	–	3	1	1	2	2	3
12	Roseau (MN)	–	–	–	–	–	–	2	–	–	–	–	–	–	–	–	–	–	–	–	–	–	–	–	–	1	3	1	–	–	1	4
11	St. John's Prep (MA)	–	–	1	1	1	–	–	–	–	–	–	–	–	–	–	–	–	–	–	–	–	1	–	–	–	–	–	2	–	–	5
14	St. Sebastian's (MA)	–	–	–	1	–	–	–	–	–	1	–	–	4	1	1	–	–	1	–	–	–	1	2	2	–	–	–	–	–	–	–
21	Shattuck-St. Mary's (MN)	–	–	1	4	1	3	3	3	1	1	2	–	1	–	–	–	–	–	–	1	–	–	–	–	–	–	–	–	–	–	–

Schools with 10 players selected: Burnsville (MN), Duluth East (MN), Hibbing (MN), Matignon (MA), Thayer Academy (MA).

U.S. College and High School Firsts

Jets first-rounder Kyle Connor, shown here at the 2015 NHL Scouting Combine, was the first of 31 USHL players selected in the 2015 Draft.

1967 – First U.S. College Player Drafted • Michigan Tech center Al Karlander was selected 17th overall by the Detroit Red Wings.

1979 – First U.S. College First- Round Selection • Minnesota-born defenseman Mike Ramsey (currently an assistant coach with the Minnesota Wild) was selected 11th overall by the Buffalo Sabres.

1980 – First U.S. High School Player Drafted • Center Jay North of Bloomington-Jefferson H.S. was taken 62nd overall by the Buffalo Sabres in 1980.

1981 – First U.S. High School First- Round Selection • Center Bob Carpenter of St. John's prep school was selected third overall by Washington in 1981.

1983 – First U.S. High School Player Drafted First Overall • Minnesota North Stars selected left winger Brian Lawton from Mount St. Charles H.S. first overall in 1983.

1986 – First U.S. College Player Drafted First Overall • Detroit selected right winger Joe Murphy from Michigan State first overall in 1986.

2003 – Most U.S. College Players Selected in the First Round • The 2003 draft saw seven U.S. college players selected in the first round, the most in Draft history. Six were selected in the first round in 2000 and four in 2001 and 2002. In addition, many players drafted in the first round from the USA U-18 and U-17 teams, high school and prep school programs, U.S. junior and Tier-2 Canadian junior go on to play college hockey.

2013 – Players Born in 22 States Selected • Minnesota, Massachusetts, Michigan and New York led the way, but players born from Alaska to Florida were selected in in 2013.

2014 – 30 USHL Players Selected • 12 of these players were part of the U.S. National Team Development Program's Under-18 squad.

2015 – 31 USHL Players Selected

2015 – Three U.S. College Players selected in top eight of the Draft.

European Leagues
Ranked by total number of players drafted

Total	Country	'15	'14	'13	'12	'11	'10	'09	'08	'07	'06	'05	'04	'03	'02	'01	'00	'99	'98	'97	'96	'95	'94	'93	'92	'91	'90	'89	'88	'87	'86	'85	'69 to '84
629	Sweden	18	30	26	23	25	21	23	19	16	18	15	18	19	24	14	24	24	19	14	16	8	17	18	11	11	9	14	15	9	16	9	88
569	KHL/Russia/CIS/USSR	12	7	8	7	6	4	6	9	7	16	16	4	11	15	24	32	33	46	29	22	16	17	27	35	31	45	25	14	18	11	2	2
432	CzRep/Slovakia	10	5	—	3	5	1	3	2	4	11	15	24	20	21	28	28	20	20	17	14	21	18	15	17	9	21	8	5	11	6	8	42
374	Finland	12	7	10	8	10	7	8	6	4	13	8	14	12	26	29	19	17	12	11	7	12	8	9	8	6	9	3	7	6	10	4	52
53	Switzerland	2	2	2	1	1	1	—	1	1	3	—	4	5	4	5	7	3	2	3	1	—	1	2	—	1	—	—	—	—	—	—	7
49	Germany	—	—	—	3	1	1	4	2	1	4	1	7	1	—	1	3	1	1	3	2	1	—	—	2	1	—	1	—	—	—	—	7
10	Norway	1	—	—	1	—	1	—	—	—	—	—	—	—	—	—	—	—	—	—	—	—	2	—	—	2	—	—	—	—	—	—	—
6	Denmark	—	—	1	—	1	—	—	—	—	—	—	—	—	—	—	—	—	—	—	—	1	—	—	—	—	—	—	—	—	—	—	1
2	Japan	—	—	—	—	—	—	—	—	—	1	—	—	—	—	—	—	—	—	—	—	—	1	—	—	—	—	—	—	—	—	—	—
2	Poland	—	—	—	—	—	—	—	—	—	—	—	1	—	—	—	—	—	—	—	—	—	—	—	—	—	—	—	—	—	—	—	1
1	Belarus	—	—	—	1	—	—	—	—	—	—	—	—	—	—	—	—	—	—	—	—	—	—	—	—	—	—	—	—	—	—	—	—
1	Hungary	—	—	—	—	—	—	—	—	—	—	—	—	—	—	1	—	—	—	—	—	—	—	—	—	—	—	—	—	—	—	—	—
1	Latvia	—	—	—	—	—	—	—	—	—	—	—	—	—	—	1	—	—	—	—	—	—	—	—	—	—	—	—	—	—	—	—	—
1	Scotland	—	—	—	—	—	—	—	—	—	—	—	—	—	—	—	—	—	—	—	—	—	—	—	—	—	—	—	1	—	—	—	—

Czech Republic and Slovakia

Total	Club	'15	'14	'13	'12	'11	'10	'09	'08	'07	'06	'05	'04	'03	'02	'01	'00	'99	'98	'97	'96	'95	'94	'93	'92	'91	'90	'89	'88	'87	'86	'85	'69 to '84
9	Brno	—	1	—	—	—	—	—	—	—	—	—	—	—	—	—	1	—	—	—	—	1	—	2	—	3	—	1	—	—	—	—	—
33	Ceske Budejovice	—	—	—	1	—	1	—	2	2	1	2	—	2	3	1	1	2	1	3	2	1	—	2	1	—	1	—	—	—	—	—	4
3	Chomutov	1	1	—	—	—	—	—	—	—	—	—	—	—	—	—	—	—	—	—	—	—	—	—	—	—	—	—	—	—	—	—	1
3	Havirov	—	—	—	—	—	—	—	—	—	—	—	—	—	—	—	—	—	—	—	—	—	—	—	—	—	—	—	—	—	—	—	—
28	Jihlava	—	—	—	—	—	—	—	—	—	—	—	—	—	1	—	—	2	2	1	1	—	1	2	3	1	1	3	—	1	—	—	9
4	Karlovy Vary	—	—	—	—	—	—	1	1	1	—	—	—	—	1	—	—	—	—	—	—	—	—	—	—	—	—	—	—	—	—	—	—
24	Kladno	1	—	—	—	—	3	1	1	1	—	1	1	—	2	—	—	2	—	2	1	—	2	1	—	1	—	—	—	—	—	—	4
18	Kosice	2	—	—	—	—	—	1	1	—	—	1	1	1	1	—	—	—	—	—	—	—	—	—	—	—	—	—	—	—	—	—	5
6	Liberec	1	1	—	—	—	—	1	1	—	2	—	—	—	—	—	—	—	—	—	—	—	—	—	—	—	—	—	—	—	—	—	—
34	Litvinov	—	—	—	—	—	3	2	—	1	—	1	1	2	2	4	2	3	1	2	2	—	—	—	—	—	—	—	—	—	—	—	6
6	Martin	—	—	—	—	—	—	—	—	—	—	—	—	—	—	—	—	—	2	—	—	—	1	—	—	—	—	—	—	—	—	—	—
7	Nitra	—	—	—	—	—	—	—	1	—	1	—	—	—	—	—	1	—	1	—	—	—	—	—	—	—	—	—	—	—	—	—	—
7	Olomouc	—	—	—	—	—	—	—	—	—	—	—	—	—	—	—	2	1	—	2	—	1	—	—	—	—	—	—	—	—	—	—	—
16	Pardubice	2	—	—	—	—	—	—	—	—	3	1	—	—	—	—	—	—	—	—	—	—	—	—	—	—	—	—	—	2	2	—	—
16	Plzen	1	—	—	1	—	—	—	—	—	—	—	2	1	—	—	3	—	1	1	—	—	—	—	—	—	—	—	—	—	—	—	—
3	Presov	—	—	—	—	—	—	—	—	—	1	—	—	—	—	—	—	—	—	—	—	—	—	—	—	—	—	—	—	—	—	—	—
31	Slavia Praha	—	1	—	1	1	—	—	1	1	2	2	5	3	2	5	4	—	—	—	—	—	—	—	—	—	—	—	—	—	—	—	1
22	Slovan Bratis.	—	—	—	—	—	—	—	3	1	—	2	2	1	1	1	—	3	—	—	1	—	—	—	—	1	1	1	4				
29	Sparta Praha	—	—	—	—	1	—	—	—	2	4	1	2	1	—	1	1	—	1	1	—	2	1	2	1	1	1	3					
31	Trencin	—	—	—	1	—	—	—	1	1	4	3	—	2	3	2	—	1	2	1	—	2	2	1	1	—	1						
12	Trinec	2	—	—	—	1	—	1	1	—	1	1	1	1	2	—	—	2															
19	Vitkovice	—	—	—	—	1	1	2	—	2	—	1	1	—	1	1	3	1	—	—	2												
14	Vsetin	—	—	—	—	1	1	—	1	1	3	2	2	1	—	1	2																
21	Zlin[1]	—	—	—	—	—	—	1	2	—	2	—	2	2	1	—	1	2	—	1													
8	Zvolen	—	—	—	—	1	—	—	2	2	—	1	1	—	1																		

Former club names: [1]–Gottwaldov. **Teams with two players selected:** Ingstav Brno, IS Banska Bystrica, Dubnica, Michalovce, Partizan Liptovsky Mikulas, VTJ Pisek, Skalica, Spisska Nova Ves, Topolcany. **Teams with one player selected:** Banik Sokolov, Havlickuv Brod, Ostrava, KC SKP Poprad, Povazska Bystrica, HK Trnava, KHM Zvolen, Slovak U20, Slovak U18.

Finland

Total	Club	'15	'14	'13	'12	'11	'10	'09	'08	'07	'06	'05	'04	'03	'02	'01	'00	'99	'98	'97	'96	'95	'94	'93	'92	'91	'90	'89	'88	'87	'86	'85	'69 to '84
19	Assat	1	1	—	1	—	—	—	—	2	—	—	—	1	—	—	1	—	—	—	1	1	1	1	—	1	—	1	—	—	—	—	7
26	Blues Espoo	1	1	1	1	1	3	1	—	—	1	1	—	1	2	—	1	2	1	1	—	—	—	—	—	—	—	—	—	—	—	—	—
43	HIFK Helsinki	—	1	1	1	—	4	1	2	—	5	2	2	4	2	1	—	1	—	2	—	1	—	1	—	—	—	1	—	—	—	1	9
14	HPK	1	—	1	—	—	—	—	1	1	3	1	1	1	—	—	2	—	—	1	—	—	—	—	—	—	—	—	—	—	—	—	—
40	Ilves	1	—	—	1	2	1	1	3	3	—	—	2	4	3	1	2	—	3	—	1	—	—	3	—	2	—	—	1	—	—	—	9
46	Jokerit	—	1	4	3	1	—	—	2	1	2	6	4	3	3	1	1	1	—	1	3	—	2	—	1	1	—	4					
16	JyP Jyvaskyla	3	—	—	1	—	—	—	1	—	2	1	—	3	1	2	—	1	—	—	—	—	—	—	—	—	—	—	—	—	—	—	—
19	KalPa	2	2	1	1	1	—	1	1	—	—	1	—	2	1	—	—	2	—	—	1	—	—	—	—	—	—	—	—	—	—	—	—
31	Karpat	2	—	1	1	1	1	—	—	—	2	2	3	3	—	1	1	—	—	1	1	—	2	2	—	3							
3	Kiekoo-67	—	—	—	—	—	—	—	—	—	—	—	—	—	3	—	—	—	—	—	—	—	—	—	—	—	—	—	—	—	—	—	—
20	Lukko	—	—	—	—	—	—	1	1	—	1	1	1	3	1	2	—	1	—	—	1	—	—	—	—	—	—	—	—	—	—	1	5
10	Pelicans	—	—	—	1	—	—	—	—	1	1	1	2	—	1	—	—	—	—	—	—	—	—	—	—	—	—	—	—	—	—	—	3
7	SaiPa	—	—	—	—	1	1	—	1	—	—	1	—	1	—	—	—	—	—	—	—	—	—	—	—	—	—	—	—	—	—	—	1
26	Tappara	1	—	—	2	2	—	1	2	2	2	1	—	2	1	1	—	—	1	—	1	4	—	—	—	—	—	—	—	—	1	4	3
39	TPS Turku	1	1	1	—	2	—	—	1	1	1	3	1	3	1	3	1	3	2	3	—	1	1	—	—	—	—	—	—	—	1	1	7

Teams with two players selected: KooKoo Kouvola, K-Vantaa, Sapko Savonlinna, Sport Vaasa, TuTo.
Teams with one player selected: Ahmat Hyvinkaa, Hermes Kokkola, Junkkarit Kalajoki, GrIFK Kauniainen, LeKi, S-Kiekko Seinajoki.

Chosen 178th overall from the WHL's Brandon Wheat Kings in 2010, Ottawa's Mark Stone (top) was a Calder Trophy nominee in 2014-15. Sweden's Filip Forsberg was selected 11th by Washington in 2012. He was among the top rookie scorers in 2014-15.

Note: International draft selections played outside North America in their draft year.

European-born players drafted from the OHL, QMJHL, WHL, U.S. colleges or other North American leagues are not counted as International players.

For analysis by birthplace, see the following page.

2016 NHL Draft

June 24-25, 2016

First Niagara Center
Buffalo, New York

Kontinental Hockey League/Russia/CIS/USSR

Total	Club	'15	'14	'13	'12	'11	'10	'09	'08	'07	'06	'05	'04	'03	'02	'01	'00	'99	'98	'97	'96	'95	'94	'93	'92	'91	'90	'89	'88	'87	'86	'85	'69 to '84
10	Ak Bars Kazan[1]	1	–	–	–	–	1	–	–	–	–	2	–	2	1	1	1	–	–	–	1												
18	Atlant Moscow Reg.[2]	–	1	–	1	–	–	–	–	1	1	1	–	3	–	–	1	–	2	1	3	1	–	–	1								
16	Avangard Omsk	1	–	–	–	1	1	6	1	–	–	–	1	–	3																		
5	Avto. Yekaterinburg[3]	1	–	–	–	1	–	–	–	1																							
5	CSK VVS Samara	–	–	–	–	1	1	–	1	–	1	–	1																				
81	CSKA Moscow	–	–	2	2	–	–	2	2	3	2	4	5	–	–	5	1	2	5	2	5	3	7	4	3	8	5	1	1	1			6
65	Dynamo Moscow	1	–	–	–	1	–	–	1	–	2	–	6	2	4	4	1	7	4	3	12	7	4	3	2								
16	Elektrostal	–	–	–	–	–	2	9	1	–	–	3																					
10	HC CSKA	–	–	–	–	5	–	5																									
4	Kristall Saratov																				1	1											
37	Krylja Sovetov	–	–	–	1	1	2	–	4	1	1	2	1	2	3	5	2	3	4	2	1	1											
27	Lada Togliatti	1	–	–	2	1	2	–	2	2	4	1	3	1	–	–	2	1															
59	Lokomotiv Yaroslavl[4]	1	1	2	–	1	–	1	2	1	3	2	–	7	3	1	10	1	6	3	3	6	1	–	2	1							
13	Magnitogorsk	1	1	–	1	–	1	1	–	2	1	1	3																				
10	Nizhnekamsk	1	–	–	1	–	–	–	3	2	–	–	1																				
6	Nizhny Novgorod[5]	–	–	–	1	–	–	2	1	–	–	1																					
13	Novokuznetsk	1	1	–	1	1	–	–	–	1	1	–	1	4	1																		
12	Pardaugava Riga[6]	2	–	–	–	–	–	–	–	1	4	1	–	2	1	–	1																
5	Perm	–	–	–	–	1	1	1	–	–	1	1																					
20	Severstal Cherepovets[7]	–	1	–	1	–	2	–	–	2	1	–	2	6	–	–	1	1	–	1	1												
14	SKA St. Petersburg[8]	1	–	–	–	–	2	2	2	–	–	1	–	2	–	–	2																
13	Sokol Kiev	–	–	–	–	–	–	1	–	2	–	1	3	2	1	1	–	1															
26	Spartak Moscow	–	1	–	–	–	2	–	6	–	1	–	1	6	4	1	–	1	1														
7	THC Tver	–	–	–	–	1	–	3	–	1	2																						
5	Tivali Minsk[9]	–	–	–	1	–	–	1	2	–	1																						
26	Traktor Chelyabinsk	–	1	–	2	1	–	1	1	1	2	–	1	1	–	1	2	7	2	–	2												
14	Ufa	–	–	–	1	–	–	1	–	1	–	1	2	1	2	–	1																
9	Ust-Kamenogorsk	–	–	–	–	1	–	1	2	–	1	2	1	1																			

Former club names: [1] Ital Kazan, [2] Khimik Voskresensk, [3] Dynamo-Erergiya Yekaterinburg, [4] Torpedo Yaroslavl, [5] Torpedo Gorky, [6] Dynamo Riga,HC Riga, [7] Metallurg Cherepovets, [8] SKA Leningrad, [9] Dynamo Minsk.

Teams with two players selected: Dizelist Penza, Mechel Chelyabinsk, Neftyanik Almetjevsk, Vityaz Podolsk, Yunost Minsk.

Teams with one player selected: Amur Khabarovsk, Argus Moscow, HC CSKA Moscow 2, Dynamo Khazov, Dynamo-81 Riga, Gazovik Tyumen, HK Gomel, Izohets St. Petersburg, Kapitan Stupino, Khimik Novopolotsk, Metalurgs Liepaja, Mostovik Kurgan, Omsk 2, Riga Jr., Spartak St. Petersburg, Sibir Novosibirsk, Slovan Bratislava (SVK), Stalkers-Juniors, HK Zelenograd.

Sweden

Total	Club	'15	'14	'13	'12	'11	'10	'09	'08	'07	'06	'05	'04	'03	'02	'01	'00	'99	'98	'97	'96	'95	'94	'93	'92	'91	'90	'89	'88	'87	'86	'85	'69 to '84
32	AIK Solna	1	–	2	–	1	4	–	–	–	–	–	–	–	1	1	–	3	1	1	–	1	–	1	1	1	1	–	–	4			9
4	Almtuna	–	–	–	1	1	1	–	–	–	–	–	–	–	–	–	–	–	–	–	–	–	–	–	–	–	–	–	–				2
9	Bjorkloven	–	–	–	–	–	–	1	–	2	1	–	–	–	–	–	–	–	–	–	–	–	–	1	–	1	1						3
3	Boden	–	–	–	–	–	–	–	–	–	–	–	–	–	–	–	–	–	1	–	–	–	–	1	–	1							1
46	Brynas Gavle	2	3	1	3	1	4	3	4	1	1	–	2	–	2	1	1	2	1	1	–	1	–	–	4	–	–						8
58	Djurgarden	2	3	4	2	3	2	1	–	1	1	2	–	2	1	4	1	–	2	2	3	–	1	1	2	1	–	2	1	–			10
3	Falun	–	–	–	–	–	–	–	–	–	–	–	–	–	–	–	–	–	1	–	1	1	–	–									
43	Farjestad	2	–	2	2	3	–	–	–	2	1	–	1	6	3	–	2	1	2	1	–	1	–	1	–	1				2			10
70	Frolunda	2	8	4	3	3	1	3	4	5	3	3	4	2	3	3	4	2	1	–	1	3	–	1	1	1	1	1	1	–			–
3	Grums	–	–	–	–	–	–	–	–	1	1	–	–	–	1																		
10	Hammarby	–	–	–	–	–	–	1	–	3	–	1	–	–	1	1	–	–	–	1	1												2
8	Huddinge	–	–	–	–	–	–	1	1	–	1	–	1	1	1	–	–	1															
32	HV 71	3	2	–	1	3	1	–	1	2	1	–	1	1	–	3	1	3	–	2	–	–	1	–	1	–	–						1
34	Leksand	–	–	1	1	1	–	1	–	1	1	–	2	–	5	–	2	1	–	3	2	–	2	–	1	2	1	1	2	5			
20	Linkoping	3	3	3	1	3	–	1	1	1	1	1	–	–	–	–	–	–	1														
19	Lulea	1	1	1	–	1	–	–	–	–	1	–	2	–	1	–	–	–	–	–	1	–	–	1	1	1	1						2
22	Malmo	–	–	1	–	2	–	1	1	1	1	1	4	–	1	1	–	2	–	1	1	1	–	1									
49	MODO	1	3	2	3	1	2	1	–	–	1	–	3	–	3	7	–	3	3	–	3	–	5	2	2	–	–	1	1				
9	Mora	–	–	1	1	–	1	–	–	1	–	1	–	1	–	–	–	–	–	–	–	1	–						–	1			
3	Morrum	–	–	–	–	–	–	–	–	2	1	–	–	–	–	–	–	–	–	–	1												
4	Nacka	–	–	–	–	–	–	–	–	–	1	–	–	–	1	1						1											
6	Orebro	–	–	–	–	–	–	–	–	–	–	–	–	–	–	–	–	–	–	–	1	–	–	1					1	–	1		3
4	Ostersund	–	–	1	–	1	–	–	–	–	–	–	–	–	–	–	–	–	–	–	–	–	1										
3	Pitea	–	–	–	–	–	–	–	–	–	–	–	–	–	–	–	1	–	1	–	–	–	–	1									1
16	Rogle	1	–	2	2	1	–	–	–	–	–	–	–	–	–	1	–	1	1	2	–	–	–	–	2	1	–						
22	Skelleftea	–	5	–	1	1	2	3	–	–	–	–	–	–	–	–	–	1	–	–	–	1	–	1	–	1	–	1	1				7
31	Sodertalje	–	1	1	1	1	2	–	3	1	2	1	2	1	3	1	2	1	–	1	–	1	–	–	1	–	2	–	2	2			6
3	Stocksund	–	–	–	–	–	–	–	–	–	–	–	–	–	–	–	–	–	–	–	–	–	–	–	–	–	–						1
4	Team Kiruna	–	–	–	–	–	–	–	–	–	–	–	–	–	–	1	–	1	–	–	–	–	–	–	1								2
12	Timra	–	–	1	–	1	–	2	–	–	1	–	–	1	–	1	–	1	–	1	–	–	–	–	–	1				1			3
3	Tingsryd	–	–	1	–	1	–	–	–	–	–	–	–	–	–	–	–	–	1														
4	Troja/Ljungby	–	–	–	–	–	–	–	1	–	1	–	–	–	–	1	1																
17	Vasteras	–	–	–	–	1	1	3	–	1	1	1	–	–	–	–	–	–	–	–	1	1	1	1	2	2	–	1	–				
3	Vita Hasten	–	–	–	–	1	–	1	–	–	1	–	–	–	–	–	–	–	–	–	–	–	–	–	–	–							

Teams with two players selected: Bofors, Skare. Teams with one player selected: Arboga, Arvika, Danderyd Hockey, Fagersta, Jamtland, Karskoga, Kumla, Skovde, S/G Hockey 83 Gavle, Sunne, Talje, Tunabro, Uppsala, Vallentuna, Vasby.

European Draft Firsts

1969 – First European (and Finn) • LW Tommi Salmelainen, 66th overall by St. Louis.

1974 – First Swede • C Per-Arne Alexandersson, 49th overall by Toronto. Four other Swedish-born players were selected that year, including defenseman Stefan Persson, 214th overall by the NY Islanders, who became the first European-trained player to be part of a Stanley Cup winner with the Islanders in 1980.

1975 – First Russian • LW Viktor Khatulev, 160th overall by Philadelphia.

1976 – First European Taken in the First Round • Swedish D Bjorn Johansson, 5th overall by the California Seals.

1976 – First Swiss • C Jacques Soguel, 121st overall by St. Louis.

1978 – First Czechoslovak • LW Ladislav Svozil, 194th overall by Detroit.

1978 – First Germans • G Bernard Engelbrecht, 196th overall by the Atlanta Flames and C Gerd Truntschka, 200th overall by St. Louis.

1989 – First European Taken First Overall • Swedish C Mats Sundin, 1st overall by Quebec in 1989.

2015 Draft Analysis

BY BIRTHPLACE

Country of Origin

Country	Players Drafted
Canada	78
USA	56
Sweden	19
Russia	17
Finland	13
Czech Republic	11
Slovakia	5
Switzerland	4
Latvia	3
Belarus	1
China	1
Germany	1
Netherlands	1
Ukraine	1
Total	**211**

Canadian-Born Players

Province	Players Drafted
Ontario	27
Quebec	21
British Columbia	13
Alberta	9
Saskatchewan	6
Manitoba	1
Prince Edward Island	1
Total	**78**

U.S.-Born Players

State	Players Drafted
Massachusetts	11
Michigan	7
Minnesota	7
Illinois	5
New York	5
Wisconsin	4
Colorado	3
California	2
Ohio	2
Texas	2
Washington	2
Alaska	1
Indiana	1
Nebraska	1
New Hampshire	1
Oregon	1
Utah	1
Total	**56**

BY BIRTH YEAR

Year	Players Drafted
1997	135
1996	62
1995	11
1994	3

BY POSITION

Position	Players Drafted
Defense	73
Center	52
Left wing	38
Right wing	24
Goaltender	24

Notes on 2015 First-Round Selections

1. EDMONTON • **CONNOR McDAVID** *(KAW-nuhr muhk-DAY-vihd)*, C. A highly skilled player with excellent vision, hockey sense, anticipation and timing, Connor McDavid can do it all at top speed. McDavid was granted exceptional player status by Hockey Canada to enter the 2012 OHL Priority Selection as a 15-year-old and became rookie of the year in 2012-13. In 2014-15 he was the OHL and CHL player of the year after collecting 44 goals and 76 assists for 120 points in just 47 games for the Erie Otters. He was a tournament All-Star as Canada won gold at the 2015 World Junior Championships.

2. BUFFALO • **JACK EICHEL** *(JAK IGH-kuhl)*, C. A dominating center with smarts and speed, Jack Eichel has elite skills. As a freshman at Boston University in 2014-15, Eichel won the Hobey Baker Award, leading all NCAA Division I skaters with 71 points (26 goals, 45 assists) in 40 games. He helped lead the Terriers to their first conference title in six years and reach the finals of the NCAA Frozen Four. A graduate of the U.S. National Team Development program, Eichel played at the World Junior Championships and the World Championships in 2015.

3. ARIZONA • **DYLAN STROME** *(DIH-luhn STROHM)*, C. A skilled and driven player with a competitive edge, Dylan Strome is not a physical player but he doesn't shy away from traffic. Strome led the OHL in scoring with the Erie Otters in 2014-15, collecting 45 goals and 84 assists for 129 points in 68 games, clinching the title with six points (two goals, four assists) in the final game. He also won the OHL trophy for sportsmanship. Brother Ryan Strome plays for the Islanders.

4. TORONTO • **MITCH MARNER** *(MIHTCH MAHR-nuhr)*, C. Only 5'11" and 160 pounds at the Draft, Mitch Marner has a high-end skill set with puckhandling and playmaking ability. He's also an excellent skater with good quickness and agility who doesn't shy away from traffic. Still only 17 in 2014-15, he finished second in the OHL in scoring with 126 points (44 goals, 82 assists) for the London Knights. Marner won a gold medal for Canada at the 2014 Ivan Hlinka Memorial.

5. CAROLINA • **NOAH HANIFIN** *(NOH-uh HAN-ih-fihn)*, D. An exceptional skater and gifted offensive player, Noah Hanifin is a defenseman who excels at the transition game. At age 17 when the 2014-15 season began, he was the youngest player in Boston College history. Hanifin captained Team USA to gold at the 2014 U-17 Hockey Challenge and won gold at the U-18 World Championship as well. He also played at the 2015 World Junior Championships.

6. NEW JERSEY • **PAVEL ZACHA** *(PAH-vehl zah-KUH)*, C. At 6'3" and 210 pounds, Pavel Zacha is a physical presence with high-end skill. He plays a strong two-way game and is an excellent competitor. Zacha was mentored by former NHLer Peter Nedved with Liberec in the Czech Republic in 2013-14 before coming to North America with the Sarnia Sting in 2014-15. His many international tournaments include winning a silver medal at the 2014 U-18 World Championship.

7. PHILADELPHIA • **IVAN PROVOROV** *(IGH-vuhn PROH-voh-rawv)*, D. A physical defenseman who is composed with the puck, Ivan Provorov has excellent vision on the ice and a good hockey IQ. He led all WHL rookies with 61 points (15 goals, 46 assists) for the Brandon Wheat Kings in 2014-15 and helped Brandon reach the WHL final. Provorov was the youngest member of Russia's silver medal-winning team at the 2015 World Junior Championships.

8. COLUMBUS • **ZACHARY WERENSKI** *(ZA-kuh-ree wuh-REHN-skee)*, D. A great skater who thinks the game well, Zachary Werenski remains calm under pressure. Starring at age 17 with Michigan in 2014-15, Werenski was named to the All Big-Ten Hockey First Team as well as to the All Big-Ten Freshman Team. Internationally, he won gold at the 2014 U-17 World Challenge and represented the United States at the World Junior Championships in 2015.

9. SAN JOSE • **TIMO MEIER** *(TEE-moh MIGH-uhr)*, RW. A solid and strong skater with and without the puck, Timo Meier has high-end hockey sense and reads the play very well. Meier led the Halifax Moosehead with 44 goals in 2014-15, setting a club record with 23 power-play goals and leading the QMJHL with 10 game-winning goals. He has represented Switzerland at several international tournaments, including the 2015 World Junior Championships.

10. COLORADO • **MIKKO RANTANEN** *(MEE-koh ran-TA-nehn)*, RW. At 6'4" and 211 pounds, Mikko Rantanen is a physically strong power forward with good speed and quickness. He also has good playmaking ability and a hard shot. Rantanen played for TPS of the Finnish elite league in 2014-15 and scored four goals in five games for Finland at the 2015 World Junior Championships. He also played at the U-18 World Championship in 2014.

11. FLORIDA • **LAWSON CROUSE** *(LAW-suhn KROWS)*, LW. A big (6'4", 215 pounds), powerful player who protects the puck, Lawson Crouse has good hands and sees the ice well. Crouse is known as "The Sherrif" for the way he looks after his teammates with the Kingston Frontenacs. Crouse made the OHL All-Rookie Second Team in 2013-14 and led Kingston in goals (29) and points (51) in 2014-15. He won a gold medal with Team Canada at the 2015 World Junior Championships and bronze at the 2014 U-18 Championship.

12. DALLAS • **DENIS GURIANOV** *(DEH-nihs goo-REE-an-awv)*, RW. A dynamic player who is full of surprises, Denis Gurianov is a strong, tough, power forward who goes to the net. He protects the puck well and is difficult to stop at full speed. Gurianov spent most of his time with Togliatti's junior team in 2014-15 and led all Russian players with six goals and seven points in five games at the 2015 U-18 World Championship. He won a bronze medal at the 2014 U-17 World Challenge and World Junior A challenge.

13. BOSTON • **JAKUB ZBORIL** *(JAY-kuhb zuh-BAW-rihl)*, D. A solid, two-way defenseman who models his game on Nicklas Lidstrom, Jakub Zboril plays well with and without the puck. He finished third among rookie defensemen in the QMJHL with 33 points (13 goals, 20 assists) for the Saint John Sea Dogs in 2014-15, setting a new club record for goals by a rookie blueliner. He won a silver medal with the Czech Republic at the 2015 Ivan Hlinka tournament and at the 2014 Under-18 World Championship.

14. BOSTON • **JAKE DeBRUSK** *(JAYK duh-BRUHSK)*, LW. The son of former NHL player Louie DeBrusk, Jake DeBrusk is a skilled player who is not afraid to go to the front of the net. He is a tireless worker who competes hard and has an excellent work ethic. DeBrusk led the Swift Current Broncos with 42 goals and 81 points in 2014-15 under coach Mark Lamb, who was a teammate of his father with the Edmonton Oilers. He plays in all situations.

15. BOSTON • **ZACHARY SENYSHYN** *(ZA-kuh-ree SEH-nih-shihn)*, RW. A strong skater with good finish around the net, Zachary Senyshyn has excellent puck skills. He finished second among OHL rookies with 26 goals and 45 points for the Sault Ste. Marie Greyhounds in 2014-15 and posted a plus-minus rating of +30 to earn a spot on the Second All-Rookie Team. In 2013-14, he led all 16-year-olds in scoring in the Central Canada Hockey League with 22 goals in 57 games as a member of the Smiths Falls Bears.

16. NY ISLANDERS • **MATHEW BARZAL** *(MA-thew BAHR-zahl)*, C. An excellent skater who is smart and poised with the puck, Mathew Barzal has great vision and puck skills. Despite an injury, he had 57 points (12 goals, 45 assists) in 44 games in 2014-15 with the Seattle Thunderbirds, who had made him the first choice in the 2012 WHL Bantam Draft. Barzal won gold for Canada at the 2015 Ivan Hlinka tourney and bronze at the 2014 U-18 World Championship.

17. WINNIPEG • **KYLE CONNOR** *(KIGH-uhl KAW-nuhr)*, LW. A gifted puckhandler who skates with a good stride and quickness, Kyle Connor is a solid two-way player. In his third year in the USHL in 2014-15, he led the league with 80 points (34 goals, 46 assists), helping the Youngstown Phantoms set a league record with a 17-game winning streak en route to winning USHL player of the year. He won a gold medal in 2014 with Team USA at the U-18 World Championship.

18. OTTAWA • **THOMAS CHABOT** *(TAW-muhs shuh-BAWT)*, D. An excellent skater who is smooth and fluid, Thomas Chabot is a smart player with the puck. He is a two-way defenseman who led Saint John Sea Dogs blueliners with 41 points (12 goals, 29 assists) in the QMJHL in 2014-15, nearly doubling his total from the previous season. As a member of Team Canada at the 2015 U-18 World Championship, he had five points (one goal, four assists) in five games and won a bronze medal.

19. DETROIT • **EVGENY SVECHNIKOV** *(ehv-GEH-nee svech-NIH-kawv)*, LW. A skilled skater who is strong on the puck, Evgeny Svechnikov plays a physical game. He finished second among QMJHL rookies with 78 points (32 goals, 46 assists) with Cape Breton in 2014-15. In 2013-14, Svechnikov had 27 points (14 goals, 13 assists) in 29 games to help Bars Kazan win their conference in Russia's junior league. He played at the U-18 World Championship in 2013 and 2014.

20. MINNESOTA • **JOEL ERIKSSON EK** *(JOHL AIR-ihk-suhn EHK)*, C. A competitive player with great speed, Joel Eriksson Ek has a good, strong shot and is an excellent puckhandler. He is creative on offense and reliable on defense. Eriksson Ek split the 2014-15 season between Farjestad's junior team and the elite league club, leading the junior league with 21 goals in 25 games. He represented Sweden at the 2015 U-18 World Championship and the 2014 Ivan Hlinka tournament.

21. OTTAWA • **COLIN WHITE** *(KAWL-ihn WIGHT)*, C. A strong two-way player with good hockey sense, Colin White is a solid competitor with high-end skill. He is a graduate of the U.S. National Team Development program who scored the gold medal-clinching goal in overtime at the 2015 U-18 World Championship and had a hat trick versus Canada in the semi-finals. He had 18 points (10 goals, eight assists) in six games to help the U.S. win the U-17 World Challenge in 2014. He is committed to Boston College for 2015-16.

22. WASHINGTON • **ILYA SAMSONOV** *(IHL-yah sam-SAWN-awv)*, G. A big goalie at 6'3" and 203 pounds, Ilya Samsonov plays at the top of the crease and effectively squares to the shooter. He shows good instincts, is well balanced and can make acrobatic saves. Samsonov played most of the 2014-15 season with the Magnitogorsk junior team and earned top goalie honors at the 2015 U-18 Five Nations tournament. He had a 46-save shutout in the bronze medal game at the 2014 U-17 World Challenge.

23. VANCOUVER • **BROCK BOESER** *(BRAWK BEH-suhr)*, RW. A strong skating forward who is very effective at getting to open space, Brock Boeser possesses a hard, accurate shot and has the ability to create opportunities off the rush. He tied for the lead in the USHL with 35 goals for the Waterloo Blackhawks in 2014-15. Boeser won gold with the U.S. team at the 2014 World Junior A challenge and captained his team to a bronze medal at the 2014 Ivan Hlinka tournament. He has committed to North Dakota for 2015-16.

24. PHILADELPHIA • **TRAVIS KONECNY** *(TRA-vihs koh-NEH-kee)*, C. A highly skilled forward who never stops working, Travis Konecny skates well and has excellent speed. Despite being only 5'10" and 177 pounds he battles hard and is not afraid to take the puck to the net. He was the OHL rookie of the year in 2013-14 after leading all rookies in goals (26) and points (70) and was captain of the Ottawa 67's in 2014-15. He scored a key game-winning goal to help Canada earn a bronze medal at the 2014 U-18 World Championship.

25. WINNIPEG • **JACK ROSLOVIC** *(JAK raws-LOH-vihk)*, C. A smart player with good quickness and energy, Jack Roslovic is a graduate of the U.S. National Team Development Program. He scored the tying goal in the third period to spark the U.S. to a 2-1 overtime win over Finland in the gold medal game of the 2015 U-18 World Championship and also won gold at the 2014 U-17 World Challenge. He is committed to Miami University for 2015-16.

26. MONTREAL • **NOAH JUULSEN** *(NOH-uh JOOL-suhn)*, D. A competitive player with good puck skills, Noah Juulsen has a good shot and is good on the power-play. He was the top-scoring defenseman with 52 points (nine goals, 43 assists) for the Everett Silvertips, who finished atop the U.S. Division in the WHL in 2014-15. His plus-minus rating of +22 ranked second on the club. Juulsen helped Team Pacific win a silver medal at the 2014 U-17 World Challenge.

27. ANAHEIM • **JACOB LARSSON** *(JAY-kuhb LAHR-suhn)*, D. A mobile defenseman with good size, Jacob Larsson makes smart plays and finds the open man well. He plays a surprisingly mature game. Larsson split his time between Frolunda's elite league and junior teams in 2014-15 after being named the top defenseman in Sweden's U-18 league in 2013-14. He played at the 2015 U-18 World Championship and at the Ivan Hlinka tournament in 2014.

28. NY ISLANDERS • **ANTHONY BEAUVILLIER** *(AN-thuh-NEE boh-VIHL-yay)*, LW. A skilled player who plays at a high pace, Anthony Beauvillier was in the top 10 in goals (42), assists (52) and points (94) in the QMJHL with Shawinigan in 2014-15 and led the league with 922 face-off wins. He was a captain opposite Connor McDavid in the 2015 Top Prospects Game. Beauvillier won gold at the 2014 Ivan Hlinka tourney and bronze at the 2015 U-18 World Championship.

29. COLUMBUS • **GABRIEL CARLSSON** *(GAY-bree-ehl KAHR-suhn)*, D. A strong, tall (6'4") shutdown defenseman, Gabriel Carlsson is a smart player who can make a good first pass. He played the majority of the 2014-15 season with Linkoping's junior team but also saw action in the Swedish elite league. He represented his country at the 2015 U-18 World Championship and at the Ivan Hlinka tournament and U-17 World Challenge in 2014.

30. ARIZONA • **NICHOLAS MERKLEY** *(NIH-koh-las MUHR-klee)*, RW. Although he doesn't have great size (5'11", 191 pounds), Nicholas Merkley is a highly competitive player with excellent offensive skill. He led Kelowna with 90 points (20 goals, 70 assists) in 2014-15 and led WHL playoffs with 22 assists to help the Rockets win the league championship. He was the top rookie in the WHL in 2013-14 and won a gold medal with Team Canada at the 2014 Ivan Hlinka tournament.

1: Connor McDavid
C – Edmonton

2: Jack Eichel
C – Buffalo

3: Dylan Strome
C – Arizona

4: Mitch Marner
C – Toronto

5: Noah Hanifin
D – Carolina

6: Pavel Zacha
C – New Jersey

7: Ivan Provorov
D – Philadelphia

8: Zachary Werenski
D – Columbus

9: Timo Meier
RW – San Jose

10: Mikko Rantanen
RW – Colorado

Players selected first through tenth in the 2015 NHL Draft.

2015 NHL DRAFT

Pick	Claimed by	Amateur Club	Position

FIRST ROUND
Pick	Claimed by	Amateur Club	Pos
1	EDM	Connor McDavid — Erie	C
2	BUF	Jack Eichel — Boston University	C
3	ARI	Dylan Strome — Erie	C
4	TOR	Mitch Marner — London	C
5	CAR	Noah Hanifin — Boston College	D
6	N.J.	Pavel Zacha — Sarnia	C
7	PHI	Ivan Provorov — Brandon	D
8	CBJ	Zachary Werenski — U of Michigan	D
9	S.J.	Timo Meier — Halifax	RW
10	COL	Mikko Rantanen — TPS	RW
11	FLA	Lawson Crouse — Kingston	LW
12	DAL	Denis Gurianov — Togliatti Jr.	RW
13	BOS	Jakub Zboril — Saint John	D
14	BOS	Jake DeBrusk — Swift Current	LW
15	BOS	Zachary Senyshyn — Sault Ste. Marie	RW
16	NYI	Mathew Barzal — Seattle	C
17	WPG	Kyle Connor — Youngstown	LW
18	OTT	Thomas Chabot — Saint John	D
19	DET	Evgeny Svechnikov — Cape Breton	LW
20	MIN	Joel Eriksson Ek — Farjestad	C
21	OTT	Colin White — USA U-18	C
22	WSH	Ilya Samsonov — Magnitogorsk Jr.	G
23	VAN	Brock Boeser — Waterloo	RW
24	PHI	Travis Konecny — Ottawa	C
25	WPG	Jack Roslovic — USA U-18	C
26	MTL	Noah Juulsen — Everett	D
27	ANA	Jacob Larsson — Frolunda	D
28	NYI	Anthony Beauvillier — Shawinigan	LW
29	CBJ	Gabriel Carlsson — Linkoping Jr.	D
30	ARI	Nicholas Merkley — Kelowna	RW

SECOND ROUND
31	S.J.	Jeremy Roy — Sherbrooke	D
32	ARI	Christian Fischer — USA U-18	RW
33	T.B.	Mitchell Stephens — Saginaw	C
34	TOR	Travis Dermott — Erie	D
35	CAR	Sebastian Aho — Karpat	LW
36	OTT	Gabriel Gagne — Victoriaville	RW
37	BOS	Brandon Carlo — Tri-City	D
38	CBJ	Paul Bittner — Portland	LW
39	COL	AJ Greer — Boston University	LW
40	COL	Nicolas Meloche — Baie-Comeau	D
41	NYR	Ryan Gropp — Seattle	LW
42	N.J.	MacKenzie Blackwood — Barrie	G
43	L.A.	Erik Cernak — Kosice	D
44	T.B.	Matthew Spencer — Peterborough	D
45	BOS	Jakob Forsbacka-Karlsson — Omaha	C
46	PIT	Daniel Sprong — Charlottetown	RW
47	WPG	Jansen Harkins — Prince George	C
48	OTT	Filip Chlapik — Charlottetown	C
49	DAL	Roope Hintz — Ilves	LW
50	MIN	Jordan Greenway — USA U-18	LW
51	BUF	Brendan Guhle — Prince Albert	D
52	BOS	Jeremy Lauzon — Rouyn-Noranda	D
53	CGY	Rasmus Andersson — Barrie	D
54	CHI	Graham Knott — Niagara	LW
55	NSH	Yakov Trenin — Gatineau	LW
56	STL	Vince Dunn — Niagara	D
57	WSH	Jonas Siegenthaler — Zurich	D
58	CBJ	Kevin Stenlund — HV 71 Jr.	C
59	ANA	Julius Nattinen — JyP-Akatemia	C
60	CGY	Oliver Kylington — Farjestad	D
61	TOR	Jeremy Bracco — USA U-18	RW

THIRD ROUND
62	NYR	Robin Kovacs — AIK	RW
63	ARI	Kyle Capobianco — Sudbury	D
64	T.B.	Dennis Yan — Shawinigan	LW
65	TOR	Andrew Nielsen — Lethbridge	D
66	VAN	Guillaume Brisebois — Acadie-Bathurst	D
67	N.J.	Blake Speers — Sault Ste. Marie	C
68	TOR	Martins Dzierkals — Riga Jr.	LW
69	CBJ	Keegan Kolesar — Seattle	RW
70	PHI	Felix Sandstrom — Brynas Jr.	G
71	COL	Jean-Christophe Beaudin — Rouyn-Noranda	C
72	T.B.	Anthony Cirelli — Oshawa	C
73	DET	Vili Saarijarvi — Green Bay	D
74	L.A.	Alexander Dergachyov — St. Petersburg Jr.	C
75	BOS	Daniel Vladar — Kladno Jr.	G
76	ARI	Adin Hill — Portland	G
77	FLA	Samuel Montembeault — Blainville-Boisbriand	G
78	WPG	Erik Foley — Cedar Rapids	LW
79	NYR	Sergey Zborovskiy — Regina	D
80	ANA	Brent Gates — Green Bay	C
81	ARI	Brendan Warren — USA U-18	LW
82	NYI	Mitchell Vande Sompel — Oshawa	D
83	ARI	Jens Looke — Brynas	RW
84	ANA	Deven Sideroff — Kamloops	RW
85	NSH	Thomas Novak — Waterloo	C
86	S.J.	Mike Robinson — Lawrence Academy	G
87	MTL	Lukas Vejdemo — Djurgarden Jr.	C
88	FLA	Thomas Schemitsch — Owen Sound	D
89	NYR	Aleksi Saarela — Assat	C
90	PHI	Matej Tomek — Topeka	G
91	CHI	Dennis Gilbert — Chicago	D

FOURTH ROUND
92	BUF	William Borgen — Moorhead	D
93	CAR	Callum Booth — Quebec	G
94	STL	Adam Musil — Red Deer	C
95	TOR	Jesper Lindgren — MODO Jr.	D
96	CAR	Nicolas Roy — Chicoutimi	C
97	N.J.	Colton White — Sault Ste. Marie	D
98	PHI	Samuel Dove-McFalls — Saint John	LW
99	L.A.	Austin Wagner — Regina	LW
100	NSH	Anthony Richard — Val-d'Or	C
101	COL	Andrei Mironov — Dynamo Moscow	D
102	FLA	Denis Malgin — Zurich	C
103	DAL	Chris Martenet — London	D
104	PHI	Mikhail Vorobyov — Ufa Jr.	C
105	BOS	Jesse Gabrielle — Regina	LW
106	S.J.	Adam Helewka — Spokane	LW
107	OTT	Christian Wolanin — Muskegon	D
108	WPG	Michael Spacek — Pardubice	C
109	OTT	Filip Ahl — HV 71 Jr.	LW
110	DET	Joren Van Pottelberghe — Linkoping U18	G
111	MIN	Ales Stezka — Liberec Jr.	G
112	NYI	Parker Wotherspoon — Tri-City	D
113	NYR	Brad Morrison — Prince George	C
114	VAN	Dmitry Zhukenov — Omsk Jr.	C
115	NSH	Alexandre Carrier — Gatineau	D
116	STL	Glenn Gawdin — Swift Current	C
117	EDM	Caleb Jones — USA-U-18	D
118	T.B.	Jonne Tammela — KalPa	RW
119	NYR	Daniel Bernhardt — Djurgarden Jr.	RW
120	T.B.	Mathieu Joseph — Saint John	RW
121	CHI	Ryan Shea — Boston College H.S.	D

FIFTH ROUND
122	BUF	Devante Stephens — Kelowna	D
123	ARI	Conor Garland — Moncton	RW
124	EDM	Ethan Bear — Seattle	D
125	TOR	Dmytro Timashov — Quebec	LW
126	CAR	Luke Stevens — Noble & Greenough	LW
127	STL	Niko Mikkola — KalPa Jr.	D
128	PHI	David Kase — Chomutov	LW
129	CBJ	Sam Ruopp — Prince George	D
130	S.J.	Karlis Cukste — Riga Jr.	D
131	MTL	Matthew Bradley — Medicine Hat	C
132	FLA	Karch Bachman — Culver Academy	LW
133	DAL	Joseph Cecconi — Muskegon	D
134	L.A.	Matt Schmalz — Sudbury	RW
135	MIN	Kirill Kaprizov — Novokuznetsk	C
136	CGY	Pavel Karnaukhov — Calgary	C
137	PIT	Dominik Simon — Plzen	C
138	CAR	Spencer Smallman — Saint John	RW
139	OTT	Christian Jaros — Lulea	D
140	DET	Chase Pearson — Youngstown	C
141	CBJ	Veeti Vainio — Blues Jr.	D
142	S.J.	Rudolfs Balcers — Stavanger	LW
143	WSH	Connor Hobbs — Regina	D
144	VAN	Carl Neill — Sherbrooke	D
145	NSH	Karel Vejmelka — Pardubice Jr.	G
146	STL	Luke Opilka — USA U-18	G
147	NYI	Ryan Pilon — Brandon	D
148	ANA	Troy Terry — USA U-18	C/RW
149	VAN	Adam Gaudette — Cedar Rapids	C
150	T.B.	Ryan Zuhlsdorf — Sioux City	D
151	CHI	Radovan Bondra — Kosice	LW

SIXTH ROUND
152	BUF	Giorgio Estephan — Lethbridge	C
153	T.B.	Kristian Oldham — Omaha	G
154	EDM	John Marino — South Shore	D
155	TOR	Stephen Desrocher — Oshawa	D
156	CAR	Jake Massie — Kimball Union	D
157	N.J.	Brett Seney — Merrimack	LW
158	PHI	Cooper Marody — Sioux Falls	C
159	CBJ	Vladislav Gavrikov — Yaroslavl	D
160	S.J.	Adam Parsells — Wausau West	D
161	COL	Sergei Boikov — Drummondville	D
162	FLA	Christopher Wilkie — Tri-City	RW
163	DAL	Markus Ruusu — JyP Jr.	G
164	CHI	Roy Radke — Barrie	RW
165	BOS	Cameron Hughes — U of Wisconsin	C
166	CGY	Andrew Mangiapane — Barrie	LW
167	PIT	Frederik Tiffels — Western Michigan	LW
168	WPG	Mason Appleton — Tri-City	C
169	CAR	David Cotton — Cushing Academy	C
170	DET	Patrick Holway — Boston Advantage U18	D
171	MIN	Nicholas Boka — USA U-18	D
172	NYI	Andong Song — Lawrenceville	D
173	WSH	Colby Williams — Regina	D
174	VAN	Lukas Jasek — Trinec	RW
175	NSH	Tyler Moy — Harvard	C
176	STL	Liam Dunda — Owen Sound	LW
177	MTL	Simon Bourque — Rimouski	D
178	ANA	Steven Ruggiero — USA U-18	D
179	ANA	Garrett Metcalf — Madison	G
180	T.B.	Bokondji Imama — Saint John	LW
181	CHI	Joni Tuulola — HPK	D

Pick	Claimed by	Amateur Club	Position

SEVENTH ROUND

Pick	Claimed by	Amateur Club	Position
182	BUF	Ivan Chukarov	Minnesota Wilderness	D
183	ARI	Erik Kallgren	Linkoping Jr.	G
184	NYR	Adam Huska	Green Bay	G
185	TOR	Nikita Korostelev	Sarnia	RW
186	CAR	Steven Lorentz	Peterborough	C/LW
187	L.A.	Chaz Reddekopp	Victoria	D
188	PHI	Ivan Fedotov	Nizhnekamsk Jr.	G
189	CBJ	Markus Nutivaara	Karpat.	D
190	S.J.	Marcus Vela	Langley	C
191	COL	Gustav Olhaver	Rogle Jr.	C
192	FLA	Patrick Shea	Kimball Union	C
193	S.J.	John Kupsky	Lone Star	G
194	L.A.	Matt Roy	Michigan Tech	LW
195	BOS	Jack Becker	Mahtomedi	C
196	CGY	Riley Bruce	North Bay	D
197	PIT	Nikita Pavlychev	Des Moines	C
198	WPG	Sami Niku	JyP-Akatemia	D
199	OTT	Joel Daccord	Cushing Academy	G
200	DET	Adam Marsh	Saint John	LW
201	MIN	Gustav Bouramman	Sault Ste. Marie	D
202	NYI	Petter Hansson	Linkoping Jr.	D
203	WPG	Matteo Gennaro	Prince Albert	C
204	MIN	Jack Sadek	Lakeville North	D
205	NSH	Evan Smith	Austin	G
206	FLA	Ryan Bednard	Johnstown	G
207	MTL	Jeremiah Addison	Ottawa	LW
208	EDM	Miroslav Svoboda	Trinec Jr.	G
209	EDM	Ziyat Paigin	Kazan	D
210	VAN	Tate Olson	Prince George	D
211	CHI	John Dahlstrom	Frolunda Jr.	LW

First Two Rounds, 2014–2012

2014

Note: Names in *italics* have not appeared in an NHL regular-season or playoff game.

FIRST ROUND

Pick	Claimed by	Amateur Club	Position
1	FLA	Aaron Ekblad	Barrie	D
2	BUF	Sam Reinhart	Kootenay	C
3	EDM	Leon Draisaitl	Prince Albert	C
4	CGY	Sam Bennett	Kingston	C
5	NYI	*Michael Dal Colle*	Oshawa	LW
6	VAN	*Jake Virtanen*	Calgary	RW
7	CAR	*Haydn Fleury*	Red Deer	D
8	TOR	*William Nylander*	MODO Ornskoldsvik	C/RW
9	WPG	*Nick Ehlers*	Halifax	LW
10	ANA	*Nicholas Ritchie*	Peterborough	LW
11	NSH	*Kevin Fiala*	HV 71 Jr.	LW
12	ARI	*Brendan Perlini*	Niagara	LW
13	WSH	*Jakub Vrana*	Linkoping	L/RW
14	DAL	*Julius Honka*	Swift Current	D
15	DET	*Dylan Larkin*	USA U-18	C
16	CBJ	*Sonny Milano*	USA U-18	LW
17	PHI	*Travis Sanheim*	Calgary	D
18	MIN	*Alex Tuch*	USA U-18	RW
19	T.B.	*Anthony DeAngelo*	Sarnia	D
20	CHI	*Nick Schmaltz*	Green Bay	C
21	STL	*Robby Fabbri*	Guelph	C
22	PIT	*Kasperi Kapanen*	KalPa	RW
23	COL	*Conner Bleackley*	Red Deer	C
24	VAN	*Jared McCann*	Sault Ste. Marie	C
25	BOS	David Pastrnak	Sodertalje	RW
26	MTL	*Nikita Scherbak*	Saskatoon	RW
27	S.J.	*Nikolay Goldobin*	Sarnia	RW
28	NYI	*Joshua Ho-Sang*	Windsor	C/RW
29	L.A.	*Adrian Kempe*	MODO Ornskoldsvik	LW
30	N.J.	*John Quenneville*	Brandon	C

SECOND ROUND

Pick	Claimed by	Amateur Club	Position
31	BUF	*Brendan Lemieux*	Barrie	LW
32	FLA	*Jayce Hawryluk*	Brandon	C
33	STL	*Ivan Barbashev*	Moncton	C/LW
34	CGY	*Mason McDonald*	Charlottetown	G
35	T.B.	*Dominik Masin*	Slavia Jr.	D
36	VAN	*Thatcher Demko*	Boston College	G
37	CAR	*Alex Nedeljkovic*	Plymouth	G
38	ANA	*Marcus Pettersson*	Skelleftea Jr.	D
39	WSH	*Vitek Vanecek*	Liberec Jr.	G
40	OTT	*Andreas Englund*	Djurgarden	D
41	N.J.	*Joshua Jacobs*	Indiana	D
42	NSH	*Vladislav Kamenev*	Magnitogorsk 2	LW
43	ARI	*Ryan MacInnis*	Kitchener	C
44	BUF	*Eric Cornel*	Peterborough	C
45	DAL	*Brett Pollock*	Edmonton	LW
46	S.J.	*Julius Bergman*	Frolunda Jr.	D
47	CBJ	*Ryan Collins*	USA U-18	D
48	PHI	*Nicolas Aube-Kubel*	Val-d'Or	RW
49	BUF	*Vaclav Karabacek*	Gatineau	RW
50	L.A.	*Roland McKeown*	Kingston	D
51	NSH	*Jack Dougherty*	USA U-18	D
52	STL	*Maxim Letunov*	Youngstown	C
53	S.J.	*Noah Rod*	Geneve Jr.	RW
54	CGY	*Hunter Smith*	Oshawa	RW
55	ANA	*Brandon Montour*	Waterloo	D
56	BOS	*Ryan Donato*	Dexter School	C
57	T.B.	*Johnathan MacLeod*	USA U-18	D
58	ARI	*Christian Dvorak*	London	LW
59	NYR	*Brandon Halverson*	Sault Ste. Marie	G
60	L.A.	*Alex Lintuniemi*	Ottawa	D

2013

FIRST ROUND

Pick	Claimed by	Amateur Club	Position
1	COL	Nathan MacKinnon	Halifax	C
2	FLA	Aleksander Barkov	Tappara	C
3	T.B.	Jonathan Drouin	Halifax	LW
4	NSH	Seth Jones	Portland	D
5	CAR	Elias Lindholm	Brynas	C
6	CGY	Sean Monahan	Ottawa	C
7	EDM	Darnell Nurse	Sault Ste. Marie	D
8	BUF	Rasmus Ristolainen	TPS Turku	D
9	VAN	Bo Horvat	London	C
10	DAL	Valeri Nichushkin	Chelyabinsk	RW
11	PHI	*Samuel Morin*	Rimouski	D
12	PHX	Max Domi	London	C/LW
13	WPG	*Joshua Morrissey*	Prince Albert	D
14	CBJ	Alexander Wennberg	Djurgarden	C
15	NYI	Ryan Pulock	Brandon	D
16	BUF	Nikita Zadorov	London	D
17	OTT	Curtis Lazar	Edmonton	C/RW
18	S.J.	Mirco Mueller	Everett	D
19	CBJ	Kerby Rychel	Windsor	LW
20	DET	Anthony Mantha	Val-d'Or	RW
21	TOR	Frederik Gauthier	Rimouski	C
22	CGY	Emile Poirier	Gatineau	LW
23	WSH	Andre Burakovsky	Malmo	LW
24	VAN	*Hunter Shinkaruk*	Medicine Hat	C/LW
25	MTL	*Michael McCarron*	USA U-18	RW
26	ANA	Shea Theodore	Seattle	D
27	CBJ	Marko Dano	Bratislava	C
28	CGY	*Morgan Klimchuk*	Regina	LW
29	DAL	Jason Dickinson	Guelph	C
30	CHI	Ryan Hartman	Plymouth	RW

SECOND ROUND

Pick	Claimed by	Amateur Club	Position
31	FLA	*Ian McCoshen*	Waterloo	D
32	COL	*Chris Bigras*	Owen Sound	D
33	T.B.	*Adam Erne*	Quebec	LW
34	MTL	*Jacob de la Rose*	Leksand	LW
35	BUF	*J.T. Compher*	USA U-18	LW
36	MTL	*Zachary Fucale*	Halifax	G
37	L.A.	*Valentin Zykov*	Baie-Comeau	LW
38	BUF	*Connor Hurley*	Edina High	C
39	PHX	*Laurent Dauphin*	Chicoutimi	C
40	DAL	*Remi Elie*	London	LW
41	PHI	*Robert Hagg*	MODO Jr.	D
42	N.J.	*Steven Santini*	USA U-18	D
43	WPG	*Nicolas Petan*	Portland	C
44	PIT	*Tristan Jarry*	Edmonton	G
45	ANA	*Nick Sorensen*	Quebec	RW
46	MIN	*Gustav Olofsson*	Green Bay	D
47	STL	*Thomas Vannelli*	Minnetonka	D
48	DET	*Zach Nastasiuk*	Owen Sound	RW
49	S.J.	*Gabryel Boudreau*	Baie-Comeau	LW
50	CBJ	*Dillon Heatherington*	Swift Current	D
51	CHI	*Carl Dahlstrom*	Linkoping Jr.	D
52	BUF	*Justin Bailey*	Kitchener	RW
53	WSH	*Madison Bowey*	Kelowna	D
54	DAL	*Philippe Desrosiers*	Rimouski	G
55	MTL	*Artturi Lehkonen*	Kalpa	LW
56	EDM	*Marc-Olivier Roy*	Blainville-Boisbriand	C
57	STL	*William Carrier*	Cape Breton	LW
58	DET	*Tyler Bertuzzi*	Guelph	LW
59	WPG	*Eric Comrie*	Tri-City	G
60	BOS	*Linus Arnesson*	Djurgarden	D
61	WSH	*Zachary Sanford*	Islanders	LW

2012

FIRST ROUND

Pick	Claimed by	Amateur Club	Position
1	EDM	Nail Yakupov	Sarnia	RW
2	CBJ	Ryan Murray	Everett	D
3	MTL	Alex Galchenyuk	Sarnia	C
4	NYI	Griffin Reinhart	Edmonton	D
5	TOR	Morgan Rielly	Moose Jaw	D
6	ANA	Hampus Lindholm	Rogle Jr.	D
7	MIN	Mathew Dumba	Red Deer	D
8	PIT	Derrick Pouliot	Portland	D
9	WPG	Jacob Trouba	USA U-18	D
10	T.B.	Slater Koekkoek	Peterborough	D
11	WSH	Filip Forsberg	Leksand	RW
12	BUF	Mikhail Grigorenko	Quebec	C
13	DAL	Radek Faksa	Kitchener	C
14	BUF	Zemgus Girgensons	Dubuque	C
15	OTT	Cody Ceci	Ottawa	D
16	WSH	Thomas Wilson	Plymouth	RW
17	S.J.	Tomas Hertl	Slavia	C
18	CHI	Teuvo Teravainen	Jokerit	LW
19	T.B.	Andrey Vasilevskiy	Ufa 2	G
20	PHI	Scott Laughton	Oshawa	C
21	CGY	Mark Jankowski	Stanstead College	C
22	PIT	Olli Maatta	London	D
23	FLA	Michael Matheson	Dubuque	D
24	BOS	Malcolm Subban	Belleville	G
25	STL	Jordan Schmaltz	Green Bay	D
26	VAN	Brendan Gaunce	Belleville	C
27	PHX	Henrik Samuelsson	Edmonton	C
28	NYR	Brady Skjei	USA U-18	D
29	N.J.	Stefan Matteau	USA U-18	C
30	L.A.	Tanner Pearson	Barrie	LW

SECOND ROUND

Pick	Claimed by	Amateur Club	Position
31	CBJ	Oscar Dansk	Brynas Jr.	G
32	EDM	Mitchell Moroz	Edmonton	LW
33	MTL	Sebastian Collberg	Frolunda	RW
34	NYI	Ville Pokka	Karpat	D
35	TOR	Matthew Finn	Guelph	D
36	ANA	Nicolas Kerdiles	USA U-18	LW
37	NSH	Pontus Aberg	Djurgarden	LW
38	CAR	Phillip Di Giuseppe	U.of Michigan	C
39	WPG	Lukas Sutter	Saskatoon	C
40	T.B.	Dylan Blujus	Brampton	D
41	COL	Mitchell Heard	Plymouth	C
42	CHY	Patrick Sieloff	USA U-18	D
43	DAL	Ludwig Bystrom	MODO Jr.	D
44	BUF	Jake McCabe	U. of Wisconsin	D
45	PHI	Anthony Stolarz	Corpus Christi	G
46	MIN	Raphael Bussieres	Baie-Comeau	LW
47	CAR	Brock McGinn	Guelph	LW
48	CHI	Dillon Fournier	Rouyn-Noranda	D
49	DET	Martin Frk	Halifax	RW
50	NSH	Colton Sissons	Kelowna	C
51	MTL	Dalton Thrower	Saskatoon	D
52	PIT	Teddy Blueger	Shattuck-St. Mary's	C
53	T.B.	Brian Hart	Exeter	RW
54	DAL	Mike Winther	Prince Albert	C
55	S.J.	Chris Tierney	London	C
56	STL	Samuel Kurker	St. John's Prep	RW
57	VAN	Alexandre Mallet	Rimouski	LW
58	PHX	Jordan Martinook	Vancouver	LW
59	NYR	Cristoval "Boo" Nieves	Kent School	C
60	N.J.	Damon Severson	Kelowna	D
61	DAL	Devin Shore	Whitby	C

Selected fourth overall at the 2013 NHL Draft, Seth Jones played 77 games as a 19-year-old rookie for Nashville in 2013-14 and a full 82 games in 2014-15. His 159 NHL games played are the largest number played amongst players selected in 2013.

First Round and Other Notable Selections, 2011–1969

Note: Names in *italics* have not appeared in an NHL regular-season or playoff game.

2011

FIRST ROUND

Pick	Claimed by	Player	Amateur Club	Position
1	EDM	Ryan Nugent-Hopkins	Red Deer	C
2	COL	Gabriel Landeskog	Kitchener	LW
3	FLA	Jonathan Huberdeau	Saint John	C
4	N.J.	Adam Larsson	Skelleftea	D
5	NYI	Ryan Strome	Niagara	C
6	OTT	Mika Zibanejad	Djurgarden	C
7	WPG	Mark Scheifele	Barrie	C
8	PHI	Sean Couturier	Drummondville	C
9	BOS	Dougie Hamilton	Niagara	D
10	MIN	Jonas Brodin	Farjestad	D
11	COL	Duncan Siemens	Saskatoon	D
12	CAR	Ryan Murphy	Kitchener	D
13	CGY	Sven Baertschi	Portland	LW
14	DAL	Jamieson Oleksiak	Northeastern	D
15	NYR	J.T. Miller	USA U-18	C
16	BUF	Joel Armia	Assat	RW
17	MTL	Nathan Beaulieu	Saint John	D
18	*CHI*	*Mark McNeill*	*Prince Albert*	*C*
19	EDM	Oscar Klefbom	Farjestad	D
20	PHX	Connor Murphy	USA U-18	D
21	OTT	Stefan Noesen	Plymouth	RW
22	*TOR*	*Tyler Biggs*	*USA U-18*	*RW*
23	PIT	Joe Morrow	Portland	D
24	OTT	Matt Puempel	Peterborough	LW
25	TOR	Stuart Percy	Mississauga St. Michael's	D
26	CHI	Phillip Danault	Victoriaville	LW
27	T.B.	Vladislav Namestnikov	London	C
28	*MIN*	*Zack Phillips*	*Saint John*	*C*
29	VAN	Nicklas Jensen	Oshawa	LW/RW
30	ANA	Rickard Rakell	Plymouth	RW

OTHER NOTABLE SELECTIONS

Pick	Claimed by	Player	Amateur Club	Position
35	DET	Tomas Jurco	Saint John	RW
37	CBJ	Boone Jenner	Oshawa	C
43	CHI	Brandon Saad	Saginaw	LW
58	T.B.	Nikita Kucherov	CSKA2	LW
96	OTT	Jean-Gabriel Pageau	Gatineau	C
104	CGY	Johnny Gaudreau	Dubuque	LW
139	CHI	Andrew Shaw	Owen Sound	C
208	T.B.	Ondrej Palat	Drummondville	LW

2010

FIRST ROUND

Pick	Claimed by	Player	Amateur Club	Position
1	EDM	Taylor Hall	Windsor	LW
2	BOS	Tyler Seguin	Plymouth	C
3	FLA	Erik Gudbranson	Kingston	D
4	CBJ	Ryan Johansen	Portland	C
5	NYI	Nino Niederreiter	Portland	RW
6	T.B.	Brett Connolly	Prince George	RW
7	CAR	Jeff Skinner	Kitchener	C
8	ATL	Alexander Burmistrov	Barrie	C
9	MIN	Mikael Granlund	HIFK Helsinki	C/W
10	NYR	Dylan McIlrath	Moose Jaw	D
11	DAL	Jack Campbell	USA U-18	G
12	ANA	Cam Fowler	Windsor	D
13	PHX	Brandon Gormley	Moncton	D
14	STL	Jaden Schwartz	Tri-City	C
15	*L.A.*	*Derek Forbort*	*USA U-18*	*D*
16	STL	Vladimir Tarasenko	Novosibirsk	RW
17	COL	Joey Hishon	Owen Sound	C
18	NSH	Austin Watson	Peterborough	LW
19	FLA	Nick Bjugstad	Blaine	C
20	PIT	Beau Bennett	Penticton	RW
21	DET	Riley Sheahan	U. of Notre Dame	C
22	MTL	Jarred Tinordi	USA U-18	D
23	BUF	Mark Pysyk	Edmonton	D
24	CHI	Kevin Hayes	Nobles	RW
25	FLA	Quinton Howden	Moose Jaw	C
26	WSH	Evgeny Kuznetsov	Chelyabinsk	C
27	PHX	Mark Visentin	Niagara	G
28	S.J.	Charlie Coyle	South Shore	C/RW
29	ANA	Emerson Etem	Medicine Hat	RW
30	NYI	Brock Nelson	Warroad	C

OTHER NOTABLE SELECTIONS

Pick	Claimed by	Player	Amateur Club	Position
37	CAR	Justin Faulk	USA U-18	D
42	ANA	Devante Smith-Pelly	Mississauga	RW
47	L.A.	Tyler Toffoli	Ottawa	C
147	MTL	Brendan Gallagher	Vancouver	RW

2009

FIRST ROUND

Pick	Claimed by	Player	Amateur Club	Position
1	NYI	John Tavares	London	C
2	T.B.	Victor Hedman	MODO Ornskoldsvik	D
3	COL	Matt Duchene	Brampton	C
4	ATL	Evander Kane	Vancouver	C
5	L.A.	Brayden Schenn	Brandon	C
6	PHX	Oliver Ekman-Larsson	Leksand	D
7	TOR	Nazem Kadri	London	C
8	DAL	Scott Glennie	Brandon	RW
9	OTT	Jared Cowen	Spokane	D
10	EDM	Magnus Paajarvi-Svensson	Timra	LW
11	NSH	Ryan Ellis	Windsor	D
12	NYI	Calvin De Haan	Oshawa	D
13	BUF	Zack Kassian	Peterborough	RW
14	FLA	Dmitry Kulikov	Drummondville	D
15	ANA	Peter Holland	Guelph	C
16	MIN	Nick Leddy	Eden Prairie	D
17	STL	David Rundblad	Skelleftea	D
18	MTL	Louis Leblanc	Omaha	C
19	NYR	Chris Kreider	Andover	C
20	N.J.	Jacob Josefson	Djurgarden	C
21	CBJ	John Moore	Chicago Steel	D
22	VAN	Jordan Schroeder	U. of Minnesota	C
23	CGY	Tim Erixon	Skelleftea	D
24	WSH	Marcus Johansson	Farjestad	C
25	BOS	Jordan Caron	Rimouski	RW
26	ANA	Kyle Palmieri	USA U-18	C/RW
27	*CAR*	*Philippe Paradis*	*Shawinigan*	*C*
28	CHI	Dylan Olsen	Camrose	D
29	T.B.	Carter Ashton	Lethbridge	RW
30	PIT	Simon Despres	Saint John	D

OTHER NOTABLE SELECTIONS

Pick	Claimed by	Player	Amateur Club	Position
33	COL	Ryan O'Reilly	Erie	C
35	L.A.	Kyle Clifford	Barrie	LW
39	OTT	Jakob Silfverberg	Brynas	LW
46	OTT	Robin Lehner	Frolunda Jr.	G
60	DET	Thomas Tatar	Zvolen	LW
85	WSH	Cody Eakin	Swift Current	C
92	NYI	Casey Cizikas	St. Michael's	C
98	NSH	Craig Smith	Waterloo	C
104	BUF	Marcus Foligno	Sudbury	LW
149	CHI	Marcus Kruger	Djurgarden	C
186	L.A.	Jordan Nolan	Sault Ste. Marie	C

2008

FIRST ROUND

Pick	Claimed by	Player	Amateur Club	Position
1	T.B.	Steven Stamkos	Sarnia	C
2	L.A.	Drew Doughty	Guelph	D
3	ATL	Zach Bogosian	Peterborough	D
4	STL	Alex Pietrangelo	Niagara	D
5	TOR	Luke Schenn	Kelowna	D
6	CBJ	Nikita Filatov	CSKA 2	LW
7	NSH	Colin Wilson	Boston University	C
8	PHX	Mikkel Boedker	Kitchener	LW
9	NYI	Joshua Bailey	Windsor	C
10	VAN	Cody Hodgson	Brampton	C
11	*CHI*	*Kyle Beach*	*Everett*	*C*
12	BUF	Tyler Myers	Kelowna	D
13	L.A.	Colten Teubert	Regina	D
14	CAR	Zach Boychuk	Lethbridge	C
15	OTT	Erik Karlsson	Frolunda Jr.	D
16	BOS	Joe Colborne	Camrose	C
17	ANA	Jake Gardiner	Minnetonka	D
18	*NSH*	*Chet Pickard*	*Tri-City*	*G*
19	PHI	Luca Sbisa	Lethbridge	D
20	NYR	Michael Del Zotto	Oshawa	D
21	*WSH*	*Anton Gustafsson*	*Frolunda Jr.*	*C*
22	EDM	Jordan Eberle	Regina	C
23	MIN	Tyler Cuma	Ottawa	D
24	N.J.	Mattias Tedenby	HV 71 Jonkoping	LW
25	CGY	Greg Nemisz	Windsor	C
26	BUF	Tyler Ennis	Medicine Hat	C
27	WSH	John Carlson	Indiana	D
28	PHX	Viktor Tikhonov	Cherepovets	W
29	*ATL*	*Daultan Leveille*	*St. Catharines*	*C*
30	DET	Thomas McCollum	Guelph	G

OTHER NOTABLE SELECTIONS

Pick	Claimed by	Player	Amateur Club	Position
32	L.A.	Slava Voynov	Chelyabinsk	D
38	NSH	Roman Josi	Bern	D
51	NYR	Derek Stepan	Shattuck-St. Mary's	C
53	NYI	Travis Hamonic	Moose Jaw	D
79	OTT	Zack Smith	Swift Current	C
93	WSH	Braden Holtby	Saskatoon	G
111	NYR	Dale Weise	Swift Current	RW
114	CGY	T.J. Brodie	Saginaw	D
148	NYI	Matt Martin	Sarnia	LW
156	NYI	Jared Spurgeon	Spokane	D
186	S.J.	Jason Demers	Victoriaville	D

2007

FIRST ROUND

Pick	Claimed by	Player	Amateur Club	Position
1	CHI	Patrick Kane	London	RW
2	PHI	James van Riemsdyk	USA U-18	LW
3	PHX	Kyle Turris	Burnaby	C
4	L.A.	Thomas Hickey	Seattle	D
5	WSH	Karl Alzner	Calgary	D
6	EDM	Sam Gagner	London	C/W
7	CBJ	Jakub Voracek	Halifax	RW
8	BOS	Zach Hamill	Everett	C
9	S.J.	Logan Couture	Ottawa	C
10	FLA	Keaton Ellerby	Kamloops	D
11	CAR	Brandon Sutter	Red Deer	C/RW
12	MTL	Ryan McDonagh	Cretin-Derham	D
13	STL	Lars Eller	Frolunda Jr.	C
14	COL	Kevin Shattenkirk	USA U-18	D
15	EDM	Alex Plante	Calgary	D
16	MIN	Colton Gillies	Saskatoon	C
17	*NYR*	*Alexei Cherepanov*	*Omsk*	*RW*
18	STL	Ian Cole	USA U-18	D
19	*ANA*	*Logan MacMillan*	*Halifax*	*C*
20	*PIT*	*Angelo Esposito*	*Quebec*	*C*
21	EDM	Riley Nash	Salmon Arm	C
22	MTL	Max Pacioretty	Sioux City	LW
23	NSH	Jonathon Blum	Vancouver	D
24	CGY	Mikael Backlund	Vasteras	C
25	*VAN*	*Patrick White*	*Tri-City*	*C*
26	STL	David Perron	Lewiston	LW
27	DET	Brendan Smith	St. Michael's	D
28	S.J.	Nicholas Petrecki	Omaha	D
29	OTT	Jim O'Brien	U. of Minnesota	C
30	*PHX*	*Nick Ross*	*Regina*	*D*

OTHER NOTABLE SELECTIONS

Pick	Claimed by	Player	Amateur Club	Position
43	MTL	P.K. Subban	Belleville	D
55	COL	T.J. Galiardi	Dartmouth	LW
58	NSH	Nick Spaling	Kitchener	C
61	L.A.	Wayne Simmonds	Owen Sound	RW
77	T.B.	Alex Killorn	Deerfield	C
95	L.A.	Alec Martinez	Miami University	D
117	N.J.	Matt Halischuk	Kitchener	RW
129	DAL	Jamie Benn	Victoria	LW
168	NYR	Carl Hagelin	Sodertalje Jr	LW
173	S.J.	Nick Bonino	Boston U.	C
194	TOR	Carl Gunnarsson	Linkoping	D

2006

FIRST ROUND

Pick	Claimed by	Player	Amateur Club	Position
1	STL	Erik Johnson	USA U-18	D
2	PIT	Jordan Staal	Peterborough	C
3	CHI	Jonathan Toews	U. of North Dakota	C
4	WSH	Nicklas Backstrom	Brynas Gavle	C
5	BOS	Phil Kessel	U. of Minnesota	C
6	CBJ	Derick Brassard	Drummondville	C
7	NYI	Kyle Okposo	Des Moines	RW
8	PHX	Peter Mueller	Everett	C
9	MIN	James Sheppard	Cape Breton	C
10	FLA	Michael Frolik	Kladno	C
11	L.A.	Jonathan Bernier	Lewiston	G
12	ATL	Bryan Little	Barrie	C
13	TOR	Jiri Tlusty	Kladno	C
14	VAN	Michael Grabner	Spokane	RW
15	T.B.	Riku Helenius	Ilves Tampere	G
16	S.J.	Ty Wishart	Prince George	D
17	L.A.	Trevor Lewis	Des Moines	C
18	COL	Chris Stewart	Kingston	RW
19	*ANA*	*Mark Mitera*	*U. of Michigan*	*D*
20	*MTL*	*David Fischer*	*Apple Valley*	*D*
21	NYR	Bobby Sanguinetti	Owen Sound	D
22	PHI	Claude Giroux	Gatineau	RW
23	WSH	Simeon Varlamov	Yaroslavl 2	G
24	*BUF*	*Dennis Persson*	*Vasteras*	*D*
25	STL	Patrik Berglund	Vasteras	C
26	CGY	Leland Irving	Everett	G
27	DAL	Ivan Vishnevskiy	Rouyn-Noranda	D
28	OTT	Nick Foligno	Sudbury	LW
29	PHX	Chris Summers	USA U-18	D
30	N.J.	Matthew Corrente	Saginaw	D

OTHER NOTABLE SELECTIONS

Pick	Claimed by	Player	Amateur Club	Position
34	WSH	Michal Neuvirth	Sparta Jr.	G
44	TOR	Nikolai Kulemin	Magnitogorsk	W
46	BUF	Jhonas Enroth	Sodertalje	G
50	BOS	Milan Lucic	Vancouver	LW
54	NYR	Artem Anisimov	Yaroslavl	C
69	CBJ	Steve Mason	London	G
71	BOS	Brad Marchand	Moncton	C
72	MIN	Cal Clutterbuck	Oshawa	RW
99	TOR	James Reimer	Red Deer	G
112	ANA	Matt Beleskey	Belleville	LW
160	NYI	Andrew MacDonald	Moncton	D
161	TOR	Viktor Stalberg	Frolunda	LW
177	WSH	Mathieu Perreault	Acadie-Bathurst	C
189	CBJ	Derek Dorsett	Medicine Hat	RW

2005

FIRST ROUND

Pick	Claimed by		Amateur Club	Position
1	PIT	Sidney Crosby	Rimouski	C
2	ANA	Bobby Ryan	Owen Sound	RW
3	CAR	Jack Johnson	USA U-18	D
4	MIN	Benoit Pouliot	Sudbury	LW
5	MTL	Carey Price	Tri-City	G
6	CBJ	Gilbert Brule	Vancouver	C
7	CHI	Jack Skille	USA U-18	RW
8	S.J.	Devin Setoguchi	Saskatoon	RW
9	OTT	Brian Lee	Moorhead	D
10	VAN	Luc Bourdon	Val d'Or	D
11	L.A.	Anze Kopitar	Sodertalje Jr.	C
12	NYR	Marc Staal	Sudbury	D
13	*BUF*	*Marek Zagrapan*	*Chicoutimi*	*C*
14	*WSH*	*Sasha Pokulok*	*Cornell*	*D*
15	NYI	Ryan O'Marra	Erie	C
16	*ATL*	*Alex Bourret*	*Lewiston*	*RW*
17	PHX	Martin Hanzal	Ceske Budejovice	C
18	NSH	Ryan Parent	Guelph	D
19	DET	Jakub Kindl	Kitchener	D
20	FLA	Kenndal McArdle	Moose Jaw	LW
21	TOR	Tuukka Rask	Ilves Jr.	G
22	BOS	Matt Lashoff	Kitchener	D
23	N.J.	Nicklas Bergfors	Sodertalje	RW
24	STL	T.J. Oshie	Warroad	C
25	EDM	Andrew Cogliano	St. Mike's Jr. A	C
26	CGY	Matt Pelech	Sarnia	D
27	WSH	Joe Finley	Sioux Falls	D
28	DAL	Matt Niskanen	Virginia	D
29	PHI	Steve Downie	Windsor	RW
30	T.B.	Vladimir Mihalik	Presov	D

OTHER NOTABLE SELECTIONS

Pick	Claimed by		Amateur Club	Position
33	DAL	James Neal	Plymouth	LW
35	S.J.	Marc-Edouard Vlasic	Quebec	D
41	ATL	Ondrej Pavelec	Poldi Kladno Jr.	G
42	DET	Justin Abdelkader	Cedar Rapids	LW
44	COL	Paul Stastny	U. of Denver	C
45	MTL	Guillaume Latendresse	Drummondville	RW
51	VAN	Mason Raymond	Camrose	LW
62	PIT	Kris Letang	Val d'Or	D
72	L.A.	Jonathan Quick	Avon Old Farms	G
85	STL	Ben Bishop	Texas	G
105	PHX	Keith Yandle	Cushing Academy	D
230	NSH	Patric Hornqvist	Vasby	RW

2004

FIRST ROUND

Pick	Claimed by		Amateur Club	Position
1	WSH	Alex Ovechkin	Dynamo Moscow	LW
2	PIT	Evgeni Malkin	Magnitogorsk	C
3	CHI	Cam Barker	Medicine Hat	D
4	CAR	Andrew Ladd	Calgary	LW
5	PHX	Blake Wheeler	Breck	RW
6	NYR	Al Montoya	U. of Michigan	G
7	FLA	Rostislav Olesz	Vitkovice	C
8	CBJ	Alexandre Picard	Lewiston	LW
9	ANA	Ladislav Smid	Liberec	D
10	ATL	Boris Valabik	Kitchener	D
11	L.A.	Lauri Tukonen	Blues Espoo	RW
12	*MIN*	*A.J. Thelen*	*Michigan State*	*D*
13	BUF	Drew Stafford	U. of North Dakota	RW
14	EDM	Devan Dubnyk	Kamloops	G
15	NSH	Alexander Radulov	Tver	LW
16	NYI	Petteri Nokelainen	SaiPa	C
17	STL	Marek Schwarz	Sparta Praha	G
18	MTL	Kyle Chipchura	Prince Albert	C
19	NYR	Lauri Korpikoski	TPS Turku Jr.	LW
20	N.J.	Travis Zajac	Salmon Arm	C
21	COL	Wojtek Wolski	Brampton	LW
22	S.J.	Lukas Kaspar	Litvinov	RW
23	OTT	Andrej Meszaros	Trencin	D
24	CGY	Kris Chucko	Salmon Arm	LW
25	EDM	Rob Schremp	London	C
26	VAN	Cory Schneider	Phillips-Andover	G
27	WSH	Jeff Schultz	Calgary	D
28	DAL	Mark Fistric	Vancouver	D
29	WSH	Mike Green	Saskatoon	D
30	*T.B.*	*Andy Rogers*	*Calgary*	*D*

OTHER NOTABLE SELECTIONS

Pick	Claimed by		Amateur Club	Position
32	CHI	Dave Bolland	London	C
47	NYI	Blake Comeau	Kelowna	LW
53	FLA	David Booth	Michigan State	LW
56	DAL	Nicklas Grossmann	Sodertalje	D
60	NYR	Brandon Dubinsky	Portland	C
63	BOS	David Krejci	Kladno Jr.	C
70	CGY	Brandon Prust	London	LW
91	VAN	Alexander Edler	Jamtland	D
97	DET	Johan Franzen	Linkoping	C
127	NYR	Ryan Callahan	Guelph	RW
134	BOS	Kris Versteeg	Lethbridge	RW
150	MTL	Mikhail Grabovski	Nizhnekamsk	C
180	STL	Roman Polak	Vitkovice Jr.	D
214	CHI	Troy Brouwer	Moose Jaw	RW
227	NYI	Chris Campoli	Erie	D
258	NSH	Pekka Rinne	Karpat	G
262	MTL	Mark Streit	Zurich	D
265	PHX	Daniel Winnik	New Hampshire	D

2003

FIRST ROUND

Pick	Claimed by		Amateur Club	Position
1	PIT	Marc-Andre Fleury	Cape Breton	G
2	CAR	Eric Staal	Peterborough	C
3	FLA	Nathan Horton	Oshawa	C
4	CBJ	Nikolai Zherdev	CSKA Moscow	W
5	BUF	Thomas Vanek	U. of Minnesota	LW
6	S.J.	Milan Michalek	Budejovice	RW
7	NSH	Ryan Suter	USA U-18	D
8	ATL	Braydon Coburn	Portland	D
9	CGY	Dion Phaneuf	Red Deer	D
10	MTL	Andrei Kostitsyn	CSKA 2	RW
11	PHI	Jeff Carter	Sault Ste. Marie	C
12	NYR	Hugh Jessiman	Dartmouth	RW
13	L.A.	Dustin Brown	Guelph	RW
14	CHI	Brent Seabrook	Lethbridge	D
15	NYI	Robert Nilsson	Leksand	RW
16	S.J.	Steve Bernier	Moncton	RW
17	N.J.	Zach Parise	North Dakota	C
18	WSH	Eric Fehr	Brandon	RW
19	ANA	Ryan Getzlaf	Calgary	C
20	MIN	Brent Burns	Brampton	RW
21	BOS	Mark Stuart	Colorado College	D
22	EDM	Marc-Antoine Pouliot	Rimouski	C
23	VAN	Ryan Kesler	Ohio State	C
24	PHI	Mike Richards	Kitchener	C
25	FLA	Anthony Stewart	Kingston	C
26	L.A.	Brian Boyle	St. Sebastian's H.S.	C
27	L.A.	Jeff Tambellini	U. of Michigan	LW
28	ANA	Corey Perry	London	RW
29	OTT	Patrick Eaves	Boston College	RW
30	STL	Shawn Belle	Tri-City	D

OTHER NOTABLE SELECTIONS

Pick	Claimed by		Amateur Club	Position
33	DAL	Loui Eriksson	Vastra Frolunda Jr.	LW
37	NSH	Kevin Klein	St. Michael's	D
45	BOS	Patrice Bergeron	Acadie-Bathurst	C
47	S.J.	Matt Carle	River City	D
49	NSH	Shea Weber	Kelowna	D
52	CHI	Corey Crawford	Moncton	G
61	MTL	Maxim Lapierre	Montreal	C
62	STL	David Backes	Lincoln	C
64	DET	Jimmy Howard	U. of Maine	G
205	S.J.	Joe Pavelski	Waterloo Jr. A	C
214	EDM	Kyle Brodziak	Moose Jaw	C
239	ATL	Tobias Enstrom	MODO Ornskolsvik	D
245	CHI	Dustin Byfuglien	Prince George	RW
263	PIT	Matt Moulson	Cornell	LW
271	MTL	Jaroslav Halak	Bratislava Jr.	G
291	OTT	Brian Elliott	Ajax	G

2002

FIRST ROUND

Pick	Claimed by		Amateur Club	Position
1	CBJ	Rick Nash	London	LW
2	ATL	Kari Lehtonen	Jokerit	G
3	FLA	Jay Bouwmeester	Medicine Hat	D
4	PHI	Joni Pitkanen	Karpat	D
5	PIT	Ryan Whitney	Boston University	D
6	NSH	Scottie Upshall	Kamloops	RW
7	ANA	Joffrey Lupul	Medicine Hat	C
8	MIN	Pierre-Marc Bouchard	Chicoutimi	C
9	FLA	Petr Taticek	Sault Ste. Marie	C
10	CGY	Eric Nystrom	U. of Michigan	LW
11	BUF	Keith Ballard	U. of Minnesota	D
12	WSH	Steve Eminger	Kitchener	D
13	WSH	Alexander Semin	Chelyabinsk	LW
14	MTL	Christopher Higgins	Yale	C
15	*EDM*	*Jesse Niinimaki*	*Ilves Tampere*	*C*
16	OTT	Jakub Klepis	Portland	C
17	WSH	Boyd Gordon	Red Deer	RW
18	L.A.	Denis Grebeshkov	Yaroslavl	D
19	*PHX*	*Jakub Koreis*	*Plzen*	*C*
20	BUF	Dan Paille	Guelph	LW
21	CHI	Anton Babchuk	Elektrostal	D
22	NYI	Sean Bergenheim	Jokerit	C
23	PHX	Ben Eager	Oshawa	LW
24	TOR	Alexander Steen	Vastra Frolunda	C
25	CAR	Cam Ward	Red Deer	G
26	*DAL*	*Martin Vagner*	*Hull*	*D*
27	*S.J.*	*Mike Morris*	*St. Sebastian's H.S.*	*RW*
28	COL	Jonas Johansson	HV 71 Jonkoping Jr.	RW
29	BOS	Hannu Toivonen	HPK Jr.	G
30	ATL	Jim Slater	Michigan State	C

OTHER NOTABLE SELECTIONS

Pick	Claimed by		Amateur Club	Position
36	EDM	Jarret Stoll	Kootenay	C
38	MIN	Josh Harding	Regina	G
43	DAL	Trevor Daley	Sault Ste. Marie	D
44	EDM	Matt Greene	Green Bay	D
54	CHI	Duncan Keith	Michigan State	D
57	TOR	Matt Stajan	Belleville	C
58	DET	Jiri Hudler	Vsetin	C
63	DET	Tomas Fleischmann	Vitkovice Jr.	LW
67	FLA	Gregory Campbell	Plymouth	LW
90	CGY	Matthew Lomardi	Victoriaville	C
95	DET	Valtteri Filppula	Jokerit Jr.	C
234	PIT	Maxime Talbot	Hull	C
241	BUF	Dennis Wideman	London	D
291	DET	Jonathan Ericsson	Hasten Jr.	D

2001

FIRST ROUND

Pick	Claimed by		Amateur Club	Position
1	ATL	Ilya Kovalchuk	Spartak	LW
2	OTT	Jason Spezza	Windsor	C
3	T.B.	Alexander Svitov	Avangard Omsk	C
4	FLA	Stephen Weiss	Plymouth	C
5	ANA	Stanislav Chistov	Avangard Omsk	LW
6	MIN	Mikko Koivu	TPS Turku	C
7	MTL	Mike Komisarek	U. of Michigan	D
8	CBJ	Pascal Leclaire	Halifax	G
9	CHI	Tuomo Ruutu	Jokerit	C/LW
10	NYR	Dan Blackburn	Kootenay	G
11	PHX	Fredrik Sjostrom	Vastra Frolunda	RW
12	NSH	Dan Hamhuis	Prince George	D
13	EDM	Ales Hemsky	Hull	RW
14	CGY	Chuck Kobasew	Boston College	C
15	*CAR*	*Igor Knyazev*	*Spartak*	*D*
16	VAN	R.J. Umberger	Ohio State	C
17	TOR	Carlo Colaiacovo	Erie	D
18	*L.A.*	*Jens Karlsson*	*Vastra Frolunda*	*RW*
19	BOS	Shaone Morrisonn	Kamloops	D
20	S.J.	Marcel Goc	Schwenningen	C
21	PIT	Colby Armstrong	Red Deer	RW
22	BUF	Jiri Novotny	Budejovice	C
23	OTT	Tim Gleason	Windsor	D
24	FLA	Lukas Krajicek	Peterborough	D
25	MTL	Alexander Perezhogin	Avangard Omsk	C
26	DAL	Jason Bacashihua	Chicago Freeze	G
27	PHI	Jeff Woywitka	Red Deer	D
28	*N.J.*	*Adrian Foster*	*Saskatoon*	*C*
29	CHI	Adam Munro	Erie	G
30	L.A.	Dave Steckel	Ohio State	C

OTHER NOTABLE SELECTIONS

Pick	Claimed by		Amateur Club	Position
32	BUF	Derek Roy	Kitchener	C
40	NYR	Fedor Tyutin	St. Petersburg	D
49	L.A.	Michael Cammalleri	U. of Michigan	C
55	BUF	Jason Pominville	Shawinigan	RW
71	MTL	Tomas Plekanec	Kladno	LW
73	CHI	Craig Anderson	Guelph	G
95	PHI	Patrick Sharp	U. of Vermont	C
98	NSH	Jordin Tootoo	Brandon	RW
99	OTT	Ray Emery	Sault Ste. Marie	G
106	S.J.	Christoph Ehrhoff	Krefeld	D
151	VAN	Kevin Bieksa	Bowling Green	D
161	DAL	Mike Smith	Sudbury	G
172	PHI	Dennis Seidenberg	Mannheim	D
176	NSH	Marek Zidlicky	HIFK Helsinki	D
192	DAL	Jussi Jokinen	Karpat Jr.	F
193	OTT	Brooks Laich	Moose Jaw	C
221	WSH	Johnny Oduya	Victoriaville	D
241	BOS	Milan Jurcina	Halifax	D
264	ANA	P-A Parenteau	Chicoutimi	C

2000

FIRST ROUND

Pick	Claimed by		Amateur Club	Position
1	NYI	Rick DiPietro	Boston University	G
2	ATL	Dany Heatley	U. of Wisconsin	RW
3	MIN	Marian Gaborik	Dukla Trencin	RW
4	CBJ	Rostislav Klesla	Brampton	D
5	NYI	Raffi Torres	Brampton	LW
6	NSH	Scott Hartnell	Prince Albert	LW
7	BOS	Lars Jonsson	Leksand	D
8	T.B.	Nikita Alexeev	Erie	RW
9	CGY	Brent Krahn	Calgary	G
10	CHI	Mikhail Yakubov	Lada Togliatti	C
11	CHI	Pavel Vorobiev	Yaroslavl	RW
12	ANA	Alexei Smirnov	Tver	LW
13	MTL	Ron Hainsey	U. of Mass-Lowell	D
14	COL	Vaclav Nedorost	Budejovice	C
15	*BUF*	*Artem Kryukov*	*Yaroslavl*	*C*
16	MTL	Marcel Hossa	Portland	LW
17	EDM	Alexei Mikhnov	Yaroslavl	LW
18	PIT	Brooks Orpik	Boston College	D
19	PHX	Krys Kolanos	Boston College	C
20	L.A.	Alexander Frolov	Yaroslavl 2	LW
21	OTT	Anton Volchenkov	HK Moscow	D
22	N.J.	David Hale	Sioux City	D
23	VAN	Nathan Smith	Swift Current	C
24	TOR	Brad Boyes	Erie	C
25	DAL	Steve Ott	Windsor	C
26	WSH	Brian Sutherby	Moose Jaw	C
27	BOS	Martin Samuelsson	MoDo Ornskoldsvik	RW
28	PHI	Justin Williams	Plymouth	RW
29	DET	Niklas Kronwall	Djurgarden	D
30	STL	Jeff Taffe	U. of Minnesota	C

OTHER NOTABLE SELECTIONS

Pick	Claimed by		Amateur Club	Position
33	MIN	Nick Schultz	Prince Albert	D
44	ANA	Ilya Bryzgalov	Lada Togliatti	G
46	CGY	Jarret Stoll	Kootenay	C
55	OTT	Antoine Vermette	Victoriaville	C
60	DAL	Dan Ellis	Omaha	G
62	COL	Paul Martin	Elk River H.S.	D
95	NYR	Dominic Moore	Harvard	C
118	L.A.	Lubomir Visnovsky	Bratislava	D
155	CGY	Travis Moen	Kelowna	LW
159	COL	John-Michael Liles	Michigan State	D
205	NYR	Henrik Lundqvist	Vastre Frolunda Jr.	G
215	BUF	Matthew Lombardi	Victoriaville	C

1999

FIRST ROUND

Pick	Claimed by	Amateur Club	Position
1	ATL	Patrik Stefan	Long Beach	C
2	VAN	Daniel Sedin	MoDo Ornskoldsvik	LW
3	VAN	Henrik Sedin	MoDo Ornskoldsvik	C
4	NYR	Pavel Brendl	Calgary	RW
5	NYI	Tim Connolly	Erie	C
6	NSH	Brian Finley	Barrie	G
7	WSH	Kris Beech	Calgary	C
8	NYI	Taylor Pyatt	Sudbury	LW
9	NYR	Jamie Lundmark	Moose Jaw	C
10	NYI	Branislav Mezei	Belleville	D
11	CGY	Oleg Saprykin	Seattle	LW
12	FLA	Denis Shvidki	Barrie	RW
13	EDM	Jani Rita	Jokerit	LW
14	S.J.	Jeff Jillson	U. of Michigan	D
15	*PHX*	*Scott Kelman*	*Seattle*	*C*
16	CAR	David Tanabe	U. of Wisconsin	D
17	STL	Barret Jackman	Regina	D
18	PIT	Konstantin Koltsov	Cherepovets	RW
19	PHX	Kirill Safronov	St. Petersburg	D
20	BUF	Barrett Heisten	U. of Maine	LW
21	BOS	Nick Boynton	Ottawa	D
22	PHI	Maxime Ouellet	Quebec	G
23	CHI	Steve McCarthy	Kootenay	D
24	*TOR*	*Luca Cereda*	*Ambri*	*C*
25	COL	Mikhail Kuleshov	Cherepovets	LW
26	OTT	Martin Havlat	Trinec	LW
27	*N.J.*	*Ari Ahonen*	*JyP HT Jr.*	*G*
28	NYI	Kristian Kudroc	Michalovce	D

OTHER NOTABLE SELECTIONS

Pick	Claimed by	Amateur Club	Position
44	ANA	Jordan Leopold	U. of Minnesota	D
91	EDM	Mike Comrie	U. of Michigan	C
94	OTT	Chris Kelly	London	C
115	PIT	Ryan Malone	Omaha	LW
138	BUF	Ryan Miller	Soo	G
165	CHI	Michael Leighton	Windsor	G
191	NSH	Martin Erat	ZPS Zlin Jr.	LW
210	DET	Henrik Zetterberg	Timra	LW
212	COL	Radim Vrbata	Hull	RW

1998

FIRST ROUND

Pick	Claimed by	Amateur Club	Position
1	T.B.	Vincent Lecavalier	Rimouski	C
2	NSH	David Legwand	Plymouth	C
3	S.J.	Brad Stuart	Regina	D
4	VAN	Bryan Allen	Oshawa	D
5	ANA	Vitaly Vishnevski	Yaroslavl 2	D
6	CGY	Rico Fata	London	RW
7	NYR	Manny Malhotra	Guelph	C
8	CHI	Mark Bell	Ottawa	C
9	NYI	Mike Rupp	Erie	RW
10	TOR	Nik Antropov	Ust-Kamenogorsk	C
11	CAR	Jeff Heerema	Sarnia	RW
12	COL	Alex Tanguay	Halifax	LW
13	*EDM*	*Michael Henrich*	*Barrie*	*RW*
14	PHX	Patrick DesRochers	Sarnia	G
15	OTT	Mathieu Chouinard	Shawinigan	G
16	MTL	Eric Chouinard	Quebec	LW
17	COL	Martin Skoula	Barrie	D
18	BUF	Dmitri Kalinin	Chelyabinsk	D
19	COL	Robyn Regehr	Kamloops	D
20	COL	Scott Parker	Kelowna	RW
21	L.A.	Mathieu Biron	Shawinigan	D
22	PHI	Simon Gagne	Quebec	LW
23	PIT	Milan Kraft	Keramika Plzen Jr.	C
24	STL	Christian Backman	Vastra Frolunda Jr.	D
25	DET	Jiri Fischer	Hull	D
26	N.J.	Mike Van Ryn	U. of Michigan	D
27	N.J.	Scott Gomez	Tri-City	C

OTHER NOTABLE SELECTIONS

Pick	Claimed by	Amateur Club	Position
29	S.J.	Jonathan Cheechoo	Belleville	RW
44	OTT	Mike Fisher	Sudbury	C
45	MTL	Mike Ribeiro	Rouyn-Noranda	C
64	T.B.	Brad Richards	Rimouski	C
68	VAN	Jarkko Ruutu	HIFK Helsinki	RW
71	CAR	Erik Cole	Clarkson	LW
75	MTL	Francois Beauchemin	Laval	D
82	N.J.	Brian Gionta	Boston College	RW
99	EDM	Shawn Horcoff	Michigan State	C
117	FLA	Jaroslav Spacek	Farjestad	D
134	PIT	Rob Scuderi	Boston College	D
145	S.J.	Mikael Samuelsson	Sodertalje	LW
161	OTT	Chris Neil	North Bay	RW
162	MTL	Andrei Markov	Khimik Voskresensk	D
164	BUF	Ales Kotalik	Ceske Budejovice Jr.	RW
171	DET	Pavel Datsyuk	Yekateringburg	C
216	MTL	Michael Ryder	Hull	RW
230	NSH	Karlis Skrastins	TPS Turku	D

1997

FIRST ROUND

Pick	Claimed by	Amateur Club	Position
1	BOS	Joe Thornton	Sault Ste. Marie	C
2	S.J.	Patrick Marleau	Seattle	C
3	L.A.	Olli Jokinen	HIFK Helsinki	C
4	NYI	Roberto Luongo	Val-d'Or	G
5	NYI	Eric Brewer	Prince George	D
6	CGY	Daniel Tkaczuk	Barrie	C
7	T.B.	Paul Mara	Sudbury	D
8	BOS	Sergei Samsonov	Detroit	LW
9	WSH	Nick Boynton	Ottawa	D
10	VAN	Brad Ference	Spokane	D
11	MTL	Jason Ward	Erie	RW
12	OTT	Marian Hossa	Dukla Trencin	RW
13	CHI	Daniel Cleary	Belleville	RW
14	EDM	Michel Riesen	Biel-Bienne	RW
15	*L.A.*	*Matt Zultek*	*Ottawa*	*LW*
16	CHI	Ty Jones	Spokane	RW
17	PIT	Robert Dome	Las Vegas (IHL)	RW
18	ANA	Mikael Holmqvist	Djurgarden	C
19	*NYR*	*Stefan Cherneski*	*Brandon*	*RW*
20	FLA	Mike Brown	Red Deer	LW
21	BUF	Mika Noronen	Tappara Tampere	G
22	CAR	Nikos Tselios	Belleville	D
23	S.J.	Scott Hannan	Kelowna	D
24	N.J.	J-F Damphousse	Moncton	G
25	DAL	Brenden Morrow	Portland	LW
26	*COL*	*Kevin Grimes*	*Kingston*	*D*

OTHER NOTABLE SELECTIONS

Pick	Claimed by	Amateur Club	Position
47	FLA	Kristian Huselius	Farjestad	LW
48	BUF	Henrik Tallinder	AIK Solna	D
69	BUF	Maxim Afinogenov	Dynamo Moscow	RW
78	COL	Ville Nieminen	Tappara Tampere	RW
83	L.A.	Joe Corvo	U. of Western Michigan	D
121	EDM	Jason Chimera	Medicine Hat	LW
144	VAN	Matt Cooke	Windsor	C
156	BUF	Brian Campbell	Ottawa	D
177	STL	Ladislav Nagy	Dragon Presov	LW
190	TOR	Shawn Thornton	Peterborough	RW
208	PIT	Andrew Ference	Portland	D

1996

FIRST ROUND

Pick	Claimed by	Amateur Club	Position
1	OTT	Chris Phillips	Prince Albert	D
2	S.J.	Andrei Zyuzin	Salavat Yulayev Ufa	D
3	NYI	J.P. Dumont	Val-d'Or	RW
4	WSH	Alexandre Volchkov	Barrie	C
5	DAL	Ric Jackman	Sault Ste. Marie	D
6	EDM	Boyd Devereaux	Kitchener	C
7	BUF	Erik Rasmussen	U. of Minnesota	LW/C
8	BOS	Johnathan Aitken	Medicine Hat	D
9	ANA	Ruslan Salei	Las Vegas (IHL)	D
10	N.J.	Lance Ward	Red Deer	D
11	PHX	Dan Focht	Tri-City	D
12	VAN	Josh Holden	Regina	C
13	CGY	Derek Morris	Regina	D
14	STL	Marty Reasoner	Boston College	C
15	PHI	Dainius Zubrus	Pembroke Jr. A	RW
16	T.B.	Mario Larocque	Hull	D
17	WSH	Jaroslav Svejkovsky	Tri-City	RW
18	MTL	Matt Higgins	Moose Jaw	C
19	EDM	Matthieu Descoteaux	Shawinigan	D
20	FLA	Marcus Nilson	Djurgarden	LW
21	S.J.	Marco Sturm	Landshut	LW
22	*NYR*	*Jeff Brown*	*Sarnia*	*D*
23	*PIT*	*Craig Hillier*	*Ottawa*	*G*
24	PHX	Danny Briere	Drummondville	C
25	COL	Peter Ratchuk	Shattuck-St. Mary's	D
26	DET	Jesse Wallin	Red Deer	D

OTHER NOTABLE SELECTIONS

Pick	Claimed by	Amateur Club	Position
27	BUF	Cory Sarich	Saskatoon	D
35	ANA	Matt Cullen	St. Cloud State	C
49	N.J.	Colin White	Hull	D
56	NYI	Zdeno Chara	Dukla Trencin	D
59	EDM	Tom Poti	Cushing Academy	D
79	COL	Mark Parrish	St. Cloud State	RW
89	CGY	Toni Lydman	Reipas Lahti	D
96	L.A.	Eric Belanger	Beauport	C
176	COL	Samuel Pahlsson	MoDo Ornskoldsvik	C
179	T.B.	Pavel Kubina	Vitkovice	D
199	N.J.	Willie Mitchell	Melfort Jr. A.	D
204	TOR	Tomas Kaberle	Kladno	D
223	HFD	Craig Adams	Harvard	RW
239	OTT	Sami Salo	TPS Turku	D

1995

FIRST ROUND

Pick	Claimed by	Amateur Club	Position
1	OTT	Bryan Berard	Detroit	D
2	NYI	Wade Redden	Brandon	D
3	L.A.	Aki Berg	Kiekko-67 Turku	D
4	ANA	Chad Kilger	Kingston	C
5	T.B.	Daymond Langkow	Tri-City	C
6	EDM	Steve Kelly	Prince Albert	C
7	WPG	Shane Doan	Kamloops	RW
8	MTL	Terry Ryan	Tri-City	LW
9	BOS	Kyle McLaren	Tacoma	D
10	FLA	Radek Dvorak	Ceske Budejovice	RW
11	DAL	Jarome Iginla	Kamloops	RW
12	*S.J.*	*Teemu Riihijarvi*	*Kiekko-Espoo*	*LW*
13	HFD	Jean-Sebastien Giguere	Halifax	G
14	BUF	Jay McKee	Niagara Falls	D
15	TOR	Jeff Ware	Oshawa	D
16	BUF	Martin Biron	Beauport	G
17	WSH	Brad Church	Prince Albert	LW
18	N.J.	Petr Sykora	Detroit	RW
19	CHI	Dmitri Nabokov	Krylja Sovetov	C/LW
20	CGY	Denis Gauthier	Drummondville	D
21	BOS	Sean Brown	Belleville	D
22	PHI	Brian Boucher	Tri-City	G
23	WSH	Miika Elomo	Kiekko-67 Turku	LW
24	PIT	Aleksey Morozov	Krylja Sovetov	RW
25	COL	Marc Denis	Chicoutimi	G
26	DET	Maxim Kuznetsov	Dynamo Moscow	D

OTHER NOTABLE SELECTIONS

Pick	Claimed by	Amateur Club	Position
31	EDM	Georges Laraque	St-Jean	RW
49	STL	Jochen Hecht	Mannheim	C
67	WPG	Brad Isbister	Portland	LW
79	N.J.	Alyn McCauley	Ottawa	C
87	HFD	Sami Kapanen	HIFK Helsinki	RW
90	S.J.	Vesa Toskala	Ilves Tampere	G
91	NYR	Marc Savard	Oshawa	C
101	STL	Michal Handzus	Banska Bystrica	C
116	S.J.	Miikka Kiprusoff	TPS Turku Jr.	G
122	N.J.	Chris Mason	Prince George	G
144	VAN	Brent Sopel	Swift Current	D
164	MTL	Stephane Robidas	Shawinigan	D
177	BOS	P.J. Axelsson	Vastra Frolunda	LW
192	FLA	Filip Kuba	Vitkovice Jr.	D
223	TOR	Danny Markov	Moscow Spartak	D

1994

FIRST ROUND

Pick	Claimed by	Amateur Club	Position
1	FLA	Ed Jovanovski	Windsor	D
2	ANA	Oleg Tverdovsky	Krylja Sovetov	D
3	OTT	Radek Bonk	Las Vegas (IHL)	C
4	EDM	Jason Bonsignore	Niagara Falls	C
5	HFD	Jeff O'Neill	Guelph	RW
6	EDM	Ryan Smyth	Moose Jaw	LW
7	L.A.	Jamie Storr	Owen Sound	G
8	T.B.	Jason Wiemer	Portland	C
9	NYI	Brett Lindros	Kingston	RW
10	WSH	Nolan Baumgartner	Kamloops	D
11	S.J.	Jeff Friesen	Regina	LW
12	QUE	Wade Belak	Saskatoon	D/RW
13	VAN	Mattias Ohlund	Pitea	D
14	CHI	Ethan Moreau	Niagara Falls	LW
15	*WSH*	*Alexander Kharlamov*	*CSKA Moscow*	*C*
16	TOR	Eric Fichaud	Chictoutimi	G
17	BUF	Wayne Primeau	Owen Sound	C
18	MTL	Brad Brown	North Bay	D
19	CGY	Chris Dingman	Brandon	LW
20	DAL	Jason Botterill	U. of Michigan	LW
21	*BOS*	*Evgeni Ryabchikov*	*Molot Perm*	*G*
22	*QUE*	*Jeffrey Kealty*	*Catholic Memorial H.S.*	*D*
23	DET	Yan Golubovsky	Dynamo 2	D
24	PIT	Chris Wells	Seattle	C
25	N.J.	Vadim Sharifijanov	Salavat Yulayev Ufa	LW
26	NYR	Dan Cloutier	Sault Ste. Marie	G

OTHER NOTABLE SELECTIONS

Pick	Claimed by	Amateur Club	Position
29	OTT	Stan Neckar	Ceske Budejovice	D
44	MTL	Jose Theodore	St-Jean	G
49	DET	Mathieu Dandenault	Sherbrooke	RW/D
50	PIT	Richard Park	Belleville	C
51	N.J.	Patrik Elias	Kladno	C
64	TOR	Fredrik Modin	Timra	LW
71	N.J.	Sheldon Souray	Tri-City	D
72	QUE	Chris Drury	Fairfield Prep	C
87	QUE	Milan Hejduk	Pardubice	RW
90	NYI	Brad Lukowich	Kamloops	D
124	DAL	Marty Turco	Cambridge Jr. A	G
133	OTT	Daniel Alfredsson	Vastra Frolunda	RW
217	QUE	Tim Thomas	U. of Vermont	G
218	PHI	Johan Hedberg	Leksand	G
219	S.J.	Evgeni Nabokov	Ust-Kamenogorsk	G
226	MTL	Tomas Vokoun	Kladno	G
233	N.J.	Steve Sullivan	Sault Ste. Marie	RW
249	WSH	Richard Zednik	Banska Bystricia	RW
257	DET	Tomas Holmstrom	Bodens IK	LW
286	NYR	Kim Johnsson	Malmo	D

Pick	Claimed by	Amateur Club	Position

1993

FIRST ROUND

Pick	Claimed by	Amateur Club	Position
1	OTT	Alexandre Daigle	Victoriaville	C
2	HFD	Chris Pronger	Peterborough	D
3	T.B.	Chris Gratton	Kingston	C
4	ANA	Paul Kariya	U. of Maine	LW
5	FLA	Rob Niedermayer	Medicine Hat	C
6	S.J.	Viktor Kozlov	Dynamo Moscow	C
7	EDM	Jason Arnott	Oshawa	C
8	NYR	Niklas Sundstrom	MoDo Ornskoldsvik	RW
9	DAL	Todd Harvey	Detroit	RW/C
10	QUE	Jocelyn Thibault	Sherbrooke	G
11	WSH	Brendan Witt	Seattle	D
12	TOR	Kenny Jonsson	Rogle Angelholm	D
13	N.J.	Denis Pederson	Prince Albert	C/RW
14	QUE	Adam Deadmarsh	Portland	RW
15	WPG	Mats Lindgren	Skelleftea	C/LW
16	EDM	Nick Stajduhar	London	D
17	WSH	Jason Allison	London	C
18	*CGY*	*Jesper Mattsson*	*Malmo*	*C*
19	TOR	Landon Wilson	Dubuque	RW
20	VAN	Mike Wilson	Sudbury	D
21	MTL	Saku Koivu	TPS Turku	C
22	DET	Anders Eriksson	MoDo Ornskoldsvik	D
23	NYI	Todd Bertuzzi	Guelph	RW
24	*CHI*	*Eric Lecompte*	*Hull*	*LW*
25	BOS	Kevyn Adams	Miami of Ohio	C
26	PIT	Stefan Bergkvist	Leksand	D

OTHER NOTABLE SELECTIONS

Pick	Claimed by	Amateur Club	Position
32	N.J.	Jay Pandolfo	Boston University	LW
35	DAL	Jamie Langenbrunner	Cloquet	C
39	N.J.	Brendan Morrison	Spokane	C
40	NYI	Bryan McCabe	Spokane	D
41	FLA	Kevin Weekes	Owen Sound	G
71	PHI	Vinny Prospal	Ceske Budejovice	C
72	HFD	Marek Malik	Vitkovice	D
89	STL	Jamal Myers	Western Mich.	RW
90	CHI	Eric Daze	Beauport	RW
111	EDM	Miroslav Satan	Dukla Trencin	LW
118	NYI	Tommy Salo	Vasteras	G
124	VAN	Scott Walker	Owen Sound	RW
151	MTL	Darcy Tucker	Kamloops	RW
156	PIT	Patrick Lalime	Shawinigan	G
164	NYR	Todd Marchant	Clarkson	C
174	WSH	Andrew Brunette	Owen Sound	LW
188	HFD	Manny Legace	Niagara Falls	G
207	BOS	Hal Gill	Nashoba H.S.	D
219	STL	Mike Grier	St. Sebastian's H.S.	RW
227	OTT	Pavol Demitra	Dukla Trencin	LW
250	L.A.	Kimmo Timonen	KalPa Kuopio	D

1992

FIRST ROUND

Pick	Claimed by	Amateur Club	Position
1	T.B.	Roman Hamrlik	ZPS Zlin	D
2	OTT	Alexei Yashin	Dynamo Moscow	C
3	S.J.	Mike Rathje	Medicine Hat	D
4	QUE	Todd Warriner	Windsor	LW
5	NYI	Darius Kasparaitis	Dynamo Moscow	D
6	CGY	Cory Stillman	Windsor	LW
7	*PHI*	*Ryan Sittler*	*Nichols H.S.*	*LW*
8	TOR	Brandon Convery	Sudbury	C
9	HFD	Robert Petrovicky	Dukla Trencin	C
10	S.J.	Andrei Nazarov	Dynamo Moscow	LW
11	BUF	David Cooper	Medicine Hat	D
12	CHI	Sergei Krivokrasov	CSKA Moscow	RW
13	EDM	Joe Hulbig	St. Sebastian's H.S.	LW
14	WSH	Sergei Gonchar	Traktor Chelyabinsk	D
15	PHI	Jason Bowen	Tri-City	D
16	BOS	Dmitri Kvartalnov	San Diego (IHL)	LW
17	WPG	Sergei Bautin	Dynamo Moscow	D
18	N.J.	Jason Smith	Regina	D
19	PIT	Martin Straka	Skoda Plzen	C
20	MTL	David Wilkie	Kamloops	D
21	*VAN*	*Libor Polasek*	*Vitkovice*	*C*
22	*DET*	*Curtis Bowen*	*Ottawa*	*LW*
23	TOR	Grant Marshall	Ottawa	RW
24	NYR	Peter Ferraro	Waterloo Jr. A	LW

OTHER NOTABLE SELECTIONS

Pick	Claimed by	Amateur Club	Position
32	WSH	Jim Carey	Catholic Memorial	G
33	MTL	Valeri Bure	Spokane	RW
38	STL	Igor Korolev	Dynamo Moscow	C
40	VAN	Michael Peca	Ottawa	C
42	N.J.	Sergei Brylin	CSKA Moscow	C
46	DET	Darren McCarty	Belleville	RW
48	NYR	Mattias Norstrom	AIK Solna	D
52	QUE	Manny Fernandez	Laval	G
65	EDM	Kirk Maltby	Owen Sound	RW
68	MTL	Craig Rivet	Kingston	D
88	MIN	Jere Lehtinen	Kiekko-Espoo	RW
117	VAN	Adrian Aucoin	Boston University	D
158	STL	Ian Laperriere	Drummondville	C/RW
186	N.J.	Stephane Yelle	Oshawa	C
204	WPG	Nikolai Khabibulin	CSKA Moscow	G
220	QUE	Anson Carter	Wexford Jr. A	C

1991

FIRST ROUND

Pick	Claimed by	Amateur Club	Position
1	QUE	Eric Lindros	Oshawa	C
2	S.J.	Pat Falloon	Spokane	RW
3	N.J.	Scott Niedermayer	Kamloops	D
4	NYI	Scott Lachance	Boston University	D
5	WPG	Aaron Ward	U. of Michigan	D
6	PHI	Peter Forsberg	MoDo Ornskoldsvik	C
7	VAN	Alek Stojanov	Hamilton	RW
8	MIN	Richard Matvichuk	Saskatoon	D
9	HFD	Patrick Poulin	St-Hyacinthe	C
10	DET	Martin Lapointe	Laval	RW
11	N.J.	Brian Rolston	Det. Compuware Jr. A	C/RW
12	EDM	Tyler Wright	Swift Current	C
13	BUF	Philippe Boucher	Granby	D
14	WSH	Pat Peake	Detroit	C
15	NYR	Alex Kovalev	Dynamo Moscow	RW
16	PIT	Markus Naslund	MoDo Ornskoldsvik	LW
17	*MTL*	*Brent Bilodeau*	*Seattle*	*D*
18	BOS	Glen Murray	Sudbury	RW
19	CGY	Niklas Sundblad	AIK Solna	RW
20	EDM	Martin Rucinsky	Litvinov	LW
21	WSH	Trevor Halverson	North Bay	LW
22	CHI	Dean McAmmond	Prince Albert	LW

OTHER NOTABLE SELECTIONS

Pick	Claimed by	Amateur Club	Position
23	S.J.	Ray Whitney	Spokane	LW
26	NYI	Ziggy Palffy	AC Nitra	RW
27	STL	Steve Staios	Niagara Falls	D
30	S.J.	Sandis Ozolinsh	Dynamo Riga	D
40	BOS	Jozef Stumpel	AC Nitra	C
47	TOR	Yanic Perreault	Trois-Rivieres	C
54	DET	Chris Osgood	Medicine Hat	G
58	WSH	Steve Konowalchuk	Portland	LW
59	HFD	Michael Nylander	Huddinge	C
76	DET	Mike Knuble	Kalamazoo Jr. A	RW
81	L.A.	Alexei Zhitnik	Sokol Kiev	D
106	BOS	Mariusz Czerkawski	GKS Tychy	RW
122	PHI	Dmitry Yushkevich	Yaroslavl	D
123	BUF	Sean O'Donnell	Sudbury	D
171	MTL	Brian Savage	Miami of Ohio	LW
203	WPG	Igor Ulanov	Khimik Voskresensk	D

1990

FIRST ROUND

Pick	Claimed by	Amateur Club	Position
1	QUE	Owen Nolan	Cornwall	RW
2	VAN	Petr Nedved	Seattle	C
3	DET	Keith Primeau	Niagara Falls	C
4	PHI	Mike Ricci	Peterborough	C
5	PIT	Jaromir Jagr	Kladno	RW
6	NYI	Scott Scissons	Saskatoon	C
7	L.A.	Darryl Sydor	Kamloops	D
8	MIN	Derian Hatcher	North Bay	D
9	WSH	John Slaney	Cornwall	D
10	TOR	Drake Berehowsky	Kingston	D
11	CGY	Trevor Kidd	Brandon	G
12	MTL	Turner Stevenson	Seattle	RW

Originally selected by Los Angeles with the 250th pick in the 1993 NHL Draft, Kimmo Timonen remained in Finland until traded to Nashville in 1998. A high-scoring defenseman with the Predators and the Flyers, Timonen retired after winning the Stanley Cup with Chicago in 2015.

Pick	Claimed by	Amateur Club	Position
13 NYR	*Michael Stewart*	*Michigan State*	*D*
14 BUF	Brad May	Niagara Falls	LW
15 HFD	Mark Greig	Lethbridge	RW
16 CHI	Karl Dykhuis	Hull	D
17 EDM	*Scott Allison*	*Prince Albert*	*C*
18 VAN	Shawn Antoski	North Bay	LW
19 WPG	Keith Tkachuk	Malden Catholic H.S.	LW
20 N.J.	Martin Brodeur	St-Hyacinthe	G
21 BOS	Bryan Smolinski	Michigan State	C

OTHER NOTABLE SELECTIONS

Pick	Claimed by	Amateur Club	Position
25 PHI	Chris Simon	Ottawa	LW
31 TOR	Felix Potvin	Chicoutimi	G
34 NYR	Doug Weight	Lake Superior State	C
36 HFD	Geoff Sanderson	Swift Current	C
45 DET	Vyacheslav Kozlov	Khimik Voskresensk	RW
77 WPG	Alexei Zhamnov	Dynamo Moscow	C
85 NYR	Sergei Zubov	CSKA Moscow	D
113 MIN	Roman Turek	Plzen	G
123 MTL	Craig Conroy	Northwood Prep	C
133 L.A.	Robert Lang	CHZ Litvinov	C
156 WSH	Peter Bondra	Kosice	RW
158 QUE	Alexander Karpovtsev	VSZ Dynamo	D
177 WSH	Ken Klee	Bowling Green	D
244 NYR	Sergei Nemchinov	Krylja Sovetov	LW

1989

FIRST ROUND

Pick	Claimed by	Amateur Club	Position
1 QUE	Mats Sundin	Nacka	C
2 NYI	Dave Chyzowski	Kamloops	LW
3 TOR	Scott Thornton	Belleville	C
4 WPG	Stu Barnes	Tri-City	C
5 N.J.	Bill Guerin	Springfield Jr. B	RW
6 CHI	Adam Bennett	Sudbury	D
7 MIN	Doug Zmolek	John Marshall H.S.	D
8 VAN	Jason Herter	North Dakota	D
9 STL	Jason Marshall	Vernon Jr. A	D
10 HFD	Bobby Holik	Dukla Jihlava	C
11 DET	Mike Sillinger	Regina	C
12 TOR	Rob Pearson	Belleville	RW
13 MTL	Lindsay Vallis	Seattle	D
14 BUF	Kevin Haller	Regina	D
15 EDM	*Jason Soules*	*Niagara Falls*	*D*
16 PIT	Jamie Heward	Regina	D
17 BOS	Shayne Stevenson	Kitchener	RW
18 N.J.	Jason Miller	Medicine Hat	C
19 WSH	Olaf Kolzig	Tri-City	G
20 NYR	Steven Rice	Kitchener	RW
21 TOR	Steve Bancroft	Belleville	D

OTHER NOTABLE SELECTIONS

Pick	Claimed by	Amateur Club	Position
22 QUE	Adam Foote	Sault Ste. Marie	D
23 NYI	Travis Green	Spokane	C
30 MTL	Patrice Brisebois	Laval	D
53 DET	Nicklas Lidstrom	Vasteras	D
62 WPG	Kris Draper	Canadian National	C
70 CGY	Robert Reichel	Litvinov	C
109 WPG	Dan Bylsma	Bowling Green	RW
74 DET	Sergei Fedorov	CSKA Moscow	C
113 VAN	Pavel Bure	CSKA Moscow	RW
116 DET	Dallas Drake	Northern Michigan	C
183 BUF	Donald Audette	Laval	RW
191 NYI	Vladimir Malakhov	CSKA Moscow	D
196 MIN	Arturs Irbe	Dynamo Riga	G
221 DET	Vladimir Konstantinov	CSKA Moscow	D

1988

FIRST ROUND

Pick	Claimed by	Amateur Club	Position
1 MIN	Mike Modano	Prince Albert	C
2 VAN	Trevor Linden	Medicine Hat	RW
3 QUE	Curtis Leschyshyn	Saskatoon	D
4 PIT	Darrin Shannon	Windsor	LW
5 QUE	Daniel Dore	Drummondville	RW
6 TOR	Scott Pearson	Kingston	LW
7 L.A.	Martin Gelinas	Hull	LW
8 CHI	Jeremy Roenick	Thayer Academy	C
9 STL	Rod Brind'Amour	Notre Dame Jr. A	C
10 WPG	Teemu Selanne	Jokerit	RW
11 HFD	Chris Govedaris	Toronto	LW
12 N.J.	Corey Foster	Peterborough	D
13 BUF	Joel Savage	Victoria	RW
14 PHI	Claude Boivin	Drummondville	LW
15 WSH	Reggie Savage	Victoriaville	C
16 NYI	*Kevin Cheveldayoff*	*Brandon*	*D*
17 DET	*Kory Kocur*	*Saskatoon*	*RW*
18 BOS	Rob Cimetta	Toronto	W
19 EDM	Francois Leroux	St-Jean	D
20 MTL	Eric Charron	Trois-Rivieres	D
21 CGY	Jason Muzzatti	Michigan State	G

Theoren Fleury was selected by Calgary with the 166th pick in the 1987 Draft. Among players selected in that year, only Joe Sakic, Brendan Shanahan and Pierre Turgeon have more goals, points and assists than the 455, 633 and 1,088 that Fleury accumulated in 15 NHL seasons.

OTHER NOTABLE SELECTIONS

Pick	Claimed by	Amateur Club	Position
27 TOR	Tie Domi	Peterborough	RW
67 PIT	Mark Recchi	Kamloops	RW
68 NYR	Tony Amonte	Thayer Academy	RW
70 L.A.	Rob Blake	Bowling Green	D
76 BUF	Keith Carney	Mount St. Charles H.S.	D
81 BOS	Joe Juneau	RPI	C
89 BUF	Alexander Mogilny	CSKA Moscow	LW
97 BUF	Rob Ray	Cornwall	RW
120 WSH	Dmitri Khristich	Kiev Sokol	RW
129 QUE	Valeri Kamensky	CSKA Moscow	LW
198 STL	Bret Hedican	North St. Paul H.S.	D
234 QUE	Claude Lapointe	Laval	LW/C

1987

FIRST ROUND

Pick	Claimed by	Amateur Club	Position
1 BUF	Pierre Turgeon	Granby	C
2 N.J.	Brendan Shanahan	London	LW
3 BOS	Glen Wesley	Portland	D
4 L.A.	Wayne McBean	Medicine Hat	D
5 PIT	Chris Joseph	Seattle	D
6 MIN	Dave Archibald	Portland	C/LW
7 TOR	Luke Richardson	Peterborough	D
8 CHI	Jimmy Waite	Chicoutimi	G
9 QUE	Bryan Fogarty	Kingston	D
10 NYR	Jay More	New Westminster	D
11 DET	Yves Racine	Longueuil	D
12 STL	Keith Osborne	North Bay	RW
13 NYI	Dean Chynoweth	Medicine Hat	D
14 BOS	Stephane Quintal	Granby	D
15 QUE	Joe Sakic	Swift Current	C
16 WPG	Bryan Marchment	Belleville	D
17 MTL	Andrew Cassels	Ottawa	C
18 HFD	Jody Hull	Peterborough	RW
19 CGY	*Bryan Deasley*	*U. of Michigan*	*LW*
20 PHI	Darren Rumble	Kitchener	D
21 EDM	*Peter Soberlak*	*Swift Current*	*LW*

OTHER NOTABLE SELECTIONS

Pick	Claimed by	Amateur Club	Position
33 MTL	John LeClair	Bellows Academy	LW
38 MTL	Eric Desjardins	Granby	D
44 MTL	Mathieu Schneider	Cornwall	D
71 TOR	Joe Sacco	Medford H.S.	RW
110 PIT	Shawn McEachern	Matignon H.S.	RW
114 QUE	Garth Snow	Mount St. Charles H.S.	G
118 NYI	Rob DiMaio	Medicine Hat	RW
149 N.J.	Jim Dowd	Brick H.S.	C
166 CGY	Theoren Fleury	Moose Jaw	RW

1986

FIRST ROUND

Pick	Claimed by	Amateur Club	Position
1 DET	Joe Murphy	Michigan State	RW
2 L.A.	Jimmy Carson	Verdun	C
3 N.J.	Neil Brady	Medicine Hat	C
4 PIT	Zarley Zalapski	Canadian National	D
5 BUF	Shawn Anderson	Canadian National	D
6 TOR	Vincent Damphousse	Laval	C
7 VAN	Dan Woodley	Portland	RW
8 WPG	Pat Elynuik	Prince Albert	RW
9 NYR	Brian Leetch	Avon Old Farms H.S.	D
10 STL	Jocelyn Lemieux	Laval	RW
11 HFD	Scott Young	Boston University	RW
12 MIN	Warren Babe	Lethbridge	LW
13 BOS	Craig Janney	Boston College	C
14 CHI	Everett Sanipass	Verdun	LW
15 MTL	Mark Pederson	Medicine Hat	LW
16 CGY	*George Pelawa*	*Bemidji H.S.*	*RW*
17 NYI	Tom Fitzgerald	Austin Prep	RW
18 QUE	Ken McRae	Sudbury	C
19 WSH	Jeff Greenlaw	Canadian National	LW
20 PHI	Kerry Huffman	Guelph	D
21 EDM	Kim Issel	Prince Albert	RW

OTHER NOTABLE SELECTIONS

Pick	Claimed by	Amateur Club	Position
22 DET	Adam Graves	Windsor	LW
29 WPG	Teppo Numminen	Tappara Tampere	D
57 MTL	Jyrki Lumme	Ilves Tampere	D
67 PIT	Rob Brown	Kamloops	RW
72 NYR	Mark Janssens	Regina	C
81 QUE	Ron Tugnutt	Peterborough	G
85 DET	Johan Garpenlov	Nacka	LW
114 NYR	Darren Turcotte	North Bay	C
141 MTL	Lyle Odelein	Moose Jaw	D

1985

FIRST ROUND

Pick	Claimed by	Amateur Club	Position
1 TOR	Wendel Clark	Saskatoon	LW/D
2 PIT	Craig Simpson	Michigan State	LW
3 N.J.	Craig Wolanin	Kitchener	D
4 VAN	Jim Sandlak	London	RW
5 HFD	Dana Murzyn	Calgary	D
6 NYI	Brad Dalgarno	Hamilton	RW
7 NYR	Ulf Dahlen	Ostersund	RW
8 DET	Brent Fedyk	Regina	LW
9 L.A.	Craig Duncanson	Sudbury	LW
10 L.A.	Dan Gratton	Oshawa	C
11 CHI	Dave Manson	Prince Albert	D
12 MTL	Jose Charbonneau	Drummondville	RW
13 NYI	Derek King	Sault Ste. Marie	LW
14 BUF	Calle Johansson	Vastra Frolunda	D
15 QUE	David Latta	Kitchener	LW

Pick	Claimed by		Amateur Club	Position
16	MTL	Tom Chorske	Minneapolis SW H.S.	LW
17	*CGY*	*Chris Biotti*	*Belmont Hill H.S.*	*D*
18	WPG	Ryan Stewart	Kamloops	C
19	WSH	Yvon Corriveau	Toronto	LW
20	EDM	Scott Metcalfe	Kingston	LW
21	PHI	Glen Seabrooke	Peterborough	C

OTHER NOTABLE SELECTIONS

Pick	Claimed by		Amateur Club	Position
24	N.J.	Sean Burke	Toronto	G
27	CGY	Joe Nieuwendyk	Cornell	C
28	NYR	Mike Richter	Northwood Prep	G
32	N.J.	Eric Weinrich	North Yarmouth Academy	D
35	BUF	Benoit Hogue	St-Jean	C
50	DET	Steve Chiasson	Guelph	D
52	BOS	Bill Ranford	New Westminster	G
81	WPG	Fredrik Olausson	Farjestad	D
113	DET	Randy McKay	Michigan Tech	RW
157	BOS	Randy Burridge	Peterborough	LW
188	EDM	Kelly Buchberger	Moose Jaw	RW
189	PHI	Gord Murphy	Oshawa	D
214	VAN	Igor Larionov	CSKA Moscow	C

1984

FIRST ROUND

Pick	Claimed by		Amateur Club	Position
1	PIT	Mario Lemieux	Laval	C
2	N.J.	Kirk Muller	Guelph	LW
3	CHI	Eddie Olczyk	Team USA	C
4	TOR	Al Iafrate	Belleville	D
5	MTL	Petr Svoboda	CHZ Litvinov	D
6	L.A.	Craig Redmond	U. of Denver	D
7	DET	Shawn Burr	Kitchener	LW/C
8	MTL	Shayne Corson	Brantford	LW
9	PIT	Doug Bodger	Kamloops	D
10	VAN	J.J. Daigneault	Longueuil	D
11	HFD	Sylvain Cote	Quebec	D
12	CGY	Gary Roberts	Ottawa	LW
13	*MIN*	*David Quinn*	*Kent H.S.*	*D*
14	NYR	Terry Carkner	Peterborough	D
15	QUE	Trevor Stienburg	Guelph	RW
16	PIT	Roger Belanger	Kingston	C
17	WSH	Kevin Hatcher	North Bay	D
18	BUF	Mikael Andersson	Vastra Frolunda	LW
19	BOS	Dave Pasin	Prince Albert	RW
20	*NYI*	*Duncan MacPherson*	*Saskatoon*	*D*
21	EDM	Selmar Odelein	Regina	D

OTHER NOTABLE SELECTIONS

Pick	Claimed by		Amateur Club	Position
25	TOR	Todd Gill	Windsor	D
27	PHI	Scott Mellanby	Henry Carr Jr. B	RW
29	MTL	Stephane Richer	Granby	RW
36	QUE	Jeff Brown	Sudbury	D
51	MTL	Patrick Roy	Granby	G
59	WSH	Michal Pivonka	Czech Nationals	C
80	WSH	Kris King	Peterborough	LW
107	N.J.	Kirk McLean	Oshawa	G
117	CGY	Brett Hull	Penticton Jr. A	RW
119	NYR	Kjell Samuelsson	Leksand	D
166	BOS	Don Sweeney	St. Paul's H.S.	D
171	L.A.	Luc Robitaille	Hull	LW
180	CGY	Gary Suter	U. of Wisconsin	D

1983

FIRST ROUND

Pick	Claimed by		Amateur Club	Position
1	MIN	Brian Lawton	Mount St. Charles H.S.	LW
2	HFD	Sylvain Turgeon	Hull	LW
3	NYI	Pat LaFontaine	Verdun	C
4	DET	Steve Yzerman	Peterborough	C
5	BUF	Tom Barrasso	Acton-Boxborough	G
6	N.J.	John MacLean	Oshawa	RW
7	TOR	Russ Courtnall	Victoria	RW
8	WPG	Andrew McBain	North Bay	RW
9	VAN	Cam Neely	Portland	RW
10	BUF	Normand Lacombe	New Hampshire	RW
11	BUF	Adam Creighton	Ottawa	C
12	NYR	Dave Gagner	Brantford	C
13	CGY	Dan Quinn	Belleville	C
14	WPG	Bobby Dollas	Laval	D
15	PIT	Bob Errey	Peterborough	LW
16	NYI	Gerald Diduck	Lethbridge	D
17	MTL	Alfie Turcotte	Portland	C
18	CHI	Bruce Cassidy	Ottawa	D
19	EDM	Jeff Beukeboom	Sault Ste. Marie	D
20	HFD	David Jensen	Lawrence Academy	C
21	BOS	Nevin Markwart	Regina	LW

OTHER NOTABLE SELECTIONS

Pick	Claimed by		Amateur Club	Position
26	MTL	Claude Lemieux	Trois-Rivieres	RW
27	MTL	Sergio Momesso	Shawinigan	LW
41	PHI	Peter Zezel	Toronto	C
46	DET	Bob Probert	Brantford	LW
59	CHI	Marc Bergevin	Chicoutimi	D
82	EDM	Esa Tikkanen	HIFK Helsinki	LW
88	DET	Petr Klima	Dukla Jihlava	W
112	L.A.	Kevin Stevens	Silver Lake H.S.	LW
125	PHI	Rick Tocchet	Sault Ste. Marie	RW
139	BUF	Christian Ruuttu	Assat Pori	C
150	N.J.	Viacheslav Fetisov	CSKA Moscow	D
207	CHI	Dominik Hasek	Pardubice	G
223	BUF	Uwe Krupp	Koln	D
241	CGY	Sergei Makarov	CSKA Moscow	RW

1982

FIRST ROUND

Pick	Claimed by		Amateur Club	Position
1	BOS	Gord Kluzak	Billings	D
2	MIN	Brian Bellows	Kitchener	LW
3	TOR	Gary Nylund	Portland	D
4	PHI	Ron Sutter	Lethbridge	C
5	WSH	Scott Stevens	Kitchener	D
6	BUF	Phil Housley	South St. Paul H.S.	D
7	CHI	Ken Yaremchuk	Portland	C
8	N.J.	Rocky Trottier	Nanaimo	RW
9	BUF	Paul Cyr	Victoria	LW
10	PIT	Rich Sutter	Lethbridge	RW
11	VAN	Michel Petit	Sherbrooke	D
12	WPG	Jim Kyte	Cornwall	D
13	QUE	David Shaw	Kitchener	D
14	HFD	Paul Lawless	Windsor	LW
15	NYR	Chris Kontos	Toronto	LW/C
16	BUF	Dave Andreychuk	Oshawa	LW
17	DET	Murray Craven	Medicine Hat	LW
18	N.J.	Ken Daneyko	Seattle	D
19	*MTL*	*Alain Heroux*	*Chicoutimi*	*LW*
20	EDM	Jim Playfair	Portland	D
21	NYI	Pat Flatley	U. of Wisconsin	RW

OTHER NOTABLE SELECTIONS

Pick	Claimed by		Amateur Club	Position
36	NYR	Tomas Sandstrom	Farjestad	RW
43	N.J.	Pat Verbeek	Sudbury	RW
45	TOR	Ken Wregget	Lethbridge	G
56	HFD	Kevin Dineen	U. of Denver	RW
67	HFD	Ulf Samuelsson	Leksand	D
75	WPG	Dave Ellett	Ottawa Jr. A	D
80	MIN	Bob Rouse	Nanaimo	D
88	HFD	Ray Ferraro	Penticton Jr. A	C
119	PHI	Ron Hextall	Brandon	G
120	NYR	Tony Granato	Northwood Prep	RW
134	STL	Doug Gilmour	Cornwall	C
140	PHI	Dave Brown	Saskatoon	RW
183	NYR	Kelly Miller	Michigan State	LW

1981

FIRST ROUND

Pick	Claimed by		Amateur Club	Position
1	WPG	Dale Hawerchuk	Cornwall	C
2	L.A.	Doug Smith	Ottawa	C
3	WSH	Bob Carpenter	St. John's Prep	C
4	HFD	Ron Francis	Sault Ste. Marie	C
5	COL	Joe Cirella	Oshawa	D
6	TOR	Jim Benning	Portland	D
7	MTL	Mark Hunter	Brantford	RW
8	EDM	Grant Fuhr	Victoria	G
9	NYR	James Patrick	Prince Albert	D
10	VAN	Garth Butcher	Regina	D
11	QUE	Randy Moller	Lethbridge	D
12	CHI	Tony Tanti	Oshawa	RW
13	MIN	Ron Meighan	Niagara Falls	D
14	BOS	Normand Leveille	Chicoutimi	LW
15	CGY	Al MacInnis	Kitchener	D
16	PHI	Steve Smith	Sault Ste. Marie	D
17	*BUF*	*Jiri Dudacek*	*Kladno*	*RW*
18	MTL	Gilbert Delorme	Chicoutimi	D
19	*MTL*	*Jan Ingman*	*Farjestad*	*LW*
20	*STL*	*Marty Ruff*	*Lethbridge*	*D*
21	NYI	Paul Boutilier	Sherbrooke	D

OTHER NOTABLE SELECTIONS

Pick	Claimed by		Amateur Club	Position
22	WPG	Scott Arniel	Cornwall	LW
40	MTL	Chris Chelios	Moose Jaw	D
56	CGY	Mike Vernon	Calgary	G
72	NYR	John Vanbiesbrouck	Sault Ste. Marie	G
107	DET	Gerard Gallant	Sherbrooke	LW
108	COL	Bruce Driver	U. of Wisconsin	D
111	EDM	Steve Smith	London	D
145	MTL	Tom Kurvers	Minnesota-Duluth	D
152	WSH	Gaetan Duchesne	Quebec	LW

1980

FIRST ROUND

Pick	Claimed by		Amateur Club	Position
1	MTL	Doug Wickenheiser	Regina	C
2	WPG	Dave Babych	Portland	D
3	CHI	Denis Savard	Montreal	C
4	L.A.	Larry Murphy	Peterborough	D
5	WSH	Darren Veitch	Regina	D
6	EDM	Paul Coffey	Kitchener	D
7	VAN	Rick Lanz	Oshawa	D
8	HFD	Fred Arthur	Cornwall	D
9	PIT	Mike Bullard	Brantford	C
10	L.A.	Jim Fox	Ottawa	RW
11	DET	Mike Blaisdell	Regina	RW
12	STL	Rik Wilson	Kingston	D
13	CGY	Denis Cyr	Montreal	RW
14	*NYR*	*Jim Malone*	*Toronto*	*C*
15	CHI	Jerome Dupont	Toronto	D
16	MIN	Brad Palmer	Victoria	LW
17	NYI	Brent Sutter	Red Deer Jr. A	C
18	BOS	Barry Pederson	Victoria	C
19	COL	Paul Gagne	Windsor	LW
20	BUF	Steve Patrick	Brandon	RW
21	PHI	Mike Stothers	Kingston	D

OTHER NOTABLE SELECTIONS

Pick	Claimed by		Amateur Club	Position
37	MIN	Don Beaupre	Sudbury	G
38	NYI	Kelly Hrudey	Medicine Hat	G
57	CHI	Troy Murray	St. Albert Jr. A	C
61	MTL	Craig Ludwig	North Dakota	D
69	EDM	Jari Kurri	Jokerit	RW
73	L.A.	Bernie Nicholls	Kingston	C
80	NYI	Greg Gilbert	Toronto	LW
81	BOS	Steve Kasper	Verdun	C
106	COL	Aaron Broten	U. of Minnesota	LW/C
120	CHI	Steve Larmer	Niagara Falls	RW
124	MTL	Mike McPhee	RPI	LW
128	WPG	Brian Mullen	U.S. Jr. National	RW
132	EDM	Andy Moog	Billings	G
181	CGY	Hakan Loob	Farjestad	RW

1979

FIRST ROUND

Pick	Claimed by		Amateur Club	Position
1	COL	Rob Ramage	London	D
2	STL	Perry Turnbull	Portland	C
3	DET	Mike Foligno	Sudbury	RW
4	WSH	Mike Gartner	Niagara Falls	RW
5	VAN	Rick Vaive	Sherbrooke	RW
6	MIN	Craig Hartsburg	Sault Ste. Marie	D
7	CHI	Keith Brown	Portland	D
8	BOS	Raymond Bourque	Verdun	D
9	TOR	Laurie Boschman	Brandon	C
10	MIN	Tom McCarthy	Oshawa	LW
11	BUF	Mike Ramsey	U. of Minnesota	D
12	ATL	Paul Reinhart	Kitchener	D
13	NYR	Doug Sulliman	Kitchener	RW
14	PHI	Brian Propp	Brandon	LW
15	BOS	Brad McCrimmon	Brandon	D
16	L.A.	Jay Wells	Kingston	D
17	NYI	Duane Sutter	Lethbridge	RW
18	HFD	Ray Allison	Brandon	RW
19	WPG	Jimmy Mann	Sherbrooke	RW
20	QUE	Michel Goulet	Quebec	LW
21	EDM	Kevin Lowe	Quebec	D

OTHER NOTABLE SELECTIONS

Pick	Claimed by		Amateur Club	Position
32	BUF	Lindy Ruff	Lethbridge	D/LW
37	MTL	Mats Naslund	Brynas Gavle	LW
40	WPG	Dave Christian	North Dakota	RW
41	QUE	Dale Hunter	Sudbury	C
42	MIN	Neal Broten	U. of Minnesota	C
44	MTL	Guy Carbonneau	Chicoutimi	C
48	EDM	Mark Messier	St. Albert Jr. A	C
54	ATL	Tim Hunter	Seattle	RW
57	BOS	Keith Crowder	Peterborough	RW
58	MTL	Rick Wamsley	Brantford	G
66	DET	John Ogrodnick	New Westminster	LW
69	EDM	Glenn Anderson	U. of Denver	RW
75	ATL	Jim Peplinski	Toronto	RW
83	QUE	Anton Stastny	Slovan Bratislava	LW
89	VAN	Dirk Graham	Regina	RW/LW
103	WPG	Thomas Steen	Leksand	C
120	BOS	Mike Krushelnyski	Montreal	LW/C

1978

FIRST ROUND

Pick	Claimed by		Amateur Club	Position
1	MIN	Bobby Smith	Ottawa	C
2	WSH	Ryan Walter	Seattle	C/LW
3	STL	Wayne Babych	Portland	RW
4	VAN	Bill Derlago	Brandon	C
5	COL	Mike Gillis	Kingston	LW
6	PHI	Behn Wilson	Kingston	D
7	PHI	Ken Linseman	Kingston	C
8	MTL	Danny Geoffrion	Cornwall	RW
9	DET	Willie Huber	Hamilton	D
10	CHI	Tim Higgins	Ottawa	RW
11	ATL	Brad Marsh	London	D
12	DET	Brent Peterson	Portland	C
13	BUF	Larry Playfair	Portland	D
14	PHI	Danny Lucas	Sault Ste. Marie	RW
15	NYI	Steve Tambellini	Lethbridge	C
16	BOS	Al Secord	Hamilton	LW
17	MTL	Dave Hunter	Sudbury	LW
18	WSH	Tim Coulis	Hamilton	LW

OTHER NOTABLE SELECTIONS

Pick	Claimed by		Amateur Club	Position
19	MIN	Steve Payne	Ottawa	LW
21	TOR	Joel Quenneville	Windsor	D
22	VAN	Curt Fraser	Victoria	LW
26	NYR	Don Maloney	Kitchener	LW
32	BUF	Tony McKegney	Kingston	LW
35	PHI	Pelle Lindberg	AIK Solna	G
40	VAN	Stan Smyl	New Westminster	RW
54	MIN	Curt Giles	Minnesota-Duluth	D
55	WSH	Bengt Gustafsson	Farjestad	RW
93	NYR	Tom Laidlaw	Northern Michigan	D
103	MTL	Keith Acton	Peterborough	C
109	STL	Paul MacLean	Hull	RW
153	BOS	Craig MacTavish	U. of Mass-Lowell	C
173	STL	Risto Siltanen	Ilves Tampere	D
179	CHI	Darryl Sutter	Lethbridge	LW
231	MTL	Chris Nilan	Northeastern	RW

1977

FIRST ROUND

Pick	Claimed by		Amateur Club	Position
1	DET	Dale McCourt	St. Catharines	C
2	COL	Barry Beck	New Westminster	D
3	WSH	Robert Picard	Montreal	D
4	VAN	Jere Gillis	Sherbrooke	LW
5	Cle.	Mike Crombeen	Kingston	RW
6	CHI	Doug Wilson	Ottawa	D
7	MIN	Brad Maxwell	New Westminster	D
8	NYR	Lucien DeBlois	Sorel	C
9	STL	Scott Campbell	London	D
10	MTL	Mark Napier	Toronto	RW
11	TOR	John Anderson	Toronto	RW
12	TOR	Trevor Johansen	Toronto	D
13	NYR	Ron Duguay	Sudbury	C/RW
14	BUF	Ric Seiling	St. Catharines	RW/C
15	NYI	Mike Bossy	Laval	RW
16	BOS	Dwight Foster	Kitchener	RW
17	PHI	Kevin McCarthy	Winnipeg	D
18	MTL	Norm Dupont	Montreal	LW

OTHER NOTABLE SELECTIONS

Pick	Claimed by		Amateur Club	Position
25	MIN	Dave Semenko	Brandon	LW
33	NYI	John Tonelli	Toronto	LW
36	MTL	Rod Langway	New Hampshire	D
40	VAN	Glen Hanlon	Brandon	G
54	MTL	Gordie Roberts	Victoria	D
66	PIT	Mark Johnson	U. of Wisconsin	C
102	PIT	Greg Millen	Peterborough	G
135	PHI	Pete Peeters	Medicine Hat	G
162	MTL	Craig Laughlin	Clarkson	RW

1976

FIRST ROUND

Pick	Claimed by		Amateur Club	Position
1	WSH	Rick Green	London	D
2	PIT	Blair Chapman	Saskatoon	RW
3	MIN	Glen Sharpley	Hull	C
4	DET	Fred Williams	Saskatoon	C
5	CAL	Bjorn Johansson	Orebro	D
6	NYR	Don Murdoch	Medicine Hat	RW
7	STL	Bernie Federko	Saskatoon	C
8	ATL	Dave Shand	Peterborough	D
9	CHI	Real Cloutier	Quebec	RW
10	ATL	Harold Phillipoff	New Westminster	LW
11	K.C.	Paul Gardner	Oshawa	C
12	MTL	Peter Lee	Ottawa	RW
13	MTL	Rod Schutt	Sudbury	LW
14	NYI	Alex McKendry	Sudbury	W
15	WSH	Greg Carroll	Medicine Hat	C
16	BOS	Clayton Pachal	New Westminster	C/LW
17	PHI	Mark Suzor	Kingston	D
18	*MTL*	*Bruce Baker*	*Ottawa*	*RW*

OTHER NOTABLE SELECTIONS

Pick	Claimed by		Amateur Club	Position
19	PIT	Greg Malone	Oshawa	C
20	STL	Brian Sutter	Lethbridge	LW
22	DET	Reed Larson	Minnesota-Duluth	D
30	TOR	Randy Carlyle	Sudbury	D
45	CHI	Thomas Gradin	MoDo Ornskoldsvik	C
47	PIT	Morris Lukowich	Medicine Hat	LW
56	STL	Mike Liut	Bowling Green	G
64	ATL	Kent Nilsson	Djurgarden	C
68	NYI	Ken Morrow	Bowling Green	D
133	MTL	Ron Wilson	St. Catharines	D

1975

FIRST ROUND

Pick	Claimed by		Amateur Club	Position
1	PHI	Mel Bridgman	Victoria	C
2	K.C.	Barry Dean	Medicine Hat	LW
3	CAL	Ralph Klassen	Saskatoon	C
4	MIN	Bryan Maxwell	Medicine Hat	D
5	DET	Rick Lapointe	Victoria	D
6	TOR	Don Ashby	Calgary	C
7	CHI	Greg Vaydik	Medicine Hat	C
8	ATL	Richard Mulhern	Sherbrooke	D
9	*MTL*	*Robin Sadler*	*Edmonton*	*D*
10	VAN	Rick Blight	Brandon	RW
11	NYI	Pat Price	Saskatoon	D
12	NYR	Wayne Dillon	Toronto	C
13	PIT	Gord Laxton	New Westminster	G
14	BOS	Doug Halward	Peterborough	D
15	MTL	Pierre Mondou	Montreal	C
16	L.A.	Tim Young	Ottawa	C
17	BUF	Bob Sauve	Laval	G
18	WSH	Alex Forsyth	Kingston	C

OTHER NOTABLE SELECTIONS

Pick	Claimed by		Amateur Club	Position
21	CAL	Dennis Maruk	London	C
22	MTL	Brian Engblom	U. of Wisconsin	D
24	TOR	Doug Jarvis	Peterborough	C
42	TOR	Bruce Boudreau	Toronto	C
43	CHI	Mike O'Connell	Kingston	D
57	CAL	Greg Smith	Colorado College	D
80	ATL	Willi Plett	St. Catharines	RW
108	PHI	Paul Holmgren	U. of Minnesota	RW
210	L.A.	Dave Taylor	Clarkson	RW

1974

FIRST ROUND

Pick	Claimed by		Amateur Club	Position
1	WSH	Greg Joly	Regina	D
2	K.C.	Wilf Paiement	St. Catharines	RW
3	CAL	Rick Hampton	St. Catharines	LW/D
4	NYI	Clark Gillies	Regina	LW
5	MTL	Cam Connor	Flin Flon	RW
6	MIN	Doug Hicks	Flin Flon	D
7	MTL	Doug Risebrough	Kitchener	C
8	PIT	Pierre Larouche	Sorel	C
9	DET	Bill Lochead	Oshawa	LW
10	MTL	Rick Chartraw	Kitchener	D/RW
11	BUF	Lee Fogolin Jr.	Oshawa	D
12	MTL	Mario Tremblay	Montreal	RW
13	TOR	Jack Valiquette	Sault Ste. Marie	C
14	NYR	Dave Maloney	Kitchener	D
15	MTL	Gord McTavish	Sudbury	C
16	CHI	Grant Mulvey	Calgary	RW
17	CAL	Ron Chipperfield	Brandon	C
18	*BOS*	*Don Larway*	*Swift Current*	*RW*

OTHER NOTABLE SELECTIONS

Pick	Claimed by		Amateur Club	Position
22	NYI	Bryan Trottier	Swift Current	C
25	BOS	Mark Howe	Toronto	D
29	BUF	Danny Gare	Calgary	RW
31	TOR	Tiger Williams	Swift Current	LW
32	NYR	Ron Greschner	New Westminster	D
38	K.C.	Bob Bourne	Saskatoon	C
39	CAL	Charlie Simmer	Sault Ste. Marie	LW
52	CHI	Bob Murray	Cornwall	D
70	CHI	Terry Ruskowski	Swift Current	C
77	VAN	Mike Rogers	Calgary	C
85	TOR	Mike Palmateer	Toronto	G
125	PHI	Reggie Lemelin	Sherbrooke	G
199	MTL	Dave Lumley	New Hampshire	RW
214	NYI	Stefan Persson	Brynas Gavle	D

1973

FIRST ROUND

Pick	Claimed by		Amateur Club	Position
1	NYI	Denis Potvin	Ottawa	D
2	ATL	Tom Lysiak	Medicine Hat	C
3	VAN	Dennis Ververgaert	London	RW
4	TOR	Lanny McDonald	Medicine Hat	RW
5	STL	John Davidson	Calgary	G
6	BOS	Andre Savard	Quebec	C
7	PIT	Blaine Stoughton	Flin Flon	RW
8	MTL	Bob Gainey	Peterborough	LW
9	VAN	Bob Dailey	Toronto	D
10	TOR	Bob Neely	Peterborough	LW
11	DET	Terry Richardson	New Westminster	G
12	BUF	Morris Titanic	Sudbury	LW
13	CHI	Darcy Rota	Edmonton	LW
14	NYR	Rick Middleton	Oshawa	RW
15	TOR	Ian Turnbull	Ottawa	D
16	ATL	Vic Mercredi	New Westminster	C

OTHER NOTABLE SELECTIONS

Pick	Claimed by		Amateur Club	Position
21	ATL	Eric Vail	Sudbury	LW
27	PIT	Colin Campbell	Peterborough	D
30	NYR	Pat Hickey	Hamilton	LW
33	NYI	Dave Lewis	Saskatoon	D
49	NYI	Andre St. Laurent	Montreal	C
85	ATL	Ken Houston	Chatham Jr. B	RW
129	NYI	Bob Lorimer	Michigan Tech	D
130	CAL	Larry Patey	Braintree H.S.	C
134	PIT	Gord Lane	New Westminster	D

1972

FIRST ROUND

Pick	Claimed by		Amateur Club	Position
1	NYI	Billy Harris	Toronto	RW
2	ATL	Jacques Richard	Quebec	LW
3	VAN	Don Lever	Niagara Falls	LW
4	MTL	Steve Shutt	Toronto	LW
5	BUF	Jim Schoenfeld	Niagara Falls	D
6	MTL	Michel Larocque	Ottawa	G
7	PHI	Bill Barber	Kitchener	LW
8	MTL	Dave Gardner	Toronto	C
9	STL	Wayne Merrick	Ottawa	C
10	*NYR*	*Al Blanchard*	*Kitchener*	*LW*
11	TOR	George Ferguson	Toronto	C
12	MIN	Jerry Byers	Kitchener	LW
13	CHI	Phil Russell	Edmonton	D
14	MTL	John Van Boxmeer	Guelph	D
15	NYR	Bob MacMillan	St. Catharines	RW
16	BOS	Mike Bloom	St. Catharines	LW

OTHER NOTABLE SELECTIONS

Pick	Claimed by		Amateur Club	Position
17	NYI	Lorne Henning	New Westminster	C
23	PHI	Tom Bladon	Edmonton	D
33	NYI	Bob Nystrom	Calgary	RW
39	PHI	Jimmy Watson	Calgary	D
55	PHI	Al MacAdam	U. of PEI	RW
85	BUF	Peter McNab	U. of Denver	C
97	NYI	Richard Brodeur	Cornwall	G
139	TOR	Pat Boutette	Minnesota-Duluth	C/RW
144	NYI	Garry Howatt	Flin Flon	LW

1971

FIRST ROUND

Pick	Claimed by		Amateur Club	Position
1	MTL	Guy Lafleur	Quebec	RW
2	DET	Marcel Dionne	St. Catharines	C
3	VAN	Jocelyn Guevremont	Montreal	D
4	STL	Gene Carr	Flin Flon	C
5	BUF	Rick Martin	Montreal	LW
6	BOS	Ron Jones	Edmonton	D
7	MTL	Chuck Arnason	Flin Flon	RW
8	PHI	Larry Wright	Regina	C
9	PHI	Pierre Plante	Drummondville	RW
10	NYR	Steve Vickers	Toronto	LW
11	MTL	Murray Wilson	Ottawa	LW
12	*CHI*	*Dan Spring*	*Edmonton*	*C*
13	NYR	Steve Durbano	Toronto	D
14	BOS	Terry O'Reilly	Oshawa	RW

OTHER NOTABLE SELECTIONS

Pick	Claimed by		Amateur Club	Position
17	VAN	Bobby Lalonde	Montreal	C
19	BUF	Craig Ramsay	Peterborough	LW
20	MTL	Larry Robinson	Kitchener	D
22	TOR	Rick Kehoe	Hamilton	RW
33	BUF	Bill Hajt	Saskatoon	D
48	L.A.	Neil Komadoski	Winnipeg	D
55	NYR	Jerry Butler	Hamilton	RW

1970

FIRST ROUND

Pick	Claimed by		Amateur Club	Position
1	BUF	Gilbert Perreault	Montreal	C
2	VAN	Dale Tallon	Toronto	D
3	BOS	Reggie Leach	Flin Flon	RW
4	BOS	Rick MacLeish	Peterborough	C
5	*MTL*	*Ray Martyniuk*	*Flin Flon*	*G*
6	MTL	Chuck Lefley	Canadian National	LW
7	PIT	Greg Polis	Estevan	LW
8	TOR	Darryl Sittler	London	C
9	BOS	Ron Plumb	Peterborough	D
10	CAL	Chris Oddleifson	Winnipeg	C
11	NYR	Norm Gratton	Montreal	LW
12	DET	Serge Lajeunesse	Montreal	D/RW
13	BOS	Bob Stewart	Oshawa	D
14	CHI	Dan Maloney	London	LW

OTHER NOTABLE SELECTIONS

Pick	Claimed by		Amateur Club	Position
18	PHI	Bill Clement	Ottawa	C
20	MIN	Fred Barrett	Toronto	D
22	TOR	Errol Thompson	Charlottetown Sr.	LW
25	NYR	Mike Murphy	Toronto	RW
27	BOS	Dan Bouchard	London	G
32	PHI	Bob Kelly	Oshawa	LW
40	DET	Yvon Lambert	Drummondville	LW
59	L.A.	Billy Smith	Cornwall	G
70	CHI	Gilles Meloche	Verdun	G
88	OAK	Terry Murray	Ottawa	D
103	TOR	Ron Low	Dauphin Jr. A.	G

1969

FIRST ROUND

Pick	Claimed by		Amateur Club	Position
1	MTL	Rejean Houle	Montreal	RW
2	MTL	Marc Tardif	Montreal	LW
3	BOS	Don Tannahill	Niagara Falls	LW
4	BOS	Frank Spring	Edmonton	RW
5	MIN	Dick Redmond	St. Catharines	D
6	*PHI*	*Bob Currier*	*Cornwall*	*C*
7	OAK	Tony Featherstone	Peterborough	RW
8	NYR	Andre Dupont	Montreal	D
9	*TOR*	*Ernie Moser*	*Estevan*	*RW*
10	DET	Jim Rutherford	Hamilton	G
11	BOS	Ivan Boldirev	Oshawa	C
12	NYR	Pierre Jarry	Ottawa	LW
13	CHI	J.P. Bordeleau	Montreal	RW

OTHER NOTABLE SELECTIONS

Pick	Claimed by		Amateur Club	Position
17	PHI	Bobby Clarke	Flin Flon	C
18	OAK	Ron Stackhouse	Peterborough	D
25	MIN	Gilles Gilbert	London	G
26	PIT	Michel Briere	Shawinigan	C
51	L.A.	Butch Goring	Dauphin Jr. A.	C
52	PHI	Dave Schultz	Sorel	LW
55	TOR	Brian Spencer	Swift Current	LW
64	PHI	Don Saleski	Regina	RW

NHL All-Stars

Active Players' All-Star Selection Records

	Total	First Team Selections			Second Team Selections
GOALTENDER					
Henrik Lundqvist	2	(1)	2011-12.	(1)	2012-13.
Roberto Luongo	2	(0)		(2)	2003-04; 2006-07.
Ryan Miller	1	(1)	2009-10.	(0)	
Sergei Bobrovsky	1	(1)	2012-13.	(0)	
Tuukka Rask	1	(1)	2013-14.	(0)	
Carey Price	1	(1)	2014-15.	(0)	
Steve Mason	1	(0)		(1)	2008-09.
Ilya Bryzgalov	1	(0)		(1)	2009-10.
Pekka Rinne	1	(0)		(1)	2010-11.
Jonathan Quick	1	(0)		(1)	2011-12.
Semyon Varlamov	1	(0)		(1)	2013-14.
Devan Dubnyk	1	(0)		(1)	2014-15.
DEFENSE					
Zdeno Chara	7	(3)	2003-04; 2008-09; 2013-14.	(4)	2005-06; 2007-08; 2010-11; 2011-12.
Shea Weber	4	(2)	2010-11; 2011-12.	(2)	2013-14; 2014-15.
Mike Green	2	(2)	2008-09; 2009-10.	(0)	
Duncan Keith	2	(2)	2009-10; 2013-14.	(0)	
Erik Karlsson	2	(2)	2011-12; 2014-15.	(0)	
P.K. Subban	2	(2)	2012-13; 2014-15.	(0)	
Sergei Gonchar	2	(0)		(2)	2001-02; 2002-03.
Dan Boyle	2	(0)		(2)	2006-07; 2008-09.
Alex Pietrangelo	2	(0)		(2)	2011-12; 2013-14.
Drew Doughty	2	(0)		(2)	2009-10; 2014-15.
Dion Phaneuf	1	(1)	2007-08.	(0)	
Ryan Suter	1	(1)	2012-13	(0)	
Brian Campbell	1	(0)		(1)	2007-08.
Lubomir Visnovsky	1	(0)		(1)	2010-11.
Francois Beauchemin	1	(0)		(1)	2012-13.
Kris Letang	1	(0)		(1)	2012-13.
CENTER					
Sidney Crosby	5	(3)	2006-07; 2012-13, 2013-14.	(2)	2009-10; 2014-15.
Evgeni Malkin	3	(3)	2007-08; 2008-09; 2011-12.	(0)	
Joe Thornton	3	(1)	2005-06.	(2)	2002-03; 2007-08.
Henrik Sedin	2	(2)	2009-10; 2010-11.	(0)	
Steven Stamkos	2	(0)		(2)	2010-11; 2011-12.
John Tavares	1	(1)	2014-15.	(0)	
Eric Staal	1	(0)		(1)	2005-06.
Vincent Lecavalier	1	(0)		(1)	2006-07.
Pavel Datsyuk	1	(0)		(1)	2008-09.
Jonathan Toews	1	(0)		(1)	2012-13.
Ryan Getzlaf	1	(0)		(1)	2013-14.
RIGHT WING					
Jaromir Jagr	8	(7)	1994-95; 1995-96; 1997-98 1998-99; 1999-00; 2000-01; 2005-06.	(1)	1996-97.
Jarome Iginla	4	(3)	2001-02; 2007-08; 2008-09.	(1)	2003-04.
Corey Perry	2	(2)	2010-11; 2013-14.	(0)	
Alex Ovechkin	2	(1)	2012-13.	(1)	2013-14.
Dany Heatley	1	(1)	2006-07.	(0)	
Patrick Kane	1	(1)	2009-10.	(0)	
James Neal	1	(1)	2011-12.	(0)	
Jakub Voracek	1	(1)	2014-15.	(0)	
Daniel Alfredsson	1	(0)		(1)	2005-06.
Marian Hossa	1	(0)		(1)	2008-09.
Marian Gaborik	1	(0)		(1)	2011-12.
Vladimir Tarasenko	1	(0)		(1)	2014-15.
LEFT WING					
Alex Ovechkin	8	(6)	2005-06; 2006-07; 2007-08; 2008-09; 2009-10; 2014-15.	(2)	2010-11; 2012-13.
Daniel Sedin	2	(1)	2010-11	(1)	2009-10.
Jamie Benn	2	(1)	2013-14.	(1)	2014-15
Patrik Elias	1	(1)	2000-01.	(0)	
Chris Kunitz	1	(1)	2012-13.	(0)	
Dany Heatley	1	(0)		(1)	2005-06.
Thomas Vanek	1	(0)		(1)	2006-07.
Henrik Zetterberg	1	(0)		(1)	2007-08.
Zach Parise	1	(0)		(1)	2008-09.
Joe Pavelski	1	(0)		(1)	2013-14.

Leading NHL All-Stars 1930-31 to 2014-15

Player	Pos.	Team(s)	Total Selections	First Team Selections	Second Team Selections	NHL Seasons
Gordie Howe	RW	Detroit	21	12	9	26
Raymond Bourque	D	Bos., Col.	19	13	6	22
Wayne Gretzky	C	Edm., L.A., NYR	15	8	7	20
Maurice Richard	RW	Montreal	14	8	6	18
Bobby Hull	LW	Chicago	12	10	2	16
Nicklas Lidstrom	D	Detroit	12	10	2	20
Doug Harvey	D	Mtl., NYR	11	10	1	19
Glenn Hall	G	Det., Chi., St.L.	11	7	4	18
* Alex Ovechkin	LW/RW	Washington	10	7	3	10
Jean Beliveau	C	Montreal	10	6	4	20
Earl Seibert	D	NYR, Chi.	10	4	6	15
Bobby Orr	D	Boston	9	8	1	12
Ted Lindsay	LW	Detroit	9	8	1	17
Mario Lemieux	C	Pittsburgh	9	5	4	17
Frank Mahovlich	LW	Tor., Det., Mtl.	9	3	6	18
Eddie Shore	D	Boston	8	7	1	14
* Jaromir Jagr	RW	Pit., NYR	8	7	1	21
Phil Esposito	C	Boston	8	6	2	18
Red Kelly	D	Detroit	8	6	2	20
Stan Mikita	C	Chicago	8	6	2	22
Mike Bossy	RW	NY Islanders	8	5	3	10
Pierre Pilote	D	Chicago	8	5	3	14
Luc Robitaille	LW	Los Angeles	8	5	3	19
Paul Coffey	D	Edm., Pit., Det.	8	4	4	21
Frank Brimsek	G	Boston	8	2	6	10
Denis Potvin	D	NY Islanders	7	5	2	15
Brad Park	D	NYR, Bos.	7	5	2	17
Chris Chelios	D	Mtl., Chi., Det.	7	5	2	25
Al MacInnis	D	Cgy., St.L.	7	4	3	23
* Zdeno Chara	D	Ott., Bos.	7	3	4	17
Jacques Plante	G	Mtl., Tor.	7	3	4	18
Bill Gadsby	D	Chi., NYR, Det.	7	3	4	20
Martin Brodeur	G	New Jersey	7	3	4	22
Terry Sawchuk	G	Detroit	7	3	4	21
Bill Durnan	G	Montreal	6	6	0	7
Dominik Hasek	G	Buffalo	6	6	0	15
Guy Lafleur	RW	Montreal	6	6	0	17
Ken Dryden	G	Montreal	6	5	1	8
Patrick Roy	G	Mtl., Col.	6	4	2	19
Dit Clapper	RW/D	Boston	6	3	3	20
Larry Robinson	D	Montreal	6	3	3	20
Tim Horton	D	Toronto	6	3	3	24
Borje Salming	D	Toronto	6	1	5	17
Bill Cowley	C	Boston	5	4	1	13
Busher Jackson	LW	Toronto	5	4	1	15
Mark Messier	LW/C	Edm., NYR	5	4	1	25
Charlie Conacher	RW	Toronto	5	3	2	12
Jack Stewart	D	Detroit	5	3	2	12
Toe Blake	LW	Montreal	5	3	2	14
Elmer Lach	C	Montreal	5	3	2	14
Bill Quackenbush	D	Det., Bos.	5	3	2	14
Michel Goulet	LW	Quebec	5	3	2	15
Paul Kariya	LW	Anaheim	5	3	2	15
Tony Esposito	G	Chicago	5	3	2	16
Ken Reardon	D	Montreal	5	2	3	7
Syl Apps	C	Toronto	5	2	3	10
Ed Giacomin	G	NY Rangers	5	2	3	13
John LeClair	LW	Mtl., Phi.	5	2	3	16
Brian Leetch	D	NY Rangers	5	2	3	17
Jari Kurri	RW	Edmonton	5	2	3	17
Scott Stevens	D	Wsh., N.J.	5	2	3	21
Martin St. Louis	RW	Tampa Bay	5	1	4	16

* Active

Position Leaders in All-Star Selections

Position	Player	Total	First Team	Second Team	NHL Seasons	Career
GOALTENDER	Glenn Hall	11	7	4	18	1952-53 to 1970-71
	Frank Brimsek	8	2	6	10	1938-39 to 1949-50
	Jacques Plante	7	3	4	18	1952-53 to 1972-73
	Terry Sawchuk	7	3	4	21	1949-50 to 1969-70
	Martin Brodeur	7	3	4	22	1991-92 to 2014-15
	Bill Durnan	6	6	0	7	1943-44 to 1949-50
	Dominik Hasek	6	6	0	15	1990-91 to 2007-08
	Ken Dryden	6	5	1	8	1970-71 to 1978-79
	Patrick Roy	6	4	2	19	1984-85 to 2002-03
DEFENSE	Raymond Bourque	19	13	6	22	1979-80 to 2000-01
	Nicklas Lidstrom	12	10	2	20	1991-92 to 2011-12
	Doug Harvey	11	10	1	20	1947-48 to 1968-69
	Earl Seibert	10	4	6	15	1931-32 to 1945-46
	Bobby Orr	9	8	1	12	1966-67 to 1978-79
	Eddie Shore	8	7	1	14	1926-27 to 1939-40
	Red Kelly	8	6	2	20	1947-48 to 1966-67
	Pierre Pilote	8	5	3	14	1955-56 to 1968-69
	Paul Coffey	8	4	4	21	1980-81 to 2000-01
CENTER	Wayne Gretzky	15	8	7	20	1979-80 to 1998-99
	Jean Beliveau	10	6	4	20	1950-51 to 1970-71
	Mario Lemieux	9	5	4	18	1984-85 to 2005-06
	Phil Esposito	8	6	2	18	1963-64 to 1980-81
	Stan Mikita	8	6	2	22	1958-59 to 1979-80
RIGHT WING	Gordie Howe	21	12	9	26	1946-47 to 1979-80
	Maurice Richard	14	8	6	18	1942-43 to 1959-60
	* Jaromir Jagr	8	7	1	21	1990-91 to 2014-15
	Mike Bossy	8	5	3	10	1977-78 to 1986-87
	Guy Lafleur	6	6	0	17	1971-72 to 1990-91
LEFT WING	Bobby Hull	12	10	2	16	1957-58 to 1979-80
	Ted Lindsay	9	8	1	17	1944-45 to 1964-65
	Frank Mahovlich	9	3	6	18	1956-57 to 1973-74
	* Alex Ovechkin	8	6	2	10	2005-06 to 2014-15
	Luc Robitaille	8	5	3	19	1986-87 to 2005-06

* active player

All-Star Teams

1930-2015

Voting for the NHL All-Star Team is conducted among the representatives of the Professional Hockey Writers' Association at the end of the season.

Following is a list of the First and Second All-Star Teams since their inception in 1930-31.

First Team		Second Team	First Team		Second Team	First Team		Second Team
2014-15			**2005-06**			**1996-97**		
Carey Price, Mtl.	G	Devan Dubnyk, Min.	Miikka Kiprusoff, Cgy.	G	Martin Brodeur, N.J.	Dominik Hasek, Buf.	G	Martin Brodeur, N.J.
Erik Karlsson, Ott.	D	Drew Doughty, L.A.	Nicklas Lidstrom, Det.	D	Zdeno Chara, Ott.	Brian Leetch, NYR	D	Chris Chelios, Chi.
P.K. Subban, Mtl.	D	Shea Weber, Nsh.	Scott Niedermayer, Ana.	D	Sergei Zubov, Dal.	Sandis Ozolinsh, Col.	D	Scott Stevens, N.J.
John Tavares, NYI	C	Sidney Crosby, Pit.	Joe Thornton, Bos., S.J.	C	Eric Staal, Car.	Mario Lemieux, Pit.	C	Wayne Gretzky, NYR
Jakub Voracek, Phi.	RW	Vladimir Tarasenko, St.L.	Jaromir Jagr, NYR	RW	Daniel Alfredsson, Ott.	Teemu Selanne, Ana.	RW	Jaromir Jagr, Pit.
Alex Ovechkin, Wsh.	LW	Jamie Benn, Dal.	Alex Ovechkin, Wsh.	LW	Dany Heatley, Ott.	Paul Kariya, Ana.	LW	John LeClair, Phi.
2013-14			**2004-05**			**1995-96**		
Tuukka Rask, Bos.	G	Semyon Varlamov, Col.	*Season Cancelled*			Jim Carey, Wsh.	G	Chris Osgood, Det.
Duncan Keith, Chi.	D	Shea Weber, Nsh.				Chris Chelios, Chi.	D	V. Konstantinov, Det.
Zdeno Chara, Bos.	D	Alex Pietrangelo, St.L.				Raymond Bourque, Bos.	D	Brian Leetch, NYR
Sidney Crosby, Pit.	C	Ryan Getzlaf, Ana.				Mario Lemieux, Pit.	C	Eric Lindros, Phi.
Corey Perry, Ana.	RW	Alex Ovechkin, Wsh.				Jaromir Jagr, Pit.	RW	Alexander Mogilny, Van.
Jamie Benn, Dal.	LW	Joe Pavelski, S.J.				Paul Kariya, Ana.	LW	John LeClair, Phi.
2012-13			**2003-04**			**1994-95**		
Sergei Bobrovsky, CBJ	G	Henrik Lundqvist, NYR	Martin Brodeur, N.J.	G	Roberto Luongo, Fla.	Dominik Hasek, Buf.	G	Ed Belfour, Chi.
P.K. Subban, Mtl.	D	Kris Letang, Pit.	Scott Niedermayer, N.J.	D	Chris Pronger, St.L.	Paul Coffey, Det.	D	Raymond Bourque, Bos.
Ryan Suter, Min.	D	Francois Beauchemin, Ana.	Zdeno Chara, Ott.	D	Bryan McCabe, Tor.	Chris Chelios, Chi.	D	Larry Murphy, Pit.
Sidney Crosby, Pit.	C	Jonathan Toews, Chi.	Joe Sakic, Col.	C	Mats Sundin, Tor.	Eric Lindros, Phi.	C	Alexei Zhamnov, Wpg.
Alex Ovechkin, Wsh.	RW	Martin St. Louis, T.B.	Martin St. Louis, T.B.	RW	Jarome Iginla, Cgy.	Jaromir Jagr, Pit.	RW	Theoren Fleury, Cgy.
Chris Kunitz, Pit.	LW	Alex Ovechkin, Wsh.	Markus Naslund, Van.	LW	Ilya Kovalchuk, Atl.	John LeClair, Mtl., Phi.	LW	Keith Tkachuk, Wpg.
2011-12			**2002-03**			**1993-94**		
Henrik Lundqvist, NYR	G	Jonathan Quick, L.A.	Martin Brodeur, N.J.	G	Marty Turco, Dal.	Dominik Hasek, Buf.	G	John Vanbiesbrouck, Fla.
Erik Karlsson, Ott.	D	Zdeno Chara, Bos.	Al MacInnis, St.L.	D	Sergei Gonchar, Wsh.	Raymond Bourque, Bos.	D	Al MacInnis, Cgy.
Shea Weber, Nsh.	D	Alex Pietrangelo, St. L.	Nicklas Lidstrom, Det.	D	Derian Hatcher, Dal.	Scott Stevens, N.J.	D	Brian Leetch, NYR
Evgeni Malkin, Pit.	C	Steven Stamkos, T.B.	Peter Forsberg, Col.	C	Joe Thornton, Bos.	Sergei Fedorov, Det.	C	Wayne Gretzky, L.A.
James Neal, Pit.	RW	Marian Gaborik, NYR	Todd Bertuzzi, Van.	RW	Milan Hejduk, Col.	Pavel Bure, Van.	RW	Cam Neely, Bos.
Ilya Kovalchuk, N.J.	LW	Ray Whitney, Phx.	Markus Naslund, Van.	LW	Paul Kariya, Ana.	Brendan Shanahan, St.L.	LW	Adam Graves, NYR
2010-11			**2001-02**			**1992-93**		
Tim Thomas, Bos.	G	Pekka Rinne, Nsh.	Patrick Roy, Col.	G	Jose Theodore, Mtl.	Ed Belfour, Chi.	G	Tom Barrasso, Pit.
Nicklas Lidstrom, Det.	D	Zdeno Chara, Bos.	Nicklas Lidstrom, Det.	D	Rob Blake, Col.	Chris Chelios, Chi.	D	Larry Murphy, Pit.
Shea Weber, Nsh.	D	Lubomir Visnovsky, Ana.	Chris Chelios, Det.	D	Sergei Gonchar, Wsh.	Raymond Bourque, Bos.	D	Al Iafrate, Wsh.
Henrik Sedin, Van.	C	Steven Stamkos, T.B.	Joe Sakic, Col.	C	Mats Sundin, Tor.	Mario Lemieux, Pit.	C	Pat LaFontaine, Buf.
Corey Perry, Ana.	RW	Martin St. Louis, T.B.	Jarome Iginla, Cgy.	RW	Bill Guerin, Bos.	Teemu Selanne, Wpg.	RW	Alexander Mogilny, Buf.
Daniel Sedin, Van.	LW	Alex Ovechkin, Wsh.	Markus Naslund, Van.	LW	Brendan Shanahan, Det.	Luc Robitaille, L.A.	LW	Kevin Stevens, Pit.
2009-10			**2000-01**			**1991-92**		
Ryan Miller, Buf.	G	Ilya Bryzgalov, Phx.	Dominik Hasek, Buf.	G	Roman Cechmanek, Phi.	Patrick Roy, Mtl.	G	Kirk McLean, Van.
Duncan Keith, Chi.	D	Drew Doughty, L.A..	Nicklas Lidstrom, Det.	D	Rob Blake, L.A., Col.	Brian Leetch, NYR	D	Phil Housley, Wpg.
Mike Green, Wsh.	D	Nicklas Lidstrom, Det.	Raymond Bourque, Col.	D	Scott Stevens, N.J.	Raymond Bourque, Bos.	D	Scott Stevens, N.J.
Henrik Sedin, Van.	C	Sidney Crosby, Pit.	Joe Sakic, Col.	C	Mario Lemieux, Pit.	Mark Messier, NYR	C	Mario Lemieux, Pit.
Patrick Kane, Chi.	RW	Martin St. Louis, T.B.	Jaromir Jagr, Pit.	RW	Pavel Bure, Fla.	Brett Hull, St.L.	RW	Mark Recchi, Pit., Phi.
Alex Ovechkin, Wsh.	LW	Daniel Sedin, Van.	Patrik Elias, N.J.	LW	Luc Robitaille, L.A.	Kevin Stevens, Pit.	LW	Luc Robitaille, L.A.
2008-09			**1999-2000**			**1990-91**		
Tim Thomas, Bos.	G	Steve Mason, CBJ	Olaf Kolzig, Wsh.	G	Roman Turek, St.L.	Ed Belfour, Chi.	G	Patrick Roy, Mtl.
Zdeno Chara, Bos	D	Nicklas Lidstrom, Det.	Chris Pronger, St.L.	D	Rob Blake, L.A.	Raymond Bourque, Bos.	D	Chris Chelios, Chi.
Mike Green, Wsh.	D	Dan Boyle, S.J.	Nicklas Lidstrom, Det.	D	Eric Desjardins, Phi.	Al MacInnis, Cgy.	D	Brian Leetch, NYR
Evgeni Malkin, Pit.	C	Pavel Datsyuk, Det.	Steve Yzerman, Det.	C	Mike Modano, Dal.	Wayne Gretzky, L.A.	C	Adam Oates, St.L.
Jarome Iginla, Cgy.	RW	Marian Hossa, Det.	Jaromir Jagr, Pit.	RW	Pavel Bure, Fla.	Brett Hull, St.L.	RW	Cam Neely, Bos.
Alex Ovechkin, Wsh.	LW	Zach Parise, N.J.	Brendan Shanahan, Det.	LW	Paul Kariya, Ana.	Luc Robitaille, L.A.	LW	Kevin Stevens, Pit.
2007-08			**1998-99**			**1989-90**		
Evgeni Nabokov, S.J.	G	Martin Brodeur, N.J.	Dominik Hasek, Buf.	G	Byron Dafoe, Bos.	Patrick Roy, Mtl.	G	Daren Puppa, Buf.
Nicklas Lidstrom, Det.	D	Brian Campbell, Buf., S.J.	Al MacInnis, St.L.	D	Raymond Bourque, Bos.	Raymond Bourque, Bos.	D	Paul Coffey, Pit.
Dion Phaneuf, Cgy.	D	Zdeno Chara, Bos.	Nicklas Lidstrom, Det.	D	Eric Desjardins, Phi.	Al MacInnis, Cgy.	D	Doug Wilson, Chi.
Evgeni Malkin, Pit.	C	Joe Thornton, S.J.	Peter Forsberg, Col.	C	Alexei Yashin, Ott.	Mark Messier, Edm.	C	Wayne Gretzky, L.A.
Jarome Iginla, Cgy.	RW	Alex Kovalev, Mtl.	Jaromir Jagr, Pit.	RW	Teemu Selanne, Ana.	Brett Hull, St.L.	RW	Cam Neely, Bos.
Alex Ovechkin, Wsh.	LW	Henrik Zetterberg, Det.	Paul Kariya, Ana.	LW	John LeClair, Phi.	Luc Robitaille, L.A.	LW	Brian Bellows, Min.
2006-07			**1997-98**			**1988-89**		
Martin Brodeur, N.J.	G	Roberto Luongo, Van.	Dominik Hasek, Buf.	G	Martin Brodeur, N.J.	Patrick Roy, Mtl.	G	Mike Vernon, Cgy.
Nicklas Lidstrom, Det.	D	Chris Pronger, Ana.	Nicklas Lidstrom, Det.	D	Chris Pronger, St.L.	Chris Chelios, Mtl.	D	Al MacInnis, Cgy.
Scott Niedermayer, Ana.	D	Dan Boyle, T.B.	Rob Blake, L.A.	D	Scott Niedermayer, N.J.	Paul Coffey, Pit.	D	Raymond Bourque, Bos.
Sidney Crosby, Pit.	C	Vincent Lecavalier, T.B.	Peter Forsberg, Col.	C	Wayne Gretzky, NYR	Mario Lemieux, Pit.	C	Wayne Gretzky, L.A.
Dany Heatley, Ott.	RW	Martin St. Louis, T.B.	Jaromir Jagr, Pit.	RW	Teemu Selanne, Ana.	Joe Mullen, Cgy.	RW	Jari Kurri, Edm.
Alex Ovechkin, Wsh.	LW	Thomas Vanek, Buf.	John LeClair, Phi.	LW	Keith Tkachuk, Phx.	Luc Robitaille, L.A.	LW	Gerard Gallant, Det.

1987-88

First Team	Pos.	Second Team
Grant Fuhr, Edm.	G	Patrick Roy, Mtl.
Raymond Bourque, Bos.	D	Gary Suter, Cgy.
Scott Stevens, Wsh.	D	Brad McCrimmon, Cgy.
Mario Lemieux, Pit.	C	Wayne Gretzky, Edm.
Hakan Loob, Cgy.	RW	Cam Neely, Bos.
Luc Robitaille, L.A.	LW	Michel Goulet, Que.

1986-87

First Team	Pos.	Second Team
Ron Hextall, Phi.	G	Mike Liut, Hfd.
Raymond Bourque, Bos.	D	Larry Murphy, Wsh.
Mark Howe, Phi.	D	Al MacInnis, Cgy.
Wayne Gretzky, Edm.	C	Mario Lemieux, Pit.
Jari Kurri, Edm.	RW	Tim Kerr, Phi.
Michel Goulet, Que.	LW	Luc Robitaille, L.A.

1985-86

First Team	Pos.	Second Team
John Vanbiesbrouck, NYR	G	Bob Froese, Phi.
Paul Coffey, Edm.	D	Larry Robinson, Mtl.
Mark Howe, Phi.	D	Raymond Bourque, Bos.
Wayne Gretzky, Edm.	C	Mario Lemieux, Pit.
Mike Bossy, NYI	RW	Jari Kurri, Edm.
Michel Goulet, Que.	LW	Mats Naslund, Mtl.

1984-85

First Team	Pos.	Second Team
Pelle Lindbergh, Phi.	G	Tom Barrasso, Buf.
Paul Coffey, Edm.	D	Rod Langway, Wsh.
Raymond Bourque, Bos.	D	Doug Wilson, Chi.
Wayne Gretzky, Edm.	C	Dale Hawerchuk, Wpg.
Jari Kurri, Edm.	RW	Mike Bossy, NYI
John Ogrodnick, Det.	LW	John Tonelli, NYI

1983-84

First Team	Pos.	Second Team
Tom Barrasso, Buf.	G	Pat Riggin, Wsh.
Rod Langway, Wsh.	D	Paul Coffey, Edm.
Raymond Bourque, Bos.	D	Denis Potvin, NYI
Wayne Gretzky, Edm.	C	Bryan Trottier, NYI
Mike Bossy, NYI	RW	Jari Kurri, Edm.
Michel Goulet, Que.	LW	Mark Messier, Edm.

1982-83

First Team	Pos.	Second Team
Pete Peeters, Bos.	G	Roland Melanson, NYI
Mark Howe, Phi.	D	Raymond Bourque, Bos.
Rod Langway, Wsh.	D	Paul Coffey, Edm.
Wayne Gretzky, Edm.	C	Denis Savard, Chi.
Mike Bossy, NYI	RW	Lanny McDonald, Cgy.
Mark Messier, Edm.	LW	Michel Goulet, Que.

1981-82

First Team	Pos.	Second Team
Billy Smith, NYI	G	Grant Fuhr, Edm.
Doug Wilson, Chi.	D	Paul Coffey, Edm.
Raymond Bourque, Bos.	D	Brian Engblom, Mtl.
Wayne Gretzky, Edm.	C	Bryan Trottier, NYI
Mike Bossy, NYI	RW	Rick Middleton, Bos.
Mark Messier, Edm.	LW	John Tonelli, NYI

1980-81

First Team	Pos.	Second Team
Mike Liut, St.L.	G	Mario Lessard, L.A.
Denis Potvin, NYI	D	Larry Robinson, Mtl.
Randy Carlyle, Pit.	D	Raymond Bourque, Bos.
Wayne Gretzky, Edm.	C	Marcel Dionne, L.A.
Mike Bossy, NYI	RW	Dave Taylor, L.A.
Charlie Simmer, L.A.	LW	Bill Barber, Phi.

1979-80

First Team	Pos.	Second Team
Tony Esposito, Chi.	G	Don Edwards, Buf.
Larry Robinson, Mtl.	D	Borje Salming, Tor.
Raymond Bourque, Bos.	D	Jim Schoenfeld, Buf.
Marcel Dionne, L.A.	C	Wayne Gretzky, Edm.
Guy Lafleur, Mtl.	RW	Danny Gare, Buf.
Charlie Simmer, L.A.	LW	Steve Shutt, Mtl.

1978-79

First Team	Pos.	Second Team
Ken Dryden, Mtl.	G	Glenn Resch, NYI
Denis Potvin, NYI	D	Borje Salming, Tor.
Larry Robinson, Mtl.	D	Serge Savard, Mtl.
Bryan Trottier, NYI	C	Marcel Dionne, L.A.
Guy Lafleur, Mtl.	RW	Mike Bossy, NYI
Clark Gillies, NYI	LW	Bill Barber, Phi.

1977-78

First Team	Pos.	Second Team
Ken Dryden, Mtl.	G	Don Edwards, Buf.
Denis Potvin, NYI	D	Larry Robinson, Mtl.
Brad Park, Bos.	D	Borje Salming, Tor.
Bryan Trottier, NYI	C	Darryl Sittler, Tor.
Guy Lafleur, Mtl.	RW	Mike Bossy, NYI
Clark Gillies, NYI	LW	Steve Shutt, Mtl.

1976-77

First Team	Pos.	Second Team
Ken Dryden, Mtl.	G	Rogie Vachon, L.A.
Larry Robinson, Mtl.	D	Denis Potvin, NYI
Borje Salming, Tor.	D	Guy Lapointe, Mtl.
Marcel Dionne, L.A.	C	Gilbert Perreault, Buf.
Guy Lafleur, Mtl.	RW	Lanny McDonald, Tor.
Steve Shutt, Mtl.	LW	Rick Martin, Buf.

1975-76

First Team	Pos.	Second Team
Ken Dryden, Mtl.	G	Glenn Resch, NYI
Denis Potvin, NYI	D	Borje Salming, Tor.
Brad Park, Bos.	D	Guy Lapointe, Mtl.
Bobby Clarke, Phi.	C	Gilbert Perreault, Buf.
Guy Lafleur, Mtl.	RW	Reggie Leach, Phi.
Bill Barber, Phi.	LW	Rick Martin, Buf.

1974-75

First Team	Pos.	Second Team
Bernie Parent, Phi.	G	Rogie Vachon, L.A.
Bobby Orr, Bos.	D	Guy Lapointe, Mtl.
Denis Potvin, NYI	D	Borje Salming, Tor.
Bobby Clarke, Phi.	C	Phil Esposito, Bos.
Guy Lafleur, Mtl.	RW	René Robert, Buf.
Rick Martin, Buf.	LW	Steve Vickers, NYR

1973-74

First Team	Pos.	Second Team
Bernie Parent, Phi.	G	Tony Esposito, Chi.
Bobby Orr, Bos.	D	Bill White, Chi.
Brad Park, NYR	D	Barry Ashbee, Phi.
Phil Esposito, Bos.	C	Bobby Clarke, Phi.
Ken Hodge, Bos.	RW	Mickey Redmond, Det.
Rick Martin, Buf.	LW	Wayne Cashman, Bos.

1972-73

First Team	Pos.	Second Team
Ken Dryden, Mtl.	G	Tony Esposito, Chi.
Bobby Orr, Bos.	D	Brad Park, NYR
Guy Lapointe, Mtl.	D	Bill White, Chi.
Phil Esposito, Bos.	C	Bobby Clarke, Phi.
Mickey Redmond, Det.	RW	Yvan Cournoyer, Mtl.
Frank Mahovlich, Mtl.	LW	Dennis Hull, Chi.

1971-72

First Team	Pos.	Second Team
Tony Esposito, Chi.	G	Ken Dryden, Mtl.
Bobby Orr, Bos.	D	Bill White, Chi.
Brad Park, NYR	D	Pat Stapleton, Chi.
Phil Esposito, Bos.	C	Jean Ratelle, NYR
Rod Gilbert, NYR	RW	Yvan Cournoyer, Mtl.
Bobby Hull, Chi.	LW	Vic Hadfield, NYR

1970-71

First Team	Pos.	Second Team
Ed Giacomin, NYR	G	Jacques Plante, Tor.
Bobby Orr, Bos.	D	Brad Park, NYR
J.C. Tremblay, Mtl.	D	Pat Stapleton, Chi.
Phil Esposito, Bos.	C	Dave Keon, Tor.
Ken Hodge, Bos.	RW	Yvan Cournoyer, Mtl.
John Bucyk, Bos.	LW	Bobby Hull, Chi.

1969-70

First Team	Pos.	Second Team
Tony Esposito, Chi.	G	Ed Giacomin, NYR
Bobby Orr, Bos.	D	Carl Brewer, Det.
Brad Park, NYR	D	Jacques Laperriere, Mtl.
Phil Esposito, Bos.	C	Stan Mikita, Chi.
Gordie Howe, Det.	RW	John McKenzie, Bos.
Bobby Hull, Chi.	LW	Frank Mahovlich, Det.

1968-69

First Team	Pos.	Second Team
Glenn Hall, St.L.	G	Ed Giacomin, NYR
Bobby Orr, Bos.	D	Ted Green, Bos.
Tim Horton, Tor.	D	Ted Harris, Mtl.
Phil Esposito, Bos.	C	Jean Béliveau, Mtl.
Gordie Howe, Det.	RW	Yvan Cournoyer, Mtl.
Bobby Hull, Chi.	LW	Frank Mahovlich, Det.

1967-68

First Team	Pos.	Second Team
Gump Worsley, Mtl.	G	Ed Giacomin, NYR
Bobby Orr, Bos.	D	J.C. Tremblay, Mtl.
Tim Horton, Tor.	D	Jim Neilson, NYR
Stan Mikita, Chi.	C	Phil Esposito, Bos.
Gordie Howe, Det.	RW	Rod Gilbert, NYR
Bobby Hull, Chi.	LW	John Bucyk, Bos.

1966-67

First Team	Pos.	Second Team
Ed Giacomin, NYR	G	Glenn Hall, Chi.
Pierre Pilote, Chi.	D	Tim Horton, Tor.
Harry Howell, NYR	D	Bobby Orr, Bos.
Stan Mikita, Chi.	C	Norm Ullman, Det.
Kenny Wharram, Chi.	RW	Gordie Howe, Det.
Bobby Hull, Chi.	LW	Don Marshall, NYR

1965-66

First Team	Pos.	Second Team
Glenn Hall, Chi.	G	Gump Worsley, Mtl.
Jacques Laperriere, Mtl.	D	Allan Stanley, Tor.
Pierre Pilote, Chi.	D	Pat Stapleton, Chi.
Stan Mikita, Chi.	C	Jean Beliveau, Mtl.
Gordie Howe, Det.	RW	Bobby Rousseau, Mtl.
Bobby Hull, Chi.	LW	Frank Mahovlich, Tor.

1964-65

First Team	Pos.	Second Team
Roger Crozier, Det.	G	Charlie Hodge, Mtl.
Pierre Pilote, Chi.	D	Bill Gadsby, Det.
Jacques Laperriere, Mtl.	D	Carl Brewer, Tor.
Norm Ullman, Det.	C	Stan Mikita, Chi.
Claude Provost, Mtl.	RW	Gordie Howe, Det.
Bobby Hull, Chi.	LW	Frank Mahovlich, Tor.

1963-64

First Team	Pos.	Second Team
Glenn Hall, Chi.	G	Charlie Hodge, Mtl.
Pierre Pilote, Chi.	D	Moose Vasko, Chi.
Tim Horton, Tor.	D	Jacques Laperriere, Mtl.
Stan Mikita, Chi.	C	Jean Béliveau, Mtl.
Kenny Wharram, Chi.	RW	Gordie Howe, Det.
Bobby Hull, Chi.	LW	Frank Mahovlich, Tor.

1962-63

First Team	Pos.	Second Team
Glenn Hall, Chi.	G	Terry Sawchuk, Det.
Pierre Pilote, Chi.	D	Tim Horton, Tor.
Carl Brewer, Tor.	D	Moose Vasko, Chi.
Stan Mikita, Chi.	C	Henri Richard, Mtl.
Gordie Howe, Det.	RW	Andy Bathgate, NYR
Frank Mahovlich, Tor.	LW	Bobby Hull, Chi.

1961-62

First Team	Pos.	Second Team
Jacques Plante, Mtl.	G	Glenn Hall, Chi.
Doug Harvey, NYR	D	Carl Brewer, Tor.
Jean-Guy Talbot, Mtl.	D	Pierre Pilote, Chi.
Stan Mikita, Chi.	C	Dave Keon, Tor.
Andy Bathgate, NYR	RW	Gordie Howe, Det.
Bobby Hull, Chi.	LW	Frank Mahovlich, Tor.

1960-61

First Team	Pos.	Second Team
Johnny Bower, Tor.	G	Glenn Hall, Chi.
Doug Harvey, Mtl.	D	Allan Stanley, Tor.
Marcel Pronovost, Det.	D	Pierre Pilote, Chi.
Jean Béliveau, Mtl.	C	Henri Richard, Mtl.
Bernie Geoffrion, Mtl.	RW	Gordie Howe, Det.
Frank Mahovlich, Tor.	LW	Dickie Moore, Mtl.

1959-60

First Team	Pos.	Second Team
Glenn Hall, Chi.	G	Jacques Plante, Mtl.
Doug Harvey, Mtl.	D	Allan Stanley, Tor.
Marcel Pronovost, Det.	D	Pierre Pilote, Chi.
Jean Béliveau, Mtl.	C	Bronco Horvath, Bos.
Gordie Howe, Det.	RW	Bernie Geoffrion, Mtl.
Bobby Hull, Chi.	LW	Dean Prentice, NYR

1958-59

First Team	Pos.	Second Team
Jacques Plante, Mtl.	G	Terry Sawchuk, Det.
Tom Johnson, Mtl.	D	Marcel Pronovost, Det.
Bill Gadsby, NYR	D	Doug Harvey, Mtl.
Jean Béliveau, Mtl.	C	Henri Richard, Mtl.
Andy Bathgate, NYR	RW	Gordie Howe, Det.
Dickie Moore, Mtl.	LW	Alex Delvecchio, Det.

1957-58

First Team	Pos.	Second Team
Glenn Hall, Chi.	G	Jacques Plante, Mtl.
Doug Harvey, Mtl.	D	Fern Flaman, Bos.
Bill Gadsby, NYR	D	Marcel Pronovost, Det.
Henri Richard, Mtl.	C	Jean Béliveau, Mtl.
Gordie Howe, Det.	RW	Andy Bathgate, NYR
Dickie Moore, Mtl.	LW	Camille Henry, NYR

1956-57

First Team	Pos.	Second Team
Glenn Hall, Det.	G	Jacques Plante, Mtl.
Doug Harvey, Mtl.	D	Fern Flaman, Bos.
Red Kelly, Det.	D	Bill Gadsby, NYR
Jean Béliveau, Mtl.	C	Ed Litzenberger, Chi.
Gordie Howe, Det.	RW	Maurice Richard, Mtl.
Ted Lindsay, Det.	LW	Real Chevrefils, Bos.

1955-56

First Team	Pos.	Second Team
Jacques Plante, Mtl.	G	Glenn Hall, Det.
Doug Harvey, Mtl.	D	Red Kelly, Det.
Bill Gadsby, NYR	D	Tom Johnson, Mtl.
Jean Béliveau, Mtl.	C	Tod Sloan, Tor.
Maurice Richard, Mtl.	RW	Gordie Howe, Det.
Ted Lindsay, Det.	LW	Bert Olmstead, Mtl.

First Team		Second Team

1954-55

Harry Lumley, Tor.	G	Terry Sawchuk, Det.
Doug Harvey, Mtl.	D	Bob Goldham, Det.
Red Kelly, Det.	D	Fern Flaman, Bos.
Jean Béliveau, Mtl.	C	Ken Mosdell, Mtl.
Maurice Richard, Mtl.	RW	Bernie Geoffrion, Mtl.
Sid Smith, Tor.	LW	Danny Lewicki, NYR

1953-54

Harry Lumley, Tor.	G	Terry Sawchuk, Det.
Red Kelly, Det.	D	Bill Gadsby, Chi.
Doug Harvey, Mtl.	D	Tim Horton, Tor.
Ken Mosdell, Mtl.	C	Ted Kennedy, Tor.
Gordie Howe, Det.	RW	Maurice Richard, Mtl.
Ted Lindsay, Det.	LW	Ed Sandford, Bos.

1952-53

Terry Sawchuk, Det.	G	Gerry McNeil, Mtl.
Red Kelly, Det.	D	Bill Quackenbush, Bos.
Doug Harvey, Mtl.	D	Bill Gadsby, Chi.
Fleming MacKell, Bos.	C	Alex Delvecchio, Det.
Gordie Howe, Det.	RW	Maurice Richard, Mtl.
Ted Lindsay, Det.	LW	Bert Olmstead, Mtl.

1951-52

Terry Sawchuk, Det.	G	Jim Henry, Bos.
Red Kelly, Det.	D	Hy Buller, NYR
Doug Harvey, Mtl.	D	Jimmy Thomson, Tor.
Elmer Lach, Mtl.	C	Milt Schmidt, Bos.
Gordie Howe, Det.	RW	Maurice Richard, Mtl.
Ted Lindsay, Det.	LW	Sid Smith, Tor.

1950-51

Terry Sawchuk, Det.	G	Chuck Rayner, NYR
Red Kelly, Det.	D	Jimmy Thomson, Tor.
Bill Quackenbush, Bos.	D	Leo Reise Jr., Det.
Milt Schmidt, Bos.	C	Sid Abel, Det.
		Ted Kennedy, Tor. (tied)
Gordie Howe, Det.	RW	Maurice Richard, Mtl.
Ted Lindsay, Det.	LW	Sid Smith, Tor.

1949-50

Bill Durnan, Mtl.	G	Chuck Rayner, NYR
Gus Mortson, Tor.	D	Leo Reise Jr., Det.
Ken Reardon, Mtl.	D	Red Kelly, Det.
Sid Abel, Det.	C	Ted Kennedy, Tor.
Maurice Richard, Mtl.	RW	Gordie Howe, Det.
Ted Lindsay, Det.	LW	Tony Leswick, NYR

1948-49

Bill Durnan, Mtl.	G	Chuck Rayner, NYR
Bill Quackenbush, Det.	D	Glen Harmon, Mtl.
Jack Stewart, Det.	D	Ken Reardon, Mtl.
Sid Abel, Det.	C	Doug Bentley, Chi.
Maurice Richard, Mtl.	RW	Gordie Howe, Det.
Roy Conacher, Chi.	LW	Ted Lindsay, Det.

1947-48

Turk Broda, Tor.	G	Frank Brimsek, Bos.
Bill Quackenbush, Det.	D	Ken Reardon, Mtl.
Jack Stewart, Det.	D	Neil Colville, NYR
Elmer Lach, Mtl.	C	Buddy O'Connor, NYR
Maurice Richard, Mtl.	RW	Bud Poile, Chi.
Ted Lindsay, Det.	LW	Gaye Stewart, Chi.

1946-47

Bill Durnan, Mtl.	G	Frank Brimsek, Bos.
Ken Reardon, Mtl.	D	Jack Stewart, Det.
Butch Bouchard, Mtl.	D	Bill Quackenbush, Det.
Milt Schmidt, Bos.	C	Max Bentley, Chi.
Maurice Richard, Mtl.	RW	Bobby Bauer, Bos.
Doug Bentley, Chi.	LW	Woody Dumart, Bos.

1945-46

Bill Durnan, Mtl.	G	Frank Brimsek, Bos.
Jack Crawford, Bos.	D	Ken Reardon, Mtl.
Butch Bouchard, Mtl.	D	Jack Stewart, Det.
Max Bentley, Chi.	C	Elmer Lach, Mtl.
Maurice Richard, Mtl.	RW	Bill Mosienko, Chi.
Gaye Stewart, Tor.	LW	Toe Blake, Mtl.
Dick Irvin, Mtl.	Coach	Johnny Gottselig, Chi.

First Team		Second Team

1944-45

Bill Durnan, Mtl.	G	Mike Karakas, Chi.
Butch Bouchard, Mtl.	D	Glen Harmon, Mtl.
Flash Hollett, Det.	D	Babe Pratt, Tor.
Elmer Lach, Mtl.	C	Bill Cowley, Bos.
Maurice Richard, Mtl.	RW	Bill Mosienko, Chi.
Toe Blake, Mtl.	LW	Syd Howe, Det.
Dick Irvin, Mtl.	Coach	Jack Adams, Det.

1943-44

Bill Durnan, Mtl.	G	Paul Bibeault, Tor.
Earl Seibert, Chi.	D	Butch Bouchard, Mtl.
Babe Pratt, Tor.	D	Dit Clapper, Bos.
Bill Cowley, Bos.	C	Elmer Lach, Mtl.
Lorne Carr, Tor.	RW	Maurice Richard, Mtl.
Doug Bentley, Chi.	LW	Herb Cain, Bos.
Dick Irvin, Mtl.	Coach	Hap Day, Tor.

1942-43

Johnny Mowers, Det.	G	Frank Brimsek, Bos.
Earl Seibert, Chi.	D	Jack Crawford, Bos.
Jack Stewart, Det.	D	Flash Hollett, Bos.
Bill Cowley, Bos.	C	Syl Apps, Tor.
Lorne Carr, Tor.	RW	Bryan Hextall, NYR
Doug Bentley, Chi.	LW	Lynn Patrick, NYR
Jack Adams, Det.	Coach	Art Ross, Bos.

1941-42

Frank Brimsek, Bos.	G	Turk Broda, Tor.
Earl Seibert, Chi.	D	Pat Egan, Bro.
Tom Anderson, Bro.	D	Bucko McDonald, Tor.
Syl Apps, Tor.	C	Phil Watson, NYR
Bryan Hextall, NYR	RW	Gordie Drillon, Tor.
Lynn Patrick, NYR	LW	Sid Abel, Det.
Frank Boucher, NYR	Coach	Paul Thompson, Chi.

1940-41

Turk Broda, Tor.	G	Frank Brimsek, Bos.
Dit Clapper, Bos.	D	Earl Seibert, Chi.
Wally Stanowski, Tor.	D	Ott Heller, NYR
Bill Cowley, Bos.	C	Syl Apps, Tor.
Bryan Hextall, NYR	RW	Bobby Bauer, Bos.
Sweeney Schriner, Tor.	LW	Woody Dumart, Bos.
Cooney Weiland, Bos.	Coach	Dick Irvin, Mtl.

1939-40

Dave Kerr, NYR	G	Frank Brimsek, Bos.
Dit Clapper, Bos.	D	Art Coulter, NYR
Ebbie Goodfellow, Det.	D	Earl Seibert, Chi.
Milt Schmidt, Bos.	C	Neil Colville, NYR
Bryan Hextall, NYR	RW	Bobby Bauer, Bos.
Toe Blake, Mtl.	LW	Woody Dumart, Bos.
Paul Thompson, Chi.	Coach	Frank Boucher, NYR

1938-39

Frank Brimsek, Bos.	G	Earl Robertson, NYA
Eddie Shore, Bos.	D	Earl Seibert, Chi.
Dit Clapper, Bos.	D	Art Coulter, NYR
Syl Apps, Tor.	C	Neil Colville, NYR
Gordie Drillon, Tor.	RW	Bobby Bauer, Bos.
Toe Blake, Mtl.	LW	Johnny Gottselig, Chi.
Art Ross, Bos.	Coach	Red Dutton, NYA

1937-38

Tiny Thompson, Bos.	G	Dave Kerr, NYR
Eddie Shore, Bos.	D	Art Coulter, NYR
Babe Siebert, Mtl.	D	Earl Seibert, Chi.
Bill Cowley, Bos.	C	Syl Apps, Tor.
Cecil Dillon, NYR	RW	
Gordie Drillon, Tor. (tied)		
Paul Thompson, Chi.	LW	Toe Blake, Mtl.
Lester Patrick, NYR	Coach	Art Ross, Bos.

1936-37

Normie Smith, Det.	G	Wilf Cude, Mtl.
Babe Siebert, Mtl.	D	Earl Seibert, Mtl.
Ebbie Goodfellow, Det.	D	Lionel Conacher, Mtl. M.
Marty Barry, Det.	C	Art Chapman, NYA
Larry Aurie, Det.	RW	Cecil Dillon, NYR
Busher Jackson, Tor.	LW	Sweeney Schriner, NYA
Jack Adams, Det.	Coach	Cecil Hart, Mtl.

First Team		Second Team

1935-36

Tiny Thompson, Bos.	G	Wilf Cude, Mtl.
Eddie Shore, Bos.	D	Earl Seibert, Chi.
Babe Siebert, Bos.	D	Ebbie Goodfellow, Det.
Hooley Smith, Mtl. M.	C	Bill Thoms, Tor.
Charlie Conacher, Tor.	RW	Cecil Dillon, NYR
Sweeney Schriner, NYA	LW	Paul Thompson, Chi.
Lester Patrick, NYR	Coach	Tommy Gorman, Mtl. M.

1934-35

Lorne Chabot, Chi.	G	Tiny Thompson, Bos.
Eddie Shore, Bos.	D	Cy Wentworth, Mtl. M.
Earl Seibert, NYR	D	Art Coulter, Chi.
Frank Boucher, NYR	C	Cooney Weiland, Det.
Charlie Conacher, Tor.	RW	Dit Clapper, Bos.
Busher Jackson, Tor.	LW	Aurel Joliat, Mtl.
Lester Patrick, NYR	Coach	Dick Irvin, Tor.

1933-34

Charlie Gardiner, Chi.	G	Roy Worters, NYA
King Clancy, Tor.	D	Eddie Shore, Bos.
Lionel Conacher, Chi.	D	Ching Johnson, NYR
Frank Boucher, NYR	C	Joe Primeau, Tor.
Charlie Conacher, Tor.	RW	Bill Cook, NYR
Busher Jackson, Tor.	LW	Aurel Joliat, Mtl.
Lester Patrick, NYR	Coach	Dick Irvin, Tor.

1932-33

John Ross Roach, Det.	G	Charlie Gardiner, Chi.
Eddie Shore, Bos.	D	King Clancy, Tor.
Ching Johnson, NYR	D	Lionel Conacher, Mtl. M.
Frank Boucher, NYR	C	Howie Morenz, Mtl.
Bill Cook, NYR	RW	Charlie Conacher, Tor.
Baldy Northcott, Mtl. M.	LW	Busher Jackson, Tor.
Lester Patrick, NYR	Coach	Dick Irvin, Tor.

1931-32

Charlie Gardiner, Chi.	G	Roy Worters, NYA
Eddie Shore, Bos.	D	Sylvio Mantha, Mtl.
Ching Johnson, NYR	D	King Clancy, Tor.
Howie Morenz, Mtl.	C	Hooley Smith, Mtl. M.
Bill Cook, NYR	RW	Charlie Conacher, Tor.
Busher Jackson, Tor.	LW	Aurel Joliat, Mtl.
Lester Patrick, NYR	Coach	Dick Irvin, Tor.

1930-31

Charlie Gardiner, Chi.	G	Tiny Thompson, Bos.
Eddie Shore, Bos.	D	Sylvio Mantha, Mtl.
King Clancy, Tor.	D	Ching Johnson, NYR
Howie Morenz, Mtl.	C	Frank Boucher, NYR
Bill Cook, NYR	RW	Dit Clapper, Bos.
Aurel Joliat, Mtl.	LW	Bun Cook, NYR
Lester Patrick, NYR	Coach	Dick Irvin, Chi.

Intense rivals during their All-Star playing days, Eddie Shore (left) and King Clancy clown around at the piano at the B'nai Brith Sports Dinner in Boston in 1964.

NHL ALL-ROOKIE TEAM

Voting for the NHL All-Rookie Team is conducted among the representatives of the Professional Hockey Writers' Association at the end of the season. The rookie all-star team was first selected for the 1982-83 season.

2014-15
Goal: Jake Allen, St. Louis
Defense: Aaron Ekblad, Florida
Defense: John Klingberg, Dallas
Forward: Filip Forsberg, Nashville
Forward: Johnny Gaudreau, Calgary
Forward: Mark Stone, Ottawa

2013-14
Goal: Frederik Andersen, Anaheim
Defense: Torey Krug, Boston
Defense: Hampus Lindholm, Anaheim
Forward: Tyler Johnson, Tampa Bay
Forward: Nathan MacKinnon, Colorado
Forward: Ondrej Palat, Tampa Bay

2012-13
Goal: Jake Allen, St. Louis
Defense: Jonas Brodin, Minnesota
Defense: Justin Schultz, Edmonton
Forward: Brendan Gallagher, Montreal
Forward: Jonathan Huberdeau, Florida
Forward: Brandon Saad, Chicago

2011-12
Goal: Jhonas Enroth, Buffalo
Defense: Justin Faulk, Carolina
Defense: Jake Gardiner, Toronto
Forward: Adam Henrique, New Jersey
Forward: Gabriel Landeskog, Colorado
Forward: Ryan Nugent-Hopkins, Edmonton

2010-11
Goal: Corey Crawford, Chicago
Defense: John Carlson, Washington
Defense: P.K. Subban, Montreal
Forward: Logan Couture, San Jose
Forward: Michael Grabner, NY Islanders
Forward: Jeff Skinner, Carolina

2009-10
Goal: Jimmy Howard, Detroit
Defense: Tyler Myers, Buffalo
Defense: Michael Del Zotto, NY Rangers
Forward: John Tavares, NY Islanders
Forward: Matt Duchene, Colorado
Forward: Niclas Bergfors, N.J., Atl.

2008-09
Goal: Steve Mason, Columbus
Defense: Drew Doughty, Los Angeles
Defense: Luke Schenn, Toronto
Forward: Patrik Berglund, St. Louis
Forward: Bobby Ryan, Anaheim
Forward: Kris Versteeg, Chicago

2007-08
Goal: Carey Price, Montreal
Defense: Tobias Enstrom, Atlanta
Defense: Tom Gilbert, Edmonton
Forward: Nicklas Backstrom, Washington
Forward: Patrick Kane, Chicago
Forward: Jonathan Toews, Chicago

2006-07
Goal: Mike Smith, Dallas
Defense: Matt Carle, San Jose
Defense: Marc-Edouard Vlasic, San Jose
Forward: Evgeni Malkin, Pittsburgh
Forward: Jordan Staal, Pittsburgh
Forward: Paul Stastny, Colorado

2005-06
Goal: Henrik Lundqvist, NY Rangers
Defense: Andrej Meszaros, Ottawa
Defense: Dion Phaneuf, Calgary
Forward: Brad Boyes, Boston
Forward: Sidney Crosby, Pittsburgh
Forward: Alex Ovechkin, Washington

2004-05

Season Cancelled

2003-04
Goal: Andrew Raycroft, Boston
Defense: John-Michael Liles, Colorado
Defense: Joni Pitkanen, Philadelphia
Forward: Trent Hunter, NY Islanders
Forward: Ryan Malone, Pittsburgh
Forward: Michael Ryder, Montreal

2002-03
Goal: Sebastien Caron, Pittsburgh
Defense: Jay Bouwmeester, Florida
Defense: Barret Jackman, St. Louis
Forward: Tyler Arnason, Chicago
Forward: Rick Nash, Columbus
Forward: Henrik Zetterberg, Detroit

2001-02
Goal: Dan Blackburn, NY Rangers
Defense: Nick Boynton, Boston
Defense: Rostislav Klesla, Columbus
Forward: Dany Heatley, Atlanta
Forward: Ilya Kovalchuk, Atlanta
Forward: Kristian Huselius, Florida

2000-01
Goal: Evgeni Nabokov, San Jose
Defense: Lubomir Visnovsky, Los Angeles
Defense: Colin White, New Jersey
Forward: Martin Havlat, Ottawa
Forward: Brad Richards, Tampa Bay
Forward: Shane Willis, Carolina

1999-2000
Goal: Brian Boucher, Philadelphia
Defense: Brian Rafalski, New Jersey
Defense: Brad Stuart, San Jose
Forward: Simon Gagne, Philadelphia
Forward: Scott Gomez, New Jersey
Forward: Michael York, NY Rangers

1998-99
Goal: Jamie Storr, Los Angeles
Defense: Tom Poti, Edmonton
Defense: Sami Salo, Ottawa
Forward: Chris Drury, Colorado
Forward: Milan Hejduk, Colorado
Forward: Marian Hossa, Ottawa

1997-98
Goal: Jamie Storr, Los Angeles
Defense: Mattias Ohlund, Vancouver
Defense: Derek Morris, Calgary
Forward: Sergei Samsonov, Boston
Forward: Patrik Elias, New Jersey
Forward: Mike Johnson, Toronto

1996-97
Goal: Patrick Lalime, Pittsburgh
Defense: Bryan Berard, NY Islanders
Defense: Janne Niinimaa, Philadelphia
Forward: Jarome Iginla, Calgary
Forward: Jim Campbell, St. Louis
Forward: Sergei Berezin, Toronto

1995-96
Goal: Corey Hirsch, Vancouver
Defense: Ed Jovanovski, Florida
Defense: Kyle McLaren, Boston
Forward: Daniel Alfredsson, Ottawa
Forward: Eric Daze, Chicago
Forward: Petr Sykora, New Jersey

1994-95
Goal: Jim Carey, Washington
Defense: Chris Therien, Philadelphia
Defense: Kenny Jonsson, Toronto
Forward: Peter Forsberg, Quebec
Forward: Jeff Friesen, San Jose
Forward: Paul Kariya, Anaheim

1993-94
Goal: Martin Brodeur, New Jersey
Defense: Chris Pronger, Hartford
Defense: Boris Mironov, Wpg./Edm.
Forward: Jason Arnott, Edmonton
Forward: Mikael Renberg, Philadelphia
Forward: Oleg Petrov, Montreal

1992-93
Goal: Felix Potvin, Toronto
Defense: Vladimir Malakhov, NY Islanders
Defense: Scott Niedermayer, New Jersey
Forward: Eric Lindros, Philadelphia
Forward: Teemu Selanne, Winnipeg
Forward: Joe Juneau, Boston

1991-92
Goal: Dominik Hasek, Chicago
Defense: Nicklas Lidstrom, Detroit
Defense: Vladimir Konstantinov, Detroit
Forward: Kevin Todd, New Jersey
Forward: Tony Amonte, NY Rangers
Forward: Gilbert Dionne, Montreal

1990-91
Goal: Ed Belfour, Chicago
Defense: Eric Weinrich, New Jersey
Defense: Rob Blake, Los Angeles
Forward: Sergei Fedorov, Detroit
Forward: Ken Hodge, Boston
Forward: Jaromir Jagr, Pittsburgh

1989-90
Goal: Bob Essensa, Winnipeg
Defense: Brad Shaw, Hartford
Defense: Geoff Smith, Edmonton
Forward: Mike Modano, Minnesota
Forward: Sergei Makarov, Calgary
Forward: Rod Brind'Amour, St. Louis

1988-89
Goal: Peter Sidorkiewicz, Hartford
Defense: Brian Leetch, NY Rangers
Defense: Zarley Zalapski, Pittsburgh
Forward: Trevor Linden, Vancouver
Forward: Tony Granato, NY Rangers
Forward: David Volek, NY Islanders

1987-88
Goal: Darren Pang, Chicago
Defense: Glen Wesley, Boston
Defense: Calle Johansson, Buffalo
Forward: Joe Nieuwendyk, Calgary
Forward: Ray Sheppard, Buffalo
Forward: Iain Duncan, Winnipeg

1986-87
Goal: Ron Hextall, Philadelphia
Defense: Steve Duchesne, Los Angeles
Defense: Brian Benning, St. Louis
Forward: Jimmy Carson, Los Angeles
Forward: Jim Sandlak, Vancouver
Forward: Luc Robitaille, Los Angeles

1985-86
Goal: Patrick Roy, Montreal
Defense: Gary Suter, Calgary
Defense: Dana Murzyn, Hartford
Forward: Mike Ridley, NY Rangers
Forward: Kjell Dahlin, Montreal
Forward: Wendel Clark, Toronto

1984-85
Goal: Steve Penney, Montreal
Defense: Chris Chelios, Montreal
Defense: Bruce Bell, Quebec
Forward: Mario Lemieux, Pittsburgh
Forward: Tomas Sandstrom, NY Rangers
Forward: Warren Young, Pittsburgh

1983-84
Goal: Tom Barrasso, Buffalo
Defense: Thomas Eriksson, Philadelphia
Defense: Jamie Macoun, Calgary
Forward: Steve Yzerman, Detroit
Forward: Hakan Loob, Calgary
Forward: Sylvain Turgeon, Hartford

1982-83
Goal: Pelle Lindbergh, Philadelphia
Defense: Scott Stevens, Washington
Defense: Phil Housley, Buffalo
Forward: Dan Daoust, Mtl./Tor.
Forward: Steve Larmer, Chicago
Forward: Mats Naslund, Montreal

2015 All-Star Game Summary

JANUARY 25, 2015 at Columbus   Team Toews 17, Team Foligno 12

PLAYERS ON ICE: Team Toews — Roberto Luongo, Jaroslav Halak, Corey Crawford, Aaron Ekblad, Mark Giordano, Shea Weber, Brent Seabrook, Filip Forsberg, Johnny Gaudreau, Ryan Getzlaf, Jonathan Toews, Ryan Suter, Patrik Elias, Justin Faulk, Patrice Bergeron, Rick Nash, Tyler Sequin, Vladimir Tarasenko, John Tavares, Jakub Voracek..

Team Foligno — Brian Elliott, Marc-Andre Fleury, Carey Price, Duncan Keith, Bobby Ryan, Drew Doughty, Alex Ovechkin, Anze Kopitar, Radim Vrbata, Ryan Johansen. Kevin Shattenkirk, Oliver Ekman-Larsson, Zemgus Girgensons, Claude Giroux, Dustin Byfuglien, Nick Foligno, Phil Kessel, Brent Burns, Patrick Kane, Steven Stamkos, Ryan Nugent-Hopkins..

SUMMARY

First Period

1.	Team Foligno	Vrbata	(Nugent-Hopkins)	3:09
2.	Team Toews	Getzlaf	(Tarasenko, Faulk)	6:33
3.	Team Toews	Voracek	(Toews, Ekblad)	9:51
4.	Team Foligno	Johansen	(Foligno, Shattenkirk)	11:05
5.	Team Toews	Bergeron	(Seguin, Elias)	12:17
6.	Team Foligno	Shattenkirk	(Nugent-Hopkins, Vrbata)	14:48
7.	Team Foligno	Johansen	(Ovechkin, Byfuglien)	16:24
8.	Team Toews	Tavares	(Bergeron, Ekblad)	19:03

PENALTIES: None

Second Period

9.	Team Toews	Suter	(Tarasenko, Seguin)	0:24
10.	Team Foligno	Giroux	(Kane)	0:32
11.	Team Toews	Seguin	(Getzlaf, Tarasenko)	1:22
12.	Team Foligno	Stamkos	(Keith)	2:27
13.	Team Toews	Nash	(Toews, Voracek)	4:08
14.	Team Toews	Forsberg	(Gaudreau, Elias)	5:56
15.	Team Toews	Tavares	(Bergeron, Faulk)	8:16
16.	Team Toews	Voracek	(Toews, Ekblad)	9:22
17.	Team Foligno	Foligno	(Johansen, Ovechkin)	11:59
18.	Team Foligno	Stamkos	(Ryan)	16:35
19.	Team Toews	Tavares	(Bergeron)	19:00

PENALTIES: None

Third Period

20.	Team Toews	Nash	(Giordano, Voracek)	1:29
21.	Team Foligno	Kane	(Giroux, Doughty)	2:15
22.	Team Toews	Tavares	(Bergeron, Seabrook)	6:13
23.	Team Toews	Voracek	(Toews, Ekblad)	7:30
24.	Team Foligno	Ryan	(Stamkos, Ekman-Larsson)	8:23
25.	Team Toews	Seguin	(Tarasenko, Weber)	9:26
26.	Team Foligno	Kane	(Burns, Giroux)	13:09
27.	Team Toews	Toews	(Suter)	14:21
28.	Team Toews	Forsberg	(Gaudreau, Voracek)	16:40
29.	Team Foligno	Burns	(Ovechkin, Johansen)	18:20

PENALTIES: None

SHOTS ON GOAL BY:

Team Toews	16	16	15	**47**
Team Foligno	17	18	10	**45**

	Goaltenders:	Time	SA	GA	ENG	Dec
Team Toews	Luongo	20:00	17	4	0	
Team Toews	Crawford	20:00	18	4	0	W
Team Toews	Halak	20:00	10	4	0	
Team Foligno	Price	20:00	16	4	0	
Team Foligno	Fleury	20:00	16	7	0	L
Team Foligno	Elliott	20:00	15	6	0	

PP Conversions: Team Toews 0/0; Team Foligno 0/0.

Referees: Chris Rooney, Chris Lee
Linesmen: Tony Sericolo, Steve Miller
Attendance: 18,901

All-Star Game Results

Year	Venue	Score	Coaches	Attendance
2015	Columbus	Team Toews 17, Team Foligno 12	Peter Laviolette, Darryl Sutter	18,901
2012	Ottawa	Team Chara 12, Team Alfredsson 9	Claude Julien, Tortorella/MacLellan	20,510
2011	Carolina	Team Lidstrom 11, Team Staal 10	Joel Quenneville, Peter Laviolette	18,680
2009	Montreal	East 12, West 11	Claude Julien, Todd McLellan	21,273
2008	Atlanta	East 8, West 7	John Paddock, Mike Babcock	18,644
2007	Dallas	West 12, East 9	Lindy Ruff, Randy Carlyle	18,532
2004	Minnesota	East 6, West 4	Pat Quinn, Dave Lewis	19,434
2003	Florida	West 6, East 5	Marc Crawford, Jacques Martin	19,250
2002	Los Angeles	World 8, North America 5	Scotty Bowman, Pat Quinn	18,118
2001	Colorado	North America 14, World 12	Joel Quenneville, Jacques Martin	18,646
2000	Toronto	World 9, North America 4	Scotty Bowman, Pat Quinn	19,300
1999	Tampa Bay	North America 8, World 6	Lindy Ruff, Ken Hitchcock	19,758
1998	Vancouver	North America 8, World 7	Jacques Lemaire, Ken Hitchcock	18,422
1997	San Jose	East 11, West 7	Doug MacLean, Ken Hitchcock	17,422
1996	Boston	East 5, West 4	Doug MacLean, Scotty Bowman	17,565
1994	NY Rangers	East 9, West 8	Jacques Demers, Barry Melrose	18,200
1993	Montreal	Wales 16, Campbell 6	Scotty Bowman, Mike Keenan	17,137
1992	Philadelphia	Campbell 10, Wales 6	Bob Gainey, Scotty Bowman	17,380
1991	Chicago	Campbell 11, Wales 5	John Muckler, Mike Milbury	18,472
1990	Pittsburgh	Wales 12, Campbell 7	Pat Burns, Terry Crisp	16,236
1989	Edmonton	Campbell 9, Wales 5	Glen Sather, Terry O'Reilly	17,503
1988	St. Louis	Wales 6, Campbell 5 OT	Mike Keenan, Glen Sather	17,878
1986	Hartford	Wales 4, Campbell 3 OT	Mike Keenan, Glen Sather	15,100
1985	Calgary	Wales 6, Campbell 4	Al Arbour, Glen Sather	16,825
1984	New Jersey	Wales 7, Campbell 6	Al Arbour, Glen Sather	18,939
1983	NY Islanders	Campbell 9, Wales 3	Roger Neilson, Al Arbour	15,230
1982	Washington	Wales 4, Campbell 2	Al Arbour, Glen Sonmor	18,130
1981	Los Angeles	Campbell 4, Wales 1	Pat Quinn, Scotty Bowman	15,761
1980	Detroit	Wales 6, Campbell 3	Scotty Bowman, Al Arbour	21,002
1978	Buffalo	Wales 3, Campbell 2 OT	Scotty Bowman, Fred Shero	16,433
1977	Vancouver	Wales 4, Campbell 3	Scotty Bowman, Fred Shero	15,607
1976	Philadelphia	Wales 7, Campbell 5	Floyd Smith, Fred Shero	16,436
1975	Montreal	Wales 7, Campbell 1	Bep Guidolin, Fred Shero	16,080
1974	Chicago	West 6, East 4	Billy Reay, Scotty Bowman	16,426
1973	NY Rangers	East 5, West 4	Tom Johnson, Billy Reay	16,986
1972	Minnesota	East 3, West 2	Al MacNeil, Billy Reay	15,423
1971	Boston	West 2, East 1	Scotty Bowman, Harry Sinden	14,790
1970	St. Louis	East 4, West 1	Claude Ruel, Scotty Bowman	16,587
1969	Montreal	East 3, West 3	Toe Blake, Scotty Bowman	16,260
1968	Toronto	Toronto 4, All-Stars 3	Punch Imlach, Toe Blake	15,753
1967	Montreal	Montreal 3, All-Stars 0	Toe Blake, Sid Abel	14,284
1965	Montreal	All-Stars 5, Montreal 2	Billy Reay, Toe Blake	13,529
1964	Toronto	All-Stars 3, Toronto 2	Sid Abel, Punch Imlach	14,232
1963	Toronto	All-Stars 3, Toronto 3	Sid Abel, Punch Imlach	14,034
1962	Toronto	Toronto 4, All-Stars 1	Punch Imlach, Rudy Pilous	14,236
1961	Chicago	All-Stars 3, Chicago 1	Sid Abel, Rudy Pilous	14,534
1960	Montreal	All-Stars 2, Montreal 1	Punch Imlach, Toe Blake	13,949
1959	Montreal	Montreal 6, All-Stars 1	Toe Blake, Punch Imlach	13,818
1958	Montreal	Montreal 6, All-Stars 3	Toe Blake, Milt Schmidt	13,989
1957	Montreal	All-Stars 5, Montreal 3	Milt Schmidt, Toe Blake	13,003
1956	Montreal	All-Stars 1, Montreal 1	Jim Skinner, Toe Blake	13,095
1955	Detroit	Detroit 3, All-Stars 1	Jim Skinner, Dick Irvin	10,111
1954	Detroit	All-Stars 2, Detroit 2	King Clancy, Jim Skinner	10,689
1953	Montreal	All-Stars 3, Montreal 1	Lynn Patrick, Dick Irvin	14,153
1952	Detroit	1st Team 1, 2nd Team 1	Tommy Ivan, Dick Irvin	10,680
1951	Toronto	1st Team 2, 2nd Team 2	Joe Primeau, Dick Irvin	11,469
1950	Detroit	Detroit 7, All-Stars 1	Tommy Ivan, Lynn Patrick	9,166
1949	Toronto	All-Stars 3, Toronto 1	Tommy Ivan, Hap Day	13,541
1948	Chicago	All-Stars 3, Toronto 1	Tommy Ivan, Hap Day	12,794
1947	Toronto	All-Stars 4, Toronto 3	Dick Irvin, Hap Day	14,169

There was no All-Star contest during the calendar year of 1966 because the game was moved from the start of season to mid-season. In 1979, the Challenge Cup series between the Soviet Union and Team NHL replaced the All-Star Game. In 1987, Rendez-Vous '87, two games between the Soviet Union and Team NHL replaced the All-Star Game. In 1995, 2005 and 2013 the All-Star Game was not played due to a labour disruption affecting the NHL. In 2006, 2010 and 2014 the All-Star Game was not played because of NHL players' participation in the Olympics.

NHL ALL-STAR GAME MVP

2015	Ryan Johansen, CBJ	1994	Mike Richter, NYR
2012	Marian Gaborik, NYR	1993	Mike Gartner, NYR
2011	Patrick Sharp, Chi.	1992	Brett Hull, St.L.
2009	Alex Kovalev, Mtl.	1991	Vincent Damphousse, Tor.
2008	Eric Staal, Car.	1990	Mario Lemieux, Pit.
2007	Daniel Briere, Buf.	1989	Wayne Gretzky, L.A.
2004	Joe Sakic, Col..	1988	Mario Lemieux, Pit.
2003	Dany Heatley, Atl.	1986	Grant Fuhr, Edm.
2002	Eric Daze, Chi.	1985	Mario Lemieux, Pit.
2001	Bill Guerin, Bos.	1984	Don Maloney, NYR
2000	Pavel Bure, Fla.	1983	Wayne Gretzky, Edm.
1999	Wayne Gretzky, NYR	1982	Mike Bossy, NYI
1998	Teemu Selanne, Ana.	1981	Mike Liut, St.L.
1997	Mark Recchi, Mtl.	1980	Reggie Leach, Phi.
1996	Raymond Bourque, Bos.	1978	Billy Smith, NYI

1977	Rick Martin, Buf.
1976	Pete Mahovlich, Mtl.
1975	Syl Apps Jr., Pit.
1974	Garry Unger, St.L.
1973	Greg Polis, Pit.
1972	Bobby Orr, Bos.
1971	Bobby Hull, Chi.
1970	Bobby Hull, Chi.
1969	Frank Mahovlich, Det.
1968	Bruce Gamble, Tor.
1967	Henri Richard, Mtl.
1965	Gordie Howe, Det.
1964	Jean Beliveau, Mtl.
1963	Frank Mahovlich, Tor.
1962	Eddie Shack, Tor.

All-Star Game Records 1947 through 2015

TEAM RECORDS

MOST GOALS, BOTH TEAMS, ONE GAME:
- **29** — Team Toews 17, Team Foligno 12, 2015 at Columbus
- 26 — North America 14, World 12, 2001 at Colorado
- 23 — East 12, West 11, 2009 at Montreal
- 22 — Wales 16, Campbell 6, 1993 at Montreal
- 21 — West 12, East 9, 2007 at Dallas
  - — Team Lidstrom 11, Team Staal 10, 2011 at Carolina
  - — Team Chara 12, Team Alfredsson 9, 2012 at Ottawa

FEWEST GOALS, BOTH TEAMS, ONE GAME:
- **2** — First Team All-Stars 1, Second Team All-Stars 1, 1952 at Detroit
  - — NHL All-Stars 1, Montreal Canadiens 1, 1956 at Montreal
- 3 — NHL All-Stars 1, Montreal Canadiens 1, 1960 at Montreal
  - — Montreal Canadiens 3, NHL All-Stars 0, 1967 at Montreal
  - — West 2, East 1, 1971 at Boston

MOST GOALS, ONE TEAM, ONE GAME:
- **17** — Team Toews 17, Team Foligno 12, 2015 at Columbus
- 16 — Wales 16, Campbell 6, 1993 at Montreal
- 14 — North America 14, World 12, 2001 at Colorado
- 12 — Wales 12, Campbell 7, 1990 at Pittsburgh
  - — World 12, North America 14, 2001 at Colorado
  - — West 12, East 9, 2007 at Dallas
  - — East 12, West 11, 2009 at Montreal
  - — Team Chara 12, Team Alfredsson 9, 2012 at Ottawa
  - — Team Foligno 12, Team Toews 17, 2015 at Columbus

FEWEST GOALS, ONE TEAM, ONE GAME:
- **0** — NHL All-Stars 0, Montreal Canadiens 3, 1967 at Montreal
- 1 — 17 times (1981, 1975, 1971, 1970, 1962, 1961, 1960, 1959, both teams 1956, 1955, 1953, both teams 1952, 1950, 1949, 1948)

MOST SHOTS, BOTH TEAMS, ONE GAME (SINCE 1955):
- **102** — 1994 at NY Rangers - East 9 (56 shots), West 8 (46 shots)
- — 2009 at Montreal - East 12 (48 shots), West 11 (54 shots)
- 98 — 2001 at Colorado - North America 14 (53 shots), World 12 (45 shots)
- 94 — 2012 at Ottawa - Team Chara 12 (44 shots), Team Alfredsson 9 (50 shots)

FEWEST SHOTS, BOTH TEAMS, ONE GAME (SINCE 1955):
- **52** — 1978 at Buffalo - Campbell 2 (12 shots), Wales 3 (40 shots)
- 53 — 1960 at Montreal - NHL All-Stars 2 (27 shots), Montreal Canadiens 1 (26 shots)
- 55 — 1956 at Montreal - NHL All-Stars 1 (28 shots), Montreal Canadiens 1 (27 shots)
- — 1971 at Boston - West 2 (28 shots), East 1 (27 shots)

MOST SHOTS, ONE TEAM, ONE GAME (SINCE 1955):
- **56** — 1994 at NY Rangers - East (9-8 vs. West)
- 54 — 2009 at Montreal - East (12-11 vs. West)
- 53 — 2001 at Colorado - North America (14-12 vs. World)
- 51 — 2008 at Atlanta - West (7-8 vs. East)

FEWEST SHOTS, ONE TEAM, ONE GAME (SINCE 1955):
- **12** — 1978 at Buffalo - Campbell (2-3 vs. Wales)
- 17 — 1970 at St. Louis - West (1-4 vs. East)
- 23 — 1961 at Chicago - Chicago Black Hawks (1-3 vs. NHL All-Stars)
- 24 — 1976 at Philadelphia - Campbell (5-7 vs. Wales)

MOST POWER-PLAY GOALS, BOTH TEAMS, ONE GAME (SINCE 1950):
- **3** — 1953 at Montreal - NHL All-Stars 3 (2 power-play goals), Montreal Canadiens 1 (1 power-play goal)
- — 1954 at Detroit - NHL All-Stars 2 (1 power-play goal) Detroit Red Wings 2 (2 power-play goals)
- — 1958 at Montreal - NHL All-Stars 3 (1 power-play goal) Montreal Canadiens 6 (2 power-play goals)

FEWEST POWER-PLAY GOALS, BOTH TEAMS, ONE GAME (SINCE 1950):
- **0** — 28 times (1952, 1959, 1960, 1967, 1968, 1969, 1972, 1973, 1976, 1980, 1981, 1984, 1985, 1992, 1994, 1996, 1999, 2000, 2001, 2002, 2003, 2004, 2007, 2008, 2009, 2011, 2012, 2015)

FASTEST TWO GOALS, BOTH TEAMS, FROM START OF GAME:
- **0:37** — 1970 at St. Louis — Jacques Laperriere of East scored at 0:20 and Dean Prentice of West scored at 0:37. Final score: East 4, West 1.
- 1:20 — 2008 at Atlanta — Rick Nash of West scored at 0:12 and Eric Staal of East scored at 1:20. Final score: East 8, West 7.
- 2:15 — 1998 at Vancouver — Teemu Selanne scored at 0:53 and Jaromir Jagr scored at 2:15 for World. Final score: North America 8, World 7.

FASTEST TWO GOALS, BOTH TEAMS:
- **0:08** — 1997 at San Jose — Owen Nolan scored at 18:54 and 19:02 of second period for West. Final score: East 11, West 7.
- — 2015 at Columbus — Ryan Suter scored at 0:24 of second period for Team Toews and Claude Giroux scored at 0:32 for Team Foligno. Final score: Team Toews 17, Team Foligno 12.
- 0:10 — 1976 at Philadelphia — Dennis Ververgaert scored at 4:33 and at 4:43 of third period for Campbell. Final score: Wales 7, Campbell 5.

FASTEST THREE GOALS, BOTH TEAMS:
0:48 — 2007 at Dallas — Martin Havlat scored at 19:00 of third period for West; Sheldon Souray scored at 19:25 for East; Dion Phaneuf scored at 19:48 for West. Final score: West 12, East 9.

0:58 — 2015 at Columbus — Ryan Suter scored at 0:24 of second period for Team Toews; Claude Giroux scored at 0:32 for Team Foligno; Tyler Seguin scored at 1:22 for Team Toews. Final score: Team Toews 17, Team Foligno 12.

1:08 — 1993 at Montreal — all by Wales — Mike Gartner scored at 3:15 and at 3:37 of first period; Peter Bondra scored at 4:23. Final score: Wales 16, Campbell 6.

FASTEST FOUR GOALS, BOTH TEAMS:
2:03 — 2015 at Columbus — Ryan Suter scored at 0:24 of second period for Team Toews; Claude Giroux scored at 0:32 for Team Foligno; Tyler Seguin scored at 1:22 for Team Toews; Steven Stamkos scored at 2:27 for Team Foligno. Final score: Team Toews 17, Team Foligno 12.

2:16 — 2012 at Ottawa — Marian Hossa scored at 12:04 of third period for Team Chara; Zdeno Chara scored at 12:20 of third period for Team Chara; Corey Perry scored at 13:26 of third period for Team Chara; Daniel Sedin scored at 14:20 of third period for Team Alfredsson. Final score: Team Chara 12, Team Alfredsson 9.

2:24 — 1997 at San Jose — Brendan Shanahan scored at 16:38 of second period for West; Dale Hawerchuk scored at 17:28 for East; Owen Nolan scored at 18:54 and 19:02 for West. Final score: East 11, West 7.

FASTEST TWO GOALS, ONE TEAM, FROM START OF GAME:
2:15 — 1998 at Vancouver — World — Teemu Selanne scored at 0:53 and Jaromir Jagr scored at 2:15. Final score: North America 8, World 7.

2:48 — 2011 at Carolina — Team Staal — Alex Ovechkin scored at 0:50 and Paul Stastny scored at 2:48. Final score: Team Lidstrom 11, Team Staal 10.

3:37 — 1993 at Montreal — Wales — Mike Gartner scored at 3:15 and at 3:37. Final score: Wales 16, Campbell 6.

FASTEST TWO GOALS, ONE TEAM:
0:08 — 1997 at San Jose — West — Owen Nolan scored at 18:54 and at 19:02 of second period. Final score: East 11, West 7.

0:10 — 1976 at Philadelphia — Campbell — Dennis Ververgaert scored at 4:33 and at 4:43 of third period. Final score: Wales 7, Campbell 5.

0:14 — 1989 at Edmonton — Campbell — Steve Yzerman and Gary Leeman scored at 17:21 and 17:35 of second period. Final score: Campbell 9, Wales 5.

FASTEST THREE GOALS, ONE TEAM:
1:08 — 1993 at Montreal — Wales — Mike Gartner scored at 3:15 and 3:37 of first period; Peter Bondra scored at 4:23. Final score: Wales 16, Campbell 6.

1:22 — 2012 at Ottawa — Team Chara — Marian Hossa scored at 12:04 of third period; Zdeno Chara scored at 12:20; Corey Perry scored at 13:26. Final score: Team Chara 12, Team Alfredsson 9.

1:32 — 1980 at Detroit — Wales — Ron Stackhouse scored at 11:40 of third period; Craig Hartsburg scored at 12:40; Reed Larson scored at 13:12. Final score: Wales 6, Campbell 3.

FASTEST FOUR GOALS, ONE TEAM:
2:57 — 2002 at Los Angeles — World — Sergei Fedorov scored at 16:59 of third period; Markus Naslund scored at 18:17; Alex Zhamnov scored at 19:12; Sami Kapanen scored at 19:56. Final score: World 8, North America 5.

3:29 — 2012 at Ottawa — Team Chara — Marian Hossa scored at 12:04 of third period; Zdeno Chara scored at 12:20; Corey Perry scored at 13:26; Joffrey Lupul scored at 15:33. Final score: Team Chara 12, Team Alfredsson 9.

4:17 — 2007 at Dallas — Brian Rolston scored at 8:30 of second period; Rick Nash scored at 10:40; Martin Havlat scored at 11:34; Yanic Perreault scored at 12:47. Final score: West 12, East 9.

MOST GOALS, BOTH TEAMS, ONE PERIOD:
11 — 2015 at Columbus — Third Period — Team Toews (7), Team Foligno (4), Final score: Team Toews 17, Team Foligno 12.

10 — 1997 at San Jose — Second period — East (6), West (4). Final score: East 11, West 7.

— 2001 at Colorado — Second period — North America (6), World (4). Final score: North America 14, World 12.

— 2001 at Colorado — Third period — North America (5), World (5). Final score: North America 14, World 12.

— 2009 at Montreal — Second period — West (6), East (4). Final score: East 12, West 11.

MOST GOALS, ONE TEAM, ONE PERIOD:
7 — 1990 at Pittsburgh — First period — Wales. Final score: Wales 12, Campbell 7.

— 2015 at Columbus — Second period — Team Toews. Final score: Team Toews 17, Team Foligno 12.

6 — 1983 at NY Islanders — Third period — Campbell. Final score: Campbell 9, Wales 3.

— 1992 at Philadelphia — Second period — Campbell. Final score: Campbell 10, Wales 6.

— 1993 at Montreal — First period — Wales. Final score: Wales 16, Campbell 6.

— 1993 at Montreal — Second period — Wales. Final score: Wales 16, Campbell 6.

— 1997 at San Jose — Second period — East. Final score: East 11, West 7.

— 2001 at Colorado — Second period — North America. Final score: North America 14, World 12.

— 2007 at Dallas — Second period — West. Final score: West 12, East 9.

— 2009 at Montreal — Second period — West. Final score: East 12, West 11.

— 2012 at Ottawa — Third period — Team Chara. Final score: Team Chara 12, Team Alfredsson 9.

— 2015 at Columbus — Third period — Team Toews. Final score: Team Toews 17, Team Foligno 12.

MOST SHOTS, BOTH TEAMS, ONE PERIOD:
42 — 2009 at Montreal — Second period — West (21), East (21). Final score: East 12, West 11.

40 — 2012 at Ottawa — Third period — Team Alfredsson (21), Team Chara (19). Final score: Team Chara 12, Team Alfredsson 9.

39 — 1994 at NY Rangers — Second period — West (21), East (18). Final score: East 9, West 8.

— 2001 at Colorado — Third period — World (23), North America (16). Final score: North America 14, World 12.

36 — 1990 at Pittsburgh — Third period — Campbell (22), Wales (14). Final score: Wales 12, Campbell 7.

— 1994 at NY Rangers — First period — East (19), West (17). Final score: East 9, West 8.

— 2002 at Los Angeles — Third period — North America (20), World (16). Final score: World 8, North America 5.

MOST SHOTS, ONE TEAM, ONE PERIOD:
23 — 2001 at Colorado — Third period — World. Final score: North America 14, World 12.

22 — 1990 at Pittsburgh — Third period — Campbell. Final score: Wales 12, Campbell 7.

— 1991 at Chicago — Third period — Wales. Final score: Campbell 11, Wales 5.

— 1993 at Montreal — First period — Wales. Final score: Wales 16, Campbell 6.

FEWEST SHOTS, BOTH TEAMS, ONE PERIOD:
9 — 1971 at Boston — Third period — East (2), West (7). Final score: West 2, East 1.

— 1980 at Detroit — Second period — Campbell (4), Wales (5). Final score: Wales 6, Campbell 3.

13 — 1982 at Washington — Third period — Campbell (6), Wales (7). Final score: Wales 4, Campbell 2.

14 — 1978 at Buffalo — First period — Campbell (7), Wales (7). Final score: Wales 3, Campbell 2.

— 1986 at Hartford — First period — Campbell (6), Wales (8). Final score: Wales 4, Campbell 3.

FEWEST SHOTS, ONE TEAM, ONE PERIOD:
2 — 1971 at Boston — Third period — East. Final score: West 2, East 1.

— 1978 at Buffalo — Second period — Campbell. Final score: Wales 3, Campbell 2.

3 — 1978 at Buffalo — Third period — Campbell. Final score: Wales 3, Campbell 2.

4 — 1955 at Detroit — First period — NHL All-Stars. Final score: Detroit Red Wings 3, NHL All-Stars 1.

— 1980 at Detroit — Second period — Campbell. Final score: Wales 6, Campbell 3.

Linemates Patrice Bergeron and Patrik Elias congratulate John Tavares, who tied a record with four goals during the highest-scoring All-Star Game in NHL history in 2015. Team Toews beat Team Foligno 17-12.

INDIVIDUAL RECORDS

Games

MOST GAMES PLAYED:
23 — Gordie Howe, 1948 through 1980
19 — Raymond Bourque, 1981 through 2001
18 — Wayne Gretzky, 1980 through 1999
15 — Frank Mahovlich, 1959 through 1974
— Mark Messier, 1982 through 2004

Goals

MOST GOALS, CAREER:
13 — Wayne Gretzky in 18GP
— Mario Lemieux in 10GP
10 — Gordie Howe in 23GP
9 — Teemu Selanne in 10GP
— Rick Nash in 6GP

MOST GOALS, ONE GAME:
4 — Wayne Gretzky, Campbell, 1983
— Mario Lemieux, Wales, 1990
— Vince Damphousse, Campbell, 1991
— Mike Gartner, Wales, 1993
— Dany Heatley, East, 2003
— John Tavares, Team Toews, 2015
3 — Ted Lindsay, Detroit, 1950
— Mario Lemieux, Wales, 1988
— Pierre Turgeon, Wales, 1993
— Mark Recchi, East, 1997
— Owen Nolan, West, 1997
— Teemu Selanne, World, 1998
— Pavel Bure, World, 2000
— Bill Guerin, North America, 2001
— Joe Sakic, West, 2004
— Rick Nash, West, 2008
— Marian Gaborik, Team Chara, 2012
— Jakub Voracek, Team Toews, 2015

MOST GOALS, ONE PERIOD:
4 — Wayne Gretzky, Campbell, Third period, 1983
3 — Mario Lemieux, Wales, First period, 1990
— Vincent Damphousse, Campbell, Third period, 1991
— Mike Gartner, Wales, First period, 1993

Assists

MOST ASSISTS, CAREER:
16 — Joe Sakic in 12GP
14 — Mark Messier in 15GP
13 — Raymond Bourque in 19GP

MOST ASSISTS, ONE GAME:
5 — Mats Naslund, Wales, 1988
4 — Raymond Bourque, Wales, 1985
— Adam Oates, Campbell, 1991
— Adam Oates, Wales, 1993
— Mark Recchi, Wales, 1993
— Pierre Turgeon, East, 1994
— Fredrik Modin, World, 2001
— Joe Sakic, West, 2007
— Daniel Briere, East, 2007
— Marian Hossa, East, 2007
— Shea Weber, Team Lidstrom, 2011
— Aaron Ekblad, Team Toews, 2015
— Jonathan Toews, Team Toews, 2015
— Patrice Bergeron, Team Toews, 2015
— Vladimir Tarasenko, Team Toews, 2015

MOST ASSISTS, ONE PERIOD:
4 — Adam Oates, Wales, First period, 1993
3 — Mark Messier, Campbell, Third period, 1983
3 — Marian Hossa, East, Third period, 2007

Points

MOST POINTS, CAREER:
25 — Wayne Gretzky (13G-12A in 18GP)
23 — Mario Lemieux (13G-10A in 10GP)
22 — Joe Sakic (6G-16A in 12GP)
20 — Mark Messier (6G-14A in 15GP)
19 — Gordie Howe (10G-9A in 23GP)

MOST POINTS, ONE GAME:
6 — Mario Lemieux, Wales, 1988 (3G-3A)
— Jakub Voracek, Team Toews, 2015 (3G-3A)
5 — Mats Naslund, Wales, 1988 (5A)
— Adam Oates, Campbell, 1991 (1G-4A)
— Mike Gartner, Wales, 1993 (4G-1A)
— Mark Recchi, Wales, 1993 (1G-4A)
— Pierre Turgeon, Wales, 1993 (3G-2A)
— Bill Guerin, North America, 2001 (3G-2A)
— Dany Heatley, East, 2003 (4G-1A)
— Daniel Briere, East, 2007 (1G-4A)
— Patrice Bergeron, Team Toews, 2015 (1G-4A)
— Jonathan Toews, Team Toews, 2015 (1G-4A)

MOST POINTS, ONE PERIOD:
4 — Wayne Gretzky, Campbell, Third period, 1983 (4G)
— Mike Gartner, Wales, First period, 1993 (3G-1A)
— Adam Oates, Wales, First period, 1993 (4A)
3 — Gordie Howe, NHL All-Stars, Second period, 1965 (1G-2A)
— Pete Mahovlich, Wales, First period, 1976 (1G-2A)
— Mark Messier, Campbell, Third period, 1983 (3A)
— Mario Lemieux, Wales, Second period, 1988 (1G-2A)
— Mario Lemieux, Wales, First period, 1990 (3G)
— Vince Damphousse, Campbell, Third period, 1991 (3G)
— Mark Recchi, Wales, Second period, 1993 (1G-2A)
— Tony Amonte, North America, Second period, 2001 (2G-1A)
— Daniel Alfredsson, East, Second period, 2004 (2G-1A)
— Marian Hossa, East, Third period, 2007 (3A)
— Jakub Voracek, Team Toews, Third period, 2015 (1G-2A)

Power-Play Goals

MOST POWER-PLAY GOALS, CAREER:
6 — Gordie Howe in 23GP
3 — Bobby Hull in 12GP
— Maurice Richard in 13GP

Fastest Goals

FASTEST GOAL FROM START OF GAME:
0:12 — Rick Nash, West, 2008
0:19 — Ted Lindsay, Detroit, 1950
0:20 — Jacques Laperriere, East, 1970
0:21 — Mario Lemieux, Wales, 1990
0:35 — Vincent Damphousse, North America, 2002

FASTEST GOAL FROM START OF A PERIOD:
0:12 — Rick Nash, West, 2008 (first period)
0:17 — Raymond Bourque, North America, 1999 (second period)
0:19 — Ted Lindsay, Detroit, 1950 (first period)
— Rick Tocchet, Wales, 1993 (second period)
0:20 — Jacques Laperriere, East, 1970 (first period)

FASTEST TWO GOALS, ONE PLAYER, FROM START OF GAME:
3:37 — Mike Gartner, Wales, 1993, at 3:15 and 3:37.
4:00 — Teemu Selanne, World, 1998, at 0:53 and 4:00
5:25 — Wally Hergesheimer, NHL All-Stars, 1953, at 4:06 and 5:25.

FASTEST TWO GOALS, ONE PLAYER, FROM START OF A PERIOD:
3:37 — Mike Gartner, Wales, 1993, at 3:15 and 3:37 of first period.
4:00 — Teemu Selanne, World, 1998, at 0:53 and 4:00 of first period.
4:43 — Dennis Ververgaert, Campbell, 1976, at 4:33 and 4:43 of third period.

FASTEST TWO GOALS, ONE PLAYER:
0:08 — Owen Nolan, West, 1997. Scored at 18:54 and 19:02 of second period.
0:10 — Dennis Ververgaert, Campbell, 1976. Scored at 4:33 and 4:43 of third period.
0:22 — Mike Gartner, Wales, 1993. Scored at 3:15 and 3:37 of first period.

Penalties

MOST PENALTY MINUTES:
25 — Gordie Howe in 23GP
21 — Gus Mortson in 9GP
16 — Harry Howell in 7GP

Goaltenders

MOST GAMES PLAYED:
13 — Glenn Hall from 1955 through 1969
11 — Terry Sawchuk from 1950 through 1968
— Patrick Roy from 1988 through 2003
9 — Martin Brodeur from 1996 through 2007
8 — Jacques Plante from 1956 through 1970

MOST MINUTES PLAYED:
540 — Glenn Hall in 13GP
467 — Terry Sawchuk in 11GP
370 — Jacques Plante in 8GP
250 — Patrick Roy in 11GP
209 — Turk Broda in 4GP

MOST GOALS AGAINST:
31 — Patrick Roy in 11GP
22 — Martin Brodeur in 9GP
— Glenn Hall in 13GP
21 — Mike Vernon in 5GP
19 — Terry Sawchuk in 11GP

BEST GOALS-AGAINST-AVERAGE AMONG THOSE WITH AT LEAST TWO GAMES PLAYED:
0.68 — Gilles Villemure in 3GP
1.49 — Gerry McNeil in 3GP
1.50 — Johnny Bower in 4GP
1.51 — Frank Brimsek in 3GP
1.64 — Gump Worsley in 4GP

Hockey Hall of Fame

(Year of induction is listed after each Honoured Members name)

Location: Brookfield Place, at the corner of Front and Yonge Streets in the heart of downtown Toronto. Easy access from all major highways running into Toronto. Close to TTC subway and Union Station.

Telephone: administration (416) 360-7735; information (416) 360-7765.

Public Hours of Operation: Open every day except Christmas Day, New Year's Day and Induction Day (November 9, 2015). Please call our information number (above) or visit our website (below) for times.

The Hockey Hall of Fame can be booked for private functions after hours.

Website address: www.hhof.com

History: The Hockey Hall of Fame was established in 1943. Members were first honoured in 1945. On August 26, 1961, the Hockey Hall of Fame opened its doors to the public in a building located on the grounds of the Canadian National Exhibition in Toronto. The Hockey Hall of Fame relocated to its current location and welcomed the hockey world on June 18, 1993.

Honour Roll: There are 388 Honoured Members in the Hockey Hall of Fame. 268 have been inducted as players including four women, 104 as builders and 16 as Referees/Linesmen. In addition, there are 94 media honourees.

Founding/Premier Sponsors: Cisco Systems, Imperial Oil, International Ice Hockey Federation, National Hockey League, National Hockey League Players' Association, PepsiCo Canada, Scotiabank, The Toronto Sun, Tim Hortons, The Sports Network (TSN/RDS).

Two of the best defensemen of their generation, Nicklas Lidstrom and Chris Pronger, shake hands after Detroit eliminated Anaheim in the 2009 Western Conference Semifinal. Lidstrom is a seven-time winner of the Norris Trophy. Pronger won the Norris and the Hart Trophy in 2000.

PLAYERS

* Abel, Sidney Gerald 1969
* Adams, John James "Jack" 1959
  Anderson, Glenn 2008
* Apps, Charles Joseph Sylvanus "Syl" 1961
  Armstrong, George Edward 1975
* Bailey, Irvine Wallace "Ace" 1975
* Bain, Donald H. "Dan" 1949
* Baker, Hobart "Hobey" 1945
  Barber, William Charles "Bill" 1990
* Barry, Martin J. "Marty" 1965
  Bathgate, Andrew James "Andy" 1978
* Bauer, Robert Theodore "Bobby" 1996
  Belfour, Ed 2011
* Béliveau, Jean Arthur 1972
* Benedict, Clinton S. 1965
* Bentley, Douglas Wagner 1964
* Bentley, Maxwell H. L. 1966
* Blake, Hector "Toe" 1966
  Blake, Rob 2014
  Boivin, Leo Joseph 1986
* Boon, Richard R. "Dickie" 1952
  Bossy, Michael 1991
* Bouchard, Emile Joseph "Butch" 1966
* Boucher, Frank 1958
* Boucher, George "Buck" 1960
  Bourque, Raymond 2004
  Bower, John William 1976
  Bowie, Russell 1947
* Brimsek, Francis Charles 1966
* Broadbent, Harry L. "Punch" 1962
* Broda, Walter Edward "Turk" 1967
  Bucyk, John Paul 1981
* Burch, Billy 1974
  Bure, Pavel 2012
* Cameron, Harold Hugh "Harry" 1962
  Cheevers, Gerald Michael "Gerry" 1985
  Chelios, Chris 2013
  Ciccarelli, Dino 2010
* Clancy, Francis Michael "King" 1958
* Clapper, Aubrey "Dit" 1947
  Clarke, Robert "Bobby" 1987
* Cleghorn, Sprague 1958
  Coffey, Paul 2004
* Colville, Neil MacNeil 1967
* Conacher, Charles W. 1961
* Conacher, Lionel Pretoria 1994
* Conacher, Roy Gordon 1998
* Connell, Alex 1958
* Cook, Fred "Bun" 1995
* Cook, William Osser 1952
* Coulter, Arthur Edmund 1974
  Cournoyer, Yvan Serge 1982
* Cowley, William Mailes 1968

* Crawford, Samuel Russell "Rusty" 1962
* Darragh, John Proctor "Jack" 1962
* Davidson, Allan M. "Scotty" 1950
* Day, Clarence Henry "Hap" 1961
  Delvecchio, Alex 1977
* Denneny, Cyril "Cy" 1959
  Dionne, Marcel 1992
* Drillon, Gordon Arthur 1975
* Drinkwater, Charles Graham 1950
  Dryden, Kenneth Wayne 1983
  Duff, Dick 2006
* Dumart, Woodrow "Woody" 1992
* Dunderdale, Thomas 1974
* Durnan, William Ronald 1964
* Dutton, Mervyn A. "Red" 1958
* Dye, Cecil Henry "Babe" 1970
  Esposito, Anthony James "Tony" 1988
  Esposito, Philip Anthony 1984
* Farrell, Arthur F. 1965
  Federko, Bernie 2002
  Fedorov, Sergei 2015
  Fetisov, Viacheslav 2001
* Flaman, Ferdinand Charles "Fern" 1990
  Forsberg, Peter 2014
* Foyston, Frank 1958
  Francis, Ron 2007
* Fredrickson, Frank 1958
  Fuhr, Grant 2003
  Gadsby, William Alexander 1970
  Gainey, Bob 1992
* Gardiner, Charles Robert "Chuck" 1945
* Gardiner, Herbert Martin "Herb" 1958
* Gardner, James Henry "Jimmy" 1962
  Gartner, Michael Alfred 2001
* Geoffrion, Jos. A. Bernard "Boom Boom" 1972
* Gerard, Eddie 1945
  Giacomin, Edward "Eddie" 1987
  Gilbert, Rodrigue Gabriel "Rod" 1982
  Gillies, Clark 2002
  Gilmour, Doug 2011
* Gilmour, Hamilton Livingstone "Billy" 1962
* Goheen, Frank Xavier "Moose" 1952
* Goodfellow, Ebenezer R. "Ebbie" 1963
  Goulet, Michel 1998
  Granato, Cammi 2010
* Grant, Michael "Mike" 1950
* Green, Wilfred "Shorty" 1962
  Gretzky, Wayne Douglas 1999
* Griffis, Silas Seth "Si" 1950
* Hainsworth, George 1961
  Hall, Glenn Henry 1975

* Hall, Joseph Henry 1961
* Harvey, Douglas Norman 1973
  Hasek, Dominik 2014
  Hawerchuk, Dale Martin 2001
* Hay, George 1958
  Heaney, Geraldine 2013
* Hern, William Milton "Riley" 1962
* Hextall, Bryan Aldwyn 1969
* Holmes, Harry "Hap" 1972
* Hooper, Charles Thomas "Tom" 1962
* Horner, George Reginald "Red" 1965
* Horton, Miles Gilbert "Tim" 1977
  Housley, Phil 2015
  Howe, Gordon 1972
  Howe, Mark 2011
* Howe, Sydney Harris 1965
  Howell, Henry Vernon "Harry" 1979
  Hull, Brett 2009
  Hull, Robert Marvin 1983
* Hutton, John Bower "Bouse" 1962
* Hyland, Harry M. 1962
* Irvin, James Dickenson "Dick" 1958
* Jackson, Harvey "Busher" 1971
  James, Angela 2010
* Johnson, Ernest "Moose" 1952
* Johnson, Ivan "Ching" 1958
* Johnson, Thomas Christian 1970
* Joliat, Aurel 1947
* Keats, Gordon "Duke" 1958
  Kelly, Leonard Patrick "Red" 1969
* Kennedy, Theodore Samuel "Teeder" 1966
  Keon, David Michael 1986
* Kharlamov, Valeri 2005
  Kurri, Jari 2001
* Lach, Elmer James 1966
  Lafleur, Guy Damien 1988
  LaFontaine, Pat 2003
* Lalonde, Edouard Charles "Newsy" 1950
  Langway, Rod Corry 2002
  Laperriere, Jacques 1987
  Lapointe, Guy 1993
  Laprade, Edgar 1993
  Larionov, Igor 2008
* Laviolette, Jean Baptiste "Jack" 1962
* Lehman, Hugh 1958
  Lemaire, Jacques Gerard 1984
  Lemieux, Mario 1997
* LeSueur, Percy 1961
  Leetch, Brian 2009
* Lewis, Herbert A. 1989
  Lidstrom, Nicklas 2015
  Lindsay, Robert Blake Theodore "Ted" 1966
* Lumley, Harry 1980

  MacInnis, Al 2007
* MacKay, Duncan "Mickey" 1952
  Mahovlich, Frank William 1981
* Malone, Joseph "Joe" 1950
* Mantha, Sylvio 1960
* Marshall, John "Jack" 1965
* Maxwell, Fred G. "Steamer" 1962
  McDonald, Lanny 1992
* McGee, Frank 1945
* McGimsie, William George "Billy" 1962
* McNamara, George 1958
  Messier, Mark 2007
  Mikita, Stanley 1983
  Modano, Mike 2014
  Moore, Richard Winston "Dickie" 1974
* Moran, Patrick Joseph "Paddy" 1958
* Morenz, Howie 1945
* Mosienko, William "Billy" 1965
  Mullen, Joseph P. 2000
  Murphy, Larry 2004
  Neely, Cam 2005
  Niedermayer, Scott 2013
  Nieuwendyk, Joe 2011
* Nighbor, Frank 1947
* Noble, Edward Reginald "Reg" 1962
  Oates, Adam 2012
* O'Connor, Herbert William "Buddy" 1988
* Oliver, Harry 1967
  Olmstead, Murray Bert "Bert" 1985
  Orr, Robert Gordon 1979
  Parent, Bernard Marcel 1984
  Park, Douglas Bradford "Brad" 1988
* Patrick, Joseph Lynn 1980
* Patrick, Lester 1947
  Perreault, Gilbert 1990
* Phillips, Tommy 1945
  Pilote, Joseph Albert Pierre Paul 1975
* Pitre, Didier "Pit" 1962
* Plante, Joseph Jacques Omer 1978
  Potvin, Denis 1991
* Pratt, Walter "Babe" 1966
* Primeau, A. Joseph 1963
  Pronger, Chris 2015
* Pronovost, Joseph René Marcel 1978
  Pulford, Bob 1991
* Pulford, Harvey 1945
* Quackenbush, Hubert George "Bill" 1976
* Rankin, Frank 1961
  Ratelle, Joseph Gilbert Yvan Jean "Jean" 1985
* Rayner, Claude Earl "Chuck" 1973
* Reardon, Kenneth Joseph 1966

Richard, Joseph Henri 1979
* Richard, Joseph Henri Maurice "Rocket" 1961
* Richardson, George Taylor 1950
* Roberts, Gordon 1971
Robinson, Larry 1995
Robitaille, Luc 2009
* Ross, Arthur Howey 1949
Roy, Patrick 2006
Ruggiero, Angela 2015
* Russell, Blair 1965
* Russell, Ernest 1965
* Ruttan, J.D. "Jack" 1962
Sakic, Joe 2012
Salming, Borje Anders 1996
Savard, Denis Joseph 2000
Savard, Serge 1986
* Sawchuk, Terrance Gordon "Terry" 1971
* Scanlan, Fred 1965
Schmidt, Milton Conrad "Milt" 1961
* Schriner, David "Sweeney" 1962
* Seibert, Earl Walter 1963
* Seibert, Oliver Levi 1961
Shanahan, Brendan 2013
* Shore, Edward W. "Eddie" 1947
Shutt, Stephen 1993
* Siebert, Albert C. "Babe" 1964
* Simpson, Harold Edward "Bullet Joe" 1962
Sittler, Darryl Glen 1989
* Smith, Alfred E. 1962
Smith, Clint 1991
* Smith, Reginald "Hooley" 1972
* Smith, Thomas James 1973
Smith, William John "Billy" 1993
* Stanley, Allan Herbert 1981
* Stanley, Russell "Barney" 1962
Stastny, Peter 1998
Stevens, Scott 2007
* Stewart, John Sherratt "Black Jack" 1964
* Stewart, Nelson "Nels" 1952
* Stuart, Bruce 1961
* Stuart, Hod 1945
Sundin, Mats 2012
* Taylor, Frederick "Cyclone" (O.B.E.) 1947
* Thompson, Cecil R. "Tiny" 1959

Tretiak, Vladislav 1989
* Trihey, Col. Harry J. 1950
Trottier, Bryan 1997
Ullman, Norman V. Alexander "Norm" 1982
* Vezina, Georges 1945
* Walker, John Phillip "Jack" 1960
* Walsh, Martin "Marty" 1962
* Watson, Harry E. 1962
* Watson, Harry 1994
* Weiland, Ralph "Cooney" 1971
* Westwick, Harry 1962
* Whitcroft, Fred 1962
* Wilson, Gordon Allan "Phat" 1962
* Worsley, Lorne John "Gump" 1980
* Worters, Roy 1969
Yzerman, Steve 2009

BUILDERS

* Adams, Charles 1960
* Adams, Weston W. 1972
* Ahearn, Thomas Franklin "Frank" 1962
* Ahearne, John Francis "Bunny" 1977
* Allan, Sir Montagu (C.V.O.) 1945
* Allen, Keith 1992
Arbour, Alger Joseph "Al" 1996
* Ballard, Harold Edwin 1977
* Bauer, Father David 1989
* Bickell, John Paris 1978
Bowman, Scotty 1991
* Brooks, Herb 2006
* Brown, George V. 1961
* Brown, Walter A. 1962
* Buckland, Frank 1975
* Burns, Pat 2014
Bush, Walter 2000
* Butterfield, Jack Arlington 1980
* Calder, Frank 1947
* Campbell, Angus D. 1964
* Campbell, Clarence Sutherland 1966
* Cattarinich, Joseph 1977
* Chynoweth, Ed 2008
Costello, Murray 2005
* Dandurand, Joseph Viateur "Leo" 1963
Devellano, Jim 2010
* Dilio, Francis Paul 1964

* Dudley, George S. 1958
* Dunn, James A. 1968
Fletcher, Cliff 2004
Francis, Emile 1982
* Gibson, Dr. John L. "Jack" 1976
* Gorman, Thomas Patrick "Tommy" 1963
Gregory, Jim 2007
* Griffiths, Frank A. 1993
* Hanley, William 1986
* Hay, Charles 1974
Hay, William "Bill", 2015
* Hendy, James C. 1968
* Hewitt, Foster 1965
* Hewitt, William Abraham 1947
* Hotchkiss, Harley 2006
* Hume, Fred J. 1962
* Illitch, Mike 2003
* Imlach, George "Punch" 1984
* Ivan, Thomas N. 1974
* Jennings, William M. 1975
* Johnson, Bob 1992
* Juckes, Gordon W. 1979
Karmanos, Jr., Peter 2015
* Kilpatrick, Gen. John Reed 1960
Kilrea, Brian Blair 2003
* Knox, Seymour H. III 1993
Lamoriello, Lou 2009
* Leader, George Alfred 1969
* LeBel, Robert 1970
* Lockhart, Thomas F. 1965
* Loicq, Paul 1961
* Mariucci, John 1985
* Mathers, Frank 1992
* McLaughlin, Major Frederic 1963
* Milford, John "Jake" 1984
* Molson, Hon. Hartland de Montarville 1973
Morrison, Ian "Scotty" 1999
* Murray, Monsignor Athol 1998
* Neilson, Roger 2002
* Nelson, Francis 1947
* Norris, Bruce A. 1969
* Norris, Sr., James 1958
* Norris, James Dougan 1962
* Northey, William M. 1947
* O'Brien, John Ambrose 1962
O'Neill, Brian 1994
* Page, Fred 1993

Patrick, Craig 2001
* Patrick, Frank 1950
* Pickard, Allan W. 1958
* Pilous, Rudy 1985
* Poile, Norman "Bud" 1990
* Pollock, Samuel Patterson Smyth 1978
* Raymond, Sen. Donat 1958
* Robertson, John Ross 1947
* Robinson, Claude C. 1947
* Ross, Philip D. 1976
* Sabetzki, Dr. Gunther 1995
Sather, Glen 1997
* Seaman, Daryl "Doc" 2010
* Selke, Frank J. 1960
* Shero, Fred 2013
Sinden, Harry James 1983
* Smith, Frank D. 1962
* Smythe, Conn 1958
Snider, Edward M. 1988
* Stanley of Preston, Lord (G.C.B.) 1945
* Sutherland, Cap. James T. 1947
* Tarasov, Anatoli V. 1974
Torrey, Bill 1995
* Turner, Lloyd 1958
* Tutt, William Thayer 1978
* Voss, Carl Potter 1974
* Waghorne, Fred 1961
* Wirtz, Arthur Michael 1971
* Wirtz, William W. "Bill" 1976
Ziegler, John A. Jr. 1987

REFEREES/LINESMEN

Armstrong, Neil 1991
* Ashley, John George 1981
* Chadwick, William L. 1964
* D'Amico, John 1993
* Elliott, Chaucer 1961
* Hayes, George William 1988
* Hewitson, Robert W. 1963
* Ion, Fred J. "Mickey" 1961
McCreary, Bill 2014
Pavelich, Matt 1987
* Rodden, Michael J. "Mike" 1962
Scapinello, Ray 2008
* Smeaton, J. Cooper 1961
* Storey, Roy Alvin "Red" 1967
* Udvari, Frank Joseph 1973
Van Hellemond, Andy 1999

Phil Housley (left) ranks fourth all-time in scoring among NHL defensemen and trails only Mike Modano for points among American-born players. Sergei Fedorov (center) was a three-time Stanley Cup champion who also won the Hart Trophy in 1994. He was the first Russian to score 1,000 points in the NHL. Angela Ruggiero (right) was the youngest member of the U.S. team that won the first Olympic gold medal in women's hockey in 1998. She also won four World Championship golds and three player-of-the-year awards at Harvard University.

Elmer Ferguson Memorial Award Winners

In recognition of distinguished members of the hockey-writing profession whose words have brought honor to journalism and to hockey. Selected by the Professional Hockey Writers' Association.

Allen, Kevin, USA Today 2014
* Barton, Charlie, Buffalo-Courier Express 1985
* Beauchamp, Jacques, Montreal Matin/Journal de Montréal 1984
* Brennan, Bill, Detroit News 1987
* Burchard, Jim, New York World Telegram 1984
* Burnett, Red, Toronto Star 1984
* Carroll, Dink, Montreal Gazette 1984
* Coleman, Jim, Southam Newspapers 1984
Conway, Russ, Eagle-Tribune 1999
* Damata, Ted, Chicago Tribune 1984
de Foy, Marc, Le Journal de Montreal/ruefrontenac.com 2010
* Delano, Hugh, New York Post 1991
Desjardins, Marcel, Montréal La Presse 1984
Duhatschek, Eric, Calgary Herald/Globe and Mail 2001
* Dulmage, Jack, Windsor Star 1984
* Dunnell, Milt, Toronto Star 1984
Dupont, Kevin Paul, Boston Globe 2002
Elliott, Helene, Los Angeles Times 2005
Farber, Michael, Montreal Gazette/Sports Illustrated 2003
* Fay, Dave, Washington Times 2007
* Ferguson, Elmer, Montreal Herald/Star 1984
* Fitzgerald, Tom, Boston Globe 1984
* Frayne, Trent, Toronto Telegram/Globe and Mail/Sun 1984
Gatecliff, Jack, St. Catharines Standard 1995
Greenberg, Jay, Kansas City Star/Philadelphia Daily News/Sports Illustrated 2013
* Gross, George, Toronto Telegram/Sun 1985
* Johnston, Dick, Buffalo News 1986
Jones, Terry, Edmonton Sun 2011
* Kelley, Jim, Buffalo News 2004
* Laney, Al, New York Herald-Tribune 1984
* Larochelle, Claude, Le Soleil 1989
L'Esperance, Zotique, Journal de Montréal/ le Petit Journal 1985
MacGregor, Roy, Globe and Mail 2012
* MacLeod, Rex, Toronto Globe and Mail/Star 1987
Matheson, Jim, Edmonton Journal 2000
* Mayer, Charles, Journal de Montréal/la Patrie 1985
McKenzie, Bob, The Hockey News/Toronto Star/TSN 2015
* McKenzie, Ken, The Hockey News 1997
Molinari, Dave, Pittsburgh Post-Gazette 2009
* Monahan, Leo, Boston Daily Record/Record-American/ Herald American 1986
* Moriarty, Tim, UPI/Newsday 1986
Morrison, Scott, Toronto Sun/Rogers Sportsnet 2006
* Nichols, Joe, New York Times 1984
* O'Brien, Andy, Weekend Magazine 1985
Olan, Ben, New York Associated Press 1987
Orr, Frank, Toronto Star 1989
* O'Meara, Basil, Montreal Star 1984
Pedneault, Yvon, La Presse/Journal de Montréal 1998
* Proudfoot, Jim, Toronto Star 1988
Raymond, Bertrand, Journal de Montréal 1990
* Rosa, Fran, Boston Globe 1987
Stevens, Neil, Canadian Press 2008
Strachan, Al, Globe and Mail/Toronto Sun 1993
* Vipond, Jim, Toronto Globe and Mail 1984
Walter, Lewis, Detroit Times 1984
* Young, Scott, Toronto Globe and Mail/Telegram 1988

United States Hockey Hall of Fame

On May 11, 2007, the U.S. Hockey Hall of Fame and USA Hockey came to a historic agreement that transferred rights to the selection process and induction event associated with the Hall, including the Wayne Gretzky International Award, to USA Hockey. As part of the agreement, the U.S. Hockey Hall of Fame Museum, located in Eveleth, Minnesota, formed a separate Board of Directors to govern the national shrine for American Hockey.

There are 169 enshrined members in the U.S. Hockey Hall of Fame (www.ushockeyhalloffame.com). New members are inducted annually and must have made extraordinary contributions to hockey in the United States during the course of their career. A special Wayne Gretzky International Award pays tribute to international individuals who have made major contributions to hockey in the USA.

The United States Hockey Hall of Fame Museum was opened on June 21, 1973. It is dedicated to honoring the sport of ice hockey in the United States by preserving those previous memories and legends of the game. It is located in Eveleth, Minnesota, 60 miles north of Duluth on Highway 53. For further information, call 800-443-7825 or 218-744-5167, or visit www.ushockeyhall.com.

INDIVIDUALS

Players

* Abel, Clarence "Taffy" 1973
Amonte, Tony 2009
* Baker, Hobey 1973
Barrasso, Tom 2009
* Bartholome, Earl 1977
Berglund, Art 2010
* Bessone, Peter 1978
* Blake, Bob 1985
Boucha, Henry 1995
* Brimsek, Frank 1973
* Brink, Milton "Curly" 2006
Broten, Aaron 2007
Broten, Neal 2000
Bye Dietz, Karyn 2014
Carpenter, Bobby 2007
Cavanagh, Joe 1994
* Chaisson, Ray 1974
* Chase, John P. 1973
Chellios, Chris 2011
Christian, David 2001
* Christian, Roger 1989
Christian, William "Bill" 1984
Christiansen, Keith "Huffer" 2005
Cleary, Bill 1976
Cleary, Bob 1981
* Conroy, Tony 1975
Coppo, Paul 2004
Curley, Cindy 2013
Curran, Mike 1998
* Dahlstrom, Carl "Cully" 1973
* Desjardins, Vic 1974
* Desmond, Dick 1988
* Dill, Bob 1979
Dougherty, Richard "Dick" 2003
Drury, Chris 2015
* Everett, Doug 1974
Fusco, Mark 2002
Fusco, Scott 2002
Ftorek, Robbie 1991
Gambucci, Gary 2006
* Garrison, John 1973
Garrity, Jack 1986
* Goheen, Frank "Moose" 1973
Granato, Cammi 2008
Grant, Wally 1994
Guerin, Bill 2012
* Harding, Francis "Austie" 1975
Hatcher, Derian 2010
Hatcher, Kevin 2010
Housley, Phil 2004
Howe, Mark 2003
Hull, Brett 2008
* Iglehart, Stewart 1975
Johnson, Mark 2004
Johnson, Paul 2001
* Johnson, Virgil 1974
* Kahler, Nick 1980
* Karakas, Mike 1973
Kirrane, Jack 1987
LaFontaine, Pat 2003
* Lane, Myles 1973
Langevin, Dave 1993
Langway, Rod 1999
Larson, Reed 1996
LeClair, John 2009
Leetch, Brian 2008

* Linder, Joe 1975
* LoPresti, Sam 1973
MacDonald, Lane 2005
* Mariucci, John 1973
* Matchefts, John 1991
* Mather, Bruce 1998
Mayasich, John 1976
McCartan, Jack 1983
Modano, Mike 2012
* Moe, Bill 1974
Morrow, Ken 1995
* Moseley, Fred 1975
Mullen, Joe 1998
* Murray, Sr. Hugh "Muzz" 1987
* Nelson, Hubert "Hub" 1978
* Nyrop, Bill 1997
Olczyk, Eddie 2012
* Olson, Eddie 1974
* Owen, Jr. George 1973
Palazzari, Doug 2000
* Palmer, Winthrop "Ding" 1973
Paradise, Bob 1989
* Purpur, Clifford "Fido" 1974
Rafalski, Brian 2014
Ramsey, Mike 2001
Richter, Mike 2008
Riley, Joe 2002
* Riley, Bill 1977
Roberts, Gordie 1999
* Roberts, Moe 2005
Roenick, Jeremy 2010
* Romnes, Elwin "Doc" 1973
* Rondeau, Dick 1985
Ruggiero, Angela 2015
Schneider, Mathieu 2015
Sheehy, Tim 1997
Suter, Gary 2011
Tkachuk, Keith 2011
Vanbiesbrouck, John 2007
* Watson, Sid 1999
Weight, Doug 2013
* Williams, Tommy 1981
* Winters, Frank "Coddy" 1973
* Yakel, Ken 1986

Coaches

* Almquist, Oscar 1983
* Bessone, Amo 1992
* Brooks, Herb 1990
Ceglarski, Len 1992
* Cunniff, John 2003
* Fullerton, Jim 1992
Gambucci, Sergio 1996
* Gordon, Malcom K. 1973
* Harkness, Ned 1994
* Heyliger, Vic 1974
* Holt, Jr. Charlie 1997
Ikola, Willard 1990
* Jeremiah, Eddie 1973
* Johnson, Bob 1991
* Kelly, John "Snooks" 1974
Kelley, John "Jack" 1993
* MacInnes, John 2007
* Marvin, Cal 1982
Mason, Ron 2013
* Pleban, Connie 1990
Riley, Jack 1979

* Ross, Larry 1988
Sauer, Jeff 2014
* Stewart, Bill 1982
* Thompson, Cliff 1973
Vairo, Lou 2014
Williamson, Murray 2005
* Winsor, Alfred "Ralph" 1973
Woog, Doug 2002

Administrators

* Brown, George 1973
* Brown, Walter 1973
Bush, Walter 1980
* Clark, Don 1978
* Claypool, Jim 1995
DeGregorio, Ron 2015
* Gibson, John "Doc" 1973
Ilitch, Mike 2004
* Jennings, William M. "Bill" 1981
Karmanos, Peter 2013
Lamoriello, Lou 2012
* Lockhart, Tom 1973
Patrick, Craig 1996
Pleau, Larry 2000
* Ridder, Bob 1976
Snider, Ed 2011
Trumble, Hal 1985
* Tutt, Thayer 1973
* Wirtz, Bill 1984
* Wright, Lyle 1973

Player/Administrators

Milbury, Mike 2006
Nanne, Lou 1998

Referee

* Chadwick, Bill 1974

Support Personnel

Emrick, Mike "Doc" 2011
Nagobads, Dr. V. George 2010
* Schulz, Charles M. 1993
* Zamboni, Frank 2009

TEAMS

1960 Olympic Team (Men's) 2000
1980 Olympic Team (Men's) 2003
1998 Olympic Team (Women's) 2009

WAYNE GRETZKY INTERNATIONAL AWARD

Wayne Gretzky 1999
The Howe Family 2000
Scotty Morrison 2001
Scotty Bowman 2002
Bobby Hull 2003
* Herb Brooks 2004
* Anatoli Tarasov 2008
Murray Costello 2012

* Deceased

New honoree Mathieu Schneider (right) stands next to his Montreal Canadiens teammate and 2009 inductee John LeClair prior to game one of the 1993 Stanley Cup Final against the Los Angeles Kings.

International Ice Hockey Federation Hall of Fame

The IIHF Hall of Fame was founded in 1997. It now boasts 201 greats from 23 countries.

Candidates for election as Honoured Members in the player category shall be chosen on the basis of their playing ability, sportsmanship, character and their contribution to their team or teams and to the game of ice hockey in general.

Candidates for election as Honoured Members in the builder category shall be chosen on the basis of their coaching, managerial or executive ability, where applicable, their sportsmanship and character, and their contribution to their organization or organizations and to the game of ice hockey in general.

Candidates for election as Honoured Members in the referee or linesman category shall be chosen on the basis of their officiating ability, sportsmanship, character and their contribution to the game of ice hockey in general. The Paul Loicq Award, named for the longtime former IIHF president, is presented to honor a person for his service to the international hockey community.

Inductees' names are followed by their country and year of induction.

PLAYERS

Alexandrov, Veniamin, RUS, 2007
Balderis, Helmut, LAT, 1998
Ball, Rudi, GER, 2004
Bergqvist, Sven, SWE, 1999
Bjorn, Lars, SWE, 1998
Bobrov, Vsevolod, RUS, 1997
Bourbonnais, Roger, CAN, 1999
Bouzek, Vladimir, CZE, 2007
Bozon, Phillippe, FRA 2008
Bubnik, Vlastimil, CZE, 1997
Bure, Pavel, RUS 2012
Bye, Karyn, USA, 2011
Bykov, Vyachslav, RUS, 2014
Cattini, Ferdinand, SUI, 1998
Cattini, Hans, SUI, 1998
Cerny, Josef, CZE, 2007
Christian, Bill, USA, 1998
Cleary, Bill, USA, 1997
Cosby, Gerry, USA, 1997
Craig, Jim, USA, 1999
Curran, Mike, USA, 1999
Davydov, Vitaly, RUS, 2004
Drobny, Jaroslav, CZE, 1997
Dzurilla, Vladimir, SVK, 1998
Erhardt, Carl, G.B., 1998
Fetisov, Viacheslav, RUS, 2005
Firsov, Anatoli, RUS, 1998
Forsberg, Peter, SWE, 2013
Golonka, Josef, SVK, 1998
Goyette, Danielle, CAN, 2013
Granato, Cammi, USA 2008
Gretzky, Wayne, CAN, 2000
Gruth, Henryk, POL, 2006
Gustafsson, Bengt-Ake, SWE, 2003
Gut, Karel, CZE, 1998
Hasek, Dominik, CZE, 2015
Heaney, Geraldine, CAN 2008
Hedberg, Anders, SWE, 1997
Hegen, Dieter, GER 2010
Helminen, Raimo, FIN 2012
Henderson, Paul, CAN, 2013
Hiti, Rudi, SLO, 2009
Hlinka, Ivan, CZE, 2002
Holecek, Jiri, CZE, 1998
Holik, Jiri, CZE, 1999
Holmqvist, Leif, SWE, 1999
Housley, Phil, USA 2012
Huck, Fran, CAN, 1999
Irbe, Arturs, LAT 2010
Jaenecke, Gustav, GER, 1998
James, Angela, CAN 2008
Johnson, Mark, USA, 1999
Johnston, Marshall, CAN, 1998
Jonsson, Tomas, SWE, 2000
Jutila, Timo, FIN, 2003
Kasatonov, Alexei, RUS, 2009
Keinonen, Matti, FIN, 2002
Kharlamov, Valeri, RUS, 1998
Khomutov, Andrei, RUS, 2014
Kiessling, Udo, GER, 2000
Kolliker, Jakob, SUI, 2007
Konovalenko, Viktor, RUS, 2007
Krutov, Vladimir, RUS 2010
Kuhnhackl, Erich, GER, 1997
Kurri, Jari, FIN, 2000
Kuzkin, Viktor, RUS, 2005
Lacarriere, Jacques, FRA, 1998
Larionov, Igor RUS 2008
Lemieux, Mario CAN 2008
Lidstrom, Nicklas, SWE, 2014
Loktev, Konstantin, RUS, 2007
Loob, Hakan, SWE, 1998

Lundquist, Vic, CAN, 1997
Lundstrom, Tord, SWE, 2011
Machac, Oldrich, CZE, 1999
MacKenzie, Barry, CAN, 1999
Makarov, Sergei, RUS, 2001
Malecek, Josef, CZE, 2003
Maltsev, Alexander, RUS, 1999
Marjamaki, Pekka, FIN, 1998
Martin, Seth, CAN, 1997
Martinec, Vladimir, CZE, 2001
Mayasich, John, USA, 1997
Mayorov, Boris, RUS, 1999
McCartan, Jack, USA, 1998
McLeod, Jackie, CAN, 1999
Mikhailov, Boris, RUS, 2000
Modry, Bohumil, CZE, 2011
Nanne, Lou, USA, 2004
Naslund, Mats, SWE, 2005
Nedomansky, Vaclav, CZE, 1997
Niedermayer, Scott, CAN, 2015
Nieminen-Valila, Riika, FIN, 2010
Nilsson, Kent, SWE, 2006
Nilsson, Nisse, SWE, 2002
Novy, Milan, CZE, 2012
Numminen, Teppo, FIN, 2013
O'Malley, Terry, CAN, 1998
Oksanen, Lasse, FIN, 1999
Pana, Eduard, ROU, 1998
Patton, Peter, G.B., 2002
Peltonen, Esa, FIN, 2007
Petrov, Vladimir, RUS, 2006
Pettersson, Ronald, SWE, 2004
Pospisil, Frantisek, CZE, 1999
Puschnig, Josef, AUT, 1999
Ragulin, Alexander, RUS, 1997
Rampf, Hans, GER, 2001
Reichel, Robert, CZE, 2015
Rooth, Maria, SWE, 2015
Rundqvist, Thomas, SWE, 2007
Salei, Ruslan, BLR, 2014
Salming, Borje, SWE, 1998
Schloder, Alois, GER, 2005
Sinden, Harry, CAN, 1997
Sologubov, Nikolai, RUS, 2004
Starshinov, Vyacheslav, RUS, 2007
Stastny, Peter, SVK, 2000
Sterner, Ulf, SWE, 2001
Stoltz, Roland, SWE, 1999
Suchy, Jan, CZE, 2009
Sundin, Mats, SWE, 2013
Tikal, Frantisek, CZE, 2004
Torriani, Bibi, SUI, 1997
Tretiak, Vladislav, RUS, 1997
Trojak, Ladislav, SVK, 2011
Tumba (Johansson), Sven, SWE, 1997
Tureanu, Doru, ROU, 2011
Valtonen, Jorma, FIN, 1999
Vasiliev, Valeri, RUS, 1998
Wahlsten, Vladimir, FIN, 2006
Watson, Harry, CAN, 1998
Yakushev, Alexander, RUS, 2003
Ylonen, Urpo, FIN, 1997
Yzerman, Steve, CAN, 2014
Zabrodsky, Vladimir, CZE, 1997
Ziesche, Joachim, GER, 1999

BUILDERS

Ahearne, Bunny, G.B., 1997
Aljancic Sr., Ernest, SLO, 2002
Bauer, Father David, CAN, 1997
Berglund, Art USA 2008
Berglund, Curt, SWE, 2003
Bokac, Ludek, CZE, 2007
Brooks, Herb, USA, 1999
Brown, Walter, USA, 1997
Buckna, Mike, CAN, 2004
Bush, Walter Jr. USA, 2009
Calcaterra, Enrico, ITA, 1999
Chernyshev, Arkady, RUS, 1999
Costello, Murray, CAN, 2014
Dimitriev, Igor, RUS, 2007
Dobida, Hans, AUT, 2007
Edvinsson, Jan-Ake SWE, 2013
Eklow, Rudolf, SWE, 1999
Fagerlund, Rickard SWE 2010
Grunander, Arne, SWE, 1997
Henschel, Heinz, GER, 2003
Hewitt, William, CAN, 1998
Holmes, Derek, CAN, 1999
Horsky, Ladislav, SVK, 2004
Hviid, Jorgen, DEN, 2005
Johannessen, Tore, NOR, 1999
Juckes, Gordon, CAN, 1997
Kawabuchi, Tsutomu, JPN, 2004
Khorozov, Anatoli, UKR, 2006
King, Dave, CAN, 2001
Kostka, Vladimir, CZE, 1997
LeBel, Bob, CAN, 1997
Lindblad, Harry, FIN, 1999
Loicq, Paul, BEL, 1997
Luhti, Cesar W., SUI, 1998
Magnus, Louis, FRA, 1997
Murray, Andy CAN 2012
Numminen, Kalevi, FIN, 2011
Pasztor, Gyorgy, HUN, 2001
Renwick, Gordon, CAN, 2002
Ridder, Bob, USA, 1998
Rider, Fran, CAN, 2015
Riley, Jack, USA, 1998
Sabetzki, Dr. Gunther, GER, 1997
Starovoitov, Andrei, RUS, 1997
Starsi, Jan, SVK, 1999
Stromberg, Arne, SWE, 1998
Stubb, Goran, FIN, 2000
Subrt, Miroslav, CZE, 2004
Tarasov, Anatoli, RUS, 1997
Tikhonov, Viktor, RUS, 1998
Tomita, Shoichi, JPN, 2006
Trumble, Hal, USA, 1999
Tsutsumi, Yoshiaki, JPN, 1999
Tutt, Thayer, USA, 2002
Unsinn, Xaver, GER, 1998
Wasservogel, Walter, AUT, 1997
Yurzinov, Vladimir, RUS, 2002

REFEREES

Adamec, Quido, CZE, 2005
Dahlberg, Ove, SWE, 2004
Karandin, Yuri, RUS, 2004
Kompalla, Josef, GER, 2003
Schell, Laszlo, HUN, 2009
Wiitala, Unto, FIN, 2003

RICHARD "BIBI" TORRIANI AWARD

Topatigh, Lucio, ITA, 2015

PAUL LOICQ AWARD

Montag, Wolf-Dieter, GER, 1998
Neumayer, Roman, GER, 1999
Kukushkin, Vsevolod, RUS, 2000
Kataoka, Isao, JPN, 2001
Marsh, Pat, G.B., 2002
Nagobads, George, USA, 2003
Kukulowicz, Aggie, CAN, 2004
Hrabcek, Rita, AUS, 2005
Tovland, Bo, SWE, 2006
Nadin, Bob, CAN, 2007
Okolicany, Juraj, SVK 2008
Griebel, Harald, GER, 2009
Vairo, Lou, USA 2010
Korolev, Yuri, RUS, 2011
Angus, Kent, CAN, 2012
Miller, Gord, CAN, 2013
Aubry, Mark, CAN, 2014
Scheier-Schneider, Monique, LUX, 2015

CENTENNIAL ALL-STAR TEAM (1908-2008)

Goaltender: Vladislav Tretiak, RUS
Defenseman: Viacheslav Fetisov, RUS
Defenseman: Borje Salming, SWE
Winger: Valeri Kharlamov, RUS
Winger: Sergei Makarov, RUS
Center: Wayne Gretzky, CAN

TRIPLE GOLD CLUB

(Olympics, World Championship, Stanley Cup)
Tomas Jonsson, SWE
Mats Naslund, SWE
Hakan Loob, SWE
Valeri Kamensky, RUS
Alexei Gusarov, RUS
Peter Forsberg, SWE
Vyacheslav Fetisov, RUS
Igor Larionov, RUS
Alexander Mogilny, RUS
Vladimir Malakhov, RUS
Rob Blake, CAN
Joe Sakic, CAN
Brendan Shanahan, CAN
Scott Niedermayer, CAN
Jaromir Jagr, CZE
Jiri Slegr, CZE
Nicklas Lidstrom, SWE
Fredrik Modin, SWE
Chris Pronger, CAN
Niklas Kronwall, SWE
Henrik Zetterberg, SWE
Mikael Samuelsson, SWE
Eric Staal, CAN
Jonathan Toews, CAN
Mike Babcock (coach), CAN
Patrice Bergeron, CAN
Sidney Crosby, CAN

MILESTONE TROPHY

1954 Soviet Union World Championship team, 2013

Results

2015

Stanley Cup Playoffs

NOTE: *A1, C2, M3 etc. indicate a team's regular-season finish in its division (Atlantic and Metropolitan in the Eastern Conference, Central and Pacific in the Western Conference). W1 and W2 indicate wildcard playoff qualifiers. Regular-season standings are found on page 135.*

FIRST-ROUND (FR)
(Best-of-seven series)

Eastern Conference

Series 'A' – A1 vs. W1

Wed. Apr. 15	Ottawa 3	at	Montreal 4
Fri. Apr. 17	Ottawa 2	at	Montreal 3 *
Sun. Apr. 19	Montreal 2	at	Ottawa 1 **
Wed. Apr. 22	Montreal 0	at	Ottawa 1
Fri. Apr. 24	Ottawa 5	at	Montreal 1
Sun. Apr. 26	Montreal 2	at	Ottawa 0

* Alex Galchenyuk scored at 3:40 of overtime
** Dale Weise scored at 8:47 of overtime
(Montreal won series 4-2)

Series 'B' – A2 vs. A3

Thu. Apr. 16	Detroit 3	at	Tampa Bay 2
Sat. Apr. 18	Detroit 1	at	Tampa Bay 5
Tue. Apr. 21	Tampa Bay 0	at	Detroit 3
Thu. Apr. 23	Tampa Bay 3	at	Detroit 2 *
Sat. Apr. 25	Detroit 4	at	Tampa Bay 0
Mon. Apr. 27	Tampa Bay 5	at	Detroit 2
Wed. Apr. 29	Detroit 0	at	Tampa Bay 2

* Tyler Johnson scored at 2:25 of overtime
(Tampa Bay won series 4-3)

Series 'C' – M1 vs. W2

Thu. Apr. 16	Pittsburgh 1	at	NY Rangers 2
Sat. Apr. 18	Pittsburgh 4	at	NY Rangers 3
Mon. Apr. 20	NY Rangers 2	at	Pittsburgh 1
Wed. Apr. 22	NY Rangers 2	at	Pittsburgh 1 *
Fri. Apr. 24	Pittsburgh 1	at	NY Rangers 2 **

* Kevin Hayes scored at 3:14 of overtime
** Carl Hagelin scored at 10:52 of overtime
(NY Rangers won series 4-1)

Series 'D' – M2 vs. M3

Wed. Apr. 15	NY Islanders 4	at	Washington 1
Fri. Apr. 17	NY Islanders 3	at	Washington 4
Sun. Apr. 19	Washington 1	at	NY Islanders 2
Tue. Apr. 21	Washington 2	at	NY Islanders 1 *
Thu. Apr. 23	NY Islanders 1	at	Washington 5
Sat. Apr. 25	Washington 1	at	NY Islanders 3
Mon. Apr. 27	NY Islanders 1	at	Washington 2

* John Tavares scored at 0:15 of overtime
** Nicklas Backstrom scored at 11:09 of overtime
(Washington won series 4-3)

Western Conference

Series 'E' – C1 vs. W1

Thu. Apr. 16	Minnesota 4	at	St. Louis 2
Sat. Apr. 18	Minnesota 1	at	St. Louis 4
Mon. Apr. 20	St. Louis 0	at	Minnesota 3
Wed. Apr. 22	St. Louis 6	at	Minnesota 1
Fri. Apr. 24	Minnesota 4	at	St. Louis 1
Sun. Apr. 26	St. Louis 1	at	Minnesota 4

(Minnesota won series 4-2)

Series 'F' – C2 vs. C3

Wed. Apr. 15	Chicago 4	at	Nashville 3 *
Fri. Apr. 17	Chicago 2	at	Nashville 6
Sun. Apr. 19	Nashville 2	at	Chicago 4
Tue. Apr. 21	Nashville 2	at	Chicago 3 **
Thu. Apr. 23	Chicago 2	at	Nashville 5
Sat. Apr. 25	Nashville 3	at	Chicago 4

* Duncan Keith scored at 27:49 of overtime
** Brent Seabrook scored at 41:00 of overtime
(Chicago won series 4-2)

Series 'G' – P1 vs. W2

Thu. Apr. 16	Winnipeg 2	at	Anaheim 4
Sat. Apr. 18	Winnipeg 1	at	Anaheim 2
Mon. Apr. 20	Anaheim 5	at	Winnipeg 4 *
Wed. Apr. 22	Anaheim 5	at	Winnipeg 2

* Rickard Rakell scored at 5:12 of overtime
(Anaheim won series 4-0)

Series 'H' – P2 vs. P3

Wed. Apr. 15	Calgary 2	at	Vancouver 1
Fri. Apr. 17	Calgary 1	at	Vancouver 4
Sun. Apr. 19	Vancouver 2	at	Calgary 4
Tue. Apr. 21	Vancouver 1	at	Calgary 3
Thu. Apr. 23	Calgary 1	at	Vancouver 2
Sat. Apr. 25	Vancouver 4	at	Calgary 7

(Calgary won series 4-2)

SECOND-ROUND (SR)
(Best-of-seven series)

Eastern Conference

Series 'I' – A1 vs. A2

Fri. May 1	Tampa Bay 2	at	Montreal 1 *
Sun. May 3	Tampa Bay 6	at	Montreal 2
Wed. May 6	Montreal 1	at	Tampa Bay 2
Thu. May 7	Montreal 6	at	Tampa Bay 2
Sat. May 9	Tampa Bay 1	at	Montreal 2
Tue. May 12	Montreal 1	at	Tampa Bay 4

* Nikita Kucherov scored at 22:06 of overtime
(Tampa Bay won series 4-2)

Series 'J' – M1 vs. M2

Thu. Apr. 30	Washington 2	at	NY Rangers 1
Sat. May 2	Washington 2	at	NY Rangers 3
Mon. May 4	NY Rangers 0	at	Washington 1
Wed. May 6	NY Rangers 1	at	Washington 2
Fri. May 8	Washington 1	at	NY Rangers 2 *
Sun. May 10	NY Rangers 4	at	Washington 3
Wed. May 13	Washington 1	at	NY Rangers 2 **

* Ryan McDonagh scored at 9:37 of overtime
** Derek Stepan scored at 11:24 of overtime
(NY Rangers won series 4-3)

Western Conference

Series 'K' – C3 vs. W1

Fri. May 1	Minnesota 3	at	Chicago 4
Sun. May 3	Minnesota 1	at	Chicago 4
Tue. May 5	Chicago 1	at	Minnesota 0
Thu. May 7	Chicago 4	at	Minnesota 3

(Chicago won series 4-0)

Series 'L' – P1 vs. P3

Thu. Apr 30	Calgary 1	at	Anaheim 6
Sun. May 3	Calgary 0	at	Anaheim 3
Tue. May 5	Anaheim 3	at	Calgary 4 *
Fri. May 8	Anaheim 4	at	Calgary 2
Sun. May 10	Calgary 2	at	Anaheim 3 **

* Mikael Backlund scored at 4:24 of overtime
** Corey Perry scored at 2:26 of overtime
(Anaheim won series 4-1)

CONFERENCE FINALS (CF)
(Best-of-seven series)

Eastern Conference

Series 'M' – A2 vs. M1

Sat. May 16	Tampa Bay 1	at	NY Rangers 2
Mon. May 18	Tampa Bay 6	at	NY Rangers 2
Wed. May 20	NY Rangers 5	at	Tampa Bay 6 *
Fri. May 22	NY Rangers 5	at	Tampa Bay 1
Sun. May 24	Tampa Bay 2	at	NY Rangers 0
Tue. May 26	NY Rangers 7	at	Tampa Bay 3
Fri. May 29	Tampa Bay 2	at	NY Rangers 0

* Nikita Kucherov scored at 3:33 of overtime
(Tampa Bay won series 4-3)

Western Conference

Series 'N' – C3 vs. P1

Sun. May 17	Chicago 1	at	Anaheim 4
Tue. May 19	Chicago 3	at	Anaheim 2 *
Thu. May 21	Anaheim 2	at	Chicago 1
Sat. May 23	Anaheim 4	at	Chicago 5 **
Mon. May 25	Chicago 4	at	Anaheim 5 ***
Wed. May 27	Anaheim 2	at	Chicago 5
Sat. May 30	Chicago 5	at	Anaheim 3

* Marcus Kruger scored at 56:12 of overtime
** Antoine Vermette scored at 25:37 of overtime
*** Matt Beleskey scored at 0:45 of overtime
(Chicago won series 4-3)

STANLEY CUP FINAL (F)
(Best-of-seven series)

Series 'O' – A2 vs. C3

Wed. June 3	Chicago 2	at	Tampa Bay 1
Sat. June 6	Chicago 3	at	Tampa Bay 4
Mon. June 8	Tampa Bay 3	at	Chicago 2
Wed. June 10	Tampa Bay 1	at	Chicago 2
Sat. June 13	Chicago 2	at	Tampa Bay 1
Mon. June 15	Tampa Bay 0	at	Chicago 2

(Chicago won series 4-2)

Team Playoff Records

	GP	W	L	GF	GA	%
Chicago	23	16	7	69	60	.696
Tampa Bay	26	14	12	65	62	.538
Anaheim	16	11	5	57	42	.688
NY Rangers	19	11	8	45	41	.579
Washington	14	7	7	28	28	.500
Montreal	12	6	6	25	29	.500
Calgary	11	5	6	27	33	.455
Minnesota	10	4	6	24	27	.400
NY Islanders	7	3	4	15	16	.429
Detroit	7	3	4	15	17	.429
Nashville	6	2	4	21	19	.333
Ottawa	6	2	4	12	12	.333
St. Louis	6	2	4	14	17	.333
Vancouver	6	2	4	14	18	.333
Pittsburgh	5	1	4	8	11	.200
Winnipeg	4	0	4	9	16	.000

Individual Leaders

Abbreviations: GP – games played; **G** – goals; **A** – assists; **PTS** – points; **+/–** – difference between Goals For (**GF**) scored when a player is on the ice with his team at even strength or shorthanded and Goals Against (**GA**) scored when the same player is on the ice with his team at even strength or on a power play; **PIM** – penalties in minutes; **PP** – power play goals; **SH** – shorthanded goals; **GW** – game-winning goals; **OT** – overtime goals; **S** – shots on goal; **S%** – percentage of shots resulting in goals; **Mins** – minutes played; **GA** – goals against; **Avg.** – goals against average; **W** – wins; **L** – losses; **SA** – shots against; **Sv%** – save percentage; **SO** – shutouts.

Playoff Scoring Leaders

Player	Team	GP	G	A	PTS	+/–	PIM	PP	SH	GW	OT	S	S%
Tyler Johnson	Tampa Bay	26	13	10	23	7	24	2	1	4	1	60	21.7
Patrick Kane	Chicago	23	11	12	23	7	0	2	0	3	0	64	17.2
Nikita Kucherov	Tampa Bay	26	10	12	22	7	14	3	0	3	2	57	17.5
Jonathan Toews	Chicago	23	10	11	21	7	8	3	1	0	0	61	16.4
Duncan Keith	Chicago	23	3	18	21	16	4	0	0	3	1	59	5.1
Ryan Getzlaf	Anaheim	16	2	18	20	6	6	2	0	0	0	48	4.2
Corey Perry	Anaheim	16	10	8	18	6	14	2	0	2	1	64	15.6
Alex Killorn	Tampa Bay	26	9	9	18	3	12	1	0	2	0	66	13.6
Steven Stamkos	Tampa Bay	26	7	11	18	2	20	2	0	1	0	65	10.8
Jakob Silfverberg	Anaheim	16	4	14	18	6	16	1	0	1	0	41	9.8
Marian Hossa	Chicago	23	4	13	17	7	10	1	1	2	0	69	5.8
Derick Brassard	NY Rangers	19	9	7	16	9	20	2	0	1	0	55	16.4
Ondrej Palat	Tampa Bay	26	8	8	16	5	12	4	0	0	0	43	18.6
Patrick Sharp	Chicago	23	5	10	15	2	8	1	0	0	0	64	7.8
Rick Nash	NY Rangers	19	5	9	14	8	4	2	0	0	0	69	7.2
Valtteri Filppula	Tampa Bay	26	4	10	14	–6	4	2	0	1	0	31	12.9
Brad Richards	Chicago	23	3	11	14	4	8	1	0	0	0	50	6.0
Victor Hedman	Tampa Bay	26	1	13	14	11	6	1	0	0	0	64	1.6
Ryan Kesler	Anaheim	16	7	6	13	2	24	1	0	1	0	33	21.2
Derek Stepan	NY Rangers	19	5	7	12	–1	10	2	0	1	1	48	10.4
Andrew Shaw	Chicago	23	5	7	12	–4	36	2	0	0	0	45	11.1

Playoff Defensemen Scoring Leaders

Player	Team	GP	G	A	PTS	+/–	PIM	PP	SH	GW	OT	S	S%
Duncan Keith	Chicago	23	3	18	21	16	4	0	0	3	1	59	5.1
Victor Hedman	Tampa Bay	26	1	13	14	11	6	1	0	0	0	64	1.6
Brent Seabrook	Chicago	23	7	4	11	5	10	1	0	1	1	44	15.9
Sami Vatanen	Anaheim	16	3	8	11	5	8	0	0	0	0	35	8.6
Keith Yandle	NY Rangers	19	2	9	11	7	10	0	0	0	0	32	6.3
Dan Boyle	NY Rangers	19	3	7	10	–3	2	1	0	1	0	32	9.4
Cam Fowler	Anaheim	16	2	8	10	5	2	0	0	0	0	28	7.1
Hampus Lindholm	Anaheim	16	2	8	10	2	10	0	0	0	0	21	9.5
Ryan Mcdonagh	NY Rangers	19	3	6	9	2	8	2	0	2	1	33	9.1
Anton Stralman	Tampa Bay	26	1	8	9	1	8	0	0	0	0	52	1.9
Francois Beauchemin	Anaheim	16	0	9	9	4	2	0	0	0	0	25	0.0
P.K. Subban	Montreal	12	1	7	8	1	31	0	0	0	0	36	2.8
Kevin Shattenkirk	St. Louis	6	0	8	8	2	2	0	0	0	0	13	0.0
Kris Russell	Calgary	11	2	5	7	–9	7	1	0	1	0	13	15.4
Jason Garrison	Tampa Bay	23	2	5	7	–2	8	1	0	1	0	31	6.5
Simon Despres	Anaheim	16	1	6	7	4	6	0	0	1	0	17	5.9
Dennis Wideman	Calgary	11	0	7	7	–2	12	0	0	0	0	18	0.0

GOALTENDING LEADERS

(Minimum 7 games played)

Goals Against Average

Goaltender	Team	GP	Mins	GA	Avg.
Braden Holtby	Washington	13	806	23	1.71
Henrik Lundqvist	NY Rangers	19	1166	41	2.11
Petr Mrazek	Detroit	7	398	14	2.11
Ben Bishop	Tampa Bay	25	1459	53	2.18
Carey Price	Montreal	12	752	28	2.23

Wins

Goaltender	Team	GP	Mins	W	L
Corey Crawford	Chicago	20	1223	13	6
Ben Bishop	Tampa Bay	25	1459	13	11
Frederik Andersen	Anaheim	16	1050	11	5
Henrik Lundqvist	NY Rangers	19	1166	11	8
Carey Price	Montreal	12	752	6	6
Braden Holtby	Washington	13	806	6	7

Save Percentage

Goaltender	Team	GP	Mins	GA	SA	Sv%	W	L
Braden Holtby	Washington	13	806	23	412	.944	6	7
Henrik Lundqvist	NY Rangers	19	1166	41	570	.928	11	8
Jaroslav Halak	NY Islanders	7	418	16	215	.926	3	4
Petr Mrazek	Detroit	7	398	14	186	.925	3	4
Corey Crawford	Chicago	20	1223	47	616	.924	13	6

Shutouts

Goaltender	Team	GP	Mins	SO	W	L
Ben Bishop	Tampa Bay	25	1459	3	13	11
Petr Mrazek	Detroit	7	398	2	3	4
Corey Crawford	Chicago	20	1223	2	13	6
Craig Anderson	Ottawa	4	247	1	2	2
Devan Dubnyk	Minnesota	10	570	1	4	6
Carey Price	Montreal	12	752	1	6	6
Braden Holtby	Washington	13	806	1	6	7
Frederik Andersen	Anaheim	16	1050	1	11	5

Goals

Player	Team	GP	G
Tyler Johnson	Tampa Bay	26	13
Patrick Kane	Chicago	23	11
Corey Perry	Anaheim	16	10
Jonathan Toews	Chicago	23	10
Nikita Kucherov	Tampa Bay	26	10
Derick Brassard	NY Rangers	19	9
Alex Killorn	Tampa Bay	26	9
Matt Beleskey	Anaheim	16	8
Brandon Saad	Chicago	23	8
Ondrej Palat	Tampa Bay	26	8
5 Players tied with			7

Assists

Player	Team	GP	A
Ryan Getzlaf	Anaheim	16	18
Duncan Keith	Chicago	23	18
Jakob Silfverberg	Anaheim	16	14
Marian Hossa	Chicago	23	13
Victor Hedman	Tampa Bay	26	13
Patrick Kane	Chicago	23	12
Nikita Kucherov	Tampa Bay	26	12
Brad Richards	Chicago	23	11
Jonathan Toews	Chicago	23	11
Steven Stamkos	Tampa Bay	26	11

Power-play Goals

Player	Team	GP	PP
Colin Wilson	Nashville	6	4
Ondrej Palat	Tampa Bay	26	4
Jiri Hudler	Calgary	11	3
Matt Beleskey	Anaheim	16	3
Patrick Maroon	Anaheim	16	3
Jonathan Toews	Chicago	23	3
Nikita Kucherov	Tampa Bay	26	3

Shorthanded Goals

Player	Team	GP	SH
Alexander Steen	St. Louis	6	1
Luke Glendening	Detroit	7	1
Zach Parise	Minnesota	10	1
Max Pacioretty	Montreal	11	1
Joe Colborne	Calgary	11	1
Lars Eller	Montreal	12	1
Marian Hossa	Chicago	23	1
Jonathan Toews	Chicago	23	1
Brandon Saad	Chicago	23	1
*Cedric Paquette	Tampa Bay	24	1
Brian Boyle	Tampa Bay	25	1
Tyler Johnson	Tampa Bay	26	1

Overtime Goals

Player	Team	GP	OT
Nikita Kucherov	Tampa Bay	26	2
17 players tied with			1

Game-winning Goals

Player	Team	GP	GW
Tyler Johnson	Tampa Bay	26	4
Matt Beleskey	Anaheim	16	3
Antoine Vermette	Chicago	20	3
Duncan Keith	Chicago	23	3
Patrick Kane	Chicago	23	3
Nikita Kucherov	Tampa Bay	26	3

Shots

Player	Team	GP	S
Rick Nash	NY Rangers	19	69
Marian Hossa	Chicago	23	69
Alex Killorn	Tampa Bay	26	66
Steven Stamkos	Tampa Bay	26	65
Corey Perry	Anaheim	16	64
Patrick Sharp	Chicago	23	64
Patrick Kane	Chicago	23	64
Victor Hedman	Tampa Bay	26	64

Plus/Minus

Player	Team	GP	+/–
Duncan Keith	Chicago	23	16
Victor Hedman	Tampa Bay	26	11
Andrew Cogliano	Anaheim	16	9
Derick Brassard	NY Rangers	19	9
Rick Nash	NY Rangers	19	8

* — rookie

TEAMS' PLAYOFF HOME/ROAD RECORD

Team	HOME GP	W	L	GF	GA	Win %	ROAD GP	W	L	GF	GA	Win %
Chicago	11	9	2	36	23	.818	12	7	5	33	37	.583
Tampa Bay	13	6	7	33	40	.462	13	8	5	32	22	.615
Anaheim	9	7	2	32	19	.778	7	4	3	25	23	.571
NY Rangers	11	6	5	19	23	.545	8	5	3	26	18	.625
Washington	7	5	2	18	14	.714	7	2	5	10	14	.286
Montreal	6	3	3	13	19	.500	6	3	3	12	10	.500
Calgary	5	4	1	20	14	.800	6	1	5	7	19	.167
Minnesota	5	2	3	11	12	.400	5	2	3	13	15	.400
NY Islanders	3	2	1	6	4	.667	4	1	3	9	12	.250
Detroit	3	1	2	7	8	.333	4	2	2	8	9	.500
Nashville	3	2	1	14	8	.667	3	0	3	7	11	.000
Ottawa	3	1	2	2	4	.333	3	1	2	10	8	.333
St. Louis	3	1	2	7	9	.333	3	1	2	7	8	.333
Vancouver	3	2	1	7	4	.667	3	0	3	7	14	.000
Pittsburgh	2	0	2	2	4	.000	3	1	2	6	7	.333
Winnipeg	2	0	2	6	10	.000	2	0	2	3	6	.000
Totals	**89**	**51**	**38**	**233**	**215**	**.573**	**89**	**38**	**51**	**215**	**233**	**.427**

TEAMS' POWER-PLAY RECORD

Abbreviations: ADV-total advantages; **PPGF**-power play goals for; **%** arrived by dividing number of power-play goals by total advantages.

	HOME Team	GP	ADV	PPGF	%	ROAD Team	GP	ADV	PPGF	%	OVERALL Team	GP	ADV	PPGF	%
1	WPG	2	6	2	33.3	OTT	3	12	5	41.7	MIN	10	23	7	30.4
2	ST.L.	3	7	2	28.6	MIN	5	12	5	41.7	NSH	6	22	6	27.3
3	NSH	3	14	4	28.6	VAN	3	7	2	28.6	ANA	16	45	12	26.7
4	ANA	9	29	8	27.6	NYR	8	22	6	27.3	OTT	6	20	5	25.0
5	CGY	5	20	5	25.0	PIT	3	8	2	25.0	NYR	19	62	13	21.0
6	T.B.	13	41	8	19.5	NSH	3	8	2	25.0	T.B.	26	85	17	20.0
7	MIN	5	11	2	18.2	ANA	7	16	4	25.0	CGY	11	36	7	19.4
8	NYR	11	40	7	17.5	CHI	12	36	9	25.0	VAN	6	16	3	18.8
9	DET	3	15	2	13.3	DET	4	14	3	21.4	ST.L.	6	11	2	18.2
10	VAN	3	9	1	11.1	T.B.	13	44	9	20.5	CHI	23	67	12	17.9
11	CHI	11	31	3	9.7	WSH	7	15	2	13.3	DET	7	29	5	17.2
12	WSH	7	13	1	7.7	CGY	6	16	2	12.5	WPG	4	13	2	15.4
13	MTL	6	19	1	5.3	MTL	6	17	1	5.9	PIT	5	13	2	15.4
14	PIT	2	5	0	.0	WPG	2	7	0	.0	WSH	14	28	3	10.7
15	OTT	3	8	0	.0	ST.L.	3	4	0	.0	MTL	12	36	2	5.6
16	NYI	3	8	0	.0	NYI	4	6	0	.0	NYI	7	14	0	.0
	Totals	**89**	**276**	**46**	**16.7**		**89**	**244**	**52**	**21.3**		**89**	**520**	**98**	**18.8**

TEAMS' PENALTY KILLING RECORD

Abbreviations: TSH – Total times shorthanded; **PPGA** – power-play goals against; **%** arrived by dividing times shorthanded minus power-play goals against by times shorthanded.

	HOME Team	GP	TSH	PPGA	%	ROAD Team	GP	TSH	PPGA	%	OVERALL Team	GP	TSH	PPGA	%
1	PIT	2	5	0	100.0	NYR	8	21	2	90.5	OTT	6	20	1	95.0
2	WPG	2	4	0	100.0	OTT	3	10	1	90.0	DET	7	30	2	93.3
3	OTT	3	10	0	100.0	WSH	7	20	2	90.0	WSH	14	32	3	90.6
4	DET	3	12	0	100.0	DET	4	18	2	88.9	PIT	5	20	3	85.0
5	WSH	7	12	1	91.7	T.B.	13	45	5	88.9	NYI	7	13	2	84.6
6	NYI	3	7	1	85.7	NSH	3	8	1	87.5	NSH	6	19	3	84.2
7	ANA	9	31	5	83.9	ANA	7	26	4	84.6	ANA	16	57	9	84.2
8	VAN	3	6	1	83.3	NYI	4	6	1	83.3	T.B.	26	85	15	82.4
9	NSH	3	11	2	81.8	MTL	6	16	3	81.3	NYR	19	50	10	80.0
10	CHI	11	26	6	76.9	CHI	12	36	7	80.6	CHI	23	62	13	79.0
11	T.B.	13	40	10	75.0	PIT	3	15	3	80.0	MIN	10	17	4	76.5
12	NYR	11	29	8	72.4	ST.L.	3	5	1	80.0	CGY	11	34	9	73.5
13	MIN	5	7	2	71.4	MIN	5	10	2	80.0	WPG	4	11	3	72.7
14	CGY	5	13	4	69.2	CGY	6	21	5	76.2	VAN	6	18	5	72.2
15	MTL	6	24	9	62.5	VAN	3	12	4	66.7	MTL	12	40	12	70.0
16	ST.L.	3	7	3	57.1	WPG	2	7	3	57.1	ST.L.	6	12	4	66.7
	Totals	**89**	**244**	**52**	**78.7**		**89**	**276**	**46**	**83.3**		**89**	**520**	**98**	**81.2**

SHORTHAND GOALS

GOALS FOR Team	GP	GF	GOALS AGAINST Team	GP	GA
CHI	23	3	CHI	23	0
T.B	26	3	WSH	14	0
MTL	12	2	MTL	12	0
STL	6	1	CGY	11	0
DET	7	1	NYI	7	0
MIN	10	1	NSH	6	0
CGY	11	1	VAN	6	0
WPG	4	0	PIT	5	0
PIT	5	0	WPG	4	0
OTT	6	0	NYR	19	1
NSH	6	0	OTT	6	1
VAN	6	0	STL	6	1
NYI	7	0	T.B	26	2
WSH	14	0	ANA	16	2
ANA	16	0	DET	7	2
NYR	19	0	MIN	10	3
Totals	**89**	**12**		**89**	**12**

TEAM PENALTIES

Abbreviations: GP – games played; **PEN** – total penalty minutes, including bench penalties; **BMI** – total bench minor minutes; **AVG** – average penalty minutes/game arrived by dividing total penalty minutes less bench minor minutes by games played.

Team	GP	PEN	BMI	AVG
Minnesota	10	38	0	3.8
Chicago	23	162	10	7.0
Winnipeg	4	28	0	7.0
Washington	14	106	0	7.6
NY Rangers	19	151	0	7.9
St. Louis	6	48	0	8.0
Anaheim	16	142	6	8.9
Pittsburgh	5	46	0	9.2
Tampa Bay	26	255	12	9.8
Nashville	6	62	0	10.3
Detroit	7	82	2	11.7
NY Islanders	7	83	0	11.9
Ottawa	6	82	4	13.7
Montreal	12	174	0	14.5
Calgary	11	211	2	19.2
Vancouver	6	132	0	22.0
Totals	**89**	**1802**	**36**	**20.2**

Duncan Keith celebrates his goal to open the scoring in game six of the Stanley Cup Final. Keith had three goals and 18 assists in the playoffs and led all players with 715:37 of total ice time for an average of 31:06 per game in 23 games played.

Stanley Cup Record Book

History: The Stanley Cup, the oldest trophy competed for by professional athletes in North America, was donated by Frederick Arthur, Lord Stanley of Preston and son of the Earl of Derby, in 1893. Lord Stanley purchased the trophy for 10 guineas ($50 at that time) for presentation to the amateur hockey champions of Canada. Since 1906, when Canadian teams began to pay their players openly, the Stanley Cup has been the symbol of professional hockey supremacy. It has been contested only by NHL teams since 1926-27 and has been under the exclusive control of the NHL since 1947.

Stanley Cup Standings

1918-2015

(ranked by Cup wins)

Teams	Cup Wins	Yrs.	Series	Wins	Losses	Games	Wins	Losses	Ties	Goals For	Goals Against	Winning %
Montreal[1,2]	24	82	151	92	58	743	427	308	8	2237	1894	.580
Toronto[3]	14	65	110	58	52	531	254	273	4	1368	1449	.482
Detroit	11	63	120	68	52	617	324	292	1	1740	1563	.526
Boston	6	69	120	57	63	609	299	304	6	1764	1736	.496
Chicago	6	60	110	56	54	528	261	262	5	1516	1607	.499
Edmonton	5	20	49	34	15	251	152	99	0	938	763	.606
NY Rangers	4	57	105	52	53	498	237	253	8	1353	1383	.484
NY Islanders	4	23	49	30	19	253	139	114	0	824	755	.549
Pittsburgh	3	30	58	31	27	316	168	148	0	981	950	.532
New Jersey[4]	3	22	44	25	19	254	136	118	0	688	622	.535
Philadelphia	2	37	78	43	35	421	217	204	0	1276	1250	.515
Los Angeles	2	28	47	21	26	246	110	136	0	731	828	.447
Colorado[5]	2	22	45	25	20	256	135	121	0	746	725	.527
Dallas[6]	1	30	57	28	29	313	156	157	0	915	930	.498
Calgary[7]	1	27	42	16	26	219	99	120	0	675	734	.452
Carolina[8]	1	13	22	10	12	127	59	68	0	323	358	.465
Anaheim	1	11	24	14	10	134	76	58	0	361	339	.567
Tampa Bay	1	8	17	10	7	99	51	48	0	256	263	.515
St. Louis	0	39	63	24	39	334	148	186	0	920	1026	.443
Buffalo	0	29	50	21	29	256	124	132	0	763	765	.484
Vancouver	0	27	43	16	27	229	101	128	0	634	735	.441
Washington	0	25	39	14	25	226	103	123	0	642	657	.456
Arizona[9]	0	19	23	4	19	119	41	78	0	310	422	.345
San Jose	0	16	31	14	17	181	87	94	0	454	531	.481
Ottawa[10]	0	15	24	9	15	132	61	71	0	310	322	.462
Nashville	0	8	10	2	8	56	21	35	0	136	153	.375
Florida	0	4	7	3	4	38	16	22	0	94	100	.421
Minnesota	0	6	10	4	6	57	22	35	0	130	151	.386
Columbus	0	2	2	0	2	10	2	8	0	25	39	.200
Winnipeg[11]	0	2	2	0	2	8	0	8	0	15	33	.000

1. Includes Stanley Cup championship won in 1916 prior to the formation of the NHL.
2. 1919 final incomplete due to influenza epidemic.
3. Includes Stanley Cup championship won by Toronto Blueshirts in 1914 prior to the formation of the NHL.
4. Includes totals of Colorado Rockies 1976-82.
5. Includes totals of Quebec Nordiques 1979-95.
6. Includes totals of Minnesota North Stars 1967-93.
7. Includes totals of Atlanta Flames 1972-80.
8. Includes totals of Hartford Whalers 1979-97.
9. Includes totals of Phoenix Coyotes, 1997-2014 and Winnipeg Jets, 1979-96
10. Modern Ottawa Senators franchise only, 1992 to date.
11. Includes totals of Atlanta Thrashers 1999-2011.

Stanley Cup Winners Prior to Formation of NHL in 1917

Season	Champions	Manager	Coach
1916-17	Seattle Metropolitans	Pete Muldoon	Pete Muldoon
1915-16	Montreal Canadiens	George Kennedy	George Kennedy
1914-15	Vancouver Millionaires	Frank Patrick	Frank Patrick
1913-14	Toronto Blueshirts	Jack Marshall	Scotty Davidson*
1912-13**	Quebec Bulldogs	M.J. Quinn	Joe Malone*
1911-12	Quebec Bulldogs	M.J. Quinn	Charley Nolan
1910-11	Ottawa Senators		Percy LeSueur
1909-10	Montreal Wanderers (Mar. 1910)	Dickie Boon	Pud Glass*
1909-10	Ottawa Senators (Jan. 1910)		Bruce Stuart*
1908-09	Ottawa Senators		Bruce Stuart*
1907-08	Montreal Wanderers	Dickie Boon	Cecil Blachford*
1906-07	Montreal Wanderers (Mar. 25, 1907)	Dickie Boon	Lester Patrick*
1906-07	Kenora Thistles (Jan./Mar. 18, 1907)	F.A. Hudson	Tom Phillips*
1905-06	Montreal Wanderers (Mar. 1906)	Cecil Blachford*	
1905-06	Ottawa Silver Seven (Feb. 1906)		Alf Smith
1904-05	Ottawa Silver Seven		Alf Smith
1903-04	Ottawa Silver Seven		Alf Smith
1902-03	Ottawa Silver Seven (Mar. 1903)		Alf Smith
1902-03	Montreal A.A.A. (Feb. 1903)		Clare McKerrow
1901-02	Montreal A.A.A. (Mar. 1902)		Clare McKerrow
1901-02	Winnipeg Victorias (Jan. 1902)		
1900-01	Winnipeg Victorias		Dan Bain*
1899-1900	Montreal Shamrocks		Harry Trihey*
1898-99	Montreal Shamrocks (Mar. 1899)		Harry Trihey*
1898-99	Montreal Victorias (Feb. 1899)		Graham Drinkwater*
1897-98	Montreal Victorias		Frank Richardson*
1896-97	Montreal Victorias		Mike Grant*
1895-96	Montreal Victorias (Dec. 1896)		Mike Grant*
1895-96	Winnipeg Victorias (Feb. 1896)		Jack Armytage*
1894-95	Montreal Victorias		Mike Grant*
1893-94	Montreal A.A.A.		
1892-93	Montreal A.A.A.		

* In the early years the teams were frequently run by the Captain. *Indicates Captain
** Victoria defeated Quebec in challenge series. No official recognition.

Stanley Cup Winners

Year	W-L-T in Finals	Winner	Coach	Finalist	Coach
2015	4-2	Chicago	Joel Quenneville	Tampa Bay	Jon Cooper
2014	4-1	Los Angeles	Darryl Sutter	NY Rangers	Alain Vigneault
2013	4-2	Chicago	Joel Quenneville	Boston	Claude Julien
2012	4-2	Los Angeles	Darryl Sutter	New Jersey	Peter DeBoer
2011	4-3	Boston	Claude Julien	Vancouver	Alain Vigneault
2010	4-2	Chicago	Joel Quenneville	Philadelphia	Peter Laviolette
2009	4-3	Pittsburgh	Dan Bylsma	Detroit	Mike Babcock
2008	4-2	Detroit	Mike Babcock	Pittsburgh	Michel Therrien
2007	4-1	Anaheim	Randy Carlyle	Ottawa	Bryan Murray
2006	4-3	Carolina	Peter Laviolette	Edmonton	Craig MacTavish
2005	....	....	....	....	....
2004	4-3	Tampa Bay	John Tortorella	Calgary	Darryl Sutter
2003	4-3	New Jersey	Pat Burns	Anaheim	Mike Babcock
2002	4-1	Detroit	Scotty Bowman	Carolina	Paul Maurice
2001	4-3	Colorado	Bob Hartley	New Jersey	Larry Robinson
2000	4-2	New Jersey	Larry Robinson	Dallas	Ken Hitchcock
1999	4-2	Dallas	Ken Hitchcock	Buffalo	Lindy Ruff
1998	4-0	Detroit	Scotty Bowman	Washington	Ron Wilson
1997	4-0	Detroit	Scotty Bowman	Philadelphia	Terry Murray
1996	4-0	Colorado	Marc Crawford	Florida	Doug MacLean
1995	4-0	New Jersey	Jacques Lemaire	Detroit	Scotty Bowman
1994	4-3	NY Rangers	Mike Keenan	Vancouver	Pat Quinn
1993	4-1	Montreal	Jacques Demers	Los Angeles	Barry Melrose
1992	4-0	Pittsburgh	Scotty Bowman	Chicago	Mike Keenan
1991	4-2	Pittsburgh	Bob Johnson	Minnesota	Bob Gainey
1990	4-1	Edmonton	John Muckler	Boston	Mike Milbury
1989	4-2	Calgary	Terry Crisp	Montreal	Pat Burns
1988	4-0	Edmonton	Glen Sather	Boston	Terry O'Reilly
1987	4-3	Edmonton	Glen Sather	Philadelphia	Mike Keenan
1986	4-1	Montreal	Jean Perron	Calgary	Bob Johnson
1985	4-1	Edmonton	Glen Sather	Philadelphia	Mike Keenan
1984	4-1	Edmonton	Glen Sather	NY Islanders	Al Arbour
1983	4-0	NY Islanders	Al Arbour	Edmonton	Glen Sather
1982	4-0	NY Islanders	Al Arbour	Vancouver	Roger Neilson
1981	4-1	NY Islanders	Al Arbour	Minnesota	Glen Sonmor
1980	4-2	NY Islanders	Al Arbour	Philadelphia	Pat Quinn
1979	4-1	Montreal	Scotty Bowman	NY Rangers	Fred Shero
1978	4-2	Montreal	Scotty Bowman	Boston	Don Cherry
1977	4-0	Montreal	Scotty Bowman	Boston	Don Cherry
1976	4-0	Montreal	Scotty Bowman	Philadelphia	Fred Shero
1975	4-2	Philadelphia	Fred Shero	Buffalo	Floyd Smith
1974	4-2	Philadelphia	Fred Shero	Boston	Bep Guidolin
1973	4-2	Montreal	Scotty Bowman	Chicago	Billy Reay
1972	4-2	Boston	Tom Johnson	NY Rangers	Emile Francis
1971	4-3	Montreal	Al MacNeil	Chicago	Billy Reay
1970	4-0	Boston	Harry Sinden	St. Louis	Scotty Bowman
1969	4-0	Montreal	Claude Ruel	St. Louis	Scotty Bowman
1968	4-0	Montreal	Toe Blake	St. Louis	Scotty Bowman
1967	4-2	Toronto	Punch Imlach	Montreal	Toe Blake
1966	4-2	Montreal	Toe Blake	Detroit	Sid Abel
1965	4-3	Montreal	Toe Blake	Chicago	Billy Reay
1964	4-3	Toronto	Punch Imlach	Detroit	Sid Abel
1963	4-1	Toronto	Punch Imlach	Detroit	Sid Abel
1962	4-2	Toronto	Punch Imlach	Chicago	Rudy Pilous
1961	4-2	Chicago	Rudy Pilous	Detroit	Sid Abel
1960	4-0	Montreal	Toe Blake	Toronto	Punch Imlach
1959	4-1	Montreal	Toe Blake	Toronto	Punch Imlach
1958	4-2	Montreal	Toe Blake	Boston	Milt Schmidt
1957	4-1	Montreal	Toe Blake	Boston	Milt Schmidt
1956	4-1	Montreal	Toe Blake	Detroit	Jimmy Skinner
1955	4-3	Detroit	Jimmy Skinner	Montreal	Dick Irvin
1954	4-3	Detroit	Tommy Ivan	Montreal	Dick Irvin
1953	4-1	Montreal	Dick Irvin	Boston	Lynn Patrick
1952	4-0	Detroit	Tommy Ivan	Montreal	Dick Irvin
1951	4-1	Toronto	Joe Primeau	Montreal	Dick Irvin
1950	4-3	Detroit	Tommy Ivan	NY Rangers	Lynn Patrick
1949	4-0	Toronto	Hap Day	Detroit	Tommy Ivan
1948	4-0	Toronto	Hap Day	Detroit	Tommy Ivan
1947	4-2	Toronto	Hap Day	Montreal	Dick Irvin
1946	4-1	Montreal	Dick Irvin	Boston	Dit Clapper
1945	4-3	Toronto	Hap Day	Detroit	Jack Adams
1944	4-0	Montreal	Dick Irvin	Chicago	Paul Thompson
1943	4-0	Detroit	Jack Adams	Boston	Art Ross
1942	4-3	Toronto	Hap Day	Detroit	Jack Adams
1941	4-0	Boston	Cooney Weiland	Detroit	Ebbie Goodfellow
1940	4-2	NY Rangers	Frank Boucher	Toronto	Dick Irvin
1939	4-1	Boston	Art Ross	Toronto	Dick Irvin
1938	3-1	Chicago	Bill Stewart	Toronto	Dick Irvin
1937	3-2	Detroit	Jack Adams	NY Rangers	Lester Patrick
1936	3-1	Detroit	Jack Adams	Toronto	Dick Irvin
1935	3-0	Mtl. Maroons	Tommy Gorman	Toronto	Dick Irvin
1934	3-1	Chicago	Tommy Gorman	Detroit	Herbie Lewis
1933	3-1	NY Rangers	Lester Patrick	Toronto	Dick Irvin
1932	3-0	Toronto	Dick Irvin	NY Rangers	Lester Patrick
1931	3-2	Montreal	Cecil Hart	Chicago	Dick Irvin
1930	2-0	Montreal	Cecil Hart	Boston	Art Ross
1929	2-0	Boston	Art Ross	NY Rangers	Lester Patrick
1928	3-2	NY Rangers	Lester Patrick	Mtl. Maroons	Eddie Gerard
1927	2-0-2	Ottawa	Dave Gill	Boston	Art Ross
		The National Hockey League assumed control of Stanley Cup competition after 1926			
1926	3-1	Mtl. Maroons	Eddie Gerard	Victoria	Lester Patrick
1925	3-1	Victoria	Lester Patrick	Montreal	Leo Dandurand
1924	2-0	Montreal	Leo Dandurand	Cgy. Tigers	Eddie Oatman
1923	2-0	Ottawa	Pete Green	Edm. Eskimos	Ken McKenzie
1922	3-2	Tor. St. Pats	George O'Donoghue	Van. Millionaires	Lloyd Cook/Frank Patrick
1921	3-2	Ottawa	Pete Green	Van. Millionaires	Lloyd Cook/Frank Patrick
1920	3-2	Ottawa	Pete Green	Seattle	Pete Muldoon
1919	2-2-1	No decision - series between Montreal and Seattle cancelled due to influenza epidemic			
1918	3-2	Tor. Arenas	Dick Carroll	Van. Millionaires	Frank Patrick

Championship Trophies

PRINCE OF WALES TROPHY

Beginning with the 1993-94 season, the club which advances to the Stanley Cup Final as the winner of the Eastern Conference Championship is presented with the Prince of Wales Trophy.

History: His Royal Highness, the Prince of Wales, donated the trophy to the National Hockey League in 1925. It was originally awarded to the winner of the first game played in Madison Square Garden, December 15, 1925 (Montreal Canadiens 3 at NY Americans 1). It was then awarded to the NHL playoff champion in 1925-26 and 1926-27. From 1927-28 through 1937-38, the award was presented to the regular-season champion of the American Division of the NHL. (The team finishing first in the Canadian Division received the O'Brien Trophy during these years.) From 1938-39, when the NHL reverted to one section, to 1966-67, it was presented to the team winning the NHL regular-season championship. With expansion in 1967-68, it again became a divisional trophy, awarded to the regular-season champions of the East Division through to the end of the 1973-74 season. Beginning in 1974-75, it was awarded to the regular-season winner of the conference bearing the name of the trophy. From 1981-82 to 1992-93 the trophy was presented to the playoff champion in the Wales Conference. Since 1993-94, the trophy has been presented to the playoff champion in the Eastern Conference.

2014-15 Winner: Tampa Bay Lightning

The Tampa Bay Lightning won the Prince of Wales Trophy on May 29, 2015 after defeating the New York Rangers 2-0 in game 7 of the Eastern Conference Finals. Before defeating the Rangers, Tampa Bay had series wins over the Detroit Red Wings and the Montreal Canadiens.

PRINCE OF WALES TROPHY WINNERS

2014-15	Tampa Bay	1982-83	NY Islanders	1951-52	Detroit
2013-14	NY Rangers	1981-82	NY Islanders	1950-51	Detroit
2012-13	Boston	1980-81	Montreal	1949-50	Detroit
2011-12	New Jersey	1979-80	Buffalo	1948-49	Detroit
2010-11	Boston	1978-79	Montreal	1947-48	Toronto
2009-10	Philadelphia	1977-78	Montreal	1946-47	Montreal
2008-09	Pittsburgh	1976-77	Montreal	1945-46	Montreal
2007-08	Pittsburgh	1975-76	Montreal	1944-45	Montreal
2006-07	Ottawa	1974-75	Buffalo	1943-44	Montreal
2005-06	Carolina	1973-74	Boston	1942-43	Detroit
2003-04	Tampa Bay	1972-73	Montreal	1941-42	NY Rangers
2002-03	New Jersey	1971-72	Boston	1940-41	Boston
2001-02	Carolina	1970-71	Boston	1939-40	Boston
2000-01	New Jersey	1969-70	Chicago	1938-39	Boston
99-2000	New Jersey	1968-69	Montreal	1937-38	Boston
1998-99	Buffalo	1967-68	Montreal	1936-37	Detroit
1997-98	Washington	1966-67	Chicago	1935-36	Detroit
1996-97	Philadelphia	1965-66	Montreal	1934-35	Boston
1995-96	Florida	1964-65	Detroit	1933-34	Detroit
1994-95	New Jersey	1963-64	Montreal	1932-33	Boston
1993-94	NY Rangers	1962-63	Toronto	1931-32	NY Rangers
1992-93	Montreal	1961-62	Montreal	1930-31	Boston
1991-92	Pittsburgh	1960-61	Montreal	1929-30	Boston
1990-91	Pittsburgh	1959-60	Montreal	1928-29	Boston
1989-90	Boston	1958-59	Montreal	1927-28	Boston
1988-89	Montreal	1957-58	Montreal	1926-27	Ottawa
1987-88	Boston	1956-57	Detroit	1925-26	Mtl. Maroons
1986-87	Philadelphia	1955-56	Montreal	Dec. 15/25	Montreal
1985-86	Montreal	1954-55	Detroit	1923-24	Montreal*
1984-85	Philadelphia	1953-54	Detroit		
1983-84	NY Islanders	1952-53	Detroit		

* Engraved by Montreal Canadiens in 1925-26.

CLARENCE S. CAMPBELL BOWL

Beginning with the 1993-94 season, the club which advances to the Stanley Cup Final as the winner of the Western Conference Championship is presented with the Clarence S. Campbell Bowl.

History: Presented by the member clubs in 1968 for perpetual competition by the National Hockey League in recognition of the services of Clarence S. Campbell, President of the NHL from 1946 to 1977. From 1967-68 through 1973-74, the trophy was awarded to the regular-season champions of the West Division. Beginning in 1974-75, it was awarded to the regular-season winner of the conference bearing the name of the trophy. From 1981-82 to 1992-93 the trophy was presented to the playoff champion in the Campbell Conference. Since 1993-94, the trophy has been presented to the playoff champion in the Western Conference. The trophy itself is a hallmark piece made of sterling silver and was crafted by a British silversmith in 1878.

2014-15 Winner: Chicago Blackhawks

The Chicago Blackhawks won the Clarence S. Campbell Bowl on May 30, 2015 after defeating the Anaheim Ducks 5-3 in game 7 of the Western Conference Finals. Before defeating the Ducks, Chicago had series wins over the Nashville Predators and the Minnesota Wild.

CLARENCE S. CAMPBELL BOWL WINNERS

2014-15	Chicago	1997-98	Detroit	1981-82	Vancouver
2013-14	Los Angeles	1996-97	Detroit	1980-81	NY Islanders
2012-13	Chicago	1995-96	Colorado	1979-80	Philadelphia
2011-12	Los Angeles	1994-95	Detroit	1978-79	NY Islanders
2010-11	Vancouver	1993-94	Vancouver	1977-78	NY Islanders
2009-10	Chicago	1992-93	Los Angeles	1976-77	Philadelphia
2008-09	Detroit	1991-92	Chicago	1975-76	Philadelphia
2007-08	Detroit	1990-91	Minnesota	1974-75	Philadelphia
2006-07	Anaheim	1989-90	Edmonton	1973-74	Philadelphia
2005-06	Edmonton	1988-89	Calgary	1972-73	Chicago
2003-04	Calgary	1987-88	Edmonton	1971-72	Chicago
2002-03	Anaheim	1986-87	Edmonton	1970-71	Chicago
2001-02	Detroit	1985-86	Calgary	1969-70	St. Louis
2000-01	Colorado	1984-85	Edmonton	1968-69	St. Louis
99-2000	Dallas	1983-84	Edmonton	1967-68	Philadelphia
1998-99	Dallas	1982-83	Edmonton		

Prince of Wales Trophy

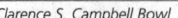

Clarence S. Campbell Bowl

Stanley Cup

Stanley Cup Winners

Rosters and Final Series Scores

2014-15 — Chicago Blackhawks — Jonathan Toews (Captain), Bryan Bickell, Daniel Carcillo, Corey Crawford, Kyle Cumiskey, Scott Darling, Andrew Desjardins, Niklas Hjalmarsson, Marian Hossa, Patrick Kane, Duncan Keith, Marcus Kruger, Joakim Nordstrom, Johnny Oduya, Brad Richards, Michal Rozsival, David Rundblad, Brandon Saad, Brent Seabrook, Patrick Sharp, Andrew Shaw, Teuvo Teravainen, Kimmo Timonen, Trevor van Riemsdyk, Antoine Vermette, Kris Versteeg, W. Rockwell Wirtz (Chairman), John McDonough (President/CEO), Jay Blunk (Executive Vice President), Stan Bowman (Vice President/General Manager), Al MacIsaac (Vice President, Hockey Operations), Norm Maciver (Assistant General Manager), Scotty Bowman (Senior Advisor), Joel Quenneville (Head Coach), Mike Kitchen, Kevin Dineen (Assistant Coaches), Jimmy Waite (Goaltending Coach), Mike Gapski (Head Athletic Trainer), Troy Parchman (Equipment Manager), Jeff Thomas (Assistant Athletic Trainer), Pawel Prylinski (Massage Therapist), Jim Heintzelman (Equipment Assistant), Paul Goodman (Strength and Conditioning Coach), Matt Meacham (Video Coach), Pierre Gauthier (Director, Player Personnel), Mark Kelley (Senior Director, Amateur Scouting), Barry Smith (Director, Player Development), Ryan Stewart (Director, Pro Scouting), Ron Anderson (Director, Player Recruitment), Tony Ommen (Senior Director, Team Services), Mark Bernard (General Manager, Minor League Affiliates), Dr. Michael Terry (Head Team Physician).

Scores: June 3, at Tampa Bay — Chicago 2, Tampa Bay 1; June 6, at Tampa Bay — Tampa Bay 4, Chicago 1; June 8, at Chicago — Tampa Bay 3, Chicago 2; June 10, at Chicago — Chicago 2, Tampa Bay 1; June 13, at Tampa Bay — Chicago 2, Tampa Bay 1; June 15, at Chicago —Chicago 2, Tampa Bay 0.

2013-14 — Los Angeles Kings — Dustin Brown (Captain), Jeff Carter, Kyle Clifford, Drew Doughty, Marian Gaborik, Matt Greene, Martin Jones, Dwight King, Anze Kopitar, Trevor Lewis, Alec Martinez, Willie Mitchell, Jake Muzzin, Jordan Nolan, Tanner Pearson, Jonathan Quick, Robyn Regehr, Mike Richards, Jeff Schultz, Jarret Stoll, Tyler Toffoli, Slava Voynov, Justin Williams, Philip Anschutz (Owner), Nancy Anschutz (Owner), Daniel Beckerman (Alternate Governor), Dean Lombardi (President/General Manager), Luc Robitaille (President, Business Operations), Robert Blake (Assistant General Manager), Jeffrey Solomon (Vice President/Hockey Operations and Legal Affairs), Michael Futa (Director of Amateur Scouting), Darryl Sutter (Head Coach), John Stevens (Assistant Coach), Davis Payne (Assistant Coach), Bill Ranford (Goaltending Coach), Kelly Cheeseman (Chief Operating Officer), Michael Altieri (Vice President, Communications and Broadcasting), Jack Ferreira (Special Assistant to the General Manager), Mike O'Connell (Development Coach), Nelson Emerson (Player Development), Alyn McCauley (Pro Scout), Mark Yannetti (Director of Amateur Scouting), Lee Callans (Scouting Operations Coordinator), Brent McEwen, Tony Gasparini (Amateur Scouts), Mike Donnelly (Collegiate Scout), Marshall Dickerson (Director of Team Operations), Zach Ziegler (Video Coordinator), Darren Granger (Head Equipment Manager), Chris Kingsley (Head Athletic Trainer), Dana C. Bryson (Assistant Equipment Manager), Myles Hirayama (Assistant Athletic Trainer).

Scores: June 4, at Los Angeles — Los Angeles 3, NY Rangers 2; June 7, at Los Angeles — Los Angeles 5. NY Rangers 4; June 9, at New York — Los Angeles 3, NY Rangers 0; June 11, at New York — NY Rangers 2, Los Angeles 1; June 13, at Los Angeles — Los Angeles 3, NY Rangers 2.

2012-13 — Chicago Blackhawks — Jonathan Toews (Captain), Bryan Bickell, Dave Bolland, Brandon Bollig, Sheldon Brookbank, Daniel Carcillo, Corey Crawford, Ray Emery, Michael Frolik, Michal Handzus, Niklas Hjalmarsson, Marian Hossa, Patrick Kane, Duncan Keith, Marcus Kruger, Nick Leddy, Jamal Mayers, Johnny Oduya, Michal Rozsival, Brandon Saad, Brent Seabrook, Patrick Sharp, Andrew Shaw, Ben Smith, Viktor Stalberg, W. Rockwell Wirtz (Chairman), John McDonough (President/CEO),
Jay Blunk (Executive Vice President), Stan Bowman (Vice President/General Manager), Al MacIsaac (Vice President/Assistant to the President), Norm Maciver (Assistant General Manager), Scotty Bowman (Senior Advisor), Joel Quenneville (Head Coach), Mike Kitchen, Jamie Kompon (Assistant Coaches), Stephane Waite (Goaltending Coach), Mike Gapski (Head Athletic Trainer), Troy Parchman (Equipment Manager), Jeff Thomas (Assistant Athletic Trainer), Clint Reif (Assistant Equipment Manager), Pawel Prylinski (Massage Therapist), Jim Heintzelman (Equipment Assistant), Paul Goodman (Strength and Conditioning Coach), Tim Campbell (Video Coach), Pierre Gauthier (Director, Player Personnel), Mark Kelley (Director, Amateur Scouting), Barry Smith (Director, Player Development), Ryan Stewart (Director, Pro Scouting), Ron Anderson (Director, Player Recruitment), Tony Ommen (Senior Director, Team Services), Mark Bernard (General Manager, Minor League Affiliates), Dr. Michael Terry (Head Team Physician).

***Scores:** June 12, at Chicago — Chicago 4, Boston 3; June 15, at Chicago — Boston 2, Chicago 1; June 17, at Boston — Boston 2, Chicago 0; June 19, at Boston — Chicago 6, Boston 5; June 22, at Chicago — Chicago 3, Boston 1; June 24, at Boston — Chicago 3, Boston 2.*

2011-12 — Los Angeles Kings — Dustin Brown (Captain), Jonathan Bernier, Jeff Carter, Kyle Clifford, Drew Doughty, Davis Drewiske, Colin Fraser, Simon Gagne, Matt Greene, Dwight King, Anze Kopitar, Trevor Lewis, Alec Martinez, Willie Mitchell, Jordan Nolan, Dustin Penner, Jonathan Quick, Mike Richards, Brad Richardson, Robert Scuderi, Jarret Stoll, Slava Voynov, Kevin Westgarth, Justin Williams, Philip Anschutz (Owner), Nancy Anschutz (Owner), Timothy Leiweke (Governor), Daniel Beckerman (Chief Financial Officer), Ted Fikre (Chief Legal Officer), Dean Lombardi (President/General Manager), Luc Robitaille (President, Business Operations), Ron Hextall (Vice President/Assistant General Manager), Jeffrey Solomon (Vice President/Hockey Operations and Legal Affairs), Darryl Sutter (Head Coach), John Stevens (Assistant Coach), Jamie Kompon (Assistant Coach), Bill Ranford (Goaltending Coach), Chris McGowan (Chief Operating Officer), Michael Altieri (Vice President, Communications and Content), Jack Ferreira (Special Assistant to the General Manager), Mike O'Connell (Player Development), Nelson Emerson (Player Development), Rob Laird (Senior Pro Scout), Michael Futa (Director of Amateur Scouting), Mark Yannetti (Director of Amateur Scouting), Lee Callans (Scouting Operations Coordinator), Marshall Dickerson (Director of Team Operations), Ryan Colville (Video Coordinator), Darren Granger (Head Equipment Manager), Chris Kingsley (Head Athletic Trainer), Dana C. Bryson (Assistant Equipment Manager), Myles Hirayama (Assistant Athletic Trainer).

***Scores:** May 30, at New Jersey — Los Angeles 2, New Jersey 1; June 2, at New Jersey — Los Angeles 2, New Jersey 1; June 4, at Los Angeles — Los Angeles 4, New Jersey 0; June 5, at Los Angeles — New Jersey 3, Los Angeles 1; June 9, at New Jersey — New Jersey 2, Los Angeles 1; June 11, at Los Angeles — Los Angeles 6, New Jersey 1.*

2010-11 — Boston Bruins — Zdeno Chara (Captain), Patrice Bergeron, Johnny Boychuk, Gregory Campbell, Andrew Ference, Nathan Horton, Tomas Kaberle, Chris Kelly, David Krejci, Milan Lucic, Brad Marchand, Adam McQuaid, Daniel Paille, Rich Peverley, Tuukka Rask, Mark Recchi, Michael Ryder, Marc Savard, Tyler Seguin, Dennis Seidenberg, Tim Thomas, Shawn Thornton, Jeremy and Margaret Jacobs, Charlie Jacobs, Louis Jacobs, Jerry Jacobs Jr. (Ownership), Cam Neely (President), Peter Chiarelli (General Manager), Jim Benning, Don Sweeney (Assistant General Managers), Claude Julien (Head Coach), Doug Jarvis, Geoff Ward, Doug Houda (Assistant Coaches), Bob Essensa (Goaltending Coach), Harry Sinden (Senior Advisor), John Bucyk (Team Road Service Coordinator), Scott Bradley (Director of Player Personnel), Wayne Smith (Director of Amateur Scouting), John Weisbrod (Director of Collegiate Scouting), Adam Creighton, Tom McVie (Scouts), Dale Hamilton-Powers (Director of Administration), Matt Chmura (Director of Communications), Ryan Nadeau (Manager of Hockey Administration), Don DelNegro (Athletic Trainer), John Whitesides (Strength and Conditioning Coach), Keith Robinson (Equipment Manager), Derek Repucci (Assistant Trainer and Massage Therapist), Jim "Beets" Johnson (Assistant Equipment Manager), Scott Waugh (Physical Therapist).

***Scores:** June 1, at Vancouver — Vancouver 1, Boston 0; June 4, at Vancouver — Vancouver 3, Boston 2; June 6, at Boston — Boston 8, Vancouver 1; June 8, at Boston — Boston 4, Vancouver 0; June 10, at Vancouver — Vancouver 1, Boston 0; June 13, at Boston — Boston 5, Vancouver 2; June 15, at Vancouver — Boston 4, Vancouver 0.*

2009-10 — Chicago Blackhawks — Jonathan Toews (Captain), Dave Bolland, Nick Boynton, Troy Brouwer, Adam Burish, Dustin Byfuglien, Brian Campbell, Ben Eager, Colin Fraser, Jordan Hendry, Niklas Hjalmarsson, Marian Hossa, Cristobal Huet, Patrick Kane, Duncan Keith, Tomas Kopecky, Andrew Ladd, John Madden, Antti Niemi, Brent Seabrook, Patrick Sharp, Brent Sopel, Kris Versteeg, W. Rockwell Wirtz (Chairman), John McDonough (President), Jay Blunk (Senior VP, Business Operations), Stan Bowman (General Manager), Kevin Cheveldayoff (Assistant General Manager), Al MacIsaac (Senior Director, Hockey Administration/Assistant to the President), Scotty Bowman, Dale Tallon (Senior Advisors, Hockey Operations), Joel Quenneville (Head Coach), John Torchetti, Mike Haviland (Assistant Coaches), Stephane Waite (Goaltending Coach), Paul Goodman (Strength and Conditioning Coach), Brad Aldrich (Video Coach), Paul Vincent (Skating Coach), Marc Bergevin (Director, Player Personnel), Mark Bernard (G.M., Minor League Affiliations), Norm Maciver (Director, Player Development), Mark Kelley (Director, Amateur Scouting), Ron Anderson (Director, Player Recruitment), Michel Dumas (Chief Amateur Scout), Tony Ommen (Director Team Services), Dr. Michael Terry (Head Team Physician), Mike Gapski (Head Athletic Trainer), Troy Parchman (Equipment Manager), Pawel Prylinski (Massage Therapist), Jeff Thomas (Assistant Athletic Trainer), Clint Reif (Assistant Equipment Manager), Jim Heintzelman (Equipment Assistant).

***Scores:** May 29, at Chicago — Chicago 6, Philadelphia 5; May 31, at Chicago — Chicago 2, Philadelphia 1; June 2 at Philadelphia — Philadelphia 4, Chicago 3; June 4 at Philadelphia — Philadelphia 5, Chicago 3; June 6, at Chicago — Chicago 7, Philadelphia 4; June 9 at Philadelphia — Chicago 4, Philadelphia 3.*

2008-09 — Pittsburgh Penguins — Sidney Crosby (Captain), Craig Adams, Philippe Boucher, Matt Cooke, Pascal Dupuis, Mark Eaton, Ruslan Fedotenko, Marc-Andre Fleury, Mathieu Garon, Hal Gill, Eric Godard, Alex Goligoski, Sergei Gonchar, Bill Guerin, Tyler Kennedy, Chris Kunitz, Kris Letang, Evgeni Malkin, Brooks Orpik, Miroslav Satan, Rob Scuderi, Jordan Staal, Petr Sykora, Maxime Talbot, Mike Zigomanis, Mario Lemieux (Co-owner/Chairman), Ron Burkle (Co-owner), Bill Kassling, Tom Grealish, Tony Liberati (Directors), Ken Sawyer (Chief Executive Officer), David Morehouse (President), Ray Shero (Executive Vice President amd General Manager), Chuck Fletcher (Assistant General Manager), Ed Johnston (Senior Advisor, Hockey Operations), Jason Botterill (Director of Hockey Administration), Dan Bylsma (Head Coach), Mike Yeo (Assistant Coach), Tom Fitzgerald (Director of Player Development), GIlles Meloche (Goaltending Coach), Mike Kadar (Strength and Conditioning Coach), Travis Ramsay (Video Coordinator), Chris Stewart (Head Athletic Trainer), Scott Adams (Assistant Athletic Trainer), Mark Mortland (Physical Therapist), Dana Heinze (Equipment Manager), Paul DeFazio, Danny Kroll (Assistant Equipment Managers), Frank Buonomo (Senior Director of Team Services and Communications), Tom McMillan (Vice President, Communications), Dan MacKinnon (Director of Professional Scouting), Jay Heinbuck (Director of Amateur Scouting).

***Scores:** May 30, at Detroit — Detroit 3, Pittsburgh 1; May 31 at Detroit — Detroit 3, Pittsburgh 1; June 2, at Pittsburgh — Pittsburgh 4, Detroit 2; June 4, at Pittsburgh — Pittsburgh 4, Detroit 2; June 6 at Detroit — Detroit 5, Pittsburgh 0; June 9, at Pittsburgh — Pittsburgh 2, Detroit 1; June 12, at Detroit — Pittsburgh 2, Detroit 1.*

2007-08 — Detroit Red Wings — Nicklas Lidstrom (Captain), Chris Chelios, Daniel Cleary, Pavel Datsyuk, Aaron Downey, Dallas Drake, Kris Draper, Valtteri Filppula, Johan Franzen, Dominik Hasek, Darren Helm, Tomas Holmstrom, Jiri Hudler, Tomas Kopecky, Niklas Kronwall, Brett Lebda, Andreas Lilja, Kirk Maltby, Darren McCarty, Derek Meech, Chris Osgood, Brian Rafalski, Mikael Samuelsson, Brad Stuart, Henrik Zetterberg, Michael Ilitch (Owner/Governor), Marian Ilitch (Owner/Secretary-Treasurer), Christopher Ilitch (Vice President/Alternate Governor), Denise Ilitch, Ronald Ilitch, Michael Ilitch Jr., Lisa Ilitch Murray, Atanas Ilitch, Carole Ilitch. Jim Devellano (Senior Vice President/Alternate Governor), Ken Holland (General Manager/Alternate Governor), Steve Yzerman (Vice President/Alternate Governor), Jim Nill (Assistant General Manager), Ryan Martin (Director, Hockey Operations), Scotty Bowman (Consultant), Mike Babcock (Head Coach), Todd McLellan (Associate Coach), Paul MacLean (Assistant Coach), Jim Bedard (Goaltending Consultant), Jay Woodcroft (Video Coordinator), Mark Howe (Director, Pro Scouting), Joe McDonnell (Director, Amateur Scouting), Hakan Andersson (Director, Amateur Scouting Europe), Piet Van Zant (Athletic Trainer), Paul Boyer (Equipment Manager), Russ Baumann, Christopher Scoppetto (Assistant Athletic Trainers).

***Scores:** May 24, at Detroit — Detroit 4, Pittsburgh 0; May 26, at Detroit — Detroit 3, Pittsburgh 0; May 28, at Pittsburgh — Pittsburgh 3, Detroit 2; May 31, at Pittsburgh — Detroit 2, Pittsburgh 1; June 2, at Detroit — Pittsburgh 4, Detroit 3; June 4, at Pittsburgh — Detroit 3, Pittsburgh 2.*

2006-07 — Anaheim Ducks — Scott Niedermayer (Captain), Rob Niedermayer, Chris Pronger, Teemu Selanne, Sean O'Donnell, Brad May, Todd Marchant, Jean-Sebastien Giguere, Andy McDonald, Samuel Pahlsson, Shawn Thornton, Ric Jackman, Joe DiPenta, Kent Huskins, Chris Kunitz, George Parros, Joe Motzko, Ilya Bryzgalov, Francois Beauchemin, Travis Moen, Ryan Carter, Drew Miller, Ryan Shannon, Dustin Penner, Ryan Getzlaf, Corey Perry; Henry Samueli, Susan Samueli (Owners), Michael Schulman (CEO), Brian Burke (Executive Vice President/General Manager), Tim Ryan (Executive Vice President/COO), Bob Wagner (Senior Vice President/Chief Marketing Officer), Bob Murray (Senior Vice President-Hockey Operations), David McNab (Assistant General Manager), Al Coates (Senior Advisor to GM), Randy Carlyle (Head Coach), Dave Farrish, Newell Brown (Assistant Coaches), Francois Allaire (Goaltending Consultant), Sean Skahan (Strength and Conditioning Coach), Joe Trotta (Video Coordinator), Tim Clark (Head Trainer), Mark O'Neill (Equipment Manager), John Allaway (Assistant Equipment Manager), James Partida (Massage Therapist), Rick Paterson (Director of Professional Scouting), Alain Chainey (Director of Amateur Scouting).

***Scores:** May 28, at Anaheim - Anaheim 3, Ottawa 2; May 30, at Anaheim - Anaheim 1, Ottawa 0; June 2, at Ottawa - Ottawa 5, Anaheim 3; June 4, at Ottawa - Anaheim 3, Ottawa 2; June 6, at Anaheim - Anaheim 6, Ottawa 2.*

2005-06 — Carolina Hurricanes — Rod Brind'Amour (Captain), Glen Wesley, Cory Stillman, Kevyn Adams, Craig Adams, Anton Babchuk, Erik Cole, Mike Commodore, Matt Cullen, Martin Gerber, Bret Hedican, Andrew Hutchinson, Frantisek Kaberle, Andrew Ladd, Chad LaRose, Mark Recchi, Eric Staal, Oleg Tverdovsky, Josef Vasicek, Niclas Wallin, Aaron Ward, Cam Ward, Doug Weight, Ray Whitney, Justin Williams; Peter Karmanos Jr., Thomas Thewes (Owners), Jim Rutherford (President/General Manager), Jason Karmanos (Vice President/Assistant General Manager), Mike Amendola (Chief Financial Officer), Peter Laviolette (Head Coach), Kevin McCarthy, Jeff Daniels (Assistant Coaches), Greg Stefan (Goaltending Coach), Chris Huffine (Video Coordinator), Skip Cunningham, Wally Tatomir, Bob Gorman (Equipment Managers), Peter Friesen (Head Athletic Therapist/Strength and Conditioning Coach), Chris Stewart (Associate Athletic Trainer), Brian Tatum (Team Services Manager), Kelly Kirwin (Event Coordinator-Hockey Operations), Mike Sundheim (Director of Media Relations), Kyle Hanlin (Manager of Media Relations), Sheldon Ferguson (Director of Amateur Scouting), Marshall Johnston (Director of Professional Scouting), Claude Larose, Ron Smith (Professional Scouts), Bert Marshall, Tony MacDonald, Martin Madden (Amateur Scouts), Tom Rowe (Lowell (AHL) - Coach).

***Scores:** June 5, at Carolina - Carolina 5, Edmonton 4; June 7, at Carolina - Carolina 5, Edmonton 0; June 10, at Edmonton - Edmonton 2, Carolina 1; June 12, at Edmonton - Carolina 2, Edmonton 1; June 14, at Carolina - Edmonton 4, Carolina 3; June 17, at Edmonton - Edmonton 4, Carolina 0; June 19, at Carolina - Carolina 3, Edmonton 1.*

2003-04 — Tampa Bay Lightning — Dave Andreychuk (Captain), Fredrik Modin, Vincent Lecavalier, Martin St. Louis, Brad Richards, Nikolai Khabibulin, Pavel Kubina, Dan Boyle, Ruslan Fedotenko, Darryl Sydor, Cory Sarich, Tim Taylor, Cory Stillman, Jassen Cullimore, John Grahame, Chris Dingman, Nolan Pratt, Brad Lukowich, Andre Roy, Dmitry Afanasenkov, Martin Cibak, Ben Clymer, Darren Rumble, Stan Neckar, Eric Perrin; William Davidson (Owner), Tom Wilson (Governor), Ron Campbell (President), Jay Feaster (General Manager), John Tortorella (Head Coach), Craig Ramsay (Associate Coach), Jeff Reese (Assistant Coach), Nigel Kirwan (Video Coach), Eric Lawson (Strength and Conditioning Coach), Tom Mulligan (Trainer), Adam Rambo (Assistant Trainer), Ray Thill (Equipment Manager), Dana Heinze, Jim Pickard (Assistant Equipment Managers), Mike Griebel (Massage Therapist), Bill Barber (Director of Player Personnel), Jake Goertzen (Head Scout), Phil Thibodeau (Director of Team Services), Ryan Belec (Assistant to the GM), Rick Paterson (Chief Pro Scout), Kari Kettunen, Glen Zacharias, Steve Baker, Dave Heitz, Yuri Yanchenkov, (Scouts), Bill Wickett (Senior Vice President - Communications), Sean Henry (Executive Vice President/COO).

***Scores:** May 25, at Tampa Bay - Calgary 4, Tampa Bay 1; May 27, at Tampa Bay - Tampa Bay 4, Calgary 1; May 29, at Calgary - Calgary 3, Tampa Bay 0; May 31, at Calgary - Tampa Bay 1, Calgary 0; June 3, at Tampa Bay - Calgary 3, Tampa Bay 2; June 5, at Calgary - Tampa Bay 3, Calgary 2; June 7, at Tampa Bay - Tampa Bay 2, Calgary 1.*

2002-03 — New Jersey Devils — Tommy Albelin, Jiri Bicek, Martin Brodeur, Sergei Brylin, Ken Daneyko, Patrik Elias, Jeff Friesen, Brian Gionta, Scott Gomez, Jamie Langenbrunner, John Madden, Grant Marshall, Jim McKenzie, Scott Niedermayer, Joe Nieuwendyk, Jay Pandolfo, Brian Rafalski, Pascal Rheaume, Mike Rupp, Corey Schwab, Richard Smehlik, Scott Stevens (Captain), Turner Stevenson, Oleg Tverdovsky, Colin White; Raymond Chambers, Lewis Catz (Owners), Peter Simon (Chairman), Lou Lamoriello (CEO/President/General Manager), Pat Burns (Head Coach), Bob Carpenter, John MacLean (Assistant Coaches), Jacques Caron

(Goaltending Coach), Larry Robinson (Special Assignment Coach), David Conte (Director - Scouting), Claude Carrier (Assistant Director - Scouting), Chris Lamoriello (Scout/Albany (AHL) - General Manager), Milt Fisher, Dan Labraaten, Marcel Pronovost (Scouts), Bob Hoffmeyer, Jan Ludvig (Pro Scouts), Dr. Barry Fisher (Orthopedist), Chris Modrzynski (Executive Vice President), Terry Farmer (Vice President - Ticket Operations), Vladimir Bure (Fitness Consultant), Taran Singleton (Hockey Operations), Bill Murray (Medical Trainer), Michael Vasalani (Strength and Conditioning Coordinator), Rick Matthews (Equipment Manager), Juergen Merz (Massage Therapist), Alex Abasto (Assistant Equipment Manager).

Scores: *May 27, at New Jersey - New Jersey 3, Anaheim 0; May 29, at New Jersey - New Jersey 3, Anaheim 0; May 31, at Anaheim - Anaheim 3, New Jersey 2; June 2, at Anaheim - Anaheim 1, New Jersey 0; June 5, at New Jersey - New Jersey 6, Anaheim 3; June 7, at Anaheim - Anaheim 5, New Jersey 2; June 9, at New Jersey - New Jersey 3, Anaheim 0.*

2001-02 — Detroit Red Wings — Steve Yzerman (Captain), Dominik Hasek, Manny Legace, Chris Chelios, Mathieu Dandenault, Steve Duchesne, Jiri Fischer, Nicklas Lidstrom, Fredrik Olausson, Jiri Slegr, Pavel Datsyuk, Boyd Devereaux, Kris Draper, Sergei Fedorov, Tomas Holmstrom, Brett Hull, Igor Larionov, Kirk Maltby, Darren McCarty, Luc Robitaille, Brendan Shanahan, Jason Williams; Michael Ilitch (Owner/Governor), Marian Ilitch (Owner/Secretary Treasurer), Christoper Ilitch (Vice President), Denise Ilitch (Alternate Governor), Ronald Ilitch, Michael Ilitch Jr., Lisa Ilitch Murray, Atanas Ilitch, Carole Ilitch, Jim Devellano (Senior Vice President), Ken Holland (General Manager), Jim Nill (Assistant General Manager), Scotty Bowman (Head Coach), Dave Lewis, Barry Smith (Associate Coaches), Jim Bedard (Goaltending Consultant), Joe Kocur (Video Coordinator), John Wharton (Athletic Trainer), Piet Van Zant (Assistant Athletic Trainer), Paul Boyer (Equipment Manager), Paul MacDonald (Senior Director of Finance), Nancy Beard (Executive Assistant), Dan Belisle, Mark Howe, Bob McCammon (Pro Scouts), Hakan Andersson (Director of European Scouting), Bruce Haralson, Mark Leach, Joe McDonnell, Glenn Merkosky (Scouts).

Scores: *June 4, at Detroit - Carolina 3, Detroit 2; June 6, at Detroit - Detroit 3, Carolina 1; June 8, at Carolina - Detroit 3, Carolina 2; June 10, at Carolina - Detroit 3, Carolina 0; June 13, at Detroit - Detroit 3, Carolina 1.*

2000-01 — Colorado Avalanche — David Aebischer, Rob Blake, Raymond Bourque, Greg de Vries, Chris Dingman, Chris Drury, Adam Foote, Peter Forsberg, Milan Hejduk, Dan Hinote, Jon Klemm, Eric Messier, Bryan Muir, Ville Nieminen, Scott Parker, Shjon Podein, Nolan Pratt, Dave Reid, Steve Reinprecht, Patrick Roy, Joe Sakic (Captain), Martin Skoula, Alex Tanguay, Stephane Yelle; E. Stanley Kroenke (Owner/Governor), Pierre Lacroix (President/ General Manager), Bob Hartley (Head Coach), Jacques Cloutier, Bryan Trottier (Assistant Coaches), Paul Fixter (Video Coach), Francois Giguere (Vice President - Hockey Operations), Brian MacDonald (Assistant General Manager), Michel Goulet (Vice President - Player Personnel), Jean Martineau (Vice President - Communications and Team Services), Pat Karns (Head Athletic Trainer), Matthew Sokolowski (Assistant Athletic Trainer), Wayne Flemming, Mark Miller (Equipment Managers), Dave Randolph (Assistant Equipment Manager), Paul Goldberg (Strength and Conditioning Coach), Gregorio Pradera (Massage Therapist), Brad Smith (Pro Scout), Jim Hammett (Chief Scout), Garth Joy, Steve Lyons, Joni Lehto, Orval Tessier (Scouts), Charlotte Grahame (Director of Hockey Administration).

Scores: *May 26, at Colorado - Colorado 5, New Jersey 0; May 29, at Colorado - New Jersey 2, Colorado 1; May 31, at New Jersey - Colorado 3, New Jersey 1; June 2, at New Jersey - New Jersey 3, Colorado 2; June 4, at Colorado - New Jersey 4, Colorado 1; June 7, at New Jersey - Colorado 4, New Jersey 0; June 9, at Colorado - Colorado 3, New Jersey 1.*

1999-2000 — New Jersey Devils — Jason Arnott, Brad Bombardir, Martin Brodeur, Steve Brule, Sergei Brylin, Ken Daneyko, Patrik Elias, Scott Gomez, Bobby Holik, Steve Kelly, Claude Lemieux, John Madden, Vladimir Malakhov, Randy McKay, Alexander Mogilny, Sergei Nemchinov, Scott Niedermayer, Krzysztof Oliwa, Jay Pandolfo, Brian Rafalski, Ken Sutton, Scott Stevens (Captain), Petr Sykora, Chris Terreri, Colin White; Dr. John J. McMullen (Owner/Chairman), Peter S. McMullen (Owner), Lou Lamoriello (President/General Manager), Larry Robinson (Head Coach), Viacheslav Fetisov (Assistant Coach), Jacques Caron (Goaltending Coach), Bob Carpenter (Assistant Coach), John Cuniff (Albany (AHL) - Coach), David Conte (Director of Scouting), Claude Carrier (Assistant Director of Scouting), Milt Fisher, Dan Labraaten, Marcel Pronovost (Scouts), Bob Hoffmeyer (Pro Scout), Dr. Barry Fisher (Orthopedist), Dennis Gendron (Albany (AHL) - Assistant Coach), Robbie Ftorek (Coach), Vladimir Bure (Consultant), Taran Singleton, Marie Carnevale, Callie Smith (Hockey Operations), Bill Murray (Medical Trainer), Michael Vasalani (Strength and Conditioning Coordinator), Dana McGuane (Equipment Manager), Juergen Merz (Massage Therapist), Harry Bricker, Lou Centanni Jr. (Assistant Equipment Managers).

Scores: *May 30, at New Jersey - New Jersey 7, Dallas 3; June 1, at New Jersey - Dallas 2, New Jersey 1; June 3, at Dallas - New Jersey 2, Dallas 1; June 5, at Dallas - New Jersey 3, Dallas 1; June 8, at New Jersey - Dallas 1 - New Jersey 0; June 10, at Dallas, New Jersey 2 - Dallas 1.*

1998-99 — Dallas Stars — Derian Hatcher (Captain), Mike Modano, Joe Nieuwendyk, Craig Ludwig, Sergei Zubov, Ed Belfour, Guy Carbonneau, Shawn Chambers, Benoit Hogue, Tony Hrkac, Brett Hull, Mike Keane, Jamie Langenbrunner, Jere Lehtinen, Grant Marshall, Richard Matvichuk, Derek Plante, Dave Reid, Brent Severyn, Jon Sim, Brian Skrudland, Blake Sloan, Darryl Sydor, Roman Turek, Pat Verbeek; Thomas Hicks (Chairman/Owner), Jim Lites (President), Bob Gainey (Vice President - Hockey Operations/General Manager), Doug Armstrong (Assistant General Manager), Craig Button (Director of Player Personnel), Ken Hitchcock (Head Coach), Doug Jarvis, Rick Wilson (Assistant Coaches), Rick McLaughlin (Vice President/Chief Financial Officer), Jeff Cogen (Vice President - Marketing and Promotion), Bill Strong (Vice President - Marketing and Broadcasting), Tim Bernhardt (Director of Amateur Scouting), Doug Overton (Director of Pro Scouting), Bob Gernander (Chief Scout), Stu MacGregor (Western Scout), Dave Suprenant (Medical Trainer), Dave Smith, Rich Matthews (Equipment Managers), J.J. McQueen (Strength and Conditioning Coach), Rick St. Croix (Goaltending Consultant), Dan Stuchal (Director of Team Services), Larry Kelly (Director of Public Relations).

Scores: *June 8, at Dallas - Buffalo 3, Dallas 2; June 10, at Dallas - Dallas 4, Buffalo 2; June 12, at Buffalo - Dallas 2, Buffalo 1; June 15, at Buffalo - Buffalo 2, Dallas 1; June 17, at Dallas - Dallas 2, Buffalo 0; June 19, at Buffalo - Dallas 2, Buffalo 1.*

1997-98 — Detroit Red Wings — Steve Yzerman (Captain), Doug Brown, Mathieu Dandenault, Kris Draper, Anders Eriksson, Sergei Fedorov, Viacheslav Fetisov, Brent Gilchrist, Kevin Hodson, Tomas Holmstrom, Mike Knuble, Joe Kocur, Vladimir Konstantinov, Vyacheslav Kozlov, Martin Lapointe, Igor Larionov, Nicklas Lidstrom, Jamie Macoun, Kirk Maltby, Darren McCarty, Dmitri Mironov, Larry Murphy, Chris Osgood, Bob Rouse, Brendan Shanahan, Aaron Ward; Mike Ilitch, (Owner/Chairman), Marian Ilitch (Owner), Atanas Ilitch, Christopher Ilitch (Vice Presidents), Denise Ilitch, Ronald Ilitch, Michael Ilitch Jr., Lisa Ilitch Murray, Carole Ilitch Trepeck, Jim Devellano (Senior Vice President), Ken Holland (General Manager), Don Waddell (Assistant General Manager), Scotty Bowman (Head Coach), Barry Smith, Dave Lewis (Associate Coaches), Jim Nill (Director of Player Development), Dan Belisle, Mark Howe (Pro Scouts), Jim Bedard (Goaltending Consultant), Hakan Andersson (Director of European Scouting), Mark Leach (USA Scout), Joe McDonnell (Eastern Scout), Bruce Haralson (Western Scout), John Wharton (Athletic Trainer), Paul Boyer (Equipment Manager), Tim Abbott (Assistant Equipment Manager), Bob Huddleston (Masseur), Sergei Mnatsakanov, Wally Crossman (Dressing Room Assistant).

Scores: *June 9, at Detroit — Detroit 2, Washington 1; June 11, at Detroit — Detroit 5, Washington 4; June 13, at Washington — Detroit 2, Washington 1; June 16, at Washington — Detroit 4, Washington 1.*

1996-97 — Detroit Red Wings — Steve Yzerman (Captain), Doug Brown, Mathieu Dandenault, Kris Draper, Sergei Fedorov, Viacheslav Fetisov, Kevin Hodson, Tomas Holmstrom, Joe Kocur, Vladimir Konstantinov, Vyacheslav Kozlov, Martin Lapointe, Igor Larionov, Nicklas Lidstrom, Kirk Maltby, Darren McCarty, Larry Murphy, Chris Osgood, Jamie Pushor, Bob Rouse, Tomas Sandstrom, Brendan Shanahan, Tim Taylor, Mike Vernon, Aaron Ward; Mike Ilitch (Owner/Chairman), Marian Ilitch (Owner), Atanas Ilitch, Christopher Ilitch (Vice Presidents), Denise Ilitch Lites, Ronald Ilitch, Michael Ilitch Jr., Lisa Ilitch Murray, Carole Ilitch Trepeck, Jim Devellano (Senior Vice President), Scotty Bowman (Head Coach/Director of Player Personnel), Ken Holland (Assistant General Manager), Barry Smith, Dave Lewis (Associate Coaches), Mike Krushelnyski (Assistant Coach), Jim Nill (Director of Player Development), Dan Belisle, Bruce Haralson, Mark Howe (Scouts), Hakan Andersson (Director of European Scouting), John Wharton (Athletic Trainer), Wally Crossman (Dressing Room Assistant), Mark Leach (Scout), Paul Boyer (Equipment Manager), Tim Abbott (Assistant Equipment Manager), Sergei Mnatsakanov (Masseur), Joe McDonnell (Scout).

Scores: *May 31, at Philadelphia — Detroit 4, Philadelphia 2; June 3, at Philadelphia — Detroit 4, Philadelphia 2; June 5, at Detroit — Detroit 6, Philadelphia 1; June 7, at Detroit — Detroit 2, Philadelphia 1.*

1995-96 — Colorado Avalanche — Rene Corbet, Adam Deadmarsh, Stephane Fiset, Adam Foote, Peter Forsberg, Alexei Gusarov, Dave Hannan, Valeri Kamensky, Mike Keane, Jon Klemm, Uwe Krupp, Sylvain Lefebvre, Claude Lemieux, Curtis Leschyshyn, Troy Murray, Sandis Ozolinsh, Mike Ricci, Patrick Roy, Warren Rychel, Joe Sakic (Captain), Chris Simon, Craig Wolanin, Stephane Yelle, Scott Young; Charlie Lyons (Chairman/CEO), Pierre Lacroix (Executive Vice President/General Manager), Marc Crawford (Head Coach), Joel Quenneville, Jacques Cloutier (Assistant Coaches), Francois Giguere (Assistant General Manager), Michel Goulet (Director of Player Personnel), Dave Draper (Chief Scout), Jean Martineau (Director of Public Relations), Pat Karns (Trainer), Matthew Sokolowski (Assistant Trainer), Rob McLean (Equipment Manager), Mike Kramer, Brock Gibbins (Assistant Equipment Managers), Skip Allen (Strength and Conditioning Coach), Paul Fixter (Video Coordinator), Leo Vyssokov (Massage Therapist).

Scores: *June 4, at Colorado — Colorado 3, Florida 1; June 6, at Colorado — Colorado 8, Florida 1; June 8, at Florida — Colorado 3, Florida 2; June 10, at Florida — Colorado 1, Florida 0.*

1994-95 — New Jersey Devils — Tommy Albelin, Martin Brodeur, Neal Broten, Sergei Brylin, Bob Carpenter, Shawn Chambers, Tom Chorske, Danton Cole, Ken Daneyko, Kevin Dean, Jim Dowd, Bruce Driver, Bill Guerin, Bobby Holik, Claude Lemieux, John MacLean, Chris McAlpine, Randy McKay, Scott Niedermayer, Mike Peluso, Stephane Richer, Brian Rolston, Scott Stevens (Captain), Chris Terreri, Valeri Zelepukin; Dr. John J. McMullen (Owner/Chairman), Peter S. McMullen (Owner), Lou Lamoriello (President/General Manager), Jacques Lemaire (Head Coach), Jacques Caron (Goaltender Coach), Dennis Gendron, Larry Robinson (Assistant Coaches), Robbie Ftorek (Albany (AHL) - Coach), Alex Abasto (Assistant Equipment Manager), Bob Huddleston (Massage Therapist), David Nichols (Equipment Manager), Ted Schuch (Medical Trainer), Michael Vasalani (Strength and Conditioning Coach), David Conte (Director of Scouting), Milt Fisher, Claude Carrier, Dan Labraaten, Marcel Pronovost (Scouts).

Scores: *June 17, at Detroit — New Jersey 2, Detroit 1; June 20, at Detroit — New Jersey 4, Detroit 2; June 22, at New Jersey — New Jersey 5, Detroit 2; June 24, at New Jersey — New Jersey 5, Detroit 2.*

1993-94 — New York Rangers — Mark Messier (Captain), Brian Leetch, Kevin Lowe, Adam Graves, Steve Larmer, Glenn Anderson, Jeff Beukeboom, Greg Gilbert, Glenn Healy, Mike Hudson, Alexander Karpovtsev, Joe Kocur, Alex Kovalev, Nick Kypreos, Doug Lidster, Stephane Matteau, Craig MacTavish, Sergei Nemchinov, Brian Noonan, Esa Tikkanen, Mike Richter, Jay Wells, Sergei Zubov, Ed Olczyk, Mike Hartman; Neil Smith (President/General Manager/Governor), Robert Gutkowski, Stanley Jaffe, Kenneth Munoz (Governors), Larry Pleau (Assistant General Manager), Mike Keenan (Head Coach), Colin Campbell (Associate Coach), Dick Todd (Assistant Coach), Matthew Loughren (Manager - Team Operations), Barry Watkins (Director - Communications), Christer Rockstrom, Tony Feltrin, Martin Madden, Herb Hammond, Darwin Bennett (Scouts), Dave Smith, Joe Murphy, Mike Folga, Bruce Lifrieri (Trainers).

Scores: *May 31, at New York — Vancouver 3, NY Rangers 2; June 2, at New York — NY Rangers 3, Vancouver 1; June 4, at Vancouver — NY Rangers 5, Vancouver 1; June 7, at Vancouver — NY Rangers 4, Vancouver 2; June 9, at New York — Vancouver 6, at NY Rangers 3; June 11, at Vancouver — Vancouver 4, NY Rangers 1; June 14, at New York — NY Rangers 3, Vancouver 2.*

1992-93 — Montreal Canadiens — Guy Carbonneau (Captain), Patrick Roy, Andre Racicot, Rob Ramage, Kirk Muller, Mike Keane, Kevin Haller, Paul DiPietro, John LeClair, Denis Savard, Benoit Brunet, Brian Bellows, Lyle Odelein, Vincent Damphousse, Gary Leeman, Mathieu Schneider, Eric Desjardins, Jesse Belanger, Ed Ronan, Mario Roberge, Donald Dufresne, Todd Ewen, Sean Hill, Patrice Brisebois, Gilbert Dionne, Stephan Lebeau, J.J. Daigneault; Ronald Corey (President), Serge Savard (Managing Director/Vice President - Hockey), Jacques Demers (Head Coach), Jacques Laperriere, Charles Thiffault (Assistant Coaches), Francois Allaire (Goaltending Instructor), Jean Béliveau (Senior Vice President - Corporate Affairs), Jacques Lemaire (Assistant to the Managing Director), André Boudrias (Assistant to the Managing Director/Director of Scouting), Gaeten Lefebvre (Athletic Trainer), John Shipman (Assistant to the Athletic Trainer), Eddy Palchak (Equipment Manager), Pierre Gervais, Robert Boulanger (Assistants to the Equipment Manager).

Scores: *June 1, at Montreal — Los Angeles 4, Montreal 1; June 3, at Montreal — Montreal 3, Los Angeles 2; June 5, at Los Angeles — Montreal 4, Los Angeles 3; June 7, at Los Angeles — Montreal 3, Los Angeles 2; June 9, at Montreal — Montreal 4, Los Angeles 1.*

1991-92 — Pittsburgh Penguins — Mario Lemieux (Captain), Ron Francis, Bryan Trottier, Kevin Stevens, Bob Errey, Phil Bourque, Troy Loney, Rick Tocchet, Joe Mullen, Jaromir Jagr, Jiri Hrdina, Shawn McEachern, Ulf Samuelsson, Kjell Samuelsson, Larry Murphy, Gordie Roberts, Jim Paek, Paul Stanton, Tom Barrasso, Ken Wregget, Jay Caufield, Jamie Leach, Wendell Young, Grant Jennings, Peter Taglianetti, Jock Callander, Dave Michayluk, Mike Needham, Jeff Chychrun, Ken Priestlay, Jeff Daniels; Morris Belzberg, Howard Baldwin, Thomas Ruta (Owners), Donn Patton (Executive

Vice President/Chief Financial Officer), Paul Martha (Executive Vice President/General Counsel), Craig Patrick (Executive Vice President/General Manager), Bob Johnson (Head Coach), Scotty Bowman (Director of Player Development/Coach), Barry Smith, Rick Kehoe, Pierre McGuire, Gilles Meloche, Rick Paterson (Assistant Coaches), Steve Latin (Equipment Manager), Skip Thayer (Trainer), John Welday (Strength and Conditioning Coach), Greg Malone, Les Binkley, Charlie Hodge, John Gill, Ralph Cox (Scouts).

Scores: *May 26, at Pittsburgh — Pittsburgh 5, Chicago 4; May 28, at Pittsburgh — Pittsburgh 3, Chicago 1; May 30, at Chicago — Pittsburgh 1, Chicago 0; June 1, at Chicago — Pittsburgh 6, Chicago 5.*

1990-91 — Pittsburgh Penguins — Mario Lemieux (Captain), Paul Coffey, Randy Hillier, Bob Errey, Tom Barrasso, Phil Bourque, Jay Caufield, Ron Francis, Randy Gilhen, Jiri Hrdina, Jaromir Jagr, Grant Jennings, Troy Loney, Joe Mullen, Larry Murphy, Jim Paek, Frank Pietrangelo, Barry Pederson, Mark Recchi, Gordie Roberts, Ulf Samuelsson, Paul Stanton, Kevin Stevens, Peter Taglianetti, Bryan Trottier, Scott Young, Wendell Young; Edward J. DeBartolo Sr. (Owner), Marie D. DeBartolo York (President), Paul Martha (Vice President/General Counsel), Craig Patrick (General Manager), Scotty Bowman (Director of Player Development and Recruitment), Bob Johnson (Head Coach), Rick Kehoe, Rick Paterson, Barry Smith (Assistant Coaches), Gilles Meloche (Goaltending Coach/Scout), Steve Latin (Equipment Manager), Skip Thayer (Trainer), John Welday (Strength and Conditioning Coach), Greg Malone (Scout).

Scores: *May 15, at Pittsburgh — Minnesota 5, Pittsburgh 4; May 17, at Pittsburgh — Pittsburgh 4, Minnesota 1; May 19, at Minnesota — Minnesota 3, Pittsburgh 1; May 21, at Minnesota — Pittsburgh 5, Minnesota 3; May 23, at Pittsburgh — Pittsburgh 6, Minnesota 4; May 25, at Minnesota — Pittsburgh 8, Minnesota 0.*

1989-90 — Edmonton Oilers — Mark Messier (Captain), Jari Kurri, Kevin Lowe, Steve Smith, Jeff Beukeboom, Mark Lamb, Joe Murphy, Glenn Anderson, Adam Graves, Craig MacTavish, Kelly Buchberger, Craig Simpson, Martin Gelinas, Randy Gregg, Charlie Huddy, Geoff Smith, Reijo Ruotsalainen, Craig Muni, Bill Ranford, Dave Brown, Pokey Reddick, Petr Klima, Esa Tikkanen, Grant Fuhr; Peter Pocklington (Owner), Glen Sather (President/General Manager), John Muckler (Head Coach), Ted Green (Co-Coach), Ron Low (Assistant Coach), Bruce MacGregor (Assistant General Manager), Barry Fraser (Director of Player Personnel), Bill Tuele (Director of Public Relations), Werner Baum (Vice President), Dr. Gordon Cameron (Medical Chief of Staff), Dr. David Reid (Team Physician), Ken Lowe (Athletic Therapist), Barrie Stafford (Athletic Trainer), Stuart Poirier (Massage Therapist), Lyle Kulchisky (Assistant Trainer), John Blackwell (Cape Breton (AHL) - Director of Operations), Ace Bailey, Ed Chadwick, Lorne Davis, Harry Howell, Albert Reeves, Matti Vaisanen (Scouts).

Scores: *May 15, at Boston — Edmonton 3, Boston 2; May 18, at Boston — Edmonton 7, Boston 2; May 20, at Edmonton — Boston 2, Edmonton 1; May 22, at Edmonton — Edmonton 5, Boston 1; May 24, at Boston — Edmonton 4, Boston 1.*

1988-89 — Calgary Flames — Lanny McDonald (Co- Captain), Jim Peplinski (Co-Captain), Tim Hunter, Mike Vernon, Rick Wamsley, Al MacInnis, Brad McCrimmon, Dana Murzyn, Ric Nattress, Joe Mullen, Gary Roberts, Colin Patterson, Hakan Loob, Theoren Fleury, Jiri Hrdina, Gary Suter, Mark Hunter, Joe Nieuwendyk, Brian MacLellan, Joel Otto, Jamie Macoun, Doug Gilmour, Rob Ramage; Norman Green, Harley Hotchkiss, Norman Kwong, Sonia Scurfield, B.J. Seaman, D.K. Seaman (Owners), Cliff Fletcher (President/General Manager), Al MacNeil (Assistant General Manager), Al Coates (Assistant to the President), Terry Crisp (Head Coach), Doug Risebrough, Tom Watt (Assistant Coaches), Glenn Hall (Goaltending Consultant), Jim Murray (Trainer), Al Murray (Assistant Trainer), Bob Stewart (Equipment Manager).

Scores: *May 14, at Calgary — Calgary 3, Montreal 2; May 17, at Calgary— Montreal 4, Calgary 2; May 19, at Montreal — Montreal 4, Calgary 3; May 21, at Montreal — Calgary 4, Montreal 2; May 23, at Calgary — Calgary 3, Montreal 2; May 25, at Montreal — Calgary 4, Montreal 2.*

1987-88 — Edmonton Oilers — Wayne Gretzky (Captain), Keith Acton, Glenn Anderson, Jeff Beukeboom, Geoff Courtnall, Grant Fuhr, Randy Gregg, Dave Hannan, Charlie Huddy, Mike Krushelnyski, Jari Kurri, Normand Lacombe, Kevin Lowe, Craig MacTavish, Kevin McClelland, Marty McSorley, Mark Messier, Craig Muni, Bill Ranford, Craig Simpson, Steve Smith, Esa Tikkanen; Peter Pocklington (Owner), Glen Sather (General Manager/Coach), John Muckler (Co-Coach), Ted Green (Assistant Coach), Bruce MacGregor (Assistant General Manager), Barry Fraser (Director of Player Personnel), Bill Tuele (Director of Public Relations), Dr. Gordon Cameron (Team Doctor), Peter Millar (Athletic Therapist), Juergen Merz (Massage Therapist), Barrie Stafford (Trainer), Lyle Kulchisky (Assistant Trainer).

Scores: *May 18, at Edmonton — Edmonton 2, Boston 1; May 20, at Edmonton — Edmonton 4, Boston 2; May 22, at Boston — Edmonton 6, Boston 3; May 24, at Boston — Boston 3, Edmonton 3 (suspended due to power failure); May 26, at Edmonton — Edmonton 6, Boston 3.*

1986-87 — Edmonton Oilers — Wayne Gretzky (Captain), Glenn Anderson, Jeff Beukeboom, Kelly Buchberger, Paul Coffey, Grant Fuhr, Randy Gregg, Charlie Huddy, Dave Hunter, Mike Krushelnyski, Jari Kurri, Moe Lemay, Kevin Lowe, Craig MacTavish, Kevin McClelland, Marty McSorley, Mark Messier, Andy Moog, Craig Muni, Kent Nilsson, Jaroslav Pouzar, Reijo Ruotsalainen, Steve Smith, Esa Tikkanen; Peter Pocklington (Owner), Glen Sather (General Manager/Coach), Bruce MacGregor (Assistant General Manager), John Muckler (Co-Coach), Ted Green, Ron Low (Assistant Coaches), Barry Fraser (Director of Player Personnel), Garnet Bailey, Ed Chadwick, Lorne Davis, Matti Vaisanen (Scouts), Peter Millar (Athletic Therapist), Juergen Merz (Massage Therapist), Dr. Gordon Cameron (Team Doctor), Barrie Stafford (Trainer), Lyle Kulchisky (Assistant Trainer).

Scores: *May 17, at Edmonton — Edmonton 4, Philadelphia 2; May 20, at Edmonton — Edmonton 3, Philadelphia 2; May 22, at Philadelphia — Philadelphia 5, Edmonton 3; May 24, at Philadelphia — Edmonton 4, Philadelphia 1; May 26, at Edmonton — Philadelphia 4, Edmonton 3; May 28, at Philadelphia — Philadelphia 3, Edmonton 2; May 31, at Edmonton — Edmonton 3, Philadelphia 1.*

1985-86 — Montreal Canadiens — Bob Gainey (Captain), Doug Soetaert, Patrick Roy, Rick Green, David Maley, Ryan Walter, Serge Boisvert, Mario Tremblay, Bobby Smith, Craig Ludwig, Tom Kurvers, Kjell Dahlin, Larry Robinson, Guy Carbonneau, Chris Chelios, Petr Svoboda, Mats Naslund, Lucien DeBlois, Steve Rooney, Gaston Gingras, Mike Lalor, Chris Nilan, John Kordic, Claude Lemieux, Mike McPhee, Brian Skrudland, Stephane Richer; Ronald Corey (President), Serge Savard (General Manager), Jean Perron (Coach), Jacques Laperrière (Assistant Coach), Jean Béliveau, Francois-Xavier Seigneur, Fred Steer (Vice Presidents), Jacques Lemaire, André Boudrias (Assistant General Managers), Claude Ruel (Player Development), Yves Belanger (Athletic Therapist), Gaetan Lefebvre (Assistant Athletic Therapist), Eddy Palchak (Trainer), Sylvain Toupin (Assistant Trainer).

Scores: *May 16, at Calgary — Calgary 5, Montreal 2; May 18, at Calgary — Montreal 3, Calgary 2; May 20, at Montreal — Montreal 5, Calgary 3; May 22, at Montreal — Montreal 1, Calgary 0; May 24, at Calgary — Montreal 4, Calgary 3.*

1984-85 — Edmonton Oilers — Wayne Gretzky (Captain), Glenn Anderson, Billy Carroll, Paul Coffey, Lee Fogolin Jr., Grant Fuhr, Randy Gregg, Charlie Huddy, Pat Hughes, Dave Hunter, Don Jackson, Mike Krushelnyski, Jari Kurri, Willy Lindstrom, Kevin Lowe, Dave Lumley, Kevin McClelland, Larry Melnyk, Mark Messier, Andy Moog, Mark Napier, Jaroslav Pouzar, Dave Semenko, Esa Tikkanen; Peter Pocklington (Owner), Glen Sather (General Manager/Coach), Bruce MacGregor (Assistant General Manager), John Muckler, Ted Green (Assistant Coaches), Barry Fraser (Director of Player Personnel/Chief Scout), Garnet Bailey, Ed Chadwick, Lorne Davis, Matti Vaisanen (Scouts), Peter Millar (Athletic Therapist), Dr. Gordon Cameron (Team Doctor), Barrie Stafford (Trainer), Lyle Kulchisky (Assistant Trainer).

Scores: *May 21, at Philadelphia — Philadelphia 4, Edmonton 1; May 23, at Philadelphia — Edmonton 3, Philadelphia 1; May 25, at Edmonton — Edmonton 4, Philadelphia 3; May 28, at Edmonton — Edmonton 5, Philadelphia 3; May 30, at Edmonton — Edmonton 8, Philadelphia 3.*

1983-84 — Edmonton Oilers — Wayne Gretzky (Captain), Glenn Anderson, Paul Coffey, Pat Conacher, Lee Fogolin Jr., Grant Fuhr, Randy Gregg, Charlie Huddy, Pat Hughes, Dave Hunter, Don Jackson, Jari Kurri, Willy Lindstrom, Ken Linseman, Kevin Lowe, Dave Lumley, Kevin McClelland, Mark Messier, Andy Moog, Jaroslav Pouzar, Dave Semenko; Peter Pocklington (Owner), Glen Sather (General Manager/Coach), Bruce MacGregor (Assistant General Manager), John Muckler, Ted Green (Assistant Coaches), Barry Fraser (Director of Player Personnel/Chief Scout), Pete Millar (Athletic Therapist), Barrie Stafford (Trainer), Lyle Kulchisky (Assistant Trainer).

Scores: *May 10, at New York — Edmonton 1, NY Islanders 0; May 12, at New York — NY Islanders 6, Edmonton 1; May 15, at Edmonton — Edmonton 7, NY Islanders 2; May 17, at Edmonton — Edmonton 7, NY Islanders 2; May 19, at Edmonton — Edmonton 5, NY Islanders 2.*

1982-83 — New York Islanders — Denis Potvin (Captain), Mike Bossy, Bob Bourne, Paul Boutilier, Billy Carroll, Greg Gilbert, Clark Gillies, Butch Goring, Mats Hallin, Tomas Jonsson, Anders Kallur, Gord Lane, Dave Langevin, Mike McEwen, Roland Melanson, Wayne Merrick, Ken Morrow, Bob Nystrom, Stefan Persson, Billy Smith, Brent Sutter, Duane Sutter, John Tonelli, Bryan Trottier; Bill Torrey (President/General Manager), John Pickett Jr. (Chairman), Gerry Ehman (Assistant General Manager/Director of Scouting), Al Arbour (Coach), Lorne Henning (Assistant Coach), Ron Waske (Trainer), Jim Pickard (Assistant Trainer).

Scores: *May 10, at Edmonton — NY Islanders 2, Edmonton 0; May 12, at Edmonton — NY Islanders 6, Edmonton 3; May 14, at New York — NY Islanders 5, Edmonton 1; May 17, at New York — NY Islanders 4, Edmonton 2*

1981-82 — New York Islanders — Denis Potvin (Captain), Mike Bossy, Bob Bourne, Billy Carroll, Greg Gilbert, Clark Gillies, Butch Goring, Tomas Jonsson, Anders Kallur, Gord Lane, Dave Langevin, Hector Marini, Mike McEwen, Roland Melanson, Wayne Merrick, Ken Morrow, Bob Nystrom, Stefan Persson, Billy Smith, Brent Sutter, Duane Sutter, John Tonelli, Bryan Trottier; Bill Torrey (President/General Manager), John Pickett Jr. (Chairman), Jim Devellano (Assistant General Manager/Director of Scouting), Al Arbour (Coach), Lorne Henning (Assistant Coach), Gerry Ehman (Head Scout), Ron Waske (Trainer), Jim Pickard (Assistant Trainer).

Scores: *May 8, at New York — NY Islanders 6, Vancouver 5; May 11, at New York — NY Islanders 6, Vancouver 4; May 13, at Vancouver — NY Islanders 3, Vancouver 0; May 16, at Vancouver — NY Islanders 3, Vancouver 1*

1980-81 — New York Islanders — Denis Potvin (Captain), Mike Bossy, Bob Bourne, Billy Carroll, Clark Gillies, Butch Goring, Garry Howatt, Anders Kallur, Gord Lane, Dave Langevin, Bob Lorimer, Hector Marini, Mike McEwen, Roland Melanson, Wayne Merrick, Ken Morrow, Bob Nystrom, Stefan Persson, Jean Potvin, Billy Smith, Duane Sutter, John Tonelli, Bryan Trottier; Bill Torrey (President/General Manager), John Pickett Jr. (Chairman), Al Arbour (Coach), Lorne Henning (Player/Assistant Coach), Jim Devellano (Chief Scout), Gerry Ehman, Mario Saraceno, Harry Boyd (Scouts), Ron Waske (Trainer), Jim Pickard (Assistant Trainer).

Scores: *May 12, at New York — NY Islanders 6, Minnesota 3; May 14, at New York — NY Islanders 6, Minnesota 3; May 17, at Minnesota — NY Islanders 7, Minnesota 5; May 19, at Minnesota— Minnesota 4, NY Islanders 2; May 21, at New York — NY Islanders 5, Minnesota 1.*

1979-80 — New York Islanders — Denis Potvin (Captain), Mike Bossy, Bob Bourne, Clark Gillies, Butch Goring, Lorne Henning, Garry Howatt, Anders Kallur, Gord Lane, Dave Langevin, Bob Lorimer, Alex McKendry, Wayne Merrick, Ken Morrow, Bob Nystrom, Stefan Persson, Jean Potvin, Glenn Resch, Billy Smith, Duane Sutter, Steve Tambellini, John Tonelli, Bryan Trottier; Bill Torrey (President/General Manager), John Pickett Jr. (Chairman), Al Arbour (Coach), Billy MacMillan (Assistant Coach), Jim Devellano (Chief Scout), Gerry Ehman, Mario Saraceno, Harry Boyd (Scouts), Ron Waske (Trainer), Jim Pickard (Assistant Trainer).

Scores: *May 13, at Philadelphia — NY Islanders 4, Philadelphia 3; May 15, at Philadelphia — Philadelphia 8, NY Islanders 3; May 17, at New York — NY Islanders 6, Philadelphia 2; May 19, at New York — NY Islanders 5, Philadelphia 2; May 22, at Philadelphia — Philadelphia 6, NY Islanders 3; May 24, at New York — NY Islanders 5, Philadelphia 4.*

1978-79 — Montreal Canadiens — Yvan Cournoyer (Captain), Guy Lafleur, Ken Dryden, Rick Chartraw, Brian Engblom, Bob Gainey, Mario Tremblay, Guy Lapointe, Doug Risebrough, Réjean Houle, Pat Hughes, Michel Larocque, Doug Jarvis, Yvon Lambert, Pierre Larouche, Gilles Lupien, Rod Langway, Jacques Lemaire, Pierre Mondou, Larry Robinson, Mark Napier, Serge Savard, Steve Shutt, Cam Connor, Richard Sévigny; Jacques Courtois (President), Sam Pollock (Director), Irving Grundman (Vice President/Managing Director), Jean Beliveau (Vice President - Corporate Affairs), Scotty Bowman (Coach), Claude Ruel (Director of Player Development), Al MacNeil (Director of Player Personnel), Morgan McCammon (Director), Ron Caron (Director of Recruitment), Eddy Palchak (Trainer), Pierre Meilleur (Assistant Trainer).

Scores: *May 13, at Montreal — NY Rangers 4, Montreal 1; May 15, at Montreal — Montreal 6, NY Rangers 2; May 17, at New York — Montreal 4, NY Rangers 1; May 19, at New York — Montreal 4, NY Rangers 3; May 21, at Montreal — Montreal 4, NY Rangers 1.*

1977-78 — Montreal Canadiens — Yvan Cournoyer (Captain), Guy Lafleur, Ken Dryden, Michel Larocque, Rick Chartraw, Réjean Houle, Pierre Larouche, Brian Engblom, Yvon Lambert, Jacques Lemaire, Bob Gainey, Guy Lapointe, Doug Jarvis, Gilles Lupien, Pierre Mondou, Larry Robinson, Bill Nyrop, Murray Wilson, Serge Savard, Steve Shutt, Mario Tremblay, Pierre Bouchard, Doug Risebrough; Jacques Courtois (President), Sam Pollock (Vice President/General Manager), Jean Beliveau (Vice President/Director of Corporate Relations), Scotty Bowman (Coach), Peter Bronfman, Edward Bronfman (Directors), Al MacNeil (Director of Player Development), Eddy Palchak (Trainer), Pierre Meilleur (Assistant Trainer), Claude Ruel (Director of Player Development), Floyd Curry, Ron Caron (Assistant General Managers).

Scores: *May 13, at Montreal — Montreal 4, Boston 1; May 16, at Montreal — Montreal 3, Boston 2; May 18, at Boston — Boston 4, Montreal 0; May 21, at Boston — Boston 4, Montreal 3; May 23, at Montreal — Montreal 4, Boston 1; May 25, at Boston — Montreal 4, Boston 1.*

1976-77 — Montreal Canadiens — Yvan Cournoyer (Captain), Larry Robinson, Guy Lafleur, Pierre Bouchard, Rejean Houle, Yvon Lambert, Bob Gainey, Jacques Lemaire, Guy Lapointe, Ken Dryden, Rick Chartraw, Bill Nyrop, Michel Larocque, Pierre Mondou, Serge Savard, Steve Shutt, Mario Tremblay, Murray Wilson, Doug Jarvis, Mike Polich, Jimmy Roberts, Pete Mahovlich, Doug Risebrough, Jacques Courtois

(President), Sam Pollock (Vice President/General Manager), Jean Beliveau (Vice President/Director of Corporate Relations), Scotty Bowman (Coach), Peter Bronfman, Edward Bronfman (Directors), Claude Ruel (Director of Player Development), Floyd Curry, Ron Caron (Assistant General Managers), Pierre Meilleur (Assistant Trainer), Eddy Palchak (Trainer).

Scores: *May 7, at Montreal — Montreal 7, Boston 3; May 10, at Montreal — Montreal 3, Boston 0; May 12, at Boston — Montreal 4, Boston 2; May 14, at Boston — Montreal 2, Boston 1.*

1975-76 — Montreal Canadiens — Yvan Cournoyer (Captain), Bob Gainey, Larry Robinson, Pierre Bouchard, Rick Chartraw, Ken Dryden, Pete Mahovlich, Guy Lafleur, Yvon Lambert, Michel Larocque, Serge Savard, Doug Jarvis, Jacques Lemaire, Guy Lapointe, Jimmy Roberts, Doug Risebrough, Steve Shutt, Murray Wilson, Mario Tremblay, Bill Nyrop; Jacques Courtois (President), Jean Beliveau (Vice President), Peter Bronfman (Chairman), Edward Bronfman (Director), Sam Pollock (Vice President/General Manager), Scotty Bowman (Coach), Eddy Palchak (Trainer), Pierre Meilleur (Assistant Trainer), Claude Ruel (Director of Player Development).

Scores: *May 9, at Montreal — Montreal 4, Philadelphia 3; May 11, at Montreal — Montreal 2, Philadelphia 1; May 13, at Philadelphia — Montreal 3, Philadelphia 2; May 16, at Philadelphia — Montreal 5, Philadelphia 3.*

1974-75 — Philadelphia Flyers — Bobby Clarke (Captain), Bernie Parent, Bobby Taylor, Wayne Stephenson, Ed Van Impe, Don Saleski, Tom Bladon, Larry Goodenough, Bill Barber, Gary Dornhoefer, Dave Schultz, Joe Watson, Ross Lonsberry, André Dupont, Terry Crisp, Orest Kindrachuk, Bill Clement, Bob Kelly, Rick MacLeish, Jimmy Watson, Reggie Leach, Ted Harris; Ed Snider (Chairman), Joe Scott (President), Eugene Dixon Jr. (Vice Chairman), Fred Shero (Coach), Keith Allen (Vice President/General Manager), Lou Scheinfeld (Vice President), Mike Nykoluk (Assistant Coach), Marcel Pelletier (Player Personnel Director), Barry Ashbee (Assistant Coach), Frank Lewis (Trainer), Jim McKenzie (Assistant Trainer).

Scores: *May 15, at Philadelphia — Philadelphia 4, Buffalo 1; May 18, at Philadelphia — Philadelphia 2, Buffalo 1; May 20, at Buffalo — Buffalo 5, Philadelphia 4; May 22, at Buffalo — Buffalo 4, Philadelphia 2; May 25, at Philadelphia — Philadelphia 5, Buffalo 1; May 27, at Buffalo — Philadelphia 2, Buffalo 0.*

1973-74 — Philadelphia Flyers — Bobby Clarke (Captain), Bernie Parent, Bobby Taylor, Bill Clement, Ross Lonsberry, Bill Barber, Orest Kindrachuk, Ed Van Impe, Don Saleski, Gary Dornhoefer, Barry Ashbee, Jimmy Watson, Dave Schultz, André Dupont, Bruce Cowick, Rick MacLeish, Terry Crisp, Bill Flett, Simon Nolet, Joe Watson, Bob Kelly, Tom Bladon; Ed Snider (Chairman), Joe Scott (President), Eugene Dixon Jr. (Vice Chairman), Fred Shero (Coach), Keith Allen (Vice President/General Manager), Mike Nykoluk (Assistant Coach), Marcel Pelletier (Player Personnel Director), Frank Lewis (Trainer), Jim McKenzie (Assistant Trainer).

Scores: *May 7, at Boston — Boston 3, Philadelphia 2; May 9, at Boston — Philadelphia 3, Boston 2; May 12, at Philadelphia — Philadelphia 4, Boston 1; May 14, at Philadelphia — Philadelphia 4, Boston 2; May 16, at Boston — Boston 5, Philadelphia 1; May 19, at Philadelphia — Philadelphia 1, Boston 0.*

1972-73 — Montreal Canadiens — Henri Richard (Captain), Jacques Laperrière, Ken Dryden, Yvan Cournoyer, Jacques Lemaire, Marc Tardif, Serge Savard, Pete Mahovlich, Guy Lapointe, Réjean Houle, Claude Larose, Pierre Bouchard, Frank Mahovlich, Jimmy Roberts, Chuck Lefley, Guy Lafleur, Bob Murdoch, Michel Plasse, Murray Wilson, Larry Robinson, Steve Shutt; Jacques Courtois (President), Jean Beliveau (Vice President), Peter Bronfman (Chairman), Sam Pollock (Vice President/General Manager), Edward Bronfman (Executive Director), Scotty Bowman (Coach), Bob Williams (Trainer).

Scores: *April 29, at Montreal — Montreal 8, Chicago 3; May 1, at Montreal — Montreal 4, Chicago 1; May 3, at Chicago — Chicago 7, Montreal 4; May 6, at Chicago — Montreal 4, Chicago 0; May 8, at Montreal — Chicago 8, Montreal 7; May 10, at Chicago — Montreal 6, Chicago 4.*

1971-72 — Boston Bruins — Bobby Orr, Gerry Cheevers, Eddie Johnston, Dallas Smith, Derek Sanderson, Carol Vadnais, Phil Esposito, Fred Stanfield, Don Awrey, Ted Green, Ken Hodge, John Bucyk, Wayne Cashman, John McKenzie, Ed Westfall, Mike Walton, Garnet Bailey, Don Marcotte; Weston Adams (Chairman), Weston Adams Jr. (President), Shelby Davis (Vice President), Charles Mulcahy (Junior Vice President/General Counsel), Eddie Powers (Vice President/Treasurer), Milt Schmidt (General Manager), Tom Johnson (Coach), Dan Canney (Trainer), John Forristall (Assistant Trainer).

Scores: *April 30, at Boston — Boston 6, NY Rangers 5; May 2, at Boston — Boston 2, NY Rangers 1; May 4, at New York — NY Rangers 5, Boston 2; May 7, at New York — Boston 3, NY Rangers 2; May 9, at Boston — NY Rangers 3, Boston 2; May 11, at New York — Boston 3, NY Rangers 0.*

1970-71 — Montreal Canadiens — Jean Béliveau (Captain), Pierre Bouchard, Yvan Cournoyer, John Ferguson, Jacques Laperrière, Terry Harper, Réjean Houle, Guy Lapointe, Claude Larose, Marc Tardif, Chuck Lefley, Jacques Lemaire, Frank Mahovlich, Henri Richard, Phil Roberto, Pete Mahovlich, Bob Murdoch, Serge Savard (37GP – injured), Bobby Sheehan, Leon Rochefort, J.C. Tremblay, Ken Dryden, Rogie Vachon; David Molson (President), William Molson, Peter Molson (Vice Presidents), Sam Pollock (Vice President/General Manager), Ron Caron (Assistant General Manager), Al MacNeil (Coach), Yves Belanger (Trainer), Phil Langlois, Eddie Palchak (Assistant Trainers).

Scores: *May 4, at Chicago — Chicago 2, Montreal 1; May 6, at Chicago — Chicago 5, Montreal 3; May 9, at Montreal — Montreal 4, Chicago 2; May 11, at Montreal — Montreal 5, Chicago 2; May 13, at Chicago — Chicago 2, Montreal 0; May 16, at Montreal — Montreal 4, Chicago 3; May 18, at Chicago — Montreal 3, Chicago 2.*

1969-70 — Boston Bruins — Don Awrey, John Bucyk, Garnet Bailey, Wayne Carleton, Wayne Cashman, Gary Doak, Phil Esposito, Ted Green, Ken Hodge, Bobby Orr, Don Marcotte, John McKenzie, Derek Sanderson, Dallas Smith, Rick Smith, Bill Speer, Fred Stanfield, Ed Westfall, Gerry Cheevers, Eddie Johnston, John Adams, Jim Lorentz, Ron Murphy, Bill Lesuk, Ivan Boldirev, Danny Schock; Weston Adams Sr. (Chairman), Weston Adams Jr. (President), Charles Mulcahy, Eddie Powers, Shelby Davis (Vice Presidents), Harry Sinden (Coach), Milt Schmidt (General Manager), Tom Johnson (Assistant General Manager), Dan Canney (Trainer), John Forristall (Assistant Trainer).

Scores: *May 3, at St. Louis — Boston 6, St. Louis 1; May 5, at St. Louis — Boston 6, St. Louis 2; May 7, at Boston — Boston 4, St. Louis 1; May 10, at Boston — Boston 4, St. Louis 3.*

1968-69 — Montreal Canadiens — Jean Béliveau (Captain), Ralph Backstrom, Jacques Lemaire, Dick Duff, Christian Bordeleau, Mickey Redmond, Yvan Cournoyer, Henri Richard, Bobby Rousseau, John Ferguson, Serge Savard, Terry Harper, Gilles Tremblay, Ted Harris, J.C. Tremblay, Larry Hillman, Jacques Laperrière, Claude Provost, Tony Esposito, Rogie Vachon, Gump Worsley; David Molson (President), William Molson, Peter Molson (Vice Presidents), Sam Pollock (Vice President/General Manager), Claude Ruel (Coach), Larry Aubut (Trainer), Eddie Palchak (Assistant Trainer).

Scores: *April 27, at Montreal — Montreal 3, St. Louis 1; April 29, at Montreal — Montreal 3, St. Louis 1; May 1, at St. Louis — Montreal 4, St. Louis 0; May 4, at St. Louis — Montreal 2, St. Louis 1.*

1967-68 — Montreal Canadiens — Jean Béliveau (Captain), Ralph Backstrom, Yvan Cournoyer, Dick Duff, John Ferguson, Danny Grant, Terry Harper, Ted Harris, Serge Savard, Jacques Laperrière, Claude Larose, Jacques Lemaire, Claude Provost, Mickey Redmond, Henri Richard, Bobby Rousseau, Gilles Tremblay, J.C. Tremblay, Carol Vadnais, Rogie Vachon, Ernie Wakely, Gump Worsley; Hartland Molson (Chairman), David Molson (President), Sam Pollock (Vice President/General Manager), Toe Blake (Coach), Larry Aubut (Trainer), Eddie Palchak (Assistant Trainer).

Scores: *May 5, at St. Louis — Montreal 3, St. Louis 2; May 7, at St. Louis — Montreal 1, St. Louis 0; May 9, at Montreal — Montreal 4, St. Louis 3; May 11, at Montreal — Montreal 3, St. Louis 2.*

1966-67 — Toronto Maple Leafs — George Armstrong (Captain), Bob Baun, Johnny Bower, Brian Conacher, Ron Ellis, Aut Erickson, Larry Hillman, Tim Horton, Red Kelly, Larry Jeffrey, Dave Keon, Frank Mahovlich, Milan Marcetta, Jim Pappin, Marcel Pronovost, Bob Pulford, Terry Sawchuk, Eddie Shack, Allan Stanley, Pete Stemkowski, Mike Walton; Stafford Smythe (President), Harold Ballard (Executive Vice President), John Bassett (Chairman), Punch Imlach (General Manager/Coach), King Clancy (Assistant Coach/Assistant General Manager), Bob Davidson (Chief Scout), John Anderson (Business Manager), Bob Haggert (Trainer), Tom Nayler (Assistant Trainer), Karl Elieff (Physiotherapist), Richard Smythe (Mascot).

Scores: *April 20, at Montreal — Toronto 2, Montreal 6; April 22, at Montreal — Toronto 3, Montreal 0; April 25, at Toronto — Toronto 3, Montreal 2; April 27, at Toronto — Toronto 2, Montreal 6; April 29, at Montreal — Toronto 4, Montreal 1; May 2, at Toronto — Toronto 3, Montreal 1.*

1965-66 — Montreal Canadiens — Jean Béliveau (Captain), Ralph Backstrom, Dave Balon, Yvan Cournoyer, Bobby Rousseau, Dick Duff, John Ferguson, Terry Harper, Ted Harris, Charlie Hodge, Jacques Laperrière, Claude Larose, Noel Price, Claude Provost, Henri Richard, Jimmy Roberts, Leon Rochefort, Jean-Guy Talbot, Gilles Tremblay, J.C. Tremblay, Gump Worsley; Hartland Molson (Chairman), David Molson (President), Sam Pollock (General Manager), Toe Blake (Coach), Andy Galley (Trainer), Larry Aubut (Assistant Trainer).

Scores: *April 24, at Montreal — Detroit 3, Montreal 2; April 26, at Montreal — Detroit 5, Montreal 2; April 28, at Detroit — Montreal 4, Detroit 2; May 1, at Detroit — Montreal 2, Detroit 1; May 3, at Montreal — Montreal 5, Detroit 1; May 5, at Detroit — Montreal 3, Detroit 2.*

1964-65 — Montreal Canadiens — Jean Béliveau (Captain), Ralph Backstrom, Dave Balon, Red Berenson, Yvan Cournoyer, Dick Duff, John Ferguson, Jean Gauthier, Charlie Hodge, Terry Harper, Ted Harris, Jacques Laperrière, Claude Larose, Garry Peters, Noel Picard, Claude Provost, Henri Richard, Jimmy Roberts, Bobby Rousseau, Jean-Guy Talbot, Gilles Tremblay, J.C. Tremblay, Ernie Wakely, Bryan Watson, Gump Worsley; Hartland Molson (Chairman), David Molson (President), Maurice Richard (Assistant to the President), Sam Pollock (General Manager), Toe Blake (Coach), Andy Galley (Trainer), Larry Aubut (Assistant Trainer).

Scores: *April 17, at Montreal — Montreal 3, Chicago 2; April 20, at Montreal — Montreal 2, Chicago 0; April 22, at Chicago — Montreal 1, Chicago 3; April 25, at Chicago — Montreal 1, Chicago 5; April 7, at Montreal — Montreal 6, Chicago 0; April 29, at Chicago — Montreal 1, Chicago 2; May 1, at Montreal — Montreal 4, Chicago 0.*

1963-64 — Toronto Maple Leafs — George Armstrong (Captain), Andy Bathgate, Bob Baun, Johnny Bower, Carl Brewer, Gerry Ehman, Billy Harris, Larry Hillman, Dave Keon, Tim Horton, Red Kelly, Frank Mahovlich, Don McKenney, Jim Pappin, Bob Pulford, Eddie Shack, Don Simmons, Allan Stanley, Ron Stewart, Al Arbour, Ed Litzenberger; Stafford Smythe (President), Harold Ballard (Executive Vice President), John Bassett (Chairman), Punch Imlach (Coach/General Manager), King Clancy (Assistant Coach/Assistant General Manager), Bob Haggert (Trainer), Tom Nayler (Assistant Trainer), Hugh Hoult (Stick Boy).

Scores *April 11, at Toronto — Toronto 3, Detroit 2; April 14, at Toronto — Toronto 3, Detroit 4; April 16, at Detroit — Toronto 3, Detroit 4; April 18, at Detroit — Toronto 4, Detroit 2; April 21, at Toronto — Toronto 1, Detroit 2; April 23, at Detroit — Toronto 4, Detroit 3; April 25, at Toronto — Toronto 4, Detroit 0.*

1962-63 — Toronto Maple Leafs — George Armstrong (Captain), Bob Baun, Johnny Bower, Carl Brewer, Kent Douglas, Dick Duff, Billy Harris, Larry Hillman, Tim Horton, Red Kelly, Dave Keon, Ed Litzenberger, John MacMillan, Frank Mahovlich, Bob Nevin, Bob Pulford, Eddie Shack, Don Simmons, Allan Stanley, Ron Stewart; Stafford Smythe (President), Harold Ballard (Executive Vice President), John Bassett (Chairman), Punch Imlach (Coach/General Manager), King Clancy (Assistant Coach/Assistant General Manager), Bob Haggert (Trainer), Tom Nayler (Assistant Trainer), Hugh Hoult (Stick Boy).

Scores: *April 9, at Toronto — Toronto 4, Detroit 2; April 11, at Toronto — Toronto 4, Detroit 2; April 14, at Detroit — Toronto 2, Detroit 3; April 16, at Detroit — Toronto 4, Detroit 2; April 18, at Toronto — Toronto 3, Detroit 1.*

1961-62 — Toronto Maple Leafs — George Armstrong (Captain), Al Arbour, Bob Baun, Johnny Bower, Carl Brewer, Dick Duff, Billy Harris, Larry Hillman, Dave Keon, Tim Horton, Red Kelly, Ed Litzenberger, John MacMillan, Frank Mahovlich, Bob Nevin, Bert Olmstead, Bob Pulford, Eddie Shack, Allan Stanley, Don Simmons, Ron Stewart; Stafford Smythe (President), Harold Ballard (Executive Vice President), John Bassett (Vice President), Conn Smythe (Chairman), Punch Imlach (Coach/General Manager), King Clancy (Assistant Coach), Bob Davidson (Chief Scout), Bob Haggert (Trainer), Tom Nayler (Assistant Trainer), Hugh Hoult (Stick Boy).

Scores: *April 10, at Toronto — Toronto 4, Chicago 1; April 12, at Toronto — Toronto 3, Chicago 2; April 15, at Chicago — Toronto 0, Chicago 3; April 17, at Chicago — Toronto 1, Chicago 4; April 19, at Toronto —Toronto 8, Chicago 4; April 22, at Chicago — Toronto 2, Chicago 1.*

1960-61 — Chicago Black Hawks — Ed Litzenberger (Captain), Al Arbour, Earl Balfour, Murray Balfour, Glenn Hall, Jack Evans, Roy Edwards, Denis DeJordy, Bill Hay, Wayne Hicks, Reggie Fleming, Wayne Hillman, Bobby Hull, Chico Maki, Ab McDonald, Moose Vasko, Stan Mikita, Ron Murphy, Eric Nesterenko, Pierre Pilote, Tod Sloan, Dollard St. Laurent, Kenny Wharram; Arthur Wirtz (President), Arthur Wirtz Jr. (Vice President), James Norris (Chairman), Tommy Ivan (General Manager), Rudy Pilous (Coach), Nick Garen, Walter Humeniuk (Trainers).

Scores: *April 6, at Chicago — Chicago 3, Detroit 2; April 8, at Detroit — Detroit 3, Chicago 1; April 10, at Chicago — Chicago 3, Detroit 1; April 12, at Detroit — Detroit 2, Chicago 1; April 14, at Chicago — Chicago 6, Detroit 3; April 16, at Detroit — Chicago 5, Detroit 1.*

1959-60 — Montreal Canadiens — Maurice Richard (Captain), Ralph Backstrom, Marcel Bonin, Jean Béliveau, Bernie Geoffrion, Phil Goyette, Doug Harvey, Bill Hicke, Charlie Hodge, Tom Johnson, Albert Langlois, Don Marshall, Dickie Moore, Ab McDonald, Jacques Plante, Henri Richard, André Pronovost, Claude Provost, Bob Turner, Jean-Guy Talbot; Senator Hartland Molson (President), Frank Selke (Managing Director), Ken Reardon (Vice President), Sam Pollock (Personnel Director), Toe Blake (Coach), Hector Dubois, Larry Aubut (Trainers).

Scores: *April 7, at Montreal — Montreal 4, Toronto 2; April 9, at Montreal — Montreal 2, Toronto 1; April 12, at Toronto — Montreal 5, Toronto 2; April 14, at Toronto — Montreal 4, Toronto 0.*

1958-59 — Montreal Canadiens — Maurice Richard (Captain), Ralph Backstrom, Marcel Bonin, Jean Béliveau, Ian Cushenan, Bernie Geoffrion, Charlie Hodge, Phil Goyette, Doug Harvey, Bill Hicke, Tom Johnson, Albert Langlois, Don Marshall, Ab McDonald, Dickie Moore, Jacques Plante, Ken Mosdell, André Pronovost, Claude Provost, Henri Richard, Jean-Guy Talbot, Bob Turner; Senator Hartland Molson (President), Frank Selke (Managing Director), Ken Reardon (Vice President), Sam Pollock (Personnel Director), Toe Blake (Coach), Hector Dubois, Larry Aubut (Trainers).

Scores: *April 9, at Montreal — Montreal 5, Toronto 3; April 11, at Montreal — Montreal 3, Toronto 1; April 14, at Toronto — Toronto 3, Montreal 2; April 16, at Toronto — Montreal 3, Toronto 2; April 18, at Montreal — Montreal 5, Toronto 3.*

1957-58 — Montreal Canadiens — Maurice Richard (Captain), Jean Béliveau, Marcel Bonin, Floyd Curry, Connie Broden, Bernie Geoffrion, Phil Goyette, Doug Harvey, Charlie Hodge, Tom Johnson, Albert Langlois, Don Marshall, Ab McDonald, Gerry McNeil, Dickie Moore, Bert Olmstead, Jacques Plante, André Pronovost, Henri Richard, Claude Provost, Dollard St. Laurent, Jean-Guy Talbot, Bob Turner; Senator Hartland Molson (President), Frank Selke (Managing Director), Ken Reardon (Vice President), Toe Blake (Coach), Hector Dubois, Larry Aubut (Trainers).

Scores: *April 8, at Montreal —Montreal 2, Boston 1; April 10, at Montreal — Boston 5, Montreal 2; April 13, at Boston — Montreal 3, Boston 0; April 15, at Boston — Boston 3, Montreal 1; April 17, at Montreal — Montreal 3, Boston 2; April 20, at Boston — Montreal 5, Boston 3.*

1956-57 — Montreal Canadiens — Maurice Richard (Captain), Jean Béliveau, Connie Broden, Floyd Curry, Bernie Geoffrion, Phil Goyette, Doug Harvey, Tom Johnson, Don Marshall, Gerry McNeil, Dickie Moore, Bert Olmstead, Jacques Plante, André Pronovost, Claude Provost, Henri Richard, Dollard St. Laurent, Jean-Guy Talbot, Bob Turner; William Northey (President), Donat Raymond (Chairman), Ken Reardon (Vice President), Frank Selke (Managing Director), Toe Blake (Coach), Hector Dubois, Larry Aubut (Trainers).

Scores: *April 6, at Montreal — Montreal 5, Boston 1; April 9, at Montreal — Montreal 1, Boston 0; April 11, at Boston — Montreal 4, Boston 2; April 14, at Boston — Boston 2, Montreal 0; April 16, at Montreal — Montreal 5, Boston 1.*

1955-56 — Montreal Canadiens — Butch Bouchard (Captain), Bob Turner, Jean Béliveau, Bert Olmstead, Floyd Curry, Bernie Geoffrion, Jacques Plante, Doug Harvey, Claude Provost, Charlie Hodge, Henri Richard, Tom Johnson, Maurice Richard, Jackie LeClair, Dollard St. Laurent, Don Marshall, Jean-Guy Talbot, Dickie Moore, Ken Mosdell; Donat Raymond (President), Frank Selke (Managing Director), D'Alton Coleman, William Northey (Vice Presidents), Ken Reardon (Assistant Manager), Toe Blake (Coach), Hector Dubois, Gaston Bettez (Trainers).

Scores: *March 31, at Montreal — Montreal 6, Detroit 4; April 3, at Montreal — Montreal 5, Detroit 1; April 5, at Detroit — Detroit 3, Montreal 1; April 8, at Detroit — Montreal 3, Detroit 0; April 10, at Montreal — Montreal 3, Detroit 1.*

1954-55 — Detroit Red Wings — Dutch Reibel, Terry Sawchuk, Jim Hay, Vic Stasiuk, Johnny Wilson, Gordie Howe, Red Kelly, Tony Leswick, Ted Lindsay (Captain), Marty Pavelich, Marcel Pronovost, Marcel Bonin, Alex Delvecchio, Bill Dineen, Bob Goldham, Benny Woit, Larry Hillman, Glen Skov; Bruce Norris (President), Marguerite Norris (President), Jack Adams (Manager), Jimmy Skinner (Coach), John Mitchell (Chief Scout), Fred Huber (Publicity Director), Carl Mattson, Lefty Wilson (Trainers).

Scores: *April 3, at Detroit — Detroit 4, Montreal 2; April 5, at Detroit — Detroit 7, Montreal 1; April 7, at Montreal — Montreal 4, Detroit 2; April 9, at Montreal — Montreal 5, Detroit 3; April 10, at Detroit — Detroit 5, Montreal 1; April 12, at Montreal — Montreal 6, Detroit 3; April 14, at Detroit — Detroit 3, Montreal 1.*

1953-54 — Detroit Red Wings — Marty Pavelich, Jimmy Peters, Marcel Pronovost, Metro Prystai, Dutch Reibel, Terry Sawchuk, Bob Goldham, Gordie Howe, Earl Johnson, Red Kelly, Tony Leswick, Ted Lindsay (Captain), Keith Allen, Al Arbour, Alex Delvecchio, Bill Dineen, Gilles Dube, Dave Gatherum, Glen Skov, Johnny Wilson, Benny Woit; Bruce Norris (Owner), Marguerite Norris (President), Jack Adams (Manager), Tommy Ivan (Coach), John Mitchell (Chief Scout), Fred Huber (Publicity Director), Carl Mattson, Lefty Wilson (Trainers), Wally Crossman (Assistant Trainer).

Scores: April 4, at Detroit — Detroit 3, Montreal 1; April 6, at Detroit — Montreal 3, Detroit 1; April 8, at Montreal — Detroit 5, Montreal 2; April 10, at Montreal — Detroit 2, Montreal 0; April 11, at Detroit — Montreal 1, Detroit 0; April 13, at Montreal — Montreal 4, Detroit 1; April 16, at Detroit — Detroit 2, Montreal 1.

1952-53 — Montreal Canadiens — Floyd Curry, Bernie Geoffrion, Bert Olmstead, Paul Meger, Dick Gamble, Dickie Moore, Tom Johnson, Bud MacPherson, Billy Reay, Ken Mosdell, Paul Masnick, John McCormack, Butch Bouchard (Captain), Maurice Richard, Elmer Lach, Gerry McNeil, Doug Harvey, Dollard St. Laurent, Jacques Plante, Lorne Davis, Calum MacKay, Eddie Mazur, Donat Raymond (President), Dalton Coleman (Director), William Northey (Special Advisor), Frank Selke (Manager), Dick Irvin (Coach), Hector Dubois, Gaston Bettez (Trainers).

Scores: *April 9, at Montreal — Montreal 4, Boston 2; April 11, at Montreal — Boston 4, Montreal 1; April 12, at Boston — Montreal 3, Boston 0; April 14, at Boston — Montreal 7, Boston 3; April 16, at Montreal — Montreal 1, Boston 0.*

1951-52 — Detroit Red Wings — Metro Prystai, Leo Reise Jr., Terry Sawchuk, Enio Sclisizzi, Glen Skov, Vic Stasiuk, Gordie Howe, Red Kelly, Tony Leswick, Ted Lindsay, Marty Pavelich, Marcel Pronovost, Sid Abel (Captain), Alex Delvecchio, Fred Glover, Bob Goldham, Glenn Hall, Benny Woit, Johnny Wilson, Larry Zeidel; James Norris (President), Bruce Norris (Owner), Jack Adams (Manager), Tommy Ivan (Coach), Fred Huber (Publicity Director), Carson Cooper (Scout), Carl Mattson, Lefty Wilson (Trainers), Wally Crossman (Assistant Trainer).

Scores: *April 10, at Montreal — Detroit 3, Montreal 1; April 12, at Montreal — Detroit 2, Montreal 1; April 13, at Detroit — Detroit 3, Montreal 0; April 15, at Detroit — Detroit 3, Montreal 0.*

1950-51 — Toronto Maple Leafs — Bill Barilko, Max Bentley, Hugh Bolton, Turk Broda, Fern Flaman, Cal Gardner, Bob Hassard, Bill Juzda, Ted Kennedy (Captain), Joe Klukay, Danny Lewicki, Fleming MacKell, Howie Meeker, Gus Mortson, John McCormack, Al Rollins, Tod Sloan, Sid Smith, Jimmy Thomson, Ray Timgren, Harry Watson; Joe Primeau (Coach), Bill MacBrien (Chairman), Conn Smythe (President/Manager), Hap Day (Assistant Manager), George McCullagh, J.Y. Murdoch (Vice Presidents), J.P. Bickell, Ed Bickle (Directors), Tim Daly (Trainer), Archie Campbell, Tommy Naylor (Assistant Trainers), Dr. Norman Delarue, Dr. James Murray, Dr. Horace MacIntyre (Club Doctors), Ed Fitkin (Publicity Director), Squib Walker (Chief Scout).

Scores: *April 11, at Toronto — Toronto 3, Montreal 2; April 14, at Toronto — Montreal 3, Toronto 2; April 17, at Montreal — Toronto 2, Montreal 1; April 19, at Montreal — Toronto 3, Montreal 2; April 21, at Toronto — Toronto 3, Montreal 2.*

1949-50 — Detroit Red Wings — Sid Abel (Captain), Pete Babando, Steve Black, Joe Carveth, Gerry Couture, Al Dewsbury, Lee Fogolin, George Gee, Gordie Howe, Red Kelly, Ted Lindsay, Harry Lumley, Clare Martin, Jim McFadden, Max McNab, Marty Pavelich, Jimmy Peters, Marcel Pronovost, Leo Reise Jr., Jack Stewart, Johnny Wilson, Larry Wilson, Doug McKay; James Norris (President), James Norris Jr. (Vice President), Arthur Wirtz (Secretary Treasurer), Jack Adams (Manager), Tommy Ivan (Coach), Fred Huber Jr. (Publicity Director), Carson Cooper (Head Scout), Carl Mattson (Trainer), Walter Humeniuk (Assistant Trainer).

Scores: *April 11, at Detroit — Detroit 4, NY Rangers 1; April 13, at Toronto* — NY Rangers 3, Detroit 1; April 15, at Toronto* — Detroit 4, NY Rangers 0; April 18, at Detroit — NY Rangers 4, Detroit 3; April 20, at Detroit — NY Rangers 2, Detroit 1; April 22, at Detroit — Detroit 5, NY Rangers 4; April 23, at Detroit — Detroit 4, NY Rangers 3.*

**Ice was unavailable in Madison Square Garden and NY Rangers elected to play second and third games on Toronto ice.*

1948-49 — Toronto Maple Leafs — Bill Barilko, Max Bentley, Garth Boesch, Turk Broda, Bob Dawes, Bill Ezinicki, Cal Gardner, Bill Juzda, Ted Kennedy (Captain), Joe Klukay, Vic Lynn, Howie Meeker, Don Metz, Fleming MacKell, Gus Mortson, Sid Smith, Harry Taylor, Ray Timgren, Jimmy Thomson, Harry Watson; Hap Day (Coach), Bill MacBrien (Chairman), Conn Smythe (President/Manager), George McCullagh, J.Y. Murdoch (Vice Presidents), J.P. Bickell, Ed Bickle (Directors), Tim Daly (Trainer), Archie Campbell (Assistant Trainer), Dr. Norman Delarue, Dr. James Murray, Dr. Horace MacIntyre (Club Doctors), Ed Fitkin (Publicity Director), Squib Walker (Chief Scout), Kerry Day (Mascot).

Scores: *April 8, at Detroit — Toronto 3, Detroit 2; April 10, at Detroit — Toronto 3, Detroit 1; April 13, at Toronto — Toronto 3, Detroit 1; April 16, at Toronto — Toronto 3, Detroit 1.*

1947-48 — Toronto Maple Leafs — Syl Apps (Captain), Bill Barilko, Max Bentley, Garth Boesch, Turk Broda, Les Costello, Bill Ezinicki, Ted Kennedy, Joe Klukay, Vic Lynn, Howie Meeker, Nick Metz, Don Metz, Gus Mortson, Phil Samis, Sid Smith, Wally Stanowski, Jimmy Thomson, Harry Watson; Hap Day (Coach), Conn Smythe (Manager), Tim Daly (Trainer).

Scores: *April 7, at Toronto — Toronto 5, Detroit 3; April 10, at Toronto — Toronto 4, Detroit 2; April 11, at Detroit — Toronto 2, Detroit 0; April 14, at Detroit — Toronto 7, Detroit 2.*

1946-47 — Toronto Maple Leafs — Turk Broda, Garth Boesch, Gus Mortson, Jimmy Thomson, Wally Stanowski, Bill Barilko, Harry Watson, Bud Poile, Ted Kennedy, Syl Apps (Captain), Don Metz, Nick Metz, Bill Ezinicki, Vic Lynn, Howie Meeker, Gaye Stewart, Joe Klukay, Gus Bodnar, Bob Goldham; Conn Smythe (Manager), Hap Day (Coach), Tim Daly (Trainer).

Scores: *April 8, at Montreal — Montreal 6, Toronto 0; April 10, at Montreal — Toronto 4, Montreal 0; April 12, at Toronto — Toronto 4, Montreal 2; April 15, at Toronto — Toronto 2, Montreal 1; April 17, at Montreal — Montreal 3, Toronto 1; April 19, at Toronto — Toronto 2, Montreal 1.*

1945-46 — Montreal Canadiens — Elmer Lach, Toe Blake (Captain), Maurice Richard, Bob Fillion, Dutch Hiller, Murph Chamberlain, Ken Mosdell, Buddy O'Connor, Glen Harmon, Jimmy Peters, Butch Bouchard, Billy Reay, Ken Reardon, Leo Lamoureux, Frank Eddolls, Gerry Plamondon, Joe Benoit, Bill Durnan; Tommy Gorman (Manager), Dick Irvin (Coach), Ernie Cook (Trainer).

Scores: *March 30, at Montreal — Montreal 4, Boston 3; April 2, at Montreal — Montreal 3, Boston 2; April 4, at Boston — Montreal 4, Boston 2; April 7, at Boston — Boston 3, Montreal 2; April 9, at Montreal — Montreal 6, Boston 3.*

1944-45 — Toronto Maple Leafs — Don Metz, Frank McCool, Wally Stanowski, Reg Hamilton, Moe Morris, John McCreedy, Tom O'Neill, Ted Kennedy, Babe Pratt, Gus Bodnar, Art Jackson, Jack McLean, Mel Hill, Nick Metz, Bob Davidson (Captain), Sweeney Schriner, Lorne Carr, Pete Backor, Ross Johnstone; Conn Smythe (Manager), Frank Selke (Business Manager), Hap Day (Coach), Tim Daly (Trainer).

Scores: *April 6, at Detroit — Toronto 1, Detroit 0; April 8, at Detroit — Toronto 2, Detroit 0; April 12, at Toronto — Toronto 1, Detroit 0; April 14, at Toronto — Detroit 5, Toronto 3; April 19, at Detroit — Detroit 2, Toronto 0; April 21, at Toronto — Detroit 1, Toronto 0; April 22, at Detroit — Toronto 2, Detroit 1.*

1943-44 — Montreal Canadiens — Toe Blake (Captain), Maurice Richard, Elmer Lach, Ray Getliffe, Murph Chamberlain, Phil Watson, Butch Bouchard, Glen Harmon, Buddy O'Connor, Gerry Heffernan, Mike McMahon, Leo Lamoureux, Fern Majeau, Bob Fillion, Bill Durnan; Tommy Gorman (Manager), Dick Irvin (Coach), Ernie Cook (Trainer).

Scores: *April 4, at Montreal — Montreal 5, Chicago 1; April 6, at Chicago — Montreal 3, Chicago 1; April 9, at Chicago — Montreal 3, Chicago 2; April 13, at Montreal — Montreal 5, Chicago 4.*

1942-43 — Detroit Red Wings — Jack Stewart, Jimmy Orlando, Sid Abel (captain), Alex Motter, Harry Watson, Joe Carveth, Mud Bruneteau, Eddie Wares, Johnny Mowers, Cully Simon, Don Grosso, Carl Liscombe, Connie Brown, Syd Howe, Les Douglas, Harold Jackson, Joe Fisher, Adam Brown; Jack Adams (Manager), Ebbie Goodfellow (Playing Coach), Honey Walker (Trainer).

Scores: *April 1, at Detroit — Detroit 6, Boston 2; April 4, at Detroit — Detroit 4, Boston 3; April 7, at Boston — Detroit 4, Boston 0; April 8, at Boston — Detroit 2, Boston 0.*

1941-42 — Toronto Maple Leafs — Wally Stanowski, Syl Apps (Captain), Bob Goldham, Gordie Drillon, Hank Goldup, Ernie Dickens, Sweeney Schriner, Bucko McDonald, Bob Davidson, Nick Metz, Bingo Kampman, Don Metz, Gaye Stewart, Turk Broda, John McCreedy, Lorne Carr, Pete Langelle, Billy Taylor, Reg Hamilton; Conn Smythe (Manager), Hap Day (Coach), Frank Selke (Business Manager), Tim Daly (Trainer).

Scores: *April 4, at Toronto — Detroit 3, Toronto 2; April 7, at Toronto — Detroit 4, Toronto 2; April 9, at Detroit — Detroit 5, Toronto 2; April 12, at Detroit — Toronto 4, Detroit 3; April 14, at Toronto — Toronto 9, Detroit 3; April 16, at Detroit — Toronto 3, Detroit 0; April 18, at Toronto — Toronto 3, Detroit 1.*

1940-41 — Boston Bruins — Bill Cowley, Des Smith, Dit Clapper (Captain), Frank Brimsek, Flash Hollett, Jack Crawford, Bobby Bauer, Pat McReavy, Herb Cain, Mel Hill, Milt Schmidt, Woody Dumart, Roy Conacher, Terry Reardon, Art Jackson, Eddie Wiseman, Jack Shewchuck; Art Ross (Manager), Cooney Weiland (Coach), Win Green (Trainer).

Scores: *April 6, at Boston — Detroit 2, Boston 3; April 8, at Boston — Detroit 1, Boston 2; April 10, at Detroit — Boston 4, Detroit 2; April 12, at Detroit — Boston 3, Detroit 1.*

1939-40 — New York Rangers — Dave Kerr, Art Coulter (Captain), Ott Heller, Alex Shibicky, Mac Colville, Neil Colville, Phil Watson, Lynn Patrick, Clint Smith, Muzz Patrick, Babe Pratt, Bryan Hextall, Kilby MacDonald, Dutch Hiller, Alf Pike, Stan Smith; Lester Patrick (Manager), Frank Boucher (Coach), Harry Westerby (Trainer).

Scores: *April 2, at New York — NY Rangers 2, Toronto 1; April 3, at New York — NY Rangers 6, Toronto 2; April 6, at Toronto — NY Rangers 1, Toronto 2; April 9, at Toronto — NY Rangers 0, Toronto 3; April 11, at Toronto — NY Rangers 2, Toronto 1; April 13, at Toronto — NY Rangers 3, Toronto 2.*

1938-39 — Boston Bruins — Bobby Bauer, Mel Hill, Flash Hollett, Roy Conacher, Gord Pettinger, Charlie Sands, Milt Schmidt, Woody Dumart, Jack Crawford, Ray Getliffe, Frank Brimsek, Eddie Shore, Dit Clapper, Bill Cowley, Jack Portland, Red Hamill, Harry Frost, Cooney Weiland (Captain); Art Ross (Manager/Coach), Win Green (Trainer).

Scores: *April 6, at Boston — Toronto 1, Boston 2; April 9, at Boston — Toronto 3, Boston 2; April 11, at Toronto — Toronto 1, Boston 3; April 13, at Toronto — Toronto 0, Boston 2; April 16, at Boston — Toronto 1, Boston 3.*

1937-38 — Chicago Black Hawks — Art Wiebe, Carl Voss, Harold Jackson, Mike Karakas, Mush March, Jack Shill, Earl Seibert, Cully Dahlstrom, Alex Levinsky, Johnny Gottselig (Captain), Lou Trudel, Pete Palangio, Bill MacKenzie, Doc Romnes, Paul Thompson, Roger Jenkins, Alfie Moore, Bert Connelly, Virgil Johnson, Paul Goodman; Bill Tobin (Vice President), Bill Stewart (Coach), Eddie Froelich (Trainer).

Scores: *April 5, at Toronto — Chicago 3, Toronto 1; April 7, at Toronto — Chicago 1, Toronto 5; April 10, at Chicago — Chicago 2, Toronto 1; April 12, at Chicago — Chicago 4, Toronto 1.*

1936-37 — Detroit Red Wings — Normie Smith, Pete Kelly, Larry Aurie, Herbie Lewis, Hec Kilrea, Mud Bruneteau, Syd Howe, Wally Kilrea, Jimmy Franks, Bucko McDonald, Gord Pettinger, Ebbie Goodfellow, John Gallagher, Ralph Bowman, John Sorrell, Marty Barry, Earl Robertson, John Sherf, Howie Mackie, Rolly Roulston, Doug Young (Captain); Jack Adams (Manager/Coach), Honey Walker (Trainer).

Scores: *April 6, at New York — Detroit 1, NY Rangers 5; April 8, at Detroit — Detroit 4, NY Rangers 2; April 11, at Detroit — Detroit 0, NY Rangers 1; April 13, at Detroit — Detroit 1, NY Rangers 0; April 15, at Detroit — Detroit 3, NY Rangers 0.*

1935-36 — Detroit Red Wings — John Sorrell, Syd Howe, Marty Barry, Herbie Lewis, Mud Bruneteau, Wally Kilrea, Hec Kilrea, Gord Pettinger, Bucko McDonald, Ralph Bowman, Pete Kelly, Doug Young (Captain), Ebbie Goodfellow, Normie Smith, Larry Aurie; Jack Adams (Manager/Coach), Honey Walker (Trainer).

Scores: *April 5, at Detroit — Detroit 3, Toronto 1; April 7, at Detroit — Detroit 9, Toronto 4; April 9, at Toronto — Detroit 3, Toronto 4; April 11, at Toronto — Detroit 3, Toronto 2.*

1934-35 — Montreal Maroons — Lionel Conacher, Cy Wentworth, Alec Connell, Toe Blake, Stewart Evans, Earl Robinson, Bill Miller, Dave Trottier, Jimmy Ward, Baldy Northcott, Hooley Smith (Captain), Russ Blinco, Al Shields, Sammy McManus, Gus Marker, Bob Gracie, Herb Cain, Dutch Gainor; Tommy Gorman (Manager/Coach), Bill O'Brien (Trainer).

Scores: *April 4, at Toronto — Mtl. Maroons 3, Toronto 2; April 6, at Toronto — Mtl. Maroons 3, Toronto 1; April 9, at Montreal — Mtl. Maroons 4, Toronto 1.*

1933-34 — Chicago Black Hawks — Clarence Abel, Rosie Couture, Lou Trudel, Lionel Conacher, Paul Thompson, Leroy Goldsworthy, Art Coulter, Roger Jenkins, Don McFadyen, Tom Cook, Doc Romnes, Johnny Gottselig, Mush March, Johnny Sheppard, Charlie Gardiner (Captain), Bill Kendall, Jack Leswick; Tommy Gorman (Manager/Coach), Eddie Froelich (Trainer).

Scores: *April 3, at Detroit — Chicago 2, Detroit 1; April 5, at Detroit — Chicago 4, Detroit 1; April 8, at Chicago — Detroit 5, Chicago 2; April 10, at Chicago — Chicago 1, Detroit 0.*

1932-33 — New York Rangers — Ching Johnson, Butch Keeling, Frank Boucher, Art Somers, Babe Siebert, Bun Cook, Andy Aitkenhead, Ott Heller, Oscar Asmundson, Gord Pettinger, Doug Brennan, Cecil Dillon, Bill Cook (Captain), Murray Murdoch, Earl Seibert; Lester Patrick (Manager/Coach), Harry Westerby (Trainer).

Scores: *April 4, at New York — NY Rangers 5, Toronto 1; April 8, at Toronto — NY Rangers 3, Toronto 1; April 11, at Toronto — Toronto 3, NY Rangers 2; April 13, at Toronto — NY Rangers 1, Toronto 0.*

1931-32 — Toronto Maple Leafs — Charlie Conacher, Busher Jackson, King Clancy, Andy Blair, Red Horner, Lorne Chabot, Alex Levinsky, Joe Primeau, Harold Darragh, Baldy Cotton, Frank Finnigan, Hap Day (Captain), Ace Bailey, Bob Gracie, Fred Robertson, Earl Miller; Conn Smythe (Manager), Dick Irvin (Coach), Tim Daly (Trainer).

Scores: *April 5, at New York — Toronto 6, NY Rangers 4; April 7, at Boston* — Toronto 6, NY Rangers 2; April 9, at Toronto — Toronto 6, NY Rangers 4.*

1930-31 — Montreal Canadiens — George Hainsworth, Wildor Larochelle, Marty Burke, Sylvio Mantha (Captain), Howie Morenz, Johnny Gagnon, Aurel Joliat, Armand Mondou, Pit Lepine, Albert Leduc, Georges Mantha, Art Lesieur, Nick Wasnie, Gus Rivers, Jean Pusie; Léo Dandurand (Manager), Cecil Hart (Coach), Ed Dufour (Trainer).

Scores: *April 3, at Chicago — Montreal 2, Chicago 1; April 5, at Chicago — Chicago 2, Montreal 1; April 9, at Montreal — Chicago 3, Montreal 2; April 11, at Montreal — Montreal 4, Chicago 2; April 14, at Montreal — Montreal 2, Chicago 0.*

1929-30 — Montreal Canadiens — George Hainsworth, Marty Burke, Sylvio Mantha (Captain), Howie Morenz, Bert McCaffrey, Aurel Joliat, Albert Leduc, Pit Lepine, Wildor Larochelle, Nick Wasnie, Gerry Carson, Armand Mondou, Georges Mantha, Gus Rivers; Léo Dandurand (Manager), Cecil Hart (Coach), Ed Dufour (Trainer).

Scores: *April 1, at Boston — Montreal 3, Boston 0; April 3, at Montreal — Montreal 4, Boston 3.*

1928-29 — Boston Bruins — Tiny Thompson, Eddie Shore, Lionel Hitchman (Captain), Percy Galbraith, Mickey MacKay, Red Green, Dutch Gainor, Harry Oliver, Eddie Rodden, Dit Clapper, Cooney Weiland, Lloyd Klein, Cy Denneny, Bill Carson, George Owen, Myles Lane; Art Ross (Manager/Coach), Win Green (Trainer).

Scores: *March 28, at Boston — Boston 2, NY Rangers 0; March 29, at New York — Boston 2, NY Rangers 1.*

1927-28 — New York Rangers — Lorne Chabot, Clarence Abel, Leo Bourgeault, Ching Johnson, Bill Cook (Captain), Bun Cook, Frank Boucher, Bill Boyd, Murray Murdoch, Paul Thompson, Alex Gray, Joe Miller, Patsy Callighen; Lester Patrick (Manager/Coach), Harry Westerby (Trainer).

Scores: *April 5, at Montreal — Mtl. Maroons 2, NY Rangers 0; April 7, at Montreal — NY Rangers 2, Mtl. Maroons 1; April 10, at Montreal — Mtl. Maroons 2, NY Rangers 0; April 12, at Montreal — NY Rangers 1, Mtl. Maroons 0; April 14, at Montreal — NY Rangers 2, Mtl. Maroons 1.*

1926-27 — Ottawa Senators — Alec Connell, King Clancy, George Boucher (Captain), Ed Gorman, Frank Finnigan, Alex Smith, Hec Kilrea, Hooley Smith, Cy Denneny, Frank Nighbor, Jack Adams, Milt Halliday; Dave Gill (Manager/Coach).

Scores: *April 7, at Boston — Ottawa 0, Boston 0; April 9, at Boston — Ottawa 3, Boston 1; April 11, at Ottawa — Boston 1, Ottawa 1; April 13, at Ottawa — Ottawa 3, Boston 1.*

1925-26 — Montreal Maroons — Clint Benedict, Reg Noble, Frank Carson, Dunc Munro (Captain), Nels Stewart, Punch Broadbent, Babe Siebert, Chuck Dinsmore, Merlyn Phillips, Hobie Kitchen, Sam Rothschild, Albert Holway, George Horne, Bernie Brophy; Eddie Gerard (Manager/Coach), Bill O'Brien (Trainer).

Scores: *March 30, at Montreal — Mtl. Maroons 3, Victoria 0; April 1, at Montreal — Mtl. Maroons 3, Victoria 0; April 3, at Montreal — Victoria 3, Mtl. Maroons 2; April 6, at Montreal — Mtl. Maroons 2, Victoria 0.*

The series in the spring of 1926 ended the annual playoffs between the champions of the East and the champions of the West. Since 1926-27 the annual playoffs in the National Hockey League have decided the Stanley Cup champions.

1924-25 — Victoria Cougars — Hap Holmes, Clem Loughlin (Captain), Gord Fraser, Frank Fredrickson, Jack Walker, Gizzy Hart, Harold Halderson, Frank Foyston, Wally Elmer, Harry Meeking, Jocko Anderson; Lester Patrick (Manager/Coach).

Scores: *March 21, at Victoria — Victoria 5, Montreal 2; March 23, at Vancouver — Victoria 3, Montreal 1; March 27, at Victoria — Montreal 4, Victoria 2; March 30, at Victoria — Victoria 6, Montreal 1.*

1923-24 — Montreal Canadiens — Georges Vezina, Sprague Cleghorn (Captain), Billy Coutu, Howie Morenz, Aurel Joliat, Billy Boucher, Odie Cleghorn, Sylvio Mantha, Bobby Boucher, Billy Bell, Billy Cameron, Joe Malone, Charles Fortier; Leo Dandurand (Manager/Coach).

Scores: *March 22, at Montreal — Montreal 6, Cgy. Tigers 1; March 25, at Ottawa* — Montreal 3, Cgy. Tigers 0.*

** Game transferred to Ottawa to benefit from artificial ice surface.*

1922-23 — Ottawa Senators — George Boucher, Lionel Hitchman, Frank Nighbor, King Clancy, Harry Helman, Clint Benedict, Jack Darragh, Eddie Gerard (Captain), Cy Denneny, Punch Broadbent; Tommy Gorman (Manager), Pete Green (Coach), F. Dolan (Trainer).

Scores: *March 29, at Vancouver — Ottawa 2, Edm. Eskimos 1; March 31, at Vancouver — Ottawa 1, Edm. Eskimos 0.*

1921-22 — Toronto St. Patricks — Ted Stackhouse, Corb Denneny, Rod Smylie, Lloyd Andrews, John Ross Roach, Harry Cameron, Billy Stuart, Babe Dye, Ken Randall, Reg Noble (Captain), Eddie Gerard (borrowed for one game from Ottawa), Stan Jackson, Ivan Mitchell; Charlie Querrie (Manager), George O'Donoghue (Coach).

Scores: *March 17, at Toronto — Van. Millionaires 4, Toronto 3; March 21, at Toronto — Toronto 2, Van. Millionaires 1; March 23, at Toronto — Van. Millionaires 3, Toronto 0; March 25, at Toronto — Toronto 6, Van. Millionaires 0; March 28, at Toronto — Toronto 5, Van. Millionaires 1.*

1920-21 — Ottawa Senators — Jack MacKell, Jack Darragh, Morley Bruce, George Boucher, Eddie Gerard (Captain), Clint Benedict, Sprague Cleghorn, Frank Nighbor, Punch Broadbent, Cy Denneny, Leth Graham; Tommy Gorman (Manager), Pete Green (Coach), F. Dolan (Trainer).

Scores: *March 21, at Vancouver — Van. Millionaires 2, Ottawa 1; March 24, at Vancouver — Ottawa 4, Van. Millionaires 3; March 28, at Vancouver — Ottawa 3, Van. Millionaires 2; March 31, at Vancouver — Van. Millionaires 3, Ottawa 2; April 4, at Vancouver — Ottawa 2, Van. Millionaires 1*

1919-20 — Ottawa Senators — Jack MacKell, Jack Darragh, Morley Bruce, Horace Merrill, George Boucher, Eddie Gerard (Captain), Clint Benedict, Sprague Cleghorn, Frank Nighbor, Punch Broadbent, Cy Denneny, Tommy Gorman (Manager), Pete Green (Coach).

Scores: *March 22, at Ottawa — Ottawa 3, Seattle 2; March 24, at Ottawa — Ottawa 3, Seattle 0; March 27, at Ottawa — Seattle 3, Ottawa 1; March 30, at Toronto* — Seattle 5, Ottawa 2; April 1, at Toronto* — Ottawa 6, Seattle 1.*

* Games transferred to Toronto to benefit from artificial ice surface.

1918-19 — No decision, Series halted by Spanish influenza epidemic, illness of several players and death of Joe Hall of Montreal Canadiens from the flu. Five games had been played when the series was halted, each team having won two and tied one. Final scores are listed below.

Scores: *March 19, at Seattle — Seattle 7, Montreal 0; March 22, at Seattle — Montreal 4, Seattle 2; March 24, at Seattle — Seattle 7, Montreal 2; March 26, at Seattle — Montreal 0, Seattle 0; March 30, at Seattle — Montreal 4, Seattle 3.*

1917-18 — Toronto Arenas — Rusty Crawford, Harry Meeking, Ken Randall (Captain), Corb Denneny, Harry Cameron, Jack Adams, Alf Skinner, Harry Mummery, Hap Holmes, Reg Noble, Sammy Hebert, Jack Marks, Jack Coughlin; Charlie Querrie (Manager), Dick Carroll (Coach), Frank Carroll (Trainer).

Scores: *March 20, at Toronto — Toronto 5, Van. Millionaires 3; March 23, at Toronto — Van. Millionaires 6, Toronto 4; March 26, at Toronto — Toronto 6, Van. Millionaires 3; March 28, at Toronto — Van. Millionaires 8, Toronto 1; March 30, at Toronto — Toronto 2, Van. Millionaires 1.*

1916-17 — Seattle Metropolitans — Hap Holmes, Ed Carpenter, Cully Wilson, Jack Walker, Bernie Morris, Frank Foyston, Roy Rickey, Jim Riley, Bobby Rowe (Captain); Peter Muldoon (Manager).

Scores: *March 17, at Seattle — Montreal 8, Seattle 4; March 20, at Seattle — Seattle 6, Montreal 1; March 23, at Seattle — Seattle 4, Montreal 1; March 26, at Seattle — Seattle 9, Montreal 1.*

1915-16 — Montreal Canadiens — Georges Vezina, Bert Corbeau, Jack Laviolette, Newsy Lalonde, Louis Berlinquette, Goldie Prodger, Howard McNamara (Captain), Didier Pitre, Skene Ronan, Amos Arbour, Skinner Poulin, Jack Fournier; George Kennedy (Manager).

Scores: *March 20, at Montreal — Portland 2, Montreal 0; March 22, at Montreal — Montreal 2, Portland 1; March 25, at Montreal — Montreal 6, Portland 3; March 28, at Montreal — Portland 6, Montreal 5; March 30, at Montreal — Montreal 2, Portland 1.*

1914-15 — Vancouver Millionaires — Ken Mallen, Frank Nighbor, Cyclone Taylor, Hugh Lehman, Lloyd Cook, Mickey MacKay, Barney Stanley, Jim Seaborn, Si Griffis (Captain), Johnny Matz; Frank Patrick (Playing Manager).

Scores: *March 22, at Vancouver — Van. Millionaires 6, Ottawa 2; March 24, at Vancouver — Van. Millionaires 8, Ottawa 3; March 26, at Vancouver — Van. Millionaires 12, Ottawa 3.*

1913-14 — Toronto Blueshirts — Con Corbeau, Roy McGiffin, Jack Walker, George McNamara, Cully Wilson, Frank Foyston, Harry Cameron, Hap Holmes, Scotty Davidson (Captain), Harriston; Jack Marshall (Playing Manager), Frank Carroll, Dick Carroll (Trainers).

Scores: *March 14, at Toronto — Toronto 5, Victoria 2; March 17, at Toronto — Toronto 6, Victoria 5; March 19, at Toronto — Toronto 2, Victoria 1.*

Prior to 1914, teams could challenge the Stanley Cup champions for the title, thus there was more than one Championship Series played in most of the seasons between 1894 and 1913.

1912-13 — Quebec Bulldogs — Joe Malone (Captain), Joe Hall, Paddy Moran, Harry Mummery, Tommy Smith, Jack Marks, Rusty Crawford, Billy Creighton, Jeff Malone, Rocket Power; M.J. Quinn (Manager), D. Beland (Trainer).

Scores: *March 8, at Quebec — Que. Bulldogs 14, Sydney 3; March 10, at Quebec — Que. Bulldogs 6, Sydney 2.*

Victoria challenged Quebec but the Bulldogs refused to put the Stanley Cup in competition so the two teams played an exhibition series with Victoria winning two games to one by scores of 7-5, 3-6, 6-1. It was the first meeting between the Eastern champions and the Western champions. The following year, and until the Western Hockey League disbanded after the 1926 playoffs, the Cup went to the winner of the series between East and West.

1911-12 — Quebec Bulldogs — Goldie Prodger, Joe Hall, Walter Rooney, Paddy Moran, Jack Marks, Jack McDonald, Eddie Oatman, George Leonard, Joe Malone (Captain); Charley Nolan (Coach), M.J. Quinn (Manager), D. Beland (Trainer).

Scores: *March 11, at Quebec — Que. Bulldogs 9, Moncton 3; March 13, at Quebec — Que. Bulldogs 8, Moncton 0.*

1910-11 — Ottawa Senators — Hamby Shore, Percy LeSueur (Captain), Jack Darragh, Bruce Stuart, Marty Walsh, Bruce Ridpath, Fred Lake, Dubbie Kerr, Alex Currie, Horace Gaul.

Scores: March 13, at Ottawa — Ottawa 7, Galt 4; March 16, at Ottawa — Ottawa 13, Port Arthur 4.

1909-10 — (March) — Montreal Wanderers — Cecil Blachford, Moose Johnson, Ernie Russell, Riley Hern, Harry Hyland, Jack Marshall, Pud Glass, Jimmy Gardner; Dickie Boon (Manager).

Scores: March 12, at Montreal — Mtl. Wanderers 7, Berlin (Kitchener) 3.

By winning the 1910 NHA title, the Montreal Wanderers took possession of the Stanley Cup from Ottawa and accepted a challenge from Berlin, 1910 champions of the OPHL

1909-10 — (January) — Ottawa Senators — Dubbie Kerr, Fred Lake, Percy LeSueur, Ken Mallen, Bruce Ridpath, Gord Roberts, Hamby Shore, Bruce Stuart (Captain), Marty Walsh.

The Senators accepted two challenges as defending Cup champions. The first was against Galt in a 2-game, total-goals series, and the second was against Edmonton, also a 2-game, total-goals series.

Scores: January 5, at Ottawa — Ottawa 12, Galt 3; January 7, at Ottawa — Ottawa 3, Galt 1; January 18, at Ottawa — Ottawa 8, Edm. Eskimos 4; January 20, at Ottawa — Ottawa 13, Edm. Eskimos 7.

1908-09 — Ottawa Senators — Fred Lake, Percy LeSueur, Cyclone Taylor, Billy Gilmour, Dubbie Kerr, Edgar Dey, Marty Walsh, Bruce Stuart (Captain).

Ottawa, as champions of the Eastern Canada Hockey Association took over the Stanley Cup in 1909 and, although a challenge was accepted by the Cup trustees from Winnipeg Shamrocks, games could not be arranged because of the lateness of the season. No other challenges were made in 1909.

1907-08 — Montreal Wanderers — Riley Hern, Art Ross, Walter Smaill, Pud Glass, Bruce Stuart, Ernie Russell, Moose Johnson, Cecil Blachford (Captain), Tom Hooper, Larry Gilmour, Ernie Liffiton; Dickie Boon (Manager).

Scores: Wanderers accepted four challenges for the Cup: January 9, at Montreal — Mtl. Wanderers 9, Ott. Victorias 3; January 13, at Montreal — Mtl. Wanderers 13, Ott. Victorias 1; March 10, at Montreal — Mtl. Wanderers 11, Wpg. Maple Leafs 5; March 12, at Montreal — Mtl. Wanderers 9, Wpg. Maple Leafs 3; March 14, at Montreal — Mtl. Wanderers 6, Toronto (OPHL) 4. At start of following season, 1908-09, Wanderers were challenged by Edmonton. Results: December 28, at Montreal — Mtl. Wanderers 7, Edm. Eskimos 3; December 30, at Montreal — Edm. Eskimos 7, Mtl. Wanderers 6. Total goals: Mtl. Wanderers 13, Edm. Eskimos 10.

1906-07 — (March 25) — Montreal Wanderers — Billy Strachan, Riley Hern, Lester Patrick (Captain), Hod Stuart, Pud Glass, Ernie Russell, Cecil Blachford, Moose Johnson, Rod Kennedy, Jack Marshall; Dickie Boon (Manager).

Scores: March 16, at Winnipeg — Kenora 8, Brandon 6; March 18, at Winnipeg — Kenora 4, Brandon 1; March 23, at Winnipeg — Mtl. Wanderers 7, Kenora 2; March 25, at Winnipeg — Kenora 6, Mtl. Wanderers 5. Total goals: Mtl. Wanderers 12, Kenora 8.

1906-07 — (January) — Kenora Thistles — Eddie Giroux, Art Ross, Si Griffis, Tom Hooper, Billy McGimsie, Roxy Beaudro, Tommy Phillips (Captain), Joe Hall, Russell Phillips.

Scores: January 17, at Montreal — Kenora 4, Mtl. Wanderers 2; Jan. 21, at Montreal — Kenora 8, Mtl. Wanderers 6.

1906-07 — (December) — Montreal Wanderers — Riley Hern, Billy Strachan, Rod Kennedy, Lester Patrick (Captain), Pud Glass, Ernie Russell, Moose Johnson, Cecil Blachford, Dickie Boon (Manager).

1905-06 — (March) — Montreal Wanderers — Henri Menard, Billy Strachan, Rod Kennedy, Lester Patrick, Pud Glass, Ernie Russell, Moose Johnson, Cecil Blachford (Captain), Josh Arnold; Dickie Boon (Manager).

Scores: March 14, at Montreal — Mtl. Wanderers 9, Ottawa 1; March 17, at Ottawa — Ottawa 9, Mtl. Wanderers 3. Total goals: Mtl. Wanderers 12, Ottawa 10. Wanderers accepted a challenge from New Glasgow, N.S., prior to the start of the 1906-07 season. Results: December 27, at Montreal — Mtl. Wanderers 10, New Glasgow 3; December 29, at Montreal — Mtl. Wanderers 7, New Glasgow 2.

1905-06 — (February) — Ottawa Silver Seven — Harvey Pulford (Captain), Arthur Moore, Harry Westwick, Frank McGee, Alf Smith (Playing Coach), Billy Gilmour, Billy Hague, Harry Smith, Tommy Smith, Coo Dion, Jack Ebbs.

Scores: February 27, at Ottawa — Ottawa 16, Queen's University 7; February 28, at Ottawa — Ottawa 12, Queen's University 7; March 6, at Ottawa — Ottawa 6, Smiths Falls 5; March 8, at Ottawa — Ottawa 8, Smiths Falls 2.

1904-05 — Ottawa Silver Seven — Dave Finnie, Harvey Pulford (Captain), Arthur Moore, Harry Westwick, Frank McGee, Alf Smith (Playing Coach), Billy Gilmour, Frank White, Horace Gaul, Hamby Shore, Bones Allen.

Scores: January 13, at Ottawa — Ottawa 9, Dawson City 2; January 16, at Ottawa — Ottawa 23, Dawson City 2; March 7, at Ottawa — Ottawa 9, Rat Portage 3; March 9, at Ottawa — Ottawa 4, Rat Portage 2; March 11, at Ottawa — Ottawa 5, Rat Portage 4.

1903-04 — Ottawa Silver Seven — Suddy Gilmour, Arthur Moore, Frank McGee, Bouse Hutton, Billy Gilmour, Jim McGee, Harry Westwick, Harvey Pulford (Captain), Scott, Alf Smith (Playing Coach).

Scores: December 30, at Ottawa — Ottawa 9, Wpg. Rowing Club 1; January 1, at Ottawa — Wpg. Rowing Club 6, Ottawa 2; January 4, at Ottawa — Ottawa 2, Wpg. Rowing Club 0. February 23, at Ottawa — Ottawa 6, Tor. Marlboros 3; February 25, at Ottawa — Ottawa 11, Tor. Marlboros 2; March 2, at Montreal — Ottawa 5, Mtl. Wanderers 5. Following the tie game, a new two-game series was ordered to be played in Ottawa but the Wanderers refused unless the tie game was replayed in Montreal. When no settlement could be reached, the series was abandoned and Ottawa retained the Cup and accepted a two-game challenge from Brandon. Results: (both games at Ottawa), March 9, Ottawa 6, Brandon 3; March 11, Ottawa 9, Brandon 3.

1902-03 — (March) — Ottawa Silver Seven — Suddy Gilmour, Percy Sims, Bouse Hutton, Dave Gilmour, Billy Gilmour, Harry Westwick, Frank McGee, F.H. Wood, A.A. Fraser, Charles Spittal, Harvey Pulford (Captain), Arthur Moore; Alf Smith (Coach).

Scores: March 7, at Montreal — Ottawa 1, Mtl. Victorias 1; March 10, at Ottawa — Ottawa 8, Mtl. Victorias 0. Total goals: Ottawa 9, Mtl. Victorias 1; March 12, at Ottawa — Ottawa 6, Rat Portage 2; March 14, at Ottawa — Ottawa 4, Rat Portage 2.

1902-03 — (February) — Montreal AAA — Tom Hodge, Dickie Boon, Billy Nicholson, Tommy Phillips, Art Hooper, Billy Bellingham, Jack Marshall, Jimmy Gardner, Cecil Blachford, George Smith.

Scores: January 29, at Montreal — Mtl. AAA 8, Wpg. Victorias 1; January 31, at Montreal — Wpg. Victorias 2, Mtl. AAA 2; February 2, at Montreal — Wpg. Victorias 4, Mtl. AAA 2; February 4, at Montreal — Mtl. AAA 5, Wpg. Victorias 1.

1901-02 — (March) — Montreal AAA — Tom Hodge, Dickie Boon, Billy Nicholson, Art Hooper, Billy Bellingham, Jack Marshall, Roland Elliot, Jimmy Gardner.

Scores: March 13, at Winnipeg — Wpg. Victorias 1, Mtl. AAA 0; March 15, at Winnipeg — Mtl. AAA 5, Wpg. Victorias 0; March 17, at Winnipeg — Mtl. AAA 2, Wpg. Victorias 1.

1901-02 — (January) — Winnipeg Victorias — Burke Wood, Tony Gingras, Charles Johnstone, Rod Flett, Magnus Flett, Dan Bain (Captain), Fred Scanlon, F. Cadham, Art Brown.

Scores: January 21, at Winnipeg — Wpg. Victorias 5, Tor Wellingtons 3; January 23, at Winnipeg — Wpg. Victorias 5, Tor. Wellingtons 3.

1900-01 — Winnipeg Victorias — Burke Wood, Jack Marshall, Tony Gingras, Charles Johnstone, Rod Flett, Magnus Flett, Dan Bain (Captain), Art Brown, George Carruthers.

Scores: January 29, at Montreal — Wpg. Victorias 4, Mtl. Shamrocks 3; January 31, at Montreal — Wpg. Victorias 2, Mtl. Shamrocks 1.

1899-1900 — Montreal Shamrocks — oe McKenna, Frank Tansey, Frank Wall, Art Farrell, Fred Scanlon, Harry Trihey (Captain), Jack Brannen.

Scores: February 12, at Montreal — Mtl. Shamrocks 4, Wpg. Victorias 3; February 14, at Montreal — Wpg. Victorias 3, Mtl. Shamrocks 2; February 16, at Montreal — Mtl. Shamrocks 5, Wpg. Victorias 4; March 6, at Montreal — Mtl. Shamrocks 10, Halifax 2; March 7, at Montreal — Mtl. Shamrocks 11, Halifax 0.

1898-99 — (March) — Montreal Shamrocks — Joe McKenna, Frank Tansey, Frank Wall, Harry Trihey (Captain), Art Farrell, Fred Scanlon, Jack Brannen, John Dobby, Charles Hoerner.

Scores: March 14, at Montreal — Mtl. Shamrocks 6, Queen's University 2.

1898-99 — (February) — Montreal Victorias — Gordon Lewis, Mike Grant, Graham Drinkwater (Captain), Cam Davidson, Bob McDougall, Ernie McLea, Frank Richardson, Jack Ewing, Russell Bowie, Douglas Acer, Fred McRobie.

Scores: February 15, at Montreal — Mtl. Victorias 2, Wpg. Victorias 1; February 18, at Montreal — Mtl. Victorias 3, Wpg. Victorias 2.

1897-98 — Montreal Victorias — Gordon Lewis, Hartland McDougall, Mike Grant, Graham Drinkwater, Cam Davidson, Bob McDougall, Ernie McLea, Frank Richardson (Captain), Jack Ewing.

1896-97 — Montreal Victorias — Gordon Lewis, Harold Henderson, Mike Grant (Captain), Cam Davidson, Graham Drinkwater, Bob McDougall, Ernie McLea, Shirley Davidson, Hartland McDougall, Jack Ewing, Percy Molson, David Gillilan, Harry Massey.

Scores: December 27, at Montreal — Mtl. Victorias 15, Ott. Capitals 2.

1895-96 — (December) — Montreal Victorias — Harold Henderson, Mike Grant (Captain), Bob McDougall, Graham Drinkwater, Shirley Davidson, Hartland McDougall, Ernie McLea, Cam Davidson, David Gillilan, Stanley Willett, Gordon Lewis, W. Wallace.

Scores: December 30, at Winnipeg — Mtl. Victorias 6, Wpg. Victorias 5.

1895-96 — (February) — Winnipeg Victorias — Whitey Merritt, Rod Flett, Fred Higginbotham, Jack Armytage (Captain), Tote Campbell, Dan Bain, Charles Johnstone, Attie Howard.

Scores: February 14, at Montreal — Wpg. Victorias 2, Mtl. Victorias 0.

1894-95 — Montreal Victorias — Robert Jones, Harold Henderson, Mike Grant (Captain), Shirley Davidson, Hartland McDougall, Bob McDougall, Norman Rankin, Graham Drinkwater, Roland Elliot, William Pullan, Arthur Fenwick, A. McDougall.

1893-94 — Montreal AAA — Herb Collins, Allan Cameron, George James, Billy Barlow, Clare Mussen, Archie Hodgson, Haviland Routh, Alex Irving, James Stewart, E. O'Brien, Toad Wand, Alex Kingan.

Scores: March 17, at Mtl. Victorias — Mtl. AAA 3, Mtl. Victorias 2; March 22, at Montreal — Mtl. AAA 3, Ott. Capitals 1.

1892-93 — Montreal AAA — Tom Paton, James Stewart, Allan Cameron, Haviland Routh, Archie Hodgson, Billy Barlow, Alex Irving, Alex Kingan, G.S. Low.

The Montreal Shamrocks unseated the Montreal Victorias as Stanley Cup champions when they finished first in the Canadian Amateur Hockey League standings in 1898-99. The Shamrocks were champions again in 1899-1900.

All-Time NHL Playoff Formats

1917-18 — The regular-season was split into two halves. The winners of both halves faced each other in a two-game, total-goals series for the NHL championship and the right to meet the PCHA champion in the best-of-five Stanley Cup Final.

1918-19 — Same as 1917-18, except that the NHL championship was a best-of-seven series.

1919-20 — Same as 1917-1918, except that Ottawa won both halves of the split regular-season schedule to earn an automatic berth into the best-of-five Stanley Cup Final against the PCHA champions.

1921-22 — The top two teams at the conclusion of the regular-season faced each other in a two-game, total-goals series for the NHL championship. The NHL champion then moved on to play the winner of the PCHA-WCHL playoff series in the best-of-five Stanley Cup Final.

1922-23 — The top two teams at the conclusion of the regular-season faced each other in a two-game, total-goals series for the NHL championship. The NHL champion then moved on to play the PCHA champion in the best-of-three Stanley Cup Semi-Finals, and the winner of the Semi-Finals played the WCHL champion, which had been given a bye, in the best-of-three Stanley Cup Final.

1923-24 — The top two teams at the conclusion of the regular-season faced each other in a two-game, total-goals series for the NHL championship. The NHL champion then moved on to play the loser of the PCHA-WCHL playoff (the winner of the PCHA-WCHL playoff earned a bye into the Stanley Cup Final) in the best-of-three Stanley Cup Semi-Finals. The winner of this series met the PCHA-WCHL playoff winner in the best-of-three Stanley Cup Final.

1924-25 — The first place team (Hamilton) at the conclusion of the regular-season was supposed to play the winner of a two-game, total-goals series between the second (Toronto) and third (Montreal) place clubs. However, Hamilton refused to abide by this new format, demanding greater compensation than offered by the League. Thus, Toronto and Montreal played their two-game, total-goals series, and the winner (Montreal) earned the NHL title and then played the WCHL champion (Victoria) in the best-of-five Stanley Cup Final.

1925-26 — The format which was intended for 1924-25 went into effect. The winner of the two-game, total-goals series between the second and third place teams squared off against the first place team in the two-game, total-goals NHL championship series. The NHL champion then moved on to play the WHL champion in the best-of-five Stanley Cup Final.

After the 1925-26 season, the NHL was the only major professional hockey league still in existence and consequently took over sole control of the Stanley Cup competition.

1926-27 — The 10-team league was divided into two divisions — Canadian and American — of five teams apiece. In each division, the winner of the two-game, total-goals series between the second and third place teams faced the first place team in a two-game, total-goals series for the division title. The two division title winners then met in the best-of-five Stanley Cup Final.

1928-29 — Both first place teams in the two divisions played each other in a best-of-five series. Both second place teams in the two divisions played each other in a two-game, total-goals series as did the two third place teams. The winners of these latter two series then played each other in a best-of-three series for the right to meet the winner of the series between the two first place clubs. This Stanley Cup Final was a best-of-three.

- Series A: First in Canadian Division vs. first in American (best-of-five)
- Series B: Second in Canadian Division vs. second in American (two-game, total-goals)
- Series C: Third in Canadian Division vs. third in American (two-game, total-goals)
- Series D: Winner of Series B vs. winner of Series C (best-of-three)
- Series E: Winner of Series A vs. winner of Series D (best-of-three) for Stanley Cup

1930-31 — Same as 1928-29, except that Series D was changed to a two-game, total-goals format and Series E was changed to best-of-five.

1936-37 — Same as 1930-31, except that Series B, C and D were each best-of-three.

1938-39 — With the NHL reduced to seven teams, the two-division system was replaced by one seven-team league. Based on final regular-season standings, the following playoff format was adopted:

- Series A: First vs. Second (best-of-seven)
- Series B: Third vs. Fourth (best-of-three)
- Series C: Fifth vs. Sixth (best-of-three)
- Series D: Winner of Series B vs. winner of Series C (best-of-three)
- Series E: Winner of Series A vs. winner of Series D (best-of-seven)

1942-43 — With the NHL reduced to six teams (the "original six"), only the top four finishers qualified for playoff action. The best-of-seven Semi-Finals pitted Team #1 vs. Team #3 and Team #2 vs. Team #4. The winners of each Semi-Final series met in the best-of-seven Stanley Cup Final.

1967-68 — When it doubled in size from 6 to 12 teams, the NHL once again was divided into two divisions — East and West — of six teams apiece. The top four clubs in each division qualified for the playoffs (all series were best-of-seven):

- Series A: Team #1 (East) vs. Team #3 (East)
- Series B: Team #2 (East) vs. Team #4 (East)
- Series C: Team #1 (West) vs. Team #3 (West)
- Series D: Team #2 (West) vs. Team #4 (West)
- Series E: Winner of Series A vs. winner of Series B
- Series F: Winner of Series C vs. winner of Series D
- Series G: Winner of Series E vs. Winner of Series F

1970-71 — Same as 1967-68 except that Series E matched the winners of Series A and D, and Series F matched the winners of Series B and C.

1971-72 — Same as 1970-71, except that Series A and C matched Team #1 vs. Team #4, and Series B and D matched Team #2 vs. Team #3.

1974-75 — With the League now expanded to 18 teams in four divisions, a completely new playoff format was introduced. First, the #2 and #3 teams in each of the four divisions were pooled together in the Preliminary round. These eight (#2 and #3) clubs were ranked #1 to #8 based on regular-season record:

- Series A: Team #1 vs. Team #8 (best-of-three)
- Series B: Team #2 vs. Team #7 (best-of-three)
- Series C: Team #3 vs. Team #6 (best-of-three)
- Series D: Team #4 vs. Team #5 (best-of-three)

The winners of this Preliminary round then pooled together with the four division winners, which had received byes into this Quarter-Final round. These eight teams were again ranked #1 to #8 based on regular-season record:

- Series E: Team #1 vs. Team #8 (best-of-seven)
- Series F: Team #2 vs. Team #7 (best-of-seven)
- Series G: Team #3 vs. Team #6 (best-of-seven)
- Series H: Team #4 vs. Team #5 (best-of-seven)

The four Quarter-Finals winners, which moved on to the Semi-Finals, were then ranked #1 to #4 based on regular season record:

- Series I: Team #1 vs. Team #4 (best-of-seven)
- Series J: Team #2 vs. Team #3 (best-of-seven)
- Series K: Winner of Series I vs. winner of Series J (best-of-seven)

1977-78 — Same as 1974-75, except that the Preliminary round consisted of the #2 teams in the four divisions and the next four teams based on regular-season record (not their standings within their divisions).

1979-80 — With the addition of four WHA franchises, the League expanded its playoff structure to include 16 of its 21 teams. The four first place teams in the four divisions automatically earned playoff berths. Among the 17 other clubs, the top 12, according to regular-season record, also earned berths. All 16 teams were then pooled together and ranked #1 to #16 based on regular-season record:

- Series A: Team #1 vs. Team #16 (best-of-five)
- Series B: Team #2 vs. Team #15 (best-of-five)
- Series C: Team #3 vs. Team #14 (best-of-five)
- Series D: Team #4 vs. Team #13 (best-of-five)
- Series E: Team #5 vs. Team #12 (best-of-five)
- Series F: Team #6 vs. Team #11 (best-of-five)
- Series G: Team #7 vs. Team #10 (best-of-five)
- Series H: Team #8 vs. Team # 9 (best-of-five)

The eight Preliminary round winners, ranked #1 to #8 based on regular-season record, moved on to the Quarter-Finals:

- Series I: Team #1 vs. Team #8 (best-of-seven)
- Series J: Team #2 vs. Team #7 (best-of-seven)
- Series K: Team #3 vs. Team #6 (best-of-seven)
- Series L: Team #4 vs. Team #5 (best-of-seven)

The four Quarter-Finals winners, ranked #1 to #4 based on regular-season record, moved on to the semi-finals:

- Series M: Team #1 vs. Team #4 (best-of-seven)
- Series N: Team #2 vs. Team #3 (best-of-seven)
- Series O: Winner of Series M vs. winner of Series N (best-of-seven)

1981-82 — The first four teams in each division earned playoff berths. In each division, the first-place team opposed the fourth-place team and the second-place team opposed the third-place team in a best-of-five Division Semi-Final series (DSF). In each division, the two winners of the DSF met in a best-of-seven Division Final series (DF). The two DF winners in each conference met in a best-of-seven Conference Final series (CF). In the Prince of Wales Conference, the Adams Division winner opposed the Patrick Division winner; in the Clarence Campbell Conference, the Smythe Division winner opposed the Norris Division winner. The two CF winners met in a best-of-seven Stanley Cup Final (F) series.

1986-87 — Division Semi-Final series changed from best-of-five to best-of-seven.

1993-94 — The NHL's playoff draw is conference-based rather than division-based. At the conclusion of the regular season, the top eight teams in each of the Eastern and Western Conferences qualify for the playoffs. The teams that finish in first place in each of the League's divisions are seeded first and second in each conference's playoff draw and are assured of home ice advantage in the first two playoff rounds. The remaining teams are seeded based on their regular-season point totals. In each conference, the team seeded #1 plays #8; #2 vs. #7; #3 vs. #6; and #4 vs. #5. All series are best-of-seven with home ice rotating on a 2-2-1-1-1 basis, with the exception of matchups between Central and Pacific Division teams. These matchups will be played on a 2-3-2 basis to reduce travel. In a 2-3-2 series, the team with the most points will have its choice to start the series at home or on the road. The Eastern Conference champion will face the Western Conference champion in the Stanley Cup Final.

1994-95 — Same as 1993-94, except that in first, second or third-round playoff series involving Central and Pacific Division teams, the team with the better record has the choice of using either a 2-3-2 or a 2-2-1-1-1 format. When a 2-3-2 format is selected, the higher-ranked team also has the choice of playing games 1, 2, 6 and 7 at home or playing games 3, 4 and 5 at home. The format for the Stanley Cup Final remains 2-2-1-1-1.

1998-99 — The NHL's clubs are re-aligned into two conferences each consisting of three divisions. The number of teams qualifying for the Stanley Cup Playoffs remains unchanged at 16.

First-round playoff berths will be awarded to the first-place team in each division as well as to the next five best teams based on regular-season point totals in each conference. The three division winners in each conference will be seeded first through third, in order of points, for the playoffs and the next five best teams, in order of points, will be seeded fourth through eighth. In each conference, the team seeded #1 will play #8; #2 vs. #7; #3 vs. #6; and #4 vs. #5 in the quarterfinal round. Home-ice in the Conference Quarter-Finals is granted to those teams seeded first through fourth in each conference.

In the Conference Semi-Finals and Conference Finals, teams will be re-seeded according to the same criteria as the Conference Quarter-Finals. Higher seeded teams will have home-ice advantage.

Home ice advantage for the Stanley Cup Final is awarded to the team with the higher number of points in the regular season.

All series remain best-of-seven.

2013-14 — The NHL club's are realigned into two conferences each comprised of two divisions. The number of teams qualifying for the Stanley Cup Playoffs remains unchanged at 16. These 16 playoff teams are seeded and placed in four divisional brackets. Eastern and Western Conference teams are on opposite sides of the draw and do not cross over until the Stanley Cup Final.

Twelve of the 16 berths in the first round of the playoffs are awarded to the top three finishers in each of the four divisions. These clubs are ranked as the first three "seeds" in each divisional bracket. Four additional "wild card" berths are awarded to the next two highest-placed finishers in each conference regardless of division. Each divisional bracket is comprised of the top three finishers in one division plus a wild card team. Wild cards are seeded fourth in their respective divisional brackets.

In each conference, the wild card team with fewer regular-season points is placed in the bracket that includes the first-place finisher with the most regular-season points. The wild card team with more regular-season points is placed in the bracket that includes the first-place finisher with the second-highest number of regular-season points.

In the first round of the playoffs in each bracket, the team seeded #1 plays #4 and the team seeded #2 plays #3. In the second round, the winners of these two first-round series meet.

The two advancing teams in the East and the two advancing teams in the West meet in the Conference Finals.

The Eastern and Western Conference champions meet in the Stanley Cup Final.

Home ice advantage for the Stanley Cup Final is awarded to the team with the higher number of points in the regular season.

All series remain best-of-seven.

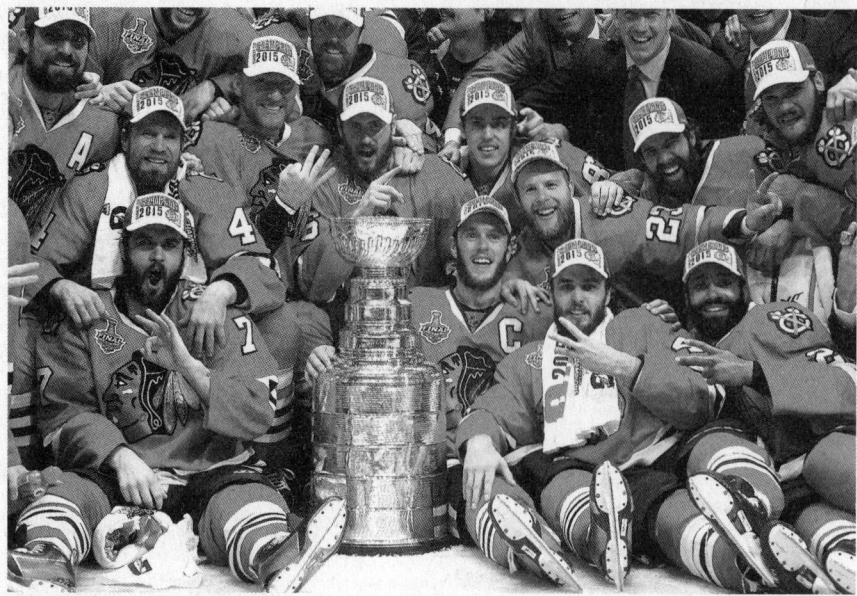

Chicago won the Stanley Cup for the third time in six seasons in 2015. The Blackhawks were nine and two at the United Center in the playoffs and won the Stanley Cup on home ice for the first time since 1938.

Team Records

1918-2015

GAMES PLAYED

MOST GAMES PLAYED BY ALL TEAMS, ONE PLAYOFF YEAR:
93 — 2014. There were 48 FR, 27 SR, 13 CF and 5 F Games.
92 — 1991. There were 51 DSF, 24 DF, 11 CF and 6 F games.
90 — **1994.** There were 48 CQF, 23 CSF, 12 CF and 7 F games.
— 2002. There were 47 CQF, 25 CSF, 13 CF and 5 F games.

MOST GAMES PLAYED, ONE TEAM, ONE PLAYOFF YEAR:
26 — Philadelphia Flyers, 1987. Won DSF 4-2 vs. NY Rangers, DF 4-3 vs. NY Islanders, CF 4-2 vs. Montreal, and lost F 4-3 vs. Edmonton.
— **Calgary Flames,** 2004. Won DSF 4-3 vs. Vancouver, DF 4-2 vs. Detroit, CF 4-2 vs. San Jose, and lost F 4-3 vs. Tampa Bay.
— **Los Angeles Kings,** 2014. Won FR 4-3 vs. San Jose, SR 4-3 vs. Anaheim, CF 4-3 vs. Chicago, and won F 4-1 vs. NY Rangers.
— **Tampa Bay Lightning,** 2015. Won FR 4-3 vs. Detroit, SR 4-2 vs. Montreal, CF 4-3 vs. NY Rangers, and lost F 4-2 vs. Chicago.
25 — New Jersey Devils, 2001. Won CQF 4-2 vs. Carolina, CSF 4-3 vs. Toronto, CF 4-1 vs. Pittsburgh, and lost F 4-3 vs. Colorado.
— Carolina Hurricanes, 2006. Won CQF 4-2 vs. Montreal, CSF 4-1 vs. New Jersey, CF 4-3 vs. Buffalo, and F 4-3 vs. Edmonton.
— Boston Bruins, 2011. Won CQF 4-3 vs. Montreal, CSF 4-0 vs. Philadelphia, CF 4-3 vs. Tampa Bay, and F 4-3 vs. Vancouver.
— Vancouver Canucks, 2011. Won CQF 4-3 vs. Chicago, CSF 4-2 vs. Nashville, CF 4-1 vs. San Jose, and lost F 4-3 vs. Boston.
— New York Rangers, 2014. Won FR 4-3 vs. Philadelphia, SR 4-3 vs. Pittsburgh, CF 4-2 vs. Montreal, and lost F 4-1 vs. Los Angeles.

PLAYOFF APPEARANCES

MOST STANLEY CUP CHAMPIONSHIPS (since 1893):
24 — Montreal Canadiens
(1916-24-30-31-44-46-53-56-57-58-59-60-65-66-68-69-71-73-76-77-78-79-86-93)
14 — Toronto Maple Leafs (1914-18-22-32-42-45-47-48-49-51-62-63-64-67)
11 — Detroit Red Wings (1936-37-43-50-52-54-55-97-98-2002-08)

MOST CONSECUTIVE STANLEY CUP CHAMPIONSHIPS:
5 — Montreal Canadiens (1956-57-58-59-60)
4 — Montreal Canadiens (1976-77-78-79)
— New York Islanders (1980-81-82-83)

MOST FINAL SERIES APPEARANCES:
32 — Montreal Canadiens in 98-year history.
24 — Detroit Red Wings in 89-year history.
21 — Toronto Maple Leafs in 98-year history.

MOST CONSECUTIVE FINAL SERIES APPEARANCES:
10 — Montreal Canadiens (1951-60, inclusive)
5 — Montreal Canadiens (1965-69, inclusive)
— New York Islanders (1980-84, inclusive)

MOST YEARS IN PLAYOFFS:
82 — Montreal Canadiens in 98-year history.
69 — Boston Bruins in 91-year history.
65 — Toronto Maple Leafs in 98-year history.

MOST CONSECUTIVE PLAYOFF APPEARANCES:
29 — Boston Bruins (1968-96, inclusive)
28 — Chicago Blackhawks (1970-97, inclusive)
25 — St. Louis Blues (1980-2004, inclusive)
24 — Montreal Canadiens (1971-94, inclusive)
— Detroit Red Wings (1991-2015 inclusive)

TEAM WINS

MOST HOME WINS, ONE TEAM, ONE PLAYOFF YEAR:
12 — New Jersey Devils, 2003 in 13 home games.
11 — Edmonton Oilers, 1988 in 11 home games.
— Detroit Red Wings, 2009 in 13 home games.
— Chicago Blackhawks, 2013 in 13 home games.
10 — Edmonton Oilers, 1985 in 10 home games.
— Montreal Canadiens, 1986 in 11 home games.
— Montreal Canadiens, 1993 in 11 home games.
— Carolina Hurricanes, 2006 in 14 home games.
— Anaheim Ducks, 2007 in 12 home games.
— Boston Bruins, 2011 in 13 home games.
— Vancouver Canucks, 2011 in 14 home games.

MOST HOME WINS, ALL TEAMS, ONE PLAYOFF YEAR:
59 — 2013. Of 86 games played, home teams won 59 (30 CQF, 20 CSF, 6 CF and 3 in F).
57 — 1991. Of 92 games played, home teams won 57 (29 DSF, 17 DF, 8 CF and 3 in F).

MOST ROAD WINS, ONE TEAM, ONE PLAYOFF YEAR:
10 — New Jersey Devils, 1995. Won three at Boston in CQF; two at Pittsburgh in CSF; three at Philadelphia in CF; and two at Detroit in F.
— **New Jersey Devils,** 2000. Won two at Florida in CQF; two at Toronto in CSF; three at Philadelphia in CF; and three at Dallas in F.
— **Calgary Flames,** 2004. Won three at Vancouver in DSF; two at Detroit in DF; three at San Jose in CF; and two at Tampa Bay in F.
— **Los Angeles Kings,** 2012. Won three at Vancouver in CQF; two at St. Louis in CSF; three at Phoenix in CF; and two at New Jersey in F.
8 — New York Islanders, 1980. Won two at Los Angeles in PR; three at Boston in QF; two at Buffalo in SF; and one at Philadelphia in F.
— Philadelphia Flyers, 1987. Won two at NY Rangers in DSF; two at NY Islanders in DF; three at Montreal in CF; and one at Edmonton in F.
— Edmonton Oilers, 1990. Won one at Winnipeg in DSF; two at Los Angeles in DF; two at Chicago in CF and three at Boston in F.
— Pittsburgh Penguins, 1992. Won two at Washington in DSF; two at NY Rangers in DF; two at Boston in CF; and two at Chicago in F.
— Vancouver Canucks, 1994. Won three at Calgary in CQF; two at Dallas in CSF; one at Toronto in CF; and two at NY Rangers in F.
— Colorado Avalanche, 1996. Won two at Vancouver in CQF; two at Chicago in CSF; two at Detroit in CF; and two at Florida in F.
— Detroit Red Wings, 1998. Won two at Phoenix in CQF; three at St. Louis in CSF; one at Dallas in CF; and two at Washington in F.
— Colorado Avalanche, 1999. Won three at San Jose in CQF; three at Detroit in CSF; and two at Dallas in CF.
— New Jersey Devils, 2001. Won two at Carolina in CQF; two at Toronto in CSF; two at Pittsburgh in CF; and two at Colorado in F.
— Detroit Red Wings, 2002. Won three at Vancouver in CQF; one at St. Louis in CSF; two at Colorado in CF; and two at Carolina in F.
— Chicago Blackhawks, 2010. Won two at Nashville in CQF; three at Vancouver in CSF; two at San Jose in CF; and one at Philadelphia in F.
— Los Angeles Kings, 2014. Won two at San Jose in FR; three at Anaheim in SR; two at Chicago in CF; and one at NY Rangers in F.
— Tampa Bay Lightning, 2015. Won two at Detroit in FR; two at Montreal in SR; three at NY Rangers in CF; and one at Chicago in F.

MOST ROAD WINS, ALL TEAMS, ONE PLAYOFF YEAR:
47 — **2012.** Of 86 games played, road teams won 47 (30 CQF, 7 CSF, 7 CF, 3 F).

MOST OVERTIME WINS, ONE TEAM, ONE PLAYOFF YEAR:
10 — **Montreal Canadiens, 1993.** Won two vs. Quebec in DSF; three vs. Buffalo in DF; two vs. NY Islanders in CF; and three vs. Los Angeles in F.
7 — Carolina Hurricanes, 2002. Won two vs. New Jersey in CQF; one vs. Montreal in CSF; three vs. Toronto in CF; and one vs. Detroit in F.
— Anaheim Mighty Ducks, 2003. Won two vs. Detroit in CQF; two vs. Dallas in CSF; one vs. Minnesota in CF; and two vs. New Jersey in F.

MOST OVERTIME WINS AT HOME, ONE TEAM, ONE PLAYOFF YEAR:
4 — **St. Louis Blues, 1968.** Won one vs. Philadelphia in QF; three vs. Minnesota in SF.
— **Montreal Canadiens, 1993.** Won one vs. Quebec in DSF; one vs. Buffalo in DF, one vs. NY Islanders in CF; one vs. Los Angeles in F.
— **Chicago Blackhawks, 2013.** Won one vs. Minnesota in CQF; one vs. Detroit in CSF; one vs. Los Angeles in CF; one vs. Boston in F.

MOST OVERTIME WINS ON THE ROAD, ONE TEAM, ONE PLAYOFF YEAR:
6 — **Montreal Canadiens, 1993.** Won one vs. Quebec in DSF; two vs. Buffalo in DF; one vs. NY Islanders in CF; two vs. Los Angeles in F.

TEAM LOSSES

MOST LOSSES, ONE TEAM, ONE PLAYOFF YEAR:
12 — **New York Rangers, 2014.** Lost three vs. Philadelphia in FR; three vs. Pittsburgh in SR; two vs. Montreal in CF; four vs. Los Angeles in F.
— **Tampa Bay Lightning, 2015.** Lost three vs. Detroit in FR; two vs. Montreal in SR; three vs. NY Rangers in CF; four vs. Chicago in F.
11 — Philadelphia Flyers, 1987. Lost two vs. NY Rangers in DSF; three vs. NY Islanders in DF; two vs. Montreal in CF; four vs. Edmonton in F.
— Calgary Flames, 2004. Lost three vs. Vancouver in CQF; two vs. Detroit in CSF; two vs. San Jose in CF; four vs. Tampa Bay in F.

MOST HOME LOSSES, ONE TEAM, ONE PLAYOFF YEAR:
7 — **Calgary Flames, 2004.** Lost two vs. Vancouver in CQF; one vs. Detroit in CSF; two vs. San Jose in CF; two vs. Tampa Bay in F.
— **Tampa Bay Lightning, 2015.** Lost two vs. Detroit in FR; one vs. Montreal in SR; two vs. NY Rangers in CF; two vs. Chicago in F.
6 — Philadelphia Flyers, 1987. Lost one vs. NY Rangers in DSF; two vs. NY Islanders in DF; two vs. Montreal in CF; one vs. Edmonton in F.
— Washington Capitals, 1998. Lost two vs. Boston in CF; two vs. Buffalo in CF; two vs. Detroit in F.
— Colorado Avalanche, 1999. Lost two vs. San Jose in CQF; two vs. Detroit in CSF; two vs. Dallas in CF.
— New Jersey Devils, 2001. Lost one vs. Carolina in CQF; two vs. Toronto in CSF; one vs. Pittsburgh in CF; two vs Colorado in F.
— Minnesota Wild, 2003. Lost two vs. Colorado in CQF; two vs. Vancouver in CSF; two vs. Anaheim in CF.

Chicago captain Keith Magnuson and goalie Tony Esposito were stars with the team when the Blackhawks lost an NHL-record 16 consecutive playoff games from 1975 to 1980.

MOST ROAD LOSSES, ONE TEAM, ONE PLAYOFF YEAR:
8 — **Los Angeles Kings, 2013.** Lost two at St. Louis in CQF; three at San Jose in CSF; three at Chicago in CF.
7 — New Jersey Devils, 2003. Lost one at Boston in CQF; one at Tampa Bay in CSF; two at Ottawa in CF; three at Anaheim in F.
— Philadelphia Flyers, 2010. Lost one at New Jersey in CQF; two at Boston in CSF; one at Montreal in CF; three at Chicago in F.
— New York Rangers, 2014. Lost two at Philadelphia in FR; one at Pittsburgh in SR; one at Montreal in CF; three at Los Angeles in F.

MOST OVERTIME LOSSES, ONE TEAM, ONE PLAYOFF YEAR:
4 — **Montreal Canadiens, 1951.** Lost four vs. Toronto in F.
— **St. Louis Blues, 1968.** Lost one vs. Philadelphia in QF; one vs. Minnesota in SF; two vs. Montreal in F.
— **New York Rangers, 1979.** Lost one vs. Philadelphia in QF; two vs. NY Islanders in SF; one vs. Montreal in F.
— **Los Angeles Kings, 1991.** Lost one vs. Vancouver in DSF; three vs. Edmonton in DF.
— **Los Angeles Kings, 1993.** Lost one vs. Toronto in CF; three vs. Montreal in F.
— **New Jersey Devils, 1994.** Lost one vs. Buffalo in CQF; one vs. Boston in CSF; two vs. NY Rangers in CF.
— **Chicago Blackhawks, 1995.** Lost one vs. Toronto in CQF; three vs. Detroit in CF.
— **Philadelphia Flyers, 1996.** Lost two vs. Tampa Bay in CQF; two vs. Florida in CSF.
— **Dallas Stars, 1999.** Lost two vs. St. Louis in CSF; one vs. Colorado in CF; one vs. Buffalo in F.
— **Detroit Red Wings, 2002.** Lost one vs. Vancouver in CQF; two vs. Colorado in CF; one vs. Carolina in F.
— **New Jersey Devils, 2003.** Lost two vs. Ottawa in CF; two vs. Anaheim in F.
— **Washington Capitals, 2012.** Lost two vs. Boston in CQF; two vs. NY Rangers in CSF.
— **New York Rangers, 2014.** Lost one vs. Montreal in CF; three vs. Los Angeles in F.

MOST OVERTIME LOSSES AT HOME, ONE TEAM, ONE PLAYOFF YEAR:
4 — **Detroit Red Wings, 2002.** Lost one vs. Vancouver in CQF; two vs. Colorado in CF; one vs. Carolina in F.

MOST OVERTIME LOSSES ON THE ROAD, ONE TEAM, ONE PLAYOFF YEAR:
3 — **Los Angeles Kings, 1991.** Lost one at Vancouver in DSF; two at Edmonton in DF.
— **Chicago Blackhawks, 1995.** Lost one at Toronto in CQF; two at Detroit in CF.
— **St. Louis Blues, 1996.** Lost two at Toronto in CQF; one at Detroit in CSF.
— **Dallas Stars, 1999.** Lost two at St. Louis in CSF; one at Colorado in CF.
— **New Jersey Devils, 2003.** Lost one at Ottawa in CF; two at Anaheim in F.
— **Los Angeles Kings, 2013.** Lost two at St. Louis in CQF; one at Chicago in CF.
— **New York Rangers, 2013.** Lost two at Washington in CQF; one at Boston in CSF.
— **New York Rangers, 2014.** Lost three at Los Angeles in F.
— **Washington Capitals, 2015.** Lost one at NY Islanders in FR; two at NY Rangers in SR.

PLAYOFF WINNING STREAKS

LONGEST PLAYOFF WINNING STREAK:
14 — **Pittsburgh Penguins.** Streak started May 9, 1992 as Pittsburgh won the first of three straight games in DF vs. NY Rangers. Continued with four wins vs. Boston in 1992 CF and four wins vs. Chicago in 1992 F. Pittsburgh then won the first three games of 1993 DSF vs. New Jersey. New Jersey ended the streak April 25, 1993, at New Jersey with a 4-1 win vs. Pittsburgh in the fourth game of 1993 DSF.
12 — Edmonton Oilers. Streak started May 15, 1984 as Edmonton won the first of three straight games in F vs. NY Islanders. Continued with three wins vs. Los Angeles in 1985 DSF and four wins vs. Winnipeg in 1985 DF. Edmonton then won the first two games of 1985 CF vs. Chicago. Chicago ended the streak May 9, 1985, at Chicago with a 5-2 win vs. Edmonton in the third game of 1985 CF.

MOST CONSECUTIVE WINS, ONE TEAM, ONE PLAYOFF YEAR:
11 — **Chicago Blackhawks** in 1992. Chicago won last three games of DSF vs. St. Louis to win series 4-2, defeated Detroit 4-0 in DF and Edmonton 4-0 in CF.
— **Pittsburgh Penguins** in 1992. Pittsburgh won last three games of DF vs. NY Rangers to win series 4-2, defeated Boston 4-0 in CF and Chicago 4-0 in F.
— **Montreal Canadiens** in 1993. Montreal won last four games of DSF vs. Quebec to win series 4-2, defeated Buffalo 4-0 in DF and won first three games of CF vs. NY Islanders.

PLAYOFF LOSING STREAKS

LONGEST PLAYOFF LOSING STREAK:
16 — **Chicago Black Hawks.** Streak started April 20, 1975 at Chicago with a 6-2 loss in fourth game of QF vs. Buffalo, won by Buffalo 4-1. Continued with four consecutive losses vs. Montreal, in 1976 QF and two straight losses vs. NY Islanders in 1977 best-of-three PR. Chicago then lost four games vs. Boston in 1978 QF and four games vs. NY Islanders in 1979 QF. Chicago ended the streak April 8, 1980, at Chicago with a 3-2 win vs. St. Louis in the opening game of 1980 PR.
14 — Los Angeles Kings. Streak started June 3, 1993 at Montreal with a 3-2 loss in second game of F vs. Montreal, won by Montreal 4-1. Los Angeles failed to qualify for the playoffs for the next four years. Then Los Angeles lost four games vs. St. Louis in 1998 CQF; missed the 1999 playoffs and lost four games vs. Detroit in 2000 CQF. Los Angeles then lost the first two games of 2001 CQF vs. Detroit. Los Angeles ended the streak April 15, 2001, at Los Angeles with a 2-1 win vs. Detroit in the third game of 2001 CQF.

MOST GOALS IN A SERIES, ONE TEAM

MOST GOALS, ONE TEAM, ONE PLAYOFF SERIES:
44 — Edmonton Oilers in 1985. Edmonton won best-of-seven CF 4-2, outscoring Chicago 44-25.
35 — Edmonton Oilers in 1983. Edmonton won best-of-seven DF 4-1, outscoring Calgary 35-13.
— Calgary Flames in 1995. Calgary lost best-of-seven CQF 4-3, outscoring San Jose 35-26.

MOST GOALS, ONE TEAM, TWO-GAME SERIES:
11 — Buffalo Sabres in 1977. Buffalo won best-of-three PR 2-0, outscoring Minnesota 11-3.
— **Toronto Maple Leafs** in 1978. Toronto won best-of-three PR 2-0, outscoring Los Angeles 11-3.

MOST GOALS, ONE TEAM, THREE-GAME SERIES:
23 — Chicago Blackhawks in 1985. Chicago won best-of-five DSF 3-0, outscoring Detroit 23-8.
20 — Minnesota North Stars in 1981. Minnesota won best-of-five PR 3-0, outscoring Boston 20-13.
— NY Islanders in 1981. NY Islanders won best-of-five PR 3-0, outscoring Toronto 20-4.

MOST GOALS, ONE TEAM, FOUR-GAME SERIES:
28 — Boston Bruins in 1972. Boston won best-of-seven SF 4-0, outscoring St. Louis 28-8.

MOST GOALS, ONE TEAM, FIVE-GAME SERIES:
35 — Edmonton Oilers in 1983. Edmonton won best-of-seven DF 4-1, outscoring Calgary 35-13.
32 — Edmonton Oilers in 1987. Edmonton won best-of-seven DSF 4-1, outscoring Los Angeles 32-20.
30 — Calgary Flames in 1988. Calgary won best-of-seven DSF 4-1, outscoring Los Angeles 30-18.

MOST GOALS, ONE TEAM, SIX-GAME SERIES:
44 — Edmonton Oilers in 1985. Edmonton won best-of-seven CF 4-2, outscoring Chicago 44-25.
33 — Montreal Canadiens in 1973. Montreal won best-of-seven F 4-2, outscoring Chicago 33-23.
— Chicago Blackhawks in 1985. Chicago won best-of-seven DF 4-2, outscoring Minnesota 33-29.
— Los Angeles Kings in 1993. Los Angeles won best-of-seven DSF 4-2, outscoring Calgary 33-28.

MOST GOALS, ONE TEAM, SEVEN-GAME SERIES:
35 — Calgary Flames in 1995. Calgary lost best-of-seven CQF 4-3, outscoring San Jose 35-26.
33 — Philadelphia Flyers in 1976. Philadelphia won best-of-seven QF 4-3, outscoring Toronto 33-23.
— Boston Bruins in 1983. Boston won best-of-seven DF 4-3, outscoring Buffalo 33-23.
— Edmonton Oilers in 1984. Edmonton won best-of-seven DF 4-3, outscoring Calgary 33-27.

FEWEST GOALS IN A SERIES, ONE TEAM

FEWEST GOALS, ONE TEAM, TWO-GAME SERIES:
0 — Toronto St. Patricks in 1921. Toronto lost two-game, total-goals NHL F 7-0 vs. Ottawa.
— **New York Americans** in 1929. NY Americans lost two-game, total-goals QF 1-0 vs. NY Rangers.
— **New York Rangers** in 1931. NY Rangers lost two-game, total-goals SF 3-0 vs. Chicago.
— **Chicago Black Hawks** in 1935. Chicago lost two-game, total-goals SF 1-0 vs. Mtl. Maroons.
— **Montreal Maroons** in 1937. Mtl. Maroons lost best-of-three SF 2-0, outscored by NY Rangers 5-0.
— **New York Americans** in 1939. NY Americans lost best-of-three QF 2-0, outscored by Toronto 5-0.

FEWEST GOALS, ONE TEAM, THREE-GAME SERIES:
1 — Montreal Maroons in 1936. Mtl. Maroons lost best-of-five SF 3-0, outscored by Detroit 6-1.

FEWEST GOALS, ONE TEAM, FOUR-GAME SERIES:
1 — Minnesota Wild in 2003. Minnesota lost best-of-seven CF 4-0, outscored by Anaheim 9-1.

FEWEST GOALS, ONE TEAM, FIVE-GAME SERIES:
2 — Philadelphia Flyers in 2002. Philadelphia lost best-of-seven CQF 4-1, outscored by Ottawa 11-2.

FEWEST GOALS, ONE TEAM, SIX-GAME SERIES:
5 — Boston Bruins in 1951. Boston lost best-of-seven SF 4-1 with 1 tie, outscored by Toronto 17-5.

FEWEST GOALS, ONE TEAM, SEVEN-GAME SERIES:
8 — Vancouver Canucks, in 2011. Vancouver lost best-of-seven F 4-3; outscored by Boston 23-8.
9 — Detroit Red Wings, in 1945. Detroit lost best-of-seven F 4-3; tied with Toronto in scoring 9-9.
— Toronto Maple Leafs, in 1945. Toronto won best-of-seven F 4-3; tied with Detroit in scoring 9-9.

During the Stanley Cup Final in 2011, Tim Thomas and the Boston Bruins held Henrik Sedin and the Vancouver Canucks to just eight goals, marking the fewest goals scored by an NHL team in a seven-game series.

MOST GOALS IN A SERIES, BOTH TEAMS

MOST GOALS, BOTH TEAMS, ONE PLAYOFF SERIES:
69 — Edmonton Oilers (44), Chicago Black Hawks (25) in 1985. Edmonton won best-of-seven CF 4-2.
62 — Chicago Black Hawks (33), Minnesota North Stars (29) in 1985. Chicago won best-of-seven DF 4-2.
61 — Los Angeles Kings (33), Calgary Flames (28) in 1993. Los Angeles won best-of-seven DSF 4-2.
— Calgary Flames (35), San Jose Sharks (26) in 1995. San Jose won best-of-seven CQF 4-3.

MOST GOALS, BOTH TEAMS, TWO-GAME SERIES:
17 — Toronto Arenas (10), Montreal Canadiens (7) in 1918. Toronto won two-game total-goals NHL F.
15 — Boston Bruins (10), Chicago Black Hawks (5) in 1927. Boston won two-game total-goals QF.
— Pittsburgh Penguins (9), St. Louis Blues (6) in 1975. Pittsburgh won best-of-three PR 2-0.

MOST GOALS, BOTH TEAMS, THREE-GAME SERIES:
33 — Minnesota North Stars (20), Boston Bruins (13) in 1981. Minnesota won best-of-five PR 3-0.
31 — Chicago Black Hawks (23), Detroit Red Wings (8) in 1985. Chicago won best-of-five DSF 3-0.
28 — Toronto Maple Leafs (18), New York Rangers (10) in 1932. Toronto won best-of-five F 3-0.

MOST GOALS, BOTH TEAMS, FOUR-GAME SERIES:
36 — Boston Bruins (28), St. Louis Blues (8) in 1972. Boston won best-of-seven SF 4-0.
— **Minnesota North Stars (18), Toronto Maple Leafs (18)** in 1983. Minnesota won best-of-five DSF 3-1.
— **Edmonton Oilers (25), Chicago Black Hawks (11)** in 1983. Edmonton won best-of-seven CF 4-0.
35 — New York Rangers (23), Los Angeles Kings (12) in 1981. NY Rangers won best-of-five PR 3-1.

MOST GOALS, BOTH TEAMS, FIVE-GAME SERIES:
- **52 — Edmonton Oilers (32), Los Angeles Kings (20)** in 1987. Edmonton won best-of-seven DSF 4-1.
- 50 — Los Angeles Kings (27), Edmonton Oilers (23) in 1982. Los Angeles won best-of-five DSF 3-2.
- 48 — Edmonton Oilers (35), Calgary Flames (13) in 1983. Edmonton won best-of-seven DF 4-1.
- — Calgary Flames (30), Los Angeles Kings (18) in 1988. Calgary won best-of-seven DSF 4-1.

MOST GOALS, BOTH TEAMS, SIX-GAME SERIES:
- **69 — Edmonton Oilers (44), Chicago Black Hawks (25)** in 1985. Edmonton won best-of-seven CF 4-2.
- 62 — Chicago Black Hawks (33), Minnesota North Stars (29) in 1985. Chicago won best-of-seven DF 4-2.
- 61 — Los Angeles Kings (33), Calgary Flames (28) in 1993. Los Angeles won best-of-seven DSF 4-2.

MOST GOALS, BOTH TEAMS, SEVEN-GAME SERIES:
- **61 — Calgary Flames (35), San Jose Sharks (26)** in 1995. San Jose won best-of-seven CQF 4-3.
- 60 — Edmonton Oilers (33), Calgary Flames (27) in 1984. Edmonton won best-of-seven DF 4-3.

FEWEST GOALS IN A SERIES, BOTH TEAMS

FEWEST GOALS, BOTH TEAMS, TWO-GAME SERIES:
- **1 — New York Rangers (1), New York Americans (0)** in 1929. NY Rangers won two-game total-goals QF.
- — **Montreal Maroons (1), Chicago Black Hawks (0)** in 1935. Mtl. Maroons won two-game total-goals SF.

FEWEST GOALS, BOTH TEAMS, THREE-GAME SERIES:
- **7 — Boston Bruins (5), Montreal Canadiens (2)** in 1929. Boston won best-of-five SF 3-0.
- — **Detroit Red Wings (6), Montreal Maroons (1)** in 1936. Detroit won best-of-five SF 3-0.

FEWEST GOALS, BOTH TEAMS, FOUR-GAME SERIES:
- **9 — Toronto Maple Leafs (7), Boston Bruins (2)** in 1935. Toronto won best-of-five SF 3-1.

FEWEST GOALS, BOTH TEAMS, FIVE-GAME SERIES:
- **11 — Montreal Maroons (6), New York Rangers (5)** in 1928. NY Rangers won best-of-five F 3-2.

FEWEST GOALS, BOTH TEAMS, SIX-GAME SERIES:
- **16 — Carolina Hurricanes (10), Toronto Maple Leafs (6)** in 2002. Carolina won best-of-seven CF 4-2.

FEWEST GOALS, BOTH TEAMS, SEVEN-GAME SERIES:
- **18 — Toronto Maple Leafs (9), Detroit Red Wings (9)** in 1945. Toronto won best-of-seven F 4-3.

MOST GOALS IN A GAME OR PERIOD

MOST GOALS, ONE TEAM, ONE GAME:
- **13 — Edmonton Oilers** April 9, 1987, vs. Los Angeles at Edmonton. Edmonton won 13-3.
- 12 — Los Angeles Kings, April 10, 1990, vs. Calgary at Los Angeles. Los Angeles won 12-4.
- 11 — Montreal Canadiens, March 30, 1944, vs. Toronto at Montreal. Montreal won 11-0.
- — Edmonton Oilers, May 4, 1985, vs. Chicago at Edmonton. Edmonton won 11-2.

MOST GOALS, ONE TEAM, ONE PERIOD:
- **7 — Montreal Canadiens,** March 30, 1944, vs. Toronto at Montreal, third period. Montreal won 11-0.

MOST GOALS, BOTH TEAMS, ONE GAME:
- **18 — Los Angeles Kings (10), Edmonton Oilers (8),** April 7, 1982, at Edmonton. Los Angeles won best-of-five DSF 3-2.
- 17 — Pittsburgh Penguins (10), Philadelphia Flyers (7), April 25, 1989, at Pittsburgh. Pittsburgh won best-of-seven DF 4-3.
- 16 — Edmonton Oilers (13), Los Angeles Kings (3), April 9, 1987, at Edmonton. Edmonton won best-of-seven DSF 4-1.
- — Los Angeles Kings (12), Calgary Flames (4), April 10, 1990, at Los Angeles. Los Angeles won best-of-seven DF 4-2.

MOST GOALS, BOTH TEAMS, ONE PERIOD:
- **9 — New York Rangers (6), Philadelphia Flyers (3),** April 24, 1979, third period, at Philadelphia. NY Rangers won 8-3.
- — **Los Angeles Kings (5), Calgary Flames (4),** April 10, 1990, second period, at Los Angeles. Los Angeles won 12-4.
- 8 — Chicago Black Hawks (5), Montreal Canadiens (3), May 8, 1973, second period, at Montreal. Chicago won 8-7.
- — Chicago Black Hawks (5), Edmonton Oilers (3), May 12, 1985, first period, at Chicago. Chicago won 8-6.
- — Edmonton Oilers (6), Winnipeg Jets (2), April 6, 1988, third period, at Edmonton. Edmonton won 7-4.
- — Hartford Whalers (5), Montreal Canadiens (3), April 10, 1988, third period, at Montreal. Hartford won 7-5.
- — Vancouver Canucks (5), New York Rangers (3), June 9, 1994, third period, at NY Rangers. Vancouver won 6-3.
- — Pittsburgh Penguins (5), Ottawa Senators (3), April 20, 2010, second period, at Ottawa. Pittsburgh won 7-4.

TEAM POWER-PLAY GOALS

MOST POWER-PLAY GOALS BY ALL TEAMS, ONE PLAYOFF YEAR:
- **199 — 1988** in 83 games.

MOST POWER-PLAY GOALS, ONE TEAM, ONE PLAYOFF YEAR:
- **35 — Minnesota North Stars,** 1991 in 23 games.
- 32 — Edmonton Oilers, 1988 in 18 games.
- 31 — New York Islanders, 1981 in 18 games.

MOST POWER-PLAY GOALS, ONE TEAM, ONE SERIES:
- **15 — New York Islanders** in 1980 F vs. Philadelphia. NY Islanders won series 4-2.
- — **Minnesota North Stars** in 1991 DSF vs. Chicago. Minnesota won series 4-2.
- 13 — New York Islanders in 1981 QF vs. Edmonton. NY Islanders won series 4-2.
- — Calgary Flames in 1986 CF vs. St. Louis. Calgary won series 4-3.
- 12 — Toronto Maple Leafs in 1976 QF vs. Philadelphia. Philadelphia won series 4-3.
- — Quebec Nordiques in 1987 CQF vs. Hartford. Quebec won series 4-3.
- — Colorado Avalanche in 1997 CQF vs. Chicago. Colorado won series 4-2.
- — Philadelphia Flyers in 2012 CQF vs. Pittsburgh. Philadelphia won series 4-2.

MOST POWER-PLAY GOALS, BOTH TEAMS, ONE SERIES:
- **21 — New York Islanders (15), Philadelphia Flyers (6)** in 1980 best-of-seven F won by NY Islanders 4-2.
- — **New York Islanders (13), Edmonton Oilers (8)** in 1981 best-of-seven QF won by NY Islanders 4-2.
- — **Philadelphia Flyers (11), Pittsburgh Penguins (10)** in 1989 best-of-seven DF won by Philadelphia 4-3.
- — **Minnesota North Stars (15), Chicago Black Hawks (6)** in 1991 best-of-seven DSF won by Minnesota 4-2.
- — **Philadelphia Flyers (12), Pittsburgh Penguins (9)** in 2012 best-of-seven CQF won by Philadelphia 4-2.
- 20 — Toronto Maple Leafs (12), Philadelphia Flyers (8) in 1976 best-of-seven QF won by Philadelphia 4-3.

MOST POWER-PLAY GOALS, ONE TEAM, ONE GAME:
- **6 — Boston Bruins,** April 2, 1969, at Boston vs. Toronto. Boston won 10-0.

MOST POWER-PLAY GOALS, BOTH TEAMS, ONE GAME:
- **8 — Minnesota North Stars (4), St. Louis Blues (4),** April 24, 1991, at Minnesota. Minnesota won 8-4.
- 7 — Minnesota North Stars (4), Edmonton Oilers (3), April 28, 1984, at Minnesota. Edmonton won 8-5.
- — Philadelphia Flyers (4), New York Rangers (3), April 13, 1985, at NY Rangers. Philadelphia won 6-5.
- — Chicago Black Hawks (5), Edmonton Oilers (2), May 14, 1985, at Edmonton. Edmonton won 10-5.
- — Edmonton Oilers (5), Los Angeles Kings (2), April 9, 1987, at Edmonton. Edmonton won 13-3.
- — Vancouver Canucks (4), Calgary Flames (3), April 9, 1989, at Vancouver. Vancouver won 5-3.
- — Pittsburgh Penguins (4), Philadelphia Flyers (3), April 18, 2012, at Philadelphia. Pittsburgh won 10-5.

MOST POWER-PLAY GOALS, ONE TEAM, ONE PERIOD:
- **4 — Toronto Maple Leafs,** March 26, 1936, second period vs. Boston at Toronto. Toronto won 8-3.
- — **Minnesota North Stars,** April 28, 1984, second period vs. Edmonton at Minnesota. Edmonton won 8-5.
- — **Boston Bruins,** April 11, 1991, third period vs. Hartford at Boston. Boston won 6-1.
- — **Minnesota North Stars,** April 24, 1991, second period vs. St. Louis at Minnesota. Minnesota won 8-4.
- — **St. Louis Blues,** April 27, 1998, third period at Los Angeles. St. Louis won 4-3.

MOST POWER-PLAY GOALS, BOTH TEAMS, ONE PERIOD:
- **5 — Minnesota North Stars (4), Edmonton Oilers (1),** April 28, 1984, at Minnesota. Edmonton won 8-5.
- — **Vancouver Canucks (3), Calgary Flames (2),** April 9, 1989, at Vancouver. Vancouver won 5-3.
- — **Minnesota North Stars (4), St. Louis Blues (1),** April 24, 1991, at Minnesota. Minnesota won 8-4.

TEAM SHORTHAND GOALS

MOST SHORTHAND GOALS BY ALL TEAMS, ONE PLAYOFF YEAR:
- **33 — 1988,** in 83 games.

MOST SHORTHAND GOALS, ONE TEAM, ONE PLAYOFF YEAR:
- **10 — Edmonton Oilers,** 1983, in 16 games.
- 9 — New York Islanders, 1981, in 19 games.
- 8 — Philadelphia Flyers, 1989, in 19 games.

MOST SHORTHAND GOALS, ONE TEAM, ONE SERIES:
- **6 — Calgary Flames** in 1995 vs. San Jose in best-of-seven CQF won by San Jose 4-3.
- — **Vancouver Canucks** in 1995 vs. St. Louis in best-of-seven CQF won by Vancouver 4-3.
- 5 — New York Rangers in 1979 vs. Philadelphia in best-of-seven QF won by NY Rangers 4-1.
- — Edmonton Oilers in 1983 vs. Calgary in best-of-seven DF won by Edmonton 4-1.

MOST SHORTHAND GOALS, BOTH TEAMS, ONE SERIES:
- **7 — Boston Bruins (4), New York Rangers (3),** in 1958 SF won by Boston 4-2.
- — **Edmonton Oilers (5), Calgary Flames (2),** in 1983 DF won by Edmonton 4-1.
- — **Vancouver Canucks (6), St. Louis Blues (1),** in 1995 CQF won by Vancouver 4-3.

MOST SHORTHAND GOALS, ONE TEAM, ONE GAME:
3 — **Boston Bruins,** April 11, 1981, at Minnesota North Stars. Minnesota won 6-3.
— **New York Islanders,** April 17, 1983, at NY Rangers. NY Rangers won 7-6.
— **Edmonton Oilers,** April 17, 1983, at Calgary Flames. Edmonton won 10-2.

MOST SHORTHAND GOALS, BOTH TEAMS, ONE GAME:
4 — **Boston Bruins (3), Minnesota North Stars (1),** April 11, 1981, at Minnesota. Minnesota won 6-3.
— **New York Islanders (3), New York Rangers (1),** April 17, 1983, at NY Rangers. NY Rangers won 7-6.
3 — Toronto Maple Leafs (2), Detroit Red Wings (1), April 5, 1947, at Toronto. Toronto won 6-1.
— New York Rangers (2), Boston Bruins (1), April 1, 1958, at Boston. NY Rangers won 5-2.
— Minnesota North Stars (2), Philadelphia Flyers (1), May 4, 1980, at Minnesota. Philadelphia won 5-3.
— Winnipeg Jets (2), Edmonton Oilers (1), April 9, 1988, at Winnipeg. Winnipeg won 6-4.
— New York Islanders (2), New Jersey Devils (1), April 14, 1988, at New Jersey. New Jersey won 6-5.
— Toronto Maple Leafs (2), San Jose Sharks (1), May 8, 1994, at San Jose. Toronto won 8-3.
— Montreal Canadiens (2), New Jersey Devils (1), April 17, 1997, at New Jersey. New Jersey won 5-2.
— Dallas Stars (2), San Jose Sharks (1), May 5, 2000, at San Jose. Dallas won 5-4.
— Detroit Red Wings (2), Calgary Flames (1), April 21, 2007, at Detroit. Detroit won 5-1.

MOST SHORTHAND GOALS, ONE TEAM, ONE PERIOD:
2 — **Toronto Maple Leafs,** April 5, 1947, first period vs. Detroit at Toronto. Toronto won 6-1.
— **Toronto Maple Leafs,** April 13, 1965, first period vs. Montreal at Toronto. Montreal won 4-3.
— **Boston Bruins,** April 20, 1969, first period vs. Montreal at Boston. Boston won 3-2.
— **Boston Bruins,** April 8, 1970, second period vs. NY Rangers at Boston. Boston won 8-2.
— **Boston Bruins,** April 30, 1972, first period vs. NY Rangers at Boston. Boston won 6-5.
— **Chicago Black Hawks,** May 3, 1973, first period vs. Montreal at Chicago. Chicago won 7-4.
— **Montreal Canadiens,** April 23, 1978, first period at Detroit. Montreal won 8-0.
— **New York Islanders,** April 8, 1980, second period vs. Los Angeles at NY Islanders. NY Islanders won 8-1.
— **Los Angeles Kings,** April 9, 1980, first period at NY Islanders. Los Angeles won 6-3.
— **Boston Bruins,** April 13, 1980, second period at Pittsburgh. Boston won 8-3.
— **Minnesota North Stars,** May 4, 1980, second period vs. Philadelphia at Minnesota. Philadelphia won 5-3.
— **Boston Bruins,** April 11, 1981, third period at Minnesota North Stars. Minnesota won 6-3.
— **New York Islanders,** May 12, 1981, first period vs. Minnesota North Stars at NY Islanders. NY Islanders won 6-3.
— **Montreal Canadiens,** April 7, 1982, third period vs. Quebec at Montreal. Montreal won 5-1.
— **Edmonton Oilers,** April 24, 1983, third period vs. Chicago at Edmonton. Edmonton won 8-4.
— **Winnipeg Jets,** April 14, 1985, second period at Calgary. Winnipeg won 5-3.
— **Boston Bruins,** April 6, 1988, first period vs. Buffalo at Boston. Boston won 7-3.
— **New York Islanders,** April 14, 1988, third period at New Jersey. New Jersey won 6-5.
— **Detroit Red Wings,** April 29, 1993, second period at Toronto. Detroit won 7-3.
— **Toronto Maple Leafs,** May 8, 1994, third period at San Jose. Toronto won 8-3.
— **Calgary Flames,** May 11, 1995, first period at San Jose. Calgary won 9-2.
— **Vancouver Canucks,** May 15, 1995, second period at St. Louis. Vancouver won 6-5.
— **Montreal Canadiens,** April 17, 1997, second period at New Jersey. New Jersey won 5-2.
— **Philadelphia Flyers,** April 26, 1997, first period vs. Pittsburgh at Philadelphia. Philadelphia won 6-3.
— **Phoenix Coyotes,** April 24, 1998, second period at Detroit. Phoenix won 7-4.
— **Buffalo Sabres,** April 27, 1998, second period vs. Philadelphia at Buffalo. Buffalo won 6-1.
— **San Jose Sharks,** April 30, 1999, third period at Colorado. San Jose won 7-3.
— **Detroit Red Wings,** April 27, 2002, second period at Vancouver. Detroit won 6-4.
— **Detroit Red Wings,** April 21, 2007, second period at Detroit. Detroit won 5-1.

MOST SHORTHAND GOALS, BOTH TEAMS, ONE PERIOD:
3 — **Toronto Maple Leafs (2), Detroit Red Wings (1),** April 5, 1947, first period at Toronto. Toronto won 6-1.
— **Toronto Maple Leafs (2), San Jose Sharks (1),** May 8, 1994, third period at San Jose. Toronto won 8-3.

FASTEST GOALS

FASTEST FIVE GOALS, BOTH TEAMS:
3:06 — **Minnesota North Stars, Chicago Black Hawks,** April 21, 1985, at Chicago. Keith Brown scored for Chicago at 1:12 of the second period; Ken Yaremchuk, Chicago, 1:27; Dino Ciccarelli, Minnesota, 2:48; Tony McKegney, Minnesota, 4:07; and Curt Fraser, Chicago, 4:18. Chicago won 6-2 and won best-of-seven DF 4-2.
3:20 — Minnesota North Stars, Philadelphia Flyers, April 29, 1980, at Philadelphia. Paul Shmyr scored for Minnesota at 13:20 of the first period; Steve Christoff, Minnesota, 13:59; Ken Linseman, Philadelphia, 14:54; Tom Gorence, Philadelphia, 15:36; and Ken Linseman, Philadelphia, 16:40. Minnesota won 6-5. Philadelphia won best-of-seven SF 4-1.
3:58 — Detroit Red Wings, Phoenix Coyotes, April 16, 2010, at Phoenix. Henrik Zetterberg scored for Detroit at 6:27 of the second period; Wojtek Wolski, Phoenix, 7:05; Pavel Datsyuk, Detroit, 8:20; Matthew Lombardi, Phoenix, 9:09; Valtteri Filppula, Detroit, 10:25. Detroit won 7-4 and won best-of-seven CQF 4-3.

FASTEST FIVE GOALS, ONE TEAM:
3:36 — **Montreal Canadiens,** March 30, 1944, at Montreal vs. Toronto. Toe Blake scored at 7:58 and 8:37 of the third period; Maurice Richard, 9:17; Ray Getliffe, 10:33; and Buddy O'Connor, 11:34. Canadiens won 11-0 and won best-of-seven SF 4-1.

FASTEST FOUR GOALS, BOTH TEAMS:
1:33 — **Toronto Maple Leafs, Philadelphia Flyers,** April 20, 1976, at Philadelphia. Don Saleski scored for Philadelphia at 10:04 of the second period; Bob Neely, Toronto, 10:42; Gary Dornhoefer, Philadelphia, 11:24; and Don Saleski, Philadelphia, 11:37. Philadelphia won 7-1 and won best-of-seven SF 4-3.
1:34 — Calgary Flames, Montreal Canadiens, May 20, 1986, at Montreal. Joel Otto scored for Calgary at 17:59 of the first period; Bobby Smith, Montreal, 18:25; Mats Naslund, Montreal, 19:17; and Bob Gainey, Montreal, 19:33. Montreal won 5-3 and won best-of-seven F 4-1.
1:38 — Boston Bruins, Philadelphia Flyers, April 26, 1977, at Philadelphia. Gregg Sheppard scored for Boston at 14:01 of the second period; Mike Milbury, Boston, 15:01; Gary Dornhoefer, Philadelphia, 15:16; and Jean Ratelle, Boston, 15:39. Boston won 5-4 and won best-of-seven SF 4-0.

FASTEST FOUR GOALS, ONE TEAM:
2:35 — **Montreal Canadiens,** March 30, 1944, at Montreal. Toe Blake scored at 7:58 and 8:37 of the third period; Maurice Richard, 9:17; and Ray Getliffe, 10:33. Montreal won 11-0 and won best-of-seven SF 4-1.

FASTEST THREE GOALS, BOTH TEAMS:
0:21 — **Chicago Black Hawks, Edmonton Oilers,** May 7, 1985, at Edmonton. Behn Wilson scored for Chicago at 19:22 of the third period; Jari Kurri, Edmonton, 19:36; and Glenn Anderson, Edmonton, 19:43. Edmonton won 7-3 and won best-of-seven CF 4-2.
0:27 — Phoenix Coyotes, Detroit Red Wings, April 24, 1998, at Detroit. Jeremy Roenick scored for Phoenix at 13:24 of the second period; Mathieu Dandenault, Detroit, 13:32; and Keith Tkachuk, Phoenix, 13:51. Phoenix won 7-4. Detroit won best-of-seven CQF 4-2.
0:30 — Pittsburgh Penguins, Chicago Blackhawks, June 1, 1992, at Chicago. Dirk Graham scored for Chicago at 6:21 of the first period; Kevin Stevens, Pittsburgh, 6:33; and Dirk Graham, Chicago, 6:51. Pittsburgh won 6-5 and won best-of-seven F 4-0.

FASTEST THREE GOALS, ONE TEAM:
0:23 — **Toronto Maple Leafs,** April 12, 1979, at Toronto vs. Atlanta Flames. Darryl Sittler scored at 4:04 and 4:16 of the first period; and Ron Ellis, 4:27. Toronto won 7-4 and won best-of-three PR 2-0.
0:37 — Anaheim Ducks, May 23, 2015, at Chicago. Ryan Kesler scored at 8:42 of the third period; Matt Belesky, 9:05; and Corey Perry, 9:19. Chicago won 5-4 and won best-of-seven CF 4-3.
0:38 — New York Rangers, April 12, 1986, at NY Rangers vs. Philadelphia. Jim Weimer scored at 12:29 of the third period; Bob Brooke, 12:43; and Ron Greschner, 13:07. NY Rangers won 5-2 and won best-of-five DSF 3-2.
— Colorado Avalanche, April 18, 2001, at Vancouver. Peter Forsberg scored at 9:11 of the third period; Joe Sakic, 9:28; and Eric Messier, 9:49. Colorado won 5-1 and won best-of-seven CQF 4-0.

FASTEST TWO GOALS, BOTH TEAMS:
0:05 — **Pittsburgh Penguins, Buffalo Sabres,** April 14, 1979, at Buffalo. Gilbert Perreault scored for Buffalo at 12:59 of the first period; and Jim Hamilton, Pittsburgh, 13:04. Pittsburgh won 4-3 and won best-of-three PR 2-1.
0:06 — Philadelphia Flyers, Pittsburgh Penguins, April 13, 2012 at Pittsburgh. Claude Giroux scored for Philadelphia at 11:04 of the second period; and Chris Kunitz, Pittsburgh, 11:10. Philadelphia won 8-5. Philadelphia won best-of-seven CQF 4-2.
0:08 — St. Louis Blues, Minnesota North Stars, April 9, 1989, at Minnesota. Bernie Federko scored for St. Louis at 2:28 of the third period; and Perry Berezan, Minnesota, 2:36. Minnesota won 5-4. St. Louis won best-of-seven DSF 4-1.
— Phoenix Coyotes, Detroit Red Wings, April 24, 1998, at Detroit. Jeremy Roenick scored for Phoenix at 13:24 of the second period; and Mathieu Dandenault, Detroit, 13:32. Phoenix won 7-4. Detroit won best-of-seven CQF 4-2.

FASTEST TWO GOALS, ONE TEAM:
0:05 — **Detroit Red Wings,** April 11, 1965, at Detroit vs. Chicago. Norm Ullman scored at 17:35 and 17:40 of the second period. Detroit won 4-2. Chicago won best-of-seven SF 4-3.

Marcus Kruger turns away to begin celebrating after ending the longest overtime game of the 2015 playoffs. Kruger scored at 16:12 of the third extra session to give Chicago a 3-2 win over Anaheim on May 19, 2015.

OVERTIME

SHORTEST OVERTIME:
0:09 — Montreal Canadiens, Calgary Flames, May 18, 1986, at Calgary. Montreal won 3-2 on Brian Skrudland's goal at 0:09 of the first overtime period. Montreal won best-of-seven F 4-1.
0:11 — New York Islanders, New York Rangers, April 11, 1975, at NY Rangers. NY Islanders won 4-3 on J.P. Parise's goal at 0:11 of the first overtime period. NY Islanders won best-of-three PR 2-1.
— Vancouver Canucks, Boston Bruins, June 4, 2011, at Vancouver. Vancouver won 3-2 on Alexandre Burrows' goal at 0:11 of the first overtime period. Boston won best-of-seven F 4-3.

LONGEST OVERTIME:
116:30 — Detroit Red Wings, Montreal Maroons, March 24, 1936, at Montreal. Mtl. Maroons won 1-0 on Mud Bruneteau's goal at 16:30 of the sixth overtime period. Detroit won best-of-five SF 3-0.

MOST OVERTIME GAMES, ONE PLAYOFF YEAR:
28 — 1993. Of 85 games played, 28 went into overtime.
27 — 2013. Of 86 games played, 27 went into overtime.
26 — 2001. Of 86 games played, 26 went into overtime.
— 2014. Of 93 games played, 26 went into overtime.

FEWEST OVERTIME GAMES, ONE PLAYOFF YEAR:
0 — 1963. None of the 16 games went into overtime, the only year since 1926 that no overtime was required in any playoff series.

MOST OVERTIME GAMES, ONE SERIES:
5 — Toronto Maple Leafs, Montreal Canadiens in 1951. Toronto won best-of-seven F 4-1.
— **Phoenix Coyotes, Chicago Blackhawks** in 2012. Phoenix won best-of-seven CQF 4-2.
4 — Toronto Maple Leafs, Boston Bruins in 1933. Toronto won best-of-five SF 3-2.
— Boston Bruins, New York Rangers in 1939. Boston won best-of-seven SF 4-3.
— St. Louis Blues, Minnesota North Stars in 1968. St. Louis won best-of-seven SF 4-3.
— Dallas Stars, St. Louis Blues in 1999. Dallas won best-of-seven CSF 4-2.
— Dallas Stars, Edmonton Oilers in 2001. Dallas won best-of-seven CQF 4-2.
— Dallas Stars, San Jose Sharks in 2008. Dallas won best-of-seven CSF 4-2
— Washington Capitals, Boston Bruins in 2012. Washington won best-of-seven CQF 4-3
— Detroit Red Wings, Anaheim Ducks in 2013. Detroit won best-of-seven CQF 4-3
— Minnesota Wild, Colorado Avalanche in 2014. Minnesota won best-of-seven FR 4-3
— Chicago Blackhawks, St. Louis Blues in 2014. Chicago won best-of-seven FR 4-2

TEAM HAT-TRICKS

MOST HAT-TRICKS, BY ALL TEAMS, ONE PLAYOFF YEAR:
12 — 1983 in 66 games.
— **1988** in 83 games.
11 — 1985 in 70 games.
— 1992 in 86 games.

MOST HAT-TRICKS, ONE TEAM, ONE PLAYOFF YEAR:
6 — Edmonton Oilers in 16 games, 1983.
— **Edmonton Oilers** in 18 games, 1985.

SHUTOUTS

MOST SHUTOUTS, ONE PLAYOFF YEAR, ALL TEAMS:
25 — 2002. Of 90 games played, Detroit had 6; Ottawa had 4; Carolina, Colorado, St. Louis and Toronto had 3 each; while Los Angeles, New Jersey and Philadelphia had 1 each.
23 — 2004. Of 89 games played, Tampa Bay and Calgary had 5 each; Toronto and San Jose had 3 each; while Boston, Colorado, Detroit, Montreal, Nashville, NY Islanders and Philadelphia had 1 each.
19 — 2001. Of 86 games played, Colorado and New Jersey had 4 each, Toronto had 3, Pittsburgh and Los Angeles had 2 each, while Buffalo, Washington, Detroit and San Jose had 1 each.

FEWEST SHUTOUTS, ONE PLAYOFF YEAR, ALL TEAMS:
0 — 1959. 18 games played.

MOST SHUTOUTS, BOTH TEAMS, ONE SERIES:
5 — Toronto Maple Leafs (3), Detroit Red Wings (2), in 1945. Toronto won best-of-seven F 4-3.
— **Toronto Maple Leafs (3), Detroit Red Wings (2),** in 1950. Detroit won best-of-seven SF 4-3.

TEAM PENALTIES

FEWEST PENALTIES, BOTH TEAMS, BEST-OF-SEVEN SERIES:
19 — Detroit Red Wings, Toronto Maple Leafs in 1945. Detroit received 10 minors, Toronto received 9 minors. Toronto won best-of-seven F 4-3.

FEWEST PENALTIES, ONE TEAM, BEST-OF-SEVEN SERIES:
9 — Toronto Maple Leafs in 1945 vs. Detroit. Toronto received 9 minors. Toronto won best-of-seven F 4-3.

MOST PENALTIES, BOTH TEAMS, ONE SERIES:
218 — New Jersey Devils, Washington Capitals in 1988. New Jersey received 97 minors, 11 majors, 9 misconducts and 1 match penalty. Washington received 80 minors, 11 majors, 8 misconducts and 1 match penalty. New Jersey won best-of-seven DF 4-3.

MOST PENALTY MINUTES, BOTH TEAMS, ONE SERIES:
654 — New Jersey Devils (349), Washington Capitals (305) in 1988. New Jersey won best-of-seven DF 4-3.

MOST PENALTIES, ONE TEAM, ONE SERIES:
118 — New Jersey Devils in 1988 vs. Washington. New Jersey received 97 minors, 11 majors, 9 misconducts and 1 match penalty. New Jersey won best-of-seven DF 4-3.

MOST PENALTY MINUTES, ONE TEAM, ONE SERIES:
349 — New Jersey Devils in 1988 vs. Washington. New Jersey won best-of-seven DF 4-3.

MOST PENALTIES, BOTH TEAMS, ONE GAME:
66 — Detroit Red Wings (33), St. Louis Blues (33), April 12, 1991, at St. Louis. St. Louis won 6-1.
63 — Minnesota North Stars (34), Chicago Blackhawks (29), April 6, 1990, at Chicago. Chicago won 5-3.
62 — New Jersey Devils (32), Washington Capitals (30), April 22, 1988, at New Jersey. New Jersey won 10-4.

MOST PENALTY MINUTES, BOTH TEAMS, ONE GAME:
298 — Detroit Red Wings (152), St. Louis Blues (146), April 12, 1991, at St. Louis. Detroit received 33 penalties; St. Louis received 33 penalties. St. Louis won 6-1.
267 — New York Rangers (142), Los Angeles Kings (125), April 9, 1981, at Los Angeles. NY Rangers received 31 penalties; Los Angeles received 28 penalties. Los Angeles won 5-4.

MOST PENALTIES, ONE TEAM, ONE GAME:
34 — Minnesota North Stars, April 6, 1990, at Chicago. Chicago won 5-3.
33 — Detroit Red Wings, April 12, 1991, at St. Louis. St. Louis won 6-1.
— St. Louis Blues, April 12, 1991, at St. Louis vs. Detroit. St. Louis won 6-1.

MOST PENALTY MINUTES, ONE TEAM, ONE GAME:
152 — Detroit Red Wings, April 12, 1991, at St. Louis. St. Louis won 6-1.
146 — St. Louis Blues, April 12, 1991, at St. Louis vs. Detroit. St. Louis won 6-1.
142 — New York Rangers, April 9, 1981, at Los Angeles. Los Angeles won 5-4.

MOST PENALTIES, BOTH TEAMS, ONE PERIOD:
43 — New York Rangers (24), Los Angeles Kings (19), April 9, 1981, first period at Los Angeles. Los Angeles won 5-4.

MOST PENALTY MINUTES, BOTH TEAMS, ONE PERIOD:
248 — New York Islanders (124), Boston Bruins (124), April 17, 1980, first period at Boston. NY Islanders won 5-4.

MOST PENALTIES, ONE TEAM, ONE PERIOD:
24 — New York Rangers, April 9, 1981, first period at Los Angeles. Los Angeles won 5-4.

Individual Records

GAMES PLAYED

MOST YEARS IN PLAYOFFS:
24 — Chris Chelios, Montreal, Chicago, Detroit (1984-97 inclusive; 1999-2004 inclusive, 2006-2009 inclusive)
21 — Raymond Bourque, Boston, Colorado (1980-96 inclusive; 98-2001 inclusive)
20 — Gordie Howe, Detroit, Hartford
— Larry Robinson, Montreal, Los Angeles
— Larry Murphy, Los Angeles, Washington, Minnesota, Pittsburgh, Toronto, Detroit
— Scott Stevens, Washington, St. Louis, New Jersey
— Steve Yzerman, Detroit
— Nicklas Lidstrom, Detroit

MOST CONSECUTIVE YEARS IN PLAYOFFS:
20 — Larry Robinson, Montreal, Los Angeles (1973-92, inclusive).
— **Nicklas Lidstrom, Detroit** (1992-2004 inclusive; 2006-2012 inclusive)
19 — Brett Hull, Calgary, St. Louis, Dallas, Detroit (1986-2004, inclusive).
18 — Larry Murphy, Los Angeles, Washington, Minnesota, Pittsburgh, Toronto, Detroit (1984-2001, inclusive).
17 — Brad Park, NY Rangers, Boston, Detroit (1969-85, inclusive).
— Raymond Bourque, Boston (1980-96, inclusive).
— Kris Draper, Detroit (1994-2004 inclusive; 2006-2011 inclusive)

MOST PLAYOFF GAMES:
266 — Chris Chelios, Montreal, Chicago, Detroit
263 — Nicklas Lidstrom, Detroit
247 — Patrick Roy, Montreal, Colorado
236 — Mark Messier, Edmonton, NY Rangers
234 — Claude Lemieux, Montreal, New Jersey, Colorado, Phoenix, Dallas, San Jose

GOALS

MOST GOALS IN PLAYOFFS, CAREER:
122 — Wayne Gretzky, Edmonton, Los Angeles, St. Louis, NY Rangers
109 — Mark Messier, Edmonton, NY Rangers
106 — Jari Kurri, Edmonton, Los Angeles, NY Rangers, Anaheim
103 — Brett Hull, Calgary, St. Louis, Dallas, Detroit
93 — Glenn Anderson, Edmonton, Toronto, NY Rangers, St. Louis

MOST GOALS, ONE PLAYOFF YEAR:
19 — Reggie Leach, Philadelphia, 1976. 16 games.
— **Jari Kurri, Edmonton,** 1985. 18 games.
18 — Joe Sakic, Colorado, 1996. 22 games.
17 — Newsy Lalonde, Montreal, 1919. 10 games.
— Mike Bossy, NY Islanders, 1981. 18 games.
— Steve Payne, Minnesota, 1981. 19 games.
— Mike Bossy, NY Islanders, 1982. 19 games.
— Mike Bossy, NY Islanders, 1983. 19 games
— Wayne Gretzky, Edmonton, 1985. 18 games.
— Kevin Stevens, Pittsburgh, 1991. 24 games.

MOST GOALS IN ONE SERIES (OTHER THAN FINAL):
12 — Jari Kurri, Edmonton, in 1985 CF, 6 games vs. Chicago.
11 — Newsy Lalonde, Montreal, in 1919 NHL F, 5 games vs. Ottawa.
10 — Tim Kerr, Philadelphia, in 1989 DF, 7 games vs. Pittsburgh.
9 — Reggie Leach, Philadelphia, in 1976 SF, 5 games vs. Boston.
— Bill Barber, Philadelphia, in 1980 SF, 5 games vs. Minnesota.
— Mike Bossy, NY Islanders, in 1983 CF, 6 games vs. Boston.
— Mario Lemieux, Pittsburgh, in 1989 DF, 7 games vs. Philadelphia.
— John Druce, Washington, in 1990 DF, 5 games vs. NY Rangers.
— Johan Franzen, Detroit, in 2008 CSF, 4 games vs. Colorado.

MOST GOALS IN FINAL SERIES (NHL PLAYERS ONLY):
9 — Babe Dye, Toronto, in 1922, 5 games vs. Van. Millionaires.
8 — Alf Skinner, Toronto, in 1918, 5 games vs. Van. Millionaires.
7 — Jean Beliveau, Montreal, in 1956, 5 games vs. Detroit.
— Mike Bossy, NY Islanders, in 1982, 4 games vs. Vancouver.
— Wayne Gretzky, Edmonton, in 1985, 5 games vs. Philadelphia.

MOST GOALS, ONE GAME:
5 — Newsy Lalonde, Montreal, March 1, 1919, at Montreal. Final score: Montreal 6, Ottawa 3.
— **Maurice Richard, Montreal,** March 23, 1944, at Montreal. Final score: Montreal 5, Toronto 1.
— **Darryl Sittler, Toronto,** April 22, 1976, at Toronto. Final score: Toronto 8, Philadelphia 5.
— **Reggie Leach, Philadelphia,** May 6, 1976, at Philadelphia. Final score: Philadelphia 6, Boston 3.
— **Mario Lemieux, Pittsburgh,** April 25, 1989, at Pittsburgh. Final score: Pittsburgh 10, Philadelphia 7.

MOST GOALS, ONE PERIOD:
4 — Tim Kerr, Philadelphia, April 13, 1985, at NY Rangers, second period. Final score: Philadelphia 6, NY Rangers 5.
— **Mario Lemieux, Pittsburgh,** April 25, 1989, at Pittsburgh vs. Philadelphia, first period. Final score: Pittsburgh 10, Philadelphia 7.

ASSISTS

MOST ASSISTS IN PLAYOFFS, CAREER:
260 — Wayne Gretzky, Edmonton, Los Angeles, St. Louis, NY Rangers
186 — Mark Messier, Edmonton, NY Rangers
139 — Raymond Bourque, Boston, Colorado
137 — Paul Coffey, Edmonton, Pittsburgh, Los Angeles, Detroit, Philadelphia, Carolina
129 — Nicklas Lidstrom, Detroit

MOST ASSISTS, ONE PLAYOFF YEAR:
31 — Wayne Gretzky, Edmonton, 1988. 19 games.
30 — Wayne Gretzky, Edmonton, 1985. 18 games.
29 — Wayne Gretzky, Edmonton, 1987. 21 games.
28 — Mario Lemieux, Pittsburgh, 1991. 23 games.
26 — Wayne Gretzky, Edmonton, 1983. 16 games.

MOST ASSISTS IN ONE SERIES (OTHER THAN FINAL):
14 — Rick Middleton, Boston, in 1983 DF, 7 games vs. Buffalo.
— **Wayne Gretzky, Edmonton,** in 1985 CF, 6 games vs. Chicago.
13 — Wayne Gretzky, Edmonton, in 1987 DSF, 5 games vs. Los Angeles.
— Doug Gilmour, Toronto, in 1994 CSF, 7 games vs. San Jose.
11 — Al MacInnis, Calgary, in 1984 DF, 7 games vs. Edmonton.
— Mark Messier, Edmonton, in 1989 DSF, 7 games vs. Los Angeles.
— Mike Ridley, Washington, in 1992 DSF, 7 games vs. Pittsburgh.
— Ron Francis, Pittsburgh, in 1995 CQF, 7 games vs. Washington.
— Henrik Sedin, Vancouver, in 2011 CF, 5 games vs. San Jose.

MOST ASSISTS IN FINAL SERIES:
10 — Wayne Gretzky, Edmonton, in 1988, 4 games plus suspended game vs. Boston.
9 — Jacques Lemaire, Montreal, in 1973, 6 games vs. Chicago.
— Wayne Gretzky, Edmonton, in 1985, 7 games vs. Philadelphia.
— Larry Murphy, Pittsburgh, in 1991, 6 games vs. Minnesota.
— Daniel Briere, Philadelphia, in 2010, 6 games vs. Chicago.

MOST ASSISTS, ONE GAME:
6 — Mikko Leinonen, NY Rangers, April 8, 1982, at NY Rangers. Final score: NY Rangers 7, Philadelphia 3.
— **Wayne Gretzky, Edmonton,** April 9, 1987, at Edmonton. Final score: Edmonton 13, Los Angeles 3.
5 — Toe Blake, Montreal, March 23, 1944, at Montreal. Final score: Montreal 5, Toronto 1.
— Maurice Richard, Montreal, March 27, 1956, at Montreal. Final score: Montreal 7, NY Rangers 0.
— Bert Olmstead, Montreal, March 30, 1957, at Montreal. Final score: Montreal 8, NY Rangers 3.
— Don McKenney, Boston, April 5, 1958, at Boston. Final score: Boston 8, NY Rangers 2.
— Stan Mikita, Chicago, April 4, 1973, at Chicago. Final score: Chicago 7, St. Louis 1.
— Wayne Gretzky, Edmonton, April 8, 1981, at Montreal. Final score: Edmonton 6, Montreal 3.
— Paul Coffey, Edmonton, May 14, 1985, at Edmonton. Final score: Edmonton 10, Chicago 5.
— Doug Gilmour, St. Louis, April 15, 1986, at Minnesota. Final score: St. Louis 6, Minnesota 3.
— Risto Siltanen, Quebec, April 14, 1987, at Hartford. Final score: Quebec 7, Hartford 5.
— Patrik Sundstrom, New Jersey, April 22, 1988, at New Jersey. Final score: New Jersey 10, Washington 4.
— Geoff Courtnall, St. Louis, April 23, 1998, at St. Louis. Final score: St. Louis 8, Los Angeles 3.

MOST ASSISTS, ONE PERIOD:
3 — Three assists by one player in one period of a playoff game has been recorded on 87 occasions. Duncan Keith of the Chicago Blackhawks is the most recent to equal this mark with 3 assists in the second period at Chicago, May 27, 2015. Final score: Chicago 5, Anaheim 2.
— Wayne Gretzky has had 3 assists in one period 5 times; Raymond Bourque, 3 times; Toe Blake, Jean Beliveau, Doug Harvey and Bobby Orr, twice each. Joe Primeau of Toronto was the first player to be credited with 3 assists in one period of a playoff game; third period at Boston vs. NY Rangers, April 7, 1932. Final score: Toronto 6, NY Rangers 2.

POINTS

MOST POINTS IN PLAYOFFS, CAREER:
382 — Wayne Gretzky, Edmonton, Los Angeles, St. Louis, NY Rangers, 122G, 260A
295 — Mark Messier, Edmonton, NY Rangers, 109G, 186A
233 — Jari Kurri, Edmonton, Los Angeles, NY Rangers, Anaheim, 106G, 127A
214 — Glenn Anderson, Edmonton, Toronto, NY Rangers, St. Louis, 93G, 121A
199 — Jaromir Jagr, Pittsburgh, Washington, NY Rangers, Philadelphia, Boston, 78G, 121A

MOST POINTS, ONE PLAYOFF YEAR:
47 — Wayne Gretzky, Edmonton, in 1985. 17 goals, 30 assists in 18 games.
44 — Mario Lemieux, Pittsburgh, in 1991. 16 goals, 28 assists in 23 games.
43 — Wayne Gretzky, Edmonton, in 1988. 12 goals, 31 assists in 19 games.
40 — Wayne Gretzky, Los Angeles, in 1993. 15 goals, 25 assists in 24 games.
38 — Wayne Gretzky, Edmonton, in 1983. 12 goals, 26 assists in 16 games.

MOST POINTS IN ONE SERIES (OTHER THAN FINAL):
19 — Rick Middleton, Boston, in 1983 DF, 7 games vs. Buffalo. 5 goals, 14 assists.
18 — Wayne Gretzky, Edmonton, in 1985 CF, 6 games vs. Chicago. 4 goals, 14 assists.
17 — Mario Lemieux, Pittsburgh, in 1992 DSF, 6 games vs. Washington. 7 goals, 10 assists.
16 — Barry Pederson, Boston, in 1983 DF, 7 games vs. Buffalo. 7 goals, 9 assists.
— Doug Gilmour, Toronto, in 1994 CSF, 7 games vs. San Jose. 3 goals, 13 assists.
15 — Jari Kurri, Edmonton, in 1985 CF, 6 games vs. Chicago. 12 goals, 3 assists.
— Wayne Gretzky, Edmonton, in 1987 DSF, 5 games vs. Los Angeles. 2 goals, 13 assists.
— Tim Kerr, Philadelphia, in 1989 DF, 7 games vs. Pittsburgh. 10 goals, 5 assists.
— Mario Lemieux, Pittsburgh, in 1991 CF, 6 games vs. Boston. 6 goals, 9 assists.

MOST POINTS IN FINAL SERIES:
13 — **Wayne Gretzky, Edmonton,** in 1988, 4 games plus suspended game vs. Boston. 3 goals, 10 assists.
12 — Gordie Howe, Detroit, in 1955, 7 games vs. Montreal. 5 goals, 7 assists.
— Yvan Cournoyer, Montreal, in 1973, 6 games vs. Chicago. 6 goals, 6 assists.
— Jacques Lemaire, Montreal, in 1973, 6 games vs. Chicago. 3 goals, 9 assists.
— Mario Lemieux, Pittsburgh, in 1991, 5 games vs. Minnesota. 5 goals, 7 assists.
— Daniel Briere, Philadelphia, in 2010, 6 games vs. Chicago. 3 goals, 9 assists.

MOST POINTS, ONE GAME:
8 — **Patrik Sundstrom, New Jersey,** April 22, 1988, at New Jersey in 10-4 win over Washington. Sundstrom had 3 goals, 5 assists.
— **Mario Lemieux, Pittsburgh,** April 25, 1989, at Pittsburgh in 10-7 win over Philadelphia. Lemieux had 5 goals, 3 assists.
7 — Wayne Gretzky, Edmonton, April 17, 1983, at Calgary in 10-2 win. Gretzky had 4 goals, 3 assists.
— Wayne Gretzky, Edmonton, April 25,1985, at Winnipeg in 8-3 win. Gretzky had 3 goals, 4 assists.
— Wayne Gretzky, Edmonton, April 9, 1987, at Edmonton in 13-3 win over Los Angeles. Gretzky had 1 goal, 6 assists.
6 — Dickie Moore, Montreal, March 25, 1954, at Montreal in 8-1 win over Boston. Moore had 2 goals, 4 assists.
— Phil Esposito, Boston, April 2, 1969, at Boston in 10-0 win over Toronto. Esposito had 4 goals, 2 assists.
— Darryl Sittler, Toronto, April 22, 1976, at Toronto in 8-5 win over Philadelphia. Sittler had 5 goals, 1 assist.
— Guy Lafleur, Montreal, April 11, 1977, at Montreal in 7-2 win over St. Louis. Lafleur had 3 goals, 3 assists.
— Mikko Leinonen, NY Rangers, April 8, 1982, at NY Rangers in 7-3 win over Philadelphia. Leinonen had 6 assists.
— Paul Coffey, Edmonton, May 14, 1985, at Edmonton in 10-5 win over Chicago. Coffey had 1 goal, 5 assists.
— John Anderson, Hartford, April 12, 1986, at Hartford in 9-4 win over Quebec. Anderson had 2 goals, 4 assists.
— Mario Lemieux, Pittsburgh, April 23, 1992, at Pittsburgh in 6-4 win over Washington. Lemieux had 3 goals, 3 assists.
— Geoff Courtnall, St. Louis, April 23, 1998, at St. Louis in 8-3 win over Los Angeles. Courtnall had 1 goal, 5 assists.
— Patrick Elias, New Jersey, April 22, 2006, at New Jersey in 6-1 win over NY Rangers. Elias had 2 goals, 4 assists.
— Johan Franzen, Detroit, May 6, 2010, at Detroit in 7-1 win over San Jose. Franzen had 4 goals, 2 assists.
— Claude Giroux, Philadelphia, April 13, 2012, at Pittsburgh in 8-5 win. Giroux had 3 goals, 3 assists.

MOST POINTS, ONE PERIOD:
4 — **Maurice Richard,** Montreal, March 29, 1945, at Montreal, third period, in 10-3 win vs. Toronto. 3 goals, 1 assist.
— **Dickie Moore,** Montreal, March 25, 1954, at Montreal, first period, in 8-1 win vs. Boston. 2 goals, 2 assists.
— **Barry Pederson,** Boston, April 8, 1982, at Boston, second period, in 7-3 win vs. Buffalo. 3 goals, 1 assist.
— **Peter McNab,** Boston, April 11, 1982, at Buffalo, second period, in 5-2 win vs. Buffalo. 1 goal, 3 assists.
— **Tim Kerr,** Philadelphia, April 13, 1985, at NY Rangers, second period, in 6-5 win vs. NY Rangers. 4 goals.
— **Ken Linseman,** Boston, April 14, 1985, at Boston, second period, in 7-6 win vs. Montreal. 2 goals, 2 assists.
— **Wayne Gretzky,** Edmonton, April 12, 1987, at Los Angeles, third period, in 6-3 win vs. Los Angeles. 1 goal, 3 assists.
— **Glenn Anderson,** Edmonton, April 6, 1988, at Edmonton, third period, in 7-4 win vs. Winnipeg. 3 goals, 1 assist.
— **Mario Lemieux,** Pittsburgh, April 25, 1989, at Pittsburgh, first period, in 10-7 win vs. Philadelphia. 4 goals.
— **Dave Gagner,** Minnesota North Stars, April 8, 1991, at Minnesota, first period, in 6-5 loss vs. Chicago. 2 goals, 2 assists.
— **Mario Lemieux,** Pittsburgh, April 23, 1992, at Pittsburgh, second period, in 6-4 win vs. Washington. 2 goals, 2 assists.
— **Alexander Mogilny,** New Jersey, April 28, 2001, at New Jersey, second period, in 6-5 win vs. Toronto. 1 goal, 3 assists.
— **Brad Richards,** Dallas, April 27, 2008, at San Jose, third period, in 5-2 win vs. San Jose. 1 goal, 3 assists.
— **Johan Franzen,** Detroit, May 6, 2010, at Detroit, first period, in 7-1 win over San Jose. 3 goals, 1 assist.
— **Tyler Seguin,** Boston, May 17, 2011, at Boston, second period, in 6-5 win over Tampa Bay. 2 goals, 2 assists.
— **Jeff Carter,** Los Angeles, May 21, 2014, at Chicago, third period, in 6-2 win over Chicago. 3 goals, 1 assist.

POWER-PLAY GOALS

MOST POWER-PLAY GOALS IN PLAYOFFS, CAREER:
38 — **Brett Hull, St. Louis, Dallas, Detroit**
35 — Mike Bossy, NY Islanders
34 — Dino Ciccarelli, Minnesota, Washington, Detroit
— Wayne Gretzky, Edmonton, Los Angeles, St. Louis, NY Rangers
30 — Nicklas Lidstrom, Detroit

MOST POWER-PLAY GOALS, ONE PLAYOFF YEAR:
9 — **Mike Bossy, NY Islanders,** 1981. 18 games vs. Toronto, Edmonton, NY Rangers and Minnesota.
— **Cam Neely, Boston,** 1991. 19 games vs. Hartford, Montreal and Pittsburgh.
8 — Tim Kerr, Philadelphia, 1989. 19 games.
— John Druce, Washington, 1990. 15 games.
— Brian Propp, Minnesota, 1991. 23 games.
— Mario Lemieux, Pittsburgh, 1992. 15 games.

MOST POWER-PLAY GOALS, ONE PLAYOFF SERIES:
6 — **Chris Kontos, Los Angeles,** 1989 DSF vs. Edmonton, won by Los Angeles 4-3.
5 — Andy Bathgate, Detroit, 1966 SF vs. Chicago, won by Detroit 4-2.
— Denis Potvin, NY Islanders, 1981 QF vs. Edmonton, won by NY Islanders 4-2.
— Ken Houston, Calgary, 1981 QF vs. Philadelphia, won by Calgary 4-3.
— Rick Vaive, Chicago, 1988 DSF vs. St. Louis, won by St. Louis 4-1.
— Tim Kerr, Philadelphia, 1989 DF vs. Pittsburgh, won by Philadelphia 4-3.
— Mario Lemieux, Pittsburgh, 1989 DF vs. Philadelphia, won by Philadelphia 4-3.
— John Druce, Washington, 1990 DF vs. NY Rangers, won by Washington 4-1.
— Pat LaFontaine, Buffalo, 1992 DSF vs. Boston, won by Boston 4-3.
— Adam Graves, NY Rangers, 1996 CQF vs Montreal, won by NY Rangers 4-2.

MOST POWER-PLAY GOALS, ONE GAME:
3 — **Syd Howe, Detroit,** March 23, 1939, at Detroit vs. Montreal. Detroit won 7-3.
— **Sid Smith, Toronto,** April 10, 1949, at Detroit. Toronto won 3-1.
— **Phil Esposito, Boston,** April 2, 1969, at Boston vs. Toronto. Boston won 10-0.
— **John Bucyk, Boston,** April 21, 1974, at Boston vs. Chicago. Boston won 8-6.
— **Denis Potvin, NY Islanders,** April 17, 1981, at NY Islanders vs. Edmonton. NY Islanders won 6-3.
— **Tim Kerr, Philadelphia,** April 13, 1985, at NY Rangers. Philadelphia won 6-5.
— **Jari Kurri, Edmonton,** April 9, 1987, at Edmonton vs. Los Angeles. Edmonton won 13-3.
— **Mark Johnson, New Jersey,** April 22, 1988, at New Jersey vs. Washington. New Jersey won 10-4.
— **Dino Ciccarelli, Detroit,** April 29, 1993, at Toronto. Detroit won 7-3.
— **Dino Ciccarelli, Detroit,** May 11, 1995, at Dallas. Detroit won 5-1.
— **Valeri Kamensky, Colorado,** April 24, 1997, at Colorado vs. Chicago. Colorado won 7-0.
— **Jonathan Toews, Chicago** May 7, 2010, at Vancouver. Chicago won 7-4.

MOST POWER-PLAY GOALS, ONE PERIOD:
3 — **Tim Kerr, Philadelphia,** April 13, 1985, at NY Rangers, second period in 6-5 win.
2 — Two power-play goals have been scored by one player in one period on 63 occasions. Charlie Conacher of Toronto was the first to score two power-play goals in one period, setting the mark with two power-play goals in the second period at Toronto vs. Boston, March 26, 1936. Final score: Toronto 8, Boston 3. Logan Couture of the San Jose Sharks is the most recent to equal this mark with two power-play goals in the third period at San Jose, May 5, 2013. Final score: San Jose 5, Vancouver 2.

SHORTHAND GOALS

MOST SHORTHAND GOALS IN PLAYOFFS, CAREER:
12 — **Mark Messier, Edmonton, NY Rangers**
11 — Wayne Gretzky, Edmonton, Los Angeles, St. Louis
10 — Jari Kurri, Edmonton, Los Angeles, NY Rangers
8 — Ed Westfall, Boston, NY Islanders
— Hakan Loob, Calgary

MOST SHORTHAND GOALS, ONE PLAYOFF YEAR:
3 — **Derek Sanderson, Boston,** 1969. 1 vs. Toronto in QF, won by Boston 4-0; 2 vs. Montreal in SF, won by Montreal, 4-2.
— **Bill Barber, Philadelphia,** 1980. All vs. Minnesota in SF, won by Philadelphia 4-1.
— **Lorne Henning, NY Islanders,** 1980. 1 vs. Boston in QF, won by NY Islanders 4-1; 1 vs. Buffalo in SF, won by NY Islanders 4-2, 1 vs. Philadelphia in F, won by NY Islanders 4-2.
— **Wayne Gretzky, Edmonton,** 1983. 2 vs. Winnipeg in DSF, won by Edmonton 3-0; 1 vs. Calgary in DF, won by Edmonton 4-1.
— **Wayne Presley, Chicago,** 1989. All vs. Detroit in DSF, won by Chicago 4-2.
— **Todd Marchant, Edmonton,** 1997. 1 vs. Dallas in CQF, won by Edmonton 4-3; 2 vs. Colorado in CSF, won by Colorado 4-1.

Blackhawks captain Jonathan Toews was the only player during the 2015 playoffs who scored a power-play goal (he had three) and a shorthand goal (he was one of 12 players with one).

MOST SHORTHAND GOALS, ONE PLAYOFF SERIES:
  3 — **Bill Barber, Philadelphia,** 1980 SF vs. Minnesota, won by Philadelphia 4-1.
  — **Wayne Presley, Chicago,** 1989 DSF vs. Detroit, won by Chicago 4-2.
  2 — Mac Colville, NY Rangers, 1940 SF vs. Boston, won by NY Rangers 4-2.
  — Jerry Toppazzini, Boston, 1958 SF vs. NY Rangers, won by Boston 4-2.
  — Dave Keon, Toronto, 1963 F vs. Detroit, won by Toronto 4-1.
  — Bob Pulford, Toronto, 1964 F vs. Detroit, won by Toronto 4-3.
  — Serge Savard, Montreal, 1968 F vs. St. Louis, won by Montreal 4-0.
  — Derek Sanderson, Boston, 1969 SF vs. Montreal, won by Montreal 4-2.
  — Bryan Trottier, NY Islanders, 1980 PR vs. Los Angeles, won by NY Islanders 3-1.
  — Bobby Lalonde, Boston, 1981 PR vs. Minnesota, won by Minnesota 3-0.
  — Butch Goring, NY Islanders, 1981 SF vs. NY Rangers, won by NY Islanders 4-0.
  — Wayne Gretzky, Edmonton, 1983 DSF vs. Winnipeg, won by Edmonton 3-0.
  — Mark Messier, Edmonton, 1983 DF vs. Calgary, won by Edmonton 4-1.
  — Jari Kurri, Edmonton, 1983 CF vs. Chicago, won by Edmonton 4-0.
  — Wayne Gretzky, Edmonton, 1985 DF vs. Winnipeg, won by Edmonton 4-0.
  — Kevin Lowe, Edmonton, 1987 F vs. Philadelphia, won by Edmonton 4-3.
  — Bob Gould, Washington, 1988 DSF vs. Philadelphia, won by Washington 4-3.
  — Dave Poulin, Philadelphia, 1989 DF vs. Pittsburgh, won by Philadelphia 4-3.
  — Russ Courtnall, Montreal, 1991 DF vs. Boston, won by Boston 4-3.
  — Sergei Fedorov, Detroit, 1992 DSF vs. Minnesota, won by Detroit 4-3.
  — Mark Messier, NY Rangers, 1992 DSF vs. New Jersey, won by NY Rangers 4-3.
  — Tom Fitzgerald, NY Islanders, 1993 DF vs. Pittsburgh, won by NY Islanders 4-3.
  — Mark Osborne, Toronto, 1994 CSF vs. San Jose, won by Toronto 4-3.
  — Tony Amonte, Chicago, 1997 CQF vs. Colorado, won by Colorado 4-2.
  — Brian Rolston, New Jersey, 1997 CQF vs. Montreal, won by New Jersey 4-1.
  — Rod Brind'Amour, Philadelphia, 1997 CQF vs. Pittsburgh, won by Philadelphia 4-1.
  — Todd Marchant, Edmonton, 1997 CSF vs. Colorado, won by Colorado 4-1.
  — Jeremy Roenick, Phoenix, 1998 CQF vs. Detroit, won by Detroit 4-2.
  — Vincent Damphousse, San Jose, 1999 CQF vs. Colorado, won by Colorado 4-2.
  — Dixon Ward, Buffalo, 1999 CF vs. Toronto, won by Buffalo 4-1.
  — Curtis Brown, Buffalo, 2001 CSF vs. Pittsburgh, won by Pittsburgh 4-3.
  — John Madden, New Jersey, 2006 CQF vs. NY Rangers, won by New Jersey 4-0.
  — David Legwand, Nashville, 2011 CSF vs. Vancouver, won by Vancouver 4-2.
  — Maxime Talbot, Philadelphia, 2012 CQF vs. Pittsburgh, won by Philadelphia 4-2.
  — Dustin Brown, Los Angeles, 2012 CQF vs. Vancouver, won by Los Angeles 4-1.
  — Pascal Dupuis, Pittsburgh, 2013 CSF vs. Ottawa, won by Pittsburgh 4-1.

MOST SHORTHAND GOALS, ONE GAME:
  2 — **Dave Keon, Toronto,** April 18, 1963, at Toronto, in 3-1 win vs. Detroit.
  — **Bryan Trottier, NY Islanders,** April 8, 1980, at NY Islanders, in 8-1 win vs. Los Angeles.
  — **Bobby Lalonde, Boston,** April 11, 1981, at Minnesota, in 6-3 loss vs. Minnesota.
  — **Wayne Gretzky, Edmonton,** April 6, 1983, at Edmonton, in 6-3 win vs. Winnipeg.
  — **Jari Kurri, Edmonton,** April 24, 1983, at Edmonton, in 8-3 win vs. Chicago.
  — **Wayne Gretzky, Edmonton,** April 25, 1985, at Winnipeg, in 8-3 win by Edmonton.
  — **Mark Messier, NY Rangers,** April 21, 1992, at NY Rangers, in 7-3 loss vs. New Jersey.
  — **Tom Fitzgerald, NY Islanders,** May 8, 1993, at NY Islanders, in 6-5 win vs. Pittsburgh.
  — **Rod Brind'Amour, Philadelphia,** April 26, 1997, at Philadelphia, in 6-3 win vs. Pittsburgh.
  — **Jeremy Roenick, Phoenix,** April 24, 1998, at Detroit, in 7-4 win by Phoenix.
  — **Vincent Damphousse, San Jose,** April 30, 1999, at Colorado, in 7-3 win by San Jose.
  — **John Madden, New Jersey,** April 24, 2006, at New Jersey, in 4-1 win vs. NY Rangers.
  — **Dustin Brown, Los Angeles,** April 13, 2012, at Vancouver, in 4-2 win vs. Vancouver.

MOST SHORTHAND GOALS, ONE PERIOD:
  2 — **Bryan Trottier, NY Islanders,** April 8, 1980, second period, at NY Islanders, in 8-1 win vs. Los Angeles.
  — **Bobby Lalonde, Boston,** April 11, 1981, third period, at Minnesota, in 6-3 loss vs. Minnesota.
  — **Jari Kurri, Edmonton,** April 24, 1983, third period, at Edmonton, in 8-4 win vs. Chicago.
  — **Rod Brind'Amour, Philadelphia,** April 26, 1997, first period, at Philadelphia, in 6-3 win vs. Pittsburgh.
  — **Jeremy Roenick, Phoenix,** April 24, 1998, second period, at Detroit, in 7-4 win by Phoenix.
  — **Vincent Damphousse, San Jose,** April 30, 1999, third period, at Colorado, in 7-3 win vs. Colorado.

GAME-WINNING GOALS

MOST GAME-WINNING GOALS IN PLAYOFFS, CAREER:
  24 — **Wayne Gretzky, Edmonton, Los Angeles, St. Louis, NY Rangers**
  — **Brett Hull, St. Louis, Dallas, Detroit**
  19 — Claude Lemieux, Montreal, New Jersey, Colorado
  — Joe Sakic, Colorado
  18 — Maurice Richard, Montreal

MOST GAME-WINNING GOALS, ONE PLAYOFF YEAR:
  7 — **Brad Richards, Tampa Bay,** 2004. 23 games.
  6 — Joe Sakic, Colorado, 1996. 22 games.
  — Joe Nieuwendyk, Dallas, 1999. 23 games.
  5 — Mike Bossy, NY Islanders, 1983. 19 games.
  — Jari Kurri, Edmonton, 1987. 21 games.
  — Bobby Smith, Minnesota, 1991. 23 games.
  — Mario Lemieux, Pittsburgh, 1992. 15 games.
  — Fernando Pisani, Edmonton, 2006. 24 games.
  — Johan Franzen, Detroit, 2008. 16 games.
  — Dustin Byfuglien, Chicago, 2010. 22 games.

MOST GAME-WINNING GOALS, ONE PLAYOFF SERIES:
  4 — **Mike Bossy, NY Islanders,** 1983 CF vs. Boston, won by NY Islanders 4-2.

OVERTIME GOALS

MOST OVERTIME GOALS IN PLAYOFFS, CAREER:
  8 — **Joe Sakic, Colorado** (2 in 1996; 1 in 1998; 1 in 2001; 2 in 2004; 1 in 2006; 1 in 2008)
  6 — Maurice Richard, Montreal
  5 — Glenn Anderson, Edmonton, Toronto, St. Louis
  4 — Bob Nystrom, NY Islanders
  — Dale Hunter, Quebec, Washington
  — Wayne Gretzky, Edmonton, Los Angeles
  — Stephane Richer, Montreal, New Jersey
  — Joe Murphy, Edmonton, Chicago
  — Esa Tikkanen, Edmonton, NY Rangers
  — Jaromir Jagr, Pittsburgh
  — Kirk Muller, Montreal, Dallas
  — Jeremy Roenick, Chicago, Philadelphia
  — Chris Drury, Colorado, Buffalo
  — Jamie Langenbrunner, Dallas, New Jersey
  — Patrick Kane, Chicago
  — Patrick Marleau, San Jose
  — Martin St. Louis, Tampa Bay, NY Rangers

MOST OVERTIME GOALS, ONE PLAYOFF YEAR:
  3 — **Mel Hill, Boston,** 1939. All vs. NY Rangers in best-of-seven SF, won by Boston 4-3.
  — **Maurice Richard, Montreal,** 1951. 2 vs. Detroit in best-of-seven SF, won by Montreal 4-2; 1 vs. Toronto best-of-seven F, won by Toronto 4-1.

MOST OVERTIME GOALS, ONE PLAYOFF SERIES:
  3 — **Mel Hill, Boston,** 1939, SF vs. NY Rangers, won by Boston 4-3. Hill scored at 59:25 of overtime March 21 for a 2-1 win; at 8:24 of overtime, March 23 for a 3-2 win; and at 48:00 of overtime, April 2 for a 2-1 win.

SCORING BY A DEFENSEMAN

MOST GOALS BY A DEFENSEMAN, ONE PLAYOFF YEAR:
  12 — **Paul Coffey, Edmonton,** 1985. 18 games.
  11 — Brian Leetch, NY Rangers, 1994. 23 games.
  9 — Bobby Orr, Boston, 1970. 14 games.
  — Brad Park, Boston, 1978. 15 games.
  8 — Denis Potvin, NY Islanders, 1981. 18 games.
  — Raymond Bourque, Boston, 1983. 17 games.
  — Denis Potvin, NY Islanders, 1983. 20 games.
  — Paul Coffey, Edmonton, 1984. 19 games.

MOST GOALS BY A DEFENSEMAN, ONE GAME:
  3 — **Bobby Orr, Boston,** April 11, 1971, at Montreal.
  Final score: Boston 5, Montreal 2.
  — **Dick Redmond, Chicago,** April 4, 1973, at Chicago.
  Final score: Chicago 7, St. Louis 1.
  — **Denis Potvin, NY Islanders,** April 17, 1981, at NY Islanders.
  Final score: NY Islanders 6, Edmonton 3.
  — **Paul Reinhart, Calgary,** April 14, 1983, at Edmonton.
  Final score: Edmonton 6, Calgary 3.
  — **Doug Halward, Vancouver,** April 7, 1984, at Vancouver.
  Final score: Vancouver 7, Calgary 0.
  — **Paul Reinhart, Calgary,** April 8, 1984, at Vancouver.
  Final score: Calgary 5, Vancouver 1.
  — **Al Iafrate, Washington,** April 26, 1993, at Washington.
  Final score: Washington 6, NY Islanders 4.
  — **Eric Desjardins, Montreal,** June 3, 1993, at Montreal.
  Final score: Montreal 3, Los Angeles 2.
  — **Gary Suter, Chicago,** April 24, 1994, at Chicago.
  Final score: Chicago 4, Toronto 3.
  — **Brian Leetch, NY Rangers,** May 22, 1995, at Philadelphia.
  Final score: Philadelphia 4, NY Rangers 3.
  — **Andy Delmore, Philadelphia,** May 7, 2000, at Philadelphia.
  Final score: Philadelphia 6, Pittsburgh 3.

MOST ASSISTS BY A DEFENSEMAN, ONE PLAYOFF YEAR:
  25 — **Paul Coffey, Edmonton,** 1985. 18 games.
  24 — Al MacInnis, Calgary, 1989. 22 games.
  23 — Brian Leetch, NY Rangers, 1994. 23 games.
  19 — Bobby Orr, Boston, 1972. 15 games.
  18 — Raymond Bourque, Boston, 1988. 23 games.
  — Raymond Bourque, Boston, 1991. 19 games.
  — Larry Murphy, Pittsburgh, 1991. 23 games.
  — Chris Pronger, Philadelphia, 2010. 23 games.
  — Duncan Keith, Chicago, 2015. 23 games.

MOST ASSISTS BY A DEFENSEMAN, ONE GAME:
  5 — **Paul Coffey, Edmonton,** May 14, 1985, at Edmonton vs. Chicago. Edmonton won 10-5.
  — **Risto Siltanen, Quebec,** April 14, 1987, at Hartford. Quebec won 7-5.

MOST POINTS BY A DEFENSEMAN, ONE PLAYOFF YEAR:
  37 — **Paul Coffey, Edmonton,** 1985. 12 goals, 25 assists in 18 games.
  34 — Brian Leetch, NY Rangers, 1994. 11 goals, 23 assists in 23 games.
  31 — Al MacInnis, Calgary, 1989. 7 goals, 24 assists in 22 games.
  25 — Denis Potvin, NY Islanders, 1981. 8 goals, 17 assists in 18 games.
  — Raymond Bourque, Boston, 1991. 7 goals, 18 assists in 19 games.

MOST POINTS BY A DEFENSEMAN, ONE GAME:
6 — **Paul Coffey, Edmonton,** May 14, 1985, at Edmonton vs. Chicago. 1 goal, 5 assists. Edmonton won 10-5.
5 — Eddie Bush, Detroit, April 9, 1942, at Detroit vs. Toronto. 1 goal, 4 assists. Detroit won 5-2.
— Bob Dailey, Philadelphia, May 1, 1980, at Philadelphia vs. Minnesota. 1 goal, 4 assists. Philadelphia won 7-0.
— Denis Potvin, NY Islanders, April 17, 1981, at NY Islanders vs. Edmonton. 3 goals, 2 assists. NY Islanders won 6-3.
— Risto Siltanen, Quebec, April 14, 1987, at Hartford. 5 assists. Quebec won 7-5.

SCORING BY A ROOKIE

MOST GOALS BY A ROOKIE, ONE PLAYOFF YEAR:
14 — **Dino Ciccarelli, Minnesota,** 1981. 19 games.
11 — Jeremy Roenick, Chicago, 1990. 20 games.
— Brad Marchand, Boston, 2011. 25 games.
10 — Claude Lemieux, Montreal, 1986. 20 games.
9 — Pat Flatley, NY Islanders, 1984. 21 games

MOST ASSISTS BY A ROOKIE, ONE PLAYOFF YEAR:
14 — **Ville Leino, Philadelphia,** 2010. 19 games.
13 — Don Maloney, NY Rangers, 1979. 18 games.

MOST POINTS BY A ROOKIE, ONE PLAYOFF YEAR:
21 — **Dino Ciccarelli, Minnesota,** 1981. 14 goals, 7 assists in 19 games.
— **Ville Leino, Philadelphia,** 2010. 7 goals, 14 assists in 19 games.
20 — Don Maloney, NY Rangers, 1979. 7 goals, 13 assists in 18 games.

THREE-OR-MORE-GOAL GAMES

MOST THREE-OR-MORE-GOAL GAMES IN PLAYOFFS, CAREER:
10 — **Wayne Gretzky, Edmonton, Los Angeles, NY Rangers.** Eight three-goal games; two four-goal games.
7 — Maurice Richard, Montreal. Four three-goal games; two four-goal games; one five-goal game.
— Jari Kurri, Edmonton. Six three-goal games; one four-goal game.
6 — Dino Ciccarelli, Minnesota, Washington, Detroit. Five three-goal games; one four-goal game.
5 — Mike Bossy, NY Islanders. Four three-goal games; one four-goal game.

MOST THREE-OR-MORE-GOAL GAMES, ONE PLAYOFF YEAR:
4 — **Jari Kurri, Edmonton,** 1985. 1 four-goal game, 3 three-goal games.
3 — Mark Messier, Edmonton, 1983. 3 three-goal games.
— Mike Bossy, NY Islanders, 1983. 1 four-goal game, 2 three-goal games
2 — Newsy Lalonde, Montreal, 1919. 1 three-goal game, 1 four-goal game.
— Maurice Richard, Montreal, 1944. 1 five-goal game; 1 three-goal game.
— Doug Bentley, Chicago, 1944. 2 three-goal games.
— Norm Ullman, Detroit, 1964. 2 three-goal games.
— Phil Esposito, Boston, 1970. 2 three-goal games.
— Pit Martin, Chicago, 1973. 2 three-goal games.
— Rick MacLeish, Philadelphia, 1975. 2 three-goal games.
— Lanny McDonald, Toronto, 1977. 1 four-goal game; 1 three-goal game.
— Wayne Gretzky, Edmonton, 1981. 2 three-goal games.
— Wayne Gretzky, Edmonton, 1983. 2 four-goal games.
— Wayne Gretzky, Edmonton, 1985. 2 three-goal games.
— Petr Klima, Detroit, 1988. 2 three-goal games.
— Cam Neely, Boston, 1991. 2 three-goal games.
— Wayne Gretzky, NY Rangers, 1997. 2 three-goal games.
— Daniel Alfredsson, Ottawa, 1998. 2 three-goal games.
— Patrick Marleau, San Jose, 2004. 2 three-goal games.
— Johan Franzen, Detroit, 2008. 2 three-goal games.

MOST THREE-OR-MORE-GOAL GAMES, ONE PLAYOFF SERIES:
3 — **Jari Kurri, Edmonton,** 1985 CF vs. Chicago, won by Edmonton 4-2. Kurri scored 3 goals May 7 at Edmonton in 7-3 win, 3 goals May 14 at Edmonton in 10-5 win and 4 goals May 16 at Chicago in 8-2 win.
2 — Doug Bentley, Chicago, 1944 SF vs. Detroit, won by Chicago 4-1. Bentley scored 3 goals March 28 at Chicago in 7-1 win and 3 goals March 30 at Detroit in 5-2 win.
— Norm Ullman, Detroit, 1964 SF vs. Chicago, won by Detroit 4-3. Ullman scored 3 goals March 29 at Chicago in 5-4 win and 3 goals April 7 at Detroit in 7-2 win.
— Mark Messier, Edmonton, 1983 DF vs. Calgary, won by Edmonton 4-1. Messier scored 4 goals April 14 at Edmonton in 6-3 win and 3 goals April 17 at Calgary in 10-2 win.
— Mike Bossy, NY Islanders, 1983 CF vs. Boston, won by NY Islanders 4-2. Bossy scored 3 goals May 3 at NY Islanders in 8-3 win and 4 goals May 7 at New York in 8-4 win.
— Johan Franzen, Detroit, 2008 CSF vs. Colorado, won by Detroit 4-0. Franzen scored 3 goals Apr. 26 at Detroit in 5-1 win and 3 goals May 1 at Colorado in 8-2 win.

SCORING STREAKS

LONGEST CONSECUTIVE GOAL-SCORING STREAK, ONE PLAYOFF YEAR:
10 Games — **Reggie Leach, Philadelphia,** 1976. Streak started April 17 at Toronto and ended May 9 at Montreal. He scored one goal in each of eight games; two in one game; and five in another; a total of 15 goals.

LONGEST CONSECUTIVE POINT-SCORING STREAK, ONE PLAYOFF YEAR:
18 games — **Bryan Trottier, NY Islanders,** 1981. 11 goals, 18 assists, 29 points.
17 games — Wayne Gretzky, Edmonton, 1988. 12 goals, 29 assists, 41 points.
— Al MacInnis, Calgary, 1989. 7 goals, 19 assists, 26 points.

LONGEST CONSECUTIVE POINT-SCORING STREAK, MORE THAN ONE PLAYOFF YEAR:
27 games — **Bryan Trottier, NY Islanders,** 1980, 1981 and 1982. 7 games in 1980 (3 goals, 5 assists, 8 points), 18 games in 1981 (11 goals, 18 assists, 29 points), and two games in 1982 (2 goals, 3 assists, 5 points). Total points, 42.
19 games — Wayne Gretzky, Edmonton, Los Angeles, 1988 and 1989. 17 games in 1988 (12 goals, 29 assists, 41 points with Edmonton), 2 games in 1989 (1 goal, 2 assists, 3 points with Los Angeles). Total points, 44.
— Al MacInnis, Calgary, 1989 and 1990. 17 games in 1989 (7 goals, 19 assists, 26 points), and two games in 1990 (2 goals, 1 assist, 3 points). Total points, 29.

FASTEST GOALS

FASTEST GOAL FROM START OF GAME:
0:06 — **Don Kozak, Los Angeles,** April 17, 1977, at Los Angeles vs. Boston and goaltender Gerry Cheevers. Los Angeles won 7-4.
0:07 — Bob Gainey, Montreal, May 5, 1977, at NY Islanders vs. goaltender Glenn Resch. Montreal won 2-1.
— Terry Murray, Philadelphia, April 12, 1981, at Quebec vs. goaltender Dan Bouchard. Quebec won 4-3 in overtime.

FASTEST GOAL FROM START OF PERIOD (OTHER THAN FIRST):
0:06 — **Pelle Eklund, Philadelphia,** April 25, 1989, at Pittsburgh vs. goaltender Tom Barrasso, second period. Pittsburgh won 10-7.
0:08 — Tomas Jurco, Detroit, April 16, 2015, at Tampa Bay vs. goaltender Ben Bishop, second period. Detroit won 3-2.
0:09 — Bill Collins, Minnesota, April 9, 1968, at Minnesota vs. Los Angeles and goaltender Wayne Rutledge, third period. Minnesota won 7-5.
— Dave Balon, Minnesota, April 25, 1968, at St. Louis vs. goaltender Glenn Hall, third period. Minnesota won 5-1.
— Murray Oliver, Minnesota, April 8, 1971, at St. Louis vs. goaltender Ernie Wakely, third period. St. Louis won 4-2.
— Clark Gillies, NY Islanders, April 15, 1977, at Buffalo vs. goaltender Don Edwards, third period. NY Islanders won 4-3.
— Eric Vail, Atlanta, April 11, 1978, at Atlanta vs. Detroit and goaltender Ron Low, third period. Detroit won 5-3.
— Stan Smyl, Vancouver, April 10, 1979, at Philadelphia vs. goaltender Wayne Stephenson, third period. Vancouver won 3-2.
— Wayne Gretzky, Edmonton, April 6, 1983, at Edmonton vs. Winnipeg and goaltender Brian Hayward, second period. Edmonton won 6-3.
— Mark Messier, Edmonton, April 16, 1984, at Calgary vs. goaltender Don Edwards, third period. Edmonton won 5-3.
— Brian Skrudland, Montreal, May 18, 1986, at Calgary vs. goaltender Mike Vernon, first overtime period. Montreal won 3-2.

FASTEST TWO GOALS:
0:05 — **Norm Ullman, Detroit,** April 11, 1965, at Detroit vs. Chicago and goaltender Glenn Hall. Ullman scored at 17:35 and 17:40 of second period. Detroit won 4-2.

FASTEST TWO GOALS FROM START OF A GAME:
1:08 — **Dick Duff, Toronto,** April 9, 1963, at Toronto vs. Detroit and goaltender Terry Sawchuk. Duff scored at 0:49 and 1:08. Toronto won 4-2.

FASTEST TWO GOALS FROM START OF A PERIOD:
0:35 — **Pat LaFontaine, NY Islanders,** May 19, 1984, at Edmonton vs. goaltender Andy Moog. LaFontaine scored at 0:13 and 0:35 of third period. Edmonton won 5-2.

PENALTIES

MOST PENALTY MINUTES IN PLAYOFFS, CAREER:
729 — **Dale Hunter, Quebec, Washington, Colorado**
541 — Chris Nilan, Montreal, NY Rangers, Boston
529 — Claude Lemieux, Montreal, New Jersey, Colorado, Phoenix, Dallas
471 — Rick Tocchet, Philadelphia, Pittsburgh, Boston, Phoenix
466 — Willi Plett, Atlanta, Calgary, Minnesota, Boston

MOST PENALTIES, ONE GAME:
8 — **Forbes Kennedy, Toronto,** April 2, 1969, at Boston. Kennedy was assessed 4 minors, 2 majors, 1 10-minute misconduct, 1 game misconduct. Boston won 10-0.
— **Kim Clackson, Pittsburgh,** April 14, 1980, at Boston. Clackson was assessed 5 minors, 2 majors, 1 10-minute misconduct. Boston won 6-2.

MOST PENALTY MINUTES, ONE GAME:
42 — **Dave Schultz, Philadelphia,** April 22, 1976, at Toronto. Schultz was assessed 1 minor, 2 majors, 1 10-minute misconduct, and 2 game-misconducts. Toronto won 8-5.
— **Derek Engelland, Calgary,** April 17, 2015, at Vancouver. Engelland was assessed 1 minor, 2 majors, and 3 game-misconducts. Vancouver won 4-1.

MOST PENALTIES, ONE PERIOD:
6 — **Ed Hospodar, NY Rangers,** April 9, 1981, at Los Angeles, first period. Hospodar was assessed 2 minors, 1 major, 1 10-minute misconduct, and 2 game misconducts. Los Angeles won 5-4.
— **Deryk Engelland, Calgary,** April 17, 2015, at Vancouver, third period. Engelland was assessed 1 minor, 2 majors, and 3 game misconducts. Vancouver won 4-1.

MOST PENALTY MINUTES, ONE PERIOD:
42 — **Deryk Engelland, Calgary,** April 17, 2015, at Vancouver, third period. Engelland was assessed 1 minor, 2 majors, and 3 game misconducts. Vancouver won 4-1.
39 — Ed Hospodar, NY Rangers, April 9, 1981, at Los Angeles, first period. Hospodar was assessed 2 minors, 1 major, 1 10-minute misconduct, and 2 game misconducts. Los Angeles won 5-4.

GOALTENDING

MOST PLAYOFF GAMES APPEARED IN BY A GOALTENDER, CAREER:
247 — Patrick Roy, Montreal, Colorado
205 — Martin Brodeur, New Jersey
161 — Ed Belfour, Chicago, Dallas, Toronto
150 — Grant Fuhr, Edmonton, Buffalo, St. Louis
138 — Mike Vernon, Calgary, Detroit, San Jose, Florida

MOST MINUTES PLAYED BY A GOALTENDER, CAREER:
15,209 — Patrick Roy, Montreal, Colorado
12,719 — Martin Brodeur, New Jersey
9,945 — Ed Belfour, Chicago, Dallas, Toronto
8,834 — Grant Fuhr, Edmonton, Buffalo, St. Louis
8,214 — Mike Vernon, Calgary, Detroit, San Jose, Florida

MOST MINUTES PLAYED BY A GOALTENDER, ONE PLAYOFF YEAR:
1,655 — Miikka Kiprusoff, Calgary, 2004. 26 games.
1,605 — Jonathan Quick, Los Angeles, 2014, 26 games
1,544 — Kirk McLean, Vancouver, 1994. 24 games.
— Ed Belfour, Dallas, 1999. 23 games.
1,542 — Tim Thomas, Boston, 2011. 25 games.

MOST SHUTOUTS IN PLAYOFFS, CAREER:
24 — Martin Brodeur, New Jersey
23 — Patrick Roy, Montreal, Colorado
16 — Curtis Joseph, St. Louis, Edmonton, Toronto, Detroit

MOST SHUTOUTS, ONE PLAYOFF YEAR:
7 — Martin Brodeur, New Jersey, 2003. 24 games.
6 — Dominik Hasek, Detroit, 2002. 23 games.
5 — Jean-Sebastien Giguere, Anaheim, 2003. 21 games.
— Nikolai Khabibulin, Tampa Bay, 2004. 23 games.
— Miikka Kiprusoff, Calgary, 2004. 26 games.

MOST SHUTOUTS, ONE PLAYOFF SERIES:
3 — Clint Benedict, Mtl. Maroons, 1926 F vs. Victoria. 4 games.
— Dave Kerr, NY Rangers, 1940 SF vs. Boston. 6 games.
— Frank McCool, Toronto, 1945 F vs. Detroit. 7 games.
— Turk Broda, Toronto, 1950 SF vs. Detroit. 7 games.
— Felix Potvin, Toronto, 1994 CQF vs. Chicago. 6 games.
— Martin Brodeur, New Jersey, 1995 CQF vs. Boston. 5 games.
— Brent Johnson, St. Louis, 2002 CQF vs. Chicago. 5 games.
— Patrick Lalime, Ottawa, 2002 CQF vs. Philadelphia. 5 games.
— Jean-Sebastien Giguere, Anaheim, 2003 CF vs. Minnesota. 4 games.
— Martin Brodeur, New Jersey, 2003 F vs. Anaheim. 7 games.
— Ed Belfour, Toronto, 2004 CQF vs. Ottawa. 7 games.
— Nikolai Khabibulin, Tampa Bay, 2004 CQF vs. NY Islanders. 5 games.
— Marty Turco, Dallas, 2007 CQF vs. Vancouver. 7 games.
— Michael Leighton, Philadelphia, 2010 CF vs. Montreal. 5 games.

MOST WINS BY A GOALTENDER, CAREER:
151 — Patrick Roy, Montreal, Colorado
113 — Martin Brodeur, New Jersey
92 — Grant Fuhr, Edmonton, Buffalo, St. Louis
88 — Billy Smith, NY Islanders
— Ed Belfour, Chicago, Dallas, Toronto

MOST WINS BY A GOALTENDER, ONE PLAYOFF YEAR:
16 — Sixteen wins by a goaltender in one playoff year has been recorded on 22 occasions. Jonathan Quick of the Los Angeles Kings is the most recent to equal this mark, posting a record of 16 wins and 10 losses in 2014. It was first accomplished by Grant Fuhr in 1988.

MOST CONSECUTIVE WINS BY A GOALTENDER, MORE THAN ONE PLAYOFF YEAR:
14 — Tom Barrasso, Pittsburgh, 1992, 1993; 3 wins vs. NY Rangers in 1992 DF, won by Pittsburgh 4-2; 4 wins vs. Boston in 1992 CF, won by Pittsburgh 4-0; 4 wins vs. Chicago in 1992 F, won by Pittsburgh 4-0; 3 wins vs. New Jersey in 1993 DSF, won by Pittsburgh 4-1.

MOST CONSECUTIVE WINS BY A GOALTENDER, ONE PLAYOFF YEAR:
11 — Ed Belfour, Chicago, 1992. 3 wins vs. St. Louis in DSF, won by Chicago 4-2; 4 wins vs. Detroit in DF, won by Chicago 4-0; and 4 wins vs. Edmonton in CF, won by Chicago 4-0.
— Tom Barrasso, Pittsburgh, 1992. 3 wins vs. NY Rangers in DF, won by Pittsburgh 4-2; 4 wins vs. Boston in CF, won by Pittsburgh 4-0; and 4 wins vs. Chicago in F, won by Pittsburgh 4-0.
— Patrick Roy, Montreal, 1993. 4 wins vs. Quebec in DSF, won by Montreal 4-2; 4 wins vs. Buffalo in DF, won by Montreal 4-0; and 3 wins vs. NY Islanders in CF, won by Montreal 4-1.

LONGEST SHUTOUT SEQUENCE:
270:08 — George Hainsworth, Montreal, 1930. Hainsworth's shutout streak began after Murray Murdoch scored a goal for the NY Rangers at 15:34 of the first period in the first game of a SF series on March 28, 1930. Hainsworth did not allow another goal in the final 113:18 of that game, won by Montreal 2-1 at 8:52 of the fourth overtime period. Hainsworth then shutout the NY Rangers in the next and final game of the series on March 30, 1930, won by Montreal 2-0. The streak continued with a 3-0 win over Boston in the opening game of the F series on April 1, 1930. His streak ended on April 3, 1930 when Boston's Eddie Shore scored at 16:50 of the second period in the second game of the F series.

MOST CONSECUTIVE SHUTOUTS:
3 — Clint Benedict, Mtl. Maroons, 1926. Benedict shut out Ottawa 1-0, March 27; he then shut out Victoria twice, 3-0, March 30; 3-0, April 1. Mtl. Maroons won NHL F vs. Ottawa 2 goals to 1 and won the best-of-five F vs. Victoria 3-1.
— John Ross Roach, NY Rangers, 1929. Roach shut out NY Americans twice, 0-0, March 19; 1-0, March 21; he then shut out Toronto 1-0, March 24. NY Rangers won QF vs. NY Americans 1 goal to 0 and won the best-of-three SF vs. Toronto 2-0.
— Frank McCool, Toronto, 1945. McCool shut out Detroit three times, 1-0, April 6; 2-0, April 8; 1-0, April 12. Toronto won the best-of-seven F 4-3.
— Brent Johnson, St. Louis, 2002. Johnson shut out Chicago three times; 2-0, April 20; 4-0, April 21; 1-0, April 23. St. Louis won the best-of-seven CQF 4-1.
— Patrick Lalime, Ottawa, 2002. Lalime shut out Philadelphia three times; 3-0, April 20; 2-0, April 22; 3-0, April 24. Ottawa won the best-of-seven CQF 4-1.
— Jean-Sebastien Giguere, Anaheim, 2003. Giguere shut out Minnesota three times, 1-0, May 10; 2-0, May 12; 4-0, May 14. Anaheim won the best-of-seven CF 4-0.
— Ilya Bryzgalov, Anaheim, 2006. Bryzgalov shut out Calgary, 3-0, May 3; he then shut out Colorado 5-0, May 5; and 3-0, May 7. Anaheim won best-of-seven CQF vs. Calgary 4-3 and won best-of-seven CSF vs. Colorado 4-0.

Early Playoff Records

1893-1918
Team Records

MOST GOALS, BOTH TEAMS, ONE GAME:
25 — Ottawa Silver Seven, Dawson City at Ottawa, Jan. 16, 1905. Ottawa 23, Dawson City 2. Ottawa won best-of-three series 2-0.

MOST GOALS, ONE TEAM, ONE GAME:
23 — Ottawa Silver Seven at Ottawa, Jan. 16, 1905. Ottawa defeated Dawson City 23-2.

MOST GOALS, BOTH TEAMS, BEST-OF-THREE SERIES:
42 — Ottawa Silver Seven, Queen's University at Ottawa, 1906. Ottawa defeated Queen's 16-7, Feb. 27, and 12-7, Feb. 28.

MOST GOALS, ONE TEAM, BEST-OF-THREE SERIES:
32 — Ottawa Silver Seven in 1905 at Ottawa. Defeated Dawson City 9-2, Jan. 13, and 23-2, Jan. 16.

MOST GOALS, BOTH TEAMS, BEST-OF-FIVE SERIES:
39 — Toronto Arenas, Vancouver Millionaires at Toronto, 1918. Toronto won 5-3, Mar. 20; 6-3, Mar. 26; 2-1, Mar. 30. Vancouver won 6-4, Mar. 23, and 8-1, Mar. 28. Toronto scored 18 goals; Vancouver 21.

MOST GOALS, ONE TEAM, BEST-OF-FIVE SERIES:
26 — Vancouver Millionaires in 1915 at Vancouver. Defeated Ottawa Senators 6-2, Mar. 22; 8-3, Mar. 24; and 12-3, Mar. 26.

Individual Records

MOST GOALS IN PLAYOFFS:
63 — Frank McGee, Ottawa Silver Seven, in 22 playoff games. Seven goals in four games, 1903; 21 goals in eight games, 1904; 18 goals in four games, 1905; 17 goals in six games, 1906.

MOST GOALS, ONE PLAYOFF SERIES:
15 — Frank McGee, Ottawa Silver Seven, in two games in 1905 at Ottawa. Scored one goal, Jan. 13, in 9-2 victory over Dawson City and 14 goals, Jan. 16, in 23-2 victory.

MOST GOALS, ONE PLAYOFF GAME:
14 — Frank McGee, Ottawa Silver Seven, at Ottawa, Jan. 16, 1905, in 23-2 victory over Dawson City.

FASTEST THREE GOALS:
40 Seconds — Marty Walsh, Ottawa Senators, at Ottawa, March 16, 1911, at 3:00, 3:10, and 3:40 of third period. Ottawa defeated Port Arthur 13-4.

All-Time Playoff Goal Leaders since 1918

(45 or more goals)

Player	Teams	Yrs.	GP	G
Wayne Gretzky	Edm., L.A., St.L., NYR	16	208	**122**
Mark Messier	Edm., NYR, Van.	17	236	**109**
Jari Kurri	Edm., L.A., NYR, Ana., Col.	15	200	**106**
Brett Hull	Cgy., St.L., Dal., Det., Phx.	19	202	**103**
Glenn Anderson	Edm., Tor., NYR, St.L.	15	225	**93**
Mike Bossy	NYI	10	129	**85**
Joe Sakic	Que., Col.	13	172	**84**
Maurice Richard	Mtl.	15	133	**82**
Claude Lemieux	Mtl., N.J., Col., Phx., Dal., S.J.	18	234	**80**
Jean Beliveau	Mtl.	17	162	**79**
*Jaromir Jagr	Pit., Wsh., NYR, Phi., Dal., Bos., N.J., Fla.	17	202	**78**
Mario Lemieux	Pit.	8	107	**76**
Dino Ciccarelli	Min., Wsh., Det., T.B., Fla.	14	141	**73**
Esa Tikkanen	Edm., NYR, St.L., N.J., Van., Fla., Wsh.	13	186	**72**
Bryan Trottier	NYI, Pit.	17	221	**71**
Steve Yzerman	Det.	20	196	**70**
Gordie Howe	Det., Hfd.	20	157	**68**
Joe Nieuwendyk	Cgy., Dal., N.J., Tor., Fla.	16	158	**66**
Denis Savard	Chi., Mtl., T.B.	16	169	**66**
Yvan Cournoyer	Mtl.	12	147	**64**
Peter Forsberg	Que., Col., Phi., Nsh.	13	151	**64**
Brian Propp	Phi., Bos., Min., Hfd.	13	160	**64**
Bobby Smith	Min., Mtl.	13	184	**64**
Bobby Hull	Chi., Wpg., Hfd.	14	119	**62**
Phil Esposito	Chi., Bos., NYR	15	130	**61**
Jacques Lemaire	Mtl.	11	145	**61**
Mark Recchi	Pit., Phi., Mtl., Car., Atl., T.B., Bos.	14	189	**61**
Joe Mullen	St.L., Cgy., Pit., Bos.	15	143	**60**
*Patrick Marleau	S.J.	14	147	**60**
Doug Gilmour	St.L., Cgy., Tor., N.J., Chi., Buf., Mtl.	17	182	**60**
Brendan Shanahan	N.J., St.L., Hfd., Det., NYR	19	184	**60**
Stan Mikita	Chi.	18	155	**59**
Paul Coffey	Edm., Pit., L.A., Det., Hfd., Phi., Chi., Car., Bos.	16	194	**59**
Guy Lafleur	Mtl., NYR, Que.	14	128	**58**
Bernie Geoffrion	Mtl., NYR	16	132	**58**
Luc Robitaille	L.A., Pit., NYR, Det.	15	159	**58**
Mike Modano	Min., Dal., Det.	16	176	**58**
Cam Neely	Van., Bos.	9	93	**57**
*Henrik Zetterberg	Det.	11	132	**56**
Steve Larmer	Chi., NYR	13	140	**56**
Denis Potvin	NYI	14	185	**56**
Rick MacLeish	Phi., Hfd., Pit., Det.	11	114	**54**
Steve Thomas	Tor., Chi., NYI, N.J., Ana., Det.	16	174	**54**
Nicklas Lidstrom	Det.	19	263	**54**
*Daniel Briere	Phx., Buf., Phi., Mtl., Col.	9	124	**53**
Bill Barber	Phi.	11	129	**53**
Stephane Richer	Mtl., N.J., T.B., St.L., Pit.	13	134	**53**
Jeremy Roenick	Chi., Phx., Phi., L.A., S.J.	17	154	**53**
Rick Tocchet	Phi., Pit., L.A., Bos., Wsh., Phx.	13	145	**52**
Sergei Fedorov	Det., Ana., CBJ, Wsh.	15	183	**52**
Daniel Alfredsson	Ott., Det.	14	124	**51**
Frank Mahovlich	Tor., Det., Mtl.	14	137	**51**
Brian Bellows	Min., Mtl., T.B., Ana., Wsh.	13	143	**51**
Rod Brind'Amour	St.L., Phi., Car.	12	159	**51**
Steve Shutt	Mtl., L.A.	12	99	**50**
Henri Richard	Mtl.	18	180	**49**
*Marian Hossa	Ott., Atl., Pit., Det., Chi.	14	194	**49**
*Patrick Kane	Chi.	6	116	**48**
Reggie Leach	Bos., Cal., Phi., Det.	8	94	**47**
Ted Lindsay	Det., Chi.	16	133	**47**
Chris Drury	Col., Cgy., Buf., NYR	9	135	**47**
Clark Gillies	NYI, Buf.	13	164	**47**
Kevin Stevens	Pit., Bos., L.A., NYR, Phi.	7	103	**46**
Dickie Moore	Mtl., Tor., St.L.	14	135	**46**
Ron Francis	Hfd., Pit., Car., Tor.	17	171	**46**
Tomas Holmstrom	Det.	14	180	**46**
Rick Middleton	NYR, Bos.	12	114	**45**
Alex Kovalev	NYR, Pit., Mtl., Ott., Fla.	11	123	**45**
*Patrik Elias	N.J.	13	162	**45**

* Active

All-Time Playoff Assist Leaders since 1918

(65 or more assists)

Player	Teams	Yrs.	GP	A
Wayne Gretzky	Edm., L.A., St.L., NYR	16	208	**260**
Mark Messier	Edm., NYR, Van.	17	236	**186**
Raymond Bourque	Bos., Col.	21	214	**139**
Paul Coffey	Edm., Pit., L.A., Det., Hfd., Phi., Chi., Car., Bos.	16	194	**137**
Nicklas Lidstrom	Det.	19	263	**129**
Doug Gilmour	St.L., Cgy., Tor., N.J., Chi., Buf., Mtl.	17	182	**128**
Jari Kurri	Edm., L.A., NYR, Ana., Col.	15	200	**127**
Sergei Fedorov	Det., Ana., CBJ, Wsh.	15	183	**124**
Al MacInnis	Cgy., St.L.	19	177	**121**
*Jaromir Jagr	Pit., Wsh., NYR, Phi., Dal., Bos., N.J., Fla.	17	202	**121**
Glenn Anderson	Edm., Tor., NYR, St.L.	15	225	**121**
Larry Robinson	Mtl., L.A.	20	227	**116**
Steve Yzerman	Det.	20	196	**115**
Larry Murphy	L.A., Wsh., Min., Pit., Tor., Det.	20	215	**115**
Adam Oates	Det., St.L., Bos., Wsh., Phi., Ana., Edm.	15	163	**114**
Bryan Trottier	NYI, Pit.	17	221	**113**
Chris Chelios	Mtl., Chi., Det., Atl.	24	266	**113**
Denis Savard	Chi., Mtl., T.B.	16	169	**109**
Denis Potvin	NYI	14	185	**108**
Peter Forsberg	Que., Col., Phi., Nsh.	13	151	**107**
Joe Sakic	Que., Col.	13	172	**104**
Jean Beliveau	Mtl.	17	162	**97**
Ron Francis	Hfd., Pit., Car., Tor.	17	171	**97**
Mario Lemieux	Pit.	8	107	**96**
Bobby Smith	Min., Mtl.	13	184	**96**
Chris Pronger	Hfd., St.L., Edm., Ana., Phi.	14	173	**95**
*Marian Hossa	Ott., Atl., Pit., Det., Chi.	14	194	**95**
Sergei Zubov	NYR, Pit., Dal.	13	164	**93**
Gordie Howe	Det., Hfd.	20	157	**92**
Scott Stevens	Wsh., St.L., N.J.	20	233	**92**
Stan Mikita	Chi.	18	155	**91**
Brad Park	NYR, Bos., Det.	17	161	**90**
Mike Modano	Min., Dal., Det.	16	176	**88**
Brett Hull	Cgy., St.L., Dal., Det., Phx.	19	202	**87**
Craig Janney	Bos., St.L., S.J., Wpg., Phx., T.B., NYI	11	120	**86**
Mark Recchi	Pit., Phi., Mtl., Car., Atl., T.B., Bos.	14	189	**86**
Brian Propp	Phi., Bos., Min., Hfd.	13	160	**84**
*Patrik Elias	N.J.	13	162	**80**
Henri Richard	Mtl.	18	180	**80**
Jacques Lemaire	Mtl.	11	145	**78**
Claude Lemieux	Mtl., N.J., Col., Phx., Dal., S.J.	18	234	**78**
Ken Linseman	Phi., Edm., Bos., Tor.	11	113	**77**
Bobby Clarke	Phi.	13	136	**77**
Guy Lafleur	Mtl., NYR, Que.	14	128	**76**
Phil Esposito	Chi., Bos., NYR	15	130	**76**
*Joe Thornton	Bos., S.J.	13	132	**76**
Dale Hunter	Que., Wsh., Col.	18	186	**76**
*Sidney Crosby	Pit.	7	100	**75**
Mike Bossy	NYI	10	129	**75**
Steve Larmer	Chi., NYR	13	140	**75**
John Tonelli	NYI, Cgy., L.A., Chi., Que.	13	172	**75**
Brendan Shanahan	N.J., St.L., Hfd., Det., NYR	19	184	**74**
Scott Niedermayer	N.J., Ana.	15	202	**73**
Peter Stastny	Que., N.J., St.L.	12	93	**72**
Bernie Nicholls	L.A., NYR, Edm., N.J., Chi., S.J.	13	118	**72**
*Scott Gomez	N.J., NYR, Mtl., S.J., Fla.	10	149	**72**
Brian Bellows	Min., Mtl., T.B., Ana., Wsh.	13	143	**71**
*Pavel Datsyuk	Det.	12	152	**71**
Brian Rafalski	N.J., Det.	10	165	**71**
Gilbert Perreault	Buf.	11	90	**70**
Geoff Courtnall	Bos., Edm., Wsh., St.L., Van.	15	156	**70**
Brian Leetch	NYR, Tor., Bos.	8	95	**69**
Dale Hawerchuk	Wpg., Buf., St.L., Phi.	15	97	**69**
*Evgeni Malkin	Pit.	7	101	**69**
Alex Delvecchio	Det.	14	121	**69**
Jeremy Roenick	Chi., Phx., Phi., L.A., S.J.	17	154	**69**
Luc Robitaille	L.A., Pit., NYR, Det.	15	159	**69**
*Sergei Gonchar	Wsh., Bos., Pit., Ott., Dal., Mtl.	13	141	**68**
*Brad Richards	T.B., Dal., NYR, Chi.	9	141	**68**
*Ryan Getzlaf	Ana.	8	97	**67**
Bobby Hull	Chi., Wpg., Hfd.	14	119	**67**
Sandis Ozolinsh	S.J., Col., Car., Fla., Ana., NYR	10	137	**67**
Frank Mahovlich	Tor., Det., Mtl.	14	137	**67**
Igor Larionov	Van., S.J., Det., Fla., N.J.	13	150	**67**
Bobby Orr	Bos., Chi.	8	74	**66**
Bernie Federko	St.L., Det.	11	91	**66**
*Patrick Kane	Chi.	6	116	**66**
Jean Ratelle	NYR, Bos.	15	123	**66**
Charlie Huddy	Edm., L.A., Buf., St.L.	14	183	**66**
Trevor Linden	Van., NYI, Mtl., Wsh.	12	124	**65**

All-Time Playoff Point Leaders since 1918

(115 or more points)

Player	Teams	Yrs.	GP	G	A	Pts.
Wayne Gretzky	Edm., L.A., St.L., NYR	16	208	122	260	**382**
Mark Messier	Edm., NYR, Van.	17	236	109	186	**295**
Jari Kurri	Edm., L.A., NYR, Ana., Col.	15	200	106	127	**233**
Glenn Anderson	Edm., Tor., NYR, St.L.	15	225	93	121	**214**
*Jaromir Jagr	Pit., Wsh., NYR, Phi., Dal., Bos., N.J., Fla.	17	202	78	121	**199**
Paul Coffey	Edm., Pit., L.A., Det., Hfd., Phi., Chi., Car., Bos.	16	194	59	137	**196**
Brett Hull	Cgy., St.L., Dal., Det., Phx.	19	202	103	87	**190**
Joe Sakic	Que., Col.	13	172	84	104	**188**
Doug Gilmour	St.L., Cgy., Tor., N.J., Chi., Buf., Mtl.	17	182	60	128	**188**
Steve Yzerman	Det.	20	196	70	115	**185**
Bryan Trottier	NYI, Pit.	17	221	71	113	**184**
Nicklas Lidstrom	Det.	19	263	54	129	**183**
Raymond Bourque	Bos., Col.	21	214	41	139	**180**
Jean Beliveau	Mtl.	17	162	79	97	**176**
Sergei Fedorov	Det., Ana., CBJ, Wsh.	15	183	52	124	**176**
Denis Savard	Chi., Mtl., T.B.	16	169	66	109	**175**
Mario Lemieux	Pit.	8	107	76	96	**172**
Peter Forsberg	Que., Col., Phi., Nsh.	13	151	64	107	**171**
Denis Potvin	NYI	14	185	56	108	**164**
Mike Bossy	NYI	10	129	85	75	**160**
Gordie Howe	Det., Hfd.	20	157	68	92	**160**
Al MacInnis	Cgy., St.L.	19	177	39	121	**160**
Bobby Smith	Min., Mtl.	13	184	64	96	**160**
Claude Lemieux	Mtl., N.J., Col., Phx., Dal., S.J.	18	234	80	78	**158**
Adam Oates	Det., St.L., Bos., Wsh., Phi., Ana., Edm.	15	163	42	114	**156**
Larry Murphy	L.A., Wsh., Min., Pit., Tor., Det.	20	215	37	115	**152**
Stan Mikita	Chi.	18	155	59	91	**150**
Brian Propp	Phi., Bos., Min., Hfd.	13	160	64	84	**148**
Mark Recchi	Pit., Phi., Mtl., Car., Atl., T.B., Bos.	14	189	61	86	**147**
Mike Modano	Min., Dal., Det.	16	176	58	88	**146**
*Marian Hossa	Ott., Atl., Pit., Det., Chi.	14	194	49	95	**144**
Larry Robinson	Mtl., L.A.	20	227	28	116	**144**
Chris Chelios	Mtl., Chi., Det., Atl.	24	266	31	113	**144**
Ron Francis	Hfd., Pit., Car., Tor.	17	171	46	97	**143**
Jacques Lemaire	Mtl.	11	145	61	78	**139**
Phil Esposito	Chi., Bos., NYR	15	130	61	76	**137**
Guy Lafleur	Mtl., NYR, Que.	14	128	58	76	**134**
Brendan Shanahan	N.J., St.L., Hfd., Det., NYR	19	184	60	74	**134**
Esa Tikkanen	Edm., NYR, St.L., N.J., Van., Fla., Wsh.	13	186	72	60	**132**
Steve Larmer	Chi., NYR	13	140	56	75	**131**
Bobby Hull	Chi., Wpg., Hfd.	14	119	62	67	**129**
Henri Richard	Mtl.	18	180	49	80	**129**
Yvan Cournoyer	Mtl.	12	147	64	63	**127**
Luc Robitaille	L.A., Pit., NYR, Det.	15	159	58	69	**127**
Maurice Richard	Mtl.	15	133	82	44	**126**
Brad Park	NYR, Bos., Det.	17	161	35	90	**125**
*Patrik Elias	N.J.	13	162	45	80	**125**
Brian Bellows	Min., Mtl., T.B., Ana., Wsh.	13	143	51	71	**122**
Jeremy Roenick	Chi., Phx., Phi., L.A., S.J.	17	154	53	69	**122**
Chris Pronger	Hfd., St.L., Edm., Ana., Phi.	14	173	26	95	**121**
Ken Linseman	Phi., Edm., Bos., Tor.	11	113	43	77	**120**
*Henrik Zetterberg	Det.	11	132	56	63	**119**
Bobby Clarke	Phi.	13	136	42	77	**119**
*Sidney Crosby	Pit.	7	100	43	75	**118**
Bernie Geoffrion	Mtl., NYR	16	132	58	60	**118**
Frank Mahovlich	Tor., Det., Mtl.	14	137	51	67	**118**
Dino Ciccarelli	Min., Wsh., Det., T.B., Fla.	14	141	73	45	**118**
Dale Hunter	Que., Wsh., Col.	18	186	42	76	**118**
Scott Stevens	Wsh., St.L., N.J.	20	233	26	92	**118**
Sergei Zubov	NYR, Pit., Dal.	13	164	24	93	**117**
*Daniel Briere	Phx., Buf., Phi., Mtl., Col.	9	124	53	63	**116**
Joe Nieuwendyk	Cgy., Dal., N.J., Tor., Fla.	16	158	66	50	**116**
John Tonelli	NYI, Cgy., L.A., Chi., Que.	13	172	40	75	**115**

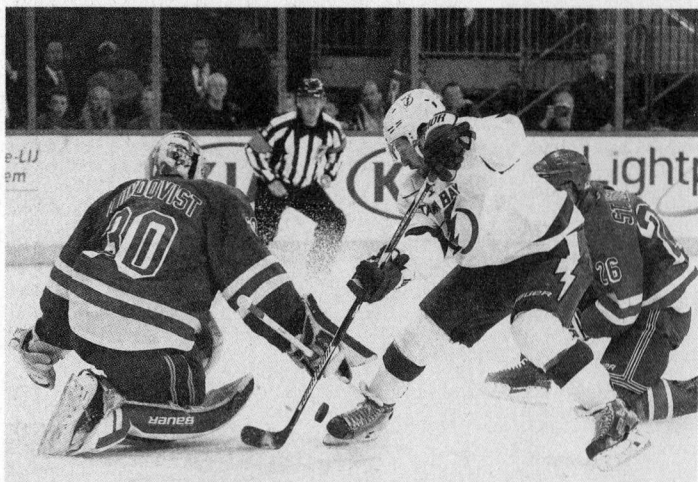

Tampa Bay's Tyler Johnson beats the Rangers' Henrik Lundqvist during game two of the Eastern Conference Final. Johnson led all playoff scorers with 13 goals and tied Chicago's Patrick Kane with 23 points.

Leading Playoff Scorers, 1918–2015

Season	Player, Team	Games Played	Goals	Assists	Points
2014-15	Tyler Johnson, Tampa Bay	26	13	10	23
	Patrick Kane, Chicago	23	11	12	23
2013-14	Anze Kopitar, Los Angeles	26	5	21	26
2012-13	David Krejci, Boston	22	9	17	26
2011-12	Dustin Brown, Los Angeles	20	8	12	20
	Anze Kopitar, Los Angeles	20	8	12	20
2010-11	David Krejci, Boston	25	12	11	23
2009-10	Daniel Briere, Philadelphia	23	12	18	30
2008-09	Evgeni Malkin, Pittsburgh	24	14	22	36
2007-08	Henrik Zetterberg, Detroit	22	13	14	27
	Sidney Crosby, Pittsburgh	20	6	21	27
2006-07	Daniel Alfredsson, Ottawa	20	14	8	22
	Dany Heatley, Ottawa	20	7	15	22
	Jason Spezza, Ottawa	20	7	15	22
2005-06	Eric Staal, Carolina	25	9	19	28
2004-05	*Season Cancelled*				
2003-04	Brad Richards, Tampa Bay	23	12	14	26
2002-03	Jamie Langenbrunner, New Jersey	24	11	7	18
	Scott Niedermayer, New Jersey	24	2	16	18
2001-02	Peter Forsberg, Colorado	20	9	18	27
2000-01	Joe Sakic, Colorado	21	13	13	26
99-2000	Brett Hull, Dallas	23	11	13	24
1998-99	Peter Forsberg, Colorado	19	8	16	24
1997-98	Steve Yzerman, Detroit	22	6	18	24
1996-97	Eric Lindros, Philadelphia	19	12	14	26
1995-96	Joe Sakic, Colorado	22	18	16	34
1994-95	Sergei Fedorov, Detroit	17	7	17	24
1993-94	Brian Leetch, NY Rangers	23	11	23	34
1992-93	Wayne Gretzky, Los Angeles	24	15	25	40
1991-92	Mario Lemieux, Pittsburgh	15	16	18	34
1990-91	Mario Lemieux, Pittsburgh	23	16	28	44
1989-90	Craig Simpson, Edmonton	22	16	15	31
	Mark Messier, Edmonton	22	9	22	31
1988-89	Al MacInnis, Calgary	22	7	24	31
1987-88	Wayne Gretzky, Edmonton	19	12	31	43
1986-87	Wayne Gretzky, Edmonton	21	5	29	34
1985-86	Doug Gilmour, St. Louis	19	9	12	21
	Bernie Federko, St. Louis	19	7	14	21
1984-85	Wayne Gretzky, Edmonton	18	17	30	47
1983-84	Wayne Gretzky, Edmonton	19	13	22	35
1982-83	Wayne Gretzky, Edmonton	16	12	26	38
1981-82	Bryan Trottier, NY Islanders	19	6	23	29
1980-81	Mike Bossy, NY Islanders	18	17	18	35
1979-80	Bryan Trottier, NY Islanders	21	12	17	29
1978-79	Jacques Lemaire, Montreal	16	11	12	23
	Guy Lafleur, Montreal	16	10	13	23
1977-78	Guy Lafleur, Montreal	15	10	11	21
	Larry Robinson, Montreal	15	4	17	21
1976-77	Guy Lafleur, Montreal	14	9	17	26
1975-76	Reggie Leach, Philadelphia	16	19	5	24
1974-75	Rick MacLeish, Philadelphia	17	11	9	20
1973-74	Rick MacLeish, Philadelphia	17	13	9	22
1972-73	Yvan Cournoyer, Montreal	17	15	10	25
1971-72	Phil Esposito, Boston	15	9	15	24
	Bobby Orr, Boston	15	5	19	24
1970-71	Frank Mahovlich, Montreal	20	14	13	27
1969-70	Phil Esposito, Boston	14	13	14	27
1968-69	Phil Esposito, Boston	10	8	10	18
1967-68	Bill Goldsworthy, Minnesota	14	8	7	15
1966-67	Jim Pappin, Toronto	12	7	8	15
1965-66	Norm Ullman, Detroit	12	6	9	15
1964-65	Bobby Hull, Chicago	14	10	7	17
1963-64	Gordie Howe, Detroit	14	9	10	19
1962-63	Gordie Howe, Detroit	11	7	9	16
	Norm Ullman, Detroit	11	4	12	16
1961-62	Stan Mikita, Chicago	12	6	15	21
1960-61	Gordie Howe, Detroit	11	4	11	15
	Pierre Pilote, Chicago	12	3	12	15
1959-60	Henri Richard, Montreal	8	3	9	12
	Bernie Geoffrion, Montreal	8	2	10	12
1958-59	Dickie Moore, Montreal	11	5	12	17
1957-58	Fleming MacKell, Boston	12	5	14	19
1956-57	Bernie Geoffrion, Montreal	10	11	7	18
1955-56	Jean Béliveau, Montreal	10	12	7	19
1954-55	Gordie Howe, Detroit	11	9	11	20
1953-54	Dickie Moore, Montreal	11	5	8	13
1952-53	Ed Sandford, Boston	11	8	3	11
1951-52	Ted Lindsay, Detroit	8	5	2	7
	Floyd Curry, Montreal	11	4	3	7
	Metro Prystai, Detroit	8	2	5	7
	Gordie Howe, Detroit	8	2	5	7
1950-51	Maurice Richard, Montreal	11	9	4	13
	Max Bentley, Toronto	11	2	11	13
1949-50	Pentti Lund, NY Rangers	12	6	5	11
1948-49	Gordie Howe, Detroit	11	8	3	11
1947-48	Ted Kennedy, Toronto	9	8	6	14
1946-47	Maurice Richard, Montreal	10	6	5	11
1945-46	Elmer Lach, Montreal	9	5	12	17
1944-45	Joe Carveth, Detroit	14	5	6	11
1943-44	Toe Blake, Montreal	9	7	11	18
1942-43	Carl Liscombe, Detroit	10	6	8	14
1941-42	Don Grosso, Detroit	12	8	6	14
	Syl Apps, Toronto	13	5	9	14
1940-41	Milt Schmidt, Boston	11	5	6	11
1939-40	Phil Watson, NY Rangers	12	3	6	9
	Neil Colville, NY Rangers	12	2	7	9
1938-39	Bill Cowley, Boston	12	3	11	14
1937-38	Johnny Gottselig, Chicago	10	5	3	8
	Gordie Drillon, Toronto	7	7	1	8
1936-37	Marty Barry, Detroit	10	4	7	11
1935-36	Frank Boll, Toronto	9	7	3	10
1934-35	Baldy Northcott, Mtl. Maroons	7	4	1	5
	Busher Jackson, Toronto	7	3	2	5
	Cy Wentworth, Mtl. Maroons	7	3	2	5
	Charlie Conacher, Toronto	7	1	4	5
1933-34	Larry Aurie, Detroit	9	3	7	10
1932-33	Cecil Dillon, NY Rangers	8	8	2	10
1931-32	Frank Boucher, NY Rangers	7	3	6	9
1930-31	Cooney Weiland, Boston	5	6	3	9
1929-30	Marty Barry, Boston	6	3	3	6
	Cooney Weiland, Boston	6	1	5	6
1928-29	Andy Blair, Toronto	4	3	0	3
	Butch Keeling, NY Rangers	6	3	0	3
	Ace Bailey, Toronto	4	1	2	3
1927-28	Frank Boucher, NY Rangers	9	7	3	10
1926-27	Harry Oliver, Boston	8	4	2	6
	Percy Galbraith, Boston	8	3	3	6
1925-26	Nels Stewart, Mtl. Maroons	8	6	3	9
1924-25	Howie Morenz, Montreal	6	7	1	8
1923-24	Howie Morenz, Montreal	6	7	3	10
1922-23	Punch Broadbent, Ottawa	8	6	1	7
1921-22	Babe Dye, Toronto	7	11	1	12
1920-21	Cy Denneny, Ottawa	7	4	2	6
1919-20	Frank Nighbor, Ottawa	5	6	1	7
	Jack Darragh, Ottawa	5	6	1	7
1918-19	Newsy Lalonde, Montreal	10	17	2	19
1917-18	Alf Skinner, Toronto	7	8	3	11

Three-or-more-Goal Games, Playoffs 1918–2015

Player	Team	Date	City	Total Goals	Opposing Goaltender	Score
Wayne Gretzky (10)	Edm.	Apr. 11/81	Edm.	3	Richard Sevigny	Edm. 6 Mtl. 2
		Apr. 19/81	Edm.	3	Billy Smith	Edm. 5 NYI 2
		Apr. 6/83	Edm.	4	Brian Hayward	Edm. 6 Wpg. 3
		Apr. 17/83	Cgy.	4	Reggie Lemelin	Edm. 10 Cgy. 2
		Apr. 25/85	Wpg.	3	Brian Hayward (2) / Marc Behrend (1)	Edm. 8 Wpg. 3
		May 25/85	Edm.	3	Pelle Lindbergh	Edm. 4 Phi. 3
		Apr. 24/86	Cgy.	3	Mike Vernon	Edm. 7 Cgy. 4
	L.A.	May 29/93	Tor.	3	Felix Potvin	L.A. 5 Tor. 4
	NYR	Apr. 23/97	NYR	3	John Vanbiesbrouck	NYR 3 Fla. 2
		May 18/97	Phi.	3	Garth Snow	NYR 5 Phi. 4
Maurice Richard (7)	Mtl.	Mar. 23/44	Mtl.	5	Paul Bibeault	Mtl. 5 Tor. 1
		Apr. 6/44	Chi.	3	Mike Karakas	Mtl. 3 Chi. 1
		Mar. 29/45	Mtl.	4	Frank McCool	Mtl. 10 Tor. 3
		Apr. 14/53	Bos.	3	Gord Henry	Mtl. 7 Bos. 3
		Mar. 20/56	Mtl.	3	Gump Worsley	Mtl. 7 NYR 1
		Apr. 6/57	Mtl.	4	Don Simmons	Mtl. 5 Bos. 1
		Apr. 1/58	Mtl.	3	Terry Sawchuk	Mtl. 4 Det. 3
Jari Kurri (7)	Edm.	Apr. 4/84	Edm.	3	Doug Soetaert (1) / Mike Veisor (2)	Edm. 9 Wpg. 2
		Apr. 25/85	Wpg.	3	Brian Hayward (2) / Marc Behrend (1)	Edm. 8 Wpg. 3
		May 7/85	Edm.	3	Murray Bannerman	Edm. 7 Chi. 3
		May 14/85	Edm.	3	Murray Bannerman	Edm. 10 Chi. 5
		May 16/85	Chi.	4	Murray Bannerman	Edm. 8 Chi. 2
		May 9/87	Edm.	4	Rollie Melanson (2) / Darren Eliot (2)	Edm. 13 L.A. 3
		May 18/90	Bos.	3	Andy Moog (2) / Reggie Lemelin (1)	Edm. 7 Bos. 2
Dino Ciccarelli (6)	Min.	May 5/81	Min.	3	Pat Riggin	Min. 7 Cgy. 4
		Apr. 10/82	Min.	3	Murray Bannerman	Min. 7 Chi. 1
	Wsh.	Apr. 5/90	N.J.	3	Sean Burke	Wsh. 5 N.J. 4
		Apr. 25/92	Pit.	4	Tom Barrasso (1) / Ken Wregget (3)	Wsh. 7 Pit. 2
	Det.	Apr. 29/93	Tor.	3	Felix Potvin (2) / Daren Puppa (1)	Det. 7 Tor. 3
		May 11/95	Dal.	3	Andy Moog (2) / Darcy Wakaluk (1)	Det. 5 Dal. 1
Mike Bossy (5)	NYI	Apr. 16/79	NYI	3	Tony Esposito	NYI 6 Chi. 2
		May 8/82	NYI	3	Richard Brodeur	NYI 6 Van. 5
		Apr. 10/83	Wsh.	3	Al Jensen	NYI 6 Wsh. 3
		May 3/83	NYI	3	Pete Peeters	NYI 8 Bos. 3
		May 7/83	NYI	3	Pete Peeters	NYI 8 Bos. 4
Phil Esposito (4)	Bos.	Apr. 2/69	Bos.	4	Bruce Gamble	Bos. 10 Tor. 0
		Apr. 8/70	Bos.	3	Ed Giacomin	Bos. 8 NYR 2
		Apr. 19/70	Chi.	3	Tony Esposito	Bos. 6 Chi. 3
		Apr. 8/75	Bos.	3	Tony Esposito (2) / Michel Dumas (1)	Bos. 8 Chi. 2
Mark Messier (4)	Edm.	Apr. 14/83	Edm.	4	Reggie Lemelin	Edm. 6 Cgy. 3
		Apr. 17/83	Cgy.	3	Reggie Lemelin (1) / Don Edwards (2)	Edm. 10 Cgy. 2
		Apr. 26/83	Edm.	3	Murray Bannerman	Edm. 8 Chi. 2
	NYR	May 25/94	N.J.	3	Martin Brodeur (2) / ENG (1)	NYR 4 N.J. 2
Steve Yzerman (4)	Det.	Apr. 6/89	Det.	3	Alain Chevrier	Chi. 5 Det. 4
		Apr. 4/91	St.L.	3	Vincent Riendeau (2) / Pat Jablonski (1)	Det. 6 St.L. 3
		May 8/96	St.L.	3	Jon Casey	St.L. 5 Det. 4
		Apr. 21/99	Det.	3	Guy Hebert (2) / Pat Jablonski (1)	Det. 5 Ana. 3
Bernie Geoffrion (3)	Mtl.	Mar. 27/52	Mtl.	3	Jim Henry	Mtl. 4 Bos. 0
		Apr. 7/55	Mtl.	3	Terry Sawchuk	Mtl. 4 Det. 2
		Mar. 30/57	Mtl.	3	Gump Worsley	Mtl. 8 NYR 3
Norm Ullman (3)	Det.	Mar. 29/64	Chi.	3	Glenn Hall	Det. 5 Chi. 4
		Apr. 7/64	Det.	3	Glenn Hall (2) / Denis DeJordy (1)	Det. 7 Chi. 2
		Apr. 11/65	Det.	3	Glenn Hall	Det. 4 Chi. 2
John Bucyk (3)	Bos.	May 3/70	St.L.	3	Jacques Plante (1) / Ernie Wakely (2)	Bos. 6 St.L. 1
		Apr. 20/72	Bos.	3	Jacques Caron (1) / Ernie Wakely (2)	Bos. 10 St.L. 2
		Apr. 21/74	Bos.	3	Tony Esposito	Bos. 8 Chi. 6
Rick MacLeish (3)	Phi.	Apr. 11/74	Phi.	3	Phil Myre	Phi. 5 Atl. 1
		Apr. 13/75	Phi.	3	Gord McRae	Phi. 6 Tor. 3
		May 13/75	Phi.	3	Glenn Resch	Phi. 4 NYI 1
Denis Savard (3)	Chi.	Apr. 19/82	Chi.	3	Mike Liut	Chi. 7 StL. 4
		Apr. 10/86	Chi.	4	Ken Wregget	Tor. 6 Chi. 4
		Apr. 9/88	St.L.	3	Greg Millen	Chi. 6 St.L. 3
Tim Kerr (3)	Phi.	Apr. 13/85	NYR	3	Glen Hanlon	Phi. 6 NYR 5
		Apr. 20/87	Phi.	3	Kelly Hrudey	Phi. 4 NYI 2
		Apr. 19/89	Pit.	3	Tom Barrasso	Phi. 4 Pit. 2
Cam Neely (3)	Bos.	Apr. 9/87	Mtl.	3	Patrick Roy	Mtl. 4 Bos. 3
		Apr. 5/91	Bos.	3	Peter Sidorkiewicz	Bos. 4 Hfd. 3
		Apr. 25/91	Bos.	3	Patrick Roy	Bos. 4 Mtl. 1
Petr Klima (3)	Det.	Apr. 7/88	Tor.	3	Allan Bester (2) / Ken Wregett (1)	Det. 6 Tor. 2
		Apr. 21/88	St.L.	3	Greg Millen	Det. 6 St.L. 0
	Edm.	May 4/91	Edm.	3	Jon Casey	Edm. 7 Min. 2
Esa Tikkanen (3)	Edm.	May 22/88	Edm.	3	Reggie Lemelin	Edm. 6 Bos. 3
		Apr. 16/91	Cgy.	3	Mike Vernon	Edm. 5 Cgy. 4
	L.A.	Apr. 26/92	L.A.	3	Kelly Hrudey (2) / Tom Askey (1)	Edm. 5 L.A. 2
Mike Gartner (3)	NYR	Apr. 13/90	NYR	3	Mark Fitzpatrick (2) / Glenn Healy (1)	NYR 6 NYI 5
		Apr. 27/92	NYR	3	Chris Terreri	NYR 8 N.J. 5
	Tor.	Apr. 25/96	Tor.	3	Jon Casey	Tor. 5 St.L. 4
Mario Lemieux (3)	Pit.	Apr. 25/89	Pit.	5	Ron Hextall	Pit. 10 Phi. 7
		Apr. 23/92	Pit.	3	Don Beaupre	Pit. 6 Wsh. 4
		May 11/96	Pit.	3	Mike Richter	Pit. 7 NYR 3
Patrick Marleau (3)	S.J.	Apr. 10/04	S.J.	3	Chris Osgood	S.J. 3 St.L. 1
		Apr. 22/04	S.J.	3	David Aebischer	S.J. 5 Col. 2
		Apr. 27/06	S.J.	3	Chris Mason	Nsh. 4 S.J. 5
Johan Franzen (3)	Det.	Apr. 26/08	Det.	3	Jose Theodore (2) / Peter Budaj (1)	Det. 5 Col. 1
		May 1/08	Col.	3	Jose Theodore (1) / Peter Budaj (1)	Det. 8 Col. 2
		May 6/10	Det.	4	Evgeni Nabokov (3) / Thomas Greiss (1)	Det. 7 S.J. 1
Newsy Lalonde (2)	Mtl.	Mar. 1/19	Mtl.	5	Clint Benedict	Mtl. 6 Ott. 3
		Mar. 22/19	Sea.	4	Hap Holmes	Mtl. 4 Sea. 2
Howie Morenz (2)	Mtl.	Mar. 22/24	Mtl.	3	Charles Reid	Mtl. 6 Cgy.T. 1
		Mar. 27/25	Mtl.	3	Hap Holmes	Mtl. 4 Vic. 2
Doug Bentley (2)	Chi.	Mar. 28/44	Chi.	3	Connie Dion	Chi. 7 Det. 1
		Mar. 30/44	Det.	3	Connie Dion	Chi. 5 Det. 2
Toe Blake (2)	Mtl.	Mar. 22/38	Mtl.	3	Mike Karakas	Mtl. 6 Chi. 4
		Mar. 26/46	Mtl.	3	Mike Karakas	Mtl. 7 Chi. 2
Ted Kennedy (2)	Tor.	Mar. 14/45	Tor.	3	Harry Lumley	Det. 5 Tor. 3
		Mar. 27/48	Tor.	4	Frank Brimsek	Tor. 5 Bos. 3
F. St. Marseille (2)	St.L.	Apr. 28/70	St.L.	3	Al Smith	St.L. 5 Pit. 0
		Apr. 6/72	Min.	3	Cesare Maniago	Min. 5 St.L. 5
Bobby Hull (2)	Chi.	Apr. 7/63	Det.	3	Terry Sawchuk	Det. 7 Chi. 4
		Apr. 9/72	Pit.	3	Jim Rutherford	Chi. 6 Pit. 5
Pit Martin (2)	Chi.	Apr. 4/73	Chi.	3	Wayne Stephenson	Chi. 7 St.L. 1
		May 10/73	Chi.	3	Ken Dryden	Chi. 6 Mtl. 4
Yvan Cournoyer (2)	Mtl.	Apr. 5/73	Mtl.	3	Dave Dryden	Mtl. 7 Buf. 3
		Apr. 11/74	Mtl.	3	Ed Giacomin	Mtl. 4 NYR 1
Guy Lafleur (2)	Mtl.	May 1/75	Mtl.	3	Roger Crozier (1) / Gerry Desjardins (2)	Mtl. 7 Buf. 0
		Apr. 11/77	Mtl.	3	Ed Staniowski	Mtl. 7 St.L. 2
Lanny McDonald (2)	Tor.	Apr. 9/77	Pit.	3	Denis Herron	Tor. 5 Pit. 2
		Apr. 17/77	Tor.	4	Wayne Stephenson	Phi. 6 Tor. 5
Bill Barber (2)	Phi.	May 4/80	Min.	3	Gilles Meloche	Phi. 5 Min. 3
		Apr. 9/81	Phi.	3	Dan Bouchard	Phi. 8 Que. 5
Bryan Trottier (2)	NYI	Apr. 8/80	NYI	3	Doug Keans	NYI 8 L.A. 1
		Apr. 9/81	NYI	3	Michel Larocque	NYI 5 Tor. 1
Butch Goring (2)	L.A.	Apr. 9/77	L.A.	3	Phil Myre	L.A. 4 Atl. 1
	NYI	May 17/81	Min.	3	Gilles Meloche	NYI 7 Min. 5
Paul Reinhart (2)	Cgy.	Apr. 14/83	Edm.	3	Andy Moog	Edm. 6 Cgy. 3
		Apr. 8/84	Van.	3	Richard Brodeur	Cgy. 5 Van. 1
Brian Propp (2)	Phi.	Apr. 22/81	Phi.	3	Pat Riggin	Phi. 9 Cgy. 4
		Apr. 21/85	Phi.	3	Billy Smith	Phi. 5 NYI 2
Peter Stastny (2)	Que.	Apr. 5/83	Bos.	3	Pete Peeters	Bos. 4 Que. 3
		Apr. 11/87	Que.	3	Mike Liut (2) / Steve Weeks (1)	Que. 5 Hfd. 1
Michel Goulet (2)	Que.	Apr. 23/85	Que.	3	Steve Penney	Que. 7 Mtl. 6
		Apr. 12/87	Que.	3	Mike Liut	Que. 4 Hfd. 1
Glenn Anderson (2)	Edm.	Apr. 26/83	Edm.	4	Murray Bannerman	Edm. 8 Chi. 2
		Apr. 6/88	Wpg.	3	Daniel Berthiaume	Edm. 7 Wpg. 4
Peter Zezel (2)	Phi.	Apr. 13/86	NYR	3	John Vanbiesbrouck	Phi. 7 NYR 1
	St.L.	Apr. 11/89	St.L.	3	Jon Casey (2) / Kari Takko (1)	St.L. 6 Min. 1
Geoff Courtnall (2)	Van.	Apr. 4/91	L.A.	3	Kelly Hrudey	Van. 5 L.A. 5
		Apr. 30/92	Van.	3	Rick Tabaracci	Van. 5 Win. 0
Joe Sakic (2)	Que.	May 6/95	Que.	3	Mike Richter	Que. 5 NYR 4
	Col.	Apr. 25/96	Col.	3	Corey Hirsch	Col. 5 Van. 4
Daniel Alfredsson (2)	Ott.	Apr. 28/98	Ott.	3	Martin Brodeur	Ott. 4 N.J. 3
		May 11/98	Ott.	3	Olaf Kolzig	Ott. 4 Wsh. 3
David Krejci (2)	Bos.	May 25/11	T.B.	3	Dwayne Roloson	T.B. 5 Bos. 4
	Bos.	May 8/13	Bos.	3	James Reimer	Bos. 4 Tor. 3
Sidney Crosby (2)	Pit.	May 4/09	Wsh.	3	Semyon Varlamov	Wsh. 4 Pit. 3
	Pit.	May 24/13	Pit.	3	Craig Anderson	Pit. 6 Ott. 2
Patrick Kane (2)	Chi.	May 11/09	Chi.	3	Roberto Luongo	Chi. 7 Van. 5
	Chi.	June 8/13	Chi.	3	Jonathan Quick	Chi. 4 L.A. 2
Evgeni Malkin (2)	Pit.	May 21/09	Pit.	3	Cam Ward	Pit. 7 Car. 4
	Pit.	Apr. 28/14	CBJ	3	Sergei Bobrovsky	Pit. 4 CBJ 3
Jeff Carter (2)	L.A.	May 15/12	Phx.	3	Mike Smith	L.A. 4 Phx. 0
	L.A.	May 21/14	L.A.	3	Corey Crawford	L.A. 6 Chi.2
Harry Meeking	Tor.	Mar. 11/18	Tor.	3	Georges Vezina	Tor. 7 Mtl. 3
Alf Skinner	Tor.	Mar. 28/18	Tor.	3	Hugh Lehman	Van.M. 6 Tor. 4
Joe Malone	Mtl.	Feb. 23/19	Mtl.	3	Clint Benedict	Mtl. 8 Ott. 4
Odie Cleghorn	Mtl.	Feb. 27/19	Ott.	3	Clint Benedict	Mtl. 5 Ott. 3
Jack Darragh	Ott.	Apr. 1/20	Tor.	3	Hap Holmes	Ott. 6 Sea. 1
George Boucher	Ott.	Mar. 10/21	Ott.	3	Jake Forbes	Ott. 5 Tor. 0
Babe Dye	Tor.	Mar. 28/22	Tor.	4	Hugh Lehman	Tor. 5 Van.M. 1
Percy Galbraith	Bos.	Mar. 31/27	Bos.	3	Hugh Lehman	Bos. 4 Chi. 4
Busher Jackson	Tor.	Apr. 5/32	NYR	3	John Ross Roach	Tor. 6 NYR 4
Frank Boucher	NYR	Apr. 9/32	Tor.	3	Lorne Chabot	Tor. 6 NYR 4
Charlie Conacher	Tor.	Mar. 26/36	Tor.	3	Tiny Thompson	Tor. 8 Bos. 3

Three-or-more-Goal Games, Playoffs *— continued*

Player	Team	Date	City	Total Goals	Opposing Goaltender	Score	
Syd Howe	Det.	Mar. 23/39	Det.	3	Claude Bourque	Det. 7	Mtl. 3
Bryan Hextall	NYR	Apr. 3/40	NYR	3	Turk Broda	NYR 6	Tor. 2
Joe Benoit	Mtl.	Mar. 22/41	Mtl.	3	Sam LoPresti	Mtl. 4	Chi. 3
Syl Apps	Tor.	Mar. 25/41	Tor.	3	Frank Brimsek	Tor. 7	Bos. 2
Jack McGill	Bos.	Mar. 29/42	Bos.	3	Johnny Mowers	Det. 6	Bos. 4
Don Metz	Tor.	Apr. 14/42	Tor.	3	Johnny Mowers	Tor. 9	Det. 3
Mud Bruneteau	Det.	Apr. 1/43	Det.	3	Frank Brimsek	Det. 6	Bos. 2
Don Grosso	Det.	Apr. 7/43	Bos.	3	Frank Brimsek	Det. 4	Bos. 0
Carl Liscombe	Det.	Apr. 3/45	Bos.	4	Paul Bibeault	Det. 5	Bos. 3
Billy Reay	Mtl.	Apr. 1/47	Bos.	4	Frank Brimsek	Mtl. 5	Bos. 1
Gerry Plamondon	Mtl.	Mar. 24/49	Det.	3	Harry Lumley	Mtl. 4	Det. 3
Sid Smith	Tor.	Apr. 10/49	Det.	3	Harry Lumley	Tor. 3	Det. 1
Pentti Lund	NYR	Apr. 2/50	NYR	3	Bill Durnan	NYR 4	Mtl. 1
Ted Lindsay	Det.	Apr. 5/55	Det.	4	Charlie Hodge (1)		
					Jacques Plante (3)	Det. 7	Mtl. 1
Gordie Howe	Det.	Apr. 10/55	Det.	3	Jacques Plante	Det. 5	Mtl. 1
Phil Goyette	Mtl.	Mar. 25/58	Mtl.	3	Terry Sawchuk	Mtl. 8	Det. 1
Jerry Toppazzini	Bos.	Apr. 5/58	Bos.	3	Gump Worsley	Bos. 8	NYR 2
Bob Pulford	Tor.	Apr. 19/62	Tor.	3	Glenn Hall	Tor. 8	Chi. 4
Dave Keon	Tor.	Apr. 9/64	Mtl.	3	Charlie Hodge (2)	Tor. 3	Mtl. 1
					ENG (1)		
Henri Richard	Mtl.	Apr. 20/67	Mtl.	3	Terry Sawchuk (2)		
					Johnny Bower (1)	Mtl. 6	Tor. 2
Rosaire Paiement	Phi.	Apr. 13/68	Phi.	3	Glenn Hall (1)		
					Seth Martin (2)	Phi. 6	St.L. 1
Jean Beliveau	Mtl.	Apr. 20/68	Mtl.	3	Denis DeJordy	Mtl. 4	Chi. 1
Red Berenson	St.L.	Apr. 15/69	St.L.	3	Gerry Desjardins	St.L. 4	L.A. 0
Ken Schinkel	Pit.	Apr. 11/70	Oak.	3	Gary Smith	Pit. 5	Oak. 2
Jim Pappin	Chi.	Apr. 11/71	Phi.	3	Bruce Gamble	Chi. 6	Phi. 2
Bobby Orr	Bos.	Apr. 11/71	Mtl.	3	Ken Dryden	Bos. 5	Mtl. 2
Jacques Lemaire	Mtl.	Apr. 20/71	Mtl.	3	Gump Worsley	Mtl. 7	Min. 2
Vic Hadfield	NYR	Apr. 22/71	NYR	3	Tony Esposito	NYR 4	Chi. 1
Fred Stanfield	Bos.	Apr. 18/72	Bos.	3	Jacques Caron	Bos. 6	St.L. 1
Ken Hodge	Bos.	Apr. 30/72	Bos.	3	Ed Giacomin	Bos. 6	NYR 5
Dick Redmond	Chi.	Apr. 4/73	Chi.	3	Wayne Stephenson	Chi. 7	St.L. 1
Steve Vickers	NYR	Apr. 10/73	Bos.	3	Ross Brooks (2)		
					Eddie Johnston (1)	NYR 6	Bos. 3
Tom Williams	L.A.	Apr. 14/74	L.A.	3	Mike Veisor	L.A. 5	Chi. 1
Marcel Dionne	L.A.	Apr. 15/76	L.A.	3	Gilles Gilbert	L.A. 6	Bos. 4
Don Saleski	Phi.	Apr. 20/76	Phi.	3	Wayne Thomas	Phi. 7	Tor. 1
Darryl Sittler	Tor.	Apr. 22/76	Tor.	5	Bernie Parent	Tor. 8	Phi. 5
Reggie Leach	Phi.	May 6/76	Phi.	5	Gilles Gilbert	Phi. 6	Bos. 3
Jim Lorentz	Buf.	Apr. 7/77	Min.	3	Pete LoPresti (2)		
					Gary Smith (1)	Buf. 7	Min. 1
Bobby Schmautz	Bos.	Apr. 11/77	Bos.	3	Rogie Vachon	Bos. 8	L.A. 3
Billy Harris	NYI	Apr. 23/77	Mtl.	3	Ken Dryden	Mtl. 4	NYI 3
George Ferguson	Tor.	Apr. 11/78	Tor.	3	Rogie Vachon	Tor. 7	L.A. 3
Jean Ratelle	Bos.	May 3/79	Bos.	3	Ken Dryden	Bos. 4	Mtl. 3
Stan Jonathan	Bos.	May 8/79	Bos.	3	Ken Dryden	Bos. 5	Mtl. 2
Ron Duguay	NYR	Apr. 20/80	NYR	3	Pete Peeters	NYR 4	Phi. 2
Steve Shutt	Mtl.	Apr. 22/80	Mtl.	3	Gilles Meloche	Mtl. 6	Min. 2
Gilbert Perreault	Buf.	May 6/80	NYI	3	Billy Smith (2)		
					ENG (1)	Buf. 7	NYI 4
Paul Holmgren	Phi.	May 15/80	Phi.	3	Billy Smith	Phi. 8	NYI 3
Steve Payne	Min.	Apr. 8/81	Bos.	3	Rogie Vachon	Min. 5	Bos. 4
Denis Potvin	NYI	Apr. 17/81	NYI	3	Andy Moog	NYI 6	Edm. 3
Barry Pederson	Bos.	Apr. 8/82	Bos.	3	Don Edwards	Bos. 7	Buf. 3
Duane Sutter	NYI	Apr. 15/83	NYI	3	Glen Hanlon	NYI 5	NYR 0
Doug Halward	Van.	Apr. 7/84	Van.	3	Reggie Lemelin (2)		
					Don Edwards (1)	Van. 7	Cgy. 0
Jorgen Pettersson	St.L.	Apr. 8/84	Det.	3	Eddie Mio	St.L. 3	Det. 2
Clark Gillies	NYI	May 12/84	NYI	3	Grant Fuhr	NYI 6	Edm. 1
Ken Linseman	Bos.	Apr. 14/85	Bos.	3	Steve Penney	Bos. 7	Mtl. 6
Dave Andreychuk	Buf.	Apr. 14/85	Buf.	3	Dan Bouchard	Buf. 7	Que. 4
Greg Paslawski	St.L.	Apr. 15/86	Min.	3	Don Beaupre	St.L. 6	Min. 3
Doug Risebrough	Cgy.	May 4/86	Cgy.	3	Rick Wamsley	Cgy. 8	St.L. 2
Mike McPhee	Mtl.	Apr. 11/87	Bos.	3	Doug Keans	Mtl. 5	Bos. 4
John Ogrodnick	Que.	Apr. 14/87	Hfd.	3	Mike Liut	Que. 7	Hfd. 5
Pelle Eklund	Phi.	May 10/87	Mtl.	3	Patrick Roy (1)		
					Brian Hayward (2)	Phi. 6	Mtl. 3
John Tucker	Buf.	Apr. 9/88	Bos.	4	Andy Moog	Buf. 6	Bos. 2
Tony Hrkac	St.L.	Apr. 10/88	St.L.	4	Darren Pang	St.L. 6	Chi. 5
Hakan Loob	Cgy.	Apr. 10/88	Cgy.	3	Glenn Healy	Cgy. 7	L.A. 3
Ed Olczyk	Tor.	Apr. 12/88	Tor.	3	Greg Stefan (2)		
					Glen Hanlon (1)	Tor. 6	Det. 5
Aaron Broten	N.J.	Apr. 20/88	N.J.	3	Pete Peeters	N.J. 5	Wsh. 2
Mark Johnson	N.J.	Apr. 22/88	Wsh.	4	Pete Peeters	N.J. 10	Wsh. 4
Patrik Sundstrom	N.J.	Apr. 22/88	Wsh.	3	Pete Peeters (2)		
					Clint Malarchuk (1)	N.J. 10	Wsh. 4
Bob Brooke	Min.	Apr. 5/89	St.L.	3	Greg Millen	St.L. 4	Min. 3
Chris Kontos	L.A.	Apr. 6/89	L.A.	3	Grant Fuhr	L.A. 5	Edm. 2
Wayne Presley	Chi.	Apr. 13/89	Chi.	3	Greg Stefan (1)		
					Glen Hanlon (2)	Chi. 7	Det. 1
Tony Granato	L.A.	Apr. 10/90	L.A.	3	Mike Vernon (1)		
					Rick Wamsley (2)	L.A. 12	Cgy. 4
Tomas Sandstrom	L.A.	Apr. 10/90	L.A.	3	Mike Vernon (1)		
					Rick Wamsley (2)	L.A. 12	Cgy. 4
Dave Taylor	L.A.	Apr. 10/90	L.A.	3	Mike Vernon (1)		
					Rick Wamsley (2)	L.A. 12	Cgy. 4
Bernie Nicholls	NYR	Apr. 19/90	NYR	3	Mike Liut	NYR 7	Wsh. 3
John Druce	Wsh.	Apr. 21/90	NYR	3	John Vanbiesbrouck	Wsh. 6	NYR 3
Adam Oates	St.L.	Apr. 12/91	St.L.	3	Tim Chevaldae	St.L. 6	Det. 1
Luc Robitaille	L.A.	Apr. 26/91	L.A.	3	Grant Fuhr	L.A. 5	Edm. 2
Ray Sheppard	Det.	Apr. 24/92	Min.	3	Jon Casey	Min. 5	Det. 2
Pavel Bure	Van.	Apr. 28/92	Wpg.	3	Rick Tabaracci	Van. 8	Wpg. 3
Joe Murphy	Edm.	May 6/92	Edm.	3	Kirk McLean	Edm. 5	Van. 2
Ron Francis	Pit.	May 9/92	Pit.	3	Mike Richter (2)		
					John V'brouck (1)	Pit. 5	NYR. 4
Kevin Stevens	Pit.	May 21/92	Bos.	4	Andy Moog	Pit. 5	Bos. 2
Dirk Graham	Chi.	Jun. 1/92	Chi.	3	Tom Barrasso	Pit. 6	Chi. 5
Brian Noonan	Chi.	Apr. 18/93	Chi.	3	Curtis Joseph	St.L. 4	Chi. 3
Dale Hunter	Wsh.	Apr. 20/93	Wsh.	3	Glenn Healy	NYI 5	Wsh. 4
Teemu Selanne	Wpg.	Apr. 23/93	Wpg.	3	Kirk McLean	Wpg. 5	Van. 4
Ray Ferraro	NYI	Apr. 26/93	Wsh.	4	Don Beaupre	Wsh. 6	NYI 4
Al Iafrate	Wsh.	Apr. 26/93	Wsh.	3	Glenn Healy (2)		
					Mark Fitzpatrick (1)	Wsh. 6	NYI 4
Paul DiPietro	Mtl.	Apr. 28/93	Mtl.	3	Ron Hextall	Mtl. 6	Que. 2
Wendel Clark	Tor.	May 27/93	L.A.	3	Kelly Hrudey	L.A. 5	Tor. 4
Eric Desjardins	Mtl.	Jun. 3/93	Mtl.	3	Kelly Hrudey	Mtl. 3	L.A. 2
Tony Amonte	Chi.	Apr. 23/94	Chi.	4	Felix Potvin	Chi. 5	Tor. 4
Gary Suter	Chi.	Apr. 24/94	Chi.	3	Felix Potvin	Chi. 4	Tor. 3
Ulf Dahlen	S.J.	May 6/94	S.J.	3	Felix Potvin	S.J. 5	Tor. 2
Mike Sullivan	Cgy.	May 11/95	S.J.	3	Arturs Irbe (2)		
					Wade Flaherty (1)	Cgy. 9	S.J. 2
Theoren Fleury	Cgy.	May 13/95	S.J.	4	Arturs Irbe (3)		
					ENG (1)	Cgy. 6	S.J. 4
Brendan Shanahan	St.L.	May 13/95	Van.	3	Kirk McLean	St.L. 5	Van. 2
John LeClair	Phi.	May 21/95	Phi.	3	Mike Richter	Phi. 5	NYR 4
Brian Leetch	NYR	May 22/95	Phi.	3	Ron Hextall	Phi. 4	NYR 3
Trevor Linden	Van.	Apr. 25/96	Col.	3	Patrick Roy	Col. 5	Van. 4
Jaromir Jagr	Pit.	May 11/96	Pit.	3	Mike Richter	Pit. 7	NYR 3
Peter Forsberg	Col.	Jun. 6/96	Col.	3	John Vanbiesbrouck	Col. 8	Fla. 1
Valeri Zelepukin	N.J.	Apr. 22/97	Mtl.	3	Jocelyn Thibault	N.J. 6	Mtl. 4
Valeri Kamensky	Col.	Apr. 24/97	Col.	3	Jeff Hackett (2)		
					Chris Terreri (1)	Col. 7	Chi. 0
Eric Lindros	Phi.	May 20/97	NYR	3	Mike Richter	Phi. 6	NYR 3
Matthew Barnaby	Buf.	May 10/98	Buf.	3	Andy Moog (2)	Buf. 6	Mtl. 3
					ENG (1)		
Martin Straka	Pit.	Apr. 25/99	Pit.	3	Martin Brodeur	Pit. 4	N.J. 2
Martin Lapointe	Det.	Apr. 15/00	Det.	3	Stephane Fiset (2)	Det. 8	L.A. 5
					Jamie Storr (1)		
Doug Weight	Edm.	Apr. 16/00	Edm.	3	Ed Belfour	Edm. 5	Dal. 2
Bill Guerin	Edm.	Apr. 18/00	Edm.	3	Ed Belfour	Dal. 4	Edm. 3
Scott Young	St.L.	Apr. 23/00	S.J.	3	Steve Shields	St.L. 6	S.J. 2
Andy Delmore	Phi.	May 7/00	Phi.	3	Ron Tugnutt (2)	Phi. 6	Pit. 3
					Peter Skudra (1)		
Brett Hull	Det.	Apr. 27/02	Van.	3	Peter Skudra	Det. 6	Van. 4
Keith Tkachuk	St.L.	May 7/02	St.L.	3	Dominik Hasek	St.L. 6	Det. 1
Darren McCarty	Det.	May 18/02	Det.	3	Patrick Roy	Det. 5	Col. 3
Alexander Mogilny	Tor.	Apr. 9/03	Phi.	3	Roman Cechmanek (2)	Tor. 5	Phi. 3
					ENG (1)		
Mike Sillinger	St.L.	Apr. 12/04	St.L.	3	Evgeni Nabokov (2)	St.L. 4	S.J. 1
					ENG (1)		
Keith Primeau	Phi.	May 2/04	Phi.	3	Ed Belfour (2)	Phi. 7	Tor. 2
					Trevor Kidd (1)		
J.P. Dumont	Buf.	Apr. 24/06	Buf.	3	Antero Niittymaki (1)	Phi. 2	Buf. 8
					Robert Esche (2)		
John Madden	N.J.	Apr. 24/06	N.J.	3	Kevin Weekes	NYR 1	N.J. 4
Jason Pominville	Buf.	Apr. 24/06	Buf.	3	Antero Niittymaki (2)	Phi. 2	Buf. 8
					Robert Esche (1)		
Joffrey Lupul	Ana.	May 9/06	Col.	4	Jose Theodore	Ana. 4	Col. 3
Michael Nylander	NYR	Apr. 17/07	NYR	3	Kari Lehtonen	NYR 7	Atl. 0
Andy McDonald	Ana.	Apr. 25/07	Ana.	3	Dany Sabourin (1)	Ana. 5	Van. 1
					Roberto Luongo (2)		
Pavel Datsyuk	Det.	May 12/08	Dal.	3	Marty Turco	Det. 5	Dal. 2
Alex Ovechkin	Wsh.	May 4/09	Wsh.	3	Marc-Andre Fleury	Wsh. 4	Pit. 3
Henrik Zetterberg	Det.	Apr. 16/10	Phx.	3	Ilya Bryzgalov	Det. 7	Phx. 4
Andrei Kostitsyn	Mtl.	Apr. 17/10	Wsh.	3	Jose Theodore (1)	Wsh. 6	Mtl. 5
					Semyon Varlamov (2)		
Nicklas Backstrom	Wsh.	Apr. 17/10	Wsh.	3	Jaroslav Halak	Wsh. 6	Mtl. 5
Dustin Byfuglien	Chi.	May 5/10	Van.	3	Roberto Luongo	Chi. 5	Van. 2
Jonathan Toews	Chi.	May 7/10	Van.	3	Roberto Luongo	Chi. 7	Van. 4
Devin Setoguchi	S.J.	May 4/11	Det.	3	Jimmy Howard	S.J. 4	Det. 3
Sean Couturier	Phi.	Apr. 13/12	Pit.	3	Marc-Andre Fleury	Phi. 8	Pit. 5
Claude Giroux	Phi.	Apr. 13/12	Pit.	3	Marc-Andre Fleury	Phi. 8	Pit. 5
Jordan Staal	Pit.	Apr. 18/12	Phi.	3	Ilya Bryzgalov (1)	Pit. 10	Phi. 3
					Sergei Bobrovsky (2)		
Jean-Gabriel Pageau	Ott.	May 5/13	Ott.	3	Carey Price	Ott. 6	Mtl. 1
James Neal	Pit.	May 24/13	Pit.	3	Craig Anderson	Pit. 6	Ott. 2
Wayne Simmonds	Phi.	Apr. 29/14	Phi.	3	Henrik Lundqvist	Phi. 5	NYR 2
Rene Bourque	Mtl.	May 27/14	Mtl.	3	Henrik Lundqvist (1)	Mtl. 7	NYR 4
					Cam Talbot (2)		
Vladimir Tarasenko	St.L.	Apr. 18/15	St.L.	3	Devan Dubnyk (2)	St.L. 4	Min. 1
					ENG (1)		
Filip Forsberg	Nsh.	Apr. 23/15	Nsh.	3	Scott Darling (2)	Nsh. 5	Chi. 2
					ENG (1)		
Tyler Johnson	T.B.	May 18/15	NYR	3	Henrik Lundqvist	T.B. 6	NYR 2
Derick Brassard	NYR	May 26/15	T.B.	3	Ben Bishop (2)	NYR 7	T.B. 3
					ENG (1)		

Overtime Games since 1918

Abbreviations: Teams/Cities: — **Ana.** - Anaheim; **Atl.** - Atlanta; **Bos.** - Boston; **Buf.** - Buffalo; **Cgy.** - Calgary; **Cgy. T.** - Calgary Tigers (Western Canada Hockey League); **Car.** - Carolina; **Chi.** - Chicago; **Col.** - Colorado; **CBJ** - Columbus; **Dal.** - Dallas; **Det.** - Detroit; **Edm.** - Edmonton; **Edm. E.** - Edmonton Eskimos (WCHL); **Fla.** - Florida; **Hfd.** - Hartford; **L.A.** - Los Angeles; **Min.** - Minnesota; **Mtl.** - Montreal; **Mtl. M.** - Montreal Maroons; **Nsh.** - Nashville; **N.J.** - New Jersey; **NYA** - NY Americans; **NYI** - New York Islanders; **NYR** - New York Rangers; **Oak.** - Oakland; **Ott.** - Ottawa; **Phi.** - Philadelphia; **Phx.** - Phoenix; **Pit.** - Pittsburgh; **Que.** - Quebec; **St.L.** - St. Louis; **Sea.** - Seattle Metropolitans (Pacific Coast Hockey Association); **S.J.** - San Jose; **T.B.** - Tampa Bay; **Tor.** - Toronto; **Van.** - Vancouver; **Van. M.** - Vancouver Millionaires (PCHA); **Vic.** - Victoria Cougars (WCHL); **Wpg.** - Winnipeg; **Wsh.** - Washington.

SERIES — **CF** - conference final; **CQF** - conference quarter-final; **CSF** - conference semi-final; **DF** - division final; **DSF** - division semi-final; **F** - final; **FR** - first round; **PR** - preliminary round; **QF** - quarter-final; **SF** - semi-final; **SR** - second round.

Date	City	Series	Score		Scorer	Overtime	Series Winner
Mar. 26/19	Sea.	F	Mtl. 0	Sea. 0	no scorer	20:00	....
Mar. 29/19	Sea.	F	Mtl. 4	Sea. 3	Jack McDonald	15:57	....
Mar. 21/22	Tor.	F	Tor. 2	Van. M. 1	Babe Dye	4:50	Tor.
Mar. 29/23	Van.	F	Ott. 2	Edm. E. 1	Cy Denneny	2:08	Ott.
Mar. 31/27	Mtl.	QF	Mtl. 1	Mtl. M. 0	Howie Morenz	12:05	Mtl.
Apr. 7/27	Bos.	F	Ott. 0	Bos. 0	no scorer	20:00	Ott.
Apr. 11/27	Ott.	F	Bos. 1	Ott. 1	no scorer	20:00	Ott.
Apr. 3/28	Mtl.	QF	Mtl. M. 1	Mtl. 0	Russell Oatman	8:20	Mtl. M.
Apr. 7/28	Mtl.	F	NYR 2	Mtl. M. 1	Frank Boucher	7:05	NYR
Mar. 21/29	NYR	QF	NYR 1	NYA 0	Butch Keeling	29:50	NYR
Mar. 26/29	Tor.	SF	NYR 2	Tor. 1	Frank Boucher	2:03	NYR
Mar. 20/30	Mtl.	SF	Bos. 2	Mtl. M. 1	Harry Oliver	45:35	Bos.
Mar. 25/30	Bos.	SF	Mtl. M. 1	Bos. 0	Archie Wilcox	26:27	Bos.
Mar. 26/30	Mtl.	QF	Chi. 2	Mtl. 2	Howie Morenz (Mtl.)	51:43	Mtl.
Mar. 28/30	Mtl.	SF	Mtl. 2	NYR 1	Gus Rivers	68:52	Mtl.
Mar. 24/31	Bos.	SF	Bos. 5	Mtl. 4	Cooney Weiland	18:56	Mtl.
Mar. 26/31	Chi.	QF	Chi. 2	Tor. 1	Stew Adams	19:20	Chi.
Mar. 28/31	Mtl.	SF	Mtl. 4	Bos. 3	Georges Mantha	5:10	Mtl.
Apr. 1/31	Mtl.	SF	Mtl. 3	Bos. 2	Wildor Larochelle	19:00	Mtl.
Apr. 5/31	Chi.	F	Chi. 2	Mtl. 1	Johnny Gottselig	24:50	Mtl.
Apr. 9/31	Mtl.	F	Chi. 3	Mtl. 2	Cy Wentworth	53:50	Mtl.
Mar. 26/32	Mtl.	SF	NYR 4	Mtl. 3	Fred Cook	59:32	NYR
Apr. 2/32	Tor.	SF	Tor. 3	Mtl. M. 2	Bob Gracie	17:59	Tor.
Mar. 25/33	Bos.	SF	Bos. 2	Tor. 1	Marty Barry	14:14	Tor.
Mar. 28/33	Bos.	SF	Tor. 1	Bos. 0	Busher Jackson	15:03	Tor.
Mar. 30/33	Tor.	SF	Bos. 2	Tor. 1	Eddie Shore	4:23	Tor.
Apr. 3/33	Tor.	SF	Tor. 1	Bos. 0	Ken Doraty	104:46	Tor.
Apr. 13/33	Tor.	F	NYR 1	Tor. 0	Bill Cook	7:33	NYR
Mar. 22/34	Tor.	SF	Det. 2	Tor. 1	Herbie Lewis	1:33	Det.
Mar. 25/34	Chi.	QF	Chi. 1	Mtl. 1	Mush March (Chi.)	11:05	Chi.
Apr. 3/34	Det.	F	Chi. 2	Det. 1	Paul Thompson	21:10	Chi.
Apr. 10/34	Chi.	F	Chi. 1	Det. 0	Mush March	30:05	Chi.
Mar. 23/35	Bos.	SF	Bos. 1	Tor. 0	Dit Clapper	33:26	Tor.
Mar. 26/35	Chi.	QF	Mtl. M. 1	Chi. 0	Baldy Northcott	4:02	Mtl. M.
Mar. 30/35	Tor.	SF	Tor. 2	Bos. 1	Pep Kelly	1:36	Tor.
Apr. 4/35	Tor.	F	Mtl. M. 3	Tor. 2	Dave Trottier	5:28	Mtl. M.
Mar. 24/36	Mtl.	SF	Det. 1	Mtl. M. 0	Mud Bruneteau	116:30	Det.
Apr. 9/36	Tor.	F	Tor. 4	Det. 3	Buzz Boll	0:31	Det.
Mar. 25/37	NYR	QF	NYR 2	Tor. 1	Babe Pratt	13:05	NYR
Apr. 1/37	Mtl.	SF	Det. 2	Mtl. 1	Hec Kilrea	51:49	Det.
Mar. 22/38	NYR	QF	NYA 2	NYR 1	John Sorrell	21:25	NYA
Mar. 24/38	Tor.	SF	Tor. 1	Bos. 0	George Parsons	21:31	Tor.
Mar. 26/38	Mtl.	QF	Chi. 3	Mtl. 2	Paul Thompson	11:49	Chi.
Mar. 27/38	NYR	QF	NYA 3	NYR 2	Lorne Carr	60:40	NYA
Mar. 29/38	Bos.	SF	Tor. 3	Bos. 2	Gordie Drillon	10:04	Tor.
Mar. 31/38	Chi.	SF	Chi. 1	NYA 0	Cully Dahlstrom	33:01	Chi.
Mar. 21/39	NYR	SF	Bos. 2	NYR 1	Mel Hill	59:25	Bos.
Mar. 23/39	Bos.	SF	Bos. 3	NYR 2	Mel Hill	8:24	Bos.
Mar. 26/39	Det.	QF	Det. 1	Mtl. 0	Marty Barry	7:47	Det.
Mar. 30/39	Bos.	SF	NYR 2	Bos. 1	Clint Smith	17:19	Bos.
Apr. 1/39	Tor.	SF	Tor. 5	Det. 4	Gordie Drillon	5:42	Tor.
Apr. 2/39	Bos.	SF	Bos. 2	NYR 1	Mel Hill	48:00	Bos.
Apr. 9/39	Bos.	F	Tor. 3	Bos. 2	Doc Romnes	10:38	Bos.
Mar. 19/40	Det.	QF	Det. 2	NYA 1	Syd Howe	0:25	Det.
Mar. 19/40	Tor.	QF	Tor. 3	Chi. 2	Syl Apps	6:35	Tor.
Apr. 2/40	NYR	F	NYR 2	Tor. 1	Alf Pike	15:30	NYR
Apr. 11/40	Tor.	F	NYR 2	Tor. 1	Muzz Patrick	31:43	NYR
Apr. 13/40	Tor.	F	NYR 3	Tor. 2	Bryan Hextall	2:07	NYR
Mar. 20/41	Det.	QF	Det. 2	NYR 1	Syd Howe	12:01	Det.
Mar. 22/41	Mtl.	QF	Mtl. 4	Chi. 3	Charlie Sands	34:04	Chi.
Mar. 29/41	Bos.	SF	Tor. 2	Bos. 1	Pete Langelle	17:31	Bos.
Mar. 30/41	Chi.	SF	Det. 2	Chi. 1	Gus Giesebrecht	9:15	Det.
Mar. 22/42	Chi.	QF	Bos. 2	Chi. 1	Des Smith	6:51	Bos.
Mar. 21/43	Bos.	SF	Bos. 5	Mtl. 4	Don Gallinger	12:30	Bos.
Mar. 23/43	Det.	SF	Tor. 3	Det. 2	Jack McLean	70:18	Det.
Mar. 25/43	Mtl.	SF	Bos. 3	Mtl. 2	Busher Jackson	3:20	Bos.
Mar. 30/43	Tor.	SF	Det. 3	Tor. 2	Adam Brown	9:21	Det.
Mar. 30/43	Bos.	SF	Bos. 5	Mtl. 4	Ab DeMarco	3:41	Bos.
Apr. 13/44	Mtl.	F	Mtl. 5	Chi. 4	Toe Blake	9:12	Mtl.
Mar. 27/45	Tor.	SF	Tor. 4	Mtl. 3	Gus Bodnar	12:36	Tor.
Mar. 29/45	Det.	SF	Det. 3	Bos. 2	Mud Bruneteau	17:12	Det.
Apr. 21/45	Tor.	F	Det. 1	Tor. 0	Eddie Bruneteau	14:16	Tor.
Mar. 28/46	Bos.	SF	Bos. 4	Det. 3	Don Gallinger	9:51	Bos.
Mar. 30/46	Mtl.	F	Mtl. 4	Bos. 3	Maurice Richard	9:08	Mtl.
Apr. 2/46	Mtl.	F	Mtl. 3	Bos. 2	Jimmy Peters	16:55	Mtl.
Apr. 7/46	Bos.	F	Bos. 3	Mtl. 2	Terry Reardon	15:13	Mtl.
Mar. 26/47	Tor.	SF	Tor. 3	Det. 2	Howie Meeker	3:05	Tor.
Mar. 27/47	Mtl.	SF	Mtl. 2	Bos. 1	Ken Mosdell	5:38	Mtl.
Apr. 3/47	Mtl.	SF	Mtl. 4	Bos. 3	John Quilty	36:40	Mtl.
Apr. 15/47	Tor.	F	Tor. 2	Mtl. 1	Syl Apps	16:36	Tor.
Mar. 24/48	Tor.	SF	Tor. 5	Bos. 4	Nick Metz	17:03	Tor.
Mar. 22/49	Det.	SF	Det. 2	Mtl. 1	Max McNab	44:52	Det.
Mar. 24/49	Det.	SF	Mtl. 4	Det. 3	Gerry Plamondon	2:59	Det.
Mar. 26/49	Tor.	SF	Bos. 5	Tor. 4	Woody Dumart	16:14	Tor.
Apr. 8/49	Det.	F	Tor. 3	Det. 2	Joe Klukay	17:31	Tor.
Apr. 4/50	Tor.	SF	Det. 2	Tor. 1	Leo Reise Jr.	20:38	Det.
Apr. 4/50	Mtl.	SF	Mtl. 3	NYR 2	Elmer Lach	15:19	NYR
Apr. 9/50	Det.	SF	Det. 1	Tor. 0	Leo Reise Jr.	8:39	Det.
Apr. 18/50	Det.	F	NYR 4	Det. 3	Don Raleigh	8:34	Det.
Apr. 20/50	Det.	F	NYR 2	Det. 1	Don Raleigh	1:38	Det.
Apr. 23/50	Det.	F	Det. 4	NYR 3	Pete Babando	28:31	Det.
Mar. 27/51	Det.	SF	Mtl. 3	Det. 2	Maurice Richard	61:09	Mtl.
Mar. 29/51	Det.	SF	Mtl. 1	Det. 0	Maurice Richard	42:20	Mtl.
Mar. 31/51	Tor.	SF	Bos. 1	Tor. 1	no scorer	20:00	Tor.
Apr. 11/51	Tor.	F	Tor. 3	Mtl. 2	Sid Smith	5:51	Tor.
Apr. 14/51	Tor.	F	Mtl. 3	Tor. 2	Maurice Richard	2:55	Tor.
Apr. 17/51	Mtl.	F	Tor. 2	Mtl. 1	Ted Kennedy	4:47	Tor.
Apr. 19/51	Mtl.	F	Tor. 3	Mtl. 2	Harry Watson	5:15	Tor.
Apr. 21/51	Tor.	F	Tor. 3	Mtl. 2	Bill Barilko	2:53	Tor.
Apr. 6/52	Bos.	SF	Mtl. 3	Bos. 2	Paul Masnick	27:49	Mtl.
Mar. 29/53	Bos.	SF	Bos. 2	Det. 1	Jack McIntyre	12:29	Bos.
Mar. 29/53	Chi.	SF	Chi. 2	Mtl. 1	Al Dewsbury	5:18	Mtl.
Apr. 16/53	Mtl.	F	Mtl. 1	Bos. 0	Elmer Lach	1:22	Mtl.
Apr. 1/54	Det.	SF	Det. 4	Tor. 3	Ted Lindsay	21:01	Det.
Apr. 11/54	Det.	F	Mtl. 1	Det. 0	Ken Mosdell	5:45	Det.
Apr. 16/54	Det.	F	Det. 2	Mtl. 1	Tony Leswick	4:29	Det.
Mar. 29/55	Bos.	SF	Mtl. 4	Bos. 3	Don Marshall	3:05	Mtl.
Mar. 24/56	Tor.	SF	Det. 5	Tor. 4	Ted Lindsay	4:22	Det.
Mar. 28/57	NYR	SF	NYR 4	Mtl. 3	Andy Hebenton	13:38	Mtl.
Apr. 4/57	Mtl.	SF	Mtl. 4	NYR 3	Maurice Richard	1:11	Mtl.
Mar. 27/58	NYR	SF	Bos. 4	NYR 3	Jerry Toppazzini	4:46	Bos.
Mar. 30/58	Det.	SF	Mtl. 2	Det. 1	André Pronovost	11:52	Mtl.
Apr. 17/58	Mtl.	F	Mtl. 3	Bos. 2	Maurice Richard	5:45	Mtl.
Mar. 28/59	Tor.	SF	Tor. 3	Bos. 2	Gerry Ehman	5:02	Tor.
Mar. 31/59	Tor.	SF	Tor. 3	Bos. 2	Frank Mahovlich	11:21	Tor.
Apr. 14/59	Tor.	F	Tor. 3	Mtl. 2	Dick Duff	10:06	Mtl.
Mar. 26/60	Mtl.	SF	Mtl. 4	Chi. 3	Doug Harvey	8:38	Mtl.
Mar. 27/60	Det.	SF	Tor. 5	Det. 4	Frank Mahovlich	43:00	Tor.
Mar. 29/60	Det.	SF	Det. 2	Tor. 1	Gerry Melnyk	1:54	Tor.
Mar. 22/61	Tor.	SF	Tor. 3	Det. 2	George Armstrong	24:51	Det.
Mar. 26/61	Chi.	SF	Chi. 2	Mtl. 1	Murray Balfour	52:12	Chi.
Apr. 5/62	Tor.	SF	Tor. 3	NYR 2	Red Kelly	24:23	Tor.
Apr. 2/64	Det.	SF	Chi. 3	Det. 2	Murray Balfour	8:21	Det.
Apr. 14/64	Tor.	F	Det. 4	Tor. 3	Larry Jeffrey	7:52	Tor.
Apr. 23/64	Det.	F	Tor. 4	Det. 3	Bob Baun	1:43	Tor.
Apr. 6/65	Tor.	SF	Tor. 3	Mtl. 2	Dave Keon	4:17	Mtl.
Apr. 13/65	Tor.	SF	Mtl. 4	Tor. 3	Claude Provost	16:33	Mtl.
May 5/66	Det.	F	Mtl. 3	Det. 2	Henri Richard	2:20	Mtl.
Apr. 13/67	NYR	SF	Mtl. 2	NYR 1	John Ferguson	6:28	Mtl.
Apr. 25/67	Tor.	F	Tor. 3	Mtl. 2	Bob Pulford	28:26	Tor.
Apr. 10/68	St.L.	QF	St.L. 3	Phi. 2	Larry Keenan	24:10	St.L.
Apr. 16/68	St.L.	QF	Phi. 2	St.L. 1	Don Blackburn	31:18	St.L.
Apr. 16/68	Min.	QF	Min. 4	L.A. 3	Milan Marcetta	9:11	Min.
Apr. 22/68	Min.	SF	Min. 3	St.L. 2	Parker MacDonald	3:41	St.L.
Apr. 27/68	St.L.	SF	St.L. 4	Min. 3	Gary Sabourin	1:32	St.L.
Apr. 28/68	Mtl.	SF	Mtl. 4	Chi. 3	Jacques Lemaire	2:14	Mtl.
Apr. 29/68	St.L.	SF	St.L. 3	Min. 2	Bill McCreary	17:27	St.L.
May 3/68	St.L.	SF	St.L. 2	Min. 1	Ron Schock	22:50	St.L.
May 5/68	St.L.	F	Mtl. 3	St.L. 2	Jacques Lemaire	1:41	Mtl.
May 9/68	Mtl.	F	Mtl. 4	St.L. 3	Bobby Rousseau	1:13	Mtl.
Apr. 2/69	Oak.	QF	L.A. 5	Oak. 4	Ted Irvine	0:19	L.A.
Apr. 10/69	Mtl.	SF	Mtl. 3	Bos. 2	Ralph Backstrom	0:42	Mtl.
Apr. 13/69	Mtl.	SF	Mtl. 4	Bos. 3	Mickey Redmond	4:55	Mtl.
Apr. 24/69	Bos.	SF	Mtl. 2	Bos. 1	Jean Béliveau	31:28	Mtl.
Apr. 12/70	Oak.	QF	Pit. 3	Oak. 2	Michel Briere	8:28	Pit.
May 10/70	Bos.	F	Bos. 4	St.L. 3	Bobby Orr	0:40	Bos.
Apr. 15/71	Tor.	QF	NYR 2	Tor. 1	Bob Nevin	9:07	NYR
Apr. 18/71	Chi.	SF	NYR 2	Chi. 1	Pete Stemkowski	1:37	Chi.
Apr. 27/71	Chi.	SF	Chi. 3	NYR 2	Bobby Hull	6:35	Chi.
Apr. 29/71	NYR	SF	NYR 3	Chi. 2	Pete Stemkowski	41:29	Chi.
May 4/71	Chi.	F	Chi. 2	Mtl. 1	Jim Pappin	21:11	Mtl.
Apr. 6/72	Bos.	QF	Tor. 4	Bos. 3	Jim Harrison	2:58	Bos.
Apr. 6/72	Min.	QF	Min. 6	St.L. 5	Bill Goldsworthy	1:36	St.L.
Apr. 9/72	Pit.	QF	Chi. 6	Pit. 5	Pit Martin	0:12	Chi.
Apr. 16/72	Min.	QF	St.L. 2	Min. 1	Kevin O'Shea	10:07	St.L.
Apr. 1/73	Mtl.	QF	Buf. 3	Mtl. 2	René Robert	9:18	Mtl.
Apr. 10/73	Phi.	QF	Phi. 3	Min. 2	Gary Dornhoefer	8:35	Phi.
Apr. 14/73	Mtl.	SF	Phi. 5	Mtl. 4	Rick MacLeish	2:56	Mtl.
Apr. 17/73	Mtl.	SF	Mtl. 4	Phi. 3	Larry Robinson	6:45	Mtl.
Apr. 14/74	Tor.	QF	Bos. 4	Tor. 3	Ken Hodge	1:27	Bos.
Apr. 14/74	Atl.	QF	Phi. 4	Atl. 3	Dave Schultz	5:40	Phi.
Apr. 16/74	Mtl.	QF	NYR 3	Mtl. 2	Ron Harris	4:07	NYR
Apr. 23/74	Chi.	SF	Chi. 4	Bos. 3	Jim Pappin	3:48	Bos.
Apr. 28/74	NYR	SF	NYR 2	Phi. 1	Rod Gilbert	4:20	Phi.
May 9/74	Bos.	F	Phi. 3	Bos. 2	Bobby Clarke	12:01	Phi.
Apr. 8/75	L.A.	PR	L.A. 3	Tor. 2	Mike Murphy	8:53	Tor.
Apr. 10/75	Tor.	PR	Tor. 3	L.A. 2	Blaine Stoughton	10:19	Tor.
Apr. 10/75	Chi.	PR	Chi. 4	Bos. 3	Ivan Boldirev	7:33	Chi.
Apr. 11/75	NYR	PR	NYI 4	NYR 3	J.P. Parise	0:11	NYI
Apr. 17/75	Chi.	QF	Chi. 5	Buf. 4	Stan Mikita	2:31	Buf.
Apr. 19/75	Tor.	QF	Phi. 4	Tor. 3	André Dupont	1:45	Phi.
Apr. 22/75	Mtl.	QF	Mtl. 5	Van. 4	Guy Lafleur	17:06	Mtl.
Apr. 27/75	Buf.	SF	Buf. 6	Mtl. 5	Danny Gare	4:42	Buf.
May 1/75	Phi.	SF	Phi. 5	NYI 4	Bobby Clarke	2:56	Phi.
May 6/75	Buf.	SF	Buf. 5	Mtl. 4	René Robert	5:56	Buf.
May 7/75	NYI	SF	NYI 4	Phi. 3	Jude Drouin	1:53	Phi.
May 20/75	Buf.	F	Buf. 5	Phi. 4	René Robert	18:29	Phi.
Apr. 8/76	Buf.	PR	Buf. 3	St.L. 2	Danny Gare	11:43	Buf.
Apr. 9/76	Buf.	PR	Buf. 2	St.L. 1	Don Luce	14:27	Buf.
Apr. 13/76	Bos.	QF	L.A. 3	Bos. 2	Butch Goring	0:27	Bos.
Apr. 13/76	Buf.	QF	Buf. 3	NYI 2	Danny Gare	14:04	NYI
Apr. 22/76	L.A.	QF	L.A. 4	Bos. 3	Butch Goring	18:28	Bos.
Apr. 29/76	Phi.	SF	Phi. 2	Bos. 1	Reggie Leach	13:38	Phi.
Apr. 15/77	Tor.	QF	Phi. 4	Tor. 3	Rick MacLeish	2:55	Phi.
Apr. 17/77	Tor.	QF	Phi. 6	Tor. 5	Reggie Leach	19:10	Phi.
Apr. 24/77	Phi.	SF	Bos. 4	Phi. 3	Rick Middleton	2:57	Bos.
Apr. 26/77	Phi.	SF	Bos. 5	Phi. 4	Terry O'Reilly	30:07	Bos.
May 3/77	Mtl.	SF	NYI 4	Mtl. 3	Billy Harris	3:58	Mtl.
May 14/77	Bos.	F	Mtl. 2	Bos. 1	Jacques Lemaire	4:32	Mtl.
Apr. 11/78	Phi.	PR	Phi. 3	Col. 2	Mel Bridgman	0:23	Phi.
Apr. 13/78	NYR	PR	NYR 4	Buf. 3	Don Murdoch	1:37	Buf.
Apr. 19/78	Bos.	QF	Bos. 4	Chi. 3	Terry O'Reilly	1:50	Bos.
Apr. 19/78	NYI	QF	NYI 3	Tor. 2	Mike Bossy	2:50	Tor.

Overtime Games since 1918 — *continued*

Date	City	Series	Score		Scorer	Overtime	Series Winner
Apr. 21/78	Chi.	QF	Bos. 4	Chi. 3	Peter McNab	10:17	Bos.
Apr. 25/78	NYI	QF	NYI 2	Tor. 1	Bob Nystrom	8:02	Tor.
Apr. 29/78	NYI	QF	Tor. 2	NYI 1	Lanny McDonald	4:13	Tor.
May 2/78	Bos.	SF	Bos. 3	Phi. 2	Rick Middleton	1:43	Bos.
May 16/78	Mtl.	F	Mtl. 3	Bos. 2	Guy Lafleur	13:09	Mtl.
May 21/78	Bos.	F	Bos. 4	Mtl. 3	Bobby Schmautz	6:22	Mtl.
Apr. 12/79	L.A.	PR	NYR 2	L.A. 1	Phil Esposito	6:11	NYR
Apr. 14/79	Buf.	PR	Pit. 4	Buf. 3	George Ferguson	0:47	Pit.
Apr. 16/79	Phi.	QF	Phi. 3	NYR 2	Ken Linseman	0:44	NYR
Apr. 18/79	NYI	QF	NYI 1	Chi. 0	Mike Bossy	2:31	NYI
Apr. 21/79	Tor.	QF	Mtl. 4	Tor. 3	Cam Connor	25:25	Mtl.
Apr. 22/79	Tor.	QF	Mtl. 5	Tor. 4	Larry Robinson	4:14	Mtl.
Apr. 28/79	NYI	SF	NYI 4	NYR 3	Denis Potvin	8:02	NYR
May 3/79	NYR	SF	NYI 3	NYR 2	Bob Nystrom	3:40	NYR
May 3/79	Bos.	SF	Bos. 4	Mtl. 3	Jean Ratelle	3:46	Mtl.
May 10/79	Mtl.	SF	Mtl. 5	Bos. 4	Yvon Lambert	9:33	Mtl.
May 19/79	Mtl.	F	Mtl. 4	NYR 3	Serge Savard	7:25	Mtl.
Apr. 8/80	NYR	PR	NYR 2	Atl. 1	Steve Vickers	0:33	NYR
Apr. 8/80	Phi.	PR	Phi. 4	Edm. 3	Bobby Clarke	8:06	Phi.
Apr. 8/80	Chi.	PR	Chi. 3	St.L. 2	Doug Lecuyer	12:34	Chi.
Apr. 11/80	Hfd.	PR	Mtl. 4	Hfd. 3	Yvon Lambert	0:29	Mtl.
Apr. 11/80	Tor.	PR	Min. 4	Tor. 3	Al MacAdam	0:32	Min.
Apr. 11/80	L.A.	PR	NYI 4	L.A. 3	Ken Morrow	6:55	NYI
Apr. 11/80	Edm.	PR	Phi. 3	Edm. 2	Ken Linseman	23:56	Phi.
Apr. 16/80	Bos.	QF	NYI 2	Bos. 1	Clark Gillies	1:02	NYI
Apr. 17/80	Bos.	QF	NYI 5	Bos. 4	Bob Bourne	1:24	NYI
Apr. 21/80	NYI	QF	Bos. 4	NYI 3	Terry O'Reilly	17:13	NYI
May 1/80	Buf.	SF	NYI 2	Buf. 1	Bob Nystrom	21:20	NYI
May 13/80	Phi.	F	NYI 4	Phi. 3	Denis Potvin	4:07	NYI
May 24/80	NYI	F	NYI 5	Phi. 4	Bob Nystrom	7:11	NYI
Apr. 8/81	Buf.	PR	Buf. 3	Van. 2	Alan Haworth	5:00	Buf.
Apr. 8/81	Bos.	PR	Min. 5	Bos. 4	Steve Payne	3:34	Min.
Apr. 11/81	Chi.	PR	Cgy. 5	Chi. 4	Willi Plett	35:17	Cgy.
Apr. 12/81	Que.	PR	Que. 4	Phi. 3	Dale Hunter	0:37	Phi.
Apr. 14/81	St.L.	PR	St.L. 4	Pit. 3	Mike Crombeen	25:16	St.L.
Apr. 16/81	Buf.	QF	Min. 4	Buf. 3	Steve Payne	0:22	Min.
Apr. 20/81	Min.	QF	Buf. 5	Min. 4	Craig Ramsay	16:32	Min.
Apr. 20/81	Edm.	QF	NYI 5	Edm. 4	Ken Morrow	5:41	NYI
Apr. 7/82	Min.	DSF	Chi. 3	Min. 2	Greg Fox	3:34	Chi.
Apr. 8/82	Edm.	DSF	Edm. 3	L.A. 2	Wayne Gretzky	6:20	L.A.
Apr. 8/82	Van.	DSF	Van. 2	Cgy. 1	Tiger Williams	14:20	Van.
Apr. 10/82	Pit.	DSF	Pit. 2	NYI 1	Rick Kehoe	4:14	NYI
Apr. 10/82	L.A.	DSF	L.A. 6	Edm. 5	Daryl Evans	2:35	L.A.
Apr. 13/82	Mtl.	DSF	Que. 3	Mtl. 2	Dale Hunter	0:22	Que.
Apr. 13/82	NYI	DSF	NYI 4	Pit. 3	John Tonelli	6:19	NYI
Apr. 16/82	Van.	DF	L.A. 3	Van. 2	Steve Bozek	4:33	Van.
Apr. 18/82	Que.	DF	Que. 3	Bos. 2	Wilf Paiement	11:44	Que.
Apr. 18/82	NYR	DF	NYI 4	NYR 3	Bryan Trottier	3:00	NYI
Apr. 18/82	L.A.	DF	Van. 4	L.A. 3	Colin Campbell	1:23	Van.
Apr. 21/82	St.L.	DF	St.L. 3	Chi. 2	Bernie Federko	3:28	Chi.
Apr. 23/82	Que.	DF	Bos. 6	Que. 5	Peter McNab	10:54	Que.
Apr. 27/82	Chi.	CF	Van. 2	Chi. 1	Jim Nill	28:58	Van.
May 1/82	Que.	CF	NYI 5	Que. 4	Wayne Merrick	16:52	NYI
May 8/82	NYI	F	NYI 6	Van. 5	Mike Bossy	19:58	NYI
Apr. 5/83	Bos.	DSF	Bos. 4	Que. 3	Barry Pederson	1:46	Bos.
Apr. 6/83	Cgy.	DSF	Cgy. 4	Van. 3	Eddy Beers	12:27	Cgy.
Apr. 7/83	Min.	DSF	Min. 5	Tor. 4	Bobby Smith	5:03	Min.
Apr. 10/83	Tor.	DSF	Min. 5	Tor. 4	Dino Ciccarelli	8:05	Min.
Apr. 10/83	Van.	DSF	Cgy. 4	Van. 3	Greg Meredith	1:06	Cgy.
Apr. 18/83	Min.	DF	Chi. 4	Min. 3	Rich Preston	10:34	Chi.
Apr. 24/83	Bos.	DF	Bos. 3	Buf. 2	Brad Park	1:52	Bos.
Apr. 5/84	Edm.	DSF	Edm. 5	Wpg. 4	Randy Gregg	0:21	Edm.
Apr. 7/84	Det.	DSF	St.L. 4	Det. 3	Mark Reeds	37:07	St.L.
Apr. 8/84	Det.	DSF	St.L. 3	Det. 2	Jorgen Pettersson	2:42	St.L.
Apr. 10/84	NYI	DSF	NYI 3	NYR 2	Ken Morrow	8:56	NYI
Apr. 13/84	Min.	DF	St.L. 4	Min. 3	Doug Gilmour	16:16	Min.
Apr. 13/84	Edm.	DF	Cgy. 6	Edm. 5	Carey Wilson	3:42	Edm.
Apr. 13/84	NYI	DF	NYI 5	Wsh. 4	Anders Kallur	7:35	NYI
Apr. 16/84	Mtl.	DF	Que. 4	Mtl. 3	Bo Berglund	3:00	Mtl.
Apr. 20/84	Cgy.	DF	Cgy. 5	Edm. 4	Lanny McDonald	1:04	Edm.
Apr. 22/84	Min.	DF	Min. 4	St.L. 3	Steve Payne	6:00	Min.
Apr. 10/85	Phi.	DSF	Phi. 5	NYR 4	Mark Howe	8:01	Phi.
Apr. 10/85	Wsh.	DSF	Wsh. 4	NYI 3	Alan Haworth	2:28	NYI
Apr. 10/85	Edm.	DSF	Edm. 3	L.A. 2	Lee Fogolin	3:01	Edm.
Apr. 10/85	Wpg.	DSF	Wpg. 5	Cgy. 4	Brian Mullen	7:56	Wpg.
Apr. 11/85	Wsh.	DSF	Wsh. 2	NYI 1	Mike Gartner	21:23	NYI
Apr. 13/85	L.A.	DSF	Edm. 4	L.A. 3	Glenn Anderson	0:46	Edm.
Apr. 18/85	Mtl.	DF	Que. 2	Mtl. 1	Mark Kumpel	12:23	Que.
Apr. 23/85	Que.	DF	Que. 7	Mtl. 6	Dale Hunter	18:36	Que.
Apr. 25/85	Min.	DF	Chi. 7	Min. 6	Darryl Sutter	21:57	Chi.
Apr. 28/85	Chi.	DF	Min. 5	Chi. 4	Dennis Maruk	1:14	Chi.
Apr. 30/85	Min.	DF	Chi. 6	Min. 5	Darryl Sutter	15:41	Chi.
May 2/85	Mtl.	DF	Que. 3	Mtl. 2	Peter Stastny	2:22	Que.
May 5/85	Que.	CF	Que. 2	Phi. 1	Peter Stastny	6:20	Phi.
Apr. 9/86	Que.	DSF	Hfd. 3	Que. 2	Sylvain Turgeon	2:36	Hfd.
Apr. 12/86	Wpg.	DSF	Cgy. 4	Wpg. 3	Lanny McDonald	8:25	Cgy.
Apr. 17/86	Wsh.	DF	NYR 4	Wsh. 3	Brian MacLellan	1:16	NYR
Apr. 20/86	Edm.	DF	Edm. 6	Cgy. 5	Glenn Anderson	1:04	Cgy.
Apr. 23/86	Hfd.	DF	Hfd. 2	Mtl. 1	Kevin Dineen	1:07	Mtl.
Apr. 23/86	NYR	DF	NYR 6	Wsh. 5	Bob Brooke	2:40	NYR
Apr. 26/86	St L.	DF	St L. 4	Tor. 3	Mark Reeds	7:11	St L.
Apr. 29/86	Mtl.	DF	Mtl. 2	Hfd. 1	Claude Lemieux	5:55	Mtl.
May 5/86	NYR	CF	Mtl. 4	NYR 3	Claude Lemieux	9:41	Mtl.
May 12/86	St L.	CF	St L. 6	Cgy. 5	Doug Wickenheiser	7:30	Cgy.
May 18/86	Cgy.	F	Mtl. 3	Cgy. 2	Brian Skrudland	0:09	Mtl.
Apr. 8/87	Hfd.	DSF	Hfd. 3	Que. 2	Paul MacDermid	2:20	Que.
Apr. 9/87	Mtl.	DSF	Mtl. 4	Bos. 3	Mats Naslund	2:38	Mtl.
Apr. 9/87	St.L.	DSF	Tor. 3	St.L. 2	Rick Lanz	10:17	Tor.
Apr. 11/87	Wpg.	DSF	Cgy. 3	Wpg. 2	Mike Bullard	3:53	Wpg.
Apr. 11/87	Chi.	DSF	Det. 4	Chi. 3	Shawn Burr	4:51	Det.
Apr. 16/87	Que.	DSF	Que. 5	Hfd. 4	Peter Stastny	6:05	Que.
Apr. 18/87	Wsh.	DSF	NYI 3	Wsh. 2	Pat LaFontaine	68:47	NYI
Apr. 21/87	Edm.	DF	Edm. 3	Wpg. 2	Glenn Anderson	0:36	Edm.
Apr. 26/87	Que.	DF	Mtl. 3	Que. 2	Mats Naslund	5:30	Mtl.
Apr. 27/87	Tor.	DF	Tor. 3	Det. 2	Mike Allison	9:31	Det.
May 4/87	Phi.	CF	Phi. 4	Mtl. 3	Ilkka Sinislao	9:11	Phi.
May 20/87	Edm.	F	Edm. 3	Phi. 2	Jari Kurri	6:50	Edm.
Apr. 6/88	NYI	DSF	NYI 4	N.J. 3	Pat LaFontaine	6:11	N.J.
Apr. 10/88	Phi.	DSF	Phi. 5	Wsh. 4	Murray Craven	1:18	Wsh.
Apr. 10/88	N.J.	DSF	NYI 5	N.J. 4	Brent Sutter	15:07	N.J.
Apr. 10/88	Buf.	DSF	Buf. 6	Bos. 5	John Tucker	5:32	Bos.
Apr. 12/88	Det.	DSF	Tor. 6	Det. 5	Ed Olczyk	0:34	Det.
Apr. 16/88	Wsh.	DSF	Wsh. 5	Phi. 4	Dale Hunter	5:57	Wsh.
Apr. 21/88	Cgy.	DF	Edm. 5	Cgy. 4	Wayne Gretzky	7:54	Edm.
May 4/88	Bos.	CF	N.J. 3	Bos. 2	Doug Brown	17:46	Bos.
May 9/88	Det.	CF	Edm. 4	Det. 3	Jari Kurri	11:02	Edm.
Apr. 5/89	St.L.	DSF	St.L. 4	Min. 3	Brett Hull	11:55	St.L.
Apr. 5/89	Cgy.	DSF	Van. 4	Cgy. 3	Paul Reinhart	2:47	Cgy.
Apr. 6/89	St.L.	DSF	St.L. 4	Min. 3	Rick Meagher	5:30	St.L.
Apr. 6/89	Det.	DSF	Chi. 5	Det. 4	Duane Sutter	14:36	Chi.
Apr. 8/89	Hfd.	DSF	Mtl. 5	Hfd. 4	Stephane Richer	5:01	Mtl.
Apr. 8/89	Phi.	DSF	Wsh. 4	Phi. 3	Kelly Miller	0:51	Phi.
Apr. 9/89	Hfd.	DSF	Mtl. 4	Hfd. 3	Russ Courtnall	15:12	Mtl.
Apr. 15/89	Cgy.	DSF	Cgy. 4	Van. 3	Joel Otto	19:21	Cgy.
Apr. 18/89	Cgy.	DF	Cgy. 4	L.A. 3	Doug Gilmour	7:47	Cgy.
Apr. 19/89	Mtl.	DF	Mtl. 3	Bos. 2	Bobby Smith	12:24	Mtl.
Apr. 20/89	St.L.	DF	St.L. 5	Chi. 4	Tony Hrkac	33:49	Chi.
Apr. 21/89	Phi.	DF	Pit. 4	Phi. 3	Phil Bourque	12:08	Phi.
May 8/89	Chi.	CF	Cgy. 2	Chi. 1	Al MacInnis	15:05	Cgy.
May 9/89	Mtl.	CF	Phi. 2	Mtl. 1	Dave Poulin	5:02	Mtl.
May 19/89	Mtl.	F	Mtl. 4	Cgy. 3	Ryan Walter	38:08	Cgy.
Apr. 5/90	N.J.	DSF	Wsh. 5	N.J. 4	Dino Ciccarelli	5:34	Wsh.
Apr. 6/90	Edm.	DSF	Edm. 3	Wpg. 2	Mark Lamb	4:21	Edm.
Apr. 8/90	Tor.	DSF	St.L. 6	Tor. 5	Sergio Momesso	6:04	St.L.
Apr. 8/90	L.A.	DSF	L.A. 2	Cgy. 1	Tony Granato	8:37	L.A.
Apr. 9/90	Mtl.	DSF	Mtl. 2	Buf. 1	Brian Skrudland	12:35	Mtl.
Apr. 9/90	NYI	DSF	NYI 4	NYR 3	Brent Sutter	20:59	NYR
Apr. 10/90	Wpg.	DSF	Wpg. 4	Edm. 3	Dave Ellett	21:08	Edm.
Apr. 14/90	L.A.	DSF	L.A. 4	Cgy. 3	Mike Krushelnyski	23:14	L.A.
Apr. 15/90	Hfd.	DSF	Hfd. 3	Bos. 2	Kevin Dineen	12:30	Bos.
Apr. 21/90	Bos.	DF	Bos. 5	Mtl. 4	Garry Galley	3:42	Bos.
Apr. 24/90	L.A.	DF	Edm. 6	L.A. 5	Joe Murphy	4:42	Edm.
Apr. 25/90	Wsh.	DF	Wsh. 4	NYR 3	Rod Langway	0:34	Wsh.
Apr. 27/90	NYR	DF	Wsh. 2	NYR 1	John Druce	6:48	Wsh.
May 15/90	Bos.	F	Edm. 3	Bos. 2	Petr Klima	55:13	Edm.
Apr. 4/91	Chi.	DSF	Min. 4	Chi. 3	Brian Propp	4:14	Min.
Apr. 5/91	Pit.	DSF	Pit. 5	N.J. 4	Jaromir Jagr	8:52	Pit.
Apr. 6/91	L.A.	DSF	L.A. 3	Van. 2	Wayne Gretzky	11:08	L.A.
Apr. 8/91	Van.	DSF	Van. 2	L.A. 1	Cliff Ronning	3:12	L.A.
Apr. 11/91	NYR	DSF	Wsh. 5	NYR 4	Dino Ciccarelli	6:44	Wsh.
Apr. 11/91	Mtl.	DSF	Mtl. 4	Buf. 3	Russ Courtnall	5:56	Mtl.
Apr. 14/91	Edm.	DSF	Cgy. 2	Edm. 1	Theoren Fleury	4:40	Edm.
Apr. 16/91	Cgy.	DSF	Edm. 5	Cgy. 4	Esa Tikkanen	6:58	Edm.
Apr. 18/91	L.A.	DF	L.A. 4	Edm. 3	Luc Robitaille	2:13	Edm.
Apr. 19/91	Bos.	DF	Mtl. 4	Bos. 3	Stephane Richer	0:27	Bos.
Apr. 19/91	Pit.	DF	Pit. 7	Wsh. 6	Kevin Stevens	8:10	Pit.
Apr. 20/91	L.A.	DF	Edm. 4	L.A. 3	Petr Klima	24:48	Edm.
Apr. 22/91	Edm.	DF	Edm. 4	L.A. 3	Esa Tikkanen	20:48	Edm.
Apr. 27/91	Mtl.	DF	Mtl. 3	Bos. 2	Shayne Corson	17:47	Bos.
Apr. 28/91	Edm.	DF	Edm. 4	L.A. 3	Craig MacTavish	16:57	Edm.
May 3/91	Bos.	CF	Bos. 5	Pit. 4	Vladimir Ruzicka	8:14	Pit.
Apr. 21/92	Bos.	DSF	Bos. 3	Buf. 2	Adam Oates	11:14	Bos.
Apr. 22/92	Min.	DSF	Det. 5	Min. 4	Yves Racine	1:15	Det.
Apr. 22/92	St.L.	DSF	St.L. 5	Chi. 4	Brett Hull	23:33	Chi.
Apr. 25/92	Buf.	DSF	Bos. 5	Buf. 4	Ted Donato	2:08	Bos.
Apr. 28/92	Min.	DSF	Det. 1	Min. 0	Sergei Fedorov	16:13	Det.
Apr. 29/92	Hfd.	DSF	Hfd. 2	Mtl. 1	Yvon Corriveau	0:24	Mtl.
May 1/92	Mtl.	DSF	Mtl. 3	Hfd. 2	Russ Courtnall	25:26	Mtl.
May 3/92	Van.	DF	Edm. 4	Van. 3	Joe Murphy	8:36	Edm.
May 5/92	Mtl.	DF	Bos. 3	Mtl. 2	Peter Douris	3:12	Bos.
May 7/92	Pit.	DF	NYR 6	Pit. 5	Kris King	1:29	Pit.
May 9/92	Pit.	DF	Pit. 5	NYR 4	Ron Francis	2:47	Pit.
May 17/92	Pit.	CF	Pit. 4	Bos. 3	Jaromir Jagr	9:44	Pit.
May 20/92	Edm.	CF	Chi. 4	Edm. 3	Jeremy Roenick	2:45	Chi.
Apr. 18/93	Bos.	DSF	Buf. 5	Bos. 4	Bob Sweeney	11:03	Buf.
Apr. 18/93	Que.	DSF	Que. 3	Mtl. 2	Scott Young	16:49	Mtl.
Apr. 20/93	Wsh.	DSF	NYI 5	Wsh. 4	Brian Mullen	34:50	NYI
Apr. 22/93	Mtl.	DSF	Mtl. 2	Que. 1	Vincent Damphousse	10:30	Mtl.
Apr. 22/93	Buf.	DSF	Buf. 4	Bos. 3	Yuri Khmylev	1:05	Buf.
Apr. 22/93	NYI	DSF	NYI 4	Wsh. 3	Ray Ferraro	4:46	NYI
Apr. 24/93	Buf.	DSF	Buf. 6	Bos. 5	Brad May	4:48	Buf.
Apr. 24/93	NYI	DSF	NYI 4	Wsh. 3	Ray Ferraro	25:40	NYI
Apr. 25/93	St.L.	DSF	St.L. 4	Chi. 3	Craig Janney	10:43	St.L.
Apr. 26/93	Que.	DSF	Mtl. 5	Que. 4	Kirk Muller	8:17	Mtl.
Apr. 27/93	Det.	DSF	Tor. 5	Det. 4	Mike Foligno	2:05	Tor.
Apr. 27/93	Van.	DSF	Wpg. 4	Van. 3	Teemu Selanne	6:18	Van.
Apr. 29/93	Wpg.	DSF	Van. 4	Wpg. 3	Greg Adams	4:30	Van.
May 1/93	Det.	DSF	Tor. 4	Det. 3	Nikolai Borschevsky	2:35	Tor.
May 3/93	Tor.	DF	Tor. 2	St.L. 1	Doug Gilmour	23:16	Tor.
May 4/93	Mtl.	DF	Mtl. 4	Buf. 3	Guy Carbonneau	2:50	Mtl.
May 5/93	Tor.	DF	St.L. 2	Tor. 1	Jeff Brown	23:03	Tor.
May 6/93	Buf.	DF	Mtl. 4	Buf. 3	Gilbert Dionne	8:28	Mtl.
May 8/93	Buf.	DF	Mtl. 4	Buf. 3	Kirk Muller	11:37	Mtl.
May 11/93	Van.	DF	L.A. 4	Van. 3	Gary Shuchuk	26:31	L.A.
May 14/93	Pit.	DF	NYI 4	Pit. 3	Dave Volek	5:16	NYI
May 18/93	Mtl.	CF	Mtl. 4	NYI 3	Stephan Lebeau	26:21	Mtl.
May 20/93	NYI	CF	Mtl. 2	NYI 1	Guy Carbonneau	12:34	Mtl.
May 25/93	Tor.	CF	Tor. 3	L.A. 2	Glenn Anderson	19:20	L.A.
May 27/93	L.A.	CF	L.A. 5	Tor. 4	Wayne Gretzky	1:41	L.A.
Jun. 3/93	Mtl.	F	Mtl. 3	L.A. 2	Eric Desjardins	0:51	Mtl.
Jun. 5/93	L.A.	F	Mtl. 4	L.A. 3	John LeClair	0:34	Mtl.
Jun. 7/93	L.A.	F	Mtl. 3	L.A. 2	John LeClair	14:37	Mtl.
Apr. 20/94	Tor.	CQF	Tor. 1	Chi. 0	Todd Gill	2:15	Tor.
Apr. 22/94	St.L.	CQF	Dal. 5	St.L. 4	Paul Cavallini	8:34	Dal.

Overtime Games since 1918 — *continued*

Date	City	Series	Score		Scorer	Overtime	Series Winner
Apr. 24/94	Chi.	CQF	Chi. 4	Tor. 3	Jeremy Roenick	1:23	Tor.
Apr. 25/94	Bos.	CQF	Mtl. 2	Bos. 1	Kirk Muller	17:18	Bos.
Apr. 26/94	Cgy.	CQF	Van. 2	Cgy. 1	Geoff Courtnall	7:15	Van.
Apr. 27/94	Buf.	CQF	Buf. 1	N.J. 0	Dave Hannan	65:43	N.J.
Apr. 28/94	Van.	CQF	Van. 3	Cgy. 2	Trevor Linden	16:43	Van.
Apr. 30/94	Cgy.	CQF	Van. 4	Cgy. 3	Pavel Bure	22:20	Van.
May 3/94	N.J.	CSF	Bos. 6	N.J. 5	Don Sweeney	9:08	N.J.
May 7/94	Bos.	CSF	N.J. 5	Bos. 4	Stephane Richer	14:19	N.J.
May 8/94	Van.	CSF	Van. 2	Dal. 1	Sergio Momesso	11:01	Van.
May 12/94	Tor.	CSF	Tor. 3	S.J. 2	Mike Gartner	8:53	Tor.
May 15/94	NYR	CF	N.J. 4	NYR 3	Stephane Richer	35:23	NYR
May 16/94	Tor.	CF	Tor. 3	Van. 2	Peter Zezel	16:55	Van.
May 19/94	N.J.	CF	NYR 3	N.J. 2	Stephane Matteau	26:13	NYR
May 24/94	Van.	CF	Van. 4	Tor. 3	Greg Adams	20:14	Van.
May 27/94	NYR	CF	NYR 2	N.J. 1	Stephane Matteau	24:24	NYR
May 31/94	NYR	F	Van. 3	NYR 2	Greg Adams	19:26	NYR
May 7/95	Phi.	CQF	Phi. 4	Buf. 3	Karl Dykhuis	10:06	Phi.
May 9/95	Cgy.	CQF	S.J. 5	Cgy. 4	Ulf Dahlen	12:21	S.J.
May 12/95	NYR	CQF	NYR 3	Que. 2	Steve Larmer	8:09	NYR
May 12/95	N.J.	CQF	N.J. 1	Bos. 0	Randy McKay	8:51	N.J.
May 14/95	Pit.	CQF	Pit. 6	Wsh. 5	Luc Robitaille	4:30	Pit.
May 15/95	St.L.	CQF	Van. 6	St.L. 5	Cliff Ronning	1:48	Van.
May 17/95	Tor.	CQF	Tor. 5	Chi. 4	Randy Wood	10:00	Chi.
May 19/95	Cgy.	CQF	S.J. 5	Cgy. 4	Ray Whitney	21:54	S.J.
May 21/95	Phi.	CSF	Phi. 5	NYR 4	Eric Desjardins	7:03	Phi.
May 21/95	Chi.	CSF	Chi. 2	Van. 1	Joe Murphy	9:04	Chi.
May 22/95	Phi.	CSF	Phi. 4	NYR 3	Kevin Haller	0:25	Phi.
May 25/95	Van.	CSF	Chi. 3	Van. 2	Chris Chelios	6:22	Chi.
May 26/95	N.J.	CSF	N.J. 2	Pit. 1	Neal Broten	18:36	N.J.
May 27/95	Van.	CSF	Chi. 4	Van. 3	Chris Chelios	5:35	Chi.
Jun. 1/95	Det.	CF	Det. 2	Chi. 1	Nicklas Lidstrom	1:01	Det.
Jun. 6/95	Chi.	CF	Det. 4	Chi. 3	Vladimir Konstantinov	29:25	Det.
Jun. 7/95	N.J.	CF	Phi. 3	N.J. 2	Eric Lindros	4:19	N.J.
Jun. 11/95	Det.	CF	Det. 2	Chi. 1	Vyacheslav Kozlov	22:25	Det.
Apr. 16/96	NYR	CQF	Mtl. 3	NYR 2	Vincent Damphousse	5:04	NYR
Apr. 18/96	Tor.	CQF	Tor. 5	St.L. 4	Mats Sundin	4:02	St.L.
Apr. 18/96	Phi.	CQF	T.B. 2	Phi. 1	Brian Bellows	9:05	Phi.
Apr. 21/96	St.L.	CQF	St.L. 3	Tor. 2	Glenn Anderson	1:24	St.L.
Apr. 21/96	T.B.	CQF	T.B. 5	Phi. 4	Alexander Selivanov	2:04	Phi.
Apr. 23/96	Cgy.	CQF	Chi. 2	Cgy. 1	Joe Murphy	50:02	Chi.
Apr. 24/96	Wsh.	CQF	Pit. 3	Wsh. 2	Petr Nedved	79:15	Pit.
Apr. 25/96	Col.	CQF	Col. 5	Van. 4	Joe Sakic	0:51	Col.
Apr. 25/96	Tor.	CQF	Tor. 5	St.L. 4	Mike Gartner	7:31	St.L.
May 2/96	Col.	CSF	Chi. 3	Col. 2	Jeremy Roenick	6:29	Col.
May 6/96	Chi.	CSF	Chi. 4	Col. 3	Sergei Krivokrasov	0:46	Col.
May 8/96	St.L.	CSF	St.L. 5	Det. 4	Igor Kravchuk	3:23	Det.
May 8/96	Chi.	CSF	Col. 3	Chi. 2	Joe Sakic	44:33	Col.
May 9/96	Fla.	CSF	Fla. 4	Phi. 3	Dave Lowry	4:06	Fla.
May 12/96	Phi.	CSF	Fla. 2	Phi. 1	Mike Hough	28:05	Fla.
May 13/96	Chi.	CSF	Col. 4	Chi. 3	Sandis Ozolinsh	25:18	Col.
May 16/96	Det.	CSF	Det. 1	St.L. 0	Steve Yzerman	21:15	Det.
May 19/96	Det.	CF	Col. 3	Det. 2	Mike Keane	17:31	Col.
Jun. 10/96	Fla.	F	Col. 1	Fla. 0	Uwe Krupp	44:31	Col.
Apr. 20/97	Chi.	CQF	Chi. 4	Col. 3	Sergei Krivokrasov	31:03	Col.
Apr. 20/97	Edm.	CQF	Edm. 4	Dal. 3	Kelly Buchberger	9:15	Edm.
Apr. 22/97	NYR	CQF	NYR 4	Fla. 3	Esa Tikkanen	16:29	NYR
Apr. 23/97	Ott.	CQF	Ott. 1	Buf. 0	Daniel Alfredsson	2:34	Buf.
Apr. 24/97	Mtl.	CQF	Mtl. 4	N.J. 3	Patrice Brisebois	47:37	N.J.
Apr. 25/97	Fla.	CQF	NYR 3	Fla. 2	Esa Tikkanen	12:02	NYR
Apr. 25/97	Dal.	CQF	Edm. 1	Dal. 0	Ryan Smyth	20:22	Edm.
Apr. 27/97	Phx.	CQF	Ana. 3	Phx. 2	Paul Kariya	7:29	Ana.
Apr. 29/97	Buf.	CQF	Buf. 3	Ott. 2	Derek Plante	5:24	Buf.
Apr. 29/97	Dal.	CQF	Edm. 4	Dal. 3	Todd Marchant	12:26	Edm.
May 2/97	Det.	CSF	Det. 2	Ana. 1	Martin Lapointe	0:59	Det.
May 4/97	Det.	CSF	Det. 3	Ana. 2	Vyacheslav Kozlov	41:31	Det.
May 8/97	Ana.	CSF	Det. 3	Ana. 2	Brendan Shanahan	37:03	Det.
May 9/97	Phi.	CSF	Buf. 5	Phi. 4	Ed Ronan	6:24	Phi.
May 9/97	Edm.	CSF	Col. 3	Edm. 2	Claude Lemieux	8:35	Col.
May 11/97	N.J.	CSF	NYR 2	N.J. 1	Adam Graves	14:08	NYR
Apr. 22/98	N.J.	CQF	Ott. 2	N.J. 1	Bruce Gardiner	5:58	Ott.
Apr. 23/98	Pit.	CQF	Mtl. 3	Pit. 2	Benoit Brunet	18:43	Mtl.
Apr. 24/98	Wsh.	CQF	Bos. 4	Wsh. 3	Darren Van Impe	20:54	Wsh.
Apr. 26/98	Ott.	CQF	Ott. 2	N.J. 1	Alexei Yashin	2:47	Ott.
Apr. 26/98	Bos.	CQF	Wsh. 3	Bos. 2	Joe Juneau	26:31	Wsh.
Apr. 26/98	Edm.	CQF	Col. 5	Edm. 4	Joe Sakic	15:25	Edm.
Apr. 28/98	S.J.	CQF	S.J. 1	Dal. 0	Andrei Zyuzin	6:31	Dal.
May 1/98	Phi.	CQF	Buf. 3	Phi. 2	Michal Grosek	5:40	Buf.
May 2/98	S.J.	CQF	Dal. 3	S.J. 2	Mike Keane	3:43	Dal.
May 3/98	Bos.	CQF	Wsh. 3	Bos. 2	Brian Bellows	15:24	Wsh.
May 3/98	Buf.	CSF	Buf. 3	Mtl. 2	Geoff Sanderson	2:37	Buf.
May 11/98	Edm.	CSF	Dal. 1	Edm. 0	Benoit Hogue	13:07	Dal.
May 12/98	Mtl.	CSF	Buf. 5	Mtl. 4	Michael Peca	21:24	Buf.
May 12/98	St.L.	CSF	Det. 3	St.L. 2	Brendan Shanahan	31:12	Det.
May 25/98	Wsh.	CF	Wsh. 3	Buf. 2	Todd Krygier	3:01	Wsh.
May 28/98	Buf.	CF	Wsh. 4	Buf. 3	Peter Bondra	9:37	Wsh.
Jun. 3/98	Dal.	CF	Dal. 3	Det. 2	Jamie Langenbrunner	0:46	Det.
Jun. 4/98	Buf.	CF	Wsh. 3	Buf. 2	Joe Juneau	6:24	Wsh.
Jun. 11/98	Det.	F	Det. 5	Wsh. 4	Kris Draper	15:24	Det.
Apr. 23/99	Ott.	CQF	Buf. 3	Ott. 2	Miroslav Satan	30:35	Buf.
Apr. 24/99	Car.	CQF	Car. 3	Bos. 2	Ray Sheppard	17:05	Bos.
Apr. 24/99	Phx.	CQF	Phx. 4	St.L. 3	Shane Doan	8:58	St.L.
Apr. 26/99	S.J.	CQF	Col. 2	S.J. 1	Milan Hejduk	7:53	Col.
Apr. 27/99	Edm.	CQF	Dal. 3	Edm. 2	Joe Nieuwendyk	57:34	Dal.
Apr. 30/99	Tor.	CQF	Tor. 2	Phi. 1	Yanic Perreault	11:51	Tor.
Apr. 30/99	Car.	CQF	Bos. 4	Car. 3	Anson Carter	34:45	Bos.
Apr. 30/99	Phx.	CQF	St.L. 2	Phx. 1	Scott Young	5:43	St.L.
May 2/99	Pit.	CQF	Pit. 3	N.J. 2	Jaromir Jagr	8:59	Pit.
May 3/99	S.J.	CQF	Col. 3	S.J. 2	Milan Hejduk	13:12	Col.
May 4/99	Phx.	CQF	St.L. 1	Phx. 0	Pierre Turgeon	17:59	St.L.
May 7/99	Col.	CSF	Det. 3	Col. 2	Kirk Maltby	4:18	Col.
May 8/99	Dal.	CSF	Dal. 5	St.L. 4	Joe Nieuwendyk	8:22	Dal.
May 10/99	St.L.	CSF	St.L. 3	Dal. 2	Pavol Demitra	2:43	Dal.
May 12/99	St.L.	CSF	St.L. 3	Dal. 2	Pierre Turgeon	5:52	Dal.

Date	City	Series	Score		Scorer	Overtime	Series Winner
May 13/99	Pit.	CSF	Tor. 3	Pit. 2	Sergei Berezin	2:18	Tor.
May 17/99	Pit.	CSF	Tor. 4	Pit. 3	Garry Valk	1:57	Tor.
May 17/99	St.L.	CSF	Dal. 2	St.L. 1	Mike Modano	2:21	Dal.
May 28/99	Col.	CF	Col. 3	Dal. 2	Chris Drury	19:29	Dal.
Jun. 8/99	Dal.	F	Buf. 3	Dal. 2	Jason Woolley	15:30	Dal.
Jun. 19/99	Buf.	F	Dal. 2	Buf. 1	Brett Hull	54:51	Dal.
Apr. 15/00	Pit.	CQF	Pit. 2	Wsh. 1	Jaromir Jagr	5:49	Pit.
Apr. 18/00	Buf.	CQF	Buf. 3	Phi. 2	Stu Barnes	4:42	Phi.
Apr. 22/00	Tor.	CQF	Tor. 2	Ott. 1	Steve Thomas	14:47	Tor.
May 2/00	Pit.	CSF	Phi. 4	Pit. 3	Andy Delmore	11:01	Phi.
May 3/00	Det.	CSF	Col. 3	Det. 2	Chris Drury	10:21	Col.
May 4/00	Pit.	CSF	Phi. 2	Pit. 1	Keith Primeau	92:01	Phi.
May 23/00	Dal.	CF	Dal. 3	Col. 2	Joe Nieuwendyk	12:10	Dal.
Jun. 8/00	N.J.	F	Dal. 1	N.J. 0	Mike Modano	46:21	N.J.
Jun. 10/00	Dal.	F	N.J. 2	Dal. 1	Jason Arnott	28:20	N.J.
Apr. 11/01	Dal.	CQF	Dal. 2	Edm. 1	Jamie Langenbrunner	2:08	Dal.
Apr. 13/01	Ott.	CQF	Tor. 1	Ott. 0	Mats Sundin	10:49	Tor.
Apr. 14/01	Phi.	CQF	Buf. 4	Phi. 3	Jay McKee	18:02	Buf.
Apr. 15/01	Edm.	CQF	Dal. 3	Edm. 2	Benoit Hogue	19:48	Dal.
Apr. 16/01	Tor.	CQF	Tor. 3	Ott. 2	Cory Cross	2:16	Tor.
Apr. 16/01	Van.	CQF	Col. 4	Van. 3	Peter Forsberg	2:50	Col.
Apr. 17/01	Buf.	CQF	Buf. 4	Phi. 3	Curtis Brown	6:13	Buf.
Apr. 17/01	Edm.	CQF	Edm. 2	Dal. 1	Mike Comrie	17:19	Dal.
Apr. 18/01	Car.	CQF	Car. 3	N.J. 2	Rod Brind'Amour	:46	N.J.
Apr. 18/01	Pit.	CQF	Wsh. 4	Pit. 3	Jeff Halpern	4:01	Pit.
Apr. 18/01	L.A.	CQF	L.A. 4	Det. 3	Eric Belanger	2:36	L.A.
Apr. 19/01	Dal.	CQF	Dal. 4	Edm. 3	Kirk Muller	8:01	Dal.
Apr. 19/01	St.L.	CQF	St.L. 3	S.J. 2	Bryce Salvador	9:54	St.L.
Apr. 23/01	Pit.	CQF	Pit. 4	Wsh. 3	Martin Straka	13:04	Pit.
Apr. 23/01	L.A.	CQF	L.A. 3	Det. 2	Adam Deadmarsh	4:48	L.A.
Apr. 26/01	Col.	CSF	L.A. 4	Col. 3	Jaroslav Modry	14:23	Col.
Apr. 28/01	N.J.	CSF	N.J. 6	Tor. 5	Randy McKay	5:31	N.J.
May 1/01	Tor.	CSF	N.J. 3	Tor. 2	Brian Rafalski	7:00	N.J.
May 1/01	St.L.	CSF	St.L. 3	Dal. 2	Cory Stillman	29:26	St.L.
May 5/01	Buf.	CSF	Buf. 3	Pit. 2	Stu Barnes	8:34	Pit.
May 6/01	L.A.	CSF	L.A. 1	Col. 0	Glen Murray	22:41	Col.
May 8/01	Pit.	CSF	Pit. 3	Buf. 2	Martin Straka	11:29	Pit.
May 10/01	Buf.	CSF	Pit. 3	Buf. 2	Darius Kasparaitis	13:01	Pit.
May 16/01	St.L.	CF	St.L. 4	Col. 3	Scott Young	30:27	Col.
May 18/01	St.L.	CF	Col. 4	St.L. 3	Stephane Yelle	4:23	Col.
May 21/01	Col.	CF	Col. 2	St.L. 1	Joe Sakic	:24	Col.
Apr. 17/02	Phi.	CQF	Phi. 1	Ott. 0	Ruslan Fedotenko	7:47	Ott.
Apr. 17/02	Det.	CQF	Van. 4	Det. 3	Henrik Sedin	13:59	Det.
Apr. 19/02	Car.	CQF	Car. 2	N.J. 1	Bates Battaglia	15:26	Car.
Apr. 24/02	Car.	CQF	Car. 3	N.J. 2	Josef Vasicek	8:16	Car.
Apr. 25/02	Col.	CQF	L.A. 1	Col. 0	Craig Johnson	2:19	Col.
Apr. 26/02	Phi.	CQF	Ott. 2	Phi. 1	Martin Havlat	7:33	Ott.
May 4/02	Tor.	CSF	Tor. 3	Ott. 2	Gary Roberts	44:30	Tor.
May 7/02	Mtl.	CSF	Mtl. 2	Car. 1	Donald Audette	2:26	Car.
May 9/02	Mtl.	CSF	Car. 4	Mtl. 3	Niclas Wallin	3:14	Car.
May 13/02	S.J.	CSF	Col. 2	S.J. 1	Peter Forsberg	2:47	Col.
May 19/02	Car.	CF	Car. 2	Tor. 1	Niclas Wallin	13:42	Car.
May 20/02	Det.	CF	Col. 4	Det. 3	Chris Drury	2:17	Det.
May 21/02	Tor.	CF	Car. 2	Tor. 1	Jeff O'Neill	6:01	Car.
May 22/02	Col.	CF	Det. 2	Col. 1	Fredrik Olausson	12:44	Det.
May 27/02	Det.	CF	Col. 2	Det. 1	Peter Forsberg	6:24	Det.
May 28/02	Tor.	CF	Car. 2	Tor. 1	Martin Gelinas	8:05	Car.
Jun. 4/02	Det.	F	Car. 3	Det. 2	Ron Francis	:58	Det.
Jun. 8/02	Car.	F	Det. 3	Car. 2	Igor Larionov	54:47	Det.
Apr. 10/03	Det.	CQF	Ana. 2	Det. 1	Paul Kariya	43:18	Ana.
Apr. 14/03	NYI	CQF	Ott. 3	NYI 2	Todd White	22:25	Ott.
Apr. 14/03	Tor.	CQF	Tor. 4	Phi. 3	Tomas Kaberle	27:20	Phi.
Apr. 15/03	Wsh.	CQF	T.B. 4	Wsh. 3	Vincent Lecavalier	2:29	T.B.
Apr. 16/03	Tor.	CQF	Phi. 3	Tor. 2	Mark Recchi	53:54	Phi.
Apr. 16/03	Ana.	CQF	Ana. 3	Det. 2	Steve Rucchin	6:53	Ana.
Apr. 20/03	Wsh.	CQF	T.B. 2	Wsh. 1	Martin St. Louis	44:03	T.B.
Apr. 21/03	Tor.	CQF	Tor. 2	Phi. 1	Travis Green	30:51	Phi.
Apr. 21/03	Min.	CQF	Min. 3	Col. 2	Richard Park	4:22	Min.
Apr. 22/03	Col.	CQF	Min. 3	Col. 2	Andrew Brunette	3:25	Min.
Apr. 24/03	Dal.	CSF	Ana. 4	Dal. 3	Petr Sykora	80:48	Ana.
Apr. 25/03	Van.	CSF	Van. 4	Min. 3	Trent Klatt	3:42	Min.
Apr. 26/03	N.J.	CSF	N.J. 3	T.B. 2	Jamie Langenbrunner	2:09	N.J.
Apr. 26/03	Dal.	CSF	Ana. 3	Dal. 2	Mike Leclerc	1:44	Ana.
Apr. 29/03	Phi.	CSF	Ott. 3	Phi. 2	Wade Redden	6:43	Ott.
May 2/03	Min.	CSF	Van. 3	Min. 2	Brent Sopel	15:52	Min.
May 2/03	N.J.	CSF	N.J. 2	T.B. 1	Grant Marshall	51:12	N.J.
May 10/03	Min.	CF	Ana. 1	Min. 0	Petr Sykora	28:06	Ana.
May 10/03	Ott.	CF	Ott. 3	N.J. 2	Shaun Van Allen	3:08	N.J.
May 21/03	N.J.	CF	Ott. 2	N.J. 1	Chris Phillips	15:51	N.J.
May 31/03	Ana.	F	Ana. 3	N.J. 2	Ruslan Salei	6:59	N.J.
Jun. 2/03	Ana.	F	Ana. 1	N.J. 0	Steve Thomas	0:39	N.J.
Apr. 8/04	S.J.	CQF	S.J. 1	St.L. 0	Niko Dimitrakos	9:16	S.J.
Apr. 9/04	Bos.	CQF	Bos. 2	Mtl. 1	Patrice Bergeron	1:26	Mtl.
Apr. 12/04	Dal.	CQF	Dal. 4	Col. 3	Steve Ott	2:11	Col.
Apr. 13/04	Mtl.	CQF	Bos. 4	Mtl. 3	Glen Murray	29:27	Mtl.
Apr. 14/04	Dal.	CQF	Col. 3	Dal. 2	Marek Svatos	25:21	Col.
Apr. 16/04	T.B.	CQF	T.B. 3	NYI 2	Martin St. Louis	4:07	T.B.
Apr. 17/04	Cgy.	CQF	Van. 5	Cgy. 4	Brendan Morrison	42:28	Cgy.
Apr. 18/04	Ott.	CQF	Ott. 2	Tor. 1	Mike Fisher	21:47	Tor.
Apr. 19/04	Van.	CQF	Cgy. 3	Van. 2	Martin Gelinas	1:25	Cgy.
Apr. 22/04	Det.	CSF	Cgy. 2	Det. 1	Marcus Nilson	2:39	Cgy.
Apr. 27/04	Mtl.	CSF	T.B. 4	Mtl 3	Brad Richards	1:05	T.B.
Apr. 28/04	Col	CSF	Col. 1	S.J. 0	Joe Sakic	5:15	S.J.
May 1/04	S.J.	CSF	Col. 2	S.J. 1	Joe Sakic	1:54	S.J.
May 3/04	Cgy	CSF	Cgy. 1	Det. 0	Martin Gelinas	19:13	Cgy.
May 4/04	Phi.	CSF	Phi. 3	Tor. 2	Jeremy Roenick	7:39	Phi.
May 9/04	S.J.	CF	Cgy. 4	S.J. 3	Steve Montador	18:43	Cgy.
May 20/04	Phi.	CF	Phi. 5	T.B. 4	Simon Gagne	18:18	T.B.
Jun. 3/04	T.B.	F	Cgy. 3	T.B. 2	Oleg Saprykin	14:40	T.B.
Jun. 5/04	Cgy.	F	T.B. 3	Cgy. 2	Martin St. Louis	20:33	T.B.
Apr. 21/06	Det.	CQF	Det. 3	Edm. 2	Kirk Maltby	22:39	Edm.
Apr. 21/06	Cgy.	CQF	Cgy. 2	Ana. 1	Darren McCarty	9:45	Ana.
Apr. 22/06	Buf.	CQF	Buf. 3	Phi. 2	Daniel Briere	27:31	Buf.

Overtime Games since 1918 — *continued*

Date	City	Series	Score		Scorer	Overtime	Series Winner
Apr. 24/06	Car.	CQF	Mtl. 6	Car. 5	Michael Ryder	22:32	Car.
Apr. 24/06	Dal.	CQF	Col. 5	Dal. 4	Joe Sakic	4:36	Col.
Apr. 25/06	Edm.	CQF	Edm. 4	Det. 3	Jarret Stoll	28:44	Edm.
Apr. 26/06	Mtl.	CQF	Car. 2	Mtl. 1	Eric Staal	3:38	Car.
Apr. 26/06	Col.	CQF	Col. 4	Dal. 3	Alex Tanguay	1:09	Col.
Apr. 27/06	Ana.	CQF	Ana. 3	Cgy. 2	Sean O'Donnell	1:36	Ana.
Apr. 30/06	Dal.	CQF	Col. 3	Dal. 2	Andrew Brunette	13:55	Col.
May 2/06	Mtl.	CQF	Car. 2	Mtl. 1	Cory Stillman	1:19	Car.
May 5/06	Ott.	CSF	Buf. 7	Ott. 6	Chris Drury	0:18	Buf.
May 8/06	Car.	CSF	Car. 3	N.J. 2	Niclas Wallin	3:09	Car.
May 9/06	Col.	CSF	Ana. 4	Col. 3	Joffrey Lupul	16:30	Ana.
May 10/06	Buf.	CSF	Buf. 3	Ott. 2	J.P. Dumont	5:05	Buf.
May 10/06	Edm.	CSF	Edm. 3	S.J. 2	Shawn Horcoff	42:24	Edm.
May 13/06	Ott.	CSF	Buf. 3	Ott. 2	Jason Pominville	2:26	Buf.
May 28/06	Car.	CF	Car. 4	Buf. 3	Cory Stillman	8:46	Car.
May 30/06	Buf.	CF	Buf. 2	Car. 1	Daniel Briere	4:22	Car.
June 14/06	Car.	F	Edm. 4	Car. 3	Fernando Pisani	3:31	Car.
Apr. 11/07	Nsh.	CQF	S.J. 5	Nsh. 4	Patrick Rissmiller	28:14	S.J.
Apr. 11/07	Van.	CQF	Van. 5	Dal. 4	Henrik Sedin	78:06	Van.
Apr. 15/07	Dal.	CQF	Van. 2	Dal. 1	Taylor Pyatt	7:47	Van.
Apr. 18/07	T.B.	CQF	N.J. 4	T.B. 3	Scott Gomez	12:54	N.J.
Apr. 19/07	Van.	CQF	Dal. 1	Van. 0	Brenden Morrow	6:22	Van.
Apr. 22/07	Cgy.	CQF	Det. 2	Cgy. 1	Johan Franzen	24:23	Det.
Apr. 27/07	Ana.	CSF	Van. 2	Ana. 1	Jeff Cowan	27:49	Ana.
Apr. 28/07	N.J.	CSF	N.J. 3	Ott. 2	Jamie Langenbrunner	21:55	Ott.
Apr. 29/07	NYR	CSF	NYR 2	Buf. 1	Michal Rozsival	36:43	Buf.
May 1/07	Van.	CSF	Ana. 3	Van. 2	Travis Moen	2:07	Ana.
May 2/07	S.J.	CSF	Det. 3	S.J. 2	Mathieu Schneider	16:04	Det.
May 3/07	Ana.	CSF	Ana. 2	Van. 1	Scott Niedermayer	24:30	Ana.
May 4/07	Buf.	CSF	Buf. 2	NYR 1	Maxim Afinogenov	4:39	Buf.
May 12/07	Buf.	CF	Ott. 4	Buf. 3	Joe Corvo	24:58	Ott.
May 13/07	Det.	CF	Ana. 4	Det. 3	Scott Niedermayer	14:17	Ana.
May 19/07	Buf.	CF	Ott. 3	Buf. 2	Daniel Alfredsson	9:32	Ott.
May 20/07	Det.	CF	Ana. 2	Det. 1	Teemu Selanne	11:57	Ana.
Apr. 9/08	Min.	CQF	Col. 3	Min. 2	Joe Sakic	11:11	Col.
Apr. 11/08	Min.	CQF	Min. 3	Col. 2	Keith Carney	1:14	Col.
Apr. 12/08	Mtl.	CQF	Mtl. 3	Bos. 2	Alex Kovalev	2:30	Mtl.
Apr. 13/08	Mtl.	CQF	Bos. 2	Mtl.1	Marc Savard	9:25	Mtl.
Apr. 13/08	NYR	CQF	N.J. 4	NYR 3	John Madden	6:01	NYR
Apr. 14/08	Col.	CQF	Min. 3	Col. 2	Pierre-Marc Bouchard	11:58	Col.
Apr. 17/08	Phi.	CQF	Phi. 4	Wsh. 3	Mike Knuble	26:40	Phi.
Apr. 18/08	Det.	CQF	Det. 2	Nsh. 1	Johan Franzen	1:48	Det.
Apr. 22/08	Wsh.	CQF	Phi. 3	Wsh. 2	Joffrey Lupul	6:06	Phi.
Apr. 24/08	Mtl.	CSF	Mtl. 4	Phi. 3	Tom Kostopoulos	0:48	Phi.
Apr. 25/08	S.J.	CSF	Dal. 3	S.J. 2	Brenden Morrow	4:39	Dal.
Apr. 29/08	Dal.	CSF	Dal. 2	S.J. 1	Mattias Norstrom	4:37	Dal.
May 2/08	S.J.	CSF	S.J. 3	Dal. 2	Joe Pavelski	1:05	Dal.
May 4/08	Pit.	CSF	Pit. 3	NYR 2	Marian Hossa	7:10	Pit.
May 4/08	Dal.	CSF	Dal. 2	S.J. 1	Brenden Morrow	69:03	Dal.
June 2/08	Det.	F	Pit. 3	Det. 2	Petr Sykora	49:57	Det.
Apr. 16/09	Chi.	CQF	Chi. 3	Cgy. 2	Martin Havlat	0:12	Chi.
Apr. 17/09	Pit.	CQF	Pit. 3	Phi. 2	Bill Guerin	18:29	Pit.
Apr. 17/09	N.J.	CQF	Car. 2	N.J. 1	Tim Gleason	2:40	Car.
Apr. 19/09	Car.	CQF	N.J. 3	Car. 2	Travis Zajac	4:58	Car.
Apr. 21/09	St.L.	CQF	Van. 3	St.L. 2	Alex Burrows	19:41	Van.
Apr. 25/09	S.J.	CQF	S.J. 3	Ana. 2	Patrick Marleau	6:02	Ana.
May 3/09	Det.	CSF	Ana. 4	Det. 3	Todd Marchant	41:15	Det.
May 6/09	Pit.	CSF	Pit. 3	Wsh. 2	Kris Letang	11:23	Pit.
May 6/09	Car.	CSF	Car. 3	Bos. 2	Jussi Jokinen	2:48	Car.
May 7/09	Chi.	CSF	Chi. 2	Van. 1	Andrew Ladd	2:52	Chi.
May 9/09	Wsh.	CSF	Pit. 4	Wsh. 3	Evgeni Malkin	3:28	Pit.
May 11/09	Pit.	CSF	Wsh. 5	Pit. 4	David Steckel	6:22	Pit.
May 14/09	Bos.	CSF	Car. 3	Bos. 2	Scott Walker	18:46	Car.
May 19/09	Det.	CF	Det. 3	Chi. 2	Mikael Samuelsson	5:14	Det.
May 22/09	Chi.	CF	Chi. 4	Det. 3	Patrick Sharp	1:52	Det.
May 27/09	Det.	CF	Det. 2	Chi. 1	Darren Helm	3:58	Det.
Apr. 15/10	Wsh.	CQF	Mtl. 3	Wsh. 2	Tomas Plekanec	13:19	Mtl.
Apr. 15/10	Van.	CQF	Van. 3	L.A. 2	Mikael Samuelsson	8:52	Van.
Apr. 16/10	S.J.	CQF	S.J. 6	Col. 5	Devin Setoguchi	5:22	S.J.
Apr. 17/10	Wsh.	CQF	Wsh. 6	Mtl. 5	Nicklas Backstrom	0:31	Mtl.
Apr. 17/10	Van.	CQF	L.A. 3	Van. 2	Anze Kopitar	7:28	Van.
Apr. 18/10	Phi.	CQF	Phi. 3	N.J. 2	Daniel Carcillo	3:35	Phi.
Apr. 18/10	Col.	CQF	Col. 1	S.J. 0	Ryan O'Reilly	0:51	S.J.
Apr. 20/10	Col.	CQF	S.J. 2	Col. 1	Joe Pavelski	10:24	S.J.
Apr. 21/10	Bos.	CQF	Bos. 3	Buf. 2	Miroslav Satan	27:41	Bos.
Apr. 22/10	Pit.	CQF	Ott. 4	Pit. 3	Matt Carkner	47:06	Pit.
Apr. 24/10	Chi.	CQF	Chi. 5	Nsh. 4	Marian Hossa	4:07	Chi.
Apr. 24/10	Ott.	CQF	Pit. 4	Ott. 3	Pascal Dupuis	9:56	Pit.
May 1/10	Bos.	CSF	Bos. 5	Phi. 4	Marc Savard	13:52	Phi.
May 4/10	Det.	CSF	S.J. 4	Det. 3	Patrick Marleau	7:07	S.J.
May 7/10	Phi.	CSF	Phi. 5	Bos. 4	Simon Gagne	14:40	Phi.
May 21/10	Chi.	CF	Chi. 3	S.J. 2	Dustin Byfuglien	12:24	Chi.
June 2/10	Phi.	F	Phi. 4	Chi. 3	Claude Giroux	5:59	Chi.
June 9/10	Phi.	F	Chi. 4	Phi. 3	Patrick Kane	4:06	Chi.
Apr. 13/11	Wsh.	CQF	Wsh. 2	NYR 1	Alexander Semin	18:24	Wsh.
Apr. 14/11	S.J.	CQF	S.J. 3	L.A. 2	Joe Pavelski	14:44	S.J.
Apr. 20/11	L.A.	CQF	S.J. 6	L.A. 5	Devin Setoguchi	3:09	S.J.
Apr. 20/11	NYR	CQF	Wsh. 4	NYR 3	Jason Chimera	32:36	Wsh.
Apr. 20/11	T.B.	CQF	Pit. 3	T.B. 2	James Neal	23:38	T.B.
Apr. 21/11	Mtl.	CQF	Bos. 5	Mtl. 4	Michael Ryder	1:59	Bos.
Apr. 22/11	Phi.	CQF	Buf. 4	Phi. 3	Tyler Ennis	5:31	Phi.
Apr. 22/11	Ana.	CQF	Nsh. 4	Ana. 3	Jerred Smithson	1:57	Nsh.
Apr. 23/11	Bos.	CQF	Bos. 2	Mtl. 1	Nathan Horton	29:03	Bos.
Apr. 24/11	Buf.	CQF	Phi. 5	Buf. 4	Ville Leino	4:43	Phi.
Apr. 24/11	Chi.	CQF	Chi. 4	Van. 3	Ben Smith	15:30	Van.
Apr. 25/11	L.A.	CQF	S.J. 4	L.A. 3	Joe Thornton	2:22	S.J.
Apr. 26/11	Van.	CQF	Van. 2	Chi. 3	Alexandre Burrows	5:22	Van.
Apr. 27/11	Bos.	CQF	Bos. 4	Mtl. 3	Nathan Horton	5:43	Bos.
Apr. 29/11	S.J.	CSF	S.J. 2	Det. 1	Benn Ferriero	7:03	S.J.
Apr. 30/11	Van.	CSF	Nsh. 2	Van. 1	Matt Halischuk	34:51	Van.
May 1/11	Wsh.	CSF	T.B. 3	Wsh. 2	Vincent Lecavalier	6:19	T.B.
May 2/11	Phi.	CSF	Bos. 3	Phi. 2	David Krejci	14:00	Bos.
May 3/11	Nsh.	CSF	Van. 3	Nsh. 2	Ryan Kesler	10:49	Van.
May 4/11	Det.	CSF	S.J. 4	Det. 3	Devin Setoguchi	9:21	S.J.
May 24/11	Van.	CF	Van. 3	S.J. 2	Kevin Bieksa	30:18	Van.
June 4/11	Van.	F	Van. 3	Bos. 2	Alexandre Burrows	0:11	Bos.
Apr. 11/12	Pit.	CQF	Phi. 4	Pit. 3	Jakub Voracek	2:23	Phi.
Apr. 12/12	Bos.	CQF	Bos. 1	Wsh. 0	Chris Kelly	1:18	Wsh.
Apr. 12/12	St. L.	CQF	S.J. 3	St. L. 2	Martin Havlat	23:34	St. L.
Apr. 12/12	Phx.	CQF	Phx. 3	Chi. 2	Martin Hanzal	9:29	Phx.
Apr. 14/12	Bos.	CQF	Wsh. 2	Bos. 1	Nicklas Backstrom	2:56	Wsh.
Apr. 14/12	NYR	CQF	Ott. 3	NYR 2	Chris Neil	1:17	NYR
Apr. 14/12	Phx.	CQF	Chi. 4	Phx. 3	Bryan Bickell	10:36	Phx.
Apr. 17/12	Chi.	CQF	Phx. 3	Chi. 2	Mikkel Boedker	13:15	Phx.
Apr. 18/12	Ott.	CQF	Ott. 3	NYR 2	Kyle Turris	2:42	NYR
Apr. 19/12	Chi.	CQF	Phx. 3	Chi. 2	Mikkel Boedker	2:15	Phx.
Apr. 21/12	Phx.	CQF	Chi. 2	Phx. 1	Jonathan Toews	2:44	Phx.
Apr. 22/12	Wsh.	CQF	Bos. 4	Wsh. 3	Tyler Seguin	3:17	Wsh.
Apr. 22/12	Van.	CQF	L.A. 2	Van. 1	Jarret Stoll	4:27	L.A.
Apr. 24/12	N.J.	CQF	N.J. 3	Fla. 2	Travis Zajac	5:39	N.J.
Apr. 25/12	Bos.	CQF	Wsh. 2	Bos. 1	Joel Ward	2:57	Wsh.
Apr. 26/12	Fla.	CQF	N.J. 3	Fla. 2	Adam Henrique	23:47	N.J.
Apr. 27/12	Phx.	CSF	Phx. 4	Nsh. 2	Ray Whitney	14:04	Phx.
Apr. 29/12	Phi.	CSF	Phi. 4	N.J. 3	Daniel Briere	4:36	N.J.
May 2/12	Wsh.	CSF	NYR 2	Wsh. 1	Marian Gaborik	54:41	NYR
May 3/12	N.J.	CSF	N.J. 4	Phi. 3	Alexei Ponikarovsky	17:21	N.J.
May 7/12	NYR	CSF	NYR 3	Wsh. 2	Marc Staal	1:35	NYR
May 22/12	Phx.	CF	L.A. 4	Phx. 3	Dustin Penner	17:42	L.A.
May 25/12	N.J.	CF	N.J. 2	NYR 1	Adam Henrique	1:03	N.J.
May 30/12	N.J.	F	L.A. 2	N.J. 1	Anze Kopitar	8:13	L.A.
June 2/12	N.J.	F	L.A. 2	N.J. 1	Jeff Carter	13:42	L.A.
Apr. 30/13	Chi.	CQF	Chi. 2	Min. 1	Bryan Bickell	16:35	Chi.
Apr. 30/13	St.L.	CQF	St.L. 2	L.A. 1	Alex Steen	13:26	L.A.
May 2/13	Ana.	CQF	Det. 5	Ana. 4	Gustav Nyquist	1:21	Det.
May 3/13	Van.	CQF	S.J. 3	Van. 2	RaffiTorres	5:31	S.J.
May 4/13	Wsh.	CQF	Wsh. 1	NYR 0	Mike Green	8:00	NYR
May 5/13	NYI	CQF	Pit. 5	NYI 4	Chris Kunitz	8:44	Pit.
May 5/13	Min.	CQF	Min. 3	Chi.2	Jason Zucker	2:15	Chi.
May 6/13	Det.	CQF	Det. 3	Ana. 2	Damien Brunner	15:10	Det.
May 7/13	Ott.	CQF	Ott. 3	Mtl. 2	Kyle Turris	2:32	Ott.
May 7/13	S.J.	CQF	S.J. 4	Van. 3	Patrick Marleau	13:18	S.J.
May 8/13	Tor.	CQF	Bos. 4	Tor. 3	David Krejci	13:06	Bos.
May 8/13	Ana.	CQF	Ana. 3	Det. 2	Nick Bonino	1:54	Det.
May 8/13	St.L.	CQF	L.A. 3	St.L. 2	Slava Voynov	8:00	L.A.
May 10/13	Wsh.	CQF	Wsh. 2	NYR 1	Mike Ribeiro	9:24	NYR
May 10/13	Det.	CQF	Det. 4	Ana. 3	Henrik Zetterberg	1:04	Det.
May 11/13	NYI	CQF	Pit. 4	NYI 3	Brooks Orpik	7:49	Pit.
May 13/13	Bos.	CQF	Bos. 5	Tor. 4	Patrice Bergeron	6:05	Bos.
May 16/13	Bos.	CSF	Bos. 3	NYR 2	Brad Marchand	15:40	Bos.
May 18/13	S.J.	CSF	S.J. 2	L.A. 1	Logan Couture	1:29	L.A.
May 19/13	Ott.	CSF	Ott. 2	Pit. 1	Colin Greening	27:39	Pit.
May 23/13	NYR	CSF	NYR 4	Bos. 3	Chris Kreider	7:03	Bos.
May 29/13	Chi.	CSF	Chi. 2	Det. 1	Brent Seabrook	3:35	Chi.
June 5/13	Bos.	CF	Bos.2	Pit. 1	Patrice Bergeron	35:19	Bos.
June 8/13	Chi.	CF	Chi. 4	L.A. 3	Patrick Kane	31:40	Chi.
June 12/13	Chi.	F	Chi. 4	Bos. 3	Andrew Shaw	52:08	Chi.
June 15/13	Chi.	F	Bos.2	Chi. 1	Daniel Paille	13:48	Chi.
June 19/13	Bos.	F	Chi. 6	Bos. 5	Brent Seabrook	9:51	Chi.
Apr. 16/14	T.B.	CQF	Mtl. 5	T.B. 4	Dale Weise	18:08	Mtl.
Apr. 17/14	St.L.	CQF	St.L. 4	Chi. 3	Alexander Steen	40:26	Chi.
Apr. 17/14	Col.	CQF	Col. 5	Min. 4	Paul Stastny	7:27	Min.
Apr. 19/14	St.L.	CQF	St.L. 4	Chi. 3	Barret Jackman	5:50	Chi.
Apr. 19/14	Pit.	CQF	CBJ 4	Pit. 3	Matt Calvert	21:10	Pit.
Apr. 21/14	Min.	CQF	Min. 1	Col. 0	Mikael Granlund	5:08	Min.
Apr. 22/14	L.A.	CQF	S.J. 4	L.A. 3	Patrick Marleau	6:20	L.A.
Apr. 23/14	CBJ	CQF	CBJ 4	Pit. 3	Nick Foligno	2:49	Pit.
Apr. 23/14	Chi.	CQF	Chi. 4	St.L. 3	Patrick Kane	11:17	Chi.
Apr. 24/14	Det.	CQF	Bos. 3	Det. 2	Jarome Iginla	13:32	Bos.
Apr. 25/14	St.L.	CQF	Chi. 3	St.L. 2	Jonathan Toews	7:36	Chi.
Apr. 26/14	Col.	CQF	Col. 4	Min. 3	Nathan MacKinnon	3:27	Min.
Apr. 27/14	Dal.	CQF	Ana. 5	Dal. 4	Nick Bonino	2:47	Ana.
Apr. 30/14	Col.	CQF	Min. 5	Col. 4	Nino Niederreiter	5:02	Min.
May 1/14	Bos.	CSF	Mtl. 4	Bos. 3	P.K. Subban	24:17	Mtl.
May 2/14	Pit.	CSF	NYR 3	Pit. 2	Derick Brassard	3:06	NYR
May 3/14	Ana.	CSF	L.A. 3	Ana. 2	Marian Gaborik	12:07	L.A.
May 8/14	Mtl.	CSF	Bos. 1	Mtl. 0	Matt Fraser	1:19	Mtl.
May 13/14	MIN	CSF	Chi. 2	Min. 1	Patrick Kane	9:42	Chi.
May 22/14	NYR	CF	Mtl. 3	NYR 2	Alex Galchenyuk	1:12	NYR
May 25/14	NYR	CF	NYR 3	Mtl. 2	Martin St. Louis	6:02	NYR
May 28/14	Chi.	CF	Chi. 5	L.A. 4	Michal Handzus	22:04	L.A.
June 1/14	Chi.	CF	L.A. 5	Chi. 4	Alec Martinez	5:47	L.A.
June 4/14	L.A.	F	L.A. 3	NYR 2	Justin Williams	4:36	L.A.
June 7/14	L.A.	F	L.A. 5	NYR 4	Dustin Brown	30:26	L.A.
June 13/14	L.A.	F	L.A. 3	NYR 2	Alec Martinez	34:43	L.A.
Apr. 15/15	Nsh.	FR	Chi. 4	Nsh. 3	Duncan Keith	27:49	Chi.
Apr. 17/15	Mtl.	FR	Mtl. 3	Ott. 2	Alex Galchenyuk	3:40	Mtl.
Apr. 19/15	NYI	FR	NYI 2	Wsh. 1	John Tavares	0:15	Wsh.
Apr. 19/15	Ott.	FR	Mtl. 2	Ott. 1	Dale Weise	8:47	Mtl.
Apr. 20/15	Wpg.	FR	Ana. 5	Wpg. 4	Rickard Rakell	5:12	Ana.
Apr. 21/15	NYI	FR	Wsh. 2	NYI 1	Nicklas Backstrom	11:09	Wsh.
Apr. 21/15	Chi.	FR	Chi. 3	Nsh. 2	Brent Seabrook	41:00	Chi.
Apr. 22/15	Pit.	FR	NYR 2	Pit. 1	Kevin Hayes	3:14	NYR
Apr. 23/15	Det.	FR	T.B. 3	Det. 2	Tyler Johnson	2:25	T.B.
Apr. 24/15	NYR	FR	NYR 2	Pit. 1	Carl Hagelin	10:52	NYR
May 1/15	Mtl.	SR	T.B. 2	Mtl. 1	Nikita Kucherov	22.06	T.B.
May 5/15	Cgy.	SR	Cgy. 4	Ana. 3	Mikael Backlund	4:24	Ana.
May 8/15	NYR	SR	NYR 2	Wsh. 1	Ryan McDonagh	9:37	NYR
May 10/15	Ana.	SR	Ana. 3	Cgy. 2	Corey Perry	2:26	Ana.
May 13/15	NYR	SR	NYR 2	Wsh. 1	Derek Stepan	11:24	NYR
May 19/15	Ana.	CF	Chi. 3	Ana. 2	Marcus Kruger	56:12	Chi.
May 20/15	T.B.	CF	T.B. 6	NYR 5	Nikita Kucherov	3:33	T.B.
May 23/15	Chi.	CF	Chi. 5	Ana. 4	Antoine Vermette	25:37	Chi.
May 25/15	Ana.	CF	Ana. 5	Chi. 4	Matt Beleskey	0:45	Chi.

Overtime Record of Current Teams

(Listed by number of OT games played)

	Overall				Home					Road				
Team	GP	W	L	T	GP	W	L	T	Last OT Game	GP	W	L	T	Last OT Game
Montreal	147	80	64	3	68	40	27	1	May 1/15	79	40	37	2	Apr. 19/15
Boston	128	56	69	3	60	30	29	1	May 1/14	68	26	40	2	May 8/14
Toronto	110	56	53	1	70	37	32	1	May 8/13	40	19	21	0	May 13/13
Detroit	99	43	56	0	59	22	37	0	Apr. 23/15	40	21	19	0	May 29/13
Chicago	98	54	42	2	49	30	18	1	May 23/15	49	24	24	1	May 25/15
NY Rangers	89	40	49	0	38	19	19	0	May 13/15	51	21	30	0	May 20/15
Philadelphia	74	36	38	0	34	19	15	0	Apr. 29/12	40	17	23	0	May 3/12
Colorado[2]	66	37	29	0	29	14	15	0	Apr. 30/14	37	23	14	0	Apr. 21/14
Dallas[1]	66	29	37	0	33	13	20	0	Apr. 27/14	33	16	17	0	May 2/08
St. Louis	60	31	29	0	35	23	12	0	Apr. 25/14	25	8	17	0	Apr. 23/14
Buffalo	59	32	27	0	33	20	13	0	Apr. 24/11	26	12	14	0	Apr. 22/11
Los Angeles	55	28	27	0	25	14	11	0	June 13/14	30	13	17	0	June 1/14
Vancouver	54	26	28	0	26	11	15	0	May 3/13	28	15	13	0	May 7/13
Washington	53	23	30	0	22	9	13	0	May 10/13	31	14	17	0	May 13/15
Pittsburgh	48	24	24	0	28	13	15	0	Apr. 22/15	20	11	9	0	Apr. 24/15
New Jersey[4]	47	18	29	0	21	9	12	0	June 2/12	26	9	17	0	Apr. 29/12
NY Islanders	44	30	14	0	22	15	7	0	Apr. 21/15	22	15	7	0	Apr. 16/04
Calgary[3]	43	18	25	0	20	7	13	0	May 5/15	23	11	12	0	May 10/15
Edmonton	42	24	18	0	23	13	10	0	May 10/06	19	11	8	0	June 14/06
San Jose	37	20	17	0	17	9	8	0	May 18/13	20	11	9	0	Apr. 22/14
Carolina[5]	34	21	13	0	20	12	8	0	May 6/09	14	9	5	0	May 14/09
Anaheim	34	20	14	0	14	8	6	0	May 25/15	20	12	9	0	May 23/15
Ottawa	30	16	14	0	13	7	6	0	Apr. 19/15	17	9	8	0	Apr. 17/15
Phoenix[6]	20	8	12	0	14	5	9	0	May 22/12	6	3	3	0	Apr. 19/12
Tampa Bay	17	11	6	0	6	3	3	0	May 20/15	11	8	3	0	May 1/15
Minnesota	15	7	8	0	8	4	4	0	May 13/14	7	3	4	0	Apr. 30/14
Nashville	9	2	7	0	3	0	3	0	Apr. 15/15	6	2	4	0	Apr. 21/15
Florida	7	2	5	0	4	1	3	0	Apr. 26/12	3	1	2	0	Apr. 24/12
Columbus	2	2	0	0	1	1	0	0	Apr. 23/14	1	1	0	0	Apr. 17/14
Winnipeg[7]	1	0	1	0	1	0	1	0	Apr. 20/15	0	0	0	0	

[1] Totals include those of Minnesota North Stars 1967-93.
[2] Totals include those of Quebec Nordiques 1979-95.
[3] Totals include those of Atlanta Flames 1972-80.
[4] Totals include those of Kansas City Scouts 1974-76 and Colorado Rockies 1977-82.
[5] Totals include those of Hartford Whalers 1979-97.
[6] Totals include those of Winnipeg Jets 1979-96.
[7] Totals include those of Atlanta Thrashers 1999-2011.

Derek Stepan celebrates his goal at 11:24 of overtime in game seven of the Eastern Conference Semifinals as the New York Rangers rallied from a three-games-to-one deficit to eliminate the Washington Capitals.

Ten Longest Overtime Games

Date	City	Series	Score		Scorer	Overtime	Series Winner
Mar. 24/36	Mtl.	SF	Det. 1	Mtl. M. 0	Mud Bruneteau	116:30	Det.
Apr. 3/33	Tor.	SF	Tor. 1	Bos. 0	Ken Doraty	104:46	Tor.
May 4/00	Pit.	CSF	Phi. 2	Pit. 1	Keith Primeau	92:01	Phi.
Apr. 24/03	Dal.	CSF	Ana. 4	Dal. 3	Petr Sykora	80:48	Ana.
Apr. 24/96	Wsh.	CQF	Pit. 3	Wsh. 2	Petr Nedved	79:15	Pit.
Apr. 11/07	Van.	CQF	Van. 5	Dal. 4	Henrik Sedin	78:06	Van.
Mar. 23/43	Det.	SF	Tor. 3	Det. 2	Jack McLean	70:18	Det.
May 4/08	Dal.	CSF	Dal. 2	S.J. 1	Brenden Morrow	69:03	Dal.
Mar. 28/30	Mtl.	SF	Mtl. 2	NYR 1	Gus Rivers	68:52	Mtl.
Apr. 18/87	Wsh.	DSF	NYI 3	Wsh. 2	Pat LaFontaine	68:47	NYI

Penalty Shots in Stanley Cup Playoff Games

Date	Player, Team	Goaltender, Team	Scored	Final Score	Series
Mar. 21/22	Babe Dye, Toronto	Hugh Lehman, Vancouver	No	Van. 1 at Tor. 2*	F
Mar. 25/37	Lionel Conacher, Mtl. Maroons	Tiny Thompson, Boston	No	Mtl. M. 0 at Bos. 4	QF
Apr. 15/37	Alex Shibicky, NY Rangers	Earl Robertson, Detroit	No	NYR 0 at Det. 3	F
Mar. 24/38	Mush March, Chicago	Wilf Cude, Montreal	No	Mtl. 0 at Chi. 4	QF
Mar. 29/38	Lorne Carr, NY Americans	Mike Karakas, Chicago	No	Chi. 1 at NYA 3	SF
Apr. 10/38	Art Wiebe, Chicago	Turk Broda, Toronto	No	Tor. 1 at Chi. 2	F
Mar. 24/42	Charlie Sands, Montreal	Johnny Mowers, Detroit	No	Det. 0 at Mtl. 5	QF
Apr. 13/44	Virgil Johnson, Chicago	Bill Durnan, Montreal	No	Chi. 4 at Mtl. 5*	F
Apr. 9/68	Wayne Connelly, Minnesota	Terry Sawchuk, Los Angeles	Yes	L.A. 5 at Min. 7	QF
Apr. 27/68	Jim Roberts, St. Louis	Cesare Maniago, Minnesota	No	St.L. 4 at Min. 3	SF
May 16/71	Frank Mahovlich, Montreal	Tony Esposito, Chicago	No	Chi. 3 at Mtl. 4	F
May 7/75	Bill Barber, Philadelphia	Glenn Resch, NY Islanders	No	Phi. 3 at NYI 4*	SF
Apr. 20/79	Mike Walton, Chicago	Glenn Resch, NY Islanders	No	NYI 4 at Chi. 0	QF
Apr. 9/81	Peter McNab, Boston	Don Beaupre, Minnesota	No	Min. 5 at Bos. 4*	PR
Apr. 17/81	Anders Hedberg, NY Rangers	Mike Liut, St. Louis	Yes	NYR 6 at St.L. 4	QF
Apr. 9/83	Denis Potvin, NY Islanders	Pat Riggin, Washington	No	NYI 6 at Wsh. 2	DSF
Apr. 28/84	Wayne Gretzky, Edmonton	Don Beaupre, Minnesota	Yes	Edm. 8 at Min. 5	CF
May 1/84	Mats Naslund, Montreal	Billy Smith, NY Islanders	No	Mtl. 1 at NYI 3	CF
Apr. 14/85	Bob Carpenter, Washington	Billy Smith, NY Islanders	No	Wsh. 4 at NYI. 6	DF
May 28/85	Ron Sutter, Philadelphia	Grant Fuhr, Edmonton	No	Phi. 3 at Edm. 5	F
May 30/85	Dave Poulin, Philadelphia	Grant Fuhr, Edmonton	No	Phi. 3 at Edm. 8	F
Apr. 9/88	John Tucker, Buffalo	Andy Moog, Boston	Yes	Bos. 2 at Buf. 6	DSF
Apr. 9/88	Petr Klima, Detroit	Allan Bester, Toronto	Yes	Det. 6 at Tor. 3	DSF
Apr. 8/89	Neal Broten, Minnesota	Greg Millen, St. Louis	Yes	St.L. 5 at Min. 3	DSF
Apr. 4/90	Al MacInnis, Calgary	Kelly Hrudey, Los Angeles	Yes	L.A. 5 at Cgy. 3	DSF
Apr. 5/90	Randy Wood, NY Islanders	Mike Richter, NY Rangers	No	NYI 1 at NYR 2	DSF
May 3/90	Kelly Miller, Washington	Andy Moog, Boston	No	Wsh. 3 at Bos. 5	CF
May 18/90	Petr Klima, Edmonton	Reggie Lemelin, Boston	No	Edm. 7 at Bos. 2	F
Apr. 6/91	Basil McRae, Minnesota	Ed Belfour, Chicago	Yes	Min. 2 at Chi. 5	DSF
Apr. 10/91	Steve Duchesne, Los Angeles	Kirk McLean, Vancouver	Yes	L.A. 6 at Van. 1	DSF
May 11/92	Jaromir Jagr, Pittsburgh	John Vanbiesbrouck, NYR	Yes	Pit. 3 at NYR 2	DF
May 13/92	Shawn McEachern, Pittsburgh	John Vanbiesbrouck, NYR	No	NYR 1 at Pit. 5	DF
June 7/94	Pavel Bure, Vancouver	Mike Richter, NYR	No	NYR 4 at Van. 2	F
May 9/95	Patrick Poulin, Chicago	Felix Potvin, Toronto	No	Tor. 3 at Chi. 0	CQF
May 10/95	Michal Pivonka, Washington	Tom Barrasso, Pittsburgh	No	Pit. 2 at Wsh. 6	CQF
Apr. 24/96	Joe Juneau, Washington	Ken Wregget, Pittsburgh	No	Pit. 3 at Wsh. 2**	CQF
May 11/97	Eric Lindros, Philadelphia	Steve Shields, Buffalo	Yes	Phi. 6 at Buf. 3	CSF
Apr. 23/98	Aleksey Morozov, Pittsburgh	Andy Moog, Montreal	No	Mtl. 3 at Pit. 2**	CQF
Apr. 22/99	Mats Sundin, Toronto	John Vanbiesbrouck, Phi.	No	Phi. 3 at Tor. 0	CQF
May 29/99	Mats Sundin, Toronto	Dominik Hasek, Buffalo	Yes	Tor. 2 at Buf. 5	CF
Apr. 16/00	Eric Desjardins, Philadelphia	Dominik Hasek, Buffalo	No	Phi. 2 at Buf. 0	CQF
Apr. 11/01	Mark Recchi, Philadelphia	Dominik Hasek, Buffalo	No	Buf. 2 at Phi. 1	CQF
May 2/01	Martin Straka, Pittsburgh	Dominik Hasek, Buffalo	No	Buf. 5 at Pit. 2	CSF
May 12/01	Joe Sakic, Colorado	Roman Turek, St. Louis	Yes	St.L. 1 at Col. 4	CF
Apr. 21/02	Todd Bertuzzi, Vancouver	Dominik Hasek, Detroit	No	Det. 3 at Van. 1	CQF
Apr. 24/02	Shawn Bates, NY Islanders	Curtis Joseph, Toronto	Yes	Tor. 3 at NYI 4	CQF
Apr. 26/02	Mike Johnson, Phoenix	Evgeni Nabokov, San Jose	Yes	Phx. 1 at S.J. 4	CQF
Apr. 15/03	Dainius Zubrus, Washington	Nikolai Khabibulin, Tampa Bay	No	T.B. 4 at Wsh. 3	CQF
Apr. 21/03	Robert Reichel, Toronto	Roman Cechmanek, Philadelphia	No	Phi. 1 at Tor. 2	CQF
Apr. 7/04	Steve Sullivan, Nashville	Manny Legace, Detroit	No	Nsh. 1 at Det. 3	CQF
Apr. 28/06	Derek Roy, Buffalo	Robert Esche, Philadelphia	No	Buf. 4 at Phi. 5	CQF
June 5/06	Chris Pronger, Edmonton***	Cam Ward, Carolina	Yes	Edm. 4 at Car. 5	F
Apr. 21/07	Daniel Cleary, Detroit	Miikka Kiprusoff, Calgary	Yes	Cgy. 1 at Det. 5	CQF
June 6/07	Antoine Vermette, Ottawa	J.S. Giguere, Anaheim	No	Ott. 2 at Ana. 6	F
Apr. 9/08	Ryan Smyth, Colorado	Niklas Backstrom, Minnesota	No	Col. 3 at Min. 2	CQF
Apr. 15/08	Mike Richards, Philadelphia	Cristobal Huet, Washington	Yes	Wsh. 3 at Phi. 6	CQF
Apr. 18/08	John Madden, New Jersey	Henrik Lundqvist, NY Rangers	No	NYR 5 at N.J. 3	CQF
Apr. 24/08	Andrei Kostitsyn, Montreal	Martin Biron, Philadelphia	No	Phi. 3 at Mtl. 4	CSF
Apr. 29/08	Niklas Hagman, Dallas	Evgeni Nabokov, San Jose	No	S.J. 1 at Dal. 2	CSF
May 1/08	Evgeni Malkin, Pittsburgh	Henrik Lundqvist, NY Rangers	No	Pit. 0 at NYR 3	CSF
Apr. 20/10	Martin Erat, Nashville	Antti Niemi, Chicago	Yes	Chi. 1 at Nsh. 4	CQF
May 4/10	Henrik Zetterberg, Detroit	Evgeni Nabokov, San Jose	No	S.J. 4 at Det. 3	CSF
May 8/10	Joe Pavelski, San Jose	Jimmy Howard, Detroit	No	S.J. 2 at Det. 1	CSF
May 12/10	Ville Leino, Philadelphia	Tuukka Rask, Boston	No	Phi. 2 at Bos. 1	CSF
Apr. 24/11	Michael Frolik, Chicago	Cory Schneider, Vancouver	Yes	Van. 3 at Chi. 4	CQF
Apr. 25/11	Chris Connor, Pittsburgh	Dwayne Roloson, Tampa Bay	No	Pit. 3 at T.B. 4	CQF
Apr. 26/11	Alexandre Burrows, Vancouver	Corey Crawford, Chicago	No	Chi. 1 at Van. 2	CQF
Apr. 18/12	Dustin Brown, Los Angeles	Cory Schneider, Vancouver	No	Van. 3 at L.A. 1	CQF
May 27/13	Michael Frolik, Chicago	Jimmy Howard, Detroit	Yes	Chi. 4 at Det. 3	CSF
May 16/14	Corey Perry, Anaheim	Jonathan Quick, Los Angeles	No	L.A. 6 at Ana. 2	FR
May 6/15	Carl Hagelin, NY Rangers	Braden Holtby, Washington	No	NYR 1 at Wsh 2	FR

* Game was decided in overtime, but shot taken during regulation time.
** Shot taken in overtime.
*** First penalty shot scored in Stanley Cup Final history

All-Time Playoff NHL Coaching Register

Playoffs, 1917-2015

Coach	Team	Games Coached	Wins	Losses	T	Years	Cup Wins	Career
Abel, Sid	Chicago	7	3	4		1		
	Detroit	69	29	40		8		
	Totals	76	32	44		9		1952-76
Adams, Jack	Detroit	105	52	52	1	15	3	1927-47
Allen, Keith	Philadelphia	11	3	8		2		1967-69
Arbour, Al	St. Louis	11	4	7		1		
	NY Islanders	198	119	79		15	4	
	Totals	209	123	86		16	4	1970-08
Babcock, Mike	Anaheim	21	15	6		1		
	Detroit	123	67	56		10	1	
	Totals	144	82	62		11	1	2002-15
Barber, Bill	Philadelphia	11	3	8		2		2000-02
Berenson, Red	St. Louis	14	5	9		2		1979-82
Bergeron, Michel	Quebec	68	31	37		7		1980-90
Berry, Bob	Los Angeles	10	2	8		3		
	Montreal	8	2	6		2		
	St. Louis	15	7	8		2		
	Totals	33	11	22		7		1978-94
Berube, Craig	Philadelphia	7	3	4		1		2013-15
Beverley, Nick	Toronto	6	2	4		1		1995-96
Blackburn, Don	Hartford	3	0	3		1		1979-81
Blair, Wren	Minnesota	14	7	7		1		1967-70
Blake, Toe	Montreal	119	82	37		13	8	1955-68
Boileau, Marc	Pittsburgh	9	5	4		1		1973-76
Boivin, Leo	St. Louis	3	1	2		1		1975-78
Boucher, Frank	NY Rangers	27	13	14		4	1	1939-54
Boucher, George	Mtl. Maroons	2	0	2	0	1		1930-50
Boucher, Guy	Tampa Bay	18	11	7		1		2010-13
Boudreau, Bruce	Washington	37	17	20		4		
	Anaheim	36	21	15		3		
	Totals	73	38	35		7		2007-15
Bowman, Scotty	St. Louis	52	26	26		4		
	Montreal	98	70	28		8	5	
	Buffalo	36	18	18		5		
	Pittsburgh	33	23	10		2	1	
	Detroit	134	86	48		9	3	
	Totals	353	223	130		28	9	1967-02
Bowness, Rick	Boston	15	8	7		1		1988-05
Brooks, Herb	NY Rangers	24	12	12		3		
	New Jersey	5	1	4		1		
	Pittsburgh	11	6	5		1		
	Totals	40	19	21		5		1981-00
Brophy, John	Toronto	19	9	10		2		1986-89
Burns, Charlie	Minnesota	6	2	4		1		1969-75
Burns, Pat	Montreal	56	30	26		4		
	Toronto	46	23	23		3		
	Boston	18	8	10		2		
	New Jersey	29	17	12		2	1	
	Totals	149	78	71		11	1	1988-05
Bylsma, Dan	Pittsburgh	78	43	35		6	1	2008-14
Cameron, Dave	Ottawa	6	2	4		1		2014-15
Campbell, Colin	NY Rangers	36	18	18		3		1994-96
Capuano, Jack	NY Islanders	13	5	8		2		2010-15
Carbonneau, Guy	Montreal	12	5	7		1		2006-09
Carlyle, Randy	Anaheim	62	36	26		5	1	
	Toronto	7	3	4		1		
	Totals	69	39	30		6	1	2005-15
Carpenter, Doug	Toronto	5	1	4		1		1984-91
Carroll, Dick	Toronto	2	1	1	0	1	1	1917-19
Carroll, Frank	Toronto	2	0	2	0	1		1920-21
Cassidy, Bruce	Washington	6	2	4		1		2002-04
Cheevers, Gerry	Boston	34	15	19		4		1980-85
Cherry, Don	Boston	55	31	24		5		1974-80
Clancy, King	Toronto	14	2	12		3		1937-56
Clapper, Dit	Boston	25	8	17		4		1945-49
Cleghorn, Odie	Pittsburgh	4	1	2	1	2		1925-29
Cleghorn, Sprague	Mtl. Maroons	4	1	1	2	1		1931-32
Clouston, Cory	Ottawa	6	2	4		1		2008-11
Constantine, Kevin	San Jose	25	11	14		2		
	Pittsburgh	19	8	11		2		
	New Jersey	6	2	4		1		
	Totals	50	21	29		5		1993-02
Cooper, Jon	Tampa Bay	30	14	16		2		2012-15
Crawford, Marc	Quebec	6	2	4		1		
	Colorado	46	29	17		3	1	
	Vancouver	27	12	15		3		
	Totals	79	43	36		7	1	1994-11
Creighton, Fred	Atlanta	9	2	7		4		1974-80
Crisp, Terry	Calgary	37	22	15		3	1	
	Tampa Bay	6	2	4		1		
	Totals	43	24	19		4	1	1987-98
Crozier, Joe	Buffalo	6	2	4		1		1971-81
Cunniff, John	New Jersey	6	2	4		1		1982-91
Curry, Alex	Ottawa	2	0	1	1	1		1925-26
Dandurand, Leo	Montreal	8	5	3	0	4	1	1921-35
Day, Hap	Toronto	80	49	31		9	5	1940-50
DeBoer, Peter	New Jersey	24	14	10		1		2008-15
Demers, Jacques	St. Louis	33	16	17		3		
	Detroit	38	20	18		3		
	Montreal	27	19	8		2	1	
	Totals	98	55	43		8	1	1979-99
Desjardins, Willie	Vancouver	6	2	4		1		2014-15
Dineen, Kevin	Florida	7	3	4		1		2011-14
Dudley, Rick	Buffalo	12	4	8		2		1989-04
Dugal, Jules	Montreal	3	1	2		1		1938-39
Duncan, Art	Toronto	2	0	1	1	1		1926-32
Dutton, Red	NY Americans	11	4	7		3		1936-40
Esposito, Phil	NY Rangers	10	2	8		2		1986-89
Evans, Jack	Hartford	16	8	8		2		1975-88
Ferguson, John	Winnipeg	3	0	3		1		1975-86
Francis, Bob	Phoenix	10	2	8		2		1999-04
Francis, Emile	NY Rangers	75	34	41		9		
	St. Louis	14	5	9		2		
	Totals	89	39	50		11		1965-83
Ftorek, Robbie	Los Angeles	16	5	11		2		
	New Jersey	7	3	4		1		
	Boston	6	2	4		1		
	Totals	29	10	19		4		1987-03
Gainey, Bob	Minnesota	30	17	13		2		
	Dallas	14	6	8		2		
	Montreal	10	2	8		2		
	Totals	54	25	29		6		1990-09
Geoffrion, Bernie	Atlanta	4	0	4		1		1968-80
Gerard, Eddie	Mtl. Maroons	21	8	8	5	5	1	1917-35
Gill, David	Ottawa	8	3	2	3	2	1	1926-29
Glover, Fred	Oakland	11	3	8		2		1968-74
Gordon, Jackie	Minnesota	25	11	14		2		1970-75
Goring, Butch	Boston	3	0	3		1		1985-01
Gorman, Tommy	NY Americans	2	0	1	1	1		
	Chicago	8	6	1		1	1	
	Mtl. Maroons	15	7	6	2	3	1	
	Totals	25	13	8	4	5	2	1925-38
Gottselig, Johnny	Chicago	4	0	4		1		1944-48
Granato, Tony	Colorado	18	9	9		2		2002-09
Green, Pete	Ottawa	8	3	4	1	4	3	1919-25
Green, Ted	Edmonton	16	8	8		2		1991-94
Guidolin, Bep	Boston	21	11	10		2		1972-76
Harris, Ted	Minnesota	2	0	2		1		1975-78
Hart, Cecil	Montreal	37	16	17	4	8	2	1926-39
Hartley, Bob	Colorado	80	49	31		4	1	
	Atlanta	4	0	4		1		
	Calgary	11	5	6		1		
	Totals	95	54	41		6	1	1998-15
Hartsburg, Craig	Chicago	16	8	8		2		
	Anaheim	4	0	4		1		
	Totals	20	8	12		3		1995-09
Harvey, Doug	NY Rangers	6	2	4		1		1961-62
Hay, Don	Phoenix	7	3	4		1		1996-01
Helmer, Rosie	NY Americans	5	2	3	0	1		1935-36
Henning, Lorne	Minnesota	5	2	3		1		1985-01
Hitchcock, Ken	Dallas	80	47	33		5	1	
	Philadelphia	37	19	18		3		
	Columbus	4	0	4		1		
	St. Louis	27	10	17		4		
	Totals	148	76	72		13	1	1995-15
Hlinka, Ivan	Pittsburgh	18	9	9		1		2000-02
Holmgren, Paul	Philadelphia	19	10	9		1		1988-96
Hunter, Dale	Washington	14	7	7		1		2011-12
Imlach, Punch	Toronto	92	44	48		11	4	1958-80
Inglis, Bill	Buffalo	3	1	2		1		1978-79
Irvin, Dick	Chicago	9	5	3	1	1		
	Toronto	66	33	32	1	9	1	
	Montreal	115	62	53		14	3	
	Totals	190	100	88	2	24	4	1928-56
Ivan, Tommy	Detroit	67	36	31		7	3	1947-58
Johnson, Bob	Calgary	52	25	27		5		
	Pittsburgh	24	16	8		1	1	
	Totals	76	41	35		6	1	1982-91
Johnson, Tom	Boston	22	15	7		2	1	1970-73
Johnston, Eddie	Chicago	7	3	4		1		
	Pittsburgh	46	22	24		5		
	Totals	53	25	28		6		1979-97
Johnston, Mike	Pittsburgh	5	1	4		1		2014-15
Julien, Claude	Montreal	11	4	7		1		
	Boston	97	57	40		7	1	
	Totals	108	61	47		8	1	2002-15
Kasper, Steve	Boston	5	1	4		1		1995-97
Keenan, Mike	Philadelphia	57	32	25		4		
	Chicago	60	33	27		4		
	NY Rangers	23	16	7		1	1	
	St. Louis	20	10	10		2		
	Calgary	13	5	8		2		
	Totals	173	96	77		13	1	1984-09
Kelly, Pat	Colorado	2	0	2		1		1977-79
Kelly, Red	Los Angeles	18	7	11		2		
	Pittsburgh	14	6	8		2		
	Toronto	30	11	19		4		
	Totals	62	24	38		8		1967-77
King, Dave	Calgary	20	8	12		3		1992-03
Kromm, Bobby	Detroit	7	3	4		1		1977-80
Laflamme, Jerry	Mtl. Maroons	4	1	3	0	1		1929-30
Lalonde, Newsy	Montreal	11	5	4	2	4		
	Ottawa	2	0	1	1	1		
	Totals	13	5	5	3	5		1917-35
Lamoriello, Lou	New Jersey	20	10	10		2		2005-07
Laviolette, Peter	NY Islanders	12	4	8		2		
	Carolina	25	16	9		1	1	
	Philadelphia	45	23	22		3		
	Nashville	6	2	4		1		
	Totals	88	45	43		7	1	2001-15
Lemaire, Jacques	Montreal	27	15	12		2		
	New Jersey	61	35	26		5	1	
	Minnesota	29	11	18		3		
	Totals	117	61	56		10	1	1983-11
Lewis, Dave	Detroit	16	6	10		2		1998-07

Coach	Team	Games Coached	Wins	Losses	Ties	Years	Cup Wins	Career
Ley, Rick	Hartford	13	5	8		2		
	Vancouver	11	4	7		1		
	Totals	24	9	15		3		1989-96
Long, Barry	Winnipeg	11	3	8		2		1983-86
Loughlin, Clem	Chicago	4	1	2	1	2		1934-37
Low, Ron	Edmonton	28	10	18		3		1994-02
Lowe, Kevin	Edmonton	5	1	4		1		1999-00
MacLean, Doug	Florida	27	13	14		2		1995-04
MacLean, Paul	Ottawa	17	8	9		2		2011-15
MacNeil, Al	Montreal	20	12	8		1	1	
	Atlanta	4	1	3		1		
	Calgary	19	9	10		2		
	Totals	43	22	21		4	1	1970-03
MacTavish, Craig	Edmonton	36	19	17		3		2000-15
Magnuson, Keith	Chicago	3	0	3		1		1980-82
Mahoney, Bill	Minnesota	16	7	9		1		1983-85
Maloney, Dan	Toronto	10	6	4		1		
	Winnipeg	15	5	10		2		
	Totals	25	11	14		3		1984-89
Maloney, Phil	Vancouver	7	1	6		2		1973-77
Martin, Jacques	St. Louis	16	7	9		2		
	Ottawa	69	31	38		8		
	Montreal	26	12	14		2		
	Totals	111	50	61		12		1986-12
Maurice, Paul	Carolina	53	25	28		4		
	Winnipeg	4	0	4		1		
	Totals	57	25	32		5		1995-15
McCammon, Bob	Philadelphia	10	1	9		3		
	Vancouver	7	3	4		1		
	Totals	17	4	13		4		1978-91
McLellan, John	Toronto	11	3	8		2		1969-73
McLellan, Todd	San Jose	62	30	32		6		2008-15
McVie, Tom	New Jersey	14	6	8		2		1975-92
Melrose, Barry	Los Angeles	24	13	11		1		1992-09
Milbury, Mike	Boston	40	23	17		2		1989-99
Muckler, John	Edmonton	40	25	15		2	1	
	Buffalo	27	11	16		4		
	Totals	67	36	31		6	1	1968-00
Muldoon, Pete	Chicago	2	0	1	1	1		1926-27
Murdoch, Bob	Chicago	5	1	4		1		
	Winnipeg	7	3	4		1		
	Totals	12	4	8		2		1987-91
Murphy, Mike	Los Angeles	5	1	4		1		1986-98
Murray, Andy	Los Angeles	24	10	14		3		
	St. Louis	4	0	4		1		
	Totals	28	10	18		4		1999-10
Murray, Bryan	Washington	53	24	29		7		
	Detroit	25	10	15		3		
	Ottawa	34	18	16		3		
	Totals	112	52	60		13		1981-08
Murray, Terry	Washington	39	18	21		4		
	Philadelphia	46	28	18		3		
	Florida	4	0	4		1		
	Los Angeles	12	4	8		2		
	Totals	101	50	51		10		1989-12
Neale, Harry	Vancouver	14	3	11		4		1978-86
Neilson, Roger	Toronto	19	8	11		2		
	Buffalo	8	4	4		1		
	Vancouver	21	12	9		2		
	NY Rangers	29	13	16		3		
	Philadelphia	29	14	15		3		
	Totals	106	51	55		11		1977-02
Nolan, Ted	Buffalo	12	5	7		2		
	NY Islanders	5	1	4		1		
	Totals	17	6	11		2		1995-15
Nykoluk, Mike	Toronto	7	1	6		2		1980-84
Oates, Adam	Washington	7	3	4		1		2012-14
O'Connell, Mike	Boston	5	1	4		1		2002-03
O'Donoghue, George	Toronto	2	1	0	1	1	1	1921-23
Oliver, Murray	Minnesota	9	4	5		1		1982-83
O'Reilly, Terry	Boston *	37	17	19	1	3		1986-89

* Playoff game May 24, 1988 suspended due to power failure. Score tied.

Coach	Team	Games Coached	Wins	Losses	Ties	Years	Cup Wins	Career
Paddock, John	Winnipeg	13	5	8		2		1991-08
Page, Pierre	Minnesota	12	4	8		2		
	Quebec	6	2	4		1		
	Calgary	4	0	4		1		
	Totals	22	6	16		4		1988-98
Patrick, Craig	NY Rangers	17	7	10		2		
	Pittsburgh	5	1	4		1		
	Totals	22	8	14		3		1980-97
Patrick, Frank	Boston	6	2	4	0	2		1934-36
Patrick, Lester	NY Rangers	65	32	26	7	12	2	1926-39
Patrick, Lynn	NY Rangers	12	7	5		1		
	Boston *	28	9	18	1	4		
	Totals	40	16	23	1	5		1948-76

* Playoff game March 31, 1951 suspended due to Toronto city curfew. Score tied.

Coach	Team	Games Coached	Wins	Losses	Ties	Years	Cup Wins	Career
Perron, Jean	Montreal	48	30	18		3	1	1985-89
Perry, Don	Los Angeles	10	4	6		1		1981-84
Pilous, Rudy	Chicago	41	19	22		5	1	1957-63
Plager, Barclay	St. Louis	4	1	3		1		1977-83
Playfair, Jim	Calgary	6	2	4		1		2006-07
Pleau, Larry	Hartford	10	2	8		2		1980-89
Polano, Nick	Detroit	7	1	6		2		1982-85
Powers, Eddie	Toronto	2	0	2	0	1		1924-26
Primeau, Joe	Toronto *	15	8	6	1	2	1	1950-53

* Playoff game March 31, 1951 suspended due to Toronto city curfew. Score tied.

Coach	Team	Games Coached	Wins	Losses	Ties	Years	Cup Wins	Career
Pronovost, Marcel	Buffalo	8	3	5		1		1977-79
Pulford, Bob	Los Angeles	26	10	16		4		
	Chicago	45	17	28		6		
	Totals	71	27	44		10		1972-00
Quenneville, Joel	St. Louis	68	34	34		7		
	Colorado	19	8	11		2		
	Chicago	117	73	44		7	3	
	Totals	204	115	89		16	3	1996-15
Quinn, Pat	Philadelphia	39	22	17		3		
	Los Angeles	3	0	3		1		
	Vancouver	61	31	30		5		
	Toronto	80	41	39		6		
	Totals	183	94	89		15		1978-10
Reay, Billy	Chicago	116	56	60		12		1957-77
Renney, Tom	NY Rangers	24	11	13		3		1996-12
Richards, Todd	Columbus	6	2	4		1		2009-15
Risebrough, Doug	Calgary	7	3	4		1		1990-92
Roberts, Jim	Hartford	7	3	4		1		1981-97
Robinson, Larry	Los Angeles	4	0	4		1		
	New Jersey	48	31	17		2	1	
	Totals	52	31	21		3	1	1995-06
Ross, Art	Boston	70	32	33	5	12	2	1917-45
Roy, Patrick	Colorado	7	3	4		1		2013-15
Ruel, Claude	Montreal	27	18	9		3	1	1968-81
Ruff, Lindy	Buffalo	101	57	44		9		
	Dallas	6	2	4		1		
	Totals	107	59	48		9		1997-15
Sacco, Joe	Colorado	6	2	4		1		2009-13
Sather, Glen	Edmonton *	127	89	37	1	10	4	1979-04

* Playoff game May 24, 1988 suspended due to power failure. Score tied.

Coach	Team	Games Coached	Wins	Losses	Ties	Years	Cup Wins	Career
Sator, Ted	NY Rangers	16	8	8		1		
	Buffalo	11	3	8		2		
	Totals	27	11	16		3		1985-89
Schinkel, Ken	Pittsburgh	6	2	4		2		1972-77
Schmidt, Milt	Boston	34	15	19		4		1954-76
Schoenfeld, Jim	New Jersey	20	11	9		1		
	Washington	24	10	14		3		
	Phoenix	13	5	8		2		
	Totals	57	26	31		6		1985-99
Shero, Fred	Philadelphia	83	48	35		6	2	
	NY Rangers	27	15	12		2		
	Totals	110	63	47		8	2	1971-81
Simpson, Terry	NY Islanders	20	9	11		2		
	Winnipeg	6	2	4		1		
	Totals	26	11	15		3		1986-96
Sinden, Harry	Boston	43	24	19		5	1	1966-85
Skinner, Jimmy	Detroit	26	14	12		3	1	1954-58
Smith, Alf	Ottawa	5	1	4	0	1		1918-19
Smith, Floyd	Buffalo	32	16	16		3		1971-80
Smythe, Conn	Toronto	4	2	2	0	1		1927-32
Sonmor, Glen	Minnesota	47	26	21		4		1978-87
Stasiuk, Vic	Philadelphia	4	0	4		1		1969-73
Stevens, John	Philadelphia	23	11	12		2		2006-12
Stewart, Bill	Chicago	10	7	3		1	1	1937-39
Stewart, Ron	Los Angeles	2	0	2		1		1975-78
Sutter, Brent	New Jersey	12	4	8		2		2007-12
Sutter, Brian	St. Louis	41	20	21		4		
	Boston	22	7	15		3		
	Chicago	5	1	4		1		
	Totals	68	28	40		8		1988-05
Sutter, Darryl	Chicago	26	11	15		3		
	San Jose	42	18	24		5		
	Calgary	33	18	15		2		
	Los Angeles	64	41	23		3	2	
	Totals	165	88	77		13	2	1992-15
Talbot, Jean-Guy	St. Louis	5	1	4		1		
	NY Rangers	3	1	2		1		
	Totals	8	2	6		2		1972-78
Tessier, Orval	Chicago	18	9	9		2		1982-85
Therrien, Michel	Montreal	47	24	23		4		
	Pittsburgh	25	15	10		2		
	Totals	72	39	33		6		2000-15
Thompson, Paul	Chicago	19	7	12		4		1938-45
Tippett, Dave	Dallas	47	21	26		5		
	Phoenix/Arizona	27	12	15		3		
	Totals	74	33	41		8		2002-15
Tobin, Bill	Chicago	4	1	2	1	2		1929-32
Tortorella, John	NY Rangers	44	19	25		4		
	Tampa Bay	45	24	21		4	1	
	Totals	89	43	46		8	1	1999-14
Tremblay, Mario	Montreal	11	3	8		2		1995-97
Trotz, Barry	Nashville	50	19	31		7		
	Washington	14	7	7		1		
	Totals	64	26	38		8		1998-15
Ubriaco, Gene	Pittsburgh	11	7	4		1		1988-90
Vigneault, Alain	Montreal	10	4	6		1		
	Vancouver	68	33	35		6		
	NY Rangers	44	24	20		2		
	Totals	122	61	61		9		1997-15
Watson, Phil	NY Rangers	16	4	12		3		1955-63
Watt, Tom	Winnipeg	7	1	6		2		
	Vancouver	3	0	3		1		
	Totals	10	1	9		3		1981-92
Webster, Tom	Los Angeles	28	12	16		3		1986-92
Weiland, Cooney	Boston	17	10	7		2	1	1939-41
White, Bill	Chicago	2	0	2		1		1976-77
Wilson, Johnny	Pittsburgh	12	4	8		1		1969-80
Wilson, Ron	Anaheim	11	4	7		1		
	Washington	32	15	17		4		
	San Jose	52	28	24		4		
	Totals	95	47	48		9		1993-12
Yeo, Mike	Minnesota	28	11	17		3		2011-15
Young, Garry	St. Louis	2	0	2		1		1972-76

How to Use the Prospect, NHL Player and Goaltender Registers

Demographics: Position, shooting side (catching hand for goaltenders), height, weight, place and date of birth as well as NHL Draft information, if any, is located on this line.

Major and tier-II junior, NCAA, minor pro, European and NHL clubs form a permanent part of each player's data panel. If a player sees action with more than one club in any of the above categories, a separate line is included for each one.

Olympic Team statistics are also listed.

Asterisks (*) indicates league leader in individual statistical categories.

Players' NHL organization as of August 14, 2015. This includes players under contract, unsigned draft choices and other players on reserve lists. Free agents as of this date show a blank here.

The complete career data panels of players with NHL experience who announced their retirement before the start of the 2015-16 season are included in the Player Register and Goaltender Register.

These newly-retired players also show a blank here.

Each NHL club's minor-pro affiliates are listed on page 14.

									Regular Season										Playoffs							
Season	Club	League	GP	G	A	Pts	PIM	PP	SH	GW	S	S%	+/–	TF	F%	Min	GP	G	A	Pts	PIM	PP	SH	GW	Min

RICHARDS, Brad   (RIH-chuhrds, BRAD)   **DET**

Center. Shoots left. 6', 196 lbs.   Born, Murray Harbour, PE, May 2, 1980. Tampa Bay's 2nd choice, 64th overall, in 1998 Entry Draft.

Season	Club	League	GP	G	A	Pts	PIM	PP	SH	GW	S	S%	+/–	TF	F%	Min	GP	G	A	Pts	PIM	PP	SH	GW	Min
1996-97	Notre Dame	SJHL	63	39	48	87	73																		
1997-98	Rimouski Oceanic	QMJHL	68	33	82	115	44										19	8	24	32	2				
1998-99	Rimouski Oceanic	QMJHL	59	39	92	131	55										11	9	12	21	6				
99-2000	Rimouski Oceanic	QMJHL	63	*71	*115	186	69										13	13	*24	*37	16				
2000-01	Tampa Bay	NHL	82	21	41	62	14	7	0	3	179	11.7	-10	955	41.4	16:54									
2001-02	Tampa Bay	NHL	82	20	42	62	13	5	0	0	251	8.0	-18	911	41.2	19:48									
2002-03	Tampa Bay	NHL	80	17	57	74	24	4	0	2	277	6.1	3	1007	47.5	19:56	11	0		5	2	0	0	0	22:21
2003-04♦	Tampa Bay	NHL	82	26	53	79	12	5	1	6	244	10.7	13	1167	46.7	20:26	23	12	14	*26	4	*7	0	*7	23:28
2004-05	Ak Bars Kazan	Russ	6	2	5	7	16																		
2005-06	Tampa Bay	NHL	82	23	68	91	32	7	4	0	282	8.2	0	1288	50.2	22:45	5	3	5	8	6	0	0	0	24:11
	Canada	Olympics	6	2	2	4	6																		
2006-07	Tampa Bay	NHL	82	25	45	70	23	12	1	3	272	9.2	-19	1580	51.4	24:07	6	3	5	8	0	0	0	0	25:39
2007-08	Tampa Bay	NHL	62	18	33	51	15	9	1	4	228	7.9	-25	944	48.1	24:17									
	Dallas	NHL	12	2	9	11	0	0	1	0	21	9.5	-2	130	56.2	19:15	18	3	12	15	0	0	0	0	21:06
2008-09	Dallas	NHL	56	16	32	48	6	5	0	2	180	8.9	-4	911	50.6	20:29									
2009-10	Dallas	NHL	80	24	67	91	14	13	0	2	284	8.5	-12	1140	51.5	20:52									
2010-11	Dallas	NHL	72	28	49	77	24	7	0	3	272	10.3	1	990	50.6	21:43									
2011-12	NY Rangers	NHL	82	25	41	66	22	7	0	9	229	10.9	-1	1316	51.8	20:16	20	6	9	15	8	2	0	0	22:12
2012-13	NY Rangers	NHL	46	11	23	34	14	3	0	1	110	10.0	8	773	50.6	18:49	10	1	0	1	2	0	0	0	14:43
2013-14	NY Rangers	NHL	82	20	31	51	18	5	0	2	259	7.7	-8	1029	49.8	18:41	25	5	7	12	4	2	0	2	17:01
2014-15♦	Chicago	NHL	76	12	25	37	12	2	0	3	199	6.0	5	825	48.4	14:53	23	3	11	14	8	1	0	0	16:44
	NHL Totals		1058	288	616	904	243	91	8	40	3287	8.8		14966	48.9	20:15	141	36	68	104	58	14	0	9	20:09

QMJHL First All-Star Team (2000) • Canadian Major Junior First All-Star Team (2000) • Canadian Major Junior Player of the Year (2000) • Memorial Cup All-Star Team (2000) • Stafford Smythe Memorial Trophy (Memorial Cup - MVP) (2000) • NHL All-Rookie Team (2001) • Lady Byng Memorial Trophy (2004) • Conn Smythe Trophy (2004)
Played in NHL All-Star Game (2011)

Signed as a free agent by **Kazan** (Russia), November 8, 2004. Traded to **Dallas** by **Tampa Bay** with Johan Holmqvist for Jussi Jokinen, Jeff Halpern, Mike Smith and Dallas' 4th round choice (later traded to Minnesota, later traded to Edmonton – Edmonton selected Kyle Bigos) in 2009 Entry Draft, February 26, 2008. Signed as a free agent by **NY Rangers**, July 2, 2011. Signed as a free agent by **Chicago**, July 1, 2014. Signed as a free agent by **Detroit**, July 1, 2015.

Diamond (♦) indicates member of Stanley Cup-winning team.

"Did not play" Indicates that a player did not participate in a professional, junior or college league for an entire season.

Birthplace reflects the world map at the time a player was born. The Czech Republic and Slovakia became independent on January 1, 1993. Previously, players were born in Czechoslovakia. The Russian Republic was established on January 1, 1992. Previously, players were born in the USSR. Germany was unified on October 3, 1990. Previously, players were born in either East or West Germany. Former Soviet Republics (Belarus, Estonia, Kazakhstan, Latvia, Lithuania, Ukraine) achieved independence between August 20 and December 25, 1991.

All trades, free agent signings and other transactions involving NHL clubs are listed here and are presented in chronological order. First draft selection for players who re-enter the NHL Draft is noted here as well. Also listed are other special notes. These are highlighted with a bullet (•).

Dates for trades or free agent signings often differ depending upon source. Signings can be reported based on when contracts are filed with NHL Central Registry or on the date a club announces that it has made a trade or come to terms with a free agent.

All-Star Team selections and awards are listed below player's year-by-year data.

NHL All-Star Game appearances are listed above trade notes.

Pronunciation of Player Names

United Press International phonetic style.

AY	long A as in mate
A	short A as in cat
AI	nasal A as on air
AH	short A as in father
AW	broad A as in talk
EE	long E as in meat
EH	short E as in get
UH	hollow E as in the
AY	French long E with acute accent as in Pathe
IH	middle E as in pretty
EW	EW dipthong as in few
IGH	long I as in time
EE	French long I as in machine
IH	short I as in pity
OH	long O as in note
AH	short O as in hot
AW	broad O as in fought
OI	OI dipthong as in noise
OO	long double OO as in fool
U	short double O as in foot
OW	OW dipthong as in how
EW	long U as in mule
OO	long U as in rule
U	middle U as in put
UH	short U as in shut or hurt
K	hard C as in cat
S	soft C as in cease
SH	soft CH as in machine
CH	hard CH or TCH as in catch
Z	hard S as in bells
S	soft S as in sun
G	hard G as in gang
J	soft G as in general
ZH	soft J as in French version of Joliet
KH	gutteral CH as in Scottish version of Loch

THIS 84TH EDITION OF THE *NHL Official Guide & Record Book* includes additional statistical categories for forwards and defensemen in the National Hockey League. These categories are, from left to right in the sample panel above, power-play goals (PP), shorthand goals (SH), game-winning goals (GW), shots on goal (S), percentage of shots that score (%), plus-minus rating (+/–), total faceoffs taken (TF), faceoff winning percentage (F%), and average time-on-ice per game played (Min).

To integrate this data, the Player Register is split into two sections. The Prospect Register presents data on players who have yet to play in the NHL. The NHL Player Register, containing more information and a photo of each player, lists all active players who have appeared in an NHL regular-season or playoff game at any time.

Goaltenders, whether prospects or active NHLers, are included in one register. With the addition of the shootout to NHL regular-season play, the column formerly used to record tie games for goaltenders has been renamed "O/T." For NHL goaltenders beginning in 2005-06, it lists overtime losses and shootout losses; previous to 2005-06, it lists tie games.

Registers (with their starting page) are presented in the following order: Prospects (275), NHL Players (344), Goaltenders (587), Retired Players (614) and Retired Goaltenders (658).

League abbreviations, page 670. Late additions to the Registers, page 663.

Some information is unavailable at press time. Readers are encouraged to contribute. See page 5 for contact names and addresses.

2015-16 Prospect Register

Note: The 2015-16 Prospect Register lists forwards and defensemen only. Goaltenders are listed separately. The Prospect Register lists every player drafted in the 2015 Entry Draft, players on NHL Reserve Lists and other players who have not yet played in the NHL. Trades and roster changes are current as of August 14, 2015.

Abbreviations: GP – games played; **G** – goals; **A** – assists; **Pts** – points; **PIM** – penalties in minutes; ***** – league-leading total.

NHL Player Register begins on page 344.
Goaltender Register begins on page 587.
Retired Player Index begins on page 612.
Retired Goaltender Index begins on page 657.
League Abbreviations are listed on page 670.

ABELTSHAUSER, Konrad   (ah-behlts-HAHW-zuhr, KAWN-rad)   ST.L.

Defense. Shoots left. 6'5", 225 lbs.   Born, Bad Tolz, Germany, September 2, 1992.
(San Jose's 6th choice, 163rd overall, in 2010 Entry Draft).

			Regular Season					Playoffs			
Season	Club	League	GP	G	A	Pts	PIM	GP	G	A	Pts	PIM
2007-08	EC Bad Tolz Jr.	Ger-Jr.	36	1	10	11	32	8	0	6	6	2
2008-09	EC Bad Tolz Jr.	Ger-Jr.	36	16	28	44	26	4	1	0	1	0
2009-10	Halifax	QMJHL	48	5	20	25	28	....	....	....	....	....
2010-11	Halifax	QMJHL	58	8	19	27	47	4	3	0	3	0
2011-12	Halifax	QMJHL	57	8	36	44	30	15	5	11	16	16
2012-13	Halifax	QMJHL	56	7	47	54	22	17	7	13	20	12
2013-14	Worcester Sharks	AHL	57	6	15	21	18	....	....	....	....	....
2014-15	Worcester Sharks	AHL	50	3	16	19	19	....	....	....	....	....
	Allen Americans	ECHL	6	5	2	7	4	25	5	11	16	12

QMJHL Second All-Star Team (2013) • Memorial Cup All-Star Team (2013)
Traded to **St. Louis** by **San Jose** for future considerations, June 29, 2015.

ABERG, Pontus   (AW-buhrg, PAWN-tuhs)   NSH

Left wing. Shoots right. 5'11", 189 lbs.   Born, Stockholm, Sweden, September 23, 1993.
(Nashville's 1st choice, 37th overall, in 2012 Entry Draft).

			Regular Season					Playoffs			
Season	Club	League	GP	G	A	Pts	PIM	GP	G	A	Pts	PIM
2008-09	Djurgarden U18	Swe-U18	27	6	3	9	8	....	....	....	....	....
2009-10	Djurgarden U18	Swe-U18	36	29	33	62	24	5	4	7	11	4
	Djurgarden Jr.	Swe-Jr.	11	0	1	1	4	....	....	....	....	....
2010-11	Djurgarden U18	Swe-U18	8	11	7	18	27	3	0	2	2	2
	Djurgarden Jr.	Swe-Jr.	41	13	17	30	16	4	2	3	5	2
	Djurgarden	Sweden	1	0	0	0	0	....	....	....	....	....
2011-12	Djurgarden Jr.	Swe-Jr.	6	4	2	6	0	1	1	0	1	0
	Djurgarden	Sweden	47	8	7	15	6	....	....	....	....	....
	Djurgarden	Sweden-Q	7	1	0	1	0	....	....	....	....	....
2012-13	Djurgarden	Sweden-2	58	15	29	44	8	....	....	....	....	....
	Djurgarden Jr.	Swe-Jr.	3	1	3	4	2	1	0	0	0	0
2013-14	Farjestad	Sweden	52	15	16	31	41	13	2	2	4	4
2014-15	Milwaukee	AHL	69	16	18	34	28	....	....	....	....	....

ACCIARI, Noel   (A-char-ee, NOHL)   BOS

Center. Shoots right. 5'10", 208 lbs.   Born, Johnston, RI, March 31, 1992.

			Regular Season					Playoffs			
Season	Club	League	GP	G	A	Pts	PIM	GP	G	A	Pts	PIM
2009-10	Kent Prep School	High-CT	26	18	20	38	....	....	....	....	....	....
2010-11	Kent Prep School	High-CT	27	31	21	52	....	....	....	....	....	....
2011-12	Providence College	H-East			DID NOT PLAY – FRESHMAN							
2012-13	Providence College	H-East	33	6	5	11	36	....	....	....	....	....
2013-14	Providence College	H-East	39	11	11	22	20	....	....	....	....	....
2014-15	Providence College	H-East	41	15	17	32	26	....	....	....	....	....

Signed as a free agent by **Boston**, June 8, 2015.

ACOLATSE, Sena   (ah-koh-LAWT-say, SEH-na)   FLA

Defense. Shoots right. 6', 210 lbs.   Born, Hayward, CA, November 28, 1990.

			Regular Season					Playoffs			
Season	Club	League	GP	G	A	Pts	PIM	GP	G	A	Pts	PIM
2006-07	Seattle	WHL	45	0	4	4	61	11	0	0	0	8
2007-08	Seattle	WHL	71	7	24	31	107	12	1	2	3	12
2008-09	Seattle	WHL	70	7	14	21	143	5	1	1	2	0
2009-10	Seattle	WHL	39	13	9	22	35	....	....	....	....	....
	Saskatoon Blades	WHL	30	3	10	13	25	7	1	1	2	17
2010-11	Saskatoon Blades	WHL	1	0	0	0	2	....	....	....	....	....
	Prince George	WHL	66	15	48	63	128	4	3	4	7	4
	Worcester Sharks	AHL	1	0	0	0	0	....	....	....	....	....
2011-12	Worcester Sharks	AHL	65	8	13	21	89	....	....	....	....	....
2012-13	Worcester Sharks	AHL	50	4	17	21	62	....	....	....	....	....
2013-14	Worcester Sharks	AHL	41	5	12	17	66	....	....	....	....	....
2014-15	Adirondack Flames	AHL	38	6	13	19	68	....	....	....	....	....

Signed as a free agent by **San Jose**, March 4, 2011. Signed as a free agent by **Calgary**, July 3, 2014. Signed as a free agent by **Florida**, July 1, 2015.

ADDISON, Jeremiah   (a-DIH-suhn, jair-ih-MY-uh)   MTL

Left wing. Shoots left. 5'11", 184 lbs.   Born, Brampton, ON, October 21, 1996.
(Montreal's 5th choice, 207th overall, in 2015 Entry Draft).

			Regular Season					Playoffs			
Season	Club	League	GP	G	A	Pts	PIM	GP	G	A	Pts	PIM
2011-12	Toronto Marlboros	GTHL		28	18	46	37	....	....	....	....	....
	Brampton Capitals	ON-Jr.A	1	1	0	1	0	....	....	....	....	....
2012-13	Saginaw Spirit	OHL	68	6	10	16	42	4	0	0	0	0
2013-14	Saginaw Spirit	OHL	61	7	10	17	52	5	0	0	0	0
2014-15	Ottawa 67's	OHL	63	19	28	47	49	6	6	4	10	7

AHL, Filip   (AHL, FIHL-ihp)   OTT

Left wing. Shoots left. 6'4", 214 lbs.   Born, Jonkoping, Sweden, June 12, 1997.
(Ottawa's 6th choice, 109th overall, in 2015 Entry Draft).

			Regular Season					Playoffs			
Season	Club	League	GP	G	A	Pts	PIM	GP	G	A	Pts	PIM
2011-12	HV 71 U18	Swe-U18	6	0	1	1	0	....	....	....	....	....
2012-13	HV 71 U18	Swe-U18	33	10	16	26	45	....	....	....	....	....
	HV 71 Jr.	Swe-Jr.	1	0	1	1	2	....	....	....	....	....
2013-14	HV 71 U18	Swe-U18	9	9	6	15	6	....	....	....	....	....
	HV 71 Jonkoping	Sweden	1	0	0	0	0	2	0	0	0	0
	HV 71 Jr.	Swe-Jr.	24	10	9	19	10	5	2	2	4	2
	HV 71 Jonkoping	Sweden	1	0	0	0	0	2	0	0	0	0
2014-15	HV 71 U18	Swe-U18	1	0	1	1	0	4	5	4	9	0
	HV 71 Jr.	Swe-Jr.	34	20	22	42	53	6	3	2	5	4
	HV 71 Jonkoping	Sweden	15	0	2	2	0	....	....	....	....	....

AHO, Sebastian   (AH-hoh, seh-BAS-t'yehn)   CAR

Left wing. Shoots left. 5'11", 172 lbs.   Born, Rauma, Finland, July 26, 1997.
(Carolina's 2nd choice, 35th overall, in 2015 Entry Draft).

			Regular Season					Playoffs			
Season	Club	League	GP	G	A	Pts	PIM	GP	G	A	Pts	PIM
2011-12	Karpat Oulu U18	Fin-U18	4	0	2	2	4	....	....	....	....	....
2012-13	Karpat Oulu U18	Fin-U18	38	28	32	60	32	....	....	....	....	....
	Karpat Oulu Jr.	Fin-Jr.	5	2	2	4	0	5	0	1	1	2
2013-14	Karpat Oulu U18	Fin-U18	2	3	3	6	0	....	....	....	....	....
	Karpat Oulu Jr.	Fin-Jr.	44	25	34	59	18	12	4	8	12	10
	Karpat Oulu	Finland	3	0	1	1	0	....	....	....	....	....
2014-15	Karpat Oulu Jr.	Fin-Jr.	10	1	9	10	4	5	1	4	5	2
	Assat Pori	Finland	3	0	2	2	0	....	....	....	....	....
	Karpat Oulu	Finland	27	4	7	11	8	10	1	2	3	2

ALDERSON, Brandon   (AHL-duhr-suhn, BRAN-duhn)   PHI

Right wing. Shoots right. 6'4", 202 lbs.   Born, Oakville, ON, January 22, 1992.

			Regular Season					Playoffs			
Season	Club	League	GP	G	A	Pts	PIM	GP	G	A	Pts	PIM
2007-08	Lon. Jr. Knights	Minor-ON	52	26	27	53	....	....	....	....	....	....
2008-09	Oakville Rangers	Minor-ON			STATISTICS NOT AVAILABLE							
	Oakville Blades	ON-Jr.A	1	1	1	2	0	....	....	....	....	....
2009-10	Sarnia Sting	OHL	67	13	11	24	30	....	....	....	....	....
2010-11	Sarnia Sting	OHL	68	11	19	30	63	....	....	....	....	....
2011-12	Sault Ste. Marie	OHL	65	17	22	39	81	....	....	....	....	....
2012-13	Sault Ste. Marie	OHL	67	28	36	64	64	6	1	3	4	4
	Adirondack	AHL	9	0	2	2	2	....	....	....	....	....
2013-14	Adirondack	AHL	71	14	7	21	42	....	....	....	....	....
2014-15	Lehigh Valley	AHL	35	3	4	7	57	....	....	....	....	....
	Reading Royals	ECHL	35	7	8	15	40	5	1	0	1	14

Signed as a free agent by **Philadelphia**, March 1, 2013.

ALM, Johan (AHLM, YOH-hahn) **NSH**

Defense. Shoots left. 6'3", 209 lbs. Born, Skelleftea, Sweden, January 28, 1992.

			Regular Season					Playoffs				
Season	Club	League	GP	G	A	Pts	PIM	GP	G	A	Pts	PIM
2007-08	Skelleftea U18	Swe-U18	20	0	2	2	16	....	....	....	....	....
	Skelleftea Jr.	Swe-Jr.	1	0	0	0	0	....	....	....	....	....
2008-09	Skelleftea AIK U18	Swe-U18	8	2	3	5	0	4	0	0	0	12
	Skelleftea AIK Jr.	Swe-Jr.	27	1	1	2	10	6	0	1	1	0
2009-10	Frolunda U18	Swe-U18	5	1	0	1	16	6	0	0	0	4
	Frolunda Jr.	Swe-Jr.	37	1	10	11	14	3	0	0	0	0
	Frolunda	Sweden	2	0	0	0	0	....	....	....	....	....
2010-11	Skelleftea AIK Jr.	Swe-Jr.	22	3	13	16	34	5	0	0	0	4
	Pitea HC	Sweden-3	1	0	0	0	2	....	....	....	....	....
	Skelleftea AIK	Sweden	13	0	1	1	6	3	0	0	0	0
2011-12	Skelleftea AIK Jr.	Swe-Jr.	10	2	2	4	6	....	....	....	....	....
	VIK Vasteras HK	Sweden-2	14	0	2	2	8	....	....	....	....	....
	Skelleftea AIK	Sweden	36	0	6	6	12	....	....	....	....	....
2012-13	Skelleftea AIK	Sweden	55	3	5	8	42	6	0	3	3	8
2013-14	Skelleftea AIK	Sweden	30	1	6	7	14	11	0	3	3	24
2014-15	Milwaukee	AHL	44	0	11	11	18	....	....	....	....	....

Signed as a free agent by **Nashville**, May 28, 2014.

AMADIO, Michael (uh-MA-dee-oh, MIGH-kuhl) **L.A.**

Center. Shoots right. 6'1", 192 lbs. Born, Sault Ste. Marie, ON, May 13, 1996.
(Los Angeles' 4th choice, 90th overall, in 2014 Entry Draft).

			Regular Season					Playoffs				
Season	Club	League	GP	G	A	Pts	PIM	GP	G	A	Pts	PIM
2010-11	Soo Greyhounds	Minor-ON	39	60	*74	*134	16	6	10	*9	19	2
2011-12	Soo North Stars	Minor-ON	29	32	30	62	12	11	5	9	14	6
2012-13	Brampton	OHL	63	6	13	19	8	5	0	0	0	0
2013-14	North Bay	OHL	64	12	26	38	14	22	4	5	9	2
2014-15	North Bay	OHL	68	24	47	71	18	15	6	9	15	4

AMOROSA, Terrance (a-moh-ROH-suh, TAIR-uhns) **PHI**

Defense. Shoots left. 6'1", 204 lbs. Born, Kirkland, QC, November 13, 1994.
(Philadelphia's 4th choice, 132nd overall, in 2013 Entry Draft).

			Regular Season					Playoffs				
Season	Club	League	GP	G	A	Pts	PIM	GP	G	A	Pts	PIM
2010-11	West Island Royals	Minor-QC	31	5	15	20	6	....	....	....	....	....
2011-12	Holderness School	High-NH	29	6	9	15	....	....	....	....	....	....
2012-13	Holderness School	High-NH	27	9	13	22	....	....	....	....	....	....
2013-14	Sioux City	USHL	50	2	13	15	10	6	0	0	0	2
2014-15	Clarkson Knights	ECAC	18	1	4	5	10	....	....	....	....	....

ANDERSEN, Niclas (AN-duhr-suhn, NIHK-luhs) **PIT**

Defense. Shoots left. 6'1", 207 lbs. Born, Grums, Sweden, April 28, 1988.
(Los Angeles' 6th choice, 114th overall, in 2006 Entry Draft).

			Regular Season					Playoffs				
Season	Club	League	GP	G	A	Pts	PIM	GP	G	A	Pts	PIM
2003-04	Grums IK	Sweden-3	30	4	5	9	45	....	....	....	....	....
2004-05	Leksands IF Jr.	Swe-Jr.	26	3	2	5	91	5	0	2	2	2
2005-06	Leksands IF U18	Swe-U18	3	0	3	3	8	2	0	0	0	10
	Leksands IF Jr.	Swe-Jr.	36	5	6	11	214	....	....	....	....	....
	Leksands IF	Sweden-Q	3	0	0	0	2	....	....	....	....	....
	Leksands IF	Sweden	8	0	0	0	8	....	....	....	....	....
2006-07	Leksands IF Jr.	Swe-Jr.	4	1	1	2	47	....	....	....	....	....
	Leksands IF	Sweden-2	35	0	5	5	38	....	....	....	....	....
2007-08	AIK IF Solna	Sweden-2	3	1	1	2	2	....	....	....	....	....
	Brynas IF Gavle Jr.	Swe-Jr.	5	0	1	1	35	....	....	....	....	....
	Brynas IF Gavle	Sweden	38	0	3	3	26	....	....	....	....	....
	Brynas IF Gavle	Sweden-Q	10	1	2	3	10	....	....	....	....	....
2008-09	Brynas IF Gavle	Sweden	55	0	8	8	60	4	0	0	0	4
2009-10	Brynas IF Gavle	Sweden	42	3	3	6	28	....	....	....	....	....
2010-11	Brynas IF Gavle	Sweden	51	4	4	8	42	5	0	0	0	0
2011-12	Brynas IF Gavle	Sweden	55	1	7	8	48	17	1	2	3	8
2012-13	Cherepovets	KHL	51	1	5	6	20	10	0	0	0	0
2013-14	Cherepovets	KHL	50	3	5	8	32	4	0	1	1	4
2014-15	Brynas IF Gavle	Sweden	54	5	17	22	32	4	0	0	0	4

Signed as a free agent by **Pittsburgh**, June 15, 2015.

ANDERSSON, Calle (AN-duhr-suhn, KAHL-leh) **NYR**

Defense. Shoots right. 6'2", 211 lbs. Born, Malmo, Sweden, May 16, 1994.
(NY Rangers' 3rd choice, 119th overall, in 2012 Entry Draft).

			Regular Season					Playoffs				
Season	Club	League	GP	G	A	Pts	PIM	GP	G	A	Pts	PIM
2009-10	Malmo U18	Swe-U18	29	1	2	3	34	....	....	....	....	....
2010-11	Malmo U18	Swe-U18	21	2	5	7	38	....	....	....	....	....
	Malmo Jr.	Swe-Jr.	25	2	4	6	24	....	....	....	....	....
2011-12	Farjestad U18	Swe-U18	10	3	6	9	0	1	0	1	1	2
	Farjestad Jr.	Swe-Jr.	49	12	24	36	56	6	2	3	5	2
2012-13	Malmo	Sweden-2	9	0	2	2	4	....	....	....	....	....
	Farjestad	Sweden	34	1	1	2	6	....	....	....	....	....
	Farjestad Jr.	Swe-Jr.	22	11	16	27	14	4	1	0	1	4
2013-14	Malmo Jr.	Swe-Jr.	8	4	1	5	26	2	0	0	0	0
	IK Pantern Malmo	Sweden-3	2	1	0	1	0	....	....	....	....	....
	Malmo	Sweden-2	49	3	10	13	10	....	....	....	....	....
2014-15	EV Zug	Swiss	18	1	2	3	6	....	....	....	....	....
	HC Lugano	Swiss	30	5	12	17	16	6	0	3	3	0

ANDERSSON, Peter (AN-duhr-suhn, PEE-tuhr) **VAN**

Defense. Shoots left. 6'3", 194 lbs. Born, Kvidinge, Sweden, April 13, 1991.
(Vancouver's 5th choice, 143rd overall, in 2009 Entry Draft).

			Regular Season					Playoffs				
Season	Club	League	GP	G	A	Pts	PIM	GP	G	A	Pts	PIM
2007-08	Frolunda U18	Swe-U18	12	2	3	5	18	5	0	1	1	14
	Frolunda Jr.	Swe-Jr.	8	0	2	2	4	1	0	0	0	0
	Frolunda	Sweden	1	0	0	0	0	....	....	....	....	....
2008-09	Frolunda U18	Swe-U18	5	0	1	1	4	5	1	1	2	2
	Frolunda Jr.	Swe-Jr.	36	3	5	8	42	4	0	1	1	0
2009-10	Frolunda Jr.	Swe-Jr.	1	1	0	1	0	....	....	....	....	....
	Frolunda	Sweden	21	1	4	5	4	....	....	....	....	....
	Boras HC	Sweden-2	10	2	4	6	12	....	....	....	....	....
2010-11	Frolunda	Sweden	27	0	0	0	8	....	....	....	....	....
	Boras HC	Sweden-2	30	2	2	4	24	....	....	....	....	....
	Frolunda Jr.	Swe-Jr.	....	....	....	....	....	7	1	3	4	2
2011-12	Orebro HK	Sweden-2	40	7	2	9	20	....	....	....	....	....
2012-13	Chicago Wolves	AHL	42	1	7	8	16	....	....	....	....	....
2013-14	Utica Comets	AHL	58	2	11	13	26	....	....	....	....	....
2014-15	Utica Comets	AHL	51	2	8	10	20	17	1	7	8	12

ANDERSSON, Rasmus (AN-duhr-suhn, RAZ-muhs) **CGY**

Defense. Shoots right. 6'2", 212 lbs. Born, Malmo, Sweden, October 27, 1996.
(Calgary's 1st choice, 53rd overall, in 2015 Entry Draft).

			Regular Season					Playoffs				
Season	Club	League	GP	G	A	Pts	PIM	GP	G	A	Pts	PIM
2010-11	Malmo U18	Swe-U18	17	0	1	1	22	....	....	....	....	....
2011-12	Malmo U18	Swe-U18	23	6	16	22	47	5	1	1	2	18
	Malmo Jr.	Swe-Jr.	13	0	3	3	6	3	0	0	0	0
2012-13	Malmo U18	Swe-U18	1	0	2	2	0	2	0	2	2	2
	Malmo Jr.	Swe-Jr.	8	5	1	6	48	1	0	0	0	2
	Malmo	Sweden-2	38	3	8	11	22	....	....	....	....	....
2013-14	Malmo Jr.	Swe-Jr.	8	1	4	5	12	....	....	....	....	....
	Malmo	Sweden-2	53	3	10	13	26	....	....	....	....	....
2014-15	Barrie Colts	OHL	67	12	52	64	88	9	1	3	4	6

OHL Second All-Star Team (2015)

ANDRONOV, Sergei (an-DROH-nahv, SAIR-gay) **ST.L.**

Right wing. Shoots left. 6'2", 190 lbs. Born, Penza, USSR, July 19, 1989.
(St. Louis' 3rd choice, 78th overall, in 2009 Entry Draft).

			Regular Season					Playoffs				
Season	Club	League	GP	G	A	Pts	PIM	GP	G	A	Pts	PIM
2006-07	Lada Togliatti	Russia	3	0	0	0	2	....	....	....	....	....
2007-08	Lada Togliatti 2	Russia-3	16	10	2	12	16	8	7	2	9	0
	Lada Togliatti	Russia	38	2	5	7	2	4	1	0	1	6
2008-09	Lada Togliatti 2	Russia-3	7	5	2	[illegible]	6	3	0	2	2	32
	Lada Togliatti	KHL	47	9	5	[illegible]	22	5	0	1	1	8
2009-10	Lada Togliatti	KHL	33	5	9	14	20	....	....	....	....	....
	CSKA Moscow	KHL	19	5	3	8	6	3	0	0	0	0
2010-11	CSKA Moscow	KHL	53	5	2	7	14	....	....	....	....	....
	CSKA Jr.	Russia-Jr.	7	3	2	5	29	16	6	5	11	4
2011-12	CSKA Moscow	KHL	29	1	3	4	4	5	1	0	1	0
2012-13	Peoria Rivermen	AHL	59	8	11	19	32	....	....	....	....	....
2013-14	Chicago Wolves	AHL	53	13	13	26	24	5	0	0	0	2
2014-15	CSKA Moscow	KHL	45	6	6	12	22	....	....	....	....	....

ANGELLO, Anthony (AN-gehl-oh, an-THUH-nee) **PIT**

Center. Shoots right. 6'4", 197 lbs. Born, Albany, NY, March 6, 1996.
(Pittsburgh's 3rd choice, 145th overall, in 2014 Entry Draft).

			Regular Season					Playoffs				
Season	Club	League	GP	G	A	Pts	PIM	GP	G	A	Pts	PIM
2011-12	Syracuse Jr. Stars	EmJHL	36	11	21	32	18	4	0	1	1	4
	Fayette.-Manlius	High-NY	18	32	31	63	....	1	1	2	3	....
2012-13	Syracuse Jr. Stars	EmJHL	40	31	29	60	60	3	1	3	4	2
	Fayette.-Manlius	High-NY	16	34	32	65	....	....	....	....	....	....
2013-14	Omaha Lancers	USHL	58	11	10	21	85	4	0	1	1	4
2014-15	Omaha Lancers	USHL	56	19	16	35	90	3	1	1	2	4

• Signed Letter of Intent to attend **Cornell University** (ECAC) in fall of 2015.

APPLETON, Mason (A-puhl-tuhn, MAY-suhn) **WPG**

Center. Shoots right. 6'2", 185 lbs. Born, Green Bay, WI, January 15, 1996.
(Winnipeg's 6th choice, 168th overall, in 2015 Entry Draft).

			Regular Season					Playoffs				
Season	Club	League	GP	G	A	Pts	PIM	GP	G	A	Pts	PIM
2010-11	Ashwaubenon	High-WI	23	15	23	38	12	3	2	5	7	0
2011-12	Notre Dame Acad.	High-WI	24	10	32	42	15	6	2	3	5	0
2012-13	Notre Dame Acad.	High-WI	23	15	21	36	19	5	5	4	9	0
2013-14	Team Wisconsin	UMHSEL	21	1	9	10	16	3	1	0	1	0
	Notre Dame Acad.	High-WI	23	26	34	60	6	5	4	6	10	14
2014-15	Tri-City Storm	USHL	54	12	28	40	84	7	4	4	8	12

• Signed Letter of Intent to attend **Michigan State University** (Big Ten) in fall of 2015.

ARCHIBALD, Josh (AHR-chih-bawld, JAWSH) **PIT**

Wing. Shoots right. 5'10", 176 lbs. Born, Regina, SK, October 6, 1992.
(Pittsburgh's 4th choice, 174th overall, in 2011 Entry Draft).

			Regular Season					Playoffs				
Season	Club	League	GP	G	A	Pts	PIM	GP	G	A	Pts	PIM
2009-10	Brainerd	High-MN	25	20	30	50	72	2	2	5	7	2
2010-11	Team North	UMHSEL	21	8	7	15	49	3	0	2	2	6
	Brainerd	High-MN	25	27	46	73	40	2	3	2	5	0
2011-12	Nebraska-Omaha	WCHA	36	10	5	15	33	....	....	....	....	....
2012-13	Nebraska-Omaha	WCHA	39	19	17	36	34	....	....	....	....	....
2013-14	Nebraska-Omaha	NCHC	37	*29	14	43	62	....	....	....	....	....
	Wilkes-Barre	AHL	7	1	0	1	13	2	1	0	1	0
2014-15	Wilkes-Barre	AHL	45	5	8	13	24	3	0	1	1	0
	Wheeling Nailers	ECHL	9	7	4	11	4	....	....	....	....	....

NCHC First All-Star Team (2014) • NCHC Player of the Year (2014) • NCAA West First All-American Team (2014)

ARNESSON, Linus (AHR-neh-suhn, LEE-nuhs) **BOS**

Defense. Shoots left. 6'1", 198 lbs. Born, Stockholm, Sweden, September 21, 1994.
(Boston's 1st choice, 60th overall, in 2013 Entry Draft).

			Regular Season					Playoffs				
Season	Club	League	GP	G	A	Pts	PIM	GP	G	A	Pts	PIM
2009-10	Djurgarden U18	Swe-U18	22	2	6	8	14	....	....	....	....	....
2010-11	Djurgarden U18	Swe-U18	21	2	6	8	12	5	1	1	2	0
	Djurgarden Jr.	Swe-Jr.	8	0	0	0	2	....	....	....	....	....
2011-12	Djurgarden U18	Swe-U18	9	0	3	3	8	4	0	2	2	2
	Djurgarden Jr.	Swe-Jr.	40	2	13	15	20	3	0	1	1	2
	Djurgarden	Sweden	3	0	0	0	0	....	....	....	....	....
2012-13	Djurgarden Jr.	Swe-Jr.	13	1	3	4	22	1	0	0	0	0
	Djurgarden	Sweden-2	35	0	1	1	8	....	....	....	....	....
2013-14	Djurgarden	Sweden-2	50	1	5	6	38	....	....	....	....	....
2014-15	Djurgarden	Sweden	41	0	5	5	28	2	0	0	0	0
	Providence Bruins	AHL	11	1	3	4	6	....	....	....	....	....

ARONSON, Taylor (AIR-uhn-suhn, TAY-luhr) **NSH**

Defense. Shoots right. 6'1", 205 lbs. Born, Placentia, CA, December 30, 1991.
(Nashville's 2nd choice, 78th overall, in 2010 Entry Draft).

			Regular Season					Playoffs				
Season	Club	League	GP	G	A	Pts	PIM	GP	G	A	Pts	PIM
2008-09	L.A. Jr. Kings	T1EHL	45	9	16	25	68	....	....	....	....	....
2009-10	Portland	WHL	71	5	25	30	65	11	2	7	9	13
2010-11	Portland	WHL	71	5	32	37	81	21	0	2	2	20
2011-12	Milwaukee	AHL	14	0	1	1	8	....	....	....	....	....
	Cincinnati	ECHL	40	6	12	18	49	....	....	....	....	....
2012-13	Milwaukee	AHL	12	0	2	2	4	....	....	....	....	....
	Cincinnati	ECHL	38	1	12	13	12	2	0	0	0	0
2013-14	Cincinnati	ECHL	65	6	32	38	57	24	0	7	7	18
2014-15	Milwaukee	AHL	73	3	29	32	27	....	....	....	....	....

ATHANASIOU, Andreas (ath-an-AYZH-yew, an–DRAY-uhs) **DET**

Center/Left wing. Shoots left. 6'2", 192 lbs. Born, London, ON, August 6, 1994.
(Detroit's 3rd choice, 110th overall, in 2012 Entry Draft).

			Regular Season					Playoffs				
Season	Club	League	GP	G	A	Pts	PIM	GP	G	A	Pts	PIM
2009-10	Toronto Titans	GTHL	56	24	34	58	32	....	....	....	....	....
2010-11	London Knights	OHL	57	11	11	22	21	6	0	0	0	0
2011-12	London Knights	OHL	63	22	15	37	22	11	1	4	5	0
2012-13	Barrie Colts	OHL	66	29	38	67	30	22	12	13	25	11
2013-14	Barrie Colts	OHL	66	49	46	95	52	11	3	9	12	2
	Grand Rapids	AHL	2	1	2	3	0	6	0	1	1	6
2014-15	Grand Rapids	AHL	55	16	16	32	25	16	5	4	9	6

ATYUSHOV, Vitali (a-tew-SHAWF, vih-TAL-ee) **OTT**

Defense. Shoots left. 6'1", 205 lbs. Born, Penza, USSR, July 4, 1979.
(Ottawa's 8th choice, 276th overall, in 2002 Entry Draft).

			Regular Season					Playoffs				
Season	Club	League	GP	G	A	Pts	PIM	GP	G	A	Pts	PIM
1997-98	Krylja Sovetov	Russia	4	0	0	0	2	....	....	....	....	....
1998-99	Dizelist Penza 2	Russia-4	2	1	1	2	2	....	....	....	....	....
	Dizelist Penza	Russia-2	22	0	0	0	22	....	....	....	....	....
	Krylja Sovetov	Russia	17	1	0	1	20	....	....	....	....	....
	Krylja Sovetov	Russia-Q	21	0	5	5	50	....	....	....	....	....
99-2000	Perm	Russia	38	4	0	4	50	3	0	0	0	12
2000-01	Perm	Russia	44	3	9	12	32	....	....	....	....	....
2001-02	Perm	Russia	51	4	8	12	66	....	....	....	....	....
2002-03	Ak Bars Kazan	Russia	33	0	9	9	12	2	0	0	0	0
2003-04	Magnitogorsk	Russia	56	5	9	14	26	14	2	3	5	6
2004-05	Magnitogorsk	Russia	58	6	18	24	42	5	2	0	2	0
2005-06	Magnitogorsk	Russia	51	7	12	19	64	11	2	0	2	4
2006-07	Magnitogorsk	Russia	54	7	20	27	46	15	3	9	12	10
2007-08	Magnitogorsk	Russia	56	10	33	43	32	10	1	4	5	2
2008-09	Magnitogorsk	KHL	55	8	27	35	34	12	1	6	7	8
2009-10	Magnitogorsk	KHL	49	5	17	22	45	10	1	3	4	6
2010-11	Magnitogorsk	KHL	46	6	14	20	36	20	0	7	7	16
2011-12	Ufa	KHL	49	4	14	18	26	6	0	3	3	4
2012-13	Ufa	KHL	40	0	13	13	20	14	1	3	4	0
2013-14	Mytischi	KHL	40	0	7	7	18	3	0	0	0	0
2014-15	Chelyabinsk	KHL	53	1	8	9	26	6	0	1	1	4

AUBE-KUBEL, Nicolas (oh-BAY-koo-BEHL, NIH-koh-las) **PHI**

Right wing. Shoots right. 5'11", 200 lbs. Born, Slave Lake, AB, May 10, 1996.
(Philadelphia's 2nd choice, 48th overall, in 2014 Entry Draft).

			Regular Season					Playoffs				
Season	Club	League	GP	G	A	Pts	PIM	GP	G	A	Pts	PIM
2009-10	Mortagne	Minor-QC	34	12	20	32	12	....	....	....	....	....
2010-11	Mortagne	Minor-QC	22	10	3	13	6	....	....	....	....	....
2011-12	Antoine-Girouard	QAAA	41	11	13	24	36	11	7	9	16	12
2012-13	Val-d'Or Foreurs	QMJHL	64	10	17	27	26	10	1	0	1	8
2013-14	Val-d'Or Foreurs	QMJHL	65	22	31	53	61	24	4	9	13	20
2014-15	Val-d'Or Foreurs	QMJHL	61	38	42	80	81	17	5	10	15	22

AUBRY, Louis-Marc (AW-bree, LOO-ee-MAHRK) **DET**

Center. Shoots left. 6'4", 208 lbs. Born, Arthabaska, QC, November 11, 1991.
(Detroit's 3rd choice, 81st overall, in 2010 Entry Draft).

			Regular Season					Playoffs				
Season	Club	League	GP	G	A	Pts	PIM	GP	G	A	Pts	PIM
2007-08	Trois-Rivieres	QAAA	20	9	20	29	30	7	1	1	2	20
2008-09	Montreal	QMJHL	65	10	12	22	53	10	2	2	4	8
2009-10	Montreal	QMJHL	66	15	18	33	69	7	1	1	2	6
2010-11	Montreal	QMJHL	35	13	12	25	26	10	5	1	6	2
2011-12	Grand Rapids	AHL	62	5	11	16	39	....	....	....	....	....
2012-13	Grand Rapids	AHL	64	4	8	12	60	14	0	1	1	0
2013-14	Grand Rapids	AHL	38	2	2	4	16	....	....	....	....	....
	Toledo Walleye	ECHL	18	7	8	15	10	....	....	....	....	....
2014-15	Grand Rapids	AHL	67	5	11	16	52	16	3	0	3	16

AUDETTE, Daniel (AW-deht, DAN-yehl) **MTL**

Center. Shoots left. 5'8", 176 lbs. Born, Buffalo, NY, May 6, 1996.
(Montreal's 4th choice, 147th overall, in 2014 Entry Draft).

			Regular Season					Playoffs				
Season	Club	League	GP	G	A	Pts	PIM	GP	G	A	Pts	PIM
2009-10	Laurentides	Minor-QC	28	19	30	49	20	6	4	2	6	6
2010-11	Laurentides	Minor-QC	21	18	14	32	34	....	....	....	....	....
	Esther-Blondin	QAAA	4	0	0	0	6	2	0	0	0	0
2011-12	Esther-Blondin	QAAA	39	25	35	60	57	13	7	16	23	20
2012-13	Sherbrooke	QMJHL	54	10	19	29	65	4	0	2	2	6
2013-14	Sherbrooke	QMJHL	68	21	55	76	79	....	....	....	....	....
2014-15	Sherbrooke	QMJHL	60	29	44	73	64	6	2	4	6	0

AUGER, Justin (AW-guhr, JUHS-tihn) **L.A.**

Right wing. Shoots right. 6'7", 227 lbs. Born, Kitchener, ON, May 14, 1994.
(Los Angeles' 2nd choice, 103rd overall, in 2013 Entry Draft).

			Regular Season					Playoffs				
Season	Club	League	GP	G	A	Pts	PIM	GP	G	A	Pts	PIM
2009-10	Waterloo Wolves	Minor-ON	30	20	11	31	16	14	5	6	11	6
	Waterloo Wolves	Other	20	10	11	21	6	....	....	....	....	....
2010-11	Waterloo Siskins	ON-Jr.B	42	22	15	37	57	4	2	5	7	2
2011-12	Guelph Storm	OHL	58	7	7	14	39	6	0	0	0	0
2012-13	Guelph Storm	OHL	68	16	17	33	39	5	0	0	0	0
2013-14	Guelph Storm	OHL	53	11	12	23	61	20	2	5	7	15
2014-15	Manchester	AHL	70	13	16	29	59	19	1	1	2	8

AUSMUS, Gage (AWZ-muhs, GAYJ) **S.J.**

Defense. Shoots left. 6'1", 210 lbs. Born, Billings, MT, April 22, 1995.
(San Jose's 5th choice, 151st overall, in 2013 Entry Draft).

			Regular Season					Playoffs				
Season	Club	League	GP	G	A	Pts	PIM	GP	G	A	Pts	PIM
2010-11	Team Great Plains	UMHSEL	14	2	0	2	10	1	0	0	0	0
	E. Grand Forks	High-MN	15	3	8	11	10	2	1	0	1	0
2011-12	USNTDP	USHL	36	2	3	5	42	1	0	0	0	0
	USNTDP	U-17	17	0	1	1	18	....	....	....	....	....
2012-13	USNTDP	USHL	26	2	5	7	20	....	....	....	....	....
	USNTDP	U-18	40	0	7	7	34	....	....	....	....	....
2013-14	North Dakota	NCHC	21	2	1	3	13	....	....	....	....	....
2014-15	North Dakota	NCHC	42	2	4	6	36	....	....	....	....	....

AUSTIN, Brady (AWZ-tihn, BRAY-dee) **BUF**

Defense. Shoots left. 6'4", 242 lbs. Born, Bobcaygeon, ON, June 16, 1993.
(Buffalo's 7th choice, 193rd overall, in 2012 Entry Draft).

			Regular Season					Playoffs				
Season	Club	League	GP	G	A	Pts	PIM	GP	G	A	Pts	PIM
2008-09	Cent. Ont. Wolves	Minor-ON	60	25	27	52	72	....	....	....	....	....
2009-10	Erie Otters	OHL	64	5	10	15	24	4	0	0	0	0
2010-11	Erie Otters	OHL	59	1	12	13	47	7	0	0	0	0
2011-12	Belleville Bulls	OHL	68	6	20	26	59	6	1	0	1	0
2012-13	Belleville Bulls	OHL	64	8	15	23	22	17	0	5	5	6
2013-14	Belleville Bulls	OHL	7	1	4	5	6	....	....	....	....	....
	London Knights	OHL	60	8	20	28	36	4	1	2	3	2
2014-15	Rochester	AHL	66	1	9	10	31	....	....	....	....	....
	Elmira Jackals	ECHL	1	0	0	0	0	....	....	....	....	....

BACHMAN, Karch (BAHK-muhn, KAHRCH) **FLA**

Left wing. Shoots left. 5'11", 175 lbs. Born, Fort Wayne, IN, March 10, 1997.
(Florida's 5th choice, 132nd overall, in 2015 Entry Draft).

			Regular Season					Playoffs				
Season	Club	League	GP	G	A	Pts	PIM	GP	G	A	Pts	PIM
2012-13	Culver Academy	High-IN	25	14	14	28	10	....	....	....	....	....
2013-14	Culver Academy	High-IN	41	36	15	51	28	....	....	....	....	....
	Tri-City Storm	USHL	2	0	0	0	0	....	....	....	....	....
2014-15	Culver Academy	High-IN	32	19	24	43	10	....	....	....	....	....
	USNTDP	U-18	2	0	0	0	0	....	....	....	....	....
	Tri-City Storm	USHL	2	0	0	0	0	....	....	....	....	....

• Signed Letter of Intent to attend **University of Miami** (NCHC) in fall of 2016.

BACKMAN, Mattias (BAK-man, mah-TIGH-uhs) **DAL**

Defense. Shoots left. 6'2", 169 lbs. Born, Linkoping, Sweden, October 3, 1992.
(Detroit's 7th choice, 146th overall, in 2011 Entry Draft).

			Regular Season					Playoffs				
Season	Club	League	GP	G	A	Pts	PIM	GP	G	A	Pts	PIM
2007-08	Linkopings HC U18	Swe-U18	21	0	2	2	14	....	....	....	....	....
2008-09	Linkopings HC U18	Swe-U18	30	5	8	13	16	1	0	1	1	0
	Linkopings HC Jr.	Swe-Jr.	2	0	0	0	2	....	....	....	....	....
2009-10	Linkopings HC U18	Swe-U18	2	2	1	3	4	3	0	0	0	2
	Linkopings HC	Sweden	5	0	0	0	2	....	....	....	....	....
	Linkopings HC Jr.	Swe-Jr.	33	4	5	9	38	6	1	0	1	10
	Linkopings HC	Sweden	5	0	0	0	2	....	....	....	....	....
2010-11	Linkopings HC Jr.	Swe-Jr.	27	2	18	20	34	3	0	2	2	4
	Linkopings HC	Sweden	6	0	0	0	4	....	....	....	....	....
	Mjolby HC	Sweden-3	2	1	2	3	2	....	....	....	....	....
2011-12	Linkopings HC	Sweden	42	1	7	8	14	....	....	....	....	....
	Linkopings HC Jr.	Swe-Jr.	6	1	1	2	0	6	2	6	8	4
2012-13	Linkopings HC	Sweden	52	2	24	26	34	10	2	4	6	4
2013-14	Linkopings HC	Sweden	54	6	15	21	16	13	0	7	7	6
	Grand Rapids	AHL	2	0	0	0	0	10	1	5	6	2
2014-15	Grand Rapids	AHL	18	0	4	4	6	....	....	....	....	....
	Linkopings HC	Sweden	25	4	13	17	4	9	0	3	3	6
	Texas Stars	AHL	1	0	0	0	0	2	0	1	1	0

Signed as a free agent by **Linkoping** (Sweden), December 24, 2014. Traded to **Dallas** by **Detroit** with Mattias Janmark and Detroit's 2nd round choice (Roope Hintz) in 2015 Entry Draft for Erik Cole and Dallas' 3rd round choice (Vili Saarijarvi) in 2015 Entry Draft, March 1, 2015.

BACKMAN, Sean (BAK-man, SHAWN)

Right wing. Shoots right. 5'9", 170 lbs. Born, Cos Cob, CT, April 29, 1986.

			Regular Season					Playoffs				
Season	Club	League	GP	G	A	Pts	PIM	GP	G	A	Pts	PIM
2002-03	Avon Old Farms	High-CT	25	9	14	23	....	....	....	....	....	....
2003-04	Avon Old Farms	High-CT	28	15	14	29	....	....	....	....	....	....
2004-05	Avon Old Farms	High-CT	27	15	10	25	....	....	....	....	....	....
2005-06	Green Bay	USHL	57	29	27	56	30	....	....	....	....	....
2006-07	Yale	ECAC	29	18	13	31	38	....	....	....	....	....
2007-08	Yale	ECAC	32	18	9	27	16	....	....	....	....	....
2008-09	Yale	ECAC	32	20	13	33	44	....	....	....	....	....
2009-10	Yale	ECAC	29	21	14	35	12	....	....	....	....	....
2010-11	Texas Stars	AHL	67	7	16	23	20	6	0	0	0	6
	Idaho Steelheads	ECHL	5	2	2	4	4	....	....	....	....	....
2011-12	Bridgeport	AHL	66	7	11	18	20	3	0	0	0	0
2012-13	Bridgeport	AHL	67	11	10	21	40	....	....	....	....	....
2013-14	Manchester	AHL	71	10	16	26	24	4	1	0	1	0
2014-15	Manchester	AHL	76	19	25	44	34	19	5	12	17	8

ECAC Second All-Star Team (2009) • ECAC First All-Star Team (2010) • NCAA East Second All-American Team (2010)

Signed as a free agent by **Dallas**, March 30, 2010. Signed as a free agent by **NY Islanders**, August 8, 2011. Signed as a free agent by **Manchester** (AHL), August 21, 2013.

BADDOCK, Brandon (BA-dawk, BRAN-duhn) **N.J.**

Left wing. Shoots left. 6'4", 210 lbs. Born, Vermilion, AB, March 29, 1995.
(New Jersey's 6th choice, 161st overall, in 2014 Entry Draft).

			Regular Season					Playoffs				
Season	Club	League	GP	G	A	Pts	PIM	GP	G	A	Pts	PIM
2008-09	Wainwright	Minor-AB	27	16	11	27	18	....	....	....	....	....
2009-10	Lloydminster Heat	AMBHL	33	11	10	21	22	....	....	....	....	....
2010-11	Lloydminster Rage	Minor-AB	38	27	23	50	116	....	....	....	....	....
2011-12	Lloydminster	AJHL	41	2	1	3	91	1	0	0	0	0
	Edmonton	WHL	1	0	0	0	0	....	....	....	....	....
2012-13	Edmonton	WHL	59	7	4	11	73	22	0	1	1	12
2013-14	Edmonton	WHL	56	6	11	17	128	13	1	0	1	6
2014-15	Edmonton	WHL	71	19	21	40	136	5	1	0	1	10

BAILEY, Justin (BAY-lee, JUHS-tihn) BUF

Right wing. Shoots right. 6'3", 207 lbs. Born, Buffalo, NY, July 1, 1995.
(Buffalo's 5th choice, 52nd overall, in 2013 Entry Draft).

			Regular Season					Playoffs				
Season	Club	League	GP	G	A	Pts	PIM	GP	G	A	Pts	PIM
2010-11	Buffalo Regals	T1EHL	12	4	1	5	0	....	....	....	....	....
	Buffalo Regals	Minor-NY	10	5	12	17	12	....	....	....	....	....
2011-12	Long Island Royals	AYHL	22	21	13	34	52	....	....	....	....	....
	Indiana Ice	USHL	2	1	0	1	0	....	....	....	....	....
2012-13	Kitchener Rangers	OHL	57	17	19	36	34	10	1	2	3	4
2013-14	Kitchener Rangers	OHL	54	25	18	43	20	....	....	....	....	....
2014-15	Kitchener Rangers	OHL	35	22	19	41	32	....	....	....	....	....
	Sault Ste. Marie	OHL	22	12	16	28	12	14	7	7	14	6

BAILEY, Matt (BAY-lee, MAT) ANA

Right wing. Shoots left. 6'1", 197 lbs. Born, Winnipeg, MB, April 5, 1991.

			Regular Season					Playoffs				
Season	Club	League	GP	G	A	Pts	PIM	GP	G	A	Pts	PIM
2006-07	Eastman Selects	MMHL	32	8	9	17	26	....	....	....	....	....
2007-08	Neepawa Natives	MJHL	56	13	15	28	63	....	....	....	....	....
2008-09	Tri-City Storm	USHL	58	10	14	24	49	....	....	....	....	....
2009-10	Sioux Falls	USHL	59	14	33	47	69	3	2	0	2	2
2010-11	Alaska-Anchorage	WCHA	30	10	10	20	23	....	....	....	....	....
2011-12	Alaska-Anchorage	WCHA	34	10	7	17	30	....	....	....	....	....
2012-13	Alaska-Anchorage	WCHA	36	7	12	19	65	....	....	....	....	....
2013-14	Alaska-Anchorage	WCHA	38	20	18	38	49	....	....	....	....	....
	Norfolk Admirals	AHL	11	2	1	3	8	10	0	2	2	10
2014-15	Norfolk Admirals	AHL	56	6	4	10	31	....	....	....	....	....

WCHA First All-Star Team (2014)

Signed as a free agent by **Anaheim**, March 25, 2014.

BAILLARGEON, Robert (ba-LAIR-zhee-awn, RAW-buhrt) OTT

Center. Shoots right. 6', 177 lbs. Born, Springfield, MA, November 26, 1993.
(Ottawa's 5th choice, 136th overall, in 2012 Entry Draft).

			Regular Season					Playoffs				
Season	Club	League	GP	G	A	Pts	PIM	GP	G	A	Pts	PIM
2009-10	Cushing	High-MA	32	15	30	45	....	....	....	....	....	....
2010-11	Cushing	High-MA	32	30	34	64	....	....	....	....	....	....
2011-12	Indiana Ice	USHL	54	14	34	48	36	6	4	2	6	2
2012-13	Indiana Ice	USHL	25	6	9	15	30	....	....	....	....	....
	Omaha Lancers	USHL	30	12	14	26	18	....	....	....	....	....
2013-14	Boston University	H-East	35	10	17	27	20	....	....	....	....	....
2014-15	Boston University	H-East	30	3	13	16	14	....	....	....	....	....

BALCERS, Rudolfs (BAHL-suhrs, ROO-dawlfs) S.J.

Left wing. Shoots left. 5'11", 165 lbs. Born, Liepaja, Latvia, April 8, 1997.
(San Jose's 6th choice, 142nd overall, in 2015 Entry Draft).

			Regular Season					Playoffs				
Season	Club	League	GP	G	A	Pts	PIM	GP	G	A	Pts	PIM
2012-13	Lorenskog IK U18	Nor-U18	26	20	17	37	26	2	3	1	4	2
	Lorenskog IK Jr.	Norway-Jr.	2	1	1	2	0	4	0	1	1	0
2013-14	Viking U18	Nor-U18	22	35	23	58	20	3	3	2	5	0
	Viking	Norway-2	10	6	3	9	4	....	....	....	....	....
	Stavanger Oilers	Norway	2	0	1	1	0	....	....	....	....	....
2014-15	Stavanger Jr.	Norway-Jr.	7	6	3	9	2	12	14	9	23	14
	Stavanger Oilers	Norway	36	8	13	21	8	....	....	....	....	....
	Stavanger U18	Nor-U18	....	....	....	....	....	1	0	0	0	0

BALISY, Chase (BAL-ih-see, CHAYS) FLA

Center. Shoots left. 5'11", 179 lbs. Born, Fullerton, CA, February 2, 1992.
(Nashville's 6th choice, 170th overall, in 2011 Entry Draft).

			Regular Season					Playoffs				
Season	Club	League	GP	G	A	Pts	PIM	GP	G	A	Pts	PIM
2007-08	Tor. Jr. Canadiens	GTHL	80	40	110	150	....	....	....	....	....	....
2008-09	USNTDP	NAHL	42	8	14	22	8	9	0	3	3	0
	USNTDP	U-17	16	4	10	14	6	....	....	....	....	....
2009-10	USNTDP	U-17	2	0	1	1	2	....	....	....	....	....
	USNTDP	USHL	28	5	6	11	8	....	....	....	....	....
	USNTDP	U-18	35	4	10	14	6	....	....	....	....	....
2010-11	Western Mich.	CCHA	42	12	18	30	12	....	....	....	....	....
2011-12	Western Mich.	CCHA	41	13	24	37	35	....	....	....	....	....
2012-13	Western Mich.	CCHA	38	11	14	25	12	....	....	....	....	....
2013-14	Western Mich.	NCHC	40	13	24	37	14	....	....	....	....	....
2014-15	St. John's IceCaps	AHL	73	21	23	44	30	....	....	....	....	....

CCHA All-Rookie Team (2011) • NCHC Second All-Star Team (2014)

Signed as a free agent by **Florida**, June 1, 2015.

BAPTISTE, Nicholas (Bap-TEEST, NIH-koh-las) BUF

Right wing. Shoots right. 6'1", 199 lbs. Born, Ottawa, ON, August 4, 1995.
(Buffalo's 6th choice, 69th overall, in 2013 Entry Draft).

			Regular Season					Playoffs				
Season	Club	League	GP	G	A	Pts	PIM	GP	G	A	Pts	PIM
2010-11	Ott. Senators MM	Minor-ON	24	22	33	55	26	....	....	....	....	....
	Ott. Senators M.M.	Other	18	17	15	32	12	....	....	....	....	....
	Cumberland	ON-Jr.A	2	1	0	1	0	....	....	....	....	....
2011-12	Sudbury Wolves	OHL	64	8	19	27	42	4	0	0	0	2
2012-13	Sudbury Wolves	OHL	66	21	27	48	44	9	3	1	4	6
2013-14	Sudbury Wolves	OHL	65	45	44	89	59	5	1	4	5	8
2014-15	Sudbury Wolves	OHL	12	6	5	11	8	....	....	....	....	....
	Erie Otters	OHL	41	26	27	53	18	20	12	11	23	10

BARBASHEV, Ivan (bahr-BUH-shawv, ee-VAHN) ST.L.

Center. Shoots left. 6', 180 lbs. Born, Moscow, Russia, December 14, 1995.
(St. Louis' 2nd choice, 33rd overall, in 2014 Entry Draft).

			Regular Season					Playoffs				
Season	Club	League	GP	G	A	Pts	PIM	GP	G	A	Pts	PIM
2011-12	Dyn'o Moscow Jr.	Russia-Jr.	38	8	2	10	18	4	2	2	4	25
2012-13	Moncton Wildcats	QMJHL	68	18	44	62	36	5	1	2	3	0
2013-14	Moncton Wildcats	QMJHL	48	25	43	68	27	6	4	6	10	8
2014-15	Moncton Wildcats	QMJHL	57	45	50	95	59	16	13	11	24	14

QMJHL All-Rookie Team (2013)

BARBER, Riley (BAHR-buhr, RIGH-lee) WSH

Right wing. Shoots right. 6', 194 lbs. Born, Livonia, MI, February 7, 1994.
(Washington's 7th choice, 167th overall, in 2012 Entry Draft).

			Regular Season					Playoffs				
Season	Club	League	GP	G	A	Pts	PIM	GP	G	A	Pts	PIM
2009-10	Det. Compuware	T1EHL	38	16	22	38	28	5	2	3	5	0
	Det. Compuware	Other	6	1	4	5	8	....	....	....	....	....
2010-11	Dubuque	USHL	57	14	14	28	48	11	2	0	2	6
2011-12	USNTDP	USHL	24	5	6	11	59	....	....	....	....	....
	USNTDP	U-18	36	16	9	25	26	....	....	....	....	....
2012-13	Miami U.	CCHA	40	15	24	39	22	....	....	....	....	....
2013-14	Miami U.	NCHC	38	19	25	44	28	....	....	....	....	....
2014-15	Miami U.	NCHC	38	20	20	40	12	....	....	....	....	....

CCHA All-Rookie Team (2013) • CCHA Rookie of the Year (2013) • CCHA First All-Star Team (2013) • NCHC Second All-Star Team (2014)

BARDREAU, Cole (BAHR-droh, KOHL) PHI

Forward. Shoots right. 5'10", 193 lbs. Born, Fairport, NY, July 22, 1993.

			Regular Season					Playoffs				
Season	Club	League	GP	G	A	Pts	PIM	GP	G	A	Pts	PIM
2008-09	Rochester Alliance	Minor-NY	35	28	48	76	....	....	....	....	....	....
	Fairport	High-NY	16	16	16	32	....	....	....	....	....	....
2009-10	USNTDP	USHL	35	4	8	12	25	....	....	....	....	....
	USNTDP	U-17	18	4	0	4	36	....	....	....	....	....
2010-11	USNTDP	USHL	24	4	7	11	23	....	....	....	....	....
	USNTDP	U-18	36	7	8	15	22	....	....	....	....	....
2011-12	Cornell Big Red	ECAC	34	4	4	8	18	....	....	....	....	....
2012-13	Cornell Big Red	ECAC	13	2	5	7	12	....	....	....	....	....
2013-14	Cornell Big Red	ECAC	26	7	9	16	14	....	....	....	....	....
2014-15	Cornell Big Red	ECAC	30	5	17	22	38	....	....	....	....	....
	Lehigh Valley	AHL	15	1	1	2	2	....	....	....	....	....

Signed as a free agent by **Philadelphia**, March 12, 2015.

BARZAL, Mathew (BAHR-zahl, MA-thew) NYI

Center. Shoots right. 6', 178 lbs. Born, Coquitlam, BC, May 26, 1997.
(NY Islanders' 1st choice, 16th overall, in 2015 Entry Draft).

			Regular Season					Playoffs				
Season	Club	League	GP	G	A	Pts	PIM	GP	G	A	Pts	PIM
2011-12	Burnaby W.C.	Minor-BC	51	55	98	153	....	....	....	....	....	....
2012-13	Van. NE Chiefs	BCMML	34	29	*74	*103	34	3	3	3	6	8
2013-14	Seattle	WHL	59	14	40	54	20	9	1	5	6	4
2014-15	Seattle	WHL	44	12	45	57	20	6	4	4	8	4

BASHKIROV, Ruslan (bash-KIHR-ahv, roos-LAHN) OTT

Left wing. Shoots left. 5'11", 193 lbs. Born, Moscow, USSR, March 7, 1989.
(Ottawa's 2nd choice, 60th overall, in 2007 Entry Draft).

			Regular Season					Playoffs				
Season	Club	League	GP	G	A	Pts	PIM	GP	G	A	Pts	PIM
2005-06	Spartak Moscow 2	Russia-3	35	16	9	25	44	....	....	....	....	....
2006-07	Quebec Remparts	QMJHL	64	30	37	67	117	5	1	3	4	6
2007-08	Mytischi	Russia	4	0	0	0	0	....	....	....	....	....
	Kristall Elektrostal	Russia-2	12	4	0	4	22	....	....	....	....	....
2008-09	Lada Togliatti	KHL	2	0	0	0	2	....	....	....	....	....
	Rys Podolsk	Russia-2	48	9	8	17	20	3	1	3	4	2
2009-10	Perm	Russia-2	37	10	8	18	12	10	2	3	5	4
2010-11	Perm	Russia-2	8	1	0	1	2	....	....	....	....	....
	HK Ryazan	Russia-2	28	8	10	18	18	3	0	0	0	12
2011-12	HK Ryazan	Russia-2	20	5	5	10	14	....	....	....	....	....
2012-13	HK Ryazan	Russia-2	17	7	1	8	4	....	....	....	....	....
2013-14	HK Ryazan	Russia-2	48	19	27	46	16	....	....	....	....	....
2014-15	Amur Khabarovsk	KHL	46	6	4	10	41	....	....	....	....	....

BEACH, Cody (BEECH, KOH-dee) ST.L.

Right wing. Shoots right. 6'5", 190 lbs. Born, Nanaimo, BC, August 8, 1992.
(St. Louis' 6th choice, 134th overall, in 2010 Entry Draft).

			Regular Season					Playoffs				
Season	Club	League	GP	G	A	Pts	PIM	GP	G	A	Pts	PIM
2007-08	Okanagan Rockets	BCMML	37	8	17	25	68	6	1	3	4	16
2008-09	Calgary Hitmen	WHL	3	0	0	0	2	....	....	....	....	....
	Okanagan Rockets	BCMML	23	10	13	23	58	2	1	0	1	2
2009-10	Calgary Hitmen	WHL	51	3	11	14	157	19	1	7	8	34
2010-11	Calgary Hitmen	WHL	17	5	10	15	73	....	....	....	....	....
	Moose Jaw	WHL	40	6	28	34	163	....	....	....	....	....
2011-12	Moose Jaw	WHL	58	15	41	56	*229	13	4	6	10	29
2012-13	Peoria Rivermen	AHL	23	2	5	7	71	....	....	....	....	....
	Evansville IceMen	ECHL	24	2	7	9	81	....	....	....	....	....
2013-14	Chicago Wolves	AHL	34	5	6	11	109	....	....	....	....	....
	Kalamazoo Wings	ECHL	7	2	1	3	14	....	....	....	....	....
2014-15	Chicago Wolves	AHL	41	2	7	9	210	4	0	0	0	6
	Alaska Aces	ECHL	6	0	0	0	26	....	....	....	....	....

BEAR, Ethan (BAIR, EE-thuhn) EDM

Defense. Shoots right. 5'11", 200 lbs. Born, Regina, SK, June 26, 1997.
(Edmonton's 3rd choice, 124th overall, in 2015 Entry Draft).

			Regular Season					Playoffs				
Season	Club	League	GP	G	A	Pts	PIM	GP	G	A	Pts	PIM
2012-13	Yorkton Harvest	SMHL	38	7	28	35	30	5	1	1	2	0
	Seattle	WHL	1	0	0	0	0	....	....	....	....	....
2013-14	Seattle	WHL	58	6	13	19	18	9	2	2	4	6
2014-15	Seattle	WHL	69	13	25	38	23	6	1	2	3	0

BEATTIE, Matthew (BAY-tee, MA-thew) VAN

Left wing. Shoots right. 6'3", 173 lbs. Born, Morristown, NJ, December 14, 1992.
(Vancouver's 5th choice, 207th overall, in 2012 Entry Draft).

			Regular Season					Playoffs				
Season	Club	League	GP	G	A	Pts	PIM	GP	G	A	Pts	PIM
2008-09	N.J. Rockets	AYHL	29	4	7	11	12	....	....	....	....	....
2009-10	Pingry Big Blue	High-NJ	25	33	34	67	10	....	....	....	....	....
	N.J. Renegades	MtJHL	38	4	10	14	60	4	2	0	2	0
2010-11	Pingry Big Blue	High-NJ	25	40	54	94	10	....	....	....	....	....
	N.J. Jr. Titans	MtJHL	38	23	24	47	34	2	2	0	2	0
2011-12	Exeter	High-NH	28	39	34	73	18	....	....	....	....	....
2012-13	Yale	ECAC	15	0	0	0	8	....	....	....	....	....
2013-14	Yale	ECAC	22	4	2	6	17	....	....	....	....	....
2014-15	Yale	ECAC	16	0	3	3	4	....	....	....	....	....

BEAUDIN, Jean-Christophe (boh-DEHN, SHAWN-krihs-TAWF) COL

Center. Shoots right. 6'1", 181 lbs. Born, Longueuil, QC, March 25, 1997.
(Colorado's 4th choice, 71st overall, in 2015 Entry Draft).

			Regular Season					Playoffs				
Season	Club	League	GP	G	A	Pts	PIM	GP	G	A	Pts	PIM
2012-13	Antoine-Girouard	QAAA	26	3	8	11	8	13	1	1	2	8
2013-14	Antoine-Girouard	QAAA	40	19	28	47	42	3	0	0	0	0
	Rouyn-Noranda	QMJHL	4	0	0	0	0	2	0	0	0	0
2014-15	Rouyn-Noranda	QMJHL	68	14	39	53	29	6	1	4	5	4

BEAUPRE, Gabriel (boh-PRAY, gay-BREE-ehl) COL

Defense. Shoots left. 6'2", 195 lbs. Born, Levis, QC, November 23, 1992.
(Colorado's 5th choice, 153rd overall, in 2011 Entry Draft).

			Regular Season					Playoffs				
Season	Club	League	GP	G	A	Pts	PIM	GP	G	A	Pts	PIM
2007-08	Levis	QAAA	45	2	6	8	52	3	0	0	0	6
2008-09	Val-d'Or Foreurs	QMJHL	52	0	3	3	48	....	....	....	....	....
2009-10	Val-d'Or Foreurs	QMJHL	56	2	5	7	94	6	1	1	2	8
2010-11	Val-d'Or Foreurs	QMJHL	66	3	15	18	73	4	0	1	1	4
2011-12	Val-d'Or Foreurs	QMJHL	62	6	15	21	102	4	0	0	0	6
2012-13	Val-d'Or Foreurs	QMJHL	4	0	0	0	6	....	....	....	....	....
	Denver Cutthroats	CHL	28	3	5	8	23	....	....	....	....	....
	Lake Erie Monsters	AHL	43	1	4	5	67	....	....	....	....	....
2013-14	Lake Erie Monsters	AHL	65	3	5	8	99	....	....	....	....	....
2014-15	Lake Erie Monsters	AHL	35	1	3	4	23	....	....	....	....	....
	Fort Wayne	ECHL	11	2	5	7	18	....	....	....	....	....

BEAUVILLIER, Anthony (boh-VIHL-yay, AN-thuh-NEE) NYI

Left wing. Shoots left. 5'11", 173 lbs. Born, Sorel-Tracy, QC, June 8, 1997.
(NY Islanders' 2nd choice, 28th overall, in 2015 Entry Draft).

			Regular Season					Playoffs				
Season	Club	League	GP	G	A	Pts	PIM	GP	G	A	Pts	PIM
2011-12	Antoine-Girouard	Minor-QC	27	27	13	40	52	....	....	....	....	....
	Antoine-Girouard	QAAA	9	1	1	2	4	1	0	0	0	0
2012-13	Antoine-Girouard	QAAA	41	*39	25	*64	22	13	5	10	15	24
2013-14	Shawinigan	QMJHL	64	9	24	33	26	4	0	0	0	8
2014-15	Shawinigan	QMJHL	67	42	52	94	72	7	2	5	7	14

QMJHL Second All-Star Team (2015)

BECKER, Jack (BEH-kuhr, JAK) BOS

Center. Shoots right. 6'3", 191 lbs. Born, Duluth, MN, June 24, 1997.
(Boston's 10th choice, 195th overall, in 2015 Entry Draft).

			Regular Season					Playoffs				
Season	Club	League	GP	G	A	Pts	PIM	GP	G	A	Pts	PIM
2012-13	Mahtomedi	High-MN	25	10	17	27	20	2	1	0	1	2
2013-14	Mahtomedi	High-MN	25	23	13	36	20	3	2	3	5	0
2014-15	Team Northeast	UMHSEL	17	9	4	13	10	3	0	0	0	0
	Mahtomedi	High-MN	23	22	25	47	16	6	8	9	17	4
	Sioux Falls	USHL	2	0	1	1	0	....	....	....	....	....

• Signed Letter of Intent to attend **University of Wisconsin** (Big Ten) in fall of 2016.

BELPEDIO, Louis (BEHL-pee-dee-oh, LOO-ee) MIN

Defense. Shoots right. 5'11", 198 lbs. Born, Skokie, IL, May 14, 1996.
(Minnesota's 2nd choice, 80th overall, in 2014 Entry Draft).

			Regular Season					Playoffs				
Season	Club	League	GP	G	A	Pts	PIM	GP	G	A	Pts	PIM
2011-12	Culver Academy	High-IN	36	3	13	16	20	....	....	....	....	....
2012-13	USNTDP	USHL	38	0	4	4	23	....	....	....	....	....
	USNTDP	U-17	18	1	7	8	10	....	....	....	....	....
2013-14	USNTDP	USHL	26	5	10	15	24	....	....	....	....	....
	USNTDP	U-18	34	2	6	8	22	....	....	....	....	....
2014-15	Miami U.	NCHC	40	6	13	19	28	....	....	....	....	....

NCHC All-Rookie Team (2015)

BENNETT, Mac (BEH-neht, MAK) MTL

Defense. Shoots left. 6', 194 lbs. Born, Narragansett, RI, March 25, 1991.
(Montreal's 3rd choice, 79th overall, in 2009 Entry Draft).

			Regular Season					Playoffs				
Season	Club	League	GP	G	A	Pts	PIM	GP	G	A	Pts	PIM
2006-07	Hotchkiss School	High-CT	25	7	6	13	....	....	....	....	....	....
2007-08	Hotchkiss School	High-CT	25	6	9	15	....	....	....	....	....	....
2008-09	Neponset Valley	Minor-MA	16	5	19	24	....	....	....	....	....	....
	Hotchkiss School	High-CT	15	4	11	15	....	....	....	....	....	....
2009-10	Cedar Rapids	USHL	53	9	15	24	34	2	1	0	1	0
2010-11	U. of Michigan	CCHA	32	2	10	12	21	....	....	....	....	....
2011-12	U. of Michigan	CCHA	41	4	17	21	18	....	....	....	....	....
2012-13	U. of Michigan	CCHA	32	6	12	18	4	....	....	....	....	....
2013-14	U. of Michigan	Big Ten	31	2	12	14	10	....	....	....	....	....
2014-15	Hamilton Bulldogs	AHL	59	4	8	12	10	....	....	....	....	....

USHL All-Rookie Team (2010) • Big Ten Second All-Star Team (2014)

BENNING, Matthew (BENH-ihng, MA-thew) BOS

Defense. Shoots right. 6', 203 lbs. Born, Edmonton, AB, May 25, 1994.
(Boston's 5th choice, 175th overall, in 2012 Entry Draft).

			Regular Season					Playoffs				
Season	Club	League	GP	G	A	Pts	PIM	GP	G	A	Pts	PIM
2008-09	St. Albert Sabres	AMBHL	33	2	15	17	44	....	....	....	....	....
2009-10	St. Albert Raiders	AMHL	33	7	14	21	32	4	1	0	1	2
2010-11	Spruce Grove	AJHL	43	0	7	7	65	13	0	1	1	20
2011-12	Spruce Grove	AJHL	44	4	14	18	87	11	2	1	3	16
2012-13	Dubuque	USHL	57	10	16	26	73	10	1	1	2	6
2013-14	Northeastern	H-East	33	3	10	13	28	....	....	....	....	....
2014-15	Northeastern	H-East	36	0	24	24	36	....	....	....	....	....

BERGMAN, Julius (BUHRG-muhn, YOO-lee-uhs) S.J.

Defense. Shoots right. 6'1", 195 lbs. Born, Stockholm, Sweden, November 2, 1995.
(San Jose's 2nd choice, 46th overall, in 2014 Entry Draft).

			Regular Season					Playoffs				
Season	Club	League	GP	G	A	Pts	PIM	GP	G	A	Pts	PIM
2010-11	Karlskrona HK Jr.	Swe-Jr.	14	5	4	9	6	1	0	1	1	0
	Karlskrona HK	Sweden-3	5	0	0	0	0	4	0	0	0	0
2011-12	Karlskrona HK	Sweden-3	36	3	6	9	47	10	1	0	1	12
2012-13	Karlskrona HK U18	Swe-U18	1	1	0	1	16	....	....	....	....	....
	Karlskrona HK Jr.	Swe-Jr.	1	0	0	0	0	....	....	....	....	....
	Karlskrona HK	Sweden-2	23	0	0	0	16	....	....	....	....	....
	Frolunda U18	Swe-U18	2	1	1	2	2	3	0	3	3	6
	Frolunda Jr.	Swe-Jr.	15	1	5	6	6	6	1	2	3	8
2013-14	Frolunda Jr.	Swe-Jr.	45	13	21	34	54	3	0	1	1	8
	Frolunda	Sweden	1	0	0	0	4	....	....	....	....	....
2014-15	London Knights	OHL	60	13	29	42	78	10	4	2	6	6
	Worcester Sharks	AHL	1	0	0	0	2	....	....	....	....	....

BERKOVITZ, Matthew (BUHR-koh-vihts, MA-thew) ANA

Defense. Shoots left. 6'1", 180 lbs. Born, Green Bay, WI, February 16, 1996.
(Anaheim's 4th choice, 123rd overall, in 2014 Entry Draft).

			Regular Season					Playoffs				
Season	Club	League	GP	G	A	Pts	PIM	GP	G	A	Pts	PIM
2010-11	Ashwaubenon	High-WI	23	7	22	29	10	3	2	2	4	0
2011-12	Ashwaubenon	High-WI	23	8	13	21	6	1	3	1	4	0
2012-13	Ashwaubenon	High-WI	23	11	14	25	14	....	....	....	....	....
2013-14	Team Wisconsin	UMHSEL	21	3	10	13	0	3	0	0	0	2
	Ashwaubenon	High-WI	24	11	26	37	12	3	0	4	4	0
2014-15	Sioux City	USHL	20	0	0	0	12	....	....	....	....	....
	Green Bay	USHL	23	0	4	4	6	....	....	....	....	....

• Signed Letter of Intent to attend **University of Wisconsin** (Big Ten) in fall of 2015.

BERNHARDT, Daniel (buhrn-HAHRT, DAN-yuhl) NYR

Right wing. Shoots left. 6'2", 187 lbs. Born, Stockholm, Sweden, April 11, 1996.
(NY Rangers' 6th choice, 119th overall, in 2015 Entry Draft).

			Regular Season					Playoffs				
Season	Club	League	GP	G	A	Pts	PIM	GP	G	A	Pts	PIM
2011-12	Nacka HK U18	Swe-U18	16	4	4	8	2	....	....	....	....	....
2012-13	Djurgarden U18	Swe-U18	35	16	9	25	6	9	2	2	4	0
2013-14	Djurgarden U18	Swe-U18	38	25	38	63	28	4	1	2	3	4
	Djurgarden Jr.	Swe-Jr.	11	0	0	0	2	1	0	0	0	0
2014-15	Djurgarden Jr.	Swe-Jr.	44	26	35	61	22	7	2	2	4	0
	Djurgarden	Sweden	2	0	0	0	0	....	....	....	....	....

BERTSCHY, Christoph (BAIRT-chee, KRIHS-tawf) MIN

Center. Shoots right. 5'10", 189 lbs. Born, Friburg, Switz., April 5, 1994.
(Minnesota's 6th choice, 158th overall, in 2012 Entry Draft).

			Regular Season					Playoffs				
Season	Club	League	GP	G	A	Pts	PIM	GP	G	A	Pts	PIM
2007-08	Fribourg U17	Swiss-U17	3	0	0	0	0	....	....	....	....	....
	Ecole U17	Swiss-U17	2	0	0	0	2	....	....	....	....	....
2008-09	Fribourg U17	Swiss-U17	34	3	4	7	50	....	....	....	....	....
2009-10	SC Bern Future Jr.	Swiss-Jr.	4	0	1	1	0	....	....	....	....	....
	SC Bern U17	Swiss-U17	29	25	15	40	46	9	4	7	11	10
2010-11	SC Bern Future Jr.	Swiss-Jr.	36	16	16	32	34	1	0	0	0	4
	SC Bern U17	Swiss-U17	4	7	4	11	2	9	8	15	23	10
2011-12	SC Bern Future Jr.	Swiss-Jr.	13	7	15	22	22	....	....	....	....	....
	SC Bern	Swiss	31	8	7	15	8	17	1	1	2	8
2012-13	SC Bern Future Jr.	Swiss-Jr.	2	2	1	3	2	....	....	....	....	....
	SC Bern	Swiss	41	4	2	6	18	20	2	1	3	2
2013-14	SC Bern	Swiss	43	6	10	16	14	....	....	....	....	....
2014-15	SC Bern	Swiss	44	14	16	30	26	7	1	2	3	0

BERTUZZI, Tyler (buhr-TOO-zee, TIGH-luhr) DET

Left wing. Shoots left. 6'1", 187 lbs. Born, Sudbury, ON, February 24, 1995.
(Detroit's 3rd choice, 58th overall, in 2013 Entry Draft).

			Regular Season					Playoffs				
Season	Club	League	GP	G	A	Pts	PIM	GP	G	A	Pts	PIM
2010-11	Sud. Wolves MM	Minor-ON	32	20	45	65	58	....	....	....	....	....
	Sud. Wolves Mid.	Minor-ON	3	1	1	2	12	2	0	0	0	12
2011-12	Guelph Storm	OHL	61	6	11	17	117	6	0	2	2	7
2012-13	Guelph Storm	OHL	43	13	9	22	68	5	0	0	0	14
2013-14	Guelph Storm	OHL	29	9	26	35	49	18	10	7	17	24
2014-15	Guelph Storm	OHL	68	43	55	98	91	9	6	2	8	10
	Grand Rapids	AHL	2	1	0	1	0	14	7	5	12	10

OHL Second All-Star Team (2015)

BESSE, Grant (BEH-see, GRANT) ANA

Right wing. Shoots left. 5'10", 175 lbs. Born, Edina, MN, July 14, 1994.
(Anaheim's 4th choice, 147th overall, in 2013 Entry Draft).

			Regular Season					Playoffs				
Season	Club	League	GP	G	A	Pts	PIM	GP	G	A	Pts	PIM
2009-10	Benilde	High-MN	25	27	19	46	12	2	3	1	4	0
2010-11	Team Northwest	UMHSEL	21	9	11	20	16	3	1	1	2	0
	Benilde	High-MN	25	29	19	48	16	2	4	1	5	2
2011-12	Team Northwest	UMHSEL	21	15	17	32	16	6	3	3	6	4
	Benilde	High-MN	25	40	35	75	20	6	12	6	18	2
2012-13	Team Northwest	UMHSEL	4	2	0	2	0	....	....	....	....	....
	Benilde	High-MN	25	44	25	69	16	3	4	3	7	2
	Omaha Lancers	USHL	7	4	0	4	0	....	....	....	....	....
2013-14	U. of Wisconsin	Big Ten	36	8	6	14	12	....	....	....	....	....
2014-15	U. of Wisconsin	Big Ten	32	11	11	22	6	....	....	....	....	....

BETKER, Ben (BEHT-kuhr, BEHN) EDM

Defense. Shoots left. 6'5", 204 lbs. Born, Cranbrook, BC, September 29, 1994.
(Edmonton's 9th choice, 158th overall, in 2013 Entry Draft).

			Regular Season					Playoffs				
Season	Club	League	GP	G	A	Pts	PIM	GP	G	A	Pts	PIM
2010-11	Kootenay Ice	BCMML	38	1	12	13	56	....	....	....	....	....
2011-12	Westside Warriors	BCHL	59	5	13	18	52	....	....	....	....	....
	Portland	WHL	1	0	0	0	0	....	....	....	....	....
2012-13	Everett Silvertips	WHL	68	1	5	6	100	6	0	1	1	8
2013-14	Everett Silvertips	WHL	68	7	14	21	102	5	0	1	1	8
2014-15	Everett Silvertips	WHL	64	6	25	31	63	9	1	2	3	16

BIGGS, Tyler (BIHGZ, TIGH-luhr) PIT

Right wing. Shoots right. 6'2", 205 lbs. Born, Binghamton, NY, April 30, 1993.
(Toronto's 1st choice, 22nd overall, in 2011 Entry Draft).

			Regular Season					Playoffs				
Season	Club	League	GP	G	A	Pts	PIM	GP	G	A	Pts	PIM
2008-09	Tor. Jr. Canadiens	GTHL	72	40	47	87	....	....	....	....	....	....
	Tor. Canadiens	ON-Jr.A	3	0	0	0	2	....	....	....	....	....
2009-10	USNTDP	USHL	24	6	5	11	54	....	....	....	....	....
	USNTDP	U-17	20	10	4	14	31	....	....	....	....	....
	USNTDP	U-18	9	0	0	0	6	....	....	....	....	....
2010-11	USNTDP	USHL	20	7	4	11	41	....	....	....	....	....
	USNTDP	U-18	35	12	8	20	120	....	....	....	....	....
2011-12	Miami U.	CCHA	37	9	8	17	63	....	....	....	....	....
2012-13	Oshawa Generals	OHL	60	26	27	53	55	9	0	1	1	13
	Toronto Marlies	AHL	4	1	0	1	0	1	0	0	0	0
2013-14	Toronto Marlies	AHL	57	7	2	9	39	3	0	0	0	4
2014-15	Toronto Marlies	AHL	47	2	3	5	56	....	....	....	....	....
	Orlando	ECHL	8	4	2	6	16	....	....	....	....	....

Traded to **Pittsburgh** by **Toronto** with Phil Kessel, Tim Erixon and future considerations for Nick Spaling, Kasperi Kapanen, Scott Harrington, New Jersey's 3rd round choice (previously acquired) in 2016 Entry Draft and future considerations, July 1, 2015.

BIGRAS, Chris (bee-GRAH, KRIHS) COL

Defense. Shoots left. 6'1", 190 lbs. Born, Orillia, ON, February 22, 1995.
(Colorado's 2nd choice, 32nd overall, in 2013 Entry Draft).

			Regular Season					Playoffs				
Season	Club	League	GP	G	A	Pts	PIM	GP	G	A	Pts	PIM
2010-11	Barrie Colts	Minor-ON	43	7	25	32	20	....	....	....	....	....
2011-12	Owen Sound	OHL	49	3	16	19	33	5	2	3	5	0
2012-13	Owen Sound	OHL	68	8	30	38	34	12	0	2	2	8
2013-14	Owen Sound	OHL	55	4	23	27	46	5	1	2	3	4
2014-15	Owen Sound	OHL	62	20	51	71	52	5	1	2	3	4
	Lake Erie Monsters	AHL	7	0	4	4	2	....	....	....	....	....

OHL First All-Star Team (2015)

BIRD, Tyler (BUHRD, TIGH-luhr) CBJ

Right wing. Shoots right. 6'1", 188 lbs. Born, Boston, MA, August 14, 1996.
(Columbus' 6th choice, 137th overall, in 2014 Entry Draft).

			Regular Season					Playoffs				
Season	Club	League	GP	G	A	Pts	PIM	GP	G	A	Pts	PIM
2010-11	St. John's Prep	High-MA	25	3	4	7	....	....	....	....	....	....
2011-12	St. John's Prep	High-MA	24	8	12	20	....	....	....	....	....	....
	Valley Jr. Warriors	EmJHL	17	5	3	8	8	....	....	....	....	....
2012-13	St. John's Prep	High-MA	24	12	15	27	....	....	....	....	....	....
2013-14	Kimball Union	High-NH	37	33	27	60	....	....	....	....	....	....
2014-15	Brown U.	ECAC	27	2	2	4	4	....	....	....	....	....

BIRKS, Dane (BURKS, DAYN) PIT

Defense. Shoots right. 6'32", 183 lbs. Born, Merritt, BC, August 29, 1995.
(Pittsburgh's 4th choice, 164th overall, in 2013 Entry Draft).

			Regular Season					Playoffs				
Season	Club	League	GP	G	A	Pts	PIM	GP	G	A	Pts	PIM
2010-11	Williams Lake	Minor-BC	STATISTICS NOT AVAILABLE									
2011-12	Creston Valley	KIJHL	47	3	21	24	72	6	0	1	1	20
	Trail Smoke Eaters	BCHL	10	0	0	0	12	....	....	....	....	....
2012-13	Merritt	BCHL	52	5	15	20	28	5	0	1	1	6
2013-14	Merritt	BCHL	50	4	17	21	57	1	0	0	0	0
2014-15	Michigan Tech	WCHA	DID NOT PLAY – FRESHMAN									

BISCHOFF, Jake (BIHSH-awf, JAYK) NYI

Defense. Shoots left. 6'1", 194 lbs. Born, Cambridge, MN, July 25, 1994.
(NY Islanders' 7th choice, 185th overall, in 2012 Entry Draft).

			Regular Season					Playoffs				
Season	Club	League	GP	G	A	Pts	PIM	GP	G	A	Pts	PIM
2010-11	Grand Rapids	High-MN	24	5	18	23	12	3	0	6	6	2
2011-12	Team North	UMHSEL	24	5	8	13	4	....	....	....	....	....
	Grand Rapids	High-MN	24	11	27	38	17	1	0	2	2	0
	Omaha Lancers	USHL	10	0	1	1	2	....	....	....	....	....
2012-13	Grand Rapids	High-MN	16	7	11	18	4	3	1	6	7	4
	Omaha Lancers	USHL	12	0	2	2	0	....	....	....	....	....
2013-14	U. of Minnesota	Big Ten	28	3	4	7	8	....	....	....	....	....
2014-15	U. of Minnesota	Big Ten	36	3	8	11	0	....	....	....	....	....

BISHOP, Clark (BIH-shuhp, KLAHRK) CAR

Center. Shoots left. 6', 194 lbs. Born, St. John's, NL, March 29, 1996.
(Carolina's 6th choice, 127th overall, in 2014 Entry Draft).

			Regular Season					Playoffs				
Season	Club	League	GP	G	A	Pts	PIM	GP	G	A	Pts	PIM
2011-12	St. John's Priv.	Minor-NF	23	18	20	38	45	....	....	....	....	....
2012-13	Cape Breton	QMJHL	58	8	14	22	33	....	....	....	....	....
2013-14	Cape Breton	QMJHL	56	14	19	33	54	4	1	0	1	8
2014-15	Cape Breton	QMJHL	38	19	16	35	54	7	5	3	8	4

BITTNER, Paul (BIHT-nuhr, PAWL) CBJ

Left wing. Shoots left. 6'5", 204 lbs. Born, Crookston, MN, November 4, 1996.
(Columbus' 3rd choice, 38th overall, in 2015 Entry Draft).

			Regular Season					Playoffs				
Season	Club	League	GP	G	A	Pts	PIM	GP	G	A	Pts	PIM
2011-12	Team Northeast	MEPDL	16	6	3	9	0	2	2	1	3	0
	Crookston Pirates	High-MN	25	15	6	21	10	1	0	0	0	0
2013-14	Portland	WHL	63	22	27	49	27	21	6	6	12	11
2014-15	Portland	WHL	66	34	37	71	52	17	4	8	12	6

BJORK, Anders (B'YOHRK, AN-duhrz) BOS

Left wing. Shoots left. 6', 186 lbs. Born, Mequon, WI, August 5, 1996.
(Boston's 4th choice, 146th overall, in 2014 Entry Draft).

			Regular Season					Playoffs				
Season	Club	League	GP	G	A	Pts	PIM	GP	G	A	Pts	PIM
2011-12	Chicago Mission	HPHL	29	14	9	23	8	....	....	....	....	....
2012-13	USNTDP	USHL	38	8	7	15	28	....	....	....	....	....
	USNTDP	U-17	18	4	5	9	20	....	....	....	....	....
2013-14	USNTDP	USHL	26	9	12	21	0	....	....	....	....	....
	USNTDP	U-18	35	12	9	21	10	....	....	....	....	....
2014-15	U. of Notre Dame	H-East	41	7	15	22	14	....	....	....	....	....

BJORKSTRAND, Oliver (bih-YOHRK-strand, AWL-ih-vuhr) CBJ

Right wing. Shoots right. 6', 177 lbs. Born, Herning, Denmark, April 10, 1995.
(Columbus' 5th choice, 89th overall, in 2013 Entry Draft).

			Regular Season					Playoffs				
Season	Club	League	GP	G	A	Pts	PIM	GP	G	A	Pts	PIM
2009-10	Herning IK U17	Den-U17	10	7	9	16	2	....	....	....	....	....
2010-11	Herning IK U17	Den-U17	19	28	26	54	39	....	....	....	....	....
	Herning IK Jr.	Den-Jr.	11	13	6	19	2	6	1	7	8	0
	Herning IK II	Den-2	....	....	....	....	....	1	0	0	0	0
2011-12	Herning IK II	Den-2	5	1	2	3	0	....	....	....	....	....
	Herning Blue Fox	Denmark	36	13	13	26	10	10	1	2	3	4
2012-13	Portland	WHL	65	31	32	63	10	21	8	11	19	4
2013-14	Portland	WHL	69	50	59	109	36	21	*16	17	*33	8
2014-15	Portland	WHL	59	*63	55	*118	35	17	13	12	25	10

WHL West First All-Star Team (2014, 2015) • WHL Player of the Year (2015)

BLACK, Graham (BLAK, GRAY-uhm) N.J.

Center. Shoots left. 6', 190 lbs. Born, Regina, SK, January 13, 1993.
(New Jersey's 5th choice, 135th overall, in 2012 Entry Draft).

			Regular Season					Playoffs				
Season	Club	League	GP	G	A	Pts	PIM	GP	G	A	Pts	PIM
2009-10	Reg. Pat Cdns.	SMHL	42	22	27	49	40	....	....	....	....	....
2010-11	Reg. Pat Cdns.	SMHL	43	*47	29	*76	48	5	7	3	10	20
	Swift Current	WHL	6	1	1	2	0	....	....	....	....	....
2011-12	Swift Current	WHL	71	17	33	50	49	....	....	....	....	....
2012-13	Swift Current	WHL	68	24	26	50	33	5	1	3	4	2
2013-14	Swift Current	WHL	69	34	63	97	43	6	2	2	4	6
	Albany Devils	AHL	2	0	0	0	0	....	....	....	....	....
2014-15	Albany Devils	AHL	46	7	7	14	16	....	....	....	....	....

BLACKWELL, Colin (BLAK-wehl, KAWL-ihn) S.J.

Center. Shoots right. 5'9", 190 lbs. Born, Lawrence, MA, March 28, 1993.
(San Jose's 6th choice, 194th overall, in 2011 Entry Draft).

			Regular Season					Playoffs				
Season	Club	League	GP	G	A	Pts	PIM	GP	G	A	Pts	PIM
2007-08	St. John's Prep	High-MA	....	2	0	2	....	....	....	....	....	....
2008-09	St. John's Prep	High-MA	....	18	10	28	....	....	....	....	....	....
2009-10	St. John's Prep	High-MA	....	17	19	36	....	....	....	....	....	....
2010-11	St. John's Prep	High-MA	25	33	33	66	....	....	....	....	....	....
2011-12	Harvard Crimson	ECAC	34	5	14	19	46	....	....	....	....	....
2012-13	Harvard Crimson	ECAC	21	3	11	14	10	....	....	....	....	....
2013-14	Harvard Crimson	ECAC	DID NOT PLAY – INJURED									
2014-15	Harvard Crimson	ECAC	11	5	1	6	6	....	....	....	....	....

• Missed 2013-14 and majority of 2014-15 due to post-concussion syndrome.

BLAIS, Samuel (BLAY, SAM-yewl) ST.L.

Left wing. Shoots left. 5'11", 164 lbs. Born, Montmagny, QC, June 17, 1996.
(St. Louis' 9th choice, 176th overall, in 2014 Entry Draft).

			Regular Season					Playoffs				
Season	Club	League	GP	G	A	Pts	PIM	GP	G	A	Pts	PIM
2010-11	Rive-Sud Bantam	Minor-QC	29	20	18	38	....	....	....	....	....	....
	Rive-Sud Express	Minor-QC	3	1	1	2	....	....	....	....	....	....
2011-12	Rive-Sud Express	Minor-QC	23	10	16	26	18	7	2	6	8	4
2012-13	Trois-Rivieres	QAAA	42	16	24	40	18	10	8	4	12	4
2013-14	Levis	QAAA	21	12	23	35	12	....	....	....	....	....
	Victoriaville Tigres	QMJHL	25	4	10	14	0	4	0	1	1	0
2014-15	Victoriaville Tigres	QMJHL	61	34	48	82	50	4	2	3	5	4

BLANDISI, Joseph (blan-DEE-zee, JOH-sehf) N.J.

Center/Right wing. Shoots left. 6', 205 lbs. Born, Markham, ON, July 18, 1994.
(Colorado's 4th choice, 162nd overall, in 2012 Entry Draft).

			Regular Season					Playoffs				
Season	Club	League	GP	G	A	Pts	PIM	GP	G	A	Pts	PIM
2010-11	Vaughan Kings	GTHL	41	51	41	92	....	....	....	....	....	....
	Vaughan Vipers	ON-Jr.A	7	2	0	2	14	....	....	....	....	....
2011-12	Owen Sound	OHL	68	17	14	31	72	5	0	1	1	8
2012-13	Owen Sound	OHL	37	7	18	25	49	....	....	....	....	....
	Ottawa 67's	OHL	26	8	18	26	68	....	....	....	....	....
2013-14	Ottawa 67's	OHL	37	21	16	37	57	....	....	....	....	....
	Barrie Colts	OHL	10	3	10	13	16	....	....	....	....	....
2014-15	Barrie Colts	OHL	68	*52	60	112	126	9	6	8	14	22

Signed as a free agent by **New Jersey**, January 14, 2015.

BLEACKLEY, Conner (BLEEK-lee, KAW-nuhr) COL

Center. Shoots right. 6', 192 lbs. Born, High River, AB, February 7, 1996.
(Colorado's 1st choice, 23rd overall, in 2014 Entry Draft).

			Regular Season					Playoffs				
Season	Club	League	GP	G	A	Pts	PIM	GP	G	A	Pts	PIM
2009-10	Okotoks Oilers	AMBHL	33	9	12	21	20	....	....	....	....	....
2010-11	Okotoks Oilers	AMBHL	29	36	32	68	62	....	....	....	....	....
	Keystone Raiders	Minor-AB	5	7	2	9	4	....	....	....	....	....
2011-12	UFA Bisons	AMHL	26	13	17	30	41	2	0	0	0	0
	Red Deer Rebels	WHL	16	2	0	2	6	....	....	....	....	....
2012-13	Red Deer Rebels	WHL	66	9	9	18	28	9	2	1	3	0
2013-14	Red Deer Rebels	WHL	71	29	39	68	48	....	....	....	....	....
2014-15	Red Deer Rebels	WHL	51	27	22	49	49	5	1	1	2	4

BLIDH, Anton (BLIHD, AN-tawn) BOS

Left wing. Shoots left. 6', 200 lbs. Born, Molnlycke, Sweden, March 14, 1995.
(Boston's 5th choice, 180th overall, in 2013 Entry Draft).

			Regular Season					Playoffs				
Season	Club	League	GP	G	A	Pts	PIM	GP	G	A	Pts	PIM
2010-11	Frolunda U18	Swe-U18	12	2	1	3	8	1	0	0	0	25
2011-12	Frolunda U18	Swe-U18	38	13	19	32	28	4	2	0	2	4
2012-13	Frolunda U18	Swe-U18	8	5	2	7	14	3	1	3	4	0
	Frolunda Jr.	Swe-Jr.	43	17	10	27	80	6	1	2	3	0
2013-14	Frolunda Jr.	Swe-Jr.	27	11	14	25	20	....	....	....	....	....
	Karlskrona HK	Sweden-2	11	1	1	2	6	....	....	....	....	....
	Frolunda	Sweden	24	0	5	5	2	6	1	2	3	0
2014-15	Frolunda Jr.	Swe-Jr.	1	1	1	2	2	....	....	....	....	....
	Frolunda	Sweden	48	5	0	5	26	13	1	0	1	4

BLOMQVIST, Axel (BLAWM-kvihst, AX-uhl) WPG

Right wing. Shoots left. 6'6", 217 lbs. Born, Osby, Sweden, January 30, 1995.

			Regular Season					Playoffs				
Season	Club	League	GP	G	A	Pts	PIM	GP	G	A	Pts	PIM
2011-12	Rogle U18	Swe-U18	38	27	19	46	67	7	1	2	3	16
	Rogle Jr.	Swe-Jr.	4	1	0	1	0	....	....	....	....	....
2012-13	Lethbridge	WHL	59	7	26	33	66	....	....	....	....	....
2013-14	Lethbridge	WHL	19	8	5	13	10	....	....	....	....	....
	Victoria Royals	WHL	46	16	27	43	14	9	0	1	1	6
2014-15	Victoria Royals	WHL	34	14	15	29	10	....	....	....	....	....
	Moose Jaw	WHL	27	11	19	30	16	....	....	....	....	....

Signed as a free agent by **Winnipeg**, October 1, 2013.

BLOMSTRAND, Ludwig (BLAWM-strand, LUHD-wihg) VAN

Left wing. Shoots left. 6'1", 198 lbs. Born, Uppsala, Sweden, March 8, 1993.
(Vancouver's 5th choice, 120th overall, in 2011 Entry Draft).

			Regular Season					Playoffs				
Season	Club	League	GP	G	A	Pts	PIM	GP	G	A	Pts	PIM
2008-09	Almtuna U18	Swe-U18	10	3	0	3	8	....	....	....	....	....
	Gimo IF Hockey	Sweden-4	26	17	10	27	18	....	....	....	....	....
2009-10	Djurgarden U18	Swe-U18	35	9	19	28	24	5	0	2	2	0
2010-11	Djurgarden U18	Swe-U18	9	2	11	13	4	5	1	3	4	10
	Djurgarden Jr.	Swe-Jr.	35	3	4	7	14	3	0	0	0	2
2011-12	Djurgarden Jr.	Swe-Jr.	41	16	15	31	62	....	....	....	....	....
	Djurgarden	Sweden	18	0	1	1	4	....	....	....	....	....
	Djurgarden	Sweden-Q	8	0	0	0	0	....	....	....	....	....
2012-13	Djurgarden Jr.	Swe-Jr.	7	2	1	3	0	....	....	....	....	....
	Djurgarden	Sweden-2	14	0	0	0	8	....	....	....	....	....
	Almtuna	Sweden-2	30	13	6	19	12	....	....	....	....	....
	Chicago Wolves	AHL	8	1	1	2	2	....	....	....	....	....
2013-14	Utica Comets	AHL	7	0	0	0	2	....	....	....	....	....
	Kalamazoo Wings	ECHL	46	14	13	27	14	5	1	1	2	0
2014-15	Kalamazoo Wings	ECHL	53	33	12	45	32	5	2	1	3	4

BLUEGER, Teddy (BLEW-guhr, TEH-dee) PIT

Center. Shoots left. 6', 185 lbs. Born, Riga, Latvia, August 15, 1994.
(Pittsburgh's 3rd choice, 52nd overall, in 2012 Entry Draft).

			Regular Season					Playoffs				
Season	Club	League	GP	G	A	Pts	PIM	GP	G	A	Pts	PIM
2009-10	Shattuck Midget	High-MN	53	20	40	60	84	....	....	....	....	....
2010-11	Shattuck Midget	High-MN	54	24	42	66	32	....	....	....	....	....
2011-12	Shattuck	High-MN	51	24	64	88	63	....	....	....	....	....
2012-13	Minnesota State	WCHA	37	6	13	19	40	....	....	....	....	....
2013-14	Minnesota State	WCHA	40	4	22	26	55	....	....	....	....	....
2014-15	Minnesota State	WCHA	37	10	18	28	26	....	....	....	....	....

BLUJUS, Dylan (BLOO-juhs, DIH-luhn) T.B.

Defense. Shoots right. 6'3", 191 lbs. Born, Buffalo, NY, January 22, 1994.
(Tampa Bay's 3rd choice, 40th overall, in 2012 Entry Draft).

			Regular Season					Playoffs				
Season	Club	League	GP	G	A	Pts	PIM	GP	G	A	Pts	PIM
2009-10	Buffalo Regals	Minor-NY	47	5	17	22	36	....	....	....	....	....
2010-11	Brampton	OHL	67	4	22	26	26	4	0	0	0	0
2011-12	Brampton	OHL	66	7	27	34	38	8	1	4	5	4
2012-13	Brampton	OHL	68	2	27	29	57	5	2	2	4	2
2013-14	North Bay	OHL	55	4	26	30	56	22	4	6	10	20
2014-15	Syracuse Crunch	AHL	67	4	18	22	18	3	0	0	0	4

BODIE, Mat (BOH-dee, MAT) NYR

Defense. Shoots left. 6', 175 lbs. Born, East St. Paul, MB, March 7, 1990.

			Regular Season					Playoffs				
Season	Club	League	GP	G	A	Pts	PIM	GP	G	A	Pts	PIM
2006-07	Wpg. Thrashers	MMHL	36	4	38	42	64	....	....	....	....	....
2007-08	Wpg. Thrashers	MMHL	34	11	28	39	42	....	....	....	....	....
2008-09	Powell River Kings	BCHL	53	1	41	42	41	18	2	12	14	20
2009-10	Powell River Kings	BCHL	51	8	34	42	37	23	9	22	31	23
2010-11	Union College	ECAC	40	6	26	32	18	....	....	....	....	....
2011-12	Union College	ECAC	39	8	21	29	32	....	....	....	....	....
2012-13	Union College	ECAC	35	6	18	24	32	....	....	....	....	....
2013-14	Union College	ECAC	40	8	31	39	57	....	....	....	....	....
2014-15	Hartford Wolf Pack	AHL	75	5	27	32	42	15	3	4	7	6

ECAC All-Rookie Team (2011) • ECAC First All-Star Team (2012, 2014) • NCAA East Second All-American Team (2012) • NCAA East First All-American Team (2014)

Signed as a free agent by **NY Rangers**, April 15, 2014.

BOESER, Brock (BEH-suhr, BRAWK) VAN

Right wing. Shoots right. 6'1", 191 lbs. Born, Burnsville, MN, February 25, 1997.
(Vancouver's 1st choice, 23rd overall, in 2015 Entry Draft).

			Regular Season					Playoffs				
Season	Club	League	GP	G	A	Pts	PIM	GP	G	A	Pts	PIM
2012-13	Burnsville Blaze	High-MN	16	12	17	29	4	3	0	5	5	2
2013-14	Team Southeast	UMHSEL	14	9	5	14	21	3	3	0	3	0
	Burnsville Blaze	High-MN	24	21	25	46	25	2	2	2	4	0
	Sioux City	USHL	8	3	2	5	2	8	1	0	1	0
2014-15	Waterloo	USHL	57	*35	33	68	30	....	....	....	....	....

USHL All-Rookie Team (2015) • USHL First All-Star Team (2015)

• Signed Letter of Intent to attend **University of North Dakota** (NCHC) in fall of 2015.

BOIKOV, Sergei (boi-KAWV, sair-GAY) COL

Defense. Shoots left. 6'2", 195 lbs. Born, Khabarovsk, Russia, January 24, 1996.
(Colorado's 6th choice, 161st overall, in 2015 Entry Draft).

			Regular Season					Playoffs				
Season	Club	League	GP	G	A	Pts	PIM	GP	G	A	Pts	PIM
2012-13	Novokuznetsk Jr.	Russia-Jr.	3	0	0	0	6	....	....	....	....	....
2013-14	Drummondville	QMJHL	68	2	10	12	89	11	0	1	1	8
2014-15	Drummondville	QMJHL	64	3	18	21	64	....	....	....	....	....

BOKA, Nicholas (BOH-kah, NIH-koh-las) MIN

Defense. Shoots right. 6'1", 197 lbs. Born, Commerce, MI, September 8, 1997.
(Minnesota's 5th choice, 171st overall, in 2015 Entry Draft).

			Regular Season					Playoffs				
Season	Club	League	GP	G	A	Pts	PIM	GP	G	A	Pts	PIM
2012-13	Det. Comp. U18	HPHL	24	5	13	18	70	....	....	....	....	....
	Det. Comp. U18	Other	23	6	4	10	....	3	1	1	2	4
2013-14	USNTDP	USHL	32	4	7	11	104	....	....	....	....	....
	USNTDP	U-17	20	2	6	8	36	....	....	....	....	....
2014-15	USNTDP	USHL	20	3	1	4	68	....	....	....	....	....
	USNTDP	U-18	34	2	5	7	28	....	....	....	....	....

• Signed Letter of Intent to attend **University of Michigan** (Big Ten) in fall of 2015.

BONDRA, Radovan (BAWN-druh, RA-doh-van) CHI

Left wing. Shoots left. 6'4", 218 lbs. Born, Trebisov, Slovakia, January 27, 1997.
(Chicago's 4th choice, 151st overall, in 2015 Entry Draft).

			Regular Season					Playoffs				
Season	Club	League	GP	G	A	Pts	PIM	GP	G	A	Pts	PIM
2010-11	HK Trebisov U18	Svk-U18	20	8	6	14	10	....	....	....	....	....
2011-12	HC Kosice U18	Svk-U18	41	14	10	24	12	....	....	....	....	....
2012-13	Slovakia U20 B	Slovak-2	8	0	1	1	0	....	....	....	....	....
	HC Kosice U18	Svk-U18	38	37	25	62	26	2	0	0	0	4
	HC Kosice Jr.	Slovak-Jr.	....	....	....	....	....	1	0	0	0	0
2013-14	Slovakia U18	Slovak-2	35	5	4	9	20	....	....	....	....	....
	HC Kosice U18	Svk-U18	7	5	5	10	0	....	....	....	....	....
	HC Kosice Jr.	Slovak-Jr.	8	3	2	5	2	4	0	1	1	0
2014-15	HK VSR SR 20	Slovakia	4	0	0	0	2	....	....	....	....	....
	SR 18	Slovak-2	17	6	6	12	47	....	....	....	....	....
	HC Kosice	Slovakia	15	2	2	4	6	15	1	2	3	4

BORGEN, William (BOHR-guhn, WIHL-yuhm) BUF

Defense. Shoots right. 6'2", 188 lbs. Born, Moorhead, MN, December 19, 1996.
(Buffalo's 3rd choice, 92nd overall, in 2015 Entry Draft).

			Regular Season					Playoffs				
Season	Club	League	GP	G	A	Pts	PIM	GP	G	A	Pts	PIM
2012-13	Moorhead Spuds	High-MN	24	3	16	19	22	6	1	3	4	2
2013-14	Team Great Plains	UMHSEL	13	4	3	7	8	3	0	1	1	2
	Moorhead Spuds	High-MN	24	6	10	16	35	3	2	3	5	2
2014-15	Team Great Plains	UMHSEL	17	1	6	7	41	3	0	2	2	2
	Moorhead Spuds	High-MN	24	5	21	26	64	3	1	1	2	6
	Omaha Lancers	USHL	18	1	7	8	0	3	0	0	0	0

• Signed Letter of Intent to attend **St. Cloud State University** (NCHC) in fall of 2016.

BOURAMMAN, Gustav (BOO-ruh-muhn, GUHS-tav) MIN

Defense. Shoots right. 6', 185 lbs. Born, Stockholm, Sweden, January 24, 1997.
(Minnesota's 6th choice, 201st overall, in 2015 Entry Draft).

			Regular Season					Playoffs				
Season	Club	League	GP	G	A	Pts	PIM	GP	G	A	Pts	PIM
2011-12	Nacka HK U18	Swe-U18	7	0	4	4	2	....	....	....	....	....
2012-13	Nacka HK U18 1	Swe-U18	1	0	0	0	0	1	2	2	4	2
	Nacka HK	Sweden-3	1	0	0	0	0	....	....	....	....	....
2013-14	Lulea HF U18	Swe-U18	16	8	17	25	12	5	0	3	3	2
	Lulea HF Jr.	Swe-Jr.	16	2	1	3	12	....	....	....	....	....
2014-15	Sault Ste. Marie	OHL	67	5	39	44	14	11	1	3	4	4

BOURKE, Troy (BOHRK, TROI) COL

Left wing. Shoots left. 5'10", 170 lbs. Born, Edmonton, AB, March 30, 1994.
(Colorado's 2nd choice, 72nd overall, in 2012 Entry Draft).

			Regular Season					Playoffs				
Season	Club	League	GP	G	A	Pts	PIM	GP	G	A	Pts	PIM
2007-08	PAC Spruce Grove	AMBHL	33	13	15	28	26	2	0	0	0	0
2008-09	PAC Spruce Grove	AMBHL	33	*45	38	*83	38	7	5	6	11	10
2009-10	St. Albert Raiders	AMHL	34	27	26	53	24	5	2	0	2	4
	Prince George	WHL	5	3	0	3	4	....	....	....	....	....
2010-11	Prince George	WHL	68	19	23	42	20	4	0	1	1	0
2011-12	Prince George	WHL	71	18	38	56	56	....	....	....	....	....
2012-13	Prince George	WHL	63	15	35	50	37	....	....	....	....	....
2013-14	Prince George	WHL	69	29	56	85	62	....	....	....	....	....
	Lake Erie Monsters	AHL	15	3	4	7	6	....	....	....	....	....
2014-15	Lake Erie Monsters	AHL	61	9	13	22	22	....	....	....	....	....

BOURQUE, Simon (BOHRK, SIGH-muhn) MTL

Defense. Shoots left. 6', 184 lbs. Born, Longueuil, QC, January 12, 1997.
(Montreal's 4th choice, 177th overall, in 2015 Entry Draft).

			Regular Season					Playoffs				
Season	Club	League	GP	G	A	Pts	PIM	GP	G	A	Pts	PIM
2012-13	C.C. Lemoyne	QAAA	42	5	13	18	24	9	1	2	3	6
2013-14	Rimouski Oceanic	QMJHL	55	3	6	9	26	11	0	2	2	2
2014-15	Rimouski Oceanic	QMJHL	68	10	28	38	69	17	1	4	5	18

BOWEY, Madison (BOW-ee, MA-dih-suhn) WSH

Defense. Shoots right. 6'1", 195 lbs. Born, Winnipeg, MB, April 22, 1995.
(Washington's 2nd choice, 53rd overall, in 2013 Entry Draft).

			Regular Season					Playoffs				
Season	Club	League	GP	G	A	Pts	PIM	GP	G	A	Pts	PIM
2010-11	Winnipeg Wild	MMHL	41	16	22	38	35	6	2	0	2	10
	Kelowna Rockets	WHL	3	0	1	1	4	1	0	0	0	0
2011-12	Kelowna Rockets	WHL	57	8	13	21	39	4	1	0	1	4
2012-13	Kelowna Rockets	WHL	69	12	18	30	75	11	0	4	4	14
2013-14	Kelowna Rockets	WHL	72	21	39	60	93	14	5	9	14	14
2014-15	Kelowna Rockets	WHL	58	17	43	60	66	19	7	12	19	24

WHL West Second All-Star Team (2014) • WHL West First All-Star Team (2015) • Memorial Cup All-Star Team (2015)

BOYD, Travis (BOID, TRA-vihs) WSH

Center. Shoots right. 5'10", 185 lbs. Born, Hopkins, MN, September 14, 1993.
(Washington's 3rd choice, 177th overall, in 2011 Entry Draft).

			Regular Season					Playoffs				
Season	Club	League	GP	G	A	Pts	PIM	GP	G	A	Pts	PIM
2008-09	Hopkins Royals	High-MN	26	26	25	51	....	....	....	....	....	....
2009-10	USNTDP	USHL	35	8	10	18	18	....	....	....	....	....
	USNTDP	U-17	17	2	4	6	4	....	....	....	....	....
	USNTDP	U-18	1	0	0	0	0	....	....	....	....	....
2010-11	USNTDP	USHL	24	5	13	18	10	....	....	....	....	....
	USNTDP	U-18	36	8	12	20	6	....	....	....	....	....
2011-12	U. of Minnesota	WCHA	35	1	8	9	4	....	....	....	....	....
2012-13	U. of Minnesota	WCHA	40	3	11	14	8	....	....	....	....	....
2013-14	U. of Minnesota	Big Ten	41	9	23	32	18	....	....	....	....	....
2014-15	U. of Minnesota	Big Ten	32	19	22	41	10	....	....	....	....	....
	Hershey Bears	AHL	2	1	1	2	0	....	....	....	....	....

BOYLE, Timothy (BOIL, TIH-moh-thee) OTT

Defense. Shoots right. 6'2", 185 lbs. Born, Hingham, MA, March 21, 1993.
(Ottawa's 4th choice, 106th overall, in 2012 Entry Draft).

			Regular Season					Playoffs				
Season	Club	League	GP	G	A	Pts	PIM	GP	G	A	Pts	PIM
2010-11	Nobles	High-MA	27	3	25	28	20	....	....	....	....	....
2011-12	Cape Cod Whalers	Minor-MA	33	5	15	20	....	....	....	....	....	....
	Nobles	High-MA	24	6	12	18	10	....	....	....	....	....
2012-13	Union College	ECAC	15	0	2	2	25	....	....	....	....	....
2013-14	South Shore Kings	USPHL	37	5	16	21	87	....	....	....	....	....
2014-15	Endicott College	NCAA-3	18	3	8	11	24	....	....	....	....	....

BOZON, Tim (boh-ZAWN, TIHM) MTL

Left wing. Shoots left. 6'1", 207 lbs. Born, St. Louis, MO, March 24, 1994.
(Montreal's 4th choice, 64th overall, in 2012 Entry Draft).

			Regular Season					Playoffs				
Season	Club	League	GP	G	A	Pts	PIM	GP	G	A	Pts	PIM
2007-08	Geneve U17	Swiss-U17	4	4	2	6	0	....	....	....	....	....
2008-09	Geneve U17	Swiss-U17	29	15	8	23	18	....	....	....	....	....
2009-10	Kloten Flyers U17	Swiss-U17	30	26	29	55	22	10	2	4	6	10
	Kloten Flyers Jr.	Swiss-Jr.	3	2	0	2	4	....	....	....	....	....
2010-11	Kloten Flyers Jr.	Swiss-Jr.	3	1	0	1	0	....	....	....	....	....
	HC Lugano U17	Swiss-U17	8	8	9	17	18	5	2	1	3	22
	HC Lugano Jr.	Swiss-Jr.	27	16	13	29	24	3	1	1	2	2
2011-12	Kamloops Blazers	WHL	71	36	35	71	40	11	5	0	5	11
2012-13	Kamloops Blazers	WHL	69	36	55	91	58	8	4	2	6	10
2013-14	Kamloops Blazers	WHL	13	3	4	7	13	....	....	....	....	....
	Kootenay Ice	WHL	50	30	32	62	34	....	....	....	....	....
2014-15	Kootenay Ice	WHL	57	35	28	63	19	7	3	6	9	6
	Hamilton Bulldogs	AHL	1	0	0	0	0	....	....	....	....	....

BRACCO, Jeremy (BRA-koh, JAIR-ih-mee) TOR

Right wing. Shoots right. 5'10", 173 lbs. Born, Manhasset, NY, March 17, 1997.
(Toronto's 3rd choice, 61st overall, in 2015 Entry Draft).

			Regular Season					Playoffs				
Season	Club	League	GP	G	A	Pts	PIM	GP	G	A	Pts	PIM
2012-13	N.J. Rockets	MtJHL	10	9	15	24	....	....	....	....	....	....
	N.J. Rockets	AtJHL	30	16	34	50	24	4	2	4	6	0
2013-14	USNTDP	USHL	34	9	28	37	10	....	....	....	....	....
	USNTDP	U-17	20	7	30	37	10	....	....	....	....	....
2014-15	USNTDP	USHL	24	14	18	32	6	....	....	....	....	....
	USNTDP	U-18	41	16	46	62	4	....	....	....	....	....

• Signed Letter of Intent to attend **Boston College** (Hockey East) in fall of 2015.

BRADLEY, Matthew (BRAD-lee, MA-thew) MTL

Center. Shoots right. 5'11", 190 lbs. Born, Vancouver, BC, January 22, 1997.
(Montreal's 3rd choice, 131st overall, in 2015 Entry Draft).

			Regular Season					Playoffs				
Season	Club	League	GP	G	A	Pts	PIM	GP	G	A	Pts	PIM
2012-13	Valley West Hawks	BCMML	25	10	18	28	28	3	1	5	6	0
2013-14	Valley West Hawks	BCMML	37	39	32	71	94	5	7	6	13	10
	Surrey Eagles	BCHL	8	0	0	0	0	....	....	....	....	....
	Medicine Hat	WHL	....	....	....	....	....	17	0	0	0	0
2014-15	Medicine Hat	WHL	71	17	23	40	24	10	0	2	2	2

BRASSARD, Austen (bruh-SAHRD, AWS-tuhn) WPG

Right wing. Shoots right. 6'2", 188 lbs. Born, Windsor, ON, January 14, 1993.
(Winnipeg's 5th choice, 149th overall, in 2011 Entry Draft).

			Regular Season					Playoffs				
Season	Club	League	GP	G	A	Pts	PIM	GP	G	A	Pts	PIM
2008-09	Wind. Jr. Spitfires	Minor-ON	69	55	66	121	111	....	....	....	....	....
2009-10	Windsor Spitfires	OHL	37	4	8	12	36	....	....	....	....	....
	Belleville Bulls	OHL	26	6	11	17	9	....	....	....	....	....
2010-11	Belleville Bulls	OHL	67	19	15	34	78	4	1	0	1	4
2011-12	Belleville Bulls	OHL	64	27	24	51	71	6	1	1	2	6
2012-13	Belleville Bulls	OHL	62	14	19	33	94	17	6	6	12	22
2013-14	St. John's IceCaps	AHL	29	3	2	5	26	....	....	....	....	....
2014-15	St. John's IceCaps	AHL	75	6	12	18	60	....	....	....	....	....

BRASSART, Brady (BRAS-uhrt, BRAY-dee) MIN

Right wing. Shoots right. 6'1", 208 lbs. Born, Vernon, BC, June 15, 1993.

			Regular Season					Playoffs				
Season	Club	League	GP	G	A	Pts	PIM	GP	G	A	Pts	PIM
2008-09	Van. NW Giants	BCMML	40	24	31	55	60	5	4	3	7	2
2009-10	Spokane Chiefs	WHL	53	9	6	15	16	7	0	1	1	4
2010-11	Spokane Chiefs	WHL	65	8	24	32	70	9	1	2	3	10
2011-12	Calgary Hitmen	WHL	70	25	34	59	106	5	0	0	0	8
2012-13	Calgary Hitmen	WHL	65	35	43	78	88	17	9	1	10	22
2013-14	Calgary Hitmen	WHL	70	35	50	85	94	6	3	6	9	8
	Iowa Wild	AHL	9	1	0	1	4	....	....	....	....	....
2014-15	Iowa Wild	AHL	72	8	13	21	22	....	....	....	....	....

Signed as a free agent by **Minnesota**, March 1, 2014.

BRICKLEY, Connor (BRIH-klee, KAW-nuhr) FLA

Center. Shoots left. 6', 203 lbs. Born, Malden, MA, February 25, 1992.
(Florida's 6th choice, 50th overall, in 2010 Entry Draft).

			Regular Season					Playoffs				
Season	Club	League	GP	G	A	Pts	PIM	GP	G	A	Pts	PIM
2008-09	Belmont Hill	High-MA	30	17	18	35	60	....	....	....	....	....
2009-10	Des Moines	USHL	52	22	21	43	68	....	....	....	....	....
	USNTDP	U-18	14	2	5	7	6	....	....	....	....	....
2010-11	U. of Vermont	H-East	35	4	9	13	33	....	....	....	....	....
2011-12	U. of Vermont	H-East	23	9	3	12	16	....	....	....	....	....
2012-13	U. of Vermont	H-East	24	3	5	8	31	....	....	....	....	....
2013-14	U. of Vermont	H-East	35	5	10	15	49	....	....	....	....	....
	San Antonio	AHL	8	1	1	2	4	....	....	....	....	....
2014-15	San Antonio	AHL	73	22	25	47	66	3	1	1	2	0

BRISEBOIS, Guillaume (BREEZ-b'wah, GEE-OHM) VAN

Defense. Shoots left. 6'2", 175 lbs. Born, St. Hillaire, QC, July 21, 1997.
(Vancouver's 2nd choice, 66th overall, in 2015 Entry Draft).

			Regular Season					Playoffs				
Season	Club	League	GP	G	A	Pts	PIM	GP	G	A	Pts	PIM
2012-13	Antoine-Girouard	QAAA	40	5	17	22	10	11	1	4	5	4
2013-14	Acadie-Bathurst	QMJHL	60	3	16	19	26	4	1	2	3	2
2014-15	Acadie-Bathurst	QMJHL	63	4	24	28	34	....	....	....	....	....

BRISEBOIS, Mathieu (BREEZ-bwah, MA-tyew) CHI

Defense. Shoots right. 5'11", 197 lbs. Born, Mont St-Hilaire, QC, April 17, 1992.

			Regular Season					Playoffs				
Season	Club	League	GP	G	A	Pts	PIM	GP	G	A	Pts	PIM
2008-09	Antoine-Girouard	QAAA	38	7	14	21	40	5	0	4	4	2
2009-10	Sherbrooke	QJHL	32	7	9	16	32	....	....	....	....	....
	Lewiston	QMJHL	31	0	7	7	22	3	0	0	0	4
2010-11	Rouyn-Noranda	QMJHL	47	3	15	18	32	....	....	....	....	....
2011-12	Rouyn-Noranda	QMJHL	68	17	39	56	106	4	1	0	1	12
2012-13	Rouyn-Noranda	QMJHL	64	19	54	73	103	14	3	12	15	24
2013-14	Portland Pirates	AHL	28	1	2	3	30	....	....	....	....	....
	Rockford IceHogs	AHL	13	2	5	7	19	....	....	....	....	....
2014-15	Rockford IceHogs	AHL	1	0	0	0	0	....	....	....	....	....
	Indy Fuel	ECHL	31	2	12	14	25	....	....	....	....	....
	Rapid City Rush	ECHL	36	9	21	30	44	13	1	4	5	14

QMJHL Second All-Star Team (2013)

Signed as a free agent by **Phoenix**, March 6, 2013. Traded to **Chicago** by **Phoenix** with David Rundblad for Chicago's 2nd round choice (Christian Dvorak) in 2014 Entry Draft, March 4, 2014.

BROADHURST, Alex (BRAWD-hurst, AL-ehx) CBJ

Center. Shoots left. 5'11", 188 lbs. Born, Orland Park, IL, March 7, 1993.
(Chicago's 10th choice, 199th overall, in 2011 Entry Draft).

			Regular Season					Playoffs				
Season	Club	League	GP	G	A	Pts	PIM	GP	G	A	Pts	PIM
2006-07	Chicago Mission	MWEHL	31	20	29	49	10	....	....	....	....	....
2007-08	Chicago Fury	MWEHL	31	4	4	8	6	....	....	....	....	....
2008-09	Team Illinois	T1EHL	31	8	18	26	22	....	....	....	....	....
2009-10	Chicago Mission	T1EHL	48	16	29	45	26	....	....	....	....	....
2010-11	Green Bay	USHL	55	13	20	33	22	11	3	6	9	4
2011-12	Green Bay	USHL	53	26	47	73	40	7	7	6	13	4
2012-13	London Knights	OHL	65	23	40	63	36	21	10	18	28	22
2013-14	Rockford IceHogs	AHL	75	16	29	45	32	....	....	....	....	....
2014-15	Rockford IceHogs	AHL	29	6	8	14	4	7	0	1	1	2

USHL First All-Star Team (2012)

Traded to **Columbus** by **Chicago** with Brandon Saad and Michael Paliotta for Artem Anisimov, Jeremy Morin, Corey Tropp, Marko Dano and Columbus' 4th round choice in 2016 Entry Draft, June 30, 2015.

BROADHURST, Terry (BRAWD-hurst, TAIR-ee)

Left wing. Shoots left. 5'11", 162 lbs. Born, Orland Park, IL, November 30, 1988.

			Regular Season					Playoffs				
Season	Club	League	GP	G	A	Pts	PIM	GP	G	A	Pts	PIM
2007-08	Sioux Falls	USHL	56	7	16	23	12	3	2	1	3	0
2008-09	Sioux City	USHL	60	27	31	58	30	4	2	1	3	2
2009-10	Nebraska-Omaha	CCHA	42	13	11	24	10	....	....	....	....	....
2010-11	Nebraska-Omaha	WCHA	30	11	19	30	14	....	....	....	....	....
2011-12	Nebraska-Omaha	WCHA	38	16	20	36	6	....	....	....	....	....
	Rockford IceHogs	AHL	8	0	2	2	0	....	....	....	....	....
2012-13	Rockford IceHogs	AHL	31	5	8	13	12	....	....	....	....	....
	Toledo Walleye	ECHL	36	12	19	31	14	....	....	....	....	....
2013-14	Rockford IceHogs	AHL	73	16	28	44	16	....	....	....	....	....
2014-15	Chicago Wolves	AHL	58	8	18	26	14	3	0	0	0	0

CCHA All-Rookie Team (2010)

Signed as a free agent by **Chicago**, March 19, 2012.

BRODEUR, Mathieu (broh-DUHR, MA-tyew)

Defense. Shoots left. 6'6", 220 lbs. Born, Laval, QC, June 21, 1990.
(Phoenix's 5th choice, 76th overall, in 2008 Entry Draft).

			Regular Season					Playoffs				
Season	Club	League	GP	G	A	Pts	PIM	GP	G	A	Pts	PIM
2006-07	Laurentides	QAAA	44	5	7	12	58	15	2	4	6	18
2007-08	Cape Breton	QMJHL	69	1	6	7	27	11	0	0	0	6
2008-09	Cape Breton	QMJHL	61	3	12	15	15	11	1	3	4	4
2009-10	Cape Breton	QMJHL	65	4	25	29	31	5	0	0	0	9
	San Antonio	AHL	2	0	1	1	0	....	....	....	....	....
2010-11	San Antonio	AHL	4	0	0	0	2	....	....	....	....	....
	Las Vegas	ECHL	52	0	1	1	43	....	....	....	....	....
2011-12	Portland Pirates	AHL	43	2	4	6	29	....	....	....	....	....
2012-13	Portland Pirates	AHL	65	3	16	19	47	3	0	0	0	2
2013-14	Portland Pirates	AHL	62	3	9	12	49	....	....	....	....	....
2014-15	Chicago Wolves	AHL	69	4	11	15	33	3	1	0	1	2

BRODZINSKI, Jonny (brawd-ZIHN-skee, JAW-nee) **L.A.**

Center. Shoots right. 6', 202 lbs. Born, Ham Lake, MN, June 19, 1993.
(Los Angeles' 5th choice, 148th overall, in 2013 Entry Draft).

			Regular Season					Playoffs				
Season	Club	League	GP	G	A	Pts	PIM	GP	G	A	Pts	PIM
2009-10	Blaine Bengals	High-MN	25	22	20	42	18	5	0	6	6	0
2010-11	Team Northwest	UMHSEL	21	11	14	25	10	3	2	3	5	2
	Blaine Bengals	High-MN	25	27	25	52	16	5	4	4	8	2
	Fargo Force	USHL	10	2	3	5	2	2	0	0	0	0
2011-12	Fargo Force	USHL	58	10	12	22	18	6	1	1	2	0
2012-13	St. Cloud State	WCHA	42	22	11	33	10	....	....	....	....	....
2013-14	St. Cloud State	NCHC	38	21	20	41	16	....	....	....	....	....
2014-15	St. Cloud State	NCHC	40	21	17	38	49	....	....	....	....	....

NCHC First All-Star Team (2015)

BRODZINSKI, Michael (brawd-ZIHN-skee, MIGH-kuhl) **S.J.**

Defense. Shoots right. 5'11", 180 lbs. Born, Coon Rapids, MN, May 28, 1995.
(San Jose's 4th choice, 141st overall, in 2013 Entry Draft).

			Regular Season					Playoffs				
Season	Club	League	GP	G	A	Pts	PIM	GP	G	A	Pts	PIM
2009-10	Blaine Bengals	High-MN	24	2	3	5	12	5	1	0	1	0
2010-11	Team Northeast	UMHSEL	21	3	8	11	20	2	0	1	1	2
	Blaine Bengals	High-MN	25	9	14	23	22	5	5	3	8	0
2011-12	Team Northwest	UMHSEL	20	4	10	14	51	3	1	1	2	0
	Blaine Bengals	High-MN	25	13	20	33	26	3	3	0	3	17
	Muskegon	USHL	3	0	1	1	0	....	....	....	....	....
2012-13	Muskegon	USHL	61	16	17	33	47	3	0	1	1	0
2013-14	U. of Minnesota	Big Ten	26	6	7	13	12	....	....	....	....	....
2014-15	U. of Minnesota	Big Ten	36	4	10	14	16	....	....	....	....	....

BROWN, Christopher (BROWN, KRIHS-tuh-fuhr) **BUF**

Center. Shoots right. 6', 179 lbs. Born, Pontiac, MI, February 22, 1996.
(Buffalo's 8th choice, 151st overall, in 2014 Entry Draft).

			Regular Season					Playoffs				
Season	Club	League	GP	G	A	Pts	PIM	GP	G	A	Pts	PIM
2010-11	Cranbrook Cranes	High-MI	25	3	7	10	6	....	....	....	....	....
2011-12	Cranbrook Cranes	High-MI	26	17	17	34	2	....	....	....	....	....
2012-13	Michigan White	Other	16	5	9	14	0	....	....	....	....	....
	Cranbrook Cranes	High-MI	31	23	27	50	6	....	....	....	....	....
2013-14	Michigan Orange	Other	11	*11	6	*17	0	....	....	....	....	....
	Cranbrook Cranes	High-MI	28	26	*58	*84	21	....	....	....	....	....
	Green Bay	USHL	2	0	0	0	0	....	....	....	....	....
2014-15	Green Bay	USHL	43	13	19	32	22	....	....	....	....	....
	Tri-City Storm	USHL	15	0	5	5	2	6	0	0	0	0

• Signed Letter of Intent to attend **Boston College** (Hockey East) in fall of 2015.

BROWN, Connor (BROWN, KAW-nuhr) **TOR**

Right wing. Shoots right. 5'11", 160 lbs. Born, Etobicoke, ON, January 14, 1994.
(Toronto's 4th choice, 156th overall, in 2012 Entry Draft).

			Regular Season					Playoffs				
Season	Club	League	GP	G	A	Pts	PIM	GP	G	A	Pts	PIM
2009-10	Toronto Marlboros	GTHL	80	25	44	69	16	....	....	....	....	....
2010-11	St. Michael's	ON-Jr.A	49	17	22	39	18	3	0	1	1	0
2011-12	Erie Otters	OHL	68	25	28	53	14	....	....	....	....	....
2012-13	Erie Otters	OHL	63	28	41	69	39	....	....	....	....	....
2013-14	Erie Otters	OHL	68	45	*83	*128	22	14	8	10	18	8
2014-15	Toronto Marlies	AHL	76	21	40	61	10	5	1	3	4	2

OHL All-Rookie Team (2012) • OHL First All-Star Team (2014) • AHL All-Rookie Team (2015)

BROWN, Josh (BROWN, JAWSH) **FLA**

Defense. Shoots right. 6'5", 213 lbs. Born, London, ON, January 21, 1994.
(Florida's 7th choice, 152nd overall, in 2013 Entry Draft).

			Regular Season					Playoffs				
Season	Club	League	GP	G	A	Pts	PIM	GP	G	A	Pts	PIM
2010-11	Whitby Fury	ON-Jr.A	35	6	4	10	59	....	....	....	....	....
2011-12	Oshawa Generals	OHL	46	0	4	4	49	2	0	0	0	0
2012-13	Oshawa Generals	OHL	68	0	16	16	79	9	1	4	5	11
2013-14	Oshawa Generals	OHL	56	2	10	12	83	9	0	0	0	18
2014-15	Oshawa Generals	OHL	60	4	17	21	92	21	2	2	4	30

BRUCE, Riley (BROOS, RIGH-lee) **CGY**

Defense. Shoots right. 6'6", 205 lbs. Born, Carp, ON, July 16, 1997.
(Calgary's 5th choice, 196th overall, in 2015 Entry Draft).

			Regular Season					Playoffs				
Season	Club	League	GP	G	A	Pts	PIM	GP	G	A	Pts	PIM
2012-13	Ott. Valley Titans	Minor-ON	29	1	4	5	42	....	....	....	....	....
	Gloucester	ON-Jr.A	8	0	0	0	4	....	....	....	....	....
2013-14	North Bay	OHL	57	0	4	4	39	15	0	1	1	9
2014-15	North Bay	OHL	52	0	3	3	32	15	1	0	1	6

BRUTON, Chris (BRUH-tuhn, KRIHS)

Right wing. Shoots right. 5'11", 195 lbs. Born, Calgary, AB, January 23, 1987.

			Regular Season					Playoffs				
Season	Club	League	GP	G	A	Pts	PIM	GP	G	A	Pts	PIM
2004-05	Spokane Chiefs	WHL	62	11	17	28	55	....	....	....	....	....
2005-06	Spokane Chiefs	WHL	66	12	14	26	111	....	....	....	....	....
2006-07	Spokane Chiefs	WHL	63	9	12	21	103	6	1	1	2	6
2007-08	Spokane Chiefs	WHL	67	26	37	63	99	21	3	7	10	6
2008-09	Acadia University	AUAA	26	15	14	29	62	....	....	....	....	....
2009-10	Acadia University	AUAA	24	11	13	24	20	....	....	....	....	....
2010-11	Acadia University	AUAA	19	8	13	21	36	....	....	....	....	....
2011-12	Alaska Aces	ECHL	27	6	7	13	60	4	0	3	3	19
	Peoria Rivermen	AHL	38	2	3	5	66	....	....	....	....	....
2012-13	Peoria Rivermen	AHL	69	4	6	10	134	....	....	....	....	....
2013-14	Bridgeport	AHL	41	2	2	4	91	....	....	....	....	....
2014-15	Grand Rapids	AHL	52	2	2	4	124	....	....	....	....	....

Signed as a free agent by **NY Islanders**, May 21, 2013. Signed as a free agent by **Grand Rapids** (AHL), September 30, 2014. Signed as a free agent by **Braehead** (Britain), July 30, 2015.

BUCHNEVICH, Pavel (buhtch-NY'AY-vihch, PAH-vehl) **NYR**

Left wing. Shoots left. 6'1", 176 lbs. Born, Cherepovets, Russia, April 17, 1995.
(NY Rangers' 2nd choice, 75th overall, in 2013 Entry Draft).

			Regular Season					Playoffs				
Season	Club	League	GP	G	A	Pts	PIM	GP	G	A	Pts	PIM
2011-12	Cherepovets Jr.	Russia-Jr.	45	15	29	44	55	10	4	3	7	4
2012-13	Cherepovets Jr.	Russia-Jr.	24	8	15	23	36	3	1	4	5	12
	Cherepovets	KHL	12	1	1	2	0	6	0	0	0	0
2013-14	Cherepovets Jr.	Russia-Jr.	2	0	2	2	2	7	4	5	9	12
	Cherepovets	KHL	40	7	11	18	12	6	1	1	2	9
2014-15	Cherepovets	KHL	48	13	17	30	16	....	....	....	....	....

BUCKLES, Matt (BUH-kuhlz, MAT) **FLA**

Center. Shoots right. 6'1", 225 lbs. Born, Toronto, ON, May 5, 1995.
(Florida's 5th choice, 98th overall, in 2013 Entry Draft).

			Regular Season					Playoffs				
Season	Club	League	GP	G	A	Pts	PIM	GP	G	A	Pts	PIM
2010-11	Don Mills Flyers	GTHL	39	16	15	31	66	....	....	....	....	....
2011-12	Tor. Patriots	ON-Jr.A	46	15	21	36	76	21	5	6	11	20
2012-13	St. Michael's	ON-Jr.A	50	40	31	71	107	17	7	10	17	54
2013-14	Cornell Big Red	ECAC	29	4	0	4	39	....	....	....	....	....
2014-15	Cornell Big Red	ECAC	29	8	3	11	33	....	....	....	....	....

BUDISH, Zach (BOO-dihsh, ZAK)

Right wing. Shoots right. 6'3", 223 lbs. Born, Edina, MN, May 9, 1991.
(Nashville's 2nd choice, 41st overall, in 2009 Entry Draft).

			Regular Season					Playoffs				
Season	Club	League	GP	G	A	Pts	PIM	GP	G	A	Pts	PIM
2006-07	Edina Hornets	High-MN	31	22	25	47	....	....	....	....	....	....
2007-08	Edina Hornets	High-MN	30	26	37	63	....	....	....	....	....	....
2008-09	Team Southwest	UMHSEL	15	14	13	27	12	....	....	....	....	....
	Edina Hornets	High-MN	DID NOT PLAY – INJURED									
2009-10	U. of Minnesota	WCHA	39	7	10	17	45	....	....	....	....	....
2010-11	U. of Minnesota	WCHA	7	2	4	6	2	....	....	....	....	....
2011-12	U. of Minnesota	WCHA	43	12	23	35	43	....	....	....	....	....
2012-13	U. of Minnesota	WCHA	40	14	22	36	14	....	....	....	....	....
	Milwaukee	AHL	9	1	3	4	0	3	0	0	0	2
2013-14	Milwaukee	AHL	41	3	6	9	22	....	....	....	....	....
	Cincinnati	ECHL	16	3	6	9	6	24	6	5	11	12
2014-15	Milwaukee	AHL	43	6	8	14	18	....	....	....	....	....
	Cincinnati	ECHL	30	8	15	23	20	....	....	....	....	....

• Missed remainder of 2008-09 due to knee injury in football.

BUNTING, Michael (BUHN-tihng, MIGH-kuhl) **ARI**

Left wing. Shoots left. 5'11", 183 lbs. Born, Toronto, ON, September 17, 1995.
(Arizona's 5th choice, 117th overall, in 2014 Entry Draft).

			Regular Season					Playoffs				
Season	Club	League	GP	G	A	Pts	PIM	GP	G	A	Pts	PIM
2012-13	Don Mills Flyers	GTHL	28	27	12	39	44	....	....	....	....	....
2013-14	Sault Ste. Marie	OHL	48	15	27	42	34	9	5	1	6	4
2014-15	Sault Ste. Marie	OHL	57	37	37	74	39	14	9	5	14	10

BURLON, Brandon (BUHR-lohn, BRAN-duhn) **N.J.**

Defense. Shoots left. 6', 190 lbs. Born, Nobleton, ON, March 5, 1990.
(New Jersey's 2nd choice, 52nd overall, in 2008 Entry Draft).

			Regular Season					Playoffs				
Season	Club	League	GP	G	A	Pts	PIM	GP	G	A	Pts	PIM
2005-06	Vaughan Kings	GTHL	55	19	29	48	38	....	....	....	....	....
2006-07	St. Michael's	ON-Jr.A	45	4	19	23	46	4	0	1	1	4
2007-08	St. Michael's	ON-Jr.A	32	7	17	24	41	10	2	4	6	8
2008-09	U. of Michigan	CCHA	33	5	10	15	14	....	....	....	....	....
2009-10	U. of Michigan	CCHA	45	3	11	14	24	....	....	....	....	....
2010-11	U. of Michigan	CCHA	38	5	13	18	28	....	....	....	....	....
2011-12	Albany Devils	AHL	57	1	8	9	21	....	....	....	....	....
2012-13	Albany Devils	AHL	53	1	16	17	25	....	....	....	....	....
2013-14	Albany Devils	AHL	54	5	6	11	39	....	....	....	....	....
2014-15	Albany Devils	AHL	72	8	28	36	93	....	....	....	....	....

CCHA All-Rookie Team (2009)

BURROUGHS, Kyle (BUHR-ohz, KIGHL) **NYI**

Defense. Shoots right. 6', 203 lbs. Born, Vancouver, BC, July 12, 1995.
(NY Islanders' 7th choice, 196th overall, in 2013 Entry Draft).

			Regular Season					Playoffs				
Season	Club	League	GP	G	A	Pts	PIM	GP	G	A	Pts	PIM
2010-11	Valley West Hawks	BCMML	36	11	25	36	58	4	0	4	4	2
	Aldergrove	PIJHL	4	0	1	1	18	....	....	....	....	....
	Regina Pats	WHL	1	0	0	0	0	....	....	....	....	....
2011-12	Regina Pats	WHL	55	2	6	8	54	5	1	1	2	0
2012-13	Regina Pats	WHL	70	5	28	33	91	....	....	....	....	....
2013-14	Regina Pats	WHL	58	8	32	40	72	4	0	1	1	8
	Bridgeport	AHL	9	0	0	0	2	....	....	....	....	....
2014-15	Regina Pats	WHL	36	5	17	22	47	....	....	....	....	....
	Medicine Hat	WHL	30	2	15	17	38	10	0	3	3	6

BUSSIERES, Raphael (boo-SEE-air, ra-FIGH-ehl) **MIN**

Left wing. Shoots left. 6'2", 202 lbs. Born, Longueuil, QC, November 5, 1993.
(Minnesota's 2nd choice, 46th overall, in 2012 Entry Draft).

			Regular Season					Playoffs				
Season	Club	League	GP	G	A	Pts	PIM	GP	G	A	Pts	PIM
2008-09	C.C. Lemoyne	QAAA	41	12	11	23	22	16	7	7	14	2
2009-10	C.C. Lemoyne	QAAA	9	10	15	25	4	....	....	....	....	....
	Moncton Wildcats	QMJHL	20	1	2	3	8	....	....	....	....	....
	Baie-Comeau	QMJHL	24	6	8	14	13	....	....	....	....	....
2010-11	Baie-Comeau	QMJHL	66	17	22	39	39	....	....	....	....	....
2011-12	Baie-Comeau	QMJHL	56	21	23	44	60	5	3	5	8	11
2012-13	Baie-Comeau	QMJHL	60	29	39	68	43	19	4	12	16	18
2013-14	Iowa Wild	AHL	61	5	14	19	51	....	....	....	....	....
2014-15	Iowa Wild	AHL	9	0	0	0	0	....	....	....	....	....
	Alaska Aces	ECHL	19	3	13	16	15	....	....	....	....	....

BUTCHER, Will (BUH-chuhr, WIHL) COL

Defense. Shoots left. 5'10", 190 lbs. Born, Madison, WI, January 6, 1995.
(Colorado's 5th choice, 123rd overall, in 2013 Entry Draft).

			Regular Season					Playoffs				
Season	Club	League	GP	G	A	Pts	PIM	GP	G	A	Pts	PIM
2010-11	Madison Capitols	T1EHL	34	10	20	30	2	....	....	....	....	....
	Dubuque	USHL	2	0	2	2	0	....	....	....	....	....
2011-12	USNTDP	USHL	31	2	8	10	4	....	....	....	....	....
	USNTDP	U-17	17	6	17	23	4	....	....	....	....	....
	USNTDP	U-18	8	0	0	0	2	....	....	....	....	....
2012-13	USNTDP	USHL	26	3	10	13	2	....	....	....	....	....
	USNTDP	U-18	41	8	16	24	6	....	....	....	....	....
2013-14	U. of Denver	NCHC	38	8	8	16	8	....	....	....	....	....
2014-15	U. of Denver	NCHC	38	4	14	18	8	....	....	....	....	....

BYRON, Blaine (BIGH-ruhn, BLAYN) PIT

Center. Shoots left. 6', 172 lbs. Born, Ottawa, ON, February 21, 1995.
(Pittsburgh's 5th choice, 179th overall, in 2013 Entry Draft).

			Regular Season					Playoffs				
Season	Club	League	GP	G	A	Pts	PIM	GP	G	A	Pts	PIM
2009-10	U.C. Cyclones	Minor-ON	28	16	23	39	14	12	6	11	17	8
2010-11	U.C. Cyclones MM	Minor-ON	30	18	30	48	12	....	....	....	....	....
	U.C. Cyclones Mid.	Minor-ON	6	2	1	3	2	....	....	....	....	....
	Kemptville 73's	ON-Jr.A	9	1	1	2	2	....	....	....	....	....
2011-12	Kemptville 73's	ON-Jr.A	42	12	27	39	20	....	....	....	....	....
2012-13	Kemptville 73's	ON-Jr.A	24	7	16	23	8	....	....	....	....	....
	Smiths Falls Bears	ON-Jr.A	27	5	24	29	16	5	0	1	1	0
2013-14	U. of Maine	H-East	32	8	8	16	4	....	....	....	....	....
2014-15	U. of Maine	H-East	39	12	15	27	6	....	....	....	....	....

BYSTROM, Ludwig (B'YEW-struhm, LOOD-wihg) DAL

Defense. Shoots left. 6', 175 lbs. Born, Ornskoldsvik, Sweden, July 20, 1994.
(Dallas' 2nd choice, 43rd overall, in 2012 Entry Draft).

			Regular Season					Playoffs				
Season	Club	League	GP	G	A	Pts	PIM	GP	G	A	Pts	PIM
2009-10	MODO U18	Swe-U18	24	4	0	4	10	5	0	1	1	0
2010-11	MODO U18	Swe-U18	9	1	5	6	10	3	0	0	0	10
	MODO Jr.	Swe-Jr.	37	1	10	11	28	6	1	2	3	6
	MODO	Sweden	1	0	0	0	0	....	....	....	....	....
2011-12	MODO U18	Swe-U18	1	1	0	1	2	1	0	0	0	10
	MODO Jr.	Swe-Jr.	34	7	22	29	101	8	1	3	4	4
	MODO	Sweden	20	0	1	1	8	1	0	0	0	0
2012-13	MODO	Sweden	30	3	3	6	2	....	....	....	....	....
	Orebro HK	Sweden-2	9	0	0	0	2	....	....	....	....	....
	MODO Jr.	Swe-Jr.	8	1	2	3	4	7	1	5	6	4
2013-14	Farjestad	Sweden	51	3	8	11	24	10	0	0	0	2
2014-15	Texas Stars	AHL	12	0	3	3	4	....	....	....	....	....
	Farjestad Jr.	Swe-Jr.	1	0	0	0	0	....	....	....	....	....
	Timra IK	Sweden-2	5	0	1	1	6	....	....	....	....	....
	Farjestad	Sweden	38	1	4	5	18	3	0	0	0	4

CALNAN, Chris (KAL-nan, KRIHS) CHI

Right wing. Shoots right. 6'2", 203 lbs. Born, Boston, MA, May 5, 1994.
(Chicago's 3rd choice, 79th overall, in 2012 Entry Draft).

			Regular Season					Playoffs				
Season	Club	League	GP	G	A	Pts	PIM	GP	G	A	Pts	PIM
2010-11	Neponset Valley	Minor-MA	11	7	11	18	28	....	....	....	....	....
	Nobles	High-MA	27	14	11	25	8	....	....	....	....	....
2011-12	Cape Cod Whalers	Minor-MA	32	21	28	49	....	....	....	....	....	....
	Nobles	High-MA	27	28	27	55	13	....	....	....	....	....
2012-13	South Shore Kings	EJHL	31	27	22	49	35	2	2	0	2	2
2013-14	Boston College	H-East	37	4	9	13	23	....	....	....	....	....
2014-15	Boston College	H-East	37	11	5	16	8	....	....	....	....	....

CAMARA, Anthony (kuh-MAR-uh, an-THUH-nee) BOS

Left wing. Shoots left. 6', 192 lbs. Born, Toronto, ON, September 4, 1993.
(Boston's 3rd choice, 81st overall, in 2011 Entry Draft).

			Regular Season					Playoffs				
Season	Club	League	GP	G	A	Pts	PIM	GP	G	A	Pts	PIM
2008-09	Miss. Senators	GTHL	50	31	25	56	94	....	....	....	....	....
2009-10	Saginaw Spirit	OHL	65	6	6	12	96	6	1	1	2	5
2010-11	Saginaw Spirit	OHL	64	8	9	17	132	12	0	1	1	25
2011-12	Saginaw Spirit	OHL	35	7	12	19	76	....	....	....	....	....
	Barrie Colts	OHL	31	9	5	14	59	13	2	3	5	22
2012-13	Barrie Colts	OHL	50	36	24	60	91	16	9	7	16	*42
2013-14	Providence Bruins	AHL	58	9	13	22	50	....	....	....	....	....
2014-15	Providence Bruins	AHL	59	3	5	8	32	....	....	....	....	....

CAMERANESI, Tony (kam-uhr-ihn-EHS-ee, TOH-nee) TOR

Center. Shoots right. 5'10", 189 lbs. Born, Maple Grove, MN, August 12, 1993.
(Toronto's 5th choice, 130th overall, in 2011 Entry Draft).

			Regular Season					Playoffs				
Season	Club	League	GP	G	A	Pts	PIM	GP	G	A	Pts	PIM
2009-10	Wayzata	High-MN	25	16	29	45	6	2	2	1	3	0
2010-11	Team Northwest	UMHSEL	21	16	17	33	18	3	2	4	6	2
	Wayzata	High-MN	25	15	39	54	26	3	2	7	9	4
2011-12	Waterloo	USHL	55	18	24	42	47	10	1	5	6	4
2012-13	U. Minn-Duluth	WCHA	38	14	20	34	28	....	....	....	....	....
2013-14	U. Minn-Duluth	NCHC	36	7	14	21	19	....	....	....	....	....
2014-15	U. Minn-Duluth	NCHC	40	9	21	30	16	....	....	....	....	....

WCHA All-Rookie Team (2013)

CAMMARATA, Taylor (kam-a-RAT-ta, TAY-luhr) NYI

Center/Left wing. Shoots left. 5'7", 160 lbs. Born, Minneapolis, MN, May 13, 1995.
(NY Islanders' 3rd choice, 76th overall, in 2013 Entry Draft).

			Regular Season					Playoffs				
Season	Club	League	GP	G	A	Pts	PIM	GP	G	A	Pts	PIM
2009-10	Shattuck Bantam	High-MN	58	92	78	170	8	....	....	....	....	....
2010-11	Shattuck Midget	High-MN	54	71	68	139	6	....	....	....	....	....
2011-12	Waterloo	USHL	60	27	42	69	6	15	8	8	16	6
2012-13	Waterloo	USHL	59	*38	55	*93	49	5	2	3	5	0
2013-14	U. of Minnesota	Big Ten	39	10	17	27	6	....	....	....	....	....
2014-15	U. of Minnesota	Big Ten	39	3	24	27	10	....	....	....	....	....

USHL All-Rookie Team (2012) • USHL Second All-Star Team (2012) • USHL Rookie of the Year (2012) • USHL First All-Star Team (2013) • USHL Player of the Year (2013)

CAMPBELL, Colin (KAM-buhl, KAWL-lihn) DET

Right wing. Shoots right. 6'1", 207 lbs. Born, Pickering, ON, April 17, 1991.

			Regular Season					Playoffs				
Season	Club	League	GP	G	A	Pts	PIM	GP	G	A	Pts	PIM
2006-07	Tor. Red Wings	GTHL	42	9	12	21	38	....	....	....	....	....
2007-08	Tor. Red Wings	GTHL	30	10	15	25	10	....	....	....	....	....
	Pickering Panthers	ON-Jr.A	1	0	0	0	2	....	....	....	....	....
2008-09	Vaughan Vipers	ON-Jr.A	47	24	42	66	39	9	7	2	9	0
2009-10	Vaughan Vipers	ON-Jr.A	46	32	44	76	55	5	3	2	5	6
2010-11	Lake Superior	CCHA	37	4	3	7	12	....	....	....	....	....
2011-12	Lake Superior	CCHA	37	9	16	25	22	....	....	....	....	....
2012-13	Lake Superior	CCHA	9	0	3	3	4	....	....	....	....	....
2013-14	Lake Superior	WCHA	36	14	15	29	26	....	....	....	....	....
	Grand Rapids	AHL	13	1	0	1	5	3	0	0	0	2
2014-15	Grand Rapids	AHL	44	2	3	5	29	7	0	1	1	2

Signed as a free agent by **Detroit**, March 17, 2014.

CAMPBELL, Evan (KAM-buhl, EH-vuhn) EDM

Left wing. Shoots left. 6'1", 175 lbs. Born, Port Coquitlam, BC, March 1, 1993.
(Edmonton's 8th choice, 128th overall, in 2013 Entry Draft).

			Regular Season					Playoffs				
Season	Club	League	GP	G	A	Pts	PIM	GP	G	A	Pts	PIM
2009-10	Van. NE Chiefs	BCMML	39	14	14	28	64	4	1	1	2	2
2010-11	Kerry Park	VIJHL	41	14	22	36	28	5	2	1	3	4
	Cowichan Valley	BCHL	1	0	0	0	0	....	....	....	....	....
2011-12	Coquitlam Express	BCHL	17	1	1	2	17	....	....	....	....	....
	Langley Rivermen	BCHL	31	11	8	19	18	....	....	....	....	....
2012-13	Langley Rivermen	BCHL	51	20	46	66	46	4	2	0	2	6
2013-14	U. Mass Lowell	H-East	33	9	2	11	18	....	....	....	....	....
2014-15	U. Mass Lowell	H-East	34	12	15	27	29	....	....	....	....	....

CANNONE, Pat (ka-NOHN, PAT) ST.L.

Right wing. Shoots right. 5'11", 192 lbs. Born, Bayport, NY, August 9, 1986.

			Regular Season					Playoffs				
Season	Club	League	GP	G	A	Pts	PIM	GP	G	A	Pts	PIM
2004-05	N.E. Jr. Falcons	EJHL	49	26	28	54	50	....	....	....	....	....
2005-06	N.E. Jr. Falcons	EJHL	45	22	31	53	52	3	1	3	4	2
2006-07	Cedar Rapids	USHL	59	18	37	55	46	6	1	7	8	6
2007-08	Miami U.	CCHA	42	6	24	30	20	....	....	....	....	....
2008-09	Miami U.	CCHA	41	11	24	35	16	....	....	....	....	....
2009-10	Miami U.	CCHA	44	14	17	31	22	....	....	....	....	....
2010-11	Miami U.	CCHA	39	14	23	37	25	....	....	....	....	....
	Binghamton	AHL	2	1	1	2	2	....	....	....	....	....
2011-12	Binghamton	AHL	76	19	24	43	32	....	....	....	....	....
2012-13	Binghamton	AHL	74	10	15	25	41	3	0	0	0	4
2013-14	Chicago Wolves	AHL	59	16	18	34	16	9	0	2	2	4
2014-15	Chicago Wolves	AHL	64	14	33	47	18	5	0	6	6	0

Signed as a free agent by **Ottawa**, April 8, 2011. Traded to **St. Louis** by **Ottawa** for future considerations, July 8, 2013.

CAPOBIANCO, Kyle (ka-poh-bee-AHN-koh, KIGH-uhl) ARI

Defense. Shoots left. 6'1", 178 lbs. Born, Mississauga, ON, August 13, 1997.
(Arizona's 4th choice, 63rd overall, in 2015 Entry Draft).

			Regular Season					Playoffs				
Season	Club	League	GP	G	A	Pts	PIM	GP	G	A	Pts	PIM
2012-13	Oakville Rangers	Minor-ON	40	7	24	31	38	....	....	....	....	....
	Oakville Rangers	Other	31	7	18	25	36	....	....	....	....	....
	Oakville Blades	ON-Jr.A	3	0	1	1	12	....	....	....	....	....
2013-14	Sudbury Wolves	OHL	53	0	11	11	18	5	0	0	0	0
2014-15	Sudbury Wolves	OHL	68	10	30	40	54	....	....	....	....	....

CAREY, Greg (KAIR-ee, GREHG) ARI

Left wing. Shoots left. 6', 195 lbs. Born, Hamilton, ON, April 5, 1990.

			Regular Season					Playoffs				
Season	Club	League	GP	G	A	Pts	PIM	GP	G	A	Pts	PIM
2005-06	Ham. Jr. Bulldogs	Minor-ON	58	66	35	101	14	....	....	....	....	....
2006-07	Glanbrook	ON-Jr.C	35	17	16	33	24	6	0	1	1	4
2007-08	Burlington	ON-Jr.A	46	10	12	22	16	3	0	0	0	0
2008-09	Burlington	ON-Jr.A	45	31	34	65	24	8	5	5	10	22
2009-10	Burlington	ON-Jr.A	48	*72	42	114	46	10	7	4	11	13
2010-11	St. Lawrence	ECAC	40	23	17	40	24	....	....	....	....	....
2011-12	St. Lawrence	ECAC	36	15	22	37	22	....	....	....	....	....
2012-13	St. Lawrence	ECAC	38	*28	23	*51	38	....	....	....	....	....
2013-14	St. Lawrence	ECAC	38	18	*39	*57	39	....	....	....	....	....
	Portland Pirates	AHL	13	1	1	2	4	....	....	....	....	....
2014-15	Gwinnett	ECHL	30	15	12	27	6	....	....	....	....	....
	Portland Pirates	AHL	29	2	4	6	18	....	....	....	....	....

ECAC All-Rookie Team (2011) • ECAC First All-Star Team (2013, 2014) • NCAA East Second All-American Team (2013) • NCAA East First All-American Team (2014)

Signed as a free agent by **Phoenix**, March 20, 2014.

CARLO, Brandon (KAHR-loh, BRAN-duhn) BOS

Defense. Shoots right. 6'5", 203 lbs. Born, Colorado Springs, CO, November 26, 1996.
(Boston's 4th choice, 37th overall, in 2015 Entry Draft).

			Regular Season					Playoffs				
Season	Club	League	GP	G	A	Pts	PIM	GP	G	A	Pts	PIM
2011-12	Col. T-birds U16	T1EHL	40	6	11	17	20	....	....	....	....	....
2012-13	Col. T-birds U16	T1EHL	41	10	37	47	58	4	1	2	3	6
	Tri-City Americans	WHL	....	....	....	....	....	5	1	0	1	8
2013-14	Tri-City Americans	WHL	71	3	10	13	66	5	0	1	1	8
2014-15	Tri-City Americans	WHL	63	4	21	25	90	4	0	1	1	4

CARLSSON, Gabriel (KAHR-suhn, GA-bree-ehl) CBJ

Defense. Shoots left. 6'4", 183 lbs. Born, Orebro, Sweden, January 2, 1997.
(Columbus' 2nd choice, 29th overall, in 2015 Entry Draft).

			Regular Season					Playoffs				
Season	Club	League	GP	G	A	Pts	PIM	GP	G	A	Pts	PIM
2012-13	Orebro HK U18	Swe-U18	16	1	5	6	4	....	....	....	....	....
	Orebro HUF U18	Swe-U18	2	2	0	2	0	....	....	....	....	....
2013-14	Linkopings HC U18	Swe-U18	40	4	15	19	14	5	0	0	0	4
2014-15	Linkopings HC U18	Swe-U18	7	2	3	5	2	....	....	....	....	....
	Linkopings HC Jr.	Swe-Jr.	39	0	7	7	14	3	0	2	2	2
	Linkopings HC	Sweden	7	0	2	2	0	10	0	1	1	2

CARPENTER, Ryan (KAHR-pehn-tuhr, RIGH-uhn) **S.J.**

Right wing. Shoots right. 6', 190 lbs. Born, Oviedo, FL, January 18, 1991.

			Regular Season					Playoffs				
Season	Club	League	GP	G	A	Pts	PIM	GP	G	A	Pts	PIM
2007-08	Det. Vic. Honda	MWEHL	31	15	14	29	26	....	....	....	....	....
	Det. Vic. Honda	Other	3	0	1	1	0	....	....	....	....	....
2008-09	Det. Honeybaked	T1EHL	46	19	13	32	26	4	0	1	1	0
2009-10	Sioux City	USHL	58	10	12	22	45	....	....	....	....	....
2010-11	Sioux City	USHL	59	13	32	45	30	3	2	1	3	2
2011-12	Bowling Green	CCHA	44	11	19	30	31	....	....	....	....	....
2012-13	Bowling Green	CCHA	41	18	15	33	20	....	....	....	....	....
2013-14	Bowling Green	WCHA	15	8	8	16	0	....	....	....	....	....
2014-15	Worcester Sharks	AHL	74	12	22	34	40	4	1	2	3	2

CCHA Second All-Star Team (2013)

Signed as a free agent by **San Jose**, March 26, 2014.

CARR, Daniel (KARR, DAHN-yehl) **MTL**

Left wing. Shoots left. 6', 193 lbs. Born, Sherwood Park, AB, November 1, 1991.

			Regular Season					Playoffs				
Season	Club	League	GP	G	A	Pts	PIM	GP	G	A	Pts	PIM
2005-06	Leduc Oil Kings	AMBHL	34	29	56	85	34	9	8	8	16	....
2006-07	Leduc Oil Kings	Minor-AB	30	17	30	47	42	....	....	....	....	....
2007-08	St. Albert Steel	AJHL	62	16	11	27	36	5	0	0	0	0
2008-09	St. Albert Steel	AJHL	59	27	28	55	81	4	2	2	4	2
2009-10	St. Albert Steel	AJHL	30	24	30	54	15	....	....	....	....	....
	Powell River Kings	BCHL	22	10	17	27	14	23	15	11	26	10
2010-11	Union College	ECAC	40	20	15	35	28	....	....	....	....	....
2011-12	Union College	ECAC	41	20	20	40	30	....	....	....	....	....
2012-13	Union College	ECAC	40	16	16	32	26	....	....	....	....	....
2013-14	Union College	ECAC	39	22	28	50	28	....	....	....	....	....
2014-15	Hamilton Bulldogs	AHL	76	24	15	39	21	....	....	....	....	....

ECAC All-Rookie Team (2011) • ECAC First All-Star Team (2014) • NCAA East Second All-American Team (2014)

Signed as a free agent by **Montreal**, April 25, 2014.

CARRICK, Trevor (KAIR-ihk, TREH-vuhr) **CAR**

Defense. Shoots left. 6'2", 186 lbs. Born, Stouffville, ON, July 4, 1994.
(Carolina's 5th choice, 115th overall, in 2012 Entry Draft).

			Regular Season					Playoffs				
Season	Club	League	GP	G	A	Pts	PIM	GP	G	A	Pts	PIM
2009-10	Markham Majors	GTHL	49	6	23	29	48	....	....	....	....	....
	Upper Canada	ON-Jr.A	2	0	1	1	2	....	....	....	....	....
2010-11	Stouffville Spirit	ON-Jr.A	40	6	13	19	44	19	2	11	13	10
2011-12	St. Michael's	OHL	68	6	13	19	64	6	1	0	1	7
2012-13	Mississauga	OHL	56	10	21	31	56	6	0	2	2	11
2013-14	Mississauga	OHL	41	16	15	31	65	....	....	....	....	....
	Sudbury Wolves	OHL	29	6	14	20	52	5	1	2	3	10
2014-15	Charlotte	AHL	76	7	25	32	94	....	....	....	....	....

CARRIER, Alexandre (kair-EE-ay, Al-ehx-AHN-druh) **NSH**

Defense. Shoots right. 5'11", 174 lbs. Born, Quebec City, QC, October 8, 1996.
(Nashville's 4th choice, 115th overall, in 2015 Entry Draft).

			Regular Season					Playoffs				
Season	Club	League	GP	G	A	Pts	PIM	GP	G	A	Pts	PIM
2011-12	Antoine-Girouard	QAAA	40	5	25	30	30	11	1	1	2	2
2012-13	Gatineau	QMJHL	50	2	5	7	28	9	1	0	1	6
2013-14	Gatineau	QMJHL	67	3	25	28	29	9	1	4	5	4
2014-15	Gatineau	QMJHL	68	12	43	55	64	11	2	3	5	18

QMJHL Second All-Star Team (2015)

CARRIER, William (kair-ree-AY, WIHL-yuhm) **BUF**

Left wing. Shoots left. 6'1", 202 lbs. Born, La Salle, QC, December 20, 1994.
(St. Louis' 2nd choice, 57th overall, in 2013 Entry Draft).

			Regular Season					Playoffs				
Season	Club	League	GP	G	A	Pts	PIM	GP	G	A	Pts	PIM
2009-10	Lac St-Louis Royals	Minor-QC			STATISTICS NOT AVAILABLE							
	Lac St-Louis Lions	QAAA	3	0	0	0	2	....	....	....	....	....
2010-11	Cape Breton	QMJHL	61	8	4	12	54	4	0	0	0	2
2011-12	Cape Breton	QMJHL	66	27	43	70	65	4	3	3	6	4
2012-13	Cape Breton	QMJHL	34	16	26	42	41	....	....	....	....	....
2013-14	Cape Breton	QMJHL	39	12	29	41	42	....	....	....	....	....
	Drummondville	QMJHL	27	10	14	24	45	4	1	3	4	6
2014-15	Rochester	AHL	63	7	14	21	38	....	....	....	....	....

Traded to **Buffalo** by **St. Louis** with Jaroslav Halak, Chris Stewart, St. Louis' 1st round choice (later traded to Winnipeg – Winnipeg selected Jack Roslovic) in 2015 Entry Draft and St. Louis' 3rd round choice in 2016 Entry Draft for Ryan Miller and Steve Ott, February 28, 2014.

CARROLL, Austin (KAIR-uhl, AW-stuhn) **CGY**

Right wing. Shoots right. 6'4", 225 lbs. Born, Calgary, AB, March 26, 1994.
(Calgary's 6th choice, 184th overall, in 2014 Entry Draft).

			Regular Season					Playoffs				
Season	Club	League	GP	G	A	Pts	PIM	GP	G	A	Pts	PIM
2009-10	P.F. Chang's U16	T1EHL	12	3	0	3	30	....	....	....	....	....
2010-11	Coquitlam Express	BCHL	42	6	5	11	28	4	0	0	0	4
2011-12	Victoria Royals	WHL	62	8	12	20	80	4	2	0	2	6
2012-13	Victoria Royals	WHL	67	15	27	42	152	4	1	1	2	2
2013-14	Victoria Royals	WHL	70	34	23	57	114	9	5	3	8	16
2014-15	Victoria Royals	WHL	69	38	39	77	124	10	1	8	9	8

CASSELS, Cole (KA-suhlz, KOHL) **VAN**

Center. Shoots right. 6'1", 184 lbs. Born, Columbus, OH, May 4, 1995.
(Vancouver's 3rd choice, 85th overall, in 2013 Entry Draft).

			Regular Season					Playoffs				
Season	Club	League	GP	G	A	Pts	PIM	GP	G	A	Pts	PIM
2009-10	Cleveland Barons	T1EHL	31	6	22	28	46	....	....	....	....	....
2010-11	Ohio Blue Jackets	T1EHL	37	11	23	34	61	....	....	....	....	....
	Ohio Blue Jackets	Minor-OH	11	11	21	32	....	....	....	....	....	....
2011-12	Oshawa Generals	OHL	64	3	8	11	31	6	1	0	1	6
2012-13	Oshawa Generals	OHL	64	15	28	43	61	9	1	0	1	14
2013-14	Oshawa Generals	OHL	61	24	49	73	90	12	6	11	17	16
2014-15	Oshawa Generals	OHL	54	30	51	81	100	21	10	21	31	14

CASTO, Chris (KAS-toh, KRIHS) **BOS**

Defense. Shoots right. 6'1", 200 lbs. Born, St. Paul, MN, December 27, 1991.

			Regular Season					Playoffs				
Season	Club	League	GP	G	A	Pts	PIM	GP	G	A	Pts	PIM
2010-11	Lincoln Stars	USHL	58	6	19	25	40	2	0	0	0	0
2011-12	U. Minn-Duluth	WCHA	41	2	11	13	14	....	....	....	....	....
2012-13	U. Minn-Duluth	WCHA	36	3	6	9	16	....	....	....	....	....
	Providence Bruins	AHL	4	0	0	0	0	12	0	2	2	13
2013-14	Providence Bruins	AHL	52	3	8	11	23	12	0	2	2	13
	South Carolina	ECHL	1	0	0	0	0	....	....	....	....	....
2014-15	Providence Bruins	AHL	62	1	11	12	35	5	0	0	0	2

Signed as a free agent by **Boston**, March 26, 2013.

CATENACCI, Daniel (ka-tehn-AH-chee, DAN-yehl) **BUF**

Center. Shoots left. 5'9", 191 lbs. Born, Richmond Hill, ON, March 9, 1993.
(Buffalo's 2nd choice, 77th overall, in 2011 Entry Draft).

			Regular Season					Playoffs				
Season	Club	League	GP	G	A	Pts	PIM	GP	G	A	Pts	PIM
2008-09	York Simcoe	Minor-ON	39	42	45	87	152	....	....	....	....	....
	Villanova Knights	ON-Jr.A	1	1	0	1	2	....	....	....	....	....
2009-10	Sault Ste. Marie	OHL	65	10	20	30	68	5	1	1	2	6
2010-11	Sault Ste. Marie	OHL	67	26	45	71	117	....	....	....	....	....
2011-12	Owen Sound	OHL	67	33	39	72	114	5	1	3	4	8
2012-13	Owen Sound	OHL	67	38	41	79	115	12	3	6	9	32
	Rochester	AHL	2	1	2	3	0	....	....	....	....	....
2013-14	Rochester	AHL	76	10	10	20	32	2	0	0	0	0
2014-15	Rochester	AHL	68	15	14	29	60	....	....	....	....	....

CAVE, Colby (KOHL-bee, KAYV) **BOS**

Center. Shoots left. 6'1", 199 lbs. Born, Battleford, SK, December 26, 1994.

			Regular Season					Playoffs				
Season	Club	League	GP	G	A	Pts	PIM	GP	G	A	Pts	PIM
2009-10	Battlefords Stars	SMHL	42	15	21	36	40	....	....	....	....	....
2010-11	Battlefords Stars	SMHL	44	14	22	36	28	....	....	....	....	....
	Battlefords	SJHL	3	0	1	1	0	....	....	....	....	....
	Swift Current	WHL	1	0	0	0	0	....	....	....	....	....
2011-12	Swift Current	WHL	70	6	10	16	36	....	....	....	....	....
2012-13	Swift Current	WHL	72	21	20	41	39	5	2	2	4	8
2013-14	Swift Current	WHL	72	33	37	70	30	6	0	2	2	0
2014-15	Swift Current	WHL	72	35	40	75	52	4	2	0	2	2
	Providence Bruins	AHL	1	0	0	0	0	....	....	....	....	....

Signed as a free agent by **Boston**, April 7, 2015.

CECCONI, Joseph (seh-KOH-nee, JOH-sehf) **DAL**

Defense. Shoots right. 6'2", 209 lbs. Born, Youngstown, NY, May 23, 1997.
(Dallas' 4th choice, 133rd overall, in 2015 Entry Draft).

			Regular Season					Playoffs				
Season	Club	League	GP	G	A	Pts	PIM	GP	G	A	Pts	PIM
2012-13	Buf. Jr. Sabres U16	T1EHL	40	1	8	9	14	4	1	0	1	0
	Buf. Jr. Sabres U18	T1EHL	4	0	0	0	2	3	0	0	0	2
2013-14	Buf. Jr. Sabres U16	T1EHL	34	10	9	19	31	....	....	....	....	....
	Muskegon	USHL	28	2	4	6	8	....	....	....	....	....
2014-15	Muskegon	USHL	60	3	14	17	35	12	0	2	2	8

• Signed Letter of Intent to attend **University of Michigan** (Big Ten) in fall of 2015.

CEDERHOLM, Anton (SEH-duhr-holm, an-TAWN) **VAN**

Defense. Shoots left. 6'2", 204 lbs. Born, Helsingborg, Sweden, February 21, 1995.
(Vancouver's 5th choice, 145th overall, in 2013 Entry Draft).

			Regular Season					Playoffs				
Season	Club	League	GP	G	A	Pts	PIM	GP	G	A	Pts	PIM
2009-10	Jonstorps IF U18	Swe-U18	12	1	3	4	14	....	....	....	....	....
	Jonstorps IF Jr.	Swe-Jr.	3	0	0	0	4	....	....	....	....	....
2010-11	Rogle U18	Swe-U18	31	4	8	12	18	4	0	1	1	2
	Rogle Jr.	Swe-Jr.	2	0	0	0	0	....	....	....	....	....
2011-12	Rogle U18	Swe-U18	8	1	3	4	45	....	....	....	....	....
	Rogle Jr.	Swe-Jr.	41	3	5	8	71	....	....	....	....	....
2012-13	Rogle U18	Swe-U18	8	0	1	1	10	3	0	1	1	6
	Rogle Jr.	Swe-Jr.	36	5	8	13	64	2	0	0	0	0
	Rogle	Sweden	12	0	0	0	6	....	....	....	....	....
2013-14	Portland	WHL	71	4	12	16	95	21	2	3	5	16
2014-15	Portland	WHL	68	9	10	19	84	17	1	1	2	6

CEHLARIK, Peter (T'SECH-lahr-ihk, PEE-tuhr) **BOS**

Left wing. Shoots left. 6'3", 202 lbs. Born, Zilina, Slovakia, August 2, 1995.
(Boston's 2nd choice, 90th overall, in 2013 Entry Draft).

			Regular Season					Playoffs				
Season	Club	League	GP	G	A	Pts	PIM	GP	G	A	Pts	PIM
2008-09	MsHK Zilina U18	Svk-U18	1	0	0	0	0	....	....	....	....	....
2009-10	Zilina U18	Svk-U18	28	4	4	8	4	....	....	....	....	....
2010-11	MsHK Zilina U18	Svk-U18	40	15	18	33	8	....	....	....	....	....
2011-12	MsHK Zilina U18	Svk-U18	6	6	2	8	16	....	....	....	....	....
	MsHK Zilina Jr.	Slovak-Jr.	4	1	2	3	2	....	....	....	....	....
	Lulea HF U18	Swe-U18	24	15	15	30	0	4	2	0	2	0
	Lulea HF Jr.	Swe-Jr.	8	2	2	4	2	1	3	0	3	0
2012-13	Lulea HF U18	Swe-U18	10	8	9	17	0	....	....	....	....	....
	Lulea HF Jr.	Swe-Jr.	38	17	20	37	10	3	0	1	1	2
	Lulea HF	Sweden	8	3	3	6	0	6	1	0	1	0
2013-14	Lulea HF	Sweden	32	2	2	4	4	2	0	0	0	0
	Lulea HF Jr.	Swe-Jr.	4	5	2	7	0	....	....	....	....	....
	Asploven	Sweden-2	18	5	8	13	6	....	....	....	....	....
2014-15	Lulea HF Jr.	Swe-Jr.	1	0	0	0	0	....	....	....	....	....
	Lulea HF	Sweden	46	6	13	19	6	8	1	1	2	2

CERNAK, Erik (CHAIR-nak, AIR-ihk) **L.A.**

Defense. Shoots right. 6'3", 203 lbs. Born, Kosice, Slovakia, May 28, 1997.
(Los Angeles' 1st choice, 43rd overall, in 2015 Entry Draft).

			Regular Season					Playoffs				
Season	Club	League	GP	G	A	Pts	PIM	GP	G	A	Pts	PIM
2011-12	HC Kosice U18	Svk-U18	37	5	4	9	61	....	....	....	....	....
2012-13	Slovakia U20 B	Slovak-2	8	2	0	2	18	....	....	....	....	....
	Bratislava U18	Svk-U18	....	....	....	....	....	1	0	2	2	0
	Bratislava Jr.	Slovak-Jr.	30	4	6	10	18	12	0	1	1	8
2013-14	Slovakia U20	Slovakia	20	2	1	3	2	....	....	....	....	....
	HC Kosice Jr.	Slovak-Jr.	8	1	3	4	16	....	....	....	....	....
	HC Kosice	Slovakia	13	0	0	0	0	7	0	0	0	2
2014-15	HC Kosice	Slovakia	43	5	8	13	16	7	0	1	1	6

CHABOT, Thomas (shuh-BAWT, TAW-muhs) OTT

Defense. Shoots left. 6'2", 185 lbs. Born, Sainte-Marie, QC, January 30, 1997.
(Ottawa's 1st choice, 18th overall, in 2015 Entry Draft).

			Regular Season					Playoffs				
Season	**Club**	**League**	**GP**	**G**	**A**	**Pts**	**PIM**	**GP**	**G**	**A**	**Pts**	**PIM**
2012-13	Levis	QAAA	41	6	20	26	22	4	1	1	2	8
2013-14	Saint John	QMJHL	55	1	21	22	36	....	....	....	....	....
2014-15	Saint John	QMJHL	66	12	29	41	62	5	0	1	1	6

CHARTIER, Rourke (SHAHR-t'yay, ROHRK) S.J.

Center. Shoots left. 5'10", 190 lbs. Born, Saskatoon, SK, April 3, 1996.
(San Jose's 7th choice, 149th overall, in 2014 Entry Draft).

			Regular Season					Playoffs				
Season	**Club**	**League**	**GP**	**G**	**A**	**Pts**	**PIM**	**GP**	**G**	**A**	**Pts**	**PIM**
2009-10	Sask. Outlaws	Minor-SK	51	86	45	131	....	....	....	....	....	....
2010-11	Sask. Stallions	Minor-SK	STATISTICS NOT AVAILABLE									
	Sask. Contacts	SMHL	7	2	0	2	4	1	1	1	2	0
2011-12	Sask. Contacts	SMHL	42	23	34	57	14	13	*8	5	13	2
2012-13	Kelowna Rockets	WHL	58	13	17	30	16	3	0	0	0	0
2013-14	Kelowna Rockets	WHL	72	24	34	58	8	14	6	6	12	2
2014-15	Kelowna Rockets	WHL	58	48	34	82	18	16	13	7	20	2

WHL West First All-Star Team (2015)

CHASE, Gregory (CHAYS, GREH-goh-ree) EDM

Center/Right wing. Shoots right. 6', 189 lbs. Born, Sherwood Park, AB, January 1, 1995.
(Edmonton's 10th choice, 188th overall, in 2013 Entry Draft).

			Regular Season					Playoffs				
Season	**Club**	**League**	**GP**	**G**	**A**	**Pts**	**PIM**	**GP**	**G**	**A**	**Pts**	**PIM**
2010-11	Sherwood Park	AMHL	30	24	15	39	64	12	7	3	10	36
	Calgary Hitmen	WHL	5	0	0	0	6	....	....	....	....	....
2011-12	Calgary Hitmen	WHL	60	6	22	28	41	5	1	1	2	11
2012-13	Calgary Hitmen	WHL	69	17	32	49	58	17	3	7	10	24
2013-14	Calgary Hitmen	WHL	70	35	50	85	83	6	4	5	9	2
	Oklahoma City	AHL	5	1	0	1	4	....	....	....	....	....
2014-15	Calgary Hitmen	WHL	15	2	13	15	20	....	....	....	....	....
	Victoria Royals	WHL	46	18	26	44	39	10	7	4	11	6
	Oklahoma City	AHL	....	....	....	....	....	4	0	1	1	2

CHATHAM, Connor (CHA-tuhm, KAW-nuhr) N.J.

Right wing. Shoots right. 6'2", 225 lbs. Born, Belleville, IL, October 30, 1995.
(New Jersey's 3rd choice, 71st overall, in 2014 Entry Draft).

			Regular Season					Playoffs				
Season	**Club**	**League**	**GP**	**G**	**A**	**Pts**	**PIM**	**GP**	**G**	**A**	**Pts**	**PIM**
2010-11	St. Louis Blues	T1EHL	12	2	0	2	0	....	....	....	....	....
2011-12	USNTDP	USHL	36	3	9	12	35	2	0	0	0	0
	USNTDP	U-17	17	4	4	8	10	....	....	....	....	....
2012-13	Omaha Lancers	USHL	63	18	17	35	71	....	....	....	....	....
2013-14	Plymouth Whalers	OHL	54	13	18	31	51	5	3	0	3	6
2014-15	Plymouth Whalers	OHL	48	17	20	37	47	....	....	....	....	....

CHEEK, Trevor (CHEEK, TREH-vuhr) COL

Left wing. Shoots left. 6'2", 205 lbs. Born, Beverly Hills, CA, December 29, 1992.

			Regular Season					Playoffs				
Season	**Club**	**League**	**GP**	**G**	**A**	**Pts**	**PIM**	**GP**	**G**	**A**	**Pts**	**PIM**
2010-11	Calgary Hitmen	WHL	57	10	15	25	37	....	....	....	....	....
2011-12	Calgary Hitmen	WHL	67	23	26	49	75	5	3	1	4	4
2012-13	Calgary Hitmen	WHL	1	0	1	1	0	....	....	....	....	....
	Vancouver Giants	WHL	39	18	14	32	35	....	....	....	....	....
	Edmonton	WHL	31	14	13	27	22	15	8	8	16	14
2013-14	Lake Erie Monsters	AHL	46	3	5	8	30	....	....	....	....	....
2014-15	Lake Erie Monsters	AHL	66	6	9	15	63	....	....	....	....	....

Signed as a free agent by **Colorado**, April 3, 2013.

CHLAPIK, Filip (KHLA-pihk, FIHL-ihp) OTT

Center. Shoots left. 6'1", 197 lbs. Born, Prague, Czech Rep., June 3, 1997.
(Ottawa's 4th choice, 48th overall, in 2015 Entry Draft).

			Regular Season					Playoffs				
Season	**Club**	**League**	**GP**	**G**	**A**	**Pts**	**PIM**	**GP**	**G**	**A**	**Pts**	**PIM**
2011-12	HC Liberec U18	CzR-U18	8	1	4	5	2	....	....	....	....	....
2012-13	HC Liberec U18	CzR-U18	43	19	31	50	12	5	3	1	4	2
2013-14	Sparta U18	CzR-U18	5	1	7	8	2	3	2	1	3	2
	Litomerice	CzRep-2	1	0	0	0	0	....	....	....	....	....
	Sparta Jr.	CzRep-Jr.	38	16	19	35	22	7	3	3	6	6
2014-15	Charlottetown	QMJHL	64	33	42	75	42	9	1	8	9	10

CHUDINOV, Maxim (choo-DEE-nawf, max-EEM) BOS

Defense. Shoots right. 5'11", 187 lbs. Born, Cherepovets, USSR, March 25, 1990.
(Boston's 7th choice, 195th overall, in 2010 Entry Draft).

			Regular Season					Playoffs				
Season	**Club**	**League**	**GP**	**G**	**A**	**Pts**	**PIM**	**GP**	**G**	**A**	**Pts**	**PIM**
2006-07	Cherepovets	Russia	2	0	0	0	0	3	0	0	0	2
2007-08	Cherepovets 2	Russia-3	STATISTICS NOT AVAILABLE									
	Cherepovets	Russia	18	0	0	0	10	1	0	0	0	0
2008-09	Cherepovets	KHL	26	0	0	0	14	....	....	....	....	....
2009-10	Cherepovets Jr.	Russia-Jr.	4	1	0	1	12	2	0	1	1	4
	Cherepovets	KHL	47	6	8	14	30	....	....	....	....	....
2010-11	Cherepovets	KHL	52	8	15	23	30	6	0	2	2	4
	Cherepovets Jr.	Russia-Jr.	....	....	....	....	....	5	2	2	4	8
2011-12	Cherepovets	KHL	52	9	26	35	62	6	0	2	2	10
	Cherepovets Jr.	Russia-Jr.	....	....	....	....	....	5	0	0	0	8
2012-13	SKA St. Petersburg	KHL	47	2	8	10	46	12	1	1	2	6
2013-14	SKA St. Petersburg	KHL	50	7	11	18	44	10	0	1	1	11
2014-15	SKA St. Petersburg	KHL	51	5	12	17	56	21	1	8	9	20

CHUKAROV, Ivan (choo-KAH-rawf, IGH-vuhn) BUF

Defense. Shoots left. 6'3", 203 lbs. Born, Des Plaines, IL, April 3, 1995.
(Buffalo's 6th choice, 182nd overall, in 2015 Entry Draft).

			Regular Season					Playoffs				
Season	**Club**	**League**	**GP**	**G**	**A**	**Pts**	**PIM**	**GP**	**G**	**A**	**Pts**	**PIM**
2011-12	Chi. Mission U18	HPHL	26	2	8	10	10	....	....	....	....	....
2012-13	Chi. Mission U18	HPHL	30	0	13	13	10	....	....	....	....	....
2013-14	Min. Wilderness	NAHL	44	4	8	12	28	5	1	2	3	0
2014-15	Min. Wilderness	NAHL	55	12	31	43	63	12	0	6	6	6

• Signed Letter of Intent to attend **University of Massachusetts** (Hockey East) in fall of 2015.

CIRELLI, Anthony (suh-REH-lee, AN-thuh-nee) T.B.

Center. Shoots left. 6', 160 lbs. Born, Etobicoke, ON, July 15, 1997.
(Tampa Bay's 4th choice, 72nd overall, in 2015 Entry Draft).

			Regular Season					Playoffs				
Season	**Club**	**League**	**GP**	**G**	**A**	**Pts**	**PIM**	**GP**	**G**	**A**	**Pts**	**PIM**
2012-13	Miss. Reps MM	GTHL	33	9	7	16	6	....	....	....	....	....
2013-14	Miss. Reps Midget	GTHL	31	10	18	28	6	....	....	....	....	....
	Mississauga	ON-Jr.A	1	0	0	0	0	1	0	0	0	0
2014-15	Oshawa Generals	OHL	68	13	23	36	22	21	2	8	10	4

CLAESSON, Fredrik (KLA-suhn, FREH-drihk) OTT

Defense. Shoots left. 6', 200 lbs. Born, Stockholm, Sweden, November 24, 1992.
(Ottawa's 6th choice, 126th overall, in 2011 Entry Draft).

			Regular Season					Playoffs				
Season	**Club**	**League**	**GP**	**G**	**A**	**Pts**	**PIM**	**GP**	**G**	**A**	**Pts**	**PIM**
2007-08	Hammarby U18	Swe-U18	15	1	2	3	29	....	....	....	....	....
	Hammarby	Sweden-2	2	0	0	0	2	....	....	....	....	....
2008-09	Djurgarden U18	Swe-U18	28	9	8	17	4	....	....	....	....	....
	Djurgarden Jr.	Swe-Jr.	7	0	0	0	0	....	....	....	....	....
2009-10	Djurgarden U18	Swe-U18	3	1	1	2	0	5	0	3	3	6
	Djurgarden Jr.	Swe-Jr.	22	0	4	4	18	....	....	....	....	....
2010-11	Djurgarden Jr.	Swe-Jr.	18	2	3	5	6	5	0	1	1	0
	Djurgarden	Sweden	35	2	0	2	6	7	0	1	1	0
2011-12	Djurgarden Jr.	Swe-Jr.	1	0	0	0	2	....	....	....	....	....
	Djurgarden	Sweden	47	1	6	7	8	....	....	....	....	....
	Djurgarden	Sweden-Q	10	1	1	2	0	....	....	....	....	....
2012-13	Binghamton	AHL	70	3	8	11	51	3	0	1	1	2
2013-14	Binghamton	AHL	75	3	26	29	39	4	0	0	0	4
2014-15	Binghamton	AHL	76	4	15	19	42	....	....	....	....	....

CLAPPERTON, Christopher (KLAP-uhr-yuhn, KRIHS-toh-fuhr)

Left wing. Shoots left. 5'9", 174 lbs. Born, Chandler, QC, February 22, 1994.
(Florida's 6th choice, 122nd overall, in 2013 Entry Draft).

			Regular Season					Playoffs				
Season	**Club**	**League**	**GP**	**G**	**A**	**Pts**	**PIM**	**GP**	**G**	**A**	**Pts**	**PIM**
2009-10	Ecole Notre Dame	QAAA	42	7	23	30	16	8	6	1	7	6
2010-11	Ecole Notre Dame	QAAA	32	9	20	29	28	17	10	11	21	12
2011-12	Blainville-Bois.	QMJHL	56	18	37	55	40	11	3	6	9	8
2012-13	Blainville-Bois.	QMJHL	67	34	43	77	71	15	6	14	20	20
2013-14	Blainville-Bois.	QMJHL	53	26	36	62	55	18	5	11	16	18
2014-15	Rimouski Oceanic	QMJHL	61	35	41	76	77	18	12	13	25	20

Signed as a free agent by **Toronto** (AHL), July 3, 2015.

CLIFTON, Connor (KLIHF-tuhn, KAW-nuhr) ARI

Defense. Shoots right. 5'11", 175 lbs. Born, Matawan, NJ, April 28, 1995.
(Phoenix's 4th choice, 133rd overall, in 2013 Entry Draft).

			Regular Season					Playoffs				
Season	**Club**	**League**	**GP**	**G**	**A**	**Pts**	**PIM**	**GP**	**G**	**A**	**Pts**	**PIM**
2010-11	Jersey Hitmen	EmJHL	36	4	14	18	95	7	2	2	4	10
2011-12	Jersey Hitmen	EmJHL	4	0	1	1	26	....	....	....	....	....
	Jersey Hitmen	EJHL	28	1	11	12	46	6	0	3	3	15
	USNTDP	USHL	8	1	0	1	16	....	....	....	....	....
	USNTDP	U-17	4	0	1	1	8	....	....	....	....	....
2012-13	USNTDP	USHL	25	3	6	9	90	....	....	....	....	....
	USNTDP	U-18	41	5	9	14	24	....	....	....	....	....
2013-14	Quinnipiac	ECAC	36	5	4	9	106	....	....	....	....	....
2014-15	Quinnipiac	ECAC	38	0	5	5	54	....	....	....	....	....

COLEMAN, Blake (KOHL-man, BLAYK) N.J.

Center. Shoots left. 5'11", 200 lbs. Born, Plano, TX, November 28, 1991.
(New Jersey's 3rd choice, 75th overall, in 2011 Entry Draft).

			Regular Season					Playoffs				
Season	**Club**	**League**	**GP**	**G**	**A**	**Pts**	**PIM**	**GP**	**G**	**A**	**Pts**	**PIM**
2009-10	Tri-City Storm	USHL	22	2	10	12	32	....	....	....	....	....
	Indiana Ice	USHL	36	8	8	16	24	9	0	2	2	13
2010-11	Indiana Ice	USHL	59	34	*58	*92	72	5	2	2	4	10
2011-12	Miami U.	CCHA	39	12	11	23	56	....	....	....	....	....
2012-13	Miami U.	CCHA	40	9	10	19	56	....	....	....	....	....
2013-14	Miami U.	NCHC	27	19	9	28	65	....	....	....	....	....
2014-15	Miami U.	NCHC	37	20	17	37	*99	....	....	....	....	....

USHL First All-Star Team (2011) • USHL Player of the Year (2011)

COLLBERG, Sebastian (KOHL-buhrg, seh-BAS-t'yehn) NYI

Right wing. Shoots right. 5'11", 195 lbs. Born, Mariestad, Sweden, February 23, 1994.
(Montreal's 2nd choice, 33rd overall, in 2012 Entry Draft).

			Regular Season					Playoffs				
Season	**Club**	**League**	**GP**	**G**	**A**	**Pts**	**PIM**	**GP**	**G**	**A**	**Pts**	**PIM**
2008-09	Mariestad U18	Swe-U18	16	8	8	16	4	....	....	....	....	....
	Mariestad Jr.	Swe-Jr.	21	4	4	8	10	....	....	....	....	....
2009-10	Mariestad U18	Swe-U18	15	12	15	27	8	....	....	....	....	....
	Mariestad Jr.	Swe-Jr.	26	25	14	39	16	....	....	....	....	....
	Mariestads BoIS	Sweden-3	4	1	0	1	0	....	....	....	....	....
2010-11	Frolunda U18	Swe-U18	8	9	7	16	0	4	1	1	2	0
	Frolunda Jr.	Swe-Jr.	35	21	23	44	12	7	4	5	9	0
	Frolunda	Sweden	5	0	0	0	0	....	....	....	....	....
2011-12	Frolunda U18	Swe-U18	1	1	1	2	0	4	3	3	6	4
	Frolunda Jr.	Swe-Jr.	21	9	8	17	18	2	0	0	0	0
	Frolunda	Sweden	41	0	0	0	0	....	....	....	....	....
2012-13	Frolunda Jr.	Swe-Jr.	1	0	0	0	0	2	0	0	0	0
	Orebro HK	Sweden-2	15	6	2	8	2	....	....	....	....	....
	Mariestads BoIS HC	Sweden-3	1	1	1	2	0	....	....	....	....	....
	Frolunda	Sweden	35	6	3	9	6	5	0	2	2	0
	Hamilton Bulldogs	AHL	2	0	0	0	0	....	....	....	....	....
2013-14	Frolunda Jr.	Swe-Jr.	3	5	1	6	0	1	0	1	1	2
	Frolunda	Sweden	40	3	6	9	8	1	0	0	0	0
	Sweden	Olympics	7	1	5	6	6	....	....	....	....	....
2014-15	Bridgeport	AHL	43	4	14	18	13	....	....	....	....	....
	Stockton Thunder	ECHL	6	4	3	7	0	....	....	....	....	....

Traded to **NY Islanders** by **Montreal** with Montreal's 2nd round choice (later traded to Tampa Bay – Tampa Bay selected Johnathan MacLeod) in 2014 Entry Draft for Tomas Vanek and NY Islanders' 5th round choice (Nikolas Koberstein) in 2014 Entry Draft, March 5, 2014.

COLLIER, Brendan (kawl-EE-uhr, BREHN-duhn) CAR

Left wing. Shoots left. 5'9", 176 lbs. Born, Charlestown, MA, October 8, 1993.
(Carolina's 9th choice, 189th overall, in 2012 Entry Draft).

			Regular Season					Playoffs				
Season	Club	League	GP	G	A	Pts	PIM	GP	G	A	Pts	PIM
2009-10	Malden Catholic	High-MA	24	19	24	43	....	....	....	....	....	....
2010-11	Malden Catholic	High-MA	25	30	45	75	....	....	....	....	....	....
2011-12	Malden Catholic	High-MA	25	26	38	64	....	....	....	....	....	....
2012-13	Valley Junior	EJHL	43	14	28	42	27	6	1	5	6	4
2013-14	Boston University	H-East	28	1	3	4	8	....	....	....	....	....
2014-15	Northeastern	H-East	35	2	6	8	2	....	....	....	....	....

COLLINS, Ryan (KAWL-ihnz, RIGH-uhn) CBJ

Defense. Shoots right. 6'5", 216 lbs. Born, Bloomington, MN, May 6, 1996.
(Columbus' 2nd choice, 47th overall, in 2014 Entry Draft).

			Regular Season					Playoffs				
Season	Club	League	GP	G	A	Pts	PIM	GP	G	A	Pts	PIM
2011-12	Benilde	High-MN	23	1	3	4	6	6	0	1	1	2
2012-13	USNTDP	USHL	38	0	4	4	12	....	....	....	....	....
	USNTDP	U-17	18	2	3	5	8	....	....	....	....	....
2013-14	USNTDP	USHL	26	0	2	2	10	....	....	....	....	....
	USNTDP	U-18	33	1	4	5	16	....	....	....	....	....
2014-15	U. of Minnesota	Big Ten	32	1	8	9	14	....	....	....	....	....

COMPHER, JT (KUHM-fuhr, JAY-TEE) COL

Left wing. Shoots right. 6', 182 lbs. Born, Northbrook, IL, April 8, 1995.
(Buffalo's 3rd choice, 35th overall, in 2013 Entry Draft).

			Regular Season					Playoffs				
Season	Club	League	GP	G	A	Pts	PIM	GP	G	A	Pts	PIM
2010-11	Team Illinois	T1EHL	34	17	22	39	56	....	....	....	....	....
2011-12	USNTDP	USHL	32	13	14	27	37	....	....	....	....	....
	USNTDP	U-17	17	8	15	23	18	....	....	....	....	....
	USNTDP	U-18	9	4	3	7	4	....	....	....	....	....
2012-13	USNTDP	USHL	21	7	17	24	23	....	....	....	....	....
	USNTDP	U-18	31	11	15	26	18	....	....	....	....	....
2013-14	U. of Michigan	Big Ten	35	11	20	31	22	....	....	....	....	....
2014-15	U. of Michigan	Big Ten	34	12	12	24	40	....	....	....	....	....

Big Ten All-Rookie Team (2014) • Big Ten Second All-Star Team (2014) • Big Ten Rookie of the Year (2014)

Traded to **Colorado** by **Buffalo** with Nikita Zadorov, Mikhail Grigorenko and Buffalo's 2nd round choice (later traded to San Jose – San Jose selected Jeremy Roy) in 2015 Entry Draft for Ryan O'Reilly and Jamie McGinn, June 26, 2015.

COMRIE, Adam (KAWM-ree, A-duhm)

Defense. Shoots left. 6'4", 215 lbs. Born, Kanata, ON, July 31, 1990.
(Florida's 3rd choice, 80th overall, in 2008 Entry Draft).

			Regular Season					Playoffs				
Season	Club	League	GP	G	A	Pts	PIM	GP	G	A	Pts	PIM
2006-07	Ohio	USHL	19	6	4	10	28	....	....	....	....	....
	Omaha Lancers	USHL	38	1	6	7	27	5	0	0	0	4
2007-08	Saginaw Spirit	OHL	58	10	18	28	90	4	0	0	0	4
2008-09	Saginaw Spirit	OHL	52	9	21	30	70	8	0	2	2	8
2009-10	Guelph Storm	OHL	68	14	26	40	79	5	1	2	3	4
2010-11	Rochester	AHL	44	0	5	5	18	....	....	....	....	....
	Cincinnati	ECHL	13	4	4	8	18	2	1	0	1	2
2011-12	Cincinnati	ECHL	4	3	3	6	2	....	....	....	....	....
	Greenville	ECHL	3	1	0	1	2	1	0	0	0	2
2012-13	Reading Royals	ECHL	45	17	16	33	106	....	....	....	....	....
	Worcester Sharks	AHL	24	3	12	15	24	....	....	....	....	....
2013-14	Worcester Sharks	AHL	56	3	16	19	38	....	....	....	....	....
2014-15	Reading Royals	ECHL	21	7	7	14	28	7	2	2	4	10
	Lehigh Valley	AHL	40	5	13	18	50	....	....	....	....	....

Signed as a free agent by **Greenville** (ECHL), March 19, 2012. Signed as a free agent by **Reading** (ECHL), August 3, 2012. Signed as a free agent by **Worcester** (AHL), February 8, 2013. Signed as a free agent by **San Jose**, July 10, 2013. Signed as a free agent by **Reading** (ECHL), October 6, 2014. • Re-assigned to **Lehigh Valley** by **San Jose**, December 27, 2014.

CONNOR, Kyle (KAW-nuhr, KIGH-uhl) WPG

Left wing. Shoots left. 6'1", 175 lbs. Born, Clinton Twp., MI, December 9, 1996.
(Winnipeg's 1st choice, 17th overall, in 2015 Entry Draft).

			Regular Season					Playoffs				
Season	Club	League	GP	G	A	Pts	PIM	GP	G	A	Pts	PIM
2011-12	Det. B. Tire U16	T1EHL	40	14	39	53	14	7	1	5	6	2
2012-13	Youngstown	USHL	62	17	24	41	16	9	0	3	3	0
2013-14	Youngstown	USHL	56	31	43	74	12	....	....	....	....	....
2014-15	Youngstown	USHL	56	34	46	*80	6	4	3	1	4	0

USHL First All-Star Team (2014, 2015) • USHL Player of the Year (2015)

• Signed Letter of Intent to attend **University of Michigan** (Big Ten) in fall of 2015.

COOPER, Brian (KOO-puhr, BRIGH-uhn) ANA

Defense. Shoots left. 5'10", 197 lbs. Born, Anchorage, AK, November 1, 1993.
(Anaheim's 6th choice, 127th overall, in 2012 Entry Draft).

			Regular Season					Playoffs				
Season	Club	League	GP	G	A	Pts	PIM	GP	G	A	Pts	PIM
2009-10	Fargo Force	USHL	55	3	10	13	69	13	0	4	4	22
2010-11	Fargo Force	USHL	51	11	22	33	132	5	2	0	2	18
2011-12	Fargo Force	USHL	55	6	18	24	92	6	1	2	3	8
2012-13	Nebraska-Omaha	WCHA	32	0	2	2	45	....	....	....	....	....
2013-14	Nebraska-Omaha	NCHC	37	2	7	9	30	....	....	....	....	....
2014-15	Nebraska-Omaha	NCHC	39	5	11	16	55	....	....	....	....	....

USHL Second All-Star Team (2011, 2012)

CORBETT, Cody (KOHR-beht, KOH-dee) COL

Defense. Shoots left. 6'1", 204 lbs. Born, Stillwater, MN, December 14, 1993.

			Regular Season					Playoffs				
Season	Club	League	GP	G	A	Pts	PIM	GP	G	A	Pts	PIM
2009-10	Stillwater Ponies	High-MN	24	1	4	5	2	2	0	0	0	0
2010-11	Stillwater Ponies	High-MN	24	9	12	21	14	2	0	1	1	0
2011-12	Edmonton	WHL	54	6	20	26	24	18	0	4	4	14
2012-13	Edmonton	WHL	71	7	35	42	48	20	2	8	10	14
2013-14	Edmonton	WHL	65	17	44	61	37	21	6	7	13	10
2014-15	Lake Erie Monsters	AHL	47	3	3	6	20	....	....	....	....	....

Memorial Cup All-Star Team (2014)

Signed as a free agent by **Colorado**, March 5, 2014.

CORNEL, Eric (kohr-NEHL, AIR-ihk) BUF

Center. Shoots right. 6'2", 191 lbs. Born, Peterborough, ON, April 11, 1996.
(Buffalo's 3rd choice, 44th overall, in 2014 Entry Draft).

			Regular Season					Playoffs				
Season	Club	League	GP	G	A	Pts	PIM	GP	G	A	Pts	PIM
2009-10	U.C. Cyclones MB	Minor-ON	27	29	18	47	10	11	10	15	25	4
	U.C. Cyclones Bant.	Minor-ON	1	2	1	3	0	2	1	1	2	0
2010-11	U.C. Cyclones Bant.	Minor-ON	30	21	40	61	16	....	....	....	....	....
	U.C. Cyclones MM	Minor-ON	4	1	3	4	0	....	....	....	....	....
2011-12	U.C. Cyclones MM	Minor-ON	26	18	32	50	14	5	0	5	5	4
	Kemptville 73's	ON-Jr.A	8	1	3	4	0	....	....	....	....	....
2012-13	Peterborough	OHL	63	4	12	16	13	....	....	....	....	....
2013-14	Peterborough	OHL	68	25	37	62	25	11	4	3	7	4
2014-15	Peterborough	OHL	66	14	38	52	35	5	0	1	1	2
	Rochester	AHL	6	0	1	1	0	....	....	....	....	....

COTTON, David (KAW-tuhn, DAY-vihd) CAR

Center. Shoots left. 6'2", 200 lbs. Born, Parker, TX, July 9, 1997.
(Carolina's 8th choice, 169th overall, in 2015 Entry Draft).

			Regular Season					Playoffs				
Season	Club	League	GP	G	A	Pts	PIM	GP	G	A	Pts	PIM
2012-13	Col. Rampage U16	T1EHL	4	2	1	3	2	....	....	....	....	....
	Col. T-birds U16	T1EHL	37	7	10	17	16	4	0	0	0	0
2013-14	Boston Jr. Bruins	Minor-MA	12	8	3	11	2	....	....	....	....	....
	Cushing	High-MA	32	19	32	51	....	....	....	....	....	....
2014-15	Boston Jr. Bruins	Minor-MA	13	15	9	24	4	....	....	....	....	....
	Cushing	High-MA	33	27	42	69	....	....	....	....	....	....

• Signed Letter of Intent to attend **Boston College** (Hockey East) in fall of 2016.

COUGHLIN, Liam (KAWF-lihn, LEE-uhm) CHI

Center/Left wing. Shoots left. 6'3", 201 lbs. Born, South Boston, MA , September 19, 1994.
(Edmonton's 4th choice, 130th overall, in 2014 Entry Draft).

			Regular Season					Playoffs				
Season	Club	League	GP	G	A	Pts	PIM	GP	G	A	Pts	PIM
2009-10	Walpole Express	MtJHL	29	3	5	8	....	....	....	....	....	....
2010-11	Catholic Memorial	High-MA	....	10	11	21	....	....	....	....	....	....
	S. Bos. Shamrocks	Minor-MA	STATISTICS NOT AVAILABLE									
2011-12	Catholic Memorial	High-MA	....	5	5	10	....	....	....	....	....	....
2012-13	Catholic Memorial	High-MA	....	28	20	48	....	....	....	....	....	....
2013-14	Vernon Vipers	BCHL	53	18	27	45	70	....	....	....	....	....
2014-15	Vernon Vipers	BCHL	54	20	40	60	31	11	3	7	10	2

• Signed Letter of Intent to attend **University of Vermont** (Hockey East) in fall of 2015. Traded to **Chicago** by **Edmonton** for Anders Nilsson, July 6, 2015.

COWICK, Corey (KOW-ihk, KOH-ree)

Left wing. Shoots left. 6'3", 211 lbs. Born, Gloucester, ON, August 1, 1989.
(Ottawa's 7th choice, 160th overall, in 2009 Entry Draft).

			Regular Season					Playoffs				
Season	Club	League	GP	G	A	Pts	PIM	GP	G	A	Pts	PIM
2006-07	Oshawa Generals	OHL	67	4	4	8	54	9	0	0	0	2
2007-08	Oshawa Generals	OHL	63	11	14	25	79	15	1	1	2	22
2008-09	Ottawa 67's	OHL	68	34	26	60	48	7	7	2	9	14
2009-10	Ottawa 67's	OHL	27	15	6	21	33	12	9	3	12	27
2010-11	Binghamton	AHL	30	1	3	4	20	....	....	....	....	....
	Elmira Jackals	ECHL	31	5	9	14	76	....	....	....	....	....
2011-12	Binghamton	AHL	53	5	6	11	38	....	....	....	....	....
	Elmira Jackals	ECHL	22	8	5	13	20	8	2	0	2	26
2012-13	Binghamton	AHL	72	16	19	35	85	3	0	0	0	2
2013-14	Binghamton	AHL	72	12	13	25	89	3	1	0	1	2
2014-15	Springfield Falcons	AHL	46	6	3	9	47	....	....	....	....	....

• Missed majority of 2009-10 due to pre-season shoulder injury at Kingston (OHL), August 30, 2009.

CRAMAROSSA, Joseph (kra-ma-ROH-sa, JOH-sehf) ANA

Center. Shoots left. 6', 190 lbs. Born, Toronto, ON, October 26, 1992.
(Anaheim's 4th choice, 65th overall, in 2011 Entry Draft).

			Regular Season					Playoffs				
Season	Club	League	GP	G	A	Pts	PIM	GP	G	A	Pts	PIM
2007-08	Markham Majors	GTHL	70	31	37	68	64	....	....	....	....	....
2008-09	Markham Waxers	ON-Jr.A	38	7	3	10	14	12	1	2	3	0
2009-10	St. Michael's	OHL	64	6	10	16	60	14	0	2	2	11
2010-11	St. Michael's	OHL	59	12	20	32	101	14	2	2	4	6
2011-12	St. Michael's	OHL	15	6	5	11	40	....	....	....	....	....
	Belleville Bulls	OHL	29	8	8	16	43	6	2	2	4	18
2012-13	Belleville Bulls	OHL	68	19	44	63	89	17	5	4	9	35
2013-14	Norfolk Admirals	AHL	47	1	3	4	52	2	0	0	0	0
	Utah Grizzlies	ECHL	3	0	2	2	7	....	....	....	....	....
2014-15	Norfolk Admirals	AHL	54	5	5	10	75	....	....	....	....	....

CRANE, Chris (KRAYN, KRIHS) S.J.

Right wing. Shoots right. 6'1", 190 lbs. Born, Virginia Beach, VA, December 2, 1991.
(San Jose's 8th choice, 200th overall, in 2010 Entry Draft).

			Regular Season					Playoffs				
Season	Club	League	GP	G	A	Pts	PIM	GP	G	A	Pts	PIM
2008-09	Green Bay	USHL	48	10	9	19	120	5	2	1	3	2
2009-10	Green Bay	USHL	52	15	14	29	107	12	2	3	5	27
2010-11	Ohio State	CCHA	37	4	6	10	37	....	....	....	....	....
2011-12	Ohio State	CCHA	35	14	10	24	30	....	....	....	....	....
2012-13	Ohio State	CCHA	38	6	3	9	69	....	....	....	....	....
	Worcester Sharks	AHL	8	0	0	0	6	....	....	....	....	....
2013-14	Worcester Sharks	AHL	2	0	1	1	0	....	....	....	....	....
	San Francisco Bulls	ECHL	40	7	9	16	37	....	....	....	....	....
	Ontario Reign	ECHL	27	3	4	7	54	3	1	0	1	0
2014-15	Worcester Sharks	AHL	13	1	5	6	9	....	....	....	....	....
	Missouri Mavericks	ECHL	37	11	8	19	33	....	....	....	....	....
	Allen Americans	ECHL	3	3	1	4	2	25	10	10	20	20

CRESCENZI, Andrew (kruh-SEHN-zee, AN-droo) L.A.

Center. Shoots left. 6'4", 199 lbs. Born, Thornhill, ON, July 29, 1992.

			Regular Season					Playoffs				
Season	Club	League	GP	G	A	Pts	PIM	GP	G	A	Pts	PIM
2008-09	Villanova Knights	ON-Jr.A	45	6	17	23	40	....	....	....	....	....
2009-10	Kitchener Rangers	OHL	68	8	4	12	42	20	1	2	3	11
2010-11	Kitchener Rangers	OHL	55	12	11	23	74	7	1	1	2	6
	Toronto Marlies	AHL	2	0	1	1	0	....	....	....	....	....
2011-12	Kitchener Rangers	OHL	52	24	23	47	74	15	4	7	11	20
2012-13	Toronto Marlies	AHL	15	1	1	2	17	....	....	....	....	....
	San Francisco Bulls	ECHL	23	3	11	14	28	....	....	....	....	....
2013-14	Toronto Marlies	AHL	32	1	1	2	33	....	....	....	....	....
	Manchester	AHL	14	1	1	2	8	....	....	....	....	....
2014-15	Manchester	AHL	54	7	8	15	60	18	0	3	3	19

Signed as a free agent by **Toronto**, September 24, 2010. Traded to **Los Angeles** by **Toronto** for Brandon Kozun, January 22, 2014.

CRISP, Connor (KRIHSP, KAW-nuhr) MTL

Left wing. Shoots left. 6'3", 221 lbs. Born, Alliston, ON, April 8, 1994.
(Montreal's 5th choice, 71st overall, in 2013 Entry Draft).

			Regular Season					Playoffs				
Season	Club	League	GP	G	A	Pts	PIM	GP	G	A	Pts	PIM
2009-10	York Simcoe	Minor-ON	60	31	37	68	126	....	....	....	....	....
2010-11	Erie Otters	OHL	48	5	0	5	45	7	0	0	0	4
2011-12	Erie Otters	OHL	6	0	1	1	4	....	....	....	....	....
2012-13	Erie Otters	OHL	63	22	14	36	139	....	....	....	....	....
2013-14	Sudbury Wolves	OHL	67	28	27	55	120	5	1	1	2	10
	Hamilton Bulldogs	AHL	7	2	0	2	2	....	....	....	....	....
2014-15	Hamilton Bulldogs	AHL	39	2	3	5	102	....	....	....	....	....

• Missed majority of 2011-12 with shoulder injury. • Replaced goaltender Ramis Sadikov in a game vs. Niagara (OHL), March 4, 2012. Played 58:15 and allowed 13 goals on 45 shots. (Niagara 13, Erie 4).

CROSS, Tommy (KRAWS, TAW-mee) BOS

Defense. Shoots left. 6'3", 206 lbs. Born, Hartford, CT, September 12, 1989.
(Boston's 2nd choice, 35th overall, in 2007 Entry Draft).

			Regular Season					Playoffs				
Season	Club	League	GP	G	A	Pts	PIM	GP	G	A	Pts	PIM
2004-05	Simsbury	High-CT	23	5	40	45	18	....	....	....	....	....
2005-06	Simsbury	High-CT	22	15	35	50	....	....	....	....	....	....
2006-07	Westminster	High-CT	25	8	12	20	20	....	....	....	....	....
	USNTDP	NAHL	2	0	2	2	0	....	....	....	....	....
	USNTDP	U-18	11	0	1	1	8	....	....	....	....	....
2007-08	Westminster	High-CT	25	9	12	21	....	....	....	....	....	....
	Ohio	USHL	9	0	4	4	8	....	....	....	....	....
2008-09	Boston College	H-East	24	0	8	8	24	....	....	....	....	....
2009-10	Boston College	H-East	38	5	5	10	36	....	....	....	....	....
2010-11	Boston College	H-East	28	7	11	18	45	....	....	....	....	....
2011-12	Boston College	H-East	44	5	19	24	66	....	....	....	....	....
	Providence Bruins	AHL	2	0	0	0	2	....	....	....	....	....
2012-13	South Carolina	ECHL	24	6	13	19	23	....	....	....	....	....
	Providence Bruins	AHL	42	1	10	11	23	12	0	3	3	8
2013-14	Providence Bruins	AHL	55	3	4	7	54	4	0	1	1	4
2014-15	Providence Bruins	AHL	54	4	18	22	85	4	1	0	1	4

CROUSE, Lawson (KROWS, LAW-suhn) FLA

Left wing. Shoots left. 6'4", 215 lbs. Born, Mt. Brydges, ON, June 23, 1997.
(Florida's 1st choice, 11th overall, in 2015 Entry Draft).

			Regular Season					Playoffs				
Season	Club	League	GP	G	A	Pts	PIM	GP	G	A	Pts	PIM
2012-13	Elgin-Mid. Chiefs	Minor-ON	27	22	28	50	51	7	4	5	9	10
	St. Thomas Stars	ON-Jr.B	5	0	1	1	0	....	....	....	....	....
2013-14	Kingston	OHL	63	15	12	27	64	7	0	3	3	7
2014-15	Kingston	OHL	56	29	22	51	70	4	2	1	3	18

CRUS-RYDBERG, Victor (KRUHS-RIGHD-buhrg, VIHK-tuhr) NYI

Center. Shoots right. 5'11", 202 lbs. Born, Vaxjo, Sweden, March 21, 1995.
(NY Islanders' 5th choice, 136th overall, in 2013 Entry Draft).

			Regular Season					Playoffs				
Season	Club	League	GP	G	A	Pts	PIM	GP	G	A	Pts	PIM
2009-10	Tingsryds AIF U18	Swe-U18	15	12	7	19	12	....	....	....	....	....
	Tingsryds AIF Jr.	Swe-Jr.	2	0	0	0	0	....	....	....	....	....
2010-11	Tingsryds AIF U18	Swe-U18	11	1	12	13	6	3	1	2	3	0
	Tingsryds AIF Jr.	Swe-Jr.	30	6	9	15	8	....	....	....	....	....
2011-12	Linkopings HC U18	Swe-U18	30	17	20	37	26	3	1	2	3	0
	Linkopings HC Jr.	Swe-Jr.	10	0	2	2	6	....	....	....	....	....
2012-13	Linkopings HC U18	Swe-U18	4	4	2	6	4	2	0	0	0	0
	Linkopings HC Jr.	Swe-Jr.	35	12	23	35	24	4	2	0	2	0
	Linkopings HC	Sweden	1	0	0	0	0	....	....	....	....	....
2013-14	Plymouth Whalers	OHL	62	12	26	38	20	5	1	2	3	6
	Bridgeport	AHL	7	0	0	0	0	....	....	....	....	....
2014-15	Plymouth Whalers	OHL	55	15	30	45	34	....	....	....	....	....

CUKSTE, Karlis (CHUHK-steh, KAHR-lihs) S.J.

Defense. Shoots left. 6'2", 205 lbs. Born, Riga, Latvia, June 17, 1997.
(San Jose's 5th choice, 130th overall, in 2015 Entry Draft).

			Regular Season					Playoffs				
Season	Club	League	GP	G	A	Pts	PIM	GP	G	A	Pts	PIM
2013-14	SK Riga U18	Latvia-Jr.	22	9	14	23	16	....	....	....	....	....
2014-15	HS Prizma U18	Latvia-U18	3	2	2	4	0	....	....	....	....	....
	HK Riga Jr.	Russia-Jr.	56	7	8	15	40	3	0	0	0	0

CULKIN, Ryan (KUHL-kin, RIGH-uhn) CGY

Defense. Shoots left. 6'2", 195 lbs. Born, Montreal, QC, December 15, 1993.
(Calgary's 5th choice, 124th overall, in 2012 Entry Draft).

			Regular Season					Playoffs				
Season	Club	League	GP	G	A	Pts	PIM	GP	G	A	Pts	PIM
2009-10	Deux Rives	Minor-QC	STATISTICS NOT AVAILABLE									
	Lac St-Louis Lions	QAAA	13	2	2	4	4	21	1	1	2	4
2010-11	Quebec Remparts	QMJHL	40	6	5	11	12	18	0	5	5	4
2011-12	Quebec Remparts	QMJHL	60	6	19	25	28	10	0	7	7	8
2012-13	Quebec Remparts	QMJHL	67	5	40	45	46	11	2	4	6	10
2013-14	Quebec Remparts	QMJHL	38	5	31	36	26	....	....	....	....	....
	Drummondville	QMJHL	27	3	11	14	18	11	2	9	11	6
2014-15	Adirondack Flames	AHL	37	1	17	18	18	....	....	....	....	....

CZARNIK, Austin (ZAHR-nihk, AW-stuhn) BOS

Center. Shoots right. 5'9", 167 lbs. Born, Washington, MI, December 12, 1992.

			Regular Season					Playoffs				
Season	Club	League	GP	G	A	Pts	PIM	GP	G	A	Pts	PIM
2007-08	Det. Belle Tire U16	MWEHL	31	7	14	21	8	....	....	....	....	....
	Det. Belle Tire U16	Other	36	23	31	54	10	....	....	....	....	....
2008-09	USNTDP	NAHL	42	16	18	34	12	9	4	2	6	10
	USNTDP	U-17	14	4	12	16	6	....	....	....	....	....
2009-10	USNTDP	USHL	26	10	18	28	25	....	....	....	....	....
	USNTDP	U-18	35	12	14	26	2	....	....	....	....	....
2010-11	Green Bay	USHL	46	20	14	34	33	11	3	1	4	2
2011-12	Miami U.	CCHA	40	10	27	37	31	....	....	....	....	....
2012-13	Miami U.	CCHA	42	14	*26	*40	24	....	....	....	....	....
2013-14	Miami U.	NCHC	37	13	*34	*47	28	....	....	....	....	....
2014-15	Miami U.	NCHC	40	9	*36	*45	36	....	....	....	....	....
	Providence Bruins	AHL	3	0	2	2	4	....	....	....	....	....

Signed as a free agent by **Boston**, April 1, 2015.

D'AGOSTINO, Nick (DA-goh-STEE-noh, NIHK)

Defense. Shoots left. 6'2", 203 lbs. Born, Mississauga, ON, June 24, 1990.
(Pittsburgh's 4th choice, 210th overall, in 2008 Entry Draft).

			Regular Season					Playoffs				
Season	Club	League	GP	G	A	Pts	PIM	GP	G	A	Pts	PIM
2006-07	Tor. Young Nats	GTHL	30	5	21	26	....	5	0	4	4	....
	Young Nats	Other	8	1	5	6	....	....	....	....	....	....
2007-08	St. Michael's	ON-Jr.A	46	5	18	23	22	12	0	3	3	8
2008-09	St. Michael's	ON-Jr.A	43	9	24	33	34	6	2	3	5	8
2009-10	Cornell Big Red	ECAC	32	4	14	18	6	....	....	....	....	....
2010-11	Cornell Big Red	ECAC	32	7	10	17	20	....	....	....	....	....
2011-12	Cornell Big Red	ECAC	34	8	12	20	24	....	....	....	....	....
2012-13	Cornell Big Red	ECAC	34	6	11	17	30	....	....	....	....	....
2013-14	Wilkes-Barre	AHL	48	1	9	10	15	....	....	....	....	....
	Wheeling Nailers	ECHL	7	0	3	3	0	....	....	....	....	....
2014-15	Wilkes-Barre	AHL	50	0	10	10	10	2	0	0	0	0
	Wheeling Nailers	ECHL	5	1	3	4	2	....	....	....	....	....

ECAC All-Rookie Team (2010) • ECAC Second All-Star Team (2012)

DAHLSTROM, Carl (DAL-struhm, KAHRL) CHI

Defense. Shoots left. 6'2", 200 lbs. Born, Stockholm, Sweden, January 28, 1995.
(Chicago's 2nd choice, 51st overall, in 2013 Entry Draft).

			Regular Season					Playoffs				
Season	Club	League	GP	G	A	Pts	PIM	GP	G	A	Pts	PIM
2010-11	Djurgarden U18	Swe-U18	1	0	0	0	0	....	....	....	....	....
2011-12	Djurgarden U18	Swe-U18	37	2	13	15	4	4	0	3	3	0
2012-13	Linkopings HC U18	Swe-U18	3	2	2	4	2	2	0	0	0	2
	Linkopings HC Jr.	Swe-Jr.	37	5	8	13	12	5	1	1	2	4
2013-14	Linkopings HC Jr.	Swe-Jr.	23	2	12	14	6	....	....	....	....	....
	Linkopings HC	Sweden	12	0	1	1	0	14	1	2	3	2
2014-15	Linkopings HC	Sweden	55	3	3	6	12	11	0	1	1	4

DAHLSTROM, John (DAL-struhm, JAWN) CHI

Left wing. Shoots left. 6', 189 lbs. Born, Kungsbacka, Sweden, January 22, 1997.
(Chicago's 7th choice, 211th overall, in 2015 Entry Draft).

			Regular Season					Playoffs				
Season	Club	League	GP	G	A	Pts	PIM	GP	G	A	Pts	PIM
2012-13	Frolunda U18	Swe-U18	3	0	1	1	0	....	....	....	....	....
2013-14	Frolunda U18	Swe-U18	39	16	24	40	8	5	0	3	3	2
2014-15	Frolunda U18	Swe-U18	14	14	5	19	6	2	0	1	1	0
	Frolunda Jr.	Swe-Jr.	28	20	15	35	2	8	5	0	5	0
	Frolunda	Sweden	2	0	0	0	0	....	....	....	....	....

DAL COLLE, Michael (DAL-KOHL, MIGH-kuhl) NYI

Left wing. Shoots left. 6'3", 194 lbs. Born, Richmond Hill, ON, June 20, 1996.
(NY Islanders' 1st choice, 5th overall, in 2014 Entry Draft).

			Regular Season					Playoffs				
Season	Club	League	GP	G	A	Pts	PIM	GP	G	A	Pts	PIM
2011-12	Vaughan Kings	GTHL	42	44	34	78	....	....	....	....	....	....
	Vaughan Kings	Other	5	4	7	11	0	....	....	....	....	....
	St. Michael's	ON-Jr.A	4	0	0	0	0	1	0	0	0	0
	The Hill Academy	High-ON	STATISTICS NOT AVAILABLE									
2012-13	Oshawa Generals	OHL	63	15	33	48	18	9	2	3	5	6
2013-14	Oshawa Generals	OHL	67	39	56	95	34	12	8	12	20	0
2014-15	Oshawa Generals	OHL	56	42	51	93	18	21	8	23	31	2

OHL All-Rookie Team (2013) • OHL Second All-Star Team (2014) • Memorial Cup All-Star Team (2015)

DARCY, Cameron (DAHR-see, KAM-ruhn) T.B.

Center. Shoots right. 6', 185 lbs. Born, South Boston, MA, March 2, 1994.
(Tampa Bay's 7th choice, 185th overall, in 2014 Entry Draft).

			Regular Season					Playoffs				
Season	Club	League	GP	G	A	Pts	PIM	GP	G	A	Pts	PIM
2007-08	Dexter School	High-MA	16	3	6	9	....	....	....	....	....	....
2008-09	Dexter School	High-MA	26	16	16	32	....	....	....	....	....	....
2009-10	Dexter School	High-MA	27	21	25	46	....	....	....	....	....	....
2010-11	USNTDP	USHL	37	9	4	13	20	2	0	0	0	2
	USNTDP	U-17	14	5	3	8	8	....	....	....	....	....
2011-12	USNTDP	USHL	24	4	2	6	8	....	....	....	....	....
	USNTDP	U-18	36	1	4	5	8	....	....	....	....	....
2012-13	Northeastern	H-East	9	0	2	2	8	....	....	....	....	....
	Muskegon	USHL	45	12	19	31	40	3	1	0	1	4
2013-14	Cape Breton	QMJHL	65	35	47	82	51	4	1	2	3	2
2014-15	Cape Breton	QMJHL	19	1	13	14	14	....	....	....	....	....
	Sherbrooke	QMJHL	37	20	25	45	34	6	5	4	9	8

QMJHL Second All-Star Team (2014)

DAUPHIN, Laurent (daw-PHEHN, LOHR-awnt) ARI

Center. Shoots left. 6', 180 lbs. Born, Repenigny, QC, March 27, 1995.
(Phoenix's 2nd choice, 39th overall, in 2013 Entry Draft).

			Regular Season					Playoffs				
Season	Club	League	GP	G	A	Pts	PIM	GP	G	A	Pts	PIM
2010-11	Esther-Blondin	QAAA	41	16	25	41	28	3	0	1	1	0
2011-12	Esther-Blondin	QAAA	40	17	45	62	48	13	12	14	*26	12
2012-13	Chicoutimi	QMJHL	62	25	32	57	50	6	2	2	4	8
2013-14	Chicoutimi	QMJHL	52	24	30	54	56	....	....	....	....	....
2014-15	Chicoutimi	QMJHL	56	31	44	75	74	5	5	3	8	12
	Portland Pirates	AHL	4	1	0	1	2	5	0	2	2	0

DE HAAS, James (dih-HAHZ, JAYMZ) DET

Defense. Shoots left. 6'4", 210 lbs. Born, Mississauga, ON, May 3, 1994.
(Detroit's 5th choice, 170th overall, in 2012 Entry Draft).

			Regular Season					Playoffs				
Season	Club	League	GP	G	A	Pts	PIM	GP	G	A	Pts	PIM
2010-11	Toronto Marlboros	GTHL	70	12	18	30	40	....	....	....	....	....
2011-12	Tor. Patriots	ON-Jr.A	45	10	19	29	32	21	5	7	12	10
2012-13	Penticton Vees	BCHL	53	5	19	24	19	15	3	6	9	8
2013-14	Clarkson Knights	ECAC	38	6	7	13	18	....	....	....	....	....
2014-15	Clarkson Knights	ECAC	36	6	9	15	18	....	....	....	....	....

ECAC All-Rookie Team (2014)

DE JONG, Nolan (deh JAWNG, NOH-luhn) MIN

Defense. Shoots left. 6'2", 199 lbs. Born, Victoria, BC, April 25, 1995.
(Minnesota's 6th choice, 197th overall, in 2013 Entry Draft).

			Regular Season					Playoffs				
Season	Club	League	GP	G	A	Pts	PIM	GP	G	A	Pts	PIM
2009-10	Saanich Braves	Minor-BC	STATISTICS NOT AVAILABLE									
	South Island	BCMML	5	0	0	0	2	....	....	....	....	....
2010-11	South Island	BCMML	35	3	7	10	69	3	0	2	2	4
2011-12	Victoria Grizzlies	BCHL	56	2	15	17	20	....	....	....	....	....
2012-13	Victoria Grizzlies	BCHL	51	5	19	24	16	10	2	2	4	6
2013-14	U. of Michigan	Big Ten	29	0	5	5	12	....	....	....	....	....
2014-15	U. of Michigan	Big Ten	23	0	9	9	14	....	....	....	....	....

De LEO, Chase (duh-LEE-oh, CHAYS) WPG

Center. Shoots left. 5'9", 185 lbs. Born, La Mirada, CA, October 25, 1995.
(Winnipeg's 3rd choice, 99th overall, in 2014 Entry Draft).

			Regular Season					Playoffs				
Season	Club	League	GP	G	A	Pts	PIM	GP	G	A	Pts	PIM
2009-10	LA Selects U14	Minor-CA	28	27	56	83	....	....	....	....	....	....
2010-11	LA Selects U16	Minor-CA	35	20	19	39	28	....	....	....	....	....
2011-12	Portland	WHL	69	14	16	30	25	22	0	*1	1	2
2012-13	Portland	WHL	71	18	38	56	24	21	5	12	17	15
2013-14	Portland	WHL	72	39	42	81	36	21	10	9	19	6
2014-15	Portland	WHL	67	39	45	84	30	17	7	12	19	10

DEA, Jean-Sebastien (DAY, ZHAWN-suh-BAS-t'yehn) PIT

Center. Shoots right. 6'11", 175 lbs. Born, Laval, QC, February 8, 1994.

			Regular Season					Playoffs				
Season	Club	League	GP	G	A	Pts	PIM	GP	G	A	Pts	PIM
2010-11	C.C. Lemoyne	QAAA	42	26	29	55	26	5	6	3	9	6
2011-12	Rouyn-Noranda	QMJHL	50	17	15	32	42	4	1	2	3	0
2012-13	Rouyn-Noranda	QMJHL	68	45	40	85	59	14	12	9	21	24
2013-14	Rouyn-Noranda	QMJHL	65	49	26	75	53	9	6	3	9	12
	Wilkes-Barre	AHL	1	0	0	0	0	....	....	....	....	....
2014-15	Wilkes-Barre	AHL	43	10	11	21	16	4	0	0	0	2
	Wheeling Nailers	ECHL	14	4	3	7	6	....	....	....	....	....

Signed as a free agent by **Pittsburgh**, September 17, 2013.

DeANGELO, Anthony (dee-AN-gehl-oh, an-THUH-nee) T.B.

Defense. Shoots right. 5'11", 177 lbs. Born, Sewell, NJ, October 24, 1995.
(Tampa Bay's 1st choice, 19th overall, in 2014 Entry Draft).

			Regular Season					Playoffs				
Season	Club	League	GP	G	A	Pts	PIM	GP	G	A	Pts	PIM
2008-09	Mercer Chiefs	AYHL	29	31	29	60	176	....	....	....	....	....
2009-10	Westchester	Minor-NY	STATISTICS NOT AVAILABLE									
	Westchester	Other	7	5	2	7	0	....	....	....	....	....
2010-11	Cedar Rapids	USHL	28	1	14	15	19	....	....	....	....	....
2011-12	Sarnia Sting	OHL	68	6	17	23	46	6	1	0	1	2
2012-13	Sarnia Sting	OHL	62	9	49	58	60	4	1	2	3	8
2013-14	Sarnia Sting	OHL	51	15	56	71	90	....	....	....	....	....
2014-15	Sarnia Sting	OHL	29	10	28	38	64	....	....	....	....	....
	Sault Ste. Marie	OHL	26	15	36	51	51	13	0	16	16	18

OHL First All-Star Team (2015)

DEBLOUW, Matthew (deh-BLOW, MA-thew) CGY

Center. Shoots left. 6'1", 190 lbs. Born, Chesterfield, MI, September 17, 1993.
(Calgary's 7th choice, 186th overall, in 2012 Entry Draft).

			Regular Season					Playoffs				
Season	Club	League	GP	G	A	Pts	PIM	GP	G	A	Pts	PIM
2008-09	Detroit Belle Tire	T1EHL	31	11	16	27	50	4	3	1	4	0
2009-10	Det. Lit. Caesars	T1EHL	48	23	21	44	91	....	....	....	....	....
	Det. Lit. Ceasars	Other	3	1	0	1	8	....	....	....	....	....
2010-11	Muskegon	USHL	33	2	4	6	51	6	3	5	8	6
2011-12	Muskegon	USHL	58	11	23	34	50	....	....	....	....	....
2012-13	Michigan State	CCHA	42	10	11	21	34	....	....	....	....	....
2013-14	Michigan State	Big Ten	23	0	4	4	17	....	....	....	....	....
2014-15	Michigan State	Big Ten	35	8	5	13	28	....	....	....	....	....

DeBRUSK, Jake (duh-BRUHSK, JAYK) BOS

Left wing. Shoots left. 6', 183 lbs. Born, Edmonton, AB, October 17, 1996.
(Boston's 2nd choice, 14th overall, in 2015 Entry Draft).

			Regular Season					Playoffs				
Season	Club	League	GP	G	A	Pts	PIM	GP	G	A	Pts	PIM
2011-12	SSAC Bulldogs	AMMHL	26	13	20	33	24	5	2	4	6	10
2012-13	SSAC Athletics	AMHL	34	25	27	52	26	14	7	2	9	10
2013-14	Swift Current	WHL	72	15	24	39	21	6	3	1	4	0
2014-15	Swift Current	WHL	72	42	39	81	40	3	0	0	0	10

DELNOV, Alexander (dehl-NAWV, al-ehx-AN-duhr) FLA

Left wing. Shoots left. 6', 189 lbs. Born, Moscow, Russia, January 14, 1994.
(Florida's 3rd choice, 114th overall, in 2012 Entry Draft).

			Regular Season					Playoffs				
Season	Club	League	GP	G	A	Pts	PIM	GP	G	A	Pts	PIM
2011-12	Mytischi Jr.	Russia-Jr.	47	11	11	22	16	5	0	0	0	2
2012-13	Seattle	WHL	69	20	29	49	33	7	2	2	4	0
	San Antonio	AHL	6	0	0	0	0	....	....	....	....	....
2013-14	Seattle	WHL	71	29	34	63	42	9	4	0	4	8
2014-15	Khanty-Mansiisk	KHL	2	0	0	0	2	....	....	....	....	....

DeMELO, Dylan (dih-MEH-loh, DIH-luhn) S.J.

Defense. Shoots right. 6'1", 195 lbs. Born, London, ON, May 1, 1993.
(San Jose's 5th choice, 179th overall, in 2011 Entry Draft).

			Regular Season					Playoffs				
Season	Club	League	GP	G	A	Pts	PIM	GP	G	A	Pts	PIM
2008-09	Lon. Jr. Knights	Minor-ON	74	11	34	45	46	....	....	....	....	....
2009-10	Mississauga	ON-Jr.A	36	9	20	29	24	....	....	....	....	....
	St. Michael's	OHL	20	0	1	1	12	....	....	....	....	....
2010-11	St. Michael's	OHL	67	3	24	27	70	20	1	4	5	15
2011-12	St. Michael's	OHL	67	7	40	47	70	6	1	1	2	13
	Worcester Sharks	AHL	4	0	1	1	2	....	....	....	....	....
2012-13	Mississauga	OHL	64	15	35	50	68	6	1	3	4	6
	Worcester Sharks	AHL	10	0	4	4	6	....	....	....	....	....
2013-14	Worcester Sharks	AHL	68	2	22	24	51	....	....	....	....	....
2014-15	Worcester Sharks	AHL	65	5	17	22	32	4	1	2	3	6

DEMPSEY, Mitchell (DEHMP-see, MIH-chuhl) BOS

Left wing. Shoots left. 6'3", 206 lbs. Born, Cambridge, ON, February 27, 1995.
(Boston's 6th choice, 210th overall, in 2013 Entry Draft).

			Regular Season					Playoffs				
Season	Club	League	GP	G	A	Pts	PIM	GP	G	A	Pts	PIM
2010-11	Camb. Hawks MM	Minor-ON	29	17	27	44	38	7	6	0	6	8
	Camb. Hawks MM	Other	19	15	7	22	30	....	....	....	....	....
	Camb. Hawks Mid.	Minor-ON	....	....	....	....	....	2	0	0	0	0
2011-12	Plymouth Whalers	OHL	34	1	4	5	29	5	0	0	0	0
2012-13	Sault Ste. Marie	OHL	36	1	4	5	17	....	....	....	....	....
2013-14	Kingston	ON-Jr.A	15	0	5	5	30	2	1	0	1	12
	Sault Ste. Marie	OHL	2	0	1	1	0	....	....	....	....	....
	Kitchener Rangers	OHL	6	0	0	0	10	....	....	....	....	....
2014-15	Saint John	QMJHL	60	8	17	25	47	3	0	0	0	4

DERGACHEV, Alexander (duhr-GAH-chy'awv, al-ehx-AN-duhr) L.A.

Center. Shoots left. 6'4", 200 lbs. Born, Langepas, Russia, September 27, 1996.
(Los Angeles' 2nd choice, 74th overall, in 2015 Entry Draft).

			Regular Season					Playoffs				
Season	Club	League	GP	G	A	Pts	PIM	GP	G	A	Pts	PIM
2012-13	Almetjevsk Jr.	Rus.-Jr. B	12	1	1	2	24	7	0	2	2	4
2013-14	St. Petersburg Jr.	Russia-Jr.	46	12	9	21	30	10	1	1	2	2
2014-15	St. Petersburg Jr.	Russia-Jr.	45	10	29	39	52	19	11	7	18	10

DERMOTT, Travis (DUHR-mawt, TRA-vihs) TOR

Defense. Shoots left. 6', 197 lbs. Born, Newmarket, ON, December 22, 1996.
(Toronto's 2nd choice, 34th overall, in 2015 Entry Draft).

			Regular Season					Playoffs				
Season	Club	League	GP	G	A	Pts	PIM	GP	G	A	Pts	PIM
2011-12	York Simcoe	Minor-ON	17	2	6	8	12	....	....	....	....	....
	York Simcoe	Other	2	0	1	1	0	....	....	....	....	....
2012-13	Newmarket	ON-Jr.A	53	1	14	15	24	24	4	11	15	14
2013-14	Erie Otters	OHL	67	3	25	28	45	14	0	5	5	8
2014-15	Erie Otters	OHL	61	8	37	45	53	20	5	12	17	22

OHL All-Rookie Team (2014)

DESCHENEAU, Jaedon (deh-SHAY-noh, JAY-duhn) ST.L.

Right wing. Shoots right. 5'9", 186 lbs. Born, Leduc, AB, February 22, 1995.
(St. Louis' 7th choice, 124th overall, in 2014 Entry Draft).

			Regular Season					Playoffs				
Season	Club	League	GP	G	A	Pts	PIM	GP	G	A	Pts	PIM
2008-09	Beaumont Braves	Minor-AB	27	28	39	67	20	....	....	....	....	....
2009-10	Leduc Oil Kings	AMBHL	33	31	*46	77	38	6	5	5	10	5
	Leduc Oil Kings	Minor-AB	1	0	0	0	0	....	....	....	....	....
2010-11	Leduc Oil Kings	AMHL	31	15	20	35	40	16	7	*10	*17	2
2011-12	Kootenay Ice	WHL	54	3	11	14	24	4	0	0	0	0
2012-13	Kootenay Ice	WHL	69	30	48	78	22	5	0	1	1	2
2013-14	Kootenay Ice	WHL	70	44	54	98	54	13	10	*10	20	6
2014-15	Kootenay Ice	WHL	70	34	47	81	58	7	5	5	10	4

WHL East Second All-Star Team (2014)

DESROCHER, Stephen (duh-ROH-shay, STEE-vehn) TOR

Defense. Shoots left. 6'4", 198 lbs. Born, Toronto, ON, January 26, 1996.
(Toronto's 8th choice, 155th overall, in 2015 Entry Draft).

			Regular Season					Playoffs				
Season	Club	League	GP	G	A	Pts	PIM	GP	G	A	Pts	PIM
2011-12	Mississauga Rebels	GTHL	64	4	22	26	30	....	....	....	....	....
2012-13	Vaughan Midget	GTHL	30	8	16	24	30	....	....	....	....	....
	Oakville Blades	ON-Jr.A	7	0	1	1	4	....	....	....	....	....
2013-14	Oshawa Generals	OHL	43	4	4	8	6	12	1	2	3	6
2014-15	Oshawa Generals	OHL	66	10	13	23	41	21	4	8	12	14

Di GIUSEPPE, Phillip (DEE-joo-SEH-pee, FIHL-ihp) CAR

Left wing. Shoots left. 6', 200 lbs. Born, Toronto, ON, October 9, 1993.
(Carolina's 1st choice, 38th overall, in 2012 Entry Draft).

			Regular Season					Playoffs				
Season	Club	League	GP	G	A	Pts	PIM	GP	G	A	Pts	PIM
2008-09	Vaughan Kings	GTHL	41	16	17	33	19	....	....	....	....	....
2009-10	Villanova Knights	ON-Jr.A	56	16	31	47	44	6	1	3	4	0
2010-11	Villanova Knights	ON-Jr.A	49	24	39	63	25	10	6	10	16	6
2011-12	U. of Michigan	CCHA	40	11	15	26	18	....	....	....	....	....
2012-13	U. of Michigan	CCHA	40	9	19	28	32	....	....	....	....	....
2013-14	U. of Michigan	Big Ten	35	13	11	24	29	....	....	....	....	....
	Charlotte	AHL	3	0	1	1	6	....	....	....	....	....
2014-15	Charlotte	AHL	76	11	19	30	20	....	....	....	....	....

DI PAULI, Thomas (DEE-paw-LEE, TAW-muhs) WSH

Center. Shoots left. 5'11", 188 lbs. Born, Woodbridge, IL, April 29, 1994.
(Washington's 4th choice, 100th overall, in 2012 Entry Draft).

			Regular Season					Playoffs				
Season	Club	League	GP	G	A	Pts	PIM	GP	G	A	Pts	PIM
2009-10	Chicago Mission	T1EHL	30	18	15	33	10	....	....	....	....	....
	Chicago Mission	Other	19	11	26	37	....	....	....	....	....	....
2010-11	USNTDP	USHL	32	4	11	15	16	2	0	1	1	0
	USNTDP	U-17	17	4	9	12	10	....	....	....	....	....
2011-12	USNTDP	USHL	21	6	5	11	6	....	....	....	....	....
	USNTDP	U-18	34	5	5	10	16	....	....	....	....	....
2012-13	U. of Notre Dame	CCHA	41	5	7	12	31	....	....	....	....	....
2013-14	U. of Notre Dame	H-East	26	3	2	5	12	....	....	....	....	....
2014-15	U. of Notre Dame	H-East	41	8	21	29	24	....	....	....	....	....

DIABY, Jonathan (dee-AH-bee, JAWN-ah-thuhn) NSH

Defense. Shoots left. 6'5", 223 lbs. Born, Montreal, QC, November 16, 1994.
(Nashville's 2nd choice, 64th overall, in 2013 Entry Draft).

			Regular Season					Playoffs				
Season	Club	League	GP	G	A	Pts	PIM	GP	G	A	Pts	PIM
2009-10	Esther-Blondin	QAAA	39	1	5	6	60	....	....	....	....	....
2010-11	Esther-Blondin	QAAA	30	2	9	11	79	....	....	....	....	....
	Victoriaville Tigres	QMJHL	19	0	0	0	19	3	0	0	0	0
2011-12	Victoriaville Tigres	QMJHL	51	1	8	9	64	4	0	0	0	11
2012-13	Victoriaville Tigres	QMJHL	67	4	22	26	117	9	0	1	1	20
2013-14	Victoriaville Tigres	QMJHL	38	9	19	28	80	5	1	4	5	4
	Milwaukee	AHL	4	0	1	1	5	....	....	....	....	....
2014-15	Milwaukee	AHL	52	0	2	2	94	....	....	....	....	....
	Cincinnati	ECHL	2	0	1	1	2	....	....	....	....	....

DICKINSON, Jason (DIH-kihn-suhn, JAY-suhn) DAL

Center. Shoots left. 6'1", 185 lbs. Born, Georgetown, ON, July 4, 1995.
(Dallas' 2nd choice, 29th overall, in 2013 Entry Draft).

			Regular Season					Playoffs				
Season	Club	League	GP	G	A	Pts	PIM	GP	G	A	Pts	PIM
2010-11	Halton Hurricanes	Minor-ON	59	45	34	79	22	....	....	....	....	....
2011-12	Guelph Storm	OHL	63	13	22	35	24	6	3	2	5	6
2012-13	Guelph Storm	OHL	66	18	29	47	31	5	1	1	2	0
2013-14	Guelph Storm	OHL	68	26	52	78	42	20	8	16	24	6
2014-15	Guelph Storm	OHL	56	27	44	71	32	9	4	4	8	10
	Texas Stars	AHL	2	0	3	3	0	3	0	0	0	2

DIDIER, Josiah (DIH-dee-ay, joh-SIGH-uh) MTL

Defense. Shoots right. 6'2", 202 lbs. Born, Littleton, CO, April 8, 1993.
(Montreal's 2nd choice, 97th overall, in 2011 Entry Draft).

			Regular Season					Playoffs				
Season	Club	League	GP	G	A	Pts	PIM	GP	G	A	Pts	PIM
2009-10	Colorado T-birds	Minor-CO	19	3	15	18	12	....	....	....	....	....
	Colorado T-birds	Other	9	5	2	7	12	....	....	....	....	....
2010-11	Cedar Rapids	USHL	58	8	13	21	81	8	0	2	2	7
2011-12	U. of Denver	WCHA	41	0	3	3	36	....	....	....	....	....
2012-13	U. of Denver	WCHA	31	0	7	7	48	....	....	....	....	....
2013-14	U. of Denver	NCHC	36	1	7	8	61	....	....	....	....	....
2014-15	U. of Denver	NCHC	40	3	8	11	58	....	....	....	....	....
	Hamilton Bulldogs	AHL	8	0	1	1	5	....	....	....	....	....

DIETZ, Darren (DEETZ, DAIR-uhn) MTL

Defense. Shoots right. 6'1", 213 lbs. Born, Medicine Hat, AB, July 17, 1993.
(Montreal's 4th choice, 138th overall, in 2011 Entry Draft).

			Regular Season					Playoffs				
Season	Club	League	GP	G	A	Pts	PIM	GP	G	A	Pts	PIM
2008-09	Medicine Hat	AMHL	34	0	4	4	62	....	....	....	....	....
2009-10	Lethbridge	AMHL	33	9	15	24	105	5	4	3	7	14
	Saskatoon Blades	WHL	8	1	1	2	4	3	0	0	0	2
2010-11	Saskatoon Blades	WHL	68	8	19	27	66	10	1	4	5	15
2011-12	Saskatoon Blades	WHL	72	15	29	44	118	3	0	1	1	5
2012-13	Saskatoon Blades	WHL	72	24	34	58	100	4	1	1	2	2
2013-14	Hamilton Bulldogs	AHL	34	0	5	5	49	....	....	....	....	....
2014-15	Hamilton Bulldogs	AHL	71	4	13	17	64	....	....	....	....	....

WHL East First All-Star Team (2013)

DiGIACINTO, Cristiano (dehGEE-a-SIHN-toh,krihs-tee-AH-no) T.B.

Left wing. Shoots left. 5'11", 186 lbs. Born, Hamilton, ON, January 10, 1996.
(Tampa Bay's 6th choice, 170th overall, in 2014 Entry Draft).

			Regular Season					Playoffs				
Season	Club	League	GP	G	A	Pts	PIM	GP	G	A	Pts	PIM
2011-12	Ham. Reps MM	Minor-ON	15	6	6	12	48	8	0	2	2	32
	Ham. Reps Mid.	Minor-ON	....	....	....	....	....	2	1	0	1	6
2012-13	Hamilton Huskies	Minor-ON	29	22	19	41	52	5	3	3	6	6
2013-14	Hamilton	ON-Jr.A	9	8	3	11	37	....	....	....	....	....
	Windsor Spitfires	OHL	50	17	11	28	101	2	0	0	0	9
2014-15	Windsor Spitfires	OHL	63	21	24	45	100	....	....	....	....	....

DJOOS, Christian (YEW-uhs, KRIHS-t'yehn) WSH

Defense. Shoots left. 5'11", 158 lbs. Born, Gothenburg, Sweden, August 6, 1994.
(Washington's 8th choice, 195th overall, in 2012 Entry Draft).

			Regular Season					Playoffs				
Season	Club	League	GP	G	A	Pts	PIM	GP	G	A	Pts	PIM
2009-10	Brynas U18	Swe-U18	35	4	12	16	66	4	1	1	2	4
2010-11	Brynas U18	Swe-U18	38	11	34	45	34	5	0	5	5	4
	Brynas IF Gavle Jr.	Swe-Jr.	11	0	1	1	0	....	....	....	....	....
2011-12	Brynas U18	Swe-U18	7	5	8	13	4	5	1	0	1	2
	Brynas IF Gavle Jr.	Swe-Jr.	40	3	21	24	22	2	0	0	0	0
	Brynas IF Gavle	Sweden	1	0	0	0	0	....	....	....	....	....
2012-13	Brynas IF Gavle Jr.	Swe-Jr.	2	0	2	2	2	....	....	....	....	....
	Brynas IF Gavle	Sweden	47	2	6	8	38	4	0	0	0	0
2013-14	Brynas IF Gavle Jr.	Swe-Jr.	1	0	1	1	0	1	0	0	0	0
	Brynas IF Gavle	Sweden	47	1	12	13	4	5	1	2	3	0
2014-15	Brynas IF Gavle	Sweden	50	5	12	17	22	7	1	1	2	8
	Hershey Bears	AHL	1	0	1	1	0	....	....	....	....	....

DOHERTY, Taylor (DOHR-eh-tee, TAY-luhr)

Defense. Shoots right. 6'8", 235 lbs. Born, Cambridge, ON, March 2, 1991.
(San Jose's 2nd choice, 57th overall, in 2009 Entry Draft).

			Regular Season					Playoffs				
Season	Club	League	GP	G	A	Pts	PIM	GP	G	A	Pts	PIM
2006-07	Cambridge Hawks	Minor-ON	70	10	37	47	169	....	....	....	....	....
2007-08	Kingston	OHL	64	6	14	20	118	....	....	....	....	....
2008-09	Kingston	OHL	68	2	18	20	140	....	....	....	....	....
2009-10	Kingston	OHL	63	16	28	44	114	5	1	4	5	0
2010-11	Kingston	OHL	68	14	39	53	86	5	0	3	3	12
	Worcester Sharks	AHL	3	0	0	0	0	....	....	....	....	....
2011-12	Worcester Sharks	AHL	63	0	6	6	76	....	....	....	....	....
2012-13	Worcester Sharks	AHL	40	1	9	10	67	....	....	....	....	....
2013-14	Worcester Sharks	AHL	69	4	11	15	111	....	....	....	....	....
2014-15	Worcester Sharks	AHL	59	2	5	7	93	....	....	....	....	....

DOMI, Max (DOH-mee, MAX) ARI

Center/Left wing. Shoots left. 5'10", 198 lbs. Born, Winnipeg, MB, March 2, 1995.
(Phoenix's 1st choice, 12th overall, in 2013 Entry Draft).

			Regular Season					Playoffs				
Season	Club	League	GP	G	A	Pts	PIM	GP	G	A	Pts	PIM
2010-11	Don Mills Flyers	GTHL	30	27	30	57	45	....	....	....	....	....
	St. Michael's	ON-Jr.A	2	1	1	2	0	....	....	....	....	....
2011-12	London Knights	OHL	62	21	28	49	48	19	4	5	9	10
2012-13	London Knights	OHL	64	39	48	87	71	21	11	21	32	26
2013-14	London Knights	OHL	61	34	59	93	90	9	4	6	10	8
2014-15	London Knights	OHL	57	32	70	102	66	9	5	4	9	16

OHL First All-Star Team (2015)

DONATO, Ryan (duh-NAT-toh, RIGH-uhn) BOS

Center. Shoots left. 6', 180 lbs. Born, Boston, MA, April 9, 1996.
(Boston's 2nd choice, 56th overall, in 2014 Entry Draft).

			Regular Season					Playoffs				
Season	Club	League	GP	G	A	Pts	PIM	GP	G	A	Pts	PIM
2011-12	Cape Cod U16	Minor-MA	12	6	2	8	4	....	....	....	....	....
	Dexter School	High-MA	26	14	22	36	....	....	....	....	....	....
2012-13	Cape Cod U16	Minor-MA	12	*18	14	*32	6	....	....	....	....	....
	Dexter School	High-MA	28	29	31	60	....	....	....	....	....	....
2013-14	Cape Cod Whalers	Minor-MA	9	8	9	17	33	....	....	....	....	....
	Dexter School	High-MA	30	37	41	78	....	....	....	....	....	....
	USNTDP	U-18	4	1	0	1	0	....	....	....	....	....
2014-15	Omaha Lancers	USHL	8	5	5	10	4	3	1	0	1	15
	South Shore Kings	USPHL	13	5	5	10	4	....	....	....	....	....

• Signed Letter of Intent to attend **Harvard University** (ECAC) in fall of 2015.

DONNAY, Troy (duh-NAY, TROI) NYR

Defense. Shoots right. 6'7", 205 lbs. Born, Flint, MI, February 18, 1994.

			Regular Season					Playoffs				
Season	Club	League	GP	G	A	Pts	PIM	GP	G	A	Pts	PIM
2009-10	Detroit Belle Tire	T1EHL	37	1	10	11	69	....	....	....	....	....
2010-11	London Knights	OHL	25	0	1	1	12	....	....	....	....	....
2011-12	London Knights	OHL	23	0	3	3	16	....	....	....	....	....
	Erie Otters	OHL	27	1	4	5	28	....	....	....	....	....
2012-13	Erie Otters	OHL	68	1	7	8	48	....	....	....	....	....
2013-14	Erie Otters	OHL	66	2	17	19	92	14	1	1	2	12
2014-15	Erie Otters	OHL	45	4	19	23	53	19	0	5	5	21

Signed as a free agent by **NY Rangers**, July 31, 2013.

DONSKOI, Joonas (DAWN-skoy, YOH-nuhs) S.J.

Right wing. Shoots right. 6', 195 lbs. Born, Raahe, Finland, April 13, 1992.
(Florida's 10th choice, 99th overall, in 2010 Entry Draft).

			Regular Season					Playoffs				
Season	Club	League	GP	G	A	Pts	PIM	GP	G	A	Pts	PIM
2007-08	Karpat Oulu U18	Fin-U18	30	18	20	38	26	5	3	4	7	0
2008-09	Karpat Oulu U18	Fin-U18	4	2	5	7	0	6	6	7	13	0
	Karpat Oulu Jr.	Fin-Jr.	32	7	17	24	12	....	....	....	....	....
2009-10	Suomi U20	Finland-2	4	1	0	1	0	....	....	....	....	....
	Karpat Oulu Jr.	Fin-Jr.	18	14	15	29	2	12	5	10	15	4
	Karpat Oulu	Finland	18	2	2	4	4	....	....	....	....	....
	Karpat Oulu U18	Fin-U18	....	....	....	....	....	1	1	1	2	0
2010-11	Suomi U20	Finland-2	2	1	0	1	0	....	....	....	....	....
	Karpat Oulu	Finland	52	16	11	27	10	3	1	0	1	0
2011-12	Karpat Oulu	Finland	52	8	17	25	12	6	3	3	6	0
2012-13	Karpat Oulu	Finland	31	4	10	14	8	3	0	1	1	2
2013-14	Karpat Oulu	Finland	60	11	26	37	10	16	4	2	6	4
2014-15	Karpat Oulu	Finland	58	19	30	49	10	19	6	16	22	6

Signed as a free agent by **San Jose**, May 19. 2015.

DOTCHIN, Jake (DAW-CHIHN, JAYK) T.B.

Defense. Shoots right. 6'2", 207 lbs. Born, Cambridge, ON, March 24, 1994.
(Tampa Bay's 7th choice, 161st overall, in 2012 Entry Draft).

			Regular Season					Playoffs				
Season	Club	League	GP	G	A	Pts	PIM	GP	G	A	Pts	PIM
2009-10	Cambridge Hawks	Minor-ON	30	8	19	27	60	11	4	6	10	26
	Cambridge Hawks	Other	11	5	10	15	6	....	....	....	....	....
2010-11	Cambridge	ON-Jr.B	41	5	10	15	88	5	1	3	4	8
2011-12	Owen Sound	OHL	64	3	16	19	77	5	0	3	3	8
2012-13	Owen Sound	OHL	38	2	12	14	39	....	....	....	....	....
	Barrie Colts	OHL	28	2	6	8	42	17	1	4	5	25
2013-14	Barrie Colts	OHL	63	11	25	36	121	11	3	2	5	13
2014-15	Syracuse Crunch	AHL	55	6	14	20	114	3	0	0	0	0

DOTY, Jacob (DOH-tee, JAY-kuhb) ST.L.

Right wing. Shoots right. 6'3", 220 lbs. Born, Billings, MT, June 19, 1993.

			Regular Season					Playoffs				
Season	Club	League	GP	G	A	Pts	PIM	GP	G	A	Pts	PIM
2008-09	Yellowstone	NORPAC	35	4	7	11	70	6	0	0	0	0
2009-10	Yellowstone	NORPAC	39	20	23	43	142	8	3	4	7	29
	Seattle	WHL	5	0	0	0	11	....	....	....	....	....
2010-11	Seattle	WHL	70	4	3	7	176	....	....	....	....	....
2011-12	Seattle	WHL	55	2	5	7	107	....	....	....	....	....
2012-13	Medicine Hat	WHL	72	11	17	28	90	8	0	1	1	11
2013-14	Medicine Hat	WHL	68	10	13	23	83	17	1	2	3	26
2014-15	Chicago Wolves	AHL	14	2	4	6	22	1	0	0	0	2
	Alaska Aces	ECHL	49	3	8	11	94	....	....	....	....	....

Signed as a free agent by **St. Louis**, September 27, 2013.

DOUGHERTY, Jack (DAWR-ih-tee, JAK) NSH

Defense. Shoots right. 6'1", 186 lbs. Born, St. Paul, MN, May 25, 1996.
(Nashville's 3rd choice, 51st overall, in 2014 Entry Draft).

			Regular Season					Playoffs				
Season	Club	League	GP	G	A	Pts	PIM	GP	G	A	Pts	PIM
2011-12	St. Thomas Acad.	High-MN	24	0	9	9	8	6	1	0	1	0
2012-13	Team Southeast	UMHSEL	19	2	9	11	30	3	0	2	2	4
	St. Thomas Acad.	High-MN	25	3	21	24	16	6	2	9	11	2
2013-14	USNTDP	USHL	23	4	8	12	34	....	....	....	....	....
	USNTDP	U-18	32	3	9	12	31	....	....	....	....	....
2014-15	U. of Wisconsin	Big Ten	33	2	7	9	29	....	....	....	....	....

DOVE-McFALLS, Samuel (DUHV-mihk-FAWLZ, SAM-yuhl) PHI

Left wing. Shoots left. 6'2", 197 lbs. Born, Montreal, QC, April 10, 1997.
(Philadelphia's 5th choice, 98th overall, in 2015 Entry Draft).

			Regular Season					Playoffs				
Season	**Club**	**League**	**GP**	**G**	**A**	**Pts**	**PIM**	**GP**	**G**	**A**	**Pts**	**PIM**
2012-13	Lac St-Louis Tigres	Minor-QC	28	15	26	41	26	....	....	....	....	....
2013-14	Saint John	QMJHL	52	6	4	10	52	....	....	....	....	....
2014-15	Saint John	QMJHL	66	14	20	34	73	5	1	0	1	4

DOWD, Nic (DOWD, NIHK) L.A.

Center. Shoots right. 6'2", 197 lbs. Born, Huntsville, AL, May 27, 1990.
(Los Angeles' 10th choice, 198th overall, in 2009 Entry Draft).

			Regular Season					Playoffs				
Season	**Club**	**League**	**GP**	**G**	**A**	**Pts**	**PIM**	**GP**	**G**	**A**	**Pts**	**PIM**
2007-08	Culver Academy	High-IN	45	15	31	46	38	....	....	....	....	....
2008-09	St. Louis Bandits	NAHL	3	0	0	0	2	....	....	....	....	....
	Wenatchee Wild	NAHL	43	16	33	49	71	13	8	*14	*22	34
2009-10	Indiana Ice	USHL	46	16	23	39	48	9	2	4	6	2
2010-11	St. Cloud State	WCHA	36	5	13	18	34	....	....	....	....	....
2011-12	St. Cloud State	WCHA	39	11	13	24	36	....	....	....	....	....
2012-13	St. Cloud State	WCHA	42	14	25	39	41	....	....	....	....	....
2013-14	St. Cloud State	NCHC	38	22	18	40	32	....	....	....	....	....
	Manchester	AHL	7	0	3	3	0	4	1	0	1	0
2014-15	Manchester	AHL	75	9	32	41	44	19	7	6	13	10

NCHC First All-Star Team (2014) • NCAA West First All-American Team (2014)

DOWNING, Grayson (DOW-nihng, GRAY-suhn) MIN

Center. Shoots left. 6', 200 lbs. Born, Abbotsford, BC, April 18, 1992.

			Regular Season					Playoffs				
Season	**Club**	**League**	**GP**	**G**	**A**	**Pts**	**PIM**	**GP**	**G**	**A**	**Pts**	**PIM**
2007-08	Fraser Valley	BCMML	32	15	25	40	32	2	1	1	2	2
2008-09	Westside Warriors	BCHL	37	13	10	23	21	6	0	0	0	0
2009-10	Westside Warriors	BCHL	43	18	18	36	28	11	6	4	10	8
2010-11	Westside Warriors	BCHL	52	24	36	70	30	9	2	7	9	4
2011-12	New Hampshire	H-East	34	10	13	23	12	....	....	....	....	....
2012-13	New Hampshire	H-East	38	15	16	31	44	....	....	....	....	....
2013-14	New Hampshire	H-East	34	10	12	22	46	....	....	....	....	....
2014-15	New Hampshire	H-East	38	21	15	36	18	....	....	....	....	....
	Iowa Wild	AHL	5	0	4	4	4	....	....	....	....	....

Signed as a free agent by **Minnesota**, March 24, 2015.

DOWNING, Michael (DOW-nihng, MIGH-kuhl) FLA

Defense. Shoots left. 6'3", 204 lbs. Born, Canton, MI, May 19, 1995.
(Florida's 4th choice, 97th overall, in 2013 Entry Draft).

			Regular Season					Playoffs				
Season	**Club**	**League**	**GP**	**G**	**A**	**Pts**	**PIM**	**GP**	**G**	**A**	**Pts**	**PIM**
2009-10	Det. Vic. Honda	T1EHL	30	4	6	10	36	....	....	....	....	....
2010-11	Catholic Central	High-MI	26	7	16	23	18	....	....	....	....	....
2011-12	USNTDP	U-17	7	0	1	1	0	....	....	....	....	....
	Dubuque	USHL	54	4	10	14	68	5	1	1	2	4
2012-13	Dubuque	USHL	52	3	20	23	107	11	0	3	3	6
2013-14	U. of Michigan	Big Ten	34	2	10	12	60	....	....	....	....	....
2014-15	U. of Michigan	Big Ten	36	6	16	22	*76	....	....	....	....	....

Big Ten All-Rookie Team (2014)

DRAEGER, John (DRAY-guhr, JAWN) MIN

Defense. Shoots right. 6'2", 188 lbs. Born, Edina, MN, December 2, 1993.
(Minnesota's 3rd choice, 68th overall, in 2012 Entry Draft).

			Regular Season					Playoffs				
Season	**Club**	**League**	**GP**	**G**	**A**	**Pts**	**PIM**	**GP**	**G**	**A**	**Pts**	**PIM**
2009-10	Shattuck U16	High-MN	53	1	9	10	57	....	....	....	....	....
2010-11	Shat.-St. Mary's	High-MN	54	3	8	11	18	....	....	....	....	....
2011-12	Shat.-St. Mary's	High-MN	57	11	30	41	36	....	....	....	....	....
2012-13	Michigan State	CCHA	42	1	9	10	22	....	....	....	....	....
2013-14	Michigan State	Big Ten	24	0	8	8	16	....	....	....	....	....
2014-15	Michigan State	Big Ten	28	1	3	4	6	....	....	....	....	....

DRAKE, David (DRAYK, DAY-vihd) PHI

Defense. Shoots left. 6'3", 185 lbs. Born, Naperville, IL, January 7, 1995.
(Philadelphia's 6th choice, 192nd overall, in 2013 Entry Draft).

			Regular Season					Playoffs				
Season	**Club**	**League**	**GP**	**G**	**A**	**Pts**	**PIM**	**GP**	**G**	**A**	**Pts**	**PIM**
2011-12	Indiana Jr. Ice	NAPHL	18	1	4	5	22	5	1	3	4	0
	Indiana Jr. Ice	HPHL	6	2	0	2	2	....	....	....	....	....
2012-13	Chicago Fury	T1EHL	40	2	4	6	16	2	0	0	0	0
	Des Moines	USHL	12	1	0	1	6	....	....	....	....	....
2013-14	Des Moines	USHL	51	0	5	5	26	....	....	....	....	....
2014-15	U. of Connecticut	H-East	32	1	4	5	14	....	....	....	....	....

DUDEK, J.D. (DOO-dehk, JAY-DEE) N.J.

Center. Shoots right. 5'11", 180 lbs. Born, Derry, NH, January 29, 1996.
(New Jersey's 5th choice, 152nd overall, in 2014 Entry Draft).

			Regular Season					Playoffs				
Season	**Club**	**League**	**GP**	**G**	**A**	**Pts**	**PIM**	**GP**	**G**	**A**	**Pts**	**PIM**
2010-11	Pinkerton	High-NH	....	14	25	39	8	....	....	....	....	....
2011-12	Pinkerton	High-NH	....	20	34	54	48	....	....	....	....	....
2012-13	Kimball Union	High-NH	30	17	25	42	....	....	....	....	....	....
2013-14	Kimball Union	High-NH	25	9	35	44	....	....	....	....	....	....
	Islanders H.C.	USPHL	2	0	0	0	12	....	....	....	....	....
2014-15	Dubuque	USHL	41	6	6	12	66	....	....	....	....	....
	Chicago Steel	USHL	13	4	2	6	6	....	....	....	....	....

• Signed Letter of Intent to attend **Boston College** (Hockey East) in fall of 2015.

DUKE, Reid (DOOK, REED) MIN

Center. Shoots right. 6', 189 lbs. Born, Calgary, AB, January 28, 1996.
(Minnesota's 7th choice, 169th overall, in 2014 Entry Draft).

			Regular Season					Playoffs				
Season	**Club**	**League**	**GP**	**G**	**A**	**Pts**	**PIM**	**GP**	**G**	**A**	**Pts**	**PIM**
2009-10	Calgary Royals	AMBHL	33	10	13	23	50	....	....	....	....	....
2010-11	Calgary Royals	AMBHL	30	28	36	64	79	....	....	....	....	....
	Cgy Royals Gold	Minor-AB	6	5	4	9	4	....	....	....	....	....
2011-12	Calgary Royals	AMHL	29	13	16	29	24	2	0	0	0	0
	Lethbridge	WHL	12	2	4	6	8	....	....	....	....	....
2012-13	Lethbridge	WHL	57	8	16	24	30	....	....	....	....	....
2013-14	Lethbridge	WHL	62	15	25	40	91	....	....	....	....	....
2014-15	Lethbridge	WHL	1	0	0	0	0	....	....	....	....	....
	Brandon	WHL	52	20	31	51	66	6	0	1	1	4

DUNDA, Liam (DUHN-duh, LEE-uhm) ST.L.

Left wing. Shoots left. 6'4", 212 lbs. Born, Issaquah, WA, September 15, 1997.
(St. Louis' 6th choice, 176th overall, in 2015 Entry Draft).

			Regular Season					Playoffs				
Season	**Club**	**League**	**GP**	**G**	**A**	**Pts**	**PIM**	**GP**	**G**	**A**	**Pts**	**PIM**
2012-13	Don Mills Flyers	GTHL	54	20	21	41	82	....	....	....	....	....
2013-14	Plymouth Whalers	OHL	50	1	3	4	56	5	0	0	0	2
2014-15	Plymouth Whalers	OHL	21	2	3	5	22	....	....	....	....	....
	Owen Sound	OHL	32	0	4	4	36	5	0	1	1	2

DUNN, Vince (DUHN-duh, VIHNS) ST.L.

Defense. Shoots left. 6', 187 lbs. Born, Lindsay, ON, October 29, 1996.
(St. Louis' 1st choice, 56th overall, in 2015 Entry Draft).

			Regular Season					Playoffs				
Season	**Club**	**League**	**GP**	**G**	**A**	**Pts**	**PIM**	**GP**	**G**	**A**	**Pts**	**PIM**
2011-12	Peter. Petes MM	Minor-ON	26	0	14	14	8	....	....	....	....	....
2012-13	Thorold	ON-Jr.B	48	5	23	28	35	13	3	5	8	10
2013-14	Niagara Ice Dogs	OHL	63	5	28	33	45	7	0	1	1	2
2014-15	Niagara Ice Dogs	OHL	68	18	38	56	59	8	6	4	10	22

DUNN, Vincent (DUHN, VIHN-sehnt) OTT

Center. Shoots left. 6', 193 lbs. Born, Hull, QC, September 14, 1995.
(Ottawa's 5th choice, 138th overall, in 2013 Entry Draft).

			Regular Season					Playoffs				
Season	**Club**	**League**	**GP**	**G**	**A**	**Pts**	**PIM**	**GP**	**G**	**A**	**Pts**	**PIM**
2010-11	Gatineau Intrepide	QAAA	41	22	26	48	122	3	1	1	2	6
2011-12	Val-d'Or Foreurs	QMJHL	56	5	8	13	94	3	1	0	1	5
2012-13	Val-d'Or Foreurs	QMJHL	53	25	27	52	98	10	0	3	3	19
2013-14	Gatineau	QMJHL	50	31	20	51	156	9	3	6	9	26
	Binghamton	AHL	1	0	0	0	0	....	....	....	....	....
2014-15	Rimouski Oceanic	QMJHL	46	19	13	32	153	....	....	....	....	....

DUPUY, Jean (DOO-pwee, ZHAWN) BUF

Left wing. Shoots left. 6'2", 207 lbs. Born, Orleans, ON, October 6, 1994.

			Regular Season					Playoffs				
Season	**Club**	**League**	**GP**	**G**	**A**	**Pts**	**PIM**	**GP**	**G**	**A**	**Pts**	**PIM**
2011-12	Kingston	OHL	50	3	5	8	25	....	....	....	....	....
2012-13	Kingston	OHL	42	4	3	7	79	4	0	0	0	9
2013-14	Kingston	OHL	3	1	0	1	5	....	....	....	....	....
	Sault Ste. Marie	OHL	45	9	8	17	41	9	3	1	4	2
2014-15	Sault Ste. Marie	OHL	54	18	28	46	52	10	4	2	6	9

Signed as a free agent by **Buffalo**, November 28, 2014.

DVORAK, Christian (duh-VOHR-ak, KRIHS-t'yen) ARI

Left wing. Shoots left. 6', 187 lbs. Born, Frankfort, IL, February 2, 1996.
(Arizona's 3rd choice, 58th overall, in 2014 Entry Draft).

			Regular Season					Playoffs				
Season	**Club**	**League**	**GP**	**G**	**A**	**Pts**	**PIM**	**GP**	**G**	**A**	**Pts**	**PIM**
2009-10	Chicago Mission	T1EHL	31	33	17	50	14	....	....	....	....	....
2010-11	Chi. Mission Bant.	T1EHL	22	10	14	24	0	....	....	....	....	....
2011-12	Chicago Mission	HPHL	29	21	24	45	2	....	....	....	....	....
2012-13	Chi. Mission U18	HPHL	31	19	33	52	4	....	....	....	....	....
	Chi. Mission U18	Other	27	16	24	40	4	....	....	....	....	....
	Chicago Steel	USHL	9	2	3	5	2	....	....	....	....	....
2013-14	London Knights	OHL	33	6	8	14	0	....	....	....	....	....
2014-15	London Knights	OHL	66	41	68	109	24	10	5	8	13	0
	Portland Pirates	AHL	2	1	1	2	4	5	0	1	1	0

DZIERKALS, Martins (d'zee-KAHLZ, MAHR-tihnsh) TOR

Left wing. Shoots left. 5'11", 169 lbs. Born, Riga, Latvia, April 4, 1997.
(Toronto's 5th choice, 68th overall, in 2015 Entry Draft).

			Regular Season					Playoffs				
Season	**Club**	**League**	**GP**	**G**	**A**	**Pts**	**PIM**	**GP**	**G**	**A**	**Pts**	**PIM**
2012-13	SK Saga U18	Latvia-U18	20	28	31	59	16	....	....	....	....	....
2013-14	SK Saga U18	Latvia-Jr.	23	35	33	68	43	....	....	....	....	....
2014-15	Ogre/Saga U18	Latvia	6	5	5	10	12	....	....	....	....	....
	HK Riga Jr.	Russia-Jr.	32	10	18	28	49	3	1	0	1	2

DZINGEL, Ryan (ZIHN-guhl, RIGH-uhn) OTT

Center. Shoots left. 6', 188 lbs. Born, Wheaton, IL, March 9, 1992.
(Ottawa's 10th choice, 204th overall, in 2011 Entry Draft).

			Regular Season					Playoffs				
Season	**Club**	**League**	**GP**	**G**	**A**	**Pts**	**PIM**	**GP**	**G**	**A**	**Pts**	**PIM**
2006-07	Chicago Mission	MWEHL	31	12	8	20	26	....	....	....	....	....
2007-08	Team Illinois	MWEHL	31	6	14	20	20	....	....	....	....	....
2008-09	Team Illinois	T1EHL	31	18	15	33	30	....	....	....	....	....
2009-10	Team Illinois	T1EHL	31	19	27	46	28	....	....	....	....	....
	Lincoln Stars	USHL	36	11	15	26	38	....	....	....	....	....
2010-11	Lincoln Stars	USHL	54	23	44	67	8	2	1	0	1	2
2011-12	Ohio State	CCHA	33	7	17	24	32	....	....	....	....	....
2012-13	Ohio State	CCHA	40	16	22	38	22	....	....	....	....	....
2013-14	Ohio State	Big Ten	37	*22	24	*46	34	....	....	....	....	....
	Binghamton	AHL	9	2	5	7	9	1	0	0	0	0
2014-15	Binghamton	AHL	66	17	17	34	50	....	....	....	....	....

Big Ten First All-Star Team (2014) • NCAA West First All-American Team (2014)

DZIURZYNSKI, Darian (z'yuhr-ZIHN-skee, dair-EE-uhn)

Left wing. Shoots left. 6'1", 204 lbs. Born, Lloydminster, AB, March 30, 1991.
(Phoenix's 6th choice, 141st overall, in 2011 Entry Draft).

			Regular Season					Playoffs				
Season	**Club**	**League**	**GP**	**G**	**A**	**Pts**	**PIM**	**GP**	**G**	**A**	**Pts**	**PIM**
2007-08	Lloydminster	AMHL	26	20	15	35	98	....	....	....	....	....
	Saskatoon Blades	WHL	33	3	1	4	18	....	....	....	....	....
	Lloydminster	AJHL	2	0	0	0	0	....	....	....	....	....
2008-09	Saskatoon Blades	WHL	64	10	15	25	96	7	0	1	1	6
2009-10	Saskatoon Blades	WHL	70	14	15	29	156	7	3	6	9	9
2010-11	Saskatoon Blades	WHL	72	35	22	57	125	10	3	3	6	18
2011-12	Saskatoon Blades	WHL	4	3	0	3	4	....	....	....	....	....
	Brandon	WHL	61	27	16	43	106	9	2	2	4	16
2012-13	Portland Pirates	AHL	59	9	7	16	87	3	1	0	1	0
2013-14	Portland Pirates	AHL	54	2	7	9	183	....	....	....	....	....
2014-15	Portland Pirates	AHL	68	15	3	18	51	2	0	0	0	2

EBERT, Nick (EE-buhrt, NIHK) **L.A.**

Defense. Shoots right. 6', 217 lbs. Born, Livingston, NJ, May 11, 1994.
(Los Angeles' 6th choice, 211th overall, in 2012 Entry Draft).

			Regular Season					Playoffs				
Season	Club	League	GP	G	A	Pts	PIM	GP	G	A	Pts	PIM
2007-08	N. Jersey Bant.	AYHL	25	9	9	18	24	....	....	....	....	....
2008-09	N. Jersey Bant.	AYHL	2	0	0	0	0	....	....	....	....	....
	N. Jersey Mid.	AYHL	26	10	15	25	23	....	....	....	....	....
2009-10	Waterloo	USHL	53	6	12	18	26	3	1	0	1	0
2010-11	Windsor Spitfires	OHL	64	11	30	41	44	18	1	2	3	6
2011-12	Windsor Spitfires	OHL	66	6	33	39	58	4	0	2	2	8
2012-13	Windsor Spitfires	OHL	68	11	27	38	58	....	....	....	....	....
	Ontario Reign	ECHL	4	0	3	3	2	10	2	5	7	0
2013-14	Windsor Spitfires	OHL	27	4	16	20	18	....	....	....	....	....
	Guelph Storm	OHL	38	9	25	34	31	20	5	11	16	8
2014-15	Manchester	AHL	45	8	6	14	18	2	0	0	0	0

OHL All-Rookie Team (2011)

EDMUNDSON, Joel (EHD-muhnd-suhn, JOHL) **ST.L.**

Defense. Shoots left. 6'4", 207 lbs. Born, Brandon, MB, June 28, 1993.
(St. Louis' 3rd choice, 46th overall, in 2011 Entry Draft).

			Regular Season					Playoffs				
Season	Club	League	GP	G	A	Pts	PIM	GP	G	A	Pts	PIM
2008-09	Brandon	MMHL	41	5	18	23	58	6	2	4	6	4
2009-10	Brandon	MMHL	44	10	25	35	54	7	0	5	5	10
2010-11	Moose Jaw	WHL	71	2	18	20	95	6	0	0	0	2
2011-12	Moose Jaw	WHL	56	4	19	23	91	14	3	2	5	12
2012-13	Moose Jaw	WHL	29	2	6	8	70	....	....	....	....	....
	Kamloops Blazers	WHL	34	7	10	17	71	15	3	5	8	29
2013-14	Chicago Wolves	AHL	64	4	4	8	108	5	0	0	0	16
2014-15	Chicago Wolves	AHL	30	4	8	12	49	5	2	0	2	2

EHLERS, Nikolaj (EH-luhrs, NIH-koh-ligh) **WPG**

Left wing. Shoots left. 6', 175 lbs. Born, Aalborg, Denmark, February 14, 1996.
(Winnipeg's 1st choice, 9th overall, in 2014 Entry Draft).

			Regular Season					Playoffs				
Season	Club	League	GP	G	A	Pts	PIM	GP	G	A	Pts	PIM
2009-10	Biel U17	Swiss-U17	1	0	0	0	0	1	0	0	0	0
2010-11	Biel U17	Swiss-U17	28	19	11	30	8	7	7	9	16	6
2011-12	Biel U17	Swiss-U17	7	4	5	9	12	10	5	8	13	6
	Biel Jr.	Swiss-Jr.	32	19	19	38	12	....	....	....	....	....
2012-13	Biel Jr.	Swiss-Jr.	34	30	23	53	36	....	....	....	....	....
	EHC Biel-Bienne	Swiss	11	1	1	2	0	7	0	3	3	0
2013-14	Halifax	QMJHL	63	49	55	104	51	16	11	17	28	18
2014-15	Halifax	QMJHL	51	37	64	101	67	14	10	21	31	14

QMJHL Second All-Star Team (2014) • Canadian Major Junior Rookie of the Year (2014) • QMJHL First All-Star Team (2015)

EHN, Christoffer (EHN, KRIHS-toh-fuhr) **DET**

Center. Shoots left. 6'3", 181 lbs. Born, Linkoping, Sweden, April 5, 1996.
(Detroit's 3rd choice, 106th overall, in 2014 Entry Draft).

			Regular Season					Playoffs				
Season	Club	League	GP	G	A	Pts	PIM	GP	G	A	Pts	PIM
2010-11	Skara IK U18	Swe-U18	13	9	11	20	0	3	2	1	3	2
2011-12	Skovde IK U18	Swe-U18	25	7	4	11	16	....	....	....	....	....
	Skovde IK Jr.	Swe-Jr.	14	4	0	4	4	....	....	....	....	....
2012-13	Frolunda U18	Swe-U18	33	9	22	1	16	3	1	0	1	2
2013-14	Frolunda U18	Swe-U18	15	8	10	18	4	5	1	3	4	0
	Frolunda	Sweden	2	0	0	0	0	....	....	....	....	....
	Frolunda Jr.	Swe-Jr.	45	4	7	11	14	3	3	0	3	0
2014-15	Frolunda Jr.	Swe-Jr.	40	12	24	36	61	....	....	....	....	....
	IK Oskarshamn	Sweden-2	4	0	0	0	0	....	....	....	....	....
	Frolunda	Sweden	6	0	0	0	2	10	0	0	0	2

EICHEL, Jack (IGH-kuhl, JAK) **BUF**

Center. Shoots right. 6'2", 199 lbs. Born, North Chelmsford, MA, October 28, 1996.
(Buffalo's 1st choice, 2nd overall, in 2015 Entry Draft).

			Regular Season					Playoffs				
Season	Club	League	GP	G	A	Pts	PIM	GP	G	A	Pts	PIM
2010-11	Bos. Jr. Bruins	EmJHL	40	15	21	36	16	7	2	5	7	6
2011-12	Bos. Jr. Bruins	EmJHL	36	39	47	86	36	5	3	1	4	0
	Bos. Jr. Bruins	EJHL	3	0	0	0	0	....	....	....	....	....
2012-13	USNTDP	USHL	35	13	14	27	14	....	....	....	....	....
	USNTDP	U-17	16	15	8	23	10	....	....	....	....	....
	USNTDP	U-18	7	1	1	2	6	....	....	....	....	....
2013-14	USNTDP	USHL	24	20	25	45	20	....	....	....	....	....
	USNTDP	U-18	29	18	24	42	22	....	....	....	....	....
2014-15	Boston University	H-East	40	*26	*45	*71	28	....	....	....	....	....

Hockey East All-Rookie Team (2015) • Hockey East First All-Star Team (2015) • Hockey East Rookie of the Year (2015) • Hockey East Player of the Year (2015) • NCAA East First All-American Team (2015) • Hobey Baker Memorial Award (Top U.S. Collegiate Player) (2015)

EISERMAN, Shane (IGH-zuhr-muhn, SHAYN) **OTT**

Center/Left wing. Shoots left. 6'2", 209 lbs. Born, Beverly, MA, October 10, 1995.
(Ottawa's 3rd choice, 100th overall, in 2014 Entry Draft).

			Regular Season					Playoffs				
Season	Club	League	GP	G	A	Pts	PIM	GP	G	A	Pts	PIM
2010-11	St. John's Prep	High-MA	25	24	28	52		....	....	....	....	....
	Valley Jr. Warriors	Minor-MA	10	9	5	14	6	....	....	....	....	....
2011-12	Cushing	High-MA	30	18	26	44		....	....	....	....	....
2012-13	USNTDP	USHL	22	4	3	7	29	....	....	....	....	....
	USNTDP	U-18	39	7	8	15	18	....	....	....	....	....
2013-14	Dubuque	USHL	53	16	24	40	71	7	0	2	2	10
2014-15	New Hampshire	H-East	35	4	11	15	28	....	....	....	....	....

ELGESTAL, Kevin (EHL-geh-stohl, KEH-vuhn) **WSH**

Right wing. Shoots right. 6'1", 176 lbs. Born, Gothenburg, Sweden, May 29, 1996.
(Washington's 6th choice, 194th overall, in 2014 Entry Draft).

			Regular Season					Playoffs				
Season	Club	League	GP	G	A	Pts	PIM	GP	G	A	Pts	PIM
2011-12	Frolunda U18	Swe-U18	28	7	3	10	4	....	....	....	....	....
2012-13	Frolunda U18	Swe-U18	35	19	20	39	56	3	0	0	0	14
	Frolunda Jr.	Swe-Jr.	5	1	0	1	2	....	....	....	....	....
2013-14	Frolunda U18	Swe-U18	5	4	5	9	8	5	2	1	3	6
	Frolunda	Sweden	2	0	1	1	0	....	....	....	....	....
	Frolunda Jr.	Swe-Jr.	44	13	22	35	34	3	1	0	1	2
2014-15	Frolunda Jr.	Swe-Jr.	33	10	16	26	65	6	2	5	7	29

ELIE, Remi (EH-lee, REH-mee) **DAL**

Left wing. Shoots left. 6'1", 205 lbs. Born, Cornwall, ON, April 16, 1995.
(Dallas' 3rd choice, 40th overall, in 2013 Entry Draft).

			Regular Season					Playoffs				
Season	Club	League	GP	G	A	Pts	PIM	GP	G	A	Pts	PIM
2010-11	E. Ont. Wild MM	Minor-ON	29	15	24	39	43	5	3	3	6	6
	E. Ont. Wild Mid.	Minor-ON	2	0	2	2	2	1	1	0	1	4
2011-12	Hawkesbury	ON-Jr.A	59	21	25	46	39	9	5	4	9	12
2012-13	London Knights	OHL	65	7	10	17	34	21	4	4	8	8
2013-14	London Knights	OHL	6	1	2	3	4	....	....	....	....	....
	Belleville Bulls	OHL	61	28	37	65	44	....	....	....	....	....
2014-15	Belleville Bulls	OHL	35	14	20	34	24	....	....	....	....	....
	Erie Otters	OHL	28	16	26	42	14	20	4	20	24	20

ELLIS, Morgan (EHL-ihs, MOHR-guhn) **MTL**

Defense. Shoots right. 6'1", 204 lbs. Born, Summerside, PE, April 30, 1992.
(Montreal's 3rd choice, 117th overall, in 2010 Entry Draft).

			Regular Season					Playoffs				
Season	Club	League	GP	G	A	Pts	PIM	GP	G	A	Pts	PIM
2007-08	Charlottetown	NBPEI	33	3	4	7	28	7	0	2	2	10
	Charlottetown	Other	16	2	6	8	16	....	....	....	....	....
2008-09	Cape Breton	QMJHL	52	0	6	6	45	10	0	1	1	4
2009-10	Cape Breton	QMJHL	60	4	25	29	56	5	1	0	1	10
2010-11	Cape Breton	QMJHL	65	8	28	36	65	4	0	0	0	8
2011-12	Cape Breton	QMJHL	34	7	18	25	18	....	....	....	....	....
	Shawinigan	QMJHL	26	8	19	27	38	11	4	7	11	6
2012-13	Hamilton Bulldogs	AHL	71	4	4	8	57	....	....	....	....	....
2013-14	Hamilton Bulldogs	AHL	59	3	7	10	36	....	....	....	....	....
2014-15	Hamilton Bulldogs	AHL	27	3	6	9	13	....	....	....	....	....
	Wheeling Nailers	ECHL	39	13	13	26	22	5	0	2	2	0

QMJHL Second All-Star Team (2012)

ELSON, Turner (EHL-suhn, TUHR-nuhr) **CGY**

Left wing. Shoots left. 5'11", 180 lbs. Born, St. Albert, AB, September 13, 1992.

			Regular Season					Playoffs				
Season	Club	League	GP	G	A	Pts	PIM	GP	G	A	Pts	PIM
2008-09	St. Albert Raiders	AMHL	33	11	12	23	77	2	0	0	0	4
2009-10	Red Deer Rebels	WHL	66	9	8	17	94	4	0	0	0	4
2010-11	Red Deer Rebels	WHL	68	16	15	31	124	9	0	4	4	23
2011-12	Red Deer Rebels	WHL	55	21	25	46	59	....	....	....	....	....
	Abbotsford Heat	AHL	1	0	0	0	2	....	....	....	....	....
2012-13	Red Deer Rebels	WHL	64	26	31	57	60	9	5	4	9	6
	Abbotsford Heat	AHL	2	0	0	0	0	....	....	....	....	....
2013-14	Abbotsford Heat	AHL	37	2	1	3	19	....	....	....	....	....
	Alaska Aces	ECHL	18	5	10	15	18	21	7	4	11	16
2014-15	Adirondack Flames	AHL	59	17	13	30	52	....	....	....	....	....

Signed as a free agent by **Calgary**, September 22, 2011.

EMANUELSSON, Petter (EE-man-yew EHL-suhn, PEH-tuhr) **S.J.**

Right wing. Shoots right. 6', 200 lbs. Born, Kiruna, Sweden, August 7, 1991.

			Regular Season					Playoffs				
Season	Club	League	GP	G	A	Pts	PIM	GP	G	A	Pts	PIM
2007-08	Skelleftea U18	Swe-U18	27	18	17	35	0	....	....	....	....	....
	Skelleftea Jr.	Swe-Jr.	2	0	0	0	0	2	0	0	0	0
2008-09	Skelleftea AIK U18	Swe-U18	9	5	9	14	2	8	5	3	8	4
	Skelleftea AIK Jr.	Swe-Jr.	36	7	12	19	4	5	2	2	4	4
2009-10	Skelleftea AIK Jr.	Swe-Jr.	22	5	9	14	2	....	....	....	....	....
	Skelleftea AIK	Sweden	1	0	1	1	0	....	....	....	....	....
2010-11	Skelleftea AIK	Sweden	4	0	0	0	0	....	....	....	....	....
	Sundsvall	Sweden-2	5	2	1	3	0	....	....	....	....	....
	Skelleftea AIK Jr.	Swe-Jr.	40	21	28	49	14	5	3	3	6	0
2011-12	Skelleftea AIK Jr.	Swe-Jr.	6	2	3	5	0	....	....	....	....	....
	Pitea HC	Sweden-3	27	16	9	25	10	....	....	....	....	....
	Skelleftea AIK	Sweden	17	1	0	1	4	....	....	....	....	....
2012-13	Skelleftea AIK	Sweden	54	9	9	18	8	13	6	2	8	0
2013-14	Skelleftea AIK	Sweden	44	6	9	15	2	9	2	1	3	0
2014-15	Worcester Sharks	AHL	6	4	0	4	0	....	....	....	....	....

Signed as a free agent by **San Jose**, June 11, 2013. • Missed majority of 2014-15 due to shoulder injury vs. Portland (AHL), October 26, 2014.

ENGLUND, Andreas (EHNG-luhnd, ahn-DRAY-uhs) **OTT**

Defense. Shoots left. 6'3", 189 lbs. Born, Stockholm, Sweden, January 21, 1996.
(Ottawa's 1st choice, 40th overall, in 2014 Entry Draft).

			Regular Season					Playoffs				
Season	Club	League	GP	G	A	Pts	PIM	GP	G	A	Pts	PIM
2011-12	Djurgarden U18	Swe-U18	27	0	4	4	6	4	0	0	0	0
2012-13	Djurgarden U18	Swe-U18	32	3	5	8	46	9	0	0	0	0
	Djurgarden Jr.	Swe-Jr.	2	0	0	0	0	....	....	....	....	....
2013-14	Djurgarden U18	Swe-U18	1	1	0	1	0	....	....	....	....	....
	Djurgarden Jr.	Swe-Jr.	33	5	5	10	26	....	....	....	....	....
	Djurgarden	Sweden-2	29	1	1	2	20	....	....	....	....	....
2014-15	Djurgarden	Sweden	49	2	3	5	32	2	0	0	0	0

ENGVALL, Pierre (EHNG-vuhl, pee-AIHR) **TOR**

Left wing. Shoots left. 6'4", 196 lbs. Born, Ljungby, Sweden, May 31, 1996.
(Toronto's 6th choice, 188th overall, in 2014 Entry Draft).

			Regular Season					Playoffs				
Season	Club	League	GP	G	A	Pts	PIM	GP	G	A	Pts	PIM
2011-12	Troja U18	Swe-U18	25	9	4	13	10	....	....	....	....	....
2012-13	Frolunda U18	Swe-U18	30	18	16	34	22	3	0	1	1	2
	Frolunda Jr.	Swe-Jr.	4	2	0	2	0	....	....	....	....	....
2013-14	Frolunda U18	Swe-U18	16	11	25	36	8	5	1	0	1	6
	IF Troja-Ljungby	Sweden-2	1	0	0	0	0	....	....	....	....	....
	Frolunda Jr.	Swe-Jr.	39	17	18	35	42	3	0	1	1	0
2014-15	Frolunda Jr.	Swe-Jr.	38	17	34	51	50	8	5	1	6	10
	IK Oskarshamn	Sweden-2	10	0	0	0	0	....	....	....	....	....
	Frolunda	Sweden	2	0	0	0	0	....	....	....	....	....

ERIKSSON EK, Joel (AIR-ihk-suhn EHK, JOHL) **MIN**

Center. Shoots left. 6'2", 185 lbs. Born, Karlstad, Sweden, January 29, 1997.
(Minnesota's 1st choice, 20th overall, in 2015 Entry Draft).

			Regular Season					Playoffs				
Season	Club	League	GP	G	A	Pts	PIM	GP	G	A	Pts	PIM
2012-13	Farjestad U18	Swe-U18	26	1	6	7	10	....	....	....	....	....
2013-14	Farjestad U18	Swe-U18	33	22	18	40	22	5	2	6	8	2
	Farjestad Jr.	Swe-Jr.	13	2	2	4	4	4	1	1	2	2
2014-15	Farjestad Jr.	Swe-Jr.	25	21	11	32	20	6	5	5	10	6
	Farjestad	Sweden	34	4	2	6	4	3	0	0	0	2

ERNE, Adam (UHR-nee, A-duhm) T.B.

Left wing. Shoots left. 6'1", 210 lbs. Born, New Haven, CT, April 20, 1995.
(Tampa Bay's 2nd choice, 33rd overall, in 2013 Entry Draft).

			Regular Season					Playoffs				
Season	Club	League	GP	G	A	Pts	PIM	GP	G	A	Pts	PIM
2009-10	L.A. Selects	Minor-CA	STATISTICS NOT AVAILABLE									
2010-11	Indiana Ice	USHL	45	10	8	18	49	3	0	1	1	0
2011-12	Quebec Remparts	QMJHL	64	28	27	55	32	11	2	4	6	10
2012-13	Quebec Remparts	QMJHL	68	28	44	72	67	11	5	5	10	19
2013-14	Quebec Remparts	QMJHL	48	21	41	62	65	1	1	0	1	2
	Syracuse Crunch	AHL	8	1	3	4	2	....	....	....	....	....
2014-15	Quebec Remparts	QMJHL	60	41	45	86	102	22	21	9	30	17

ESTEPHAN, Giorgio (EHS-teh-fan, johr-JEE-oh) BUF

Center. Shoots right. 6', 196 lbs. Born, Edmonton, AB, February 3, 1997.
(Buffalo's 5th choice, 152nd overall, in 2015 Entry Draft).

			Regular Season					Playoffs				
Season	Club	League	GP	G	A	Pts	PIM	GP	G	A	Pts	PIM
2012-13	SSAC Athletics	AMHL	32	17	30	47	12	14	5	6	11	6
	Lethbridge	WHL	3	1	0	1	0	....	....	....	....	....
2013-14	Lethbridge	WHL	64	12	12	24	18	....	....	....	....	....
2014-15	Lethbridge	WHL	64	23	28	51	18	....	....	....	....	....

EVANS, Jake (EN-vuhnz, JAYK) MTL

Center/Right wing. Shoots right. 6', 186 lbs. Born, Toronto, ON, June 2, 1996.
(Montreal's 6th choice, 207th overall, in 2014 Entry Draft).

			Regular Season					Playoffs				
Season	Club	League	GP	G	A	Pts	PIM	GP	G	A	Pts	PIM
2011-12	Mississauga Rebels	GTHL	77	34	55	89	38	....	....	....	....	....
	St. Michael's	ON-Jr.A	5	2	2	4	0	....	....	....	....	....
2012-13	St. Michael's	ON-Jr.A	50	12	32	44	45	24	8	9	17	14
2013-14	St. Michael's	ON-Jr.A	49	16	47	63	79	5	0	5	5	8
2014-15	U. of Notre Dame	H-East	41	7	10	17	22	....	....	....	....	....

EWANYK, Travis (ee-WAHN-ihk, TRA-vihs) OTT

Left wing. Shoots left. 6'1", 200 lbs. Born, North Vancouver, BC, March 29, 1993.
(Edmonton's 5th choice, 74th overall, in 2011 Entry Draft).

			Regular Season					Playoffs				
Season	Club	League	GP	G	A	Pts	PIM	GP	G	A	Pts	PIM
2007-08	St. Albert Sabres	AMBHL	30	12	19	31	66	2	0	1	1	2
2008-09	St. Albert Raiders	AMHL	33	7	12	19	14	2	0	0	0	4
	Edmonton	WHL	2	0	0	0	0	3	0	0	0	0
2009-10	Edmonton	WHL	42	1	4	5	45	....	....	....	....	....
2010-11	Edmonton	WHL	72	16	11	27	126	4	0	0	0	13
2011-12	Edmonton	WHL	11	1	3	4	8	20	3	2	5	10
2012-13	Edmonton	WHL	58	8	15	23	119	22	6	4	10	26
2013-14	Oklahoma City	AHL	68	7	5	12	100	3	0	1	1	4
2014-15	Oklahoma City	AHL	69	3	5	8	120	....	....	....	....	....

Traded to **Ottawa** by **Edmonton** with Pittsburgh's 4th round choice (previously acquired, Ottawa selected Christian Wolanin) in 2015 Entry Draft for Eric Gryba, June 27, 2015.

FABBRI, Robby (FAB-ree, RAW-bee) ST.L.

Center. Shoots left. 5'10", 170 lbs. Born, Mississauga, ON, January 22, 1996.
(St. Louis' 1st choice, 21st overall, in 2014 Entry Draft).

			Regular Season					Playoffs				
Season	Club	League	GP	G	A	Pts	PIM	GP	G	A	Pts	PIM
2009-10	Mississauga Rebels	GTHL	71	58	45	103	102	....	....	....	....	....
2010-11	Mississauga Rebels	GTHL	75	66	68	134	68	....	....	....	....	....
2011-12	Mississauga Rebels	GTHL	69	62	56	118	92	....	....	....	....	....
	Tor. Canadiens	ON-Jr.A	1	0	3	3	0	1	0	0	0	0
2012-13	Guelph Storm	OHL	59	10	23	33	38	5	0	1	1	4
2013-14	Guelph Storm	OHL	58	45	42	87	55	16	13	15	28	12
2014-15	Guelph Storm	OHL	30	25	26	51	40	9	1	3	4	17
	Chicago Wolves	AHL	3	1	3	4	2	3	0	0	0	0

OHL Playoff MVP (2013)

FAITH, Tanner (FAYTH, TA-nuhr) MIN

Defense. Shoots right. 6'4", 219 lbs. Born, Terrace, BC, October 5, 1995.
(Minnesota's 4th choice, 139th overall, in 2014 Entry Draft).

			Regular Season					Playoffs				
Season	Club	League	GP	G	A	Pts	PIM	GP	G	A	Pts	PIM
2009-10	Notre Dame	SMBHL	20	4	13	17	8	5	0	3	3	0
2010-11	Notre Dame	SMHL	29	4	5	9	32	....	....	....	....	....
	Kootenay Ice	WHL	4	0	0	0	2	....	....	....	....	....
2011-12	Notre Dame	SMHL	21	3	5	8	32	....	....	....	....	....
2012-13	Kootenay Ice	WHL	55	2	6	8	35	5	0	0	0	2
2013-14	Kootenay Ice	WHL	10	0	1	1	9	....	....	....	....	....
2014-15	Kootenay Ice	WHL	19	1	5	6	29	....	....	....	....	....

FAKSA, Radek (FAK-suh, RA-dehk) DAL

Center. Shoots left. 6'3", 210 lbs. Born, Vitkov, Czech Rep., January 9, 1994.
(Dallas' 1st choice, 13th overall, in 2012 Entry Draft).

			Regular Season					Playoffs				
Season	Club	League	GP	G	A	Pts	PIM	GP	G	A	Pts	PIM
2007-08	HC Trinec U17	CzR-U17	2	0	1	1	0	1	0	0	0	0
2008-09	HC Trinec U17	CzR-U17	44	16	21	37	32	9	0	2	2	8
2009-10	HC Trinec U18	CzR-U18	36	19	19	38	52	....	....	....	....	....
	HC Trinec Jr.	CzRep-Jr.	3	0	0	0	2	....	....	....	....	....
2010-11	HC Trinec U18	CzR-U18	28	19	30	49	32	2	1	0	1	10
	HC Trinec Jr.	CzRep-Jr.	24	9	6	15	12	2	2	2	4	4
2011-12	Kitchener Rangers	OHL	62	29	37	66	47	13	2	4	6	10
2012-13	Kitchener Rangers	OHL	39	9	22	31	26	10	4	2	6	4
	Texas Stars	AHL	2	0	1	1	0	....	....	....	....	....
2013-14	Kitchener Rangers	OHL	30	16	11	27	22	....	....	....	....	....
	Sudbury Wolves	OHL	29	5	16	21	26	5	1	2	3	10
	Texas Stars	AHL	6	1	2	3	6	21	4	0	4	8
2014-15	Texas Stars	AHL	32	4	6	10	12	....	....	....	....	....

OHL All-Rookie Team (2012)

FASCHING, Hudson (FA-SHIHNG, HUHD-suhn) BUF

Right wing. Shoots right. 6'2", 216 lbs. Born, Milwaukee, WI, July 28, 1995.
(Los Angeles' 3rd choice, 118th overall, in 2013 Entry Draft).

			Regular Season					Playoffs				
Season	Club	League	GP	G	A	Pts	PIM	GP	G	A	Pts	PIM
2009-10	Apple Valley	High-MN	25	20	16	36	12	6	4	2	6	0
2010-11	Team Southeast	UMHSEL	18	7	8	15	12	3	1	3	4	4
	Apple Valley	High-MN	25	16	29	45	14	3	2	3	5	2
2011-12	USNTDP	USHL	37	7	14	21	38	1	1	1	2	2
	USNTDP	U-17	16	8	5	13	12	....	....	....	....	....
	USNTDP	U-18	1	0	0	0	0	....	....	....	....	....
2012-13	USNTDP	USHL	25	4	7	11	8	....	....	....	....	....
	USNTDP	U-18	40	7	18	25	50	....	....	....	....	....
2013-14	U. of Minnesota	Big Ten	40	14	16	30	22	....	....	....	....	....
2014-15	U. of Minnesota	Big Ten	38	12	14	26	24	....	....	....	....	....

Big Ten All-Rookie Team (2014)

Traded to **Buffalo** by **Los Angeles** with Nicolas Deslauriers for Brayden McNabb, Jonathan Parker, Los Angeles' 2nd round choice (previously acquired, Los Angeles selected Alex Lintuniemi) in 2014 Entry Draft and Los Angeles' 2nd round choice (previously acquired, Los Angeles selected Erik Cernak) in 2015 Entry Draft, March 5, 2014.

FAUST, Joe (FOWST, JOH) N.J.

Defense. Shoots right. 6', 205 lbs. Born, Edina, MN, November 15, 1991.
(New Jersey's 3rd choice, 114th overall, in 2010 Entry Draft).

			Regular Season					Playoffs				
Season	Club	League	GP	G	A	Pts	PIM	GP	G	A	Pts	PIM
2007-08	Bloomington-Jeff.	High-MN	28	4	14	18	10	....	....	....	....	....
2008-09	Bloomington-Jeff.	High-MN	28	14	26	40	12	....	....	....	....	....
2009-10	Team Southeast	UMHSEL	24	3	6	9	....	....	....	....	....	....
	Bloomington-Jeff.	High-MN	25	12	28	40	18	3	2	4	6	2
2010-11	U. of Wisconsin	WCHA	20	1	1	2	8	....	....	....	....	....
2011-12	U. of Wisconsin	WCHA	37	2	3	5	16	....	....	....	....	....
2012-13	U. of Wisconsin	WCHA	42	1	0	1	14	....	....	....	....	....
2013-14	U. of Wisconsin	Big Ten	37	2	12	14	8	....	....	....	....	....
2014-15	Albany Devils	AHL	26	1	3	4	18	....	....	....	....	....

FAZLEEV, Radel (faz-L'YAY-ehv, rah-DEHL) PHI

Left wing. Shoots left. 6', 194 lbs. Born, Kazan, Russia, January 7, 1996.
(Philadelphia's 5th choice, 168th overall, in 2014 Entry Draft).

			Regular Season					Playoffs				
Season	Club	League	GP	G	A	Pts	PIM	GP	G	A	Pts	PIM
2012-13	Bars Kazan Jr.	Russia-Jr.	9	0	0	0	0	....	....	....	....	....
	Irbis Kazan Jr.	Rus.-Jr. B	23	7	10	17	8	5	1	2	3	4
2013-14	Calgary Hitmen	WHL	38	5	20	25	12	6	3	4	7	0
2014-15	Calgary Hitmen	WHL	71	18	33	51	36	17	4	10	14	6

FEJES, Hunter (FAY-jihs, HUHN -tuhr) ARI

Left wing. Shoots left. 6'1", 204 lbs. Born, Anchorage, AK, May 31, 1994.
(Phoenix's 6th choice, 178th overall, in 2012 Entry Draft).

			Regular Season					Playoffs				
Season	Club	League	GP	G	A	Pts	PIM	GP	G	A	Pts	PIM
2010-11	Shat.-St. Mary's	High-MN	49	14	14	28	12	....	....	....	....	....
2011-12	Shat.-St. Mary's	High-MN	55	38	40	78	20	....	....	....	....	....
2012-13	Colorado College	WCHA	41	8	6	14	8	....	....	....	....	....
2013-14	Colorado College	NCHC	26	0	1	1	29	....	....	....	....	....
2014-15	Colorado College	NCHC	35	5	14	19	31	....	....	....	....	....

FIDLER, Miguel (FIHD-luhr, mi-G'WEHL) FLA

Left wing. Shoots left. 6', 200 lbs. Born, Edina, MN, March 17, 1996.
(Florida's 5th choice, 143rd overall, in 2014 Entry Draft).

			Regular Season					Playoffs				
Season	Club	League	GP	G	A	Pts	PIM	GP	G	A	Pts	PIM
2011-12	Edina Hornets	High-MN	25	2	9	11	42	5	4	3	7	0
2012-13	Metro Southwest	MEPDL	....	4	5	9	....	....	....	....	....	....
	Edina Hornets	High-MN	23	5	6	11	28	6	3	1	4	4
2013-14	Team Southwest	UMHSEL	20	5	4	9	32	3	3	4	7	10
	Edina Hornets	High-MN	25	16	25	41	24	5	4	5	9	4
2014-15	Lincoln Stars	USHL	45	5	16	21	55	....	....	....	....	....
	Madison Capitols	USHL	15	2	4	6	8	....	....	....	....	....

• Signed Letter of Intent to attend **Ohio State University** (Big Ten) in fall of 2015.

FIEGL, Jared (FEE-guhl, JAIR-uhd) ARI

Left wing. Shoots left. 6'1", 206 lbs. Born, Parker, CO, January 23, 1996.
(Arizona's 8th choice, 191st overall, in 2014 Entry Draft).

			Regular Season					Playoffs				
Season	Club	League	GP	G	A	Pts	PIM	GP	G	A	Pts	PIM
2010-11	Col. Rampage	T1EHL	36	6	0	6	14	....	....	....	....	....
2011-12	Col. Rampage	T1EHL	30	11	11	22	28	....	....	....	....	....
	U.S. Youth Oly.	Other	6	1	1	2	8	....	....	....	....	....
2012-13	USNTDP	USHL	38	4	4	8	29	....	....	....	....	....
	USNTDP	U-17	18	3	5	8	8	....	....	....	....	....
2013-14	USNTDP	USHL	16	0	0	0	10	....	....	....	....	....
	USNTDP	U-18	29	2	4	6	16	....	....	....	....	....
2014-15	Cornell Big Red	ECAC	26	1	0	1	39	....	....	....	....	....

FINN, Matt (FIHN, MAT) TOR

Defense. Shoots left. 6'1", 199 lbs. Born, Toronto, ON, February 24, 1994.
(Toronto's 2nd choice, 35th overall, in 2012 Entry Draft).

			Regular Season					Playoffs				
Season	Club	League	GP	G	A	Pts	PIM	GP	G	A	Pts	PIM
2009-10	Toronto Marlboros	GTHL	79	22	35	57	94	....	....	....	....	....
2010-11	Guelph Storm	OHL	60	3	18	21	23	5	0	3	3	0
2011-12	Guelph Storm	OHL	61	10	38	48	58	6	0	2	2	10
2012-13	Guelph Storm	OHL	41	11	20	31	24	....	....	....	....	....
2013-14	Guelph Storm	OHL	66	14	47	61	42	20	5	9	14	6
2014-15	Toronto Marlies	AHL	28	1	2	3	24	....	....	....	....	....
	Orlando	ECHL	8	1	1	2	4	....	....	....	....	....

Memorial Cup All-Star Team (2014)

FISCHER, Christian (FIH-shuhr, KRIHS-ch'yehn) **ARI**

Right wing. Shoots right. 6'1", 212 lbs. Born, Chicago, IL, April 15, 1997.
(Arizona's 3rd choice, 32nd overall, in 2015 Entry Draft).

			Regular Season					Playoffs				
Season	Club	League	GP	G	A	Pts	PIM	GP	G	A	Pts	PIM
2012-13	Chi. Mission U16	HPHL	25	12	14	26	10	....	....	....	....	....
2013-14	USNTDP	USHL	34	11	12	23	6	....	....	....	....	....
	USNTDP	U-17	20	8	11	19	19	....	....	....	....	....
2014-15	USNTDP	USHL	25	15	15	30	10	....	....	....	....	....
	USNTDP	U-18	41	16	19	35	12	....	....	....	....	....

• Signed Letter of Intent to attend **University of Notre Dame** (Hockey East) in fall of 2015.

FITZGERALD, Ryan (fihtz-JAIR-uhld, RIGH-uhn) **BOS**

Center. Shoots right. 5'9", 172 lbs. Born, Boca Raton, FL, October 19, 1994.
(Boston's 3rd choice, 120th overall, in 2013 Entry Draft).

			Regular Season					Playoffs				
Season	Club	League	GP	G	A	Pts	PIM	GP	G	A	Pts	PIM
2009-10	Malden Catholic	High-MA	24	17	30	47	....	....	....	....	....	....
2010-11	Malden Catholic	High-MA	24	28	44	72	....	....	....	....	....	....
2011-12	Malden Catholic	High-MA	19	31	20	51	....	....	....	....	....	....
2012-13	Valley Junior	EJHL	26	14	16	30	50	6	3	3	6	8
	USNTDP	U-18	5	1	0	1	8	....	....	....	....	....
2013-14	Boston College	H-East	40	13	16	29	22	....	....	....	....	....
2014-15	Boston College	H-East	38	17	8	25	54	....	....	....	....	....

FLEURY, Haydn (FLUH-ree, HAY-duhn) **CAR**

Defense. Shoots left. 6'3", 207 lbs. Born, Carlyle, SK, July 8, 1996.
(Carolina's 1st choice, 7th overall, in 2014 Entry Draft).

			Regular Season					Playoffs				
Season	Club	League	GP	G	A	Pts	PIM	GP	G	A	Pts	PIM
2009-10	Cam. Red Wings	AMBHL	33	1	8	9	36	....	....	....	....	....
2010-11	Notre Dame	SMBHL	21	7	19	26	30	....	....	....	....	....
	Notre Dame Argos	SMHL	3	0	1	1	0	....	....	....	....	....
2011-12	Notre Dame Argos	SMHL	39	6	15	21	60	8	1	4	5	8
	Red Deer Rebels	WHL	4	0	0	0	0	....	....	....	....	....
2012-13	Red Deer Rebels	WHL	66	4	15	19	21	9	0	2	2	4
2013-14	Red Deer Rebels	WHL	70	8	38	46	46	....	....	....	....	....
2014-15	Red Deer Rebels	WHL	63	6	22	28	63	5	1	1	2	2
	Charlotte	AHL	1	1	0	1	0	....	....	....	....	....

FLICK, Rob (FLIHK, RAWB) **FLA**

Center. Shoots left. 6'2", 208 lbs. Born, London, ON, March 28, 1991.
(Chicago's 7th choice, 120th overall, in 2010 Entry Draft).

			Regular Season					Playoffs				
Season	Club	League	GP	G	A	Pts	PIM	GP	G	A	Pts	PIM
2007-08	Lon. Jr. Knights	Minor-ON	57	32	29	61	160	....	....	....	....	....
	London Nationals	ON-Jr.B	8	0	1	1	25	....	....	....	....	....
2008-09	St. Michael's	OHL	48	4	4	8	69	10	1	1	2	14
2009-10	St. Michael's	OHL	65	15	19	34	157	16	2	2	4	*44
2010-11	St. Michael's	OHL	68	27	30	57	167	20	8	8	16	34
2011-12	Rockford IceHogs	AHL	45	7	6	13	91	....	....	....	....	....
	Toledo Walleye	ECHL	17	4	6	10	43	....	....	....	....	....
2012-13	Rockford IceHogs	AHL	51	3	2	5	97	....	....	....	....	....
	Providence Bruins	AHL	5	0	0	0	7	....	....	....	....	....
2013-14	Providence Bruins	AHL	53	2	5	7	92	....	....	....	....	....
2014-15	Providence Bruins	AHL	65	19	5	24	77	5	0	0	0	8

Traded to **Boston** by **Chicago** for Max Sauve, April 3, 2013. Signed as a free agent by **Florida**, July 2, 2015.

FLORENTINO, Anthony (flohr-ehn-TEE-noh, AN-thuh-nee) **BUF**

Defense. Shoots right. 6', 207 lbs. Born, Boston, MA, January 30, 1995.
(Buffalo's 9th choice, 143rd overall, in 2013 Entry Draft).

			Regular Season					Playoffs				
Season	Club	League	GP	G	A	Pts	PIM	GP	G	A	Pts	PIM
2010-11	South Shore Kings	EmJHL	7	0	1	1	26	....	....	....	....	....
	South Kent School	High-CT	24	5	10	15	....	....	....	....	....	....
2011-12	South Kent School	High-CT	36	5	14	19	....	....	....	....	....	....
	USNTDP	U-17	3	0	2	2	4	....	....	....	....	....
2012-13	South Kent	High-CT	62	21	32	53	68	....	....	....	....	....
2013-14	Providence College	H-East	30	5	6	11	16	....	....	....	....	....
2014-15	Providence College	H-East	40	3	12	15	25	....	....	....	....	....

FOEGELE, Warren (FOH-GEHL, WAHR-ihn) **CAR**

Left wing. Shoots left. 6'2", 191 lbs. Born, Markham, ON, April 1, 1996.
(Carolina's 3rd choice, 67th overall, in 2014 Entry Draft).

			Regular Season					Playoffs				
Season	Club	League	GP	G	A	Pts	PIM	GP	G	A	Pts	PIM
2011-12	Markham Waxers	Minor-ON	28	10	8	18	38	....	....	....	....	....
	St. Andrew's	MPHL	5	0	1	1	0	2	0	0	0	0
	St. Andrew's	CISSA	1	0	0	0	0	....	....	....	....	....
2012-13	St. Andrew's	MPHL	13	7	10	*17	12	3	2	*5	*7	2
	St. Andrew's	CISAA	15	9	10	19	20	5	3	2	5	6
	St. Andrew's	High-ON	22	16	9	25	8	....	....	....	....	....
2013-14	St. Andrew's	MPHL	13	12	*17	*29	14	3	*6	5	*11	2
	St. Andrew's	CISAA	14	17	6	23	15	5	5	4	9	10
	St. Andrew's	High-ON	17	18	17	35	26	....	....	....	....	....
2014-15	New Hampshire	H-East	34	5	11	16	26	....	....	....	....	....

FOGARTY, Steven (FOH-guhr-tee, STEE-vehn) **NYR**

Center. Shoots right. 6'2", 194 lbs. Born, Chambersburg, PA, April 19, 1993.
(NY Rangers' 2nd choice, 72nd overall, in 2011 Entry Draft).

			Regular Season					Playoffs				
Season	Club	League	GP	G	A	Pts	PIM	GP	G	A	Pts	PIM
2009-10	Edina Hornets	High-MN	25	18	12	30	4	6	3	7	10	2
2010-11	Team Southwest	UMHSEL	19	10	4	14	10	3	2	5	7	4
	Edina Hornets	High-MN	24	23	17	40	12	6	3	8	11	0
	Chicago Steel	USHL	6	2	0	2	2	....	....	....	....	....
2011-12	Penticton Vees	BCHL	60	33	48	81	32	15	4	4	8	12
2012-13	U. of Notre Dame	CCHA	41	5	5	10	4	....	....	....	....	....
2013-14	U. of Notre Dame	H-East	33	3	8	11	10	....	....	....	....	....
2014-15	U. of Notre Dame	H-East	39	9	12	21	6	....	....	....	....	....

FOLEY, Erik (FOH-lee, AIR-ihk) **WPG**

Left wing. Shoots left. 6', 192 lbs. Born, Mansfield, MA, June 30, 1997.
(Winnipeg's 4th choice, 78th overall, in 2015 Entry Draft).

			Regular Season					Playoffs				
Season	Club	League	GP	G	A	Pts	PIM	GP	G	A	Pts	PIM
2012-13	Neponset Valley	Minor-MA	12	4	10	14	2	....	....	....	....	....
	Tabor Academy	High-MA	27	9	19	28	....	....	....	....	....	....
2013-14	Cape Cod Whalers	Minor-MA	10	8	4	12	2	....	....	....	....	....
	Tabor Academy	High-MA	28	17	20	37	....	....	....	....	....	....
	Cedar Rapids	USHL	1	0	0	0	2	2	0	0	0	0
2014-15	Cedar Rapids	USHL	55	27	27	54	80	3	1	0	1	6

USHL All-Rookie Team (2015)

• Signed Letter of Intent to attend **Providence College** (Hockey East) in fall of 2015.

FORBORT, Derek (FOHR-bohrt, DAIR-ihk) **L.A.**

Defense. Shoots left. 6'4", 219 lbs. Born, Duluth, MN, March 4, 1992.
(Los Angeles' 1st choice, 15th overall, in 2010 Entry Draft).

			Regular Season					Playoffs				
Season	Club	League	GP	G	A	Pts	PIM	GP	G	A	Pts	PIM
2008-09	Duluth East	High-MN	25	7	21	28	....	....	....	....	....	....
	USNTDP	NAHL	2	0	1	1	6	....	....	....	....	....
	USNTDP	U-17	7	1	4	5	4	....	....	....	....	....
2009-10	USNTDP	USHL	26	4	10	14	26	....	....	....	....	....
	USNTDP	U-18	39	1	13	14	20	....	....	....	....	....
2010-11	North Dakota	WCHA	38	0	15	15	26	....	....	....	....	....
2011-12	North Dakota	WCHA	35	2	11	13	28	....	....	....	....	....
2012-13	North Dakota	WCHA	42	4	13	17	22	....	....	....	....	....
	Manchester	AHL	6	0	1	1	0	4	0	0	0	4
2013-14	Manchester	AHL	74	1	16	17	42	3	0	0	0	0
2014-15	Manchester	AHL	67	4	11	15	52	19	0	6	6	12

FORSBACKA-KARLSSON, Jakob (forz-BAH-kuh KAHRL-suhn, YA-kuhb) **BOS**

Center. Shoots right. 6'1", 184 lbs. Born, Stockholm, Sweden, October 31, 1996.
(Boston's 5th choice, 45th overall, in 2015 Entry Draft).

			Regular Season					Playoffs				
Season	Club	League	GP	G	A	Pts	PIM	GP	G	A	Pts	PIM
2011-12	Nacka HK U18	Swe-U18	26	13	19	32	16	....	....	....	....	....
2012-13	Linkopings HC U18	Swe-U18	17	15	20	35	16	2	0	0	0	0
	Linkopings HC Jr.	Swe-Jr.	31	9	7	16	26	5	0	2	2	4
2013-14	Omaha Lancers	USHL	60	11	22	33	26	4	0	1	1	4
2014-15	Omaha Lancers	USHL	50	15	38	53	38	....	....	....	....	....

• Signed Letter of Intent to attend **Boston College** (Hockey East) in fall of 2015.

FORSLING, Gustav (FOHRZ-lihng, GOO-stahv) **CHI**

Defense. Shoots left. 6', 183 lbs. Born, Linkoping, Sweden, June 12, 1996.
(Vancouver's 5th choice, 126th overall, in 2014 Entry Draft).

			Regular Season					Playoffs				
Season	Club	League	GP	G	A	Pts	PIM	GP	G	A	Pts	PIM
2011-12	Linkopings HC U18	Swe-U18	27	5	3	8	10	3	0	1	1	0
2012-13	Linkopings HC U18	Swe-U18	31	7	8	15	20	2	0	0	0	0
	Linkopings HC Jr.	Swe-Jr.	14	0	1	1	8	1	0	0	0	0
2013-14	Linkopings HC U18	Swe-U18	5	3	3	6	2	5	1	0	1	0
	Linkopings HC Jr.	Swe-Jr.	44	6	12	18	36	2	1	3	4	2
2014-15	Linkopings HC	Sweden	38	3	3	6	8	....	....	....	....	....

Traded to **Chicago** by **Vancouver** for Adam Clendening, January 29, 2015.

FOURNIER, Dillon (FOHR-n'yay, DIHL-uhn) **CHI**

Defense. Shoots left. 6'2", 186 lbs. Born, Montreal, QC, June 15, 1994.
(Chicago's 2nd choice, 48th overall, in 2012 Entry Draft).

			Regular Season					Playoffs				
Season	Club	League	GP	G	A	Pts	PIM	GP	G	A	Pts	PIM
2009-10	Lac St-Louis Lions	QAAA	39	0	12	12	24	21	0	3	3	40
2010-11	Lewiston	QMJHL	60	3	11	14	38	11	0	2	2	15
2011-12	Rouyn-Noranda	QMJHL	52	9	29	38	59	....	....	....	....	....
2012-13	Rouyn-Noranda	QMJHL	59	6	18	24	61	14	4	8	12	14
2013-14	Rouyn-Noranda	QMJHL	36	13	19	32	54	....	....	....	....	....
2014-15	Rockford IceHogs	AHL	21	0	3	3	16	....	....	....	....	....
	Indy Fuel	ECHL	34	2	5	7	13	....	....	....	....	....

FOURNIER, Stefan (FOHR-n'yay, STEH-fan) **MTL**

Right wing. Shoots right. 6'3", 226 lbs. Born, Dorval, QC, April 30, 1992.

			Regular Season					Playoffs				
Season	Club	League	GP	G	A	Pts	PIM	GP	G	A	Pts	PIM
2007-08	Lac St-Louis Lions	QAAA	19	10	17	27	18	....	....	....	....	....
2008-09	Acadie-Bathurst	QMJHL	40	2	1	3	18	....	....	....	....	....
2009-10	Lewiston	QMJHL	52	12	13	25	54	4	1	2	3	2
2010-11	Lewiston	QMJHL	67	20	27	47	69	15	4	6	10	22
2011-12	Victoriaville Tigres	QMJHL	64	32	33	65	96	4	1	1	2	2
2012-13	Halifax	QMJHL	66	35	37	72	100	17	*16	13	29	31
2013-14	Hamilton Bulldogs	AHL	40	2	5	7	86	....	....	....	....	....
	Wheeling Nailers	ECHL	1	0	0	0	0	....	....	....	....	....
2014-15	Hamilton Bulldogs	AHL	14	0	1	1	14	....	....	....	....	....
	Wheeling Nailers	ECHL	12	0	5	5	22	....	....	....	....	....

Signed as a free agent by **Montreal**, July 6, 2013.

FOX, Dane (FAWX, DAYN) **VAN**

Left wing. Shoots left. 6', 185 lbs. Born, Chatham, ON, October 13, 1993.

			Regular Season					Playoffs				
Season	Club	League	GP	G	A	Pts	PIM	GP	G	A	Pts	PIM
2008-09	Chatham-Kent	Minor-ON	30	25	22	47	76	8	8	10	18	36
2009-10	Strathroy Rockets	ON-Jr.B	23	11	10	21	103	....	....	....	....	....
	London Knights	OHL	26	1	6	7	13	2	0	1	1	0
2010-11	London Knights	OHL	51	11	12	23	55	6	1	0	1	6
2011-12	London Knights	OHL	34	13	19	32	54	....	....	....	....	....
	Erie Otters	OHL	34	13	19	32	54	....	....	....	....	....
2012-13	Erie Otters	OHL	37	19	17	36	78	....	....	....	....	....
2013-14	Erie Otters	OHL	67	*64	43	107	122	14	8	11	19	26
2014-15	Kalamazoo Wings	ECHL	70	30	15	45	110	3	0	1	1	4

Signed as a free agent by **Vancouver**, December 28, 2014.

FRANKLIN, C.J. (FRANK-lihn, SEE-JAY) WPG

Left wing. Shoots left. 5'11", 193 lbs. Born, St. Paul, MN, March 17, 1994.
(Winnipeg's 5th choice, 129th overall, in 2014 Entry Draft).

			Regular Season					Playoffs				
Season	Club	League	GP	G	A	Pts	PIM	GP	G	A	Pts	PIM
2009-10	Forest Lake	High-MN	25	18	19	37	18	2	1	2	3	0
2010-11	Forest Lake	High-MN	25	23	10	33	22	1	0	0	0	0
2011-12	Team Northeast	UMHSEL	20	7	5	12	22	3	2	3	5	0
	Forest Lake	High-MN	25	15	23	38	26	2	0	4	4	2
2012-13	Sioux Falls	USHL	62	32	28	60	60	10	1	3	4	7
2013-14	Sioux Falls	USHL	53	22	29	51	43	3	2	1	3	4
2014-15	Minnesota State	WCHA	37	9	19	28	21	....	....	....	....	....

WCHA All-Rookie Team (2015)

FRIEDMAN, Mark (FREED-muhn, MAHRK) PHI

Defense. Shoots right. 5'11", 194 lbs. Born, Toronto, ON, December 25, 1995.
(Philadelphia's 3rd choice, 86th overall, in 2014 Entry Draft).

			Regular Season					Playoffs				
Season	Club	League	GP	G	A	Pts	PIM	GP	G	A	Pts	PIM
2010-11	Don Mills Flyers	GTHL	37	7	5	12	40	....	....	....	....	....
	North York	ON-Jr.A	2	0	0	0	0	....	....	....	....	....
2011-12	North York	ON-Jr.A	48	9	18	27	44	4	1	3	4	0
2012-13	Waterloo	USHL	64	8	27	35	44	5	2	3	5	2
2013-14	Waterloo	USHL	51	10	30	40	30	12	0	7	7	4
2014-15	Bowling Green	WCHA	39	2	17	19	75	....	....	....	....	....

USHL Second All-Star Team (2014) • WCHA All-Rookie Team (2015)

FRIESEN, Alex (FREE-zuhn, AL-ehx) VAN

Center. Shoots left. 5'9", 186 lbs. Born, Niagara-on-the-Lake, ON, January 30, 1991.
(Vancouver's 3rd choice, 172nd overall, in 2010 Entry Draft).

			Regular Season					Playoffs				
Season	Club	League	GP	G	A	Pts	PIM	GP	G	A	Pts	PIM
2006-07	N.F. Thunder	Minor-ON	69	45	67	112	66	....	....	....	....	....
2007-08	Niagara Ice Dogs	OHL	46	5	9	14	26	10	0	2	2	6
2008-09	Niagara Ice Dogs	OHL	64	11	22	33	94	12	3	7	10	25
2009-10	Niagara Ice Dogs	OHL	60	23	37	60	94	5	1	6	7	8
2010-11	Niagara Ice Dogs	OHL	60	26	40	66	61	14	2	8	10	19
2011-12	Niagara Ice Dogs	OHL	62	26	45	71	106	20	8	14	22	18
2012-13	Chicago Wolves	AHL	42	1	4	5	22	....	....	....	....	....
	Kalamazoo Wings	ECHL	10	0	4	4	2	....	....	....	....	....
2013-14	Utica Comets	AHL	54	6	14	20	32	....	....	....	....	....
2014-15	Utica Comets	AHL	60	10	20	30	57	23	4	6	10	12

FRK, Martin (FRIHK, MAHR-tihn) DET

Right wing. Shoots right. 6'1", 194 lbs. Born, Pelhrimov, Czech Rep., October 5, 1993.
(Detroit's 1st choice, 49th overall, in 2012 Entry Draft).

			Regular Season					Playoffs				
Season	Club	League	GP	G	A	Pts	PIM	GP	G	A	Pts	PIM
2006-07	Karlovy Vary U17	CzR-U17	5	0	1	1	0	....	....	....	....	....
2007-08	Karlovy Vary U17	CzR-U17	44	25	17	42	56	2	1	0	1	4
2008-09	Karlovy Vary U17	CzR-U17	22	26	12	38	85	....	....	....	....	....
	Karlovy Vary Jr.	CzRep-Jr.	16	8	12	20	6	....	....	....	....	....
2009-10	Karlovy Vary U18	CzR-U18	8	9	4	13	41	....	....	....	....	....
	Karlovy Vary Jr.	CzRep-Jr.	41	28	30	58	186	6	2	3	5	4
2010-11	Halifax	QMJHL	62	22	28	50	75	4	0	2	2	8
2011-12	Halifax	QMJHL	34	16	13	29	41	17	5	6	11	26
2012-13	Halifax	QMJHL	56	35	49	84	84	17	13	20	33	32
2013-14	Grand Rapids	AHL	50	3	9	12	22	4	0	0	0	0
	Toledo Walleye	ECHL	15	5	8	13	10	....	....	....	....	....
2014-15	Grand Rapids	AHL	32	6	6	12	16	2	0	2	2	0
	Toledo Walleye	ECHL	29	23	15	38	16	14	9	4	13	10

Memorial Cup All-Star Team (2013)

FROESE, Byron (FRAYZ, BIGH-ruhn) TOR

Center. Shoots right. 6', 190 lbs. Born, Winkler, MB, March 12, 1991.
(Chicago's 4th choice, 119th overall, in 2009 Entry Draft).

			Regular Season					Playoffs				
Season	Club	League	GP	G	A	Pts	PIM	GP	G	A	Pts	PIM
2007-08	Pembina Valley	MMHL	23	14	20	34	8	11	7	7	14	8
2008-09	Everett Silvertips	WHL	72	19	38	57	30	5	0	3	3	4
2009-10	Everett Silvertips	WHL	70	29	32	61	37	7	3	2	5	0
2010-11	Red Deer Rebels	WHL	70	43	38	81	37	9	5	2	7	4
2011-12	Rockford IceHogs	AHL	57	4	6	10	17	....	....	....	....	....
	Toledo Walleye	ECHL	3	1	1	2	2	....	....	....	....	....
2012-13	Rockford IceHogs	AHL	9	0	2	2	4	....	....	....	....	....
	Toledo Walleye	ECHL	38	12	21	33	12	6	2	4	6	6
2013-14	Rockford IceHogs	AHL	28	0	5	5	14	....	....	....	....	....
	Cincinnati	ECHL	25	11	10	21	20	23	8	17	25	20
2014-15	San Antonio	AHL	3	0	0	0	2	....	....	....	....	....
	Cincinnati	ECHL	17	8	16	24	14	....	....	....	....	....
	Toronto Marlies	AHL	46	18	24	42	26	5	1	3	4	4

Signed to a PTO (professional tryout) contract by **San Antonio** (AHL, September 30, 2014. Signed as a free agent by **Toronto** (AHL), January 7, 2015. Signed as a free agent by **Toronto**, July 3, 2015.

GABRIEL, Kurtis (GAY-bree-uhl, KUHR-tihs) MIN

Right wing. Shoots right. 6'4", 214 lbs. Born, Newmarket, ON, April 20, 1993.
(Minnesota's 2nd choice, 81st overall, in 2013 Entry Draft).

			Regular Season					Playoffs				
Season	Club	League	GP	G	A	Pts	PIM	GP	G	A	Pts	PIM
2009-10	Markham Waxers	Minor-ON	50	16	23	39	....	....	....	....	....	....
2010-11	Owen Sound	OHL	40	1	3	4	20	....	....	....	....	....
2011-12	Owen Sound	OHL	65	4	13	17	72	3	0	0	0	0
2012-13	Owen Sound	OHL	67	13	15	28	100	12	3	2	5	34
2013-14	Owen Sound	OHL	60	15	36	51	99	5	0	1	1	22
2014-15	Iowa Wild	AHL	67	7	9	16	125	....	....	....	....	....

GABRIELLE, Jesse (GAY-bree-ehl, JEH-see) BOS

Left wing. Shoots left. 5'11", 205 lbs. Born, Edmonton, AB, June 17, 1997.
(Boston's 8th choice, 105th overall, in 2015 Entry Draft).

			Regular Season					Playoffs				
Season	Club	League	GP	G	A	Pts	PIM	GP	G	A	Pts	PIM
2012-13	Team Southeast	UMHSEL	3	0	0	0	0	....	....	....	....	....
	Team Southeast	MEPDL	13	6	5	11	....	....	....	....	....	....
	Eagan Wildcats	High-MN	25	15	28	43	22	3	0	4	4	0
	Brandon	WHL	2	0	0	0	7	....	....	....	....	....
2013-14	Brandon	WHL	49	12	14	26	68	9	3	3	6	22
2014-15	Brandon	WHL	33	13	12	25	69	....	....	....	....	....
	Regina Pats	WHL	33	10	9	19	43	9	1	3	4	8

GAGNE, Gabriel (GAH-n'yay, gah-BREE-ehl) OTT

Right wing. Shoots right. 6'5", 190 lbs. Born, Laval, QC, November 11, 1996.
(Ottawa's 3rd choice, 36th overall, in 2015 Entry Draft).

			Regular Season					Playoffs				
Season	Club	League	GP	G	A	Pts	PIM	GP	G	A	Pts	PIM
2011-12	Nord Selects	Minor-QC	STATISTICS NOT AVAILABLE									
	Saint-Eustache	QAAA	3	0	0	0	0	....	....	....	....	....
2012-13	Saint-Eustache	QAAA	41	15	11	26	38	4	1	2	3	4
	Victoriaville Tigres	QMJHL	1	0	0	0	0	1	0	0	0	0
2013-14	Victoriaville Tigres	QMJHL	67	16	21	37	14	5	0	2	2	4
2014-15	Victoriaville Tigres	QMJHL	67	35	24	59	39	4	2	1	3	4

GAGNE, Kevin (gahn-YAY, KEH-vihn) ANA

Defense. Shoots left. 5'8", 176 lbs. Born, Edmundston, NB, April 14, 1992.

			Regular Season					Playoffs				
Season	Club	League	GP	G	A	Pts	PIM	GP	G	A	Pts	PIM
2008-09	Saint John	QMJHL	48	3	3	6	20	4	0	0	0	0
2009-10	Saint John	QMJHL	63	4	25	29	40	5	0	1	1	2
2010-11	Saint John	QMJHL	59	6	26	32	34	19	2	5	7	4
2011-12	Saint John	QMJHL	68	9	26	35	10	17	2	13	15	2
2012-13	Saint John	QMJHL	31	11	23	34	14	....	....	....	....	....
	Rimouski Oceanic	QMJHL	31	6	31	37	22	6	1	1	2	0
	Norfolk Admirals	AHL	5	0	1	1	0	....	....	....	....	....
2013-14	Norfolk Admirals	AHL	71	3	19	22	25	8	0	1	1	0
2014-15	Norfolk Admirals	AHL	57	2	6	8	16	....	....	....	....	....

QMJHL First All-Star Team (2013) • QMJHL Defenseman of the Year (2013)

Signed as a free agent by **Anaheim**, March 6, 2013.

GALIMOV, Emil (ga-LEE-mawv, eh-MIHL) S.J.

Left wing. Shoots left. 6'1", 170 lbs. Born, Nizhnekamsk, Russia, May 9, 1992.
(San Jose's 7th choice, 207th overall, in 2013 Entry Draft).

			Regular Season					Playoffs				
Season	Club	League	GP	G	A	Pts	PIM	GP	G	A	Pts	PIM
2009-10	Nizhnekamsk Jr.	Russia-Jr.	32	6	4	10	69	1	0	1	1	0
2010-11	Nizhnekamsk Jr.	Russia-Jr.	27	11	7	18	34	5	3	0	3	27
	Nizhnekamsk	KHL	18	1	1	2	4	....	....	....	....	....
2011-12	Nizhnekamsk Jr.	Russia-Jr.	9	5	4	9	33	....	....	....	....	....
	Nizhnekamsk	KHL	8	0	0	0	2	....	....	....	....	....
	Loko Yaroslavl Jr.	Russia-Jr.	8	4	5	9	2	....	....	....	....	....
	Yaroslavl	Russia-2	17	9	4	13	12	10	2	3	5	10
2012-13	Loko Yaroslavl Jr.	Russia-Jr.	2	1	1	2	2	....	....	....	....	....
	Yaroslavl-VHL	Russia-2	5	4	1	5	4	....	....	....	....	....
	Yaroslavl	KHL	33	7	13	20	10	6	0	2	2	6
2013-14	Yaroslavl	KHL	43	7	5	12	24	18	1	3	4	8
2014-15	Yaroslavl	KHL	54	9	9	18	28	6	0	2	2	8

GALLACHER, Ben (gal-lah-CHUR, BEHN) FLA

Defense. Shoots left. 5'11", 191 lbs. Born, Calgary, AB, September 11, 1992.
(Florida's 9th choice, 93rd overall, in 2010 Entry Draft).

			Regular Season					Playoffs				
Season	Club	League	GP	G	A	Pts	PIM	GP	G	A	Pts	PIM
2008-09	Camrose Kodiaks	AJHL	43	4	6	10	58	9	0	1	1	4
2009-10	Camrose Kodiaks	AJHL	34	3	19	22	61	11	1	1	2	43
2010-11	Camrose Kodiaks	AJHL	37	5	22	27	119	18	3	5	8	52
2011-12	Ohio State	CCHA	24	1	11	12	30	....	....	....	....	....
2012-13	Green Bay	USHL	42	4	15	19	72	3	0	0	0	0
2013-14	Massachusetts	H-East	34	1	10	11	30	....	....	....	....	....
2014-15	Massachusetts	H-East	32	2	8	10	42	....	....	....	....	....

GANLY, Tyler (GAN-lee, TIGH-luhr) CAR

Defense. Shoots right. 6'2", 204 lbs. Born, Mississauga, ON, March 22, 1995.
(Carolina's 4th choice, 156th overall, in 2013 Entry Draft).

			Regular Season					Playoffs				
Season	Club	League	GP	G	A	Pts	PIM	GP	G	A	Pts	PIM
2010-11	Tor. Jr. Canadiens	GTHL	84	14	30	44	44	....	....	....	....	....
	Tor. Canadiens	ON-Jr.A	2	0	1	1	0	....	....	....	....	....
2011-12	Tor. Jr. Canadiens	GTHL	39	9	15	24	60	10	2	4	6	4
	Tor. Jr. Canadiens	Other	24	3	10	13	18	....	....	....	....	....
	Brampton Capitals	ON-Jr.A	7	0	1	1	0	....	....	....	....	....
2012-13	Sault Ste. Marie	OHL	62	0	17	17	64	6	0	0	0	0
2013-14	Sault Ste. Marie	OHL	67	3	18	21	62	9	0	2	2	8
2014-15	Sault Ste. Marie	OHL	38	2	14	16	33	14	2	7	9	4

GARDINER, Max (GAHR-dih-nuhr, MAX) ST.L.

Center. Shoots left. 6'3", 204 lbs. Born, Edina, MN, May 7, 1992.
(St. Louis' 4th choice, 74th overall, in 2010 Entry Draft).

			Regular Season					Playoffs				
Season	Club	League	GP	G	A	Pts	PIM	GP	G	A	Pts	PIM
2007-08	Minnetonka High	High-MN	27	9	12	21	16	....	....	....	....	....
2008-09	Minnetonka High	High-MN	28	15	28	43	8	....	....	....	....	....
2009-10	Team Southwest	UMHSEL	22	6	6	12	....	....	....	....	....	....
	Minnetonka High	High-MN	17	17	26	43	14	6	5	6	11	0
2010-11	U. of Minnesota	WCHA	17	1	2	3	24	....	....	....	....	....
2011-12	Dubuque	USHL	50	12	14	26	29	5	1	3	4	2
2012-13	Penn State	NCAA	27	3	19	22	22	....	....	....	....	....
2013-14	Penn State	Big Ten	22	0	1	1	8	....	....	....	....	....
2014-15	Penn State	Big Ten	33	5	2	7	12	....	....	....	....	....

GARLAND, Conor (GAHR-luhnd, KAW-nuhr) ARI

Right wing. Shoots right. 5'8", 163 lbs. Born, Scituate, MA, March 11, 1996.
(Arizona's 8th choice, 123rd overall, in 2015 Entry Draft).

			Regular Season					Playoffs				
Season	Club	League	GP	G	A	Pts	PIM	GP	G	A	Pts	PIM
2011-12	Bos. Jr. Bruins	EmJHL	40	42	52	94	53	5	3	6	9	14
	Boston Jr. Bruins	Other	2	1	5	6	0	....	....	....	....	....
2012-13	Muskegon	USHL	6	1	2	3	2	....	....	....	....	....
	Moncton Wildcats	QMJHL	26	6	11	17	16	5	0	0	0	0
2013-14	Moncton Wildcats	QMJHL	51	24	30	54	39	6	2	3	5	2
2014-15	Moncton Wildcats	QMJHL	67	35	*94	*129	66	16	3	22	25	17

QMJHL First All-Star Team (2015) • QMJHL Player of the Year (2015)

GATES, Brent (GAYTZ, BREHNT) ANA

Center. Shoots left. 6'2", 196 lbs. Born, Seattle, WA, August 12, 1997.
(Anaheim's 3rd choice, 80th overall, in 2015 Entry Draft).

			Regular Season					Playoffs				
Season	Club	League	GP	G	A	Pts	PIM	GP	G	A	Pts	PIM
2012-13	Det. Comp. U16	HPHL	26	10	9	19	10	....	....	....	....	....
2013-14	Green Bay	USHL	50	11	4	15	16	2	0	0	0	2
2014-15	Green Bay	USHL	33	10	17	27	18	....	....	....	....	....

• Signed Letter of Intent to attend **University of Minnesota** (Big Ten) in fall of 2015.

GAUDETTE, Adam (gaw-DEHT, A-duhm) VAN

Center. Shoots right. 6'1", 170 lbs. Born, Braintree, MA, October 3, 1996.
(Vancouver's 5th choice, 149th overall, in 2015 Entry Draft).

			Regular Season					Playoffs				
Season	Club	League	GP	G	A	Pts	PIM	GP	G	A	Pts	PIM
2012-13	Bos. Adv. U16	T1EHL	6	2	2	4	2	....	....	....	....	....
	Thayer Academy	High-MA	11	2	3	5	....	....	....	....	....	....
2013-14	Thayer Academy	High-MA	27	29	38	67	....	....	....	....	....	....
2014-15	Cedar Rapids	USHL	50	13	17	30	55	3	0	0	0	4

• Signed Letter of Intent to attend **Northeastern University** (Hockey East) in fall of 2016.

GAUNCE, Brendan (GAWNS, BREHN-duhn) VAN

Center. Shoots left. 6'2", 207 lbs. Born, Markham, ON, March 25, 1994.
(Vancouver's 1st choice, 26th overall, in 2012 Entry Draft).

			Regular Season					Playoffs				
Season	Club	League	GP	G	A	Pts	PIM	GP	G	A	Pts	PIM
2009-10	Markham Waxers	Minor-ON	86	55	93	*148	54	....	....	....	....	....
	Markham Waxers	ON-Jr.A	1	0	0	0	0	....	....	....	....	....
2010-11	Belleville Bulls	OHL	65	11	25	36	40	4	0	0	0	4
2011-12	Belleville Bulls	OHL	68	28	40	68	68	6	1	2	3	2
2012-13	Belleville Bulls	OHL	60	33	27	60	44	17	8	14	22	10
2013-14	Belleville Bulls	OHL	22	10	16	26	27	....	....	....	....	....
	Erie Otters	OHL	43	21	25	46	32	14	5	11	16	16
2014-15	Utica Comets	AHL	74	11	18	29	31	21	4	5	9	12

GAUTHIER, Frederik (GOH-t'yay, frehd-RIHK) TOR

Center. Shoots left. 6'5", 230 lbs. Born, St-Lin, QC, April 26, 1995.
(Toronto's 1st choice, 21st overall, in 2013 Entry Draft).

			Regular Season					Playoffs				
Season	Club	League	GP	G	A	Pts	PIM	GP	G	A	Pts	PIM
2010-11	Esther-Blondin	QAAA	37	7	14	21	6	3	0	0	0	0
2011-12	Esther-Blondin	QAAA	39	26	25	51	28	13	13	11	24	6
2012-13	Rimouski Oceanic	QMJHL	62	22	38	60	26	6	0	2	2	2
2013-14	Rimouski Oceanic	QMJHL	54	18	34	52	27	11	3	6	9	6
2014-15	Rimouski Oceanic	QMJHL	37	16	16	32	21	20	2	14	16	4

QMJHL All-Rookie Team (2013)

GAVRIKOV, Vladislav (GAV-rih-kawv, vla-dih-SLAV) CBJ

Defense. Shoots left. 6'3", 205 lbs. Born, Yaroslavl, Russia, November 21, 1995.
(Columbus' 8th choice, 159th overall, in 2015 Entry Draft).

			Regular Season					Playoffs				
Season	Club	League	GP	G	A	Pts	PIM	GP	G	A	Pts	PIM
2011-12	Loko Yaroslavl Jr.	Russia-Jr.	8	1	1	2	4	2	0	0	0	0
2012-13	Loko Yaroslavl Jr.	Russia-Jr.	47	3	3	6	18	....	....	....	....	....
2013-14	Loko Yaroslavl Jr.	Russia-Jr.	45	3	9	12	28	7	0	2	2	4
2014-15	Loko Yaroslavl Jr.	Russia-Jr.	16	1	6	7	16	5	0	0	0	2
	HK Ryazan	Russia-2	11	1	2	3	4	....	....	....	....	....
	Yaroslavl	KHL	16	0	1	1	4	4	0	0	0	0

GAVRUS, Artur (GAV-ruhs, ahr-TUHR) N.J.

Center/Left wing. Shoots left. 5'10", 175 lbs. Born, Ratichi, Belarus, January 3, 1994.
(New Jersey's 7th choice, 180th overall, in 2012 Entry Draft).

			Regular Season					Playoffs				
Season	Club	League	GP	G	A	Pts	PIM	GP	G	A	Pts	PIM
2009-10	Neman Grodno 2	Belarus-2	41	14	12	26	22	....	....	....	....	....
2010-11	Neman Grodno 2	Belarus-2	19	4	4	8	18	....	....	....	....	....
2011-12	Owen Sound	OHL	45	15	22	37	18	1	0	0	0	0
2012-13	Neman Grodno	Belarus	15	5	7	12	0	....	....	....	....	....
	Neman Grodno 2	Belarus-2	2	0	3	3	0	....	....	....	....	....
	Owen Sound	OHL	21	8	6	14	11	12	3	5	8	2
2013-14	Dynamo Minsk	KHL	30	1	3	4	8	....	....	....	....	....
2014-15	Dynamo Minsk	KHL	36	5	4	9	12	....	....	....	....	....
	Molodechno	Belarus	4	2	4	6	2	....	....	....	....	....
	Bobruisk Jr.	Russia-Jr.	....	....	....	....	....	3	1	1	2	12

GAWDIN, Glenn (GAW-dihn, GLEHN) ST.L.

Center. Shoots right. 6'1", 191 lbs. Born, Richmond, BC, March 25, 1997.
(St. Louis' 3rd choice, 116th overall, in 2015 Entry Draft).

			Regular Season					Playoffs				
Season	Club	League	GP	G	A	Pts	PIM	GP	G	A	Pts	PIM
2011-12	Seafair Islanders	Minor-BC	43	58	32	90	34	....	....	....	....	....
	Greater Van.	BCMML	....	....	....	....	....	4	1	0	1	0
2012-13	Greater Van.	BCMML	37	17	29	46	49	6	7	4	11	14
	Swift Current	WHL	2	0	0	0	0	....	....	....	....	....
2013-14	Swift Current	WHL	66	10	12	22	34	6	0	0	0	2
2014-15	Swift Current	WHL	72	15	39	54	59	4	1	1	2	0

GEERTSEN, Mason (GEERT-suhn, MAY-suhn) COL

Defense. Shoots left. 6'4", 205 lbs. Born, Drayton Valley, AB, April 19, 1995.
(Colorado's 4th choice, 93rd overall, in 2013 Entry Draft).

			Regular Season					Playoffs				
Season	Club	League	GP	G	A	Pts	PIM	GP	G	A	Pts	PIM
2010-11	Sherwood Park	AMHL	31	3	7	10	84	10	1	2	3	24
	Edmonton	WHL	3	0	0	0	4	....	....	....	....	....
2011-12	Edmonton	WHL	34	0	3	3	70	....	....	....	....	....
2012-13	Edmonton	WHL	15	0	4	4	32	....	....	....	....	....
	Vancouver Giants	WHL	58	2	8	10	98	....	....	....	....	....
2013-14	Vancouver Giants	WHL	66	4	19	23	126	4	0	0	0	14
2014-15	Vancouver Giants	WHL	69	13	25	38	107	....	....	....	....	....
	Lake Erie Monsters	AHL	9	0	0	0	2	....	....	....	....	....

GELINAS, Guillaume (ZHEHL-ih-nuh, GEE-AWM) MIN

Defense. Shoots left. 5'10", 203 lbs. Born, Quebec, QC, June 14, 1993.

			Regular Season					Playoffs				
Season	Club	League	GP	G	A	Pts	PIM	GP	G	A	Pts	PIM
2008-09	St-Francois	QAAA	45	4	10	14	42	3	0	0	0	18
2009-10	St-Francois	QAAA	34	10	22	32	44	4	0	2	2	2
	Val-d'Or Foreurs	QMJHL	16	0	1	1	6	....	....	....	....	....
2010-11	Val-d'Or Foreurs	QMJHL	60	4	17	21	53	4	0	0	0	6
2011-12	Val-d'Or Foreurs	QMJHL	64	10	24	34	43	4	1	0	1	6
2012-13	Val-d'Or Foreurs	QMJHL	68	6	39	45	111	6	1	2	3	2
2013-14	Val-d'Or Foreurs	QMJHL	67	23	69	92	81	24	11	23	34	20
2014-15	Iowa Wild	AHL	37	2	2	4	22	....	....	....	....	....

QMJHL First All-Star Team (2014)

Signed as a free agent by **Minnesota**, July 1, 2014.

GENDRON, Miles (GEHN-druhn, MIGH-uhlz) OTT

Defense. Shoots left. 6'3", 190 lbs. Born, Oakville, ON, June 28, 1996.
(Ottawa's 2nd choice, 70th overall, in 2014 Entry Draft).

			Regular Season					Playoffs				
Season	Club	League	GP	G	A	Pts	PIM	GP	G	A	Pts	PIM
2010-11	The Rivers School	High-MA	24	2	6	8	....	....	....	....	....	....
2011-12	The Rivers School	High-MA	24	7	9	16	....	....	....	....	....	....
2012-13	The Rivers School	High-MA	29	12	18	30	....	....	....	....	....	....
2013-14	Neponset Valley	Minor-MA	11	1	8	9	4	....	....	....	....	....
	The Rivers School	High-MA	22	6	13	19	....	....	....	....	....	....
2014-15	Penticton Vees	BCHL	54	5	12	17	42	22	0	12	12	4

• Signed Letter of Intent to attend **University of Connecticut** (Atlantic Hockey) in fall of 2015.

GENNARO, Matteo (jeh-NAIR-oh, muh-TAY-oh) WPG

Center. Shoots left. 6'2", 193 lbs. Born, St. Albert, AB, March 30, 1997.
(Winnipeg's 8th choice, 203rd overall, in 2015 Entry Draft).

			Regular Season					Playoffs				
Season	Club	League	GP	G	A	Pts	PIM	GP	G	A	Pts	PIM
2012-13	St. Albert Raiders	AMHL	30	9	12	21	32	4	0	2	2	2
2013-14	Prince Albert	WHL	60	5	10	15	14	3	0	0	0	0
2014-15	Prince Albert	WHL	72	16	15	31	44	....	....	....	....	....

GERNAT, Martin (GAIR-naht, MAR-tihn) EDM

Defense. Shoots left. 6'4", 202 lbs. Born, Presov, Slovakia, April 11, 1993.
(Edmonton's 8th choice, 122nd overall, in 2011 Entry Draft).

			Regular Season					Playoffs				
Season	Club	League	GP	G	A	Pts	PIM	GP	G	A	Pts	PIM
2008-09	P.H.K. Presov U18	Svk-U18	41	6	28	34	36	....	....	....	....	....
2009-10	HC Kosice U18	Svk-U18	36	4	21	25	20	5	0	3	3	2
	HC Kosice Jr.	Slovak-Jr.	....	....	....	....	....	2	0	0	0	2
2010-11	HC Kosice U18	Svk-U18	8	3	4	7	22	1	0	0	0	2
	HC Kosice Jr.	Slovak-Jr.	28	3	15	18	20	12	3	3	6	10
2011-12	Edmonton	WHL	60	9	46	55	46	20	7	6	13	8
2012-13	Edmonton	WHL	23	3	10	13	14	22	6	11	17	6
2013-14	Oklahoma City	AHL	57	4	17	21	26	1	0	0	0	0
	Bakersfield	ECHL	3	0	1	1	6	....	....	....	....	....
2014-15	Oklahoma City	AHL	54	1	8	9	32	....	....	....	....	....

GERSICH, Shane (GUHR-sihch, SHAYN) WSH

Center/Left wing. Shoots left. 5'11", 175 lbs. Born, Chaska, MN, July 10, 1996.
(Washington's 4th choice, 134th overall, in 2014 Entry Draft).

			Regular Season					Playoffs				
Season	Club	League	GP	G	A	Pts	PIM	GP	G	A	Pts	PIM
2011-12	Holy Family Cath.	High-MN	20	30	30	60	21	1	0	0	0	0
	U.S. Youth Oly.	Other	6	3	1	4	6	....	....	....	....	....
2012-13	Holy Family Cath.	High-MN	24	28	34	62	35	1	0	0	0	2
	Omaha Lancers	USHL	6	1	0	1	19	....	....	....	....	....
2013-14	USNTDP	USHL	26	8	8	16	4	....	....	....	....	....
	USNTDP	U-18	35	8	8	16	14	....	....	....	....	....
2014-15	Omaha Lancers	USHL	52	27	23	50	32	3	1	1	2	0

• Signed Letter of Intent to attend **University of North Dakota** (NCHC) in fall of 2015.

GILBERT, Dennis (GIHL-buhrt, DEH-nihs) CHI

Defense. Shoots left. 6'2", 199 lbs. Born, Buffalo, NY, October 30, 1996.
(Chicago's 2nd choice, 91st overall, in 2015 Entry Draft).

			Regular Season					Playoffs				
Season	Club	League	GP	G	A	Pts	PIM	GP	G	A	Pts	PIM
2011-12	St. Joseph's	High-NY	27	4	5	9	1.5	....	....	....	....	....
2012-13	St. Joseph's	High-NY	28	12	8	20	21	....	....	....	....	....
2013-14	Buffalo Jr. Sabres	ON-Jr.A	35	4	13	17	36	10	0	3	3	8
2014-15	Chicago Steel	USHL	59	4	23	27	89	....	....	....	....	....

USHL All-Rookie Team (2015)

• Signed Letter of Intent to attend **University of Notre Dame** (Hockey East) in fall of 2015.

GILMOUR, Adam (GIHL-mohr, A-duhm) MIN

Center. Shoots right. 6'4", 192 lbs. Born, Albany, NY, January 29, 1994.
(Minnesota's 4th choice, 98th overall, in 2012 Entry Draft).

			Regular Season					Playoffs				
Season	Club	League	GP	G	A	Pts	PIM	GP	G	A	Pts	PIM
2010-11	Nobles	High-MA	27	11	16	27	8	....	....	....	....	....
2011-12	Cape Cod Whalers	Minor-MA	30	19	26	45		....	....	....	....	....
	Nobles	High-MA	26	26	30	56	28	....	....	....	....	....
2012-13	Muskegon	USHL	64	19	28	47	12	3	1	0	1	10
2013-14	Boston College	H-East	40	7	13	20	10	....	....	....	....	....
2014-15	Boston College	H-East	38	9	18	27	22	....	....	....	....	....

GILMOUR, John (GIHL-mohr, JAWN) CGY

Defense. Shoots left. 5'11", 180 lbs. Born, Montreal, QC, May 17, 1993.
(Calgary's 8th choice, 198th overall, in 2013 Entry Draft).

			Regular Season					Playoffs				
Season	Club	League	GP	G	A	Pts	PIM	GP	G	A	Pts	PIM
2010-11	Gilmour Acad.	MPHL	13	4	7	11	8	3	0	2	2	0
	Gilmour Acad.	High-OH	46	....	....	31	....	....	....	....	....	....
2011-12	Cedar Rapids	USHL	58	10	14	24	14	2	0	1	1	0
2012-13	Providence College	H-East	38	4	9	13	35	....	....	....	....	....
2013-14	Providence College	H-East	39	5	13	18	22	....	....	....	....	....
2014-15	Providence College	H-East	30	4	7	11	10	....	....	....	....	....

GIMAYEV, Sergei (gih-MIGH-ehv, SAIR-gay) OTT

Defense. Shoots left. 6'1", 183 lbs. Born, Moscow, USSR, February 16, 1984.
(Ottawa's 6th choice, 166th overall, in 2003 Entry Draft).

			Regular Season					Playoffs				
Season	Club	League	GP	G	A	Pts	PIM	GP	G	A	Pts	PIM
2001-02	CSKA Moscow 2	Russia-3	36	0	10	10	50	....	....	....	....	....
2002-03	Cherepovets	Russia	11	0	0	0	4	....	....	....	....	....
2003-04	Cherepovets	Russia	50	1	3	4	32	....	....	....	....	....
2004-05	Cherepovets	Russia	5	0	1	1	2	....	....	....	....	....
	Sibir Novosibirsk	Russia	31	1	6	7	34	....	....	....	....	....
2005-06	Dynamo Moscow	Russia	46	1	3	4	36	2	0	0	0	0
2006-07	Dynamo Moscow	Russia	23	0	2	2	28	2	0	0	0	6
2007-08	Cherepovets	Russia	39	1	0	1	30	8	1	1	2	4
2008-09	Barys Astana	KHL	45	0	2	2	79	....	....	....	....	....
2009-10	Barys Astana	KHL	54	6	6	12	73	3	0	0	0	8
2010-11	Barys Astana	KHL	52	5	3	8	44	4	0	0	0	4
2011-12	Ufa	KHL	43	1	4	5	27	3	0	0	0	0
2012-13	CSKA Moscow	KHL	43	1	0	1	22	2	0	0	0	2
2013-14	CSKA Moscow	KHL	33	0	3	3	12	4	0	0	0	2
2014-15	Novosibirsk	KHL	53	0	4	4	55	16	0	3	3	6

GIRARD, Felix (zhih-RAHRD, FEE-lihx) NSH

Center. Shoots right. 5'10", 185 lbs. Born, Quebec, QC, May 9, 1994.
(Nashville's 3rd choice, 95th overall, in 2013 Entry Draft).

			Regular Season					Playoffs				
Season	Club	League	GP	G	A	Pts	PIM	GP	G	A	Pts	PIM
2009-10	St-Francois	QAAA	41	7	11	18	68	3	1	1	2	15
2010-11	Baie-Comeau	QMJHL	64	5	12	17	37	....	....	....	....	....
2011-12	Baie-Comeau	QMJHL	60	6	15	21	63	8	2	1	3	14
2012-13	Baie-Comeau	QMJHL	58	23	38	61	58	19	4	11	15	42
2013-14	Baie-Comeau	QMJHL	58	11	32	43	130	21	4	8	12	43
2014-15	Milwaukee	AHL	61	4	5	9	54	....	....	....	....	....

GLAZACHEV, Konstantin (GLAH-zuh-chehv, KAWN-stan-tihn) NSH

Left wing. Shoots right. 6', 186 lbs. Born, Arkhangelsk, USSR, February 18, 1985.
(Nashville's 2nd choice, 35th overall, in 2003 Entry Draft).

			Regular Season					Playoffs				
Season	Club	League	GP	G	A	Pts	PIM	GP	G	A	Pts	PIM
2001-02	Yaroslavl 2	Russia-3	7	5	6	11	6	....	....	....	....	....
2002-03	Yaroslavl 2	Russia-3	STATISTICS NOT AVAILABLE									
	Yaroslavl	Russia	13	3	4	7	4	4	0	0	0	0
2003-04	Yaroslavl 2	Russia-3	9	6	5	11	8	....	....	....	....	....
	Yaroslavl	Russia	35	4	3	7	4	2	0	0	0	0
2004-05	Sibir Novosibirsk	Russia	24	4	9	13	6	....	....	....	....	....
	Yaroslavl	Russia	9	0	3	3	2	....	....	....	....	....
	Yaroslavl 2	Russia-3	20	17	9	26	14	....	....	....	....	....
2005-06	Yaroslavl	Russia	29	7	4	11	8	9	0	2	2	0
2006-07	Yaroslavl	Russia	14	4	1	5	10	....	....	....	....	....
	Yaroslavl 2	Russia-3	4	2	5	7	0	....	....	....	....	....
	Amur Khabarovsk	Russia	22	4	7	11	14	....	....	....	....	....
2007-08	Novokuznetsk	Russia	50	7	9	16	10	....	....	....	....	....
2008-09	Barys Astana	KHL	56	28	24	52	30	3	3	0	3	2
2009-10	Barys Astana	KHL	42	16	17	33	18	2	0	0	0	0
2010-11	Dynamo Minsk	KHL	52	12	23	35	28	7	2	4	6	2
2011-12	Magnitogorsk	KHL	18	3	7	10	6	....	....	....	....	....
	Ak Bars Kazan	KHL	27	3	5	8	10	6	0	1	1	0
2012-13	SKA St. Petersburg	KHL	6	0	1	1	4	....	....	....	....	....
	Sibir Novosibirsk	KHL	16	5	3	8	0	....	....	....	....	....
	Khanty-Mansiisk	KHL	19	6	13	19	4	4	0	1	1	2
2013-14	Dynamo Moscow	KHL	32	9	5	14	12	2	0	0	0	0
2014-15	Dynamo Moscow	KHL	37	6	8	14	10	2	0	0	0	0

GLOVER, Jack (GLUH-vuhr, JAK) WPG

Defense. Shoots right. 6'3", 190 lbs. Born, Golden Valley, MN, May 17, 1996.
(Winnipeg's 2nd choice, 69th overall, in 2014 Entry Draft).

			Regular Season					Playoffs				
Season	Club	League	GP	G	A	Pts	PIM	GP	G	A	Pts	PIM
2011-12	Benilde	High-MN	22	2	14	16	2	5	0	2	2	2
	U.S. Youth Oly.	Other	6	1	1	2	2	....	....	....	....	....
2012-13	USNTDP	USHL	37	1	5	6	24	....	....	....	....	....
	USNTDP	U-17	19	5	9	14	8	....	....	....	....	....
2013-14	USNTDP	USHL	24	1	9	10	12	....	....	....	....	....
	USNTDP	U-18	33	1	17	18	18	....	....	....	....	....
2014-15	U. of Minnesota	Big Ten	22	0	3	3	6	....	....	....	....	....

GOLDOBIN, Nikolay (gohl-DOH-bihn, NIH-koh-ligh) S.J.

Right wing. Shoots left. 5'10", 185 lbs. Born, Moscow, Russia, October 7, 1995.
(San Jose's 1st choice, 27th overall, in 2014 Entry Draft).

			Regular Season					Playoffs				
Season	Club	League	GP	G	A	Pts	PIM	GP	G	A	Pts	PIM
2011-12	Chekhov Jr.	Russia-Jr.	50	13	9	22	8	9	2	1	3	0
2012-13	Sarnia Sting	OHL	68	30	38	68	12	4	0	1	1	0
	Sarnia Sting	OHL	68	30	38	68	12	4	0	1	1	0
2013-14	Sarnia Sting	OHL	67	38	56	94	21	....	....	....	....	....
2014-15	HIFK Helsinki	Finland	38	11	10	21	12	8	1	5	6	2
	Worcester Sharks	AHL	9	3	2	5	4	4	0	0	0	0

GONCHAROV, Maxim (gohn-CHAR-ahv, mahx-EEM) ARI

Defense. Shoots right. 6'3", 215 lbs. Born, Moscow, USSR, June 15, 1989.
(Phoenix's 6th choice, 123rd overall, in 2007 Entry Draft).

			Regular Season					Playoffs				
Season	Club	League	GP	G	A	Pts	PIM	GP	G	A	Pts	PIM
2005-06	CSKA Moscow 2	Russia-3	STATISTICS NOT AVAILABLE									
2006-07	CSKA Moscow 2	Russia-3	STATISTICS NOT AVAILABLE									
	CSKA Moscow	Russia	18	0	0	0	10	5	0	0	0	2
2007-08	CSKA Moscow	Russia	47	3	2	5	38	6	0	2	2	0
	CSKA Moscow 2	Russia-3	4	0	2	2	35	3	0	0	0	8
2008-09	CSKA Moscow	KHL	47	7	8	15	50	7	0	0	0	4
2009-10	CSKA Moscow	KHL	51	4	13	17	52	3	1	0	1	2
2010-11	San Antonio	AHL	61	6	9	15	65	....	....	....	....	....
2011-12	Portland Pirates	AHL	45	1	3	4	37	....	....	....	....	....
2012-13	Portland Pirates	AHL	45	2	13	15	114	1	0	0	0	4
2013-14	CSKA Moscow	KHL	21	3	4	7	24	....	....	....	....	....
	Omsk	KHL	27	3	3	6	100	2	0	0	0	2
2014-15	Omsk	KHL	15	1	0	1	16	12	0	1	1	29

Signed as a free agent by **CSKA Moscow** (KHL), June 3, 2013. Signed as a free agent by **Omsk** (KHL), November 5, 2013.

GORTZ, Max (GUHRTS, MAX) NSH

Right wing. Shoots right. 6'3", 196 lbs. Born, Hoor, Sweden, January 28, 1993.
(Nashville's 8th choice, 172nd overall, in 2012 Entry Draft).

			Regular Season					Playoffs				
Season	Club	League	GP	G	A	Pts	PIM	GP	G	A	Pts	PIM
2008-09	Malmo U18	Swe-U18	10	2	0	2	2	....	....	....	....	....
2009-10	Malmo U18	Swe-U18	23	8	23	31	2	....	....	....	....	....
	Malmo Jr.	Swe-Jr.	26	1	3	4	6	....	....	....	....	....
2010-11	Malmo U18	Swe-U18	8	2	1	3	6	....	....	....	....	....
	Malmo Jr.	Swe-Jr.	40	9	9	18	14	5	2	0	2	2
2011-12	Farjestad Jr.	Swe-Jr.	28	17	18	35	6	6	4	3	7	0
	Farjestad	Sweden	18	2	3	5	0	2	0	0	0	2
2012-13	Farjestad Jr.	Swe-Jr.	8	7	1	8	0	4	2	3	5	0
	Farjestad	Sweden	50	9	6	15	4	9	0	2	2	0
2013-14	Farjestad Jr.	Swe-Jr.	4	3	2	5	2	....	....	....	....	....
	Farjestad	Sweden	22	2	2	4	2	....	....	....	....	....
	Frolunda	Sweden	18	6	0	6	2	7	3	2	5	0
2014-15	Frolunda	Sweden	53	14	14	28	6	12	3	1	4	0

GOULBOURNE, Tyrell (GOHL-buhrn, tigh-REHL) PHI

Left wing. Shoots left. 6', 200 lbs. Born, Edmonton, AB, January 26, 1994.
(Philadelphia's 3rd choice, 72nd overall, in 2013 Entry Draft).

			Regular Season					Playoffs				
Season	Club	League	GP	G	A	Pts	PIM	GP	G	A	Pts	PIM
2009-10	CAC Gregg's Dist.	AMHL	31	13	13	26	85	2	0	0	0	2
	Kelowna Rockets	WHL	5	0	1	1	0	....	....	....	....	....
2010-11	CAC Gregg's Dist.	AMHL	26	10	16	26	69	....	....	....	....	....
	Kelowna Rockets	WHL	13	1	0	1	27	6	0	0	0	6
2011-12	Kelowna Rockets	WHL	63	6	8	14	109	4	0	0	0	2
2012-13	Kelowna Rockets	WHL	64	14	13	27	135	11	1	2	3	15
2013-14	Kelowna Rockets	WHL	68	17	20	37	114	14	2	3	5	23
2014-15	Kelowna Rockets	WHL	62	22	23	45	76	12	1	1	2	23

GOURDE, Yanni (GOHRD, YAH-nee) T.B.

Left wing. Shoots left. 5'9", 170 lbs. Born, St-Narcisse, QC, December 15, 1991.

			Regular Season					Playoffs				
Season	Club	League	GP	G	A	Pts	PIM	GP	G	A	Pts	PIM
2007-08	Rive-Sud Express	Minor-QC	STATISTICS NOT AVAILABLE									
	Levis	QAAA	2	0	0	0	0	....	....	....	....	....
2008-09	Jonquiere Elites	QAAA	41	23	30	53	50	4	1	5	6	6
	Victoriaville Tigres	QMJHL	4	0	1	1	0	....	....	....	....	....
2009-10	Victoriaville Tigres	QMJHL	59	11	17	28	36	16	2	3	5	20
2010-11	Victoriaville Tigres	QMJHL	68	26	42	68	48	9	4	6	10	12
2011-12	Victoriaville Tigres	QMJHL	68	37	87	124	70	4	1	2	3	6
	Worcester Sharks	AHL	4	1	2	3	0	....	....	....	....	....
2012-13	Worcester Sharks	AHL	54	8	6	14	41	....	....	....	....	....
	San Francisco Bulls	ECHL	8	4	6	10	9	....	....	....	....	....
2013-14	Worcester Sharks	AHL	25	4	20	24	26	....	....	....	....	....
	Kalamazoo Wings	ECHL	30	15	19	34	19	....	....	....	....	....
	Syracuse Crunch	AHL	18	2	6	8	16	....	....	....	....	....
2014-15	Syracuse Crunch	AHL	76	29	28	57	61	3	1	1	2	10

Signed as a free agent by **Tampa Bay**, March 10, 2014.

GRAHAM, Jesse (GRAY-uhm, JEH-see) NYI

Defense. Shoots right. 6', 185 lbs. Born, Oshawa, ON, May 13, 1994.
(NY Islanders' 6th choice, 155th overall, in 2012 Entry Draft).

			Regular Season					Playoffs				
Season	Club	League	GP	G	A	Pts	PIM	GP	G	A	Pts	PIM
2009-10	Tor. Young Nats	GTHL	84	14	74	88	38	....	....	....	....	....
2010-11	Niagara Ice Dogs	OHL	63	1	17	18	22	14	1	8	9	8
2011-12	Niagara Ice Dogs	OHL	68	4	37	41	36	20	1	9	10	20
2012-13	Niagara Ice Dogs	OHL	68	4	35	39	48	5	0	3	3	6
2013-14	Niagara Ice Dogs	OHL	24	6	11	17	21	....	....	....	....	....
	Saginaw Spirit	OHL	42	5	32	37	22	5	0	3	3	2
	Bridgeport	AHL	7	1	3	4	2	....	....	....	....	....
2014-15	Bridgeport	AHL	39	3	16	19	20	....	....	....	....	....
	Florida Everblades	ECHL	23	1	13	14	10	12	1	5	6	4

OHL All-Rookie Team (2011)

GRAVEL, Kevin (gra-VEHL, KEH-vihn) L.A.

Defense. Shoots left. 6'4", 204 lbs. Born, Kingsford, MI, March 6, 1992.
(Los Angeles' 4th choice, 148th overall, in 2010 Entry Draft).

			Regular Season					Playoffs				
Season	Club	League	GP	G	A	Pts	PIM	GP	G	A	Pts	PIM
2008-09	Marquette	NAHL	58	3	11	14	29	....	....	....	....	....
	USNTDP	U-17	3	0	1	1	4	....	....	....	....	....
2009-10	Sioux City	USHL	53	3	3	6	36	....	....	....	....	....
2010-11	St. Cloud State	WCHA	36	1	5	6	4	....	....	....	....	....
2011-12	St. Cloud State	WCHA	37	1	7	8	12	....	....	....	....	....
2012-13	St. Cloud State	WCHA	42	1	11	12	25	....	....	....	....	....
2013-14	St. Cloud State	NCHC	38	10	13	23	2	....	....	....	....	....
	Manchester	AHL	5	0	0	0	2	....	....	....	....	....
2014-15	Manchester	AHL	58	6	9	15	23	19	0	5	5	0

GRAVES, Ryan (GRAVZ, RIGH-uhn) **NYR**

Defense. Shoots left. 6'4", 220 lbs. Born, Yarmouth, NS, May 21, 1995.
(NY Rangers' 4th choice, 110th overall, in 2013 Entry Draft).

			Regular Season					Playoffs				
Season	Club	League	GP	G	A	Pts	PIM	GP	G	A	Pts	PIM
2010-11	South Shore	NSMHL	32	5	7	12	58	5	0	6	6	8
	Yarmouth	MJrHL	1	0	0	0	2	3	0	0	0	2
2011-12	P.E.I. Rocket	QMJHL	62	2	7	9	34	....	....	....	....	....
2012-13	P.E.I. Rocket	QMJHL	68	3	13	16	90	6	0	0	0	6
2013-14	Charlottetown	QMJHL	39	3	9	12	52	....	....	....	....	....
	Val-d'Or Foreurs	QMJHL	26	2	8	10	16	24	1	7	8	24
2014-15	Quebec Remparts	QMJHL	50	15	24	39	49	21	5	6	11	25

Memorial Cup All-Star Team (2015)

GREENWAY, Jordan (GREEN-way, JOHR-duhn) **MIN**

Left wing. Shoots left. 6'6", 218 lbs. Born, Canton, NY, February 16, 1997.
(Minnesota's 2nd choice, 50th overall, in 2015 Entry Draft).

			Regular Season					Playoffs				
Season	Club	League	GP	G	A	Pts	PIM	GP	G	A	Pts	PIM
2012-13	Shattuck U16	High-MN	46	23	39	62	96	....	....	....	....	....
2013-14	USNTDP	USHL	33	10	16	26	61	....	....	....	....	....
	USNTDP	U-17	19	6	9	15	55	....	....	....	....	....
2014-15	USNTDP	USHL	22	5	15	20	16	....	....	....	....	....
	USNTDP	U-18	31	4	19	23	34	....	....	....	....	....

• Signed Letter of Intent to attend **Boston College** (Hockey East) in fall of 2015.

GREER, AJ (GREER, AY-JAY) **COL**

Left wing. Shoots left. 6'3", 204 lbs. Born, Joliette, QC, December 14, 1996.
(Colorado's 2nd choice, 39th overall, in 2015 Entry Draft).

			Regular Season					Playoffs				
Season	Club	League	GP	G	A	Pts	PIM	GP	G	A	Pts	PIM
2011-12	Esther-Blondin	QAAA	42	15	13	28	75	13	7	3	10	4
2012-13	Kimball Union	High-NH	30	16	19	35	....	....	....	....	....	....
2013-14	Boston Jr. Bruins	Minor-MA	8	2	4	6	0	....	....	....	....	....
	Kimball Union	High-NH	34	24	39	63	....	....	....	....	....	....
	Des Moines	USHL	2	2	1	3	2	....	....	....	....	....
2014-15	Boston University	H-East	37	3	4	7	18	....	....	....	....	....

GREGOIRE, Jeremy (greh-G'WAHR, JAIR-ih-mee) **MTL**

Center. Shoots right. 6', 191 lbs. Born, Sherbrooke, QC, September 5, 1995.
(Montreal's 8th choice, 176th overall, in 2013 Entry Draft).

			Regular Season					Playoffs				
Season	Club	League	GP	G	A	Pts	PIM	GP	G	A	Pts	PIM
2009-10	Magog	QAAA	28	4	8	12	22	10	3	1	4	6
2010-11	Magog	QAAA	38	28	25	53	42	13	8	8	16	10
2011-12	Chicoutimi	QMJHL	61	15	15	30	59	18	2	4	6	14
2012-13	Chicoutimi	QMJHL	35	7	8	15	71	....	....	....	....	....
	Baie-Comeau	QMJHL	27	12	5	17	29	18	9	7	16	27
2013-14	Baie-Comeau	QMJHL	65	35	34	69	84	22	9	14	23	35
2014-15	Baie-Comeau	QMJHL	32	20	21	41	59	....	....	....	....	....

GRENIER, Alexandre (GREHN-yay, al-ehx-AHN-druh) **VAN**

Right wing. Shoots right. 6'5", 200 lbs. Born, Laval, QC, September 5, 1991.
(Vancouver's 3rd choice, 90th overall, in 2011 Entry Draft).

			Regular Season					Playoffs				
Season	Club	League	GP	G	A	Pts	PIM	GP	G	A	Pts	PIM
2009-10	St-Jerome	QJHL	51	26	28	54	63	7	1	3	4	2
2010-11	St-Jerome	QJHL	33	25	35	60	34	....	....	....	....	....
	Quebec Remparts	QMJHL	31	9	15	24	6	15	8	8	16	4
2011-12	Halifax	QMJHL	64	25	39	64	42	17	4	12	16	19
2012-13	Salzburg	Austria	25	5	8	13	21	....	....	....	....	....
	Chicago Wolves	AHL	4	0	0	0	2	....	....	....	....	....
	Kalamazoo Wings	ECHL	37	10	21	31	51	....	....	....	....	....
2013-14	Utica Comets	AHL	68	17	22	39	56	....	....	....	....	....
2014-15	Utica Comets	AHL	67	17	26	43	71	23	6	9	15	25

Signed as a free agent by **Salzburg** (Austria), June 1, 2012.

GROPP, Ryan (GRAWP, RIGH-uhn) **NYR**

Left wing. Shoots left. 6'2", 187 lbs. Born, Kamloops, BC, September 16, 1996.
(NY Rangers' 1st choice, 41st overall, in 2015 Entry Draft).

			Regular Season					Playoffs				
Season	Club	League	GP	G	A	Pts	PIM	GP	G	A	Pts	PIM
2011-12	Okanagan H.A.	High-BC	41	21	30	51	60	1	0	1	1	0
	St. Andrew's	CISSA	8	3	5	8	20	2	1	1	2	0
	Penticton Vees	BCHL	2	1	0	1	0	....	....	....	....	....
2012-13	Penticton Vees	BCHL	50	12	19	31	26	15	4	5	9	4
2013-14	Penticton Vees	BCHL	10	3	5	8	2	....	....	....	....	....
	Seattle	WHL	59	18	24	42	22	9	1	3	4	0
2014-15	Seattle	WHL	67	30	28	58	44	6	1	7	8	8

GRZELCYK, Matthew (GRIHZ-lihk, MA-thew) **BOS**

Defense. Shoots left. 5'9", 174 lbs. Born, Charlestown, MA, January 5, 1994.
(Boston's 2nd choice, 85th overall, in 2012 Entry Draft).

			Regular Season					Playoffs				
Season	Club	League	GP	G	A	Pts	PIM	GP	G	A	Pts	PIM
2009-10	Belmont Hill	High-MA	31	2	18	20	30	....	....	....	....	....
2010-11	USNTDP	USHL	36	1	9	10	28	2	0	0	0	2
	USNTDP	U-17	17	1	7	8	10	....	....	....	....	....
2011-12	USNTDP	USHL	24	1	10	11	6	....	....	....	....	....
	USNTDP	U-18	36	2	19	21	16	....	....	....	....	....
2012-13	Boston University	H-East	38	3	20	23	26	....	....	....	....	....
2013-14	Boston University	H-East	19	3	8	11	16	....	....	....	....	....
2014-15	Boston University	H-East	41	10	28	38	36	....	....	....	....	....

Hockey East All-Rookie Team (2013) • Hockey East First All-Star Team (2015) • NCAA East First All-American Team (2015)

GUDBRANSON, Alex (guhd-BRAN-suhn, AL-ehx) **MIN**

Defense. Shoots right. 6'2", 234 lbs. Born, Orleans, ON, September 3, 1994.

			Regular Season					Playoffs				
Season	Club	League	GP	G	A	Pts	PIM	GP	G	A	Pts	PIM
2010-11	Kingston	OHL	62	3	11	14	37	5	0	1	1	0
2011-12	Kingston	OHL	50	2	7	9	52	....	....	....	....	....
2012-13	Sault Ste. Marie	OHL	65	3	11	14	62	6	0	0	0	15
2013-14	Sault Ste. Marie	OHL	66	7	8	15	76	9	1	3	4	18
2014-15	Iowa Wild	AHL	46	1	3	4	17	....	....	....	....	....

Signed as a free agent by **Minnesota**, September 23, 2014.

GUENTZEL, Jake (GUHNT-zuhl, JAYK) **PIT**

Center. Shoots left. 5'10", 167 lbs. Born, Omaha, NE, October 6, 1994.
(Pittsburgh's 2nd choice, 77th overall, in 2013 Entry Draft).

			Regular Season					Playoffs				
Season	Club	League	GP	G	A	Pts	PIM	GP	G	A	Pts	PIM
2010-11	Team Northwest	UMHSEL	15	6	5	11	4	3	0	0	0	0
	Hill-Murray	High-MN	25	15	28	43	10	3	4	2	6	4
2011-12	Team Southeast	UMHSEL	21	14	27	41	8	3	0	3	3	0
	Hill-Murray	High-MN	25	21	46	67	16	6	2	6	8	0
2012-13	Sioux City	USHL	60	29	44	73	24	....	....	....	....	....
2013-14	Nebraska-Omaha	NCHC	37	7	27	34	16	....	....	....	....	....
2014-15	Nebraska-Omaha	NCHC	36	14	25	39	34	....	....	....	....	....

USHL All-Rookie Team (2013) • USHL Second All-Star Team (2013) • USHL Rookie of the Year (2013) • NCHC All-Rookie Team (2014)

GUHLE, Brendan (GOO-lee, BREHN-duhn) **BUF**

Defense. Shoots left. 6'1", 186 lbs. Born, Edmonton, AB, July 29, 1997.
(Buffalo's 2nd choice, 51st overall, in 2015 Entry Draft).

			Regular Season					Playoffs				
Season	Club	League	GP	G	A	Pts	PIM	GP	G	A	Pts	PIM
2012-13	Sherwood Park	AMHL	32	3	8	11	34	9	1	4	5	10
2013-14	Prince Albert	WHL	51	0	10	10	29	4	1	1	2	0
2014-15	Prince Albert	WHL	72	5	27	32	36	....	....	....	....	....

GUPTILL, Alexander (GUP-tihl, al-ehx-AN-duhr) **OTT**

Left wing. Shoots left. 6'3", 190 lbs. Born, Burlington, ON, March 5, 1992.
(Dallas' 3rd choice, 77th overall, in 2010 Entry Draft).

			Regular Season					Playoffs				
Season	Club	League	GP	G	A	Pts	PIM	GP	G	A	Pts	PIM
2008-09	Brampton Capitals	ON-Jr.A	49	30	34	64	28	3	0	1	1	0
2009-10	Brampton Capitals	ON-Jr.A	10	6	5	11	24	....	....	....	....	....
	Orangeville	ON-Jr.A	19	13	13	26	26	2	1	0	1	2
2010-11	Waterloo	USHL	43	13	12	25	53	2	0	0	0	0
2011-12	U. of Michigan	CCHA	41	16	17	33	48	....	....	....	....	....
2012-13	U. of Michigan	CCHA	38	16	20	36	32	....	....	....	....	....
2013-14	U. of Michigan	Big Ten	31	12	13	25	20	....	....	....	....	....
	Texas Stars	AHL	5	0	2	2	6	....	....	....	....	....
2014-15	Binghamton	AHL	61	9	9	18	74	....	....	....	....	....

CCHA All-Rookie Team (2012) • CCHA Rookie of the Year (2012)

Traded to **Ottawa** by **Dallas** with Alex Chiasson, Nicholas Paul and Dallas' 2nd round choice (later traded to New Jersey – New Jersey selected Mackenzie Blackwood) in 2015 Entry Draft for Jason Spezza and Ludwig Karlsson, July 1, 2014.

GURJANOV, Denis (goo-REE-an-awv, deh-NEEZ) **DAL**

Right wing. Shoots left. 6'3", 192 lbs. Born, Togliatti, Russia, June 7, 1997.
(Dallas' 1st choice, 12th overall, in 2015 Entry Draft).

			Regular Season					Playoffs				
Season	Club	League	GP	G	A	Pts	PIM	GP	G	A	Pts	PIM
2013-14	Ladja Togliatti Jr.	Russia-Jr.	37	7	9	16	6	....	....	....	....	....
2014-15	Lada Togliatti	KHL	8	0	1	1	2	....	....	....	....	....
	Ladja Togliatti Jr.	Russia-Jr.	23	15	10	25	39	4	3	1	4	12

GUSEV, Nikita (GOO-sehv, nih-KEE-tuh) **T.B.**

Left wing. Shoots right. 5'9", 163 lbs. Born, Moscow, Russia, July 8, 1992.
(Tampa Bay's 8th choice, 202nd overall, in 2012 Entry Draft).

			Regular Season					Playoffs				
Season	Club	League	GP	G	A	Pts	PIM	GP	G	A	Pts	PIM
2009-10	CSKA Jr.	Russia-Jr.	48	17	40	57	14	5	1	2	3	0
2010-11	CSKA Jr.	Russia-Jr.	38	22	37	59	14	16	17	10	27	6
	CSKA Moscow	KHL	18	1	0	1	2	....	....	....	....	....
2011-12	CSKA Jr.	Russia-Jr.	34	30	46	76	26	19	16	17	33	0
	CSKA Moscow	KHL	15	2	1	3	0	1	0	0	0	0
2012-13	CSKA Moscow	KHL	6	0	1	1	0	....	....	....	....	....
	THK Tver	Russia-2	15	7	6	13	2	....	....	....	....	....
	Amur Khabarovsk	KHL	24	4	8	12	6	12	1	4	5	6
2013-14	Khanty-Mansiisk	KHL	44	8	6	14	10	6	3	3	6	0
2014-15	Khanty-Mansiisk	KHL	55	21	16	37	12	....	....	....	....	....

GUSTAFSSON, Erik (GOOS-tahf-suhn, AIR-ihk) **CHI**

Defense. Shoots left. 6', 176 lbs. Born, Nynashamn, Sweden, March 14, 1992.
(Edmonton's 5th choice, 93rd overall, in 2012 Entry Draft).

			Regular Season					Playoffs				
Season	Club	League	GP	G	A	Pts	PIM	GP	G	A	Pts	PIM
2008-09	Djurgarden U18	Swe-U18	33	2	8	10	22	2	0	0	0	0
2009-10	Djurgarden Jr.	Swe-Jr.	24	0	8	8	26	....	....	....	....	....
	Djurgarden U18	Swe-U18	27	7	13	20	54	3	0	0	0	0
2010-11	Djurgarden Jr.	Swe-Jr.	38	2	21	23	104	4	0	1	1	6
2011-12	Djurgarden Jr.	Swe-Jr.	21	3	11	14	14	....	....	....	....	....
	Djurgarden	Sweden	41	3	4	7	16	....	....	....	....	....
	Djurgarden	Sweden-Q	10	0	1	1	6	....	....	....	....	....
2012-13	Djurgarden	Sweden-2	55	8	16	24	82	....	....	....	....	....
2013-14	Frolunda	Sweden	50	2	18	20	16	....	....	....	....	....
2014-15	Frolunda	Sweden	55	4	25	29	22	12	1	2	3	31

Signed as a free agent by **Chicago**, April 30, 2015.

HAAR, Garrett (HAHR, GAIR-eht) **WSH**

Defense. Shoots left. 6', 197 lbs. Born, Huntington Beach, CA, August 16, 1993.
(Washington's 4th choice, 207th overall, in 2011 Entry Draft).

			Regular Season					Playoffs				
Season	Club	League	GP	G	A	Pts	PIM	GP	G	A	Pts	PIM
2008-09	L.A. Selects	Minor-CA	STATISTICS NOT AVAILABLE									
2009-10	Russell Stover	T1EHL	42	4	34	38	28	....	....	....	....	....
2010-11	Fargo Force	USHL	51	7	16	23	38	5	1	2	3	2
2011-12	Western Mich.	CCHA	36	1	7	8	32	....	....	....	....	....
2012-13	Western Mich.	CCHA	22	3	6	9	12	....	....	....	....	....
2013-14	Portland	WHL	61	7	38	45	55	21	0	3	3	21
2014-15	South Carolina	ECHL	35	4	12	16	16	....	....	....	....	....

CCHA All-Rookie Team (2012)

HACHE, Justin (ha-SHAY, JUHS-tihn) **ARI**

Defense. Shoots left. 6'2", 202 lbs. Born, Petit-Rocher, NB, January 10, 1994.
(Phoenix's 8th choice, 208th overall, in 2012 Entry Draft).

			Regular Season					Playoffs				
Season	Club	League	GP	G	A	Pts	PIM	GP	G	A	Pts	PIM
2008-09	Miramichi	NBPEI	33	0	4	4	8	3	0	1	1	0
2009-10	Miramichi	NBPEI	31	6	16	22	31	9	0	5	5	4
2010-11	Shawinigan	QMJHL	37	3	12	15	17	10	0	2	2	4
2011-12	Shawinigan	QMJHL	60	2	16	18	46	11	1	0	1	2
2012-13	Cape Breton	QMJHL	68	7	26	33	61	....	....	....	....	....
2013-14	Cape Breton	QMJHL	57	5	41	46	53	3	0	1	1	0
	Portland Pirates	AHL	6	0	0	0	2	....	....	....	....	....
2014-15	Portland Pirates	AHL	60	0	6	6	18	....	....	....	....	....

QMJHL Second All-Star Team (2014)

HAGEL, Marc (HAY-guhl, MAHRK) **MIN**

Right wing. Shoots right. 6', 196 lbs. Born, Hamilton, ON, September 12, 1988.

			Regular Season					Playoffs				
Season	Club	League	GP	G	A	Pts	PIM	GP	G	A	Pts	PIM
2008-09	Princeton	ECAC	26	3	2	5	14	....	....	....	....	....
2009-10	Princeton	ECAC	31	7	4	11	8	....	....	....	....	....
2010-11	Princeton	ECAC	4	0	0	0	0	....	....	....	....	....
2011-12	Princeton	ECAC	32	7	12	19	33	....	....	....	....	....
2012-13	Miami U.	CCHA	42	6	13	19	37	....	....	....	....	....
	Lake Erie Monsters	AHL	6	0	2	2	0	....	....	....	....	....
2013-14	Iowa Wild	AHL	46	8	7	15	35	....	....	....	....	....
	South Carolina	ECHL	21	9	8	17	11	2	0	0	0	4
2014-15	Iowa Wild	AHL	67	12	21	33	36	....	....	....	....	....

• Missed majority of 2010-11 due to various injuries. Signed as a free agent by **Minnesota**, July 1, 2015.

HAGG, Robert (HAG, RAW-buhrt) **PHI**

Defense. Shoots left. 6'2", 201 lbs. Born, Uppsala, Sweden, February 8, 1995.
(Philadelphia's 2nd choice, 41st overall, in 2013 Entry Draft).

			Regular Season					Playoffs				
Season	Club	League	GP	G	A	Pts	PIM	GP	G	A	Pts	PIM
2008-09	Gimo IF Hockey	Sweden-4	23	0	0	0	6	....	....	....	....	....
2009-10	Gimo IF	Sweden-4	32	7	9	16	28	....	....	....	....	....
2010-11	Tierps HK	Sweden-3	30	2	9	11	30	....	....	....	....	....
	MODO U18	Swe-U18	2	0	0	0	2	....	....	....	....	....
2011-12	MODO U18	Swe-U18	5	1	4	5	10	1	0	0	0	0
	MODO Jr.	Swe-Jr.	44	4	13	17	46	8	1	1	2	2
2012-13	MODO Jr.	Swe-Jr.	28	11	13	24	24	7	1	1	2	4
	MODO	Sweden	27	0	1	1	2	1	0	0	0	0
	MODO U18	Swe-U18	....	....	....	....	....	2	1	1	2	0
2013-14	MODO Jr.	Swe-Jr.	8	1	6	7	6	2	1	0	1	2
	MODO	Sweden	50	1	5	6	47	2	0	0	0	4
	Sweden	Olympics	7	1	0	1	12					
	Adirondack	AHL	10	1	3	4	10	....	....	....	....	....
2014-15	Lehigh Valley	AHL	69	3	17	20	42	....	....	....	....	....

HAGGERTY, Ryan (HA-guhr-tee, RIGH-uhn) **CHI**

Right wing. Shoots right. 6', 201 lbs. Born, Stamford, CT, March 4, 1993.

			Regular Season					Playoffs				
Season	Club	League	GP	G	A	Pts	PIM	GP	G	A	Pts	PIM
2008-09	Trinity Cath.	High-CT	25	27	31	58	....	....	....	....	....	....
	Seacoast Kings	Minor-CT	23	17	21	38	....	....	....	....	....	....
2009-10	USNTDP	USHL	37	5	6	11	38	....	....	....	....	....
	USNTDP	U-17	15	5	3	8	6	....	....	....	....	....
	USNTDP	U-18	2	0	0	0	0	....	....	....	....	....
2010-11	USNTDP	USHL	23	7	8	15	9	....	....	....	....	....
	USNTDP	U-18	31	4	10	14	13	....	....	....	....	....
2011-12	RPI Engineers	ECAC	35	7	8	15	30	....	....	....	....	....
2012-13	RPI Engineers	ECAC	36	12	14	26	30	....	....	....	....	....
2013-14	RPI Engineers	ECAC	35	*28	15	43	42	....	....	....	....	....
2014-15	Hartford Wolf Pack	AHL	76	15	18	33	34	14	2	4	6	4

ECAC First All-Star Team (2014) • NCAA East Second All-American Team (2014)

Signed as a free agent by **NY Rangers**, March 12, 2014. Traded to **Chicago** by **NY Rangers** for Antti Raanta, June 27, 2015.

HAKANPAA, Jani (HAHK-an-pah, YAH-nee) **ST.L.**

Defense. Shoots right. 6'5", 218 lbs. Born, Kirkkonummi, Finland, March 31, 1992.
(St. Louis' 5th choice, 104th overall, in 2010 Entry Draft).

			Regular Season					Playoffs				
Season	Club	League	GP	G	A	Pts	PIM	GP	G	A	Pts	PIM
2007-08	K-Vantaa U18	Fin-U18	2	0	1	1	2	2	0	0	0	0
2008-09	K-Vantaa U18	Fin-U18	10	3	4	7	14	....	....	....	....	....
2009-10	K-Vantaa U18	Fin-U18	32	3	16	19	69	6	0	2	2	6
2010-11	Suomi U20	Finland-2	8	1	2	3	31	....	....	....	....	....
	Blues Espoo Jr.	Fin-Jr.	36	3	20	23	61	12	3	2	5	10
2011-12	Blues Espoo Jr.	Fin-Jr.	5	0	4	4	0	....	....	....	....	....
	Blues Espoo	Finland	41	5	7	12	30	....	....	....	....	....
2012-13	Peoria Rivermen	AHL	14	1	3	4	6	....	....	....	....	....
	Blues Espoo	Finland	34	2	3	5	34	....	....	....	....	....
2013-14	Chicago Wolves	AHL	54	4	4	8	33	3	0	1	1	0
2014-15	Chicago Wolves	AHL	64	1	7	8	47	4	0	1	1	6
	Quad City	ECHL	2	1	0	1	0	....	....	....	....	....

HAMILTON, Wacey (HAM-ihl-tuhn, WAY-see)

Center. Shoots left. 5'11", 185 lbs. Born, Calgary, AB, September 10, 1990.

			Regular Season					Playoffs				
Season	Club	League	GP	G	A	Pts	PIM	GP	G	A	Pts	PIM
2006-07	Camrose Kodiaks	AJHL	49	11	6	17	38	5	1	1	2	8
2007-08	Medicine Hat	WHL	63	13	19	32	95	5	1	0	1	6
2008-09	Medicine Hat	WHL	37	4	13	17	64	11	1	3	4	24
2009-10	Medicine Hat	WHL	67	24	47	71	100	12	3	5	8	23
2010-11	Medicine Hat	WHL	67	20	53	73	113	15	4	8	12	20
2011-12	Binghamton	AHL	74	5	6	11	46	....	....	....	....	....
	Elmira Jackals	ECHL	2	0	2	2	2	....	....	....	....	....
2012-13	Binghamton	AHL	38	4	4	8	17	3	0	0	0	4
2013-14	Binghamton	AHL	63	4	16	20	73	4	0	1	1	0
2014-15	Utica Comets	AHL	41	5	10	15	27	22	2	2	4	25

Signed as a free agent by **Ottawa**, March 8, 2011. Signed to a PTO (professional tryout) contract by **Utica** (AHL), October 9, 2014. Signed as a free agent by **Utica** (AHL), November 18, 2014.

HANIFIN, Noah (HAN-ih-fihn, NOH-uh) **CAR**

Defense. Shoots left. 6'3", 206 lbs. Born, Boston, MA, January 25, 1997.
(Carolina's 1st choice, 5th overall, in 2015 Entry Draft).

			Regular Season					Playoffs				
Season	Club	League	GP	G	A	Pts	PIM	GP	G	A	Pts	PIM
2010-11	St. Sebastian's	High-MA	27	2	9	11	....	....	....	....	....	....
2011-12	Bos. Adv. U18	T1EHL	9	1	1	2	5	....	....	....	....	....
	St. Sebastian's	High-MA	28	5	24	29	....	....	....	....	....	....
2012-13	Cape Cod Whalers	Minor-MA	10	1	2	3	19	....	....	....	....	....
	St. Sebastian's	High-MA	28	10	24	34	....	....	....	....	....	....
2013-14	USNTDP	USHL	31	6	14	20	18	....	....	....	....	....
	USNTDP	U-17	20	3	17	20	16	....	....	....	....	....
	USNTDP	U-18	8	1	4	5	4	....	....	....	....	....
2014-15	Boston College	H-East	37	5	18	23	16	....	....	....	....	....

Hockey East All-Rookie Team (2015) • Hockey East Second All-Star Team (2015)

HANLEY, Joel (HAN-lee, JOHL) **MTL**

Defense. Shoots right. 6', 180 lbs. Born, Keswick, ON, June 8, 1991.

			Regular Season					Playoffs				
Season	Club	League	GP	G	A	Pts	PIM	GP	G	A	Pts	PIM
2007-08	Georgina Ice	ON-Jr.C	38	8	22	30	45	9	3	5	8	6
	Newmarket	ON-Jr.A	2	0	0	0	0	....	....	....	....	....
2008-09	Newmarket	ON-Jr.A	50	14	24	38	61	....	....	....	....	....
2009-10	Newmarket	ON-Jr.A	23	5	15	20	11	....	....	....	....	....
2010-11	Massachusetts	H-East	28	3	15	18	24	....	....	....	....	....
2011-12	Massachusetts	H-East	36	7	18	25	18	....	....	....	....	....
2012-13	Massachusetts	H-East	33	5	11	16	46	....	....	....	....	....
2013-14	Massachusetts	H-East	34	2	14	16	39	....	....	....	....	....
	Portland Pirates	AHL	15	0	5	5	6	....	....	....	....	....
2014-15	Portland Pirates	AHL	63	2	15	17	34	5	0	1	1	0
	Gwinnett	ECHL	3	1	0	1	0	....	....	....	....	....

Signed to PTO (professional tryout) contract by **Portland** (AHL), March 11, 2014. Signed as a free agent by **Montreal**, July 1, 2015.

HANNIKAINEN, Markus (hah-nih-KAY-nehn, MAHR-kuhs) **CBJ**

Left wing. Shoots left. 6'2", 189 lbs. Born, Helsinki, Finland, March 26, 1993.

			Regular Season					Playoffs				
Season	Club	League	GP	G	A	Pts	PIM	GP	G	A	Pts	PIM
2010-11	Jokerit U18	Fin-U18	7	1	4	5	2	2	0	4	4	0
	Jokerit Helsinki Jr.	Fin-Jr.	36	7	12	19	12	9	1	1	2	2
2011-12	Jokerit Helsinki Jr.	Fin-Jr.	16	6	7	13	12	12	5	5	10	2
	Kiekko-Vantaa	Finland-2	10	2	0	2	4	....	....	....	....	....
	Jokerit Helsinki	Finland	15	0	0	0	4	....	....	....	....	....
2012-13	Jokerit Helsinki Jr.	Fin-Jr.	11	7	7	14	4	....	....	....	....	....
	Kiekko-Vantaa	Finland-2	21	3	6	9	4	....	....	....	....	....
	Jokerit Helsinki	Finland	20	0	1	1	4	1	0	0	0	0
2013-14	Jokerit Helsinki Jr.	Fin-Jr.	4	3	0	3	0	4	1	3	4	0
	HPK Hameenlinna	Finland	4	0	0	0	4	....	....	....	....	....
	Kiekko-Vantaa	Finland-2	15	2	5	7	2	....	....	....	....	....
	Jokerit Helsinki	Finland	18	3	3	6	4	2	1	0	1	0
2014-15	JYP Jyvaskyla	Finland	60	19	27	51	22	....	....	....	....	....

Signed as a free agent by **Columbus**, April 20, 2015.

HANSSON, Petter (HAN-suhn, PEH-tuhr) **NYI**

Defense. Shoots left. 6'1", 187 lbs. Born, Gislaved, Sweden, May 16, 1996.
(NY Islanders' 7th choice, 202nd overall, in 2015 Entry Draft).

			Regular Season					Playoffs				
Season	Club	League	GP	G	A	Pts	PIM	GP	G	A	Pts	PIM
2011-12	Gislaveds SK U18	Swe-U18	9	2	3	5	0	....	....	....	....	....
	Gislaveds SK Jr.	Swe-Jr.	6	0	3	3	0	....	....	....	....	....
	Gislaveds SK	Sweden-3	22	0	0	0	0	....	....	....	....	....
2012-13	Linkopings HC U18	Swe-U18	40	1	12	13	16	2	0	0	0	0
	Linkopings HC Jr.	Swe-Jr.	1	0	0	0	0	....	....	....	....	....
2013-14	Linkopings HC U18	Swe-U18	26	1	15	16	8	5	4	0	4	2
	Linkopings HC Jr.	Swe-Jr.	19	1	3	4	6	1	0	1	1	0
2014-15	Linkopings HC Jr.	Swe-Jr.	38	15	19	34	32	1	0	0	0	0
	Linkopings HC	Sweden	15	0	1	1	2	1	0	0	0	0

HANSSON, Niklas (HAN-suhn, NIHK-luhs) **DAL**

Defense. Shoots right. 6'1", 180 lbs. Born, Helsingborg, Sweden, January 8, 1995.
(Dallas' 5th choice, 68th overall, in 2013 Entry Draft).

			Regular Season					Playoffs				
Season	Club	League	GP	G	A	Pts	PIM	GP	G	A	Pts	PIM
2010-11	Jonstorps IF U18	Swe-U18	2	0	0	0	0	....	....	....	....	....
	Jonstorps IF Jr.	Swe-Jr.	1	0	0	0	0	....	....	....	....	....
	Jonstorps IF	Sweden-4	18	0	2	2	2	....	....	....	....	....
	Rogle U18	Swe-U18	5	0	0	0	0	....	....	....	....	....
2011-12	Rogle U18	Swe-U18	33	3	28	31	14	5	1	3	4	0
	Rogle Jr.	Swe-Jr.	18	2	1	3	6	7	0	2	2	0
2012-13	Rogle U18	Swe-U18	7	3	3	6	4	3	0	1	1	0
	Rogle Jr.	Swe-Jr.	39	3	20	23	47	2	0	0	0	0
	Rogle	Sweden	9	0	0	0	4	....	....	....	....	....
	Rogle	Sweden-Q	6	0	1	1	0	....	....	....	....	....
2013-14	Rogle Jr.	Swe-Jr.	12	4	8	12	2	....	....	....	....	....
	Rogle	Sweden-2	63	3	20	23	22	....	....	....	....	....
2014-15	Rogle	Sweden-2	52	2	21	23	12	5	1	1	2	2
	Rogle Jr.	Swe-Jr.	....	....	....	....	....	1	2	0	2	2

HARGROVE, Colton (HAHR-grohv, KOHL-tuhn) **BOS**

Left wing. Shoots left. 6'1", 213 lbs. Born, Dallas, TX, June 25, 1992.
(Boston's 6th choice, 205th overall, in 2012 Entry Draft).

			Regular Season					Playoffs				
Season	Club	League	GP	G	A	Pts	PIM	GP	G	A	Pts	PIM
2009-10	Dallas Stars	T1EHL	16	5	6	11	16	....	....	....	....	....
	St. Louis Blues	T1EHL	30	14	10	24	72	....	....	....	....	....
2010-11	Fargo Force	USHL	56	13	14	27	109	5	0	3	3	2
2011-12	Fargo Force	USHL	54	16	22	38	140	6	0	0	0	10
2012-13	Western Mich.	CCHA	32	9	1	10	29	....	....	....	....	....
2013-14	Western Mich.	NCHC	39	11	13	24	38	....	....	....	....	....
2014-15	Western Mich.	NCHC	34	14	14	28	80	....	....	....	....	....

HARKINS, Jansen (HAHR-kihnz, YAN-suhn) **WPG**

Center. Shoots left. 6'1", 186 lbs. Born, North Vancouver, BC, May 23, 1997.
(Winnipeg's 3rd choice, 47th overall, in 2015 Entry Draft).

			Regular Season					Playoffs				
Season	Club	League	GP	G	A	Pts	PIM	GP	G	A	Pts	PIM
2011-12	North Shore W.C.	Minor-BC	74	83	70	153	....	....	....	....	....	....
	Van. NW Giants	BCMML	6	2	5	7	0	3	0	0	0	0
2012-13	Van. NW Giants	BCMML	37	14	45	59	14	8	1	*9	10	14
	Prince George	WHL	5	0	0	0	2	....	....	....	....	....
2013-14	Prince George	WHL	67	10	24	34	18	....	....	....	....	....
2014-15	Prince George	WHL	70	20	59	79	45	5	0	4	4	2

HARPER, Shane (HAHR-puhr, SHAYN) **FLA**

Right wing. Shoots right. 5'11", 193 lbs. Born, Valencia, CA, February 1, 1989.

			Regular Season					Playoffs				
Season	Club	League	GP	G	A	Pts	PIM	GP	G	A	Pts	PIM
2005-06	Everett Silvertips	WHL	62	6	4	10	8	5	1	0	1	0
2006-07	Everett Silvertips	WHL	58	3	12	15	23	8	1	2	3	0
2007-08	Everett Silvertips	WHL	71	17	26	43	18	4	0	2	2	0
2008-09	Everett Silvertips	WHL	72	32	34	66	10	5	0	4	4	0
2009-10	Everett Silvertips	WHL	72	42	38	80	38	7	6	4	10	6
	Adirondack	AHL	5	1	0	1	2	....	....	....	....	....
2010-11	Adirondack	AHL	20	1	2	3	4	....	....	....	....	....
	Greenville	ECHL	48	22	23	45	20	11	4	6	10	2
2011-12	Adirondack	AHL	70	13	14	27	43	....	....	....	....	....
2012-13	Adirondack	AHL	48	5	5	10	35	....	....	....	....	....
	Trenton Titans	ECHL	15	14	13	27	2	....	....	....	....	....
2013-14	Chicago Wolves	AHL	63	13	20	33	8	9	2	3	5	0
2014-15	Chicago Wolves	AHL	75	32	18	50	14	5	0	4	4	4

WHL West Second All-Star Team (2010)

Signed as a free agent by **Philadelphia**, March 4, 2010. Traded to **NY Islanders** by **Philadelphia** with Philadelphia's 4th round choice (Devon Toews) in 2014 Entry Draft for Mark Streit, June 12, 2013. Signed as a free agent by **Florida**, July 1, 2015.

HARPUR, Ben (HAHR-puhr, BEHN) **OTT**

Defense. Shoots left. 6'6", 218 lbs. Born, Hamilton, ON, January 12, 1995.
(Ottawa's 4th choice, 108th overall, in 2013 Entry Draft).

			Regular Season					Playoffs				
Season	Club	League	GP	G	A	Pts	PIM	GP	G	A	Pts	PIM
2010-11	N.F. Canucks	Minor-ON	43	6	12	18	111	....	....	....	....	....
2011-12	Guelph Storm	OHL	34	1	3	4	22	....	....	....	....	....
2012-13	Guelph Storm	OHL	67	3	12	15	59	5	0	0	0	2
2013-14	Guelph Storm	OHL	67	3	13	16	69	20	1	4	5	12
2014-15	Guelph Storm	OHL	28	4	16	20	40	....	....	....	....	....
	Barrie Colts	OHL	29	1	10	11	22	9	2	4	6	6

HARRISON, Tim (HAIR-ih-suhn, TIHM) **CGY**

Right wing. Shoots right. 6'3", 175 lbs. Born, Duxbury, MA, January 11, 1994.
(Calgary's 6th choice, 157th overall, in 2013 Entry Draft).

			Regular Season					Playoffs				
Season	Club	League	GP	G	A	Pts	PIM	GP	G	A	Pts	PIM
2009-10	Duxbury	High-MA	....	2	5	7	....	....	....	....	....	....
2010-11	Duxbury	High-MA	....	9	9	18	....	....	....	....	....	....
2011-12	Dexter School	High-MA	21	13	13	26	....	....	....	....	....	....
2012-13	Dexter School	High-MA	28	24	27	51	....	....	....	....	....	....
2013-14	Colgate	ECAC	34	0	5	5	20	....	....	....	....	....
2014-15	Colgate	ECAC	37	7	4	11	24	....	....	....	....	....

HARSTAD, Aaron (HAHR-stad, AIR-uhn) **WPG**

Defense. Shoots left. 6'2", 199 lbs. Born, Stevens Point, WI, April 27, 1992.
(Winnipeg's 7th choice, 187th overall, in 2011 Entry Draft).

			Regular Season					Playoffs				
Season	Club	League	GP	G	A	Pts	PIM	GP	G	A	Pts	PIM
2008-09	Team Wisconsin	UMHSEL	3	0	2	2	6	....	....	....	....	....
	Stevens Point High	High-WI	18	22	19	41	....	....	....	....	....	....
	Green Bay	USHL	10	0	0	0	2	5	0	0	0	6
2009-10	Green Bay	USHL	47	2	6	8	61	11	0	3	3	9
2010-11	Green Bay	USHL	51	7	14	21	73	11	2	2	4	26
2011-12	Colorado College	WCHA	29	0	6	6	27	....	....	....	....	....
2012-13	Colorado College	WCHA	31	2	4	6	10	....	....	....	....	....
2013-14	Colorado College	NCHC	37	2	7	9	37	....	....	....	....	....
2014-15	Colorado College	NCHC	30	5	4	9	32	....	....	....	....	....
	St. John's IceCaps	AHL	5	0	0	0	0	....	....	....	....	....

HART, Brian (HAHRT, BRIGH-uhn) **T.B.**

Right wing. Shoots right. 6'2", 203 lbs. Born, Cumberland, ME, November 25, 1993.
(Tampa Bay's 4th choice, 53rd overall, in 2012 Entry Draft).

			Regular Season					Playoffs				
Season	Club	League	GP	G	A	Pts	PIM	GP	G	A	Pts	PIM
2008-09	Greely Rangers	High-ME	20	28	21	39	....	....	....	....	....	....
2009-10	Brewster Academy	High-NH	28	27	24	51	....	....	....	....	....	....
2010-11	Exeter	High-NH	27	29	32	61	12	....	....	....	....	....
2011-12	Exeter	High-NH	29	31	34	65	20	....	....	....	....	....
2012-13	Harvard Crimson	ECAC	30	5	13	18	10	....	....	....	....	....
2013-14	Harvard Crimson	ECAC	31	6	9	15	22	....	....	....	....	....
2014-15	Harvard Crimson	ECAC	37	7	10	17	21	....	....	....	....	....

HATHAWAY, Garnet (HATH-UH-way, GAHR-neht) **CGY**

Right wing. Shoots right. 6'2", 210 lbs. Born, Kennebunkport, ME, November 23, 1991.

			Regular Season					Playoffs				
Season	Club	League	GP	G	A	Pts	PIM	GP	G	A	Pts	PIM
2008-09	Andover	High-MA	26	16	13	29	....	....	....	....	....	....
2009-10	Andover	High-MA	28	17	20	37	....	....	....	....	....	....
2010-11	Brown U.	ECAC	31	5	9	14	42	....	....	....	....	....
2011-12	Brown U.	ECAC	26	3	5	8	48	....	....	....	....	....
2012-13	Brown U.	ECAC	33	6	15	21	47	....	....	....	....	....
2013-14	Brown U.	ECAC	31	6	9	15	41	....	....	....	....	....
	Abbotsford Heat	AHL	8	0	0	0	10	1	0	0	0	10
2014-15	Adirondack Flames	AHL	72	19	17	36	77	....	....	....	....	....

Signed as a free agent by **Abbotsford** (AHL), March 14, 2014. Signed as a free agent by **Calgary**, April 13, 2015.

HAWRYLUK, Jayce (HAW-rih-luhk, JAYS) **FLA**

Center. Shoots right. 5'10", 190 lbs. Born, Yorkton, SK, January 1, 1996.
(Florida's 2nd choice, 32nd overall, in 2014 Entry Draft).

			Regular Season					Playoffs				
Season	Club	League	GP	G	A	Pts	PIM	GP	G	A	Pts	PIM
2010-11	Russell Rams	Minor-MB	54	138	126	264	....	....	....	....	....	....
2011-12	Parkland Rangers	MMHL	40	31	36	67	138	....	....	....	....	....
2012-13	Brandon	WHL	61	18	25	43	46	....	....	....	....	....
2013-14	Brandon	WHL	59	24	40	64	44	8	5	7	12	14
2014-15	Brandon	WHL	54	30	35	65	69	16	10	9	19	24

HAYDEN, John (HAY-duhn, JAWN) **CHI**

Center. Shoots right. 6'2", 223 lbs. Born, Chicago, IL, February 14, 1995.
(Chicago's 3rd choice, 74th overall, in 2013 Entry Draft).

			Regular Season					Playoffs				
Season	Club	League	GP	G	A	Pts	PIM	GP	G	A	Pts	PIM
2010-11	Brunswick Bruins	High-CT	26	21	9	30	....	....	....	....	....	....
2011-12	USNTDP	USHL	36	8	7	15	51	2	0	2	2	2
	USNTDP	U-17	17	3	6	9	12	....	....	....	....	....
2012-13	USNTDP	USHL	24	11	9	20	51	....	....	....	....	....
	USNTDP	U-18	29	6	8	14	29	....	....	....	....	....
2013-14	Yale	ECAC	33	6	10	16	18	....	....	....	....	....
2014-15	Yale	ECAC	29	7	11	18	10	....	....	....	....	....

HAYDON, Aaron (HAY-duhn, AIR-uhn) **DAL**

Defense. Shoots right. 6'4", 195 lbs. Born, Plymouth, MI, January 6, 1996.
(Dallas' 7th choice, 154th overall, in 2014 Entry Draft).

			Regular Season					Playoffs				
Season	Club	League	GP	G	A	Pts	PIM	GP	G	A	Pts	PIM
2009-10	Detroit Belle Tire	T1EHL	29	5	15	20	50	....	....	....	....	....
2010-11	Detroit Belle Tire	T1EHL	27	2	4	6	79	....	....	....	....	....
2011-12	Detroit Belle Tire	T1EHL	40	2	9	11	93	....	....	....	....	....
	Belle Tire U16	Minor-MI	....	....	....	....	....	7	3	3	6	28
2012-13	Niagara Ice Dogs	OHL	42	4	6	10	39	3	0	1	1	2
2013-14	Niagara Ice Dogs	OHL	61	5	11	16	112	7	0	0	0	10
2014-15	Niagara Ice Dogs	OHL	60	8	17	25	104	11	0	2	2	15

HEARD, Mitchell (HUHRD, MIH-chuhl)

Center. Shoots left. 6'1", 200 lbs. Born, Bowmanville, ON, March 12, 1992.
(Colorado's 1st choice, 41st overall, in 2012 Entry Draft).

			Regular Season					Playoffs				
Season	Club	League	GP	G	A	Pts	PIM	GP	G	A	Pts	PIM
2008-09	Clarington Toros	Minor-ON	36	....	....	31	48	....	....	....	....	....
2009-10	Bowmanville	ON-Jr.A	22	17	13	30	24	22	6	13	19	34
	Plymouth Whalers	OHL	16	2	1	3	4	....	....	....	....	....
2010-11	Plymouth Whalers	OHL	66	20	30	50	67	11	1	2	3	10
2011-12	Plymouth Whalers	OHL	57	29	28	57	111	13	4	7	11	26
2012-13	Plymouth Whalers	OHL	32	17	19	36	34	14	8	5	13	37
	Lake Erie Monsters	AHL	23	1	3	4	72	....	....	....	....	....
2013-14	Lake Erie Monsters	AHL	63	4	8	12	167	....	....	....	....	....
2014-15	Lake Erie Monsters	AHL	51	6	6	12	137	....	....	....	....	....
	Fort Wayne	ECHL	12	10	6	16	15	10	3	6	9	22

HEATHERINGTON, Dillon (HEH-thuhr-ihng-tuhn, DIH-luhn) **CBJ**

Defense. Shoots left. 6'4", 220 lbs. Born, Calgary, AB, May 9, 1995.
(Columbus' 4th choice, 50th overall, in 2013 Entry Draft).

			Regular Season					Playoffs				
Season	Club	League	GP	G	A	Pts	PIM	GP	G	A	Pts	PIM
2010-11	Calgary Flames	AMHL	31	0	11	11	44	4	0	0	0	2
	Swift Current	WHL	1	0	0	0	0	....	....	....	....	....
2011-12	Swift Current	WHL	57	2	8	10	63	....	....	....	....	....
2012-13	Swift Current	WHL	71	4	23	27	80	5	0	3	3	0
2013-14	Swift Current	WHL	70	6	29	35	63	6	0	1	1	8
2014-15	Swift Current	WHL	48	1	14	15	48	4	0	0	0	4
	Springfield Falcons	AHL	3	0	1	1	0	....	....	....	....	....

HEINEN, Danton (HIGH-nehn, DAN-tuhn) **BOS**

Center/Left wing. Shoots left. 6'1", 186 lbs. Born, Langley, BC, July 5, 1995.
(Boston's 3rd choice, 116th overall, in 2014 Entry Draft).

			Regular Season					Playoffs				
Season	Club	League	GP	G	A	Pts	PIM	GP	G	A	Pts	PIM
2011-12	Valley West Hawks	BCMML	39	19	24	43	6	2	2	0	2	0
2012-13	Richmond	PJHL	43	21	28	49	4	15	6	8	14	2
	Merritt	BCHL	2	0	2	2	0	....	....	....	....	....
2013-14	Surrey Eagles	BCHL	57	29	33	62	8	6	2	5	7	2
2014-15	U. of Denver	NCHC	40	16	29	*45	10	....	....	....	....	....

NCHC Second All-Star Team (2015) • NCHC Rookie of the Year (2015)

HELEWKA, Adam (huh-LOO-kuh, A-duhm) **S.J.**

Left wing. Shoots left. 6'1", 201 lbs. Born, Burnaby, BC, July 21, 1995.
(San Jose's 4th choice, 106th overall, in 2015 Entry Draft).

			Regular Season					Playoffs				
Season	Club	League	GP	G	A	Pts	PIM	GP	G	A	Pts	PIM
2011-12	Van. NW Giants	BCMML	40	24	29	53	74	5	5	4	9	0
2012-13	Spokane Chiefs	WHL	60	10	17	27	12	9	1	2	3	2
2013-14	Spokane Chiefs	WHL	62	23	27	50	32	4	0	0	0	4
2014-15	Spokane Chiefs	WHL	69	44	43	87	59	6	3	2	5	12

WHL West Second All-Star Team (2015)

HELGESEN, Kenton (HEHL-geh-suhn, KEHN-tuhn) **ANA**

Defense. Shoots left. 6'3", 197 lbs. Born, Grand Prarie, AB, March 19, 1994.
(Anaheim's 7th choice, 187th overall, in 2012 Entry Draft).

			Regular Season					Playoffs				
Season	Club	League	GP	G	A	Pts	PIM	GP	G	A	Pts	PIM
2008-09	Grand Prairie Storm	AMBHL	33	10	14	24	82	....	....	....	....	....
2009-10	Grand Prairie	AMHL	35	0	9	9	54	....	....	....	....	....
2010-11	Grande Prairie	AJHL	42	1	5	6	39	2	0	0	0	0
2011-12	Calgary Hitmen	WHL	58	3	11	14	63	5	0	0	0	2
2012-13	Calgary Hitmen	WHL	70	0	20	20	116	3	0	1	1	0
2013-14	Calgary Hitmen	WHL	71	10	41	51	67	6	1	1	2	4
2014-15	Calgary Hitmen	WHL	67	21	24	45	51	17	6	7	13	8

HENLEY, Samuel (HEHN-lee, SAM-yewl) **COL**

Center. Shoots left. 6'4", 210 lbs. Born, Val-d'Or, QC, July 25, 1993.

			Regular Season					Playoffs				
Season	Club	League	GP	G	A	Pts	PIM	GP	G	A	Pts	PIM
2008-09	Amos Forestiers	QAAA	13	1	4	5	2	6	1	2	3	0
2009-10	Lewiston	QMJHL	63	4	9	13	22	4	0	1	1	2
2010-11	Lewiston	QMJHL	64	13	18	31	37	15	0	2	2	4
2011-12	Val-d'Or Foreurs	QMJHL	63	13	14	27	71	4	1	2	3	9
2012-13	Val-d'Or Foreurs	QMJHL	58	22	23	45	59	10	1	2	3	6
2013-14	Val-d'Or Foreurs	QMJHL	51	30	39	69	42	24	8	20	28	25
2014-15	Lake Erie Monsters	AHL	54	6	4	10	47	....	....	....	....	....

Signed as a free agent by **Colorado**, May 5, 2014.

HERBERT, Caleb (HUHR-buhrt, KAY-lehb) **WSH**

Center. Shoots right. 5'11", 185 lbs. Born, St. Paul, MN, October 12, 1991.
(Washington's 4th choice, 142nd overall, in 2010 Entry Draft).

			Regular Season					Playoffs				
Season	Club	League	GP	G	A	Pts	PIM	GP	G	A	Pts	PIM
2007-08	Bloomington-Jeff.	High-MN	6	4	3	7	6	....	....	....	....	....
2008-09	Bloomington-Jeff.	High-MN	27	29	24	53	36	....	....	....	....	....
2009-10	Team Southeast	UMHSEL	24	14	8	22	....	....	....	....	....	....
	Bloomington-Jeff.	High-MN	25	26	28	54	42	3	4	4	8	2
2010-11	Sioux City	USHL	51	23	27	50	61	3	0	0	0	4
2011-12	U. Minn-Duluth	WCHA	41	14	19	33	30	....	....	....	....	....
2012-13	U. Minn-Duluth	WCHA	35	6	19	25	53	....	....	....	....	....
2013-14	U. Minn-Duluth	NCHC	36	12	19	31	85	....	....	....	....	....
	Hershey Bears	AHL	7	2	1	3	4	....	....	....	....	....
2014-15	Hershey Bears	AHL	12	0	2	2	4	....	....	....	....	....
	South Carolina	ECHL	42	19	9	28	84	27	3	11	14	26

HERZOG, Fabrice (HUHR-tsawg, fah-BREES) **TOR**

Right wing. Shoots left. 6'2", 176 lbs. Born, Frauenfeld, Switz., December 9, 1994.
(Toronto's 3rd choice, 142nd overall, in 2013 Entry Draft).

			Regular Season					Playoffs				
Season	Club	League	GP	G	A	Pts	PIM	GP	G	A	Pts	PIM
2007-08	Oberthurgau II U17	Swiss-U17	8	6	3	9	4	....	....	....	....	....
2008-09	Oberthurgau U17	Swiss-U17	17	1	1	2	0	2	0	0	0	0
	SC Herisau U17	Swiss-U17	5	0	0	0	2	....	....	....	....	....
2009-10	Oberthurgau U17	Swiss-U17	32	6	7	13	12	6	6	0	6	6
2010-11	Oberthurgau U17	Swiss-U17	27	22	14	36	14	6	6	3	9	0
	Oberthurgau	Swiss-3	2	0	0	0	0	....	....	....	....	....
	Oberthurgau II U17	Swiss-5	1	0	1	1	2	....	....	....	....	....
2011-12	EV Zug Jr.	Swiss-Jr.	35	18	14	32	45	10	6	2	8	6
2012-13	EV Zug Jr.	Swiss-Jr.	32	28	17	45	26	4	3	2	5	2
	EV Zug	Swiss	20	2	2	4	6	....	....	....	....	....
2013-14	Quebec Remparts	QMJHL	61	32	26	58	34	5	3	2	5	4
	Toronto Marlies	AHL	5	0	0	0	0	....	....	....	....	....
2014-15	EV Zug	Swiss	43	6	3	9	16	6	0	3	3	0

HEXTALL, Brett (HEHX-tahl, BREHT)

Center. Shoots right. 5'10", 190 lbs. Born, Philadelphia, PA, April 2, 1988.
(Phoenix's 7th choice, 159th overall, in 2008 Entry Draft).

			Regular Season					Playoffs				
Season	Club	League	GP	G	A	Pts	PIM	GP	G	A	Pts	PIM
2006-07	Penticton Vees	BCHL	59	18	27	45	156	11	2	2	4	8
2007-08	Penticton Vees	BCHL	54	24	48	72	52	15	*12	3	15	12
2008-09	North Dakota	WCHA	42	12	24	36	91	....	....	....	....	....
2009-10	North Dakota	WCHA	34	14	12	26	88	....	....	....	....	....
2010-11	North Dakota	WCHA	39	13	16	29	63	....	....	....	....	....
2011-12	Portland Pirates	AHL	72	7	8	15	59	....	....	....	....	....
2012-13	Portland Pirates	AHL	66	9	6	15	79	3	0	0	0	4
2013-14	Portland Pirates	AHL	59	11	12	23	83	....	....	....	....	....
2014-15	Lehigh Valley	AHL	63	6	8	14	119	....	....	....	....	....

HICKETTS, Joe (HIH-kehts, JOH) **DET**

Defense. Shoots left. 5'8", 175 lbs. Born, Kamloops, BC, May 4, 1996.

			Regular Season					Playoffs				
Season	Club	League	GP	G	A	Pts	PIM	GP	G	A	Pts	PIM
2012-13	Victoria Royals	WHL	67	6	18	24	45	6	0	1	1	2
2013-14	Victoria Royals	WHL	36	6	18	24	12	9	0	2	2	9
2014-15	Victoria Royals	WHL	62	12	52	64	48	10	0	5	5	10

WHL West Second All-Star Team (2015)

Signed as a free agent by **Detroit**, September 24, 2014.

HICKEY, Brandon (HIH-kee, BRAN-duhn) **CGY**

Defense. Shoots left. 6'2", 190 lbs. Born, Edmonton, AB, April 13, 1996.
(Calgary's 4th choice, 64th overall, in 2014 Entry Draft).

			Regular Season					Playoffs				
Season	Club	League	GP	G	A	Pts	PIM	GP	G	A	Pts	PIM
2009-10	Leduc Roughnecks	Minor-AB	31	6	13	19	44	....	....	....	....	....
2010-11	Leduc Oil Kings	AMBHL	28	6	12	18	52	2	0	1	1	0
	Leduc Oil Kings	Minor-AB	1	0	0	0	0	....	....	....	....	....
2011-12	Leduc Oil Kings	AMHL	19	4	7	11	12	9	0	1	1	0
	Spruce Grove	AJHL	2	0	0	0	2	....	....	....	....	....
2012-13	Spruce Grove	AJHL	55	1	6	7	11	16	0	0	0	12
2013-14	Spruce Grove	AJHL	49	4	18	22	29	13	0	5	5	4
2014-15	Boston University	H-East	41	6	11	17	18	....	....	....	....	....

HICKMAN, Justin HIHK-muhn, JUHS-tihn **BOS**

Right wing. Shoots right. 6'2", 224 lbs. Born, Kelowna, BC, March 18, 1994.

			Regular Season					Playoffs				
Season	Club	League	GP	G	A	Pts	PIM	GP	G	A	Pts	PIM
2009-10	Okanagan Rockets	BCMML	38	13	12	25	58	1	0	0	0	23
2010-11	Seattle	WHL	46	0	2	2	51	....	....	....	....	....
2011-12	Seattle	WHL	71	12	10	22	106	....	....	....	....	....
2012-13	Seattle	WHL	70	12	22	34	115	6	0	1	1	11
2013-14	Seattle	WHL	67	22	24	46	154	9	2	1	3	12
	Bridgeport	AHL	5	1	0	1	4	....	....	....	....	....
2014-15	Seattle	WHL	31	9	19	28	40	....	....	....	....	....

Signed to ATO (amateur tryout) contract by **Bridgeport** (AHL), April 11, 2014. Signed as a free agent by **Boston**, March 4, 2015.

HINOSTROZA, Vincent (hihn-oh-STROH-za, VIHN-sihnt) **CHI**

Center. Shoots right. 5'9", 158 lbs. Born, Chicago, IL, April 3, 1994.
(Chicago's 6th choice, 169th overall, in 2012 Entry Draft).

			Regular Season					Playoffs				
Season	Club	League	GP	G	A	Pts	PIM	GP	G	A	Pts	PIM
2009-10	Chicago Mission	T1EHL	34	13	21	34	38	....	....	....	....	....
2010-11	Waterloo	USHL	50	8	14	22	36	....	....	....	....	....
2011-12	Waterloo	USHL	55	20	24	44	56	1	0	0	0	0
2012-13	Waterloo	USHL	46	25	35	60	14	5	4	3	7	8
2013-14	U. of Notre Dame	H-East	34	8	24	32	4	....	....	....	....	....
2014-15	U. of Notre Dame	H-East	42	11	33	44	48	....	....	....	....	....

Hockey East First All-Star Team (2015)

HINTZ, Roope (HIHNTZ, ROO-peh) **DAL**

Left wing. Shoots left. 6'2", 185 lbs. Born, Tampere, Finland, November 17, 1996.
(Dallas' 2nd choice, 49th overall, in 2015 Entry Draft).

			Regular Season					Playoffs				
Season	Club	League	GP	G	A	Pts	PIM	GP	G	A	Pts	PIM
2011-12	Ilves Tampere U18	Fin-U18	18	3	6	9	2	....	....	....	....	....
2012-13	Tampa Bay Juniors	EmJHL	20	20	15	35	0	....	....	....	....	....
	Bismarck Bobcats	NAHL	2	0	0	0	0	....	....	....	....	....
	Ilves Tampere U18	Fin-U18	9	4	9	13	0	....	....	....	....	....
2013-14	Ilves Tampere U18	Fin-U18	1	2	0	2	0	7	3	6	9	4
	Ilves Tampere Jr.	Fin-Jr.	29	18	20	38	16	5	0	0	0	2
	Ilves Tampere	Finland	7	0	0	0	2	....	....	....	....	....
2014-15	Ilves Tampere	Finland	42	5	12	17	10	2	0	0	0	0
	Ilves Tampere Jr.	Fin-Jr.	....	....	....	....	....	6	1	1	2	0

HOBBS, Connor (HAWBZ, KAW-nuhr) **WSH**

Defense. Shoots right. 6'1", 187 lbs. Born, Regina, SK, January 4, 1997.
(Washington's 3rd choice, 143rd overall, in 2015 Entry Draft).

			Regular Season					Playoffs				
Season	Club	League	GP	G	A	Pts	PIM	GP	G	A	Pts	PIM
2012-13	Saskatoon Blazers	SMHL	38	6	10	16	68	7	1	3	4	14
2013-14	Saskatoon Blazers	SMHL	33	11	12	23	84	....	....	....	....	....
	Medicine Hat	WHL	10	1	2	3	4	....	....	....	....	....
2014-15	Medicine Hat	WHL	12	1	1	2	15	....	....	....	....	....
	Nipawin Hawks	SJHL	4	0	0	0	4	....	....	....	....	....
	Regina Pats	WHL	33	1	15	16	21	8	2	0	2	7

HODGES, Steven (HAW-juhz, STEE-vehn) **FLA**

Center. Shoots left. 6', 185 lbs. Born, Yellowknife, NT, May 5, 1994.
(Florida's 2nd choice, 84th overall, in 2012 Entry Draft).

			Regular Season					Playoffs				
Season	Club	League	GP	G	A	Pts	PIM	GP	G	A	Pts	PIM
2008-09	South Delta Storm	Minor-BC	60	62	80	142	....	....	....	....	....	....
	Greater Van.	BCMML	1	0	0	0	0	....	....	....	....	....
2009-10	Fraser Valley	BCMML	37	17	17	34	84	....	....	....	....	....
	Chilliwack Bruins	WHL	5	0	2	2	0	....	....	....	....	....
2010-11	Chilliwack Bruins	WHL	58	5	6	11	44	3	0	0	0	0
2011-12	Victoria Royals	WHL	72	21	25	46	62	4	0	4	4	4
2012-13	Victoria Royals	WHL	60	28	23	51	67	6	2	4	6	2
2013-14	Victoria Royals	WHL	52	21	26	47	65	9	4	6	10	9
2014-15	San Antonio	AHL	23	1	1	2	4	....	....	....	....	....
	Cincinnati	ECHL	28	8	7	15	32	....	....	....	....	....

HOEFFEL, Mike (HOH-fuhl, MIGHK)

Left wing. Shoots left. 6'4", 205 lbs. Born, North Oaks, MN, April 9, 1989.
(New Jersey's 1st choice, 57th overall, in 2007 Entry Draft).

			Regular Season					Playoffs				
Season	Club	League	GP	G	A	Pts	PIM	GP	G	A	Pts	PIM
2004-05	Hill-Murray	High-MN	26	24	19	43	10	....	....	....	....	....
2005-06	Hill-Murray	High-MN	30	27	46	73	20	....	....	....	....	....
2006-07	USNTDP	U-18	33	10	2	12	18	....	....	....	....	....
	USNTDP	NAHL	11	6	5	11	10	....	....	....	....	....
2007-08	U. of Minnesota	WCHA	45	9	10	19	22	....	....	....	....	....
2008-09	U. of Minnesota	WCHA	35	12	8	20	38	....	....	....	....	....
2009-10	U. of Minnesota	WCHA	34	14	10	24	22	....	....	....	....	....
2010-11	U. of Minnesota	WCHA	35	13	11	24	24	....	....	....	....	....
	Albany Devils	AHL	10	2	0	2	6	....	....	....	....	....
2011-12	Albany Devils	AHL	50	5	4	9	28	....	....	....	....	....
2012-13	Albany Devils	AHL	52	5	5	10	37	....	....	....	....	....
2013-14	Albany Devils	AHL	53	7	12	19	40	....	....	....	....	....
2014-15	Springfield Falcons	AHL	62	9	9	18	39	....	....	....	....	....

HOFMANN, Gregory (HAWF-muhn, GREH-goh-ree) **CAR**

Center. Shoots left. 6', 200 lbs. Born, Tramelan, Switz., November 13, 1992.
(Carolina's 4th choice, 103rd overall, in 2011 Entry Draft).

			Regular Season					Playoffs				
Season	Club	League	GP	G	A	Pts	PIM	GP	G	A	Pts	PIM
2006-07	Chaux-de-Fonds Jr.	Swiss-Jr.	2	0	0	0	0	....	....	....	....	....
2007-08	HC Luzern U17	Swiss-U17	6	2	5	7	14	....	....	....	....	....
	Ambri U17	Swiss-U17	22	14	11	25	64	5	4	3	7	20
	Ambri Jr.	Swiss-Jr.	11	4	1	5	6	8	0	0	0	2
2008-09	Ambri U17	Swiss-U17	20	9	16	25	42	....	....	....	....	....
	Ambri Jr.	Swiss-Jr.	22	10	7	17	26	2	0	0	0	2
2009-10	Ambri Jr.	Swiss-Jr.	34	25	30	55	20	3	1	2	3	6
	HC Ambri-Piotta	Swiss	1	0	0	0	0	1	0	0	0	0
2010-11	Ambri Jr.	Swiss-Jr.	2	2	0	2	2	....	....	....	....	....
	HC Ambri-Piotta	Swiss	41	3	9	12	2	12	0	2	2	2
	HC Ambri-Piotta	Swiss-Q	....	....	....	....	....	5	1	2	3	2
2011-12	HC Ambri-Piotta	Swiss	34	5	1	6	6	8	1	0	1	0
	HC Ambri-Piotta	Swiss-Q	....	....	....	....	....	4	1	1	2	2
	Ambri Jr.	Swiss-Jr.	7	3	1	4	2	2	2	0	2	0
2012-13	HC Davos	Swiss	49	16	11	27	20	7	0	2	2	0
2013-14	HC Davos	Swiss	41	7	10	17	30	....	....	....	....	....
2014-15	HC Davos	Swiss	47	11	14	25	18	13	3	2	5	2

HOLLAND, Rhett (HAW-luhnd, REHT) ARI

Defense. Shoots right. 6'2", 220 lbs. Born, Calgary, AB, September 25, 1993.
(Phoenix's 4th choice, 102nd overall, in 2012 Entry Draft).

			Regular Season					Playoffs				
Season	Club	League	GP	G	A	Pts	PIM	GP	G	A	Pts	PIM
2007-08	Calgary Royals	AMBHL	33	0	5	5	75	3	0	0	0	0
2008-09	Calgary Royals	AMHL	30	1	3	4	66	4	0	0	0	0
2009-10	Okotoks Oilers	AJHL	57	3	8	11	91	7	0	1	1	6
2010-11	Okotoks Oilers	AJHL	31	2	9	11	117	....	....	....	....	....
2011-12	Okotoks Oilers	AJHL	47	3	7	10	223	8	0	1	1	18
2012-13	Michigan State	CCHA	3	0	0	0	15	....	....	....	....	....
2013-14	Michigan State	Big Ten	31	0	4	4	49	....	....	....	....	....
2014-15	Michigan State	Big Ten	35	1	3	4	18	....	....	....	....	....

HOLLOWAY, Bud (HAHL-OH-way, BUHD) MTL

Left wing. Shoots right. 6', 200 lbs. Born, Wapella, SK, March 1, 1988.
(Los Angeles' 5th choice, 86th overall, in 2006 Entry Draft).

			Regular Season					Playoffs				
Season	Club	League	GP	G	A	Pts	PIM	GP	G	A	Pts	PIM
2003-04	Yorkton Harvest	SMHL	43	15	21	36	22	....	....	....	....	....
	Seattle	WHL	2	0	0	0	0	....	....	....	....	....
2004-05	Seattle	WHL	67	4	11	15	27	12	0	1	1	0
2005-06	Seattle	WHL	72	21	13	34	18	7	3	2	5	4
2006-07	Seattle	WHL	71	27	38	65	50	11	3	3	6	8
2007-08	Seattle	WHL	70	43	40	83	55	12	5	5	10	4
2008-09	Manchester	AHL	38	7	5	12	6	....	....	....	....	....
	Ontario Reign	ECHL	23	14	8	22	8	7	5	9	14	8
2009-10	Manchester	AHL	75	19	28	47	26	16	7	7	14	9
2010-11	Manchester	AHL	78	28	33	61	58	7	4	7	11	10
2011-12	Skelleftea AIK	Sweden	55	21	28	49	32	19	10	*13	*23	4
2012-13	Skelleftea AIK	Sweden	55	20	*51	*71	36	13	4	5	9	18
2013-14	Skelleftea AIK	Sweden	53	10	23	33	26	11	3	5	8	6
2014-15	SC Bern	Swiss	42	13	24	37	24	11	4	4	8	4

Signed as a free agent by **Skelleftea** (Sweden), July 25, 2011. Signed as a free agent by **Montreal**, July 1, 2015.

HOLMSTROM, Axel (HOHLM-struhm, AX-uhl) DET

Center. Shoots left. 6', 198 lbs. Born, Arvidsjaur, Sweden, June 29, 1996.
(Detroit's 6th choice, 196th overall, in 2014 Entry Draft).

			Regular Season					Playoffs				
Season	Club	League	GP	G	A	Pts	PIM	GP	G	A	Pts	PIM
2011-12	Skelleftea AIK U18	Swe-U18	1	0	2	2	0	4	1	1	2	0
2012-13	Skelleftea AIK U18	Swe-U18	31	16	48	64	6	8	3	8	11	4
	Skelleftea AIK Jr.	Swe-Jr.	10	2	1	3	0	4	0	1	1	0
2013-14	Skelleftea AIK Jr.	Swe-Jr.	33	15	23	38	12	2	0	0	0	0
	Skelleftea AIK	Sweden	4	0	0	0	0	....	....	....	....	....
	Skelleftea AIK U18	Swe-U18	....	....	....	....	....	3	1	3	4	0
2014-15	Skelleftea AIK Jr.	Swe-Jr.	3	0	4	4	0	....	....	....	....	....
	Skelleftea AIK	Sweden	44	10	10	20	4	15	7	*11	*18	0

HOLWAY, Patrick (HAWL-way, PA-trihk) DET

Defense. Shoots right. 6'4", 200 lbs. Born, Cohasset, MA, October 1, 1996.
(Detroit's 5th choice, 170th overall, in 2015 Entry Draft).

			Regular Season					Playoffs				
Season	Club	League	GP	G	A	Pts	PIM	GP	G	A	Pts	PIM
2011-12	Bos. Adv. U16	T1EHL	40	2	6	8	18	....	....	....	....	....
2012-13	Bos. Adv. U16	T1EHL	41	4	15	19	43	4	0	3	3	2
	Bos. Adv. U18	T1EHL	1	0	0	0	0	....	....	....	....	....
2013-14	Bos. Adv. U18	T1EHL	34	8	11	19	51	....	....	....	....	....
2014-15	Bos. Adv. U18	T1EHL	28	8	17	25	34	....	....	....	....	....

• Signed Letter of Intent to attend **University of Maine** (Hockey East) in fall of 2016.

HOLZAPFEL, Riley (HOHL-za-fehl, RIGH-lee) PIT

Center. Shoots left. 6', 190 lbs. Born, Regina, SK, August 18, 1988.
(Atlanta's 2nd choice, 43rd overall, in 2006 Entry Draft).

			Regular Season					Playoffs				
Season	Club	League	GP	G	A	Pts	PIM	GP	G	A	Pts	PIM
2004-05	Moose Jaw	WHL	63	15	13	28	32	5	1	2	3	8
2005-06	Moose Jaw	WHL	64	19	38	57	46	22	7	9	16	20
2006-07	Moose Jaw	WHL	72	39	43	82	94	....	....	....	....	....
2007-08	Moose Jaw	WHL	49	18	23	41	43	6	3	5	8	12
	Chicago Wolves	AHL	1	0	0	0	0	....	....	....	....	....
2008-09	Chicago Wolves	AHL	73	13	19	32	38	....	....	....	....	....
2009-10	Chicago Wolves	AHL	60	7	16	23	30	14	0	3	3	6
2010-11	Chicago Wolves	AHL	68	12	15	27	20	....	....	....	....	....
2011-12	St. John's IceCaps	AHL	29	8	7	15	8	....	....	....	....	....
	Syracuse Crunch	AHL	28	8	14	22	34	4	0	1	1	4
2012-13	Wilkes-Barre	AHL	76	21	30	51	93	15	4	6	10	8
2013-14	HV 71 Jonkoping	Sweden	48	10	12	22	49	4	0	0	0	0
2014-15	HV 71 Jonkoping	Sweden	49	7	6	13	14	6	0	0	0	0

WHL East First All-Star Team (2007)

• Transferred to **Winnipeg** after **Atlanta** franchise relocated, June 21, 2011. Traded to **Anaheim** by **Winnipeg** for Maxime Macenauer, February 13, 2012. Signed as a free agent by **Pittsburgh**, July 1. 2012. Signed as a free agent by **Jonkoping** (Sweden), July 4, 2013.

HONKA, Julius (HOHN-kuh, YOO-lee-uhs) DAL

Defense. Shoots right. 5'11", 185 lbs. Born, Jyvaskyla, Finland, December 3, 1995.
(Dallas' 1st choice, 14th overall, in 2014 Entry Draft).

			Regular Season					Playoffs				
Season	Club	League	GP	G	A	Pts	PIM	GP	G	A	Pts	PIM
2011-12	JyP Jyvaskyla U18	Fin-U18	35	8	7	15	32	....	....	....	....	....
	JyP Jyvaskyla Jr.	Fin-Jr.	2	0	0	0	0	....	....	....	....	....
2012-13	JyP Jyvaskyla Jr.	Fin-Jr.	42	4	11	15	47	4	0	0	0	25
2013-14	Swift Current	WHL	62	16	40	56	52	6	2	0	2	6
2014-15	Texas Stars	AHL	68	8	23	31	55	3	1	1	2	4

WHL East Second All-Star Team (2014)

HO-SANG, Joshua (HOH-SANG, JAW-shoo-wah) NYI

Center/Right wing. Shoots right. 6', 173 lbs. Born, Toronto, ON, January 22, 1996.
(NY Islanders' 2nd choice, 28th overall, in 2014 Entry Draft).

			Regular Season					Playoffs				
Season	Club	League	GP	G	A	Pts	PIM	GP	G	A	Pts	PIM
2011-12	Toronto Marlboros	GTHL	30	31	48	79	24	....	....	....	....	....
2012-13	Windsor Spitfires	OHL	63	14	30	44	22	....	....	....	....	....
2013-14	Windsor Spitfires	OHL	67	32	53	85	44	4	1	2	3	10
2014-15	Windsor Spitfires	OHL	11	3	16	19	8	....	....	....	....	....
	Niagara Ice Dogs	OHL	49	14	48	62	38	11	1	15	16	18

HRIVIK, Marek (huh-RIHV-ihk, MAIR-ehk) NYR

Left wing. Shoots left. 6'2", 200 lbs. Born, Zilina, Slovakia, August 28, 1991.

			Regular Season					Playoffs				
Season	Club	League	GP	G	A	Pts	PIM	GP	G	A	Pts	PIM
2007-08	MsHK Zilina Jr.	Slovak-Jr.	47	17	17	34	24	....	....	....	....	....
2009-10	Moncton Wildcats	QMJHL	66	26	29	55	14	21	5	12	17	8
2010-11	Moncton Wildcats	QMJHL	59	38	41	79	18	4	0	6	6	11
2011-12	Moncton Wildcats	QMJHL	54	29	41	70	8	4	1	2	3	0
	Connecticut Whale	AHL	8	1	0	1	0	9	5	4	9	10
2012-13	Connecticut Whale	AHL	40	7	19	26	10	....	....	....	....	....
2013-14	Hartford Wolf Pack	AHL	74	13	14	27	22	....	....	....	....	....
2014-15	Hartford Wolf Pack	AHL	72	12	21	33	12	15	3	6	9	6

Signed as a free agent by **NY Rangers**, May 30, 2012.

HUDON, Charles (OO-dawn, CHAR-uhlz) MTL

Left wing. Shoots left. 5'10", 191 lbs. Born, Alma, QC, June 23, 1994.
(Montreal's 6th choice, 122nd overall, in 2012 Entry Draft).

			Regular Season					Playoffs				
Season	Club	League	GP	G	A	Pts	PIM	GP	G	A	Pts	PIM
2009-10	Saint-Eustache	QAAA	40	23	24	47	32	6	4	5	9	4
2010-11	Chicoutimi	QMJHL	63	23	37	60	42	4	0	3	3	4
2011-12	Chicoutimi	QMJHL	59	25	41	66	50	18	6	5	11	16
2012-13	Chicoutimi	QMJHL	56	30	41	71	66	6	5	5	10	8
	Hamilton Bulldogs	AHL	9	1	2	3	4	....	....	....	....	....
2013-14	Chicoutimi	QMJHL	33	14	27	41	57	....	....	....	....	....
	Baie-Comeau	QMJHL	24	12	23	35	26	22	10	11	21	30
2014-15	Hamilton Bulldogs	AHL	75	19	38	57	68	....	....	....	....	....

QMJHL All-Rookie Team (2011) • QMJHL Rookie of the Year (2011) • AHL All-Rookie Team (2015)

HUGHES, Cameron (HEWZ, KAM-ruhn) BOS

Center. Shoots left. 6', 163 lbs. Born, Edmonton, AB, October 9, 1996.
(Boston's 9th choice, 165th overall, in 2015 Entry Draft).

			Regular Season					Playoffs				
Season	Club	League	GP	G	A	Pts	PIM	GP	G	A	Pts	PIM
2011-12	CAC Canadiens	AMHL	32	8	23	31	24	....	....	....	....	....
2012-13	Spruce Grove	AJHL	60	11	20	31	42	14	3	6	9	11
2013-14	Spruce Grove	AJHL	52	21	36	57	58	18	1	16	17	2
2014-15	U. of Wisconsin	Big Ten	34	3	10	13	35	....	....	....	....	....

HUGHES, Tommy (HEWZ, TAW-mee) NYR

Defense. Shoots right. 6'2", 225 lbs. Born, London, ON, April 7, 1992.

			Regular Season					Playoffs				
Season	Club	League	GP	G	A	Pts	PIM	GP	G	A	Pts	PIM
2009-10	Lon. Knights Mid.	Minor-ON	27	5	15	20	38	10	3	5	8	12
	London Nationals	ON-Jr.B	2	0	0	0	0	....	....	....	....	....
	London Knights	OHL	7	0	0	0	0	....	....	....	....	....
2010-11	London Nationals	ON-Jr.B	24	2	11	13	54	....	....	....	....	....
	London Knights	OHL	39	0	6	6	39	6	0	0	0	12
2011-12	London Knights	OHL	56	2	8	10	64	19	1	3	4	20
2012-13	London Knights	OHL	67	1	15	16	66	20	1	1	2	19
2013-14	Hartford Wolf Pack	AHL	72	2	7	9	34	....	....	....	....	....
2014-15	Hartford Wolf Pack	AHL	42	1	6	7	27	15	1	2	3	4

Signed as a free agent by **NY Rangers**, April 1, 2013.

HURLEY, Connor (HUHR-lee, KAW-nuhr) BUF

Center. Shoots left. 6'2", 178 lbs. Born, Eagan, MN, September 15, 1995.
(Buffalo's 4th choice, 38th overall, in 2013 Entry Draft).

			Regular Season					Playoffs				
Season	Club	League	GP	G	A	Pts	PIM	GP	G	A	Pts	PIM
2009-10	Shattuck Bantam	High-MN	58	20	39	59	14	....	....	....	....	....
2010-11	Hastings Raiders	High-MN	26	10	26	36	24	....	....	....	....	....
2011-12	Edina Hornets	High-MN	25	22	26	48	10	5	4	6	10	2
2012-13	Edina Hornets	High-MN	25	15	28	43	8	6	5	4	9	2
	Team Southwest	UMHSEL	11	3	13	16	12	....	....	....	....	....
	Muskegon	USHL	11	1	7	8	4	3	0	1	1	4
	USNTDP	U-18	10	1	1	2	4	....	....	....	....	....
2013-14	Muskegon	USHL	21	3	11	14	14	....	....	....	....	....
	Green Bay	USHL	35	10	26	36	18	4	2	2	4	2
2014-15	U. of Notre Dame	H-East	41	4	10	14	6	....	....	....	....	....

HUTTON, Ben (HUH-tuhn, BEHN) VAN

Defense. Shoots left. 6'3", 200 lbs. Born, Prescott, ON, April 20, 1993.
(Vancouver's 3rd choice, 147th overall, in 2012 Entry Draft).

			Regular Season					Playoffs				
Season	Club	League	GP	G	A	Pts	PIM	GP	G	A	Pts	PIM
2008-09	U.C. Cyclones	Minor-ON	54	6	21	27	20	....	....	....	....	....
	Kemptville 73's	ON-Jr.A	4	0	0	0	2	....	....	....	....	....
2009-10	Kemptville 73's	ON-Jr.A	60	16	18	34	6	4	0	0	0	2
2010-11	Kemptville 73's	ON-Jr.A	61	8	27	35	28	....	....	....	....	....
2011-12	Kemptville 73's	ON-Jr.A	35	7	20	27	25	....	....	....	....	....
	Nepean Raiders	ON-Jr.A	22	4	12	16	6	18	5	8	13	6
2012-13	U. of Maine	H-East	34	4	11	15	18	....	....	....	....	....
2013-14	U. of Maine	H-East	35	15	14	29	8	....	....	....	....	....
2014-15	U. of Maine	H-East	39	9	12	21	14	....	....	....	....	....
	Utica Comets	AHL	4	1	0	1	2	....	....	....	....	....

Hockey East First All-Star Team (2014) • NCAA East Second All-American Team (2014)

HYMAN, Zach (HIGH-muhn, ZAK) TOR

Center. Shoots right. 6', 197 lbs. Born, Toronto, ON, June 9, 1992.
(Florida's 11th choice, 123rd overall, in 2010 Entry Draft).

			Regular Season					Playoffs				
Season	Club	League	GP	G	A	Pts	PIM	GP	G	A	Pts	PIM
2008-09	Hamilton	ON-Jr.A	49	13	24	37	24	5	2	2	4	4
2009-10	Hamilton	ON-Jr.A	49	35	40	75	30	11	7	9	16	4
2010-11	Hamilton	ON-Jr.A	43	42	60	102	24	7	3	5	8	6
2011-12	U. of Michigan	CCHA	41	2	7	9	12	....	....	....	....	....
2012-13	U. of Michigan	CCHA	38	4	5	9	8	....	....	....	....	....
2013-14	U. of Michigan	Big Ten	35	7	10	17	12	....	....	....	....	....
2014-15	U. of Michigan	Big Ten	37	*22	32	*54	10	....	....	....	....	....

CJHL Player of the Year (2011) • NCAA West First All-American Team (2015)

Traded to **Toronto** by **Florida** with future considerations for Greg McKegg, June 19, 2015.

IACOPELLI, Matt (YA-koh-peh-lee, MAT) **CHI**

Right wing. Shoots left. 6'1", 207 lbs. Born, Woodhaven, MI, May 15, 1994.
(Chicago's 2nd choice, 83rd overall, in 2014 Entry Draft).

			Regular Season					Playoffs				
Season	Club	League	GP	G	A	Pts	PIM	GP	G	A	Pts	PIM
2011-12	Det. L.C.	HPHL	17	5	5	10	6	....	....	....	....	....
	Texas Tornado	NAHL	1	0	0	0	0	....	....	....	....	....
2012-13	Det. B. Tire U18	T1EHL	39	26	20	46	65	5	0	2	2	6
	Springfield-IL	NAHL	4	3	1	4	0	....	....	....	....	....
2013-14	Muskegon	USHL	58	*41	22	63	47	....	....	....	....	....
2014-15	Muskegon	USHL	56	23	14	37	38	11	5	2	7	10

USHL First All-Star Team (2014)

• Signed Letter of Intent to attend **Western Michigan University** (NCHC) in fall of 2015.

IKONEN, Henri (EEH-koh-nehn, AWN-ree) **T.B.**

Left wing. Shoots left. 5'11", 184 lbs. Born, Savonlinna, Finland, April 17, 1994.
(Tampa Bay's 4th choice, 154th overall, in 2013 Entry Draft).

			Regular Season					Playoffs				
Season	Club	League	GP	G	A	Pts	PIM	GP	G	A	Pts	PIM
2008-09	SaPKo U18	Fin-U18	3	1	2	3	0	....	....	....	....	....
2009-10	SaPKo U18	Fin-U18	5	6	4	10	12	....	....	....	....	....
	SapKo Jr.	Fin-Jr.	14	13	8	21	8	4	3	0	3	4
2010-11	KalPa Kuopio U18	Fin-U18	10	5	6	11	28	4	1	3	4	0
	KalPa Kuopio Jr.	Fin-Jr.	33	9	13	22	10	....	....	....	....	....
2011-12	KalPa Kuopio U18	Fin-U18	6	6	9	15	2	....	....	....	....	....
	KalPa Kuopio Jr.	Fin-Jr.	37	17	28	45	18	9	8	6	14	2
	KalPa Kuopio	Finland	8	0	1	1	4	....	....	....	....	....
2012-13	Kingston	OHL	61	22	29	51	30	4	1	0	1	4
2013-14	Kingston	OHL	54	25	45	70	49	7	1	5	6	8
	Syracuse Crunch	AHL	6	0	2	2	2	....	....	....	....	....
2014-15	Syracuse Crunch	AHL	59	5	8	13	43	3	0	0	0	0

IMAMA, Boko (ih-MA-ma, BOH-KOH) **T.B.**

Left wing. Shoots left. 6'1", 214 lbs. Born, Montreal, QC, August 3, 1996.
(Tampa Bay's 9th choice, 180th overall, in 2015 Entry Draft).

			Regular Season					Playoffs				
Season	Club	League	GP	G	A	Pts	PIM	GP	G	A	Pts	PIM
2011-12	Laval-Montreal	QAAA	43	7	9	16	30	....	....	....	....	....
2012-13	Baie-Comeau	QMJHL	44	3	3	6	34	5	0	0	0	9
2013-14	Baie-Comeau	QMJHL	59	7	8	15	101	14	0	4	4	14
2014-15	Baie-Comeau	QMJHL	36	10	9	19	89	....	....	....	....	....
	Saint John	QMJHL	23	3	6	9	48	5	0	1	1	6

IRVING, Aaron (UHR-vihng, AIR-uhn) **NSH**

Defense. Shoots right. 6'1", 185 lbs. Born, Edmonton, AB, March 3, 1996.
(Nashville's 7th choice, 162nd overall, in 2014 Entry Draft).

			Regular Season					Playoffs				
Season	Club	League	GP	G	A	Pts	PIM	GP	G	A	Pts	PIM
2009-10	South Side AC	Minor-AB	29	13	18	31	62	....	....	....	....	....
	SSAC Lions	AMBHL	1	0	0	0	2	8	0	2	2	2
2010-11	SSAC Lions	AMBHL	33	6	12	18	48	....	....	....	....	....
	SSAC Bulldogs	Minor-AB	1	1	1	2	4	....	....	....	....	....
2011-12	SSAC Athletics	AMHL	31	3	15	18	80	6	1	2	3	12
2012-13	Bonnyville Pontiacs	AJHL	43	1	6	7	57	9	0	0	0	11
	Edmonton	WHL	5	0	0	0	6	....	....	....	....	....
2013-14	Edmonton	WHL	63	9	21	30	88	21	0	2	2	10
2014-15	Edmonton	WHL	65	6	7	13	58	5	0	0	0	2

IVERSON, Keegan (IGH-vuhr-suhn, KEE-guhn) **NYR**

Center/Right wing. Shoots right. 6'1", 219 lbs. Born, Minneapolis, MN, April 5, 1996.
(NY Rangers' 2nd choice, 85th overall, in 2014 Entry Draft).

			Regular Season					Playoffs				
Season	Club	League	GP	G	A	Pts	PIM	GP	G	A	Pts	PIM
2010-11	Breck Mustangs	High-MN	24	10	9	19	43	6	2	4	6	14
2011-12	Breck Mustangs	High-MN	23	13	23	36	33	6	5	4	9	2
	Portland	WHL	1	0	0	0	0	1	0	0	0	0
2012-13	Portland	WHL	47	6	4	10	69	17	0	2	2	0
	USNTDP	U-17	6	1	1	2	8	....	....	....	....	....
2013-14	Portland	WHL	67	22	20	42	70	21	4	4	8	12
2014-15	Portland	WHL	68	15	24	39	91	17	2	7	9	27

JACKSON, Jacob (JAK-suhn, JAY-kuhb) **S.J.**

Center. Shoots left. 5'11", 190 lbs. Born, Maplewood, MN, December 5, 1994.
(San Jose's 6th choice, 201st overall, in 2013 Entry Draft).

			Regular Season					Playoffs				
Season	Club	League	GP	G	A	Pts	PIM	GP	G	A	Pts	PIM
2010-11	Tartan School	High-MN	25	15	10	25	18	1	1	0	1	0
2011-12	Tartan School	High-MN	25	24	19	43	28	2	1	0	1	2
2012-13	Tartan School	High-MN	25	29	27	56	10	1	3	0	3	0
	Team Northeast	UMHSEL	21	10	4	14	10	....	....	....	....	....
	Waterloo	USHL	2	1	0	1	0	....	....	....	....	....
2013-14	Des Moines	USHL	42	2	6	8	20	....	....	....	....	....
2014-15	Michigan Tech	WCHA	DID NOT PLAY – FRESHMAN									

JACOBS, Colin (JAY-kuhbz, KAWL-ihn) **BUF**

Center. Shoots right. 6'1", 204 lbs. Born, Coppell, TX, January 20, 1993.
(Buffalo's 3rd choice, 107th overall, in 2011 Entry Draft).

			Regular Season					Playoffs				
Season	Club	League	GP	G	A	Pts	PIM	GP	G	A	Pts	PIM
2007-08	Dallas Ice Jets	Minor-TX	51	61	50	111	88	....	....	....	....	....
2008-09	Dallas Stars U16	Minor-TX	50	36	36	72	147	....	....	....	....	....
	Seattle	WHL	2	0	0	0	0	4	2	1	3	0
2009-10	Seattle	WHL	72	13	13	26	119	....	....	....	....	....
2010-11	Seattle	WHL	68	22	22	44	69	....	....	....	....	....
2011-12	Seattle	WHL	44	9	10	19	46	....	....	....	....	....
2012-13	Prince George	WHL	66	25	28	53	98	....	....	....	....	....
	Rochester	AHL	11	1	2	3	0	....	....	....	....	....
2013-14	Rochester	AHL	24	0	2	2	29	....	....	....	....	....
	Elmira Jackals	ECHL	20	2	3	5	31	....	....	....	....	....
2014-15	Rochester	AHL	9	1	1	2	19	....	....	....	....	....
	Elmira Jackals	ECHL	40	5	8	13	113	....	....	....	....	....

JACOBS, Joshua (JAY-kuhbz, JAW-shoo-wah) **N.J.**

Defense. Shoots right. 6'2", 195 lbs. Born, Shelby Township, MI, February 15, 1996.
(New Jersey's 2nd choice, 41st overall, in 2014 Entry Draft).

			Regular Season					Playoffs				
Season	Club	League	GP	G	A	Pts	PIM	GP	G	A	Pts	PIM
2010-11	Detroit Belle Tire	T1EHL	31	9	19	28	24	....	....	....	....	....
2011-12	Det. Honeybaked	HPHL	24	3	14	17	20	....	....	....	....	....
	Det. Honeybaked	Minor-MI	....	....	....	....	....	7	0	3	3	0
2012-13	Indiana Ice	USHL	48	2	13	15	52	....	....	....	....	....
2013-14	Indiana Ice	USHL	56	5	18	23	46	12	3	2	5	2
2014-15	Michigan State	Big Ten	35	0	9	9	26	....	....	....	....	....

JANKOWSKI, Mark (jan-KOW-skee, MAHRK) **CGY**

Center. Shoots left. 6'3", 190 lbs. Born, Hamilton, ON, September 13, 1994.
(Calgary's 1st choice, 21st overall, in 2012 Entry Draft).

			Regular Season					Playoffs				
Season	Club	League	GP	G	A	Pts	PIM	GP	G	A	Pts	PIM
2009-10	St. Cath. Falcons	Minor-ON	33	11	14	25	14	....	....	....	....	....
2010-11	Stanstead Coll.	MPHL	13	5	4	9	10	2	2	1	3	2
	Stanstead Coll.	High-QU	50	24	37	61	10	....	....	....	....	....
2011-12	Stanstead Coll.	MPHL	13	*19	11	*30	12	3	3	*4	*7	0
	Stanstead Coll.	High-QU	41	31	26	57	22	....	....	....	....	....
2012-13	Providence College	H-East	34	7	11	18	10	....	....	....	....	....
2013-14	Providence College	H-East	39	13	12	25	14	....	....	....	....	....
2014-15	Providence College	H-East	37	8	19	27	14	....	....	....	....	....

JANMARK, Mattias (YAN-mahrk, mah-TEE-uhs) **DAL**

Center. Shoots left. 6'1", 189 lbs. Born, Stockholm, Sweden, December 8, 1992.
(Detroit's 4th choice, 79th overall, in 2013 Entry Draft).

			Regular Season					Playoffs				
Season	Club	League	GP	G	A	Pts	PIM	GP	G	A	Pts	PIM
2007-08	SDE U18	Swe-U18	15	3	4	7	10	....	....	....	....	....
2008-09	SDE U18	Swe-U18	22	16	21	37	36	....	....	....	....	....
	AIK IF Solna U18	Swe-U18	12	2	6	8	4	7	5	5	10	2
2009-10	AIK IF Solna U18	Swe-U18	33	13	22	35	12	1	0	0	0	0
	AIK IF Solna Jr.	Swe-Jr.	13	4	7	11	6	4	0	1	1	0
2010-11	AIK IF Solna Jr.	Swe-Jr.	40	11	17	28	34	....	....	....	....	....
2011-12	AIK Solna Jr.	Swe-Jr.	40	23	38	61	30	3	0	0	0	4
	AIK Solna	Sweden	18	0	0	0	2	3	0	0	0	0
2012-13	AIK Solna	Sweden	55	14	17	31	32	....	....	....	....	....
2013-14	AIK Solna	Sweden	45	18	12	30	56	....	....	....	....	....
	AIK Solna	Sweden-Q	10	1	3	4	24	....	....	....	....	....
2014-15	Frolunda	Sweden	55	13	23	36	30	13	4	3	7	4
	Texas Stars	AHL	....	....	....	....	....	1	0	0	0	0

Traded to **Dallas** by **Detroit** with Mattias Backman and Detroit's 2nd round choice (Roope Hintz) in 2015 Entry Draft for Erik Cole and Dallas' 3rd round choice (Vili Saarijarvi) in 2015 Entry Draft, March 1, 2015.

JARDINE, Sam (jar-DEEN, SAM) **CHI**

Defense. Shoots left. 6'2", 209 lbs. Born, Lacombe, AB, August 12, 1993.
(Chicago's 9th choice, 169th overall, in 2011 Entry Draft).

			Regular Season					Playoffs				
Season	Club	League	GP	G	A	Pts	PIM	GP	G	A	Pts	PIM
2008-09	Red Deer Chiefs	Minor-AB	32	6	21	27	36	....	....	....	....	....
	Red Deer	AMHL	4	0	1	1	0	....	....	....	....	....
2009-10	Red Deer	AMHL	34	9	15	24	18	....	....	....	....	....
	Camrose Kodiaks	AJHL	3	0	0	0	2	....	....	....	....	....
2010-11	Camrose Kodiaks	AJHL	50	6	16	22	56	23	4	7	11	24
2011-12	Camrose Kodiaks	AJHL	51	11	19	30	83	4	0	2	2	19
2012-13	Ohio State	CCHA	28	0	7	7	48	....	....	....	....	....
2013-14	Ohio State	Big Ten	36	1	12	13	41	....	....	....	....	....
2014-15	Ohio State	Big Ten	33	2	10	12	29	....	....	....	....	....

JAROS, Christian (YA-ruhsh, KRIHS-ch'yehn) **OTT**

Defense. Shoots right. 6'3", 217 lbs. Born, Kosice, Slovakia, April 2, 1996.
(Ottawa's 7th choice, 139th overall, in 2015 Entry Draft).

			Regular Season					Playoffs				
Season	Club	League	GP	G	A	Pts	PIM	GP	G	A	Pts	PIM
2010-11	HC Kosice U18	Svk-U18	2	0	0	0	0	....	....	....	....	....
	HK Trebisov U18	Svk-U18	5	0	0	0	0	....	....	....	....	....
2011-12	HC Kosice U18	Svk-U18	38	4	10	14	26	....	....	....	....	....
2012-13	HC Kosice U18	Svk-U18	15	3	17	20	16	2	0	0	0	0
2013-14	Lulea HF U18	Swe-U18	34	11	14	25	44	5	0	2	2	6
	Lulea HF Jr.	Swe-Jr.	3	1	3	4	0	....	....	....	....	....
2014-15	Lulea HF Jr.	Swe-Jr.	23	4	8	12	74	3	0	1	1	6
	Asploven	Sweden-2	6	0	1	1	0	....	....	....	....	....
	Lulea HF	Sweden	25	0	1	1	6	....	....	....	....	....

JARVINEN, Joonas (yar-VIH-nehen, YOH-nuhs) **NSH**

Defense. Shoots left. 6'3", 212 lbs. Born, Turku, Finland, January 5, 1989.

			Regular Season					Playoffs				
Season	Club	League	GP	G	A	Pts	PIM	GP	G	A	Pts	PIM
2004-05	TPS Turku U18	Fin-U18	2	0	0	0	2	....	....	....	....	....
2005-06	TPS Turku U18	Fin-U18	34	2	4	6	50	....	....	....	....	....
	TPS Turku Jr.	Fin-Jr.	2	0	0	0	0	....	....	....	....	....
2006-07	TPS Turku U18	Fin-U18	4	0	1	1	6	6	3	3	6	5
	TPS Turku Jr.	Fin-Jr.	37	2	4	6	26	5	2	1	3	2
2007-08	Suomi U20	Finland-2	3	0	0	0	2	....	....	....	....	....
	TPS Turku Jr.	Fin-Jr.	10	5	1	6	12	....	....	....	....	....
	TPS Turku	Finland	50	1	3	4	14	2	0	1	1	0
2008-09	Suomi U20	Finland-2	3	1	0	1	10	....	....	....	....	....
	TPS Turku Jr.	Fin-Jr.	3	1	1	2	4	1	0	0	0	2
	TPS Turku	Finland	53	1	0	1	16	8	1	0	1	6
2009-10	TPS Turku	Finland	50	2	3	5	70	15	1	3	4	16
2010-11	TPS Turku	Finland	50	4	7	11	85	....	....	....	....	....
2011-12	Pelicans Lahti	Finland	57	5	18	23	125	17	3	3	6	16
2012-13	Milwaukee	AHL	75	2	9	11	124	4	0	0	0	2
2013-14	Milwaukee	AHL	54	4	8	12	68	3	0	0	0	2
2014-15	HK Sochi	KHL	39	0	1	1	59	4	0	0	0	2

Signed as a free agent by **Nashville**, May 30, 2012. Signed as a free agent by **Sochi** (KHL), June 17, 2014.

JASEK, Lukas (YAH-shehk, LOO-kuhs) **VAN**

Right wing. Shoots right. 6'1", 172 lbs. Born, Trinec, Czech Rep., August 28, 1997.
(Vancouver's 6th choice, 174th overall, in 2015 Entry Draft).

			Regular Season					Playoffs				
Season	Club	League	GP	G	A	Pts	PIM	GP	G	A	Pts	PIM
2011-12	HC Trinec U18	CzR-U18	9	2	4	6	2	....	....	....	....	....
2012-13	HC Trinec U18	CzR-U18	38	21	29	50	4	9	2	7	9	0
	HC Trinec Jr.	CzRep-Jr.	2	0	0	0	0	....	....	....	....	....
2013-14	Sodertalje SK U18	Swe-U18	15	5	7	12	4	....	....	....	....	....
	Sodertalje SK Jr.	Swe-Jr.	25	2	2	4	10	....	....	....	....	....
2014-15	HC Trinec Jr.	CzRep-Jr.	24	10	17	27	6	....	....	....	....	....
	HC Ocelari Trinec	CzRep	27	0	2	2	4	1	0	0	0	0
	HC Trinec U18	CzR-U18	....	....	....	....	....	2	1	1	2	6

JENKINS, Kyle (JEHN-kihnz, KIGHL) **CAR**

Defense. Shoots left. 6'1", 175 lbs. Born, Brampton, ON, April 22, 1996.
(Carolina's 7th choice, 187th overall, in 2014 Entry Draft).

			Regular Season					Playoffs				
Season	Club	League	GP	G	A	Pts	PIM	GP	G	A	Pts	PIM
2009-10	Mississauga Rebels	GTHL	75	10	22	32	30	....	....	....	....	....
2010-11	Mississauga Rebels	GTHL	78	8	37	45	24	....	....	....	....	....
2011-12	Mississauga Rebels	GTHL	77	15	30	45	44	....	....	....	....	....
2012-13	Oakville Blades	ON-Jr.A	46	9	20	29	47	6	1	2	3	16
	Sault Ste. Marie	OHL	1	0	0	0	0	....	....	....	....	....
2013-14	Sault Ste. Marie	OHL	63	7	18	25	28	9	1	0	1	8
2014-15	Sault Ste. Marie	OHL	38	5	19	24	26	....	....	....	....	....
	Peterborough	OHL	32	2	10	12	10	5	1	1	2	2

JENSEN, Nick (JEHN-suhn, NIHK) **DET**

Defense. Shoots right. 6', 190 lbs. Born, St. Paul, MN, September 21, 1990.
(Detroit's 5th choice, 150th overall, in 2009 Entry Draft).

			Regular Season					Playoffs				
Season	Club	League	GP	G	A	Pts	PIM	GP	G	A	Pts	PIM
2006-07	Rogers Royals	High-MN	21	20	17	37	....	....	....	....	....	....
2007-08	Rogers Royals	High-MN	14	14	13	27	....	....	....	....	....	....
2008-09	Green Bay	USHL	52	5	17	22	27	7	0	1	1	2
2009-10	Green Bay	USHL	53	6	21	27	35	12	2	6	8	6
2010-11	St. Cloud State	WCHA	38	5	18	23	18	....	....	....	....	....
2011-12	St. Cloud State	WCHA	39	6	26	32	4	....	....	....	....	....
2012-13	St. Cloud State	WCHA	42	4	27	31	14	....	....	....	....	....
2013-14	Grand Rapids	AHL	45	0	9	9	8	10	0	1	1	2
	Toledo Walleye	ECHL	3	0	0	0	0	....	....	....	....	....
2014-15	Grand Rapids	AHL	75	6	21	27	15	16	0	3	3	4

WCHA First All-Star Team (2013) • NCAA West First All-American Team (2013)

JENYS, Pavel (YEH-nihsh, PAH-vehl) **MIN**

Center. Shoots left. 6'3", 203 lbs. Born, Brno, Czech Republic, April 2, 1996.
(Minnesota's 8th choice, 199th overall, in 2014 Entry Draft).

			Regular Season					Playoffs				
Season	Club	League	GP	G	A	Pts	PIM	GP	G	A	Pts	PIM
2010-11	Brno U18	CzR-U18	3	1	0	1	0	....	....	....	....	....
2011-12	Brno U18	CzR-U18	33	8	9	17	18	2	0	0	0	2
2012-13	Brno U18	CzR-U18	9	6	9	15	6	3	0	2	2	2
	Brno Jr.	CzRep-Jr.	29	7	8	15	12	....	....	....	....	....
	HC Kometa Brno	CzRep	1	0	0	0	0	....	....	....	....	....
2013-14	Brno Jr.	CzRep-Jr.	26	13	6	19	35	....	....	....	....	....
	HC Kometa Brno	CzRep	29	2	0	2	4	....	....	....	....	....
	Brno U18	CzR-U18	....	....	....	....	....	10	10	3	13	6
2014-15	Sudbury Wolves	OHL	63	15	30	45	45	....	....	....	....	....
	Iowa Wild	AHL	8	0	3	3	0	....	....	....	....	....

JEVPALOVS, Nikita (yehv-PAH-lahf, nih-KEE-tuh) **S.J.**

Right wing. Shoots right. 6'1", 210 lbs. Born, Riga, Latvia, September 9, 1994.

			Regular Season					Playoffs				
Season	Club	League	GP	G	A	Pts	PIM	GP	G	A	Pts	PIM
2012-13	Blainville-Bois.	QMJHL	60	18	21	39	36	15	3	5	8	2
2013-14	Blainville-Bois.	QMJHL	61	28	26	54	32	20	10	6	16	8
2014-15	Blainville-Bois.	QMJHL	64	49	51	100	30	5	1	5	6	4

QMJHL Second All-Star Team (2015)

Signed as a free agent by **San Jose**, January 26, 2015.

JOHANSSON, Emil (yoh-HAHN-suhn, eh-MIHL) **BOS**

Defense. Shoots left. 6', 189 lbs. Born, Vaxjo, Sweden, May 6, 1996.
(Boston's 5th choice, 206th overall, in 2014 Entry Draft).

			Regular Season					Playoffs				
Season	Club	League	GP	G	A	Pts	PIM	GP	G	A	Pts	PIM
2010-11	Aseda IF Jr.	Swe-Jr.	....	0	3	3	22	....	....	....	....	....
	Aseda IF	Sweden-4	31	1	2	3	12	....	....	....	....	....
2011-12	Aseda IF	Sweden-4	14	4	0	4	14	....	....	....	....	....
2012-13	HV 71 U18	Swe-U18	32	5	12	17	14	....	....	....	....	....
	HV 71 Jr.	Swe-Jr.	1	1	1	2	0	....	....	....	....	....
2013-14	HV 71 U18	Swe-U18	6	2	3	5	20	....	....	....	....	....
	HV 71 Jr.	Swe-Jr.	42	2	7	9	28	....	....	....	....	....
2014-15	HV 71 Jr.	Swe-Jr.	11	0	2	2	10	3	0	0	0	2
	HV 71 Jonkoping	Sweden	35	0	1	1	12	6	0	0	0	4

JOHNS, Stephen (JAWNZ, STEE-vehn) **DAL**

Defense. Shoots right. 6'3", 229 lbs. Born, Ellwood City, PA, April 18, 1992.
(Chicago's 5th choice, 60th overall, in 2010 Entry Draft).

			Regular Season					Playoffs				
Season	Club	League	GP	G	A	Pts	PIM	GP	G	A	Pts	PIM
2007-08	Pittsburgh Hornets	MWEHL	26	4	7	11	24	....	....	....	....	....
	Pittsburgh Hornets	Minor-PA	50	12	22	34	46	....	....	....	....	....
2008-09	USNTDP	NAHL	31	3	5	8	30	....	....	....	....	....
	USNTDP	U-17	16	2	6	8	20	....	....	....	....	....
2009-10	USNTDP	USHL	23	1	7	8	29	....	....	....	....	....
	USNTDP	U-18	39	2	9	11	38	....	....	....	....	....
2010-11	U. of Notre Dame	CCHA	44	2	11	13	*98	....	....	....	....	....
2011-12	U. of Notre Dame	CCHA	39	4	6	10	71	....	....	....	....	....
2012-13	U. of Notre Dame	CCHA	41	1	13	14	62	....	....	....	....	....
2013-14	U. of Notre Dame	H-East	40	8	12	20	69	....	....	....	....	....
	Rockford IceHogs	AHL	8	1	4	5	4	....	....	....	....	....
2014-15	Rockford IceHogs	AHL	51	4	17	21	44	8	3	4	7	4

Hockey East Second All-Star Team (2014)

Traded to **Dallas** by **Chicago** with Patrick Sharp for Trevor Daley and Ryan Garbutt, July 12, 2015.

JOHNSON, Andreas (JAWN-suhn, ahn-DRAY-uhs) **TOR**

Left wing. Shoots left. 5'10", 183 lbs. Born, Gavle, Sweden, November 21, 1994.
(Toronto's 5th choice, 202nd overall, in 2013 Entry Draft).

			Regular Season					Playoffs				
Season	Club	League	GP	G	A	Pts	PIM	GP	G	A	Pts	PIM
2009-10	Frolunda U18	Swe-U18	5	1	1	2	0	....	....	....	....	....
2010-11	Frolunda U18	Swe-U18	27	23	22	45	26	5	3	1	4	2
	Frolunda Jr.	Swe-Jr.	30	9	5	14	4	3	0	1	1	0
2011-12	Frolunda U18	Swe-U18	6	9	5	14	4	4	2	4	6	4
	Frolunda Jr.	Swe-Jr.	42	19	13	32	75	2	0	0	0	0
2012-13	Frolunda Jr.	Swe-Jr.	42	23	31	54	54	4	1	1	2	12
	Frolunda	Sweden	7	1	0	1	0	5	0	0	0	0
2013-14	Frolunda Jr.	Swe-Jr.	4	1	4	5	0	....	....	....	....	....
	Frolunda	Sweden	44	15	9	24	2	7	1	0	1	4
2014-15	Frolunda	Sweden	55	22	13	35	34	8	2	2	4	4

JOHNSON, Ben (JAWN-suhn, BEHN) **N.J.**

Right wing. Shoots left. 6', 195 lbs. Born, Hancock, MI, June 7, 1994.
(New Jersey's 3rd choice, 90th overall, in 2012 Entry Draft).

			Regular Season					Playoffs				
Season	Club	League	GP	G	A	Pts	PIM	GP	G	A	Pts	PIM
2009-10	Calumet High	High-MI	....	....	....	59	....	....	....	....	....	....
	Ojibway Eagles	Minor-MI	21	8	11	19	....	....	....	....	....	....
	Marquette	Minor-MI	2	0	1	1	2	....	....	....	....	....
2010-11	Calumet High	High-MI	30	37	40	77	....	....	....	....	....	....
	Det. Lit. Caesars	T1EHL	13	3	2	5	16	....	....	....	....	....
	Det. Lit. Caesars	Other	9	3	1	4	0	....	....	....	....	....
	Fargo Force	USHL	5	0	0	0	2	....	....	....	....	....
	USNTDP	USHL	2	1	0	1	0	....	....	....	....	....
	USNTDP	U-17	2	3	1	4	0	....	....	....	....	....
2011-12	Windsor Spitfires	OHL	68	18	20	38	44	4	0	2	2	0
2012-13	Windsor Spitfires	OHL	64	20	17	37	32	....	....	....	....	....
2013-14	Windsor Spitfires	OHL	59	28	25	53	30	4	4	2	6	2
	Albany Devils	AHL	5	0	1	1	0	....	....	....	....	....
2014-15	Albany Devils	AHL	28	1	1	2	8	....	....	....	....	....
	Orlando	ECHL	12	2	6	8	0	4	2	2	4	0

• Re-assigned to **Orlando** (ECHL) by **New Jersey**, March 2, 2015.

JOHNSON, Luke (JAWN-suhn, LOOK) **CHI**

Center. Shoots right. 5'9", 151 lbs. Born, Grand Forks, ND, September 19, 1994.
(Chicago's 6th choice, 134th overall, in 2013 Entry Draft).

			Regular Season					Playoffs				
Season	Club	League	GP	G	A	Pts	PIM	GP	G	A	Pts	PIM
2008-09	Gr. Forks R.R.R.	High-ND	27	9	17	26	....	....	....	....	....	....
2009-10	Grand Forks C.K.	High-ND	27	17	29	46	....	....	....	....	....	....
2010-11	Team Great Plains	UMHSEL	20	9	12	21	26	3	0	1	1	0
	Grand Forks C.K.	High-ND	25	17	25	42	....	....	....	....	....	....
2011-12	Lincoln Stars	USHL	55	20	35	55	52	8	1	1	2	2
2012-13	Lincoln Stars	USHL	57	19	27	46	32	5	0	0	0	0
2013-14	North Dakota	NCHC	42	8	13	21	26	....	....	....	....	....
2014-15	North Dakota	NCHC	42	11	13	24	54	....	....	....	....	....

JOHNSON, Steven (JAWN-suhn, STEE-vehn) **L.A.**

Defense. Shoots left. 6', 185 lbs. Born, Excelsior, MN, June 27, 1994.
(Los Angeles' 5th choice, 120th overall, in 2014 Entry Draft).

			Regular Season					Playoffs				
Season	Club	League	GP	G	A	Pts	PIM	GP	G	A	Pts	PIM
2010-11	Minnetonka High	High-MN	25	0	8	8	0	2	0	0	0	0
2011-12	Minnetonka High	High-MN	25	2	2	4	0	3	2	0	2	2
2012-13	Aberdeen Wings	NAHL	59	6	7	13	32	....	....	....	....	....
2013-14	USNTDP	USHL	56	5	26	31	6	4	0	2	2	0
2014-15	U. of Minnesota	Big Ten	11	0	1	1	4	....	....	....	....	....

JOHNSTON, Ross (JAWN-stuhn, RAWS) **NYI**

Left wing. Shoots left. 6'4", 225 lbs. Born, Charlottetown, PEI, February 18, 1994.

			Regular Season					Playoffs				
Season	Club	League	GP	G	A	Pts	PIM	GP	G	A	Pts	PIM
2010-11	Charlottetown	NBPEI	34	20	*37	57	109	5	5	3	8	20
	Summerside	MJrHL	2	2	1	3	4	....	....	....	....	....
2011-12	Summerside	MJrHL	23	12	17	29	55	....	....	....	....	....
	Moncton Wildcats	QMJHL	38	2	5	7	55	2	0	0	0	8
2012-13	Moncton Wildcats	QMJHL	53	12	15	27	96	3	0	0	0	4
2013-14	Victoriaville Tigres	QMJHL	60	10	15	25	139	5	0	3	3	6
2014-15	Charlottetown	QMJHL	44	18	14	32	124	10	4	7	11	28
	Bridgeport	AHL	2	0	0	0	0	....	....	....	....	....

Signed as a free agent by **NY Islanders**, March 31, 2015.

JONES, Caleb (JOHNZ, KA-lehb) **EDM**

Defense. Shoots left. 6', 194 lbs. Born, Arlington, TX, June 6, 1997.
(Edmonton's 2nd choice, 117th overall, in 2015 Entry Draft).

			Regular Season					Playoffs				
Season	Club	League	GP	G	A	Pts	PIM	GP	G	A	Pts	PIM
2012-13	Dal. Stars MM	T1EHL	40	2	17	19	36	4	0	1	1	2
2013-14	USNTDP	USHL	33	0	7	7	57	....	....	....	....	....
	USNTDP	U-17	19	1	7	8	33	....	....	....	....	....
2014-15	USNTDP	USHL	25	2	6	8	28	....	....	....	....	....
	USNTDP	U-18	40	4	13	17	22	....	....	....	....	....

JONES, Kellen (JOHNZ, KEHL-ehn)

Left wing. Shoots left. 5'9", 164 lbs. Born, Montrose, BC, August 16, 1990.
(Edmonton's 11th choice, 202nd overall, in 2010 Entry Draft).

			Regular Season					Playoffs				
Season	Club	League	GP	G	A	Pts	PIM	GP	G	A	Pts	PIM
2006-07	Beaver Valley	KIJHL	50	32	35	67	48	13	8	4	12	6
	Vernon Vipers	BCHL	2	0	1	1	0	16	3	5	8	8
2007-08	Vernon Vipers	BCHL	60	12	55	67	30	10	7	4	11	8
2008-09	Vernon Vipers	BCHL	51	15	37	52	16	17	6	12	18	8
2009-10	Vernon Vipers	BCHL	41	12	41	53	18	19	5	14	19	14
2010-11	Quinnipiac	ECAC	38	8	14	22	33	....	....	....	....	....
2011-12	Quinnipiac	ECAC	36	14	22	36	39	....	....	....	....	....
2012-13	Quinnipiac	ECAC	43	13	14	27	24	....	....	....	....	....
2013-14	Quinnipiac	ECAC	40	18	24	42	27	....	....	....	....	....
	Oklahoma City	AHL	5	0	1	1	0	....	....	....	....	....
2014-15	Oklahoma City	AHL	49	5	10	15	10	10	2	1	3	0
	Bakersfield	ECHL	27	7	18	25	12	....	....	....	....	....

ECAC Second All-Star Team (2014)

JORG, Mauro (YOHRG, MAHW-roh) **N.J.**

Right wing. Shoots left. 6', 200 lbs. Born, Chur, Switz., April 29, 1990.
(New Jersey's 5th choice, 204th overall, in 2010 Entry Draft).

			Regular Season					Playoffs				
Season	Club	League	GP	G	A	Pts	PIM	GP	G	A	Pts	PIM
2006-07	HC Lugano Jr.	Swiss-Jr.	4	2	3	5	6	....	....	....	....	....
	EHC Arosa	Swiss-3	7	4	1	5	8	1	0	0	0	2
	EHC Chur	Swiss-2	20	1	1	2	0	....	....	....	....	....
2007-08	Switzerland U20	Swiss-2	1	0	0	0	0	....	....	....	....	....
	EHC Chur Jr.	Swiss-Jr.	4	4	1	5	18	....	....	....	....	....
	EHC Chur	Swiss-2	40	11	9	20	33	....	....	....	....	....
	HC Lugano Jr.	Swiss-Jr.	8	5	2	7	12	....	....	....	....	....
	HC Lugano	Swiss	....	....	....	....	....	1	0	0	0	0
2008-09	HC Lugano	Swiss	47	3	3	6	6	7	0	0	0	0
	Switzerland U20	Swiss-2	5	1	0	1	0	....	....	....	....	....
	HC Ceresio Lugano	Swiss-3	1	0	0	0	0	....	....	....	....	....
	HC Lugano Jr.	Swiss-Jr.	3	0	3	3	0	2	0	3	3	4
2009-10	HC Lugano	Swiss	44	1	7	8	14	4	0	0	0	0
	HC Lugano Jr.	Swiss-Jr.	1	0	0	0	0	....	....	....	....	....
	EHC Visp	Swiss-2	....	....	....	....	....	7	0	1	1	0
2010-11	HC Lugano	Swiss	50	3	9	12	26	4	0	0	0	2
2011-12	HC Lugano	Swiss	48	4	3	7	8	6	0	2	2	0
	Sierre	Swiss-2	2	3	1	4	2	....	....	....	....	....
2012-13	Rapperswil	Swiss	48	4	6	10	10	12	0	4	4	4
2013-14	Rapperswil	Swiss	52	6	11	17	31	6	2	0	2	0
2014-15	HC Davos	Swiss	49	14	8	22	14	14	2	2	4	2

JOSEPH, Mathieu (JOH-seph, MA-tyew) **T.B.**

Right wing. Shoots right. 6'1", 166 lbs. Born, Laval, QC, February 9, 1997.
(Tampa Bay's 6th choice, 120th overall, in 2015 Entry Draft).

			Regular Season					Playoffs				
Season	Club	League	GP	G	A	Pts	PIM	GP	G	A	Pts	PIM
2012-13	Antoine-Girouard	Minor-QC	34	26	23	49	61	....	....	....	....	....
	Antoine-Girouard	QAAA	3	0	1	1	2	2	0	1	1	0
2013-14	Antoine-Girouard	QAAA	32	11	25	36	68	....	....	....	....	....
	Saint John	QMJHL	30	1	10	11	10	....	....	....	....	....
2014-15	Saint John	QMJHL	59	21	21	42	46	5	1	2	3	4

JOSEPHS, Troy (JOH-sehfs, TROI) **PIT**

Center. Shoots left. 6'1", 184 lbs. Born, Whitby, ON, May 9, 1994.
(Pittsburgh's 6th choice, 209th overall, in 2013 Entry Draft).

			Regular Season					Playoffs				
Season	Club	League	GP	G	A	Pts	PIM	GP	G	A	Pts	PIM
2009-10	Whitby Wildcats	Minor-ON	70	27	25	52	52	4	0	0	0	6
2010-11	PEAC Panthers	High-ON	52	29	38	67	38	....	....	....	....	....
	Pickering Panthers	ON-Jr.A	7	4	1	5	4	....	....	....	....	....
2011-12	St. Michael's	ON-Jr.A	41	11	13	24	10	5	0	0	0	2
2012-13	St. Michael's	ON-Jr.A	42	17	20	37	64	24	7	13	20	38
2013-14	Clarkson Knights	ECAC	33	2	3	5	60	....	....	....	....	....
2014-15	Clarkson Knights	ECAC	36	3	14	17	14	....	....	....	....	....

JOSHUA, Dakota (JAW-shoo-wuh, duh-KOH-tuh) **TOR**

Center. Shoots left. 6'2", 182 lbs. Born, Dearborn, MI, May 15, 1996.
(Toronto's 4th choice, 128th overall, in 2014 Entry Draft).

			Regular Season					Playoffs				
Season	Club	League	GP	G	A	Pts	PIM	GP	G	A	Pts	PIM
2012-13	Det. H-Baked U16	HPHL	18	12	10	22	18	....	....	....	....	....
	Det. H-Baked U18	HPHL	11	0	0	0	0	....	....	....	....	....
	USNTDP	USHL	6	2	0	2	2	....	....	....	....	....
	Sioux Falls	USHL	1	0	1	1	0	....	....	....	....	....
2013-14	Sioux Falls	USHL	55	17	21	38	58	3	0	0	0	8
2014-15	Sioux Falls	USHL	52	20	24	44	74	11	4	9	13	38

• Signed Letter of Intent to attend **Ohio State University** (Big Ten) in fall of 2015.

JUULSEN, Noah (JOOL-suhn, NOH-uh) **MTL**

Defense. Shoots right. 6'1", 171 lbs. Born, Surrey, BC, April 2, 1997.
(Montreal's 1st choice, 26th overall, in 2015 Entry Draft).

			Regular Season					Playoffs				
Season	Club	League	GP	G	A	Pts	PIM	GP	G	A	Pts	PIM
2012-13	Fraser Valley	BCMML	35	6	19	25	24	....	....	....	....	....
	Everett Silvertips	WHL	1	0	0	0	0	....	....	....	....	....
2013-14	Everett Silvertips	WHL	59	2	8	10	32	3	0	0	0	2
2014-15	Everett Silvertips	WHL	68	9	43	52	42	6	0	1	1	8

KADEYKIN, Alexander (ka-DAY-kihn, al-ehx-AN-duhr) **DET**

Center. Shoots left. 6'3", 213 lbs. Born, Elektrostal, Russia, October 4, 1993.
(Detroit's 7th choice, 201st overall, in 2014 Entry Draft).

			Regular Season					Playoffs				
Season	Club	League	GP	G	A	Pts	PIM	GP	G	A	Pts	PIM
2008-09	Elektrostal 2	Russia-4	12	2	4	6	0	....	....	....	....	....
2010-11	Mytischi Jr.	Russia-Jr.	48	10	19	29	42	6	1	1	2	2
2011-12	Mytischi Jr.	Russia-Jr.	60	22	36	58	20	12	7	9	16	22
2012-13	Mytischi Jr.	Russia-Jr.	26	14	29	43	4	8	4	7	11	6
	Mytischi	KHL	2	0	0	0	0	2	0	0	0	0
2013-14	Mytischi Jr.	Russia-Jr.	1	1	0	1	2	3	0	3	3	2
	Mytischi	KHL	54	8	15	23	24	3	0	0	0	0
2014-15	Mytischi	KHL	9	0	1	1	2	....	....	....	....	....
	SKA St. Petersburg	KHL	20	4	4	8	2	....	....	....	....	....

KALININ, Sergey (kah-LIH-nihn, sair-GAY) **N.J.**

Right wing. Shoots left. 6'3", 190 lbs. Born, Omsk, Russia, March 17, 1991.

			Regular Season					Playoffs				
Season	Club	League	GP	G	A	Pts	PIM	GP	G	A	Pts	PIM
2008-09	Avangard Omsk 2	Russia-3	41	5	13	18	16	....	....	....	....	....
2009-10	Omsk Jr.	Russia-Jr.	54	14	22	36	52	8	1	1	2	2
	Omsk	KHL	1	0	0	0	0	....	....	....	....	....
2010-11	Omsk Jr.	Russia-Jr.	5	1	4	5	4	....	....	....	....	....
	Omsk	KHL	24	0	1	1	0	8	0	1	1	0
2011-12	Omsk	KHL	53	9	9	18	20	19	2	1	3	10
2012-13	Omsk	KHL	26	2	6	8	10	6	1	0	1	4
2013-14	Omsk	KHL	51	8	9	17	32	11	2	5	7	4
2014-15	Omsk	KHL	58	12	13	25	49	6	0	0	0	2

Signed as a free agent by **New Jersey**, May 29, 2015.

KAMENEV, Vladislav (KA-men-ehv, vla-dih-SLAHV) **NSH**

Left wing. Shoots left. 6'2", 203 lbs. Born, Orsk, Russia, August 12, 1996.
(Nashville's 2nd choice, 42nd overall, in 2014 Entry Draft).

			Regular Season					Playoffs				
Season	Club	League	GP	G	A	Pts	PIM	GP	G	A	Pts	PIM
2012-13	Magnitogorsk Jr.	Russia-Jr.	36	9	6	15	22	3	0	0	0	0
2013-14	Yuzhny Ural Orsk	Russia-2	3	0	1	1	2	1	0	0	0	0
	Magnitogorsk	KHL	16	1	0	1	2	....	....	....	....	....
	Magnitogorsk Jr.	Russia-Jr.	15	4	6	10	12	5	1	2	3	4
2014-15	Magnitogorsk	KHL	41	6	4	10	10	10	1	0	1	0

KANTOR, Michael (KAN-tohr, MIGH-kuhl) **NYR**

Right wing. Shoots right. 6'1", 196 lbs. Born, Lake Forest, IL, February 2, 1992.

			Regular Season					Playoffs				
Season	Club	League	GP	G	A	Pts	PIM	GP	G	A	Pts	PIM
2009-10	Albert Lea	NAHL	24	2	3	5	108	....	....	....	....	....
	Saginaw Spirit	OHL	29	4	8	12	71	6	0	0	0	10
2010-11	Saginaw Spirit	OHL	35	8	5	13	85	....	....	....	....	....
	Sault Ste. Marie	OHL	17	3	4	7	35	....	....	....	....	....
2011-12	Sault Ste. Marie	OHL	34	2	8	10	76	....	....	....	....	....
	Sudbury Wolves	OHL	26	6	13	19	60	....	....	....	....	....
2012-13	Sudbury Wolves	OHL	56	20	13	33	93	9	2	2	4	12
2013-14	Hartford Wolf Pack	AHL	27	0	0	0	113	....	....	....	....	....
	Greenville	ECHL	3	0	3	3	12	....	....	....	....	....
2014-15	Hartford Wolf Pack	AHL	1	0	0	0	14	....	....	....	....	....
	Greenville	ECHL	2	1	1	2	0	....	....	....	....	....

Signed as a free agent by **NY Rangers**, April 20, 2013.

KANZIG, Keegan (KAN-zihg, KEE-guhn) **CGY**

Defense. Shoots left. 6'7", 245 lbs. Born, Athabasca, AB, February 26, 1995.
(Calgary's 4th choice, 67th overall, in 2013 Entry Draft).

			Regular Season					Playoffs				
Season	Club	League	GP	G	A	Pts	PIM	GP	G	A	Pts	PIM
2010-11	Ft. Saskatchewan	AMHL	31	4	8	12	82	3	0	0	0	18
2011-12	Victoria Royals	WHL	63	0	2	2	66	4	0	0	0	8
2012-13	Victoria Royals	WHL	70	0	7	7	159	6	1	0	1	10
2014-15	Victoria Royals	WHL	21	0	6	6	51	....	....	....	....	....
	Calgary Hitmen	WHL	49	3	13	16	*115	17	0	3	3	31

KAPANEN, Kasperi (KA-puh-nihn, kas-PAIR-ee) **TOR**

Right wing. Shoots right. 6', 178 lbs. Born, Kuopio, Finland, July 23, 1996.
(Pittsburgh's 1st choice, 22nd overall, in 2014 Entry Draft).

			Regular Season					Playoffs				
Season	Club	League	GP	G	A	Pts	PIM	GP	G	A	Pts	PIM
2011-12	KalPa Kuopio U18	Fin-U18	27	13	11	24	8	2	0	0	0	0
2012-13	KalPa Kuopio U18	Fin-U18	3	3	3	6	0	....	....	....	....	....
	KalPa Kuopio Jr.	Fin-Jr.	36	14	15	29	16	....	....	....	....	....
	KalPa Kuopio	Finland	13	4	0	4	2	4	0	1	1	2
2013-14	KalPa Kuopio U18	Fin-U18	2	5	1	6	0	4	6	1	7	0
	KalPa Kuopio	Finland	47	7	7	14	10	....	....	....	....	....
2014-15	KalPa Kuopio	Finland	41	11	10	21	14	6	0	5	5	2
	Wilkes-Barre	AHL	4	1	1	2	0	7	3	2	5	0

Traded to **Toronto** by **Pittsburgh** with Nick Spaling, Scott Harrington, New Jersey's 3rd round choice (previously acquired) in 2016 Entry Draft and future considerations for Phil Kessel, Tyler Biggs, Tim Erixon and future considerations, July 1, 2015.

KAPRIZOV, Kirill (kah-PREE-zawf, kih-REEL) **MIN**

Left wing. Shoots left. 5'9", 185 lbs. Born, Novokuznetsk, Russia, April 26, 1997.
(Minnesota's 4th choice, 135th overall, in 2015 Entry Draft).

			Regular Season					Playoffs				
Season	Club	League	GP	G	A	Pts	PIM	GP	G	A	Pts	PIM
2013-14	Novokuznetsk Jr.	Russia-Jr.	52	18	16	34	30	8	1	2	3	2
2014-15	Novokuznetsk	KHL	31	4	4	8	6	....	....	....	....	....
	Novokuznetsk Jr.	Russia-Jr.	3	0	2	2	2	3	0	0	0	2

KARABACEK, Vaclav (kahr-ah-BAH-chehk, VATS-lav) **BUF**

Right wing. Shoots right. 6', 198 lbs. Born, Brandys nad Labem, Czech Rep., May 2, 1996.
(Buffalo's 4th choice, 49th overall, in 2014 Entry Draft).

			Regular Season					Playoffs				
Season	Club	League	GP	G	A	Pts	PIM	GP	G	A	Pts	PIM
2011-12	HC Letnany U18	CzR-U18	25	15	14	29	18	....	....	....	....	....
2012-13	EC Salzburg U18	Austria-U18	21	26	19	45	55	....	....	....	....	....
	EC Salzburg Jr. II	Austria-Jr.	5	2	1	3	2	....	....	....	....	....
2013-14	Gatineau	QMJHL	65	21	26	47	40	9	6	6	12	10
2014-15	Gatineau	QMJHL	31	11	14	25	44	....	....	....	....	....
	Baie-Comeau	QMJHL	28	6	9	15	18	....	....	....	....	....

KARJALAINEN, Miro (kah-ree-uh-LIGH-nuhn, MEE-roh) **DAL**

Defense. Shoots right. 6'5", 205 lbs. Born, Espoo, Finland, May 23, 1996.
(Dallas' 6th choice, 135th overall, in 2014 Entry Draft).

			Regular Season					Playoffs				
Season	Club	League	GP	G	A	Pts	PIM	GP	G	A	Pts	PIM
2012-13	K-Vantaa U18	Fin-U18	2	0	0	0	0	....	....	....	....	....
	EKS Espoo U17	Fin-U17	1	0	0	0	25	....	....	....	....	....
	EKS Espoo U18	Fin-U18	4	4	2	6	2	....	....	....	....	....
	EKS Espoo	Finland-5	2	0	0	0	0	....	....	....	....	....
2013-14	K-Vantaa U18	Fin-U18	1	0	0	0	0	....	....	....	....	....
	Jokerit U18	Fin-U18	38	1	7	8	57	11	2	3	5	6
2014-15	HIFK Helsinki Jr.	Fin-Jr.	10	0	1	1	8	3	2	0	2	0

KARLSSON, Anton (KAHRL-suhn, AN-tawn) **ARI**

Left wing. Shoots left. 6'1", 192 lbs. Born, Lerum, Sweden, August 3, 1996.
(Arizona's 4th choice, 87th overall, in 2014 Entry Draft).

			Regular Season					Playoffs				
Season	Club	League	GP	G	A	Pts	PIM	GP	G	A	Pts	PIM
2010-11	Frolunda U18	Swe-U18	4	0	1	1	0	....	....	....	....	....
2011-12	Frolunda U18	Swe-U18	28	12	19	31	32	....	....	....	....	....
2012-13	Frolunda U18	Swe-U18	23	20	19	39	64	3	1	3	4	0
	Frolunda Jr.	Swe-Jr.	17	4	4	8	4	3	1	1	2	0
2013-14	Frolunda U18	Swe-U18	5	2	5	7	10	5	3	3	6	2
	Mora IK	Sweden-2	9	0	0	0	2	....	....	....	....	....
	Frolunda Jr.	Swe-Jr.	28	12	10	22	88	3	0	2	2	2
2014-15	Skelleftea AIK	Sweden	6	0	1	1	0	....	....	....	....	....
	Skelleftea AIK Jr.	Swe-Jr.	16	8	6	14	37	....	....	....	....	....
	Frolunda	Sweden	9	0	1	1	2	....	....	....	....	....
	Frolunda Jr.	Swe-Jr.	16	6	9	15	4	8	3	7	10	6

KARLSSON, Erik (KAHRL-suhn, AIR-ihk) CAR

Center/Left wing. Shoots left. 6', 170 lbs. Born, Lerum, Sweden, July 28, 1994.
(Carolina's 4th choice, 99th overall, in 2012 Entry Draft).

			Regular Season					Playoffs				
Season	Club	League	GP	G	A	Pts	PIM	GP	G	A	Pts	PIM
2009-10	Frolunda U18	Swe-U18	13	2	3	5	2	1	0	0	0	27
2010-11	Frolunda U18	Swe-U18	26	20	22	42	12	4	1	1	2	4
	Frolunda Jr.	Swe-Jr.	29	4	9	13	41	7	1	1	2	4
2011-12	Frolunda U18	Swe-U18	4	3	7	10	8	4	2	3	5	4
	Frolunda Jr.	Swe-Jr.	47	14	19	33	70	2	0	0	0	0
2012-13	Frolunda	Sweden	5	0	0	0	0	....	....	....	....	....
	Karlskrona HK	Sweden-2	2	0	1	1	0	....	....	....	....	....
	Frolunda Jr.	Swe-Jr.	40	10	25	35	48	6	1	5	6	0
2013-14	Frolunda Jr.	Swe-Jr.	9	5	10	15	2	....	....	....	....	....
	Frolunda	Sweden	41	5	1	6	6	6	1	0	1	0
2014-15	Frolunda	Sweden	53	1	2	3	6	7	0	0	0	2

KARLSTROM, Marcus (KAHRL-struhm, MAHR-kuhs) WPG

Defense. Shoots right. 6'2", 168 lbs. Born, Trangsund, Sweden, January 6, 1995.
(Winnipeg's 10th choice, 194th overall, in 2013 Entry Draft).

			Regular Season					Playoffs				
Season	Club	League	GP	G	A	Pts	PIM	GP	G	A	Pts	PIM
2010-11	SDE U18	Swe-U18	3	0	1	1	2	....	....	....	....	....
2011-12	AIK Solna U18	Swe-U18	38	1	7	8	20	....	....	....	....	....
2012-13	AIK Solna U18	Swe-U18	40	14	30	44	38	5	0	1	1	2
	AIK Solna Jr.	Swe-Jr.	5	1	0	1	0	....	....	....	....	....
2013-14	AIK Solna	Sweden	1	0	0	0	0	....	....	....	....	....
	AIK Solna Jr.	Swe-Jr.	44	10	17	27	38	2	0	0	0	2
2014-15	Mora IK	Sweden-2	29	0	2	2	4	....	....	....	....	....
	Visby-Roma HK	Sweden-3	14	1	5	6	6	....	....	....	....	....
	Mora IK Jr.	Swe-Jr.	15	3	2	5	8	2	0	5	5	0

KARNAUKHOV, Pavel (kahr-nuh-OO-kawf, PAH-vehl) CGY

Center. Shoots left. 6'3", 200 lbs. Born, Minsk, Belarus, March 15, 1997.
(Calgary's 3rd choice, 136th overall, in 2015 Entry Draft).

			Regular Season					Playoffs				
Season	Club	League	GP	G	A	Pts	PIM	GP	G	A	Pts	PIM
2013-14	CSKA Jr.	Russia-Jr.	48	13	16	29	56	11	3	2	5	4
2014-15	Calgary Hitmen	WHL	69	20	22	42	51	17	6	5	11	10

KASE, David (kah-SHEH, DAY-vihd) PHI

Right wing. Shoots left. 5'11", 164 lbs. Born, Kadan, Czech Rep., January 28, 1997.
(Philadelphia's 7th choice, 128th overall, in 2015 Entry Draft).

			Regular Season					Playoffs				
Season	Club	League	GP	G	A	Pts	PIM	GP	G	A	Pts	PIM
2011-12	Chomutov U18	CzR-U18	13	3	2	5	2	1	0	0	0	0
2012-13	Chomutov U18	CzR-U18	25	5	21	26	8	....	....	....	....	....
	KLH Chomutov Jr.	CzRep-Jr.	4	0	1	1	0	....	....	....	....	....
2013-14	Chomutov U18	CzR-U18	14	9	22	31	4	3	1	2	3	0
	KLH Chomutov Jr.	CzRep-Jr.	35	11	19	30	10	11	2	1	3	8
2014-15	KLH Chomutov Jr.	CzRep-Jr.	8	7	8	15	2	9	5	7	12	12
	Pirati Chomutov	CzRep-2	30	7	7	14	10	1	0	0	0	0

KASE, Ondrej (kah-SHEH, AWN-dray) ANA

Left wing. Shoots left. 6', 165 lbs. Born, Kadan, Czech Rep., November 8, 1995.
(Anaheim's 5th choice, 205th overall, in 2014 Entry Draft).

			Regular Season					Playoffs				
Season	Club	League	GP	G	A	Pts	PIM	GP	G	A	Pts	PIM
2010-11	Chomutov U18	CzR-U18	8	3	3	6	2	....	....	....	....	....
2011-12	Chomutov U18	CzR-U18	38	18	26	44	14	2	0	2	2	0
2012-13	Chomutov U18	CzR-U18	14	10	16	26	6	....	....	....	....	....
	KLH Chomutov Jr.	CzRep-Jr.	22	9	7	16	18	3	0	0	0	2
	SK Kadan	CzRep-2	9	2	1	3	2	4	1	0	1	0
2013-14	KLH Chomutov Jr.	CzRep-Jr.	7	5	10	15	12	1	0	2	2	0
	SK Kadan	CzRep-2	5	3	1	4	0	....	....	....	....	....
	Pirati Chomutov	CzRep	43	5	5	10	10	....	....	....	....	....
	Pirati Chomutov	CzRep-Q	10	2	3	5	0	....	....	....	....	....
2014-15	KLH Chomutov Jr.	CzRep-Jr.	3	1	7	8	0	....	....	....	....	....
	Pirati Chomutov	CzRep-2	49	10	17	27	8	11	6	5	11	4

KEA, Justin (KEE-a, JUHS-tihn) BUF

Center. Shoots left. 6'4", 221 lbs. Born, Woodville, ON, February 7, 1994.
(Buffalo's 4th choice, 73rd overall, in 2012 Entry Draft).

			Regular Season					Playoffs				
Season	Club	League	GP	G	A	Pts	PIM	GP	G	A	Pts	PIM
2009-10	Cent. Ont. Wolves	Minor-ON	51	22	22	44	44	....	....	....	....	....
2010-11	Saginaw Spirit	OHL	62	4	2	6	49	10	0	1	1	0
2011-12	Saginaw Spirit	OHL	65	3	11	14	76	12	1	4	5	2
2012-13	Saginaw Spirit	OHL	68	22	26	48	102	4	1	0	1	7
2013-14	Saginaw Spirit	OHL	58	22	27	49	97	5	1	3	4	0
	Rochester	AHL	1	0	0	0	0	....	....	....	....	....
2014-15	Rochester	AHL	26	2	0	2	56	....	....	....	....	....
	Elmira Jackals	ECHL	35	5	7	12	65	....	....	....	....	....

KELLY, Dan (KEHL-lee, DAN) N.J.

Defense. Shoots left. 6'1", 210 lbs. Born, Morrisonville, NY, May 17, 1989.

			Regular Season					Playoffs				
Season	Club	League	GP	G	A	Pts	PIM	GP	G	A	Pts	PIM
2003-04	Beekmantown	High-NY	STATISTICS NOT AVAILABLE									
2004-05	Pembroke	ON-Jr.A	50	2	12	14	80	11	0	1	1	2
2005-06	Pembroke	ON-Jr.A	46	2	15	17	95	11	0	3	3	18
	Kitchener Rangers	OHL	9	0	3	3	8	....	....	....	....	....
2006-07	Kitchener Rangers	OHL	59	0	19	19	79	9	1	1	2	10
2007-08	Kitchener Rangers	OHL	65	1	17	18	61	8	0	2	2	4
2008-09	Kitchener Rangers	OHL	44	4	11	15	30	....	....	....	....	....
2009-10	Kitchener Rangers	OHL	58	6	21	27	99	20	4	9	13	23
2010-11	Albany Devils	AHL	61	2	5	7	71	....	....	....	....	....
2011-12	Albany Devils	AHL	54	2	4	6	93	....	....	....	....	....
2012-13	Albany Devils	AHL	47	2	6	8	62	....	....	....	....	....
2013-14	Albany Devils	AHL	71	3	14	17	86	1	0	0	0	2
2014-15	Albany Devils	AHL	64	1	10	11	130	....	....	....	....	....

Signed as a free agent by **New Jersey**, May 19, 2010.

KEMPE, Adrian (KEHM-peh, AY-dree-uhn) L.A.

Left wing. Shoots left. 6'1", 187 lbs. Born, Kramfors, Sweden, September 13, 1996.
(Los Angeles' 1st choice, 29th overall, in 2014 Entry Draft).

			Regular Season					Playoffs				
Season	Club	League	GP	G	A	Pts	PIM	GP	G	A	Pts	PIM
2010-11	Kramfors U18	Swe-U18	25	1	7	8	10	3	1	0	1	0
2011-12	Djurgarden U18	Swe-U18	34	10	10	20	24	4	0	2	2	0
2012-13	MODO U18	Swe-U18	3	1	1	2	2	2	0	2	2	0
	MODO Jr.	Swe-Jr.	39	6	7	13	36	7	1	0	1	4
2013-14	MODO Jr.	Swe-Jr.	20	3	16	19	32	5	1	1	2	6
	MODO	Sweden	45	5	6	11	12	2	0	1	1	0
	MODO U18	Swe-U18	....	....	....	....	....	4	5	3	8	6
2014-15	MODO	Sweden	50	5	12	17	42	....	....	....	....	....
	MODO	Sweden-Q	....	....	....	....	....	4	1	2	3	2
	Manchester	AHL	3	0	0	0	2	17	8	1	9	2

KEMPPAINEN, Joonas (kehm-PIGH-nehn, YOH-nuhs) BOS

Center. Shoots left. 6'3", 223 lbs. Born, Kajaani, Finland, April 7, 1988.

			Regular Season					Playoffs				
Season	Club	League	GP	G	A	Pts	PIM	GP	G	A	Pts	PIM
2006-07	Assat Pori Jr.	Fin-Jr.	27	7	17	24	8	3	1	1	2	0
	Assat Pori	Finland	43	1	3	4	4	....	....	....	....	....
2007-08	Assat Pori Jr.	Fin-Jr.	18	2	11	13	6	12	3	4	7	4
	Assat Pori	Finland	22	1	1	2	0	....	....	....	....	....
	Jukurit Mikkeli	Finland-2	8	1	5	6	2	....	....	....	....	....
2008-09	HPK Hameenlinna	Finland	54	7	15	22	20	6	1	0	1	2
2009-10	HPK Hameenlinna	Finland	55	7	19	26	12	17	0	1	1	....
2010-11	Karpat Oulu	Finland	60	2	5	7	10	3	1	1	2	0
2011-12	Karpat Oulu	Finland	60	9	14	23	43	1	0	0	0	0
2012-13	Karpat Oulu	Finland	60	7	7	14	14	3	1	0	1	0
2013-14	Karpat Oulu	Finland	51	17	14	31	6	16	0	4	4	12
2014-15	Karpat Oulu	Finland	59	11	21	32	18	19	10	14	*24	2

Signed as a free agent by **Boston**, May 21, 2015.

KERANEN, Michael (kair-A-nehn, mih-KIGH-ehl) MIN

Right wing. Shoots left. 6'1", 191 lbs. Born, Stockholm, Sweden, January 4, 1990.

			Regular Season					Playoffs				
Season	Club	League	GP	G	A	Pts	PIM	GP	G	A	Pts	PIM
2006-07	Tappara U18	Fin-U18	18	0	1	1	16	....	....	....	....	....
	Ilves Tampere U18	Fin-U18	12	1	4	5	10	2	0	0	0	0
2007-08	Ilves Tampere U18	Fin-U18	35	13	28	41	30	....	....	....	....	....
	Ilves Tampere Jr.	Fin-Jr.	1	0	0	0	0	....	....	....	....	....
2008-09	Ilves Tampere Jr.	Fin-Jr.	35	6	6	12	22	....	....	....	....	....
2009-10	Ilves Tampere Jr.	Fin-Jr.	41	22	28	50	50	9	4	7	11	6
	Ilves Tampere	Finland	1	0	0	0	0	....	....	....	....	....
2010-11	Ilves Tampere Jr.	Fin-Jr.	4	3	4	7	0	6	4	2	6	2
	LeKi Lempaala	Finland-2	9	7	4	11	4	....	....	....	....	....
	Ilves Tampere	Finland	42	5	6	11	45	....	....	....	....	....
2011-12	Ilves Tampere	Finland	44	6	5	11	20	....	....	....	....	....
	Ilves Tampere	Finland-Q	....	....	....	....	....	5	0	0	0	2
2012-13	Ilves Tampere	Finland	56	13	14	27	10	....	....	....	....	....
	Ilves Tampere	Finland-Q	....	....	....	....	....	5	1	4	5	0
2013-14	Ilves Tampere	Finland	52	17	35	*52	47	....	....	....	....	....
2014-15	Iowa Wild	AHL	70	10	27	37	22	....	....	....	....	....

Signed as a free agent by **Minnesota**, June 5, 2014.

KERDILES, Nicolas (kair-DEE-lihs, NIH-koh-las) ANA

Left wing. Shoots left. 6'2", 201 lbs. Born, Lewisville, TX, January 11, 1994.
(Anaheim's 2nd choice, 36th overall, in 2012 Entry Draft).

			Regular Season					Playoffs				
Season	Club	League	GP	G	A	Pts	PIM	GP	G	A	Pts	PIM
2009-10	L.A. Selects	T1EHL	37	25	29	54	48	....	....	....	....	....
	L.A. Selects	Other	31	40	27	67	30	....	....	....	....	....
2010-11	USNTDP	USHL	32	12	8	20	52	....	....	....	....	....
	USNTDP	U-17	14	7	5	12	12	....	....	....	....	....
	USNTDP	U-18	14	1	4	5	2	....	....	....	....	....
2011-12	USNTDP	USHL	18	4	9	13	18	....	....	....	....	....
	USNTDP	U-18	36	18	17	35	20	....	....	....	....	....
2012-13	U. of Wisconsin	WCHA	32	11	22	33	37	....	....	....	....	....
2013-14	U. of Wisconsin	Big Ten	28	15	23	38	33	....	....	....	....	....
	Norfolk Admirals	AHL	6	1	3	4	2	10	3	1	4	2
2014-15	Norfolk Admirals	AHL	51	9	17	26	43	....	....	....	....	....

Big Ten Second All-Star Team (2014)

KERFOOT, Alexander (KUHR-fut, al-ehx-AN-duhr) N.J.

Center. Shoots left. 5'10", 155 lbs. Born, Vancouver, BC, August 11, 1994.
(New Jersey's 6th choice, 150th overall, in 2012 Entry Draft).

			Regular Season					Playoffs				
Season	Club	League	GP	G	A	Pts	PIM	GP	G	A	Pts	PIM
2009-10	Van. NW Giants	BCMML	26	7	14	21	4	....	....	....	....	....
2010-11	Van. NW Giants	BCMML	38	36	*72	*108	58	5	6	6	*12	6
	Coquitlam Express	BCHL	5	0	0	0	0	1	0	0	0	0
2011-12	Coquitlam Express	BCHL	51	25	44	69	24	6	4	0	4	6
2012-13	Coquitlam Express	BCHL	16	8	11	19	16	....	....	....	....	....
2013-14	Harvard Crimson	ECAC	25	8	6	14	8	....	....	....	....	....
2014-15	Harvard Crimson	ECAC	27	8	22	30	12	....	....	....	....	....

KERO, Tanner (KAIR-oh, TA-nuhr) CHI

Left wing. Shoots left. 6', 185 lbs. Born, Southfield, MI, July 24, 1992.

			Regular Season					Playoffs				
Season	Club	League	GP	G	A	Pts	PIM	GP	G	A	Pts	PIM
2009-10	Marquette	NAHL	57	32	19	51	39	3	1	0	1	0
2010-11	Fargo Force	USHL	55	14	23	37	22	5	1	0	1	2
2011-12	Michigan Tech	WCHA	39	9	7	16	14	....	....	....	....	....
2012-13	Michigan Tech	WCHA	33	11	13	24	27	....	....	....	....	....
2013-14	Michigan Tech	WCHA	40	15	10	25	16	....	....	....	....	....
2014-15	Michigan Tech	WCHA	41	20	26	*46	10	....	....	....	....	....
	Rockford IceHogs	AHL	6	5	0	5	0	6	2	1	3	0

WCHA First All-Star Team (2015) • WCHA Player of the Year (2015) • NCAA West First All-American Team (2015)

Signed as a free agent by **Chicago**, April 2, 2015.

KESSY, Kale (KEH-see, KAYL) EDM

Left wing. Shoots left. 6'3", 212 lbs. Born, Shaunavon, SK, December 4, 1992.
(Phoenix's 5th choice, 111th overall, in 2011 Entry Draft).

			Regular Season					Playoffs				
Season	Club	League	GP	G	A	Pts	PIM	GP	G	A	Pts	PIM
2008-09	Medicine Hat	AMHL	33	17	12	29	42	....	....	....	....	....
	Medicine Hat	WHL	9	0	0	0	2	....	....	....	....	....
2009-10	Medicine Hat	WHL	70	11	18	29	123	12	1	3	4	10
2010-11	Medicine Hat	WHL	65	10	14	24	129	14	3	3	6	37
2011-12	Medicine Hat	WHL	49	4	12	16	151	2	0	1	1	2
2012-13	Medicine Hat	WHL	2	2	0	2	17	....	....	....	....	....
	Vancouver Giants	WHL	27	7	9	16	45	....	....	....	....	....
	Kamloops Blazers	WHL	31	12	13	25	44	15	11	3	14	21
2013-14	Oklahoma City	AHL	54	2	4	6	88	....	....	....	....	....
	Bakersfield	ECHL	3	1	0	1	0	....	....	....	....	....
2014-15	Oklahoma City	AHL	17	3	3	6	61	....	....	....	....	....

Traded to **Edmonton** by **Phoenix** for Tobias Rieder, March 30, 2013. • Missed majority of 2014-15 due to knee injury at Oklahoma City (AHL), December 2, 2014.

KHAIRA, Jujhar (KAIR-a, JOO-jahr) EDM

Left wing. Shoots left. 6'3", 214 lbs. Born, Surrey, BC, August 13, 1994.
(Edmonton's 3rd choice, 63rd overall, in 2012 Entry Draft).

			Regular Season					Playoffs				
Season	Club	League	GP	G	A	Pts	PIM	GP	G	A	Pts	PIM
2009-10	Cloverdale Colts	Minor-BC	STATISTICS NOT AVAILABLE									
2010-11	Prince George	BCHL	58	10	32	42	21	....	....	....	....	....
2011-12	Prince George	BCHL	54	29	50	79	69	4	0	2	2	2
2012-13	Michigan Tech	WCHA	37	6	19	25	49	....	....	....	....	....
2013-14	Everett Silvertips	WHL	59	16	27	43	59	5	3	1	4	8
	Oklahoma City	AHL	6	0	0	0	2	3	1	0	1	0
2014-15	Oklahoma City	AHL	51	4	6	10	62	8	3	1	4	4

KICHTON, Brenden (KIHCH-tuhn, BREHN-duhn) WPG

Defense. Shoots right. 5'10", 185 lbs. Born, Edmonton, AB, June 18, 1992.
(Winnipeg's 9th choice, 190th overall, in 2013 Entry Draft).

			Regular Season					Playoffs				
Season	Club	League	GP	G	A	Pts	PIM	GP	G	A	Pts	PIM
2007-08	St. Albert	AMHL	35	10	16	26	14	1	0	0	0	2
2008-09	Spokane Chiefs	WHL	57	1	8	9	12	8	0	0	0	0
2009-10	Spokane Chiefs	WHL	70	4	15	19	21	7	0	0	0	4
2010-11	Spokane Chiefs	WHL	64	23	58	81	31	17	1	10	11	2
2011-12	Spokane Chiefs	WHL	71	17	57	74	49	1	0	1	1	0
2012-13	Spokane Chiefs	WHL	71	22	63	85	30	9	2	5	7	6
2013-14	St. John's IceCaps	AHL	76	10	38	48	14	21	2	5	7	2
2014-15	St. John's IceCaps	AHL	65	8	21	29	32	....	....	....	....	....

• Re-entered NHL Entry Draft. Originally NY Islanders' 7th choice, 127th overall, in 2011 Entry Draft.

WHL West Second All-Star Team (2011) • WHL West First All-Star Team (2012, 2013) • AHL All-Rookie Team (2014)

KIRKLAND, Justin (KUHRK-luhnd, JUHS-tihn) NSH

Left wing. Shoots left. 6'2", 175 lbs. Born, Winnipeg, MB, August 2, 1996.
(Nashville's 4th choice, 62nd overall, in 2014 Entry Draft).

			Regular Season					Playoffs				
Season	Club	League	GP	G	A	Pts	PIM	GP	G	A	Pts	PIM
2009-10	Cam. Red Wings	AMBHL	32	5	2	7	42	....	....	....	....	....
2010-11	Cam. Red Wings	AMBHL	33	18	22	40	46	....	....	....	....	....
2011-12	Notre Dame Argos	SMHL	43	13	22	35	26	8	5	4	9	8
	Kelowna Rockets	WHL	6	0	1	1	0	....	....	....	....	....
2012-13	Notre Dame Argos	SMHL	44	25	24	49	42	3	0	2	2	2
	Notre Dame	SJHL	1	0	0	0	0	....	....	....	....	....
	Kelowna Rockets	WHL	6	2	0	2	6	6	0	1	1	0
2013-14	Kelowna Rockets	WHL	68	17	31	48	40	14	5	5	10	20
2014-15	Kelowna Rockets	WHL	50	21	30	51	25	9	3	2	5	0

KITSYN, Maxim (KIHT-sihn, max-EEM) L.A.

Left wing. Shoots right. 6'3", 202 lbs. Born, Novokuznetsk, USSR, December 24, 1991.
(Los Angeles' 5th choice, 158th overall, in 2010 Entry Draft).

			Regular Season					Playoffs				
Season	Club	League	GP	G	A	Pts	PIM	GP	G	A	Pts	PIM
2007-08	Novokuznetsk 2	Russia-3	4	1	0	1	0	....	....	....	....	....
2008-09	Novokuznetsk 2	Russia-3	STATISTICS NOT AVAILABLE									
	Novokuznetsk	KHL	31	5	2	7	26	....	....	....	....	....
2009-10	Novokuznetsk Jr.	Russia-Jr.	11	6	12	18	26	17	9	12	21	42
	Novokuznetsk	KHL	21	1	1	2	12	....	....	....	....	....
2010-11	Novokuznetsk Jr.	Russia-Jr.	3	1	1	2	2	....	....	....	....	....
	Novokuznetsk	KHL	18	3	4	7	8	....	....	....	....	....
	St. Michael's	OHL	32	9	17	26	24	20	10	9	19	14
2011-12	Novokuznetsk	KHL	32	1	2	3	13	....	....	....	....	....
	Yermak Angarsk	Russia-2	6	2	2	4	0	4	0	0	0	4
	Novokuznetsk Jr.	Russia-Jr.	10	7	1	8	10	7	3	3	6	8
2012-13	Nizhny Novgorod	KHL	8	0	0	0	4	1	0	0	0	2
	HK Sarov	Russia-2	29	9	3	12	63	5	1	1	2	4
2013-14	Manchester	AHL	20	3	1	4	2	....	....	....	....	....
	Ontario Reign	ECHL	33	14	16	30	27	4	1	0	1	2
2014-15	Ontario Reign	ECHL	57	26	17	43	155	19	4	7	11	19
	Manchester	AHL	7	1	0	1	0	....	....	....	....	....

KIVIHALME, Teemu (kih-vih-HAHL-meh, TEE-moo) NSH

Defense. Shoots left. 5'11", 161 lbs. Born, Cloquet, MN, June 17, 1995.
(Nashville's 6th choice, 140th overall, in 2013 Entry Draft).

			Regular Season					Playoffs				
Season	Club	League	GP	G	A	Pts	PIM	GP	G	A	Pts	PIM
2010-11	Burnsville Blaze	High-MN	25	3	11	14	12	....	....	....	....	....
	Team North	UMHSEL	5	0	0	0	2	....	....	....	....	....
2011-12	Burnsville Blaze	High-MN	28	9	22	31	25	....	....	....	....	....
	Team Southeast	UMHSEL	2	1	0	1	0	....	....	....	....	....
2012-13	Team Southeast	UMHSEL	20	3	4	7	8	3	0	2	2	2
	Burnsville Blaze	High-MN	28	9	22	31	24	3	0	1	1	2
	Fargo Force	USHL	4	0	1	1	0	....	....	....	....	....
2013-14	Fargo Force	USHL	47	3	9	12	12	....	....	....	....	....
2014-15	Colorado College	NCHC	35	5	6	11	10	....	....	....	....	....

KLIMCHUK, Morgan (KLIHM-chuhk, MOHR-guhn) CGY

Left wing. Shoots left. 6', 185 lbs. Born, Regina, SK, March 2, 1995.
(Calgary's 3rd choice, 28th overall, in 2013 Entry Draft).

			Regular Season					Playoffs				
Season	Club	League	GP	G	A	Pts	PIM	GP	G	A	Pts	PIM
2010-11	Calgary Buffaloes	AMHL	32	27	23	50	12	2	0	0	0	0
	Regina Pats	WHL	5	0	1	1	0	....	....	....	....	....
2011-12	Regina Pats	WHL	67	18	18	36	27	5	0	1	1	2
2012-13	Regina Pats	WHL	72	36	40	76	20	....	....	....	....	....
2013-14	Regina Pats	WHL	57	30	44	74	27	4	3	2	5	2
	Abbotsford Heat	AHL	4	0	0	0	4	....	....	....	....	....
2014-15	Regina Pats	WHL	27	14	16	30	12	....	....	....	....	....
	Brandon	WHL	33	20	30	50	12	13	3	10	13	2

KNIGHT, Jared (NIGHT, JAIR-uhd) MIN

Center. Shoots right. 5'11", 203 lbs. Born, Battle Creek, MI, January 16, 1992.
(Boston's 2nd choice, 32nd overall, in 2010 Entry Draft).

			Regular Season					Playoffs				
Season	Club	League	GP	G	A	Pts	PIM	GP	G	A	Pts	PIM
2007-08	Det. Compuware	MWEHL	22	8	21	29	21	....	....	....	....	....
	Det. Compuware	Other	5	1	2	3	8	....	....	....	....	....
2008-09	London Knights	OHL	67	15	15	30	60	14	3	0	3	2
2009-10	London Knights	OHL	63	36	21	57	39	12	10	7	17	12
2010-11	London Knights	OHL	68	25	45	70	39	6	4	2	6	2
	Providence Bruins	AHL	3	0	2	2	2	....	....	....	....	....
2011-12	London Knights	OHL	52	26	26	52	28	15	4	4	8	9
2012-13	South Carolina	ECHL	2	0	0	0	0	....	....	....	....	....
	Providence Bruins	AHL	10	1	2	3	8	6	1	1	2	6
2013-14	Providence Bruins	AHL	58	5	14	19	18	9	0	1	1	16
2014-15	Providence Bruins	AHL	36	1	2	3	38	....	....	....	....	....
	Iowa Wild	AHL	16	3	4	7	4	....	....	....	....	....

Traded to **Minnesota** by **Boston** for Zack Phillips, March 2, 2015.

KNOTT, Graham (NAWT, GRAY-uhm) CHI

Left wing. Shoots left. 6'3", 188 lbs. Born, Etobicoke, ON, January 13, 1997.
(Chicago's 1st choice, 54th overall, in 2015 Entry Draft).

			Regular Season					Playoffs				
Season	Club	League	GP	G	A	Pts	PIM	GP	G	A	Pts	PIM
2012-13	York Simcoe	Minor-ON	25	8	8	16	22	....	....	....	....	....
	Aurora Tigers	ON-Jr.A	1	0	0	0	0	....	....	....	....	....
2013-14	Niagara Ice Dogs	OHL	64	8	14	22	18	7	0	1	1	0
2014-15	Niagara Ice Dogs	OHL	59	25	18	43	33	11	2	2	4	2

KOBERSTEIN, Nikolas (KOH-burh-steen, NIH-koh-las) MTL

Defense. Shoots right. 6'2", 185 lbs. Born, Ponoka, AB, January 19, 1996.
(Montreal's 3rd choice, 125th overall, in 2014 Entry Draft).

			Regular Season					Playoffs				
Season	Club	League	GP	G	A	Pts	PIM	GP	G	A	Pts	PIM
2009-10	PAC Saints	AMBHL	33	0	11	11	8	....	....	....	....	....
2010-11	PAC Saints	AMBHL	28	4	19	23	24	....	....	....	....	....
	PAC Saints	Minor-AB	1	0	0	0	0	....	....	....	....	....
2011-12	PAC Saints	Minor-AB	37	9	23	32	71	....	....	....	....	....
	St. Albert Raiders	AMHL	6	0	3	3	2	....	....	....	....	....
2012-13	St. Albert Raiders	AMHL	34	1	11	12	34	4	0	0	0	4
2013-14	Olds Grizzlys	AJHL	51	5	13	18	153	9	0	2	2	24
2014-15	Sioux Falls	USHL	30	1	0	1	75	....	....	....	....	....
	Bloomington	USHL	31	3	8	11	63	....	....	....	....	....

• Signed Letter of Intent to attend **University of Alaska** (WCHA) in fall of 2015.

KOLESAR, Keegan (KOHL-uh-sahr, KEE-guhn) CBJ

Right wing. Shoots right. 6'2", 217 lbs. Born, Brandon, MB, April 8, 1997.
(Columbus' 5th choice, 69th overall, in 2015 Entry Draft).

			Regular Season					Playoffs				
Season	Club	League	GP	G	A	Pts	PIM	GP	G	A	Pts	PIM
2012-13	Wpg. Thrashers	MMHL	41	21	17	38	26	11	3	4	7	4
	Seattle	WHL	1	0	0	0	0	2	0	0	0	0
2013-14	Seattle	WHL	60	2	6	8	45	9	0	2	2	2
2014-15	Seattle	WHL	64	19	19	38	85	....	....	....	....	....

KOLTSOV, Kirill (kohlt-SAHV, kih-RIHL) VAN

Defense. Shoots left. 5'11", 183 lbs. Born, Chelyabinsk, USSR, February 1, 1983.
(Vancouver's 1st choice, 49th overall, in 2002 Entry Draft).

			Regular Season					Playoffs				
Season	Club	League	GP	G	A	Pts	PIM	GP	G	A	Pts	PIM
1998-99	Streetsville Derbys	ON-Jr.A	20	5	7	12	4	....	....	....	....	....
99-2000	Omsk 2	Russia-3	27	0	7	7	30	....	....	....	....	....
	Avangard Omsk	Russia	2	0	0	0	0	....	....	....	....	....
2000-01	Avangard Omsk	Russia	39	0	1	1	20	16	1	3	4	12
2001-02	Avangard Omsk	Russia	41	1	5	6	34	11	1	0	1	8
2002-03	Avangard Omsk	Russia	45	4	8	12	54	12	1	3	4	8
2003-04	Manitoba Moose	AHL	74	7	25	32	62	....	....	....	....	....
2004-05	Manitoba Moose	AHL	28	3	14	17	42	....	....	....	....	....
	Avangard Omsk	Russia	22	2	2	4	46	10	0	1	1	18
2005-06	Avangard Omsk	Russia	43	9	8	17	98	13	4	5	9	10
2006-07	Avangard Omsk	Russia	51	9	31	40	46	9	3	3	6	12
2007-08	Ufa	Russia	50	5	18	23	42	11	0	6	6	6
2008-09	Ufa	KHL	49	5	20	25	81	3	0	0	0	2
2009-10	Ufa	KHL	45	6	16	22	40	11	1	5	6	18
2010-11	Ufa	KHL	50	5	20	25	60	21	2	9	11	14
2011-12	SKA St. Petersburg	KHL	52	3	32	35	72	15	1	9	10	14
2012-13	Ufa	KHL	36	3	10	13	36	14	0	8	8	8
2013-14	Ufa	KHL	48	11	24	35	42	15	1	9	10	2
2014-15	Ufa	KHL	60	18	30	48	30	5	0	0	0	2

KONECNY, Travis (koh-NEH-kee, TRA-vihs) PHI

Center. Shoots right. 5'10", 177 lbs. Born, London, ON, March 11, 1997.
(Philadelphia's 2nd choice, 24th overall, in 2015 Entry Draft).

			Regular Season					Playoffs				
Season	Club	League	GP	G	A	Pts	PIM	GP	G	A	Pts	PIM
2011-12	Elgin-Middl. Bant.	Minor-ON	63	78	74	152	137	....	....	....	....	....
	Elgin-Mid. Chiefs	Minor-ON	3	3	4	7	0	....	....	....	....	....
2012-13	Elgin-Mid. Chiefs	Minor-ON	27	31	35	66	72	11	7	11	18	42
	Elgin-Mid. Chiefs	Other	16	15	15	30	....	....	....	....	....	....
2013-14	Ottawa 67's	OHL	63	26	44	70	18	....	....	....	....	....
2014-15	Ottawa 67's	OHL	60	29	39	68	34	5	3	7	10	6

OHL All-Rookie Team (2014) • OHL Rookie of the Year (2014) • E.J. McGuire Award of Excellence (2015)

KOROSTELEV, Nikita (kuh-RUH-stih-lee-AWV, nih-KEE-ta) **TOR**

Right wing. Shoots right. 6'1", 195 lbs. Born, Moscow, Russia, February 8, 1997.
(Toronto's 9th choice, 185th overall, in 2015 Entry Draft).

			Regular Season					Playoffs				
Season	**Club**	**League**	**GP**	**G**	**A**	**Pts**	**PIM**	**GP**	**G**	**A**	**Pts**	**PIM**
2012-13	Tor. Jr. Can. MM	GTHL	13	12	14	26	....	....	....	....	....	....
	Tor. Jr. Can. Midg.	GTHL	1	0	0	0	0	1	1	0	1	0
2013-14	Sarnia Sting	OHL	60	17	21	38	23	....	....	....	....	....
2014-15	Sarnia Sting	OHL	55	24	29	53	18	5	1	2	3	4

KOSMACHUK, Scott (KAWZ-muh-chuk, SKAWT) **WPG**

Right wing. Shoots right. 5'11", 192 lbs. Born, Richmond Hill, ON, January 24, 1994.
(Winnipeg's 3rd choice, 70th overall, in 2012 Entry Draft).

			Regular Season					Playoffs				
Season	**Club**	**League**	**GP**	**G**	**A**	**Pts**	**PIM**	**GP**	**G**	**A**	**Pts**	**PIM**
2009-10	Toronto Marlboros	GTHL	79	39	33	72	108	....	....	....	....	....
2010-11	Guelph Storm	OHL	68	6	15	21	25	6	1	0	1	5
2011-12	Guelph Storm	OHL	67	30	29	59	110	6	2	3	5	12
2012-13	Guelph Storm	OHL	68	35	30	65	105	5	1	0	1	13
2013-14	Guelph Storm	OHL	68	49	52	101	83	20	10	18	28	27
2014-15	St. John's IceCaps	AHL	70	14	14	28	62	....	....	....	....	....

OHL Second All-Star Team (2014)

KOSOV, Yaroslav (KAW-sawf, YAHR-oh-slahv) **FLA**

Center. Shoots left. 6'3", 220 lbs. Born, Magnitogorsk, Russia, July 5, 1993.
(Florida's 8th choice, 124th overall, in 2011 Entry Draft).

			Regular Season					Playoffs				
Season	**Club**	**League**	**GP**	**G**	**A**	**Pts**	**PIM**	**GP**	**G**	**A**	**Pts**	**PIM**
2010-11	Magnitogorsk Jr.	Russia-Jr.	42	11	10	21	22	17	6	1	7	0
2011-12	Magnitogorsk Jr.	Russia-Jr.	12	6	4	10	6	6	0	0	0	0
	Magnitogorsk	KHL	27	4	5	9	6	7	0	0	0	0
2012-13	Magnitogorsk	KHL	40	4	3	7	10	5	0	0	0	0
	Magnitogorsk Jr.	Russia-Jr.	....	....	....	....	....	3	0	1	1	0
2013-14	Magnitogorsk Jr.	Russia-Jr.	2	1	2	3	0	....	....	....	....	....
	Yuzhny Ural Orsk	Russia-2	2	1	1	2	2	....	....	....	....	....
	Magnitogorsk	KHL	32	2	2	4	0	21	2	1	3	0
2014-15	Magnitogorsk	KHL	52	4	5	9	14	5	0	0	0	4

KOSTALEK, Jan (kawsh-TAH-lehk, YAHN) **WPG**

Defense. Shoots right. 6'1", 186 lbs. Born, Prague, Czech Rep., February 17, 1995.
(Winnipeg's 7th choice, 114th overall, in 2013 Entry Draft).

			Regular Season					Playoffs				
Season	**Club**	**League**	**GP**	**G**	**A**	**Pts**	**PIM**	**GP**	**G**	**A**	**Pts**	**PIM**
2010-11	Sparta U18	CzR-U18	39	2	9	11	34	5	0	0	0	8
	Sparta Jr.	CzRep-Jr.	1	0	0	0	0	....	....	....	....	....
2011-12	Sparta U18	CzR-U18	7	0	13	13	12	3	1	3	4	2
	Sparta Jr.	CzRep-Jr.	32	3	4	7	30	4	0	0	0	2
	HC Sparta Praha	CzRep	10	0	0	0	4	....	....	....	....	....
2012-13	Rimouski Oceanic	QMJHL	48	5	13	18	53	6	0	1	1	2
2013-14	Rimouski Oceanic	QMJHL	55	5	22	27	40	6	0	3	3	4
2014-15	Rimouski Oceanic	QMJHL	57	7	36	43	35	20	8	13	21	10

QMJHL All-Rookie Team (2013) • QMJHL First All-Star Team (2015)

KOUDYS, Patrick (KOO-dihs, PAT-rihk) **WSH**

Defense. Shoots left. 6'4", 210 lbs. Born, Hamilton, ON, November 15, 1992.
(Washington's 2nd choice, 147th overall, in 2011 Entry Draft).

			Regular Season					Playoffs				
Season	**Club**	**League**	**GP**	**G**	**A**	**Pts**	**PIM**	**GP**	**G**	**A**	**Pts**	**PIM**
2008-09	Welland Tigers	Minor-ON	52	1	11	12	48	....	....	....	....	....
2009-10	Burlington	ON-Jr.A	50	5	28	33	42	12	0	1	1	16
2010-11	RPI Engineers	ECAC	31	1	2	3	14	....	....	....	....	....
2011-12	RPI Engineers	ECAC	27	1	1	2	22	....	....	....	....	....
2012-13	Muskegon	USHL	64	1	14	15	95	3	0	0	0	0
2013-14	Penn State	Big Ten	36	2	6	8	26	....	....	....	....	....
2014-15	Penn State	Big Ten	36	1	7	8	35	....	....	....	....	....

KOVACS, Robin (KOH-vach, RAW-bihn) **NYR**

Right wing. Shoots left. 6', 176 lbs. Born, Stockholm, Sweden, November 16, 1996.
(NY Rangers' 2nd choice, 62nd overall, in 2015 Entry Draft).

			Regular Season					Playoffs				
Season	**Club**	**League**	**GP**	**G**	**A**	**Pts**	**PIM**	**GP**	**G**	**A**	**Pts**	**PIM**
2010-11	Flemingsberg U18 2	Swe-U18		7	6	8	14	24	....	....	....	....
....												
	Flemingsberg U18 1	Swe-U18		13	6	5	11	10	....	....	....	....
....												
2011-12	AIK Solna U18	Swe-U18	35	12	16	28	61	....	....	....	....	....
2012-13	AIK Solna U18	Swe-U18	36	32	32	64	83	5	4	4	8	8
	AIK Solna Jr.	Swe-Jr.	6	2	2	4	4	1	0	0	0	0
	AIK Solna	Sweden	1	0	0	0	0	....	....	....	....	....
2013-14	AIK Solna U18	Swe-U18	7	2	5	7	51	....	....	....	....	....
	AIK Solna Jr.	Swe-Jr.	40	15	13	28	87	2	1	1	2	6
	AIK Solna	Sweden	3	0	0	0	0	....	....	....	....	....
2014-15	AIK Solna Jr.	Swe-Jr.	9	5	5	10	8	....	....	....	....	....
	AIK Solna	Sweden-2	62	19	16	35	67	....	....	....	....	....

KRAMER, Darren (KRAY-muhr, DAIR-uhn)

Center. Shoots left. 6'1", 210 lbs. Born, Peace River, AB, November 19, 1991.
(Ottawa's 7th choice, 156th overall, in 2011 Entry Draft).

			Regular Season					Playoffs				
Season	**Club**	**League**	**GP**	**G**	**A**	**Pts**	**PIM**	**GP**	**G**	**A**	**Pts**	**PIM**
2007-08	Peace River Royals	Minor-AB	30	26	22	48	58	9	9	8	17	18
	Peace River	NWJHL	1	0	0	0	0	....	....	....	....	....
2008-09	Grande Prairie	AJHL	38	4	0	4	220	14	1	0	1	45
2009-10	Grande Prairie	AJHL	58	19	11	30	*311	9	2	2	4	23
2010-11	Grande Prairie	AJHL	10	4	1	5	28	....	....	....	....	....
	Spokane Chiefs	WHL	68	7	7	14	*306	17	5	3	8	21
2011-12	Spokane Chiefs	WHL	71	22	18	40	200	12	3	3	6	20
2012-13	Binghamton	AHL	21	1	0	1	83	....	....	....	....	....
	Elmira Jackals	ECHL	19	3	7	10	127	....	....	....	....	....
2013-14	Binghamton	AHL	45	2	2	4	178	3	0	0	0	2
2014-15	Binghamton	AHL	70	5	12	17	*284	....	....	....	....	....

KRASKOVSKY, Pavel (kras-KOHV-skee, PAH-vehl) **WPG**

Center. Shoots left. 6'4", 187 lbs. Born, Yaroslavl, Russia, September 11, 1996.
(Winnipeg's 6th choice, 164th overall, in 2014 Entry Draft).

			Regular Season					Playoffs				
Season	**Club**	**League**	**GP**	**G**	**A**	**Pts**	**PIM**	**GP**	**G**	**A**	**Pts**	**PIM**
2012-13	Loko Yaroslavl Jr.	Russia-Jr.	19	2	3	5	0	....	....	....	....	....
2013-14	Loko Yaroslavl Jr.	Russia-Jr.	39	10	17	27	16	7	0	0	0	2
	Yaroslavl	KHL	8	1	0	1	14	....	....	....	....	....
2014-15	Yaroslavl	KHL	3	0	0	0	0	....	....	....	....	....
	Loko Yaroslavl Jr.	Russia-Jr.	38	11	19	30	56	15	4	9	13	8

KRISTO, Danny (KRIHS-toh, DAN-ee) **ST.L.**

Right wing. Shoots right. 6', 195 lbs. Born, Edina, MN, June 18, 1990.
(Montreal's 1st choice, 56th overall, in 2008 Entry Draft).

			Regular Season					Playoffs				
Season	**Club**	**League**	**GP**	**G**	**A**	**Pts**	**PIM**	**GP**	**G**	**A**	**Pts**	**PIM**
2006-07	USNTDP	U-17	14	4	5	9	0	....	....	....	....	....
	USNTDP	NAHL	39	8	10	18	34	6	0	1	1	2
2007-08	USNTDP	U-18	43	18	14	32	18	....	....	....	....	....
	USNTDP	NAHL	14	4	4	8	6	....	....	....	....	....
2008-09	Omaha Lancers	USHL	50	22	35	57	18	3	3	0	3	2
2009-10	North Dakota	WCHA	41	15	21	36	8	....	....	....	....	....
2010-11	North Dakota	WCHA	34	8	20	28	18	....	....	....	....	....
2011-12	North Dakota	WCHA	42	19	26	45	33	....	....	....	....	....
2012-13	North Dakota	WCHA	40	*26	26	52	24	....	....	....	....	....
	Hamilton Bulldogs	AHL	9	0	3	3	2	....	....	....	....	....
2013-14	Hartford Wolf Pack	AHL	65	25	18	43	18	....	....	....	....	....
2014-15	Hartford Wolf Pack	AHL	72	22	24	46	35	15	3	3	6	2

WCHA All-Rookie Team (2010) • WCHA Rookie of the Year (2010) • WCHA First All-Star Team (2013) • NCAA West First All-American Team (2013)

Traded to **NY Rangers** by **Montreal** for Christian Thomas, July 2, 2013. Signed as a free agent by **St. Louis**, July 2, 2015.

KUBALIK, Dominik (koo-BAH-lihk, DOHM-ihn-ihk) **L.A.**

Left wing. Shoots left. 6'2", 179 lbs. Born, Plzen, Czech Rep., August 21, 1995.
(Los Angeles' 7th choice, 191st overall, in 2013 Entry Draft).

			Regular Season					Playoffs				
Season	**Club**	**League**	**GP**	**G**	**A**	**Pts**	**PIM**	**GP**	**G**	**A**	**Pts**	**PIM**
2010-11	HC Plzen U18	CzR-U18	42	38	21	59	32	6	4	2	6	2
2011-12	HC Plzen U18	CzR-U18	20	22	16	38	12	2	3	0	3	2
	HC Plzen Jr.	CzRep-Jr.	24	11	6	17	22	2	1	2	3	0
	HC Plzen 1929	CzRep	8	1	0	1	0	....	....	....	....	....
2012-13	Sudbury Wolves	OHL	67	17	17	34	25	9	3	3	6	4
2013-14	Sudbury Wolves	OHL	36	13	10	23	35	....	....	....	....	....
	Kitchener Rangers	OHL	23	5	1	6	11	....	....	....	....	....
2014-15	HC Skoda Plzen	CzRep	35	3	4	7	35	4	1	1	2	2

KUHNHACKL, Tom (koon-HAH-kuhl, TAWM) **PIT**

Center. Shoots left. 6'2", 196 lbs. Born, Landshut, Germany, January 21, 1992.
(Pittsburgh's 3rd choice, 110th overall, in 2010 Entry Draft).

			Regular Season					Playoffs				
Season	**Club**	**League**	**GP**	**G**	**A**	**Pts**	**PIM**	**GP**	**G**	**A**	**Pts**	**PIM**
2007-08	EV Landshut Jr.	Ger-Jr.	30	21	20	41	102	3	1	0	1	2
2008-09	EV Landshut Jr.	Ger-Jr.	6	4	3	7	31	7	5	5	10	27
	Landshut Cann.	German-2	42	11	10	21	34	6	1	0	1	6
2009-10	EV Landshut Jr.	Ger-Jr.	2	1	3	4	0	3	4	4	8	12
	Landshut Cann.	German-2	38	12	9	21	38	6	0	0	0	2
	Augsburg	Germany	4	0	0	0	0	....	....	....	....	....
2010-11	Windsor Spitfires	OHL	63	39	29	68	47	18	11	12	23	10
2011-12	Windsor Spitfires	OHL	4	1	3	4	6	....	....	....	....	....
	Niagara Ice Dogs	OHL	30	7	18	25	29	20	6	5	11	14
2012-13	Wilkes-Barre	AHL	11	2	2	4	6	....	....	....	....	....
	Wheeling Nailers	ECHL	2	1	0	1	2	....	....	....	....	....
2013-14	Wilkes-Barre	AHL	48	8	2	10	22	2	0	0	0	2
	Wheeling Nailers	ECHL	16	7	7	14	12	10	6	0	6	6
2014-15	Wilkes-Barre	AHL	72	12	18	30	19	8	0	2	2	0

KUJAWINSKI, Ryan (koo-juh-WIHN-skee, RIGH-uhn) **N.J.**

Center. Shoots left. 6'2", 200 lbs. Born, Kirkland Lake, ON, March 30, 1995.
(New Jersey's 2nd choice, 73rd overall, in 2013 Entry Draft).

			Regular Season					Playoffs				
Season	**Club**	**League**	**GP**	**G**	**A**	**Pts**	**PIM**	**GP**	**G**	**A**	**Pts**	**PIM**
2010-11	Sud. Wolves MM	Minor-ON	24	35	21	56	24	....	....	....	....	....
	Sud. Wolves Mid.	Minor-ON	2	1	1	2	0	3	4	6	10	4
2011-12	Sarnia Sting	OHL	29	1	5	6	2	....	....	....	....	....
	Kingston	OHL	30	15	15	30	15	....	....	....	....	....
2012-13	Kingston	OHL	66	17	31	48	40	4	2	0	2	2
2013-14	Kingston	OHL	45	23	18	41	39	7	1	1	2	2
2014-15	Kingston	OHL	27	13	10	23	18	....	....	....	....	....
	North Bay	OHL	34	21	15	36	12	15	6	3	9	11

KUKAN, Dean (KOO-kahn, DEEN) **CBJ**

Defense. Shoots left. 6'2", 198 lbs. Born, Volketswil, Switzerland, July 8, 1993.

			Regular Season					Playoffs				
Season	**Club**	**League**	**GP**	**G**	**A**	**Pts**	**PIM**	**GP**	**G**	**A**	**Pts**	**PIM**
2009-10	GCK Zurich Jr.	Swiss-Jr.	13	1	5	6	2	9	0	4	4	2
	GCK Lions Zurich	Swiss-2	29	0	6	6	14	....	....	....	....	....
2010-11	GCK Zurich Jr.	Swiss-Jr.	2	0	1	1	0	10	0	0	0	6
	ZSC Lions Zurich	Swiss	37	1	2	3	4	....	....	....	....	....
	GCK Lions Zurich	Swiss-2	2	0	0	0	0	....	....	....	....	....
2011-12	Lulea HF Jr.	Swe-Jr.	42	5	16	21	8	3	0	2	2	2
	Lulea HF	Sweden	3	0	0	0	0	....	....	....	....	....
2012-13	Lulea HF Jr.	Swe-Jr.	11	2	1	3	2	....	....	....	....	....
	Asploven	Sweden-2	2	0	0	0	4	....	....	....	....	....
	Tingsryds AIF	Sweden-2	16	0	2	2	2	....	....	....	....	....
	Lulea HF	Sweden	16	1	3	4	0	15	0	1	1	0
2013-14	Lulea HF	Sweden	54	4	8	12	12	6	1	1	2	....
2014-15	Lulea HF	Sweden	52	3	10	13	14	9	0	2	2	0

Signed as a free agent by **Columbus**, June 1, 2015.

KULYASH, Denis (kuh-L'YASH, DEH-nihs) NSH

Defense. Shoots left. 6'3", 199 lbs. Born, Omsk, USSR, May 31, 1983.
(Nashville's 9th choice, 243rd overall, in 2004 Entry Draft).

			Regular Season					Playoffs				
Season	Club	League	GP	G	A	Pts	PIM	GP	G	A	Pts	PIM
2003-04	CSK VVS Samara 2	Russia-3	STATISTICS NOT AVAILABLE									
	CSKA Moscow	Russia	10	1	0	1	8	....	....	....	....	....
2004-05	CSKA Moscow	Russia	59	8	10	18	58	....	....	....	....	....
2005-06	Dynamo Moscow	Russia	44	12	5	17	117	4	0	2	2	6
2006-07	Dynamo Moscow	Russia	48	3	9	12	58	2	0	0	0	2
2007-08	CSKA Moscow	Russia	53	9	13	22	79	6	1	1	2	34
2008-09	CSKA Moscow	KHL	56	16	10	26	62	8	2	1	3	20
2009-10	CSKA Moscow	KHL	35	11	10	21	34	....	....	....	....	....
	Omsk	KHL	6	1	1	2	6	3	0	0	0	4
2010-11	Omsk	KHL	48	11	15	26	45	14	3	3	6	12
2011-12	Ak Bars Kazan	KHL	44	6	12	18	40	12	0	1	1	37
2012-13	Ak Bars Kazan	KHL	44	4	9	13	66	18	2	5	7	6
2013-14	Omsk	KHL	51	11	11	22	57	11	2	4	6	8
2014-15	Omsk	KHL	58	10	17	27	58	11	2	0	2	0

KURALY, Sean (KUH-ra-lee, SHAWN) BOS

Center. Shoots left. 6'2", 205 lbs. Born, Lewiston, NY, January 20, 1993.
(San Jose's 3rd choice, 133rd overall, in 2011 Entry Draft).

			Regular Season					Playoffs				
Season	Club	League	GP	G	A	Pts	PIM	GP	G	A	Pts	PIM
2009-10	Ohio Blue Jackets	T1EHL	37	19	30	49	24	....	....	....	....	....
	Indiana Ice	USHL	5	1	2	3	0	....	....	....	....	....
2010-11	Indiana Ice	USHL	51	8	21	29	45	5	1	1	2	4
2011-12	Indiana Ice	USHL	54	32	38	70	48	6	3	3	6	4
2012-13	Miami U.	CCHA	40	6	6	12	41	....	....	....	....	....
2013-14	Miami U.	NCHC	38	12	17	29	59	....	....	....	....	....
2014-15	Miami U.	NCHC	40	19	10	29	38	....	....	....	....	....

USHL Second All-Star Team (2012)

Traded to **Boston** by **San Jose** with San Jose's 1st round choice in 2016 Entry Draft for Martin Jones, June 30, 2015.

KURKER, Sam (KUHR-kuhr, SAM) ST.L.

Right wing. Shoots right. 6'2", 202 lbs. Born, Boston, MA, April 8, 1994.
(St. Louis' 2nd choice, 56th overall, in 2012 Entry Draft).

			Regular Season					Playoffs				
Season	Club	League	GP	G	A	Pts	PIM	GP	G	A	Pts	PIM
2010-11	Bos. Little Bruins	Minor-MA	STATISTICS NOT AVAILABLE									
	St. John's Prep	High-MA	25	20	17	37	24	....	....	....	....	....
2011-12	Bos. Little Bruins	Minor-MA	STATISTICS NOT AVAILABLE									
	St. John's Prep	High-MA	24	32	28	60	23	....	....	....	....	....
	USNTDP	U-18	2	0	0	0	2	....	....	....	....	....
2012-13	Boston University	H-East	35	3	2	5	61	....	....	....	....	....
2013-14	Boston University	H-East	12	1	0	1	14	....	....	....	....	....
	Indiana Ice	USHL	24	6	8	14	45	12	3	3	6	6
2014-15	Sioux City	USHL	56	24	25	49	86	5	0	2	2	18

KURTZ, John (KUHRTZ, JAWN)

Left wing. Shoots left. 6'2", 210 lbs. Born, Oakville, ON, May 16, 1989.

			Regular Season					Playoffs				
Season	Club	League	GP	G	A	Pts	PIM	GP	G	A	Pts	PIM
2005-06	Burlington	ON-Jr.A	42	7	11	18	34	4	0	0	0	2
2006-07	Windsor Spitfires	OHL	58	8	7	15	31	....	....	....	....	....
2007-08	Sudbury Wolves	OHL	63	12	16	28	41	....	....	....	....	....
2008-09	Sudbury Wolves	OHL	68	21	33	54	44	6	1	1	2	2
2009-10	Sudbury Wolves	OHL	62	30	16	46	59	4	0	1	1	2
	Syracuse Crunch	AHL	6	1	0	1	7	....	....	....	....	....
2010-11	Syracuse Crunch	AHL	49	4	2	6	102	....	....	....	....	....
	Elmira Jackals	ECHL	8	1	2	3	0	....	....	....	....	....
2011-12	Syracuse Crunch	AHL	12	1	0	1	40	....	....	....	....	....
	Elmira Jackals	ECHL	19	3	5	8	30	....	....	....	....	....
2012-13	Norfolk Admirals	AHL	59	3	5	8	103	....	....	....	....	....
2013-14	Norfolk Admirals	AHL	73	5	7	12	112	9	1	0	1	9
2014-15	Norfolk Admirals	AHL	72	4	5	9	188	....	....	....	....	....

Signed as a free agent by **Anaheim**, April 10, 2013.

KYLINGTON, Oliver (CHIH-lihng-tuhn, AW-lih-vuhr) CGY

Defense. Shoots left. 6', 185 lbs. Born, Stockholm, Sweden, May 19, 1997.
(Calgary's 2nd choice, 60th overall, in 2015 Entry Draft).

			Regular Season					Playoffs				
Season	Club	League	GP	G	A	Pts	PIM	GP	G	A	Pts	PIM
2011-12	Djurgarden U18	Swe-U18	13	0	3	3	4	....	....	....	....	....
2012-13	Sodertalje SK U18	Swe-U18	3	0	0	0	0	....	....	....	....	....
	Sodertalje SK Jr.	Swe-Jr.	39	3	10	13	12	3	0	1	1	0
2013-14	Farjestad U18	Swe-U18	2	1	2	3	2	....	....	....	....	....
	Farjestad Jr.	Swe-Jr.	21	5	16	21	22	2	3	0	3	0
	Farjestad	Sweden	32	2	4	6	6	12	0	2	2	2
2014-15	Farjestad Jr.	Swe-Jr.	10	4	3	7	2	6	0	5	5	6
	AIK Solna	Sweden-2	17	4	3	7	6	....	....	....	....	....
	Farjestad	Sweden	18	2	3	5	4	....	....	....	....	....

LABANC, Kevin (luh-BAHNK, KEH-vuhn) S.J.

Right wing. Shoots right. 5'10", 185 lbs. Born, Brooklyn, NY, December 12, 1995.
(San Jose's 8th choice, 171st overall, in 2014 Entry Draft).

			Regular Season					Playoffs				
Season	Club	League	GP	G	A	Pts	PIM	GP	G	A	Pts	PIM
2009-10	N.J. Colonials	AYHL	37	18	41	59	24	....	....	....	....	....
2010-11	N.J. Rockets	AtJHL	5	0	1	1	2	....	....	....	....	....
	N.J. Rockets	MtJHL	36	13	33	46	16	2	1	0	1	0
2011-12	USNTDP	USHL	33	3	8	11	10	2	0	0	0	2
	USNTDP	U-17	17	2	9	11	12	....	....	....	....	....
2012-13	USNTDP	USHL	26	3	6	9	8	....	....	....	....	....
	USNTDP	U-18	41	7	8	15	12	....	....	....	....	....
2013-14	Barrie Colts	OHL	65	11	24	35	30	11	3	4	7	4
2014-15	Barrie Colts	OHL	68	31	76	107	55	9	2	4	6	8

LABATE, Joseph (luh-BA-tay, JOH-sehf) VAN

Center. Shoots left. 6'4", 190 lbs. Born, Burnsville, MN, April 16, 1993.
(Vancouver's 4th choice, 101st overall, in 2011 Entry Draft).

			Regular Season					Playoffs				
Season	Club	League	GP	G	A	Pts	PIM	GP	G	A	Pts	PIM
2009-10	Holy Angels	High-MN	25	29	29	58	26	2	0	1	1	2
2010-11	Team Southeast	UMHSEL	5	2	6	8	2	3	4	2	6	0
	Holy Angels	High-MN	25	27	22	49	42	1	2	1	3	0
2011-12	U. of Wisconsin	WCHA	37	5	15	20	24	....	....	....	....	....
2012-13	U. of Wisconsin	WCHA	41	9	14	23	51	....	....	....	....	....
2013-14	U. of Wisconsin	Big Ten	37	11	11	22	22	....	....	....	....	....
2014-15	U. of Wisconsin	Big Ten	35	6	12	18	46	....	....	....	....	....
	Utica Comets	AHL	2	0	0	0	2	....	....	....	....	....

LABBE, Dylan (la-BAY, DIH-luhn) MIN

Defense. Shoots left. 6'2", 205 lbs. Born, St-George, QC, January 9, 1995.
(Minnesota's 3rd choice, 107th overall, in 2013 Entry Draft).

			Regular Season					Playoffs				
Season	Club	League	GP	G	A	Pts	PIM	GP	G	A	Pts	PIM
2011-12	Levis	QAAA	38	13	11	24	30	4	0	1	1	0
	Shawinigan	QMJHL	6	0	0	0	7	4	0	1	1	0
2012-13	Shawinigan	QMJHL	61	7	21	28	57	....	....	....	....	....
2013-14	Iowa Wild	AHL	11	1	2	3	4	....	....	....	....	....
	Shawinigan	QMJHL	63	9	18	27	20	3	0	0	0	2
2014-15	Shawinigan	QMJHL	63	15	36	51	43	7	1	7	8	15
	Iowa Wild	AHL	3	0	0	0	0	....	....	....	....	....

LABRIE, Hubert (la-BREE, hew-BAIR)

Defense. Shoots left. 5'11", 190 lbs. Born, Victoriaville, QC, July 12, 1991.

			Regular Season					Playoffs				
Season	Club	League	GP	G	A	Pts	PIM	GP	G	A	Pts	PIM
2006-07	Trois-Rivieres	QAAA	34	3	9	12	96	8	1	1	2	18
2007-08	Gatineau	QMJHL	61	2	15	17	79	19	1	3	4	26
2008-09	Gatineau	QMJHL	55	1	3	4	82	5	0	0	0	14
2009-10	Gatineau	QMJHL	67	4	16	20	99	11	3	4	7	20
2010-11	Gatineau	QMJHL	9	3	4	7	8	24	4	8	12	30
2011-12	Texas Stars	AHL	33	2	1	3	18	....	....	....	....	....
	Idaho Steelheads	ECHL	8	1	4	5	0	6	0	0	0	4
2012-13	Texas Stars	AHL	27	0	3	3	45	....	....	....	....	....
	Idaho Steelheads	ECHL	22	2	3	5	46	17	0	1	1	21
2013-14	Texas Stars	AHL	40	2	5	7	49	4	0	0	0	6
	Idaho Steelheads	ECHL	4	0	0	0	7	....	....	....	....	....
2014-15	Springfield Falcons	AHL	46	1	8	9	65	....	....	....	....	....

Signed as a free agent by **Dallas**, September 18, 2009.

LADUE, Paul (la-DOO, PAWL) L.A.

Defense. Shoots right. 6'1", 186 lbs. Born, Grand Forks, ND, September 6, 1992.
(Los Angeles' 5th choice, 181st overall, in 2012 Entry Draft).

			Regular Season					Playoffs				
Season	Club	League	GP	G	A	Pts	PIM	GP	G	A	Pts	PIM
2009-10	Grand Forks C.K.	High-ND	25	....	....	30	....	....	....	....	....	....
2010-11	Alexandria Blizzard	NAHL	56	3	19	22	58	3	0	2	2	2
2011-12	Lincoln Stars	USHL	56	9	25	34	27	8	1	2	3	2
2012-13	Lincoln Stars	USHL	62	12	37	49	20	5	1	1	2	0
2013-14	North Dakota	NCHC	41	6	15	21	23	....	....	....	....	....
2014-15	North Dakota	NCHC	41	5	17	22	31	....	....	....	....	....

USHL First All-Star Team (2013) • NCHC All-Rookie Team (2014)

LAFFERTY, Sam (LAF-fuhr-tee, SAM) PIT

Center/Left wing. Shoots right. 6'1", 184 lbs. Born, Hollidaysburg, PA, March 6, 1995.
(Pittsburgh's 2nd choice, 113th overall, in 2014 Entry Draft).

			Regular Season					Playoffs				
Season	Club	League	GP	G	A	Pts	PIM	GP	G	A	Pts	PIM
2011-12	Deerfield Academy	High-MA	25	8	8	16	....	....	....	....	....	....
2012-13	Deerfield Academy	High-MA	24	9	15	24	....	....	....	....	....	....
2013-14	Boston Jr. Bruins	Minor-MA	11	2	9	11	2	....	....	....	....	....
	Deerfield Academy	High-MA	25	21	34	55	....	....	....	....	....	....
2014-15	Brown U.	ECAC	31	4	8	12	16	....	....	....	....	....

LAGANIERE, Antoine (LA-GAH-n'yay, an-TWAHN)

Center. Shoots left. 6'4", 196 lbs. Born, L'Ile-Cadieux, QC, July 5, 1990.

			Regular Season					Playoffs				
Season	Club	League	GP	G	A	Pts	PIM	GP	G	A	Pts	PIM
2005-06	Chateauguay	QAAA	44	14	12	26	8	19	11	10	21	14
2006-07	Chateauguay	QAAA	44	20	23	43	30	3	2	2	4	2
2007-08	Deerfield Academy	High-MA	25	8	30	38	14	....	....	....	....	....
2008-09	Deerfield Academy	High-MA	....	12	16	28	....	....	....	....	....	....
2009-10	Yale	ECAC	25	7	3	10	18	....	....	....	....	....
2010-11	Yale	ECAC	25	5	8	13	14	....	....	....	....	....
2011-12	Yale	ECAC	35	19	14	33	45	....	....	....	....	....
2012-13	Yale	ECAC	37	15	14	29	58	....	....	....	....	....
2013-14	Norfolk Admirals	AHL	72	10	8	18	36	4	0	0	0	2
2014-15	Norfolk Admirals	AHL	73	14	7	21	42	....	....	....	....	....

Signed as a free agent by **Anaheim**, April 16, 2013. Signed as a free agent by **San Diego** (AHL), July 8, 2015.

LAGESSON, William (lah-GUH-suhn, WIHL-yuhm) EDM

Defense. Shoots left. 6'2", 196 lbs. Born, Gothenburg, Sweden, February 22, 1996.
(Edmonton's 2nd choice, 91st overall, in 2014 Entry Draft).

			Regular Season					Playoffs				
Season	Club	League	GP	G	A	Pts	PIM	GP	G	A	Pts	PIM
2011-12	Frolunda U18	Swe-U18	25	0	3	3	2	2	0	0	0	0
2012-13	Frolunda U18	Swe-U18	32	4	15	19	74	3	1	2	3	4
	Frolunda Jr.	Swe-Jr.	6	0	0	0	0	2	0	0	0	0
2013-14	Frolunda U18	Swe-U18	4	0	1	1	0	5	2	2	4	10
	Frolunda Jr.	Swe-Jr.	44	8	12	20	30	3	0	1	1	2
2014-15	Dubuque	USHL	52	2	14	16	79	8	1	1	2	4

LALEGGIA, Joey (lah-lehj-EE-a, JOH-ee) **EDM**

Defense. Shoots left. 5'9", 182 lbs. Born, Burnaby, BC, June 24, 1992.
(Edmonton's 6th choice, 123rd overall, in 2012 Entry Draft).

			Regular Season					Playoffs				
Season	Club	League	GP	G	A	Pts	PIM	GP	G	A	Pts	PIM
2006-07	Burnaby W.C.	Minor-BC	65	7	37	44	58	....	....	....	....	....
2007-08	Van. NW Giants	BCMML	40	7	34	41	32	2	0	1	1	0
2008-09	Van. NW Giants	BCMML	40	15	39	54	67	5	2	4	6	0
	Penticton Vees	BCHL	2	0	0	0	0	....	....	....	....	....
2009-10	Penticton Vees	BCHL	54	13	52	65	19	16	2	10	12	8
2010-11	Penticton Vees	BCHL	58	20	62	82	47	9	1	9	10	12
2011-12	U. of Denver	WCHA	43	11	27	38	35	....	....	....	....	....
2012-13	U. of Denver	WCHA	39	11	18	29	31	....	....	....	....	....
2013-14	U. of Denver	NCHC	37	12	13	25	36	....	....	....	....	....
2014-15	U. of Denver	NCHC	37	15	25	40	56	....	....	....	....	....
	Oklahoma City	AHL	5	1	1	2	2	2	0	0	0	0

WCHA All-Rookie Team (2012) • WCHA Rookie of the Year (2012) • WCHA Second All-Star Team (2013) • NCHC First All-Star Team (2014, 2015) • NCAA West Second All-American Team (2014) • NCHC Player of the Year (2015) • NCAA West First All-American Team (2015)

LAMARCHE, Maxim (la-MARSH, MAX-eem) **PHI**

Defense. Shoots right. 6'3", 218 lbs. Born, Laval, QC, July 11, 1992.

			Regular Season					Playoffs				
Season	Club	League	GP	G	A	Pts	PIM	GP	G	A	Pts	PIM
2007-08	Laval-Bourassa	QAAA	45	3	13	16	46	5	0	4	4	12
2008-09	Laval-Bourassa	QAAA	44	6	21	27	36	19	1	13	14	6
2009-10	Victoriaville Tigres	QMJHL	33	3	10	13	21	....	....	....	....	....
	Baie-Comeau	QMJHL	29	3	1	4	20	....	....	....	....	....
2010-11	Baie-Comeau	QMJHL	67	4	24	28	98	....	....	....	....	....
2011-12	Baie-Comeau	QMJHL	68	4	21	25	67	8	0	4	4	12
2012-13	Baie-Comeau	QMJHL	55	9	34	43	63	19	3	8	11	28
2013-14	Adirondack	AHL	12	0	1	1	7	....	....	....	....	....
	Elmira Jackals	ECHL	50	3	5	8	38	....	....	....	....	....
2014-15	Reading Royals	ECHL	60	9	23	32	56	7	1	2	3	16
	Lehigh Valley	AHL	7	0	1	1	4	....	....	....	....	....

Signed as a free agent by **Philadelphia**, May 31, 2013.

LAMMIKKO, Juho (lah-MIH-koh, YOO-hoh) **FLA**

Left wing. Shoots left. 6'3", 203 lbs. Born, Noormarkku, Finland, January 29, 1996.
(Florida's 3rd choice, 65th overall, in 2014 Entry Draft).

			Regular Season					Playoffs				
Season	Club	League	GP	G	A	Pts	PIM	GP	G	A	Pts	PIM
2011-12	Assat Pori U18	Fin-U18	2	0	1	1	0	....	....	....	....	....
	Assat Pori Jr.	Fin-Jr.	2	0	1	1	0	....	....	....	....	....
2012-13	Assat Pori U18	Fin-U18	31	21	32	53	22	9	5	6	11	12
	Assat Pori Jr.	Fin-Jr.	15	0	1	1	10	....	....	....	....	....
2013-14	Assat Pori Jr.	Fin-Jr.	37	17	25	42	32	11	3	5	8	28
	Assat Pori	Finland	20	0	1	1	0	....	....	....	....	....
2014-15	Kingston	OHL	64	18	26	44	36	4	1	1	2	8

LANDRY, Jon (LAN-dree, JAWN)

Defense. Shoots left. 6'2", 212 lbs. Born, Montreal, QC, May 1, 1983.

			Regular Season					Playoffs				
Season	Club	League	GP	G	A	Pts	PIM	GP	G	A	Pts	PIM
99-2000	Lac St-Louis Lions	QAAA	42	17	27	44	32	7	2	5	7	10
2000-01	St. Paul's School	High-NH	26	10	23	33	....	....	....	....	....	....
2001-02	St. Paul's School	High-NH	STATISTICS NOT AVAILABLE									
2002-03	Bowdoin College	NCAA-3	23	11	14	25	14	....	....	....	....	....
2003-04	Bowdoin College	NCAA-3	24	13	20	33	20	....	....	....	....	....
2004-05	Bowdoin College	NCAA-3	24	11	14	25	16	....	....	....	....	....
2005-06	Bowdoin College	NCAA-3	27	16	22	38	37	....	....	....	....	....
	Portland Pirates	AHL	2	0	0	0	2	....	....	....	....	....
2006-07	Augusta Lynx	ECHL	2	1	0	1	2	....	....	....	....	....
	Arizona Sundogs	CHL	41	7	7	14	41	14	0	0	0	4
2007-08	Arizona Sundogs	CHL	60	9	33	42	70	17	3	6	9	14
2008-09	Arizona Sundogs	CHL	64	11	31	42	63	....	....	....	....	....
2009-10	Arizona Sundogs	CHL	38	9	22	31	54	....	....	....	....	....
	Kolner Haie	Germany	9	0	2	2	20	....	....	....	....	....
2010-11	Braehead Clan	Britain	54	18	40	58	67	....	....	....	....	....
2011-12	Colorado Eagles	ECHL	35	12	18	30	44	....	....	....	....	....
	Bridgeport	AHL	34	2	18	20	27	2	0	0	0	0
2012-13	Bridgeport	AHL	72	8	25	33	57	....	....	....	....	....
2013-14	Iowa Wild	AHL	50	0	18	18	32	....	....	....	....	....
2014-15	Hershey Bears	AHL	64	3	11	14	38	5	1	0	1	0

Signed as a free agent by **Koln** (Germany), January 29, 2010. Signed as a free agent by **Braehead** (Britain), July 13, 2010. Signed as a free agent by **Colorado** (ECHL), September 21, 2011. Signed to a PTO (professional tryout) contract by **Bridgeport** (AHL), January 12, 2012. Signed as a free agent by **Bridgeport** (AHL), February 24, 2012. Signed as a free agent by **NY Islanders**, July 1, 2012. Signed as a free agent by **Minnesota**, July 9, 2013. Signed as a free agent by **Washington**, July 1, 2014.

LANE, Phil (LAYN, FIHL)

Right wing. Shoots right. 6'2", 203 lbs. Born, Rochester, NY, May 29, 1992.
(Phoenix's 3rd choice, 52nd overall, in 2010 Entry Draft).

			Regular Season					Playoffs				
Season	Club	League	GP	G	A	Pts	PIM	GP	G	A	Pts	PIM
2008-09	Buffalo Jr. Sabres	ON-Jr.A	45	18	24	42	72	5	0	0	0	6
2009-10	Brampton	OHL	64	18	14	32	52	11	3	0	3	14
2010-11	Brampton	OHL	54	17	17	34	113	4	0	1	1	2
2011-12	Brampton	OHL	53	15	26	41	94	8	4	1	5	7
2012-13	Portland Pirates	AHL	70	14	8	22	61	3	0	1	1	9
2013-14	Portland Pirates	AHL	39	3	3	6	49	....	....	....	....	....
2014-15	Portland Pirates	AHL	53	3	7	10	39	5	1	1	2	2

LANE, Tanner (LAYN, TA-nuhr) **WPG**

Center. Shoots left. 6'2", 193 lbs. Born, Detroit Lakes, MN, August 13, 1992.
(Atlanta's 7th choice, 160th overall, in 2010 Entry Draft).

			Regular Season					Playoffs				
Season	Club	League	GP	G	A	Pts	PIM	GP	G	A	Pts	PIM
2007-08	Detroit Lakes	High-MN	26	24	20	44	28	....	....	....	....	....
2008-09	Detroit Lakes	High-MN	26	26	26	52	50	....	....	....	....	....
2009-10	Team Great Plains	UMHSEL	21	8	7	15	....	....	....	....	....	....
	Detroit Lakes	High-MN	25	49	41	*90	62	1	0	0	0	2
2010-11	Fargo Force	USHL	57	4	9	13	48	5	0	0	0	0
2011-12	Fargo Force	USHL	12	1	8	9	10	....	....	....	....	....
	Omaha Lancers	USHL	48	12	20	32	38	4	0	0	0	2
2012-13	Nebraska-Omaha	WCHA	31	2	4	6	8	....	....	....	....	....
2013-14	Nebraska-Omaha	NCHC	34	5	4	9	12	....	....	....	....	....
2014-15	Nebraska-Omaha	NCHC	35	2	6	8	18	....	....	....	....	....

• Transferred to **Winnipeg** after **Atlanta** franchise relocated, June 21, 2011.

LANG, Chase (LANG, CHAYS) **MIN**

Center. Shoots left. 6'1", 193 lbs. Born, Nanaimo, BC, September 13, 1996.
(Minnesota's 6th choice, 167th overall, in 2014 Entry Draft).

			Regular Season					Playoffs				
Season	Club	League	GP	G	A	Pts	PIM	GP	G	A	Pts	PIM
2010-11	PoE Academy	High-BC	53	32	48	80	50	....	....	....	....	....
2011-12	North Island	BCMML	40	29	32	61	52	....	....	....	....	....
	Alberni Valley	BCHL	5	0	0	0	2	....	....	....	....	....
2012-13	Calgary Hitmen	WHL	44	4	7	11	10	5	0	0	0	0
2013-14	Calgary Hitmen	WHL	68	10	15	25	52	6	0	3	3	13
2014-15	Calgary Hitmen	WHL	63	25	31	56	61	10	4	3	7	10

LANGLOIS, Jeremy (LANG-LOYS, JAIR-ih-mee) **S.J.**

Right wing. Shoots right. 6', 175 lbs. Born, Tempe, AZ, June 2, 1990.

			Regular Season					Playoffs				
Season	Club	League	GP	G	A	Pts	PIM	GP	G	A	Pts	PIM
2006-07	Phoenix	WSHL	45	32	41	73	51	6	2	2	4	6
2007-08	Phoenix	WSHL	47	30	54	84	47	6	4	10	14	2
2008-09	Jersey Hitmen	EJHL	45	35	47	*82	16	7	*6	*5	*11	4
2009-10	Quinnipiac	ECAC	40	8	12	20	18	....	....	....	....	....
2010-11	Quinnipiac	ECAC	39	18	5	23	16	....	....	....	....	....
2011-12	Quinnipiac	ECAC	35	17	9	26	18	....	....	....	....	....
2012-13	Quinnipiac	ECAC	42	13	18	31	32	....	....	....	....	....
2013-14	Springfield Falcons	AHL	5	0	0	0	0	....	....	....	....	....
	Evansville IceMen	ECHL	49	16	36	52	15	....	....	....	....	....
	Bridgeport	AHL	7	2	2	4	2	....	....	....	....	....
	Stockton Thunder	ECHL	7	3	5	8	0	3	4	5	9	0
2014-15	Worcester Sharks	AHL	42	16	10	26	8	4	0	1	1	15

Signed as a free agent by **Springfield** (AHL), July 2, 2013. Signed as a free agent by **Worcester** (AHL), August 28, 2014. Signed as a free agent by **San Jose**, June 27, 2015.

LARKIN, Dylan (LAHR-kihn, DIH-luhn) **DET**

Center. Shoots left. 6'1", 190 lbs. Born, Waterford, MI, July 30, 1996.
(Detroit's 1st choice, 15th overall, in 2014 Entry Draft).

			Regular Season					Playoffs				
Season	Club	League	GP	G	A	Pts	PIM	GP	G	A	Pts	PIM
2011-12	Detroit Belle Tire	T1EHL	25	18	18	36	24	....	....	....	....	....
2012-13	USNTDP	USHL	37	7	7	14	40	....	....	....	....	....
	USNTDP	U-17	18	6	7	13	14	....	....	....	....	....
2013-14	USNTDP	USHL	26	17	9	26	24	....	....	....	....	....
	USNTDP	U-18	34	14	17	31	32	....	....	....	....	....
2014-15	U. of Michigan	Big Ten	35	15	32	47	38	....	....	....	....	....
	Grand Rapids	AHL	....	....	....	....	....	6	3	2	5	6

NCAA West Second All-American Team (2015)

LARKIN, Thomas (LAHR-kihn, TAW-muhs)

Defense. Shoots right. 6'5", 206 lbs. Born, London, England, December 31, 1990.
(Columbus' 4th choice, 137th overall, in 2009 Entry Draft).

			Regular Season					Playoffs				
Season	Club	League	GP	G	A	Pts	PIM	GP	G	A	Pts	PIM
2006-07	Exeter	High-NH	28	1	7	8	5	....	....	....	....	....
2007-08	Exeter	High-NH	29	6	15	21	18	....	....	....	....	....
2008-09	Exeter	High-NH	35	14	38	52	30	....	....	....	....	....
	Bos. Little Bruins	Minor-MA	18	1	1	2	10	....	....	....	....	....
2009-10	Colgate	ECAC	33	3	16	19	32	....	....	....	....	....
2010-11	Colgate	ECAC	41	5	6	11	41	....	....	....	....	....
2011-12	Colgate	ECAC	37	4	10	14	48	....	....	....	....	....
2012-13	Colgate	ECAC	36	3	11	14	55	....	....	....	....	....
	Springfield Falcons	AHL	7	1	0	1	2	....	....	....	....	....
2013-14	Evansville IceMen	ECHL	33	3	17	20	60	....	....	....	....	....
	Springfield Falcons	AHL	19	0	2	2	48	1	0	0	0	0
2014-15	Springfield Falcons	AHL	62	5	12	17	89	....	....	....	....	....

LARSSON, Jacob (LAHR-suhn, YA-kuhb) **ANA**

Defense. Shoots left. 6'2", 185 lbs. Born, Ljungby, Sweden, April 29, 1997.
(Anaheim's 1st choice, 27th overall, in 2015 Entry Draft).

			Regular Season					Playoffs				
Season	Club	League	GP	G	A	Pts	PIM	GP	G	A	Pts	PIM
2012-13	Troja U18	Swe-U18	10	0	0	0	0	2	0	1	1	2
	Troja Jr.	Swe-Jr.	19	5	5	10	2	....	....	....	....	....
2013-14	Frolunda U18	Swe-U18	38	9	16	25	55	5	2	4	6	8
	Frolunda Jr.	Swe-Jr.	13	0	0	0	0	3	0	0	0	0
2014-15	Frolunda U18	20 Elit	3	1	1	2	0	2	0	1	1	0
	Frolunda Jr.	Swe-Jr.	30	8	11	19	49	8	0	4	4	6
	Frolunda	Sweden	20	1	2	3	6	....	....	....	....	....

LAURIDSEN, Markus (LAW-rihd-suhn, MAHR-kuhs)

Defense. Shoots left. 6'1", 205 lbs. Born, Gentofte, Denmark, February 28, 1991.

			Regular Season					Playoffs				
Season	Club	League	GP	G	A	Pts	PIM	GP	G	A	Pts	PIM
2010-11	Green Bay	USHL	44	5	5	10	16	11	0	4	4	0
2011-12	Green Bay	USHL	58	6	24	30	32	11	3	1	4	8
2012-13	Lake Erie Monsters	AHL	36	0	12	12	16	....	....	....	....	....
	Denver Cutthroats	CHL	30	6	9	15	14	....	....	....	....	....
2013-14	Lake Erie Monsters	AHL	39	3	9	12	14	....	....	....	....	....
2014-15	Lake Erie Monsters	AHL	62	5	11	16	22	....	....	....	....	....

Signed as a free agent by **Lake Erie** (AHL), September 28, 2012. Signed as a free agent by **Colorado**, March 22, 2013. Signed as a free agent by **AIK Solna** (Sweden-2), June 16, 2015.

LAUZON, Jeremy (LOH-zawn, JAIR-ih-mee) BOS

Defense. Shoots left. 6'2", 204 lbs. Born, Val d'Or, QC, April 28, 1997.
(Boston's 6th choice, 52nd overall, in 2015 Entry Draft).

			Regular Season					Playoffs				
Season	Club	League	GP	G	A	Pts	PIM	GP	G	A	Pts	PIM
2012-13	Amos Forestiers	QAAA	41	4	11	15	52	....	....	....	....	....
2013-14	Rouyn-Noranda	QMJHL	55	5	11	16	64	9	2	2	4	4
2014-15	Rouyn-Noranda	QMJHL	60	15	21	36	88	....	....	....	....	....

LEBLANC, Chris (luh-BLAWNK, KRIHS) OTT

Right wing. Shoots right. 6'4", 202 lbs. Born, Winthrop, MA , September 12, 1993.
(Ottawa's 6th choice, 161st overall, in 2013 Entry Draft).

			Regular Season					Playoffs				
Season	Club	League	GP	G	A	Pts	PIM	GP	G	A	Pts	PIM
2008-09	Winthrop Vikings	High-MA	20	6	10	16	18	....	....	....	....	....
2009-10	Winthrop Vikings	High-MA	20	13	18	31	32	3	3	3	6	6
2010-11	Winthrop Vikings	High-MA	....	21	25	46	....	....	....	....	....	....
2011-12	Winthrop Vikings	High-MA	....	24	22	46	....	....	....	....	....	....
2012-13	South Shore Kings	EJHL	44	13	20	33	38	2	1	0	1	0
2013-14	Merrimack College	H-East	23	6	6	12	8	....	....	....	....	....
2014-15	Merrimack College	H-East	28	5	4	9	18	....	....	....	....	....

LeBLANC, Olivier (luh-BLAWNK, oh-lih-VEE-ay) CBJ

Defense. Shoots left. 6', 172 lbs. Born, Quebec, QC, February 17, 1996.
(Columbus' 7th choice, 197th overall, in 2014 Entry Draft).

			Regular Season					Playoffs				
Season	Club	League	GP	G	A	Pts	PIM	GP	G	A	Pts	PIM
2011-12	Sem. St-Francois	QAAA	40	3	12	15	24	20	1	4	5	6
2012-13	Saint John	QMJHL	60	4	14	18	41	4	0	0	0	4
2013-14	Saint John	QMJHL	56	7	26	33	58	....	....	....	....	....
2014-15	Saint John	QMJHL	37	4	18	22	63	....	....	....	....	....
	Cape Breton	QMJHL	21	3	9	12	18	....	....	....	....	....

LEDUC, Jerome (leh-DOOK, jah-ROHM) BUF

Defense. Shoots right. 6'1", 192 lbs. Born, Quebec, QC, July 30, 1992.
(Buffalo's 2nd choice, 68th overall, in 2010 Entry Draft).

			Regular Season					Playoffs				
Season	Club	League	GP	G	A	Pts	PIM	GP	G	A	Pts	PIM
2007-08	Sem. St-Francois	QAAA	43	10	12	22	10	17	2	6	8	26
2008-09	Rouyn-Noranda	QMJHL	52	1	16	17	8	6	0	2	2	5
2009-10	Rouyn-Noranda	QMJHL	68	20	26	46	16	11	2	4	6	2
2010-11	Rimouski Oceanic	QMJHL	61	18	38	56	26	5	1	2	3	6
2011-12	Rimouski Oceanic	QMJHL	62	28	46	74	41	21	9	10	19	12
2012-13	Rochester	AHL	48	3	4	7	8	3	0	0	0	0
2013-14	Rochester	AHL	51	3	7	10	22	4	0	1	1	0
	Gwinnett	ECHL	8	1	3	4	2	....	....	....	....	....
2014-15	Rochester	AHL	76	6	19	25	59	....	....	....	....	....

QMJHL First All-Star Team (2012)

LEDUC, Loic (luh-DOOK, LOYK) NYI

Defense. Shoots right. 6'7", 234 lbs. Born, Mercier, QC, June 14, 1994.
(NY Islanders' 4th choice, 103rd overall, in 2012 Entry Draft).

			Regular Season					Playoffs				
Season	Club	League	GP	G	A	Pts	PIM	GP	G	A	Pts	PIM
2009-10	Lac St-L. Patriotes	Minor-QC	STATISTICS NOT AVAILABLE									
	Chateauguay	QAAA	1	0	0	0	0	....	....	....	....	....
2010-11	Cape Breton	QMJHL	36	1	3	4	27	2	0	0	0	0
2011-12	Cape Breton	QMJHL	65	2	8	10	99	4	0	1	1	4
2012-13	Cape Breton	QMJHL	38	0	2	2	50	....	....	....	....	....
2013-14	Cape Breton	QMJHL	37	3	5	8	58	....	....	....	....	....
	Rimouski Oceanic	QMJHL	26	3	4	7	44	11	0	2	2	27
2014-15	Stockton Thunder	ECHL	44	3	2	5	85	....	....	....	....	....
	Colorado Eagles	ECHL	11	1	1	2	10	4	0	0	0	2

LEHKONEN, Artturi (lehch-KOH-nehn, AHR-tu-ree) MTL

Left wing. Shoots left. 6', 174 lbs. Born, Piikkio, Finland, April 7, 1995.
(Montreal's 4th choice, 55th overall, in 2013 Entry Draft).

			Regular Season					Playoffs				
Season	Club	League	GP	G	A	Pts	PIM	GP	G	A	Pts	PIM
2010-11	TPS Turku U18	Fin-U18	28	23	15	38	43	13	8	6	14	4
	TPS Turku Jr.	Fin-Jr.	2	0	1	1	0	....	....	....	....	....
2011-12	TPS Turku U18	Fin-U18	3	4	6	10	0	4	3	4	7	2
	TPS Turku Jr.	Fin-Jr.	40	28	26	54	54	....	....	....	....	....
	TPS Turku	Finland	18	2	2	4	8	2	0	0	0	0
2012-13	KalPa Kuopio	Finland	45	14	16	30	12	4	2	1	3	2
2013-14	KalPa Kuopio	Finland	33	7	13	20	4	....	....	....	....	....
2014-15	Frolunda	Sweden	47	8	8	16	12	13	3	3	6	0

LEIER, Taylor (LEER, TAY-luhr) PHI

Left wing. Shoots left. 5'10", 174 lbs. Born, Saskatoon, SK, February 15, 1994.
(Philadelphia's 5th choice, 117th overall, in 2012 Entry Draft).

			Regular Season					Playoffs				
Season	Club	League	GP	G	A	Pts	PIM	GP	G	A	Pts	PIM
2008-09	Saskatoon Bobcats	Minor-SK	STATISTICS NOT AVAILABLE									
	Sask. Contacts	SMHL	2	2	0	2	0	....	....	....	....	....
2009-10	Sask. Contacts	SMHL	41	17	24	41	30	11	5	2	7	0
2010-11	Sask. Contacts	SMHL	44	31	43	74	32	9	7	6	13	8
2011-12	Portland	WHL	72	13	24	37	36	22	5	2	7	12
2012-13	Portland	WHL	64	27	35	62	63	21	9	7	16	12
2013-14	Portland	WHL	62	37	42	79	42	21	6	20	26	10
2014-15	Lehigh Valley	AHL	73	13	18	31	18	....	....	....	....	....

LEIPSIC, Brendan (LIGHP-sihk, BREHN-duhn) TOR

Left wing. Shoots left. 5'10", 180 lbs. Born, Winnipeg, MB, May 19, 1994.
(Nashville's 4th choice, 89th overall, in 2012 Entry Draft).

			Regular Season					Playoffs				
Season	Club	League	GP	G	A	Pts	PIM	GP	G	A	Pts	PIM
2009-10	Winnipeg Wild	MMHL	40	23	40	63	36	7	2	2	4	17
2010-11	Portland	WHL	68	16	17	33	50	21	3	4	7	14
2011-12	Portland	WHL	65	28	30	58	82	20	7	8	15	28
2012-13	Portland	WHL	68	*49	71	*120	103	21	10	14	24	41
2013-14	Portland	WHL	60	39	52	91	111	20	14	19	33	49
2014-15	Milwaukee	AHL	47	7	28	35	16	....	....	....	....	....
	Toronto Marlies	AHL	27	7	12	19	6	5	1	2	3	14

WHL West Second All-Star Team (2013)

Traded to **Toronto** by **Nashville** with Olli Jokinen and Nashville's 1st round choice (later traded to Philadelphia – Philadelphia selected Travis Konecny) in 2015 Entry Draft for Cody Franson and Mike Santorelli, February 15, 2015.

LEMIEUX, Brendan (luh-M'YEW, BREHN-duhn) WPG

Left wing. Shoots left. 6', 213 lbs. Born, Denver, CO, March 15, 1996.
(Buffalo's 2nd choice, 31st overall, in 2014 Entry Draft).

			Regular Season					Playoffs				
Season	Club	League	GP	G	A	Pts	PIM	GP	G	A	Pts	PIM
2011-12	Toronto Marlboros	GTHL	26	9	23	32	....	....	....	....	....	....
	The Hill Academy	High-ON	STATISTICS NOT AVAILABLE									
2012-13	Green Bay	USHL	11	1	1	2	34	....	....	....	....	....
	Barrie Colts	OHL	42	6	8	14	52	21	2	0	2	35
2013-14	Barrie Colts	OHL	65	27	26	53	145	11	7	3	10	16
2014-15	Barrie Colts	OHL	57	41	19	60	145	5	1	2	3	12

Traded to **Winnipeg** by **Buffalo** with Tyler Myers, Drew Stafford, Joel Armia and St. Louis' 1st round choice (previously acquired, Winnipeg selected Jack Roslovic) in 2015 Entry Draft for Evander Kane, Zach Bogosian and Jason Kasdorf, February 11, 2015.

LERNOUT, Brett (luhr-NOWT, BREHT) MTL

Defense. Shoots right. 6'4", 210 lbs. Born, Winnipeg, MB, September 24, 1995.
(Montreal's 2nd choice, 73rd overall, in 2014 Entry Draft).

			Regular Season					Playoffs				
Season	Club	League	GP	G	A	Pts	PIM	GP	G	A	Pts	PIM
2009-10	Winnipeg Sharks	Minor-MB	25	1	6	7	27	....	....	....	....	....
2010-11	Winnipeg Warriors	Minor-MB	31	3	12	15	67	....	....	....	....	....
2011-12	Winnipeg Wild	MMHL	44	8	27	35	62	9	1	4	5	16
	Steinbach Pistons	MJHL	6	0	1	1	0	....	....	....	....	....
	Saskatoon Blades	WHL	2	0	0	0	0	....	....	....	....	....
2012-13	Saskatoon Blades	WHL	18	0	0	0	15	....	....	....	....	....
	Swift Current	WHL	41	1	1	2	43	....	0	0	0	0
2013-14	Swift Current	WHL	72	8	14	22	103	6	0	1	1	0
2014-15	Swift Current	WHL	72	14	28	42	68	4	1	0	1	4
	Hamilton Bulldogs	AHL	6	0	0	0	2	....	....	....	....	....

LESLIE, Zachary (LEHS-lee, za-KAH-ree) L.A.

Defense. Shoots left. 6', 183 lbs. Born, Ottawa, ON, January 31, 1994.
(Los Angeles' 6th choice, 178th overall, in 2013 Entry Draft).

			Regular Season					Playoffs				
Season	Club	League	GP	G	A	Pts	PIM	GP	G	A	Pts	PIM
2009-10	Ott. Jr. 67's MM	Minor-ON	29	10	24	34	36	11	2	6	8	12
	Ott. Jr. 67's Mid.	Minor-ON	5	1	1	2	2	3	0	2	2	4
	Gloucester	ON-Jr.A	1	0	0	0	0	....	....	....	....	....
2010-11	Gloucester	ON-Jr.A	56	13	22	35	26	9	1	3	4	4
2011-12	Guelph Storm	OHL	65	2	15	17	54	5	0	0	0	4
2012-13	Guelph Storm	OHL	68	12	28	40	58	5	0	1	1	4
2013-14	Guelph Storm	OHL	60	14	36	50	39	20	1	9	10	22
2014-15	Guelph Storm	OHL	57	11	37	48	57	....	....	....	....	....

LETUNOV, Maxim (leh-too-NAWV, max-EEM) ARI

Center. Shoots left. 6'2", 168 lbs. Born, Moscow, Russia, February 20, 1996.
(St. Louis' 3rd choice, 52nd overall, in 2014 Entry Draft).

			Regular Season					Playoffs				
Season	Club	League	GP	G	A	Pts	PIM	GP	G	A	Pts	PIM
2012-13	Dallas Midget	EHL Midget	40	29	37	66	6	4	2	2	4	6
2013-14	Youngstown	USHL	60	19	24	43	42	....	....	....	....	....
2014-15	Youngstown	USHL	58	25	39	64	18	4	0	1	1	0

Traded to **Arizona** by **St. Louis** for Zbynek Michalek and future considerations, March 2, 2015.

LEWINGTON, Tyler (LOO-ihng-tuhn, TIGH-luhr) WSH

Defense. Shoots right. 6'1", 189 lbs. Born, Edmonton, AB, December 5, 1994.
(Washington's 6th choice, 204th overall, in 2013 Entry Draft).

			Regular Season					Playoffs				
Season	Club	League	GP	G	A	Pts	PIM	GP	G	A	Pts	PIM
2010-11	Sherwood Park	AMHL	34	4	22	26	46	13	1	8	9	4
2011-12	Medicine Hat	WHL	44	0	3	3	46	8	0	1	1	2
2012-13	Medicine Hat	WHL	69	2	24	26	131	8	1	0	1	14
2013-14	Medicine Hat	WHL	68	7	31	38	121	18	0	3	3	26
2014-15	Medicine Hat	WHL	69	9	36	45	113	9	1	1	2	10

LINDBERG, Tobias (LIHND-buhrg, toh-BEE-uhs) OTT

Right wing. Shoots left. 6'3", 215 lbs. Born, Stockholm, Sweden, July 22, 1995.
(Ottawa's 3rd choice, 102nd overall, in 2013 Entry Draft).

			Regular Season					Playoffs				
Season	Club	League	GP	G	A	Pts	PIM	GP	G	A	Pts	PIM
2010-11	SDE U18	Swe-U18	9	0	2	2	18	....	....	....	....	....
2011-12	Djurgarden U18	Swe-U18	39	19	20	39	42	4	2	0	2	20
	Djurgarden Jr.	Swe-Jr.	1	0	0	0	0	3	0	1	1	0
2012-13	Djurgarden U18	Swe-U18	14	9	12	21	6	9	4	10	14	24
	Djurgarden Jr.	Swe-Jr.	43	9	13	22	30	2	0	2	2	2
	Djurgarden	Sweden-2	6	0	1	1	4	....	....	....	....	....
2013-14	Djurgarden Jr.	Swe-Jr.	38	7	15	22	93	4	2	1	3	12
	Djurgarden	Sweden-2	3	0	0	0	0	....	....	....	....	....
2014-15	Oshawa Generals	OHL	67	32	46	78	14	21	7	12	19	8

LINDBLOM, Oskar (LIHND-blawm, AWS-kuhr) PHI

Left wing. Shoots left. 6'1", 200 lbs. Born, Gavle, Sweden, August 15, 1996.
(Philadelphia's 4th choice, 138th overall, in 2014 Entry Draft).

			Regular Season					Playoffs				
Season	Club	League	GP	G	A	Pts	PIM	GP	G	A	Pts	PIM
2011-12	Brynas U18	Swe-U18	30	12	14	26	8	1	0	1	1	0
2012-13	Brynas U18	Swe-U18	33	31	28	59	14	8	4	5	9	2
	Brynas IF Gavle Jr.	Swe-Jr.	3	1	0	1	0	....	....	....	....	....
2013-14	Brynas U18	Swe-U18	6	8	5	13	0	....	....	....	....	....
	Brynas IF Gavle	Sweden	4	0	0	0	0	....	....	....	....	....
	Brynas IF Gavle Jr.	Swe-Jr.	43	13	20	33	28	7	6	1	7	6
2014-15	Brynas IF Gavle	Sweden	37	8	7	15	16	7	1	1	2	0

LINDELL, Esa (lihn-DEHL, EH-suh) DAL

Defense. Shoots left. 6'3", 210 lbs. Born, Vantaa, Finland, May 23, 1994.
(Dallas' 5th choice, 74th overall, in 2012 Entry Draft).

			Regular Season					Playoffs				
Season	Club	League	GP	G	A	Pts	PIM	GP	G	A	Pts	PIM
2009-10	Jokerit U18	Fin-U18	3	0	1	1	2	....	....	....	....	....
2010-11	Jokerit U18	Fin-U18	14	5	7	12	10	4	0	1	1	4
	Jokerit Helsinki Jr.	Fin-Jr.	....	....	....	....	....	3	1	1	2	2
2011-12	Jokerit Helsinki Jr.	Fin-Jr.	48	21	30	51	16	11	2	5	7	6
	Kiekko-Vantaa	Finland-2	2	0	0	0	0	....	....	....	....	....
2012-13	Jokerit Helsinki Jr.	Fin-Jr.	11	5	4	9	6	....	....	....	....	....
	Kiekko-Vantaa	Finland-2	22	4	6	10	16	....	....	....	....	....
	Jokerit Helsinki	Finland	19	0	0	0	4	....	....	....	....	....
2013-14	Kiekko-Vantaa	Finland-2	11	2	3	5	8	....	....	....	....	....
	Jokerit Helsinki	Finland	44	2	3	5	10	2	0	0	0	0
2014-15	Assat Pori	Finland	57	14	21	35	28	2	0	0	0	0
	Texas Stars	AHL	5	0	1	1	2	....	....	....	....	....

LINDGREN, Jesper (LIHND-gruhn, YEHS-puhr) TOR

Defense. Shoots right. 6', 161 lbs. Born, Umea, Sweden, May 19, 1997.
(Toronto's 6th choice, 95th overall, in 2015 Entry Draft).

			Regular Season					Playoffs				
Season	Club	League	GP	G	A	Pts	PIM	GP	G	A	Pts	PIM
2012-13	Bjorkloven U18	Swe-U18	35	1	15	16	8	....	....	....	....	....
2013-14	MODO U18	Swe-U18	35	7	25	32	34	5	0	0	0	0
	MODO Jr.	Swe-Jr.	8	1	3	4	2	....	....	....	....	....
2014-15	MODO U18	Swe-U18	6	0	9	9	8	3	1	1	2	0
	MODO Jr.	Swe-Jr.	39	6	27	33	39	4	0	1	1	2
	MODO	Sweden	4	0	1	1	0	....	....	....	....	....

LINDHOLM, Anton (LIHND-hohlm, AN-tawn) COL

Defense. Shoots left. 5'11", 191 lbs. Born, Skelleftea, Sweden, November 29, 1994.
(Colorado's 5th choice, 144th overall, in 2014 Entry Draft).

			Regular Season					Playoffs				
Season	Club	League	GP	G	A	Pts	PIM	GP	G	A	Pts	PIM
2009-10	Skelleftea AIK U18	Swe-U18	14	1	2	3	29	....	....	....	....	....
2010-11	Skelleftea AIK U18	Swe-U18	37	9	15	24	36	7	0	2	2	4
	Skelleftea AIK Jr.	Swe-Jr.	3	0	0	0	4	....	....	....	....	....
2011-12	Skelleftea AIK U18	Swe-U18	4	0	0	0	2	2	0	0	0	2
	Skelleftea AIK	Sweden	1	0	0	0	0	....	....	....	....	....
	Skelleftea AIK Jr.	Swe-Jr.	43	1	3	4	20	3	0	1	1	0
2012-13	Skelleftea AIK Jr.	Swe-Jr.	37	1	9	10	24	5	1	0	1	2
	Skelleftea AIK	Sweden	2	0	0	0	2	....	....	....	....	....
2013-14	Skelleftea AIK Jr.	Swe-Jr.	39	1	5	6	34	....	....	....	....	....
	Pitea HC	Sweden-3	1	0	1	1	0	....	....	....	....	....
	Skelleftea AIK	Sweden	7	0	0	0	4	14	1	2	3	4
2014-15	Malmo	Sweden-2	5	1	2	3	2	....	....	....	....	....
	Skelleftea AIK	Sweden	35	0	7	7	35	15	1	4	5	8

LINDO, Jaden (LIHN-doh, JAY-duhn) PIT

Right wing. Shoots right. 6'2", 211 lbs. Born, Brampton, ON, January 11, 1996.
(Pittsburgh's 4th choice, 173rd overall, in 2014 Entry Draft).

			Regular Season					Playoffs				
Season	Club	League	GP	G	A	Pts	PIM	GP	G	A	Pts	PIM
2011-12	Toronto Marlboros	GTHL	....	15	20	35	34	....	....	....	....	....
2012-13	Owen Sound	OHL	63	5	17	22	55	12	0	1	1	2
2013-14	Owen Sound	OHL	40	9	9	18	41	....	....	....	....	....
2014-15	Owen Sound	OHL	49	7	2	9	34	5	0	0	0	11

LINTUNIEMI, Alex (LIHN-too-nee-EH-mee, AL-ehx) L.A.

Defense. Shoots left. 6'3", 218 lbs. Born, Helsinki, Finland, September 23, 1995.
(Los Angeles' 3rd choice, 60th overall, in 2014 Entry Draft).

			Regular Season					Playoffs				
Season	Club	League	GP	G	A	Pts	PIM	GP	G	A	Pts	PIM
2010-11	HIFK Helsinki U18	Fin-U18	24	3	11	14	6	3	0	1	1	2
2011-12	Jokerit U18	Fin-U18	37	4	17	21	24	11	2	5	7	8
	Jokerit Helsinki Jr.	Fin-Jr.	3	0	1	1	0	....	....	....	....	....
2012-13	Jokerit Helsinki Jr.	Fin-Jr.	38	4	10	14	76	....	....	....	....	....
	Kiekko-Vantaa	Finland-2	11	1	2	3	6	....	....	....	....	....
	Jokerit U18	Fin-U18	....	....	....	....	....	10	4	4	8	6
2013-14	Ottawa 67's	OHL	68	4	17	21	26	....	....	....	....	....
2014-15	Ottawa 67's	OHL	58	7	29	36	22	6	1	2	3	2
	Manchester	AHL	4	0	1	1	0	....	....	....	....	....

LIPON, J.C. (lih-PAWN, JAY-SEE) WPG

Right wing. Shoots right. 6', 183 lbs. Born, Regina, SK, July 10, 1993.
(Winnipeg's 5th choice, 91st overall, in 2013 Entry Draft).

			Regular Season					Playoffs				
Season	Club	League	GP	G	A	Pts	PIM	GP	G	A	Pts	PIM
2008-09	Reg. Pat Cdns.	SMHL	43	4	9	13	26	5	2	1	3	4
2009-10	Kamloops Blazers	WHL	53	3	10	13	38	3	0	0	0	0
2010-11	Kamloops Blazers	WHL	65	3	18	21	111	....	....	....	....	....
2011-12	Kamloops Blazers	WHL	69	19	46	65	111	10	2	7	9	20
2012-13	Kamloops Blazers	WHL	61	36	53	89	115	15	6	17	23	20
2013-14	St. John's IceCaps	AHL	72	9	32	41	136	14	0	1	1	4
2014-15	St. John's IceCaps	AHL	75	5	21	26	163	....	....	....	....	....

LODGE, Jimmy (LAWDG, JIHM-ee) WPG

Center. Shoots right. 6'1", 172 lbs. Born, Downington, PA, March 5, 1995.
(Winnipeg's 4th choice, 84th overall, in 2013 Entry Draft).

			Regular Season					Playoffs				
Season	Club	League	GP	G	A	Pts	PIM	GP	G	A	Pts	PIM
2010-11	Toronto Titans	GTHL	29	18	25	43	44	....	....	....	....	....
2011-12	Saginaw Spirit	OHL	45	8	4	12	10	11	0	0	0	0
2012-13	Saginaw Spirit	OHL	64	28	39	67	28	4	1	2	3	7
2013-14	Saginaw Spirit	OHL	59	19	27	46	49	5	2	2	4	2
2014-15	Saginaw Spirit	OHL	18	10	8	18	8	....	....	....	....	....
	Mississauga	OHL	40	18	27	45	45	....	....	....	....	....
	St. John's IceCaps	AHL	1	0	0	0	0	....	....	....	....	....

LOOKE, Jens (LOH-keh, YEHNZ) ARI

Right wing. Shoots right. 6'1", 180 lbs. Born, Gavle, Sweden, April 11, 1997.
(Arizona's 7th choice, 83rd overall, in 2015 Entry Draft).

			Regular Season					Playoffs				
Season	Club	League	GP	G	A	Pts	PIM	GP	G	A	Pts	PIM
2011-12	Brynas U18	Swe-U18	1	0	0	0	0	....	....	....	....	....
2012-13	Brynas U18	Swe-U18	34	16	14	30	2	8	2	6	8	2
2013-14	Brynas U18	Swe-U18	32	15	25	40	14	5	3	4	7	2
	Brynas IF Gavle Jr.	Swe-Jr.	7	2	0	2	0	2	0	1	1	0
2014-15	Brynas U18	Swe-U18	1	1	4	5	0	4	3	3	6	0
	Brynas IF Gavle Jr.	Swe-Jr.	18	10	8	18	4	2	1	1	2	2
	Brynas IF Gavle	Sweden	43	2	4	6	2	7	0	0	0	0

LOOV, Viktor (LUHV, VIHK-tohr) TOR

Defense. Shoots left. 6'1", 209 lbs. Born, Sodertalje, Sweden, November 16, 1992.
(Toronto's 6th choice, 209th overall, in 2012 Entry Draft).

			Regular Season					Playoffs				
Season	Club	League	GP	G	A	Pts	PIM	GP	G	A	Pts	PIM
2008-09	Sodertalje SK U18	Swe-U18	17	0	3	3	8	4	0	1	1	6
2009-10	Sodertalje SK U18	Swe-U18	21	4	14	18	32	2	0	0	0	4
	Sodertalje SK Jr.	Swe-Jr.	12	0	4	4	8	....	....	....	....	....
2010-11	Sodertalje SK Jr.	Swe-Jr.	42	4	19	23	36	2	0	0	0	2
	Sodertalje SK	Sweden-Q	1	0	0	0	0	....	....	....	....	....
2011-12	Sodertalje SK Jr.	Swe-Jr.	5	0	3	3	2	4	2	0	2	2
	Sodertalje SK	Sweden-2	50	3	3	6	42	....	....	....	....	....
2012-13	Sodertalje SK	Sweden-2	50	2	9	11	57	....	....	....	....	....
2013-14	MODO	Sweden	42	5	7	12	20	2	0	0	0	0
2014-15	Toronto Marlies	AHL	74	6	15	21	44	3	0	1	1	12

LORENTZ, Steven (LAWR-ehntz, STEE-vehn) CAR

Center/Left wing. Shoots left. 6'3", 191 lbs. Born, Kitchener, ON, April 13, 1996.
(Carolina's 9th choice, 186th overall, in 2015 Entry Draft).

			Regular Season					Playoffs				
Season	Club	League	GP	G	A	Pts	PIM	GP	G	A	Pts	PIM
2011-12	Wat. Wolves MM	Minor-ON	56	19	28	47	24	....	....	....	....	....
2012-13	Wat. Wolves Mid.	Minor-ON	31	17	17	34	24	16	8	15	23	10
	Waterloo Siskins	ON-Jr.B	3	0	0	0	2	....	....	....	....	....
2013-14	Peterborough	OHL	64	7	11	18	18	11	2	0	2	0
2014-15	Peterborough	OHL	59	16	21	37	15	5	0	1	1	2

LOUIS, Anthony (LOO-ihs, AN-thuh-nee) CHI

Center. Shoots left. 5'9", 151 lbs. Born, Wheaton, IL, February 10, 1995.
(Chicago's 7th choice, 181st overall, in 2013 Entry Draft).

			Regular Season					Playoffs				
Season	Club	League	GP	G	A	Pts	PIM	GP	G	A	Pts	PIM
2010-11	Team Illinois	T1EHL	35	33	27	60	18	....	....	....	....	....
2011-12	USNTDP	USHL	32	16	6	22	12	....	....	....	....	....
	USNTDP	U-17	17	12	8	20	6	....	....	....	....	....
	USNTDP	U-18	7	0	1	1	2	....	....	....	....	....
2012-13	USNTDP	USHL	24	10	15	25	10	....	....	....	....	....
	USNTDP	U-18	38	12	14	26	10	....	....	....	....	....
2013-14	Miami U.	NCHC	36	12	13	25	10	....	....	....	....	....
2014-15	Miami U.	NCHC	37	9	27	36	8	....	....	....	....	....

LOUIS, Mark (LEW-ihs, MAHRK)

Defense. Shoots right. 6'4", 225 lbs. Born, Ponoka, AB, April 18, 1987.

			Regular Season					Playoffs				
Season	Club	League	GP	G	A	Pts	PIM	GP	G	A	Pts	PIM
2003-04	Brandon	WHL	39	0	1	1	18	....	....	....	....	....
2004-05	Brandon	WHL	66	2	10	12	94	12	0	2	2	12
2005-06	Brandon	WHL	58	1	7	8	61	6	0	0	0	4
2006-07	Brandon	WHL	72	2	6	8	113	11	0	0	0	8
2007-08	Brandon	WHL	6	0	2	2	15	....	....	....	....	....
	Red Deer Rebels	WHL	62	5	14	19	78	....	....	....	....	....
2008-09	St. FX University	AUAA	3	0	0	0	8	....	....	....	....	....
2009-10	St. FX University	AUAA	11	0	2	2	36	....	....	....	....	....
2010-11	St. FX University	AUAA	27	1	1	2	48	....	....	....	....	....
2011-12	Portland Pirates	AHL	23	0	4	4	72	....	....	....	....	....
2012-13	Portland Pirates	AHL	61	0	3	3	111	2	0	0	0	0
2013-14	Portland Pirates	AHL	56	1	4	5	89	....	....	....	....	....
2014-15	Portland Pirates	AHL	34	0	3	3	77	....	....	....	....	....
	Bridgeport	AHL	7	0	0	0	18	....	....	....	....	....

Signed as a free agent by **Phoenix**, April 30, 2012. Traded to **NY Islanders** by **Arizona** for David Leggio, March 2, 2015.

LOVERDE, Vincent (LOH-vuhr-dee, VIHN-sehnt) L.A.

Defense. Shoots right. 5'11", 209 lbs. Born, Chicago, IL, April 14, 1989.

			Regular Season					Playoffs				
Season	Club	League	GP	G	A	Pts	PIM	GP	G	A	Pts	PIM
2004-05	Chicago Y.A.	MWEHL	28	3	12	15	38	....	....	....	....	....
2005-06	Waterloo	USHL	53	5	6	11	78	....	....	....	....	....
2006-07	Waterloo	USHL	46	4	17	21	96	9	1	2	3	31
2007-08	Miami U.	CCHA	42	0	8	8	20	....	....	....	....	....
2008-09	Miami U.	CCHA	38	1	7	8	40	....	....	....	....	....
2009-10	Miami U.	CCHA	40	3	8	11	48	....	....	....	....	....
2010-11	Miami U.	CCHA	39	2	7	9	28	....	....	....	....	....
2011-12	Ontario Reign	ECHL	64	5	19	24	54	5	0	1	1	0
2012-13	Ontario Reign	ECHL	27	7	10	17	15	....	....	....	....	....
	Manchester	AHL	51	2	11	13	30	4	0	0	0	2
2013-14	Manchester	AHL	70	2	18	20	46	4	0	0	0	0
2014-15	Manchester	AHL	63	9	11	20	63	19	2	8	10	27

Signed as a free agent by **Ontario** (ECHL), October 21, 2011. Signed to a PTO (professional tryout) contract by **Manchester** (AHL), November 9, 2012. Signed as a free agent by **Los Angeles**, May 15, 2014.

LOWRY, Joel (LOW-ree, JOHL) L.A.

Left wing. Shoots left. 6'2", 185 lbs. Born, Calgary, AB, November 15, 1991.
(Los Angeles' 5th choice, 140th overall, in 2011 Entry Draft).

			Regular Season					Playoffs				
Season	Club	League	GP	G	A	Pts	PIM	GP	G	A	Pts	PIM
2008-09	Calgary Buffaloes	AMHL	32	14	16	30	32	15	5	6	11	20
	Okotoks Oilers	AJHL	3	0	0	0	0	....	....	....	....	....
2009-10	Victoria Grizzlies	BCHL	57	15	29	44	55	6	1	4	5	2
2010-11	Victoria Grizzlies	BCHL	42	24	43	67	35	12	5	12	17	6
2011-12	Cornell Big Red	ECAC	35	6	16	22	47	....	....	....	....	....
2012-13	Cornell Big Red	ECAC	33	12	11	23	55	....	....	....	....	....
2013-14	Cornell Big Red	ECAC	32	7	17	24	39	....	....	....	....	....
2014-15	Cornell Big Red	ECAC	11	4	4	8	14	....	....	....	....	....

LUCIA, Mario (LOO-chee-a, MAR-ee-oh) MIN

Left wing. Shoots left. 6'3", 202 lbs. Born, Fairbanks, AK, August 25, 1993.
(Minnesota's 3rd choice, 60th overall, in 2011 Entry Draft).

			Regular Season					Playoffs				
Season	Club	League	GP	G	A	Pts	PIM	GP	G	A	Pts	PIM
2009-10	Wayzata	High-MN	25	15	25	40	6	2	0	2	2	0
2010-11	Team Northwest	UMHSEL	10	6	6	12	4	1	0	0	0	0
	Wayzata	High-MN	24	25	22	47	14	3	5	2	7	2
	USNTDP	USHL	6	3	0	3	0	....	....	....	....	....
	USNTDP	U-18	9	1	1	2	0	....	....	....	....	....
2011-12	Penticton Vees	BCHL	56	42	51	93	42	15	6	10	16	2
2012-13	U. of Notre Dame	CCHA	32	12	11	23	18	....	....	....	....	....
2013-14	U. of Notre Dame	H-East	40	16	15	31	12	....	....	....	....	....
2014-15	U. of Notre Dame	H-East	42	21	11	32	22	....	....	....	....	....

CCHA All-Rookie Team (2013)

LUUKKO, Nick (LOO-koh, NIHK) PHI

Defense. Shoots right. 6'2", 180 lbs. Born, West Chester, PA, November 29, 1991.
(Philadelphia's 4th choice, 179th overall, in 2010 Entry Draft).

			Regular Season					Playoffs				
Season	Club	League	GP	G	A	Pts	PIM	GP	G	A	Pts	PIM
2008-09	Team Comcast	AYHL	3	0	1	1	2	....	....	....	....	....
	The Gunnery	High-CT	34	4	11	15	....	....	....	....	....	....
2009-10	The Gunnery	High-CT	....	3	22	25	....	....	....	....	....	....
2010-11	Dubuque	USHL	45	7	10	17	20	11	1	4	5	2
2011-12	U. of Vermont	H-East	17	0	3	3	4	....	....	....	....	....
2012-13	U. of Vermont	H-East	36	3	7	10	26	....	....	....	....	....
2013-14	U. of Vermont	H-East	37	3	5	8	28	....	....	....	....	....
2014-15	U. of Vermont	H-East	41	2	12	14	14	....	....	....	....	....
	Lehigh Valley	AHL	6	0	0	0	0	....	....	....	....	....

LYAMIN, Kirill (L'YAH-mihn, kih-RIHL) OTT

Defense. Shoots left. 6'2", 211 lbs. Born, Moscow, USSR, January 13, 1986.
(Ottawa's 2nd choice, 58th overall, in 2004 Entry Draft).

			Regular Season					Playoffs				
Season	Club	League	GP	G	A	Pts	PIM	GP	G	A	Pts	PIM
2001-02	Moscow 18	Exhib.	5	0	3	3	4	....	....	....	....	....
2002-03	CSKA Moscow 2	Russia-3	5	0	0	0	10	....	....	....	....	....
	Moscow 18	Exhib.	5	0	0	0	6	....	....	....	....	....
2003-04	CSKA Moscow 2	Russia-3	STATISTICS NOT AVAILABLE									
	CSKA Moscow	Russia	28	0	3	3	12	....	....	....	....	....
2004-05	CSKA Moscow 2	Russia-3	STATISTICS NOT AVAILABLE									
2005-06	CSKA Moscow	Russia	25	0	1	1	28	2	0	0	0	0
2006-07	CSKA Moscow	Russia	47	1	7	8	48	12	1	0	1	8
2007-08	Mytischi	Russia	40	1	6	7	77	3	0	0	0	0
2008-09	Spartak Moscow	KHL	54	1	7	8	82	6	0	0	0	4
2009-10	Spartak Moscow	KHL	48	3	9	12	52	9	0	1	1	8
2010-11	Cherepovets	KHL	49	3	9	12	66	6	1	2	3	8
2011-12	Omsk	KHL	49	1	4	5	53	19	0	5	5	12
2012-13	Omsk	KHL	37	3	1	4	32	12	1	0	1	6
2013-14	Omsk	KHL	52	3	11	14	22	11	1	3	4	4
2014-15	Omsk	KHL	57	2	8	10	28	12	0	2	2	2

LYYTINEN, Joonas (LEE'YOO-tih-nehn, YOH-nuhs) NSH

Defense. Shoots left. 6', 154 lbs. Born, Espoo, Finland, April 4, 1995.
(Nashville's 6th choice, 132nd overall, in 2014 Entry Draft).

			Regular Season					Playoffs				
Season	Club	League	GP	G	A	Pts	PIM	GP	G	A	Pts	PIM
2010-11	KalPa Kuopio U18	Fin-U18	7	1	1	2	6	1	0	1	1	0
2011-12	KalPa Kuopio U18	Fin-U18	32	8	10	18	40	3	0	0	0	2
	KalPa Kuopio Jr.	Fin-Jr.	5	1	3	4	6	....	....	....	....	....
2012-13	KalPa Kuopio U18	Fin-U18	3	0	2	2	4	....	....	....	....	....
	KalPa Kuopio Jr.	Fin-Jr.	31	4	9	13	30	3	0	0	0	4
2013-14	KalPa Kuopio Jr.	Fin-Jr.	24	7	17	24	32	....	....	....	....	....
	KalPa Kuopio	Finland	30	3	6	9	24	....	....	....	....	....
2014-15	KalPa Kuopio	Finland	52	8	9	17	34	6	0	0	0	6

MacDERMID, Kurtis (MAK-DUHR-mihd, KUHR-this) L.A.

Defense. Shoots left. 6'5", 222 lbs. Born, Sauble Beach, ON, March 25, 1994.

			Regular Season					Playoffs				
Season	Club	League	GP	G	A	Pts	PIM	GP	G	A	Pts	PIM
2010-11	Owen Sound	ON-Jr.B	51	6	16	22	124	....	....	....	....	....
2011-12	Owen Sound	ON-Jr.B	20	3	6	9	80	....	....	....	....	....
	Owen Sound	OHL	9	0	2	2	7	....	....	....	....	....
2012-13	Owen Sound	OHL	65	1	7	8	110	12	0	3	3	11
2013-14	Owen Sound	OHL	38	5	12	17	*90	....	....	....	....	....
	Erie Otters	OHL	28	2	1	3	*75	12	0	3	3	29
2014-15	Erie Otters	OHL	61	8	32	40	129	12	0	5	5	23

Signed as a free agent by **Los Angeles**, September 12, 2012.

MACEACHERN, Mackenzie (MAK-EHK-uhrn, muh-KEHN-zee) ST.L.

Left wing. Shoots left. 6'2", 190 lbs. Born, Royal Oak, MI, March 9, 1994.
(St. Louis' 3rd choice, 67th overall, in 2012 Entry Draft).

			Regular Season					Playoffs				
Season	Club	League	GP	G	A	Pts	PIM	GP	G	A	Pts	PIM
2010-11	Brother Rice	High-MI	30	23	41	64	12	....	....	....	....	....
2011-12	Brother Rice	High-MI	29	42	48	90	16	....	....	....	....	....
	Michigan D.H.L.	Other	18	7	8	15	8	....	....	....	....	....
2012-13	Chicago Steel	USHL	50	8	13	21	35	....	....	....	....	....
2013-14	Michigan State	Big Ten	36	8	4	12	14	....	....	....	....	....
2014-15	Michigan State	Big Ten	35	11	15	26	10	....	....	....	....	....

MacINNIS, Ryan (muh-KIH-nihs, RIGH-uhn) ARI

Center. Shoots left. 6'3", 182 lbs. Born, St. Louis, MO, February 14, 1996.
(Arizona's 2nd choice, 43rd overall, in 2014 Entry Draft).

			Regular Season					Playoffs				
Season	Club	League	GP	G	A	Pts	PIM	GP	G	A	Pts	PIM
2011-12	St. Louis Blues	T1EHL	34	27	20	47	18	....	....	....	....	....
	U.S. Youth Oly.	Other	6	4	2	6	4	....	....	....	....	....
2012-13	USNTDP	USHL	41	8	6	14	6	....	....	....	....	....
	USNTDP	U-17	11	7	4	11	0	....	....	....	....	....
2013-14	Kitchener Rangers	OHL	66	16	21	37	18	....	....	....	....	....
2014-15	Kitchener Rangers	OHL	67	25	37	62	28	6	3	5	8	6

MacKENZIE, Matt (muh-KEHN-zee, MAT)

Defense. Shoots right. 6'1", 180 lbs. Born, New Westminster, BC, October 15, 1991.
(Buffalo's 4th choice, 83rd overall, in 2010 Entry Draft).

			Regular Season					Playoffs				
Season	Club	League	GP	G	A	Pts	PIM	GP	G	A	Pts	PIM
2006-07	Van. NW Giants	BCMML	40	5	11	16	64	....	....	....	....	....
2007-08	Calgary Hitmen	WHL	39	2	6	8	8	6	1	2	3	2
2008-09	Calgary Hitmen	WHL	49	3	9	12	24	16	0	2	2	4
2009-10	Calgary Hitmen	WHL	64	6	34	40	62	23	6	10	16	31
2010-11	Calgary Hitmen	WHL	40	2	21	23	50	....	....	....	....	....
	Tri-City Americans	WHL	33	5	10	15	36	10	1	4	5	6
2011-12	Rochester	AHL	20	0	4	4	16	....	....	....	....	....
	Gwinnett	ECHL	5	0	2	2	11	....	....	....	....	....
2012-13	Greenville	ECHL	2	1	0	1	2	....	....	....	....	....
	Rochester	AHL	30	0	4	4	66	2	0	1	1	2
2013-14	Rochester	AHL	64	2	8	10	84	1	0	0	0	2
2014-15	Rochester	AHL	47	2	4	6	77	....	....	....	....	....
	Elmira Jackals	ECHL	8	1	1	2	13	....	....	....	....	....

MacLEOD, Johnathan (muh-KLOWD, JAWN-ah-thuhn) T.B.

Defense. Shoots right. 6'2", 200 lbs. Born, Lowell, MA, June 2, 1996.
(Tampa Bay's 3rd choice, 57th overall, in 2014 Entry Draft).

			Regular Season					Playoffs				
Season	Club	League	GP	G	A	Pts	PIM	GP	G	A	Pts	PIM
2011-12	Kimball Union	High-NH	31	0	13	13	22	....	....	....	....	....
2012-13	USNTDP	USHL	33	0	2	2	71	....	....	....	....	....
	USNTDP	U-17	13	0	3	3	22	....	....	....	....	....
2013-14	USNTDP	USHL	19	1	4	5	36	....	....	....	....	....
	USNTDP	U-18	32	4	3	7	38	....	....	....	....	....
2014-15	Boston University	H-East	37	2	7	9	58	....	....	....	....	....

MacMILLAN, Mark (muhk-MIHL-uhn, MAHRK) MTL

Center. Shoots left. 6', 182 lbs. Born, Penticton, BC, January 23, 1992.
(Montreal's 2nd choice, 113th overall, in 2010 Entry Draft).

			Regular Season					Playoffs				
Season	Club	League	GP	G	A	Pts	PIM	GP	G	A	Pts	PIM
2008-09	Okanagan Prep	Minor-BC	50	16	21	37	34	....	....	....	....	....
2009-10	Alberni Valley	BCHL	59	26	54	80	44	13	5	9	14	16
2010-11	Penticton Vees	BCHL	40	21	36	57	43	3	0	5	5	6
2011-12	North Dakota	WCHA	42	7	16	23	26	....	....	....	....	....
2012-13	North Dakota	WCHA	42	13	12	25	28	....	....	....	....	....
2013-14	North Dakota	NCHC	38	10	16	26	26	....	....	....	....	....
2014-15	North Dakota	NCHC	29	16	9	25	27	....	....	....	....	....

NCHC First All-Star Team (2015)

MADAISKY, Austin (muh-DAY-skee, AW-stuhn) CBJ

Defense. Shoots right. 6'2", 185 lbs. Born, Surrey, BC, January 30, 1992.
(Columbus' 6th choice, 124th overall, in 2010 Entry Draft).

			Regular Season					Playoffs				
Season	Club	League	GP	G	A	Pts	PIM	GP	G	A	Pts	PIM
2007-08	Valley West Hawks	BCMML	35	6	23	29	38	....	....	....	....	....
2008-09	Calgary Hitmen	WHL	48	2	7	9	16	2	0	0	0	2
2009-10	Calgary Hitmen	WHL	39	5	13	18	46	....	....	....	....	....
	Kamloops Blazers	WHL	26	2	7	9	28	4	3	3	6	6
2010-11	Kamloops Blazers	WHL	55	7	20	27	104	....	....	....	....	....
2011-12	Kamloops Blazers	WHL	70	13	37	50	87	9	0	7	7	12
2012-13	Evansville IceMen	ECHL	11	2	4	6	2	....	....	....	....	....
	Springfield Falcons	AHL	6	0	0	0	2	....	....	....	....	....
2013-14	Springfield Falcons	AHL	38	4	4	8	10	....	....	....	....	....
	Evansville IceMen	ECHL	8	0	2	2	0	....	....	....	....	....
2014-15	Springfield Falcons	AHL	53	12	23	35	28	....	....	....	....	....

WHL West Second All-Star Team (2012)

MAENALANEN, Saku (mai-NA-lah-nehn, SA-koo) NSH

Right wing. Shoots left. 6'3", 185 lbs. Born, Tornio, Finland, May 29, 1994.
(Nashville's 5th choice, 125th overall, in 2013 Entry Draft).

			Regular Season					Playoffs				
Season	Club	League	GP	G	A	Pts	PIM	GP	G	A	Pts	PIM
2010-11	Laser U18	Fin-U18	26	27	38	65	20	....	....	....	....	....
	Karpat Oulu U18	Fin-U18	1	0	0	0	2	....	....	....	....	....
2011-12	Karpat Oulu U18	Fin-U18	41	14	35	49	72	12	8	4	12	6
2012-13	Karpat Oulu Jr.	Fin-Jr.	45	23	35	58	43	5	5	2	7	18
2013-14	Karpat Oulu	Finland	25	4	3	7	0	....	....	....	....	....
	Jokipojat Joensuu	Finland-2	15	9	6	15	4	....	....	....	....	....
	Karpat Oulu Jr.	Fin-Jr.	5	3	3	6	2	12	4	4	8	10
2014-15	Karpat Oulu Jr.	Fin-Jr.	6	2	6	8	2	....	....	....	....	....
	Hokki Kajaani	Finland-2	17	5	8	13	6	10	2	4	6	22
	Pelicans Lahti	Finland	8	1	0	1	0	....	....	....	....	....
	Karpat Oulu	Finland	20	4	1	5	2	7	0	1	1	0

MAGYAR, Nick (MAG-YAHR, NIHK) COL

Right wing. Shoots right. 6'2", 194 lbs. Born, Cleveland, OH, May 29, 1996.
(Colorado's 3rd choice, 93rd overall, in 2014 Entry Draft).

			Regular Season					Playoffs				
Season	Club	League	GP	G	A	Pts	PIM	GP	G	A	Pts	PIM
2009-10	Cleveland Barons	T1EHL	31	25	30	55	33	....	....	....	....	....
2010-11	Cle. Barons Bant.	T1EHL	31	18	27	45	20	....	....	....	....	....
	Cle. Barons U18	T1EHL	2	0	0	0	0	....	....	....	....	....
2011-12	Cle. Barons U16	T1EHL	36	30	34	64	14	....	....	....	....	....
2012-13	Cle. Barons U18	T1EHL	31	13	21	34	64	3	0	0	0	0
	Sioux City	USHL	27	1	5	6	6	....	....	....	....	....
	USNTDP	USHL	4	0	0	0	2	....	....	....	....	....
2013-14	Kitchener Rangers	OHL	66	20	26	46	20	....	....	....	....	....
2014-15	Kitchener Rangers	OHL	65	16	16	32	18	6	1	2	3	2

MAKELA, Aleksi (ma-KIH-luh, A-LEHK-see) DAL

Defense. Shoots left. 6'1", 200 lbs. Born, Tampere, Finland, February 8, 1995.
(Dallas' 9th choice, 182nd overall, in 2013 Entry Draft).

			Regular Season					Playoffs				
Season	Club	League	GP	G	A	Pts	PIM	GP	G	A	Pts	PIM
2011-12	Ilves Tampere U17	Fin-U17	2	0	2	2	2	9	4	6	10	10
	Ilves Tampere U18	Fin-U18	35	4	10	14	10	3	1	0	1	2
	Ilves Tampere Jr.	Fin-Jr.	4	0	0	0	2	....	....	....	....	....
2012-13	Ilves Tampere U18	Fin-U18	8	0	9	9	4	....	....	....	....	....
	Ilves Tampere Jr.	Fin-Jr.	37	8	9	17	42	....	....	....	....	....
	Ilves Tampere	Finland	7	1	1	2	4	....	....	....	....	....
	Ilves Tampere	Finland-Q	....	....	....	....	....	3	0	1	1	0
2013-14	Ilves Tampere	Finland	9	0	0	0	4	....	....	....	....	....
	LeKi Lempaala	Finland-2	3	0	0	0	2	....	....	....	....	....
	Ilves Tampere Jr.	Fin-Jr.	25	3	11	14	16	2	0	0	0	2
2014-15	Ilves Tampere	Finland	30	0	6	6	22	....	....	....	....	....
	LeKi Lempaala	Finland-2	7	0	0	0	4	....	....	....	....	....

MALGIN, Denis (mahl-GEEN, deh-NEEZ) FLA

Center. Shoots right. 5'9", 176 lbs. Born, Olten, Switzerland, January 18, 1997.
(Florida's 4th choice, 102nd overall, in 2015 Entry Draft).

			Regular Season					Playoffs				
Season	Club	League	GP	G	A	Pts	PIM	GP	G	A	Pts	PIM
2010-11	Zurich U17 II	Swiss-U17	16	13	9	22	6	....	....	....	....	....
2011-12	ZSC Zurich U17	Swiss-U17	25	17	19	36	34	8	2	7	9	2
2012-13	Zurich U17	Swiss-U17	7	6	10	16	16	5	4	5	9	4
	GCK Zurich Jr.	Swiss-Jr.	25	15	11	26	14	3	1	1	2	2
2013-14	GCK Zurich Jr.	Swiss-Jr.	....	....	....	....	....	7	5	1	6	8
	GCK Lions Zurich	Swiss-2	38	6	13	19	14	....	....	....	....	....
2014-15	GCK Lions Zurich	Swiss-2	24	6	6	12	4	....	....	....	....	....
	ZSC Lions Zurich	Swiss	23	2	6	8	8	18	4	2	6	4
	GCK Zurich Jr.	Swiss-Jr.	....	....	....	....	....	5	1	8	9	4

MALONE, Sean (ma-LOHN, SHAWN) BUF

Center. Shoots left. 6', 190 lbs. Born, Buffalo, NY, April 30, 1995.
(Buffalo's 10th choice, 159th overall, in 2013 Entry Draft).

			Regular Season					Playoffs				
Season	Club	League	GP	G	A	Pts	PIM	GP	G	A	Pts	PIM
2010-11	Nichols	High-NY	14	3	9	12	4	3	3	3	6	0
	Buffalo Saints	Minor-NY	STATISTICS NOT AVAILABLE									
2011-12	Nichols	High-NY	15	17	18	35	6	1	0	1	1	0
	Nichols	Other	16	17	17	34	....	....	....	....	....	....
	Buffalo Saints	Minor-NY	....	27	27	54	....	....	....	....	....	....
2012-13	USNTDP	USHL	15	5	8	13	17	....	....	....	....	....
	USNTDP	U-18	35	9	11	20	2	....	....	....	....	....
2013-14	Harvard Crimson	ECAC	31	6	14	20	16	....	....	....	....	....
2014-15	Harvard Crimson	ECAC	21	8	10	18	12	....	....	....	....	....

MANGIAPANE, Andrew (MAN-gee-AH-pah-nee, an-DROO) CGY

Left wing. Shoots left. 5'10", 170 lbs. Born, Bolton, ON, April 4, 1996.
(Calgary's 4th choice, 166th overall, in 2015 Entry Draft).

			Regular Season					Playoffs				
Season	Club	League	GP	G	A	Pts	PIM	GP	G	A	Pts	PIM
2011-12	Miss. Senators	GTHL	46	22	17	39	44	....	....	....	....	....
2012-13	Tor. Jr. Can. Midg.	GTHL	32	14	22	36	22	7	5	2	7	8
	Tor. Canadiens	ON-Jr.A	4	0	0	0	2	....	....	....	....	....
2013-14	Barrie Colts	OHL	68	24	27	51	28	11	2	5	7	8
2014-15	Barrie Colts	OHL	68	43	61	104	54	9	6	4	10	12

OHL All-Rookie Team (2014)

MANTHA, Anthony (MAN-tha, AN-thuh-nee) DET

Right wing. Shoots left. 6'5", 214 lbs. Born, Longueuil, QC, September 16, 1994.
(Detroit's 1st choice, 20th overall, in 2013 Entry Draft).

			Regular Season					Playoffs				
Season	Club	League	GP	G	A	Pts	PIM	GP	G	A	Pts	PIM
2010-11	C.C. Lemoyne	QAAA	37	20	24	44	42	3	0	1	1	12
	Val-d'Or Foreurs	QMJHL	2	0	0	0	0	....	....	....	....	....
2011-12	Val-d'Or Foreurs	QMJHL	63	22	29	51	39	4	2	2	4	6
2012-13	Val-d'Or Foreurs	QMJHL	67	*50	39	89	71	9	5	7	12	13
2013-14	Val-d'Or Foreurs	QMJHL	57	*57	63	*120	75	24	*24	14	38	*52
2014-15	Grand Rapids	AHL	62	15	18	33	64	16	2	2	4	16

QMJHL Second All-Star Team (2013) • QMJHL First All-Star Team (2014) • QMJHL Player of the Year (2014) • Canadian Major Junior Player of the Year (2014)

MANTHA, Ryan (MAN-thuh, RIGH-uhn) NYR

Defense. Shoots right. 6'5", 225 lbs. Born, Clarkston, MI, June 18, 1996.
(NY Rangers' 3rd choice, 104th overall, in 2014 Entry Draft).

			Regular Season					Playoffs				
Season	Club	League	GP	G	A	Pts	PIM	GP	G	A	Pts	PIM
2010-11	Det. L.C. Bant.	T1EHL	28	4	10	14	29	....	....	....	....	....
	Det. L.C. U16	T1EHL	4	0	0	0	2	....	....	....	....	....
2011-12	Detroit Belle Tire	T1EHL	38	8	14	22	41	6	0	1	1	19
2012-13	Sioux City	USHL	52	1	6	7	48	....	....	....	....	....
2013-14	Sioux City	USHL	29	1	5	6	51	....	....	....	....	....
	Indiana Ice	USHL	24	2	7	9	20	10	0	3	3	11
2014-15	Niagara Ice Dogs	OHL	52	10	15	25	45	11	1	5	6	6

MARCANTUONI, Matia (mark-an-TEW-oh-nee, mah-TEE-ah) PIT

Center/Right wing. Shoots right. 6', 200 lbs. Born, Woodbridge, ON, February 22, 1994.
(Pittsburgh's 6th choice, 92nd overall, in 2012 Entry Draft).

			Regular Season					Playoffs				
Season	Club	League	GP	G	A	Pts	PIM	GP	G	A	Pts	PIM
2009-10	Toronto Marlboros	GTHL	77	39	33	72	64	....	....	....	....	....
	St. Michael's	ON-Jr.A	2	2	0	2	2	....	....	....	....	....
2010-11	Kitchener Rangers	OHL	42	11	16	27	26	7	0	0	0	0
2011-12	Kitchener Rangers	OHL	24	9	5	14	10	....	....	....	....	....
2012-13	Kitchener Rangers	OHL	64	7	18	25	34	10	1	1	2	6
2013-14	Kitchener Rangers	OHL	54	15	17	32	29	....	....	....	....	....
	Wilkes-Barre	AHL	1	0	0	0	2	....	....	....	....	....
2014-15	Wheeling Nailers	ECHL	11	4	6	10	6	....	....	....	....	....
	Wilkes-Barre	AHL	59	4	10	14	20	4	0	0	0	2

• Missed majority of 2011-12 due to shoulder injury vs. Erie (OHL), January 7, 2012.

MARCHMENT, Jake (MARCH-muhnt, JAYK) L.A.

Center. Shoots right. 6'3", 215 lbs. Born, Ajax, ON, May 20, 1995.
(Los Angeles' 7th choice, 157th overall, in 2014 Entry Draft).

			Regular Season					Playoffs				
Season	Club	League	GP	G	A	Pts	PIM	GP	G	A	Pts	PIM
2010-11	Clarington Toros	Minor-ON	36	18	14	32	22	....	....	....	....	....
	Cobourg Cougars	ON-Jr.A	3	1	0	1	2	....	....	....	....	....
2011-12	Clarington Toros	Minor-ON	23	8	12	20	12	12	8	11	19	22
	Clarington Toros	Other	15	16	3	19	10	....	....	....	....	....
2012-13	Wellington Dukes	ON-Jr.A	49	7	13	20	50	5	1	1	2	7
2013-14	Belleville Bulls	OHL	57	10	22	32	53	....	....	....	....	....
2014-15	Belleville Bulls	OHL	22	6	6	12	16	....	....	....	....	....
	Erie Otters	OHL	29	4	7	11	26	19	8	6	14	4

MARINO, John (muh-REE-noh, JAWN) EDM

Defense. Shoots right. 6'1", 171 lbs. Born, Brockton, MA, May 21, 1997.
(Edmonton's 4th choice, 154th overall, in 2015 Entry Draft).

			Regular Season					Playoffs				
Season	Club	League	GP	G	A	Pts	PIM	GP	G	A	Pts	PIM
2012-13	South Shore Kings	EJHL	37	3	31	34	12	6	0	3	3	6
2013-14	South Shore U18	USPHL	12	1	4	5	12	....	....	....	....	....
	South Shore Kings	USPHL	34	6	11	17	16	5	0	2	2	2
2014-15	South Shore Kings	USPHL	49	4	24	28	42	5	0	2	2	6

• Signed Letter of Intent to attend **Harvard University** (ECAC) in fall of 2016.

MARNER, Mitch (MAHR-nuhr, MIHTCH) TOR

Center. Shoots right. 5'11", 160 lbs. Born, Markham, ON, May 5, 1997.
(Toronto's 1st choice, 4th overall, in 2015 Entry Draft).

			Regular Season					Playoffs				
Season	Club	League	GP	G	A	Pts	PIM	GP	G	A	Pts	PIM
2012-13	Don Mills Flyers	GTHL	55	41	45	86	34	....	....	....	....	....
	St. Michael's	ON-Jr.A	6	1	3	4	0	14	3	1	4	0
2013-14	London Knights	OHL	64	13	46	59	24	9	3	6	9	4
	London Knights	M-Cup	....	....	....	....	....	3	0	1	1	2
2014-15	London Knights	OHL	63	44	82	126	53	7	9	7	16	8

OHL First All-Star Team (2015)

MARODY, Cooper (mah-ROH-dee, KOO-puhr) PHI

Center. Shoots right. 6', 177 lbs. Born, Brighton, MI, December 20, 1996.
(Philadelphia's 8th choice, 158th overall, in 2015 Entry Draft).

			Regular Season					Playoffs				
Season	Club	League	GP	G	A	Pts	PIM	GP	G	A	Pts	PIM
2011-12	St. Mary's Prep	High-MI	7	1	3	4	2	....	....	....	....	....
2012-13	St. Mary's Prep	High-MI	26	19	23	42	20	....	....	....	....	....
	St. Mary's Prep	Other	2	1	2	3	0	....	....	....	....	....
2013-14	Muskegon	USHL	58	9	21	30	36	....	....	....	....	....
2014-15	Muskegon	USHL	14	2	7	9	4	....	....	....	....	....
	Sioux Falls	USHL	38	20	29	49	28	12	1	11	12	10

• Signed Letter of Intent to attend **University of Michigan** (Big Ten) in fall of 2015.

MARSH, Adam (MAHRSH, A-duhm) DET

Left wing. Shoots left. 6', 160 lbs. Born, Chicago, IL, August 22, 1997.
(Detroit's 6th choice, 200th overall, in 2015 Entry Draft).

			Regular Season					Playoffs				
Season	Club	League	GP	G	A	Pts	PIM	GP	G	A	Pts	PIM
2012-13	Chi. Americans	HPHL	23	3	0	3	16	....	....	....	....	....
2013-14	Chi. Americans	HPHL	6	6	2	8	6	....	....	....	....	....
	Chi. Americans	Other	14	9	7	16	26	....	....	....	....	....
2014-15	Saint John	QMJHL	60	24	20	44	57	....	....	....	....	....

MARTEL, Danick (MAHR-tehl, dah-NEEK) PHI

Center. Shoots left. 5'8", 166 lbs. Born, Drummondville, QC, December 12, 1994.

			Regular Season					Playoffs				
Season	Club	League	GP	G	A	Pts	PIM	GP	G	A	Pts	PIM
2010-11	Magog	QAAA	41	10	8	18	60	13	7	4	11	8
2011-12	Magog	QAAA	41	23	29	52	83	7	6	3	9	10
	Blainville-Bois.	QMJHL	1	0	0	0	0	....	....	....	....	....
2012-13	Blainville-Bois.	QMJHL	68	19	22	41	50	15	3	4	7	16
2013-14	Blainville-Bois.	QMJHL	63	32	28	60	42	11	8	1	9	8
2014-15	Blainville-Bois.	QMJHL	64	48	54	102	85	6	4	3	7	8
	Lehigh Valley	AHL	5	1	2	3	4	....	....	....	....	....

QMJHL First All-Star Team (2015)

Signed as a free agent by **Philadelphia**, March 10, 2015.

MARTENET, Chris (MAHR-tih-neht, KRIHS) DAL

Defense. Shoots left. 6'7", 198 lbs. Born, Waukesha, WI, September 25, 1996.
(Dallas' 3rd choice, 103rd overall, in 2015 Entry Draft).

			Regular Season					Playoffs				
Season	Club	League	GP	G	A	Pts	PIM	GP	G	A	Pts	PIM
2011-12	Shattuck Midget	High-MN	37	1	16	17	34	....	....	....	....	....
2012-13	Shattuck Midget	High-MN	43	8	22	30	20	....	....	....	....	....
2013-14	Indiana Ice	USHL	35	0	5	5	20	2	0	0	0	0
2014-15	London Knights	OHL	64	7	9	16	49	10	0	0	0	2

MARTI, Christian (MAHR-tee, KRIHS-t'yen) PHI

Defense. Shoots left. 6'3", 214 lbs. Born, Bulach, Switzerland, March 29, 1993.

			Regular Season					Playoffs				
Season	Club	League	GP	G	A	Pts	PIM	GP	G	A	Pts	PIM
2009-10	Kloten Flyers U17	Swiss-U17	28	11	14	25	86	10	2	6	8	26
	Kloten Flyers Jr.	Swiss-Jr.	2	0	0	0	0	....	....	....	....	....
2010-11	Kloten Flyers Jr.	Swiss-Jr.	38	3	6	9	22	11	0	0	0	28
2011-12	Kloten Flyers Jr.	Swiss-Jr.	12	4	6	10	24	3	1	0	1	0
	Kloten Flyers	Swiss	41	0	2	2	6	5	0	0	0	2
2012-13	Blainville-Bois.	QMJHL	46	5	9	14	35	15	1	3	4	6
2013-14	Geneve	Swiss	50	4	8	12	24	12	1	4	5	8
2014-15	Geneve	Swiss	32	1	7	8	20	....	....	....	....	....

Signed as a free agent by **Philadelphia**, May 1, 2015.

MARTIN, Brycen (MAR-tihn, BRIGH-suhn) **BUF**

Defense. Shoots left. 6'1", 199 lbs. Born, Calgary, AB, May 9, 1996.
(Buffalo's 6th choice, 74th overall, in 2014 Entry Draft).

			Regular Season					Playoffs				
Season	Club	League	GP	G	A	Pts	PIM	GP	G	A	Pts	PIM
2009-10	Calgary Bisons	AMBHL	33	2	22	24	18	13	0	6	6	4
2010-11	Calgary Bisons	AMBHL	31	6	36	42	60	....	....	....	....	....
	CBHA Rangers	Minor-AB	1	0	0	0	0	....	....	....	....	....
2011-12	Calgary Buffaloes	AMHL	25	6	11	17	65	5	0	2	2	8
	Swift Current	WHL	3	0	0	0	0	....	....	....	....	....
2012-13	Swift Current	WHL	67	2	17	19	32	5	0	0	0	0
2013-14	Swift Current	WHL	72	6	31	37	42	6	0	2	2	4
2014-15	Swift Current	WHL	39	2	14	16	22	....	....	....	....	....
	Saskatoon Blades	WHL	30	5	17	22	19	....	....	....	....	....
	Rochester	AHL	2	0	0	0	0	....	....	....	....	....

MARTINDALE, Ryan (MAHR-tihn-dayl, RIGH-uhn)

Center. Shoots left. 6'3", 202 lbs. Born, Oshawa, ON, October 27, 1991.
(Edmonton's 5th choice, 61st overall, in 2010 Entry Draft).

			Regular Season					Playoffs				
Season	Club	League	GP	G	A	Pts	PIM	GP	G	A	Pts	PIM
2006-07	Whitby Wildcats	Minor-ON	79	65	67	132	....	....	....	....	....	....
2007-08	Ottawa 67's	OHL	64	9	8	17	18	4	0	0	0	2
2008-09	Ottawa 67's	OHL	53	23	24	47	14	7	2	1	3	7
2009-10	Ottawa 67's	OHL	61	19	41	60	37	12	4	5	9	6
2010-11	Ottawa 67's	OHL	65	34	49	83	30	4	3	2	5	2
2011-12	Oklahoma City	AHL	16	0	2	2	4	....	....	....	....	....
	Stockton Thunder	ECHL	34	6	9	15	10	....	....	....	....	....
2012-13	Stockton Thunder	ECHL	5	2	0	2	0	....	....	....	....	....
	Oklahoma City	AHL	41	6	8	14	10	2	0	0	0	5
2013-14	Oklahoma City	AHL	22	3	7	10	8	....	....	....	....	....
	San Antonio	AHL	37	5	9	14	14	....	....	....	....	....
2014-15	San Antonio	AHL	45	8	5	13	6	....	....	....	....	....
	Syracuse Crunch	AHL	19	8	6	14	4	3	0	0	0	0

Traded to **Florida** by **Edmonton** for Steve Pinizzotto, January 16, 2014.

MARTINSEN, Andreas (MAHR-tihn-sehn, an-DRAY-uhs) **COL**

Left wing. Shoots left. 6'3", 220 lbs. Born, Baerum, Norway, June 13, 1990.

			Regular Season					Playoffs				
Season	Club	League	GP	G	A	Pts	PIM	GP	G	A	Pts	PIM
2009-10	Leksands IF	Sweden-2	22	3	2	5	8	....	....	....	....	....
	Leksands IF Jr.	Swe-Jr.	8	2	3	5	37	....	....	....	....	....
2012-13	Dusseldorf	Germany	52	6	16	22	72	....	....	....	....	....
2013-14	Dusseldorfer EG	Germany	42	9	8	17	124	....	....	....	....	....
2014-15	Dusseldorfer EG	Germany	50	18	23	41	99	12	1	4	5	8

Signed as a free agent by **Colorado**, May 15, 2015.

MASIN, Dominik (MAH-shihn, DOHM-ihn-ihk) **T.B.**

Defense. Shoots left. 6'2", 189 lbs. Born, Mestec Kralove, Czech Rep., February 1, 1996.
(Tampa Bay's 2nd choice, 35th overall, in 2014 Entry Draft).

			Regular Season					Playoffs				
Season	Club	League	GP	G	A	Pts	PIM	GP	G	A	Pts	PIM
2010-11	Slavia U18	CzR-U18	16	1	2	3	18	3	0	1	1	2
2011-12	Slavia U18	CzR-U18	34	0	3	3	26	....	....	....	....	....
2012-13	Slavia U18	CzR-U18	12	3	3	6	41	2	0	0	0	4
	HC Slavia Praha Jr.	CzRep-Jr.	25	1	2	3	16	....	....	....	....	....
2013-14	HC Slavia Praha Jr.	CzRep-Jr.	39	2	19	21	102	5	1	1	2	33
	Slavia U18	CzR-U18	....	....	....	....	....	2	1	0	1	2
2014-15	Peterborough	OHL	48	7	19	26	70	....	....	....	....	....

MASSIE, Jake (MA-see, JAYK) **CAR**

Defense. Shoots left. 6'1", 178 lbs. Born, Montreal, QC, January 21, 1997.
(Carolina's 7th choice, 156th overall, in 2015 Entry Draft).

			Regular Season					Playoffs				
Season	Club	League	GP	G	A	Pts	PIM	GP	G	A	Pts	PIM
2012-13	John Rennie	High-QU	24	1	4	5	....	....	....	....	....	....
2013-14	John Rennie	High-QU	30	9	14	23	....	....	....	....	....	....
2014-15	Boston Jr. Bruins	Minor-MA	14	6	5	11	20	....	....	....	....	....
	Kimball Union	High-NH	34	5	15	20	....	....	....	....	....	....

• Signed Letter of Intent to attend **University of Massachusetts** (Hockey East) in fall of 2015.

MATHERS, Derek (MA-thurz, DAIR-ihk) **PHI**

Right wing. Shoots right. 6'3", 226 lbs. Born, Strathroy, ON, August 4, 1993.
(Philadelphia's 6th choice, 206th overall, in 2011 Entry Draft).

			Regular Season					Playoffs				
Season	Club	League	GP	G	A	Pts	PIM	GP	G	A	Pts	PIM
2008-09	Elgin-Mid. Chiefs	Minor-ON	30	2	5	7	60	....	....	....	....	....
2009-10	Strathroy Rockets	ON-Jr.B	43	2	5	7	53	5	0	3	3	4
2010-11	Peterborough	OHL	55	1	4	5	*171	....	....	....	....	....
2011-12	Peterborough	OHL	65	9	8	17	177	....	....	....	....	....
	Adirondack	AHL	9	0	0	0	26	....	....	....	....	....
2012-13	Peterborough	OHL	64	10	19	29	125	....	....	....	....	....
	Adirondack	AHL	12	1	0	1	24	....	....	....	....	....
2013-14	Adirondack	AHL	34	2	0	2	105	....	....	....	....	....
2014-15	Lehigh Valley	AHL	40	0	2	2	147	....	....	....	....	....
	Reading Royals	ECHL	3	0	1	1	14	....	....	....	....	....

MATHESON, Michael (MA-thuh-suhn, MIGH-kuhl) **FLA**

Defense. Shoots left. 6'2", 192 lbs. Born, Pointe-Claire, QC, February 27, 1994.
(Florida's 1st choice, 23rd overall, in 2012 Entry Draft).

			Regular Season					Playoffs				
Season	Club	League	GP	G	A	Pts	PIM	GP	G	A	Pts	PIM
2009-10	Lac St-Louis Lions	QAAA	30	5	6	11	33	17	6	7	13	10
2010-11	Lac St-Louis Lions	QAAA	35	14	24	38	72	15	7	18	25	16
2011-12	Dubuque	USHL	53	11	16	27	84	5	4	1	5	4
2012-13	Boston College	H-East	36	8	17	25	78	....	....	....	....	....
2013-14	Boston College	H-East	38	3	18	21	49	....	....	....	....	....
2014-15	Boston College	H-East	38	3	22	25	26	....	....	....	....	....
	San Antonio	AHL	5	0	2	2	8	....	....	....	....	....

Hockey East All-Rookie Team (2013) • Hockey East First All-Star Team (2014) • NCAA East Second All-American Team (2014)

MAYO, Dysin (MAY-oh, DIGH-sihn) **ARI**

Defense. Shoots right. 6', 185 lbs. Born, Victoria, BC, August 17, 1996.
(Arizona's 6th choice, 133rd overall, in 2014 Entry Draft).

			Regular Season					Playoffs				
Season	Club	League	GP	G	A	Pts	PIM	GP	G	A	Pts	PIM
2010-11	PoE Academy	High-BC	51	8	33	41	30	....	....	....	....	....
	PoE Academy	CSSHL	....	....	....	....	....	4	0	2	2	0
2011-12	PoE Academy	NAPHL	17	3	1	4	12	5	0	1	1	6
	Victoria Cougars	VIJHL	1	0	1	1	0	....	....	....	....	....
2012-13	Edmonton	WHL	42	1	4	5	12	19	0	4	4	2
2013-14	Edmonton	WHL	63	7	28	35	50	21	3	12	15	10
2014-15	Edmonton	WHL	72	14	37	51	75	5	0	2	2	2

MCCANN, Jared (muh-KAN, JAIR-uhd) **VAN**

Center. Shoots left. 6', 185 lbs. Born, London, ON, May 31, 1996.
(Vancouver's 2nd choice, 24th overall, in 2014 Entry Draft).

			Regular Season					Playoffs				
Season	Club	League	GP	G	A	Pts	PIM	GP	G	A	Pts	PIM
2009-10	Elgin-Middl. Bant.	Minor-ON	62	61	69	130	91	....	....	....	....	....
2010-11	Elgin-Middl. Bant.	Minor-ON	78	81	98	179	84	....	....	....	....	....
	Elgin-Middl. MM	Minor-ON	3	0	0	0	0	3	3	0	3	0
2011-12	Lon. Knights MM	Minor-ON	29	33	26	59	22	11	9	11	20	4
	Lon. Knights MM	Other	27	19	33	52	6	....	....	....	....	....
	London Nationals	ON-Jr.B	4	1	0	1	2	4	2	1	3	0
2012-13	Sault Ste. Marie	OHL	64	21	23	44	35	1	0	0	0	0
2013-14	Sault Ste. Marie	OHL	64	27	35	62	51	9	2	5	7	4
2014-15	Sault Ste. Marie	OHL	56	34	47	81	27	14	6	10	16	12

McCARRON, Michael (muh-KAIR-uhn, MIGH-kuhl) **MTL**

Right wing. Shoots right. 6'6", 235 lbs. Born, Grosse Pointe, MI, March 7, 1995.
(Montreal's 1st choice, 25th overall, in 2013 Entry Draft).

			Regular Season					Playoffs				
Season	Club	League	GP	G	A	Pts	PIM	GP	G	A	Pts	PIM
2009-10	Det. Honeybaked	T1EHL	29	12	20	32	44	....	....	....	....	....
2010-11	Det. Honeybaked	T1EHL	38	6	12	18	88	....	....	....	....	....
2011-12	USNTDP	USHL	35	3	14	17	112	1	0	1	1	2
	USNTDP	U-17	17	3	6	9	14	....	....	....	....	....
2012-13	USNTDP	USHL	19	5	5	10	84	....	....	....	....	....
	USNTDP	U-18	40	11	16	27	98	....	....	....	....	....
2013-14	London Knights	OHL	66	14	20	34	120	9	3	2	5	22
2014-15	London Knights	OHL	25	22	19	41	58	....	....	....	....	....
	Oshawa Generals	OHL	31	6	21	27	70	21	9	9	18	33

Memorial Cup All-Star Team (2015)

McCARTHY, Chris (muh-KAHR-thee, KRIHS) **NYR**

Left wing. Shoots right. 6'1", 206 lbs. Born, Collegeville, PA, July 30, 1991.

			Regular Season					Playoffs				
Season	Club	League	GP	G	A	Pts	PIM	GP	G	A	Pts	PIM
2007-08	Berkshire Bears	High-MA	29	19	18	37	12	....	....	....	....	....
2008-09	USNTDP	NAHL	19	4	7	11	22	9	0	1	1	4
	USNTDP	U-18	31	7	11	18	22	....	....	....	....	....
2009-10	U. of Vermont	H-East	35	6	11	17	23	....	....	....	....	....
2010-11	U. of Vermont	H-East	36	8	12	20	20	....	....	....	....	....
2011-12	U. of Vermont	H-East	5	1	3	4	4	....	....	....	....	....
2012-13	U. of Vermont	H-East	36	13	18	31	10	....	....	....	....	....
2013-14	U. of Vermont	H-East	38	18	24	42	12	....	....	....	....	....
	Hartford Wolf Pack	AHL	8	1	0	1	2	....	....	....	....	....
2014-15	Hartford Wolf Pack	AHL	5	1	0	1	0	....	....	....	....	....
	Greenville	ECHL	63	15	24	39	12	....	....	....	....	....

Hockey East Second All-Star Team (2014)

Signed as a free agent by **NY Rangers**, April 2, 2014.

MCCORMICK, Max (muh-KOHR-mihk, MAX) **OTT**

Left wing. Shoots left. 5'11", 185 lbs. Born, De Pere, WI, May 1, 1992.
(Ottawa's 8th choice, 171st overall, in 2011 Entry Draft).

			Regular Season					Playoffs				
Season	Club	League	GP	G	A	Pts	PIM	GP	G	A	Pts	PIM
2007-08	Notre Dame Acad.	High-WI	16	19	20	39	....	....	....	....	....	....
2008-09	Team Wisconsin	UMHSEL	STATISTICS NOT AVAILABLE									
	Notre Dame Acad.	High-WI	18	19	38	57	....	....	....	....	....	....
2009-10	Team Wisconsin	UMHSEL	24	....	....	24	....	....	....	....	....	....
	Notre Dame Acad.	High-WI	29	38	37	75	74	....	....	....	....	....
2010-11	Sioux City	USHL	55	21	21	42	102	3	1	2	3	4
2011-12	Ohio State	CCHA	27	10	12	22	31	....	....	....	....	....
2012-13	Ohio State	CCHA	40	15	16	31	26	....	....	....	....	....
2013-14	Ohio State	Big Ten	37	11	24	35	40	....	....	....	....	....
2014-15	Binghamton	AHL	62	10	10	20	133	....	....	....	....	....

CCHA All-Rookie Team (2012)

McCOSHEN, Ian (muh-KOH-shuhn, EE-uhn) **FLA**

Defense. Shoots left. 6'3", 215 lbs. Born, Anaheim, CA, August 5, 1995.
(Florida's 2nd choice, 31st overall, in 2013 Entry Draft).

			Regular Season					Playoffs				
Season	Club	League	GP	G	A	Pts	PIM	GP	G	A	Pts	PIM
2009-10	Shattuck Bantam	High-MN	58	21	35	56	46	....	....	....	....	....
2010-11	Waterloo	USHL	42	0	6	6	38	2	0	0	0	0
2011-12	Waterloo	USHL	55	8	12	20	43	15	4	3	7	6
2012-13	Waterloo	USHL	53	11	33	44	48	5	2	2	4	4
2013-14	Boston College	H-East	35	5	8	13	48	....	....	....	....	....
2014-15	Boston College	H-East	35	6	10	16	63	....	....	....	....	....

USHL First All-Star Team (2013)

McDAVID, Connor (muhk-DAY-vihd, KAW-nuhr) **EDM**

Center. Shoots left. 6'1", 195 lbs. Born, Richmond Hill, ON, January 13, 1997.
(Edmonton's 1st choice, 1st overall, in 2015 Entry Draft).

			Regular Season					Playoffs				
Season	Club	League	GP	G	A	Pts	PIM	GP	G	A	Pts	PIM
2011-12	Toronto Marlboros	GTHL	33	27	50	77	....	14	11	15	26	....
	Toronto Marlboros	Other	41	41	65	106	....	....	....	....	....	....
	PEAC Piranhas	Other	17	31	32	63	....	....	....	....	....	....
2012-13	Erie Otters	OHL	63	25	41	66	36	....	....	....	....	....
2013-14	Erie Otters	OHL	56	28	71	99	20	14	4	15	19	2
2014-15	Erie Otters	OHL	47	44	76	120	48	20	21	28	49	12

OHL All-Rookie Team (2013) • OHL Rookie of the Year (2013) • OHL Second All-Star Team (2014) • OHL First All-Star Team (2015) • OHL Player of the Year (2015) • OHL Playoff MVP (2015)

McENENY, Evan (muhk-EHN-ehn-ee, EH-vuhn) VAN

Defense. Shoots left. 6'3", 214 lbs. Born, Hamilton, ON, May 22, 1994.

			Regular Season					Playoffs				
Season	Club	League	GP	G	A	Pts	PIM	GP	G	A	Pts	PIM
2009-10	Ham. Jr. Bulldogs	Minor-ON	59	13	37	50	50	....	....	....	....	....
	Burlington	ON-Jr.A	4	0	1	1	0	....	....	....	....	....
2010-11	Kitchener Rangers	OHL	44	0	4	4	14	4	0	0	0	0
2011-12	Kitchener Rangers	OHL	2	0	2	2	4	....	....	....	....	....
2012-13	Kitchener Rangers	OHL	65	6	28	34	42	10	1	3	4	14
2013-14	Kitchener Rangers	OHL	15	2	5	7	23	....	....	....	....	....
	Kingston	OHL	46	5	30	35	55	7	1	1	2	6
	Utica Comets	AHL	1	0	0	0	2	....	....	....	....	....
2014-15	Kingston	OHL	68	9	36	45	71	4	1	1	2	0

• Missed majority of 2011-12 due to knee injury at Sarnia (OHL), September 23, 2011. Signed as a free agent by **Vancouver**, September 13, 2012.

McFARLAND, John (muhk-FAHR-luhnd, JAWN) FLA

Left wing. Shoots right. 6', 211 lbs. Born, Richmond Hill, ON, April 2, 1992.
(Florida's 4th choice, 33rd overall, in 2010 Entry Draft).

			Regular Season					Playoffs				
Season	Club	League	GP	G	A	Pts	PIM	GP	G	A	Pts	PIM
2007-08	Tor. Jr. Canadiens	GTHL	76	96	69	165	176	....	....	....	....	....
2008-09	Sudbury Wolves	OHL	58	21	31	52	36	6	1	3	4	2
2009-10	Sudbury Wolves	OHL	64	20	30	50	70	4	3	0	3	2
2010-11	Sudbury Wolves	OHL	12	6	4	10	13	....	....	....	....	....
	Saginaw Spirit	OHL	37	19	9	28	33	12	5	4	9	6
2011-12	Saginaw Spirit	OHL	36	20	21	41	18	....	....	....	....	....
	Ottawa 67's	OHL	12	4	5	9	10	....	....	....	....	....
2012-13	San Antonio	AHL	43	5	9	14	10	....	....	....	....	....
	Cincinnati	ECHL	23	12	13	25	12	12	4	5	9	6
2013-14	San Antonio	AHL	45	10	14	24	17	....	....	....	....	....
	Cincinnati	ECHL	20	8	5	13	4	....	....	....	....	....
2014-15	San Antonio	AHL	46	10	9	19	8	3	1	0	1	6

McGINN, Brock (muh-GIHN, BRAWK) CAR

Left wing. Shoots left. 6', 185 lbs. Born, Fergus, ON, February 2, 1994.
(Carolina's 2nd choice, 47th overall, in 2012 Entry Draft).

			Regular Season					Playoffs				
Season	Club	League	GP	G	A	Pts	PIM	GP	G	A	Pts	PIM
2009-10	Guelph Jr. Storm	Minor-ON	STATISTICS NOT AVAILABLE									
	Orangeville	ON-Jr.A	3	0	0	0	0	1	0	0	0	0
2010-11	Guelph Storm	OHL	68	10	4	14	38	6	0	0	0	2
2011-12	Guelph Storm	OHL	33	12	7	19	25	6	1	1	2	8
2012-13	Guelph Storm	OHL	68	28	26	54	71	3	2	2	4	11
	Charlotte	AHL	4	0	0	0	0	2	0	0	0	2
2013-14	Guelph Storm	OHL	58	43	42	85	45	12	6	6	12	21
2014-15	Charlotte	AHL	73	15	12	27	38	....	....	....	....	....

McKEE, Mike (muh-KEE, MIGHK) DET

Defense. Shoots left. 6'5", 250 lbs. Born, Newmarket, ON, August 17, 1993.
(Detroit's 4th choice, 140th overall, in 2012 Entry Draft).

			Regular Season					Playoffs				
Season	Club	League	GP	G	A	Pts	PIM	GP	G	A	Pts	PIM
2008-09	South Central	Minor-ON	25	8	6	14	74	....	....	....	....	....
2009-10	Kent Prep School	High-CT	26	3	8	11	22	....	....	....	....	....
2010-11	Kent Prep School	High-CT	27	8	14	22	50	....	....	....	....	....
2011-12	Lincoln Stars	USHL	59	2	17	19	237	8	0	0	0	44
2012-13	Lincoln Stars	USHL	42	3	18	21	*292	5	0	4	4	18
2013-14	Western Mich.	NCHC	21	1	0	1	54	....	....	....	....	....
2014-15	Western Mich.	NCHC	34	2	1	3	82	....	....	....	....	....

McKEOWN, Roland (muh-KOW-uhn, ROH-luhnd) CAR

Defense. Shoots right. 6'1", 195 lbs. Born, Listowel, ON, January 20, 1996.
(Los Angeles' 2nd choice, 50th overall, in 2014 Entry Draft).

			Regular Season					Playoffs				
Season	Club	League	GP	G	A	Pts	PIM	GP	G	A	Pts	PIM
2011-12	Toronto Marlboros	GTHL	28	10	25	35	30	....	....	....	....	....
2012-13	Kingston	OHL	61	7	22	29	33	4	0	0	0	4
2013-14	Kingston	OHL	62	11	32	43	61	7	1	3	4	8
2014-15	Kingston	OHL	65	7	25	32	57	4	0	1	1	9
	Charlotte	AHL	4	0	1	1	0	....	....	....	....	....

OHL All-Rookie Team (2013)

Traded to **Carolina** by **Los Angeles** with Los Angeles' 1st round choice in 2016 Entry Draft for Andrej Sekera, February 25, 2015.

McNALLY, Patrick (muhk-NAL-ee, PAT-rihk) S.J.

Defense. Shoots left. 6'2", 190 lbs. Born, Glen Head, NY, December 4, 1991.
(Vancouver's 1st choice, 115th overall, in 2010 Entry Draft).

			Regular Season					Playoffs				
Season	Club	League	GP	G	A	Pts	PIM	GP	G	A	Pts	PIM
2008-09	Suffolk PAL S.S.	MtJHL	52	25	41	66	72	....	....	....	....	....
2009-10	Milton Academy	High-MA	28	14	21	35	....	....	....	....	....	....
2010-11	Milton Academy	High-MA	28	22	29	51	....	....	....	....	....	....
2011-12	Harvard Crimson	ECAC	34	6	22	28	40	....	....	....	....	....
2012-13	Harvard Crimson	ECAC	7	1	2	3	6	....	....	....	....	....
2013-14	Harvard Crimson	ECAC	20	1	7	8	12	....	....	....	....	....
2014-15	Harvard Crimson	ECAC	21	6	15	21	10	....	....	....	....	....

ECAC All-Rookie Team (2012) • ECAC First All-Star Team (2015)

• Left Harvard (ECAC) for academic reasons, December 12, 2012. Traded to **San Jose** by **Vancouver** for Tampa Bay's 7th round choice (previously acquired, later traded to Vancouver – Vancouver selected Tate Olson) in 2015 Entry Draft, June 27, 2015.

MCNEILL, Mark (muhk-NEEL, MAHRK) CHI

Right wing. Shoots right. 6'2", 214 lbs. Born, Langley, BC, February 22, 1993.
(Chicago's 1st choice, 18th overall, in 2011 Entry Draft).

			Regular Season					Playoffs				
Season	Club	League	GP	G	A	Pts	PIM	GP	G	A	Pts	PIM
2008-09	SSAC Athletics	AMHL	33	21	18	39	38	4	2	0	2	2
	Prince Albert	WHL	4	0	0	0	0	....	....	....	....	....
2009-10	Prince Albert	WHL	68	9	15	24	27	....	....	....	....	....
2010-11	Prince Albert	WHL	70	32	49	81	53	6	2	3	5	2
2011-12	Prince Albert	WHL	69	31	40	71	48	....	....	....	....	....
	Rockford IceHogs	AHL	7	0	0	0	12	....	....	....	....	....
2012-13	Prince Albert	WHL	65	25	42	67	43	4	1	3	4	4
	Rockford IceHogs	AHL	5	0	0	0	0	....	....	....	....	....
2013-14	Rockford IceHogs	AHL	76	18	19	37	46	....	....	....	....	....
2014-15	Rockford IceHogs	AHL	63	23	21	44	23	8	2	2	4	2

McNEILL, Reid (muhk-NEEL, REED) PIT

Defense. Shoots left. 6'4", 215 lbs. Born, London, ON, April 29, 1992.
(Pittsburgh's 6th choice, 170th overall, in 2010 Entry Draft).

			Regular Season					Playoffs				
Season	Club	League	GP	G	A	Pts	PIM	GP	G	A	Pts	PIM
2008-09	Lambeth Lancers	ON-Jr.D	16	0	4	4	12	....	....	....	....	....
	Lucas High School	High-ON	STATISTICS NOT AVAILABLE									
2009-10	London Nationals	ON-Jr.B	20	0	7	7	6	....	....	....	....	....
	London Knights	OHL	53	2	3	5	32	12	0	1	1	0
2010-11	London Knights	OHL	62	2	4	6	70	6	0	0	0	4
2011-12	Barrie Colts	OHL	51	3	9	12	60	13	0	0	0	22
2012-13	Wilkes-Barre	AHL	3	0	0	0	0	12	0	1	1	12
	Wheeling Nailers	ECHL	44	2	4	6	90	....	....	....	....	....
2013-14	Wilkes-Barre	AHL	55	1	4	5	119	10	1	2	3	14
2014-15	Wilkes-Barre	AHL	54	2	5	7	121	8	0	1	1	11

McPHERSON, Corbin (muhk-FUHR-suhn, KOHR-bihn)

Defense. Shoots right. 6'4", 210 lbs. Born, Folsom, CA, September 7, 1988.
(New Jersey's 3rd choice, 87th overall, in 2007 Entry Draft).

			Regular Season					Playoffs				
Season	Club	League	GP	G	A	Pts	PIM	GP	G	A	Pts	PIM
2005-06	San Jose Jr. Sharks	Minor-CA	59	5	16	21	45	....	....	....	....	....
2006-07	Cowichan Valley	BCHL	45	4	10	14	63	18	1	3	4	14
2007-08	Cowichan Valley	BCHL	55	3	14	17	84	....	....	....	....	....
2008-09	Colgate	ECAC	37	0	5	5	50	....	....	....	....	....
2009-10	Colgate	ECAC	35	2	6	8	20	....	....	....	....	....
2010-11	Colgate	ECAC	41	4	6	10	36	....	....	....	....	....
2011-12	Colgate	ECAC	39	4	6	10	28	....	....	....	....	....
	Albany Devils	AHL	9	0	1	1	2	....	....	....	....	....
2012-13	Albany Devils	AHL	72	2	5	7	43	....	....	....	....	....
2013-14	Albany Devils	AHL	69	0	10	10	41	4	0	0	0	6
2014-15	Albany Devils	AHL	73	1	8	9	68	....	....	....	....	....

MEDVEDEV, Evgeni (mehd-VEH-dehv, ehv-GEH-nee) PHI

Defense. Shoots left. 6'3", 187 lbs. Born, Chelyabinsk, Russia, August 27, 1987.

			Regular Season					Playoffs				
Season	Club	League	GP	G	A	Pts	PIM	GP	G	A	Pts	PIM
2002-03	Mechel	Russia	11	0	0	0	6	....	....	....	....	....
2003-04	Chelyabinsk	Russia-2	34	7	11	18	24	....	....	....	....	....
2004-05	Chelyabinsk	Russia-2	44	5	6	11	42	5	1	0	1	8
2005-06	Cherepovets	Russia	49	4	5	9	54	2	0	0	0	6
2006-07	Cherepovets	Russia	50	10	10	20	115	3	0	0	0	6
2007-08	Ak Bars Kazan	Russia	41	6	20	26	89	8	2	1	3	4
2008-09	Ak Bars Kazan	KHL	48	8	11	19	64	21	2	5	7	32
2009-10	Ak Bars Kazan	KHL	48	2	10	12	40	17	2	3	5	6
2010-11	Ak Bars Kazan	KHL	49	4	16	20	26	9	0	3	3	6
2011-12	Ak Bars Kazan	KHL	45	5	19	24	36	6	0	1	1	6
2012-13	Ak Bars Kazan	KHL	49	6	20	26	44	18	0	7	7	12
2013-14	Ak Bars Kazan	KHL	50	3	21	24	55	5	1	0	1	31
	Russia	Olympics	5	0	1	1	2	....	....	....	....	....
2014-15	Ak Bars Kazan	KHL	43	3	13	16	26	14	1	3	4	12

Signed as a free agent by **Philadelphia**, May 20, 2015.

MEGALINSKY, Dmitri (meh-gahl-IHN-skee, dih-MEE-tree) OTT

Defense. Shoots left. 6'2", 212 lbs. Born, Perm, USSR, April 15, 1985.
(Ottawa's 7th choice, 186th overall, in 2005 Entry Draft).

			Regular Season					Playoffs				
Season	Club	League	GP	G	A	Pts	PIM	GP	G	A	Pts	PIM
2003-04	HK Voronezh	Russia-2	42	4	8	12	159	....	....	....	....	....
	Yaroslavl	Russia	1	0	0	0	0	....	....	....	....	....
	Yaroslavl 2	Russia-3	11	0	4	4	16	....	....	....	....	....
2004-05	Yaroslavl	Russia	1	0	0	0	2	....	....	....	....	....
	Yaroslavl 2	Russia-3	30	6	12	18	82	....	....	....	....	....
2005-06	Yaroslavl 2	Russia-3	12	4	10	14	6	....	....	....	....	....
	Yaroslavl	Russia	20	0	1	1	8	8	0	0	0	6
2006-07	Khimik	Russia-2	33	4	7	11	34	7	0	1	1	16
2007-08	Vityaz Chekhov	Russia	25	2	7	9	20	....	....	....	....	....
2008-09	Vityaz Chekhov	KHL	52	2	5	7	72	....	....	....	....	....
2009-10	Vityaz Chekhov	KHL	52	4	16	20	98	....	....	....	....	....
2010-11	Vityaz Chekhov	KHL	27	0	3	3	18	....	....	....	....	....
2011-12	Novokuznetsk	KHL	46	2	11	13	34	....	....	....	....	....
2012-13	Novokuznetsk	KHL	38	5	9	14	18	....	....	....	....	....
2013-14	Spartak Moscow	KHL	19	0	0	0	6	....	....	....	....	....
	Avtomobilist	KHL	28	4	6	10	22	4	1	0	1	0
2014-15	Avtomobilist	KHL	40	3	6	9	22	5	0	1	1	4

MEGAN, Wade (MEE-guhn, WAYD)

Center. Shoots left. 6'1", 195 lbs. Born, Canton, NY, July 22, 1990.
(Florida's 6th choice, 138th overall, in 2009 Entry Draft).

			Regular Season					Playoffs				
Season	Club	League	GP	G	A	Pts	PIM	GP	G	A	Pts	PIM
2007-08	Kent Prep School	High-CT	34	24	29	53	....	....	....	....	....	....
2008-09	Kent Prep School	High-CT	32	27	36	63	18	....	....	....	....	....
	Neponset Valley	Minor-MA	16	8	8	16	....	....	....	....	....	....
2009-10	Boston University	H-East	35	5	7	12	22	....	....	....	....	....
2010-11	Boston University	H-East	39	8	5	13	32	....	....	....	....	....
2011-12	Boston University	H-East	39	20	9	29	57	....	....	....	....	....
2012-13	Boston University	H-East	38	16	13	29	50	....	....	....	....	....
	San Antonio	AHL	13	1	0	1	0	....	....	....	....	....
2013-14	San Antonio	AHL	43	11	6	17	18	....	....	....	....	....
	Cincinnati	ECHL	16	13	7	20	11	22	10	3	13	12
2014-15	San Antonio	AHL	59	8	5	13	44	3	0	0	0	0
	Cincinnati	ECHL	5	4	3	7	12	....	....	....	....	....

Signed as a free agent by **Portland** (AHL), June 9, 2015.

MEGNA, Jaycob (MEHG-na, JAY-kuhb) ANA

Defense. Shoots left. 6'5", 218 lbs. Born, Plantation, FL, December 10, 1992.
(Anaheim's 8th choice, 210th overall, in 2012 Entry Draft).

			Regular Season					Playoffs				
Season	Club	League	GP	G	A	Pts	PIM	GP	G	A	Pts	PIM
2009-10	Team Illinois	T1EHL	48	1	12	13	8	....	....	....	....	....
	Team Illinois	Other	25	1	19	20	4	....	....	....	....	....
2010-11	Muskegon	USHL	55	1	17	18	24	6	0	3	3	0
2011-12	Nebraska-Omaha	WCHA	35	2	3	5	8	....	....	....	....	....
2012-13	Nebraska-Omaha	WCHA	38	2	5	7	14	....	....	....	....	....
2013-14	Nebraska-Omaha	NCHC	32	0	10	10	18	....	....	....	....	....
	Norfolk Admirals	AHL	2	0	0	0	2	....	....	....	....	....
2014-15	Norfolk Admirals	AHL	32	1	4	5	4	....	....	....	....	....

WCHA All-Rookie Team (2012)

MEIER, Timo (MIGH-uhr, TEE-moh) **S.J.**

Right wing. Shoots left. 6'1", 210 lbs. Born, St. Gallen, Switzerland, October 8, 1996.
(San Jose's 1st choice, 9th overall, in 2015 Entry Draft).

			Regular Season					Playoffs				
Season	Club	League	GP	G	A	Pts	PIM	GP	G	A	Pts	PIM
2009-10	SC Herisau U17	Swiss-U17	20	15	9	24	18	....	....	....	....	....
2010-11	Pikes U17	Swiss-U17	23	7	2	9	8	2	0	0	0	2
2011-12	Pikes U17	Swiss-U17	29	23	23	46	22	10	10	6	16	8
	Pikes II	Swiss-6	1	2	2	4	0	....	....	....	....	....
2012-13	Rapperswil U17	Swiss-U17	10	11	17	28	2	2	1	2	3	0
	Rapperswil Jr.	Swiss-Jr.	39	16	22	38	60	....	....	....	....	....
2013-14	Halifax	QMJHL	66	17	17	34	48	12	1	3	4	8
2014-15	Halifax	QMJHL	61	44	46	90	59	14	10	11	21	18

QMJHL Second All-Star Team (2015)

MELEN, Hampus (MEH-lehn, HAHM-puhs) **DET**

Right wing. Shoots left. 6'2", 165 lbs. Born, Karlskrona, Sweden, February 28, 1995.
(Detroit's 8th choice, 199th overall, in 2013 Entry Draft).

			Regular Season					Playoffs				
Season	Club	League	GP	G	A	Pts	PIM	GP	G	A	Pts	PIM
2010-11	Karlskrona HK U18	Swe-U18	6	3	8	11	4	....	....	....	....	....
	Karlskrona HK U20	Swe-Jr.	2	0	3	3	0	2	1	1	2	0
2011-12	Tingsryds AIF U18	Swe-U18	26	9	22	31	16	....	....	....	....	....
2012-13	Tingsryds AIF U18	Swe-U18	24	18	22	40	59	....	....	....	....	....
	Tingsryds AIF Jr.	Swe-Jr.	5	0	0	0	2	....	....	....	....	....
2013-14	Tingsryds AIF Jr.	Swe-Jr.	11	0	5	5	14	....	....	....	....	....
2014-15	Karlskrona HK U18	Swe-U18	1	1	1	2	0	....	....	....	....	....
	Vaxjo Jr.	Swe-Jr.	13	1	8	9	6	....	....	....	....	....
	Karlskrona HK Jr.	Swe-Jr.	15	12	14	26	41	2	2	0	2	0

MELINDY, James (muh-LIHN-dee, JAYMZ) **ARI**

Defense. Shoots right. 6'3", 203 lbs. Born, Goulds, NL, December 11, 1993.
(Phoenix's 3rd choice, 88th overall, in 2012 Entry Draft).

			Regular Season					Playoffs				
Season	Club	League	GP	G	A	Pts	PIM	GP	G	A	Pts	PIM
2008-09	Notre Dame Argos	SMHL	40	1	8	9	32	....	....	....	....	....
2009-10	Notre Dame	SMHL	41	8	19	27	92	13	0	2	2	14
2010-11	Moncton Wildcats	QMJHL	40	4	1	5	17	5	0	0	0	0
2011-12	Moncton Wildcats	QMJHL	61	9	18	27	74	4	2	1	3	12
2012-13	Moncton Wildcats	QMJHL	67	4	20	24	90	5	0	0	0	4
	Portland Pirates	AHL	2	0	0	0	0	....	....	....	....	....
2013-14	Portland Pirates	AHL	38	2	0	2	34	....	....	....	....	....
2014-15	Portland Pirates	AHL	9	0	0	0	6	....	....	....	....	....
	Gwinnett	ECHL	47	2	7	9	69	....	....	....	....	....

MELOCHE, Nicolas (meh-LAWSH, NIH-koh-las) **COL**

Defense. Shoots right. 6'3", 204 lbs. Born, LaSalle, QC, July 18, 1997.
(Colorado's 3rd choice, 40th overall, in 2015 Entry Draft).

			Regular Season					Playoffs				
Season	Club	League	GP	G	A	Pts	PIM	GP	G	A	Pts	PIM
2012-13	Saint-Eustache	QAAA	38	9	17	26	58	1	0	1	1	0
2013-14	Baie-Comeau	QMJHL	54	6	19	25	47	22	0	8	8	8
2014-15	Baie-Comeau	QMJHL	44	10	24	34	99	12	4	6	10	22

MERKLEY, Nick (MUHR-klee, NIHK) **ARI**

Right wing. Shoots right. 5'11", 191 lbs. Born, Calgary, AB, May 23, 1997.
(Arizona's 2nd choice, 30th overall, in 2015 Entry Draft).

			Regular Season					Playoffs				
Season	Club	League	GP	G	A	Pts	PIM	GP	G	A	Pts	PIM
2011-12	Calgary Bisons	AMBHL	32	41	32	73	42	9	9	4	13	14
2012-13	Calgary Buffaloes	AMHL	30	14	19	33	95	11	4	6	10	16
	Kelowna Rockets	WHL	1	0	0	0	0	7	0	3	3	0
2013-14	Kelowna Rockets	WHL	66	25	33	58	46	14	4	13	17	12
2014-15	Kelowna Rockets	WHL	72	20	70	90	79	19	5	22	27	18

WHL West Second All-Star Team (2015) • Memorial Cup All-Star Team (2015)

MERMIS, Dakota (MUHR-mihs, da-KOH-tah) **ARI**

Defense. Shoots left. 6', 190 lbs. Born, Alton, IL, January 5, 1994.

			Regular Season					Playoffs				
Season	Club	League	GP	G	A	Pts	PIM	GP	G	A	Pts	PIM
2009-10	St.L. Blues U18	T1EHL	48	11	26	37	76	....	....	....	....	....
	Lincoln Stars	USHL	2	0	1	1	0	....	....	....	....	....
2010-11	USNTDP	USHL	36	4	4	8	53	2	0	0	0	0
	USNTDP	U-17	17	1	4	5	20	....	....	....	....	....
2011-12	Green Bay	USHL	60	5	22	27	98	12	0	1	1	20
2012-13	U. of Denver	WCHA	19	1	3	4	14	....	....	....	....	....
	London Knights	OHL	27	2	9	11	34	21	1	3	4	21
2013-14	London Knights	OHL	66	5	20	25	76	9	1	3	4	12
2014-15	London Knights	OHL	36	1	10	11	36	....	....	....	....	....
	Oshawa Generals	OHL	30	5	14	19	50	21	1	14	15	14

Signed as a free agent by **Arizona**, July 1, 2015.

MERSCH, Michael (MUHRSH, MIGH-kuhl) **L.A.**

Left wing. Shoots left. 6'2", 224 lbs. Born, Park Ridge, IL, October 2, 1992.
(Los Angeles' 4th choice, 110th overall, in 2011 Entry Draft).

			Regular Season					Playoffs				
Season	Club	League	GP	G	A	Pts	PIM	GP	G	A	Pts	PIM
2007-08	Team Illinois	MWEHL	31	13	16	29	46	....	....	....	....	....
	Team Illinois	Other	....	22	24	46	29	....	....	....	....	....
2008-09	USNTDP	NAHL	42	15	13	28	50	9	5	2	7	4
	USNTDP	U-17	14	7	4	11	4	....	....	....	....	....
2009-10	USNTDP	USHL	26	4	4	8	22	....	....	....	....	....
	USNTDP	U-18	23	0	6	6	8	....	....	....	....	....
2010-11	U. of Wisconsin	WCHA	41	8	11	19	32	....	....	....	....	....
2011-12	U. of Wisconsin	WCHA	37	14	16	30	37	....	....	....	....	....
2012-13	U. of Wisconsin	WCHA	42	23	13	36	22	....	....	....	....	....
2013-14	U. of Wisconsin	Big Ten	37	*22	13	35	18	....	....	....	....	....
	Manchester	AHL	7	2	1	3	2	4	0	1	1	2
2014-15	Manchester	AHL	76	22	23	45	25	18	13	9	22	8

Big Ten First All-Star Team (2014) • NCAA West Second All-American Team (2014)

MEURS, Garrett (MEWRZ, GAIR-eht) **COL**

Center. Shoots right. 5'11", 180 lbs. Born, Wingham, ON, January 12, 1993.
(Colorado's 4th choice, 123rd overall, in 2011 Entry Draft).

			Regular Season					Playoffs				
Season	Club	League	GP	G	A	Pts	PIM	GP	G	A	Pts	PIM
2008-09	Huron-Perth	Minor-ON	67	52	43	95	67	....	....	....	....	....
2009-10	Plymouth Whalers	OHL	62	16	18	34	22	9	1	2	3	0
2010-11	Plymouth Whalers	OHL	68	10	31	41	61	11	1	2	3	8
2011-12	Plymouth Whalers	OHL	67	20	33	53	67	....	....	....	....	....
2012-13	Plymouth Whalers	OHL	68	32	33	65	66	15	7	7	14	22
2013-14	Lake Erie Monsters	AHL	64	6	8	14	74	....	....	....	....	....
2014-15	Lake Erie Monsters	AHL	20	0	0	0	8	....	....	....	....	....
	Fort Wayne	ECHL	30	12	10	22	42	10	3	3	6	16

MIDDLETON, Jacob (MIH-duhl-tuhn, JAY-kuhb) **L.A.**

Defense. Shoots left. 6'2", 205 lbs. Born, Stratford, ON, January 2, 1996.
(Los Angeles' 10th choice, 210th overall, in 2014 Entry Draft).

			Regular Season					Playoffs				
Season	Club	League	GP	G	A	Pts	PIM	GP	G	A	Pts	PIM
2010-11	Huron-Perth MM	Minor-ON	4	0	0	0	0	1	0	0	0	0
2011-12	Huron-Perth MM	Minor-ON	25	7	16	23	26	8	1	7	8	16
	Huron-Perth Mid.	Minor-ON	2	1	0	1	4	....	....	....	....	....
	Stratford Cullitons	ON-Jr.B	4	0	3	3	0	....	....	....	....	....
2012-13	Owen Sound	OHL	14	0	1	1	7	....	....	....	....	....
	Ottawa 67's	OHL	15	1	3	4	18	....	....	....	....	....
2013-14	Ottawa 67's	OHL	65	2	21	23	64	....	....	....	....	....
2014-15	Ottawa 67's	OHL	64	4	23	27	62	6	1	1	2	4

MIKKOLA, Niko (mih-KOH-luh, NEE-koh) **ST.L.**

Defense. Shoots left. 6'4", 185 lbs. Born, Kiiminki, Finland, April 27, 1996.
(St. Louis' 4th choice, 127th overall, in 2015 Entry Draft).

			Regular Season					Playoffs				
Season	Club	League	GP	G	A	Pts	PIM	GP	G	A	Pts	PIM
2012-13	KalPa Kuopio U18	Fin-U18	12	0	0	0	6	....	....	....	....	....
2013-14	KalPa Kuopio U18	Fin-U18	46	4	13	17	103	8	0	2	2	6
2014-15	KalPa Kuopio Jr.	Fin-Jr.	37	9	14	23	80	....	....	....	....	....
	KalPa Kuopio	Finland	10	0	1	1	4	....	....	....	....	....
	Hokki Kajaani	Finland-2	5	1	0	1	8	7	0	1	1	2

MILANO, Sonny (mih-LA-noh, SUH-nee) **CBJ**

Left wing. Shoots left. 6', 199 lbs. Born, Massapequa, NY, May 12, 1996.
(Columbus' 1st choice, 16th overall, in 2014 Entry Draft).

			Regular Season					Playoffs				
Season	Club	League	GP	G	A	Pts	PIM	GP	G	A	Pts	PIM
2011-12	Cleveland Barons	T1EHL	40	44	43	87	10	....	....	....	....	....
2012-13	USNTDP	USHL	38	10	12	22	12	....	....	....	....	....
	USNTDP	U-17	18	10	15	25	8	....	....	....	....	....
2013-14	USNTDP	USHL	25	14	25	39	21	....	....	....	....	....
	USNTDP	U-18	33	15	33	48	8	....	....	....	....	....
2014-15	Plymouth Whalers	OHL	50	22	46	68	24	....	....	....	....	....
	Springfield Falcons	AHL	10	0	5	5	0	....	....	....	....	....

MILLER, Colin (MIH-luhr, KAW-lihn) **BOS**

Defense. Shoots right. 6'1", 201 lbs. Born, Sault Ste. Marie, ON, October 29, 1992.
(Los Angeles' 3rd choice, 151st overall, in 2012 Entry Draft).

			Regular Season					Playoffs				
Season	Club	League	GP	G	A	Pts	PIM	GP	G	A	Pts	PIM
2008-09	Soo North Stars	Minor-ON	32	6	15	21	42	10	2	7	9	14
2009-10	Soo Thunderbirds	NOJHL	46	7	23	30	38	14	5	9	14	6
2010-11	Sault Ste. Marie	OHL	66	3	19	22	44	....	....	....	....	....
2011-12	Sault Ste. Marie	OHL	54	8	20	28	79	....	....	....	....	....
2012-13	Sault Ste. Marie	OHL	54	20	35	55	78	6	1	6	7	0
2013-14	Manchester	AHL	65	5	12	17	35	3	0	0	0	6
2014-15	Manchester	AHL	70	19	33	52	82	19	2	8	10	12

AHL Second All-Star Team (2015)

Traded to **Boston** by **Los Angeles** with Martin Jones and Los Angeles' 1st round choice (Jakub Zboril) in 2015 Entry Draft for Milan Lucic, June 26, 2015.

MIRNOV, Igor (mihr-NAWF, EE-gohr) **OTT**

Left wing. Shoots left. 6', 187 lbs. Born, Chita, USSR, September 19, 1984.
(Ottawa's 2nd choice, 67th overall, in 2003 Entry Draft).

			Regular Season					Playoffs				
Season	Club	League	GP	G	A	Pts	PIM	GP	G	A	Pts	PIM
2001-02	Dyn'o Moscow 2	Russia-3	30	33	17	50	34	....	....	....	....	....
	Dynamo Moscow	Russia	6	0	0	0	0	....	....	....	....	....
2002-03	Dynamo Moscow	Russia	50	3	7	10	49	5	0	0	0	2
2003-04	Dynamo Moscow	Russia	53	11	10	21	26	3	0	0	0	2
2004-05	Dynamo Moscow	Russia	55	13	13	26	50	9	2	4	6	0
2005-06	Dynamo Moscow	Russia	32	8	10	18	36	4	0	2	2	4
2006-07	Dynamo Moscow	Russia	49	21	25	46	54	3	2	1	3	4
2007-08	Dynamo Moscow	Russia	24	3	3	6	16	....	....	....	....	....
	Magnitogorsk	Russia	23	9	6	15	20	13	3	1	4	4
2008-09	Magnitogorsk	KHL	39	11	8	19	24	11	2	7	9	8
2009-10	Mytischi	KHL	20	2	4	6	0	....	....	....	....	....
	MVD	KHL	10	1	3	4	4	....	....	....	....	....
	Sibir Novosibirsk	KHL	12	7	5	12	8	....	....	....	....	....
2010-11	Sibir Novosibirsk	KHL	53	16	25	41	30	4	0	2	2	2
2011-12	Ufa	KHL	50	14	10	24	14	5	0	1	1	6
2012-13	Ufa	KHL	49	21	16	37	32	14	2	3	5	2
2013-14	Ufa	KHL	48	18	13	31	14	18	8	2	10	0
2014-15	Ak Bars Kazan	KHL	57	10	20	30	14	20	2	6	8	10

MIRONOV, Andrei (mih-RAW-nawv, AWN-dray) **COL**

Defense. Shoots left. 6'3", 194 lbs. Born, Moscow, Russia, July 29, 1994.
(Colorado's 5th choice, 101st overall, in 2015 Entry Draft).

			Regular Season					Playoffs				
Season	Club	League	GP	G	A	Pts	PIM	GP	G	A	Pts	PIM
2011-12	Dyn'o Moscow Jr.	Russia-Jr.	59	1	8	9	87	2	0	0	0	0
2012-13	Dynamo Moscow	KHL	40	0	5	5	26	18	1	2	3	8
	Dyn'o Moscow Jr.	Russia-Jr.	6	0	1	1	0	1	0	0	0	4
2013-14	Dynamo Moscow	KHL	46	3	7	10	16	7	0	1	1	6
	Dyn'o Moscow Jr.	Russia-Jr.	3	0	1	1	2	....	....	....	....	....
2014-15	Dynamo Moscow	KHL	52	5	3	8	20	11	0	1	1	6
	Dynamo Balashikha	Russia-2	1	0	0	0	2	....	....	....	....	....

MISKOVIC, Zach (MIHS-koh-vihch, ZAK)

Defense. Shoots right. 6'1", 190 lbs. Born, River Forest, IL, May 8, 1985.

			Regular Season					Playoffs				
Season	Club	League	GP	G	A	Pts	PIM	GP	G	A	Pts	PIM
2002-03	Cedar Rapids	USHL	60	2	6	8	91	7	0	0	0	12
2003-04	Cedar Rapids	USHL	60	6	15	21	139	4	1	1	2	2
2004-05	Cedar Rapids	USHL	60	4	16	20	149	8	1	0	1	14
2005-06	St. Lawrence	ECAC	40	1	15	16	30	....	....	....	....	....
2006-07	St. Lawrence	ECAC	39	2	10	12	48	....	....	....	....	....
2007-08	St. Lawrence	ECAC	37	8	12	20	36	....	....	....	....	....
2008-09	St. Lawrence	ECAC	38	16	9	25	32	....	....	....	....	....
2009-10	Hershey Bears	AHL	59	6	20	26	25	6	1	1	2	0
2010-11	Hershey Bears	AHL	58	7	9	16	58	5	0	0	0	8
2011-12	Hershey Bears	AHL	35	0	3	3	26	3	0	2	2	0
2012-13	Chicago Wolves	AHL	15	2	1	3	9	....	....	....	....	....
	San Antonio	AHL	27	4	9	13	22	....	....	....	....	....
2013-14	San Antonio	AHL	10	0	2	2	2	....	....	....	....	....
	Cincinnati	ECHL	6	2	2	4	2	....	....	....	....	....
	Rockford IceHogs	AHL	15	0	7	7	10	....	....	....	....	....
	Iowa Wild	AHL	19	1	0	1	16	....	....	....	....	....
2014-15	Rockford IceHogs	AHL	42	2	6	8	40	2	1	0	1	2

ECAC First All-Star Team (2009) • NCAA East First All-American Team (2009)

Signed as a free agent by **Washington**, March 25, 2009. Signed as a free agent by **Chicago** (AHL), August 13, 2012. Signed as a free agent by **San Antonio** (AHL), February 14, 2013. Signed as a free agent by **Rockford** (AHL), January 8, 2014. Traded to **Iowa** (AHL) by **Rockford** (AHL) for future considerations, February 26, 2014. Signed as a free agent by **Rockford** (AHL), July 2, 2014.

MISTELE, Matthew (MIHS-teh-lee, MA-thew) L.A.

Left wing. Shoots left. 6'1", 190 lbs. Born, Whitby, ON, October 17, 1995.
(Los Angeles' 8th choice, 180th overall, in 2014 Entry Draft).

			Regular Season					Playoffs				
Season	Club	League	GP	G	A	Pts	PIM	GP	G	A	Pts	PIM
2010-11	Whitby Wildcats	Minor-ON	60	43	34	77	50	....	....	....	....	....
2011-12	Plymouth Whalers	OHL	28	3	2	5	33	12	2	3	5	11
2012-13	Plymouth Whalers	OHL	68	34	26	60	69	9	3	2	5	8
2013-14	Plymouth Whalers	OHL	55	18	19	37	59	5	0	2	2	2
2014-15	Plymouth Whalers	OHL	35	24	18	42	19	....	....	....	....	....
	Oshawa Generals	OHL	25	13	9	22	15	21	13	3	16	18

MITCHELL, Garrett (MIH-chuhl, GAIR-reht) WSH

Right wing. Shoots right. 5'11", 183 lbs. Born, Regina, SK, September 2, 1991.
(Washington's 6th choice, 175th overall, in 2009 Entry Draft).

			Regular Season					Playoffs				
Season	Club	League	GP	G	A	Pts	PIM	GP	G	A	Pts	PIM
2006-07	Reg. Pat Cdns.	SMHL	42	14	11	25	140	....	....	....	....	....
	Regina Pats	WHL	4	0	1	1	2	....	....	....	....	....
2007-08	Regina Pats	WHL	62	8	5	13	73	6	1	0	1	6
2008-09	Regina Pats	WHL	71	10	5	15	140	....	....	....	....	....
2009-10	Regina Pats	WHL	57	15	16	31	110	....	....	....	....	....
	Hershey Bears	AHL	1	0	0	0	0	....	....	....	....	....
2010-11	Regina Pats	WHL	70	18	34	52	140	....	....	....	....	....
	Hershey Bears	AHL	2	0	0	0	5	....	....	....	....	....
2011-12	Hershey Bears	AHL	65	6	9	15	85	5	1	0	1	0
	South Carolina	ECHL	2	0	0	0	7	....	....	....	....	....
2012-13	Hershey Bears	AHL	75	15	15	30	94	5	1	0	1	4
2013-14	Hershey Bears	AHL	17	0	2	2	44	....	....	....	....	....
2014-15	Hershey Bears	AHL	64	4	4	8	121	10	1	2	3	10

MITCHELL, Zack (MIH-chuhl, ZAK) MIN

Right wing. Shoots right. 6', 193 lbs. Born, Caledon, ON, January 7, 1993.

			Regular Season					Playoffs				
Season	Club	League	GP	G	A	Pts	PIM	GP	G	A	Pts	PIM
2008-09	Toronto Marlboros	GTHL	77	42	48	90	74	....	....	....	....	....
2009-10	Guelph Storm	OHL	59	3	7	10	25	5	2	0	2	0
2010-11	Guelph Storm	OHL	61	9	10	19	24	6	1	6	7	2
2011-12	Guelph Storm	OHL	67	37	38	75	32	6	2	2	4	2
2012-13	Guelph Storm	OHL	68	22	34	56	34	5	1	1	2	4
2013-14	Guelph Storm	OHL	67	31	52	83	40	20	12	18	30	12
2014-15	Iowa Wild	AHL	76	17	18	35	12	....	....	....	....	....

Signed as a free agent by **Minnesota**, March 4, 2014.

MOLIN, Emil (moh-LEEN, eh-MIHL) DAL

Right wing. Shoots left. 6', 180 lbs. Born, Gavle, Sweden, February 3, 1993.
(Dallas' 3rd choice, 105th overall, in 2011 Entry Draft).

			Regular Season					Playoffs				
Season	Club	League	GP	G	A	Pts	PIM	GP	G	A	Pts	PIM
2009-10	Brynas U18	Swe-U18	38	22	35	57	24	4	2	6	8	0
2010-11	Brynas U18	Swe-U18	36	31	50	81	60	5	3	5	8	0
	Brynas IF Gavle Jr.	Swe-Jr.	9	0	1	1	2	1	0	0	0	0
2011-12	Brynas IF Gavle Jr.	Swe-Jr.	29	15	27	42	45	1	0	1	1	0
	Brynas IF Gavle	Sweden	34	1	4	5	0	10	0	1	1	0
2012-13	Mora IK	Sweden-2	8	0	0	0	2	....	....	....	....	....
	Brynas IF Gavle Jr.	Swe-Jr.	15	5	6	11	37	2	0	1	1	0
	Brynas IF Gavle	Sweden	34	1	2	3	0	1	0	0	0	0
2013-14	Almtuna	Sweden-2	1	0	0	0	0	....	....	....	....	....
	Rogle	Sweden-2	35	5	16	21	4	....	....	....	....	....
	Brynas IF Gavle	Sweden	21	0	3	3	0	....	....	....	....	....
2014-15	Rogle	Sweden-2	55	1	12	13	2	5	0	0	0	0

MONTOUR, Brandon (MAWN-toor, BRAN-duhn) ANA

Defense. Shoots right. 6', 172 lbs. Born, Brantford, ON, April 11, 1994.
(Anaheim's 3rd choice, 55th overall, in 2014 Entry Draft).

			Regular Season					Playoffs				
Season	Club	League	GP	G	A	Pts	PIM	GP	G	A	Pts	PIM
2009-10	Cambridge Hawks	Minor-ON	30	4	14	18	12	11	0	2	2	6
2010-11	Camb. Hawks Mid.	Minor-ON	19	3	8	11	38	....	....	....	....	....
	Brantford	ON-Jr.B	37	1	13	14	22	10	0	3	3	6
2011-12	Brantford	ON-Jr.B	51	14	22	36	65	19	6	12	18	30
2012-13	Caledonia Corvairs	ON-Jr.B	49	18	49	67	94	12	4	11	15	22
2013-14	Waterloo	USHL	60	14	48	62	36	12	6	*10	*16	10
2014-15	Massachusetts	H-East	21	3	17	20	30	....	....	....	....	....
	Norfolk Admirals	AHL	14	1	9	10	8	....	....	....	....	....

USHL First All-Star Team (2014) • USHL Player of the Year (2014) • Hockey East All-Rookie Team (2015)

MORIN, Samuel (moh-REHN, SAM-yewl) PHI

Defense. Shoots left. 6'7", 227 lbs. Born, Lac-Beauport, QC, July 12, 1995.
(Philadelphia's 1st choice, 11th overall, in 2013 Entry Draft).

			Regular Season					Playoffs				
Season	Club	League	GP	G	A	Pts	PIM	GP	G	A	Pts	PIM
2010-11	Levis	QAAA	36	0	12	12	40	4	0	0	0	4
2011-12	Rimouski Oceanic	QMJHL	62	0	8	8	57	10	0	1	1	8
2012-13	Rimouski Oceanic	QMJHL	46	4	12	16	117	6	1	6	7	16
2013-14	Rimouski Oceanic	QMJHL	54	7	24	31	121	11	4	4	8	30
2014-15	Rimouski Oceanic	QMJHL	38	5	27	32	68	19	1	10	11	28

MOROZ, Mitchell (maw-RAWZ, MIH-chuhl) EDM

Left wing. Shoots left. 6'2", 214 lbs. Born, Edmonton, AB, May 3, 1994.
(Edmonton's 2nd choice, 32nd overall, in 2012 Entry Draft).

			Regular Season					Playoffs				
Season	Club	League	GP	G	A	Pts	PIM	GP	G	A	Pts	PIM
2007-08	Cgy. N. Sabres	AMBHL	31	5	7	12	40	2	0	2	2	12
2008-09	Cgy. N. Sabres	AMBHL	31	20	16	36	50	....	....	....	....	....
2009-10	Edge School	High-AB	43	20	23	43	80	....	....	....	....	....
	Edmonton	WHL	7	0	1	1	2	....	....	....	....	....
2010-11	Calgary Northstars	AMHL	22	10	4	14	34	2	0	0	0	0
	Edmonton	WHL	1	0	0	0	0	....	....	....	....	....
2011-12	Edmonton	WHL	66	16	9	25	131	20	4	4	8	24
2012-13	Edmonton	WHL	69	13	21	34	140	22	2	5	7	41
2013-14	Edmonton	WHL	70	35	28	63	156	21	6	13	19	40
2014-15	Oklahoma City	AHL	66	5	4	9	169	6	0	1	1	6

MORRISON, Brad (MOHR-ih-suhn, BRAD) NYR

Center. Shoots left. 6', 160 lbs. Born, Prince George, BC, January 4, 1997.
(NY Rangers' 5th choice, 113th overall, in 2015 Entry Draft).

			Regular Season					Playoffs				
Season	Club	League	GP	G	A	Pts	PIM	GP	G	A	Pts	PIM
2012-13	Cariboo Cougars	BCMML	38	20	30	50	26	4	1	0	1	2
	Prince George	WHL	5	1	2	3	4	....	....	....	....	....
2013-14	Prince George	WHL	55	12	9	21	12	....	....	....	....	....
2014-15	Prince George	WHL	67	23	27	50	30	5	2	5	7	4

MORRISON, Kenney (MOHR-ih-suhn, KEHN-nee) CGY

Defense. Shoots . 6'3", 208 lbs. Born, Lloydminster, AB, February 13, 1992.

			Regular Season					Playoffs				
Season	Club	League	GP	G	A	Pts	PIM	GP	G	A	Pts	PIM
2008-09	Lloydminster	AMHL	34	0	7	7	14	....	....	....	....	....
2009-10	Lloydminster	AMHL	35	7	18	25	52	10	2	7	9	10
	Lloydminster	AJHL	1	0	0	0	2	....	....	....	....	....
2010-11	Alberni Valley	BCHL	55	8	27	35	26	4	0	2	2	2
2011-12	Omaha Lancers	USHL	57	15	20	35	44	3	0	0	0	0
2012-13	Western Mich.	CCHA	38	7	13	20	32	....	....	....	....	....
2013-14	Western Mich.	NCHC	40	4	15	19	83	....	....	....	....	....
2014-15	Western Mich.	NCHC	37	5	10	15	36	....	....	....	....	....
	Adirondack Flames	AHL	10	2	4	6	4	....	....	....	....	....

Signed as a free agent by **Calgary**, March 19, 2015.

MORRISSEY, Josh (MOHR-ih-see, JAWSH) WPG

Defense. Shoots left. 6', 176 lbs. Born, Calgary, AB, March 28, 1995.
(Winnipeg's 1st choice, 13th overall, in 2013 Entry Draft).

			Regular Season					Playoffs				
Season	Club	League	GP	G	A	Pts	PIM	GP	G	A	Pts	PIM
2008-09	Calgary Royals	AMBHL	33	6	18	24	56	....	....	....	....	....
2009-10	Calgary Royals	AMBHL	32	21	28	49	108	....	....	....	....	....
2010-11	Calgary Royals	AMHL	30	17	22	39	11	6	1	3	4	10
	Prince Albert	WHL	5	0	0	0	4	....	....	....	....	....
2011-12	Prince Albert	WHL	68	10	28	38	60	....	....	....	....	....
2012-13	Prince Albert	WHL	70	15	32	47	91	4	0	1	1	9
2013-14	Prince Albert	WHL	59	28	45	73	59	4	1	2	3	6
	St. John's IceCaps	AHL	8	0	1	1	2	20	2	7	9	20
2014-15	Prince Albert	WHL	27	7	14	21	28	....	....	....	....	....
	Kelowna Rockets	WHL	20	6	11	17	34	13	2	12	14	24

Canadian Major Junior Scholastic Player of the Year (2013) • WHL East First All-Star Team (2014) • WHL West Second All-Star Team (2015)

MOSES, Steve (MOH-zehs, STEEV) NSH

Right wing. Shoots right. 5'9", 170 lbs. Born, Leominster, MA, August 9, 1989.

			Regular Season					Playoffs				
Season	Club	League	GP	G	A	Pts	PIM	GP	G	A	Pts	PIM
2007-08	Bos. Jr. Bruins	EJHL	45	11	36	47	22	4	1	3	4	0
2008-09	New Hampshire	H-East	33	5	8	13	6	....	....	....	....	....
2009-10	New Hampshire	H-East	39	6	18	24	20	....	....	....	....	....
2010-11	New Hampshire	H-East	39	14	12	26	23	....	....	....	....	....
2011-12	New Hampshire	H-East	37	22	13	35	16	....	....	....	....	....
	Connecticut Whale	AHL	8	2	0	2	2	1	0	0	0	0
2012-13	Jokerit Helsinki	Finland	55	22	16	38	24	2	0	0	0	0
2013-14	Jokerit Helsinki	Finland	42	12	11	23	14	1	0	0	0	4
2014-15	Jokerit	KHL	60	*36	21	57	20	10	5	2	7	6

Signed to a ATO (amateur tryout) contract by **Connecticut** (AHL), March 23, 2012. Signed as a free agent by **Nashville**, April 9, 2015.

MOTTE, Tyler (MAWT, TIGH-luhr) CHI

Center. Shoots left. 5'8", 192 lbs. Born, Port Huron, MI, March 10, 1995.
(Chicago's 5th choice, 121st overall, in 2013 Entry Draft).

			Regular Season					Playoffs				
Season	Club	League	GP	G	A	Pts	PIM	GP	G	A	Pts	PIM
2010-11	Det. Honeybaked	T1EHL	34	23	14	37	20	....	....	....	....	....
2011-12	USNTDP	USHL	36	15	13	28	32	2	2	0	2	0
	USNTDP	U-17	17	8	3	11	30	....	....	....	....	....
	USNTDP	U-18	2	1	0	1	0	....	....	....	....	....
2012-13	USNTDP	USHL	26	11	6	17	6	....	....	....	....	....
	USNTDP	U-18	41	15	13	28	44	....	....	....	....	....
2013-14	U. of Michigan	Big Ten	34	9	9	18	22	....	....	....	....	....
2014-15	U. of Michigan	Big Ten	35	9	22	31	14	....	....	....	....	....

MOUTREY, Nick (MOO-tree, NIHK) CBJ

Center/Left wing. Shoots left. 6'2", 222 lbs. Born, Toronto, ON, June 24, 1995.
(Columbus' 6th choice, 105th overall, in 2013 Entry Draft).

			Regular Season					Playoffs				
Season	Club	League	GP	G	A	Pts	PIM	GP	G	A	Pts	PIM
2010-11	York Simcoe	Minor-ON	69	43	46	89	46	....	....	....	....	....
2011-12	Saginaw Spirit	OHL	66	2	7	9	46	12	0	0	0	4
2012-13	Saginaw Spirit	OHL	65	16	27	43	44	4	0	0	0	12
2013-14	Saginaw Spirit	OHL	68	15	26	41	82	5	0	3	3	2
2014-15	Saginaw Spirit	OHL	36	15	26	41	40	....	....	....	....	....
	North Bay	OHL	26	10	12	22	14	15	7	6	13	12

MOY, Tyler (MOY, TIGH-luhr) NSH

Center. Shoots right. 6'1", 195 lbs. Born, La Jolla, CA, July 18, 1995.
(Nashville's 6th choice, 175th overall, in 2015 Entry Draft).

			Regular Season					Playoffs				
Season	Club	League	GP	G	A	Pts	PIM	GP	G	A	Pts	PIM
2012-13	Omaha Lancers	USHL	64	4	19	23	22	....	....	....	....	....
2013-14	Harvard Crimson	ECAC	27	4	6	10	2	....	....	....	....	....
2014-15	Harvard Crimson	ECAC	37	12	15	27	16	....	....	....	....	....

MOZIK, Vojtech (MOH-zihk, VOI-tehk) N.J.

Defense. Shoots right. 6'2", 195 lbs. Born, Praha, Czech Rep., December 26, 1992.

			Regular Season					Playoffs				
Season	Club	League	GP	G	A	Pts	PIM	GP	G	A	Pts	PIM
2009-10	Ml. Boleslav U18	CzR-U18	50	9	23	32	83	2	0	0	0	14
	Ml. Boleslav Jr.	CzRep-Jr.	3	0	1	1	2	....	....	....	....	....
2010-11	Ml. Boleslav Jr.	CzRep-Jr.	52	3	12	15	48	....	....	....	....	....
2011-12	Ml. Boleslav Jr.	CzRep-Jr.	11	0	3	3	14	....	....	....	....	....
	BK Mlada Boleslav	CzRep	39	3	5	8	16	....	....	....	....	....
	BK Mlada Boleslav	CzRep-Q	....	....	....	....	....	7	0	2	2	8
2012-13	BK Mlada Boleslav	CzRep-2	5	0	0	0	2	....	....	....	....	....
	HC Skoda Plzen	CzRep	28	0	1	1	20	....	....	....	....	....
2013-14	HC Skoda Plzen	CzRep	51	8	6	14	60	6	0	1	1	2
2014-15	HC Skoda Plzen	CzRep	51	10	19	29	94	4	1	1	2	6

Signed as a free agent by **New Jersey**, June 15, 2015.

MUIR, Aidan (MEWR, AY-duhn) EDM

Wing. Shoots right. 6'3", 182 lbs. Born, Brampton, ON, August 21, 1995.
(Edmonton's 7th choice, 113th overall, in 2013 Entry Draft).

			Regular Season					Playoffs				
Season	Club	League	GP	G	A	Pts	PIM	GP	G	A	Pts	PIM
2011-12	Det. Vic. Honda	T1EHL	40	13	7	20	8	4	3	4	7	8
2012-13	Det. Vic. Honda	T1EHL	37	17	23	40	41	3	0	1	1	0
2013-14	Indiana Ice	USHL	54	14	27	41	60	10	1	1	2	2
2014-15	Western Mich.	NCHC	36	6	9	15	4	....	....	....	....	....

MULLEN, Patrick (MUHL-uhn, PA-trihk) OTT

Defense. Shoots right. 5'11", 185 lbs. Born, Pittsburgh, PA, May 6, 1986.

			Regular Season					Playoffs				
Season	Club	League	GP	G	A	Pts	PIM	GP	G	A	Pts	PIM
2004-05	Sioux City	USHL	60	14	23	37	8	....	....	....	....	....
2005-06	U. of Denver	WCHA	37	7	10	17	24	....	....	....	....	....
2006-07	U. of Denver	WCHA	37	5	12	17	20	....	....	....	....	....
2007-08	U. of Denver	WCHA	40	4	18	22	65	....	....	....	....	....
2008-09	U. of Denver	WCHA	38	4	21	25	39	....	....	....	....	....
2009-10	Manchester	AHL	44	4	6	10	16	2	0	0	0	2
	Ontario Reign	ECHL	1	0	0	0	0	....	....	....	....	....
2010-11	Manchester	AHL	67	3	17	20	32	7	0	1	1	4
2011-12	Manchester	AHL	69	13	28	41	45	4	1	2	3	8
2012-13	Chicago Wolves	AHL	2	0	0	0	0	....	....	....	....	....
2013-14	Utica Comets	AHL	46	7	13	20	23	....	....	....	....	....
	Binghamton	AHL	20	1	11	12	12	4	0	2	2	6
2014-15	Binghamton	AHL	54	5	24	29	32	....	....	....	....	....

Signed as a free agent by **Los Angeles**, April 3, 2009. Signed as a free agent by **Vancouver**, July 5, 2012. Traded to **Ottawa** by **Vancouver** for Jeff Costello, March 4, 2014.

MURPHY, Wade (MUHR-fee, WAYD) NSH

Right wing. Shoots right. 5'11", 176 lbs. Born, Victoria, BC, October 22, 1993.
(Nashville's 9th choice, 185th overall, in 2013 Entry Draft).

			Regular Season					Playoffs				
Season	Club	League	GP	G	A	Pts	PIM	GP	G	A	Pts	PIM
2008-09	South Island	BCMML	39	9	9	18	40	4	0	0	0	2
2009-10	Saanich Braves	VIJHL	STATISTICS NOT AVAILABLE									
	Victoria Grizzlies	BCHL	6	3	1	4	2	....	....	....	....	....
2010-11	Victoria Grizzlies	BCHL	56	7	9	16	30	8	2	1	3	6
2011-12	Victoria Grizzlies	BCHL	38	22	40	62	58	....	....	....	....	....
	Penticton Vees	BCHL	22	14	15	29	8	15	*9	9	*18	6
2012-13	Penticton Vees	BCHL	50	23	47	70	50	15	5	6	11	12
2013-14	North Dakota	NCHC	19	0	3	3	8	....	....	....	....	....
2014-15	North Dakota	NCHC	16	0	1	1	6	....	....	....	....	....

MUSIL, Adam (mew-SEEL, A-duhm) ST.L.

Center. Shoots right. 6'3", 202 lbs. Born, Ottawa, ON, March 26, 1997.
(St. Louis' 2nd choice, 94th overall, in 2015 Entry Draft).

			Regular Season					Playoffs				
Season	Club	League	GP	G	A	Pts	PIM	GP	G	A	Pts	PIM
2012-13	Greater Van.	BCMML	32	16	28	44	30	6	1	2	3	6
	Red Deer Rebels	WHL	3	0	0	0	0	3	0	0	0	2
2013-14	Red Deer Rebels	WHL	60	11	18	29	36	....	....	....	....	....
2014-15	Red Deer Rebels	WHL	66	15	24	39	71	....	....	....	....	....

NAKLADAL, Jakub (nahk-LA-dahl, YA-kuhb) CGY

Defense. Shoots right. 6'2", 203 lbs. Born, Hradec Kralove, Czech Rep., December 30, 1987.

			Regular Season					Playoffs				
Season	Club	League	GP	G	A	Pts	PIM	GP	G	A	Pts	PIM
2007-08	Pardubice	CzRep	14	1	2	3	20	....	....	....	....	....
	HC Vrchlabi	CzRep-2	11	0	1	1	6	....	....	....	....	....
2008-09	Pardubice	CzRep	42	2	7	9	38	....	....	....	....	....
	HC Chrudim	CzRep-2	3	0	0	0	4	1	0	0	0	2
2009-10	Pardubice	CzRep	45	5	9	15	58	13	1	3	4	26
2010-11	Pardubice	CzRep	45	5	6	11	32	9	1	2	3	18
2011-12	Pardubice	CzRep	12	2	3	5	4	....	....	....	....	....
	Ufa	KHL	32	1	7	8	30	6	1	0	1	20
2012-13	Spartak Moscow	KHL	37	0	4	4	26	....	....	....	....	....
	HC Lev Praha	KHL	14	1	4	5	8	4	0	0	0	2
2013-14	HC Lev Praha	KHL	34	0	3	3	26	....	....	....	....	....
2014-15	TPS Turku	Finland	50	3	12	15	63	....	....	....	....	....

Signed as a free agent by **Calgary**, May 19, 2015.

NAKYVA, Kristian (nah-KEE-va, KRIHS-ch'yehn) NSH

Defense. Shoots left. 6', 198 lbs. Born, Helsinki, Finland, November 18, 1990.

			Regular Season					Playoffs				
Season	Club	League	GP	G	A	Pts	PIM	GP	G	A	Pts	PIM
2007-08	Blues Espoo U18	Fin-U18	4	1	3	4	0	....	....	....	....	....
	Blues Espoo Jr.	Fin-Jr.	42	4	10	14	14	2	0	0	0	0
2008-09	Suomi U20	Finland-2	9	0	0	0	2	....	....	....	....	....
	Blues Jr.	Finland-Jr.	37	8	17	25	28	8	3	3	6	6
	Blues Espoo	Finland	6	0	2	2	2	....	....	....	....	....
2009-10	Suomi U20	Finland-2	11	1	1	2	12	....	....	....	....	....
	Blues Espoo Jr.	Fin-Jr.	25	9	12	21	56	....	....	....	....	....
	TuTo Turku	Finland-2	5	0	0	0	2	....	....	....	....	....
	Blues Espoo	Finland	7	0	0	0	4	....	....	....	....	....
2010-11	Blues Espoo Jr.	Fin-Jr.	11	3	2	5	14	13	2	12	14	6
	Jukurit Mikkeli	Finland-2	16	0	7	7	8	....	....	....	....	....
	Kiekko-Vantaa	Finland-2	5	0	2	2	6	....	....	....	....	....
	Blues Espoo	Finland	16	0	1	1	8	....	....	....	....	....
2011-12	JYP-Akatemia	Finland-2	2	2	1	3	2	....	....	....	....	....
	JYP Jyvaskyla	Finland	55	7	16	23	20	13	0	5	5	4
2012-13	JYP Jyvaskyla	Finland	59	6	22	28	52	11	1	3	4	6
2013-14	JYP Jyvaskyla	Finland	57	7	19	26	40	6	1	2	3	2
2014-15	Lulea HF	Sweden	55	10	19	29	42	9	1	3	4	6

Signed as a free agent by **Nashville**, April 24, 2015.

NANNE, Louis (NA-nee, LOO-ee) MIN

Left wing. Shoots left. 5'10", 178 lbs. Born, Edina, MN, June 18, 1994.
(Minnesota's 7th choice, 188th overall, in 2012 Entry Draft).

			Regular Season					Playoffs				
Season	Club	League	GP	G	A	Pts	PIM	GP	G	A	Pts	PIM
2009-10	Edina Hornets	High-MN	20	3	0	3	4	6	1	1	2	2
2010-11	Edina Hornets	High-MN	21	11	12	23	10	6	2	4	6	2
2011-12	Team Southwest	UMHSEL	23	7	13	20	12	....	....	....	....	....
	Edina Hornets	High-MN	24	12	8	20	30	4	3	4	7	4
2012-13	Penticton Vees	BCHL	45	19	22	41	16	15	6	6	12	4
2013-14	Sioux Falls	USHL	37	4	5	9	12	3	1	0	1	0
2014-15	RPI Engineers	ECAC	31	5	5	10	12	....	....	....	....	....

NANNE, Tyler (NA-nee, TIGH-luhr) NYR

Defense. Shoots right. 5'10", 174 lbs. Born, Edina, MN, March 17, 1996.
(NY Rangers' 7th choice, 142nd overall, in 2014 Entry Draft).

			Regular Season					Playoffs				
Season	Club	League	GP	G	A	Pts	PIM	GP	G	A	Pts	PIM
2011-12	Edina Hornets	High-MN	25	5	10	15	10	5	2	5	7	4
2012-13	Edina Hornets	High-MN	25	9	10	19	6	6	1	3	4	4
	Lincoln Stars	USHL	2	0	0	0	0	....	....	....	....	....
2013-14	Team Southwest	UMHSEL	20	2	6	8	18	3	0	3	3	4
	Edina Hornets	High-MN	25	7	20	27	41	5	5	6	11	11
	Sioux Falls	USHL	4	0	2	2	4	3	0	0	0	0
	USNTDP	U-18	1	0	0	0	2	....	....	....	....	....
2014-15	Sioux Falls	USHL	14	1	2	3	14	....	....	....	....	....
	Madison Capitols	USHL	29	7	6	13	32	....	....	....	....	....

• Signed Letter of Intent to attend **Ohio State University** (Big Ten) in fall of 2015.

NANTEL, Julien (nan-TEHL, JOO-lee-ehn) COL

Center. Shoots left. 6', 193 lbs. Born, Laval, QC, September 6, 1996.
(Colorado's 7th choice, 204th overall, in 2014 Entry Draft).

			Regular Season					Playoffs				
Season	Club	League	GP	G	A	Pts	PIM	GP	G	A	Pts	PIM
2011-12	Laval-Montreal	QAAA	40	11	17	28	8	....	....	....	....	....
2012-13	Laval-Montreal	QAAA	36	19	21	40	18	17	6	11	17	6
	Rouyn-Noranda	QMJHL	4	1	0	1	0	....	....	....	....	....
2013-14	Rouyn-Noranda	QMJHL	68	14	20	34	18	9	0	4	4	2
2014-15	Rouyn-Noranda	QMJHL	64	26	35	61	34	6	3	1	4	2

NASTASIUK, Zach (nas-TAYZ-ee-uhk, ZAK) DET

Right wing. Shoots right. 6'2", 200 lbs. Born, Barrie, ON, March 30, 1995.
(Detroit's 2nd choice, 48th overall, in 2013 Entry Draft).

			Regular Season					Playoffs				
Season	Club	League	GP	G	A	Pts	PIM	GP	G	A	Pts	PIM
2010-11	Barrie Colts	Minor-ON	41	17	23	40	38	....	....	....	....	....
	Orangeville Flyers	ON-Jr.A	1	0	0	0	0	....	....	....	....	....
2011-12	Owen Sound	OHL	68	11	8	19	15	5	1	0	1	0
2012-13	Owen Sound	OHL	62	20	20	40	32	12	4	7	11	0
2013-14	Owen Sound	OHL	62	24	27	51	26	5	3	1	4	2
	Grand Rapids	AHL	5	0	0	0	0	7	0	1	1	0
2014-15	Owen Sound	OHL	64	35	42	77	34	5	1	0	1	4
	Grand Rapids	AHL	6	0	0	0	0	4	0	0	0	0

NATTINEN, Julius (na-TIH-nehn, YOO-lee-uhs) ANA

Center. Shoots left. 6'2", 191 lbs. Born, Jyvaskyla, Finland, January 14, 1997.
(Anaheim's 2nd choice, 59th overall, in 2015 Entry Draft).

			Regular Season					Playoffs				
Season	Club	League	GP	G	A	Pts	PIM	GP	G	A	Pts	PIM
2011-12	JyP Jyvaskyla U18	Fin-U18	9	3	2	5	2	....	....	....	....	....
2012-13	JyP Jyvaskyla U18	Fin-U18	20	16	11	27	8	....	....	....	....	....
	JyP Jyvaskyla Jr.	Fin-Jr.	24	5	10	15	6	5	1	0	1	2
2013-14	JyP Jyvaskyla U18	Fin-U18	4	1	7	8	2	....	....	....	....	....
	JyP Jyvaskyla Jr.	Fin-Jr.	32	5	22	27	14	....	....	....	....	....
	JYP Jyvaskyla	Finland	1	0	0	0	2	....	....	....	....	....
	JYP-Akatemia	Finland-2	5	0	0	0	0	....	....	....	....	....
2014-15	JYP Jyvaskyla	Finland	9	0	3	3	0	....	....	....	....	....
	JYP-Akatemia	Finland-2	39	11	18	29	8	6	0	0	0	2

NEDOMLEL, Richard (NEHD-oh-muh-lehl, rih-CHUHRD) DET

Defense. Shoots left. 6'4", 234 lbs. Born, Prague, Czech Rep., July 1, 1993.
(Detroit's 8th choice, 175th overall, in 2011 Entry Draft).

			Regular Season					Playoffs				
Season	Club	League	GP	G	A	Pts	PIM	GP	G	A	Pts	PIM
2008-09	Chomutov U17	CzR-U17	17	0	3	3	47	....	....	....	....	....
	Slavia U17	CzR-U17	25	0	4	4	18	9	1	1	2	4
2009-10	Slavia U18	CzR-U18	44	9	10	19	221	4	1	0	1	54
2010-11	Swift Current	WHL	66	0	10	10	107	....	....	....	....	....
2011-12	Swift Current	WHL	72	10	36	46	83	....	....	....	....	....
2012-13	Swift Current	WHL	72	7	21	28	105	5	0	1	1	2
2013-14	Grand Rapids	AHL	3	0	0	0	2	....	....	....	....	....
	Toledo Walleye	ECHL	60	8	10	18	150	....	....	....	....	....
2014-15	Toledo Walleye	ECHL	49	3	11	14	56	12	0	2	2	10

NEILL, Carl (NEEL, KAHRL) VAN

Defense. Shoots right. 6'3", 206 lbs. Born, Blainville, QC, July 6, 1996.
(Vancouver's 4th choice, 144th overall, in 2015 Entry Draft).

			Regular Season					Playoffs				
Season	Club	League	GP	G	A	Pts	PIM	GP	G	A	Pts	PIM
2011-12	Saint-Eustache	QAAA	42	2	19	21	34	....	....	....	....	....
2012-13	Sherbrooke	QMJHL	61	3	17	20	30	4	1	1	2	8
2013-14	Sherbrooke	QMJHL	65	4	18	22	58	....	....	....	....	....
2014-15	Sherbrooke	QMJHL	63	14	26	40	77	6	1	5	6	4

NEJEZCHLEB, Richard (NEE'YEHZ-khlehb, RIH-khurd) NYR

Right wing. Shoots left. 6'2", 203 lbs. Born, Prague, Czech Rep., May 2, 1994.
(NY Rangers' 5th choice, 122nd overall, in 2014 Entry Draft).

			Regular Season					Playoffs				
Season	Club	League	GP	G	A	Pts	PIM	GP	G	A	Pts	PIM
2008-09	Slavia U17	CzR-U17	6	0	1	1	8	....	....	....	....	....
2009-10	Slavia U18	CzR-U18	32	5	11	16	12	4	0	3	3	2
2010-11	Slavia U18	CzR-U18	36	22	16	38	56	3	1	1	2	31
	HC Slavia Praha Jr.	CzRep-Jr.	10	1	7	8	4	....	....	....	....	....
2011-12	Slavia U18	CzR-U18	3	4	2	6	6	....	....	....	....	....
	HC Slavia Praha Jr.	CzRep-Jr.	24	11	12	23	14	1	0	0	0	0
2012-13	Brandon	WHL	35	11	13	24	34	....	....	....	....	....
	Brandon	WHL	35	11	13	24	34	....	....	....	....	....
2013-14	Brandon	WHL	66	32	25	57	75	9	5	4	9	13
2014-15	Brandon	WHL	2	1	1	2	0	....	....	....	....	....
	Tri-City Americans	WHL	47	19	30	49	62	4	1	0	1	8

NEVINS, Jack (NEH-vihns, JAK) BUF

Left wing. Shoots left. 6'2", 204 lbs. Born, Stittsville, ON, September 18, 1993.

			Regular Season					Playoffs				
Season	Club	League	GP	G	A	Pts	PIM	GP	G	A	Pts	PIM
2009-10	Almonte Thunder	ON-Jr.B	37	5	7	12	44	4	0	0	0	8
2010-11	Almonte Thunder	ON-Jr.B	9	6	3	9	10	....	....	....	....	....
	Kemptville 73's	ON-Jr.A	37	1	3	4	50	....	....	....	....	....
2011-12	Sarnia Sting	OHL	36	4	1	5	60	....	....	....	....	....
	Kingston	OHL	23	1	5	6	25	....	....	....	....	....
2012-13	London Knights	OHL	2	0	0	0	0	....	....	....	....	....
	P.E.I. Rocket	QMJHL	51	8	7	15	103	....	....	....	....	....
2013-14	Charlottetown	QMJHL	41	14	22	36	98	....	....	....	....	....
	Rouyn-Noranda	QMJHL	23	5	7	12	61	9	5	3	8	14
	Hamilton Bulldogs	AHL	3	0	1	1	15	....	....	....	....	....
2014-15	Hamilton Bulldogs	AHL	32	0	0	0	88	....	....	....	....	....
	Rochester	AHL	13	0	0	0	10	....	....	....	....	....

Signed as a free agent by **Montreal**, December 4, 2013. Traded to **Buffalo** by **Montreal** with a 7th round choice in 2016 Entry Draft for Torrey Mitchell, March 2, 2015.

NICHOLLS, Josh (NIH-kuhls, JAWSH) NYR

Right wing. Shoots right. 6'2", 189 lbs. Born, Tsawwassen, BC, April 27, 1992.
(Toronto's 7th choice, 182nd overall, in 2010 Entry Draft).

			Regular Season					Playoffs				
Season	Club	League	GP	G	A	Pts	PIM	GP	G	A	Pts	PIM
2007-08	Greater Van.	BCMML	39	18	30	48	68	2	0	0	0	20
2008-09	Saskatoon Blades	WHL	63	9	16	25	37	7	2	0	2	4
2009-10	Saskatoon Blades	WHL	71	18	30	48	55	10	0	5	5	6
2010-11	Saskatoon Blades	WHL	71	34	53	87	47	10	4	2	6	6
2011-12	Saskatoon Blades	WHL	56	30	38	68	24	4	2	1	3	2
2012-13	Saskatoon Blades	WHL	71	47	38	85	43	4	0	1	1	9
2013-14	Hartford Wolf Pack	AHL	6	0	0	0	0	....	....	....	....	....
	Greenville	ECHL	63	20	22	42	20	18	6	9	15	14
2014-15	Hartford Wolf Pack	AHL	5	0	1	1	0	....	....	....	....	....
	Greenville	ECHL	53	21	22	43	20	....	....	....	....	....

Signed as a free agent by **NY Rangers**, March 5, 2013.

NIELSEN, Andrew (NEEL-sehn, an-DROO) TOR

Defense. Shoots right. 6'4", 207 lbs. Born, Red Deer, AB, November 13, 1996.
(Toronto's 4th choice, 65th overall, in 2015 Entry Draft).

			Regular Season					Playoffs				
Season	Club	League	GP	G	A	Pts	PIM	GP	G	A	Pts	PIM
2012-13	Red Deer Elks	Minor-AB	33	8	17	25	124	5	0	4	4	16
2013-14	Red Deer Chiefs	AMHL	35	3	15	18	34	11	0	5	5	8
	Lethbridge	WHL	1	0	0	0	0	....	....	....	....	....
2014-15	Lethbridge	WHL	59	7	17	24	101	....	....	....	....	....

NIEVES, Cristoval (noo-EH-vehz, KRIHS-TOH-vahl) NYR

Center. Shoots left. 6'3", 200 lbs. Born, Syracuse, NY, January 23, 1994.
(NY Rangers' 2nd choice, 59th overall, in 2012 Entry Draft).

			Regular Season					Playoffs				
Season	Club	League	GP	G	A	Pts	PIM	GP	G	A	Pts	PIM
2009-10	Syracuse Nationals	Minor-NY	60	30	42	72	....	....	....	....	....	....
2010-11	Kent Prep School	High-CT	22	11	28	39	6	....	....	....	....	....
2011-12	Kent Prep School	High-CT	26	7	32	39	24	....	....	....	....	....
	Indiana Ice	USHL	13	2	8	10	2	....	....	....	....	....
2012-13	U. of Michigan	CCHA	40	8	21	29	18	....	....	....	....	....
2013-14	U. of Michigan	Big Ten	34	3	19	22	18	....	....	....	....	....
2014-15	U. of Michigan	Big Ten	35	7	21	28	18	....	....	....	....	....

NIKU, Sami (NEE-koo, SA-mee) WPG

Defense. Shoots left. 6'1", 182 lbs. Born, Haapavesi, Finland, October 10, 1996.
(Winnipeg's 7th choice, 198th overall, in 2015 Entry Draft).

			Regular Season					Playoffs				
Season	Club	League	GP	G	A	Pts	PIM	GP	G	A	Pts	PIM
2011-12	JyP Jyvaskyla U18	Fin-U18	17	1	1	2	0	....	....	....	....	....
2012-13	JyP Jyvaskyla U18	Fin-U18	3	2	1	3	0	....	....	....	....	....
	JyP Jyvaskyla Jr.	Fin-Jr.	30	0	8	8	22	6	0	0	0	2
2013-14	JyP Jyvaskyla U18	Fin-U18	1	0	3	3	0	....	....	....	....	....
	JyP Jyvaskyla Jr.	Fin-Jr.	20	4	10	14	20	....	....	....	....	....
	JYP-Akatemia	Finland-2	30	0	3	3	16	....	....	....	....	....
2014-15	JYP Jyvaskyla	Finland	12	0	1	1	6	....	....	....	....	....
	JYP-Akatemia	Finland-2	39	3	22	25	24	6	0	5	5	4

NILSSON, Tom (NIHL-suhn, TAWM) TOR

Defense. Shoots right. 6', 176 lbs. Born, Tyreso, Sweden, August 19, 1993.
(Toronto's 4th choice, 100th overall, in 2011 Entry Draft).

			Regular Season					Playoffs				
Season	Club	League	GP	G	A	Pts	PIM	GP	G	A	Pts	PIM
2009-10	Mora IK U18	Swe-U18	35	11	9	20	30	....	....	....	....	....
	Mora IK Jr.	Swe-Jr.	3	0	0	0	0	....	....	....	....	....
2010-11	Mora IK U18	Swe-U18	11	1	7	8	10	1	0	0	0	12
	Mora IK Jr.	Swe-Jr.	37	2	6	8	26	....	....	....	....	....
	Mora IK	Sweden-2	16	0	1	1	12	....	....	....	....	....
2011-12	Mora IK	Sweden-2	44	4	6	10	45	....	....	....	....	....
	Mora IK Jr.	Swe-Jr.	10	0	2	2	2	2	0	1	1	0
2012-13	Mora IK	Sweden-2	42	1	3	4	18	....	....	....	....	....
	Mora IK Jr.	Swe-Jr.	3	0	0	0	0	2	3	2	5	0
2013-14	Frolunda	Sweden	50	2	2	4	22	7	0	0	0	2
2014-15	Toronto Marlies	AHL	44	1	5	6	26	4	0	0	0	2

NOGIER, Nelson (NOH-jay, NEHL-suhn) WPG

Defense. Shoots right. 6'3", 204 lbs. Born, Saskatoon, SK, May 27, 1996.
(Winnipeg's 4th choice, 101st overall, in 2014 Entry Draft).

			Regular Season					Playoffs				
Season	Club	League	GP	G	A	Pts	PIM	GP	G	A	Pts	PIM
2011-12	Sask. Contacts	SMHL	43	3	10	13	42	13	0	3	3	4
	Saskatoon Blades	WHL	4	0	0	0	0	....	....	....	....	....
2012-13	Sask. Contacts	SMHL	7	2	7	9	4	....	....	....	....	....
	Saskatoon Blades	WHL	55	0	4	4	8	3	0	1	1	0
2013-14	Saskatoon Blades	WHL	37	1	5	6	25	....	....	....	....	....
2014-15	Saskatoon Blades	WHL	32	1	7	8	42	....	....	....	....	....
	Red Deer Rebels	WHL	38	2	9	11	42	5	0	1	1	4

NOONAN, Garrett (NOO-nuhn, GAIR-eht) NSH

Defense. Shoots left. 6', 205 lbs. Born, Norfolk, MA, January 28, 1991.
(Nashville's 4th choice, 112th overall, in 2011 Entry Draft).

			Regular Season					Playoffs				
Season	Club	League	GP	G	A	Pts	PIM	GP	G	A	Pts	PIM
2008-09	Catholic Memorial	High-MA	30	12	22	34	....	....	....	....	....	....
2009-10	Vernon Vipers	BCHL	58	2	16	18	60	19	3	3	6	16
2010-11	Boston University	H-East	38	4	11	15	89	....	....	....	....	....
2011-12	Boston University	H-East	38	16	11	27	64	....	....	....	....	....
2012-13	Boston University	H-East	34	6	13	19	94	....	....	....	....	....
2013-14	Boston University	H-East	34	4	16	20	42	....	....	....	....	....
2014-15	Milwaukee	AHL	40	4	5	9	17	....	....	....	....	....
	Cincinnati	ECHL	23	1	9	10	22	....	....	....	....	....

Hockey East Second All-Star Team (2012)

NOREAU, Samuel (noh-ROH, SAM-yewl) NYR

Defense. Shoots right. 6'5", 227 lbs. Born, Montreal, QC, January 31, 1993.
(NY Rangers' 5th choice, 136th overall, in 2011 Entry Draft).

			Regular Season					Playoffs				
Season	Club	League	GP	G	A	Pts	PIM	GP	G	A	Pts	PIM
2008-09	Lac St-Louis Tigres	Minor-QC	33	5	20	25	8	....	....	....	....	....
2009-10	Lac St-Louis Lions	QAAA	24	2	3	5	10	....	....	....	....	....
	Baie-Comeau	QMJHL	34	1	3	4	17	....	....	....	....	....
2010-11	Baie-Comeau	QMJHL	67	5	5	10	141	....	....	....	....	....
2011-12	Baie-Comeau	QMJHL	58	5	12	17	92	8	0	0	0	18
2012-13	Baie-Comeau	QMJHL	66	7	25	32	64	15	2	1	3	12
2013-14	Hartford Wolf Pack	AHL	5	0	0	0	6	....	....	....	....	....
	Greenville	ECHL	61	1	9	10	90	14	0	4	4	29
2014-15	Hartford Wolf Pack	AHL	4	0	0	0	13	....	....	....	....	....
	Greenville	ECHL	67	2	9	11	114	....	....	....	....	....

NORELL, Robin (NOH-REHL, RAW-bihn) CHI

Defense. Shoots left. 5'10", 195 lbs. Born, Stockholm, Sweden, February 18, 1995.
(Chicago's 4th choice, 111th overall, in 2013 Entry Draft).

			Regular Season					Playoffs				
Season	Club	League	GP	G	A	Pts	PIM	GP	G	A	Pts	PIM
2010-11	Djurgarden U18	Swe-U18	4	0	0	0	0	....	....	....	....	....
2011-12	Djurgarden U18	Swe-U18	37	2	9	11	24	4	0	0	0	2
	Djurgarden Jr.	Swe-Jr.	....	....	....	....	....	1	0	0	0	0
2012-13	Djurgarden U18	Swe-U18	30	10	7	17	16	9	2	1	3	6
	Djurgarden Jr.	Swe-Jr.	33	1	4	5	4	2	0	0	0	2
2013-14	Djurgarden Jr.	Swe-Jr.	1	0	0	0	0	....	....	....	....	....
	Djurgarden	Sweden-2	32	0	6	6	10	....	....	....	....	....
2014-15	Djurgarden	Sweden	48	3	6	9	12	2	0	0	0	0
	Rockford IceHogs	AHL	....	....	....	....	....	3	0	0	0	2

NOSEK, Tomas (NOH-shehk, toh-MAHSH) DET

Left wing. Shoots left. 6'3", 210 lbs. Born, Pardubice, Czech Rep., September 1, 1992.

			Regular Season					Playoffs				
Season	Club	League	GP	G	A	Pts	PIM	GP	G	A	Pts	PIM
2011-12	Pardubice	CzRep	27	0	4	4	2	....	....	....	....	....
2012-13	Pardubice	CzRep	50	5	9	14	18	3	1	1	2	2
	Hr. Kralove	CzRep-2	5	4	1	5	2	....	....	....	....	....
2013-14	Pardubice	CzRep	52	19	25	44	36	10	3	3	6	*44
2014-15	Grand Rapids	AHL	55	11	23	34	22	12	2	5	7	4

Signed as a free agent by **Detroit**, June 14, 2014.

NOVAK, Thomas (NOH-vak, TAW-muhs) NSH

Center. Shoots left. 6'1", 179 lbs. Born, St. Paul, MN, April 28, 1997.
(Nashville's 2nd choice, 85th overall, in 2015 Entry Draft).

			Regular Season					Playoffs				
Season	Club	League	GP	G	A	Pts	PIM	GP	G	A	Pts	PIM
2011-12	St. Thomas Acad.	High-MN	25	14	20	34	0	6	4	5	9	2
2012-13	St. Thomas Acad.	High-MN	25	25	22	47	6	6	3	7	10	0
2013-14	Team Southeast	UMHSEL	19	11	22	33	8	3	0	2	2	0
	St. Thomas Acad.	High-MN	25	26	44	70	8	3	4	4	8	2
	USNTDP	USHL	2	0	0	0	0	....	....	....	....	....
2014-15	Waterloo	USHL	46	14	34	48	12	....	....	....	....	....

• Signed Letter of Intent to attend **University of Minnesota** (Big Ten) in fall of 2015.

NUTIVAARA, Markus (noo-tih-VAH-ruh, MAHR-kuhs) CBJ

Defense. Shoots left. 6', 185 lbs. Born, Oulu, Finland, June 6, 1994.
(Columbus' 9th choice, 189th overall, in 2015 Entry Draft).

			Regular Season					Playoffs				
Season	Club	League	GP	G	A	Pts	PIM	GP	G	A	Pts	PIM
2010-11	Ahmat U18	Fin-U18	22	10	13	23	43	....	....	....	....	....
	Ahmat Haukipudas	Finland-4	3	0	0	0	2	....	....	....	....	....
2011-12	Karpat Oulu U18	Fin-U18	41	10	20	30	14	9	2	4	6	4
2012-13	Pelicans Lahti Jr.	Fin-Jr.	42	4	11	15	14	....	....	....	....	....
2013-14	Karpat Oulu Jr.	Fin-Jr.	19	2	9	11	10	12	1	4	5	2
	Jokipojat Joensuu	Finland-2	11	0	3	3	4	....	....	....	....	....
2014-15	Karpat Oulu Jr.	Fin-Jr.	7	2	6	8	0	5	3	2	5	0
	Hokki Kajaani	Finland-2	2	0	2	2	2	....	....	....	....	....
	Karpat Oulu	Finland	35	0	2	2	4	16	1	5	6	0

NYBERG, John (NIGH-buhrg, JAWN) DAL

Defense. Shoots left. 6'2", 190 lbs. Born, Harryda, Sweden, July 14, 1996.
(Dallas' 8th choice, 165th overall, in 2014 Entry Draft).

			Regular Season					Playoffs				
Season	Club	League	GP	G	A	Pts	PIM	GP	G	A	Pts	PIM
2011-12	Frolunda U18	Swe-U18	12	0	0	0	0	....	....	....	....	....
2012-13	Frolunda U18	Swe-U18	40	4	10	14	36	3	0	0	0	2
2013-14	Frolunda U18	Swe-U18	33	11	27	38	22	5	2	0	2	12
	Frolunda Jr.	Swe-Jr.	19	1	3	4	0	....	....	....	....	....
2014-15	Mora IK	Sweden-2	4	0	0	0	0	....	....	....	....	....
	IK Oskarshamn	Sweden-2	9	0	1	1	2	....	....	....	....	....
	Frolunda Jr.	Swe-Jr.	25	7	10	17	26	8	1	1	2	16
	Frolunda	Sweden	17	0	1	1	2	....	....	....	....	....

NYGREN, Magnus (NEW-grihn, MAG-nuhs) MTL

Defense. Shoots right. 6'1", 193 lbs. Born, Karlstad, Sweden, June 7, 1990.
(Montreal's 3rd choice, 113th overall, in 2011 Entry Draft).

			Regular Season					Playoffs				
Season	Club	League	GP	G	A	Pts	PIM	GP	G	A	Pts	PIM
2006-07	Farjestad U18	Swe-U18	7	0	4	4	4	8	1	2	3	6
2007-08	Farjestad U18	Swe-U18	31	9	19	28	61	8	2	6	8	12
2008-09	Skare Jr.	Swe-Jr.	2	2	3	5	0	....	....	....	....	....
	Skare BK Karlstad	Sweden-3	41	7	21	28	32	3	1	0	1	2
2009-10	Skare BK	Sweden-3	24	9	18	27	10	....	....	....	....	....
	Farjestad	Sweden	9	0	0	0	4	....	....	....	....	....
	Mora IK	Sweden-2	21	2	5	7	10	2	0	1	1	2
2010-11	Bofors	Sweden-2	35	5	6	11	10	....	....	....	....	....
	Farjestad	Sweden	22	4	11	15	4	14	3	7	10	6
2011-12	Farjestad Jr.	Swe-Jr.	1	1	0	1	2	....	....	....	....	....
	Bofors	Sweden-2	3	1	1	2	4	....	....	....	....	....
	Farjestad	Sweden	50	7	11	18	6	10	2	0	2	0
2012-13	Farjestad	Sweden	51	13	19	32	49	10	1	3	4	10
2013-14	Farjestad	Sweden	25	12	8	20	8	15	2	3	5	6
	Hamilton Bulldogs	AHL	16	1	7	8	14	....	....	....	....	....
2014-15	Hamilton Bulldogs	AHL	15	4	6	10	2	....	....	....	....	....

• Missed majority of 2014-15 due to head injury vs. Lake Erie (AHL), November 29, 2014. Signed as a free agent by **Farjestad** (Sweden), May 8, 2015.

NYLANDER, William (NIGH-lan-duhr, WIHL-yuhm) TOR

Center. Shoots right. 6', 182 lbs. Born, Calgary, AB, May 1, 1996.
(Toronto's 1st choice, 8th overall, in 2014 Entry Draft).

			Regular Season					Playoffs				
Season	Club	League	GP	G	A	Pts	PIM	GP	G	A	Pts	PIM
2011-12	SDE U18	Swe-U18	18	12	14	26	14	....	....	....	....	....
	Sodertalje SK U18	Swe-U18	9	7	5	12	2	....	....	....	....	....
	Sodertalje SK Jr.	Swe-Jr.	8	1	3	4	2	4	0	5	5	2
2012-13	Sodertalje SK U18	Swe-U18	1	2	1	3	2	....	....	....	....	....
	Sodertalje SK Jr.	Swe-Jr.	27	15	28	43	14	....	....	....	....	....
	Sodertalje SK	Sweden-2	18	6	3	9	6	....	....	....	....	....
2013-14	Sodertalje SK	Sweden-2	17	11	8	19	6	....	....	....	....	....
	Rogle	Sweden-2	18	4	4	8	10	....	....	....	....	....
	MODO Jr.	Swe-Jr.	3	0	3	3	4	5	3	5	8	2
	MODO	Sweden	22	1	6	7	6	2	0	0	0	0
	MODO U18	Swe-U18	....	....	....	....	....	4	3	4	7	4
2014-15	MODO	Sweden	21	8	12	20	6	....	....	....	....	....
	Toronto Marlies	AHL	37	14	18	32	4	5	0	3	3	0

• Loaned to **MODO** (Sweden) by **Toronto**, October 6, 2014.

O'BRIEN, Andrew (oh-BRIGH-uhn, an-DROO) ANA

Defense. Shoots left. 6'4", 205 lbs. Born, Hamilton, ON, November 21, 1992.
(Anaheim's 5th choice, 108th overall, in 2012 Entry Draft).

			Regular Season					Playoffs				
Season	Club	League	GP	G	A	Pts	PIM	GP	G	A	Pts	PIM
2008-09	Humber Valley	Minor-ON	STATISTICS NOT AVAILABLE									
	Milton Icehawks	ON-Jr.A	2	0	0	0	0	....	....	....	....	....
2009-10	Dixie Beehives	ON-Jr.A	44	3	4	7	45	....	....	....	....	....
2010-11	Chicoutimi	QMJHL	55	1	9	10	33	4	1	1	2	6
2011-12	Chicoutimi	QMJHL	68	8	21	29	95	18	1	9	10	31
2012-13	Rouyn-Noranda	QMJHL	67	2	16	18	113	14	0	4	4	22
2013-14	Norfolk Admirals	AHL	4	0	0	0	4	....	....	....	....	....
	Utah Grizzlies	ECHL	24	2	3	5	70	3	0	0	0	0
2014-15	Norfolk Admirals	AHL	62	4	10	14	118	....	....	....	....	....

O'DONOGHUE, Dan (OH-dawn-A-hew, DAN) ARI

Left wing. Shoots left. 6'5", 207 lbs. Born, Port Jefferson Station, NY, January 28, 1991.

			Regular Season					Playoffs				
Season	Club	League	GP	G	A	Pts	PIM	GP	G	A	Pts	PIM
2007-08	Long Island Bant.	AYHL	21	14	13	27	10	....	....	....	....	....
2008-09	New York Bobcats	AtJHL	39	17	18	35	32	....	....	....	....	....
2009-10	Des Moines	USHL	39	6	2	8	42	....	....	....	....	....
	New York Bobcats	AtJHL	10	6	6	12	8	4	3	2	5	4
2010-11	Mercyhurst	AH	37	10	10	20	22	....	....	....	....	....
2011-12	Mercyhurst	AH	39	8	12	20	39	....	....	....	....	....
2012-13	Mercyhurst	AH	41	12	24	36	33	....	....	....	....	....
2013-14	Mercyhurst	AH	38	15	28	43	41	....	....	....	....	....
2014-15	Portland Pirates	AHL	16	0	0	0	2	....	....	....	....	....
	Gwinnett	ECHL	23	4	4	8	19	....	....	....	....	....

AH Second All-Star Team (2014)

Signed as a free agent by **Phoenix**, April 14, 2014.

O'GARA, Rob (OH-GAR-uh, RAWB) BOS

Defense. Shoots left. 6'4", 207 lbs. Born, Massapequa, NY, July 6, 1993.
(Boston's 5th choice, 151st overall, in 2011 Entry Draft).

			Regular Season					Playoffs				
Season	Club	League	GP	G	A	Pts	PIM	GP	G	A	Pts	PIM
2007-08	Long Island Bant.	AYHL	27	1	6	7	22	....	....	....	....	....
2008-09	Long Island Mid.	AYHL	17	1	4	5	16	....	....	....	....	....
2009-10	Long Island Mid.	AYHL	33	8	17	25	48	....	....	....	....	....
2010-11	Milton Academy	High-MA	30	2	7	9	22	....	....	....	....	....
2011-12	Milton Academy	High-MA	STATISTICS NOT AVAILABLE									
2012-13	Yale	ECAC	37	0	7	7	32	....	....	....	....	....
2013-14	Yale	ECAC	33	4	7	11	30	....	....	....	....	....
2014-15	Yale	ECAC	33	6	15	21	31	....	....	....	....	....

ECAC First All-Star Team (2015) • NCAA East First All-American Team (2015)

OLEKSUK, Travis (oh-LEHK-suhk, TRA-vihs)

Center. Shoots left. 6', 200 lbs. Born, Thunder Bay, ON, February 3, 1989.

			Regular Season					Playoffs				
Season	Club	League	GP	G	A	Pts	PIM	GP	G	A	Pts	PIM
2006-07	Sioux City	USHL	56	6	16	22	35	7	0	2	2	0
2007-08	Sioux City	USHL	60	14	30	44	27	4	1	2	3	2
2008-09	U. Minn-Duluth	WCHA	18	0	5	5	10	....	....	....	....	....
2009-10	U. Minn-Duluth	WCHA	33	10	14	24	24	....	....	....	....	....
2010-11	U. Minn-Duluth	WCHA	42	14	19	33	33	....	....	....	....	....
2011-12	U. Minn-Duluth	WCHA	41	21	32	53	6	....	....	....	....	....
2012-13	Worcester Sharks	AHL	60	3	10	13	12	....	....	....	....	....
2013-14	Worcester Sharks	AHL	74	19	21	40	20	....	....	....	....	....
2014-15	Worcester Sharks	AHL	69	10	17	27	18	4	0	1	1	2

Signed as a free agent by **San Jose**, March 30, 2012.

OLHAVER, Gustav (OH-luh-vuhr, GUHS-tav) COL

Center. Shoots left. 6'6", 213 lbs. Born, Angelholm, Sweden, July 3, 1997.
(Colorado's 7th choice, 191st overall, in 2015 Entry Draft).

			Regular Season					Playoffs				
Season	Club	League	GP	G	A	Pts	PIM	GP	G	A	Pts	PIM
2012-13	Rogle U18	Swe-U18	4	0	1	1	0	....	....	....	....	....
2013-14	Rogle U18	Swe-U18	37	19	8	27	16	....	....	....	....	....
	Rogle Jr.	Swe-Jr.	5	1	0	1	2	....	....	....	....	....
2014-15	Rogle U18	Swe-U18	18	14	11	25	8	....	....	....	....	....
	Rogle Jr.	Swe-Jr.	41	6	6	12	10	6	0	0	0	2

OLLAS MATTSSON, Adam (OH-luhs MAT-suhn, A-duhm) CGY

Defense. Shoots left. 6'4", 209 lbs. Born, Stockholm, Sweden, July 30, 1996.
(Calgary's 5th choice, 175th overall, in 2014 Entry Draft).

			Regular Season					Playoffs				
Season	Club	League	GP	G	A	Pts	PIM	GP	G	A	Pts	PIM
2010-11	Varmdo Jr.	Swe-Jr.	1	0	0	0	0	....	....	....	....	....
2011-12	Djurgarden U18	Swe-U18	1	0	0	0	0	....	....	....	....	....
2012-13	Djurgarden U18	Swe-U18	32	0	8	8	44	8	0	1	1	6
2013-14	Djurgarden U18	Swe-U18	3	0	1	1	0	3	1	0	1	2
	Djurgarden	Sweden-2	6	0	2	2	4	....	....	....	....	....
	Djurgarden Jr.	Swe-Jr.	33	1	8	9	42	4	0	2	2	2
2014-15	Djurgarden Jr.	Swe-Jr.	19	1	6	7	42	7	0	2	2	29
	Djurgarden	Sweden	34	0	2	2	4	1	0	0	0	0

OLOFSSON, Fredrik (OH-lawf-suhn, FREHD-rihk) CHI

Left wing. Shoots left. 6'1", 197 lbs. Born, Helsingborg, Sweden, May 27, 1996.
(Chicago's 4th choice, 98th overall, in 2014 Entry Draft).

			Regular Season					Playoffs				
Season	Club	League	GP	G	A	Pts	PIM	GP	G	A	Pts	PIM
2011-12	Col. T-birds Ban.	T1EHL	56	28	37	65	26					
	Col. T-birds U16	T1EHL	4	2	1	3	4					
2012-13	Col. T-birds U16	T1EHL	31	26	43	69	8	4	1	4	5	2
	Green Bay	USHL	8	0	0	0	0					
2013-14	Green Bay	USHL	28	2	4	6	21					
	Chicago Steel	USHL	24	4	11	15	24					
2014-15	Chicago Steel	USHL	57	27	33	60	14					

• Signed Letter of Intent to attend **University of Nebraska-Omaha** (NCAA) in fall of 2015.

OLOFSSON, Gustav (OH-lawf-suhn, GOO-stahv) MIN

Defense. Shoots left. 6'3", 197 lbs. Born, Boras, Sweden, December 1, 1994.
(Minnesota's 1st choice, 46th overall, in 2013 Entry Draft).

			Regular Season					Playoffs				
Season	Club	League	GP	G	A	Pts	PIM	GP	G	A	Pts	PIM
2010-11	Col. T-birds U16	T1EHL	35	5	10	15	18	....	....	....	....	....
2011-12	Col. T-birds U18	T1EHL	38	5	25	30	10	....	....	....	....	....
	Green Bay	USHL	3	0	1	1	0	....	....	....	....	....
2012-13	Green Bay	USHL	63	2	21	23	59	4	0	0	0	0
2013-14	Colorado College	NCHC	30	4	4	8	20	....	....	....	....	....
	Iowa Wild	AHL	8	1	0	1	2	....	....	....	....	....
	Sweden	Olympics	7	1	4	5	2	....	....	....	....	....
2014-15	Iowa Wild	AHL	1	0	0	0	0	....	....	....	....	....

USHL All-Rookie Team (2013)

OLOFSSON, Victor (OH-lawf-suhn, VIHK-tuhr) BUF

Right wing. Shoots left. 5'11", 173 lbs. Born, Ornskoldsvik, Sweden, July 18, 1995.
(Buffalo's 9th choice, 181st overall, in 2014 Entry Draft).

			Regular Season					Playoffs				
Season	Club	League	GP	G	A	Pts	PIM	GP	G	A	Pts	PIM
2010-11	MODO U18	Swe-U18	3	1	0	1	0	....	....	....	....	....
2011-12	MODO U18	Swe-U18	39	19	15	34	4	2	1	0	1	0
2012-13	MODO U18	Swe-U18	37	31	24	55	6	4	1	2	3	0
	MODO Jr.	Swe-Jr.	7	2	3	5	0	6	0	1	1	0
2013-14	MODO Jr.	Swe-Jr.	44	32	21	53	16	5	4	5	9	2
	MODO	Sweden	11	0	0	0	0	....	....	....	....	....
2014-15	MODO Jr.	Swe-Jr.	6	1	3	4	0	5	3	5	8	0
	MODO	Sweden	39	10	8	18	4	....	....	....	....	....
	Timra IK	Sweden-2	8	2	0	2	0	....	....	....	....	....

OLSEN, Ryan (OHL-suhn, RIGH-uhn) WPG

Center. Shoots right. 6'2", 200 lbs. Born, Delta, BC, March 25, 1994.
(Winnipeg's 5th choice, 160th overall, in 2012 Entry Draft).

			Regular Season					Playoffs				
Season	Club	League	GP	G	A	Pts	PIM	GP	G	A	Pts	PIM
2008-09	South Delta Storm	Minor-BC	60	65	67	132	....	....	....	....	....	....
2009-10	Greater Van.	BCMML	38	24	23	47	32	5	2	1	3	20
	Saskatoon Blades	WHL	5	0	0	0	2	....	....	....	....	....
2010-11	Saskatoon Blades	WHL	63	7	7	14	39	3	0	0	0	4
2011-12	Saskatoon Blades	WHL	67	15	17	32	64	4	0	0	0	4
2012-13	Kelowna Rockets	WHL	69	32	24	56	87	11	1	5	6	14
2013-14	Kelowna Rockets	WHL	71	30	34	64	73	14	4	3	7	8
2014-15	St. John's IceCaps	AHL	60	4	5	9	47	....	....	....	....	....

OLSON, Brett (OHL-suhn, BREHT) FLA

Center. Shoots right. 6', 185 lbs. Born, Superior, WI, February 19, 1987.

			Regular Season					Playoffs				
Season	Club	League	GP	G	A	Pts	PIM	GP	G	A	Pts	PIM
2005-06	Sioux City	USHL	6	0	1	1	4	....	....	....	....	....
	Waterloo	USHL	44	9	5	14	14	....	....	....	....	....
2006-07	Waterloo	USHL	52	9	13	22	82	9	3	4	7	4
2007-08	Waterloo	USHL	49	17	37	54	50	11	3	7	10	10
2008-09	Michigan Tech	WCHA	38	10	13	23	41	....	....	....	....	....
2009-10	Michigan Tech	WCHA	32	18	12	30	45	....	....	....	....	....
2010-11	Michigan Tech	WCHA	18	4	6	10	25	....	....	....	....	....
2011-12	Michigan Tech	WCHA	39	10	20	30	45	....	....	....	....	....
2012-13	Abbotsford Heat	AHL	70	8	10	18	31	....	....	....	....	....
2013-14	Abbotsford Heat	AHL	75	17	27	44	38	4	1	0	1	2
2014-15	San Antonio	AHL	76	14	31	45	58	3	0	1	1	0

Signed as a free agent by **Florida**, July 4, 2014.

OLSON, Tate (OHL-suhn, TAYT) VAN

Defense. Shoots left. 6'3", 174 lbs. Born, Saskatoon, SK, March 21, 1997.
(Vancouver's 7th choice, 210th overall, in 2015 Entry Draft).

			Regular Season					Playoffs				
Season	Club	League	GP	G	A	Pts	PIM	GP	G	A	Pts	PIM
2012-13	Sask. Contacts	SMHL	29	7	9	16	24	11	0	2	2	6
2013-14	Prince George	WHL	52	2	8	10	17	....	....	....	....	....
2014-15	Prince George	WHL	68	5	19	24	69	5	3	0	3	0

O'NEILL, Will (oh-NEEL, WIHL) PIT

Defense. Shoots left. 6'1", 190 lbs. Born, Boston, MA, April 28, 1988.
(Atlanta's 8th choice, 210th overall, in 2006 Entry Draft).

			Regular Season					Playoffs				
Season	Club	League	GP	G	A	Pts	PIM	GP	G	A	Pts	PIM
2004-05	Tabor	High-MA	....	1	16	17	....	....	....	....	....	....
2005-06	Tabor	High-MA	28	5	25	30	38	....	....	....	....	....
2006-07	Omaha Lancers	USHL	57	4	9	13	73	5	0	0	0	8
2007-08	Omaha Lancers	USHL	58	5	19	24	95	14	1	6	7	38
2008-09	U. of Maine	H-East	34	4	12	16	82	....	....	....	....	....
2009-10	U. of Maine	H-East	39	8	23	31	69	....	....	....	....	....
2010-11	U. of Maine	H-East	28	4	17	21	44	....	....	....	....	....
2011-12	U. of Maine	H-East	40	3	30	33	68	....	....	....	....	....
	St. John's IceCaps	AHL	7	1	2	3	9	....	....	....	....	....
2012-13	St. John's IceCaps	AHL	59	3	18	21	32	....	....	....	....	....
2013-14	St. John's IceCaps	AHL	68	9	26	35	80	18	3	*13	16	27
2014-15	St. John's IceCaps	AHL	72	10	38	48	74	....	....	....	....	....

• Transferred to **Winnipeg** after **Atlanta** franchise relocated, June 21, 2011. Signed as a free agent by **Pittsburgh**, July 2, 2015.

O'NEILL, Brian (oh-NEEL, BRIGH-uhn) L.A.

Right wing. Shoots right. 5'9", 174 lbs. Born, Yardley, PA, June 1, 1988.

			Regular Season					Playoffs				
Season	Club	League	GP	G	A	Pts	PIM	GP	G	A	Pts	PIM
2007-08	Chicago Steel	USHL	60	23	38	61	40	7	3	2	5	10
2008-09	Yale	ECAC	30	12	14	26	37	....	....	....	....	....
2009-10	Yale	ECAC	34	16	29	45	20	....	....	....	....	....
2010-11	Yale	ECAC	36	20	26	46	39	....	....	....	....	....
2011-12	Yale	ECAC	35	21	25	46	26	....	....	....	....	....
	Manchester	AHL	12	1	1	2	4	4	0	1	1	6
2012-13	Manchester	AHL	49	3	12	15	18	4	1	0	1	2
2013-14	Manchester	AHL	60	26	21	47	39	....	....	....	....	....
2014-15	Manchester	AHL	71	22	*58	*80	55	19	10	10	20	12

ECAC All-Rookie Team (2009) • ECAC First All-Star Team (2011, 2012) • NCAA East Second All-American Team (2012) • AHL Second All-Star Team (2015) • John P. Sollenberger Trophy (AHL - Top Scorer) (2015) • Les Cunningham Award (AHL – MVP) (2015)

Signed as a free agent by **Los Angeles**, March 15, 2012.

O'REGAN, Daniel (oh-REE-guhn, DAN-yehl) S.J.

Center. Shoots right. 5'9", 175 lbs. Born, Berlin, Germany, January 30, 1994.
(San Jose's 4th choice, 138th overall, in 2012 Entry Draft).

			Regular Season					Playoffs				
Season	Club	League	GP	G	A	Pts	PIM	GP	G	A	Pts	PIM
2010-11	Cape Cod U16	Minor-MA	22	16	16	32	....	....	....	....	....	....
	St. Sebastian's	High-MA	27	25	25	50	10	....	....	....	....	....
2011-12	Cape Cod Whalers	Minor-MA	19	15	18	33	....	....	....	....	....	....
	St. Sebastian's	High-MA	27	21	35	56	8	....	....	....	....	....
	USNTDP	USHL	7	3	2	5	0	....	....	....	....	....
	USNTDP	U-18	7	1	4	5	2	....	....	....	....	....
2012-13	Boston University	H-East	39	16	22	38	16	....	....	....	....	....
2013-14	Boston University	H-East	35	10	12	22	14	....	....	....	....	....
2014-15	Boston University	H-East	41	23	27	50	26	....	....	....	....	....

Hockey East All-Rookie Team (2013) • Hockey East Second All-Star Team (2015)

PAIGIN, Ziyat (pigh-GEEN, zee-YAT) EDM

Defense. Shoots left. 6'6", 209 lbs. Born, Penza, Russia, February 8, 1995.
(Edmonton's 6th choice, 209th overall, in 2015 Entry Draft).

			Regular Season					Playoffs				
Season	Club	League	GP	G	A	Pts	PIM	GP	G	A	Pts	PIM
2011-12	Irbis Kazan Jr.	Rus.-Jr. B	35	6	12	18	38	4	0	0	0	0
2012-13	Bars Kazan Jr.	Russia-Jr.	46	3	9	12	16	4	0	0	0	2
	Irbis Kazan Jr.	Rus.-Jr. B	8	1	1	2	6	....	....	....	....	....
2013-14	Bars Kazan Jr.	Russia-Jr.	47	3	8	11	14	12	0	1	1	2
2014-15	Bars Kazan	Russia-2	3	0	1	1	4	....	....	....	....	....
	Ak Bars Kazan	KHL	33	1	1	2	2	2	0	0	0	0

PALMQUIST, Zach (PAHM-kwihst, ZAK) MIN

Defense. Shoots left. 6', 188 lbs. Born, South St. Paul, MN, December 9, 1990.

			Regular Season					Playoffs				
Season	Club	League	GP	G	A	Pts	PIM	GP	G	A	Pts	PIM
2008-09	South St. Paul	High-MN	25	14	24	38	32	....	....	....	....	....
	Waterloo	USHL	12	0	3	3	18	2	0	0	0	2
2009-10	Waterloo	USHL	53	9	27	36	60	3	0	0	0	0
2010-11	Waterloo	USHL	59	4	14	18	67	2	0	1	1	0
2011-12	Minnesota State	WCHA	38	6	13	19	31	....	....	....	....	....
2012-13	Minnesota State	WCHA	41	7	18	25	20	....	....	....	....	....
2013-14	Minnesota State	WCHA	41	4	19	23	36	....	....	....	....	....
2014-15	Minnesota State	WCHA	40	8	21	29	20	....	....	....	....	....
	Iowa Wild	AHL	8	0	3	3	4	....	....	....	....	....

WCHA First All-Star Team (2014, 2015) • NCAA West Second All-American Team (2015)

Signed as a free agent by **Minnesota**, March 30, 2015.

PANARIN, Artemi (pah-NAHR-ihn, ahr-TEHM-ee) CHI

Left wing. Shoots right. 5'11", 170 lbs. Born, Korkino, USSR, October 30, 1991.

			Regular Season					Playoffs				
Season	Club	League	GP	G	A	Pts	PIM	GP	G	A	Pts	PIM
2008-09	Vityaz Chekhov 2	Russia-3	62	29	39	68	70	13	4	5	9	28
	Vityaz Chekhov	KHL	5	0	1	1	2	....	....	....	....	....
2009-10	Chekhov Jr.	Russia-Jr.	38	20	24	44	55	4	1	2	3	12
	Vityaz Chekhov	KHL	20	1	8	9	16	....	....	....	....	....
2010-11	Chekhov Jr.	Russia-Jr.	13	5	12	17	22	....	....	....	....	....
	Vityaz Chekhov	KHL	40	5	16	21	8	....	....	....	....	....
2011-12	Vityaz Chekhov	KHL	38	12	14	26	49	....	....	....	....	....
	Ak Bars Kazan	KHL	12	1	4	5	4	3	0	0	0	0
2012-13	Vityaz Chekhov	KHL	40	11	7	18	22	....	....	....	....	....
	SKA St. Petersburg	KHL	3	0	1	1	2	14	2	7	9	0
2013-14	SKA St. Petersburg	KHL	51	20	20	40	30	4	0	0	0	2
2014-15	SKA St. Petersburg	KHL	54	26	36	62	37	20	5	*15	20	4

Signed as a free agent by **Chicago**, May 1, 2015.

PARADIS, Philippe (PAIR-a-dee, fihl-EEP) T.B.

Center. Shoots left. 6'2", 205 lbs. Born, Dolbeau, QC, January 2, 1991.
(Carolina's 1st choice, 27th overall, in 2009 Entry Draft).

			Regular Season					Playoffs				
Season	Club	League	GP	G	A	Pts	PIM	GP	G	A	Pts	PIM
2006-07	Jonquiere Elites	QAAA	38	5	12	17	76	3	1	1	2	6
2007-08	Shawinigan	QMJHL	45	11	12	23	44	3	0	0	0	0
2008-09	Shawinigan	QMJHL	66	19	31	50	74	21	6	6	12	20
2009-10	Shawinigan	QMJHL	63	24	20	44	104	6	2	1	3	4
	Toronto Marlies	AHL	4	0	2	2	0	....	....	....	....	....
2010-11	P.E.I. Rocket	QMJHL	59	23	30	53	85	5	1	1	2	8
	Rockford IceHogs	AHL	4	1	0	1	2	....	....	....	....	....
2011-12	Rockford IceHogs	AHL	58	5	11	16	39	....	....	....	....	....
2012-13	Rockford IceHogs	AHL	36	1	7	8	100	....	....	....	....	....
	Toledo Walleye	ECHL	5	0	0	0	9	....	....	....	....	....
	Syracuse Crunch	AHL	8	0	1	1	11	18	3	1	4	23
2013-14	Syracuse Crunch	AHL	56	6	9	15	118	....	....	....	....	....
2014-15	Syracuse Crunch	AHL	34	8	7	15	49	....	....	....	....	....

Traded to **Toronto** by **Carolina** for Jiri Tlusty, December 3, 2009. Traded to **Chicago** by **Toronto** with Viktor Stalberg and Chris Didomenico for Kris Versteeg and Bill Sweatt, June 30, 2010. Traded to **Tampa Bay** by **Chicago** for Kirill Gotovets, April 2, 2013.

PARAYKO, Colton (pa-RAY-koh, KOHL-tuhn) ST.L.

Defense. Shoots right. 6'5", 214 lbs. Born, St. Albert, AB, May 12, 1993.
(St. Louis' 4th choice, 86th overall, in 2012 Entry Draft).

			Regular Season					Playoffs				
Season	Club	League	GP	G	A	Pts	PIM	GP	G	A	Pts	PIM
2008-09	St. Albert Flyers	Minor-AB	33	1	16	17	10	2	0	2	2	0
2009-10	St. Albert	Minor-AB	33	5	8	13	10	....	....	....	....	....
2010-11	Fort McMurray	AJHL	42	3	9	12	12	12	2	1	3	2
2011-12	Fort McMurray	AJHL	53	9	33	42	65	21	3	9	12	14
2012-13	Alaska	CCHA	33	4	13	17	23	....	....	....	....	....
2013-14	Alaska	WCHA	37	7	19	26	16	....	....	....	....	....
2014-15	Alaska	WCHA	34	6	17	23	16	....	....	....	....	....
	Chicago Wolves	AHL	17	4	3	7	6	5	0	0	0	6

WCHA First All-Star Team (2014, 2015) • NCAA West Second All-American Team (2014, 2015)

PARKES, Trevor (PAHRKS, TREH-vuhr)

Right wing. Shoots right. 6'2", 188 lbs. Born, Fort Erie, ON, May 13, 1991.

			Regular Season					Playoffs				
Season	Club	League	GP	G	A	Pts	PIM	GP	G	A	Pts	PIM
2008-09	Fort Erie Meteors	ON-Jr.B	52	23	20	43	34	5	0	1	1	2
2009-10	Montreal	QMJHL	66	27	20	47	34	....	....	....	....	....
2010-11	Montreal	QMJHL	60	33	29	62	32	10	6	2	8	12
2011-12	Grand Rapids	AHL	44	2	6	8	23	....	....	....	....	....
	Toledo Walleye	ECHL	4	4	0	4	2	....	....	....	....	....
2012-13	Grand Rapids	AHL	36	3	6	9	35	....	....	....	....	....
	Toledo Walleye	ECHL	19	14	16	30	6	6	3	2	5	6
2013-14	Grand Rapids	AHL	36	6	3	9	27	3	1	0	1	12
	Toledo Walleye	ECHL	27	17	17	34	20	....	....	....	....	....
2014-15	Worcester Sharks	AHL	20	3	6	9	14	....	....	....	....	....
	Greenville	ECHL	39	15	18	33	24	....	....	....	....	....

Signed as a free agent by **Detroit**, September 23, 2010. Signed to a PTO (professional tryout) contract by **Worcester** (AHL), February 3, 2015. Signed as a free agent by **San Jose** (AHL), July 16, 2015.

PARKS, Michael (PARKS, MIGH-kuhl) **PHI**

Right wing. Shoots right. 5'11", 188 lbs. Born, O'Fallon, MO, February 15, 1992.
(Philadelphia's 3rd choice, 149th overall, in 2010 Entry Draft).

			Regular Season					Playoffs				
Season	Club	League	GP	G	A	Pts	PIM	GP	G	A	Pts	PIM
2008-09	St. Louis Selects	Other	46	38	47	85	26	....	....	....	....	....
2009-10	Cedar Rapids	USHL	51	11	11	22	57	5	0	1	1	0
2010-11	Cedar Rapids	USHL	56	25	17	42	42	8	3	1	4	6
2011-12	North Dakota	WCHA	42	12	10	22	38	....	....	....	....	....
2012-13	North Dakota	WCHA	25	7	1	8	31	....	....	....	....	....
2013-14	North Dakota	NCHC	42	12	18	30	28	....	....	....	....	....
2014-15	North Dakota	NCHC	42	12	20	32	44	....	....	....	....	....

NCHC Second All-Star Team (2014)

PARSELLS, Adam (pahr-SEHLZ, A-duhm) **S.J.**

Defense. Shoots left. 6'6", 195 lbs. Born, Wausau, WI, January 3, 1997.
(San Jose's 7th choice, 160th overall, in 2015 Entry Draft).

			Regular Season					Playoffs				
Season	Club	League	GP	G	A	Pts	PIM	GP	G	A	Pts	PIM
2011-12	Wausau West	High-WI	23	1	0	1	2	6	0	0	0	0
2012-13	Team Wisconsin	MEPDL	12	2	2	4	....	....	....	....	....	....
	Wausau West	High-WI	24	2	8	10	6	4	0	3	3	6
2013-14	Team Wisconsin	UMHSEL	2	0	0	0	0	....	....	....	....	....
	Wausau West	High-WI	23	1	12	13	39	4	2	3	5	2
	Green Bay	USHL	1	0	0	0	0	....	....	....	....	....
2014-15	Team Wisconsin	UMHSEL	18	3	1	4	16	3	0	1	1	0
	Wausau West	High-WI	23	7	15	22	28	6	0	2	2	0
	Green Bay	USHL	3	0	0	0	0	....	....	....	....	....

• Signed Letter of Intent to attend **University of Wisconsin** (Big Ten) in fall of 2016.

PARSHIN, Denis (PAHR-shihn, DEH-nihs) **COL**

Right wing. Shoots left. 5'10", 165 lbs. Born, Rybinsk, USSR, February 1, 1986.
(Colorado's 3rd choice, 72nd overall, in 2004 Entry Draft).

			Regular Season					Playoffs				
Season	Club	League	GP	G	A	Pts	PIM	GP	G	A	Pts	PIM
2002-03	CSKA Moscow 2	Russia-3	4	1	0	1	2	....	....	....	....	....
2003-04	CSKA Moscow	Russia	27	2	4	6	4	....	....	....	....	....
	CSKA Moscow 2	Russia-3	STATISTICS NOT AVAILABLE									
2004-05	CSKA Moscow	Russia	42	3	4	7	18	....	....	....	....	....
2005-06	CSKA Moscow 2	Russia-3	STATISTICS NOT AVAILABLE									
	CSKA Moscow	Russia	37	2	8	10	22	6	0	2	2	2
2006-07	CSKA Moscow	Russia	54	18	14	32	24	12	2	2	4	8
2007-08	CSKA Moscow	Russia	56	12	23	35	46	6	1	0	1	0
2008-09	CSKA Moscow	KHL	48	13	14	27	34	8	1	0	1	6
2009-10	CSKA Moscow	KHL	56	21	22	43	28	3	0	1	1	6
2010-11	CSKA Moscow	KHL	49	16	17	33	32	....	....	....	....	....
2011-12	CSKA Moscow	KHL	32	12	12	24	24	5	1	1	2	6
2012-13	CSKA Moscow	KHL	9	1	1	2	2	....	....	....	....	....
	Ufa	KHL	29	5	7	12	20	....	....	....	....	....
2013-14	Nizhny Novgorod	KHL	46	15	18	33	36	7	1	3	4	0
2014-15	Omsk	KHL	60	25	31	56	40	3	0	1	1	0

PASHNIN, Mikhail (pahsh-NIHN, mih-KHIGH-eel) **NYR**

Defense. Shoots left. 6'1", 191 lbs. Born, Chelyabinsk, USSR, May 11, 1989.
(NY Rangers' 7th choice, 200th overall, in 2009 Entry Draft).

			Regular Season					Playoffs				
Season	Club	League	GP	G	A	Pts	PIM	GP	G	A	Pts	PIM
2005-06	Mechel 2	Russia-3	25	0	5	5	30	....	....	....	....	....
2006-07	Mechel 2	Russia-3	12	1	3	4	26	....	....	....	....	....
	Mechel	Russia-2	41	0	2	2	40	4	0	0	0	8
2007-08	Mechel 2	Russia-3	8	4	1	5	12	....	....	....	....	....
	Mechel	Russia-2	49	2	5	7	58	....	....	....	....	....
2008-09	Mechel 2	Russia-3	3	0	1	1	4	....	....	....	....	....
	Mechel	Russia-2	35	2	4	6	40	7	0	2	2	8
2009-10	CSKA Moscow	KHL	44	1	4	5	52	1	0	0	0	0
	CSKA Jr.	Russia-Jr.	4	0	3	3	2	4	1	1	2	20
2010-11	CSKA Moscow	KHL	42	2	2	4	38	....	....	....	....	....
	CSKA Jr.	Russia-Jr.	10	2	2	4	14	16	1	4	5	60
2011-12	CSKA Moscow	KHL	50	3	2	5	68	5	0	1	1	20
2012-13	Yaroslavl	KHL	32	1	1	2	75	6	0	0	0	6
2013-14	Yaroslavl	KHL	32	0	3	3	114	16	0	1	1	14
2014-15	Yaroslavl	KHL	32	0	2	2	22	5	0	0	0	29

PAUL, Nicholas (PAWL, NIH-koh-las) **OTT**

Left wing. Shoots left. 6'4", 223 lbs. Born, Mississauga, ON, March 20, 1995.
(Dallas' 6th choice, 101st overall, in 2013 Entry Draft).

			Regular Season					Playoffs				
Season	Club	League	GP	G	A	Pts	PIM	GP	G	A	Pts	PIM
2010-11	Miss. Senators	GTHL	37	14	11	25	12	....	....	....	....	....
2011-12	Mississauga Reps	GTHL	33	25	32	57	....	....	....	....	....	....
	Mississauga Reps	Other	30	23	28	51	....	....	....	....	....	....
	Mississauga	ON-Jr.A	9	3	2	5	4	....	....	....	....	....
2012-13	Brampton	OHL	66	12	16	28	21	5	0	1	1	0
2013-14	North Bay	OHL	67	26	20	46	39	22	12	6	18	10
2014-15	North Bay	OHL	58	37	29	66	49	15	7	8	15	6

Traded to **Ottawa** by **Dallas** with Alex Chiasson, Alexander Guptill and Dallas' 2nd round choice (later traded to New Jersey – New Jersey selected Mackenzie Blackwood) in 2015 Entry Draft for Jason Spezza and Ludwig Karlsson, July 1, 2014.

PAULOVIC, Matej (PAWL-oh-vihch, mah-TAY) **DAL**

Left wing. Shoots right. 6'3", 195 lbs. Born, Topolcany, Slovakia, January 13, 1995.
(Dallas' 8th choice, 149th overall, in 2013 Entry Draft).

			Regular Season					Playoffs				
Season	Club	League	GP	G	A	Pts	PIM	GP	G	A	Pts	PIM
2009-10	HC Topolcany U18	Svk-U18	39	17	16	33	26	....	....	....	....	....
2010-11	HC Topolcany U18	Svk-U18	42	33	29	62	34	....	....	....	....	....
	HK Nitra Jr.	Slovak-Jr.	2	0	0	0	0	....	....	....	....	....
2011-12	Farjestad U18	Swe-U18	33	17	23	40	51	6	2	1	3	2
	Farjestad Jr.	Swe-Jr.	12	2	1	3	6	....	....	....	....	....
2012-13	Farjestad U18	Swe-U18	8	3	4	7	8	....	....	....	....	....
	Farjestad Jr.	Swe-Jr.	34	5	12	17	6	7	1	1	2	6
2013-14	Peterborough	OHL	18	2	2	4	4	....	....	....	....	....
	Muskegon	USHL	29	6	10	16	39	....	....	....	....	....
2014-15	Muskegon	USHL	51	17	33	50	79	12	3	5	8	12

PAVLYCHEV, Nikita (pav-LIH-chehv, nih-KEE-ta) **PIT**

Center. Shoots left. 6'7", 205 lbs. Born, Yaroslavl, Russia, March 23, 1997.
(Pittsburgh's 4th choice, 197th overall, in 2015 Entry Draft).

			Regular Season					Playoffs				
Season	Club	League	GP	G	A	Pts	PIM	GP	G	A	Pts	PIM
2012-13	Wilkes Barre U16	AYHL	21	10	16	26	47	2	0	3	3	10
2013-14	Wilkes Barre U18	AYHL	22	9	14	23	65	....	....	....	....	....
	Des Moines	USHL	4	0	1	1	0	....	....	....	....	....
2014-15	Des Moines	USHL	42	6	10	16	80	....	....	....	....	....

• Signed Letter of Intent to attend **Penn State University** (Big Ten) in fall of 2015.

PEARSON, Chase (PEER-suhn, CHAYS) **DET**

Center. Shoots left. 6'2", 189 lbs. Born, Cornwall, ON, August 23, 1997.
(Detroit's 4th choice, 140th overall, in 2015 Entry Draft).

			Regular Season					Playoffs				
Season	Club	League	GP	G	A	Pts	PIM	GP	G	A	Pts	PIM
2012-13	Atlanta Fire U16	NAPHL	22	11	13	24	50	4	4	6	10	10
2013-14	Cornwall Colts	ON-Jr.A	39	8	15	23	18	5	0	1	1	2
	Youngstown	USHL	2	0	0	0	0	....	....	....	....	....
2014-15	Youngstown	USHL	57	12	14	26	96	4	0	2	2	0

• Signed Letter of Intent to attend **University of Maine** (Hockey East) in fall of 2015.

PECA, Matthew (PEH-kuh, MA-thew) **T.B.**

Center. Shoots left. 5'8", 155 lbs. Born, Petawawa, ON, April 27, 1993.
(Tampa Bay's 5th choice, 201st overall, in 2011 Entry Draft).

			Regular Season					Playoffs				
Season	Club	League	GP	G	A	Pts	PIM	GP	G	A	Pts	PIM
2008-09	Ott. Valley Titans	Minor-ON	23	10	17	27	12	6	2	3	5	2
	Ottawa Valley	Other	12	7	13	20	6	....	....	....	....	....
2009-10	Pembroke	ON-Jr.A	60	21	26	47	10	15	3	3	6	6
2010-11	Pembroke	ON-Jr.A	50	26	46	72	14	14	11	10	21	6
2011-12	Quinnipiac	ECAC	39	8	31	39	12	....	....	....	....	....
2012-13	Quinnipiac	ECAC	39	15	15	30	36	....	....	....	....	....
2013-14	Quinnipiac	ECAC	40	12	26	38	16	....	....	....	....	....
2014-15	Quinnipiac	ECAC	39	7	29	36	27	....	....	....	....	....
	Syracuse Crunch	AHL	8	1	3	4	0	3	1	1	2	0

ECAC All-Rookie Team (2012) • ECAC First All-Star Team (2015)

PEDAN, Andrey (peh-DAHN, AWN-dray) **VAN**

Defense. Shoots left. 6'5", 213 lbs. Born, Kaunas, Lithuania, July 3, 1993.
(NY Islanders' 4th choice, 63rd overall, in 2011 Entry Draft).

			Regular Season					Playoffs				
Season	Club	League	GP	G	A	Pts	PIM	GP	G	A	Pts	PIM
2009-10	Dyn.Moscow U18	Rus-U18	3	2	1	3	12	....	....	....	....	....
2010-11	Guelph Storm	OHL	51	2	10	12	89	6	0	8	8	8
2011-12	Guelph Storm	OHL	63	10	30	40	152	6	1	2	3	14
2012-13	Guelph Storm	OHL	60	14	30	44	*145	5	3	1	4	16
	Bridgeport	AHL	8	0	2	2	7	....	....	....	....	....
2013-14	Bridgeport	AHL	28	5	5	10	43	....	....	....	....	....
	Stockton Thunder	ECHL	5	0	0	0	6	2	0	0	0	0
2014-15	Bridgeport	AHL	6	0	3	3	51	....	....	....	....	....
	Stockton Thunder	ECHL	2	0	1	1	2	....	....	....	....	....
	Utica Comets	AHL	42	3	11	14	70	....	....	....	....	....

Traded to **Vancouver** by **NY Islanders** for Alexandre Mallet and Vancouver's 3rd round choice in 2016 Entry Draft, November 25, 2014.

PELECH, Adam (PEHL-ehk, A-duhm) **NYI**

Defense. Shoots left. 6'3", 213 lbs. Born, Toronto, ON, August 16, 1994.
(NY Islanders' 3rd choice, 65th overall, in 2012 Entry Draft).

			Regular Season					Playoffs				
Season	Club	League	GP	G	A	Pts	PIM	GP	G	A	Pts	PIM
2009-10	Toronto Marlboros	GTHL	69	6	28	34	40	....	....	....	....	....
2010-11	Erie Otters	OHL	65	1	13	14	27	7	0	2	2	2
2011-12	Erie Otters	OHL	44	2	18	20	52	....	....	....	....	....
2012-13	Erie Otters	OHL	59	8	32	40	98	....	....	....	....	....
2013-14	Erie Otters	OHL	60	10	45	55	46	14	2	5	7	10
2014-15	Bridgeport	AHL	65	0	11	11	48	....	....	....	....	....

OHL Second All-Star Team (2014)

PELLETIER, Julien (PEHL-tyay, JOO-lee-ehn) **CBJ**

Left wing. Shoots left. 5'11", 183 lbs. Born, Buckingham, QC, June 28, 1996.
(Columbus' 5th choice, 107th overall, in 2014 Entry Draft).

			Regular Season					Playoffs				
Season	Club	League	GP	G	A	Pts	PIM	GP	G	A	Pts	PIM
2010-11	Outaouais	Minor-ON	27	8	7	15	74	....	....	....	....	....
2011-12	Gatineau Intrepide	QAAA	39	6	18	24	28	....	....	....	....	....
2012-13	Gatineau Intrepide	QAAA	34	23	20	43	44	....	....	....	....	....
	Cape Breton	QMJHL	7	1	0	1	2	....	....	....	....	....
2013-14	Cape Breton	QMJHL	67	25	25	50	28	4	1	1	2	2
2014-15	Cape Breton	QMJHL	26	5	9	14	14	....	....	....	....	....
	Rouyn-Noranda	QMJHL	27	5	10	15	16	6	0	4	4	2

PEPIN, Alexis (peh-PEHN, al-EHX-ihs) COL

Left wing. Shoots left. 6'3", 218 lbs. Born, Montreal, QC, April 24, 1996.
(Colorado's 4th choice, 114th overall, in 2014 Entry Draft).

			Regular Season					Playoffs				
Season	Club	League	GP	G	A	Pts	PIM	GP	G	A	Pts	PIM
2009-10	St. Laurent Pred.	Minor-QC	33	10	9	19	74	....	....	....	....	....
2010-11	C.C. Lemoyne	Minor-QC	34	26	13	39	54	....	....	....	....	....
	C.C. Lemoyne	QAAA	10	0	0	0	8	....	....	....	....	....
2011-12	C.C. Lemoyne	QAAA	38	22	18	40	93	....	....	....	....	....
2012-13	P.E.I. Rocket	QMJHL	64	18	12	30	78	6	1	1	2	4
2013-14	Charlottetown	QMJHL	37	8	9	17	58	....	....	....	....	....
	Gatineau	QMJHL	23	9	8	17	11	8	4	1	5	4
2014-15	Gatineau	QMJHL	24	10	4	14	20	....	....	....	....	....
	Val-d'Or Foreurs	QMJHL	23	8	5	13	36	17	4	4	8	37

PERLINI, Brendan (puhr-LEE-nee, BREHN-duhn) ARI

Left wing. Shoots left. 6'2", 205 lbs. Born, Guildford, UK, April 27, 1996.
(Arizona's 1st choice, 12th overall, in 2014 Entry Draft).

			Regular Season					Playoffs				
Season	Club	League	GP	G	A	Pts	PIM	GP	G	A	Pts	PIM
2009-10	Soo Greyhounds	Minor-ON	18	19	15	34	12	....	....	....	....	....
2010-11	Detroit Belle Tire	T1EHL	31	18	17	35	17	....	....	....	....	....
2011-12	Detroit Belle Tire	T1EHL	40	21	23	44	20	7	4	3	7	4
2012-13	Barrie Colts	OHL	32	1	1	2	4	....	....	....	....	....
	Niagara Ice Dogs	OHL	27	7	3	10	4	5	1	2	3	4
2013-14	Niagara Ice Dogs	OHL	58	34	37	71	36	7	0	1	1	6
2014-15	Niagara Ice Dogs	OHL	43	26	34	60	22	11	7	5	12	7
	Portland Pirates	AHL	....	....	....	....	....	4	1	0	1	0

PERRON, Francis (pair-AWN, FRAN-sihs) OTT

Left wing. Shoots left. 6', 166 lbs. Born, Laval, QC, April 18, 1996.
(Ottawa's 5th choice, 190th overall, in 2014 Entry Draft).

			Regular Season					Playoffs				
Season	Club	League	GP	G	A	Pts	PIM	GP	G	A	Pts	PIM
2011-12	Saint-Eustache	QAAA	14	5	13	18	14	....	....	....	....	....
2012-13	Rouyn-Noranda	QMJHL	57	7	11	18	28	5	1	1	2	7
2013-14	Rouyn-Noranda	QMJHL	68	16	39	55	32	9	1	7	8	4
2014-15	Rouyn-Noranda	QMJHL	64	29	47	76	39	6	3	4	7	14

PESCE, Brett (PEH-SHEE, BREHT) CAR

Defense. Shoots right. 6'3", 200 lbs. Born, Tarrytown, NY, November 15, 1994.
(Carolina's 2nd choice, 66th overall, in 2013 Entry Draft).

			Regular Season					Playoffs				
Season	Club	League	GP	G	A	Pts	PIM	GP	G	A	Pts	PIM
2011-12	Jersey Hitmen	EJHL	17	1	5	6	18	....	....	....	....	....
	USNTDP	U-18	6	0	0	0	2	....	....	....	....	....
2012-13	New Hampshire	H-East	38	1	5	6	10	....	....	....	....	....
2013-14	New Hampshire	H-East	41	7	14	21	6	....	....	....	....	....
2014-15	New Hampshire	H-East	31	3	13	16	32	....	....	....	....	....
	Charlotte	AHL	4	0	1	1	6	....	....	....	....	....

PETAN, Nic (peh-TAN, NIHK) WPG

Center. Shoots left. 5'9", 181 lbs. Born, Delta, BC, March 22, 1995.
(Winnipeg's 2nd choice, 43rd overall, in 2013 Entry Draft).

			Regular Season					Playoffs				
Season	Club	League	GP	G	A	Pts	PIM	GP	G	A	Pts	PIM
2010-11	Greater Van.	BCMML	35	19	30	49	36	6	3	3	6	18
	Portland	WHL	3	0	1	1	0	7	0	0	0	0
2011-12	Portland	WHL	61	14	21	35	22	22	0	0	0	4
2012-13	Portland	WHL	71	46	*74	*120	43	21	9	*19	28	16
2013-14	Portland	WHL	63	35	*78	113	69	21	7	21	28	38
2014-15	Portland	WHL	54	15	74	89	41	17	10	18	28	20

WHL West First All-Star Team (2013, 2014) • WHL West Second All-Star Team (2015)

PETERS, Alex (PEE-tuhrz, AL-ehx)) DAL

Defense. Shoots left. 6'3", 205 lbs. Born, Goderich, ON, July 2, 1996.
(Dallas' 3rd choice, 75th overall, in 2014 Entry Draft).

			Regular Season					Playoffs				
Season	Club	League	GP	G	A	Pts	PIM	GP	G	A	Pts	PIM
2011-12	Huron-Perth MM	Minor-ON	28	8	5	13	14	8	3	2	5	6
	Huron-Perth Mid.	Minor-ON	1	0	0	0	0	2	0	0	0	0
2012-13	Plymouth Whalers	OHL	58	0	12	12	31	13	0	1	1	11
2013-14	Plymouth Whalers	OHL	50	3	6	9	44	5	0	0	0	10
2014-15	Plymouth Whalers	OHL	8	0	4	4	14	....	....	....	....	....

• Missed majority of 2014-15 due to knee injury at Kingston (OHL), October 17, 2014.

PETERS, Taylor (PEE-tuhrs, TAY-luhr) DAL

Center. Shoots left. 6'2", 215 lbs. Born, Delta, BC, January 24, 1992.

			Regular Season					Playoffs				
Season	Club	League	GP	G	A	Pts	PIM	GP	G	A	Pts	PIM
2007-08	Greater Van.	BCMML	39	10	14	24	66	2	1	0	1	2
	Portland	WHL	5	2	0	2	0	....	....	....	....	....
2008-09	Portland	WHL	70	4	4	8	41	....	....	....	....	....
2009-10	Penticton Vees	BCHL	22	3	5	8	16	....	....	....	....	....
	Portland	WHL	32	4	3	7	15	2	0	0	0	0
2010-11	Portland	WHL	72	8	11	19	47	21	3	5	8	8
2011-12	Portland	WHL	72	12	26	38	60	22	1	7	8	12
2012-13	Portland	WHL	68	15	27	42	61	21	1	9	10	19
2013-14	Texas Stars	AHL	70	7	9	16	58	7	1	1	2	4
2014-15	Texas Stars	AHL	39	0	3	3	9	....	....	....	....	....
	Idaho Steelheads	ECHL	9	4	3	7	6	3	0	0	0	2

Signed as a free agent by **Dallas**, March 4, 2013.

PETERSON, Avery (PEE-tuhr-suhn, AY-vuhr-ee) MIN

Center. Shoots left. 6'3", 208 lbs. Born, Grand Rapids, MN, June 20, 1995.
(Minnesota's 5th choice, 167th overall, in 2013 Entry Draft).

			Regular Season					Playoffs				
Season	Club	League	GP	G	A	Pts	PIM	GP	G	A	Pts	PIM
2010-11	Grand Rapids	High-MN	28	8	18	26	28	3	1	3	4	8
2011-12	Grand Rapids	High-MN	25	14	32	46	46	1	0	2	2	0
2012-13	Grand Rapids	High-MN	23	23	31	54	2	3	4	4	8	0
	Team North	UMHSEL	21	5	10	15	19	....	....	....	....	....
	Sioux City	USHL	8	1	3	4	7	....	....	....	....	....
2013-14	Sioux City	USHL	27	6	15	21	16	....	....	....	....	....
2014-15	Nebraska-Omaha	NCHC	39	11	10	21	18	....	....	....	....	....

PETERSON, Judd (PEE-tuhr-suhn, JUHD) BUF

Center/Right wing. Shoots right. 6', 189 lbs. Born, Duluth, MN, September 27, 1993.
(Buffalo's 8th choice, 204th overall, in 2012 Entry Draft).

			Regular Season					Playoffs				
Season	Club	League	GP	G	A	Pts	PIM	GP	G	A	Pts	PIM
2009-10	Duluth Marshall	High-MN	23	15	14	29	24	2	1	0	1	0
2010-11	Team North	UMHSEL	24	8	3	11	22	....	....	....	....	....
	Duluth Marshall	High-MN	25	24	19	43	40	2	1	2	3	0
2011-12	Team North	UMHSEL	16	4	2	6	22	....	....	....	....	....
	Duluth Marshall	High-MN	25	41	33	74	30	5	6	3	9	2
2012-13	Cedar Rapids	USHL	46	11	15	26	38	....	....	....	....	....
2013-14	Cedar Rapids	USHL	47	16	15	31	43	2	0	0	0	0
2014-15	St. Cloud State	NCHC	37	4	3	7	20	....	....	....	....	....

PETROV, Kirill (peh-TRAWF, kih-RIHL) NYI

Right wing. Shoots left. 6'3", 198 lbs. Born, Kazan, USSR, April 13, 1990.
(NY Islanders' 7th choice, 73rd overall, in 2008 Entry Draft).

			Regular Season					Playoffs				
Season	Club	League	GP	G	A	Pts	PIM	GP	G	A	Pts	PIM
2005-06	Ak Bars Kazan 2	Russia-3		STATISTICS NOT AVAILABLE								
2006-07	Ak Bars Kazan 2	Russia-3		STATISTICS NOT AVAILABLE								
	Ak Bars Kazan	Russia	9	1	1	2	8	3	0	0	0	2
2007-08	Ak Bars Kazan	Russia	47	4	6	10	54	8	1	1	2	0
2008-09	Ak Bars Kazan 2	Russia-3	9	4	10	14	26	....	....	....	....	....
	Ak Bars Kazan	KHL	6	1	0	1	2	....	....	....	....	....
2009-10	Ak Bars Kazan	KHL	8	0	0	0	4	3	0	1	1	0
	Bars Kazan Jr.	Russia-Jr.	4	2	1	3	4	....	....	....	....	....
	Almetjevsk	Russia-2	22	7	13	20	48	13	12	7	19	24
2010-11	Ak Bars Kazan	KHL	2	0	0	0	0	....	....	....	....	....
	Bars Kazan Jr.	Russia-Jr.	3	1	1	2	4	....	....	....	....	....
	Khanty-Mansiisk	KHL	47	8	11	19	20	6	2	2	4	8
2011-12	Ak Bars Kazan	KHL	52	16	13	29	8	12	3	2	5	8
2012-13	Ak Bars Kazan	KHL	47	12	8	20	26	18	4	1	5	6
2013-14	Ak Bars Kazan	KHL	53	14	15	29	29	6	1	2	3	0
2014-15	Ak Bars Kazan	KHL	47	5	10	15	41	17	2	1	3	12

PETTERSSON, Emil (PEH-tuhr-suhn, eh-MIHL) NSH

Center. Shoots left. 6'1", 158 lbs. Born, Sundsvall, Sweden, January 14, 1994.
(Nashville's 7th choice, 155th overall, in 2013 Entry Draft).

			Regular Season					Playoffs				
Season	Club	League	GP	G	A	Pts	PIM	GP	G	A	Pts	PIM
2010-11	Timra IK U18	Swe-U18	34	10	16	26	26	5	0	1	1	0
2011-12	Timra IK U18	Swe-U18	31	19	22	41	94	3	1	4	5	10
	Timra IK Jr.	Swe-Jr.	17	4	2	6	10	3	1	1	2	2
2012-13	Timra IK Jr.	Swe-Jr.	44	13	31	44	38	2	0	0	0	2
	Timra IK	Sweden	2	0	0	0	0	....	....	....	....	....
	Timra IK	Sweden-Q	2	1	0	1	0	....	....	....	....	....
2013-14	Timra IK	Sweden-2	44	6	8	14	12	....	....	....	....	....
	Timra IK Jr.	Swe-Jr.	12	10	9	19	12	2	2	0	2	4
2014-15	Timra IK	Sweden-2	52	12	23	35	16	....	....	....	....	....
	MODO	Sweden	2	1	0	1	2	....	....	....	....	....
	MODO	Sweden-Q	....	....	....	....	....	4	1	3	4	0

PETTERSSON, Jesper (PEH-tuhr-suhn, YEHS-puhr) PHI

Defense. Shoots right. 5'8", 192 lbs. Born, Stockholm, Sweden, July 16, 1994.
(Philadelphia's 6th choice, 198th overall, in 2014 Entry Draft).

			Regular Season					Playoffs				
Season	Club	League	GP	G	A	Pts	PIM	GP	G	A	Pts	PIM
2008-09	Flem'sberg U18 2	Swe-U18	22	6	7	13	42	....	....	....	....	....
	Flemingsberg U18	Swe-U18	6	0	2	2	2	....	....	....	....	....
2009-10	Flemingsberg U18	Swe-U18	24	6	7	13	20	....	....	....	....	....
	Flemingsberg Jr.	Swe-Jr.	7	0	3	3	8	....	....	....	....	....
2010-11	Linkopings HC U18	Swe-U18	32	5	6	11	94	5	1	1	2	6
	Linkopings HC Jr.	Swe-Jr.	3	0	0	0	0	....	....	....	....	....
2011-12	Linkopings HC U18	Swe-U18	1	0	0	0	0	....	....	....	....	....
	Linkopings HC Jr.	Swe-Jr.	41	3	13	16	30	....	....	....	....	....
2012-13	Linkopings HC Jr.	Swe-Jr.	18	3	9	12	14	....	....	....	....	....
	Linkopings HC	Sweden	14	1	2	3	6	....	....	....	....	....
2013-14	Linkopings HC Jr.	Swe-Jr.	7	2	4	6	29	1	0	0	0	2
	Linkopings HC	Sweden	48	0	1	1	30	3	0	0	0	0
2014-15	Lehigh Valley	AHL	51	2	5	7	35	....	....	....	....	....

PETTERSSON, Marcus (PEH-tuhr-suhn, MAHR-kuhs) ANA

Defense. Shoots left. 6'4", 167 lbs. Born, Skelleftea, Sweden, May 8, 1996.
(Anaheim's 2nd choice, 38th overall, in 2014 Entry Draft).

			Regular Season					Playoffs				
Season	Club	League	GP	G	A	Pts	PIM	GP	G	A	Pts	PIM
2010-11	Skelleftea AIK U18	Swe-U18	2	0	0	0	0	....	....	....	....	....
2011-12	Skelleftea AIK U18	Swe-U18	33	5	7	12	12	7	1	3	4	14
2012-13	Skelleftea AIK U18	Swe-U18	2	0	0	0	0	9	2	7	9	4
	Skelleftea AIK Jr.	Swe-Jr.	37	4	8	12	16	2	0	0	0	0
2013-14	Skelleftea AIK Jr.	Swe-Jr.	38	4	14	18	38	2	0	0	0	2
	Skelleftea AIK	Sweden	10	0	0	0	2	....	....	....	....	....
	Skelleftea AIK U18	Swe-U18	....	....	....	....	....	3	0	1	1	4
2014-15	Vita Hasten	Sweden-2	15	3	3	6	22	4	0	1	1	2
	Skelleftea AIK Jr.	Swe-Jr.	20	2	8	10	20	1	0	0	0	2
	Skelleftea AIK	Sweden	14	0	0	0	0	....	....	....	....	....

PETTIT, Kyle (PEH-tiht, KIGHL) VAN

Center. Shoots left. 6'3", 200 lbs. Born, Komoka, ON, January 19, 1996.
(Vancouver's 6th choice, 156th overall, in 2014 Entry Draft).

			Regular Season					Playoffs				
Season	Club	League	GP	G	A	Pts	PIM	GP	G	A	Pts	PIM
2011-12	Lon. Knights MM	Minor-ON	30	14	18	32	14	11	4	4	8	12
2012-13	Erie Otters	OHL	67	3	3	6	21	....	....	....	....	....
2013-14	Erie Otters	OHL	53	5	5	10	24	9	0	0	0	2
2014-15	Erie Otters	OHL	60	16	11	27	10	3	0	0	0	2

PHILLIPS, Zack (FIHL-ihps, ZAK) **BOS**

Center. Shoots right. 6', 194 lbs. Born, Fredericton, NB, October 28, 1992.
(Minnesota's 2nd choice, 28th overall, in 2011 Entry Draft).

			Regular Season					Playoffs				
Season	Club	League	GP	G	A	Pts	PIM	GP	G	A	Pts	PIM
2008-09	Lawrence	High-MA	30	19	29	48	....	....	....	....	....	....
2009-10	Saint John	QMJHL	65	16	28	44	31	21	2	4	6	4
2010-11	Saint John	QMJHL	67	38	57	95	16	17	9	15	24	8
2011-12	Saint John	QMJHL	60	30	50	80	32	17	9	23	32	4
2012-13	Houston Aeros	AHL	71	8	19	27	10	5	0	1	1	2
2013-14	Iowa Wild	AHL	76	12	21	33	16	....	....	....	....	....
2014-15	Iowa Wild	AHL	49	7	8	15	14	....	....	....	....	....
	Providence Bruins	AHL	16	3	8	11	0	2	0	0	0	4

George Parsons Trophy (Memorial Cup – Most Sportsmanlike Player) (2012)

Traded to **Boston** by **Minnesota** for Jared Knight, March 2, 2015.

PICCINICH, J.J. (pih-SIH-nihch, JAY-JAY) **TOR**

Right wing. Shoots right. 6', 190 lbs. Born, Paramus, NJ, June 12, 1996.
(Toronto's 3rd choice, 103rd overall, in 2014 Entry Draft).

			Regular Season					Playoffs				
Season	Club	League	GP	G	A	Pts	PIM	GP	G	A	Pts	PIM
2011-12	N.J. Avalanche	AYHL	22	*23	19	*42	16	....	....	....	....	....
2012-13	Youngstown	USHL	63	3	12	15	4	9	1	1	2	0
2013-14	Youngstown	USHL	60	27	31	58	31	....	....	....	....	....
	USNTDP	U-18	1	0	0	0	0	....	....	....	....	....
2014-15	Boston University	H-East	25	1	3	4	2	....	....	....	....	....

PIETILA, Blake (pee-EH-tihl-a, BLAYK) **N.J.**

Left wing. Shoots left. 6', 195 lbs. Born, Milford, MI, February 20, 1993.
(New Jersey's 5th choice, 129th overall, in 2011 Entry Draft).

			Regular Season					Playoffs				
Season	Club	League	GP	G	A	Pts	PIM	GP	G	A	Pts	PIM
2008-09	Det. Compuware	T1EHL	31	8	11	19	8	5	1	5	6	0
2009-10	USNTDP	USHL	28	5	3	8	27	....	....	....	....	....
	USNTDP	U-17	18	1	6	7	10	....	....	....	....	....
	USNTDP	U-18	1	0	0	0	0	....	....	....	....	....
2010-11	USNTDP	USHL	24	4	5	9	20	....	....	....	....	....
	USNTDP	U-18	13	10	4	14	33	....	....	....	....	....
2011-12	Michigan Tech	WCHA	39	10	14	24	46	....	....	....	....	....
2012-13	Michigan Tech	WCHA	35	14	10	24	44	....	....	....	....	....
2013-14	Michigan Tech	WCHA	39	8	20	28	84	....	....	....	....	....
2014-15	Michigan Tech	WCHA	40	14	16	30	56	....	....	....	....	....

PILON, Ryan (PEE-lawn, RIGH-uhn) **NYI**

Defense. Shoots left. 6'3", 206 lbs. Born, Prince Albert, SK, October 10, 1996.
(NY Islanders' 5th choice, 147th overall, in 2015 Entry Draft).

			Regular Season					Playoffs				
Season	Club	League	GP	G	A	Pts	PIM	GP	G	A	Pts	PIM
2011-12	Beardy's	SMHL	32	8	16	24	56	2	0	1	1	2
	Lethbridge	WHL	2	0	0	0	0	....	....	....	....	....
2012-13	Lethbridge	WHL	57	5	23	28	63	....	....	....	....	....
2013-14	Lethbridge	WHL	17	3	4	7	25	....	....	....	....	....
	Brandon	WHL	49	4	25	29	21	9	1	3	4	11
2014-15	Brandon	WHL	68	11	41	52	40	19	1	11	12	10

PINHO, Brian (PIHN-oh, BRIGH-uhn) **WSH**

Center. Shoots right. 6', 173 lbs. Born, Beverly, MA, May 11, 1995.
(Washington's 5th choice, 174th overall, in 2013 Entry Draft).

			Regular Season					Playoffs				
Season	Club	League	GP	G	A	Pts	PIM	GP	G	A	Pts	PIM
2010-11	Valley Jr. Warriors	Minor-MA	10	4	4	8	8	....	....	....	....	....
	Valley Jr. Warriors	EmJHL	6	4	1	5	2	....	....	....	....	....
2011-12	St. John's Prep	High-MA	24	20	37	57	....	....	....	....	....	....
	Valley Jr. Warriors	Minor-MA	10	0	10	10	2	....	....	....	....	....
2012-13	St. John's Prep	High-MA	24	15	27	42	....	....	....	....	....	....
2013-14	Indiana Ice	USHL	59	28	28	56	21	12	2	4	6	0
2014-15	Providence College	H-East	39	6	12	18	6	....	....	....	....	....

PLACHTA, Matthias (PLAK-tuh, mah-TIGH-uhs) **ARI**

Left wing. Shoots left. 6'2", 220 lbs. Born, Freiburg, Germany, May 16, 1991.

			Regular Season					Playoffs				
Season	Club	League	GP	G	A	Pts	PIM	GP	G	A	Pts	PIM
2008-09	Heil./Mann. Jr.	Ger-Jr.	26	17	22	39	26	8	6	6	12	6
	Heilbronner Falken	German-2	10	0	0	0	2	3	1	0	1	0
2009-10	Adler Mannheim	Germany	3	0	0	0	0	....	....	....	....	....
	Heilbronner Falken	German-2	43	6	8	14	59	6	0	0	0	2
2010-11	Heilbronner Falken	German-2	4	1	2	3	4	....	....	....	....	....
	Adler Mannheim	Germany	45	7	7	14	8	6	0	0	0	2
2011-12	Adler Mannheim	Germany	49	4	3	7	32	14	0	1	1	6
2012-13	Adler Mannheim	Germany	42	12	10	22	14	6	2	3	5	2
2013-14	Adler Mannheim	Germany	45	4	8	12	40	3	0	0	0	2
2014-15	Adler Mannheim	Germany	47	14	21	35	75	15	5	4	9	6

Signed as a free agent by **Arizona**, May 28, 2015.

PLATZER, Kyle (PLAT-zuhr, KIGHL) **EDM**

Center. Shoots right. 5'11", 182 lbs. Born, Waterloo, ON, March 4, 1995.
(Edmonton's 6th choice, 96th overall, in 2013 Entry Draft).

			Regular Season					Playoffs				
Season	Club	League	GP	G	A	Pts	PIM	GP	G	A	Pts	PIM
2010-11	Wat. Wolves MM	Minor-ON	30	20	22	42	20	13	6	7	13	16
	Wat. Wolves Mid.	Minor-ON	8	2	2	4	8	....	....	....	....	....
	Waterloo Siskins	ON-Jr.B	2	0	0	0	0	....	....	....	....	....
2011-12	Waterloo Siskins	ON-Jr.B	50	31	24	55	70	6	4	6	10	6
	London Knights	OHL	4	0	1	1	0	....	....	....	....	....
2012-13	London Knights	OHL	65	5	17	22	15	21	2	4	6	8
2013-14	London Knights	OHL	39	9	8	17	14	....	....	....	....	....
	Owen Sound	OHL	27	13	6	19	12	5	1	2	3	6
2014-15	Owen Sound	OHL	68	34	47	81	46	5	1	4	5	4
	Oklahoma City	AHL	4	2	1	3	0	3	0	0	0	0

PLOTNIKOV, Sergei (ploht-NIH-kauf, sair-GAY) **PIT**

Left wing. Shoots left. 6'2", 205 lbs. Born, Komsomolsk-na-Amur, Russia, June 3, 1990.

			Regular Season					Playoffs				
Season	Club	League	GP	G	A	Pts	PIM	GP	G	A	Pts	PIM
2008-09	Yermak Angarsk	Russia-2	26	2	3	5	36	4	2	1	3	2
2009-10	Amur Khabarovsk	KHL	43	6	6	12	30	....	....	....	....	....
2010-11	Khabarovsk Jr.	Russia-Jr.	16	12	22	34	32	8	1	5	6	47
	Amur Khabarovsk	KHL	45	5	8	13	36	....	....	....	....	....
2011-12	Amur Khabarovsk	KHL	53	13	7	20	70	4	0	0	0	8
2012-13	Yaroslavl	KHL	50	14	16	30	54	5	1	2	3	4
2013-14	Yaroslavl	KHL	53	15	20	35	88	18	4	10	14	30
2014-15	Yaroslavl	KHL	56	15	21	36	71	5	1	0	1	33

Signed as a free agent by **Pittsburgh**, July 1, 2015.

POCHIRO, Zach (puh-CHUHR-oh, ZAK) **ST.L.**

Left wing. Shoots right. 6'1", 155 lbs. Born, St. Louis, MO, March 6, 1994.
(St. Louis' 3rd choice, 112th overall, in 2013 Entry Draft).

			Regular Season					Playoffs				
Season	Club	League	GP	G	A	Pts	PIM	GP	G	A	Pts	PIM
2010-11	L.A. Jr. Kings	T1EHL	31	22	12	34	128	....	....	....	....	....
2011-12	Wichita Falls	NAHL	52	18	16	34	154	....	....	....	....	....
2012-13	Prince George	WHL	65	15	24	39	105	....	....	....	....	....
2013-14	Prince George	WHL	63	27	39	66	123	....	....	....	....	....
	Kalamazoo Wings	ECHL	9	0	2	2	0	....	....	....	....	....
2014-15	Prince George	WHL	41	19	23	42	69	5	4	2	6	6
	Alaska Aces	ECHL	8	0	2	2	13	....	....	....	....	....

POGANSKI, Austin (POH-gan-skee, AW-stuhn) **ST.L.**

Right wing. Shoots right. 6'1", 198 lbs. Born, St. Cloud, MN, February 16, 1996.
(St. Louis' 6th choice, 110th overall, in 2014 Entry Draft).

			Regular Season					Playoffs				
Season	Club	League	GP	G	A	Pts	PIM	GP	G	A	Pts	PIM
2010-11	St. Cloud Cath.	High-MN	25	22	13	35	6	2	0	3	3	0
2011-12	St. Cloud Cath.	High-MN	25	22	27	49	6	2	2	1	3	0
2012-13	Team Great Plains	UMHSEL	19	8	12	20	6	3	2	2	4	0
	St. Cloud Cath.	High-MN	23	25	22	47	14	3	10	9	19	2
	USNTDP	U-17	11	7	0	7	2	....	....	....	....	....
	Tri-City Storm	USHL	2	1	1	2	0	....	....	....	....	....
2013-14	Tri-City Storm	USHL	55	19	12	31	57	....	....	....	....	....
2014-15	North Dakota	NCHC	38	4	10	14	19	....	....	....	....	....

POINT, Brayden (POYNT, BRAY-duhn) **T.B.**

Center. Shoots right. 5'10", 163 lbs. Born, Calgary, AB, March 13, 1996.
(Tampa Bay's 4th choice, 79th overall, in 2014 Entry Draft).

			Regular Season					Playoffs				
Season	Club	League	GP	G	A	Pts	PIM	GP	G	A	Pts	PIM
2009-10	Calgary Bisons	AMBHL	33	21	12	33	26	12	7	5	12	31
2010-11	Calgary Bisons	AMBHL	33	42	*60	*102	12	....	....	....	....	....
2011-12	Calgary Buffaloes	AMHL	32	19	22	41	22	5	1	0	1	2
	Canmore Eagles	AJHL	4	2	1	3	0	....	....	....	....	....
	Moose Jaw	WHL	5	1	0	1	0	14	7	3	10	2
2012-13	Moose Jaw	WHL	67	*24	33	57	26	....	....	....	....	....
2013-14	Moose Jaw	WHL	72	36	55	91	53	....	....	....	....	....
2014-15	Moose Jaw	WHL	60	38	49	87	46	....	....	....	....	....
	Syracuse Crunch	AHL	9	2	2	4	2	2	0	0	0	0

WHL East First All-Star Team (2015)

POKKA, Ville (POH-ka, VIHL-ee) **CHI**

Defense. Shoots right. 6', 214 lbs. Born, Tornio, Finland, June 3, 1994.
(NY Islanders' 2nd choice, 34th overall, in 2012 Entry Draft).

			Regular Season					Playoffs				
Season	Club	League	GP	G	A	Pts	PIM	GP	G	A	Pts	PIM
2009-10	Karpat Oulu U18	Fin-U18	25	0	7	7	10	5	0	0	0	4
2010-11	Karpat Oulu Jr.	Fin-Jr.	33	6	16	22	18	....	....	....	....	....
	Karpat Oulu	Finland	2	0	0	0	2	....	....	....	....	....
	Kiekko-Laser Oulu	Finland-2	3	0	3	3	0	....	....	....	....	....
	Karpat Oulu U18	Fin-U18	3	0	2	2	0	9	0	7	7	8
2011-12	Karpat Oulu Jr.	Fin-Jr.	4	3	4	7	2	....	....	....	....	....
	Karpat Oulu	Finland	35	0	3	3	12	9	0	3	3	2
2012-13	Karpat Oulu Jr.	Fin-Jr.	3	0	0	0	4	....	....	....	....	....
	Karpat Oulu	Finland	47	6	6	12	8	3	0	2	2	0
2013-14	Karpat Oulu	Finland	54	6	21	27	16	16	2	9	11	10
2014-15	Rockford IceHogs	AHL	68	8	22	30	16	8	0	3	3	0

AHL All-Rookie Team (2015)

Traded to **Chicago** by **NY Islanders** with T.J. Brennan and Anders Nilsson for Nick Leddy and Kent Simpson, October 4, 2014.

POLLOCK, Brett (PAW-luhk, BREHT) **DAL**

Left wing. Shoots left. 6'2", 195 lbs. Born, Regina, SK, March 17, 1996.
(Dallas' 2nd choice, 45th overall, in 2014 Entry Draft).

			Regular Season					Playoffs				
Season	Club	League	GP	G	A	Pts	PIM	GP	G	A	Pts	PIM
2009-10	Sherwood Park	Minor-AB	31	13	17	30	26	....	....	....	....	....
	Sherwood Park	AMBHL	1	0	0	0	0	....	....	....	....	....
2010-11	Sherwood Park	AMBHL	33	20	17	37	46	....	....	....	....	....
	Sherwood Park	Minor-AB	3	1	1	2	2	....	....	....	....	....
2011-12	Sherwood Park	AMHL	34	8	17	25	54	1	0	0	0	19
2012-13	Edmonton	WHL	40	2	2	4	2	....	....	....	....	....
2013-14	Edmonton	WHL	71	25	30	55	36	21	11	8	19	10
2014-15	Edmonton	WHL	70	32	30	62	88	5	3	2	5	4

POOLMAN, Tucker (POOL-MAN, TUH-kuhr) **WPG**

Defense. Shoots right. 6'3", 214 lbs. Born, East Grand Forks, MN, June 8, 1993.
(Winnipeg's 8th choice, 127th overall, in 2013 Entry Draft).

			Regular Season					Playoffs				
Season	Club	League	GP	G	A	Pts	PIM	GP	G	A	Pts	PIM
2008-09	E. Grand Forks	High-MN	25	3	4	7	2	....	....	....	....	....
2009-10	E. Grand Forks	High-MN	25	3	7	10	10	2	0	2	2	0
2010-11	Team Great Plains	UMHSEL	16	2	3	5	4	3	0	2	2	0
	E. Grand Forks	High-MN	23	5	17	22	13	2	0	0	0	0
2011-12	Wichita Falls	NAHL	59	7	22	29	29	....	....	....	....	....
2012-13	Omaha Lancers	USHL	64	14	14	28	49	....	....	....	....	....
2013-14	Omaha Lancers	USHL	58	15	26	41	23	4	1	3	4	4
2014-15	North Dakota	NCHC	40	8	10	18	16	....	....	....	....	....

USHL First All-Star Team (2014)

POPE, David (POHP, DAY-vihd) DET

Left wing. Shoots left. 6'2", 187 lbs. Born, Edmonton, AB, September 27, 1994.
(Detroit's 5th choice, 109th overall, in 2013 Entry Draft).

			Regular Season					Playoffs				
Season	Club	League	GP	G	A	Pts	PIM	GP	G	A	Pts	PIM
2007-08	Calgary Bisons	AMBHL	27	3	13	16	10	....	....	....	....	....
2008-09	Notre Dame	Minor-SK	26	28	22	50	12	5	5	3	8	0
2009-10	K of C Pats	AMHL	27	2	8	10	12	....	....	....	....	....
2010-11	PoE Academy	High-BC	STATISTICS NOT AVAILABLE									
	PoE Academy	CSSHL	10	8	8	16	2	5	4	4	8	2
2011-12	Cowichan Valley	BCHL	24	2	5	7	12	....	....	....	....	....
	Westside Warriors	BCHL	20	6	12	18	19	....	....	....	....	....
2012-13	West Kelowna	BCHL	42	17	22	39	20	7	4	1	5	2
2013-14	West Kelowna	BCHL	45	27	23	50	20	6	2	4	6	2
2014-15	Nebraska-Omaha	NCHC	33	8	6	14	6	....	....	....	....	....

POSSLER, Gustav (POHS-luhr, GOO-stahv) BUF

Right wing. Shoots left. 6', 183 lbs. Born, Sodertalje, Sweden, November 11, 1994.
(Buffalo's 8th choice, 130th overall, in 2013 Entry Draft).

			Regular Season					Playoffs				
Season	Club	League	GP	G	A	Pts	PIM	GP	G	A	Pts	PIM
2009-10	Bjorkloven U18	Swe-U18	25	9	16	25	24	....	....	....	....	....
2010-11	Lulea HF U18	Swe-U18	18	21	15	36	16	....	....	....	....	....
	Lulea HF Jr.	Swe-Jr.	4	0	0	0	0	....	....	....	....	....
	MODO U18	Swe-U18	13	6	7	13	2	3	2	2	4	4
	MODO Jr.	Swe-Jr.	1	1	1	2	0	3	0	0	0	0
2011-12	MODO U18	Swe-U18	10	9	4	13	6	1	0	0	0	0
	MODO Jr.	Swe-Jr.	37	23	17	40	14	8	2	1	3	4
	MODO	Sweden	2	1	0	1	0	....	....	....	....	....
2012-13	MODO Jr.	Swe-Jr.	36	19	21	40	28	7	4	4	8	4
	MODO	Sweden	7	1	0	1	2	....	....	....	....	....
	Mora IK	Sweden-2	3	0	0	0	0	....	....	....	....	....
2013-14	MODO	Sweden	22	8	7	15	4	....	....	....	....	....
2014-15	MODO	Sweden	47	9	12	21	8	....	....	....	....	....
	MODO	Sweden-Q	....	....	....	....	....	4	0	2	2	0

PRAPAVESSIS, Michael (pra-PA-veh-sihs, MIGH-kuhl) DAL

Defense. Shoots left. 6'1", 180 lbs. Born, Mississauga, ON, January 7, 1996.
(Dallas' 4th choice, 105th overall, in 2014 Entry Draft).

			Regular Season					Playoffs				
Season	Club	League	GP	G	A	Pts	PIM	GP	G	A	Pts	PIM
2011-12	Mississauga Rebels	GTHL	63	7	20	27	20	....	....	....	....	....
2012-13	Mississauga Rebels	GTHL	26	3	6	9	4	....	....	....	....	....
	Tor. Patriots	ON-Jr.A	25	2	9	11	2	6	0	3	3	2
2013-14	Tor. Patriots	ON-Jr.A	47	5	50	55	2	19	2	13	15	4
2014-15	RPI Engineers	ECAC	41	1	7	8	12	....	....	....	....	....

PRESS, Robin (PREHS, RAW-bihn) CHI

Defense. Shoots right. 6'3", 209 lbs. Born, Uppsala, Sweden, December 21, 1994.
(Chicago's 8th choice, 211th overall, in 2013 Entry Draft).

			Regular Season					Playoffs				
Season	Club	League	GP	G	A	Pts	PIM	GP	G	A	Pts	PIM
2010-11	Almtuna U18	Swe-U18	31	7	6	13	8	....	....	....	....	....
2011-12	Almtuna U18	Swe-U18	28	8	16	24	52	....	....	....	....	....
	Almtuna Jr.	Swe-Jr.	24	15	20	35	26	....	....	....	....	....
	Almtuna	Sweden-2	9	0	1	1	4	....	....	....	....	....
2012-13	Sodertalje SK Jr.	Swe-Jr.	26	7	9	16	16	3	0	2	2	0
	Sodertalje SK	Sweden-2	49	2	3	5	14	....	....	....	....	....
2013-14	Sodertalje SK	Sweden-2	51	4	11	15	20	....	....	....	....	....
	Sodertalje SK Jr.	Swe-Jr.	10	6	7	13	6	4	0	3	3	4
2014-15	Sodertalje SK Jr.	Swe-Jr.	1	0	1	1	0	....	....	....	....	....
	Sodertalje SK	Sweden-2	61	17	20	37	12	....	....	....	....	....
	Rockford IceHogs	AHL	2	0	0	0	0	4	0	0	0	0

PROKHORKIN, Nikolay (proh-KHOHR-kihn, nih-koh-LIGH) L.A.

Left wing. Shoots left. 6'2", 191 lbs. Born, Chelyabinsk, Russia, September 17, 1993.
(Los Angeles' 2nd choice, 121st overall, in 2012 Entry Draft).

			Regular Season					Playoffs				
Season	Club	League	GP	G	A	Pts	PIM	GP	G	A	Pts	PIM
2010-11	CSKA Jr.	Russia-Jr.	46	23	17	40	42	16	3	5	8	10
	CSKA Moscow	KHL	6	0	0	0	0	....	....	....	....	....
2011-12	CSKA Jr.	Russia-Jr.	15	9	17	26	47	16	2	9	11	14
	CSKA Moscow	KHL	15	1	1	2	4	4	0	1	1	2
2012-13	Manchester	AHL	8	0	1	1	6	....	....	....	....	....
	THK Tver	Russia-2	5	2	2	4	4	....	....	....	....	....
	CSKA Moscow	KHL	14	2	1	3	10	9	3	1	4	0
2013-14	CSKA Moscow	KHL	52	19	18	37	47	4	1	1	2	16
2014-15	CSKA Moscow	KHL	41	9	11	20	15	4	0	0	0	2

PROVOROV, Ivan (PROH-voh-rawv, ih-VAHN) PHI

Defense. Shoots left. 6', 200 lbs. Born, Yaroslavl, Russia, January 13, 1997.
(Philadelphia's 1st choice, 7th overall, in 2015 Entry Draft).

			Regular Season					Playoffs				
Season	Club	League	GP	G	A	Pts	PIM	GP	G	A	Pts	PIM
2011-12	Wilkes Barre Bant.	AYHL	27	28	33	61	39	....	....	....	....	....
2012-13	Wilkes Barre U16	AYHL	24	14	22	36	47	....	....	....	....	....
	Wilkes Barre U16	Other	27	28	33	61	....	....	....	....	....	....
2013-14	Cedar Rapids	USHL	56	6	13	19	32	....	....	....	....	....
2014-15	Brandon	WHL	60	15	46	61	42	19	2	11	13	10

WHL East First All-Star Team (2015)

PULOCK, Ryan (POO-lawk, RIGH-uhn) NYI

Defense. Shoots right. 6'2", 212 lbs. Born, Dauphin, MB, October 6, 1994.
(NY Islanders' 1st choice, 15th overall, in 2013 Entry Draft).

			Regular Season					Playoffs				
Season	Club	League	GP	G	A	Pts	PIM	GP	G	A	Pts	PIM
2009-10	Parkland Rangers	MMHL	39	9	10	19	8	3	0	1	1	0
2010-11	Brandon	WHL	63	8	34	42	4	6	2	4	6	2
2011-12	Brandon	WHL	71	19	41	60	20	9	3	2	5	0
2012-13	Brandon	WHL	61	14	31	45	22	....	....	....	....	....
2013-14	Brandon	WHL	66	23	40	63	18	9	2	2	4	6
	Bridgeport	AHL	3	0	1	1	2	....	....	....	....	....
2014-15	Bridgeport	AHL	54	17	12	29	6	....	....	....	....	....

WHL East First All-Star Team (2012, 2014) • AHL All-Rookie Team (2015)

QUENNEVILLE, John (KWEHN-vihl, JAWN) N.J.

Center. Shoots left. 6'1", 200 lbs. Born, Edmonton, AB, April 16, 1996.
(New Jersey's 1st choice, 30th overall, in 2014 Entry Draft).

			Regular Season					Playoffs				
Season	Club	League	GP	G	A	Pts	PIM	GP	G	A	Pts	PIM
2009-10	Sherwood Park	AMBHL	29	15	15	30	51	....	....	....	....	....
2010-11	SSAC Lions	AMBHL	33	35	40	75	52	2	2	2	4	0
	SSAC Bulldogs	Minor-AB	2	1	3	4	0	....	....	....	....	....
2011-12	SSAC Athletics	AMHL	30	15	18	33	40	6	2	1	3	20
	Sherwood Park	AJHL	9	0	3	3	0	2	2	0	2	0
2012-13	Brandon	WHL	47	8	11	19	14	....	....	....	....	....
2013-14	Brandon	WHL	61	25	33	58	71	9	5	8	13	10
2014-15	Brandon	WHL	57	17	30	47	63	19	10	9	19	18

QUENNEVILLE, Peter (KWEHN-vihl, PEE-tuhr) CBJ

Center/Right wing. Shoots right. 5'11", 183 lbs. Born, Edmonton, AB, March 9, 1994.
(Columbus' 8th choice, 195th overall, in 2013 Entry Draft).

			Regular Season					Playoffs				
Season	Club	League	GP	G	A	Pts	PIM	GP	G	A	Pts	PIM
2009-10	Edmonton MLAC	AMHL	33	13	11	24	10	....	....	....	....	....
2010-11	Sherwood Park	AJHL	54	6	16	22	8	3	0	0	0	0
2011-12	Sherwood Park	AJHL	53	31	50	81	22	10	4	4	8	10
2012-13	Dubuque	USHL	63	33	37	70	18	9	6	3	9	2
2013-14	Quinnipiac	ECAC	5	0	4	4	2	....	....	....	....	....
	Brandon	WHL	44	21	31	52	10	8	1	3	4	4
2014-15	Brandon	WHL	72	27	48	75	20	19	10	10	20	4

USHL Second All-Star Team (2013)

QUINE, Alan (KWIH-nee, AL-uhn) NYI

Center. Shoots left. 6', 196 lbs. Born, Orleans, ON, February 25, 1993.
(NY Islanders' 6th choice, 166th overall, in 2013 Entry Draft).

			Regular Season					Playoffs				
Season	Club	League	GP	G	A	Pts	PIM	GP	G	A	Pts	PIM
2008-09	Tor. Jr. Canadiens	GTHL	35	26	26	52	8	....	....	....	....	....
	Tor. Canadiens	ON-Jr.A	2	1	1	2	0	....	....	....	....	....
2009-10	Kingston	OHL	64	11	17	28	8	7	1	2	3	0
2010-11	Kingston	OHL	17	4	7	11	2	....	....	....	....	....
	Peterborough	OHL	52	22	20	42	6	....	....	....	....	....
2011-12	Peterborough	OHL	65	30	40	70	21	....	....	....	....	....
	Grand Rapids	AHL	3	0	1	1	0	....	....	....	....	....
2012-13	Peterborough	OHL	26	9	17	26	14	....	....	....	....	....
	Belleville Bulls	OHL	28	14	27	41	6	17	8	7	15	6
2013-14	Bridgeport	AHL	61	8	19	27	23	....	....	....	....	....
	Stockton Thunder	ECHL	7	2	6	8	2	8	3	1	4	0
2014-15	Bridgeport	AHL	75	23	38	61	34	....	....	....	....	....

• Re-entered NHL Entry Draft. Originally Detroit's 4th choice, 85th overall, in 2011 Entry Draft.

RADKE, Roy (RAD-kee, ROY) CHI

Right wing. Shoots right. 6'2", 200 lbs. Born, Chicago, IL, December 10, 1996.
(Chicago's 5th choice, 164th overall, in 2015 Entry Draft).

			Regular Season					Playoffs				
Season	Club	League	GP	G	A	Pts	PIM	GP	G	A	Pts	PIM
2013-14	Shat.-St. Mary's	High-MN	49	19	21	40	46	....	....	....	....	....
2014-15	Barrie Colts	OHL	64	9	9	18	29	9	4	0	4	2

RAFIKOV, Rushan (ra-FIH-kawv, roo-SHAN) CGY

Defense. Shoots left. 6'2", 181 lbs. Born, Saratov, Russia, May 15, 1995.
(Calgary's 7th choice, 187th overall, in 2013 Entry Draft).

			Regular Season					Playoffs				
Season	Club	League	GP	G	A	Pts	PIM	GP	G	A	Pts	PIM
2011-12	Loko Yaroslavl Jr.	Russia-Jr.	24	4	2	6	14	3	0	1	1	25
2012-13	Loko Yaroslavl Jr.	Russia-Jr.	53	1	9	10	38	....	....	....	....	....
2013-14	Loko Yaroslavl Jr.	Russia-Jr.	47	8	12	20	46	7	0	0	0	2
2014-15	HK Ryazan	Russia-2	35	1	17	18	16	5	1	2	3	0
	Loko Yaroslavl Jr.	Russia-Jr.	2	1	0	1	0	14	4	4	8	22

RAMSEY, Jack (RAM-zee, JAK) CHI

Right wing. Shoots right. 6'3", 185 lbs. Born, Farmington, MI, November 2, 1995.
(Chicago's 9th choice, 208th overall, in 2014 Entry Draft).

			Regular Season					Playoffs				
Season	Club	League	GP	G	A	Pts	PIM	GP	G	A	Pts	PIM
2011-12	Metro Northwest	MEPDL	13	5	5	10	0	....	....	....	....	....
	Team Southeast	UMHSEL	4	0	1	1	0	....	....	....	....	....
	Team Northeast	UMHSEL	1	0	1	1	0	1	0	0	0	0
2012-13	Minnetonka High	High-MN	22	8	18	26	2	2	1	0	1	4
2013-14	Penticton Vees	BCHL	57	9	16	25	27	11	1	7	8	0
2014-15	Penticton Vees	BCHL	54	17	21	38	24	22	3	6	9	4

• Signed Letter of Intent to attend **University of Minnesota** (Big Ten) in fall of 2015.

RANDELL, Tyler (RAN-duhl, TIGH-luhr) BOS

Right wing. Shoots right. 6'1", 197 lbs. Born, Scarborough, ON, June 15, 1991.
(Boston's 4th choice, 176th overall, in 2009 Entry Draft).

			Regular Season					Playoffs				
Season	Club	League	GP	G	A	Pts	PIM	GP	G	A	Pts	PIM
2006-07	Brampton	Minor-ON	63	53	38	91	81	....	....	....	....	....
2007-08	Belleville Bulls	OHL	62	5	6	11	24	19	0	0	0	0
2008-09	Belleville Bulls	OHL	36	10	5	15	60	....	....	....	....	....
	Kitchener Rangers	OHL	37	14	8	22	39	....	....	....	....	....
2009-10	Kitchener Rangers	OHL	47	9	12	21	88	20	1	4	5	19
2010-11	Kitchener Rangers	OHL	68	20	12	32	160	7	0	0	0	7
2011-12	Kitchener Rangers	OHL	17	9	1	10	21	6	7	1	8	14
	Providence Bruins	AHL	30	2	0	2	45	....	....	....	....	....
2012-13	Providence Bruins	AHL	23	0	0	0	56	....	....	....	....	....
	South Carolina	ECHL	22	2	2	4	46	....	....	....	....	....
2013-14	Providence Bruins	AHL	43	4	7	11	93	8	1	0	1	6
2014-15	Providence Bruins	AHL	74	11	9	20	120	5	0	0	0	4

RANTANEN, Mikko (ran-TA-nehn, MEE-koh) **COL**

Right wing. Shoots left. 6'4", 211 lbs. Born, Nousiainen, Finland, October 29, 1996.
(Colorado's 1st choice, 10th overall, in 2015 Entry Draft).

			Regular Season					Playoffs				
Season	Club	League	GP	G	A	Pts	PIM	GP	G	A	Pts	PIM
2011-12	TPS Turku U18	Fin-U18	22	5	8	13	6	7	1	1	2	2
2012-13	TPS Turku U18	Fin-U18	5	2	6	8	0	1	1	0	1	0
	TPS Turku Jr.	Fin-Jr.	35	10	14	24	14	9	2	4	6	4
	TPS Turku	Finland	15	2	1	3	4	....	....	....	....	....
2013-14	TPS Turku U18	Fin-U18	2	0	2	2	0	....	....	....	....	....
	TPS Turku Jr.	Fin-Jr.	17	5	13	18	8	3	2	1	3	0
	TPS Turku	Finland	37	5	4	9	10	....	....	....	....	....
2014-15	TPS Turku	Finland	56	9	19	28	22	....	....	....	....	....
	TPS Turku Jr.	Fin-Jr.	....	....	....	....	....	7	6	8	14	2

RASMUSSEN, Dennis (rahz-MOO-suhn, DEH-nihs) **CHI**

Center. Shoots left. 6'3", 205 lbs. Born, Vasteras, Sweden, July 3, 1990.

			Regular Season					Playoffs				
Season	Club	League	GP	G	A	Pts	PIM	GP	G	A	Pts	PIM
2007-08	Vasteras Jr.	Swe-Jr.	39	8	11	19	38	3	1	2	3	8
2008-09	Vasteras Jr.	Swe-Jr.	40	19	25	44	18	3	1	3	4	0
	VIK Vasteras HK	Sweden-2	20	5	2	7	4	....	....	....	....	....
2009-10	Vasteras Jr.	Swe-Jr.	3	1	3	4	29	5	1	4	5	2
	VIK Vasteras HK	Sweden-2	44	4	13	17	20	....	....	....	....	....
2010-11	VIK Vasteras HK	Sweden-2	54	13	25	38	16	....	....	....	....	....
2011-12	Vaxjo Lakers HC	Sweden	55	8	9	17	10	....	....	....	....	....
2012-13	Vaxjo Lakers HC	Sweden	42	16	12	28	28	....	....	....	....	....
2013-14	Vaxjo Lakers HC	Sweden	52	16	24	40	20	12	2	4	6	6
2014-15	Rockford IceHogs	AHL	73	13	14	27	30	7	0	0	0	2

Signed as a free agent by **Chicago**, June 10, 2014.

RAU, Kyle (ROW, KIGHL) **FLA**

Center. Shoots left. 5'8", 178 lbs. Born, Hoffman Estates, IL, October 24, 1992.
(Florida's 7th choice, 91st overall, in 2011 Entry Draft).

			Regular Season					Playoffs				
Season	Club	League	GP	G	A	Pts	PIM	GP	G	A	Pts	PIM
2009-10	Eden Prairie Eagles	High-MN	25	38	39	77	12	3	2	2	4	0
2010-11	Team Southwest	UMHSEL	19	16	7	23	14	3	0	0	0	0
	Eden Prairie Eagles	High-MN	25	33	36	69	16	6	8	4	12	2
	Sioux Falls	USHL	11	4	6	10	15	10	*7	5	*12	4
2011-12	U. of Minnesota	WCHA	40	18	25	43	29	....	....	....	....	....
2012-13	U. of Minnesota	WCHA	40	15	25	40	22	....	....	....	....	....
2013-14	U. of Minnesota	Big Ten	41	14	26	40	16	....	....	....	....	....
2014-15	U. of Minnesota	Big Ten	39	20	21	41	18	....	....	....	....	....
	San Antonio	AHL	7	2	1	3	0	1	0	0	0	2

WCHA All-Rookie Team (2012) • Big Ten Second All-Star Team (2014) • NCAA West Second All-American Team (2014)

REDDEKOPP, Chaz (REH-deh-kawp, CHAZ) **L.A.**

Defense. Shoots left. 6'3", 219 lbs. Born, Abbotsford, BC, January 1, 1997.
(Los Angeles' 5th choice, 187th overall, in 2015 Entry Draft).

			Regular Season					Playoffs				
Season	Club	League	GP	G	A	Pts	PIM	GP	G	A	Pts	PIM
2012-13	PoE Academy	CSSHL	10	3	10	13	22	2	1	1	2	0
	PoE Academy	NAPHL	21	3	10	13	15	4	1	3	4	4
	Victoria Royals	WHL	1	0	0	0	0	....	....	....	....	....
2013-14	Victoria Royals	WHL	40	1	8	9	33	2	0	0	0	0
2014-15	Victoria Royals	WHL	72	5	16	21	53	10	0	2	2	12

REGNER, Brent (REHG-nuhr, BREHNT) **FLA**

Defense. Shoots right. 5'11", 189 lbs. Born, Westlock, AB, May 17, 1989.
(Columbus' 7th choice, 137th overall, in 2008 Entry Draft).

			Regular Season					Playoffs				
Season	Club	League	GP	G	A	Pts	PIM	GP	G	A	Pts	PIM
2004-05	Ft. Saskatchewan	AMHL	36	2	13	15	24	....	....	....	....	....
2005-06	Ft. Saskatchewan	AMHL	36	9	25	34	30	14	1	7	8	2
	Vancouver Giants	WHL	1	0	0	0	0	....	....	....	....	....
2006-07	Vancouver Giants	WHL	64	1	5	6	19	22	0	6	6	10
2007-08	Vancouver Giants	WHL	72	8	39	47	45	10	0	10	10	10
2008-09	Vancouver Giants	WHL	70	15	52	67	42	17	2	11	13	6
2009-10	Syracuse Crunch	AHL	50	4	16	20	22	....	....	....	....	....
2010-11	Springfield Falcons	AHL	56	6	13	19	17	....	....	....	....	....
2011-12	Springfield Falcons	AHL	75	2	29	31	26	....	....	....	....	....
2012-13	Peoria Rivermen	AHL	66	3	15	18	22	....	....	....	....	....
	Evansville IceMen	ECHL	2	1	0	1	0	....	....	....	....	....
	Chicago Wolves	AHL	7	0	1	1	7	....	....	....	....	....
2013-14	Chicago Wolves	AHL	63	3	21	24	36	9	2	4	6	6
2014-15	Chicago Wolves	AHL	71	6	23	29	29	3	1	1	2	0

WHL West Second All-Star Team (2009)

Signed as a free agent by **St. Louis**, July 3, 2014. Signed as a free agent by **Florida**, July 1, 2015.

REHILL, Ryan (REE-hihl, RIGH-uhn) **N.J.**

Defense. Shoots right. 6'3", 215 lbs. Born, Edmonton, AB, November 7, 1995.
(New Jersey's 4th choice, 131st overall, in 2014 Entry Draft).

			Regular Season					Playoffs				
Season	Club	League	GP	G	A	Pts	PIM	GP	G	A	Pts	PIM
2008-09	Edm. MLAC	AMBHL	33	0	6	6	18	....	....	....	....	....
2009-10	Edm. MLAC	AMBHL	33	6	17	23	56	....	....	....	....	....
	Edm. MLAC Leafs	Minor-AB	7	0	3	3	2	....	....	....	....	....
2010-11	Edm. MLAC Leafs	Minor-AB	4	0	1	1	19	....	....	....	....	....
	Edm. MLAC	AMHL	29	1	6	7	50	....	....	....	....	....
2011-12	South Side AC	Minor-AB	18	6	12	18	70	....	....	....	....	....
	Edm. MLAC	AMHL	21	1	3	4	24	....	....	....	....	....
	Beverly Warriors	CapJHL	6	0	0	0	14	3	0	1	1	16
2012-13	Kamloops Blazers	WHL	46	0	3	3	104	9	0	0	0	2
2013-14	Kamloops Blazers	WHL	72	4	16	20	*182	....	....	....	....	....
2014-15	Kamloops Blazers	WHL	68	7	13	20	128	....	....	....	....	....

REILLY, Mike (RIGH-lee, MIGHK) **MIN**

Defense. Shoots left. 6'2", 187 lbs. Born, Chicago, IL, July 13, 1993.
(Columbus' 3rd choice, 98th overall, in 2011 Entry Draft).

			Regular Season					Playoffs				
Season	Club	League	GP	G	A	Pts	PIM	GP	G	A	Pts	PIM
2009-10	Holy Angels	High-MN	24	4	29	33	19	2	3	2	5	0
2010-11	Shat.-St. Mary's	High-MN	54	14	34	48	30	....	....	....	....	....
2011-12	Penticton Vees	BCHL	51	24	59	83	42	15	1	8	9	10
2012-13	U. of Minnesota	WCHA	37	3	11	14	14	....	....	....	....	....
2013-14	U. of Minnesota	Big Ten	41	9	24	33	18	....	....	....	....	....
2014-15	U. of Minnesota	Big Ten	39	6	*36	42	44	....	....	....	....	....

Big Ten First All-Star Team (2014) • NCAA West First All-American Team (2014, 2015)

Signed as a free agent by **Minnesota**, July 1, 2015.

REWAY, Martin (rih-VIGH, MAR-tihn) **MTL**

Left wing. Shoots left. 5'8", 170 lbs. Born, Prague, Czech Rep., January 24, 1995.
(Montreal's 7th choice, 116th overall, in 2013 Entry Draft).

			Regular Season					Playoffs				
Season	Club	League	GP	G	A	Pts	PIM	GP	G	A	Pts	PIM
2008-09	Dolny Kubin U18	Svk-U18	13	8	12	20	10	....	....	....	....	....
	MHC Martin U18	Svk-U18	2	0	0	0	0	....	....	....	....	....
2009-10	Dolny Kubin U18	Svk-U18	26	32	38	70	24	....	....	....	....	....
2010-11	MHC Martin U18	Svk-U18	20	13	22	35	65	....	....	....	....	....
	MHC Martin Jr.	Slovak-Jr.	10	5	5	10	0	....	....	....	....	....
2011-12	Sparta U18	CzR-U18	25	21	39	60	42	9	8	16	24	12
	Sparta Jr.	CzRep-Jr.	5	2	4	6	2	....	....	....	....	....
2012-13	Gatineau	QMJHL	47	22	28	50	56	10	1	11	12	20
2013-14	Gatineau	QMJHL	43	20	42	62	48	9	5	10	15	16
2014-15	HC Sparta Praha	CzRep	34	9	28	37	54	8	1	6	7	20

RICHARD, Anthony (rih-SHAHRD, AN-thuh-nee) **NSH**

Center. Shoots left. 5'10", 163 lbs. Born, Trois-Rivieres, QC, December 20, 1996.
(Nashville's 3rd choice, 100th overall, in 2015 Entry Draft).

			Regular Season					Playoffs				
Season	Club	League	GP	G	A	Pts	PIM	GP	G	A	Pts	PIM
2011-12	Trois-Rivieres	QAAA	41	11	17	28	50	8	3	5	8	14
2012-13	Trois-Rivieres	QAAA	12	9	6	15	8	....	....	....	....	....
	Val-d'Or Foreurs	QMJHL	42	6	2	8	15	9	0	1	1	5
2013-14	Val-d'Or Foreurs	QMJHL	66	25	27	52	49	24	10	7	17	12
2014-15	Val-d'Or Foreurs	QMJHL	66	43	48	91	78	17	12	10	22	10

RICHARD, Tanner (rih-SHARD, TA-nuhr) **T.B.**

Center. Shoots left. 6', 176 lbs. Born, Markham, ON, April 6, 1993.
(Tampa Bay's 5th choice, 71st overall, in 2012 Entry Draft).

			Regular Season					Playoffs				
Season	Club	League	GP	G	A	Pts	PIM	GP	G	A	Pts	PIM
2010-11	Rapperswil	Swiss	4	0	0	0	0	4	0	1	1	0
2011-12	Guelph Storm	OHL	43	13	35	48	46	6	1	4	5	6
2012-13	Guelph Storm	OHL	52	11	51	62	94	5	0	3	3	6
	Syracuse Crunch	AHL	8	0	3	3	6	....	....	....	....	....
2013-14	Syracuse Crunch	AHL	65	2	15	17	95	....	....	....	....	....
2014-15	Syracuse Crunch	AHL	70	13	25	38	135	2	1	0	1	2

RILEY, Blair (RIGH-lee, BLAIR)

Left wing. Shoots right. 6', 217 lbs. Born, Kamloops, BC, November 1, 1985.

			Regular Season					Playoffs				
Season	Club	League	GP	G	A	Pts	PIM	GP	G	A	Pts	PIM
2002-03	Merritt	BCHL	19	9	4	13	17	....	....	....	....	....
2003-04	Merritt	BCHL	60	22	42	64	214	5	2	0	2	10
2004-05	Nanaimo Clippers	BCHL	61	41	26	67	91	13	6	9	15	45
2005-06	Nanaimo Clippers	BCHL	59	41	38	79	79	5	1	1	2	7
2006-07	Ferris State	CCHA	34	3	6	9	44	....	....	....	....	....
2007-08	Ferris State	CCHA	36	14	10	24	90	....	....	....	....	....
2008-09	Ferris State	CCHA	37	7	9	16	70	....	....	....	....	....
2009-10	Ferris State	CCHA	40	18	20	38	58	....	....	....	....	....
	Springfield Falcons	AHL	3	0	0	0	2	....	....	....	....	....
2010-11	San Antonio	AHL	4	1	0	1	0	....	....	....	....	....
	Peoria Rivermen	AHL	8	0	2	2	7	....	....	....	....	....
	Las Vegas	ECHL	59	20	20	40	114	5	4	1	5	0
2011-12	Chicago Express	ECHL	15	7	9	16	8	....	....	....	....	....
	Bridgeport	AHL	55	7	4	11	77	3	0	0	0	2
2012-13	Bridgeport	AHL	74	7	8	15	165	....	....	....	....	....
2013-14	St. John's IceCaps	AHL	71	7	14	21	133	21	3	3	6	18
2014-15	St. John's IceCaps	AHL	70	8	10	18	116	....	....	....	....	....

Signed as a free agent by **NY Islanders**, June 1, 2012. Signed as a free agent by **St. John's** (AHL), July 16, 2013.

RISSLING, Jaynen (RIHZ-lihng, JAY-nehn) **NSH**

Defense. Shoots left. 6'4", 223 lbs. Born, Edmonton, AB, September 21, 1993.
(Washington's 9th choice, 197th overall, in 2012 Entry Draft).

			Regular Season					Playoffs				
Season	Club	League	GP	G	A	Pts	PIM	GP	G	A	Pts	PIM
2007-08	CAC Lehigh	AMBHL	33	7	13	20	54	2	0	2	2	2
2008-09	CAC Gregg's Dist.	AMHL	33	3	11	14	68	5	0	0	0	22
2009-10	Calgary Hitmen	WHL	36	0	8	8	19	9	1	2	3	4
2010-11	Calgary Hitmen	WHL	67	5	16	21	95	....	....	....	....	....
2011-12	Calgary Hitmen	WHL	55	5	18	23	124	5	0	0	0	0
2012-13	Calgary Hitmen	WHL	61	5	23	28	122	17	0	6	6	18
2013-14	Calgary Hitmen	WHL	54	8	29	37	105	6	0	2	2	12
2014-15	Milwaukee	AHL	5	0	0	0	4	....	....	....	....	....
	Cincinnati	ECHL	37	1	2	3	76	....	....	....	....	....

Traded to **Nashville** by **Washington** for Nashville's 7th round choice (later traded to Winnipeg – Winnipeg selected Matt Ustaski) in 2014 Entry Draft, April 19, 2014.

RITCHIE, Nick (RIH-chee, NIHK) **ANA**

Left wing. Shoots left. 6'2", 226 lbs. Born, Orangeville, ON, December 5, 1995.
(Anaheim's 1st choice, 10th overall, in 2014 Entry Draft).

			Regular Season					Playoffs				
Season	Club	League	GP	G	A	Pts	PIM	GP	G	A	Pts	PIM
2010-11	Toronto Marlboros	GTHL	68	50	45	95	119	....	....	....	....	....
	Georgetown	ON-Jr.A	1	0	0	0	0	....	....	....	....	....
2011-12	Peterborough	OHL	63	16	23	39	60	....	....	....	....	....
2012-13	Peterborough	OHL	41	18	17	35	50	....	....	....	....	....
2013-14	Peterborough	OHL	61	39	35	74	136	11	5	5	10	24
2014-15	Peterborough	OHL	25	14	18	32	69	....	....	....	....	....
	Sault Ste. Marie	OHL	23	15	15	30	44	14	13	13	26	28

ROACH, Alex (ROHCH, AL-ehx) L.A.

Defense. Shoots left. 6'5", 221 lbs. Born, Quesnel, BC, April 19, 1993.

			Regular Season					Playoffs				
Season	Club	League	GP	G	A	Pts	PIM	GP	G	A	Pts	PIM
2009-10	Cariboo Cougars	BCMML	40	6	15	21	68	4	0	2	2	16
	Quesnel	BCHL	4	0	0	0	2	....	....	....	....	....
2010-11	Calgary Hitmen	WHL	61	4	12	16	77	....	....	....	....	....
2011-12	Calgary Hitmen	WHL	61	4	14	18	78	5	1	2	3	2
2012-13	Calgary Hitmen	WHL	62	15	34	49	72	17	2	4	6	12
2013-14	Calgary Hitmen	WHL	56	12	32	44	59	6	1	1	2	8
	Ontario Reign	ECHL	5	0	3	3	0	....	....	....	....	....
2014-15	Ontario Reign	ECHL	60	2	14	16	51	19	2	4	6	28

WHL East Second All-Star Team (2013)

Signed as a free agent by **Los Angeles**, September 26, 2011.

ROBERTSON, Dennis (RAW-buhrt-suhn, DEH-nihs) CAR

Defense. Shoots left. 6'1", 215 lbs. Born, Fort St. John, BC, May 24, 1991.
(Toronto's 7th choice, 173rd overall, in 2011 Entry Draft).

			Regular Season					Playoffs				
Season	Club	League	GP	G	A	Pts	PIM	GP	G	A	Pts	PIM
2006-07	Okanagan Prep	Minor-BC	62	15	15	30	78	....	....	....	....	....
2007-08	Summerland Sting	KIJHL	50	9	18	27	66	4	2	1	3	12
2008-09	Langley Chiefs	BCHL	55	1	11	12	64	4	0	1	1	4
2009-10	Langley Chiefs	BCHL	53	9	25	34	83	10	2	2	4	14
2010-11	Brown U.	ECAC	30	6	11	17	48	....	....	....	....	....
2011-12	Brown U.	ECAC	32	2	14	16	72	....	....	....	....	....
2012-13	Brown U.	ECAC	36	3	17	20	69	....	....	....	....	....
2013-14	Brown U.	ECAC	30	6	11	17	78	....	....	....	....	....
	Charlotte	AHL	1	0	0	0	0	....	....	....	....	....
2014-15	Charlotte	AHL	57	3	14	17	70	....	....	....	....	....

ECAC All-Rookie Team (2011)

Traded to **Carolina** by **Toronto** with John-Michael Liles for Tim Gleason, January 1, 2014.

ROBINSON, Buddy (RAW-bihn-suhn, BUH-dee) OTT

Right wing. Shoots right. 6'5", 232 lbs. Born, Bellmawr, NJ, September 30, 1991.

			Regular Season					Playoffs				
Season	Club	League	GP	G	A	Pts	PIM	GP	G	A	Pts	PIM
2009-10	Hamilton	ON-Jr.A	49	11	12	23	62	....	....	....	....	....
2010-11	Hamilton	ON-Jr.A	32	15	23	38	39	....	....	....	....	....
	Nepean Raiders	ON-Jr.A	19	5	19	24	20	....	....	....	....	....
2011-12	Lake Superior	CCHA	39	5	5	10	37	....	....	....	....	....
2012-13	Lake Superior	CCHA	38	8	8	16	48	....	....	....	....	....
	Binghamton	AHL	6	2	2	4	8	2	0	0	0	0
2013-14	Binghamton	AHL	69	15	16	31	49	4	0	0	0	4
	Elmira Jackals	ECHL	1	0	0	0	0	....	....	....	....	....
2014-15	Binghamton	AHL	75	12	22	34	69	....	....	....	....	....

Signed as a free agent by **Ottawa**, March 25, 2013.

ROD, Noah (RAWD, NOH-uh) S.J.

Right wing. Shoots left. 5'10", 188 lbs. Born, La Chaux-de-Fonds, Switz., June 7, 1996.
(San Jose's 3rd choice, 53rd overall, in 2014 Entry Draft).

			Regular Season					Playoffs				
Season	Club	League	GP	G	A	Pts	PIM	GP	G	A	Pts	PIM
2009-10	Lausanne U17 II	Swiss-U17	2	1	0	1	2	....	....	....	....	....
2010-11	Lausanne HC U17	Swiss-U17	7	0	0	0	2	....	....	....	....	....
	Lausanne U17 II	Swiss-U17	3	1	3	4	2	....	....	....	....	....
2011-12	Geneve U17	Swiss-U17	26	11	24	35	46	6	2	4	6	8
	Geneve U17 II	Swiss-U17	1	1	0	1	0	....	....	....	....	....
	Geneve Jr.	Swiss-Jr.	18	0	2	2	16	....	....	....	....	....
2012-13	Geneve U17	Swiss-U17	6	3	7	10	10	5	4	1	5	4
	Geneve Jr.	Swiss-Jr.	39	19	19	38	96	....	....	....	....	....
2013-14	Geneve Jr.	Swiss-Jr.	31	16	21	37	58	2	0	1	1	29
	Geneve	Swiss	28	1	2	3	8	12	1	3	4	4
2014-15	Geneve	Swiss	38	1	3	4	22	10	2	1	3	6

RODRIGUES, Evan (rawd-REE-gehz, EH-vuhn) BUF

Left wing. Shoots right. 5'10", 174 lbs. Born, Etobicoke, ON, July 28, 1993.

			Regular Season					Playoffs				
Season	Club	League	GP	G	A	Pts	PIM	GP	G	A	Pts	PIM
2008-09	Toronto Marlboros	GTHL	73	39	54	93	80	....	....	....	....	....
2009-10	Georgetown	ON-Jr.A	56	20	31	51	22	11	4	2	6	2
2010-11	Georgetown	ON-Jr.A	37	21	33	54	42	5	1	3	4	0
2011-12	Boston University	H-East	36	2	10	12	24	....	....	....	....	....
2012-13	Boston University	H-East	38	14	20	34	28	....	....	....	....	....
2013-14	Boston University	H-East	31	5	9	14	20	....	....	....	....	....
2014-15	Boston University	H-East	41	21	40	61	31	....	....	....	....	....

Hockey East Second All-Star Team (2013, 2015)

Signed as a free agent by **Buffalo**, April 22, 2015.

ROSLOVIC, Jack (raws-LOH-vihk, JAK) WPG

Center. Shoots right. 6'1", 182 lbs. Born, Columbus, OH, January 29, 1997.
(Winnipeg's 2nd choice, 25th overall, in 2015 Entry Draft).

			Regular Season					Playoffs				
Season	Club	League	GP	G	A	Pts	PIM	GP	G	A	Pts	PIM
2012-13	Ohio B-Jack. U16	T1EHL	40	23	30	53	22	4	3	2	5	0
	Ohio B-Jack. Midg.	T1EHL	4	0	0	0	2	....	....	....	....	....
2013-14	USNTDP	USHL	34	4	10	14	14	....	....	....	....	....
	USNTDP	U-17	20	9	8	17	16	....	....	....	....	....
2014-15	USNTDP	USHL	25	11	27	38	8	....	....	....	....	....
	USNTDP	U-18	40	16	26	42	20	....	....	....	....	....

• Signed Letter of Intent to attend **University of Miami** (NCHC) in fall of 2015.

ROSS, Garret (RAWS, GAIR-eht) CHI

Left wing. Shoots left. 6', 173 lbs. Born, Dearborn Heights, MI, May 26, 1992.
(Chicago's 4th choice, 139th overall, in 2012 Entry Draft).

			Regular Season					Playoffs				
Season	Club	League	GP	G	A	Pts	PIM	GP	G	A	Pts	PIM
2007-08	Det. Honda U18	MWEHL	16	18	8	26	6	....	....	....	....	....
	Det. Belle Tire U16	MWEHL	30	7	13	20	32	....	....	....	....	....
	Det. Belle Tire U16	Other	4	1	1	2	6	....	....	....	....	....
2008-09	Det. Vic. Honda	T1EHL	46	28	28	56	40	4	2	3	5	0
2009-10	Saginaw Spirit	OHL	43	7	4	11	103	6	0	0	0	12
2010-11	Saginaw Spirit	OHL	53	6	9	15	111	12	3	1	4	8
2011-12	Saginaw Spirit	OHL	60	25	29	54	93	12	6	4	10	23
2012-13	Saginaw Spirit	OHL	61	44	46	90	114	4	0	3	3	8
	Rockford IceHogs	AHL	2	0	0	0	5	....	....	....	....	....
2013-14	Rockford IceHogs	AHL	74	15	19	34	78	....	....	....	....	....
2014-15	Rockford IceHogs	AHL	69	21	22	43	100	8	2	1	3	2

OHL Second All-Star Team (2013)

ROY, Eric (ROI, AIR-ihk) CGY

Defense. Shoots left. 6'3", 180 lbs. Born, Meadow Lake, SK, October 24, 1994.
(Calgary's 5th choice, 135th overall, in 2013 Entry Draft).

			Regular Season					Playoffs				
Season	Club	League	GP	G	A	Pts	PIM	GP	G	A	Pts	PIM
2009-10	Prince Albert	SMHL	40	9	25	34	30	8	5	3	8	8
2010-11	Brandon	WHL	49	4	15	19	15	6	0	3	3	0
2011-12	Brandon	WHL	69	11	42	53	55	9	1	2	3	9
2012-13	Brandon	WHL	72	17	22	39	37	....	....	....	....	....
2013-14	Brandon	WHL	66	11	33	44	51	8	1	2	3	4
2014-15	Brandon	WHL	66	5	40	45	55	19	3	12	15	20

ROY, Jeremy (WAH, JAIR-ih-mee) S.J.

Defense. Shoots right. 6', 190 lbs. Born, Longueuil, QC, May 14, 1997.
(San Jose's 2nd choice, 31st overall, in 2015 Entry Draft).

			Regular Season					Playoffs				
Season	Club	League	GP	G	A	Pts	PIM	GP	G	A	Pts	PIM
2011-12	Antoine-Girouard	QAAA	41	7	25	32	22	11	1	2	3	2
2012-13	Antoine-Girouard	QAAA	42	12	42	54	18	13	4	11	15	6
2013-14	Sherbrooke	QMJHL	64	14	30	44	23	....	....	....	....	....
2014-15	Sherbrooke	QMJHL	46	5	38	43	37	6	1	4	5	0

ROY, Kevin (ROY, KEH-vihn) ANA

Center. Shoots left. 5'9", 174 lbs. Born, Greenfield Park, QC, May 20, 1993.
(Anaheim's 4th choice, 97th overall, in 2012 Entry Draft).

			Regular Season					Playoffs				
Season	Club	League	GP	G	A	Pts	PIM	GP	G	A	Pts	PIM
2009-10	Deerfield Academy	High-MA	27	12	16	28	....	....	....	....	....	....
2010-11	Deerfield Academy	High-MA	18	19	15	34	6	....	....	....	....	....
2011-12	Lincoln Stars	USHL	59	54	50	104	50	8	7	3	10	4
2012-13	Northeastern	H-East	29	17	17	34	24	....	....	....	....	....
2013-14	Northeastern	H-East	37	19	27	46	30	....	....	....	....	....
2014-15	Northeastern	H-East	35	19	25	44	28	....	....	....	....	....

USHL All-Rookie Team (2012) • USHL First All-Star Team (2012) • USHL Player of the Year (2012) • Hockey East All-Rookie Team (2013) • Hockey East Second All-Star Team (2014) • Hockey East First All-Star Team (2015) • NCAA East Second All-American Team (2015)

ROY, Matt (ROI, MAT) L.A.

Defense. Shoots right. 6', 200 lbs. Born, Canton, MI, March 1, 1995.
(Los Angeles' 6th choice, 194th overall, in 2015 Entry Draft).

			Regular Season					Playoffs				
Season	Club	League	GP	G	A	Pts	PIM	GP	G	A	Pts	PIM
2010-11	Det. V. Honda U16	T1EHL	35	3	10	13	24	....	....	....	....	....
	Det. V. Honda U16	Other	11	2	2	4	14	....	....	....	....	....
2011-12	Det. V. Honda U18	T1EHL	37	1	8	9	28	7	2	0	2	5
2012-13	Det. V. Honda U18	T1EHL	41	12	21	33	62	4	0	2	2	4
	Indiana Ice	USHL	10	1	2	3	4	....	....	....	....	....
2013-14	Indiana Ice	USHL	24	4	5	9	21	12	2	4	6	4
2014-15	Michigan Tech	WCHA	36	0	9	9	22	....	....	....	....	....

ROY, Nicolas (WAH, NIH-koh-las) CAR

Center. Shoots right. 6'4", 197 lbs. Born, Amos, QC, February 5, 1997.
(Carolina's 4th choice, 96th overall, in 2015 Entry Draft).

			Regular Season					Playoffs				
Season	Club	League	GP	G	A	Pts	PIM	GP	G	A	Pts	PIM
2011-12	Amos Forestiers	QAAA	43	13	18	31	30	....	....	....	....	....
2012-13	Amos Forestiers	QAAA	27	15	18	33	24	....	....	....	....	....
2013-14	Chicoutimi	QMJHL	63	16	25	41	19	4	0	2	2	8
2014-15	Chicoutimi	QMJHL	68	16	34	50	40	5	2	3	5	8

RUGGIERO, Steven (roo-zhee-AIR-oh, STEE-vehn) ANA

Defense. Shoots left. 6'3", 200 lbs. Born, Kings Park, NY, January 1, 1997.
(Anaheim's 6th choice, 178th overall, in 2015 Entry Draft).

			Regular Season					Playoffs				
Season	Club	League	GP	G	A	Pts	PIM	GP	G	A	Pts	PIM
2012-13	NY Metro F.M.	MtJHL	20	2	7	9	16	4	0	0	0	4
	Long Island Gulls	AYHL	1	0	0	0	0	....	....	....	....	....
2013-14	Long Island Gulls	AYHL	2	0	0	0	0	....	....	....	....	....
	Youngstown	USHL	41	1	4	5	22	....	....	....	....	....
2014-15	USNTDP	USHL	25	0	7	7	16	....	....	....	....	....
	USNTDP	U-18	41	1	7	8	28	....	....	....	....	....

• Signed Letter of Intent to attend **Providence College** (Hockey East) in fall of 2015.

RUOPP, Harrison (ROO-awp, HAIR-ih-suhn) PIT

Defense. Shoots right. 6'3", 192 lbs. Born, Zehner, SK, March 17, 1993.
(Phoenix's 4th choice, 84th overall, in 2011 Entry Draft).

			Regular Season					Playoffs				
Season	Club	League	GP	G	A	Pts	PIM	GP	G	A	Pts	PIM
2007-08	Balgonie	Minor-SK	26	9	11	20	37	7	0	3	3	4
2008-09	Reg. Pat Cdns.	SMHL	36	0	1	1	46	5	0	1	1	4
2009-10	Prince Albert	WHL	33	0	0	0	38	....	....	....	....	....
2010-11	Prince Albert	WHL	54	0	9	9	98	6	0	0	0	9
2011-12	Prince Albert	WHL	62	2	7	9	127	....	....	....	....	....
2012-13	Prince Albert	WHL	65	1	15	16	132	4	0	0	0	4
2013-14	Wilkes-Barre	AHL	21	0	0	0	34	1	0	0	0	2
	Wheeling Nailers	ECHL	19	0	3	3	42	....	....	....	....	....
2014-15	Wilkes-Barre	AHL	7	0	0	0	9	....	....	....	....	....
	Wheeling Nailers	ECHL	30	0	1	1	58	4	0	0	0	2

Traded to **Pittsburgh** by **Phoenix** with Marc Cheverie and Philadelphia's 3rd round choice (previously acquired, Pittsburgh selected Oskar Sundqvist) in 2012 Entry Draft for Zbynek Michalek, June 22, 2012.

RUOPP, Sam (ROO-awp, SAM) CBJ

Defense. Shoots left. 6'4", 191 lbs. Born, Regina, SK, June 3, 1996.
(Columbus' 6th choice, 129th overall, in 2015 Entry Draft).

			Regular Season					Playoffs				
Season	Club	League	GP	G	A	Pts	PIM	GP	G	A	Pts	PIM
2011-12	Reg. Pat Cdns.	SMHL	41	0	10	10	44	....	....	....	....	....
2012-13	Reg. Pat Cdns.	SMHL	37	3	11	14	34	8	0	2	2	4
	Prince George	WHL	6	0	0	0	0	....	....	....	....	....
2013-14	Prince George	WHL	64	5	11	16	55	....	....	....	....	....
2014-15	Prince George	WHL	64	3	23	26	140	5	1	2	3	4

RUPERT, Ryan (ROO-puhrt, RIGH-uhn) TOR

Center. Shoots left. 5'8", 186 lbs. Born, Grand Bend, ON, June 2, 1994.
(Toronto's 5th choice, 157th overall, in 2012 Entry Draft).

			Regular Season					Playoffs				
Season	Club	League	GP	G	A	Pts	PIM	GP	G	A	Pts	PIM
2008-09	Lambton Jr. Sting	Minor-ON	27	21	20	41	53	11	3	3	6	14
2009-10	Elgin-Mid. Chiefs	Minor-ON	30	22	27	49	40	15	11	10	21	22
	Elgin-Mid. Chiefs	Other	11	3	11	14	38	....	....	....	....	....
	Lambton Shores	ON-Jr.B	4	0	2	2	12	....	....	....	....	....
2010-11	Lambton Shores	ON-Jr.B	25	15	21	36	107	....	....	....	....	....
	London Knights	OHL	39	9	18	27	30	6	2	1	3	6
2011-12	London Knights	OHL	63	17	31	48	120	19	9	6	15	31
2012-13	London Knights	OHL	54	11	35	46	75	21	11	9	20	12
2013-14	London Knights	OHL	68	21	52	73	54	9	3	7	10	10
2014-15	Toronto Marlies	AHL	57	15	12	27	39	5	0	1	1	2
	Orlando	ECHL	17	5	9	14	28	....	....	....	....	....

RUSSO, Robbie (ROO-soh, RAW-bee)

Defense. Shoots right. 6', 189 lbs. Born, Westmount, IL, February 15, 1993.
(NY Islanders' 5th choice, 95th overall, in 2011 Entry Draft).

			Regular Season					Playoffs				
Season	Club	League	GP	G	A	Pts	PIM	GP	G	A	Pts	PIM
2008-09	Chicago Mission	T1EHL	46	5	17	22	10	....	....	....	....	....
	Chicago Mission	Other	....	5	3	8	10	....	....	....	....	....
2009-10	USNTDP	USHL	34	3	17	20	36	....	....	....	....	....
	USNTDP	U-17	18	4	7	11	22	....	....	....	....	....
2010-11	USNTDP	USHL	24	0	6	6	11	....	....	....	....	....
	USNTDP	U-18	36	4	20	24	16	....	....	....	....	....
2011-12	U. of Notre Dame	CCHA	40	4	11	15	14	....	....	....	....	....
2012-13	U. of Notre Dame	CCHA	41	5	18	23	40	....	....	....	....	....
2013-14	U. of Notre Dame	H-East	21	4	11	15	8	....	....	....	....	....
2014-15	U. of Notre Dame	H-East	40	15	26	41	20	....	....	....	....	....

CCHA All-Rookie Team (2012) • Hockey East First All-Star Team (2015) • NCAA East Second All-American Team (2015)

RUTKOWSKI, Troy (ruht-KOW-skee, TROI) OTT

Defense. Shoots right. 6'2", 218 lbs. Born, Edmonton, AB, April 29, 1992.
(Colorado's 6th choice, 137th overall, in 2010 Entry Draft).

			Regular Season					Playoffs				
Season	Club	League	GP	G	A	Pts	PIM	GP	G	A	Pts	PIM
2007-08	SSAC Athletics	AMHL	36	6	16	22	28	....	....	....	....	....
2008-09	Portland	WHL	64	6	9	15	34	....	....	....	....	....
2009-10	Portland	WHL	71	12	31	43	70	13	4	3	7	8
2010-11	Portland	WHL	72	10	37	47	65	21	4	9	13	16
2011-12	Portland	WHL	72	13	32	45	37	22	1	9	10	10
2012-13	Portland	WHL	72	20	46	66	43	21	4	10	14	14
2013-14	Binghamton	AHL	12	1	0	1	2	....	....	....	....	....
	Elmira Jackals	ECHL	41	0	9	9	10	....	....	....	....	....
2014-15	Binghamton	AHL	15	2	2	4	14	....	....	....	....	....
	Evansville IceMen	ECHL	54	6	18	24	28	....	....	....	....	....

WHL West Second All-Star Team (2013)

Signed as a free agent by **Ottawa**, March 14, 2013.

RYAN, Derek (RIGH-uhn, DAIR-ihk) CAR

Center. Shoots right. 5'10", 170 lbs. Born, Spokane, WA, December 29, 1986.

			Regular Season					Playoffs				
Season	Club	League	GP	G	A	Pts	PIM	GP	G	A	Pts	PIM
2003-04	Spokane Chiefs	WHL	1	1	0	1	0	4	1	0	1	0
2004-05	Spokane Chiefs	WHL	71	14	32	46	39	....	....	....	....	....
2005-06	Spokane Chiefs	WHL	72	24	37	61	50	....	....	....	....	....
2006-07	Spokane Chiefs	WHL	72	28	31	59	50	6	3	2	5	2
	Kalamazoo Wings	UHL	3	0	2	2	0	13	4	1	5	8
2007-08	U. of Alberta	CIS	44	15	23	38	48	....	....	....	....	....
2008-09	U. of Alberta	CIS	39	23	28	51	22	....	....	....	....	....
2009-10	U. of Alberta	CIS	42	19	33	52	40	....	....	....	....	....
2010-11	U. of Alberta	CIS	40	29	37	66	20	....	....	....	....	....
2011-12	Szekesfehervar	Austria	50	25	24	49	20	6	1	3	4	6
2012-13	EC VSV Villach	Austria	54	27	39	66	22	7	3	8	11	6
2013-14	EC VSV Villach	Austria	54	38	46	84	50	....	....	....	....	....
2014-15	Orebro HK	Sweden	55	15	*45	*60	18	6	0	1	1	2

Signed as a free agent by **Carolina**, June 15, 2015.

RYAN, Joakim (RIGHN, YOH-ah-kihm) S.J.

Defense. Shoots left. 5'11", 185 lbs. Born, Rumson, NJ, June 17, 1993.
(San Jose's 6th choice, 198th overall, in 2012 Entry Draft).

			Regular Season					Playoffs				
Season	Club	League	GP	G	A	Pts	PIM	GP	G	A	Pts	PIM
2009-10	N.J. Devils Youth	AYHL	32	13	23	36	34	....	....	....	....	....
2010-11	Dubuque	USHL	53	3	29	32	26	11	2	3	5	2
2011-12	Cornell Big Red	ECAC	34	7	10	17	20	....	....	....	....	....
2012-13	Cornell Big Red	ECAC	34	3	20	23	12	....	....	....	....	....
2013-14	Cornell Big Red	ECAC	32	8	16	24	27	....	....	....	....	....
2014-15	Cornell Big Red	ECAC	23	1	13	14	27	....	....	....	....	....
	Worcester Sharks	AHL	7	0	2	2	2	....	....	....	....	....

ECAC Second All-Star Team (2014) • ECAC First All-Star Team (2015)

RYAN, Kenny (RIGH-uhn, KEHN-nee)

Right wing. Shoots right. 6', 200 lbs. Born, Franklin Village, MI, July 10, 1991.
(Toronto's 2nd choice, 50th overall, in 2009 Entry Draft).

			Regular Season					Playoffs				
Season	Club	League	GP	G	A	Pts	PIM	GP	G	A	Pts	PIM
2006-07	Det. Honeybaked	MWEHL	31	16	17	33	34	....	....	....	....	....
	Det. Honeybaked	Other	34	17	24	41	....	....	....	....	....	....
2007-08	USNTDP	NAHL	36	10	8	18	53	....	....	....	....	....
	USNTDP	U-17	13	0	5	5	12	....	....	....	....	....
2008-09	USNTDP	NAHL	16	4	9	13	12	....	....	....	....	....
	USNTDP	U-18	46	23	13	36	38	....	....	....	....	....
2009-10	Windsor Spitfires	OHL	52	14	21	35	33	19	3	2	5	14
2010-11	Windsor Spitfires	OHL	63	21	37	58	42	18	4	8	12	25
2011-12	Toronto Marlies	AHL	16	1	0	1	9	....	....	....	....	....
	Reading Royals	ECHL	32	13	10	23	18	5	3	2	5	27
2012-13	Toronto Marlies	AHL	59	9	12	21	38	9	0	0	0	13
2013-14	Toronto Marlies	AHL	50	5	11	16	60	14	1	4	5	2
2014-15	Lake Erie Monsters	AHL	73	12	17	29	34	....	....	....	....	....

SAARELA, Aleksi (sah'ah-REH-lah, al-EHX-ay) NYR

Center. Shoots left. 5'11", 198 lbs. Born, Helsinki, Finland, January 7, 1997.
(NY Rangers' 4th choice, 89th overall, in 2015 Entry Draft).

			Regular Season					Playoffs				
Season	Club	League	GP	G	A	Pts	PIM	GP	G	A	Pts	PIM
2012-13	Lukko Rauma U18	Fin-U18	16	17	19	36	14	....	....	....	....	....
	Lukko Rauma Jr.	Fin-Jr.	22	8	10	18	6	10	2	6	8	2
	Lukko Rauma	Finland	3	1	1	2	0	....	....	....	....	....
2013-14	Lukko Rauma Jr.	Fin-Jr.	17	6	16	22	8	....	....	....	....	....
	Lukko Rauma	Finland	12	0	2	2	2	....	....	....	....	....
2014-15	Assat Pori	Finland	51	6	6	12	18	2	0	1	1	0

SAARI, Santeri (sah-AH-RI, SAHN-tair-ee) ST.L.

Defense. Shoots left. 6'3", 206 lbs. Born, Helsinki, Finland, October 18, 1994.
(St. Louis' 4th choice, 173rd overall, in 2013 Entry Draft).

			Regular Season					Playoffs				
Season	Club	League	GP	G	A	Pts	PIM	GP	G	A	Pts	PIM
2009-10	Jokerit U18	Fin-U18	1	0	0	0	0	....	....	....	....	....
2010-11	Jokerit U18	Fin-U18	14	0	1	1	24	9	0	2	2	4
	Jokerit Helsinki Jr.	Fin-Jr.	3	0	0	0	2	....	....	....	....	....
2011-12	Jokerit U18	Fin-U18	33	7	17	24	48	11	3	2	5	2
	Jokerit Helsinki Jr.	Fin-Jr.	13	2	2	4	10	....	....	....	....	....
2012-13	Jokerit Helsinki Jr.	Fin-Jr.	46	5	18	23	34	....	....	....	....	....
	Jokerit Helsinki	Finland	2	0	0	0	0	....	....	....	....	....
	Kiekko-Vantaa	Finland-2	7	0	0	0	6	....	....	....	....	....
2013-14	Jokerit Helsinki Jr.	Fin-Jr.	7	1	5	6	4	....	....	....	....	....
	Kiekko-Vantaa	Finland-2	25	1	0	1	12	....	....	....	....	....
2014-15	Jokerit	KHL	9	1	0	1	6	....	....	....	....	....
	Bofors	Sweden-2	18	0	5	5	12	....	....	....	....	....
	Kiekko-Vantaa	Finland-2	1	0	0	0	0	....	....	....	....	....
	HPK Hameenlinna	Finland	13	2	1	3	4	....	....	....	....	....

SAARIJARVI, Vili (sah'ah-rih-YAHR-vee, VIH-lee) DET

Defense. Shoots right. 5'10", 163 lbs. Born, Rovaniemi, Finland, May 15, 1997.
(Detroit's 2nd choice, 73rd overall, in 2015 Entry Draft).

			Regular Season					Playoffs				
Season	Club	League	GP	G	A	Pts	PIM	GP	G	A	Pts	PIM
2012-13	Karpat Oulu U18	Fin-U18	38	5	25	30	24	3	0	1	1	2
	Karpat Oulu Jr.	Fin-Jr.	3	0	1	1	0	2	0	0	0	4
2013-14	Karpat Oulu U18	Fin-U18	8	3	7	10	2	....	....	....	....	....
	Karpat Oulu Jr.	Fin-Jr.	40	7	21	28	10	12	1	0	1	6
2014-15	Green Bay	USHL	57	6	17	23	14	....	....	....	....	....

SABOURIN, Scott (SA-boo-rihn, SKAWT) L.A.

Right wing. Shoots right. 6'3", 206 lbs. Born, Orleans, ON, July 30, 1992.

			Regular Season					Playoffs				
Season	Club	League	GP	G	A	Pts	PIM	GP	G	A	Pts	PIM
2007-08	Ottawa Jr. 67's	Minor-ON	25	12	3	15	39	8	1	3	4	14
2008-09	Brockville Braves	ON-Jr.A	57	9	8	17	64	9	1	2	3	4
2009-10	Kanata Stallions	ON-Jr.A	43	4	2	6	64	....	....	....	....	....
	Oshawa Generals	OHL	4	0	1	1	2	....	....	....	....	....
2010-11	Oshawa Generals	OHL	42	6	4	10	75	10	1	2	3	15
2011-12	Oshawa Generals	OHL	55	10	9	19	111	6	0	0	0	10
2012-13	Oshawa Generals	OHL	65	30	20	50	142	9	4	3	7	12
	Manchester	AHL	5	0	1	1	4	3	0	0	0	7
2013-14	Manchester	AHL	69	12	14	26	115	4	0	0	0	0
2014-15	Manchester	AHL	51	5	6	11	138	....	....	....	....	....

Signed as a free agent by **Manchester** (AHL), April 10, 2013. Signed as a free agent by **Los Angeles**, October 7, 2013.

SADEK, Jack (SAY-dehk, JAK) MIN

Defense. Shoots right. 6'2", 185 lbs. Born, Lakeville, MN, April 19, 1997.
(Minnesota's 7th choice, 204th overall, in 2015 Entry Draft).

			Regular Season					Playoffs				
Season	Club	League	GP	G	A	Pts	PIM	GP	G	A	Pts	PIM
2012-13	Lakeville North	High-MN	25	2	1	3	18	5	0	3	3	4
2013-14	Lakeville North	High-MN	25	4	9	13	16	6	2	2	4	6
2014-15	Team Southeast	UMHSEL	21	3	6	9	48	3	1	1	2	16
	Lakeville North	High-MN	25	5	20	25	36	6	2	6	8	2

• Signed Letter of Intent to attend **University of Minnesota** (Big Ten) in fall of 2015.

SADOWY, Dylan (sa-DOH-way, DIH-luhn) S.J.

Left wing. Shoots left. 5'11", 185 lbs. Born, Brampton, ON, April 2, 1996.
(San Jose's 5th choice, 81st overall, in 2014 Entry Draft).

			Regular Season					Playoffs				
Season	Club	League	GP	G	A	Pts	PIM	GP	G	A	Pts	PIM
2011-12	Vaughan Kings	GTHL	53	33	45	78	....	....	....	....	....	....
2012-13	Saginaw Spirit	OHL	61	2	6	8	45	3	0	1	1	7
2013-14	Saginaw Spirit	OHL	68	27	9	36	69	5	4	0	4	2
2014-15	Saginaw Spirit	OHL	65	42	32	74	66	4	0	0	0	4

ST. CROIX, Michael (SAYNT KR'WAH, MIGH-kuhl) NYR

Center. Shoots right. 5'11", 180 lbs. Born, Winnipeg, MB, April 10, 1993.
(NY Rangers' 3rd choice, 106th overall, in 2011 Entry Draft).

			Regular Season					Playoffs				
Season	Club	League	GP	G	A	Pts	PIM	GP	G	A	Pts	PIM
2008-09	Winnipeg Wild	MMHL	41	*56	47	*103	10	9	8	12	20	4
	Edmonton	WHL	2	1	1	2	0	....	....	....	....	....
2009-10	Edmonton	WHL	66	18	28	46	30	....	....	....	....	....
2010-11	Edmonton	WHL	68	27	48	75	48	4	1	0	1	9
2011-12	Edmonton	WHL	72	45	60	105	49	20	7	12	19	6
2012-13	Edmonton	WHL	72	37	55	92	36	22	13	13	26	14
2013-14	Hartford Wolf Pack	AHL	13	0	0	0	2	....	....	....	....	....
	Greenville	ECHL	53	17	31	48	12	18	4	11	15	6
2014-15	Greenville	ECHL	59	15	26	41	44	....	....	....	....	....

WHL East Second All-Star Team (2012) • WHL East First All-Star Team (2013)

SALMINEN, Saku (SAL-mih-nehn, SA-koo) T.B.

Center. Shoots left. 6'3", 198 lbs. Born, Helsinki, Finland, October 20, 1994.
(Tampa Bay's 5th choice, 184th overall, in 2013 Entry Draft).

			Regular Season					Playoffs				
Season	Club	League	GP	G	A	Pts	PIM	GP	G	A	Pts	PIM
2009-10	HIFK Helsinki U18	Fin-U18	25	8	10	18	22	11	4	1	5	2
2010-11	HIFK Helsinki U18	Fin-U18	16	7	9	16	30	4	0	1	1	6
	HIFK Helsinki Jr.	Fin-Jr.	13	2	2	4	2	....	....	....	....	....
2011-12	Jokerit U18	Fin-U18	2	1	1	2	2	2	0	0	0	2
	Jokerit Helsinki Jr.	Fin-Jr.	44	9	17	26	16	12	0	1	1	2
2012-13	Jokerit Helsinki Jr.	Fin-Jr.	4	1	2	3	2	....	....	....	....	....
	Jokerit Helsinki	Finland	13	1	1	2	12	....	....	....	....	....
	Kiekko-Vantaa	Finland-2	12	1	4	5	0	4	1	5	6	2
2013-14	Kiekko-Vantaa	Finland-2	13	0	2	2	16	....	....	....	....	....
	Jokerit Helsinki Jr.	Fin-Jr.	....	....	....	....	....	4	1	2	3	2
2014-15	HPK Hameenlinna	Finland	36	3	5	8	4	....	....	....	....	....

SANDLAK, Carter (SAND-lahk, KAR-tuhr) CAR

Left wing. Shoots left. 6'2", 200 lbs. Born, Vancouver, BC, May 18, 1993.

			Regular Season					Playoffs				
Season	Club	League	GP	G	A	Pts	PIM	GP	G	A	Pts	PIM
2008-09	Lon. Knights MM	Minor-ON	30	13	18	31	*112	11	5	7	12	20
	Lon. Jr. Knights	Minor-ON	4	0	1	1	2	....	....	....	....	....
2009-10	Guelph Storm	OHL	61	7	8	15	59	5	0	1	1	13
2010-11	Guelph Storm	OHL	22	4	3	7	25	....	....	....	....	....
	Belleville Bulls	OHL	34	9	7	16	44	4	0	1	1	7
2011-12	Belleville Bulls	OHL	34	6	7	13	52	6	0	2	2	6
2012-13	Belleville Bulls	OHL	60	9	14	23	98	15	4	3	7	34
2013-14	Plymouth Whalers	OHL	61	24	24	48	95	1	1	0	1	4
2014-15	Charlotte	AHL	44	2	2	4	69	....	....	....	....	....
	Florida Everblades	ECHL	3	0	3	3	14	....	....	....	....	....

Signed as a free agent by **Carolina**, December 6, 2013.

SANFORD, Zachary (SAN-fohrd, za-KAH-ree) WSH

Left wing. Shoots left. 6'3", 185 lbs. Born, Salem, MA, November 9, 1994.
(Washington's 3rd choice, 61st overall, in 2013 Entry Draft).

			Regular Season					Playoffs				
Season	Club	League	GP	G	A	Pts	PIM	GP	G	A	Pts	PIM
2009-10	Pinkerton	High-NH	23	14	11	25	48	....	....	....	....	....
2010-11	Pinkerton	High-NH	21	15	16	31	39	....	....	....	....	....
2011-12	Pinkerton	High-NH	21	36	33	69	40	....	....	....	....	....
2012-13	Islanders H.C.	EJHL	37	12	24	36	22	7	4	4	8	8
2013-14	Waterloo	USHL	52	17	18	35	60	12	5	7	12	8
2014-15	Boston College	H-East	38	7	17	24	30	....	....	....	....	....

SANHEIM, Travis (SAN-highm, TRA-vihs) PHI

Defense. Shoots left. 6'3", 198 lbs. Born, Elkhorn, MB, March 29, 1996.
(Philadelphia's 1st choice, 17th overall, in 2014 Entry Draft).

			Regular Season					Playoffs				
Season	Club	League	GP	G	A	Pts	PIM	GP	G	A	Pts	PIM
2010-11	Elkhorn Bm AA	Minor-MB	STATISTICS NOT AVAILABLE									
2011-12	Yellowhead Chiefs	MMHL	44	15	24	39	14	2	0	1	1	2
2012-13	Yellowhead Chiefs	MMHL	43	12	23	35	44	4	2	3	5	2
	Winkler Flyers	MJHL	....	....	....	....	....	6	0	1	1	2
2013-14	Calgary Hitmen	WHL	67	5	24	29	14	6	1	1	2	6
2014-15	Calgary Hitmen	WHL	67	15	50	65	52	17	5	13	18	10

WHL East First All-Star Team (2015)

SANTINI, Steven (san-TEE-nee, STEE-vehn) N.J.

Defense. Shoots right. 6'2", 205 lbs. Born, Bronxville, NY, March 7, 1995.
(New Jersey's 1st choice, 42nd overall, in 2013 Entry Draft).

			Regular Season					Playoffs				
Season	Club	League	GP	G	A	Pts	PIM	GP	G	A	Pts	PIM
2010-11	NY Apple Core	EJHL	44	3	14	17	26	5	0	1	1	0
2011-12	USNTDP	USHL	36	1	4	5	41	2	0	1	1	0
	USNTDP	U-17	17	1	3	4	28	....	....	....	....	....
2012-13	USNTDP	USHL	25	0	5	5	6	....	....	....	....	....
	USNTDP	U-18	41	0	10	10	38	....	....	....	....	....
2013-14	Boston College	H-East	35	3	8	11	52	....	....	....	....	....
2014-15	Boston College	H-East	22	1	4	5	20	....	....	....	....	....

SANVIDO, Patrick (SAN-vee-doh, PAHT-rihk) DAL

Defense. Shoots left. 6'5", 230 lbs. Born, Guelph, ON, June 28, 1996.
(Dallas' 9th choice, 195th overall, in 2014 Entry Draft).

			Regular Season					Playoffs				
Season	Club	League	GP	G	A	Pts	PIM	GP	G	A	Pts	PIM
2011-12	Guelph Jr. Storm	Minor-ON	30	3	13	16	34	....	....	....	....	....
	Guelph Jr. Storm	Other	26	3	14	17	34	....	....	....	....	....
2012-13	Windsor Spitfires	OHL	60	0	6	6	40	....	....	....	....	....
2013-14	Windsor Spitfires	OHL	64	1	7	8	82	4	0	0	0	7
2014-15	Windsor Spitfires	OHL	59	3	8	11	62	....	....	....	....	....

SARAULT, Charles (sah-ROH, CHAR-uhlz) ANA

Center. Shoots left. 5'11", 184 lbs. Born, Ottawa, ON, February 20, 1992.

			Regular Season					Playoffs				
Season	Club	League	GP	G	A	Pts	PIM	GP	G	A	Pts	PIM
2008-09	Kingston	OHL	68	2	7	9	22	....	....	....	....	....
2009-10	Kingston	OHL	62	4	12	16	31	6	1	3	4	4
2010-11	Kingston	OHL	68	13	25	38	32	5	1	1	2	0
2011-12	Sarnia Sting	OHL	68	20	67	87	32	6	0	4	4	4
2012-13	Sarnia Sting	OHL	68	22	*86	108	28	4	1	3	4	4
	Norfolk Admirals	AHL	11	0	6	6	0	....	....	....	....	....
2013-14	Norfolk Admirals	AHL	43	6	8	14	16	....	....	....	....	....
	Utah Grizzlies	ECHL	8	3	8	11	2	5	2	2	4	2
2014-15	Norfolk Admirals	AHL	51	8	7	15	24	....	....	....	....	....

OHL Second All-Star Team (2013)

Signed as a free agent by **Anaheim**, March 5, 2013.

SAUTNER, Ashton (SAWT-nuhr, ASH-tuhn) VAN

Defense. Shoots left. 6', 192 lbs. Born, Flaxcombe, SK, May 27, 1994.

			Regular Season					Playoffs				
Season	Club	League	GP	G	A	Pts	PIM	GP	G	A	Pts	PIM
2009-10	Moose Jaw	SMHL	42	1	10	11	24	4	0	2	2	6
2010-11	Moose Jaw	SMHL	42	12	23	35	43	6	1	2	3	12
2011-12	Edmonton	WHL	59	2	10	12	38	19	0	2	2	10
2012-13	Edmonton	WHL	62	2	10	12	28	14	3	2	5	10
2013-14	Edmonton	WHL	72	8	34	42	26	20	3	9	12	8
2014-15	Edmonton	WHL	72	12	39	51	38	5	0	1	1	6

Signed as a free agent by **Vancouver**, March 14. 2015.

SCARLETT, Reece (SKAR-leht, REES) N.J.

Defense. Shoots right. 6'1", 185 lbs. Born, Edmonton, AB, March 31, 1993.
(New Jersey's 6th choice, 159th overall, in 2011 Entry Draft).

			Regular Season					Playoffs				
Season	Club	League	GP	G	A	Pts	PIM	GP	G	A	Pts	PIM
2007-08	Sherwood Park	AMBHL	33	14	16	30	48	12	4	5	9	26
	Sherwood Park	Minor-AB	3	1	0	1	4	....	....	....	....	....
2008-09	Sherwood Park	AMHL	34	4	13	17	60	11	2	6	8	4
	Swift Current	WHL	1	0	0	0	0	....	....	....	....	....
2009-10	Swift Current	WHL	65	1	9	10	49	4	0	2	2	4
2010-11	Swift Current	WHL	72	6	18	24	59	....	....	....	....	....
2011-12	Swift Current	WHL	71	9	40	49	74	....	....	....	....	....
2012-13	Swift Current	WHL	67	9	40	49	66	5	0	3	3	10
2013-14	Albany Devils	AHL	48	6	14	20	18	....	....	....	....	....
2014-15	Albany Devils	AHL	57	2	23	25	27	....	....	....	....	....

SCHEMITSCH, Thomas (SHEHM-ihtch, TAW-muhs) FLA

Defense. Shoots right. 6'3", 205 lbs. Born, Thornhill, ON, October 26, 1996.
(Florida's 3rd choice, 88th overall, in 2015 Entry Draft).

			Regular Season					Playoffs				
Season	Club	League	GP	G	A	Pts	PIM	GP	G	A	Pts	PIM
2011-12	Miss. Senators	GTHL	33	6	11	17	18	....	....	....	....	....
2012-13	Tor. Titans Midg.	GTHL	30	12	15	27	....	....	....	....	....	....
	Tor. Patriots	ON-Jr.A	4	0	0	0	0	1	0	0	0	0
2013-14	Owen Sound	OHL	63	6	11	17	26	5	1	0	1	2
2014-15	Owen Sound	OHL	68	14	35	49	36	5	0	2	2	2

SCHEMPP, Kyle (SHEHMP, KIGHL) NYI

Center. Shoots left. 5'11", 178 lbs. Born, Saginaw, MI, January 13, 1994.
(NY Islanders' 6th choice, 155th overall, in 2014 Entry Draft).

			Regular Season					Playoffs				
Season	Club	League	GP	G	A	Pts	PIM	GP	G	A	Pts	PIM
2009-10	Det. Comp. U16	T1EHL	35	5	16	21	32	....	....	....	....	....
	Det. Comp. U16	Other	6	3	3	6	2	....	....	....	....	....
2010-11	Det. Comp. U18	T1EHL	40	21	9	30	16	....	....	....	....	....
	Det. Comp. U18	Other	13	4	4	8	17	....	....	....	....	....
2011-12	Traverse City	NAHL	59	13	22	35	29	4	0	1	1	0
2012-13	Sioux Falls	USHL	64	14	27	41	28	10	0	5	5	2
2013-14	Ferris State	WCHA	43	10	15	25	12	....	....	....	....	....
2014-15	Ferris State	WCHA	37	10	6	16	22	....	....	....	....	....

SCHERBAK, Nikita (shair-BAK, nih-KEE-tuh) MTL

Right wing. Shoots left. 6'2", 204 lbs. Born, Moscow, Russia, December 30, 1995.
(Montreal's 1st choice, 26th overall, in 2014 Entry Draft).

			Regular Season					Playoffs				
Season	Club	League	GP	G	A	Pts	PIM	GP	G	A	Pts	PIM
2012-13	Stupino Jr.	Russia-Jr.	50	7	7	14	14	....	....	....	....	....
2013-14	Saskatoon Blades	WHL	65	28	50	78	46	....	....	....	....	....
2014-15	Everett Silvertips	WHL	65	27	55	82	60	11	3	5	8	10

SCHMALTZ, Jordan (SHMAHLTZ, JOHR-dahn) ST.L.

Defense. Shoots right. 6'2", 190 lbs. Born, Madison, WI, October 8, 1993.
(St. Louis' 1st choice, 25th overall, in 2012 Entry Draft).

			Regular Season					Playoffs				
Season	Club	League	GP	G	A	Pts	PIM	GP	G	A	Pts	PIM
2008-09	Chi. Mission U16	T1EHL	25	3	10	13	33	....	....	....	....	....
2009-10	Chicago Mission	T1EHL	39	10	21	31	30	....	....	....	....	....
2010-11	Sioux City	USHL	53	13	31	44	22	3	0	1	1	4
2011-12	Sioux City	USHL	9	3	3	6	9	....	....	....	....	....
	Green Bay	USHL	46	7	28	35	20	12	2	5	7	8
2012-13	North Dakota	WCHA	42	3	9	12	31	....	....	....	....	....
2013-14	North Dakota	NCHC	41	6	18	24	12	....	....	....	....	....
2014-15	North Dakota	NCHC	42	4	24	28	8	....	....	....	....	....

USHL All-Rookie Team (2011) • USHL First All-Star Team (2011, 2012) • NCHC Second All-Star Team (2014, 2015)

SCHMALTZ, Nick (SHMAHLTZ, NIHK) CHI

Center. Shoots right. 5'10", 177 lbs. Born, Madison, WI, February 23, 1996.
(Chicago's 1st choice, 20th overall, in 2014 Entry Draft).

			Regular Season					Playoffs				
Season	Club	League	GP	G	A	Pts	PIM	GP	G	A	Pts	PIM
2011-12	Chicago Mission	HPHL	13	9	11	20	4	....	....	....	....	....
	Green Bay	USHL	11	1	3	4	2	....	....	....	....	....
2012-13	Green Bay	USHL	64	18	34	52	15	4	1	1	2	0
2013-14	Green Bay	USHL	55	18	45	63	16	4	1	2	3	17
	USNTDP	U-18	2	0	0	0	0	....	....	....	....	....
2014-15	North Dakota	NCHC	38	5	21	26	12	....	....	....	....	....

NCHC All-Rookie Team (2015)

SCHMALZ, Matt (SCHMAWLZ, MAT) L.A.

Right wing. Shoots right. 6'6", 209 lbs. Born, Dunnville, ON, March 21, 1996.
(Los Angeles' 4th choice, 134th overall, in 2015 Entry Draft).

			Regular Season					Playoffs				
Season	Club	League	GP	G	A	Pts	PIM	GP	G	A	Pts	PIM
2011-12	Southern Tier	Minor-ON	35	23	18	41	40	....	....	....	....	....
	Southern Tier	Other	26	12	23	35	22	....	....	....	....	....
2012-13	Kitchener Rangers	OHL	25	1	0	1	8	....	....	....	....	....
	Sudbury Wolves	OHL	24	3	6	9	13	4	0	1	1	2
2013-14	Sudbury Wolves	OHL	66	3	5	8	60	5	0	0	0	0
2014-15	Sudbury Wolves	OHL	66	24	16	40	68	....	....	....	....	....

SCHNEIDER, Cole (SHNIGH-duhr, KOHL) OTT

Left wing. Shoots left. 6'1", 198 lbs. Born, Williamsville, NY, August 26, 1990.

			Regular Season					Playoffs				
Season	Club	League	GP	G	A	Pts	PIM	GP	G	A	Pts	PIM
2008-09	Mahoning Valley	NAHL	42	17	16	33	12	14	3	7	10	2
2009-10	Topeka	NAHL	29	25	14	39	18	9	7	4	11	20
2010-11	U. of Connecticut	AH	37	13	20	33	30	....	....	....	....	....
2011-12	U. of Connecticut	AH	38	23	22	45	35	....	....	....	....	....
	Binghamton	AHL	11	0	2	2	0	....	....	....	....	....
2012-13	Binghamton	AHL	60	17	18	35	37	3	0	0	0	0
2013-14	Binghamton	AHL	69	20	34	54	22	4	0	2	2	0
2014-15	Binghamton	AHL	69	29	29	58	14	....	....	....	....	....

Signed as a free agent by **Ottawa**, March 14, 2012.

SCHOENBORN, Alex (SHAYN-bohrn, AL-ehx) S.J.

Right wing. Shoots right. 6', 200 lbs. Born, Minot, ND, December 12, 1995.
(San Jose's 4th choice, 72nd overall, in 2014 Entry Draft).

			Regular Season					Playoffs				
Season	Club	League	GP	G	A	Pts	PIM	GP	G	A	Pts	PIM
2010-11	Minot Magicians	High-ND	27	23	22	45	48	....	....	....	....	....
2011-12	Om. Lancers U16	NAPHL	17	10	24	34	47	4	6	4	10	8
	Om. Lancers U16	Other	42	29	44	73	99	....	....	....	....	....
	Lincoln Stars	USHL	3	0	0	0	2	....	....	....	....	....
2012-13	Portland	WHL	20	1	1	2	22	....	....	....	....	....
	Wenatchee Wild	NAHL	10	0	1	1	34	....	....	....	....	....
2013-14	Portland	WHL	72	18	18	36	121	21	3	2	5	41
2014-15	Portland	WHL	49	15	18	33	66	17	3	1	4	18

SDAO, Michael (S'DAY-oh, MIGH-kuhl) OTT

Defense. Shoots left. 6'4", 227 lbs. Born, Bloomington, MN, July 3, 1989.
(Ottawa's 9th choice, 191st overall, in 2009 Entry Draft).

			Regular Season					Playoffs				
Season	Club	League	GP	G	A	Pts	PIM	GP	G	A	Pts	PIM
2005-06	Culver Academy	High-IN	40	1	6	7	38	....	....	....	....	....
2006-07	Culver Academy	High-IN	43	1	6	7	85	....	....	....	....	....
2007-08	Lincoln Stars	USHL	53	3	6	9	178	8	0	1	1	20
2008-09	Lincoln Stars	USHL	51	3	7	10	162	7	0	0	0	*33
2009-10	Princeton	ECAC	30	5	4	9	48	....	....	....	....	....
2010-11	Princeton	ECAC	27	3	7	10	65	....	....	....	....	....
2011-12	Princeton	ECAC	30	10	10	20	87	....	....	....	....	....
2012-13	Princeton	ECAC	31	8	7	15	36	....	....	....	....	....
	Binghamton	AHL	12	1	0	1	23	....	....	....	....	....
2013-14	Binghamton	AHL	61	6	5	11	171	....	....	....	....	....
2014-15	Binghamton	AHL	33	2	2	4	89	....	....	....	....	....

ECAC Second All-Star Team (2012)

• Missed majority of 2014-15 as a healthy reserve.

SEDLAK, Lukas (SEHD-lak, LOO-kuhsh) CBJ

Center. Shoots left. 6', 198 lbs. Born, Ceske Budejovice, Czech Rep., February 25, 1993.
(Columbus' 5th choice, 158th overall, in 2011 Entry Draft).

			Regular Season					Playoffs				
Season	Club	League	GP	G	A	Pts	PIM	GP	G	A	Pts	PIM
2007-08	C. Budejovice U17	CzR-U17	6	0	2	2	4	2	0	0	0	2
2008-09	C. Budejovice U17	CzR-U17	44	12	17	29	14	4	0	0	0	4
2009-10	C. Budejovice U18	CzR-U18	37	29	27	56	76	4	5	1	6	39
	C. Budejovice Jr.	CzRep-Jr.	11	4	8	12	4	....	....	....	....	....
2010-11	C. Budejovice Jr.	CzRep-Jr.	47	14	13	27	65	....	....	....	....	....
	C. Budejovice U18	CzR-U18	....	....	....	....	....	1	0	1	1	0
2011-12	Chicoutimi	QMJHL	50	17	28	45	57	18	5	3	8	18
2012-13	Chicoutimi	QMJHL	48	15	19	34	64	6	1	4	5	8
2013-14	Springfield Falcons	AHL	54	8	6	14	26	4	0	1	1	0
2014-15	Springfield Falcons	AHL	51	6	10	16	30	....	....	....	....	....

SEGALLA, Ryan (seh-GAL-ah, RIGH-uhn) PIT

Defense. Shoots left. 6'1", 195 lbs. Born, Boston, MA, December 29, 1994.
(Pittsburgh's 3rd choice, 119th overall, in 2013 Entry Draft).

			Regular Season					Playoffs				
Season	Club	League	GP	G	A	Pts	PIM	GP	G	A	Pts	PIM
2009-10	Bridgewater	EmJHL	41	9	18	27	52	2	1	0	1	0
2010-11	Salisbury School	High-CT	26	3	10	13	30	....	....	....	....	....
	South Shore	Minor-CT	11	1	0	1	4	4	0	0	0	6
2011-12	Salisbury School	High-CT	28	6	6	12	36	....	....	....	....	....
2012-13	Salisbury School	High-CT	28	10	8	18	28	....	....	....	....	....
	Mid Fairfield Blues	Minor-CT		STATISTICS NOT AVAILABLE								
2013-14	U. of Connecticut	AH	34	1	13	14	47	....	....	....	....	....
2014-15	U. of Connecticut	H-East	31	2	3	5	54	....	....	....	....	....

SENEY, Brett (SEE-nee, BREHT) N.J.

Left wing. Shoots left. 5'9", 160 lbs. Born, London, ON, February 28, 1996.
(New Jersey's 5th choice, 157th overall, in 2015 Entry Draft).

			Regular Season					Playoffs				
Season	Club	League	GP	G	A	Pts	PIM	GP	G	A	Pts	PIM
2011-12	Lon. Knights MM	Minor-ON	29	20	26	46	20	11	6	13	19	6
	Lon. Knights Mid.	Minor-ON	1	1	1	2	2	1	0	0	0	2
2012-13	Kingston	ON-Jr.A	49	3	7	10	18	15	2	0	2	8
2013-14	Kingston	ON-Jr.A	49	26	43	69	67	11	5	7	12	12
2014-15	Merrimack College	H-East	34	11	15	26	55	....	....	....	....	....

SENYSHYN, Zach (SEH-nih-shihn, ZAK) BOS

Right wing. Shoots right. 6'1", 192 lbs. Born, Ottawa, ON, March 30, 1997.
(Boston's 3rd choice, 15th overall, in 2015 Entry Draft).

			Regular Season					Playoffs				
Season	Club	League	GP	G	A	Pts	PIM	GP	G	A	Pts	PIM
2012-13	Ott. Senators MM	Minor-ON	27	22	11	33	21	11	6	6	12	0
2013-14	Smiths Falls Bears	ON-Jr.A	57	22	10	32	8	16	4	6	10	0
	Sault Ste. Marie	OHL	4	1	1	2	0	....	....	....	....	....
2014-15	Sault Ste. Marie	OHL	66	26	19	45	17	14	4	3	7	2

SERGEEV, Dmitrii (sair-GAY-ehf, dih-MEE-tree) ST.L.

Defense. Shoots right. 6'3", 200 lbs. Born, Chelyabinsk, Russia, March 26, 1996.

			Regular Season					Playoffs				
Season	Club	League	GP	G	A	Pts	PIM	GP	G	A	Pts	PIM
2013-14	Kitchener Rangers	OHL	49	2	7	9	22	....	....	....	....	....
2014-15	Kitchener Rangers	OHL	54	5	23	28	44	6	0	2	2	8

Signed as a free agent by **St. Louis**, September 28, 2014.

SERVILLE, Brennan (SUHR-vihl, BREH-nuhn) WPG

Defense. Shoots right. 6'3", 184 lbs. Born, Scarborough, ON, June 2, 1993.
(Winnipeg's 3rd choice, 78th overall, in 2011 Entry Draft).

			Regular Season					Playoffs				
Season	Club	League	GP	G	A	Pts	PIM	GP	G	A	Pts	PIM
2008-09	Ajax Pickering	Minor-ON	56	4	15	19	28	....	....	....	....	....
2009-10	Stouffville Spirit	ON-Jr.A	43	3	12	15	26	4	1	2	3	0
2010-11	Stouffville Spirit	ON-Jr.A	36	3	27	30	29	19	2	10	12	20
2011-12	U. of Michigan	CCHA	34	0	8	8	4	....	....	....	....	....
2012-13	U. of Michigan	CCHA	29	1	2	3	16	....	....	....	....	....
2013-14	U. of Michigan	Big Ten	33	0	3	3	14	....	....	....	....	....
2014-15	U. of Michigan	Big Ten	33	0	7	7	12	....	....	....	....	....

SEXTON, Ben (SEHKS-tuhn, BEHN) BOS

Center. Shoots right. 5'11", 182 lbs. Born, Ottawa, ON, June 6, 1991.
(Boston's 5th choice, 206th overall, in 2009 Entry Draft).

			Regular Season					Playoffs				
Season	Club	League	GP	G	A	Pts	PIM	GP	G	A	Pts	PIM
2007-08	Nepean Raiders	ON-Jr.A	48	15	15	30	71	6	1	5	6	4
2008-09	Nepean Raiders	ON-Jr.A	38	14	21	35	54	11	3	9	12	22
2009-10	Penticton Vees	BCHL	50	13	29	42	83	5	1	2	3	4
2010-11	Clarkson Knights	ECAC	12	5	3	8	12	....	....	....	....	....
2011-12	Clarkson Knights	ECAC	27	8	21	29	44	....	....	....	....	....
2012-13	Clarkson Knights	ECAC	28	5	15	20	70	....	....	....	....	....
2013-14	Clarkson Knights	ECAC	35	6	22	28	88	....	....	....	....	....
	Providence Bruins	AHL	9	1	1	2	9	....	....	....	....	....
2014-15	Providence Bruins	AHL	35	3	9	12	57	5	0	0	0	2

• Missed majority of 2010-11 due to arm injury vs. Colgate (ECAC), November 5, 2010.

SHAFIGULIN, Grigory (sha-fih-GOO-lihn, grih-GOH-ree) NSH

Center. Shoots left. 6'2", 185 lbs. Born, Chelyabinsk, USSR, January 13, 1985.
(Nashville's 8th choice, 98th overall, in 2003 Entry Draft).

			Regular Season					Playoffs				
Season	Club	League	GP	G	A	Pts	PIM	GP	G	A	Pts	PIM
2000-01	Chelyabinsk 2	Russia-3	6	3	2	5	8	....	....	....	....	....
2001-02	Yaroslavl 2	Russia-3	19	2	2	4	12	....	....	....	....	....
2002-03	Yaroslavl 2	Russia-3	33	18	12	30	46	7	0	4	4	31
	Yaroslavl	Russia	11	0	1	1	4	8	0	0	0	4
2003-04	Yaroslavl 2	Russia-3	11	3	8	11	22	....	....	....	....	....
	Yaroslavl	Russia	29	3	0	3	4	2	0	0	0	0
2004-05	Yaroslavl 2	Russia-3	1	0	2	2	0	....	....	....	....	....
	Yaroslavl	Russia	46	5	6	11	49	9	0	0	0	10
2005-06	Yaroslavl	Russia	32	3	6	9	20	3	0	0	0	6
	Yaroslavl 2	Russia-3	7	1	3	4	18	....	....	....	....	....
2006-07	Yaroslavl	Russia	54	5	16	21	46	7	3	0	3	14
2007-08	Ak Bars Kazan	Russia	39	5	5	10	112	8	1	0	1	4
2008-09	Ak Bars Kazan	KHL	28	4	5	9	18	....	....	....	....	....
	Vityaz Chekhov	KHL	14	3	5	8	6	....	....	....	....	....
2009-10	Nizhny Novgorod	KHL	40	5	12	17	62	....	....	....	....	....
2010-11	Dynamo Moscow	KHL	20	1	5	6	16	....	....	....	....	....
2011-12	Dynamo Moscow	KHL	37	8	8	16	14	9	0	0	0	6
2012-13	Dynamo Moscow	KHL	27	3	1	4	6	2	0	0	0	0
2013-14	Dynamo Moscow	KHL	8	1	0	1	8	....	....	....	....	....
2014-15	Magnitogorsk	KHL	9	0	0	0	14	....	....	....	....	....
	Amur Khabarovsk	KHL	26	1	7	8	19	....	....	....	....	....

SHAW, Logan (SHAW, LOH-guhn) FLA

Right wing. Shoots right. 6'3", 202 lbs. Born, Glace Bay, NS, October 5, 1992.
(Florida's 5th choice, 76th overall, in 2011 Entry Draft).

			Regular Season					Playoffs				
Season	Club	League	GP	G	A	Pts	PIM	GP	G	A	Pts	PIM
2007-08	Cape Breton	NSMHL	34	17	22	39	55	10	3	9	12	8
	Cape Breton	Other	2	1	0	1	0	....	....	....	....	....
2008-09	Cape Breton	QMJHL	49	5	3	8	22	8	0	0	0	0
2009-10	Cape Breton	QMJHL	67	9	15	24	31	5	0	0	0	4
2010-11	Cape Breton	QMJHL	68	26	20	46	37	4	0	1	1	4
2011-12	Cape Breton	QMJHL	37	14	12	26	27	....	....	....	....	....
	Quebec Remparts	QMJHL	23	6	9	15	19	11	6	5	11	12
2012-13	Quebec Remparts	QMJHL	67	26	42	68	37	11	3	5	8	8
2013-14	San Antonio	AHL	46	1	7	8	24	....	....	....	....	....
	Cincinnati	ECHL	20	8	10	18	8	24	5	1	6	4
2014-15	San Antonio	AHL	69	13	12	25	25	2	0	0	0	0

SHEA, Patrick (SHAY, PA-trihk) FLA

Center. Shoots right. 5'10", 186 lbs. Born, Marshfield, MA, March 25, 1997.
(Florida's 7th choice, 192nd overall, in 2015 Entry Draft).

			Regular Season					Playoffs				
Season	Club	League	GP	G	A	Pts	PIM	GP	G	A	Pts	PIM
2011-12	Marshfield Rams	High-MA	12	2	14	16	....	....	....	....	....	....
2012-13	Marshfield Rams	High-MA	16	8	20	28	....	....	....	....	....	....
2013-14	Cape Cod U16	Minor-MA	11	6	8	14	2	....	....	....	....	....
	Marshfield Rams	High-MA	21	19	36	55	....	....	....	....	....	....
2014-15	Boston Jr. Bruins	Minor-MA	11	5	7	12	20	....	....	....	....	....
	Kimball Union	High-NH	33	19	20	39	....	....	....	....	....	....

• Signed Letter of Intent to attend **University of Maine** (Hockey East) in fall of 2015.

SHEA, Ryan (SHAY, RIGH-uhn) **CHI**

Defense. Shoots left. 6', 177 lbs. Born, Milton, MA, February 11, 1997.
(Chicago's 3rd choice, 121st overall, in 2015 Entry Draft).

			Regular Season					Playoffs				
Season	Club	League	GP	G	A	Pts	PIM	GP	G	A	Pts	PIM
2012-13	Bos. College High	High-MA	23	3	9	12	....	....	....	....	....	....
2013-14	Cape Cod U16	Minor-MA	12	1	7	8	4	....	....	....	....	....
	Bos. College High	High-MA	19	5	16	21	....	....	....	....	....	....
2014-15	Cape Cod U18	Minor-MA	14	3	6	9	0	....	....	....	....	....
	Bos. College High	High-MA	22	6	29	35	....	....	....	....	....	....
	Youngstown	USHL	2	0	0	0	0	....	....	....	....	....

• Signed Letter of Intent to attend **Northeastern University** (Hockey East) in fall of 2016.

SHEARY, Conor (SHEER-ee, KAW-nuhr) **PIT**

Left wing. Shoots left. 5'9", 175 lbs. Born, Melrose, MA, June 8, 1992.

			Regular Season					Playoffs				
Season	Club	League	GP	G	A	Pts	PIM	GP	G	A	Pts	PIM
2007-08	Cushing	High-MA	29	2	2	4	....	....	....	....	....	....
2008-09	Cushing	High-MA	31	16	27	43	....	....	....	....	....	....
2009-10	Cushing	High-MA	31	31	41	72	....	....	....	....	....	....
2010-11	Massachusetts	H-East	34	6	8	14	12	....	....	....	....	....
2011-12	Massachusetts	H-East	36	12	23	35	10	....	....	....	....	....
2012-13	Massachusetts	H-East	34	11	16	27	29	....	....	....	....	....
2013-14	Massachusetts	H-East	34	9	19	28	2	....	....	....	....	....
	Wilkes-Barre	AHL	2	0	0	0	0	15	6	5	11	0
2014-15	Wilkes-Barre	AHL	58	20	25	45	8	8	5	7	12	2

Signed as a free agent by **Pittsburgh**, July 1, 2015.

SHERMAN, Wiley (SHUHR-man, WIGH-lee) **BOS**

Defense. Shoots left. 6'6", 200 lbs. Born, Greenwich, CT, May 24, 1995.
(Boston's 4th choice, 150th overall, in 2013 Entry Draft).

			Regular Season					Playoffs				
Season	Club	League	GP	G	A	Pts	PIM	GP	G	A	Pts	PIM
2010-11	Hotchkiss School	High-CT	23	0	4	4	....	....	....	....	....	....
2011-12	Hotchkiss School	High-CT	24	2	5	7	....	....	....	....	....	....
2012-13	Hotchkiss School	High-CT	26	4	6	10	32	....	....	....	....	....
	Mid Fairfield Blues	Minor-CT	20	2	5	7	....	....	....	....	....	....
2013-14	Hotchkiss School	High-CT	26	5	12	17	40	....	....	....	....	....
	Mid Fairfield Blues	Minor-CT	STATISTICS NOT AVAILABLE									
2014-15	Harvard Crimson	ECAC	37	0	3	3	4	....	....	....	....	....

SHERWOOD, Kole (SHUHR-wud, KOHL) **CBJ**

Right wing. Shoots right. 6', 189 lbs. Born, Columbus, OH, January 22, 1997.

			Regular Season					Playoffs				
Season	Club	League	GP	G	A	Pts	PIM	GP	G	A	Pts	PIM
2012-13	Ohio B-Jack. U16	T1EHL	40	13	11	24	19	4	1	3	4	2
2013-14	Ohio B-Jack. U16	T1EHL	34	24	18	42	17	....	....	....	....	....
2014-15	Ohio B-Jack. U16	T1EHL	31	22	26	48	29	4	1	3	4	16
	Youngstown	USHL	3	1	1	2	0	....	....	....	....	....

Signed as a free agent by **Columbus**, July 7, 2015.

SHIELDS, David (SHEELDZ, DAY-vihd) **ST.L.**

Defense. Shoots right. 6'3", 204 lbs. Born, Buffalo, NY, January 27, 1991.
(St. Louis' 5th choice, 168th overall, in 2009 Entry Draft).

			Regular Season					Playoffs				
Season	Club	League	GP	G	A	Pts	PIM	GP	G	A	Pts	PIM
2006-07	Maksymum	Minor-NY	37	4	16	20	60	....	....	....	....	....
2007-08	Erie Otters	OHL	60	1	3	4	31	....	....	....	....	....
2008-09	Erie Otters	OHL	61	1	16	17	28	5	0	0	0	5
2009-10	Erie Otters	OHL	68	7	12	19	42	4	0	0	0	12
2010-11	Erie Otters	OHL	61	6	21	27	48	7	1	4	5	4
2011-12	Peoria Rivermen	AHL	48	0	4	4	10	....	....	....	....	....
	Alaska Aces	ECHL	12	1	5	6	2	3	0	2	2	0
2012-13	Peoria Rivermen	AHL	59	0	5	5	41	....	....	....	....	....
2013-14	Chicago Wolves	AHL	55	5	10	15	21	3	0	0	0	2
2014-15	Chicago Wolves	AHL	42	0	6	6	10	....	....	....	....	....

SHINKARUK, Hunter (shinh-KA-ruhk, HUHN-tuhr) **VAN**

Center/Left wing. Shoots left. 5'10", 181 lbs. Born, Calgary, AB, October 13, 1994.
(Vancouver's 2nd choice, 24th overall, in 2013 Entry Draft).

			Regular Season					Playoffs				
Season	Club	League	GP	G	A	Pts	PIM	GP	G	A	Pts	PIM
2007-08	Calgary Royals	AMBHL	33	10	30	40	24	3	2	2	4	0
2008-09	Calgary Royals	AMBHL	27	32	31	63	10	10	11	11	22	6
2009-10	Calgary Royals	AMHL	3	0	1	1	0	....	....	....	....	....
2010-11	Medicine Hat	WHL	63	14	28	42	24	14	4	5	9	0
2011-12	Medicine Hat	WHL	66	49	42	91	38	8	2	9	11	6
2012-13	Medicine Hat	WHL	64	37	49	86	44	8	3	3	6	8
2013-14	Medicine Hat	WHL	18	5	11	16	29	....	....	....	....	....
2014-15	Utica Comets	AHL	74	16	15	31	28	23	4	2	6	4

WHL East Second All-Star Team (2013)

• Missed majority of 2009-10 season due to leg injury at Fort Saskatchewan.. • Missed majority of 2013-14 due to recurring hip injury and resulting surgery, January 7, 2014..

SHORE, Devin (SHOHR, DEH-vihn) **DAL**

Center. Shoots left. 6'1", 205 lbs. Born, Ajax, ON, July 19, 1994.
(Dallas' 4th choice, 61st overall, in 2012 Entry Draft).

			Regular Season					Playoffs				
Season	Club	League	GP	G	A	Pts	PIM	GP	G	A	Pts	PIM
2009-10	Ajax-Pickering	Minor-ON	68	40	48	88	35	....	....	....	....	....
2010-11	The Hill Academy	High-ON	61	33	62	95	18	....	....	....	....	....
2011-12	Whitby Fury	ON-Jr.A	41	29	29	58	26	23	7	25	32	10
2012-13	U. of Maine	H-East	38	6	20	26	10	....	....	....	....	....
2013-14	U. of Maine	H-East	35	14	29	43	38	....	....	....	....	....
2014-15	U. of Maine	H-East	39	14	21	35	20	....	....	....	....	....
	Texas Stars	AHL	19	4	2	6	4	3	1	0	1	0

Hockey East First All-Star Team (2014) • NCAA East Second All-American Team (2014) • Hockey East Second All-Star Team (2015)

SHORE, Quentin (SHOHR, KWEHN-tihn) **OTT**

Center. Shoots right. 6'2", 190 lbs. Born, Denver, CO, May 25, 1994.
(Ottawa's 7th choice, 168th overall, in 2013 Entry Draft).

			Regular Season					Playoffs				
Season	Club	League	GP	G	A	Pts	PIM	GP	G	A	Pts	PIM
2009-10	Col. Thunderbirds	T1EHL	33	13	13	26	10	....	....	....	....	....
2010-11	USNTDP	USHL	33	3	6	9	14	2	0	0	0	0
	USNTDP	U-17	17	1	8	9	14	....	....	....	....	....
2011-12	USNTDP	USHL	24	8	2	10	15	....	....	....	....	....
	USNTDP	U-18	36	9	8	17	16	....	....	....	....	....
2012-13	U. of Denver	WCHA	39	10	9	22	1	....	....	....	....	....
2013-14	U. of Denver	NCHC	33	7	18	25	16	....	....	....	....	....
2014-15	U. of Denver	NCHC	39	10	16	26	18	....	....	....	....	....

SIDEROFF, Deven (SIH-duhr-awf, DEH-vuhn) **ANA**

Right wing. Shoots right. 5'11", 171 lbs. Born, Kamloops, BC, April 14, 1997.
(Anaheim's 4th choice, 84th overall, in 2015 Entry Draft).

			Regular Season					Playoffs				
Season	Club	League	GP	G	A	Pts	PIM	GP	G	A	Pts	PIM
2012-13	Okanagan H.A.	High-BC	STATISTICS NOT AVAILABLE									
	Okanagan H.A.	CSSHL	12	4	8	12	22	1	0	0	0	0
	Kamloops Blazers	WHL	2	1	1	2	0	....	....	....	....	....
2013-14	Okanagan H.A.	High-BC	15	12	13	25	26	....	....	....	....	....
	Okanagan H.A.	CSSHL	24	18	23	41	40	3	2	6	8	6
	Kamloops Blazers	WHL	12	2	4	6	6	....	....	....	....	....
2014-15	Kamloops Blazers	WHL	64	17	25	42	25	....	....	....	....	....

SIEBENALER, Blake (SEE-beh-nay-luhr, BLAYK) **CBJ**

Defense. Shoots right. 6'1", 201 lbs. Born, Toledo, OH, February 27, 1996.
(Columbus' 4th choice, 77th overall, in 2014 Entry Draft).

			Regular Season					Playoffs				
Season	Club	League	GP	G	A	Pts	PIM	GP	G	A	Pts	PIM
2010-11	Ft. Wayne Car.	High-IN	14	15	11	26	0	4	3	3	6	0
	Ft. Wayne Car.	Other	15	10	6	16	10	....	....	....	....	....
2011-12	Cle. Barons U16	T1EHL	40	5	7	12	6	....	....	....	....	....
2012-13	Det. B. Tire U16	T1EHL	39	9	9	18	22	4	2	1	3	0
	Belle Tire U16	Minor-MI	....	....	....	....	....	7	2	2	4	0
	USNTDP	U-17	4	0	0	0	0	....	....	....	....	....
	Indiana Ice	USHL	11	1	2	3	8	....	....	....	....	....
2013-14	Niagara Ice Dogs	OHL	68	6	24	30	24	7	1	3	4	2
2014-15	Niagara Ice Dogs	OHL	66	12	25	37	30	11	0	1	1	8

SIEGENTHALER, Jonas (zee-GEHN-tahl-uhr, YOH-nuhs) **WSH**

Defense. Shoots left. 6'3", 220 lbs. Born, Zurich, Switzerland, May 6, 1997.
(Washington's 2nd choice, 57th overall, in 2015 Entry Draft).

			Regular Season					Playoffs				
Season	Club	League	GP	G	A	Pts	PIM	GP	G	A	Pts	PIM
2010-11	Zurich U17 II	Swiss-U17	17	6	4	10	24	....	....	....	....	....
	ZSC Zurich U17	Swiss-U17	2	0	0	0	0	5	0	0	0	4
2011-12	ZSC Zurich U17	Swiss-U17	29	3	9	12	103	8	0	2	2	50
	ZSC Zurich Jr.	Swiss-Jr.	2	0	0	0	0	....	....	....	....	....
	GCK Zurich Jr.	Swiss-Jr.	7	0	2	2	4	....	....	....	....	....
2012-13	Zurich U17	Swiss-U17	5	1	7	8	20	5	0	2	2	31
	GCK Zurich Jr.	Swiss-Jr.	34	2	12	14	54	7	0	1	1	8
2013-14	GCK Zurich Jr.	Swiss-Jr.	....	....	....	....	....	7	0	0	0	2
	GCK Lions Zurich	Swiss-2	40	2	6	8	24	....	....	....	....	....
	ZSC Lions Zurich	Swiss	6	0	0	0	2	....	....	....	....	....
2014-15	GCK Lions Zurich	Swiss-2	10	1	7	8	10	....	....	....	....	....
	ZSC Lions Zurich	Swiss	41	0	3	3	39	18	0	2	2	4

SIELOFF, Patrick (SEE-lawf, PAT-rihk) **CGY**

Defense. Shoots left. 6'1", 210 lbs. Born, Ann Arbor, MI, May 15, 1994.
(Calgary's 2nd choice, 42nd overall, in 2012 Entry Draft).

			Regular Season					Playoffs				
Season	Club	League	GP	G	A	Pts	PIM	GP	G	A	Pts	PIM
2009-10	Det. Compuware	T1EHL	37	2	8	10	52	5	0	3	3	0
	Det. Compuware	Other	6	0	3	3	2	....	....	....	....	....
2010-11	USNTDP	USHL	36	1	3	4	66	2	0	0	0	2
	USNTDP	U-17	17	2	3	5	10	....	....	....	....	....
2011-12	USNTDP	USHL	24	0	2	2	55	....	....	....	....	....
	USNTDP	U-18	36	3	5	8	58	....	....	....	....	....
2012-13	Windsor Spitfires	OHL	45	3	8	11	85	....	....	....	....	....
2013-14	Abbotsford Heat	AHL	2	0	0	0	0	....	....	....	....	....
2014-15	Adirondack Flames	AHL	48	2	3	5	78	....	....	....	....	....

• Missed majority of 2013-14 due to broken cheekbone in pre-seaon game vs. Ottawa, September 20, 2013.

SIKURA, Dylan (SIH-koo-ruh, DIH-luhn) **CHI**

Center. Shoots left. 5'9", 158 lbs. Born, Aurora, ON, June 1, 1995.
(Chicago's 7th choice, 178th overall, in 2014 Entry Draft).

			Regular Season					Playoffs				
Season	Club	League	GP	G	A	Pts	PIM	GP	G	A	Pts	PIM
2011-12	Aurora Tigers	ON-Jr.A	44	6	12	18	2	9	2	0	2	0
2012-13	Aurora Tigers	ON-Jr.A	46	8	20	28	28	6	0	1	1	0
2013-14	Aurora Tigers	ON-Jr.A	41	17	47	64	16	21	10	11	21	28
2014-15	Northeastern	H-East	25	5	2	7	0	....	....	....	....	....

SIMON, Dominik (see-MAWN, DOHM-ihn-ihk) **PIT**

Center. Shoots left. 5'11", 176 lbs. Born, Prague, Czech Rep., August 8, 1994.
(Pittsburgh's 2nd choice, 137th overall, in 2015 Entry Draft).

			Regular Season					Playoffs				
Season	Club	League	GP	G	A	Pts	PIM	GP	G	A	Pts	PIM
2009-10	Sparta U18	CzR-U18	4	1	1	2	0	....	....	....	....	....
2010-11	Sparta U18	CzR-U18	38	24	16	40	10	5	2	1	3	4
2011-12	Sparta U18	CzR-U18	14	17	13	30	12	7	3	5	8	4
	Sparta Jr.	CzRep-Jr.	34	11	10	21	2	....	....	....	....	....
2012-13	Sparta Jr.	CzRep-Jr.	11	9	8	17	2	7	7	0	7	2
	HC Sparta Praha	CzRep	18	1	1	2	0	....	....	....	....	....
	Litomerice	CzRep-2	25	9	10	19	24	....	....	....	....	....
2013-14	HC Sparta Praha	CzRep	46	7	4	11	4	10	1	1	2	6
	Litomerice	CzRep-2	3	0	1	1	12	....	....	....	....	....
2014-15	HC Skoda Plzen	CzRep	52	18	12	30	20	4	1	2	3	4

SIMPSON, Dillon (SIHMP-suhn, DIH-luhn) **EDM**

Defense. Shoots left. 6'1", 194 lbs. Born, Edmonton, AB, February 10, 1993.
(Edmonton's 6th choice, 92nd overall, in 2011 Entry Draft).

			Regular Season					Playoffs				
Season	Club	League	GP	G	A	Pts	PIM	GP	G	A	Pts	PIM
2007-08	Southgate	AMBHL	33	7	31	38	32	4	4	2	6	2
2008-09	SSAC Athletics	AMHL	34	3	12	15	8	4	0	0	0	0
	Spruce Grove	AJHL	1	0	0	0	0	1	0	0	0	2
2009-10	Spruce Grove	AJHL	58	12	29	41	19	16	0	6	6	6
2010-11	North Dakota	WCHA	30	2	8	10	8	....	....	....	....	....
2011-12	North Dakota	WCHA	42	2	16	18	8	....	....	....	....	....
2012-13	North Dakota	WCHA	42	5	19	24	12	....	....	....	....	....
2013-14	North Dakota	NCHC	42	7	16	23	20	....	....	....	....	....
2014-15	Oklahoma City	AHL	71	3	14	17	14	10	0	0	0	0

NCHC First All-Star Team (2014)

SINITSYN, Dmitry (sih-NIHT-sihn, dih-MEE-tree) **DAL**

Defense. Shoots left. 6'2", 205 lbs. Born, Moscow, Russia, June 17, 1994.
(Dallas' 9th choice, 183rd overall, in 2012 Entry Draft).

			Regular Season					Playoffs				
Season	Club	League	GP	G	A	Pts	PIM	GP	G	A	Pts	PIM
2010-11	Dallas Stars U16	T1EHL	36	11	20	31	18	....	....	....	....	....
	Dallas Stars U16	Other	21	13	8	21	26	....	....	....	....	....
2011-12	Zelenograd Jr.	Rus.-Jr. B	7	0	0	0	10	....	....	....	....	....
	U. Mass Lowell	H-East	DID NOT PLAY – FRESHMAN									
2012-13	U. Mass Lowell	H-East	13	2	0	2	4	....	....	....	....	....
2013-14	Regina Pats	WHL	69	10	34	44	63	4	0	0	0	6
2014-15	Dynamo Moscow	KHL	15	0	1	1	8	4	1	0	0	0

SJALIN, Pontus (SHA-lihn, PAWN-tuhs) **MIN**

Defense. Shoots left. 6', 175 lbs. Born, Ostersund, Sweden, June 12, 1996.
(Minnesota's 5th choice, 160th overall, in 2014 Entry Draft).

			Regular Season					Playoffs				
Season	Club	League	GP	G	A	Pts	PIM	GP	G	A	Pts	PIM
2011-12	Ostersunds IK U18	Swe-U18	19	2	5	7	8	....	....	....	....	....
2012-13	Ostersunds IK U18	Swe-U18	24	8	5	13	22	....	....	....	....	....
	Ostersunds IK Jr.	Swe-Jr.	4	2	4	6	2	....	....	....	....	....
	Ostersunds IK	Sweden-3	1	1	0	1	0	....	....	....	....	....
2013-14	Ostersunds IK U18	Swe-U18	6	1	2	3	0	....	....	....	....	....
	Ostersunds IK Jr.	Swe-Jr.	8	1	3	4	4	....	....	....	....	....
	Ostersunds IK	Sweden-3	21	3	1	4	8	4	0	0	0	0
2014-15	Leksands IF Jr.	Swe-Jr.	37	3	16	19	18	3	0	3	3	6
	Ostersunds IK	Sweden-3	1	0	0	0	0	....	....	....	....	....
	Leksands IF	Sweden	2	0	0	0	0	....	....	....	....	....

SKJEI, Brady (SHAY, BRAY-dee) **NYR**

Defense. Shoots left. 6'3", 206 lbs. Born, Lakeville, MN, March 26, 1994.
(NY Rangers' 1st choice, 28th overall, in 2012 Entry Draft).

			Regular Season					Playoffs				
Season	Club	League	GP	G	A	Pts	PIM	GP	G	A	Pts	PIM
2009-10	Lakeville North	High-MN	25	7	16	23	24	5	4	2	6	6
2010-11	USNTDP	USHL	36	1	5	6	14	2	0	0	0	0
	USNTDP	U-17	17	4	9	13	10	....	....	....	....	....
2011-12	USNTDP	USHL	24	3	9	12	12	....	....	....	....	....
	USNTDP	U-18	36	1	10	11	24	....	....	....	....	....
2012-13	U. of Minnesota	WCHA	36	1	2	3	14	....	....	....	....	....
2013-14	U. of Minnesota	Big Ten	40	6	8	14	30	....	....	....	....	....
2014-15	U. of Minnesota	Big Ten	33	1	9	10	32	....	....	....	....	....
	Hartford Wolf Pack	AHL	8	0	0	0	0	15	1	2	3	16

SLAVIN, Jaccob (SLA-vihn, JAY-kuhb) **CAR**

Defense. Shoots left. 6'2", 205 lbs. Born, Denver, CO, May 1, 1994.
(Carolina's 6th choice, 120th overall, in 2012 Entry Draft).

			Regular Season					Playoffs				
Season	Club	League	GP	G	A	Pts	PIM	GP	G	A	Pts	PIM
2010-11	Col. Thunderbirds	T1EHL	34	5	21	26	12	....	....	....	....	....
	Chicago Steel	USHL	17	1	0	1	10	....	....	....	....	....
2011-12	Chicago Steel	USHL	60	3	27	30	12	....	....	....	....	....
2012-13	Chicago Steel	USHL	62	5	28	33	6	....	....	....	....	....
2013-14	Colorado College	NCHC	32	5	20	25	11	....	....	....	....	....
2014-15	Colorado College	NCHC	34	5	12	17	2	....	....	....	....	....

NCHC All-Rookie Team (2014) • NCHC Rookie of the Year (2014) • NCHC Second All-Star Team (2014) • NCHC First All-Star Team (2015)

SLEPYSHEV, Anton (SLEHP-ih-shehv, an-TAWN) **EDM**

Left wing. Shoots left. 6'2", 194 lbs. Born, Penza, Russia, May 13, 1994.
(Edmonton's 4th choice, 88th overall, in 2013 Entry Draft).

			Regular Season					Playoffs				
Season	Club	League	GP	G	A	Pts	PIM	GP	G	A	Pts	PIM
2009-10	Dizel Penza 2	Russia-3	39	12	9	21	10	4	1	1	2	4
2010-11	Dizel Penza 2	Russia-3	20	8	4	12	10	....	....	....	....	....
2011-12	Novokuznetsk Jr.	Russia-Jr.	13	7	2	9	6	3	1	0	1	0
	Novokuznetsk	KHL	39	4	3	7	2	....	....	....	....	....
2012-13	Novokuznetsk Jr.	Russia-Jr.	1	0	0	0	0	....	....	....	....	....
	Novokuznetsk	KHL	15	3	0	3	2	....	....	....	....	....
	Ufa	KHL	11	4	2	6	2	14	0	0	0	0
	Tolpar Ufa Jr.	Russia-Jr.	....	....	....	....	....	3	0	1	1	12
2013-14	Tolpar Ufa Jr.	Russia-Jr.	2	2	2	4	0	....	....	....	....	....
	Ufa	KHL	36	3	5	8	4	18	2	1	3	6
2014-15	Ufa	KHL	58	15	10	25	12	5	0	2	2	0

SMALLMAN, Spencer (SMAWL-muhn, SPEHN-suhr) **CAR**

Right wing. Shoots right. 6', 201 lbs. Born, Summerside, PE, September 9, 1996.
(Carolina's 6th choice, 138th overall, in 2015 Entry Draft).

			Regular Season					Playoffs				
Season	Club	League	GP	G	A	Pts	PIM	GP	G	A	Pts	PIM
2011-12	Fredericton	NBPEI	34	16	25	41	4	10	4	*13	17	2
2012-13	Saint John	QMJHL	42	2	4	6	14	4	0	0	0	0
2013-14	Saint John	QMJHL	66	12	23	35	42	....	....	....	....	....
2014-15	Saint John	QMJHL	66	23	33	56	73	5	1	3	4	4

SMITH, Dalton (SMIHTH, DAHL-tuhn)

Left wing. Shoots left. 6'2", 206 lbs. Born, Markham, ON, June 30, 1992.
(Columbus' 2nd choice, 34th overall, in 2010 Entry Draft).

			Regular Season					Playoffs				
Season	Club	League	GP	G	A	Pts	PIM	GP	G	A	Pts	PIM
2007-08	Osh. Generals MM	Minor-ON	62	22	38	60	192	....	....	....	....	....
2008-09	Whitby Fury	ON-Jr.A	40	10	13	23	109	4	2	1	3	12
	Ottawa 67's	OHL	17	2	5	7	8	7	0	0	0	0
2009-10	Ottawa 67's	OHL	62	21	23	44	129	12	3	3	6	27
2010-11	Ottawa 67's	OHL	64	12	17	29	124	4	2	2	4	12
2011-12	Ottawa 67's	OHL	53	15	10	25	67	18	4	4	8	46
2012-13	Springfield Falcons	AHL	67	3	6	9	128	1	0	0	0	12
2013-14	Springfield Falcons	AHL	50	4	5	9	99	....	....	....	....	....
	Syracuse Crunch	AHL	19	2	1	3	51	....	....	....	....	....
2014-15	Syracuse Crunch	AHL	62	11	6	17	79	2	0	0	0	4

Traded to **Tampa Bay** by **Columbus** with Jon Marchessault for Matt Taormina and Dana Tyrell, March 5, 2014.

SMITH, Gemel (SMIHTH, juh-MEHL) **DAL**

Center. Shoots left. 5'10", 200 lbs. Born, Toronto, ON, April 16, 1994.
(Dallas' 6th choice, 104th overall, in 2012 Entry Draft).

			Regular Season					Playoffs				
Season	Club	League	GP	G	A	Pts	PIM	GP	G	A	Pts	PIM
2009-10	North York	GTHL	52	31	51	82	....	....	....	....	....	....
2010-11	Owen Sound	OHL	66	8	8	16	14	21	1	2	3	2
2011-12	Owen Sound	OHL	68	21	39	60	51	5	1	2	3	10
2012-13	Owen Sound	OHL	61	23	29	52	54	12	7	3	10	10
2013-14	Owen Sound	OHL	40	26	22	48	37	....	....	....	....	....
	London Knights	OHL	29	11	16	27	10	9	3	9	12	9
2014-15	Texas Stars	AHL	68	10	17	27	38	....	....	....	....	....

SMITH, Hunter (SMIHTH, HUHN-tuhr) **CGY**

Right wing. Shoots right. 6'7", 220 lbs. Born, Windsor, ON, September 11, 1995.
(Calgary's 3rd choice, 54th overall, in 2014 Entry Draft).

			Regular Season					Playoffs				
Season	Club	League	GP	G	A	Pts	PIM	GP	G	A	Pts	PIM
2010-11	Wind. Jr. Spitfires	Minor-ON	30	15	15	30	64	9	8	0	8	18
	Wind. Jr. Spitfires	Other	10	8	6	14	10	....	....	....	....	....
2011-12	LaSalle Vipers	ON-Jr.B	41	5	9	14	109	4	1	2	3	2
	Windsor Spitfires	OHL	15	1	0	1	19	2	0	0	0	0
2012-13	Oshawa Generals	OHL	30	0	1	1	22	3	0	0	0	0
2013-14	Oshawa Generals	OHL	64	16	24	40	100	12	3	8	11	25
2014-15	Oshawa Generals	OHL	57	23	26	49	122	21	9	9	18	38

SNUGGERUD, Luc (snuh-GUH-rood, LEWK) **CHI**

Defense. Shoots left. 6', 183 lbs. Born, Edina, MN, September 18, 1995.
(Chicago's 5th choice, 141st overall, in 2014 Entry Draft).

			Regular Season					Playoffs				
Season	Club	League	GP	G	A	Pts	PIM	GP	G	A	Pts	PIM
2011-12	Team Southwest	UMHSEL	19	1	12	13	8	3	0	1	1	0
	Eden Prairie Eagles	High-MN	25	5	15	20	14	1	0	0	0	0
2012-13	Team Southeast	UMHSEL	21	1	8	9	14	3	1	2	3	0
	Eden Prairie Eagles	High-MN	25	5	33	38	24	2	0	4	4	2
2013-14	Team Southeast	UMHSEL	19	5	16	21	8	3	0	2	2	2
	Eden Prairie Eagles	High-MN	25	8	30	38	19	6	1	9	10	2
	Muskegon	USHL	3	1	2	3	0	....	....	....	....	....
	Omaha Lancers	USHL	4	0	2	2	6	4	0	1	1	4
2014-15	Nebraska-Omaha	NCHC	39	2	14	16	18	....	....	....	....	....

NCHC All-Rookie Team (2015)

SOBERG, Markus (SHOH-buhrg, MAHR-kuhs) **CBJ**

Right wing. Shoots right. 6', 176 lbs. Born, Oslo, Norway, April 22, 1995.
(Columbus' 7th choice, 165th overall, in 2013 Entry Draft).

			Regular Season					Playoffs				
Season	Club	League	GP	G	A	Pts	PIM	GP	G	A	Pts	PIM
2009-10	Manglerud U17	Nor-U17	8	10	8	18	14	2	2	1	3	10
2010-11	MODO U18	Swe-U18	10	7	7	14	18	....	....	....	....	....
	Manglerud U17	Nor-U17	13	22	20	42	106	7	9	7	16	6
	Manglerud Jr.	Nor-U19	14	21	15	36	22	3	4	0	4	4
2011-12	Frolunda U18	Swe-U18	27	26	16	42	26	4	1	2	3	6
	Frolunda Jr.	Swe-Jr.	25	5	5	10	14	....	....	....	....	....
2012-13	Frolunda U18	Swe-U18	7	4	1	5	10	2	3	4	7	0
	Frolunda Jr.	Swe-Jr.	36	10	16	26	20	6	5	1	6	4
2013-14	Frolunda	Sweden	1	0	0	0	0	....	....	....	....	....
	Frolunda Jr.	Swe-Jr.	45	21	17	38	40	3	1	0	1	6
2014-15	Windsor Spitfires	OHL	61	13	17	30	26	....	....	....	....	....

SODERBERG, Andreas (SOH-duhr-buhrg, ahn-DRAY-uhs) **CHI**

Defense. Shoots left. 6'3", 205 lbs. Born, Skelleftea, Sweden, June 16, 1996.
(Chicago's 6th choice, 148th overall, in 2014 Entry Draft).

			Regular Season					Playoffs				
Season	Club	League	GP	G	A	Pts	PIM	GP	G	A	Pts	PIM
2011-12	Skelleftea AIK U18	Swe-U18	10	0	2	2	0	....	....	....	....	....
2012-13	Skelleftea AIK U18	Swe-U18	39	7	18	25	24	9	0	3	3	2
2013-14	Skelleftea AIK U18	Swe-U18	12	1	2	3	20	3	1	0	1	0
	Skelleftea AIK Jr.	Swe-Jr.	36	1	5	6	14	2	1	0	1	0
2014-15	Skelleftea AIK Jr.	Swe-Jr.	44	1	6	7	34	5	0	0	0	6

SOIN, Sergei (SOY-ihn, SAIR-gay) **NSH**

Center/Left wing. Shoots left. 6', 185 lbs. Born, Moscow, USSR, March 31, 1982.
(Colorado's 3rd choice, 50th overall, in 2000 Entry Draft).

			Regular Season					Playoffs				
Season	Club	League	GP	G	A	Pts	PIM	GP	G	A	Pts	PIM
1997-98	Krylja Sovetov 2	Russia-3	2	0	0	0	0	....	....	....	....	....
1998-99	Krylja Sovetov	Russia	34	1	4	5	12	....	....	....	....	....
99-2000	Krylja Sovetov 2	Russia-3	8	2	3	5	12	....	....	....	....	....
	Krylja Sovetov	Russia-2	32	8	8	16	28	14	0	2	2	6
2000-01	Krylja Sovetov 2	Russia-3	8	2	3	5	12	....	....	....	....	....
	Krylja Sovetov	Russia-2	19	6	3	9	8	11	2	2	4	2
2001-02	Krylja Sovetov 2	Russia-3	5	2	6	8	20	....	....	....	....	....
	Krylja Sovetov	Russia	41	5	7	12	8	....	....	....	....	....
2002-03	Krylja Sovetov	Russia	49	8	6	14	40	....	....	....	....	....
2003-04	CSKA Moscow	Russia	49	1	6	7	32	....	....	....	....	....
2004-05	CSKA Moscow	Russia	19	3	3	6	10	....	....	....	....	....
2005-06	Cherepovets	Russia	48	5	12	17	36	4	1	1	2	0
2006-07	Cherepovets	Russia	52	12	12	24	78	5	2	1	3	0
2007-08	Cherepovets	Russia	52	9	11	20	22	7	1	1	2	4
2008-09	Cherepovets	KHL	51	7	19	26	38	....	....	....	....	....
2009-10	Cherepovets	KHL	52	7	13	20	30	....	....	....	....	....
2010-11	Cherepovets	KHL	54	4	10	14	26	6	1	0	1	0
2011-12	Dynamo Moscow	KHL	52	10	12	22	61	21	0	1	1	22
2012-13	Dynamo Moscow	KHL	35	5	4	9	10	21	4	7	11	26
2013-14	Dynamo Moscow	KHL	19	7	6	13	24	2	0	0	0	6
2014-15	Dynamo Moscow	KHL	40	3	6	9	30	11	3	2	5	8

Traded to **Nashville** by **Colorado** for Tomas Slovak, June 21, 2003.

SOLEWAY, Jedd (SOHL-way, JEHD) **ARI**

Center. Shoots right. 6'2", 220 lbs. Born, Vernon, BC, May 12, 1994.
(Phoenix's 6th choice, 193rd overall, in 2013 Entry Draft).

			Regular Season					Playoffs				
Season	Club	League	GP	G	A	Pts	PIM	GP	G	A	Pts	PIM
2010-11	Okanagan Rockets	BCMML	40	16	17	33	97	....	....	....	....	....
2011-12	Vernon Vipers	BCHL	58	13	12	25	50	....	....	....	....	....
2012-13	Vernon Vipers	BCHL	26	5	12	17	29	....	....	....	....	....
	Penticton Vees	BCHL	22	14	15	29	33	15	5	6	11	6
2013-14	U. of Wisconsin	Big Ten	35	1	7	8	28	....	....	....	....	....
2014-15	U. of Wisconsin	Big Ten	35	7	2	9	48	....	....	....	....	....

SOMERBY, Doyle (SUH-muhr-bee, DOIL) **NYI**

Defense. Shoots left. 6'6", 221 lbs. Born, Marblehead, MA, July 4, 1994.
(NY Islanders' 5th choice, 125th overall, in 2012 Entry Draft).

			Regular Season					Playoffs				
Season	Club	League	GP	G	A	Pts	PIM	GP	G	A	Pts	PIM
2009-10	St. Mary's High	High-MA	24	2	3	5	....	....	....	....	....	....
2010-11	Kimball Union	High-NH	32	2	5	7	18	....	....	....	....	....
2011-12	Kimball Union	High-NH	34	4	20	24	26	....	....	....	....	....
2012-13	Muskegon	USHL	10	2	0	2	6	....	....	....	....	....
2013-14	Boston University	H-East	34	1	3	4	49	....	....	....	....	....
2014-15	Boston University	H-East	39	1	6	7	45	....	....	....	....	....

SONG, Andong (SAWNG, AN-dawng) **NYI**

Defense. Shoots left. 6', 168 lbs. Born, Beijing, China, January 31, 1997.
(NY Islanders' 6th choice, 172nd overall, in 2015 Entry Draft).

			Regular Season					Playoffs				
Season	Club	League	GP	G	A	Pts	PIM	GP	G	A	Pts	PIM
2012-13	Lawrenceville	High-NJ	24	3	5	8	....					
2013-14	Lawrenceville	High-NJ	17	0	7	7	....					
2014-15	Lawrenceville	High-NJ	26	3	7	10	....					

SORENSEN, Nick (SOHR-ehn-sehn, NIHK) **ANA**

Right wing. Shoots right. 6'1", 182 lbs. Born, Holback, Denmark, October 23, 1994.
(Anaheim's 2nd choice, 45th overall, in 2013 Entry Draft).

			Regular Season					Playoffs				
Season	Club	League	GP	G	A	Pts	PIM	GP	G	A	Pts	PIM
2009-10	Rogle U18	Swe-U18	30	22	17	39	22	2	0	0	0	0
2010-11	Rogle U18	Swe-U18	6	7	3	10	4	4	1	0	1	2
	Rogle Jr.	Swe-Jr.	30	18	11	29	34	....	....	....	....	....
	Rogle	Sweden-2	6	0	0	0	2	....	....	....	....	....
2011-12	Quebec Remparts	QMJHL	8	5	4	9	2	....	....	....	....	....
2012-13	Quebec Remparts	QMJHL	46	20	27	47	18	8	7	3	10	10
2013-14	Quebec Remparts	QMJHL	44	31	30	61	43	5	6	3	9	8
	Sweden	Olympics	7	2	4	6	4	....	....	....	....	....
2014-15	Skelleftea AIK	Sweden	14	1	3	4	4	8	0	0	0	2

SOSHNIKOV, Nikita (sohsh-NIH-kauf, nih-kee-tuh) **TOR**

Right wing. Shoots left. 5'11", 183 lbs. Born, Nizhny Tagil, Russia, October 14, 1993.

			Regular Season					Playoffs				
Season	Club	League	GP	G	A	Pts	PIM	GP	G	A	Pts	PIM
2013-14	Mytischi	KHL	33	2	3	5	27	....	....	....	....	....
2014-15	Mytischi	KHL	57	14	18	32	22	....	....	....	....	....

Signed as a free agent by **Toronto**, March 20, 2015.

SOUCY, Carson (SOO-SEE, KAR-suhn) **MIN**

Defense. Shoots left. 6'5", 209 lbs. Born, Viking, AB, July 27, 1994.
(Minnesota's 4th choice, 137th overall, in 2013 Entry Draft).

			Regular Season					Playoffs				
Season	Club	League	GP	G	A	Pts	PIM	GP	G	A	Pts	PIM
2009-10	Lloydminster	Minor-AB	34	1	7	8	58	....	....	....	....	....
2010-11	Lloydminster	AMHL	34	3	8	11	20	2	0	0	0	2
2011-12	Lloydminster	AMHL	30	9	20	29	100	3	0	4	4	10
	Spruce Grove	AJHL	7	0	0	0	4	....	....	....	....	....
2012-13	Spruce Grove	AJHL	35	5	10	15	71	16	1	1	2	30
2013-14	U. Minn-Duluth	NCHC	34	0	6	6	60	....	....	....	....	....
2014-15	U. Minn-Duluth	NCHC	40	6	8	14	40	....	....	....	....	....

SPACEK, Michael (SHPAH-chehk, MIGH-kuhl) **WPG**

Right wing. Shoots right. 5'11", 189 lbs. Born, Marianske Lazne, Czech Rep., April 9, 1997.
(Winnipeg's 5th choice, 108th overall, in 2015 Entry Draft).

			Regular Season					Playoffs				
Season	Club	League	GP	G	A	Pts	PIM	GP	G	A	Pts	PIM
2011-12	HC Pardubice U18	CzR-U18	7	4	1	5	6	....	....	....	....	....
2012-13	HC Pardubice U18	CzR-U18	39	28	22	50	69	2	0	0	0	2
2013-14	HC Pardubice U18	CzR-U18	6	4	5	9	8	....	....	....	....	....
	HC Pardubice Jr.	CzRep-Jr.	31	15	13	28	56	....	....	....	....	....
	Pardubice	CzRep	4	0	0	0	0	....	....	....	....	....
2014-15	HC Pardubice Jr.	CzRep-Jr.	5	2	5	7	38	....	....	....	....	....
	Pardubice	CzRep	40	5	7	12	12	4	0	0	0	0
	HC Pardubice U18	CzR-U18	....	....	....	....	....	4	3	3	6	12

SPEERS, Blake (SPEERZ, BLAYK) **N.J.**

Center. Shoots right. 5'11", 185 lbs. Born, Sault Ste. Marie, ON, January 2, 1997.
(New Jersey's 3rd choice, 67th overall, in 2015 Entry Draft).

			Regular Season					Playoffs				
Season	Club	League	GP	G	A	Pts	PIM	GP	G	A	Pts	PIM
2012-13	Soo Thunder	Minor-ON	61	43	70	113	56	....	....	....	....	....
2013-14	Sault Ste. Marie	OHL	62	19	21	40	12	9	0	3	3	0
2014-15	Sault Ste. Marie	OHL	57	24	43	67	12	14	3	6	9	4

OHL All-Rookie Team (2014)

SPENCER, Matthew (SPEHN-suhr, MA-thew) **T.B.**

Defense. Shoots right. 6'2", 203 lbs. Born, Guelph, ON, March 24, 1997.
(Tampa Bay's 2nd choice, 44th overall, in 2015 Entry Draft).

			Regular Season					Playoffs				
Season	Club	League	GP	G	A	Pts	PIM	GP	G	A	Pts	PIM
2012-13	Oakville Rangers	Minor-ON	40	9	27	36	34	....	....	....	....	....
	Oakville Rangers	Other	31	8	12	20	42	....	....	....	....	....
	Oakville Blades	ON-Jr.A	3	0	0	0	2	1	0	0	0	0
2013-14	Peterborough	OHL	64	1	14	15	33	11	0	4	4	19
2014-15	Peterborough	OHL	67	6	24	30	64	5	1	0	1	2

SPINNER, Steven (SPIH-nuhr, STEE-vehn) **WSH**

Right wing. Shoots right. 6', 202 lbs. Born, Eden Prairie, MN, December 15, 1995.
(Washington's 5th choice, 159th overall, in 2014 Entry Draft).

			Regular Season					Playoffs				
Season	Club	League	GP	G	A	Pts	PIM	GP	G	A	Pts	PIM
2011-12	Eden Prairie Eagles	High-MN	24	20	10	30	21	1	0	0	0	0
2012-13	Team Southeast	UMHSEL	20	10	11	21	28	3	1	4	5	0
	Eden Prairie Eagles	High-MN	23	15	26	41	29	2	4	1	5	4
2013-14	Team Southeast	UMHSEL	20	7	13	20	24	3	3	3	6	4
	Eden Prairie Eagles	High-MN	25	17	22	39	42	6	6	5	11	4
	Muskegon	USHL	3	2	1	3	0	....	....	....	....	....
	Omaha Lancers	USHL	8	0	2	2	14	4	0	0	0	0
2014-15	Omaha Lancers	USHL	56	22	20	42	28	3	0	1	1	6

• Signed Letter of Intent to attend **University of Nebraska Omaha** (NCHC) in fall of 2015.

SPRONG, Daniel (SPRAWNG, DAN-yuhl) **PIT**

Right wing. Shoots right. 6', 180 lbs. Born, Amsterdam, Netherlands, March 17, 1997.
(Pittsburgh's 1st choice, 46th overall, in 2015 Entry Draft).

			Regular Season					Playoffs				
Season	Club	League	GP	G	A	Pts	PIM	GP	G	A	Pts	PIM
2012-13	Lac St-Louis Tigres	Minor-QC	30	48	56	104	36	3	5	3	8	0
2013-14	Charlottetown	QMJHL	67	30	38	68	20	4	4	1	5	0
2014-15	Charlottetown	QMJHL	68	39	49	88	18	10	7	4	11	6

STARRETT, Beau (STAIR-eht, BOH) **CHI**

Center. Shoots left. 6'5", 212 lbs. Born, Framingham, MA, November 1, 1995.
(Chicago's 3rd choice, 88th overall, in 2014 Entry Draft).

			Regular Season					Playoffs				
Season	Club	League	GP	G	A	Pts	PIM	GP	G	A	Pts	PIM
2011-12	Catholic Memorial	High-MA	....	2	5	7	....	....	....	....	....	....
2012-13	South Shore Kings	EmJHL	18	11	11	22	20	....	....	....	....	....
	Catholic Memorial	High-MA	....	9	9	18	....	....	....	....	....	....
2013-14	South Shore Kings	USPHL	48	11	36	47	94	....	....	....	....	....
	South Shore Kings	Other	3	0	3	3	2	....	....	....	....	....
2014-15	South Shore Kings	USPHL	7	2	3	5	6	....	....	....	....	....

• Signed Letter of Intent to attend **Cornell University** (ECAC) in fall of 2015. • Missed majority of 2014-15 due to recurring shoulder injury.

STENLUND, Kevin (STEHN-luhnd, KEH-vihn) **CBJ**

Center. Shoots right. 6'4", 200 lbs. Born, Huddinge, Sweden, September 20, 1996.
(Columbus' 4th choice, 58th overall, in 2015 Entry Draft).

			Regular Season					Playoffs				
Season	Club	League	GP	G	A	Pts	PIM	GP	G	A	Pts	PIM
2011-12	Botkyrka U18	Swe-U18	16	24	15	39	44	5	4	4	8	20
	Botkyrka Jr.	Swe-Jr.	2	0	0	0	0	5	3	0	3	4
	Botkyrka	Sweden-4	1	0	0	0	0	....	....	....	....	....
2012-13	HV 71 U18	Swe-U18	5	1	2	3	0	....	....	....	....	....
2013-14	HV 71 U18	Swe-U18	9	8	3	11	4	....	....	....	....	....
	HV 71 Jr.	Swe-Jr.	29	4	5	9	16	7	1	1	2	0
2014-15	HV 71 Jr.	Swe-Jr.	36	14	22	36	16	6	1	3	4	4
	HV 71 Jonkoping	Sweden	17	1	0	1	2	....	....	....	....	....

STEPAN, Zach (STEH-pan, ZAK) **NSH**

Center. Shoots left. 6', 165 lbs. Born, Hastings, MN, January 6, 1994.
(Nashville's 5th choice, 112th overall, in 2012 Entry Draft).

			Regular Season					Playoffs				
Season	Club	League	GP	G	A	Pts	PIM	GP	G	A	Pts	PIM
2009-10	Shattuck U16	High-MN	40	19	23	42	20	....	....	....	....	....
2010-11	Shat.-St. Mary's	High-MN	54	25	39	64	20	....	....	....	....	....
2011-12	Shat.-St. Mary's	High-MN	50	22	43	65	20	....	....	....	....	....
2012-13	Waterloo	USHL	56	32	46	78	50	5	3	1	4	0
2013-14	Minnesota State	WCHA	35	9	12	21	39	....	....	....	....	....
2014-15	Minnesota State	WCHA	34	3	9	12	12	....	....	....	....	....

STEPHENS, Devante (STEE-vehnz, Deh-VAHN-tay) **BUF**

Defense. Shoots left. 6'1", 171 lbs. Born, Surrey, BC, January 2, 1997.
(Buffalo's 4th choice, 122nd overall, in 2015 Entry Draft).

			Regular Season					Playoffs				
Season	Club	League	GP	G	A	Pts	PIM	GP	G	A	Pts	PIM
2013-14	Valley West Hawks	BCMML	22	6	14	20	32	5	0	2	2	10
2014-15	Kelowna Rockets	WHL	64	4	7	11	33	17	0	4	4	8

STEPHENS, Mitchell (STEE-vehnz, mih-CHUHL) **T.B.**

Center. Shoots right. 5'11", 188 lbs. Born, Peterborough, ON, February 5, 1997.
(Tampa Bay's 1st choice, 33rd overall, in 2015 Entry Draft).

			Regular Season					Playoffs				
Season	Club	League	GP	G	A	Pts	PIM	GP	G	A	Pts	PIM
2012-13	Toronto Marlboros	GTHL	58	44	40	84	12	....	....	....	....	....
2013-14	Saginaw Spirit	OHL	57	9	12	21	8	5	0	2	2	2
2014-15	Saginaw Spirit	OHL	62	22	26	48	44	4	0	0	0	0

STEPHENSON, Chandler (STEE-vehn-suhn, CHAND-luhr) **WSH**

Center/Left wing. Shoots left. 5'11", 190 lbs. Born, Saskatoon, SK, April 22, 1994.
(Washington's 3rd choice, 77th overall, in 2012 Entry Draft).

			Regular Season					Playoffs				
Season	Club	League	GP	G	A	Pts	PIM	GP	G	A	Pts	PIM
2008-09	Sask. Generals	Minor-SK	46	49	61	110	72	....	....	....	....	....
	Saskatoon Blazers	SMHL	9	2	1	3	2	....	....	....	....	....
2009-10	Sask. Contacts	SMHL	42	17	37	54	34	11	5	14	19	4
2010-11	Regina Pats	WHL	60	7	12	19	6	....	....	....	....	....
2011-12	Regina Pats	WHL	55	22	20	42	24	5	1	3	4	0
2012-13	Regina Pats	WHL	46	14	31	45	37	....	....	....	....	....
2013-14	Regina Pats	WHL	69	30	59	89	65	4	0	4	4	0
	Hershey Bears	AHL	2	1	0	1	0	....	....	....	....	....
2014-15	Hershey Bears	AHL	54	7	7	14	10	10	1	4	5	2

WHL East Second All-Star Team (2014)

STEVENS, Luke (STEE-vehnz, LOOK) **CAR**

Left wing. Shoots left. 6'3", 195 lbs. Born, Bellair, CA, February 11, 1997.
(Carolina's 5th choice, 126th overall, in 2015 Entry Draft).

			Regular Season					Playoffs				
Season	Club	League	GP	G	A	Pts	PIM	GP	G	A	Pts	PIM
2013-14	Cape Cod U16	Minor-MA	11	5	5	10	2	....	....	....	....	....
	Nobles	High-MA	28	15	7	22	....	....	....	....	....	....
2014-15	Cape Cod U18	Minor-MA	14	5	12	17	0	....	....	....	....	....
	Nobles	High-MA	23	11	18	29	....	....	....	....	....	....

• Signed Letter of Intent to attend **Yale University** (ECAC) in fall of 2016.

STEVENSON, Dustin (STEE-vehn-suhn, DUHS-tihn)

Defense. Shoots left. 6'5", 215 lbs. Born, Gull Lake, SK, August 12, 1989.

			Regular Season					Playoffs				
Season	Club	League	GP	G	A	Pts	PIM	GP	G	A	Pts	PIM
2007-08	La Ronge	SJHL	53	2	11	13	63	6	0	2	2	2
2008-09	La Ronge	SJHL	53	15	24	39	124	....	....	....	....	....
2009-10	La Ronge	SJHL	56	11	36	47	134	....	....	....	....	....
2010-11	South Carolina	ECHL	63	3	9	12	44	....	....	....	....	....
2011-12	South Carolina	ECHL	72	0	7	7	113	9	1	2	3	6
2012-13	Reading Royals	ECHL	65	0	10	10	103	22	1	8	9	14
2013-14	Wilkes-Barre	AHL	7	0	0	0	7	....	....	....	....	....
	Wheeling Nailers	ECHL	57	5	21	26	115	10	1	3	4	12
2014-15	Adirondack Flames	AHL	45	3	8	11	94	....	....	....	....	....

Signed as a free agent by **Washington**, April 5, 2010. Signed as a free agent by **Wilkes-Barre** (AHL), August 8, 2013. Signed as a free agent by **Adirondack** (AHL), October 9, 2014. Signed as a free agent by **Stockton** (AHL), July 15, 2015.

STEWART, Mackenze (STEW-uhrt, muh-KEHN-zee) **VAN**

Defense. Shoots left. 6'3", 216 lbs. Born, Red Deer, AB, August 10, 1995.
(Vancouver's 7th choice, 186th overall, in 2014 Entry Draft).

			Regular Season					Playoffs				
Season	Club	League	GP	G	A	Pts	PIM	GP	G	A	Pts	PIM
2009-10	Calgary Blazers	Minor-AB	STATISTICS NOT AVAILABLE									
	Calgary Northstars	AMBHL	1	0	0	0	0	....	....	....	....	....
2010-11	Edge Maroon	Minor-AB	12	0	5	5	0	....	....	....	....	....
	Edge Maroon	CSSHL	24	3	10	13	8	6	0	1	1	2
	Edge School	MPHL	1	1	0	1	0	....	....	....	....	....
2011-12	High River Flyers	HJHL	13	1	1	2	8	....	....	....	....	....
	Okotoks Bisons	HJHL	12	3	6	9	12	....	....	....	....	....
	Calgary Blazers	CgJHL	STATISTICS NOT AVAILABLE									
2012-13	Prince Albert	WHL	6	0	0	0	2	....	....	....	....	....
	Calgary Mustangs	AJHL	33	1	4	5	65	3	0	0	0	17
2013-14	Prince Albert	WHL	55	5	4	9	69	4	0	1	1	2
2014-15	Prince Albert	WHL	66	5	6	11	114	....	....	....	....	....

STORM, Ben (STOHRM, BEHN) **COL**

Defense. Shoots left. 6'6", 220 lbs. Born, Laurium, MI, March 30, 1994.
(Colorado's 6th choice, 153rd overall, in 2013 Entry Draft).

			Regular Season					Playoffs				
Season	Club	League	GP	G	A	Pts	PIM	GP	G	A	Pts	PIM
2009-10	Calumet High	High-MI	29	13	14	27	35	....	....	....	....	....
2010-11	Calumet High	High-MI	30	11	19	30	34	....	....	....	....	....
2011-12	Calumet High	High-MI	26	15	20	35	24	....	....	....	....	....
2012-13	Muskegon	USHL	52	2	10	12	82	3	0	0	0	2
2013-14	St. Cloud State	NCHC	30	0	1	1	14	....	....	....	....	....
2014-15	St. Cloud State	NCHC	33	2	3	5	14	....	....	....	....	....

STOYKEWYCH, Peter (STOY-kuh-wihch, PEE-tuhr) **WPG**

Defense. Shoots left. 6'2", 190 lbs. Born, Winnipeg, MB, July 14, 1992.
(Atlanta's 9th choice, 199th overall, in 2010 Entry Draft).

			Regular Season					Playoffs				
Season	Club	League	GP	G	A	Pts	PIM	GP	G	A	Pts	PIM
2007-08	Winnipeg Wild	MMHL	39	1	21	22	22	....	....	....	....	....
2008-09	Wpg. South Blues	MJHL	28	2	7	9	....	....	....	....	....	....
2009-10	Wpg. South Blues	MJHL	56	6	25	31	63	4	1	0	1	16
2010-11	Des Moines	USHL	58	5	10	15	77	....	....	....	....	....
2011-12	Colorado College	WCHA	26	0	3	3	14	....	....	....	....	....
2012-13	Colorado College	WCHA	42	2	9	11	20	....	....	....	....	....
2013-14	Colorado College	NCHC	37	1	8	9	46	....	....	....	....	....
2014-15	Colorado College	NCHC	34	3	8	11	42	....	....	....	....	....
	St. John's IceCaps	AHL	6	0	1	1	11	....	....	....	....	....

• Transferred to **Winnipeg** after **Atlanta** franchise relocated, June 21, 2011.

STRANSKY, Matej (STRAHN-skee, MAH-tay) **DAL**

Right wing. Shoots right. 6'3", 210 lbs. Born, Ostrava, Czech Rep., July 11, 1993.
(Dallas' 5th choice, 165th overall, in 2011 Entry Draft).

			Regular Season					Playoffs				
Season	Club	League	GP	G	A	Pts	PIM	GP	G	A	Pts	PIM
2006-07	HC Vitkovice U17	CzR-U17	1	0	0	0	0	....	....	....	....	....
2007-08	HC Vitkovice U17	CzR-U17	43	5	14	19	22	3	1	1	2	2
2008-09	HC Vitkovice U17	CzR-U17	46	40	23	63	68	7	5	5	10	6
2009-10	HC Vitkovice U18	CzR-U18	43	17	33	50	112	2	1	2	3	4
	HC Vitkovice Jr.	CzRep-Jr.	11	2	1	3	4	....	....	....	....	....
2010-11	Saskatoon Blades	WHL	71	14	12	26	53	10	3	6	9	8
2011-12	Saskatoon Blades	WHL	70	39	42	81	75	4	1	1	2	2
2012-13	Saskatoon Blades	WHL	72	40	45	85	88	4	0	0	0	4
2013-14	Texas Stars	AHL	65	9	14	23	53	21	1	4	5	10
2014-15	Texas Stars	AHL	70	7	12	19	60	2	0	0	0	0

STROME, Dylan (STROHM, DIH-luhn) **ARI**

Center. Shoots left. 6'3", 185 lbs. Born, Mississauga, ON, March 7, 1997.
(Arizona's 1st choice, 3rd overall, in 2015 Entry Draft).

			Regular Season					Playoffs				
Season	Club	League	GP	G	A	Pts	PIM	GP	G	A	Pts	PIM
2012-13	Toronto Marlboros	GTHL	60	65	78	143	8	....	....	....	....	....
2013-14	Erie Otters	OHL	60	10	29	39	11	14	3	6	9	0
2014-15	Erie Otters	OHL	68	45	*84	*129	32	20	10	12	22	12

OHL Second All-Star Team (2015)

SUBBAN, Jordan (soo-BAN, JOHR-duhn) **VAN**

Defense. Shoots right. 5'9", 175 lbs. Born, Rexdale, ON, March 3, 1995.
(Vancouver's 4th choice, 115th overall, in 2013 Entry Draft).

			Regular Season					Playoffs				
Season	Club	League	GP	G	A	Pts	PIM	GP	G	A	Pts	PIM
2010-11	Toronto Marlboros	GTHL	68	21	43	64	64	....	....	....	....	....
2011-12	Belleville Bulls	OHL	56	5	15	20	31	5	0	0	0	4
2012-13	Belleville Bulls	OHL	68	15	36	51	47	17	2	3	5	20
2013-14	Belleville Bulls	OHL	66	12	30	42	63	....	....	....	....	....
2014-15	Belleville Bulls	OHL	63	25	27	52	62	4	3	0	3	2

SULLIVAN, Colin (SUHL-ih-vuhn, KAWL-ihn) **MTL**

Defense. Shoots right. 6'1", 197 lbs. Born, Milford, CT, March 26, 1993.
(Montreal's 6th choice, 198th overall, in 2011 Entry Draft).

			Regular Season					Playoffs				
Season	Club	League	GP	G	A	Pts	PIM	GP	G	A	Pts	PIM
2009-10	Avon Old Farms	High-CT	29	1	8	9	16	....	....	....	....	....
2010-11	Avon Old Farms	High-CT	27	3	12	15	14	....	....	....	....	....
2011-12	Avon Old Farms	High-CT	24	7	9	16	24	....	....	....	....	....
2012-13	Boston College	H-East	32	0	1	1	6	....	....	....	....	....
2013-14	Green Bay	USHL	41	2	6	8	46	4	0	0	0	2
2014-15	Miami U.	NCHC	9	0	1	1	4	....	....	....	....	....

SUMMERS, Kelly (SUH-muhrz, KEH-lee) **OTT**

Defense. Shoots right. 6'2", 201 lbs. Born, Renfrew, ON, April 29, 1996.
(Ottawa's 4th choice, 189th overall, in 2014 Entry Draft).

			Regular Season					Playoffs				
Season	Club	League	GP	G	A	Pts	PIM	GP	G	A	Pts	PIM
2011-12	Ott. Valley Titans	Minor-ON	30	9	22	31	20	8	3	6	9	....
	Carleton Place	ON-Jr.A	2	0	0	0	0	....	....	....	....	....
2012-13	Carleton Place	ON-Jr.A	59	13	20	33	14	12	1	1	2	4
2013-14	Carleton Place	ON-Jr.A	56	17	43	60	12	16	5	8	13	4
2014-15	Clarkson Knights	ECAC	33	6	4	10	4	....	....	....	....	....

ECAC All-Rookie Team (2015)

SUNDQVIST, Oscar (SUHND-qvihst, AWS-kuhr) **PIT**

Center. Shoots right. 6'3", 209 lbs. Born, Boden, Sweden, March 23, 1994.
(Pittsburgh's 4th choice, 81st overall, in 2012 Entry Draft).

			Regular Season					Playoffs				
Season	Club	League	GP	G	A	Pts	PIM	GP	G	A	Pts	PIM
2010-11	Skelleftea AIK Jr.	Swe-Jr.	1	0	0	0	0	....	....	....	....	....
	Skelleftea AIK U18	Swe-U18	38	19	16	35	100	8	1	0	1	29
2011-12	Skelleftea AIK Jr.	Swe-Jr.	2	1	0	1	0	....	....	....	....	....
	Skelleftea AIK U18	Swe-U18	39	21	32	53	129	7	5	5	10	14
2012-13	Skelleftea AIK	Sweden	14	1	0	1	8	....	....	....	....	....
	Skelleftea AIK Jr.	Swe-Jr.	38	17	16	33	48	5	3	2	5	4
2013-14	Skelleftea AIK	Sweden	51	6	10	16	16	13	4	2	6	16
	Sweden	Olympics	7	2	0	2	4	....	....	....	....	....
2014-15	Skelleftea AIK	Sweden	41	9	10	19	34	15	1	4	5	18

SVECHNIKOV, Evgeni (svech-NIH-kawv, ehv-GEH-nee) **DET**

Left wing. Shoots left. 6'3", 205 lbs. Born, Neftegorsk, Russia, October 31, 1996.
(Detroit's 1st choice, 19th overall, in 2015 Entry Draft).

			Regular Season					Playoffs				
Season	Club	League	GP	G	A	Pts	PIM	GP	G	A	Pts	PIM
2012-13	Irbis Kazan Jr.	Rus.-Jr. B	6	2	2	4	6	....	....	....	....	....
	Bars Kazan Jr.	Russia-Jr.	34	9	9	18	34	4	1	1	2	2
2013-14	Ak Bars Kazan	KHL	3	0	0	0	0	....	....	....	....	....
	Bars Kazan Jr.	Russia-Jr.	29	14	13	27	68	6	4	1	5	14
2014-15	Cape Breton	QMJHL	55	32	46	78	70	7	1	6	7	14

SVEDBERG, Viktor (SVEHD-buhrg, VIHK-tuhr) **CHI**

Defense. Shoots left. 6'8", 238 lbs. Born, Gothenburg, Sweden, May 24, 1991.

			Regular Season					Playoffs				
Season	Club	League	GP	G	A	Pts	PIM	GP	G	A	Pts	PIM
2009-10	Frolunda Jr.	Swe-Jr.	40	4	10	14	85	....	....	....	....	....
2010-11	Frolunda Jr.	Swe-Jr.	41	5	17	22	73	7	0	1	1	10
	Frolunda	Sweden	9	0	0	0	0	....	....	....	....	....
2011-12	Frolunda Jr.	Swe-Jr.	6	1	2	3	4	....	....	....	....	....
	Frolunda	Sweden	55	3	2	5	20	6	0	0	0	0
2012-13	Frolunda Jr.	Swe-Jr.	1	0	0	0	2	....	....	....	....	....
	Frolunda	Sweden	51	0	2	2	24	6	0	0	0	4
2013-14	Rockford IceHogs	AHL	35	2	7	9	26	....	....	....	....	....
2014-15	Rockford IceHogs	AHL	49	3	11	14	41	8	0	4	4	8

Signed as a free agent by **Rockford** (AHL), May 16, 2013. Signed as a free agent by **Chicago**, October 19, 2013. • Missed remainder of 2013-14 due to shoulder injury vs. Chicago (AHL), February 14, 2014.

TAMBELLINI, Adam (tam-buh-LEE-nee, A-duhm) NYR

Center. Shoots left. 6'3", 195 lbs. Born, Port Moody, BC, November 1, 1994.
(NY Rangers' 1st choice, 65th overall, in 2013 Entry Draft).

			Regular Season					Playoffs				
Season	Club	League	GP	G	A	Pts	PIM	GP	G	A	Pts	PIM
2008-09	Southgate	AMBHL	33	6	13	19	4	11	1	3	4	2
2009-10	SSAC Bulldogs	Minor-AB	34	27	24	51	20	6	6	4	10	10
2010-11	SSAC Athletics	AMHL	33	22	25	47	4	5	4	2	6	0
	Sherwood Park	AJHL	3	1	0	1	0	....	....	....	....	....
2011-12	Vernon Vipers	BCHL	55	27	29	56	28	....	....	....	....	....
2012-13	Vernon Vipers	BCHL	36	22	17	39	18	....	....	....	....	....
	Surrey Eagles	BCHL	16	14	12	26	8	17	*10	8	*18	6
2013-14	North Dakota	NCHC	16	2	2	4	31	....	....	....	....	....
	Calgary Hitmen	WHL	31	17	22	39	10	6	5	4	9	2
2014-15	Calgary Hitmen	WHL	71	47	39	86	30	16	13	13	26	10

WHL East Second All-Star Team (2015)

TAMMELA, Jonne (tah-MEH-lah, YOH-nay) T.B.

Right wing. Shoots left. 5'11", 185 lbs. Born, Ylivieska, Finland, August 5, 1997.
(Tampa Bay's 5th choice, 118th overall, in 2015 Entry Draft).

			Regular Season					Playoffs				
Season	Club	League	GP	G	A	Pts	PIM	GP	G	A	Pts	PIM
2012-13	JyP Jyvaskyla U18	Fin-U18	21	12	10	22	16	....	....	....	....	....
	JyP Jyvaskyla Jr.	Fin-Jr.	10	1	2	3	18	3	1	0	1	0
2013-14	KalPa Kuopio U18	Fin-U18	3	2	3	5	2	8	6	4	10	0
	KalPa Kuopio Jr.	Fin-Jr.	24	5	11	16	12	....	....	....	....	....
2014-15	KalPa Kuopio Jr.	Fin-Jr.	26	11	16	27	26	....	....	....	....	....
	KalPa Kuopio	Finland	32	4	0	4	6	4	0	0	0	4

TAYLOR, Jeff (TAY-luhr, JEHF) PIT

Defense. Shoots left. 5'11", 181 lbs. Born, Albany, NY, April 13, 1994.
(Pittsburgh's 5th choice, 203rd overall, in 2014 Entry Draft).

			Regular Season					Playoffs				
Season	Club	League	GP	G	A	Pts	PIM	GP	G	A	Pts	PIM
2010-11	Albany	High-NY	36	7	28	35	....	....	....	....	....	....
2011-12	Albany	High-NY	26	10	28	38	....	....	....	....	....	....
2012-13	Dubuque	USHL	57	5	22	27	16	11	0	5	5	4
2013-14	Union College	ECAC	41	3	13	16	18	....	....	....	....	....
2014-15	Union College	ECAC	34	4	27	31	28	....	....	....	....	....

TELEGIN, Ivan (tuh-LEH-gihn, ih-VUHN) WPG

Left wing. Shoots left. 6'4", 185 lbs. Born, Novokuznetsk, Russia, February 28, 1992.
(Atlanta's 3rd choice, 101st overall, in 2010 Entry Draft).

			Regular Season					Playoffs				
Season	Club	League	GP	G	A	Pts	PIM	GP	G	A	Pts	PIM
2008-09	Novokuznetsk 2	Russia-3	STATISTICS NOT AVAILABLE									
2009-10	Saginaw Spirit	OHL	51	26	18	44	20	6	1	1	2	6
2010-11	Saginaw Spirit	OHL	59	20	41	61	35	12	2	8	10	8
2011-12	Barrie Colts	OHL	46	35	29	64	26	13	5	9	14	6
2012-13	St. John's IceCaps	AHL	34	3	7	10	8	....	....	....	....	....
2013-14			DID NOT PLAY – SUSPENDED									
2014-15	CSKA Moscow	KHL	31	3	1	4	29	3	0	0	0	2

• Transferred to **Winnipeg** after **Atlanta** franchise relocated, June 21, 2011. • Missed remainder of 2012-13 • Suspended by **Winnipeg** for failing to report to **St. John's** (AHL), September 29, 2013. • Suspension was lifted by **Winnipeg**, January 30, 2013 but missed remainder of 2013-14 due to various injuries. • Loaned to **CSKA Moscow** (KHL) by **Winnipeg**, January 13, 2014

TERRY, Troy (TAIR-ee, TROY) ANA

Center/Right wing. Shoots right. 5'11", 160 lbs. Born, Denver, CO, September 10, 1997.
(Anaheim's 5th choice, 148th overall, in 2015 Entry Draft).

			Regular Season					Playoffs				
Season	Club	League	GP	G	A	Pts	PIM	GP	G	A	Pts	PIM
2012-13	Col. T-birds U16	T1EHL	41	14	35	49	6	2	0	0	0	0
2013-14	Col. T-birds U16	T1EHL	31	16	25	41	0	....	....	....	....	....
	Indiana Ice	USHL	1	0	0	0	0	....	....	....	....	....
2014-15	USNTDP	USHL	25	6	8	14	4	....	....	....	....	....
	USNTDP	U-18	41	13	17	30	4	....	....	....	....	....

• Signed Letter of Intent to attend **University of Denver** (NCHC) in fall of 2015.

TESINK, Ryan (TEH-sihnk, RIGH-uhn) ST.L.

Center. Shoots left. 6', 172 lbs. Born, Saint John, NB, May 21, 1993.
(St. Louis' 7th choice, 162nd overall, in 2011 Entry Draft).

			Regular Season					Playoffs				
Season	Club	League	GP	G	A	Pts	PIM	GP	G	A	Pts	PIM
2008-09	Holderness School	High-NH	28	4	13	17	....	....	....	....	....	....
2009-10	Woodstock	MJrHL	44	10	19	29	96	14	4	6	10	12
2010-11	Saint John	QMJHL	59	8	27	35	38	19	3	2	5	10
2011-12	Saint John	QMJHL	36	13	27	40	54	17	7	6	13	24
2012-13	Saint John	QMJHL	35	16	21	37	75	....	....	....	....	....
	Blainville-Bois.	QMJHL	6	1	3	4	6	4	1	0	1	23
2013-14	Blainville-Bois.	QMJHL	47	13	23	36	71	14	7	6	13	28
2014-15	Alaska Aces	ECHL	36	2	9	11	39	....	....	....	....	....

THEODORE, Shea (THEE-oh-dohr, SHAY) ANA

Defense. Shoots left. 6'2", 182 lbs. Born, Langley, BC, August 3, 1995.
(Anaheim's 1st choice, 26th overall, in 2013 Entry Draft).

			Regular Season					Playoffs				
Season	Club	League	GP	G	A	Pts	PIM	GP	G	A	Pts	PIM
2010-11	Fraser Valley	BCMML	35	5	24	29	28	....	....	....	....	....
	Seattle	WHL	4	0	0	0	2	....	....	....	....	....
2011-12	Seattle	WHL	69	4	31	35	30	....	....	....	....	....
2012-13	Seattle	WHL	71	19	31	50	32	7	0	2	2	4
2013-14	Seattle	WHL	70	22	57	79	39	9	0	5	5	4
	Norfolk Admirals	AHL	4	0	0	0	0	4	1	2	3	2
2014-15	Seattle	WHL	43	13	35	48	16	6	3	6	9	0
	Norfolk Admirals	AHL	9	4	7	11	2	....	....	....	....	....

WHL West First All-Star Team (2014, 2015)

THOMAS, Ben (TAW-muhs, BEHN) T.B.

Defense. Shoots right. 6'1", 190 lbs. Born, Calgary, AB, May 28, 1996.
(Tampa Bay's 5th choice, 119th overall, in 2014 Entry Draft).

			Regular Season					Playoffs				
Season	Club	League	GP	G	A	Pts	PIM	GP	G	A	Pts	PIM
2009-10	CNHA Blazers	Minor-AB	28	1	3	4	20	2	0	1	1	0
	Calgary Northstars	AMBHL	1	0	0	0	0	....	....	....	....	....
2010-11	Calgary Northstars	AMBHL	32	1	10	11	46	....	....	....	....	....
2011-12	Calgary Northstars	AMHL	34	2	15	17	46	6	0	0	0	8
2012-13	Calgary Mustangs	AJHL	12	1	0	1	4	....	....	....	....	....
	Calgary Canucks	AJHL	31	4	3	7	33	....	....	....	....	....
	Calgary Hitmen	WHL	7	0	0	0	0	1	0	0	0	0
2013-14	Calgary Hitmen	WHL	72	7	24	31	39	6	1	5	6	13
2014-15	Calgary Hitmen	WHL	60	7	24	31	28	17	0	4	4	2

THOMPSON, Garrett (TAWM-suhn, GAIR-eht)

Left wing. Shoots left. 6'3", 205 lbs. Born, Traverse City, MI, March 7, 1990.

			Regular Season					Playoffs				
Season	Club	League	GP	G	A	Pts	PIM	GP	G	A	Pts	PIM
2006-07	Soo Indians	MWEHL	26	6	4	10	30	....	....	....	....	....
	Soo Indians	Other	3	1	0	1	0	....	....	....	....	....
2007-08	Traverse City	NAHL	24	5	2	7	27	....	....	....	....	....
2008-09	Traverse City	NAHL	40	11	12	23	26	5	0	2	2	2
2009-10	Traverse City	NAHL	57	24	26	50	75	10	6	4	10	2
2010-11	Ferris State	CCHA	18	4	2	6	2	....	....	....	....	....
2011-12	Ferris State	CCHA	41	11	12	23	20	....	....	....	....	....
2012-13	Ferris State	CCHA	37	11	15	26	22	....	....	....	....	....
2013-14	Ferris State	WCHA	43	16	16	32	42	....	....	....	....	....
	Binghamton	AHL	7	1	2	3	0	2	0	0	0	0
2014-15	Binghamton	AHL	65	6	8	14	33	....	....	....	....	....

WCHA Second All-Star Team (2014)

Signed as a free agent by **Ottawa**, April 2, 2014.

THOMPSON, Keaton (TAWM-suhn, KEE-tuhn) ANA

Defense. Shoots left. 6', 182 lbs. Born, Edina, MN, September 14, 1995.
(Anaheim's 3rd choice, 87th overall, in 2013 Entry Draft).

			Regular Season					Playoffs				
Season	Club	League	GP	G	A	Pts	PIM	GP	G	A	Pts	PIM
2010-11	Team Great Plains	UMHSEL	16	0	1	1	12	3	0	2	2	4
	Fargo Force	USHL	13	0	0	0	4	2	0	0	0	5
2011-12	USNTDP	USHL	35	4	9	13	17	2	0	0	0	2
	USNTDP	U-17	17	1	8	9	14	....	....	....	....	....
2012-13	USNTDP	USHL	26	3	6	9	18	....	....	....	....	....
	USNTDP	U-18	41	1	12	13	22	....	....	....	....	....
2013-14	North Dakota	NCHC	26	3	5	8	12	....	....	....	....	....
2014-15	North Dakota	NCHC	36	3	8	11	14	....	....	....	....	....

THOMPSON, Paul (TAWM-suhn, PAWL) N.J.

Right wing. Shoots right. 6'1", 205 lbs. Born, Methuen, MA, November 30, 1988.

			Regular Season					Playoffs				
Season	Club	League	GP	G	A	Pts	PIM	GP	G	A	Pts	PIM
2005-06	N.H. Jr. Monarchs	EJHL	38	13	17	30	20	....	....	....	....	....
2006-07	N.H. Jr. Monarchs	EJHL	44	45	38	83	56	....	....	....	....	....
2007-08	New Hampshire	H-East	35	6	6	12	22	....	....	....	....	....
2008-09	New Hampshire	H-East	27	4	5	9	22	....	....	....	....	....
2009-10	New Hampshire	H-East	39	19	20	39	24	....	....	....	....	....
2010-11	New Hampshire	H-East	39	28	24	*52	30	....	....	....	....	....
	Wilkes-Barre	AHL	6	1	2	3	2	4	0	1	1	2
2011-12	Wheeling Nailers	ECHL	1	1	1	2	0	....	....	....	....	....
	Wilkes-Barre	AHL	67	10	15	25	37	12	2	1	3	2
2012-13	Wilkes-Barre	AHL	58	20	9	29	84	15	3	3	6	21
2013-14	Wilkes-Barre	AHL	39	4	3	7	50	....	....	....	....	....
	Springfield Falcons	AHL	30	4	4	8	50	5	0	0	0	5
2014-15	Albany Devils	AHL	73	33	22	55	67	....	....	....	....	....

Hockey East First All-Star Team (2011) • Hockey East Player of the Year (2011) • NCAA East First All-American Team (2011)

Signed as a free agent by **Pittsburgh**, March 28, 2011. Traded to **Columbus** by **Pittsburgh** for Spencer Machacek, February 6, 2014. Signed as a free agent by **New Jersey**, July 1, 2015.

THOMSON, Ben (TAWM-suhn, BEHN) N.J.

Left wing. Shoots left. 6'4", 210 lbs. Born, Brampton, ON, January 16, 1993.
(New Jersey's 4th choice, 96th overall, in 2012 Entry Draft).

			Regular Season					Playoffs				
Season	Club	League	GP	G	A	Pts	PIM	GP	G	A	Pts	PIM
2008-09	Mississauga Reps	GTHL	20	13	25	38	88	....	....	....	....	....
2009-10	Kitchener Rangers	OHL	46	6	6	12	30	11	0	1	1	6
2010-11	Kitchener Rangers	OHL	68	6	13	19	107	7	0	1	1	0
2011-12	Kitchener Rangers	OHL	67	11	31	42	137	16	5	5	10	36
2012-13	Kitchener Rangers	OHL	67	15	17	32	119	10	1	2	3	18
2013-14	Kitchener Rangers	OHL	12	3	3	6	34	....	....	....	....	....
	North Bay	OHL	43	24	15	39	56	22	5	9	14	*64
2014-15	Albany Devils	AHL	67	8	8	16	97	....	....	....	....	....

THROWER, Dalton (THROW-uhr, DAHL-tuhn) MTL

Defense. Shoots right. 6'1", 212 lbs. Born, Squamish, BC, December 20, 1993.
(Montreal's 3rd choice, 51st overall, in 2012 Entry Draft).

			Regular Season					Playoffs				
Season	Club	League	GP	G	A	Pts	PIM	GP	G	A	Pts	PIM
2008-09	Van. NW Giants	BCMML	31	8	11	19	72	5	1	0	1	6
2009-10	Saskatoon Blades	WHL	55	0	7	7	61	8	0	1	1	2
2010-11	Saskatoon Blades	WHL	68	6	14	20	91	10	2	1	3	11
2011-12	Saskatoon Blades	WHL	66	18	36	54	103	4	0	1	1	4
2012-13	Saskatoon Blades	WHL	54	6	21	27	89	4	0	0	0	6
2013-14	Vancouver Giants	WHL	42	12	27	39	70	....	....	....	....	....
2014-15	Brampton Beast	ECHL	37	3	3	6	107	....	....	....	....	....

TIFFELS, Frederik (TIH-fuhlz, FREHD-uhr-ihk) PIT

Left wing. Shoots left. 6', 200 lbs. Born, Cologne, Germany, May 20, 1995.
(Pittsburgh's 3rd choice, 167th overall, in 2015 Entry Draft).

			Regular Season					Playoffs				
Season	Club	League	GP	G	A	Pts	PIM	GP	G	A	Pts	PIM
2010-11	Heil./Mann. Jr.	Ger-Jr.	36	9	23	32	12	4	0	0	0	2
2011-12	Heil./Mann. Jr.	Ger-Jr.	36	6	22	28	6	8	3	5	8	0
2012-13	Muskegon	USHL	50	3	22	25	10	3	1	0	1	0
2013-14	Muskegon	USHL	13	3	2	5	4	....	....	....	....	....
	Fargo Force	USHL	12	1	4	5	2	....	....	....	....	....
	Cedar Rapids	USHL	31	9	18	27	4	4	1	0	1	2
2014-15	Western Mich.	NCHC	32	11	10	21	14	....	....	....	....	....

TIMASHOV, Dmytro (tihm-ah-SHAWV, dih-mih-TROH) TOR

Left wing. Shoots left. 5'9", 192 lbs. Born, Kirovograd, Ukraine, October 1, 1996.
(Toronto's 7th choice, 125th overall, in 2015 Entry Draft).

			Regular Season					Playoffs				
Season	Club	League	GP	G	A	Pts	PIM	GP	G	A	Pts	PIM
2011-12	SDE U18	Swe-U18	17	10	13	23	37	....	....	....	....	....
	Djurgarden U18	Swe-U18	17	2	4	6	4	4	0	0	0	0
2012-13	Djurgarden U18	Swe-U18	11	4	5	9	8	....	....	....	....	....
	Djurgarden Jr.	Swe-Jr.	22	4	6	10	8	....	....	....	....	....
	MODO U18	Swe-U18	2	2	1	3	0	2	0	1	1	0
	MODO Jr.	Swe-Jr.	16	5	7	12	4	7	0	1	1	0
2013-14	MODO Jr.	Swe-Jr.	40	12	29	41	18	6	0	1	1	8
	MODO	Sweden	3	0	1	1	0	....	....	....	....	....
	Mora IK	Sweden-2	6	0	1	1	2	....	....	....	....	....
	IF Bjorkloven Umea	Sweden-2	4	0	0	0	25	....	....	....	....	....
	MODO U18	Swe-U18	....	....	....	....	....	4	2	5	7	2
2014-15	Quebec Remparts	QMJHL	66	19	71	90	54	22	3	15	18	18

QMJHL All-Rookie Team (2015) • QMJHL Rookie of the Year (2015)

TOEWS, Devon (TAYVZ, deh-VAWN) NYI

Defense. Shoots left. 6'1", 181 lbs. Born, Abbotsford, BC, February 21, 1994.
(NY Islanders' 5th choice, 108th overall, in 2014 Entry Draft).

			Regular Season					Playoffs				
Season	Club	League	GP	G	A	Pts	PIM	GP	G	A	Pts	PIM
2008-09	Abbotsford Hawks	Minor-BC	61	8	56	64	60	....	....	....	....	....
2009-10	Fraser Valley	BCMML	39	2	5	7	60	....	....	....	....	....
	Yale Lions	High-BC	3	2	9	11	0	3	3	8	11	2
2010-11	Fraser Valley	BCMML	39	12	25	37	62	....	....	....	....	....
	Yale Lions	High-BC	4	6	8	14	0	....	....	....	....	....
	Abbotsford Pilots	PIJHL	5	1	1	2	0	13	1	5	6	2
2011-12	Surrey Eagles	BCHL	54	7	22	29	42	12	5	7	12	15
2012-13	Surrey Eagles	BCHL	48	10	37	47	55	17	0	9	9	10
	Surrey Eagles	RB-Cup	....	....	....	....	....	5	1	6	7	6
2013-14	Quinnipiac	ECAC	37	1	16	17	10	....	....	....	....	....
2014-15	Quinnipiac	ECAC	31	4	16	20	16	....	....	....	....	....

TOLCHINSKY, Sergey (tohl-CHIHN-skee, SIHR-gay) CAR

Left wing. Shoots left. 5'8", 170 lbs. Born, Moscow, Russia, February 3, 1995.

			Regular Season					Playoffs				
Season	Club	League	GP	G	A	Pts	PIM	GP	G	A	Pts	PIM
2011-12	CSKA Jr.	Russia-Jr.	51	19	15	34	26	15	2	2	4	6
2012-13	Sault Ste. Marie	OHL	62	26	25	51	12	6	2	2	4	4
2013-14	Sault Ste. Marie	OHL	66	31	60	91	22	9	2	4	6	4
	Charlotte	AHL	1	0	0	0	0	....	....	....	....	....
2014-15	Sault Ste. Marie	OHL	61	30	65	95	10	14	4	10	14	2

Signed as a free agent by **Carolina**, August 22, 2013.

TOMMERNES, Henrik (TOHM-uhr-nehs, HEHN-rihk) VAN

Defense. Shoots left. 6'1", 176 lbs. Born, Karlstad, Sweden, August 28, 1990.
(Vancouver's 8th choice, 210th overall, in 2011 Entry Draft).

			Regular Season					Playoffs				
Season	Club	League	GP	G	A	Pts	PIM	GP	G	A	Pts	PIM
2006-07	Farjestad U18	Swe-U18	14	3	6	9	32	8	3	4	7	4
2007-08	Farjestad U18	Swe-U18	22	4	16	20	10	8	0	3	3	10
2008-09	Frolunda Jr.	Swe-Jr.	40	10	22	32	52	5	2	6	8	8
	Frolunda	Sweden	11	0	0	0	0	....	....	....	....	....
2009-10	Frolunda Jr.	Swe-Jr.	4	1	1	2	4	....	....	....	....	....
	Boras HC	Sweden-2	23	5	9	14	43	....	....	....	....	....
	Frolunda	Sweden	27	0	3	3	10	7	0	1	1	2
2010-11	Frolunda	Sweden	47	3	17	20	24	....	....	....	....	....
2011-12	Frolunda	Sweden	44	5	9	14	36	6	1	3	4	4
2012-13	Frolunda	Sweden	54	5	11	16	28	6	1	4	5	6
2013-14	Utica Comets	AHL	54	4	14	18	14	....	....	....	....	....
2014-15	Utica Comets	AHL	23	3	8	11	8	....	....	....	....	....
	Tappara Tampere	Finland	22	2	8	10	18	20	2	5	7	8

Signed as a free agent by **Tappara Tampere** (Finland), January 11, 2015. Signed as a free agent by **Frolunda** (Sweden), April 29, 2015.

TONINATO, Dominic (toh-nee-NAH-toh, DOHM-ihn-ihk) TOR

Center. Shoots left. 6'1", 185 lbs. Born, Duluth, MN, March 9, 1994.
(Toronto's 3rd choice, 126th overall, in 2012 Entry Draft).

			Regular Season					Playoffs				
Season	Club	League	GP	G	A	Pts	PIM	GP	G	A	Pts	PIM
2009-10	Duluth East	High-MN	25	4	7	11	6	6	4	4	8	6
2010-11	Team North	UMHSEL	24	11	8	19	12	....	....	....	....	....
	Duluth East	High-MN	23	24	27	51	12	6	6	4	10	0
2011-12	Team North	UMHSEL	24	10	15	25	30	....	....	....	....	....
	Duluth East	High-MN	25	27	34	61	28	6	6	6	12	4
	Fargo Force	USHL	4	1	0	1	2	....	....	....	....	....
2012-13	Fargo Force	USHL	64	29	41	70	50	12	3	3	6	6
2013-14	U. Minn-Duluth	NCHC	35	7	8	15	51	....	....	....	....	....
2014-15	U. Minn-Duluth	NCHC	34	16	10	26	58	....	....	....	....	....

USHL Second All-Star Team (2013)

TOUSIGNANT, Mathieu (TOO-saynt, ma-t'yoo) CGY

Center. Shoots left. 6', 182 lbs. Born, St-Etienne De Lauzon, QC, November 21, 1989.

			Regular Season					Playoffs				
Season	Club	League	GP	G	A	Pts	PIM	GP	G	A	Pts	PIM
2004-05	Magog	QAAA	8	2	1	3	0	....	....	....	....	....
2005-06	Magog	QAAA	43	22	36	58	50	13	6	9	15	26
	Baie-Comeau	QMJHL	1	0	1	1	2	....	....	....	....	....
2006-07	Baie-Comeau	QMJHL	70	8	25	33	93	9	2	2	4	9
2007-08	Baie-Comeau	QMJHL	36	14	20	34	68	....	....	....	....	....
	P.E.I. Rocket	QMJHL	27	8	14	22	61	4	2	4	6	14
2008-09	P.E.I. Rocket	QMJHL	35	14	24	38	72	....	....	....	....	....
	Chicoutimi	QMJHL	33	15	24	39	73	4	1	1	2	11
2009-10	Texas Stars	AHL	45	4	3	7	62	....	....	....	....	....
	Idaho Steelheads	ECHL	20	6	11	17	53	13	1	2	3	27
2010-11	Texas Stars	AHL	78	10	13	23	120	5	1	0	1	0
2011-12	Texas Stars	AHL	35	2	5	7	32	....	....	....	....	....
2012-13	Idaho Steelheads	ECHL	28	4	15	19	77	....	....	....	....	....
	Texas Stars	AHL	18	1	0	1	10	....	....	....	....	....
	St. John's IceCaps	AHL	5	0	1	1	17	....	....	....	....	....
2013-14	Milwaukee	AHL	76	8	13	21	158	3	0	0	0	2
2014-15	Adirondack Flames	AHL	70	5	14	19	136	....	....	....	....	....

Signed as a free agent by **Dallas**, March 24, 2010. • Missed majority of 2011-12 due to various injuries and as a healthy reserve. Signed as a free agent by **Adirondack** (AHL), July 3, 2014.

TRENIN, Yakov (TREH-nihn, YA-kawv) NSH

Left wing. Shoots left. 6'2", 194 lbs. Born, Chelyabinsk, Russia, January 13, 1997.
(Nashville's 1st choice, 55th overall, in 2015 Entry Draft).

			Regular Season					Playoffs				
Season	Club	League	GP	G	A	Pts	PIM	GP	G	A	Pts	PIM
2013-14	Chelyabinsk Jr.	Russia-Jr.	22	7	7	14	12	4	0	1	1	2
2014-15	Gatineau	QMJHL	58	18	49	67	34	11	3	8	11	10

TROOCK, Branden (TROOK, BRAN-duhn) DAL

Right wing. Shoots right. 6'3", 215 lbs. Born, Edmonton, AB, March 20, 1994.
(Dallas' 7th choice, 134th overall, in 2012 Entry Draft).

			Regular Season					Playoffs				
Season	Club	League	GP	G	A	Pts	PIM	GP	G	A	Pts	PIM
2008-09	CAC Lehigh	AMBHL	32	21	28	49	82	....	....	....	....	....
2009-10	CAC Gregg's Dist.	AMHL	27	19	18	37	38	2	0	3	3	2
	Seattle	WHL	9	2	4	6	4	....	....	....	....	....
2010-11			DID NOT PLAY – INJURED									
2011-12	Seattle	WHL	58	14	12	26	83	....	....	....	....	....
2012-13	Seattle	WHL	19	5	6	11	19	....	....	....	....	....
2013-14	Seattle	WHL	58	24	34	58	69	9	4	3	7	8
	Texas Stars	AHL	1	0	0	0	0	1	0	0	0	0
2014-15	Texas Stars	AHL	49	6	9	15	27	....	....	....	....	....
	Idaho Steelheads	ECHL	5	1	1	2	2	....	....	....	....	....

• Missed remainder of 2009-10 and all of 2010-11 due to head injury, playing for Team Alberta, in Western Canada Under-16 Challenge Tournament, October 31, 2009. • Missed majority of 2012-13 due to shoulder injury vs. Lethbridge (WHL), January 20, 2013.

TRYAMKIN, Nikita (tree-AM-kihn, nih-KEE-tuh) VAN

Defense. Shoots left. 6'7", 228 lbs. Born, Yekaterinburg, Russia, August 30, 1994.
(Vancouver's 4th choice, 66th overall, in 2014 Entry Draft).

			Regular Season					Playoffs				
Season	Club	League	GP	G	A	Pts	PIM	GP	G	A	Pts	PIM
2011-12	Avtomobilist Jr.	Russia-Jr.	60	3	9	12	82	9	0	0	0	8
2012-13	Avtomobilist Jr.	Russia-Jr.	28	8	10	18	58	8	1	2	3	40
	Avtomobilist	KHL	32	3	1	4	12	8	2	0	2	8
2013-14	Avtomobilist Jr.	Russia-Jr.	2	2	1	3	4	1	0	0	0	0
	Avtomobilist	KHL	45	1	6	7	38	4	0	0	0	2
2014-15	Avtomobilist Jr.	Russia-Jr.	3	1	3	4	8	1	0	0	0	12
	Avtomobilist	KHL	58	1	5	6	37	5	0	0	0	12

TSCHANTZ, Dwyer (SHAHNTZ, DWIGH-uhr) ST.L.

Right wing. Shoots right. 6'5", 209 lbs. Born, Wilmington, DE, March 22, 1995.
(St. Louis' 10th choice, 202nd overall, in 2014 Entry Draft).

			Regular Season					Playoffs				
Season	Club	League	GP	G	A	Pts	PIM	GP	G	A	Pts	PIM
2010-11	Phi. Jr. Flyers	T1EHL	36	9	11	20	22	....	....	....	....	....
2011-12	Team Comcast	T1EHL	37	17	15	32	28	....	....	....	....	....
2012-13	Team Comcast	T1EHL	40	20	32	52	28	4	0	0	0	22
	USNTDP	USHL	1	0	0	0	0	....	....	....	....	....
2013-14	Indiana Ice	USHL	52	24	20	44	58	8	0	3	3	7
2014-15	Cornell Big Red	ECAC	19	2	3	5	14	....	....	....	....	....

TUCH, Alex (TUHK, AL-ehx) MIN

Right wing. Shoots right. 6'4", 225 lbs. Born, Syracuse, NY, May 10, 1996.
(Minnesota's 1st choice, 18th overall, in 2014 Entry Draft).

			Regular Season					Playoffs				
Season	Club	League	GP	G	A	Pts	PIM	GP	G	A	Pts	PIM
2011-12	Syracuse Jr. Stars	EmJHL	40	44	57	*101	26	4	1	3	4	4
2012-13	USNTDP	USHL	38	4	6	10	24	....	....	....	....	....
	USNTDP	U-17	18	7	9	16	8	....	....	....	....	....
2013-14	USNTDP	USHL	26	13	19	32	36	....	....	....	....	....
	USNTDP	U-18	35	16	15	31	36	....	....	....	....	....
2014-15	Boston College	H-East	37	14	14	28	28	....	....	....	....	....

Hockey East All-Rookie Team (2015)

TURGEON, Dominic (TUHR-zhawn, DOHM-ihn-ihk) DET

Center. Shoots left. 6'2", 196 lbs. Born, Pointe-Claire, QC, February 25, 1996.
(Detroit's 2nd choice, 63rd overall, in 2014 Entry Draft).

			Regular Season					Playoffs				
Season	Club	League	GP	G	A	Pts	PIM	GP	G	A	Pts	PIM
2010-11	Col. T-Birds U14	Minor-CO	76	44	72	116	12	....	....	....	....	....
2011-12	Col. T-birds U16	T1EHL	40	25	15	40	4	....	....	....	....	....
	Col. T-Birds U16	Minor-CO	22	9	17	26	4	....	....	....	....	....
	Portland	WHL	1	0	0	0	0	....	....	....	....	....
2012-13	Portland	WHL	54	3	5	8	2	5	0	0	0	0
	USNTDP	U-17	7	0	3	3	0	....	....	....	....	....
2013-14	Portland	WHL	65	10	21	31	31	21	2	6	8	18
2014-15	Portland	WHL	67	18	25	43	36	17	8	1	9	0

TUULOLA, Joni (TOO'oo-oh-luh, YOH-nee) CHI

Defense. Shoots left. 6'3", 180 lbs. Born, Hameenlinna, Finland, January 1, 1996.
(Chicago's 6th choice, 181st overall, in 2015 Entry Draft).

			Regular Season					Playoffs				
Season	Club	League	GP	G	A	Pts	PIM	GP	G	A	Pts	PIM
2010-11	HPK U18	Fin-U18	3	0	1	1	2	....	....	....	....	....
2011-12	HPK U18	Fin-U18	24	1	7	8	28	....	....	....	....	....
2012-13	HPK U18	Fin-U18	41	10	21	31	26	7	0	1	1	25
	HPK Jr.	Fin-Jr.	6	1	0	1	4	....	....	....	....	....
2013-14	HPK U18	Fin-U18	10	3	9	12	2	1	0	0	0	2
	HPK Jr.	Fin-Jr.	47	8	16	24	34	3	0	0	0	0
	HPK Hameenlinna	Finland	2	1	0	1	0	2	0	0	0	0
2014-15	HPK Jr.	Fin-Jr.	6	0	4	4	2	....	....	....	....	....
	HPK Hameenlinna	Finland	32	5	5	10	8	....	....	....	....	....

TVRDON, Marek (T'VAIR-doin, MAIR-ehk) DET

Right wing. Shoots left. 6'3", 220 lbs. Born, Nitra, Slovakia, January 31, 1993.
(Detroit's 5th choice, 115th overall, in 2011 Entry Draft).

			Regular Season					Playoffs				
Season	Club	League	GP	G	A	Pts	PIM	GP	G	A	Pts	PIM
2007-08	HK Ardo Nitra U18	Svk-U18	20	5	4	9	10	....	....	....	....	....
2008-09	HK Nitra U18	Svk-U18	58	50	33	83	113	....	....	....	....	....
	HK Nitra Jr.	Slovak-Jr.	....	....	....	....	....	1	0	0	0	0
2009-10	HK Nitra Jr.	Slovak-Jr.	45	25	31	56	90	....	....	....	....	....
	HK Nitra	Slovakia	6	0	0	0	2	1	0	0	0	0
2010-11	Vancouver Giants	WHL	12	6	5	11	14	....	....	....	....	....
2011-12	Vancouver Giants	WHL	60	31	43	74	62	6	3	3	6	0
2012-13	Vancouver Giants	WHL	18	8	14	22	16	....	....	....	....	....
2013-14	Kelowna Rockets	WHL	29	11	16	27	24	14	5	8	13	14
	Grand Rapids	AHL	1	0	0	0	0	....	....	....	....	....
	Toledo Walleye	ECHL	22	9	4	13	6	....	....	....	....	....
2014-15	Grand Rapids	AHL	51	10	19	29	16	13	2	4	6	2
	Toledo Walleye	ECHL	24	6	18	24	14	....	....	....	....	....

TYNAN, TJ (TIGH-nuhn, TEE-JAY) CBJ

Center. Shoots right. 5'8", 165 lbs. Born, Orland Park, IL, February 25, 1992.
(Columbus' 2nd choice, 66th overall, in 2011 Entry Draft).

			Regular Season					Playoffs				
Season	Club	League	GP	G	A	Pts	PIM	GP	G	A	Pts	PIM
2009-10	Des Moines	USHL	60	17	*55	72	55	....	....	....	....	....
2010-11	U. of Notre Dame	CCHA	44	23	31	54	36	....	....	....	....	....
2011-12	U. of Notre Dame	CCHA	39	13	28	41	38	....	....	....	....	....
2012-13	U. of Notre Dame	CCHA	41	10	18	28	28	....	....	....	....	....
2013-14	U. of Notre Dame	H-East	40	8	30	38	30	....	....	....	....	....
	Springfield Falcons	AHL	3	0	0	0	2	....	....	....	....	....
2014-15	Springfield Falcons	AHL	75	13	35	48	48	....	....	....	....	....

USHL All-Rookie Team (2010) • CCHA All-Rookie Team (2011) • CCHA Second All-Star Team (2011) • CCHA Rookie of the Year (2011) • CCHA First All-Star Team (2012)

TYRVAINEN, Antti (TUHR-va-nihn, AHN-tee) EDM

Left wing. Shoots left. 5'10", 198 lbs. Born, Seinajoki, Finland, April 3, 1989.

			Regular Season					Playoffs				
Season	Club	League	GP	G	A	Pts	PIM	GP	G	A	Pts	PIM
2006-07	Pelicans Lahti Jr.	Fin-Jr.	19	1	4	5	51	....	....	....	....	....
2007-08	Pelicans Lahti Jr.	Fin-Jr.	41	5	13	18	56	....	....	....	....	....
2008-09	Pelicans Lahti Jr.	Fin-Jr.	27	9	9	18	104	....	....	....	....	....
	HeKi Heinola	Finland-2	3	0	0	0	25	....	....	....	....	....
	Pelicans Lahti	Finland	5	0	0	0	0	1	0	0	0	0
2009-10	Pelicans Lahti	Finland	32	8	3	11	85	....	....	....	....	....
2010-11	Pelicans Lahti	Finland	52	14	9	23	186	....	....	....	....	....
	Pelicans Lahti	Finland-Q	....	....	....	....	....	4	3	2	5	24
2011-12	Oklahoma City	AHL	55	6	13	19	71	14	0	1	1	20
2012-13	Oklahoma City	AHL	32	3	2	5	65	16	3	3	6	28
2013-14	Jokerit Helsinki	Finland	41	5	9	14	142	2	0	0	0	10
2014-15	Ilves Tampere	Finland	46	10	10	20	89	2	1	0	1	18

Signed as a free agent by **Edmonton**, June 15, 2011. Signed as a free agent by **Jokerit Helsinki** (Finland), June 6, 2013. Signed as a free agent by **Ilves Tampere** (Finland), April 24, 2014.

ULLY, Cole (YEW-lee, KOHL) DAL

Left wing. Shoots left. 5'11", 170 lbs. Born, Calgary, AB, February 20, 1995.
(Dallas' 7th choice, 131st overall, in 2013 Entry Draft).

			Regular Season					Playoffs				
Season	Club	League	GP	G	A	Pts	PIM	GP	G	A	Pts	PIM
2010-11	Calgary Flames	AMHL	32	17	17	34	20	2	0	0	0	0
	Kamloops Blazers	WHL	1	0	1	1	0	....	....	....	....	....
2011-12	Kamloops Blazers	WHL	55	9	11	20	2	6	1	1	2	2
2012-13	Kamloops Blazers	WHL	62	22	28	50	37	15	1	7	8	4
2013-14	Kamloops Blazers	WHL	69	30	42	72	34	....	....	....	....	....
2014-15	Kamloops Blazers	WHL	69	34	60	94	32	....	....	....	....	....
	Texas Stars	AHL	2	0	1	1	0	....	....	....	....	....

WHL West First All-Star Team (2015)

USTASKI, Matt (YEW-staz-kee, MAT) WPG

Center. Shoots left. 6'6", 228 lbs. Born, Glenview, IL, May 27, 1994.
(Winnipeg's 7th choice, 192nd overall, in 2014 Entry Draft).

			Regular Season					Playoffs				
Season	Club	League	GP	G	A	Pts	PIM	GP	G	A	Pts	PIM
2011-12	Lake Forest	MPHL	13	3	6	9	2	3	1	0	1	17
	Lake Forest	High-IL	....	10	12	22	....	....	....	....	....	....
2012-13	Langley Rivermen	BCHL	55	11	16	27	38	....	....	....	....	....
2013-14	Langley Rivermen	BCHL	54	29	20	49	30	....	....	....	....	....
2014-15	U. of Wisconsin	Big Ten	24	4	4	8	20	....	....	....	....	....

VAHATALO, Julius (vah-hah-TAL-oh, YOO-lee-uhs) DET

Center. Shoots left. 6'5", 191 lbs. Born, Vahto, Finland, March 23, 1995.
(Detroit's 5th choice, 166th overall, in 2014 Entry Draft).

			Regular Season					Playoffs				
Season	Club	League	GP	G	A	Pts	PIM	GP	G	A	Pts	PIM
2010-11	TuTo Turku U18	Fin-U18	27	4	9	13	35	....	....	....	....	....
2011-12	TuTo Turku U17	Fin-U17	5	1	0	1	4	....	....	....	....	....
	TuTo Turku U18	Fin-U18	6	3	3	6	2	....	....	....	....	....
	TPS Turku U18	Fin-U18	17	5	12	17	14	6	2	4	6	0
	TPS Turku Jr.	Fin-Jr.	8	1	1	2	0	....	....	....	....	....
2012-13	TPS Turku U18	Fin-U18	13	11	13	24	8	1	0	2	2	0
	TPS Turku Jr.	Fin-Jr.	8	0	4	4	2	....	....	....	....	....
2013-14	TPS Turku Jr.	Fin-Jr.	33	18	21	39	6	3	0	0	0	0
	TPS Turku	Finland	18	3	0	3	0	....	....	....	....	....
2014-15	TPS Turku Jr.	Fin-Jr.	12	7	9	16	6	12	7	6	13	0
	TPS Turku	Finland	36	1	1	2	8	....	....	....	....	....

VAINIO, Veeti (VIGH-n'yoh, vee-eh-TAY) CBJ

Defense. Shoots right. 6'2", 181 lbs. Born, Espoo, Finland, June 16, 1997.
(Columbus' 7th choice, 141st overall, in 2015 Entry Draft).

			Regular Season					Playoffs				
Season	Club	League	GP	G	A	Pts	PIM	GP	G	A	Pts	PIM
2012-13	Blues Espoo U18	Fin-U18	27	2	9	11	30	....	....	....	....	....
2013-14	Blues Espoo U18	Fin-U18	4	1	3	4	10	2	1	1	2	4
	Blues Ak U18	Fin-U18	1	1	2	3	0	....	....	....	....	....
	Blues Espoo Jr.	Fin-Jr.	35	9	14	23	46	11	5	5	10	2
2014-15	Blues Espoo	Finland	2	0	1	1	0	1	0	0	0	0
	Blues Espoo Jr.	Fin-Jr.	42	13	31	44	42	5	2	5	7	4

VAINONEN, Mikko (VIGH-noh-nehn, MEE-koh) NSH

Defense. Shoots left. 6'3", 222 lbs. Born, Helsinki, Finland, April 11, 1994.
(Nashville's 6th choice, 118th overall, in 2012 Entry Draft).

			Regular Season					Playoffs				
Season	Club	League	GP	G	A	Pts	PIM	GP	G	A	Pts	PIM
2009-10	HIFK Helsinki U18	Fin-U18	1	0	1	1	0	....	....	....	....	....
2010-11	HIFK Helsinki U18	Fin-U18	24	4	10	14	24	1	0	0	0	0
	HIFK Helsinki Jr.	Fin-Jr.	8	1	2	3	12	4	0	0	0	6
2011-12	HIFK Helsinki U18	Fin-U18	2	0	1	1	8	1	0	0	0	2
	HIFK Helsinki Jr.	Fin-Jr.	38	7	11	18	44	10	0	1	1	12
	HIFK Helsinki	Finland	8	0	0	0	2	....	....	....	....	....
2012-13	Kingston	OHL	55	4	18	22	42	4	2	1	3	2
2013-14	Kingston	OHL	57	4	14	18	73	7	1	3	4	8
	Milwaukee	AHL	2	0	0	0	0	....	....	....	....	....
2014-15	Cincinnati	ECHL	31	0	5	5	16	....	....	....	....	....
	SaiPa	Finland	19	0	1	1	14	7	0	2	2	33

• Loaned to **SaiPa** (Finland) by **Nashville**, January 15, 2015.

VAIVE, Justin (VIGHV, JUHS-tihn) NYI

Left wing. Shoots left. 6'4", 210 lbs. Born, Buffalo, NY, July 8, 1989.
(Anaheim's 4th choice, 92nd overall, in 2007 Entry Draft).

			Regular Season					Playoffs				
Season	Club	League	GP	G	A	Pts	PIM	GP	G	A	Pts	PIM
2004-05	Toronto Marlboros	GTHL	72	38	64	102	....	....	....	....	....	....
2005-06	USNTDP	U-17	13	3	5	8	18	....	....	....	....	....
	USNTDP	NAHL	24	4	8	12	34	5	1	1	2	6
2006-07	USNTDP	U-18	43	7	8	15	49	....	....	....	....	....
	USNTDP	NAHL	15	4	1	5	22	....	....	....	....	....
2007-08	Miami U.	CCHA	41	3	7	10	65	....	....	....	....	....
2008-09	Miami U.	CCHA	37	6	6	12	44	....	....	....	....	....
2009-10	Miami U.	CCHA	43	5	3	8	51	....	....	....	....	....
2010-11	Miami U.	CCHA	39	9	7	16	48	....	....	....	....	....
2011-12	Cincinnati	ECHL	40	6	12	18	65	....	....	....	....	....
	San Antonio	AHL	15	0	0	0	10	....	....	....	....	....
2012-13	San Antonio	AHL	41	2	2	4	38	....	....	....	....	....
	Cincinnati	ECHL	6	2	2	4	10	15	1	2	3	21
2013-14	Hartford Wolf Pack	AHL	27	1	4	5	31	....	....	....	....	....
	Greenville	ECHL	13	10	8	18	20	13	6	5	11	14
2014-15	Hartford Wolf Pack	AHL	62	14	18	32	94	8	0	1	1	10

Signed as a free agent by **San Antonio** (AHL), July, 2012. Signed as a free agent by **Florida**, July, 2012. Signed as a free agent by **NY Islanders**, July 2, 2015.

VALENTINE, Scott (VAL-ehn-tighn, SKAWT) NSH

Defense. Shoots left. 6'2", 201 lbs. Born, Ottawa, ON, May 2, 1991.
(Anaheim's 7th choice, 166th overall, in 2009 Entry Draft).

			Regular Season					Playoffs				
Season	Club	League	GP	G	A	Pts	PIM	GP	G	A	Pts	PIM
2007-08	Hawkesbury	ON-Jr.A	51	2	15	17	81	11	3	4	7	18
	London Knights	OHL	3	0	0	0	2	....	....	....	....	....
2008-09	London Knights	OHL	17	0	0	0	20	....	....	....	....	....
	Oshawa Generals	OHL	26	1	8	9	51	....	....	....	....	....
2009-10	Oshawa Generals	OHL	63	5	14	19	82	....	....	....	....	....
2010-11	Oshawa Generals	OHL	62	4	32	36	106	9	1	1	2	28
2011-12	Milwaukee	AHL	63	2	10	12	69	2	0	0	0	0
2012-13	Milwaukee	AHL	64	6	4	10	74	2	0	0	0	2
2013-14	Milwaukee	AHL	65	2	9	11	59	....	....	....	....	....
2014-15	Idaho Steelheads	ECHL	12	0	6	6	20	....	....	....	....	....
	Texas Stars	AHL	48	3	7	10	77	....	....	....	....	....

Signed as a free agent by **Nashville**, September 30. 2011. Signed as a free agent by **Texas** (AHL), November 19, 2014.

VALIEV, Rinat (va-LEE'yev, rin-NAT) TOR

Defense. Shoots left. 6'2", 208 lbs. Born, Nizhnekamsk, Russia, May 11, 1995.
(Toronto's 2nd choice, 68th overall, in 2014 Entry Draft).

			Regular Season					Playoffs				
Season	Club	League	GP	G	A	Pts	PIM	GP	G	A	Pts	PIM
2011-12	Bars Kazan Jr.	Russia-Jr.	15	1	1	2	10	1	1	0	1	0
	Irbis Kazan Jr.	Rus.-Jr. B	26	2	7	9	38	4	0	2	2	6
2012-13	Bars Kazan Jr.	Russia-Jr.	6	0	0	0	0	....	....	....	....	....
	Indiana Ice	USHL	36	6	7	13	43	....	....	....	....	....
2013-14	Kootenay Ice	WHL	55	5	23	28	68	13	1	8	9	16
2014-15	Kootenay Ice	WHL	52	9	37	46	53	7	3	2	5	0
	Toronto Marlies	AHL	2	0	0	0	0	....	....	....	....	....

WHL East Second All-Star Team (2015)

VANCE, Troy (VANS, TROI) DAL

Defense. Shoots right. 6'4", 225 lbs. Born, Goshen, NY, August 2, 1993.
(Dallas' 4th choice, 135th overall, in 2011 Entry Draft).

			Regular Season					Playoffs				
Season	Club	League	GP	G	A	Pts	PIM	GP	G	A	Pts	PIM
2010-11	Phi. Revolution	EmJHL	9	1	9	10	10	....	....	....	....	....
	Phi. Revolution	EJHL	18	1	2	3	33	....	....	....	....	....
	Victoriaville Tigres	QMJHL	23	1	3	4	21	9	1	3	4	4
2011-12	Victoriaville Tigres	QMJHL	57	4	20	24	45	4	0	2	2	4
2012-13	Victoriaville Tigres	QMJHL	39	3	15	18	41	....	....	....	....	....
	P.E.I. Rocket	QMJHL	28	1	7	8	16	6	0	2	2	2
2013-14	Charlottetown	QMJHL	59	8	21	29	48	4	1	2	3	2
	Elmira Jackals	ECHL	4	1	1	2	2	....	....	....	....	....
2014-15	Idaho Steelheads	ECHL	47	2	8	10	15	....	....	....	....	....
	Missouri Mavericks	ECHL	14	1	0	1	11	....	....	....	....	....

VANDE SOMPEL, Mitchell (VAN-duh SUHM-puhl, mih-CHUHL) NYI

Defense. Shoots left. 5'10", 182 lbs. Born, London, ON, February 11, 1997.
(NY Islanders' 3rd choice, 82nd overall, in 2015 Entry Draft).

			Regular Season					Playoffs				
Season	Club	League	GP	G	A	Pts	PIM	GP	G	A	Pts	PIM
2012-13	Lon. Knights MM	Minor-ON	23	9	23	32	16	14	8	10	18	4
	Lon. Knights Mid.	Minor-ON	....	....	....	....	....	1	0	0	0	0
	St. Thomas Stars	ON-Jr.B	2	0	1	1	0	....	....	....	....	....
2013-14	Oshawa Generals	OHL	47	5	15	20	18	12	1	2	3	0
2014-15	Oshawa Generals	OHL	58	12	51	63	38	21	5	9	14	4

OHL All-Rookie Team (2014)

VANIER, Alexis (VAN-yay, al-EHX-ihs) S.J.

Defense. Shoots left. 6'5", 215 lbs. Born, St. Catherine, QC, December 21, 1995.
(San Jose's 6th choice, 102nd overall, in 2014 Entry Draft).

			Regular Season					Playoffs				
Season	Club	League	GP	G	A	Pts	PIM	GP	G	A	Pts	PIM
2009-10	C.C. Lemoyne	Minor-QC	32	4	8	12	76	....	....	....	....	....
2010-11	C.C. Lemoyne	Minor-QC	34	0	9	9	92	....	....	....	....	....
2011-12	C.C. Lemoyne	QAAA	34	4	10	14	110	....	....	....	....	....
2012-13	Baie-Comeau	QMJHL	53	0	8	8	66	6	0	0	0	11
2013-14	Baie-Comeau	QMJHL	61	15	21	36	52	....	....	....	....	....
2014-15	Baie-Comeau	QMJHL	29	4	7	11	43	....	....	....	....	....
	Sherbrooke	QMJHL	19	1	10	11	14	....	....	....	....	....

VANNELLI, Thomas (vuh-NEHL-ee, TAW-muhs) ST.L.

Defense. Shoots right. 6'2", 165 lbs. Born, Minneapolis, MN, January 26, 1995.
(St. Louis' 1st choice, 47th overall, in 2013 Entry Draft).

			Regular Season					Playoffs				
Season	Club	League	GP	G	A	Pts	PIM	GP	G	A	Pts	PIM
2011-12	Minnetonka High	High-MN	25	6	14	20	8	3	1	4	5	0
2012-13	Team Northwest	UMHSEL	20	4	10	14	16	3	0	0	0	0
	Minnetonka High	High-MN	25	8	23	31	14	2	2	2	4	0
	USNTDP	USHL	11	1	1	2	4	....	....	....	....	....
	USNTDP	U-18	9	2	1	3	0	....	....	....	....	....
2013-14	Medicine Hat	WHL	60	14	27	41	34	18	2	6	8	10
2014-15	Medicine Hat	WHL	44	12	23	35	52	10	0	4	4	2

VATRANO, Frank (vuh-TRAH-noh, FRANK) BOS

Left wing. Shoots left. 5'9", 201 lbs. Born, East Longmeadow, MA, March 14, 1994.

			Regular Season					Playoffs				
Season	Club	League	GP	G	A	Pts	PIM	GP	G	A	Pts	PIM
2009-10	Bos. Jr. Bruins	EJHL	8	0	2	2	2	....	....	....	....	....
2010-11	USNTDP	USHL	34	11	4	15	22	2	1	0	1	0
	USNTDP	U-17	17	7	7	14	28	....	....	....	....	....
2011-12	USNTDP	USHL	24	7	11	18	8	....	....	....	....	....
	USNTDP	U-18	36	9	8	17	16	....	....	....	....	....
2012-13	USNTDP	USHL	1	0	1	1	2	....	....	....	....	....
	USNTDP	U-18	4	0	3	3	19	....	....	....	....	....
	Bos. Jr. Bruins	EJHL	19	13	9	22	20	....	....	....	....	....
2013-14	U. Mass Lowell	H-East	1	0	0	0	0	....	....	....	....	....
2014-15	U. Mass Lowell	H-East	36	18	10	28	28	....	....	....	....	....
	Providence Bruins	AHL	5	1	0	1	0	....	....	....	....	....

Signed as a free agent by **Boston**, March 13, 2015.

VEILLEUX, Yannick (VAY-yew, YA-nihk) ST.L.

Left wing. Shoots left. 6'2", 206 lbs. Born, Saint-Hippolyte, QC, February 22, 1993.
(St. Louis' 5th choice, 102nd overall, in 2011 Entry Draft).

			Regular Season					Playoffs				
Season	Club	League	GP	G	A	Pts	PIM	GP	G	A	Pts	PIM
2008-09	Saint-Eustache	QAAA	43	21	13	34	44	5	1	4	5	23
2009-10	Shawinigan	QMJHL	55	3	6	9	17	6	0	0	0	6
2010-11	Shawinigan	QMJHL	68	19	29	48	40	12	2	5	7	14
2011-12	Shawinigan	QMJHL	59	27	31	58	69	11	5	6	11	17
2012-13	Moncton Wildcats	QMJHL	65	34	39	73	102	4	2	0	2	10
	Peoria Rivermen	AHL	8	2	1	3	0	....	....	....	....	....
2013-14	Kalamazoo Wings	ECHL	62	16	23	39	65	6	3	0	3	4
	Chicago Wolves	AHL	4	0	1	1	5	....	....	....	....	....
2014-15	Chicago Wolves	AHL	64	9	4	13	83	5	0	0	0	2

VEJDEMO, Lukas (vay-DEH-moh, LOO-kuhs) MTL

Center. Shoots left. 6', 188 lbs. Born, Stockholm, Sweden, January 25, 1996.
(Montreal's 2nd choice, 87th overall, in 2015 Entry Draft).

			Regular Season					Playoffs				
Season	Club	League	GP	G	A	Pts	PIM	GP	G	A	Pts	PIM
2011-12	SDE U18	Swe-U18	32	9	10	19	8	2	0	0	0	0
2012-13	Djurgarden U18	Swe-U18	39	12	30	42	10	9	2	3	5	2
	Djurgarden Jr.	Swe-Jr.	5	0	0	0	0	1	0	0	0	0
2013-14	Djurgarden U18	Swe-U18	20	11	20	31	34	4	1	1	2	4
	Djurgarden Jr.	Swe-Jr.	3	1	0	1	2	1	0	0	0	0
2014-15	Djurgarden Jr.	Swe-Jr.	34	23	25	48	51	7	4	2	6	4
	Djurgarden	Sweden	3	0	0	0	0	....	....	....	....	....

VELA, Marcus (VEH-lah, MAHR-kuhs) S.J.

Center. Shoots right. 6'1", 204 lbs. Born, Burnaby, BC, March 3, 1997.
(San Jose's 8th choice, 190th overall, in 2015 Entry Draft).

			Regular Season					Playoffs				
Season	Club	League	GP	G	A	Pts	PIM	GP	G	A	Pts	PIM
2012-13	Burnaby Bulldogs	Minor-BC	30	25	55	80	....	....	....	....	....	....
2013-14	Langley Rivermen	BCHL	54	11	11	22	41	12	1	4	5	6
2014-15	Langley Rivermen	BCHL	50	20	26	46	57	3	0	1	1	4

• Signed Letter of Intent to attend **University of New Hampshire** (Hockey East) in fall of 2015.

VERHAEGHE, Carter (vuhr-HAY-GEE, KAR-tuhr) TOR

Center. Shoots left. 6'1", 181 lbs. Born, Waterdown, ON, August 14, 1995.
(Toronto's 2nd choice, 82nd overall, in 2013 Entry Draft).

			Regular Season					Playoffs				
Season	Club	League	GP	G	A	Pts	PIM	GP	G	A	Pts	PIM
2010-11	Ham. Jr. Bulldogs	Minor-ON	45	34	30	64	28	....	....	....	....	....
2011-12	Niagara Ice Dogs	OHL	62	4	12	16	10	19	1	2	3	2
2012-13	Niagara Ice Dogs	OHL	67	18	26	44	22	5	2	2	4	6
2013-14	Niagara Ice Dogs	OHL	65	28	54	82	60	6	2	2	4	6
	Toronto Marlies	AHL	2	0	1	1	0	....	....	....	....	....
2014-15	Niagara Ice Dogs	OHL	68	33	49	82	38	11	6	8	14	4

VERMIN, Joel (VAIR-mihn, JOHL) T.B.

Right wing. Shoots left. 5'11", 192 lbs. Born, Bern, Switz., February 5, 1992.
(Tampa Bay's 6th choice, 186th overall, in 2013 Entry Draft).

			Regular Season					Playoffs				
Season	Club	League	GP	G	A	Pts	PIM	GP	G	A	Pts	PIM
2007-08	SC Bern U17	Swiss-U17	32	24	21	45	22	13	2	8	10	2
	SC Bern Future Jr.	Swiss-Jr.	4	0	0	0	6	....	....	....	....	....
2008-09	SC Bern U17	Swiss-U17	28	29	25	54	50	8	7	9	16	12
	SC Bern Future Jr.	Swiss-Jr.	13	3	5	8	2	....	....	....	....	....
2009-10	SC Bern Future Jr.	Swiss-Jr.	34	28	27	55	59	7	3	8	11	2
	SC Bern	Swiss	12	0	0	0	0	....	....	....	....	....
2010-11	SC Bern Future Jr.	Swiss-Jr.	6	4	6	10	2	....	....	....	....	....
	SC Bern	Swiss	36	1	7	8	6	11	3	3	6	0
2011-12	SC Bern	Swiss	33	11	10	21	0	17	2	3	5	2
2012-13	SC Bern	Swiss	47	13	22	35	14	19	3	6	9	8
2013-14	SC Bern	Swiss	55	8	14	22	18	....	....	....	....	....
	Syracuse Crunch	AHL	8	1	0	1	0	....	....	....	....	....
2014-15	Syracuse Crunch	AHL	73	12	21	33	16	3	0	1	1	0

VESEL, Tyler (VEH-suhl, TIGH-luhr) EDM

Center. Shoots right. 5'11", 180 lbs. Born, Duluth, MN, April 14, 1994.
(Edmonton's 5th choice, 153rd overall, in 2014 Entry Draft).

			Regular Season					Playoffs				
Season	Club	League	GP	G	A	Pts	PIM	GP	G	A	Pts	PIM
2011-12	Shat.-St. Mary's	UMHSEL	15	4	7	11	2	....	....	....	....	....
	Shattuck	High-MN	57	29	45	74	4	....	....	....	....	....
2012-13	Shat.-St. Mary's	UMHSEL	15	11	6	17	6	....	....	....	....	....
	Shattuck	High-MN	55	32	45	77	16	....	....	....	....	....
2013-14	Omaha Lancers	USHL	49	33	38	71	22	4	3	1	4	0
2014-15	Nebraska-Omaha	NCHC	39	8	15	23	2	....	....	....	....	....

USHL Second All-Star Team (2014)

VESEY, Jimmy (VEE-ZEE, JIHM-mee) NSH

Left wing. Shoots left. 6'1", 194 lbs. Born, Boston, MA, May 26, 1993.
(Nashville's 3rd choice, 66th overall, in 2012 Entry Draft).

			Regular Season					Playoffs				
Season	Club	League	GP	G	A	Pts	PIM	GP	G	A	Pts	PIM
2009-10	Belmont Hill	High-MA	30	13	17	30	....	....	....	....	....	....
2010-11	Belmont Hill	High-MA	32	23	12	35	90	....	....	....	....	....
2011-12	South Shore Kings	EJHL	45	*48	43	*91	52	6	5	3	8	2
2012-13	Harvard Crimson	ECAC	27	11	7	18	25	....	....	....	....	....
2013-14	Harvard Crimson	ECAC	31	13	9	22	14	....	....	....	....	....
2014-15	Harvard Crimson	ECAC	37	*32	26	*58	21	....	....	....	....	....

ECAC All-Rookie Team (2013) • ECAC First All-Star Team (2015) • ECAC Player of the Year (2015) • NCAA East First All-American Team (2015)

VESEY, Nolan (VEE-ZEE, NOH-luhn) TOR

Left wing. Shoots left. 6'1", 195 lbs. Born, North Reading, MA, March 28, 1995.
(Toronto's 5th choice, 158th overall, in 2014 Entry Draft).

			Regular Season					Playoffs				
Season	Club	League	GP	G	A	Pts	PIM	GP	G	A	Pts	PIM
2012-13	Austin Prep	High-MA	24	21	13	34	....	....	....	....	....	....
2013-14	South Shore Kings	USPHL	48	26	40	66	30	5	0	2	2	2
	South Shore U18	USPHL	1	2	1	3	0	....	....	....	....	....
2014-15	U. of Maine	H-East	36	10	13	23	37	....	....	....	....	....

VIRTANEN, Jake (vuhr-TA-nehn, JAYK) VAN

Right wing. Shoots right. 6'1", 212 lbs. Born, Abbotsford, BC, August 17, 1996.
(Vancouver's 1st choice, 6th overall, in 2014 Entry Draft).

			Regular Season					Playoffs				
Season	Club	League	GP	G	A	Pts	PIM	GP	G	A	Pts	PIM
2010-11	Abbotsford Hawks	Minor-BC	62	70	49	119	153	....	....	....	....	....
	Yale Lions	High-BC	....	....	....	....	....	1	1	1	2	....
2011-12	Fraser Valley	BCMML	39	17	22	39	120	....	....	....	....	....
	Yale Lions	High-BC	6	10	3	13	....	....	....	....	....	....
	Calgary Hitmen	WHL	9	3	1	4	4	5	0	0	0	4
2012-13	Calgary Hitmen	WHL	62	16	18	34	67	15	2	4	6	27
2013-14	Calgary Hitmen	WHL	71	45	26	71	100	6	1	3	4	4
2014-15	Calgary Hitmen	WHL	50	21	31	52	82	14	5	8	13	28
	Utica Comets	AHL	....	....	....	....	....	10	0	1	1	6

VOROBYEV, Mikhail (voh-roh-bee-AWV, mih-KIGH-ehl) PHI

Center. Shoots left. 6'2", 194 lbs. Born, Ufa, Russia, January 5, 1997.
(Philadelphia's 6th choice, 104th overall, in 2015 Entry Draft).

			Regular Season					Playoffs				
Season	Club	League	GP	G	A	Pts	PIM	GP	G	A	Pts	PIM
2013-14	Tolpar Ufa Jr.	Russia-Jr.	4	0	3	3	0	....	....	....	....	....
2014-15	Tolpar Ufa Jr.	Russia-Jr.	39	8	12	20	40	8	3	0	3	2

VRANA, Jakub (vuh-RA-nuh, YA-kuhb) WSH

Right wing. Shoots left. 5'11", 185 lbs. Born, Prague, Czech Rep., February 28, 1996.
(Washington's 1st choice, 13th overall, in 2014 Entry Draft).

			Regular Season					Playoffs				
Season	Club	League	GP	G	A	Pts	PIM	GP	G	A	Pts	PIM
2010-11	HC Letnany U18	CzR-U18	26	19	10	29	10	....	....	....	....	....
2011-12	Linkopings HC U18	Swe-U18	32	28	17	45	6	3	2	2	4	12
	Linkopings HC Jr.	Swe-Jr.	3	1	0	1	2	....	....	....	....	....
2012-13	Linkopings HC U18	Swe-U18	3	3	2	5	2	2	1	0	1	12
	Linkopings HC Jr.	Swe-Jr.	32	20	12	32	49	5	1	0	1	0
	Linkopings HC	Sweden	5	0	0	0	0	....	....	....	....	....
2013-14	Linkopings HC U18	Swe-U18	1	0	0	0	0	3	1	2	3	4
	Linkopings HC Jr.	Swe-Jr.	24	14	11	25	26	....	....	....	....	....
	Linkopings HC	Sweden	24	2	1	3	2	14	1	1	2	6
2014-15	Linkopings HC	Sweden	44	12	12	24	12	11	4	1	5	2
	Hershey Bears	AHL	3	0	5	5	0	10	2	4	6	2

WAGNER, Austin (WAG-nuhr, AW-stuhn) L.A.

Left wing. Shoots left. 6'1", 178 lbs. Born, Calgary, AB, June 23, 1997.
(Los Angeles' 3rd choice, 99th overall, in 2015 Entry Draft).

			Regular Season					Playoffs				
Season	Club	League	GP	G	A	Pts	PIM	GP	G	A	Pts	PIM
2012-13	Calgary Northstars	AMHL	28	7	3	10	30	2	0	0	0	15
	Regina Pats	WHL	1	0	0	0	0	....	....	....	....	....
2013-14	Regina Pats	WHL	42	1	1	2	18	2	0	0	0	0
2014-15	Regina Pats	WHL	61	20	19	39	53	9	1	2	3	8

WALCOTT, Daniel (WAWL-kawt, DAN-yehl) T.B.

Defense. Shoots left. 5'11", 165 lbs. Born, Ile Perrot, QC, February 19, 1994.
(NY Rangers' 6th choice, 140th overall, in 2014 Entry Draft).

			Regular Season					Playoffs				
Season	Club	League	GP	G	A	Pts	PIM	GP	G	A	Pts	PIM
2011-12	New Trier Trevians	High-IL	STATISTICS NOT AVAILABLE									
2012-13	Lindenwood Lions	NCAA-2	33	4	9	13	30	....	....	....	....	....
2013-14	Blainville-Bois.	QMJHL	67	10	29	39	71	19	4	6	10	18
2014-15	Blainville-Bois.	QMJHL	54	7	34	41	40	6	1	3	4	4
	Hartford Wolf Pack	AHL	1	0	0	0	0	....	....	....	....	....

QMJHL First All-Star Team (2015)

Traded to **Tampa Bay** by **NY Rangers** for NY Rangers' 7th round choice (previously acquired, later traded to Edmonton – Edmonton selected Ziyat Paigin) in 2015 Entry Draft, June 1, 2015.

WALKER, Geoff (WAW-kuhr, JEHF) T.B.

Right wing. Shoots right. 6'3", 225 lbs. Born, Charlottetown, PE, December 9, 1987.

			Regular Season					Playoffs				
Season	Club	League	GP	G	A	Pts	PIM	GP	G	A	Pts	PIM
2004-05	Gatineau	QMJHL	45	11	6	17	27	....	....	....	....	....
2005-06	Gatineau	QMJHL	15	0	2	2	18	....	....	....	....	....
	P.E.I. Rocket	QMJHL	34	15	11	26	49	6	2	1	3	6
2006-07	P.E.I. Rocket	QMJHL	65	30	50	80	105	7	4	5	9	6
2007-08	P.E.I. Rocket	QMJHL	69	38	52	90	59	4	4	3	7	4
	Texas Brahmas	CHL	....	....	....	....	....	5	0	0	0	9
2008-09	Ontario Reign	ECHL	68	21	27	48	39	7	3	5	8	0
2009-10	Manchester	AHL	37	5	9	14	55	....	....	....	....	....
	Ontario Reign	ECHL	26	7	16	23	20	....	....	....	....	....
2010-11	Wilkes-Barre	AHL	70	11	19	30	102	12	1	3	4	8
2011-12	Wilkes-Barre	AHL	68	18	26	44	114	12	1	4	5	4
2012-13	Lake Erie Monsters	AHL	51	5	15	20	55	....	....	....	....	....
2013-14	Syracuse Crunch	AHL	43	6	2	8	56	....	....	....	....	....
	Florida Everblades	ECHL	6	6	3	9	2	....	....	....	....	....
2014-15	Ontario Reign	ECHL	35	12	14	26	31	....	....	....	....	....
	Missouri Mavericks	ECHL	25	6	11	17	20	....	....	....	....	....

Signed as a free agent by **Wilkes-Barre** (AHL), September 3, 2010. Signed as a free agent by **Colorado**, July 1, 2012. Signed as a free agent by **Tampa Bay**, July 5, 2013. Signed as a free agent by **Ontario** (ECHL), September 23, 2014. Traded to **Missouri** (ECHL) by **Ontario** (ECHL) for David Rutherford, January 22, 2015.

WALKER, Luke (WAW-kuhr, LEWK) COL

Right wing. Shoots right. 6'1", 174 lbs. Born, New Haven, CT, February 19, 1990.
(Colorado's 7th choice, 139th overall, in 2010 Entry Draft).

			Regular Season					Playoffs				
Season	Club	League	GP	G	A	Pts	PIM	GP	G	A	Pts	PIM
2006-07	Okanagan Prep	Minor-BC	52	50	42	92	87	....	....	....	....	....
2007-08	Portland	WHL	70	9	12	21	84	....	....	....	....	....
2008-09	Portland	WHL	71	29	23	52	84	....	....	....	....	....
2009-10	Portland	WHL	61	27	30	57	103	13	6	4	10	17
2010-11	Lake Erie Monsters	AHL	75	10	8	18	40	5	1	1	2	0
2011-12	Lake Erie Monsters	AHL	61	9	18	27	26	....	....	....	....	....
2012-13	Lake Erie Monsters	AHL	47	12	13	25	51	....	....	....	....	....
2013-14	Medvescak Zagreb	KHL	36	1	2	3	20	1	0	0	0	0
2014-15	EC Graz	Austria	51	19	12	31	28	....	....	....	....	....

Signed as a free agent by **Zagreb** (KHL), June 24, 2013. Signed as a free agent by **Graz** (Austria), July 31, 2014.

WALKER, Nathan (WAW-kuhr, NAY-thuhn) WSH

Left wing. Shoots left. 5'11", 180 lbs. Born, Cardiff, Wales, February 7, 1994.
(Washington's 3rd choice, 89th overall, in 2014 Entry Draft).

			Regular Season					Playoffs				
Season	Club	League	GP	G	A	Pts	PIM	GP	G	A	Pts	PIM
2007-08	HC Vitkovice U17	CzR-U17	1	0	0	0	2	....	....	....	....	....
2008-09	HC Vitkovice U17	CzR-U17	33	6	9	15	12	5	1	0	1	4
2009-10	HC Vitkovice U18	CzR-U18	28	22	20	42	47	2	2	2	4	4
	HC Vitkovice Jr.	CzRep-Jr.	23	5	5	10	16	1	0	0	0	0
	Sydney Ice Dogs	Australia	4	0	1	1	0	....	....	....	....	....
2010-11	HC Vitkovice U18	CzR-U18	10	4	10	14	22	....	....	....	....	....
	HC Vitkovice Jr.	CzRep-Jr.	37	20	22	42	20	....	....	....	....	....
	Sydney Ice Dogs	Australia	3	1	1	2	6	....	....	....	....	....
2011-12	HC Vitkovice Jr.	CzRep-Jr.	14	14	6	20	16	3	0	1	1	0
	HC Vitkovice Steel	CzRep	34	4	5	9	8	1	0	0	0	2
	HC Olomouc	CzRep-2	2	0	1	1	4	5	0	0	0	6
	HC Vitkovice U18	CzR-U18	....	....	....	....	....	3	4	1	5	14
2012-13	Youngstown	USHL	29	7	20	27	63	....	....	....	....	....
	HC Vitkovice Jr.	CzRep-Jr.	13	12	12	24	42	....	....	....	....	....
	HC Vitkovice Steel	CzRep	20	0	1	1	27	....	....	....	....	....
	Salith Sumperk	CzRep-2	3	0	1	1	2	....	....	....	....	....
2013-14	Hershey Bears	AHL	43	5	6	11	40	....	....	....	....	....
2014-15	Hershey Bears	AHL	28	1	3	4	30	....	....	....	....	....
	South Carolina	ECHL	6	2	2	4	0	....	....	....	....	....

WALLMARK, Lucas (VAWL-mahrk, LOO-kuhs) CAR

Center. Shoots left. 6', 176 lbs. Born, Umea, Sweden, September 5, 1995.
(Carolina's 5th choice, 97th overall, in 2014 Entry Draft).

			Regular Season					Playoffs				
Season	Club	League	GP	G	A	Pts	PIM	GP	G	A	Pts	PIM
2009-10	Tegs SK Umea U18	Swe-U18	16	3	6	9	37	....	....	....	....	....
	Bjorkloven U18	Swe-U18	10	1	3	4	0	....	....	....	....	....
2010-11	Skelleftea AIK U18	Swe-U18	36	18	49	67	18	2	1	0	1	0
2011-12	Skelleftea AIK U18	Swe-U18	2	1	1	2	0	3	3	2	5	2
	Skelleftea AIK Jr.	Swe-Jr.	37	11	26	37	14	3	1	2	3	4
2012-13	Skelleftea AIK Jr.	Swe-Jr.	14	5	11	16	18	....	....	....	....	....
	Skelleftea AIK	Sweden	2	0	0	0	0	....	....	....	....	....
	Karlskrona HK	Sweden-2	23	5	10	15	6	....	....	....	....	....
2013-14	Asploven	Sweden-2	11	1	7	8	6	....	....	....	....	....
	Lulea HF	Sweden	41	3	7	10	2	1	0	0	0	0
2014-15	Lulea HF	Sweden	50	5	13	18	14	9	0	5	5	2

WALMAN, Jake (WAWL-muhn, JAYK) ST.L.

Defense. Shoots left. 6'1", 170 lbs. Born, Toronto, ON, February 20, 1996.
(St. Louis' 4th choice, 82nd overall, in 2014 Entry Draft).

			Regular Season					Playoffs				
Season	Club	League	GP	G	A	Pts	PIM	GP	G	A	Pts	PIM
2011-12	North York	GTHL	33	10	12	22	18	....	....	....	....	....
2012-13	Tor. Jr. Canadiens	GTHL	30	6	12	18	8	7	1	1	2	16
2013-14	Tor. Canadiens	ON-Jr.A	43	7	26	33	87	....	....	....	....	....
2014-15	Providence College	H-East	41	1	15	16	44	....	....	....	....	....

WANNSTROM, Sebastian (VAN-strohm, seh-BAS-t'yehn) ST.L.

Right wing. Shoots right. 6'1", 180 lbs. Born, Gavle, Sweden, March 3, 1991.
(St. Louis' 3rd choice, 44th overall, in 2010 Entry Draft).

			Regular Season					Playoffs				
Season	Club	League	GP	G	A	Pts	PIM	GP	G	A	Pts	PIM
2006-07	Brynas U18	Swe-U18	11	0	4	4	4	3	0	0	0	4
2007-08	Brynas U18	Swe-U18	5	0	1	1	4	5	1	3	4	2
	Brynas IF Gavle Jr.	Swe-Jr.	15	0	4	4	8	....	....	....	....	....
2008-09	Brynas U18	Swe-U18	9	6	12	18	12	2	0	3	3	0
	Brynas IF Gavle Jr.	Swe-Jr.	32	11	9	20	4	6	0	0	0	0
2009-10	Brynas IF Gavle Jr.	Swe-Jr.	35	30	27	57	55	5	2	3	5	0
	Brynas IF Gavle	Sweden	18	0	0	0	2	1	0	0	0	0
2010-11	Brynas IF Gavle Jr.	Swe-Jr.	7	5	4	9	0	1	0	0	0	10
	Leksands IF	Sweden-2	2	0	0	0	0	....	....	....	....	....
	Brynas IF Gavle	Sweden	45	0	2	2	6	5	0	0	0	0
2011-12	Brynas IF Gavle Jr.	Swe-Jr.	5	2	1	3	2	....	....	....	....	....
	Brynas IF Gavle	Sweden	43	8	7	15	20	17	2	5	7	4
2012-13	Peoria Rivermen	AHL	16	1	2	3	4	....	....	....	....	....
	Evansville IceMen	ECHL	14	6	1	7	12	....	....	....	....	....
	Brynas IF Gavle	Sweden	9	0	0	0	8	4	0	0	0	2
2013-14	Kalamazoo Wings	ECHL	4	3	2	5	2	....	....	....	....	....
	Chicago Wolves	AHL	37	5	5	10	20	6	1	2	3	6
2014-15	Chicago Wolves	AHL	36	3	9	12	12	....	....	....	....	....

WARNER, Hunter (WAHR-nuhr, HUHN-tuhr) MIN

Defense. Shoots right. 6'4", 221 lbs. Born, Cambridge, MN, September 21, 1995.

			Regular Season					Playoffs				
Season	Club	League	GP	G	A	Pts	PIM	GP	G	A	Pts	PIM
2011-12	Eden Prairie Eagles	High-MN	25	1	8	9	37	1	0	1	1	0
2012-13	Eden Prairie Eagles	High-MN	23	3	7	10	58	2	0	1	1	4
	Waterloo	USHL	6	0	1	1	7	....	....	....	....	....
2013-14	Waterloo	USHL	7	0	0	0	2	....	....	....	....	....
	Fargo Force	USHL	43	2	10	12	125	....	....	....	....	....
2014-15	Prince Albert	WHL	24	0	3	3	25	....	....	....	....	....

Signed as a free agent by **Minnesota**, September 23, 2014.

WARREN, Brendan (WAW-rehn, BREHN-duhn) ARI

Left wing. Shoots left. 6', 191 lbs. Born, Carleton, MI, May 7, 1997.
(Arizona's 6th choice, 81st overall, in 2015 Entry Draft).

			Regular Season					Playoffs				
Season	Club	League	GP	G	A	Pts	PIM	GP	G	A	Pts	PIM
2012-13	Det. Comp. U18	HPHL	26	10	14	24	13	....	....	....	....	....
	Det. Comp. U18	Other	....	....	....	....	....	3	0	1	1	2
2013-14	USNTDP	USHL	33	6	13	19	41	....	....	....	....	....
	USNTDP	U-17	20	8	13	21	24	....	....	....	....	....
2014-15	USNTDP	USHL	20	7	6	13	33	....	....	....	....	....
	USNTDP	U-18	41	12	13	25	16	....	....	....	....	....

• Signed Letter of Intent to attend **University of Michigan** (Big Ten) in fall of 2015.

WATSON, Clifford (WAWT-suhn, KLIHF-uhrd) S.J.

Defense. Shoots left. 6'2", 185 lbs. Born, Sheboygan, WI, December 21, 1993.
(San Jose's 5th choice, 168th overall, in 2012 Entry Draft).

			Regular Season					Playoffs				
Season	Club	League	GP	G	A	Pts	PIM	GP	G	A	Pts	PIM
2009-10	Appleton United	High-WI	23	5	12	17	34	....	....	....	....	....
2010-11	Team Wisconsin	UMHSEL	24	1	15	16	28	....	....	....	....	....
	Appleton United	High-WI	21	18	22	40	44	1	0	0	0	0
2011-12	Sioux City	USHL	58	0	8	8	53	2	0	0	0	0
2012-13	Sioux City	USHL	62	3	8	11	65	....	....	....	....	....
2013-14	Michigan Tech	WCHA	40	0	4	4	30	....	....	....	....	....
2014-15	Michigan Tech	WCHA	40	3	10	13	47	....	....	....	....	....

WATSON, Spencer (WAWT-suhn, SPEHN-suhr) L.A.

Right wing. Shoots right. 5'10", 173 lbs. Born, London, ON, April 25, 1996.
(Los Angeles' 9th choice, 209th overall, in 2014 Entry Draft).

			Regular Season					Playoffs				
Season	Club	League	GP	G	A	Pts	PIM	GP	G	A	Pts	PIM
2011-12	Lon. Knights MM	Minor-ON	30	43	24	67	26	11	12	6	18	10
	Lon. Knights Mid.	Minor-ON	2	3	0	3	0	....	....	....	....	....
	London Nationals	ON-Jr.B	2	0	0	0	0	7	3	1	4	2
2012-13	Kingston	OHL	63	23	20	43	18	2	1	1	2	0
2013-14	Kingston	OHL	65	33	35	68	16	7	1	4	5	0
2014-15	Kingston	OHL	41	20	28	48	10	4	0	1	1	0

OHL All-Rookie Team (2013)

WEAL, Jordan (WEEL, JOHR-dahn) L.A.

Center. Shoots right. 5'10", 179 lbs. Born, North Vancouver, BC, April 15, 1992.
(Los Angeles' 3rd choice, 70th overall, in 2010 Entry Draft).

			Regular Season					Playoffs				
Season	Club	League	GP	G	A	Pts	PIM	GP	G	A	Pts	PIM
2007-08	Van. NW Giants	BCMML	40	*39	*61	*100	44	2	0	2	2	2
	Regina Pats	WHL	3	0	1	1	0	4	0	0	0	0
2008-09	Regina Pats	WHL	65	16	54	70	26	....	....	....	....	....
2009-10	Regina Pats	WHL	72	35	67	102	54	....	....	....	....	....
2010-11	Regina Pats	WHL	72	43	53	96	70	....	....	....	....	....
	Manchester	AHL	7	0	1	1	0	....	....	....	....	....
2011-12	Regina Pats	WHL	70	41	75	116	36	5	1	4	5	0
	Manchester	AHL	2	0	0	0	0	....	....	....	....	....
2012-13	Manchester	AHL	63	15	18	33	38	4	0	2	2	4
2013-14	Manchester	AHL	76	23	47	70	42	4	0	3	3	2
2014-15	Manchester	AHL	73	20	49	69	56	19	10	12	22	16

WHL East First All-Star Team (2012) • AHL Second All-Star Team (2015)

WEEGAR, MacKenzie (WEE-guhr, muh-KEHN-zee) FLA

Defense. Shoots right. 6', 212 lbs. Born, Ottawa, ON, January 7, 1994.
(Florida's 8th choice, 206th overall, in 2013 Entry Draft).

			Regular Season					Playoffs				
Season	Club	League	GP	G	A	Pts	PIM	GP	G	A	Pts	PIM
2010-11	Winchester Hawks	ON-Jr.B	40	10	23	33	94	13	3	6	9	83
	Nepean Raiders	ON-Jr.A	5	0	2	2	0	....	....	....	....	....
2011-12	Nepean Raiders	ON-Jr.A	53	13	37	50	61	18	2	4	6	24
2012-13	Halifax	QMJHL	62	8	36	44	58	17	0	5	5	10
2013-14	Halifax	QMJHL	61	12	47	59	97	16	5	17	22	14
2014-15	San Antonio	AHL	31	2	8	10	40	....	....	....	....	....
	Cincinnati	ECHL	21	1	12	13	13	....	....	....	....	....

QMJHL All-Rookie Team (2013) • QMJHL Second All-Star Team (2014)

WEGWERTH, Joe (WEHG-wuhrth, JOH) FLA

Right wing. Shoots left. 6'3", 232 lbs. Born, Burnsville, MN, June 16, 1996.
(Florida's 4th choice, 92nd overall, in 2014 Entry Draft).

			Regular Season					Playoffs				
Season	Club	League	GP	G	A	Pts	PIM	GP	G	A	Pts	PIM
2011-12	Brewster Bulldogs	EmJHL	34	17	35	52	52	....	....	....	....	....
	U.S. Youth Oly.	Other	6	2	2	4	18	....	....	....	....	....
2012-13	USNTDP	USHL	16	3	1	4	32	....	....	....	....	....
	USNTDP	U-17	11	4	5	9	2	....	....	....	....	....
2013-14	USNTDP	USHL	25	2	1	3	78	....	....	....	....	....
	USNTDP	U-18	35	1	5	6	49	....	....	....	....	....
2014-15	Green Bay	USHL	35	5	16	21	59	....	....	....	....	....
	Cedar Rapids	USHL	24	4	5	9	38	3	1	2	3	4

• Signed Letter of Intent to attend **University of Notre Dame** (Hockey East) in fall of 2015.

WELINSKI, Andy (wehl-IHN-skee, AN-dee) ANA

Defense. Shoots right. 6'1", 196 lbs. Born, Duluth, MN, April 27, 1993.
(Anaheim's 5th choice, 83rd overall, in 2011 Entry Draft).

			Regular Season					Playoffs				
Season	Club	League	GP	G	A	Pts	PIM	GP	G	A	Pts	PIM
2009-10	Duluth East	High-MN	19	3	12	15	16	6	2	7	9	2
2010-11	Green Bay	USHL	51	6	8	14	14	11	2	0	2	4
2011-12	Green Bay	USHL	54	15	22	37	37	7	1	1	2	4
2012-13	U. Minn-Duluth	WCHA	38	4	14	18	24	....	....	....	....	....
2013-14	U. Minn-Duluth	NCHC	36	5	14	19	51	....	....	....	....	....
2014-15	U. Minn-Duluth	NCHC	40	9	12	21	24	....	....	....	....	....

USHL First All-Star Team (2012) • WCHA All-Rookie Team (2013) • NCHC Second All-Star Team (2015)

WERENSKI, Zachary (wuh-REHN-skee, ZA-kuh-ree) CBJ

Defense. Shoots left. 6'2", 209 lbs. Born, Grosse Pointe, MI, July 19, 1997.
(Columbus' 1st choice, 8th overall, in 2015 Entry Draft).

			Regular Season					Playoffs				
Season	Club	League	GP	G	A	Pts	PIM	GP	G	A	Pts	PIM
2011-12	Det. B. Tire U16	T1EHL	35	8	20	28	18	7	3	5	8	4
2012-13	Det. L.C. U18	HPHL	28	7	14	21	18	....	....	....	....	....
2013-14	USNTDP	USHL	35	6	13	19	17	....	....	....	....	....
	USNTDP	U-17	16	2	11	13	25	....	....	....	....	....
2014-15	U. of Michigan	Big Ten	35	9	16	25	8	....	....	....	....	....

WESLEY, Josh (WEHZ-lee, JAWSH) CAR

Defense. Shoots right. 6'3", 200 lbs. Born, Hartford, CT, April 9, 1996.
(Carolina's 4th choice, 96th overall, in 2014 Entry Draft).

			Regular Season					Playoffs				
Season	Club	League	GP	G	A	Pts	PIM	GP	G	A	Pts	PIM
2011-12	Car. Jr. Hurricanes	NAPHL	18	7	6	13	10	5	1	6	7	14
2012-13	USNTDP	USHL	38	0	1	1	14	....	....	....	....	....
	USNTDP	U-17	18	0	6	6	6	....	....	....	....	....
2013-14	Plymouth Whalers	OHL	68	1	8	9	62	5	0	1	1	2
2014-15	Plymouth Whalers	OHL	63	5	5	10	67	....	....	....	....	....
	Charlotte	AHL	1	0	0	0	0	....	....	....	....	....

WESTLUND, David (WEHST-luhnd, DAY-vihd) ARI

Defense. Shoots left. 6'3", 207 lbs. Born, Ostersund, Sweden, February 5, 1995.
(Arizona's 7th choice, 163rd overall, in 2014 Entry Draft).

			Regular Season					Playoffs				
Season	Club	League	GP	G	A	Pts	PIM	GP	G	A	Pts	PIM
2010-11	Brynas U18	Swe-U18	8	0	0	0	4	....	....	....	....	....
2011-12	Brynas U18	Swe-U18	37	5	12	17	63	6	0	0	0	6
2012-13	Brynas U18	Swe-U18	19	3	5	8	63	7	1	2	3	6
	Brynas IF Gavle Jr.	Swe-Jr.	32	1	5	6	59	2	0	0	0	4
2013-14	Brynas IF Gavle Jr.	Swe-Jr.	33	5	5	10	61	7	0	2	2	10
	Brynas IF Gavle	Sweden	21	0	1	1	0	....	....	....	....	....
2014-15	Brynas IF Gavle Jr.	Swe-Jr.	12	4	4	8	41	3	1	3	4	4
	Brynas IF Gavle	Sweden	53	0	2	2	8	3	0	0	0	0

WESTLUND, Wilhelm (WEHST-luhnd, WIHL-hehlm) COL

Defense. Shoots left. 6', 178 lbs. Born, Stockholm, Sweden, March 15, 1995.
(Colorado's 7th choice, 183rd overall, in 2013 Entry Draft).

			Regular Season					Playoffs				
Season	Club	League	GP	G	A	Pts	PIM	GP	G	A	Pts	PIM
2009-10	SDE U18	Swe-U18	2	0	1	1	0	....	....	....	....	....
2010-11	Farjestad U18	Swe-U18	35	2	11	13	18	....	....	....	....	....
2011-12	Farjestad U18	Swe-U18	13	4	5	9	8	2	1	0	1	2
	Farjestad Jr.	Swe-Jr.	33	3	4	7	12	6	0	0	0	0
2012-13	Farjestad U18	Swe-U18	1	0	0	0	0	....	....	....	....	....
	Farjestad Jr.	Swe-Jr.	33	3	12	15	76	5	0	3	3	2
	Farjestad	Sweden	26	1	0	1	0	6	0	0	0	0
2013-14	Farjestad	Sweden	11	0	0	0	0	....	....	....	....	....
	Farjestad Jr.	Swe-Jr.	34	2	15	17	16	6	2	5	7	2
2014-15	Vita Hasten	Sweden-2	45	2	9	11	18	4	1	0	1	0
	Djurgarden Jr.	Swe-Jr.	....	....	....	....	....	4	2	2	4	4

WHITE, Colin (WIGHT, KAWL-ihn) OTT

Center. Shoots right. 6'1", 192 lbs. Born, Boston, MA, January 30, 1997.
(Ottawa's 2nd choice, 21st overall, in 2015 Entry Draft).

			Regular Season					Playoffs				
Season	Club	League	GP	G	A	Pts	PIM	GP	G	A	Pts	PIM
2011-12	Nobles	High-MA	29	16	18	44	....	....	....	....	....	....
2012-13	Cape Cod Whalers	Minor-MA	9	3	6	9	0	....	....	....	....	....
	Nobles	High-MA	22	18	14	32	10	....	....	....	....	....
2013-14	USNTDP	USHL	35	14	14	28	50	....	....	....	....	....
	USNTDP	U-17	20	20	19	39	35	....	....	....	....	....
2014-15	USNTDP	USHL	20	4	13	17	10	....	....	....	....	....
	USNTDP	U-18	34	19	19	38	18	....	....	....	....	....

• Signed Letter of Intent to attend **Boston College** (Hockey East) in fall of 2015.

WHITE, Colton (WIGHT, KOHL-tuhn) N.J.

Defense. Shoots left. 6', 180 lbs. Born, London, ON, May 3, 1997.
(New Jersey's 4th choice, 97th overall, in 2015 Entry Draft).

			Regular Season					Playoffs				
Season	Club	League	GP	G	A	Pts	PIM	GP	G	A	Pts	PIM
2011-12	Lon. Knights Bant.	Minor-ON	STATISTICS NOT AVAILABLE									
	Lon. Knights MM	Minor-ON	6	0	1	1	4	4	0	0	0	0
2012-13	Lon. Knights MM	Minor-ON	27	7	13	20	22	16	3	4	7	6
2013-14	Sault Ste. Marie	OHL	57	0	5	5	2	9	0	1	1	0
2014-15	Sault Ste. Marie	OHL	67	6	16	22	30	14	0	2	2	0

WIDEMAN, Chris (WIGHD-muhn, KRIHS) OTT

Defense. Shoots right. 5'10", 180 lbs. Born, St. Louis, MO, January 7, 1990.
(Ottawa's 4th choice, 100th overall, in 2009 Entry Draft).

			Regular Season					Playoffs				
Season	Club	League	GP	G	A	Pts	PIM	GP	G	A	Pts	PIM
2006-07	St.L. AAA Blues	Minor-MO	62	9	21	30	122	....	....	....	....	....
	St. Louis Bandits	NAHL	1	0	0	0	0	7	0	1	1	4
2007-08	Cedar Rapids	USHL	53	2	12	14	51	1	0	0	0	0
2008-09	Miami U.	CCHA	39	0	26	26	56	....	....	....	....	....
2009-10	Miami U.	CCHA	44	5	17	22	63	....	....	....	....	....
2010-11	Miami U.	CCHA	39	3	20	23	32	....	....	....	....	....
2011-12	Miami U.	CCHA	41	4	20	24	40	....	....	....	....	....
2012-13	Binghamton	AHL	60	2	16	18	46	3	1	2	3	2
	Elmira Jackals	ECHL	5	0	5	5	7	....	....	....	....	....
2013-14	Binghamton	AHL	73	9	42	51	101	4	1	0	1	6
2014-15	Binghamton	AHL	75	19	42	61	116	....	....	....	....	....

CCHA All-Rookie Team (2009) • CCHA Second All-Star Team (2011) • AHL First All-Star Team (2015) • Eddie Shore Award (AHL – Outstanding Defenseman) (2015)

WIKSTRAND, Mikael (VIHK-strand, mih-kigh-EHL) OTT

Defense. Shoots left. 6'1", 185 lbs. Born, Karlstad, Sweden, November 5, 1993.
(Ottawa's 7th choice, 196th overall, in 2012 Entry Draft).

			Regular Season					Playoffs				
Season	Club	League	GP	G	A	Pts	PIM	GP	G	A	Pts	PIM
2007-08	Ore U18	Swe-U18	14	0	4	4	6	....	....	....	....	....
2008-09	Ore U18	Swe-U18	9	0	2	2	31	1	1	1	2	....
	IFK Ore Furudal	Sweden-5	3	0	0	0	....	....	....	....	....	....
2009-10	Mora IK U18	Swe-U18	23	10	11	21	26	....	....	....	....	....
	Mora IK Jr.	Swe-Jr.	14	1	2	3	8	....	....	....	....	....
2010-11	Mora IK U18	Swe-U18	4	1	2	3	6	3	1	3	4	4
	Mora IK Jr.	Swe-Jr.	16	3	5	8	6	....	....	....	....	....
	Mora IK	Sweden-2	37	0	1	1	8	....	....	....	....	....
2011-12	Mora IK Jr.	Swe-Jr.	11	3	4	7	2	2	1	3	4	2
	Mora IK	Sweden-2	47	2	1	3	14	....	....	....	....	....
2012-13	Mora IK Jr.	Swe-Jr.	2	0	1	1	0	....	....	....	....	....
	Mora IK	Sweden-2	45	11	14	25	35	....	....	....	....	....
2013-14	Mora IK	Sweden-2	27	4	16	20	14	....	....	....	....	....
	Frolunda	Sweden	19	4	7	11	4	7	1	1	2	0
2014-15	Frolunda	Sweden	46	5	15	20	10	13	0	5	5	8

WILKIE, Chris (WIHL-kee, KRIHS) FLA

Right wing. Shoots right. 6', 199 lbs. Born, Omaha, NE, July 10, 1996.
(Florida's 6th choice, 162nd overall, in 2015 Entry Draft).

			Regular Season					Playoffs				
Season	Club	League	GP	G	A	Pts	PIM	GP	G	A	Pts	PIM
2010-11	Om. Lancers U16	NAPHL	20	3	5	8	0	4	0	0	0	2
2011-12	Om. Lancers U16	NAPHL	18	22	26	48	8	4	3	10	13	6
	Lincoln Stars	USHL	1	0	0	0	0	....	....	....	....	....
2012-13	USNTDP	USHL	38	7	7	14	38	....	....	....	....	....
	USNTDP	U-17	18	6	11	17	2	....	....	....	....	....
2013-14	Tri-City Storm	USHL	57	17	19	36	39	....	....	....	....	....
2014-15	Tri-City Storm	USHL	59	*35	20	55	66	7	3	3	6	22

USHL Second All-Star Team (2015)

• Signed Letter of Intent to attend **University of North Dakota** (NCHC) in fall of 2015.

WILLCOX, Reece (WIHL-cawx, REES) PHI

Defense. Shoots right. 6'3", 202 lbs. Born, Surrey, BC, March 20, 1994.
(Philadelphia's 6th choice, 141st overall, in 2012 Entry Draft).

			Regular Season					Playoffs				
Season	Club	League	GP	G	A	Pts	PIM	GP	G	A	Pts	PIM
2009-10	Surrey Thunder	Minor-BC	STATISTICS NOT AVAILABLE									
	West Valley Hawks	BCMML	9	1	3	4	0	....	....	....	....	....
2010-11	Merritt	BCHL	53	5	9	14	16	4	1	2	3	0
2011-12	Merritt	BCHL	52	5	18	23	26	9	2	2	4	6
2012-13	Cornell Big Red	ECAC	34	0	5	5	8	....	....	....	....	....
2013-14	Cornell Big Red	ECAC	32	2	5	7	10	....	....	....	....	....
2014-15	Cornell Big Red	ECAC	21	1	3	4	10	....	....	....	....	....

WILLIAMS, Colby (WIHL-yuhmz, KOHL-bee) WSH

Defense. Shoots right. 5'11", 191 lbs. Born, Regina, SK, January 26, 1995.
(Washington's 4th choice, 173rd overall, in 2015 Entry Draft).

			Regular Season					Playoffs				
Season	Club	League	GP	G	A	Pts	PIM	GP	G	A	Pts	PIM
2010-11	Reg. Pat Cdns.	SMHL	35	4	14	18	54	....	....	....	....	....
	Regina Pats	WHL	2	0	0	0	0	....	....	....	....	....
2011-12	Reg. Pat Cdns.	SMHL	43	7	24	31	144	....	....	....	....	....
	Melville	SJHL	....	....	....	....	....	6	0	0	0	0
	Regina Pats	WHL	1	0	0	0	2	....	....	....	....	....
2012-13	Regina Pats	WHL	59	0	19	19	70	....	....	....	....	....
2013-14	Regina Pats	WHL	66	9	23	32	82	4	0	0	0	8
2014-15	Regina Pats	WHL	64	11	30	41	95	9	3	5	8	12

WHL East Second All-Star Team (2015)

WILLIAMSON, Mike (WIHL-yuhm-suhn, MIGHK) VAN

Defense. Shoots left. 6'3", 187 lbs. Born, Leduc, AB, September 5, 1993.
(Vancouver's 6th choice, 175th overall, in 2013 Entry Draft).

			Regular Season					Playoffs				
Season	Club	League	GP	G	A	Pts	PIM	GP	G	A	Pts	PIM
2008-09	Leduc Oil Kings	Minor-AB	27	6	18	24	36	....	....	....	....	....
2009-10	Leduc Oil Kings	AMHL	31	7	3	10	72	10	0	3	3	8
	Drayton Valley	AJHL	4	0	0	0	0	....	....	....	....	....
2010-11	Leduc Oil Kings	AMHL	32	6	13	19	70	15	3	1	4	33
	Spruce Grove	AJHL	1	0	0	0	2	....	....	....	....	....
2011-12	Spruce Grove	AJHL	41	9	9	18	73	11	4	2	6	14
2012-13	Spruce Grove	AJHL	23	1	10	11	35	15	1	3	4	21
2013-14	Penn State	Big Ten	27	2	4	6	38	....	....	....	....	....
2014-15	Penn State	Big Ten	16	1	1	2	8	....	....	....	....	....

WILLMAN, Max (WIHL-muhn, MAX) BUF

Center. Shoots left. 6', 181 lbs. Born, Barnstable, MA, February 13, 1995.
(Buffalo's 7th choice, 121st overall, in 2014 Entry Draft).

			Regular Season					Playoffs				
Season	Club	League	GP	G	A	Pts	PIM	GP	G	A	Pts	PIM
2009-10	Barnstable	High-MA	....	4	3	7	....	....	....	....	....	....
2010-11	Barnstable	High-MA	....	13	9	22	....	....	....	....	....	....
2011-12	Barnstable	High-MA	....	19	16	35	....	....	....	....	....	....
2012-13	Barnstable	High-MA	....	19	13	32	....	....	....	....	....	....
2013-14	Springfield Rifles	Minor-MA	11	5	13	18	6	....	....	....	....	....
	Williston North.	High-MA	25	21	23	44	....	....	....	....	....	....
2014-15	Brown U.	ECAC	30	1	2	3	12	....	....	....	....	....

WITTCHOW, Eddie (WIHT-chow, EH-dee) FLA

Defense. Shoots left. 6'3", 189 lbs. Born, Burnsville, MN, October 31, 1992.
(Florida's 9th choice, 154th overall, in 2011 Entry Draft).

			Regular Season					Playoffs				
Season	Club	League	GP	G	A	Pts	PIM	GP	G	A	Pts	PIM
2009-10	Burnsville Blaze	High-MN	25	2	5	7	20	2	0	1	1	0
2010-11	Burnsville Blaze	High-MN	25	9	14	23	28	3	2	1	3	2
2011-12	Waterloo	USHL	60	5	13	18	74	7	0	4	4	4
2012-13	U. of Wisconsin	WCHA	29	0	3	3	28	....	....	....	....	....
2013-14	U. of Wisconsin	Big Ten	37	1	6	7	26	....	....	....	....	....
2014-15	U. of Wisconsin	Big Ten	25	0	0	0	43	....	....	....	....	....

USHL All-Rookie Team (2012)

WOHLBERG, David (WOHL-buhrg, DAY-vihd)

Center. Shoots left. 6'1", 192 lbs. Born, Southfield, MI, July 18, 1990.
(New Jersey's 7th choice, 172nd overall, in 2008 Entry Draft).

			Regular Season					Playoffs				
Season	Club	League	GP	G	A	Pts	PIM	GP	G	A	Pts	PIM
2006-07	USNTDP	U-17	12	2	6	8	42	....	....	....	....	....
	USNTDP	NAHL	45	10	10	20	99	6	1	4	5	22
2007-08	USNTDP	U-18	37	9	7	16	48	....	....	....	....	....
	USNTDP	NAHL	22	10	5	15	27	....	....	....	....	....
2008-09	U. of Michigan	CCHA	40	15	15	30	51	....	....	....	....	....
2009-10	U. of Michigan	CCHA	44	10	17	27	76	....	....	....	....	....
2010-11	U. of Michigan	CCHA	37	15	6	21	42	....	....	....	....	....
2011-12	U. of Michigan	CCHA	41	16	17	33	30	....	....	....	....	....
	Albany Devils	AHL	6	1	0	1	0	....	....	....	....	....
2013-14	Albany Devils	AHL	62	5	7	12	41	1	0	0	0	0
2014-15	Albany Devils	AHL	49	5	7	12	18	....	....	....	....	....

CCHA All-Rookie Team (2009) • CCHA Rookie of the Year (2009)

WOLANIN, Christian (woh-LA-nihn, KRIHS-ch'yehn) OTT

Defense. Shoots left. 6'2", 185 lbs. Born, Quebec City, QC, March 17, 1995.
(Ottawa's 5th choice, 107th overall, in 2015 Entry Draft).

			Regular Season					Playoffs				
Season	Club	League	GP	G	A	Pts	PIM	GP	G	A	Pts	PIM
2010-11	Det. L.C. U16	T1EHL	34	13	13	26	30	....	....	....	....	....
	Det. L.C. U16	Other	14	3	6	9	35	....	....	....	....	....
2011-12	Det. L.C. U18	HPHL	22	3	10	13	28	....	....	....	....	....
	Det. L.C. U18	Other	....	....	....	....	....	7	1	3	4	2
2012-13	Green Bay	USHL	54	0	8	8	70	4	1	0	1	2
2013-14	Green Bay	USHL	23	1	4	5	30	....	....	....	....	....
	Muskegon	USHL	32	5	16	21	44	....	....	....	....	....
2014-15	Muskegon	USHL	56	14	27	41	107	12	3	5	8	20

USHL Second All-Star Team (2015)

• Signed Letter of Intent to attend **University of North Dakota** (NCHC) in fall of 2015.

WOOD, Kyle (WUD, KIGHL) COL

Defense. Shoots right. 6'5", 210 lbs. Born, Waterloo, ON, May 4, 1996.
(Colorado's 2nd choice, 84th overall, in 2014 Entry Draft).

			Regular Season					Playoffs				
Season	Club	League	GP	G	A	Pts	PIM	GP	G	A	Pts	PIM
2011-12	Wat. Wolves MM	Minor-ON	30	9	11	20	54	14	3	13	16	6
	Waterloo Siskins	ON-Jr.B	2	0	0	0	0	5	0	2	2	4
2012-13	Orangeville Flyers	ON-Jr.A	46	6	11	17	10	....	....	....	....	....
	Brampton	OHL	16	1	1	2	8	5	0	0	0	2
2013-14	North Bay	OHL	33	2	10	12	21	22	2	8	10	6
2014-15	North Bay	OHL	67	16	24	40	18	15	1	10	11	2

WOOD, Miles (WUD, MIGH-uhlz) N.J.

Left wing. Shoots left. 6'1", 180 lbs. Born, Buffalo, NY, September 13, 1995.
(New Jersey's 3rd choice, 100th overall, in 2013 Entry Draft).

			Regular Season					Playoffs				
Season	Club	League	GP	G	A	Pts	PIM	GP	G	A	Pts	PIM
2010-11	Salem Ice Dogs	EmJHL	13	4	5	9	8	2	0	0	0	0
2011-12	Salem Ice Dogs	EmJHL	14	8	1	9	28	....	....	....	....	....
2012-13	Cape Cod Whalers	Minor-MA	6	0	0	0	0	....	....	....	....	....
	Nobles	High-MA	15	8	10	18	18	....	....	....	....	....
2013-14	Nobles	High-MA	27	29	24	53	....	....	....	....	....	....
2014-15	Nobles	High-MA	17	17	18	35	....	....	....	....	....	....

WOTHERSPOON, Parker (WAW-thuhr-spoon, PAHR-kuhr) NYI

Defense. Shoots left. 6', 171 lbs. Born, Surrey, BC, August 24, 1997.
(NY Islanders' 4th choice, 112th overall, in 2015 Entry Draft).

			Regular Season					Playoffs				
Season	Club	League	GP	G	A	Pts	PIM	GP	G	A	Pts	PIM
2011-12	Cloverdale Colts	Minor-BC	45	15	34	49	....	8	1	4	5	....
2012-13	Valley West Hawks	BCMML	37	7	19	22	118	....	....	....	....	....
	Tri-City Americans	WHL	5	0	0	0	4	2	0	0	0	0
2013-14	Tri-City Americans	WHL	62	2	16	18	74	5	0	2	2	2
2014-15	Tri-City Americans	WHL	72	9	33	42	93	4	0	1	1	4

WUTHRICH, Austin (wuhth-RIHCH, AW-stuhn) WSH

Right wing. Shoots right. 6'1", 190 lbs. Born, Bakersfield, CA, August 11, 1993.
(Washington's 5th choice, 107th overall, in 2012 Entry Draft).

			Regular Season					Playoffs				
Season	Club	League	GP	G	A	Pts	PIM	GP	G	A	Pts	PIM
2008-09	South Anchorage	High-AK	26	15	12	27	12	....	....	....	....	....
2009-10	Team Illinois	T1EHL	31	9	8	17	22	....	....	....	....	....
	USNTDP	USHL	15	2	2	4	10	....	....	....	....	....
	USNTDP	U-17	10	0	1	1	6	....	....	....	....	....
2010-11	USNTDP	USHL	16	3	4	7	38	2	0	0	0	17
	USNTDP	U-18	2	0	1	1	2	....	....	....	....	....
2011-12	U. of Notre Dame	CCHA	36	7	10	17	34	....	....	....	....	....
2012-13	U. of Notre Dame	CCHA	33	5	4	9	18	....	....	....	....	....
2013-14	U. of Notre Dame	H-East	40	6	7	13	20	....	....	....	....	....
2014-15	U. of Notre Dame	H-East	37	10	7	17	44	....	....	....	....	....

YAKIMOWICZ, C.J. (yah-KIHM-oh-wihtz, SEE-JAY) ST.L.

Right wing. Shoots right. 6'2", 210 lbs. Born, Wilkes Barre, PA, January 26, 1996.
(St. Louis' 8th choice, 172nd overall, in 2014 Entry Draft).

			Regular Season					Playoffs				
Season	Club	League	GP	G	A	Pts	PIM	GP	G	A	Pts	PIM
2011-12	Wilkes Barre	MtJHL	37	11	13	24	26	....	....	....	....	....
2012-13	Wilkes Barre	MtJHL	31	13	22	35	80	....	....	....	....	....
2013-14	Wilkes Barre U16	AYHL	10	6	7	13	60	....	....	....	....	....
	USNTDP	USHL	4	0	1	1	2	....	....	....	....	....
	London Knights	OHL	33	3	4	7	45	9	2	0	2	4
2014-15	London Knights	OHL	63	13	20	33	95	10	1	1	2	20

YAN, Dennis (YAN, DEH-nihs) T.B.

Left wing. Shoots left. 6'1", 184 lbs. Born, Portland, OR, April 14, 1997.
(Tampa Bay's 3rd choice, 64th overall, in 2015 Entry Draft).

			Regular Season					Playoffs				
Season	Club	League	GP	G	A	Pts	PIM	GP	G	A	Pts	PIM
2011-12	Lambton Jr. Sting	Minor-ON	30	22	11	33	26	12	10	7	17	24
2012-13	Det. B.T. MajMid.	T1EHL	40	30	15	45	47	5	5	1	6	6
2013-14	USNTDP	USHL	30	6	5	11	49	....	....	....	....	....
	USNTDP	U-17	18	6	11	17	10	....	....	....	....	....
2014-15	Shawinigan	QMJHL	59	33	31	64	71	7	7	1	8	6

YOUNG, Gus (YUHNG, GUHS)

Defense. Shoots left. 6'2", 200 lbs. Born, Dedham, MA, July 10, 1991.
(Colorado's 7th choice, 184th overall, in 2009 Entry Draft).

			Regular Season					Playoffs				
Season	Club	League	GP	G	A	Pts	PIM	GP	G	A	Pts	PIM
2006-07	Nobles	High-MA	31	3	10	13	14	....	....	....	....	....
2007-08	Bos. Little Bruins	Minor-MA	11	0	6	6	....	....	....	....	....	....
	Nobles	High-MA	29	6	9	15	....	....	....	....	....	....
2008-09	Cape Cod Whalers	Minor-MA	14	3	11	14	....	....	....	....	....	....
	Nobles	High-MA	29	5	29	34	16	....	....	....	....	....
2009-10	Cape Cod Whalers	Minor-MA	33	13	27	40	....	....	....	....	....	....
	Nobles	High-MA	29	12	26	38	10	....	....	....	....	....
2010-11	Yale	ECAC	5	0	1	1	4	....	....	....	....	....
2011-12	Yale	ECAC	35	3	9	12	36	....	....	....	....	....
2012-13	Yale	ECAC	37	2	7	9	58	....	....	....	....	....
2013-14	Yale	ECAC	33	7	11	18	28	....	....	....	....	....
2014-15	Worcester Sharks	AHL	64	5	10	15	37	4	0	0	0	0

NCAA Championship All-Tournament Team (2013)

• Missed majority of 2010-11 as a healthy reserve. Signed as a free agent by **Worcester** (AHL), October 9, 2014. Signed as a free agent by **San Jose** (AHL), July 10, 2015.

ZAAR, Daniel (ZAHR, DAN-yehl) CBJ

Right wing. Shoots right. 5'11", 175 lbs. Born, Helsingborg, Sweden, April 24, 1994.
(Columbus' 5th choice, 152nd overall, in 2012 Entry Draft).

			Regular Season					Playoffs				
Season	Club	League	GP	G	A	Pts	PIM	GP	G	A	Pts	PIM
2009-10	Jonstorps IF U18	Swe-U18	17	12	11	23	10	....	....	....	....	....
	Jonstorps IF Jr.	Swe-Jr.	4	3	3	6	4	....	....	....	....	....
	Jonstorps IF	Sweden-4	....	....	....	....	....	4	1	1	2	0
2010-11	Rogle U18	Swe-U18	23	16	18	34	4	4	0	4	4	4
	Rogle Jr.	Swe-Jr.	26	3	3	6	14	3	0	0	0	0
2011-12	Rogle U18	Swe-U18	7	6	6	12	0	5	5	4	9	6
	Rogle Jr.	Swe-Jr.	44	14	24	38	28	7	5	3	8	8
2012-13	Rogle Jr.	Swe-Jr.	17	11	8	19	6	1	0	0	0	2
	Bofors	Sweden-2	21	2	8	10	4	....	....	....	....	....
	Rogle	Sweden	25	2	1	3	0	....	....	....	....	....
	Rogle	Sweden-Q	7	1	0	1	2	....	....	....	....	....
2013-14	Rogle	Sweden-2	68	22	36	58	44	....	....	....	....	....
2014-15	Lulea HF	Sweden	55	9	18	27	18	9	2	2	4	6

ZACHA, Pavel (zah-KHUH, PAH-vehl) N.J.

Center. Shoots left. 6'3", 210 lbs. Born, Brno, Czech Rep., April 6, 1997.
(New Jersey's 1st choice, 6th overall, in 2015 Entry Draft).

			Regular Season					Playoffs				
Season	Club	League	GP	G	A	Pts	PIM	GP	G	A	Pts	PIM
2010-11	HC Liberec U18	CzR-U18	3	1	0	1	0	....	....	....	....	....
2011-12	HC Liberec U18	CzR-U18	36	10	15	25	20	7	2	3	5	6
	HC Liberec Jr.	CzRep-Jr.	1	0	0	0	0	....	....	....	....	....
2012-13	HC Liberec U18	CzR-U18	6	6	7	13	4	1	1	0	1	10
	Benatky	CzRep-2	1	0	0	0	0	....	....	....	....	....
	HC Liberec Jr.	CzRep-Jr.	39	14	26	40	26	5	2	2	4	0
2013-14	HC Liberec Jr.	CzRep-Jr.	10	6	11	17	64	3	1	1	2	4
	Benatky	CzRep-2	12	4	5	9	6	....	....	....	....	....
	Liberec	CzRep	38	4	4	8	10	3	0	0	0	0
2014-15	Sarnia Sting	OHL	37	16	18	34	56	5	2	1	3	10

OHL All-Rookie Team (2015)

ZAJAC, Darcy

(ZAY-jak, DAHR-see)

Center. Shoots right. 6'1", 205 lbs.   Born, Winnipeg, MB, September 23, 1986.

Season	Club	League	GP	G	A	Pts	PIM	GP	G	A	Pts	PIM
						Regular Season					Playoffs	
2004-05	Salmon Arm	BCHL	60	12	21	33	75	....	....	....	....	....
2005-06	Salmon Arm	BCHL	57	37	43	80	76	....	....	....	....	....
2006-07	North Dakota	WCHA	41	8	2	10	18	....	....	....	....	....
2007-08	North Dakota	WCHA	41	3	5	8	46	....	....	....	....	....
2008-09	North Dakota	WCHA	43	5	12	17	32	....	....	....	....	....
2009-10	North Dakota	WCHA	41	8	11	19	49	....	....	....	....	....
	Adirondack	AHL	2	0	0	0	4	....	....	....	....	....
2010-11	Albany Devils	AHL	40	4	5	9	60	....	....	....	....	....
	Trenton Devils	ECHL	32	6	17	23	35	....	....	....	....	....
2011-12	Albany Devils	AHL	66	8	16	24	86	....	....	....	....	....
2012-13	Albany Devils	AHL	67	9	8	17	86	....	....	....	....	....
2013-14	Albany Devils	AHL	19	1	5	6	43	4	0	0	0	0
2014-15	Albany Devils	AHL	71	8	15	23	83	....	....	....	....	....

Signed as a free agent by **Adirondack** (AHL), April 8, 2010. Signed as a free agent by **Albany** (AHL), June 26, 2010. Signed as a free agent by **New Jersey**, July 6, 2013.

ZAMORSKY, Petr

(za-MOHR-skee, PEE-tuhr)   **NYR**

Defense. Shoots right. 6', 190 lbs.   Born, Zlin, Czech Rep., August 3, 1992.

Season	Club	League	GP	G	A	Pts	PIM	GP	G	A	Pts	PIM
						Regular Season					Playoffs	
2011-12	PSG Zlin	CzRep	37	1	4	5	34	12	0	0	0	0
2012-13	PSG Zlin	CzRep	37	8	5	13	30	16	0	4	4	34
2013-14	PSG Zlin	CzRep	44	7	11	18	80	14	4	5	9	24
2014-15	Blues Espoo	Finland	25	3	3	6	18	....	....	....	....	....
	Orebro HK	Sweden	10	1	4	5	8	6	2	2	4	4

Signed as a free agent by **NY Rangers**, June 10, 2014.

ZBORIL, Jakub

(zuh-BAW-rihl, YA-kuhb)   **BOS**

Defense. Shoots left. 6', 200 lbs.   Born, Brno, Czech Rep., February 21, 1997.
(Boston's 1st choice, 13th overall, in 2015 Entry Draft).

Season	Club	League	GP	G	A	Pts	PIM	GP	G	A	Pts	PIM
						Regular Season					Playoffs	
2010-11	Brno U18	CzR-U18	2	0	0	0	0	....	....	....	....	....
2011-12	Brno U18	CzR-U18	35	2	4	6	69	2	0	0	0	0
2012-13	Brno U18	CzR-U18	27	4	5	9	70	3	0	2	2	8
2013-14	Brno U18	CzR-U18	2	1	1	2	0	10	3	5	8	14
	Brno Jr.	CzRep-Jr.	36	5	16	21	57	....	....	....	....	....
2014-15	Saint John	QMJHL	44	13	20	33	73	5	1	2	3	18

ZBOROVSKIY, Sergei

(z'bohr-AWV-skee, SAIR-gay)   **NYR**

Defense. Shoots left. 6'4", 190 lbs.   Born, Moscow, Russia, February 21, 1997.
(NY Rangers' 3rd choice, 79th overall, in 2015 Entry Draft).

Season	Club	League	GP	G	A	Pts	PIM	GP	G	A	Pts	PIM
						Regular Season					Playoffs	
2013-14	Dyn'o Moscow Jr.	Russia-Jr.	4	0	0	0	2	....	....	....	....	....
2014-15	Regina Pats	WHL	71	3	16	19	70	6	0	1	1	13

ZHARKOV, Daniil

(zharh-KAWV, da-NEEL)   **EDM**

Left wing. Shoots left. 6'4", 208 lbs.   Born, St. Petersburg, Russia, February 6, 1994.
(Edmonton's 4th choice, 91st overall, in 2012 Entry Draft).

Season	Club	League	GP	G	A	Pts	PIM	GP	G	A	Pts	PIM
						Regular Season					Playoffs	
2010-11	Tri-City Storm	USHL	36	8	3	11	27	....	....	....	....	....
	Ser. Ljvy Jr.	Russia-Jr.	12	1	2	3	16	....	....	....	....	....
2011-12	Belleville Bulls	OHL	50	23	13	36	25	6	1	2	3	2
2012-13	Belleville Bulls	OHL	59	25	18	43	24	17	4	8	12	21
2013-14	Nizhny Novgorod	KHL	49	2	3	5	35	....	....	....	....	....
	HK Sarov	Russia-2	6	1	1	2	2	....	....	....	....	....
2014-15	Nizhny Novgorod	KHL	9	0	0	0	4	....	....	....	....	....
	HK Sarov	Russia-2	39	4	5	9	22	....	....	....	....	....
	Nizh. Novgorod Jr.	Russia-Jr.	1	0	0	0	0	3	1	0	1	4

ZHUKENOV, Dmitri

(zhoo-KEH-nawv, dih-MEE-tree)   **VAN**

Center. Shoots right. 5'11", 169 lbs.   Born, Omsk, Russia, March 24, 1997.
(Vancouver's 3rd choice, 114th overall, in 2015 Entry Draft).

Season	Club	League	GP	G	A	Pts	PIM	GP	G	A	Pts	PIM
						Regular Season					Playoffs	
2014-15	Omsk Jr.	Russia-Jr.	35	3	16	19	42	4	0	2	2	0

ZLOBIN, Anton

(ZLOH-bihn, an-TAWN)   **PIT**

Right wing. Shoots right. 5'11", 209 lbs.   Born, Moscow, Russia, February 22, 1993.
(Pittsburgh's 9th choice, 173rd overall, in 2012 Entry Draft).

Season	Club	League	GP	G	A	Pts	PIM	GP	G	A	Pts	PIM
						Regular Season					Playoffs	
2010-11	Shawinigan	QMJHL	59	23	22	45	28	12	5	1	6	2
2011-12	Shawinigan	QMJHL	66	40	36	76	50	11	3	7	10	2
2012-13	Val-d'Or Foreurs	QMJHL	61	29	62	91	43	10	2	8	10	4
2013-14	Wilkes-Barre	AHL	46	8	11	19	16	15	6	4	10	4
	Wheeling Nailers	ECHL	10	5	6	11	4	....	....	....	....	....
2014-15	Wilkes-Barre	AHL	6	0	0	0	0	....	....	....	....	....

• Missed majority of 2014-15 due to upper-body injury at Norwich (AHL), October 31, 2014.

ZUHLSDORF, Ryan

(ZOHLZ-dohrf, RIGH-uhn)   **T.B.**

Defense. Shoots left. 5'11", 188 lbs.   Born, Edina, MN, July 1, 1997.
(Tampa Bay's 7th choice, 150th overall, in 2015 Entry Draft).

Season	Club	League	GP	G	A	Pts	PIM	GP	G	A	Pts	PIM
						Regular Season					Playoffs	
2013-14	Team Southwest	UMHSEL	2	0	0	0	0	....	....	....	....	....
	Team Northeast	UMHSEL	2	0	1	1	0	5	0	1	1	2
	Team Southeast	UMHSEL	12	2	3	5	10	5	0	1	1	2
	Edina Hornets	High-MN	25	1	11	12	6	5	0	4	4	0
2014-15	Sioux City	USHL	56	3	19	22	58	5	0	2	2	0

• Signed Letter of Intent to attend **University of Minnesota** (Big Ten) in fall of 2016.

ZYKOV, Valentin

(ZIH-kawv, val-ehn-TEEN)   **L.A.**

Left wing. Shoots right. 6', 212 lbs.   Born, St. Petersburg, Russia, May 15, 1995.
(Los Angeles' 1st choice, 37th overall, in 2013 Entry Draft).

Season	Club	League	GP	G	A	Pts	PIM	GP	G	A	Pts	PIM
						Regular Season					Playoffs	
2011-12	CSKA Jr.	Russia-Jr.	52	5	6	11	105	18	0	2	2	4
2012-13	Baie-Comeau	QMJHL	67	40	35	75	60	19	10	9	19	18
2013-14	Baie-Comeau	QMJHL	53	23	40	63	70	22	7	15	22	14
2014-15	Baie-Comeau	QMJHL	16	6	12	18	22	....	....	....	....	....
	Gatineau	QMJHL	26	15	13	28	38	11	3	4	7	20

QMJHL All-Rookie Team (2013) • QMJHL Rookie of the Year (2013) • Canadian Major Junior Rookie of the Year (2013)

2015-16 NHL Player Register

Note: The 2015-16 NHL Player Register lists forwards and defensemen only. Goaltenders are listed separately. The NHL Player Register lists every active skater who played in the NHL in 2014-15 plus additional players with NHL experience. Trades and roster changes are current as of August 14, 2015.

Abbreviations: GP – games played; **G** – goals; **A** – assists; **Pts** – points; **PIM** – penalties in minutes; **PP** – power-play goals; **SH** – shorthanded goals; **GW** – game-winning goals; **S** – shots; **S%** – shooting percentage; **+/–** – plus/minus; **TF** – total faceoffs taken; **F%** – faceoff winning percentage; **Min** – average time on ice per game; ***** – league-leading total ♦ – member of Stanley Cup-winning team.

Prospect Register begins on page 275.
Goaltender Register begins on page 587.
Retired Player Index begins on page 612.
Retired Goaltender Index begins on page 657.
League abbreviations are listed on page 670.

| | | | | | | Regular Season | | | | | | | | | | | | | | Playoffs | | | | | | |
Season	Club	League	GP	G	A	Pts	PIM	PP	SH	GW	S	S%	+/-	TF	F%	Min	GP	G	A	Pts	PIM	PP	SH	GW	Min

ABBOTT, Spencer
(A-buht, SPEHN-suhr)

Right wing. Shoots right. 5'9", 170 lbs. Born, Hamilton, ON, April 30, 1988.

Season	Club	League	GP	G	A	Pts	PIM	PP	SH	GW	S	S%	+/-	TF	F%	Min	GP	G	A	Pts	PIM	PP	SH	GW	Min
2005-06	Sherwood Saints	High-ON	STATISTICS NOT AVAILABLE																						
	Hamilton Reps	Minor-ON	STATISTICS NOT AVAILABLE																						
	Hamilton	ON-Jr.A	11	1	0	1	0	....	....	....	....	....	....	....	....	....	1	0	0	0	0	....	....	....	....
2006-07	Hamilton	ON-Jr.A	49	32	43	75	22	....	....	....	....	....	....	....	....	....	19	4	5	9	12	....	....	....	....
2007-08	Hamilton	ON-Jr.A	48	42	41	83	42	....	....	....	....	....	....	....	....	....	5	2	4	6	2	....	....	....	....
2008-09	U. of Maine	H-East	38	7	9	16	8	....	....	....	....	....	....	....	....	....									
2009-10	U. of Maine	H-East	38	9	19	28	6	....	....	....	....	....	....	....	....	....									
2010-11	U. of Maine	H-East	36	17	23	40	16	....	....	....	....	....	....	....	....	....									
2011-12	U. of Maine	H-East	39	21	41	62	34	....	....	....	....	....	....	....	....	....									
	Toronto Marlies	AHL	3	0	1	1	0	....	....	....	....	....	....	....	....	....	5	0	0	0	0	....	....	....	....
2012-13	Toronto Marlies	AHL	55	13	20	33	10	....	....	....	....	....	....	....	....	....	5	2	3	5	2	....	....	....	....
2013-14	**Toronto**	**NHL**	1	0	0	0	0	0	0	0	2	0.0	–2	0	0.0	5:16	....	....	....	....	....	....	....	....	....
	Toronto Marlies	AHL	64	17	52	69	16	....	....	....	....	....	....	....	....	....	11	4	7	11	2	....	....	....	....
2014-15	Toronto Marlies	AHL	46	7	17	24	10	....	....	....	....	....	....	....	....	....									
	Rockford IceHogs	AHL	19	12	9	21	6	....	....	....	....	....	....	....	....	....	8	3	3	6	2	....	....	....	....
	NHL Totals		1	0	0	0	0	0	0	0	2	0.0		0	0.0	5:16	....	....	....	....	....	....	....	....	....

Hockey East First All-Star Team (2012) • NCAA East First All-American Team (2012) • AHL Second All-Star Team (2014)
Signed as a free agent by **Toronto**, March 28, 2012. Traded to **Chicago** by **Toronto** for T.J. Brennan, February 26, 2015. Signed as a free agent by **Frolunda** (Sweden), June 16, 2015.

ABDELKADER, Justin
(abdehl-KAY-duhr, JUHS-tihn)   **DET**

Left wing. Shoots left. 6'2", 218 lbs. Born, Muskegon, MI, February 25, 1987. Detroit's 2nd choice, 42nd overall, in 2005 Entry Draft.

Season	Club	League	GP	G	A	Pts	PIM	PP	SH	GW	S	S%	+/-	TF	F%	Min	GP	G	A	Pts	PIM	PP	SH	GW	Min
2003-04	Muskegon M.S.	High-MI	28	37	43	80	....	....	....	....	....	....	....	....	....	....									
2004-05	Cedar Rapids	USHL	60	27	25	52	86	....	....	....	....	....	....	....	....	....	11	0	4	4	8	....	....	....	....
2005-06	Michigan State	CCHA	44	10	12	22	83	....	....	....	....	....	....	....	....	....									
2006-07	Michigan State	CCHA	38	15	18	33	91	....	....	....	....	....	....	....	....	....									
2007-08	Michigan State	CCHA	42	19	21	40	107	....	....	....	....	....	....	....	....	....									
	Detroit	**NHL**	2	0	0	0	2	0	0	0	6	0.0	0	12	41.7	12:13	....	....	....	....	....	....	....	....	....
2008-09	**Detroit**	**NHL**	2	0	0	0	0	0	0	0	2	0.0	0	7	57.1	9:18	10	2	1	3	0	0	0	0	6:58
	Grand Rapids	AHL	76	24	28	52	102	....	....	....	....	....	....	....	....	....	10	6	2	8	23	....	....	....	....
2009-10	**Detroit**	**NHL**	50	3	3	6	35	0	0	0	79	3.8	–11	318	46.5	10:35	11	1	1	2	*36	0	0	0	7:30
	Grand Rapids	AHL	33	11	13	24	86	....	....	....	....	....	....	....	....	....									
2010-11	**Detroit**	**NHL**	74	7	12	19	61	0	0	1	129	5.4	15	430	52.8	12:18	11	0	0	0	22	0	0	0	13:27
2011-12	**Detroit**	**NHL**	81	8	14	22	62	0	0	1	121	6.6	4	452	52.9	12:19	5	0	0	0	2	0	0	0	12:31
2012-13	**Detroit**	**NHL**	48	10	3	13	34	0	0	0	96	10.4	6	125	52.0	14:49	12	2	1	3	33	0	1	0	16:57
2013-14	**Detroit**	**NHL**	70	10	18	28	31	1	0	3	147	6.8	2	55	41.8	15:17	5	0	2	2	6	0	0	0	15:48
2014-15	**Detroit**	**NHL**	71	23	21	44	72	8	0	5	154	14.9	3	154	46.7	17:55	5	0	2	2	6	0	0	0	16:44
	NHL Totals		398	61	71	132	297	9	0	10	734	8.3		1414	50.8	13:54	59	5	7	12	105	0	1	0	12:21

NCAA Championship All-Tournament Team (2007) • NCAA Championship Tournament MVP (2007) • AHL All-Rookie Team (2009)

ACTON, Will
(AK-tuhn, WIHL)   **VAN**

Center. Shoots left. 6'2", 190 lbs. Born, Stouffville, ON, July 16, 1987.

Season	Club	League	GP	G	A	Pts	PIM	PP	SH	GW	S	S%	+/-	TF	F%	Min	GP	G	A	Pts	PIM	PP	SH	GW	Min
2004-05	Stouffville Spirit	ON-Jr.A	41	5	8	13	28	....	....	....	....	....	....	....	....	....									
2005-06	Stouffville Spirit	ON-Jr.A	48	11	20	31	38	....	....	....	....	....	....	....	....	....	30	9	17	26	71	....	....	....	....
2006-07	Stouffville Spirit	ON-Jr.A	33	16	13	29	63	....	....	....	....	....	....	....	....	....	8	6	3	9	12	....	....	....	....
2007-08	Lake Superior	CCHA	36	6	7	13	22	....	....	....	....	....	....	....	....	....									
2008-09	Lake Superior	CCHA	38	7	9	16	53	....	....	....	....	....	....	....	....	....									
2009-10	Lake Superior	CCHA	36	10	14	24	39	....	....	....	....	....	....	....	....	....									
2010-11	Lake Superior	CCHA	34	9	15	24	18	....	....	....	....	....	....	....	....	....									
	Toronto Marlies	AHL	5	0	0	0	0	....	....	....	....	....	....	....	....	....									
	Reading Royals	ECHL	1	0	0	0	0	....	....	....	....	....	....	....	....	....									
2011-12	Toronto Marlies	AHL	69	7	9	16	58	....	....	....	....	....	....	....	....	....	17	1	1	2	9	....	....	....	....
2012-13	Toronto Marlies	AHL	67	8	11	19	60	....	....	....	....	....	....	....	....	....	9	4	2	6	12	....	....	....	....
2013-14	**Edmonton**	**NHL**	30	3	2	5	21	0	0	1	18	16.7	–2	195	50.3	8:08	....	....	....	....	....	....	....	....	....
	Oklahoma City	AHL	47	12	11	23	74	....	....	....	....	....	....	....	....	....	3	0	1	1	0	....	....	....	....
2014-15	**Edmonton**	**NHL**	3	0	0	0	5	0	0	0	2	0.0	–2	8	50.0	10:43									
	Oklahoma City	AHL	6	1	1	2	2	....	....	....	....	....	....	....	....	....									
	Utica Comets	AHL	45	11	8	19	26	....	....	....	....	....	....	....	....	....	9	1	2	3	2	....	....	....	....
	NHL Totals		33	3	2	5	26	0	0	1	20	15.0		203	50.2	8:22	....	....	....	....	....	....	....	....	....

Signed as a free agent by **Edmonton**, July 6, 2013. Traded to **Vancouver** by **Edmonton** Kellan Lain, November 20, 2014.

ADAM, Luke
(A-duhm, LEWK) **NYR**

Center. Shoots left. 6'2", 206 lbs. Born, St. John's, NL, June 18, 1990. Buffalo's 3rd choice, 44th overall, in 2008 Entry Draft.

			Regular Season														Playoffs								
Season	Club	League	GP	G	A	Pts	PIM	PP	SH	GW	S	S%	+/-	TF	F%	Min	GP	G	A	Pts	PIM	PP	SH	GW	Min
2006-07	St. John's	QMJHL	63	6	9	15	51	....	....	....	....	....	....	....	....	....	4	0	2	2	4	....	....	....	....
2007-08	St. John's	QMJHL	70	36	30	66	72	....	....	....	....	....	....	....	....	....	6	3	5	8	8	....	....	....	....
2008-09	Montreal	QMJHL	47	22	27	49	59	....	....	....	....	....	....	....	....	....	....	....	....	....	....	....	....	....	....
2009-10	Cape Breton	QMJHL	56	49	41	90	75	....	....	....	....	....	....	....	....	....	5	3	1	4	2	....	....	....	....
	Portland Pirates	AHL	....	....	....	....	....	....	....	....	....	....	....	....	....	....	3	0	2	2	0	....	....	....	....
2010-11	**Buffalo**	**NHL**	**19**	**3**	**1**	**4**	**12**	**0**	**0**	**1**	**31**	**9.7**	**-6**	**119**	**34.5**	**11:13**	....	....	....	....	....	....	....	....	....
	Portland Pirates	AHL	57	29	33	62	46	....	....	....	....	....	....	....	....	....	12	4	3	7	14	....	....	....	....
2011-12	**Buffalo**	**NHL**	**52**	**10**	**10**	**20**	**14**	**0**	**0**	**0**	**89**	**11.2**	**-6**	**259**	**44.0**	**12:24**	....	....	....	....	....	....	....	....	....
	Rochester	AHL	27	4	9	13	18	....	....	....	....	....	....	....	....	....	3	0	1	1	4	....	....	....	....
2012-13	Rochester	AHL	67	15	22	37	57	....	....	....	....	....	....	....	....	....	3	0	0	0	2	....	....	....	....
	Buffalo	**NHL**	**4**	**1**	**0**	**1**	**2**	**0**	**0**	**0**	**2**	**50.0**	**1**	**1**	**100.0**	**9:48**	....	....	....	....	....	....	....	....	....
2013-14	**Buffalo**	**NHL**	**12**	**1**	**0**	**1**	**4**	**0**	**0**	**0**	**16**	**6.3**	**0**	**26**	**38.5**	**12:50**	....	....	....	....	....	....	....	....	....
	Rochester	AHL	59	29	20	49	48	....	....	....	....	....	....	....	....	....	5	2	2	4	4	....	....	....	....
2014-15	Rochester	AHL	27	8	12	20	24	....	....	....	....	....	....	....	....	....	....	....	....	....	....	....	....	....	....
	Columbus	**NHL**	**3**	**0**	**0**	**0**	**4**	**0**	**0**	**0**	**0**	**0.0**	**0**	**0**	**0.0**	**6:27**	....	....	....	....	....	....	....	....	....
	Springfield	AHL	46	8	14	22	38	....	....	....	....	....	....	....	....	....	....	....	....	....	....	....	....	....	....
	NHL Totals		**90**	**15**	**11**	**26**	**36**	**0**	**0**	**1**	**138**	**10.9**		**405**	**41.0**	**11:54**	....	....	....	....	....	....	....	....	....

QMJHL First All-Star Team (2010) • AHL All-Rookie Team (2011) • Dudley "Red" Garrett Memorial Award (AHL – Rookie of the Year) (2011)

Traded to **Columbus** by **Buffalo** for Jerry D'Amigo, December 16, 2014. Signed as a free agent by **NY Rangers**, July 3, 2015.

ADAMS, Craig
(A-duhmz, KRAYG)

Right wing. Shoots right. 6', 200 lbs. Born, Seria, Brunei, April 26, 1977. Hartford's 9th choice, 223rd overall, in 1996 Entry Draft.

Season	Club	League	GP	G	A	Pts	PIM	PP	SH	GW	S	S%	+/-	TF	F%	Min	GP	G	A	Pts	PIM	PP	SH	GW	Min
1995-96	Harvard Crimson	ECAC	34	8	9	17	56	....	....	....	....	....	....	....	....	....	....	....	....	....	....	....	....	....	....
1996-97	Harvard Crimson	ECAC	32	6	4	10	36	....	....	....	....	....	....	....	....	....	....	....	....	....	....	....	....	....	....
1997-98	Harvard Crimson	ECAC	12	6	6	12	12	....	....	....	....	....	....	....	....	....	....	....	....	....	....	....	....	....	....
1998-99	Harvard Crimson	ECAC	31	9	14	23	53	....	....	....	....	....	....	....	....	....	....	....	....	....	....	....	....	....	....
99-2000	Cincinnati	IHL	73	12	12	24	124	....	....	....	....	....	....	....	....	....	8	0	1	1	14	....	....	....	....
2000-01	**Carolina**	**NHL**	**44**	**1**	**0**	**1**	**20**	**0**	**0**	**0**	**15**	**6.7**	**-7**	**4**	**25.0**	**4:30**	**3**	**0**	**0**	**0**	**0**	**0**	**0**	**0**	**3:45**
	Cincinnati	IHL	4	0	1	1	9	....	....	....	....	....	....	....	....	....	1	0	0	0	2	....	....	....	....
2001-02	**Carolina**	**NHL**	**33**	**0**	**1**	**1**	**38**	**0**	**0**	**0**	**17**	**0.0**	**2**	**9**	**33.3**	**5:54**	**1**	**0**	**0**	**0**	**0**	**0**	**0**	**0**	**7:41**
	Lowell	AHL	22	5	4	9	51	....	....	....	....	....	....	....	....	....	....	....	....	....	....	....	....	....	....
2002-03	**Carolina**	**NHL**	**81**	**6**	**12**	**18**	**71**	**1**	**0**	**1**	**107**	**5.6**	**-11**	**20**	**35.0**	**12:12**	....	....	....	....	....	....	....	....	....
2003-04	**Carolina**	**NHL**	**80**	**7**	**10**	**17**	**69**	**0**	**1**	**0**	**110**	**6.4**	**-5**	**20**	**45.0**	**13:41**	....	....	....	....	....	....	....	....	....
2004-05	HC Milano	Italy	30	15	14	29	57	....	....	....	....	....	....	....	....	....	15	4	7	11	26	....	....	....	....
2005-06♦	**Carolina**	**NHL**	**67**	**10**	**11**	**21**	**51**	**1**	**1**	**2**	**68**	**14.7**	**1**	**13**	**53.9**	**12:18**	**25**	**0**	**0**	**0**	**10**	**0**	**0**	**0**	**8:16**
	Lowell	AHL	13	4	3	7	20	....	....	....	....	....	....	....	....	....	....	....	....	....	....	....	....	....	....
2006-07	**Carolina**	**NHL**	**82**	**7**	**7**	**14**	**54**	**0**	**1**	**1**	**71**	**9.9**	**-9**	**36**	**30.6**	**10:04**	....	....	....	....	....	....	....	....	....
2007-08	**Carolina**	**NHL**	**40**	**2**	**3**	**5**	**34**	**0**	**0**	**0**	**31**	**6.5**	**-8**	**11**	**27.3**	**9:48**	....	....	....	....	....	....	....	....	....
	Chicago	**NHL**	**35**	**2**	**4**	**6**	**24**	**0**	**1**	**1**	**32**	**6.3**	**-8**	**30**	**53.3**	**11:56**	....	....	....	....	....	....	....	....	....
2008-09	**Chicago**	**NHL**	**36**	**2**	**4**	**6**	**22**	**1**	**0**	**0**	**38**	**5.3**	**-3**	**16**	**37.5**	**8:43**	....	....	....	....	....	....	....	....	....
	♦ **Pittsburgh**	**NHL**	**9**	**0**	**1**	**1**	**0**	**0**	**0**	**0**	**9**	**0.0**	**0**	**5**	**40.0**	**8:34**	**24**	**3**	**2**	**5**	**16**	**0**	**0**	**0**	**9:45**
2009-10	**Pittsburgh**	**NHL**	**82**	**0**	**10**	**10**	**72**	**0**	**0**	**0**	**84**	**0.0**	**-5**	**562**	**43.8**	**11:06**	**13**	**2**	**1**	**3**	**15**	**0**	**0**	**1**	**10:38**
2010-11	**Pittsburgh**	**NHL**	**80**	**4**	**11**	**15**	**76**	**0**	**2**	**1**	**90**	**4.4**	**-5**	**465**	**41.7**	**12:11**	**7**	**1**	**0**	**1**	**2**	**0**	**0**	**0**	**13:06**
2011-12	**Pittsburgh**	**NHL**	**82**	**5**	**13**	**18**	**34**	**0**	**0**	**0**	**76**	**6.6**	**-6**	**292**	**45.2**	**11:17**	**5**	**0**	**0**	**0**	**19**	**0**	**0**	**0**	**8:39**
2012-13	**Pittsburgh**	**NHL**	**48**	**3**	**6**	**9**	**28**	**0**	**1**	**0**	**46**	**6.5**	**-1**	**98**	**52.0**	**11:10**	**15**	**0**	**1**	**1**	**10**	**0**	**0**	**0**	**12:02**
2013-14	**Pittsburgh**	**NHL**	**82**	**5**	**6**	**11**	**46**	**0**	**0**	**0**	**73**	**6.8**	**-16**	**139**	**43.9**	**12:28**	**13**	**1**	**1**	**2**	**2**	**0**	**1**	**0**	**10:42**
2014-15	**Pittsburgh**	**NHL**	**70**	**1**	**6**	**7**	**44**	**0**	**0**	**1**	**51**	**2.0**	**-1**	**40**	**42.5**	**9:45**	....	....	....	....	....	....	....	....	....
	NHL Totals		**951**	**55**	**105**	**160**	**683**	**3**	**7**	**7**	**918**	**6.0**		**1760**	**43.5**	**10:55**	**106**	**7**	**5**	**12**	**74**	**0**	**1**	**1**	**9:55**

• Rights transferred to **Carolina** after **Hartford** franchise relocated, June 25, 1997. • Missed majority of 1997-98 due to shoulder injury vs. University of Wisconsin (WCHA), December 27, 1997. Signed as a free agent by **Milano**, (Italy), July 28, 2004. Signed as a free agent by **Anaheim**, August 25, 2005. Traded to **Carolina** by **Anaheim** for Bruno St. Jacques, October 3, 2005. Traded to **Chicago** by **Carolina** for future considerations, January 17, 2008. Claimed on waivers by **Pittsburgh** from **Chicago**, March 4, 2009.

AGOSTINO, Kenny
(a-goh-STEE-noh, KEHN-nee) **CGY**

Left wing. Shoots left. 6'1", 200 lbs. Born, Morristown, NJ, April 30, 1992. Pittsburgh's 4th choice, 140th overall, in 2010 Entry Draft.

Season	Club	League	GP	G	A	Pts	PIM	PP	SH	GW	S	S%	+/-	TF	F%	Min	GP	G	A	Pts	PIM	PP	SH	GW	Min
2007-08	Delbarton	High-NJ	....	24	48	72	....	....	....	....	....	....	....	....	....	....	....	....	....	....	....	....	....	....	....
2008-09	Delbarton	High-NJ	STATISTICS NOT AVAILABLE					....	....	....	....	....	....	....	....	....	....	....	....	....	....	....	....	....	....
2009-10	Delbarton	High-NJ	27	50	33	83	40	....	....	....	....	....	....	....	....	....	....	....	....	....	....	....	....	....	....
	USNTDP	U-18	2	0	0	0	2	....	....	....	....	....	....	....	....	....	....	....	....	....	....	....	....	....	....
2010-11	Yale	ECAC	31	11	14	25	30	....	....	....	....	....	....	....	....	....	....	....	....	....	....	....	....	....	....
2011-12	Yale	ECAC	33	14	20	34	32	....	....	....	....	....	....	....	....	....	....	....	....	....	....	....	....	....	....
2012-13	Yale	ECAC	37	17	24	41	32	....	....	....	....	....	....	....	....	....	....	....	....	....	....	....	....	....	....
2013-14	Yale	ECAC	33	14	18	32	46	....	....	....	....	....	....	....	....	....	....	....	....	....	....	....	....	....	....
	Calgary	**NHL**	**8**	**1**	**1**	**2**	**0**	**0**	**0**	**0**	**12**	**8.3**	**-2**	**0**	**0.0**	**11:06**	....	....	....	....	....	....	....	....	....
2014-15	Adirondack	AHL	67	15	28	43	52	....	....	....	....	....	....	....	....	....	....	....	....	....	....	....	....	....	....
	NHL Totals		**8**	**1**	**1**	**2**	**0**	**0**	**0**	**0**	**12**	**8.3**		**0**	**0.0**	**11:06**	....	....	....	....	....	....	....	....	....

ECAC Second All-Star Team (2013)

Traded to **Calgary** by **Pittsburgh** with Ben Hanowski and Pittsburgh's 1st round choice (Morgan Klimchuk) in 2013 Entry Draft for Jarome Iginla, March 28, 2013.

AGOZZINO, Andrew
(a-guh-ZEEN-oh, AN-droo) **COL**

Left wing. Shoots left. 5'10", 187 lbs. Born, Kleinburg, ON, January 3, 1991.

Season	Club	League	GP	G	A	Pts	PIM	PP	SH	GW	S	S%	+/-	TF	F%	Min	GP	G	A	Pts	PIM	PP	SH	GW	Min
2007-08	Niagara Ice Dogs	OHL	50	12	10	22	47	....	....	....	....	....	....	....	....	....	....	....	....	....	....	....	....	....	....
2008-09	Niagara Ice Dogs	OHL	67	27	29	56	88	....	....	....	....	....	....	....	....	....	12	6	5	11	24	....	....	....	....
2009-10	Niagara Ice Dogs	OHL	66	37	29	66	95	....	....	....	....	....	....	....	....	....	5	3	2	5	15	....	....	....	....
	Peoria Rivermen	AHL	2	0	0	0	0	....	....	....	....	....	....	....	....	....	....	....	....	....	....	....	....	....	....
2010-11	Niagara Ice Dogs	OHL	68	43	31	74	73	....	....	....	....	....	....	....	....	....	14	6	7	13	19	....	....	....	....
2011-12	Niagara Ice Dogs	OHL	67	40	48	88	67	....	....	....	....	....	....	....	....	....	20	11	7	18	16	....	....	....	....
2012-13	Lake Erie	AHL	76	20	32	52	73	....	....	....	....	....	....	....	....	....	....	....	....	....	....	....	....	....	....
2013-14	Lake Erie	AHL	75	17	32	49	73	....	....	....	....	....	....	....	....	....	....	....	....	....	....	....	....	....	....
2014-15	**Colorado**	**NHL**	**1**	**0**	**1**	**1**	**0**	**0**	**0**	**0**	**1**	**0.0**	**1**	**2**	**0.0**	**9:45**	....	....	....	....	....	....	....	....	....
	Lake Erie	AHL	74	30	34	64	55	....	....	....	....	....	....	....	....	....	....	....	....	....	....	....	....	....	....
	NHL Totals		**1**	**0**	**1**	**1**	**0**	**0**	**0**	**0**	**1**	**0.0**		**2**	**0.0**	**9:45**	....	....	....	....	....	....	....	....	....

Signed to a ATO (amateur tryout) contract by **Peoria** (AHL), April 8, 2010. Signed as a free agent by **Lake Erie** (AHL), August 28, 2012. Signed as a free agent by **Colorado**, March 22, 2013.

AKESON, Jason
(AK-uh-suhn, JAY-suhn) **BUF**

Right wing. Shoots right. 5'10", 190 lbs. Born, Orleans, ON, June 3, 1990.

Season	Club	League	GP	G	A	Pts	PIM	PP	SH	GW	S	S%	+/-	TF	F%	Min	GP	G	A	Pts	PIM	PP	SH	GW	Min
2006-07	Cumberland	ON-Jr.A	54	17	36	53	40	....	....	....	....	....	....	....	....	....	....	....	....	....	....	....	....	....	....
2007-08	Cumberland	ON-Jr.A	34	18	43	61	14	....	....	....	....	....	....	....	....	....	....	....	....	....	....	....	....	....	....
	Kitchener Rangers	OHL	13	0	2	2	4	....	....	....	....	....	....	....	....	....	16	0	1	1	0	....	....	....	....
2008-09	Kitchener Rangers	OHL	56	20	44	64	16	....	....	....	....	....	....	....	....	....	....	....	....	....	....	....	....	....	....
2009-10	Kitchener Rangers	OHL	65	24	56	80	24	....	....	....	....	....	....	....	....	....	20	8	11	19	14	....	....	....	....
2010-11	Kitchener Rangers	OHL	67	24	*84	*108	23	....	....	....	....	....	....	....	....	....	7	3	6	9	0	....	....	....	....
2011-12	Adirondack	AHL	76	14	41	55	26	....	....	....	....	....	....	....	....	....	....	....	....	....	....	....	....	....	....
2012-13	Adirondack	AHL	62	20	33	53	27	....	....	....	....	....	....	....	....	....	....	....	....	....	....	....	....	....	....
	Trenton Titans	ECHL	14	2	8	10	7	....	....	....	....	....	....	....	....	....	....	....	....	....	....	....	....	....	....
	Philadelphia	**NHL**	**1**	**1**	**0**	**1**	**0**	**0**	**0**	**0**	**2**	**50.0**	**2**	**0**	**0.0**	**12:23**	....	....	....	....	....	....	....	....	....
2013-14	**Philadelphia**	**NHL**	**1**	**0**	**1**	**1**	**0**	**0**	**0**	**0**	**2**	**0.0**	**1**	**0**	**0.0**	**13:22**	**7**	**2**	**1**	**3**	**4**	**1**	**0**	**0**	**13:00**
	Adirondack	AHL	70	24	40	64	42	....	....	....	....	....	....	....	....	....	....	....	....	....	....	....	....	....	....

			Regular Season													Playoffs								
Season	Club	League	GP	G	A	Pts	PIM	PP	SH	GW	S	S%	+/-	TF	F%	Min	GP	G	A	Pts	PIM	PP	SH	GW	Min
2014-15	**Philadelphia**	**NHL**	**13**	**0**	**0**	**0**	**8**	**0**	**0**	**0**	**9**	**0.0**	**−1**	**2**	**50.0**	**8:03**	....	....	....	....	....	....	....	....	....
	Lehigh Valley	AHL	57	23	30	53	25	....	....	....	....	....	....	....	....	....	....	....	....	....	....	....	....	....	....
	NHL Totals		**15**	**1**	**1**	**2**	**8**	**0**	**0**	**0**	**13**	**7.7**		**2**	**50.0**	**8:42**	**7**	**2**	**1**	**3**	**4**	**1**	**0**	**0**	**13:00**

OHL Second All-Star Team (2011)

Signed as a free agent by **Philadelphia**, March 2, 2011. Signed as a free agent by **Buffalo**, July 1, 2015.

ALBERT, John (AL-buhrt, JAWN) WPG

Center. Shoots left. 5'11", 190 lbs. Born, Cleveland, OH, January 19, 1989. Atlanta's 3rd choice, 175th overall, in 2007 Entry Draft.

Season	Club	League	GP	G	A	Pts	PIM	PP	SH	GW	S	S%	+/-	TF	F%	Min	GP	G	A	Pts	PIM	PP	SH	GW	Min
2004-05	Cleveland Barons	MWEHL	67	34	60	94	....	....	....	....	....	....	....	....	....	....	....	....	....	....	....	....	....	....	....
	Cleveland Barons	NAHL	3	0	0	0	0	....	....	....	....	....	....	....	....	....	....	....	....	....	....	....	....	....	....
2005-06	USNTDP	U-17	19	8	15	23	25	....	....	....	....	....	....	....	....	....	....	....	....	....	....	....	....	....	....
	USNTDP	NAHL	36	8	15	23	23	....	....	....	....	....	....	....	....	....	....	....	....	....	....	....	....	....	....
2006-07	USNTDP	U-18	41	8	16	24	10	....	....	....	....	....	....	....	....	....	....	....	....	....	....	....	....	....	....
	USNTDP	NAHL	15	4	9	13	4	....	....	....	....	....	....	....	....	....	....	....	....	....	....	....	....	....	....
2007-08	Ohio State	CCHA	41	4	17	21	10	....	....	....	....	....	....	....	....	....	....	....	....	....	....	....	....	....	....
2008-09	Ohio State	CCHA	42	11	28	39	20	....	....	....	....	....	....	....	....	....	....	....	....	....	....	....	....	....	....
2009-10	Ohio State	CCHA	39	6	24	30	20	....	....	....	....	....	....	....	....	....	....	....	....	....	....	....	....	....	....
2010-11	Ohio State	CCHA	37	12	22	34	18	....	....	....	....	....	....	....	....	....	....	....	....	....	....	....	....	....	....
2011-12	St. John's IceCaps	AHL	64	9	18	27	28	....	....	....	....	....	....	....	....	....	15	3	2	5	8	....	....	....	....
2012-13	St. John's IceCaps	AHL	24	3	2	5	10	....	....	....	....	....	....	....	....	....	....	....	....	....	....	....	....	....	....
2013-14	**Winnipeg**	**NHL**	**9**	**1**	**0**	**1**	**0**	**0**	**0**	**0**	**5**	**20.0**	**−3**	**21**	**42.9**	**5:07**	....	....	....	....	....	....	....	....	....
	St. John's IceCaps	AHL	63	28	17	45	20	....	....	....	....	....	....	....	....	....	21	1	6	7	18	....	....	....	....
2014-15	St. John's IceCaps	AHL	66	16	26	42	26	....	....	....	....	....	....	....	....	....	....	....	....	....	....	....	....	....	....
	NHL Totals		**9**	**1**	**0**	**1**	**0**	**0**	**0**	**0**	**5**	**20.0**		**21**	**42.9**	**5:07**	....	....	....	....	....	....	....	....	....

• Transferred to **Winnipeg** after **Atlanta** franchise relocated, June 21, 2011.

ALIU, Akim (ah-lee-OO, a-KEEM)

Right wing. Shoots right. 6'4", 225 lbs. Born, Okene, Nigeria, April 24, 1989. Chicago's 3rd choice, 56th overall, in 2007 Entry Draft.

Season	Club	League	GP	G	A	Pts	PIM	PP	SH	GW	S	S%	+/-	TF	F%	Min	GP	G	A	Pts	PIM	PP	SH	GW	Min
2004-05	Tor. Marlboros	GTHL	68	35	50	85	197	....	....	....	....	....	....	....	....	....	....	....	....	....	....	....	....	....	....
2005-06	Windsor Spitfires	OHL	18	3	4	7	25	....	....	....	....	....	....	....	....	....	....	....	....	....	....	....	....	....	....
	Sudbury Wolves	OHL	29	7	6	13	54	....	....	....	....	....	....	....	....	....	6	0	1	1	7	....	....	....	....
2006-07	Sudbury Wolves	OHL	53	20	22	42	104	....	....	....	....	....	....	....	....	....	21	1	5	6	50	....	....	....	....
2007-08	London Knights	OHL	60	28	33	61	133	....	....	....	....	....	....	....	....	....	5	2	1	3	15	....	....	....	....
	Rockford IceHogs	AHL	2	0	0	0	2	....	....	....	....	....	....	....	....	....	....	....	....	....	....	....	....	....	....
2008-09	London Knights	OHL	16	8	10	18	30	....	....	....	....	....	....	....	....	....	....	....	....	....	....	....	....	....	....
	Sudbury Wolves	OHL	29	10	16	26	61	....	....	....	....	....	....	....	....	....	6	2	1	3	14	....	....	....	....
	Rockford IceHogs	AHL	5	2	0	2	14	....	....	....	....	....	....	....	....	....	1	1	0	1	0	....	....	....	....
2009-10	Rockford IceHogs	AHL	48	11	6	17	69	....	....	....	....	....	....	....	....	....	....	....	....	....	....	....	....	....	....
	Toledo Walleye	ECHL	13	5	9	14	18	....	....	....	....	....	....	....	....	....	2	1	1	2	16	....	....	....	....
2010-11	Chicago Wolves	AHL	43	4	5	9	53	....	....	....	....	....	....	....	....	....	....	....	....	....	....	....	....	....	....
	Gwinnett	ECHL	16	12	8	20	22	....	....	....	....	....	....	....	....	....	....	....	....	....	....	....	....	....	....
	Peoria Rivermen	AHL	16	5	4	9	20	....	....	....	....	....	....	....	....	....	2	1	0	1	6	....	....	....	....
2011-12	Colorado Eagles	ECHL	10	2	4	6	28	....	....	....	....	....	....	....	....	....	....	....	....	....	....	....	....	....	....
	Calgary	**NHL**	**2**	**2**	**1**	**3**	**12**	**0**	**0**	**0**	**3**	**66.7**	**3**	**0**	**0.0**	**11:02**	....	....	....	....	....	....	....	....	....
	Abbotsford Heat	AHL	42	10	4	14	59	....	....	....	....	....	....	....	....	....	5	0	1	1	28	....	....	....	....
2012-13	Abbotsford Heat	AHL	42	4	7	11	111	....	....	....	....	....	....	....	....	....	....	....	....	....	....	....	....	....	....
	Calgary	**NHL**	**5**	**0**	**0**	**0**	**14**	**0**	**0**	**0**	**2**	**0.0**	**−2**	**0**	**0.0**	**10:52**	....	....	....	....	....	....	....	....	....
2013-14	Hamilton	AHL	14	3	1	4	18	....	....	....	....	....	....	....	....	....	....	....	....	....	....	....	....	....	....
	Hartford	AHL	9	1	0	1	7	....	....	....	....	....	....	....	....	....	....	....	....	....	....	....	....	....	....
	AIK Solna	Sweden	2	1	0	1	6	....	....	....	....	....	....	....	....	....	....	....	....	....	....	....	....	....	....
	AIK Solna	Sweden-Q	1	0	0	0	0	....	....	....	....	....	....	....	....	....	....	....	....	....	....	....	....	....	....
2014-15	Rochester	AHL	10	3	1	4	51	....	....	....	....	....	....	....	....	....	....	....	....	....	....	....	....	....	....
	Bakersfield	ECHL	15	2	7	9	24	....	....	....	....	....	....	....	....	....	....	....	....	....	....	....	....	....	....
	Oklahoma City	AHL	1	0	0	0	0	....	....	....	....	....	....	....	....	....	....	....	....	....	....	....	....	....	....
	NHL Totals		**7**	**2**	**1**	**3**	**26**	**0**	**0**	**0**	**5**	**40.0**		**0**	**0.0**	**10:55**	....	....	....	....	....	....	....	....	....

Traded to **Atlanta** by **Chicago** with Brent Sopel, Dustin Byfuglien and Ben Eager for Marty Reasoner, Joey Crabb, Jeremy Morin and New Jersey's 1st (previously acquired, Chicago selected Kevin Hayes) and 2nd (previously acquired, Chicago selected Justin Holl) round choices in 2010 Entry Draft, June 24, 2010. • Transferred to **Winnipeg** after **Atlanta** franchise relocated, June 21, 2011. Traded to **Calgary** by **Winnipeg** for John Negrin, January 29, 2012. Signed to a PTO (professional tryout) contract by **Hamilton** (AHL), September 20, 2013. Signed to a PTO (professional tryout) contract by **Hartford** (AHL), December 16, 2013. Signed as a free agent by **Solna** (Sweden), February 26, 2014. Signed to a PTO (professional tryout) contract by **Rochester** (AHL), October 10, 2014. Signed as a free agent by **Bakersfield** (ECHL), January 23, 2015. • Loaned to **Oklahoma City** (AHL) by **Bakersfield** (ECHL), March 3, 2015.

ALLEN, Bryan (AL-luhn, BRIGH-uhn)

Defense. Shoots left. 6'5", 223 lbs. Born, Kingston, ON, August 21, 1980. Vancouver's 1st choice, 4th overall, in 1998 Entry Draft.

Season	Club	League	GP	G	A	Pts	PIM	PP	SH	GW	S	S%	+/-	TF	F%	Min	GP	G	A	Pts	PIM	PP	SH	GW	Min
1995-96	Ernestown Jets	ON-Jr.C	36	1	16	17	71	....	....	....	....	....	....	....	....	....	....	....	....	....	....	....	....	....	....
1996-97	Oshawa Generals	OHL	60	2	4	6	76	....	....	....	....	....	....	....	....	....	18	1	3	4	26	....	....	....	....
1997-98	Oshawa Generals	OHL	48	6	13	19	126	....	....	....	....	....	....	....	....	....	5	0	5	5	18	....	....	....	....
1998-99	Oshawa Generals	OHL	37	7	15	22	77	....	....	....	....	....	....	....	....	....	15	0	3	3	26	....	....	....	....
99-2000	Oshawa Generals	OHL	3	0	2	2	12	....	....	....	....	....	....	....	....	....	3	0	0	0	13	....	....	....	....
	Syracuse Crunch	AHL	9	1	1	2	11	....	....	....	....	....	....	....	....	....	2	0	0	0	2	....	....	....	....
2000-01	**Vancouver**	**NHL**	**6**	**0**	**0**	**0**	**0**	**0**	**0**	**0**	**2**	**0.0**	**0**	**0**	**0.0**	**9:20**	**2**	**0**	**0**	**0**	**2**	**0**	**0**	**0**	**13:47**
	Kansas City	IHL	75	5	20	25	99	....	....	....	....	....	....	....	....	....	....	....	....	....	....	....	....	....	....
2001-02	**Vancouver**	**NHL**	**11**	**0**	**0**	**0**	**6**	**0**	**0**	**0**	**4**	**0.0**	**1**	**0**	**0.0**	**10:47**	....	....	....	....	....	....	....	....	....
	Manitoba Moose	AHL	68	7	18	25	121	....	....	....	....	....	....	....	....	....	5	0	1	1	8	....	....	....	....
2002-03	**Vancouver**	**NHL**	**48**	**5**	**3**	**8**	**73**	**0**	**0**	**1**	**43**	**11.6**	**8**	**0**	**0.0**	**12:56**	**1**	**0**	**0**	**0**	**2**	**0**	**0**	**0**	**10:35**
	Manitoba Moose	AHL	7	0	1	1	4	....	....	....	....	....	....	....	....	....	....	....	....	....	....	....	....	....	....
2003-04	**Vancouver**	**NHL**	**74**	**2**	**5**	**7**	**94**	**0**	**0**	**0**	**70**	**2.9**	**−10**	**0**	**0.0**	**16:51**	**4**	**0**	**0**	**0**	**2**	**0**	**0**	**0**	**14:37**
2004-05	Voskresensk	Russia	19	0	3	3	34	....	....	....	....	....	....	....	....	....	....	....	....	....	....	....	....	....	....
2005-06	**Vancouver**	**NHL**	**77**	**7**	**10**	**17**	**115**	**1**	**0**	**0**	**88**	**8.0**	**4**	**0**	**0.0**	**20:27**	....	....	....	....	....	....	....	....	....
2006-07	**Florida**	**NHL**	**82**	**4**	**21**	**25**	**112**	**0**	**0**	**0**	**99**	**4.0**	**7**	**1**	**0.0**	**21:36**	....	....	....	....	....	....	....	....	....
2007-08	**Florida**	**NHL**	**73**	**2**	**14**	**16**	**67**	**0**	**0**	**0**	**67**	**3.0**	**5**	**0**	**0.0**	**21:17**	....	....	....	....	....	....	....	....	....
2008-09	**Florida**	**NHL**	**2**	**0**	**1**	**1**	**0**	**0**	**0**	**0**	**5**	**0.0**	**2**	**0**	**0.0**	**27:11**	....	....	....	....	....	....	....	....	....
2009-10	**Florida**	**NHL**	**74**	**4**	**9**	**13**	**99**	**0**	**1**	**2**	**78**	**5.1**	**−8**	**0**	**0.0**	**19:10**	....	....	....	....	....	....	....	....	....
2010-11	**Florida**	**NHL**	**53**	**4**	**8**	**12**	**63**	**0**	**0**	**1**	**50**	**8.0**	**−5**	**0**	**0.0**	**19:13**	....	....	....	....	....	....	....	....	....
	Carolina	**NHL**	**19**	**0**	**5**	**5**	**19**	**0**	**0**	**0**	**8**	**0.0**	**4**	**0**	**0.0**	**15:51**	....	....	....	....	....	....	....	....	....
2011-12	**Carolina**	**NHL**	**82**	**1**	**13**	**14**	**76**	**0**	**0**	**1**	**87**	**1.1**	**−1**	**0**	**0.0**	**19:10**	....	....	....	....	....	....	....	....	....
2012-13	**Anaheim**	**NHL**	**41**	**0**	**6**	**6**	**34**	**0**	**0**	**0**	**25**	**0.0**	**1**	**0**	**0.0**	**18:44**	**7**	**0**	**1**	**1**	**2**	**0**	**0**	**0**	**17:22**
2013-14	**Anaheim**	**NHL**	**68**	**0**	**10**	**10**	**75**	**0**	**0**	**0**	**60**	**0.0**	**20**	**0**	**0.0**	**17:33**	**13**	**1**	**0**	**1**	**28**	**0**	**0**	**0**	**18:21**
2014-15	**Anaheim**	**NHL**	**6**	**0**	**1**	**1**	**4**	**0**	**0**	**0**	**4**	**0.0**	**0**	**0**	**0.0**	**18:13**	....	....	....	....	....	....	....	....	....
	Norfolk Admirals	AHL	2	0	0	0	0	....	....	....	....	....	....	....	....	....	....	....	....	....	....	....	....	....	....
	Montreal	**NHL**	**5**	**0**	**1**	**1**	**2**	**0**	**0**	**0**	**2**	**0.0**	**−2**	**0**	**0.0**	**12:44**	....	....	....	....	....	....	....	....	....
	Hamilton	AHL	35	1	5	6	24	....	....	....	....	....	....	....	....	....	....	....	....	....	....	....	....	....	....
	NHL Totals		**721**	**29**	**107**	**136**	**839**	**1**	**1**	**5**	**692**	**4.2**		**1**	**0.0**	**18:38**	**27**	**1**	**1**	**2**	**36**	**0**	**0**	**0**	**16:55**

OHL First All-Star Team (1999)

• Missed majority of 1999-2000 due to knee injury in training camp, September 21, 1999. Signed as a free agent by **Voskresensk** (Russia), December 20, 2004. Traded to **Florida** by **Vancouver** with Todd Bertuzzi and Alex Auld for Roberto Luongo, Lukas Krajicek and Florida's 6th round choice (Sergei Shirokov) in 2006 Entry Draft, June 23, 2006. • Missed majority of 2008-09 due to off-season arthroscopic knee surgery and follow-up cartilage surgery, October 27, 2008. Traded to **Carolina** by **Florida** for Sergei Samsonov, February 28, 2011. Signed as a free agent by **Anaheim**, July 1, 2012. Traded to **Montreal** by **Anaheim** for Rene Bourque, November 20, 2014.

ALLEN, Conor
(AL-uhn, KAW-nuhr) **NSH**

Defense. Shoots left. 6'1", 210 lbs. Born, Chicago, IL, January 31, 1990.

Season	Club	League	GP	G	A	Pts	PIM	PP	SH	GW	S	S%	+/-	TF	F%	Min	GP	G	A	Pts	PIM	PP	SH	GW	Min
			Regular Season														Playoffs								
2008-09	St. Louis Bandits	NAHL	46	5	10	15	48	....	....	....	....	....	....	....	....	....	12	1	4	5	15	....	....	....	....
2009-10	Sioux Falls	USHL	48	7	8	15	69	....	....	....	....	....	....	....	....	....	....	....	....	....	....	....	....	....	....
2010-11	Massachusetts	H-East	31	2	4	6	29	....	....	....	....	....	....	....	....	....	....	....	....	....	....	....	....	....	....
2011-12	Massachusetts	H-East	35	7	7	14	28	....	....	....	....	....	....	....	....	....	....	....	....	....	....	....	....	....	....
2012-13	Massachusetts	H-East	33	5	14	19	53	....	....	....	....	....	....	....	....	....	....	....	....	....	....	....	....	....	....
	Connecticut	AHL	1	0	0	0	0	....	....	....	....	....	....	....	....	....	....	....	....	....	....	....	....	....	....
2013-14	**NY Rangers**	**NHL**	**3**	**0**	**0**	**0**	**0**	**0**	**0**	**0**	**2**	**0.0**	**–1**	**0**	**0.0**	**14:26**	....	....	....	....	....	....	....	....	....
	Hartford	AHL	72	6	25	31	71	....	....	....	....	....	....	....	....	....	....	....	....	....	....	....	....	....	....
2014-15	**NY Rangers**	**NHL**	**4**	**0**	**0**	**0**	**4**	**0**	**0**	**0**	**2**	**0.0**	**–1**	**0**	**0.0**	**12:12**	....	....	....	....	....	....	....	....	....
	Hartford	AHL	72	11	23	34	113	....	....	....	....	....	....	....	....	....	12	1	1	2	10	....	....	....	....
	NHL Totals		**7**	**0**	**0**	**0**	**4**	**0**	**0**	**0**	**4**	**0.0**		**0**	**0.0**	**13:10**	....	....	....	....	....	....	....	....	....

Signed as a free agent by **NY Rangers**, March 29, 2013. Signed as a free agent by **Nashville**, July 2, 2015.

ALT, Mark
(AHLT, MAHRK) **PHI**

Defense. Shoots right. 6'4", 201 lbs. Born, Kansas City, MO, October 18, 1991. Carolina's 3rd choice, 53rd overall, in 2010 Entry Draft.

Season	Club	League	GP	G	A	Pts	PIM	PP	SH	GW	S	S%	+/-	TF	F%	Min	GP	G	A	Pts	PIM	PP	SH	GW	Min
2007-08	Cretin-Derham	High-MN	17	1	5	6	4	....	....	....	....	....	....	....	....	....	....	....	....	....	....	....	....	....	....
2008-09	Cretin-Derham	High-MN	26	11	16	27	10	....	....	....	....	....	....	....	....	....	....	....	....	....	....	....	....	....	....
2009-10	Cretin-Derham	High-MN	22	6	9	15	12	....	....	....	....	....	....	....	....	....	2	0	5	5	2	....	....	....	....
	Team Northeast	UMHSEL	24	13	9	22	....	....	....	....	....	....	....	....	....	....	....	....	....	....	....	....	....	....	....
2010-11	U. of Minnesota	WCHA	35	2	8	10	22	....	....	....	....	....	....	....	....	....	....	....	....	....	....	....	....	....	....
2011-12	U. of Minnesota	WCHA	43	5	17	22	43	....	....	....	....	....	....	....	....	....	....	....	....	....	....	....	....	....	....
2012-13	U. of Minnesota	WCHA	39	0	7	7	20	....	....	....	....	....	....	....	....	....	....	....	....	....	....	....	....	....	....
	Adirondack	AHL	6	1	1	2	2	....	....	....	....	....	....	....	....	....	....	....	....	....	....	....	....	....	....
2013-14	Adirondack	AHL	75	4	22	26	31	....	....	....	....	....	....	....	....	....	....	....	....	....	....	....	....	....	....
2014-15	**Philadelphia**	**NHL**	**1**	**0**	**0**	**0**	**0**	**0**	**0**	**0**	**0**	**0.0**	**–1**	**0**	**0.0**	**9:25**	....	....	....	....	....	....	....	....	....
	Lehigh Valley	AHL	44	2	8	10	18	....	....	....	....	....	....	....	....	....	....	....	....	....	....	....	....	....	....
	NHL Totals		**1**	**0**	**0**	**0**	**0**	**0**	**0**	**0**	**0**	**0.0**		**0**	**0.0**	**9:25**	....	....	....	....	....	....	....	....	....

Traded to **Philadelphia** by **Carolina** with Brian Boucher for Luke Pither, January 13, 2013.

ALZNER, Karl
(ALZ-nuhr, KARL) **WSH**

Defense. Shoots left. 6'2", 217 lbs. Born, Burnaby, BC, September 24, 1988. Washington's 1st choice, 5th overall, in 2007 Entry Draft.

Season	Club	League	GP	G	A	Pts	PIM	PP	SH	GW	S	S%	+/-	TF	F%	Min	GP	G	A	Pts	PIM	PP	SH	GW	Min
2002-03	Burnaby W.C.	Minor-BC	64	17	31	48	24	....	....	....	....	....	....	....	....	....	....	....	....	....	....	....	....	....	....
2003-04	Richmond	PIJHL	41	3	9	12	8	....	....	....	....	....	....	....	....	....	13	0	2	2	0	....	....	....	....
	Calgary Hitmen	WHL	1	0	0	0	0	....	....	....	....	....	....	....	....	....	....	....	....	....	....	....	....	....	....
2004-05	Calgary Hitmen	WHL	66	0	10	10	19	....	....	....	....	....	....	....	....	....	12	0	3	3	9	....	....	....	....
2005-06	Calgary Hitmen	WHL	70	4	20	24	28	....	....	....	....	....	....	....	....	....	13	1	3	4	4	....	....	....	....
2006-07	Calgary Hitmen	WHL	63	8	39	47	32	....	....	....	....	....	....	....	....	....	18	1	12	13	4	....	....	....	....
2007-08	Calgary Hitmen	WHL	60	7	29	36	15	....	....	....	....	....	....	....	....	....	16	6	2	8	4	....	....	....	....
2008-09	**Washington**	**NHL**	**30**	**1**	**4**	**5**	**2**	**0**	**0**	**0**	**31**	**3.2**	**–1**	**0**	**0.0**	**19:25**	....	....	....	....	....	....	....	....	....
	Hershey Bears	AHL	48	4	16	20	10	....	....	....	....	....	....	....	....	....	10	0	2	2	2	....	....	....	....
2009-10	**Washington**	**NHL**	**21**	**0**	**5**	**5**	**8**	**0**	**0**	**0**	**16**	**0.0**	**–2**	**0**	**0.0**	**16:24**	**1**	**0**	**0**	**0**	**0**	**0**	**0**	**0**	**15:09**
	Hershey Bears	AHL	56	3	18	21	10	....	....	....	....	....	....	....	....	....	20	3	7	10	4	....	....	....	....
2010-11	**Washington**	**NHL**	**82**	**2**	**10**	**12**	**24**	**0**	**0**	**0**	**64**	**3.1**	**14**	**0**	**0.0**	**20:01**	**9**	**0**	**1**	**1**	**0**	**0**	**0**	**0**	**22:44**
2011-12	**Washington**	**NHL**	**82**	**1**	**16**	**17**	**29**	**0**	**0**	**0**	**56**	**1.8**	**12**	**0**	**0.0**	**20:52**	**14**	**0**	**2**	**2**	**0**	**0**	**0**	**0**	**24:53**
2012-13	**Washington**	**NHL**	**48**	**1**	**4**	**5**	**14**	**0**	**0**	**0**	**39**	**2.6**	**–6**	**0**	**0.0**	**20:57**	**7**	**1**	**1**	**2**	**2**	**0**	**0**	**0**	**22:18**
2013-14	**Washington**	**NHL**	**82**	**2**	**16**	**18**	**26**	**0**	**0**	**1**	**95**	**2.1**	**–7**	**0**	**0.0**	**20:32**	....	....	....	....	....	....	....	....	....
2014-15	**Washington**	**NHL**	**82**	**5**	**16**	**21**	**20**	**0**	**0**	**0**	**72**	**6.9**	**14**	**0**	**0.0**	**19:26**	**14**	**2**	**2**	**4**	**6**	**0**	**0**	**1**	**20:14**
	NHL Totals		**427**	**12**	**71**	**83**	**123**	**0**	**0**	**1**	**373**	**3.2**		**0**	**0.0**	**20:03**	**45**	**3**	**6**	**9**	**8**	**0**	**0**	**1**	**22:23**

WHL East Second All-Star Team (2007) • Canadian Major Junior Second All-Star Team (2007) • WHL East First All-Star Team (2008) • WHL Defenseman of the Year (2008) • WHL Player of the Year (2008) • Canadian Major Junior First All-Star Team (2008) • Canadian Major Junior Defenseman of the Year (2008)

ANDERSON, Josh
(AN-duhr-suhn, JAWSH) **CBJ**

Right wing. Shoots right. 6'3", 212 lbs. Born, Burlington, ON, May 7, 1994. Columbus' 4th choice, 95th overall, in 2012 Entry Draft.

Season	Club	League	GP	G	A	Pts	PIM	PP	SH	GW	S	S%	+/-	TF	F%	Min	GP	G	A	Pts	PIM	PP	SH	GW	Min
2010-11	Burlington Eagles	Minor-ON	58	41	35	76	....	....	....	....	....	....	....	....	....	....	....	....	....	....	....	....	....	....	....
	Burlington	ON-Jr.A	4	0	2	2	0	....	....	....	....	....	....	....	....	....	1	0	0	0	0	....	....	....	....
2011-12	London Knights	OHL	64	12	10	22	34	....	....	....	....	....	....	....	....	....	19	2	3	5	4	....	....	....	....
2012-13	London Knights	OHL	68	23	26	49	77	....	....	....	....	....	....	....	....	....	19	1	2	3	23	....	....	....	....
2013-14	London Knights	OHL	59	27	25	52	81	....	....	....	....	....	....	....	....	....	9	5	4	9	14	....	....	....	....
2014-15	**Columbus**	**NHL**	**6**	**0**	**1**	**1**	**2**	**0**	**0**	**0**	**10**	**0.0**	**–1**	**0**	**0.0**	**13:27**	....	....	....	....	....	....	....	....	....
	Springfield	AHL	52	7	10	17	76	....	....	....	....	....	....	....	....	....	....	....	....	....	....	....	....	....	....
	NHL Totals		**6**	**0**	**1**	**1**	**2**	**0**	**0**	**0**	**10**	**0.0**		**0**	**0.0**	**13:27**	....	....	....	....	....	....	....	....	....

ANDERSSON, Joakim
(AN-duhr-suhn, YOH-ah-kihm) **DET**

Center. Shoots left. 6'1", 211 lbs. Born, Munkedal, Sweden, February 5, 1989. Detroit's 2nd choice, 88th overall, in 2007 Entry Draft.

Season	Club	League	GP	G	A	Pts	PIM	PP	SH	GW	S	S%	+/-	TF	F%	Min	GP	G	A	Pts	PIM	PP	SH	GW	Min
2004-05	Munkedals BK	Sweden-5	STATISTICS NOT AVAILABLE																						
2005-06	Frolunda U18	Swe-U18	1	0	0	0	0	....	....	....	....	....	....	....	....	....	2	0	1	1	0	....	....	....	....
	Frolunda Jr.	Swe-Jr.	35	9	11	20	10	....	....	....	....	....	....	....	....	....	7	2	5	7	4	....	....	....	....
2006-07	Frolunda U18	Swe-U18	2	1	2	3	2	....	....	....	....	....	....	....	....	....	6	3	2	5	28	....	....	....	....
	Frolunda Jr.	Swe-Jr.	41	20	26	46	60	....	....	....	....	....	....	....	....	....	8	0	7	7	4	....	....	....	....
	Frolunda	Sweden	1	0	0	0	0	....	....	....	....	....	....	....	....	....	....	....	....	....	....	....	....	....	....
2007-08	Boras HC	Sweden-2	33	6	17	23	26	....	....	....	....	....	....	....	....	....	....	....	....	....	....	....	....	....	....
	Frolunda Jr.	Swe-Jr.	6	8	2	10	30	....	....	....	....	....	....	....	....	....	5	6	3	9	4	....	....	....	....
	Frolunda	Sweden	9	1	0	1	2	....	....	....	....	....	....	....	....	....	4	1	1	2	0	....	....	....	....
2008-09	Boras HC	Sweden-2	4	2	2	4	2	....	....	....	....	....	....	....	....	....	....	....	....	....	....	....	....	....	....
	Frolunda	Sweden	49	6	6	12	22	....	....	....	....	....	....	....	....	....	11	0	0	0	4	....	....	....	....
	Grand Rapids	AHL	1	0	1	1	2	....	....	....	....	....	....	....	....	....	10	1	2	3	4	....	....	....	....
2009-10	Frolunda	Sweden	55	6	12	18	42	....	....	....	....	....	....	....	....	....	7	1	2	3	0	....	....	....	....
2010-11	Grand Rapids	AHL	79	7	15	22	30	....	....	....	....	....	....	....	....	....	....	....	....	....	....	....	....	....	....
2011-12	**Detroit**	**NHL**	**5**	**0**	**0**	**0**	**0**	**0**	**0**	**0**	**3**	**0.0**	**1**	**6**	**83.3**	**6:40**	....	....	....	....	....	....	....	....	....
	Grand Rapids	AHL	73	21	30	51	34	....	....	....	....	....	....	....	....	....	....	....	....	....	....	....	....	....	....
2012-13	Grand Rapids	AHL	36	10	17	27	55	....	....	....	....	....	....	....	....	....	10	3	5	8	0	....	....	....	....
	Detroit	**NHL**	**38**	**3**	**5**	**8**	**8**	**0**	**0**	**0**	**43**	**7.0**	**2**	**310**	**46.5**	**12:05**	**14**	**1**	**4**	**5**	**10**	**0**	**0**	**0**	**13:20**
2013-14	**Detroit**	**NHL**	**65**	**8**	**9**	**17**	**12**	**0**	**0**	**1**	**78**	**10.3**	**–11**	**671**	**51.4**	**13:50**	**1**	**0**	**0**	**0**	**0**	**0**	**0**	**0**	**8:17**
2014-15	**Detroit**	**NHL**	**68**	**3**	**5**	**8**	**22**	**0**	**0**	**1**	**74**	**4.1**	**–4**	**375**	**51.2**	**11:38**	**7**	**1**	**1**	**2**	**2**	**0**	**0**	**0**	**9:45**
	NHL Totals		**176**	**14**	**19**	**33**	**42**	**0**	**0**	**2**	**198**	**7.1**		**1362**	**50.4**	**12:24**	**22**	**2**	**5**	**7**	**12**	**0**	**0**	**0**	**11:58**

ANDREOFF, Andy
(an-DRAY-awf, AN-dee) **L.A.**

Left wing. Shoots left. 6'1", 206 lbs. Born, Pickering, ON, May 17, 1991. Los Angeles' 2nd choice, 80th overall, in 2011 Entry Draft.

Season	Club	League	GP	G	A	Pts	PIM	PP	SH	GW	S	S%	+/-	TF	F%	Min	GP	G	A	Pts	PIM	PP	SH	GW	Min
2006-07	Ajax Pickering	Minor-ON	48	17	21	38	58	....	....	....	....	....	....	....	....	....	....	....	....	....	....	....	....	....	....
2007-08	Pickering Panthers	ON-Jr.A	40	12	15	27	58	....	....	....	....	....	....	....	....	....	....	....	....	....	....	....	....	....	....
	Oshawa Generals	OHL	25	0	1	1	8	....	....	....	....	....	....	....	....	....	9	0	0	0	2	....	....	....	....
2008-09	Oshawa Generals	OHL	66	11	14	25	37	....	....	....	....	....	....	....	....	....	....	....	....	....	....	....	....	....	....
2009-10	Oshawa Generals	OHL	67	15	33	48	70	....	....	....	....	....	....	....	....	....	....	....	....	....	....	....	....	....	....
2010-11	Oshawa Generals	OHL	66	33	42	75	109	....	....	....	....	....	....	....	....	....	10	3	8	11	16	....	....	....	....
2011-12	Oshawa Generals	OHL	57	22	36	58	88	....	....	....	....	....	....	....	....	....	6	1	3	4	4	....	....	....	....
	Manchester	AHL	5	1	0	1	4	....	....	....	....	....	....	....	....	....	4	2	0	2	2	....	....	....	....
2012-13	Manchester	AHL	69	13	13	26	111	....	....	....	....	....	....	....	....	....	4	0	3	3	0	....	....	....	....
2013-14	Manchester	AHL	76	11	24	35	133	....	....	....	....	....	....	....	....	....	4	1	2	3	2	....	....	....	....

			Regular Season														Playoffs								
Season	Club	League	GP	G	A	Pts	PIM	PP	SH	GW	S	S%	+/-	TF	F%	Min	GP	G	A	Pts	PIM	PP	SH	GW	Min
2014-15	Los Angeles	NHL	18	2	1	3	18	0	0	1	14	14.3	1	61	52.5	8:34	....	....	....	....	....	....	....	....	....
	Manchester	AHL	7	5	5	10	11	....	....	....	....	....	....	....	....	....	....	....	....	....	....	....	....	....	....
	NHL Totals		18	2	1	3	18	0	0	1	14	14.3		61	52.5	8:34	....	....	....	....	....	....	....	....	....

ANDRIGHETTO, Sven

(an-drih-GEH-toh, SVEHN) **MTL**

Right wing. Shoots left. 5'10", 186 lbs. Born, Zurich, Switz., March 21, 1993. Montreal's 6th choice, 86th overall, in 2013 Entry Draft.

Season	Club	League	GP	G	A	Pts	PIM	PP	SH	GW	S	S%	+/-	TF	F%	Min	GP	G	A	Pts	PIM	PP	SH	GW	Min
2007-08	Zurich II U17	Swiss-U17	17	10	13	23	26	....	....	....	....	....	....	....	....	....	....	....	....	....	....	....	....	....	....
	Zurich U17	Swiss-U17	1	0	0	0	0	....	....	....	....	....	....	....	....	....	....	....	....	....	....	....	....	....	....
2008-09	Zurich U17	Swiss-U17	28	14	11	25	40	....	....	....	....	....	....	....	....	....	10	3	2	5	8	....	....	....	....
	Dubendorf Jr.	Swiss-Jr.	4	1	4	5	0	....	....	....	....	....	....	....	....	....	....	....	....	....	....	....	....	....	....
2009-10	Zurich U17	Swiss-U17	22	24	31	55	14	....	....	....	....	....	....	....	....	....	10	16	8	24	18	....	....	....	....
	GCK Zurich Jr.	Swiss-Jr.	14	3	4	7	4	....	....	....	....	....	....	....	....	....	....	....	....	....	....	....	....	....	....
2010-11	GCK Lions Zurich	Swiss-2	36	11	12	23	20	....	....	....	....	....	....	....	....	....	....	....	....	....	....	....	....	....	....
	EHC Visp	Swiss-2	2	0	0	0	0	....	....	....	....	....	....	....	....	....	17	1	2	3	12	....	....	....	....
2011-12	Rouyn-Noranda	QMJHL	62	36	38	74	50	....	....	....	....	....	....	....	....	....	4	0	2	2	4	....	....	....	....
2012-13	Rouyn-Noranda	QMJHL	53	31	67	98	45	....	....	....	....	....	....	....	....	....	14	8	22	30	14	....	....	....	....
2013-14	Hamilton	AHL	64	17	27	44	40	....	....	....	....	....	....	....	....	....	....	....	....	....	....	....	....	....	....
2014-15	Montreal	NHL	12	2	1	3	0	0	0	0	12	16.7	0	15	20.0	9:25	....	....	....	....	....	....	....	....	....
	Hamilton	AHL	60	14	29	43	42	....	....	....	....	....	....	....	....	....	....	....	....	....	....	....	....	....	....
	NHL Totals		12	2	1	3	0	0	0	0	12	16.7		15	20.0	9:25	....	....	....	....	....	....	....	....	....

ANGELIDIS, Mike

(AN-gehl-EE-dihs, MIGHK) **T.B.**

Left wing. Shoots left. 6'1", 212 lbs. Born, Woodbridge, ON, June 27, 1985.

Season	Club	League	GP	G	A	Pts	PIM	PP	SH	GW	S	S%	+/-	TF	F%	Min	GP	G	A	Pts	PIM	PP	SH	GW	Min
2002-03	Owen Sound	OHL	65	7	10	17	81	....	....	....	....	....	....	....	....	....	4	1	1	2	0	....	....	....	....
2003-04	Owen Sound	OHL	66	9	9	18	118	....	....	....	....	....	....	....	....	....	7	4	1	5	4	....	....	....	....
2004-05	Owen Sound	OHL	41	9	10	19	126	....	....	....	....	....	....	....	....	....	8	3	2	5	10	....	....	....	....
2005-06	Owen Sound	OHL	68	53	25	78	167	....	....	....	....	....	....	....	....	....	11	5	9	14	38	....	....	....	....
2006-07	Albany River Rats	AHL	27	4	5	9	44	....	....	....	....	....	....	....	....	....	4	0	0	0	10	....	....	....	....
	Florida Everblades	ECHL	24	10	8	18	54	....	....	....	....	....	....	....	....	....	....	....	....	....	....	....	....	....	....
2007-08	Albany River Rats	AHL	74	11	16	27	151	....	....	....	....	....	....	....	....	....	7	0	2	2	6	....	....	....	....
2008-09	Albany River Rats	AHL	67	15	10	25	142	....	....	....	....	....	....	....	....	....	....	....	....	....	....	....	....	....	....
2009-10	Albany River Rats	AHL	67	12	12	24	119	....	....	....	....	....	....	....	....	....	8	2	4	6	12	....	....	....	....
2010-11	Norfolk Admirals	AHL	80	20	18	38	169	....	....	....	....	....	....	....	....	....	3	0	0	0	2	....	....	....	....
2011-12	Tampa Bay	NHL	6	1	0	1	5	0	0	0	8	12.5	–1	7	57.1	6:30	....	....	....	....	....	....	....	....	....
	Norfolk Admirals	AHL	54	14	13	27	135	....	....	....	....	....	....	....	....	....	18	1	5	6	35	....	....	....	....
2012-13	Syracuse Crunch	AHL	71	11	13	24	158	....	....	....	....	....	....	....	....	....	18	2	4	6	49	....	....	....	....
	Tampa Bay	NHL	1	0	0	0	0	0	0	0	0	0.0	0	7	42.9	7:22	....	....	....	....	....	....	....	....	....
2013-14	Syracuse Crunch	AHL	75	12	21	33	161	....	....	....	....	....	....	....	....	....	....	....	....	....	....	....	....	....	....
2014-15	Tampa Bay	NHL	3	0	0	0	12	0	0	0	0	0.0	0	19	36.8	7:21	....	....	....	....	....	....	....	....	....
	Syracuse Crunch	AHL	64	20	18	38	138	....	....	....	....	....	....	....	....	....	3	0	1	1	6	....	....	....	....
	NHL Totals		10	1	0	1	17	0	0	0	8	12.5		33	42.4	6:50	....	....	....	....	....	....	....	....	....

OHL First All-Star Team (2006) • Canadian Major Junior Humanitarian Player of the Year (2006)

Signed as a free agent by **Carolina**, July 27, 2006. Signed as a free agent by **Tampa Bay**, August 3, 2010.

ANISIMOV, Artem

(a-NEE-see-mawv, AHR-tehm) **CHI**

Center. Shoots left. 6'4", 200 lbs. Born, Yaroslavl, USSR, May 24, 1988. NY Rangers' 2nd choice, 54th overall, in 2006 Entry Draft.

Season	Club	League	GP	G	A	Pts	PIM	PP	SH	GW	S	S%	+/-	TF	F%	Min	GP	G	A	Pts	PIM	PP	SH	GW	Min
2004-05	Yaroslavl 2	Russia-3	24	3	5	8	10	....	....	....	....	....	....	....	....	....	....	....	....	....	....	....	....	....	....
2005-06	Yaroslavl 2	Russia-3	32	15	12	27	28	....	....	....	....	....	....	....	....	....	....	....	....	....	....	....	....	....	....
	Yaroslavl	Russia	10	0	1	1	4	....	....	....	....	....	....	....	....	....	....	....	....	....	....	....	....	....	....
2006-07	Yaroslavl 2	Russia-3	2	2	0	2	0	....	....	....	....	....	....	....	....	....	....	....	....	....	....	....	....	....	....
	Yaroslavl	Russia	39	2	8	10	26	....	....	....	....	....	....	....	....	....	7	3	2	5	4	....	....	....	....
2007-08	Hartford	AHL	74	16	27	43	30	....	....	....	....	....	....	....	....	....	5	1	0	1	2	....	....	....	....
2008-09	NY Rangers	NHL	1	0	0	0	0	0	0	0	1	0.0	0	5	40.0	9:27	1	0	0	0	0	0	0	0	5:35
	Hartford	AHL	80	37	44	81	50	....	....	....	....	....	....	....	....	....	6	2	0	2	0	....	....	....	....
2009-10	NY Rangers	NHL	82	12	16	28	32	1	0	2	124	9.7	–2	690	44.9	12:54	....	....	....	....	....	....	....	....	....
2010-11	NY Rangers	NHL	82	18	26	44	20	3	0	2	190	9.5	3	688	44.5	16:12	5	1	0	1	0	0	0	0	15:10
2011-12	NY Rangers	NHL	79	16	20	36	34	4	1	1	132	12.1	12	345	46.7	15:24	20	3	7	10	4	0	0	0	13:52
2012-13	Yaroslavl	KHL	36	12	17	29	22	....	....	....	....	....	....	....	....	....	....	....	....	....	....	....	....	....	....
	Columbus	NHL	35	11	7	18	12	1	0	3	68	16.2	–6	509	48.9	16:25	....	....	....	....	....	....	....	....	....
2013-14	Columbus	NHL	81	22	17	39	20	3	2	5	162	13.6	–2	965	49.3	16:36	6	1	2	3	4	1	0	0	17:28
	Russia	Olympics	5	0	0	0	2	....	....	....	....	....	....	....	....	....	....	....	....	....	....	....	....	....	....
2014-15	Columbus	NHL	52	7	20	27	8	0	0	2	88	8.0	–6	229	44.5	16:23	....	....	....	....	....	....	....	....	....
	NHL Totals		412	86	106	192	126	12	3	15	765	11.2		3431	46.8	15:30	32	5	9	14	8	1	0	0	14:29

Traded to **Columbus** by **NY Rangers** with Brandon Dubinsky, Tim Erixon and NY Rangers' 1st round choice (Kerby Rychel) in 2013 Entry Draft for Rick Nash, Steven Delisle and Columbus' 3rd round choice (Pavel Buchnevich) in 2013 Entry Draft, July 23, 2012. Signed as a free agent by **Yaroslavl** (KHL), September 20, 2012. Traded to **Chicago** by **Columbus** with Jeremy Morin, Corey Tropp, Marko Dano and Columbus' 4th round choice in 2016 Entry Draft for Brandon Saad, Michael Paliotta and Alex Broadhurst, June 30, 2015.

ARCHIBALD, Darren

(ahr-CHIH-bawld, DAIR-ehn) **VAN**

Right wing. Shoots left. 6'3", 210 lbs. Born, Newmarket, ON, February 9, 1990.

Season	Club	League	GP	G	A	Pts	PIM	PP	SH	GW	S	S%	+/-	TF	F%	Min	GP	G	A	Pts	PIM	PP	SH	GW	Min
2007-08	Stouffville Spirit	ON-Jr.A	49	21	27	48	46	....	....	....	....	....	....	....	....	....	15	9	9	18	35	....	....	....	....
2008-09	Barrie Colts	OHL	68	25	24	49	35	....	....	....	....	....	....	....	....	....	5	4	3	7	2	....	....	....	....
2009-10	Barrie Colts	OHL	57	26	33	59	62	....	....	....	....	....	....	....	....	....	16	5	5	10	16	....	....	....	....
2010-11	Barrie Colts	OHL	24	18	12	30	21	....	....	....	....	....	....	....	....	....	....	....	....	....	....	....	....	....	....
	Niagara Ice Dogs	OHL	37	23	13	36	30	....	....	....	....	....	....	....	....	....	14	10	4	14	6	....	....	....	....
2011-12	Chicago Wolves	AHL	20	1	0	1	10	....	....	....	....	....	....	....	....	....	....	....	....	....	....	....	....	....	....
	Kalamazoo Wings	ECHL	49	14	31	45	59	....	....	....	....	....	....	....	....	....	14	2	4	6	21	....	....	....	....
2012-13	Kalamazoo Wings	ECHL	18	6	7	13	29	....	....	....	....	....	....	....	....	....	....	....	....	....	....	....	....	....	....
	Chicago Wolves	AHL	55	12	10	22	47	....	....	....	....	....	....	....	....	....	....	....	....	....	....	....	....	....	....
2013-14	Vancouver	NHL	16	1	2	3	0	0	0	0	11	9.1	1	1	0.0	7:48	....	....	....	....	....	....	....	....	....
	Utica Comets	AHL	59	10	12	22	102	....	....	....	....	....	....	....	....	....	....	....	....	....	....	....	....	....	....
2014-15	Utica Comets	AHL	70	14	10	24	107	....	....	....	....	....	....	....	....	....	6	1	2	3	2	....	....	....	....
	NHL Totals		16	1	2	3	0	0	0	0	11	9.1		1	0.0	7:48	....	....	....	....	....	....	....	....	....

Signed as a free agent by **Vancouver**, December 13, 2010.

ARCOBELLO, Mark

(ahr-koh-BEHL-oh, MAHRK) **TOR**

Right wing. Shoots right. 5'10", 185 lbs. Born, Milford, CT, August 12, 1988.

Season	Club	League	GP	G	A	Pts	PIM	PP	SH	GW	S	S%	+/-	TF	F%	Min	GP	G	A	Pts	PIM	PP	SH	GW	Min
2006-07	Yale	ECAC	29	10	14	24	49	....	....	....	....	....	....	....	....	....	....	....	....	....	....	....	....	....	....
2007-08	Yale	ECAC	34	7	14	21	40	....	....	....	....	....	....	....	....	....	....	....	....	....	....	....	....	....	....
2008-09	Yale	ECAC	34	17	18	35	68	....	....	....	....	....	....	....	....	....	....	....	....	....	....	....	....	....	....
2009-10	Yale	ECAC	34	15	21	36	46	....	....	....	....	....	....	....	....	....	....	....	....	....	....	....	....	....	....
2010-11	Stockton Thunder	ECHL	33	7	13	20	10	....	....	....	....	....	....	....	....	....	....	....	....	....	....	....	....	....	....
	Oklahoma City	AHL	26	11	11	22	4	....	....	....	....	....	....	....	....	....	6	1	1	2	0	....	....	....	....
2011-12	Oklahoma City	AHL	73	17	26	43	28	....	....	....	....	....	....	....	....	....	14	5	8	13	6	....	....	....	....
2012-13	Oklahoma City	AHL	74	22	46	68	48	....	....	....	....	....	....	....	....	....	17	12	8	20	14	....	....	....	....
	Edmonton	NHL	1	0	0	0	0	0	0	0	0	0.0	0	10	30.0	18:15	....	....	....	....	....	....	....	....	....
2013-14	Edmonton	NHL	41	4	14	18	8	1	0	1	70	5.7	–7	404	51.0	15:04	....	....	....	....	....	....	....	....	....
	Oklahoma City	AHL	15	10	18	28	6	....	....	....	....	....	....	....	....	....	....	....	....	....	....	....	....	....	....

			Regular Season														Playoffs								
Season	Club	League	GP	G	A	Pts	PIM	PP	SH	GW	S	S%	+/-	TF	F%	Min	GP	G	A	Pts	PIM	PP	SH	GW	Min
2014-15	**Edmonton**	**NHL**	**36**	**7**	**5**	**12**	**12**	**0**	**0**	**0**	**54**	**13.0**	**–7**	**526**	**47.9**	**15:23**	....	....	....	....	....	....	....	....	....
	Nashville	**NHL**	**4**	**1**	**0**	**1**	**0**	**0**	**0**	**0**	**3**	**33.3**	**0**	**3**	**66.7**	**10:35**	....	....	....	....	....	....	....	....	....
	Pittsburgh	**NHL**	**10**	**0**	**2**	**2**	**2**	**0**	**0**	**0**	**13**	**0.0**	**1**	**7**	**28.6**	**12:05**	....	....	....	....	....	....	....	....	....
	Arizona	**NHL**	**27**	**9**	**7**	**16**	**6**	**1**	**0**	**2**	**59**	**15.3**	**–4**	**403**	**53.4**	**15:41**	....	....	....	....	....	....	....	....	....
	NHL Totals		**119**	**21**	**28**	**49**	**28**	**2**	**0**	**3**	**199**	**10.6**		**1353**	**50.3**	**14:56**	....	....	....	....	....	....	....	....	....

ECAC First All-Star Team (2009) • NCAA East Second All-American Team (2009)

Signed as a free agent by **Oklahoma City** (AHL), September 27, 2010. • Re-assigned to **Stockton** (ECHL) by **Oklahoma City** (AHL), October 13, 2010. Signed as a free agent by **Edmonton**, April 1, 2011. Traded to **Nashville** by **Edmonton** for Derek Roy, December 29, 2014. Claimed on waivers by **Pittsburgh** from **Nashville**, January 14, 2015. Claimed on waivers by **Arizona** from **Pittsburgh**, February 11, 2015. Signed as a free agent by **Toronto**, July 1, 2015.

ARMIA, Joel

(AHR-mee-uh, JOHL) **WPG**

Right wing. Shoots right. 6'3", 205 lbs. Born, Pori, Finland, May 31, 1993. Buffalo's 1st choice, 16th overall, in 2011 Entry Draft.

Season	Club	League	GP	G	A	Pts	PIM	PP	SH	GW	S	S%	+/-	TF	F%	Min	GP	G	A	Pts	PIM	PP	SH	GW	Min
2008-09	Assat Pori U18	Fin-U18	8	3	1	4	2	....	....	....	....	....	....	....	....	....	....	....	....	....	....	....	....	....	....
2009-10	Assat Pori U18	Fin-U18	9	7	9	16	31	....	....	....	....	....	....	....	....	....	6	6	3	9	8	....	....	....	....
	Assat Pori Jr.	Fin-Jr.	27	15	6	21	32	....	....	....	....	....	....	....	....	....	5	1	1	2	0	....	....	....	....
2010-11	Suomi U20	Finland-2	4	0	3	3	6	....	....	....	....	....	....	....	....	....	....	....	....	....	....	....	....	....	....
	Assat Pori	Finland	48	18	11	29	24	....	....	....	....	....	....	....	....	....	5	2	0	2	4	....	....	....	....
2011-12	Assat Pori	Finland	54	18	20	38	64	....	....	....	....	....	....	....	....	....	3	0	2	2	0	....	....	....	....
2012-13	Assat Pori	Finland	47	19	14	33	32	....	....	....	....	....	....	....	....	....	16	3	5	8	20	....	....	....	....
2013-14	Rochester	AHL	54	7	20	27	30	....	....	....	....	....	....	....	....	....	5	3	3	6	9	....	....	....	....
2014-15	**Buffalo**	**NHL**	**1**	**0**	**0**	**0**	**0**	**0**	**0**	**0**	**0**	**0.0**	**0**	**0**	**0.0**	**14:47**	....	....	....	....	....	....	....	....	....
	Rochester	AHL	33	10	15	25	39	....	....	....	....	....	....	....	....	....	....	....	....	....	....	....	....	....	....
	St. John's IceCaps	AHL	21	2	6	8	22	....	....	....	....	....	....	....	....	....	....	....	....	....	....	....	....	....	....
	NHL Totals		**1**	**0**	**0**	**0**	**0**	**0**	**0**	**0**	**0**	**0.0**		**0**	**0.0**	**14:47**	....	....	....	....	....	....	....	....	....

Traded to **Winnipeg** by **Buffalo** with Tyler Myers, Drew Stafford, Brendan Lemieux and St. Louis' 1st round choice (previously acquired, Winnipeg selected Jack Roscovic) in 2015 Entry Draft for Evander Kane, Zach Bogosian and Jason Kasdorf, February 11, 2015.

ARNOLD, Bill

(AHR-nohld, BIHL) **CGY**

Center. Shoots right. 6', 218 lbs. Born, Boston, MA, May 13, 1992. Calgary's 4th choice, 108th overall, in 2010 Entry Draft.

Season	Club	League	GP	G	A	Pts	PIM	PP	SH	GW	S	S%	+/-	TF	F%	Min	GP	G	A	Pts	PIM	PP	SH	GW	Min
2008-09	Nobles	High-MA	29	28	27	55	....	....	....	....	....	....	....	....	....	....	....	....	....	....	....	....	....	....	....
	Bos. Little Bruins	Minor-MA	33	26	21	47	24	....	....	....	....	....	....	....	....	....	....	....	....	....	....	....	....	....	....
2009-10	USNTDP	USHL	26	8	15	23	20	....	....	....	....	....	....	....	....	....	....	....	....	....	....	....	....	....	....
	USNTDP	U-18	38	12	16	28	30	....	....	....	....	....	....	....	....	....	....	....	....	....	....	....	....	....	....
2010-11	Boston College	H-East	39	10	10	20	38	....	....	....	....	....	....	....	....	....	....	....	....	....	....	....	....	....	....
2011-12	Boston College	H-East	42	17	19	36	46	....	....	....	....	....	....	....	....	....	....	....	....	....	....	....	....	....	....
2012-13	Boston College	H-East	38	17	18	35	40	....	....	....	....	....	....	....	....	....	....	....	....	....	....	....	....	....	....
2013-14	Boston College	H-East	40	14	39	53	51	....	....	....	....	....	....	....	....	....	....	....	....	....	....	....	....	....	....
	Calgary	**NHL**	**1**	**0**	**0**	**0**	**0**	**0**	**0**	**0**	**0**	**0.0**	**–1**	**9**	**55.6**	**13:35**	....	....	....	....	....	....	....	....	....
2014-15	Adirondack	AHL	61	15	23	38	30	....	....	....	....	....	....	....	....	....	....	....	....	....	....	....	....	....	....
	NHL Totals		**1**	**0**	**0**	**0**	**0**	**0**	**0**	**0**	**0**	**0.0**		**9**	**55.6**	**13:35**	....	....	....	....	....	....	....	....	....

Hockey East All-Rookie Team (2011)

ARVIDSSON, Viktor

(AHR-vihd-suhn, VIHK-tuhr) **NSH**

Right wing. Shoots right. 5'9", 177 lbs. Born, Skelleftea, Sweden, April 8, 1993. Nashville's 5th choice, 112th overall, in 2014 Entry Draft.

Season	Club	League	GP	G	A	Pts	PIM	PP	SH	GW	S	S%	+/-	TF	F%	Min	GP	G	A	Pts	PIM	PP	SH	GW	Min
2008-09	Skelleftea AIK U18	Swe-U18	14	7	7	14	16	....	....	....	....	....	....	....	....	....	5	1	2	3	4	....	....	....	....
2009-10	Skelleftea AIK U18	Swe-U18	40	52	48	100	60	....	....	....	....	....	....	....	....	....	3	1	1	2	0	....	....	....	....
	Skelleftea AIK Jr.	Swe-Jr.	2	0	1	1	2	....	....	....	....	....	....	....	....	....	2	1	0	1	0	....	....	....	....
2010-11	Skelleftea AIK U18	Swe-U18	4	7	7	14	18	....	....	....	....	....	....	....	....	....	7	4	6	10	4	....	....	....	....
	Skelleftea AIK Jr.	Swe-Jr.	40	15	19	34	51	....	....	....	....	....	....	....	....	....	5	3	3	6	4	....	....	....	....
	Skelleftea AIK	Sweden	3	0	0	0	0	....	....	....	....	....	....	....	....	....	....	....	....	....	....	....	....	....	....
2011-12	Skelleftea AIK Jr.	Swe-Jr.	43	25	17	42	18	....	....	....	....	....	....	....	....	....	3	0	0	0	0	....	....	....	....
	Skelleftea AIK	Sweden	4	0	0	0	0	....	....	....	....	....	....	....	....	....	....	....	....	....	....	....	....	....	....
2012-13	Skelleftea AIK Jr.	Swe-Jr.	4	3	1	4	0	....	....	....	....	....	....	....	....	....	....	....	....	....	....	....	....	....	....
	Skelleftea AIK	Sweden	49	7	5	12	12	....	....	....	....	....	....	....	....	....	13	6	2	8	2	....	....	....	....
2013-14	Skelleftea AIK	Sweden	50	16	24	40	59	....	....	....	....	....	....	....	....	....	14	4	12	16	4	....	....	....	....
2014-15	**Nashville**	**NHL**	**6**	**0**	**0**	**0**	**0**	**0**	**0**	**0**	**9**	**0.0**	**0**	**0**	**0.0**	**10:15**	....	....	....	....	....	....	....	....	....
	Milwaukee	AHL	70	22	33	55	43	....	....	....	....	....	....	....	....	....	....	....	....	....	....	....	....	....	....
	NHL Totals		**6**	**0**	**0**	**0**	**0**	**0**	**0**	**0**	**9**	**0.0**		**0**	**0.0**	**10:15**	....	....	....	....	....	....	....	....	....

AHL All-Rookie Team (2015)

ASHTON, Carter

(ASH-tuhn, KAHR-tuhr)

Right wing. Shoots left. 6'3", 215 lbs. Born, Winnipeg, MB, April 1, 1991. Tampa Bay's 2nd choice, 29th overall, in 2009 Entry Draft.

Season	Club	League	GP	G	A	Pts	PIM	PP	SH	GW	S	S%	+/-	TF	F%	Min	GP	G	A	Pts	PIM	PP	SH	GW	Min
2006-07	Sask. Contacts	SMHL	41	28	38	66	99	....	....	....	....	....	....	....	....	....	....	....	....	....	....	....	....	....	....
	Lethbridge	WHL	2	0	0	0	0	....	....	....	....	....	....	....	....	....	....	....	....	....	....	....	....	....	....
2007-08	Lethbridge	WHL	40	5	4	9	21	....	....	....	....	....	....	....	....	....	19	0	1	1	12	....	....	....	....
2008-09	Lethbridge	WHL	70	30	20	50	93	....	....	....	....	....	....	....	....	....	11	1	2	3	15	....	....	....	....
2009-10	Lethbridge	WHL	28	13	13	26	52	....	....	....	....	....	....	....	....	....	....	....	....	....	....	....	....	....	....
	Regina Pats	WHL	37	11	14	25	57	....	....	....	....	....	....	....	....	....	....	....	....	....	....	....	....	....	....
	Norfolk Admirals	AHL	11	1	0	1	6	....	....	....	....	....	....	....	....	....	....	....	....	....	....	....	....	....	....
2010-11	Regina Pats	WHL	29	16	11	27	44	....	....	....	....	....	....	....	....	....	....	....	....	....	....	....	....	....	....
	Tri-City	WHL	33	17	27	44	62	....	....	....	....	....	....	....	....	....	10	3	5	8	4	....	....	....	....
	Norfolk Admirals	AHL	....	....	....	....	....	....	....	....	....	....	....	....	....	....	2	0	0	0	0	....	....	....	....
2011-12	Norfolk Admirals	AHL	56	19	16	35	58	....	....	....	....	....	....	....	....	....	....	....	....	....	....	....	....	....	....
	Toronto	**NHL**	**15**	**0**	**0**	**0**	**13**	**0**	**0**	**0**	**22**	**0.0**	**–10**	**2**	**50.0**	**10:25**	....	....	....	....	....	....	....	....	....
	Toronto Marlies	AHL	7	2	1	3	8	....	....	....	....	....	....	....	....	....	6	1	2	3	8	....	....	....	....
2012-13	Toronto Marlies	AHL	53	11	8	19	67	....	....	....	....	....	....	....	....	....	9	3	2	5	4	....	....	....	....
2013-14	**Toronto**	**NHL**	**32**	**0**	**3**	**3**	**19**	**0**	**0**	**0**	**23**	**0.0**	**1**	**23**	**52.2**	**6:16**	....	....	....	....	....	....	....	....	....
	Toronto Marlies	AHL	24	16	7	23	30	....	....	....	....	....	....	....	....	....	12	4	5	9	16	....	....	....	....
2014-15	**Toronto**	**NHL**	**7**	**0**	**0**	**0**	**0**	**0**	**0**	**0**	**4**	**0.0**	**–3**	**5**	**20.0**	**6:13**	....	....	....	....	....	....	....	....	....
	Toronto Marlies	AHL	12	4	4	8	8	....	....	....	....	....	....	....	....	....	....	....	....	....	....	....	....	....	....
	Syracuse Crunch	AHL	29	3	11	14	61	....	....	....	....	....	....	....	....	....	3	0	0	0	7	....	....	....	....
	NHL Totals		**54**	**0**	**3**	**3**	**32**	**0**	**0**	**0**	**49**	**0.0**		**30**	**46.7**	**7:25**	....	....	....	....	....	....	....	....	....

Traded to **Toronto** by **Tampa Bay** for Keith Aulie, February 27, 2012. • Missed remainder of 2014-15 as a healthy reserve and due to a 20-game suspension for violating terms of the NHL/NHLPA Program for Performance Enhancing Substances, November 6, 2014. Traded to **Tampa Bay** by **Toronto** with David Broll for future considerations, February 6, 2015. Signed as a free agent by **Nizhny Novgorod** (KHL), July 21, 2015.

ATKINSON, Cam

(AT-kihn-suhn, KAM) **CBJ**

Right wing. Shoots right. 5'8", 174 lbs. Born, Riverside, CT, June 5, 1989. Columbus' 8th choice, 157th overall, in 2008 Entry Draft.

Season	Club	League	GP	G	A	Pts	PIM	PP	SH	GW	S	S%	+/-	TF	F%	Min	GP	G	A	Pts	PIM	PP	SH	GW	Min
2005-06	Avon Old Farms	High-CT	25	15	20	35	16	....	....	....	....	....	....	....	....	....	....	....	....	....	....	....	....	....	....
2006-07	Avon Old Farms	High-CT	27	28	24	52	12	....	....	....	....	....	....	....	....	....	....	....	....	....	....	....	....	....	....
2007-08	Avon Old Farms	High-CT	28	26	37	63	10	....	....	....	....	....	....	....	....	....	....	....	....	....	....	....	....	....	....
2008-09	Boston College	H-East	36	7	12	19	28	....	....	....	....	....	....	....	....	....	....	....	....	....	....	....	....	....	....
2009-10	Boston College	H-East	42	*30	23	53	30	....	....	....	....	....	....	....	....	....	....	....	....	....	....	....	....	....	....
2010-11	Boston College	H-East	39	*31	21	*52	28	....	....	....	....	....	....	....	....	....	....	....	....	....	....	....	....	....	....
	Springfield	AHL	5	3	2	5	0	....	....	....	....	....	....	....	....	....	....	....	....	....	....	....	....	....	....
2011-12	**Columbus**	**NHL**	**27**	**7**	**7**	**14**	**14**	**1**	**0**	**0**	**66**	**10.6**	**1**	**1**	**0.0**	**15:23**	....	....	....	....	....	....	....	....	....
	Springfield	AHL	51	29	15	44	31	....	....	....	....	....	....	....	....	....	....	....	....	....	....	....	....	....	....
2012-13	Springfield	AHL	33	17	21	38	14	....	....	....	....	....	....	....	....	....	....	....	....	....	....	....	....	....	....
	Columbus	**NHL**	**35**	**9**	**9**	**18**	**4**	**1**	**0**	**1**	**91**	**9.9**	**9**	**0**	**0.0**	**15:35**	....	....	....	....	....	....	....	....	....

			Regular Season														Playoffs								
Season	Club	League	GP	G	A	Pts	PIM	PP	SH	GW	S	S%	+/-	TF	F%	Min	GP	G	A	Pts	PIM	PP	SH	GW	Min
2013-14	Columbus	NHL	79	21	19	40	18	4	1	5	216	9.7	–4	0	0.0	15:47	6	1	2	3	0	0	0	0	16:45
2014-15	Columbus	NHL	78	22	18	40	22	7	1	7	212	10.4	–2	9	44.4	16:59									
	NHL Totals		219	59	53	112	58	13	2	13	585	10.1		10	40.0	16:08	6	1	2	3	0	0	0	0	16:45

Hockey East Second All-Star Team (2010) • NCAA Championship All-Tournament Team (2010) • Hockey East First All-Star Team (2011) • NCAA East First All-American Team (2011)

AUCOIN, Keith

(oh-KOIN, KEETH)

Center. Shoots right. 5'8", 171 lbs. Born, Waltham, MA, November 6, 1978.

Season	Club	League	GP	G	A	Pts	PIM	PP	SH	GW	S	S%	+/-	TF	F%	Min	GP	G	A	Pts	PIM	PP	SH	GW	Min
1997-98	Norwich U.	ECAC-3	26	19	14	33																			
1998-99	Norwich U.	ECAC-3	31	33	39	72																			
99-2000	Norwich U.	ECAC-3	31	36	41	77	14																		
2000-01	Norwich U.	ECAC-3	28	26	30	56	26																		
2001-02	Lowell	AHL	30	6	10	16	8																		
	Florida Everblades	ECHL	1	0	2	2	0																		
	BC Icemen	UHL	44	23	35	58	42										10	3	5	8	4				
2002-03	Providence Bruins	AHL	78	25	49	74	71										4	0	1	1	6				
2003-04	Cincinnati	AHL	80	18	30	48	64										9	0	3	3	4				
2004-05	Memphis	CHL	5	4	5	9	10																		
	Providence Bruins	AHL	72	21	45	66	49										17	4	*14	18	18				
2005-06	**Carolina**	**NHL**	**7**	**0**	**1**	**1**	**4**	**0**	**0**	**0**	**3**	**0.0**	**–4**	**4**	**100.0**	**5:19**									
	Lowell	AHL	72	29	56	85	68																		
2006-07	**Carolina**	**NHL**	**8**	**0**	**1**	**1**	**0**	**0**	**0**	**0**	**6**	**0.0**	**1**	**29**	**65.5**	**6:17**									
	Albany River Rats	AHL	65	27	72	99	108										5	1	3	4	7				
2007-08	**Carolina**	**NHL**	**38**	**5**	**8**	**13**	**10**	**0**	**0**	**0**	**65**	**7.7**	**3**	**327**	**37.9**	**13:28**									
	Albany River Rats	AHL	38	8	37	45	38																		
2008-09	**Washington**	**NHL**	**12**	**2**	**4**	**6**	**4**	**1**	**0**	**0**	**15**	**13.3**	**5**	**83**	**39.8**	**10:19**									
	Hershey Bears	AHL	70	25	*71	96	73										21	5	*18	23	16				
2009-10	**Washington**	**NHL**	**9**	**1**	**4**	**5**	**0**	**0**	**0**	**0**	**4**	**25.0**	**–2**	**56**	**55.4**	**8:48**									
	Hershey Bears	AHL	72	35	*71	*106	49										21	2	*23	25	2				
2010-11	**Washington**	**NHL**	**1**	**0**	**0**	**0**	**0**	**0**	**0**	**0**	**0**	**0.0**	**0**	**3**	**33.3**	**11:47**									
	Hershey Bears	AHL	53	18	54	72	49										6	2	6	8	2				
2011-12	**Washington**	**NHL**	**27**	**3**	**8**	**11**	**0**	**0**	**0**	**1**	**21**	**14.3**	**4**	**121**	**47.1**	**11:04**	**14**	**0**	**2**	**2**	**2**	**0**	**0**	**0**	**10:21**
	Hershey Bears	AHL	43	11	59	70	34																		
2012-13	Toronto Marlies	AHL	34	10	27	37	40																		
	NY Islanders	**NHL**	**41**	**6**	**6**	**12**	**4**	**1**	**0**	**1**	**50**	**12.0**	**–1**	**344**	**48.6**	**12:30**	**6**	**0**	**3**	**3**	**10**	**0**	**0**	**0**	**12:19**
2013-14	**St. Louis**	**NHL**	**2**	**0**	**0**	**0**	**0**	**0**	**0**	**0**	**1**	**0.0**	**–3**	**15**	**60.0**	**13:19**									
	Chicago Wolves	AHL	62	11	32	43	24										9	2	4	6	2				
2014-15	HC Ambri-Piotta	Swiss	47	7	24	31	22										6	3	4	7	4				
	NHL Totals		**145**	**17**	**32**	**49**	**22**	**2**	**0**	**2**	**165**	**10.3**		**982**	**45.3**	**11:23**	**20**	**0**	**5**	**5**	**12**	**0**	**0**	**0**	**10:56**

ECAC-3 First All-Star Team (2000, 2001) • ECAC-3 Player of the Year (2000, 2001) • AHL Second All-Star Team (2006, 2007, 2011) • AHL First All-Star Team (2009, 2010, 2012) • John B. Sollenberger Trophy (AHL – Leading Scorer) (2010) • Les Cunningham Award (AHL – MVP) (2010)

Signed as a free agent by **Lowell** (AHL), June 19, 2001. Signed as a free agent by **Providence** (AHL), August 2, 2002. Signed as a free agent by **Anaheim**, August 29, 2003. Signed to a PTO (professional tryout) contract by **Providence** (AHL), November 4, 2004, Signed as a free agent by **Providence** (AHL), December 9, 2004. Signed as a free agent by **Carolina**, August 4, 2005. Signed as a free agent by **Washington**, July 3, 2008. Signed as a free agent by **Toronto**, July 24, 2012. Claimed on waivers by **NY Islanders** from **Toronto**, January 17, 2013. Signed as a free agent by **St. Louis**, July 5, 2013. Signed as a free agent by **Ambri-Piotta** (Swiss), June 13, 2014.

AULIE, Keith

(AW-lee, KEETH)

Defense. Shoots left. 6'6", 228 lbs. Born, Rouleau, SK, June 11, 1989. Calgary's 3rd choice, 116th overall, in 2007 Entry Draft.

Season	Club	League	GP	G	A	Pts	PIM	PP	SH	GW	S	S%	+/-	TF	F%	Min	GP	G	A	Pts	PIM	PP	SH	GW	Min
2004-05	Notre Dame	SMHL	38	2	7	9	53																		
2005-06	Brandon	WHL	38	0	2	2	32										4	0	0	0	4				
2006-07	Brandon	WHL	66	1	8	9	82										11	0	2	2	14				
2007-08	Brandon	WHL	72	5	12	17	81										6	0	3	3	11				
2008-09	Brandon	WHL	58	6	27	33	83										12	2	7	9	12				
2009-10	Abbotsford Heat	AHL	43	2	4	6	32																		
	Toronto Marlies	AHL	5	0	0	0	6																		
2010-11	**Toronto**	**NHL**	**40**	**2**	**0**	**2**	**32**	**0**	**0**	**0**	**32**	**6.3**	**–1**	**0**	**0.0**	**19:08**									
	Toronto Marlies	AHL	36	3	6	9	61																		
2011-12	**Toronto**	**NHL**	**17**	**0**	**2**	**2**	**16**	**0**	**0**	**0**	**14**	**0.0**	**–2**	**0**	**0.0**	**16:07**									
	Toronto Marlies	AHL	23	0	1	1	30																		
	Tampa Bay	**NHL**	**19**	**0**	**1**	**1**	**13**	**0**	**0**	**0**	**4**	**0.0**	**–5**	**0**	**0.0**	**11:02**									
	Norfolk Admirals	AHL	3	0	2	2	0										18	1	5	6	10				
2012-13	Syracuse Crunch	AHL	20	3	3	6	34																		
	Tampa Bay	**NHL**	**45**	**2**	**5**	**7**	**60**	**0**	**0**	**0**	**37**	**5.4**	**1**	**0**	**0.0**	**12:49**									
2013-14	**Tampa Bay**	**NHL**	**15**	**0**	**1**	**1**	**9**	**0**	**0**	**0**	**6**	**0.0**	**–3**	**0**	**0.0**	**9:49**	**1**	**0**	**0**	**0**	**0**	**0**	**0**	**0**	**12:22**
2014-15	**Edmonton**	**NHL**	**31**	**0**	**1**	**1**	**66**	**0**	**0**	**0**	**25**	**0.0**	**–3**	**0**	**0.0**	**14:18**									
	Oklahoma City	AHL	8	0	1	1	0																		
	NHL Totals		**167**	**4**	**10**	**14**	**196**	**0**	**0**	**0**	**118**	**3.4**		**0**	**0.0**	**14:28**	**1**	**0**	**0**	**0**	**0**	**0**	**0**	**0**	**12:22**

WHL East First All-Star Team (2009)

Traded to **Toronto** by **Calgary** with Dion Phaneuf and Fredrik Sjostrom for Matt Stajan, Niklas Hagman, Jamal Mayers and Ian White, January 31, 2010. Traded to **Tampa Bay** by **Toronto** for Carter Ashton, February 27, 2012. • Missed majority of 2013-14 due to hand injury vs. Ottawa, December 5, 2013 and as a healthy reserve. Signed as a free agent by **Edmonton**, July 1, 2014. • Missed majority of 2014-15 as a healthy reserve.

BACKES, David

(BA-kuhs, DAY-vihd) **ST.L.**

Center. Shoots right. 6'3", 221 lbs. Born, Blaine, MN, May 1, 1984. St. Louis' 2nd choice, 62nd overall, in 2003 Entry Draft.

Season	Club	League	GP	G	A	Pts	PIM	PP	SH	GW	S	S%	+/-	TF	F%	Min	GP	G	A	Pts	PIM	PP	SH	GW	Min
99-2000	Spring Lake Park	High-MN	24	17	20	37																			
2000-01	Spring Lake Park	High-MN	24	29	46	75																			
2001-02	Chicago Steel	USHL	25	31	36	67											2	1	1	2					
	Lincoln Stars	USHL	30	11	10	21	54										3	0	0	0	2				
2002-03	Lincoln Stars	USHL	57	28	41	69	126										7	4	1	5	17				
2003-04	Minnesota State	WCHA	39	16	21	37	66																		
2004-05	Minnesota State	WCHA	38	17	23	40	55																		
2005-06	Minnesota State	WCHA	38	13	29	42	91																		
	Peoria Rivermen	AHL	12	5	5	10	10										3	1	1	2	8				
2006-07	**St. Louis**	**NHL**	**49**	**10**	**13**	**23**	**37**	**2**	**0**	**2**	**89**	**11.2**	**6**	**26**	**46.2**	**13:25**									
	Peoria Rivermen	AHL	31	10	3	13	47																		
2007-08	**St. Louis**	**NHL**	**72**	**13**	**18**	**31**	**99**	**3**	**0**	**2**	**129**	**10.1**	**–11**	**67**	**44.8**	**14:41**									
2008-09	**St. Louis**	**NHL**	**82**	**31**	**23**	**54**	**165**	**6**	**2**	**1**	**208**	**14.9**	**–3**	**477**	**44.4**	**17:41**	**4**	**1**	**2**	**3**	**10**	**0**	**0**	**0**	**22:56**
2009-10	**St. Louis**	**NHL**	**79**	**17**	**31**	**48**	**106**	**5**	**0**	**3**	**163**	**10.4**	**–4**	**1065**	**47.3**	**18:18**									
	United States	Olympics	6	1	2	3	2																		
2010-11	**St. Louis**	**NHL**	**82**	**31**	**31**	**62**	**93**	**5**	**0**	**2**	**211**	**14.7**	**32**	**1138**	**44.5**	**19:42**									
2011-12	**St. Louis**	**NHL**	**82**	**24**	**30**	**54**	**101**	**8**	**2**	**4**	**234**	**10.3**	**15**	**1353**	**48.6**	**20:00**	**9**	**2**	**2**	**4**	**18**	**0**	**0**	**0**	**20:19**
2012-13	**St. Louis**	**NHL**	**48**	**6**	**22**	**28**	**62**	**1**	**0**	**1**	**100**	**6.0**	**5**	**912**	**52.3**	**19:37**	**6**	**1**	**2**	**3**	**0**	**0**	**0**	**0**	**20:32**
2013-14	**St. Louis**	**NHL**	**74**	**27**	**30**	**57**	**119**	**10**	**0**	**5**	**165**	**16.4**	**14**	**1201**	**51.7**	**19:33**	**4**	**0**	**1**	**1**	**2**	**0**	**0**	**0**	**23:26**
	United States	Olympics	6	3	1	4	6																		
2014-15	**St. Louis**	**NHL**	**80**	**26**	**32**	**58**	**104**	**10**	**0**	**3**	**183**	**14.2**	**7**	**1130**	**54.6**	**18:38**	**6**	**1**	**1**	**2**	**2**	**0**	**0**	**0**	**19:06**
	NHL Totals		**648**	**185**	**230**	**415**	**886**	**50**	**4**	**23**	**1482**	**12.5**		**7369**	**49.4**	**18:08**	**29**	**5**	**8**	**13**	**32**	**0**	**0**	**0**	**20:54**

USHL First All-Star Team (2003) • WCHA All-Rookie Team (2004) • WCHA Second All-Star Team (2006) • NCAA West Second All-American Team (2006)

Played in NHL All-Star Game (2011)

BACKLUND, Mikael
(BAHK-luhnd, mih-KIGH-ehl) **CGY**

Center. Shoots left. 6', 198 lbs. Born, Vasteras, Sweden, March 17, 1989. Calgary's 1st choice, 24th overall, in 2007 Entry Draft.

			Regular Season														Playoffs								
Season	Club	League	GP	G	A	Pts	PIM	PP	SH	GW	S	S%	+/-	TF	F%	Min	GP	G	A	Pts	PIM	PP	SH	GW	Min
2004-05	Vasteras U18	Swe-U18	14	5	6	11	14										4	2	1	3	2				
2005-06	Vasteras Jr.	Swe-Jr.	25	15	16	31	30																		
	VIK Vasteras HK	Sweden-2	12	2	2	4	14																		
2006-07	Vasteras U18	Swe-U18	2	2	1	3	2										1	0	0	0	10				
	Vasteras Jr.	Swe-Jr.	7	5	4	9	8										5	1	0	1	4				
	VIK Vasteras HK	Sweden-2	18	1	2	3	14																		
2007-08	Vasteras Jr.	Swe-Jr.	9	7	6	13	20																		
	VIK Vasteras HK	Sweden-2	46	11	4	15	28										5	4	3	7	0				
2008-09	Vasteras Jr.	Swe-Jr.	2	3	2	5	0																		
	VIK Vasteras HK	Sweden-2	17	4	4	8	39																		
	Calgary	**NHL**	**1**	**0**	**0**	**0**	**0**	**0**	**0**	**0**	**1**	**0.0**	**0**	**7**	**28.6**	**10:44**									
	Kelowna Rockets	WHL	28	12	18	30	26										19	*13	10	23	26				
2009-10	**Calgary**	**NHL**	**23**	**1**	**9**	**10**	**6**	**0**	**0**	**0**	**47**	**2.1**	**5**	**191**	**53.4**	**12:36**									
	Abbotsford Heat	AHL	54	15	17	32	26										13	1	8	9	14				
2010-11	**Calgary**	**NHL**	**73**	**10**	**15**	**25**	**18**	**2**	**0**	**1**	**144**	**6.9**	**4**	**664**	**48.0**	**12:05**									
	Abbotsford Heat	AHL	1	0	0	0	0																		
2011-12	**Calgary**	**NHL**	**41**	**4**	**7**	**11**	**16**	**2**	**0**	**2**	**85**	**4.7**	**–13**	**496**	**45.4**	**15:23**									
2012-13	VIK Vasteras HK	Sweden-2	23	12	18	30	22																		
	Calgary	**NHL**	**32**	**8**	**8**	**16**	**29**	**2**	**0**	**1**	**88**	**9.1**	**–6**	**407**	**47.7**	**15:07**									
2013-14	**Calgary**	**NHL**	**76**	**18**	**21**	**39**	**32**	**5**	**4**	**3**	**178**	**10.1**	**4**	**1322**	**47.5**	**18:32**									
2014-15	**Calgary**	**NHL**	**52**	**10**	**17**	**27**	**14**	**0**	**2**	**2**	**103**	**9.7**	**4**	**875**	**48.3**	**17:45**	**11**	**1**	**1**	**2**	**8**	**0**	**0**	**1**	**18:52**
	NHL Totals		**298**	**51**	**77**	**128**	**115**	**11**	**6**	**9**	**646**	**7.9**		**3962**	**47.8**	**15:32**	**11**	**1**	**1**	**2**	**8**	**0**	**0**	**1**	**18:52**

Signed as a free agent by **Vasteras** (Sweden-2), October 4, 2012.

BACKSTROM, Nicklas
(BAK-struhm, NIHK-luhs) **WSH**

Center. Shoots left. 6'1", 208 lbs. Born, Gavle, Sweden, November 23, 1987. Washington's 1st choice, 4th overall, in 2006 Entry Draft.

Season	Club	League	GP	G	A	Pts	PIM	PP	SH	GW	S	S%	+/-	TF	F%	Min	GP	G	A	Pts	PIM	PP	SH	GW	Min
2001-02	Brynas U18	Swe-U18	2	0	0	0	0																		
2002-03	Brynas U18	Swe-U18	STATISTICS NOT AVAILABLE																						
2003-04	Brynas U18	Swe-U18	6	9	5	14	4										3	0	3	3	0				
	Brynas IF Gavle Jr.	Swe-Jr.	21	2	6	8	2										5	0	0	0	4				
2004-05	Brynas IF Gavle Jr.	Swe-Jr.	29	17	17	34	24																		
	Brynas IF Gavle	Sweden	19	0	0	0	2																		
2005-06	Brynas IF Gavle	Sweden	46	10	16	26	30										4	1	0	1	2				
	Brynas IF Gavle Jr.	Swe-Jr.															1	0	0	0	2				
2006-07	Brynas IF Gavle	Sweden	45	12	28	40	46										7	3	3	6	6				
2007-08	**Washington**	**NHL**	**82**	**14**	**55**	**69**	**24**	**3**	**0**	**4**	**153**	**9.2**	**13**	**874**	**46.3**	**19:00**	**7**	**4**	**2**	**6**	**2**	**3**	**0**	**0**	**20:26**
2008-09	**Washington**	**NHL**	**82**	**22**	**66**	**88**	**46**	**14**	**0**	**1**	**174**	**12.6**	**16**	**1171**	**48.7**	**19:57**	**14**	**3**	**12**	**15**	**8**	**2**	**0**	**0**	**21:40**
2009-10	**Washington**	**NHL**	**82**	**33**	**68**	**101**	**50**	**11**	**0**	**4**	**222**	**14.9**	**37**	**1336**	**49.9**	**20:27**	**7**	**5**	**4**	**9**	**4**	**0**	**0**	**1**	**21:03**
	Sweden	Olympics	4	1	5	6	0																		
2010-11	**Washington**	**NHL**	**77**	**18**	**47**	**65**	**40**	**4**	**1**	**2**	**202**	**8.9**	**24**	**1315**	**52.5**	**20:36**	**9**	**0**	**2**	**2**	**4**	**0**	**0**	**0**	**23:18**
2011-12	**Washington**	**NHL**	**42**	**14**	**30**	**44**	**24**	**3**	**0**	**4**	**95**	**14.7**	**–4**	**691**	**51.1**	**19:10**	**13**	**2**	**6**	**8**	**18**	**0**	**0**	**1**	**21:31**
2012-13	Dynamo Moscow	KHL	19	10	15	25	10																		
	Washington	**NHL**	**48**	**8**	**40**	**48**	**20**	**3**	**0**	**1**	**82**	**9.8**	**8**	**840**	**51.4**	**19:54**	**7**	**1**	**2**	**3**	**0**	**0**	**0**	**0**	**19:47**
2013-14	**Washington**	**NHL**	**82**	**18**	**61**	**79**	**54**	**6**	**1**	**1**	**196**	**9.2**	**–20**	**1415**	**50.5**	**19:48**									
	Sweden	Olympics	5	0	4	4	0																		
2014-15	**Washington**	**NHL**	**82**	**18**	***60**	**78**	**40**	**3**	**0**	**3**	**153**	**11.8**	**5**	**1609**	**53.6**	**20:32**	**14**	**3**	**5**	**8**	**2**	**1**	**0**	**1**	**21:36**
	NHL Totals		**577**	**145**	**427**	**572**	**298**	**47**	**2**	**20**	**1277**	**11.4**		**9251**	**50.7**	**19:58**	**71**	**18**	**33**	**51**	**38**	**6**	**0**	**3**	**21:28**

NHL All-Rookie Team (2008)

Signed as a free agent by **Dynamo Moscow** (KHL), October 18, 2012.

BAERTSCHI, Sven
(BEHR-chee, SVEHN) **VAN**

Left wing. Shoots left. 5'11", 187 lbs. Born, Langenthal, Switzerland, October 5, 1992. Calgary's 1st choice, 13th overall, in 2011 Entry Draft.

Season	Club	League	GP	G	A	Pts	PIM	PP	SH	GW	S	S%	+/-	TF	F%	Min	GP	G	A	Pts	PIM	PP	SH	GW	Min
2006-07	Langenthal U17	Swiss-U17	13	15	23	38	16																		
2007-08	Langenthal U17	Swiss-U17	17	16	22	38	22																		
	SC Langenthal Jr.	Swiss-Jr.	18	3	3	6	4										7	1	2	3	4				
2008-09	Langenthal U17	Swiss-U17	3	4	4	8	0																		
	SC Langenthal Jr.	Swiss-Jr.	37	21	32	53	40										6	4	3	7	35				
	SC Langenthal	Swiss-2	2	0	0	0	0																		
2009-10	SC Langenthal Jr.	Swiss-Jr.	2	3	0	3	2																		
	EV Zug Jr.	Swiss-Jr.	9	10	13	23	4										2	3	1	4	2				
	SC Langenthal	Swiss-2	37	6	6	12	8										7	0	3	3	4				
2010-11	Portland	WHL	66	34	51	85	74										21	10	17	27	16				
2011-12	Portland	WHL	47	33	61	94	36										22	14	20	34	10				
	Calgary	**NHL**	**5**	**3**	**0**	**3**	**4**	**0**	**0**	**0**	**10**	**30.0**	**2**	**0**	**0.0**	**11:08**									
2012-13	**Calgary**	**NHL**	**20**	**3**	**7**	**10**	**6**	**0**	**0**	**0**	**28**	**10.7**	**0**	**1**	**100.0**	**13:24**									
	Abbotsford Heat	AHL	32	10	16	26	16																		
2013-14	**Calgary**	**NHL**	**26**	**2**	**9**	**11**	**6**	**1**	**0**	**0**	**30**	**6.7**	**–4**	**0**	**0.0**	**14:07**									
	Abbotsford Heat	AHL	41	13	16	29	18										4	0	1	1	6				
2014-15	**Calgary**	**NHL**	**15**	**0**	**4**	**4**	**6**	**0**	**0**	**0**	**11**	**0.0**	**–3**	**0**	**0.0**	**9:13**									
	Adirondack	AHL	36	8	17	25	6																		
	Vancouver	**NHL**	**3**	**2**	**0**	**2**	**4**	**0**	**0**	**0**	**4**	**50.0**	**0**	**0**	**0.0**	**12:02**	**2**	**0**	**0**	**0**	**0**	**0**	**0**	**0**	**9:40**
	Utica Comets	AHL	15	7	8	15	4										21	8	7	15	6				
	NHL Totals		**69**	**10**	**20**	**30**	**26**	**1**	**0**	**0**	**83**	**12.0**		**1**	**100.0**	**12:32**	**2**	**0**	**0**	**0**	**0**	**0**	**0**	**0**	**9:40**

WHL West Second All-Star Team (2012)

Traded to **Vancouver** by **Calgary** for Vancouver's 2nd round choice (Rasmus Andersson) in 2015 Entry Draft, March 2, 2015.

BAGNALL, Drew
(BAG-nuhl, DROO)

Defense. Shoots left. 6'3", 220 lbs. Born, Oakbank, MB, October 26, 1983. Dallas' 9th choice, 195th overall, in 2003 Entry Draft.

Season	Club	League	GP	G	A	Pts	PIM	PP	SH	GW	S	S%	+/-	TF	F%	Min	GP	G	A	Pts	PIM	PP	SH	GW	Min
2000-01	Battlefords	SJHL	58	7	20	27	205																		
2001-02	Battlefords	SJHL	60	16	23	39	247																		
2002-03	Battlefords	SJHL	55	17	46	63	248										4	0	1	1	4				
2003-04	St. Lawrence	ECAC	40	5	13	18	61																		
2004-05	St. Lawrence	ECAC	37	7	12	19	68																		
2005-06	St. Lawrence	ECAC	24	1	9	10	32																		
2006-07	St. Lawrence	ECAC	39	6	19	25	74																		
2007-08	Manchester	AHL	54	1	11	12	115										4	0	0	0	4				
	Reading Royals	ECHL	10	1	2	3	32																		
2008-09	Manchester	AHL	79	0	6	6	150																		
2009-10	Manchester	AHL	58	2	10	12	113										16	0	3	3	21				
2010-11	**Minnesota**	**NHL**	**2**	**0**	**0**	**0**	**4**	**0**	**0**	**0**	**1**	**0.0**	**–2**	**0**	**0.0**	**13:00**									
	Houston Aeros	AHL	72	0	2	2	112										24	1	1	2	22				
2011-12	Houston Aeros	AHL	72	2	12	14	98										4	0	0	0	8				
2012-13	Houston Aeros	AHL	47	1	5	6	88										5	0	0	0	6				
2013-14	Rochester	AHL	51	0	6	6	88																		
2014-15	Rochester	AHL	41	3	9	12	62																		
	NHL Totals		**2**	**0**	**0**	**0**	**4**	**0**	**0**	**0**	**1**	**0.0**		**0**	**0.0**	**13:00**									

Traded to **Florida** by **Dallas** with Dallas' 2nd round compensatory choice (later traded to Phoenix – Phoenix selected Enver Lisin) in 2004 Entry Draft for Valeri Bure, March 8, 2004. Signed as a free agent by **Los Angeles**, August 23, 2007. Signed as a free agent by **Minnesota**, July 2, 2010. Signed as a free agent by **Buffalo**, July 6, 2013.

BAILEY, Casey
(BAY-lee, KAY-see) **TOR**

Forward. Shoots right. 6'3", 195 lbs. Born, Anchorage, AK, October 27, 1991.

			Regular Season														Playoffs								
Season	Club	League	GP	G	A	Pts	PIM	PP	SH	GW	S	S%	+/-	TF	F%	Min	GP	G	A	Pts	PIM	PP	SH	GW	Min
2008-09	Anchorage	Minor-AK	16	15	16	31	50	....	....	....	....	....	....	....	....	....	....	....	....	....	....	....	....	....	....
2009-10	Alberni Valley	BCHL	51	13	11	24	43	....	....	....	....	....	....	....	....	....	13	0	2	2	2	....	....	....	....
2010-11	Alberni Valley	BCHL	60	28	30	58	74	....	....	....	....	....	....	....	....	....	4	4	3	7	4	....	....	....	....
2011-12	Omaha Lancers	USHL	60	27	33	60	83	....	....	....	....	....	....	....	....	....	4	2	2	4	6	....	....	....	....
2012-13	Penn State	NCAA	27	14	13	27	34	....	....	....	....	....	....	....	....	....	....	....	....	....	....	....	....	....	....
2013-14	Penn State	Big Ten	32	9	4	13	20	....	....	....	....	....	....	....	....	....	....	....	....	....	....	....	....	....	....
2014-15	Penn State	Big Ten	37	*22	18	40	37	....	....	....	....	....	....	....	....	....	....	....	....	....	....	....	....	....	....
	Toronto	**NHL**	**6**	**1**	**0**	**1**	**2**	0	0	0	9	11.1	1	0	0.0	9:02	....	....	....	....	....	....	....	....	....
	NHL Totals		**6**	**1**	**0**	**1**	**2**	0	0	0	9	11.1		0	0.0	9:02	....	....	....	....	....	....	....	....	....

Signed as a free agent by **Toronto**, March 21, 2015.

BAILEY, Josh
(BAY-lee, JAWSH) **NYI**

Center. Shoots left. 6'1", 194 lbs. Born, Bowmanville, ON, October 2, 1989. NY Islanders' 1st choice, 9th overall, in 2008 Entry Draft.

Season	Club	League	GP	G	A	Pts	PIM	PP	SH	GW	S	S%	+/-	TF	F%	Min	GP	G	A	Pts	PIM	PP	SH	GW	Min
2004-05	Clarington Toros	Minor-ON	69	53	59	112	38	....	....	....	....	....	....	....	....	....	....	....	....	....	....	....	....	....	....
2005-06	Owen Sound	OHL	55	7	19	26	8	....	....	....	....	....	....	....	....	....	11	0	0	0	0	....	....	....	....
2006-07	Owen Sound	OHL	27	11	15	26	8	....	....	....	....	....	....	....	....	....	....	....	....	....	....	....	....	....	....
	Windsor Spitfires	OHL	42	11	24	35	16	....	....	....	....	....	....	....	....	....	....	....	....	....	....	....	....	....	....
2007-08	Windsor Spitfires	OHL	67	29	67	96	32	....	....	....	....	....	....	....	....	....	5	1	5	6	2	....	....	....	....
2008-09	**NY Islanders**	**NHL**	**68**	**7**	**18**	**25**	**16**	3	0	0	74	9.5	-14	807	41.1	15:29	....	....	....	....	....	....	....	....	....
2009-10	**NY Islanders**	**NHL**	**73**	**16**	**19**	**35**	**18**	3	1	2	112	14.3	5	426	40.1	15:09	....	....	....	....	....	....	....	....	....
2010-11	**NY Islanders**	**NHL**	**70**	**11**	**17**	**28**	**37**	5	0	2	102	10.8	-13	615	44.4	17:50	....	....	....	....	....	....	....	....	....
	Bridgeport	AHL	11	6	11	17	4	....	....	....	....	....	....	....	....	....	....	....	....	....	....	....	....	....	....
2011-12	**NY Islanders**	**NHL**	**80**	**13**	**19**	**32**	**32**	1	3	1	104	12.5	-10	736	43.9	15:13	....	....	....	....	....	....	....	....	....
2012-13	Bietigheim	German-2	6	3	8	11	16	....	....	....	....	....	....	....	....	....	....	....	....	....	....	....	....	....	....
	NY Islanders	**NHL**	**38**	**11**	**8**	**19**	**6**	0	0	1	76	14.5	7	75	46.7	16:23	6	0	3	3	0	0	0	0	20:14
2013-14	**NY Islanders**	**NHL**	**77**	**8**	**30**	**38**	**26**	2	0	1	98	8.2	-8	228	49.6	15:50	....	....	....	....	....	....	....	....	....
2014-15	**NY Islanders**	**NHL**	**70**	**15**	**26**	**41**	**12**	2	0	1	140	10.7	3	66	45.5	16:47	7	2	3	5	0	0	0	0	17:26
	NHL Totals		**476**	**81**	**137**	**218**	**147**	16	4	8	706	11.5		2953	43.2	16:03	13	2	6	8	0	0	0	0	18:43

Signed as a free agent by **Bietigheim** (German-2), November 9, 2012.

BALLARD, Keith
(BAL-uhrd, KEETH)

Defense. Shoots left. 5'11", 199 lbs. Born, Baudette, MN, November 26, 1982. Buffalo's 1st choice, 11th overall, in 2002 Entry Draft.

Season	Club	League	GP	G	A	Pts	PIM	PP	SH	GW	S	S%	+/-	TF	F%	Min	GP	G	A	Pts	PIM	PP	SH	GW	Min
99-2000	USNTDP	U-18	6	1	1	2	4	....	....	....	....	....	....	....	....	....	....	....	....	....	....	....	....	....	....
	USNTDP	USHL	58	12	21	33	119	....	....	....	....	....	....	....	....	....	....	....	....	....	....	....	....	....	....
2000-01	Omaha Lancers	USHL	56	22	29	51	168	....	....	....	....	....	....	....	....	....	10	1	6	7	8	....	....	....	....
2001-02	U. of Minnesota	WCHA	41	10	13	23	42	....	....	....	....	....	....	....	....	....	....	....	....	....	....	....	....	....	....
2002-03	U. of Minnesota	WCHA	41	12	29	41	78	....	....	....	....	....	....	....	....	....	....	....	....	....	....	....	....	....	....
2003-04	U. of Minnesota	WCHA	37	11	25	36	83	....	....	....	....	....	....	....	....	....	....	....	....	....	....	....	....	....	....
2004-05	Utah Grizzlies	AHL	60	2	18	20	88	....	....	....	....	....	....	....	....	....	....	....	....	....	....	....	....	....	....
2005-06	**Phoenix**	**NHL**	**82**	**8**	**31**	**39**	**99**	1	3	1	102	7.8	-18	0	0.0	19:59	....	....	....	....	....	....	....	....	....
2006-07	**Phoenix**	**NHL**	**69**	**5**	**22**	**27**	**59**	2	0	0	79	6.3	-7	0	0.0	22:00	....	....	....	....	....	....	....	....	....
2007-08	**Phoenix**	**NHL**	**82**	**6**	**15**	**21**	**85**	2	1	1	105	5.7	7	0	0.0	21:16	....	....	....	....	....	....	....	....	....
2008-09	**Florida**	**NHL**	**82**	**6**	**28**	**34**	**72**	1	0	1	106	5.7	14	1	0.0	22:23	....	....	....	....	....	....	....	....	....
2009-10	**Florida**	**NHL**	**82**	**8**	**20**	**28**	**88**	1	0	1	90	8.9	-7	0	0.0	22:24	....	....	....	....	....	....	....	....	....
2010-11	**Vancouver**	**NHL**	**65**	**2**	**5**	**7**	**53**	0	0	0	53	3.8	10	0	0.0	15:54	10	0	0	0	6	0	0	0	14:14
2011-12	**Vancouver**	**NHL**	**47**	**1**	**6**	**7**	**64**	0	0	0	41	2.4	0	0	0.0	15:33	4	0	1	1	2	0	0	0	14:40
2012-13	**Vancouver**	**NHL**	**36**	**0**	**2**	**2**	**29**	0	0	0	35	0.0	-2	0	0.0	15:28	....	....	....	....	....	....	....	....	....
2013-14	**Minnesota**	**NHL**	**45**	**2**	**7**	**9**	**37**	0	0	0	29	6.9	-7	0	0.0	13:37	3	0	0	0	0	0	0	0	10:45
2014-15	**Minnesota**	**NHL**	**14**	**0**	**1**	**1**	**26**	0	0	0	5	0.0	-3	0	0.0	12:03	....	....	....	....	....	....	....	....	....
	NHL Totals		**604**	**38**	**137**	**175**	**612**	7	4	4	645	5.9		1	0.0	19:20	17	0	1	1	8	0	0	0	13:43

USHL First All-Star Team (2001) • WCHA All-Rookie Team (2002) • WCHA First All-Star Team (2003, 2004) • NCAA West First All-American Team (2004)

Traded to **Colorado** by **Buffalo** for Steve Reinprecht, July 3, 2003. Traded to **Phoenix** by **Colorado** with Derek Morris for Ossi Vaananen, Chris Gratton and Phoenix's 2nd round choice (Paul Stastny) in 2005 Entry Draft, March 9, 2004. Traded to **Florida** by **Phoenix** with Nick Boynton and Ottawa's 2nd round choice (previously acquired, later traded back to Phoenix - Phoenix selected Jared Staal) in 2008 Entry Draft for Olli Jokinen, June 20, 2008. Traded to **Vancouver** by **Florida** with Victor Oreskovich for Steve Bernier, Michael Grabner and Vancouver's 1st round choice (Quinton Howden) in 2010 Entry Draft, June 25, 2010. Signed as a free agent by **Minnesota**, July 5, 2013. • Missed majority of 2014-15 due to head injury vs. NY Islanders, December 9, 2014.

BANCKS, Carter
(BANKS, KAHR-tuhr)

Left wing. Shoots left. 5'11", 180 lbs. Born, Marysville, BC, August 9, 1989.

Season	Club	League	GP	G	A	Pts	PIM	PP	SH	GW	S	S%	+/-	TF	F%	Min	GP	G	A	Pts	PIM	PP	SH	GW	Min
2005-06	Kimberley	KIJHL	50	24	49	73	57	....	....	....	....	....	....	....	....	....	13	5	7	12	6	....	....	....	....
	Lethbridge	WHL	2	0	0	0	0	....	....	....	....	....	....	....	....	....	6	0	0	0	4	....	....	....	....
2006-07	Lethbridge	WHL	67	11	20	31	64	....	....	....	....	....	....	....	....	....	....	....	....	....	....	....	....	....	....
2007-08	Lethbridge	WHL	70	15	30	45	56	....	....	....	....	....	....	....	....	....	19	6	4	10	19	....	....	....	....
2008-09	Lethbridge	WHL	53	13	34	47	68	....	....	....	....	....	....	....	....	....	3	0	0	0	4	....	....	....	....
2009-10	Lethbridge	WHL	70	19	36	55	96	....	....	....	....	....	....	....	....	....	....	....	....	....	....	....	....	....	....
	Abbotsford Heat	AHL	9	0	0	0	0	....	....	....	....	....	....	....	....	....	13	0	1	1	7	....	....	....	....
2010-11	Abbotsford Heat	AHL	29	5	14	19	16	....	....	....	....	....	....	....	....	....	....	....	....	....	....	....	....	....	....
2011-12	Abbotsford Heat	AHL	55	2	8	10	57	....	....	....	....	....	....	....	....	....	8	0	0	0	14	....	....	....	....
2012-13	Abbotsford Heat	AHL	59	5	7	12	53	....	....	....	....	....	....	....	....	....	....	....	....	....	....	....	....	....	....
	Calgary	**NHL**	**2**	**0**	**0**	**0**	**0**	0	0	0	0	0.0	0	0	0.0	14:41	....	....	....	....	....	....	....	....	....
2013-14	Abbotsford Heat	AHL	72	3	8	11	53	....	....	....	....	....	....	....	....	....	4	0	0	0	0	....	....	....	....
2014-15	Utica Comets	AHL	57	6	8	14	44	....	....	....	....	....	....	....	....	....	10	0	0	0	4	....	....	....	....
	NHL Totals		**2**	**0**	**0**	**0**	**0**	0	0	0	0	0.0		0	0.0	14:41	....	....	....	....	....	....	....	....	....

Signed to a ATO (amateur tryout) contract by **Abbotsford** (AHL), March 18, 2010. Signed as a free agent by **Calgary**, July 1, 2011. Signed to a PTO (professional tryout) contract by **Utica** (AHL), September 27, 2014.

BARBERIO, Mark
(bahr-BAIR-ee-oh, MAHRK) **MTL**

Defense. Shoots left. 6'1", 199 lbs. Born, Montreal, QC, March 23, 1990. Tampa Bay's 5th choice, 152nd overall, in 2008 Entry Draft.

Season	Club	League	GP	G	A	Pts	PIM	PP	SH	GW	S	S%	+/-	TF	F%	Min	GP	G	A	Pts	PIM	PP	SH	GW	Min
2005-06	Lac St-Louis Lions	QAAA	43	2	12	14	80	....	....	....	....	....	....	....	....	....	10	1	7	8	26	....	....	....	....
2006-07	Cape Breton	QMJHL	41	2	8	10	42	....	....	....	....	....	....	....	....	....	....	....	....	....	....	....	....	....	....
	Moncton Wildcats	QMJHL	19	1	6	7	21	....	....	....	....	....	....	....	....	....	7	0	2	2	8	....	....	....	....
2007-08	Moncton Wildcats	QMJHL	70	11	35	46	75	....	....	....	....	....	....	....	....	....	....	....	....	....	....	....	....	....	....
2008-09	Moncton Wildcats	QMJHL	66	15	30	45	42	....	....	....	....	....	....	....	....	....	10	0	4	4	8	....	....	....	....
2009-10	Moncton Wildcats	QMJHL	65	17	43	60	72	....	....	....	....	....	....	....	....	....	21	5	17	22	12	....	....	....	....
2010-11	Norfolk Admirals	AHL	68	9	22	31	28	....	....	....	....	....	....	....	....	....	6	1	0	1	4	....	....	....	....
2011-12	Norfolk Admirals	AHL	74	13	48	61	39	....	....	....	....	....	....	....	....	....	18	2	7	9	12	....	....	....	....
2012-13	Syracuse Crunch	AHL	73	8	34	42	44	....	....	....	....	....	....	....	....	....	18	3	12	15	18	....	....	....	....
	Tampa Bay	**NHL**	**2**	**0**	**0**	**0**	**0**	0	0	0	1	0.0	-2	0	0.0	15:30	....	....	....	....	....	....	....	....	....
2013-14	**Tampa Bay**	**NHL**	**49**	**5**	**5**	**10**	**28**	1	0	0	54	9.3	10	0	0.0	14:35	2	0	0	0	6	0	0	0	9:04
2014-15	**Tampa Bay**	**NHL**	**52**	**1**	**6**	**7**	**16**	0	0	0	53	1.9	-4	0	0.0	16:47	1	0	0	0	0	0	0	0	8:44
	NHL Totals		**103**	**6**	**11**	**17**	**44**	1	0	0	108	5.6		0	0.0	15:42	3	0	0	0	6	0	0	0	8:57

QMJHL All-Rookie Team (2007) • QMJHL Second All-Star Team (2010) • AHL First All-Star Team (2012) • Eddie Shore Award (AHL - Outstanding Defenseman) (2012) • AHL Second All-Star Team (2013)

Signed as a free agent by **Montreal**, July 1, 2015.

BARKER, Cam

(BAR-kuhr, KAM)

Defense. Shoots left. 6'3", 223 lbs. Born, Winnipeg, MB, April 4, 1986. Chicago's 1st choice, 3rd overall, in 2004 Entry Draft.

			Regular Season														Playoffs								
Season	Club	League	GP	G	A	Pts	PIM	PP	SH	GW	S	S%	+/-	TF	F%	Min	GP	G	A	Pts	PIM	PP	SH	GW	Min
2001-02	Gloucester	ON-Jr.A	32	1	8	9	77	....	....	....	....	....	....	....	....	....	....	....	....	....	....	....	....	....	....
	Cornwall Colts	ON-Jr.A	18	3	13	16	66	....	....	....	....	....	....	....	....	....	13	0	2	2	26	....	....	....	....
	Medicine Hat	WHL	3	0	1	1	0	....	....	....	....	....	....	....	....	....	....	....	....	....	....	....	....	....	....
2002-03	Medicine Hat	WHL	64	10	37	47	79	....	....	....	....	....	....	....	....	....	11	3	4	7	17	....	....	....	....
2003-04	Medicine Hat	WHL	69	21	44	65	105	....	....	....	....	....	....	....	....	....	20	3	9	12	18	....	....	....	....
2004-05	Medicine Hat	WHL	52	15	33	48	99	....	....	....	....	....	....	....	....	....	12	3	3	6	16	....	....	....	....
2005-06	**Chicago**	**NHL**	**1**	**0**	**0**	**0**	**0**	**0**	**0**	**0**	**1**	**0.0**	**0**	**0**	**0.0**	**11:02**	....	....	....	....	....	....	....	....	....
	Medicine Hat	WHL	26	5	13	18	63	....	....	....	....	....	....	....	....	....	13	4	8	12	*59	....	....	....	....
2006-07	**Chicago**	**NHL**	**35**	**1**	**7**	**8**	**44**	**1**	**0**	**0**	**38**	**2.6**	**-12**	**0**	**0.0**	**19:19**	....	....	....	....	....	....	....	....	....
	Norfolk Admirals	AHL	34	5	10	15	53	....	....	....	....	....	....	....	....	....	6	1	3	4	13	....	....	....	....
2007-08	**Chicago**	**NHL**	**45**	**6**	**12**	**18**	**52**	**2**	**0**	**0**	**42**	**14.3**	**-3**	**0**	**0.0**	**17:12**	....	....	....	....	....	....	....	....	....
	Rockford IceHogs	AHL	29	8	11	19	67	....	....	....	....	....	....	....	....	....	....	....	....	....	....	....	....	....	....
2008-09	**Chicago**	**NHL**	**68**	**6**	**34**	**40**	**65**	**5**	**0**	**1**	**101**	**5.9**	**-6**	**1**	**0.0**	**18:20**	**17**	**3**	**6**	**9**	**2**	**0**	**0**	**0**	**16:39**
	Rockford IceHogs	AHL	7	3	2	5	6	....	....	....	....	....	....	....	....	....	....	....	....	....	....	....	....	....	....
2009-10	**Chicago**	**NHL**	**51**	**4**	**10**	**14**	**58**	**3**	**0**	**1**	**74**	**5.4**	**7**	**0**	**0.0**	**13:06**	....	....	....	....	....	....	....	....	....
	Minnesota	**NHL**	**19**	**1**	**6**	**7**	**10**	**1**	**0**	**0**	**31**	**3.2**	**-2**	**0**	**0.0**	**22:02**	....	....	....	....	....	....	....	....	....
2010-11	**Minnesota**	**NHL**	**52**	**1**	**4**	**5**	**34**	**0**	**0**	**1**	**44**	**2.3**	**-10**	**0**	**0.0**	**16:24**	....	....	....	....	....	....	....	....	....
2011-12	**Edmonton**	**NHL**	**25**	**2**	**0**	**2**	**23**	**1**	**0**	**1**	**35**	**5.7**	**0**	**0**	**0.0**	**18:22**	....	....	....	....	....	....	....	....	....
2012-13	Texas Stars	AHL	23	3	5	8	24	....	....	....	....	....	....	....	....	....	....	....	....	....	....	....	....	....	....
	Vancouver	**NHL**	**14**	**0**	**2**	**2**	**4**	**0**	**0**	**0**	**19**	**0.0**	**-3**	**0**	**0.0**	**14:12**	....	....	....	....	....	....	....	....	....
2013-14	Barys Astana	KHL	26	2	10	12	26	....	....	....	....	....	....	....	....	....	10	1	2	3	10	....	....	....	....
2014-15	Bratislava	KHL	18	0	9	9	19	....	....	....	....	....	....	....	....	....	....	....	....	....	....	....	....	....	....
	NHL Totals		**310**	**21**	**75**	**96**	**290**	**13**	**0**	**4**	**385**	**5.5**		**1**	**0.0**	**17:07**	**17**	**3**	**6**	**9**	**2**	**0**	**0**	**0**	**16:39**

Traded to **Minnesota** by **Chicago** for Kim Johnsson and Nick Leddy, February 12, 2010. Signed as a free agent by **Edmonton**, July 1, 2011. • Missed majority of 2011-12 due to ankle injury at Boston, November 11, 2011. Signed as a free agent by **Texas** (AHL), September 28, 2012. Signed as a free agent by **Vancouver**, January 13, 2012. • Missed majority of 2012-13 a a healthy reserve. Signed as a free agent by **Astana** (KHL), November 5, 2013. Signed as a free agent by **Bratislava** (KHL), December 23, 2014.

BARKOV, Aleksander

(bar-KAWV, al-ehx-AN-duhr) **FLA**

Center. Shoots left. 6'3", 213 lbs. Born, Tampere, Finland, September 2, 1995. Florida's 1st choice, 2nd overall, in 2013 Entry Draft.

Season	Club	League	GP	G	A	Pts	PIM	PP	SH	GW	S	S%	+/-	TF	F%	Min	GP	G	A	Pts	PIM	PP	SH	GW	Min
2010-11	Tappara U18	Fin-U18	11	7	8	15	8	....	....	....	....	....	....	....	....	....	2	3	0	3	0	....	....	....	....
	Tappara Jr.	Fin-Jr.	25	5	12	17	6	....	....	....	....	....	....	....	....	....	....	....	....	....	....	....	....	....	....
2011-12	Tappara Jr.	Fin-Jr.	5	2	3	5	2	....	....	....	....	....	....	....	....	....	....	....	....	....	....	....	....	....	....
	Tappara Tampere	Finland	32	7	9	16	4	....	....	....	....	....	....	....	....	....	....	....	....	....	....	....	....	....	....
2012-13	Tappara Tampere	Finland	53	21	27	48	8	....	....	....	....	....	....	....	....	....	5	0	5	5	2	....	....	....	....
2013-14	**Florida**	**NHL**	**54**	**8**	**16**	**24**	**10**	**3**	**0**	**1**	**87**	**9.2**	**-3**	**819**	**48.8**	**17:06**	....	....	....	....	....	....	....	....	....
	Finland	Olympics	2	0	1	1	2	....	....	....	....	....	....	....	....	....	....	....	....	....	....	....	....	....	....
2014-15	**Florida**	**NHL**	**71**	**16**	**20**	**36**	**16**	**3**	**0**	**3**	**123**	**13.0**	**-4**	**1002**	**46.1**	**17:30**	....	....	....	....	....	....	....	....	....
	NHL Totals		**125**	**24**	**36**	**60**	**26**	**6**	**0**	**4**	**210**	**11.4**		**1821**	**47.3**	**17:20**	....	....	....	....	....	....	....	....	....

BARRIE, Tyson

(BAIR-ree, TIGH-suhn) **COL**

Defense. Shoots right. 5'10", 190 lbs. Born, Victoria, BC, July 26, 1991. Colorado's 4th choice, 64th overall, in 2009 Entry Draft.

Season	Club	League	GP	G	A	Pts	PIM	PP	SH	GW	S	S%	+/-	TF	F%	Min	GP	G	A	Pts	PIM	PP	SH	GW	Min
2006-07	Juan de Fuca	Minor-BC	72	43	87	130	....	....	....	....	....	....	....	....	....	....	....	....	....	....	....	....	....	....	....
	Kelowna Rockets	WHL	7	0	3	3	2	....	....	....	....	....	....	....	....	....	....	....	....	....	....	....	....	....	....
2007-08	Kelowna Rockets	WHL	64	9	34	43	32	....	....	....	....	....	....	....	....	....	7	1	3	4	0	....	....	....	....
2008-09	Kelowna Rockets	WHL	68	12	40	52	31	....	....	....	....	....	....	....	....	....	22	4	14	18	12	....	....	....	....
2009-10	Kelowna Rockets	WHL	63	19	53	72	31	....	....	....	....	....	....	....	....	....	12	3	8	11	6	....	....	....	....
2010-11	Kelowna Rockets	WHL	54	11	47	58	34	....	....	....	....	....	....	....	....	....	10	2	9	11	8	....	....	....	....
2011-12	**Colorado**	**NHL**	**10**	**0**	**0**	**0**	**0**	**0**	**0**	**0**	**15**	**0.0**	**-2**	**0**	**0.0**	**17:39**	....	....	....	....	....	....	....	....	....
	Lake Erie	AHL	49	5	27	32	24	....	....	....	....	....	....	....	....	....	....	....	....	....	....	....	....	....	....
2012-13	Lake Erie	AHL	38	7	22	29	7	....	....	....	....	....	....	....	....	....	....	....	....	....	....	....	....	....	....
	Colorado	**NHL**	**32**	**2**	**11**	**13**	**10**	**1**	**0**	**1**	**58**	**3.4**	**-11**	**0**	**0.0**	**21:35**	....	....	....	....	....	....	....	....	....
2013-14	**Colorado**	**NHL**	**64**	**13**	**25**	**38**	**20**	**4**	**0**	**5**	**101**	**12.9**	**17**	**0**	**0.0**	**18:33**	**3**	**0**	**2**	**2**	**0**	**0**	**0**	**0**	**18:17**
	Lake Erie	AHL	6	0	3	3	0	....	....	....	....	....	....	....	....	....	....	....	....	....	....	....	....	....	....
2014-15	**Colorado**	**NHL**	**80**	**12**	**41**	**53**	**26**	**2**	**0**	**0**	**139**	**8.6**	**5**	**0**	**0.0**	**21:22**	....	....	....	....	....	....	....	....	....
	NHL Totals		**186**	**27**	**77**	**104**	**56**	**7**	**0**	**6**	**313**	**8.6**		**0**	**0.0**	**20:14**	**3**	**0**	**2**	**2**	**0**	**0**	**0**	**0**	**18:17**

Canadian Major Junior All-Rookie Team (2008) • WHL West First All-Star Team (2010, 2011) • WHL Defenseman of the Year (2010) • Canadian Major Junior Second All-Star Team (2010)

BARTKOWSKI, Matt

(bahrt-KOW-skee, MATT) **VAN**

Defense. Shoots left. 6'1", 196 lbs. Born, Pittsburgh, PA, June 4, 1988. Florida's 5th choice, 190th overall, in 2008 Entry Draft.

Season	Club	League	GP	G	A	Pts	PIM	PP	SH	GW	S	S%	+/-	TF	F%	Min	GP	G	A	Pts	PIM	PP	SH	GW	Min
2006-07	Lincoln Stars	USHL	57	3	6	9	95	....	....	....	....	....	....	....	....	....	3	0	0	0	2	....	....	....	....
2007-08	Lincoln Stars	USHL	60	4	37	41	135	....	....	....	....	....	....	....	....	....	8	1	4	5	10	....	....	....	....
2008-09	Ohio State	CCHA	41	5	15	20	46	....	....	....	....	....	....	....	....	....	....	....	....	....	....	....	....	....	....
2009-10	Ohio State	CCHA	39	6	12	18	*99	....	....	....	....	....	....	....	....	....	....	....	....	....	....	....	....	....	....
2010-11	**Boston**	**NHL**	**6**	**0**	**0**	**0**	**4**	**0**	**0**	**0**	**2**	**0.0**	**-1**	**0**	**0.0**	**9:10**	....	....	....	....	....	....	....	....	....
	Providence Bruins	AHL	69	5	18	23	42	....	....	....	....	....	....	....	....	....	....	....	....	....	....	....	....	....	....
2011-12	**Boston**	**NHL**	**3**	**0**	**0**	**0**	**0**	**0**	**0**	**0**	**0**	**0.0**	**-2**	**0**	**0.0**	**6:08**	....	....	....	....	....	....	....	....	....
	Providence Bruins	AHL	50	3	19	22	38	....	....	....	....	....	....	....	....	....	....	....	....	....	....	....	....	....	....
2012-13	Providence Bruins	AHL	56	3	21	24	56	....	....	....	....	....	....	....	....	....	5	0	5	5	4	....	....	....	....
	Boston	**NHL**	**11**	**0**	**2**	**2**	**6**	**0**	**0**	**0**	**9**	**0.0**	**0**	**0**	**0.0**	**13:29**	**7**	**1**	**1**	**2**	**4**	**0**	**0**	**0**	**19:47**
2013-14	**Boston**	**NHL**	**64**	**0**	**18**	**18**	**30**	**0**	**0**	**0**	**91**	**0.0**	**22**	**0**	**0.0**	**19:32**	**8**	**0**	**1**	**1**	**10**	**0**	**0**	**0**	**20:21**
2014-15	**Boston**	**NHL**	**47**	**0**	**4**	**4**	**37**	**0**	**0**	**0**	**67**	**0.0**	**-6**	**0**	**0.0**	**16:56**	....	....	....	....	....	....	....	....	....
	NHL Totals		**131**	**0**	**24**	**24**	**77**	**0**	**0**	**0**	**169**	**0.0**		**0**	**0.0**	**17:19**	**15**	**1**	**2**	**3**	**14**	**0**	**0**	**0**	**20:05**

CCHA All-Rookie Team (2009) • USHL First All-Star Team (2008)

Traded to **Boston** by **Florida** with Dennis Seidenberg for Byron Bitz, Craig Weller and Tampa Bay's 2nd round choice (previously acquired, Florida selected Alexander Petrovic) in 2010 Entry Draft, March 3, 2010. Signed as a free agent by **Vancouver**, July 1, 2015.

BARTLEY, Victor

(BAR-tlee, WAYD) **NSH**

Defense. Shoots left. 6', 203 lbs. Born, Ottawa, ON, February 17, 1988.

Season	Club	League	GP	G	A	Pts	PIM	PP	SH	GW	S	S%	+/-	TF	F%	Min	GP	G	A	Pts	PIM	PP	SH	GW	Min
2003-04	Delta Ice Hawks	PIJHL	42	2	25	27	66	....	....	....	....	....	....	....	....	....	....	....	....	....	....	....	....	....	....
	Kamloops Blazers	WHL	3	0	0	0	0	....	....	....	....	....	....	....	....	....	....	....	....	....	....	....	....	....	....
2004-05	Kamloops Blazers	WHL	68	4	6	10	58	....	....	....	....	....	....	....	....	....	5	0	3	3	4	....	....	....	....
2005-06	Kamloops Blazers	WHL	65	3	24	27	114	....	....	....	....	....	....	....	....	....	....	....	....	....	....	....	....	....	....
2006-07	Kamloops Blazers	WHL	67	4	39	43	104	....	....	....	....	....	....	....	....	....	4	0	2	2	8	....	....	....	....
2007-08	Kamloops Blazers	WHL	36	3	15	18	51	....	....	....	....	....	....	....	....	....	....	....	....	....	....	....	....	....	....
	Regina Pats	WHL	25	7	17	24	42	....	....	....	....	....	....	....	....	....	6	1	3	4	8	....	....	....	....
2008-09	Regina Pats	WHL	72	15	31	46	97	....	....	....	....	....	....	....	....	....	....	....	....	....	....	....	....	....	....
	Providence Bruins	AHL	10	0	0	0	6	....	....	....	....	....	....	....	....	....	....	....	....	....	....	....	....	....	....
2009-10	Bridgeport	AHL	8	2	0	2	6	....	....	....	....	....	....	....	....	....	....	....	....	....	....	....	....	....	....
	Utah Grizzlies	ECHL	21	2	11	13	21	....	....	....	....	....	....	....	....	....	....	....	....	....	....	....	....	....	....
2010-11	Rogle	Sweden-2	52	11	23	34	56	....	....	....	....	....	....	....	....	....	....	....	....	....	....	....	....	....	....
2011-12	Milwaukee	AHL	76	9	30	39	64	....	....	....	....	....	....	....	....	....	1	1	0	1	0	....	....	....	....
2012-13	Milwaukee	AHL	54	7	19	26	35	....	....	....	....	....	....	....	....	....	2	0	1	1	0	....	....	....	....
	Nashville	**NHL**	**24**	**0**	**7**	**7**	**6**	**0**	**0**	**0**	**19**	**0.0**	**2**	**0**	**0.0**	**19:33**	....	....	....	....	....	....	....	....	....
2013-14	**Nashville**	**NHL**	**50**	**1**	**5**	**6**	**23**	**0**	**0**	**0**	**21**	**4.8**	**0**	**0**	**0.0**	**15:22**	....	....	....	....	....	....	....	....	....
2014-15	**Nashville**	**NHL**	**37**	**0**	**10**	**10**	**26**	**0**	**0**	**0**	**28**	**0.0**	**1**	**0**	**0.0**	**13:26**	**4**	**0**	**0**	**0**	**2**	**0**	**0**	**0**	**11:21**
	NHL Totals		**111**	**1**	**22**	**23**	**55**	**0**	**0**	**0**	**68**	**1.5**		**0**	**0.0**	**15:37**	**4**	**0**	**0**	**0**	**2**	**0**	**0**	**0**	**11:21**

Signed as a free agent by **Rogle** (Sweden-2), May 26, 2010. Signed as a free agent by **Nashville**, May 24, 2011. • Missed majority of 2014-15 as a healthy reserve.

BASS, Cody
(BAS, KOH-dee) **NSH**

Center. Shoots right. 6', 203 lbs. Born, Owen Sound, ON, January 7, 1987. Ottawa's 3rd choice, 95th overall, in 2005 Entry Draft.

			Regular Season														Playoffs								
Season	Club	League	GP	G	A	Pts	PIM	PP	SH	GW	S	S%	+/-	TF	F%	Min	GP	G	A	Pts	PIM	PP	SH	GW	Min
2003-04	Mississauga	OHL	61	3	7	10	30	....	....	....	....	....	....	....	....	....	24	2	3	5	21	....	....	....	....
2004-05	Mississauga	OHL	66	11	17	28	103	....	....	....	....	....	....	....	....	....	5	1	1	2	8	....	....	....	....
2005-06	Mississauga	OHL	67	16	25	41	152	....	....	....	....	....	....	....	....	....	....	....	....	....	....	....	....	....	....
	Binghamton	AHL	9	1	0	1	2	....	....	....	....	....	....	....	....	....	....	....	....	....	....	....	....	....	....
2006-07	Mississauga	OHL	23	5	11	16	37	....	....	....	....	....	....	....	....	....	....	....	....	....	....	....	....	....	....
	Saginaw Spirit	OHL	30	5	24	29	49	....	....	....	....	....	....	....	....	....	6	1	2	3	10	....	....	....	....
	Binghamton	AHL	5	0	2	2	9	....	....	....	....	....	....	....	....	....	....	....	....	....	....	....	....	....	....
2007-08	**Ottawa**	**NHL**	**21**	**2**	**2**	**4**	**19**	**0**	**1**	**1**	**12**	**16.7**	**-1**	**73**	**43.8**	**5:19**	**4**	**1**	**0**	**1**	**6**	**0**	**0**	**0**	**8:21**
	Binghamton	AHL	24	3	5	8	44	....	....	....	....	....	....	....	....	....	....	....	....	....	....	....	....	....	....
2008-09	**Ottawa**	**NHL**	**12**	**0**	**0**	**0**	**15**	**0**	**0**	**0**	**5**	**0.0**	**-2**	**50**	**42.0**	**5:41**	....	....	....	....	....	....	....	....	....
	Binghamton	AHL	18	1	1	2	41	....	....	....	....	....	....	....	....	....	....	....	....	....	....	....	....	....	....
2009-10	Binghamton	AHL	57	5	6	11	109	....	....	....	....	....	....	....	....	....	....	....	....	....	....	....	....	....	....
2010-11	**Ottawa**	**NHL**	**1**	**0**	**0**	**0**	**0**	**0**	**0**	**0**	**0**	**0.0**	**0**	**0**	**0.0**	**7:09**	....	....	....	....	....	....	....	....	....
	Binghamton	AHL	58	6	9	15	111	....	....	....	....	....	....	....	....	....	18	2	2	4	24	....	....	....	....
2011-12	**Columbus**	**NHL**	**14**	**0**	**1**	**1**	**32**	**0**	**0**	**0**	**13**	**0.0**	**0**	**8**	**62.5**	**9:05**	....	....	....	....	....	....	....	....	....
	Springfield	AHL	23	5	6	11	43	....	....	....	....	....	....	....	....	....	....	....	....	....	....	....	....	....	....
2012-13	Springfield	AHL	18	2	5	7	54	....	....	....	....	....	....	....	....	....	8	2	2	4	26	....	....	....	....
2013-14	**Columbus**	**NHL**	**1**	**0**	**0**	**0**	**5**	**0**	**0**	**0**	**0**	**0.0**	**0**	**0**	**0.0**	**2:43**	....	....	....	....	....	....	....	....	....
	Springfield	AHL	58	8	10	18	132	....	....	....	....	....	....	....	....	....	4	0	0	0	4	....	....	....	....
2014-15	Rockford IceHogs	AHL	61	6	8	14	165	....	....	....	....	....	....	....	....	....	8	0	1	1	31	....	....	....	....
	NHL Totals		**49**	**2**	**3**	**5**	**71**	**0**	**1**	**1**	**30**	**6.7**		**131**	**44.3**	**6:28**	**4**	**1**	**0**	**1**	**6**	**0**	**0**	**0**	**8:21**

Yanick Dupre Memorial Award (AHL - Outstanding Humanitarian Contribution) (2011)

• Missed remainder of 2008-09 due to shoulder injury at Calgary, December 27, 2008. Signed as a free agent by **Columbus**, July 13, 2011. • Missed majority of 2011-12 due to shoulder injury at Springfield (AHL) practice, December 19, 2011. • Missed majority of 2012-13 due to shoulder injury vs. Portland (AHL), October 28, 2012. Signed as a free agent by **Chicago**, July 1, 2014. Signed as a free agent by **Nashville**, July 4, 2015.

BAUN, Kyle
(BAHN, KIGH-uhl) **CHI**

Right wing. Shoots right. 6'2", 209 lbs. Born, Toronto, ON, May 4, 1992.

Season	Club	League	GP	G	A	Pts	PIM	PP	SH	GW	S	S%	+/-	TF	F%	Min	GP	G	A	Pts	PIM	PP	SH	GW	Min
2008-09	Toronto Titans	GTHL	STATISTICS NOT AVAILABLE																						
	Tor. Canadiens	ON-Jr.A	1	0	1	1	0	....	....	....	....	....	....	....	....	....	....	....	....	....	....	....	....	....	....
2009-10	Tor. Canadiens	ON-Jr.A	45	5	10	15	27	....	....	....	....	....	....	....	....	....	7	0	0	0	6	....	....	....	....
2010-11	Cornwall Colts	ON-Jr.A	56	19	23	42	44	....	....	....	....	....	....	....	....	....	16	7	1	8	26	....	....	....	....
2011-12	Cornwall Colts	ON-Jr.A	42	29	32	61	50	....	....	....	....	....	....	....	....	....	17	8	12	20	16	....	....	....	....
2012-13	Colgate	ECAC	36	14	10	24	30	....	....	....	....	....	....	....	....	....	....	....	....	....	....	....	....	....	....
2013-14	Colgate	ECAC	39	11	15	26	53	....	....	....	....	....	....	....	....	....	....	....	....	....	....	....	....	....	....
2014-15	Colgate	ECAC	38	14	15	29	68	....	....	....	....	....	....	....	....	....	....	....	....	....	....	....	....	....	....
	Chicago	**NHL**	**3**	**0**	**0**	**0**	**0**	**0**	**0**	**0**	**4**	**0.0**	**-1**	**0**	**0.0**	**12:32**	....	....	....	....	....	....	....	....	....
	NHL Totals		**3**	**0**	**0**	**0**	**0**	**0**	**0**	**0**	**4**	**0.0**		**0**	**0.0**	**12:32**	....	....	....	....	....	....	....	....	....

ECAC All-Rookie Team (2013)

Signed as a free agent by **Chicago**, March 26, 2015.

BEAGLE, Jay
(BEE-guhl, JAY) **WSH**

Right wing. Shoots right. 6'3", 215 lbs. Born, Calgary, AB, October 16, 1985.

Season	Club	League	GP	G	A	Pts	PIM	PP	SH	GW	S	S%	+/-	TF	F%	Min	GP	G	A	Pts	PIM	PP	SH	GW	Min
2003-04	Calgary Royals	AJHL	58	10	27	37	100	....	....	....	....	....	....	....	....	....	....	....	....	....	....	....	....	....	....
2004-05	Calgary Royals	AJHL	64	28	42	70	114	....	....	....	....	....	....	....	....	....	....	....	....	....	....	....	....	....	....
2005-06	Alaska Anchorage	WCHA	31	4	6	10	40	....	....	....	....	....	....	....	....	....	....	....	....	....	....	....	....	....	....
2006-07	Alaska Anchorage	WCHA	36	10	10	20	93	....	....	....	....	....	....	....	....	....	....	....	....	....	....	....	....	....	....
	Idaho Steelheads	ECHL	8	2	8	10	4	....	....	....	....	....	....	....	....	....	18	1	2	3	22	....	....	....	....
2007-08	Hershey Bears	AHL	64	19	18	37	41	....	....	....	....	....	....	....	....	....	5	0	1	1	2	....	....	....	....
2008-09	**Washington**	**NHL**	**3**	**0**	**0**	**0**	**2**	**0**	**0**	**0**	**5**	**0.0**	**-3**	**13**	**38.5**	**7:36**	**4**	**0**	**0**	**0**	**0**	**0**	**0**	**0**	**3:33**
	Hershey Bears	AHL	47	4	5	9	37	....	....	....	....	....	....	....	....	....	18	1	3	4	16	....	....	....	....
2009-10	**Washington**	**NHL**	**7**	**1**	**1**	**2**	**2**	**0**	**0**	**0**	**10**	**10.0**	**-1**	**31**	**54.8**	**9:16**	....	....	....	....	....	....	....	....	....
	Hershey Bears	AHL	66	16	19	35	25	....	....	....	....	....	....	....	....	....	21	2	6	8	0	....	....	....	....
2010-11	**Washington**	**NHL**	**31**	**2**	**1**	**3**	**8**	**0**	**0**	**2**	**27**	**7.4**	**-2**	**105**	**55.2**	**10:30**	....	....	....	....	....	....	....	....	....
	Hershey Bears	AHL	34	8	6	14	26	....	....	....	....	....	....	....	....	....	....	....	....	....	....	....	....	....	....
2011-12	**Washington**	**NHL**	**41**	**4**	**1**	**5**	**23**	**0**	**0**	**0**	**49**	**8.2**	**-2**	**215**	**57.7**	**11:51**	**12**	**1**	**1**	**2**	**4**	**0**	**0**	**0**	**18:26**
2012-13	**Washington**	**NHL**	**48**	**2**	**6**	**8**	**14**	**0**	**0**	**1**	**56**	**3.6**	**-1**	**444**	**56.1**	**12:06**	**7**	**1**	**0**	**1**	**4**	**0**	**0**	**0**	**9:39**
2013-14	**Washington**	**NHL**	**62**	**4**	**5**	**9**	**28**	**0**	**0**	**0**	**60**	**6.7**	**-9**	**573**	**51.7**	**11:15**	....	....	....	....	....	....	....	....	....
2014-15	**Washington**	**NHL**	**62**	**10**	**10**	**20**	**20**	**0**	**0**	**2**	**84**	**11.9**	**6**	**384**	**56.5**	**12:49**	**14**	**1**	**4**	**5**	**4**	**0**	**0**	**1**	**15:48**
	NHL Totals		**254**	**23**	**24**	**47**	**97**	**0**	**0**	**5**	**291**	**7.9**		**1765**	**54.7**	**11:42**	**37**	**3**	**5**	**8**	**12**	**0**	**0**	**1**	**14:10**

Signed as a free agent by **Washington**, March 26, 2008.

BEAUCHEMIN, Francois
(boh-sheh-MEH, frahn-SWUH) **COL**

Defense. Shoots left. 6'1", 208 lbs. Born, Sorel, QC, June 4, 1980. Montreal's 3rd choice, 75th overall, in 1998 Entry Draft.

Season	Club	League	GP	G	A	Pts	PIM	PP	SH	GW	S	S%	+/-	TF	F%	Min	GP	G	A	Pts	PIM	PP	SH	GW	Min
1995-96	Richelieu Riverains	QAAA	40	9	23	32	59	....	....	....	....	....	....	....	....	....	4	1	7	8	0	....	....	....	....
1996-97	Laval Titan	QMJHL	66	7	20	27	112	....	....	....	....	....	....	....	....	....	3	0	0	0	2	....	....	....	....
1997-98	Laval Titan	QMJHL	70	12	35	47	132	....	....	....	....	....	....	....	....	....	16	1	3	4	23	....	....	....	....
1998-99	Acadie-Bathurst	QMJHL	31	4	17	21	53	....	....	....	....	....	....	....	....	....	23	2	16	18	55	....	....	....	....
99-2000	Acadie-Bathurst	QMJHL	38	11	36	47	64	....	....	....	....	....	....	....	....	....	....	....	....	....	....	....	....	....	....
	Moncton Wildcats	QMJHL	33	8	31	39	35	....	....	....	....	....	....	....	....	....	16	2	11	13	14	....	....	....	....
2000-01	Quebec Citadelles	AHL	56	3	6	9	44	....	....	....	....	....	....	....	....	....	....	....	....	....	....	....	....	....	....
2001-02	Quebec Citadelles	AHL	56	8	11	19	88	....	....	....	....	....	....	....	....	....	3	0	1	1	0	....	....	....	....
	Mississippi	ECHL	7	1	3	4	2	....	....	....	....	....	....	....	....	....	....	....	....	....	....	....	....	....	....
2002-03	**Montreal**	**NHL**	**1**	**0**	**0**	**0**	**0**	**0**	**0**	**0**	**1**	**0.0**	**-1**	**0**	**0.0**	**17:11**	....	....	....	....	....	....	....	....	....
	Hamilton	AHL	75	7	21	28	92	....	....	....	....	....	....	....	....	....	23	1	9	10	16	....	....	....	....
2003-04	Hamilton	AHL	77	9	27	36	57	....	....	....	....	....	....	....	....	....	10	2	4	6	18	....	....	....	....
2004-05	Syracuse Crunch	AHL	72	3	27	30	55	....	....	....	....	....	....	....	....	....	....	....	....	....	....	....	....	....	....
2005-06	**Columbus**	**NHL**	**11**	**0**	**2**	**2**	**11**	**0**	**0**	**0**	**16**	**0.0**	**-6**	**0**	**0.0**	**17:16**	....	....	....	....	....	....	....	....	....
	Anaheim	**NHL**	**61**	**8**	**26**	**34**	**41**	**4**	**0**	**3**	**121**	**6.6**	**8**	**1**	**0.0**	**24:14**	**16**	**3**	**6**	**9**	**11**	**3**	**0**	**0**	**27:26**
2006-07♦	**Anaheim**	**NHL**	**71**	**7**	**21**	**28**	**49**	**2**	**0**	**0**	**128**	**5.5**	**7**	**1**	**0.0**	**25:28**	**20**	**4**	**4**	**8**	**16**	**4**	**0**	**0**	**30:33**
2007-08	**Anaheim**	**NHL**	**82**	**2**	**19**	**21**	**59**	**0**	**0**	**2**	**144**	**1.4**	**-9**	**1**	**0.0**	**25:32**	**6**	**0**	**0**	**0**	**26**	**0**	**0**	**0**	**21:02**
2008-09	**Anaheim**	**NHL**	**20**	**4**	**1**	**5**	**12**	**0**	**0**	**2**	**45**	**8.9**	**-3**	**0**	**0.0**	**24:54**	**13**	**1**	**0**	**1**	**15**	**0**	**0**	**0**	**21:25**
2009-10	**Toronto**	**NHL**	**82**	**5**	**21**	**26**	**33**	**4**	**0**	**1**	**170**	**2.9**	**-13**	**4**	**75.0**	**25:28**	....	....	....	....	....	....	....	....	....
2010-11	**Toronto**	**NHL**	**54**	**2**	**10**	**12**	**16**	**0**	**0**	**0**	**76**	**2.6**	**-4**	**0**	**0.0**	**23:45**	....	....	....	....	....	....	....	....	....
	Anaheim	**NHL**	**27**	**3**	**2**	**5**	**16**	**1**	**0**	**0**	**30**	**10.0**	**-4**	**1**	**0.0**	**21:42**	**6**	**0**	**2**	**2**	**2**	**0**	**0**	**0**	**23:32**
2011-12	**Anaheim**	**NHL**	**82**	**8**	**14**	**22**	**48**	**3**	**0**	**1**	**139**	**5.8**	**-14**	**2**	**50.0**	**25:33**	....	....	....	....	....	....	....	....	....
2012-13	**Anaheim**	**NHL**	**48**	**6**	**18**	**24**	**22**	**1**	**0**	**0**	**74**	**8.1**	**19**	**0**	**0.0**	**23:27**	**7**	**2**	**4**	**6**	**4**	**1**	**0**	**0**	**25:22**
2013-14	**Anaheim**	**NHL**	**70**	**4**	**13**	**17**	**39**	**1**	**0**	**1**	**100**	**4.0**	**26**	**0**	**0.0**	**23:06**	**13**	**0**	**4**	**4**	**2**	**0**	**0**	**0**	**23:58**
2014-15	**Anaheim**	**NHL**	**64**	**11**	**12**	**23**	**48**	**2**	**0**	**1**	**110**	**10.0**	**17**	**1**	**100.0**	**22:45**	**16**	**0**	**9**	**9**	**2**	**0**	**0**	**0**	**25:25**
	NHL Totals		**673**	**60**	**159**	**219**	**394**	**18**	**0**	**11**	**1154**	**5.2**		**11**	**45.5**	**24:16**	**97**	**10**	**29**	**39**	**78**	**8**	**0**	**0**	**25:41**

QMJHL All-Rookie Team (1997) • QMJHL Second All-Star Team (2000) • NHL Second All-Star Team (2013)

Claimed on waivers by **Columbus** from **Montreal**, September 15, 2004. Traded to **Anaheim** by **Columbus** with Tyler Wright for Sergei Fedorov and Anaheim's 5th round choice (Maxime Frechette) in 2006 Entry Draft, November 15, 2005. • Missed remainder of 2008-09 due to knee injury vs. Nashville, November 14, 2008. Signed as a free agent by **Toronto**, July 6, 2009. Traded to **Anaheim** by **Toronto** for Joffrey Lupul, Jake Gardiner and Anaheim's 4th round choice (later traded to San Jose – San Jose selected Fredrik Bergvik) in 2013 Entry Draft, February 9, 2011. Signed as a free agent by **Colorado**, July 1, 2015.

BEAULIEU, Nathan
(BOI-loh, NAY-thun) **MTL**

Defense. Shoots left. 6'2", 201 lbs. Born, Strathroy, ON, December 5, 1992. Montreal's 1st choice, 17th overall, in 2011 Entry Draft.

			Regular Season															Playoffs								
Season	Club	League	GP	G	A	Pts	PIM	PP	SH	GW	S	S%	+/-	TF	F%	Min	GP	G	A	Pts	PIM	PP	SH	GW	Min
2007-08	Saint John Vito's	NBPEI	33	1	14	15	45	....	....	....	....	....	....	....	....	....	4	1	2	3	6	....	....	....	....
2008-09	Saint John	QMJHL	49	2	8	10	14	....	....	....	....	....	....	....	....	....	4	0	0	0	2	....	....	....	....
2009-10	Saint John	QMJHL	66	12	33	45	40	....	....	....	....	....	....	....	....	....	21	4	12	16	22	....	....	....	....
2010-11	Saint John	QMJHL	65	12	33	45	52	....	....	....	....	....	....	....	....	....	19	4	13	17	26	....	....	....	....
2011-12	Saint John	QMJHL	53	11	41	52	100	....	....	....	....	....	....	....	....	....	17	4	11	15	32	....	....	....	....
2012-13	Hamilton	AHL	67	7	24	31	63	....	....	....	....	....	....	....	....	....	....	....	....	....	....	....	....	....	....
	Montreal	**NHL**	**6**	**0**	**2**	**2**	**0**	**0**	**0**	**0**	**8**	**0.0**	**5**	**0**	**0.0**	**15:22**	....	....	....	....	....	....	....	....	....
2013-14	**Montreal**	**NHL**	**17**	**0**	**2**	**2**	**8**	**0**	**0**	**0**	**15**	**0.0**	**6**	**0**	**0.0**	**13:14**	**7**	**0**	**2**	**2**	**2**	**0**	**0**	**0**	**10:46**
	Hamilton	AHL	57	7	20	27	33	....	....	....	....	....	....	....	....	....	....	....	....	....	....	....	....	....	....
2014-15	**Montreal**	**NHL**	**64**	**1**	**8**	**9**	**45**	**0**	**0**	**0**	**62**	**1.6**	**6**	**0**	**0.0**	**15:42**	**5**	**0**	**1**	**1**	**0**	**0**	**0**	**0**	**12:55**
	Hamilton	AHL	8	2	2	4	9	....	....	....	....	....	....	....	....	....	....	....	....	....	....	....	....	....	....
	NHL Totals		**87**	**1**	**12**	**13**	**53**	**0**	**0**	**0**	**85**	**1.2**		**0**	**0.0**	**15:12**	**12**	**0**	**3**	**3**	**2**	**0**	**0**	**0**	**11:40**

Memorial Cup All-Star Team (2011)

BECK, Taylor
(BEHK, TAY-luhr) **TOR**

Right wing. Shoots right. 6'2", 206 lbs. Born, St. Catharines, ON, May 13, 1991. Nashville's 4th choice, 70th overall, in 2009 Entry Draft.

2006-07	N.F. Thunder	Minor-ON	69	64	75	139	76	....	....	....	....	....	....	....	....	....	....	....	....	....	....	....	....	....	....
2007-08	Guelph Storm	OHL	56	7	14	21	43	....	....	....	....	....	....	....	....	....	7	0	0	0	4	....	....	....	....
2008-09	Guelph Storm	OHL	67	22	36	58	36	....	....	....	....	....	....	....	....	....	4	0	0	0	2	....	....	....	....
2009-10	Guelph Storm	OHL	61	39	54	93	54	....	....	....	....	....	....	....	....	....	5	3	3	6	2	....	....	....	....
2010-11	Guelph Storm	OHL	62	42	53	95	60	....	....	....	....	....	....	....	....	....	6	3	5	8	10	....	....	....	....
	Milwaukee	AHL	4	0	1	1	0	....	....	....	....	....	....	....	....	....	8	2	0	2	2	....	....	....	....
2011-12	Milwaukee	AHL	74	16	24	40	32	....	....	....	....	....	....	....	....	....	3	0	1	1	2	....	....	....	....
2012-13	Milwaukee	AHL	50	11	30	41	28	....	....	....	....	....	....	....	....	....	2	0	1	1	2	....	....	....	....
	Nashville	**NHL**	**16**	**3**	**4**	**7**	**2**	**1**	**0**	**0**	**39**	**7.7**	**0**	**9**	**66.7**	**16:06**	....	....	....	....	....	....	....	....	....
2013-14	**Nashville**	**NHL**	**7**	**0**	**0**	**0**	**6**	**0**	**0**	**0**	**9**	**0.0**	**–2**	**0**	**0.0**	**12:50**	....	....	....	....	....	....	....	....	....
	Milwaukee	AHL	65	17	32	49	38	....	....	....	....	....	....	....	....	....	3	0	0	0	2	....	....	....	....
2014-15	**Nashville**	**NHL**	**62**	**8**	**8**	**16**	**18**	**2**	**0**	**3**	**78**	**10.3**	**–4**	**10**	**50.0**	**11:56**	**5**	**0**	**0**	**0**	**2**	**0**	**0**	**0**	**12:55**
	NHL Totals		**85**	**11**	**12**	**23**	**26**	**3**	**0**	**3**	**126**	**8.7**		**19**	**57.9**	**12:47**	**5**	**0**	**0**	**0**	**2**	**0**	**0**	**0**	**12:55**

OHL Second All-Star Team (2010)

Traded to **Toronto** by **Nashville** for Jamie Devane, July 12, 2015.

BELESKEY, Matt
(beh-LEH-skee, MAT) **BOS**

Left wing. Shoots left. 6', 200 lbs. Born, Windsor, ON, June 7, 1988. Anaheim's 4th choice, 112th overall, in 2006 Entry Draft.

2003-04	Collingwood	ON-Jr.A	46	8	13	21	110	....	....	....	....	....	....	....	....	....	8	1	7	8	18	....	....	....	....
2004-05	Belleville Bulls	OHL	68	10	13	23	118	....	....	....	....	....	....	....	....	....	5	0	0	0	18	....	....	....	....
2005-06	Belleville Bulls	OHL	61	20	20	40	119	....	....	....	....	....	....	....	....	....	6	1	2	3	10	....	....	....	....
2006-07	Belleville Bulls	OHL	66	27	41	68	124	....	....	....	....	....	....	....	....	....	15	4	10	14	18	....	....	....	....
2007-08	Belleville Bulls	OHL	62	41	49	90	106	....	....	....	....	....	....	....	....	....	21	12	21	33	23	....	....	....	....
2008-09	**Anaheim**	**NHL**	**2**	**0**	**0**	**0**	**0**	**0**	**0**	**0**	**0**	**0.0**	**0**	**2**	**0.0**	**11:10**	....	....	....	....	....	....	....	....	....
	Iowa Chops	AHL	58	11	24	35	58	....	....	....	....	....	....	....	....	....	....	....	....	....	....	....	....	....	....
2009-10	**Anaheim**	**NHL**	**60**	**11**	**7**	**18**	**35**	**0**	**0**	**3**	**123**	**8.9**	**–10**	**20**	**40.0**	**13:59**	....	....	....	....	....	....	....	....	....
	San Antonio	AHL	12	1	4	5	19	....	....	....	....	....	....	....	....	....	....	....	....	....	....	....	....	....	....
	Toronto Marlies	AHL	3	1	1	2	2	....	....	....	....	....	....	....	....	....	....	....	....	....	....	....	....	....	....
2010-11	**Anaheim**	**NHL**	**35**	**3**	**7**	**10**	**36**	**0**	**0**	**0**	**58**	**5.2**	**–10**	**8**	**37.5**	**12:59**	**6**	**1**	**0**	**1**	**4**	**0**	**0**	**0**	**11:14**
	Syracuse Crunch	AHL	27	11	13	24	39	....	....	....	....	....	....	....	....	....	....	....	....	....	....	....	....	....	....
2011-12	**Anaheim**	**NHL**	**70**	**4**	**11**	**15**	**72**	**0**	**0**	**0**	**75**	**5.3**	**–2**	**26**	**42.3**	**10:16**	....	....	....	....	....	....	....	....	....
2012-13	Coventry Blaze	Britain	26	12	21	33	39	....	....	....	....	....	....	....	....	....	....	....	....	....	....	....	....	....	....
	Anaheim	**NHL**	**42**	**8**	**5**	**13**	**56**	**2**	**0**	**1**	**61**	**13.1**	**2**	**19**	**31.6**	**12:01**	**7**	**2**	**1**	**3**	**2**	**1**	**0**	**0**	**11:01**
2013-14	**Anaheim**	**NHL**	**55**	**9**	**15**	**24**	**64**	**0**	**0**	**2**	**112**	**8.0**	**8**	**18**	**44.4**	**12:26**	**5**	**2**	**2**	**4**	**8**	**1**	**0**	**1**	**14:34**
	Norfolk Admirals	AHL	3	1	0	1	0	....	....	....	....	....	....	....	....	....	....	....	....	....	....	....	....	....	....
2014-15	**Anaheim**	**NHL**	**65**	**22**	**10**	**32**	**39**	**4**	**0**	**8**	**145**	**15.2**	**13**	**19**	**42.1**	**14:29**	**16**	**8**	**1**	**9**	**2**	**3**	**0**	**3**	**16:00**
	NHL Totals		**329**	**57**	**55**	**112**	**302**	**6**	**0**	**14**	**574**	**9.9**		**112**	**39.3**	**12:39**	**34**	**13**	**4**	**17**	**16**	**5**	**0**	**4**	**13:55**

Signed as a free agent by **Coventry** (Britain), October 9, 2012. Signed as a free agent by **Boston**, July 1, 2015.

BELLEMARE, Pierre-Edouard
(BEHL-mahr, PEE-air-EHD-wawrd) **PHI**

Left wing. Shoots left. 5'11", 198 lbs. Born, Paris, France, March 6, 1985.

2002-03	HC Rouen	France	11	0	1	1	6	....	....	....	....	....	....	....	....	....	....	....	....	....	....	....	....	....	....
2003-04	HC Rouen	France	22	10	10	20	16	....	....	....	....	....	....	....	....	....	4	1	1	2	4	....	....	....	....
2004-05	HC Rouen	France	28	4	15	19	20	....	....	....	....	....	....	....	....	....	12	7	5	12	6	....	....	....	....
2005-06	HC Rouen	France	26	12	17	29	24	....	....	....	....	....	....	....	....	....	9	2	7	9	6	....	....	....	....
2006-07	Leksands IF	Sweden-2	44	8	11	19	24	....	....	....	....	....	....	....	....	....	10	1	0	1	4	....	....	....	....
2007-08	Leksands IF Jr.	Swe-Jr.	2	1	0	1	14	....	....	....	....	....	....	....	....	....	....	....	....	....	....	....	....	....	....
	Leksands IF	Sweden-2	40	14	15	29	12	....	....	....	....	....	....	....	....	....	10	2	3	5	4	....	....	....	....
2008-09	Leksands IF	Sweden-2	41	31	18	49	113	....	....	....	....	....	....	....	....	....	10	5	5	10	6	....	....	....	....
2009-10	Skelleftea AIK	Sweden	49	9	5	14	16	....	....	....	....	....	....	....	....	....	12	2	7	9	8	....	....	....	....
2010-11	Skelleftea AIK	Sweden	53	10	8	18	20	....	....	....	....	....	....	....	....	....	16	1	4	5	0	....	....	....	....
2011-12	Skelleftea AIK	Sweden	55	19	17	36	40	....	....	....	....	....	....	....	....	....	15	4	8	12	12	....	....	....	....
2012-13	Skelleftea AIK	Sweden	29	6	16	22	47	....	....	....	....	....	....	....	....	....	9	0	1	1	2	....	....	....	....
2013-14	Skelleftea AIK	Sweden	52	20	15	35	32	....	....	....	....	....	....	....	....	....	14	9	5	14	6	....	....	....	....
2014-15	**Philadelphia**	**NHL**	**81**	**6**	**6**	**12**	**18**	**0**	**0**	**1**	**113**	**5.3**	**–3**	**761**	**47.3**	**12:50**	....	....	....	....	....	....	....	....	....
	NHL Totals		**81**	**6**	**6**	**12**	**18**	**0**	**0**	**1**	**113**	**5.3**		**761**	**47.3**	**12:50**	....	....	....	....	....	....	....	....	....

Signed as a free agent by **Philadelphia**, June 11, 2014.

BELLEMORE, Brett
(BEHL-mohr, BREHT)

Defense. Shoots right. 6'4", 225 lbs. Born, Windsor, ON, June 25, 1988. Carolina's 5th choice, 162nd overall, in 2007 Entry Draft.

2005-06	Plymouth Whalers	OHL	46	0	0	0	16	....	....	....	....	....	....	....	....	....	10	0	0	0	0	....	....	....	....
2006-07	Plymouth Whalers	OHL	50	0	12	12	50	....	....	....	....	....	....	....	....	....	20	0	5	5	28	....	....	....	....
2007-08	Plymouth Whalers	OHL	56	6	18	24	70	....	....	....	....	....	....	....	....	....	4	0	2	2	8	....	....	....	....
	Albany River Rats	AHL	4	0	0	0	6	....	....	....	....	....	....	....	....	....	5	0	0	0	6	....	....	....	....
2008-09	Plymouth Whalers	OHL	29	2	10	12	39	....	....	....	....	....	....	....	....	....	11	1	2	3	16	....	....	....	....
	Albany River Rats	AHL	6	0	0	0	4	....	....	....	....	....	....	....	....	....	....	....	....	....	....	....	....	....	....
2009-10	Albany River Rats	AHL	75	1	6	7	81	....	....	....	....	....	....	....	....	....	8	0	1	1	2	....	....	....	....
2010-11	Charlotte	AHL	71	2	8	10	74	....	....	....	....	....	....	....	....	....	16	1	1	2	12	....	....	....	....
2011-12	Charlotte	AHL	76	1	9	10	60	....	....	....	....	....	....	....	....	....	....	....	....	....	....	....	....	....	....
2012-13	Charlotte	AHL	68	2	11	13	87	....	....	....	....	....	....	....	....	....	5	0	1	1	6	....	....	....	....
	Carolina	**NHL**	**8**	**0**	**2**	**2**	**7**	**0**	**0**	**0**	**3**	**0.0**	**–2**	**0**	**0.0**	**13:46**	....	....	....	....	....	....	....	....	....
2013-14	**Carolina**	**NHL**	**64**	**2**	**6**	**8**	**45**	**0**	**0**	**0**	**54**	**3.7**	**–1**	**0**	**0.0**	**17:28**	....	....	....	....	....	....	....	....	....
2014-15	**Carolina**	**NHL**	**49**	**2**	**8**	**10**	**27**	**0**	**0**	**1**	**26**	**7.7**	**1**	**0**	**0.0**	**16:23**	....	....	....	....	....	....	....	....	....
	NHL Totals		**121**	**4**	**16**	**20**	**79**	**0**	**0**	**1**	**83**	**4.8**		**0**	**0.0**	**16:47**	....	....	....	....	....	....	....	....	....

BELOV, Anton
(BEE-lawv, AN-tawn)

Defense. Shoots left. 6'4", 218 lbs. Born, Ryazan, USSR, July 29, 1986.

2004-05	CSKA Moscow 2	Russia-3	20	1	7	8	14	....	....	....	....	....	....	....	....	....	....	....	....	....	....	....	....	....	....
	CSKA Moscow	Russia	31	0	0	0	14	....	....	....	....	....	....	....	....	....	....	....	....	....	....	....	....	....	....
2005-06	CSKA Moscow 2	Russia-3	6	1	2	3	2	....	....	....	....	....	....	....	....	....	....	....	....	....	....	....	....	....	....
	CSKA Moscow	Russia	18	0	2	2	35	....	....	....	....	....	....	....	....	....	1	0	0	0	0	....	....	....	....
2006-07	CSKA Moscow	Russia	49	4	4	8	42	....	....	....	....	....	....	....	....	....	12	1	3	4	8	....	....	....	....
2007-08	CSKA Moscow	Russia	54	1	4	5	69	....	....	....	....	....	....	....	....	....	6	1	1	2	16	....	....	....	....
2008-09	Omsk	KHL	38	1	4	5	71	....	....	....	....	....	....	....	....	....	5	1	0	1	4	....	....	....	....

			Regular Season														Playoffs								
Season	Club	League	GP	G	A	Pts	PIM	PP	SH	GW	S	S%	+/-	TF	F%	Min	GP	G	A	Pts	PIM	PP	SH	GW	Min
2009-10	Omsk	KHL	39	1	10	11	48	....	....	....	....	....	....	....	....	....	....	....	....	....	....	....	....	....	....
2010-11	Omsk	KHL	54	4	12	16	26	....	....	....	....	....	....	....	....	....	8	1	2	3	4	....	....	....	....
2011-12	Omsk	KHL	50	0	6	6	30	....	....	....	....	....	....	....	....	....	18	1	2	3	12	....	....	....	....
2012-13	Omsk	KHL	46	9	17	26	30	....	....	....	....	....	....	....	....	....	12	1	3	4	24	....	....	....	....
2013-14	**Edmonton**	**NHL**	**57**	**1**	**6**	**7**	**34**	**0**	**0**	**0**	**54**	**1.9**	**–12**	**0**	**0.0**	**16:41**	....	....	....	....	....	....	....	....	....
	Russia	Olympics	5	1	0	1	0	....	....	....	....	....	....	....	....	....	....	....	....	....	....	....	....	....	....
2014-15	St. Petersburg	KHL	36	3	5	8	12	....	....	....	....	....	....	....	....	....	20	1	6	7	13	....	....	....	....
	NHL Totals		**57**	**1**	**6**	**7**	**34**	**0**	**0**	**0**	**54**	**1.9**		**0**	**0.0**	**16:41**	....	....	....	....	....	....	....	....	....

Signed as a free agent by **Edmonton**, May 30, 2013. Signed as a free agent by **St. Petersburg** (KHL), April 16, 2014.

BENN, Jamie

(BEHN, JAY-mee) **DAL**

Left wing. Shoots left. 6'2", 210 lbs. Born, Victoria, BC, July 18, 1989. Dallas' 5th choice, 129th overall, in 2007 Entry Draft.

2004-05	Peninsula Eagles	Minor-BC	STATISTICS NOT AVAILABLE																						
	Peninsula	VIJHL	4	1	2	3	2	....	....	....	....	....	....	....	....	....	2	0	0	0	0	....	....	....	....
2005-06	Peninsula	VIJHL	38	31	24	55	92	....	....	....	....	....	....	....	....	....	7	5	7	10	20	....	....	....	....
	Victoria Salsa	BCHL	6	0	0	0	0	....	....	....	....	....	....	....	....	....	....	....	....	....	....	....	....	....	....
2006-07	Victoria Grizzlies	BCHL	53	42	23	65	78	....	....	....	....	....	....	....	....	....	11	5	4	9	12	....	....	....	....
2007-08	Victoria Grizzlies	BCHL	2	0	0	0	2	....	....	....	....	....	....	....	....	....	....	....	....	....	....	....	....	....	....
	Kelowna Rockets	WHL	51	33	32	65	68	....	....	....	....	....	....	....	....	....	7	3	8	11	4	....	....	....	....
2008-09	Kelowna Rockets	WHL	56	46	36	82	71	....	....	....	....	....	....	....	....	....	19	*13	*20	*33	18	....	....	....	....
2009-10	**Dallas**	**NHL**	**82**	**22**	**19**	**41**	**45**	**2**	**0**	**3**	**182**	**12.1**	**–1**	**236**	**46.2**	**14:42**	....	....	....	....	....	....	....	....	....
	Texas Stars	AHL	....	....	....	....	....	....	....	....	....	....	....	....	....	....	24	*14	12	26	22	....	....	....	....
2010-11	**Dallas**	**NHL**	**69**	**22**	**34**	**56**	**52**	**6**	**4**	**3**	**177**	**12.4**	**–5**	**195**	**43.1**	**18:01**	....	....	....	....	....	....	....	....	....
2011-12	**Dallas**	**NHL**	**71**	**26**	**37**	**63**	**55**	**2**	**1**	**7**	**203**	**12.8**	**15**	**751**	**46.2**	**18:04**	....	....	....	....	....	....	....	....	....
2012-13	Hamburg Freezers	Germany	19	7	13	20	30	....	....	....	....	....	....	....	....	....	....	....	....	....	....	....	....	....	....
	Dallas	**NHL**	**41**	**12**	**21**	**33**	**40**	**3**	**0**	**3**	**110**	**10.9**	**–12**	**709**	**46.1**	**19:55**	....	....	....	....	....	....	....	....	....
2013-14	**Dallas**	**NHL**	**81**	**34**	**45**	**79**	**64**	**5**	**1**	**3**	**279**	**12.2**	**21**	**778**	**52.8**	**19:09**	**6**	**4**	**1**	**5**	**4**	**1**	**1**	**1**	**21:10**
	Canada	Olympics	6	2	0	2	4	....	....	....	....	....	....	....	....	....	....	....	....	....	....	....	....	....	....
2014-15	**Dallas**	**NHL**	**82**	**35**	**52**	***87**	**64**	**10**	**2**	**6**	**253**	**13.8**	**1**	**576**	**51.7**	**19:57**	....	....	....	....	....	....	....	....	....
	NHL Totals		**426**	**151**	**208**	**359**	**320**	**28**	**8**	**25**	**1204**	**12.5**		**3245**	**48.6**	**18:09**	**6**	**4**	**1**	**5**	**4**	**1**	**1**	**1**	**21:10**

WHL West First All-Star Team (2009) • Ed Chynoweth Trophy (Memorial Cup - Leading Scorer) (2009) • NHL First All-Star Team (2014) • NHL Second All-Star Team (2015) • Art Ross Trophy (2015)
Played in NHL All-Star Game (2012)
Signed as a free agent by **Hamburg** (Germany), October 3, 2012.

BENN, Jordie

(BEHN, JOHR-dee) **DAL**

Defense. Shoots left. 6'2", 200 lbs. Born, Victoria, BC, July 26, 1987.

2004-05	Peninsula	VIJHL	45	5	21	26	35	....	....	....	....	....	....	....	....	....	....	....	....	....	....	....	....	....	....
	Victoria Salsa	BCHL	4	0	1	1	6	....	....	....	....	....	....	....	....	....	1	0	0	0	2	....	....	....	....
2005-06	Victoria Salsa	BCHL	55	5	20	25	61	....	....	....	....	....	....	....	....	....	16	1	5	6	6	....	....	....	....
2006-07	Victoria Grizzlies	BCHL	53	4	37	41	62	....	....	....	....	....	....	....	....	....	11	1	7	8	22	....	....	....	....
2007-08	Victoria Grizzlies	BCHL	60	15	32	47	78	....	....	....	....	....	....	....	....	....	11	2	8	10	8	....	....	....	....
2008-09	Victoria	ECHL	55	1	11	12	26	....	....	....	....	....	....	....	....	....	3	0	0	0	0	....	....	....	....
2009-10	Allen Americans	CHL	45	9	9	18	55	....	....	....	....	....	....	....	....	....	20	2	9	11	12	....	....	....	....
2010-11	Texas Stars	AHL	60	2	10	12	39	....	....	....	....	....	....	....	....	....	1	0	0	0	0	....	....	....	....
2011-12	**Dallas**	**NHL**	**3**	**0**	**2**	**2**	**0**	**0**	**0**	**0**	**1**	**0.0**	**1**	**0**	**0.0**	**13:57**	....	....	....	....	....	....	....	....	....
	Texas Stars	AHL	62	9	23	32	33	....	....	....	....	....	....	....	....	....	....	....	....	....	....	....	....	....	....
2012-13	Texas Stars	AHL	43	7	14	21	33	....	....	....	....	....	....	....	....	....	7	0	2	2	10	....	....	....	....
	Dallas	**NHL**	**26**	**1**	**5**	**6**	**10**	**1**	**0**	**0**	**31**	**3.2**	**–4**	**0**	**0.0**	**17:19**	....	....	....	....	....	....	....	....	....
2013-14	**Dallas**	**NHL**	**78**	**3**	**17**	**20**	**30**	**1**	**0**	**0**	**91**	**3.3**	**16**	**1**	**100.0**	**19:09**	**6**	**0**	**3**	**3**	**2**	**0**	**0**	**0**	**21:57**
2014-15	**Dallas**	**NHL**	**73**	**2**	**14**	**16**	**34**	**0**	**0**	**0**	**70**	**2.9**	**–5**	**1**	**0.0**	**18:04**	....	....	....	....	....	....	....	....	....
	NHL Totals		**180**	**6**	**38**	**44**	**74**	**2**	**0**	**0**	**193**	**3.1**		**2**	**50.0**	**18:22**	**6**	**0**	**3**	**3**	**2**	**0**	**0**	**0**	**21:57**

Signed as a free agent by **Texas** (AHL), October 8, 2010. Signed as a free agent by **Dallas**, July 1, 2011.

BENNETT, Beau

(BEH-neht, BOH) **PIT**

Right wing. Shoots right. 6'2", 195 lbs. Born, Gardena, CA, November 27, 1991. Pittsburgh's 1st choice, 20th overall, in 2010 Entry Draft.

2008-09	L.A. Jr. Kings	T1EHL	46	25	33	58	10	....	....	....	....	....	....	....	....	....	....	....	....	....	....	....	....	....	....
2009-10	Penticton Vees	BCHL	56	41	79	*120	20	....	....	....	....	....	....	....	....	....	15	5	9	14	6	....	....	....	....
2010-11	U. of Denver	WCHA	37	9	16	25	18	....	....	....	....	....	....	....	....	....	....	....	....	....	....	....	....	....	....
2011-12	U. of Denver	WCHA	10	4	9	13	25	....	....	....	....	....	....	....	....	....	....	....	....	....	....	....	....	....	....
2012-13	Wilkes-Barre	AHL	39	7	21	28	18	....	....	....	....	....	....	....	....	....	....	....	....	....	....	....	....	....	....
	Pittsburgh	**NHL**	**26**	**3**	**11**	**14**	**6**	**1**	**0**	**2**	**30**	**10.0**	**7**	**4**	**25.0**	**12:18**	**6**	**1**	**0**	**1**	**0**	**1**	**0**	**1**	**11:05**
2013-14	**Pittsburgh**	**NHL**	**21**	**3**	**4**	**7**	**0**	**0**	**0**	**1**	**27**	**11.1**	**–2**	**2**	**100.0**	**13:51**	**12**	**1**	**4**	**5**	**8**	**1**	**0**	**0**	**12:24**
	Wilkes-Barre	AHL	3	0	1	1	0	....	....	....	....	....	....	....	....	....	....	....	....	....	....	....	....	....	....
2014-15	**Pittsburgh**	**NHL**	**49**	**4**	**8**	**12**	**16**	**0**	**0**	**1**	**81**	**4.9**	**–1**	**2**	**0.0**	**12:29**	**2**	**0**	**0**	**0**	**0**	**0**	**0**	**0**	**8:02**
	Wilkes-Barre	AHL	2	0	5	5	0	....	....	....	....	....	....	....	....	....	....	....	....	....	....	....	....	....	....
	NHL Totals		**96**	**10**	**23**	**33**	**22**	**1**	**0**	**4**	**138**	**7.2**		**8**	**37.5**	**12:44**	**20**	**2**	**4**	**6**	**8**	**2**	**0**	**1**	**11:34**

• Missed majority of 2013-14 due to wrist injury vs. Boston, November 22, 2013.

BENNETT, Sam

(BEH-neht, SAM) **CGY**

Center. Shoots left. 6'1", 185 lbs. Born, Holland Landing, ON, June 20, 1996. Calgary's 1st choice, 4th overall, in 2014 Entry Draft.

2011-12	Tor. Marlboros	GTHL	37	33	36	69	34	....	....	....	....	....	....	....	....	....	....	....	....	....	....	....	....	....	....
2012-13	Kingston	OHL	60	18	22	40	87	....	....	....	....	....	....	....	....	....	4	0	3	3	2	....	....	....	....
2013-14	Kingston	OHL	57	36	55	91	118	....	....	....	....	....	....	....	....	....	7	5	4	9	18	....	....	....	....
2014-15	Kingston	OHL	11	11	13	24	14	....	....	....	....	....	....	....	....	....	4	0	3	3	4	....	....	....	....
	Calgary	**NHL**	**1**	**0**	**1**	**1**	**0**	**0**	**0**	**0**	**1**	**0.0**	**–1**	**6**	**16.7**	**16:00**	**11**	**3**	**1**	**4**	**8**	**0**	**0**	**1**	**14:01**
	NHL Totals		**1**	**0**	**1**	**1**	**0**	**0**	**0**	**0**	**1**	**0.0**		**6**	**16.7**	**16:00**	**11**	**3**	**1**	**4**	**8**	**0**	**0**	**1**	**14:01**

• Missed majority of 2014-15 due to recurring shoulder injury and resulting surgery, October 14, 2014.

BENOIT, Andre

(behn-WAH, AWN-dray)

Defense. Shoots left. 5'11", 191 lbs. Born, St. Albert, ON, January 6, 1984.

2000-01	Kitchener Rangers	OHL	65	16	19	35	37	....	....	....	....	....	....	....	....	....	....	....	....	....	....	....	....	....	....
2001-02	Kitchener Rangers	OHL	62	13	32	45	77	....	....	....	....	....	....	....	....	....	4	1	0	1	8	....	....	....	....
2002-03	Kitchener Rangers	OHL	65	22	45	67	77	....	....	....	....	....	....	....	....	....	21	1	16	17	16	....	....	....	....
2003-04	Kitchener Rangers	OHL	65	24	51	75	67	....	....	....	....	....	....	....	....	....	5	1	1	2	6	....	....	....	....
2004-05	Kitchener Rangers	OHL	67	24	53	77	72	....	....	....	....	....	....	....	....	....	15	5	13	18	6	....	....	....	....
2005-06	Hamilton	AHL	70	7	19	26	60	....	....	....	....	....	....	....	....	....	....	....	....	....	....	....	....	....	....
2006-07	Hamilton	AHL	64	10	21	31	41	....	....	....	....	....	....	....	....	....	22	2	11	13	22	....	....	....	....
2007-08	Tappara Tampere	Finland	54	12	26	38	96	....	....	....	....	....	....	....	....	....	11	2	3	5	10	....	....	....	....
2008-09	Sodertalje SK	Sweden	54	4	16	20	34	....	....	....	....	....	....	....	....	....	....	....	....	....	....	....	....	....	....
	Sodertalje SK	Sweden-Q	10	0	2	2	10	....	....	....	....	....	....	....	....	....	....	....	....	....	....	....	....	....	....
2009-10	Hamilton	AHL	78	6	30	36	63	....	....	....	....	....	....	....	....	....	19	3	11	14	8	....	....	....	....
2010-11	**Ottawa**	**NHL**	**8**	**0**	**1**	**1**	**6**	**0**	**0**	**0**	**17**	**0.0**	**–1**	**0**	**0.0**	**16:50**	....	....	....	....	....	....	....	....	....
	Binghamton	AHL	73	11	44	55	53	....	....	....	....	....	....	....	....	....	23	3	*15	18	14	....	....	....	....
2011-12	Spartak Moscow	KHL	53	5	12	17	34	....	....	....	....	....	....	....	....	....	....	....	....	....	....	....	....	....	....
2012-13	Binghamton	AHL	34	9	16	25	28	....	....	....	....	....	....	....	....	....	....	....	....	....	....	....	....	....	....
	Ottawa	**NHL**	**33**	**3**	**7**	**10**	**8**	**1**	**0**	**2**	**50**	**6.0**	**–3**	**0**	**0.0**	**16:25**	**5**	**0**	**3**	**3**	**0**	**0**	**0**	**0**	**15:28**

			Regular Season														Playoffs								
Season	Club	League	GP	G	A	Pts	PIM	PP	SH	GW	S	S%	+/-	TF	F%	Min	GP	G	A	Pts	PIM	PP	SH	GW	Min
2013-14	**Colorado**	**NHL**	**79**	**7**	**21**	**28**	**26**	**1**	**0**	**2**	**113**	**6.2**	**2**	**0**	**0.0**	**20:13**	**7**	**0**	**1**	**1**	**6**	**0**	**0**	**0**	**21:17**
2014-15	**Buffalo**	**NHL**	**59**	**1**	**8**	**9**	**20**	**0**	**1**	**0**	**45**	**2.2**	**–19**	**0**	**0.0**	**18:09**	....	....	....	....	....	....	....	....	....
	NHL Totals		**179**	**11**	**37**	**48**	**60**	**2**	**1**	**4**	**225**	**4.9**		**0**	**0.0**	**18:41**	**12**	**0**	**4**	**4**	**6**	**0**	**0**	**0**	**18:52**

AHL Second All-Star Team (2011)

Signed as a free agent by **Montreal**, January 9, 2006. Signed as a free agent by **Tappara Tampere** (Finland), June 21, 2007. Signed as a free agent by **Sodertalje** (Sweden), April 7, 2008. Signed as a free agent by **Montreal**, May 13, 2009. Signed as a free agent by **Ottawa**, August 6, 2010. Signed as a free agent by **Spartak Moscow** (KHL), August 11, 2011. Signed as a free agent by **Ottawa**, July 2, 2012. Signed as a free agent by **Colorado**, July 5, 2013. Signed as a free agent by **Buffalo**, July 23, 2014.

BERGENHEIM, Sean

(BUHR-gehn-highm, SHAWN)

Left wing. Shoots left. 5'10", 201 lbs. Born, Helsinki, Finland, February 8, 1984. NY Islanders' 1st choice, 22nd overall, in 2002 Entry Draft.

Season	Club	League	GP	G	A	Pts	PIM	PP	SH	GW	S	S%	+/-	TF	F%	Min	GP	G	A	Pts	PIM	PP	SH	GW	Min
99-2000	Jokerit U18	Fin-U18	30	22	11	33	34	....	....	....	....	....	....	....	....	....	3	1	0	1	0	....	....	....	....
	Jokerit U18	Fin-U18	17	10	8	18	14	....	....	....	....	....	....	....	....	....	3	1	0	1	2	....	....	....	....
2000-01	Jokerit U18	Fin-U18	1	1	0	1	4	....	....	....	....	....	....	....	....	....	6	9	5	14	8	....	....	....	....
	Jokerit Helsinki Jr.	Fin-Jr.	18	6	4	10	26	....	....	....	....	....	....	....	....	....	2	0	0	0	4	....	....	....	....
2001-02	Jokerit U18	Fin-U18	....	....	....	....	....	....	....	....	....	....	....	....	....	....	5	6	2	8	18	....	....	....	....
	Jokerit Helsinki Jr.	Fin-Jr.	23	11	19	30	36	....	....	....	....	....	....	....	....	....	1	0	0	0	2	....	....	....	....
	Kiekko-Vantaa	Finland-2	4	0	0	0	52	....	....	....	....	....	....	....	....	....	....	....	....	....	....	....	....	....	....
	Jokerit Helsinki	Finland	28	2	2	4	4	....	....	....	....	....	....	....	....	....	....	....	....	....	....	....	....	....	....
2002-03	Jokerit Helsinki Jr.	Fin-Jr.	2	3	0	3	2	....	....	....	....	....	....	....	....	....	....	....	....	....	....	....	....	....	....
	Jokerit Helsinki	Finland	38	3	3	6	4	....	....	....	....	....	....	....	....	....	2	0	0	0	0	....	....	....	....
2003-04	**NY Islanders**	**NHL**	**18**	**1**	**1**	**2**	**4**	**0**	**1**	**0**	**12**	**8.3**	**–4**	**2**	**50.0**	**8:55**	....	....	....	....	....	....	....	....	....
	Jokerit Helsinki	Finland	20	2	2	4	18	....	....	....	....	....	....	....	....	....	3	1	1	2	0	....	....	....	....
	Bridgeport	AHL	....	....	....	....	....	....	....	....	....	....	....	....	....	....	7	2	3	5	10	....	....	....	....
2004-05	Bridgeport	AHL	61	15	14	29	69	....	....	....	....	....	....	....	....	....	....	....	....	....	....	....	....	....	....
2005-06	**NY Islanders**	**NHL**	**28**	**4**	**5**	**9**	**20**	**0**	**0**	**1**	**63**	**6.3**	**–11**	**14**	**28.6**	**13:17**	....	....	....	....	....	....	....	....	....
	Bridgeport	AHL	55	25	22	47	112	....	....	....	....	....	....	....	....	....	7	0	2	2	24	....	....	....	....
2006-07	Yaroslavl	Russia	9	1	4	5	26	....	....	....	....	....	....	....	....	....	....	....	....	....	....	....	....	....	....
	Frolunda	Sweden	36	16	17	33	80	....	....	....	....	....	....	....	....	....	....	....	....	....	....	....	....	....	....
2007-08	**NY Islanders**	**NHL**	**78**	**10**	**12**	**22**	**62**	**1**	**0**	**1**	**155**	**6.5**	**–3**	**15**	**60.0**	**11:15**	....	....	....	....	....	....	....	....	....
2008-09	**NY Islanders**	**NHL**	**59**	**15**	**9**	**24**	**64**	**0**	**4**	**5**	**152**	**9.9**	**–2**	**22**	**40.9**	**14:15**	....	....	....	....	....	....	....	....	....
2009-10	**NY Islanders**	**NHL**	**63**	**10**	**13**	**23**	**45**	**0**	**2**	**0**	**133**	**7.5**	**1**	**17**	**29.4**	**14:04**	....	....	....	....	....	....	....	....	....
2010-11	**Tampa Bay**	**NHL**	**80**	**14**	**15**	**29**	**56**	**2**	**0**	**1**	**182**	**7.7**	**0**	**51**	**49.0**	**13:59**	**16**	**9**	**2**	**11**	**8**	**0**	**0**	**1**	**14:09**
2011-12	**Florida**	**NHL**	**62**	**17**	**6**	**23**	**48**	**5**	**1**	**2**	**185**	**9.2**	**–5**	**11**	**27.3**	**16:25**	**7**	**3**	**3**	**6**	**4**	**1**	**0**	**0**	**16:14**
2012-13	HIFK Helsinki	Finland	2	1	0	1	0	....	....	....	....	....	....	....	....	....	....	....	....	....	....	....	....	....	....
2013-14	**Florida**	**NHL**	**62**	**16**	**13**	**29**	**40**	**3**	**0**	**3**	**190**	**8.4**	**–16**	**4**	**50.0**	**16:30**	....	....	....	....	....	....	....	....	....
2014-15	**Florida**	**NHL**	**39**	**8**	**10**	**18**	**34**	**0**	**0**	**2**	**84**	**9.5**	**2**	**5**	**40.0**	**14:09**	....	....	....	....	....	....	....	....	....
	Minnesota	**NHL**	**17**	**1**	**0**	**1**	**6**	**0**	**0**	**0**	**24**	**4.2**	**–4**	**1**	**0.0**	**10:45**	**3**	**0**	**0**	**0**	**0**	**0**	**0**	**0**	**10:09**
	NHL Totals		**506**	**96**	**84**	**180**	**379**	**11**	**8**	**15**	**1180**	**8.1**		**142**	**42.3**	**13:54**	**26**	**12**	**5**	**17**	**12**	**1**	**0**	**1**	**14:15**

Signed as a free agent by **Yaroslavl** (Russia), August 5, 2006. Signed as a free agent by **Frolunda** (Sweden), November 3, 2006. Signed as a free agent by **Tampa Bay**, August 17, 2010. Signed as a free agent by **Florida**, July 1, 2011. Signed as a free agent by **HIFK Helsinki** (Finland), September 25, 2012. • Suspended by **Florida** due to hip injury with **HIFK Helsinki** (Finland) during NHL lockout, January 16, 2013. Traded to **Minnesota** by **Florida** with Florida's 7th round choice in 2016 Entry Draft for Minnesota's 3rd round choice in 2016 Entry Draft, February 24, 2015.

BERGERON, Patrice

(BUHR-zhuhr-uhn, pa-TREES) **BOS**

Center. Shoots right. 6'2", 194 lbs. Born, Ancienne-Lorette, QC, July 24, 1985. Boston's 2nd choice, 45th overall, in 2003 Entry Draft.

Season	Club	League	GP	G	A	Pts	PIM	PP	SH	GW	S	S%	+/-	TF	F%	Min	GP	G	A	Pts	PIM	PP	SH	GW	Min
2000-01	Ste-Foy	QAAA	5	1	2	3	0	....	....	....	....	....	....	....	....	....									
2001-02	St-Francois	QAAA	38	25	37	62	18	....	....	....	....	....	....	....	....	....	8	6	4	10	10	....	....	....	....
	Acadie-Bathurst	QMJHL	4	0	1	1	0	....	....	....	....	....	....	....	....	....	....	....	....	....	....	....	....	....	....
2002-03	Acadie-Bathurst	QMJHL	70	23	50	73	62	....	....	....	....	....	....	....	....	....	11	6	9	15	6	....	....	....	....
2003-04	**Boston**	**NHL**	**71**	**16**	**23**	**39**	**22**	**7**	**0**	**2**	**133**	**12.0**	**5**	**699**	**49.4**	**16:21**	**7**	**1**	**3**	**4**	**0**	**0**	**0**	**1**	**17:13**
2004-05	Providence Bruins	AHL	68	21	40	61	59	....	....	....	....	....	....	....	....	....	16	5	7	12	4	....	....	....	....
2005-06	**Boston**	**NHL**	**81**	**31**	**42**	**73**	**22**	**12**	**1**	**6**	**310**	**10.0**	**3**	**1447**	**54.7**	**20:36**	....	....	....	....	....	....	....	....	....
2006-07	**Boston**	**NHL**	**77**	**22**	**48**	**70**	**26**	**14**	**0**	**6**	**224**	**9.8**	**–28**	**1560**	**51.2**	**20:49**	....	....	....	....	....	....	....	....	....
2007-08	**Boston**	**NHL**	**10**	**3**	**4**	**7**	**2**	**2**	**0**	**0**	**24**	**12.5**	**2**	**175**	**50.3**	**18:10**	....	....	....	....	....	....	....	....	....
2008-09	**Boston**	**NHL**	**64**	**8**	**31**	**39**	**16**	**1**	**1**	**1**	**155**	**5.2**	**2**	**1025**	**54.5**	**17:59**	**11**	**0**	**5**	**5**	**11**	**0**	**0**	**0**	**17:56**
2009-10	**Boston**	**NHL**	**73**	**19**	**33**	**52**	**28**	**0**	**1**	**4**	**184**	**10.3**	**6**	**1342**	**58.0**	**18:54**	**13**	**4**	**7**	**11**	**2**	**0**	**0**	**1**	**20:23**
	Canada	Olympics	7	0	1	1	2	....	....	....	....	....	....	....	....	....	....	....	....	....	....	....	....	....	....
2010-11•	**Boston**	**NHL**	**80**	**22**	**35**	**57**	**26**	**3**	**2**	**4**	**211**	**10.4**	**20**	**1439**	**56.6**	**17:53**	**23**	**6**	**14**	**20**	**28**	**0**	***2**	**1**	**18:42**
2011-12	**Boston**	**NHL**	**81**	**22**	**42**	**64**	**20**	**5**	**2**	**3**	**191**	**11.5**	**36**	**1641**	**59.3**	**18:35**	**7**	**0**	**2**	**2**	**8**	**0**	**0**	**0**	**19:38**
2012-13	HC Lugano	Swiss	21	11	18	29	8	....	....	....	....	....	....	....	....	....	....	....	....	....	....	....	....	....	....
	Boston	**NHL**	**42**	**10**	**22**	**32**	**18**	**2**	**0**	**3**	**125**	**8.0**	**24**	**884**	**62.1**	**19:18**	**22**	**9**	**6**	**15**	**13**	**4**	**0**	**2**	**20:44**
2013-14	**Boston**	**NHL**	**80**	**30**	**32**	**62**	**43**	**7**	**1**	**7**	**243**	**12.3**	**38**	**1732**	**58.6**	**17:59**	**12**	**3**	**6**	**9**	**4**	**0**	**0**	**0**	**19:42**
	Canada	Olympics	6	0	2	2	4	....	....	....	....	....	....	....	....	....	....	....	....	....	....	....	....	....	....
2014-15	**Boston**	**NHL**	**81**	**23**	**32**	**55**	**44**	**4**	**1**	**4**	**234**	**9.8**	**2**	**1951**	**60.2**	**18:08**	....	....	....	....	....	....	....	....	....
	NHL Totals		**740**	**206**	**344**	**550**	**267**	**57**	**9**	**40**	**2034**	**10.1**		**13895**	**56.8**	**18:39**	**95**	**23**	**43**	**66**	**66**	**4**	**2**	**5**	**19:24**

QAAA Second All-Star Team (2002) • Frank J. Selke Trophy (2012, 2014, 2015) • King Clancy Memorial Trophy (2013) • NHL Foundation Player Award (2014)

Played in NHL All-Star Game (2015)

• Missed majority of 2007-08 due to head injury vs. Philadelphia, October 27, 2007. Signed as a free agent by **Lugano** (Swiss), October 2, 2012.

BERGLUND, Patrik

(BUHRG-luhnd, PAT-rihk) **ST.L.**

Center. Shoots left. 6'3", 217 lbs. Born, Vasteras, Sweden, June 2, 1988. St. Louis' 2nd choice, 25th overall, in 2006 Entry Draft.

Season	Club	League	GP	G	A	Pts	PIM	PP	SH	GW	S	S%	+/-	TF	F%	Min	GP	G	A	Pts	PIM	PP	SH	GW	Min
2002-03	Vasteras U18	Swe-U18	1	0	1	1	0	....	....	....	....	....	....	....	....	....	....	....	....	....	....	....	....	....	....
2003-04	Vasteras U18	Swe-U18	10	4	1	5	18	....	....	....	....	....	....	....	....	....	....	....	....	....	....	....	....	....	....
2004-05	Vasteras U18	Swe-U18	5	2	1	3	4	....	....	....	....	....	....	....	....	....	3	0	1	1	6	....	....	....	....
	Vasteras Jr.	Swe-Jr.	25	5	5	10	14	....	....	....	....	....	....	....	....	....	....	....	....	....	....	....	....	....	....
2005-06	Vasteras Jr.	Swe-Jr.	27	17	12	29	38	....	....	....	....	....	....	....	....	....	....	....	....	....	....	....	....	....	....
	VIK Vasteras HK	Sweden-2	21	3	1	4	4	....	....	....	....	....	....	....	....	....	....	....	....	....	....	....	....	....	....
2006-07	VIK Vasteras HK	Sweden-2	35	21	27	48	30	....	....	....	....	....	....	....	....	....	1	0	0	0	2	....	....	....	....
	Vasteras Jr.	Swe-Jr.	....	....	....	....	....	....	....	....	....	....	....	....	....	....	5	4	5	9	6	....	....	....	....
2007-08	VIK Vasteras HK	Sweden-2	46	22	32	54	26	....	....	....	....	....	....	....	....	....	5	1	2	3	6	....	....	....	....
2008-09	**St. Louis**	**NHL**	**76**	**21**	**26**	**47**	**16**	**7**	**0**	**1**	**143**	**14.7**	**19**	**540**	**39.8**	**14:43**	**4**	**0**	**0**	**0**	**2**	**0**	**0**	**0**	**10:11**
2009-10	**St. Louis**	**NHL**	**71**	**13**	**13**	**26**	**16**	**6**	**0**	**4**	**129**	**10.1**	**–5**	**504**	**43.7**	**13:30**	....	....	....	....	....	....	....	....	....
2010-11	**St. Louis**	**NHL**	**81**	**22**	**30**	**52**	**26**	**8**	**0**	**1**	**175**	**12.6**	**–3**	**974**	**46.2**	**17:11**	....	....	....	....	....	....	....	....	....
2011-12	**St. Louis**	**NHL**	**82**	**19**	**19**	**38**	**30**	**0**	**2**	**3**	**188**	**10.1**	**4**	**1168**	**48.5**	**17:58**	**9**	**3**	**4**	**7**	**6**	**2**	**0**	**0**	**20:08**
2012-13	VIK Vasteras HK	Sweden-2	30	20	12	32	20	....	....	....	....	....	....	....	....	....	....	....	....	....	....	....	....	....	....
	St. Louis	**NHL**	**48**	**17**	**8**	**25**	**12**	**5**	**2**	**3**	**74**	**23.0**	**–2**	**603**	**46.3**	**16:50**	**6**	**1**	**1**	**2**	**2**	**0**	**0**	**0**	**17:46**
2013-14	**St. Louis**	**NHL**	**78**	**14**	**18**	**32**	**38**	**2**	**0**	**2**	**144**	**9.7**	**10**	**783**	**47.6**	**16:10**	**4**	**0**	**0**	**0**	**0**	**0**	**0**	**0**	**15:06**
	Slovenia	Olympics	6	2	1	3	4	....	....	....	....	....	....	....	....	....	....	....	....	....	....	....	....	....	....
2014-15	**St. Louis**	**NHL**	**77**	**12**	**15**	**27**	**26**	**0**	**0**	**0**	**145**	**8.3**	**–2**	**329**	**48.6**	**14:35**	**6**	**2**	**2**	**4**	**0**	**0**	**0**	**0**	**13:58**
	NHL Totals		**513**	**118**	**129**	**247**	**164**	**28**	**4**	**14**	**998**	**11.8**		**4901**	**46.2**	**15:51**	**29**	**6**	**7**	**13**	**10**	**2**	**0**	**0**	**16:18**

NHL All-Rookie Team (2009)

Signed as a free agent by **Vasteras** (Sweden-2), September 18, 2012.

BERNIER, Steve

(BUHRN-yay, STEEV)

Right wing. Shoots right. 6'3", 215 lbs. Born, Quebec City, QC, March 31, 1985. San Jose's 2nd choice, 16th overall, in 2003 Entry Draft.

Season	Club	League	GP	G	A	Pts	PIM	PP	SH	GW	S	S%	+/-	TF	F%	Min	GP	G	A	Pts	PIM	PP	SH	GW	Min
1998-99	Quebec AA Aces	QAHA	28	33	23	56	24	....	....	....	....	....	....	....	....	....	....	....	....	....	....	....	....	....	....
99-2000	Quebec AA Aces	QAHA	26	12	23	35	42	....	....	....	....	....	....	....	....	....	....	....	....	....	....	....	....	....	....
2000-01	Ste-Foy	QAAA	39	17	35	52	48	....	....	....	....	....	....	....	....	....	16	9	17	26	8	....	....	....	....
2001-02	Moncton Wildcats	QMJHL	66	31	28	59	51	....	....	....	....	....	....	....	....	....	....	....	....	....	....	....	....	....	....
2002-03	Moncton Wildcats	QMJHL	71	49	52	101	90	....	....	....	....	....	....	....	....	....	2	1	0	1	2	....	....	....	....
2003-04	Moncton Wildcats	QMJHL	66	36	46	82	80	....	....	....	....	....	....	....	....	....	20	7	10	17	17	....	....	....	....
2004-05	Moncton Wildcats	QMJHL	68	35	36	71	114	....	....	....	....	....	....	....	....	....	12	6	13	19	22	....	....	....	....
2005-06	**San Jose**	**NHL**	**39**	**14**	**13**	**27**	**35**	**2**	**1**	**1**	**75**	**18.7**	**4**	**8**	**62.5**	**14:08**	**11**	**1**	**5**	**6**	**8**	**1**	**0**	**1**	**15:17**
	Cleveland Barons	AHL	49	20	23	43	33	....	....	....	....	....	....	....	....	....	....	....	....	....	....	....	....	....	....

			Regular Season														Playoffs								
Season	Club	League	GP	G	A	Pts	PIM	PP	SH	GW	S	S%	+/-	TF	F%	Min	GP	G	A	Pts	PIM	PP	SH	GW	Min
2006-07	**San Jose**	**NHL**	**62**	**15**	**16**	**31**	**29**	**6**	**0**	**4**	**104**	**14.4**	**5**	**18**	**27.8**	**13:35**	**11**	**0**	**1**	**1**	**2**	**0**	**0**	**0**	**10:39**
	Worcester Sharks	AHL	10	3	4	7	2	....	....	....	....	....	....	....	....	....	....	....	....	....	....	....	....	....	....
2007-08	**San Jose**	**NHL**	**59**	**13**	**10**	**23**	**62**	**4**	**0**	**0**	**96**	**13.5**	**–2**	**10**	**50.0**	**13:07**	....	....	....	....	....	....	....	....	....
	Buffalo	**NHL**	**17**	**3**	**6**	**9**	**2**	**0**	**0**	**0**	**35**	**8.6**	**1**	**5**	**20.0**	**14:06**	....	....	....	....	....	....	....	....	....
2008-09	**Vancouver**	**NHL**	**81**	**15**	**17**	**32**	**27**	**2**	**0**	**4**	**137**	**10.9**	**4**	**21**	**23.8**	**13:50**	**10**	**2**	**2**	**4**	**7**	**2**	**0**	**2**	**15:00**
2009-10	**Vancouver**	**NHL**	**59**	**11**	**11**	**22**	**21**	**3**	**0**	**0**	**95**	**11.6**	**0**	**34**	**20.6**	**14:10**	**12**	**4**	**1**	**5**	**0**	**2**	**0**	**0**	**9:59**
2010-11	**Florida**	**NHL**	**68**	**5**	**10**	**15**	**21**	**3**	**0**	**0**	**97**	**5.2**	**–14**	**17**	**23.5**	**13:02**	....	....	....	....	....	....	....	....	....
2011-12	Albany Devils	AHL	17	3	3	6	8	....	....	....	....	....	....	....	....	....	....	....	....	....	....	....	....	....	....
	New Jersey	**NHL**	**32**	**1**	**5**	**6**	**16**	**0**	**0**	**0**	**23**	**4.3**	**6**	**15**	**20.0**	**11:58**	**24**	**2**	**5**	**7**	**27**	**0**	**0**	**0**	**10:21**
2012-13	**New Jersey**	**NHL**	**47**	**8**	**7**	**15**	**17**	**2**	**0**	**1**	**88**	**9.1**	**–7**	**10**	**50.0**	**13:46**	....	....	....	....	....	....	....	....	....
2013-14	**New Jersey**	**NHL**	**78**	**3**	**9**	**12**	**33**	**0**	**0**	**1**	**104**	**2.9**	**–15**	**18**	**33.3**	**12:27**	....	....	....	....	....	....	....	....	....
2014-15	**New Jersey**	**NHL**	**67**	**16**	**16**	**32**	**28**	**4**	**0**	**2**	**107**	**15.0**	**2**	**2**	**50.0**	**12:56**	....	....	....	....	....	....	....	....	....
	Albany Devils	AHL	9	1	4	5	17	....	....	....	....	....	....	....	....	....	....	....	....	....	....	....	....	....	....
	NHL Totals		**609**	**104**	**120**	**224**	**291**	**26**	**1**	**13**	**961**	**10.8**		**158**	**29.7**	**13:20**	**68**	**9**	**14**	**23**	**44**	**5**	**0**	**3**	**11:49**

QMJHL All-Rookie Team (2002) • QMJHL Second All-Star Team (2003, 2004) • Canadian Major Junior Second All-Star Team (2003)

Traded to **Buffalo** by **San Jose** with San Jose's 1st round choice (Tyler Ennis) in 2008 Entry Draft for Brian Campbell and Buffalo's 7th round choice (Drew Daniels) in 2008 Entry Draft, February 26, 2008. Traded to **Vancouver** by **Buffalo** for Los Angeles' 3rd round choice (previously acquired, Buffalo selected Brayden McNabb) in 2009 Entry Draft and Vancouver's 2nd round choice (later traded to Columbus – Columbus selected Petr Straka) in 2010 Entry Draft, July 4, 2008. Traded to **Florida** by **Vancouver** with Michael Grabner and Vancouver's 1st round choice (Quinton Howden) in 2010 Entry Draft for Keith Ballard and Victor Oreskovich, June 25, 2010. Signed as a free agent by **Albany** (AHL), October 26, 2011. Signed as a free agent by **New Jersey**, January 30, 2012.

BICKEL, Stu

(BIH-kuhl, STEW)

Defense. Shoots right. 6'4", 210 lbs. Born, Chanhassen, MN, October 2, 1986.

2004-05	Green Bay	USHL	13	0	0	0	20	....	....	....	....	....	....	....	....	....	....	....	....	....	....	....	....	....	....
2005-06	Green Bay	USHL	14	0	0	0	25	....	....	....	....	....	....	....	....	....	....	....	....	....	....	....	....	....	....
2006-07	Sioux Falls	USHL	57	2	11	13	*215	....	....	....	....	....	....	....	....	....	8	0	3	3	29	....	....	....	....
2007-08	U. of Minnesota	WCHA	45	1	6	7	*92	....	....	....	....	....	....	....	....	....	....	....	....	....	....	....	....	....	....
2008-09	Iowa Chops	AHL	21	0	1	1	51	....	....	....	....	....	....	....	....	....	....	....	....	....	....	....	....	....	....
2009-10	San Antonio	AHL	36	2	2	4	38	....	....	....	....	....	....	....	....	....	....	....	....	....	....	....	....	....	....
	Bakersfield	ECHL	24	1	12	13	50	....	....	....	....	....	....	....	....	....	9	0	2	2	14	....	....	....	....
2010-11	Syracuse Crunch	AHL	6	0	3	3	14	....	....	....	....	....	....	....	....	....	....	....	....	....	....	....	....	....	....
	Elmira Jackals	ECHL	1	0	0	0	0	....	....	....	....	....	....	....	....	....	....	....	....	....	....	....	....	....	....
	Connecticut	AHL	54	2	7	9	135	....	....	....	....	....	....	....	....	....	6	0	1	1	6	....	....	....	....
2011-12	**NY Rangers**	**NHL**	**51**	**0**	**9**	**9**	**108**	**0**	**0**	**0**	**22**	**0.0**	**2**	**1**	**100.0**	**10:26**	**18**	**0**	**0**	**0**	**16**	**0**	**0**	**0**	**5:10**
	Connecticut	AHL	27	1	3	4	80	....	....	....	....	....	....	....	....	....	....	....	....	....	....	....	....	....	....
2012-13	Connecticut	AHL	10	0	1	1	18	....	....	....	....	....	....	....	....	....	....	....	....	....	....	....	....	....	....
	NY Rangers	**NHL**	**16**	**0**	**0**	**0**	**49**	**0**	**0**	**0**	**2**	**0.0**	**–2**	**0**	**0.0**	**5:31**	....	....	....	....	....	....	....	....	....
2013-14	Hartford	AHL	24	1	7	8	85	....	....	....	....	....	....	....	....	....	....	....	....	....	....	....	....	....	....
2014-15	**Minnesota**	**NHL**	**9**	**0**	**1**	**1**	**46**	**0**	**0**	**0**	**3**	**0.0**	**1**	**0**	**0.0**	**5:26**	....	....	....	....	....	....	....	....	....
	Iowa Wild	AHL	43	3	8	11	93	....	....	....	....	....	....	....	....	....	....	....	....	....	....	....	....	....	....
	NHL Totals		**76**	**0**	**10**	**10**	**203**	**0**	**0**	**0**	**27**	**0.0**		**1**	**100.0**	**8:49**	**18**	**0**	**0**	**0**	**16**	**0**	**0**	**0**	**5:10**

Signed as a free agent by **Anaheim**, July 2, 2008. Traded to **NY Rangers** by **Anaheim** for Nigel Williams, November 23, 2010. • Missed majority of 2012-13 and 2013-14 as a healthy reserve. Signed as a free agent by **Minnesota**, July 1, 2014.

BICKELL, Bryan

(BIH-kuhl, BRIGH-uhn) **CHI**

Left wing. Shoots left. 6'4", 223 lbs. Born, Bowmanville, ON, March 9, 1986. Chicago's 3rd choice, 41st overall, in 2004 Entry Draft.

2000-01	Tor. Red Wings	GTHL	68	24	26	50	20	....	....	....	....	....	....	....	....	....	5	3	1	4	4	....	....	....	....
2001-02	Tor. Red Wings	GTHL	65	31	41	72	76	....	....	....	....	....	....	....	....	....	2	2	2	4	0	....	....	....	....
2002-03	Ottawa 67's	OHL	50	7	10	17	4	....	....	....	....	....	....	....	....	....	20	5	3	8	12	....	....	....	....
2003-04	Ottawa 67's	OHL	59	20	16	36	76	....	....	....	....	....	....	....	....	....	7	3	0	3	11	....	....	....	....
2004-05	Ottawa 67's	OHL	66	22	32	54	95	....	....	....	....	....	....	....	....	....	21	5	12	17	32	....	....	....	....
2005-06	Ottawa 67's	OHL	41	28	22	50	41	....	....	....	....	....	....	....	....	....	....	....	....	....	....	....	....	....	....
	Windsor Spitfires	OHL	26	17	16	33	19	....	....	....	....	....	....	....	....	....	7	5	5	10	10	....	....	....	....
2006-07	**Chicago**	**NHL**	**3**	**2**	**0**	**2**	**0**	**0**	**0**	**0**	**10**	**20.0**	**1**	**0**	**0.0**	**11:49**	....	....	....	....	....	....	....	....	....
	Norfolk Admirals	AHL	48	10	15	25	66	....	....	....	....	....	....	....	....	....	2	0	0	0	0	....	....	....	....
2007-08	**Chicago**	**NHL**	**4**	**0**	**0**	**0**	**2**	**0**	**0**	**0**	**3**	**0.0**	**–1**	**0**	**0.0**	**9:08**	....	....	....	....	....	....	....	....	....
	Rockford IceHogs	AHL	73	19	20	39	52	....	....	....	....	....	....	....	....	....	12	2	3	5	11	....	....	....	....
2008-09	Rockford IceHogs	AHL	42	6	8	14	60	....	....	....	....	....	....	....	....	....	4	0	2	2	4	....	....	....	....
2009-10	**Chicago**	**NHL**	**16**	**3**	**1**	**4**	**5**	**0**	**0**	**1**	**20**	**15.0**	**4**	**2**	**0.0**	**9:36**	**4**	**0**	**1**	**1**	**2**	**0**	**0**	**0**	**13:14**
	Rockford IceHogs	AHL	65	16	15	31	58	....	....	....	....	....	....	....	....	....	....	....	....	....	....	....	....	....	....
2010-11	**Chicago**	**NHL**	**78**	**17**	**20**	**37**	**40**	**2**	**0**	**2**	**130**	**13.1**	**6**	**12**	**25.0**	**13:50**	**5**	**2**	**2**	**4**	**0**	**0**	**0**	**0**	**13:05**
2011-12	**Chicago**	**NHL**	**71**	**9**	**15**	**24**	**48**	**0**	**0**	**0**	**84**	**10.7**	**–3**	**1**	**0.0**	**12:08**	**6**	**2**	**0**	**2**	**4**	**1**	**0**	**1**	**16:46**
2012-13	Orli Znojmo	Austria	28	9	18	27	14	....	....	....	....	....	....	....	....	....	....	....	....	....	....	....	....	....	....
	♦ Chicago	**NHL**	**48**	**9**	**14**	**23**	**25**	**0**	**0**	**2**	**82**	**11.0**	**12**	**6**	**33.3**	**12:48**	**23**	**9**	**8**	**17**	**14**	**1**	**0**	**2**	**15:22**
2013-14	**Chicago**	**NHL**	**59**	**11**	**4**	**15**	**28**	**0**	**0**	**2**	**93**	**11.8**	**–6**	**2**	**50.0**	**11:21**	**19**	**7**	**3**	**10**	**8**	**2**	**0**	**0**	**16:17**
2014-15	**♦ Chicago**	**NHL**	**80**	**14**	**14**	**28**	**38**	**1**	**0**	**3**	**113**	**12.4**	**5**	**2**	**0.0**	**12:05**	**18**	**0**	**5**	**5**	**14**	**0**	**0**	**0**	**14:33**
	NHL Totals		**359**	**65**	**68**	**133**	**186**	**3**	**0**	**10**	**535**	**12.1**		**25**	**24.0**	**12:18**	**75**	**20**	**19**	**39**	**42**	**4**	**0**	**3**	**15:15**

Signed as a free agent by **Znojmo** (Austria), October 3, 2012.

BIEGA, Alex

(bee-AY-guh, AL-ehx) **VAN**

Defense. Shoots right. 5'10", 187 lbs. Born, Montreal, QC, April 4, 1988. Buffalo's 5th choice, 147th overall, in 2006 Entry Draft.

2003-04	West Island Lions	QAAA	36	7	16	23	56	....	....	....	....	....	....	....	....	....	9	0	9	9	15	....	....	....	....
2004-05	Salisbury School	High-CT	27	9	22	31	45	....	....	....	....	....	....	....	....	....	....	....	....	....	....	....	....	....	....
2005-06	Salisbury School	High-CT	28	10	17	27	51	....	....	....	....	....	....	....	....	....	....	....	....	....	....	....	....	....	....
2006-07	Harvard Crimson	ECAC	33	6	12	18	36	....	....	....	....	....	....	....	....	....	....	....	....	....	....	....	....	....	....
2007-08	Harvard Crimson	ECAC	34	3	19	22	28	....	....	....	....	....	....	....	....	....	....	....	....	....	....	....	....	....	....
2008-09	Harvard Crimson	ECAC	31	4	16	20	46	....	....	....	....	....	....	....	....	....	....	....	....	....	....	....	....	....	....
2009-10	Harvard Crimson	ECAC	33	2	8	10	30	....	....	....	....	....	....	....	....	....	....	....	....	....	....	....	....	....	....
2010-11	Portland Pirates	AHL	61	3	15	18	52	....	....	....	....	....	....	....	....	....	12	1	1	2	6	....	....	....	....
2011-12	Rochester	AHL	65	5	18	23	47	....	....	....	....	....	....	....	....	....	2	0	2	2	6	....	....	....	....
2012-13	Rochester	AHL	72	5	20	25	59	....	....	....	....	....	....	....	....	....	3	0	2	2	2	....	....	....	....
2013-14	Utica Comets	AHL	73	3	19	22	53	....	....	....	....	....	....	....	....	....	....	....	....	....	....	....	....	....	....
2014-15	**Vancouver**	**NHL**	**7**	**1**	**0**	**1**	**0**	**0**	**0**	**1**	**7**	**14.3**	**–2**	**0**	**0.0**	**15:48**	....	....	....	....	....	....	....	....	....
	Utica Comets	AHL	62	3	16	19	24	....	....	....	....	....	....	....	....	....	23	0	4	4	16	....	....	....	....
	NHL Totals		**7**	**1**	**0**	**1**	**0**	**0**	**0**	**1**	**7**	**14.3**		**0**	**0.0**	**15:48**	....	....	....	....	....	....	....	....	....

ECAC All-Rookie Team (2007)

Signed as a free agent by **Vancouver**, July 6, 2013.

BIEGA, Danny

(bee-AY-guh, DAN-ee) **CAR**

Defense. Shoots right. 6', 205 lbs. Born, Montreal, QC, September 29, 1991. Carolina's 4th choice, 67th overall, in 2010 Entry Draft.

2006-07	Lac St-Louis Lions	QAAA	39	8	18	26	76	....	....	....	....	....	....	....	....	....	16	1	5	6	52	....	....	....	....
2007-08	Salisbury School	High-CT	26	4	13	17	....	....	....	....	....	....	....	....	....	....	....	....	....	....	....	....	....	....	....
2008-09	Salisbury School	High-CT	29	8	14	22	....	....	....	....	....	....	....	....	....	....	....	....	....	....	....	....	....	....	....
2009-10	Harvard Crimson	ECAC	32	5	4	9	47	....	....	....	....	....	....	....	....	....	....	....	....	....	....	....	....	....	....
2010-11	Harvard Crimson	ECAC	34	11	19	30	34	....	....	....	....	....	....	....	....	....	....	....	....	....	....	....	....	....	....
2011-12	Harvard Crimson	ECAC	34	10	25	35	41	....	....	....	....	....	....	....	....	....	....	....	....	....	....	....	....	....	....
2012-13	Harvard Crimson	ECAC	32	2	9	11	43	....	....	....	....	....	....	....	....	....	....	....	....	....	....	....	....	....	....
	Charlotte	AHL	1	0	0	0	0	....	....	....	....	....	....	....	....	....	3	0	2	2	8	....	....	....	....
2013-14	Charlotte	AHL	65	3	15	18	22	....	....	....	....	....	....	....	....	....	....	....	....	....	....	....	....	....	....
2014-15	**Carolina**	**NHL**	**10**	**0**	**2**	**2**	**0**	**0**	**0**	**0**	**7**	**0.0**	**–5**	**0**	**0.0**	**16:09**	....	....	....	....	....	....	....	....	....
	Charlotte	AHL	69	2	12	14	89	....	....	....	....	....	....	....	....	....	....	....	....	....	....	....	....	....	....
	NHL Totals		**10**	**0**	**2**	**2**	**0**	**0**	**0**	**0**	**7**	**0.0**		**0**	**0.0**	**16:08**	....	....	....	....	....	....	....	....	....

ECAC Second All-Star Team (2011) • ECAC First All-Star Team (2012) • NCAA East First All-American Team (2012)

BIEKSA, Kevin
(BEE-ehks-ah, KEH-vihn) **ANA**

Defense. Shoots right. 6'1", 198 lbs. Born, Grimsby, ON, June 16, 1981. Vancouver's 4th choice, 151st overall, in 2001 Entry Draft.

			Regular Season														Playoffs								
Season	Club	League	GP	G	A	Pts	PIM	PP	SH	GW	S	S%	+/-	TF	F%	Min	GP	G	A	Pts	PIM	PP	SH	GW	Min
1997-98	Stoney Creek	ON-Jr.B	STATISTICS NOT AVAILABLE																						
	Burlington	ON-Jr.A	27	0	3	3	10	....	....	....	....	....	....	....	....	....	....	....	....	....	....	....	....	....	....
1998-99	Burlington	ON-Jr.A	49	8	29	37	83	....	....	....	....	....	....	....	....	....	....	....	....	....	....	....	....	....	....
99-2000	Burlington	ON-Jr.A	49	6	27	33	139	....	....	....	....	....	....	....	....	....	....	....	....	....	....	....	....	....	....
2000-01	Bowling Green	CCHA	35	4	9	13	90	....	....	....	....	....	....	....	....	....	....	....	....	....	....	....	....	....	....
2001-02	Bowling Green	CCHA	40	5	10	15	68	....	....	....	....	....	....	....	....	....	....	....	....	....	....	....	....	....	....
2002-03	Bowling Green	CCHA	34	8	17	25	92	....	....	....	....	....	....	....	....	....	....	....	....	....	....	....	....	....	....
2003-04	Bowling Green	CCHA	38	7	15	22	66	....	....	....	....	....	....	....	....	....	....	....	....	....	....	....	....	....	....
	Manitoba Moose	AHL	4	0	2	2	2	....	....	....	....	....	....	....	....	....	....	....	....	....	....	....	....	....	....
2004-05	Manitoba Moose	AHL	80	12	27	39	192	....	....	....	....	....	....	....	....	....	14	1	1	2	52	....	....	....	....
2005-06	**Vancouver**	**NHL**	**39**	**0**	**6**	**6**	**77**	**0**	**0**	**0**	**38**	**0.0**	**–1**	**0**	**0.0**	**16:06**	....	....	....	....	....	....	....	....	....
	Manitoba Moose	AHL	23	3	17	20	71	....	....	....	....	....	....	....	....	....	13	0	10	10	38	....	....	....	....
2006-07	**Vancouver**	**NHL**	**81**	**12**	**30**	**42**	**134**	**6**	**0**	**2**	**203**	**5.9**	**1**	**0**	**0.0**	**24:16**	**9**	**0**	**0**	**0**	**20**	**0**	**0**	**0**	**28:01**
2007-08	**Vancouver**	**NHL**	**34**	**2**	**10**	**12**	**90**	**1**	**0**	**1**	**64**	**3.1**	**–11**	**0**	**0.0**	**23:24**	....	....	....	....	....	....	....	....	....
	Manitoba Moose	AHL	1	0	1	1	2	....	....	....	....	....	....	....	....	....	....	....	....	....	....	....	....	....	....
2008-09	**Vancouver**	**NHL**	**72**	**11**	**32**	**43**	**97**	**5**	**0**	**2**	**153**	**7.2**	**–4**	**0**	**0.0**	**23:29**	**10**	**0**	**5**	**5**	**14**	**0**	**0**	**0**	**24:08**
2009-10	**Vancouver**	**NHL**	**55**	**3**	**19**	**22**	**85**	**1**	**0**	**0**	**95**	**3.2**	**–5**	**0**	**0.0**	**21:49**	**12**	**3**	**5**	**8**	**14**	**1**	**0**	**1**	**22:37**
2010-11	**Vancouver**	**NHL**	**66**	**6**	**16**	**22**	**73**	**1**	**0**	**2**	**105**	**5.7**	**32**	**0**	**0.0**	**22:28**	**25**	**5**	**5**	**10**	**51**	**1**	**0**	**1**	**25:40**
2011-12	**Vancouver**	**NHL**	**78**	**8**	**36**	**44**	**94**	**2**	**0**	**2**	**166**	**4.8**	**12**	**1**	**0.0**	**23:38**	**5**	**1**	**0**	**1**	**6**	**0**	**0**	**1**	**24:46**
2012-13	**Vancouver**	**NHL**	**36**	**6**	**6**	**12**	**48**	**2**	**0**	**1**	**77**	**7.8**	**6**	**0**	**0.0**	**21:56**	**4**	**1**	**0**	**1**	**8**	**0**	**0**	**0**	**25:51**
2013-14	**Vancouver**	**NHL**	**76**	**4**	**20**	**24**	**104**	**1**	**0**	**1**	**167**	**2.4**	**–8**	**1**	**100.0**	**22:46**	....	....	....	....	....	....	....	....	....
2014-15	**Vancouver**	**NHL**	**60**	**4**	**10**	**14**	**77**	**0**	**0**	**1**	**99**	**4.0**	**0**	**0**	**0.0**	**20:50**	**6**	**0**	**0**	**0**	**9**	**0**	**0**	**0**	**18:19**
	NHL Totals		**597**	**56**	**185**	**241**	**879**	**19**	**0**	**12**	**1167**	**4.8**		**2**	**50.0**	**22:25**	**71**	**10**	**15**	**25**	**122**	**2**	**0**	**3**	**24:34**

AHL All-Rookie Team (2005)

Traded to **Anaheim** by **Vancouver** for Anaheim's 2nd round choice in 2016 Entry Draft, June 30, 2015.

BILLINS, Chad
(BIHL-uhns, CHAD) **CGY**

Defense. Shoots left. 5'10", 175 lbs. Born, Marysville, MI, May 26, 1989.

Season	Club	League	GP	G	A	Pts	PIM	PP	SH	GW	S	S%	+/-	TF	F%	Min	GP	G	A	Pts	PIM	PP	SH	GW	Min
2005-06	Det. Caesers	MWEHL	22	1	4	5	18	....	....	....	....	....	....	....	....	....	3	0	1	1	6	....	....	....	....
	Alpena IceDiggers	NAHL	1	0	0	0	0	....	....	....	....	....	....	....	....	....	....	....	....	....	....	....	....	....	....
2006-07	Alpena IceDiggers	NAHL	61	7	18	25	98	....	....	....	....	....	....	....	....	....	3	0	0	0	0	....	....	....	....
2007-08	Waterloo	USHL	60	10	26	36	81	....	....	....	....	....	....	....	....	....	11	5	4	9	0	....	....	....	....
2008-09	Ferris State	CCHA	27	2	9	11	38	....	....	....	....	....	....	....	....	....	....	....	....	....	....	....	....	....	....
2009-10	Ferris State	CCHA	40	3	8	11	26	....	....	....	....	....	....	....	....	....	....	....	....	....	....	....	....	....	....
2010-11	Ferris State	CCHA	39	5	11	16	20	....	....	....	....	....	....	....	....	....	....	....	....	....	....	....	....	....	....
2011-12	Ferris State	CCHA	43	7	22	29	24	....	....	....	....	....	....	....	....	....	....	....	....	....	....	....	....	....	....
2012-13	Grand Rapids	AHL	76	10	27	37	40	....	....	....	....	....	....	....	....	....	24	2	12	14	12	....	....	....	....
2013-14	**Calgary**	**NHL**	**10**	**0**	**3**	**3**	**0**	**0**	**0**	**0**	**3**	**0.0**	**–3**	**0**	**0.0**	**12:13**	....	....	....	....	....	....	....	....	....
	Abbotsford Heat	AHL	65	10	31	41	40	....	....	....	....	....	....	....	....	....	4	0	2	2	2	....	....	....	....
2014-15	CSKA Moscow	KHL	21	2	4	6	8	....	....	....	....	....	....	....	....	....	....	....	....	....	....	....	....	....	....
	Lulea HF	Sweden	23	1	5	6	4	....	....	....	....	....	....	....	....	....	9	1	1	2	2	....	....	....	....
	NHL Totals		**10**	**0**	**3**	**3**	**0**	**0**	**0**	**0**	**3**	**0.0**		**0**	**0.0**	**12:13**	....	....	....	....	....	....	....	....	....

NCAA West Second All-American Team (2012)

Signed as a free agent by **Calgary**, July 5, 2013. Signed as a free agent by **CSKA Moscow** (KHL), June 30, 2014. Signed as a free agent by **Lulea** (Sweden), December 20, 2014.

BISSONNETTE, Paul
(bih-sawn-EHT, PAWL)

Left wing. Shoots left. 6'3", 220 lbs. Born, Welland, ON, March 11, 1985. Pittsburgh's 5th choice, 121st overall, in 2003 Entry Draft.

Season	Club	League	GP	G	A	Pts	PIM	PP	SH	GW	S	S%	+/-	TF	F%	Min	GP	G	A	Pts	PIM	PP	SH	GW	Min
2001-02	North Bay	OHL	57	3	3	6	21	....	....	....	....	....	....	....	....	....	5	0	0	0	2	....	....	....	....
2002-03	Saginaw Spirit	OHL	67	7	16	23	57	....	....	....	....	....	....	....	....	....	....	....	....	....	....	....	....	....	....
2003-04	Saginaw Spirit	OHL	67	5	14	19	96	....	....	....	....	....	....	....	....	....	....	....	....	....	....	....	....	....	....
2004-05	Saginaw Spirit	OHL	28	1	6	7	46	....	....	....	....	....	....	....	....	....	....	....	....	....	....	....	....	....	....
	Owen Sound	OHL	35	2	11	13	46	....	....	....	....	....	....	....	....	....	8	1	3	4	2	....	....	....	....
2005-06	Wilkes-Barre	AHL	55	1	5	6	60	....	....	....	....	....	....	....	....	....	11	0	1	1	4	....	....	....	....
	Wheeling Nailers	ECHL	14	3	7	10	4	....	....	....	....	....	....	....	....	....	....	....	....	....	....	....	....	....	....
2006-07	Wilkes-Barre	AHL	3	0	0	0	6	....	....	....	....	....	....	....	....	....	....	....	....	....	....	....	....	....	....
	Wheeling Nailers	ECHL	65	10	32	42	115	....	....	....	....	....	....	....	....	....	....	....	....	....	....	....	....	....	....
2007-08	Wilkes-Barre	AHL	46	3	5	8	145	....	....	....	....	....	....	....	....	....	7	0	0	0	11	....	....	....	....
	Wheeling Nailers	ECHL	22	3	14	17	43	....	....	....	....	....	....	....	....	....	....	....	....	....	....	....	....	....	....
2008-09	**Pittsburgh**	**NHL**	**15**	**0**	**1**	**1**	**22**	**0**	**0**	**0**	**4**	**0.0**	**–1**	**0**	**0.0**	**3:31**	....	....	....	....	....	....	....	....	....
	Wilkes-Barre	AHL	57	9	7	16	176	....	....	....	....	....	....	....	....	....	8	0	2	2	9	....	....	....	....
2009-10	**Phoenix**	**NHL**	**41**	**3**	**2**	**5**	**117**	**0**	**0**	**1**	**25**	**12.0**	**–2**	**0**	**0.0**	**5:52**	....	....	....	....	....	....	....	....	....
2010-11	**Phoenix**	**NHL**	**48**	**1**	**0**	**1**	**71**	**0**	**0**	**0**	**18**	**5.6**	**6**	**3**	**66.7**	**5:15**	**1**	**0**	**0**	**0**	**0**	**0**	**0**	**0**	**4:05**
2011-12	**Phoenix**	**NHL**	**31**	**1**	**0**	**1**	**41**	**0**	**0**	**1**	**15**	**6.7**	**–4**	**1**	**0.0**	**6:04**	**3**	**0**	**0**	**0**	**15**	**0**	**0**	**0**	**2:41**
2012-13	Cardiff Devils	Britain	11	6	15	21	8	....	....	....	....	....	....	....	....	....	....	....	....	....	....	....	....	....	....
	Phoenix	**NHL**	**28**	**0**	**6**	**6**	**36**	**0**	**0**	**0**	**13**	**0.0**	**2**	**0**	**0.0**	**5:25**	....	....	....	....	....	....	....	....	....
2013-14	**Phoenix**	**NHL**	**39**	**2**	**6**	**8**	**53**	**0**	**0**	**0**	**25**	**8.0**	**6**	**3**	**33.3**	**4:45**	....	....	....	....	....	....	....	....	....
2014-15	Portland Pirates	AHL	8	0	0	0	0	....	....	....	....	....	....	....	....	....	....	....	....	....	....	....	....	....	....
	Manchester	AHL	48	1	6	7	167	....	....	....	....	....	....	....	....	....	11	0	0	0	5	....	....	....	....
	NHL Totals		**202**	**7**	**15**	**22**	**340**	**0**	**0**	**2**	**100**	**7.0**		**7**	**42.9**	**5:18**	**4**	**0**	**0**	**0**	**15**	**0**	**0**	**0**	**3:02**

Claimed on waivers by **Phoenix** from **Pittsburgh**, September 30, 2009. • Missed majority of 2011-12 as a healthy reserve. Signed as a free agent by **Cardiff** (Britain), November 1, 2012. Signed to a PTO (professional tryout) contract by **Portland** (AHL), October 28, 2014. Signed to a PTO (professional tryout) contract by **Manchester** (AHL), December 9, 2014. Signed as a free agent by **Ontario** (AHL), July 8, 2015.

BITETTO, Anthony
(bih-TEH-toh, AN-thuh-nee) **NSH**

Defense. Shoots left. 6'1", 210 lbs. Born, Island Park, NY, July 15, 1990. Nashville's 4th choice, 168th overall, in 2010 Entry Draft.

Season	Club	League	GP	G	A	Pts	PIM	PP	SH	GW	S	S%	+/-	TF	F%	Min	GP	G	A	Pts	PIM	PP	SH	GW	Min
2007-08	NY Apple Core	EmJHL	12	4	10	14	32	....	....	....	....	....	....	....	....	....	....	....	....	....	....	....	....	....	....
	NY Apple Core	EJHL	17	2	6	8	28	....	....	....	....	....	....	....	....	....	....	....	....	....	....	....	....	....	....
2008-09	NY Apple Core	EJHL	30	2	9	11	50	....	....	....	....	....	....	....	....	....	....	....	....	....	....	....	....	....	....
	Indiana Ice	USHL	24	1	3	4	29	....	....	....	....	....	....	....	....	....	13	0	3	3	6	....	....	....	....
2009-10	Indiana Ice	USHL	58	11	29	40	99	....	....	....	....	....	....	....	....	....	9	2	2	4	19	....	....	....	....
2010-11	Northeastern	H-East	38	3	17	20	66	....	....	....	....	....	....	....	....	....	....	....	....	....	....	....	....	....	....
2011-12	Northeastern	H-East	34	4	11	15	34	....	....	....	....	....	....	....	....	....	....	....	....	....	....	....	....	....	....
	Milwaukee	AHL	....	....	....	....	....	....	....	....	....	....	....	....	....	....	1	0	0	0	0	....	....	....	....
2012-13	Cincinnati	ECHL	23	1	2	3	16	....	....	....	....	....	....	....	....	....	....	....	....	....	....	....	....	....	....
	Milwaukee	AHL	34	1	5	6	35	....	....	....	....	....	....	....	....	....	....	....	....	....	....	....	....	....	....
2013-14	Milwaukee	AHL	73	11	25	36	85	....	....	....	....	....	....	....	....	....	3	0	0	0	8	....	....	....	....
2014-15	**Nashville**	**NHL**	**7**	**0**	**0**	**0**	**7**	**0**	**0**	**0**	**2**	**0.0**	**–1**	**1**	**100.0**	**11:47**	....	....	....	....	....	....	....	....	....
	Milwaukee	AHL	70	4	26	30	96	....	....	....	....	....	....	....	....	....	....	....	....	....	....	....	....	....	....
	NHL Totals		**7**	**0**	**0**	**0**	**7**	**0**	**0**	**0**	**2**	**0.0**		**1**	**100.0**	**11:47**	....	....	....	....	....	....	....	....	....

USHL Second All-Star Team (2010) • Hockey East All-Rookie Team (2011)

BJUGSTAD, Nick
(BYOOG-stad, NIHK) **FLA**

Center. Shoots right. 6'6", 218 lbs. Born, Minneapolis, MN, July 17, 1992. Florida's 2nd choice, 19th overall, in 2010 Entry Draft.

Season	Club	League	GP	G	A	Pts	PIM	PP	SH	GW	S	S%	+/-	TF	F%	Min	GP	G	A	Pts	PIM	PP	SH	GW	Min
2007-08	Blaine Bengals	High-MN	24	6	14	20	10	....	....	....	....	....	....	....	....	....	....	....	....	....	....	....	....	....	....
2008-09	Blaine Bengals	High-MN	25	26	25	51	20	....	....	....	....	....	....	....	....	....	....	....	....	....	....	....	....	....	....
2009-10	Team Northwest	UMHSEL	23	13	8	21	18	....	....	....	....	....	....	....	....	....	....	....	....	....	....	....	....	....	....
	Blaine Bengals	High-MN	25	29	31	60	24	....	....	....	....	....	....	....	....	....	5	6	3	9	2	....	....	....	....
	USNTDP	U-18	4	0	0	0	0	....	....	....	....	....	....	....	....	....	....	....	....	....	....	....	....	....	....
2010-11	U. of Minnesota	WCHA	29	8	12	20	51	....	....	....	....	....	....	....	....	....	....	....	....	....	....	....	....	....	....
2011-12	U. of Minnesota	WCHA	40	25	17	42	28	....	....	....	....	....	....	....	....	....	....	....	....	....	....	....	....	....	....
2012-13	U. of Minnesota	WCHA	40	21	15	36	28	....	....	....	....	....	....	....	....	....	....	....	....	....	....	....	....	....	....
	Florida	**NHL**	**11**	**1**	**0**	**1**	**2**	**0**	**0**	**0**	**17**	**5.9**	**–8**	**132**	**40.2**	**15:13**	....	....	....	....	....	....	....	....	....

			Regular Season														Playoffs								
Season	Club	League	GP	G	A	Pts	PIM	PP	SH	GW	S	S%	+/-	TF	F%	Min	GP	G	A	Pts	PIM	PP	SH	GW	Min
2013-14	**Florida**	**NHL**	**76**	**16**	**22**	**38**	**16**	**0**	**1**	**4**	**185**	**8.6**	**–14**	**1123**	**48.9**	**16:13**	....	....	....	....	....	....	....	....	....
2014-15	**Florida**	**NHL**	**72**	**24**	**19**	**43**	**38**	**7**	**0**	**3**	**207**	**11.6**	**–7**	**994**	**48.9**	**16:35**	....	....	....	....	....	....	....	....	....
	NHL Totals		**159**	**41**	**41**	**82**	**56**	**7**	**1**	**7**	**409**	**10.0**		**2249**	**48.4**	**16:19**	....	....	....	....	....	....	....	....	....

WCHA First All-Star Team (2012) • NCAA West Second All-American Team (2012)

BLACKER, Jesse

(BLA-kuhr, JEH-see)

Defense. Shoots right. 6'2", 190 lbs. Born, Toronto, ON, April 19, 1991. Toronto's 3rd choice, 58th overall, in 2009 Entry Draft.

2006-07	Tor. Red Wings	GTHL	43	9	25	34	86	....	....	....	....	....	....	....	....	....	....	....	....	....	....	....	....	....	....
2007-08	Chatham	ON-Jr.B	8	1	2	3	25	....	....	....	....	....	....	....	....	....	....	....	....	....	....	....	....	....	....
	Windsor Spitfires	OHL	17	0	4	4	6	....	....	....	....	....	....	....	....	....	5	0	1	1	2	....	....	....	....
2008-09	Windsor Spitfires	OHL	67	4	17	21	54	....	....	....	....	....	....	....	....	....	20	0	4	4	18	....	....	....	....
2009-10	Windsor Spitfires	OHL	9	0	3	3	12	....	....	....	....	....	....	....	....	....	....	....	....	....	....	....	....	....	....
	Owen Sound	OHL	48	6	24	30	62	....	....	....	....	....	....	....	....	....	....	....	....	....	....	....	....	....	....
	Toronto Marlies	AHL	6	0	1	1	0	....	....	....	....	....	....	....	....	....	....	....	....	....	....	....	....	....	....
2010-11	Owen Sound	OHL	62	10	44	54	83	....	....	....	....	....	....	....	....	....	22	5	11	16	14	....	....	....	....
2011-12	Toronto Marlies	AHL	58	1	15	16	73	....	....	....	....	....	....	....	....	....	6	0	1	1	4	....	....	....	....
2012-13	Toronto Marlies	AHL	61	4	7	11	33	....	....	....	....	....	....	....	....	....	4	0	1	1	0	....	....	....	....
2013-14	Toronto Marlies	AHL	5	1	0	1	4	....	....	....	....	....	....	....	....	....	....	....	....	....	....	....	....	....	....
	Norfolk Admirals	AHL	50	5	19	24	19	....	....	....	....	....	....	....	....	....	10	1	0	1	10	....	....	....	....
2014-15	**Anaheim**	**NHL**	**1**	**0**	**0**	**0**	**0**	**0**	**0**	**0**	**0**	**0.0**	**–2**	**0**	**0.0**	**6:03**	....	....	....	....	....	....	....	....	....
	Norfolk Admirals	AHL	15	0	5	5	9	....	....	....	....	....	....	....	....	....	....	....	....	....	....	....	....	....	....
	San Antonio	AHL	40	6	12	18	24	....	....	....	....	....	....	....	....	....	2	0	1	1	2	....	....	....	....
	NHL Totals		**1**	**0**	**0**	**0**	**0**	**0**	**0**	**0**	**0**	**0.0**		**0**	**0.0**	**6:03**	....	....	....	....	....	....	....	....	....

Traded to **Anaheim** by **Toronto** with Toronto's 2nd round choice (Marcus Pettersson) in 2014 Entry Draft and Anaheim's 7th round choice (previously acquired, Anaheim selected Ondrej Kase) in 2014 Entry Draft for Peter Holland and Brad Staubitz, November 16, 2013. Traded to **Florida** by **Anaheim** with future considerations for Colby Robak, December 4, 2014. Signed as a free agent by **Texas** (AHL), July 7, 2015.

BLANCHARD, Nicolas

(BLAN-shard, NIHK-oh-las)

Left wing. Shoots left. 6'3", 205 lbs. Born, Granby, QC, May 31, 1987. Carolina's 8th choice, 192nd overall, in 2005 Entry Draft.

2003-04	Antoine-Girouard	QAAA	42	24	28	52	28	....	....	....	....	....	....	....	....	....	13	9	6	15	4	....	....	....	....
2004-05	Chicoutimi	QMJHL	69	13	26	39	31	....	....	....	....	....	....	....	....	....	17	2	2	4	10	....	....	....	....
2005-06	Chicoutimi	QMJHL	60	15	29	44	51	....	....	....	....	....	....	....	....	....	9	1	2	3	4	....	....	....	....
2006-07	Chicoutimi	QMJHL	62	22	35	57	41	....	....	....	....	....	....	....	....	....	4	0	2	2	8	....	....	....	....
	Albany River Rats	AHL	7	1	2	3	2	....	....	....	....	....	....	....	....	....	5	0	0	0	2	....	....	....	....
2007-08	Albany River Rats	AHL	64	11	12	23	70	....	....	....	....	....	....	....	....	....	7	0	2	2	2	....	....	....	....
2008-09	Albany River Rats	AHL	55	7	12	19	132	....	....	....	....	....	....	....	....	....	....	....	....	....	....	....	....	....	....
2009-10	Albany River Rats	AHL	76	14	8	22	171	....	....	....	....	....	....	....	....	....	8	0	0	0	13	....	....	....	....
2010-11	Charlotte	AHL	72	8	10	18	101	....	....	....	....	....	....	....	....	....	16	2	3	5	16	....	....	....	....
2011-12	Charlotte	AHL	68	9	12	21	103	....	....	....	....	....	....	....	....	....	....	....	....	....	....	....	....	....	....
2012-13	Charlotte	AHL	61	4	5	9	124	....	....	....	....	....	....	....	....	....	3	0	1	1	7	....	....	....	....
	Carolina	**NHL**	**9**	**0**	**0**	**0**	**20**	**0**	**0**	**0**	**6**	**0.0**	**–2**	**1**	**100.0**	**8:41**	....	....	....	....	....	....	....	....	....
2013-14	Charlotte	AHL	65	7	8	15	111	....	....	....	....	....	....	....	....	....	....	....	....	....	....	....	....	....	....
2014-15	St. John's IceCaps	AHL	63	3	11	14	81	....	....	....	....	....	....	....	....	....	....	....	....	....	....	....	....	....	....
	NHL Totals		**9**	**0**	**0**	**0**	**20**	**0**	**0**	**0**	**6**	**0.0**		**1**	**100.0**	**8:41**	....	....	....	....	....	....	....	....	....

BLUM, Jonathon

(BLUHM, JAWN-ah-thuhn) **MIN**

Defense. Shoots right. 6'1", 188 lbs. Born, Long Beach, CA, January 30, 1989. Nashville's 1st choice, 23rd overall, in 2007 Entry Draft.

2004-05	California Wave	Minor-CA	55	15	50	65	65	....	....	....	....	....	....	....	....	....	....	....	....	....	....	....	....	....	....
2005-06	Vancouver Giants	WHL	61	7	17	24	25	....	....	....	....	....	....	....	....	....	18	1	7	8	16	....	....	....	....
2006-07	Vancouver Giants	WHL	72	8	43	51	48	....	....	....	....	....	....	....	....	....	22	3	6	9	8	....	....	....	....
2007-08	Vancouver Giants	WHL	64	18	45	63	44	....	....	....	....	....	....	....	....	....	10	3	4	7	10	....	....	....	....
2008-09	Vancouver Giants	WHL	51	16	50	66	30	....	....	....	....	....	....	....	....	....	17	7	11	18	6	....	....	....	....
	Milwaukee	AHL	....	....	....	....	....	....	....	....	....	....	....	....	....	....	5	0	0	0	0	....	....	....	....
2009-10	Milwaukee	AHL	80	11	30	41	32	....	....	....	....	....	....	....	....	....	7	1	7	8	0	....	....	....	....
2010-11	**Nashville**	**NHL**	**23**	**3**	**5**	**8**	**8**	**1**	**0**	**1**	**18**	**16.7**	**8**	**0**	**0.0**	**17:45**	**12**	**0**	**2**	**2**	**0**	**0**	**0**	**0**	**18:51**
	Milwaukee	AHL	54	7	27	34	20	....	....	....	....	....	....	....	....	....	1	0	0	0	0	....	....	....	....
2011-12	**Nashville**	**NHL**	**33**	**3**	**4**	**7**	**6**	**0**	**0**	**1**	**25**	**12.0**	**–14**	**0**	**0.0**	**17:56**	....	....	....	....	....	....	....	....	....
	Milwaukee	AHL	48	4	22	26	36	....	....	....	....	....	....	....	....	....	3	0	1	1	4	....	....	....	....
2012-13	Milwaukee	AHL	34	1	11	12	16	....	....	....	....	....	....	....	....	....	....	....	....	....	....	....	....	....	....
	Nashville	**NHL**	**35**	**1**	**6**	**7**	**6**	**0**	**0**	**0**	**26**	**3.8**	**–1**	**0**	**0.0**	**14:18**	....	....	....	....	....	....	....	....	....
2013-14	**Minnesota**	**NHL**	**15**	**0**	**1**	**1**	**0**	**0**	**0**	**0**	**11**	**0.0**	**–1**	**0**	**0.0**	**11:40**	....	....	....	....	....	....	....	....	....
	Iowa Wild	AHL	54	7	22	29	23	....	....	....	....	....	....	....	....	....	....	....	....	....	....	....	....	....	....
2014-15	**Minnesota**	**NHL**	**4**	**0**	**1**	**1**	**2**	**0**	**0**	**0**	**3**	**0.0**	**–3**	**0**	**0.0**	**9:52**	....	....	....	....	....	....	....	....	....
	Iowa Wild	AHL	66	12	25	37	18	....	....	....	....	....	....	....	....	....	....	....	....	....	....	....	....	....	....
	NHL Totals		**110**	**7**	**17**	**24**	**22**	**1**	**0**	**2**	**83**	**8.4**		**0**	**0.0**	**15:36**	**12**	**0**	**2**	**2**	**0**	**0**	**0**	**0**	**18:51**

WHL West Second All-Star Team (2008) • WHL West First All-Star Team (2009) • WHL Defenseman of the Year (2009) • Canadian Major Junior First All-Star Team (2009) • Canadian Major Junior Defenseman of the Year (2009)

Signed as a free agent by **Minnesota**, July 12, 2013. Signed as a free agent by **Vladivostok** (KHL), August 9, 2015.

BLUNDEN, Mike

(BLUHN-dehn, MIGHK) **T.B.**

Right wing. Shoots right. 6'4", 211 lbs. Born, Toronto, ON, December 15, 1986. Chicago's 2nd choice, 43rd overall, in 2005 Entry Draft.

2001-02	Gloucester	Minor-ON	32	23	12	35	52	....	....	....	....	....	....	....	....	....	....	....	....	....	....	....	....	....	....
	Gloucester	ON-Jr.A	2	0	0	0	2	....	....	....	....	....	....	....	....	....	....	....	....	....	....	....	....	....	....
2002-03	Erie Otters	OHL	63	10	7	17	55	....	....	....	....	....	....	....	....	....	....	....	....	....	....	....	....	....	....
2003-04	Erie Otters	OHL	52	22	17	39	53	....	....	....	....	....	....	....	....	....	3	0	0	0	0	....	....	....	....
2004-05	Erie Otters	OHL	61	22	19	41	75	....	....	....	....	....	....	....	....	....	2	0	0	0	2	....	....	....	....
2005-06	Erie Otters	OHL	60	46	38	84	63	....	....	....	....	....	....	....	....	....	....	....	....	....	....	....	....	....	....
	Norfolk Admirals	AHL	11	1	5	6	2	....	....	....	....	....	....	....	....	....	1	0	0	0	0	....	....	....	....
2006-07	**Chicago**	**NHL**	**9**	**0**	**0**	**0**	**10**	**0**	**0**	**0**	**10**	**0.0**	**–5**	**1**	**0.0**	**11:23**	....	....	....	....	....	....	....	....	....
	Norfolk Admirals	AHL	17	4	5	9	15	....	....	....	....	....	....	....	....	....	....	....	....	....	....	....	....	....	....
2007-08	**Chicago**	**NHL**	**1**	**0**	**0**	**0**	**0**	**0**	**0**	**0**	**1**	**0.0**	**–1**	**0**	**0.0**	**7:51**	....	....	....	....	....	....	....	....	....
	Rockford IceHogs	AHL	74	16	21	37	83	....	....	....	....	....	....	....	....	....	12	1	3	4	35	....	....	....	....
2008-09	Rockford IceHogs	AHL	37	3	7	10	42	....	....	....	....	....	....	....	....	....	....	....	....	....	....	....	....	....	....
	Syracuse Crunch	AHL	39	9	12	21	68	....	....	....	....	....	....	....	....	....	....	....	....	....	....	....	....	....	....
2009-10	**Columbus**	**NHL**	**40**	**2**	**2**	**4**	**59**	**0**	**0**	**0**	**40**	**5.0**	**3**	**90**	**32.2**	**8:07**	....	....	....	....	....	....	....	....	....
	Syracuse Crunch	AHL	25	7	9	16	43	....	....	....	....	....	....	....	....	....	....	....	....	....	....	....	....	....	....
2010-11	**Columbus**	**NHL**	**1**	**0**	**0**	**0**	**0**	**0**	**0**	**0**	**2**	**0.0**	**–1**	**10**	**50.0**	**10:31**	....	....	....	....	....	....	....	....	....
	Springfield	AHL	37	12	9	21	41	....	....	....	....	....	....	....	....	....	....	....	....	....	....	....	....	....	....
2011-12	**Montreal**	**NHL**	**39**	**2**	**2**	**4**	**27**	**0**	**0**	**0**	**34**	**5.9**	**–1**	**5**	**40.0**	**9:22**	....	....	....	....	....	....	....	....	....
	Hamilton	AHL	17	3	5	8	12	....	....	....	....	....	....	....	....	....	....	....	....	....	....	....	....	....	....
2012-13	Hamilton	AHL	54	10	12	22	76	....	....	....	....	....	....	....	....	....	....	....	....	....	....	....	....	....	....
	Montreal	**NHL**	**5**	**0**	**0**	**0**	**4**	**0**	**0**	**0**	**5**	**0.0**	**–1**	**0**	**0.0**	**8:21**	**1**	**0**	**0**	**0**	**10**	**0**	**0**	**0**	**8:12**
2013-14	**Montreal**	**NHL**	**7**	**0**	**0**	**0**	**5**	**0**	**0**	**0**	**2**	**0.0**	**–2**	**0**	**0.0**	**6:08**	....	....	....	....	....	....	....	....	....
	Hamilton	AHL	68	18	19	37	79	....	....	....	....	....	....	....	....	....	....	....	....	....	....	....	....	....	....
2014-15	**Tampa Bay**	**NHL**	**2**	**0**	**0**	**0**	**2**	**0**	**0**	**0**	**0**	**0.0**	**–1**	**0**	**0.0**	**9:47**	....	....	....	....	....	....	....	....	....
	Syracuse Crunch	AHL	33	13	9	22	28	....	....	....	....	....	....	....	....	....	....	....	....	....	....	....	....	....	....
	NHL Totals		**104**	**4**	**4**	**8**	**107**	**0**	**0**	**0**	**94**	**4.3**		**106**	**34.0**	**8:48**	**1**	**0**	**0**	**0**	**10**	**0**	**0**	**0**	**8:12**

• Missed majority of 2006-07 due to shoulder injury vs. Hershey (AHL), December 10, 2006. Traded to **Columbus** by **Chicago** for Adam Pineault, January 10, 2008. • Missed remainder of 2010-11 due to shoulder injury vs. Worcester (AHL), January 14, 2011. Traded to **Montreal** by **Columbus** for Ryan Russell, July 7, 2011. Signed as a free agent by **Tampa Bay**, July 1, 2014. • Missed majority of 2014-15 due to knee injury vs. Rochester (AHL), January 30, 2015.

BODIE, Troy

(BOH-dee, TROI)

Right wing. Shoots right. 6'5", 226 lbs. Born, Portage La Prairie, MB, January 25, 1985. Edmonton's 12th choice, 278th overall, in 2003 Entry Draft.

			Regular Season														Playoffs								
Season	Club	League	GP	G	A	Pts	PIM	PP	SH	GW	S	S%	+/-	TF	F%	Min	GP	G	A	Pts	PIM	PP	SH	GW	Min
2001-02	Central Plains	MMMHL	40	22	21	43	10	....	....	....	....	....	....	....	....	....	....	....	....	....	....	....	....	....	....
2002-03	Kelowna Rockets	WHL	35	4	4	8	36	....	....	....	....	....	....	....	....	....	11	1	1	2	2	....	....	....	....
2003-04	Kelowna Rockets	WHL	71	8	12	20	112	....	....	....	....	....	....	....	....	....	17	7	3	10	6	....	....	....	....
2004-05	Kelowna Rockets	WHL	72	24	24	48	96	....	....	....	....	....	....	....	....	....	24	4	13	17	26	....	....	....	....
2005-06	Kelowna Rockets	WHL	72	28	25	53	117	....	....	....	....	....	....	....	....	....	12	5	4	9	8	....	....	....	....
2006-07	Hamilton	AHL	20	0	1	1	29	....	....	....	....	....	....	....	....	....	....	....	....	....	....	....	....	....	....
	Stockton Thunder	ECHL	46	21	17	38	80	....	....	....	....	....	....	....	....	....	6	0	2	2	6	....	....	....	....
2007-08	Springfield	AHL	62	9	6	15	108	....	....	....	....	....	....	....	....	....	....	....	....	....	....	....	....	....	....
2008-09	**Anaheim**	**NHL**	**4**	**0**	**0**	**0**	**0**	**0**	**0**	**0**	**5**	**0.0**	**0**	**2**	**50.0**	**8:09**	....	....	....	....	....	....	....	....	....
	Iowa Chops	AHL	71	15	12	27	105	....	....	....	....	....	....	....	....	....	....	....	....	....	....	....	....	....	....
2009-10	**Anaheim**	**NHL**	**44**	**5**	**2**	**7**	**80**	**0**	**1**	**1**	**58**	**8.6**	**–8**	**1**	**0.0**	**11:15**	....	....	....	....	....	....	....	....	....
	San Antonio	AHL	16	2	1	3	43	....	....	....	....	....	....	....	....	....	....	....	....	....	....	....	....	....	....
	Toronto Marlies	AHL	16	6	4	10	13	....	....	....	....	....	....	....	....	....	....	....	....	....	....	....	....	....	....
2010-11	**Anaheim**	**NHL**	**9**	**0**	**1**	**1**	**7**	**0**	**0**	**0**	**5**	**0.0**	**–3**	**0**	**0.0**	**9:43**	....	....	....	....	....	....	....	....	....
	Carolina	**NHL**	**50**	**1**	**2**	**3**	**54**	**0**	**0**	**0**	**39**	**2.6**	**–4**	**1**	**0.0**	**6:19**	....	....	....	....	....	....	....	....	....
2011-12	Syracuse Crunch	AHL	69	5	10	15	119	....	....	....	....	....	....	....	....	....	4	0	0	0	0	....	....	....	....
2012-13	Norfolk Admirals	AHL	47	4	8	12	111	....	....	....	....	....	....	....	....	....	....	....	....	....	....	....	....	....	....
	Portland Pirates	AHL	5	3	1	4	7	....	....	....	....	....	....	....	....	....	2	0	0	0	2	....	....	....	....
2013-14	**Toronto**	**NHL**	**47**	**3**	**7**	**10**	**26**	**0**	**0**	**0**	**50**	**6.0**	**6**	**7**	**28.6**	**8:38**	....	....	....	....	....	....	....	....	....
	Toronto Marlies	AHL	17	4	4	8	9	....	....	....	....	....	....	....	....	....	....	....	....	....	....	....	....	....	....
2014-15	**Toronto**	**NHL**	**5**	**0**	**0**	**0**	**5**	**0**	**0**	**0**	**1**	**0.0**	**0**	**0**	**0.0**	**4:37**	....	....	....	....	....	....	....	....	....
	Toronto Marlies	AHL	58	8	7	15	77	....	....	....	....	....	....	....	....	....	3	1	0	1	2	....	....	....	....
	NHL Totals		**159**	**9**	**12**	**21**	**172**	**0**	**1**	**1**	**158**	**5.7**		**11**	**27.3**	**8:33**	....	....	....	....	....	....	....	....	....

Signed as a free agent by **Anaheim**, July 22, 2008. Claimed on waivers by **Carolina** from **Anaheim**, November 16, 2010. Signed as a free agent by **Anaheim**, October 12, 2011. Signed as a free agent by **Norfolk** (AHL), September 21, 2012. • Loaned to **Portland** (AHL) by **Norfolk** (AHL), April 10, 2013. Signed as a free agent by **Toronto**, July 10, 2013.

BODNARCHUK, Andrew

(BAWD-nahr-chuhk, AN-droo) **CBJ**

Defense. Shoots left. 5'10", 189 lbs. Born, Drumheller, AB, July 11, 1988. Boston's 5th choice, 128th overall, in 2006 Entry Draft.

Season	Club	League	GP	G	A	Pts	PIM	PP	SH	GW	S	S%	+/-	TF	F%	Min	GP	G	A	Pts	PIM	PP	SH	GW	Min
2003-04	Dartmouth	NSMHL	58	16	23	39	81	....	....	....	....	....	....	....	....	....	....	....	....	....	....	....	....	....	....
2004-05	St. Paul's School	High-NH	36	3	15	18	....	....	....	....	....	....	....	....	....	....	....	....	....	....	....	....	....	....	....
2005-06	Halifax	QMJHL	68	6	17	23	136	....	....	....	....	....	....	....	....	....	11	0	2	2	22	....	....	....	....
2006-07	Halifax	QMJHL	63	16	41	57	96	....	....	....	....	....	....	....	....	....	12	1	10	11	25	....	....	....	....
	Providence Bruins	AHL	....	....	....	....	....	....	....	....	....	....	....	....	....	....	1	0	0	0	0	....	....	....	....
2007-08	Halifax	QMJHL	65	10	33	43	89	....	....	....	....	....	....	....	....	....	14	0	9	9	16	....	....	....	....
2008-09	Providence Bruins	AHL	62	1	8	9	33	....	....	....	....	....	....	....	....	....	15	0	2	2	22	....	....	....	....
2009-10	**Boston**	**NHL**	**5**	**0**	**0**	**0**	**2**	**0**	**0**	**0**	**0**	**0.0**	**–2**	**0**	**0.0**	**7:19**	....	....	....	....	....	....	....	....	....
	Providence Bruins	AHL	70	5	10	15	51	....	....	....	....	....	....	....	....	....	....	....	....	....	....	....	....	....	....
2010-11	Providence Bruins	AHL	75	1	15	16	91	....	....	....	....	....	....	....	....	....	....	....	....	....	....	....	....	....	....
2011-12	Providence Bruins	AHL	63	5	12	17	44	....	....	....	....	....	....	....	....	....	....	....	....	....	....	....	....	....	....
2012-13	Manchester	AHL	69	5	15	20	77	....	....	....	....	....	....	....	....	....	4	0	0	0	0	....	....	....	....
2013-14	Manchester	AHL	73	8	24	32	89	....	....	....	....	....	....	....	....	....	4	0	0	0	0	....	....	....	....
2014-15	Manchester	AHL	61	5	20	25	84	....	....	....	....	....	....	....	....	....	19	0	6	6	14	....	....	....	....
	NHL Totals		**5**	**0**	**0**	**0**	**2**	**0**	**0**	**0**	**0**	**0.0**		**0**	**0.0**	**7:19**	....	....	....	....	....	....	....	....	....

QMJHL All-Rookie Team (2006)

Signed as a free agent by **Los Angeles**, July 6, 2012. Signed as a free agent by **Columbus**, July 2, 2015.

BOEDKER, Mikkel

(BAWD-kuhr, MIH-kehl) **ARI**

Left wing. Shoots left. 6', 211 lbs. Born, Brondby, Denmark, December 16, 1989. Phoenix's 1st choice, 8th overall, in 2008 Entry Draft.

Season	Club	League	GP	G	A	Pts	PIM	PP	SH	GW	S	S%	+/-	TF	F%	Min	GP	G	A	Pts	PIM	PP	SH	GW	Min
2004-05	Rodovre IK	Den-2	1	0	1	1	0	....	....	....	....	....	....	....	....	....	....	....	....	....	....	....	....	....	....
2005-06	Frolunda U18	Swe-U18	5	2	0	2	0	....	....	....	....	....	....	....	....	....	2	0	1	1	0	....	....	....	....
	Frolunda Jr.	Swe-Jr.	37	9	8	17	22	....	....	....	....	....	....	....	....	....	2	1	2	3	0	....	....	....	....
2006-07	Frolunda U18	Swe-U18	3	3	2	5	2	....	....	....	....	....	....	....	....	....	6	5	4	9	2	....	....	....	....
	Frolunda Jr.	Swe-Jr.	39	19	30	49	14	....	....	....	....	....	....	....	....	....	8	6	5	11	6	....	....	....	....
	Frolunda	Sweden	2	0	0	0	0	....	....	....	....	....	....	....	....	....	....	....	....	....	....	....	....	....	....
2007-08	Kitchener Rangers	OHL	62	29	44	73	14	....	....	....	....	....	....	....	....	....	20	9	*26	35	2	....	....	....	....
2008-09	**Phoenix**	**NHL**	**78**	**11**	**17**	**28**	**18**	**2**	**0**	**3**	**116**	**9.5**	**–6**	**8**	**12.5**	**15:32**	....	....	....	....	....	....	....	....	....
2009-10	**Phoenix**	**NHL**	**14**	**1**	**2**	**3**	**0**	**0**	**0**	**0**	**7**	**14.3**	**2**	**0**	**0.0**	**8:43**	....	....	....	....	....	....	....	....	....
	San Antonio	AHL	64	11	27	38	4	....	....	....	....	....	....	....	....	....	....	....	....	....	....	....	....	....	....
2010-11	**Phoenix**	**NHL**	**34**	**4**	**10**	**14**	**8**	**0**	**0**	**0**	**39**	**10.3**	**11**	**5**	**60.0**	**10:54**	**4**	**0**	**1**	**1**	**2**	**0**	**0**	**0**	**8:58**
	San Antonio	AHL	36	12	22	34	8	....	....	....	....	....	....	....	....	....	....	....	....	....	....	....	....	....	....
2011-12	**Phoenix**	**NHL**	**82**	**11**	**13**	**24**	**12**	**0**	**0**	**2**	**86**	**12.8**	**–2**	**2**	**50.0**	**13:38**	**16**	**4**	**4**	**8**	**0**	**0**	**0**	**2**	**16:56**
2012-13	Lukko Rauma	Finland	29	21	12	33	10	....	....	....	....	....	....	....	....	....	....	....	....	....	....	....	....	....	....
	Phoenix	**NHL**	**48**	**7**	**19**	**26**	**12**	**3**	**0**	**2**	**83**	**8.4**	**0**	**11**	**9.1**	**18:29**	....	....	....	....	....	....	....	....	....
2013-14	**Phoenix**	**NHL**	**82**	**19**	**32**	**51**	**20**	**5**	**0**	**1**	**166**	**11.4**	**–9**	**7**	**42.9**	**17:25**	....	....	....	....	....	....	....	....	....
2014-15	**Arizona**	**NHL**	**45**	**14**	**14**	**28**	**6**	**3**	**0**	**2**	**79**	**17.7**	**–10**	**2**	**0.0**	**17:29**	....	....	....	....	....	....	....	....	....
	NHL Totals		**383**	**67**	**107**	**174**	**76**	**13**	**0**	**10**	**576**	**11.6**		**35**	**25.7**	**15:28**	**20**	**4**	**5**	**9**	**2**	**0**	**0**	**2**	**15:20**

Signed as a free agent by **Rauma** (Finland), September 27, 2012.

BOGOSIAN, Zach

(buh-GOH-zhuhn, ZAK) **BUF**

Defense. Shoots right. 6'3", 215 lbs. Born, Massena, NY, July 15, 1990. Atlanta's 1st choice, 3rd overall, in 2008 Entry Draft.

Season	Club	League	GP	G	A	Pts	PIM	PP	SH	GW	S	S%	+/-	TF	F%	Min	GP	G	A	Pts	PIM	PP	SH	GW	Min
2005-06	Cushing	High-MA	36	1	16	17	....	....	....	....	....	....	....	....	....	....	....	....	....	....	....	....	....	....	....
2006-07	Peterborough	OHL	67	7	26	33	63	....	....	....	....	....	....	....	....	....	....	....	....	....	....	....	....	....	....
2007-08	Peterborough	OHL	60	11	50	61	72	....	....	....	....	....	....	....	....	....	5	0	3	3	8	....	....	....	....
2008-09	**Atlanta**	**NHL**	**47**	**9**	**10**	**19**	**47**	**2**	**1**	**1**	**90**	**10.0**	**11**	**0**	**0.0**	**18:06**	....	....	....	....	....	....	....	....	....
	Chicago Wolves	AHL	5	1	0	1	0	....	....	....	....	....	....	....	....	....	....	....	....	....	....	....	....	....	....
2009-10	**Atlanta**	**NHL**	**81**	**10**	**13**	**23**	**61**	**3**	**1**	**0**	**155**	**6.5**	**–18**	**0**	**0.0**	**21:25**	....	....	....	....	....	....	....	....	....
2010-11	**Atlanta**	**NHL**	**71**	**5**	**12**	**17**	**29**	**0**	**0**	**1**	**155**	**3.2**	**–27**	**0**	**0.0**	**22:24**	....	....	....	....	....	....	....	....	....
2011-12	**Winnipeg**	**NHL**	**65**	**5**	**25**	**30**	**71**	**1**	**0**	**0**	**150**	**3.3**	**–3**	**0**	**0.0**	**23:19**	....	....	....	....	....	....	....	....	....
2012-13	**Winnipeg**	**NHL**	**33**	**5**	**9**	**14**	**29**	**0**	**0**	**0**	**85**	**5.9**	**–5**	**0**	**0.0**	**23:07**	....	....	....	....	....	....	....	....	....
2013-14	**Winnipeg**	**NHL**	**55**	**3**	**8**	**11**	**48**	**0**	**0**	**0**	**134**	**2.2**	**3**	**0**	**0.0**	**22:55**	....	....	....	....	....	....	....	....	....
2014-15	**Winnipeg**	**NHL**	**41**	**3**	**10**	**13**	**40**	**0**	**0**	**0**	**74**	**4.1**	**1**	**0**	**0.0**	**22:10**	....	....	....	....	....	....	....	....	....
	Buffalo	**NHL**	**21**	**0**	**7**	**7**	**38**	**0**	**0**	**0**	**51**	**0.0**	**–7**	**0**	**0.0**	**26:34**	....	....	....	....	....	....	....	....	....
	NHL Totals		**414**	**40**	**94**	**134**	**363**	**6**	**2**	**2**	**894**	**4.5**		**0**	**0.0**	**22:11**	....	....	....	....	....	....	....	....	....

OHL First All-Star Team (2008)

• Transferred to **Winnipeg** after **Atlanta** franchise relocated, June 21, 2011. Traded to **Buffalo** by **Winnipeg** with Evander Kane and Jason Kasdorf for Tyler Myers, Drew Stafford, Joel Armia, Brendan Lemieux and St. Louis' 1st round choice (previously acquired, Winnipeg selected Jack Roslovic) in 2015 Entry Draft, February 11, 2015.

BOLDUC, Alexandre

(bohl-DUHK, ahl-ehx-AHN-druh)

Center. Shoots left. 6'3", 200 lbs. Born, Montreal, QC, June 26, 1985. St. Louis' 6th choice, 127th overall, in 2003 Entry Draft.

Season	Club	League	GP	G	A	Pts	PIM	PP	SH	GW	S	S%	+/-	TF	F%	Min	GP	G	A	Pts	PIM	PP	SH	GW	Min
2000-01	Notre Dame	SMHL	61	17	35	52	....	....	....	....	....	....	....	....	....	....	....	....	....	....	....	....	....	....	....
2001-02	Rouyn-Noranda	QMJHL	64	6	14	20	69	....	....	....	....	....	....	....	....	....	4	1	1	2	4	....	....	....	....
2002-03	Rouyn-Noranda	QMJHL	66	14	29	43	131	....	....	....	....	....	....	....	....	....	4	0	2	2	2	....	....	....	....
2003-04	Rouyn-Noranda	QMJHL	65	23	35	58	115	....	....	....	....	....	....	....	....	....	11	3	4	7	18	....	....	....	....
2004-05	Rouyn-Noranda	QMJHL	33	7	10	17	46	....	....	....	....	....	....	....	....	....	....	....	....	....	....	....	....	....	....
	Shawinigan	QMJHL	29	7	11	18	14	....	....	....	....	....	....	....	....	....	3	0	0	0	0	....	....	....	....
2005-06	Manitoba Moose	AHL	29	3	7	10	35	....	....	....	....	....	....	....	....	....	....	....	....	....	....	....	....	....	....
	Bakersfield	ECHL	24	10	6	16	56	....	....	....	....	....	....	....	....	....	11	4	4	8	28	....	....	....	....
2006-07	Manitoba Moose	AHL	32	4	5	9	35	....	....	....	....	....	....	....	....	....	5	0	0	0	8	....	....	....	....
	Bakersfield	ECHL	16	7	17	24	42	....	....	....	....	....	....	....	....	....	6	2	4	6	9	....	....	....	....
2007-08	Manitoba Moose	AHL	70	18	19	37	93	....	....	....	....	....	....	....	....	....	6	1	0	1	6	....	....	....	....

			Regular Season														Playoffs								
Season	Club	League	GP	G	A	Pts	PIM	PP	SH	GW	S	S%	+/-	TF	F%	Min	GP	G	A	Pts	PIM	PP	SH	GW	Min
2008-09	Vancouver	NHL	7	0	1	1	4	0	0	0	7	0.0	1	13	38.5	7:20									
	Manitoba Moose	AHL	63	12	21	33	116										13	5	4	9	14				
2009-10	Vancouver	NHL	15	0	0	0	13	0	0	0	14	0.0	–3	87	54.0	9:58									
	Manitoba Moose	AHL	13	2	1	3	20																		
2010-11	Vancouver	NHL	24	2	2	4	21	0	0	1	21	9.5	1	97	45.4	7:26	3	0	0	0	0	0	0	0	3:38
	Manitoba Moose	AHL	26	6	9	15	28										14	4	0	4	20				
2011-12	Phoenix	NHL	2	0	0	0	2	0	0	0	1	0.0	–1	1	100.0	7:10									
	Portland Pirates	AHL	23	3	12	15	30																		
2012-13	Portland Pirates	AHL	56	24	27	51	90										1	1	1	2	2				
	Phoenix	NHL	14	0	0	0	2	0	0	0	17	0.0	–4	21	33.3	7:38									
2013-14	Chicago Wolves	AHL	59	18	19	37	82																		
2014-15	Arizona	NHL	3	0	0	0	2	0	0	0	3	0.0	–1	19	52.6	10:40									
	Portland Pirates	AHL	62	23	29	52	106										2	0	0	0	0				
	NHL Totals		65	2	3	5	44	0	0	1	63	3.2		238	47.9	8:11	3	0	0	0	0	0	0	0	3:39

Signed as a free agent by **Vancouver**, July 2, 2008. • Missed majority of 2009-10 due to shoulder injury at Los Angeles, October 29, 2009. Signed as a free agent by **Phoenix**, July 2, 2011. • Missed majority of 2011-12 due to recurring upper body injury. Signed as a free agent by **St. Louis**, July 6, 2013. Signed as a free agent by **Arizona**, July 1, 2014. Signed as a free agent by **Chelyabinsk** (KHL), June 3, 2015.

BOLL, Jared (BOWL, JAIR-ehd) CBJ

Right wing. Shoots right. 6'3", 214 lbs. Born, Charlotte, NC, May 13, 1986. Columbus' 4th choice, 101st overall, in 2005 Entry Draft.

Season	Club	League	GP	G	A	Pts	PIM	PP	SH	GW	S	S%	+/-	TF	F%	Min	GP	G	A	Pts	PIM	PP	SH	GW	Min
2003-04	Lincoln Stars	USHL	57	6	8	14	*176																		
2004-05	Lincoln Stars	USHL	59	23	24	47	*294										4	1	3	4	25				
2005-06	Plymouth Whalers	OHL	65	19	22	41	205										13	2	4	6	21				
2006-07	Plymouth Whalers	OHL	66	28	27	55	198										20	6	4	10	*66				
2007-08	Columbus	NHL	75	5	5	10	226	0	0	3	63	7.9	–4	6	33.3	8:01									
2008-09	Columbus	NHL	75	4	10	14	180	1	0	0	73	5.5	–6	4	0.0	8:54	1	0	0	0	0	0	0	0	5:17
2009-10	Columbus	NHL	68	4	3	7	149	0	0	0	56	7.1	–8	3	0.0	7:12									
2010-11	Columbus	NHL	73	7	5	12	182	0	0	2	66	10.6	–2	6	0.0	7:40									
2011-12	Columbus	NHL	54	2	1	3	126	0	0	0	35	5.7	–8	5	60.0	8:07									
2012-13	TuTo Turku	Finland-2	5	2	1	3	31																		
	Columbus	NHL	43	2	4	6	100	0	0	0	19	10.5	1	9	44.4	8:05									
2013-14	Columbus	NHL	28	1	1	2	62	0	0	0	12	8.3	–6	1	0.0	7:38	2	0	0	0	0	0	0	0	6:35
2014-15	Columbus	NHL	72	1	4	5	109	0	0	0	28	3.6	–13	2	0.0	7:16									
	NHL Totals		488	26	33	59	1134	1	0	5	352	7.4		36	25.0	7:52	3	0	0	0	0	0	0	0	6:09

Signed as a free agent by **TuTo Turku** (Finland-2), November 15, 2012. • Missed majority of 2013-14 due to recurring ankle injury and tendon surgery, November 25, 2013.

BOLLAND, Dave (BOHL-uhnd, DAYV) FLA

Center. Shoots right. 6', 184 lbs. Born, Mimico, ON, June 5, 1986. Chicago's 2nd choice, 32nd overall, in 2004 Entry Draft.

Season	Club	League	GP	G	A	Pts	PIM	PP	SH	GW	S	S%	+/-	TF	F%	Min	GP	G	A	Pts	PIM	PP	SH	GW	Min
2000-01	Tor. Red Wings	GTHL	95	79	67	146																			
2001-02	Tor. Red Wings	GTHL	36	35	35	70	40																		
2002-03	London Knights	OHL	64	7	10	17	21										14	2	1	3	2				
2003-04	London Knights	OHL	65	37	30	67	58										15	3	10	13	18				
2004-05	London Knights	OHL	66	34	51	85	97										18	11	14	25	30				
2005-06	London Knights	OHL	59	*57	73	130	104										15	*15	9	24	41				
2006-07	Chicago	NHL	1	0	0	0	0	0	0	0	1	0.0	–1	11	36.4	11:17									
	Norfolk Admirals	AHL	65	17	32	49	53										6	0	4	4	17				
2007-08	Chicago	NHL	39	4	13	17	28	0	0	0	49	8.2	6	385	46.5	13:43									
	Rockford IceHogs	AHL	16	6	4	10	22										7	0	0	0	8				
2008-09	Chicago	NHL	81	19	28	47	52	2	2	4	111	17.1	19	1177	44.4	16:27	17	4	8	12	24	1	1	1	18:43
2009-10♦	Chicago	NHL	39	6	10	16	28	1	0	0	52	11.5	5	555	49.4	17:22	22	8	8	16	30	2	2	1	18:40
2010-11	Chicago	NHL	61	15	22	37	34	4	0	1	102	14.7	11	1008	45.1	17:39	4	2	4	6	4	0	0	0	19:58
2011-12	Chicago	NHL	76	19	18	37	47	7	3	2	126	15.1	0	1203	48.4	16:30	6	0	3	3	2	0	0	0	19:30
2012-13♦	Chicago	NHL	35	7	7	14	22	1	0	1	46	15.2	–7	518	46.1	16:20	18	3	3	6	24	0	0	1	13:31
2013-14	Toronto	NHL	23	8	4	12	24	1	1	2	33	24.2	–1	337	45.1	14:28									
2014-15	Florida	NHL	53	6	17	23	48	0	1	0	76	7.9	4	931	44.5	16:21									
	NHL Totals		408	84	119	203	283	16	7	10	596	14.1		6125	46.1	16:19	67	17	26	43	84	3	3	3	17:27

OHL First All-Star Team (2006) • Canadian Major Junior First All-Star Team (2006)

• Missed majority of 2009-10 due to recurring back injury and resulting surgery, November 10, 2009. Traded to **Toronto** by **Chicago** for Toronto's 2nd round choice (Carl Dahlstrom) in 2013 Entry Draft, Anaheim's 4th round choice (previously acquired, later traded to San Jose – San Jose selected Fredrik Bergvik) in 2013 Entry Draft and Toronto's 4th round choice (Frederik Olofsson) in 2014 Entry Draft, June 30, 2013. • Missed majority of 2013-14 due to ankle injury at Vancouver, November 2, 2013. Signed as a free agent by **Florida**, July 1, 2014.

BOLLIG, Brandon (BOH-lihg, BRAN-duhn) CGY

Left wing. Shoots left. 6'2", 223 lbs. Born, St. Charles, MO, January 31, 1987.

Season	Club	League	GP	G	A	Pts	PIM	PP	SH	GW	S	S%	+/-	TF	F%	Min	GP	G	A	Pts	PIM	PP	SH	GW	Min
2005-06	Lincoln Stars	USHL	58	8	8	16	175										9	1	2	3	12				
2006-07	Lincoln Stars	USHL	57	14	12	26	207										4	0	2	2	2				
2007-08	Lincoln Stars	USHL	58	15	16	31	211										8	2	4	6	40				
2008-09	St. Lawrence	ECAC	36	6	7	13	51																		
2009-10	St. Lawrence	ECAC	42	7	18	25	83																		
	Rockford IceHogs	AHL	3	1	1	2	7																		
2010-11	Rockford IceHogs	AHL	55	4	0	4	115																		
2011-12	Chicago	NHL	18	0	0	0	58	0	0	0	16	0.0	–2	0	0.0	5:53	4	1	0	1	19	0	0	0	6:01
	Rockford IceHogs	AHL	53	3	6	9	163																		
2012-13	Rockford IceHogs	AHL	35	5	4	9	157																		
	♦ Chicago	NHL	25	0	0	0	51	0	0	0	34	0.0	–1	3	0.0	8:01	5	0	0	0	2	0	0	0	8:51
2013-14	Chicago	NHL	82	7	7	14	92	0	0	1	109	6.4	–1	1	100.0	10:17	15	0	1	1	16	0	0	0	6:24
2014-15	Calgary	NHL	62	1	4	5	88	0	0	0	67	1.5	–9	5	60.0	8:36	11	2	0	2	38	0	0	0	6:53
	NHL Totals		187	8	11	19	289	0	0	1	226	3.5		9	44.4	9:00	35	3	1	4	75	0	0	0	6:52

Signed as a free agent by **Chicago**, April 3, 2010. Traded to **Calgary** by **Chicago** for Pittsburgh's 3rd round choice (previously acquired, Chicago selected Matt Iacopelli) in 2014 Entry Draft, June 28, 2014.

BONINO, Nick (boh-NEE-noh, NIHK) PIT

Center. Shoots left. 6'1", 196 lbs. Born, Hartford, CT, April 20, 1988. San Jose's 6th choice, 173rd overall, in 2007 Entry Draft.

Season	Club	League	GP	G	A	Pts	PIM	PP	SH	GW	S	S%	+/-	TF	F%	Min	GP	G	A	Pts	PIM	PP	SH	GW	Min
2003-04	Farmington	High-CT	24	44	23	67	10																		
2004-05	Farmington	High-CT	24	68	23	91	12																		
2005-06	Avon Old Farms	High-CT	25	26	30	56	10																		
2006-07	Avon Old Farms	High-CT	26	24	42	66	14																		
2007-08	Boston University	H-East	39	16	13	29	10																		
2008-09	Boston University	H-East	44	18	32	50	30																		
2009-10	Boston University	H-East	33	11	27	38	12																		
	Anaheim	NHL	9	1	1	2	6	1	0	0	14	7.1	0	78	43.6	14:13									
2010-11	Anaheim	NHL	26	0	0	0	4	0	0	0	23	0.0	–3	166	47.0	9:48	4	0	0	0	2	0	0	0	11:36
	Syracuse Crunch	AHL	50	12	33	45	32																		
2011-12	Anaheim	NHL	50	5	13	18	8	0	0	0	63	7.9	1	454	43.0	12:29									
	Syracuse Crunch	AHL	19	6	16	22	2																		
2012-13	Neumarkt/Egna	Italy-2	19	26	26	52	14																		
	Anaheim	NHL	27	5	8	13	8	1	0	0	37	13.5	–3	295	46.8	15:53	7	3	1	4	4	2	0	2	16:38
2013-14	Anaheim	NHL	77	22	27	49	22	7	0	2	159	13.8	14	1194	48.8	16:14	13	4	4	8	8	1	0	1	17:44
2014-15	Vancouver	NHL	75	15	24	39	22	1	0	6	149	10.1	7	1245	47.4	16:55	6	1	2	3	4	0	0	0	16:35
	NHL Totals		264	48	73	121	70	10	0	8	445	10.8		3432	47.1	14:59	30	8	7	15	18	3	0	3	16:26

NCAA Championship All-Tournament Team (2009)

Traded to **Anaheim** by **San Jose** with Timo Pielmeier and San Jose's 4th round choice (Andrew O'Brien) in 2012 Entry Draft for Travis Moen and Kent Huskins, March 4, 2009. Signed as a free agent by **Neumarkt/Egna** (Italy-2), October 16, 2012. Traded to **Vancouver** by **Anaheim** with Luca Sbisa and Anaheim's 1st (Jared McCann) and 3rd (later traded to NY Rangers – NY Rangers selected Keegan Iverson) round choices in 2014 Entry Draft for Ryan Kesler and Vancouver's 3rd round choice (Deven Sideroff) in 2015 Entry Draft, June 27, 2014. Traded to **Pittsburgh** by **Vancouver** with Adam Clendening and Anaheim's 2nd round choice (previously acquired) in 2016 Entry Draft for Brandon Sutter and Pittsburgh's 3rd round compensatory choice in 2016 Entry Draft, July 28, 2015.

BOOTH, David

(BOOTH, DAY-vihd)

Left wing. Shoots left. 6', 212 lbs. Born, Detroit, MI, November 24, 1984. Florida's 3rd choice, 53rd overall, in 2004 Entry Draft.

			Regular Season														Playoffs								
Season	Club	League	GP	G	A	Pts	PIM	PP	SH	GW	S	S%	+/-	TF	F%	Min	GP	G	A	Pts	PIM	PP	SH	GW	Min
2000-01	Det. Compuware	NAHL	42	17	13	30	44										2	1	0	1	2				
2001-02	USNTDP	U-18	40	12	6	18	17																		
	USNTDP	USHL	12	4	3	7	6																		
	USNTDP	NAHL	6	1	3	4	18																		
2002-03	Michigan State	CCHA	39	17	19	36	53																		
2003-04	Michigan State	CCHA	30	8	10	18	30																		
2004-05	Michigan State	CCHA	29	7	9	16	30																		
2005-06	Michigan State	CCHA	37	13	22	35	50																		
2006-07	**Florida**	**NHL**	**48**	**3**	**7**	**10**	**12**	**0**	**0**	**1**	**86**	**3.5**	**0**	**11**	**36.4**	**9:34**									
	Rochester	AHL	25	7	7	14	26										6	0	2	2	4				
2007-08	**Florida**	**NHL**	**73**	**22**	**18**	**40**	**26**	**1**	**0**	**6**	**228**	**9.6**	**13**	**38**	**34.2**	**16:10**									
2008-09	**Florida**	**NHL**	**72**	**31**	**29**	**60**	**38**	**11**	**0**	**5**	**246**	**12.6**	**10**	**17**	**41.2**	**17:05**									
2009-10	**Florida**	**NHL**	**28**	**8**	**8**	**16**	**23**	**0**	**0**	**1**	**95**	**8.4**	**–3**	**10**	**20.0**	**18:08**									
2010-11	**Florida**	**NHL**	**82**	**23**	**17**	**40**	**26**	**8**	**0**	**3**	**280**	**8.2**	**–31**	**48**	**50.0**	**18:54**									
2011-12	**Florida**	**NHL**	**6**	**0**	**1**	**1**	**2**	**0**	**0**	**0**	**14**	**0.0**	**–6**	**0**	**0.0**	**15:30**									
	Vancouver	**NHL**	**56**	**16**	**13**	**29**	**32**	**3**	**0**	**1**	**145**	**11.0**	**1**	**18**	**50.0**	**14:52**	**5**	**0**	**1**	**1**	**0**	**0**	**0**	**0**	**16:07**
2012-13	**Vancouver**	**NHL**	**12**	**1**	**2**	**3**	**4**	**0**	**0**	**0**	**27**	**3.7**	**–3**	**1**	**100.0**	**12:45**									
2013-14	**Vancouver**	**NHL**	**66**	**9**	**10**	**19**	**18**	**0**	**0**	**0**	**117**	**7.7**	**1**	**23**	**56.5**	**13:28**									
	Utica Comets	AHL	3	0	1	1	0																		
2014-15	**Toronto**	**NHL**	**59**	**7**	**6**	**13**	**25**	**0**	**0**	**2**	**107**	**6.5**	**–8**	**13**	**46.2**	**11:56**									
	Toronto Marlies	AHL	2	1	0	1	2																		
	NHL Totals		**502**	**120**	**111**	**231**	**206**	**23**	**0**	**19**	**1345**	**8.9**		**179**	**44.1**	**15:08**	**5**	**0**	**1**	**1**	**0**	**0**	**0**	**0**	**16:07**

CCHA All-Rookie Team (2003)

• Missed majority of 2009-10 due to head injury at Philadelphia, October 24, 2009. Traded to **Vancouver** by **Florida** with Steve Reinprecht and Vancouver's 3rd round choice (previously acquired, Vancouver selected Cole Cassels) in 2013 Entry Draft for Mikael Samuelsson and Marco Sturm, October 22, 2011. • Missed majority of 2012-13 due to recurring groin injury and ankle injury vs. Detroit, March 16, 2013. Signed as a free agent by **Toronto**, July 22, 2014.

BORDELEAU, Patrick

(BOHR-duh-loh, PAT-rihk) **COL**

Left wing. Shoots left. 6'6", 225 lbs. Born, Montreal, QC, March 23, 1986. Minnesota's 6th choice, 114th overall, in 2004 Entry Draft.

			Regular Season														Playoffs								
Season	Club	League	GP	G	A	Pts	PIM	PP	SH	GW	S	S%	+/-	TF	F%	Min	GP	G	A	Pts	PIM	PP	SH	GW	Min
2002-03	Gatineau	QAAA	39	8	13	21	50										6	0	1	1	6				
2003-04	Val-d'Or Foreurs	QMJHL	68	7	11	18	97										7	1	1	2	8				
2004-05	Val-d'Or Foreurs	QMJHL	63	14	24	38	51																		
2005-06	Val-d'Or Foreurs	QMJHL	67	23	33	56	87										5	1	0	1	7				
2006-07	Drummondville	QMJHL	3	0	2	2	6																		
	Acadie-Bathurst	QMJHL	17	7	12	19	26																		
2007-08	Charlotte	ECHL	10	1	2	3	11																		
	Wheeling Nailers	ECHL	3	0	1	1	0																		
	Pensacola	ECHL	38	7	11	18	60																		
2008-09	Augusta Lynx	ECHL	18	4	6	10	57																		
	Albany River Rats	AHL	6	0	2	2	21																		
	Florida Everblades	ECHL	29	4	9	13	81																		
	Springfield	AHL	4	0	0	0	4																		
	Lake Erie	AHL	3	0	1	1	17																		
	Milwaukee	AHL	2	0	0	0	0																		
2009-10	Lake Erie	AHL	60	1	2	3	106																		
2010-11	Lake Erie	AHL	72	2	10	12	125										7	0	0	0	6				
2011-12	Lake Erie	AHL	52	4	4	8	96																		
2012-13	Lake Erie	AHL	29	2	5	7	91																		
	Colorado	**NHL**	**46**	**2**	**3**	**5**	**70**	**0**	**0**	**0**	**24**	**8.3**	**–7**	**2**	**0.0**	**6:13**									
2013-14	**Colorado**	**NHL**	**82**	**6**	**5**	**11**	**115**	**0**	**0**	**1**	**37**	**16.2**	**–1**	**3**	**33.3**	**6:53**	**7**	**0**	**0**	**0**	**10**	**0**	**0**	**0**	**5:43**
2014-15	**Colorado**	**NHL**	**1**	**0**	**0**	**0**	**0**	**0**	**0**	**0**	**0**	**0.0**	**0**	**0**	**0.0**	**6:46**									
	NHL Totals		**129**	**8**	**8**	**16**	**185**	**0**	**0**	**1**	**61**	**13.1**		**5**	**20.0**	**6:39**	**7**	**0**	**0**	**0**	**10**	**0**	**0**	**0**	**5:43**

Signed to a PTO (professional tryout) contract by **Albany** (AHL), December 5, 2008. Signed as a free agent by **Florida** (ECHL), December 11, 2008. Signed to a PTO (professional tryout) contract by **Springfield** (AHL), January 5, 2009. Signed to a PTO (professional tryout) contract by **Lake Erie** (AHL), March 31, 2009. Signed to a PTO (professional tryout) contract by **Milwaukee** (AHL), April 6, 2009. Signed as a free agent by **Colorado**, July 1, 2011. • Missed majority of 2014-15 due to back surgery, October 7, 2014 and knee injury vs. Buffalo, December 20, 2014.

BOROWIECKI, Mark

(BOHR-vee-YHET-skee, MAHRK) **OTT**

Defense. Shoots left. 6'2", 215 lbs. Born, Ottawa, ON, July 12, 1989. Ottawa's 6th choice, 139th overall, in 2008 Entry Draft.

			Regular Season														Playoffs								
Season	Club	League	GP	G	A	Pts	PIM	PP	SH	GW	S	S%	+/-	TF	F%	Min	GP	G	A	Pts	PIM	PP	SH	GW	Min
2006-07	Smiths Falls Bears	ON-Jr.A	53	3	25	28	85										6	0	0	0	10				
2007-08	Smiths Falls Bears	ON-Jr.A	46	2	24	26	80										15	1	10	11	22				
2008-09	Clarkson Knights	ECAC	33	1	1	2	24																		
2009-10	Clarkson Knights	ECAC	35	8	11	19	55																		
2010-11	Clarkson Knights	ECAC	31	3	8	11	67																		
	Binghamton	AHL	9	0	0	0	6										21	0	2	2	8				
2011-12	**Ottawa**	**NHL**	**2**	**0**	**0**	**0**	**2**	**0**	**0**	**0**	**1**	**0.0**	**–1**	**0**	**0.0**	**12:30**									
	Binghamton	AHL	73	5	17	22	127																		
2012-13	Binghamton	AHL	53	4	10	14	157										3	1	0	1	4				
	Ottawa	**NHL**	**6**	**0**	**0**	**0**	**18**	**0**	**0**	**0**	**1**	**0.0**	**1**	**0**	**0.0**	**13:00**									
2013-14	**Ottawa**	**NHL**	**13**	**1**	**0**	**1**	**48**	**0**	**0**	**0**	**6**	**16.7**	**–2**	**0**	**0.0**	**12:35**									
	Binghamton	AHL	50	2	6	8	158										4	0	0	0	4				
2014-15	**Ottawa**	**NHL**	**63**	**1**	**10**	**11**	**107**	**0**	**0**	**0**	**30**	**3.3**	**15**	**0**	**0.0**	**15:55**	**6**	**0**	**0**	**0**	**6**	**0**	**0**	**0**	**16:24**
	NHL Totals		**84**	**2**	**10**	**12**	**175**	**0**	**0**	**0**	**38**	**5.3**		**0**	**0.0**	**15:06**	**6**	**0**	**0**	**0**	**6**	**0**	**0**	**0**	**16:24**

BORTUZZO, Robert

(bohr-TOOZ-oh, RAW-buhrt) **ST.L.**

Defense. Shoots right. 6'4", 215 lbs. Born, Thunder Bay, ON, March 18, 1989. Pittsburgh's 3rd choice, 78th overall, in 2007 Entry Draft.

			Regular Season														Playoffs								
Season	Club	League	GP	G	A	Pts	PIM	PP	SH	GW	S	S%	+/-	TF	F%	Min	GP	G	A	Pts	PIM	PP	SH	GW	Min
2005-06	F-Wm. North Stars	ON-Jr.A	40	4	18	22																			
2006-07	Kitchener Rangers	OHL	63	2	12	14	67										9	1	2	3	8				
2007-08	Kitchener Rangers	OHL	52	3	15	18	61										18	0	8	8	14				
2008-09	Kitchener Rangers	OHL	23	1	16	17	24																		
2009-10	Wilkes-Barre	AHL	75	2	10	12	109										4	0	0	0	0				
2010-11	Wilkes-Barre	AHL	79	4	22	26	111										12	0	1	1	6				
2011-12	**Pittsburgh**	**NHL**	**6**	**0**	**0**	**0**	**2**	**0**	**0**	**0**	**3**	**0.0**	**1**	**0**	**0.0**	**10:54**									
	Wilkes-Barre	AHL	51	3	9	12	61										12	0	1	1	13				
2012-13	Wilkes-Barre	AHL	31	1	3	4	34																		
	Pittsburgh	**NHL**	**15**	**2**	**2**	**4**	**27**	**0**	**0**	**0**	**10**	**20.0**	**3**	**0**	**0.0**	**13:17**									
2013-14	**Pittsburgh**	**NHL**	**54**	**0**	**10**	**10**	**74**	**0**	**0**	**0**	**50**	**0.0**	**–3**	**1**	**0.0**	**15:29**	**8**	**0**	**1**	**1**	**4**	**0**	**0**	**0**	**13:14**
2014-15	**Pittsburgh**	**NHL**	**38**	**2**	**4**	**6**	**68**	**0**	**0**	**0**	**37**	**5.4**	**–6**	**1**	**100.0**	**15:28**									
	St. Louis	**NHL**	**13**	**1**	**1**	**2**	**25**	**0**	**0**	**0**	**19**	**5.3**	**–3**	**0**	**0.0**	**14:06**									
	NHL Totals		**126**	**5**	**17**	**22**	**196**	**0**	**0**	**0**	**119**	**4.2**		**2**	**50.0**	**14:51**	**8**	**0**	**1**	**1**	**4**	**0**	**0**	**0**	**13:14**

Traded to **St. Louis** by **Pittsburgh** with a 7th round choice in 2016 Entry Draft for Ian Cole, March 2, 2015.

BOUCHARD, Pierre-Marc

(BOO-shahrd, PEE-air- MAHRK)

Center. Shoots left. 5'11", 171 lbs. Born, Sherbrooke, QC, April 27, 1984. Minnesota's 1st choice, 8th overall, in 2002 Entry Draft.

			Regular Season														Playoffs								
Season	Club	League	GP	G	A	Pts	PIM	PP	SH	GW	S	S%	+/-	TF	F%	Min	GP	G	A	Pts	PIM	PP	SH	GW	Min
1998-99	Mtl.-Bourassa	QAHA	28	23	41	64																			
99-2000	C.C. Lemoyne	QAAA	42	28	*45	*74	20										9	4	8	12	6				
2000-01	Chicoutimi	QMJHL	67	38	57	95	20										6	5	8	13	0				
2001-02	Chicoutimi	QMJHL	69	46	*94	*140	54										4	2	3	5	4				
2002-03	**Minnesota**	**NHL**	**50**	**7**	**13**	**20**	**18**	**5**	**0**	**1**	**53**	**13.2**	**1**	**474**	**40.7**	**13:16**	**5**	**0**	**1**	**1**	**2**	**0**	**0**	**0**	**13:15**
2003-04	**Minnesota**	**NHL**	**61**	**4**	**18**	**22**	**22**	**2**	**0**	**0**	**60**	**6.7**	**–7**	**60**	**50.0**	**14:00**									
2004-05	Houston Aeros	AHL	67	12	42	54	46										5	0	1	1	0				
2005-06	**Minnesota**	**NHL**	**80**	**17**	**42**	**59**	**28**	**7**	**0**	**3**	**118**	**14.4**	**3**	**15**	**46.7**	**15:15**									
2006-07	**Minnesota**	**NHL**	**82**	**20**	**37**	**57**	**14**	**5**	**0**	**3**	**173**	**11.6**	**13**	**18**	**33.3**	**15:59**	**5**	**1**	**1**	**2**	**0**	**0**	**0**	**0**	**14:48**

Season	Club	League	GP	G	A	Pts	PIM	PP	SH	GW	S	S%	+/-	TF	F%	Min	GP	G	A	Pts	PIM	PP	SH	GW	Min
			Regular Season														Playoffs								
2007-08	**Minnesota**	**NHL**	**81**	**13**	**50**	**63**	**34**	**6**	**0**	**4**	**129**	**10.1**	**11**	**10**	**40.0**	**16:51**	**6**	**2**	**2**	**4**	**2**	**1**	**0**	**1**	**17:47**
2008-09	**Minnesota**	**NHL**	**71**	**16**	**30**	**46**	**20**	**2**	**0**	**1**	**142**	**11.3**	**–5**	**19**	**57.9**	**16:59**									
2009-10	**Minnesota**	**NHL**	**1**	**0**	**0**	**0**	**2**	**0**	**0**	**0**	**0**	**0.0**	**0**	**3**	**33.3**	**10:44**									
2010-11	**Minnesota**	**NHL**	**59**	**12**	**26**	**38**	**14**	**0**	**0**	**2**	**98**	**12.2**	**–3**	**43**	**39.5**	**15:43**									
2011-12	**Minnesota**	**NHL**	**37**	**9**	**13**	**22**	**18**	**2**	**0**	**3**	**84**	**10.7**	**–1**	**16**	**25.0**	**16:19**									
2012-13	**Minnesota**	**NHL**	**43**	**8**	**12**	**20**	**8**	**0**	**0**	**2**	**71**	**11.3**	**3**	**7**	**14.3**	**13:57**	**5**	**1**	**1**	**2**	**0**	**0**	**0**	**0**	**14:36**
2013-14	**NY Islanders**	**NHL**	**28**	**4**	**5**	**9**	**12**	**1**	**0**	**1**	**51**	**7.8**	**–9**	**5**	**60.0**	**13:57**									
	Bridgeport	AHL	20	6	11	17	4																		
	Rockford IceHogs	AHL	24	3	17	20	10																		
2014-15	EV Zug	Swiss	49	17	34	51	16										6	3	2	5	0				
	NHL Totals		**593**	**110**	**246**	**356**	**190**	**30**	**0**	**20**	**979**	**11.2**		**670**	**41.3**	**15:26**	**21**	**4**	**5**	**9**	**4**	**1**	**0**	**1**	**15:14**

QMJHL Rookie of the Year (2001) • QMJHL First All-Star Team (2002) • Canadian Major Junior First All-Star Team (2002) • Canadian Major Junior Player of the Year (2002)

• Missed majority of 2009-10 due to post-concussion syndrome. Signed as a free agent by **NY Islanders**, July 5, 2013. Traded to **Chicago** by **NY Islanders** with Peter Regin for Chicago's 4th round choice (later traded to Washington, later traded to NY Rangers – NY Rangers selected Igor Shesterkin) in 2014 Entry Draft, February 6, 2014. Signed as a free agent by **Zug** (Swiss), July 8, 2014.

BOUCHER, Reid (BOO-shay, REED) N.J.

Left wing. Shoots left. 5'10", 190 lbs. Born, Lansing, MI, September 8, 1993. New Jersey's 4th choice, 99th overall, in 2011 Entry Draft.

Season	Club	League	GP	G	A	Pts	PIM	PP	SH	GW	S	S%	+/-	TF	F%	Min	GP	G	A	Pts	PIM	PP	SH	GW	Min
2008-09	Lansing Capitals	Minor-MI	64	79	41	120	119																		
2009-10	USNTDP	USHL	24	10	4	14	22																		
	USNTDP	U-17	17	7	9	16	16																		
	USNTDP	U-18	1	0	0	0	0																		
2010-11	USNTDP	USHL	24	14	6	20	13																		
	USNTDP	U-18	35	12	8	20	120																		
2011-12	Sarnia Sting	OHL	67	28	22	50	19										6	2	1	3	4				
	Albany Devils	AHL	1	0	0	0	0																		
2012-13	Sarnia Sting	OHL	68	*62	33	95	53										4	2	3	5	4				
	Albany Devils	AHL	11	3	2	5	6																		
2013-14	**New Jersey**	**NHL**	**23**	**2**	**5**	**7**	**4**	**0**	**0**	**0**	**27**	**7.4**	**2**	**3**	**33.3**	**11:21**									
	Albany Devils	AHL	56	22	16	38	10										4	1	0	1	0				
2014-15	**New Jersey**	**NHL**	**11**	**1**	**0**	**1**	**0**	**0**	**0**	**0**	**20**	**5.0**	**–4**	**0**	**0.0**	**11:08**									
	Albany Devils	AHL	62	15	15	30	36																		
	NHL Totals		**34**	**3**	**5**	**8**	**4**	**0**	**0**	**0**	**47**	**6.4**		**3**	**33.3**	**11:17**									

OHL First All-Star Team (2013)

BOULTON, Eric (BOHL-tuhn, AIR-ihk)

Left wing. Shoots left. 6', 225 lbs. Born, Halifax, NS, August 17, 1976. NY Rangers' 12th choice, 234th overall, in 1994 Entry Draft.

Season	Club	League	GP	G	A	Pts	PIM	PP	SH	GW	S	S%	+/-	TF	F%	Min	GP	G	A	Pts	PIM	PP	SH	GW	Min
1992-93	Cole Harbour	MJrHL	44	12	15	27	212																		
1993-94	Oshawa Generals	OHL	45	4	3	7	149										5	0	0	0	16				
1994-95	Oshawa Generals	OHL	27	7	5	12	125																		
	Sarnia Sting	OHL	24	3	7	10	134										4	0	1	1	10				
1995-96	Sarnia Sting	OHL	66	14	29	43	243										9	0	3	3	29				
1996-97	Binghamton	AHL	23	2	3	5	67										3	0	0	0	4				
	Charlotte	ECHL	44	14	11	25	325										3	0	1	1	6				
1997-98	Charlotte	ECHL	53	11	16	27	202										4	1	0	1	0				
	Fort Wayne	IHL	8	0	2	2	42																		
1998-99	Kentucky	AHL	34	3	3	6	154										10	0	1	1	36				
	Florida Everblades	ECHL	26	9	13	22	143																		
	Houston Aeros	IHL	7	1	0	1	41																		
99-2000	Rochester	AHL	76	2	2	4	276										18	2	1	3	53				
2000-01	**Buffalo**	**NHL**	**35**	**1**	**2**	**3**	**94**	**0**	**0**	**0**	**20**	**5.0**	**–1**	**2**	**0.0**	**5:42**									
2001-02	**Buffalo**	**NHL**	**35**	**2**	**3**	**5**	**129**	**0**	**0**	**1**	**21**	**9.5**	**–1**	**0**	**0.0**	**6:08**									
2002-03	**Buffalo**	**NHL**	**58**	**1**	**5**	**6**	**178**	**0**	**0**	**0**	**33**	**3.0**	**1**	**6**	**33.3**	**6:35**									
2003-04	**Buffalo**	**NHL**	**44**	**1**	**2**	**3**	**110**	**0**	**0**	**0**	**20**	**5.0**	**–2**	**1**	**0.0**	**4:52**									
2004-05	Columbia Inferno	ECHL	48	23	16	39	124										4	2	3	5	8				
2005-06	**Atlanta**	**NHL**	**51**	**4**	**5**	**9**	**87**	**0**	**0**	**0**	**28**	**14.3**	**–4**	**2**	**50.0**	**4:54**									
2006-07	**Atlanta**	**NHL**	**45**	**3**	**4**	**7**	**49**	**0**	**0**	**0**	**42**	**7.1**	**2**	**2**	**50.0**	**6:16**	**4**	**0**	**0**	**0**	**24**	**0**	**0**	**0**	**5:04**
2007-08	**Atlanta**	**NHL**	**74**	**4**	**5**	**9**	**127**	**0**	**0**	**0**	**64**	**6.3**	**–10**	**4**	**25.0**	**7:27**									
2008-09	**Atlanta**	**NHL**	**76**	**3**	**10**	**13**	**176**	**0**	**0**	**0**	**71**	**4.2**	**–3**	**4**	**25.0**	**7:33**									
2009-10	**Atlanta**	**NHL**	**62**	**2**	**6**	**8**	**113**	**1**	**0**	**0**	**39**	**5.1**	**–1**	**4**	**50.0**	**6:51**									
2010-11	**Atlanta**	**NHL**	**69**	**6**	**4**	**10**	**87**	**0**	**0**	**1**	**51**	**11.8**	**1**	**3**	**0.0**	**8:57**									
2011-12	**New Jersey**	**NHL**	**51**	**0**	**0**	**0**	**115**	**0**	**0**	**0**	**25**	**0.0**	**–12**	**3**	**33.3**	**6:35**									
	Albany Devils	AHL	2	0	0	0	0																		
2012-13	**NY Islanders**	**NHL**	**15**	**0**	**0**	**0**	**36**	**0**	**0**	**0**	**5**	**0.0**	**–4**	**0**	**0.0**	**5:40**									
2013-14	**NY Islanders**	**NHL**	**23**	**2**	**2**	**4**	**88**	**0**	**0**	**0**	**21**	**9.5**	**0**	**0**	**0.0**	**6:25**									
2014-15	**NY Islanders**	**NHL**	**10**	**2**	**0**	**2**	**30**	**0**	**0**	**0**	**9**	**22.2**	**–1**	**0**	**0.0**	**7:12**									
	NHL Totals		**648**	**31**	**48**	**79**	**1419**	**1**	**0**	**2**	**449**	**6.9**		**31**	**29.0**	**6:43**	**4**	**0**	**0**	**0**	**24**	**0**	**0**	**0**	**5:04**

Signed as a free agent by **Buffalo**, September 14, 1999. Signed as a free agent by **Columbia** (ECHL), November 24, 2004. Signed as a free agent by **Atlanta**, August 8, 2005. • Transferred to **Winnipeg** after **Atlanta** franchise relocated, June 21, 2011. Signed as a free agent by **New Jersey**, July 15, 2011. Signed as a free agent by **NY Islanders**, July 2, 2012. • Missed majority of 2012-13 as a healthy reserve. • Missed majority of 2013-14 due to hand injury at Winnipeg, March 4, 2014 and as a healthy reserve. • Missed majority of 2014-15 due to recurring lower-body injury and as a healthy reserve.

BOUMA, Lance (BOW-ma, LANTZ) CGY

Center. Shoots left. 6'1", 210 lbs. Born, Provost, AB, March 25, 1990. Calgary's 3rd choice, 78th overall, in 2008 Entry Draft.

Season	Club	League	GP	G	A	Pts	PIM	PP	SH	GW	S	S%	+/-	TF	F%	Min	GP	G	A	Pts	PIM	PP	SH	GW	Min
2005-06	Wainwright	RAMHL	37	21	29	50																			
	Vancouver Giants	WHL	5	1	3	4	0																		
2006-07	Vancouver Giants	WHL	49	3	5	8	31										22	3	3	6	12				
2007-08	Vancouver Giants	WHL	71	12	23	35	93										10	0	1	1	8				
2008-09	Vancouver Giants	WHL	48	9	16	25	116										17	7	5	12	30				
2009-10	Vancouver Giants	WHL	57	14	29	43	134										16	4	13	17	*47				
	Abbotsford Heat	AHL															5	1	0	1	2				
2010-11	**Calgary**	**NHL**	**16**	**0**	**1**	**1**	**2**	**0**	**0**	**0**	**9**	**0.0**	**–1**	**3**	**0.0**	**5:52**									
	Abbotsford Heat	AHL	61	12	8	20	53																		
2011-12	**Calgary**	**NHL**	**27**	**1**	**2**	**3**	**11**	**0**	**0**	**0**	**26**	**3.8**	**–5**	**22**	**50.0**	**10:10**									
	Abbotsford Heat	AHL	31	3	3	6	53																		
2012-13	Abbotsford Heat	AHL	3	1	0	1	2																		
2013-14	**Calgary**	**NHL**	**78**	**5**	**10**	**15**	**41**	**0**	**1**	**0**	**82**	**6.1**	**–4**	**85**	**25.9**	**12:36**									
2014-15	**Calgary**	**NHL**	**78**	**16**	**18**	**34**	**54**	**0**	**0**	**4**	**104**	**15.4**	**10**	**74**	**39.2**	**14:01**	**2**	**0**	**0**	**0**	**2**	**0**	**0**	**0**	**14:16**
	NHL Totals		**199**	**22**	**31**	**53**	**108**	**0**	**1**	**4**	**221**	**10.0**		**184**	**33.7**	**12:17**	**2**	**0**	**0**	**0**	**2**	**0**	**0**	**0**	**14:16**

• Missed majority of 2012-13 due to knee injury vs. Chicago (AHL), October 19, 2012.

BOURNIVAL, Michael (boor-nee-VAHL, MIGH-kuhl) MTL

Left wing. Shoots left. 5'11", 195 lbs. Born, Shawinigan, QC, May 31, 1992. Colorado's 3rd choice, 71st overall, in 2010 Entry Draft.

Season	Club	League	GP	G	A	Pts	PIM	PP	SH	GW	S	S%	+/-	TF	F%	Min	GP	G	A	Pts	PIM	PP	SH	GW	Min
2007-08	Trois-Rivieres	QAAA	52	33	23	56	66										7	3	3	6	10				
2008-09	Shawinigan	QMJHL	46	11	11	22	29										21	1	3	4	12				
2009-10	Shawinigan	QMJHL	58	24	38	62	37										6	2	2	4	6				
2010-11	Shawinigan	QMJHL	56	28	36	64	28										12	5	8	13	10				
2011-12	Shawinigan	QMJHL	41	30	26	56	27										11	1	6	7	12				
2012-13	Hamilton	AHL	69	10	20	30	26																		
2013-14	**Montreal**	**NHL**	**60**	**7**	**7**	**14**	**18**	**1**	**0**	**1**	**78**	**9.0**	**–6**	**61**	**45.9**	**10:19**	**14**	**0**	**1**	**1**	**0**	**0**	**0**	**0**	**10:16**
	Hamilton	AHL	3	2	1	3	2																		
2014-15	**Montreal**	**NHL**	**29**	**3**	**2**	**5**	**4**	**0**	**0**	**1**	**27**	**11.1**	**3**	**5**	**80.0**	**7:53**									
	Hamilton	AHL	12	3	6	9	8																		
	NHL Totals		**89**	**10**	**9**	**19**	**22**	**1**	**0**	**2**	**105**	**9.5**		**66**	**48.5**	**9:32**	**14**	**0**	**1**	**1**	**0**	**0**	**0**	**0**	**10:16**

Traded to **Montreal** by **Colorado** for Ryan O'Byrne, November 11, 2010. • Missed majority of 2014-15 due to shoulder injury at Buffalo, November 5, 2014 and as a healthy reserve.

BOURQUE, Chris

(BOHRK, KRIHS) **WSH**

Center. Shoots left. 5'8", 174 lbs. Born, Boston, MA, January 29, 1986. Washington's 4th choice, 33rd overall, in 2004 Entry Draft.

			Regular Season														Playoffs								
Season	Club	League	GP	G	A	Pts	PIM	PP	SH	GW	S	S%	+/-	TF	F%	Min	GP	G	A	Pts	PIM	PP	SH	GW	Min
2002-03	Cushing	High-MA	28	31	26	57	49	....	....	....	....	....	....	....	....	....	....	....	....	....	....	....	....	....	....
2003-04	Cushing	High-MA	31	37	53	90	96	....	....	....	....	....	....	....	....	....	....	....	....	....	....	....	....	....	....
2004-05	Boston University	H-East	35	10	13	23	50	....	....	....	....	....	....	....	....	....	....	....	....	....	....	....	....	....	....
	Portland Pirates	AHL	6	1	1	2	2	....	....	....	....	....	....	....	....	....	....	....	....	....	....	....	....	....	....
2005-06	Hershey Bears	AHL	52	8	28	36	40	....	....	....	....	....	....	....	....	....	1	0	0	0	0	....	....	....	....
2006-07	Hershey Bears	AHL	76	25	33	58	49	....	....	....	....	....	....	....	....	....	19	2	6	8	18	....	....	....	....
2007-08	**Washington**	**NHL**	**4**	**0**	**0**	**0**	**2**	**0**	**0**	**0**	**4**	**0.0**	**0**	**1**	**0.0**	**8:42**	....	....	....	....	....	....	....	....	....
	Hershey Bears	AHL	73	28	35	63	56	....	....	....	....	....	....	....	....	....	5	1	3	4	8	....	....	....	....
2008-09	**Washington**	**NHL**	**8**	**1**	**0**	**1**	**0**	**0**	**0**	**0**	**11**	**9.1**	**0**	**0**	**0.0**	**9:46**	....	....	....	....	....	....	....	....	....
	Hershey Bears	AHL	69	21	52	73	57	....	....	....	....	....	....	....	....	....	22	5	16	21	30	....	....	....	....
2009-10	**Pittsburgh**	**NHL**	**20**	**0**	**3**	**3**	**10**	**0**	**0**	**0**	**20**	**0.0**	**–4**	**0**	**0.0**	**9:35**	....	....	....	....	....	....	....	....	....
	Washington	**NHL**	**1**	**0**	**0**	**0**	**0**	**0**	**0**	**0**	**1**	**0.0**	**–2**	**0**	**0.0**	**9:37**	....	....	....	....	....	....	....	....	....
	Hershey Bears	AHL	49	22	48	70	26	....	....	....	....	....	....	....	....	....	21	7	20	*27	10	....	....	....	....
2010-11	Mytischi	KHL	8	1	0	1	0	....	....	....	....	....	....	....	....	....	....	....	....	....	....	....	....	....	....
	HC Lugano	Swiss	39	14	19	33	24	....	....	....	....	....	....	....	....	....	2	1	4	5	0	....	....	....	....
2011-12	Hershey Bears	AHL	73	27	*66	*93	42	....	....	....	....	....	....	....	....	....	5	1	3	4	0	....	....	....	....
2012-13	Providence Bruins	AHL	39	10	28	38	34	....	....	....	....	....	....	....	....	....	12	5	9	14	14	....	....	....	....
	Boston	**NHL**	**18**	**1**	**3**	**4**	**6**	**0**	**0**	**1**	**24**	**4.2**	**–6**	**1**	**0.0**	**12:05**	....	....	....	....	....	....	....	....	....
2013-14	Ak Bars Kazan	KHL	11	2	0	2	6	....	....	....	....	....	....	....	....	....	....	....	....	....	....	....	....	....	....
	EHC Biel-Bienne	Swiss	25	7	8	15	14	....	....	....	....	....	....	....	....	....	6	3	2	5	4	....	....	....	....
2014-15	Hartford	AHL	73	29	37	66	68	....	....	....	....	....	....	....	....	....	15	4	13	17	12	....	....	....	....
	NHL Totals		**51**	**2**	**6**	**8**	**18**	**0**	**0**	**1**	**60**	**3.3**		**2**	**0.0**	**10:25**	....	....	....	....	....	....	....	....	....

Hockey East All-Rookie Team (2005) • Jack A. Butterfield Trophy (AHL – Playoff MVP) (2010) • AHL First All-Star Team (2012, 2015) • John P. Sollenberger Trophy (AHL - Top Scorer) (2012)

Claimed on waivers by **Pittsburgh** from **Washington**, September 30, 2009. Claimed on waivers by **Washington** from **Pittsburgh**, December 5, 2009. Signed as a free agent by **Mytischi** (KHL), June 23, 2010. Signed as a free agent by **Lugano** (Swiss), October 4, 2010. Traded to **Boston** by **Washington** for Zach Hamill, May 26, 2012. Signed as a free agent by **Kazan** (KHL), June 18, 2013. Signed as a free agent by **Biel-Bienne** (Swiss), November 29, 2013. Signed as a free agent by **NY Rangers**, July 1, 2014. Signed as a free agent by **Washington**, July 2, 2015.

BOURQUE, Gabriel

(BOHRK, gah-BREE-ehl) **NSH**

Left wing. Shoots left. 5'10", 195 lbs. Born, Rimouski, QC, September 23, 1990. Nashville's 9th choice, 132nd overall, in 2009 Entry Draft.

Season	Club	League	GP	G	A	Pts	PIM	PP	SH	GW	S	S%	+/-	TF	F%	Min	GP	G	A	Pts	PIM	PP	SH	GW	Min
2006-07	Ecole Notre Dame	QAAA	43	15	35	50	115	....	....	....	....	....	....	....	....	....	13	8	16	24	14	....	....	....	....
2007-08	Baie-Comeau	QMJHL	65	10	18	28	38	....	....	....	....	....	....	....	....	....	5	0	0	0	0	....	....	....	....
2008-09	Baie-Comeau	QMJHL	60	22	39	61	82	....	....	....	....	....	....	....	....	....	5	0	2	2	16	....	....	....	....
2009-10	Baie-Comeau	QMJHL	30	13	25	38	61	....	....	....	....	....	....	....	....	....	....	....	....	....	....	....	....	....	....
	Moncton Wildcats	QMJHL	25	3	11	14	37	....	....	....	....	....	....	....	....	....	21	19	10	29	18	....	....	....	....
2010-11	Milwaukee	AHL	78	18	18	36	19	....	....	....	....	....	....	....	....	....	13	7	6	13	4	....	....	....	....
2011-12	**Nashville**	**NHL**	**43**	**7**	**12**	**19**	**6**	**0**	**0**	**1**	**59**	**11.9**	**–2**	**1**	**0.0**	**12:47**	**10**	**3**	**2**	**5**	**4**	**0**	**0**	**1**	**13:00**
	Milwaukee	AHL	25	2	14	16	23	....	....	....	....	....	....	....	....	....	....	....	....	....	....	....	....	....	....
2012-13	Milwaukee	AHL	15	7	5	12	4	....	....	....	....	....	....	....	....	....	....	....	....	....	....	....	....	....	....
	Nashville	**NHL**	**34**	**11**	**5**	**16**	**4**	**3**	**1**	**2**	**50**	**22.0**	**6**	**6**	**66.7**	**15:50**	....	....	....	....	....	....	....	....	....
2013-14	**Nashville**	**NHL**	**74**	**9**	**17**	**26**	**8**	**0**	**0**	**1**	**108**	**8.3**	**–5**	**1**	**0.0**	**13:50**	....	....	....	....	....	....	....	....	....
2014-15	**Nashville**	**NHL**	**69**	**3**	**10**	**13**	**10**	**0**	**0**	**0**	**76**	**3.9**	**–13**	**6**	**50.0**	**12:01**	**5**	**0**	**0**	**0**	**2**	**0**	**0**	**0**	**15:26**
	NHL Totals		**220**	**30**	**44**	**74**	**28**	**3**	**1**	**4**	**293**	**10.2**		**14**	**50.0**	**13:22**	**15**	**3**	**2**	**5**	**6**	**0**	**0**	**1**	**13:48**

BOURQUE, Rene

(BOHRK, reh-NAY) **CBJ**

Right wing. Shoots left. 6'2", 217 lbs. Born, Lac La Biche, AB, December 10, 1981.

Season	Club	League	GP	G	A	Pts	PIM	PP	SH	GW	S	S%	+/-	TF	F%	Min	GP	G	A	Pts	PIM	PP	SH	GW	Min
1998-99	Notre Dame	SMHL	42	22	19	41	84	....	....	....	....	....	....	....	....	....	3	1	0	1	6	....	....	....	....
	Notre Dame	SJHL	5	1	0	0	0	....	....	....	....	....	....	....	....	....	1	0	0	0	0	....	....	....	....
2000-01	U. of Wisconsin	WCHA	32	10	5	15	18	....	....	....	....	....	....	....	....	....	....	....	....	....	....	....	....	....	....
2001-02	U. of Wisconsin	WCHA	38	12	7	19	26	....	....	....	....	....	....	....	....	....	....	....	....	....	....	....	....	....	....
2002-03	U. of Wisconsin	WCHA	40	19	8	27	54	....	....	....	....	....	....	....	....	....	....	....	....	....	....	....	....	....	....
2003-04	U. of Wisconsin	WCHA	42	16	20	36	74	....	....	....	....	....	....	....	....	....	....	....	....	....	....	....	....	....	....
2004-05	Norfolk Admirals	AHL	78	33	27	60	105	....	....	....	....	....	....	....	....	....	6	1	0	1	8	....	....	....	....
2005-06	**Chicago**	**NHL**	**77**	**16**	**18**	**34**	**56**	**4**	**0**	**2**	**180**	**8.9**	**3**	**11**	**36.4**	**15:20**	....	....	....	....	....	....	....	....	....
2006-07	**Chicago**	**NHL**	**44**	**7**	**10**	**17**	**38**	**2**	**1**	**1**	**82**	**8.5**	**–4**	**9**	**22.2**	**16:01**	....	....	....	....	....	....	....	....	....
	Norfolk Admirals	AHL	1	0	0	0	0	....	....	....	....	....	....	....	....	....	....	....	....	....	....	....	....	....	....
2007-08	**Chicago**	**NHL**	**62**	**10**	**14**	**24**	**42**	**0**	**5**	**2**	**103**	**9.7**	**6**	**8**	**25.0**	**15:16**	....	....	....	....	....	....	....	....	....
2008-09	**Calgary**	**NHL**	**58**	**21**	**19**	**40**	**70**	**0**	**1**	**0**	**149**	**14.1**	**18**	**18**	**50.0**	**16:05**	**5**	**1**	**0**	**1**	**22**	**0**	**0**	**0**	**17:06**
2009-10	**Calgary**	**NHL**	**73**	**27**	**31**	**58**	**88**	**6**	**4**	**5**	**215**	**12.6**	**7**	**25**	**32.0**	**18:19**	....	....	....	....	....	....	....	....	....
2010-11	**Calgary**	**NHL**	**80**	**27**	**23**	**50**	**42**	**6**	**1**	**6**	**218**	**12.4**	**–17**	**24**	**29.2**	**17:45**	....	....	....	....	....	....	....	....	....
2011-12	**Calgary**	**NHL**	**38**	**13**	**3**	**16**	**41**	**3**	**0**	**1**	**91**	**14.3**	**–3**	**13**	**69.2**	**17:10**	....	....	....	....	....	....	....	....	....
	Montreal	**NHL**	**38**	**5**	**3**	**8**	**27**	**0**	**1**	**0**	**67**	**7.5**	**–16**	**7**	**42.9**	**18:29**	....	....	....	....	....	....	....	....	....
2012-13	**Montreal**	**NHL**	**27**	**7**	**6**	**13**	**32**	**2**	**0**	**1**	**63**	**11.1**	**–1**	**1**	**0.0**	**16:20**	**5**	**2**	**1**	**3**	**10**	**1**	**0**	**0**	**16:08**
2013-14	**Montreal**	**NHL**	**63**	**9**	**7**	**16**	**32**	**3**	**0**	**2**	**118**	**7.6**	**–1**	**8**	**50.0**	**14:11**	**17**	**8**	**3**	**11**	**27**	**0**	**0**	**2**	**14:40**
2014-15	**Montreal**	**NHL**	**13**	**0**	**2**	**2**	**6**	**0**	**0**	**0**	**18**	**0.0**	**–9**	**5**	**60.0**	**12:21**	....	....	....	....	....	....	....	....	....
	Hamilton	AHL	4	2	2	4	4	....	....	....	....	....	....	....	....	....	....	....	....	....	....	....	....	....	....
	Anaheim	**NHL**	**30**	**2**	**6**	**8**	**12**	**1**	**0**	**0**	**44**	**4.5**	**–4**	**5**	**20.0**	**12:08**	....	....	....	....	....	....	....	....	....
	Columbus	**NHL**	**8**	**4**	**0**	**4**	**4**	**1**	**0**	**1**	**23**	**17.4**	**–2**	**0**	**0.0**	**15:00**	....	....	....	....	....	....	....	....	....
	NHL Totals		**611**	**148**	**142**	**290**	**490**	**28**	**13**	**21**	**1371**	**10.8**		**134**	**38.8**	**16:08**	**27**	**11**	**4**	**15**	**59**	**1**	**0**	**2**	**15:24**

AHL All-Rookie Team (2005) • Dudley "Red" Garrett Memorial Trophy (AHL - Top Rookie) (2005)

Signed as a free agent by **Chicago**, July 29, 2004. Traded to **Calgary** by **Chicago** for Calgary's 2nd round choice (later traded to Toronto – Toronto selected Brad Ross) in 2010 Entry Draft, July 1, 2008. Traded to **Montreal** by **Calgary** with Patrick Holland and Calgary's 2nd round choice (Zachary Fucale) in 2013 Entry Draft for Mike Cammalleri, Karri Ramo and Montreal's 5th round choice (Ryan Culkin) in 2012 Entry Draft, January 12, 2012. Traded to **Anaheim** by **Montreal** for Bryan Allen, November 20, 2014. Traded to **Columbus** by **Anaheim** with William Karlsson and Anaheim's 2nd round choice (Kevin Stenlund) in 2015 Entry Draft for James Wisniewski and Detroit's 3rd round choice (previously acquired, Anaheim selected Brent Gates) in 2015 Entry Draft, March 2, 2015.

BOURQUE, Ryan

(BOHRK, RIGH-uhn) **NYR**

Center. Shoots left. 5'9", 170 lbs. Born, Boxford, MA, January 3, 1991. NY Rangers' 3rd choice, 80th overall, in 2009 Entry Draft.

Season	Club	League	GP	G	A	Pts	PIM	PP	SH	GW	S	S%	+/-	TF	F%	Min	GP	G	A	Pts	PIM	PP	SH	GW	Min
2006-07	Cushing	High-MA	29	19	31	50	....	....	....	....	....	....	....	....	....	....	....	....	....	....	....	....	....	....	....
2007-08	USNTDP	NAHL	34	11	9	20	14	....	....	....	....	....	....	....	....	....	....	....	....	....	....	....	....	....	....
	USNTDP	U-17	7	4	3	7	10	....	....	....	....	....	....	....	....	....	....	....	....	....	....	....	....	....	....
	USNTDP	U-18	27	4	12	16	18	....	....	....	....	....	....	....	....	....	....	....	....	....	....	....	....	....	....
2008-09	USNTDP	NAHL	14	7	9	16	10	....	....	....	....	....	....	....	....	....	....	....	....	....	....	....	....	....	....
	USNTDP	U-18	43	14	24	38	48	....	....	....	....	....	....	....	....	....	....	....	....	....	....	....	....	....	....
2009-10	Quebec Remparts	QMJHL	44	19	24	43	20	....	....	....	....	....	....	....	....	....	9	3	7	10	6	....	....	....	....
2010-11	Quebec Remparts	QMJHL	49	26	33	59	22	....	....	....	....	....	....	....	....	....	18	5	11	16	8	....	....	....	....
2011-12	Connecticut	AHL	69	6	8	14	10	....	....	....	....	....	....	....	....	....	9	2	1	3	4	....	....	....	....
2012-13	Connecticut	AHL	53	8	7	15	11	....	....	....	....	....	....	....	....	....	....	....	....	....	....	....	....	....	....
2013-14	Hartford	AHL	74	21	16	37	22	....	....	....	....	....	....	....	....	....	....	....	....	....	....	....	....	....	....
2014-15	**NY Rangers**	**NHL**	**1**	**0**	**0**	**0**	**0**	**0**	**0**	**0**	**1**	**0.0**	**–1**	**0**	**0.0**	**11:49**	....	....	....	....	....	....	....	....	....
	Hartford	AHL	73	12	20	32	27	....	....	....	....	....	....	....	....	....	5	0	1	1	2	....	....	....	....
	NHL Totals		**1**	**0**	**0**	**0**	**0**	**0**	**0**	**0**	**1**	**0.0**		**0**	**0.0**	**11:49**	....	....	....	....	....	....	....	....	....

BOUWMEESTER, Jay

(BOW-mee-stuhr, JAY) **ST.L.**

Defense. Shoots left. 6'4", 212 lbs. Born, Edmonton, AB, September 27, 1983. Florida's 1st choice, 3rd overall, in 2002 Entry Draft.

Season	Club	League	GP	G	A	Pts	PIM	PP	SH	GW	S	S%	+/-	TF	F%	Min	GP	G	A	Pts	PIM	PP	SH	GW	Min
1998-99	Edmonton SSAC	AMHL	32	14	29	43	36	....	....	....	....	....	....	....	....	....	....	....	....	....	....	....	....	....	....
	Medicine Hat	WHL	8	2	1	3	2	....	....	....	....	....	....	....	....	....	....	....	....	....	....	....	....	....	....
99-2000	Medicine Hat	WHL	64	13	21	34	26	....	....	....	....	....	....	....	....	....	....	....	....	....	....	....	....	....	....
2000-01	Medicine Hat	WHL	61	14	39	53	44	....	....	....	....	....	....	....	....	....	....	....	....	....	....	....	....	....	....
2001-02	Medicine Hat	WHL	61	11	50	61	42	....	....	....	....	....	....	....	....	....	....	....	....	....	....	....	....	....	....
2002-03	**Florida**	**NHL**	**82**	**4**	**12**	**16**	**14**	**2**	**0**	**0**	**110**	**3.6**	**–29**	**0**	**0.0**	**20:09**	....	....	....	....	....	....	....	....	....
2003-04	**Florida**	**NHL**	**61**	**2**	**18**	**20**	**30**	**0**	**0**	**0**	**85**	**2.4**	**–15**	**0**	**0.0**	**23:02**	....	....	....	....	....	....	....	....	....
	San Antonio	AHL	2	0	1	1	2	....	....	....	....	....	....	....	....	....	....	....	....	....	....	....	....	....	....

			Regular Season														Playoffs								
Season	Club	League	GP	G	A	Pts	PIM	PP	SH	GW	S	S%	+/-	TF	F%	Min	GP	G	A	Pts	PIM	PP	SH	GW	Min
2004-05	San Antonio	AHL	64	4	13	17	50	....	....	....	....	....	....	....	....	....	....	....	....	....	....	....	....	....	....
	Chicago Wolves	AHL	18	6	3	9	12	....	....	....	....	....	....	....	....	....	18	0	0	0	14	....	....	....	....
2005-06	Florida	NHL	82	5	41	46	79	0	0	0	189	2.6	1	1	0.0	25:29	....	....	....	....	....	....	....	....	....
	Canada	Olympics	6	0	0	0	0	....	....	....	....	....	....	....	....	....	....	....	....	....	....	....	....	....	....
2006-07	Florida	NHL	82	12	30	42	66	3	0	3	174	6.9	23	0	0.0	26:09	....	....	....	....	....	....	....	....	....
2007-08	Florida	NHL	82	15	22	37	72	4	0	0	182	8.2	–5	0	0.0	27:28	....	....	....	....	....	....	....	....	....
2008-09	Florida	NHL	82	15	27	42	68	9	0	2	182	8.2	–2	0	0.0	26:59	....	....	....	....	....	....	....	....	....
2009-10	Calgary	NHL	82	3	26	29	48	1	0	0	130	2.3	–4	0	0.0	25:55	....	....	....	....	....	....	....	....	....
2010-11	Calgary	NHL	82	4	20	24	44	1	0	1	121	3.3	–2	0	0.0	25:59	....	....	....	....	....	....	....	....	....
2011-12	Calgary	NHL	82	5	24	29	26	2	0	1	107	4.7	–21	0	0.0	25:57	....	....	....	....	....	....	....	....	....
2012-13	Calgary	NHL	33	6	9	15	16	1	0	0	55	10.9	–11	0	0.0	25:10	....	....	....	....	....	....	....	....	....
	St. Louis	NHL	14	1	6	7	6	0	0	0	24	4.2	5	0	0.0	23:24	6	0	1	1	0	0	0	0	25:08
2013-14	St. Louis	NHL	82	4	33	37	20	1	0	0	152	2.6	26	4	75.0	24:03	6	0	1	1	2	0	0	0	25:52
	Canada	Olympics	6	0	1	1	0	....	....	....	....	....	....	....	....	....	....	....	....	....	....	....	....	....	....
2014-15	St. Louis	NHL	72	2	11	13	24	0	0	0	92	2.2	7	0	0.0	22:40	6	0	0	0	2	0	0	0	20:28
	NHL Totals		918	78	279	357	513	24	0	7	1603	4.9		5	60.0	24:57	18	0	2	2	4	0	0	0	23:49

WHL East First All-Star Team (2002) • NHL All-Rookie Team (2003)

Played in NHL All-Star Game (2007, 2009)

• Loaned to **Chicago** (AHL) by **Florida** for cash, March 8, 2005. Traded to **Calgary** by **Florida** for Jordan Leopold and Phoenix's 3rd round choice (previously acquired, Florida selected Josh Birkholz) in 2009 Entry Draft, June 27, 2009. Traded to **St. Louis** by **Calgary** for Mark Cundari, Reto Berra and St. Louis' 1st round choice (Emile Poirier) in 2013 Entry Draft, April 1, 2013.

BOWMAN, Drayson

(BOH-muhn, DRAY-suhn)

Center/Left wing. Shoots left. 6'1", 195 lbs. Born, Grand Rapids, MI, March 8, 1989. Carolina's 2nd choice, 72nd overall, in 2007 Entry Draft.

Season	Club	League	GP	G	A	Pts	PIM	PP	SH	GW	S	S%	+/-	TF	F%	Min	GP	G	A	Pts	PIM	PP	SH	GW	Min
2004-05	Kimberley	KIJHL	47	29	30	59	108	....	....	....	....	....	....	....	....	....	....	....	....	....	....	....	....	....	....
	Spokane Chiefs	WHL	4	0	0	0	0	....	....	....	....	....	....	....	....	....	....	....	....	....	....	....	....	....	....
2005-06	Spokane Chiefs	WHL	72	17	17	34	51	....	....	....	....	....	....	....	....	....	....	....	....	....	....	....	....	....	....
2006-07	Spokane Chiefs	WHL	61	24	19	43	55	....	....	....	....	....	....	....	....	....	6	2	5	7	4	....	....	....	....
2007-08	Spokane Chiefs	WHL	66	42	40	82	62	....	....	....	....	....	....	....	....	....	21	11	9	20	8	....	....	....	....
2008-09	Spokane Chiefs	WHL	62	47	36	83	107	....	....	....	....	....	....	....	....	....	12	8	5	13	8	....	....	....	....
2009-10	Carolina	NHL	9	2	0	2	4	1	0	0	17	11.8	–1	0	0.0	12:01	....	....	....	....	....	....	....	....	....
	Albany River Rats	AHL	56	17	15	32	29	....	....	....	....	....	....	....	....	....	8	3	6	9	12	....	....	....	....
2010-11	Carolina	NHL	23	0	1	1	12	0	0	0	28	0.0	0	0	0.0	9:49	....	....	....	....	....	....	....	....	....
	Charlotte	AHL	51	12	18	30	53	....	....	....	....	....	....	....	....	....	15	2	6	8	6	....	....	....	....
2011-12	Carolina	NHL	37	6	7	13	4	0	0	0	70	8.6	2	0	0.0	13:21	....	....	....	....	....	....	....	....	....
	Charlotte	AHL	42	13	13	26	45	....	....	....	....	....	....	....	....	....	....	....	....	....	....	....	....	....	....
2012-13	Charlotte	AHL	37	14	8	22	21	....	....	....	....	....	....	....	....	....	....	....	....	....	....	....	....	....	....
	Carolina	NHL	37	3	2	5	17	0	0	0	68	4.4	–7	10	40.0	11:42	....	....	....	....	....	....	....	....	....
2013-14	Carolina	NHL	70	4	8	12	16	0	0	0	80	5.0	–2	10	60.0	10:21	....	....	....	....	....	....	....	....	....
2014-15	Montreal	NHL	3	0	0	0	0	0	0	0	0	0.0	0	0	0.0	6:31	....	....	....	....	....	....	....	....	....
	Hamilton	AHL	62	14	19	33	33	....	....	....	....	....	....	....	....	....	....	....	....	....	....	....	....	....	....
	NHL Totals		179	15	18	33	53	1	0	0	263	5.7		20	50.0	11:12	....	....	....	....	....	....	....	....	....

WHL West Second All-Star Team (2008, 2009) • Memorial Cup All-Star Team (2008)

Signed as a free agent by **Montreal**, October 2, 2014.

BOYCHUK, Johnny

(BOY-chuhk, JAW-nee) **NYI**

Defense. Shoots right. 6'2", 225 lbs. Born, Edmonton, AB, January 19, 1984. Colorado's 2nd choice, 61st overall, in 2002 Entry Draft.

Season	Club	League	GP	G	A	Pts	PIM	PP	SH	GW	S	S%	+/-	TF	F%	Min	GP	G	A	Pts	PIM	PP	SH	GW	Min
1998-99	Edm. Cycle	AMBHL	36	8	20	28	59	....	....	....	....	....	....	....	....	....	....	....	....	....	....	....	....	....	....
99-2000	Edm. Cycle	AMHL	35	6	17	23	59	....	....	....	....	....	....	....	....	....	....	....	....	....	....	....	....	....	....
	Calgary Hitmen	WHL	1	0	0	0	0	....	....	....	....	....	....	....	....	....	....	....	....	....	....	....	....	....	....
2000-01	Calgary Hitmen	WHL	66	4	8	12	61	....	....	....	....	....	....	....	....	....	12	1	1	2	17	....	....	....	....
2001-02	Calgary Hitmen	WHL	70	8	32	40	85	....	....	....	....	....	....	....	....	....	7	1	1	2	6	....	....	....	....
2002-03	Calgary Hitmen	WHL	40	8	18	26	58	....	....	....	....	....	....	....	....	....	....	....	....	....	....	....	....	....	....
	Moose Jaw	WHL	27	5	17	22	32	....	....	....	....	....	....	....	....	....	13	2	6	8	29	....	....	....	....
2003-04	Moose Jaw	WHL	62	13	20	33	71	....	....	....	....	....	....	....	....	....	10	1	9	10	9	....	....	....	....
2004-05	Hershey Bears	AHL	80	3	12	15	69	....	....	....	....	....	....	....	....	....	....	....	....	....	....	....	....	....	....
2005-06	Lowell	AHL	74	6	26	32	73	....	....	....	....	....	....	....	....	....	....	....	....	....	....	....	....	....	....
2006-07	Albany River Rats	AHL	80	10	18	28	125	....	....	....	....	....	....	....	....	....	5	1	1	2	4	....	....	....	....
2007-08	Colorado	NHL	4	0	0	0	0	0	0	0	3	0.0	1	1	0.0	8:57	....	....	....	....	....	....	....	....	....
	Lake Erie	AHL	60	8	18	26	63	....	....	....	....	....	....	....	....	....	....	....	....	....	....	....	....	....	....
2008-09	Boston	NHL	1	0	0	0	0	0	0	0	0	0.0	0	0	0.0	14:48	....	....	....	....	....	....	....	....	....
	Providence Bruins	AHL	78	20	46	66	61	....	....	....	....	....	....	....	....	....	16	3	5	8	19	....	....	....	....
2009-10	Boston	NHL	51	5	10	15	43	0	0	0	96	5.2	10	0	0.0	17:39	13	2	4	6	6	1	0	0	26:10
	Providence Bruins	AHL	2	1	0	1	0	....	....	....	....	....	....	....	....	....	....	....	....	....	....	....	....	....	....
2010-11 •	Boston	NHL	69	3	13	16	45	1	0	1	154	1.9	15	0	0.0	20:30	25	3	6	9	12	0	0	1	20:38
2011-12	Boston	NHL	77	5	10	15	53	0	0	2	171	2.9	27	0	0.0	20:37	7	1	2	3	4	1	0	0	22:16
2012-13	Salzburg	Austria	15	2	6	8	2	....	....	....	....	....	....	....	....	....	....	....	....	....	....	....	....	....	....
	Boston	NHL	44	1	5	6	12	0	0	0	75	1.3	5	0	0.0	20:24	22	6	1	7	10	0	0	1	23:56
2013-14	Boston	NHL	75	5	18	23	45	0	0	1	142	3.5	31	0	0.0	21:12	12	1	1	2	2	0	0	0	22:17
2014-15	NY Islanders	NHL	72	9	26	35	14	5	0	1	192	4.7	15	2	100.0	21:41	7	0	2	2	2	0	0	0	26:00
	NHL Totals		393	28	82	110	212	6	0	5	833	3.4		3	66.7	20:22	86	13	16	29	36	2	0	2	23:07

AHL First All-Star Team (2009) • Eddie Shore Award (AHL – Outstanding Defenseman) (2009)

Traded to **Boston** by **Colorado** for Matt Hendricks, June 24, 2008. Signed as a free agent by **Salzburg** (Austria), November 16, 2012. Traded to **NY Islanders** by **Boston** for Philadelphia's 2nd round choice (previously acquired, Boston selected Brandon Carlo) in 2015 Entry Draft and future considerations, October 4, 2014.

BOYCHUK, Zach

(BOY-chuhk, ZAK) **CAR**

Center. Shoots left. 5'10", 185 lbs. Born, Airdrie, AB, October 4, 1989. Carolina's 1st choice, 14th overall, in 2008 Entry Draft.

Season	Club	League	GP	G	A	Pts	PIM	PP	SH	GW	S	S%	+/-	TF	F%	Min	GP	G	A	Pts	PIM	PP	SH	GW	Min
2004-05	UFA Bisons	AMHL	36	13	14	27	18	....	....	....	....	....	....	....	....	....	16	10	5	15	....	....	....	....	....
2005-06	Lethbridge	WHL	64	18	33	51	30	....	....	....	....	....	....	....	....	....	6	0	5	5	2	....	....	....	....
2006-07	Lethbridge	WHL	69	31	60	91	52	....	....	....	....	....	....	....	....	....	....	....	....	....	....	....	....	....	....
2007-08	Lethbridge	WHL	61	33	39	72	80	....	....	....	....	....	....	....	....	....	18	*13	8	21	6	....	....	....	....
2008-09	Carolina	NHL	2	0	0	0	0	0	0	0	0	0.0	0	1	0.0	12:03	....	....	....	....	....	....	....	....	....
	Lethbridge	WHL	43	28	29	57	22	....	....	....	....	....	....	....	....	....	11	7	6	13	12	....	....	....	....
	Albany River Rats	AHL	2	0	1	1	2	....	....	....	....	....	....	....	....	....	....	....	....	....	....	....	....	....	....
2009-10	Carolina	NHL	31	3	6	9	2	0	0	0	37	8.1	1	9	55.6	10:45	....	....	....	....	....	....	....	....	....
	Albany River Rats	AHL	52	15	21	36	24	....	....	....	....	....	....	....	....	....	8	2	3	5	4	....	....	....	....
2010-11	Carolina	NHL	23	4	3	7	4	1	0	1	44	9.1	–2	5	20.0	10:43	....	....	....	....	....	....	....	....	....
	Charlotte	AHL	60	22	43	65	48	....	....	....	....	....	....	....	....	....	16	3	6	9	14	....	....	....	....
2011-12	Carolina	NHL	16	0	2	2	0	0	0	0	10	0.0	–3	4	50.0	8:55	....	....	....	....	....	....	....	....	....
	Charlotte	AHL	64	21	23	44	46	....	....	....	....	....	....	....	....	....	....	....	....	....	....	....	....	....	....
2012-13	Charlotte	AHL	49	23	20	43	16	....	....	....	....	....	....	....	....	....	5	3	3	6	4	....	....	....	....
	Carolina	NHL	1	0	0	0	0	0	0	0	0	0.0	0	0	0.0	10:13	....	....	....	....	....	....	....	....	....
	Pittsburgh	NHL	7	0	0	0	2	0	0	0	6	0.0	–2	0	0.0	11:37	....	....	....	....	....	....	....	....	....
	Nashville	NHL	5	1	1	2	4	0	0	0	8	12.5	1	0	0.0	13:42	....	....	....	....	....	....	....	....	....
2013-14	Carolina	NHL	11	1	3	4	0	0	0	0	15	6.7	2	1	0.0	10:12	....	....	....	....	....	....	....	....	....
	Charlotte	AHL	69	*36	38	74	55	....	....	....	....	....	....	....	....	....	....	....	....	....	....	....	....	....	....
2014-15	Carolina	NHL	31	3	3	6	4	0	0	0	35	8.6	0	0	0.0	10:38	....	....	....	....	....	....	....	....	....
	Charlotte	AHL	39	12	12	24	14	....	....	....	....	....	....	....	....	....	....	....	....	....	....	....	....	....	....
	NHL Totals		127	12	18	30	16	1	0	1	155	7.7		20	40.0	10:37	....	....	....	....	....	....	....	....	....

WHL East Second All-Star Team (2007, 2008) • AHL Second All-Star Team (2014) • Willie Marshall Award (AHL – Top Goal-scorer) (2014)

Claimed on waivers by **Pittsburgh** from **Carolina**, January 29, 2013. Claimed on waivers by **Nashville** from **Pittsburgh**, March 5, 2013. Signed as a free agent by **Carolina**, August 20, 2013.

BOYES, Brad

(BOIZ, BRAD)

Right wing. Shoots right. 6', 195 lbs. Born, Mississauga, ON, April 17, 1982. Toronto's 1st choice, 24th overall, in 2000 Entry Draft.

			Regular Season														Playoffs								
Season	Club	League	GP	G	A	Pts	PIM	PP	SH	GW	S	S%	+/-	TF	F%	Min	GP	G	A	Pts	PIM	PP	SH	GW	Min
1997-98	Mississauga Reps	MTHL	44	27	50	77	....	....	....	....	....	....	....	....	....	....	....	....	....	....	....	....	....	....	....
1998-99	Erie Otters	OHL	59	24	36	60	30	....	....	....	....	....	....	....	....	....	5	1	2	3	10	....	....	....	....
99-2000	Erie Otters	OHL	68	36	46	82	38	....	....	....	....	....	....	....	....	....	13	6	8	14	10	....	....	....	....
2000-01	Erie Otters	OHL	59	45	45	90	42	....	....	....	....	....	....	....	....	....	15	10	13	23	8	....	....	....	....
2001-02	Erie Otters	OHL	47	36	41	77	42	....	....	....	....	....	....	....	....	....	21	22	*19	41	27	....	....	....	....
2002-03	St. John's	AHL	65	23	28	51	45	....	....	....	....	....	....	....	....	....	....	....	....	....	....	....	....	....	....
	Cleveland Barons	AHL	15	7	6	13	21	....	....	....	....	....	....	....	....	....	....	....	....	....	....	....	....	....	....
2003-04	**San Jose**	**NHL**	**1**	**0**	**0**	**0**	**2**	**0**	**0**	**0**	**0**	**0.0**	**–2**	**0**	**0.0**	**13:03**	....	....	....	....	....	....	....	....	....
	Cleveland Barons	AHL	61	25	35	60	38	....	....	....	....	....	....	....	....	....	....	....	....	....	....	....	....	....	....
	Providence Bruins	AHL	17	6	6	12	13	....	....	....	....	....	....	....	....	....	2	1	0	1	0	....	....	....	....
2004-05	Providence Bruins	AHL	80	33	42	75	58	....	....	....	....	....	....	....	....	....	16	8	7	15	23	....	....	....	....
2005-06	**Boston**	**NHL**	**82**	**26**	**43**	**69**	**30**	**8**	**0**	**3**	**203**	**12.8**	**11**	**265**	**53.6**	**15:46**	....	....	....	....	....	....	....	....	....
2006-07	**Boston**	**NHL**	**62**	**13**	**21**	**34**	**25**	**1**	**1**	**1**	**139**	**9.4**	**–17**	**220**	**44.1**	**16:04**	....	....	....	....	....	....	....	....	....
	St. Louis	**NHL**	**19**	**4**	**8**	**12**	**4**	**0**	**0**	**1**	**43**	**9.3**	**0**	**93**	**58.1**	**17:25**	....	....	....	....	....	....	....	....	....
2007-08	**St. Louis**	**NHL**	**82**	**43**	**22**	**65**	**20**	**11**	**0**	**9**	**207**	**20.8**	**1**	**236**	**44.5**	**17:57**	....	....	....	....	....	....	....	....	....
2008-09	**St. Louis**	**NHL**	**82**	**33**	**39**	**72**	**26**	**16**	**0**	**11**	**220**	**15.0**	**–20**	**315**	**49.2**	**19:08**	**4**	**2**	**1**	**3**	**0**	**1**	**0**	**0**	**21:34**
2009-10	**St. Louis**	**NHL**	**82**	**14**	**28**	**42**	**26**	**2**	**0**	**3**	**197**	**7.1**	**1**	**311**	**44.4**	**16:47**	....	....	....	....	....	....	....	....	....
2010-11	**St. Louis**	**NHL**	**62**	**12**	**29**	**41**	**30**	**4**	**0**	**2**	**132**	**9.1**	**11**	**135**	**41.5**	**17:10**	....	....	....	....	....	....	....	....	....
	Buffalo	**NHL**	**21**	**5**	**9**	**14**	**6**	**2**	**0**	**1**	**46**	**10.9**	**2**	**185**	**43.2**	**16:28**	**7**	**1**	**0**	**1**	**0**	**1**	**0**	**0**	**14:23**
2011-12	**Buffalo**	**NHL**	**65**	**8**	**15**	**23**	**6**	**2**	**0**	**0**	**100**	**8.0**	**2**	**267**	**47.2**	**13:10**	....	....	....	....	....	....	....	....	....
2012-13	**NY Islanders**	**NHL**	**48**	**10**	**25**	**35**	**16**	**1**	**0**	**1**	**97**	**10.3**	**–6**	**16**	**25.0**	**18:13**	**6**	**0**	**3**	**3**	**2**	**0**	**0**	**0**	**19:06**
2013-14	**Florida**	**NHL**	**78**	**21**	**15**	**36**	**28**	**2**	**1**	**1**	**176**	**11.9**	**–6**	**69**	**53.6**	**17:03**	....	....	....	....	....	....	....	....	....
2014-15	**Florida**	**NHL**	**78**	**14**	**24**	**38**	**20**	**5**	**0**	**4**	**151**	**9.3**	**11**	**173**	**56.1**	**15:39**	....	....	....	....	....	....	....	....	....
	NHL Totals		**762**	**203**	**278**	**481**	**239**	**54**	**2**	**37**	**1711**	**11.9**		**2285**	**47.7**	**16:43**	**17**	**3**	**4**	**7**	**2**	**2**	**0**	**0**	**17:44**

Canadian Major Junior Scholastic Player of the Year (2000) • OHL Second All-Star Team (2001) • OHL First All-Star Team (2002) • OHL Playoff MVP (2002) • Canadian Major Junior Second All-Star Team (2002) • Canadian Major Junior Sportsman of the Year (2002) • AHL All-Rookie Team (2003) • AHL Second All-Star Team (2004) • NHL All-Rookie Team (2006)

Traded to **San Jose** by **Toronto** with Alyn McCauley and Toronto's 1st round choice (later traded to Boston – Boston selected Mark Stuart) in 2003 Entry Draft for Owen Nolan, March 5, 2003. Traded to **Boston** by **San Jose** for Jeff Jillson, March 9, 2004. Traded to **St. Louis** by **Boston** for Dennis Wideman, February 27, 2007. Traded to **Buffalo** by **St. Louis** for Buffalo's 2nd round choice (Joel Edmundson) in 2011 Entry Draft, February 27, 2011. Signed as a free agent by **NY Islanders**, July 1, 2012. Signed as a free agent by **Florida**, September 29, 2013.

BOYLE, Brian

(BOIL, BRIGH-uhn) **T.B.**

Center. Shoots left. 6'7", 244 lbs. Born, Hingham, MA, December 18, 1984. Los Angeles' 2nd choice, 26th overall, in 2003 Entry Draft.

			Regular Season														Playoffs								
Season	Club	League	GP	G	A	Pts	PIM	PP	SH	GW	S	S%	+/-	TF	F%	Min	GP	G	A	Pts	PIM	PP	SH	GW	Min
2000-01	St. Sebastian's	High-MA	25	20	19	39	23	....	....	....	....	....	....	....	....	....	....	....	....	....	....	....	....	....	....
2001-02	St. Sebastian's	High-MA	28	21	26	47	22	....	....	....	....	....	....	....	....	....	....	....	....	....	....	....	....	....	....
2002-03	St. Sebastian's	High-MA	31	32	31	62	46	....	....	....	....	....	....	....	....	....	....	....	....	....	....	....	....	....	....
2003-04	Boston College	H-East	35	5	3	8	36	....	....	....	....	....	....	....	....	....	....	....	....	....	....	....	....	....	....
2004-05	Boston College	H-East	40	19	8	27	64	....	....	....	....	....	....	....	....	....	....	....	....	....	....	....	....	....	....
2005-06	Boston College	H-East	42	22	*30	52	90	....	....	....	....	....	....	....	....	....	....	....	....	....	....	....	....	....	....
2006-07	Boston College	H-East	42	19	*34	*53	*104	....	....	....	....	....	....	....	....	....	....	....	....	....	....	....	....	....	....
	Manchester	AHL	2	0	0	0	2	....	....	....	....	....	....	....	....	....	16	3	5	8	13	....	....	....	....
2007-08	**Los Angeles**	**NHL**	**8**	**4**	**1**	**5**	**4**	**0**	**0**	**0**	**19**	**21.1**	**4**	**80**	**46.3**	**13:38**	....	....	....	....	....	....	....	....	....
	Manchester	AHL	70	31	31	62	87	....	....	....	....	....	....	....	....	....	....	....	....	....	....	....	....	....	....
2008-09	**Los Angeles**	**NHL**	**28**	**4**	**1**	**5**	**42**	**0**	**0**	**1**	**36**	**11.1**	**–9**	**225**	**45.3**	**10:08**	....	....	....	....	....	....	....	....	....
	Manchester	AHL	42	10	11	21	73	....	....	....	....	....	....	....	....	....	....	....	....	....	....	....	....	....	....
2009-10	**NY Rangers**	**NHL**	**71**	**4**	**2**	**6**	**47**	**0**	**0**	**1**	**73**	**5.5**	**–6**	**323**	**38.7**	**8:25**	....	....	....	....	....	....	....	....	....
2010-11	**NY Rangers**	**NHL**	**82**	**21**	**14**	**35**	**74**	**4**	**1**	**2**	**218**	**9.6**	**2**	**1101**	**48.5**	**15:44**	**5**	**0**	**0**	**0**	**6**	**0**	**0**	**0**	**21:30**
2011-12	**NY Rangers**	**NHL**	**82**	**11**	**15**	**26**	**59**	**0**	**0**	**2**	**165**	**6.7**	**2**	**1215**	**51.8**	**15:14**	**17**	**3**	**3**	**6**	**15**	**0**	**0**	**2**	**16:44**
2012-13	**NY Rangers**	**NHL**	**38**	**2**	**3**	**5**	**29**	**0**	**0**	**1**	**56**	**3.6**	**–13**	**381**	**56.4**	**14:13**	**11**	**3**	**2**	**5**	**2**	**1**	**0**	**0**	**18:50**
2013-14	**NY Rangers**	**NHL**	**82**	**6**	**12**	**18**	**56**	**1**	**0**	**1**	**137**	**4.4**	**1**	**578**	**52.9**	**12:46**	**25**	**3**	**5**	**8**	**19**	**0**	**1**	**0**	**13:18**
2014-15	**Tampa Bay**	**NHL**	**82**	**15**	**9**	**24**	**54**	**0**	**3**	**5**	**140**	**10.7**	**3**	**905**	**50.8**	**13:00**	**25**	**1**	**1**	**2**	**10**	**0**	**1**	**0**	**13:40**
	NHL Totals		**473**	**67**	**57**	**124**	**365**	**5**	**4**	**13**	**844**	**7.9**		**4808**	**50.1**	**13:04**	**83**	**10**	**11**	**21**	**52**	**1**	**2**	**2**	**15:20**

Hockey East First All-Star Team (2006, 2007) • NCAA East Second All-American Team (2006) • NCAA East First All-American Team (2007) • NCAA Championship All-Tournament Team (2007) • AHL All-Rookie Team (2008)

Traded to **NY Rangers** by **Los Angeles** for NY Rangers' 3rd round choice (Jordan Weal) in 2010 Entry Draft, June 27, 2009. Signed as a free agent by **Tampa Bay**, July 1, 2014.

BOYLE, Dan

(BOIL, DAN) **NYR**

Defense. Shoots right. 5'11", 190 lbs. Born, Ottawa, ON, July 12, 1976.

			Regular Season														Playoffs								
Season	Club	League	GP	G	A	Pts	PIM	PP	SH	GW	S	S%	+/-	TF	F%	Min	GP	G	A	Pts	PIM	PP	SH	GW	Min
1992-93	Gloucester	ON-Jr.A	55	22	51	73	60	....	....	....	....	....	....	....	....	....	5	0	4	4	12	....	....	....	....
1993-94	Gloucester	ON-Jr.A	53	27	54	81	155	....	....	....	....	....	....	....	....	....	15	9	17	26	36	....	....	....	....
1994-95	Miami U.	CCHA	35	8	18	26	24	....	....	....	....	....	....	....	....	....	....	....	....	....	....	....	....	....	....
1995-96	Miami U.	CCHA	36	7	20	27	70	....	....	....	....	....	....	....	....	....	....	....	....	....	....	....	....	....	....
1996-97	Miami U.	CCHA	40	11	43	54	52	....	....	....	....	....	....	....	....	....	....	....	....	....	....	....	....	....	....
1997-98	Miami U.	CCHA	37	14	26	40	58	....	....	....	....	....	....	....	....	....	....	....	....	....	....	....	....	....	....
1998-99	**Florida**	**NHL**	**22**	**3**	**5**	**8**	**6**	**1**	**0**	**1**	**31**	**9.7**	**0**	**1**	**100.0**	**18:50**	....	....	....	....	....	....	....	....	....
	Kentucky	AHL	53	8	34	42	87	....	....	....	....	....	....	....	....	....	12	3	5	8	16	....	....	....	....
99-2000	**Florida**	**NHL**	**13**	**0**	**3**	**3**	**4**	**0**	**0**	**0**	**9**	**0.0**	**–2**	**0**	**0.0**	**16:57**	....	....	....	....	....	....	....	....	....
	Louisville Panthers	AHL	58	14	38	52	75	....	....	....	....	....	....	....	....	....	4	0	2	2	8	....	....	....	....
2000-01	**Florida**	**NHL**	**69**	**4**	**18**	**22**	**28**	**1**	**0**	**0**	**83**	**4.8**	**–14**	**0**	**0.0**	**16:56**	....	....	....	....	....	....	....	....	....
	Louisville Panthers	AHL	6	0	5	5	12	....	....	....	....	....	....	....	....	....	....	....	....	....	....	....	....	....	....
2001-02	**Florida**	**NHL**	**25**	**3**	**3**	**6**	**12**	**1**	**0**	**0**	**31**	**9.7**	**–1**	**2**	**50.0**	**15:40**	....	....	....	....	....	....	....	....	....
	Tampa Bay	**NHL**	**41**	**5**	**15**	**20**	**27**	**2**	**0**	**1**	**68**	**7.4**	**–15**	**0**	**0.0**	**22:28**	....	....	....	....	....	....	....	....	....
2002-03	**Tampa Bay**	**NHL**	**77**	**13**	**40**	**53**	**44**	**8**	**0**	**1**	**136**	**9.6**	**9**	**2**	**0.0**	**24:31**	**11**	**0**	**7**	**7**	**6**	**0**	**0**	**0**	**27:45**
2003-04 ♦	**Tampa Bay**	**NHL**	**78**	**9**	**30**	**39**	**60**	**3**	**0**	**2**	**137**	**6.6**	**23**	**0**	**0.0**	**22:46**	**23**	**2**	**8**	**10**	**16**	**1**	**0**	**0**	**21:27**
2004-05	Djurgarden	Sweden	32	9	9	18	47	....	....	....	....	....	....	....	....	....	12	2	3	5	26	....	....	....	....
2005-06	**Tampa Bay**	**NHL**	**79**	**15**	**38**	**53**	**38**	**6**	**0**	**4**	**153**	**9.8**	**–8**	**1**	**0.0**	**23:26**	**5**	**1**	**3**	**4**	**6**	**0**	**0**	**0**	**25:54**
	Canada	Olympics	DID NOT PLAY																						
2006-07	**Tampa Bay**	**NHL**	**82**	**20**	**43**	**63**	**62**	**10**	**1**	**4**	**203**	**9.9**	**–5**	**1**	**0.0**	**27:03**	**6**	**0**	**1**	**1**	**2**	**0**	**0**	**0**	**28:03**
2007-08	**Tampa Bay**	**NHL**	**37**	**4**	**21**	**25**	**57**	**2**	**0**	**1**	**74**	**5.4**	**–29**	**0**	**0.0**	**27:24**	....	....	....	....	....	....	....	....	....
2008-09	**San Jose**	**NHL**	**77**	**16**	**41**	**57**	**52**	**8**	**0**	**4**	**213**	**7.5**	**6**	**1**	**0.0**	**24:46**	**6**	**2**	**2**	**4**	**8**	**1**	**0**	**0**	**23:17**
2009-10	**San Jose**	**NHL**	**76**	**15**	**43**	**58**	**70**	**6**	**0**	**3**	**180**	**8.3**	**6**	**3**	**0.0**	**26:13**	**15**	**2**	**12**	**14**	**8**	**1**	**0**	**0**	**27:11**
	Canada	Olympics	7	1	5	6	2	....	....	....	....	....	....	....	....	....	....	....	....	....	....	....	....	....	....
2010-11	**San Jose**	**NHL**	**76**	**9**	**41**	**50**	**67**	**4**	**0**	**2**	**199**	**4.5**	**2**	**2**	**0.0**	**26:14**	**18**	**4**	**12**	**16**	**8**	**2**	**0**	**1**	**26:10**
2011-12	**San Jose**	**NHL**	**81**	**9**	**39**	**48**	**57**	**3**	**0**	**2**	**252**	**3.6**	**10**	**0**	**0.0**	**25:35**	**5**	**0**	**2**	**2**	**4**	**0**	**0**	**0**	**28:23**
2012-13	**San Jose**	**NHL**	**46**	**7**	**13**	**20**	**27**	**5**	**0**	**0**	**97**	**7.2**	**3**	**0**	**0.0**	**22:48**	**11**	**3**	**5**	**8**	**2**	**1**	**0**	**1**	**22:12**
2013-14	**San Jose**	**NHL**	**75**	**12**	**24**	**36**	**32**	**6**	**0**	**1**	**154**	**7.8**	**–8**	**0**	**0.0**	**21:17**	**7**	**0**	**4**	**4**	**8**	**0**	**0**	**0**	**21:52**
2014-15	**NY Rangers**	**NHL**	**65**	**9**	**11**	**20**	**20**	**3**	**0**	**3**	**116**	**7.8**	**18**	**0**	**0.0**	**20:15**	**19**	**3**	**7**	**10**	**2**	**1**	**0**	**1**	**19:48**
	NHL Totals		**1019**	**153**	**428**	**581**	**663**	**69**	**1**	**29**	**2136**	**7.2**		**13**	**15.4**	**23:21**	**126**	**17**	**63**	**80**	**70**	**7**	**0**	**3**	**24:03**

CCHA First All-Star Team (1997, 1998) • NCAA West First All-American Team (1997, 1998) • AHL All-Rookie Team (1999) • AHL Second All-Star Team (1999, 2000) • NHL Second All-Star Team (2007, 2009)

Played in NHL All-Star Game (2009, 2011)

Signed as a free agent by **Florida**, March 30, 1998. Traded to **Tampa Bay** by **Florida** for Tampa Bay's 5th round choice (Martin Tuma) in 2003 Entry Draft, January 7, 2002. Signed as a free agent by **Djurgarden** (Sweden), November 14, 2004. • Missed majority of 2007-08 due to off-ice wrist injury, September 22, 2007 and resulting surgery, November 6, 2007. Traded to **San Jose** by **Tampa Bay** with Brad Lukowich for Matt Carle, Ty Wishart, San Jose's 1st round choice (later traded to Ottawa, later traded to NY Islanders, later traded to Columbus, later traded to Anaheim - Anaheim selected Kyle Palmieri) in 2009 Entry Draft and San Jose's 4th round choice (James Mullin) in 2010 Entry Draft, July 4, 2008. Traded to **NY Islanders** by **San Jose** for NY Islanders' 5th round choice (Rudolfs Balcers) in 2015 Entry Draft, June 5, 2014. Signed as a free agent by **NY Rangers**, July 1, 2014.

BOZAK, Tyler
(BOH-zak, TIGH-luhr) **TOR**

Center. Shoots right. 6'1", 195 lbs. Born, Regina, SK, March 19, 1986.

			Regular Season														Playoffs								
Season	Club	League	GP	G	A	Pts	PIM	PP	SH	GW	S	S%	+/-	TF	F%	Min	GP	G	A	Pts	PIM	PP	SH	GW	Min
2003-04	Reg. Pat Cdns.	SMHL	42	17	19	36	40	....	....	....	....	....	....	....	....	....	....	....	....	....	....	....	....	....	....
2004-05	Victoria Salsa	BCHL	55	15	16	31	24	....	....	....	....	....	....	....	....	....	5	0	2	2	2	....	....	....	....
2005-06	Victoria Salsa	BCHL	56	31	38	69	26	....	....	....	....	....	....	....	....	....	16	8	8	16	14	....	....	....	....
2006-07	Victoria Grizzlies	BCHL	59	45	83	128	45	....	....	....	....	....	....	....	....	....	11	4	9	13	6	....	....	....	....
2007-08	U. of Denver	WCHA	41	18	16	34	22	....	....	....	....	....	....	....	....	....	....	....	....	....	....	....	....	....	....
2008-09	U. of Denver	WCHA	19	8	15	23	10	....	....	....	....	....	....	....	....	....	....	....	....	....	....	....	....	....	....
2009-10	**Toronto**	**NHL**	**37**	**8**	**19**	**27**	**6**	**2**	**0**	**1**	**51**	**15.7**	**–5**	**648**	**55.3**	**19:14**	....	....	....	....	....	....	....	....	....
	Toronto Marlies	AHL	32	4	16	20	6	....	....	....	....	....	....	....	....	....	....	....	....	....	....	....	....	....	....
2010-11	**Toronto**	**NHL**	**82**	**15**	**17**	**32**	**14**	**6**	**1**	**4**	**120**	**12.5**	**–29**	**1441**	**54.6**	**19:17**	....	....	....	....	....	....	....	....	....
2011-12	**Toronto**	**NHL**	**73**	**18**	**29**	**47**	**22**	**4**	**0**	**1**	**109**	**16.5**	**–7**	**1198**	**52.7**	**18:51**	....	....	....	....	....	....	....	....	....
2012-13	**Toronto**	**NHL**	**46**	**12**	**16**	**28**	**6**	**4**	**1**	**3**	**61**	**19.7**	**–1**	**1063**	**52.6**	**20:19**	**5**	**1**	**1**	**2**	**4**	**0**	**1**	**0**	**21:44**
2013-14	**Toronto**	**NHL**	**58**	**19**	**30**	**49**	**14**	**5**	**1**	**1**	**90**	**21.1**	**2**	**1399**	**48.7**	**20:57**	....	....	....	....	....	....	....	....	....
2014-15	**Toronto**	**NHL**	**82**	**23**	**26**	**49**	**44**	**12**	**2**	**3**	**154**	**14.9**	**–34**	**1775**	**53.2**	**19:09**	....	....	....	....	....	....	....	....	....
	NHL Totals		**378**	**95**	**137**	**232**	**106**	**33**	**5**	**13**	**585**	**16.2**		**7524**	**52.6**	**19:33**	**5**	**1**	**1**	**2**	**4**	**0**	**1**	**0**	**21:44**

WCHA All-Rookie Team (2008)

Signed as a free agent by **Toronto**, April 3, 2009.

BRASSARD, Derick
(bruh-SAHRD, DAIR-ihk) **NYR**

Center. Shoots left. 6'1", 202 lbs. Born, Hull, QC, September 22, 1987. Columbus' 1st choice, 6th overall, in 2006 Entry Draft.

Season	Club	League	GP	G	A	Pts	PIM	PP	SH	GW	S	S%	+/-	TF	F%	Min	GP	G	A	Pts	PIM	PP	SH	GW	Min
2002-03	Gatineau	QAAA	42	7	33	40	38	....	....	....	....	....	....	....	....	....	5	0	1	1	2	....	....	....	....
2003-04	Gatineau	QAAA	29	19	47	66	104	....	....	....	....	....	....	....	....	....	4	3	7	10	6	....	....	....	....
	Drummondville	QMJHL	10	0	1	1	0	....	....	....	....	....	....	....	....	....	7	0	0	0	0	....	....	....	....
2004-05	Drummondville	QMJHL	69	25	51	76	25	....	....	....	....	....	....	....	....	....	6	1	5	6	6	....	....	....	....
2005-06	Drummondville	QMJHL	58	44	72	116	92	....	....	....	....	....	....	....	....	....	7	5	4	9	10	....	....	....	....
2006-07	Drummondville	QMJHL	14	6	19	25	24	....	....	....	....	....	....	....	....	....	12	9	15	24	12	....	....	....	....
2007-08	**Columbus**	**NHL**	**17**	**1**	**1**	**2**	**6**	**0**	**0**	**0**	**13**	**7.7**	**–4**	**80**	**42.5**	**9:03**	....	....	....	....	....	....	....	....	....
	Syracuse Crunch	AHL	42	15	36	51	51	....	....	....	....	....	....	....	....	....	13	4	9	13	10	....	....	....	....
2008-09	**Columbus**	**NHL**	**31**	**10**	**15**	**25**	**17**	**3**	**0**	**1**	**59**	**16.9**	**12**	**332**	**48.5**	**14:25**	....	....	....	....	....	....	....	....	....
2009-10	**Columbus**	**NHL**	**79**	**9**	**27**	**36**	**48**	**4**	**0**	**0**	**125**	**7.2**	**–17**	**503**	**41.8**	**14:57**	....	....	....	....	....	....	....	....	....
2010-11	**Columbus**	**NHL**	**74**	**17**	**30**	**47**	**55**	**6**	**0**	**3**	**183**	**9.3**	**–11**	**888**	**46.6**	**17:02**	....	....	....	....	....	....	....	....	....
2011-12	**Columbus**	**NHL**	**74**	**14**	**27**	**41**	**42**	**5**	**0**	**3**	**125**	**11.2**	**–20**	**617**	**45.1**	**16:20**	....	....	....	....	....	....	....	....	....
2012-13	Salzburg	Austria	6	4	1	5	6	....	....	....	....	....	....	....	....	....	....	....	....	....	....	....	....	....	....
	Columbus	**NHL**	**34**	**7**	**11**	**18**	**16**	**1**	**0**	**1**	**63**	**11.1**	**–2**	**283**	**45.6**	**16:32**	....	....	....	....	....	....	....	....	....
	NY Rangers	**NHL**	**13**	**5**	**6**	**11**	**0**	**2**	**0**	**0**	**25**	**20.0**	**3**	**163**	**52.8**	**16:38**	**12**	**2**	**10**	**12**	**2**	**1**	**0**	**1**	**18:55**
2013-14	**NY Rangers**	**NHL**	**81**	**18**	**27**	**45**	**46**	**7**	**0**	**4**	**159**	**11.3**	**2**	**977**	**48.0**	**15:48**	**23**	**6**	**6**	**12**	**8**	**0**	**0**	**2**	**15:47**
2014-15	**NY Rangers**	**NHL**	**80**	**19**	**41**	**60**	**34**	**6**	**0**	**3**	**168**	**11.3**	**9**	**1376**	**48.8**	**17:24**	**19**	**9**	**7**	**16**	**20**	**2**	**0**	**1**	**17:49**
	NHL Totals		**483**	**100**	**185**	**285**	**264**	**34**	**0**	**15**	**920**	**10.9**		**5219**	**47.0**	**15:56**	**54**	**17**	**23**	**40**	**30**	**3**	**0**	**4**	**17:11**

QMJHL First All-Star Team (2006) • Canadian Major Junior Second All-Star Team (2006)

• Missed majority of 2006-07 due to pre-season shoulder injury. • Missed majority of 2008-09 due to shoulder injury at Dallas, December 18, 2008. Signed as a free agent by **Salzburg** (Austria), November 26, 2012. Traded to **NY Rangers** by **Columbus** with Derek Dorsett, John Moore and Columbus' 6th round choice (later traded to Minnesota – Minnesota selected Chase Lang) in 2014 Entry Draft for Marian Gaborik, Blake Parlett and Steven Delisle, April 3, 2013.

BRAUN, Justin
(BRAWN, JUHS-tihn) **S.J.**

Defense. Shoots right. 6'2", 205 lbs. Born, St. Paul, MN, February 10, 1987. San Jose's 7th choice, 201st overall, in 2007 Entry Draft.

Season	Club	League	GP	G	A	Pts	PIM	PP	SH	GW	S	S%	+/-	TF	F%	Min	GP	G	A	Pts	PIM	PP	SH	GW	Min
2004-05	White Bear Lake	High-MN	STATISTICS NOT AVAILABLE																						
	Green Bay	USHL	10	0	0	0	2	....	....	....	....	....	....	....	....	....	....	....	....	....	....	....	....	....	....
2005-06	Green Bay	USHL	59	2	11	13	69	....	....	....	....	....	....	....	....	....	3	0	0	0	2	....	....	....	....
2006-07	Massachusetts	H-East	39	4	10	14	20	....	....	....	....	....	....	....	....	....	....	....	....	....	....	....	....	....	....
2007-08	Massachusetts	H-East	36	4	16	20	20	....	....	....	....	....	....	....	....	....	....	....	....	....	....	....	....	....	....
2008-09	Massachusetts	H-East	39	7	16	23	50	....	....	....	....	....	....	....	....	....	....	....	....	....	....	....	....	....	....
2009-10	Massachusetts	H-East	36	8	23	31	30	....	....	....	....	....	....	....	....	....	....	....	....	....	....	....	....	....	....
	Worcester Sharks	AHL	3	0	3	3	0	....	....	....	....	....	....	....	....	....	11	0	3	3	4	....	....	....	....
2010-11	**San Jose**	**NHL**	**28**	**2**	**9**	**11**	**2**	**2**	**0**	**0**	**44**	**4.5**	**–1**	**0**	**0.0**	**16:30**	**1**	**0**	**0**	**0**	**0**	**0**	**0**	**0**	**15:32**
	Worcester Sharks	AHL	34	5	18	23	8	....	....	....	....	....	....	....	....	....	....	....	....	....	....	....	....	....	....
2011-12	**San Jose**	**NHL**	**66**	**2**	**9**	**11**	**23**	**1**	**0**	**0**	**113**	**1.8**	**–2**	**0**	**0.0**	**16:33**	**5**	**0**	**0**	**0**	**15**	**0**	**0**	**0**	**17:55**
	Worcester Sharks	AHL	6	0	3	3	0	....	....	....	....	....	....	....	....	....	....	....	....	....	....	....	....	....	....
2012-13	Tappara Tampere	Finland	6	0	3	3	2	....	....	....	....	....	....	....	....	....	....	....	....	....	....	....	....	....	....
	San Jose	**NHL**	**41**	**0**	**7**	**7**	**6**	**0**	**0**	**0**	**48**	**0.0**	**–5**	**0**	**0.0**	**18:48**	**11**	**0**	**1**	**1**	**0**	**0**	**0**	**0**	**19:38**
2013-14	**San Jose**	**NHL**	**82**	**4**	**13**	**17**	**20**	**1**	**0**	**1**	**121**	**3.3**	**19**	**0**	**0.0**	**20:59**	**7**	**1**	**1**	**2**	**7**	**0**	**0**	**1**	**20:24**
2014-15	**San Jose**	**NHL**	**70**	**1**	**22**	**23**	**48**	**0**	**0**	**0**	**94**	**1.1**	**8**	**0**	**0.0**	**21:02**	....	....	....	....	....	....	....	....	....
	NHL Totals		**287**	**9**	**60**	**69**	**99**	**4**	**0**	**1**	**420**	**2.1**		**0**	**0.0**	**19:14**	**24**	**1**	**2**	**3**	**22**	**0**	**0**	**1**	**19:20**

Hockey East All-Rookie Team (2007) • Hockey East Second All-Star Team (2009) • Hockey East First All-Star Team (2010) • NCAA East Second All-American Team (2010)

Signed as a free agent by **Tappara Tampere** (Finland), November 23, 2012.

BREEN, Chris
(BREEN, KRIHS) **BOS**

Defense. Shoots left. 6'7", 224 lbs. Born, Uxbridge, ON, June 29, 1989.

Season	Club	League	GP	G	A	Pts	PIM	PP	SH	GW	S	S%	+/-	TF	F%	Min	GP	G	A	Pts	PIM	PP	SH	GW	Min
2005-06	Mississauga	ON-Jr.A	33	1	6	7	10	....	....	....	....	....	....	....	....	....	....	....	....	....	....	....	....	....	....
	Saginaw Spirit	OHL	25	0	0	0	10	....	....	....	....	....	....	....	....	....	....	....	....	....	....	....	....	....	....
2006-07	Saginaw Spirit	OHL	39	1	2	3	32	....	....	....	....	....	....	....	....	....	2	0	0	0	2	....	....	....	....
2007-08	Saginaw Spirit	OHL	55	0	6	6	67	....	....	....	....	....	....	....	....	....	4	0	1	1	0	....	....	....	....
2008-09	Saginaw Spirit	OHL	6	0	1	1	9	....	....	....	....	....	....	....	....	....	....	....	....	....	....	....	....	....	....
	Erie Otters	OHL	59	0	12	12	31	....	....	....	....	....	....	....	....	....	5	0	1	1	7	....	....	....	....
2009-10	Erie Otters	OHL	12	0	2	2	11	....	....	....	....	....	....	....	....	....	....	....	....	....	....	....	....	....	....
	Peterborough	OHL	53	4	8	12	36	....	....	....	....	....	....	....	....	....	4	1	0	1	5	....	....	....	....
	Abbotsford Heat	AHL	1	0	1	1	4	....	....	....	....	....	....	....	....	....	....	....	....	....	....	....	....	....	....
2010-11	Abbotsford Heat	AHL	73	4	7	11	47	....	....	....	....	....	....	....	....	....	....	....	....	....	....	....	....	....	....
2011-12	Abbotsford Heat	AHL	70	1	6	7	37	....	....	....	....	....	....	....	....	....	8	1	0	1	0	....	....	....	....
2012-13	Abbotsford Heat	AHL	60	3	4	7	55	....	....	....	....	....	....	....	....	....	....	....	....	....	....	....	....	....	....
2013-14	**Calgary**	**NHL**	**9**	**0**	**2**	**2**	**5**	**0**	**0**	**0**	**4**	**0.0**	**1**	**0**	**0.0**	**9:23**	....	....	....	....	....	....	....	....	....
	Abbotsford Heat	AHL	41	1	3	4	29	....	....	....	....	....	....	....	....	....	4	0	2	2	2	....	....	....	....
2014-15	Providence Bruins	AHL	52	2	8	10	33	....	....	....	....	....	....	....	....	....	5	0	1	1	0	....	....	....	....
	NHL Totals		**9**	**0**	**2**	**2**	**5**	**0**	**0**	**0**	**4**	**0.0**		**0**	**0.0**	**9:23**	....	....	....	....	....	....	....	....	....

Signed to an ATO (amateur tryout) contract by **Abbotsford** (AHL), March 30, 2010. Signed as a free agent by **Calgary**, May 28, 2010. Signed as a free agent by **Boston**, July 2, 2014.

BRENNAN, T.J.
(BREH-nan, TEE-JAY) **TOR**

Defense. Shoots left. 6'1", 216 lbs. Born, Willingboro, NJ, April 3, 1989. Buffalo's 1st choice, 31st overall, in 2007 Entry Draft.

Season	Club	League	GP	G	A	Pts	PIM	PP	SH	GW	S	S%	+/-	TF	F%	Min	GP	G	A	Pts	PIM	PP	SH	GW	Min
2005-06	Phi. Little Flyers	AtJHL	42	9	23	32	....	....	....	....	....	....	....	....	....	....	....	....	....	....	....	....	....	....	....
2006-07	St. John's	QMJHL	68	16	25	41	79	....	....	....	....	....	....	....	....	....	4	1	1	2	4	....	....	....	....
2007-08	St. John's	QMJHL	65	16	25	41	92	....	....	....	....	....	....	....	....	....	6	2	4	6	12	....	....	....	....
2008-09	Montreal	QMJHL	59	5	29	34	63	....	....	....	....	....	....	....	....	....	10	4	8	12	34	....	....	....	....
2009-10	Portland Pirates	AHL	65	6	17	23	64	....	....	....	....	....	....	....	....	....	4	0	1	1	2	....	....	....	....
2010-11	Portland Pirates	AHL	72	15	24	39	49	....	....	....	....	....	....	....	....	....	4	0	1	1	6	....	....	....	....
2011-12	**Buffalo**	**NHL**	**11**	**1**	**0**	**1**	**6**	**0**	**0**	**0**	**14**	**7.1**	**0**	**0**	**0.0**	**14:07**	....	....	....	....	....	....	....	....	....
	Rochester	AHL	52	16	14	30	39	....	....	....	....	....	....	....	....	....	3	2	0	2	6	....	....	....	....
2012-13	Rochester	AHL	36	14	21	35	57	....	....	....	....	....	....	....	....	....	....	....	....	....	....	....	....	....	....
	Buffalo	**NHL**	**10**	**1**	**0**	**1**	**6**	**1**	**0**	**0**	**18**	**5.6**	**–1**	**0**	**0.0**	**14:49**	....	....	....	....	....	....	....	....	....
	Florida	**NHL**	**19**	**2**	**7**	**9**	**2**	**0**	**0**	**0**	**24**	**8.3**	**–8**	**0**	**0.0**	**17:41**	....	....	....	....	....	....	....	....	....
2013-14	Toronto Marlies	AHL	76	25	47	72	115	....	....	....	....	....	....	....	....	....	14	6	8	14	10	....	....	....	....

			Regular Season														Playoffs								
Season	Club	League	GP	G	A	Pts	PIM	PP	SH	GW	S	S%	+/-	TF	F%	Min	GP	G	A	Pts	PIM	PP	SH	GW	Min
2014-15	Rockford IceHogs	AHL	54	9	27	36	59	....	....	....	....	....	....	....	....	....	....	....	....	....	....	....	....	....	....
	Toronto	**NHL**	6	0	1	1	9	0	0	0	11	0.0	–7	0	0.0	16:49	....	....	....	....	....	....	....	....	....
	Toronto Marlies	AHL	19	3	13	16	12	....	....	....	....	....	....	....	....	....	5	3	4	7	12	....	....	....	....
	NHL Totals		46	4	8	12	23	1	0	0	67	6.0		0	0.0	16:05	....	....	....	....	....	....	....	....	....

AHL First All-Star Team (2014) • Eddie Shore Award (Outstanding Defenseman – (AHL) (2014)

Traded to **Florida** by **Buffalo** for New Jersey's 5th round choice (previously acquired, later traded to Buffalo – Buffalo selected Gustav Possler) in 2013 Entry Draft, March 15, 2013. Traded to **Nashville** by **Florida** for Bobby Butler, June 14, 2013. Signed as a free agent by **Toronto**, July 5, 2013. Signed as a free agent by **NY Islanders**, July 1, 2014. Traded to **Chicago** by **NY Islanders** with Ville Pokka and Anders Nilsson for Nick Leddy and Kent Simpson, October 4, 2014. Traded to **Toronto** by **Chicago** for Spencer Abbott, February 26, 2015.

BRENT, Tim

(BREHNT, TIHM) **PHI**

Center. Shoots right. 6', 188 lbs. Born, Cambridge, ON, March 10, 1984. Anaheim's 3rd choice, 75th overall, in 2004 Entry Draft.

Season	Club	League	GP	G	A	Pts	PIM	PP	SH	GW	S	S%	+/-	TF	F%	Min	GP	G	A	Pts	PIM	PP	SH	GW	Min
99-2000	Cambridge	ON-Jr.B	40	19	16	35	42	....	....	....	....	....	....	....	....	....	....	....	....	....	....	....	....	....	....
2000-01	St. Michael's	OHL	64	9	19	28	31	....	....	....	....	....	....	....	....	....	18	2	8	10	6	....	....	....	....
2001-02	St. Michael's	OHL	61	19	40	59	52	....	....	....	....	....	....	....	....	....	14	7	12	19	20	....	....	....	....
2002-03	St. Michael's	OHL	60	24	42	66	74	....	....	....	....	....	....	....	....	....	19	7	17	24	14	....	....	....	....
2003-04	St. Michael's	OHL	53	26	41	67	105	....	....	....	....	....	....	....	....	....	18	4	13	17	24	....	....	....	....
2004-05	Cincinnati	AHL	46	5	13	18	42	....	....	....	....	....	....	....	....	....	12	0	1	1	6	....	....	....	....
2005-06	Portland Pirates	AHL	37	15	9	24	32	....	....	....	....	....	....	....	....	....	15	4	4	8	16	....	....	....	....
2006-07	**Anaheim**	**NHL**	15	1	0	1	6	0	0	0	14	7.1	–5	86	48.8	6:55	....	....	....	....	....	....	....	....	....
	Portland Pirates	AHL	48	16	14	30	40	....	....	....	....	....	....	....	....	....	....	....	....	....	....	....	....	....	....
2007-08	**Pittsburgh**	**NHL**	1	0	0	0	0	0	0	0	0	0.0	–1	5	60.0	4:34	....	....	....	....	....	....	....	....	....
	Wilkes-Barre	AHL	74	18	43	61	79	....	....	....	....	....	....	....	....	....	23	*12	15	27	10	....	....	....	....
2008-09	**Chicago**	**NHL**	2	0	0	0	2	0	0	0	0	0.0	0	10	50.0	8:21	....	....	....	....	....	....	....	....	....
	Rockford IceHogs	AHL	64	20	42	62	59	....	....	....	....	....	....	....	....	....	4	0	1	1	2	....	....	....	....
2009-10	**Toronto**	**NHL**	1	0	0	0	0	0	0	0	3	0.0	0	8	50.0	13:21	....	....	....	....	....	....	....	....	....
	Toronto Marlies	AHL	33	13	15	28	19	....	....	....	....	....	....	....	....	....	....	....	....	....	....	....	....	....	....
2010-11	**Toronto**	**NHL**	79	8	12	20	33	0	1	1	60	13.3	–4	788	52.0	11:39	....	....	....	....	....	....	....	....	....
2011-12	**Carolina**	**NHL**	79	12	12	24	27	3	1	3	71	16.9	–8	571	48.7	10:53	....	....	....	....	....	....	....	....	....
2012-13	**Carolina**	**NHL**	30	0	3	3	8	0	0	0	23	0.0	–3	240	51.7	9:48	....	....	....	....	....	....	....	....	....
2013-14	Nizhny Novgorod	KHL	18	3	8	11	16	....	....	....	....	....	....	....	....	....	....	....	....	....	....	....	....	....	....
	Magnitogorsk	KHL	33	6	12	18	59	....	....	....	....	....	....	....	....	....	20	1	0	1	37	....	....	....	....
2014-15	Magnitogorsk	KHL	42	5	10	15	30	....	....	....	....	....	....	....	....	....	10	1	2	3	8	....	....	....	....
	NHL Totals		207	21	27	48	76	3	2	4	171	12.3		1708	50.7	10:41	....	....	....	....	....	....	....	....	....

• Re-entered NHL Entry Draft. Originally Anaheim's 2nd choice, 37th overall, in 2002 Entry Draft.

Traded to **Pittsburgh** by **Anaheim** for Stephen Dixon, June 23, 2007. Traded to **Chicago** by **Pittsburgh** for Danny Richmond, July 17, 2008. Signed as a free agent by **Toronto**, July 6, 2009. • Missed majority of 2009-10 due to recurring chest injury. Signed as a free agent by **Carolina**, July 1, 2011. Signed as a free agent by **Nizhny Novgorod** (KHL), July 30, 2013. Signed as a free agent by **Magnitogorsk** (KHL), October 21, 2013. Signed as a free agent by **Philadelphia**, July 1, 2015.

BREWER, Eric

(BREW-uhr, AIR-ihk)

Defense. Shoots left. 6'4", 216 lbs. Born, Vernon, BC, April 17, 1979. NY Islanders' 2nd choice, 5th overall, in 1997 Entry Draft.

Season	Club	League	GP	G	A	Pts	PIM	PP	SH	GW	S	S%	+/-	TF	F%	Min	GP	G	A	Pts	PIM	PP	SH	GW	Min
1994-95	Kamloops	Minor-BC	40	19	19	38	62	....	....	....	....	....	....	....	....	....	....	....	....	....	....	....	....	....	....
1995-96	Prince George	WHL	63	4	10	14	25	....	....	....	....	....	....	....	....	....	....	....	....	....	....	....	....	....	....
1996-97	Prince George	WHL	71	5	24	29	81	....	....	....	....	....	....	....	....	....	15	2	4	6	16	....	....	....	....
1997-98	Prince George	WHL	34	5	28	33	45	....	....	....	....	....	....	....	....	....	11	4	2	6	19	....	....	....	....
1998-99	**NY Islanders**	**NHL**	63	5	6	11	32	2	0	0	63	7.9	–14	0	0.0	15:28	....	....	....	....	....	....	....	....	....
99-2000	**NY Islanders**	**NHL**	26	0	2	2	20	0	0	0	30	0.0	–11	0	0.0	18:33	....	....	....	....	....	....	....	....	....
	Lowell	AHL	25	2	2	4	26	....	....	....	....	....	....	....	....	....	7	0	0	0	0	....	....	....	....
2000-01	**Edmonton**	**NHL**	77	7	14	21	53	2	0	2	91	7.7	15	0	0.0	18:31	6	1	5	6	2	1	0	0	28:12
2001-02	**Edmonton**	**NHL**	81	7	18	25	45	6	0	2	165	4.2	–5	0	0.0	23:56	....	....	....	....	....	....	....	....	....
	Canada	Olympics	6	2	0	2	0	....	....	....	....	....	....	....	....	....	....	....	....	....	....	....	....	....	....
2002-03	**Edmonton**	**NHL**	80	8	21	29	45	1	0	1	147	5.4	–11	1	100.0	24:56	6	1	3	4	6	0	0	0	25:31
2003-04	**Edmonton**	**NHL**	77	7	18	25	67	3	0	1	135	5.2	–6	0	0.0	24:40	....	....	....	....	....	....	....	....	....
2004-05			DID NOT PLAY																						
2005-06	**St. Louis**	**NHL**	32	6	3	9	45	1	0	1	64	9.4	–17	0	0.0	23:28	....	....	....	....	....	....	....	....	....
2006-07	**St. Louis**	**NHL**	82	6	23	29	69	2	0	1	111	5.4	–10	0	0.0	24:32	....	....	....	....	....	....	....	....	....
2007-08	**St. Louis**	**NHL**	77	1	21	22	91	0	0	0	101	1.0	–18	0	0.0	24:38	....	....	....	....	....	....	....	....	....
2008-09	**St. Louis**	**NHL**	28	1	5	6	24	1	0	0	49	2.0	–14	0	0.0	25:07	....	....	....	....	....	....	....	....	....
2009-10	**St. Louis**	**NHL**	59	8	7	15	46	0	0	0	84	9.5	–17	0	0.0	21:27	....	....	....	....	....	....	....	....	....
2010-11	**St. Louis**	**NHL**	54	8	6	14	57	0	0	1	86	9.3	1	0	0.0	22:14	....	....	....	....	....	....	....	....	....
	Tampa Bay	**NHL**	22	1	1	2	24	0	0	0	24	4.2	5	0	0.0	21:34	18	1	6	7	14	0	0	0	25:36
2011-12	**Tampa Bay**	**NHL**	82	1	20	21	49	0	0	0	83	1.2	–5	0	0.0	23:16	....	....	....	....	....	....	....	....	....
2012-13	**Tampa Bay**	**NHL**	48	4	8	12	30	1	0	1	56	7.1	3	0	0.0	20:31	....	....	....	....	....	....	....	....	....
2013-14	**Tampa Bay**	**NHL**	77	4	13	17	59	0	0	2	83	4.8	10	0	0.0	17:33	4	0	0	0	0	0	0	0	21:47
2014-15	**Tampa Bay**	**NHL**	17	0	4	4	18	0	0	0	14	0.0	5	0	0.0	17:50	....	....	....	....	....	....	....	....	....
	Anaheim	**NHL**	9	1	1	2	6	0	0	0	7	14.3	–6	0	0.0	17:16	....	....	....	....	....	....	....	....	....
	Toronto	**NHL**	18	2	3	5	12	0	0	1	12	16.7	–4	0	0.0	20:12	....	....	....	....	....	....	....	....	....
	NHL Totals		1009	77	194	271	792	19	0	13	1405	5.5		1	100.0	21:53	34	3	14	17	22	1	0	0	25:36

WHL West Second All-Star Team (1998)

Played in NHL All-Star Game (2003)

Traded to **Edmonton** by **NY Islanders** with Josh Green and NY Islanders' 2nd round choice (Brad Winchester) in 2000 Entry Draft for Roman Hamrlik, June 24, 2000. Traded to **St. Louis** by **Edmonton** with Doug Lynch and Jeff Woywitka for Chris Pronger, August 2, 2005. • Missed majority of 2005-06 due to shoulder injuries at Columbus (November 16, 2005) and Atlanta (January 13, 2006). • Missed majority of 2008-09 due to back injury at Los Angeles, December 11, 2008. Traded to **Tampa Bay** by **St. Louis** for Brock Beukeboom and Tampa Bay's 3rd round choice (Jordan Binnington) in 2011 Entry Draft, February 18, 2011. Traded to **Anaheim** by **Tampa Bay** for Edmonton's 3rd round choice (previously acquired, Tampa Bay selected Dennis Yan) in 2015 Entry Draft, November 28, 2014. Traded to **Toronto** by **Anaheim** with Anaheim's 5th round choice in 2016 Entry Draft for Korbinian Holzer, March 2, 2015.

BRIERE, Daniel

(bree-AIR, DAN-yehl)

Center. Shoots right. 5'9", 174 lbs. Born, Gatineau, QC, October 6, 1977. Phoenix's 2nd choice, 24th overall, in 1996 Entry Draft.

Season	Club	League	GP	G	A	Pts	PIM	PP	SH	GW	S	S%	+/-	TF	F%	Min	GP	G	A	Pts	PIM	PP	SH	GW	Min
1992-93	Abitibi Regents	QAAA	42	24	30	54	28	....	....	....	....	....	....	....	....	....	3	0	3	3	8	....	....	....	....
1993-94	Gatineau	QAAA	44	56	47	103	56	....	....	....	....	....	....	....	....	....	12	13	19	32	8	....	....	....	....
1994-95	Drummondville	QMJHL	72	51	72	123	54	....	....	....	....	....	....	....	....	....	4	2	3	5	2	....	....	....	....
1995-96	Drummondville	QMJHL	67	*67	*96	*163	84	....	....	....	....	....	....	....	....	....	6	6	12	18	8	....	....	....	....
1996-97	Drummondville	QMJHL	59	52	78	130	86	....	....	....	....	....	....	....	....	....	8	7	7	14	14	....	....	....	....
1997-98	**Phoenix**	**NHL**	5	1	0	1	2	0	0	0	4	25.0	1	....	....	....	....	....	....	....	....	....	....	....	....
	Springfield	AHL	68	36	56	92	42	....	....	....	....	....	....	....	....	....	4	1	2	3	4	....	....	....	....
1998-99	**Phoenix**	**NHL**	64	8	14	22	30	2	0	2	90	8.9	–3	484	47.5	11:13	....	....	....	....	....	....	....	....	....
	Las Vegas	IHL	1	1	1	2	0	....	....	....	....	....	....	....	....	....	....	....	....	....	....	....	....	....	....
	Springfield	AHL	13	2	6	8	20	....	....	....	....	....	....	....	....	....	3	0	1	1	2	....	....	....	....
99-2000	**Phoenix**	**NHL**	13	1	1	2	0	0	0	0	9	11.1	0	65	49.2	7:41	1	0	0	0	0	0	0	0	6:16
	Springfield	AHL	58	29	42	71	56	....	....	....	....	....	....	....	....	....	....	....	....	....	....	....	....	....	....
2000-01	**Phoenix**	**NHL**	30	11	4	15	12	9	0	1	43	25.6	–2	210	50.0	10:50	....	....	....	....	....	....	....	....	....
	Springfield	AHL	30	21	25	46	30	....	....	....	....	....	....	....	....	....	....	....	....	....	....	....	....	....	....
2001-02	**Phoenix**	**NHL**	78	32	28	60	52	12	0	5	149	21.5	6	951	51.8	15:44	5	2	1	3	2	1	0	1	16:25
2002-03	**Phoenix**	**NHL**	68	17	29	46	50	4	0	3	142	12.0	–21	1108	52.5	17:02	....	....	....	....	....	....	....	....	....
	Buffalo	**NHL**	14	7	5	12	12	5	0	1	39	17.9	1	206	50.0	17:49	....	....	....	....	....	....	....	....	....
2003-04	**Buffalo**	**NHL**	82	28	37	65	70	11	0	3	194	14.4	–7	1066	47.1	18:20	....	....	....	....	....	....	....	....	....
2004-05	SC Bern	Swiss	36	16	29	45	26	....	....	....	....	....	....	....	....	....	11	1	6	7	2	....	....	....	....
2005-06	**Buffalo**	**NHL**	48	25	33	58	48	11	0	4	147	17.0	3	517	50.7	19:04	18	8	11	19	12	3	0	2	18:48
2006-07	**Buffalo**	**NHL**	81	32	63	95	89	9	0	6	234	13.7	17	1089	49.6	19:19	16	3	12	15	16	2	0	1	20:53
2007-08	**Philadelphia**	**NHL**	79	31	41	72	68	14	0	3	182	17.0	–22	1250	50.5	18:52	17	9	7	16	20	*6	0	3	18:26
2008-09	**Philadelphia**	**NHL**	29	11	14	25	26	4	0	0	54	20.4	–1	147	46.3	15:39	6	1	3	4	8	1	0	0	16:41
2009-10	**Philadelphia**	**NHL**	75	26	27	53	71	8	0	1	193	13.5	–2	120	44.2	16:35	23	12	18	*30	18	4	0	4	19:37
2010-11	**Philadelphia**	**NHL**	77	34	34	68	87	6	0	6	246	13.8	20	820	48.2	18:19	11	7	2	9	14	2	0	1	19:56
2011-12	**Philadelphia**	**NHL**	70	16	33	49	69	4	0	3	174	9.2	5	831	48.9	17:22	11	*8	5	13	4	1	0	1	17:44
2012-13	Eisbaren Berlin	Germany	21	10	24	34	24	....	....	....	....	....	....	....	....	....	....	....	....	....	....	....	....	....	....
	Philadelphia	**NHL**	34	6	10	16	10	3	0	1	87	6.9	–13	135	45.9	16:04	....	....	....	....	....	....	....	....	....

Season	Club	League	GP	G	A	Pts	PIM	PP	SH	GW	S	S%	+/-	TF	F%	Min	GP	G	A	Pts	PIM	PP	SH	GW	Min
		Regular Season															Playoffs								
2013-14	**Montreal**	**NHL**	**69**	**13**	**12**	**25**	**30**	**4**	**0**	**1**	**118**	**11.0**	**1**	**350**	**48.9**	**12:46**	**16**	**3**	**4**	**7**	**4**	**1**	**0**	**0**	**10:05**
2014-15	**Colorado**	**NHL**	**57**	**8**	**4**	**12**	**18**	**0**	**0**	**3**	**69**	**11.6**	**–7**	**24**	**54.2**	**12:07**	....	....	....	....	....	....	....	....	....
	NHL Totals		**973**	**307**	**389**	**696**	**744**	**106**	**0**	**43**	**2174**	**14.1**		**9373**	**49.6**	**16:13**	**124**	**53**	**63**	**116**	**98**	**21**	**0**	**13**	**17:45**

QMJHL All-Rookie Team (1995) • QMJHL Offensive Rookie of the Year (1995) • QMJHL Second All-Star Team (1996, 1997) • AHL All-Rookie Team (1998) • AHL First All-Star Team (1998) • Dudley "Red" Garrett Memorial Award (AHL) – Rookie of the Year) (1998)

Played in NHL All-Star Game (2007, 2011)

Traded to **Buffalo** by **Phoenix** with Phoenix's 3rd round choice (Andrej Sekera) in 2004 Entry Draft for Chris Gratton and Buffalo's 4th round choice (later traded to Edmonton – Edmonton selected Liam Reddox) in 2004 Entry Draft, March 10, 2003. Signed as a free agent by **Bern** (Swiss), September 28, 2004. Signed as a free agent by **Philadelphia**, July 1, 2007. • Missed majority of 2008-09 due to abdominal surgery (October 25, 2008) and groin surgery (January 22, 2009). Signed as a free agent by **Berlin** (Germany), October 4, 2012. Signed as a free agent by **Montreal**, July 4, 2013. Traded to **Colorado** by **Montreal** for Pierre-Alexandre Parenteau and Colorado's 5th round choice (Matthew Bradley) in 2015 Entry Draft, June 30, 2014.

BRODIE, T.J.

(BROH-dee, TEE-JAY) **CGY**

Defense. Shoots left. 6'1", 182 lbs. Born, Chatham, ON, June 7, 1990. Calgary's 5th choice, 114th overall, in 2008 Entry Draft.

Season	Club	League	GP	G	A	Pts	PIM	PP	SH	GW	S	S%	+/-	TF	F%	Min	GP	G	A	Pts	PIM	PP	SH	GW	Min
2006-07	Leamington Flyers	ON-Jr.B	43	8	38	46	104	....	....	....	....	....	....	....	....	....	5	1	2	3	12	....	....	....	....
	Saginaw Spirit	OHL	20	0	4	4	23	....	....	....	....	....	....	....	....	....	3	0	1	1	2	....	....	....	....
2007-08	Saginaw Spirit	OHL	68	4	26	30	73	....	....	....	....	....	....	....	....	....	4	0	3	3	2	....	....	....	....
2008-09	Saginaw Spirit	OHL	63	12	38	50	67	....	....	....	....	....	....	....	....	....	8	3	6	9	8	....	....	....	....
2009-10	Saginaw Spirit	OHL	19	4	19	23	20	....	....	....	....	....	....	....	....	....	....	....	....	....	....	....	....	....	....
	Barrie Colts	OHL	46	3	30	33	38	....	....	....	....	....	....	....	....	....	17	1	14	15	14	....	....	....	....
2010-11	**Calgary**	**NHL**	**3**	**0**	**0**	**0**	**2**	**0**	**0**	**0**	**1**	**0.0**	**–3**	**0**	**0.0**	**16:00**	....	....	....	....	....	....	....	....	....
	Abbotsford Heat	AHL	68	5	29	34	32	....	....	....	....	....	....	....	....	....	....	....	....	....	....	....	....	....	....
2011-12	**Calgary**	**NHL**	**54**	**2**	**12**	**14**	**14**	**1**	**0**	**2**	**44**	**4.5**	**3**	**0**	**0.0**	**16:29**	....	....	....	....	....	....	....	....	....
	Abbotsford Heat	AHL	12	1	2	3	10	....	....	....	....	....	....	....	....	....	....	....	....	....	....	....	....	....	....
2012-13	Abbotsford Heat	AHL	35	1	19	20	22	....	....	....	....	....	....	....	....	....	....	....	....	....	....	....	....	....	....
	Calgary	**NHL**	**47**	**2**	**12**	**14**	**8**	**0**	**0**	**0**	**44**	**4.5**	**–9**	**0**	**0.0**	**20:13**	....	....	....	....	....	....	....	....	....
2013-14	**Calgary**	**NHL**	**81**	**4**	**27**	**31**	**20**	**1**	**0**	**2**	**104**	**3.8**	**0**	**0**	**0.0**	**24:04**	....	....	....	....	....	....	....	....	....
2014-15	**Calgary**	**NHL**	**81**	**11**	**30**	**41**	**30**	**3**	**1**	**3**	**133**	**8.3**	**15**	**0**	**0.0**	**25:12**	**11**	**1**	**4**	**5**	**0**	**0**	**0**	**0**	**27:07**
	NHL Totals		**266**	**19**	**81**	**100**	**74**	**5**	**1**	**7**	**326**	**5.8**		**0**	**0.0**	**22:06**	**11**	**1**	**4**	**5**	**0**	**0**	**0**	**0**	**27:07**

BRODIN, Jonas

(BROH-deen, JOH-nuhs) **MIN**

Defense. Shoots left. 6'1", 194 lbs. Born, Karlstad, Sweden, July 12, 1993. Minnesota's 1st choice, 10th overall, in 2011 Entry Draft.

Season	Club	League	GP	G	A	Pts	PIM	PP	SH	GW	S	S%	+/-	TF	F%	Min	GP	G	A	Pts	PIM	PP	SH	GW	Min
2008-09	Farjestad U18	Swe-U18	22	3	8	11	10	....	....	....	....	....	....	....	....	....	4	1	1	2	4	....	....	....	....
2009-10	Skare BK Jr.	Swe-Jr.	2	0	1	1	2	....	....	....	....	....	....	....	....	....	....	....	....	....	....	....	....	....	....
	Skare BK	Sweden-3	21	1	6	7	10	....	....	....	....	....	....	....	....	....	....	....	....	....	....	....	....	....	....
	Farjestad	Sweden	3	0	0	0	2	....	....	....	....	....	....	....	....	....	....	....	....	....	....	....	....	....	....
	Farjestad U18	Swe-U18	19	6	11	17	6	....	....	....	....	....	....	....	....	....	7	3	8	11	8	....	....	....	....
2010-11	Farjestad U18	Swe-U18	2	0	1	1	2	....	....	....	....	....	....	....	....	....	....	....	....	....	....	....	....	....	....
	Farjestad	Sweden	42	0	4	4	12	....	....	....	....	....	....	....	....	....	14	2	0	2	2	....	....	....	....
2011-12	Farjestad Jr.	Swe-Jr.	1	0	0	0	0	....	....	....	....	....	....	....	....	....	....	....	....	....	....	....	....	....	....
	Farjestad	Sweden	49	0	8	8	14	....	....	....	....	....	....	....	....	....	11	2	0	2	6	....	....	....	....
2012-13	Houston Aeros	AHL	9	2	2	4	4	....	....	....	....	....	....	....	....	....	....	....	....	....	....	....	....	....	....
	Minnesota	**NHL**	**45**	**2**	**9**	**11**	**10**	**1**	**0**	**0**	**51**	**3.9**	**3**	**0**	**0.0**	**23:13**	**5**	**0**	**0**	**0**	**0**	**0**	**0**	**0**	**26:23**
2013-14	**Minnesota**	**NHL**	**79**	**8**	**11**	**19**	**22**	**3**	**0**	**0**	**74**	**10.8**	**0**	**0**	**0.0**	**23:54**	**13**	**0**	**2**	**2**	**12**	**0**	**0**	**0**	**23:38**
2014-15	**Minnesota**	**NHL**	**71**	**3**	**14**	**17**	**8**	**0**	**0**	**1**	**95**	**3.2**	**21**	**0**	**0.0**	**24:10**	**10**	**0**	**0**	**0**	**0**	**0**	**0**	**0**	**21:53**
	NHL Totals		**195**	**13**	**34**	**47**	**40**	**4**	**0**	**1**	**220**	**5.9**		**0**	**0.0**	**23:50**	**28**	**0**	**2**	**2**	**12**	**0**	**0**	**0**	**23:30**

NHL All-Rookie Team (2013)

BRODZIAK, Kyle

(brohd-ZEE-ak, KIGHL) **ST.L.**

Center. Shoots right. 6'2", 208 lbs. Born, St. Paul, AB, May 25, 1984. Edmonton's 9th choice, 214th overall, in 2003 Entry Draft.

Season	Club	League	GP	G	A	Pts	PIM	PP	SH	GW	S	S%	+/-	TF	F%	Min	GP	G	A	Pts	PIM	PP	SH	GW	Min
99-2000	Ft. Saskatchewan	AMBHL	36	23	33	56	57	....	....	....	....	....	....	....	....	....	....	....	....	....	....	....	....	....	....
	Moose Jaw	WHL	2	0	0	0	0	....	....	....	....	....	....	....	....	....	....	....	....	....	....	....	....	....	....
2000-01	Moose Jaw	WHL	57	2	8	10	47	....	....	....	....	....	....	....	....	....	3	0	0	0	0	....	....	....	....
2001-02	Moose Jaw	WHL	72	8	12	20	56	....	....	....	....	....	....	....	....	....	12	0	3	3	11	....	....	....	....
2002-03	Moose Jaw	WHL	72	32	30	62	84	....	....	....	....	....	....	....	....	....	13	5	3	8	16	....	....	....	....
2003-04	Moose Jaw	WHL	70	39	54	93	58	....	....	....	....	....	....	....	....	....	10	5	4	9	10	....	....	....	....
2004-05	Edmonton	AHL	56	6	26	32	49	....	....	....	....	....	....	....	....	....	....	....	....	....	....	....	....	....	....
2005-06	**Edmonton**	**NHL**	**10**	**0**	**0**	**0**	**4**	**0**	**0**	**0**	**7**	**0.0**	**–4**	**75**	**52.0**	**11:02**	....	....	....	....	....	....	....	....	....
	Iowa Stars	AHL	55	12	19	31	41	....	....	....	....	....	....	....	....	....	7	1	3	4	2	....	....	....	....
2006-07	**Edmonton**	**NHL**	**6**	**1**	**0**	**1**	**2**	**0**	**0**	**0**	**11**	**9.1**	**0**	**48**	**52.1**	**17:08**	....	....	....	....	....	....	....	....	....
	Wilkes-Barre	AHL	62	24	32	56	44	....	....	....	....	....	....	....	....	....	11	1	5	6	14	....	....	....	....
2007-08	**Edmonton**	**NHL**	**80**	**14**	**17**	**31**	**33**	**0**	**1**	**3**	**125**	**11.2**	**–6**	**297**	**51.5**	**12:55**	....	....	....	....	....	....	....	....	....
2008-09	**Edmonton**	**NHL**	**79**	**11**	**16**	**27**	**21**	**1**	**1**	**3**	**99**	**11.1**	**4**	**947**	**51.6**	**12:43**	....	....	....	....	....	....	....	....	....
2009-10	**Minnesota**	**NHL**	**82**	**9**	**23**	**32**	**22**	**0**	**0**	**3**	**140**	**6.4**	**–3**	**1001**	**48.4**	**15:20**	....	....	....	....	....	....	....	....	....
2010-11	**Minnesota**	**NHL**	**80**	**16**	**21**	**37**	**56**	**2**	**1**	**1**	**126**	**12.7**	**–4**	**1088**	**48.9**	**15:47**	....	....	....	....	....	....	....	....	....
2011-12	**Minnesota**	**NHL**	**82**	**22**	**22**	**44**	**66**	**5**	**0**	**0**	**160**	**13.8**	**–15**	**1429**	**49.5**	**19:04**	....	....	....	....	....	....	....	....	....
2012-13	**Minnesota**	**NHL**	**48**	**8**	**4**	**12**	**20**	**1**	**1**	**1**	**88**	**9.1**	**–18**	**763**	**49.4**	**17:21**	**5**	**0**	**2**	**2**	**4**	**0**	**0**	**0**	**20:41**
2013-14	**Minnesota**	**NHL**	**81**	**8**	**16**	**24**	**61**	**0**	**1**	**1**	**115**	**7.0**	**0**	**1223**	**48.2**	**16:13**	**12**	**3**	**3**	**6**	**2**	**0**	**0**	**0**	**13:15**
2014-15	**Minnesota**	**NHL**	**73**	**9**	**11**	**20**	**47**	**0**	**1**	**0**	**86**	**10.5**	**–6**	**687**	**49.2**	**13:03**	**10**	**0**	**0**	**0**	**2**	**0**	**0**	**0**	**12:30**
	NHL Totals		**621**	**98**	**130**	**228**	**332**	**9**	**6**	**12**	**957**	**10.2**		**7558**	**49.4**	**15:11**	**27**	**3**	**5**	**8**	**8**	**0**	**0**	**0**	**14:21**

WHL East First All-Star Team (2004) • Canadian Major Junior Second All-Star Team (2004)

Traded to **Minnesota** by **Edmonton** with Edmonton's 6th round choice (Darcy Kuemper) in 2009 Entry Draft for Dallas's 4th round choice (previously acquired, Edmonton selected Kyle Bigos) in 2009 Entry Draft and Minnesota's 5th round choice (Olivier Roy) in 2009 Entry Draft, June 27, 2009. Signed as a free agent by **St. Louis**, July 2, 2015.

BROLL, David

(BROHL, DAY-vihd) **T.B.**

Left wing. Shoots left. 6'3", 235 lbs. Born, Mississauga, ON, January 4, 1993. Toronto's 6th choice, 152nd overall, in 2011 Entry Draft.

Season	Club	League	GP	G	A	Pts	PIM	PP	SH	GW	S	S%	+/-	TF	F%	Min	GP	G	A	Pts	PIM	PP	SH	GW	Min
2008-09	Tor. Young Nats	GTHL	73	31	26	57	....	....	....	....	....	....	....	....	....	....	....	....	....	....	....	....	....	....	....
2009-10	Erie Otters	OHL	64	9	9	18	42	....	....	....	....	....	....	....	....	....	4	0	0	0	2	....	....	....	....
2010-11	Erie Otters	OHL	41	8	14	22	51	....	....	....	....	....	....	....	....	....	....	....	....	....	....	....	....	....	....
	Sault Ste. Marie	OHL	24	5	7	12	34	....	....	....	....	....	....	....	....	....	....	....	....	....	....	....	....	....	....
2011-12	Sault Ste. Marie	OHL	59	8	25	33	81	....	....	....	....	....	....	....	....	....	....	....	....	....	....	....	....	....	....
	Toronto Marlies	AHL	3	0	0	0	5	....	....	....	....	....	....	....	....	....	2	0	0	0	0	....	....	....	....
2012-13	Sault Ste. Marie	OHL	67	17	37	54	77	....	....	....	....	....	....	....	....	....	6	0	2	2	21	....	....	....	....
	Toronto Marlies	AHL	7	0	0	0	15	....	....	....	....	....	....	....	....	....	3	0	0	0	2	....	....	....	....
2013-14	**Toronto**	**NHL**	**5**	**0**	**1**	**1**	**5**	**0**	**0**	**0**	**3**	**0.0**	**1**	**0**	**0.0**	**8:11**	....	....	....	....	....	....	....	....	....
	Toronto Marlies	AHL	63	3	13	16	120	....	....	....	....	....	....	....	....	....	4	0	0	0	6	....	....	....	....
2014-15	Toronto Marlies	AHL	21	0	0	0	79	....	....	....	....	....	....	....	....	....	....	....	....	....	....	....	....	....	....
	Orlando	ECHL	16	2	7	9	9	....	....	....	....	....	....	....	....	....	....	....	....	....	....	....	....	....	....
	Syracuse Crunch	AHL	20	0	3	3	40	....	....	....	....	....	....	....	....	....	2	0	0	0	2	....	....	....	....
	NHL Totals		**5**	**0**	**1**	**1**	**5**	**0**	**0**	**0**	**3**	**0.0**		**0**	**0.0**	**8:11**	....	....	....	....	....	....	....	....	....

Traded to **Tampa Bay** by **Toronto** with Carter Ashton for future considerations, February 6, 2015.

BROOKBANK, Sheldon

(BRUK-bank, SHEHL-duhn)

Defense. Shoots right. 6'1", 202 lbs. Born, Lanigan, SK, October 3, 1980.

Season	Club	League	GP	G	A	Pts	PIM	PP	SH	GW	S	S%	+/-	TF	F%	Min	GP	G	A	Pts	PIM	PP	SH	GW	Min
2000-01	Humboldt	SJHL	59	14	35	49	281	....	....	....	....	....	....	....	....	....	....	....	....	....	....	....	....	....	....
2001-02	Grand Rapids	AHL	6	0	1	1	24	....	....	....	....	....	....	....	....	....	....	....	....	....	....	....	....	....	....
	Mississippi	ECHL	62	8	21	29	137	....	....	....	....	....	....	....	....	....	10	1	4	5	27	....	....	....	....
2002-03	Grand Rapids	AHL	69	2	11	13	136	....	....	....	....	....	....	....	....	....	15	1	3	4	28	....	....	....	....
2003-04	Cincinnati	AHL	74	2	9	11	216	....	....	....	....	....	....	....	....	....	9	0	2	2	20	....	....	....	....
2004-05	Cincinnati	AHL	60	1	11	12	181	....	....	....	....	....	....	....	....	....	11	0	0	0	40	....	....	....	....
2005-06	Milwaukee	AHL	73	9	26	35	232	....	....	....	....	....	....	....	....	....	21	1	8	9	49	....	....	....	....
2006-07	**Nashville**	**NHL**	**3**	**0**	**1**	**1**	**12**	**0**	**0**	**0**	**3**	**0.0**	**0**	**0**	**0.0**	**8:16**	....	....	....	....	....	....	....	....	....
	Milwaukee	AHL	78	15	38	53	176	....	....	....	....	....	....	....	....	....	4	0	0	0	6	....	....	....	....

Season	Club	League	Regular Season GP	G	A	Pts	PIM	PP	SH	GW	S	S%	+/-	TF	F%	Min	Playoffs GP	G	A	Pts	PIM	PP	SH	GW	Min
2007-08	New Jersey	NHL	44	0	8	8	63	0	0	0	43	0.0	0	0	0.0	15:08	....	....	....	....	....	....	....	....	....
	Lowell Devils	AHL	1	0	0	0	5	....	....	....	....	....	....	....	....	....	....	....	....	....	....	....	....	....	....
2008-09	New Jersey	NHL	15	0	0	0	25	0	0	0	6	0.0	1	0	0.0	8:51	....	....	....	....	....	....	....	....	....
	Anaheim	NHL	29	1	3	4	51	0	0	0	24	4.2	3	0	0.0	13:50	13	0	0	0	18	0	0	0	11:13
2009-10	Anaheim	NHL	66	0	9	9	114	0	0	0	60	0.0	10	0	0.0	14:58	....	....	....	....	....	....	....	....	....
2010-11	Anaheim	NHL	40	0	0	0	63	0	0	0	29	0.0	-8	0	0.0	13:20	4	0	0	0	14	0	0	0	14:35
2011-12	Anaheim	NHL	80	3	11	14	72	0	0	1	49	6.1	11	0	0.0	15:36	....	....	....	....	....	....	....	....	....
2012-13♦	Chicago	NHL	26	1	0	1	21	0	1	0	25	4.0	-2	1	0.0	12:45	1	0	0	0	0	0	0	0	6:50
2013-14	Chicago	NHL	48	2	5	7	52	0	0	1	43	4.7	2	0	0.0	12:53	7	0	2	2	0	0	0	0	14:50
2014-15	Ak Bars Kazan	KHL	35	3	4	7	37	....	....	....	....	....	....	....	....	....	9	1	0	1	4	....	....	....	....
	NHL Totals		351	7	37	44	473	0	1	2	282	2.5		1	0.0	14:05	25	0	2	2	32	0	0	0	12:36

AHL First All-Star Team (2007) • Eddie Shore Award (AHL - Outstanding Defenseman) (2007)

Signed as a free agent by **Anaheim**, July 21, 2003. Signed as a free agent by **Nashville**, August 4, 2005. Signed as a free agent by **Columbus**, July 1, 2007. Claimed on waivers by **New Jersey** from **Columbus**, October 2, 2007. Traded to **Anaheim** by **New Jersey** for David McIntyre, February 3, 2009. Signed as a free agent by **Chicago**, July 1. 2012. Signed as a free agent by **Kazan** (KHL), October 31, 2014.

BROUILLETTE, Julien

(BREE-eht, JOO-lee-ehn)

Defense. Shoots left. 5'11", 185 lbs. Born, St. Esprit, QC, December 5, 1986.

Season	Club	League	GP	G	A	Pts	PIM	PP	SH	GW	S	S%	+/-	TF	F%	Min	GP	G	A	Pts	PIM	PP	SH	GW	Min
2002-03	Cap-d-Madeleine	QAAA	41	8	20	28	26	....	....	....	....	....	....	....	....	....	....	....	....	....	....	....	....	....	....
2003-04	Trois-Rivieres	QAAA	13	5	15	20	16	....	....	....	....	....	....	....	....	....	....	....	....	....	....	....	....	....	....
	Chicoutimi	QMJHL	24	0	0	0	7	....	....	....	....	....	....	....	....	....	18	0	4	4	0	....	....	....	....
2004-05	Chicoutimi	QMJHL	65	7	11	18	61	....	....	....	....	....	....	....	....	....	17	4	4	8	23	....	....	....	....
2005-06	Chicoutimi	QMJHL	70	10	42	52	86	....	....	....	....	....	....	....	....	....	9	1	3	4	8	....	....	....	....
2006-07	Chicoutimi	QMJHL	68	10	43	53	52	....	....	....	....	....	....	....	....	....	4	1	2	3	8	....	....	....	....
2007-08	Columbia Inferno	ECHL	67	6	11	17	55	....	....	....	....	....	....	....	....	....	13	0	4	4	6	....	....	....	....
2008-09	Charlotte	ECHL	70	11	18	29	67	....	....	....	....	....	....	....	....	....	6	0	1	1	2	....	....	....	....
2009-10	Charlotte	ECHL	47	13	20	33	23	....	....	....	....	....	....	....	....	....	7	0	5	5	2	....	....	....	....
	Providence Bruins	AHL	3	0	1	1	0	....	....	....	....	....	....	....	....	....	....	....	....	....	....	....	....	....	....
	Hartford	AHL	21	1	3	4	4	....	....	....	....	....	....	....	....	....	....	....	....	....	....	....	....	....	....
2010-11	Greenville	ECHL	25	11	12	23	8	....	....	....	....	....	....	....	....	....	1	0	0	0	0	....	....	....	....
	Charlotte	AHL	1	0	0	0	0	....	....	....	....	....	....	....	....	....	....	....	....	....	....	....	....	....	....
	Lake Erie	AHL	49	2	15	17	20	....	....	....	....	....	....	....	....	....	7	1	1	2	2	....	....	....	....
2011-12	Hershey Bears	AHL	74	7	14	21	24	....	....	....	....	....	....	....	....	....	3	0	1	1	4	....	....	....	....
2012-13	Hershey Bears	AHL	61	2	5	7	35	....	....	....	....	....	....	....	....	....	5	0	3	3	0	....	....	....	....
	Reading Royals	ECHL	1	0	0	0	2	....	....	....	....	....	....	....	....	....	....	....	....	....	....	....	....	....	....
2013-14	Washington	NHL	10	1	1	2	0	0	0	1	4	25.0	3	0	0.0	15:33	....	....	....	....	....	....	....	....	....
	Hershey Bears	AHL	51	10	10	20	22	....	....	....	....	....	....	....	....	....	....	....	....	....	....	....	....	....	....
2014-15	Winnipeg	NHL	1	0	0	0	0	0	0	0	0	0.0	0	0	0.0	9:33	....	....	....	....	....	....	....	....	....
	St. John's IceCaps	AHL	49	7	11	18	16	....	....	....	....	....	....	....	....	....	....	....	....	....	....	....	....	....	....
	NHL Totals		11	1	1	2	0	0	0	1	4	25.0		0	0.0	15:00	....	....	....	....	....	....	....	....	....

Signed as a free agent by **Washington**, April 5, 2013. Signed as a free agent by **Winnipeg**, August 8, 2014.

BROUWER, Troy

(BROW-uhr, TROI) **ST.L.**

Right wing. Shoots right. 6'3", 213 lbs. Born, Vancouver, BC, August 17, 1985. Chicago's 13th choice, 214th overall, in 2004 Entry Draft.

Season	Club	League	GP	G	A	Pts	PIM	PP	SH	GW	S	S%	+/-	TF	F%	Min	GP	G	A	Pts	PIM	PP	SH	GW	Min
2001-02	Delta Ice Hawks	PIJHL	30	21	18	39	130	....	....	....	....	....	....	....	....	....	....	....	....	....	....	....	....	....	....
	Moose Jaw	WHL	13	0	0	0	7	....	....	....	....	....	....	....	....	....	....	....	....	....	....	....	....	....	....
2002-03	Moose Jaw	WHL	59	9	12	21	54	....	....	....	....	....	....	....	....	....	13	1	2	3	14	....	....	....	....
2003-04	Moose Jaw	WHL	72	23	26	49	111	....	....	....	....	....	....	....	....	....	10	3	0	3	12	....	....	....	....
2004-05	Moose Jaw	WHL	71	22	25	47	132	....	....	....	....	....	....	....	....	....	5	1	2	3	8	....	....	....	....
2005-06	Moose Jaw	WHL	72	49	53	*102	122	....	....	....	....	....	....	....	....	....	17	10	4	14	34	....	....	....	....
2006-07	Chicago	NHL	10	0	0	0	7	0	0	0	7	0.0	-7	0	0.0	9:55	....	....	....	....	....	....	....	....	....
	Norfolk Admirals	AHL	66	41	38	79	70	....	....	....	....	....	....	....	....	....	6	1	0	1	4	....	....	....	....
2007-08	Chicago	NHL	2	0	1	1	0	0	0	0	0	0.0	1	0	0.0	11:56	....	....	....	....	....	....	....	....	....
	Rockford IceHogs	AHL	75	35	19	54	154	....	....	....	....	....	....	....	....	....	12	5	4	9	16	....	....	....	....
2008-09	Chicago	NHL	69	10	16	26	50	4	1	0	126	7.9	7	20	45.0	15:05	17	0	2	2	12	0	0	0	11:51
	Rockford IceHogs	AHL	5	2	6	8	20	....	....	....	....	....	....	....	....	....	....	....	....	....	....	....	....	....	....
2009-10♦	Chicago	NHL	78	22	18	40	66	7	1	7	116	19.0	9	9	55.6	16:22	19	4	4	8	8	0	0	0	11:01
2010-11	Chicago	NHL	79	17	19	36	38	7	0	5	122	13.9	-2	25	48.0	15:06	7	0	0	0	11	0	0	0	14:25
2011-12	Washington	NHL	82	18	15	33	61	3	0	5	133	13.5	-15	83	45.8	17:11	14	2	2	4	8	1	0	1	19:01
2012-13	Washington	NHL	47	19	14	33	28	7	1	5	111	17.1	-5	232	47.8	18:32	7	1	1	2	10	0	0	0	19:34
2013-14	Washington	NHL	82	25	18	43	92	12	0	3	161	15.5	-6	436	51.2	18:51	....	....	....	....	....	....	....	....	....
2014-15	Washington	NHL	82	21	22	43	53	8	2	3	145	14.5	11	441	56.9	17:31	14	0	3	3	10	0	0	0	17:59
	NHL Totals		531	132	123	255	395	48	5	28	921	14.3		1246	52.1	16:45	78	7	12	19	59	1	0	1	14:57

WHL East First All-Star Team (2006) • Canadian Major Junior Second All-Star Team (2006) • AHL All-Rookie Team (2007) • AHL Second All-Star Team (2007)

Traded to **Washington** by **Chicago** for Washington's 1st round choice (Phillip Danault) in 2011 Entry Draft, June 24, 2011. Traded to **St. Louis** by **Washington** with Pheonix Copley and Washington's 3rd round choice in 2016 Entry Draft for T.J. Oshie, July 2, 2015.

BROWN, Chris

(BROWN, KRIHS) **WSH**

Center. Shoots right. 6'2", 215 lbs. Born, Flower Mound, TX, February 3, 1991. Phoenix's 2nd choice, 36th overall, in 2009 Entry Draft.

Season	Club	League	GP	G	A	Pts	PIM	PP	SH	GW	S	S%	+/-	TF	F%	Min	GP	G	A	Pts	PIM	PP	SH	GW	Min
2007-08	USNTDP	NAHL	43	8	6	14	66	....	....	....	....	....	....	....	....	....	3	0	0	0	0	....	....	....	....
	USNTDP	U-17	17	5	1	6	8	....	....	....	....	....	....	....	....	....	....	....	....	....	....	....	....	....	....
2008-09	USNTDP	NAHL	15	6	2	8	37	....	....	....	....	....	....	....	....	....	....	....	....	....	....	....	....	....	....
	USNTDP	U-18	47	14	16	30	83	....	....	....	....	....	....	....	....	....	....	....	....	....	....	....	....	....	....
2009-10	U. of Michigan	CCHA	45	13	15	28	58	....	....	....	....	....	....	....	....	....	....	....	....	....	....	....	....	....	....
2010-11	U. of Michigan	CCHA	42	9	14	23	59	....	....	....	....	....	....	....	....	....	....	....	....	....	....	....	....	....	....
2011-12	U. of Michigan	CCHA	38	12	17	29	66	....	....	....	....	....	....	....	....	....	....	....	....	....	....	....	....	....	....
2012-13	Portland Pirates	AHL	68	29	18	47	98	....	....	....	....	....	....	....	....	....	3	1	1	2	6	....	....	....	....
	Phoenix	NHL	5	0	0	0	2	0	0	0	6	0.0	0	0	0.0	7:38	....	....	....	....	....	....	....	....	....
2013-14	Phoenix	NHL	6	0	0	0	17	0	0	0	4	0.0	0	2	0.0	7:41	....	....	....	....	....	....	....	....	....
	Portland Pirates	AHL	51	14	21	35	68	....	....	....	....	....	....	....	....	....	....	....	....	....	....	....	....	....	....
	Washington	NHL	6	1	1	2	0	0	0	0	4	25.0	0	38	39.5	9:42	....	....	....	....	....	....	....	....	....
	Hershey Bears	AHL	12	2	3	5	2	....	....	....	....	....	....	....	....	....	....	....	....	....	....	....	....	....	....
2014-15	Washington	NHL	5	1	0	1	2	0	0	0	4	25.0	1	3	33.3	6:28	....	....	....	....	....	....	....	....	....
	Hershey Bears	AHL	64	17	11	28	70	....	....	....	....	....	....	....	....	....	9	3	2	5	10	....	....	....	....
	NHL Totals		22	2	1	3	21	0	0	0	18	11.1		43	37.2	7:57	....	....	....	....	....	....	....	....	....

CCHA All-Rookie Team (2010)

Traded to **Washington** by **Phoenix** with Rostislav Klesla and Arizona's 4th round choice (later traded to Carolina – Carolina selected Callum Booth) in 2015 Entry Draft for Martin Erat and John Mitchell, March 4, 2014.

BROWN, Dustin

(BROWN, DUHS-tihn) **L.A.**

Right wing. Shoots right. 6', 205 lbs. Born, Ithaca, NY, November 4, 1984. Los Angeles' 1st choice, 13th overall, in 2003 Entry Draft.

Season	Club	League	GP	G	A	Pts	PIM	PP	SH	GW	S	S%	+/-	TF	F%	Min	GP	G	A	Pts	PIM	PP	SH	GW	Min
1998-99	Ithaca	High-NY	18	4	13	17	....	....	....	....	....	....	....	....	....	....	....	....	....	....	....	....	....	....	....
99-2000	Ithaca	High-NY	24	33	21	54	....	....	....	....	....	....	....	....	....	....	....	....	....	....	....	....	....	....	....
2000-01	Guelph Storm	OHL	53	23	22	45	45	....	....	....	....	....	....	....	....	....	4	0	0	0	10	....	....	....	....
2001-02	Guelph Storm	OHL	63	41	32	73	56	....	....	....	....	....	....	....	....	....	9	8	5	13	14	....	....	....	....
2002-03	Guelph Storm	OHL	58	34	42	76	89	....	....	....	....	....	....	....	....	....	11	7	8	15	6	....	....	....	....
2003-04	Los Angeles	NHL	31	1	4	5	16	0	0	0	40	2.5	0	1	0.0	10:29	....	....	....	....	....	....	....	....	....
2004-05	Manchester	AHL	79	29	45	74	96	....	....	....	....	....	....	....	....	....	6	5	2	7	10	....	....	....	....
2005-06	Los Angeles	NHL	79	14	14	28	80	6	0	2	159	8.8	-10	15	66.7	13:59	....	....	....	....	....	....	....	....	....
2006-07	Los Angeles	NHL	81	17	29	46	54	13	0	1	195	8.7	-21	77	49.4	18:43	....	....	....	....	....	....	....	....	....
2007-08	Los Angeles	NHL	78	33	27	60	55	12	2	4	219	15.1	-13	40	50.0	20:18	....	....	....	....	....	....	....	....	....
2008-09	Los Angeles	NHL	80	24	29	53	64	7	0	6	292	8.2	-15	54	46.3	19:24	....	....	....	....	....	....	....	....	....
2009-10	Los Angeles	NHL	82	24	32	56	41	7	0	3	248	9.7	-6	39	43.6	19:15	6	1	4	5	6	1	0	0	18:53
	United States	Olympics	6	0	0	0	0	....	....	....	....	....	....	....	....	....	....	....	....	....	....	....	....	....	....
2010-11	Los Angeles	NHL	82	28	29	57	67	7	0	2	228	12.3	17	37	48.7	19:22	6	1	1	2	6	1	0	0	20:00

			Regular Season														Playoffs								
Season	Club	League	GP	G	A	Pts	PIM	PP	SH	GW	S	S%	+/-	TF	F%	Min	GP	G	A	Pts	PIM	PP	SH	GW	Min
2011-12♦	**Los Angeles**	**NHL**	**82**	**22**	**32**	**54**	**53**	**9**	**1**	**6**	**214**	**10.3**	**18**	**39**	**43.6**	**20:10**	**20**	***8**	***12**	***20**	**34**	**1**	***2**	**3**	**20:44**
2012-13	ZSC Lions Zurich	Swiss	16	8	5	13	26	....	....	....	....	....	....	....	....	....	....	....	....	....	....	....	....	....	....
	Los Angeles	**NHL**	**46**	**18**	**11**	**29**	**22**	**8**	**0**	**1**	**142**	**12.7**	**6**	**41**	**36.6**	**19:30**	**18**	**3**	**1**	**4**	**8**	**2**	**0**	**0**	**18:47**
2013-14♦	**Los Angeles**	**NHL**	**79**	**15**	**12**	**27**	**66**	**1**	**0**	**2**	**195**	**7.7**	**7**	**19**	**31.6**	**15:50**	**26**	**6**	**8**	**14**	**22**	**1**	**0**	**2**	**16:57**
	United States	Olympics	6	2	1	3	4	....	....	....	....	....	....	....	....	....	....	....	....	....	....	....	....	....	....
2014-15	**Los Angeles**	**NHL**	**82**	**11**	**16**	**27**	**26**	**1**	**0**	**3**	**189**	**5.8**	**–17**	**35**	**42.9**	**16:31**	....	....	....	....	....	....	....	....	....
	NHL Totals		**802**	**207**	**235**	**442**	**544**	**71**	**3**	**30**	**2121**	**9.8**		**397**	**45.6**	**17:58**	**76**	**19**	**26**	**45**	**76**	**6**	**2**	**5**	**18:47**

OHL All-Rookie Team (2001) • Canadian Major Junior Scholastic Player of the Year (2003) • NHL Foundation Player Award (2011) • Mark Messier NHL Leadership Award (2014)
Played in NHL All-Star Game (2009)
• Missed majority of 2003-04 due to ankle injury vs. Chicago, November 29, 2003. Signed as a free agent by **Zurich** (Swiss), November 1, 2012.

BROWN, J.T. (BROWN, JAY-TEE) T.B.

Right wing. Shoots right. 5'11", 170 lbs. Born, High Point, NC, July 2, 1990.

Season	Club	League	GP	G	A	Pts	PIM	PP	SH	GW	S	S%	+/-	TF	F%	Min	GP	G	A	Pts	PIM	PP	SH	GW	Min
2008-09	Waterloo	USHL	36	14	22	36	28	....	....	....	....	....	....	....	....	....	3	1	0	1	4	....	....	....	....
2009-10	Waterloo	USHL	60	34	43	77	64	....	....	....	....	....	....	....	....	....	3	1	0	1	0	....	....	....	....
2010-11	U. Minn-Duluth	WCHA	42	16	21	37	50	....	....	....	....	....	....	....	....	....	....	....	....	....	....	....	....	....	....
2011-12	U. Minn-Duluth	WCHA	39	24	23	47	59	....	....	....	....	....	....	....	....	....	....	....	....	....	....	....	....	....	....
	Tampa Bay	**NHL**	**5**	**0**	**1**	**1**	**0**	**0**	**0**	**0**	**13**	**0.0**	**2**	**0**	**0.0**	**13:51**	....	....	....	....	....	....	....	....	....
2012-13	Syracuse Crunch	AHL	51	10	18	28	27	....	....	....	....	....	....	....	....	....	18	4	5	9	18	....	....	....	....
2013-14	**Tampa Bay**	**NHL**	**63**	**4**	**15**	**19**	**6**	**0**	**0**	**0**	**113**	**3.5**	**–9**	**22**	**31.8**	**13:02**	**4**	**0**	**2**	**2**	**0**	**0**	**0**	**0**	**15:00**
	Syracuse Crunch	AHL	13	4	6	10	24	....	....	....	....	....	....	....	....	....	....	....	....	....	....	....	....	....	....
2014-15	**Tampa Bay**	**NHL**	**52**	**3**	**6**	**9**	**30**	**0**	**0**	**0**	**74**	**4.1**	**–2**	**13**	**46.2**	**10:36**	**24**	**1**	**1**	**2**	**0**	**0**	**0**	**0**	**12:21**
	NHL Totals		**120**	**7**	**22**	**29**	**36**	**0**	**0**	**0**	**200**	**3.5**		**35**	**37.1**	**12:01**	**28**	**1**	**3**	**4**	**0**	**0**	**0**	**0**	**12:43**

USHL Second All-Star Team (2010) • WCHA All-Rookie Team (2011) • NCAA Championship All-Tournament Team (2011) • NCAA Championship Tournament MVP (2011) • WCHA First All-Star Team (2012) • NCAA West Second All-American Team (2012)
Signed as a free agent by **Tampa Bay**, March 28, 2012.

BROWN, Mike (BROWN, MIGHK) S.J.

Right wing. Shoots right. 5'11", 202 lbs. Born, Chicago, IL, June 24, 1985. Vancouver's 4th choice, 159th overall, in 2004 Entry Draft.

Season	Club	League	GP	G	A	Pts	PIM	PP	SH	GW	S	S%	+/-	TF	F%	Min	GP	G	A	Pts	PIM	PP	SH	GW	Min
2000-01	Chicago Chill	USAHA	66	27	23	50	....	....	....	....	....	....	....	....	....	....	....	....	....	....	....	....	....	....	....
2001-02	USNTDP	U-17	17	6	4	10	13	....	....	....	....	....	....	....	....	....	....	....	....	....	....	....	....	....	....
	USNTDP	NAHL	46	5	11	16	56	....	....	....	....	....	....	....	....	....	....	....	....	....	....	....	....	....	....
2002-03	USNTDP	U-18	34	5	3	8	16	....	....	....	....	....	....	....	....	....	....	....	....	....	....	....	....	....	....
	USNTDP	NAHL	9	0	3	3	29	....	....	....	....	....	....	....	....	....	....	....	....	....	....	....	....	....	....
2003-04	U. of Michigan	CCHA	42	8	5	13	51	....	....	....	....	....	....	....	....	....	....	....	....	....	....	....	....	....	....
2004-05	U. of Michigan	CCHA	35	3	5	8	95	....	....	....	....	....	....	....	....	....	....	....	....	....	....	....	....	....	....
2005-06	Manitoba Moose	AHL	73	7	8	15	139	....	....	....	....	....	....	....	....	....	13	1	2	3	17	....	....	....	....
2006-07	Manitoba Moose	AHL	62	3	0	3	194	....	....	....	....	....	....	....	....	....	13	0	2	2	16	....	....	....	....
2007-08	**Vancouver**	**NHL**	**19**	**1**	**0**	**1**	**55**	**0**	**0**	**0**	**9**	**11.1**	**–2**	**0**	**0.0**	**6:19**	....	....	....	....	....	....	....	....	....
	Manitoba Moose	AHL	54	10	3	13	201	....	....	....	....	....	....	....	....	....	6	2	0	2	11	....	....	....	....
2008-09	**Vancouver**	**NHL**	**20**	**0**	**1**	**1**	**85**	**0**	**0**	**0**	**6**	**0.0**	**–5**	**2**	**0.0**	**5:29**	....	....	....	....	....	....	....	....	....
	Anaheim	**NHL**	**28**	**2**	**1**	**3**	**60**	**0**	**0**	**2**	**38**	**5.3**	**–2**	**4**	**0.0**	**10:02**	**13**	**0**	**2**	**2**	**25**	**0**	**0**	**0**	**8:28**
2009-10	**Anaheim**	**NHL**	**75**	**6**	**1**	**7**	**106**	**0**	**1**	**2**	**82**	**7.3**	**1**	**7**	**0.0**	**8:21**	....	....	....	....	....	....	....	....	....
2010-11	**Toronto**	**NHL**	**50**	**3**	**5**	**8**	**69**	**1**	**0**	**0**	**59**	**5.1**	**1**	**15**	**26.7**	**10:06**	....	....	....	....	....	....	....	....	....
2011-12	**Toronto**	**NHL**	**50**	**2**	**2**	**4**	**74**	**0**	**0**	**0**	**56**	**3.6**	**–8**	**1**	**0.0**	**9:17**	....	....	....	....	....	....	....	....	....
2012-13	**Toronto**	**NHL**	**12**	**0**	**1**	**1**	**70**	**0**	**0**	**0**	**2**	**0.0**	**1**	**1**	**0.0**	**4:39**	....	....	....	....	....	....	....	....	....
	Edmonton	**NHL**	**27**	**1**	**0**	**1**	**53**	**0**	**0**	**0**	**16**	**6.3**	**–8**	**7**	**71.4**	**8:48**	....	....	....	....	....	....	....	....	....
2013-14	**Edmonton**	**NHL**	**8**	**0**	**0**	**0**	**19**	**0**	**0**	**0**	**1**	**0.0**	**1**	**0**	**0.0**	**5:49**	....	....	....	....	....	....	....	....	....
	San Jose	**NHL**	**48**	**2**	**3**	**5**	**75**	**0**	**0**	**0**	**44**	**4.5**	**–10**	**3**	**66.7**	**7:22**	**6**	**1**	**1**	**2**	**26**	**0**	**0**	**0**	**6:57**
2014-15	**San Jose**	**NHL**	**12**	**0**	**0**	**0**	**22**	**0**	**0**	**0**	**11**	**0.0**	**0**	**7**	**57.1**	**8:12**	....	....	....	....	....	....	....	....	....
	NHL Totals		**349**	**17**	**14**	**31**	**688**	**1**	**1**	**4**	**324**	**5.2**		**47**	**31.9**	**8:18**	**19**	**1**	**3**	**4**	**51**	**0**	**0**	**0**	**7:59**

Traded to **Anaheim** by **Vancouver** for Nathan McIver, February 4, 2009. Traded to **Toronto** by **Anaheim** for Toronto's 5th round choice (Chris Wagner) in 2010 Entry Draft, June 25, 2010. Traded to **Edmonton** by **Toronto** for Edmonton's 4th round choice (later traded to Colorado – Colorado selected Nicholas Magyar) in 2014 Entry Draft, March 6, 2013. Traded to **San Jose** by **Edmonton** for San Jose's 4th round choice (Zachary Nagelvoort) in 2014 Entry Draft, October 21, 2013. • Missed majority of 2014-15 due to hand (October 11, 2014 vs. Winnipeg) and lower-body (December 9, 2014 vs. Edmonton) injuries.

BROWN, Patrick (BROWN, PAT-rihk) CAR

Left wing. Shoots right. 6'1", 210 lbs. Born, Bloomfield Hills, MI, May 29, 1992.

Season	Club	League	GP	G	A	Pts	PIM	PP	SH	GW	S	S%	+/-	TF	F%	Min	GP	G	A	Pts	PIM	PP	SH	GW	Min
2009-10	Cranbrook Cranes	High-MI	30	23	25	48	14	....	....	....	....	....	....	....	....	....	....	....	....	....	....	....	....	....	....
2010-11	Boston College	H-East	29	0	1	1	8	....	....	....	....	....	....	....	....	....	....	....	....	....	....	....	....	....	....
2011-12	Boston College	H-East	13	1	0	1	6	....	....	....	....	....	....	....	....	....	....	....	....	....	....	....	....	....	....
2012-13	Boston College	H-East	38	5	6	11	14	....	....	....	....	....	....	....	....	....	....	....	....	....	....	....	....	....	....
2013-14	Boston College	H-East	40	15	15	30	30	....	....	....	....	....	....	....	....	....	....	....	....	....	....	....	....	....	....
2014-15	**Carolina**	**NHL**	**7**	**0**	**0**	**0**	**4**	**0**	**0**	**0**	**4**	**0.0**	**–4**	**2**	**0.0**	**8:53**	....	....	....	....	....	....	....	....	....
	Charlotte	AHL	60	2	8	10	34	....	....	....	....	....	....	....	....	....	....	....	....	....	....	....	....	....	....
	NHL Totals		**7**	**0**	**0**	**0**	**4**	**0**	**0**	**0**	**4**	**0.0**		**2**	**0.0**	**8:53**	....	....	....	....	....	....	....	....	....

Signed as a free agent by **Carolina**, April 14, 2014.

BRUNNER, Damien (BROO-nuhr, DAY-mee-uhn)

Right wing. Shoots right. 5'10", 185 lbs. Born, Zurich, Switz., March 9, 1986.

Season	Club	League	GP	G	A	Pts	PIM	PP	SH	GW	S	S%	+/-	TF	F%	Min	GP	G	A	Pts	PIM	PP	SH	GW	Min
2006-07	Kloten Flyers	Swiss	42	9	9	18	22	....	....	....	....	....	....	....	....	....	11	1	0	1	4	....	....	....	....
2007-08	Kloten Flyers	Swiss	50	5	2	7	8	....	....	....	....	....	....	....	....	....	5	0	0	0	0	....	....	....	....
2008-09	Kloten Flyers	Swiss	12	0	0	0	2	....	....	....	....	....	....	....	....	....	....	....	....	....	....	....	....	....	....
	HC Thurgau	Swiss-2	3	1	3	4	4	....	....	....	....	....	....	....	....	....	....	....	....	....	....	....	....	....	....
	EV Zug	Swiss	36	12	14	26	16	....	....	....	....	....	....	....	....	....	10	3	2	5	4	....	....	....	....
2009-10	EV Zug	Swiss	47	23	35	58	22	....	....	....	....	....	....	....	....	....	13	5	5	10	6	....	....	....	....
2010-11	EV Zug	Swiss	40	19	27	46	34	....	....	....	....	....	....	....	....	....	8	4	4	8	2	....	....	....	....
2011-12	EV Zug	Swiss	45	24	36	60	48	....	....	....	....	....	....	....	....	....	9	3	11	14	6	....	....	....	....
2012-13	EV Zug	Swiss	33	25	32	57	49	....	....	....	....	....	....	....	....	....	....	....	....	....	....	....	....	....	....
	Detroit	**NHL**	**44**	**12**	**14**	**26**	**12**	**3**	**0**	**1**	**123**	**9.8**	**–6**	**5**	**40.0**	**15:35**	**14**	**5**	**4**	**9**	**4**	**0**	**0**	**1**	**13:07**
2013-14	**New Jersey**	**NHL**	**60**	**11**	**14**	**25**	**26**	**4**	**0**	**1**	**110**	**10.0**	**–11**	**8**	**12.5**	**13:32**	....	....	....	....	....	....	....	....	....
	Switzerland	Olympics	4	0	0	0	0	....	....	....	....	....	....	....	....	....	....	....	....	....	....	....	....	....	....
2014-15	**New Jersey**	**NHL**	**17**	**2**	**5**	**7**	**8**	**0**	**0**	**0**	**29**	**6.9**	**–1**	**4**	**50.0**	**15:09**	....	....	....	....	....	....	....	....	....
	HC Lugano	Swiss	20	11	5	16	30	....	....	....	....	....	....	....	....	....	3	0	1	1	0	....	....	....	....
	NHL Totals		**121**	**25**	**33**	**58**	**46**	**7**	**0**	**2**	**262**	**9.5**		**17**	**29.4**	**14:30**	**14**	**5**	**4**	**9**	**4**	**0**	**0**	**1**	**13:07**

Signed as a free agent by **Detroit**, July 1, 2012. Signed as a free agent by **Zug** (Swiss), September 17, 2012. Signed as a free agent by **New Jersey**, September 23, 2013. Signed as a free agent by **Lugano** (Swiss), December 12, 2014.

BULMER, Brett (BUHL-muhr, BREHT) MIN

Right wing. Shoots right. 6'4", 212 lbs. Born, Prince George, BC, April 26, 1992. Minnesota's 2nd choice, 39th overall, in 2010 Entry Draft.

Season	Club	League	GP	G	A	Pts	PIM	PP	SH	GW	S	S%	+/-	TF	F%	Min	GP	G	A	Pts	PIM	PP	SH	GW	Min
2007-08	Cariboo Cougars	BCMML	40	20	19	39	40	....	....	....	....	....	....	....	....	....	6	2	7	9	4	....	....	....	....
2008-09	Cariboo Cougars	BCMML	36	28	35	63	56	....	....	....	....	....	....	....	....	....	5	4	2	6	8	....	....	....	....
	Kelowna Rockets	WHL	3	0	0	0	2	....	....	....	....	....	....	....	....	....	....	....	....	....	....	....	....	....	....
2009-10	Kelowna Rockets	WHL	65	13	27	40	95	....	....	....	....	....	....	....	....	....	12	3	2	5	6	....	....	....	....
2010-11	Kelowna Rockets	WHL	57	18	31	49	109	....	....	....	....	....	....	....	....	....	10	4	2	6	4	....	....	....	....
	Houston Aeros	AHL	....	....	....	....	....	....	....	....	....	....	....	....	....	....	8	0	0	0	6	....	....	....	....
2011-12	**Minnesota**	**NHL**	**9**	**0**	**3**	**3**	**6**	**0**	**0**	**0**	**7**	**0.0**	**1**	**0**	**0.0**	**11:02**	....	....	....	....	....	....	....	....	....
	Kelowna Rockets	WHL	53	34	28	62	93	....	....	....	....	....	....	....	....	....	3	1	4	5	17	....	....	....	....
	Houston Aeros	AHL	6	1	1	2	2	....	....	....	....	....	....	....	....	....	4	1	1	2	2	....	....	....	....
2012-13	Houston Aeros	AHL	43	4	3	7	41	....	....	....	....	....	....	....	....	....	4	0	0	0	2	....	....	....	....

			Regular Season														Playoffs								
Season	Club	League	GP	G	A	Pts	PIM	PP	SH	GW	S	S%	+/-	TF	F%	Min	GP	G	A	Pts	PIM	PP	SH	GW	Min
2013-14	**Minnesota**	**NHL**	**5**	**0**	**0**	**0**	**2**	**0**	**0**	**0**	**7**	**0.0**	**–2**	**0**	**0.0**	**10:41**	....	....	....	....	....	....	....	....	....
	Iowa Wild	AHL	43	11	8	19	79	....	....	....	....	....	....	....	....	....	....	....	....	....	....	....	....	....	....
2014-15	Iowa Wild	AHL	53	4	12	16	50	....	....	....	....	....	....	....	....	....	....	....	....	....	....	....	....	....	....
	NHL Totals		**14**	**0**	**3**	**3**	**8**	**0**	**0**	**0**	**14**	**0.0**		**0**	**0.0**	**10:55**	....	....	....	....	....	....	....	....	....

BURAKOVSKY, Andre

(buhr-a-KAWV-skee, AHN-DRAY) **WSH**

Left wing. Shoots left. 6'2", 188 lbs. Born, Klagenfurt , Austria, February 9, 1995. Washington's 1st choice, 23rd overall, in 2013 Entry Draft.

Season	Club	League	GP	G	A	Pts	PIM	PP	SH	GW	S	S%	+/-	TF	F%	Min	GP	G	A	Pts	PIM	PP	SH	GW	Min
2010-11	Malmo U18	Swe-U18	27	8	9	17	6	....	....	....	....	....	....	....	....	....	....	....	....	....	....	....	....	....	....
2011-12	Malmo U18	Swe-U18	9	6	8	14	14	....	....	....	....	....	....	....	....	....	4	2	4	6	0	....	....	....	....
	Malmo Jr.	Swe-Jr.	42	17	25	42	43	....	....	....	....	....	....	....	....	....	5	1	4	5	2	....	....	....	....
	Malmo	Sweden-2	10	0	1	1	0	....	....	....	....	....	....	....	....	....	3	0	0	0	0	....	....	....	....
2012-13	Malmo U18	Swe-U18	3	6	4	10	2	....	....	....	....	....	....	....	....	....	4	3	3	6	0	....	....	....	....
	Malmo Jr.	Swe-Jr.	13	3	4	7	8	....	....	....	....	....	....	....	....	....	3	1	2	3	8	....	....	....	....
	Malmo	Sweden-2	43	4	7	11	8	....	....	....	....	....	....	....	....	....	....	....	....	....	....	....	....	....	....
2013-14	Erie Otters	OHL	57	41	46	87	35	....	....	....	....	....	....	....	....	....	14	10	3	13	2	....	....	....	....
2014-15	**Washington**	**NHL**	**53**	**9**	**13**	**22**	**10**	**2**	**0**	**2**	**65**	**13.8**	**12**	**167**	**44.3**	**12:55**	**11**	**2**	**1**	**3**	**0**	**0**	**0**	**1**	**12:25**
	Hershey Bears	AHL	13	3	4	7	6	....	....	....	....	....	....	....	....	....	1	1	0	1	0	....	....	....	....
	NHL Totals		**53**	**9**	**13**	**22**	**10**	**2**	**0**	**2**	**65**	**13.8**		**167**	**44.3**	**12:55**	**11**	**2**	**1**	**3**	**0**	**0**	**0**	**1**	**12:25**

BURISH, Adam

(BUHR-ish, A-duhm)

Right wing. Shoots right. 6'1", 195 lbs. Born, Madison, WI, January 6, 1983. Chicago's 9th choice, 282nd overall, in 2002 Entry Draft.

Season	Club	League	GP	G	A	Pts	PIM	PP	SH	GW	S	S%	+/-	TF	F%	Min	GP	G	A	Pts	PIM	PP	SH	GW	Min
2000-01	Edgewood	High-WI	22	25	30	55	22	....	....	....	....	....	....	....	....	....	....	....	....	....	....	....	....	....	....
2001-02	Green Bay	USHL	61	24	33	57	122	....	....	....	....	....	....	....	....	....	1	0	0	0	0	....	....	....	....
2002-03	U. of Wisconsin	WCHA	19	0	6	6	32	....	....	....	....	....	....	....	....	....	....	....	....	....	....	....	....	....	....
2003-04	U. of Wisconsin	WCHA	43	6	13	19	63	....	....	....	....	....	....	....	....	....	....	....	....	....	....	....	....	....	....
2004-05	U. of Wisconsin	WCHA	41	13	7	20	41	....	....	....	....	....	....	....	....	....	....	....	....	....	....	....	....	....	....
2005-06	U. of Wisconsin	WCHA	42	9	24	33	67	....	....	....	....	....	....	....	....	....	....	....	....	....	....	....	....	....	....
2006-07	**Chicago**	**NHL**	**9**	**0**	**0**	**0**	**2**	**0**	**0**	**0**	**12**	**0.0**	**–4**	**6**	**50.0**	**11:08**	....	....	....	....	....	....	....	....	....
	Norfolk Admirals	AHL	64	11	10	21	146	....	....	....	....	....	....	....	....	....	6	1	1	2	4	....	....	....	....
2007-08	**Chicago**	**NHL**	**81**	**4**	**4**	**8**	**214**	**0**	**1**	**1**	**69**	**5.8**	**–13**	**264**	**42.1**	**11:45**	....	....	....	....	....	....	....	....	....
2008-09	**Chicago**	**NHL**	**66**	**6**	**3**	**9**	**93**	**0**	**0**	**2**	**83**	**7.2**	**3**	**124**	**39.5**	**9:12**	**17**	**3**	**2**	**5**	**30**	**0**	**0**	**1**	**11:02**
2009-10♦	**Chicago**	**NHL**	**13**	**1**	**3**	**4**	**14**	**0**	**0**	**0**	**9**	**11.1**	**2**	**21**	**33.3**	**8:46**	**15**	**0**	**0**	**0**	**2**	**0**	**0**	**0**	**5:35**
2010-11	**Dallas**	**NHL**	**63**	**8**	**6**	**14**	**91**	**0**	**0**	**1**	**89**	**9.0**	**2**	**477**	**53.5**	**14:21**	....	....	....	....	....	....	....	....	....
2011-12	**Dallas**	**NHL**	**65**	**6**	**13**	**19**	**76**	**0**	**0**	**1**	**82**	**7.3**	**6**	**389**	**55.8**	**12:47**	....	....	....	....	....	....	....	....	....
2012-13	**San Jose**	**NHL**	**46**	**1**	**2**	**3**	**25**	**0**	**1**	**0**	**39**	**2.6**	**–7**	**228**	**53.5**	**10:34**	**6**	**0**	**0**	**0**	**4**	**0**	**0**	**0**	**10:15**
2013-14	**San Jose**	**NHL**	**15**	**0**	**0**	**0**	**6**	**0**	**0**	**0**	**9**	**0.0**	**–4**	**75**	**52.0**	**9:37**	....	....	....	....	....	....	....	....	....
2014-15	**San Jose**	**NHL**	**20**	**1**	**2**	**3**	**33**	**0**	**0**	**0**	**22**	**4.5**	**–6**	**107**	**53.3**	**11:09**	....	....	....	....	....	....	....	....	....
	Worcester Sharks	AHL	18	4	3	7	14	....	....	....	....	....	....	....	....	....	....	....	....	....	....	....	....	....	....
	Chicago Wolves	AHL	36	6	6	12	18	....	....	....	....	....	....	....	....	....	5	0	1	1	4	....	....	....	....
	NHL Totals		**378**	**27**	**33**	**60**	**554**	**0**	**2**	**5**	**414**	**6.5**		**1691**	**50.9**	**11:32**	**38**	**3**	**2**	**5**	**36**	**0**	**0**	**1**	**8:45**

NCAA Championship All-Tournament Team (2006)

• Missed majority of 2009-10 due to knee injury in pre-season at Minnesota, September 20, 2009. Signed as a free agent by **Dallas**, July 1, 2010. Signed as a free agent by **San Jose**, July 1, 2012. • Missed majority of 2013-14 due to recurring back injury and hand injury vs. Edmonton, March 25, 2014.

BURMISTROV, Alexander

(buhr-MIHS-trawf, al-ehx-AN-duhr) **WPG**

Center. Shoots left. 6'1", 180 lbs. Born, Kazan, Russia, October 21, 1991. Atlanta's 1st choice, 8th overall, in 2010 Entry Draft.

Season	Club	League	GP	G	A	Pts	PIM	PP	SH	GW	S	S%	+/-	TF	F%	Min	GP	G	A	Pts	PIM	PP	SH	GW	Min
2008-09	Ak Bars Kazan 2	Russia-3	34	25	25	50	54	....	....	....	....	....	....	....	....	....	....	....	....	....	....	....	....	....	....
	Ak Bars Kazan	KHL	1	0	0	0	0	....	....	....	....	....	....	....	....	....	....	....	....	....	....	....	....	....	....
2009-10	Barrie Colts	OHL	62	22	43	65	49	....	....	....	....	....	....	....	....	....	17	8	8	16	22	....	....	....	....
2010-11	**Atlanta**	**NHL**	**74**	**6**	**14**	**20**	**27**	**0**	**0**	**2**	**92**	**6.5**	**–12**	**696**	**41.5**	**13:13**	....	....	....	....	....	....	....	....	....
2011-12	**Winnipeg**	**NHL**	**76**	**13**	**15**	**28**	**42**	**1**	**1**	**0**	**123**	**10.6**	**4**	**564**	**44.0**	**16:40**	....	....	....	....	....	....	....	....	....
2012-13	**Winnipeg**	**NHL**	**44**	**4**	**6**	**10**	**14**	**0**	**0**	**0**	**55**	**7.3**	**0**	**301**	**47.2**	**15:38**	....	....	....	....	....	....	....	....	....
2013-14	Ak Bars Kazan	KHL	54	10	28	38	32	....	....	....	....	....	....	....	....	....	6	0	2	2	9	....	....	....	....
2014-15	Ak Bars Kazan	KHL	53	10	16	26	40	....	....	....	....	....	....	....	....	....	17	1	3	4	8	....	....	....	....
	NHL Totals		**194**	**23**	**35**	**58**	**83**	**1**	**1**	**2**	**270**	**8.5**		**1561**	**43.5**	**15:07**	....	....	....	....	....	....	....	....	....

• Transferred to **Winnipeg** after **Atlanta** franchise relocated, June 21, 2011. Signed as a free agent by **Kazan** (KHL), July 8, 2013. Signed as a free agent by **Winnipeg**, July 1, 2015.

BURNS, Brent

(BUHRNZ, BREHNT) **S.J.**

Defense. Shoots right. 6'5", 230 lbs. Born, Ajax, ON, March 9, 1985. Minnesota's 1st choice, 20th overall, in 2003 Entry Draft.

Season	Club	League	GP	G	A	Pts	PIM	PP	SH	GW	S	S%	+/-	TF	F%	Min	GP	G	A	Pts	PIM	PP	SH	GW	Min
2001-02	Couchiching	ON-Jr.A	46	4	7	11	16	....	....	....	....	....	....	....	....	....	....	....	....	....	....	....	....	....	....
2002-03	Brampton	OHL	68	15	25	40	14	....	....	....	....	....	....	....	....	....	11	5	6	11	6	....	....	....	....
2003-04	**Minnesota**	**NHL**	**36**	**1**	**5**	**6**	**12**	**0**	**0**	**0**	**34**	**2.9**	**–10**	**7**	**28.6**	**13:29**	....	....	....	....	....	....	....	....	....
	Houston Aeros	AHL	1	0	1	1	2	....	....	....	....	....	....	....	....	....	....	....	....	....	....	....	....	....	....
2004-05	Houston Aeros	AHL	73	11	16	27	57	....	....	....	....	....	....	....	....	....	5	0	0	0	4	....	....	....	....
2005-06	**Minnesota**	**NHL**	**72**	**4**	**12**	**16**	**32**	**1**	**0**	**1**	**73**	**5.5**	**–7**	**11**	**54.6**	**14:07**	....	....	....	....	....	....	....	....	....
2006-07	**Minnesota**	**NHL**	**77**	**7**	**18**	**25**	**26**	**3**	**0**	**3**	**108**	**6.5**	**16**	**4**	**25.0**	**15:48**	**5**	**0**	**1**	**1**	**14**	**0**	**0**	**0**	**18:59**
2007-08	**Minnesota**	**NHL**	**82**	**15**	**28**	**43**	**80**	**8**	**0**	**4**	**158**	**9.5**	**12**	**1**	**100.0**	**23:06**	**6**	**0**	**2**	**2**	**6**	**0**	**0**	**0**	**27:35**
2008-09	**Minnesota**	**NHL**	**59**	**8**	**19**	**27**	**45**	**4**	**0**	**2**	**147**	**5.4**	**–7**	**5**	**60.0**	**22:25**	....	....	....	....	....	....	....	....	....
2009-10	**Minnesota**	**NHL**	**47**	**3**	**17**	**20**	**32**	**2**	**0**	**0**	**104**	**2.9**	**–15**	**0**	**0.0**	**22:22**	....	....	....	....	....	....	....	....	....
2010-11	**Minnesota**	**NHL**	**80**	**17**	**29**	**46**	**98**	**8**	**0**	**3**	**170**	**10.0**	**–10**	**2**	**50.0**	**25:03**	....	....	....	....	....	....	....	....	....
2011-12	**San Jose**	**NHL**	**81**	**11**	**26**	**37**	**34**	**5**	**0**	**2**	**201**	**5.5**	**8**	**0**	**0.0**	**22:32**	**5**	**1**	**1**	**2**	**4**	**1**	**0**	**0**	**25:07**
2012-13	**San Jose**	**NHL**	**30**	**9**	**11**	**20**	**20**	**2**	**0**	**0**	**81**	**11.1**	**0**	**13**	**30.8**	**16:17**	**11**	**2**	**2**	**4**	**8**	**0**	**0**	**0**	**17:50**
2013-14	**San Jose**	**NHL**	**69**	**22**	**26**	**48**	**34**	**2**	**0**	**3**	**245**	**9.0**	**26**	**131**	**46.6**	**16:49**	**7**	**2**	**1**	**3**	**23**	**1**	**0**	**0**	**17:32**
2014-15	**San Jose**	**NHL**	**82**	**17**	**43**	**60**	**65**	**7**	**0**	**2**	**245**	**6.9**	**–9**	**0**	**0.0**	**23:57**	....	....	....	....	....	....	....	....	....
	NHL Totals		**715**	**114**	**234**	**348**	**478**	**42**	**0**	**20**	**1566**	**7.3**		**174**	**45.4**	**20:11**	**34**	**5**	**7**	**12**	**55**	**2**	**0**	**0**	**20:44**

NHL Foundation Player Award (2015)

Played in NHL All-Star Game (2011, 2015)

• Missed majority of 2003-04 on assignment to Team Canada and as a healthy reserve. • Missed majority of 2009-10 due to head injury vs. Phoenix, November 18, 2009. Traded to **San Jose** by **Minnesota** with Minnesota's 2nd round choice (later traded to Tampa Bay, later traded to Nashville – Nashville selected Pontius Aberg) in 2012 Entry Draft for Devin Setoguchi, Charlie Coyle and San Jose's 1st round choice (Zack Phillips) in 2011 Entry Draft, June 24, 2011.

BURROWS, Alexandre

(BUHR-ohz, al-ehx-AHN-druh) **VAN**

Left wing. Shoots left. 6'1", 188 lbs. Born, Pincourt, QC, April 11, 1981.

Season	Club	League	GP	G	A	Pts	PIM	PP	SH	GW	S	S%	+/-	TF	F%	Min	GP	G	A	Pts	PIM	PP	SH	GW	Min
99-2000	Kahnawake	QJHL	53	24	45	69	223	....	....	....	....	....	....	....	....	....	....	....	....	....	....	....	....	....	....
2000-01	Shawinigan	QMJHL	63	16	14	30	105	....	....	....	....	....	....	....	....	....	10	2	1	3	8	....	....	....	....
2001-02	Shawinigan	QMJHL	64	35	35	70	184	....	....	....	....	....	....	....	....	....	12	9	11	20	34	....	....	....	....
2002-03	Greenville	ECHL	53	9	17	26	201	....	....	....	....	....	....	....	....	....	....	....	....	....	....	....	....	....	....
	Baton Rouge	ECHL	13	4	2	6	64	....	....	....	....	....	....	....	....	....	....	....	....	....	....	....	....	....	....
2003-04	Manitoba Moose	AHL	2	0	0	0	0	....	....	....	....	....	....	....	....	....	....	....	....	....	....	....	....	....	....
	Columbia Inferno	ECHL	64	29	44	73	194	....	....	....	....	....	....	....	....	....	4	2	0	2	28	....	....	....	....
2004-05	Manitoba Moose	AHL	72	9	17	26	107	....	....	....	....	....	....	....	....	....	14	0	3	3	37	....	....	....	....
	Columbia Inferno	ECHL	4	5	1	6	4	....	....	....	....	....	....	....	....	....	....	....	....	....	....	....	....	....	....
2005-06	**Vancouver**	**NHL**	**43**	**7**	**5**	**12**	**61**	**0**	**1**	**1**	**49**	**14.3**	**5**	**19**	**47.4**	**10:24**	....	....	....	....	....	....	....	....	....
	Manitoba Moose	AHL	33	12	18	30	57	....	....	....	....	....	....	....	....	....	13	6	7	13	27	....	....	....	....
2006-07	**Vancouver**	**NHL**	**81**	**3**	**6**	**9**	**93**	**0**	**0**	**1**	**70**	**4.3**	**–7**	**16**	**43.8**	**11:26**	**11**	**1**	**0**	**1**	**14**	**0**	**0**	**0**	**10:34**
2007-08	**Vancouver**	**NHL**	**82**	**12**	**19**	**31**	**179**	**1**	**3**	**3**	**126**	**9.5**	**11**	**37**	**35.1**	**15:06**	....	....	....	....	....	....	....	....	....
2008-09	**Vancouver**	**NHL**	**82**	**28**	**23**	**51**	**150**	**0**	**4**	**3**	**175**	**16.0**	**23**	**80**	**46.3**	**16:51**	**10**	**3**	**1**	**4**	**20**	**0**	**0**	**1**	**18:48**
2009-10	**Vancouver**	**NHL**	**82**	**35**	**32**	**67**	**121**	**4**	**5**	**3**	**209**	**16.7**	**34**	**34**	**41.2**	**17:52**	**12**	**3**	**3**	**6**	**22**	**0**	**0**	**0**	**18:51**
2010-11	**Vancouver**	**NHL**	**72**	**26**	**22**	**48**	**77**	**1**	**1**	**4**	**152**	**17.1**	**26**	**14**	**42.9**	**17:02**	**25**	**9**	**8**	**17**	**34**	**1**	**1**	**2**	**20:40**
2011-12	**Vancouver**	**NHL**	**80**	**28**	**24**	**52**	**90**	**3**	**2**	**7**	**198**	**14.1**	**24**	**20**	**35.0**	**18:50**	**5**	**1**	**0**	**1**	**7**	**0**	**0**	**0**	**18:50**
2012-13	**Vancouver**	**NHL**	**47**	**13**	**11**	**24**	**54**	**1**	**0**	**2**	**140**	**9.3**	**15**	**108**	**44.4**	**18:54**	**4**	**2**	**1**	**3**	**6**	**1**	**0**	**0**	**20:36**

			Regular Season														Playoffs								
Season	Club	League	GP	G	A	Pts	PIM	PP	SH	GW	S	S%	+/-	TF	F%	Min	GP	G	A	Pts	PIM	PP	SH	GW	Min
2013-14	**Vancouver**	**NHL**	**49**	**5**	**10**	**15**	**71**	**2**	**0**	**0**	**104**	**4.8**	**-9**	**55**	**41.8**	**17:49**	....	....	....	....	....	....	....	....	....
2014-15	**Vancouver**	**NHL**	**70**	**18**	**15**	**33**	**68**	**4**	**1**	**3**	**145**	**12.4**	**0**	**14**	**42.9**	**15:29**	**3**	**0**	**2**	**2**	**21**	**0**	**0**	**0**	**14:22**
	NHL Totals		**688**	**175**	**167**	**342**	**964**	**16**	**17**	**27**	**1368**	**12.8**		**397**	**42.8**	**16:00**	**70**	**19**	**15**	**34**	**124**	**2**	**1**	**3**	**18:06**

Signed as a free agent by **Manitoba** (AHL), October 21, 2003. Signed as a free agent by **Vancouver**, November 8, 2005.

BUTLER, Bobby

(BUHT-luhr, BAW-bee)

Right wing. Shoots right. 6', 189 lbs. Born, Marlborough, MA, April 26, 1987.

Season	Club	League	GP	G	A	Pts	PIM	PP	SH	GW	S	S%	+/-	TF	F%	Min	GP	G	A	Pts	PIM	PP	SH	GW	Min
2002-03	Bos. Little Bruins	Minor-MA	35	21	27	48	12	....	....	....	....	....	....	....	....	....	....	....	....	....	....	....	....	....	....
	Bos. Jr. Bruins	EJHL	13	1	3	4	0	....	....	....	....	....	....	....	....	....	....	....	....	....	....	....	....	....	....
2003-04	Bos. Jr. Bruins	EJHL	59	15	18	33	28	....	....	....	....	....	....	....	....	....	....	....	....	....	....	....	....	....	....
2004-05	Bos. Jr. Bruins	EJHL	56	19	20	39	20	....	....	....	....	....	....	....	....	....	....	....	....	....	....	....	....	....	....
2005-06	Bos. Jr. Bruins	EJHL	61	28	30	58	48	....	....	....	....	....	....	....	....	....	....	....	....	....	....	....	....	....	....
2006-07	New Hampshire	H-East	38	9	3	12	12	....	....	....	....	....	....	....	....	....	....	....	....	....	....	....	....	....	....
2007-08	New Hampshire	H-East	38	14	12	26	20	....	....	....	....	....	....	....	....	....	....	....	....	....	....	....	....	....	....
2008-09	New Hampshire	H-East	38	9	21	30	36	....	....	....	....	....	....	....	....	....	....	....	....	....	....	....	....	....	....
2009-10	New Hampshire	H-East	39	29	24	53	20	....	....	....	....	....	....	....	....	....	....	....	....	....	....	....	....	....	....
	Ottawa	**NHL**	**2**	**0**	**0**	**0**	**0**	**0**	**0**	**0**	**2**	**0.0**	**-1**	**0**	**0.0**	**8:21**	....	....	....	....	....	....	....	....	....
2010-11	**Ottawa**	**NHL**	**36**	**10**	**11**	**21**	**10**	**1**	**0**	**3**	**73**	**13.7**	**-16**	**2**	**0.0**	**15:26**	....	....	....	....	....	....	....	....	....
	Binghamton	AHL	47	22	11	33	35	....	....	....	....	....	....	....	....	....	23	13	4	17	6	....	....	....	....
2011-12	**Ottawa**	**NHL**	**56**	**6**	**10**	**16**	**12**	**0**	**0**	**4**	**86**	**7.0**	**8**	**3**	**100.0**	**11:29**	**3**	**0**	**0**	**0**	**0**	**0**	**0**	**0**	**12:44**
2012-13	Albany Devils	AHL	37	16	11	27	8	....	....	....	....	....	....	....	....	....	....	....	....	....	....	....	....	....	....
	New Jersey	**NHL**	**14**	**1**	**1**	**2**	**0**	**1**	**0**	**0**	**13**	**7.7**	**-6**	**4**	**50.0**	**9:59**	....	....	....	....	....	....	....	....	....
	Nashville	**NHL**	**20**	**3**	**6**	**9**	**4**	**0**	**0**	**0**	**28**	**10.7**	**-2**	**1**	**0.0**	**11:23**	....	....	....	....	....	....	....	....	....
2013-14	**Florida**	**NHL**	**2**	**0**	**1**	**1**	**2**	**0**	**0**	**0**	**5**	**0.0**	**1**	**0**	**0.0**	**13:50**	....	....	....	....	....	....	....	....	....
	San Antonio	AHL	69	22	25	47	12	....	....	....	....	....	....	....	....	....	....	....	....	....	....	....	....	....	....
2014-15	San Antonio	AHL	68	27	32	59	37	....	....	....	....	....	....	....	....	....	....	....	....	....	....	....	....	....	....
	NHL Totals		**130**	**20**	**29**	**49**	**28**	**2**	**0**	**7**	**207**	**9.7**		**10**	**50.0**	**12:23**	**3**	**0**	**0**	**0**	**0**	**0**	**0**	**0**	**12:44**

Hockey East First All-Star Team (2010) • Hockey East Player of the Year (2010) • NCAA East First All-American Team (2010)

Signed as a free agent by **Ottawa**, March 29, 2010. Signed as a free agent by **New Jersey**, August 9, 2012. Claimed on waivers by **Nashville** from **New Jersey**, March 4, 2013. Traded to **Florida** by **Nashviille** for T.J. Brennan, June 14, 2013. Signed as a free agent by **MODO** (Sweden), July 15, 2015.

BUTLER, Chris

(BUHT-luhr, KRIHS) **ST.L.**

Defense. Shoots left. 6'1", 196 lbs. Born, St. Louis, MO, October 27, 1986. Buffalo's 4th choice, 96th overall, in 2005 Entry Draft.

Season	Club	League	GP	G	A	Pts	PIM	PP	SH	GW	S	S%	+/-	TF	F%	Min	GP	G	A	Pts	PIM	PP	SH	GW	Min
2003-04	Sioux City	USHL	55	3	6	9	37	....	....	....	....	....	....	....	....	....	7	0	1	1	6	....	....	....	....
2004-05	Sioux City	USHL	60	6	22	28	90	....	....	....	....	....	....	....	....	....	13	1	6	7	10	....	....	....	....
2005-06	U. of Denver	WCHA	35	7	15	22	28	....	....	....	....	....	....	....	....	....	....	....	....	....	....	....	....	....	....
2006-07	U. of Denver	WCHA	39	10	17	27	42	....	....	....	....	....	....	....	....	....	....	....	....	....	....	....	....	....	....
2007-08	U. of Denver	WCHA	41	3	14	17	38	....	....	....	....	....	....	....	....	....	....	....	....	....	....	....	....	....	....
2008-09	**Buffalo**	**NHL**	**47**	**2**	**4**	**6**	**18**	**0**	**0**	**1**	**36**	**5.6**	**11**	**0**	**0.0**	**16:43**	....	....	....	....	....	....	....	....	....
	Portland Pirates	AHL	27	2	10	12	14	....	....	....	....	....	....	....	....	....	4	0	0	0	0	....	....	....	....
2009-10	**Buffalo**	**NHL**	**59**	**1**	**20**	**21**	**22**	**0**	**0**	**0**	**61**	**1.6**	**-15**	**0**	**0.0**	**20:01**	....	....	....	....	....	....	....	....	....
2010-11	**Buffalo**	**NHL**	**49**	**2**	**7**	**9**	**26**	**0**	**0**	**0**	**52**	**3.8**	**8**	**0**	**0.0**	**18:10**	**7**	**0**	**1**	**1**	**10**	**0**	**0**	**0**	**22:59**
2011-12	**Calgary**	**NHL**	**68**	**2**	**13**	**15**	**34**	**0**	**0**	**0**	**62**	**3.2**	**-9**	**0**	**0.0**	**21:36**	....	....	....	....	....	....	....	....	....
2012-13	Karlskrona HK	Sweden-2	5	0	0	0	8	....	....	....	....	....	....	....	....	....	....	....	....	....	....	....	....	....	....
	Calgary	**NHL**	**44**	**1**	**7**	**8**	**19**	**0**	**1**	**0**	**40**	**2.5**	**-10**	**0**	**0.0**	**17:02**	....	....	....	....	....	....	....	....	....
2013-14	**Calgary**	**NHL**	**82**	**2**	**14**	**16**	**39**	**0**	**0**	**1**	**83**	**2.4**	**-23**	**0**	**0.0**	**20:16**	....	....	....	....	....	....	....	....	....
2014-15	**St. Louis**	**NHL**	**33**	**3**	**6**	**9**	**23**	**0**	**1**	**0**	**54**	**5.6**	**8**	**0**	**0.0**	**17:11**	....	....	....	....	....	....	....	....	....
	Chicago Wolves	AHL	14	1	8	9	6	....	....	....	....	....	....	....	....	....	....	....	....	....	....	....	....	....	....
	NHL Totals		**382**	**13**	**71**	**84**	**181**	**0**	**2**	**2**	**388**	**3.4**		**0**	**0.0**	**19:07**	**7**	**0**	**1**	**1**	**10**	**0**	**0**	**0**	**23:00**

USHL First All-Star Team (2005) • WCHA All-Rookie Team (2006) • WCHA Second All-Star Team (2008) • NCAA West Second All-American Team (2008)

Traded to **Calgary** by **Buffalo** with Paul Byron for Robyn Regehr, Ales Kotalik and Calgary's 2nd round choice (Jake McCabe) in 2012 Entry Draft, June 25, 2011. Signed as a free agent by **Karlskrona** (Sweden-2), November 27, 2012. Signed as a free agent by **St. Louis**, July 16, 2014.

BYERS, Dane

(BIGH-uhrs, DAYN)

Left wing. Shoots left. 6'3", 204 lbs. Born, Nipawin, SK, February 21, 1986. NY Rangers' 4th choice, 48th overall, in 2004 Entry Draft.

Season	Club	League	GP	G	A	Pts	PIM	PP	SH	GW	S	S%	+/-	TF	F%	Min	GP	G	A	Pts	PIM	PP	SH	GW	Min
2001-02	Prince Albert	SMMHL	43	5	15	20	67	....	....	....	....	....	....	....	....	....	3	2	3	5	9	....	....	....	....
2002-03	Prince Albert	WHL	49	8	6	14	46	....	....	....	....	....	....	....	....	....	....	....	....	....	....	....	....	....	....
2003-04	Prince Albert	WHL	51	9	8	17	134	....	....	....	....	....	....	....	....	....	6	1	2	3	17	....	....	....	....
2004-05	Prince Albert	WHL	65	11	9	20	181	....	....	....	....	....	....	....	....	....	17	4	6	10	18	....	....	....	....
2005-06	Prince Albert	WHL	71	21	27	48	157	....	....	....	....	....	....	....	....	....	....	....	....	....	....	....	....	....	....
	Hartford	AHL	5	0	2	2	6	....	....	....	....	....	....	....	....	....	....	....	....	....	....	....	....	....	....
2006-07	Hartford	AHL	78	17	30	47	213	....	....	....	....	....	....	....	....	....	7	2	0	2	16	....	....	....	....
2007-08	**NY Rangers**	**NHL**	**1**	**0**	**0**	**0**	**0**	**0**	**0**	**0**	**0**	**0.0**	**-1**	**0**	**0.0**	**5:05**	....	....	....	....	....	....	....	....	....
	Hartford	AHL	73	23	23	46	184	....	....	....	....	....	....	....	....	....	5	2	1	3	2	....	....	....	....
2008-09	Hartford	AHL	9	4	3	7	18	....	....	....	....	....	....	....	....	....	6	3	1	4	7	....	....	....	....
2009-10	**NY Rangers**	**NHL**	**5**	**1**	**0**	**1**	**31**	**0**	**0**	**0**	**3**	**33.3**	**1**	**0**	**0.0**	**6:21**	....	....	....	....	....	....	....	....	....
	Hartford	AHL	74	25	27	52	100	....	....	....	....	....	....	....	....	....	....	....	....	....	....	....	....	....	....
2010-11	Connecticut	AHL	16	3	6	9	25	....	....	....	....	....	....	....	....	....	....	....	....	....	....	....	....	....	....
	Springfield	AHL	48	9	16	25	95	....	....	....	....	....	....	....	....	....	....	....	....	....	....	....	....	....	....
	San Antonio	AHL	21	3	9	12	41	....	....	....	....	....	....	....	....	....	....	....	....	....	....	....	....	....	....
2011-12	**Columbus**	**NHL**	**8**	**0**	**0**	**0**	**29**	**0**	**0**	**0**	**8**	**0.0**	**0**	**0**	**0.0**	**8:05**	....	....	....	....	....	....	....	....	....
	Springfield	AHL	61	16	23	39	108	....	....	....	....	....	....	....	....	....	....	....	....	....	....	....	....	....	....
2012-13	Oklahoma City	AHL	58	6	4	10	144	....	....	....	....	....	....	....	....	....	....	....	....	....	....	....	....	....	....
	Hershey Bears	AHL	5	0	0	0	11	....	....	....	....	....	....	....	....	....	1	0	1	1	0	....	....	....	....
2013-14	Hershey Bears	AHL	73	15	22	37	211	....	....	....	....	....	....	....	....	....	....	....	....	....	....	....	....	....	....
2014-15	Hershey Bears	AHL	43	7	12	19	91	....	....	....	....	....	....	....	....	....	....	....	....	....	....	....	....	....	....
	NHL Totals		**14**	**1**	**0**	**1**	**60**	**0**	**0**	**0**	**11**	**9.1**		**0**	**0.0**	**7:15**	....	....	....	....	....	....	....	....	....

• Missed majority of 2008-09 due to knee injury vs. Worcester (AHL), October 31, 2008. Traded to **Columbus** by **NY Rangers** for Chad Kolarik, November 11, 2010. Traded to **Phoenix** by **Columbus** with Rostislav Klesla for Scottie Upshall and Sami Lepisto, February 28, 2011. Signed as a free agent by **Columbus**. July 11, 2011. Signed as a free agent by **Edmonton**, July 5, 2012. Traded to **Washington** by **Edmonton** for Garrett Stafford, April 2, 2013.

BYFUGLIEN, Dustin

(BUHF-lihn, DUHS-tihn) **WPG**

Defense. Shoots right. 6'5", 265 lbs. Born, Minneapolis, MN, March 27, 1985. Chicago's 8th choice, 245th overall, in 2003 Entry Draft.

Season	Club	League	GP	G	A	Pts	PIM	PP	SH	GW	S	S%	+/-	TF	F%	Min	GP	G	A	Pts	PIM	PP	SH	GW	Min
2001-02	Chicago Mission	MAHL	52	32	30	62	40	....	....	....	....	....	....	....	....	....	....	....	....	....	....	....	....	....	....
	Brandon	WHL	3	0	0	0	0	....	....	....	....	....	....	....	....	....	....	....	....	....	....	....	....	....	....
2002-03	Brandon	WHL	8	1	1	2	4	....	....	....	....	....	....	....	....	....	....	....	....	....	....	....	....	....	....
	Prince George	WHL	48	9	28	37	74	....	....	....	....	....	....	....	....	....	5	1	3	4	12	....	....	....	....
2003-04	Prince George	WHL	66	16	29	45	137	....	....	....	....	....	....	....	....	....	....	....	....	....	....	....	....	....	....
2004-05	Prince George	WHL	64	22	36	58	184	....	....	....	....	....	....	....	....	....	....	....	....	....	....	....	....	....	....
2005-06	**Chicago**	**NHL**	**25**	**3**	**2**	**5**	**24**	**0**	**0**	**1**	**45**	**6.7**	**-6**	**0**	**0.0**	**17:19**	....	....	....	....	....	....	....	....	....
	Norfolk Admirals	AHL	53	8	15	23	75	....	....	....	....	....	....	....	....	....	4	1	2	3	4	....	....	....	....
2006-07	**Chicago**	**NHL**	**9**	**1**	**2**	**3**	**10**	**0**	**0**	**0**	**18**	**5.6**	**-2**	**0**	**0.0**	**17:18**	....	....	....	....	....	....	....	....	....
	Norfolk Admirals	AHL	63	16	28	44	146	....	....	....	....	....	....	....	....	....	6	0	2	2	18	....	....	....	....
2007-08	**Chicago**	**NHL**	**67**	**19**	**17**	**36**	**59**	**7**	**0**	**4**	**163**	**11.7**	**-7**	**1**	**0.0**	**17:02**	....	....	....	....	....	....	....	....	....
	Rockford IceHogs	AHL	8	2	5	7	25	....	....	....	....	....	....	....	....	....	....	....	....	....	....	....	....	....	....
2008-09	**Chicago**	**NHL**	**77**	**15**	**16**	**31**	**81**	**3**	**0**	**4**	**202**	**7.4**	**7**	**11**	**18.2**	**14:52**	**17**	**3**	**6**	**9**	**26**	**1**	**0**	**0**	**17:11**
2009-10 ♦	**Chicago**	**NHL**	**82**	**17**	**17**	**34**	**94**	**6**	**0**	**3**	**211**	**8.1**	**-7**	**2**	**50.0**	**16:25**	**22**	**11**	**5**	**16**	**20**	**5**	**0**	**5**	**16:16**
2010-11	**Atlanta**	**NHL**	**81**	**20**	**33**	**53**	**93**	**8**	**0**	**6**	**347**	**5.8**	**-2**	**0**	**0.0**	**23:18**	....	....	....	....	....	....	....	....	....
2011-12	**Winnipeg**	**NHL**	**66**	**12**	**41**	**53**	**72**	**4**	**0**	**3**	**223**	**5.4**	**-8**	**0**	**0.0**	**24:07**	....	....	....	....	....	....	....	....	....
2012-13	**Winnipeg**	**NHL**	**43**	**8**	**20**	**28**	**34**	**4**	**0**	**2**	**142**	**5.6**	**-1**	**0**	**0.0**	**24:24**	....	....	....	....	....	....	....	....	....

			Regular Season														Playoffs								
Season	Club	League	GP	G	A	Pts	PIM	PP	SH	GW	S	S%	+/-	TF	F%	Min	GP	G	A	Pts	PIM	PP	SH	GW	Min
2013-14	**Winnipeg**	**NHL**	78	20	36	56	86	8	0	1	256	7.8	–20	2	0.0	23:05	....	....	....	....	....	....	....	....	....
2014-15	**Winnipeg**	**NHL**	69	18	27	45	124	5	0	3	209	8.6	5	3	0.0	22:41	4	0	1	1	4	0	0	0	23:00
	NHL Totals		597	133	211	344	677	45	0	27	1816	7.3		19	15.8	20:18	43	14	12	26	50	6	0	5	17:15

AHL Second All-Star Team (2007)

Played in NHL All-Star Game (2011, 2015)

Traded to **Atlanta** by **Chicago** with Brent Sopel, Ben Eager and Akim Aliu for Marty Reasoner, Joey Crabb, Jeremy Morin and New Jersey's 1st (previously acquired, Chicago selected Kevin Hayes) and 2nd (previously acquired, Chicago selected Justin Holl) round choices in 2010 Entry Draft, June 24, 2010. • Transferred to **Winnipeg** after **Atlanta** franchise relocated, June 21, 2011.

BYRON, Paul

(BIGH-ruhn, PAWL) **CGY**

Center. Shoots left. 5'7", 153 lbs. Born, Ottawa, ON, April 27, 1989. Buffalo's 6th choice, 179th overall, in 2007 Entry Draft.

Season	Club	League	GP	G	A	Pts	PIM	PP	SH	GW	S	S%	+/-	TF	F%	Min	GP	G	A	Pts	PIM	PP	SH	GW	Min
2005-06	Ottawa West	ON-Jr.B	33	20	23	43	33	....	....	....	....	....	....	....	....	....	7	3	8	11	4	....	....	....	....
2006-07	Gatineau	QMJHL	68	21	23	44	46	....	....	....	....	....	....	....	....	....	5	5	1	6	2	....	....	....	....
2007-08	Gatineau	QMJHL	52	37	31	68	25	....	....	....	....	....	....	....	....	....	19	*21	11	32	12	....	....	....	....
2008-09	Gatineau	QMJHL	64	33	66	99	32	....	....	....	....	....	....	....	....	....	10	2	14	16	4	....	....	....	....
2009-10	Portland Pirates	AHL	57	14	19	33	59	....	....	....	....	....	....	....	....	....	4	0	0	0	0	....	....	....	....
2010-11	**Buffalo**	**NHL**	8	1	1	2	2	0	0	0	5	20.0	0	71	40.9	10:57	....	....	....	....	....	....	....	....	....
	Portland Pirates	AHL	67	26	27	53	52	....	....	....	....	....	....	....	....	....	12	2	5	7	6	....	....	....	....
2011-12	**Calgary**	**NHL**	22	3	2	5	2	0	0	1	13	23.1	3	22	36.4	10:14	....	....	....	....	....	....	....	....	....
	Abbotsford Heat	AHL	39	7	14	21	40	....	....	....	....	....	....	....	....	....	8	1	3	4	2	....	....	....	....
2012-13	**Calgary**	**NHL**	4	0	1	1	2	0	0	0	1	0.0	–2	17	41.2	10:27	....	....	....	....	....	....	....	....	....
	Abbotsford Heat	AHL	38	6	9	15	38	....	....	....	....	....	....	....	....	....	....	....	....	....	....	....	....	....	....
2013-14	**Calgary**	**NHL**	47	7	14	21	27	2	1	1	46	15.2	6	32	21.9	14:27	....	....	....	....	....	....	....	....	....
	Abbotsford Heat	AHL	23	5	13	18	4	....	....	....	....	....	....	....	....	....	....	....	....	....	....	....	....	....	....
2014-15	**Calgary**	**NHL**	57	6	13	19	8	1	0	0	62	9.7	–2	97	35.1	14:28	....	....	....	....	....	....	....	....	....
	NHL Totals		138	17	31	48	41	3	1	2	127	13.4		239	35.6	13:28	....	....	....	....	....	....	....	....	....

QMJHL Second All-Star Team (2009)

Traded to **Calgary** by **Buffalo** with Chris Butler for Robyn Regehr, Ales Kotalik and Calgary's 2nd round choice (Jake McCabe) in 2012 Entry Draft, June 25, 2011.

CALLAHAN, Mitch

(kal-AH-han, MIHCH) **DET**

Right wing. Shoots right. 6', 196 lbs. Born, Whittier, CA, August 17, 1991. Detroit's 6th choice, 180th overall, in 2009 Entry Draft.

Season	Club	League	GP	G	A	Pts	PIM	PP	SH	GW	S	S%	+/-	TF	F%	Min	GP	G	A	Pts	PIM	PP	SH	GW	Min
2007-08	L.A. Jr. Kings	Minor-CA	52	32	37	69	62	....	....	....	....	....	....	....	....	....	....	....	....	....	....	....	....	....	....
2008-09	Kelowna Rockets	WHL	70	14	13	27	188	....	....	....	....	....	....	....	....	....	22	1	3	4	43	....	....	....	....
2009-10	Kelowna Rockets	WHL	72	20	27	47	165	....	....	....	....	....	....	....	....	....	12	2	4	6	10	....	....	....	....
2010-11	Kelowna Rockets	WHL	62	23	31	54	87	....	....	....	....	....	....	....	....	....	10	5	4	9	17	....	....	....	....
2011-12	Grand Rapids	AHL	48	6	3	9	103	....	....	....	....	....	....	....	....	....	....	....	....	....	....	....	....	....	....
2012-13	Grand Rapids	AHL	71	11	9	20	93	....	....	....	....	....	....	....	....	....	24	6	5	11	33	....	....	....	....
2013-14	**Detroit**	**NHL**	1	0	0	0	0	0	0	0	0	0.0	0	0	0.0	9:01	....	....	....	....	....	....	....	....	....
	Grand Rapids	AHL	70	26	18	44	51	....	....	....	....	....	....	....	....	....	8	1	4	5	6	....	....	....	....
2014-15	Grand Rapids	AHL	48	16	22	38	24	....	....	....	....	....	....	....	....	....	....	....	....	....	....	....	....	....	....
	NHL Totals		1	0	0	0	0	0	0	0	0	0.0		0	0.0	9:01	....	....	....	....	....	....	....	....	....

CALLAHAN, Ryan

(kal-AH-han, RIGH-uhn) **T.B.**

Right wing. Shoots right. 5'11", 190 lbs. Born, Rochester, NY, March 21, 1985. NY Rangers' 9th choice, 127th overall, in 2004 Entry Draft.

Season	Club	League	GP	G	A	Pts	PIM	PP	SH	GW	S	S%	+/-	TF	F%	Min	GP	G	A	Pts	PIM	PP	SH	GW	Min
2002-03	Guelph Storm	OHL	59	14	17	31	47	....	....	....	....	....	....	....	....	....	11	0	3	3	2	....	....	....	....
2003-04	Guelph Storm	OHL	68	36	32	68	86	....	....	....	....	....	....	....	....	....	22	*13	8	21	20	....	....	....	....
2004-05	Guelph Storm	OHL	60	28	26	54	108	....	....	....	....	....	....	....	....	....	4	1	1	2	6	....	....	....	....
2005-06	Guelph Storm	OHL	62	52	32	84	126	....	....	....	....	....	....	....	....	....	13	7	17	24	20	....	....	....	....
2006-07	**NY Rangers**	**NHL**	14	4	2	6	9	0	0	1	40	10.0	5	3	66.7	10:31	10	2	1	3	6	1	0	0	12:19
	Hartford	AHL	60	35	20	55	74	....	....	....	....	....	....	....	....	....	....	....	....	....	....	....	....	....	....
2007-08	**NY Rangers**	**NHL**	52	8	5	13	31	0	1	1	92	8.7	7	5	20.0	12:22	10	2	2	4	10	0	1	1	15:55
	Hartford	AHL	11	7	8	15	27	....	....	....	....	....	....	....	....	....	....	....	....	....	....	....	....	....	....
2008-09	**NY Rangers**	**NHL**	81	22	18	40	45	2	1	1	237	9.3	7	10	70.0	17:04	7	2	0	2	4	1	0	1	19:44
2009-10	**NY Rangers**	**NHL**	77	19	18	37	48	9	0	3	204	9.3	–12	35	48.6	19:24	....	....	....	....	....	....	....	....	....
	United States	Olympics	6	0	1	1	2	....	....	....	....	....	....	....	....	....	....	....	....	....	....	....	....	....	....
2010-11	**NY Rangers**	**NHL**	60	23	25	48	46	10	0	5	179	12.8	–7	17	11.8	19:54	....	....	....	....	....	....	....	....	....
2011-12	**NY Rangers**	**NHL**	76	29	25	54	61	13	1	9	235	12.3	–8	20	50.0	21:02	20	6	4	10	12	2	0	0	23:32
2012-13	**NY Rangers**	**NHL**	45	16	15	31	12	6	2	4	144	11.1	9	30	46.7	21:31	12	2	3	5	6	0	0	0	23:22
2013-14	**NY Rangers**	**NHL**	45	11	14	25	16	4	1	2	109	10.1	–3	19	36.8	17:57	....	....	....	....	....	....	....	....	....
	United States	Olympics	6	0	1	1	0	....	....	....	....	....	....	....	....	....	....	....	....	....	....	....	....	....	....
	Tampa Bay	**NHL**	20	6	5	11	8	3	0	1	54	11.1	4	13	46.2	20:13	4	0	0	0	0	0	0	0	20:42
2014-15	**Tampa Bay**	**NHL**	77	24	30	54	41	10	0	4	191	12.6	9	31	48.4	17:44	25	2	6	8	14	1	0	0	16:53
	NHL Totals		547	162	157	319	317	57	6	31	1485	10.9		183	44.3	18:18	88	16	16	32	52	5	1	2	19:03

OHL Second All-Star Team (2006) • AHL All-Rookie Team (2007)

Traded to **Tampa Bay** by **NY Rangers** with NY Rangers' 1st round choice (later traded to NY Islanders – NY Islanders selected Joshua Ho-Sang) in 2014 Entry Draft and NY Rangers' 1st (later traded to NY Islanders – NY Islanders selected Anthony Beauvillier) and 7th (later traded to Edmonton – Edmonton selected Ziyat Paigin) round choices in 2015 Entry Draft for Martin St. Louis and Tampa Bay's 2nd round choice (later traded to Calgary – Calgary selected Oliver Kylington) in 2015 Entry Draft, March 5, 2014.

CALVERT, Matt

(KAL-vuhrt, MAT) **CBJ**

Left wing. Shoots left. 5'11", 187 lbs. Born, Brandon, MB, December 24, 1989. Columbus' 5th choice, 127th overall, in 2008 Entry Draft.

Season	Club	League	GP	G	A	Pts	PIM	PP	SH	GW	S	S%	+/-	TF	F%	Min	GP	G	A	Pts	PIM	PP	SH	GW	Min
2005-06	Brandon	MMHL	38	24	30	54	48	....	....	....	....	....	....	....	....	....	6	3	6	9	18	....	....	....	....
2006-07	Brandon	MMHL	30	28	55	83	46	....	....	....	....	....	....	....	....	....	16	5	13	18	16	....	....	....	....
	Winkler Flyers	MJHL	1	0	0	0	15	....	....	....	....	....	....	....	....	....	....	....	....	....	....	....	....	....	....
2007-08	Brandon	WHL	72	24	40	64	53	....	....	....	....	....	....	....	....	....	6	1	2	3	2	....	....	....	....
2008-09	Brandon	WHL	58	28	39	67	58	....	....	....	....	....	....	....	....	....	12	9	8	17	22	....	....	....	....
2009-10	Brandon	WHL	68	47	52	99	70	....	....	....	....	....	....	....	....	....	15	9	7	16	15	....	....	....	....
2010-11	**Columbus**	**NHL**	42	11	9	20	12	3	0	1	50	22.0	3	9	33.3	11:06	....	....	....	....	....	....	....	....	....
	Springfield	AHL	38	13	12	25	12	....	....	....	....	....	....	....	....	....	....	....	....	....	....	....	....	....	....
2011-12	**Columbus**	**NHL**	13	0	3	3	16	0	0	0	4	0.0	–5	0	0.0	9:08	....	....	....	....	....	....	....	....	....
	Springfield	AHL	56	17	19	36	52	....	....	....	....	....	....	....	....	....	....	....	....	....	....	....	....	....	....
2012-13	Springfield	AHL	34	10	11	21	39	....	....	....	....	....	....	....	....	....	....	....	....	....	....	....	....	....	....
	Columbus	**NHL**	42	9	7	16	32	0	1	2	63	14.3	–9	6	33.3	14:11	....	....	....	....	....	....	....	....	....
2013-14	**Columbus**	**NHL**	56	9	15	24	53	2	0	1	90	10.0	–1	9	33.3	16:06	6	2	2	4	4	0	1	1	17:35
2014-15	**Columbus**	**NHL**	56	13	10	23	28	0	0	3	93	14.0	1	10	60.0	16:00	....	....	....	....	....	....	....	....	....
	NHL Totals		209	42	44	86	141	5	1	7	300	14.0		34	41.2	14:15	6	2	2	4	4	0	1	1	17:35

WHL East Second All-Star Team (2010) • Memorial Cup All-Star Team (2010)

CAMMALLERI, Mike

(kam-UH-LAIR-ee, MIGHK) **N.J.**

Left wing. Shoots left. 5'9", 190 lbs. Born, Toronto, ON, June 8, 1982. Los Angeles' 3rd choice, 49th overall, in 2001 Entry Draft.

Season	Club	League	GP	G	A	Pts	PIM	PP	SH	GW	S	S%	+/-	TF	F%	Min	GP	G	A	Pts	PIM	PP	SH	GW	Min
1997-98	Bramalea Blues	ON-Jr.A	46	36	52	88	30	....	....	....	....	....	....	....	....	....	....	....	....	....	....	....	....	....	....
1998-99	Bramalea Blues	ON-Jr.A	41	31	72	103	51	....	....	....	....	....	....	....	....	....	....	....	....	....	....	....	....	....	....
99-2000	U. of Michigan	CCHA	39	13	13	26	32	....	....	....	....	....	....	....	....	....	....	....	....	....	....	....	....	....	....
2000-01	U. of Michigan	CCHA	42	*29	32	61	24	....	....	....	....	....	....	....	....	....	....	....	....	....	....	....	....	....	....
2001-02	U. of Michigan	CCHA	29	23	21	44	28	....	....	....	....	....	....	....	....	....	....	....	....	....	....	....	....	....	....
2002-03	**Los Angeles**	**NHL**	28	5	3	8	22	2	0	2	40	12.5	–4	253	51.4	14:05	....	....	....	....	....	....	....	....	....
	Manchester	AHL	13	5	15	20	12	....	....	....	....	....	....	....	....	....	....	....	....	....	....	....	....	....	....
2003-04	**Los Angeles**	**NHL**	31	9	6	15	20	2	0	2	53	17.0	1	280	53.6	13:18	....	....	....	....	....	....	....	....	....
	Manchester	AHL	41	20	19	39	28	....	....	....	....	....	....	....	....	....	1	0	1	1	0	....	....	....	....
2004-05	Manchester	AHL	79	*46	63	109	60	....	....	....	....	....	....	....	....	....	6	1	5	6	0	....	....	....	....
2005-06	**Los Angeles**	**NHL**	80	26	29	55	50	15	0	4	206	12.6	–14	578	53.5	16:45	....	....	....	....	....	....	....	....	....
2006-07	**Los Angeles**	**NHL**	81	34	46	80	48	16	0	5	299	11.4	5	301	54.2	18:03	....	....	....	....	....	....	....	....	....
2007-08	**Los Angeles**	**NHL**	63	19	28	47	30	10	0	1	210	9.0	–16	380	54.2	18:35	....	....	....	....	....	....	....	....	....
2008-09	**Calgary**	**NHL**	81	39	43	82	44	19	0	6	255	15.3	–2	368	60.3	17:33	6	1	2	3	2	0	0	0	18:02

			Regular Season														Playoffs								
Season	Club	League	GP	G	A	Pts	PIM	PP	SH	GW	S	S%	+/-	TF	F%	Min	GP	G	A	Pts	PIM	PP	SH	GW	Min
2009-10	Montreal	NHL	65	26	24	50	16	4	0	4	218	11.9	7	51	51.0	19:31	19	*13	6	19	6	4	0	3	20:40
2010-11	Montreal	NHL	67	19	28	47	33	7	0	2	193	9.8	2	74	44.6	18:29	7	3	7	10	0	1	0	0	23:35
2011-12	Montreal	NHL	38	9	13	22	10	1	0	2	111	8.1	–6	29	34.5	17:49	....	....	....	....	....	....	....	....	....
	Calgary	NHL	28	11	8	19	16	2	0	2	64	17.2	–4	199	47.2	18:30	....	....	....	....	....	....	....	....	....
2012-13	Calgary	NHL	44	13	19	32	25	5	0	3	102	12.7	–15	496	51.0	18:03	....	....	....	....	....	....	....	....	....
2013-14	Calgary	NHL	63	26	19	45	26	6	0	8	191	13.6	–13	191	46.1	19:51	....	....	....	....	....	....	....	....	....
2014-15	New Jersey	NHL	68	27	15	42	28	9	2	8	156	17.3	2	282	42.2	18:20	....	....	....	....	....	....	....	....	....
	NHL Totals		737	263	281	544	368	98	2	49	2098	12.5		3482	51.8	17:54	32	17	15	32	8	5	0	3	20:49

CCHA First All-Star Team (2001) • NCAA West Second All-American Team (2001) • CCHA Second All-Star Team (2002) • NCAA West First All-American Team (2002) • AHL Second All-Star Team (2005) • Willie Marshall Award (AHL - Top Goal-scorer) (2005)

• Missed majority of 2002-03 due to head injury vs. San Jose, January 28, 2003. Traded to **Calgary** by **Los Angeles** with Calgary's 2nd round choice (previously acquired, Calgary selected Mitch Wahl) in 2008 Entry Draft for Calgary's 1st round choice (later traded to Anaheim – Anaheim selected Jake Gardiner) in 2008 Entry Draft and Calgary's 2nd round choice (later traded to Carolina – Carolina selected Brian Dumoulin) in 2009 Entry Draft, June 20, 2008. Signed as a free agent by **Montreal**, July 1, 2009. Traded to **Calgary** by **Montreal** with Karri Ramo and Montreal's 5th round choice (Ryan Culkin) in 2012 Entry Draft for Rene Bourque, Patrick Holland and Calgary's 2nd round choice (Zachary Fucale) in 2013 Entry Draft, January 12, 2012. Signed as a free agent by **New Jersey**, July 1, 2014.

CAMPBELL, Andrew

(KAM-buhl, AN-droo)

Defense. Shoots left. 6'4", 206 lbs. Born, Caledonia, ON, February 4, 1988. Los Angeles' 5th choice, 74th overall, in 2008 Entry Draft.

2005-06	Sault Ste. Marie	OHL	31	1	3	4	23	....	....	....	....	....	....	....	....	....	3	0	0	0	4	....	....	....	....
2006-07	Sault Ste. Marie	OHL	63	4	14	18	75	....	....	....	....	....	....	....	....	....	13	0	1	1	6	....	....	....	....
2007-08	Sault Ste. Marie	OHL	68	13	22	35	64	....	....	....	....	....	....	....	....	....	14	2	3	5	13	....	....	....	....
2008-09	Manchester	AHL	72	3	5	8	72	....	....	....	....	....	....	....	....	....	....	....	....	....	....	....	....	....	....
2009-10	Manchester	AHL	74	2	9	11	68	....	....	....	....	....	....	....	....	....	16	1	4	5	6	....	....	....	....
2010-11	Manchester	AHL	76	1	11	12	68	....	....	....	....	....	....	....	....	....	7	0	0	0	0	....	....	....	....
2011-12	Manchester	AHL	76	2	17	19	54	....	....	....	....	....	....	....	....	....	4	0	0	0	9	....	....	....	....
2012-13	Manchester	AHL	47	2	9	11	40	....	....	....	....	....	....	....	....	....	4	0	0	0	2	....	....	....	....
2013-14	Los Angeles	NHL	3	0	0	0	0	0	0	0	4	0.0	0	0	0.0	12:42	....	....	....	....	....	....	....	....	....
	Manchester	AHL	69	3	13	16	58	....	....	....	....	....	....	....	....	....	4	1	0	1	0	....	....	....	....
2014-15	Arizona	NHL	33	0	1	1	10	0	0	0	28	0.0	–13	0	0.0	17:32	....	....	....	....	....	....	....	....	....
	Portland Pirates	AHL	40	3	9	12	30	....	....	....	....	....	....	....	....	....	....	....	....	....	....	....	....	....	....
	NHL Totals		36	0	1	1	10	0	0	0	32	0.0		0	0.0	17:08	....	....	....	....	....	....	....	....	....

Signed as a free agent by **Arizona**, July 1, 2014. Signed as a free agent by **Toronto** (AHL), July 3, 2015.

CAMPBELL, Brian

(KAM-buhl, BRIGH-uhn) **FLA**

Defense. Shoots left. 5'10", 192 lbs. Born, Strathroy, ON, May 23, 1979. Buffalo's 7th choice, 156th overall, in 1997 Entry Draft.

1994-95	Petrolia Oil Barons	ON-Jr.B	49	11	27	38	43	....	....	....	....	....	....	....	....	....	....	....	....	....	....	....	....	....	....
1995-96	Ottawa 67's	OHL	66	5	22	27	23	....	....	....	....	....	....	....	....	....	4	0	1	1	2	....	....	....	....
1996-97	Ottawa 67's	OHL	66	7	36	43	12	....	....	....	....	....	....	....	....	....	24	2	11	13	8	....	....	....	....
1997-98	Ottawa 67's	OHL	66	14	39	53	31	....	....	....	....	....	....	....	....	....	13	1	14	15	0	....	....	....	....
1998-99	Ottawa 67's	OHL	62	12	75	87	27	....	....	....	....	....	....	....	....	....	9	2	10	12	6	....	....	....	....
	Rochester	AHL	....	....	....	....	....	....	....	....	....	....	....	....	....	....	2	0	0	0	0	....	....	....	....
99-2000	Buffalo	NHL	12	1	4	5	4	0	0	0	10	10.0	–2	0	0.0	15:48	....	....	....	....	....	....	....	....	....
	Rochester	AHL	67	2	24	26	22	....	....	....	....	....	....	....	....	....	21	0	3	3	0	....	....	....	....
2000-01	Buffalo	NHL	8	0	0	0	2	0	0	0	7	0.0	–2	0	0.0	15:40	....	....	....	....	....	....	....	....	....
	Rochester	AHL	65	7	25	32	24	....	....	....	....	....	....	....	....	....	4	0	1	1	0	....	....	....	....
2001-02	Buffalo	NHL	29	3	3	6	12	0	0	0	30	10.0	0	1	0.0	15:18	....	....	....	....	....	....	....	....	....
	Rochester	AHL	45	2	35	37	13	....	....	....	....	....	....	....	....	....	....	....	....	....	....	....	....	....	....
2002-03	Buffalo	NHL	65	2	17	19	20	0	0	1	90	2.2	–8	1	0.0	18:40	....	....	....	....	....	....	....	....	....
2003-04	Buffalo	NHL	53	3	8	11	12	0	0	0	45	6.7	–8	0	0.0	16:02	....	....	....	....	....	....	....	....	....
2004-05	Jokerit Helsinki	Finland	44	12	13	25	12	....	....	....	....	....	....	....	....	....	12	3	4	7	6	....	....	....	....
2005-06	Buffalo	NHL	79	12	32	44	16	5	0	5	105	11.4	–14	0	0.0	17:43	18	0	6	6	12	0	0	0	20:29
2006-07	Buffalo	NHL	82	6	42	48	35	1	0	1	92	6.5	28	0	0.0	21:53	16	3	4	7	14	2	0	0	21:39
2007-08	Buffalo	NHL	63	5	38	43	12	3	0	0	102	4.9	–1	0	0.0	25:06	....	....	....	....	....	....	....	....	....
	San Jose	NHL	20	3	16	19	8	2	0	0	40	7.5	9	0	0.0	25:07	13	1	6	7	4	0	0	0	29:19
2008-09	Chicago	NHL	82	7	45	52	22	4	0	1	108	6.5	5	0	0.0	22:34	17	2	8	10	0	2	0	0	20:29
2009-10 ♦	Chicago	NHL	68	7	31	38	18	3	0	2	131	5.3	18	0	0.0	23:13	19	1	4	5	2	0	0	0	19:35
2010-11	Chicago	NHL	65	5	22	27	6	2	0	1	84	6.0	28	0	0.0	22:59	7	1	2	3	6	0	0	0	26:26
2011-12	Florida	NHL	82	4	49	53	6	1	0	0	131	3.1	–9	0	0.0	26:54	7	1	4	5	2	1	0	1	28:00
2012-13	Florida	NHL	48	8	19	27	12	6	0	2	70	11.4	–22	0	0.0	26:25	....	....	....	....	....	....	....	....	....
2013-14	Florida	NHL	82	7	30	37	20	2	0	2	116	6.0	–6	1	0.0	26:57	....	....	....	....	....	....	....	....	....
2014-15	Florida	NHL	82	3	24	27	22	1	0	0	118	2.5	4	0	0.0	23:13	....	....	....	....	....	....	....	....	....
	NHL Totals		920	76	380	456	227	30	0	15	1279	5.9		3	0.0	22:24	97	9	34	43	40	5	0	1	22:39

OHL First All-Star Team (1999) • OHL MVP (1999) • Canadian Major Junior First All-Star Team (1999) • Canadian Major Junior Player of the Year (1999) • George Parsons Trophy (Memorial Cup - Most Sportsmanlike Player) (1999) • NHL Second All-Star Team (2008) • Lady Byng Trophy (2012)

Played in NHL All-Star Game (2007, 2008, 2009, 2012)

Signed as a free agent by **Jokerit Helsinki** (Finland), October 19, 2004. Traded to **San Jose** by **Buffalo** with Buffalo's 7th round choice (Drew Daniels) in 2008 Entry Draft for Steve Bernier and San Jose's 1st round choice (Tyler Ennis) in 2008 Entry Draft, February 26, 2008. Signed as a free agent by **Chicago**, July 1, 2008. Traded to **Florida** by **Chicago** for Rostislav Olesz, June 25, 2011.

CAMPBELL, Gregory

(KAM-buhl, GREH-goh-ree) **CBJ**

Center. Shoots left. 6', 197 lbs. Born, London, ON, December 17, 1983. Florida's 4th choice, 67th overall, in 2002 Entry Draft.

1998-99	Aylmer Aces	ON-Jr.B	49	5	9	14	44	....	....	....	....	....	....	....	....	....	....	....	....	....	....	....	....	....	....
99-2000	St. Thomas Stars	ON-Jr.B	51	12	8	20	51	....	....	....	....	....	....	....	....	....	....	....	....	....	....	....	....	....	....
2000-01	Plymouth Whalers	OHL	65	2	12	14	40	....	....	....	....	....	....	....	....	....	10	0	0	0	7	....	....	....	....
2001-02	Plymouth Whalers	OHL	65	17	36	53	105	....	....	....	....	....	....	....	....	....	6	0	2	2	13	....	....	....	....
2002-03	Kitchener Rangers	OHL	55	23	33	56	116	....	....	....	....	....	....	....	....	....	21	15	4	19	34	....	....	....	....
2003-04	Florida	NHL	2	0	0	0	5	0	0	0	0	0.0	–1	1	0.0	9:09	....	....	....	....	....	....	....	....	....
	San Antonio	AHL	76	13	16	29	73	....	....	....	....	....	....	....	....	....	....	....	....	....	....	....	....	....	....
2004-05	San Antonio	AHL	70	12	16	28	113	....	....	....	....	....	....	....	....	....	....	....	....	....	....	....	....	....	....
2005-06	Florida	NHL	64	3	6	9	40	0	0	0	59	5.1	–11	38	34.2	8:38	....	....	....	....	....	....	....	....	....
	Rochester	AHL	11	3	3	6	30	....	....	....	....	....	....	....	....	....	....	....	....	....	....	....	....	....	....
2006-07	Florida	NHL	79	6	3	9	66	0	1	0	103	5.8	–10	588	45.2	10:34	....	....	....	....	....	....	....	....	....
2007-08	Florida	NHL	81	5	13	18	72	0	2	1	113	4.4	–12	460	51.1	12:27	....	....	....	....	....	....	....	....	....
2008-09	Florida	NHL	77	13	19	32	76	1	0	1	135	9.6	0	1018	50.0	16:47	....	....	....	....	....	....	....	....	....
2009-10	Florida	NHL	60	2	15	17	53	0	0	1	84	2.4	–5	341	46.3	15:24	....	....	....	....	....	....	....	....	....
2010-11 ♦	Boston	NHL	80	13	16	29	93	1	1	1	98	13.3	11	832	51.7	13:26	25	1	3	4	4	0	0	0	10:59
2011-12	Boston	NHL	78	8	8	16	80	0	0	0	74	10.8	–3	678	50.7	12:48	7	0	2	2	0	0	0	0	10:51
2012-13	Boston	NHL	48	4	9	13	41	0	1	0	52	7.7	2	401	47.1	13:43	15	3	4	7	11	0	0	1	11:35
2013-14	Boston	NHL	82	8	13	21	47	0	1	2	84	9.5	1	749	47.8	11:54	12	0	0	0	4	0	0	0	11:18
2014-15	Boston	NHL	70	6	6	12	45	0	1	2	64	9.4	1	632	53.6	12:08	....	....	....	....	....	....	....	....	....
	NHL Totals		721	68	108	176	618	2	7	8	866	7.9		5738	49.5	12:45	59	4	9	13	19	0	0	1	11:12

Memorial Cup All-Star Team (2003) • George Parsons Trophy (Memorial Cup - Most Sportsmanlike Player) (2003) • Ed Chynoweth Trophy (Memorial Cup - Leading Scorer) (2003)

Traded to **Boston** by **Florida** with Nathan Horton for Dennis Wideman, Boston's 1st round choice (later traded to Los Angeles – Los Angeles selected Derek Forbert) in 2010 Entry Draft and Boston's 3rd round choice (Kyle Rau) in 2011 Entry Draft, June 22, 2010. Signed as a free agent by **Columbus**, July 1, 2015.

CAMPER, Carter

(KAM-puhr, KAR-tuhr) **WSH**

Right wing. Shoots right. 5'9", 176 lbs. Born, Rocky River, OH, July 6, 1988.

2004-05	Cleveland Barons	NAHL	54	14	23	37	12	....	....	....	....	....	....	....	....	....	....	....	....	....	....	....	....	....	....
2005-06	Cleveland Barons	NAHL	57	31	51	82	26	....	....	....	....	....	....	....	....	....	14	6	15	21	4	....	....	....	....
2006-07	Lincoln Stars	USHL	56	23	48	71	40	....	....	....	....	....	....	....	....	....	4	1	1	2	2	....	....	....	....
2007-08	Miami U.	CCHA	33	15	26	41	20	....	....	....	....	....	....	....	....	....	....	....	....	....	....	....	....	....	....
2008-09	Miami U.	CCHA	40	20	22	42	24	....	....	....	....	....	....	....	....	....	....	....	....	....	....	....	....	....	....
2009-10	Miami U.	CCHA	44	15	28	43	14	....	....	....	....	....	....	....	....	....	....	....	....	....	....	....	....	....	....
2010-11	Miami U.	CCHA	39	19	38	57	27	....	....	....	....	....	....	....	....	....	....	....	....	....	....	....	....	....	....
	Providence Bruins	AHL	3	1	1	2	2	....	....	....	....	....	....	....	....	....	....	....	....	....	....	....	....	....	....

			Regular Season														Playoffs								
Season	Club	League	GP	G	A	Pts	PIM	PP	SH	GW	S	S%	+/-	TF	F%	Min	GP	G	A	Pts	PIM	PP	SH	GW	Min
2011-12	Boston	NHL	3	1	0	1	0	0	0	0	1	100.0	1	14	42.9	6:42	....	....	....	....	....	....	....	....	....
	Providence Bruins	AHL	69	18	30	48	18	....	....	....	....	....	....	....	....	....	....	....	....	....	....	....	....	....	....
2012-13	Providence Bruins	AHL	57	10	37	47	6	....	....	....	....	....	....	....	....	....	12	8	5	13	0	....	....	....	....
2013-14	Providence Bruins	AHL	41	8	23	31	16	....	....	....	....	....	....	....	....	....	....	....	....	....	....	....	....	....	....
	Springfield	AHL	19	4	16	20	8	....	....	....	....	....	....	....	....	....	5	1	4	5	0	....	....	....	....
2014-15	Binghamton	AHL	75	15	37	52	16	....	....	....	....	....	....	....	....	....	....	....	....	....	....	....	....	....	....
	NHL Totals		3	1	0	1	0	0	0	0	1	100.0		14	42.9	6:42	....	....	....	....	....	....	....	....	....

CCHA All-Rookie Team (2008) • CCHA First All-Star Team (2009, 2011) • NCAA West Second All-American Team (2009, 2011)

Signed as a free agent by **Boston**, April 7, 2011. Traded to **Columbus** by **Boston** for Blake Parlett, February 7, 2014. Signed as a free agent by **Ottawa**, July 2, 2014. Signed as a free agent by **Washington**, July 1, 2015.

CARCILLO, Daniel

(KAR-sihl-oh, DAN-yuhl)

Left wing. Shoots left. 6', 200 lbs. Born, King City, ON, January 28, 1985. Pittsburgh's 4th choice, 73rd overall, in 2003 Entry Draft.

			Regular Season														Playoffs								
Season	Club	League	GP	G	A	Pts	PIM	PP	SH	GW	S	S%	+/-	TF	F%	Min	GP	G	A	Pts	PIM	PP	SH	GW	Min
2001-02	Milton Merchants	ON-Jr.B	47	15	16	31	162	....	....	....	....	....	....	....	....	....	....	....	....	....	....	....	....	....	....
2002-03	Sarnia Sting	OHL	68	29	37	66	157	....	....	....	....	....	....	....	....	....	6	0	4	4	14	....	....	....	....
2003-04	Sarnia Sting	OHL	61	30	29	59	148	....	....	....	....	....	....	....	....	....	4	1	2	3	12	....	....	....	....
2004-05	Sarnia Sting	OHL	12	2	7	9	40	....	....	....	....	....	....	....	....	....	....	....	....	....	....	....	....	....	....
	Mississauga	OHL	20	8	10	18	75	....	....	....	....	....	....	....	....	....	5	3	1	4	18	....	....	....	....
2005-06	Wilkes-Barre	AHL	51	11	13	24	311	....	....	....	....	....	....	....	....	....	11	1	0	1	47	....	....	....	....
	Wheeling Nailers	ECHL	6	3	2	5	32	....	....	....	....	....	....	....	....	....	....	....	....	....	....	....	....	....	....
2006-07	Wilkes-Barre	AHL	52	21	9	30	183	....	....	....	....	....	....	....	....	....	....	....	....	....	....	....	....	....	....
	Phoenix	NHL	18	4	3	7	74	3	0	0	32	12.5	-7	0	0.0	14:56	....	....	....	....	....	....	....	....	....
2007-08	Phoenix	NHL	57	13	11	24	*324	3	0	1	106	12.3	1	5	80.0	12:43	....	....	....	....	....	....	....	....	....
	San Antonio	AHL	5	2	1	3	16	....	....	....	....	....	....	....	....	....	....	....	....	....	....	....	....	....	....
2008-09	Phoenix	NHL	54	3	7	10	*174	2	0	0	95	3.2	-13	18	55.6	11:59	....	....	....	....	....	....	....	....	....
	Philadelphia	NHL	20	0	4	4	*80	0	0	0	35	0.0	-2	2	100.0	10:16	5	1	1	2	5	0	0	0	8:11
2009-10	Philadelphia	NHL	76	12	10	22	207	1	0	1	105	11.4	5	3	33.3	11:15	17	2	4	6	34	0	0	1	10:32
2010-11	Philadelphia	NHL	57	4	2	6	127	0	0	2	56	7.1	-14	2	50.0	7:46	11	2	1	3	30	0	0	0	8:25
2011-12	Chicago	NHL	28	2	9	11	82	0	0	0	27	7.4	10	4	50.0	11:24	....	....	....	....	....	....	....	....	....
2012-13	Chicago	NHL	23	2	1	3	11	0	0	1	23	8.7	1	1	0.0	9:00	4	0	1	1	6	0	0	0	6:41
2013-14	Los Angeles	NHL	26	1	1	2	57	0	0	1	22	4.5	-1	1	100.0	9:52	....	....	....	....	....	....	....	....	....
	NY Rangers	NHL	31	3	0	3	43	0	0	1	22	13.6	0	0	0.0	8:47	8	2	0	2	22	0	0	0	8:46
2014-15♦	Chicago	NHL	39	4	4	8	54	0	0	0	42	9.5	3	1	0.0	8:11	....	....	....	....	....	....	....	....	....
	NHL Totals		429	48	52	100	1233	9	0	7	565	8.5		37	56.8	10:32	45	7	7	14	97	0	0	1	9:06

Traded to **Phoenix** by **Pittsburgh** with Pittsburgh's 3rd round choice (later traded to NY Rangers - NY Rangers selected Tomas Kundratek) in 2008 Entry Draft for Georges Laraque, February 27, 2007. Traded to **Philadelphia** by **Phoenix** for Scottie Upshall and Philadelphia's 2nd round choice (Lucas Lessio) in 2011 Entry Draft, March 4, 2009. Signed as a free agent by **Chicago**, July 1, 2011. • Missed majority of 2011-12 due to knee injury vs. Edmonton, January 2, 2012. Traded to **Los Angeles** by **Chicago** for Los Angeles' 6th round choice (Roy Radke) in 2015 Entry Draft, July 16, 2013. Traded to **NY Rangers** by **Los Angeles** for NY Rangers' 7th round choice (Spencer Watson) in 2014 Entry Draft, January 4, 2014. Signed as a free agent by **Chicago**, October 4, 2014. • Missed majority of 2014-15 due to knee injury at St. Louis, October 25, 2014, a recurring upper-body injury and as a healthy reserve.

CAREY, Matt

(KAIR-ee, MAT)

Left wing. Shoots left. 6', 189 lbs. Born, Hamilton, ON, February 28, 1992.

			Regular Season														Playoffs								
Season	Club	League	GP	G	A	Pts	PIM	PP	SH	GW	S	S%	+/-	TF	F%	Min	GP	G	A	Pts	PIM	PP	SH	GW	Min
2007-08	Ham. Jr. Bulldogs	Minor-ON	48	13	14	27	....	....	....	....	....	....	....	....	....	....	....	....	....	....	....	....	....	....	....
2008-09	Hamilton Reps	Minor-ON	36	16	28	44	48	....	....	....	....	....	....	....	....	....	11	8	9	17	22	....	....	....	....
2009-10	Burlington	ON-Jr.A	5	0	0	0	0	....	....	....	....	....	....	....	....	....	....	....	....	....	....	....	....	....	....
	Hamilton	ON-Jr.A	20	7	6	13	20	....	....	....	....	....	....	....	....	....	10	1	2	3	20	....	....	....	....
2010-11	Hamilton	ON-Jr.A	45	25	59	84	40	....	....	....	....	....	....	....	....	....	7	3	2	5	10	....	....	....	....
2011-12	Hamilton	ON-Jr.A	23	17	21	38	8	....	....	....	....	....	....	....	....	....	....	....	....	....	....	....	....	....	....
	Tor. Canadiens	ON-Jr.A	25	16	15	31	24	....	....	....	....	....	....	....	....	....	10	9	5	14	18	....	....	....	....
2012-13	St. Lawrence	ECAC	DID NOT PLAY – FRESHMAN																						
2013-14	St. Lawrence	ECAC	38	18	19	37	47	....	....	....	....	....	....	....	....	....	....	....	....	....	....	....	....	....	....
	Chicago	NHL	2	1	0	1	2	0	0	0	1	100.0	-1	21	47.6	9:38	....	....	....	....	....	....	....	....	....
2014-15	Rockford IceHogs	AHL	67	10	11	21	43	....	....	....	....	....	....	....	....	....	2	0	0	0	0	....	....	....	....
	NHL Totals		2	1	0	1	2	0	0	0	1	100.0		21	47.6	9:38	....	....	....	....	....	....	....	....	....

ECAC All-Rookie Team (2014)

Signed as a free agent by **Chicago**, March 20, 2014.

CAREY, Paul

(KAIR-ee, PAWL) **WSH**

Center. Shoots left. 6', 190 lbs. Born, Boston, MA, September 24, 1988. Colorado's 7th choice, 135th overall, in 2007 Entry Draft.

			Regular Season														Playoffs								
Season	Club	League	GP	G	A	Pts	PIM	PP	SH	GW	S	S%	+/-	TF	F%	Min	GP	G	A	Pts	PIM	PP	SH	GW	Min
2005-06	Salisbury School	High-CT	27	14	11	25	18	....	....	....	....	....	....	....	....	....	....	....	....	....	....	....	....	....	....
2006-07	Salisbury School	High-CT	24	16	11	27	16	....	....	....	....	....	....	....	....	....	....	....	....	....	....	....	....	....	....
2007-08	Indiana Ice	USHL	60	34	32	66	32	....	....	....	....	....	....	....	....	....	4	1	2	3	2	....	....	....	....
2008-09	Boston College	H-East	24	5	4	9	8	....	....	....	....	....	....	....	....	....	....	....	....	....	....	....	....	....	....
2009-10	Boston College	H-East	41	9	12	21	29	....	....	....	....	....	....	....	....	....	....	....	....	....	....	....	....	....	....
2010-11	Boston College	H-East	38	13	13	26	18	....	....	....	....	....	....	....	....	....	....	....	....	....	....	....	....	....	....
2011-12	Boston College	H-East	44	18	12	30	30	....	....	....	....	....	....	....	....	....	....	....	....	....	....	....	....	....	....
	Lake Erie	AHL	2	0	0	0	2	....	....	....	....	....	....	....	....	....	....	....	....	....	....	....	....	....	....
2012-13	Lake Erie	AHL	72	19	22	41	29	....	....	....	....	....	....	....	....	....	....	....	....	....	....	....	....	....	....
2013-14	Colorado	NHL	12	0	0	0	0	0	0	0	6	0.0	2	0	0.0	6:26	3	0	0	0	0	0	0	0	3:46
	Lake Erie	AHL	54	8	13	21	42	....	....	....	....	....	....	....	....	....	....	....	....	....	....	....	....	....	....
2014-15	Colorado	NHL	10	0	1	1	0	0	0	0	5	0.0	2	3	0.0	7:53	....	....	....	....	....	....	....	....	....
	Lake Erie	AHL	43	13	14	27	16	....	....	....	....	....	....	....	....	....	....	....	....	....	....	....	....	....	....
	Providence Bruins	AHL	17	2	5	7	10	....	....	....	....	....	....	....	....	....	4	1	0	1	4	....	....	....	....
	NHL Totals		22	0	1	1	0	0	0	0	11	0.0		3	0.0	7:05	3	0	0	0	0	0	0	0	3:46

USHL All-Rookie Team (2008) • USHL Second All-Star Team (2008) • NCAA Championship All-Tournament Team (2012)

Traded to **Boston** by **Colorado** with Max Talbot for Jordan Caron and a 6th round choice in 2016 Entry Draft, March 2, 2015. Signed as a free agent by **Washington**, July 8, 2015.

CARKNER, Matt

(KARK-nehr, MAT)

Defense. Shoots right. 6'5", 233 lbs. Born, Winchester, ON, November 3, 1980. Montreal's 2nd choice, 58th overall, in 1999 Entry Draft.

			Regular Season														Playoffs								
Season	Club	League	GP	G	A	Pts	PIM	PP	SH	GW	S	S%	+/-	TF	F%	Min	GP	G	A	Pts	PIM	PP	SH	GW	Min
1996-97	Winchester	ON-Jr.B	29	1	18	19	....	....	....	....	....	....	....	....	....	....	....	....	....	....	....	....	....	....	....
	Brockville Braves	ON-Jr.A	7	0	0	0	37	....	....	....	....	....	....	....	....	....	9	0	1	1	6	....	....	....	....
1997-98	Peterborough	OHL	57	0	6	6	121	....	....	....	....	....	....	....	....	....	4	0	0	0	2	....	....	....	....
1998-99	Peterborough	OHL	60	2	16	18	173	....	....	....	....	....	....	....	....	....	5	0	0	0	20	....	....	....	....
99-2000	Peterborough	OHL	62	3	13	16	177	....	....	....	....	....	....	....	....	....	5	0	1	1	6	....	....	....	....
2000-01	Peterborough	OHL	53	8	8	16	128	....	....	....	....	....	....	....	....	....	7	0	3	3	25	....	....	....	....
2001-02	Cleveland Barons	AHL	74	0	3	3	335	....	....	....	....	....	....	....	....	....	....	....	....	....	....	....	....	....	....
2002-03	Cleveland Barons	AHL	39	1	4	5	104	....	....	....	....	....	....	....	....	....	....	....	....	....	....	....	....	....	....
2003-04	Cleveland Barons	AHL	60	2	11	13	115	....	....	....	....	....	....	....	....	....	9	0	3	3	39	....	....	....	....
2004-05	Cleveland Barons	AHL	73	0	10	10	192	....	....	....	....	....	....	....	....	....	....	....	....	....	....	....	....	....	....
2005-06	San Jose	NHL	1	0	1	1	2	0	0	0	0	0.0	0	0	0.0	6:01	....	....	....	....	....	....	....	....	....
	Cleveland Barons	AHL	69	10	21	31	202	....	....	....	....	....	....	....	....	....	....	....	....	....	....	....	....	....	....
2006-07	Wilkes-Barre	AHL	75	6	24	30	167	....	....	....	....	....	....	....	....	....	8	1	0	1	19	....	....	....	....
2007-08	Binghamton	AHL	67	10	15	25	218	....	....	....	....	....	....	....	....	....	....	....	....	....	....	....	....	....	....
2008-09	Ottawa	NHL	1	0	0	0	0	0	0	0	0	0.0	0	0	0.0	4:08	....	....	....	....	....	....	....	....	....
	Binghamton	AHL	67	3	18	21	210	....	....	....	....	....	....	....	....	....	....	....	....	....	....	....	....	....	....
2009-10	Ottawa	NHL	81	2	9	11	190	0	0	0	87	2.3	0	0	0.0	16:55	6	1	0	1	12	0	0	1	18:38
2010-11	Ottawa	NHL	50	1	6	7	136	0	0	0	40	2.5	0	0	0.0	14:53	....	....	....	....	....	....	....	....	....
2011-12	Ottawa	NHL	29	1	2	3	33	0	0	0	17	5.9	0	0	0.0	11:55	4	0	1	1	21	0	0	0	7:02
	Binghamton	AHL	3	0	1	1	11	....	....	....	....	....	....	....	....	....	....	....	....	....	....	....	....	....	....
2012-13	NY Islanders	NHL	22	0	2	2	46	0	0	0	19	0.0	-2	0	0.0	12:35	4	0	1	1	2	0	0	0	12:41

			Regular Season														Playoffs								
Season	Club	League	GP	G	A	Pts	PIM	PP	SH	GW	S	S%	+/-	TF	F%	Min	GP	G	A	Pts	PIM	PP	SH	GW	Min
2013-14	**NY Islanders**	**NHL**	**53**	**0**	**3**	**3**	**149**	**0**	**0**	**0**	**50**	**0.0**	**–10**	**0**	**0.0**	**11:59**	....	....	....	....	....	....	....	....	....
2014-15	Bridgeport	AHL	19	2	1	3	38	....	....	....	....	....	....	....	....	....	....	....	....	....	....	....	....	....	....
	NHL Totals		**237**	**4**	**23**	**27**	**556**	**0**	**0**	**0**	**213**	**1.9**		**0**	**0.0**	**14:16**	**14**	**1**	**2**	**3**	**35**	**0**	**0**	**1**	**13:37**

Yanick Dupre Memorial Award (AHL - Outstanding Humanitarian Contribution) (2007)

Signed as a free agent by **San Jose**, June 6, 2001. • Missed majority of 2002-03 due to knee injury vs. Utah (AHL), January 4, 2003. Signed as a free agent by **Pittsburgh**, July 23, 2006. Signed as a free agent by **Ottawa**, July 3, 2007. Signed as a free agent by **NY Islanders**, July 1. 2012. • Missed majority of 2011-12 due to knee surgery, October 3, 2011 and as a healthy reserve. • Missed majority of 2012-13 due to wrist injury vs. Pittsburgh, February 5, 2013 and as a healthy reserve. • Missed majority of 2014-15 due to off-season back surgery. Signed as a free agent by **Bridgeport** (AHL), August 11, 2015.

CARLE, Matt

(KAHRL, MAT) **T.B.**

Defense. Shoots left. 6', 205 lbs. Born, Anchorage, AK, September 25, 1984. San Jose's 4th choice, 47th overall, in 2003 Entry Draft.

99-2000	Alaska All-Stars	AASHA	42	14	28	42	....	....	....	....	....	....	....	....	....	....	....	....	....	....	....	....	....	....	....
2000-01	USNTDP	U-17	13	0	1	1	....	....	....	....	....	....	....	....	....	....	....	....	....	....	....	....	....	....	....
	USNTDP	NAHL	55	1	4	5	33	....	....	....	....	....	....	....	....	....	....	....	....	....	....	....	....	....	....
2001-02	USNTDP	U-18	45	3	13	16	30	....	....	....	....	....	....	....	....	....	....	....	....	....	....	....	....	....	....
	USNTDP	NAHL	7	1	2	3	0	....	....	....	....	....	....	....	....	....	....	....	....	....	....	....	....	....	....
	USNTDP	USHL	12	0	0	0	21	....	....	....	....	....	....	....	....	....	....	....	....	....	....	....	....	....	....
2002-03	River City Lancers	USHL	59	12	30	42	98	....	....	....	....	....	....	....	....	....	11	2	2	4	20	....	....	....	....
2003-04	U. of Denver	WCHA	30	5	20	25	33	....	....	....	....	....	....	....	....	....	....	....	....	....	....	....	....	....	....
2004-05	U. of Denver	WCHA	43	13	31	44	68	....	....	....	....	....	....	....	....	....	....	....	....	....	....	....	....	....	....
2005-06	U. of Denver	WCHA	39	11	*42	53	58	....	....	....	....	....	....	....	....	....	....	....	....	....	....	....	....	....	....
	San Jose	**NHL**	**12**	**3**	**3**	**6**	**14**	**2**	**0**	**1**	**11**	**27.3**	**–2**	**0**	**0.0**	**16:07**	**11**	**0**	**3**	**3**	**4**	**0**	**0**	**0**	**15:17**
2006-07	**San Jose**	**NHL**	**77**	**11**	**31**	**42**	**30**	**8**	**0**	**1**	**111**	**9.9**	**9**	**1**	**0.0**	**18:08**	**11**	**2**	**3**	**5**	**0**	**1**	**0**	**1**	**14:51**
	Worcester Sharks	AHL	3	0	2	2	0	....	....	....	....	....	....	....	....	....	....	....	....	....	....	....	....	....	....
2007-08	**San Jose**	**NHL**	**62**	**2**	**13**	**15**	**26**	**2**	**0**	**1**	**63**	**3.2**	**–8**	**1**	**100.0**	**16:33**	**11**	**0**	**1**	**1**	**4**	**0**	**0**	**0**	**13:56**
2008-09	**Tampa Bay**	**NHL**	**12**	**1**	**1**	**2**	**6**	**0**	**0**	**0**	**13**	**7.7**	**1**	**0**	**0.0**	**21:58**	....	....	....	....	....	....	....	....	....
	Philadelphia	**NHL**	**64**	**4**	**20**	**24**	**16**	**0**	**0**	**2**	**72**	**5.6**	**2**	**0**	**0.0**	**21:17**	**6**	**0**	**3**	**3**	**4**	**0**	**0**	**0**	**22:15**
2009-10	**Philadelphia**	**NHL**	**80**	**6**	**29**	**35**	**16**	**2**	**0**	**1**	**137**	**4.4**	**19**	**0**	**0.0**	**23:23**	**23**	**1**	**12**	**13**	**8**	**0**	**0**	**0**	**25:54**
2010-11	**Philadelphia**	**NHL**	**82**	**1**	**39**	**40**	**23**	**0**	**0**	**0**	**117**	**0.9**	**30**	**0**	**0.0**	**21:59**	**11**	**0**	**4**	**4**	**2**	**0**	**0**	**0**	**23:24**
2011-12	**Philadelphia**	**NHL**	**82**	**4**	**34**	**38**	**36**	**3**	**0**	**0**	**132**	**3.0**	**4**	**0**	**0.0**	**23:01**	**11**	**2**	**4**	**6**	**6**	**1**	**0**	**0**	**25:19**
2012-13	**Tampa Bay**	**NHL**	**48**	**5**	**17**	**22**	**4**	**2**	**0**	**0**	**66**	**7.6**	**1**	**0**	**0.0**	**23:45**	....	....	....	....	....	....	....	....	....
2013-14	**Tampa Bay**	**NHL**	**82**	**2**	**29**	**31**	**28**	**1**	**0**	**0**	**115**	**1.7**	**11**	**1**	**0.0**	**22:11**	**4**	**1**	**0**	**1**	**0**	**0**	**0**	**0**	**25:11**
2014-15	**Tampa Bay**	**NHL**	**59**	**4**	**14**	**18**	**26**	**1**	**0**	**0**	**73**	**5.5**	**12**	**0**	**0.0**	**20:29**	**25**	**0**	**3**	**3**	**4**	**0**	**0**	**0**	**16:30**
	NHL Totals		**660**	**43**	**230**	**273**	**225**	**21**	**0**	**6**	**910**	**4.7**		**3**	**33.3**	**21:10**	**113**	**6**	**33**	**39**	**32**	**2**	**0**	**1**	**20:02**

USHL First All-Star Team (2003) • USHL Defenseman of the Year (2003) • WCHA All-Rookie Team (2004) • WCHA First All-Star Team (2005, 2006) • NCAA West First All-American Team (2005, 2006) • NCAA Championship All-Tournament Team (2005) • WCHA Player of the Year (2006) • Hobey Baker Memorial Award (Top U.S. Collegiate Player) (2006) • NHL All-Rookie Team (2007)

Traded to **Tampa Bay** by **San Jose** with Ty Wishart, San Jose's 1st round choice (later traded to Ottawa, later traded to NY Islanders, later traded to Columbus, later traded to Anahaim – Anaheim selected Kyle Palmieri) in 2009 Entry Draft and San Jose's 4th round choice (James Mullin) in 2010 Entry Draft for Dan Boyle and Brad Lukowich, July 4, 2008. Traded to **Philadelphia** by **Tampa Bay** with San Jose's 3rd round choice (previously acquired, Philadelphia selected Simon Bertilsson) in 2009 Entry Draft for Steve Eminger, Steve Downie and Tampa Bay's 4th round choice (previously acquired, Tampa Bay selected Alex Hutchings) in 2009 Entry Draft, November 7, 2008. Signed as a free agent by **Tampa Bay**, July 4, 2012.

CARLSON, John

(KAHRL-suhn, JAWN) **WSH**

Defense. Shoots right. 6'3", 212 lbs. Born, Natick, MA, January 10, 1990. Washington's 2nd choice, 27th overall, in 2008 Entry Draft.

2005-06	N.J. Rockets	AtJHL	38	2	10	12	42	....	....	....	....	....	....	....	....	....	....	....	....	....	....	....	....	....	....
2006-07	N.J. Rockets	AtJHL	44	12	38	50	96	....	....	....	....	....	....	....	....	....	....	....	....	....	....	....	....	....	....
	Indiana Ice	USHL	2	0	0	0	6	....	....	....	....	....	....	....	....	....	....	....	....	....	....	....	....	....	....
2007-08	Indiana Ice	USHL	59	12	31	43	72	....	....	....	....	....	....	....	....	....	4	1	0	1	0	....	....	....	....
2008-09	London Knights	OHL	59	16	60	76	65	....	....	....	....	....	....	....	....	....	14	7	15	22	16	....	....	....	....
	Hershey Bears	AHL	....	....	....	....	....	....	....	....	....	....	....	....	....	....	16	2	1	3	0	....	....	....	....
2009-10	**Washington**	**NHL**	**22**	**1**	**5**	**6**	**8**	**0**	**0**	**0**	**21**	**4.8**	**11**	**0**	**0.0**	**15:15**	**7**	**1**	**3**	**4**	**0**	**0**	**0**	**0**	**20:14**
	Hershey Bears	AHL	48	4	35	39	26	....	....	....	....	....	....	....	....	....	13	2	4	6	8	....	....	....	....
2010-11	**Washington**	**NHL**	**82**	**7**	**30**	**37**	**44**	**1**	**0**	**3**	**144**	**4.9**	**21**	**0**	**0.0**	**22:39**	**9**	**2**	**1**	**3**	**4**	**0**	**0**	**0**	**24:23**
2011-12	**Washington**	**NHL**	**82**	**9**	**23**	**32**	**22**	**4**	**0**	**0**	**152**	**5.9**	**–15**	**1**	**0.0**	**21:52**	**14**	**2**	**3**	**5**	**8**	**1**	**0**	**0**	**24:02**
2012-13	**Washington**	**NHL**	**48**	**6**	**16**	**22**	**18**	**0**	**0**	**0**	**97**	**6.2**	**11**	**1**	**100.0**	**23:01**	**7**	**0**	**1**	**1**	**4**	**0**	**0**	**0**	**22:29**
2013-14	**Washington**	**NHL**	**82**	**10**	**27**	**37**	**22**	**5**	**0**	**0**	**208**	**4.8**	**–3**	**1**	**0.0**	**24:31**	....	....	....	....	....	....	....	....	....
	United States	Olympics	6	1	1	2	0	....	....	....	....	....	....	....	....	....	....	....	....	....	....	....	....	....	....
2014-15	**Washington**	**NHL**	**82**	**12**	**43**	**55**	**28**	**3**	**1**	**3**	**193**	**6.2**	**11**	**0**	**0.0**	**23:04**	**14**	**1**	**5**	**6**	**4**	**1**	**0**	**0**	**23:57**
	NHL Totals		**398**	**45**	**144**	**189**	**142**	**13**	**1**	**6**	**815**	**5.5**		**3**	**33.3**	**22:36**	**51**	**6**	**13**	**19**	**20**	**2**	**0**	**0**	**23:21**

USHL All-Rookie Team (2008) • USHL Second All-Star Team (2008) • OHL Second All-Star Team (2009) • Canadian Major Junior All-Rookie Team (2009) • AHL All-Rookie Team (2010) • NHL All-Rookie Team (2011)

CARON, Jordan

(kuh-RAWN, JOHR-dihn) **ST.L.**

Right wing. Shoots left. 6'3", 204 lbs. Born, Sayabec, QC, November 2, 1990. Boston's 1st choice, 25th overall, in 2009 Entry Draft.

2005-06	Notre Dame	SMHL	35	8	16	24	32	....	....	....	....	....	....	....	....	....	....	....	....	....	....	....	....	....	....
2006-07	Rimouski Oceanic	QMJHL	59	18	22	40	41	....	....	....	....	....	....	....	....	....	....	....	....	....	....	....	....	....	....
2007-08	Rimouski Oceanic	QMJHL	46	20	23	43	42	....	....	....	....	....	....	....	....	....	9	3	1	4	18	....	....	....	....
2008-09	Rimouski Oceanic	QMJHL	56	36	31	67	66	....	....	....	....	....	....	....	....	....	13	6	5	11	16	....	....	....	....
2009-10	Rimouski Oceanic	QMJHL	20	9	11	20	8	....	....	....	....	....	....	....	....	....	....	....	....	....	....	....	....	....	....
	Rouyn-Noranda	QMJHL	23	17	16	33	16	....	....	....	....	....	....	....	....	....	11	7	11	18	15	....	....	....	....
2010-11	**Boston**	**NHL**	**23**	**3**	**4**	**7**	**6**	**0**	**0**	**1**	**27**	**11.1**	**3**	**7**	**14.3**	**12:40**	....	....	....	....	....	....	....	....	....
	Providence Bruins	AHL	47	12	16	28	16	....	....	....	....	....	....	....	....	....	....	....	....	....	....	....	....	....	....
2011-12	**Boston**	**NHL**	**48**	**7**	**8**	**15**	**14**	**0**	**0**	**0**	**57**	**12.3**	**0**	**2**	**50.0**	**11:32**	**2**	**0**	**0**	**0**	**0**	**0**	**0**	**0**	**6:41**
	Providence Bruins	AHL	17	4	9	13	10	....	....	....	....	....	....	....	....	....	....	....	....	....	....	....	....	....	....
2012-13	Providence Bruins	AHL	47	11	7	18	38	....	....	....	....	....	....	....	....	....	12	2	7	9	10	....	....	....	....
	Boston	**NHL**	**17**	**1**	**2**	**3**	**4**	**0**	**0**	**0**	**20**	**5.0**	**1**	**0**	**0.0**	**9:24**	....	....	....	....	....	....	....	....	....
2013-14	**Boston**	**NHL**	**35**	**1**	**2**	**3**	**36**	**0**	**0**	**0**	**52**	**1.9**	**–8**	**4**	**25.0**	**10:55**	**7**	**1**	**0**	**1**	**4**	**0**	**0**	**0**	**7:54**
2014-15	**Boston**	**NHL**	**11**	**0**	**0**	**0**	**16**	**0**	**0**	**0**	**4**	**0.0**	**–1**	**1**	**0.0**	**7:56**	....	....	....	....	....	....	....	....	....
	Providence Bruins	AHL	23	9	10	19	10	....	....	....	....	....	....	....	....	....	....	....	....	....	....	....	....	....	....
	Colorado	**NHL**	**19**	**0**	**0**	**0**	**2**	**0**	**0**	**0**	**8**	**0.0**	**–1**	**0**	**0.0**	**8:06**	....	....	....	....	....	....	....	....	....
	NHL Totals		**153**	**12**	**16**	**28**	**78**	**0**	**0**	**1**	**168**	**7.1**		**14**	**21.4**	**10:38**	**9**	**1**	**0**	**1**	**4**	**0**	**0**	**0**	**7:38**

• Missed majority of 2013-14 as a healthy reserve. Traded to **Colorado** by **Boston** with a 6th round choice in 2016 Entry Draft for Max Talbot and Paul Carey, March 2, 2015. Signed as a free agent by **St. Louis**, July 3, 2015.

CARRICK, Connor

(KAIR-ihk, KAW-nuhr) **WSH**

Defense. Shoots right. 5'11", 185 lbs. Born, Orland Park, IL, April 13, 1994. Washington's 6th choice, 137th overall, in 2012 Entry Draft.

2009-10	Chicago Fury U18	T1EHL	22	2	4	6	2	....	....	....	....	....	....	....	....	....	....	....	....	....	....	....	....	....	....
	Chicago Fury	T1EHL	37	7	15	22	48	....	....	....	....	....	....	....	....	....	....	....	....	....	....	....	....	....	....
2010-11	USNTDP	USHL	36	1	6	7	42	....	....	....	....	....	....	....	....	....	2	0	0	0	2	....	....	....	....
	USNTDP	U-17	17	3	10	13	10	....	....	....	....	....	....	....	....	....	....	....	....	....	....	....	....	....	....
2011-12	USNTDP	USHL	21	1	4	5	30	....	....	....	....	....	....	....	....	....	....	....	....	....	....	....	....	....	....
	USNTDP	U-18	36	7	9	16	16	....	....	....	....	....	....	....	....	....	....	....	....	....	....	....	....	....	....
2012-13	Plymouth Whalers	OHL	68	12	32	44	79	....	....	....	....	....	....	....	....	....	15	2	16	18	6	....	....	....	....
2013-14	**Washington**	**NHL**	**34**	**1**	**5**	**6**	**23**	**0**	**0**	**0**	**26**	**3.8**	**–9**	**0**	**0.0**	**15:58**	....	....	....	....	....	....	....	....	....
	Hershey Bears	AHL	13	0	4	4	15	....	....	....	....	....	....	....	....	....	....	....	....	....	....	....	....	....	....
2014-15	Hershey Bears	AHL	73	8	34	42	132	....	....	....	....	....	....	....	....	....	10	2	2	4	12	....	....	....	....
	NHL Totals		**34**	**1**	**5**	**6**	**23**	**0**	**0**	**0**	**26**	**3.8**		**0**	**0.0**	**15:58**	....	....	....	....	....	....	....	....	....

CARRICK, Sam
(KAIR-ihk, SAM) **TOR**

Center. Shoots right. 6', 188 lbs. Born, Stouffville, ON, February 4, 1992. Toronto's 5th choice, 144th overall, in 2010 Entry Draft.

			Regular Season														Playoffs								
Season	Club	League	GP	G	A	Pts	PIM	PP	SH	GW	S	S%	+/-	TF	F%	Min	GP	G	A	Pts	PIM	PP	SH	GW	Min
2007-08	Tor. Red Wings	GTHL	55	40	30	70	130	....	....	....	....	....	....	....	....	....	....	....	....	....	....	....	....	....	....
2008-09	Brampton	OHL	61	10	11	21	47	....	....	....	....	....	....	....	....	....	21	1	0	1	16	....	....	....	....
2009-10	Brampton	OHL	66	21	21	42	96	....	....	....	....	....	....	....	....	....	8	2	2	4	8	....	....	....	....
2010-11	Brampton	OHL	59	16	23	39	74	....	....	....	....	....	....	....	....	....	4	0	1	1	4	....	....	....	....
2011-12	Brampton	OHL	68	37	30	67	104	....	....	....	....	....	....	....	....	....	8	4	4	8	16	....	....	....	....
2012-13	Toronto Marlies	AHL	19	2	2	4	18	....	....	....	....	....	....	....	....	....	5	0	0	0	0	....	....	....	....
	Idaho Steelheads	ECHL	50	16	21	37	70	....	....	....	....	....	....	....	....	....	....	....	....	....	....	....	....	....	....
2013-14	Toronto Marlies	AHL	62	14	21	35	115	....	....	....	....	....	....	....	....	....	14	5	4	9	10	....	....	....	....
2014-15	**Toronto**	**NHL**	**16**	**1**	**1**	**2**	**9**	**0**	**0**	**0**	**17**	**5.9**	**1**	**91**	**41.8**	**6:29**	....	....	....	....	....	....	....	....	....
	Toronto Marlies	AHL	59	9	18	27	112	....	....	....	....	....	....	....	....	....	5	1	2	3	4	....	....	....	....
	NHL Totals		**16**	**1**	**1**	**2**	**9**	**0**	**0**	**0**	**17**	**5.9**		**91**	**41.8**	**6:29**	....	....	....	....	....	....	....	....	....

CARTER, Jeff
(KAHR-tuhr, JEHF) **L.A.**

Center. Shoots right. 6'4", 210 lbs. Born, London, ON, January 1, 1985. Philadelphia's 1st choice, 11th overall, in 2003 Entry Draft.

Season	Club	League	GP	G	A	Pts	PIM	PP	SH	GW	S	S%	+/-	TF	F%	Min	GP	G	A	Pts	PIM	PP	SH	GW	Min
2000-01	Strathroy Rockets	ON-Jr.B	49	27	20	47	10	....	....	....	....	....	....	....	....	....	....	....	....	....	....	....	....	....	....
2001-02	Sault Ste. Marie	OHL	63	18	17	35	12	....	....	....	....	....	....	....	....	....	4	0	0	0	2	....	....	....	....
2002-03	Sault Ste. Marie	OHL	61	35	36	71	55	....	....	....	....	....	....	....	....	....	4	0	2	2	2	....	....	....	....
2003-04	Sault Ste. Marie	OHL	57	36	30	66	26	....	....	....	....	....	....	....	....	....	....	....	....	....	....	....	....	....	....
	Philadelphia	AHL	....	....	....	....	....	....	....	....	....	....	....	....	....	....	12	4	1	5	0	....	....	....	....
2004-05	Sault Ste. Marie	OHL	55	34	40	74	40	....	....	....	....	....	....	....	....	....	7	5	5	10	6	....	....	....	....
	Philadelphia	AHL	3	0	1	1	4	....	....	....	....	....	....	....	....	....	21	12	11	23	12	....	....	....	....
2005-06	**Philadelphia**	**NHL**	**81**	**23**	**19**	**42**	**40**	**6**	**2**	**7**	**189**	**12.2**	**10**	**683**	**48.2**	**12:04**	**6**	**0**	**0**	**0**	**10**	**0**	**0**	**0**	**13:04**
2006-07	**Philadelphia**	**NHL**	**62**	**14**	**23**	**37**	**48**	**3**	**2**	**1**	**215**	**6.5**	**-17**	**1062**	**45.4**	**19:00**	....	....	....	....	....	....	....	....	....
2007-08	**Philadelphia**	**NHL**	**82**	**29**	**24**	**53**	**55**	**7**	**2**	**5**	**260**	**11.2**	**6**	**1378**	**47.7**	**18:51**	**17**	**6**	**5**	**11**	**12**	**3**	**0**	**1**	**20:08**
2008-09	**Philadelphia**	**NHL**	**82**	**46**	**38**	**84**	**68**	**13**	**4**	***12**	**342**	**13.5**	**23**	**1725**	**48.3**	**20:57**	**6**	**1**	**0**	**1**	**8**	**0**	**0**	**0**	**20:21**
2009-10	**Philadelphia**	**NHL**	**74**	**33**	**28**	**61**	**38**	**11**	**2**	**6**	**319**	**10.3**	**2**	**1314**	**52.4**	**19:18**	**12**	**5**	**2**	**7**	**2**	**2**	**0**	**1**	**17:57**
2010-11	**Philadelphia**	**NHL**	**80**	**36**	**30**	**66**	**39**	**8**	**0**	**7**	**335**	**10.7**	**27**	**605**	**54.7**	**18:15**	**6**	**1**	**1**	**2**	**2**	**1**	**0**	**0**	**15:15**
2011-12	**Columbus**	**NHL**	**39**	**15**	**10**	**25**	**14**	**8**	**0**	**1**	**130**	**11.5**	**-11**	**740**	**51.0**	**19:38**	....	....	....	....	....	....	....	....	....
	♦ Los Angeles	**NHL**	**16**	**6**	**3**	**9**	**2**	**2**	**0**	**1**	**54**	**11.1**	**-1**	**34**	**47.1**	**18:06**	**20**	***8**	**5**	**13**	**4**	**4**	**0**	***3**	**18:02**
2012-13	**Los Angeles**	**NHL**	**48**	**26**	**7**	**33**	**16**	**8**	**0**	***8**	**133**	**19.5**	**0**	**384**	**52.6**	**17:35**	**18**	**6**	**7**	**13**	**14**	**1**	**0**	**0**	**19:37**
2013-14♦	**Los Angeles**	**NHL**	**72**	**27**	**23**	**50**	**44**	**8**	**1**	**5**	**256**	**10.5**	**8**	**644**	**52.2**	**18:57**	**26**	**10**	**15**	**25**	**4**	***4**	**0**	**1**	**18:16**
	Canada	Olympics	6	3	2	5	2	....	....	....	....	....	....	....	....	....	....	....	....	....	....	....	....	....	....
2014-15	**Los Angeles**	**NHL**	**82**	**28**	**34**	**62**	**28**	**10**	**1**	**5**	**218**	**12.8**	**7**	**1193**	**52.6**	**17:58**	....	....	....	....	....	....	....	....	....
	NHL Totals		**718**	**283**	**239**	**522**	**392**	**84**	**14**	**58**	**2451**	**11.5**		**9762**	**50.0**	**18:10**	**111**	**37**	**35**	**72**	**56**	**15**	**0**	**6**	**18:22**

OHL Second All-Star Team (2004) • OHL First All-Star Team (2005) • Canadian Major Junior Sportsman of the Year (2005) • Canadian Major Junior First All-Star Team (2005)

Played in NHL All-Star Game (2009)

Traded to **Columbus** by **Philadelphia** for Jakub Voracek and Columbus' 1st (Sean Couturier) and 3rd (Nick Cousins) round choices in 2011 Entry Draft, June 23, 2011. Traded to **Los Angeles** by **Columbus** for Jack Johnson and Los Angeles' 1st round choice (Marko Dano) in 2013 Entry Draft, February 23, 2012.

CARTER, Ryan
(KAHR-tuhr, RIGH-uhn) **MIN**

Left wing. Shoots left. 6'1", 205 lbs. Born, White Bear Lake, MN, August 3, 1983.

Season	Club	League	GP	G	A	Pts	PIM	PP	SH	GW	S	S%	+/-	TF	F%	Min	GP	G	A	Pts	PIM	PP	SH	GW	Min
2001-02	White Bear Lake	High-MN	STATISTICS NOT AVAILABLE																						
	Green Bay	USHL	1	0	0	0	2	....	....	....	....	....	....	....	....	....	....	....	....	....	....	....	....	....	....
2002-03	Green Bay	USHL	55	19	17	36	94	....	....	....	....	....	....	....	....	....	....	....	....	....	....	....	....	....	....
2003-04	Green Bay	USHL	59	22	23	45	131	....	....	....	....	....	....	....	....	....	....	....	....	....	....	....	....	....	....
2004-05	Minnesota State	WCHA	37	15	8	23	44	....	....	....	....	....	....	....	....	....	....	....	....	....	....	....	....	....	....
2005-06	Minnesota State	WCHA	39	19	16	35	71	....	....	....	....	....	....	....	....	....	....	....	....	....	....	....	....	....	....
2006-07	Portland Pirates	AHL	76	16	20	36	85	....	....	....	....	....	....	....	....	....	....	....	....	....	....	....	....	....	....
	♦ Anaheim	**NHL**	....	....	....	....	....	....	....	....	....	....	....	....	....	....	**4**	**0**	**0**	**0**	**0**	**0**	**0**	**0**	**3:12**
2007-08	**Anaheim**	**NHL**	**34**	**4**	**4**	**8**	**36**	**0**	**0**	**1**	**56**	**7.1**	**-2**	**299**	**61.5**	**10:29**	**6**	**0**	**0**	**0**	**6**	**0**	**0**	**0**	**11:03**
	Portland Pirates	AHL	13	3	2	5	38	....	....	....	....	....	....	....	....	....	....	....	....	....	....	....	....	....	....
2008-09	**Anaheim**	**NHL**	**48**	**3**	**6**	**9**	**52**	**0**	**0**	**1**	**40**	**7.5**	**3**	**304**	**48.0**	**9:06**	**10**	**2**	**3**	**5**	**0**	**1**	**0**	**0**	**12:14**
2009-10	**Anaheim**	**NHL**	**38**	**4**	**5**	**9**	**31**	**0**	**0**	**1**	**38**	**10.5**	**0**	**221**	**52.5**	**9:51**	....	....	....	....	....	....	....	....	....
2010-11	**Anaheim**	**NHL**	**18**	**1**	**2**	**3**	**22**	**0**	**0**	**0**	**23**	**4.3**	**-4**	**171**	**50.3**	**10:44**	....	....	....	....	....	....	....	....	....
	Carolina	**NHL**	**32**	**0**	**3**	**3**	**22**	**0**	**0**	**0**	**26**	**0.0**	**0**	**208**	**50.5**	**8:18**	....	....	....	....	....	....	....	....	....
	Florida	**NHL**	**12**	**2**	**1**	**3**	**22**	**0**	**0**	**0**	**14**	**14.3**	**3**	**99**	**51.5**	**13:30**	....	....	....	....	....	....	....	....	....
2011-12	**Florida**	**NHL**	**7**	**0**	**0**	**0**	**6**	**0**	**0**	**0**	**3**	**0.0**	**-1**	**39**	**46.2**	**9:19**	....	....	....	....	....	....	....	....	....
	New Jersey	**NHL**	**65**	**4**	**4**	**8**	**84**	**0**	**0**	**0**	**47**	**8.5**	**-12**	**393**	**50.1**	**10:28**	**23**	**5**	**2**	**7**	**32**	**0**	**0**	**2**	**8:43**
2012-13	**New Jersey**	**NHL**	**44**	**6**	**9**	**15**	**31**	**0**	**1**	**1**	**63**	**9.5**	**-2**	**83**	**51.8**	**13:03**	....	....	....	....	....	....	....	....	....
2013-14	**New Jersey**	**NHL**	**62**	**7**	**3**	**10**	**35**	**0**	**0**	**2**	**69**	**10.1**	**-6**	**36**	**44.4**	**11:20**	....	....	....	....	....	....	....	....	....
2014-15	**Minnesota**	**NHL**	**53**	**3**	**10**	**13**	**55**	**0**	**1**	**0**	**47**	**6.4**	**3**	**70**	**41.4**	**10:05**	**1**	**0**	**0**	**0**	**0**	**0**	**0**	**0**	**6:18**
	NHL Totals		**413**	**34**	**47**	**81**	**396**	**0**	**2**	**6**	**426**	**8.0**		**1923**	**51.5**	**10:31**	**44**	**7**	**5**	**12**	**38**	**1**	**0**	**2**	**9:16**

Signed as a free agent by **Anaheim**, July 12, 2006. • Missed majority of 2009-10 due to foot injury in pre-game skate at Columbus, November 13, 2009. Traded to **Carolina** by **Anaheim** for Stefan Chaput and Matt Kennedy, November 23, 2010. Traded to **Florida** by **Carolina** with Carolina's 5th round choice (later traded to Atlanta, later traded to San Jose – San Jose selected Sean Kuraly) in 2011 Entry Draft for Cory Stillman, February 24, 2011. Claimed on waivers by **New Jersey** from **Florida**, October 26, 2011. Signed as a free agent by **Minnesota**, October 7, 2014.

CARUSO, Michael
(kah-ROO-soh, MIGH-kuhl)

Defense. Shoots left. 6'2", 191 lbs. Born, Mississauga, ON, July 5, 1988. Florida's 3rd choice, 103rd overall, in 2006 Entry Draft.

Season	Club	League	GP	G	A	Pts	PIM	PP	SH	GW	S	S%	+/-	TF	F%	Min	GP	G	A	Pts	PIM	PP	SH	GW	Min
2004-05	Guelph Storm	OHL	56	0	3	3	31	....	....	....	....	....	....	....	....	....	4	0	0	0	2	....	....	....	....
2005-06	Guelph Storm	OHL	66	1	15	16	85	....	....	....	....	....	....	....	....	....	15	1	2	3	24	....	....	....	....
2006-07	Guelph Storm	OHL	64	4	16	20	119	....	....	....	....	....	....	....	....	....	4	0	0	0	8	....	....	....	....
2007-08	Guelph Storm	OHL	62	10	24	34	103	....	....	....	....	....	....	....	....	....	10	2	6	8	22	....	....	....	....
2008-09	Rochester	AHL	73	1	9	10	66	....	....	....	....	....	....	....	....	....	....	....	....	....	....	....	....	....	....
2009-10	Rochester	AHL	67	1	10	11	42	....	....	....	....	....	....	....	....	....	....	....	....	....	....	....	....	....	....
2010-11	Rochester	AHL	75	5	4	9	77	....	....	....	....	....	....	....	....	....	....	....	....	....	....	....	....	....	....
2011-12	San Antonio	AHL	68	5	8	13	63	....	....	....	....	....	....	....	....	....	10	0	4	4	4	....	....	....	....
2012-13	San Antonio	AHL	35	1	3	4	22	....	....	....	....	....	....	....	....	....	....	....	....	....	....	....	....	....	....
	Florida	**NHL**	**2**	**0**	**0**	**0**	**0**	**0**	**0**	**0**	**0**	**0.0**	**-1**	**0**	**0.0**	**7:55**	....	....	....	....	....	....	....	....	....
2013-14	San Antonio	AHL	35	0	2	2	32	....	....	....	....	....	....	....	....	....	....	....	....	....	....	....	....	....	....
2014-15	Reading Royals	ECHL	65	4	16	20	63	....	....	....	....	....	....	....	....	....	....	....	....	....	....	....	....	....	....
	NHL Totals		**2**	**0**	**0**	**0**	**0**	**0**	**0**	**0**	**0**	**0.0**		**0**	**0.0**	**7:55**	....	....	....	....	....	....	....	....	....

• Missed remainder of 2012-13 and majority of 2013-14 due to wrist injury vs. Montreal, January 22, 2013..

CECI, Cody
(SEE-SEE, KOH-dee) **OTT**

Defense. Shoots right. 6'3", 207 lbs. Born, Ottawa, ON, December 21, 1993. Ottawa's 1st choice, 15th overall, in 2012 Entry Draft.

Season	Club	League	GP	G	A	Pts	PIM	PP	SH	GW	S	S%	+/-	TF	F%	Min	GP	G	A	Pts	PIM	PP	SH	GW	Min
2008-09	Peter. Petes Mid.	Minor-ON	57	24	48	72	26	....	....	....	....	....	....	....	....	....	....	....	....	....	....	....	....	....	....
2009-10	Ottawa 67's	OHL	64	4	8	12	12	....	....	....	....	....	....	....	....	....	12	0	3	3	0	....	....	....	....
2010-11	Ottawa 67's	OHL	68	9	25	34	28	....	....	....	....	....	....	....	....	....	4	0	2	2	4	....	....	....	....
2011-12	Ottawa 67's	OHL	64	17	43	60	14	....	....	....	....	....	....	....	....	....	18	2	13	15	4	....	....	....	....
2012-13	Ottawa 67's	OHL	42	11	29	40	10	....	....	....	....	....	....	....	....	....	....	....	....	....	....	....	....	....	....
	Owen Sound	OHL	27	8	16	24	2	....	....	....	....	....	....	....	....	....	12	1	9	10	0	....	....	....	....
	Binghamton	AHL	3	1	1	2	0	....	....	....	....	....	....	....	....	....	3	0	0	0	0	....	....	....	....
2013-14	**Ottawa**	**NHL**	**49**	**3**	**6**	**9**	**14**	**0**	**0**	**2**	**82**	**3.7**	**-5**	**0**	**0.0**	**17:12**	....	....	....	....	....	....	....	....	....
	Binghamton	AHL	27	2	17	19	10	....	....	....	....	....	....	....	....	....	4	1	1	2	0	....	....	....	....
2014-15	**Ottawa**	**NHL**	**81**	**5**	**16**	**21**	**6**	**1**	**0**	**0**	**130**	**3.8**	**-4**	**0**	**0.0**	**19:17**	**6**	**0**	**2**	**2**	**0**	**0**	**0**	**0**	**18:00**
	NHL Totals		**130**	**8**	**22**	**30**	**20**	**1**	**0**	**2**	**212**	**3.8**		**0**	**0.0**	**18:30**	**6**	**0**	**2**	**2**	**0**	**0**	**0**	**0**	**18:00**

OHL Second All-Star Team (2012, 2013)

CHAPUT, Michael

(sha-PUT, MIGH-kuhl) **CBJ**

Center. Shoots left. 6'2", 197 lbs. Born, Ile Bizard, QC, April 9, 1992. Philadelphia's 1st choice, 89th overall, in 2010 Entry Draft.

			Regular Season														Playoffs								
Season	Club	League	GP	G	A	Pts	PIM	PP	SH	GW	S	S%	+/-	TF	F%	Min	GP	G	A	Pts	PIM	PP	SH	GW	Min
2007-08	Lac St-L. Royals	Minor-QC	STATISTICS NOT AVAILABLE																						
	Lac St-Louis Lions	QAAA	4	0	0	0	0	....	....	....	....	....	....	....	....	....	....	....	....	....	....	....	....	....	....
2008-09	Lewiston	QMJHL	29	3	7	10	34	....	....	....	....	....	....	....	....	....	....	....	....	....	....	....	....	....	....
2009-10	Lewiston	QMJHL	68	28	27	55	60	....	....	....	....	....	....	....	....	....	4	0	1	1	2	....	....	....	....
2010-11	Lewiston	QMJHL	62	25	34	59	97	....	....	....	....	....	....	....	....	....	13	7	13	20	11	....	....	....	....
2011-12	Shawinigan	QMJHL	57	21	42	63	47	....	....	....	....	....	....	....	....	....	11	4	8	12	2	....	....	....	....
2012-13	Springfield	AHL	73	13	19	32	57	....	....	....	....	....	....	....	....	....	8	1	1	2	4	....	....	....	....
2013-14	**Columbus**	**NHL**	**17**	**0**	**1**	**1**	**2**	**0**	**0**	**0**	**6**	**0.0**	**0**	**98**	**42.9**	**8:54**	....	....	....	....	....	....	....	....	....
	Springfield	AHL	55	19	26	45	51	....	....	....	....	....	....	....	....	....	5	2	1	3	6	....	....	....	....
2014-15	**Columbus**	**NHL**	**33**	**1**	**4**	**5**	**21**	**0**	**0**	**0**	**23**	**4.3**	**-8**	**294**	**48.6**	**10:12**	....	....	....	....	....	....	....	....	....
	Springfield	AHL	45	10	11	21	22	....	....	....	....	....	....	....	....	....	....	....	....	....	....	....	....	....	....
	NHL Totals		**50**	**1**	**5**	**6**	**23**	**0**	**0**	**0**	**29**	**3.4**		**392**	**47.2**	**9:45**	....	....	....	....	....	....	....	....	....

Memorial Cup All-Star Team (2012) • Ed Chynoweth Trophy (Memorial Cup - Leading Scorer) (2012) • Stafford Smythe Memorial Trophy (Memorial Cup - MVP) (2012)

• Missed majority of 2008-09 due to shoulder injury. Traded to **Columbus** by **Philadelphia** with Greg Moore for Tom Sestito, February 28, 2011.

CHARA, Zdeno

(CHAH-rah, z'DEHN-oh) **BOS**

Defense. Shoots left. 6'9", 255 lbs. Born, Trencin, Czechoslovakia, March 18, 1977. NY Islanders' 3rd choice, 56th overall, in 1996 Entry Draft.

Season	Club	League	GP	G	A	Pts	PIM	PP	SH	GW	S	S%	+/-	TF	F%	Min	GP	G	A	Pts	PIM	PP	SH	GW	Min
1994-95	Dukla Trencin U18	Svk-U18	30	22	22	44	113	....	....	....	....	....	....	....	....	....	....	....	....	....	....	....	....	....	....
	Dukla Trencin Jr.	Slovak-Jr.	2	0	0	0	0	....	....	....	....	....	....	....	....	....	....	....	....	....	....	....	....	....	....
1995-96	Dukla Trencin Jr.	Slovak-Jr.	22	1	13	14	80	....	....	....	....	....	....	....	....	....	....	....	....	....	....	....	....	....	....
	HK VTJ Piestany	Slovak-2	10	1	3	4	10	....	....	....	....	....	....	....	....	....	....	....	....	....	....	....	....	....	....
	Sparta Jr.	CzRep-Jr.	15	1	2	3	42	....	....	....	....	....	....	....	....	....	....	....	....	....	....	....	....	....	....
	HC Sparta Praha	CzRep	1	0	0	0	0	....	....	....	....	....	....	....	....	....	....	....	....	....	....	....	....	....	....
1996-97	Prince George	WHL	49	3	19	22	120	....	....	....	....	....	....	....	....	....	15	1	7	8	45	....	....	....	....
1997-98	**NY Islanders**	**NHL**	**25**	**0**	**1**	**1**	**50**	**0**	**0**	**0**	**10**	**0.0**	**1**	....	....	....	....	....	....	....	....	....	....	....	....
	Kentucky	AHL	48	4	9	13	125	....	....	....	....	....	....	....	....	....	1	0	0	0	4	....	....	....	....
1998-99	**NY Islanders**	**NHL**	**59**	**2**	**6**	**8**	**83**	**0**	**1**	**0**	**56**	**3.6**	**-8**	**0**	**0.0**	**18:54**	....	....	....	....	....	....	....	....	....
	Lowell	AHL	23	2	2	4	47	....	....	....	....	....	....	....	....	....	....	....	....	....	....	....	....	....	....
99-2000	**NY Islanders**	**NHL**	**65**	**2**	**9**	**11**	**57**	**0**	**0**	**1**	**47**	**4.3**	**-27**	**0**	**0.0**	**22:52**	....	....	....	....	....	....	....	....	....
2000-01	**NY Islanders**	**NHL**	**82**	**2**	**7**	**9**	**157**	**0**	**1**	**0**	**83**	**2.4**	**-27**	**0**	**0.0**	**22:20**	....	....	....	....	....	....	....	....	....
2001-02	Dukla Trencin	Slovakia	8	2	2	4	32	....	....	....	....	....	....	....	....	....	....	....	....	....	....	....	....	....	....
	Ottawa	**NHL**	**75**	**10**	**13**	**23**	**156**	**4**	**1**	**2**	**105**	**9.5**	**30**	**0**	**0.0**	**22:16**	**10**	**0**	**1**	**1**	**12**	**0**	**0**	**0**	**26:07**
2002-03	**Ottawa**	**NHL**	**74**	**9**	**30**	**39**	**116**	**3**	**0**	**2**	**168**	**5.4**	**29**	**0**	**0.0**	**24:57**	**18**	**1**	**6**	**7**	**14**	**0**	**0**	**0**	**25:07**
2003-04	**Ottawa**	**NHL**	**79**	**16**	**25**	**41**	**147**	**7**	**0**	**3**	**185**	**8.6**	**33**	**0**	**0.0**	**24:38**	**7**	**1**	**1**	**2**	**8**	**0**	**0**	**0**	**24:38**
2004-05	Farjestad	Sweden	33	10	15	25	132	....	....	....	....	....	....	....	....	....	13	3	5	8	82	....	....	....	....
2005-06	**Ottawa**	**NHL**	**71**	**16**	**27**	**43**	**135**	**10**	**1**	**3**	**212**	**7.5**	**17**	**24**	**41.7**	**27:11**	**10**	**1**	**3**	**4**	**23**	**1**	**0**	**0**	**27:32**
	Slovakia	Olympics	6	1	1	2	2	....	....	....	....	....	....	....	....	....	....	....	....	....	....	....	....	....	....
2006-07	**Boston**	**NHL**	**80**	**11**	**32**	**43**	**100**	**9**	**0**	**3**	**204**	**5.4**	**-21**	**1**	**0.0**	**27:58**	....	....	....	....	....	....	....	....	....
2007-08	**Boston**	**NHL**	**77**	**17**	**34**	**51**	**114**	**9**	**1**	**0**	**207**	**8.2**	**14**	**0**	**0.0**	**26:50**	**7**	**1**	**1**	**2**	**12**	**1**	**0**	**0**	**25:52**
2008-09	**Boston**	**NHL**	**80**	**19**	**31**	**50**	**95**	**11**	**0**	**3**	**216**	**8.8**	**23**	**4**	**25.0**	**26:04**	**11**	**1**	**3**	**4**	**12**	**1**	**0**	**1**	**25:11**
2009-10	**Boston**	**NHL**	**80**	**7**	**37**	**44**	**87**	**4**	**0**	**1**	**242**	**2.9**	**19**	**2**	**50.0**	**25:22**	**13**	**2**	**5**	**7**	**29**	**0**	**0**	**1**	**28:08**
	Slovakia	Olympics	7	0	3	3	6	....	....	....	....	....	....	....	....	....	....	....	....	....	....	....	....	....	....
2010-11♦	**Boston**	**NHL**	**81**	**14**	**30**	**44**	**88**	**8**	**1**	**2**	**264**	**5.3**	***33**	**0**	**0.0**	**25:26**	**24**	**2**	**7**	**9**	**34**	**1**	**0**	**0**	**27:39**
2011-12	**Boston**	**NHL**	**79**	**12**	**40**	**52**	**86**	**8**	**0**	**0**	**224**	**5.4**	**33**	**1**	**0.0**	**25:00**	**7**	**1**	**2**	**3**	**8**	**0**	**0**	**1**	**27:21**
2012-13	HC Lev Praha	KHL	25	4	6	10	24	....	....	....	....	....	....	....	....	....	....	....	....	....	....	....	....	....	....
	Boston	**NHL**	**48**	**7**	**12**	**19**	**70**	**3**	**0**	**2**	**119**	**5.9**	**14**	**1**	**0.0**	**24:56**	**22**	**3**	**12**	**15**	**20**	**0**	**0**	**0**	**29:32**
2013-14	**Boston**	**NHL**	**77**	**17**	**23**	**40**	**66**	**10**	**0**	**3**	**168**	**10.1**	**25**	**0**	**0.0**	**24:39**	**12**	**2**	**2**	**4**	**14**	**2**	**0**	**0**	**25:20**
	Slovakia	Olympics	4	0	1	1	4	....	....	....	....	....	....	....	....	....	....	....	....	....	....	....	....	....	....
2014-15	**Boston**	**NHL**	**63**	**8**	**12**	**20**	**42**	**4**	**0**	**0**	**138**	**5.8**	**0**	**1**	**100.0**	**23:21**	....	....	....	....	....	....	....	....	....
	NHL Totals		**1195**	**169**	**369**	**538**	**1649**	**90**	**6**	**25**	**2648**	**6.4**		**34**	**38.2**	**24:39**	**141**	**15**	**43**	**58**	**186**	**6**	**0**	**3**	**26:54**

AHL All-Rookie Team (1998) • NHL First All-Star Team (2004, 2009, 2014) • NHL Second All-Star Team (2006, 2008, 2011, 2012) • James Norris Memorial Trophy (2009) • Mark Messier NHL Leadership Award (2011)

Played in NHL All-Star Game (2003, 2007, 2008, 2009, 2011, 2012)

Traded to **Ottawa** by **NY Islanders** with Bill Muckalt and NY Islanders' 1st round choice (Jason Spezza) in 2001 Entry Draft for Alexei Yashin, June 23, 2001. Signed as a free agent by **Farjestad** (Sweden), September 24, 2004. Signed as a free agent by **Boston**, July 1, 2006. Signed as a free agent by **Lev Praha** (KHL), October 2, 2012.

CHIAROT, Ben

(CHAIR-awt, BEHN) **WPG**

Defense. Shoots left. 6'3", 215 lbs. Born, Hamilton, ON, May 9, 1991. Atlanta's 5th choice, 120th overall, in 2009 Entry Draft.

Season	Club	League	GP	G	A	Pts	PIM	PP	SH	GW	S	S%	+/-	TF	F%	Min	GP	G	A	Pts	PIM	PP	SH	GW	Min
2006-07	Mississauga Reps	GTHL	60	21	42	63	166	....	....	....	....	....	....	....	....	....	....	....	....	....	....	....	....	....	....
2007-08	Guelph Storm	OHL	31	0	0	0	14	....	....	....	....	....	....	....	....	....	....	....	....	....	....	....	....	....	....
2008-09	Guelph Storm	OHL	67	2	10	12	111	....	....	....	....	....	....	....	....	....	4	0	3	3	8	....	....	....	....
2009-10	Guelph Storm	OHL	41	4	9	13	106	....	....	....	....	....	....	....	....	....	....	....	....	....	....	....	....	....	....
	Sudbury Wolves	OHL	26	4	4	8	61	....	....	....	....	....	....	....	....	....	4	1	1	2	6	....	....	....	....
	Chicago Wolves	AHL	1	0	0	0	4	....	....	....	....	....	....	....	....	....	....	....	....	....	....	....	....	....	....
2010-11	Sudbury Wolves	OHL	25	5	8	13	62	....	....	....	....	....	....	....	....	....	....	....	....	....	....	....	....	....	....
	Saginaw Spirit	OHL	39	5	19	24	51	....	....	....	....	....	....	....	....	....	12	1	4	5	21	....	....	....	....
2011-12	St. John's IceCaps	AHL	18	1	1	2	19	....	....	....	....	....	....	....	....	....	....	....	....	....	....	....	....	....	....
	Colorado Eagles	ECHL	24	6	7	13	13	....	....	....	....	....	....	....	....	....	....	....	....	....	....	....	....	....	....
2012-13	St. John's IceCaps	AHL	61	1	11	12	81	....	....	....	....	....	....	....	....	....	....	....	....	....	....	....	....	....	....
2013-14	**Winnipeg**	**NHL**	**1**	**0**	**0**	**0**	**0**	**0**	**0**	**0**	**0**	**0.0**	**-3**	**0**	**0.0**	**10:47**	....	....	....	....	....	....	....	....	....
	St. John's IceCaps	AHL	65	6	14	20	96	....	....	....	....	....	....	....	....	....	21	2	3	5	16	....	....	....	....
2014-15	**Winnipeg**	**NHL**	**40**	**2**	**6**	**8**	**22**	**0**	**0**	**0**	**37**	**5.4**	**5**	**0**	**0.0**	**17:01**	**2**	**0**	**0**	**0**	**2**	**0**	**0**	**0**	**13:42**
	St. John's IceCaps	AHL	24	4	5	9	21	....	....	....	....	....	....	....	....	....	....	....	....	....	....	....	....	....	....
	NHL Totals		**41**	**2**	**6**	**8**	**22**	**0**	**0**	**0**	**37**	**5.4**		**0**	**0.0**	**16:52**	**2**	**0**	**0**	**0**	**2**	**0**	**0**	**0**	**13:42**

• Transferred to **Winnipeg** after **Atlanta** franchise relocated, June 21, 2011.

CHIASSON, Alex

(CHAY-sahn, Al-ehx) **OTT**

Right wing. Shoots right. 6'4", 209 lbs. Born, Montreal, QC, October 1, 1990. Dallas' 2nd choice, 38th overall, in 2009 Entry Draft.

Season	Club	League	GP	G	A	Pts	PIM	PP	SH	GW	S	S%	+/-	TF	F%	Min	GP	G	A	Pts	PIM	PP	SH	GW	Min
2005-06	Sem. St-Francois	QAAA	13	1	1	2	16	....	....	....	....	....	....	....	....	....	2	1	1	2	0	....	....	....	....
2006-07	Sem. St-Francois	QAAA	43	12	18	30	41	....	....	....	....	....	....	....	....	....	18	4	18	22	18	....	....	....	....
2007-08	Northwood	High-NY	45	35	46	81	....	....	....	....	....	....	....	....	....	....	....	....	....	....	....	....	....	....	....
2008-09	Des Moines	USHL	56	17	33	50	101	....	....	....	....	....	....	....	....	....	....	....	....	....	....	....	....	....	....
2009-10	Boston University	H-East	35	7	12	19	44	....	....	....	....	....	....	....	....	....	....	....	....	....	....	....	....	....	....
2010-11	Boston University	H-East	35	14	20	34	75	....	....	....	....	....	....	....	....	....	....	....	....	....	....	....	....	....	....
2011-12	Boston University	H-East	38	15	31	46	67	....	....	....	....	....	....	....	....	....	....	....	....	....	....	....	....	....	....
	Texas Stars	AHL	9	1	4	5	9	....	....	....	....	....	....	....	....	....	....	....	....	....	....	....	....	....	....
2012-13	Texas Stars	AHL	57	13	22	35	43	....	....	....	....	....	....	....	....	....	7	2	1	3	4	....	....	....	....
	Dallas	**NHL**	**7**	**6**	**1**	**7**	**0**	**1**	**0**	**1**	**13**	**46.2**	**3**	**18**	**27.8**	**14:05**	....	....	....	....	....	....	....	....	....
2013-14	**Dallas**	**NHL**	**79**	**13**	**22**	**35**	**38**	**6**	**0**	**4**	**144**	**9.0**	**-21**	**132**	**48.5**	**15:07**	**6**	**1**	**1**	**2**	**2**	**1**	**0**	**0**	**15:41**
2014-15	**Ottawa**	**NHL**	**76**	**11**	**15**	**26**	**67**	**3**	**0**	**1**	**105**	**10.5**	**-5**	**21**	**14.3**	**13:23**	**4**	**0**	**0**	**0**	**0**	**0**	**0**	**0**	**9:14**
	NHL Totals		**162**	**30**	**38**	**68**	**105**	**10**	**0**	**6**	**262**	**11.5**		**171**	**42.1**	**14:15**	**10**	**1**	**1**	**2**	**2**	**1**	**0**	**0**	**13:06**

Traded to **Ottawa** by **Dallas** with Alexander Guptill, Nicholas Paul and Dallas' 2nd round choice (later traded to New Jersey – New Jersey selected Mackenzie Blackwood) in 2015 Entry Draft for Jason Spezza and Ludwig Karlsson, July 1, 2014.

CHIMERA, Jason

(shih-MAIR-uh, JAY-suhn) **WSH**

Left wing. Shoots left. 6'3", 213 lbs. Born, Edmonton, AB, May 2, 1979. Edmonton's 5th choice, 121st overall, in 1997 Entry Draft.

			Regular Season														Playoffs								
Season	Club	League	GP	G	A	Pts	PIM	PP	SH	GW	S	S%	+/-	TF	F%	Min	GP	G	A	Pts	PIM	PP	SH	GW	Min
1994-95	Edmonton Pats	AMHL	33	27	31	58	42	....	....	....	....	....	....	....	....	....	....	....	....	....	....	....	....	....	....
1995-96	Edmonton Pats	AMHL	34	23	24	47	44	....	....	....	....	....	....	....	....	....	....	....	....	....	....	....	....	....	....
1996-97	Medicine Hat	WHL	71	16	23	39	54	....	....	....	....	....	....	....	....	....	4	0	1	1	4	....	....	....	....
1997-98	Medicine Hat	WHL	72	34	32	66	93	....	....	....	....	....	....	....	....	....	....	....	....	....	....	....	....	....	....
	Hamilton	AHL	4	0	0	0	8	....	....	....	....	....	....	....	....	....	....	....	....	....	....	....	....	....	....
1998-99	Medicine Hat	WHL	37	18	22	40	84	....	....	....	....	....	....	....	....	....	....	....	....	....	....	....	....	....	....
	Brandon	WHL	21	14	12	26	32	....	....	....	....	....	....	....	....	....	5	4	1	5	8	....	....	....	....
99-2000	Hamilton	AHL	78	15	13	28	77	....	....	....	....	....	....	....	....	....	10	0	2	2	12	....	....	....	....
2000-01	**Edmonton**	**NHL**	**1**	**0**	**0**	**0**	**0**	**0**	**0**	**0**	**0**	**0.0**	**0**	**0**	**0.0**	**6:58**	....	....	....	....	....	....	....	....	....
	Hamilton	AHL	78	29	25	54	93	....	....	....	....	....	....	....	....	....	....	....	....	....	....	....	....	....	....
2001-02	**Edmonton**	**NHL**	**3**	**1**	**0**	**1**	**0**	**0**	**0**	**0**	**3**	**33.3**	**-3**	**0**	**0.0**	**12:44**	....	....	....	....	....	....	....	....	....
	Hamilton	AHL	77	26	51	77	158	....	....	....	....	....	....	....	....	....	15	4	6	10	10	....	....	....	....
2002-03	**Edmonton**	**NHL**	**66**	**14**	**9**	**23**	**36**	**0**	**1**	**4**	**90**	**15.6**	**-2**	**11**	**54.6**	**10:46**	**2**	**0**	**2**	**2**	**0**	**0**	**0**	**0**	**10:55**
2003-04	**Edmonton**	**NHL**	**60**	**4**	**8**	**12**	**57**	**0**	**0**	**1**	**79**	**5.1**	**-1**	**22**	**31.8**	**10:07**	....	....	....	....	....	....	....	....	....
2004-05	AS Varese Hockey	Italy	15	7	3	10	34	....	....	....	....	....	....	....	....	....	5	2	1	3	31	....	....	....	....
2005-06	**Columbus**	**NHL**	**80**	**17**	**13**	**30**	**95**	**1**	**1**	**5**	**127**	**13.4**	**-10**	**16**	**50.0**	**12:41**	....	....	....	....	....	....	....	....	....
2006-07	**Columbus**	**NHL**	**82**	**15**	**21**	**36**	**91**	**2**	**2**	**2**	**151**	**9.9**	**2**	**38**	**36.8**	**15:22**	....	....	....	....	....	....	....	....	....
2007-08	**Columbus**	**NHL**	**81**	**14**	**17**	**31**	**98**	**1**	**1**	**3**	**198**	**7.1**	**-5**	**35**	**45.7**	**17:30**	....	....	....	....	....	....	....	....	....
2008-09	**Columbus**	**NHL**	**49**	**8**	**14**	**22**	**41**	**1**	**0**	**1**	**115**	**7.0**	**8**	**42**	**42.9**	**16:15**	**4**	**0**	**1**	**1**	**2**	**0**	**0**	**0**	**13:21**
2009-10	**Columbus**	**NHL**	**39**	**8**	**9**	**17**	**47**	**1**	**0**	**1**	**92**	**8.7**	**-7**	**23**	**65.2**	**14:47**	....	....	....	....	....	....	....	....	....
	Washington	**NHL**	**39**	**7**	**10**	**17**	**51**	**0**	**0**	**0**	**68**	**10.3**	**6**	**17**	**41.2**	**12:36**	**7**	**1**	**2**	**3**	**2**	**0**	**0**	**1**	**11:46**
2010-11	**Washington**	**NHL**	**81**	**10**	**16**	**26**	**64**	**2**	**0**	**1**	**162**	**6.2**	**-10**	**39**	**51.3**	**13:15**	**9**	**2**	**2**	**4**	**2**	**0**	**0**	**2**	**12:53**
2011-12	**Washington**	**NHL**	**82**	**20**	**19**	**39**	**78**	**1**	**2**	**5**	**205**	**9.8**	**4**	**62**	**48.4**	**14:26**	**14**	**4**	**3**	**7**	**6**	**0**	**0**	**1**	**13:42**
2012-13	Pirati Chomutov	CzRep	5	1	0	1	10	....	....	....	....	....	....	....	....	....	....	....	....	....	....	....	....	....	....
	Washington	**NHL**	**47**	**3**	**11**	**14**	**48**	**0**	**0**	**0**	**92**	**3.3**	**-5**	**36**	**58.3**	**12:40**	**7**	**1**	**2**	**3**	**4**	**0**	**0**	**0**	**13:40**
2013-14	**Washington**	**NHL**	**82**	**15**	**27**	**42**	**36**	**1**	**0**	**0**	**167**	**9.0**	**4**	**87**	**43.7**	**15:25**	....	....	....	....	....	....	....	....	....
2014-15	**Washington**	**NHL**	**77**	**7**	**12**	**19**	**51**	**0**	**0**	**2**	**96**	**7.3**	**-1**	**76**	**56.6**	**12:56**	**14**	**3**	**4**	**7**	**4**	**0**	**0**	**1**	**15:36**
	NHL Totals		**869**	**143**	**186**	**329**	**793**	**10**	**7**	**25**	**1645**	**8.7**		**504**	**48.2**	**13:51**	**57**	**11**	**16**	**27**	**20**	**0**	**0**	**5**	**13:40**

AHL First All-Star Team (2002)

Traded to **Phoenix** by **Edmonton** with Edmonton's 3rd round choice (later traded to Carolina, later traded to NY Rangers – NY Rangers selected Billy Ryan) in 2004 Entry Draft for New Jersey's 2nd round choice (previously acquired, Edmonton selected Geoff Paukovich) in 2004 Entry Draft and Buffalo's 4th round choice (previously acquired, Edmonton selected Liam Reddox) in 2004 Entry Draft, June 26, 2004. Signed as a free agent by **Varese** (Italy), December 15, 2004. Traded to **Columbus** by **Phoenix** with Cale Hulse and Mike Rupp for Geoff Sanderson and Tim Jackman, October 8, 2005. Traded to **Washington** by **Columbus** for Chris Clark and Milan Jurcina, December 28, 2009. Signed as a free agent by **Chomutov** (CzRep), November 14, 2012.

CHIPCHURA, Kyle

(chip-CHUHR-a, KIGHL) **ARI**

Center. Shoots left. 6'2", 203 lbs. Born, Westlock, AB, February 19, 1986. Montreal's 1st choice, 18th overall, in 2004 Entry Draft.

			Regular Season														Playoffs								
Season	Club	League	GP	G	A	Pts	PIM	PP	SH	GW	S	S%	+/-	TF	F%	Min	GP	G	A	Pts	PIM	PP	SH	GW	Min
2000-01	Spruce Grove	AMBHL	36	26	34	60	48	....	....	....	....	....	....	....	....	....	....	....	....	....	....	....	....	....	....
2001-02	Ft. Saskatchewan	AMHL	33	15	36	51	78	....	....	....	....	....	....	....	....	....	17	16	20	36	....	....	....	....	....
	Prince Albert	WHL	2	0	0	0	0	....	....	....	....	....	....	....	....	....	....	....	....	....	....	....	....	....	....
2002-03	Prince Albert	WHL	63	9	21	30	89	....	....	....	....	....	....	....	....	....	....	....	....	....	....	....	....	....	....
2003-04	Prince Albert	WHL	64	15	33	48	118	....	....	....	....	....	....	....	....	....	6	2	4	6	12	....	....	....	....
2004-05	Prince Albert	WHL	28	14	18	32	32	....	....	....	....	....	....	....	....	....	14	4	7	11	25	....	....	....	....
2005-06	Prince Albert	WHL	59	21	34	55	81	....	....	....	....	....	....	....	....	....	....	....	....	....	....	....	....	....	....
	Hamilton	AHL	8	1	2	3	6	....	....	....	....	....	....	....	....	....	....	....	....	....	....	....	....	....	....
2006-07	Hamilton	AHL	80	12	27	39	56	....	....	....	....	....	....	....	....	....	22	6	7	13	20	....	....	....	....
2007-08	**Montreal**	**NHL**	**36**	**4**	**7**	**11**	**10**	**0**	**0**	**0**	**36**	**11.1**	**-1**	**317**	**43.9**	**11:22**	....	....	....	....	....	....	....	....	....
	Hamilton	AHL	39	10	11	21	27	....	....	....	....	....	....	....	....	....	....	....	....	....	....	....	....	....	....
2008-09	**Montreal**	**NHL**	**13**	**0**	**3**	**3**	**5**	**0**	**0**	**0**	**5**	**0.0**	**-6**	**107**	**43.9**	**10:18**	....	....	....	....	....	....	....	....	....
	Hamilton	AHL	51	14	21	35	65	....	....	....	....	....	....	....	....	....	6	3	0	3	2	....	....	....	....
2009-10	**Montreal**	**NHL**	**19**	**0**	**0**	**0**	**16**	**0**	**0**	**0**	**11**	**0.0**	**-10**	**106**	**53.8**	**8:38**	....	....	....	....	....	....	....	....	....
	Anaheim	**NHL**	**55**	**6**	**6**	**12**	**56**	**0**	**1**	**1**	**43**	**14.0**	**-2**	**670**	**47.9**	**12:29**	....	....	....	....	....	....	....	....	....
2010-11	**Anaheim**	**NHL**	**40**	**0**	**2**	**2**	**32**	**0**	**0**	**0**	**23**	**0.0**	**1**	**283**	**46.6**	**8:00**	....	....	....	....	....	....	....	....	....
2011-12	**Phoenix**	**NHL**	**53**	**3**	**13**	**16**	**42**	**0**	**0**	**0**	**43**	**7.0**	**2**	**364**	**47.8**	**10:32**	**15**	**1**	**3**	**4**	**7**	**0**	**0**	**0**	**7:46**
	Portland Pirates	AHL	8	4	2	6	4	....	....	....	....	....	....	....	....	....	....	....	....	....	....	....	....	....	....
2012-13	Arizona Sundogs	CHL	10	2	11	13	4	....	....	....	....	....	....	....	....	....	....	....	....	....	....	....	....	....	....
	Phoenix	**NHL**	**46**	**5**	**9**	**14**	**50**	**0**	**0**	**0**	**37**	**13.5**	**1**	**261**	**48.3**	**9:42**	....	....	....	....	....	....	....	....	....
2013-14	**Phoenix**	**NHL**	**80**	**5**	**15**	**20**	**45**	**0**	**0**	**0**	**46**	**10.9**	**3**	**331**	**53.2**	**9:43**	....	....	....	....	....	....	....	....	....
2014-15	**Arizona**	**NHL**	**70**	**4**	**10**	**14**	**82**	**1**	**0**	**0**	**81**	**4.9**	**-23**	**916**	**51.6**	**13:24**	....	....	....	....	....	....	....	....	....
	NHL Totals		**412**	**27**	**65**	**92**	**338**	**1**	**1**	**1**	**325**	**8.3**		**3355**	**49.0**	**10:46**	**15**	**1**	**3**	**4**	**7**	**0**	**0**	**0**	**7:46**

WHL East Second All-Star Team (2006)

Traded to **Anaheim** by **Montreal** for Anaheim's 4th round choice (Magnus Nygren) in 2011 Entry Draft, December 1, 2009. • Missed majority of 2010-11 due to head injury at San Jose, October 30, 2010 and as a healthy reserve. Signed as a free agent by **Phoenix**, July 19, 2011. Signed as a free agent by **Arizona** (CHL), October 16, 2012.

CHORNEY, Taylor

(CHOHR-nee, TAY-luhr) **WSH**

Defense. Shoots left. 6'1", 189 lbs. Born, Thunder Bay, ON, April 27, 1987. Edmonton's 2nd choice, 36th overall, in 2005 Entry Draft.

			Regular Season														Playoffs								
Season	Club	League	GP	G	A	Pts	PIM	PP	SH	GW	S	S%	+/-	TF	F%	Min	GP	G	A	Pts	PIM	PP	SH	GW	Min
2003-04	Shat.-St. Mary's	High-MN	74	12	44	56	58	....	....	....	....	....	....	....	....	....	....	....	....	....	....	....	....	....	....
2004-05	Shat.-St. Mary's	High-MN	50	4	30	34	52	....	....	....	....	....	....	....	....	....	....	....	....	....	....	....	....	....	....
2005-06	North Dakota	WCHA	44	3	15	18	54	....	....	....	....	....	....	....	....	....	....	....	....	....	....	....	....	....	....
2006-07	North Dakota	WCHA	39	8	23	31	48	....	....	....	....	....	....	....	....	....	....	....	....	....	....	....	....	....	....
2007-08	North Dakota	WCHA	43	3	21	24	24	....	....	....	....	....	....	....	....	....	....	....	....	....	....	....	....	....	....
2008-09	**Edmonton**	**NHL**	**2**	**0**	**0**	**0**	**0**	**0**	**0**	**0**	**0**	**0.0**	**-4**	**0**	**0.0**	**15:43**	....	....	....	....	....	....	....	....	....
	Springfield	AHL	68	5	16	21	22	....	....	....	....	....	....	....	....	....	....	....	....	....	....	....	....	....	....
2009-10	**Edmonton**	**NHL**	**42**	**0**	**3**	**3**	**12**	**0**	**0**	**0**	**35**	**0.0**	**-21**	**0**	**0.0**	**17:24**	....	....	....	....	....	....	....	....	....
	Springfield	AHL	32	4	9	13	14	....	....	....	....	....	....	....	....	....	....	....	....	....	....	....	....	....	....
2010-11	**Edmonton**	**NHL**	**12**	**1**	**3**	**4**	**4**	**1**	**0**	**1**	**13**	**7.7**	**-5**	**0**	**0.0**	**15:59**	....	....	....	....	....	....	....	....	....
	Oklahoma City	AHL	46	3	13	16	22	....	....	....	....	....	....	....	....	....	....	....	....	....	....	....	....	....	....
2011-12	**St. Louis**	**NHL**	**2**	**0**	**0**	**0**	**0**	**0**	**0**	**0**	**1**	**0.0**	**0**	**0**	**0.0**	**11:40**	....	....	....	....	....	....	....	....	....
	Edmonton	**NHL**	**3**	**0**	**0**	**0**	**0**	**0**	**0**	**0**	**1**	**0.0**	**-1**	**0**	**0.0**	**15:48**	....	....	....	....	....	....	....	....	....
	Oklahoma City	AHL	50	6	18	24	29	....	....	....	....	....	....	....	....	....	10	0	1	1	6	....	....	....	....
2012-13	Peoria Rivermen	AHL	73	4	20	24	37	....	....	....	....	....	....	....	....	....	....	....	....	....	....	....	....	....	....
2013-14	Chicago Wolves	AHL	69	5	20	25	37	....	....	....	....	....	....	....	....	....	9	1	1	2	2	....	....	....	....
2014-15	**Pittsburgh**	**NHL**	**7**	**0**	**0**	**0**	**0**	**0**	**0**	**0**	**4**	**0.0**	**-1**	**0**	**0.0**	**12:10**	**5**	**0**	**0**	**0**	**2**	**0**	**0**	**0**	**16:35**
	Wilkes-Barre	AHL	62	4	15	19	42	....	....	....	....	....	....	....	....	....	6	1	1	2	6	....	....	....	....
	NHL Totals		**68**	**1**	**6**	**7**	**16**	**1**	**0**	**1**	**54**	**1.9**		**0**	**0.0**	**16:19**	**5**	**0**	**0**	**0**	**2**	**0**	**0**	**0**	**16:35**

WCHA Second All-Star Team (2007) • NCAA West Second All-American Team (2007) • WCHA First All-Star Team (2008)

Claimed on waivers by **St. Louis** from **Edmonton** October 11, 2011. Claimed on waivers by **Edmonton** from **St. Louis** November 10, 2011. Signed as a free agent by **St. Louis**, July 1, 2012. Signed as a free agent by **Pittsburgh**, July 1, 2014. Signed as a free agent by **Washington**, July 1, 2015.

CIZIKAS, Casey

(sih-ZEE-kuhs, KAY-see) **NYI**

Center. Shoots left. 5'11", 201 lbs. Born, Toronto, ON, February 27, 1991. NY Islanders' 5th choice, 92nd overall, in 2009 Entry Draft.

			Regular Season														Playoffs								
Season	Club	League	GP	G	A	Pts	PIM	PP	SH	GW	S	S%	+/-	TF	F%	Min	GP	G	A	Pts	PIM	PP	SH	GW	Min
2006-07	Mississauga Reps	GTHL	77	46	60	106	88	....	....	....	....	....	....	....	....	....	....	....	....	....	....	....	....	....	....
2007-08	St. Michael's	OHL	62	18	23	41	41	....	....	....	....	....	....	....	....	....	4	1	2	3	6	....	....	....	....
2008-09	St. Michael's	OHL	55	16	20	36	39	....	....	....	....	....	....	....	....	....	11	5	4	9	11	....	....	....	....
2009-10	St. Michael's	OHL	68	25	37	62	77	....	....	....	....	....	....	....	....	....	16	7	7	14	16	....	....	....	....
2010-11	St. Michael's	OHL	52	29	35	64	40	....	....	....	....	....	....	....	....	....	16	5	14	19	14	....	....	....	....
2011-12	**NY Islanders**	**NHL**	**15**	**0**	**4**	**4**	**6**	**0**	**0**	**0**	**12**	**0.0**	**1**	**115**	**40.9**	**10:36**	....	....	....	....	....	....	....	....	....
	Bridgeport	AHL	52	15	30	45	30	....	....	....	....	....	....	....	....	....	3	0	0	0	20	....	....	....	....
2012-13	Bridgeport	AHL	31	10	11	21	35	....	....	....	....	....	....	....	....	....	....	....	....	....	....	....	....	....	....
	NY Islanders	**NHL**	**45**	**6**	**9**	**15**	**14**	**0**	**0**	**1**	**45**	**13.3**	**0**	**276**	**52.2**	**10:47**	**6**	**2**	**2**	**4**	**12**	**0**	**0**	**0**	**10:46**
2013-14	**NY Islanders**	**NHL**	**80**	**6**	**10**	**16**	**30**	**1**	**0**	**1**	**79**	**7.6**	**-12**	**1011**	**48.4**	**13:22**	....	....	....	....	....	....	....	....	....
2014-15	**NY Islanders**	**NHL**	**70**	**9**	**9**	**18**	**24**	**0**	**2**	**2**	**90**	**10.0**	**-2**	**855**	**52.2**	**12:31**	**7**	**1**	**0**	**1**	**0**	**0**	**0**	**0**	**13:42**
	NHL Totals		**210**	**21**	**32**	**53**	**74**	**1**	**2**	**4**	**226**	**9.3**		**2257**	**49.9**	**12:20**	**13**	**3**	**2**	**5**	**12**	**0**	**0**	**0**	**12:21**

CLARK, Mat
(KLAHRK, MAT) **COL**

Defense. Shoots right. 6'3", 225 lbs. Born, Wheat Ridge, CO, October 17, 1990. Anaheim's 3rd choice, 37th overall, in 2009 Entry Draft.

			Regular Season														Playoffs								
Season	Club	League	GP	G	A	Pts	PIM	PP	SH	GW	S	S%	+/-	TF	F%	Min	GP	G	A	Pts	PIM	PP	SH	GW	Min
2006-07	Brampton	ON-Jr.A	47	2	7	9	50	....	....	....	....	....	....	....	....	....	8	1	1	2	19	....	....	....	....
2007-08	Brampton	ON-Jr.A	46	6	11	17	82	....	....	....	....	....	....	....	....	....	8	1	4	5	45	....	....	....	....
2008-09	Brampton	OHL	63	3	20	23	91	....	....	....	....	....	....	....	....	....	21	0	5	5	37	....	....	....	....
2009-10	Brampton	OHL	66	7	16	23	88	....	....	....	....	....	....	....	....	....	7	2	4	6	9	....	....	....	....
	Manitoba Moose	AHL	1	0	0	0	0	....	....	....	....	....	....	....	....	....	6	0	0	0	2	....	....	....	....
2010-11	Syracuse Crunch	AHL	80	2	14	16	128	....	....	....	....	....	....	....	....	....	....	....	....	....	....	....	....	....	....
2011-12	**Anaheim**	**NHL**	**2**	**0**	**0**	**0**	**0**	**0**	**0**	**0**	**2**	**0.0**	**–2**	**0**	**0.0**	**11:02**	....	....	....	....	....	....	....	....	....
	Syracuse Crunch	AHL	62	1	11	12	72	....	....	....	....	....	....	....	....	....	4	1	1	2	11	....	....	....	....
2012-13	Norfolk Admirals	AHL	71	1	9	10	79	....	....	....	....	....	....	....	....	....	....	....	....	....	....	....	....	....	....
2013-14	Norfolk Admirals	AHL	23	0	2	2	37	....	....	....	....	....	....	....	....	....	....	....	....	....	....	....	....	....	....
2014-15	**Anaheim**	**NHL**	**7**	**0**	**1**	**1**	**6**	**0**	**0**	**0**	**2**	**0.0**	**2**	**0**	**0.0**	**12:46**	....	....	....	....	....	....	....	....	....
	Norfolk Admirals	AHL	45	1	5	6	60	....	....	....	....	....	....	....	....	....	....	....	....	....	....	....	....	....	....
	Lake Erie	AHL	21	0	1	1	11	....	....	....	....	....	....	....	....	....	....	....	....	....	....	....	....	....	....
	NHL Totals		**9**	**0**	**1**	**1**	**6**	**0**	**0**	**0**	**4**	**0.0**		**0**	**0.0**	**12:23**	....	....	....	....	....	....	....	....	....

• Missed remainder of 2013-14 due to injury at Syracuse (AHL), December 6, 2013. Traded to **Colorado** by **Anaheim** for Michael Sgarbossa, March 2, 2015.

CLARKSON, David
(KLAHRK-suhn, DAYV-ihd) **CBJ**

Right wing. Shoots right. 6'1", 200 lbs. Born, Toronto, ON, March 31, 1984.

			Regular Season														Playoffs								
Season	Club	League	GP	G	A	Pts	PIM	PP	SH	GW	S	S%	+/-	TF	F%	Min	GP	G	A	Pts	PIM	PP	SH	GW	Min
2000-01	Port Hope	ON-Jr.A	47	18	14	32	118	....	....	....	....	....	....	....	....	....	....	....	....	....	....	....	....	....	....
2001-02	Aurora Tigers	ON-Jr.A	37	26	21	47	141	....	....	....	....	....	....	....	....	....	....	....	....	....	....	....	....	....	....
	Belleville Bulls	OHL	22	2	7	9	34	....	....	....	....	....	....	....	....	....	8	1	1	2	6	....	....	....	....
2002-03	Belleville Bulls	OHL	3	0	0	0	11	....	....	....	....	....	....	....	....	....	....	....	....	....	....	....	....	....	....
	Kitchener Rangers	OHL	54	17	11	28	122	....	....	....	....	....	....	....	....	....	21	4	3	7	23	....	....	....	....
2003-04	Kitchener Rangers	OHL	55	22	17	39	173	....	....	....	....	....	....	....	....	....	....	....	....	....	....	....	....	....	....
2004-05	Kitchener Rangers	OHL	51	33	21	54	145	....	....	....	....	....	....	....	....	....	15	6	2	8	40	....	....	....	....
2005-06	Albany River Rats	AHL	56	13	21	34	233	....	....	....	....	....	....	....	....	....	....	....	....	....	....	....	....	....	....
2006-07	**New Jersey**	**NHL**	**7**	**3**	**1**	**4**	**6**	**2**	**0**	**1**	**18**	**16.7**	**–1**	**1**	**0.0**	**17:02**	**3**	**0**	**0**	**0**	**2**	**0**	**0**	**0**	**6:42**
	Lowell Devils	AHL	67	20	18	38	150	....	....	....	....	....	....	....	....	....	....	....	....	....	....	....	....	....	....
2007-08	**New Jersey**	**NHL**	**81**	**9**	**13**	**22**	**183**	**0**	**0**	**1**	**151**	**6.0**	**1**	**15**	**40.0**	**12:02**	**5**	**0**	**0**	**0**	**4**	**0**	**0**	**0**	**12:20**
2008-09	**New Jersey**	**NHL**	**82**	**17**	**15**	**32**	**164**	**4**	**0**	**3**	**158**	**10.8**	**–1**	**7**	**28.6**	**12:03**	**7**	**2**	**0**	**2**	**19**	**1**	**0**	**1**	**8:32**
2009-10	**New Jersey**	**NHL**	**46**	**11**	**13**	**24**	**85**	**3**	**0**	**2**	**106**	**10.4**	**3**	**20**	**30.0**	**14:27**	**5**	**0**	**0**	**0**	**22**	**0**	**0**	**0**	**12:28**
2010-11	**New Jersey**	**NHL**	**82**	**12**	**6**	**18**	**116**	**1**	**0**	**1**	**192**	**6.3**	**–20**	**45**	**42.2**	**13:37**	....	....	....	....	....	....	....	....	....
2011-12	**New Jersey**	**NHL**	**80**	**30**	**16**	**46**	**138**	**8**	**0**	**7**	**228**	**13.2**	**–8**	**243**	**42.0**	**16:22**	**24**	**3**	**9**	**12**	**32**	**0**	**0**	***3**	**14:52**
2012-13	Salzburg	Austria	5	2	1	3	18	....	....	....	....	....	....	....	....	....	....	....	....	....	....	....	....	....	....
	New Jersey	**NHL**	**48**	**15**	**9**	**24**	**78**	**6**	**0**	**5**	**180**	**8.3**	**–6**	**25**	**24.0**	**17:36**	....	....	....	....	....	....	....	....	....
2013-14	**Toronto**	**NHL**	**60**	**5**	**6**	**11**	**93**	**1**	**0**	**1**	**102**	**4.9**	**–14**	**21**	**38.1**	**15:06**	....	....	....	....	....	....	....	....	....
2014-15	**Toronto**	**NHL**	**58**	**10**	**5**	**15**	**92**	**1**	**0**	**1**	**93**	**10.8**	**–11**	**63**	**31.8**	**13:53**	....	....	....	....	....	....	....	....	....
	Columbus	**NHL**	**3**	**0**	**0**	**0**	**14**	**0**	**0**	**0**	**2**	**0.0**	**–1**	**10**	**50.0**	**12:18**	....	....	....	....	....	....	....	....	....
	NHL Totals		**547**	**112**	**84**	**196**	**969**	**26**	**0**	**22**	**1230**	**9.1**		**450**	**38.7**	**14:12**	**44**	**5**	**9**	**14**	**79**	**1**	**0**	**4**	**12:44**

Signed as a free agent by **New Jersey**, August 12, 2005. Signed as a free agent by **Salzburg** (Austria), October 24, 2012. Signed as a free agent by **Toronto**, July 5, 2013. Traded to **Columbus** by **Toronto** for Nathan Horton, February 26, 2015.

CLEARY, Dan
(KLIH-ree, DAN) **DET**

Right wing. Shoots left. 6', 208 lbs. Born, Carbonear, NL, December 18, 1978. Chicago's 1st choice, 13th overall, in 1997 Entry Draft.

			Regular Season														Playoffs								
Season	Club	League	GP	G	A	Pts	PIM	PP	SH	GW	S	S%	+/-	TF	F%	Min	GP	G	A	Pts	PIM	PP	SH	GW	Min
1993-94	Kingston	ON-Jr.A	41	18	28	46	33	....	....	....	....	....	....	....	....	....	2	0	1	1	0	....	....	....	....
1994-95	Belleville Bulls	OHL	62	26	55	81	62	....	....	....	....	....	....	....	....	....	16	7	10	17	23	....	....	....	....
1995-96	Belleville Bulls	OHL	64	53	62	115	74	....	....	....	....	....	....	....	....	....	14	10	17	27	40	....	....	....	....
1996-97	Belleville Bulls	OHL	64	32	48	80	88	....	....	....	....	....	....	....	....	....	6	3	4	7	6	....	....	....	....
1997-98	**Chicago**	**NHL**	**6**	**0**	**0**	**0**	**0**	**0**	**0**	**0**	**4**	**0.0**	**–2**	....	....	....	....	....	....	....	....	....	....	....	....
	Belleville Bulls	OHL	30	16	31	47	14	....	....	....	....	....	....	....	....	....	10	6	*17	*23	10	....	....	....	....
	Indianapolis Ice	IHL	4	2	1	3	6	....	....	....	....	....	....	....	....	....	....	....	....	....	....	....	....	....	....
1998-99	**Chicago**	**NHL**	**35**	**4**	**5**	**9**	**24**	**0**	**0**	**0**	**49**	**8.2**	**–1**	**13**	**46.2**	**14:21**	....	....	....	....	....	....	....	....	....
	Portland Pirates	AHL	30	9	17	26	74	....	....	....	....	....	....	....	....	....	....	....	....	....	....	....	....	....	....
	Hamilton	AHL	9	0	1	1	7	....	....	....	....	....	....	....	....	....	3	0	0	0	0	....	....	....	....
99-2000	**Edmonton**	**NHL**	**17**	**3**	**2**	**5**	**8**	**0**	**0**	**1**	**18**	**16.7**	**–1**	**1**	**100.0**	**9:44**	**4**	**0**	**1**	**1**	**2**	**0**	**0**	**0**	**8:40**
	Hamilton	AHL	58	22	52	74	108	....	....	....	....	....	....	....	....	....	5	2	3	5	18	....	....	....	....
2000-01	**Edmonton**	**NHL**	**81**	**14**	**21**	**35**	**37**	**2**	**0**	**2**	**107**	**13.1**	**5**	**13**	**23.1**	**12:58**	**6**	**1**	**1**	**2**	**8**	**1**	**0**	**0**	**14:09**
2001-02	**Edmonton**	**NHL**	**65**	**10**	**19**	**29**	**51**	**2**	**1**	**1**	**75**	**13.3**	**–1**	**5**	**60.0**	**12:43**	....	....	....	....	....	....	....	....	....
2002-03	**Edmonton**	**NHL**	**57**	**4**	**13**	**17**	**31**	**0**	**0**	**1**	**89**	**4.5**	**5**	**5**	**40.0**	**11:58**	....	....	....	....	....	....	....	....	....
2003-04	**Phoenix**	**NHL**	**68**	**6**	**11**	**17**	**42**	**0**	**3**	**0**	**83**	**7.2**	**–8**	**51**	**39.2**	**13:12**	....	....	....	....	....	....	....	....	....
2004-05	Mora IK	Sweden	47	11	26	37	138	....	....	....	....	....	....	....	....	....	....	....	....	....	....	....	....	....	....
2005-06	**Detroit**	**NHL**	**77**	**3**	**12**	**15**	**40**	**0**	**0**	**1**	**106**	**2.8**	**5**	**286**	**45.8**	**10:30**	**6**	**0**	**1**	**1**	**6**	**0**	**0**	**0**	**10:44**
2006-07	**Detroit**	**NHL**	**71**	**20**	**20**	**40**	**24**	**6**	**2**	**5**	**135**	**14.8**	**6**	**411**	**51.1**	**15:28**	**18**	**4**	**8**	**12**	**30**	**1**	***2**	**0**	**16:28**
2007-08 ♦	**Detroit**	**NHL**	**63**	**20**	**22**	**42**	**33**	**5**	**0**	**3**	**177**	**11.3**	**21**	**110**	**50.9**	**17:23**	**22**	**2**	**1**	**3**	**4**	**0**	**1**	**0**	**17:50**
2008-09	**Detroit**	**NHL**	**74**	**14**	**26**	**40**	**46**	**3**	**0**	**3**	**163**	**8.6**	**0**	**121**	**55.4**	**16:56**	**23**	**9**	**6**	**15**	**12**	**0**	**0**	***3**	**16:55**
2009-10	**Detroit**	**NHL**	**64**	**15**	**19**	**34**	**29**	**2**	**0**	**2**	**140**	**10.7**	**–3**	**119**	**49.6**	**17:14**	**12**	**2**	**0**	**2**	**4**	**0**	**0**	**0**	**14:47**
2010-11	**Detroit**	**NHL**	**68**	**26**	**20**	**46**	**20**	**5**	**0**	**8**	**192**	**13.5**	**–1**	**91**	**38.5**	**16:38**	**11**	**2**	**4**	**6**	**6**	**0**	**0**	**1**	**17:09**
2011-12	**Detroit**	**NHL**	**75**	**12**	**21**	**33**	**30**	**2**	**0**	**0**	**199**	**6.0**	**2**	**51**	**41.2**	**15:59**	**5**	**0**	**0**	**0**	**2**	**0**	**0**	**0**	**15:11**
2012-13	**Detroit**	**NHL**	**48**	**9**	**6**	**15**	**40**	**5**	**1**	**0**	**93**	**9.7**	**–6**	**23**	**47.8**	**16:27**	**14**	**4**	**6**	**10**	**2**	**1**	**0**	**0**	**16:47**
2013-14	**Detroit**	**NHL**	**52**	**4**	**4**	**8**	**31**	**0**	**0**	**1**	**64**	**6.3**	**–11**	**22**	**54.6**	**13:54**	....	....	....	....	....	....	....	....	....
2014-15	**Detroit**	**NHL**	**17**	**1**	**1**	**2**	**6**	**0**	**0**	**0**	**17**	**5.9**	**–4**	**4**	**50.0**	**9:08**	....	....	....	....	....	....	....	....	....
	NHL Totals		**938**	**165**	**222**	**387**	**492**	**32**	**7**	**28**	**1711**	**9.6**		**1326**	**48.2**	**14:28**	**121**	**24**	**28**	**52**	**76**	**3**	**3**	**4**	**16:01**

OHL All-Rookie Team (1995) • OHL First All-Star Team (1996, 1997) • AHL Second All-Star Team (2000)

Traded to **Edmonton** by **Chicago** with Chad Kilger, Ethan Moreau and Christian Laflamme for Boris Mironov, Dean McAmmond and Jonas Elofsson, March 20, 1999. Signed as a free agent by **Phoenix**, July 15, 2003. Signed as a free agent by **Mora** (Sweden), September 6, 2004. Signed as a free agent by **Detroit**, October 4, 2005. • Missed majority of 2014-15 as a healthy reserve.

CLENDENING, Adam
(klehn-DEHN-ihng, A-duhm) **PIT**

Defense. Shoots right. 5'11", 187 lbs. Born, Niagara Falls, NY, October 26, 1992. Chicago's 3rd choice, 36th overall, in 2011 Entry Draft.

			Regular Season														Playoffs								
Season	Club	League	GP	G	A	Pts	PIM	PP	SH	GW	S	S%	+/-	TF	F%	Min	GP	G	A	Pts	PIM	PP	SH	GW	Min
2007-08	Tor. Marlboros	GTHL	60	8	42	50	116	....	....	....	....	....	....	....	....	....	....	....	....	....	....	....	....	....	....
2008-09	USNTDP	NAHL	34	0	9	9	38	....	....	....	....	....	....	....	....	....	....	....	....	....	....	....	....	....	....
	USNTDP	U-17	15	1	5	6	18	....	....	....	....	....	....	....	....	....	....	....	....	....	....	....	....	....	....
	USNTDP	U-18	13	1	5	6	14	....	....	....	....	....	....	....	....	....	....	....	....	....	....	....	....	....	....
2009-10	USNTDP	USHL	26	4	13	17	44	....	....	....	....	....	....	....	....	....	....	....	....	....	....	....	....	....	....
	USNTDP	U-18	39	10	22	32	76	....	....	....	....	....	....	....	....	....	....	....	....	....	....	....	....	....	....
2010-11	Boston University	H-East	39	5	21	26	80	....	....	....	....	....	....	....	....	....	....	....	....	....	....	....	....	....	....
2011-12	Boston University	H-East	38	4	29	33	64	....	....	....	....	....	....	....	....	....	....	....	....	....	....	....	....	....	....
2012-13	Rockford IceHogs	AHL	73	9	37	46	67	....	....	....	....	....	....	....	....	....	....	....	....	....	....	....	....	....	....
2013-14	Rockford IceHogs	AHL	74	12	47	59	64	....	....	....	....	....	....	....	....	....	....	....	....	....	....	....	....	....	....
2014-15	**Chicago**	**NHL**	**4**	**1**	**1**	**2**	**2**	**1**	**0**	**0**	**2**	**50.0**	**1**	**0**	**0.0**	**13:10**	....	....	....	....	....	....	....	....	....
	Rockford IceHogs	AHL	38	1	12	13	20	....	....	....	....	....	....	....	....	....	....	....	....	....	....	....	....	....	....
	Vancouver	**NHL**	**17**	**0**	**2**	**2**	**8**	**0**	**0**	**0**	**15**	**0.0**	**1**	**0**	**0.0**	**17:27**	....	....	....	....	....	....	....	....	....
	Utica Comets	AHL	11	1	4	5	28	....	....	....	....	....	....	....	....	....	23	3	5	8	26	....	....	....	....
	NHL Totals		**21**	**1**	**3**	**4**	**10**	**1**	**0**	**0**	**17**	**5.9**		**0**	**0.0**	**16:38**	....	....	....	....	....	....	....	....	....

Hockey East All-Rookie Team (2011) • Hockey East First All-Star Team (2012) • AHL Second All-Star Team (2013) • AHL First All-Star Team (2014)

Traded to **Vancouver** by **Chicago** for Gustav Forsling, January 29, 2015. Traded to **Pittsburgh** by **Vancouver** with Nick Bonino and Anaheim's 2nd round choice (previously acquired) in 2016 Entry Draft for Brandon Sutter and Pittsburgh's 3rd round compensatory choice in 2016 Entry Draft, July 28, 2015.

CLICHE, Marc-Andre

(KLEESH, MAHRK-AWN-dray) **COL**

Center. Shoots right. 6', 202 lbs. Born, Rouyn-Noranda, QC, March 23, 1987. NY Rangers' 3rd choice, 56th overall, in 2005 Entry Draft.

			Regular Season														Playoffs								
Season	Club	League	GP	G	A	Pts	PIM	PP	SH	GW	S	S%	+/-	TF	F%	Min	GP	G	A	Pts	PIM	PP	SH	GW	Min
2002-03	Amos Forestiers	QAAA	42	26	16	42	18	....	....	....	....	....	....	....	....	....	15	6	12	18	6	....	....	....	....
2003-04	Lewiston	QMJHL	52	8	10	18	17	....	....	....	....	....	....	....	....	....	7	1	2	3	0	....	....	....	....
2004-05	Lewiston	QMJHL	19	4	4	8	8	....	....	....	....	....	....	....	....	....	....	....	....	....	....	....	....	....	....
2005-06	Lewiston	QMJHL	66	37	45	82	60	....	....	....	....	....	....	....	....	....	6	2	2	4	0	....	....	....	....
2006-07	Lewiston	QMJHL	52	24	30	54	42	....	....	....	....	....	....	....	....	....	16	6	16	22	10	....	....	....	....
2007-08	Manchester	AHL	52	11	10	21	25	....	....	....	....	....	....	....	....	....	4	0	1	1	2	....	....	....	....
2008-09	Manchester	AHL	31	5	4	9	19	....	....	....	....	....	....	....	....	....	....	....	....	....	....	....	....	....	....
2009-10	**Los Angeles**	**NHL**	**1**	**0**	**0**	**0**	**0**	**0**	**0**	**0**	**0**	**0.0**	**1**	**6**	**66.7**	**7:23**	....	....	....	....	....	....	....	....	....
	Manchester	AHL	66	11	14	25	45	....	....	....	....	....	....	....	....	....	12	1	1	2	8	....	....	....	....
2010-11	Manchester	AHL	63	14	21	35	35	....	....	....	....	....	....	....	....	....	....	....	....	....	....	....	....	....	....
2011-12	Manchester	AHL	72	17	24	41	35	....	....	....	....	....	....	....	....	....	4	1	0	1	6	....	....	....	....
2012-13	Manchester	AHL	57	10	10	20	46	....	....	....	....	....	....	....	....	....	3	0	0	0	4	....	....	....	....
2013-14	**Colorado**	**NHL**	**76**	**1**	**6**	**7**	**17**	**0**	**0**	**0**	**69**	**1.4**	**-11**	**719**	**46.0**	**10:34**	**7**	**0**	**0**	**0**	**2**	**0**	**0**	**0**	**14:20**
2014-15	**Colorado**	**NHL**	**74**	**2**	**5**	**7**	**17**	**0**	**0**	**0**	**68**	**2.9**	**-2**	**735**	**51.3**	**10:36**	....	....	....	....	....	....	....	....	....
	NHL Totals		**151**	**3**	**11**	**14**	**34**	**0**	**0**	**0**	**137**	**2.2**		**1460**	**48.8**	**10:34**	**7**	**0**	**0**	**0**	**2**	**0**	**0**	**0**	**14:20**

• Missed majority of 2004-05 due to shoulder injury. Traded to **Los Angeles** by **NY Rangers** with Jason Ward, Jan Marek and NY Rangers' 3rd round choice (later traded to Buffalo - Buffalo selected Corey Fienhage) in 2008 Entry Draft for Sean Avery and John Seymour, February 5, 2007. • Missed majority of 2008-09 due to training camp shoulder injury. Claimed on waivers by **Colorado** from **Los Angeles**, September 22, 2013.

CLIFFORD, Kyle

(KLIHF-fuhrd, KIGHL) **L.A.**

Left wing. Shoots left. 6'2", 208 lbs. Born, Ayr, ON, January 13, 1991. Los Angeles' 2nd choice, 35th overall, in 2009 Entry Draft.

			Regular Season														Playoffs								
Season	Club	League	GP	G	A	Pts	PIM	PP	SH	GW	S	S%	+/-	TF	F%	Min	GP	G	A	Pts	PIM	PP	SH	GW	Min
2006-07	Cambridge	Minor-ON	70	31	49	80	119	....	....	....	....	....	....	....	....	....	....	....	....	....	....	....	....	....	....
2007-08	Barrie Colts	OHL	66	1	14	15	83	....	....	....	....	....	....	....	....	....	9	0	1	1	4	....	....	....	....
2008-09	Barrie Colts	OHL	60	16	12	28	133	....	....	....	....	....	....	....	....	....	5	0	0	0	13	....	....	....	....
2009-10	Barrie Colts	OHL	58	28	29	57	111	....	....	....	....	....	....	....	....	....	17	5	9	14	28	....	....	....	....
	Manchester	AHL	....	....	....	....	....	....	....	....	....	....	....	....	....	....	7	0	2	2	12	....	....	....	....
2010-11	**Los Angeles**	**NHL**	**76**	**7**	**7**	**14**	**141**	**0**	**0**	**0**	**69**	**10.1**	**-10**	**15**	**53.3**	**9:30**	**6**	**3**	**2**	**5**	**7**	**0**	**0**	**1**	**13:17**
2011-12♦	**Los Angeles**	**NHL**	**81**	**5**	**7**	**12**	**123**	**0**	**0**	**2**	**88**	**5.7**	**-5**	**8**	**12.5**	**9:24**	**3**	**0**	**0**	**0**	**2**	**0**	**0**	**0**	**5:01**
2012-13	Ontario Reign	ECHL	9	4	3	7	2	....	....	....	....	....	....	....	....	....	....	....	....	....	....	....	....	....	....
	Los Angeles	**NHL**	**48**	**7**	**7**	**14**	**51**	**0**	**0**	**1**	**56**	**12.5**	**1**	**9**	**11.1**	**10:36**	**14**	**0**	**2**	**2**	**8**	**0**	**0**	**0**	**10:21**
2013-14♦	**Los Angeles**	**NHL**	**71**	**3**	**5**	**8**	**81**	**0**	**0**	**0**	**74**	**4.1**	**6**	**12**	**50.0**	**10:10**	**24**	**1**	**6**	**7**	***39**	**0**	**0**	**0**	**9:47**
2014-15	**Los Angeles**	**NHL**	**80**	**6**	**9**	**15**	**87**	**0**	**0**	**1**	**117**	**5.1**	**5**	**6**	**33.3**	**10:44**	....	....	....	....	....	....	....	....	....
	NHL Totals		**356**	**28**	**35**	**63**	**483**	**0**	**0**	**4**	**404**	**6.9**		**50**	**36.0**	**10:02**	**47**	**4**	**10**	**14**	**56**	**0**	**0**	**1**	**10:06**

Signed as a free agent by **Ontario** (ECHL), November 20, 2012.

CLITSOME, Grant

(KLIHT-suhm, GRANT) **WPG**

Defense. Shoots left. 5'11", 215 lbs. Born, Gloucester, ON, April 14, 1985. Columbus' 12th choice, 271st overall, in 2004 Entry Draft.

			Regular Season														Playoffs								
Season	Club	League	GP	G	A	Pts	PIM	PP	SH	GW	S	S%	+/-	TF	F%	Min	GP	G	A	Pts	PIM	PP	SH	GW	Min
2001-02	Nepean Raiders	ON-Jr.A	43	1	6	7	20	....	....	....	....	....	....	....	....	....	1	0	0	0	....	....	....	....	....
2002-03	Nepean Raiders	ON-Jr.A	54	4	12	16	46	....	....	....	....	....	....	....	....	....	17	5	10	15	18	....	....	....	....
2003-04	Nepean Raiders	ON-Jr.A	55	13	26	39	67	....	....	....	....	....	....	....	....	....	17	1	10	11	6	....	....	....	....
2004-05	Clarkson Knights	ECAC	39	2	11	13	36	....	....	....	....	....	....	....	....	....	....	....	....	....	....	....	....	....	....
2005-06	Clarkson Knights	ECAC	34	2	17	19	20	....	....	....	....	....	....	....	....	....	....	....	....	....	....	....	....	....	....
2006-07	Clarkson Knights	ECAC	38	7	12	19	38	....	....	....	....	....	....	....	....	....	....	....	....	....	....	....	....	....	....
2007-08	Clarkson Knights	ECAC	39	5	17	22	28	....	....	....	....	....	....	....	....	....	....	....	....	....	....	....	....	....	....
	Syracuse Crunch	AHL	....	....	....	....	....	....	....	....	....	....	....	....	....	....	1	0	0	0	0	....	....	....	....
2008-09	Syracuse Crunch	AHL	73	4	15	19	74	....	....	....	....	....	....	....	....	....	....	....	....	....	....	....	....	....	....
2009-10	**Columbus**	**NHL**	**11**	**1**	**2**	**3**	**6**	**0**	**0**	**0**	**7**	**14.3**	**0**	**0**	**0.0**	**14:44**	....	....	....	....	....	....	....	....	....
	Syracuse Crunch	AHL	64	5	15	20	42	....	....	....	....	....	....	....	....	....	....	....	....	....	....	....	....	....	....
2010-11	**Columbus**	**NHL**	**31**	**4**	**15**	**19**	**16**	**2**	**0**	**0**	**50**	**8.0**	**2**	**0**	**0.0**	**21:16**	....	....	....	....	....	....	....	....	....
	Springfield	AHL	32	5	10	15	22	....	....	....	....	....	....	....	....	....	....	....	....	....	....	....	....	....	....
2011-12	**Columbus**	**NHL**	**51**	**4**	**10**	**14**	**24**	**1**	**0**	**1**	**74**	**5.4**	**-6**	**1**	**0.0**	**17:02**	....	....	....	....	....	....	....	....	....
	Winnipeg	**NHL**	**12**	**0**	**3**	**3**	**8**	**0**	**0**	**0**	**13**	**0.0**	**-3**	**0**	**0.0**	**16:54**	....	....	....	....	....	....	....	....	....
2012-13	**Winnipeg**	**NHL**	**44**	**4**	**12**	**16**	**18**	**2**	**0**	**0**	**56**	**7.1**	**10**	**0**	**0.0**	**18:50**	....	....	....	....	....	....	....	....	....
2013-14	**Winnipeg**	**NHL**	**32**	**2**	**10**	**12**	**18**	**0**	**0**	**0**	**42**	**4.8**	**-5**	**0**	**0.0**	**19:47**	....	....	....	....	....	....	....	....	....
2014-15	**Winnipeg**	**NHL**	**24**	**0**	**4**	**4**	**8**	**0**	**0**	**0**	**22**	**0.0**	**4**	**0**	**0.0**	**16:22**	....	....	....	....	....	....	....	....	....
	NHL Totals		**205**	**15**	**56**	**71**	**98**	**5**	**0**	**1**	**264**	**5.7**		**1**	**0.0**	**18:17**	....	....	....	....	....	....	....	....	....

ECAC First All-Star Team (2008) • NCAA East Second All-American Team (2008)

Claimed on waivers by **Winnipeg** from **Columbus**, February 27, 2012. • Missed majority of 2013-14 and 2014-15 due to recurring back injury.

CLOWE, Ryane

(KLOH, RIGH-uhn) **N.J.**

Left wing. Shoots left. 6'3", 225 lbs. Born, St. John's, NL, September 30, 1982. San Jose's 5th choice, 175th overall, in 2001 Entry Draft.

			Regular Season														Playoffs								
Season	Club	League	GP	G	A	Pts	PIM	PP	SH	GW	S	S%	+/-	TF	F%	Min	GP	G	A	Pts	PIM	PP	SH	GW	Min
2000-01	Rimouski Oceanic	QMJHL	32	15	10	25	43	....	....	....	....	....	....	....	....	....	11	8	1	9	12	....	....	....	....
2001-02	Rimouski Oceanic	QMJHL	53	28	45	73	120	....	....	....	....	....	....	....	....	....	7	1	6	7	2	....	....	....	....
2002-03	Rimouski Oceanic	QMJHL	17	8	19	27	44	....	....	....	....	....	....	....	....	....	....	....	....	....	....	....	....	....	....
	Montreal Rocket	QMJHL	43	18	30	48	60	....	....	....	....	....	....	....	....	....	7	3	7	10	6	....	....	....	....
2003-04	Cleveland Barons	AHL	72	11	29	40	97	....	....	....	....	....	....	....	....	....	8	3	1	4	9	....	....	....	....
2004-05	Cleveland Barons	AHL	74	27	35	62	101	....	....	....	....	....	....	....	....	....	....	....	....	....	....	....	....	....	....
2005-06	**San Jose**	**NHL**	**18**	**0**	**2**	**2**	**9**	**0**	**0**	**0**	**14**	**0.0**	**-2**	**2**	**0.0**	**9:40**	**1**	**0**	**0**	**0**	**0**	**0**	**0**	**0**	**5:06**
	Cleveland Barons	AHL	35	13	21	34	35	....	....	....	....	....	....	....	....	....	....	....	....	....	....	....	....	....	....
2006-07	**San Jose**	**NHL**	**58**	**16**	**18**	**34**	**78**	**4**	**0**	**3**	**93**	**17.2**	**4**	**5**	**60.0**	**13:11**	**11**	**4**	**2**	**6**	**17**	**0**	**0**	**1**	**15:19**
2007-08	**San Jose**	**NHL**	**15**	**3**	**5**	**8**	**22**	**2**	**0**	**0**	**22**	**13.6**	**-1**	**14**	**35.7**	**14:17**	**13**	**5**	**4**	**9**	**12**	**2**	**0**	**0**	**19:00**
2008-09	**San Jose**	**NHL**	**71**	**22**	**30**	**52**	**51**	**11**	**0**	**1**	**161**	**13.7**	**8**	**120**	**40.8**	**17:47**	**6**	**1**	**1**	**2**	**8**	**0**	**0**	**0**	**18:22**
2009-10	**San Jose**	**NHL**	**82**	**19**	**38**	**57**	**131**	**2**	**0**	**2**	**189**	**10.1**	**0**	**73**	**48.0**	**17:10**	**15**	**2**	**8**	**10**	**28**	**0**	**0**	**0**	**20:11**
2010-11	**San Jose**	**NHL**	**75**	**24**	**38**	**62**	**100**	**5**	**0**	**2**	**185**	**13.0**	**13**	**41**	**41.5**	**17:58**	**17**	**6**	**9**	**15**	**32**	**3**	**0**	**0**	**19:27**
2011-12	**San Jose**	**NHL**	**76**	**17**	**28**	**45**	**97**	**4**	**0**	**2**	**180**	**9.4**	**-5**	**20**	**30.0**	**17:52**	**5**	**0**	**3**	**3**	**0**	**0**	**0**	**0**	**19:25**
2012-13	**San Jose**	**NHL**	**28**	**0**	**11**	**11**	**79**	**0**	**0**	**0**	**65**	**0.0**	**-4**	**12**	**33.3**	**16:28**	....	....	....	....	....	....	....	....	....
	NY Rangers	**NHL**	**12**	**3**	**5**	**8**	**14**	**1**	**0**	**0**	**22**	**13.6**	**5**	**3**	**33.3**	**17:02**	**2**	**0**	**1**	**1**	**0**	**0**	**0**	**0**	**7:07**
2013-14	**New Jersey**	**NHL**	**43**	**7**	**19**	**26**	**33**	**3**	**0**	**1**	**74**	**9.5**	**-10**	**3**	**33.3**	**16:08**	....	....	....	....	....	....	....	....	....
2014-15	**New Jersey**	**NHL**	**13**	**1**	**3**	**4**	**4**	**0**	**0**	**0**	**15**	**6.7**	**-1**	**1**	**0.0**	**15:40**	....	....	....	....	....	....	....	....	....
	NHL Totals		**491**	**112**	**197**	**309**	**618**	**32**	**0**	**11**	**1020**	**11.0**		**294**	**41.2**	**16:29**	**70**	**18**	**28**	**46**	**97**	**5**	**0**	**1**	**18:13**

• Missed majority of 2007-08 due to knee injury at Columbus, October 27, 2007. Traded to **NY Rangers** by **San Jose** for NY Rangers' 2nd round choice (Gabryel Boudreau) in 2013 Entry Draft, Florida's 3rd round choice (previously acquired, later traded to Phoenix – Phoenix selected Pavel Laplante) in 2013 Entry Draft and NY Rangers' 5th round choice (Rourke Chartier) in 2014 Entry Draft, April 2, 2013. Signed as a free agent by **New Jersey**, July 5, 2013. • Missed majority of 2014-15 due to head injury at St. Louis, November 6, 2014.

CLUNE, Rich

(KLOON, RITCH)

Left wing. Shoots left. 5'11", 219 lbs. Born, Toronto, ON, April 25, 1987. Dallas' 3rd choice, 71st overall, in 2005 Entry Draft.

			Regular Season														Playoffs								
Season	Club	League	GP	G	A	Pts	PIM	PP	SH	GW	S	S%	+/-	TF	F%	Min	GP	G	A	Pts	PIM	PP	SH	GW	Min
2003-04	Sarnia Sting	OHL	58	3	13	16	72	....	....	....	....	....	....	....	....	....	5	0	1	1	0	....	....	....	....
2004-05	Sarnia Sting	OHL	68	21	13	34	103	....	....	....	....	....	....	....	....	....	....	....	....	....	....	....	....	....	....
2005-06	Sarnia Sting	OHL	61	20	32	52	126	....	....	....	....	....	....	....	....	....	....	....	....	....	....	....	....	....	....
2006-07	Barrie Colts	OHL	67	32	46	78	151	....	....	....	....	....	....	....	....	....	8	3	4	7	8	....	....	....	....
	Iowa Stars	AHL	1	0	0	0	2	....	....	....	....	....	....	....	....	....	....	....	....	....	....	....	....	....	....
2007-08	Iowa Stars	AHL	38	3	5	8	137	....	....	....	....	....	....	....	....	....	....	....	....	....	....	....	....	....	....
	Idaho Steelheads	ECHL	19	1	9	10	41	....	....	....	....	....	....	....	....	....	....	....	....	....	....	....	....	....	....
2008-09	Manchester	AHL	35	3	6	9	87	....	....	....	....	....	....	....	....	....	....	....	....	....	....	....	....	....	....
2009-10	**Los Angeles**	**NHL**	**14**	**0**	**2**	**2**	**26**	**0**	**0**	**0**	**7**	**0.0**	**1**	**5**	**40.0**	**7:17**	**4**	**0**	**0**	**0**	**5**	**0**	**0**	**0**	**5:12**
	Manchester	AHL	44	4	10	14	126	....	....	....	....	....	....	....	....	....	....	....	....	....	....	....	....	....	....
2010-11	Manchester	AHL	66	8	14	22	222	....	....	....	....	....	....	....	....	....	7	0	3	3	6	....	....	....	....
2011-12	Manchester	AHL	56	6	9	15	253	....	....	....	....	....	....	....	....	....	4	0	0	0	14	....	....	....	....
2012-13	Manchester	AHL	35	2	5	7	98	....	....	....	....	....	....	....	....	....	....	....	....	....	....	....	....	....	....
	Nashville	**NHL**	**47**	**4**	**5**	**9**	**113**	**0**	**0**	**1**	**46**	**8.7**	**3**	**2**	**0.0**	**9:24**	....	....	....	....	....	....	....	....	....
2013-14	**Nashville**	**NHL**	**58**	**3**	**4**	**7**	**166**	**0**	**0**	**1**	**29**	**10.3**	**-7**	**0**	**0.0**	**8:27**	....	....	....	....	....	....	....	....	....

			Regular Season														Playoffs								
Season	Club	League	GP	G	A	Pts	PIM	PP	SH	GW	S	S%	+/-	TF	F%	Min	GP	G	A	Pts	PIM	PP	SH	GW	Min
2014-15	Nashville	NHL	1	0	0	0	0	0	0	0	0	0.0	0	0	0.0	5:30	....	....	....	....	....	....	....	....	....
	Milwaukee	AHL	62	6	11	17	181	....	....	....	....	....	....	....	....	....	....	....	....	....	....	....	....	....	....
	NHL Totals		120	7	11	18	305	0	0	2	82	8.5		7	28.6	8:40	4	0	0	0	5	0	0	0	5:12

Traded to **Los Angeles** by **Dallas** for Lauri Tukonen, July 21, 2008. Claimed on waivers by **Nashville** from **Los Angeles**, January 15, 2013. Signed as a free agent by **Toronto** (AHL), July 5, 2015.

CLUTTERBUCK, Cal

(KLUH-tuhr-buhck, KAL) **NYI**

Right wing. Shoots right. 5'11", 215 lbs. Born, Welland, ON, November 18, 1987. Minnesota's 3rd choice, 72nd overall, in 2006 Entry Draft.

Season	Club	League	GP	G	A	Pts	PIM	PP	SH	GW	S	S%	+/-	TF	F%	Min	GP	G	A	Pts	PIM	PP	SH	GW	Min
2004-05	St. Michael's	OHL	38	10	6	16	55	....	....	....	....	....	....	....	....	....	....	....	....	....	....	....	....	....	....
	Oshawa Generals	OHL	27	9	9	18	42	....	....	....	....	....	....	....	....	....	....	....	....	....	....	....	....	....	....
2005-06	Oshawa Generals	OHL	66	35	33	68	139	....	....	....	....	....	....	....	....	....	....	....	....	....	....	....	....	....	....
2006-07	Oshawa Generals	OHL	65	35	54	89	153	....	....	....	....	....	....	....	....	....	9	8	5	13	21	....	....	....	....
2007-08	Minnesota	NHL	2	0	0	0	0	0	0	0	0	0.0	0	1	100.0	7:05	....	....	....	....	....	....	....	....	....
	Houston Aeros	AHL	73	11	13	24	97	....	....	....	....	....	....	....	....	....	5	0	0	0	14	....	....	....	....
2008-09	Minnesota	NHL	78	11	7	18	76	1	0	1	136	8.1	–5	17	11.8	13:00	....	....	....	....	....	....	....	....	....
	Houston Aeros	AHL	2	0	0	0	0	....	....	....	....	....	....	....	....	....	....	....	....	....	....	....	....	....	....
2009-10	Minnesota	NHL	74	13	8	21	52	1	2	1	136	9.6	–8	10	30.0	14:17	....	....	....	....	....	....	....	....	....
2010-11	Minnesota	NHL	76	19	15	34	79	4	0	3	191	9.9	–5	11	27.3	15:51	....	....	....	....	....	....	....	....	....
2011-12	Minnesota	NHL	74	15	12	27	103	3	*4	2	161	9.3	–4	15	33.3	16:21	....	....	....	....	....	....	....	....	....
2012-13	Minnesota	NHL	42	4	6	10	27	0	0	1	87	4.6	–5	2	50.0	13:44	5	1	1	2	4	0	0	0	15:51
2013-14	NY Islanders	NHL	73	12	7	19	50	0	3	1	172	7.0	–9	16	43.8	14:20	....	....	....	....	....	....	....	....	....
2014-15	NY Islanders	NHL	76	7	9	16	60	0	2	4	124	5.6	1	9	66.7	12:44	7	2	1	3	26	0	0	0	12:50
	NHL Totals		495	81	64	145	447	9	11	13	1007	8.0		81	34.6	14:19	12	3	2	5	30	0	0	0	14:05

Traded to **NY Islanders** by **Minnesota** with New Jersey's 3rd round choice (previously acquired, NY Islanders selected Eamon McAdam) in 2013 Entry Draft for Nino Niederreiter, June 30, 2013.

COBURN, Braydon

(KOH-buhrn, BRAY-duhn) **T.B.**

Defense. Shoots left. 6'5", 220 lbs. Born, Calgary, AB, February 27, 1985. Atlanta's 1st choice, 8th overall, in 2003 Entry Draft.

Season	Club	League	GP	G	A	Pts	PIM	PP	SH	GW	S	S%	+/-	TF	F%	Min	GP	G	A	Pts	PIM	PP	SH	GW	Min
2000-01	Notre Dame	SMHL	32	3	19	22	70	....	....	....	....	....	....	....	....	....	....	....	....	....	....	....	....	....	....
	Portland	WHL	2	0	1	1	0	....	....	....	....	....	....	....	....	....	14	0	4	4	2	....	....	....	....
2001-02	Portland	WHL	68	4	33	37	100	....	....	....	....	....	....	....	....	....	7	1	1	2	9	....	....	....	....
2002-03	Portland	WHL	53	3	16	19	147	....	....	....	....	....	....	....	....	....	7	0	1	1	8	....	....	....	....
2003-04	Portland	WHL	55	10	20	30	92	....	....	....	....	....	....	....	....	....	5	0	1	1	10	....	....	....	....
2004-05	Portland	WHL	60	12	32	44	144	....	....	....	....	....	....	....	....	....	7	1	5	6	6	....	....	....	....
	Chicago Wolves	AHL	3	0	1	1	5	....	....	....	....	....	....	....	....	....	18	0	1	1	36	....	....	....	....
2005-06	Atlanta	NHL	9	0	1	1	4	0	0	0	4	0.0	–2	0	0.0	7:43	....	....	....	....	....	....	....	....	....
	Chicago Wolves	AHL	73	6	20	26	134	....	....	....	....	....	....	....	....	....	....	....	....	....	....	....	....	....	....
2006-07	Atlanta	NHL	29	0	4	4	30	0	0	0	21	0.0	1	0	0.0	11:41	....	....	....	....	....	....	....	....	....
	Chicago Wolves	AHL	15	1	10	11	36	....	....	....	....	....	....	....	....	....	....	....	....	....	....	....	....	....	....
	Philadelphia	NHL	20	3	4	7	16	1	0	0	33	9.1	–2	0	0.0	20:58	....	....	....	....	....	....	....	....	....
2007-08	Philadelphia	NHL	78	9	27	36	74	5	0	2	113	8.0	17	0	0.0	21:14	14	0	6	6	14	0	0	0	22:25
2008-09	Philadelphia	NHL	80	7	21	28	97	3	0	0	130	5.4	7	0	0.0	24:37	6	0	3	3	7	0	0	0	26:29
2009-10	Philadelphia	NHL	81	5	14	19	54	1	0	0	122	4.1	–6	0	0.0	21:08	23	1	3	4	22	1	0	1	25:09
2010-11	Philadelphia	NHL	82	2	14	16	53	0	0	0	114	1.8	15	0	0.0	21:04	11	1	2	3	6	0	0	0	24:07
2011-12	Philadelphia	NHL	81	4	20	24	56	0	0	0	113	3.5	10	1	0.0	22:03	11	0	4	4	8	0	0	0	27:10
2012-13	Philadelphia	NHL	33	1	4	5	41	0	0	0	38	2.6	–10	0	0.0	22:37	....	....	....	....	....	....	....	....	....
2013-14	Philadelphia	NHL	82	5	12	17	63	0	1	2	122	4.1	–6	0	0.0	22:27	7	0	3	3	4	0	0	0	21:11
2014-15	Philadelphia	NHL	39	1	8	9	16	0	0	0	45	2.2	–1	0	0.0	20:14	....	....	....	....	....	....	....	....	....
	Tampa Bay	NHL	4	0	2	2	9	0	0	0	1	0.0	3	0	0.0	17:02	26	1	3	4	21	0	0	1	17:00
	NHL Totals		618	37	131	168	513	10	1	4	856	4.3		1	0.0	21:14	98	3	24	27	82	1	0	2	22:30

WHL Rookie of the Year (2002) • WHL West First All-Star Team (2004, 2005) • Canadian Major Junior Second All-Star Team (2005)

Traded to **Philadelphia** by **Atlanta** for Alexei Zhitnik, February 24, 2007. Traded to **Tampa Bay** by **Philadelphia** for Radko Gudas and Tampa Bay's 1st (later traded to Columbus – Columbus selected Gabriel Carlsson) and 3rd (Matej Tomek) round choices in 2015 Entry Draft, March 2, 2015.

COGLIANO, Andrew

(kawg-lee-A-noh, AN-droo) **ANA**

Center. Shoots left. 5'10", 181 lbs. Born, Toronto, ON, June 14, 1987. Edmonton's 1st choice, 25th overall, in 2005 Entry Draft.

Season	Club	League	GP	G	A	Pts	PIM	PP	SH	GW	S	S%	+/-	TF	F%	Min	GP	G	A	Pts	PIM	PP	SH	GW	Min
2002-03	Vaughan Kings	GTHL	58	39	54	93	122	....	....	....	....	....	....	....	....	....	....	....	....	....	....	....	....	....	....
2003-04	St. Mike's B's	ON-Jr.A	36	26	47	73	14	....	....	....	....	....	....	....	....	....	24	11	20	31	12	....	....	....	....
2004-05	St. Mike's B's	ON-Jr.A	49	36	*66	*102	33	....	....	....	....	....	....	....	....	....	25	*22	*24	*46	20	....	....	....	....
2005-06	U. of Michigan	CCHA	39	12	16	28	38	....	....	....	....	....	....	....	....	....	....	....	....	....	....	....	....	....	....
2006-07	U. of Michigan	CCHA	38	24	26	50	12	....	....	....	....	....	....	....	....	....	....	....	....	....	....	....	....	....	....
2007-08	Edmonton	NHL	82	18	27	45	20	1	2	5	98	18.4	1	542	39.5	13:40	....	....	....	....	....	....	....	....	....
2008-09	Edmonton	NHL	82	18	20	38	22	4	0	4	116	15.5	–6	702	37.2	14:24	....	....	....	....	....	....	....	....	....
2009-10	Edmonton	NHL	82	10	18	28	31	1	0	1	139	7.2	–5	379	43.0	14:11	....	....	....	....	....	....	....	....	....
2010-11	Edmonton	NHL	82	11	24	35	64	0	1	3	129	8.5	–12	1108	41.6	17:15	....	....	....	....	....	....	....	....	....
2011-12	Anaheim	NHL	82	13	13	26	15	2	0	2	115	11.3	–4	386	42.0	14:42	....	....	....	....	....	....	....	....	....
2012-13	Klagenfurter AC	Austria	7	2	4	6	2	....	....	....	....	....	....	....	....	....	....	....	....	....	....	....	....	....	....
	Anaheim	NHL	48	13	10	23	6	0	2	1	79	16.5	14	92	34.8	15:22	7	0	1	1	4	0	0	0	15:47
2013-14	Anaheim	NHL	82	21	21	42	26	0	3	5	157	13.4	13	27	40.7	15:24	13	1	6	7	8	0	1	1	14:54
2014-15	Anaheim	NHL	82	15	14	29	14	0	3	2	134	11.2	5	49	32.7	14:36	16	3	6	9	4	0	0	0	16:16
	NHL Totals		622	119	147	266	198	8	11	23	967	12.3		3285	40.2	14:55	36	4	13	17	16	0	1	1	15:41

CCHA All-Rookie Team (2006)

Traded to **Anaheim** by **Edmonton** for Anaheim's 2nd round choice (Marc-Olivier Roy) in 2013 Entry Draft, July 12, 2011. Signed as a free agent by **Klagenfurt** (Austria), November 17, 2012.

COLAIACOVO, Carlo

(koh-lee-A-KOH-voh, KAHR-loh) **BUF**

Defense. Shoots left. 6'1", 200 lbs. Born, Toronto, ON, January 27, 1983. Toronto's 1st choice, 17th overall, in 2001 Entry Draft.

Season	Club	League	GP	G	A	Pts	PIM	PP	SH	GW	S	S%	+/-	TF	F%	Min	GP	G	A	Pts	PIM	PP	SH	GW	Min
1998-99	Mississauga Reps	GTHL	44	10	12	23	28	....	....	....	....	....	....	....	....	....	....	....	....	....	....	....	....	....	....
99-2000	Erie Otters	OHL	52	4	18	22	12	....	....	....	....	....	....	....	....	....	13	2	4	6	9	....	....	....	....
2000-01	Erie Otters	OHL	62	12	27	39	59	....	....	....	....	....	....	....	....	....	14	4	7	11	16	....	....	....	....
2001-02	Erie Otters	OHL	60	13	27	40	49	....	....	....	....	....	....	....	....	....	21	7	10	17	20	....	....	....	....
2002-03	Toronto	NHL	2	0	1	1	0	0	0	0	1	0.0	0	0	0.0	13:43	....	....	....	....	....	....	....	....	....
	Erie Otters	OHL	35	14	21	35	12	....	....	....	....	....	....	....	....	....	....	....	....	....	....	....	....	....	....
2003-04	Toronto	NHL	2	0	1	1	2	0	0	0	0	0.0	1	0	0.0	13:56	....	....	....	....	....	....	....	....	....
	St. John's	AHL	62	6	25	31	50	....	....	....	....	....	....	....	....	....	....	....	....	....	....	....	....	....	....
2004-05	St. John's	AHL	49	4	20	24	59	....	....	....	....	....	....	....	....	....	5	0	1	1	2	....	....	....	....
2005-06	Toronto	NHL	21	2	5	7	17	1	0	0	21	9.5	0	1	0.0	15:26	....	....	....	....	....	....	....	....	....
	Toronto Marlies	AHL	14	5	6	11	14	....	....	....	....	....	....	....	....	....	....	....	....	....	....	....	....	....	....
2006-07	Toronto	NHL	48	8	9	17	22	0	0	1	60	13.3	5	0	0.0	17:57	....	....	....	....	....	....	....	....	....
	Toronto Marlies	AHL	5	1	5	6	4	....	....	....	....	....	....	....	....	....	....	....	....	....	....	....	....	....	....
2007-08	Toronto	NHL	28	2	4	6	10	0	0	1	30	6.7	–4	0	0.0	17:26	....	....	....	....	....	....	....	....	....
	Toronto Marlies	AHL	2	0	0	0	0	....	....	....	....	....	....	....	....	....	....	....	....	....	....	....	....	....	....
2008-09	Toronto	NHL	10	0	1	1	6	0	0	0	9	0.0	–2	0	0.0	16:52	....	....	....	....	....	....	....	....	....
	St. Louis	NHL	63	3	26	29	29	0	0	0	78	3.8	2	0	0.0	18:29	4	0	0	0	2	0	0	0	22:19
2009-10	St. Louis	NHL	67	7	25	32	60	4	1	1	74	9.5	8	1	100.0	17:18	....	....	....	....	....	....	....	....	....
2010-11	St. Louis	NHL	65	6	20	26	23	1	0	1	81	7.4	–4	0	0.0	18:08	....	....	....	....	....	....	....	....	....
2011-12	St. Louis	NHL	64	2	17	19	22	0	0	2	68	2.9	7	0	0.0	19:00	7	0	3	3	16	0	0	0	17:55
2012-13	Grand Rapids	AHL	2	0	0	0	0	....	....	....	....	....	....	....	....	....	....	....	....	....	....	....	....	....	....
	Detroit	NHL	6	0	1	1	2	0	0	0	12	0.0	–4	0	0.0	18:55	9	0	1	1	2	0	0	0	15:14

			Regular Season													Playoffs								
Season	Club	League	GP	G	A	Pts	PIM	PP	SH	GW	S	S%	+/-	TF	F%	Min	GP	G	A	Pts	PIM	PP	SH	GW	Min
2013-14	**St. Louis**	**NHL**	**25**	**1**	**3**	**4**	**18**	**0**	**0**	**0**	**18**	**5.6**	**-4**	**0**	**0.0**	**15:09**	....	....	....	....	....	....	....	....	....
2014-15	**Philadelphia**	**NHL**	**33**	**2**	**6**	**8**	**10**	**0**	**0**	**0**	**42**	**4.8**	**0**	**0**	**0.0**	**16:29**	....	....	....	....	....	....	....	....	....
	NHL Totals		**434**	**33**	**119**	**152**	**221**	**6**	**1**	**6**	**494**	**6.7**		**2**	**50.0**	**17:38**	**20**	**0**	**4**	**4**	**20**	**0**	**0**	**0**	**17:35**

OHL Second All-Star Team (2002, 2003)

• Missed remainder of 2005-06 due to head injury at Ottawa, January 23, 2006. • Missed majority of 2007-08 due to knee surgery, April 29, 2007. Traded to **St. Louis** by **Toronto** with Alexander Steen for Lee Stempniak, November 24, 2008. Signed as a free agent by **Detroit**, September 14, 2012. • Missed majority of 2012-13 due to recurring shoulder injury and as a healthy reserve. Signed as a free agent by **St. Louis**, November 12, 2013. • Missed majority of 2013-14 as a healthy reserve. Signed as a free agent by **Philadelphia**, October 30, 2014. • Missed majority of 2014-15 as a healthy reserve. Signed as a free agent by **Buffalo**, July 3, 2015.

COLBORNE, Joe

(KOHL-bohrn, JOH) **CGY**

Center. Shoots left. 6'5", 213 lbs. Born, Calgary, AB, January 30, 1990. Boston's 1st choice, 16th overall, in 2008 Entry Draft.

Season	Club	League	GP	G	A	Pts	PIM	PP	SH	GW	S	S%	+/-	TF	F%	Min	GP	G	A	Pts	PIM	PP	SH	GW	Min
2004-05	Calgary Titans	Minor-AB	44	13	13	26	28	....	....	....	....	....	....	....	....	....	....	....	....	....	....	....	....	....	....
2005-06	Notre Dame	SMHL	48	13	14	27	26	....	....	....	....	....	....	....	....	....	....	....	....	....	....	....	....	....	....
2006-07	Camrose Kodiaks	AJHL	53	20	28	48	44	....	....	....	....	....	....	....	....	....	16	5	1	6	10	....	....	....	....
2007-08	Camrose Kodiaks	AJHL	55	33	*57	90	48	....	....	....	....	....	....	....	....	....	18	8	8	*16	26	....	....	....	....
2008-09	U. of Denver	WCHA	40	10	21	31	24	....	....	....	....	....	....	....	....	....	....	....	....	....	....	....	....	....	....
2009-10	U. of Denver	WCHA	39	22	19	41	30	....	....	....	....	....	....	....	....	....	....	....	....	....	....	....	....	....	....
	Providence Bruins	AHL	6	0	2	2	2	....	....	....	....	....	....	....	....	....	....	....	....	....	....	....	....	....	....
2010-11	Providence Bruins	AHL	55	12	14	26	35	....	....	....	....	....	....	....	....	....	....	....	....	....	....	....	....	....	....
	Toronto	**NHL**	**1**	**0**	**1**	**1**	**0**	**0**	**0**	**0**	**1**	**0.0**	**1**	**9**	**33.3**	**18:41**	....	....	....	....	....	....	....	....	....
	Toronto Marlies	AHL	20	8	8	16	8	....	....	....	....	....	....	....	....	....	....	....	....	....	....	....	....	....	....
2011-12	**Toronto**	**NHL**	**10**	**1**	**4**	**5**	**4**	**0**	**0**	**0**	**7**	**14.3**	**2**	**78**	**35.9**	**13:41**	....	....	....	....	....	....	....	....	....
	Toronto Marlies	AHL	65	16	23	39	46	....	....	....	....	....	....	....	....	....	15	2	6	8	8	....	....	....	....
2012-13	Toronto Marlies	AHL	65	14	28	42	53	....	....	....	....	....	....	....	....	....	4	0	1	1	2	....	....	....	....
	Toronto	**NHL**	**5**	**0**	**0**	**0**	**2**	**0**	**0**	**0**	**4**	**0.0**	**-1**	**29**	**51.7**	**9:07**	**2**	**0**	**0**	**0**	**0**	**0**	**0**	**0**	**13:28**
2013-14	**Calgary**	**NHL**	**80**	**10**	**18**	**28**	**34**	**1**	**0**	**1**	**80**	**12.5**	**-17**	**441**	**48.5**	**14:16**	....	....	....	....	....	....	....	....	....
2014-15	**Calgary**	**NHL**	**64**	**8**	**20**	**28**	**43**	**1**	**1**	**1**	**67**	**11.9**	**7**	**336**	**52.4**	**15:25**	**11**	**1**	**2**	**3**	**20**	**0**	**1**	**0**	**17:13**
	NHL Totals		**160**	**19**	**43**	**62**	**83**	**2**	**1**	**2**	**159**	**11.9**		**893**	**48.8**	**14:34**	**13**	**1**	**2**	**3**	**20**	**0**	**1**	**0**	**16:39**

WCHA All-Rookie Team (2009)

Traded to **Toronto** by **Boston** with Boston's 1st round choice (later traded to Anaheim – Anaheim selected Rickard Rakell) in 2011 Entry Draft and Boston's 2nd round choice (later traded to Colorado, later traded to Washington, later traded to Dallas – Dallas selected Mke Winther) in 2012 Entry Draft for Tomas Kaberle, February 18, 2011. Traded to **Calgary** by **Toronto** for Calgary's 4th round choice (later traded to St. Louis – St. Louis selected Ville Husso) in 2014 Entry Draft, September 29, 2013.

COLE, Erik

(KOHL, AIR-ihk)

Left wing. Shoots left. 6'2", 205 lbs. Born, Oswego, NY, November 6, 1978. Carolina's 3rd choice, 71st overall, in 1998 Entry Draft.

Season	Club	League	GP	G	A	Pts	PIM	PP	SH	GW	S	S%	+/-	TF	F%	Min	GP	G	A	Pts	PIM	PP	SH	GW	Min
1995-96	Oswego	High-NY	40	49	41	90	....	....	....	....	....	....	....	....	....	....	....	....	....	....	....	....	....	....	....
1996-97	Des Moines	USHL	48	30	34	64	140	....	....	....	....	....	....	....	....	....	5	2	0	2	6	....	....	....	....
1997-98	Clarkson Knights	ECAC	34	11	20	31	55	....	....	....	....	....	....	....	....	....	....	....	....	....	....	....	....	....	....
1998-99	Clarkson Knights	ECAC	36	*22	20	42	50	....	....	....	....	....	....	....	....	....	....	....	....	....	....	....	....	....	....
99-2000	Clarkson Knights	ECAC	33	19	11	30	46	....	....	....	....	....	....	....	....	....	....	....	....	....	....	....	....	....	....
	Cincinnati	IHL	9	4	3	7	2	....	....	....	....	....	....	....	....	....	7	1	1	2	2	....	....	....	....
2000-01	Cincinnati	IHL	69	23	20	43	28	....	....	....	....	....	....	....	....	....	5	1	0	1	2	....	....	....	....
2001-02	**Carolina**	**NHL**	**81**	**16**	**24**	**40**	**35**	**3**	**0**	**2**	**159**	**10.1**	**-10**	**17**	**47.1**	**16:04**	**23**	**6**	**3**	**9**	**30**	**1**	**0**	**1**	**18:27**
2002-03	**Carolina**	**NHL**	**53**	**14**	**13**	**27**	**72**	**6**	**2**	**3**	**125**	**11.2**	**1**	**56**	**39.3**	**17:08**	....	....	....	....	....	....	....	....	....
2003-04	**Carolina**	**NHL**	**80**	**18**	**24**	**42**	**93**	**2**	**2**	**3**	**172**	**10.5**	**-4**	**15**	**46.7**	**18:06**	....	....	....	....	....	....	....	....	....
2004-05	Eisbaren Berlin	Germany	39	6	21	27	76	....	....	....	....	....	....	....	....	....	8	5	1	6	37	....	....	....	....
2005-06♦	**Carolina**	**NHL**	**60**	**30**	**29**	**59**	**54**	**3**	**3**	**8**	**164**	**18.3**	**19**	**19**	**36.8**	**19:18**	**2**	**0**	**0**	**0**	**0**	**0**	**0**	**0**	**15:29**
	United States	Olympics	6	1	2	3	0	....	....	....	....	....	....	....	....	....	....	....	....	....	....	....	....	....	....
2006-07	**Carolina**	**NHL**	**71**	**29**	**32**	**61**	**76**	**9**	**0**	**4**	**166**	**17.5**	**2**	**27**	**40.7**	**18:01**	....	....	....	....	....	....	....	....	....
2007-08	**Carolina**	**NHL**	**73**	**22**	**29**	**51**	**76**	**10**	**0**	**4**	**216**	**10.2**	**5**	**38**	**23.7**	**19:22**	....	....	....	....	....	....	....	....	....
2008-09	**Edmonton**	**NHL**	**63**	**16**	**11**	**27**	**63**	**5**	**0**	**1**	**145**	**11.0**	**-3**	**48**	**39.6**	**17:05**	....	....	....	....	....	....	....	....	....
	Carolina	**NHL**	**17**	**2**	**13**	**15**	**10**	**0**	**0**	**0**	**33**	**6.1**	**3**	**1**	**100.0**	**19:36**	**18**	**0**	**5**	**5**	**22**	**0**	**0**	**0**	**17:17**
2009-10	**Carolina**	**NHL**	**40**	**11**	**5**	**16**	**29**	**2**	**0**	**1**	**81**	**13.6**	**-9**	**15**	**26.7**	**16:23**	....	....	....	....	....	....	....	....	....
2010-11	**Carolina**	**NHL**	**82**	**26**	**26**	**52**	**49**	**3**	**1**	**9**	**201**	**12.9**	**-1**	**34**	**20.6**	**18:27**	....	....	....	....	....	....	....	....	....
2011-12	**Montreal**	**NHL**	**82**	**35**	**26**	**61**	**48**	**11**	**0**	**6**	**241**	**14.5**	**11**	**56**	**42.9**	**18:32**	....	....	....	....	....	....	....	....	....
2012-13	**Montreal**	**NHL**	**19**	**3**	**3**	**6**	**10**	**0**	**0**	**2**	**41**	**7.3**	**1**	**24**	**29.2**	**15:39**	....	....	....	....	....	....	....	....	....
	Dallas	**NHL**	**28**	**6**	**1**	**7**	**10**	**1**	**0**	**0**	**45**	**13.3**	**-7**	**43**	**34.9**	**16:54**	....	....	....	....	....	....	....	....	....
2013-14	**Dallas**	**NHL**	**75**	**16**	**13**	**29**	**20**	**3**	**0**	**4**	**139**	**11.5**	**-17**	**41**	**46.3**	**15:10**	**3**	**0**	**0**	**0**	**2**	**0**	**0**	**0**	**9:51**
2014-15	**Dallas**	**NHL**	**57**	**18**	**15**	**33**	**14**	**2**	**1**	**0**	**98**	**18.4**	**4**	**15**	**26.7**	**14:32**	....	....	....	....	....	....	....	....	....
	Detroit	**NHL**	**11**	**3**	**3**	**6**	**0**	**1**	**0**	**0**	**24**	**12.5**	**-2**	**1**	**100.0**	**14:39**	....	....	....	....	....	....	....	....	....
	NHL Totals		**892**	**265**	**267**	**532**	**659**	**61**	**9**	**47**	**2050**	**12.9**		**450**	**36.7**	**17:23**	**46**	**6**	**8**	**14**	**54**	**1**	**0**	**1**	**17:19**

USHL Second All-Star Team (1997) • ECAC Rookie of the Year (1998) (co-winner - Willie Mitchell) • ECAC First All-Star Team (1999) • NCAA East Second All-American Team (1999) • ECAC Second All-Star Team (2000)

Signed as a free agent by **Berlin** (Germany), October 24, 2004. Traded to **Edmonton** by **Carolina** for Joni Pitkanen, July 1, 2008. Traded to **Carolina** by **Edmonton** with Edmonton's 5th round choice (Matt Kennedy) in 2009 Entry Draft for Patrick O'Sullivan and Carolina's 2nd round choice (later traded to Buffalo, later traded to Toronto – Toronto selected Jesse Blacker) in 2009 Entry Draft, March 4, 2009. • Missed majority of 2009-10 due to leg and upper-body injuries. Signed as a free agent by **Montreal**, July 1, 2011. Traded to **Dallas** by **Montreal** for Michael Ryder and Dallas' 3rd round choice (Connor Crisp) in 2013 Entry Draft, February 26, 2013. Traded to **Detroit** by **Dallas** with Dallas' 3rd round choice (Vili Saarijarvi) in 2015 Entry Draft for Mattias Backman, Mattias Janmark and Detroit's 2nd round choice (Roope Hintz) in 2015 Entry Draft, March 1, 2015.

COLE, Ian

(KOHL, EE-an) **PIT**

Defense. Shoots left. 6'1", 219 lbs. Born, Ann Arbour, MI, February 21, 1989. St. Louis' 2nd choice, 18th overall, in 2007 Entry Draft.

Season	Club	League	GP	G	A	Pts	PIM	PP	SH	GW	S	S%	+/-	TF	F%	Min	GP	G	A	Pts	PIM	PP	SH	GW	Min
2004-05	Det. Vic. Honda	MWEHL	60	15	25	40		....	....	....	....	....	....	....	....	....	....	....	....	....	....	....	....	....	....
2005-06	USNTDP	U-17	18	2	1	3	14	....	....	....	....	....	....	....	....	....	....	....	....	....	....	....	....	....	....
	USNTDP	NAHL	40	2	8	10	75	....	....	....	....	....	....	....	....	....	12	0	3	3	14	....	....	....	....
2006-07	USNTDP	U-18	42	6	11	17	36	....	....	....	....	....	....	....	....	....	....	....	....	....	....	....	....	....	....
	USNTDP	NAHL	16	2	7	9	28	....	....	....	....	....	....	....	....	....	....	....	....	....	....	....	....	....	....
2007-08	U. of Notre Dame	CCHA	43	8	12	20	40	....	....	....	....	....	....	....	....	....	....	....	....	....	....	....	....	....	....
2008-09	U. of Notre Dame	CCHA	38	6	20	26	58	....	....	....	....	....	....	....	....	....	....	....	....	....	....	....	....	....	....
2009-10	U. of Notre Dame	CCHA	30	3	16	19	55	....	....	....	....	....	....	....	....	....	....	....	....	....	....	....	....	....	....
	Peoria Rivermen	AHL	9	1	4	5	4	....	....	....	....	....	....	....	....	....	....	....	....	....	....	....	....	....	....
2010-11	**St. Louis**	**NHL**	**26**	**1**	**3**	**4**	**35**	**0**	**0**	**0**	**22**	**4.5**	**6**	**0**	**0.0**	**17:36**	....	....	....	....	....	....	....	....	....
	Peoria Rivermen	AHL	44	5	10	15	63	....	....	....	....	....	....	....	....	....	....	....	....	....	....	....	....	....	....
2011-12	**St. Louis**	**NHL**	**26**	**1**	**5**	**6**	**22**	**0**	**0**	**0**	**18**	**5.6**	**7**	**0**	**0.0**	**15:55**	**2**	**0**	**0**	**0**	**0**	**0**	**0**	**0**	**10:26**
	Peoria Rivermen	AHL	22	1	3	4	26	....	....	....	....	....	....	....	....	....	....	....	....	....	....	....	....	....	....
2012-13	Peoria Rivermen	AHL	34	3	11	14	43	....	....	....	....	....	....	....	....	....	....	....	....	....	....	....	....	....	....
	St. Louis	**NHL**	**15**	**0**	**1**	**1**	**10**	**0**	**0**	**0**	**10**	**0.0**	**-4**	**0**	**0.0**	**17:45**	....	....	....	....	....	....	....	....	....
2013-14	**St. Louis**	**NHL**	**46**	**3**	**8**	**11**	**31**	**0**	**0**	**0**	**45**	**6.7**	**15**	**0**	**0.0**	**15:05**	....	....	....	....	....	....	....	....	....
2014-15	**St. Louis**	**NHL**	**54**	**4**	**5**	**9**	**44**	**0**	**0**	**0**	**52**	**7.7**	**16**	**0**	**0.0**	**15:03**	....	....	....	....	....	....	....	....	....
	Pittsburgh	**NHL**	**20**	**1**	**7**	**8**	**7**	**0**	**0**	**0**	**31**	**3.2**	**-2**	**0**	**0.0**	**18:29**	**5**	**0**	**2**	**2**	**8**	**0**	**0**	**0**	**23:00**
	NHL Totals		**187**	**10**	**29**	**39**	**149**	**0**	**0**	**0**	**178**	**5.6**		**0**	**0.0**	**16:07**	**7**	**0**	**2**	**2**	**8**	**0**	**0**	**0**	**19:25**

CCHA First All-Star Team (2009) • NCAA West First All-American Team (2009)

Traded to **Pittsburgh** by **St. Louis** for Robert Bortuzzo and a 7th round choice in 2016 Entry Draft, March 2, 2015.

COLLINS, Sean

(KAW-lihnz, SHAWN) **WSH**

Center. Shoots left. 6'3", 205 lbs. Born, Saskatoon, SK, December 29, 1988. Columbus' 9th choice, 187th overall, in 2008 Entry Draft.

Season	Club	League	GP	G	A	Pts	PIM	PP	SH	GW	S	S%	+/-	TF	F%	Min	GP	G	A	Pts	PIM	PP	SH	GW	Min
2006-07	Waywayseecappo	MJHL	70	20	69	89	34	....	....	....	....	....	....	....	....	....	....	....	....	....	....	....	....	....	....
2007-08	Waywayseecappo	MJHL	60	51	64	115	34	....	....	....	....	....	....	....	....	....	7	9	4	13	10	....	....	....	....
2008-09	Cornell Big Red	ECAC	33	3	3	6	16	....	....	....	....	....	....	....	....	....	....	....	....	....	....	....	....	....	....
2009-10	Cornell Big Red	ECAC	34	7	3	10	12	....	....	....	....	....	....	....	....	....	....	....	....	....	....	....	....	....	....
2010-11	Cornell Big Red	ECAC	34	7	8	15	20	....	....	....	....	....	....	....	....	....	....	....	....	....	....	....	....	....	....
2011-12	Cornell Big Red	ECAC	35	13	13	26	14	....	....	....	....	....	....	....	....	....	....	....	....	....	....	....	....	....	....
	Springfield	AHL	8	1	4	5	0	....	....	....	....	....	....	....	....	....	....	....	....	....	....	....	....	....	....
2012-13	Springfield	AHL	64	11	20	31	24	....	....	....	....	....	....	....	....	....	8	0	0	0	4	....	....	....	....
	Columbus	**NHL**	**5**	**0**	**0**	**0**	**6**	**0**	**0**	**0**	**0**	**0.0**	**-2**	**5**	**20.0**	**12:30**	....	....	....	....	....	....	....	....	....

			Regular Season														Playoffs								
Season	Club	League	GP	G	A	Pts	PIM	PP	SH	GW	S	S%	+/-	TF	F%	Min	GP	G	A	Pts	PIM	PP	SH	GW	Min
2013-14	**Columbus**	**NHL**	**6**	**0**	**1**	**1**	**0**	**0**	**0**	**0**	**6**	**0.0**	**1**	**0**	**0.0**	**8:11**									
	Springfield	AHL	67	16	25	41	34										5	0	1	1	2				
2014-15	**Columbus**	**NHL**	**8**	**0**	**2**	**2**	**2**	**0**	**0**	**0**	**4**	**0.0**	**0**	**5**	**40.0**	**10:20**									
	Springfield	AHL	64	17	19	36	28																		
	NHL Totals		**19**	**0**	**3**	**3**	**8**	**0**	**0**	**0**	**10**	**0.0**		**10**	**30.0**	**10:13**									

Signed as a free agent by **Washington**, July 1, 2015.

COMEAU, Blake (KOH-moh, BLAYK) COL

Right wing. Shoots right. 6'1", 202 lbs. Born, Meadow Lake, SK, February 18, 1986. NY Islanders' 2nd choice, 47th overall, in 2004 Entry Draft.

Season	Club	League	GP	G	A	Pts	PIM	PP	SH	GW	S	S%	+/-	TF	F%	Min	GP	G	A	Pts	PIM	PP	SH	GW	Min
2001-02	Sask. Contacts	SMHL	42	27	33	60	72																		
	Kelowna Rockets	WHL	3	0	0	0	4																		
2002-03	Kelowna Rockets	WHL	54	5	18	23	77										19	2	1	3	20				
2003-04	Kelowna Rockets	WHL	71	10	23	33	123										17	4	2	6	23				
2004-05	Kelowna Rockets	WHL	65	24	23	47	108										24	6	12	18	34				
2005-06	Kelowna Rockets	WHL	60	21	53	74	85										12	4	9	13	22				
	Bridgeport	AHL															7	0	3	3	0				
2006-07	**NY Islanders**	**NHL**	**3**	**0**	**0**	**0**	**0**	**0**	**0**	**0**	**1**	**0.0**	**0**	**0**	**0.0**	**9:25**									
	Bridgeport	AHL	61	12	31	43	46																		
2007-08	**NY Islanders**	**NHL**	**51**	**8**	**7**	**15**	**22**	**1**	**0**	**1**	**67**	**11.9**	**1**	**27**	**29.6**	**11:40**									
	Bridgeport	AHL	31	4	15	19	30																		
2008-09	**NY Islanders**	**NHL**	**53**	**7**	**18**	**25**	**32**	**2**	**0**	**0**	**78**	**9.0**	**-17**	**45**	**31.1**	**16:17**									
	Bridgeport	AHL	19	4	15	19	22										2	0	0	0	0				
2009-10	**NY Islanders**	**NHL**	**61**	**17**	**18**	**35**	**40**	**0**	**1**	**2**	**133**	**12.8**	**-2**	**21**	**47.6**	**15:25**									
2010-11	**NY Islanders**	**NHL**	**77**	**24**	**22**	**46**	**43**	**5**	**1**	**3**	**182**	**13.2**	**-17**	**112**	**31.3**	**18:41**									
2011-12	**NY Islanders**	**NHL**	**16**	**0**	**0**	**0**	**6**	**0**	**0**	**0**	**20**	**0.0**	**-11**	**8**	**25.0**	**13:04**									
	Calgary	**NHL**	**58**	**5**	**10**	**15**	**24**	**0**	**0**	**0**	**117**	**4.3**	**0**	**83**	**32.5**	**16:06**									
2012-13	**Calgary**	**NHL**	**33**	**4**	**3**	**7**	**14**	**0**	**1**	**1**	**44**	**9.1**	**-9**	**81**	**45.7**	**12:17**									
	Columbus	**NHL**	**9**	**2**	**3**	**5**	**6**	**0**	**0**	**0**	**4**	**50.0**	**5**	**5**	**60.0**	**11:41**									
2013-14	**Columbus**	**NHL**	**61**	**5**	**11**	**16**	**36**	**0**	**0**	**0**	**107**	**4.7**	**-2**	**17**	**58.8**	**12:04**	**6**	**0**	**0**	**0**	**10**	**0**	**0**	**0**	**11:51**
2014-15	**Pittsburgh**	**NHL**	**61**	**16**	**15**	**31**	**65**	**0**	**0**	**5**	**147**	**10.9**	**6**	**9**	**77.8**	**15:17**	**5**	**1**	**0**	**1**	**8**	**0**	**0**	**0**	**14:13**
	NHL Totals		**483**	**88**	**107**	**195**	**288**	**8**	**3**	**12**	**900**	**9.8**		**408**	**37.5**	**14:53**	**11**	**1**	**0**	**1**	**18**	**0**	**0**	**0**	**12:55**

WHL West First All-Star Team (2006)

Claimed on waivers by **Calgary** from **NY Islanders**, November 25, 2011. Traded to **Columbus** by **Calgary** for Columbus' 5th round choice (Eric Roy) in 2013 Entry Draft, April 3, 2013. Signed as a free agent by **Pittsburgh**, July 1, 2014. Signed as a free agent by **Colorado**, July 1, 2015.

CONACHER, Cory (KAW-nuh-kuhr, KOHR-ee)

Left wing. Shoots left. 5'8", 180 lbs. Born, Burlington, ON, December 14, 1989.

Season	Club	League	GP	G	A	Pts	PIM	PP	SH	GW	S	S%	+/-	TF	F%	Min	GP	G	A	Pts	PIM	PP	SH	GW	Min
2006-07	Burlington	ON-Jr.A	48	22	40	62	62										6	3	3	6	8				
2007-08	Canisius College	AH	20	7	10	17	24																		
2008-09	Canisius College	AH	37	12	23	35	40																		
2009-10	Canisius College	AH	35	20	33	53	36																		
2010-11	Canisius College	AH	37	23	19	42	54																		
	Rochester	AHL	2	1	0	1	2																		
	Cincinnati	ECHL	3	5	2	7	0																		
	Milwaukee	AHL	5	3	2	5	2										7	0	1	1	6				
2011-12	Norfolk Admirals	AHL	75	*39	41	80	114										18	2	13	15	28				
2012-13	**Tampa Bay**	**NHL**	**35**	**9**	**15**	**24**	**16**	**1**	**0**	**2**	**53**	**17.0**	**-3**	**3**	**0.0**	**14:22**									
	Syracuse Crunch	AHL	36	12	16	28	56																		
	Ottawa	**NHL**	**12**	**2**	**3**	**5**	**4**	**0**	**0**	**1**	**14**	**14.3**	**6**	**12**	**33.3**	**12:51**	**8**	**3**	**0**	**3**	**31**	**1**	**0**	**1**	**11:57**
2013-14	**Ottawa**	**NHL**	**60**	**4**	**16**	**20**	**34**	**0**	**0**	**1**	**73**	**5.5**	**8**	**13**	**61.5**	**12:18**									
	Buffalo	**NHL**	**19**	**3**	**3**	**6**	**16**	**1**	**0**	**1**	**27**	**11.1**	**-7**	**1**	**100.0**	**14:58**									
2014-15	**NY Islanders**	**NHL**	**15**	**1**	**2**	**3**	**14**	**0**	**0**	**0**	**23**	**4.3**	**-3**	**3**	**33.3**	**13:29**									
	Bridgeport	AHL	28	5	18	23	30																		
	Utica Comets	AHL	20	7	9	16	22										23	5	3	8	28				
	NHL Totals		**141**	**19**	**39**	**58**	**84**	**2**	**0**	**5**	**190**	**10.0**		**32**	**43.8**	**13:21**	**8**	**3**	**0**	**3**	**31**	**1**	**0**	**1**	**11:57**

AHL All-Rookie Team (2012) • AHL Second All-Star Team (2012) • Dudley "Red" Garrett Memorial Trophy (AHL - Top Rookie) (2012) • Willie Marshall Award (AHL - Top Goal-scorer) (2012) • Les Cunningham Award (AHL - MVP) (2012)

Signed to an ATO (amateur tryout) contract by **Rochester** (AHL), March 24, 2011. Signed to an ATO (amateur tryout) contract by **Cincinnati** (ECHL), March 27, 2011. Signed to an ATO (amateur tryout) contract by **Milwaukee** (AHL), April 12, 2011. Signed as a free agent by **Norfolk** (AHL), July 5, 2011. Signed as a free agent by **Tampa Bay**, March 1, 2012. Traded to **Ottawa** by **Tampa Bay** with Philadelphia's 4th round choice (previously acquired, Ottawa selected Tobias Lindberg) in 2013 Entry Draft for Ben Bishop, April 3, 2013. Claimed on waivers by **Buffalo** from **Ottawa**, March 5, 2014. Signed as a free agent by **NY Islanders**, July 1, 2014. Traded to **Vancouver** by **NY Islanders** for Dustin Jeffrey, March 2, 2015.

CONDRA, Erik (KAWN-druh, AIR-ihk) T.B.

Right wing. Shoots right. 6', 190 lbs. Born, Trenton, MI, August 6, 1986. Ottawa's 7th choice, 211th overall, in 2006 Entry Draft.

Season	Club	League	GP	G	A	Pts	PIM	PP	SH	GW	S	S%	+/-	TF	F%	Min	GP	G	A	Pts	PIM	PP	SH	GW	Min
2004-05	Lincoln Stars	USHL	60	30	30	60	56										4	0	2	2	4				
2005-06	U. of Notre Dame	CCHA	36	6	28	34	32																		
2006-07	U. of Notre Dame	CCHA	42	14	34	48	18																		
2007-08	U. of Notre Dame	CCHA	41	15	23	38	26																		
2008-09	U. of Notre Dame	CCHA	40	13	25	38	34																		
2009-10	Binghamton	AHL	80	11	27	38	61																		
2010-11	**Ottawa**	**NHL**	**26**	**6**	**5**	**11**	**12**	**1**	**0**	**2**	**48**	**12.5**	**-1**	**4**	**50.0**	**15:52**									
	Binghamton	AHL	55	17	30	47	28										23	5	12	17	8				
2011-12	**Ottawa**	**NHL**	**81**	**8**	**17**	**25**	**30**	**0**	**2**	**1**	**140**	**5.7**	**11**	**27**	**40.7**	**14:10**	**7**	**1**	**0**	**1**	**0**	**0**	**0**	**0**	**11:41**
2012-13	EV Fussen	German-3	7	8	11	19	2																		
	Riessersee	German-2	10	10	5	15	8																		
	Ottawa	**NHL**	**48**	**4**	**8**	**12**	**34**	**0**	**0**	**0**	**73**	**5.5**	**3**	**21**	**38.1**	**13:10**	**10**	**1**	**6**	**7**	**2**	**1**	**0**	**0**	**13:36**
2013-14	**Ottawa**	**NHL**	**76**	**6**	**10**	**16**	**30**	**0**	**1**	**0**	**85**	**7.1**	**0**	**15**	**6.7**	**11:39**									
2014-15	**Ottawa**	**NHL**	**68**	**9**	**14**	**23**	**30**	**0**	**1**	**1**	**106**	**8.5**	**13**	**9**	**22.2**	**14:27**	**6**	**1**	**0**	**1**	**0**	**0**	**0**	**0**	**17:31**
	NHL Totals		**299**	**33**	**54**	**87**	**136**	**1**	**4**	**4**	**452**	**7.3**		**76**	**31.6**	**13:35**	**23**	**3**	**6**	**9**	**2**	**1**	**0**	**0**	**14:02**

CCHA All-Rookie Team (2006) • CCHA Second All-Star Team (2009) • NCAA West Second All-American Team (2009)

Signed as a free agent by **Fussen** (German-3), October 16, 2012. Signed as a free agent by **Riessersee** (German-2), November 12, 2012. Signed as a free agent by **Tampa Bay**, July 1, 2015.

CONNAUTON, Kevin (kuh-NAW-tuhn, KEH-vihn) CBJ

Defense. Shoots left. 6'2", 200 lbs. Born, Edmonton, AB, February 23, 1990. Vancouver's 3rd choice, 83rd overall, in 2009 Entry Draft.

Season	Club	League	GP	G	A	Pts	PIM	PP	SH	GW	S	S%	+/-	TF	F%	Min	GP	G	A	Pts	PIM	PP	SH	GW	Min
2007-08	Spruce Grove	AJHL	56	13	32	45	59										15	5	0	5	18				
2008-09	Western Mich.	CCHA	40	7	11	18	44																		
2009-10	Vancouver Giants	WHL	69	24	48	72	107										16	3	10	13	21				
2010-11	Manitoba Moose	AHL	73	11	12	23	51										6	1	0	1	0				
2011-12	Chicago Wolves	AHL	73	13	20	33	58										5	0	1	1	8				
2012-13	Chicago Wolves	AHL	60	7	18	25	67																		
	Texas Stars	AHL	9	2	4	6	6										9	2	3	5	6				
2013-14	**Dallas**	**NHL**	**36**	**1**	**7**	**8**	**16**	**0**	**0**	**0**	**56**	**1.8**	**-6**	**0**	**0.0**	**15:20**	**4**	**0**	**0**	**0**	**16**	**0**	**0**	**0**	**10:44**
	Texas Stars	AHL	6	0	1	1	23																		
2014-15	**Dallas**	**NHL**	**8**	**0**	**2**	**2**	**6**	**0**	**0**	**0**	**10**	**0.0**	**4**	**0**	**0.0**	**12:05**									
	Columbus	**NHL**	**54**	**9**	**10**	**19**	**29**	**0**	**0**	**4**	**86**	**10.5**	**1**	**0**	**0.0**	**16:50**									
	NHL Totals		**98**	**10**	**19**	**29**	**51**	**0**	**0**	**4**	**152**	**6.6**		**0**	**0.0**	**15:53**	**4**	**0**	**0**	**0**	**16**	**0**	**0**	**0**	**10:44**

WHL West First All-Star Team (2010) • Canadian Major Junior All-Rookie Team (2010)

Traded to **Dallas** by **Vancouver** with Vancouver's 2nd round choice (Philippe Desrosiers) in 2013 Entry Draft for Derek Roy, April 2, 2013. Claimed on waivers by **Columbus** from **Dallas**, November 18, 2014.

CONNER, Chris

(KAWN-uhr, KRIHS) **PHI**

Right wing. Shoots left. 5'7", 181 lbs. Born, Westland, MI, December 23, 1983.

			Regular Season														Playoffs								
Season	Club	League	GP	G	A	Pts	PIM	PP	SH	GW	S	S%	+/-	TF	F%	Min	GP	G	A	Pts	PIM	PP	SH	GW	Min
2002-03	Michigan Tech	WCHA	38	13	24	37	8	....	....	....	....	....	....	....	....	....	....	....	....	....	....	....	....	....	....
2003-04	Michigan Tech	WCHA	38	25	14	39	12	....	....	....	....	....	....	....	....	....	....	....	....	....	....	....	....	....	....
2004-05	Michigan Tech	WCHA	37	14	10	24	6	....	....	....	....	....	....	....	....	....	....	....	....	....	....	....	....	....	....
2005-06	Michigan Tech	WCHA	38	17	12	29	18	....	....	....	....	....	....	....	....	....	....	....	....	....	....	....	....	....	....
	Iowa Stars	AHL	15	2	3	5	0	....	....	....	....	....	....	....	....	....	7	1	1	2	2	....	....	....	....
2006-07	**Dallas**	**NHL**	**11**	**1**	**2**	**3**	**4**	**0**	**0**	**0**	**18**	**5.6**	**-3**	**1**	**100.0**	**11:15**	....	....	....	....	....	....	....	....	....
	Iowa Stars	AHL	48	19	18	37	24	....	....	....	....	....	....	....	....	....	12	2	5	7	2	....	....	....	....
2007-08	**Dallas**	**NHL**	**22**	**3**	**2**	**5**	**6**	**0**	**0**	**0**	**27**	**11.1**	**0**	**1**	**100.0**	**12:00**	**1**	**0**	**0**	**0**	**0**	**0**	**0**	**0**	**4:17**
	Iowa Stars	AHL	55	13	26	39	17	....	....	....	....	....	....	....	....	....	....	....	....	....	....	....	....	....	....
2008-09	**Dallas**	**NHL**	**38**	**3**	**10**	**13**	**10**	**0**	**0**	**1**	**34**	**8.8**	**-5**	**1**	**0.0**	**10:56**	....	....	....	....	....	....	....	....	....
	Peoria Rivermen	AHL	30	16	12	28	10	....	....	....	....	....	....	....	....	....	....	....	....	....	....	....	....	....	....
2009-10	**Pittsburgh**	**NHL**	**8**	**2**	**1**	**3**	**0**	**0**	**0**	**1**	**11**	**18.2**	**-1**	**1**	**0.0**	**9:36**	**1**	**0**	**0**	**0**	**0**	**0**	**0**	**0**	**11:03**
	Wilkes-Barre	AHL	59	19	37	56	21	....	....	....	....	....	....	....	....	....	4	2	2	4	2	....	....	....	....
2010-11	**Pittsburgh**	**NHL**	**60**	**7**	**9**	**16**	**10**	**0**	**0**	**3**	**91**	**7.7**	**5**	**4**	**25.0**	**11:49**	**7**	**1**	**0**	**1**	**0**	**0**	**0**	**0**	**12:22**
	Wilkes-Barre	AHL	11	3	6	9	2	....	....	....	....	....	....	....	....	....	....	....	....	....	....	....	....	....	....
2011-12	**Detroit**	**NHL**	**8**	**1**	**2**	**3**	**0**	**0**	**0**	**0**	**10**	**10.0**	**2**	**0**	**0.0**	**10:34**	....	....	....	....	....	....	....	....	....
	Grand Rapids	AHL	57	16	37	53	22	....	....	....	....	....	....	....	....	....	....	....	....	....	....	....	....	....	....
2012-13	Portland Pirates	AHL	60	13	27	40	28	....	....	....	....	....	....	....	....	....	1	0	1	1	2	....	....	....	....
	Phoenix	**NHL**	**12**	**1**	**1**	**2**	**2**	**0**	**0**	**0**	**15**	**6.7**	**3**	**2**	**0.0**	**11:23**	....	....	....	....	....	....	....	....	....
2013-14	**Pittsburgh**	**NHL**	**19**	**4**	**1**	**5**	**2**	**0**	**0**	**0**	**17**	**23.5**	**-3**	**1**	**0.0**	**11:46**	....	....	....	....	....	....	....	....	....
	Wilkes-Barre	AHL	17	6	5	11	8	....	....	....	....	....	....	....	....	....	....	....	....	....	....	....	....	....	....
2014-15	**Washington**	**NHL**	**2**	**0**	**0**	**0**	**4**	**0**	**0**	**0**	**3**	**0.0**	**1**	**0**	**0.0**	**8:49**	....	....	....	....	....	....	....	....	....
	Hershey Bears	AHL	61	19	33	52	10	....	....	....	....	....	....	....	....	....	10	2	5	7	2	....	....	....	....
	NHL Totals		**180**	**22**	**28**	**50**	**38**	**0**	**0**	**5**	**226**	**9.7**		**11**	**27.3**	**11:24**	**9**	**1**	**0**	**1**	**0**	**0**	**0**	**0**	**11:20**

WCHA Second All-Star Team (2004)

Signed as a free agent by **Dallas**, July 13, 2006. Signed as a free agent by **Pittsburgh**, July 5. 2009. Signed as a free agent by **Detroit**, July 5, 2011. Signed as a free agent by **Phoenix**, July 2, 2012. Signed as a free agent by **Pittsburgh**, July 6, 2013. • Missed majority of 2013-14 due to hand injury at New Jersey, December 31, 2013. Signed as a free agent by **Washington**, July 1, 2014. Signed as a free agent by **Philadelphia**, July 1, 2015.

CONNOLLY, Brett

(KAW-nuh-lee, BREHT) **BOS**

Right wing. Shoots right. 6'2", 200 lbs. Born, Prince George, BC, May 2, 1992. Tampa Bay's 1st choice, 6th overall, in 2010 Entry Draft.

			Regular Season														Playoffs								
Season	Club	League	GP	G	A	Pts	PIM	PP	SH	GW	S	S%	+/-	TF	F%	Min	GP	G	A	Pts	PIM	PP	SH	GW	Min
2007-08	Cariboo Cougars	BCMML	38	16	16	32	80	....	....	....	....	....	....	....	....	....	6	4	1	5	10	....	....	....	....
	Prince George	WHL	4	0	0	0	0	....	....	....	....	....	....	....	....	....	....	....	....	....	....	....	....	....	....
2008-09	Prince George	WHL	65	30	30	60	38	....	....	....	....	....	....	....	....	....	4	0	2	2	6	....	....	....	....
2009-10	Prince George	WHL	16	10	9	19	8	....	....	....	....	....	....	....	....	....	....	....	....	....	....	....	....	....	....
2010-11	Prince George	WHL	59	46	27	73	26	....	....	....	....	....	....	....	....	....	1	0	0	0	0	....	....	....	....
2011-12	**Tampa Bay**	**NHL**	**68**	**4**	**11**	**15**	**30**	**1**	**0**	**2**	**94**	**4.3**	**-9**	**52**	**38.5**	**11:28**	....	....	....	....	....	....	....	....	....
2012-13	Syracuse Crunch	AHL	71	31	32	63	53	....	....	....	....	....	....	....	....	....	18	6	5	11	12	....	....	....	....
	Tampa Bay	**NHL**	**5**	**1**	**0**	**1**	**0**	**1**	**0**	**0**	**10**	**10.0**	**-3**	**5**	**80.0**	**10:16**	....	....	....	....	....	....	....	....	....
2013-14	**Tampa Bay**	**NHL**	**11**	**1**	**0**	**1**	**4**	**0**	**0**	**1**	**12**	**8.3**	**-5**	**52**	**48.1**	**12:01**	....	....	....	....	....	....	....	....	....
	Syracuse Crunch	AHL	66	21	36	57	50	....	....	....	....	....	....	....	....	....	....	....	....	....	....	....	....	....	....
2014-15	**Tampa Bay**	**NHL**	**50**	**12**	**3**	**15**	**38**	**2**	**0**	**2**	**74**	**16.2**	**4**	**42**	**42.9**	**11:56**	....	....	....	....	....	....	....	....	....
	Boston	**NHL**	**5**	**0**	**2**	**2**	**10**	**0**	**0**	**0**	**9**	**0.0**	**-1**	**1**	**0.0**	**14:22**	....	....	....	....	....	....	....	....	....
	NHL Totals		**139**	**18**	**16**	**34**	**82**	**4**	**0**	**5**	**199**	**9.0**		**152**	**44.1**	**11:44**	....	....	....	....	....	....	....	....	....

WHL Rookie of the Year (2009) • Canadian Major Junior All-Rookie Team (2009) • Canadian Major Junior Rookie of the Year (2009) • AHL Second All-Star Team (2013)

• Missed majority of 2009-10 due to pre-season hip injury. Traded to **Boston** by **Tampa Bay** for Boston's 2nd round choice (Matthew Spencer) in 2015 Entry Draft, March 2, 2015.

COOKE, Matt

(KUK, MAT)

Center. Shoots left. 5'11", 208 lbs. Born, Belleville, ON, September 7, 1978. Vancouver's 8th choice, 144th overall, in 1997 Entry Draft.

			Regular Season														Playoffs								
Season	Club	League	GP	G	A	Pts	PIM	PP	SH	GW	S	S%	+/-	TF	F%	Min	GP	G	A	Pts	PIM	PP	SH	GW	Min
1994-95	Wellington Dukes	ON-Jr.A	46	9	23	32	62	....	....	....	....	....	....	....	....	....	....	....	....	....	....	....	....	....	....
1995-96	Windsor Spitfires	OHL	61	8	11	19	102	....	....	....	....	....	....	....	....	....	7	1	3	4	6	....	....	....	....
1996-97	Windsor Spitfires	OHL	65	45	50	95	146	....	....	....	....	....	....	....	....	....	5	5	5	10	10	....	....	....	....
1997-98	Windsor Spitfires	OHL	23	14	19	33	50	....	....	....	....	....	....	....	....	....	....	....	....	....	....	....	....	....	....
	Kingston	OHL	25	8	13	21	49	....	....	....	....	....	....	....	....	....	12	8	8	16	20	....	....	....	....
1998-99	**Vancouver**	**NHL**	**30**	**0**	**2**	**2**	**27**	**0**	**0**	**0**	**22**	**0.0**	**-12**	**189**	**40.2**	**8:07**	....	....	....	....	....	....	....	....	....
	Syracuse Crunch	AHL	37	15	18	33	119	....	....	....	....	....	....	....	....	....	....	....	....	....	....	....	....	....	....
99-2000	**Vancouver**	**NHL**	**51**	**5**	**7**	**12**	**39**	**0**	**1**	**1**	**58**	**8.6**	**3**	**71**	**39.4**	**11:48**	....	....	....	....	....	....	....	....	....
	Syracuse Crunch	AHL	18	5	8	13	27	....	....	....	....	....	....	....	....	....	....	....	....	....	....	....	....	....	....
2000-01	**Vancouver**	**NHL**	**81**	**14**	**13**	**27**	**94**	**0**	**2**	**0**	**121**	**11.6**	**5**	**321**	**43.0**	**14:35**	**4**	**0**	**0**	**0**	**4**	**0**	**0**	**0**	**12:04**
2001-02	**Vancouver**	**NHL**	**82**	**13**	**20**	**33**	**111**	**1**	**0**	**2**	**103**	**12.6**	**4**	**28**	**32.1**	**14:03**	**6**	**3**	**2**	**5**	**0**	**1**	**0**	**0**	**15:09**
2002-03	**Vancouver**	**NHL**	**82**	**15**	**27**	**42**	**82**	**1**	**4**	**0**	**118**	**12.7**	**21**	**31**	**35.5**	**13:24**	**14**	**2**	**1**	**3**	**12**	**0**	**0**	**0**	**14:07**
2003-04	**Vancouver**	**NHL**	**53**	**11**	**12**	**23**	**73**	**1**	**1**	**4**	**79**	**13.9**	**5**	**34**	**52.9**	**14:06**	**7**	**3**	**1**	**4**	**12**	**0**	**0**	**1**	**18:23**
2004-05			DID NOT PLAY																						
2005-06	**Vancouver**	**NHL**	**45**	**8**	**10**	**18**	**71**	**0**	**0**	**2**	**67**	**11.9**	**-8**	**25**	**24.0**	**13:57**	....	....	....	....	....	....	....	....	....
2006-07	**Vancouver**	**NHL**	**81**	**10**	**20**	**30**	**64**	**1**	**0**	**3**	**133**	**7.5**	**0**	**19**	**47.4**	**15:37**	**1**	**0**	**0**	**0**	**2**	**0**	**0**	**0**	**9:51**
2007-08	**Vancouver**	**NHL**	**61**	**7**	**9**	**16**	**64**	**0**	**0**	**1**	**68**	**10.3**	**-4**	**26**	**42.3**	**13:24**	....	....	....	....	....	....	....	....	....
	Washington	**NHL**	**17**	**3**	**4**	**7**	**27**	**0**	**1**	**0**	**18**	**16.7**	**5**	**2**	**50.0**	**12:19**	**7**	**0**	**0**	**0**	**4**	**0**	**0**	**0**	**13:55**
2008-09♦	**Pittsburgh**	**NHL**	**76**	**13**	**18**	**31**	**101**	**0**	**0**	**1**	**86**	**15.1**	**0**	**19**	**36.8**	**14:13**	**24**	**1**	**6**	**7**	**22**	**0**	**0**	**0**	**15:09**
2009-10	**Pittsburgh**	**NHL**	**79**	**15**	**15**	**30**	**106**	**2**	**0**	**1**	**105**	**14.3**	**17**	**24**	**54.2**	**14:47**	**13**	**4**	**2**	**6**	**22**	**0**	**0**	**0**	**15:11**
2010-11	**Pittsburgh**	**NHL**	**67**	**12**	**18**	**30**	**129**	**0**	**3**	**2**	**95**	**12.6**	**14**	**29**	**27.6**	**15:38**	....	....	....	....	....	....	....	....	....
2011-12	**Pittsburgh**	**NHL**	**82**	**19**	**19**	**38**	**44**	**1**	**2**	**4**	**147**	**12.9**	**5**	**33**	**54.6**	**15:41**	**6**	**0**	**4**	**4**	**16**	**0**	**0**	**0**	**16:13**
2012-13	**Pittsburgh**	**NHL**	**48**	**8**	**13**	**21**	**36**	**0**	**0**	**1**	**61**	**13.1**	**-2**	**14**	**21.4**	**14:43**	**15**	**0**	**4**	**4**	**35**	**0**	**0**	**0**	**15:08**
2013-14	**Minnesota**	**NHL**	**82**	**10**	**18**	**28**	**54**	**0**	**1**	**3**	**104**	**9.6**	**8**	**26**	**38.5**	**15:24**	**6**	**0**	**3**	**3**	**8**	**0**	**0**	**0**	**16:00**
2014-15	**Minnesota**	**NHL**	**29**	**4**	**6**	**10**	**13**	**0**	**0**	**0**	**24**	**16.7**	**0**	**9**	**33.3**	**12:36**	**7**	**0**	**2**	**2**	**4**	**0**	**0**	**0**	**11:08**
	NHL Totals		**1046**	**167**	**231**	**398**	**1135**	**7**	**15**	**25**	**1409**	**11.9**		**900**	**41.0**	**14:12**	**110**	**13**	**25**	**38**	**141**	**1**	**0**	**1**	**14:50**

Traded to **Washington** by **Vancouver** for Matt Pettinger, February 26, 2008. Signed as a free agent by **Pittsburgh**, July 6, 2008. Signed as a free agent by **Minnesota**, July 5, 2013. • Missed majority of 2014-15 due to lower-body (October 28, 2014 at Boston) and (February 1, 2015 at Vancouver) injures.

COPP, Andrew

(KAWP, AN-droo) **WPG**

Center. Shoots left. 6'1", 207 lbs. Born, Ann Arbor, MI, July 8, 1994. Winnipeg's 6th choice, 104th overall, in 2013 Entry Draft.

			Regular Season														Playoffs								
Season	Club	League	GP	G	A	Pts	PIM	PP	SH	GW	S	S%	+/-	TF	F%	Min	GP	G	A	Pts	PIM	PP	SH	GW	Min
2009-10	Det. Compuware	T1EHL	38	12	15	27	12	....	....	....	....	....	....	....	....	....	....	....	....	....	....	....	....	....	....
2010-11	Det. Compuware	T1EHL	17	2	7	9	6	....	....	....	....	....	....	....	....	....	....	....	....	....	....	....	....	....	....
	USNTDP	USHL	22	1	4	5	4	....	....	....	....	....	....	....	....	....	1	0	0	0	0	....	....	....	....
	USNTDP	U-17	3	1	0	1	0	....	....	....	....	....	....	....	....	....	....	....	....	....	....	....	....	....	....
	USNTDP	U-18	5	0	0	0	0	....	....	....	....	....	....	....	....	....	....	....	....	....	....	....	....	....	....
2011-12	USNTDP	USHL	18	3	7	10	2	....	....	....	....	....	....	....	....	....	....	....	....	....	....	....	....	....	....
	USNTDP	U-17	7	3	3	6	....	....	....	....	....	....	....	....	....	....	....	....	....	....	....	....	....	....	....
	USNTDP	U-18	7	0	1	1	2	....	....	....	....	....	....	....	....	....	....	....	....	....	....	....	....	....	....
2012-13	U. of Michigan	CCHA	38	11	10	21	12	....	....	....	....	....	....	....	....	....	....	....	....	....	....	....	....	....	....
2013-14	U. of Michigan	Big Ten	33	15	14	29	26	....	....	....	....	....	....	....	....	....	....	....	....	....	....	....	....	....	....
2014-15	U. of Michigan	Big Ten	36	14	17	31	29	....	....	....	....	....	....	....	....	....	....	....	....	....	....	....	....	....	....
	Winnipeg	**NHL**	**1**	**0**	**1**	**1**	**0**	**0**	**0**	**0**	**4**	**0.0**	**2**	**9**	**66.7**	**13:16**	....	....	....	....	....	....	....	....	....
	NHL Totals		**1**	**0**	**1**	**1**	**0**	**0**	**0**	**0**	**4**	**0.0**		**9**	**66.7**	**13:16**	....	....	....	....	....	....	....	....	....

CORMIER, Patrice

(KOHR-mee-ay, pa-TREEZ) **WPG**

Center. Shoots left. 6'2", 215 lbs. Born, Moncton, NB, June 14, 1990. New Jersey's 3rd choice, 54th overall, in 2008 Entry Draft.

			Regular Season														Playoffs								
Season	Club	League	GP	G	A	Pts	PIM	PP	SH	GW	S	S%	+/-	TF	F%	Min	GP	G	A	Pts	PIM	PP	SH	GW	Min
2005-06	Dieppe	MJrHL	43	21	27	48	41	....	....	....	....	....	....	....	....	....	6	2	2	4	6	....	....	....	....
2006-07	Rimouski Oceanic	QMJHL	53	11	10	21	73	....	....	....	....	....	....	....	....	....	....	....	....	....	....	....	....	....	....
2007-08	Rimouski Oceanic	QMJHL	51	18	23	41	84	....	....	....	....	....	....	....	....	....	9	4	5	9	10	....	....	....	....
2008-09	Rimouski Oceanic	QMJHL	54	23	28	51	118	....	....	....	....	....	....	....	....	....	13	4	6	10	30	....	....	....	....

			Regular Season														Playoffs								
Season	Club	League	GP	G	A	Pts	PIM	PP	SH	GW	S	S%	+/-	TF	F%	Min	GP	G	A	Pts	PIM	PP	SH	GW	Min
2009-10	Rimouski Oceanic	QMJHL	28	11	15	26	57	....	....	....	....	....	....	....	....	....	....	....	....	....	....	....	....	....	....
	Rouyn-Noranda	QMJHL	3	0	5	5	7	....	....	....	....	....	....	....	....	....	....	....	....	....	....	....	....	....	....
	Chicago Wolves	AHL	....	....	....	....	....	....	....	....	....	....	....	....	....	....	9	0	0	0	8	....	....	....	....
2010-11	**Atlanta**	**NHL**	**21**	**1**	**1**	**2**	**4**	**0**	**0**	**0**	**27**	**3.7**	**–5**	**67**	**58.2**	**9:39**	....	....	....	....	....	....	....	....	....
	Chicago Wolves	AHL	11	2	3	5	14	....	....	....	....	....	....	....	....	....	....	....	....	....	....	....	....	....	....
2011-12	**Winnipeg**	**NHL**	**9**	**0**	**0**	**0**	**0**	**0**	**0**	**0**	**8**	**0.0**	**1**	**30**	**73.3**	**6:22**	....	....	....	....	....	....	....	....	....
	St. John's IceCaps	AHL	56	18	15	33	75	....	....	....	....	....	....	....	....	....	15	3	0	3	12	....	....	....	....
2012-13	St. John's IceCaps	AHL	35	7	4	11	69	....	....	....	....	....	....	....	....	....	....	....	....	....	....	....	....	....	....
	Winnipeg	**NHL**	**10**	**0**	**0**	**0**	**7**	**0**	**0**	**0**	**4**	**0.0**	**–3**	**6**	**16.7**	**3:53**	....	....	....	....	....	....	....	....	....
2013-14	**Winnipeg**	**NHL**	**9**	**0**	**3**	**3**	**7**	**0**	**0**	**0**	**4**	**0.0**	**2**	**46**	**56.5**	**6:58**	....	....	....	....	....	....	....	....	....
	St. John's IceCaps	AHL	61	9	17	26	98	....	....	....	....	....	....	....	....	....	21	2	5	7	22	....	....	....	....
2014-15	**Winnipeg**	**NHL**	**1**	**0**	**0**	**0**	**0**	**0**	**0**	**0**	**0**	**0.0**	**0**	**5**	**60.0**	**4:54**	....	....	....	....	....	....	....	....	....
	St. John's IceCaps	AHL	47	12	9	21	74	....	....	....	....	....	....	....	....	....	....	....	....	....	....	....	....	....	....
	NHL Totals		**50**	**1**	**4**	**5**	**18**	**0**	**0**	**0**	**43**	**2.3**		**154**	**59.1**	**7:20**	....	....	....	....	....	....	....	....	....

Traded to **Atlanta** by **New Jersey** with Johnny Oduya, Niclas Bergfors and New Jersey's 1st (later traded to Chicago - Chicago selected Kevin Hayes) and 2nd (later traded to Chicago - Chicago selected Justin Holl) round choices in 2010 Entry Draft for Ilya Kovalchuk, Anssi Salmela and Atlanta's 2nd round choice (Jonathon Merrill) in 2010 Entry Draft, February 4, 2010. • Missed majority of 2010-11 due to training camp foot injury and upper-body injury at Phoenix, February 17, 2011. • Transferred to **Winnipeg** after **Atlanta** franchise relocated, June 21, 2011.

CORNET, Philippe

(kohr-NAY, fih-LEEP)

Left wing. Shoots left. 6', 196 lbs. Born, Val-Senneville, QC, March 28, 1990. Edmonton's 3rd choice, 133rd overall, in 2008 Entry Draft.

Season	Club	League	GP	G	A	Pts	PIM	PP	SH	GW	S	S%	+/-	TF	F%	Min	GP	G	A	Pts	PIM	PP	SH	GW	Min
2006-07	Rimouski Oceanic	QMJHL	46	7	14	21	8	....	....	....	....	....	....	....	....	....	....	....	....	....	....	....	....	....	....
2007-08	Rimouski Oceanic	QMJHL	61	23	26	49	24	....	....	....	....	....	....	....	....	....	9	3	3	6	6	....	....	....	....
2008-09	Rimouski Oceanic	QMJHL	63	29	48	77	34	....	....	....	....	....	....	....	....	....	13	4	11	15	14	....	....	....	....
2009-10	Rouyn-Noranda	QMJHL	65	28	49	77	32	....	....	....	....	....	....	....	....	....	11	5	6	11	6	....	....	....	....
2010-11	Oklahoma City	AHL	60	7	16	23	8	....	....	....	....	....	....	....	....	....	....	....	....	....	....	....	....	....	....
2011-12	**Edmonton**	**NHL**	**2**	**0**	**1**	**1**	**0**	**0**	**0**	**0**	**0**	**0.0**	**0**	**0**	**0.0**	**10:35**	....	....	....	....	....	....	....	....	....
	Oklahoma City	AHL	67	24	13	37	26	....	....	....	....	....	....	....	....	....	14	2	5	7	2	....	....	....	....
2012-13	Stockton Thunder	ECHL	18	9	14	23	2	....	....	....	....	....	....	....	....	....	....	....	....	....	....	....	....	....	....
	Oklahoma City	AHL	46	15	18	33	18	....	....	....	....	....	....	....	....	....	17	2	7	9	0	....	....	....	....
2013-14	San Antonio	AHL	4	0	1	1	0	....	....	....	....	....	....	....	....	....	....	....	....	....	....	....	....	....	....
	Cincinnati	ECHL	3	0	0	0	0	....	....	....	....	....	....	....	....	....	....	....	....	....	....	....	....	....	....
	Charlotte	AHL	58	13	15	28	16	....	....	....	....	....	....	....	....	....	....	....	....	....	....	....	....	....	....
2014-15	Hershey Bears	AHL	55	9	13	22	17	....	....	....	....	....	....	....	....	....	5	0	0	0	0	....	....	....	....
	NHL Totals		**2**	**0**	**1**	**1**	**0**	**0**	**0**	**0**	**0**	**0.0**		**0**	**0.0**	**10:35**	....	....	....	....	....	....	....	....	....

Signed as a free agent by **San Antonio** (AHL), October 3, 2013. Signed as a free agent by **Hershey** (AHL), August 18, 2014.

CORRADO, Frank

(koh-RA-doh, FRANK) **VAN**

Defense. Shoots right. 6'2", 191 lbs. Born, Woodbridge, ON, March 26, 1993. Vancouver's 6th choice, 150th overall, in 2011 Entry Draft.

Season	Club	League	GP	G	A	Pts	PIM	PP	SH	GW	S	S%	+/-	TF	F%	Min	GP	G	A	Pts	PIM	PP	SH	GW	Min
2008-09	Vaughan Kings	GTHL	62	15	33	48	136	....	....	....	....	....	....	....	....	....	....	....	....	....	....	....	....	....	....
2009-10	Sudbury Wolves	OHL	63	1	8	9	46	....	....	....	....	....	....	....	....	....	4	0	1	1	0	....	....	....	....
2010-11	Sudbury Wolves	OHL	67	4	26	30	94	....	....	....	....	....	....	....	....	....	8	1	4	5	8	....	....	....	....
2011-12	Sudbury Wolves	OHL	60	3	23	26	81	....	....	....	....	....	....	....	....	....	4	0	0	0	12	....	....	....	....
	Chicago Wolves	AHL	4	0	1	1	0	....	....	....	....	....	....	....	....	....	2	0	0	0	0	....	....	....	....
2012-13	Sudbury Wolves	OHL	41	6	21	27	44	....	....	....	....	....	....	....	....	....	....	....	....	....	....	....	....	....	....
	Kitchener Rangers	OHL	28	1	17	18	45	....	....	....	....	....	....	....	....	....	10	1	1	2	6	....	....	....	....
	Chicago Wolves	AHL	3	0	2	2	0	....	....	....	....	....	....	....	....	....	....	....	....	....	....	....	....	....	....
	Vancouver	**NHL**	**3**	**0**	**0**	**0**	**0**	**0**	**0**	**0**	**4**	**0.0**	**–1**	**0**	**0.0**	**19:24**	**4**	**0**	**0**	**0**	**0**	**0**	**0**	**0**	**12:19**
2013-14	**Vancouver**	**NHL**	**15**	**1**	**0**	**1**	**4**	**0**	**0**	**0**	**20**	**5.0**	**–2**	**0**	**0.0**	**12:34**	....	....	....	....	....	....	....	....	....
	Utica Comets	AHL	59	6	11	17	46	....	....	....	....	....	....	....	....	....	....	....	....	....	....	....	....	....	....
2014-15	**Vancouver**	**NHL**	**10**	**1**	**0**	**1**	**0**	**0**	**0**	**0**	**8**	**12.5**	**–7**	**0**	**0.0**	**15:40**	....	....	....	....	....	....	....	....	....
	Utica Comets	AHL	35	7	9	16	31	....	....	....	....	....	....	....	....	....	18	1	0	1	24	....	....	....	....
	NHL Totals		**28**	**2**	**0**	**2**	**4**	**0**	**0**	**0**	**32**	**6.3**		**0**	**0.0**	**14:24**	**4**	**0**	**0**	**0**	**0**	**0**	**0**	**0**	**12:19**

CORRENTE, Matthew

(kohr-REHN-tay, MA-thew)

Defense. Shoots right. 6', 205 lbs. Born, Mississauga, ON, March 17, 1988. New Jersey's 1st choice, 30th overall, in 2006 Entry Draft.

Season	Club	League	GP	G	A	Pts	PIM	PP	SH	GW	S	S%	+/-	TF	F%	Min	GP	G	A	Pts	PIM	PP	SH	GW	Min
2004-05	Saginaw Spirit	OHL	62	6	9	15	89	....	....	....	....	....	....	....	....	....	....	....	....	....	....	....	....	....	....
2005-06	Saginaw Spirit	OHL	61	6	24	30	172	....	....	....	....	....	....	....	....	....	4	1	1	2	8	....	....	....	....
2006-07	Saginaw Spirit	OHL	29	2	13	15	67	....	....	....	....	....	....	....	....	....	....	....	....	....	....	....	....	....	....
	Mississauga	OHL	14	1	10	11	27	....	....	....	....	....	....	....	....	....	5	0	1	1	8	....	....	....	....
2007-08	Niagara Ice Dogs	OHL	21	2	13	15	64	....	....	....	....	....	....	....	....	....	10	0	5	5	33	....	....	....	....
2008-09	Lowell Devils	AHL	67	6	12	18	161	....	....	....	....	....	....	....	....	....	....	....	....	....	....	....	....	....	....
2009-10	**New Jersey**	**NHL**	**12**	**0**	**0**	**0**	**24**	**0**	**0**	**0**	**6**	**0.0**	**0**	**0**	**0.0**	**8:51**	**2**	**0**	**0**	**0**	**2**	**0**	**0**	**0**	**5:51**
	Lowell Devils	AHL	43	5	15	20	74	....	....	....	....	....	....	....	....	....	....	....	....	....	....	....	....	....	....
2010-11	**New Jersey**	**NHL**	**22**	**0**	**6**	**6**	**44**	**0**	**0**	**0**	**21**	**0.0**	**–5**	**0**	**0.0**	**13:36**	....	....	....	....	....	....	....	....	....
	Albany Devils	AHL	3	0	1	1	10	....	....	....	....	....	....	....	....	....	....	....	....	....	....	....	....	....	....
2011-12	Albany Devils	AHL	39	2	6	8	73	....	....	....	....	....	....	....	....	....	....	....	....	....	....	....	....	....	....
2012-13	Albany Devils	AHL	11	0	2	2	32	....	....	....	....	....	....	....	....	....	....	....	....	....	....	....	....	....	....
2013-14	Charlotte	AHL	72	2	9	11	136	....	....	....	....	....	....	....	....	....	....	....	....	....	....	....	....	....	....
2014-15	Syracuse Crunch	AHL	48	2	6	8	101	....	....	....	....	....	....	....	....	....	....	....	....	....	....	....	....	....	....
	San Antonio	AHL	10	1	4	5	43	....	....	....	....	....	....	....	....	....	....	....	....	....	....	....	....	....	....
	NHL Totals		**34**	**0**	**6**	**6**	**68**	**0**	**0**	**0**	**27**	**0.0**		**0**	**0.0**	**11:56**	**2**	**0**	**0**	**0**	**2**	**0**	**0**	**0**	**5:51**

• Missed majority of 2010-11 due to shoulder injury at Tampa Bay, January 14, 2011. • Missed majority of 2011-12 due to various injuries. • Missed majority of 2012-13 due to recurring shoulder injury. Signed as a free agent by **Carolina**, July 10, 2013. Signed as a free agent by **Tampa Bay**, July 8, 2014.

COTE, Jean-Philippe

(KOH-tay, ZHAWN-fihl-EEP)

Defense. Shoots left. 6'2", 216 lbs. Born, Charlesbourg, QC, April 22, 1982. Toronto's 10th choice, 265th overall, in 2000 Entry Draft.

Season	Club	League	GP	G	A	Pts	PIM	PP	SH	GW	S	S%	+/-	TF	F%	Min	GP	G	A	Pts	PIM	PP	SH	GW	Min
1998-99	Ste-Foy	QAAA	38	10	24	34	34	....	....	....	....	....	....	....	....	....	17	1	8	9	17	....	....	....	....
	Quebec Remparts	QMJHL	8	0	0	0	2	....	....	....	....	....	....	....	....	....	....	....	....	....	....	....	....	....	....
99-2000	Quebec Remparts	QMJHL	34	0	10	10	15	....	....	....	....	....	....	....	....	....	....	....	....	....	....	....	....	....	....
	Cape Breton	QMJHL	28	0	4	4	21	....	....	....	....	....	....	....	....	....	4	0	1	1	4	....	....	....	....
2000-01	Cape Breton	QMJHL	71	6	29	35	90	....	....	....	....	....	....	....	....	....	12	0	0	0	18	....	....	....	....
2001-02	Cape Breton	QMJHL	61	4	20	24	72	....	....	....	....	....	....	....	....	....	16	1	6	7	38	....	....	....	....
2002-03	Cape Breton	QMJHL	16	1	3	4	12	....	....	....	....	....	....	....	....	....	....	....	....	....	....	....	....	....	....
	Acadie-Bathurst	QMJHL	48	8	18	26	87	....	....	....	....	....	....	....	....	....	11	2	3	5	20	....	....	....	....
2003-04	Hamilton	AHL	75	2	7	9	79	....	....	....	....	....	....	....	....	....	10	0	4	4	24	....	....	....	....
2004-05	Hamilton	AHL	51	1	8	9	58	....	....	....	....	....	....	....	....	....	4	0	1	1	0	....	....	....	....
2005-06	**Montreal**	**NHL**	**8**	**0**	**0**	**0**	**4**	**0**	**0**	**0**	**2**	**0.0**	**2**	**0**	**0.0**	**11:02**	....	....	....	....	....	....	....	....	....
	Hamilton	AHL	61	3	8	11	113	....	....	....	....	....	....	....	....	....	....	....	....	....	....	....	....	....	....
2006-07	Hamilton	AHL	68	3	9	12	115	....	....	....	....	....	....	....	....	....	6	0	0	0	2	....	....	....	....
2007-08	Hamilton	AHL	79	1	12	13	112	....	....	....	....	....	....	....	....	....	....	....	....	....	....	....	....	....	....
2008-09	Wilkes-Barre	AHL	50	2	10	12	74	....	....	....	....	....	....	....	....	....	2	0	0	0	2	....	....	....	....
2009-10	Kassel Huskies	Germany	38	6	7	13	119	....	....	....	....	....	....	....	....	....	....	....	....	....	....	....	....	....	....
2010-11	Hamburg Freezers	Germany	39	3	1	4	70	....	....	....	....	....	....	....	....	....	....	....	....	....	....	....	....	....	....
2011-12	Norfolk Admirals	AHL	58	3	12	15	67	....	....	....	....	....	....	....	....	....	18	1	3	4	29	....	....	....	....
2012-13	Syracuse Crunch	AHL	74	3	14	17	143	....	....	....	....	....	....	....	....	....	18	1	5	6	29	....	....	....	....
2013-14	Syracuse Crunch	AHL	33	2	11	13	57	....	....	....	....	....	....	....	....	....	....	....	....	....	....	....	....	....	....
	Tampa Bay	**NHL**	**19**	**0**	**4**	**4**	**22**	**0**	**0**	**0**	**12**	**0.0**	**0**	**0**	**0.0**	**10:00**	....	....	....	....	....	....	....	....	....
2014-15	Syracuse Crunch	AHL	74	2	9	11	112	....	....	....	....	....	....	....	....	....	3	0	0	0	4	....	....	....	....
	NHL Totals		**27**	**0**	**4**	**4**	**26**	**0**	**0**	**0**	**14**	**0.0**		**0**	**0.0**	**10:18**	....	....	....	....	....	....	....	....	....

Signed as a free agent by **Montreal**, August 19, 2004. Signed as a free agent by **Kassel** (Germany), November 6, 2009. Signed as a free agent by **Hamburg** (Germany), March 22, 2010. Signed as a free agent by **Syracuse** (AHL), October 11, 2012. Signed as a free agent by **Tampa Bay**, December 18, 2013. Signed as a free agent by **Iserlohn** (Germany), July 17, 2015.

COUSINS, Nick
(KUH-zihnz, NIHK) **PHI**

Center. Shoots left. 5'11", 188 lbs. Born, Belleville, ON, July 20, 1993. Philadelphia's 2nd choice, 68th overall, in 2011 Entry Draft.

			Regular Season														Playoffs								
Season	Club	League	GP	G	A	Pts	PIM	PP	SH	GW	S	S%	+/-	TF	F%	Min	GP	G	A	Pts	PIM	PP	SH	GW	Min
2008-09	Quinte Red Devils	Minor-ON	71	72	67	139	....	....	....	....	....	....	....	....	....	....	....	....	....	....	....	....	....	....	....
	Trenton Hercs	ON-Jr.A	5	0	1	1	2	....	....	....	....	....	....	....	....	....	....	....	....	....	....	....	....	....	....
2009-10	Sault Ste. Marie	OHL	67	11	21	32	34	....	....	....	....	....	....	....	....	....	5	0	1	1	2	....	....	....	....
2010-11	Sault Ste. Marie	OHL	68	29	39	68	56	....	....	....	....	....	....	....	....	....	....	....	....	....	....	....	....	....	....
2011-12	Sault Ste. Marie	OHL	65	35	53	88	88	....	....	....	....	....	....	....	....	....	....	....	....	....	....	....	....	....	....
	Adirondack	AHL	1	0	0	0	0	....	....	....	....	....	....	....	....	....	....	....	....	....	....	....	....	....	....
2012-13	Sault Ste. Marie	OHL	64	27	76	103	83	....	....	....	....	....	....	....	....	....	6	3	3	6	12	....	....	....	....
	Adirondack	AHL	7	0	1	1	2	....	....	....	....	....	....	....	....	....	....	....	....	....	....	....	....	....	....
2013-14	Adirondack	AHL	74	11	18	29	47	....	....	....	....	....	....	....	....	....	....	....	....	....	....	....	....	....	....
2014-15	**Philadelphia**	**NHL**	**11**	**0**	**0**	**0**	**2**	**0**	**0**	**0**	**6**	**0.0**	**1**	**52**	**44.2**	**8:49**	....	....	....	....	....	....	....	....	....
	Lehigh Valley	AHL	64	22	34	56	73	....	....	....	....	....	....	....	....	....	....	....	....	....	....	....	....	....	....
	NHL Totals		**11**	**0**	**0**	**0**	**2**	**0**	**0**	**0**	**6**	**0.0**		**52**	**44.2**	**8:49**	....	....	....	....	....	....	....	....	....

COUTURE, Logan
(koh-TYOOR, LOH-guhn) **S.J.**

Center. Shoots left. 6'1", 200 lbs. Born, Guelph, ON, March 28, 1989. San Jose's 1st choice, 9th overall, in 2007 Entry Draft.

Season	Club	League	GP	G	A	Pts	PIM	PP	SH	GW	S	S%	+/-	TF	F%	Min	GP	G	A	Pts	PIM	PP	SH	GW	Min
2004-05	St. Thomas Stars	ON-Jr.B	48	24	22	46	....	....	....	....	....	....	....	....	....	....	....	....	....	....	....	....	....	....	....
2005-06	Ottawa 67's	OHL	65	25	39	64	52	....	....	....	....	....	....	....	....	....	6	3	4	7	0	....	....	....	....
2006-07	Ottawa 67's	OHL	54	26	52	78	24	....	....	....	....	....	....	....	....	....	5	1	7	8	4	....	....	....	....
2007-08	Ottawa 67's	OHL	51	21	37	58	37	....	....	....	....	....	....	....	....	....	4	2	1	3	0	....	....	....	....
2008-09	Ottawa 67's	OHL	62	39	48	87	46	....	....	....	....	....	....	....	....	....	7	3	7	10	6	....	....	....	....
	Worcester Sharks	AHL	4	0	0	0	7	....	....	....	....	....	....	....	....	....	12	2	1	3	11	....	....	....	....
2009-10	**San Jose**	**NHL**	**25**	**5**	**4**	**9**	**6**	**1**	**0**	**1**	**42**	**11.9**	**4**	**143**	**52.5**	**10:16**	**15**	**4**	**0**	**4**	**4**	**0**	**0**	**1**	**11:23**
	Worcester Sharks	AHL	42	20	33	53	12	....	....	....	....	....	....	....	....	....	....	....	....	....	....	....	....	....	....
2010-11	**San Jose**	**NHL**	**79**	**32**	**24**	**56**	**41**	**10**	**0**	**8**	**253**	**12.6**	**18**	**888**	**53.4**	**17:49**	**18**	**7**	**7**	**14**	**2**	**1**	**0**	**0**	**19:23**
2011-12	**San Jose**	**NHL**	**80**	**31**	**34**	**65**	**16**	**11**	**2**	**5**	**245**	**12.7**	**2**	**910**	**51.4**	**18:34**	**5**	**1**	**3**	**4**	**0**	**0**	**0**	**0**	**19:54**
2012-13	Geneve	Swiss	22	7	16	23	10	....	....	....	....	....	....	....	....	....	....	....	....	....	....	....	....	....	....
	San Jose	**NHL**	**48**	**21**	**16**	**37**	**4**	**7**	**0**	**5**	**151**	**13.9**	**7**	**489**	**51.5**	**18:06**	**11**	**5**	**6**	**11**	**0**	***5**	**0**	**3**	**20:31**
2013-14	**San Jose**	**NHL**	**65**	**23**	**31**	**54**	**20**	**4**	**2**	**6**	**233**	**9.9**	**21**	**950**	**50.4**	**18:56**	**7**	**1**	**2**	**3**	**7**	**0**	**0**	**0**	**18:36**
2014-15	**San Jose**	**NHL**	**82**	**27**	**40**	**67**	**12**	**6**	**2**	**4**	**263**	**10.3**	**–6**	**990**	**48.2**	**19:04**	....	....	....	....	....	....	....	....	....
	NHL Totals		**379**	**139**	**149**	**288**	**99**	**39**	**6**	**29**	**1187**	**11.7**		**4370**	**50.9**	**17:59**	**56**	**18**	**18**	**36**	**13**	**6**	**0**	**4**	**17:25**

AHL All-Rookie Team (2010) • NHL All-Rookie Team (2011)

Played in NHL All-Star Game (2012)

Signed as a free agent by **Geneve** (Swiss), September 18, 2012.

COUTURIER, Sean
(koo-TOO-ree-ay, SHAWN) **PHI**

Center. Shoots left. 6'3", 211 lbs. Born, Phoenix, AZ, December 7, 1992. Philadelphia's 1st choice, 8th overall, in 2011 Entry Draft.

Season	Club	League	GP	G	A	Pts	PIM	PP	SH	GW	S	S%	+/-	TF	F%	Min	GP	G	A	Pts	PIM	PP	SH	GW	Min
2007-08	Notre Dame	SMHL	40	19	37	56	32	....	....	....	....	....	....	....	....	....	10	3	8	11	10	....	....	....	....
2008-09	Drummondville	QMJHL	58	9	22	31	14	....	....	....	....	....	....	....	....	....	19	1	7	8	8	....	....	....	....
2009-10	Drummondville	QMJHL	68	41	55	*96	47	....	....	....	....	....	....	....	....	....	14	10	8	18	18	....	....	....	....
2010-11	Drummondville	QMJHL	58	36	60	96	36	....	....	....	....	....	....	....	....	....	10	6	5	11	14	....	....	....	....
2011-12	**Philadelphia**	**NHL**	**77**	**13**	**14**	**27**	**14**	**0**	**2**	**4**	**116**	**11.2**	**18**	**804**	**47.0**	**14:08**	**11**	**3**	**1**	**4**	**2**	**0**	**0**	**0**	**14:30**
2012-13	Adirondack	AHL	31	10	18	28	16	....	....	....	....	....	....	....	....	....	....	....	....	....	....	....	....	....	....
	Philadelphia	**NHL**	**46**	**4**	**11**	**15**	**10**	**0**	**0**	**0**	**75**	**5.3**	**–8**	**553**	**43.9**	**15:53**	....	....	....	....	....	....	....	....	....
2013-14	**Philadelphia**	**NHL**	**82**	**13**	**26**	**39**	**45**	**0**	**1**	**2**	**165**	**7.9**	**1**	**1353**	**47.8**	**19:05**	**7**	**0**	**0**	**0**	**6**	**0**	**0**	**0**	**19:35**
2014-15	**Philadelphia**	**NHL**	**82**	**15**	**22**	**37**	**28**	**1**	**1**	**0**	**148**	**10.1**	**4**	**1330**	**48.4**	**18:23**	....	....	....	....	....	....	....	....	....
	NHL Totals		**287**	**45**	**73**	**118**	**97**	**1**	**4**	**6**	**504**	**8.9**		**4040**	**47.3**	**17:03**	**18**	**3**	**1**	**4**	**8**	**0**	**0**	**0**	**16:29**

QMJHL Second All-Star Team (2010) • QMJHL First All-Star Team (2011) • QMJHL Player of the Year (2011)

COWEN, Jared
(KOW-ehn, JAIR-ehd) **OTT**

Defense. Shoots left. 6'5", 235 lbs. Born, Saskatoon, SK, January 25, 1991. Ottawa's 1st choice, 9th overall, in 2009 Entry Draft.

Season	Club	League	GP	G	A	Pts	PIM	PP	SH	GW	S	S%	+/-	TF	F%	Min	GP	G	A	Pts	PIM	PP	SH	GW	Min
2006-07	Sask. Contacts	SMHL	41	6	22	28	103	....	....	....	....	....	....	....	....	....	....	....	....	....	....	....	....	....	....
	Spokane Chiefs	WHL	6	0	2	2	2	....	....	....	....	....	....	....	....	....	6	0	1	1	6	....	....	....	....
2007-08	Spokane Chiefs	WHL	68	4	14	18	62	....	....	....	....	....	....	....	....	....	21	1	3	4	17	....	....	....	....
2008-09	Spokane Chiefs	WHL	48	7	14	21	45	....	....	....	....	....	....	....	....	....	....	....	....	....	....	....	....	....	....
2009-10	Spokane Chiefs	WHL	59	8	22	30	74	....	....	....	....	....	....	....	....	....	7	1	1	2	8	....	....	....	....
	Ottawa	**NHL**	**1**	**0**	**0**	**0**	**2**	**0**	**0**	**0**	**0**	**0.0**	**0**	**0**	**0.0**	**6:46**	....	....	....	....	....	....	....	....	....
2010-11	Spokane Chiefs	WHL	58	18	30	48	91	....	....	....	....	....	....	....	....	....	17	2	12	14	16	....	....	....	....
	Binghamton	AHL	....	....	....	....	....	....	....	....	....	....	....	....	....	....	10	0	4	4	0	....	....	....	....
2011-12	**Ottawa**	**NHL**	**82**	**5**	**12**	**17**	**56**	**0**	**0**	**1**	**58**	**8.6**	**–4**	**0**	**0.0**	**18:54**	**7**	**0**	**1**	**1**	**4**	**0**	**0**	**0**	**17:02**
2012-13	Binghamton	AHL	3	0	3	3	2	....	....	....	....	....	....	....	....	....	....	....	....	....	....	....	....	....	....
	Ottawa	**NHL**	**7**	**1**	**0**	**1**	**10**	**0**	**0**	**0**	**8**	**12.5**	**1**	**0**	**0.0**	**20:17**	**10**	**0**	**3**	**3**	**21**	**0**	**0**	**0**	**18:34**
2013-14	**Ottawa**	**NHL**	**68**	**6**	**9**	**15**	**45**	**0**	**0**	**2**	**68**	**8.8**	**0**	**0**	**0.0**	**20:31**	....	....	....	....	....	....	....	....	....
2014-15	**Ottawa**	**NHL**	**54**	**3**	**6**	**9**	**45**	**0**	**0**	**1**	**47**	**6.4**	**–11**	**0**	**0.0**	**18:09**	....	....	....	....	....	....	....	....	....
	NHL Totals		**212**	**15**	**27**	**42**	**158**	**0**	**0**	**4**	**181**	**8.3**		**0**	**0.0**	**19:13**	**17**	**0**	**4**	**4**	**25**	**0**	**0**	**0**	**17:56**

WHL West Second All-Star Team (2010) • WHL West First All-Star Team (2011)

• Missed majority of 2012-13 due to hip injury vs. Albany (AHL), October 6, 2012.

COYLE, Charlie
(KOYL, CHAR-lee) **MIN**

Center/Right wing. Shoots right. 6'3", 221 lbs. Born, E. Weymouth, MA, March 2, 1992. San Jose's 1st choice, 28th overall, in 2010 Entry Draft.

Season	Club	League	GP	G	A	Pts	PIM	PP	SH	GW	S	S%	+/-	TF	F%	Min	GP	G	A	Pts	PIM	PP	SH	GW	Min
2007-08	Thayer Academy	High-MA	....	14	23	37	....	....	....	....	....	....	....	....	....	....	....	....	....	....	....	....	....	....	....
2008-09	Thayer Academy	High-MA	26	20	28	48	4	....	....	....	....	....	....	....	....	....	....	....	....	....	....	....	....	....	....
2009-10	South Shore	EJHL	42	21	42	63	50	....	....	....	....	....	....	....	....	....	4	2	1	3	0	....	....	....	....
	USNTDP	U-18	4	1	0	1	2	....	....	....	....	....	....	....	....	....	....	....	....	....	....	....	....	....	....
2010-11	Boston University	H-East	37	7	19	26	34	....	....	....	....	....	....	....	....	....	....	....	....	....	....	....	....	....	....
2011-12	Boston University	H-East	16	3	11	14	20	....	....	....	....	....	....	....	....	....	....	....	....	....	....	....	....	....	....
	Saint John	QMJHL	23	15	23	38	8	....	....	....	....	....	....	....	....	....	17	15	19	34	8	....	....	....	....
2012-13	Houston Aeros	AHL	47	14	11	25	22	....	....	....	....	....	....	....	....	....	....	....	....	....	....	....	....	....	....
	Minnesota	**NHL**	**37**	**8**	**6**	**14**	**28**	**1**	**0**	**2**	**50**	**16.0**	**3**	**26**	**34.6**	**15:04**	**5**	**0**	**2**	**2**	**2**	**0**	**0**	**0**	**18:10**
2013-14	**Minnesota**	**NHL**	**70**	**12**	**18**	**30**	**33**	**2**	**0**	**2**	**135**	**8.9**	**–7**	**458**	**41.9**	**17:05**	**13**	**3**	**4**	**7**	**6**	**1**	**0**	**1**	**17:50**
2014-15	**Minnesota**	**NHL**	**82**	**11**	**24**	**35**	**39**	**1**	**0**	**4**	**120**	**9.2**	**13**	**718**	**46.5**	**14:33**	**10**	**1**	**1**	**2**	**0**	**0**	**0**	**0**	**14:22**
	NHL Totals		**189**	**31**	**48**	**79**	**100**	**4**	**0**	**8**	**305**	**10.2**		**1202**	**44.5**	**15:36**	**28**	**4**	**7**	**11**	**8**	**1**	**0**	**1**	**16:39**

Hockey East All-Rookie Team (2011) • Hockey East Rookie of the Year (2011)

Traded to **Minnesota** by **San Jose** with Devin Setoguchi and San Jose's 1st round choice (Zack Phillips) in 2011 Entry Draft for Brent Burns and Minnesota's 2nd round choice (later traded to Tampa Bay – later traded to Nashville – Nashville selected Pontius Aberg) in 2012 Entry Draft, June 24, 2011.

CRABB, Joey
(KRAB, JOH-ee)

Right wing. Shoots right. 6'1", 190 lbs. Born, Anchorage, AK, April 3, 1983. NY Rangers' 7th choice, 226th overall, in 2002 Entry Draft.

Season	Club	League	GP	G	A	Pts	PIM	PP	SH	GW	S	S%	+/-	TF	F%	Min	GP	G	A	Pts	PIM	PP	SH	GW	Min
99-2000	USNTDP	NAHL	55	13	10	23	69	....	....	....	....	....	....	....	....	....	3	1	0	1	4	....	....	....	....
2000-01	USNTDP	U-18	39	10	10	20	22	....	....	....	....	....	....	....	....	....	....	....	....	....	....	....	....	....	....
	USNTDP	USHL	21	2	3	5	18	....	....	....	....	....	....	....	....	....	....	....	....	....	....	....	....	....	....
2001-02	Green Bay	USHL	61	15	27	42	94	....	....	....	....	....	....	....	....	....	7	4	8	12	21	....	....	....	....
2002-03	Colorado College	WCHA	35	4	4	8	40	....	....	....	....	....	....	....	....	....	....	....	....	....	....	....	....	....	....
2003-04	Colorado College	WCHA	39	15	12	27	20	....	....	....	....	....	....	....	....	....	....	....	....	....	....	....	....	....	....
2004-05	Colorado College	WCHA	43	16	16	32	44	....	....	....	....	....	....	....	....	....	....	....	....	....	....	....	....	....	....
2005-06	Colorado College	WCHA	42	18	25	43	45	....	....	....	....	....	....	....	....	....	....	....	....	....	....	....	....	....	....
2006-07	Chicago Wolves	AHL	63	7	15	22	25	....	....	....	....	....	....	....	....	....	6	0	0	0	0	....	....	....	....
2007-08	Chicago Wolves	AHL	72	9	26	35	78	....	....	....	....	....	....	....	....	....	24	1	4	5	20	....	....	....	....
2008-09	**Atlanta**	**NHL**	**29**	**4**	**5**	**9**	**28**	**0**	**1**	**1**	**33**	**12.1**	**–2**	**33**	**39.4**	**12:13**	....	....	....	....	....	....	....	....	....
	Chicago Wolves	AHL	42	15	14	29	62	....	....	....	....	....	....	....	....	....	....	....	....	....	....	....	....	....	....

			Regular Season														Playoffs								
Season	Club	League	GP	G	A	Pts	PIM	PP	SH	GW	S	S%	+/-	TF	F%	Min	GP	G	A	Pts	PIM	PP	SH	GW	Min
2009-10	Chicago Wolves	AHL	79	24	29	53	59	....	....	....	....	....	....	....	....	....	14	6	5	11	12	....	....	....	....
2010-11	**Toronto**	**NHL**	**48**	**3**	**12**	**15**	**24**	**0**	**1**	**2**	**51**	**5.9**	**–1**	**22**	**22.7**	**12:59**	....	....	....	....	....	....	....	....	....
	Toronto Marlies	AHL	34	11	7	18	31	....	....	....	....	....	....	....	....	....	....	....	....	....	....	....	....	....	....
2011-12	**Toronto**	**NHL**	**67**	**11**	**15**	**26**	**33**	**0**	**2**	**4**	**75**	**14.7**	**1**	**10**	**10.0**	**13:27**	....	....	....	....	....	....	....	....	....
	Toronto Marlies	AHL	9	7	8	15	7	....	....	....	....	....	....	....	....	....	....	....	....	....	....	....	....	....	....
2012-13	Alaska Aces	ECHL	35	17	21	38	56	....	....	....	....	....	....	....	....	....	....	....	....	....	....	....	....	....	....
	Hershey Bears	AHL	12	6	6	12	6	....	....	....	....	....	....	....	....	....	5	5	0	5	2	....	....	....	....
	Washington	**NHL**	**26**	**2**	**0**	**2**	**8**	**0**	**0**	**0**	**20**	**10.0**	**–1**	**34**	**20.6**	**9:25**	....	....	....	....	....	....	....	....	....
2013-14	**Florida**	**NHL**	**9**	**0**	**1**	**1**	**7**	**0**	**0**	**0**	**5**	**0.0**	**–2**	**20**	**50.0**	**14:23**	....	....	....	....	....	....	....	....	....
	San Antonio	AHL	62	15	14	29	51	....	....	....	....	....	....	....	....	....	....	....	....	....	....	....	....	....	....
2014-15	Hartford	AHL	66	12	16	28	40	....	....	....	....	....	....	....	....	....	15	6	4	10	8	....	....	....	....
	NHL Totals		**179**	**20**	**33**	**53**	**100**	**0**	**4**	**7**	**184**	**10.9**		**119**	**30.3**	**12:35**	....	....	....	....	....	....	....	....	....

Signed as a free agent by **Atlanta**, August 31, 2006. Traded to **Chicago** by **Atlanta** with Marty Reasoner, Jeremy Morin and New Jersey's 1st (previously acquired, Chicago selected Kevin Hayes) and 2nd (previously acquired, Chicago selected Justin Holl) round choices in 2010 Entry Draft for Brent Sopel, Dustin Byfuglien, Ben Eager and Akim Aliu, June 24, 2010. Signed as a free agent by **Toronto**, July 15, 2010. Signed as a free agent by **Washington**, July 2, 2012. Signed as a free agent by **Alaska** (ECHL), September 28, 2012. Signed as a free agent by **Florida**, July 5, 2013. Traded to **NY Rangers** by **Florida** for Steven Kampfer and Andrew Yogan, October 6, 2014.

CRACKNELL, Adam

(krak-NEHL, A-duhm) **ST.L.**

Right wing. Shoots right. 6'2", 210 lbs. Born, Prince Albert, SK, July 15, 1985. Calgary's 10th choice, 279th overall, in 2004 Entry Draft.

Season	Club	League	GP	G	A	Pts	PIM	PP	SH	GW	S	S%	+/-	TF	F%	Min	GP	G	A	Pts	PIM	PP	SH	GW	Min
2002-03	Kootenay Ice	WHL	67	7	4	11	37	....	....	....	....	....	....	....	....	....	11	0	0	0	2	....	....	....	....
2003-04	Kootenay Ice	WHL	72	26	35	61	63	....	....	....	....	....	....	....	....	....	4	1	1	2	2	....	....	....	....
2004-05	Kootenay Ice	WHL	72	19	29	48	65	....	....	....	....	....	....	....	....	....	16	8	8	16	6	....	....	....	....
2005-06	Kootenay Ice	WHL	72	42	51	93	85	....	....	....	....	....	....	....	....	....	6	1	4	5	6	....	....	....	....
	Omaha	AHL	6	1	2	3	2	....	....	....	....	....	....	....	....	....	....	....	....	....	....	....	....	....	....
2006-07	Las Vegas	ECHL	31	8	14	22	35	....	....	....	....	....	....	....	....	....	8	3	3	6	6	....	....	....	....
2007-08	Quad City Flames	AHL	4	1	0	1	0	....	....	....	....	....	....	....	....	....	....	....	....	....	....	....	....	....	....
	Las Vegas	ECHL	61	29	30	59	47	....	....	....	....	....	....	....	....	....	21	9	13	22	4	....	....	....	....
2008-09	Quad City Flames	AHL	79	10	16	26	36	....	....	....	....	....	....	....	....	....	....	....	....	....	....	....	....	....	....
2009-10	Peoria Rivermen	AHL	76	17	21	38	40	....	....	....	....	....	....	....	....	....	....	....	....	....	....	....	....	....	....
2010-11	**St. Louis**	**NHL**	**24**	**3**	**4**	**7**	**8**	**0**	**0**	**0**	**26**	**11.5**	**1**	**118**	**39.0**	**8:55**	....	....	....	....	....	....	....	....	....
	Peoria Rivermen	AHL	61	6	19	25	54	....	....	....	....	....	....	....	....	....	4	2	0	2	0	....	....	....	....
2011-12	**St. Louis**	**NHL**	**2**	**1**	**0**	**1**	**0**	**0**	**0**	**0**	**1**	**100.0**	**1**	**1**	**0.0**	**7:39**	....	....	....	....	....	....	....	....	....
	Peoria Rivermen	AHL	72	23	26	49	54	....	....	....	....	....	....	....	....	....	....	....	....	....	....	....	....	....	....
2012-13	Peoria Rivermen	AHL	49	17	16	33	26	....	....	....	....	....	....	....	....	....	....	....	....	....	....	....	....	....	....
	St. Louis	**NHL**	**20**	**2**	**4**	**6**	**4**	**0**	**0**	**0**	**21**	**9.5**	**3**	**25**	**24.0**	**8:37**	**5**	**0**	**0**	**0**	**0**	**0**	**0**	**0**	**7:59**
2013-14	**St. Louis**	**NHL**	**19**	**0**	**2**	**2**	**0**	**0**	**0**	**0**	**16**	**0.0**	**0**	**27**	**37.0**	**8:11**	**5**	**1**	**0**	**1**	**2**	**0**	**0**	**0**	**12:43**
	Chicago Wolves	AHL	28	12	13	25	8	....	....	....	....	....	....	....	....	....	7	3	1	4	2	....	....	....	....
2014-15	**Columbus**	**NHL**	**17**	**0**	**1**	**1**	**2**	**0**	**0**	**0**	**17**	**0.0**	**–8**	**58**	**34.5**	**9:57**	....	....	....	....	....	....	....	....	....
	Springfield	AHL	18	3	4	7	2	....	....	....	....	....	....	....	....	....	....	....	....	....	....	....	....	....	....
	Chicago Wolves	AHL	22	7	6	13	8	....	....	....	....	....	....	....	....	....	5	1	0	1	4	....	....	....	....
	NHL Totals		**82**	**6**	**11**	**17**	**14**	**0**	**0**	**0**	**81**	**7.4**		**229**	**35.8**	**8:51**	**10**	**1**	**0**	**1**	**2**	**0**	**0**	**0**	**10:21**

WHL West Second All-Star Team (2006)

Signed as a free agent by **St. Louis**, July 23, 2009. Signed as a free agent by **Los Angeles**, July 1, 2014. Claimed on waivers by **Columbus** from **Los Angeles**, October 7, 2014. Traded to **St. Louis** by **Columbus** for future considerations, February 26, 2015.

CRAIG, Ryan

(KRAIG, RIGH-uhn)

Center. Shoots left. 6'2", 221 lbs. Born, Abbotsford, BC, January 6, 1982. Tampa Bay's 10th choice, 255th overall, in 2002 Entry Draft.

Season	Club	League	GP	G	A	Pts	PIM	PP	SH	GW	S	S%	+/-	TF	F%	Min	GP	G	A	Pts	PIM	PP	SH	GW	Min
1997-98	Abbotsford	Minor-BC	80	118	120	238	110	....	....	....	....	....	....	....	....	....	....	....	....	....	....	....	....	....	....
	Brandon	WHL	1	0	0	0	0	....	....	....	....	....	....	....	....	....	....	....	....	....	....	....	....	....	....
1998-99	Brandon	WHL	54	11	12	23	46	....	....	....	....	....	....	....	....	....	5	0	0	0	4	....	....	....	....
99-2000	Brandon	WHL	65	17	19	36	40	....	....	....	....	....	....	....	....	....	....	....	....	....	....	....	....	....	....
2000-01	Brandon	WHL	70	38	33	71	49	....	....	....	....	....	....	....	....	....	6	3	0	3	7	....	....	....	....
2001-02	Brandon	WHL	52	29	35	64	52	....	....	....	....	....	....	....	....	....	19	11	10	21	13	....	....	....	....
2002-03	Brandon	WHL	60	42	32	74	69	....	....	....	....	....	....	....	....	....	17	5	8	13	29	....	....	....	....
2003-04	Hershey Bears	AHL	61	4	8	12	24	....	....	....	....	....	....	....	....	....	....	....	....	....	....	....	....	....	....
	Pensacola	ECHL	5	3	5	8	0	....	....	....	....	....	....	....	....	....	2	0	1	1	0	....	....	....	....
2004-05	Springfield	AHL	80	27	14	41	50	....	....	....	....	....	....	....	....	....	....	....	....	....	....	....	....	....	....
2005-06	**Tampa Bay**	**NHL**	**48**	**15**	**13**	**28**	**6**	**6**	**0**	**0**	**81**	**18.5**	**–4**	**95**	**46.3**	**15:21**	**5**	**0**	**0**	**0**	**10**	**0**	**0**	**0**	**12:59**
	Springfield	AHL	28	12	10	22	14	....	....	....	....	....	....	....	....	....	....	....	....	....	....	....	....	....	....
2006-07	**Tampa Bay**	**NHL**	**72**	**14**	**13**	**27**	**55**	**4**	**0**	**2**	**130**	**10.8**	**–11**	**110**	**40.0**	**15:20**	**6**	**0**	**0**	**0**	**12**	**0**	**0**	**0**	**7:02**
2007-08	**Tampa Bay**	**NHL**	**7**	**1**	**1**	**2**	**0**	**1**	**0**	**0**	**8**	**12.5**	**–1**	**1**	**100.0**	**13:04**	....	....	....	....	....	....	....	....	....
	Norfolk Admirals	AHL	2	1	2	3	2	....	....	....	....	....	....	....	....	....	....	....	....	....	....	....	....	....	....
2008-09	**Tampa Bay**	**NHL**	**54**	**2**	**4**	**6**	**60**	**0**	**0**	**0**	**64**	**3.1**	**–7**	**222**	**49.6**	**10:16**	....	....	....	....	....	....	....	....	....
2009-10	**Tampa Bay**	**NHL**	**3**	**0**	**0**	**0**	**5**	**0**	**0**	**0**	**5**	**0.0**	**0**	**1**	**0.0**	**9:47**	....	....	....	....	....	....	....	....	....
	Norfolk Admirals	AHL	73	23	22	45	64	....	....	....	....	....	....	....	....	....	....	....	....	....	....	....	....	....	....
2010-11	**Pittsburgh**	**NHL**	**6**	**0**	**0**	**0**	**22**	**0**	**0**	**0**	**7**	**0.0**	**–3**	**5**	**60.0**	**9:49**	....	....	....	....	....	....	....	....	....
	Wilkes-Barre	AHL	71	19	29	48	84	....	....	....	....	....	....	....	....	....	12	3	4	7	12	....	....	....	....
2011-12	Wilkes-Barre	AHL	68	11	19	30	70	....	....	....	....	....	....	....	....	....	12	1	3	4	2	....	....	....	....
2012-13	Springfield	AHL	75	20	27	47	71	....	....	....	....	....	....	....	....	....	8	2	2	4	7	....	....	....	....
2013-14	**Columbus**	**NHL**	**6**	**0**	**0**	**0**	**0**	**0**	**0**	**0**	**4**	**0.0**	**–3**	**0**	**0.0**	**7:01**	....	....	....	....	....	....	....	....	....
	Springfield	AHL	55	18	15	33	52	....	....	....	....	....	....	....	....	....	5	4	1	5	4	....	....	....	....
2014-15	**Columbus**	**NHL**	**2**	**0**	**0**	**0**	**0**	**0**	**0**	**0**	**2**	**0.0**	**0**	**0**	**0.0**	**7:17**	....	....	....	....	....	....	....	....	....
	Springfield	AHL	67	17	20	37	60	....	....	....	....	....	....	....	....	....	....	....	....	....	....	....	....	....	....
	NHL Totals		**198**	**32**	**31**	**63**	**148**	**11**	**0**	**2**	**301**	**10.6**		**434**	**46.5**	**13:18**	**11**	**0**	**0**	**0**	**22**	**0**	**0**	**0**	**9:44**

WHL East First All-Star Team (2003) • Canadian Major Junior Humanitarian Player of the Year (2003)

• Missed majority of 2007-08 due to back and knee injuries. Signed as a free agent by **Pittsburgh**, July 2, 2010. Signed as a free agent by **Springfield** (AHL), July 19, 2012. Signed as a free agent by **Columbus**, July 6, 2013. Signed as a free agent by **Lake Erie** (AHL), June 29, 2015.

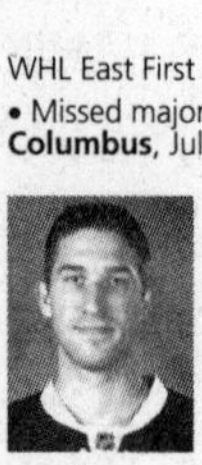

CROMBEEN, B.J.

(KRAWM-been, BEE-JAY)

Right wing. Shoots right. 6'2", 209 lbs. Born, Denver, CO, July 10, 1985. Dallas' 3rd choice, 54th overall, in 2003 Entry Draft.

Season	Club	League	GP	G	A	Pts	PIM	PP	SH	GW	S	S%	+/-	TF	F%	Min	GP	G	A	Pts	PIM	PP	SH	GW	Min
2000-01	Newmarket	ON-Jr.A	35	14	14	28	63	....	....	....	....	....	....	....	....	....	....	....	....	....	....	....	....	....	....
2001-02	Barrie Colts	OHL	60	12	13	25	118	....	....	....	....	....	....	....	....	....	20	1	1	2	31	....	....	....	....
2002-03	Barrie Colts	OHL	63	22	24	46	133	....	....	....	....	....	....	....	....	....	6	1	0	1	8	....	....	....	....
2003-04	Barrie Colts	OHL	62	21	29	50	154	....	....	....	....	....	....	....	....	....	12	5	7	12	35	....	....	....	....
2004-05	Barrie Colts	OHL	63	31	18	49	111	....	....	....	....	....	....	....	....	....	6	2	4	6	35	....	....	....	....
2005-06	Iowa Stars	AHL	52	5	7	12	97	....	....	....	....	....	....	....	....	....	5	1	0	1	9	....	....	....	....
	Idaho Steelheads	ECHL	8	5	3	8	5	....	....	....	....	....	....	....	....	....	....	....	....	....	....	....	....	....	....
2006-07	Assat Pori	Finland	55	13	9	22	152	....	....	....	....	....	....	....	....	....	....	....	....	....	....	....	....	....	....
	Idaho Steelheads	ECHL	13	7	4	11	43	....	....	....	....	....	....	....	....	....	22	5	5	10	45	....	....	....	....
2007-08	**Dallas**	**NHL**	**8**	**0**	**2**	**2**	**39**	**0**	**0**	**0**	**9**	**0.0**	**1**	**1**	**0.0**	**6:38**	**5**	**0**	**0**	**0**	**0**	**0**	**0**	**0**	**4:16**
	Iowa Stars	AHL	65	14	14	28	158	....	....	....	....	....	....	....	....	....	....	....	....	....	....	....	....	....	....
2008-09	**Dallas**	**NHL**	**15**	**1**	**4**	**5**	**26**	**0**	**0**	**0**	**12**	**8.3**	**–1**	**0**	**0.0**	**8:14**	....	....	....	....	....	....	....	....	....
	St. Louis	**NHL**	**66**	**11**	**6**	**17**	**122**	**0**	**1**	**3**	**112**	**9.8**	**–8**	**7**	**42.9**	**13:45**	**4**	**0**	**0**	**0**	**12**	**0**	**0**	**0**	**9:46**
2009-10	**St. Louis**	**NHL**	**79**	**7**	**8**	**15**	**168**	**0**	**1**	**1**	**120**	**5.8**	**–5**	**51**	**35.3**	**13:05**	....	....	....	....	....	....	....	....	....
2010-11	**St. Louis**	**NHL**	**80**	**7**	**7**	**14**	**154**	**0**	**1**	**0**	**113**	**6.2**	**–18**	**64**	**29.7**	**12:48**	....	....	....	....	....	....	....	....	....
2011-12	**St. Louis**	**NHL**	**40**	**1**	**2**	**3**	**71**	**0**	**0**	**0**	**50**	**2.0**	**–2**	**12**	**25.0**	**8:18**	**7**	**1**	**0**	**1**	**31**	**0**	**0**	**0**	**8:27**
2012-13	Orlando	ECHL	2	0	0	0	2	....	....	....	....	....	....	....	....	....	....	....	....	....	....	....	....	....	....
	Tampa Bay	**NHL**	**44**	**1**	**7**	**8**	**112**	**0**	**0**	**0**	**50**	**2.0**	**4**	**20**	**20.0**	**11:05**	....	....	....	....	....	....	....	....	....
2013-14	**Tampa Bay**	**NHL**	**55**	**3**	**7**	**10**	**79**	**0**	**0**	**1**	**60**	**5.0**	**–2**	**8**	**37.5**	**10:10**	**2**	**0**	**0**	**0**	**0**	**0**	**0**	**0**	**7:46**
2014-15	**Arizona**	**NHL**	**58**	**3**	**3**	**6**	**79**	**0**	**0**	**0**	**43**	**7.0**	**–6**	**1**	**100.0**	**8:06**	....	....	....	....	....	....	....	....	....
	NHL Totals		**445**	**34**	**46**	**80**	**850**	**0**	**3**	**5**	**569**	**6.0**		**164**	**31.1**	**11:13**	**18**	**1**	**0**	**1**	**43**	**0**	**0**	**0**	**7:30**

Signed as a free agent by **Pori** (Finland), August 2, 2006. Claimed on waivers by **St. Louis** from **Dallas**, November 18, 2008. Traded to **Tampa Bay** by **St. Louis** with St. Louis's 5th round choice (Austin Poganski) in 2014 Entry Draft for Tampa Bay's 4th round choice (later traded to Edmonton – Edmonton selected Jackson Houck) in 2013 Entry Draft and Tampa Bay's 4th round choice (Austin Poganski) in 2014 Entry Draft, July 10, 2012. Signed as a free agent by **Orlando** (ECHL), November 16, 2012. Traded to **Arizona** by **Tampa Bay** with Sam Gagner for Arizona's 6th round choice (Kristian Oldham) in 2015 Entry Draft, June 29, 2014.

CROSBY, Sidney

(KRAWZ-bee, SIHD-nee) **PIT**

Center. Shoots left. 5'11", 200 lbs. Born, Cole Harbour, NS, August 7, 1987. Pittsburgh's 1st choice, 1st overall, in 2005 Entry Draft.

			Regular Season														Playoffs								
Season	Club	League	GP	G	A	Pts	PIM	PP	SH	GW	S	S%	+/-	TF	F%	Min	GP	G	A	Pts	PIM	PP	SH	GW	Min
2001-02	Dartmouth	NSMHL	74	95	98	193	114	....	....	....	....	....	....	....	....	....	....	....	....	....	....	....	....	....	....
2002-03	Shat.-St. Mary's	High-MN	57	72	90	162	....	....	....	....	....	....	....	....	....	....	....	....	....	....	....	....	....	....	....
2003-04	Rimouski Oceanic	QMJHL	59	54	*81	*135	74	....	....	....	....	....	....	....	....	....	9	7	9	16	10	....	....	....	....
2004-05	Rimouski Oceanic	QMJHL	62	*66	*102	*168	84	....	....	....	....	....	....	....	....	....	13	*14	*17	*31	16	....	....	....	....
2005-06	Pittsburgh	NHL	81	39	63	102	110	16	0	5	278	14.0	–1	1174	45.5	20:08	....	....	....	....	....	....	....	....	....
2006-07	Pittsburgh	NHL	79	36	84	*120	60	13	0	4	250	14.4	10	1686	49.8	20:46	5	3	2	5	4	1	0	1	21:40
2007-08	Pittsburgh	NHL	53	24	48	72	39	6	0	4	173	13.9	18	1103	51.4	20:51	20	6	*21	*27	12	2	0	1	20:42
2008-09♦	Pittsburgh	NHL	77	33	70	103	76	7	0	3	238	13.9	3	1615	51.3	21:57	24	*15	16	31	14	5	0	2	20:49
2009-10	Pittsburgh	NHL	81	*51	58	109	71	13	2	6	298	17.1	15	1791	55.9	21:57	13	6	13	19	6	1	0	1	23:32
	Canada	Olympics	7	4	3	7	4	....	....	....	....	....	....	....	....	....	....	....	....	....	....	....	....	....	....
2010-11	Pittsburgh	NHL	41	32	34	66	31	10	1	3	161	19.9	20	981	55.7	21:55	....	....	....	....	....	....	....	....	....
2011-12	Pittsburgh	NHL	22	8	29	37	14	2	0	3	75	10.7	15	453	50.1	18:28	6	3	5	8	9	0	0	0	20:37
2012-13	Pittsburgh	NHL	36	15	41	56	16	3	0	1	124	12.1	26	834	54.3	21:06	14	7	8	15	8	2	0	0	23:05
2013-14	Pittsburgh	NHL	80	36	*68	*104	46	11	0	5	259	13.9	18	1887	52.5	21:58	13	1	8	9	4	0	0	1	21:19
	Canada	Olympics	6	1	2	3	0	....	....	....	....	....	....	....	....	....	....	....	....	....	....	....	....	....	....
2014-15	Pittsburgh	NHL	77	28	56	84	47	10	0	3	237	11.8	5	1597	49.9	19:58	5	2	2	4	0	0	0	0	20:09
	NHL Totals		627	302	551	853	510	91	3	37	2093	14.4		13121	51.7	21:03	100	43	75	118	57	11	0	6	21:31

QMJHL All-Rookie Team (2004) • QMJHL First All-Star Team (2004, 2005) • QMJHL Player of the Year (2004, 2005) • Canadian Major Junior First All-Star Team (2004, 2005) • Canadian Major Junior Rookie of the Year (2004) • Canadian Major Junior Player of the Year (2004, 2005) • Memorial Cup All-Star Team (2005) • Ed Chynoweth Trophy (Memorial Cup - Leading Scorer) (2005) • NHL All-Rookie Team (2006) • NHL First All-Star Team (2007, 2013, 2014) • Art Ross Trophy (2007, 2014) • Lester B. Pearson Award (2007) • Hart Memorial Trophy (2007, 2014) • NHL Second All-Star Team (2010, 2015) • Mark Messier NHL Leadership Award (2010) • Maurice "Rocket" Richard Trophy (2010) (tied with Steven Stamkos) • Ted Lindsay Award (2013, 2014)

Played in NHL All-Star Game (2007)

• Missed majority of 2010-11 and 2011-12 due to post-concussion syndrome.

CULLEN, Matt

(KUH-lehn, MAT) **PIT**

Center. Shoots left. 6'1", 200 lbs. Born, Virginia, MN, November 2, 1976. Anaheim's 2nd choice, 35th overall, in 1996 Entry Draft.

			Regular Season														Playoffs								
Season	Club	League	GP	G	A	Pts	PIM	PP	SH	GW	S	S%	+/-	TF	F%	Min	GP	G	A	Pts	PIM	PP	SH	GW	Min
1993-94	Moorhead Spuds	High-MN	STATISTICS NOT AVAILABLE																						
1994-95	Moorhead Spuds	High-MN	28	47	42	89	78	....	....	....	....	....	....	....	....	....	....	....	....	....	....	....	....	....	....
1995-96	St. Cloud State	WCHA	39	12	29	41	28	....	....	....	....	....	....	....	....	....	....	....	....	....	....	....	....	....	....
1996-97	St. Cloud State	WCHA	36	15	30	45	70	....	....	....	....	....	....	....	....	....	....	....	....	....	....	....	....	....	....
	Baltimore Bandits	AHL	6	3	3	6	7	....	....	....	....	....	....	....	....	....	3	0	2	2	0	....	....	....	....
1997-98	Anaheim	NHL	61	6	21	27	23	2	0	0	75	8.0	–4	....	....	....	....	....	....	....	....	....	....	....	....
	Cincinnati	AHL	18	15	12	27	2	....	....	....	....	....	....	....	....	....	....	....	....	....	....	....	....	....	....
1998-99	Anaheim	NHL	75	11	14	25	47	5	1	1	112	9.8	–12	1047	47.7	15:31	4	0	0	0	0	0	0	0	15:30
	Cincinnati	AHL	3	1	2	3	8	....	....	....	....	....	....	....	....	....	....	....	....	....	....	....	....	....	....
99-2000	Anaheim	NHL	80	13	26	39	24	1	0	1	137	9.5	5	1247	44.6	16:54	....	....	....	....	....	....	....	....	....
2000-01	Anaheim	NHL	82	10	30	40	38	4	0	1	159	6.3	–23	1478	48.0	18:15	....	....	....	....	....	....	....	....	....
2001-02	Anaheim	NHL	79	18	30	48	24	3	1	4	164	11.0	–1	1283	51.4	17:01	....	....	....	....	....	....	....	....	....
2002-03	Anaheim	NHL	50	7	14	21	12	1	0	1	77	9.1	–4	271	50.6	14:18	....	....	....	....	....	....	....	....	....
	Florida	NHL	30	6	6	12	22	2	1	1	54	11.1	–4	423	47.3	14:43	....	....	....	....	....	....	....	....	....
2003-04	Florida	NHL	56	6	13	19	24	1	0	2	75	8.0	–2	735	50.6	14:12	....	....	....	....	....	....	....	....	....
2004-05	SG Cortina	Italy	36	*27	33	60	64	....	....	....	....	....	....	....	....	....	18	8	14	22	32	....	....	....	....
2005-06♦	Carolina	NHL	78	25	24	49	40	8	0	5	214	11.7	4	583	52.1	16:26	25	4	14	18	12	2	0	1	15:37
2006-07	NY Rangers	NHL	80	16	25	41	52	2	3	2	217	7.4	0	1134	54.6	17:10	10	1	3	4	6	0	0	1	16:55
2007-08	Carolina	NHL	59	13	36	49	32	8	0	1	137	9.5	2	649	56.1	16:52	....	....	....	....	....	....	....	....	....
2008-09	Carolina	NHL	69	22	21	43	20	4	2	2	139	15.8	11	884	51.7	16:48	18	3	3	6	14	0	1	0	16:41
2009-10	Carolina	NHL	60	12	28	40	26	1	2	1	137	8.8	0	898	49.1	19:02	....	....	....	....	....	....	....	....	....
	Ottawa	NHL	21	4	4	8	8	1	0	1	58	6.9	–7	223	58.7	17:59	6	3	5	8	0	2	0	0	23:14
2010-11	Minnesota	NHL	78	12	27	39	34	5	4	2	150	8.0	–14	843	56.1	18:02	....	....	....	....	....	....	....	....	....
2011-12	Minnesota	NHL	73	14	21	35	24	4	0	0	164	8.5	–10	1178	53.2	18:56	....	....	....	....	....	....	....	....	....
2012-13	Minnesota	NHL	42	7	20	27	10	0	0	0	79	8.9	9	448	54.7	15:53	5	0	3	3	2	0	0	0	19:08
2013-14	Nashville	NHL	77	10	29	39	32	1	0	2	134	7.5	4	772	56.7	15:30	....	....	....	....	....	....	....	....	....
2014-15	Nashville	NHL	62	7	18	25	16	0	0	1	90	7.8	8	287	54.0	13:01	6	1	1	2	4	0	0	0	17:19
	NHL Totals		1212	219	407	626	508	53	14	28	2372	9.2		14383	51.4	16:35	74	12	29	41	38	4	1	2	17:03

WCHA Second All-Star Team (1997)

Traded to **Florida** by **Anaheim** with Pavel Trnka and Anaheim's 4th round choice (James Pemberton) in 2003 Entry Draft for Sandis Ozolinsh and Lance Ward, January 30, 2003. Signed as a free agent by **Carolina**, August 5, 2004. Signed as a free agent by **Cortina** (Italy), September 18, 2004. Signed as a free agent by **NY Rangers**, July 1, 2006. Traded to **Carolina** by **NY Rangers** for Andrew Hutchinson, Joe Barnes and Carolina's 3rd round choice (Evgeny Grachev) in 2008 Entry Draft, July 17, 2007. Traded to **Ottawa** by **Carolina** for Alexandre Picard and Ottawa's 2nd round choice (later traded to Edmonton – Edmonton selected Martin Marincin) in 2010 Entry Draft, February 12, 2010. Signed as a free agent by **Minnesota**, July 1, 2010. Signed as a free agent by **Nashville**, July 5, 2013. Signed as a free agent by **Pittsburgh**, August 6, 2015.

CUMISKEY, Kyle

(kuh-MIHS-kee, KIGHL)

Defense. Shoots left. 5'11", 187 lbs. Born, Abbotsford, BC, December 2, 1986. Colorado's 9th choice, 222nd overall, in 2005 Entry Draft.

			Regular Season														Playoffs								
Season	Club	League	GP	G	A	Pts	PIM	PP	SH	GW	S	S%	+/-	TF	F%	Min	GP	G	A	Pts	PIM	PP	SH	GW	Min
2002-03	Penticton	BCHL	59	10	11	21	36	....	....	....	....	....	....	....	....	....	....	....	....	....	....	....	....	....	....
2003-04	Kelowna Rockets	WHL	54	2	7	9	20	....	....	....	....	....	....	....	....	....	17	0	0	0	0	....	....	....	....
2004-05	Kelowna Rockets	WHL	72	4	36	40	47	....	....	....	....	....	....	....	....	....	24	0	13	13	12	....	....	....	....
2005-06	Kelowna Rockets	WHL	51	6	24	30	52	....	....	....	....	....	....	....	....	....	12	0	6	6	8	....	....	....	....
2006-07	Colorado	NHL	9	1	1	2	2	0	0	0	8	12.5	0	0	0.0	13:28	....	....	....	....	....	....	....	....	....
	Albany River Rats	AHL	63	7	26	33	32	....	....	....	....	....	....	....	....	....	5	0	2	2	6	....	....	....	....
2007-08	Colorado	NHL	38	0	5	5	16	0	0	0	19	0.0	–3	0	0.0	12:08	....	....	....	....	....	....	....	....	....
	Lake Erie	AHL	5	1	1	2	4	....	....	....	....	....	....	....	....	....	....	....	....	....	....	....	....	....	....
2008-09	Colorado	NHL	6	0	0	0	0	0	0	0	2	0.0	–2	0	0.0	8:32	....	....	....	....	....	....	....	....	....
	Lake Erie	AHL	28	5	12	17	16	....	....	....	....	....	....	....	....	....	....	....	....	....	....	....	....	....	....
2009-10	Colorado	NHL	61	7	13	20	20	2	0	1	74	9.5	0	0	0.0	19:48	6	1	1	2	2	0	0	0	22:37
2010-11	Colorado	NHL	18	1	7	8	10	0	0	0	21	4.8	–3	0	0.0	19:40	....	....	....	....	....	....	....	....	....
2011-12	Syracuse Crunch	AHL	57	6	23	29	44	....	....	....	....	....	....	....	....	....	4	0	1	1	0	....	....	....	....
2012-13	MODO	Sweden	46	7	25	32	30	....	....	....	....	....	....	....	....	....	5	1	4	5	0	....	....	....	....
2013-14	MODO	Sweden	45	4	24	28	16	....	....	....	....	....	....	....	....	....	2	0	0	0	0	....	....	....	....
2014-15	Chicago	NHL	7	0	0	0	0	0	0	0	5	0.0	–1	0	0.0	13:18	9	0	0	0	0	0	0	0	9:28
	Rockford IceHogs	AHL	54	2	18	20	10	....	....	....	....	....	....	....	....	....	....	....	....	....	....	....	....	....	....
	NHL Totals		139	9	26	35	48	2	0	1	129	7.0		0	0.0	16:28	15	1	1	2	2	0	0	0	14:44

• Missed majority of 2010-11 due to post-concussion syndrome. Traded to **Anaheim** by **Colorado** for Jake Newton and Anaheim's 7th round choice (later traded to San Jose – San Jose selected Emil Galimov) in 2013 Entry Draft, October 8, 2011. Signed as a free agent by **MODO** (Sweden), July 9, 2012. Signed as a free agent by **Chicago**, July 2, 2014.

CUNDARI, Mark

(kuhn-DAHR-ee, MAHRK) **S.J.**

Defense. Shoots left. 5'9", 195 lbs. Born, Woodbridge, ON, April 23, 1990.

			Regular Season														Playoffs								
Season	Club	League	GP	G	A	Pts	PIM	PP	SH	GW	S	S%	+/-	TF	F%	Min	GP	G	A	Pts	PIM	PP	SH	GW	Min
2005-06	Vaughan Kings	GTHL	STATISTICS NOT AVAILABLE																						
	Vaughan Vipers	ON-Jr.A	2	0	0	0	0	....	....	....	....	....	....	....	....	....	....	....	....	....	....	....	....	....	....
2006-07	Windsor Spitfires	OHL	62	6	16	22	130	....	....	....	....	....	....	....	....	....	....	....	....	....	....	....	....	....	....
2007-08	Windsor Spitfires	OHL	63	6	17	23	141	....	....	....	....	....	....	....	....	....	3	0	0	0	10	....	....	....	....
2008-09	Windsor Spitfires	OHL	60	10	22	32	143	....	....	....	....	....	....	....	....	....	20	1	8	9	38	....	....	....	....
2009-10	Windsor Spitfires	OHL	63	8	46	54	139	....	....	....	....	....	....	....	....	....	19	3	15	18	42	....	....	....	....
2010-11	Peoria Rivermen	AHL	69	10	20	30	106	....	....	....	....	....	....	....	....	....	3	0	1	1	4	....	....	....	....
2011-12	Peoria Rivermen	AHL	48	3	12	15	62	....	....	....	....	....	....	....	....	....	....	....	....	....	....	....	....	....	....
2012-13	Peoria Rivermen	AHL	56	7	18	25	80	....	....	....	....	....	....	....	....	....	....	....	....	....	....	....	....	....	....
	Calgary	NHL	4	1	2	3	2	1	0	0	8	12.5	–2	0	0.0	19:46	....	....	....	....	....	....	....	....	....
	Abbotsford Heat	AHL	2	0	3	3	13	....	....	....	....	....	....	....	....	....	....	....	....	....	....	....	....	....	....

			Regular Season														Playoffs								
Season	Club	League	GP	G	A	Pts	PIM	PP	SH	GW	S	S%	+/-	TF	F%	Min	GP	G	A	Pts	PIM	PP	SH	GW	Min
2013-14	Calgary	NHL	4	0	0	0	0	0	0	0	6	0.0	–4	0	0.0	10:47									
	Abbotsford Heat	AHL	32	4	6	10	45																		
	Chicago Wolves	AHL	24	5	8	13	28										9	1	2	3	10				
2014-15	Adirondack	AHL	50	7	22	29	64																		
	NHL Totals		8	1	2	3	2	1	0	0	14	7.1		0	0.0	15:17									

Signed as a free agent by **St. Louis**, September 24, 2008. Traded to **Calgary** by **St. Louis** with Reto Berra and St. Louis' 1st round choice (Emile Poirier) in 2013 Entry Draft for Jay Bouwmeester, April 1, 2013. Signed as a free agent by **San Jose**, July 2, 2015.

CUNNINGHAM, Craig

(KUN-ihng-ham, KRAYG) **ARI**

Left wing. Shoots right. 5'10", 184 lbs. Born, Trail, BC, September 13, 1990. Boston's 4th choice, 97th overall, in 2010 Entry Draft.

Season	Club	League	GP	G	A	Pts	PIM	PP	SH	GW	S	S%	+/-	TF	F%	Min	GP	G	A	Pts	PIM	PP	SH	GW	Min
2005-06	Beaver Valley	KIJHL	47	19	25	44	22										16	4	5	9	29				
2006-07	Vancouver Giants	WHL	48	0	5	5	38										15	0	1	1	15				
2007-08	Vancouver Giants	WHL	67	11	14	25	72										10	1	2	3	6				
2008-09	Vancouver Giants	WHL	72	28	22	50	62										17	5	9	14	12				
2009-10	Vancouver Giants	WHL	72	37	60	97	44										16	12	12	24	12				
2010-11	Vancouver Giants	WHL	36	10	35	45	31																		
	Portland	WHL	35	17	25	42	25										21	7	14	21	12				
2011-12	Providence Bruins	AHL	76	20	16	36	20																		
2012-13	Providence Bruins	AHL	75	25	21	46	26										12	3	5	8	4				
2013-14	Boston	NHL	2	0	0	0	0	0	0	0	4	0.0	0	7	42.9	9:29									
	Providence Bruins	AHL	75	25	22	47	40										12	3	4	7	6				
2014-15	Boston	NHL	32	2	1	3	2	0	1	0	31	6.5	–4	94	50.0	10:07									
	Providence Bruins	AHL	21	5	10	15	8																		
	Arizona	NHL	19	1	3	4	2	0	0	0	23	4.3	–3	42	52.4	11:05									
	NHL Totals		53	3	4	7	4	0	1	0	58	5.2		143	50.3	10:26									

WHL West First All-Star Team (2010)

Claimed on waivers by **Arizona** from **Boston**, March 2, 2015.

CZUCZMAN, Kevin

(CHUHRCH-muhn, KEH-vihn) **NYI**

Defense. Shoots left. 6'2", 209 lbs. Born, Port Elgin, ON, January 9, 1991.

Season	Club	League	GP	G	A	Pts	PIM	PP	SH	GW	S	S%	+/-	TF	F%	Min	GP	G	A	Pts	PIM	PP	SH	GW	Min
2006-07	Grey Bruce	Minor-ON	59	2	19	21	50										4	1	0	1	0				
2007-08	Grey Bruce	Minor-ON	54	6	20	26	76										4	1	2	3	6				
	Owen Sound	ON-Jr.B	2	0	0	0	0																		
2008-09	Listowel Cyclones	ON-Jr.B	2	0	0	0	0																		
	Walkerton Hawks	ON-Jr.C	35	3	20	23	49										10	2	3	5	4				
2009-10	Waterloo Siskins	ON-Jr.B	51	2	23	25	84										10	1	1	2	15				
2010-11	Newmarket	ON-Jr.A	47	4	19	23	40										10	1	3	4	13				
2011-12	Lake Superior	CCHA	40	2	11	13	26																		
2012-13	Lake Superior	CCHA	38	2	9	11	42																		
2013-14	Lake Superior	WCHA	36	10	11	21	73																		
	NY Islanders	NHL	13	0	2	2	14	0	0	0	24	0.0	–5	1	100.0	19:33									
2014-15	Bridgeport	AHL	50	1	6	7	56																		
	Florida Everblades	ECHL	9	1	0	1	4										12	0	0	0	6				
	NHL Totals		13	0	2	2	14	0	0	0	24	0.0		1	100.0	19:33									

WCHA Second All-Star Team (2014)

Signed as a free agent by **NY Islanders**, March 11, 2014.

DA COSTA, Stephane

(DA-KAWS-tuh, steh-FAN) **OTT**

Center. Shoots right. 5'11", 180 lbs. Born, Paris, France, July 11, 1989.

Season	Club	League	GP	G	A	Pts	PIM	PP	SH	GW	S	S%	+/-	TF	F%	Min	GP	G	A	Pts	PIM	PP	SH	GW	Min
2006-07	Texas Tornado	NAHL	50	23	17	40	31										10	4	3	7	6				
2007-08	Sioux City	USHL	51	12	25	37	22										4	1	2	3	8				
2008-09	Sioux City	USHL	48	31	36	67	23																		
2009-10	Merrimack	H-East	34	16	29	45	41																		
2010-11	Merrimack	H-East	33	14	31	45	42																		
	Ottawa	NHL	4	0	0	0	0	0	0	0	9	0.0	–1	21	28.6	11:25									
2011-12	Ottawa	NHL	22	3	2	5	8	0	0	0	31	9.7	–9	177	36.7	12:10									
	Binghamton	AHL	46	13	23	36	12																		
2012-13	Binghamton	AHL	57	13	25	38	26										3	0	1	1	0				
	Ottawa	NHL	9	1	1	2	0	0	0	0	15	6.7	–3	64	60.9	11:52									
2013-14	Ottawa	NHL	12	3	1	4	2	1	0	0	20	15.0	2	79	40.5	10:25									
	Binghamton	AHL	56	18	40	58	32										4	2	2	4	4				
2014-15	CSKA Moscow	KHL	46	30	32	62	12										11	4	4	8	8				
	NHL Totals		47	7	4	11	10	1	0	0	75	9.3		341	41.6	11:36									

Hockey East All-Rookie Team (2010) • Hockey East Second All-Star Team (2010, 2011) • Hockey East Rookie of the Year (2010) • NCAA Rookie of the Year (2010) • NCAA East Second All-American Team (2011)

Signed as a free agent by **Ottawa**. March 31, 2011. Signed as a free agent by **CSKA Moscw** (KHL), July 12, 2014.

D'AGOSTINI, Matt

(DAG-uh-stee-nee, MAT)

Right wing. Shoots right. 6', 198 lbs. Born, Sault Ste. Marie, ON, October 23, 1986. Montreal's 5th choice, 190th overall, in 2005 Entry Draft.

Season	Club	League	GP	G	A	Pts	PIM	PP	SH	GW	S	S%	+/-	TF	F%	Min	GP	G	A	Pts	PIM	PP	SH	GW	Min
2003-04	Soo North Stars	GNML	36	36	23	59	41																		
2004-05	Guelph Storm	OHL	59	24	22	46	29										4	0	2	2	8				
2005-06	Guelph Storm	OHL	66	25	54	79	81										15	8	20	28	16				
2006-07	Hamilton	AHL	63	21	28	49	33										22	4	9	13	18				
2007-08	Montreal	NHL	1	0	0	0	2	0	0	0	0	0.0	0	0	0.0	8:49									
	Hamilton	AHL	76	23	30	53	38																		
2008-09	Montreal	NHL	53	12	9	21	16	3	0	1	116	10.3	–17	9	33.3	13:25	3	0	0	0	0	0	0	0	11:49
	Hamilton	AHL	20	14	11	25	16																		
2009-10	Montreal	NHL	40	2	2	4	26	0	0	0	48	4.2	–12	3	66.7	9:53									
	Hamilton	AHL	3	0	1	1	2																		
	St. Louis	NHL	7	0	0	0	2	0	0	0	6	0.0	–3	7	71.4	9:13									
2010-11	St. Louis	NHL	82	21	25	46	40	6	0	5	163	12.9	8	55	38.2	14:46									
2011-12	St. Louis	NHL	55	9	9	18	27	3	0	3	101	8.9	12	29	27.6	14:01	4	1	0	1	4	0	0	0	12:16
2012-13	Riessersee	German-2	10	2	6	8	6																		
	St. Louis	NHL	16	1	1	2	2	0	0	0	19	5.3	–4	14	28.6	11:52									
	New Jersey	NHL	13	2	2	4	6	0	0	0	14	14.3	–1	4	25.0	12:51									
2013-14	Pittsburgh	NHL	8	0	1	1	4	0	0	0	11	0.0	–1	0	0.0	11:20									
	Buffalo	NHL	49	5	6	11	22	2	0	2	99	5.1	–14	15	33.3	15:26									
2014-15	Geneve	Swiss	40	14	23	37	30										12	*7	3	10	8				
	NHL Totals		324	52	55	107	147	14	0	11	577	9.0		136	36.0	13:28	7	1	0	1	4	0	0	0	12:04

Traded to **St. Louis** by **Montreal** for Aaron Palushaj, March 2, 2010. Signed as a free agent by **Riessersee** (German-2), October 8, 2012. Traded to **New Jersey** by **St. Louis** with St. Louis' 7th round choice (later traded to Florida – Florida selected Ryan Bednard) in 2015 Entry Draft for New Jersey's 5th round choice (Niko Mikkola) in 2015 Entry Draft, March 22, 2013. Signed as a free agent by **Pittsburgh**, July 10, 2013. Claimed on waivers by **Buffalo** from **Pittsburgh**, November 27, 2013. Signed as a free agent by **Geneve** (Swiss), July 18, 2014.

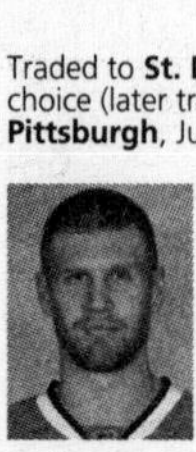

DAHLBECK, Klas

(DAHL-behk, KLAHS) **ARI**

Defense. Shoots left. 6'2", 207 lbs. Born, Katrineholm, Sweden, July 6, 1991. Chicago's 6th choice, 79th overall, in 2011 Entry Draft.

Season	Club	League	GP	G	A	Pts	PIM	PP	SH	GW	S	S%	+/-	TF	F%	Min	GP	G	A	Pts	PIM	PP	SH	GW	Min
2007-08	Vaxjo U18	Swe-U18	16	7	10	17	4																		
	Vaxjo Jr.	Swe-Jr.	22	3	4	7	14																		
2008-09	Vaxjo U18	Swe-U18	14	4	5	9	6																		
	Vaxjo Jr.	Swe-Jr.	15	4	6	10	8																		
2009-10	Linkopings HC Jr.	Swe-Jr.	39	4	7	11	8										6	1	1	2	4				
	Mjolby HC	Sweden-3	2	0	0	0	0																		
	Linkopings HC	Sweden	6	0	0	0	0										3	0	0	0	0				

			Regular Season														Playoffs								
Season	Club	League	GP	G	A	Pts	PIM	PP	SH	GW	S	S%	+/-	TF	F%	Min	GP	G	A	Pts	PIM	PP	SH	GW	Min
2010-11	Linkopings HC	Sweden	47	0	8	8	12	....	....	....	....	....	....	....	....	....	7	0	0	0	0	....	....	....	....
2011-12	Linkopings HC	Sweden	55	2	2	4	20	....	....	....	....	....	....	....	....	....	....	....	....	....	....	....	....	....	....
2012-13	Rockford IceHogs	AHL	70	1	5	6	29	....	....	....	....	....	....	....	....	....	....	....	....	....	....	....	....	....	....
2013-14	Rockford IceHogs	AHL	75	10	25	35	49	....	....	....	....	....	....	....	....	....	....	....	....	....	....	....	....	....	....
2014-15	**Chicago**	**NHL**	**4**	**1**	**0**	**1**	**2**	**0**	**0**	**0**	**4**	**25.0**	**–1**	**0**	**0.0**	**10:24**	....	....	....	....	....	....	....	....	....
	Rockford IceHogs	AHL	49	4	6	10	35	....	....	....	....	....	....	....	....	....	....	....	....	....	....	....	....	....	....
	Arizona	**NHL**	**19**	**0**	**3**	**3**	**6**	**0**	**0**	**0**	**16**	**0.0**	**–7**	**0**	**0.0**	**19:11**	....	....	....	....	....	....	....	....	....
	Portland Pirates	AHL	3	0	1	1	0	....	....	....	....	....	....	....	....	....	5	0	1	1	4	....	....	....	....
	NHL Totals		**23**	**1**	**3**	**4**	**8**	**0**	**0**	**0**	**20**	**5.0**		**0**	**0.0**	**17:40**	....	....	....	....	....	....	....	....	....

Traded to **Arizona** by **Chicago** with Chicago's 1st round choice (Nick Merkley) in 2015 Entry Draft for Antoine Vermette, February 28, 2015.

DALEY, Trevor

(DAY-lee, TREH-vuhr) **CHI**

Defense. Shoots left. 5'11", 195 lbs. Born, Toronto, ON, October 9, 1983. Dallas' 5th choice, 43rd overall, in 2002 Entry Draft.

Season	Club	League	GP	G	A	Pts	PIM	PP	SH	GW	S	S%	+/-	TF	F%	Min	GP	G	A	Pts	PIM	PP	SH	GW	Min
1998-99	Vaughan Vipers	ON-Jr.A	44	10	36	46	79	....	....	....	....	....	....	....	....	....	....	....	....	....	....	....	....	....	....
99-2000	Sault Ste. Marie	OHL	54	16	30	46	77	....	....	....	....	....	....	....	....	....	15	3	7	10	12	....	....	....	....
2000-01	Sault Ste. Marie	OHL	58	14	27	41	105	....	....	....	....	....	....	....	....	....	....	....	....	....	....	....	....	....	....
2001-02	Sault Ste. Marie	OHL	47	9	39	48	38	....	....	....	....	....	....	....	....	....	6	2	2	4	4	....	....	....	....
2002-03	Sault Ste. Marie	OHL	57	20	33	53	128	....	....	....	....	....	....	....	....	....	1	0	0	0	2	....	....	....	....
2003-04	**Dallas**	**NHL**	**27**	**1**	**5**	**6**	**14**	**1**	**0**	**0**	**34**	**2.9**	**–6**	**0**	**0.0**	**16:02**	**1**	**0**	**0**	**0**	**0**	**0**	**0**	**0**	**10:21**
	Utah Grizzlies	AHL	40	8	6	14	76	....	....	....	....	....	....	....	....	....	....	....	....	....	....	....	....	....	....
2004-05	Hamilton	AHL	78	7	27	34	109	....	....	....	....	....	....	....	....	....	4	0	1	1	2	....	....	....	....
2005-06	**Dallas**	**NHL**	**81**	**3**	**11**	**14**	**87**	**0**	**0**	**1**	**91**	**3.3**	**–2**	**0**	**0.0**	**18:40**	**3**	**0**	**0**	**0**	**0**	**0**	**0**	**0**	**11:30**
2006-07	**Dallas**	**NHL**	**74**	**4**	**8**	**12**	**63**	**0**	**0**	**1**	**68**	**5.9**	**2**	**0**	**0.0**	**19:23**	**7**	**1**	**0**	**1**	**4**	**0**	**0**	**0**	**22:26**
2007-08	**Dallas**	**NHL**	**82**	**5**	**19**	**24**	**85**	**0**	**0**	**1**	**87**	**5.7**	**–1**	**1**	**100.0**	**19:48**	**18**	**1**	**0**	**1**	**20**	**0**	**0**	**0**	**18:52**
2008-09	**Dallas**	**NHL**	**75**	**7**	**18**	**25**	**73**	**0**	**0**	**2**	**104**	**6.7**	**2**	**1**	**0.0**	**22:00**	....	....	....	....	....	....	....	....	....
2009-10	**Dallas**	**NHL**	**77**	**6**	**16**	**22**	**25**	**2**	**0**	**2**	**107**	**5.6**	**3**	**0**	**0.0**	**22:11**	....	....	....	....	....	....	....	....	....
2010-11	**Dallas**	**NHL**	**82**	**8**	**19**	**27**	**34**	**2**	**0**	**1**	**131**	**6.1**	**7**	**0**	**0.0**	**22:29**	....	....	....	....	....	....	....	....	....
2011-12	**Dallas**	**NHL**	**79**	**4**	**21**	**25**	**42**	**1**	**0**	**2**	**134**	**3.0**	**3**	**0**	**0.0**	**21:39**	....	....	....	....	....	....	....	....	....
2012-13	**Dallas**	**NHL**	**44**	**4**	**9**	**13**	**14**	**2**	**0**	**0**	**58**	**6.9**	**1**	**0**	**0.0**	**21:25**	....	....	....	....	....	....	....	....	....
2013-14	**Dallas**	**NHL**	**67**	**9**	**16**	**25**	**38**	**1**	**0**	**3**	**107**	**8.4**	**10**	**0**	**0.0**	**21:09**	**6**	**2**	**3**	**5**	**16**	**0**	**0**	**0**	**25:48**
2014-15	**Dallas**	**NHL**	**68**	**16**	**22**	**38**	**34**	**6**	**2**	**2**	**113**	**14.2**	**–13**	**0**	**0.0**	**22:53**	....	....	....	....	....	....	....	....	....
	NHL Totals		**756**	**67**	**164**	**231**	**509**	**15**	**2**	**15**	**1034**	**6.5**		**2**	**50.0**	**20:56**	**35**	**4**	**3**	**7**	**40**	**0**	**0**	**0**	**19:53**

Traded to **Chicago** by **Dallas** with Ryan Garbutt for Patrick Sharp and Stephen Johns, July 12, 2015

DALPE, Zac

(DAL-pee, ZAK) **MIN**

Right wing. Shoots right. 6'1", 195 lbs. Born, Paris, ON, November 1, 1989. Carolina's 2nd choice, 45th overall, in 2008 Entry Draft.

Season	Club	League	GP	G	A	Pts	PIM	PP	SH	GW	S	S%	+/-	TF	F%	Min	GP	G	A	Pts	PIM	PP	SH	GW	Min
2006-07	Stratford Cullitons	ON-Jr.B	52	30	43	73	68	....	....	....	....	....	....	....	....	....	....	....	....	....	....	....	....	....	....
2007-08	Penticton Vees	BCHL	46	27	36	63	14	....	....	....	....	....	....	....	....	....	15	8	9	17	4	....	....	....	....
2008-09	Ohio State	CCHA	37	13	12	25	25	....	....	....	....	....	....	....	....	....	....	....	....	....	....	....	....	....	....
2009-10	Ohio State	CCHA	39	*21	24	45	19	....	....	....	....	....	....	....	....	....	....	....	....	....	....	....	....	....	....
	Albany River Rats	AHL	9	6	2	8	0	....	....	....	....	....	....	....	....	....	8	3	3	6	0	....	....	....	....
2010-11	**Carolina**	**NHL**	**15**	**3**	**1**	**4**	**0**	**0**	**0**	**1**	**16**	**18.8**	**0**	**26**	**26.9**	**7:56**	....	....	....	....	....	....	....	....	....
	Charlotte	AHL	61	23	34	57	21	....	....	....	....	....	....	....	....	....	16	6	7	13	6	....	....	....	....
2011-12	**Carolina**	**NHL**	**16**	**1**	**2**	**3**	**4**	**0**	**0**	**0**	**20**	**5.0**	**–3**	**11**	**45.5**	**9:35**	....	....	....	....	....	....	....	....	....
	Charlotte	AHL	56	18	14	32	17	....	....	....	....	....	....	....	....	....	....	....	....	....	....	....	....	....	....
2012-13	Charlotte	AHL	54	21	21	42	12	....	....	....	....	....	....	....	....	....	5	0	0	0	4	....	....	....	....
	Carolina	**NHL**	**10**	**1**	**2**	**3**	**0**	**0**	**0**	**0**	**18**	**5.6**	**–7**	**3**	**33.3**	**12:18**	....	....	....	....	....	....	....	....	....
2013-14	**Vancouver**	**NHL**	**55**	**4**	**3**	**7**	**6**	**1**	**0**	**0**	**52**	**7.7**	**–7**	**231**	**45.9**	**7:08**	....	....	....	....	....	....	....	....	....
	Utica Comets	AHL	6	0	3	3	2	....	....	....	....	....	....	....	....	....	....	....	....	....	....	....	....	....	....
2014-15	**Buffalo**	**NHL**	**21**	**1**	**2**	**3**	**4**	**0**	**0**	**0**	**29**	**3.4**	**–11**	**33**	**60.6**	**9:17**	....	....	....	....	....	....	....	....	....
	Rochester	AHL	44	16	12	28	0	....	....	....	....	....	....	....	....	....	....	....	....	....	....	....	....	....	....
	NHL Totals		**117**	**10**	**10**	**20**	**14**	**1**	**0**	**1**	**135**	**7.4**		**304**	**45.7**	**8:24**	....	....	....	....	....	....	....	....	....

CCHA All-Rookie Team (2009) • CCHA First All-Star Team (2010) • NCAA West Second All-American Team (2010) • AHL All-Rookie Team (2011)

Traded to **Vancouver** by **Carolina** with Jeremy Welsh for Kellan Tochkin and Vancouver's 4th round choice (Josh Wesley) in 2014 Entry Draft, September 29, 2013. Signed as a free agent by **Buffalo** July 13, 2014. Signed as a free agent by **Minnesota**, July 1, 2015.

D'AMIGO, Jerry

(dah-MEE-goh, JAIR-ree) **BUF**

Right wing. Shoots left. 5'11", 213 lbs. Born, Binghamton, NY, February 19, 1991. Toronto's 6th choice, 158th overall, in 2009 Entry Draft.

Season	Club	League	GP	G	A	Pts	PIM	PP	SH	GW	S	S%	+/-	TF	F%	Min	GP	G	A	Pts	PIM	PP	SH	GW	Min
2007-08	USNTDP	NAHL	44	5	12	17	59	....	....	....	....	....	....	....	....	....	3	1	1	2	6	....	....	....	....
	USNTDP	U-17	17	5	4	9	10	....	....	....	....	....	....	....	....	....	....	....	....	....	....	....	....	....	....
2008-09	USNTDP	NAHL	11	8	6	14	4	....	....	....	....	....	....	....	....	....	....	....	....	....	....	....	....	....	....
	USNTDP	U-18	42	15	27	42	57	....	....	....	....	....	....	....	....	....	....	....	....	....	....	....	....	....	....
2009-10	RPI Engineers	ECAC	35	10	24	34	37	....	....	....	....	....	....	....	....	....	....	....	....	....	....	....	....	....	....
2010-11	Toronto Marlies	AHL	43	5	10	15	23	....	....	....	....	....	....	....	....	....	....	....	....	....	....	....	....	....	....
	Kitchener Rangers	OHL	21	12	16	28	12	....	....	....	....	....	....	....	....	....	7	6	3	9	0	....	....	....	....
2011-12	Toronto Marlies	AHL	76	15	26	41	39	....	....	....	....	....	....	....	....	....	17	8	5	13	12	....	....	....	....
2012-13	Toronto Marlies	AHL	70	17	12	29	40	....	....	....	....	....	....	....	....	....	9	1	8	9	10	....	....	....	....
2013-14	**Toronto**	**NHL**	**22**	**1**	**2**	**3**	**0**	**0**	**0**	**0**	**12**	**8.3**	**–1**	**4**	**25.0**	**8:03**	....	....	....	....	....	....	....	....	....
	Toronto Marlies	AHL	51	20	13	33	17	....	....	....	....	....	....	....	....	....	14	6	8	14	8	....	....	....	....
2014-15	Springfield	AHL	28	3	4	7	26	....	....	....	....	....	....	....	....	....	....	....	....	....	....	....	....	....	....
	Buffalo	**NHL**	**9**	**0**	**0**	**0**	**2**	**0**	**0**	**0**	**7**	**0.0**	**–4**	**0**	**0.0**	**9:44**	....	....	....	....	....	....	....	....	....
	Rochester	AHL	31	6	13	19	21	....	....	....	....	....	....	....	....	....	....	....	....	....	....	....	....	....	....
	NHL Totals		**31**	**1**	**2**	**3**	**2**	**0**	**0**	**0**	**19**	**5.3**		**4**	**25.0**	**8:32**	....	....	....	....	....	....	....	....	....

ECAC All-Rookie Team (2010) • ECAC Rookie of the Year (2010)

• Loaned to **Kitchener** (OHL) by **Toronto**, February 3, 2011. Traded to **Columbus** by **Toronto** with future considerations for Matt Frattin, July 1, 2014. Traded to **Buffalo** by **Columbus** for Luke Adam, December 16, 2014.

DANAULT, Phillip

(duh-NOH, FIHL-ihp) **CHI**

Center. Shoots left. 6', 201 lbs. Born, Victoriaville, QC, February 24, 1993. Chicago's 2nd choice, 26th overall, in 2011 Entry Draft.

Season	Club	League	GP	G	A	Pts	PIM	PP	SH	GW	S	S%	+/-	TF	F%	Min	GP	G	A	Pts	PIM	PP	SH	GW	Min
2008-09	Trois-Rivieres	QAAA	44	8	19	27	39	....	....	....	....	....	....	....	....	....	19	4	11	15	8	....	....	....	....
2009-10	Victoriaville Tigres	QMJHL	61	10	18	28	54	....	....	....	....	....	....	....	....	....	16	0	1	1	8	....	....	....	....
2010-11	Victoriaville Tigres	QMJHL	64	23	44	67	59	....	....	....	....	....	....	....	....	....	9	5	10	15	6	....	....	....	....
2011-12	Victoriaville Tigres	QMJHL	62	18	53	71	61	....	....	....	....	....	....	....	....	....	4	0	3	3	4	....	....	....	....
	Rockford IceHogs	AHL	7	0	2	2	10	....	....	....	....	....	....	....	....	....	....	....	....	....	....	....	....	....	....
2012-13	Victoriaville Tigres	QMJHL	29	14	30	44	28	....	....	....	....	....	....	....	....	....	....	....	....	....	....	....	....	....	....
	Moncton Wildcats	QMJHL	27	9	32	41	22	....	....	....	....	....	....	....	....	....	4	1	3	4	0	....	....	....	....
	Rockford IceHogs	AHL	5	0	0	0	2	....	....	....	....	....	....	....	....	....	....	....	....	....	....	....	....	....	....
2013-14	Rockford IceHogs	AHL	72	6	20	26	40	....	....	....	....	....	....	....	....	....	....	....	....	....	....	....	....	....	....
2014-15	**Chicago**	**NHL**	**2**	**0**	**0**	**0**	**0**	**0**	**0**	**0**	**2**	**0.0**	**0**	**20**	**30.0**	**9:30**	....	....	....	....	....	....	....	....	....
	Rockford IceHogs	AHL	70	13	25	38	38	....	....	....	....	....	....	....	....	....	8	3	2	5	20	....	....	....	....
	NHL Totals		**2**	**0**	**0**	**0**	**0**	**0**	**0**	**0**	**2**	**0.0**		**20**	**30.0**	**9:30**	....	....	....	....	....	....	....	....	....

DANO, Marko

(DA-noh, MAHR-koh) **CHI**

Center. Shoots left. 5'11", 183 lbs. Born, Eisenstadt , Austria, November 30, 1994. Columbus' 3rd choice, 27th overall, in 2013 Entry Draft.

Season	Club	League	GP	G	A	Pts	PIM	PP	SH	GW	S	S%	+/-	TF	F%	Min	GP	G	A	Pts	PIM	PP	SH	GW	Min
2008-09	Dukla Trencin U18	Svk-U18	5	1	0	1	14	....	....	....	....	....	....	....	....	....	....	....	....	....	....	....	....	....	....
2009-10	Dukla Trencin U18	Svk-U18	36	13	12	25	77	....	....	....	....	....	....	....	....	....	....	....	....	....	....	....	....	....	....
2010-11	Dukla Trencin U18	Svk-U18	9	13	4	17	2	....	....	....	....	....	....	....	....	....	4	2	2	4	8	....	....	....	....
	Dukla Trencin Jr.	Slovak-Jr.	28	18	22	40	86	....	....	....	....	....	....	....	....	....	8	4	2	6	14	....	....	....	....
	Dukla Trencin	Slovakia	8	0	1	1	10	....	....	....	....	....	....	....	....	....	3	0	0	0	0	....	....	....	....
2011-12	Dukla Trencin Jr.	Slovak-Jr.	3	3	1	4	18	....	....	....	....	....	....	....	....	....	3	4	2	6	4	....	....	....	....
	Dukla Trencin	Slovakia	32	4	6	10	12	....	....	....	....	....	....	....	....	....	9	0	3	3	18	....	....	....	....
2012-13	Bratislava	KHL	37	3	4	7	26	....	....	....	....	....	....	....	....	....	4	0	0	0	4	....	....	....	....
	Dukla Trencin Jr.	Slovak-Jr.	....	....	....	....	....	....	....	....	....	....	....	....	....	....	2	0	0	0	0	....	....	....	....

Season	Club	League	GP	G	A	Pts	PIM	Regular Season PP	SH	GW	S	S%	+/-	TF	F%	Min	Playoffs GP	G	A	Pts	PIM	PP	SH	GW	Min
2013-14	Bratislava	KHL	41	3	2	5	41	....	....	....	....	....	....	....	....	....	....	....	....	....	....	....	....	....	....
	Springfield	AHL	10	2	4	6	4	....	....	....	....	....	....	....	....	....	5	0	2	2	0	....	....	....	....
2014-15	**Columbus**	**NHL**	**35**	**8**	**13**	**21**	**14**	**0**	**0**	**1**	**84**	**9.5**	**12**	**37**	**43.2**	**13:15**	....	....	....	....	....	....	....	....	....
	Springfield	AHL	39	11	8	19	34	....	....	....	....	....	....	....	....	....	....	....	....	....	....	....	....	....	....
	NHL Totals		**35**	**8**	**13**	**21**	**14**	**0**	**0**	**1**	**84**	**9.5**		**37**	**43.2**	**13:15**	....	....	....	....	....	....	....	....	....

Traded to **Chicago** by **Columbus** with Artem Anisimov, Jeremy Morin, Corey Tropp and Columbus' 4th round choice in 2016 Entry Draft for Brandon Saad, Michael Paliotta and Alex Broadhurst, June 30, 2015.

DATSYUK, Pavel

(daht-SOOK, PAH-vehl) **DET**

Center. Shoots left. 5'11", 194 lbs. Born, Sverdlovsk, USSR, July 20, 1978. Detroit's 8th choice, 171st overall, in 1998 Entry Draft.

1996-97	Yekaterinburg 2	Russia-3	18	2	2	4	4	....	....	....	....	....	....	....	....	....	....	....	....	....	....	....	....	....	....
	Yekaterinburg	Russia	36	12	10	22	12	....	....	....	....	....	....	....	....	....	....	....	....	....	....	....	....	....	....
1997-98	Yekaterinburg	Russia	24	3	5	8	4	....	....	....	....	....	....	....	....	....	....	....	....	....	....	....	....	....	....
	Yekaterinburg 2	Russia-3	22	7	8	15	4	....	....	....	....	....	....	....	....	....	....	....	....	....	....	....	....	....	....
1998-99	Yekaterinburg 2	Russia-4	10	14	14	28	4	....	....	....	....	....	....	....	....	....	....	....	....	....	....	....	....	....	....
	Yekaterinburg	Russia-2	35	21	23	44	14	....	....	....	....	....	....	....	....	....	9	3	7	10	10	....	....	....	....
99-2000	Yekaterinburg	Russia	15	1	3	4	4	....	....	....	....	....	....	....	....	....	....	....	....	....	....	....	....	....	....
2000-01	Ak Bars Kazan	Russia	42	9	18	27	10	....	....	....	....	....	....	....	....	....	4	0	1	1	2	....	....	....	....
2001-02 ♦	**Detroit**	**NHL**	**70**	**11**	**24**	**35**	**4**	**2**	**0**	**1**	**79**	**13.9**	**4**	**794**	**47.7**	**13:39**	**21**	**3**	**3**	**6**	**2**	**1**	**0**	**1**	**10:40**
	Russia	Olympics	6	1	2	3	0	....	....	....	....	....	....	....	....	....	....	....	....	....	....	....	....	....	....
2002-03	**Detroit**	**NHL**	**64**	**12**	**39**	**51**	**16**	**1**	**0**	**1**	**82**	**14.6**	**20**	**778**	**48.2**	**15:28**	**4**	**0**	**0**	**0**	**0**	**0**	**0**	**0**	**18:48**
2003-04	**Detroit**	**NHL**	**75**	**30**	**38**	**68**	**35**	**8**	**1**	**4**	**136**	**22.1**	**–2**	**1314**	**54.0**	**18:16**	**12**	**0**	**6**	**6**	**2**	**0**	**0**	**0**	**17:23**
2004-05	Dynamo Moscow	Russia	47	15	17	32	16	....	....	....	....	....	....	....	....	....	10	*6	3	9	4	....	....	....	....
2005-06	**Detroit**	**NHL**	**75**	**28**	**59**	**87**	**22**	**11**	**0**	**4**	**145**	**19.3**	**26**	**1059**	**53.1**	**17:53**	**5**	**0**	**3**	**3**	**0**	**0**	**0**	**0**	**20:05**
	Russia	Olympics	8	1	7	8	10	....	....	....	....	....	....	....	....	....	....	....	....	....	....	....	....	....	....
2006-07	**Detroit**	**NHL**	**79**	**27**	**60**	**87**	**20**	**5**	**2**	**5**	**207**	**13.0**	**36**	**845**	**56.2**	**19:57**	**18**	**8**	**8**	**16**	**8**	**4**	**0**	**2**	**22:03**
2007-08 ♦	**Detroit**	**NHL**	**82**	**31**	**66**	**97**	**20**	**10**	**1**	**6**	**264**	**11.7**	***41**	**833**	**54.4**	**21:23**	**22**	**10**	**13**	**23**	**6**	**4**	**0**	**1**	**21:40**
2008-09	**Detroit**	**NHL**	**81**	**32**	**65**	**97**	**22**	**11**	**1**	**3**	**248**	**12.9**	**34**	**1135**	**56.0**	**19:13**	**16**	**1**	**8**	**9**	**9**	**1**	**0**	**0**	**20:05**
2009-10	**Detroit**	**NHL**	**80**	**27**	**43**	**70**	**18**	**9**	**0**	**3**	**203**	**13.3**	**17**	**1070**	**55.1**	**20:21**	**12**	**6**	**7**	**13**	**8**	**1**	**0**	**1**	**18:49**
	Russia	Olympics	4	1	2	3	2	....	....	....	....	....	....	....	....	....	....	....	....	....	....	....	....	....	....
2010-11	**Detroit**	**NHL**	**56**	**23**	**36**	**59**	**15**	**6**	**1**	**5**	**137**	**16.8**	**11**	**785**	**54.7**	**19:19**	**11**	**4**	**11**	**15**	**8**	**2**	**0**	**0**	**21:09**
2011-12	**Detroit**	**NHL**	**70**	**19**	**48**	**67**	**14**	**4**	**0**	**5**	**164**	**11.6**	**21**	**1249**	**56.2**	**19:34**	**5**	**1**	**2**	**3**	**2**	**0**	**0**	**0**	**21:17**
2012-13	CSKA Moscow	KHL	31	11	25	36	4	....	....	....	....	....	....	....	....	....	....	....	....	....	....	....	....	....	....
	Detroit	**NHL**	**47**	**15**	**34**	**49**	**14**	**8**	**0**	**6**	**107**	**14.0**	**21**	**887**	**55.0**	**20:11**	**14**	**3**	**6**	**9**	**4**	**0**	**0**	**0**	**20:59**
2013-14	**Detroit**	**NHL**	**45**	**17**	**20**	**37**	**6**	**6**	**0**	**2**	**126**	**13.5**	**1**	**835**	**53.4**	**20:16**	**5**	**3**	**2**	**5**	**0**	**1**	**0**	**1**	**21:13**
2014-15	**Detroit**	**NHL**	**63**	**26**	**39**	**65**	**8**	**8**	**0**	**5**	**165**	**15.8**	**12**	**1122**	**53.6**	**19:03**	**7**	**3**	**2**	**5**	**2**	**1**	**0**	**1**	**19:08**
	NHL Totals		**887**	**298**	**571**	**869**	**214**	**89**	**6**	**50**	**2063**	**14.4**		**12706**	**53.9**	**18:49**	**152**	**42**	**71**	**113**	**51**	**15**	**0**	**7**	**19:06**

Lady Byng Memorial Trophy (2006, 2007, 2008, 2009) • Frank J. Selke Trophy (2008, 2009, 2010) • NHL Second All-Star Team (2009)

Played in NHL All-Star Game (2004, 2008, 2012)

• Spent majority of 1999-2000 on **Kazan** (Russia) reserve squad. Signed as a free agent by **Dynamo Moscow** (Russia), June 19, 2004. Signed as a free agent by **CSKA Moscow** (KHL), September 22, 2012.

DAVIDSON, Brandon

(DAY-vihn-suhn, BRAN-duhn) **EDM**

Defense. Shoots left. 6'2", 214 lbs. Born, Lethbridge, AB, August 21, 1991. Edmonton's 8th choice, 162nd overall, in 2010 Entry Draft.

2008-09	Lethbridge	AMHL	31	7	14	21	52	....	....	....	....	....	....	....	....	....	7	2	5	7	14	....	....	....	....
2009-10	Regina Pats	WHL	59	1	33	34	37	....	....	....	....	....	....	....	....	....	....	....	....	....	....	....	....	....	....
2010-11	Regina Pats	WHL	72	8	43	51	71	....	....	....	....	....	....	....	....	....	....	....	....	....	....	....	....	....	....
	Oklahoma City	AHL	1	0	0	0	0	....	....	....	....	....	....	....	....	....	1	0	0	0	0	....	....	....	....
2011-12	Regina Pats	WHL	69	13	36	49	83	....	....	....	....	....	....	....	....	....	4	0	1	1	6	....	....	....	....
2012-13	Stockton Thunder	ECHL	11	7	5	12	4	....	....	....	....	....	....	....	....	....	....	....	....	....	....	....	....	....	....
	Oklahoma City	AHL	26	2	3	5	14	....	....	....	....	....	....	....	....	....	17	0	6	6	2	....	....	....	....
2013-14	Oklahoma City	AHL	68	5	8	13	58	....	....	....	....	....	....	....	....	....	3	0	1	1	0	....	....	....	....
2014-15	**Edmonton**	**NHL**	**12**	**1**	**0**	**1**	**0**	**0**	**0**	**0**	**7**	**14.3**	**–5**	**0**	**0.0**	**15:08**	....	....	....	....	....	....	....	....	....
	Oklahoma City	AHL	55	4	6	10	43	....	....	....	....	....	....	....	....	....	10	1	1	2	12	....	....	....	....
	NHL Totals		**12**	**1**	**0**	**1**	**0**	**0**	**0**	**0**	**7**	**14.3**		**0**	**0.0**	**15:08**	....	....	....	....	....	....	....	....	....

WHL East Second All-Star Team (2012) • Fred T. Hunt Memorial Award (AHL – Sportsmanship) (2013)

de HAAN, Calvin

(DUH HAWN, CAL-vihn) **NYI**

Defense. Shoots left. 6'1", 193 lbs. Born, Carp, ON, May 9, 1991. NY Islanders' 2nd choice, 12th overall, in 2009 Entry Draft.

2006-07	Ott. Valley Titans	Minor-ON	32	4	22	26	20	....	....	....	....	....	....	....	....	....	....	....	....	....	....	....	....	....	....
2007-08	Kemptville 73's	ON-Jr.A	58	3	39	42	14	....	....	....	....	....	....	....	....	....	....	....	....	....	....	....	....	....	....
2008-09	Oshawa Generals	OHL	68	8	55	63	40	....	....	....	....	....	....	....	....	....	....	....	....	....	....	....	....	....	....
2009-10	Oshawa Generals	OHL	34	5	19	24	14	....	....	....	....	....	....	....	....	....	....	....	....	....	....	....	....	....	....
2010-11	Oshawa Generals	OHL	55	6	42	48	48	....	....	....	....	....	....	....	....	....	10	1	11	12	6	....	....	....	....
2011-12	**NY Islanders**	**NHL**	**1**	**0**	**0**	**0**	**0**	**0**	**0**	**0**	**2**	**0.0**	**1**	**0**	**0.0**	**13:01**	....	....	....	....	....	....	....	....	....
	Bridgeport	AHL	56	2	14	16	24	....	....	....	....	....	....	....	....	....	3	0	2	2	2	....	....	....	....
2012-13	Bridgeport	AHL	3	0	2	2	4	....	....	....	....	....	....	....	....	....	....	....	....	....	....	....	....	....	....
2013-14	**NY Islanders**	**NHL**	**51**	**3**	**13**	**16**	**30**	**1**	**0**	**1**	**71**	**4.2**	**–7**	**0**	**0.0**	**21:01**	....	....	....	....	....	....	....	....	....
	Bridgeport	AHL	17	1	2	3	8	....	....	....	....	....	....	....	....	....	....	....	....	....	....	....	....	....	....
2014-15	**NY Islanders**	**NHL**	**65**	**1**	**11**	**12**	**24**	**0**	**1**	**0**	**92**	**1.1**	**3**	**0**	**0.0**	**19:01**	**5**	**0**	**1**	**1**	**2**	**0**	**0**	**0**	**17:21**
	NHL Totals		**117**	**4**	**24**	**28**	**54**	**1**	**1**	**1**	**165**	**2.4**		**0**	**0.0**	**19:50**	**5**	**0**	**1**	**1**	**2**	**0**	**0**	**0**	**17:21**

• Missed remainder of 2012-13 due to shoulder injury at Wilkes-Barre (AHL), October 20, 2012.

DeFAZIO, Brandon

(deh-FAZ-ee-oh, BRAN-duhn) **BOS**

Left wing. Shoots left. 6'2", 204 lbs. Born, Etobicoke, ON, September 13, 1988.

2005-06	Oakville Blades	ON-Jr.A	11	2	11	13	8	....	....	....	....	....	....	....	....	....	....	....	....	....	....	....	....	....	....
	Milton Icehawks	ON-Jr.A	36	10	6	16	38	....	....	....	....	....	....	....	....	....	....	....	....	....	....	....	....	....	....
2006-07	Oakville Blades	ON-Jr.A	46	12	33	45	135	....	....	....	....	....	....	....	....	....	....	....	....	....	....	....	....	....	....
2007-08	Clarkson Knights	ECAC	37	3	4	7	34	....	....	....	....	....	....	....	....	....	....	....	....	....	....	....	....	....	....
2008-09	Clarkson Knights	ECAC	33	7	11	18	28	....	....	....	....	....	....	....	....	....	....	....	....	....	....	....	....	....	....
2009-10	Clarkson Knights	ECAC	35	12	14	26	58	....	....	....	....	....	....	....	....	....	....	....	....	....	....	....	....	....	....
2010-11	Clarkson Knights	ECAC	36	14	12	26	56	....	....	....	....	....	....	....	....	....	....	....	....	....	....	....	....	....	....
	Wilkes-Barre	AHL	2	0	0	0	0	....	....	....	....	....	....	....	....	....	....	....	....	....	....	....	....	....	....
	Wheeling Nailers	ECHL	10	4	5	9	7	....	....	....	....	....	....	....	....	....	14	4	2	6	8	....	....	....	....
2011-12	Wilkes-Barre	AHL	66	11	5	16	104	....	....	....	....	....	....	....	....	....	12	0	0	0	6	....	....	....	....
2012-13	Bridgeport	AHL	69	11	14	25	139	....	....	....	....	....	....	....	....	....	....	....	....	....	....	....	....	....	....
2013-14	Utica Comets	AHL	76	17	17	34	106	....	....	....	....	....	....	....	....	....	....	....	....	....	....	....	....	....	....
2014-15	**Vancouver**	**NHL**	**2**	**0**	**0**	**0**	**0**	**0**	**0**	**0**	**2**	**0.0**	**0**	**0**	**0.0**	**5:57**	....	....	....	....	....	....	....	....	....
	Utica Comets	AHL	75	21	22	43	92	....	....	....	....	....	....	....	....	....	21	2	5	7	12	....	....	....	....
	NHL Totals		**2**	**0**	**0**	**0**	**0**	**0**	**0**	**0**	**2**	**0.0**		**0**	**0.0**	**5:57**	....	....	....	....	....	....	....	....	....

Signed to an ATO (amateur tryout) contract by **Pittsburgh**, April 1, 2011. Signed as a free agent by **Pittsburgh**, October 7, 2011. Signed as a free agent by **NY Islanders**, July 2, 2012. Signed as a free agent by **Vancouver**, July 12, 2013. Signed as a free agent by **Boston**, July 6, 2015.

DeKEYSER, Danny

(duh-KIGH-zuhr, DAN-ee) **DET**

Defense. Shoots left. 6'3", 190 lbs. Born, Detroit, MI, March 7, 1990.

2008-09	Trail	BCHL	58	8	17	25	12	....	....	....	....	....	....	....	....	....	3	1	0	1	4	....	....	....	....
2009-10	Sioux City	USHL	41	1	10	11	12	....	....	....	....	....	....	....	....	....	....	....	....	....	....	....	....	....	....
2010-11	Western Mich.	CCHA	42	5	12	17	43	....	....	....	....	....	....	....	....	....	....	....	....	....	....	....	....	....	....
2011-12	Western Mich.	CCHA	41	5	12	17	42	....	....	....	....	....	....	....	....	....	....	....	....	....	....	....	....	....	....
2012-13	Western Mich.	CCHA	35	2	13	15	22	....	....	....	....	....	....	....	....	....	....	....	....	....	....	....	....	....	....
	Detroit	**NHL**	**11**	**0**	**1**	**1**	**2**	**0**	**0**	**0**	**15**	**0.0**	**4**	**0**	**0.0**	**18:03**	**2**	**0**	**0**	**0**	**0**	**0**	**0**	**0**	**17:53**
	Grand Rapids	AHL	....	....	....	....	....	....	....	....	....	....	....	....	....	....	6	0	1	1	8	....	....	....	....

			Regular Season														Playoffs								
Season	Club	League	GP	G	A	Pts	PIM	PP	SH	GW	S	S%	+/-	TF	F%	Min	GP	G	A	Pts	PIM	PP	SH	GW	Min
2013-14	Detroit	NHL	65	4	19	23	30	1	1	0	84	4.8	10	0	0.0	21:38	5	0	0	0	6	0	0	0	23:11
2014-15	Detroit	NHL	80	2	29	31	42	0	0	1	89	2.2	11	0	0.0	20:56	7	1	0	1	12	0	0	0	21:22
	NHL Totals		156	6	49	55	74	1	1	1	188	3.2		0	0.0	21:01	14	1	0	1	18	0	0	0	21:31

CCHA All-Rookie Team (2011) • CCHA Second All-Star Team (2012) • CCHA First All-Star Team (2013) • NCAA West Second All-American Team (2012, 2013)
Signed as a free agent by **Detroit**, March 29, 2013.

DEL ZOTTO, Michael

(DEHL ZAW-toh, MIGH-kuhl) **PHI**

Defense. Shoots left. 6', 195 lbs. Born, Stouffville, ON, June 24, 1990. NY Rangers' 1st choice, 20th overall, in 2008 Entry Draft.

Season	Club	League	GP	G	A	Pts	PIM	PP	SH	GW	S	S%	+/-	TF	F%	Min	GP	G	A	Pts	PIM	PP	SH	GW	Min
2005-06	Markham Waxers	Minor-ON	73	30	90	120	90	....	....	....	....	....	....	....	....	....	....	....	....	....	....	....	....	....	....
2006-07	Oshawa Generals	OHL	64	10	47	57	78	....	....	....	....	....	....	....	....	....	9	3	9	12	14	....	....	....	....
2007-08	Oshawa Generals	OHL	64	16	47	63	82	....	....	....	....	....	....	....	....	....	15	2	6	8	38	....	....	....	....
2008-09	Oshawa Generals	OHL	34	7	26	33	48	....	....	....	....	....	....	....	....	....	....	....	....	....	....	....	....	....	....
	London Knights	OHL	28	6	24	30	30	....	....	....	....	....	....	....	....	....	14	3	16	19	18	....	....	....	....
2009-10	**NY Rangers**	**NHL**	**80**	**9**	**28**	**37**	**32**	**4**	**0**	**1**	**81**	**11.1**	**–20**	**0**	**0.0**	**18:58**	....	....	....	....	....	....	....	....	....
2010-11	**NY Rangers**	**NHL**	**47**	**2**	**9**	**11**	**20**	**2**	**0**	**0**	**58**	**3.4**	**–5**	**0**	**0.0**	**19:29**	....	....	....	....	....	....	....	....	....
	Connecticut	AHL	11	0	7	7	8	....	....	....	....	....	....	....	....	....	....	....	....	....	....	....	....	....	....
2011-12	**NY Rangers**	**NHL**	**77**	**10**	**31**	**41**	**36**	**1**	**1**	**2**	**113**	**8.8**	**20**	**0**	**0.0**	**22:26**	**20**	**2**	**8**	**10**	**12**	**1**	**0**	**1**	**21:39**
2012-13	Rapperswil	Swiss	9	2	5	7	10	....	....	....	....	....	....	....	....	....	....	....	....	....	....	....	....	....	....
	NY Rangers	**NHL**	**46**	**3**	**18**	**21**	**18**	**0**	**1**	**0**	**81**	**3.7**	**6**	**0**	**0.0**	**23:10**	**12**	**1**	**1**	**2**	**8**	**0**	**0**	**0**	**21:10**
2013-14	**NY Rangers**	**NHL**	**42**	**2**	**9**	**11**	**10**	**1**	**0**	**0**	**64**	**3.1**	**–5**	**0**	**0.0**	**17:45**	....	....	....	....	....	....	....	....	....
	Nashville	**NHL**	**25**	**1**	**4**	**5**	**8**	**0**	**0**	**0**	**26**	**3.8**	**–4**	**1**	**0.0**	**16:18**	....	....	....	....	....	....	....	....	....
2014-15	**Philadelphia**	**NHL**	**64**	**10**	**22**	**32**	**34**	**1**	**1**	**4**	**119**	**8.4**	**–5**	**0**	**0.0**	**21:55**	....	....	....	....	....	....	....	....	....
	NHL Totals		**381**	**37**	**121**	**158**	**158**	**9**	**3**	**7**	**542**	**6.8**		**1**	**0.0**	**20:26**	**32**	**3**	**9**	**12**	**20**	**1**	**0**	**1**	**21:28**

NHL All-Rookie Team (2010)
Signed as a free agent by **Rapperswil** (Swiss), October 31, 2012. Traded to **Nashville** by **NY Rangers** for Kevin Klein, January 22, 2014. Signed as a free agent by **Philadelphia** August 5, 2014.

DE LA ROSE, Jacob

(deh la ROHZ, YA-kuhb) **MTL**

Left wing. Shoots left. 6'3", 207 lbs. Born, Arvika, Sweden, May 20, 1995. Montreal's 2nd choice, 34th overall, in 2013 Entry Draft.

Season	Club	League	GP	G	A	Pts	PIM	PP	SH	GW	S	S%	+/-	TF	F%	Min	GP	G	A	Pts	PIM	PP	SH	GW	Min
2008-09	Nor U18	Swe-U18	11	3	14	17	4	....	....	....	....	....	....	....	....	....	....	....	....	....	....	....	....	....	....
2009-10	Farjestad U18	Swe-U18	6	0	0	0	2	....	....	....	....	....	....	....	....	....	7	0	0	0	0	....	....	....	....
2010-11	Leksands IF U18	Swe-U18	30	12	13	25	22	....	....	....	....	....	....	....	....	....	6	0	4	4	4	....	....	....	....
	Leksands IF Jr.	Swe-Jr.	2	1	0	1	0	....	....	....	....	....	....	....	....	....	....	....	....	....	....	....	....	....	....
2011-12	Leksands IF U18	Swe-U18	4	3	3	6	6	....	....	....	....	....	....	....	....	....	....	....	....	....	....	....	....	....	....
	Leksands IF Jr.	Swe-Jr.	28	4	9	13	24	....	....	....	....	....	....	....	....	....	....	....	....	....	....	....	....	....	....
	Leksands IF	Sweden-2	24	4	0	4	12	....	....	....	....	....	....	....	....	....	....	....	....	....	....	....	....	....	....
2012-13	Leksands IF Jr.	Swe-Jr.	4	1	4	5	0	....	....	....	....	....	....	....	....	....	....	....	....	....	....	....	....	....	....
	Leksands IF	Sweden-2	48	6	7	13	33	....	....	....	....	....	....	....	....	....	....	....	....	....	....	....	....	....	....
2013-14	Leksands IF	Sweden	49	7	6	13	18	....	....	....	....	....	....	....	....	....	3	0	0	0	0	....	....	....	....
	Sweden	Olympics	7	3	3	6	6	....	....	....	....	....	....	....	....	....	....	....	....	....	....	....	....	....	....
2014-15	**Montreal**	**NHL**	**33**	**4**	**2**	**6**	**12**	**0**	**1**	**0**	**38**	**10.5**	**–5**	**160**	**40.0**	**13:48**	**12**	**0**	**0**	**0**	**4**	**0**	**0**	**0**	**12:40**
	Hamilton	AHL	37	6	5	11	11	....	....	....	....	....	....	....	....	....	....	....	....	....	....	....	....	....	....
	NHL Totals		**33**	**4**	**2**	**6**	**12**	**0**	**1**	**0**	**38**	**10.5**		**160**	**40.0**	**13:48**	**12**	**0**	**0**	**0**	**4**	**0**	**0**	**0**	**12:40**

DEMERS, Jason

(duh-MAIRZ, JAY-suhn) **DAL**

Defense. Shoots right. 6'1", 195 lbs. Born, Dorval, QC, June 9, 1988. San Jose's 6th choice, 186th overall, in 2008 Entry Draft.

Season	Club	League	GP	G	A	Pts	PIM	PP	SH	GW	S	S%	+/-	TF	F%	Min	GP	G	A	Pts	PIM	PP	SH	GW	Min
2004-05	Moncton Wildcats	QMJHL	25	0	1	1	10	....	....	....	....	....	....	....	....	....	....	....	....	....	....	....	....	....	....
2005-06	Moncton Wildcats	QMJHL	21	1	3	4	15	....	....	....	....	....	....	....	....	....	....	....	....	....	....	....	....	....	....
	Victoriaville Tigres	QMJHL	33	2	13	15	58	....	....	....	....	....	....	....	....	....	5	0	2	2	10	....	....	....	....
2006-07	Victoriaville Tigres	QMJHL	69	5	19	24	98	....	....	....	....	....	....	....	....	....	6	0	0	0	2	....	....	....	....
2007-08	Victoriaville Tigres	QMJHL	67	9	55	64	91	....	....	....	....	....	....	....	....	....	6	1	5	6	6	....	....	....	....
2008-09	Worcester Sharks	AHL	78	2	31	33	54	....	....	....	....	....	....	....	....	....	12	0	4	4	6	....	....	....	....
2009-10	**San Jose**	**NHL**	**51**	**4**	**17**	**21**	**21**	**3**	**0**	**1**	**52**	**7.7**	**5**	**0**	**0.0**	**15:26**	**15**	**1**	**4**	**5**	**8**	**1**	**0**	**0**	**11:10**
	Worcester Sharks	AHL	25	4	13	17	24	....	....	....	....	....	....	....	....	....	....	....	....	....	....	....	....	....	....
2010-11	**San Jose**	**NHL**	**75**	**2**	**22**	**24**	**28**	**0**	**0**	**0**	**105**	**1.9**	**19**	**0**	**0.0**	**19:30**	**13**	**2**	**1**	**3**	**8**	**0**	**0**	**0**	**19:56**
2011-12	**San Jose**	**NHL**	**57**	**4**	**9**	**13**	**22**	**2**	**0**	**1**	**73**	**5.5**	**–8**	**0**	**0.0**	**16:51**	**3**	**0**	**0**	**0**	**2**	**0**	**0**	**0**	**15:28**
2012-13	Karpat Oulu	Finland	30	5	16	21	18	....	....	....	....	....	....	....	....	....	....	....	....	....	....	....	....	....	....
	San Jose	**NHL**	**22**	**1**	**2**	**3**	**10**	**0**	**0**	**0**	**27**	**3.7**	**–4**	**0**	**0.0**	**18:38**	**1**	**0**	**0**	**0**	**2**	**0**	**0**	**0**	**3:47**
2013-14	**San Jose**	**NHL**	**75**	**5**	**29**	**34**	**30**	**1**	**0**	**0**	**105**	**4.8**	**14**	**0**	**0.0**	**19:29**	**7**	**0**	**1**	**1**	**12**	**0**	**0**	**0**	**19:58**
2014-15	**San Jose**	**NHL**	**20**	**0**	**3**	**3**	**8**	**0**	**0**	**0**	**20**	**0.0**	**–6**	**0**	**0.0**	**18:11**	....	....	....	....	....	....	....	....	....
	Dallas	**NHL**	**61**	**5**	**17**	**22**	**63**	**2**	**0**	**2**	**79**	**6.3**	**3**	**0**	**0.0**	**19:26**	....	....	....	....	....	....	....	....	....
	NHL Totals		**361**	**21**	**99**	**120**	**182**	**8**	**0**	**4**	**461**	**4.6**		**0**	**0.0**	**18:22**	**39**	**3**	**6**	**9**	**32**	**1**	**0**	**0**	**15:49**

Signed as a free agent by **Oulu** (Finland), September 15, 2012. Traded to **Dallas** by **San Jose** with San Jose's 3rd round choice in 2016 Entry Draft for Brenden Dillon, November 21, 2014.

DESCHAMPS, Nicolas

(day-SHAWMP, NIHK-oh-las)

Center. Shoots left. 6'1", 207 lbs. Born, Lasalle, QC, January 6, 1990. Anaheim's 2nd choice, 35th overall, in 2008 Entry Draft.

Season	Club	League	GP	G	A	Pts	PIM	PP	SH	GW	S	S%	+/-	TF	F%	Min	GP	G	A	Pts	PIM	PP	SH	GW	Min
2005-06	C.C. Lemoyne	QAAA	23	5	4	9	14	....	....	....	....	....	....	....	....	....	8	0	0	0	12	....	....	....	....
2006-07	C.C. Lemoyne	QAAA	35	20	28	48	60	....	....	....	....	....	....	....	....	....	10	4	7	11	22	....	....	....	....
2007-08	Chicoutimi	QMJHL	70	24	43	67	63	....	....	....	....	....	....	....	....	....	6	2	3	5	6	....	....	....	....
2008-09	Chicoutimi	QMJHL	65	24	41	65	40	....	....	....	....	....	....	....	....	....	4	3	1	4	12	....	....	....	....
	Iowa Chops	AHL	2	0	1	1	0	....	....	....	....	....	....	....	....	....	....	....	....	....	....	....	....	....	....
2009-10	Chicoutimi	QMJHL	31	18	26	*44	20	....	....	....	....	....	....	....	....	....	....	....	....	....	....	....	....	....	....
	Moncton Wildcats	QMJHL	33	21	31	*52	20	....	....	....	....	....	....	....	....	....	15	5	9	14	10	....	....	....	....
2010-11	Syracuse Crunch	AHL	80	15	31	46	26	....	....	....	....	....	....	....	....	....	....	....	....	....	....	....	....	....	....
2011-12	Syracuse Crunch	AHL	31	5	2	7	10	....	....	....	....	....	....	....	....	....	....	....	....	....	....	....	....	....	....
	Toronto Marlies	AHL	40	7	23	30	14	....	....	....	....	....	....	....	....	....	17	3	9	12	8	....	....	....	....
2012-13	Toronto Marlies	AHL	50	7	9	16	26	....	....	....	....	....	....	....	....	....	....	....	....	....	....	....	....	....	....
	Hershey Bears	AHL	16	3	4	7	2	....	....	....	....	....	....	....	....	....	5	1	2	3	2	....	....	....	....
2013-14	**Washington**	**NHL**	**3**	**0**	**0**	**0**	**0**	**0**	**0**	**0**	**2**	**0.0**	**–1**	**0**	**0.0**	**6:49**	....	....	....	....	....	....	....	....	....
	Hershey Bears	AHL	65	15	25	40	24	....	....	....	....	....	....	....	....	....	....	....	....	....	....	....	....	....	....
2014-15	Karpat Oulu	Finland	8	1	0	1	20	....	....	....	....	....	....	....	....	....	....	....	....	....	....	....	....	....	....
	Straubing Tigers	Germany	11	2	6	8	6	....	....	....	....	....	....	....	....	....	....	....	....	....	....	....	....	....	....
	Vienna	Austria	10	0	2	2	0	....	....	....	....	....	....	....	....	....	....	....	....	....	....	....	....	....	....
	Syracuse Crunch	AHL	12	0	1	1	2	....	....	....	....	....	....	....	....	....	....	....	....	....	....	....	....	....	....
	Florida Everblades	ECHL	13	3	7	10	2	....	....	....	....	....	....	....	....	....	12	4	9	13	2	....	....	....	....
	NHL Totals		**3**	**0**	**0**	**0**	**0**	**0**	**0**	**0**	**2**	**0.0**		**0**	**0.0**	**6:49**	....	....	....	....	....	....	....	....	....

QMJHL All-Rookie Team (2008) • Canadian Major Junior All-Rookie Team (2008) • QMJHL Second All-Star Team (2010)
Traded to **Toronto** by **Anaheim** for Luca Caputi, January 3, 2012. Traded to **Washington** by **Toronto** for Kevin Marshall, March 14, 2013. Signed as a free agent by **Oulu** (Finland), July 22, 2014. Signed as a free agent by **Straubing** (Germany), October 30, 2014. Signed as a free agent by **Vienna** (Austria), December 23, 2014. Signed as a free agent by **Syracuse** (AHL), February 5, 2015. Signed as a free agent by **Florida**, (ECHL), March 10, 2015.

DESHARNAIS, David

(day-hahr-NAY, DAY-vihd) **MTL**

Center. Shoots left. 5'7", 176 lbs. Born, Laurier-Station, QC, September 14, 1986.

Season	Club	League	GP	G	A	Pts	PIM	PP	SH	GW	S	S%	+/-	TF	F%	Min	GP	G	A	Pts	PIM	PP	SH	GW	Min
2001-02	Rive-Sud Express	Minor-QC	STATISTICS NOT AVAILABLE																						
	Levis	QAAA	2	0	2	2	0	....	....	....	....	....	....	....	....	....	....	....	....	....	....	....	....	....	....
2002-03	Levis	QAAA	42	27	42	69	10	....	....	....	....	....	....	....	....	....	13	6	12	18	8	....	....	....	....
2003-04	Chicoutimi	QMJHL	70	23	28	51	12	....	....	....	....	....	....	....	....	....	18	4	7	11	8	....	....	....	....
2004-05	Chicoutimi	QMJHL	68	32	65	97	39	....	....	....	....	....	....	....	....	....	17	5	10	15	8	....	....	....	....
2005-06	Chicoutimi	QMJHL	63	33	85	118	44	....	....	....	....	....	....	....	....	....	9	2	9	11	4	....	....	....	....
2006-07	Chicoutimi	QMJHL	61	38	70	108	32	....	....	....	....	....	....	....	....	....	4	1	5	6	2	....	....	....	....
	Bridgeport	AHL	7	1	1	2	4	....	....	....	....	....	....	....	....	....	....	....	....	....	....	....	....	....	....
2007-08	Hamilton	AHL	4	0	1	1	6	....	....	....	....	....	....	....	....	....	....	....	....	....	....	....	....	....	....
	Cincinnati	ECHL	68	29	*77	*106	18	....	....	....	....	....	....	....	....	....	22	9	*24	*33	18	....	....	....	....
2008-09	Hamilton	AHL	77	24	34	58	20	....	....	....	....	....	....	....	....	....	6	1	3	4	4	....	....	....	....

								Regular Season									Playoffs								
Season	Club	League	GP	G	A	Pts	PIM	PP	SH	GW	S	S%	+/-	TF	F%	Min	GP	G	A	Pts	PIM	PP	SH	GW	Min
2009-10	Montreal	NHL	6	0	1	1	0	0	0	0	2	0.0	–1	28	57.1	8:27	....	....	....	....	....	....	....	....	....
	Hamilton	AHL	60	27	51	78	34	....	....	....	....	....	....	....	....	....	19	10	13	23	16	....	....	....	....
2010-11	Montreal	NHL	43	8	14	22	12	4	0	0	55	14.5	–3	445	49.7	12:52	5	0	1	1	2	0	0	0	11:03
	Hamilton	AHL	35	10	35	45	24	....	....	....	....	....	....	....	....	....	....	....	....	....	....	....	....	....	....
2011-12	Montreal	NHL	81	16	44	60	24	3	0	2	98	16.3	10	1371	49.5	18:24	....	....	....	....	....	....	....	....	....
2012-13	Fribourg	Swiss	16	4	12	16	12	....	....	....	....	....	....	....	....	....	....	....	....	....	....	....	....	....	....
	Montreal	NHL	48	10	18	28	26	2	0	3	66	15.2	–2	764	50.0	16:28	5	0	1	1	2	0	0	0	17:14
2013-14	Montreal	NHL	79	16	36	52	24	3	0	2	96	16.7	11	1202	50.8	17:12	17	2	6	8	6	1	0	0	18:40
2014-15	Montreal	NHL	82	14	34	48	24	2	0	4	90	15.6	22	1189	52.9	17:15	11	1	2	3	4	0	0	1	16:15
	NHL Totals		339	64	147	211	110	14	0	11	407	15.7		4999	50.8	16:41	38	3	10	13	14	1	0	1	16:47

ECHL Rookie of the Year (2008) • ECHL Leading Scorer (2008) • ECHL MVP (2008)

Signed as a free agent by **Montreal**, November 5, 2008. Signed as a free agent by **Fribourg** (Swiss), November 2, 2012.

DESJARDINS, Andrew

(deh-ZHAHR-dehn, AN-droo) **CHI**

Center. Shoots right. 6'1", 195 lbs. Born, Lively, ON, July 27, 1986.

2003-04	Sault Ste. Marie	OHL	55	3	6	9	41	....	....	....	....	....	....	....	....	....	....	....	....	....	....	....	....	....	....
2004-05	Sault Ste. Marie	OHL	68	17	17	34	49	....	....	....	....	....	....	....	....	....	7	0	0	0	2	....	....	....	....
2005-06	Sault Ste. Marie	OHL	6	12	16	28	78	....	....	....	....	....	....	....	....	....	4	2	3	5	10	....	....	....	....
2006-07	Sault Ste. Marie	OHL	65	16	26	42	96	....	....	....	....	....	....	....	....	....	13	2	5	7	18	....	....	....	....
2007-08	Laredo Bucks	CHL	64	22	37	59	112	....	....	....	....	....	....	....	....	....	11	2	4	6	21	....	....	....	....
2008-09	Phoenix	ECHL	5	2	0	2	6	....	....	....	....	....	....	....	....	....	....	....	....	....	....	....	....	....	....
	Worcester Sharks	AHL	74	8	14	22	99	....	....	....	....	....	....	....	....	....	12	4	2	6	13	....	....	....	....
2009-10	Worcester Sharks	AHL	80	19	27	46	126	....	....	....	....	....	....	....	....	....	11	2	2	4	32	....	....	....	....
2010-11	San Jose	NHL	17	1	2	3	4	0	0	0	12	8.3	–1	56	55.4	7:08	3	1	0	1	4	0	0	0	6:48
	Worcester Sharks	AHL	58	12	17	29	69	....	....	....	....	....	....	....	....	....	....	....	....	....	....	....	....	....	....
2011-12	San Jose	NHL	76	4	13	17	47	0	0	3	80	5.0	4	362	53.0	9:35	5	1	0	1	2	0	0	0	11:32
2012-13	San Jose	NHL	42	2	1	3	61	0	0	0	51	3.9	–6	72	54.2	10:07	11	0	0	0	6	0	0	0	10:58
2013-14	San Jose	NHL	81	3	14	17	86	0	0	1	95	3.2	–8	675	55.0	11:09	7	0	2	2	31	0	0	0	10:14
2014-15	San Jose	NHL	56	5	3	8	50	0	0	1	43	11.6	–2	293	49.8	10:27	....	....	....	....	....	....	....	....	....
	♦ Chicago	NHL	13	0	2	2	7	0	0	0	16	0.0	1	19	63.2	12:00	21	1	3	4	4	0	0	0	13:56
	NHL Totals		285	15	35	50	255	0	0	5	297	5.1		1477	53.6	10:14	47	3	5	8	47	0	0	0	11:58

Signed as a free agent by **Worcester** (AHL), October, 2008. Signed as a free agent by **San Jose**, June 26, 2010. Traded to **Chicago** by **San Jose** for Ben Smith and a conditional 7th round choice in 2017 Entry Draft, March 2, 2015.

DESLAURIERS, Nicolas

(duh-LOHR-ree-AY, NIH-koh-las) **BUF**

Left wing. Shoots left. 6'1", 209 lbs. Born, LaSalle, QC, February 22, 1991. Los Angeles' 3rd choice, 84th overall, in 2009 Entry Draft.

2006-07	Chateauguay	QAAA	43	2	10	12	28	....	....	....	....	....	....	....	....	....	3	1	0	1	4	....	....	....	....
2007-08	Rouyn-Noranda	QMJHL	42	2	7	9	38	....	....	....	....	....	....	....	....	....	4	0	0	0	0	....	....	....	....
2008-09	Rouyn-Noranda	QMJHL	68	11	19	30	80	....	....	....	....	....	....	....	....	....	6	2	2	4	8	....	....	....	....
2009-10	Rouyn-Noranda	QMJHL	65	9	36	45	72	....	....	....	....	....	....	....	....	....	11	2	6	8	2	....	....	....	....
2010-11	Gatineau	QMJHL	48	13	30	43	53	....	....	....	....	....	....	....	....	....	24	5	15	20	19	....	....	....	....
2011-12	Manchester	AHL	65	1	13	14	67	....	....	....	....	....	....	....	....	....	4	0	0	0	7	....	....	....	....
2012-13	Manchester	AHL	63	4	19	23	80	....	....	....	....	....	....	....	....	....	4	2	2	4	2	....	....	....	....
2013-14	Manchester	AHL	60	18	21	39	76	....	....	....	....	....	....	....	....	....	....	....	....	....	....	....	....	....	....
	Buffalo	NHL	17	1	0	1	18	0	0	0	30	3.3	–10	1	0.0	13:09	....	....	....	....	....	....	....	....	....
	Rochester	AHL	5	1	2	3	9	....	....	....	....	....	....	....	....	....	5	1	1	2	9	....	....	....	....
2014-15	Buffalo	NHL	82	5	10	15	71	0	0	1	76	6.6	–24	1	0.0	11:52	....	....	....	....	....	....	....	....	....
	NHL Totals		99	6	10	16	89	0	0	1	106	5.7		2	0.0	12:05	....	....	....	....	....	....	....	....	....

Traded to **Buffalo** by **Los Angeles** with Hudson Fasching for Brayden McNabb, Jonathan Parker, Los Angeles' 2nd round choice (previously acquired, Los Angeles selected Alex Lintuniemi) in 2014 Entry Draft and Los Angeles' 2nd round choice (previously acquired, Los Angeles selected Erik Cernak) in 2015 Entry Draft, March 5, 2014.

DESPRES, Simon

(duh-PRAY, see-MOHN) **ANA**

Defense. Shoots left. 6'4", 214 lbs. Born, Laval, QC, July 27, 1991. Pittsburgh's 1st choice, 30th overall, in 2009 Entry Draft.

2006-07	Laval-Bourassa	QAAA	42	8	31	39	36	....	....	....	....	....	....	....	....	....	5	0	2	2	8	....	....	....	....
2007-08	Saint John	QMJHL	64	1	13	14	30	....	....	....	....	....	....	....	....	....	14	0	4	4	18	....	....	....	....
2008-09	Saint John	QMJHL	66	2	30	32	74	....	....	....	....	....	....	....	....	....	4	0	4	4	2	....	....	....	....
2009-10	Saint John	QMJHL	63	9	38	47	87	....	....	....	....	....	....	....	....	....	21	2	17	19	18	....	....	....	....
2010-11	Saint John	QMJHL	47	13	28	41	54	....	....	....	....	....	....	....	....	....	19	4	8	12	16	....	....	....	....
2011-12	Pittsburgh	NHL	18	1	3	4	10	1	0	0	22	4.5	5	0	0.0	14:13	3	0	0	0	2	0	0	0	9:18
	Wilkes-Barre	AHL	44	5	10	15	45	....	....	....	....	....	....	....	....	....	10	1	1	2	2	....	....	....	....
2012-13	Wilkes-Barre	AHL	27	4	3	7	28	....	....	....	....	....	....	....	....	....	....	....	....	....	....	....	....	....	....
	Pittsburgh	NHL	33	2	5	7	20	0	0	0	33	6.1	9	0	0.0	15:07	3	0	0	0	0	0	0	0	11:07
2013-14	Pittsburgh	NHL	34	0	5	5	26	0	0	0	41	0.0	4	0	0.0	16:45	....	....	....	....	....	....	....	....	....
	Wilkes-Barre	AHL	36	6	16	22	39	....	....	....	....	....	....	....	....	....	17	2	7	9	32	....	....	....	....
2014-15	Pittsburgh	NHL	59	2	15	17	64	0	0	1	76	2.6	9	1	0.0	16:23	....	....	....	....	....	....	....	....	....
	Anaheim	NHL	16	1	5	6	22	0	0	0	27	3.7	2	0	0.0	18:40	16	1	6	7	6	0	0	1	20:46
	NHL Totals		160	6	33	39	142	1	0	1	199	3.0		1	0.0	16:11	22	1	6	7	8	0	0	1	17:53

QMJHL All-Rookie Team (2008) • QMJHL First All-Star Team (2011) • QMJHL Defenseman of the Year (2011)

Traded to **Anaheim** by **Pittsburgh** for Ben Lovejoy, March 2, 2015.

DEVANE, Jamie

(dah-VAN, JAY-mee) **NSH**

Left wing. Shoots left. 6'5", 217 lbs. Born, Mississauga, ON, February 20, 1991. Toronto's 4th choice, 68th overall, in 2009 Entry Draft.

2007-08	Vaughan Kings	GTHL	15	4	11	15	24	....	....	....	....	....	....	....	....	....	....	....	....	....	....	....	....	....	....
	Vaughan Vipers	ON-Jr.A	19	2	0	2	17	....	....	....	....	....	....	....	....	....	1	0	0	0	0	....	....	....	....
2008-09	Plymouth Whalers	OHL	64	5	12	17	92	....	....	....	....	....	....	....	....	....	11	0	0	0	17	....	....	....	....
2009-10	Plymouth Whalers	OHL	51	6	8	14	84	....	....	....	....	....	....	....	....	....	9	0	1	1	12	....	....	....	....
	Toronto Marlies	AHL	2	0	0	0	4	....	....	....	....	....	....	....	....	....	....	....	....	....	....	....	....	....	....
2010-11	Plymouth Whalers	OHL	63	18	20	38	131	....	....	....	....	....	....	....	....	....	10	2	3	5	19	....	....	....	....
2011-12	Plymouth Whalers	OHL	59	23	22	45	104	....	....	....	....	....	....	....	....	....	13	2	1	3	19	....	....	....	....
2012-13	Toronto Marlies	AHL	22	2	3	5	41	....	....	....	....	....	....	....	....	....	....	....	....	....	....	....	....	....	....
	San Francisco	ECHL	12	1	0	1	45	....	....	....	....	....	....	....	....	....	....	....	....	....	....	....	....	....	....
2013-14	Toronto	NHL	2	0	0	0	0	0	0	0	1	0.0	–1	0	0.0	5:52	....	....	....	....	....	....	....	....	....
	Toronto Marlies	AHL	55	4	4	8	146	....	....	....	....	....	....	....	....	....	2	0	0	0	2	....	....	....	....
2014-15	Toronto Marlies	AHL	39	0	2	2	62	....	....	....	....	....	....	....	....	....	....	....	....	....	....	....	....	....	....
	NHL Totals		2	0	0	0	0	0	0	0	1	0.0		0	0.0	5:52	....	....	....	....	....	....	....	....	....

• Missed majority of 2014-15 as a healthy reserve. Traded to **Nashville** by **Toronto** for Taylor Beck, July 12, 2015.

DIAZ, Raphael

(DEE-az, ra-FIGH-ehl) **NYR**

Defense. Shoots right. 5'11", 197 lbs. Born, Baar, Switz., January 9, 1986.

2001-02	EV Zug Jr.	Swiss-Jr.	4	0	1	1	0	....	....	....	....	....	....	....	....	....	....	....	....	....	....	....	....	....	....
2002-03	EV Zug Jr.	Swiss-Jr.	30	7	10	17	32	....	....	....	....	....	....	....	....	....	7	1	1	2	12	....	....	....	....
2003-04	EV Zug Jr.	Swiss-Jr.	15	6	5	11	22	....	....	....	....	....	....	....	....	....	....	....	....	....	....	....	....	....	....
	EV Zug	Swiss	38	2	1	3	16	....	....	....	....	....	....	....	....	....	5	0	0	0	2	....	....	....	....
2004-05	EV Zug	Swiss	41	1	4	5	12	....	....	....	....	....	....	....	....	....	9	0	0	0	4	....	....	....	....
2005-06	EV Zug	Swiss	35	5	2	7	34	....	....	....	....	....	....	....	....	....	7	0	0	0	4	....	....	....	....
2006-07	EV Zug	Swiss	44	2	4	6	22	....	....	....	....	....	....	....	....	....	12	0	1	1	6	....	....	....	....
2007-08	EV Zug	Swiss	50	3	11	14	44	....	....	....	....	....	....	....	....	....	7	0	0	0	4	....	....	....	....
2008-09	EV Zug	Swiss	50	4	9	13	36	....	....	....	....	....	....	....	....	....	10	1	1	2	4	....	....	....	....
2009-10	EV Zug	Swiss	49	4	27	31	22	....	....	....	....	....	....	....	....	....	13	1	5	6	10	....	....	....	....
	Switzerland	Olympics	5	0	0	0	4	....	....	....	....	....	....	....	....	....	....	....	....	....	....	....	....	....	....
2010-11	EV Zug	Swiss	45	12	27	39	26	....	....	....	....	....	....	....	....	....	10	2	4	6	4	....	....	....	....
2011-12	Montreal	NHL	59	3	13	16	30	0	0	1	61	4.9	–7	2	50.0	18:00	....	....	....	....	....	....	....	....	....

			Regular Season														Playoffs								
Season	Club	League	GP	G	A	Pts	PIM	PP	SH	GW	S	S%	+/-	TF	F%	Min	GP	G	A	Pts	PIM	PP	SH	GW	Min
2012-13	EV Zug	Swiss	32	7	22	29	12	....	....	....	....	....	....	....	....	....	....	....	....	....	....	....	....	....	....
	Montreal	**NHL**	**23**	**1**	**13**	**14**	**6**	0	0	0	34	2.9	4	0	0.0	20:33	5	0	0	0	0	0	0	0	22:22
2013-14	**Montreal**	**NHL**	**46**	**0**	**11**	**11**	**12**	0	0	0	41	0.0	-4	1	0.0	18:54	....	....	....	....	....	....	....	....	....
	Vancouver	**NHL**	**6**	**1**	**1**	**2**	**0**	0	0	0	9	11.1	-3	0	0.0	15:58	....	....	....	....	....	....	....	....	....
	Switzerland	Olympics	4	0	0	0	4	....	....	....	....	....	....	....	....	....	....	....	....	....	....	....	....	....	....
	NY Rangers	**NHL**	**11**	**1**	**1**	**2**	**4**	0	0	0	18	5.6	5	0	0.0	15:14	4	0	0	0	0	0	0	0	14:31
2014-15	**Calgary**	**NHL**	**56**	**2**	**2**	**4**	**10**	1	0	1	52	3.8	-3	0	0.0	12:01	3	0	0	0	0	0	0	0	7:53
	NHL Totals		**201**	**8**	**41**	**49**	**62**	1	0	2	215	3.7		3	33.3	16:37	12	0	0	0	0	0	0	0	16:08

Signed as a free agent by **Montreal**, May 13, 2011. Signed as a free agent by **Zug** (Swiss), September 15, 2012. Traded to **Vancouver** by **Montreal** for Dale Weise, February 3, 2014. Traded to **NY Rangers** by **Vancouver** for NY Rangers' 5th round choice (Ryan Pilon) in 2015 Entry Draft, March 5, 2014. Signed as a free agent by **Calgary**, October 6, 2014. Signed as a free agent by **NY Rangers**, July 1, 2015.

DILLON, Brenden

(DIHL-uhn, BREHN-duhn) **S.J.**

Defense. Shoots left. 6'4", 225 lbs. Born, Surrey, BC, November 13, 1990.

Season	Club	League	GP	G	A	Pts	PIM	PP	SH	GW	S	S%	+/-	TF	F%	Min	GP	G	A	Pts	PIM	PP	SH	GW	Min
2007-08	Seattle	WHL	71	1	10	11	54	....	....	....	....	....	....	....	....	....	12	0	2	2	21	....	....	....	....
2008-09	Seattle	WHL	70	0	10	10	68	....	....	....	....	....	....	....	....	....	5	0	1	1	6	....	....	....	....
2009-10	Seattle	WHL	67	2	12	14	101	....	....	....	....	....	....	....	....	....	....	....	....	....	....	....	....	....	....
2010-11	Seattle	WHL	72	8	51	59	139	....	....	....	....	....	....	....	....	....	....	....	....	....	....	....	....	....	....
	Texas Stars	AHL	10	0	0	0	8	....	....	....	....	....	....	....	....	....	6	0	2	2	7	....	....	....	....
2011-12	**Dallas**	**NHL**	**1**	**0**	**0**	**0**	**0**	0	0	0	6	0.0	0	0	0.0	19:59	....	....	....	....	....	....	....	....	....
	Texas Stars	AHL	76	6	23	29	97	....	....	....	....	....	....	....	....	....	....	....	....	....	....	....	....	....	....
2012-13	Texas Stars	AHL	37	3	11	14	45	....	....	....	....	....	....	....	....	....	....	....	....	....	....	....	....	....	....
	Dallas	**NHL**	**48**	**3**	**5**	**8**	**65**	0	0	1	75	4.0	1	0	0.0	21:23	....	....	....	....	....	....	....	....	....
2013-14	**Dallas**	**NHL**	**80**	**6**	**11**	**17**	**86**	0	2	1	97	6.2	9	0	0.0	21:06	2	0	0	0	2	0	0	0	18:13
2014-15	**Dallas**	**NHL**	**20**	**0**	**1**	**1**	**23**	0	0	0	16	0.0	-2	0	0.0	20:37	....	....	....	....	....	....	....	....	....
	San Jose	**NHL**	**60**	**2**	**7**	**9**	**54**	0	1	1	75	2.7	-11	0	0.0	19:13	....	....	....	....	....	....	....	....	....
	NHL Totals		**209**	**11**	**24**	**35**	**228**	0	3	3	269	4.1		0	0.0	20:34	2	0	0	0	2	0	0	0	18:13

Signed as a free agent by **Dallas**, March 1, 2011. Traded to **San Jose** by **Dallas** for Jason Demers and San Jose's 3rd round choice in 2016 Entry Draft, November 21, 2014.

DOAN, Shane

(DOHN, SHAYN) **ARI**

Right wing. Shoots right. 6'1", 223 lbs. Born, Halkirk, AB, October 10, 1976. Winnipeg's 1st choice, 7th overall, in 1995 Entry Draft.

Season	Club	League	GP	G	A	Pts	PIM	PP	SH	GW	S	S%	+/-	TF	F%	Min	GP	G	A	Pts	PIM	PP	SH	GW	Min
1991-92	Killam Selects	AAHA	56	80	84	164	74	....	....	....	....	....	....	....	....	....	....	....	....	....	....	....	....	....	....
1992-93	Kamloops Blazers	WHL	51	7	12	19	65	....	....	....	....	....	....	....	....	....	13	0	1	1	8	....	....	....	....
1993-94	Kamloops Blazers	WHL	52	24	24	48	88	....	....	....	....	....	....	....	....	....	....	....	....	....	....	....	....	....	....
1994-95	Kamloops Blazers	WHL	71	37	57	94	106	....	....	....	....	....	....	....	....	....	21	6	10	16	16	....	....	....	....
1995-96	**Winnipeg**	**NHL**	**74**	**7**	**10**	**17**	**101**	1	0	3	106	6.6	-9	....	....	....	6	0	0	0	6	0	0	0	....
1996-97	**Phoenix**	**NHL**	**63**	**4**	**8**	**12**	**49**	0	0	0	100	4.0	-3	....	....	....	4	0	0	0	2	0	0	0	....
1997-98	**Phoenix**	**NHL**	**33**	**5**	**6**	**11**	**35**	0	0	3	42	11.9	-3	....	....	....	6	1	0	1	6	0	0	0	....
	Springfield	AHL	39	21	21	42	64	....	....	....	....	....	....	....	....	....	....	....	....	....	....	....	....	....	....
1998-99	**Phoenix**	**NHL**	**79**	**6**	**16**	**22**	**54**	0	0	1	156	3.8	-5	6	16.7	12:42	7	2	2	4	6	0	0	2	17:58
99-2000	**Phoenix**	**NHL**	**81**	**26**	**25**	**51**	**66**	1	1	4	221	11.8	6	25	36.0	16:51	4	1	2	3	8	1	0	0	18:11
2000-01	**Phoenix**	**NHL**	**76**	**26**	**37**	**63**	**89**	6	1	6	220	11.8	0	15	40.0	19:32	....	....	....	....	....	....	....	....	....
2001-02	**Phoenix**	**NHL**	**81**	**20**	**29**	**49**	**61**	6	0	2	205	9.8	11	52	44.2	18:10	5	2	2	4	6	0	0	0	17:21
2002-03	**Phoenix**	**NHL**	**82**	**21**	**37**	**58**	**86**	7	0	2	225	9.3	3	623	39.8	18:47	....	....	....	....	....	....	....	....	....
2003-04	**Phoenix**	**NHL**	**79**	**27**	**41**	**68**	**47**	9	2	1	254	10.6	-11	55	40.0	21:46	....	....	....	....	....	....	....	....	....
2004-05				DID NOT PLAY																					
2005-06	**Phoenix**	**NHL**	**82**	**30**	**36**	**66**	**123**	17	0	7	254	11.8	-9	126	43.7	19:08	....	....	....	....	....	....	....	....	....
	Canada	Olympics	6	2	1	3	2	....	....	....	....	....	....	....	....	....	....	....	....	....	....	....	....	....	....
2006-07	**Phoenix**	**NHL**	**73**	**27**	**28**	**55**	**73**	11	0	7	209	12.9	-14	174	39.1	20:27	....	....	....	....	....	....	....	....	....
2007-08	**Phoenix**	**NHL**	**80**	**28**	**50**	**78**	**59**	9	2	5	243	11.5	4	187	41.2	20:46	....	....	....	....	....	....	....	....	....
2008-09	**Phoenix**	**NHL**	**82**	**31**	**42**	**73**	**72**	10	0	4	230	13.5	5	362	44.2	20:15	....	....	....	....	....	....	....	....	....
2009-10	**Phoenix**	**NHL**	**82**	**18**	**37**	**55**	**41**	5	0	4	234	7.7	3	153	45.8	19:10	3	1	1	2	4	0	0	0	13:22
2010-11	**Phoenix**	**NHL**	**72**	**20**	**40**	**60**	**67**	11	0	6	221	9.0	5	159	45.9	19:17	4	3	2	5	6	2	0	0	21:42
2011-12	**Phoenix**	**NHL**	**79**	**22**	**28**	**50**	**48**	5	0	5	226	9.7	-8	59	55.9	19:36	16	5	4	9	41	1	0	2	20:47
2012-13	**Phoenix**	**NHL**	**48**	**13**	**14**	**27**	**37**	5	0	2	129	10.1	6	15	26.7	18:03	....	....	....	....	....	....	....	....	....
2013-14	**Phoenix**	**NHL**	**69**	**23**	**24**	**47**	**34**	10	0	4	167	13.8	-7	12	50.0	18:56	....	....	....	....	....	....	....	....	....
2014-15	**Arizona**	**NHL**	**79**	**14**	**22**	**36**	**65**	5	0	0	189	7.4	-29	11	27.3	18:53	....	....	....	....	....	....	....	....	....
	NHL Totals		**1394**	**368**	**530**	**898**	**1207**	113	6	65	3631	10.1		2034	42.2	18:54	55	15	13	28	85	4	0	4	19:06

Memorial Cup All-Star Team (1995) • Stafford Smythe Memorial Trophy (Memorial Cup - MVP) (1995) • King Clancy Memorial Trophy (2010) • Mark Messier NHL Leadership Award (2012)

Played in NHL All-Star Game (2004, 2009)

• Transferred to **Phoenix** after **Winnipeg** franchise relocated, July 1, 1996.

DONOVAN, Matt

(DAWN-uh-vuhn, MAT) **BUF**

Defense. Shoots left. 6', 195 lbs. Born, Edmond, OK, May 9, 1990. NY Islanders' 8th choice, 96th overall, in 2008 Entry Draft.

Season	Club	League	GP	G	A	Pts	PIM	PP	SH	GW	S	S%	+/-	TF	F%	Min	GP	G	A	Pts	PIM	PP	SH	GW	Min
2006-07	Dallas Stars AAA	NTHL	....	22	46	68	54	....	....	....	....	....	....	....	....	....	....	....	....	....	....	....	....	....	....
2007-08	Cedar Rapids	USHL	59	12	18	30	41	....	....	....	....	....	....	....	....	....	3	0	1	1	4	....	....	....	....
2008-09	Cedar Rapids	USHL	57	19	32	51	43	....	....	....	....	....	....	....	....	....	5	0	4	4	2	....	....	....	....
2009-10	U. of Denver	WCHA	36	7	14	21	50	....	....	....	....	....	....	....	....	....	....	....	....	....	....	....	....	....	....
2010-11	U. of Denver	WCHA	42	9	23	32	64	....	....	....	....	....	....	....	....	....	....	....	....	....	....	....	....	....	....
	Bridgeport	AHL	6	1	4	5	10	....	....	....	....	....	....	....	....	....	....	....	....	....	....	....	....	....	....
2011-12	**NY Islanders**	**NHL**	**3**	**0**	**0**	**0**	**0**	0	0	0	6	0.0	-3	0	0.0	18:34	....	....	....	....	....	....	....	....	....
	Bridgeport	AHL	72	10	35	45	63	....	....	....	....	....	....	....	....	....	3	0	1	1	6	....	....	....	....
2012-13	Bridgeport	AHL	75	14	34	48	112	....	....	....	....	....	....	....	....	....	....	....	....	....	....	....	....	....	....
2013-14	**NY Islanders**	**NHL**	**52**	**2**	**14**	**16**	**26**	1	0	0	86	2.3	-9	0	0.0	18:04	....	....	....	....	....	....	....	....	....
	Bridgeport	AHL	27	7	14	21	25	....	....	....	....	....	....	....	....	....	....	....	....	....	....	....	....	....	....
2014-15	**NY Islanders**	**NHL**	**12**	**0**	**3**	**3**	**0**	0	0	0	12	0.0	4	0	0.0	17:34	2	0	0	0	10	0	0	0	11:21
	NHL Totals		**67**	**2**	**17**	**19**	**26**	1	0	0	104	1.9		0	0.0	18:00	2	0	0	0	10	0	0	0	11:21

USHL All-Rookie Team (2008) • USHL First All-Star Team (2009) • WCHA All-Rookie Team (2010) • WCHA Second All-Star Team (2011) • AHL All-Rookie Team (2012)

• Missed majority of 2014-15 as a healthy reserve. Signed as a free agent by **Buffalo**, July 1, 2015.

DORSETT, Derek

(DOHRS-iht, DAIR-ihk) **VAN**

Right wing. Shoots right. 6', 192 lbs. Born, Kindersley, SK, December 20, 1986. Columbus' 9th choice, 189th overall, in 2006 Entry Draft.

Season	Club	League	GP	G	A	Pts	PIM	PP	SH	GW	S	S%	+/-	TF	F%	Min	GP	G	A	Pts	PIM	PP	SH	GW	Min
2004-05	Medicine Hat	WHL	51	5	11	16	108	....	....	....	....	....	....	....	....	....	13	5	1	6	35	....	....	....	....
2005-06	Medicine Hat	WHL	68	25	23	48	*279	....	....	....	....	....	....	....	....	....	13	8	4	12	53	....	....	....	....
2006-07	Medicine Hat	WHL	61	19	45	64	206	....	....	....	....	....	....	....	....	....	17	8	8	16	56	....	....	....	....
2007-08	Syracuse Crunch	AHL	64	10	8	18	289	....	....	....	....	....	....	....	....	....	12	0	1	1	56	....	....	....	....
2008-09	**Columbus**	**NHL**	**52**	**4**	**1**	**5**	**150**	0	0	1	59	6.8	-1	9	44.4	8:53	3	0	0	0	2	0	0	0	9:11
	Syracuse Crunch	AHL	7	1	5	6	35	....	....	....	....	....	....	....	....	....	....	....	....	....	....	....	....	....	....
2009-10	**Columbus**	**NHL**	**51**	**4**	**10**	**14**	**105**	0	0	0	57	7.0	6	33	27.3	10:53	....	....	....	....	....	....	....	....	....
2010-11	**Columbus**	**NHL**	**76**	**4**	**13**	**17**	**184**	0	0	0	112	3.6	-15	51	37.3	13:12	....	....	....	....	....	....	....	....	....
2011-12	**Columbus**	**NHL**	**77**	**12**	**8**	**20**	***235**	2	1	1	137	8.8	-11	28	50.0	14:42	....	....	....	....	....	....	....	....	....
2012-13	Salzburg	Austria	4	0	1	1	25	....	....	....	....	....	....	....	....	....	....	....	....	....	....	....	....	....	....
	Columbus	**NHL**	**24**	**3**	**6**	**9**	**53**	0	0	0	38	7.9	-11	23	56.5	15:59	....	....	....	....	....	....	....	....	....
	NY Rangers	**NHL**	....	....	....	....	....	....	....	....	....	....	....	....	....	....	11	0	1	1	28	0	0	0	10:46
2013-14	**NY Rangers**	**NHL**	**51**	**4**	**4**	**8**	**128**	0	0	0	67	6.0	-1	3	0.0	11:02	23	0	1	1	19	0	0	0	9:29
2014-15	**Vancouver**	**NHL**	**79**	**7**	**18**	**25**	**175**	0	2	3	89	7.9	4	16	43.8	12:03	6	0	0	0	20	0	0	0	12:37
	NHL Totals		**410**	**38**	**60**	**98**	**1030**	2	3	5	559	6.8		163	40.5	12:19	43	0	2	2	69	0	0	0	10:13

Signed as a free agent by **Salzburg** (Austria), November 26, 2012. Traded to **NY Rangers** by **Columbus** with Derick Brassard, John Moore and Columbus' 6th round choice (later traded to Minnesota – Minnesota selected Chase Lang) in 2014 Entry Draft for Marian Gaborik, Blake Parlett and Steven Delisle, April 3, 2013. Traded to **Vancouver** by **NY Rangers** for Anaheim's 3rd round choice (previously acquired, NY Rangers selected Keegan Iverson) in 2014 Entry Draft, June 27, 2014.

DOUGHTY, Drew (DOW-tee, DROO) L.A.

Defense. Shoots right. 6'1", 201 lbs. Born, London, ON, December 8, 1989. Los Angeles' 1st choice, 2nd overall, in 2008 Entry Draft.

			Regular Season														Playoffs								
Season	Club	League	GP	G	A	Pts	PIM	PP	SH	GW	S	S%	+/-	TF	F%	Min	GP	G	A	Pts	PIM	PP	SH	GW	Min
2004-05	Lon. Jr. Knights	Minor-ON	55	19	30	49	31	....	....	....	....	....	....	....	....	....	....	....	....	....	....	....	....	....	....
2005-06	Guelph Storm	OHL	65	5	28	33	40	....	....	....	....	....	....	....	....	....	14	0	13	13	18	....	....	....	....
2006-07	Guelph Storm	OHL	67	21	53	74	76	....	....	....	....	....	....	....	....	....	4	2	3	5	8	....	....	....	....
2007-08	Guelph Storm	OHL	58	13	37	50	68	....	....	....	....	....	....	....	....	....	10	3	6	9	14	....	....	....	....
2008-09	**Los Angeles**	**NHL**	**81**	**6**	**21**	**27**	**56**	**3**	**0**	**1**	**126**	**4.8**	**–17**	**0**	**0.0**	**23:50**	....	....	....	....	....	....	....	....	....
2009-10	**Los Angeles**	**NHL**	**82**	**16**	**43**	**59**	**54**	**9**	**0**	**5**	**142**	**11.3**	**20**	**0**	**0.0**	**24:59**	**6**	**3**	**4**	**7**	**4**	**2**	**0**	**0**	**27:26**
	Canada	Olympics	7	0	2	2	2	....	....	....	....	....	....	....	....	....	....	....	....	....	....	....	....	....	....
2010-11	**Los Angeles**	**NHL**	**76**	**11**	**29**	**40**	**68**	**5**	**0**	**3**	**139**	**7.9**	**13**	**0**	**0.0**	**25:39**	**6**	**2**	**2**	**4**	**8**	**1**	**0**	**0**	**27:08**
2011-12♦	**Los Angeles**	**NHL**	**77**	**10**	**26**	**36**	**69**	**3**	**0**	**3**	**168**	**6.0**	**–2**	**0**	**0.0**	**24:54**	**20**	**4**	**12**	**16**	**14**	**1**	**0**	**0**	**26:09**
2012-13	**Los Angeles**	**NHL**	**48**	**6**	**16**	**22**	**36**	**3**	**0**	**0**	**114**	**5.3**	**4**	**0**	**0.0**	**26:24**	**18**	**2**	**3**	**5**	**8**	**1**	**0**	**0**	**27:57**
2013-14♦	**Los Angeles**	**NHL**	**78**	**10**	**27**	**37**	**64**	**6**	**0**	**2**	**177**	**5.6**	**17**	**0**	**0.0**	**25:43**	**26**	**5**	**13**	**18**	**30**	**1**	**0**	**1**	**28:45**
	Canada	Olympics	6	4	2	6	0	....	....	....	....	....	....	....	....	....	....	....	....	....	....	....	....	....	....
2014-15	**Los Angeles**	**NHL**	**82**	**7**	**39**	**46**	**56**	**1**	**0**	**2**	**219**	**3.2**	**3**	**1**	**0.0**	**29:00**	....	....	....	....	....	....	....	....	....
	NHL Totals		**524**	**66**	**201**	**267**	**403**	**30**	**0**	**16**	**1085**	**6.1**		**1**	**0.0**	**25:45**	**76**	**16**	**34**	**50**	**64**	**6**	**0**	**1**	**27:39**

OHL All-Rookie Team (2006) • OHL First All-Star Team (2007, 2008) • Canadian Major Junior First All-Star Team (2008) • NHL All-Rookie Team (2009) • NHL Second All-Star Team (2010, 2015) • Olympic All-Star Team (2014)

Played in NHL All-Star Game (2015)

DOWELL, Jake (DOW-uhl, JAYK)

Center. Shoots left. 6', 200 lbs. Born, Eau Claire, WI, March 4, 1985. Chicago's 10th choice, 140th overall, in 2004 Entry Draft.

2000-01	Eau Claire Mem.	High-WI	24	25	30	55	....	....	....	....	....	....	....	....	....	....	....	....	....	....	....	....	....	....	....
2001-02	USNTDP	U-17	11	5	1	6	14	....	....	....	....	....	....	....	....	....	....	....	....	....	....	....	....	....	....
	USNTDP	NAHL	44	5	12	17	51	....	....	....	....	....	....	....	....	....	....	....	....	....	....	....	....	....	....
2002-03	USNTDP	U-18	54	8	17	25	54	....	....	....	....	....	....	....	....	....	....	....	....	....	....	....	....	....	....
	USNTDP	NAHL	9	2	2	4	13	....	....	....	....	....	....	....	....	....	....	....	....	....	....	....	....	....	....
2003-04	U. of Wisconsin	WCHA	37	6	13	19	48	....	....	....	....	....	....	....	....	....	....	....	....	....	....	....	....	....	....
2004-05	U. of Wisconsin	WCHA	38	12	14	26	74	....	....	....	....	....	....	....	....	....	....	....	....	....	....	....	....	....	....
2005-06	U. of Wisconsin	WCHA	43	5	15	20	42	....	....	....	....	....	....	....	....	....	....	....	....	....	....	....	....	....	....
2006-07	U. of Wisconsin	WCHA	41	19	6	25	54	....	....	....	....	....	....	....	....	....	....	....	....	....	....	....	....	....	....
	Norfolk Admirals	AHL	9	2	3	5	8	....	....	....	....	....	....	....	....	....	6	0	3	3	4	....	....	....	....
2007-08	**Chicago**	**NHL**	**19**	**2**	**1**	**3**	**10**	**0**	**1**	**0**	**19**	**10.5**	**1**	**170**	**46.5**	**11:56**	....	....	....	....	....	....	....	....	....
	Rockford IceHogs	AHL	49	7	10	17	64	....	....	....	....	....	....	....	....	....	12	1	1	2	6	....	....	....	....
2008-09	**Chicago**	**NHL**	**1**	**0**	**0**	**0**	**2**	**0**	**0**	**0**	**0**	**0.0**	**1**	**12**	**66.7**	**13:37**	....	....	....	....	....	....	....	....	....
	Rockford IceHogs	AHL	75	6	14	20	128	....	....	....	....	....	....	....	....	....	4	0	0	0	0	....	....	....	....
2009-10	**Chicago**	**NHL**	**3**	**1**	**1**	**2**	**5**	**0**	**0**	**0**	**4**	**25.0**	**1**	**4**	**50.0**	**6:56**	....	....	....	....	....	....	....	....	....
	Rockford IceHogs	AHL	78	7	16	23	96	....	....	....	....	....	....	....	....	....	4	0	0	0	0	....	....	....	....
2010-11	**Chicago**	**NHL**	**79**	**6**	**15**	**21**	**63**	**0**	**0**	**0**	**74**	**8.1**	**5**	**652**	**48.9**	**11:49**	**2**	**0**	**0**	**0**	**0**	**0**	**0**	**0**	**8:23**
2011-12	**Dallas**	**NHL**	**52**	**2**	**5**	**7**	**53**	**0**	**0**	**0**	**39**	**5.1**	**–3**	**197**	**47.7**	**7:38**	....	....	....	....	....	....	....	....	....
2012-13	Houston Aeros	AHL	37	4	5	9	34	....	....	....	....	....	....	....	....	....	4	0	1	1	4	....	....	....	....
	Minnesota	**NHL**	**2**	**0**	**0**	**0**	**0**	**0**	**0**	**0**	**3**	**0.0**	**0**	**3**	**66.7**	**8:33**	....	....	....	....	....	....	....	....	....
2013-14	**Minnesota**	**NHL**	**1**	**0**	**0**	**0**	**0**	**0**	**0**	**0**	**1**	**0.0**	**–1**	**4**	**50.0**	**7:09**	....	....	....	....	....	....	....	....	....
	Iowa Wild	AHL	57	7	12	19	56	....	....	....	....	....	....	....	....	....	....	....	....	....	....	....	....	....	....
2014-15	Hamilton	AHL	76	5	10	15	75	....	....	....	....	....	....	....	....	....	....	....	....	....	....	....	....	....	....
	NHL Totals		**157**	**11**	**22**	**33**	**133**	**0**	**1**	**0**	**140**	**7.9**		**1042**	**48.6**	**10:17**	**2**	**0**	**0**	**0**	**0**	**0**	**0**	**0**	**8:23**

Fred T. Hunt Memorial Award (Sportsmanship – AHL) (2014)

Signed as a free agent by **Dallas**, July 1, 2011. Signed as a free agent by **Minnesota**, July 4, 2012. Signed as a free agent by **Hamilton** (AHL), July 28, 2014.

DOWNIE, Steve (DOW-nee, STEEV) ARI

Right wing. Shoots right. 5'11", 191 lbs. Born, Newmarket, ON, April 3, 1987. Philadelphia's 1st choice, 29th overall, in 2005 Entry Draft.

2002-03	Aurora Tigers	ON-Jr.A	34	12	13	25	55	....	....	....	....	....	....	....	....	....	....	....	....	....	....	....	....	....	....
2003-04	Windsor Spitfires	OHL	49	7	9	16	90	....	....	....	....	....	....	....	....	....	4	0	1	1	27	....	....	....	....
2004-05	Windsor Spitfires	OHL	61	21	52	73	179	....	....	....	....	....	....	....	....	....	11	4	5	9	49	....	....	....	....
2005-06	Windsor Spitfires	OHL	1	3	0	3	4	....	....	....	....	....	....	....	....	....	....	....	....	....	....	....	....	....	....
	Peterborough	OHL	34	16	34	50	109	....	....	....	....	....	....	....	....	....	19	6	15	21	38	....	....	....	....
2006-07	Peterborough	OHL	28	23	36	59	92	....	....	....	....	....	....	....	....	....	....	....	....	....	....	....	....	....	....
	Kitchener Rangers	OHL	17	12	21	33	32	....	....	....	....	....	....	....	....	....	9	8	14	22	15	....	....	....	....
	Philadelphia	AHL	1	0	0	0	0	....	....	....	....	....	....	....	....	....	....	....	....	....	....	....	....	....	....
2007-08	**Philadelphia**	**NHL**	**32**	**6**	**6**	**12**	**73**	**0**	**1**	**1**	**25**	**24.0**	**2**	**15**	**33.3**	**9:51**	**6**	**0**	**1**	**1**	**10**	**0**	**0**	**0**	**6:04**
	Philadelphia	AHL	21	5	12	17	114	....	....	....	....	....	....	....	....	....	....	....	....	....	....	....	....	....	....
2008-09	**Philadelphia**	**NHL**	**6**	**0**	**0**	**0**	**11**	**0**	**0**	**0**	**1**	**0.0**	**–4**	**13**	**15.4**	**5:57**	....	....	....	....	....	....	....	....	....
	Philadelphia	AHL	4	1	7	8	23	....	....	....	....	....	....	....	....	....	....	....	....	....	....	....	....	....	....
	Tampa Bay	**NHL**	**23**	**3**	**3**	**6**	**54**	**0**	**0**	**1**	**25**	**12.0**	**2**	**7**	**42.9**	**9:04**	....	....	....	....	....	....	....	....	....
	Norfolk Admirals	AHL	23	8	17	25	107	....	....	....	....	....	....	....	....	....	....	....	....	....	....	....	....	....	....
2009-10	**Tampa Bay**	**NHL**	**79**	**22**	**24**	**46**	**208**	**7**	**0**	**1**	**116**	**19.0**	**14**	**34**	**50.0**	**14:43**	....	....	....	....	....	....	....	....	....
2010-11	**Tampa Bay**	**NHL**	**57**	**10**	**22**	**32**	**171**	**2**	**0**	**1**	**83**	**12.0**	**8**	**96**	**44.8**	**14:31**	**17**	**2**	**12**	**14**	**40**	**0**	**0**	**1**	**12:35**
2011-12	**Tampa Bay**	**NHL**	**55**	**12**	**16**	**28**	**121**	**2**	**0**	**1**	**99**	**12.1**	**–15**	**77**	**45.5**	**15:30**	....	....	....	....	....	....	....	....	....
	Colorado	**NHL**	**20**	**2**	**11**	**13**	**16**	**0**	**0**	**1**	**41**	**4.9**	**9**	**10**	**50.0**	**17:06**	....	....	....	....	....	....	....	....	....
2012-13	**Colorado**	**NHL**	**2**	**0**	**1**	**1**	**6**	**0**	**0**	**0**	**2**	**0.0**	**1**	**1**	**100.0**	**8:54**	....	....	....	....	....	....	....	....	....
2013-14	**Colorado**	**NHL**	**11**	**1**	**6**	**7**	**36**	**1**	**0**	**1**	**26**	**3.8**	**4**	**0**	**0.0**	**16:43**	....	....	....	....	....	....	....	....	....
	Philadelphia	**NHL**	**51**	**3**	**14**	**17**	**70**	**2**	**0**	**0**	**62**	**4.8**	**–3**	**7**	**57.1**	**13:32**	....	....	....	....	....	....	....	....	....
2014-15	**Pittsburgh**	**NHL**	**72**	**14**	**14**	**28**	***238**	**3**	**0**	**2**	**104**	**13.5**	**2**	**8**	**50.0**	**12:26**	**5**	**0**	**2**	**2**	**4**	**0**	**0**	**0**	**10:40**
	NHL Totals		**408**	**73**	**117**	**190**	**1004**	**17**	**1**	**9**	**584**	**12.5**		**268**	**44.4**	**13:33**	**28**	**2**	**15**	**17**	**54**	**0**	**0**	**1**	**10:51**

Traded to **Tampa Bay** by **Philadelphia** with Steve Eminger and Tampa Bay's 4th round choice (previously acquired, Tampa Bay selected Alex Hutchings) in 2009 Entry Draft for Matt Carle and San Jose's 3rd round choice (previously acquired, Philadelphia selected Simon Bertilsson) in 2009 Entry Draft, November 7, 2008. Traded to **Colorado** by **Tampa Bay** for Kyle Quincey, February 21, 2012. • Missed majority of 2012-13 due to knee injury vs. Los Angeles, January 22, 2013. Traded to **Philadelphia** by **Colorado** for Max Talbot, October 31, 2013. Signed as a free agent by **Pittsburgh**, July 2, 2014. Signed as a free agent by **Arizona**, July 1, 2015.

DRAISAITL, Leon (DRIGH-zigh-tuhl, LEE-awn) EDM

Center. Shoots left. 6'1", 210 lbs. Born, Cologne, Germany, October 27, 1995. Edmonton's 1st choice, 3rd overall, in 2014 Entry Draft.

2010-11	Heil./Mann. Jr.	Ger-Jr.	6	0	1	1	2	....	....	....	....	....	....	....	....	....	....	....	....	....	....	....	....	....	....
2011-12	Heil./Mann. Jr.	Ger-Jr.	35	21	35	56	39	....	....	....	....	....	....	....	....	....	8	6	6	12	2	....	....	....	....
2012-13	Prince Albert	WHL	64	21	37	58	22	....	....	....	....	....	....	....	....	....	4	0	4	4	0	....	....	....	....
2013-14	Prince Albert	WHL	64	38	67	105	24	....	....	....	....	....	....	....	....	....	4	1	2	3	4	....	....	....	....
2014-15	**Edmonton**	**NHL**	**37**	**2**	**7**	**9**	**4**	**1**	**0**	**1**	**49**	**4.1**	**–17**	**315**	**40.6**	**12:42**	....	....	....	....	....	....	....	....	....
	Kelowna Rockets	WHL	32	19	34	53	25	....	....	....	....	....	....	....	....	....	19	10	18	28	12	....	....	....	....
	NHL Totals		**37**	**2**	**7**	**9**	**4**	**1**	**0**	**1**	**49**	**4.1**		**315**	**40.6**	**12:42**	....	....	....	....	....	....	....	....	....

WHL East First All-Star Team (2014) • Ed Chynoweth Trophy (Memorial Cup - Leading Scorer) (2015) • Stafford Smythe Memorial Trophy (Memorial Cup - MVP) (2015)

DRAZENOVIC, Nick (DRAY-zehn-oh-vihk, NIHK)

Center. Shoots left. 6', 192 lbs. Born, Prince George, BC, January 14, 1987. St. Louis' 6th choice, 171st overall, in 2005 Entry Draft.

2002-03	Prince George	Minor-BC	STATISTICS NOT AVAILABLE																						
	Prince George	WHL	15	4	4	8	....	....	....	....	....	....	....	....	....	....	4	0	0	0	....	....	....	....	....
2003-04	Prince George	WHL	65	7	30	37	38	....	....	....	....	....	....	....	....	....	....	....	....	....	....	....	....	....	....
2004-05	Prince George	WHL	72	18	38	56	24	....	....	....	....	....	....	....	....	....	....	....	....	....	....	....	....	....	....
2005-06	Prince George	WHL	71	30	33	63	51	....	....	....	....	....	....	....	....	....	5	0	0	0	4	....	....	....	....
2006-07	Prince George	WHL	58	18	32	50	63	....	....	....	....	....	....	....	....	....	15	9	10	19	6	....	....	....	....
2007-08	Peoria Rivermen	AHL	69	16	26	42	38	....	....	....	....	....	....	....	....	....	....	....	....	....	....	....	....	....	....
2008-09	Peoria Rivermen	AHL	76	12	21	33	43	....	....	....	....	....	....	....	....	....	5	1	0	1	2	....	....	....	....
2009-10	Peoria Rivermen	AHL	58	19	20	39	40	....	....	....	....	....	....	....	....	....	....	....	....	....	....	....	....	....	....
2010-11	**St. Louis**	**NHL**	**3**	**0**	**0**	**0**	**0**	**0**	**0**	**0**	**2**	**0.0**	**–3**	**11**	**54.6**	**8:59**	....	....	....	....	....	....	....	....	....
	Peoria Rivermen	AHL	75	23	23	46	24	....	....	....	....	....	....	....	....	....	4	0	1	1	2	....	....	....	....
2011-12	Springfield	AHL	41	13	28	41	16	....	....	....	....	....	....	....	....	....	....	....	....	....	....	....	....	....	....

			Regular Season														Playoffs								
Season	Club	League	GP	G	A	Pts	PIM	PP	SH	GW	S	S%	+/-	TF	F%	Min	GP	G	A	Pts	PIM	PP	SH	GW	Min
2012-13	Springfield	AHL	62	17	36	53	30	....	....	....	....	....	....	....	....	....	8	2	2	4	2	....	....	....	....
	Columbus	**NHL**	**8**	**0**	**0**	**0**	**4**	**0**	**0**	**0**	**5**	**0.0**	**–2**	**54**	**53.7**	**9:56**	....	....	....	....	....	....	....	....	....
2013-14	**Pittsburgh**	**NHL**	**1**	**0**	**0**	**0**	**2**	**0**	**0**	**0**	**3**	**0.0**	**–1**	**4**	**75.0**	**10:18**	....	....	....	....	....	....	....	....	....
	Wilkes-Barre	AHL	63	13	29	42	28	....	....	....	....	....	....	....	....	....	9	1	3	4	2	....	....	....	....
2014-15	Wilkes-Barre	AHL	25	8	11	19	18	....	....	....	....	....	....	....	....	....	3	0	1	1	0	....	....	....	....
	NHL Totals		**12**	**0**	**0**	**0**	**6**	**0**	**0**	**0**	**10**	**0.0**		**69**	**55.1**	**9:43**	....	....	....	....	....	....	....	....	....

Signed as a free agent by **Columbus**, July 1, 2011. Signed as a free agent by **Pittsburgh**, July 6, 2013. • Missed majority of 2014-15 due to various injuries.

DREWISKE, Davis

(droo-WIHS-kee, DAY-vihs) **PHI**

Defense. Shoots left. 6'2", 220 lbs. Born, Hudson, WI, November 22, 1984.

Season	Club	League	GP	G	A	Pts	PIM	PP	SH	GW	S	S%	+/-	TF	F%	Min	GP	G	A	Pts	PIM	PP	SH	GW	Min
2003-04	Des Moines	USHL	60	4	19	23	63	....	....	....	....	....	....	....	....	....	3	0	0	0	4	....	....	....	....
2004-05	U. of Wisconsin	WCHA	34	1	5	6	20	....	....	....	....	....	....	....	....	....	....	....	....	....	....	....	....	....	....
2005-06	U. of Wisconsin	WCHA	35	2	2	4	22	....	....	....	....	....	....	....	....	....	....	....	....	....	....	....	....	....	....
2006-07	U. of Wisconsin	WCHA	41	4	6	10	46	....	....	....	....	....	....	....	....	....	....	....	....	....	....	....	....	....	....
2007-08	U. of Wisconsin	WCHA	40	5	16	21	46	....	....	....	....	....	....	....	....	....	....	....	....	....	....	....	....	....	....
	Manchester	AHL	5	0	0	0	6	....	....	....	....	....	....	....	....	....	4	0	1	1	6	....	....	....	....
2008-09	**Los Angeles**	**NHL**	**17**	**0**	**3**	**3**	**18**	**0**	**0**	**0**	**21**	**0.0**	**1**	**0**	**0.0**	**17:19**	....	....	....	....	....	....	....	....	....
	Manchester	AHL	61	1	13	14	95	....	....	....	....	....	....	....	....	....	....	....	....	....	....	....	....	....	....
2009-10	**Los Angeles**	**NHL**	**42**	**1**	**7**	**8**	**14**	**0**	**0**	**0**	**32**	**3.1**	**–4**	**0**	**0.0**	**15:15**	....	....	....	....	....	....	....	....	....
2010-11	**Los Angeles**	**NHL**	**38**	**0**	**5**	**5**	**19**	**0**	**0**	**0**	**27**	**0.0**	**–1**	**0**	**0.0**	**14:21**	....	....	....	....	....	....	....	....	....
2011-12♦	**Los Angeles**	**NHL**	**9**	**2**	**0**	**2**	**2**	**0**	**0**	**0**	**11**	**18.2**	**0**	**0**	**0.0**	**12:34**	....	....	....	....	....	....	....	....	....
2012-13	**Los Angeles**	**NHL**	**20**	**1**	**3**	**4**	**14**	**1**	**0**	**0**	**20**	**5.0**	**3**	**1**	**100.0**	**14:28**	....	....	....	....	....	....	....	....	....
	Montreal	**NHL**	**9**	**1**	**2**	**3**	**0**	**0**	**0**	**0**	**8**	**12.5**	**0**	**0**	**0.0**	**16:50**	....	....	....	....	....	....	....	....	....
2013-14	Hamilton	AHL	21	0	3	3	8	....	....	....	....	....	....	....	....	....	....	....	....	....	....	....	....	....	....
2014-15	Hamilton	AHL	62	4	18	22	28	....	....	....	....	....	....	....	....	....	....	....	....	....	....	....	....	....	....
	NHL Totals		**135**	**5**	**20**	**25**	**67**	**1**	**0**	**0**	**119**	**4.2**		**1**	**100.0**	**15:04**	....	....	....	....	....	....	....	....	....

Signed as a free agent by **Los Angeles**, April 1, 2008. • Missed majority of 2010-11 and 2011-12 as a healthy reserve. Traded to **Montreal** by **Los Angeles** for Montreal's 5th round choice (Patrik Bartosak) in 2013 Entry Draft, April 2, 2013. • Missed majority of 2013-14 due to recurring shoulder injury. Signed as a free agent by **Philadelphia**, July 1, 2015.

DROUIN, Jonathan

(droo-EHN, JAWN-ah-thuhn) **T.B.**

Left wing. Shoots left. 5'11", 191 lbs. Born, Ste-Agathe, QC, March 28, 1995. Tampa Bay's 1st choice, 3rd overall, in 2013 Entry Draft.

Season	Club	League	GP	G	A	Pts	PIM	PP	SH	GW	S	S%	+/-	TF	F%	Min	GP	G	A	Pts	PIM	PP	SH	GW	Min
2010-11	Lac St-Louis Lions	QAAA	38	22	36	58	38	....	....	....	....	....	....	....	....	....	15	11	17	28	18	....	....	....	....
2011-12	Lac St-Louis Lions	QAAA	21	21	29	50	35	....	....	....	....	....	....	....	....	....	....	....	....	....	....	....	....	....	....
	Halifax	QMJHL	33	7	22	29	12	....	....	....	....	....	....	....	....	....	17	9	17	26	4	....	....	....	....
2012-13	Halifax	QMJHL	49	41	64	105	32	....	....	....	....	....	....	....	....	....	17	12	*23	*35	14	....	....	....	....
2013-14	Halifax	QMJHL	46	29	*79	108	43	....	....	....	....	....	....	....	....	....	16	13	*28	*41	18	....	....	....	....
2014-15	**Tampa Bay**	**NHL**	**70**	**4**	**28**	**32**	**34**	**3**	**0**	**0**	**76**	**5.3**	**3**	**21**	**52.4**	**13:14**	**6**	**0**	**0**	**0**	**2**	**0**	**0**	**0**	**10:02**
	Syracuse Crunch	AHL	2	1	2	3	0	....	....	....	....	....	....	....	....	....	....	....	....	....	....	....	....	....	....
	NHL Totals		**70**	**4**	**28**	**32**	**34**	**3**	**0**	**0**	**76**	**5.3**		**21**	**52.4**	**13:14**	**6**	**0**	**0**	**0**	**2**	**0**	**0**	**0**	**10:02**

QMJHL First All-Star Team (2013, 2014) • QMJHL Player of the Year (2013) • Canadian Major Junior Player of the Year (2013)

DUBINSKY, Brandon

(DOO-bihn-skee, BRAN-duhn) **CBJ**

Center. Shoots left. 6'2", 216 lbs. Born, Anchorage, AK, April 29, 1986. NY Rangers' 6th choice, 60th overall, in 2004 Entry Draft.

Season	Club	League	GP	G	A	Pts	PIM	PP	SH	GW	S	S%	+/-	TF	F%	Min	GP	G	A	Pts	PIM	PP	SH	GW	Min
2001-02	Alaska All-Stars	AASHA	37	14	24	38	....	....	....	....	....	....	....	....	....	....	....	....	....	....	....	....	....	....	....
2002-03	Portland	WHL	44	8	18	26	35	....	....	....	....	....	....	....	....	....	7	2	2	4	10	....	....	....	....
2003-04	Portland	WHL	71	30	48	78	137	....	....	....	....	....	....	....	....	....	5	0	2	2	6	....	....	....	....
2004-05	Portland	WHL	68	23	36	59	160	....	....	....	....	....	....	....	....	....	7	4	5	9	8	....	....	....	....
2005-06	Portland	WHL	51	21	46	67	98	....	....	....	....	....	....	....	....	....	12	5	10	15	24	....	....	....	....
	Hartford	AHL	....	....	....	....	....	....	....	....	....	....	....	....	....	....	11	5	5	10	14	....	....	....	....
2006-07	**NY Rangers**	**NHL**	**6**	**0**	**0**	**0**	**2**	**0**	**0**	**0**	**9**	**0.0**	**0**	**26**	**46.2**	**8:10**	....	....	....	....	....	....	....	....	....
	Hartford	AHL	71	21	22	43	115	....	....	....	....	....	....	....	....	....	7	1	3	4	12	....	....	....	....
2007-08	**NY Rangers**	**NHL**	**82**	**14**	**26**	**40**	**79**	**1**	**0**	**0**	**157**	**8.9**	**8**	**995**	**51.5**	**14:30**	**10**	**4**	**4**	**8**	**12**	**2**	**0**	**0**	**18:59**
2008-09	**NY Rangers**	**NHL**	**82**	**13**	**28**	**41**	**112**	**3**	**1**	**7**	**188**	**6.9**	**–6**	**870**	**53.6**	**16:38**	**7**	**1**	**3**	**4**	**18**	**0**	**0**	**1**	**18:14**
2009-10	**NY Rangers**	**NHL**	**69**	**20**	**24**	**44**	**54**	**6**	**2**	**5**	**165**	**12.1**	**9**	**675**	**51.4**	**19:33**	....	....	....	....	....	....	....	....	....
2010-11	**NY Rangers**	**NHL**	**77**	**24**	**30**	**54**	**100**	**4**	**2**	**2**	**202**	**11.9**	**–3**	**875**	**52.5**	**20:14**	**5**	**2**	**1**	**3**	**2**	**0**	**0**	**1**	**24:56**
2011-12	**NY Rangers**	**NHL**	**77**	**10**	**24**	**34**	**110**	**0**	**1**	**1**	**140**	**7.1**	**16**	**395**	**51.9**	**16:16**	**9**	**0**	**2**	**2**	**14**	**0**	**0**	**0**	**14:27**
2012-13	Alaska Aces	ECHL	17	9	7	16	22	....	....	....	....	....	....	....	....	....	....	....	....	....	....	....	....	....	....
	Columbus	**NHL**	**29**	**2**	**18**	**20**	**76**	**1**	**0**	**0**	**50**	**4.0**	**2**	**439**	**58.3**	**18:24**	....	....	....	....	....	....	....	....	....
2013-14	**Columbus**	**NHL**	**76**	**16**	**34**	**50**	**98**	**4**	**2**	**2**	**189**	**8.5**	**5**	**1107**	**52.9**	**18:47**	**6**	**1**	**5**	**6**	**6**	**0**	**0**	**0**	**20:43**
2014-15	**Columbus**	**NHL**	**47**	**13**	**23**	**36**	**43**	**0**	**1**	**1**	**100**	**13.0**	**11**	**859**	**50.8**	**18:04**	....	....	....	....	....	....	....	....	....
	NHL Totals		**545**	**112**	**207**	**319**	**674**	**19**	**9**	**18**	**1200**	**9.3**		**6241**	**52.5**	**17:34**	**37**	**8**	**15**	**23**	**52**	**2**	**0**	**2**	**18:50**

WHL West Second All-Star Team (2004, 2006)

Traded to **Columbus** by **NY Rangers** with Artem Anisimov, Tim Erixon and NY Rangers' 1st round choice (Kerby Rychel) in 2013 Entry Draft for Rick Nash, Steven Delisle and Columbus' 3rd round choice (Pavel Buchnevich) in 2013 Entry Draft, July 23, 2012. Signed as a free agent by **Alaska** (ECHL), October 1, 2012.

DUCHENE, Matt

(DOO-shayn, MAT) **COL**

Center. Shoots left. 5'11", 200 lbs. Born, Haliburton, ON, January 16, 1991. Colorado's 1st choice, 3rd overall, in 2009 Entry Draft.

Season	Club	League	GP	G	A	Pts	PIM	PP	SH	GW	S	S%	+/-	TF	F%	Min	GP	G	A	Pts	PIM	PP	SH	GW	Min
2006-07	Cent. Ont. Wolves	Minor-ON	52	69	37	106	36	....	....	....	....	....	....	....	....	....	....	....	....	....	....	....	....	....	....
2007-08	Brampton	OHL	64	30	20	50	22	....	....	....	....	....	....	....	....	....	5	1	1	2	10	....	....	....	....
2008-09	Brampton	OHL	57	31	48	79	42	....	....	....	....	....	....	....	....	....	21	14	12	26	21	....	....	....	....
2009-10	**Colorado**	**NHL**	**81**	**24**	**31**	**55**	**16**	**10**	**1**	**2**	**180**	**13.3**	**1**	**1088**	**44.0**	**17:44**	**6**	**0**	**3**	**3**	**0**	**0**	**0**	**0**	**19:20**
2010-11	**Colorado**	**NHL**	**80**	**27**	**40**	**67**	**33**	**3**	**0**	**2**	**202**	**13.4**	**–8**	**1246**	**50.4**	**18:57**	....	....	....	....	....	....	....	....	....
2011-12	**Colorado**	**NHL**	**58**	**14**	**14**	**28**	**8**	**5**	**0**	**2**	**132**	**10.6**	**–11**	**391**	**51.2**	**16:17**	....	....	....	....	....	....	....	....	....
2012-13	Frolunda	Sweden	19	4	10	14	12	....	....	....	....	....	....	....	....	....	....	....	....	....	....	....	....	....	....
	HC Ambri-Piotta	Swiss	4	2	3	5	2	....	....	....	....	....	....	....	....	....	....	....	....	....	....	....	....	....	....
	Colorado	**NHL**	**47**	**17**	**26**	**43**	**12**	**2**	**0**	**3**	**132**	**12.9**	**–12**	**893**	**54.7**	**20:55**	....	....	....	....	....	....	....	....	....
2013-14	**Colorado**	**NHL**	**71**	**23**	**47**	**70**	**19**	**5**	**0**	**6**	**217**	**10.6**	**8**	**1058**	**50.3**	**18:30**	**2**	**0**	**3**	**3**	**2**	**0**	**0**	**0**	**20:15**
	Canada	Olympics	4	0	0	0	0	....	....	....	....	....	....	....	....	....	....	....	....	....	....	....	....	....	....
2014-15	**Colorado**	**NHL**	**82**	**21**	**34**	**55**	**16**	**2**	**0**	**4**	**207**	**10.1**	**3**	**1217**	**52.2**	**18:34**	....	....	....	....	....	....	....	....	....
	NHL Totals		**419**	**126**	**192**	**318**	**104**	**27**	**1**	**19**	**1070**	**11.8**		**5893**	**50.3**	**18:25**	**8**	**0**	**6**	**6**	**2**	**0**	**0**	**0**	**19:33**

NHL All-Rookie Team (2010)

Played in NHL All-Star Game (2011)

Signed as a free agent by **Frolunda** (Sweden), October 2, 2012. Signed as a free agent by **Ambri-Piotta** (Swiss), December 9, 2012.

DUCLAIR, Anthony

(doo-KLAIR, AN-thuh-nee) **ARI**

Left wing. Shoots left. 5'11", 185 lbs. Born, Pointe-Claire, QC, August 26, 1995. NY Rangers' 3rd choice, 80th overall, in 2013 Entry Draft.

Season	Club	League	GP	G	A	Pts	PIM	PP	SH	GW	S	S%	+/-	TF	F%	Min	GP	G	A	Pts	PIM	PP	SH	GW	Min
2009-10	Laurentides	Minor-QC	59	81	47	128	32	....	....	....	....	....	....	....	....	....	....	....	....	....	....	....	....	....	....
2010-11	Lac St-Louis Lions	QAAA	34	25	32	57	36	....	....	....	....	....	....	....	....	....	14	9	14	23	20	....	....	....	....
2011-12	Quebec Remparts	QMJHL	63	31	35	66	50	....	....	....	....	....	....	....	....	....	11	3	5	8	8	....	....	....	....
2012-13	Quebec Remparts	QMJHL	55	20	30	50	22	....	....	....	....	....	....	....	....	....	11	3	5	8	12	....	....	....	....
2013-14	Quebec Remparts	QMJHL	59	50	49	99	56	....	....	....	....	....	....	....	....	....	....	....	....	....	....	....	....	....	....
2014-15	**NY Rangers**	**NHL**	**18**	**1**	**6**	**7**	**4**	**0**	**0**	**0**	**18**	**5.6**	**4**	**0**	**0.0**	**12:09**	....	....	....	....	....	....	....	....	....
	Quebec Remparts	QMJHL	26	15	19	34	24	....	....	....	....	....	....	....	....	....	22	8	18	26	18	....	....	....	....
	NHL Totals		**18**	**1**	**6**	**7**	**4**	**0**	**0**	**0**	**18**	**5.6**		**0**	**0.0**	**12:09**	....	....	....	....	....	....	....	....	....

QMJHL First All-Star Team (2014)

Traded to **Arizona** by **NY Rangers** with John Moore, Tampa Bay's 2nd round choice (previously acquired, later traded to Calgary – Calgary selected Oliver Kylington) in 2015 Entry Draft and future considerations for Keith Yandle, Chris Summers and a 4th round choice in 2016 Entry Draft, March 1, 2015.

DUCO, Mike

(DOO-koh, MIGHK)

Left wing. Shoots left. 5'10", 200 lbs. Born, Toronto, ON, July 8, 1987.

			Regular Season														Playoffs								
Season	Club	League	GP	G	A	Pts	PIM	PP	SH	GW	S	S%	+/-	TF	F%	Min	GP	G	A	Pts	PIM	PP	SH	GW	Min
2002-03	Tor. Marlboros	GTHL	32	27	33	60	160	....	....	....	....	....	....	....	....	....	....	....	....	....	....	....	....	....	....
2003-04	Stouffville Spirit	ON-Jr.A	7	3	2	5	15	....	....	....	....	....	....	....	....	....	....	....	....	....	....	....	....	....	....
	Thornhill Islanders	ON-Jr.A	37	25	30	55	50	....	....	....	....	....	....	....	....	....	....	....	....	....	....	....	....	....	....
	Kitchener Rangers	OHL	5	1	2	3	4	....	....	....	....	....	....	....	....	....	4	0	1	1	4	....	....	....	....
2004-05	Kitchener Rangers	OHL	62	24	26	50	78	....	....	....	....	....	....	....	....	....	15	0	0	0	11	....	....	....	....
2005-06	Kitchener Rangers	OHL	59	22	22	44	113	....	....	....	....	....	....	....	....	....	5	2	1	3	10	....	....	....	....
2006-07	Kitchener Rangers	OHL	54	20	20	40	121	....	....	....	....	....	....	....	....	....	9	1	1	2	12	....	....	....	....
2007-08	Kitchener Rangers	OHL	62	32	22	54	173	....	....	....	....	....	....	....	....	....	20	*16	6	22	37	....	....	....	....
2008-09	Rochester	AHL	68	14	14	28	147	....	....	....	....	....	....	....	....	....	....	....	....	....	....	....	....	....	....
2009-10	**Florida**	**NHL**	**10**	**0**	**0**	**0**	**50**	**0**	**0**	**0**	**6**	**0.0**	**-3**	**0**	**0.0**	**7:43**	....	....	....	....	....	....	....	....	....
	Rochester	AHL	59	9	10	19	111	....	....	....	....	....	....	....	....	....	7	1	0	1	18	....	....	....	....
2010-11	**Florida**	**NHL**	**2**	**0**	**0**	**0**	**10**	**0**	**0**	**0**	**0**	**0.0**	**-1**	**0**	**0.0**	**8:33**	....	....	....	....	....	....	....	....	....
	Rochester	AHL	67	20	11	31	126	....	....	....	....	....	....	....	....	....	....	....	....	....	....	....	....	....	....
2011-12	Chicago Wolves	AHL	56	11	13	24	59	....	....	....	....	....	....	....	....	....	5	0	0	0	2	....	....	....	....
	Vancouver	**NHL**	**6**	**0**	**2**	**2**	**5**	**0**	**0**	**0**	**4**	**0.0**	**1**	**0**	**0.0**	**8:03**	....	....	....	....	....	....	....	....	....
2012-13	Salzburg	Austria	15	4	2	6	7	....	....	....	....	....	....	....	....	....	6	2	0	2	4	....	....	....	....
2013-14	Toronto Marlies	AHL	17	2	3	5	32	....	....	....	....	....	....	....	....	....	....	....	....	....	....	....	....	....	....
	Orlando	ECHL	19	4	3	7	30	....	....	....	....	....	....	....	....	....	1	0	0	0	2	....	....	....	....
2014-15	Indy Fuel	ECHL	63	17	19	36	113	....	....	....	....	....	....	....	....	....	....	....	....	....	....	....	....	....	....
	NHL Totals		**18**	**0**	**2**	**2**	**65**	**0**	**0**	**0**	**10**	**0.0**		**0**	**0.0**	**7:56**									

Signed as a free agent by **Florida**, October 8, 2007. Traded to **Vancouver** by **Florida** for Sergei Shirokov, July 8, 2011. Signed as a free agent by **Salzburg** (Austria), December 9, 2012. Signed as a free agent by **Toronto** (AHL), October 3, 2013. Signed as a free agent by **Indy** (ECHL), October 6, 2014.

DUMBA, Matt

(DUHM-ba, MAT) **MIN**

Defense. Shoots right. 6', 187 lbs. Born, Regina, SK, July 25, 1994. Minnesota's 1st choice, 7th overall, in 2012 Entry Draft.

			Regular Season														Playoffs								
Season	Club	League	GP	G	A	Pts	PIM	PP	SH	GW	S	S%	+/-	TF	F%	Min	GP	G	A	Pts	PIM	PP	SH	GW	Min
2007-08	Calgary Bronks	AMBHL	33	3	8	11	26	....	....	....	....	....	....	....	....	....	2	1	1	2	2	....	....	....	....
2008-09	Calgary Bronks	AMBHL	33	20	18	38	96	....	....	....	....	....	....	....	....	....	....	....	....	....	....	....	....	....	....
2009-10	Edge School	High-AB	41	16	28	44	47	....	....	....	....	....	....	....	....	....	....	....	....	....	....	....	....	....	....
	Red Deer Rebels	WHL	6	0	2	2	4	....	....	....	....	....	....	....	....	....	2	0	0	0	4	....	....	....	....
2010-11	Red Deer Rebels	WHL	62	15	11	26	83	....	....	....	....	....	....	....	....	....	9	2	0	2	20	....	....	....	....
2011-12	Red Deer Rebels	WHL	69	20	37	57	67	....	....	....	....	....	....	....	....	....	....	....	....	....	....	....	....	....	....
2012-13	Red Deer Rebels	WHL	62	16	26	42	80	....	....	....	....	....	....	....	....	....	9	2	2	4	14	....	....	....	....
	Houston Aeros	AHL	3	0	0	0	2	....	....	....	....	....	....	....	....	....	5	0	0	0	0	....	....	....	....
2013-14	**Minnesota**	**NHL**	**13**	**1**	**1**	**2**	**2**	**1**	**0**	**0**	**12**	**8.3**	**-5**	**0**	**0.0**	**12:27**	....	....	....	....	....	....	....	....	....
	Portland	WHL	26	8	16	24	37	....	....	....	....	....	....	....	....	....	21	8	10	18	33	....	....	....	....
2014-15	**Minnesota**	**NHL**	**58**	**8**	**8**	**16**	**23**	**2**	**0**	**2**	**86**	**9.3**	**13**	**0**	**0.0**	**15:01**	**10**	**2**	**2**	**4**	**2**	**2**	**0**	**0**	**16:05**
	Iowa Wild	AHL	20	5	9	14	6	....	....	....	....	....	....	....	....	....	....	....	....	....	....	....	....	....	....
	NHL Totals		**71**	**9**	**9**	**18**	**25**	**3**	**0**	**2**	**98**	**9.2**		**0**	**0.0**	**14:32**	**10**	**2**	**2**	**4**	**2**	**2**	**0**	**0**	**16:05**

• Missed majority of 2013-14 as a healthy reserve.

DUMONT, Gabriel

(doo-MAWNT, gah-BREE-ehl) **MTL**

Center. Shoots right. 5'10", 184 lbs. Born, Ville Degelis, QC, October 6, 1990. Montreal's 5th choice, 139th overall, in 2009 Entry Draft.

			Regular Season														Playoffs								
Season	Club	League	GP	G	A	Pts	PIM	PP	SH	GW	S	S%	+/-	TF	F%	Min	GP	G	A	Pts	PIM	PP	SH	GW	Min
2005-06	Ecole Notre Dame	QAAA	29	5	16	21	50	....	....	....	....	....	....	....	....	....	9	0	1	1	12	....	....	....	....
2006-07	Ecole Notre Dame	QAAA	39	30	42	72	127	....	....	....	....	....	....	....	....	....	13	11	12	23	20	....	....	....	....
	Drummondville	QMJHL	8	1	1	2	6	....	....	....	....	....	....	....	....	....	6	0	2	2	0	....	....	....	....
2007-08	Drummondville	QMJHL	59	11	14	25	103	....	....	....	....	....	....	....	....	....	....	....	....	....	....	....	....	....	....
2008-09	Drummondville	QMJHL	51	28	21	49	63	....	....	....	....	....	....	....	....	....	19	6	13	19	32	....	....	....	....
2009-10	Drummondville	QMJHL	62	*51	42	93	127	....	....	....	....	....	....	....	....	....	14	*11	10	21	19	....	....	....	....
	Hamilton	AHL	....	....	....	....	....	....	....	....	....	....	....	....	....	....	11	2	0	2	12	....	....	....	....
2010-11	Hamilton	AHL	64	5	13	18	79	....	....	....	....	....	....	....	....	....	20	6	3	9	6	....	....	....	....
2011-12	**Montreal**	**NHL**	**3**	**0**	**0**	**0**	**0**	**0**	**0**	**0**	**1**	**0.0**	**-1**	**18**	**16.7**	**8:34**	....	....	....	....	....	....	....	....	....
	Hamilton	AHL	59	13	11	24	55	....	....	....	....	....	....	....	....	....	....	....	....	....	....	....	....	....	....
2012-13	Hamilton	AHL	55	16	15	31	83	....	....	....	....	....	....	....	....	....	....	....	....	....	....	....	....	....	....
	Montreal	**NHL**	**10**	**1**	**2**	**3**	**13**	**0**	**0**	**0**	**20**	**5.0**	**1**	**46**	**63.0**	**9:41**	**3**	**0**	**0**	**0**	**12**	**0**	**0**	**0**	**6:21**
2013-14	**Montreal**	**NHL**	**2**	**0**	**0**	**0**	**0**	**0**	**0**	**0**	**1**	**0.0**	**0**	**8**	**37.5**	**6:50**	....	....	....	....	....	....	....	....	....
	Hamilton	AHL	74	19	17	36	111	....	....	....	....	....	....	....	....	....	....	....	....	....	....	....	....	....	....
2014-15	**Montreal**	**NHL**	**3**	**0**	**0**	**0**	**0**	**0**	**0**	**0**	**4**	**0.0**	**-1**	**13**	**84.6**	**9:07**	....	....	....	....	....	....	....	....	....
	Hamilton	AHL	66	20	25	45	88	....	....	....	....	....	....	....	....	....	....	....	....	....	....	....	....	....	....
	NHL Totals		**18**	**1**	**2**	**3**	**13**	**0**	**0**	**0**	**26**	**3.8**		**85**	**54.1**	**9:05**	**3**	**0**	**0**	**0**	**12**	**0**	**0**	**0**	**6:21**

QMJHL First All-Star Team (2010) • Canadian Major Junior Second All-Star Team (2010)

DUMOULIN, Brian

(DOO-moh-lihn, BRIGH-uhn) **PIT**

Defense. Shoots left. 6'4", 219 lbs. Born, Biddeford, ME, September 6, 1991. Carolina's 2nd choice, 51st overall, in 2009 Entry Draft.

			Regular Season														Playoffs								
Season	Club	League	GP	G	A	Pts	PIM	PP	SH	GW	S	S%	+/-	TF	F%	Min	GP	G	A	Pts	PIM	PP	SH	GW	Min
2007-08	Biddeford Tigers	High-ME	24	13	48	61	10	....	....	....	....	....	....	....	....	....	....	....	....	....	....	....	....	....	....
2008-09	N.H. Jr. Monarchs	EJHL	41	7	23	30	30	....	....	....	....	....	....	....	....	....	7	0	3	3	2	....	....	....	....
2009-10	Boston College	H-East	42	1	21	22	16	....	....	....	....	....	....	....	....	....	....	....	....	....	....	....	....	....	....
2010-11	Boston College	H-East	37	3	30	33	6	....	....	....	....	....	....	....	....	....	....	....	....	....	....	....	....	....	....
2011-12	Boston College	H-East	44	7	21	28	26	....	....	....	....	....	....	....	....	....	....	....	....	....	....	....	....	....	....
2012-13	Wilkes-Barre	AHL	73	6	18	24	18	....	....	....	....	....	....	....	....	....	15	2	6	8	6	....	....	....	....
2013-14	**Pittsburgh**	**NHL**	**6**	**0**	**1**	**1**	**4**	**0**	**0**	**0**	**3**	**0.0**	**1**	**0**	**0.0**	**19:14**	....	....	....	....	....	....	....	....	....
	Wilkes-Barre	AHL	53	5	16	21	21	....	....	....	....	....	....	....	....	....	17	3	9	12	22	....	....	....	....
2014-15	**Pittsburgh**	**NHL**	**8**	**1**	**0**	**1**	**2**	**0**	**0**	**0**	**4**	**25.0**	**0**	**0**	**0.0**	**15:40**	**5**	**0**	**0**	**0**	**0**	**0**	**0**	**0**	**14:06**
	Wilkes-Barre	AHL	62	4	29	33	18	....	....	....	....	....	....	....	....	....	6	0	3	3	0	....	....	....	....
	NHL Totals		**14**	**1**	**1**	**2**	**6**	**0**	**0**	**0**	**7**	**14.3**		**0**	**0.0**	**17:12**	**5**	**0**	**0**	**0**	**0**	**0**	**0**	**0**	**14:06**

Hockey East All-Rookie Team (2010) • NCAA Championship All-Tournament Team (2010, 2012) • Hockey East First All-Star Team (2011, 2012) • NCAA East First All-American Team (2011, 2012)

Traded to **Pittsburgh** by **Carolina** with Brandon Sutter and Carolina's 1st round choice (Derrick Pouliot) in 2012 Entry Draft for Jordan Staal, June 22, 2012.

DUPUIS, Pascal

(doo-PWEE, pas-KAL) **PIT**

Left wing. Shoots left. 6'1", 205 lbs. Born, Laval, QC, April 7, 1979.

			Regular Season														Playoffs								
Season	Club	League	GP	G	A	Pts	PIM	PP	SH	GW	S	S%	+/-	TF	F%	Min	GP	G	A	Pts	PIM	PP	SH	GW	Min
1995-96	Laval-Laurentides	QAAA	41	10	15	25	103	....	....	....	....	....	....	....	....	....	14	11	11	22	24	....	....	....	....
1996-97	Rouyn-Noranda	QMJHL	44	9	15	24	20	....	....	....	....	....	....	....	....	....	....	....	....	....	....	....	....	....	....
1997-98	Rouyn-Noranda	QMJHL	42	10	19	29	36	....	....	....	....	....	....	....	....	....	....	....	....	....	....	....	....	....	....
	Shawinigan	QMJHL	25	6	11	17	10	....	....	....	....	....	....	....	....	....	6	2	0	2	4	....	....	....	....
1998-99	Shawinigan	QMJHL	57	30	42	72	118	....	....	....	....	....	....	....	....	....	6	1	8	9	18	....	....	....	....
99-2000	Shawinigan	QMJHL	61	50	55	105	164	....	....	....	....	....	....	....	....	....	13	*15	7	22	4	....	....	....	....
2000-01	**Minnesota**	**NHL**	**4**	**1**	**0**	**1**	**4**	**1**	**0**	**0**	**8**	**12.5**	**0**	**0**	**0.0**	**15:36**	....	....	....	....	....	....	....	....	....
	Cleveland	IHL	70	19	24	43	37	....	....	....	....	....	....	....	....	....	4	0	0	0	0	....	....	....	....
2001-02	**Minnesota**	**NHL**	**76**	**15**	**12**	**27**	**16**	**3**	**2**	**0**	**154**	**9.7**	**-10**	**40**	**32.5**	**15:08**	....	....	....	....	....	....	....	....	....
2002-03	**Minnesota**	**NHL**	**80**	**20**	**28**	**48**	**44**	**6**	**0**	**4**	**183**	**10.9**	**17**	**186**	**40.9**	**17:30**	**16**	**4**	**4**	**8**	**8**	**2**	**0**	**1**	**16:58**
2003-04	**Minnesota**	**NHL**	**59**	**11**	**15**	**26**	**20**	**2**	**0**	**1**	**127**	**8.7**	**5**	**129**	**45.7**	**15:48**	....	....	....	....	....	....	....	....	....
2004-05	HC Ajoie	Swiss-2	8	5	5	10	26	....	....	....	....	....	....	....	....	....	6	6	8	14	8	....	....	....	....
2005-06	**Minnesota**	**NHL**	**67**	**10**	**16**	**26**	**40**	**4**	**0**	**2**	**151**	**6.6**	**-10**	**93**	**29.0**	**16:30**	....	....	....	....	....	....	....	....	....
2006-07	**Minnesota**	**NHL**	**48**	**10**	**3**	**13**	**38**	**2**	**2**	**0**	**106**	**9.4**	**-7**	**110**	**27.3**	**15:07**	....	....	....	....	....	....	....	....	....
	NY Rangers	**NHL**	**6**	**1**	**0**	**1**	**0**	**0**	**0**	**0**	**10**	**10.0**	**-4**	**2**	**50.0**	**15:30**	....	....	....	....	....	....	....	....	....
	Atlanta	**NHL**	**17**	**3**	**2**	**5**	**4**	**0**	**0**	**1**	**40**	**7.5**	**-6**	**19**	**52.6**	**16:44**	**4**	**1**	**2**	**3**	**4**	**0**	**0**	**0**	**20:28**
2007-08	**Atlanta**	**NHL**	**62**	**10**	**5**	**15**	**24**	**0**	**3**	**1**	**111**	**9.0**	**-4**	**13**	**38.5**	**14:46**	....	....	....	....	....	....	....	....	....
	Pittsburgh	**NHL**	**16**	**2**	**10**	**12**	**8**	**0**	**0**	**0**	**32**	**6.3**	**4**	**3**	**0.0**	**16:50**	**20**	**2**	**5**	**7**	**18**	**0**	**0**	**0**	**16:14**
2008-09 ♦	**Pittsburgh**	**NHL**	**71**	**12**	**16**	**28**	**30**	**0**	**0**	**2**	**145**	**8.3**	**1**	**16**	**18.8**	**14:13**	**16**	**0**	**0**	**0**	**8**	**0**	**0**	**0**	**8:23**
2009-10	**Pittsburgh**	**NHL**	**81**	**18**	**20**	**38**	**16**	**0**	**0**	**5**	**157**	**11.5**	**5**	**33**	**39.4**	**14:11**	**13**	**2**	**6**	**8**	**4**	**0**	**0**	**1**	**16:51**
2010-11	**Pittsburgh**	**NHL**	**81**	**17**	**20**	**37**	**59**	**0**	**4**	**3**	**171**	**9.9**	**16**	**28**	**21.4**	**16:52**	**7**	**1**	**0**	**1**	**2**	**0**	**0**	**0**	**16:36**
2011-12	**Pittsburgh**	**NHL**	**82**	**25**	**34**	**59**	**34**	**0**	**3**	**8**	**214**	**11.7**	**18**	**115**	**44.4**	**16:56**	**6**	**2**	**4**	**6**	**0**	**0**	**0**	**0**	**17:08**
2012-13	**Pittsburgh**	**NHL**	**48**	**20**	**18**	**38**	**26**	**2**	**1**	**2**	**140**	**14.3**	**31**	**57**	**47.4**	**17:30**	**15**	**7**	**4**	**11**	**12**	**0**	***2**	**0**	**18:52**

			Regular Season														Playoffs								
Season	Club	League	GP	G	A	Pts	PIM	PP	SH	GW	S	S%	+/-	TF	F%	Min	GP	G	A	Pts	PIM	PP	SH	GW	Min
2013-14	**Pittsburgh**	**NHL**	**39**	**7**	**13**	**20**	**8**	**0**	**0**	**0**	**97**	**7.2**	**6**	**6**	**33.3**	**17:42**	....	....	....	....	....	....	....	....	....
2014-15	**Pittsburgh**	**NHL**	**16**	**6**	**5**	**11**	**4**	**2**	**0**	**1**	**44**	**13.6**	**2**	**1**	**100.0**	**16:39**	....	....	....	....	....	....	....	....	....
	NHL Totals		**853**	**188**	**217**	**405**	**375**	**22**	**15**	**30**	**1890**	**9.9**		**851**	**38.1**	**16:00**	**97**	**19**	**25**	**44**	**56**	**2**	**2**	**2**	**15:48**

Signed as a free agent by **Minnesota**, August 18, 2000. Signed as a free agent by **Ajoie** (Swiss-2), January 14, 2005. Traded to **NY Rangers** by **Minnesota** for Adam Hall, February 9, 2007. Traded to **Atlanta** by **NY Rangers** with NY Rangers' 3rd round choice (later traded to Pittsburgh - Pittsburgh selected Robert Bortuzzo) in 2007 Entry Draft for Alex Bourret, February 27, 2007. Traded to **Pittsburgh** by **Atlanta** with Marian Hossa for Colby Armstrong, Erik Christensen, Angelo Esposito and Pittsburgh's 1st round choice (Daulton Leveille) in 2008 Entry Draft, February 26, 2008. • Missed majority of 2013-14 due to knee inury at Ottawa, December 23, 2013. • Missed majority of 2014-15 after diagnosis of blood clot in lungs, November 19, 2014.

DWYER, Patrick

(DWIGH-uhr, PAT-rihk)

Right wing. Shoots right. 5'11", 175 lbs. Born, Spokane, WA, June 22, 1983. Atlanta's 3rd choice, 116th overall, in 2002 Entry Draft.

Season	Club	League	GP	G	A	Pts	PIM	PP	SH	GW	S	S%	+/-	TF	F%	Min	GP	G	A	Pts	PIM	PP	SH	GW	Min
2000-01	Great Falls	NWJHL	40	33	57	90	106	....	....	....	....	....	....	....	....	....	12	10	12	22	....	....	....	....	....
2001-02	Western Mich.	CCHA	38	17	17	34	26	....	....	....	....	....	....	....	....	....	....	....	....	....	....	....	....	....	....
2002-03	Western Mich.	CCHA	33	9	10	19	20	....	....	....	....	....	....	....	....	....	....	....	....	....	....	....	....	....	....
2003-04	Western Mich.	CCHA	35	13	13	26	22	....	....	....	....	....	....	....	....	....	....	....	....	....	....	....	....	....	....
2004-05	Western Mich.	CCHA	36	6	16	22	56	....	....	....	....	....	....	....	....	....	....	....	....	....	....	....	....	....	....
2005-06	Chicago Wolves	AHL	73	16	29	45	49	....	....	....	....	....	....	....	....	....	....	....	....	....	....	....	....	....	....
2006-07	Albany River Rats	AHL	79	16	25	41	39	....	....	....	....	....	....	....	....	....	5	0	1	1	5	....	....	....	....
2007-08	Albany River Rats	AHL	59	13	12	25	29	....	....	....	....	....	....	....	....	....	7	0	2	2	0	....	....	....	....
2008-09	**Carolina**	**NHL**	**13**	**1**	**0**	**1**	**0**	**0**	**0**	**0**	**9**	**11.1**	**–2**	**12**	**41.7**	**8:34**	**2**	**0**	**1**	**1**	**0**	**0**	**0**	**0**	**4:48**
	Albany River Rats	AHL	62	24	16	40	29	....	....	....	....	....	....	....	....	....	....	....	....	....	....	....	....	....	....
2009-10	**Carolina**	**NHL**	**58**	**7**	**5**	**12**	**6**	**0**	**0**	**2**	**80**	**8.8**	**–3**	**224**	**34.8**	**12:30**	....	....	....	....	....	....	....	....	....
2010-11	**Carolina**	**NHL**	**80**	**8**	**10**	**18**	**12**	**0**	**1**	**2**	**104**	**7.7**	**–6**	**238**	**33.6**	**12:35**	....	....	....	....	....	....	....	....	....
2011-12	**Carolina**	**NHL**	**73**	**5**	**7**	**12**	**23**	**0**	**2**	**0**	**120**	**4.2**	**0**	**29**	**51.7**	**15:22**	....	....	....	....	....	....	....	....	....
2012-13	**Carolina**	**NHL**	**46**	**8**	**8**	**16**	**12**	**1**	**1**	**0**	**93**	**8.6**	**–7**	**47**	**36.2**	**15:26**	....	....	....	....	....	....	....	....	....
2013-14	**Carolina**	**NHL**	**75**	**8**	**14**	**22**	**14**	**0**	**2**	**2**	**134**	**6.0**	**–2**	**24**	**37.5**	**14:39**	....	....	....	....	....	....	....	....	....
2014-15	**Carolina**	**NHL**	**71**	**5**	**7**	**12**	**10**	**0**	**0**	**0**	**77**	**6.5**	**–12**	**19**	**26.3**	**12:46**	....	....	....	....	....	....	....	....	....
	NHL Totals		**416**	**42**	**51**	**93**	**77**	**1**	**6**	**6**	**617**	**6.8**		**593**	**35.2**	**13:39**	**2**	**0**	**1**	**1**	**0**	**0**	**0**	**0**	**4:48**

CCHA All-Rookie Team (2002) • CCHA Rookie of the Year (2002)

Signed as a free agent by **Carolina**, July 7, 2006.

DZIURZYNSKI, David

(z'yuhr-ZIHN-skee, DAY-vihd) **OTT**

Center. Shoots left. 6'3", 222 lbs. Born, Lloydminster, AB, October 6, 1989.

Season	Club	League	GP	G	A	Pts	PIM	PP	SH	GW	S	S%	+/-	TF	F%	Min	GP	G	A	Pts	PIM	PP	SH	GW	Min
2007-08	Lloydminster	AJHL	52	8	12	20	82	....	....	....	....	....	....	....	....	....	3	0	0	0	4	....	....	....	....
2008-09	Lloydminster	AJHL	54	12	25	37	185	....	....	....	....	....	....	....	....	....	4	0	1	1	2	....	....	....	....
2009-10	Alberni Valley	BCHL	57	21	53	74	79	....	....	....	....	....	....	....	....	....	13	9	10	19	8	....	....	....	....
2010-11	Binghamton	AHL	75	6	14	20	57	....	....	....	....	....	....	....	....	....	14	0	3	3	4	....	....	....	....
2011-12	Binghamton	AHL	72	11	17	28	92	....	....	....	....	....	....	....	....	....	....	....	....	....	....	....	....	....	....
2012-13	Binghamton	AHL	54	4	16	20	110	....	....	....	....	....	....	....	....	....	3	0	1	1	4	....	....	....	....
	Ottawa	**NHL**	**12**	**2**	**0**	**2**	**13**	**0**	**0**	**0**	**20**	**10.0**	**–1**	**4**	**75.0**	**12:33**	....	....	....	....	....	....	....	....	....
2013-14	Binghamton	AHL	68	13	12	25	91	....	....	....	....	....	....	....	....	....	4	0	1	1	4	....	....	....	....
2014-15	Binghamton	AHL	39	4	10	14	79	....	....	....	....	....	....	....	....	....	....	....	....	....	....	....	....	....	....
	NHL Totals		**12**	**2**	**0**	**2**	**13**	**0**	**0**	**0**	**20**	**10.0**		**4**	**75.0**	**12:33**	....	....	....	....	....	....	....	....	....

Signed as a free agent by **Ottawa**, April 6, 2010. • Missed majority of 2014-15 due to recurring head injury and as a healthy reserve.

EAGER, Ben

(EE-guhr, BEHN)

Left wing. Shoots left. 6'2", 240 lbs. Born, Ottawa, ON, January 22, 1984. Phoenix's 2nd choice, 23rd overall, in 2002 Entry Draft.

Season	Club	League	GP	G	A	Pts	PIM	PP	SH	GW	S	S%	+/-	TF	F%	Min	GP	G	A	Pts	PIM	PP	SH	GW	Min
99-2000	Ott. Jr. Senators	ON-Jr.A	50	8	11	19	119	....	....	....	....	....	....	....	....	....	....	....	....	....	....	....	....	....	....
2000-01	Oshawa Generals	OHL	61	4	6	10	120	....	....	....	....	....	....	....	....	....	....	....	....	....	....	....	....	....	....
2001-02	Oshawa Generals	OHL	63	14	23	37	255	....	....	....	....	....	....	....	....	....	5	0	1	1	13	....	....	....	....
2002-03	Oshawa Generals	OHL	58	16	24	40	216	....	....	....	....	....	....	....	....	....	8	0	4	4	8	....	....	....	....
2003-04	Oshawa Generals	OHL	61	25	27	52	204	....	....	....	....	....	....	....	....	....	7	2	3	5	31	....	....	....	....
	Philadelphia	AHL	5	0	0	0	0	....	....	....	....	....	....	....	....	....	3	0	1	1	8	....	....	....	....
2004-05	Philadelphia	AHL	66	7	10	17	232	....	....	....	....	....	....	....	....	....	16	1	1	2	71	....	....	....	....
2005-06	**Philadelphia**	**NHL**	**25**	**3**	**5**	**8**	**18**	**0**	**0**	**0**	**21**	**14.3**	**0**	**0**	**0.0**	**7:24**	**2**	**0**	**0**	**0**	**26**	**0**	**0**	**0**	**7:06**
	Philadelphia	AHL	49	6	12	18	256	....	....	....	....	....	....	....	....	....	....	....	....	....	....	....	....	....	....
2006-07	**Philadelphia**	**NHL**	**63**	**6**	**5**	**11**	***233**	**0**	**0**	**0**	**48**	**12.5**	**–13**	**1**	**100.0**	**8:14**	....	....	....	....	....	....	....	....	....
	Philadelphia	AHL	3	0	0	0	21	....	....	....	....	....	....	....	....	....	....	....	....	....	....	....	....	....	....
2007-08	**Philadelphia**	**NHL**	**23**	**0**	**0**	**0**	**62**	**0**	**0**	**0**	**11**	**0.0**	**–8**	**5**	**20.0**	**5:29**	....	....	....	....	....	....	....	....	....
	Chicago	**NHL**	**9**	**0**	**2**	**2**	**27**	**0**	**0**	**0**	**5**	**0.0**	**–1**	**0**	**0.0**	**6:37**	....	....	....	....	....	....	....	....	....
2008-09	**Chicago**	**NHL**	**75**	**11**	**4**	**15**	**161**	**0**	**0**	**0**	**80**	**13.8**	**1**	**0**	**0.0**	**8:31**	**17**	**1**	**1**	**2**	***61**	**0**	**0**	**1**	**8:32**
2009-10♦	**Chicago**	**NHL**	**60**	**7**	**9**	**16**	**120**	**0**	**0**	**2**	**68**	**10.3**	**9**	**1**	**0.0**	**8:20**	**18**	**1**	**2**	**3**	**20**	**0**	**0**	**1**	**6:02**
2010-11	**Atlanta**	**NHL**	**34**	**3**	**7**	**10**	**77**	**0**	**0**	**1**	**41**	**7.3**	**4**	**2**	**0.0**	**12:15**	....	....	....	....	....	....	....	....	....
	San Jose	**NHL**	**34**	**4**	**3**	**7**	**43**	**0**	**0**	**0**	**43**	**9.3**	**0**	**0**	**0.0**	**9:02**	**10**	**1**	**0**	**1**	**41**	**0**	**0**	**0**	**4:53**
2011-12	**Edmonton**	**NHL**	**63**	**8**	**5**	**13**	**107**	**0**	**0**	**3**	**69**	**11.6**	**–1**	**2**	**0.0**	**8:32**	....	....	....	....	....	....	....	....	....
2012-13	Oklahoma City	AHL	9	0	2	2	13	....	....	....	....	....	....	....	....	....	13	1	4	5	64	....	....	....	....
	Edmonton	**NHL**	**14**	**1**	**1**	**2**	**25**	**0**	**0**	**0**	**14**	**7.1**	**–4**	**0**	**0.0**	**9:40**	....	....	....	....	....	....	....	....	....
2013-14	**Edmonton**	**NHL**	**7**	**0**	**1**	**1**	**2**	**0**	**0**	**0**	**4**	**0.0**	**1**	**2**	**50.0**	**7:13**	....	....	....	....	....	....	....	....	....
	Oklahoma City	AHL	44	6	2	8	136	....	....	....	....	....	....	....	....	....	2	0	0	0	4	....	....	....	....
2014-15	CSKA Moscow	KHL	5	0	0	0	2	....	....	....	....	....	....	....	....	....	....	....	....	....	....	....	....	....	....
	Chicago Wolves	AHL	26	0	2	2	86	....	....	....	....	....	....	....	....	....	....	....	....	....	....	....	....	....	....
	NHL Totals		**407**	**43**	**42**	**85**	**875**	**0**	**0**	**6**	**404**	**10.6**		**13**	**23.1**	**8:32**	**47**	**3**	**3**	**6**	**148**	**0**	**0**	**2**	**6:44**

Traded to **Philadelphia** by **Phoenix** with Sean Burke and Branko Radivojevic for Mike Comrie, February 9, 2004. Traded to **Chicago** by **Philadelphia** for Jim Vandermeer, December 18, 2007. Traded to **Atlanta** by **Chicago** with Brent Sopel, Dustin Byfuglien and Akim Aliu for Marty Reasoner, Joey Crabb, Jeremy Morin and New Jersey's 1st (previously acquired, Chicago selected Kevin Hayes) and 2nd (previously acquired, Chicago selected Justin Holl) round choices in 2010 Entry Draft, June 24, 2010. Traded to **San Jose** by **Atlanta** for San Jose's 5th round choice (Austen Brassard) in 2011 Entry Draft, January 18, 2011. Signed as a free agent by **Edmonton**, July 1, 2011. • Missed majority of 2012-13 due to head injury at Vancouver, January 20, 2013. Signed as a free agent by **CSKA Moscow** (KHL), July 11, 2014. Signed as a free agent by **Chicago** (AHL), December 18, 2014. • Missed majoriry of 2014-15 due to recurring head injury and as a healthy reserve.

EAKIN, Cody

(EE-kihn, KOH-dee) **DAL**

Center. Shoots left. 6', 190 lbs. Born, Winnipeg, MB, May 24, 1991. Washington's 3rd choice, 85th overall, in 2009 Entry Draft.

Season	Club	League	GP	G	A	Pts	PIM	PP	SH	GW	S	S%	+/-	TF	F%	Min	GP	G	A	Pts	PIM	PP	SH	GW	Min
2006-07	Winnipeg Wild	MMHL	38	29	35	64	62	....	....	....	....	....	....	....	....	....	7	5	4	9	10	....	....	....	....
	Swift Current	WHL	3	0	0	0	0	....	....	....	....	....	....	....	....	....	....	....	....	....	....	....	....	....	....
2007-08	Swift Current	WHL	55	11	6	17	52	....	....	....	....	....	....	....	....	....	12	3	4	7	6	....	....	....	....
2008-09	Swift Current	WHL	54	24	24	48	42	....	....	....	....	....	....	....	....	....	7	3	0	3	10	....	....	....	....
2009-10	Swift Current	WHL	70	47	44	91	71	....	....	....	....	....	....	....	....	....	4	1	1	2	2	....	....	....	....
	Hershey Bears	AHL	4	2	0	2	2	....	....	....	....	....	....	....	....	....	5	0	0	0	2	....	....	....	....
2010-11	Swift Current	WHL	30	18	21	39	24	....	....	....	....	....	....	....	....	....	....	....	....	....	....	....	....	....	....
	Kootenay Ice	WHL	26	18	26	44	19	....	....	....	....	....	....	....	....	....	19	11	16	27	14	....	....	....	....
2011-12	**Washington**	**NHL**	**30**	**4**	**4**	**8**	**4**	**0**	**0**	**0**	**31**	**12.9**	**2**	**40**	**52.5**	**9:17**	....	....	....	....	....	....	....	....	....
	Hershey Bears	AHL	43	13	14	27	10	....	....	....	....	....	....	....	....	....	5	0	1	1	0	....	....	....	....
2012-13	Texas Stars	AHL	35	12	12	24	14	....	....	....	....	....	....	....	....	....	....	....	....	....	....	....	....	....	....
	Dallas	**NHL**	**48**	**7**	**17**	**24**	**31**	**3**	**0**	**1**	**67**	**10.4**	**1**	**626**	**48.6**	**15:05**	....	....	....	....	....	....	....	....	....
2013-14	**Dallas**	**NHL**	**81**	**16**	**19**	**35**	**36**	**3**	**1**	**2**	**161**	**9.9**	**–9**	**1223**	**47.8**	**17:20**	**6**	**2**	**3**	**5**	**0**	**1**	**0**	**1**	**18:32**
2014-15	**Dallas**	**NHL**	**78**	**19**	**21**	**40**	**26**	**2**	**2**	**6**	**142**	**13.4**	**–1**	**1292**	**50.8**	**17:12**	....	....	....	....	....	....	....	....	....
	NHL Totals		**237**	**46**	**61**	**107**	**97**	**8**	**3**	**9**	**401**	**11.5**		**3181**	**49.2**	**15:49**	**6**	**2**	**3**	**5**	**0**	**1**	**0**	**1**	**18:32**

WHL East Second All-Star Team (2010, 2011)

Traded to **Dallas** by **Washington** with Boston's 2nd round choice (previously acquired, Dallas selected Mike Winther) in 2012 Entry Draft for Mike Ribeiro. June 22, 2012.

EAVES, Patrick
(EEVZ, PAT-rihk) **DAL**

Right wing. Shoots right. 6', 200 lbs. Born, Calgary, AB, May 1, 1984. Ottawa's 1st choice, 29th overall, in 2003 Entry Draft.

			Regular Season														Playoffs								
Season	Club	League	GP	G	A	Pts	PIM	PP	SH	GW	S	S%	+/-	TF	F%	Min	GP	G	A	Pts	PIM	PP	SH	GW	Min
99-2000	Shat.-St. Mary's	High-MN	50	23	24	47	....	....	....	....	....	....	....	....	....	....	....	....	....	....	....	....	....	....	....
2000-01	USNTDP	U-17	13	7	8	15	3	....	....	....	....	....	....	....	....	....	....	....	....	....	....	....	....	....	....
	USNTDP	NAHL	34	12	11	23	75	....	....	....	....	....	....	....	....	....	....	....	....	....	....	....	....	....	....
2001-02	USNTDP	U-18	32	19	21	40	87	....	....	....	....	....	....	....	....	....	....	....	....	....	....	....	....	....	....
	USNTDP	USHL	9	1	4	5	18	....	....	....	....	....	....	....	....	....	....	....	....	....	....	....	....	....	....
	USNTDP	NAHL	8	5	3	8	37	....	....	....	....	....	....	....	....	....	....	....	....	....	....	....	....	....	....
2002-03	Boston College	H-East	14	10	8	18	61	....	....	....	....	....	....	....	....	....	....	....	....	....	....	....	....	....	....
2003-04	Boston College	H-East	34	18	23	41	66	....	....	....	....	....	....	....	....	....	....	....	....	....	....	....	....	....	....
2004-05	Boston College	H-East	36	19	29	48	36	....	....	....	....	....	....	....	....	....	....	....	....	....	....	....	....	....	....
2005-06	**Ottawa**	**NHL**	**58**	**20**	**9**	**29**	**22**	**5**	**1**	**4**	**100**	**20.0**	**7**	**14**	**21.4**	**12:29**	**10**	**1**	**0**	**1**	**10**	**0**	**0**	**0**	**11:40**
	Binghamton	AHL	18	5	8	13	10	....	....	....	....	....	....	....	....	....	....	....	....	....	....	....	....	....	....
2006-07	**Ottawa**	**NHL**	**73**	**14**	**18**	**32**	**36**	**3**	**1**	**1**	**130**	**10.8**	**1**	**9**	**11.1**	**12:13**	**7**	**0**	**2**	**2**	**2**	**0**	**0**	**0**	**7:23**
2007-08	**Ottawa**	**NHL**	**26**	**4**	**6**	**10**	**6**	**1**	**0**	**1**	**59**	**6.8**	**0**	**1**	**100.0**	**12:44**	....	....	....	....	....	....	....	....	....
	Carolina	**NHL**	**11**	**1**	**4**	**5**	**4**	**1**	**0**	**0**	**22**	**4.5**	**-2**	**2**	**0.0**	**12:51**	....	....	....	....	....	....	....	....	....
2008-09	**Carolina**	**NHL**	**74**	**6**	**8**	**14**	**31**	**1**	**1**	**1**	**115**	**5.2**	**7**	**12**	**41.7**	**11:15**	**18**	**1**	**2**	**3**	**13**	**0**	**0**	**0**	**9:29**
2009-10	**Detroit**	**NHL**	**65**	**12**	**10**	**22**	**26**	**0**	**1**	**1**	**120**	**10.0**	**0**	**14**	**28.6**	**13:26**	**8**	**0**	**0**	**0**	**2**	**0**	**0**	**0**	**11:58**
2010-11	**Detroit**	**NHL**	**63**	**13**	**7**	**20**	**14**	**2**	**1**	**1**	**108**	**12.0**	**-2**	**10**	**30.0**	**12:42**	**11**	**3**	**1**	**4**	**6**	**0**	**0**	**0**	**11:24**
2011-12	**Detroit**	**NHL**	**10**	**0**	**1**	**1**	**2**	**0**	**0**	**0**	**24**	**0.0**	**0**	**5**	**40.0**	**11:03**	....	....	....	....	....	....	....	....	....
2012-13	**Detroit**	**NHL**	**34**	**2**	**6**	**8**	**4**	**0**	**0**	**1**	**42**	**4.8**	**-1**	**11**	**63.6**	**10:35**	**13**	**1**	**2**	**3**	**4**	**0**	**0**	**0**	**10:00**
2013-14	**Detroit**	**NHL**	**25**	**2**	**3**	**5**	**2**	**1**	**0**	**0**	**51**	**3.9**	**-4**	**15**	**46.7**	**11:33**	....	....	....	....	....	....	....	....	....
	Grand Rapids	AHL	8	4	2	6	8	....	....	....	....	....	....	....	....	....	....	....	....	....	....	....	....	....	....
	Nashville	**NHL**	**5**	**0**	**0**	**0**	**0**	**0**	**0**	**0**	**2**	**0.0**	**-3**	**0**	**0.0**	**9:46**	....	....	....	....	....	....	....	....	....
2014-15	**Dallas**	**NHL**	**47**	**14**	**13**	**27**	**8**	**6**	**0**	**2**	**91**	**15.4**	**12**	**5**	**40.0**	**13:43**	....	....	....	....	....	....	....	....	....
	NHL Totals		**491**	**88**	**85**	**173**	**155**	**20**	**5**	**12**	**864**	**10.2**		**98**	**35.7**	**12:19**	**67**	**6**	**7**	**13**	**37**	**0**	**0**	**0**	**10:18**

Hockey East Second All-Star Team (2004) • NCAA East Second All-American Team (2004) • Hockey East First All-Star Team (2005) • NCAA East First All-American Team (2005)

• Missed majority of 2002-03 due to neck injury vs. University of Maine (Hockey East), December 7, 2002. Traded to **Carolina** by **Ottawa** with Joe Corvo for Cory Stillman and Mike Commodore, February 11, 2008. • Missed majority of 2007-08 due to shoulder injury at Buffalo, November 21, 2007. Traded to **Boston** by **Carolina** with Carolina's 4th round choice (Craig Cunningham) in 2010 Entry Draft for Aaron Ward, July 24, 2009. Signed as a free agent by **Detroit**, August 4, 2009. • Missed majority of 2011-12 due to head injury vs. Nashville, November 26, 2012. Traded to **Nashville** by **Detroit** with Calle Jarnkrok and Detroit's 2nd round choice (later traded to San Jose – San Jose selected Julius Bergman) in 2014 Entry Draft for David Legwand, March 5, 2014. • Missed majority of 2013-14 due to pre-season knee injury and lower-body injury at Vancouver, March 19, 2014. Signed as a free agent by **Dallas**, July 1, 2014.

EBBETT, Andrew
(EH-beht, AN-droo)

Center. Shoots left. 5'9", 174 lbs. Born, Vernon, AB, January 2, 1983.

			Regular Season														Playoffs								
Season	Club	League	GP	G	A	Pts	PIM	PP	SH	GW	S	S%	+/-	TF	F%	Min	GP	G	A	Pts	PIM	PP	SH	GW	Min
2002-03	U. of Michigan	CCHA	43	9	18	27	22	....	....	....	....	....	....	....	....	....	....	....	....	....	....	....	....	....	....
2003-04	U. of Michigan	CCHA	43	9	28	37	56	....	....	....	....	....	....	....	....	....	....	....	....	....	....	....	....	....	....
2004-05	U. of Michigan	CCHA	40	6	31	37	28	....	....	....	....	....	....	....	....	....	....	....	....	....	....	....	....	....	....
2005-06	U. of Michigan	CCHA	41	14	28	42	25	....	....	....	....	....	....	....	....	....	....	....	....	....	....	....	....	....	....
2006-07	Binghamton	AHL	71	26	39	65	44	....	....	....	....	....	....	....	....	....	....	....	....	....	....	....	....	....	....
2007-08	**Anaheim**	**NHL**	**3**	**0**	**0**	**0**	**2**	**0**	**0**	**0**	**3**	**0.0**	**3**	**29**	**58.6**	**13:18**	....	....	....	....	....	....	....	....	....
	Portland Pirates	AHL	74	18	54	72	66	....	....	....	....	....	....	....	....	....	18	6	11	17	4	....	....	....	....
2008-09	**Anaheim**	**NHL**	**48**	**8**	**24**	**32**	**24**	**6**	**0**	**0**	**100**	**8.0**	**8**	**455**	**48.6**	**13:52**	**13**	**1**	**2**	**3**	**8**	**0**	**0**	**0**	**13:11**
	Iowa Chops	AHL	28	10	19	29	6	....	....	....	....	....	....	....	....	....	....	....	....	....	....	....	....	....	....
2009-10	**Anaheim**	**NHL**	**2**	**0**	**0**	**0**	**0**	**0**	**0**	**0**	**1**	**0.0**	**-1**	**17**	**35.3**	**12:55**	....	....	....	....	....	....	....	....	....
	Chicago	**NHL**	**10**	**1**	**0**	**1**	**2**	**0**	**0**	**0**	**14**	**7.1**	**1**	**72**	**50.0**	**10:43**	....	....	....	....	....	....	....	....	....
	Minnesota	**NHL**	**49**	**8**	**6**	**14**	**6**	**2**	**0**	**2**	**57**	**14.0**	**-8**	**464**	**50.0**	**13:06**	....	....	....	....	....	....	....	....	....
2010-11	**Phoenix**	**NHL**	**33**	**2**	**3**	**5**	**4**	**0**	**1**	**1**	**23**	**8.7**	**-1**	**229**	**45.4**	**10:01**	**3**	**0**	**0**	**0**	**0**	**0**	**0**	**0**	**7:58**
	San Antonio	AHL	37	11	27	38	12	....	....	....	....	....	....	....	....	....	....	....	....	....	....	....	....	....	....
2011-12	**Vancouver**	**NHL**	**18**	**5**	**1**	**6**	**6**	**1**	**0**	**2**	**27**	**18.5**	**2**	**28**	**53.6**	**9:35**	**1**	**0**	**0**	**0**	**0**	**0**	**0**	**0**	**10:21**
2012-13	Chicago Wolves	AHL	37	11	21	32	10	....	....	....	....	....	....	....	....	....	....	....	....	....	....	....	....	....	....
	Vancouver	**NHL**	**28**	**1**	**5**	**6**	**4**	**0**	**0**	**0**	**23**	**4.3**	**-1**	**267**	**39.7**	**12:19**	**2**	**0**	**0**	**0**	**0**	**0**	**0**	**0**	**4:30**
2013-14	**Pittsburgh**	**NHL**	**9**	**0**	**1**	**1**	**0**	**0**	**0**	**0**	**9**	**0.0**	**-4**	**35**	**42.9**	**11:03**	....	....	....	....	....	....	....	....	....
	Wilkes-Barre	AHL	44	13	27	40	28	....	....	....	....	....	....	....	....	....	6	2	6	8	14	....	....	....	....
2014-15	**Pittsburgh**	**NHL**	**24**	**1**	**5**	**6**	**2**	**0**	**0**	**0**	**21**	**4.8**	**1**	**86**	**45.4**	**9:00**	....	....	....	....	....	....	....	....	....
	Wilkes-Barre	AHL	44	17	27	44	12	....	....	....	....	....	....	....	....	....	8	1	6	7	2	....	....	....	....
	NHL Totals		**224**	**26**	**45**	**71**	**50**	**9**	**1**	**5**	**278**	**9.4**		**1682**	**47.0**	**11:48**	**19**	**1**	**2**	**3**	**8**	**0**	**0**	**0**	**11:18**

Signed as a free agent by **Anaheim**, May 16, 2007. Claimed on waivers by **Chicago** from **Anaheim**, October 17, 2009. Claimed on waivers by **Minnesota** from **Chicago**, November 21, 2009. Signed as a free agent by **Phoenix**, July 2, 2010. Signed as a free agent by **Vancouver**, July 5, 2011. • Missed majority of 2011-12 due to foot (November 11, 2011 at Anaheim) and collarbone (January 9, 2012 at Florida) injuries. Signed as a free agent by **Pittsburgh**, July 6, 2013. Signed as a free agent by **Bern** (Swiss), June 24, 2014.

EBERLE, Jordan
(EH-buhr-lee, JOHR-dahn) **EDM**

Center. Shoots right. 5'11", 180 lbs. Born, Regina, SK, May 15, 1990. Edmonton's 1st choice, 22nd overall, in 2008 Entry Draft.

			Regular Season														Playoffs								
Season	Club	League	GP	G	A	Pts	PIM	PP	SH	GW	S	S%	+/-	TF	F%	Min	GP	G	A	Pts	PIM	PP	SH	GW	Min
2005-06	Calgary Buffaloes	AMHL	31	14	20	34	6	....	....	....	....	....	....	....	....	....	11	7	1	8	8	....	....	....	....
2006-07	Regina Pats	WHL	66	28	27	55	32	....	....	....	....	....	....	....	....	....	6	2	5	7	2	....	....	....	....
2007-08	Regina Pats	WHL	70	42	33	75	20	....	....	....	....	....	....	....	....	....	5	2	4	6	7	....	....	....	....
2008-09	Regina Pats	WHL	61	35	39	74	20	....	....	....	....	....	....	....	....	....	....	....	....	....	....	....	....	....	....
	Springfield	AHL	9	3	6	9	4	....	....	....	....	....	....	....	....	....	....	....	....	....	....	....	....	....	....
2009-10	Regina Pats	WHL	57	50	56	106	32	....	....	....	....	....	....	....	....	....	....	....	....	....	....	....	....	....	....
	Springfield	AHL	11	6	8	14	0	....	....	....	....	....	....	....	....	....	....	....	....	....	....	....	....	....	....
2010-11	**Edmonton**	**NHL**	**69**	**18**	**25**	**43**	**22**	**4**	**2**	**5**	**158**	**11.4**	**-12**	**26**	**42.3**	**17:41**	....	....	....	....	....	....	....	....	....
2011-12	**Edmonton**	**NHL**	**78**	**34**	**42**	**76**	**10**	**10**	**0**	**4**	**180**	**18.9**	**4**	**27**	**44.4**	**17:36**	....	....	....	....	....	....	....	....	....
2012-13	Oklahoma City	AHL	34	25	26	51	10	....	....	....	....	....	....	....	....	....	....	....	....	....	....	....	....	....	....
	Edmonton	**NHL**	**48**	**16**	**21**	**37**	**16**	**3**	**0**	**3**	**133**	**12.0**	**-4**	**19**	**42.1**	**19:00**	....	....	....	....	....	....	....	....	....
2013-14	**Edmonton**	**NHL**	**80**	**28**	**37**	**65**	**18**	**7**	**1**	**4**	**200**	**14.0**	**-11**	**21**	**38.1**	**19:33**	....	....	....	....	....	....	....	....	....
2014-15	**Edmonton**	**NHL**	**81**	**24**	**39**	**63**	**24**	**6**	**0**	**2**	**183**	**13.1**	**-16**	**6**	**16.7**	**19:03**	....	....	....	....	....	....	....	....	....
	NHL Totals		**356**	**120**	**164**	**284**	**90**	**30**	**3**	**18**	**854**	**14.1**		**99**	**40.4**	**18:34**	....	....	....	....	....	....	....	....	....

WHL East First All-Star Team (2008, 2010) • WHL Player of the Year (2010) • Canadian Major Junior First All-Star Team (2010) • Canadian Major Junior Player of the Year (2010)

Played in NHL All-Star Game (2012)

EDLER, Alexander
(EHD-luhr, al-EHX-AN-duhr) **VAN**

Defense. Shoots left. 6'3", 215 lbs. Born, Ostersund, Sweden, April 21, 1986. Vancouver's 2nd choice, 91st overall, in 2004 Entry Draft.

			Regular Season														Playoffs								
Season	Club	League	GP	G	A	Pts	PIM	PP	SH	GW	S	S%	+/-	TF	F%	Min	GP	G	A	Pts	PIM	PP	SH	GW	Min
2001-02	Jamtland	Exhib.	8	0	1	1	2	....	....	....	....	....	....	....	....	....	....	....	....	....	....	....	....	....	....
2002-03	Jamtland	Exhib.	8	2	1	3	0	....	....	....	....	....	....	....	....	....	....	....	....	....	....	....	....	....	....
2003-04	Jamtland Jr.	Swe-Jr.	6	0	3	3	6	....	....	....	....	....	....	....	....	....	....	....	....	....	....	....	....	....	....
	Jamtland	Sweden-3	24	3	6	9	20	....	....	....	....	....	....	....	....	....	....	....	....	....	....	....	....	....	....
2004-05	MODO Jr.	Swe-Jr.	33	8	15	23	40	....	....	....	....	....	....	....	....	....	5	1	0	1	6	....	....	....	....
2005-06	Kelowna Rockets	WHL	62	13	40	53	44	....	....	....	....	....	....	....	....	....	12	3	5	8	12	....	....	....	....
2006-07	**Vancouver**	**NHL**	**22**	**1**	**2**	**3**	**6**	**0**	**0**	**0**	**10**	**10.0**	**3**	**0**	**0.0**	**11:27**	**3**	**0**	**0**	**0**	**2**	**0**	**0**	**0**	**11:51**
	Manitoba Moose	AHL	49	5	21	26	28	....	....	....	....	....	....	....	....	....	8	0	0	0	2	....	....	....	....
2007-08	**Vancouver**	**NHL**	**75**	**8**	**12**	**20**	**42**	**4**	**0**	**0**	**124**	**6.5**	**6**	**1**	**100.0**	**21:20**	....	....	....	....	....	....	....	....	....
	Manitoba Moose	AHL	2	0	1	1	0	....	....	....	....	....	....	....	....	....	....	....	....	....	....	....	....	....	....
2008-09	**Vancouver**	**NHL**	**80**	**10**	**27**	**37**	**54**	**5**	**0**	**1**	**145**	**6.9**	**11**	**1**	**100.0**	**21:08**	**10**	**1**	**7**	**8**	**6**	**1**	**0**	**0**	**22:09**
2009-10	**Vancouver**	**NHL**	**76**	**5**	**37**	**42**	**40**	**2**	**0**	**0**	**161**	**3.1**	**0**	**2**	**0.0**	**22:39**	**12**	**2**	**4**	**6**	**10**	**1**	**0**	**0**	**23:07**
2010-11	**Vancouver**	**NHL**	**51**	**8**	**25**	**33**	**24**	**5**	**0**	**1**	**121**	**6.6**	**13**	**2**	**0.0**	**24:17**	**25**	**2**	**9**	**11**	**8**	**0**	**0**	**0**	**24:46**
2011-12	**Vancouver**	**NHL**	**82**	**11**	**38**	**49**	**34**	**5**	**1**	**0**	**228**	**4.8**	**0**	**3**	**0.0**	**23:52**	**5**	**2**	**0**	**2**	**8**	**1**	**0**	**0**	**24:17**
2012-13	**Vancouver**	**NHL**	**45**	**8**	**14**	**22**	**37**	**5**	**0**	**0**	**113**	**7.1**	**-5**	**1**	**100.0**	**23:51**	**4**	**1**	**0**	**1**	**2**	**0**	**0**	**0**	**26:57**
2013-14	**Vancouver**	**NHL**	**63**	**7**	**15**	**22**	**50**	**4**	**0**	**0**	**178**	**3.9**	**-39**	**3**	**66.7**	**23:17**	....	....	....	....	....	....	....	....	....
	Sweden	Olympics	4	1	1	2	0	....	....	....	....	....	....	....	....	....	....	....	....	....	....	....	....	....	....
2014-15	**Vancouver**	**NHL**	**74**	**8**	**23**	**31**	**54**	**5**	**0**	**2**	**175**	**4.6**	**13**	**1**	**0.0**	**23:59**	**6**	**0**	**3**	**3**	**4**	**0**	**0**	**0**	**23:41**
	NHL Totals		**568**	**66**	**193**	**259**	**341**	**35**	**1**	**4**	**1255**	**5.3**		**14**	**35.7**	**22:29**	**65**	**8**	**23**	**31**	**40**	**3**	**0**	**0**	**23:28**

Played in NHL All-Star Game (2012)

EHRHOFF, Christian

(AIR-hawf, KRIHS-tyehn)

Defense. Shoots left. 6'2", 196 lbs. Born, Moers, West Germany, July 6, 1982. San Jose's 2nd choice, 106th overall, in 2001 Entry Draft.

			Regular Season														Playoffs								
Season	Club	League	GP	G	A	Pts	PIM	PP	SH	GW	S	S%	+/-	TF	F%	Min	GP	G	A	Pts	PIM	PP	SH	GW	Min
1998-99	Krefelder EV Jr.	Ger-Jr.	22	10	14	24	46	....	....	....	....	....	....	....	....	....	....	....	....	....	....	....	....	....	....
99-2000	EV Duisburg	German-3	41	3	12	15	50	....	....	....	....	....	....	....	....	....	....	....	....	....	....	....	....	....	....
	Krefeld Pinguine	Germany	9	1	0	1	6	....	....	....	....	....	....	....	....	....	3	0	0	0	0	....	....	....	....
2000-01	EV Duisburg	German-3	6	1	2	3	12	....	....	....	....	....	....	....	....	....	....	....	....	....	....	....	....	....	....
	Krefeld Pinguine	Germany	58	3	11	14	73	....	....	....	....	....	....	....	....	....	....	....	....	....	....	....	....	....	....
2001-02	Krefeld Pinguine	Germany	46	7	17	24	81	....	....	....	....	....	....	....	....	....	3	0	0	0	2	....	....	....	....
	Germany	Olympics	7	0	0	0	8	....	....	....	....	....	....	....	....	....	....	....	....	....	....	....	....	....	....
2002-03	Krefeld Pinguine	Germany	48	10	17	27	54	....	....	....	....	....	....	....	....	....	14	3	6	9	24	....	....	....	....
2003-04	San Jose	NHL	41	1	11	12	14	0	0	1	58	1.7	4	0	0.0	15:23	....	....	....	....	....	....	....	....	....
	Cleveland Barons	AHL	27	4	10	14	43	....	....	....	....	....	....	....	....	....	9	2	6	8	11	....	....	....	....
2004-05	Cleveland Barons	AHL	79	12	23	35	103	....	....	....	....	....	....	....	....	....	....	....	....	....	....	....	....	....	....
2005-06	San Jose	NHL	64	5	18	23	32	2	0	2	124	4.0	10	0	0.0	17:48	11	2	6	8	18	1	0	1	19:47
	Germany	Olympics	5	1	1	2	4	....	....	....	....	....	....	....	....	....	....	....	....	....	....	....	....	....	....
2006-07	San Jose	NHL	82	10	23	33	63	6	0	2	164	6.1	8	1	0.0	18:34	11	0	2	2	6	0	0	0	17:47
2007-08	San Jose	NHL	77	1	21	22	72	1	0	1	97	1.0	9	0	0.0	21:44	10	0	5	5	14	0	0	0	23:04
2008-09	San Jose	NHL	77	8	34	42	63	5	0	2	165	4.8	−12	0	0.0	21:14	6	0	0	0	2	0	0	0	24:47
2009-10	Vancouver	NHL	80	14	30	44	42	6	0	3	181	7.7	36	0	0.0	22:47	12	3	4	7	8	1	0	0	24:09
	Germany	Olympics	4	0	0	0	4	....	....	....	....	....	....	....	....	....	....	....	....	....	....	....	....	....	....
2010-11	Vancouver	NHL	79	14	36	50	52	6	0	3	209	6.7	19	0	0.0	23:59	23	2	10	12	16	1	0	0	22:26
2011-12	Buffalo	NHL	66	5	27	32	47	1	0	3	136	3.7	−2	0	0.0	23:03	....	....	....	....	....	....	....	....	....
2012-13	Krefeld Pinguine	Germany	32	8	18	26	52	....	....	....	....	....	....	....	....	....	....	....	....	....	....	....	....	....	....
	Buffalo	NHL	47	5	17	22	34	1	0	2	102	4.9	6	0	0.0	25:11	....	....	....	....	....	....	....	....	....
2013-14	Buffalo	NHL	79	6	27	33	38	1	1	2	161	3.7	−27	0	0.0	23:55	....	....	....	....	....	....	....	....	....
2014-15	Pittsburgh	NHL	49	3	11	14	26	0	0	3	110	2.7	8	0	0.0	21:46	....	....	....	....	....	....	....	....	....
	NHL Totals		741	72	255	327	483	29	1	24	1507	4.8		1	0.0	21:34	73	7	27	34	64	3	0	1	21:54

Traded to **Vancouver** by **San Jose** with Brad Lukowich for Patrick White and Daniel Rahimi, August 28, 2009. Traded to **NY Islanders** by **Vancouver** for NY Islanders' 4th round choice (later traded to Columbus – Columbus selected Josh Anderson) in 2012 Entry Draft, June 28, 2011. Traded to **Buffalo** by **NY Islanders** for Buffalo's 4th round choice (Loic Leduc) in 2012 Entry Draft, June 29, 2011. Signed as a free agent by **Krefeld** (Germany), September 17, 2012. Signed as a free agent by **Pittsburgh**, July 1, 2014.

EKBLAD, Aaron

(EHK-blad, AIR-uhn) **FLA**

Defense. Shoots right. 6'4", 216 lbs. Born, Windsor, ON, February 7, 1996. Florida's 1st choice, 1st overall, in 2014 Entry Draft.

			Regular Season														Playoffs								
Season	Club	League	GP	G	A	Pts	PIM	PP	SH	GW	S	S%	+/-	TF	F%	Min	GP	G	A	Pts	PIM	PP	SH	GW	Min
2010-11	Sun County	Minor-ON	30	4	30	34	34	....	....	....	....	....	....	....	....	....	18	5	16	21	14	....	....	....	....
	Sun County	Other	14	5	7	12	18	....	....	....	....	....	....	....	....	....	....	....	....	....	....	....	....	....	....
2011-12	Barrie Colts	OHL	63	10	19	29	34	....	....	....	....	....	....	....	....	....	13	2	3	5	8	....	....	....	....
2012-13	Barrie Colts	OHL	54	7	27	34	64	....	....	....	....	....	....	....	....	....	22	7	10	17	28	....	....	....	....
2013-14	Barrie Colts	OHL	58	23	30	53	91	....	....	....	....	....	....	....	....	....	9	2	4	6	14	....	....	....	....
2014-15	Florida	NHL	81	12	27	39	32	6	0	4	170	7.1	12	0	0.0	21:49	....	....	....	....	....	....	....	....	....
	NHL Totals		81	12	27	39	32	6	0	4	170	7.1		0	0.0	21:49	....	....	....	....	....	....	....	....	....

OHL First All-Star Team (2014) • NHL All-Rookie Team (2015) • Calder Memorial Trophy (2015)

Played in NHL All-Star Game (2015)

EKHOLM, Mattias

(EHK-hohlm, ma-TEE-uhs) **NSH**

Defense. Shoots left. 6'4", 204 lbs. Born, Borlange, Sweden, May 24, 1990. Nashville's 7th choice, 102nd overall, in 2009 Entry Draft.

			Regular Season														Playoffs								
Season	Club	League	GP	G	A	Pts	PIM	PP	SH	GW	S	S%	+/-	TF	F%	Min	GP	G	A	Pts	PIM	PP	SH	GW	Min
2006-07	Mora IK U18	Swe-U18	5	2	2	4	6	....	....	....	....	....	....	....	....	....	....	....	....	....	....	....	....	....	....
	Mora IK Jr.	Swe-Jr.	36	0	4	4	28	....	....	....	....	....	....	....	....	....	2	0	0	0	0	....	....	....	....
2007-08	Mora IK U18	Swe-U18	9	4	5	9	12	....	....	....	....	....	....	....	....	....	....	....	....	....	....	....	....	....	....
	Mora IK Jr.	Swe-Jr.	37	5	7	12	54	....	....	....	....	....	....	....	....	....	....	....	....	....	....	....	....	....	....
	Mora IK	Sweden	1	0	0	0	0	....	....	....	....	....	....	....	....	....	....	....	....	....	....	....	....	....	....
	Mora IK	Sweden-Q	6	0	0	0	2	....	....	....	....	....	....	....	....	....	....	....	....	....	....	....	....	....	....
2008-09	Mora IK Jr.	Swe-Jr.	21	3	5	8	32	....	....	....	....	....	....	....	....	....	....	....	....	....	....	....	....	....	....
	Mora IK	Sweden-2	38	2	11	13	12	....	....	....	....	....	....	....	....	....	3	0	0	0	4	....	....	....	....
2009-10	Mora IK	Sweden-2	41	1	21	22	54	....	....	....	....	....	....	....	....	....	2	0	0	0	6	....	....	....	....
2010-11	Brynas IF Gavle	Sweden	55	10	23	33	38	....	....	....	....	....	....	....	....	....	5	0	4	4	10	....	....	....	....
2011-12	Nashville	NHL	2	0	0	0	0	0	0	0	1	0.0	−1	0	0.0	12:25	....	....	....	....	....	....	....	....	....
	Brynas IF Gavle	Sweden	41	9	8	17	55	....	....	....	....	....	....	....	....	....	17	1	8	9	12	....	....	....	....
2012-13	Milwaukee	AHL	59	10	22	32	30	....	....	....	....	....	....	....	....	....	4	0	1	1	0	....	....	....	....
	Nashville	NHL	1	0	0	0	0	0	0	0	0	0.0	−1	0	0.0	16:05	....	....	....	....	....	....	....	....	....
2013-14	Nashville	NHL	62	1	8	9	10	0	0	0	58	1.7	−8	0	0.0	16:49	....	....	....	....	....	....	....	....	....
2014-15	Nashville	NHL	80	7	11	18	52	1	0	1	86	8.1	12	0	0.0	19:01	6	1	0	1	2	0	0	0	26:25
	NHL Totals		145	8	19	27	62	1	0	1	145	5.5		0	0.0	17:58	6	1	0	1	2	0	0	0	26:25

EKMAN-LARSSON, Oliver

(EHK-man-LAHR-suhn, AW-lih-vuhr) **ARI**

Defense. Shoots left. 6'2", 190 lbs. Born, Karlskrona, Sweden, July 17, 1991. Phoenix's 1st choice, 6th overall, in 2009 Entry Draft.

			Regular Season														Playoffs								
Season	Club	League	GP	G	A	Pts	PIM	PP	SH	GW	S	S%	+/-	TF	F%	Min	GP	G	A	Pts	PIM	PP	SH	GW	Min
2005-06	Tingsryds AIF Jr.	Swe-Jr.	1	0	0	0	2	....	....	....	....	....	....	....	....	....	....	....	....	....	....	....	....	....	....
2006-07	Tingsryds AIF U18	Swe-U18	23	0	3	3	28	....	....	....	....	....	....	....	....	....	....	....	....	....	....	....	....	....	....
2007-08	Tingsryds AIF U18	Swe-U18	12	2	3	5	57	....	....	....	....	....	....	....	....	....	....	....	....	....	....	....	....	....	....
	Tingsryds AIF Jr.	Swe-Jr.	7	2	4	6	16	....	....	....	....	....	....	....	....	....	....	....	....	....	....	....	....	....	....
	Tingsryds AIF	Sweden-3	27	3	5	8	10	....	....	....	....	....	....	....	....	....	....	....	....	....	....	....	....	....	....
2008-09	Leksands IF	Sweden-2	47	5	16	21	38	....	....	....	....	....	....	....	....	....	....	....	....	....	....	....	....	....	....
2009-10	Leksands IF	Sweden-2	52	11	22	33	106	....	....	....	....	....	....	....	....	....	....	....	....	....	....	....	....	....	....
2010-11	Phoenix	NHL	48	1	10	11	24	0	0	0	50	2.0	3	0	0.0	15:02	....	....	....	....	....	....	....	....	....
	San Antonio	AHL	15	3	7	10	16	....	....	....	....	....	....	....	....	....	....	....	....	....	....	....	....	....	....
2011-12	Phoenix	NHL	82	13	19	32	32	2	1	2	147	8.8	0	0	0.0	22:07	16	1	3	4	8	1	0	1	25:47
2012-13	Portland Pirates	AHL	20	7	14	21	28	....	....	....	....	....	....	....	....	....	....	....	....	....	....	....	....	....	....
	Phoenix	NHL	48	3	21	24	26	0	0	1	101	3.0	5	0	0.0	25:06	....	....	....	....	....	....	....	....	....
2013-14	Phoenix	NHL	80	15	29	44	50	8	0	6	199	7.5	−4	1	0.0	25:54	....	....	....	....	....	....	....	....	....
	Sweden	Olympics	6	0	3	3	2	....	....	....	....	....	....	....	....	....	....	....	....	....	....	....	....	....	....
2014-15	Arizona	NHL	82	23	20	43	40	10	1	7	264	8.7	−18	0	0.0	25:13	....	....	....	....	....	....	....	....	....
	NHL Totals		340	55	99	154	172	20	2	16	761	7.2		1	0.0	23:10	16	1	3	4	8	1	0	1	25:47

Played in NHL All-Star Game (2015)

ELIAS, Patrik

(ehl-EE-ahsh, PAT-rihk) **N.J.**

Center. Shoots left. 6'1", 195 lbs. Born, Trebic, Czech., April 13, 1976. New Jersey's 2nd choice, 51st overall, in 1994 Entry Draft.

			Regular Season														Playoffs								
Season	Club	League	GP	G	A	Pts	PIM	PP	SH	GW	S	S%	+/-	TF	F%	Min	GP	G	A	Pts	PIM	PP	SH	GW	Min
1992-93	Poldi Kladno	Czech	2	0	0	0	....	....	....	....	....	....	....	....	....	....	....	....	....	....	....	....	....	....	....
1993-94	HC Kladno	CzRep	15	1	2	3	....	....	....	....	....	....	....	....	....	....	11	2	2	4	....	....	....	....	....
1994-95	HC Kladno	CzRep	28	4	3	7	37	....	....	....	....	....	....	....	....	....	7	1	2	3	12	....	....	....	....
1995-96	New Jersey	NHL	1	0	0	0	0	0	0	0	2	0.0	−1	....	....	....	....	....	....	....	....	....	....	....	....
	Albany River Rats	AHL	74	27	36	63	83	....	....	....	....	....	....	....	....	....	4	1	1	2	2	....	....	....	....
1996-97	New Jersey	NHL	17	2	3	5	2	0	0	0	23	8.7	−4	....	....	....	8	2	3	5	4	1	0	0	....
	Albany River Rats	AHL	57	24	43	67	76	....	....	....	....	....	....	....	....	....	6	1	2	3	8	....	....	....	....
1997-98	New Jersey	NHL	74	18	19	37	28	5	0	6	147	12.2	18	....	....	....	4	0	1	1	0	0	0	0	....
	Albany River Rats	AHL	3	3	0	3	2	....	....	....	....	....	....	....	....	....	....	....	....	....	....	....	....	....	....
1998-99	New Jersey	NHL	74	17	33	50	34	3	0	2	157	10.8	19	99	38.4	15:50	7	0	5	5	6	0	0	0	18:07
99-2000	Trebic	CzRep-2	2	2	1	3	2	....	....	....	....	....	....	....	....	....	....	....	....	....	....	....	....	....	....
	Pardubice	CzRep	5	1	4	5	31	....	....	....	....	....	....	....	....	....	....	....	....	....	....	....	....	....	....
	♦ New Jersey	NHL	72	35	37	72	58	9	0	9	183	19.1	16	134	45.5	17:28	23	7	*13	20	9	2	1	1	17:44
2000-01	New Jersey	NHL	82	40	56	96	51	8	3	6	220	18.2	*45	155	41.3	18:44	25	9	14	23	10	3	1	2	18:14
2001-02	New Jersey	NHL	75	29	32	61	36	8	1	8	199	14.6	4	128	45.3	18:57	6	2	4	6	6	2	0	0	20:33
	Czech Republic	Olympics	4	1	1	2	0	....	....	....	....	....	....	....	....	....	....	....	....	....	....	....	....	....	....
2002-03 ♦	New Jersey	NHL	81	28	29	57	22	6	0	4	255	11.0	17	427	43.8	18:05	24	5	8	13	26	2	0	2	17:14
2003-04	New Jersey	NHL	82	38	43	81	44	9	3	9	300	12.7	26	49	36.7	18:46	5	3	2	5	2	1	0	1	18:59

								Regular Season									Playoffs								
Season	Club	League	GP	G	A	Pts	PIM	PP	SH	GW	S	S%	+/-	TF	F%	Min	GP	G	A	Pts	PIM	PP	SH	GW	Min
2004-05	Znojmo	CzRep	28	8	20	28	65	....	....	....	....	....	....	....	....	....	....	....	....	....	....	....	....	....	....
	Magnitogorsk	Russia	17	5	9	14	28	....	....	....	....	....	....	....	....	....	....	....	....	....	....	....	....	....	....
2005-06	**New Jersey**	**NHL**	**38**	**16**	**29**	**45**	**20**	**6**	**0**	**3**	**142**	**11.3**	**11**	**10**	**20.0**	**18:34**	**9**	**6**	**10**	**16**	**4**	**4**	**0**	**0**	**18:43**
	Czech Republic	Olympics	1	0	0	0	2	....	....	....	....	....	....	....	....	....	....	....	....	....	....	....	....	....	....
2006-07	**New Jersey**	**NHL**	**75**	**21**	**48**	**69**	**38**	**8**	**0**	**5**	**267**	**7.9**	**1**	**18**	**38.9**	**18:37**	**10**	**1**	**9**	**10**	**4**	**1**	**0**	**0**	**19:13**
2007-08	**New Jersey**	**NHL**	**74**	**20**	**35**	**55**	**38**	**7**	**0**	**8**	**263**	**7.6**	**10**	**776**	**45.6**	**18:28**	**5**	**4**	**2**	**6**	**4**	**3**	**0**	**0**	**20:30**
2008-09	**New Jersey**	**NHL**	**77**	**31**	**47**	**78**	**32**	**12**	**2**	**6**	**247**	**12.6**	**18**	**87**	**29.9**	**18:34**	**7**	**1**	**2**	**3**	**2**	**0**	**0**	**0**	**17:53**
2009-10	**New Jersey**	**NHL**	**58**	**19**	**29**	**48**	**40**	**3**	**1**	**4**	**145**	**13.1**	**18**	**457**	**44.9**	**17:37**	**5**	**0**	**4**	**4**	**2**	**0**	**0**	**0**	**18:41**
	Czech Republic	Olympics	5	2	2	4	2	....	....	....	....	....	....	....	....	....	....	....	....	....	....	....	....	....	....
2010-11	**New Jersey**	**NHL**	**81**	**21**	**41**	**62**	**16**	**7**	**1**	**5**	**204**	**10.3**	**–4**	**498**	**45.0**	**18:38**	....	....	....	....	....	....	....	....	....
2011-12	**New Jersey**	**NHL**	**81**	**26**	**52**	**78**	**16**	**8**	**2**	**3**	**164**	**15.9**	**–8**	**1369**	**44.1**	**19:51**	**24**	**5**	**3**	**8**	**10**	**2**	**0**	**0**	**18:30**
2012-13	**New Jersey**	**NHL**	**48**	**14**	**22**	**36**	**22**	**5**	**1**	**0**	**118**	**11.9**	**5**	**163**	**43.6**	**18:43**	....	....	....	....	....	....	....	....	....
2013-14	**New Jersey**	**NHL**	**65**	**18**	**35**	**53**	**30**	**4**	**2**	**1**	**116**	**15.5**	**–4**	**677**	**40.8**	**17:53**	....	....	....	....	....	....	....	....	....
	Czech Republic	Olympics	3	0	1	1	0	....	....	....	....	....	....	....	....	....	....	....	....	....	....	....	....	....	....
2014-15	**New Jersey**	**NHL**	**69**	**13**	**21**	**34**	**12**	**5**	**0**	**1**	**114**	**11.4**	**–20**	**673**	**39.1**	**17:39**	....	....	....	....	....	....	....	....	....
	NHL Totals		**1224**	**406**	**611**	**1017**	**539**	**113**	**16**	**80**	**3266**	**12.4**		**5720**	**43.0**	**18:18**	**162**	**45**	**80**	**125**	**89**	**21**	**2**	**6**	**18:19**

NHL All-Rookie Team (1998) • NHL First All-Star Team (2001) • Bud Light Plus/Minus Award (2001) (tied with Joe Sakic)

Played in NHL All-Star Game (2000, 2002, 2011, 2015)

Signed as a free agent by **Znojmo** (CzRep), September 6, 2004. Signed as a free agent by **Magnitogorsk** (Russia), December 9, 2004. • Missed majority of 2005-06 due to hepatitis-A virus.

ELLER, Lars

(EHL-uhr, LARZ) **MTL**

Center. Shoots left. 6'2", 209 lbs. Born, Rodovre, Denmark, May 8, 1989. St. Louis' 1st choice, 13th overall, in 2007 Entry Draft.

Season	Club	League	GP	G	A	Pts	PIM	PP	SH	GW	S	S%	+/-	TF	F%	Min	GP	G	A	Pts	PIM	PP	SH	GW	Min
2004-05	Rodovre IK Jr.	Den-Jr.	28	21	26	47	20	....	....	....	....	....	....	....	....	....	....	....	....	....	....	....	....	....	....
	Rodovre	Denmark	1	3	1	4	0	....	....	....	....	....	....	....	....	....	....	....	....	....	....	....	....	....	....
2005-06	Frolunda U18	Swe-U18	8	2	4	6	10	....	....	....	....	....	....	....	....	....	2	0	0	0	0	....	....	....	....
	Frolunda Jr.	Swe-Jr.	36	7	7	14	6	....	....	....	....	....	....	....	....	....	2	0	0	0	0	....	....	....	....
2006-07	Frolunda U18	Swe-U18	3	1	4	5	6	....	....	....	....	....	....	....	....	....	6	3	2	5	8	....	....	....	....
	Frolunda Jr.	Swe-Jr.	39	18	37	55	58	....	....	....	....	....	....	....	....	....	8	4	1	5	24	....	....	....	....
2007-08	Boras HC	Sweden-2	19	2	6	8	8	....	....	....	....	....	....	....	....	....	....	....	....	....	....	....	....	....	....
	Frolunda Jr.	Swe-Jr.	9	4	4	8	10	....	....	....	....	....	....	....	....	....	7	5	6	11	14	....	....	....	....
	Frolunda	Sweden	14	0	2	2	4	....	....	....	....	....	....	....	....	....	7	0	1	1	2	....	....	....	....
2008-09	Frolunda	Sweden	48	12	17	29	28	....	....	....	....	....	....	....	....	....	10	3	1	4	12	....	....	....	....
	Denmark	Oly-Q	3	1	1	2	8	....	....	....	....	....	....	....	....	....	....	....	....	....	....	....	....	....	....
2009-10	**St. Louis**	**NHL**	**7**	**2**	**0**	**2**	**4**	**1**	**0**	**0**	**8**	**25.0**	**2**	**19**	**47.4**	**10:49**	....	....	....	....	....	....	....	....	....
	Peoria Rivermen	AHL	70	18	39	57	84	....	....	....	....	....	....	....	....	....	....	....	....	....	....	....	....	....	....
2010-11	**Montreal**	**NHL**	**77**	**7**	**10**	**17**	**48**	**0**	**0**	**2**	**79**	**8.9**	**–4**	**431**	**42.5**	**11:08**	**7**	**0**	**2**	**2**	**4**	**0**	**0**	**0**	**13:04**
2011-12	**Montreal**	**NHL**	**79**	**16**	**12**	**28**	**66**	**2**	**2**	**2**	**129**	**12.4**	**–5**	**685**	**46.6**	**15:19**	....	....	....	....	....	....	....	....	....
2012-13	JYP Jyvaskyla	Finland	15	5	10	15	18	....	....	....	....	....	....	....	....	....	....	....	....	....	....	....	....	....	....
	Montreal	**NHL**	**46**	**8**	**22**	**30**	**45**	**1**	**0**	**1**	**84**	**9.5**	**8**	**542**	**49.3**	**14:50**	**1**	**0**	**0**	**0**	**0**	**0**	**0**	**0**	**8:43**
2013-14	**Montreal**	**NHL**	**77**	**12**	**14**	**26**	**68**	**2**	**1**	**3**	**137**	**8.8**	**–15**	**979**	**53.2**	**15:58**	**17**	**5**	**8**	**13**	**18**	**0**	**1**	**1**	**16:27**
2014-15	**Montreal**	**NHL**	**77**	**15**	**12**	**27**	**42**	**1**	**0**	**7**	**150**	**10.0**	**–6**	**784**	**51.7**	**15:30**	**12**	**1**	**2**	**3**	**4**	**0**	**1**	**0**	**15:59**
	NHL Totals		**363**	**60**	**70**	**130**	**273**	**7**	**3**	**15**	**587**	**10.2**		**3440**	**49.5**	**14:27**	**37**	**6**	**12**	**18**	**26**	**0**	**2**	**1**	**15:27**

AHL All-Rookie Team (2010)

Traded to **Montreal** by **St. Louis** with Ian Schultz for Jaroslav Halak, June 17, 2010. Signed as a free agent by **Jyvaskyla** (Finland), October 28, 2012.

ELLERBY, Keaton

(EHL-uhr-bee, KEE-tuhn)

Defense. Shoots left. 6'5", 220 lbs. Born, Strathmore, AB, November 5, 1988. Florida's 1st choice, 10th overall, in 2007 Entry Draft.

Season	Club	League	GP	G	A	Pts	PIM	PP	SH	GW	S	S%	+/-	TF	F%	Min	GP	G	A	Pts	PIM	PP	SH	GW	Min
2003-04	Okotoks Oilers	AMHA	30	7	32	39	69	....	....	....	....	....	....	....	....	....	....	....	....	....	....	....	....	....	....
2004-05	Kamloops Blazers	WHL	60	0	1	1	77	....	....	....	....	....	....	....	....	....	6	0	0	0	16	....	....	....	....
2005-06	Kamloops Blazers	WHL	68	2	6	8	121	....	....	....	....	....	....	....	....	....	....	....	....	....	....	....	....	....	....
2006-07	Kamloops Blazers	WHL	69	2	23	25	120	....	....	....	....	....	....	....	....	....	4	1	2	3	12	....	....	....	....
2007-08	Kamloops Blazers	WHL	16	0	3	3	29	....	....	....	....	....	....	....	....	....	....	....	....	....	....	....	....	....	....
	Moose Jaw	WHL	53	2	21	23	81	....	....	....	....	....	....	....	....	....	5	0	2	2	15	....	....	....	....
2008-09	Rochester	AHL	75	3	20	23	44	....	....	....	....	....	....	....	....	....	....	....	....	....	....	....	....	....	....
2009-10	**Florida**	**NHL**	**22**	**0**	**0**	**0**	**2**	**0**	**0**	**0**	**5**	**0.0**	**–1**	**0**	**0.0**	**5:26**	....	....	....	....	....	....	....	....	....
	Rochester	AHL	58	6	13	19	34	....	....	....	....	....	....	....	....	....	7	1	0	1	4	....	....	....	....
2010-11	**Florida**	**NHL**	**54**	**2**	**10**	**12**	**22**	**0**	**0**	**0**	**56**	**3.6**	**–15**	**0**	**0.0**	**16:06**	....	....	....	....	....	....	....	....	....
	Rochester	AHL	17	2	3	5	8	....	....	....	....	....	....	....	....	....	....	....	....	....	....	....	....	....	....
2011-12	**Florida**	**NHL**	**40**	**0**	**5**	**5**	**10**	**0**	**0**	**0**	**45**	**0.0**	**–3**	**0**	**0.0**	**15:23**	**1**	**0**	**0**	**0**	**2**	**0**	**0**	**0**	**8:42**
2012-13	**Florida**	**NHL**	**9**	**0**	**0**	**0**	**36**	**0**	**0**	**0**	**8**	**0.0**	**–2**	**0**	**0.0**	**15:11**	....	....	....	....	....	....	....	....	....
	Los Angeles	**NHL**	**35**	**0**	**3**	**3**	**16**	**0**	**0**	**0**	**15**	**0.0**	**5**	**0**	**0.0**	**14:17**	**5**	**0**	**0**	**0**	**0**	**0**	**0**	**0**	**10:43**
2013-14	**Winnipeg**	**NHL**	**51**	**2**	**4**	**6**	**2**	**1**	**0**	**1**	**33**	**6.1**	**4**	**0**	**0.0**	**13:55**	....	....	....	....	....	....	....	....	....
2014-15	**Winnipeg**	**NHL**	**1**	**0**	**1**	**1**	**0**	**0**	**0**	**0**	**0**	**0.0**	**–1**	**0**	**0.0**	**16:58**	....	....	....	....	....	....	....	....	....
	St. John's IceCaps	AHL	41	3	13	16	32	....	....	....	....	....	....	....	....	....	....	....	....	....	....	....	....	....	....
	NHL Totals		**212**	**4**	**23**	**27**	**88**	**1**	**0**	**1**	**162**	**2.5**		**0**	**0.0**	**14:00**	**6**	**0**	**0**	**0**	**2**	**0**	**0**	**0**	**10:23**

• Missed majority of 2011-12 as a healthy reserve. Traded to **Los Angeles** by **Florida** for New Jersey's 5th round choice (previously acquired, later traded to Buffalo – Buffalo selected Gustav Possler) in 2013 Entry Draft, February 8, 2013. Claimed on waivers by **Winnipeg** from **Los Angeles**, November 2, 2013. • Missed majority of 2014-15 as a healthy reserve. Signed as a free agent by **Astana** (KHL), July 7, 2015.

ELLIOTT, Stefan

(ehl-LEE-awt, STEH-fan) **COL**

Defense. Shoots right. 6'1", 190 lbs. Born, Vancouver, BC, January 30, 1991. Colorado's 3rd choice, 49th overall, in 2009 Entry Draft.

Season	Club	League	GP	G	A	Pts	PIM	PP	SH	GW	S	S%	+/-	TF	F%	Min	GP	G	A	Pts	PIM	PP	SH	GW	Min
2006-07	Van. NW Giants	BCMML	36	12	19	31	18	....	....	....	....	....	....	....	....	....	....	....	....	....	....	....	....	....	....
	Saskatoon Blades	WHL	1	0	0	0	0	....	....	....	....	....	....	....	....	....	....	....	....	....	....	....	....	....	....
2007-08	Saskatoon Blades	WHL	67	9	31	40	17	....	....	....	....	....	....	....	....	....	....	....	....	....	....	....	....	....	....
2008-09	Saskatoon Blades	WHL	71	16	39	55	26	....	....	....	....	....	....	....	....	....	7	1	3	4	4	....	....	....	....
2009-10	Saskatoon Blades	WHL	72	26	39	65	24	....	....	....	....	....	....	....	....	....	10	3	5	8	4	....	....	....	....
2010-11	Saskatoon Blades	WHL	71	31	50	81	14	....	....	....	....	....	....	....	....	....	10	3	5	8	0	....	....	....	....
	Lake Erie	AHL	....	....	....	....	....	....	....	....	....	....	....	....	....	....	5	0	2	2	0	....	....	....	....
2011-12	**Colorado**	**NHL**	**39**	**4**	**9**	**13**	**8**	**0**	**0**	**1**	**84**	**4.8**	**2**	**0**	**0.0**	**17:09**	....	....	....	....	....	....	....	....	....
	Lake Erie	AHL	30	5	9	14	4	....	....	....	....	....	....	....	....	....	....	....	....	....	....	....	....	....	....
2012-13	Lake Erie	AHL	44	5	8	13	6	....	....	....	....	....	....	....	....	....	....	....	....	....	....	....	....	....	....
	Colorado	**NHL**	**18**	**1**	**3**	**4**	**2**	**0**	**0**	**0**	**35**	**2.9**	**–3**	**0**	**0.0**	**17:30**	....	....	....	....	....	....	....	....	....
2013-14	**Colorado**	**NHL**	**1**	**1**	**0**	**1**	**0**	**0**	**0**	**0**	**1**	**100.0**	**0**	**0**	**0.0**	**16:51**	....	....	....	....	....	....	....	....	....
	Lake Erie	AHL	61	14	14	28	14	....	....	....	....	....	....	....	....	....	....	....	....	....	....	....	....	....	....
2014-15	**Colorado**	**NHL**	**5**	**0**	**0**	**0**	**2**	**0**	**0**	**0**	**10**	**0.0**	**–2**	**0**	**0.0**	**13:56**	....	....	....	....	....	....	....	....	....
	Lake Erie	AHL	64	19	21	40	22	....	....	....	....	....	....	....	....	....	....	....	....	....	....	....	....	....	....
	NHL Totals		**63**	**6**	**12**	**18**	**12**	**0**	**0**	**1**	**130**	**4.6**		**0**	**0.0**	**16:59**	....	....	....	....	....	....	....	....	....

Canadian Major Junior Scholastic Player of the Year (2009) • WHL East First All-Star Team (2011) • WHL Defenseman of the Year (2011)

ELLIS, Matt

(EHL-ihs, MAT)

Left wing. Shoots left. 6', 208 lbs. Born, Welland, ON, August 31, 1981.

Season	Club	League	GP	G	A	Pts	PIM	PP	SH	GW	S	S%	+/-	TF	F%	Min	GP	G	A	Pts	PIM	PP	SH	GW	Min
1998-99	St. Michael's	OHL	47	10	8	18	6	....	....	....	....	....	....	....	....	....	....	....	....	....	....	....	....	....	....
99-2000	St. Michael's	OHL	59	15	20	35	20	....	....	....	....	....	....	....	....	....	....	....	....	....	....	....	....	....	....
2000-01	St. Michael's	OHL	68	21	24	45	19	....	....	....	....	....	....	....	....	....	18	4	8	12	6	....	....	....	....
2001-02	St. Michael's	OHL	66	38	51	89	20	....	....	....	....	....	....	....	....	....	15	8	6	14	6	....	....	....	....
2002-03	Toledo Storm	ECHL	71	27	32	59	34	....	....	....	....	....	....	....	....	....	7	3	5	8	0	....	....	....	....
2003-04	Grand Rapids	AHL	64	5	10	15	23	....	....	....	....	....	....	....	....	....	4	0	0	0	2	....	....	....	....
2004-05	Grand Rapids	AHL	79	18	23	41	59	....	....	....	....	....	....	....	....	....	....	....	....	....	....	....	....	....	....
2005-06	Grand Rapids	AHL	74	20	28	48	61	....	....	....	....	....	....	....	....	....	16	4	1	5	20	....	....	....	....
2006-07	**Detroit**	**NHL**	**16**	**0**	**0**	**0**	**6**	**0**	**0**	**0**	**22**	**0.0**	**–1**	**48**	**47.9**	**5:35**	....	....	....	....	....	....	....	....	....
	Grand Rapids	AHL	65	26	23	49	44	....	....	....	....	....	....	....	....	....	7	4	3	7	4	....	....	....	....
2007-08	**Detroit**	**NHL**	**35**	**2**	**4**	**6**	**12**	**0**	**0**	**1**	**28**	**7.1**	**1**	**87**	**49.4**	**5:23**	....	....	....	....	....	....	....	....	....
	Los Angeles	**NHL**	**19**	**1**	**1**	**2**	**14**	**0**	**1**	**0**	**38**	**2.6**	**2**	**27**	**37.0**	**12:41**	....	....	....	....	....	....	....	....	....

			Regular Season														Playoffs								
Season	Club	League	GP	G	A	Pts	PIM	PP	SH	GW	S	S%	+/-	TF	F%	Min	GP	G	A	Pts	PIM	PP	SH	GW	Min
2008-09	**Buffalo**	**NHL**	**45**	**7**	**5**	**12**	**12**	**0**	**0**	**2**	**73**	**9.6**	**4**	**239**	**46.9**	**8:50**	....	....	....	....	....	....	....	....	....
	Portland Pirates	AHL	12	2	2	4	4	....	....	....	....	....	....	....	....	....	....	....	....	....	....	....	....	....	....
2009-10	**Buffalo**	**NHL**	**72**	**3**	**10**	**13**	**12**	**0**	**0**	**1**	**112**	**2.7**	**–1**	**282**	**50.0**	**9:03**	**3**	**1**	**0**	**1**	**0**	**0**	**0**	**0**	**9:44**
2010-11	**Buffalo**	**NHL**	**14**	**0**	**0**	**0**	**0**	**0**	**0**	**0**	**20**	**0.0**	**–4**	**58**	**48.3**	**10:03**	**1**	**0**	**0**	**0**	**0**	**0**	**0**	**0**	**11:32**
	Portland Pirates	AHL	52	10	21	31	12	....	....	....	....	....	....	....	....	....	11	1	5	6	4	....	....	....	....
2011-12	**Buffalo**	**NHL**	**60**	**3**	**5**	**8**	**25**	**0**	**0**	**1**	**85**	**3.5**	**–3**	**244**	**48.0**	**9:43**	....	....	....	....	....	....	....	....	....
2012-13	Rochester	AHL	32	7	5	12	6	....	....	....	....	....	....	....	....	....	3	0	0	0	2	....	....	....	....
	Buffalo	**NHL**	**6**	**0**	**0**	**0**	**0**	**0**	**0**	**0**	**8**	**0.0**	**0**	**36**	**41.7**	**6:12**	....	....	....	....	....	....	....	....	....
2013-14	**Buffalo**	**NHL**	**50**	**4**	**2**	**6**	**4**	**0**	**0**	**0**	**70**	**5.7**	**–6**	**166**	**41.6**	**9:28**	....	....	....	....	....	....	....	....	....
	Rochester	AHL	25	5	5	10	10	....	....	....	....	....	....	....	....	....	....	....	....	....	....	....	....	....	....
2014-15	**Buffalo**	**NHL**	**39**	**1**	**1**	**2**	**4**	**0**	**0**	**1**	**29**	**3.4**	**–12**	**205**	**48.8**	**8:19**	....	....	....	....	....	....	....	....	....
	Rochester	AHL	38	7	6	13	2	....	....	....	....	....	....	....	....	....	....	....	....	....	....	....	....	....	....
	NHL Totals		**356**	**21**	**28**	**49**	**89**	**0**	**1**	**6**	**485**	**4.3**		**1392**	**47.3**	**8:47**	**4**	**1**	**0**	**1**	**0**	**0**	**0**	**0**	**10:11**

Signed as a free agent by **Detroit**, May 10, 2002. Claimed on waivers by **Los Angeles** from **Detroit**, February 21, 2008. Claimed on waivers by **Buffalo** from **Los Angeles**, October 1, 2008.

ELLIS, Ryan

(EHL-ihs, RIGH-uhn) **NSH**

Defense. Shoots right. 5'10", 175 lbs. Born, Hamilton, ON, January 3, 1991. Nashville's 1st choice, 11th overall, in 2009 Entry Draft.

Season	Club	League	GP	G	A	Pts	PIM	PP	SH	GW	S	S%	+/-	TF	F%	Min	GP	G	A	Pts	PIM	PP	SH	GW	Min
2006-07	Cambridge	Minor-ON	75	37	56	93	151	....	....	....	....	....	....	....	....	....	....	....	....	....	....	....	....	....	....
2007-08	Windsor Spitfires	OHL	63	15	48	63	51	....	....	....	....	....	....	....	....	....	5	2	3	5	2	....	....	....	....
2008-09	Windsor Spitfires	OHL	57	22	*67	89	57	....	....	....	....	....	....	....	....	....	20	8	*23	31	20	....	....	....	....
2009-10	Windsor Spitfires	OHL	48	12	49	61	38	....	....	....	....	....	....	....	....	....	19	3	*30	33	14	....	....	....	....
2010-11	Windsor Spitfires	OHL	58	24	77	101	61	....	....	....	....	....	....	....	....	....	18	6	13	19	12	....	....	....	....
	Milwaukee	AHL	....	....	....	....	....	....	....	....	....	....	....	....	....	....	7	1	1	2	2	....	....	....	....
2011-12	**Nashville**	**NHL**	**32**	**3**	**8**	**11**	**4**	**2**	**0**	**2**	**34**	**8.8**	**5**	**0**	**0.0**	**14:50**	**3**	**0**	**0**	**0**	**0**	**0**	**0**	**0**	**6:54**
	Milwaukee	AHL	29	4	14	18	8	....	....	....	....	....	....	....	....	....	....	....	....	....	....	....	....	....	....
2012-13	Milwaukee	AHL	32	5	9	14	18	....	....	....	....	....	....	....	....	....	4	0	0	0	0	....	....	....	....
	Nashville	**NHL**	**32**	**2**	**4**	**6**	**15**	**2**	**0**	**0**	**48**	**4.2**	**–2**	**0**	**0.0**	**16:23**	....	....	....	....	....	....	....	....	....
2013-14	**Nashville**	**NHL**	**80**	**6**	**21**	**27**	**24**	**0**	**0**	**2**	**123**	**4.9**	**9**	**0**	**0.0**	**16:04**	....	....	....	....	....	....	....	....	....
2014-15	**Nashville**	**NHL**	**58**	**9**	**18**	**27**	**27**	**2**	**0**	**0**	**118**	**7.6**	**8**	**0**	**0.0**	**18:59**	**6**	**0**	**3**	**3**	**2**	**0**	**0**	**0**	**26:24**
	NHL Totals		**202**	**20**	**51**	**71**	**70**	**6**	**0**	**4**	**323**	**6.2**		**0**	**0.0**	**16:45**	**9**	**0**	**3**	**3**	**2**	**0**	**0**	**0**	**19:54**

Canadian Major Junior All-Rookie Team (2008) • OHL First All-Star Team (2009, 2011) • Canadian Major Junior First All-Star Team (2009) • Memorial Cup All-Star Team (2009, 2010) • OHL Second All-Star Team (2010) • Canadian Major Junior Defenseman of the Year (2011) • Canadian Major Junior Player of the Year (2011)

EMELIN, Alexei

(eh-MUH-lehn, al-EHX-ay) **MTL**

Defense. Shoots left. 6'2", 217 lbs. Born, Togliatti, USSR, April 25, 1986. Montreal's 2nd choice, 84th overall, in 2004 Entry Draft.

Season	Club	League	GP	G	A	Pts	PIM	PP	SH	GW	S	S%	+/-	TF	F%	Min	GP	G	A	Pts	PIM	PP	SH	GW	Min
2002-03	Lada Togliatti 2	Russia-3	31	1	1	2	20	....	....	....	....	....	....	....	....	....	....	....	....	....	....	....	....	....	....
2003-04	Lada Togliatti 2	Russia-3	2	0	0	0	10	....	....	....	....	....	....	....	....	....	....	....	....	....	....	....	....	....	....
	CSK VVS Samara	Russia-2	52	2	4	6	180	....	....	....	....	....	....	....	....	....	1	0	0	0	18	....	....	....	....
2004-05	Lada Togliatti	Russia	12	0	1	1	24	....	....	....	....	....	....	....	....	....	2	0	0	0	2	....	....	....	....
2005-06	Lada Togliatti	Russia	44	6	6	12	131	....	....	....	....	....	....	....	....	....	6	0	1	1	*47	....	....	....	....
2006-07	Lada Togliatti	Russia	43	2	5	7	74	....	....	....	....	....	....	....	....	....	3	0	0	0	4	....	....	....	....
2007-08	Ak Bars Kazan	Russia	56	0	5	5	123	....	....	....	....	....	....	....	....	....	10	0	1	1	10	....	....	....	....
2008-09	Ak Bars Kazan	KHL	51	0	3	3	58	....	....	....	....	....	....	....	....	....	7	1	0	1	20	....	....	....	....
2009-10	Ak Bars Kazan	KHL	46	1	6	7	50	....	....	....	....	....	....	....	....	....	22	5	8	13	24	....	....	....	....
2010-11	Ak Bars Kazan	KHL	52	11	16	27	92	....	....	....	....	....	....	....	....	....	9	0	0	0	4	....	....	....	....
2011-12	**Montreal**	**NHL**	**67**	**3**	**4**	**7**	**30**	**0**	**1**	**0**	**62**	**4.8**	**–18**	**0**	**0.0**	**17:18**	....	....	....	....	....	....	....	....	....
2012-13	Ak Bars Kazan	KHL	24	2	7	9	40	....	....	....	....	....	....	....	....	....	....	....	....	....	....	....	....	....	....
	Montreal	**NHL**	**38**	**3**	**9**	**12**	**33**	**0**	**0**	**0**	**33**	**9.1**	**2**	**0**	**0.0**	**19:40**	....	....	....	....	....	....	....	....	....
2013-14	**Montreal**	**NHL**	**59**	**3**	**14**	**17**	**59**	**1**	**0**	**0**	**58**	**5.2**	**–1**	**0**	**0.0**	**19:15**	**15**	**0**	**2**	**2**	**4**	**0**	**0**	**0**	**22:21**
	Russia	Olympics	5	0	0	0	8	....	....	....	....	....	....	....	....	....	....	....	....	....	....	....	....	....	....
2014-15	**Montreal**	**NHL**	**68**	**3**	**11**	**14**	**59**	**0**	**0**	**0**	**43**	**7.0**	**5**	**0**	**0.0**	**19:49**	**12**	**0**	**2**	**2**	**10**	**0**	**0**	**0**	**21:29**
	NHL Totals		**232**	**12**	**38**	**50**	**181**	**1**	**1**	**0**	**196**	**6.1**		**0**	**0.0**	**18:55**	**27**	**0**	**4**	**4**	**14**	**0**	**0**	**0**	**21:58**

Signed as a free agent by **Kazan** (KHL), October 13, 2012.

EMINGER, Steve

(EH-mihn-juhr, STEEV)

Defense. Shoots right. 6'2", 207 lbs. Born, Woodbridge, ON, October 31, 1983. Washington's 1st choice, 12th overall, in 2002 Entry Draft.

Season	Club	League	GP	G	A	Pts	PIM	PP	SH	GW	S	S%	+/-	TF	F%	Min	GP	G	A	Pts	PIM	PP	SH	GW	Min
1998-99	Bramalea Blues	ON-Jr.A	47	6	9	15	81	....	....	....	....	....	....	....	....	....	....	....	....	....	....	....	....	....	....
99-2000	Kitchener Rangers	OHL	50	2	14	16	74	....	....	....	....	....	....	....	....	....	5	0	0	0	0	....	....	....	....
2000-01	Kitchener Rangers	OHL	54	6	26	32	66	....	....	....	....	....	....	....	....	....	....	....	....	....	....	....	....	....	....
2001-02	Kitchener Rangers	OHL	64	19	39	58	93	....	....	....	....	....	....	....	....	....	4	0	2	2	10	....	....	....	....
2002-03	**Washington**	**NHL**	**17**	**0**	**2**	**2**	**24**	**0**	**0**	**0**	**6**	**0.0**	**–3**	**0**	**0.0**	**10:08**	....	....	....	....	....	....	....	....	....
	Kitchener Rangers	OHL	23	2	27	29	40	....	....	....	....	....	....	....	....	....	21	3	8	11	44	....	....	....	....
2003-04	**Washington**	**NHL**	**41**	**0**	**4**	**4**	**45**	**0**	**0**	**0**	**12**	**0.0**	**–11**	**0**	**0.0**	**17:32**	....	....	....	....	....	....	....	....	....
	Portland Pirates	AHL	41	0	4	4	40	....	....	....	....	....	....	....	....	....	7	0	1	1	2	....	....	....	....
2004-05	Portland Pirates	AHL	62	3	17	20	40	....	....	....	....	....	....	....	....	....	....	....	....	....	....	....	....	....	....
2005-06	**Washington**	**NHL**	**66**	**5**	**13**	**18**	**81**	**1**	**0**	**0**	**50**	**10.0**	**–12**	**1**	**100.0**	**21:21**	....	....	....	....	....	....	....	....	....
2006-07	**Washington**	**NHL**	**68**	**1**	**16**	**17**	**63**	**0**	**0**	**0**	**27**	**3.7**	**–14**	**1**	**100.0**	**18:56**	....	....	....	....	....	....	....	....	....
2007-08	**Washington**	**NHL**	**20**	**0**	**2**	**2**	**8**	**0**	**0**	**0**	**14**	**0.0**	**–4**	**0**	**0.0**	**11:08**	**5**	**1**	**0**	**1**	**2**	**0**	**0**	**0**	**16:06**
2008-09	**Philadelphia**	**NHL**	**12**	**0**	**2**	**2**	**8**	**0**	**0**	**0**	**9**	**0.0**	**0**	**0**	**0.0**	**17:53**	....	....	....	....	....	....	....	....	....
	Tampa Bay	**NHL**	**50**	**4**	**19**	**23**	**36**	**2**	**0**	**0**	**63**	**6.3**	**–4**	**1**	**0.0**	**23:33**	....	....	....	....	....	....	....	....	....
	Florida	**NHL**	**9**	**1**	**0**	**1**	**6**	**0**	**0**	**1**	**13**	**7.7**	**1**	**0**	**0.0**	**15:49**	....	....	....	....	....	....	....	....	....
2009-10	**Anaheim**	**NHL**	**63**	**4**	**12**	**16**	**30**	**0**	**0**	**1**	**45**	**8.9**	**1**	**0**	**0.0**	**19:29**	....	....	....	....	....	....	....	....	....
2010-11	**NY Rangers**	**NHL**	**65**	**2**	**4**	**6**	**22**	**0**	**0**	**1**	**23**	**8.7**	**–5**	**0**	**0.0**	**15:51**	....	....	....	....	....	....	....	....	....
2011-12	**NY Rangers**	**NHL**	**42**	**2**	**3**	**5**	**28**	**0**	**0**	**0**	**19**	**10.5**	**0**	**0**	**0.0**	**13:17**	**4**	**0**	**0**	**0**	**0**	**0**	**0**	**0**	**6:49**
2012-13	**NY Rangers**	**NHL**	**35**	**0**	**3**	**3**	**8**	**0**	**0**	**0**	**22**	**0.0**	**9**	**0**	**0.0**	**13:02**	**11**	**0**	**2**	**2**	**4**	**0**	**0**	**0**	**12:45**
	Connecticut	AHL	4	1	0	1	0	....	....	....	....	....	....	....	....	....	....	....	....	....	....	....	....	....	....
2013-14	CSKA Moscow	KHL	25	0	2	2	10	....	....	....	....	....	....	....	....	....	....	....	....	....	....	....	....	....	....
	Norfolk Admirals	AHL	33	3	4	7	24	....	....	....	....	....	....	....	....	....	10	1	1	2	14	....	....	....	....
2014-15	Providence Bruins	AHL	62	4	19	23	60	....	....	....	....	....	....	....	....	....	1	0	0	0	0	....	....	....	....
	NHL Totals		**488**	**19**	**80**	**99**	**359**	**3**	**0**	**3**	**303**	**6.3**		**3**	**66.7**	**17:39**	**20**	**1**	**2**	**3**	**6**	**0**	**0**	**0**	**12:24**

OHL Second All-Star Team (2002, 2003) • Canadian Major Junior Second All-Star Team (2002) • Memorial Cup All-Star Team (2003)

Traded to **Philadelphia** by **Washington** with Washington's 3rd round choice (Jacob Deserres) in 2008 Entry Draft for Philadelphia's 1st round choice (John Carlson) in 2008 Entry Draft, June 20, 2008. Traded to **Tampa Bay** by **Philadelphia** with Steve Downie and Tampa Bay's 4th round choice (previously acquired, Tampa Bay selected Alex Hutchings) in 2009 Entry Draft for Matt Carle and San Jose's 3rd round choice (previously acquired, Philadelphia selected Simon Bertilsson) in 2009 Entry Draft, November 7, 2008. Traded to **Florida** by **Tampa Bay** for Noah Welch and Florida's 3rd round choice (later traded to Detroit – Detroit selected Andrej Nestrasil) in 2009 Entry Draft, March 4, 2009. Signed as a free agent by **Anaheim**, September 4, 2009. Traded to **NY Rangers** by **Anaheim** for Aaron Voros and Ryan Hillier, July 9, 2010. Signed as a free agent by **CSKA Moscow** (KHL), October 21, 2013. Signed as a free agent by **Norfolk** (AHL), January 24, 2014. Signed as a free agent by **Providence** (AHL), September 5, 2014.

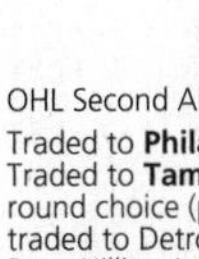

ENGELLAND, Deryk

(ehn-GUHL-uhnd, DEH-rihk) **CGY**

Defense. Shoots right. 6'2", 215 lbs. Born, Edmonton, AB, April 5, 1982. New Jersey's 11th choice, 194th overall, in 2000 Entry Draft.

Season	Club	League	GP	G	A	Pts	PIM	PP	SH	GW	S	S%	+/-	TF	F%	Min	GP	G	A	Pts	PIM	PP	SH	GW	Min
1998-99	Sicamous Eagles	KIJHL	STATISTICS NOT AVAILABLE																						
	Moose Jaw	WHL	2	0	0	0	0	....	....	....	....	....	....	....	....	....	....	....	....	....	....	....	....	....	....
99-2000	Moose Jaw	WHL	55	0	5	5	62	....	....	....	....	....	....	....	....	....	4	0	0	0	0	....	....	....	....
2000-01	Moose Jaw	WHL	65	4	11	15	157	....	....	....	....	....	....	....	....	....	4	0	0	0	10	....	....	....	....
2001-02	Moose Jaw	WHL	56	7	10	17	102	....	....	....	....	....	....	....	....	....	12	0	2	2	27	....	....	....	....
2002-03	Moose Jaw	WHL	65	3	8	11	199	....	....	....	....	....	....	....	....	....	13	1	1	2	20	....	....	....	....
2003-04	Lowell	AHL	26	0	0	0	34	....	....	....	....	....	....	....	....	....	....	....	....	....	....	....	....	....	....
	Las Vegas	ECHL	35	2	11	13	63	....	....	....	....	....	....	....	....	....	2	0	0	0	0	....	....	....	....
2004-05	Las Vegas	ECHL	72	5	16	21	138	....	....	....	....	....	....	....	....	....	....	....	....	....	....	....	....	....	....
2005-06	Hershey Bears	AHL	37	0	4	4	77	....	....	....	....	....	....	....	....	....	1	0	0	0	0	....	....	....	....
	South Carolina	ECHL	35	3	13	16	20	....	....	....	....	....	....	....	....	....	....	....	....	....	....	....	....	....	....
2006-07	Hershey Bears	AHL	44	4	6	10	95	....	....	....	....	....	....	....	....	....	14	0	0	0	14	....	....	....	....
	Reading Royals	ECHL	6	0	3	3	8	....	....	....	....	....	....	....	....	....	....	....	....	....	....	....	....	....	....
2007-08	Wilkes-Barre	AHL	80	2	15	17	141	....	....	....	....	....	....	....	....	....	23	1	3	4	14	....	....	....	....
2008-09	Wilkes-Barre	AHL	80	3	11	14	143	....	....	....	....	....	....	....	....	....	12	0	2	2	6	....	....	....	....

			Regular Season														Playoffs								
Season	Club	League	GP	G	A	Pts	PIM	PP	SH	GW	S	S%	+/-	TF	F%	Min	GP	G	A	Pts	PIM	PP	SH	GW	Min
2009-10	Pittsburgh	NHL	9	0	2	2	17	0	0	0	4	0.0	–2	0	0.0	16:08	....	....	....	....	....	....	....	....	....
	Wilkes-Barre	AHL	71	5	6	11	121	....	....	....	....	....	....	....	....	....	4	0	1	1	7	....	....	....	....
2010-11	Pittsburgh	NHL	63	3	7	10	123	0	0	0	49	6.1	–5	0	0.0	13:20	....	....	....	....	....	....	....	....	....
2011-12	Pittsburgh	NHL	73	4	13	17	56	0	0	1	86	4.7	10	0	0.0	16:09	6	0	1	1	14	0	0	0	11:30
2012-13	Rosenborg Elite	Norway	15	1	8	9	43	....	....	....	....	....	....	....	....	....	....	....	....	....	....	....	....	....	....
	Pittsburgh	NHL	42	0	6	6	54	0	0	0	31	0.0	5	0	0.0	13:55	7	0	0	0	8	0	0	0	15:28
2013-14	Pittsburgh	NHL	56	6	6	12	58	0	0	1	59	10.2	–6	0	0.0	13:03	....	....	....	....	....	....	....	....	....
2014-15	Calgary	NHL	76	2	9	11	53	0	0	0	51	3.9	–16	0	0.0	14:23	11	0	1	1	50	0	0	0	20:04
	NHL Totals		**319**	**15**	**43**	**58**	**361**	**0**	**0**	**2**	**280**	**5.4**		**0**	**0.0**	**14:20**	**24**	**0**	**2**	**2**	**72**	**0**	**0**	**0**	**16:35**

Signed as a free agent by **Calgary**, July, 2003. Signed as a free agent by **Pittsburgh**, July 16, 2007. Signed as a free agent by **Rosenborg** (Norway), October 12, 2012. Signed as a free agent by **Calgary**, July 1, 2014.

ENNIS, Tyler (EH-nihs, TIGH-luhr) BUF

Center. Shoots left. 5'9", 169 lbs. Born, Edmonton, AB, October 6, 1989. Buffalo's 2nd choice, 26th overall, in 2008 Entry Draft.

Season	Club	League	GP	G	A	Pts	PIM	PP	SH	GW	S	S%	+/-	TF	F%	Min	GP	G	A	Pts	PIM	PP	SH	GW	Min
2004-05	K of C Pats	AMHL	36	15	17	32	10	....	....	....	....	....	....	....	....	....	....	....	....	....	....	....	....	....	....
2005-06	Medicine Hat	WHL	43	3	7	10	10	....	....	....	....	....	....	....	....	....	7	0	0	0	0	....	....	....	....
2006-07	Medicine Hat	WHL	71	26	24	50	30	....	....	....	....	....	....	....	....	....	22	8	4	12	6	....	....	....	....
2007-08	Medicine Hat	WHL	70	43	48	91	42	....	....	....	....	....	....	....	....	....	5	0	4	4	6	....	....	....	....
2008-09	Medicine Hat	WHL	61	43	42	85	21	....	....	....	....	....	....	....	....	....	11	8	11	19	10	....	....	....	....
2009-10	Buffalo	NHL	10	3	6	9	6	0	0	0	23	13.0	1	31	41.9	15:20	6	1	3	4	0	0	0	0	17:09
	Portland Pirates	AHL	69	23	42	65	12	....	....	....	....	....	....	....	....	....	....	....	....	....	....	....	....	....	....
2010-11	Buffalo	NHL	82	20	29	49	30	5	0	1	210	9.5	0	9	22.2	15:40	7	2	2	4	4	0	0	1	16:38
2011-12	Buffalo	NHL	48	15	19	34	14	2	0	1	82	18.3	11	316	45.9	16:10	....	....	....	....	....	....	....	....	....
2012-13	Langnau	Swiss	9	3	5	8	0	....	....	....	....	....	....	....	....	....	....	....	....	....	....	....	....	....	....
	Buffalo	NHL	47	10	21	31	16	2	0	0	108	9.3	–14	377	41.9	17:53	....	....	....	....	....	....	....	....	....
2013-14	Buffalo	NHL	80	21	22	43	42	6	0	0	210	10.0	–25	625	38.7	18:51	....	....	....	....	....	....	....	....	....
2014-15	Buffalo	NHL	78	20	26	46	37	6	1	2	185	10.8	–19	183	36.6	19:07	....	....	....	....	....	....	....	....	....
	NHL Totals		**345**	**89**	**123**	**212**	**145**	**21**	**1**	**4**	**818**	**10.9**		**1541**	**40.7**	**17:33**	**13**	**3**	**5**	**8**	**4**	**0**	**0**	**1**	**16:52**

WHL East First All-Star Team (2008, 2009) • AHL All-Rookie Team (2010) • Dudley "Red" Garrett Memorial Award (AHL – Rookie of the Year) (2010)

Signed as a free agent by **Langnau** (Swiss), September 21, 2012.

ENSTROM, Toby (EHN-struhm, toh-BEE) WPG

Defense. Shoots left. 5'10", 180 lbs. Born, Nordingra, Sweden, November 5, 1984. Atlanta's 8th choice, 239th overall, in 2003 Entry Draft.

Season	Club	League	GP	G	A	Pts	PIM	PP	SH	GW	S	S%	+/-	TF	F%	Min	GP	G	A	Pts	PIM	PP	SH	GW	Min
99-2000	MoDo U18	Swe-U18	3	0	0	0	0	....	....	....	....	....	....	....	....	....	....	....	....	....	....	....	....	....	....
2000-01	MoDo U18	Swe-U18	16	7	6	13	18	....	....	....	....	....	....	....	....	....	....	....	....	....	....	....	....	....	....
	MoDo Jr.	Swe-Jr.	1	0	0	0	0	....	....	....	....	....	....	....	....	....	....	....	....	....	....	....	....	....	....
2001-02	MODO Jr.	Swe-Jr.	21	1	7	8	10	....	....	....	....	....	....	....	....	....	2	1	1	2	2	....	....	....	....
2002-03	MODO Jr.	Swe-Jr.	7	4	6	10	31	....	....	....	....	....	....	....	....	....	....	....	....	....	....	....	....	....	....
	MODO	Sweden	42	1	5	6	16	....	....	....	....	....	....	....	....	....	6	0	1	1	4	....	....	....	....
2003-04	MODO	Sweden	33	1	4	5	6	....	....	....	....	....	....	....	....	....	6	1	1	2	2	....	....	....	....
2004-05	MODO	Sweden	49	4	10	14	24	....	....	....	....	....	....	....	....	....	2	0	0	0	0	....	....	....	....
2005-06	MODO	Sweden	47	4	7	11	48	....	....	....	....	....	....	....	....	....	4	0	1	1	25	....	....	....	....
2006-07	MODO	Sweden	55	7	21	28	52	....	....	....	....	....	....	....	....	....	20	1	11	12	37	....	....	....	....
2007-08	Atlanta	NHL	82	5	33	38	42	4	0	0	105	4.8	–5	0	0.0	24:28	....	....	....	....	....	....	....	....	....
2008-09	Atlanta	NHL	82	5	27	32	52	2	1	1	86	5.8	14	2	50.0	23:32	....	....	....	....	....	....	....	....	....
2009-10	Atlanta	NHL	82	6	44	50	30	2	0	0	109	5.5	–5	0	0.0	22:16	....	....	....	....	....	....	....	....	....
	Sweden	Olympics	4	0	2	2	4	....	....	....	....	....	....	....	....	....	....	....	....	....	....	....	....	....	....
2010-11	Atlanta	NHL	72	10	41	51	54	6	0	0	113	8.8	–10	0	0.0	23:41	....	....	....	....	....	....	....	....	....
2011-12	Winnipeg	NHL	62	6	27	33	38	2	0	1	94	6.4	6	0	0.0	23:51	....	....	....	....	....	....	....	....	....
2012-13	Salzburg	Austria	5	1	0	1	4	....	....	....	....	....	....	....	....	....	....	....	....	....	....	....	....	....	....
	Winnipeg	NHL	22	4	11	15	8	1	0	2	21	19.0	–8	0	0.0	22:31	....	....	....	....	....	....	....	....	....
2013-14	Winnipeg	NHL	82	10	20	30	56	4	0	3	106	9.4	–9	1	100.0	23:54	....	....	....	....	....	....	....	....	....
2014-15	Winnipeg	NHL	60	4	19	23	36	1	0	0	58	6.9	13	0	0.0	23:34	4	0	1	1	0	0	0	0	20:46
	NHL Totals		**544**	**50**	**222**	**272**	**316**	**22**	**1**	**7**	**692**	**7.2**		**3**	**66.7**	**23:33**	**4**	**0**	**1**	**1**	**0**	**0**	**0**	**0**	**20:46**

NHL All-Rookie Team (2008)

• Transferred to **Winnipeg** after **Atlanta** franchise relocated, June 21, 2011. Signed as a free agent by **Salzburg** (Austria), October 22, 2012. • Missed majority of 2012-13 due to shoulder (February 15, 2013 vs. Pittsburgh) and back (April 9, 2013 vs. Buffalo) injuries.

ERAT, Martin (EE-rat, MAHR-tihn)

Right wing. Shoots left. 6', 196 lbs. Born, Trebic, Czech., August 29, 1981. Nashville's 12th choice, 191st overall, in 1999 Entry Draft.

Season	Club	League	GP	G	A	Pts	PIM	PP	SH	GW	S	S%	+/-	TF	F%	Min	GP	G	A	Pts	PIM	PP	SH	GW	Min
1997-98	HC ZPS Zlin Jr.	CzRep-Jr.	46	35	30	65	....	....	....	....	....	....	....	....	....	....	....	....	....	....	....	....	....	....	....
1998-99	HC ZPS Zlin Jr.	CzRep-Jr.	35	21	23	44	....	....	....	....	....	....	....	....	....	....	....	....	....	....	....	....	....	....	....
	Zlin	CzRep	5	0	0	0	2	....	....	....	....	....	....	....	....	....	....	....	....	....	....	....	....	....	....
99-2000	Saskatoon Blades	WHL	66	27	26	53	82	....	....	....	....	....	....	....	....	....	11	4	8	12	16	....	....	....	....
2000-01	Saskatoon Blades	WHL	31	19	35	54	48	....	....	....	....	....	....	....	....	....	....	....	....	....	....	....	....	....	....
	Red Deer Rebels	WHL	17	4	24	28	24	....	....	....	....	....	....	....	....	....	22	*15	*21	*36	32	....	....	....	....
2001-02	Nashville	NHL	80	9	24	33	32	2	0	2	84	10.7	–11	3	66.7	13:10	....	....	....	....	....	....	....	....	....
2002-03	Nashville	NHL	27	1	7	8	14	1	0	0	39	2.6	–9	1	0.0	12:47	....	....	....	....	....	....	....	....	....
	Milwaukee	AHL	45	10	22	32	41	....	....	....	....	....	....	....	....	....	6	5	4	9	4	....	....	....	....
2003-04	Nashville	NHL	76	16	33	49	38	4	0	2	137	11.7	10	31	29.0	15:00	6	0	1	1	6	0	0	0	14:09
2004-05	HC Hame Zlin	CzRep	48	20	23	43	129	....	....	....	....	....	....	....	....	....	16	*7	5	12	12	....	....	....	....
2005-06	Nashville	NHL	80	20	29	49	76	5	0	1	143	14.0	0	25	16.0	14:45	5	1	1	2	6	1	0	0	19:31
	Czech Republic	Olympics	8	1	1	2	4	....	....	....	....	....	....	....	....	....	....	....	....	....	....	....	....	....	....
2006-07	Nashville	NHL	68	16	41	57	50	5	1	3	132	12.1	13	43	44.2	18:59	3	0	1	1	0	0	0	0	14:13
2007-08	Nashville	NHL	76	23	34	57	40	4	0	6	163	14.1	–3	41	36.6	18:39	6	1	3	4	8	0	0	0	20:56
2008-09	Nashville	NHL	71	17	33	50	48	3	0	3	149	11.4	–7	38	29.0	18:34	....	....	....	....	....	....	....	....	....
2009-10	Nashville	NHL	74	21	28	49	50	5	0	2	168	12.5	–7	73	32.9	17:59	6	4	1	5	4	0	0	0	18:56
	Czech Republic	Olympics	5	0	1	1	2	....	....	....	....	....	....	....	....	....	....	....	....	....	....	....	....	....	....
2010-11	Nashville	NHL	64	17	33	50	22	7	0	3	135	12.6	14	44	43.2	18:06	10	1	5	6	6	1	0	0	19:15
2011-12	Nashville	NHL	71	19	39	58	30	5	1	3	107	17.8	12	126	47.6	18:29	10	1	3	4	6	1	0	0	18:51
2012-13	Nashville	NHL	36	4	17	21	26	1	0	1	60	6.7	–7	60	51.7	18:55	....	....	....	....	....	....	....	....	....
	Washington	NHL	9	1	2	3	4	0	0	1	9	11.1	0	2	50.0	13:55	4	0	0	0	4	0	0	0	14:32
2013-14	Washington	NHL	53	1	23	24	22	0	0	0	46	2.2	1	210	45.7	14:44	....	....	....	....	....	....	....	....	....
	Czech Republic	Olympics	5	1	0	1	0	....	....	....	....	....	....	....	....	....	....	....	....	....	....	....	....	....	....
	Phoenix	NHL	17	2	3	5	6	0	0	0	7	28.6	4	3	33.3	14:28	....	....	....	....	....	....	....	....	....
2014-15	Arizona	NHL	79	9	23	32	48	3	0	1	91	9.9	–16	6	0.0	15:52	....	....	....	....	....	....	....	....	....
	NHL Totals		**881**	**176**	**369**	**545**	**506**	**45**	**2**	**28**	**1470**	**12.0**		**706**	**41.4**	**16:37**	**50**	**8**	**15**	**23**	**40**	**3**	**0**	**0**	**18:04**

Signed as a free agent by **Zlin** (CzRep), September 5, 2004. Traded to **Washington** by **Nashville** with Michael Latta for Filip Forsberg, April 3, 2013. Traded to **Phoenix** by **Washington** with John Mitchell for Rostislav Klesla, Chris Brown and Phoenix/Arizona's 4th round choice (previously acquired, later traded to Carolina – Carolina selected Callum Booth) in 2015 Entry Draft, March 4, 2014.

ERICSSON, Jonathan (AIR-ihk-suhn, JAWN-ah-thuhn) DET

Defense. Shoots left. 6'4", 221 lbs. Born, Karlskrona, Sweden, March 2, 1984. Detroit's 10th choice, 291st overall, in 2002 Entry Draft.

Season	Club	League	GP	G	A	Pts	PIM	PP	SH	GW	S	S%	+/-	TF	F%	Min	GP	G	A	Pts	PIM	PP	SH	GW	Min
2001-02	Hasten Jr.	Swe-Jr.	STATISTICS NOT AVAILABLE																						
2002-03	Vita Hasten	Sweden-3	40	2	4	6	36	....	....	....	....	....	....	....	....	....	....	....	....	....	....	....	....	....	....
2003-04	Sodertalje SK	Sweden	42	1	0	1	12	....	....	....	....	....	....	....	....	....	....	....	....	....	....	....	....	....	....
2004-05	Sodertalje SK	Sweden	15	0	0	0	4	....	....	....	....	....	....	....	....	....	1	0	0	0	0	....	....	....	....
2005-06	Sodertalje SK Jr.	Swe-Jr.	1	0	0	0	2	....	....	....	....	....	....	....	....	....	....	....	....	....	....	....	....	....	....
	Almtuna	Sweden-2	19	2	3	5	44	....	....	....	....	....	....	....	....	....	....	....	....	....	....	....	....	....	....
	Sodertalje SK	Sweden	24	0	0	0	20	....	....	....	....	....	....	....	....	....	....	....	....	....	....	....	....	....	....
	Sodertalje SK	Sweden-Q	7	0	1	1	4	....	....	....	....	....	....	....	....	....	....	....	....	....	....	....	....	....	....
2006-07	Grand Rapids	AHL	67	5	24	29	102	....	....	....	....	....	....	....	....	....	7	0	0	0	8	....	....	....	....
2007-08	Detroit	NHL	8	1	0	1	4	1	0	0	19	5.3	–3	0	0.0	15:58	....	....	....	....	....	....	....	....	....
	Grand Rapids	AHL	69	10	24	34	83	....	....	....	....	....	....	....	....	....	....	....	....	....	....	....	....	....	....

			Regular Season														Playoffs								
Season	Club	League	GP	G	A	Pts	PIM	PP	SH	GW	S	S%	+/-	TF	F%	Min	GP	G	A	Pts	PIM	PP	SH	GW	Min
2008-09	**Detroit**	**NHL**	**19**	**1**	**3**	**4**	**15**	**0**	**0**	**0**	**25**	**4.0**	**–1**	**0**	**0.0**	**17:40**	**22**	**4**	**4**	**8**	**25**	**0**	**0**	**1**	**18:44**
	Grand Rapids	AHL	40	2	13	15	48	....	....	....	....	....	....	....	....	....	....	....	....	....	....	....	....	....	....
2009-10	**Detroit**	**NHL**	**62**	**4**	**9**	**13**	**44**	**0**	**1**	**1**	**55**	**7.3**	**–15**	**0**	**0.0**	**16:42**	**12**	**0**	**2**	**2**	**8**	**0**	**0**	**0**	**14:17**
2010-11	**Detroit**	**NHL**	**74**	**3**	**12**	**15**	**87**	**1**	**0**	**0**	**89**	**3.4**	**8**	**0**	**0.0**	**18:50**	**11**	**1**	**2**	**3**	**4**	**0**	**0**	**0**	**18:47**
2011-12	**Detroit**	**NHL**	**69**	**1**	**10**	**11**	**47**	**0**	**0**	**0**	**63**	**1.6**	**16**	**0**	**0.0**	**17:05**	**5**	**0**	**0**	**0**	**6**	**0**	**0**	**0**	**19:49**
2012-13	Vita Hasten	Sweden-3	3	0	3	3	4	....	....	....	....	....	....	....	....	....	....	....	....	....	....	....	....	....	....
	Sodertalje SK	Sweden-2	4	0	1	1	6	....	....	....	....	....	....	....	....	....	....	....	....	....	....	....	....	....	....
	Detroit	**NHL**	**45**	**3**	**10**	**13**	**29**	**0**	**0**	**1**	**34**	**8.8**	**6**	**0**	**0.0**	**21:19**	**14**	**0**	**3**	**3**	**2**	**0**	**0**	**0**	**22:33**
2013-14	**Detroit**	**NHL**	**48**	**1**	**10**	**11**	**34**	**0**	**0**	**0**	**66**	**1.5**	**2**	**0**	**0.0**	**21:15**	....	....	....	....	....	....	....	....	....
	Sweden	Olympics	6	0	1	1	8	....	....	....	....	....	....	....	....	....	....	....	....	....	....	....	....	....	....
2014-15	**Detroit**	**NHL**	**82**	**3**	**12**	**15**	**70**	**0**	**0**	**0**	**82**	**3.7**	**–5**	**0**	**0.0**	**19:35**	**7**	**0**	**4**	**4**	**8**	**0**	**0**	**0**	**19:51**
	NHL Totals		**407**	**17**	**66**	**83**	**330**	**2**	**1**	**2**	**433**	**3.9**		**0**	**0.0**	**18:49**	**71**	**5**	**15**	**20**	**53**	**0**	**0**	**1**	**18:56**

Signed as a free agent by **Vita Hasten** (Sweden-3). October 7, 2012. Signed as a free agent by **Sodertalje** (Sweden-2), October 26, 2012.

ERIKSSON, Loui (AIR-ihk-suhn, LOO-ee) BOS

Left wing. Shoots left. 6'2", 196 lbs. Born, Goteborg, Sweden, July 17, 1985. Dallas' 1st choice, 33rd overall, in 2003 Entry Draft.

Season	Club	League	GP	G	A	Pts	PIM	PP	SH	GW	S	S%	+/-	TF	F%	Min	GP	G	A	Pts	PIM	PP	SH	GW	Min
2000-01	V.Frolunda U18	Swe-U18	9	5	3	8	4	....	....	....	....	....	....	....	....	....	....	....	....	....	....	....	....	....	....
	V.Frolunda Jr.	Swe-Jr.	1	0	0	0	0	....	....	....	....	....	....	....	....	....	....	....	....	....	....	....	....	....	....
2001-02	V.Frolunda U18	Swe-U18	1	1	0	1	0	....	....	....	....	....	....	....	....	....	....	....	....	....	....	....	....	....	....
	V.Frolunda Jr.	Swe-Jr.	35	7	15	22	2	....	....	....	....	....	....	....	....	....	8	2	3	5	2	....	....	....	....
2002-03	V.Frolunda Jr.	Swe-Jr.	30	16	15	31	10	....	....	....	....	....	....	....	....	....	8	4	6	10	4	....	....	....	....
2003-04	V.Frolunda	Sweden	46	8	5	13	4	....	....	....	....	....	....	....	....	....	10	1	5	6	0	....	....	....	....
2004-05	Frolunda	Sweden	39	5	9	14	4	....	....	....	....	....	....	....	....	....	12	0	0	0	0	....	....	....	....
2005-06	Iowa Stars	AHL	78	31	29	60	27	....	....	....	....	....	....	....	....	....	7	2	5	7	0	....	....	....	....
2006-07	**Dallas**	**NHL**	**59**	**6**	**13**	**19**	**18**	**2**	**0**	**0**	**78**	**7.7**	**–3**	**9**	**44.4**	**13:11**	**4**	**0**	**1**	**1**	**0**	**0**	**0**	**0**	**15:47**
	Iowa Stars	AHL	15	5	3	8	13	....	....	....	....	....	....	....	....	....	9	2	5	7	0	....	....	....	....
2007-08	**Dallas**	**NHL**	**69**	**14**	**17**	**31**	**28**	**4**	**0**	**0**	**120**	**11.7**	**5**	**13**	**15.4**	**14:02**	**18**	**4**	**4**	**8**	**8**	**1**	**0**	**0**	**18:12**
	Iowa Stars	AHL	2	1	2	3	2	....	....	....	....	....	....	....	....	....	....	....	....	....	....	....	....	....	....
2008-09	**Dallas**	**NHL**	**82**	**36**	**27**	**63**	**14**	**7**	**1**	**4**	**178**	**20.2**	**14**	**11**	**18.2**	**19:50**	....	....	....	....	....	....	....	....	....
2009-10	**Dallas**	**NHL**	**82**	**29**	**42**	**71**	**26**	**6**	**2**	**4**	**214**	**13.6**	**–4**	**11**	**36.4**	**19:46**	....	....	....	....	....	....	....	....	....
	Sweden	Olympics	4	3	1	4	0	....	....	....	....	....	....	....	....	....	....	....	....	....	....	....	....	....	....
2010-11	**Dallas**	**NHL**	**79**	**27**	**46**	**73**	**8**	**10**	**1**	**6**	**179**	**15.1**	**10**	**4**	**25.0**	**20:34**	....	....	....	....	....	....	....	....	....
2011-12	**Dallas**	**NHL**	**82**	**26**	**45**	**71**	**12**	**5**	**2**	**3**	**187**	**13.9**	**18**	**16**	**43.8**	**19:46**	....	....	....	....	....	....	....	....	....
2012-13	HC Davos	Swiss	7	3	3	6	0	....	....	....	....	....	....	....	....	....	....	....	....	....	....	....	....	....	....
	Dallas	**NHL**	**48**	**12**	**17**	**29**	**8**	**2**	**1**	**3**	**104**	**11.5**	**-9**	**34**	**26.5**	**20:07**	....	....	....	....	....	....	....	....	....
2013-14	**Boston**	**NHL**	**61**	**10**	**27**	**37**	**6**	**2**	**0**	**2**	**115**	**8.7**	**14**	**0**	**0.0**	**16:32**	**12**	**2**	**3**	**5**	**4**	**1**	**0**	**0**	**17:39**
	Sweden	Olympics	6	2	1	3	0	....	....	....	....	....	....	....	....	....	....	....	....	....	....	....	....	....	....
2014-15	**Boston**	**NHL**	**81**	**22**	**25**	**47**	**14**	**6**	**0**	**4**	**169**	**13.0**	**1**	**12**	**33.3**	**18:29**	....	....	....	....	....	....	....	....	....
	NHL Totals		**643**	**182**	**259**	**441**	**134**	**44**	**7**	**26**	**1344**	**13.5**		**110**	**30.0**	**18:13**	**34**	**6**	**8**	**14**	**12**	**2**	**0**	**0**	**17:43**

Played in NHL All-Star Game (2011)

Signed as a free agent by **Davos** (Swiss), December 4, 2012. Traded to **Boston** by **Dallas** with Joe Morrow, Reilly Smith and Matt Fraser for Tyler Seguin, Rich Peverley and Ryan Button, July 4, 2013.

ERIXON, Tim (AIR-ihx-uhn, TIHM) PIT

Defense. Shoots left. 6'2", 190 lbs. Born, Port Chester, NY, February 24, 1991. Calgary's 1st choice, 23rd overall, in 2009 Entry Draft.

Season	Club	League	GP	G	A	Pts	PIM	PP	SH	GW	S	S%	+/-	TF	F%	Min	GP	G	A	Pts	PIM	PP	SH	GW	Min
2005-06	Skelleftea U18	Swe-U18	9	0	2	2	4	....	....	....	....	....	....	....	....	....	....	....	....	....	....	....	....	....	....
2006-07	Skelleftea U18	Swe-U18	8	2	2	4	20	....	....	....	....	....	....	....	....	....	....	....	....	....	....	....	....	....	....
	Skelleftea Jr.	Swe-Jr.	8	0	2	2	2	....	....	....	....	....	....	....	....	....	2	0	0	0	4	....	....	....	....
2007-08	Skelleftea U18	Swe-U18	4	0	1	1	10	....	....	....	....	....	....	....	....	....	....	....	....	....	....	....	....	....	....
	Skelleftea Jr.	Swe-Jr.	28	3	11	14	78	....	....	....	....	....	....	....	....	....	1	0	1	1	4	....	....	....	....
	Skelleftea AIK HK	Sweden	2	0	0	0	0	....	....	....	....	....	....	....	....	....	....	....	....	....	....	....	....	....	....
2008-09	Skelleftea AIK U18	Swe-U18	1	0	2	2	10	....	....	....	....	....	....	....	....	....	5	1	5	6	14	....	....	....	....
	Skelleftea AIK Jr.	Swe-Jr.	9	2	12	14	10	....	....	....	....	....	....	....	....	....	5	1	2	3	4	....	....	....	....
	Malmo	Sweden-2	3	0	2	2	0	....	....	....	....	....	....	....	....	....	....	....	....	....	....	....	....	....	....
	Skelleftea AIK	Sweden	45	2	5	7	12	....	....	....	....	....	....	....	....	....	9	0	0	0	4	....	....	....	....
2009-10	Skelleftea AIK	Sweden	45	7	6	13	44	....	....	....	....	....	....	....	....	....	12	1	0	1	8	....	....	....	....
2010-11	Skelleftea AIK	Sweden	48	5	19	24	40	....	....	....	....	....	....	....	....	....	18	3	5	8	12	....	....	....	....
2011-12	**NY Rangers**	**NHL**	**18**	**0**	**2**	**2**	**8**	**0**	**0**	**0**	**9**	**0.0**	**–2**	**0**	**0.0**	**13:00**	....	....	....	....	....	....	....	....	....
	Connecticut	AHL	52	3	30	33	42	....	....	....	....	....	....	....	....	....	9	0	4	4	8	....	....	....	....
2012-13	Springfield	AHL	40	5	24	29	38	....	....	....	....	....	....	....	....	....	....	....	....	....	....	....	....	....	....
	Columbus	**NHL**	**31**	**0**	**5**	**5**	**14**	**0**	**0**	**0**	**21**	**0.0**	**4**	**0**	**0.0**	**15:42**	....	....	....	....	....	....	....	....	....
2013-14	**Columbus**	**NHL**	**2**	**0**	**0**	**0**	**2**	**0**	**0**	**0**	**1**	**0.0**	**2**	**0**	**0.0**	**14:21**	....	....	....	....	....	....	....	....	....
	Springfield	AHL	40	5	33	38	16	....	....	....	....	....	....	....	....	....	5	1	1	2	4	....	....	....	....
2014-15	**Columbus**	**NHL**	**19**	**1**	**5**	**6**	**4**	**1**	**0**	**0**	**20**	**5.0**	**–3**	**0**	**0.0**	**16:58**	....	....	....	....	....	....	....	....	....
	Chicago	**NHL**	**8**	**0**	**0**	**0**	**4**	**0**	**0**	**0**	**6**	**0.0**	**1**	**0**	**0.0**	**9:59**	....	....	....	....	....	....	....	....	....
	Toronto	**NHL**	**15**	**1**	**0**	**1**	**6**	**0**	**0**	**0**	**10**	**10.0**	**–5**	**0**	**0.0**	**15:48**	....	....	....	....	....	....	....	....	....
	NHL Totals		**93**	**2**	**12**	**14**	**38**	**1**	**0**	**0**	**67**	**3.0**		**0**	**0.0**	**14:56**	....	....	....	....	....	....	....	....	....

Traded to **NY Rangers** by **Calgary** with Calgary's 5th round choice (Shane McColgan) in 2011 Entry Draft for Roman Horak, NY Rangers' 2nd round choice (Markus Granlund) in 2011 Entry Draft and Pittsburgh's 2nd round choice (previously acquired, Calgary selected Tyler Wotherspoon) in 2011 Entry Draft, June 1, 2011. Traded to **Columbus** by **NY Rangers** with Brandon Dubinsky, Artem Anisimov and NY Rangers' 1st round choice (Kerby Rychel) in 2013 Entry Draft for Rick Nash, Steven Delisle and Columbus' 3rd round choice (Pavel Buchnevich) in 2013 Entry Draft, July 23, 2012. Traded to **Chicago** by **Columbus** for Jeremy Morin, December 14, 2014. Claimed on waivers by **Toronto** from **Chicago**, March 1, 2015. Traded to **Pittsburgh** by **Toronto** with Phil Kessel, Tyler Biggs and future considerations for Nick Spaling, Kasperi Kapanen, Scott Harrington, New Jersey's 3rd round choice (previously acquired) in 2016 Entry Draft and future considerations, July 1, 2015.

ETEM, Emerson (EE-tehm, EHM-ur-suhn) NYR

Right wing. Shoots left. 6'1", 210 lbs. Born, Long Beach, CA, June 16, 1992. Anaheim's 2nd choice, 29th overall, in 2010 Entry Draft.

Season	Club	League	GP	G	A	Pts	PIM	PP	SH	GW	S	S%	+/-	TF	F%	Min	GP	G	A	Pts	PIM	PP	SH	GW	Min
2007-08	Shat.-St. Mary's	High-MN	58	13	15	28	20	....	....	....	....	....	....	....	....	....	....	....	....	....	....	....	....	....	....
2008-09	USNTDP	NAHL	40	19	14	33	16	....	....	....	....	....	....	....	....	....	9	4	4	8	4	....	....	....	....
	USNTDP	U-17	13	6	7	13	0	....	....	....	....	....	....	....	....	....	....	....	....	....	....	....	....	....	....
2009-10	Medicine Hat	WHL	72	37	28	65	26	....	....	....	....	....	....	....	....	....	12	7	3	10	0	....	....	....	....
2010-11	Medicine Hat	WHL	65	45	35	80	24	....	....	....	....	....	....	....	....	....	15	10	11	21	7	....	....	....	....
2011-12	Medicine Hat	WHL	65	*61	46	107	34	....	....	....	....	....	....	....	....	....	7	7	6	13	13	....	....	....	....
	Syracuse Crunch	AHL	2	1	0	1	2	....	....	....	....	....	....	....	....	....	4	2	0	2	0	....	....	....	....
2012-13	Norfolk Admirals	AHL	45	13	3	16	12	....	....	....	....	....	....	....	....	....	....	....	....	....	....	....	....	....	....
	Anaheim	**NHL**	**38**	**3**	**7**	**10**	**9**	**0**	**0**	**0**	**48**	**6.3**	**7**	**5**	**40.0**	**11:28**	**7**	**3**	**2**	**5**	**2**	**0**	**0**	**0**	**12:50**
2013-14	**Anaheim**	**NHL**	**29**	**7**	**4**	**11**	**4**	**1**	**1**	**2**	**44**	**15.9**	**3**	**1**	**0.0**	**12:47**	**4**	**0**	**0**	**0**	**12**	**0**	**0**	**0**	**10:22**
	Norfolk Admirals	AHL	50	24	30	54	10	....	....	....	....	....	....	....	....	....	4	0	2	2	0	....	....	....	....
2014-15	**Anaheim**	**NHL**	**45**	**5**	**5**	**10**	**4**	**0**	**0**	**0**	**77**	**6.5**	**–6**	**4**	**50.0**	**12:15**	**12**	**3**	**0**	**3**	**0**	**0**	**0**	**0**	**11:42**
	Norfolk Admirals	AHL	22	13	8	21	2	....	....	....	....	....	....	....	....	....	....	....	....	....	....	....	....	....	....
	NHL Totals		**112**	**15**	**16**	**31**	**17**	**1**	**1**	**2**	**169**	**8.9**		**10**	**40.0**	**12:07**	**23**	**6**	**2**	**8**	**14**	**0**	**0**	**0**	**11:49**

WHL East First All-Star Team (2012)

Traded to **NY Rangers** by **Anaheim** with Florida's 2nd round choice (previously acquired, NY Rangers selected Ryan Gropp) in 2015 Entry Draft for Carl Hagelin and NY Rangers' 2nd (Julius Naatinen) and 6th (Garrett Metcalf) round choices in 2015 Entry Draft, June 27, 2015.

EVERBERG, Dennis (EH-vuhr-buhrg, DEH-nihs) COL

Right wing. Shoots left. 6'4", 205 lbs. Born, Vasteras, Sweden, December 31, 1991.

Season	Club	League	GP	G	A	Pts	PIM	PP	SH	GW	S	S%	+/-	TF	F%	Min	GP	G	A	Pts	PIM	PP	SH	GW	Min
2009-10	Rogle Jr.	Swe-Jr.	36	6	12	18	55	....	....	....	....	....	....	....	....	....	2	1	0	1	2	....	....	....	....
	Rogle	Sweden	12	1	1	2	6	....	....	....	....	....	....	....	....	....	....	....	....	....	....	....	....	....	....
	Rogle	Sweden-Q	8	0	0	0	0	....	....	....	....	....	....	....	....	....	....	....	....	....	....	....	....	....	....
2010-11	Rogle Jr.	Swe-Jr.	18	4	2	6	54	....	....	....	....	....	....	....	....	....	1	1	1	2	2	....	....	....	....
	Rogle	Sweden-2	49	5	7	12	20	....	....	....	....	....	....	....	....	....	....	....	....	....	....	....	....	....	....
2011-12	Rogle Jr.	Swe-Jr.	3	0	4	4	0	....	....	....	....	....	....	....	....	....	....	....	....	....	....	....	....	....	....
	Rogle	Sweden-2	15	2	4	6	0	....	....	....	....	....	....	....	....	....	6	1	0	1	0	....	....	....	....
2012-13	Rogle	Sweden	55	5	3	8	47	....	....	....	....	....	....	....	....	....	....	....	....	....	....	....	....	....	....
	Rogle	Sweden-Q	10	0	1	1	0	....	....	....	....	....	....	....	....	....	....	....	....	....	....	....	....	....	....
2013-14	Rogle	Sweden-2	63	25	20	45	42	....	....	....	....	....	....	....	....	....	....	....	....	....	....	....	....	....	....

Season	Club	League	GP	G	A	Pts	PIM	PP	SH	GW	S	S%	+/-	TF	F%	Min	GP	G	A	Pts	PIM	PP	SH	GW	Min
2014-15	Colorado	NHL	55	3	9	12	10	0	0	0	62	4.8	-7	3	0.0	11:48	....	....	....	....	....	....	....	....	....
	Lake Erie	AHL	12	5	2	7	4	....						....			....								
	NHL Totals		55	3	9	12	10	0	0	0	62	4.8		3	0.0	11:48									

Signed as a free agent by **Colorado**, April 29, 2014.

FALK, Justin · (FAWLK, JUHS-tihn) · CBJ

Defense. Shoots left. 6'5", 215 lbs. Born, Snowflake, MB, October 11, 1988. Minnesota's 2nd choice, 110th overall, in 2007 Entry Draft.

Season	Club	League	GP	G	A	Pts	PIM	PP	SH	GW	S	S%	+/-	TF	F%	Min	GP	G	A	Pts	PIM	PP	SH	GW	Min
2004-05	Swan Valley	MJHL	56	0	8	8	46																		
	Calgary Hitmen	WHL	4	0	0	0	2											5	0	0	0	0				
2005-06	Calgary Hitmen	WHL	5	0	2	2	0																			
	Spokane Chiefs	WHL	48	0	8	8	35																			
2006-07	Spokane Chiefs	WHL	62	3	12	15	88											6	0	0	0	8				
2007-08	Spokane Chiefs	WHL	72	4	22	26	98											21	1	4	5	12				
2008-09	Houston Aeros	AHL	65	0	3	3	44											20	0	2	2	4				
2009-10	**Minnesota**	**NHL**	3	0	0	0	0	0	0	0	1	0.0	-2	0	0.0	7:33									
	Houston Aeros	AHL	69	3	6	9	87																			
2010-11	**Minnesota**	**NHL**	22	0	3	3	6	0	0	0	7	0.0	-4	0	0.0	14:09									
	Houston Aeros	AHL	55	3	11	14	41											24	0	5	5	33				
2011-12	**Minnesota**	**NHL**	47	1	8	9	54	1	0	0	46	2.2	-13	0	0.0	19:30									
2012-13	**Minnesota**	**NHL**	36	0	3	3	40	0	0	0	27	0.0	-9	0	0.0	13:13	4	0	0	0	2	0	0	0	11:33
2013-14	**NY Rangers**	**NHL**	21	0	2	2	20	0	0	0	10	0.0	-5	0	0.0	11:56									
2014-15	**Minnesota**	**NHL**	13	0	0	0	7	0	0	0	10	0.0	-6	0	0.0	9:08									
	Iowa Wild	AHL	39	1	6	7	34																			
	Columbus	**NHL**	5	1	1	2	7	0	0	0	8	12.5	-3	0	0.0	15:13									
	NHL Totals		147	2	17	19	134	1	0	0	109	1.8		0	0.0	14:46	4	0	0	0	2	0	0	0	11:33

Memorial Cup All-Star Team (2008)

Traded to **NY Rangers** by **Minnesota** for Benn Ferriero and Columbus' 6th round choice (previously acquired, Minnesota selected Chase Lang) in 2014 Entry Draft, June 30, 2013. • Missed majority of 2013-14 as a healthy reserve. Signed as a free agent by **Minnesota**, August 1, 2014. Traded to **Columbus** by **Minnesota** with Minnesota's 5th round choice (Veeti Vainio) in 2015 Entry Draft for Jordan Leopold, March 2, 2015.

FARNHAM, Bobby · (FAHRN-uhm, BAW-bee) · PIT

Left wing. Shoots left. 5'10", 188 lbs. Born, North Andover, MA, January 21, 1989.

Season	Club	League	GP	G	A	Pts	PIM	PP	SH	GW	S	S%	+/-	TF	F%	Min	GP	G	A	Pts	PIM	PP	SH	GW	Min
2008-09	Brown U.	ECAC	31	4	3	7	24																		
2009-10	Brown U.	ECAC	36	3	8	11	14																			
2010-11	Brown U.	ECAC	31	8	7	15	39																			
2011-12	Brown U.	ECAC	31	8	13	21	51																			
	Providence Bruins	AHL	3	0	0	0	4																			
	Worcester Sharks	AHL	3	0	0	0	2																			
2012-13	Wheeling Nailers	ECHL	9	3	1	4	46																			
	Wilkes-Barre	AHL	65	3	8	11	274											6	0	0	0	4				
2013-14	Wilkes-Barre	AHL	64	7	7	14	166											12	0	0	0	30				
2014-15	**Pittsburgh**	**NHL**	11	0	0	0	24	0	0	0	6	0.0	0	0	0.0	7:11									
	Wilkes-Barre	AHL	62	7	7	14	226											8	0	0	0	14				
	NHL Totals		11	0	0	0	24	0	0	0	6	0.0		0	0.0	7:11									

Signed as a free agent by **Pittsburgh**, July 6, 2013.

FAST, Jesper · (FAHST, YEHS-puhr) · NYR

Right wing. Shoots right. 6', 185 lbs. Born, Nassjo, Sweden, December 2, 1991. NY Rangers' 5th choice, 157th overall, in 2010 Entry Draft.

Season	Club	League	GP	G	A	Pts	PIM	PP	SH	GW	S	S%	+/-	TF	F%	Min	GP	G	A	Pts	PIM	PP	SH	GW	Min
2007-08	HV 71 U18	Swe-U18	30	15	11	26	14																		
	HV 71 Jr.	Swe-Jr.	3	0	0	0	2																			
2008-09	HV 71 U18	Swe-U18	3	2	2	4	2																			
	HV 71 Jr.	Swe-Jr.	37	7	7	14	16											7	2	1	3	6				
2009-10	HV 71 Jr.	Swe-Jr.	37	23	26	49	10											3	0	2	2	0				
	HV 71 Jonkoping	Sweden	2	0	0	0	0																			
2010-11	HV 71 Jonkoping	Sweden	36	7	9	16	6											3	0	0	0	0				
	HV 71 Jr.	Swe-Jr.	6	3	7	10	4											3	2	2	4	2				
2011-12	HV 71 Jonkoping	Sweden	21	5	11	16	4											5	2	1	3	0				
2012-13	HV 71 Jonkoping	Sweden	47	18	17	35	4											5	1	4	5	0				
	Connecticut	AHL	1	1	0	1	2																			
2013-14	**NY Rangers**	**NHL**	11	0	0	0	2	0	0	0	7	0.0	-5	0	0.0	11:17	3	0	1	1	0	0	0	0	9:40
	Hartford	AHL	48	17	17	34	30																			
2014-15	**NY Rangers**	**NHL**	58	6	8	14	8	0	0	0	52	11.5	-1	20	20.0	11:48	19	3	4	7	2	0	0	0	14:50
	Hartford	AHL	11	1	8	9	2																			
	NHL Totals		69	6	8	14	10	0	0	0	59	10.2		20	20.0	11:43	22	3	4	7	2	0	0	0	14:08

FAULK, Justin · (FAWLK, JUHS-tihn) · CAR

Defense. Shoots right. 6', 215 lbs. Born, South St. Paul, MN, March 20, 1992. Carolina's 2nd choice, 37th overall, in 2010 Entry Draft.

Season	Club	League	GP	G	A	Pts	PIM	PP	SH	GW	S	S%	+/-	TF	F%	Min	GP	G	A	Pts	PIM	PP	SH	GW	Min
2007-08	South St. Paul	High-MN	26	6	15	21	32																		
2008-09	USNTDP	NAHL	38	3	9	12	20											9	3	3	6	6				
	USNTDP	U-17	17	7	9	16	35																			
	USNTDP	U-18	1	0	0	0	0																			
2009-10	USNTDP	USHL	21	9	3	12	46																			
	USNTDP	U-18	39	12	9	21	20																			
2010-11	U. Minn-Duluth	WCHA	39	8	25	33	47																			
	Charlotte	AHL															13	0	2	2	2				
2011-12	**Carolina**	**NHL**	66	8	14	22	29	5	0	2	101	7.9	-16	0	0.0	22:51									
	Charlotte	AHL	12	2	4	6	11																			
2012-13	Charlotte	AHL	31	5	19	24	16																			
	Carolina	**NHL**	38	5	10	15	15	1	1	0	76	6.6	1	0	0.0	24:00									
2013-14	**Carolina**	**NHL**	76	5	27	32	37	2	0	1	152	3.3	-9	0	0.0	23:25									
	United States	Olympics	2	0	0	0	0																			
2014-15	**Carolina**	**NHL**	82	15	34	49	30	7	2	4	238	6.3	-19	0	0.0	24:26									
	NHL Totals		262	33	85	118	111	15	3	7	567	5.8		0	0.0	23:40									

WCHA All-Rookie Team (2011) • NCAA Championship All-Tournament Team (2011) • NHL All-Rookie Team (2012)
Played in NHL All-Star Game (2015)

FAYNE, Mark · (FAYN, MAHRK) · EDM

Defense. Shoots right. 6'3", 210 lbs. Born, Nashua, NH, May 15, 1987. New Jersey's 5th choice, 155th overall, in 2005 Entry Draft.

Season	Club	League	GP	G	A	Pts	PIM	PP	SH	GW	S	S%	+/-	TF	F%	Min	GP	G	A	Pts	PIM	PP	SH	GW	Min
2003-04	Nobles	High-MA	20	3	5	8	14																		
2004-05	Nobles	High-MA	24	1	17	18	16																			
2005-06	Nobles	High-MA	29	10	24	34																				
2006-07	Providence	H-East	36	5	7	12	43																			
2007-08	Providence	H-East	36	2	4	6	18																			
2008-09	Providence	H-East	33	4	5	9	30																			
2009-10	Providence	H-East	34	5	17	22	14																			
2010-11	**New Jersey**	**NHL**	57	4	10	14	27	0	0	0	77	5.2	10	0	0.0	17:50									
	Albany Devils	AHL	19	1	3	4	6																			
2011-12	**New Jersey**	**NHL**	82	4	13	17	26	0	0	1	94	4.3	-4	0	0.0	20:11	24	0	3	3	6	0	0	0	20:19
2012-13	**New Jersey**	**NHL**	31	1	5	6	16	0	1	0	34	2.9	6	0	0.0	18:06									

			Regular Season														Playoffs								
Season	Club	League	GP	G	A	Pts	PIM	PP	SH	GW	S	S%	+/-	TF	F%	Min	GP	G	A	Pts	PIM	PP	SH	GW	Min
2013-14	**New Jersey**	**NHL**	72	4	7	11	30	0	1	0	88	4.5	-5	0	0.0	18:19	....	....	....	....	....	....	....	....	....
2014-15	**Edmonton**	**NHL**	74	2	6	8	14	0	0	0	78	2.6	-21	0	0.0	17:56	....	....	....	....	....	....	....	....	....
	NHL Totals		316	15	41	56	113	0	2	1	371	4.0		0	0.0	18:36	24	0	3	3	6	0	0	0	20:19

Signed as a free agent by **Edmonton**, July 1, 2014.

FEDOTENKO, Ruslan

(feh-doh-TEHN-koh, roos-LAHN) **MIN**

Left wing. Shoots left. 6'2", 195 lbs. Born, Kiev, USSR, January 18, 1979.

Season	Club	League	GP	G	A	Pts	PIM	PP	SH	GW	S	S%	+/-	TF	F%	Min	GP	G	A	Pts	PIM	PP	SH	GW	Min
1995-96	Kiev 2	EEHL	33	9	11	20	12	....	....	....	....	....	....	....	....	....	....	....	....	....	....	....	....	....	....
	Sokol Kiev	CIS	2	0	0	0	0	....	....	....	....	....	....	....	....	....	....	....	....	....	....	....	....	....	....
1996-97	TPS Turku U18	Fin-U18	3	3	2	5	2	....	....	....	....	....	....	....	....	....	....	....	....	....	....	....	....	....	....
	TPS Turku Jr.	Fin-Jr.	11	1	1	2	2	....	....	....	....	....	....	....	....	....	....	....	....	....	....	....	....	....	....
	Kiekko-67 Turku	Finland-2	22	4	3	7	16	....	....	....	....	....	....	....	....	....	....	....	....	....	....	....	....	....	....
	Kiekko Turku	Finland-3	....	....	....	....	....	....	....	....	....	....	....	....	....	....	3	1	0	1	2	....	....	....	....
1997-98	Melfort Mustangs	SJHL	68	35	31	66	55	....	....	....	....	....	....	....	....	....	....	....	....	....	....	....	....	....	....
1998-99	Sioux City	USHL	55	43	34	77	139	....	....	....	....	....	....	....	....	....	5	5	1	6	9	....	....	....	....
99-2000	Trenton Titans	ECHL	8	5	3	8	9	....	....	....	....	....	....	....	....	....	....	....	....	....	....	....	....	....	....
	Philadelphia	AHL	67	16	34	50	42	....	....	....	....	....	....	....	....	....	2	0	0	0	0	....	....	....	....
2000-01	**Philadelphia**	**NHL**	74	16	20	36	72	3	0	4	119	13.4	8	7	71.4	14:38	6	0	1	1	4	0	0	0	11:18
	Philadelphia	AHL	8	1	0	1	8	....	....	....	....	....	....	....	....	....	....	....	....	....	....	....	....	....	....
2001-02	**Philadelphia**	**NHL**	78	17	9	26	43	0	1	3	121	14.0	15	41	43.9	13:56	5	1	0	1	2	0	0	1	14:11
	Ukraine	Olympics	1	1	0	1	4	....	....	....	....	....	....	....	....	....	....	....	....	....	....	....	....	....	....
2002-03	**Tampa Bay**	**NHL**	76	19	13	32	44	6	0	6	114	16.7	-7	90	48.9	16:01	11	0	1	1	2	0	0	0	13:58
2003-04♦	**Tampa Bay**	**NHL**	77	17	22	39	30	0	0	3	116	14.7	14	58	55.2	14:39	22	12	2	14	14	5	0	3	16:40
2004-05			DID NOT PLAY																						
2005-06	**Tampa Bay**	**NHL**	80	26	15	41	44	4	0	6	164	15.9	-4	28	42.9	15:21	5	0	0	0	20	0	0	0	14:38
2006-07	**Tampa Bay**	**NHL**	80	12	20	32	52	2	0	1	154	7.8	-3	8	25.0	16:15	4	0	0	0	4	0	0	0	17:27
2007-08	**NY Islanders**	**NHL**	67	16	17	33	40	8	0	2	121	13.2	-9	28	39.3	16:42	....	....	....	....	....	....	....	....	....
2008-09♦	**Pittsburgh**	**NHL**	65	16	23	39	44	1	0	3	117	13.7	18	18	22.2	14:06	24	7	7	14	4	0	0	0	14:31
2009-10	**Pittsburgh**	**NHL**	80	11	19	30	50	3	0	3	158	7.0	-17	28	35.7	14:39	6	0	0	0	4	0	0	0	12:31
2010-11	**NY Rangers**	**NHL**	66	10	15	25	25	0	1	0	120	8.3	9	32	37.5	15:00	5	0	2	2	4	0	0	0	20:55
2011-12	**NY Rangers**	**NHL**	73	9	11	20	16	1	0	1	94	9.6	-7	34	47.1	13:36	20	2	5	7	8	0	0	0	15:17
2012-13	Donetsk	KHL	33	8	10	18	22	....	....	....	....	....	....	....	....	....	....	....	....	....	....	....	....	....	....
	Philadelphia	**NHL**	47	4	9	13	12	0	0	1	43	9.3	8	186	36.0	12:34	....	....	....	....	....	....	....	....	....
2013-14	Donetsk	KHL	46	7	10	17	42	....	....	....	....	....	....	....	....	....	13	0	6	6	35	....	....	....	....
2014-15	Iowa Wild	AHL	13	3	0	3	6	....	....	....	....	....	....	....	....	....	....	....	....	....	....	....	....	....	....
	NHL Totals		863	173	193	366	472	28	2	33	1441	12.0		558	41.8	14:52	108	22	18	40	66	5	0	4	15:09

USHL First All-Star Team (1999)

Signed as a free agent by **Philadelphia**, August 3, 1999. Traded to **Tampa Bay** by **Philadelphia** with Tampa Bay's 2nd round choice (previously acquired, later traded to Dallas – Dallas selected Tobias Stephan) in 2002 Entry Draft and Phoenix's 2nd round choice (previously acquired, later traded to San Jose – San Jose selected Dan Spang) in 2002 Entry Draft for Tampa Bay's 1st round choice (Joni Pitkanen) in 2002 Entry Draft, June 21, 2002. Signed as a free agent by **NY Islanders**, July 4, 2007. Signed as a free agent by **Pittsburgh**, July 3, 2008. Signed as a free agent by **NY Rangers**, October 4, 2010. Signed as a free agent by **Philadelphia**, July 5, 2012. Signed as a free agent by **Donetsk** (KHL), September 16, 2012. Signed to a PTO (professional tryout) contract by **Iowa** (AHL), January 20, 2015. Signed as a free agent by **Minnesota**, July 1, 2015.

FEDUN, Taylor

(fuh-DOON, TAY-luhr) **VAN**

Defense. Shoots right. 6', 200 lbs. Born, Edmonton, AB, June 4, 1988.

Season	Club	League	GP	G	A	Pts	PIM	PP	SH	GW	S	S%	+/-	TF	F%	Min	GP	G	A	Pts	PIM	PP	SH	GW	Min
2003-04	SSAC Thunder	Minor-AB	36	8	26	34	24	....	....	....	....	....	....	....	....	....	....	....	....	....	....	....	....	....	....
	SSAC Athletics	AMHL	1	0	0	0	0	....	....	....	....	....	....	....	....	....	....	....	....	....	....	....	....	....	....
2004-05	SSAC Athletics	AMHL	36	7	13	20	68	....	....	....	....	....	....	....	....	....	....	....	....	....	....	....	....	....	....
	Ft. Saskatchewan	AJHL	1	0	1	1	0	....	....	....	....	....	....	....	....	....	....	....	....	....	....	....	....	....	....
2005-06	Ft. Saskatchewan	AJHL	60	13	18	31	72	....	....	....	....	....	....	....	....	....	3	1	1	2	4	....	....	....	....
2006-07	Spruce Grove	AJHL	50	10	33	43	103	....	....	....	....	....	....	....	....	....	10	3	5	8	31	....	....	....	....
2007-08	Princeton	ECAC	32	4	10	14	32	....	....	....	....	....	....	....	....	....	....	....	....	....	....	....	....	....	....
2008-09	Princeton	ECAC	35	3	12	15	50	....	....	....	....	....	....	....	....	....	....	....	....	....	....	....	....	....	....
2009-10	Princeton	ECAC	31	3	14	17	34	....	....	....	....	....	....	....	....	....	....	....	....	....	....	....	....	....	....
2010-11	Princeton	ECAC	29	10	12	22	38	....	....	....	....	....	....	....	....	....	....	....	....	....	....	....	....	....	....
2011-12			DID NOT PLAY – INJURED																						
2012-13	Oklahoma City	AHL	70	8	19	27	30	....	....	....	....	....	....	....	....	....	17	3	3	6	6	....	....	....	....
2013-14	**Edmonton**	**NHL**	4	2	0	2	0	0	0	0	6	33.3	-1	0	0.0	12:13	....	....	....	....	....	....	....	....	....
	Oklahoma City	AHL	65	10	28	38	51	....	....	....	....	....	....	....	....	....	3	0	1	1	4	....	....	....	....
2014-15	**San Jose**	**NHL**	7	0	4	4	4	0	0	0	12	0.0	0	0	0.0	16:59	....	....	....	....	....	....	....	....	....
	Worcester Sharks	AHL	65	6	28	34	37	....	....	....	....	....	....	....	....	....	4	1	0	1	6	....	....	....	....
	NHL Totals		11	2	4	6	4	0	0	0	18	11.1		0	0.0	15:15	....	....	....	....	....	....	....	....	....

ECAC Second All-Star Team (2010) • ECAC First All-Star Team (2011) • NCAA East Second All-American Team (2011)

Signed as a free agent by **Edmonton**, March 8, 2011. • Missed 2011-12 due to pre-season leg injury vs. Minnesota, September 30, 2011. Signed as a free agent by **San Jose**, July 2, 2014. Signed as a free agent by **Vancouver**, July 1, 2015.

FEHR, Eric

(FAIR, AIR-ihk) **PIT**

Right wing. Shoots right. 6'4", 212 lbs. Born, Winkler, MB, September 7, 1985. Washington's 1st choice, 18th overall, in 2003 Entry Draft.

Season	Club	League	GP	G	A	Pts	PIM	PP	SH	GW	S	S%	+/-	TF	F%	Min	GP	G	A	Pts	PIM	PP	SH	GW	Min
2000-01	Pembina Valley	MMMHL	36	45	13	58	30	....	....	....	....	....	....	....	....	....	....	....	....	....	....	....	....	....	....
	Brandon	WHL	4	0	0	0	0	....	....	....	....	....	....	....	....	....	....	....	....	....	....	....	....	....	....
2001-02	Brandon	WHL	63	11	16	27	29	....	....	....	....	....	....	....	....	....	12	1	1	2	0	....	....	....	....
2002-03	Brandon	WHL	70	26	29	55	76	....	....	....	....	....	....	....	....	....	17	4	8	12	26	....	....	....	....
2003-04	Brandon	WHL	71	50	34	84	129	....	....	....	....	....	....	....	....	....	7	5	0	5	16	....	....	....	....
2004-05	Brandon	WHL	71	*59	52	*111	91	....	....	....	....	....	....	....	....	....	24	16	16	*32	47	....	....	....	....
2005-06	**Washington**	**NHL**	11	0	0	0	2	0	0	0	10	0.0	0	4	25.0	5:45	....	....	....	....	....	....	....	....	....
	Hershey Bears	AHL	70	25	28	53	70	....	....	....	....	....	....	....	....	....	19	8	3	11	8	....	....	....	....
2006-07	**Washington**	**NHL**	14	2	1	3	8	0	0	1	25	8.0	3	6	16.7	10:43	....	....	....	....	....	....	....	....	....
	Hershey Bears	AHL	40	22	19	41	63	....	....	....	....	....	....	....	....	....	....	....	....	....	....	....	....	....	....
2007-08	**Washington**	**NHL**	23	1	5	6	6	0	0	0	40	2.5	4	2	0.0	10:31	5	1	0	1	0	0	0	0	9:41
	Hershey Bears	AHL	11	3	4	7	4	....	....	....	....	....	....	....	....	....	2	1	3	4	2	....	....	....	....
2008-09	**Washington**	**NHL**	61	12	13	25	22	1	0	2	134	9.0	8	3	33.3	11:15	9	0	0	0	0	0	0	0	7:22
2009-10	**Washington**	**NHL**	69	21	18	39	24	3	0	3	145	14.5	18	2	50.0	12:08	7	3	1	4	4	0	0	0	11:24
2010-11	**Washington**	**NHL**	52	10	10	20	16	3	0	1	120	8.3	0	1	0.0	12:35	5	1	0	1	0	0	0	0	13:28
2011-12	**Winnipeg**	**NHL**	35	2	1	3	12	0	0	1	54	3.7	-6	0	0.0	9:42	....	....	....	....	....	....	....	....	....
2012-13	HPK Hameenlinna	Finland	21	13	12	25	22	....	....	....	....	....	....	....	....	....	....	....	....	....	....	....	....	....	....
	Washington	**NHL**	41	9	8	17	10	2	1	2	72	12.5	14	4	0.0	13:22	7	0	0	0	6	0	0	0	15:52
2013-14	**Washington**	**NHL**	73	13	18	31	32	0	0	2	137	9.5	0	426	46.0	14:45	....	....	....	....	....	....	....	....	....
2014-15	**Washington**	**NHL**	75	19	14	33	20	1	1	4	142	13.4	8	863	52.0	14:51	4	0	0	0	2	0	0	0	9:53
	NHL Totals		454	89	88	177	152	10	2	16	879	10.1		1311	49.5	12:35	37	5	1	6	12	0	0	0	11:09

WHL East First All-Star Team (2005) • WHL Player of the Year (2005) • Canadian Major Junior Second All-Star Team (2005)

• Missed majority of 2011-12 due to shoulder surgery and as a healthy reserve. Traded to **Winnipeg** by **Washington** for Danick Paquette and Winnipeg's 4th round choice (Thomas Di Pauli) in 2012 Entry Draft, July 8, 2011. Signed as a free agent by **Hameenlinna** (Finland), October 23, 2012. Signed as a free agent by **Washington**, January 12, 2013. Signed as a free agent by **Pittsburgh**, July 28, 2015.

FERENCE, Andrew

(FAIR-ehns, AN-droo) **EDM**

Defense. Shoots left. 5'11", 187 lbs. Born, Edmonton, AB, March 17, 1979. Pittsburgh's 8th choice, 208th overall, in 1997 Entry Draft.

Season	Club	League	GP	G	A	Pts	PIM	PP	SH	GW	S	S%	+/-	TF	F%	Min	GP	G	A	Pts	PIM	PP	SH	GW	Min
1994-95	Sherwood Park	AMHL	31	4	14	18	74	....	....	....	....	....	....	....	....	....	....	....	....	....	....	....	....	....	....
	Portland	WHL	2	0	0	0	4	....	....	....	....	....	....	....	....	....	....	....	....	....	....	....	....	....	....
1995-96	Portland	WHL	72	9	31	40	159	....	....	....	....	....	....	....	....	....	7	1	3	4	12	....	....	....	....
1996-97	Portland	WHL	72	12	32	44	149	....	....	....	....	....	....	....	....	....	6	1	2	3	12	....	....	....	....
1997-98	Portland	WHL	72	11	57	68	142	....	....	....	....	....	....	....	....	....	16	2	18	20	28	....	....	....	....
1998-99	Portland	WHL	40	11	21	32	104	....	....	....	....	....	....	....	....	....	4	1	4	5	10	....	....	....	....
	Kansas City	IHL	5	1	2	3	4	....	....	....	....	....	....	....	....	....	3	0	0	0	9	....	....	....	....
99-2000	**Pittsburgh**	**NHL**	30	2	4	6	20	0	0	1	26	7.7	3	0	0.0	16:19	....	....	....	....	....	....	....	....	....
	Wilkes-Barre	AHL	44	8	20	28	58	....	....	....	....	....	....	....	....	....	....	....	....	....	....	....	....	....	....

			Regular Season														Playoffs								
Season	Club	League	GP	G	A	Pts	PIM	PP	SH	GW	S	S%	+/-	TF	F%	Min	GP	G	A	Pts	PIM	PP	SH	GW	Min
2000-01	Pittsburgh	NHL	36	4	11	15	28	1	0	1	47	8.5	6	0	0.0	18:51	18	3	7	10	16	1	0	1	22:02
	Wilkes-Barre	AHL	43	6	18	24	95	....	....	....	....	....	....	....	....	....	3	1	0	1	12	....	....	....	....
2001-02	Pittsburgh	NHL	75	4	7	11	73	1	0	0	82	4.9	−12	2	0.0	18:34	....	....	....	....	....	....	....	....	....
2002-03	Pittsburgh	NHL	22	1	3	4	36	1	0	0	22	4.5	−16	1	100.0	19:33	....	....	....	....	....	....	....	....	....
	Wilkes-Barre	AHL	1	0	0	0	2	....	....	....	....	....	....	....	....	....	....	....	....	....	....	....	....	....	....
	Calgary	NHL	16	0	4	4	6	0	0	0	17	0.0	1	0	0.0	17:38	....	....	....	....	....	....	....	....	....
2003-04	Calgary	NHL	72	4	12	16	53	1	0	0	86	4.7	5	0	0.0	18:40	26	0	3	3	25	0	0	0	24:13
2004-05	C. Budejovice	CzRep-2	19	5	6	11	45	....	....	....	....	....	....	....	....	....	12	2	7	9	10	....	....	....	....
2005-06	Calgary	NHL	82	4	27	31	85	2	0	0	111	3.6	−12	1	0.0	20:08	7	0	4	4	12	0	0	0	23:09
2006-07	Calgary	NHL	54	2	10	12	66	1	0	0	51	3.9	7	3	33.3	18:29	....	....	....	....	....	....	....	....	....
	Boston	NHL	26	1	2	3	31	0	0	0	29	3.4	−2	0	0.0	22:22	....	....	....	....	....	....	....	....	....
2007-08	Boston	NHL	59	1	14	15	50	0	0	0	71	1.4	−14	1	100.0	22:15	7	0	4	4	6	0	0	0	21:39
2008-09	Boston	NHL	47	1	15	16	40	1	0	0	72	1.4	7	0	0.0	21:32	3	0	0	0	4	0	0	0	15:30
2009-10	Boston	NHL	51	0	8	8	16	0	0	0	60	0.0	−7	0	0.0	19:42	13	0	1	1	18	0	0	0	14:58
2010-11 ♦	Boston	NHL	70	3	12	15	60	0	0	0	78	3.8	22	0	0.0	17:59	25	4	6	10	37	1	0	1	20:36
2011-12	Boston	NHL	72	6	18	24	46	0	0	1	107	5.6	9	1	100.0	18:53	7	1	3	4	0	0	0	0	21:34
2012-13	C. Budejovice	CzRep	21	2	5	7	24	....	....	....	....	....	....	....	....	....	....	....	....	....	....	....	....	....	....
	Boston	NHL	48	4	9	13	35	0	0	0	66	6.1	9	0	0.0	19:29	14	0	2	2	4	0	0	0	24:31
2013-14	Edmonton	NHL	71	3	15	18	63	0	0	1	77	3.9	−18	3	66.7	21:04	....	....	....	....	....	....	....	....	....
2014-15	Edmonton	NHL	70	3	11	14	39	0	0	0	58	5.2	−17	2	0.0	18:53	....	....	....	....	....	....	....	....	....
	NHL Totals		901	43	182	225	747	8	0	4	1060	4.1		14	42.9	19:29	120	8	30	38	122	2	0	2	21:35

WHL West First All-Star Team (1998) • WHL West Second All-Star Team (1999) • King Clancy Memorial Trophy (2014)

• Missed majority of 2002-03 due to groin (November 18, 2002 vs. Montreal) and ankle (March 20, 2003 vs. Los Angeles) injuries. Traded to **Calgary** by **Pittsburgh** for Calgary's 3rd round choice (Brian Gifford) in 2004 Entry Draft, February 9, 2003. Signed as a free agent by **Ceske Budejovice** (CzRep-2), December 1, 2004. Traded to **Boston** by **Calgary** with Chuck Kobasew for Brad Stuart, Wayne Primeau and Washington's 4th round choice (previously acquired, Calgary selected T.J. Brodie) in 2008 Entry Draft, February 10, 2007. Signed as a free agent by **Ceske Budejovice** (CzRep), September 19, 2012. Signed as a free agent by **Edmonton**, July 5, 2013.

FERLAND, Micheal

(FAIR-land, MIGH-kuhl) **CGY**

Left wing. Shoots left. 6'2", 215 lbs. Born, Swan River, MB, April 20, 1992. Calgary's 5th choice, 133rd overall, in 2010 Entry Draft.

Season	Club	League	GP	G	A	Pts	PIM	PP	SH	GW	S	S%	+/-	TF	F%	Min	GP	G	A	Pts	PIM	PP	SH	GW	Min
2007-08	Brandon	MMHL	40	12	8	20	20	....	....	....	....	....	....	....	....	....	6	3	2	5	4	....	....	....	....
2008-09	Brandon	MMHL	44	45	40	85	52	....	....	....	....	....	....	....	....	....	6	4	5	9	8	....	....	....	....
2009-10	Brandon	WHL	61	9	19	28	85	....	....	....	....	....	....	....	....	....	15	3	1	4	8	....	....	....	....
2010-11	Brandon	WHL	56	23	33	56	110	....	....	....	....	....	....	....	....	....	6	4	2	6	4	....	....	....	....
2011-12	Brandon	WHL	68	47	49	96	84	....	....	....	....	....	....	....	....	....	8	3	3	6	6	....	....	....	....
2012-13	Brandon	WHL	4	1	1	2	4	....	....	....	....	....	....	....	....	....	....	....	....	....	....	....	....	....	....
	Saskatoon Blades	WHL	26	8	21	29	18	....	....	....	....	....	....	....	....	....	4	0	0	0	2	....	....	....	....
	Abbotsford Heat	AHL	7	0	0	0	10	....	....	....	....	....	....	....	....	....	....	....	....	....	....	....	....	....	....
	Utah Grizzlies	ECHL	3	0	1	1	5	....	....	....	....	....	....	....	....	....	....	....	....	....	....	....	....	....	....
2013-14	Abbotsford Heat	AHL	25	6	12	18	31	....	....	....	....	....	....	....	....	....	....	....	....	....	....	....	....	....	....
2014-15	Calgary	NHL	26	2	3	5	16	0	0	1	34	5.9	1	0	0.0	10:31	9	3	2	5	23	0	0	0	12:34
	Adirondack	AHL	32	7	8	15	30	....	....	....	....	....	....	....	....	....	....	....	....	....	....	....	....	....	....
	NHL Totals		26	2	3	5	16	0	0	1	34	5.9		0	0.0	10:31	9	3	2	5	23	0	0	0	12:34

WHL East Second All-Star Team (2012)

FERLIN, Brian

(FUHR-lihn, BRIGH-uhn) **BOS**

Right wing. Shoots right. 6'2", 209 lbs. Born, Jacksonville, FL, June 3, 1992. Boston's 4th choice, 121st overall, in 2011 Entry Draft.

Season	Club	League	GP	G	A	Pts	PIM	PP	SH	GW	S	S%	+/-	TF	F%	Min	GP	G	A	Pts	PIM	PP	SH	GW	Min
2009-10	Indiana Ice	USHL	57	6	10	16	36	....	....	....	....	....	....	....	....	....	8	1	2	3	2	....	....	....	....
2010-11	Indiana Ice	USHL	55	25	48	73	26	....	....	....	....	....	....	....	....	....	5	1	4	5	4	....	....	....	....
2011-12	Cornell Big Red	ECAC	26	8	13	21	30	....	....	....	....	....	....	....	....	....	....	....	....	....	....	....	....	....	....
2012-13	Cornell Big Red	ECAC	34	10	14	24	55	....	....	....	....	....	....	....	....	....	....	....	....	....	....	....	....	....	....
2013-14	Cornell Big Red	ECAC	32	13	14	27	26	....	....	....	....	....	....	....	....	....	....	....	....	....	....	....	....	....	....
2014-15	Boston	NHL	7	0	1	1	0	0	0	0	6	0.0	0	1	0.0	8:48	....	....	....	....	....	....	....	....	....
	Providence Bruins	AHL	53	11	9	20	40	....	....	....	....	....	....	....	....	....	....	....	....	....	....	....	....	....	....
	NHL Totals		7	0	1	1	0	0	0	0	6	0.0		1	0.0	8:48	....	....	....	....	....	....	....	....	....

ECAC All-Rookie Team (2012) • ECAC Rookie of the Year (2012)

FERRARO, Landon

(fuh-RAHR-oh, LAN-duhn) **DET**

Center. Shoots right. 6', 186 lbs. Born, Trail, BC, August 8, 1991. Detroit's 1st choice, 32nd overall, in 2009 Entry Draft.

Season	Club	League	GP	G	A	Pts	PIM	PP	SH	GW	S	S%	+/-	TF	F%	Min	GP	G	A	Pts	PIM	PP	SH	GW	Min
2006-07	Van. NW Giants	BCMML	25	21	13	34	77	....	....	....	....	....	....	....	....	....	....	....	....	....	....	....	....	....	....
	Red Deer Rebels	WHL	4	0	0	0	0	....	....	....	....	....	....	....	....	....	1	0	0	0	0	....	....	....	....
2007-08	Red Deer Rebels	WHL	54	13	11	24	65	....	....	....	....	....	....	....	....	....	....	....	....	....	....	....	....	....	....
2008-09	Red Deer Rebels	WHL	68	37	18	55	99	....	....	....	....	....	....	....	....	....	....	....	....	....	....	....	....	....	....
2009-10	Red Deer Rebels	WHL	53	16	30	46	55	....	....	....	....	....	....	....	....	....	3	0	0	0	2	....	....	....	....
	Grand Rapids	AHL	2	0	0	0	0	....	....	....	....	....	....	....	....	....	....	....	....	....	....	....	....	....	....
2010-11	Everett Silvertips	WHL	41	10	17	27	51	....	....	....	....	....	....	....	....	....	4	0	3	3	13	....	....	....	....
2011-12	Grand Rapids	AHL	56	9	11	20	47	....	....	....	....	....	....	....	....	....	....	....	....	....	....	....	....	....	....
2012-13	Grand Rapids	AHL	72	24	23	47	44	....	....	....	....	....	....	....	....	....	24	5	11	16	11	....	....	....	....
2013-14	Detroit	NHL	4	0	0	0	2	0	0	0	2	0.0	0	0	0.0	8:59	....	....	....	....	....	....	....	....	....
	Grand Rapids	AHL	70	15	16	31	52	....	....	....	....	....	....	....	....	....	9	1	2	3	2	....	....	....	....
2014-15	Detroit	NHL	3	1	0	1	0	0	0	1	4	25.0	1	0	0.0	11:59	7	0	0	0	2	0	0	0	10:09
	Grand Rapids	AHL	70	27	15	42	61	....	....	....	....	....	....	....	....	....	....	....	....	....	....	....	....	....	....
	NHL Totals		7	1	0	1	2	0	0	1	6	16.7		0	0.0	10:16	7	0	0	0	2	0	0	0	10:09

FERRIERO, Benn

(fuh-RAIR-oh, BEHN)

Center. Shoots right. 5'11", 195 lbs. Born, Boston, MA, April 29, 1987. Phoenix's 8th choice, 196th overall, in 2006 Entry Draft.

Season	Club	League	GP	G	A	Pts	PIM	PP	SH	GW	S	S%	+/-	TF	F%	Min	GP	G	A	Pts	PIM	PP	SH	GW	Min
2001-02	Gov. Dummer	High-MA	STATISTICS NOT AVAILABLE																						
2002-03	Gov. Dummer	High-MA	....	8	10	18	....	....	....	....	....	....	....	....	....	....	....	....	....	....	....	....	....	....	....
2003-04	Gov. Dummer	High-MA	28	19	24	43	....	....	....	....	....	....	....	....	....	....	....	....	....	....	....	....	....	....	....
2004-05	Gov. Dummer	High-MA	28	15	27	42	....	....	....	....	....	....	....	....	....	....	....	....	....	....	....	....	....	....	....
2005-06	Boston College	H-East	42	16	9	25	36	....	....	....	....	....	....	....	....	....	....	....	....	....	....	....	....	....	....
2006-07	Boston College	H-East	42	23	23	46	43	....	....	....	....	....	....	....	....	....	....	....	....	....	....	....	....	....	....
2007-08	Boston College	H-East	44	17	25	42	71	....	....	....	....	....	....	....	....	....	....	....	....	....	....	....	....	....	....
2008-09	Boston College	H-East	37	8	18	26	44	....	....	....	....	....	....	....	....	....	....	....	....	....	....	....	....	....	....
2009-10	San Jose	NHL	24	2	3	5	8	0	0	0	42	4.8	4	4	75.0	11:08	....	....	....	....	....	....	....	....	....
	Worcester Sharks	AHL	58	19	31	50	20	....	....	....	....	....	....	....	....	....	11	4	2	6	4	....	....	....	....
2010-11	San Jose	NHL	33	5	4	9	9	1	0	1	56	8.9	8	11	18.2	13:05	8	1	0	1	6	0	0	1	6:54
	Worcester Sharks	AHL	43	16	17	33	16	....	....	....	....	....	....	....	....	....	....	....	....	....	....	....	....	....	....
2011-12	San Jose	NHL	35	7	1	8	8	0	0	4	68	10.3	0	12	25.0	12:03	....	....	....	....	....	....	....	....	....
	Worcester Sharks	AHL	20	9	11	20	18	....	....	....	....	....	....	....	....	....	....	....	....	....	....	....	....	....	....
2012-13	Wilkes-Barre	AHL	34	4	14	18	14	....	....	....	....	....	....	....	....	....	....	....	....	....	....	....	....	....	....
	Connecticut	AHL	23	4	8	12	17	....	....	....	....	....	....	....	....	....	....	....	....	....	....	....	....	....	....
	NY Rangers	NHL	4	0	1	1	0	0	0	0	4	0.0	0	9	22.2	9:37	....	....	....	....	....	....	....	....	....
2013-14	Vancouver	NHL	2	0	0	0	0	0	0	0	0	0.0	0	0	0.0	4:22	....	....	....	....	....	....	....	....	....
	Utica Comets	AHL	54	19	20	39	42	....	....	....	....	....	....	....	....	....	....	....	....	....	....	....	....	....	....
2014-15	Chicago Wolves	AHL	39	2	5	7	12	....	....	....	....	....	....	....	....	....	2	1	0	1	0	....	....	....	....
	NHL Totals		98	14	9	23	25	1	0	5	170	8.2		36	27.8	11:55	8	1	0	1	6	0	0	1	6:54

Hockey East All-Rookie Team (2006)

Signed as a free agent by **San Jose**, August 23, 2009. Signed as a free agent by **Pittsburgh**, July 13, 2012. Traded to **NY Rangers** by **Pittsburgh** for Chad Kolarik, January 24, 2013. Traded to **Minnesota** by **NY Rangers** with Columbus' 6th round choice (previously acquired, Minnesota selected Chase Lang) in 2014 Entry Draft for Justin Falk, June 30, 2013. Signed as a free agent by **Vancouver**, July 12, 2013. Signed as a free agent by **St. Louis**, July 16, 2014. Signed as a free agent by **Salzburg** (Austria), June 9, 2015.

FIALA, Kevin

(fee-A-lah, KEH-vuhn) **NSH**

Left wing. Shoots left. 5'10", 180 lbs. Born, St. Gallen, Switzerland, July 22, 1996. Nashville's 1st choice, 11th overall, in 2014 Entry Draft.

Season	Club	League	GP	G	A	Pts	PIM	PP	SH	GW	S	S%	+/-	TF	F%	Min	GP	G	A	Pts	PIM	PP	SH	GW	Min
			Regular Season														Playoffs								
2009-10	EHC Uzwil U17	Swiss-U17	19	19	15	34	10	....	....	....	....	....	....	....	....	....	....	....	....	....	....	....	....	....	....
2010-11	ZSC Zurich U17	Swiss-U17	25	10	10	20	14	....	....	....	....	....	....	....	....	....	7	0	2	2	0	....	....	....	....
2011-12	ZSC Zurich U17	Swiss-U17	28	34	18	52	98	....	....	....	....	....	....	....	....	....	8	6	8	14	24	....	....	....	....
	ZSC Zurich Jr.	Swiss-Jr.	7	1	4	5	8	....	....	....	....	....	....	....	....	....	4	3	2	5	18	....	....	....	....
	GCK Zurich Jr.	Swiss-Jr.	2	0	1	1	0	....	....	....	....	....	....	....	....	....	....	....	....	....	....	....	....	....	....
2012-13	Malmo U18	Swe-U18	9	6	4	10	28	....	....	....	....	....	....	....	....	....	4	4	3	7	4	....	....	....	....
	Malmo Jr.	Swe-Jr.	33	9	19	28	28	....	....	....	....	....	....	....	....	....	3	0	0	0	2	....	....	....	....
2013-14	HV 71 Jr.	Swe-Jr.	27	10	15	25	40	....	....	....	....	....	....	....	....	....	....	....	....	....	....	....	....	....	....
	HV 71 Jonkoping	Sweden	8	3	8	11	10	....	....	....	....	....	....	....	....	....	8	1	5	6	14	....	....	....	....
2014-15	HV 71 Jonkoping	Sweden	20	5	9	14	14	....	....	....	....	....	....	....	....	....	....	....	....	....	....	....	....	....	....
	Nashville	**NHL**	**1**	**0**	**0**	**0**	**0**	**0**	**0**	**0**	**3**	**0.0**	**-1**	**0**	**0.0**	**11:25**	**1**	**0**	**0**	**0**	**0**	**0**	**0**	**0**	**11:05**
	Milwaukee	AHL	33	11	9	20	18	....	....	....	....	....	....	....	....	....	....	....	....	....	....	....	....	....	....
	NHL Totals		**1**	**0**	**0**	**0**	**0**	**0**	**0**	**0**	**3**	**0.0**		**0**	**0.0**	**11:25**	**1**	**0**	**0**	**0**	**0**	**0**	**0**	**0**	**11:05**

FIDDLER, Vernon

(FIHD-luhr, VUHR-nuhn) **DAL**

Center. Shoots left. 5'11", 205 lbs. Born, Edmonton, AB, May 9, 1980.

Season	Club	League	GP	G	A	Pts	PIM	PP	SH	GW	S	S%	+/-	TF	F%	Min	GP	G	A	Pts	PIM	PP	SH	GW	Min
1997-98	Kelowna Rockets	WHL	65	10	11	21	31	....	....	....	....	....	....	....	....	....	7	0	1	1	4	....	....	....	....
1998-99	Kelowna Rockets	WHL	68	22	21	43	82	....	....	....	....	....	....	....	....	....	6	2	0	2	8	....	....	....	....
99-2000	Kelowna Rockets	WHL	64	20	28	48	60	....	....	....	....	....	....	....	....	....	5	1	3	4	4	....	....	....	....
2000-01	Kelowna Rockets	WHL	3	0	2	2	0	....	....	....	....	....	....	....	....	....	....	....	....	....	....	....	....	....	....
	Medicine Hat	WHL	67	33	38	71	100	....	....	....	....	....	....	....	....	....	....	....	....	....	....	....	....	....	....
	Arkansas	ECHL	3	0	1	1	2	....	....	....	....	....	....	....	....	....	5	3	0	3	5	....	....	....	....
2001-02	Roanoke Express	ECHL	44	27	28	55	71	....	....	....	....	....	....	....	....	....	....	....	....	....	....	....	....	....	....
	Norfolk Admirals	AHL	38	8	5	13	28	....	....	....	....	....	....	....	....	....	4	1	3	4	2	....	....	....	....
2002-03	**Nashville**	**NHL**	**19**	**4**	**2**	**6**	**14**	**0**	**0**	**1**	**20**	**20.0**	**2**	**171**	**53.8**	**9:40**	....	....	....	....	....	....	....	....	....
	Milwaukee	AHL	54	8	16	24	70	....	....	....	....	....	....	....	....	....	6	1	2	3	14	....	....	....	....
2003-04	**Nashville**	**NHL**	**17**	**0**	**0**	**0**	**23**	**0**	**0**	**0**	**8**	**0.0**	**-6**	**123**	**49.6**	**8:06**	....	....	....	....	....	....	....	....	....
	Milwaukee	AHL	47	9	15	24	72	....	....	....	....	....	....	....	....	....	22	5	3	8	36	....	....	....	....
2004-05	Milwaukee	AHL	73	20	22	42	70	....	....	....	....	....	....	....	....	....	7	0	0	0	18	....	....	....	....
2005-06	**Nashville**	**NHL**	**40**	**8**	**4**	**12**	**42**	**3**	**0**	**2**	**46**	**17.4**	**-2**	**464**	**52.6**	**13:49**	**2**	**0**	**1**	**1**	**0**	**0**	**0**	**0**	**8:48**
	Milwaukee	AHL	11	1	6	7	20	....	....	....	....	....	....	....	....	....	....	....	....	....	....	....	....	....	....
2006-07	**Nashville**	**NHL**	**72**	**11**	**15**	**26**	**40**	**0**	**1**	**1**	**90**	**12.2**	**11**	**680**	**51.6**	**13:38**	**5**	**1**	**1**	**2**	**4**	**0**	**0**	**0**	**12:21**
2007-08	**Nashville**	**NHL**	**79**	**11**	**21**	**32**	**47**	**2**	**1**	**1**	**97**	**11.3**	**-4**	**384**	**50.3**	**13:56**	**6**	**0**	**0**	**0**	**0**	**0**	**0**	**0**	**16:48**
2008-09	**Nashville**	**NHL**	**78**	**11**	**6**	**17**	**24**	**1**	**2**	**2**	**114**	**9.6**	**-13**	**612**	**54.1**	**13:58**	....	....	....	....	....	....	....	....	....
2009-10	**Phoenix**	**NHL**	**76**	**8**	**22**	**30**	**46**	**0**	**3**	**1**	**119**	**6.7**	**13**	**1121**	**52.5**	**14:21**	**6**	**1**	**1**	**2**	**14**	**0**	**0**	**0**	**14:04**
2010-11	**Phoenix**	**NHL**	**71**	**6**	**16**	**22**	**46**	**0**	**1**	**2**	**97**	**6.2**	**3**	**1224**	**53.9**	**15:33**	**4**	**0**	**0**	**0**	**0**	**0**	**0**	**0**	**9:57**
2011-12	**Dallas**	**NHL**	**82**	**8**	**13**	**21**	**60**	**0**	**0**	**1**	**123**	**6.5**	**-13**	**1049**	**50.9**	**13:59**	....	....	....	....	....	....	....	....	....
2012-13	**Dallas**	**NHL**	**46**	**4**	**13**	**17**	**48**	**1**	**0**	**0**	**56**	**7.1**	**3**	**619**	**51.5**	**12:51**	....	....	....	....	....	....	....	....	....
2013-14	**Dallas**	**NHL**	**76**	**6**	**17**	**23**	**37**	**0**	**0**	**1**	**109**	**5.5**	**3**	**982**	**52.2**	**13:17**	**6**	**1**	**2**	**3**	**24**	**0**	**0**	**0**	**14:26**
2014-15	**Dallas**	**NHL**	**80**	**13**	**16**	**29**	**34**	**3**	**1**	**2**	**132**	**9.8**	**-5**	**1097**	**51.9**	**13:08**	....	....	....	....	....	....	....	....	....
	NHL Totals		**736**	**90**	**145**	**235**	**461**	**10**	**9**	**14**	**1011**	**8.9**		**8526**	**52.3**	**13:38**	**29**	**3**	**5**	**8**	**42**	**0**	**0**	**0**	**13:29**

ECHL All-Rookie Team (2002)

Signed as a free agent by **Arkansas** (ECHL), March 31, 2001. Traded to **Roanoke** (ECHL) by **Arkansas** (ECHL) for Calvin Elfring, August 11, 2001. Signed as a free agent by **Nashville**, May 6, 2002. Signed as a free agent by **Phoenix**, July 1, 2009. Signed as a free agent by **Dallas**, July 1, 2011.

FILATOV, Nikita

(FIHL-uh-tawf, nih-KEE-ta)

Left wing. Shoots right. 6', 190 lbs. Born, Moscow, USSR, May 25, 1990. Columbus' 1st choice, 6th overall, in 2008 Entry Draft.

Season	Club	League	GP	G	A	Pts	PIM	PP	SH	GW	S	S%	+/-	TF	F%	Min	GP	G	A	Pts	PIM	PP	SH	GW	Min
2005-06	CSKA Moscow 2	Russia-3	STATISTICS NOT AVAILABLE																						
2006-07	CSKA Moscow 2	Russia-3	STATISTICS NOT AVAILABLE																						
2007-08	CSKA Moscow 2	Russia-3	23	24	23	47	62	....	....	....	....	....	....	....	....	....	11	14	9	23	28	....	....	....	....
	CSKA Moscow	Russia	5	0	0	0	0	....	....	....	....	....	....	....	....	....	....	....	....	....	....	....	....	....	....
2008-09	**Columbus**	**NHL**	**8**	**4**	**0**	**4**	**0**	**0**	**0**	**1**	**10**	**40.0**	**3**	**0**	**0.0**	**8:08**	....	....	....	....	....	....	....	....	....
	Syracuse Crunch	AHL	39	16	16	32	24	....	....	....	....	....	....	....	....	....	....	....	....	....	....	....	....	....	....
2009-10	**Columbus**	**NHL**	**13**	**2**	**0**	**2**	**8**	**0**	**0**	**1**	**11**	**18.2**	**0**	**3**	**66.7**	**8:07**	....	....	....	....	....	....	....	....	....
	CSKA Moscow	KHL	26	9	13	22	16	....	....	....	....	....	....	....	....	....	3	0	1	1	4	....	....	....	....
2010-11	**Columbus**	**NHL**	**23**	**0**	**7**	**7**	**8**	**0**	**0**	**0**	**31**	**0.0**	**3**	**0**	**0.0**	**12:19**	....	....	....	....	....	....	....	....	....
	Springfield	AHL	36	9	11	20	20	....	....	....	....	....	....	....	....	....	....	....	....	....	....	....	....	....	....
2011-12	**Ottawa**	**NHL**	**9**	**0**	**1**	**1**	**4**	**0**	**0**	**0**	**6**	**0.0**	**1**	**1**	**0.0**	**9:49**	....	....	....	....	....	....	....	....	....
	Binghamton	AHL	15	7	5	12	12	....	....	....	....	....	....	....	....	....	....	....	....	....	....	....	....	....	....
	CSKA Moscow	KHL	18	4	4	8	12	....	....	....	....	....	....	....	....	....	5	0	1	1	4	....	....	....	....
2012-13	Ufa	KHL	47	10	11	21	24	....	....	....	....	....	....	....	....	....	13	3	3	6	6	....	....	....	....
2013-14	Ufa	KHL	35	13	7	20	18	....	....	....	....	....	....	....	....	....	5	1	0	1	0	....	....	....	....
2014-15	Khanty-Mansiisk	KHL	4	1	0	1	4	....	....	....	....	....	....	....	....	....	....	....	....	....	....	....	....	....	....
	Nizhny Novgorod	KHL	38	4	11	15	14	....	....	....	....	....	....	....	....	....	4	0	1	1	2	....	....	....	....
	NHL Totals		**53**	**6**	**8**	**14**	**20**	**0**	**0**	**2**	**58**	**10.3**		**4**	**50.0**	**10:14**	....	....	....	....	....	....	....	....	....

• Loaned to **CSKA Moscow** (KHL) by **Columbus** for remainder of 2009-10 season, November 17, 2009. Traded to **Ottawa** by **Columbus** for Ottawa's 3rd round choice (Thomas Tynan) in 2011 Entry Draft, June 25, 2011. • Loaned to **CSKA Moscow** (KHL) by **Ottawa** for remainder of 2011-12 season, December 12, 2011. Signed as a free agent by **Ufa** (KHL), May 14, 2012. Signed as a free agent by **Khanty-Mansiisk** (KHL), May 14, 2014. Signed as a free agent by **Nizhny-Novgorod** (KHL), October 20, 2014.

FILPPULA, Valtteri

(FIHL-poo-luh, VAL-tuhr-ee) **T.B.**

Center. Shoots left. 6', 195 lbs. Born, Vantaa, Finland, March 20, 1984. Detroit's 3rd choice, 95th overall, in 2002 Entry Draft.

Season	Club	League	GP	G	A	Pts	PIM	PP	SH	GW	S	S%	+/-	TF	F%	Min	GP	G	A	Pts	PIM	PP	SH	GW	Min
2000-01	Jokerit U18	Fin-U18	31	18	29	47	4	....	....	....	....	....	....	....	....	....	6	4	4	8	0	....	....	....	....
	Jokerit Helsinki Jr.	Fin-Jr.	1	0	1	1	0	....	....	....	....	....	....	....	....	....	....	....	....	....	....	....	....	....	....
2001-02	Jokerit U18	Fin-U18	1	0	1	1	0	....	....	....	....	....	....	....	....	....	8	4	9	13	2	....	....	....	....
	Jokerit Helsinki Jr.	Fin-Jr.	40	8	15	23	14	....	....	....	....	....	....	....	....	....	1	0	0	0	0	....	....	....	....
2002-03	Jokerit Helsinki Jr.	Fin-Jr.	35	16	37	53	14	....	....	....	....	....	....	....	....	....	11	4	10	14	4	....	....	....	....
2003-04	Suomi U20	Finland-2	1	0	0	0	2	....	....	....	....	....	....	....	....	....	....	....	....	....	....	....	....	....	....
	Jokerit Helsinki	Finland	49	5	13	18	6	....	....	....	....	....	....	....	....	....	....	....	....	....	....	....	....	....	....
2004-05	Jokerit Helsinki	Finland	55	10	20	30	20	....	....	....	....	....	....	....	....	....	12	5	6	11	2	....	....	....	....
2005-06	**Detroit**	**NHL**	**4**	**0**	**1**	**1**	**2**	**0**	**0**	**0**	**1**	**0.0**	**1**	**21**	**47.6**	**7:19**	....	....	....	....	....	....	....	....	....
	Grand Rapids	AHL	74	20	51	71	30	....	....	....	....	....	....	....	....	....	16	7	9	16	4	....	....	....	....
2006-07	**Detroit**	**NHL**	**73**	**10**	**7**	**17**	**20**	**0**	**0**	**1**	**76**	**13.2**	**8**	**267**	**55.8**	**11:16**	**18**	**3**	**2**	**5**	**2**	**0**	**0**	**0**	**12:12**
	Grand Rapids	AHL	3	2	2	4	2	....	....	....	....	....	....	....	....	....	....	....	....	....	....	....	....	....	....
2007-08 ♦	**Detroit**	**NHL**	**78**	**19**	**17**	**36**	**28**	**3**	**0**	**3**	**122**	**15.6**	**16**	**621**	**50.6**	**16:58**	**22**	**5**	**6**	**11**	**2**	**0**	**0**	**0**	**16:40**
2008-09	**Detroit**	**NHL**	**80**	**12**	**28**	**40**	**42**	**1**	**0**	**1**	**129**	**9.3**	**9**	**785**	**52.1**	**16:06**	**23**	**3**	**13**	**16**	**8**	**1**	**0**	**1**	**17:38**
2009-10	**Detroit**	**NHL**	**55**	**11**	**24**	**35**	**24**	**1**	**1**	**1**	**114**	**9.6**	**-4**	**573**	**51.7**	**18:14**	**12**	**4**	**5**	**9**	**6**	**2**	**0**	**0**	**18:34**
	Finland	Olympics	6	3	0	3	0	....	....	....	....	....	....	....	....	....	....	....	....	....	....	....	....	....	....
2010-11	**Detroit**	**NHL**	**71**	**16**	**23**	**39**	**22**	**4**	**0**	**5**	**115**	**13.9**	**-1**	**928**	**51.5**	**16:43**	**11**	**2**	**6**	**8**	**6**	**0**	**0**	**2**	**17:47**
2011-12	**Detroit**	**NHL**	**81**	**23**	**43**	**66**	**14**	**3**	**1**	**1**	**144**	**16.0**	**18**	**373**	**51.7**	**18:16**	**5**	**0**	**2**	**2**	**2**	**0**	**0**	**0**	**19:20**
2012-13	Jokerit Helsinki	Finland	16	6	9	15	6	....	....	....	....	....	....	....	....	....	....	....	....	....	....	....	....	....	....
	Detroit	**NHL**	**41**	**9**	**8**	**17**	**6**	**3**	**0**	**0**	**78**	**11.5**	**-4**	**323**	**55.4**	**17:47**	**14**	**2**	**4**	**6**	**4**	**0**	**0**	**1**	**16:36**
2013-14	**Tampa Bay**	**NHL**	**75**	**25**	**33**	**58**	**20**	**6**	**0**	**2**	**131**	**19.1**	**5**	**1326**	**52.3**	**19:59**	**4**	**0**	**1**	**1**	**0**	**0**	**0**	**0**	**21:15**
2014-15	**Tampa Bay**	**NHL**	**82**	**12**	**36**	**48**	**24**	**2**	**0**	**0**	**91**	**13.2**	**-14**	**1185**	**52.4**	**19:01**	**26**	**4**	**10**	**14**	**4**	**2**	**0**	**1**	**19:13**
	NHL Totals		**640**	**137**	**220**	**357**	**202**	**23**	**2**	**14**	**1001**	**13.7**		**6402**	**52.2**	**17:04**	**135**	**23**	**49**	**72**	**34**	**5**	**0**	**5**	**17:13**

Signed as a free agent by **Jokerit Helsinki** (Finland), September 21, 2012. Signed as a free agent by **Tampa Bay**, July 5, 2013.

FINLEY, Joe

(FIHN-lee, JOH)

Defense. Shoots left. 6'8", 249 lbs. Born, Edina, MN, June 29, 1987. Washington's 2nd choice, 27th overall, in 2005 Entry Draft.

			Regular Season														Playoffs								
Season	Club	League	GP	G	A	Pts	PIM	PP	SH	GW	S	S%	+/-	TF	F%	Min	GP	G	A	Pts	PIM	PP	SH	GW	Min
2004-05	Sioux Falls	USHL	55	3	10	13	181	....	....	....	....	....	....	....	....	....	....	....	....	....	....	....	....	....	....
2005-06	North Dakota	WCHA	43	0	3	3	96	....	....	....	....	....	....	....	....	....	....	....	....	....	....	....	....	....	....
2006-07	North Dakota	WCHA	41	1	6	7	72	....	....	....	....	....	....	....	....	....	....	....	....	....	....	....	....	....	....
2007-08	North Dakota	WCHA	43	4	11	15	79	....	....	....	....	....	....	....	....	....	....	....	....	....	....	....	....	....	....
2008-09	North Dakota	WCHA	27	2	8	10	56	....	....	....	....	....	....	....	....	....	....	....	....	....	....	....	....	....	....
	Hershey Bears	AHL	1	0	0	0	7	....	....	....	....	....	....	....	....	....	....	....	....	....	....	....	....	....	....
2009-10	South Carolina	ECHL	17	1	3	4	43	....	....	....	....	....	....	....	....	....	....	....	....	....	....	....	....	....	....
2010-11	Hershey Bears	AHL	7	0	1	1	15	....	....	....	....	....	....	....	....	....	....	....	....	....	....	....	....	....	....
	South Carolina	ECHL	26	1	7	8	73	....	....	....	....	....	....	....	....	....	4	0	0	0	10	....	....	....	....
2011-12	Rochester	AHL	57	1	5	6	143	....	....	....	....	....	....	....	....	....	3	0	0	0	0	....	....	....	....
	Buffalo	**NHL**	**5**	**0**	**0**	**0**	**12**	**0**	**0**	**0**	**1**	**0.0**	**–3**	**0**	**0.0**	**7:48**	....	....	....	....	....	....	....	....	....
2012-13	Rochester	AHL	36	1	4	5	81	....	....	....	....	....	....	....	....	....	....	....	....	....	....	....	....	....	....
	NY Islanders	**NHL**	**16**	**0**	**1**	**1**	**20**	**0**	**0**	**0**	**2**	**0.0**	**–5**	**1**	**0.0**	**11:57**	....	....	....	....	....	....	....	....	....
2013-14	Bridgeport	AHL	29	0	2	2	50	....	....	....	....	....	....	....	....	....	....	....	....	....	....	....	....	....	....
2014-15	Hamilton	AHL	54	0	3	3	132	....	....	....	....	....	....	....	....	....	....	....	....	....	....	....	....	....	....
	NHL Totals		**21**	**0**	**1**	**1**	**32**	**0**	**0**	**0**	**3**	**0.0**		**1**	**0.0**	**10:58**	....	....	....	....	....	....	....	....	....

• Missed majority of 2009-10 due to recurring hand injury. Signed as a free agent by **Rochester**, September 18, 2011. Signed as a free agent by **Buffalo**, November 28, 2011. Claimed on waivers by **NY Islanders** from **Buffalo**, January 14, 2013. • Missed majority of 2013-14 due to recurring hand injury.

FISHER, Mike

(FIH-shuhr, MIGHK) **NSH**

Center. Shoots right. 6'1", 215 lbs. Born, Peterborough, ON, June 5, 1980. Ottawa's 2nd choice, 44th overall, in 1998 Entry Draft.

1996-97	Peterborough	ON-Jr.A	51	26	30	56	35	....	....	....	....	....	....	....	....	....	....	....	....	....	....	....	....	....	....
1997-98	Sudbury Wolves	OHL	66	24	25	49	65	....	....	....	....	....	....	....	....	....	9	2	2	4	13	....	....	....	....
1998-99	Sudbury Wolves	OHL	68	41	65	106	55	....	....	....	....	....	....	....	....	....	4	2	1	3	4	....	....	....	....
99-2000	**Ottawa**	**NHL**	**32**	**4**	**5**	**9**	**15**	**0**	**0**	**1**	**49**	**8.2**	**–6**	**356**	**47.8**	**12:57**	....	....	....	....	....	....	....	....	....
2000-01	**Ottawa**	**NHL**	**60**	**7**	**12**	**19**	**46**	**0**	**0**	**3**	**83**	**8.4**	**–1**	**709**	**50.2**	**11:38**	**4**	**0**	**1**	**1**	**4**	**0**	**0**	**0**	**13:41**
2001-02	**Ottawa**	**NHL**	**58**	**15**	**9**	**24**	**55**	**0**	**3**	**4**	**123**	**12.2**	**8**	**848**	**48.7**	**14:05**	**10**	**2**	**1**	**3**	**0**	**0**	**0**	**0**	**16:17**
2002-03	**Ottawa**	**NHL**	**74**	**18**	**20**	**38**	**54**	**5**	**1**	**3**	**142**	**12.7**	**13**	**1077**	**48.1**	**15:59**	**18**	**2**	**2**	**4**	**16**	**0**	**1**	**1**	**16:58**
2003-04	**Ottawa**	**NHL**	**24**	**4**	**6**	**10**	**39**	**1**	**0**	**0**	**47**	**8.5**	**–3**	**357**	**42.0**	**17:26**	**7**	**1**	**0**	**1**	**4**	**0**	**0**	**1**	**16:11**
2004-05	EV Zug	Swiss	21	9	18	27	34	....	....	....	....	....	....	....	....	....	9	2	3	5	10	....	....	....	....
2005-06	**Ottawa**	**NHL**	**68**	**22**	**22**	**44**	**64**	**2**	**4**	**3**	**150**	**14.7**	**23**	**883**	**50.3**	**17:09**	**10**	**2**	**2**	**4**	**12**	**0**	**1**	**0**	**18:50**
2006-07	**Ottawa**	**NHL**	**68**	**22**	**26**	**48**	**41**	**7**	**2**	**3**	**193**	**11.4**	**15**	**1191**	**52.1**	**18:25**	**20**	**5**	**5**	**10**	**24**	**2**	**1**	**1**	**17:43**
2007-08	**Ottawa**	**NHL**	**79**	**23**	**24**	**47**	**82**	**6**	**2**	**4**	**215**	**10.7**	**–10**	**1230**	**50.2**	**19:46**	....	....	....	....	....	....	....	....	....
2008-09	**Ottawa**	**NHL**	**78**	**13**	**19**	**32**	**66**	**1**	**2**	**3**	**182**	**7.1**	**0**	**1044**	**51.3**	**18:30**	....	....	....	....	....	....	....	....	....
2009-10	**Ottawa**	**NHL**	**79**	**25**	**28**	**53**	**59**	**10**	**0**	**6**	**212**	**11.8**	**1**	**1307**	**52.0**	**18:58**	**6**	**2**	**3**	**5**	**6**	**2**	**0**	**0**	**23:04**
2010-11	**Ottawa**	**NHL**	**55**	**14**	**10**	**24**	**33**	**3**	**0**	**1**	**132**	**10.6**	**–19**	**825**	**48.4**	**18:25**	....	....	....	....	....	....	....	....	....
	Nashville	**NHL**	**27**	**5**	**7**	**12**	**10**	**1**	**0**	**1**	**60**	**8.3**	**2**	**421**	**48.2**	**18:15**	**12**	**3**	**4**	**7**	**11**	**0**	**0**	**1**	**20:43**
2011-12	**Nashville**	**NHL**	**72**	**24**	**27**	**51**	**33**	**5**	**0**	**7**	**157**	**15.3**	**11**	**1217**	**48.3**	**19:18**	**10**	**1**	**3**	**4**	**8**	**0**	**0**	**0**	**20:44**
2012-13	**Nashville**	**NHL**	**38**	**10**	**11**	**21**	**27**	**1**	**0**	**0**	**68**	**14.7**	**6**	**563**	**48.9**	**19:28**	....	....	....	....	....	....	....	....	....
2013-14	**Nashville**	**NHL**	**75**	**20**	**29**	**49**	**60**	**4**	**0**	**4**	**177**	**11.3**	**–4**	**1146**	**52.0**	**19:45**	....	....	....	....	....	....	....	....	....
2014-15	**Nashville**	**NHL**	**59**	**19**	**20**	**39**	**39**	**7**	**1**	**1**	**111**	**17.1**	**4**	**1149**	**52.3**	**18:26**	**3**	**0**	**1**	**1**	**0**	**0**	**0**	**0**	**11:32**
	NHL Totals		**946**	**245**	**275**	**520**	**723**	**53**	**15**	**44**	**2101**	**11.7**		**14323**	**50.0**	**17:36**	**100**	**18**	**22**	**40**	**85**	**4**	**3**	**4**	**18:05**

NHL Foundation Player Award (2012)

• Missed majority of 1999-2000 due to knee injury vs. Boston, December 30, 1999. • Missed majority of 2003-04 due to elbow injury in practice, October 4, 2003. Signed as a free agent by **Zug** (Swiss), November 1, 2004. Traded to **Nashville** by **Ottawa** for Nashville's 1st round choice (Stefan Noesen) in 2011 Entry Draft and Nashville's 3rd round choice (Jarrod Maidens) in 2012 Entry Draft , February 10, 2011.

FISTRIC, Mark

(FIHST-rihc, MAHRK)

Defense. Shoots left. 6'2", 225 lbs. Born, Edmonton, AB, June 1, 1986. Dallas' 1st choice, 28th overall, in 2004 Entry Draft.

2000-01	Edmonton MLAC	AMBHL	34	13	13	26	144	....	....	....	....	....	....	....	....	....	....	....	....	....	....	....	....	....	....
2001-02	Edmonton MLAC	AMHL	30	8	10	18	85	....	....	....	....	....	....	....	....	....	....	....	....	....	....	....	....	....	....
	Vancouver Giants	WHL	4	0	2	2	0	....	....	....	....	....	....	....	....	....	....	....	....	....	....	....	....	....	....
2002-03	Vancouver Giants	WHL	63	2	7	9	81	....	....	....	....	....	....	....	....	....	4	0	0	0	8	....	....	....	....
2003-04	Vancouver Giants	WHL	72	1	11	12	192	....	....	....	....	....	....	....	....	....	11	0	2	2	10	....	....	....	....
2004-05	Vancouver Giants	WHL	15	1	5	6	32	....	....	....	....	....	....	....	....	....	6	1	1	2	16	....	....	....	....
2005-06	Vancouver Giants	WHL	60	7	22	29	148	....	....	....	....	....	....	....	....	....	18	1	9	10	30	....	....	....	....
2006-07	Iowa Stars	AHL	80	2	22	24	83	....	....	....	....	....	....	....	....	....	12	0	0	0	16	....	....	....	....
2007-08	**Dallas**	**NHL**	**37**	**0**	**2**	**2**	**24**	**0**	**0**	**0**	**17**	**0.0**	**3**	**0**	**0.0**	**12:44**	**9**	**0**	**0**	**0**	**6**	**0**	**0**	**0**	**14:51**
	Iowa Stars	AHL	30	1	4	5	48	....	....	....	....	....	....	....	....	....	....	....	....	....	....	....	....	....	....
2008-09	**Dallas**	**NHL**	**36**	**0**	**4**	**4**	**42**	**0**	**0**	**0**	**35**	**0.0**	**–1**	**0**	**0.0**	**15:57**	....	....	....	....	....	....	....	....	....
	Manitoba Moose	AHL	35	0	8	8	26	....	....	....	....	....	....	....	....	....	22	2	5	7	26	....	....	....	....
2009-10	**Dallas**	**NHL**	**67**	**1**	**9**	**10**	**69**	**0**	**0**	**0**	**46**	**2.2**	**27**	**0**	**0.0**	**14:56**	....	....	....	....	....	....	....	....	....
2010-11	**Dallas**	**NHL**	**57**	**2**	**3**	**5**	**44**	**0**	**0**	**1**	**26**	**7.7**	**–10**	**0**	**0.0**	**14:23**	....	....	....	....	....	....	....	....	....
	Texas Stars	AHL	3	0	0	0	2	....	....	....	....	....	....	....	....	....	....	....	....	....	....	....	....	....	....
2011-12	**Dallas**	**NHL**	**60**	**0**	**2**	**2**	**41**	**0**	**0**	**0**	**30**	**0.0**	**–3**	**1**	**100.0**	**16:31**	....	....	....	....	....	....	....	....	....
2012-13	**Edmonton**	**NHL**	**25**	**0**	**6**	**6**	**32**	**0**	**0**	**0**	**9**	**0.0**	**6**	**0**	**0.0**	**15:20**	....	....	....	....	....	....	....	....	....
2013-14	**Anaheim**	**NHL**	**34**	**1**	**4**	**5**	**28**	**0**	**0**	**0**	**22**	**4.5**	**9**	**0**	**0.0**	**15:24**	**5**	**0**	**0**	**0**	**6**	**0**	**0**	**0**	**13:25**
	Norfolk Admirals	AHL	2	0	0	0	4	....	....	....	....	....	....	....	....	....	....	....	....	....	....	....	....	....	....
2014-15	**Anaheim**	**NHL**	**9**	**0**	**0**	**0**	**4**	**0**	**0**	**0**	**1**	**0.0**	**–3**	**0**	**0.0**	**14:47**	....	....	....	....	....	....	....	....	....
	Norfolk Admirals	AHL	34	1	6	7	84	....	....	....	....	....	....	....	....	....	....	....	....	....	....	....	....	....	....
	NHL Totals		**325**	**4**	**30**	**34**	**284**	**0**	**0**	**1**	**186**	**2.2**		**1**	**100.0**	**15:04**	**14**	**0**	**0**	**0**	**12**	**0**	**0**	**0**	**14:20**

Traded to **Edmonton** by **Dallas** for Edmonton's 3rd round choice (Niklas Hansson) in 2013 Entry Draft, January 14, 2013. Signed as a free agent by **Anaheim**, August 20, 2013. • Missed majority of 2013-14 as a healthy reserve and due to lower-body injury vs. Los Angeles, March 15, 2014.

FLEISCHMANN, Tomas

(FLIGHSH-muhn, TAW-mahsh)

Left wing. Shoots left. 6'1", 192 lbs. Born, Koprivnice, Czech., May 16, 1984. Detroit's 2nd choice, 63rd overall, in 2002 Entry Draft.

99-2000	HC Vitkovice Jr.	CzRep-Jr.	46	9	13	22	6	....	....	....	....	....	....	....	....	....	....	....	....	....	....	....	....	....	....
2000-01	HC Vitkovice U17	CzR-U17	30	28	34	62	8	....	....	....	....	....	....	....	....	....	....	....	....	....	....	....	....	....	....
	HC Vitkovice Jr.	CzRep-Jr.	21	4	9	13	8	....	....	....	....	....	....	....	....	....	....	....	....	....	....	....	....	....	....
2001-02	HC Vitkovice Jr.	CzRep-Jr.	46	26	35	51	16	....	....	....	....	....	....	....	....	....	....	....	....	....	....	....	....	....	....
	TJ Novy Jicin	CzRep-3	8	3	2	5	8	....	....	....	....	....	....	....	....	....	7	3	4	7	35	....	....	....	....
2002-03	Moose Jaw	WHL	65	21	50	71	36	....	....	....	....	....	....	....	....	....	12	4	11	15	6	....	....	....	....
2003-04	Moose Jaw	WHL	60	33	42	75	32	....	....	....	....	....	....	....	....	....	10	3	4	7	10	....	....	....	....
2004-05	Portland Pirates	AHL	53	7	12	19	14	....	....	....	....	....	....	....	....	....	....	....	....	....	....	....	....	....	....
2005-06	**Washington**	**NHL**	**14**	**0**	**2**	**2**	**0**	**0**	**0**	**0**	**11**	**0.0**	**–7**	**5**	**40.0**	**6:45**	....	....	....	....	....	....	....	....	....
	Hershey Bears	AHL	57	30	33	63	32	....	....	....	....	....	....	....	....	....	20	11	*21	32	15	....	....	....	....
2006-07	**Washington**	**NHL**	**29**	**4**	**4**	**8**	**8**	**1**	**0**	**1**	**52**	**7.7**	**–6**	**14**	**35.7**	**11:38**	....	....	....	....	....	....	....	....	....
	Hershey Bears	AHL	45	22	29	51	22	....	....	....	....	....	....	....	....	....	19	5	16	21	10	....	....	....	....
2007-08	**Washington**	**NHL**	**75**	**10**	**20**	**30**	**18**	**1**	**0**	**1**	**107**	**9.3**	**–7**	**30**	**50.0**	**12:37**	**2**	**0**	**0**	**0**	**0**	**0**	**0**	**0**	**9:49**
2008-09	**Washington**	**NHL**	**73**	**19**	**18**	**37**	**20**	**7**	**0**	**4**	**131**	**14.5**	**–3**	**34**	**26.5**	**15:05**	**14**	**3**	**1**	**4**	**4**	**1**	**0**	**1**	**14:19**
2009-10	**Washington**	**NHL**	**69**	**23**	**28**	**51**	**28**	**7**	**0**	**4**	**121**	**19.0**	**9**	**371**	**43.1**	**16:02**	**6**	**0**	**1**	**1**	**6**	**0**	**0**	**0**	**13:21**
	Hershey Bears	AHL	2	0	1	1	0	....	....	....	....	....	....	....	....	....	....	....	....	....	....	....	....	....	....
	Czech Republic	Olympics	5	1	2	3	2	....	....	....	....	....	....	....	....	....	....	....	....	....	....	....	....	....	....
2010-11	**Washington**	**NHL**	**23**	**4**	**6**	**10**	**10**	**0**	**0**	**1**	**44**	**9.1**	**3**	**225**	**43.1**	**14:20**	....	....	....	....	....	....	....	....	....
	Colorado	**NHL**	**22**	**8**	**13**	**21**	**8**	**3**	**0**	**1**	**54**	**14.8**	**–1**	**11**	**18.2**	**18:28**	....	....	....	....	....	....	....	....	....
2011-12	**Florida**	**NHL**	**82**	**27**	**34**	**61**	**26**	**6**	**0**	**4**	**217**	**12.4**	**–7**	**27**	**51.9**	**19:06**	**7**	**1**	**2**	**3**	**2**	**0**	**0**	**0**	**18:44**
2012-13	**Florida**	**NHL**	**48**	**12**	**23**	**35**	**16**	**2**	**1**	**2**	**121**	**9.9**	**–10**	**20**	**50.0**	**18:44**	....	....	....	....	....	....	....	....	....
2013-14	**Florida**	**NHL**	**80**	**8**	**20**	**28**	**22**	**2**	**0**	**1**	**188**	**4.3**	**–18**	**18**	**27.8**	**17:07**	....	....	....	....	....	....	....	....	....

Season	Club	League	GP	G	A	Pts	PIM	PP	SH	GW	S	S%	+/-	TF	F%	Min	GP	G	A	Pts	PIM	PP	SH	GW	Min
			Regular Season														Playoffs								
2014-15	Florida	NHL	52	7	14	21	8	0	0	1	107	6.5	12	9	22.2	14:51	....	....	....	....	....	....	....	....	....
	Anaheim	NHL	14	1	5	6	4	0	0	0	24	4.2	0	5	40.0	14:10	6	0	1	1	0	0	0	0	10:39
	NHL Totals		581	123	187	310	168	29	1	20	1177	10.5		769	42.0	15:43	35	4	5	9	12	1	0	1	14:09

WHL East Second All-Star Team (2004)

Traded to **Washington** by **Detroit** with Detroit's 1st round choice (Mike Green) in 2004 Entry Draft and Detroit's 4th round choice (Luke Lynes) in 2006 Entry Draft for Robert Lang, February 27, 2004. Traded to **Colorado** by **Washington** for Scott Hannan, November 30, 2010. Signed as a free agent by **Florida**, July 1, 2011. Traded to **Anaheim** by **Florida** for Dany Heatley and Anaheim's 3rd round choice (Thomas Schemitsch) in 2015 Entry Draft, February 28, 2015.

FLOREK, Justin

(FLOHR-ehk, JUHS-tihn) **NYI**

Left wing. Shoots left. 6'4", 199 lbs. Born, Marquette, MI, May 18, 1990. Boston's 5th choice, 135th overall, in 2010 Entry Draft.

Season	Club	League	GP	G	A	Pts	PIM	PP	SH	GW	S	S%	+/-	TF	F%	Min	GP	G	A	Pts	PIM	PP	SH	GW	Min
2006-07	USNTDP	NAHL	47	11	10	21	40	....	....	....	....	....	....	....	....	....	6	3	0	3	4	....	....	....	....
	USNTDP	U-17	13	6	1	7	8	....	....	....	....	....	....	....	....	....	....	....	....	....	....	....	....	....	....
2007-08	USNTDP	NAHL	13	3	3	6	8	....	....	....	....	....	....	....	....	....	....	....	....	....	....	....	....	....	....
	USNTDP	U-17	1	0	0	0	2	....	....	....	....	....	....	....	....	....	....	....	....	....	....	....	....	....	....
	USNTDP	U-18	41	5	5	10	20	....	....	....	....	....	....	....	....	....	....	....	....	....	....	....	....	....	....
2008-09	Northern Mich.	CCHA	40	9	8	17	6	....	....	....	....	....	....	....	....	....	....	....	....	....	....	....	....	....	....
2009-10	Northern Mich.	CCHA	41	12	23	35	22	....	....	....	....	....	....	....	....	....	....	....	....	....	....	....	....	....	....
2010-11	Northern Mich.	CCHA	39	13	15	28	14	....	....	....	....	....	....	....	....	....	....	....	....	....	....	....	....	....	....
2011-12	Northern Mich.	CCHA	37	19	17	36	18	....	....	....	....	....	....	....	....	....	....	....	....	....	....	....	....	....	....
	Providence Bruins	AHL	8	2	2	4	2	....	....	....	....	....	....	....	....	....	....	....	....	....	....	....	....	....	....
2012-13	Providence Bruins	AHL	71	11	16	27	37	....	....	....	....	....	....	....	....	....	12	1	2	3	4	....	....	....	....
2013-14	Boston	NHL	4	1	1	2	0	0	0	0	5	20.0	1	1	0.0	11:51	6	1	0	1	4	0	0	0	11:50
	Providence Bruins	AHL	69	19	19	38	27	....	....	....	....	....	....	....	....	....	4	1	0	1	0	....	....	....	....
2014-15	Providence Bruins	AHL	73	11	24	35	33	....	....	....	....	....	....	....	....	....	5	0	0	0	2	....	....	....	....
	NHL Totals		4	1	1	2	0	0	0	0	5	20.0		1	0.0	11:51	6	1	0	1	4	0	0	0	11:50

CCHA Second All-Star Team (2012)

Signed as a free agent by **NY Islanders**, July 2, 2015.

FLYNN, Brian

(FLIHN, BRIGH-uhn) **MTL**

Right wing. Shoots right. 6'1", 180 lbs. Born, Lynnfield, MA, July 26, 1988.

Season	Club	League	GP	G	A	Pts	PIM	PP	SH	GW	S	S%	+/-	TF	F%	Min	GP	G	A	Pts	PIM	PP	SH	GW	Min
2008-09	U. of Maine	H-East	38	12	13	25	10	....	....	....	....	....	....	....	....	....	....	....	....	....	....	....	....	....	....
2009-10	U. of Maine	H-East	39	19	28	47	12	....	....	....	....	....	....	....	....	....	....	....	....	....	....	....	....	....	....
2010-11	U. of Maine	H-East	36	20	16	36	8	....	....	....	....	....	....	....	....	....	....	....	....	....	....	....	....	....	....
2011-12	U. of Maine	H-East	40	18	30	48	37	....	....	....	....	....	....	....	....	....	....	....	....	....	....	....	....	....	....
	Rochester	AHL	5	0	1	1	2	....	....	....	....	....	....	....	....	....	....	....	....	....	....	....	....	....	....
2012-13	Rochester	AHL	45	16	16	32	18	....	....	....	....	....	....	....	....	....	3	0	0	0	4	....	....	....	....
	Buffalo	NHL	26	6	5	11	0	0	1	1	49	12.2	6	60	40.0	14:41	....	....	....	....	....	....	....	....	....
2013-14	Buffalo	NHL	79	6	7	13	14	0	1	0	102	5.9	-10	389	47.3	14:25	....	....	....	....	....	....	....	....	....
2014-15	Buffalo	NHL	54	5	12	17	8	0	0	0	73	6.8	-3	330	47.6	15:53	....	....	....	....	....	....	....	....	....
	Montreal	NHL	9	0	0	0	0	0	0	0	9	0.0	-2	29	51.7	9:04	6	1	2	3	0	0	0	1	11:00
	NHL Totals		168	17	24	41	22	0	2	1	233	7.3		808	47.0	14:39	6	1	2	3	0	0	0	1	11:00

Hockey East First All-Star Team (2012)

Signed as a free agent by **Buffalo**, March 29, 2012. Traded to **Montreal** by **Buffalo** for Montreal's 5th round choice in 2016 Entry Draft, March 2, 2015.

FOLIGNO, Marcus

(foh-LEE-noh, MAHR-kuhs) **BUF**

Left wing. Shoots left. 6'3", 223 lbs. Born, Buffalo, NY, August 10, 1991. Buffalo's 3rd choice, 104th overall, in 2009 Entry Draft.

Season	Club	League	GP	G	A	Pts	PIM	PP	SH	GW	S	S%	+/-	TF	F%	Min	GP	G	A	Pts	PIM	PP	SH	GW	Min
2006-07	Sud. Nickel Cap's	Minor-ON	30	21	15	36	70	....	....	....	....	....	....	....	....	....	....	....	....	....	....	....	....	....	....
2007-08	Sudbury Wolves	OHL	66	5	6	11	38	....	....	....	....	....	....	....	....	....	....	....	....	....	....	....	....	....	....
2008-09	Sudbury Wolves	OHL	65	12	18	30	96	....	....	....	....	....	....	....	....	....	6	1	2	3	9	....	....	....	....
2009-10	Sudbury Wolves	OHL	67	14	25	39	156	....	....	....	....	....	....	....	....	....	4	1	1	2	6	....	....	....	....
2010-11	Sudbury Wolves	OHL	47	23	36	59	92	....	....	....	....	....	....	....	....	....	8	2	1	3	24	....	....	....	....
2011-12	Buffalo	NHL	14	6	7	13	9	2	0	1	23	26.1	6	3	0.0	15:49	....	....	....	....	....	....	....	....	....
	Rochester	AHL	60	16	23	39	78	....	....	....	....	....	....	....	....	....	3	2	1	3	4	....	....	....	....
2012-13	Rochester	AHL	33	10	17	27	38	....	....	....	....	....	....	....	....	....	....	....	....	....	....	....	....	....	....
	Buffalo	NHL	47	5	13	18	41	1	0	0	55	9.1	-4	75	60.0	13:38	....	....	....	....	....	....	....	....	....
2013-14	Buffalo	NHL	74	7	12	19	82	0	1	3	79	8.9	-17	301	48.5	15:04	....	....	....	....	....	....	....	....	....
2014-15	Buffalo	NHL	57	8	12	20	50	0	0	0	66	12.1	-5	132	43.2	16:14	....	....	....	....	....	....	....	....	....
	NHL Totals		192	26	44	70	182	3	1	4	223	11.7		511	48.5	15:07	....	....	....	....	....	....	....	....	....

OHL Second All-Star Team (2011)

FOLIGNO, Nick

(foh-LEE-noh, NIHK) **CBJ**

Left wing. Shoots left. 6', 210 lbs. Born, Buffalo, NY, October 31, 1987. Ottawa's 1st choice, 28th overall, in 2006 Entry Draft.

Season	Club	League	GP	G	A	Pts	PIM	PP	SH	GW	S	S%	+/-	TF	F%	Min	GP	G	A	Pts	PIM	PP	SH	GW	Min
2003-04	USNTDP	U-17	18	7	9	16	28	....	....	....	....	....	....	....	....	....	....	....	....	....	....	....	....	....	....
	USNTDP	NAHL	43	8	12	20	44	....	....	....	....	....	....	....	....	....	7	2	1	3	8	....	....	....	....
2004-05	USNTDP	U-18	4	2	1	3	0	....	....	....	....	....	....	....	....	....	....	....	....	....	....	....	....	....	....
	Sudbury Wolves	OHL	65	10	28	38	111	....	....	....	....	....	....	....	....	....	12	5	5	10	16	....	....	....	....
2005-06	Sudbury Wolves	OHL	65	24	46	70	146	....	....	....	....	....	....	....	....	....	10	1	3	4	28	....	....	....	....
2006-07	Sudbury Wolves	OHL	66	31	57	88	135	....	....	....	....	....	....	....	....	....	21	12	17	29	36	....	....	....	....
2007-08	Ottawa	NHL	45	6	3	9	20	0	0	0	44	13.6	0	49	44.9	9:10	4	1	0	1	2	0	0	0	12:50
	Binghamton	AHL	28	6	13	19	16	....	....	....	....	....	....	....	....	....	....	....	....	....	....	....	....	....	....
2008-09	Ottawa	NHL	81	17	15	32	59	7	0	2	145	11.7	-10	47	44.7	13:41	....	....	....	....	....	....	....	....	....
2009-10	Ottawa	NHL	61	9	17	26	53	2	0	2	83	10.8	6	50	34.0	14:19	6	0	1	1	2	0	0	0	17:07
2010-11	Ottawa	NHL	82	14	20	34	43	5	0	3	149	9.4	-19	138	47.1	15:35	....	....	....	....	....	....	....	....	....
2011-12	Ottawa	NHL	82	15	32	47	124	1	0	3	153	9.8	2	149	41.6	14:39	7	1	3	4	8	0	0	0	15:10
2012-13	Columbus	NHL	45	6	13	19	28	1	0	2	69	8.7	6	9	33.3	16:31	....	....	....	....	....	....	....	....	....
2013-14	Columbus	NHL	70	18	21	39	96	3	0	5	111	16.2	5	13	46.2	16:04	4	2	0	2	4	0	0	1	14:56
2014-15	Columbus	NHL	79	31	42	73	50	11	0	3	182	17.0	16	263	47.5	18:50	....	....	....	....	....	....	....	....	....
	NHL Totals		545	116	163	279	473	30	0	20	936	12.4		718	44.7	15:06	21	4	4	8	16	0	0	1	15:14

Played in NHL All-Star Game (2015)

Traded to **Columbus** by **Ottawa** for Marc Methot, July 1, 2012.

FOLIN, Christian

(FOH-lihn, KRIHS-t'yehn) **MIN**

Defense. Shoots right. 6'3", 215 lbs. Born, Molndal, Sweden, February 9, 1991.

Season	Club	League	GP	G	A	Pts	PIM	PP	SH	GW	S	S%	+/-	TF	F%	Min	GP	G	A	Pts	PIM	PP	SH	GW	Min
2007-08	Frolunda U18	Swe-U18	28	3	10	13	10	....	....	....	....	....	....	....	....	....	5	0	0	0	2	....	....	....	....
2008-09	Frolunda U18	Swe-U18	27	6	17	23	55	....	....	....	....	....	....	....	....	....	7	1	3	4	6	....	....	....	....
	Frolunda Jr.	Swe-Jr.	13	2	1	3	4	....	....	....	....	....	....	....	....	....	4	0	0	0	2	....	....	....	....
2009-10	Frolunda Jr.	Swe-Jr.	38	3	16	19	22	....	....	....	....	....	....	....	....	....	5	0	3	3	20	....	....	....	....
	Hanhals HF	Sweden-4	1	1	1	2	0	....	....	....	....	....	....	....	....	....	....	....	....	....	....	....	....	....	....
2010-11	Fargo Force	USHL	12	2	2	4	6	....	....	....	....	....	....	....	....	....	....	....	....	....	....	....	....	....	....
	Austin Bruins	NAHL	33	2	9	11	27	....	....	....	....	....	....	....	....	....	....	....	....	....	....	....	....	....	....
2011-12	Austin Bruins	NAHL	54	11	20	31	50	....	....	....	....	....	....	....	....	....	2	0	1	1	2	....	....	....	....
2012-13	U. Mass Lowell	H-East	38	6	15	21	24	....	....	....	....	....	....	....	....	....	....	....	....	....	....	....	....	....	....
2013-14	U. Mass Lowell	H-East	41	6	14	20	31	....	....	....	....	....	....	....	....	....	....	....	....	....	....	....	....	....	....
	Minnesota	NHL	1	0	1	1	0	0	0	0	0	0.0	3	0	0.0	19:26	....	....	....	....	....	....	....	....	....
2014-15	Minnesota	NHL	40	2	8	10	13	0	0	0	39	5.1	3	0	0.0	15:12	....	....	....	....	....	....	....	....	....
	Iowa Wild	AHL	13	2	2	4	4	....	....	....	....	....	....	....	....	....	....	....	....	....	....	....	....	....	....
	NHL Totals		41	2	9	11	13	0	0	0	39	5.1		0	0.0	15:18	....	....	....	....	....	....	....	....	....

Signed as a free agent by **Minnesota**, April 2, 2014.

FONTAINE, Justin

(fawn-TAYN, JUHS-tihn) **MIN**

Right wing. Shoots right. 5'10", 177 lbs. Born, Bonnyville, AB, November 6, 1987.

			Regular Season														Playoffs								
Season	Club	League	GP	G	A	Pts	PIM	PP	SH	GW	S	S%	+/-	TF	F%	Min	GP	G	A	Pts	PIM	PP	SH	GW	Min
2004-05	N.E. Panthers	Minor-AB	STATISTICS NOT AVAILABLE																						
	Bonnyville	AJHL	12	1	4	5	12	....	....	....	....	....	....	....	....	....	....	....	....	....	....	....	....	....	....
2005-06	Bonnyville	AJHL	50	26	55	81	36	....	....	....	....	....	....	....	....	....	9	1	6	7	4	....	....	....	....
2006-07	Bonnyville	AJHL	52	30	41	71	60	....	....	....	....	....	....	....	....	....	5	3	5	8	10	....	....	....	....
2007-08	U. Minn-Duluth	WCHA	35	4	8	12	8	....	....	....	....	....	....	....	....	....	....	....	....	....	....	....	....	....	....
2008-09	U. Minn-Duluth	WCHA	43	15	33	48	18	....	....	....	....	....	....	....	....	....	....	....	....	....	....	....	....	....	....
2009-10	U. Minn-Duluth	WCHA	39	21	25	46	22	....	....	....	....	....	....	....	....	....	....	....	....	....	....	....	....	....	....
2010-11	U. Minn-Duluth	WCHA	42	22	36	58	42	....	....	....	....	....	....	....	....	....	....	....	....	....	....	....	....	....	....
2011-12	Houston Aeros	AHL	73	16	39	55	32	....	....	....	....	....	....	....	....	....	4	0	0	0	0	....	....	....	....
2012-13	Houston Aeros	AHL	64	23	33	56	18	....	....	....	....	....	....	....	....	....	5	3	5	8	4	....	....	....	....
2013-14	**Minnesota**	**NHL**	**66**	**13**	**8**	**21**	**26**	**1**	**0**	**1**	**79**	**16.5**	**6**	**2**	**100.0**	**12:15**	**9**	**1**	**1**	**2**	**2**	**0**	**0**	**0**	**11:06**
2014-15	**Minnesota**	**NHL**	**71**	**9**	**22**	**31**	**12**	**0**	**0**	**2**	**104**	**8.7**	**13**	**2**	**50.0**	**11:57**	**6**	**1**	**1**	**2**	**2**	**0**	**0**	**1**	**10:45**
	NHL Totals		**137**	**22**	**30**	**52**	**38**	**1**	**0**	**3**	**183**	**12.0**		**4**	**75.0**	**12:06**	**15**	**2**	**2**	**4**	**4**	**0**	**0**	**1**	**10:58**

WCHA Second All-Star Team (2009, 2010, 2011)
Signed as a free agent by **Minnesota**, April 19, 2011.

FORSBERG, Filip

(FOHRZ-buhrg, FIHL-ihp) **NSH**

Center. Shoots right. 6'1", 186 lbs. Born, Ostervala, Sweden, August 13, 1994. Washington's 1st choice, 11th overall, in 2012 Entry Draft.

Season	Club	League	GP	G	A	Pts	PIM	PP	SH	GW	S	S%	+/-	TF	F%	Min	GP	G	A	Pts	PIM	PP	SH	GW	Min
2008-09	Leksands IF U18 2	Swe-U18	15	12	9	21	14	....	....	....	....	....	....	....	....	....	....	....	....	....	....	....	....	....	....
2009-10	Leksands IF U18	Swe-U18	31	21	16	37	22	....	....	....	....	....	....	....	....	....	4	5	3	8	0	....	....	....	....
	Leksands IF Jr.	Swe-Jr.	....	....	....	....	....	....	....	....	....	....	....	....	....	....	5	0	0	0	0	....	....	....	....
2010-11	Leksands IF U18	Swe-U18	3	1	5	6	4	....	....	....	....	....	....	....	....	....	6	2	2	4	2	....	....	....	....
	Leksands IF Jr.	Swe-Jr.	36	21	19	40	22	....	....	....	....	....	....	....	....	....	....	....	....	....	....	....	....	....	....
	Leksands IF	Sweden-2	16	1	1	2	0	....	....	....	....	....	....	....	....	....	....	....	....	....	....	....	....	....	....
2011-12	Leksands IF U18	Swe-U18	1	0	2	2	0	....	....	....	....	....	....	....	....	....	....	....	....	....	....	....	....	....	....
	Leksands IF Jr.	Swe-Jr.	6	0	1	1	2	....	....	....	....	....	....	....	....	....	....	....	....	....	....	....	....	....	....
	Leksands IF	Sweden-2	53	10	10	20	33	....	....	....	....	....	....	....	....	....	....	....	....	....	....	....	....	....	....
2012-13	Leksands IF	Sweden-2	47	20	22	42	22	....	....	....	....	....	....	....	....	....	....	....	....	....	....	....	....	....	....
	Nashville	**NHL**	**5**	**0**	**1**	**1**	**0**	**0**	**0**	**0**	**14**	**0.0**	**-5**	**1**	**0.0**	**15:29**	....	....	....	....	....	....	....	....	....
2013-14	**Nashville**	**NHL**	**13**	**1**	**4**	**5**	**4**	**1**	**0**	**0**	**20**	**5.0**	**-8**	**0**	**0.0**	**11:24**	....	....	....	....	....	....	....	....	....
	Milwaukee	AHL	47	15	19	34	14	....	....	....	....	....	....	....	....	....	3	1	1	2	0	....	....	....	....
	Sweden	Olympics	7	4	8	12	2	....	....	....	....	....	....	....	....	....	....	....	....	....	....	....	....	....	....
2014-15	**Nashville**	**NHL**	**82**	**26**	**37**	**63**	**24**	**6**	**0**	**6**	**237**	**11.0**	**15**	**7**	**42.9**	**17:20**	**6**	**4**	**2**	**6**	**4**	**1**	**0**	**0**	**20:36**
	NHL Totals		**100**	**27**	**42**	**69**	**28**	**7**	**0**	**6**	**271**	**10.0**		**8**	**37.5**	**16:28**	**6**	**4**	**2**	**6**	**4**	**1**	**0**	**0**	**20:35**

NHL All-Rookie Team (2015)
Played in NHL All-Star Game (2015)
Traded to **Nashville** by **Washington** for Martin Erat and Michael Latta, April 3, 2013.

FORTUNUS, Maxime

(fohr-TOON-uhs, MAX-eem)

Defense. Shoots right. 6'1", 198 lbs. Born, Longueil, QC, July 28, 1983.

Season	Club	League	GP	G	A	Pts	PIM	PP	SH	GW	S	S%	+/-	TF	F%	Min	GP	G	A	Pts	PIM	PP	SH	GW	Min
1998-99	C.C. Lemoyne	QAAA	39	3	10	13	18	....	....	....	....	....	....	....	....	....	17	0	9	9	8	....	....	....	....
99-2000	Baie-Comeau	QMJHL	68	6	15	21	36	....	....	....	....	....	....	....	....	....	6	0	0	0	2	....	....	....	....
2000-01	Baie-Comeau	QMJHL	71	10	31	41	106	....	....	....	....	....	....	....	....	....	11	2	4	6	6	....	....	....	....
2001-02	Baie-Comeau	QMJHL	72	11	30	41	76	....	....	....	....	....	....	....	....	....	5	0	1	1	2	....	....	....	....
2002-03	Baie-Comeau	QMJHL	69	12	32	44	44	....	....	....	....	....	....	....	....	....	12	2	4	6	6	....	....	....	....
2003-04	Baie-Comeau	QMJHL	5	1	0	1	15	....	....	....	....	....	....	....	....	....	....	....	....	....	....	....	....	....	....
	Houston Aeros	AHL	12	0	2	2	2	....	....	....	....	....	....	....	....	....	1	0	0	0	0	....	....	....	....
	Louisiana	ECHL	64	3	15	18	27	....	....	....	....	....	....	....	....	....	4	1	1	2	0	....	....	....	....
2004-05	Houston Aeros	AHL	13	0	0	0	4	....	....	....	....	....	....	....	....	....	....	....	....	....	....	....	....	....	....
	Louisiana	ECHL	59	8	16	24	26	....	....	....	....	....	....	....	....	....	....	....	....	....	....	....	....	....	....
2005-06	Manitoba Moose	AHL	76	3	10	13	36	....	....	....	....	....	....	....	....	....	13	0	0	0	10	....	....	....	....
2006-07	Manitoba Moose	AHL	72	2	18	20	64	....	....	....	....	....	....	....	....	....	13	1	4	5	10	....	....	....	....
2007-08	Manitoba Moose	AHL	65	8	13	21	28	....	....	....	....	....	....	....	....	....	6	0	1	1	4	....	....	....	....
2008-09	Manitoba Moose	AHL	58	7	12	19	18	....	....	....	....	....	....	....	....	....	22	3	7	10	2	....	....	....	....
2009-10	**Dallas**	**NHL**	**8**	**0**	**0**	**0**	**4**	**0**	**0**	**0**	**5**	**0.0**	**-6**	**0**	**0.0**	**15:09**	....	....	....	....	....	....	....	....	....
	Texas Stars	AHL	72	11	12	23	28	....	....	....	....	....	....	....	....	....	24	2	7	9	14	....	....	....	....
2010-11	Texas Stars	AHL	73	5	29	34	20	....	....	....	....	....	....	....	....	....	6	0	1	1	2	....	....	....	....
2011-12	Texas Stars	AHL	60	6	14	20	18	....	....	....	....	....	....	....	....	....	....	....	....	....	....	....	....	....	....
2012-13	Texas Stars	AHL	67	7	21	28	16	....	....	....	....	....	....	....	....	....	9	0	1	1	2	....	....	....	....
2013-14	**Dallas**	**NHL**	**1**	**0**	**1**	**1**	**0**	**0**	**0**	**0**	**0**	**0.0**	**1**	**0**	**0.0**	**16:17**	....	....	....	....	....	....	....	....	....
	Texas Stars	AHL	65	6	22	28	18	....	....	....	....	....	....	....	....	....	21	0	4	4	8	....	....	....	....
2014-15	Texas Stars	AHL	65	9	25	34	31	....	....	....	....	....	....	....	....	....	3	0	0	0	2	....	....	....	....
	NHL Totals		**9**	**0**	**1**	**1**	**4**	**0**	**0**	**0**	**5**	**0.0**		**0**	**0.0**	**15:16**	....	....	....	....	....	....	....	....	....

Signed as a free agent by **Dallas**, July 3, 2008.

FOWLER, Cam

(FOW-luhr, KAM) **ANA**

Defense. Shoots left. 6'1", 207 lbs. Born, Windsor, ON, December 5, 1991. Anaheim's 1st choice, 12th overall, in 2010 Entry Draft.

Season	Club	League	GP	G	A	Pts	PIM	PP	SH	GW	S	S%	+/-	TF	F%	Min	GP	G	A	Pts	PIM	PP	SH	GW	Min
2006-07	Det. Honeybaked	MWEHL	21	5	13	18	18	....	....	....	....	....	....	....	....	....	....	....	....	....	....	....	....	....	....
	Det. Honeybaked	Minor-MI	31	3	7	10	....	....	....	....	....	....	....	....	....	....	....	....	....	....	....	....	....	....	....
2007-08	USNTDP	NAHL	38	3	10	13	2	....	....	....	....	....	....	....	....	....	3	0	0	0	2	....	....	....	....
	USNTDP	U-17	18	0	2	2	8	....	....	....	....	....	....	....	....	....	....	....	....	....	....	....	....	....	....
	USNTDP	U-18	1	0	0	0	0	....	....	....	....	....	....	....	....	....	....	....	....	....	....	....	....	....	....
2008-09	USNTDP	NAHL	14	2	7	9	12	....	....	....	....	....	....	....	....	....	....	....	....	....	....	....	....	....	....
	USNTDP	U-18	33	6	25	31	32	....	....	....	....	....	....	....	....	....	....	....	....	....	....	....	....	....	....
2009-10	Windsor Spitfires	OHL	55	8	47	55	14	....	....	....	....	....	....	....	....	....	19	3	11	14	10	....	....	....	....
2010-11	**Anaheim**	**NHL**	**76**	**10**	**30**	**40**	**20**	**6**	**0**	**3**	**123**	**8.1**	**-25**	**0**	**0.0**	**22:08**	**6**	**1**	**3**	**4**	**2**	**1**	**0**	**0**	**22:13**
2011-12	**Anaheim**	**NHL**	**82**	**5**	**24**	**29**	**18**	**2**	**0**	**0**	**123**	**4.1**	**-28**	**1**	**100.0**	**23:16**	....	....	....	....	....	....	....	....	....
2012-13	Sodertalje SK	Sweden-2	14	2	5	7	14	....	....	....	....	....	....	....	....	....	....	....	....	....	....	....	....	....	....
	Anaheim	**NHL**	**37**	**1**	**10**	**11**	**4**	**1**	**0**	**0**	**50**	**2.0**	**-4**	**0**	**0.0**	**20:26**	**7**	**0**	**3**	**3**	**0**	**0**	**0**	**0**	**22:45**
2013-14	**Anaheim**	**NHL**	**70**	**6**	**30**	**36**	**14**	**4**	**1**	**2**	**100**	**6.0**	**15**	**0**	**0.0**	**23:52**	**13**	**0**	**4**	**4**	**4**	**0**	**0**	**0**	**23:52**
	United States	Olympics	6	1	0	1	0	....	....	....	....	....	....	....	....	....	....	....	....	....	....	....	....	....	....
2014-15	**Anaheim**	**NHL**	**80**	**7**	**27**	**34**	**14**	**1**	**1**	**2**	**87**	**8.0**	**4**	**0**	**0.0**	**21:09**	**16**	**2**	**8**	**10**	**2**	**0**	**0**	**0**	**23:08**
	NHL Totals		**345**	**29**	**121**	**150**	**70**	**14**	**2**	**7**	**483**	**6.0**		**1**	**100.0**	**22:20**	**42**	**3**	**18**	**21**	**8**	**1**	**0**	**0**	**23:10**

Memorial Cup All-Star Team (2010)
Signed as a free agent by **Sodertalje** (Sweden-2), November 14, 2012.

FRANSON, Cody

(FRAN-suhn, KOH-dee)

Defense. Shoots right. 6'5", 213 lbs. Born, Sicamous, BC, August 8, 1987. Nashville's 3rd choice, 79th overall, in 2005 Entry Draft.

Season	Club	League	GP	G	A	Pts	PIM	PP	SH	GW	S	S%	+/-	TF	F%	Min	GP	G	A	Pts	PIM	PP	SH	GW	Min
2002-03	Sicamous	Minor-BC	65	44	82	126	42	....	....	....	....	....	....	....	....	....	....	....	....	....	....	....	....	....	....
	Vancouver Giants	WHL	3	0	0	0	2	....	....	....	....	....	....	....	....	....	....	....	....	....	....	....	....	....	....
2003-04	Beaver Valley	KIJHL	48	10	22	32	70	....	....	....	....	....	....	....	....	....	....	....	....	....	....	....	....	....	....
	Trail	BCHL	2	0	1	1	0	....	....	....	....	....	....	....	....	....	....	....	....	....	....	....	....	....	....
	Vancouver Giants	WHL	2	0	0	0	0	....	....	....	....	....	....	....	....	....	....	....	....	....	....	....	....	....	....
2004-05	Vancouver Giants	WHL	64	2	11	13	44	....	....	....	....	....	....	....	....	....	4	0	1	1	0	....	....	....	....
2005-06	Vancouver Giants	WHL	71	15	40	55	61	....	....	....	....	....	....	....	....	....	18	5	15	20	12	....	....	....	....
2006-07	Vancouver Giants	WHL	59	17	34	51	88	....	....	....	....	....	....	....	....	....	19	3	4	7	10	....	....	....	....
2007-08	Milwaukee	AHL	76	11	25	36	40	....	....	....	....	....	....	....	....	....	6	0	2	2	2	....	....	....	....
2008-09	Milwaukee	AHL	76	11	41	52	47	....	....	....	....	....	....	....	....	....	11	3	5	8	8	....	....	....	....
2009-10	**Nashville**	**NHL**	**61**	**6**	**15**	**21**	**16**	**1**	**0**	**3**	**90**	**6.7**	**15**	**0**	**0.0**	**14:12**	**4**	**0**	**1**	**1**	**2**	**0**	**0**	**0**	**9:02**
	Milwaukee	AHL	6	2	5	7	4	....	....	....	....	....	....	....	....	....	....	....	....	....	....	....	....	....	....
2010-11	**Nashville**	**NHL**	**80**	**8**	**21**	**29**	**30**	**2**	**0**	**2**	**156**	**5.1**	**10**	**0**	**0.0**	**15:10**	**12**	**1**	**5**	**6**	**0**	**0**	**0**	**0**	**15:19**

			Regular Season															Playoffs								
Season	Club	League	GP	G	A	Pts	PIM	PP	SH	GW	S	S%	+/-	TF	F%	Min	GP	G	A	Pts	PIM	PP	SH	GW	Min
2011-12	**Toronto**	**NHL**	**57**	**5**	**16**	**21**	**22**	**2**	**0**	**0**	**65**	**7.7**	**–1**	**0**	**0.0**	**16:11**	....	....	....	....	....	....	....	....	....
2012-13	Brynas IF Gavle	Sweden	26	3	4	7	10	....	....	....	....	....	....	....	....	....	....	....	....	....	....	....	....	....	....
	Toronto	**NHL**	**45**	**4**	**25**	**29**	**8**	**3**	**0**	**0**	**70**	**5.7**	**4**	**0**	**0.0**	**18:47**	**7**	**3**	**3**	**6**	**0**	**1**	**0**	**0**	**22:49**
2013-14	**Toronto**	**NHL**	**79**	**5**	**28**	**33**	**30**	**1**	**0**	**0**	**115**	**4.3**	**–20**	**0**	**0.0**	**20:41**	....	....	....	....	....	....	....	....	....
2014-15	**Toronto**	**NHL**	**55**	**6**	**26**	**32**	**26**	**4**	**0**	**0**	**92**	**6.5**	**–7**	**0**	**0.0**	**21:23**	....	....	....	....	....	....	....	....	....
	Nashville	**NHL**	**23**	**1**	**3**	**4**	**2**	**1**	**0**	**0**	**35**	**2.9**	**0**	**0**	**0.0**	**15:25**	**5**	**0**	**2**	**2**	**0**	**0**	**0**	**0**	**14:36**
	NHL Totals		**400**	**35**	**134**	**169**	**134**	**14**	**0**	**5**	**623**	**5.6**		**0**	**0.0**	**17:32**	**28**	**4**	**11**	**15**	**2**	**1**	**0**	**0**	**16:10**

WHL West Second All-Star Team (2006) • WHL West First All-Star Team (2007) • Memorial Cup All-Star Team (2007) • AHL All-Rookie Team (2008) • AHL Second All-Star Team (2009)

Traded to **Toronto** by **Nashville** with Matthew Lombardi for Robert Slaney, Brett Lebda and Toronto's 4th round choice (later traded to St. Louis – St. Louis selected Zachary Pochiro) in 2013 Entry Draft, July 3, 2011. Signed as a free agent by **Gavle** (Sweden), October 1, 2012. Traded to **Nashville** by **Toronto** with Mike Santorelli for Olli Jokinen, Brendan Leipsic and Nashville's 1st round choice (later traded to Philadelphia – Philadelphia selected Travis Konecny) in 2015 Entry Draft, February 15, 2015.

FRANZEN, Johan

(FRAN-zehn, YOH-han) **DET**

Left wing. Shoots left. 6'4", 232 lbs. Born, Landsbro, Sweden, December 23, 1979. Detroit's 1st choice, 97th overall, in 2004 Entry Draft.

Season	Club	League	GP	G	A	Pts	PIM	PP	SH	GW	S	S%	+/-	TF	F%	Min	GP	G	A	Pts	PIM	PP	SH	GW	Min
2001-02	Linkopings HC	Sweden	36	2	6	8	64	....	....	....	....	....	....	....	....	....	....	....	....	....	....	....	....	....	....
2002-03	Linkopings HC	Sweden	37	2	4	6	14	....	....	....	....	....	....	....	....	....	....	....	....	....	....	....	....	....	....
2003-04	Linkopings HC	Sweden	49	12	18	30	26	....	....	....	....	....	....	....	....	....	5	0	1	1	8	....	....	....	....
2004-05	Linkopings HC	Sweden	43	7	7	14	45	....	....	....	....	....	....	....	....	....	6	2	0	2	16	....	....	....	....
2005-06	**Detroit**	**NHL**	**80**	**12**	**4**	**16**	**36**	**0**	**2**	**2**	**119**	**10.1**	**4**	**171**	**41.5**	**12:27**	**6**	**1**	**2**	**3**	**4**	**0**	**0**	**0**	**12:00**
2006-07	**Detroit**	**NHL**	**69**	**10**	**20**	**30**	**37**	**0**	**1**	**2**	**151**	**6.6**	**20**	**45**	**40.0**	**15:35**	**18**	**3**	**4**	**7**	**10**	**0**	**0**	**2**	**16:47**
2007-08♦	**Detroit**	**NHL**	**72**	**27**	**11**	**38**	**51**	**14**	**0**	**8**	**199**	**13.6**	**12**	**390**	**48.5**	**17:44**	**16**	***13**	**5**	**18**	**14**	***6**	***2**	***5**	**18:49**
2008-09	**Detroit**	**NHL**	**71**	**34**	**25**	**59**	**44**	**11**	**1**	**8**	**246**	**13.8**	**21**	**241**	**56.0**	**18:06**	**23**	**12**	**11**	**23**	**12**	**4**	**0**	**3**	**19:41**
2009-10	**Detroit**	**NHL**	**27**	**10**	**11**	**21**	**22**	**6**	**0**	**1**	**91**	**11.0**	**1**	**27**	**55.6**	**18:42**	**12**	**6**	**12**	**18**	**16**	**1**	**0**	**1**	**17:34**
	Sweden	Olympics	4	1	1	2	2	....	....	....	....	....	....	....	....	....	....	....	....	....	....	....	....	....	....
2010-11	**Detroit**	**NHL**	**76**	**28**	**27**	**55**	**58**	**10**	**0**	**5**	**248**	**11.3**	**5**	**147**	**50.3**	**17:26**	**8**	**2**	**1**	**3**	**6**	**0**	**0**	**0**	**15:47**
2011-12	**Detroit**	**NHL**	**77**	**29**	**27**	**56**	**40**	**11**	**0**	**10**	**211**	**13.7**	**23**	**179**	**44.1**	**17:42**	**5**	**1**	**0**	**1**	**8**	**0**	**0**	**1**	**16:07**
2012-13	**Detroit**	**NHL**	**41**	**14**	**17**	**31**	**41**	**6**	**0**	**1**	**116**	**12.1**	**13**	**62**	**48.4**	**18:05**	**14**	**4**	**2**	**6**	**8**	**3**	**0**	**0**	**19:30**
2013-14	**Detroit**	**NHL**	**54**	**16**	**25**	**41**	**40**	**7**	**0**	**4**	**149**	**10.7**	**6**	**225**	**52.9**	**17:39**	**5**	**0**	**2**	**2**	**2**	**0**	**0**	**0**	**18:53**
2014-15	**Detroit**	**NHL**	**33**	**7**	**15**	**22**	**30**	**4**	**0**	**3**	**74**	**9.5**	**–12**	**15**	**33.3**	**16:04**	....	....	....	....	....	....	....	....	....
	NHL Totals		**600**	**187**	**182**	**369**	**399**	**69**	**4**	**44**	**1604**	**11.7**		**1502**	**48.9**	**16:45**	**107**	**42**	**39**	**81**	**80**	**14**	**2**	**12**	**17:53**

• Missed majority of 2009-10 due to knee injury vs. Chicago, October 8, 2009. • Missed majority of 2014-15 due to upper-body injury at Edmonton, January 6, 2015.

FRASER, Colin

(FRAY-zuhr, KAW-lihn) **ST.L.**

Center. Shoots left. 6'1", 190 lbs. Born, Sicamous, BC, January 28, 1985. Philadelphia's 3rd choice, 69th overall, in 2003 Entry Draft.

Season	Club	League	GP	G	A	Pts	PIM	PP	SH	GW	S	S%	+/-	TF	F%	Min	GP	G	A	Pts	PIM	PP	SH	GW	Min
2000-01	Port Coquitlam	PIJHL	38	16	24	40	90	....	....	....	....	....	....	....	....	....	8	2	2	4	21	....	....	....	....
2001-02	Red Deer Rebels	WHL	67	11	31	42	126	....	....	....	....	....	....	....	....	....	23	2	1	3	39	....	....	....	....
2002-03	Red Deer Rebels	WHL	69	15	37	52	192	....	....	....	....	....	....	....	....	....	22	7	6	13	40	....	....	....	....
2003-04	Red Deer Rebels	WHL	70	24	29	53	174	....	....	....	....	....	....	....	....	....	19	5	9	14	24	....	....	....	....
2004-05	Red Deer Rebels	WHL	63	24	43	67	148	....	....	....	....	....	....	....	....	....	7	2	5	7	8	....	....	....	....
	Norfolk Admirals	AHL	3	0	0	0	20	....	....	....	....	....	....	....	....	....	6	1	0	1	2	....	....	....	....
2005-06	Norfolk Admirals	AHL	75	12	13	25	145	....	....	....	....	....	....	....	....	....	4	0	0	0	7	....	....	....	....
2006-07	**Chicago**	**NHL**	**1**	**0**	**0**	**0**	**2**	**0**	**0**	**0**	**0**	**0.0**	**–1**	**2**	**0.0**	**3:18**	....	....	....	....	....	....	....	....	....
	Norfolk Admirals	AHL	67	12	24	36	158	....	....	....	....	....	....	....	....	....	6	1	0	1	21	....	....	....	....
2007-08	**Chicago**	**NHL**	**5**	**0**	**0**	**0**	**7**	**0**	**0**	**0**	**4**	**0.0**	**–2**	**38**	**36.8**	**10:19**	....	....	....	....	....	....	....	....	....
	Rockford IceHogs	AHL	75	17	24	41	165	....	....	....	....	....	....	....	....	....	12	1	2	3	28	....	....	....	....
2008-09	**Chicago**	**NHL**	**81**	**6**	**11**	**17**	**55**	**0**	**1**	**0**	**67**	**9.0**	**3**	**787**	**47.8**	**10:54**	**2**	**0**	**0**	**0**	**2**	**0**	**0**	**0**	**11:31**
2009-10♦	**Chicago**	**NHL**	**70**	**7**	**12**	**19**	**44**	**0**	**0**	**0**	**92**	**7.6**	**6**	**445**	**48.8**	**9:36**	**3**	**0**	**0**	**0**	**0**	**0**	**0**	**0**	**8:24**
2010-11	**Edmonton**	**NHL**	**67**	**3**	**2**	**5**	**60**	**0**	**1**	**0**	**57**	**5.3**	**–2**	**552**	**44.6**	**10:17**	....	....	....	....	....	....	....	....	....
2011-12♦	**Los Angeles**	**NHL**	**67**	**2**	**6**	**8**	**67**	**0**	**0**	**0**	**54**	**3.7**	**–2**	**370**	**47.3**	**9:44**	**18**	**1**	**1**	**2**	**4**	**0**	**0**	**0**	**8:34**
2012-13	**Los Angeles**	**NHL**	**34**	**2**	**5**	**7**	**25**	**0**	**0**	**0**	**19**	**10.5**	**–4**	**168**	**46.4**	**9:22**	**16**	**0**	**2**	**2**	**10**	**0**	**0**	**0**	**8:27**
2013-14	**Los Angeles**	**NHL**	**33**	**0**	**2**	**2**	**30**	**0**	**0**	**0**	**22**	**0.0**	**–4**	**173**	**50.3**	**8:59**	....	....	....	....	....	....	....	....	....
	Manchester	AHL	10	3	3	6	4	....	....	....	....	....	....	....	....	....	....	....	....	....	....	....	....	....	....
2014-15	**St. Louis**	**NHL**	**1**	**0**	**0**	**0**	**0**	**0**	**0**	**0**	**1**	**0.0**	**–1**	**0**	**0.0**	**4:42**	....	....	....	....	....	....	....	....	....
	Chicago Wolves	AHL	59	9	8	17	67	....	....	....	....	....	....	....	....	....	5	1	0	1	4	....	....	....	....
	NHL Totals		**359**	**20**	**38**	**58**	**290**	**0**	**2**	**0**	**316**	**6.3**		**2535**	**47.1**	**9:57**	**39**	**1**	**3**	**4**	**16**	**0**	**0**	**0**	**8:40**

Canadian Major Junior Humanitarian Player of the Year (2005)

Traded to **Chicago** by **Philadelphia** with Jim Vandermeer and Los Angeles' 2nd round choice (previously acquired, Chicago selected Bryan Bickell) in 2004 Entry Draft for Alex Zhamnov and Washington's 4th round choice (previously acquired, Philadelphia selected R.J. Anderson) in 2004 Entry Draft, February 19, 2004. Traded to **Edmonton** by **Chicago** for Edmonton's 6th round choice (Mirko Hoefflin) in 2010 Entry Draft, June 24, 2010. Traded to **Los Angeles** by **Edmonton** with Edmonron's 7th round choice (later traded to Dallas – Dallas selected Dmitri Sinitsyn) in 2012 Entry Draft for Ryan Smyth, June 26, 2011. Signed as a free agent by **St. Louis**, September 5, 2014. Signed as a free agent by **Nuremberg** (Germany), June 16, 2015.

FRASER, Mark

(FRAY-zuhr, MAHRK)

Defense. Shoots left. 6'4", 220 lbs. Born, Ottawa, ON, September 29, 1986. New Jersey's 3rd choice, 84th overall, in 2005 Entry Draft.

Season	Club	League	GP	G	A	Pts	PIM	PP	SH	GW	S	S%	+/-	TF	F%	Min	GP	G	A	Pts	PIM	PP	SH	GW	Min
2002-03	Clarence Beavers	ON-Jr.B	STATISTICS NOT AVAILABLE																						
	Gloucester	ON-Jr.A	5	0	0	0	4	....	....	....	....	....	....	....	....	....	3	0	0	0	0	....	....	....	....
2003-04	Gloucester	ON-Jr.A	52	0	11	11	107	....	....	....	....	....	....	....	....	....	20	0	3	3	32	....	....	....	....
2004-05	Gloucester	ON-Jr.A	11	0	5	5	22	....	....	....	....	....	....	....	....	....	....	....	....	....	....	....	....	....	....
	Kitchener Rangers	OHL	58	0	8	8	96	....	....	....	....	....	....	....	....	....	15	0	3	3	26	....	....	....	....
2005-06	Kitchener Rangers	OHL	59	0	5	5	129	....	....	....	....	....	....	....	....	....	5	0	1	1	4	....	....	....	....
	Albany River Rats	AHL	4	0	0	0	2	....	....	....	....	....	....	....	....	....	....	....	....	....	....	....	....	....	....
2006-07	**New Jersey**	**NHL**	**7**	**0**	**0**	**0**	**7**	**0**	**0**	**0**	**1**	**0.0**	**–1**	**0**	**0.0**	**3:34**	....	....	....	....	....	....	....	....	....
	Lowell Devils	AHL	71	1	8	9	73	....	....	....	....	....	....	....	....	....	....	....	....	....	....	....	....	....	....
2007-08	Lowell Devils	AHL	79	1	17	18	96	....	....	....	....	....	....	....	....	....	....	....	....	....	....	....	....	....	....
2008-09	Lowell Devils	AHL	74	3	14	17	152	....	....	....	....	....	....	....	....	....	....	....	....	....	....	....	....	....	....
2009-10	**New Jersey**	**NHL**	**61**	**3**	**3**	**6**	**36**	**0**	**0**	**0**	**24**	**12.5**	**3**	**0**	**0.0**	**12:23**	**1**	**0**	**0**	**0**	**0**	**0**	**0**	**0**	**5:52**
2010-11	**New Jersey**	**NHL**	**26**	**0**	**2**	**2**	**29**	**0**	**0**	**0**	**16**	**0.0**	**2**	**0**	**0.0**	**13:59**	....	....	....	....	....	....	....	....	....
	Albany Devils	AHL	5	0	1	1	0	....	....	....	....	....	....	....	....	....	....	....	....	....	....	....	....	....	....
2011-12	**New Jersey**	**NHL**	**4**	**0**	**0**	**0**	**14**	**0**	**0**	**0**	**0**	**0.0**	**–2**	**0**	**0.0**	**14:20**	....	....	....	....	....	....	....	....	....
	Syracuse Crunch	AHL	25	0	5	5	35	....	....	....	....	....	....	....	....	....	....	....	....	....	....	....	....	....	....
	Toronto Marlies	AHL	20	0	2	2	32	....	....	....	....	....	....	....	....	....	17	0	3	3	31	....	....	....	....
2012-13	Toronto Marlies	AHL	30	2	3	5	114	....	....	....	....	....	....	....	....	....	....	....	....	....	....	....	....	....	....
	Toronto	**NHL**	**45**	**0**	**8**	**8**	**85**	**0**	**0**	**0**	**33**	**0.0**	**18**	**0**	**0.0**	**16:57**	**4**	**0**	**1**	**1**	**7**	**0**	**0**	**0**	**18:26**
2013-14	**Toronto**	**NHL**	**19**	**0**	**1**	**1**	**33**	**0**	**0**	**0**	**6**	**0.0**	**–8**	**0**	**0.0**	**15:13**	....	....	....	....	....	....	....	....	....
	Edmonton	**NHL**	**23**	**1**	**0**	**1**	**43**	**0**	**0**	**0**	**5**	**20.0**	**–7**	**0**	**0.0**	**15:30**	....	....	....	....	....	....	....	....	....
2014-15	Albany Devils	AHL	18	1	2	3	45	....	....	....	....	....	....	....	....	....	....	....	....	....	....	....	....	....	....
	New Jersey	**NHL**	**34**	**0**	**4**	**4**	**55**	**0**	**0**	**0**	**19**	**0.0**	**2**	**0**	**0.0**	**16:17**	....	....	....	....	....	....	....	....	....
	NHL Totals		**219**	**4**	**18**	**22**	**302**	**0**	**0**	**0**	**104**	**3.8**		**0**	**0.0**	**14:27**	**5**	**0**	**1**	**1**	**7**	**0**	**0**	**0**	**15:55**

• Missed majority of 2010-11 due to hand injury at Buffalo, October 13. 2010 and as a healthy reserve. Traded to **Anaheim** by **New Jersey** with Rod Pelley and New Jersey's 7th round choice (Jaycob Megna) in 2012 Entry Draft for Kurtis Foster and Timo Pielmeier, December 12, 2011. Traded to **Toronto** by **Anaheim** for Dale Mitchell, February 27, 2012. Traded to **Edmonton** by **Toronto** for Cameron Abney and Teemu Hartikainen, January 31, 2014. Signed as a free agent by **Albany** (AHL), November 3, 2014. Signed as a free agent by **New Jersey**, December 18. 2014.

FRASER, Matt

(FRAY-zuhr, MAT) **WPG**

Left wing. Shoots left. 6'1", 204 lbs. Born, Red Deer, AB, May 20, 1990.

Season	Club	League	GP	G	A	Pts	PIM	PP	SH	GW	S	S%	+/-	TF	F%	Min	GP	G	A	Pts	PIM	PP	SH	GW	Min
2005-06	Red Deer Chiefs	Minor-AB	33	31	23	54	62	....	....	....	....	....	....	....	....	....	....	....	....	....	....	....	....	....	....
	Red Deer	AMHL	1	0	1	1	0	....	....	....	....	....	....	....	....	....	....	....	....	....	....	....	....	....	....
2006-07	Red Deer	AMHL	23	8	17	25	47	....	....	....	....	....	....	....	....	....	10	1	6	7	4	....	....	....	....
	Red Deer Rebels	WHL	3	0	0	0	2	....	....	....	....	....	....	....	....	....	1	0	0	0	0	....	....	....	....
2007-08	Red Deer Rebels	WHL	5	0	0	0	2	....	....	....	....	....	....	....	....	....	....	....	....	....	....	....	....	....	....
	Kootenay Ice	WHL	63	9	11	20	48	....	....	....	....	....	....	....	....	....	8	1	1	2	0	....	....	....	....
2008-09	Kootenay Ice	WHL	63	10	14	24	123	....	....	....	....	....	....	....	....	....	4	0	2	2	12	....	....	....	....
2009-10	Kootenay Ice	WHL	65	32	24	56	117	....	....	....	....	....	....	....	....	....	6	1	1	2	12	....	....	....	....
	Peoria Rivermen	AHL	2	0	0	0	0	....	....	....	....	....	....	....	....	....	....	....	....	....	....	....	....	....	....
2010-11	Kootenay Ice	WHL	66	36	38	74	115	....	....	....	....	....	....	....	....	....	19	*17	10	27	18	....	....	....	....
2011-12	**Dallas**	**NHL**	**1**	**0**	**0**	**0**	**0**	**0**	**0**	**0**	**1**	**0.0**	**0**	**0**	**0.0**	**3:57**	....	....	....	....	....	....	....	....	....
	Texas Stars	AHL	73	37	18	55	45	....	....	....	....	....	....	....	....	....	....	....	....	....	....	....	....	....	....

			Regular Season														Playoffs								
Season	Club	League	GP	G	A	Pts	PIM	PP	SH	GW	S	S%	+/-	TF	F%	Min	GP	G	A	Pts	PIM	PP	SH	GW	Min
2012-13	Texas Stars	AHL	62	33	13	46	26	....	....	....	....	....	....	....	....	....	9	2	0	2	2	....	....	....	....
	Dallas	**NHL**	12	1	2	3	0	0	0	0	17	5.9	0	0	0.0	11:48	....	....	....	....	....	....	....	....	....
2013-14	**Boston**	**NHL**	14	2	0	2	10	0	0	0	13	15.4	0	2	50.0	9:39	4	1	1	2	0	0	0	1	11:21
	Providence Bruins	AHL	44	20	10	30	34	....	....	....	....	....	....	....	....	....	5	3	2	5	0	....	....	....	....
2014-15	**Boston**	**NHL**	24	3	0	3	7	0	0	1	29	10.3	−5	4	0.0	10:31	....	....	....	....	....	....	....	....	....
	Edmonton	**NHL**	36	5	4	9	10	1	0	0	63	7.9	−11	3	100.0	11:41	....	....	....	....	....	....	....	....	....
	NHL Totals		87	11	6	17	27	1	0	1	123	8.9		9	44.4	10:58	4	1	1	2	0	0	0	1	11:21

AHL Second All-Star Team (2013)

Signed as a free agent by **Dallas**, November 18, 2010. Traded to **Boston** by **Dallas** with Loui Eriksson, Joe Morrow and Reilly Smith for Tyler Seguin, Rich Peverley and Ryan Button, July 4, 2013. Claimed on waivers by **Edmonton** from **Boston**, December 29, 2014. Signed as a free agent by **Winnipeg**, July 2, 2015.

FRATTIN, Matt (FRA-tihn, MAT) TOR

Right wing. Shoots right. 6', 205 lbs. Born, Edmonton, AB, January 3, 1988. Toronto's 2nd choice, 99th overall, in 2007 Entry Draft.

2004-05	Gregg Distributors	AMHL	34	12	13	25	14	....	....	....	....	....	....	....	....	....	....	....	....	....	....	....	....	....	....
2005-06	Gregg Distributors	AMHL	34	20	17	37	48	....	....	....	....	....	....	....	....	....	6	5	1	6	4	....	....	....	....
	Ft. Saskatchewan	AJHL	3	2	0	2	0	....	....	....	....	....	....	....	....	....	....	....	....	....	....	....	....	....	....
2006-07	Ft. Saskatchewan	AJHL	58	49	34	83	75	....	....	....	....	....	....	....	....	....	15	5	6	11	10	....	....	....	....
2007-08	North Dakota	WCHA	43	4	11	15	18	....	....	....	....	....	....	....	....	....	....	....	....	....	....	....	....	....	....
2008-09	North Dakota	WCHA	42	13	12	25	48	....	....	....	....	....	....	....	....	....	....	....	....	....	....	....	....	....	....
2009-10	North Dakota	WCHA	24	11	8	19	21	....	....	....	....	....	....	....	....	....	....	....	....	....	....	....	....	....	....
2010-11	North Dakota	WCHA	44	*36	24	*60	42	....	....	....	....	....	....	....	....	....	....	....	....	....	....	....	....	....	....
	Toronto	**NHL**	1	0	0	0	0	0	0	0	5	0.0	−1	0	0.0	15:34	....	....	....	....	....	....	....	....	....
2011-12	**Toronto**	**NHL**	56	8	7	15	25	0	0	2	92	8.7	−4	8	25.0	13:10	....	....	....	....	....	....	....	....	....
	Toronto Marlies	AHL	23	14	4	18	20	....	....	....	....	....	....	....	....	....	13	10	3	13	6	....	....	....	....
2012-13	Toronto Marlies	AHL	21	9	8	17	14	....	....	....	....	....	....	....	....	....	....	....	....	....	....	....	....	....	....
	Toronto	**NHL**	25	7	6	13	4	0	0	3	42	16.7	6	8	62.5	13:14	6	0	2	2	0	0	0	0	13:47
2013-14	**Los Angeles**	**NHL**	40	2	4	6	11	1	0	0	60	3.3	−6	4	50.0	11:59	....	....	....	....	....	....	....	....	....
	Columbus	**NHL**	4	0	1	1	0	0	0	0	1	0.0	2	0	0.0	12:22	....	....	....	....	....	....	....	....	....
2014-15	**Toronto**	**NHL**	9	0	0	0	4	0	0	0	6	0.0	0	1	100.0	7:03	....	....	....	....	....	....	....	....	....
	Toronto Marlies	AHL	59	26	22	48	26	....	....	....	....	....	....	....	....	....	5	3	3	6	14	....	....	....	....
	NHL Totals		135	17	18	35	44	1	0	5	206	8.3		21	47.6	12:25	6	0	2	2	0	0	0	0	13:47

WCHA First All-Star Team (2011) • NCAA West First All-American Team (2011) • WCHA Player of the Year (2011)

Traded to **Los Angeles** by **Toronto** with Ben Scrivens and Toronto's 2nd round choice (later traded to Columbus, later traded back to Toronto – Toronto selected Travis Dermott) in 2015 Entry Draft for Jonathan Bernier, June 23, 2013. Traded to **Columbus** by **Los Angeles** with Los Angeles' 2nd round choice (later traded to Columbus, later traded to Detroit – Detroit selected Dominic Turgeon) in 2014 Entry Draft and Toronto's 2nd round choice (previously acquired, later traded back to Toronto – Toronto selected Travis Dermott) in 2015 Entry Draft for Marian Gaborik, March 5, 2014. Traded to **Toronto** by **Columbus** for Jerry D'Amigo and future considerations, July 1, 2014.

FRIBERG, Max (FREE-buhrg, MAX) ANA

Left wing. Shoots right. 5'11", 200 lbs. Born, Skovde, Sweden, November 20, 1992. Anaheim's 6th choice, 143rd overall, in 2011 Entry Draft.

2007-08	Skovde IK U18	Swe-U18	24	6	3	9	44	....	....	....	....	....	....	....	....	....	....	....	....	....	....	....	....	....	....
	Skovde IK Jr.	Swe-Jr.	12	1	2	3	0	....	....	....	....	....	....	....	....	....	....	....	....	....	....	....	....	....	....
2008-09	Skovde IK U18	Swe-U18	10	14	18	32	4	....	....	....	....	....	....	....	....	....	....	....	....	....	....	....	....	....	....
	Skovde IK Jr.	Swe-Jr.	17	13	7	20	18	....	....	....	....	....	....	....	....	....	....	....	....	....	....	....	....	....	....
	Skovde IK	Sweden-3	24	1	3	4	2	....	....	....	....	....	....	....	....	....	....	....	....	....	....	....	....	....	....
2009-10	Skovde IK U18	Swe-U18	5	5	6	11	2	....	....	....	....	....	....	....	....	....	....	....	....	....	....	....	....	....	....
	Skovde IK Jr.	Swe-Jr.	1	0	3	3	0	....	....	....	....	....	....	....	....	....	....	....	....	....	....	....	....	....	....
	Skovde IK	Sweden-3	36	12	18	30	22	....	....	....	....	....	....	....	....	....	....	....	....	....	....	....	....	....	....
2010-11	Skovde IK Jr.	Swe-Jr.	2	1	3	4	2	....	....	....	....	....	....	....	....	....	....	....	....	....	....	....	....	....	....
	Skovde IK	Sweden-3	34	13	27	40	6	....	....	....	....	....	....	....	....	....	....	....	....	....	....	....	....	....	....
2011-12	Timra IK Jr.	Swe-Jr.	2	2	2	4	0	....	....	....	....	....	....	....	....	....	....	....	....	....	....	....	....	....	....
	Sundsvall	Sweden-2	1	0	0	0	0	....	....	....	....	....	....	....	....	....	....	....	....	....	....	....	....	....	....
	Timra IK	Sweden	48	5	5	10	8	....	....	....	....	....	....	....	....	....	....	....	....	....	....	....	....	....	....
	Timra IK	Sweden-Q	10	3	4	7	4	....	....	....	....	....	....	....	....	....	....	....	....	....	....	....	....	....	....
2012-13	Timra IK	Sweden	55	8	8	16	12	....	....	....	....	....	....	....	....	....	....	....	....	....	....	....	....	....	....
	Timra IK	Sweden-Q	10	4	2	6	0	....	....	....	....	....	....	....	....	....	....	....	....	....	....	....	....	....	....
	Norfolk Admirals	AHL	6	1	0	1	0	....	....	....	....	....	....	....	....	....	....	....	....	....	....	....	....	....	....
2013-14	Norfolk Admirals	AHL	74	17	23	40	55	....	....	....	....	....	....	....	....	....	10	3	2	5	2	....	....	....	....
2014-15	**Anaheim**	**NHL**	1	0	0	0	0	0	0	0	0	0.0	0	0	0.0	8:47	....	....	....	....	....	....	....	....	....
	Norfolk Admirals	AHL	58	15	25	40	46	....	....	....	....	....	....	....	....	....	....	....	....	....	....	....	....	....	....
	NHL Totals		1	0	0	0	0	0	0	0	0	0.0		0	0.0	8:47	....	....	....	....	....	....	....	....	....

FROLIK, Michael (FROH-lihk, MIGH-kuhl) CGY

Left wing. Shoots left. 6'1", 198 lbs. Born, Kladno, Czech., February 17, 1988. Florida's 1st choice, 10th overall, in 2006 Entry Draft.

2002-03	HC Kladno U17	CzR-U17	46	37	21	58	36	....	....	....	....	....	....	....	....	....	9	9	1	10	18	....	....	....	....
	HC Kladno Jr.	CzRep-Jr.	....	....	....	....	....	....	....	....	....	....	....	....	....	....	1	0	0	0	2	....	....	....	....
2003-04	HC Kladno U17	CzR-U17	1	0	1	1	2	....	....	....	....	....	....	....	....	....	....	....	....	....	....	....	....	....	....
	HC Kladno Jr.	CzRep-Jr.	53	21	23	44	22	....	....	....	....	....	....	....	....	....	7	3	1	4	6	....	....	....	....
2004-05	HC Kladno U17	CzR-U17	....	....	....	....	....	....	....	....	....	....	....	....	....	....	1	1	0	1	0	....	....	....	....
	HC Kladno Jr.	CzRep-Jr.	15	9	11	20	18	....	....	....	....	....	....	....	....	....	5	1	0	1	0	....	....	....	....
	HC Rabat Kladno	CzRep	27	3	1	4	6	....	....	....	....	....	....	....	....	....	1	0	0	0	0	....	....	....	....
2005-06	HC Kladno Jr.	CzRep-Jr.	3	1	2	3	0	....	....	....	....	....	....	....	....	....	6	3	9	12	6	....	....	....	....
	HC Rabat Kladno	CzRep	48	2	7	9	32	....	....	....	....	....	....	....	....	....	....	....	....	....	....	....	....	....	....
2006-07	Rimouski Oceanic	QMJHL	52	31	42	73	40	....	....	....	....	....	....	....	....	....	....	....	....	....	....	....	....	....	....
2007-08	Rimouski Oceanic	QMJHL	45	24	41	65	22	....	....	....	....	....	....	....	....	....	9	2	4	6	12	....	....	....	....
2008-09	**Florida**	**NHL**	79	21	24	45	22	1	0	2	158	13.3	10	67	40.3	14:48	....	....	....	....	....	....	....	....	....
2009-10	**Florida**	**NHL**	82	21	22	43	43	5	0	1	219	9.6	−4	35	37.1	17:29	....	....	....	....	....	....	....	....	....
2010-11	**Florida**	**NHL**	52	8	21	29	16	1	0	1	158	5.1	2	12	41.7	16:02	....	....	....	....	....	....	....	....	....
	Chicago	**NHL**	28	3	6	9	14	0	0	0	93	3.2	0	107	40.2	14:46	7	2	3	5	2	0	0	0	17:28
2011-12	**Chicago**	**NHL**	63	5	10	15	22	0	0	0	117	4.3	−10	48	33.3	12:52	4	2	1	3	0	0	0	0	17:23
2012-13	Pirati Chomutov	CzRep	32	14	10	24	22	....	....	....	....	....	....	....	....	....	....	....	....	....	....	....	....	....	....
	♦ **Chicago**	**NHL**	45	3	7	10	8	0	0	1	98	3.1	5	40	37.5	12:31	23	3	7	10	6	0	1	1	13:09
2013-14	**Winnipeg**	**NHL**	81	15	27	42	12	1	0	2	189	7.9	8	68	63.2	16:40	....	....	....	....	....	....	....	....	....
	Czech Republic	Olympics	5	0	0	0	0	....	....	....	....	....	....	....	....	....	....	....	....	....	....	....	....	....	....
2014-15	**Winnipeg**	**NHL**	82	19	23	42	18	3	3	4	206	9.2	4	41	34.2	17:30	4	0	0	0	2	0	0	0	17:22
	NHL Totals		512	95	140	235	155	11	3	11	1238	7.7		418	42.1	15:39	38	7	11	18	10	0	1	1	14:50

QMJHL All-Rookie Team (2007)

Traded to **Chicago** by **Florida** with Alexander Salak for Jack Skille, Hugh Jessiman and David Pacan, February 9, 2011. Signed as a free agent by **Chomutov** (CzRep), September 22, 2012. Traded to **Winnipeg** by **Chicago** for Winnipeg's 3rd (John Hayden) and 5th (Luke Johnson) round choices in 2013 Entry Draft, June 30, 2013. Signed as a free agent by **Calgary**, July 1, 2015.

GABORIK, Marian (GAB-uhr-ihk, MAIR-ee-uhn) L.A.

Right wing. Shoots left. 6'1", 202 lbs. Born, Trencin, Czech., February 14, 1982. Minnesota's 1st choice, 3rd overall, in 2000 Entry Draft.

1997-98	Dukla Trencin Jr.	Slovak-Jr.	36	37	22	59	28	....	....	....	....	....	....	....	....	....	....	....	....	....	....	....	....	....	....
	Dukla Trencin	Slovakia	1	1	0	1	0	....	....	....	....	....	....	....	....	....	....	....	....	....	....	....	....	....	....
1998-99	Dukla Trencin	Slovakia	33	11	9	20	6	....	....	....	....	....	....	....	....	....	3	1	0	1	2	....	....	....	....
99-2000	Dukla Trencin	Slovakia	50	25	21	46	34	....	....	....	....	....	....	....	....	....	5	1	2	3	2	....	....	....	....
2000-01	**Minnesota**	**NHL**	71	18	18	36	32	6	0	3	179	10.1	−6	3	33.3	15:26	....	....	....	....	....	....	....	....	....
2001-02	**Minnesota**	**NHL**	78	30	37	67	34	10	0	4	221	13.6	0	4	25.0	16:47	....	....	....	....	....	....	....	....	....
2002-03	**Minnesota**	**NHL**	81	30	35	65	46	5	1	8	280	10.7	12	16	25.0	17:24	18	9	8	17	6	4	0	0	18:12
2003-04	Dukla Trencin	Slovakia	9	10	3	13	10	....	....	....	....	....	....	....	....	....	....	....	....	....	....	....	....	....	....
	Minnesota	**NHL**	65	18	22	40	20	3	0	4	220	8.2	10	11	45.5	18:17	....	....	....	....	....	....	....	....	....
2004-05	Dukla Trencin	Slovakia	29	25	27	52	46	....	....	....	....	....	....	....	....	....	12	8	9	17	26	....	....	....	....
	Farjestad	Sweden	12	6	4	10	45	....	....	....	....	....	....	....	....	....	....	....	....	....	....	....	....	....	....
2005-06	**Minnesota**	**NHL**	65	38	28	66	64	10	2	7	252	15.1	6	11	27.3	18:26	....	....	....	....	....	....	....	....	....
	Slovakia	Olympics	6	3	4	7	4	....	....	....	....	....	....	....	....	....	....	....	....	....	....	....	....	....	....
2006-07	**Minnesota**	**NHL**	48	30	27	57	40	12	1	7	196	15.3	12	4	0.0	19:38	5	3	1	4	8	1	1	1	19:32

			Regular Season														Playoffs								
Season	Club	League	GP	G	A	Pts	PIM	PP	SH	GW	S	S%	+/-	TF	F%	Min	GP	G	A	Pts	PIM	PP	SH	GW	Min
2007-08	Minnesota	NHL	77	42	41	83	63	11	1	8	278	15.1	17	21	28.6	19:36	6	0	1	1	4	0	0	0	21:51
2008-09	Minnesota	NHL	17	13	10	23	2	2	1	2	68	19.1	3	5	0.0	20:00	....	....	....	....	....	....	....	....	....
2009-10	NY Rangers	NHL	76	42	44	86	37	14	1	4	272	15.4	15	7	28.6	21:15	....	....	....	....	....	....	....	....	....
	Slovakia	Olympics	7	4	1	5	6	....	....	....	....	....	....	....	....	....	....	....	....	....	....	....	....	....	....
2010-11	NY Rangers	NHL	62	22	26	48	18	7	0	4	192	11.5	8	0	0.0	18:05	5	1	1	2	2	0	0	0	23:55
2011-12	NY Rangers	NHL	82	41	35	76	34	10	0	7	276	14.9	15	2	0.0	19:31	20	5	6	11	2	0	0	1	19:56
2012-13	NY Rangers	NHL	35	9	10	19	8	1	0	4	113	8.0	–8	2	0.0	18:40	....	....	....	....	....	....	....	....	....
	Columbus	NHL	12	3	5	8	6	0	0	1	38	7.9	5	1	100.0	18:05	....	....	....	....	....	....	....	....	....
2013-14	Columbus	NHL	22	6	8	14	6	0	0	0	47	12.8	0	0	0.0	16:25	....	....	....	....	....	....	....	....	....
	♦ Los Angeles	NHL	19	5	11	16	4	1	0	0	56	8.9	7	2	0.0	17:42	26	*14	8	22	6	3	0	1	17:46
2014-15	Los Angeles	NHL	69	27	20	47	16	11	0	2	174	15.5	7	1	100.0	16:55	....	....	....	....	....	....	....	....	....
	NHL Totals		879	374	377	751	430	103	7	65	2862	13.1		90	26.7	18:16	80	32	25	57	28	8	1	3	19:12

NHL Second All-Star Team (2012)

Played in NHL All-Star Game (2003, 2008, 2012)

Signed as a free agent by **Trencin** (Slovakia), July 5, 2004. Signed as a free agent by **Farjestad** (Sweden), December 21, 2004. • Missed majority of 2008-09 due to hip surgery, January 5, 2009. Signed as a free agent by **NY Rangers**, July 1, 2009. Traded to **Columbus** by **NY Rangers** with Blake Parlett and Steven Delisle for Derek Dorsett, Derick Brassard, John Moore and Columbus' 6th round choice (later traded to Minnesota – Minnesota selected Chase Lang) in 2014 Entry Draft, April 3, 2013. Traded to **Los Angeles** by **Columbus** for Matt Frattin, Edmonton's 3rd round choice (later traded to Detroit – Detroit selected Dominic Turgeon) in 2014 Entry Draft and Toronto's 2nd round choice (previously acquired, later traded back to Toronto – Toronto selected Travis Dermott) in 2015 Entry Draft, March 5, 2014.

GAGNER, Sam

(GAH-n'yay, SAM) **PHI**

Center. Shoots right. 5'11", 202 lbs. Born, London, ON, August 10, 1989. Edmonton's 1st choice, 6th overall, in 2007 Entry Draft.

Season	Club	League	GP	G	A	Pts	PIM	PP	SH	GW	S	S%	+/-	TF	F%	Min	GP	G	A	Pts	PIM	PP	SH	GW	Min
2001-02	Tor. Marlboros	GTHL	68	56	61	117	42	....	....	....	....	....	....	....	....	....	....	....	....	....	....	....	....	....	....
2002-03	Tor. Marlboros	GTHL	72	68	86	154	35	....	....	....	....	....	....	....	....	....	....	....	....	....	....	....	....	....	....
2003-04	Tor. Marlboros	GTHL	85	64	108	171	36	....	....	....	....	....	....	....	....	....	....	....	....	....	....	....	....	....	....
2004-05	Tor. Marlboros	GTHL	70	62	118	180	56	....	....	....	....	....	....	....	....	....	....	....	....	....	....	....	....	....	....
	Milton Icehawks	ON-Jr.A	13	5	10	15	10	....	....	....	....	....	....	....	....	....	....	....	....	....	....	....	....	....	....
2005-06	Sioux City	USHL	56	11	35	46	60	....	....	....	....	....	....	....	....	....	....	....	....	....	....	....	....	....	....
2006-07	London Knights	OHL	53	35	83	118	36	....	....	....	....	....	....	....	....	....	16	7	*22	29	22	....	....	....	....
2007-08	Edmonton	NHL	79	13	36	49	23	4	0	1	135	9.6	–21	299	41.8	15:41	....	....	....	....	....	....	....	....	....
2008-09	Edmonton	NHL	76	16	25	41	51	6	0	1	156	10.3	–1	690	42.0	16:46	....	....	....	....	....	....	....	....	....
2009-10	Edmonton	NHL	68	15	26	41	33	6	0	1	170	8.8	–8	709	47.4	16:17	....	....	....	....	....	....	....	....	....
2010-11	Edmonton	NHL	68	15	27	42	37	3	1	2	138	10.9	–17	935	43.9	17:45	....	....	....	....	....	....	....	....	....
2011-12	Edmonton	NHL	75	18	29	47	36	6	0	0	149	12.1	5	701	47.7	17:11	....	....	....	....	....	....	....	....	....
2012-13	Klagenfurter AC	Austria	21	10	10	20	8	....	....	....	....	....	....	....	....	....	....	....	....	....	....	....	....	....	....
	Edmonton	NHL	48	14	24	38	23	4	0	1	113	12.4	–6	741	43.9	19:25	....	....	....	....	....	....	....	....	....
2013-14	Edmonton	NHL	67	10	27	37	41	1	0	1	143	7.0	–29	963	46.8	18:23	....	....	....	....	....	....	....	....	....
2014-15	Arizona	NHL	81	15	26	41	28	6	0	1	183	8.2	–28	771	46.8	17:15	....	....	....	....	....	....	....	....	....
	NHL Totals		562	116	220	336	272	36	1	8	1187	9.8		5809	45.3	17:13	....	....	....	....	....	....	....	....	....

USHL All-Rookie Team (2006) • OHL All-Rookie Team (2007)

Signed as a free agent by **Klagenfurt** (Austria), October 15, 2012. Traded to **Tampa Bay** by **Edmonton** for Teddy Purcell, June 29, 2014. Traded to **Arizona** by **Tampa Bay** with B.J. Crombeen for Arizona's 6th round choice (Kristian Oldham) in 2015 Entry Draft, June 29, 2014. Traded to **Philadelphia** by **Arizona** with future considerations for Nicklas Grossmann and Chris Pronger, June 27, 2015.

GALCHENYUK, Alex

(gal-CHEHN-yuhk, AL-ehx) **MTL**

Center. Shoots left. 6'1", 198 lbs. Born, Milwaukee, WI, February 12, 1994. Montreal's 1st choice, 3rd overall, in 2012 Entry Draft.

Season	Club	League	GP	G	A	Pts	PIM	PP	SH	GW	S	S%	+/-	TF	F%	Min	GP	G	A	Pts	PIM	PP	SH	GW	Min
2009-10	Chi. Americans	T1EHL	38	44	43	87	56	....	....	....	....	....	....	....	....	....	....	....	....	....	....	....	....	....	....
2010-11	Sarnia Sting	OHL	68	31	52	83	52	....	....	....	....	....	....	....	....	....	....	....	....	....	....	....	....	....	....
2011-12	Sarnia Sting	OHL	2	0	0	0	0	....	....	....	....	....	....	....	....	....	6	2	2	4	4	....	....	....	....
2012-13	Sarnia Sting	OHL	33	27	34	61	22	....	....	....	....	....	....	....	....	....	....	....	....	....	....	....	....	....	....
	Montreal	NHL	48	9	18	27	20	0	0	2	79	11.4	14	138	42.8	12:19	5	1	2	3	0	0	0	0	13:00
2013-14	Montreal	NHL	65	13	18	31	26	3	0	2	110	11.8	–12	15	33.3	14:24	5	2	1	3	2	1	0	1	15:01
2014-15	Montreal	NHL	80	20	26	46	39	3	0	1	163	12.3	8	174	47.1	16:26	12	1	3	4	10	0	0	1	16:01
	NHL Totals		193	42	62	104	85	6	0	5	352	11.9		327	44.6	14:43	22	4	6	10	12	1	0	2	15:06

OHL All-Rookie Team (2011)

• Missed majority of 2011-12 due to pre-season knee injury vs. Windsor (OHL), September 16, 2011.

GALIARDI, TJ

(gal-ee-AR-dee, TEE-JAY)

Left wing. Shoots left. 6'2", 195 lbs. Born, Calgary, AB, April 22, 1988. Colorado's 4th choice, 55th overall, in 2007 Entry Draft.

Season	Club	League	GP	G	A	Pts	PIM	PP	SH	GW	S	S%	+/-	TF	F%	Min	GP	G	A	Pts	PIM	PP	SH	GW	Min
2004-05	Cgy. North Stars	AMHL	36	14	16	30	32	....	....	....	....	....	....	....	....	....	....	....	....	....	....	....	....	....	....
2005-06	Calgary Royals	AJHL	56	19	37	56	60	....	....	....	....	....	....	....	....	....	....	....	....	....	....	....	....	....	....
2006-07	Dartmouth	ECAC	33	14	17	31	30	....	....	....	....	....	....	....	....	....	....	....	....	....	....	....	....	....	....
2007-08	Calgary Hitmen	WHL	72	18	52	70	77	....	....	....	....	....	....	....	....	....	16	5	*19	*24	20	....	....	....	....
2008-09	Colorado	NHL	11	3	1	4	6	0	0	0	14	21.4	–4	133	42.1	16:21	....	....	....	....	....	....	....	....	....
	Lake Erie	AHL	66	10	17	27	32	....	....	....	....	....	....	....	....	....	....	....	....	....	....	....	....	....	....
2009-10	Colorado	NHL	70	15	24	39	28	2	1	3	120	12.5	6	327	50.5	18:11	6	0	2	2	6	0	0	0	20:50
2010-11	Colorado	NHL	35	7	8	15	12	0	0	1	62	11.3	–6	134	46.3	16:12	....	....	....	....	....	....	....	....	....
	Lake Erie	AHL	1	0	1	1	0	....	....	....	....	....	....	....	....	....	....	....	....	....	....	....	....	....	....
2011-12	Colorado	NHL	55	8	6	14	47	0	1	2	101	7.9	–6	162	45.1	13:33	....	....	....	....	....	....	....	....	....
	San Jose	NHL	14	1	0	1	6	0	0	0	12	8.3	–2	5	40.0	11:04	3	0	0	0	6	0	0	0	12:37
2012-13	Bietigheim	German-2	7	3	3	6	8	....	....	....	....	....	....	....	....	....	....	....	....	....	....	....	....	....	....
	San Jose	NHL	36	5	9	14	14	1	0	0	68	7.4	1	19	26.3	13:52	11	1	1	2	6	0	0	1	16:50
2013-14	Calgary	NHL	62	4	13	17	21	0	1	0	100	4.0	–13	155	40.0	14:37	....	....	....	....	....	....	....	....	....
2014-15	Winnipeg	NHL	38	1	0	1	2	0	0	0	35	2.9	–8	11	18.2	10:28	....	....	....	....	....	....	....	....	....
	NHL Totals		321	44	61	105	136	3	3	6	512	8.6		946	45.1	14:43	20	1	3	4	18	0	0	1	17:24

ECAC All-Rookie Team (2007)

• Missed majority of 2010-11 due to wrist injury vs. Calgary, November 9. 2010. Traded to **San Jose** by **Colorado** with Daniel Winnik and Anaheim's 7th round choice (previously acquired, San Jose selected Emil Galimov) in 2013 Entry Draft for Jamie McGinn, Michael Sgarbossa and Mike Connolly, February 27, 2012. Signed as a free agent by **Bietigheim** (German-2), October 4, 2012. Traded to **Calgary** by **San Jose** for Calgary's 4th round choice (Christian Wolanin) in 2015 Entry Draft, July 2, 2013. Signed as a free agent by **Winnipeg**, August 1, 2014. • Missed majority of 2014-15 as a healthy reserve. Signed as a free agent by **Malmo** (Sweden), June 9, 2015.

GALIEV, Stanislav

(gah-LEE-ehv, stan-ihs-LAHV) **WSH**

Right wing. Shoots right. 6'1", 187 lbs. Born, Moscow, Russia, January 17, 1992. Washington's 2nd choice, 86th overall, in 2010 Entry Draft.

Season	Club	League	GP	G	A	Pts	PIM	PP	SH	GW	S	S%	+/-	TF	F%	Min	GP	G	A	Pts	PIM	PP	SH	GW	Min
2008-09	Indiana Ice	USHL	60	29	35	64	46	....	....	....	....	....	....	....	....	....	13	5	4	9	8	....	....	....	....
2009-10	Saint John	QMJHL	67	15	45	60	38	....	....	....	....	....	....	....	....	....	21	8	11	19	14	....	....	....	....
2010-11	Saint John	QMJHL	64	37	28	65	40	....	....	....	....	....	....	....	....	....	19	10	17	27	12	....	....	....	....
2011-12	Saint John	QMJHL	20	13	6	19	16	....	....	....	....	....	....	....	....	....	17	16	18	34	6	....	....	....	....
2012-13	Hershey Bears	AHL	17	0	1	1	8	....	....	....	....	....	....	....	....	....	....	....	....	....	....	....	....	....	....
	Reading Royals	ECHL	46	23	24	47	32	....	....	....	....	....	....	....	....	....	10	4	7	11	0	....	....	....	....
2013-14	Hershey Bears	AHL	16	3	3	6	0	....	....	....	....	....	....	....	....	....	....	....	....	....	....	....	....	....	....
	Reading Royals	ECHL	14	5	8	13	6	....	....	....	....	....	....	....	....	....	3	1	1	2	0	....	....	....	....
2014-15	Washington	NHL	2	1	0	1	0	0	0	0	2	50.0	1	0	0.0	9:23	....	....	....	....	....	....	....	....	....
	Hershey Bears	AHL	67	25	20	45	24	....	....	....	....	....	....	....	....	....	5	1	0	1	0	....	....	....	....
	NHL Totals		2	1	0	1	0	0	0	0	2	50.0		0	0.0	9:23	....	....	....	....	....	....	....	....	....

QMJHL All-Rookie Team (2010)

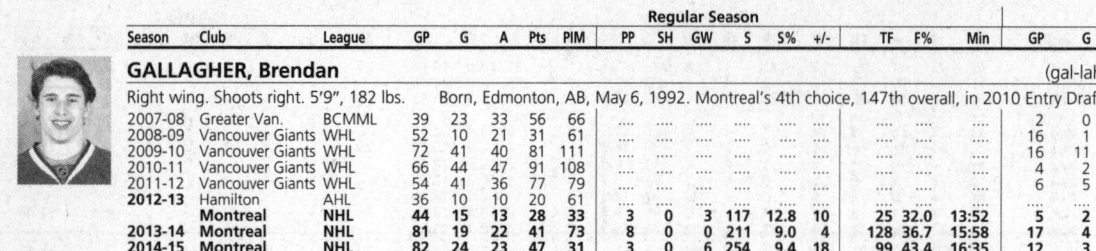

GALLAGHER, Brendan
(gal-lah-GUR, BREHN-duhn) **MTL**

Right wing. Shoots right. 5'9", 182 lbs. Born, Edmonton, AB, May 6, 1992. Montreal's 4th choice, 147th overall, in 2010 Entry Draft.

			Regular Season															Playoffs								
Season	Club	League	GP	G	A	Pts	PIM	PP	SH	GW	S	S%	+/-	TF	F%	Min	GP	G	A	Pts	PIM	PP	SH	GW	Min
2007-08	Greater Van.	BCMML	39	23	33	56	66	....	....	....	....	....	....	....	....	....	2	0	1	1	0	....	....	....	....
2008-09	Vancouver Giants	WHL	52	10	21	31	61	....	....	....	....	....	....	....	....	....	16	1	2	3	10	....	....	....	....
2009-10	Vancouver Giants	WHL	72	41	40	81	111	....	....	....	....	....	....	....	....	....	16	11	10	21	14	....	....	....	....
2010-11	Vancouver Giants	WHL	66	44	47	91	108	....	....	....	....	....	....	....	....	....	4	2	0	2	16	....	....	....	....
2011-12	Vancouver Giants	WHL	54	41	36	77	79	....	....	....	....	....	....	....	....	....	6	5	5	10	16	....	....	....	....
2012-13	Hamilton	AHL	36	10	10	20	61	....	....	....	....	....	....	....	....	....	....	....	....	....	....	....	....	....	....
	Montreal	**NHL**	**44**	**15**	**13**	**28**	**33**	**3**	**0**	**3**	**117**	**12.8**	**10**	**25**	**32.0**	**13:52**	**5**	**2**	**0**	**2**	**5**	**1**	**0**	**1**	**14:26**
2013-14	**Montreal**	**NHL**	**81**	**19**	**22**	**41**	**73**	**8**	**0**	**0**	**211**	**9.0**	**4**	**128**	**36.7**	**15:58**	**17**	**4**	**7**	**11**	**6**	**1**	**0**	**0**	**16:36**
2014-15	**Montreal**	**NHL**	**82**	**24**	**23**	**47**	**31**	**3**	**0**	**6**	**254**	**9.4**	**18**	**99**	**43.4**	**16:35**	**12**	**3**	**2**	**5**	**0**	**0**	**0**	**1**	**18:02**
	NHL Totals		**207**	**58**	**58**	**116**	**137**	**14**	**0**	**9**	**582**	**10.0**		**252**	**38.9**	**15:46**	**34**	**9**	**9**	**18**	**11**	**2**	**0**	**2**	**16:47**

WHL West First All-Star Team (2011, 2012) • NHL All-Rookie Team (2013)

GALLANT, Brett
(guh-LANT, BREHT) **CBJ**

Left wing. Shoots left. 6', 194 lbs. Born, Summerside, PEI, December 28, 1988.

Season	Club	League	GP	G	A	Pts	PIM	PP	SH	GW	S	S%	+/-	TF	F%	Min	GP	G	A	Pts	PIM	PP	SH	GW	Min
2005-06	Saint John	QMJHL	26	0	1	1	72	....	....	....	....	....	....	....	....	....	....	....	....	....	....	....	....	....	....
	Summerside	MJrHL	9	0	2	2	148	....	....	....	....	....	....	....	....	....	....	....	....	....	....	....	....	....	....
2006-07	Saint John	QMJHL	48	5	1	6	192	....	....	....	....	....	....	....	....	....	....	....	....	....	....	....	....	....	....
2007-08	Saint John	QMJHL	57	3	2	5	175	....	....	....	....	....	....	....	....	....	11	1	0	1	15	....	....	....	....
2008-09	Summerside	MJrHL	50	24	49	73	235	....	....	....	....	....	....	....	....	....	....	....	....	....	....	....	....	....	....
2009-10	Elmira Jackals	ECHL	38	1	1	2	185	....	....	....	....	....	....	....	....	....	....	....	....	....	....	....	....	....	....
	Syracuse Crunch	AHL	1	0	0	0	5	....	....	....	....	....	....	....	....	....	....	....	....	....	....	....	....	....	....
2010-11	Elmira Jackals	ECHL	13	0	0	0	80	....	....	....	....	....	....	....	....	....	....	....	....	....	....	....	....	....	....
	Reading Royals	ECHL	12	1	2	3	52	....	....	....	....	....	....	....	....	....	....	....	....	....	....	....	....	....	....
	Bridgeport	AHL	17	1	0	1	73	....	....	....	....	....	....	....	....	....	....	....	....	....	....	....	....	....	....
2011-12	Bridgeport	AHL	25	2	1	3	80	....	....	....	....	....	....	....	....	....	....	....	....	....	....	....	....	....	....
2012-13	Bridgeport	AHL	42	0	0	0	202	....	....	....	....	....	....	....	....	....	....	....	....	....	....	....	....	....	....
2013-14	**NY Islanders**	**NHL**	**4**	**0**	**0**	**0**	**17**	**0**	**0**	**0**	**3**	**0.0**	**0**	**0**	**0.0**	**6:53**	....	....	....	....	....	....	....	....	....
	Bridgeport	AHL	58	1	1	2	255	....	....	....	....	....	....	....	....	....	....	....	....	....	....	....	....	....	....
2014-15	Bridgeport	AHL	45	2	4	6	247	....	....	....	....	....	....	....	....	....	....	....	....	....	....	....	....	....	....
	NHL Totals		**4**	**0**	**0**	**0**	**17**	**0**	**0**	**0**	**3**	**0.0**		**0**	**0.0**	**6:53**	....	....	....	....	....	....	....	....	....

• Missed majority of 2011-12 due to recurring shoulder injury. Signed as a free agent by **NY Islanders**, February 5, 2013. Signed as a free agent by **Columbus**, July 2, 2015.

GARBUTT, Ryan
(GAHR-buht, RIGH-uhn) **CHI**

Center. Shoots left. 6', 195 lbs. Born, Winnipeg, MB, August 12, 1985.

Season	Club	League	GP	G	A	Pts	PIM	PP	SH	GW	S	S%	+/-	TF	F%	Min	GP	G	A	Pts	PIM	PP	SH	GW	Min
2003-04	Wpg. South Blues	MJHL	60	23	25	48	143	....	....	....	....	....	....	....	....	....	....	....	....	....	....	....	....	....	....
2004-05	Wpg. South Blues	MJHL	63	47	34	81	303	....	....	....	....	....	....	....	....	....	....	....	....	....	....	....	....	....	....
2005-06	Brown U.	ECAC	28	2	4	6	61	....	....	....	....	....	....	....	....	....	....	....	....	....	....	....	....	....	....
2006-07	Brown U.	ECAC	29	9	4	13	30	....	....	....	....	....	....	....	....	....	....	....	....	....	....	....	....	....	....
2007-08	Brown U.	ECAC	29	12	11	23	56	....	....	....	....	....	....	....	....	....	....	....	....	....	....	....	....	....	....
2008-09	Brown U.	ECAC	30	6	10	16	56	....	....	....	....	....	....	....	....	....	....	....	....	....	....	....	....	....	....
2009-10	Corpus Christi	CHL	64	22	28	50	204	....	....	....	....	....	....	....	....	....	1	0	0	0	2	....	....	....	....
2010-11	Gwinnett	ECHL	10	10	7	17	24	....	....	....	....	....	....	....	....	....	....	....	....	....	....	....	....	....	....
	Chicago Wolves	AHL	65	19	18	37	118	....	....	....	....	....	....	....	....	....	....	....	....	....	....	....	....	....	....
2011-12	**Dallas**	**NHL**	**20**	**2**	**1**	**3**	**22**	**0**	**0**	**1**	**28**	**7.1**	**−1**	**27**	**44.4**	**8:17**	....	....	....	....	....	....	....	....	....
	Texas Stars	AHL	50	16	17	33	96	....	....	....	....	....	....	....	....	....	....	....	....	....	....	....	....	....	....
2012-13	**Dallas**	**NHL**	**36**	**3**	**7**	**10**	**32**	**0**	**0**	**0**	**59**	**5.1**	**1**	**17**	**41.2**	**9:55**	....	....	....	....	....	....	....	....	....
2013-14	**Dallas**	**NHL**	**75**	**17**	**15**	**32**	**106**	**0**	**2**	**1**	**165**	**10.3**	**10**	**10**	**40.0**	**13:04**	**6**	**3**	**0**	**3**	**25**	**0**	**0**	**0**	**11:57**
2014-15	**Dallas**	**NHL**	**67**	**8**	**17**	**25**	**55**	**0**	**1**	**2**	**143**	**5.6**	**−9**	**25**	**64.0**	**13:34**	....	....	....	....	....	....	....	....	....
	NHL Totals		**198**	**30**	**40**	**70**	**215**	**0**	**3**	**4**	**395**	**7.6**		**79**	**49.4**	**12:11**	**6**	**3**	**0**	**3**	**25**	**0**	**0**	**0**	**11:57**

Signed as a free agent by **Corpus Christi** (CHL), September, 2009. Signed as a free agent by **Gwinnett** (ECHL), September 21, 2010. Signed as a free agent by **Chicago** (AHL), November 11, 2010. Signed as a free agent by **Dallas**, July 1, 2011. Traded to **Chicago** by **Dallas** with Trevor Daley for Patrick Sharp and Stephen Johns, July 12, 2015

GARDINER, Jake
(GAHR-dih-nuhr, JAYK) **TOR**

Defense. Shoots left. 6'2", 184 lbs. Born, Minnetonka, MN, July 4, 1990. Anaheim's 1st choice, 17th overall, in 2008 Entry Draft.

Season	Club	League	GP	G	A	Pts	PIM	PP	SH	GW	S	S%	+/-	TF	F%	Min	GP	G	A	Pts	PIM	PP	SH	GW	Min
2005-06	Minnetonka High	High-MN	21	2	14	16	6	....	....	....	....	....	....	....	....	....	....	....	....	....	....	....	....	....	....
2006-07	Minnetonka High	High-MN	19	10	22	32	20	....	....	....	....	....	....	....	....	....	....	....	....	....	....	....	....	....	....
	Team Southwest	UMWEHL	11	4	3	7	....	....	....	....	....	....	....	....	....	....	....	....	....	....	....	....	....	....	....
2007-08	Minnetonka High	High-MN	24	20	28	48	14	....	....	....	....	....	....	....	....	....	....	....	....	....	....	....	....	....	....
	Team Southwest	UMWEHL	11	8	7	15	....	....	....	....	....	....	....	....	....	....	....	....	....	....	....	....	....	....	....
2008-09	U. of Wisconsin	WCHA	39	3	18	21	16	....	....	....	....	....	....	....	....	....	....	....	....	....	....	....	....	....	....
2009-10	U. of Wisconsin	WCHA	41	6	7	13	20	....	....	....	....	....	....	....	....	....	....	....	....	....	....	....	....	....	....
2010-11	U. of Wisconsin	WCHA	41	10	31	41	24	....	....	....	....	....	....	....	....	....	....	....	....	....	....	....	....	....	....
	Toronto Marlies	AHL	10	0	3	3	4	....	....	....	....	....	....	....	....	....	....	....	....	....	....	....	....	....	....
2011-12	**Toronto**	**NHL**	**75**	**7**	**23**	**30**	**18**	**1**	**0**	**0**	**79**	**8.9**	**−2**	**0**	**0.0**	**21:35**	....	....	....	....	....	....	....	....	....
	Toronto Marlies	AHL	4	0	2	2	2	....	....	....	....	....	....	....	....	....	17	2	9	11	10	....	....	....	....
2012-13	Toronto Marlies	AHL	43	10	21	31	12	....	....	....	....	....	....	....	....	....	....	....	....	....	....	....	....	....	....
	Toronto	**NHL**	**12**	**0**	**4**	**4**	**0**	**0**	**0**	**0**	**12**	**0.0**	**0**	**0**	**0.0**	**20:29**	**6**	**1**	**4**	**5**	**0**	**1**	**0**	**0**	**23:01**
2013-14	**Toronto**	**NHL**	**80**	**10**	**21**	**31**	**19**	**2**	**1**	**1**	**136**	**7.4**	**−3**	**0**	**0.0**	**21:05**	....	....	....	....	....	....	....	....	....
2014-15	**Toronto**	**NHL**	**79**	**4**	**20**	**24**	**24**	**0**	**0**	**0**	**100**	**4.0**	**−23**	**0**	**0.0**	**20:58**	....	....	....	....	....	....	....	....	....
	NHL Totals		**246**	**21**	**68**	**89**	**61**	**3**	**1**	**1**	**327**	**6.4**		**0**	**0.0**	**21:10**	**6**	**1**	**4**	**5**	**0**	**1**	**0**	**0**	**23:01**

WCHA All-Rookie Team (2009) • WCHA Second All-Star Team (2011) • NCAA West Second All-American Team (2011) • NHL All-Rookie Team (2012)

Traded to **Toronto** by **Anaheim** with Joffrey Lupul and Anaheim's 4th round choice (later traded to San Jose – San Jose selected Fredrik Bergvik) in 2013 Entry Draft for Francois Beauchemin, February 9, 2011.

GARRISON, Jason
(GAIR-ih-suhn, JAY-suhn) **T.B.**

Defense. Shoots left. 6'2", 218 lbs. Born, White Rock, BC, November 13, 1984.

Season	Club	League	GP	G	A	Pts	PIM	PP	SH	GW	S	S%	+/-	TF	F%	Min	GP	G	A	Pts	PIM	PP	SH	GW	Min
2003-04	Nanaimo Clippers	BCHL	52	7	20	27	31	....	....	....	....	....	....	....	....	....	24	3	10	13	12	....	....	....	....
2004-05	Nanaimo Clippers	BCHL	57	22	40	62	42	....	....	....	....	....	....	....	....	....	....	....	....	....	....	....	....	....	....
2005-06	U. Minn-Duluth	WCHA	40	3	9	12	26	....	....	....	....	....	....	....	....	....	....	....	....	....	....	....	....	....	....
2006-07	U. Minn-Duluth	WCHA	21	1	2	3	16	....	....	....	....	....	....	....	....	....	....	....	....	....	....	....	....	....	....
2007-08	U. Minn-Duluth	WCHA	26	5	9	14	26	....	....	....	....	....	....	....	....	....	....	....	....	....	....	....	....	....	....
2008-09	**Florida**	**NHL**	**1**	**0**	**0**	**0**	**0**	**0**	**0**	**0**	**0**	**0.0**	**0**	**0**	**0.0**	**11:57**	....	....	....	....	....	....	....	....	....
	Rochester	AHL	75	8	27	35	68	....	....	....	....	....	....	....	....	....	....	....	....	....	....	....	....	....	....
2009-10	**Florida**	**NHL**	**39**	**2**	**6**	**8**	**23**	**0**	**0**	**0**	**24**	**8.3**	**5**	**0**	**0.0**	**15:08**	....	....	....	....	....	....	....	....	....
	Rochester	AHL	38	3	16	19	33	....	....	....	....	....	....	....	....	....	7	2	7	9	0	....	....	....	....
2010-11	**Florida**	**NHL**	**73**	**5**	**13**	**18**	**26**	**0**	**0**	**3**	**116**	**4.3**	**−2**	**0**	**0.0**	**22:18**	....	....	....	....	....	....	....	....	....
2011-12	**Florida**	**NHL**	**77**	**16**	**17**	**33**	**32**	**9**	**0**	**3**	**168**	**9.5**	**6**	**2**	**50.0**	**23:42**	**4**	**1**	**2**	**3**	**0**	**1**	**0**	**0**	**25:11**
2012-13	**Vancouver**	**NHL**	**47**	**8**	**8**	**16**	**28**	**3**	**0**	**2**	**94**	**8.5**	**18**	**0**	**0.0**	**21:41**	**4**	**0**	**0**	**0**	**2**	**0**	**0**	**0**	**23:44**
2013-14	**Vancouver**	**NHL**	**81**	**7**	**26**	**33**	**57**	**4**	**1**	**1**	**181**	**3.9**	**−5**	**0**	**0.0**	**20:54**	....	....	....	....	....	....	....	....	....
2014-15	**Tampa Bay**	**NHL**	**70**	**4**	**26**	**30**	**19**	**1**	**0**	**3**	**111**	**3.6**	**27**	**0**	**0.0**	**20:01**	**23**	**2**	**5**	**7**	**8**	**1**	**0**	**1**	**19:29**
	NHL Totals		**388**	**42**	**96**	**138**	**185**	**17**	**1**	**12**	**694**	**6.1**		**2**	**50.0**	**21:03**	**31**	**3**	**7**	**10**	**10**	**2**	**0**	**1**	**20:46**

Signed as a free agent by **Florida**, April 2, 2008. Signed as a free agent by **Vancouver**, July 1, 2012. Traded to **Tampa Bay** by **Vancouver** with Jeff Costello and Vancouver's 7th round choice (later traded to Minnesota – Minnesota selected Jack Sedak) in 2015 Entry Draft for Tampa Bay's 2nd round choice (later traded to Los Angeles – Los Angeles selected Roland McKeown) in 2014 Entry Draft, June 27, 2014.

GAUDET, Tyler

(GAH-deht, TIGH-luhr) **ARI**

Center. Shoots left. 6'3", 205 lbs. Born, Hamilton, ON, April 4, 1993.

			Regular Season														Playoffs								
Season	Club	League	GP	G	A	Pts	PIM	PP	SH	GW	S	S%	+/-	TF	F%	Min	GP	G	A	Pts	PIM	PP	SH	GW	Min
2010-11	Hamilton	ON-Jr.A	41	4	15	19	14	....	....	....	....	....	....	....	....	....	7	3	3	6	6	....	....	....	....
2011-12	Gatineau	QMJHL	38	3	2	5	25	....	....	....	....	....	....	....	....	....	....	....	....	....	....	....	....	....	....
	Pembroke	ON-Jr.A	22	4	12	16	6	....	....	....	....	....	....	....	....	....	11	0	3	3	2	....	....	....	....
2012-13	Pembroke	ON-Jr.A	25	10	12	22	6	....	....	....	....	....	....	....	....	....	....	....	....	....	....	....	....	....	....
	Sault Ste. Marie	OHL	34	3	5	8	10	....	....	....	....	....	....	....	....	....	6	1	0	1	10	....	....	....	....
2013-14	Sault Ste. Marie	OHL	65	26	35	61	35	....	....	....	....	....	....	....	....	....	9	2	6	8	0	....	....	....	....
	Portland Pirates	AHL	2	0	0	0	0	....	....	....	....	....	....	....	....	....	....	....	....	....	....	....	....	....	....
2014-15	**Arizona**	**NHL**	**2**	**0**	**0**	**0**	**0**	**0**	**0**	**0**	**1**	**0.0**	**–1**	**17**	**52.9**	**9:35**	....	....	....	....	....	....	....	....	....
	Portland Pirates	AHL	71	8	12	20	22	....	....	....	....	....	....	....	....	....	4	1	1	2	0	....	....	....	....
	NHL Totals		**2**	**0**	**0**	**0**	**0**	**0**	**0**	**0**	**1**	**0.0**		**17**	**52.9**	**9:35**	....	....	....	....	....	....	....	....	....

Signed as a free agent by **Phoenix**, November 4, 2013.

GAUDREAU, Johnny

(GAW-droh, JAWN-nee) **CGY**

Left wing. Shoots left. 5'9", 150 lbs. Born, Salem, NJ, August 13, 1993. Calgary's 4th choice, 104th overall, in 2011 Entry Draft.

Season	Club	League	GP	G	A	Pts	PIM	PP	SH	GW	S	S%	+/-	TF	F%	Min	GP	G	A	Pts	PIM	PP	SH	GW	Min
2009-10	Gloucester Cath.	High-NJ	14	21	27	48	....	....	....	....	....	....	....	....	....	....	....	....	....	....	....	....	....	....	....
	Team Comcast	T1EHL	48	29	29	58	16	....	....	....	....	....	....	....	....	....	....	....	....	....	....	....	....	....	....
2010-11	Dubuque	USHL	60	36	36	72	36	....	....	....	....	....	....	....	....	....	11	5	6	11	6	....	....	....	....
2011-12	Boston College	H-East	44	21	23	44	10	....	....	....	....	....	....	....	....	....	....	....	....	....	....	....	....	....	....
2012-13	Boston College	H-East	35	21	30	*51	29	....	....	....	....	....	....	....	....	....	....	....	....	....	....	....	....	....	....
2013-14	Boston College	H-East	40	*36	*44	*80	14	....	....	....	....	....	....	....	....	....	....	....	....	....	....	....	....	....	....
	Calgary	**NHL**	**1**	**1**	**0**	**1**	**0**	**0**	**0**	**0**	**1**	**100.0**	**1**	**0**	**0.0**	**15:11**	....	....	....	....	....	....	....	....	....
2014-15	**Calgary**	**NHL**	**80**	**24**	**40**	**64**	**14**	**8**	**0**	**4**	**167**	**14.4**	**11**	**8**	**37.5**	**17:43**	**11**	**4**	**5**	**9**	**6**	**2**	**0**	**0**	**19:10**
	NHL Totals		**81**	**25**	**40**	**65**	**14**	**8**	**0**	**4**	**168**	**14.9**		**8**	**37.5**	**17:41**	**11**	**4**	**5**	**9**	**6**	**2**	**0**	**0**	**19:10**

USHL All-Rookie Team (2011) • USHL Second All-Star Team (2011) • USHL Rookie of the Year (2011) • Hockey East All-Rookie Team (2012) • Hockey East First All-Star Team (2013, 2014) • Hockey East Player of the Year (2013, 2014) • NCAA East First All-American Team (2013, 2014) • Hobey Baker Memorial Award (Top U.S. Collegiate Player) (2014) • NHL All-Rookie Team (2015)

Played in NHL All-Star Game (2015)

GAUNCE, Cameron

(GAWNS, KAM-ih-RUHN) **FLA**

Defense. Shoots left. 6'1", 210 lbs. Born, Sudbury, ON, March 19, 1990. Colorado's 1st choice, 50th overall, in 2008 Entry Draft.

Season	Club	League	GP	G	A	Pts	PIM	PP	SH	GW	S	S%	+/-	TF	F%	Min	GP	G	A	Pts	PIM	PP	SH	GW	Min
2005-06	Markham Waxers	Minor-ON	72	11	60	71	122	....	....	....	....	....	....	....	....	....	....	....	....	....	....	....	....	....	....
2006-07	Markham Waxers	ON-Jr.A	45	2	12	14	68	....	....	....	....	....	....	....	....	....	11	0	3	3	26	....	....	....	....
2007-08	St. Michael's	OHL	63	10	30	40	99	....	....	....	....	....	....	....	....	....	4	0	1	1	6	....	....	....	....
2008-09	St. Michael's	OHL	67	17	47	64	110	....	....	....	....	....	....	....	....	....	11	4	6	10	20	....	....	....	....
2009-10	St. Michael's	OHL	55	6	31	37	112	....	....	....	....	....	....	....	....	....	16	0	13	13	34	....	....	....	....
2010-11	**Colorado**	**NHL**	**11**	**1**	**0**	**1**	**16**	**0**	**0**	**0**	**4**	**25.0**	**–3**	**0**	**0.0**	**12:44**	....	....	....	....	....	....	....	....	....
	Lake Erie	AHL	61	2	20	22	84	....	....	....	....	....	....	....	....	....	....	....	....	....	....	....	....	....	....
2011-12	Lake Erie	AHL	75	6	21	27	90	....	....	....	....	....	....	....	....	....	....	....	....	....	....	....	....	....	....
2012-13	Lake Erie	AHL	61	1	10	11	98	....	....	....	....	....	....	....	....	....	....	....	....	....	....	....	....	....	....
	Texas Stars	AHL	9	1	4	5	0	....	....	....	....	....	....	....	....	....	9	0	0	0	0	....	....	....	....
2013-14	**Dallas**	**NHL**	**9**	**0**	**0**	**0**	**7**	**0**	**0**	**0**	**9**	**0.0**	**1**	**0**	**0.0**	**13:50**	....	....	....	....	....	....	....	....	....
	Texas Stars	AHL	65	3	15	18	73	....	....	....	....	....	....	....	....	....	18	0	4	4	12	....	....	....	....
2014-15	Texas Stars	AHL	73	4	10	14	113	....	....	....	....	....	....	....	....	....	3	0	0	0	0	....	....	....	....
	NHL Totals		**20**	**1**	**0**	**1**	**23**	**0**	**0**	**0**	**13**	**7.7**		**0**	**0.0**	**13:14**	....	....	....	....	....	....	....	....	....

OHL Second All-Star Team (2009, 2010)

Traded to **Dallas** by **Colorado** for Tomas Vincour, April 2, 2013. Signed as a free agent by **Florida**, July 1, 2015.

GAUSTAD, Paul

(GAW-stad, PAWL) **NSH**

Center. Shoots left. 6'5", 223 lbs. Born, Fargo, ND, February 3, 1982. Buffalo's 6th choice, 220th overall, in 2000 Entry Draft.

Season	Club	League	GP	G	A	Pts	PIM	PP	SH	GW	S	S%	+/-	TF	F%	Min	GP	G	A	Pts	PIM	PP	SH	GW	Min
1998-99	Portland Hawks	USAHA	45	47	53	100	81	....	....	....	....	....	....	....	....	....	....	....	....	....	....	....	....	....	....
99-2000	Portland	WHL	56	6	8	14	110	....	....	....	....	....	....	....	....	....	....	....	....	....	....	....	....	....	....
2000-01	Portland	WHL	70	11	30	41	168	....	....	....	....	....	....	....	....	....	16	10	6	16	59	....	....	....	....
2001-02	Portland	WHL	72	36	44	80	202	....	....	....	....	....	....	....	....	....	6	3	1	4	16	....	....	....	....
2002-03	**Buffalo**	**NHL**	**1**	**0**	**0**	**0**	**0**	**0**	**0**	**0**	**0**	**0.0**	**0**	**7**	**42.9**	**5:48**	....	....	....	....	....	....	....	....	....
	Rochester	AHL	80	14	39	53	137	....	....	....	....	....	....	....	....	....	3	0	0	0	4	....	....	....	....
2003-04	Rochester	AHL	78	9	22	31	169	....	....	....	....	....	....	....	....	....	16	3	10	13	30	....	....	....	....
2004-05	Rochester	AHL	76	18	25	43	192	....	....	....	....	....	....	....	....	....	9	6	5	11	16	....	....	....	....
2005-06	**Buffalo**	**NHL**	**78**	**9**	**15**	**24**	**65**	**0**	**0**	**0**	**113**	**8.0**	**4**	**829**	**52.2**	**12:08**	**18**	**0**	**4**	**4**	**14**	**0**	**0**	**0**	**12:21**
2006-07	**Buffalo**	**NHL**	**54**	**9**	**13**	**22**	**74**	**3**	**0**	**0**	**75**	**12.0**	**11**	**386**	**52.9**	**13:19**	**7**	**0**	**1**	**1**	**2**	**0**	**0**	**0**	**11:00**
2007-08	**Buffalo**	**NHL**	**82**	**10**	**26**	**36**	**85**	**5**	**0**	**2**	**136**	**7.4**	**–4**	**1165**	**54.9**	**17:10**	....	....	....	....	....	....	....	....	....
2008-09	**Buffalo**	**NHL**	**62**	**12**	**17**	**29**	**108**	**3**	**1**	**1**	**122**	**9.8**	**4**	**858**	**52.7**	**16:06**	....	....	....	....	....	....	....	....	....
2009-10	**Buffalo**	**NHL**	**65**	**12**	**10**	**22**	**82**	**3**	**0**	**1**	**111**	**10.8**	**–7**	**1043**	**57.4**	**15:45**	**6**	**0**	**1**	**1**	**8**	**0**	**0**	**0**	**18:40**
2010-11	**Buffalo**	**NHL**	**81**	**12**	**19**	**31**	**101**	**1**	**0**	**3**	**117**	**10.3**	**7**	**1158**	**59.8**	**15:08**	**7**	**0**	**2**	**2**	**13**	**0**	**0**	**0**	**19:19**
2011-12	**Buffalo**	**NHL**	**56**	**7**	**10**	**17**	**70**	**0**	**0**	**3**	**62**	**11.3**	**–1**	**871**	**56.8**	**15:05**	....	....	....	....	....	....	....	....	....
	Nashville	**NHL**	**14**	**0**	**4**	**4**	**6**	**0**	**0**	**0**	**13**	**0.0**	**0**	**279**	**58.8**	**13:31**	**10**	**1**	**1**	**2**	**5**	**0**	**0**	**0**	**11:36**
2012-13	**Nashville**	**NHL**	**23**	**2**	**3**	**5**	**20**	**0**	**0**	**0**	**35**	**5.7**	**–1**	**449**	**59.7**	**15:13**	....	....	....	....	....	....	....	....	....
2013-14	**Nashville**	**NHL**	**75**	**10**	**11**	**21**	**61**	**0**	**0**	**0**	**74**	**13.5**	**–6**	**1200**	**58.0**	**13:48**	....	....	....	....	....	....	....	....	....
2014-15	**Nashville**	**NHL**	**73**	**4**	**10**	**14**	**60**	**0**	**0**	**1**	**54**	**7.4**	**7**	**1097**	**56.4**	**12:26**	**6**	**0**	**0**	**0**	**22**	**0**	**0**	**0**	**15:56**
	NHL Totals		**664**	**87**	**138**	**225**	**732**	**15**	**1**	**11**	**912**	**9.5**		**9342**	**56.4**	**14:32**	**54**	**1**	**9**	**10**	**64**	**0**	**0**	**0**	**14:02**

Traded to **Nashville** by **Buffalo** with Buffalo's 4th round choice (Juuse Saros) in 2013 Entry Draft for Nashville's 1st round choice (later traded to Calgary – Calgary selected Mark Jankowski) in 2012 Entry Draft, February 27, 2012. • Missed majority of 2012-13 due to recurring upper-body and shoulder injuries.

GAZDIC, Luke

(GAZ-dihk, LEWK) **EDM**

Left wing. Shoots left. 6'3", 240 lbs. Born, Toronto, ON, July 25, 1989. Dallas' 8th choice, 172nd overall, in 2007 Entry Draft.

Season	Club	League	GP	G	A	Pts	PIM	PP	SH	GW	S	S%	+/-	TF	F%	Min	GP	G	A	Pts	PIM	PP	SH	GW	Min
2004-05	North York	GTHL	38	13	16	29	24	....	....	....	....	....	....	....	....	....	....	....	....	....	....	....	....	....	....
2005-06	Wexford Raiders	ON-Jr.A	47	17	16	33	105	....	....	....	....	....	....	....	....	....	....	....	....	....	....	....	....	....	....
2006-07	Erie Otters	OHL	58	5	8	13	136	....	....	....	....	....	....	....	....	....	....	....	....	....	....	....	....	....	....
2007-08	Erie Otters	OHL	67	17	12	29	144	....	....	....	....	....	....	....	....	....	....	....	....	....	....	....	....	....	....
2008-09	Erie Otters	OHL	63	20	10	30	127	....	....	....	....	....	....	....	....	....	5	0	0	0	9	....	....	....	....
	Idaho Steelheads	ECHL	2	1	0	1	14	....	....	....	....	....	....	....	....	....	2	0	0	0	0	....	....	....	....
2009-10	Texas Stars	AHL	49	3	1	4	155	....	....	....	....	....	....	....	....	....	....	....	....	....	....	....	....	....	....
	Idaho Steelheads	ECHL	4	1	1	2	10	....	....	....	....	....	....	....	....	....	....	....	....	....	....	....	....	....	....
2010-11	Texas Stars	AHL	72	9	8	17	110	....	....	....	....	....	....	....	....	....	5	0	0	0	2	....	....	....	....
2011-12	Texas Stars	AHL	76	11	12	23	102	....	....	....	....	....	....	....	....	....	....	....	....	....	....	....	....	....	....
2012-13	Texas Stars	AHL	59	4	7	11	80	....	....	....	....	....	....	....	....	....	8	0	0	0	19	....	....	....	....
2013-14	**Edmonton**	**NHL**	**67**	**2**	**2**	**4**	**127**	**0**	**0**	**0**	**30**	**6.7**	**–8**	**3**	**100.0**	**5:48**	....	....	....	....	....	....	....	....	....
2014-15	**Edmonton**	**NHL**	**40**	**2**	**1**	**3**	**43**	**0**	**0**	**0**	**26**	**7.7**	**–4**	**0**	**0.0**	**7:23**	....	....	....	....	....	....	....	....	....
	Oklahoma City	AHL	5	2	0	2	7	....	....	....	....	....	....	....	....	....	....	....	....	....	....	....	....	....	....
	NHL Totals		**107**	**4**	**3**	**7**	**170**	**0**	**0**	**0**	**56**	**7.1**		**3**	**100.0**	**6:24**	....	....	....	....	....	....	....	....	....

Claimed on waivers by **Edmonton** from **Dallas**, September 29, 2013.

GELINAS, Eric

(ZHEHL-ih-nuh, AIR-ihk) **N.J.**

Defense. Shoots left. 6'4", 215 lbs. Born, Vanier, ON, May 8, 1991. New Jersey's 2nd choice, 54th overall, in 2009 Entry Draft.

Season	Club	League	GP	G	A	Pts	PIM	PP	SH	GW	S	S%	+/-	TF	F%	Min	GP	G	A	Pts	PIM	PP	SH	GW	Min
2006-07	C.C. Lemoyne	QAAA	44	5	14	19	50	....	....	....	....	....	....	....	....	....	10	1	4	5	14	....	....	....	....
2007-08	Lewiston	QMJHL	54	3	16	19	34	....	....	....	....	....	....	....	....	....	5	0	0	0	2	....	....	....	....
2008-09	Lewiston	QMJHL	67	10	29	39	80	....	....	....	....	....	....	....	....	....	4	0	1	1	12	....	....	....	....
2009-10	Lewiston	QMJHL	33	3	16	19	33	....	....	....	....	....	....	....	....	....	....	....	....	....	....	....	....	....	....
	Chicoutimi	QMJHL	28	3	9	12	26	....	....	....	....	....	....	....	....	....	6	1	4	5	6	....	....	....	....
2010-11	Chicoutimi	QMJHL	35	9	15	24	41	....	....	....	....	....	....	....	....	....	....	....	....	....	....	....	....	....	....
	Saint John	QMJHL	27	3	17	20	26	....	....	....	....	....	....	....	....	....	19	5	8	13	25	....	....	....	....

			Regular Season														Playoffs								
Season	Club	League	GP	G	A	Pts	PIM	PP	SH	GW	S	S%	+/-	TF	F%	Min	GP	G	A	Pts	PIM	PP	SH	GW	Min
2011-12	Albany Devils	AHL	75	16	21	37	55	....	....	....	....	....	....	....	....	....	....	....	....	....	....	....	....	....	....
2012-13	Albany Devils	AHL	57	6	16	22	46	....	....	....	....	....	....	....	....	....	....	....	....	....	....	....	....	....	....
	New Jersey	**NHL**	**1**	**0**	**0**	**0**	**0**	**0**	**0**	**0**	**1**	**0.0**	**–1**	**0**	**0.0**	**15:59**	....	....	....	....	....	....	....	....	....
2013-14	**New Jersey**	**NHL**	**60**	**7**	**22**	**29**	**22**	**5**	**0**	**2**	**124**	**5.6**	**–3**	**0**	**0.0**	**16:55**	....	....	....	....	....	....	....	....	....
	Albany Devils	AHL	13	1	4	5	10	....	....	....	....	....	....	....	....	....	4	0	1	1	0	....	....	....	....
2014-15	**New Jersey**	**NHL**	**61**	**6**	**13**	**19**	**42**	**3**	**0**	**2**	**112**	**5.4**	**–2**	**0**	**0.0**	**16:28**	....	....	....	....	....	....	....	....	....
	NHL Totals		**122**	**13**	**35**	**48**	**64**	**8**	**0**	**4**	**237**	**5.5**		**0**	**0.0**	**16:41**	....	....	....	....	....	....	....	....	....

GERBE, Nathan

(GUHR-bee, NAY-thuhn) **CAR**

Center. Shoots left. 5'5", 178 lbs. Born, Oxford, MI, July 24, 1987. Buffalo's 5th choice, 142nd overall, in 2005 Entry Draft.

Season	Club	League	GP	G	A	Pts	PIM	PP	SH	GW	S	S%	+/-	TF	F%	Min	GP	G	A	Pts	PIM	PP	SH	GW	Min
2002-03	River City Lancers	USHL	25	3	3	6	49	....	....	....	....	....	....	....	....	....	7	1	1	2	2	....	....	....	....
2003-04	USNTDP	U-17	32	14	12	26	66	....	....	....	....	....	....	....	....	....	....	....	....	....	....	....	....	....	....
	USNTDP	NAHL	26	11	7	18	87	....	....	....	....	....	....	....	....	....	....	....	....	....	....	....	....	....	....
2004-05	USNTDP	U-18	26	6	11	17	48	....	....	....	....	....	....	....	....	....	....	....	....	....	....	....	....	....	....
	USNTDP	NAHL	12	7	5	12	25	....	....	....	....	....	....	....	....	....	....	....	....	....	....	....	....	....	....
2005-06	Boston College	H-East	39	11	7	18	75	....	....	....	....	....	....	....	....	....	....	....	....	....	....	....	....	....	....
2006-07	Boston College	H-East	41	*25	22	47	76	....	....	....	....	....	....	....	....	....	....	....	....	....	....	....	....	....	....
2007-08	Boston College	H-East	43	*35	33	*68	65	....	....	....	....	....	....	....	....	....	....	....	....	....	....	....	....	....	....
2008-09	**Buffalo**	**NHL**	**10**	**0**	**1**	**1**	**4**	**0**	**0**	**0**	**24**	**0.0**	**3**	**1**	**100.0**	**13:37**	....	....	....	....	....	....	....	....	....
	Portland Pirates	AHL	57	30	26	56	63	....	....	....	....	....	....	....	....	....	5	0	0	0	4	....	....	....	....
2009-10	**Buffalo**	**NHL**	**10**	**2**	**3**	**5**	**4**	**2**	**0**	**1**	**29**	**6.9**	**1**	**3**	**33.3**	**14:39**	**2**	**1**	**1**	**2**	**0**	**0**	**0**	**0**	**14:38**
	Portland Pirates	AHL	44	11	27	38	46	....	....	....	....	....	....	....	....	....	4	1	1	2	4	....	....	....	....
2010-11	**Buffalo**	**NHL**	**64**	**16**	**15**	**31**	**34**	**2**	**0**	**3**	**171**	**9.4**	**11**	**17**	**23.5**	**13:20**	**7**	**2**	**0**	**2**	**18**	**0**	**0**	**0**	**13:20**
2011-12	**Buffalo**	**NHL**	**62**	**6**	**19**	**25**	**32**	**0**	**0**	**2**	**137**	**4.4**	**2**	**19**	**36.8**	**14:12**	....	....	....	....	....	....	....	....	....
2012-13	**Buffalo**	**NHL**	**42**	**5**	**5**	**10**	**14**	**0**	**1**	**0**	**64**	**7.8**	**–3**	**1**	**0.0**	**12:30**	....	....	....	....	....	....	....	....	....
2013-14	**Carolina**	**NHL**	**81**	**16**	**15**	**31**	**36**	**3**	**2**	**1**	**221**	**7.2**	**–6**	**6**	**33.3**	**16:24**	....	....	....	....	....	....	....	....	....
2014-15	**Carolina**	**NHL**	**78**	**10**	**18**	**28**	**34**	**2**	**0**	**2**	**235**	**4.3**	**–14**	**15**	**60.0**	**16:27**	....	....	....	....	....	....	....	....	....
	NHL Totals		**347**	**55**	**76**	**131**	**158**	**9**	**3**	**9**	**881**	**6.2**		**62**	**38.7**	**14:51**	**9**	**3**	**1**	**4**	**18**	**0**	**0**	**0**	**13:38**

Hockey East Second Alll-Star Team (2007) • NCAA Championship All-Tournament Team (2007, 2008) • Hockey East First All-Star Team (2008) • NCAA East First All-American Team (2008) • NCAA Championship Tournament MVP (2008) • AHL All-Rookie Team (2009) • Dudley ''Red'' Garrett Memorial Award (AHL – Rookie of the Year) (2009)

Signed as a free agent by **Carolina**, July 26, 2013.

GERVAIS, Bruno

(ZHUR-vay, BROO-noh)

Defense. Shoots right. 6'1", 200 lbs. Born, Longueuil, QC, October 3, 1984. NY Islanders' 6th choice, 182nd overall, in 2003 Entry Draft.

Season	Club	League	GP	G	A	Pts	PIM	PP	SH	GW	S	S%	+/-	TF	F%	Min	GP	G	A	Pts	PIM	PP	SH	GW	Min
99-2000	Antoine-Girouard	QAAA	6	0	0	0	0	....	....	....	....	....	....	....	....	....	4	0	0	0	0	....	....	....	....
2000-01	Antoine-Girouard	QAAA	40	8	27	35	46	....	....	....	....	....	....	....	....	....	7	4	2	6	8	....	....	....	....
2001-02	Acadie-Bathurst	QMJHL	65	4	12	16	42	....	....	....	....	....	....	....	....	....	16	3	2	5	8	....	....	....	....
2002-03	Acadie-Bathurst	QMJHL	72	22	28	50	73	....	....	....	....	....	....	....	....	....	11	3	5	8	14	....	....	....	....
2003-04	Acadie-Bathurst	QMJHL	23	4	6	10	28	....	....	....	....	....	....	....	....	....	....	....	....	....	....	....	....	....	....
2004-05	Bridgeport	AHL	76	8	22	30	58	....	....	....	....	....	....	....	....	....	....	....	....	....	....	....	....	....	....
2005-06	**NY Islanders**	**NHL**	**27**	**3**	**4**	**7**	**8**	**1**	**0**	**0**	**21**	**14.3**	**–1**	**0**	**0.0**	**16:47**	....	....	....	....	....	....	....	....	....
	Bridgeport	AHL	55	16	25	41	70	....	....	....	....	....	....	....	....	....	7	1	2	3	0	....	....	....	....
2006-07	**NY Islanders**	**NHL**	**51**	**0**	**6**	**6**	**28**	**0**	**0**	**0**	**47**	**0.0**	**–10**	**0**	**0.0**	**15:23**	**5**	**1**	**1**	**2**	**2**	**0**	**0**	**0**	**15:36**
	Bridgeport	AHL	3	0	0	0	6	....	....	....	....	....	....	....	....	....	....	....	....	....	....	....	....	....	....
2007-08	**NY Islanders**	**NHL**	**60**	**0**	**13**	**13**	**34**	**0**	**0**	**0**	**59**	**0.0**	**–5**	**0**	**0.0**	**20:00**	....	....	....	....	....	....	....	....	....
2008-09	**NY Islanders**	**NHL**	**69**	**3**	**16**	**19**	**33**	**0**	**0**	**1**	**82**	**3.7**	**–15**	**1**	**0.0**	**21:36**	....	....	....	....	....	....	....	....	....
2009-10	**NY Islanders**	**NHL**	**71**	**3**	**14**	**17**	**31**	**1**	**0**	**1**	**83**	**3.6**	**–15**	**0**	**0.0**	**20:01**	....	....	....	....	....	....	....	....	....
2010-11	**NY Islanders**	**NHL**	**53**	**0**	**6**	**6**	**30**	**0**	**0**	**0**	**43**	**0.0**	**–14**	**0**	**0.0**	**15:41**	....	....	....	....	....	....	....	....	....
2011-12	**Tampa Bay**	**NHL**	**50**	**6**	**7**	**13**	**8**	**1**	**0**	**0**	**57**	**10.5**	**–4**	**0**	**0.0**	**14:16**	....	....	....	....	....	....	....	....	....
2012-13	Heilbronn	German-2	9	0	3	3	18	....	....	....	....	....	....	....	....	....	....	....	....	....	....	....	....	....	....
	Philadelphia	**NHL**	**37**	**1**	**5**	**6**	**10**	**0**	**0**	**0**	**49**	**2.0**	**–17**	**0**	**0.0**	**17:08**	....	....	....	....	....	....	....	....	....
2013-14	Adirondack	AHL	59	10	16	26	24	....	....	....	....	....	....	....	....	....	....	....	....	....	....	....	....	....	....
2014-15	Lake Erie	AHL	71	3	10	13	26	....	....	....	....	....	....	....	....	....	....	....	....	....	....	....	....	....	....
	NHL Totals		**418**	**16**	**71**	**87**	**182**	**3**	**0**	**2**	**441**	**3.6**		**1**	**0.0**	**18:00**	**5**	**1**	**1**	**2**	**2**	**0**	**0**	**0**	**15:36**

QMJHL Second All-Star Team (2003)

• Missed majority of 2003-04 due to knee injury in Team Canada Jr. training camp, December 12, 2003. Traded to **Tampa Bay** by **NY Islanders** for future considerations, June 25, 2011. Signed as a free agent by **Philadelphia**, July 5, 2012. Signed as a free agent by **Heilbronn** (German-2), November 14, 2012. Signed as a free agent by **Colorado**, July 1, 2014.

GETZLAF, Ryan

(GEHTZ-laf, RIGH-uhn) **ANA**

Center. Shoots right. 6'4", 221 lbs. Born, Regina, SK, May 10, 1985. Anaheim's 1st choice, 19th overall, in 2003 Entry Draft.

Season	Club	League	GP	G	A	Pts	PIM	PP	SH	GW	S	S%	+/-	TF	F%	Min	GP	G	A	Pts	PIM	PP	SH	GW	Min
2000-01	Regina Rangers	SBHL	41	33	41	74	189	....	....	....	....	....	....	....	....	....	....	....	....	....	....	....	....	....	....
	Reg. Pat Cdns.	SMHL	8	4	3	7	8	....	....	....	....	....	....	....	....	....	....	....	....	....	....	....	....	....	....
2001-02	Calgary Hitmen	WHL	63	9	9	18	34	....	....	....	....	....	....	....	....	....	7	2	1	3	4	....	....	....	....
2002-03	Calgary Hitmen	WHL	70	29	39	68	121	....	....	....	....	....	....	....	....	....	5	1	1	2	6	....	....	....	....
2003-04	Calgary Hitmen	WHL	49	28	47	75	97	....	....	....	....	....	....	....	....	....	7	5	1	6	12	....	....	....	....
2004-05	Calgary Hitmen	WHL	51	29	25	54	102	....	....	....	....	....	....	....	....	....	12	4	13	17	18	....	....	....	....
	Cincinnati	AHL	....	....	....	....	....	....	....	....	....	....	....	....	....	....	10	1	4	5	4	....	....	....	....
2005-06	**Anaheim**	**NHL**	**57**	**14**	**25**	**39**	**22**	**10**	**0**	**1**	**116**	**12.1**	**6**	**534**	**44.0**	**12:35**	**16**	**3**	**4**	**7**	**13**	**2**	**0**	**1**	**15:49**
	Portland Pirates	AHL	17	8	25	33	36	....	....	....	....	....	....	....	....	....	1	0	0	0	4	....	....	....	....
2006-07♦	**Anaheim**	**NHL**	**82**	**25**	**33**	**58**	**66**	**11**	**1**	**6**	**203**	**12.3**	**17**	**888**	**49.4**	**15:04**	**21**	**7**	**10**	**17**	**32**	**3**	**1**	**3**	**21:43**
2007-08	**Anaheim**	**NHL**	**77**	**24**	**58**	**82**	**94**	**4**	**1**	**2**	**185**	**13.0**	**32**	**1152**	**47.3**	**19:39**	**6**	**2**	**3**	**5**	**6**	**1**	**0**	**0**	**20:29**
2008-09	**Anaheim**	**NHL**	**81**	**25**	**66**	**91**	**121**	**9**	**0**	**2**	**227**	**11.0**	**5**	**1128**	**50.2**	**20:08**	**13**	**4**	**14**	**18**	**25**	**1**	**0**	**0**	**24:08**
2009-10	**Anaheim**	**NHL**	**66**	**19**	**50**	**69**	**79**	**8**	**0**	**5**	**149**	**12.8**	**4**	**1124**	**47.4**	**21:40**	....	....	....	....	....	....	....	....	....
	Canada	Olympics	7	3	4	7	2	....	....	....	....	....	....	....	....	....	....	....	....	....	....	....	....	....	....
2010-11	**Anaheim**	**NHL**	**67**	**19**	**57**	**76**	**35**	**7**	**0**	**4**	**117**	**16.2**	**14**	**1183**	**45.8**	**21:51**	**6**	**2**	**4**	**6**	**9**	**0**	**0**	**1**	**24:01**
2011-12	**Anaheim**	**NHL**	**82**	**11**	**46**	**57**	**75**	**4**	**0**	**4**	**185**	**5.9**	**–11**	**1354**	**47.2**	**21:36**	....	....	....	....	....	....	....	....	....
2012-13	**Anaheim**	**NHL**	**44**	**15**	**34**	**49**	**41**	**4**	**3**	**3**	**99**	**15.2**	**14**	**739**	**48.0**	**20:12**	**7**	**3**	**3**	**6**	**6**	**1**	**1**	**0**	**21:28**
2013-14	**Anaheim**	**NHL**	**77**	**31**	**56**	**87**	**31**	**5**	**0**	**7**	**204**	**15.2**	**28**	**1411**	**49.0**	**21:17**	**12**	**4**	**11**	**15**	**10**	**1**	**0**	**0**	**21:26**
	Canada	Olympics	6	1	2	3	4	....	....	....	....	....	....	....	....	....	....	....	....	....	....	....	....	....	....
2014-15	**Anaheim**	**NHL**	**77**	**25**	**45**	**70**	**62**	**3**	**0**	**6**	**191**	**13.1**	**15**	**1249**	**50.6**	**20:06**	**16**	**2**	**18**	**20**	**6**	**2**	**0**	**0**	**22:25**
	NHL Totals		**710**	**208**	**470**	**678**	**626**	**65**	**5**	**40**	**1676**	**12.4**		**10762**	**48.1**	**19:29**	**97**	**27**	**67**	**94**	**107**	**11**	**2**	**5**	**21:12**

WHL East First All-Star Team (2004) • WHL East Second All-Star Team (2005) • NHL Second All-Star Team (2014)

Played in NHL All-Star Game (2008, 2009, 2015)

GIBBONS, Brian

(GIH-buhnz, BRIGH-uhn) **NYR**

Center. Shoots left. 5'8", 170 lbs. Born, Braintree, MA, February 26, 1988.

Season	Club	League	GP	G	A	Pts	PIM	PP	SH	GW	S	S%	+/-	TF	F%	Min	GP	G	A	Pts	PIM	PP	SH	GW	Min
2006-07	Salisbury School	High-CT	25	8	19	27	....	....	....	....	....	....	....	....	....	....	....	....	....	....	....	....	....	....	....
2007-08	Boston College	H-East	43	13	22	35	32	....	....	....	....	....	....	....	....	....	....	....	....	....	....	....	....	....	....
2008-09	Boston College	H-East	36	9	19	28	52	....	....	....	....	....	....	....	....	....	....	....	....	....	....	....	....	....	....
2009-10	Boston College	H-East	42	16	34	50	78	....	....	....	....	....	....	....	....	....	....	....	....	....	....	....	....	....	....
2010-11	Boston College	H-East	39	18	*33	51	79	....	....	....	....	....	....	....	....	....	....	....	....	....	....	....	....	....	....
2011-12	Wilkes-Barre	AHL	70	11	19	30	26	....	....	....	....	....	....	....	....	....	9	0	0	0	8	....	....	....	....
2012-13	Wilkes-Barre	AHL	70	8	22	30	34	....	....	....	....	....	....	....	....	....	15	3	5	8	22	....	....	....	....
2013-14	**Pittsburgh**	**NHL**	**41**	**5**	**12**	**17**	**6**	**1**	**0**	**0**	**29**	**17.2**	**5**	**22**	**40.9**	**11:57**	**8**	**2**	**1**	**3**	**2**	**0**	**1**	**0**	**10:37**
	Wilkes-Barre	AHL	28	11	19	30	43	....	....	....	....	....	....	....	....	....	10	1	2	3	18	....	....	....	....
2014-15	**Columbus**	**NHL**	**25**	**0**	**5**	**5**	**8**	**0**	**0**	**0**	**21**	**0.0**	**2**	**9**	**44.4**	**13:49**	....	....	....	....	....	....	....	....	....
	Springfield	AHL	26	3	8	11	14	....	....	....	....	....	....	....	....	....	....	....	....	....	....	....	....	....	....
	NHL Totals		**66**	**5**	**17**	**22**	**14**	**1**	**0**	**0**	**50**	**10.0**		**31**	**41.9**	**12:39**	**8**	**2**	**1**	**3**	**2**	**0**	**1**	**0**	**10:37**

Hockey East First All-Star Team (2010) • Hockey East Second All-Star Team (2011)

Signed as a free agent by **Pittsburgh**, April 4, 2011. Signed as a free agent by **Columbus**,July 4, 2014. Signed as a free agent by **NY Rangers**, July 1, 2015.

GILBERT, Tom

(GIHL-buhrt, TAWM) **MTL**

Defense. Shoots right. 6'2", 204 lbs. Born, Bloomington, MN, January 10, 1983. Colorado's 5th choice, 129th overall, in 2002 Entry Draft.

			Regular Season														Playoffs								
Season	Club	League	GP	G	A	Pts	PIM	PP	SH	GW	S	S%	+/-	TF	F%	Min	GP	G	A	Pts	PIM	PP	SH	GW	Min
99-2000	Bloomington-Jeff.	High-MN	18	7	18	25	....	....	....	....	....	....	....	....	....	....	....	....	....	....	....	....	....	....	....
2000-01	Bloomington-Jeff.	High-MN	23	20	18	38	....	....	....	....	....	....	....	....	....	....	....	....	....	....	....	....	....	....	....
	Chicago Steel	USHL	1	0	0	0	0	....	....	....	....	....	....	....	....	....	....	....	....	....	....	....	....	....	....
2001-02	Chicago Steel	USHL	57	13	15	28	62	....	....	....	....	....	....	....	....	....	4	0	0	0	4	....	....	....	....
2002-03	U. of Wisconsin	WCHA	39	7	13	20	36	....	....	....	....	....	....	....	....	....	....	....	....	....	....	....	....	....	....
2003-04	U. of Wisconsin	WCHA	39	6	15	21	36	....	....	....	....	....	....	....	....	....	....	....	....	....	....	....	....	....	....
2004-05	U. of Wisconsin	WCHA	41	8	9	17	48	....	....	....	....	....	....	....	....	....	....	....	....	....	....	....	....	....	....
2005-06	U. of Wisconsin	WCHA	43	12	19	31	32	....	....	....	....	....	....	....	....	....	....	....	....	....	....	....	....	....	....
2006-07	**Edmonton**	**NHL**	**12**	**1**	**5**	**6**	**0**	**0**	**0**	**0**	**13**	**7.7**	**-1**	**0**	**0.0**	**20:05**	....	....	....	....	....	....	....	....	....
	Wilkes-Barre	AHL	48	4	26	30	32	....	....	....	....	....	....	....	....	....	10	1	7	8	10	....	....	....	....
2007-08	**Edmonton**	**NHL**	**82**	**13**	**20**	**33**	**20**	**3**	**0**	**1**	**98**	**13.3**	**-6**	**0**	**0.0**	**22:12**	....	....	....	....	....	....	....	....	....
2008-09	**Edmonton**	**NHL**	**82**	**5**	**40**	**45**	**26**	**2**	**0**	**1**	**107**	**4.7**	**6**	**0**	**0.0**	**21:58**	....	....	....	....	....	....	....	....	....
2009-10	**Edmonton**	**NHL**	**82**	**5**	**26**	**31**	**16**	**1**	**1**	**0**	**98**	**5.1**	**-10**	**0**	**0.0**	**22:25**	....	....	....	....	....	....	....	....	....
2010-11	**Edmonton**	**NHL**	**79**	**6**	**20**	**26**	**32**	**3**	**0**	**0**	**106**	**5.7**	**-14**	**0**	**0.0**	**24:30**	....	....	....	....	....	....	....	....	....
2011-12	**Edmonton**	**NHL**	**47**	**3**	**14**	**17**	**12**	**2**	**0**	**1**	**50**	**6.0**	**-3**	**0**	**0.0**	**22:49**	....	....	....	....	....	....	....	....	....
	Minnesota	**NHL**	**20**	**0**	**5**	**5**	**8**	**0**	**0**	**0**	**22**	**0.0**	**-5**	**0**	**0.0**	**27:01**	....	....	....	....	....	....	....	....	....
2012-13	**Minnesota**	**NHL**	**43**	**3**	**10**	**13**	**18**	**1**	**0**	**0**	**36**	**8.3**	**-11**	**0**	**0.0**	**19:19**	**5**	**0**	**0**	**0**	**2**	**0**	**0**	**0**	**16:16**
2013-14	**Florida**	**NHL**	**73**	**3**	**25**	**28**	**18**	**2**	**0**	**1**	**93**	**3.2**	**-5**	**0**	**0.0**	**21:20**	....	....	....	....	....	....	....	....	....
2014-15	**Montreal**	**NHL**	**72**	**4**	**8**	**12**	**30**	**0**	**0**	**0**	**70**	**5.7**	**10**	**0**	**0.0**	**19:20**	**12**	**2**	**3**	**5**	**14**	**0**	**0**	**0**	**19:34**
	NHL Totals		**592**	**43**	**173**	**216**	**180**	**14**	**1**	**4**	**693**	**6.2**		**0**	**0.0**	**22:01**	**17**	**2**	**3**	**5**	**16**	**0**	**0**	**0**	**18:36**

WCHA First All-Star Team (2006) • NCAA West Second All-American Team (2006) • NCAA Championship All-Tournament Team (2006) • NHL All-Rookie Team (2008)

Traded to **Edmonton** by **Colorado** for Tommy Salo and Edmonton's 6th round choice (Justin Mercier) in 2005 Entry Draft, March 8, 2004. Traded to **Minnesota** by **Edmonton** for Nick Schultz, February 27, 2012. Signed as a free agent by **Florida**, September 28, 2013. Signed as a free agent by **Montreal**, July 1, 2014.

GILLIES, Colton

(GIHL-eez, KOHL-tuhn)

Left wing. Shoots left. 6'4", 208 lbs. Born, White Rock, BC, February 12, 1989. Minnesota's 1st choice, 16th overall, in 2007 Entry Draft.

			Regular Season														Playoffs								
Season	Club	League	GP	G	A	Pts	PIM	PP	SH	GW	S	S%	+/-	TF	F%	Min	GP	G	A	Pts	PIM	PP	SH	GW	Min
2004-05	North Delta Flyers	PIJHL	44	9	17	26	....	....	....	....	....	....	....	....	....	....	6	2	1	3	....	....	....	....	....
	Surrey Eagles	BCHL	3	1	0	1	0	....	....	....	....	....	....	....	....	....	....	....	....	....	....	....	....	....	....
	Saskatoon Blades	WHL	9	1	1	2	8	....	....	....	....	....	....	....	....	....	2	0	0	0	0	....	....	....	....
2005-06	Saskatoon Blades	WHL	63	6	6	12	57	....	....	....	....	....	....	....	....	....	8	0	0	0	4	....	....	....	....
2006-07	Saskatoon Blades	WHL	65	13	17	30	148	....	....	....	....	....	....	....	....	....	....	....	....	....	....	....	....	....	....
2007-08	Saskatoon Blades	WHL	58	24	23	47	97	....	....	....	....	....	....	....	....	....	....	....	....	....	....	....	....	....	....
	Houston Aeros	AHL	11	1	7	8	4	....	....	....	....	....	....	....	....	....	5	0	0	0	2	....	....	....	....
2008-09	**Minnesota**	**NHL**	**45**	**2**	**5**	**7**	**18**	**0**	**0**	**1**	**22**	**9.1**	**-2**	**2**	**50.0**	**8:14**	....	....	....	....	....	....	....	....	....
2009-10	Houston Aeros	AHL	72	7	13	20	73	....	....	....	....	....	....	....	....	....	....	....	....	....	....	....	....	....	....
2010-11	**Minnesota**	**NHL**	**7**	**1**	**0**	**1**	**2**	**0**	**0**	**0**	**3**	**33.3**	**-2**	**2**	**50.0**	**10:22**	....	....	....	....	....	....	....	....	....
	Houston Aeros	AHL	64	11	15	26	82	....	....	....	....	....	....	....	....	....	24	7	5	12	32	....	....	....	....
2011-12	**Minnesota**	**NHL**	**37**	**0**	**2**	**2**	**10**	**0**	**0**	**0**	**24**	**0.0**	**-5**	**4**	**75.0**	**9:10**	....	....	....	....	....	....	....	....	....
	Columbus	**NHL**	**38**	**2**	**4**	**6**	**25**	**0**	**0**	**0**	**24**	**8.3**	**-4**	**13**	**30.8**	**10:59**	....	....	....	....	....	....	....	....	....
2012-13	**Columbus**	**NHL**	**27**	**1**	**1**	**2**	**17**	**0**	**0**	**0**	**17**	**5.9**	**1**	**2**	**0.0**	**8:18**	....	....	....	....	....	....	....	....	....
2013-14	Rochester	AHL	65	9	14	23	49	....	....	....	....	....	....	....	....	....	5	1	1	2	11	....	....	....	....
2014-15	Bridgeport	AHL	70	5	8	13	72	....	....	....	....	....	....	....	....	....	....	....	....	....	....	....	....	....	....
	NHL Totals		**154**	**6**	**12**	**18**	**72**	**0**	**0**	**1**	**90**	**6.7**		**23**	**39.1**	**9:15**	....	....	....	....	....	....	....	....	....

Claimed on waivers by **Columbus** from **Minnesota**, January 14, 2012. Signed as a free agent by **Rochester** (AHL), October 3, 2013. Signed to a PTO (professional tryout) contract by **Bridgeport** (AHL), October 9, 2014.

GILROY, Matt

(GIHL-roy, MAT)

Defense. Shoots right. 6'1", 199 lbs. Born, North Bellmore, NY, July 30, 1984.

			Regular Season														Playoffs								
Season	Club	League	GP	G	A	Pts	PIM	PP	SH	GW	S	S%	+/-	TF	F%	Min	GP	G	A	Pts	PIM	PP	SH	GW	Min
2000-01	St. Mary's Gaels	High-NY	STATISTICS NOT AVAILABLE																						
2001-02	St. Mary's Gaels	High-NY	STATISTICS NOT AVAILABLE																						
2002-03	St. Mary's Gaels	High-NY	STATISTICS NOT AVAILABLE																						
2003-04	NY Apple Core	EJHL	STATISTICS NOT AVAILABLE																						
2004-05	Walpole Stars	EJHL	55	24	29	53	20	....	....	....	....	....	....	....	....	....	....	....	....	....	....	....	....	....	....
2005-06	Boston University	H-East	36	2	6	8	10	....	....	....	....	....	....	....	....	....	....	....	....	....	....	....	....	....	....
2006-07	Boston University	H-East	39	9	17	26	14	....	....	....	....	....	....	....	....	....	....	....	....	....	....	....	....	....	....
2007-08	Boston University	H-East	40	6	15	21	12	....	....	....	....	....	....	....	....	....	....	....	....	....	....	....	....	....	....
2008-09	Boston University	H-East	45	8	29	37	12	....	....	....	....	....	....	....	....	....	....	....	....	....	....	....	....	....	....
2009-10	**NY Rangers**	**NHL**	**69**	**4**	**11**	**15**	**23**	**0**	**0**	**1**	**82**	**4.9**	**0**	**1**	**100.0**	**16:19**	....	....	....	....	....	....	....	....	....
	Hartford	AHL	5	0	4	4	4	....	....	....	....	....	....	....	....	....	....	....	....	....	....	....	....	....	....
2010-11	**NY Rangers**	**NHL**	**58**	**3**	**8**	**11**	**14**	**0**	**0**	**1**	**75**	**4.0**	**5**	**0**	**0.0**	**14:11**	**5**	**1**	**0**	**1**	**2**	**0**	**0**	**0**	**15:40**
2011-12	**Tampa Bay**	**NHL**	**53**	**2**	**15**	**17**	**16**	**0**	**0**	**0**	**60**	**3.3**	**2**	**0**	**0.0**	**17:36**	....	....	....	....	....	....	....	....	....
	Ottawa	**NHL**	**14**	**1**	**2**	**3**	**2**	**0**	**0**	**0**	**20**	**5.0**	**0**	**0**	**0.0**	**17:08**	**3**	**0**	**0**	**0**	**0**	**0**	**0**	**0**	**12:55**
2012-13	Connecticut	AHL	34	6	9	15	14	....	....	....	....	....	....	....	....	....	....	....	....	....	....	....	....	....	....
	NY Rangers	**NHL**	**15**	**0**	**0**	**0**	**6**	**0**	**0**	**0**	**14**	**0.0**	**-3**	**0**	**0.0**	**9:33**	....	....	....	....	....	....	....	....	....
2013-14	**Florida**	**NHL**	**16**	**1**	**1**	**2**	**6**	**0**	**0**	**0**	**27**	**3.7**	**-2**	**0**	**0.0**	**16:15**	....	....	....	....	....	....	....	....	....
	San Antonio	AHL	42	10	11	21	0	....	....	....	....	....	....	....	....	....	....	....	....	....	....	....	....	....	....
2014-15	Mytischi	KHL	60	9	24	33	14	....	....	....	....	....	....	....	....	....	....	....	....	....	....	....	....	....	....
	NHL Totals		**225**	**11**	**37**	**48**	**67**	**0**	**0**	**2**	**278**	**4.0**		**1**	**100.0**	**15:40**	**8**	**1**	**0**	**1**	**2**	**0**	**0**	**0**	**14:38**

Hockey East First All-Star Team (2008, 2009) • NCAA East First All-American Team (2008, 2009) • Hobey Baker Memorial Award (Top U.S. Collegiate Player) (2009)

Signed as a free agent by **NY Rangers**, April 17, 2009. Signed as a free agent by **Tampa Bay**, July 2, 2011. Traded to **Ottawa** by **Tampa Bay** for Brian Lee, February 27, 2012. Signed as a free agent by **Connecticut** (AHL), October 7, 2012. Signed as a free agent by **Florida**, July 8, 2013. Signed as a free agent by **Atlant Mytischi** (KHL), June 26, 2014. Signed as a free agent by **Spartak Moscow** (KHL), June 4, 2015.

GIONTA, Brian

(jee-OHN-tuh, BRIGH-uhn) **BUF**

Right wing. Shoots right. 5'7", 176 lbs. Born, Rochester, NY, January 18, 1979. New Jersey's 4th choice, 82nd overall, in 1998 Entry Draft.

			Regular Season														Playoffs								
Season	Club	League	GP	G	A	Pts	PIM	PP	SH	GW	S	S%	+/-	TF	F%	Min	GP	G	A	Pts	PIM	PP	SH	GW	Min
1994-95	Rochester	EmJHL	28	*52	37	*89	....	....	....	....	....	....	....	....	....	....	....	....	....	....	....	....	....	....	....
1995-96	Niagara Scenic	ON-Jr.A	51	47	44	91	59	....	....	....	....	....	....	....	....	....	....	....	....	....	....	....	....	....	....
1996-97	Niagara Scenic	ON-Jr.A	50	57	70	127	101	....	....	....	....	....	....	....	....	....	6	6	11	17	21	....	....	....	....
1997-98	Boston College	H-East	40	30	32	62	44	....	....	....	....	....	....	....	....	....	....	....	....	....	....	....	....	....	....
1998-99	Boston College	H-East	39	27	33	60	46	....	....	....	....	....	....	....	....	....	....	....	....	....	....	....	....	....	....
99-2000	Boston College	H-East	42	*33	23	56	66	....	....	....	....	....	....	....	....	....	....	....	....	....	....	....	....	....	....
2000-01	Boston College	H-East	43	*33	21	*54	47	....	....	....	....	....	....	....	....	....	....	....	....	....	....	....	....	....	....
2001-02	**New Jersey**	**NHL**	**33**	**4**	**7**	**11**	**8**	**0**	**0**	**0**	**58**	**6.9**	**10**	**36**	**44.4**	**13:25**	**6**	**2**	**2**	**4**	**0**	**0**	**1**	**2**	**17:08**
	Albany River Rats	AHL	37	9	16	25	18	....	....	....	....	....	....	....	....	....	....	....	....	....	....	....	....	....	....
2002-03 ♦	**New Jersey**	**NHL**	**58**	**12**	**13**	**25**	**23**	**2**	**0**	**3**	**129**	**9.3**	**5**	**14**	**57.1**	**14:48**	**24**	**1**	**8**	**9**	**6**	**0**	**0**	**0**	**14:31**
2003-04	**New Jersey**	**NHL**	**75**	**21**	**8**	**29**	**36**	**0**	**0**	**8**	**174**	**12.1**	**19**	**60**	**58.3**	**14:44**	**5**	**2**	**3**	**5**	**0**	**1**	**0**	**0**	**15:41**
2004-05	Albany River Rats	AHL	15	5	7	12	10	....	....	....	....	....	....	....	....	....	....	....	....	....	....	....	....	....	....
2005-06	**New Jersey**	**NHL**	**82**	**48**	**41**	**89**	**46**	**24**	**1**	**10**	**291**	**16.5**	**18**	**73**	**38.4**	**19:49**	**9**	**3**	**4**	**7**	**2**	**1**	**1**	**2**	**20:06**
	United States	Olympics	6	4	0	4	2	....	....	....	....	....	....	....	....	....	....	....	....	....	....	....	....	....	....
2006-07	**New Jersey**	**NHL**	**62**	**25**	**20**	**45**	**36**	**11**	**0**	**4**	**194**	**12.9**	**-3**	**31**	**38.7**	**18:49**	**11**	**8**	**1**	**9**	**4**	**3**	**0**	**1**	**19:15**
2007-08	**New Jersey**	**NHL**	**82**	**22**	**31**	**53**	**46**	**8**	**1**	**4**	**257**	**8.6**	**1**	**55**	**54.6**	**18:16**	**5**	**1**	**0**	**1**	**2**	**0**	**0**	**0**	**17:52**
2008-09	**New Jersey**	**NHL**	**81**	**20**	**40**	**60**	**32**	**3**	**3**	**1**	**248**	**8.1**	**12**	**132**	**38.6**	**16:58**	**7**	**2**	**3**	**5**	**4**	**0**	**0**	**0**	**17:49**
2009-10	**Montreal**	**NHL**	**61**	**28**	**18**	**46**	**26**	**10**	**0**	**3**	**237**	**11.8**	**3**	**13**	**53.9**	**20:45**	**19**	**9**	**6**	**15**	**14**	**4**	**0**	**1**	**22:11**
2010-11	**Montreal**	**NHL**	**82**	**29**	**17**	**46**	**24**	**7**	**2**	**6**	**298**	**9.7**	**3**	**59**	**32.2**	**19:37**	**7**	**3**	**2**	**5**	**0**	**1**	**0**	**2**	**22:35**
2011-12	**Montreal**	**NHL**	**31**	**8**	**7**	**15**	**16**	**2**	**0**	**0**	**75**	**10.7**	**-7**	**33**	**42.4**	**19:26**	....	....	....	....	....	....	....	....	....
2012-13	**Montreal**	**NHL**	**48**	**14**	**12**	**26**	**8**	**5**	**0**	**3**	**112**	**12.5**	**3**	**42**	**33.3**	**18:07**	**2**	**0**	**1**	**1**	**0**	**0**	**0**	**0**	**17:10**
2013-14	**Montreal**	**NHL**	**81**	**18**	**22**	**40**	**22**	**2**	**0**	**3**	**184**	**9.8**	**1**	**60**	**38.3**	**17:51**	**17**	**1**	**6**	**7**	**2**	**0**	**1**	**0**	**17:49**
2014-15	**Buffalo**	**NHL**	**69**	**13**	**22**	**35**	**18**	**3**	**1**	**2**	**153**	**8.5**	**-13**	**169**	**40.8**	**18:03**	....	....	....	....	....	....	....	....	....
	NHL Totals		**845**	**262**	**258**	**520**	**341**	**77**	**8**	**47**	**2410**	**10.9**		**777**	**42.0**	**17:53**	**112**	**32**	**36**	**68**	**34**	**10**	**3**	**8**	**18:20**

Hockey East Rookie of the Year (1998) • Hockey East Second All-Star Team (1998) • NCAA East Second All-American Team (1998) • Hockey East First All-Star Team (1999, 2000, 2001) • NCAA East First All-American Team (1999, 2000, 2001) • Hockey East Player of the Year (2001)

Signed as a free agent by **Montreal**, July 1, 2009. • Missed majority of 2011-12 due to arm injury vs. St. Louis, January 10, 2012. Signed as a free agent by **Buffalo**, July 1, 2014.

GIONTA, Stephen

(jee-OHN-tuh, STEE-vehn) **N.J.**

Center. Shoots right. 5'7", 185 lbs. Born, Rochester, NY, October 9, 1983.

			Regular Season														Playoffs								
Season	Club	League	GP	G	A	Pts	PIM	PP	SH	GW	S	S%	+/-	TF	F%	Min	GP	G	A	Pts	PIM	PP	SH	GW	Min
99-2000	Rochester	NAHL	41	11	15	26	56	....	....	....	....	....	....	....	....	....	....	....	....	....	....	....	....	....	....
2000-01	USNTDP	USHL	16	1	2	3	12	....	....	....	....	....	....	....	....	....	....	....	....	....	....	....	....	....	....
	USNTDP	NAHL	1	0	0	0	0	....	....	....	....	....	....	....	....	....	....	....	....	....	....	....	....	....	....
2001-02	USNTDP	NAHL	22	2	5	7	33	....	....	....	....	....	....	....	....	....	....	....	....	....	....	....	....	....	....
2002-03	Boston College	H-East	33	5	10	15	36	....	....	....	....	....	....	....	....	....	....	....	....	....	....	....	....	....	....
2003-04	Boston College	H-East	41	9	15	24	36	....	....	....	....	....	....	....	....	....	....	....	....	....	....	....	....	....	....
2004-05	Boston College	H-East	38	8	11	19	44	....	....	....	....	....	....	....	....	....	....	....	....	....	....	....	....	....	....
2005-06	Boston College	H-East	37	11	21	32	66	....	....	....	....	....	....	....	....	....	....	....	....	....	....	....	....	....	....
	Albany River Rats	AHL	3	5	1	6	2	....	....	....	....	....	....	....	....	....	....	....	....	....	....	....	....	....	....
2006-07	Lowell Devils	AHL	67	7	8	15	15	....	....	....	....	....	....	....	....	....	....	....	....	....	....	....	....	....	....
2007-08	Lowell Devils	AHL	63	16	13	29	33	....	....	....	....	....	....	....	....	....	....	....	....	....	....	....	....	....	....
2008-09	Lowell Devils	AHL	52	2	9	11	30	....	....	....	....	....	....	....	....	....	....	....	....	....	....	....	....	....	....
2009-10	Lowell Devils	AHL	68	15	19	34	26	....	....	....	....	....	....	....	....	....	5	0	1	1	0	....	....	....	....
2010-11	**New Jersey**	**NHL**	**12**	**0**	**0**	**0**	**6**	**0**	**0**	**0**	**13**	**0.0**	**–3**	**0**	**0.0**	**9:00**	....	....	....	....	....	....	....	....	....
	Albany Devils	AHL	54	10	20	30	21	....	....	....	....	....	....	....	....	....	....	....	....	....	....	....	....	....	....
2011-12	**New Jersey**	**NHL**	**1**	**1**	**0**	**1**	**0**	**0**	**0**	**1**	**2**	**50.0**	**1**	**8**	**62.5**	**10:37**	**24**	**3**	**4**	**7**	**4**	**0**	**0**	**0**	**9:14**
	Albany Devils	AHL	56	6	10	16	40	....	....	....	....	....	....	....	....	....	....	....	....	....	....	....	....	....	....
2012-13	Albany Devils	AHL	11	2	3	5	4	....	....	....	....	....	....	....	....	....	....	....	....	....	....	....	....	....	....
	New Jersey	**NHL**	**48**	**4**	**10**	**14**	**14**	**0**	**0**	**0**	**58**	**6.9**	**2**	**390**	**35.1**	**13:02**	....	....	....	....	....	....	....	....	....
2013-14	**New Jersey**	**NHL**	**66**	**4**	**7**	**11**	**18**	**0**	**1**	**1**	**89**	**4.5**	**–8**	**581**	**41.0**	**12:28**	....	....	....	....	....	....	....	....	....
2014-15	**New Jersey**	**NHL**	**61**	**5**	**8**	**13**	**12**	**0**	**0**	**1**	**84**	**6.0**	**4**	**394**	**40.4**	**13:11**	....	....	....	....	....	....	....	....	....
	NHL Totals		**188**	**14**	**25**	**39**	**50**	**0**	**1**	**3**	**246**	**5.7**		**1373**	**39.3**	**12:37**	**24**	**3**	**4**	**7**	**4**	**0**	**0**	**0**	**9:14**

Signed to an ATO (amateur tryout) contract by **Albany** (AHL), April 12, 2006. Signed as a free agent by **New Jersey**, August 26, 2010.

GIORDANO, Mark

(jee-ohr-DAN-oh, MAHRK) **CGY**

Defense. Shoots left. 6', 200 lbs. Born, Toronto, ON, October 3, 1983.

Season	Club	League	GP	G	A	Pts	PIM	PP	SH	GW	S	S%	+/-	TF	F%	Min	GP	G	A	Pts	PIM	PP	SH	GW	Min
2002-03	Owen Sound	OHL	68	18	30	48	109	....	....	....	....	....	....	....	....	....	4	1	3	4	2	....	....	....	....
2003-04	Owen Sound	OHL	65	14	35	49	72	....	....	....	....	....	....	....	....	....	7	1	3	4	5	....	....	....	....
2004-05	Lowell	AHL	66	6	10	16	85	....	....	....	....	....	....	....	....	....	11	0	1	1	41	....	....	....	....
2005-06	**Calgary**	**NHL**	**7**	**0**	**1**	**1**	**8**	**0**	**0**	**0**	**5**	**0.0**	**2**	**0**	**0.0**	**12:05**	....	....	....	....	....	....	....	....	....
	Omaha	AHL	73	16	42	58	141	....	....	....	....	....	....	....	....	....	....	....	....	....	....	....	....	....	....
2006-07	**Calgary**	**NHL**	**48**	**7**	**8**	**15**	**36**	**3**	**0**	**2**	**49**	**14.3**	**7**	**0**	**0.0**	**13:27**	**4**	**1**	**0**	**1**	**0**	**1**	**0**	**0**	**12:16**
	Omaha	AHL	5	0	2	2	8	....	....	....	....	....	....	....	....	....	3	0	1	1	2	....	....	....	....
2007-08	Dynamo Moscow	Russia	50	4	8	12	89	....	....	....	....	....	....	....	....	....	9	1	5	6	35	....	....	....	....
2008-09	**Calgary**	**NHL**	**58**	**2**	**17**	**19**	**59**	**2**	**0**	**0**	**82**	**2.4**	**2**	**0**	**0.0**	**16:13**	....	....	....	....	....	....	....	....	....
2009-10	**Calgary**	**NHL**	**82**	**11**	**19**	**30**	**81**	**5**	**0**	**1**	**111**	**9.9**	**17**	**0**	**0.0**	**20:50**	....	....	....	....	....	....	....	....	....
2010-11	**Calgary**	**NHL**	**82**	**8**	**35**	**43**	**67**	**5**	**0**	**1**	**165**	**4.8**	**–8**	**0**	**0.0**	**23:08**	....	....	....	....	....	....	....	....	....
2011-12	**Calgary**	**NHL**	**61**	**9**	**18**	**27**	**75**	**5**	**0**	**0**	**125**	**7.2**	**0**	**0**	**0.0**	**23:01**	....	....	....	....	....	....	....	....	....
2012-13	**Calgary**	**NHL**	**47**	**4**	**11**	**15**	**40**	**1**	**1**	**1**	**58**	**6.9**	**–7**	**0**	**0.0**	**23:10**	....	....	....	....	....	....	....	....	....
2013-14	**Calgary**	**NHL**	**64**	**14**	**33**	**47**	**63**	**7**	**0**	**2**	**180**	**7.8**	**12**	**0**	**0.0**	**25:14**	....	....	....	....	....	....	....	....	....
2014-15	**Calgary**	**NHL**	**61**	**11**	**37**	**48**	**37**	**2**	**1**	**2**	**157**	**7.0**	**13**	**0**	**0.0**	**25:10**	....	....	....	....	....	....	....	....	....
	NHL Totals		**510**	**66**	**179**	**245**	**466**	**30**	**2**	**9**	**932**	**7.1**		**0**	**0.0**	**21:25**	**4**	**1**	**0**	**1**	**0**	**1**	**0**	**0**	**12:16**

Played in NHL All-Star Game (2015)

Signed as a free agent by **Calgary**, July 6, 2004. Signed as a free agent by **Dynamo Moscow** (Russia) August 28, 2007. Signed as a free agent by **Calgary**, July 1, 2008.

GIRARDI, Dan

(jih-RAHR-dee, DAN) **NYR**

Defense. Shoots right. 6'1", 208 lbs. Born, Welland, ON, April 29, 1984.

Season	Club	League	GP	G	A	Pts	PIM	PP	SH	GW	S	S%	+/-	TF	F%	Min	GP	G	A	Pts	PIM	PP	SH	GW	Min
99-2000	Welland Cougars	Minor-ON	47	2	16	18	14	....	....	....	....	....	....	....	....	....	....	....	....	....	....	....	....	....	....
2000-01	Welland Cougars	Minor-ON	11	1	4	5	4	....	....	....	....	....	....	....	....	....	....	....	....	....	....	....	....	....	....
	Couchiching	ON-Jr.A	27	1	11	12	27	....	....	....	....	....	....	....	....	....	....	....	....	....	....	....	....	....	....
	Barrie Colts	OHL	6	0	0	0	0	....	....	....	....	....	....	....	....	....	....	....	....	....	....	....	....	....	....
2001-02	Barrie Colts	OHL	21	0	1	1	0	....	....	....	....	....	....	....	....	....	20	0	0	0	0	....	....	....	....
2002-03	Barrie Colts	OHL	31	3	13	16	24	....	....	....	....	....	....	....	....	....	....	....	....	....	....	....	....	....	....
	Guelph Storm	OHL	36	1	13	14	20	....	....	....	....	....	....	....	....	....	11	0	9	9	14	....	....	....	....
2003-04	Guelph Storm	OHL	68	8	39	47	55	....	....	....	....	....	....	....	....	....	22	2	17	19	10	....	....	....	....
2004-05	Guelph Storm	OHL	38	5	20	25	24	....	....	....	....	....	....	....	....	....	....	....	....	....	....	....	....	....	....
	London Knights	OHL	31	4	10	14	14	....	....	....	....	....	....	....	....	....	18	0	6	6	10	....	....	....	....
2005-06	Hartford	AHL	66	8	31	39	44	....	....	....	....	....	....	....	....	....	13	4	5	9	8	....	....	....	....
	Charlotte	ECHL	7	1	4	5	6	....	....	....	....	....	....	....	....	....	....	....	....	....	....	....	....	....	....
2006-07	**NY Rangers**	**NHL**	**34**	**0**	**6**	**6**	**8**	**0**	**0**	**0**	**33**	**0.0**	**7**	**0**	**0.0**	**15:50**	**10**	**0**	**0**	**0**	**4**	**0**	**0**	**0**	**19:52**
	Hartford	AHL	45	2	22	24	16	....	....	....	....	....	....	....	....	....	....	....	....	....	....	....	....	....	....
2007-08	**NY Rangers**	**NHL**	**82**	**10**	**18**	**28**	**14**	**5**	**0**	**1**	**147**	**6.8**	**0**	**1**	**0.0**	**21:12**	**10**	**0**	**3**	**3**	**6**	**0**	**0**	**0**	**20:42**
2008-09	**NY Rangers**	**NHL**	**82**	**4**	**18**	**22**	**53**	**2**	**0**	**1**	**122**	**3.3**	**–14**	**0**	**0.0**	**21:32**	**7**	**0**	**0**	**0**	**6**	**0**	**0**	**0**	**21:04**
2009-10	**NY Rangers**	**NHL**	**82**	**6**	**18**	**24**	**53**	**1**	**1**	**1**	**108**	**5.6**	**–2**	**0**	**0.0**	**21:29**	....	....	....	....	....	....	....	....	....
2010-11	**NY Rangers**	**NHL**	**80**	**4**	**27**	**31**	**37**	**2**	**0**	**1**	**110**	**3.6**	**7**	**0**	**0.0**	**24:35**	**5**	**0**	**0**	**0**	**0**	**0**	**0**	**0**	**27:01**
2011-12	**NY Rangers**	**NHL**	**82**	**5**	**24**	**29**	**20**	**1**	**0**	**2**	**122**	**4.1**	**13**	**0**	**0.0**	**26:15**	**20**	**3**	**9**	**12**	**2**	**1**	**0**	***3**	**26:52**
2012-13	**NY Rangers**	**NHL**	**46**	**2**	**12**	**14**	**16**	**0**	**0**	**1**	**81**	**2.5**	**–1**	**0**	**0.0**	**25:25**	**12**	**2**	**2**	**4**	**2**	**2**	**0**	**0**	**25:59**
2013-14	**NY Rangers**	**NHL**	**81**	**5**	**19**	**24**	**16**	**1**	**0**	**0**	**100**	**5.0**	**6**	**0**	**0.0**	**23:07**	**25**	**1**	**6**	**7**	**10**	**0**	**0**	**0**	**24:19**
2014-15	**NY Rangers**	**NHL**	**82**	**4**	**16**	**20**	**22**	**1**	**0**	**1**	**111**	**3.6**	**12**	**0**	**0.0**	**22:42**	**19**	**0**	**4**	**4**	**4**	**0**	**0**	**0**	**21:38**
	NHL Totals		**651**	**40**	**158**	**198**	**239**	**13**	**1**	**8**	**934**	**4.3**		**1**	**0.0**	**22:46**	**108**	**6**	**24**	**30**	**34**	**3**	**0**	**3**	**23:40**

AHL All-Rookie Team (2006)

Played in NHL All-Star Game (2012)

Signed as a free agent by **NY Rangers**, July 1, 2006.

GIRGENSONS, Zemgus

(GEER-gehn-suhnz, ZEHM-guhz) **BUF**

Center. Shoots left. 6'1", 200 lbs. Born, Riga, Latvia, January 5, 1994. Buffalo's 2nd choice, 14th overall, in 2012 Entry Draft.

Season	Club	League	GP	G	A	Pts	PIM	PP	SH	GW	S	S%	+/-	TF	F%	Min	GP	G	A	Pts	PIM	PP	SH	GW	Min
2009-10	Green Mountain	EmJHL	19	17	12	29	6	....	....	....	....	....	....	....	....	....	....	....	....	....	....	....	....	....	....
	Green Mountain	EJHL	23	11	17	28	13	....	....	....	....	....	....	....	....	....	2	0	2	2	0	....	....	....	....
2010-11	Dubuque	USHL	51	21	28	49	46	....	....	....	....	....	....	....	....	....	11	3	5	8	8	....	....	....	....
2011-12	Dubuque	USHL	49	24	31	55	69	....	....	....	....	....	....	....	....	....	2	2	2	4	0	....	....	....	....
2012-13	Rochester	AHL	61	6	11	17	28	....	....	....	....	....	....	....	....	....	3	3	0	3	0	....	....	....	....
2013-14	**Buffalo**	**NHL**	**70**	**8**	**14**	**22**	**14**	**0**	**1**	**1**	**115**	**7.0**	**–6**	**240**	**41.7**	**15:19**	....	....	....	....	....	....	....	....	....
	Latvia	Olympics	5	1	1	2	2	....	....	....	....	....	....	....	....	....	....	....	....	....	....	....	....	....	....
2014-15	**Buffalo**	**NHL**	**61**	**15**	**15**	**30**	**25**	**1**	**3**	**1**	**115**	**13.0**	**–16**	**1000**	**44.0**	**19:05**	....	....	....	....	....	....	....	....	....
	NHL Totals		**131**	**23**	**29**	**52**	**39**	**1**	**4**	**2**	**230**	**10.0**		**1240**	**43.5**	**17:04**	....	....	....	....	....	....	....	....	....

USHL First All-Star Team (2012)

Played in NHL All-Star Game (2015)

GIROUX, Claude

(zhih-ROO, KLOHD) **PHI**

Right wing. Shoots right. 5'11", 185 lbs. Born, Hearst, ON, January 12, 1988. Philadelphia's 1st choice, 22nd overall, in 2006 Entry Draft.

Season	Club	League	GP	G	A	Pts	PIM	PP	SH	GW	S	S%	+/-	TF	F%	Min	GP	G	A	Pts	PIM	PP	SH	GW	Min
2004-05	Cumberland	ON-Jr.A	48	13	27	40	30	....	....	....	....	....	....	....	....	....	....	....	....	....	....	....	....	....	....
2005-06	Gatineau	QMJHL	69	39	64	103	64	....	....	....	....	....	....	....	....	....	17	5	15	20	24	....	....	....	....
2006-07	Gatineau	QMJHL	63	48	64	112	49	....	....	....	....	....	....	....	....	....	5	2	5	7	2	....	....	....	....
	Philadelphia	AHL	5	1	1	2	6	....	....	....	....	....	....	....	....	....	....	....	....	....	....	....	....	....	....
2007-08	**Philadelphia**	**NHL**	**2**	**0**	**0**	**0**	**0**	**0**	**0**	**0**	**2**	**0.0**	**–2**	**0**	**0.0**	**9:35**	....	....	....	....	....	....	....	....	....
	Gatineau	QMJHL	55	38	68	106	37	....	....	....	....	....	....	....	....	....	19	17	*34	*51	6	....	....	....	....
2008-09	**Philadelphia**	**NHL**	**42**	**9**	**18**	**27**	**14**	**2**	**0**	**0**	**67**	**13.4**	**10**	**309**	**47.3**	**15:10**	**6**	**2**	**3**	**5**	**6**	**0**	**0**	**0**	**15:57**
	Philadelphia	AHL	33	17	17	34	22	....	....	....	....	....	....	....	....	....	....	....	....	....	....	....	....	....	....
2009-10	**Philadelphia**	**NHL**	**82**	**16**	**31**	**47**	**23**	**8**	**0**	**2**	**145**	**11.0**	**–9**	**600**	**49.5**	**16:37**	**23**	**10**	**11**	**21**	**4**	**3**	**0**	**2**	**18:45**
2010-11	**Philadelphia**	**NHL**	**82**	**25**	**51**	**76**	**47**	**8**	**3**	**5**	**169**	**14.8**	**20**	**1095**	**50.1**	**19:24**	**11**	**1**	**11**	**12**	**8**	**0**	**0**	**0**	**21:57**
2011-12	**Philadelphia**	**NHL**	**77**	**28**	**65**	**93**	**29**	**6**	**0**	**5**	**242**	**11.6**	**6**	**1543**	**53.7**	**21:33**	**10**	***8**	**9**	**17**	**13**	**3**	***2**	**0**	**22:43**

			Regular Season														Playoffs								
Season	Club	League	GP	G	A	Pts	PIM	PP	SH	GW	S	S%	+/-	TF	F%	Min	GP	G	A	Pts	PIM	PP	SH	GW	Min
2012-13	Eisbaren Berlin	Germany	9	4	15	19	6	....	....	....	....	....	....	....	....	....	....	....	....	....	....	....	....	....	....
	Philadelphia	**NHL**	**48**	**13**	**35**	**48**	**22**	**6**	**1**	**2**	**137**	**9.5**	**–7**	**1182**	**54.5**	**21:10**	....	....	....	....	....	....	....	....	....
2013-14	**Philadelphia**	**NHL**	**82**	**28**	**58**	**86**	**46**	**7**	**0**	**7**	**223**	**12.6**	**7**	**1760**	**52.9**	**20:26**	**7**	**2**	**4**	**6**	**2**	**0**	**0**	**0**	**19:24**
2014-15	**Philadelphia**	**NHL**	**81**	**25**	**48**	**73**	**36**	**14**	**0**	**4**	**279**	**9.0**	**–3**	**1878**	**56.6**	**20:34**	....	....	....	....	....	....	....	....	....
	NHL Totals		**496**	**144**	**306**	**450**	**217**	**51**	**4**	**25**	**1264**	**11.4**		**8367**	**53.3**	**19:24**	**57**	**23**	**38**	**61**	**33**	**6**	**2**	**2**	**19:51**

QMJHL All-Rookie Team (2006) • QMJHL First All-Star Team (2008) • Canadian Major Junior First All-Star Team (2008)
Played in NHL All-Star Game (2011, 2012, 2015)
Signed as a free agent by **Berlin** (Germany), October 4, 2012.

GLASS, Tanner

(GLAS, TA-nuhr) **NYR**

Left wing. Shoots left. 6'1", 210 lbs. Born, Regina, SK, November 29, 1983. Florida's 13th choice, 265th overall, in 2003 Entry Draft.

Season	Club	League	GP	G	A	Pts	PIM	PP	SH	GW	S	S%	+/-	TF	F%	Min	GP	G	A	Pts	PIM	PP	SH	GW	Min
2000-01	Yorkton Mallers	SMHL	39	31	29	60	120	....	....	....	....	....	....	....	....	....	4	3	1	4	10	....	....	....	....
2001-02	Penticton	BCHL	57	11	28	39	171	....	....	....	....	....	....	....	....	....	....	....	....	....	....	....	....	....	....
2002-03	Penticton	BCHL	32	15	25	40	108	....	....	....	....	....	....	....	....	....	....	....	....	....	....	....	....	....	....
	Nanaimo Clippers	BCHL	18	8	14	22	46	....	....	....	....	....	....	....	....	....	....	....	....	....	....	....	....	....	....
2003-04	Dartmouth	ECAC	26	4	7	11	18	....	....	....	....	....	....	....	....	....	....	....	....	....	....	....	....	....	....
2004-05	Dartmouth	ECAC	33	7	8	15	32	....	....	....	....	....	....	....	....	....	....	....	....	....	....	....	....	....	....
2005-06	Dartmouth	ECAC	33	12	16	28	56	....	....	....	....	....	....	....	....	....	....	....	....	....	....	....	....	....	....
2006-07	Dartmouth	ECAC	32	8	20	28	92	....	....	....	....	....	....	....	....	....	....	....	....	....	....	....	....	....	....
	Rochester	AHL	4	0	1	1	5	....	....	....	....	....	....	....	....	....	....	....	....	....	....	....	....	....	....
2007-08	**Florida**	**NHL**	**41**	**1**	**1**	**2**	**39**	**0**	**0**	**0**	**11**	**9.1**	**–5**	**2**	**0.0**	**4:25**	....	....	....	....	....	....	....	....	....
	Rochester	AHL	43	6	5	11	84	....	....	....	....	....	....	....	....	....	....	....	....	....	....	....	....	....	....
2008-09	**Florida**	**NHL**	**3**	**0**	**0**	**0**	**7**	**0**	**0**	**0**	**1**	**0.0**	**0**	**1**	**100.0**	**6:45**	....	....	....	....	....	....	....	....	....
	Rochester	AHL	44	4	9	13	100	....	....	....	....	....	....	....	....	....	....	....	....	....	....	....	....	....	....
2009-10	**Vancouver**	**NHL**	**67**	**4**	**7**	**11**	**115**	**0**	**0**	**0**	**52**	**7.7**	**5**	**18**	**16.7**	**10:28**	**4**	**0**	**0**	**0**	**0**	**0**	**0**	**0**	**3:08**
2010-11	**Vancouver**	**NHL**	**73**	**3**	**7**	**10**	**72**	**0**	**0**	**1**	**45**	**6.7**	**–5**	**62**	**40.3**	**8:56**	**20**	**0**	**0**	**0**	**18**	**0**	**0**	**0**	**7:28**
2011-12	**Winnipeg**	**NHL**	**78**	**5**	**11**	**16**	**73**	**0**	**0**	**1**	**86**	**5.8**	**–12**	**73**	**39.7**	**13:25**	....	....	....	....	....	....	....	....	....
2012-13	B. Bystrica	Slovakia	6	0	1	1	75	....	....	....	....	....	....	....	....	....	....	....	....	....	....	....	....	....	....
	Pittsburgh	**NHL**	**48**	**1**	**1**	**2**	**62**	**1**	**0**	**0**	**38**	**2.6**	**–11**	**51**	**43.1**	**10:04**	**5**	**1**	**0**	**1**	**4**	**0**	**0**	**0**	**8:13**
2013-14	**Pittsburgh**	**NHL**	**67**	**4**	**9**	**13**	**90**	**0**	**0**	**0**	**56**	**7.1**	**–8**	**19**	**47.4**	**11:47**	**8**	**0**	**0**	**0**	**4**	**0**	**0**	**0**	**9:50**
2014-15	**NY Rangers**	**NHL**	**66**	**1**	**5**	**6**	**98**	**0**	**0**	**0**	**53**	**1.9**	**–12**	**21**	**33.3**	**10:15**	**19**	**0**	**1**	**1**	**31**	**0**	**0**	**0**	**9:21**
	NHL Totals		**443**	**19**	**41**	**60**	**556**	**1**	**0**	**2**	**342**	**5.6**		**247**	**38.9**	**10:16**	**56**	**1**	**1**	**2**	**57**	**0**	**0**	**0**	**8:12**

Signed as a free aget by **Vancouver**, July 22, 2009. Signed as a free agent by **Winnipeg**, July 2, 2011. Signed as a free agent by **Pittsburgh**, July 1, 2012. Signed as a free agent by **Banska Bystrica** (Slovakia), December 4, 2012. Signed as a free agent by **NY Rangers**, July 1, 2014.

GLEASON, Tim

(GLEE-suhn, TIHM)

Defense. Shoots left. 6', 217 lbs. Born, Clawson, MI, January 29, 1983. Ottawa's 2nd choice, 23rd overall, in 2001 Entry Draft.

Season	Club	League	GP	G	A	Pts	PIM	PP	SH	GW	S	S%	+/-	TF	F%	Min	GP	G	A	Pts	PIM	PP	SH	GW	Min
1998-99	Leamington Flyers	ON-Jr.B	52	5	26	31	76	....	....	....	....	....	....	....	....	....	....	....	....	....	....	....	....	....	....
99-2000	Windsor Spitfires	OHL	55	5	13	18	101	....	....	....	....	....	....	....	....	....	12	2	4	6	14	....	....	....	....
2000-01	Windsor Spitfires	OHL	47	8	28	36	124	....	....	....	....	....	....	....	....	....	9	1	2	3	23	....	....	....	....
2001-02	Windsor Spitfires	OHL	67	17	42	59	109	....	....	....	....	....	....	....	....	....	16	7	13	20	40	....	....	....	....
2002-03	Windsor Spitfires	OHL	45	7	31	38	75	....	....	....	....	....	....	....	....	....	7	5	2	7	17	....	....	....	....
2003-04	**Los Angeles**	**NHL**	**47**	**0**	**7**	**7**	**21**	**0**	**0**	**0**	**45**	**0.0**	**1**	**0**	**0.0**	**14:59**	....	....	....	....	....	....	....	....	....
	Manchester	AHL	22	0	8	8	19	....	....	....	....	....	....	....	....	....	6	0	1	1	4	....	....	....	....
2004-05	Manchester	AHL	67	10	14	24	112	....	....	....	....	....	....	....	....	....	5	0	0	0	4	....	....	....	....
2005-06	**Los Angeles**	**NHL**	**78**	**2**	**19**	**21**	**77**	**0**	**0**	**0**	**72**	**2.8**	**0**	**0**	**0.0**	**17:41**	....	....	....	....	....	....	....	....	....
2006-07	**Carolina**	**NHL**	**57**	**2**	**4**	**6**	**57**	**1**	**0**	**0**	**72**	**2.8**	**–10**	**0**	**0.0**	**18:53**	....	....	....	....	....	....	....	....	....
2007-08	**Carolina**	**NHL**	**80**	**3**	**16**	**19**	**84**	**0**	**0**	**0**	**98**	**3.1**	**5**	**0**	**0.0**	**18:38**	....	....	....	....	....	....	....	....	....
2008-09	**Carolina**	**NHL**	**70**	**0**	**12**	**12**	**68**	**0**	**0**	**0**	**61**	**0.0**	**3**	**0**	**0.0**	**20:40**	**18**	**1**	**4**	**5**	**32**	**0**	**0**	**1**	**20:29**
2009-10	**Carolina**	**NHL**	**61**	**5**	**14**	**19**	**78**	**1**	**1**	**0**	**76**	**6.6**	**0**	**0**	**0.0**	**21:12**	....	....	....	....	....	....	....	....	....
	United States	Olympics	6	0	0	0	0	....	....	....	....	....	....	....	....	....	....	....	....	....	....	....	....	....	....
2010-11	**Carolina**	**NHL**	**82**	**2**	**14**	**16**	**85**	**0**	**0**	**0**	**84**	**2.4**	**–11**	**0**	**0.0**	**20:58**	....	....	....	....	....	....	....	....	....
2011-12	**Carolina**	**NHL**	**82**	**1**	**17**	**18**	**71**	**0**	**0**	**0**	**65**	**1.5**	**12**	**0**	**0.0**	**20:43**	....	....	....	....	....	....	....	....	....
2012-13	**Carolina**	**NHL**	**42**	**0**	**9**	**9**	**40**	**0**	**0**	**0**	**36**	**0.0**	**–3**	**0**	**0.0**	**19:34**	....	....	....	....	....	....	....	....	....
2013-14	**Carolina**	**NHL**	**17**	**0**	**1**	**1**	**10**	**0**	**0**	**0**	**15**	**0.0**	**–7**	**0**	**0.0**	**15:54**	....	....	....	....	....	....	....	....	....
	Toronto	**NHL**	**39**	**1**	**4**	**5**	**55**	**0**	**0**	**0**	**28**	**3.6**	**–14**	**0**	**0.0**	**16:57**	....	....	....	....	....	....	....	....	....
2014-15	**Carolina**	**NHL**	**55**	**1**	**6**	**7**	**44**	**0**	**0**	**0**	**44**	**2.3**	**–18**	**0**	**0.0**	**16:39**	....	....	....	....	....	....	....	....	....
	Washington	**NHL**	**17**	**0**	**2**	**2**	**11**	**0**	**0**	**0**	**10**	**0.0**	**5**	**0**	**0.0**	**15:17**	**14**	**0**	**1**	**1**	**5**	**0**	**0**	**0**	**13:08**
	NHL Totals		**727**	**17**	**125**	**142**	**701**	**2**	**1**	**0**	**706**	**2.4**		**0**	**0.0**	**18:54**	**32**	**1**	**5**	**6**	**37**	**0**	**0**	**1**	**17:16**

Traded to **Los Angeles** by **Ottawa** for Bryan Smolinski, March 11, 2003. Traded to **Carolina** by **Los Angeles** with Eric Belanger for Oleg Tverdovsky and Jack Johnson, September 29, 2006. Traded to **Toronto** by **Carolina** for John-Michael Liles and Dennis Robertson, January 1, 2014. Signed as a free agent by **Carolina**, July 3, 2014. Traded to **Washington** by **Carolina** for Jack Hillen and Arizona's 4th round choice (previously acquired, Carolina selected Callum Booth) in 2015 Entry Draft, February 28, 2015.

GLENCROSS, Curtis

(GLEHN-kraws, KUHR-tihs)

Center. Shoots left. 6'1", 197 lbs. Born, Kindersley, SK, December 28, 1982.

Season	Club	League	GP	G	A	Pts	PIM	PP	SH	GW	S	S%	+/-	TF	F%	Min	GP	G	A	Pts	PIM	PP	SH	GW	Min
2001-02	Brooks Bandits	AJHL	....	42	26	68	....	....	....	....	....	....	....	....	....	....	....	....	....	....	....	....	....	....	....
2002-03	Alaska Anchorage	WCHA	35	11	12	23	79	....	....	....	....	....	....	....	....	....	....	....	....	....	....	....	....	....	....
2003-04	Alaska Anchorage	WCHA	37	21	13	34	79	....	....	....	....	....	....	....	....	....	....	....	....	....	....	....	....	....	....
	Cincinnati	AHL	7	2	1	3	6	....	....	....	....	....	....	....	....	....	9	1	6	7	10	....	....	....	....
2004-05	Cincinnati	AHL	51	6	3	9	63	....	....	....	....	....	....	....	....	....	12	2	0	2	10	....	....	....	....
2005-06	Portland Pirates	AHL	41	15	10	25	85	....	....	....	....	....	....	....	....	....	19	4	6	10	37	....	....	....	....
2006-07	**Anaheim**	**NHL**	**2**	**1**	**0**	**1**	**2**	**0**	**0**	**0**	**5**	**20.0**	**–1**	**0**	**0.0**	**10:43**	....	....	....	....	....	....	....	....	....
	Portland Pirates	AHL	31	6	10	16	74	....	....	....	....	....	....	....	....	....	....	....	....	....	....	....	....	....	....
	Columbus	**NHL**	**7**	**0**	**0**	**0**	**0**	**0**	**0**	**0**	**3**	**0.0**	**–4**	**2**	**0.0**	**8:43**	....	....	....	....	....	....	....	....	....
	Syracuse Crunch	AHL	29	19	16	35	53	....	....	....	....	....	....	....	....	....	....	....	....	....	....	....	....	....	....
2007-08	**Columbus**	**NHL**	**36**	**6**	**6**	**12**	**25**	**1**	**0**	**1**	**63**	**9.5**	**3**	**14**	**57.1**	**12:07**	....	....	....	....	....	....	....	....	....
	Edmonton	**NHL**	**26**	**9**	**4**	**13**	**28**	**0**	**0**	**0**	**41**	**22.0**	**5**	**11**	**45.5**	**10:19**	....	....	....	....	....	....	....	....	....
2008-09	**Calgary**	**NHL**	**74**	**13**	**27**	**40**	**42**	**1**	**1**	**3**	**152**	**8.6**	**14**	**62**	**48.4**	**14:41**	**6**	**0**	**3**	**3**	**12**	**0**	**0**	**0**	**15:00**
2009-10	**Calgary**	**NHL**	**67**	**15**	**18**	**33**	**58**	**2**	**3**	**2**	**117**	**12.8**	**11**	**24**	**37.5**	**15:43**	....	....	....	....	....	....	....	....	....
2010-11	**Calgary**	**NHL**	**79**	**24**	**19**	**43**	**59**	**3**	**2**	**4**	**149**	**16.1**	**6**	**141**	**40.4**	**16:15**	....	....	....	....	....	....	....	....	....
2011-12	**Calgary**	**NHL**	**67**	**26**	**22**	**48**	**62**	**8**	**1**	**3**	**110**	**23.6**	**–13**	**82**	**50.0**	**18:01**	....	....	....	....	....	....	....	....	....
2012-13	**Calgary**	**NHL**	**40**	**15**	**11**	**26**	**18**	**3**	**1**	**3**	**92**	**16.3**	**–8**	**46**	**43.5**	**18:14**	....	....	....	....	....	....	....	....	....
2013-14	**Calgary**	**NHL**	**38**	**12**	**12**	**24**	**12**	**3**	**0**	**2**	**77**	**15.6**	**–11**	**41**	**34.2**	**17:37**	....	....	....	....	....	....	....	....	....
2014-15	**Calgary**	**NHL**	**53**	**9**	**19**	**28**	**39**	**2**	**0**	**1**	**87**	**10.3**	**3**	**15**	**40.0**	**16:41**	....	....	....	....	....	....	....	....	....
	Washington	**NHL**	**18**	**4**	**3**	**7**	**6**	**2**	**0**	**0**	**21**	**19.0**	**–1**	**3**	**66.7**	**12:36**	**10**	**1**	**0**	**1**	**2**	**0**	**0**	**0**	**10:25**
	NHL Totals		**507**	**134**	**141**	**275**	**351**	**25**	**8**	**19**	**917**	**14.6**		**441**	**43.5**	**15:38**	**16**	**1**	**3**	**4**	**14**	**0**	**0**	**0**	**12:08**

Signed as a free agent by **Anaheim**, March 25, 2004. Traded to **Columbus** by **Anaheim** with Zenon Konopka and Anaheim's 7th round choice (Trent Vogelhuber) in 2007 Entry Draft for Mark Hartigan, Joe Motzko and Columbus' 4th round choice (Sebastian Stefaniszin) in 2007 Entry Draft, January 26, 2007. Traded to **Edmonton** by **Columbus** for Dick Tarnstrom, February 1, 2008. Signed as a free agent by **Calgary**, July 2, 2008. • Missed majority of 2013-14 due to knee (November 5, 2013 at Minnesota) and ankle (December 21, 2013 at Pittsburgh) injuries. Traded to **Washington** by **Calgary** for Washington's 2nd (later traded to Boston – Boston selected Jeremy Lauzon) and 3rd (later traded to Arizona – Arizona selected Jens Looke) round choices in 2015 Entry Draft, March 1, 2015.

GLENDENING, Luke

(glehn-DEHN-ihng , LEWK) **DET**

Right wing. Shoots right. 5'11", 195 lbs. Born, Grand Rapids, MI, April 28, 1989.

Season	Club	League	GP	G	A	Pts	PIM	PP	SH	GW	S	S%	+/-	TF	F%	Min	GP	G	A	Pts	PIM	PP	SH	GW	Min
2008-09	U. of Michigan	CCHA	35	6	4	10	33	....	....	....	....	....	....	....	....	....	....	....	....	....	....	....	....	....	....
2009-10	U. of Michigan	CCHA	45	7	14	21	39	....	....	....	....	....	....	....	....	....	....	....	....	....	....	....	....	....	....
2010-11	U. of Michigan	CCHA	44	8	10	18	26	....	....	....	....	....	....	....	....	....	....	....	....	....	....	....	....	....	....
2011-12	U. of Michigan	CCHA	41	10	11	21	24	....	....	....	....	....	....	....	....	....	....	....	....	....	....	....	....	....	....
	Providence Bruins	AHL	3	0	0	0	0	....	....	....	....	....	....	....	....	....	....	....	....	....	....	....	....	....	....
2012-13	Toledo Walleye	ECHL	27	14	7	21	27	....	....	....	....	....	....	....	....	....	....	....	....	....	....	....	....	....	....
	Grand Rapids	AHL	51	8	18	26	50	....	....	....	....	....	....	....	....	....	24	6	10	16	30	....	....	....	....

			Regular Season														Playoffs								
Season	Club	League	GP	G	A	Pts	PIM	PP	SH	GW	S	S%	+/-	TF	F%	Min	GP	G	A	Pts	PIM	PP	SH	GW	Min
2013-14	Detroit	NHL	56	1	6	7	22	0	0	0	54	1.9	-8	678	48.5	13:55	5	1	0	1	0	0	0	0	14:11
	Grand Rapids	AHL	18	5	7	12	18	....	....	....	....	....	....	....	....	....	....	....	....	....	....	....	....	....	....
2014-15	Detroit	NHL	82	12	6	18	34	1	0	2	104	11.5	5	962	51.9	14:43	7	2	1	3	8	0	1	1	15:31
	NHL Totals		138	13	12	25	56	1	0	2	158	8.2		1640	50.5	14:24	12	3	1	4	8	0	1	1	14:58

Signed as a free agent by **Detroit**, July 5, 2013.

GLENNIE, Scott

(GLEH-nee, SKAWT)

Right wing. Shoots right. 6'1", 200 lbs. Born, Winnipeg, MB, February 22, 1991. Dallas' 1st choice, 8th overall, in 2009 Entry Draft.

Season	Club	League	GP	G	A	Pts	PIM	PP	SH	GW	S	S%	+/-	TF	F%	Min	GP	G	A	Pts	PIM	PP	SH	GW	Min
2006-07	Winnipeg Wild	MMHL	38	31	37	68	64	....	....	....	....	....	....	....	....	....	7	3	3	6	16	....	....	....	....
2007-08	Brandon	WHL	61	26	32	58	50	....	....	....	....	....	....	....	....	....	6	1	0	1	7	....	....	....	....
2008-09	Brandon	WHL	55	28	42	70	25	....	....	....	....	....	....	....	....	....	12	3	15	18	11	....	....	....	....
2009-10	Brandon	WHL	66	32	57	89	50	....	....	....	....	....	....	....	....	....	15	3	7	10	14	....	....	....	....
2010-11	Brandon	WHL	70	35	56	91	58	....	....	....	....	....	....	....	....	....	6	3	7	10	6	....	....	....	....
	Texas Stars	AHL	4	0	0	0	2	....	....	....	....	....	....	....	....	....	6	1	0	1	2	....	....	....	....
2011-12	Dallas	NHL	1	0	0	0	2	0	0	0	0	0.0	0	0	0.0	9:35	....	....	....	....	....	....	....	....	....
	Texas Stars	AHL	70	12	25	37	26	....	....	....	....	....	....	....	....	....	....	....	....	....	....	....	....	....	....
2012-13	Texas Stars	AHL	37	5	9	14	10	....	....	....	....	....	....	....	....	....	9	0	0	0	8	....	....	....	....
2013-14	Texas Stars	AHL	50	15	13	28	14	....	....	....	....	....	....	....	....	....	20	6	4	10	18	....	....	....	....
2014-15	Texas Stars	AHL	69	14	25	39	47	....	....	....	....	....	....	....	....	....	3	1	0	1	0	....	....	....	....
	NHL Totals		1	0	0	0	2	0	0	0	0	0.0		0	0.0	9:35	....	....	....	....	....	....	....	....	....

GOC, Marcel

(GAWCH, MAHR-sehl) **ST.L.**

Center. Shoots left. 6'1", 197 lbs. Born, Calw, West Germany, August 24, 1983. San Jose's 1st choice, 20th overall, in 2001 Entry Draft.

Season	Club	League	GP	G	A	Pts	PIM	PP	SH	GW	S	S%	+/-	TF	F%	Min	GP	G	A	Pts	PIM	PP	SH	GW	Min
1998-99	Schwenningen Jr.	Ger-Jr.	12	23	10	33	12	....	....	....	....	....	....	....	....	....	....	....	....	....	....	....	....	....	....
99-2000	Schwenningen	Germany	51	0	3	3	4	....	....	....	....	....	....	....	....	....	11	1	1	2	2	....	....	....	....
2000-01	Schwenningen	Germany	58	13	28	41	12	....	....	....	....	....	....	....	....	....	....	....	....	....	....	....	....	....	....
	Germany	Oly-Q	3	0	0	0	0	....	....	....	....	....	....	....	....	....	....	....	....	....	....	....	....	....	....
2001-02	Schwenningen	Germany	45	8	9	17	24	....	....	....	....	....	....	....	....	....	....	....	....	....	....	....	....	....	....
	Adler Mannheim	Germany	8	0	2	2	0	....	....	....	....	....	....	....	....	....	....	....	....	....	....	....	....	....	....
2002-03	Adler Mannheim	Germany	36	6	14	20	16	....	....	....	....	....	....	....	....	....	8	1	2	3	0	....	....	....	....
2003-04	Cleveland Barons	AHL	78	16	21	37	24	....	....	....	....	....	....	....	....	....	....	....	....	....	....	....	....	....	....
	San Jose	NHL	....	....	....	....	....	....	....	....	....	....	....	....	....	....	5	1	1	2	0	0	0	1	7:08
2004-05	Cleveland Barons	AHL	76	16	34	50	28	....	....	....	....	....	....	....	....	....	....	....	....	....	....	....	....	....	....
2005-06	San Jose	NHL	81	8	14	22	22	2	0	2	96	8.3	-7	808	47.9	11:42	11	0	3	3	0	0	0	0	12:38
	Germany	Olympics	5	1	0	1	0	....	....	....	....	....	....	....	....	....	....	....	....	....	....	....	....	....	....
2006-07	San Jose	NHL	78	5	8	13	24	0	1	0	96	5.2	-2	659	55.2	12:01	11	2	1	3	4	0	0	0	14:49
2007-08	San Jose	NHL	51	5	3	8	12	0	0	0	87	5.7	-15	208	51.4	10:41	4	0	0	0	2	0	0	0	8:03
2008-09	San Jose	NHL	55	2	9	11	18	0	0	1	104	1.9	-6	570	58.3	13:55	6	0	0	0	2	0	0	0	10:33
2009-10	Nashville	NHL	73	12	18	30	14	0	0	1	118	10.2	10	912	52.1	14:41	6	0	1	1	2	0	0	0	16:07
	Germany	Olympics	4	2	1	3	0	....	....	....	....	....	....	....	....	....	....	....	....	....	....	....	....	....	....
2010-11	Nashville	NHL	51	9	15	24	6	0	1	2	111	8.1	10	693	49.9	16:02	....	....	....	....	....	....	....	....	....
2011-12	Florida	NHL	57	11	16	27	10	3	0	1	97	11.3	5	978	51.6	17:37	7	2	3	5	0	1	0	1	18:11
2012-13	Adler Mannheim	Germany	18	4	15	19	8	....	....	....	....	....	....	....	....	....	....	....	....	....	....	....	....	....	....
	Florida	NHL	42	9	10	19	8	4	0	1	92	9.8	-6	786	52.2	18:16	....	....	....	....	....	....	....	....	....
2013-14	Florida	NHL	62	11	12	23	31	0	0	1	105	10.5	-7	1090	52.8	16:59	....	....	....	....	....	....	....	....	....
	Pittsburgh	NHL	12	0	2	2	4	0	0	0	12	0.0	0	143	57.3	12:55	9	0	1	1	4	0	0	0	11:35
2014-15	Pittsburgh	NHL	43	2	4	6	4	0	0	0	43	4.7	-2	437	54.0	12:27	....	....	....	....	....	....	....	....	....
	St. Louis	NHL	31	1	2	3	4	0	0	0	34	2.9	-1	248	54.8	10:38	4	0	0	0	0	0	0	0	8:26
	NHL Totals		636	75	113	188	157	9	2	9	995	7.5		7532	52.5	14:02	63	5	10	15	14	1	0	2	12:37

Signed as a free agent by **Nashville**, August 21, 2009. Signed as a free agent by **Florida**, July 1, 2011. Signed as a free agent by **Mannheim** (Germany). September 21, 2012. Traded to **Pittsburgh** by **Florida** for Pittsburgh's 5th round choice (Miguel Fidler) in 2014 Entry Draft and Pittsburgh's 3rd round choice (Samuel Montembault) in 2015 Entry Draft, March 5, 2014. Traded to **St. Louis** by **Pittsburgh** for Maxim Lapierre, January 27, 2015.

GOLIGOSKI, Alex

(goh-lih-GAW-skee, AL-ehx) **DAL**

Defense. Shoots left. 5'11", 190 lbs. Born, Grand Rapids, MN, July 30, 1985. Pittsburgh's 3rd choice, 61st overall, in 2004 Entry Draft.

Season	Club	League	GP	G	A	Pts	PIM	PP	SH	GW	S	S%	+/-	TF	F%	Min	GP	G	A	Pts	PIM	PP	SH	GW	Min
2002-03	Grand Rapids	High-MN	28	14	20	34	22	....	....	....	....	....	....	....	....	....	....	....	....	....	....	....	....	....	....
2003-04	Grand Rapids	High-MN	26	25	31	56	16	....	....	....	....	....	....	....	....	....	....	....	....	....	....	....	....	....	....
	Sioux Falls	USHL	10	0	2	2	6	....	....	....	....	....	....	....	....	....	....	....	....	....	....	....	....	....	....
2004-05	U. of Minnesota	WCHA	33	5	15	20	44	....	....	....	....	....	....	....	....	....	....	....	....	....	....	....	....	....	....
2005-06	U. of Minnesota	WCHA	41	11	28	39	63	....	....	....	....	....	....	....	....	....	....	....	....	....	....	....	....	....	....
2006-07	U. of Minnesota	WCHA	44	9	30	39	51	....	....	....	....	....	....	....	....	....	....	....	....	....	....	....	....	....	....
2007-08	Pittsburgh	NHL	3	0	2	2	2	0	0	0	2	0.0	2	0	0.0	13:56	....	....	....	....	....	....	....	....	....
	Wilkes-Barre	AHL	70	10	28	38	53	....	....	....	....	....	....	....	....	....	23	4	24	28	18	....	....	....	....
2008-09 ♦	Pittsburgh	NHL	45	6	14	20	16	4	0	0	61	9.8	5	0	0.0	18:18	2	0	1	1	0	0	0	0	10:22
	Wilkes-Barre	AHL	26	2	16	18	16	....	....	....	....	....	....	....	....	....	9	1	5	6	10	....	....	....	....
2009-10	Pittsburgh	NHL	69	8	29	37	22	2	0	0	98	8.2	7	0	0.0	21:25	13	2	7	9	2	1	0	0	20:34
2010-11	Pittsburgh	NHL	60	9	22	31	28	4	0	4	101	8.9	20	0	0.0	20:46	....	....	....	....	....	....	....	....	....
	Dallas	NHL	23	5	10	15	12	3	0	0	61	8.2	0	0	0.0	26:04	....	....	....	....	....	....	....	....	....
2011-12	Dallas	NHL	71	9	21	30	16	2	0	1	140	6.4	0	0	0.0	22:46	....	....	....	....	....	....	....	....	....
2012-13	Dallas	NHL	47	3	24	27	18	0	0	0	80	3.8	4	0	0.0	22:23	....	....	....	....	....	....	....	....	....
2013-14	Dallas	NHL	81	6	36	42	28	3	0	0	141	4.3	9	1	0.0	24:19	6	1	3	4	8	0	0	0	28:30
2014-15	Dallas	NHL	81	4	32	36	24	0	0	0	122	3.3	0	0	0.0	23:49	....	....	....	....	....	....	....	....	....
	NHL Totals		480	50	190	240	166	18	0	5	806	6.2		1	0.0	22:25	21	3	11	14	10	1	0	0	21:52

WCHA All-Rookie Team (2005) • WCHA Second All-Star Team (2006) • WCHA First All-Star Team (2007) • NCAA West First All-American Team (2007) • AHL All-Rookie Team (2008)

Traded to **Dallas** by **Pittsburgh** for James Neal and Matt Niskanen, February 21, 2011.

GOLOUBEF, Cody

(GOH-luh-behf, KOH-dee) **CBJ**

Defense. Shoots right. 6'1", 190 lbs. Born, Mississauga, ON, November 30, 1989. Columbus' 2nd choice, 37th overall, in 2008 Entry Draft.

Season	Club	League	GP	G	A	Pts	PIM	PP	SH	GW	S	S%	+/-	TF	F%	Min	GP	G	A	Pts	PIM	PP	SH	GW	Min
2003-04	Tor. Marlboros	GTHL	89	10	27	37	44	....	....	....	....	....	....	....	....	....	....	....	....	....	....	....	....	....	....
2004-05	Tor. Marlboros	GTHL	69	14	47	61	56	....	....	....	....	....	....	....	....	....	....	....	....	....	....	....	....	....	....
2005-06	Milton Icehawks	ON-Jr.A	42	9	29	38	38	....	....	....	....	....	....	....	....	....	7	1	3	4	10	....	....	....	....
2006-07	Oakville Blades	ON-Jr.A	9	5	5	10	46	....	....	....	....	....	....	....	....	....	10	2	10	12	18	....	....	....	....
2007-08	U. of Wisconsin	WCHA	40	4	6	10	36	....	....	....	....	....	....	....	....	....	....	....	....	....	....	....	....	....	....
2008-09	U. of Wisconsin	WCHA	36	5	8	13	38	....	....	....	....	....	....	....	....	....	....	....	....	....	....	....	....	....	....
2009-10	U. of Wisconsin	WCHA	42	3	11	14	64	....	....	....	....	....	....	....	....	....	....	....	....	....	....	....	....	....	....
2010-11	Springfield	AHL	50	5	12	17	42	....	....	....	....	....	....	....	....	....	....	....	....	....	....	....	....	....	....
2011-12	Columbus	NHL	1	0	0	0	0	0	0	0	0	0.0	1	0	0.0	6:00	....	....	....	....	....	....	....	....	....
	Springfield	AHL	48	1	11	12	43	....	....	....	....	....	....	....	....	....	....	....	....	....	....	....	....	....	....
2012-13	Springfield	AHL	38	5	8	13	49	....	....	....	....	....	....	....	....	....	7	0	2	2	10	....	....	....	....
	Columbus	NHL	11	1	0	1	0	0	0	1	14	7.1	-3	0	0.0	14:49	....	....	....	....	....	....	....	....	....
2013-14	Columbus	NHL	5	0	0	0	2	0	0	0	4	0.0	0	0	0.0	9:49	....	....	....	....	....	....	....	....	....
	Springfield	AHL	62	7	21	28	98	....	....	....	....	....	....	....	....	....	5	0	0	0	6	....	....	....	....
2014-15	Columbus	NHL	36	0	9	9	19	0	0	0	23	0.0	12	0	0.0	15:34	....	....	....	....	....	....	....	....	....
	Springfield	AHL	3	0	0	0	0	....	....	....	....	....	....	....	....	....	....	....	....	....	....	....	....	....	....
	NHL Totals		53	1	9	10	21	0	0	1	41	2.4		0	0.0	14:41	....	....	....	....	....	....	....	....	....

• Missed majority of 2006-07 due to various injuries. • Missed majority of 2014-15 due to hand injury in practice, September 27, 2014 and as a healthy reserve.

GOMEZ, Scott (GOH-mehz, SKAWT)

Center. Shoots left. 5'11", 202 lbs. Born, Anchorage, AK, December 23, 1979. New Jersey's 2nd choice, 27th overall, in 1998 Entry Draft.

Season	Club	League	GP	G	A	Pts	PIM	PP	SH	GW	S	S%	+/-	TF	F%	Min	GP	G	A	Pts	PIM	PP	SH	GW	Min
			Regular Season														Playoffs								
1994-95	East High	High-AK	28	30	48	78	....	....	....	....	....	....	....	....	....	....	....	....	....	....	....	....	....	....	....
1995-96	East High	High-AK	27	*56	49	*101	....	....	....	....	....	....	....	....	....	....	....	....	....	....	....	....	....	....	....
	Anchorage	AAHL	40	*70	*67	*137	44	....	....	....	....	....	....	....	....	....	....	....	....	....	....	....	....	....	....
1996-97	South Surrey	BCHL	56	48	76	124	94	....	....	....	....	....	....	....	....	....	21	18	23	41	57	....	....	....	....
1997-98	Tri-City	WHL	45	12	37	49	57	....	....	....	....	....	....	....	....	....	....	....	....	....	....	....	....	....	....
1998-99	Tri-City	WHL	58	30	*78	108	55	....	....	....	....	....	....	....	....	....	10	6	13	19	31	....	....	....	....
99-2000 ♦	**New Jersey**	**NHL**	**82**	**19**	**51**	**70**	**78**	**7**	**0**	**1**	**204**	**9.3**	**14**	**341**	**44.6**	**16:21**	**23**	**4**	**6**	**10**	**4**	**1**	**0**	**2**	**14:08**
2000-01	**New Jersey**	**NHL**	**76**	**14**	**49**	**63**	**46**	**2**	**0**	**4**	**155**	**9.0**	**-1**	**1010**	**44.6**	**15:46**	**25**	**5**	**9**	**14**	**24**	**0**	**0**	**0**	**16:06**
2001-02	**New Jersey**	**NHL**	**76**	**10**	**38**	**48**	**36**	**1**	**0**	**1**	**156**	**6.4**	**-4**	**628**	**48.7**	**16:46**	....	....	....	....	....	....	....	....	....
2002-03 ♦	**New Jersey**	**NHL**	**80**	**13**	**42**	**55**	**48**	**2**	**0**	**4**	**205**	**6.3**	**17**	**864**	**47.5**	**16:01**	**24**	**3**	**9**	**12**	**2**	**0**	**0**	**0**	**13:45**
2003-04	**New Jersey**	**NHL**	**80**	**14**	***56**	**70**	**70**	**3**	**0**	**1**	**189**	**7.4**	**18**	**1129**	**46.2**	**16:00**	**5**	**0**	**6**	**6**	**0**	**0**	**0**	**0**	**17:14**
2004-05	Alaska Aces	ECHL	61	13	*73	*86	69	....	....	....	....	....	....	....	....	....	4	1	3	4	4	....	....	....	....
2005-06	**New Jersey**	**NHL**	**82**	**33**	**51**	**84**	**42**	**9**	**0**	**5**	**244**	**13.5**	**8**	**1434**	**52.6**	**18:47**	**9**	**5**	**4**	**9**	**6**	**4**	**0**	**1**	**18:14**
	United States	Olympics	6	1	4	5	10	....	....	....	....	....	....	....	....	....	....	....	....	....	....	....	....	....	....
2006-07	**New Jersey**	**NHL**	**72**	**13**	**47**	**60**	**42**	**4**	**0**	**1**	**248**	**5.2**	**7**	**1204**	**52.2**	**18:56**	**11**	**4**	**10**	**14**	**14**	**0**	**0**	**1**	**20:01**
2007-08	**NY Rangers**	**NHL**	**81**	**16**	**54**	**70**	**36**	**7**	**0**	**3**	**242**	**6.6**	**3**	**1165**	**52.5**	**19:54**	**10**	**4**	**7**	**11**	**8**	**1**	**0**	**0**	**20:53**
2008-09	**NY Rangers**	**NHL**	**77**	**16**	**42**	**58**	**60**	**3**	**1**	**7**	**271**	**5.9**	**-2**	**1312**	**52.4**	**21:04**	**7**	**2**	**3**	**5**	**4**	**1**	**0**	**0**	**19:58**
2009-10	**Montreal**	**NHL**	**78**	**12**	**47**	**59**	**60**	**5**	**0**	**1**	**180**	**6.7**	**1**	**1375**	**50.8**	**19:56**	**19**	**2**	**12**	**14**	**25**	**0**	**0**	**0**	**21:10**
2010-11	**Montreal**	**NHL**	**80**	**7**	**31**	**38**	**48**	**3**	**0**	**2**	**157**	**4.5**	**-15**	**1197**	**48.0**	**18:34**	**7**	**0**	**4**	**4**	**2**	**0**	**0**	**0**	**19:42**
2011-12	**Montreal**	**NHL**	**38**	**2**	**9**	**11**	**14**	**2**	**0**	**1**	**59**	**3.4**	**-9**	**333**	**49.6**	**14:08**	....	....	....	....	....	....	....	....	....
2012-13	Alaska Aces	ECHL	11	6	7	13	12	....	....	....	....	....	....	....	....	....	....	....	....	....	....	....	....	....	....
	San Jose	**NHL**	**39**	**2**	**13**	**15**	**22**	**0**	**0**	**0**	**58**	**3.4**	**-10**	**324**	**55.9**	**13:32**	**9**	**0**	**2**	**2**	**6**	**0**	**0**	**0**	**15:01**
2013-14	**Florida**	**NHL**	**46**	**2**	**10**	**12**	**24**	**0**	**0**	**0**	**56**	**3.6**	**-11**	**515**	**46.4**	**13:08**	....	....	....	....	....	....	....	....	....
2014-15	**New Jersey**	**NHL**	**58**	**7**	**27**	**34**	**23**	**0**	**0**	**1**	**70**	**10.0**	**-10**	**788**	**46.6**	**16:31**	....	....	....	....	....	....	....	....	....
	NHL Totals		**1045**	**180**	**567**	**747**	**649**	**48**	**1**	**32**	**2494**	**7.2**		**13619**	**49.5**	**17:24**	**149**	**29**	**72**	**101**	**95**	**7**	**0**	**4**	**17:08**

WHL West First All-Star Team (1999) • NHL All-Rookie Team (2000) • Calder Memorial Trophy (2000) • ECHL First All-Star Team (2005) • ECHL Leading Scorer (2005) • ECHL MVP (2005)

Played in NHL All-Star Game (2000, 2008)

Signed as a free agent by **Alaska** (ECHL), October 25, 2004. Signed as a free agent by **NY Rangers**, July 1, 2007. Traded to **Montreal** by **NY Rangers** with Tom Pyatt and Michael Busto for Chris Higgins, Ryan McDonagh and Pavel Valentenko, June 30, 2009. • Missed majority of 2011-12 due to upper body, groin and head injuries. Signed to a PTO (professional tryout) contract by **Alaska** (ECHL), September 28, 2012. Signed as a free agent by **San Jose**, January 23, 2013. Signed as a free agent by **Florida**, July 31, 2013. Signed as a free agent by **New Jersey**, December 1, 2014.

GONCHAR, Sergei (gohn-CHAR, SAIR-gay)

Defense. Shoots left. 6'2", 210 lbs. Born, Chelyabinsk, USSR, April 13, 1974. Washington's 1st choice, 14th overall, in 1992 Entry Draft.

Season	Club	League	GP	G	A	Pts	PIM	PP	SH	GW	S	S%	+/-	TF	F%	Min	GP	G	A	Pts	PIM	PP	SH	GW	Min
1990-91	Mechel	USSR-2	2	0	0	0	0	....	....	....	....	....	....	....	....	....	....	....	....	....	....	....	....	....	....
	Chelyabinsk	USSR-Q	11	0	0	0	4	....	....	....	....	....	....	....	....	....	....	....	....	....	....	....	....	....	....
1991-92	Chelyabinsk	CIS	31	1	0	1	6	....	....	....	....	....	....	....	....	....	....	....	....	....	....	....	....	....	....
1992-93	Dynamo Moscow	CIS	31	1	3	4	70	....	....	....	....	....	....	....	....	....	10	0	0	0	12	....	....	....	....
1993-94	Dynamo Moscow	CIS	44	4	5	9	36	....	....	....	....	....	....	....	....	....	....	....	....	....	....	....	....	....	....
	Portland Pirates	AHL	....	....	....	....	....	....	....	....	....	....	....	....	....	....	2	0	0	0	0	....	....	....	....
1994-95	Portland Pirates	AHL	61	10	32	42	67	....	....	....	....	....	....	....	....	....	....	....	....	....	....	....	....	....	....
	Washington	**NHL**	**31**	**2**	**5**	**7**	**22**	**0**	**0**	**0**	**38**	**5.3**	**4**	....	....	....	**7**	**2**	**2**	**4**	**2**	**0**	**0**	**1**	....
1995-96	**Washington**	**NHL**	**78**	**15**	**26**	**41**	**60**	**4**	**0**	**4**	**139**	**10.8**	**25**	....	....	....	**6**	**2**	**4**	**6**	**4**	**1**	**0**	**0**	....
1996-97	**Washington**	**NHL**	**57**	**13**	**17**	**30**	**36**	**3**	**0**	**3**	**129**	**10.1**	**-11**	....	....	....	....	....	....	....	....	....	....	....	....
1997-98	Lada Togliatti	Russia	7	3	2	5	4	....	....	....	....	....	....	....	....	....	....	....	....	....	....	....	....	....	....
	Washington	**NHL**	**72**	**5**	**16**	**21**	**66**	**2**	**0**	**0**	**134**	**3.7**	**2**	....	....	....	**21**	**7**	**4**	**11**	**30**	**3**	**1**	**2**	....
	Russia	Olympics	6	0	2	2	0	....	....	....	....	....	....	....	....	....	....	....	....	....	....	....	....	....	....
1998-99	**Washington**	**NHL**	**53**	**21**	**10**	**31**	**57**	**13**	**1**	**3**	**180**	**11.7**	**1**	**0**	**0.0**	**23:55**	....	....	....	....	....	....	....	....	....
99-2000	**Washington**	**NHL**	**73**	**18**	**36**	**54**	**52**	**5**	**0**	**3**	**181**	**9.9**	**26**	**0**	**0.0**	**21:46**	**5**	**1**	**0**	**1**	**6**	**0**	**0**	**0**	**19:58**
2000-01	**Washington**	**NHL**	**76**	**19**	**38**	**57**	**70**	**8**	**0**	**2**	**241**	**7.9**	**12**	**1**	**100.0**	**22:26**	**6**	**1**	**3**	**4**	**2**	**1**	**0**	**0**	**19:45**
2001-02	**Washington**	**NHL**	**76**	**26**	**33**	**59**	**58**	**7**	**0**	**2**	**216**	**12.0**	**-1**	**1**	**100.0**	**23:51**	....	....	....	....	....	....	....	....	....
	Russia	Olympics	6	0	0	0	2	....	....	....	....	....	....	....	....	....	....	....	....	....	....	....	....	....	....
2002-03	**Washington**	**NHL**	**82**	**18**	**49**	**67**	**52**	**7**	**0**	**2**	**224**	**8.0**	**13**	**0**	**0.0**	**26:35**	**6**	**0**	**5**	**5**	**4**	**0**	**0**	**0**	**29:00**
2003-04	**Washington**	**NHL**	**56**	**7**	**42**	**49**	**44**	**4**	**0**	**0**	**127**	**5.5**	**-20**	**0**	**0.0**	**27:57**	....	....	....	....	....	....	....	....	....
	Boston	**NHL**	**15**	**4**	**5**	**9**	**12**	**2**	**0**	**0**	**34**	**11.8**	**6**	**0**	**0.0**	**25:32**	**7**	**1**	**4**	**5**	**4**	**1**	**0**	**1**	**27:51**
2004-05	Magnitogorsk	Russia	40	2	17	19	54	....	....	....	....	....	....	....	....	....	4	1	1	2	6	....	....	....	....
2005-06	**Pittsburgh**	**NHL**	**75**	**12**	**46**	**58**	**100**	**8**	**0**	**2**	**192**	**6.3**	**-13**	**0**	**0.0**	**24:40**	....	....	....	....	....	....	....	....	....
	Russia	Olympics	8	0	2	2	8	....	....	....	....	....	....	....	....	....	....	....	....	....	....	....	....	....	....
2006-07	**Pittsburgh**	**NHL**	**82**	**13**	**54**	**67**	**72**	**10**	**1**	**3**	**191**	**6.8**	**-5**	**0**	**0.0**	**26:34**	**5**	**1**	**3**	**4**	**2**	**1**	**0**	**0**	**26:53**
2007-08	**Pittsburgh**	**NHL**	**78**	**12**	**53**	**65**	**66**	**8**	**0**	**2**	**173**	**6.9**	**13**	**0**	**0.0**	**25:55**	**20**	**1**	**13**	**14**	**8**	**1**	**0**	**0**	**25:13**
2008-09 ♦	**Pittsburgh**	**NHL**	**25**	**6**	**13**	**19**	**26**	**5**	**0**	**1**	**71**	**8.5**	**6**	**0**	**0.0**	**25:11**	**22**	**3**	**11**	**14**	**12**	**2**	**0**	**2**	**23:03**
2009-10	**Pittsburgh**	**NHL**	**62**	**11**	**39**	**50**	**49**	**6**	**0**	**3**	**138**	**8.0**	**-4**	**0**	**0.0**	**24:24**	**13**	**2**	**10**	**12**	**4**	**1**	**0**	**1**	**26:27**
	Russia	Olympics	4	1	0	1	2	....	....	....	....	....	....	....	....	....	....	....	....	....	....	....	....	....	....
2010-11	**Ottawa**	**NHL**	**67**	**7**	**20**	**27**	**20**	**5**	**0**	**0**	**107**	**6.5**	**-15**	**0**	**0.0**	**23:12**	....	....	....	....	....	....	....	....	....
2011-12	**Ottawa**	**NHL**	**74**	**5**	**32**	**37**	**55**	**2**	**0**	**1**	**131**	**3.8**	**-4**	**0**	**0.0**	**22:15**	**7**	**1**	**3**	**4**	**6**	**1**	**0**	**0**	**24:35**
2012-13	Magnitogorsk	KHL	37	3	26	29	40	....	....	....	....	....	....	....	....	....	....	....	....	....	....	....	....	....	....
	Ottawa	**NHL**	**45**	**3**	**24**	**27**	**26**	**2**	**0**	**3**	**85**	**3.5**	**4**	**0**	**0.0**	**24:00**	**10**	**0**	**6**	**6**	**14**	**0**	**0**	**0**	**23:55**
2013-14	**Dallas**	**NHL**	**76**	**2**	**20**	**22**	**20**	**1**	**0**	**1**	**89**	**2.2**	**-12**	**0**	**0.0**	**17:37**	**6**	**0**	**0**	**0**	**4**	**0**	**0**	**0**	**13:24**
2014-15	**Dallas**	**NHL**	**3**	**0**	**1**	**1**	**2**	**0**	**0**	**0**	**1**	**0.0**	**-1**	**0**	**0.0**	**13:02**	....	....	....	....	....	....	....	....	....
	Montreal	**NHL**	**45**	**1**	**12**	**13**	**16**	**0**	**0**	**0**	**45**	**2.2**	**7**	**1**	**100.0**	**18:00**	....	....	....	....	....	....	....	....	....
	NHL Totals		**1301**	**220**	**591**	**811**	**981**	**102**	**2**	**35**	**2866**	**7.7**		**3**	**100.0**	**23:40**	**141**	**22**	**68**	**90**	**102**	**12**	**1**	**7**	**24:00**

NHL Second All-Star Team (2002, 2003)

Played in NHL All-Star Game (2001, 2002, 2003, 2008)

Traded to **Boston** by **Washington** for Shaonne Morrisonn and Boston's 1st (Jeff Schultz) and 2nd (Michail Yunkov) round choices in 2004 Entry Draft, March 3, 2004. Signed as a free agent by **Magnitogorsk** (Russia), September 21, 2004. Signed as a free agent by **Pittsburgh**, August 3, 2005. Signed as a free agent by **Ottawa**, July 1, 2010. Signed as a free agent by **Magnitogorsk** (KHL), September 16, 2012. Traded to **Dallas** by **Ottawa** for Dallas' 6th round choice (Chris LeBlanc) in 2013 Entry Draft, June 7, 2013. Traded to **Montreal** by **Dallas** for Travis Moen, November 11, 2014.

GOODROW, Barclay (GUD-roh, BAHR-klee) S.J.

Right wing. Shoots left. 6'2", 215 lbs. Born, Aurora, ON, February 26, 1993.

Season	Club	League	GP	G	A	Pts	PIM	PP	SH	GW	S	S%	+/-	TF	F%	Min	GP	G	A	Pts	PIM	PP	SH	GW	Min
2008-09	York Simcoe	Minor-ON	71	67	47	114	65	....	....	....	....	....	....	....	....	....	....	....	....	....	....	....	....	....	....
	Villanova Knights	ON-Jr.A	2	2	1	3	2	....	....	....	....	....	....	....	....	....	....	....	....	....	....	....	....	....	....
2009-10	Brampton	OHL	63	6	13	19	34	....	....	....	....	....	....	....	....	....	11	1	3	4	2	....	....	....	....
2010-11	Brampton	OHL	65	24	15	39	36	....	....	....	....	....	....	....	....	....	4	0	0	0	2	....	....	....	....
2011-12	Brampton	OHL	60	26	26	52	58	....	....	....	....	....	....	....	....	....	8	1	1	2	6	....	....	....	....
2012-13	Brampton	OHL	62	38	14	52	59	....	....	....	....	....	....	....	....	....	5	2	3	5	6	....	....	....	....
2013-14	North Bay	OHL	63	33	34	67	64	....	....	....	....	....	....	....	....	....	22	*14	10	24	23	....	....	....	....
2014-15	**San Jose**	**NHL**	**60**	**4**	**8**	**12**	**35**	**0**	**0**	**2**	**68**	**5.9**	**-1**	**23**	**52.2**	**11:04**	....	....	....	....	....	....	....	....	....
	Worcester Sharks	AHL	7	2	4	6	11	....	....	....	....	....	....	....	....	....	4	0	1	1	4	....	....	....	....
	NHL Totals		**60**	**4**	**8**	**12**	**35**	**0**	**0**	**2**	**68**	**5.9**		**23**	**52.2**	**11:04**	....	....	....	....	....	....	....	....	....

Signed as a free agent by **San Jose**, March 6, 2014.

GORDON, Boyd (GOHR-duhn, BOID) ARI

Center. Shoots right. 6', 202 lbs. Born, Unity, SK, October 19, 1983. Washington's 3rd choice, 17th overall, in 2002 Entry Draft.

Season	Club	League	GP	G	A	Pts	PIM	PP	SH	GW	S	S%	+/-	TF	F%	Min	GP	G	A	Pts	PIM	PP	SH	GW	Min
1998-99	Regina Rangers	SMBHL	60	70	102	172	53	....	....	....	....	....	....	....	....	....	....	....	....	....	....	....	....	....	....
99-2000	Red Deer Rebels	WHL	66	10	26	36	24	....	....	....	....	....	....	....	....	....	4	0	1	1	16	....	....	....	....
2000-01	Red Deer Rebels	WHL	72	12	27	39	39	....	....	....	....	....	....	....	....	....	22	3	6	9	2	....	....	....	....
2001-02	Red Deer Rebels	WHL	66	22	29	51	19	....	....	....	....	....	....	....	....	....	23	10	12	22	8	....	....	....	....
2002-03	Red Deer Rebels	WHL	56	33	48	81	28	....	....	....	....	....	....	....	....	....	23	8	12	20	14	....	....	....	....
2003-04	**Washington**	**NHL**	**41**	**1**	**5**	**6**	**8**	**0**	**0**	**0**	**42**	**2.4**	**-9**	**328**	**43.0**	**13:11**	....	....	....	....	....	....	....	....	....
	Portland Pirates	AHL	43	5	17	22	16	....	....	....	....	....	....	....	....	....	7	2	1	3	0	....	....	....	....
2004-05	Portland Pirates	AHL	80	17	22	39	35	....	....	....	....	....	....	....	....	....	....	....	....	....	....	....	....	....	....
2005-06	**Washington**	**NHL**	**25**	**0**	**1**	**1**	**4**	**0**	**0**	**0**	**12**	**0.0**	**-4**	**216**	**46.3**	**11:40**	....	....	....	....	....	....	....	....	....
	Hershey Bears	AHL	58	16	22	38	23	....	....	....	....	....	....	....	....	....	21	3	5	8	10	....	....	....	....

			Regular Season														Playoffs								
Season	Club	League	GP	G	A	Pts	PIM	PP	SH	GW	S	S%	+/-	TF	F%	Min	GP	G	A	Pts	PIM	PP	SH	GW	Min
2006-07	**Washington**	**NHL**	**71**	**7**	**22**	**29**	**14**	**0**	**2**	**0**	**104**	**6.7**	**10**	**1214**	**52.1**	**15:53**	....	....	....	....	....	....	....	....	....
2007-08	**Washington**	**NHL**	**67**	**7**	**9**	**16**	**12**	**0**	**1**	**0**	**100**	**7.0**	**5**	**904**	**55.8**	**15:44**	**7**	**0**	**0**	**0**	**0**	**0**	**0**	**0**	**13:23**
2008-09	**Washington**	**NHL**	**63**	**5**	**9**	**14**	**16**	**0**	**1**	**2**	**69**	**7.2**	**–4**	**667**	**56.1**	**13:28**	**14**	**0**	**3**	**3**	**4**	**0**	**0**	**0**	**11:17**
2009-10	**Washington**	**NHL**	**36**	**4**	**6**	**10**	**12**	**0**	**0**	**0**	**40**	**10.0**	**4**	**205**	**61.0**	**10:17**	**6**	**1**	**1**	**2**	**0**	**0**	**1**	**0**	**11:02**
	Hershey Bears	AHL	2	0	2	2	0	....	....	....	....	....	....	....	....	....	....	....	....	....	....	....	....	....	....
2010-11	**Washington**	**NHL**	**60**	**3**	**6**	**9**	**16**	**0**	**1**	**1**	**77**	**3.9**	**–5**	**719**	**58.0**	**13:03**	**9**	**0**	**0**	**0**	**6**	**0**	**0**	**0**	**12:54**
2011-12	**Phoenix**	**NHL**	**75**	**8**	**15**	**23**	**10**	**0**	**1**	**2**	**114**	**7.0**	**9**	**1177**	**56.8**	**15:56**	**16**	**0**	**2**	**2**	**6**	**0**	**0**	**0**	**17:49**
2012-13	**Phoenix**	**NHL**	**48**	**4**	**10**	**14**	**8**	**0**	**0**	**0**	**59**	**6.8**	**0**	**789**	**57.3**	**15:01**	....	....	....	....	....	....	....	....	....
2013-14	**Edmonton**	**NHL**	**74**	**8**	**13**	**21**	**20**	**1**	**1**	**1**	**80**	**10.0**	**–15**	**1492**	**56.5**	**14:45**	....	....	....	....	....	....	....	....	....
2014-15	**Edmonton**	**NHL**	**68**	**6**	**7**	**13**	**17**	**1**	**1**	**1**	**65**	**9.2**	**–5**	**1218**	**55.9**	**13:20**	....	....	....	....	....	....	....	....	....
	NHL Totals		**628**	**53**	**103**	**156**	**137**	**2**	**8**	**7**	**762**	**7.0**		**8929**	**55.3**	**14:13**	**52**	**1**	**6**	**7**	**16**	**0**	**1**	**0**	**13:50**

WHL East First All-Star Team (2003)

• Missed majority of 2009-10 due to recurring back injury. Signed as a free agent by **Phoeniix**, July 1, 2011. Signed as a free agent by **Edmonton**, July 5, 2013. Traded to **Arizona** by **Edmonton** for Lauri Korpikoski, June 30, 2015.

GORGES, Josh

(JOHR-juhz, JAWSH) **BUF**

Defense. Shoots left. 6'1", 201 lbs. Born, Kelowna, BC, August 14, 1984.

Season	Club	League	GP	G	A	Pts	PIM	PP	SH	GW	S	S%	+/-	TF	F%	Min	GP	G	A	Pts	PIM	PP	SH	GW	Min
2000-01	Kelowna Rockets	WHL	57	4	6	10	24	....	....	....	....	....	....	....	....	....	6	1	1	2	4	....	....	....	....
2001-02	Kelowna Rockets	WHL	72	7	34	41	74	....	....	....	....	....	....	....	....	....	15	1	7	8	8	....	....	....	....
2002-03	Kelowna Rockets	WHL	54	11	48	59	76	....	....	....	....	....	....	....	....	....	19	3	17	20	16	....	....	....	....
2003-04	Kelowna Rockets	WHL	62	11	31	42	38	....	....	....	....	....	....	....	....	....	17	2	13	15	6	....	....	....	....
2004-05	Cleveland Barons	AHL	74	4	8	12	37	....	....	....	....	....	....	....	....	....	....	....	....	....	....	....	....	....	....
2005-06	**San Jose**	**NHL**	**49**	**0**	**6**	**6**	**31**	**0**	**0**	**0**	**25**	**0.0**	**5**	**0**	**0.0**	**17:38**	**11**	**0**	**1**	**1**	**4**	**0**	**0**	**0**	**18:56**
	Cleveland Barons	AHL	18	2	3	5	12	....	....	....	....	....	....	....	....	....	....	....	....	....	....	....	....	....	....
2006-07	**San Jose**	**NHL**	**47**	**1**	**3**	**4**	**26**	**0**	**0**	**0**	**37**	**2.7**	**–3**	**0**	**0.0**	**17:48**	....	....	....	....	....	....	....	....	....
	Worcester Sharks	AHL	7	0	1	1	2	....	....	....	....	....	....	....	....	....	....	....	....	....	....	....	....	....	....
	Montreal	**NHL**	**7**	**0**	**0**	**0**	**0**	**0**	**0**	**0**	**3**	**0.0**	**–1**	**0**	**0.0**	**12:28**	....	....	....	....	....	....	....	....	....
2007-08	**Montreal**	**NHL**	**62**	**0**	**9**	**9**	**32**	**0**	**0**	**0**	**41**	**0.0**	**0**	**0**	**0.0**	**16:20**	**12**	**0**	**3**	**3**	**0**	**0**	**0**	**0**	**18:20**
2008-09	**Montreal**	**NHL**	**81**	**4**	**19**	**23**	**37**	**2**	**0**	**0**	**63**	**6.3**	**12**	**1**	**0.0**	**20:08**	**4**	**0**	**1**	**1**	**7**	**0**	**0**	**0**	**23:46**
2009-10	**Montreal**	**NHL**	**82**	**3**	**7**	**10**	**39**	**0**	**0**	**1**	**52**	**5.8**	**2**	**0**	**0.0**	**21:01**	**19**	**0**	**2**	**2**	**14**	**0**	**0**	**0**	**22:42**
2010-11	**Montreal**	**NHL**	**36**	**1**	**6**	**7**	**18**	**1**	**0**	**1**	**20**	**5.0**	**–3**	**0**	**0.0**	**21:10**	....	....	....	....	....	....	....	....	....
2011-12	**Montreal**	**NHL**	**82**	**2**	**14**	**16**	**39**	**0**	**0**	**1**	**59**	**3.4**	**14**	**0**	**0.0**	**22:38**	....	....	....	....	....	....	....	....	....
2012-13	**Montreal**	**NHL**	**48**	**2**	**7**	**9**	**15**	**0**	**0**	**0**	**40**	**5.0**	**4**	**0**	**0.0**	**21:23**	**5**	**0**	**0**	**0**	**4**	**0**	**0**	**0**	**21:18**
2013-14	**Montreal**	**NHL**	**66**	**1**	**13**	**14**	**12**	**0**	**0**	**0**	**35**	**2.9**	**6**	**1**	**0.0**	**21:15**	**17**	**0**	**2**	**2**	**6**	**0**	**0**	**0**	**23:27**
2014-15	**Buffalo**	**NHL**	**46**	**0**	**6**	**6**	**16**	**0**	**0**	**0**	**28**	**0.0**	**–28**	**0**	**0.0**	**22:22**	....	....	....	....	....	....	....	....	....
	NHL Totals		**606**	**14**	**90**	**104**	**265**	**3**	**0**	**3**	**403**	**3.5**		**2**	**0.0**	**20:11**	**68**	**0**	**9**	**9**	**35**	**0**	**0**	**0**	**21:28**

WHL West Second All-Star Team (2003) • WHL West First All-Star Team (2004) • George Parsons Trophy (Memorial Cup - Most Sportsmanlike Player) (2004)

Signed as a free agent by **San Jose**, September 20, 2002. Traded to **Montreal** by **San Jose** with San Jose's 1st round choice (Max Pacioretty) in 2007 Entry Draft for Craig Rivet and Montreal's 5th round choice (Julien Demers) in 2008 Entry Draft, February 25, 2007. • Missed majority of 2010-11 due to knee injury at NY Islanders, December 26, 2010. Traded to **Buffalo** by **Montreal** for a 2nd round choice in 2016 Entry Draft, July 1, 2014.

GORMLEY, Brandon

(GOHRM-lee, BRAN-duhn) **ARI**

Defense. Shoots left. 6'2", 196 lbs. Born, Murray River, PE, February 18, 1992. Phoenix's 1st choice, 13th overall, in 2010 Entry Draft.

Season	Club	League	GP	G	A	Pts	PIM	PP	SH	GW	S	S%	+/-	TF	F%	Min	GP	G	A	Pts	PIM	PP	SH	GW	Min
2007-08	Notre Dame	SMHL	42	23	33	56	63	....	....	....	....	....	....	....	....	....	9	1	6	7	18	....	....	....	....
2008-09	Moncton Wildcats	QMJHL	62	7	20	27	34	....	....	....	....	....	....	....	....	....	10	1	3	4	6	....	....	....	....
2009-10	Moncton Wildcats	QMJHL	58	9	34	43	54	....	....	....	....	....	....	....	....	....	21	2	15	17	10	....	....	....	....
2010-11	Moncton Wildcats	QMJHL	47	13	35	48	42	....	....	....	....	....	....	....	....	....	5	0	1	1	6	....	....	....	....
	San Antonio	AHL	4	1	0	1	0	....	....	....	....	....	....	....	....	....	....	....	....	....	....	....	....	....	....
2011-12	Moncton Wildcats	QMJHL	26	10	17	27	18	....	....	....	....	....	....	....	....	....	....	....	....	....	....	....	....	....	....
	Shawinigan	QMJHL	9	0	5	5	4	....	....	....	....	....	....	....	....	....	7	5	2	7	8	....	....	....	....
2012-13	Portland Pirates	AHL	68	5	24	29	44	....	....	....	....	....	....	....	....	....	3	1	2	3	0	....	....	....	....
2013-14	**Phoenix**	**NHL**	**5**	**0**	**0**	**0**	**2**	**0**	**0**	**0**	**4**	**0.0**	**4**	**0**	**0.0**	**14:33**	....	....	....	....	....	....	....	....	....
	Portland Pirates	AHL	54	7	29	36	34	....	....	....	....	....	....	....	....	....	....	....	....	....	....	....	....	....	....
2014-15	**Arizona**	**NHL**	**27**	**2**	**2**	**4**	**10**	**1**	**0**	**0**	**39**	**5.1**	**–7**	**0**	**0.0**	**15:19**	....	....	....	....	....	....	....	....	....
	Portland Pirates	AHL	23	3	7	10	18	....	....	....	....	....	....	....	....	....	5	1	4	5	2	....	....	....	....
	NHL Totals		**32**	**2**	**2**	**4**	**12**	**1**	**0**	**0**	**43**	**4.7**		**0**	**0.0**	**15:12**	....	....	....	....	....	....	....	....	....

QMJHL All-Rookie Team (2009) • QMJHL Second All-Star Team (2010, 2011) • Memorial Cup All-Star Team (2012)

GOSTISBEHERE, Shayne

(gaws-TIHS-bair, SHAYN) **PHI**

Defense. Shoots left. 5'11", 186 lbs. Born, Pembroke Pines, FL, April 20, 1993. Philadelphia's 3rd choice, 78th overall, in 2012 Entry Draft.

Season	Club	League	GP	G	A	Pts	PIM	PP	SH	GW	S	S%	+/-	TF	F%	Min	GP	G	A	Pts	PIM	PP	SH	GW	Min
2010-11	South Kent	High-CT	24	7	29	36	32	....	....	....	....	....	....	....	....	....	....	....	....	....	....	....	....	....	....
2011-12	Union College	ECAC	41	5	17	22	20	....	....	....	....	....	....	....	....	....	....	....	....	....	....	....	....	....	....
2012-13	Union College	ECAC	36	8	18	26	39	....	....	....	....	....	....	....	....	....	....	....	....	....	....	....	....	....	....
2013-14	Union College	ECAC	42	9	25	34	26	....	....	....	....	....	....	....	....	....	....	....	....	....	....	....	....	....	....
	Adirondack	AHL	2	0	0	0	0	....	....	....	....	....	....	....	....	....	....	....	....	....	....	....	....	....	....
2014-15	**Philadelphia**	**NHL**	**2**	**0**	**0**	**0**	**0**	**0**	**0**	**0**	**2**	**0.0**	**–2**	**0**	**0.0**	**12:34**	....	....	....	....	....	....	....	....	....
	Lehigh Valley	AHL	5	0	5	5	0	....	....	....	....	....	....	....	....	....	....	....	....	....	....	....	....	....	....
	NHL Totals		**2**	**0**	**0**	**0**	**0**	**0**	**0**	**0**	**2**	**0.0**		**0**	**0.0**	**12:34**	....	....	....	....	....	....	....	....	....

ECAC All-Rookie Team (2012) • ECAC Second All-Star Team (2013) • NCAA East Second All-American Team (2013) • ECAC First All-Star Team (2014) • NCAA East First All-American Team (2014)

• Missed majority of 2014-15 due to knee injury at Manchester (AHL), November 7, 2014.

GRABNER, Michael

(GRAB-nuhr, MIGH-kuhl) **NYI**

Right wing. Shoots left. 6'1", 202 lbs. Born, Villach, Austria, October 5, 1987. Vancouver's 1st choice, 14th overall, in 2006 Entry Draft.

Season	Club	League	GP	G	A	Pts	PIM	PP	SH	GW	S	S%	+/-	TF	F%	Min	GP	G	A	Pts	PIM	PP	SH	GW	Min
2002-03	EC VSV Villach Jr.	Austria-Jr.	13	6	4	10	4	....	....	....	....	....	....	....	....	....	....	....	....	....	....	....	....	....	....
2003-04	EC VSV Villach Jr.	Austria-Jr.	23	32	5	37	58	....	....	....	....	....	....	....	....	....	....	....	....	....	....	....	....	....	....
	EC VSV Villach	Austria	18	2	1	3	0	....	....	....	....	....	....	....	....	....	....	....	....	....	....	....	....	....	....
	Austria	WJ18-B	5	3	1	4	4	....	....	....	....	....	....	....	....	....	....	....	....	....	....	....	....	....	....
2004-05	Spokane Chiefs	WHL	58	13	11	24	18	....	....	....	....	....	....	....	....	....	....	....	....	....	....	....	....	....	....
2005-06	Spokane Chiefs	WHL	67	36	14	50	28	....	....	....	....	....	....	....	....	....	....	....	....	....	....	....	....	....	....
2006-07	Spokane Chiefs	WHL	55	39	16	55	34	....	....	....	....	....	....	....	....	....	6	0	1	1	2	....	....	....	....
	Manitoba Moose	AHL	2	1	1	2	0	....	....	....	....	....	....	....	....	....	6	0	0	0	0	....	....	....	....
2007-08	Manitoba Moose	AHL	74	22	22	44	8	....	....	....	....	....	....	....	....	....	6	3	0	3	2	....	....	....	....
2008-09	Manitoba Moose	AHL	66	30	18	48	20	....	....	....	....	....	....	....	....	....	20	10	7	17	2	....	....	....	....
	Austria	Oly-Q	3	5	0	5	0	....	....	....	....	....	....	....	....	....	....	....	....	....	....	....	....	....	....
2009-10	**Vancouver**	**NHL**	**20**	**5**	**6**	**11**	**8**	**2**	**0**	**1**	**63**	**7.9**	**2**	**2**	**50.0**	**13:54**	**9**	**1**	**0**	**1**	**0**	**0**	**0**	**0**	**9:06**
	Manitoba Moose	AHL	38	15	11	26	6	....	....	....	....	....	....	....	....	....	....	....	....	....	....	....	....	....	....
2010-11	**NY Islanders**	**NHL**	**76**	**34**	**18**	**52**	**10**	**2**	**6**	**3**	**228**	**14.9**	**13**	**6**	**33.3**	**15:05**	....	....	....	....	....	....	....	....	....
2011-12	**NY Islanders**	**NHL**	**78**	**20**	**12**	**32**	**12**	**1**	**1**	**3**	**174**	**11.5**	**–18**	**5**	**60.0**	**15:33**	....	....	....	....	....	....	....	....	....
2012-13	EC VSV Villach	Austria	17	10	9	19	2	....	....	....	....	....	....	....	....	....	....	....	....	....	....	....	....	....	....
	NY Islanders	**NHL**	**45**	**16**	**5**	**21**	**12**	**2**	**1**	**3**	**108**	**14.8**	**4**	**22**	**45.5**	**14:48**	**6**	**1**	**3**	**4**	**0**	**0**	**0**	**0**	**12:30**
2013-14	**NY Islanders**	**NHL**	**64**	**12**	**14**	**26**	**12**	**0**	**3**	**2**	**137**	**8.8**	**–10**	**15**	**46.7**	**14:12**	....	....	....	....	....	....	....	....	....
	Austria	Olympics	4	5	1	6	0	....	....	....	....	....	....	....	....	....	....	....	....	....	....	....	....	....	....
2014-15	**NY Islanders**	**NHL**	**34**	**8**	**5**	**13**	**4**	**0**	**0**	**0**	**63**	**12.7**	**4**	**2**	**0.0**	**12:56**	**2**	**0**	**1**	**1**	**2**	**0**	**0**	**0**	**11:45**
	NHL Totals		**317**	**95**	**60**	**155**	**58**	**7**	**11**	**12**	**773**	**12.3**		**52**	**44.2**	**14:40**	**17**	**2**	**4**	**6**	**2**	**0**	**0**	**0**	**10:37**

NHL All-Rookie Team (2011)

Traded to **Florida** by **Vancouver** with Steve Bernier and Vancouver's 1st round choice (Quinton Howden) in 2010 Entry Draft for Keith Ballard and Victor Oreskovich, June 25, 2010. Claimed on waivers by **NY Islanders** from **Florida**, October 5, 2010. Signed as a free agent by **Villach** (Austria), October 4, 2012. • Missed majority of 2014-15 due to sports hernia surgery, October 9, 2014 and as a healthy reserve.

GRABOVSKI, Mikhail
(gra-BAWV-skee, mih-kigh-EHL) **NYI**

Center. Shoots left. 5'11", 183 lbs. Born, Potsdam, East Germany, January 31, 1984. Montreal's 4th choice, 150th overall, in 2004 Entry Draft.

			Regular Season														Playoffs								
Season	Club	League	GP	G	A	Pts	PIM	PP	SH	GW	S	S%	+/-	TF	F%	Min	GP	G	A	Pts	PIM	PP	SH	GW	Min
2001-02	HC Minsk	Belarus	26	10	7	17	16	....	....	....	....	....	....	....	....	....	....	....	....	....	....	....	....	....	....
	Belarus	WJC-A	6	0	1	1	2	....	....	....	....	....	....	....	....	....	....	....	....	....	....	....	....	....	....
2002-03	HC Minsk	Belarus	STATISTICS NOT AVAILABLE																						
2003-04	Nizhnekamsk	Russia	45	6	11	17	26	....	....	....	....	....	....	....	....	....	5	0	0	0	4	....	....	....	....
2004-05	Nizhnekamsk	Russia	60	16	20	36	32	....	....	....	....	....	....	....	....	....	3	2	0	2	2	....	....	....	....
	Belarus	Oly-Q	3	4	3	7	10	....	....	....	....	....	....	....	....	....	....	....	....	....	....	....	....	....	....
	Yunost-Minsk	BelOpen	....	....	....	....	....	....	....	....	....	....	....	....	....	....	5	2	4	6	6	....	....	....	....
2005-06	Dynamo Moscow	Russia	48	10	17	27	28	....	....	....	....	....	....	....	....	....	4	0	0	0	4	....	....	....	....
	Yunost-Minsk	BelOpen	8	6	8	14	10	....	....	....	....	....	....	....	....	....	....	....	....	....	....	....	....	....	....
2006-07	**Montreal**	**NHL**	**3**	**0**	**0**	**0**	**0**	**0**	**0**	**0**	**5**	**0.0**	**-2**	**31**	**41.9**	**13:18**	....	....	....	....	....	....	....	....	....
	Hamilton	AHL	66	17	37	54	34	....	....	....	....	....	....	....	....	....	20	4	7	11	21	....	....	....	....
2007-08	**Montreal**	**NHL**	**24**	**3**	**6**	**9**	**8**	**0**	**0**	**1**	**23**	**13.0**	**-4**	**154**	**33.1**	**11:14**	....	....	....	....	....	....	....	....	....
	Hamilton	AHL	12	8	12	20	6	....	....	....	....	....	....	....	....	....	....	....	....	....	....	....	....	....	....
2008-09	**Toronto**	**NHL**	**78**	**20**	**28**	**48**	**92**	**6**	**0**	**2**	**120**	**16.7**	**-8**	**957**	**44.5**	**16:13**	....	....	....	....	....	....	....	....	....
2009-10	**Toronto**	**NHL**	**59**	**10**	**25**	**35**	**10**	**2**	**1**	**3**	**126**	**7.9**	**3**	**735**	**49.8**	**16:48**	....	....	....	....	....	....	....	....	....
2010-11	**Toronto**	**NHL**	**81**	**29**	**29**	**58**	**60**	**10**	**0**	**4**	**239**	**12.1**	**14**	**1326**	**48.4**	**19:22**	....	....	....	....	....	....	....	....	....
2011-12	**Toronto**	**NHL**	**74**	**23**	**28**	**51**	**51**	**5**	**0**	**2**	**163**	**14.1**	**0**	**905**	**51.5**	**17:36**	....	....	....	....	....	....	....	....	....
2012-13	CSKA Moscow	KHL	29	12	12	24	10	....	....	....	....	....	....	....	....	....	....	....	....	....	....	....	....	....	....
	Toronto	**NHL**	**48**	**9**	**7**	**16**	**24**	**0**	**0**	**1**	**80**	**11.3**	**-10**	**638**	**50.6**	**15:34**	**7**	**0**	**2**	**2**	**2**	**0**	**0**	**0**	**19:06**
2013-14	**Washington**	**NHL**	**58**	**13**	**22**	**35**	**26**	**3**	**0**	**1**	**81**	**16.0**	**6**	**641**	**54.0**	**15:45**	....	....	....	....	....	....	....	....	....
2014-15	**NY Islanders**	**NHL**	**51**	**9**	**10**	**19**	**8**	**0**	**0**	**2**	**81**	**11.1**	**3**	**83**	**45.8**	**14:16**	**3**	**0**	**0**	**0**	**0**	**0**	**0**	**0**	**14:27**
	NHL Totals		**476**	**116**	**155**	**271**	**279**	**26**	**1**	**16**	**918**	**12.6**		**5470**	**48.8**	**16:26**	**10**	**0**	**2**	**2**	**2**	**0**	**0**	**0**	**17:42**

Traded to **Toronto** by **Montreal** for Greg Pateryn and Toronto's 2nd round choice (later traded to Chicago, later traded back to Toronto, later traded to Boston - Boston selected Jared Knight) in 2010 Entry Draft, July 3, 2008. Signed as a free agent by **CSKA Moscow** (KHL), September 25, 2012. Signed as a free agent by **Washington**, August 22, 2013. Signed as a free agent by **NY Islanders**, July 2, 2014.

GRAGNANI, Marc-Andre
(GRUH-na-nee, MAHRK-AWN-dray) **N.J.**

Defense. Shoots left. 6'2", 200 lbs. Born, Montreal, QC, March 11, 1987. Buffalo's 3rd choice, 87th overall, in 2005 Entry Draft.

Season	Club	League	GP	G	A	Pts	PIM	PP	SH	GW	S	S%	+/-	TF	F%	Min	GP	G	A	Pts	PIM	PP	SH	GW	Min
2002-03	West Island Lions	QAAA	34	3	15	18	22	....	....	....	....	....	....	....	....	....	....	....	....	....	....	....	....	....	....
2003-04	P.E.I. Rocket	QMJHL	61	2	13	15	42	....	....	....	....	....	....	....	....	....	11	0	0	0	4	....	....	....	....
2004-05	P.E.I. Rocket	QMJHL	68	10	29	39	48	....	....	....	....	....	....	....	....	....	....	....	....	....	....	....	....	....	....
2005-06	P.E.I. Rocket	QMJHL	62	16	55	71	75	....	....	....	....	....	....	....	....	....	6	1	4	5	14	....	....	....	....
2006-07	P.E.I. Rocket	QMJHL	65	22	46	68	58	....	....	....	....	....	....	....	....	....	7	5	8	13	4	....	....	....	....
2007-08	**Buffalo**	**NHL**	**2**	**0**	**0**	**0**	**4**	**0**	**0**	**0**	**1**	**0.0**	**-2**	**0**	**0.0**	**6:18**	....	....	....	....	....	....	....	....	....
	Rochester	AHL	78	14	38	52	38	....	....	....	....	....	....	....	....	....	....	....	....	....	....	....	....	....	....
2008-09	**Buffalo**	**NHL**	**4**	**0**	**0**	**0**	**2**	**0**	**0**	**0**	**3**	**0.0**	**2**	**0**	**0.0**	**15:23**	....	....	....	....	....	....	....	....	....
	Portland Pirates	AHL	76	9	42	51	59	....	....	....	....	....	....	....	....	....	5	0	2	2	4	....	....	....	....
2009-10	Portland Pirates	AHL	66	12	31	43	37	....	....	....	....	....	....	....	....	....	4	0	2	2	0	....	....	....	....
2010-11	**Buffalo**	**NHL**	**9**	**1**	**2**	**3**	**2**	**0**	**0**	**1**	**11**	**9.1**	**0**	**0**	**0.0**	**15:17**	**7**	**1**	**6**	**7**	**4**	**1**	**0**	**0**	**21:53**
	Portland Pirates	AHL	63	12	48	60	51	....	....	....	....	....	....	....	....	....	....	....	....	....	....	....	....	....	....
2011-12	**Buffalo**	**NHL**	**44**	**1**	**11**	**12**	**20**	**1**	**0**	**0**	**35**	**2.9**	**10**	**1**	**100.0**	**16:23**	....	....	....	....	....	....	....	....	....
	Vancouver	**NHL**	**14**	**1**	**2**	**3**	**6**	**0**	**0**	**0**	**12**	**8.3**	**-4**	**0**	**0.0**	**15:25**	....	....	....	....	....	....	....	....	....
2012-13	Charlotte	AHL	42	3	25	28	29	....	....	....	....	....	....	....	....	....	....	....	....	....	....	....	....	....	....
	Carolina	**NHL**	**1**	**0**	**0**	**0**	**0**	**0**	**0**	**0**	**0**	**0.0**	**0**	**0**	**0.0**	**7:53**	....	....	....	....	....	....	....	....	....
2013-14	HC Lev Praha	KHL	42	2	7	9	43	....	....	....	....	....	....	....	....	....	22	0	4	4	0	....	....	....	....
2014-15	SC Bern	Swiss	49	8	29	37	18	....	....	....	....	....	....	....	....	....	11	1	4	5	0	....	....	....	....
	NHL Totals		**74**	**3**	**15**	**18**	**34**	**1**	**0**	**1**	**62**	**4.8**		**1**	**100.0**	**15:37**	**7**	**1**	**6**	**7**	**4**	**1**	**0**	**0**	**21:54**

AHL First All-Star Team (2011) • Eddie Shore Award (AHL – Outstanding Defenseman) (2011)

Traded to **Vancouver** by **Buffalo** for Alexander Sulzer, February 27, 2012. Signed as a free agent by **Carolina**, July 11, 2012. Signed as a free agent by **Lev Praha** (KHL), May 22, 2013. Signed as a free agent by **Bern** (Swiss), July 10, 2014. Signed as a free agent by **New Jersey**, July 3, 2015.

GRANBERG, Petter
(GRAN-buhrg, PEH-tuhr) **TOR**

Defense. Shoots right. 6'3", 205 lbs. Born, Gallivare, Sweden, August 27, 1992. Toronto's 4th choice, 116th overall, in 2010 Entry Draft.

Season	Club	League	GP	G	A	Pts	PIM	PP	SH	GW	S	S%	+/-	TF	F%	Min	GP	G	A	Pts	PIM	PP	SH	GW	Min
2007-08	Skelleftea U18	Swe-U18	28	1	3	4	4	....	....	....	....	....	....	....	....	....	....	....	....	....	....	....	....	....	....
2008-09	Skelleftea AIK U18	Swe-U18	32	0	8	8	20	....	....	....	....	....	....	....	....	....	8	0	0	0	4	....	....	....	....
	Skelleftea AIK Jr.	Swe-Jr.	4	0	0	0	0	....	....	....	....	....	....	....	....	....	2	0	0	0	6	....	....	....	....
2009-10	Skelleftea AIK U18	Swe-U18	6	0	1	1	2	....	....	....	....	....	....	....	....	....	3	0	3	3	4	....	....	....	....
	Skelleftea AIK Jr.	Swe-Jr.	40	2	7	9	39	....	....	....	....	....	....	....	....	....	4	1	0	1	4	....	....	....	....
	Skelleftea AIK	Sweden	1	0	0	0	0	....	....	....	....	....	....	....	....	....	....	....	....	....	....	....	....	....	....
2010-11	Skelleftea AIK Jr.	Swe-Jr.	34	2	6	8	16	....	....	....	....	....	....	....	....	....	5	0	1	1	0	....	....	....	....
	Pitea HC	Sweden-3	1	0	0	0	0	....	....	....	....	....	....	....	....	....	....	....	....	....	....	....	....	....	....
	Skelleftea AIK	Sweden	23	0	1	1	6	....	....	....	....	....	....	....	....	....	11	0	1	1	2	....	....	....	....
2011-12	Skelleftea AIK Jr.	Swe-Jr.	5	2	4	6	6	....	....	....	....	....	....	....	....	....	....	....	....	....	....	....	....	....	....
	Sundsvall	Sweden-2	3	0	0	0	6	....	....	....	....	....	....	....	....	....	....	....	....	....	....	....	....	....	....
	Skelleftea AIK	Sweden	38	1	3	4	10	....	....	....	....	....	....	....	....	....	19	1	1	2	12	....	....	....	....
2012-13	Skelleftea AIK	Sweden	13	0	0	0	4	....	....	....	....	....	....	....	....	....	13	0	2	2	10	....	....	....	....
	Skelleftea AIK Jr.	Swe-Jr.	3	0	1	1	2	....	....	....	....	....	....	....	....	....	....	....	....	....	....	....	....	....	....
2013-14	**Toronto**	**NHL**	**1**	**0**	**0**	**0**	**0**	**0**	**0**	**0**	**0**	**0.0**	**0**	**0**	**0.0**	**11:46**	....	....	....	....	....	....	....	....	....
	Toronto Marlies	AHL	73	2	5	7	28	....	....	....	....	....	....	....	....	....	14	0	2	2	8	....	....	....	....
2014-15	**Toronto**	**NHL**	**7**	**0**	**0**	**0**	**6**	**0**	**0**	**0**	**1**	**0.0**	**1**	**0**	**0.0**	**11:27**	....	....	....	....	....	....	....	....	....
	Toronto Marlies	AHL	53	1	14	15	30	....	....	....	....	....	....	....	....	....	5	0	1	1	4	....	....	....	....
	NHL Totals		**8**	**0**	**0**	**0**	**6**	**0**	**0**	**0**	**1**	**0.0**		**0**	**0.0**	**11:29**	....	....	....	....	....	....	....	....	....

GRANLUND, Markus
(GRAN-luhnd, mahr-KUHS) **CGY**

Center. Shoots left. 5'11", 185 lbs. Born, Oulu, Finland, April 16, 1993. Calgary's 2nd choice, 45th overall, in 2011 Entry Draft.

Season	Club	League	GP	G	A	Pts	PIM	PP	SH	GW	S	S%	+/-	TF	F%	Min	GP	G	A	Pts	PIM	PP	SH	GW	Min
2008-09	Karpat Oulu U18	Fin-U18	4	1	3	4	0	....	....	....	....	....	....	....	....	....	....	....	....	....	....	....	....	....	....
2009-10	HIFK Helsinki U18	Fin-U18	11	9	20	29	6	....	....	....	....	....	....	....	....	....	....	....	....	....	....	....	....	....	....
	HIFK Helsinki Jr.	Fin-Jr.	37	17	25	42	38	....	....	....	....	....	....	....	....	....	14	2	11	13	18	....	....	....	....
2010-11	Suomi U20	Finland-2	6	3	3	6	6	....	....	....	....	....	....	....	....	....	....	....	....	....	....	....	....	....	....
	HIFK Helsinki	Finland	2	0	0	0	0	....	....	....	....	....	....	....	....	....	....	....	....	....	....	....	....	....	....
	HIFK Helsinki Jr.	Fin-Jr.	40	20	32	52	49	....	....	....	....	....	....	....	....	....	5	4	5	9	6	....	....	....	....
2011-12	Kiekko-Vantaa	Finland-2	7	2	5	7	6	....	....	....	....	....	....	....	....	....	....	....	....	....	....	....	....	....	....
	HIFK Helsinki	Finland	47	15	19	34	18	....	....	....	....	....	....	....	....	....	3	0	0	0	0	....	....	....	....
	HIFK Helsinki Jr.	Fin-Jr.	....	....	....	....	....	....	....	....	....	....	....	....	....	....	1	1	0	1	0	....	....	....	....
2012-13	HIFK Helsinki	Finland	50	10	20	30	18	....	....	....	....	....	....	....	....	....	5	1	2	3	4	....	....	....	....
2013-14	**Calgary**	**NHL**	**7**	**2**	**1**	**3**	**0**	**0**	**1**	**0**	**9**	**22.2**	**2**	**54**	**51.9**	**12:05**	....	....	....	....	....	....	....	....	....
	Abbotsford Heat	AHL	52	25	21	46	22	....	....	....	....	....	....	....	....	....	4	2	3	5	2	....	....	....	....
2014-15	**Calgary**	**NHL**	**48**	**8**	**10**	**18**	**16**	**1**	**0**	**1**	**65**	**12.3**	**-4**	**524**	**36.8**	**13:22**	**3**	**0**	**1**	**1**	**0**	**0**	**0**	**0**	**7:44**
	Adirondack	AHL	21	9	8	17	14	....	....	....	....	....	....	....	....	....	....	....	....	....	....	....	....	....	....
	NHL Totals		**55**	**10**	**11**	**21**	**16**	**1**	**1**	**1**	**74**	**13.5**		**578**	**38.2**	**13:12**	**3**	**0**	**1**	**1**	**0**	**0**	**0**	**0**	**7:44**

GRANLUND, Mikael
(GRAN-lund, mih-KIGH-ehl) **MIN**

Center. Shoots left. 5'10", 186 lbs. Born, Oulu, Finland, February 26, 1992. Minnesota's 1st choice, 9th overall, in 2010 Entry Draft.

Season	Club	League	GP	G	A	Pts	PIM	PP	SH	GW	S	S%	+/-	TF	F%	Min	GP	G	A	Pts	PIM	PP	SH	GW	Min
2007-08	Karpat Oulu U18	Fin-U18	31	22	27	49	20	....	....	....	....	....	....	....	....	....	5	3	5	8	0	....	....	....	....
2008-09	Suomi U20	Finland-2	6	4	3	7	0	....	....	....	....	....	....	....	....	....	....	....	....	....	....	....	....	....	....
	Karpat Oulu Jr.	Fin-Jr.	38	22	44	66	45	....	....	....	....	....	....	....	....	....	....	....	....	....	....	....	....	....	....
	Karpat Oulu	Finland	2	0	0	0	0	....	....	....	....	....	....	....	....	....	....	....	....	....	....	....	....	....	....
	Karpat Oulu U18	Fin-U18	....	....	....	....	....	....	....	....	....	....	....	....	....	....	3	2	4	6	2	....	....	....	....
2009-10	Suomi U20	Finland-2	1	0	0	0	0	....	....	....	....	....	....	....	....	....	....	....	....	....	....	....	....	....	....
	HIFK Helsinki	Finland	43	13	27	40	2	....	....	....	....	....	....	....	....	....	6	1	5	6	0	....	....	....	....
2010-11	HIFK Helsinki	Finland	39	8	28	36	14	....	....	....	....	....	....	....	....	....	15	5	*11	*16	4	....	....	....	....
2011-12	HIFK Helsinki	Finland	45	20	31	51	18	....	....	....	....	....	....	....	....	....	4	0	2	2	0	....	....	....	....
2012-13	Houston Aeros	AHL	29	10	18	28	8	....	....	....	....	....	....	....	....	....	5	1	1	2	4	....	....	....	....
	Minnesota	**NHL**	**27**	**2**	**6**	**8**	**6**	**0**	**0**	**0**	**36**	**5.6**	**-4**	**206**	**47.1**	**13:11**	....	....	....	....	....	....	....	....	....

			Regular Season														Playoffs								
Season	Club	League	GP	G	A	Pts	PIM	PP	SH	GW	S	S%	+/-	TF	F%	Min	GP	G	A	Pts	PIM	PP	SH	GW	Min
2013-14	**Minnesota**	**NHL**	**63**	**8**	**33**	**41**	**22**	**2**	**0**	**2**	**104**	**7.7**	**–3**	**789**	**52.6**	**17:19**	**13**	**4**	**3**	**7**	**2**	**0**	**0**	**1**	**18:01**
	Finland	Olympics	6	3	4	7	4	....	....	....	....	....	....	....	....	....	....	....	....	....	....	....	....	....	....
2014-15	**Minnesota**	**NHL**	**68**	**8**	**31**	**39**	**20**	**0**	**0**	**2**	**99**	**8.1**	**17**	**984**	**48.4**	**17:54**	**10**	**2**	**4**	**6**	**0**	**0**	**0**	**1**	**17:50**
	NHL Totals		**158**	**18**	**70**	**88**	**48**	**2**	**0**	**4**	**239**	**7.5**		**1979**	**49.9**	**16:52**	**23**	**6**	**7**	**13**	**2**	**0**	**0**	**2**	**17:56**

Olympic All-Star Team (2014)

GRANT, Alex

(GRANT, AL-ehx) **ARI**

Defense. Shoots right. 6'4", 205 lbs. Born, Antigonish, NS, January 20, 1989. Pittsburgh's 6th choice, 118th overall, in 2007 Entry Draft.

Season	Club	League	GP	G	A	Pts	PIM	PP	SH	GW	S	S%	+/-	TF	F%	Min	GP	G	A	Pts	PIM	PP	SH	GW	Min
2004-05	Antigonish	MJrHL	50	7	9	16	36	....	....	....	....	....	....	....	....	....	3	1	1	2	2	....	....	....	....
2005-06	Saint John	QMJHL	47	4	9	13	58	....	....	....	....	....	....	....	....	....	....	....	....	....	....	....	....	....	....
2006-07	Saint John	QMJHL	68	12	20	32	108	....	....	....	....	....	....	....	....	....	....	....	....	....	....	....	....	....	....
2007-08	Saint John	QMJHL	70	15	33	48	96	....	....	....	....	....	....	....	....	....	14	3	11	14	12	....	....	....	....
2008-09	Saint John	QMJHL	37	9	22	31	51	....	....	....	....	....	....	....	....	....	....	....	....	....	....	....	....	....	....
	Shawinigan	QMJHL	23	4	15	19	11	....	....	....	....	....	....	....	....	....	21	4	5	9	18	....	....	....	....
2009-10	Wilkes-Barre	AHL	14	3	2	5	28	....	....	....	....	....	....	....	....	....	2	0	0	0	0	....	....	....	....
	Wheeling Nailers	ECHL	40	7	20	27	36	....	....	....	....	....	....	....	....	....	....	....	....	....	....	....	....	....	....
2010-11	Wilkes-Barre	AHL	4	0	0	0	0	....	....	....	....	....	....	....	....	....	....	....	....	....	....	....	....	....	....
	Wheeling Nailers	ECHL	14	3	2	5	6	....	....	....	....	....	....	....	....	....	17	2	0	2	13	....	....	....	....
2011-12	Wilkes-Barre	AHL	61	10	27	37	73	....	....	....	....	....	....	....	....	....	12	2	5	7	13	....	....	....	....
2012-13	Wilkes-Barre	AHL	46	4	16	20	73	....	....	....	....	....	....	....	....	....	13	2	2	4	27	....	....	....	....
2013-14	**Anaheim**	**NHL**	**2**	**2**	**0**	**2**	**2**	**0**	**0**	**0**	**2**	**100.0**	**3**	**0**	**0.0**	**12:11**	....	....	....	....	....	....	....	....	....
	Norfolk Admirals	AHL	52	7	20	27	46	....	....	....	....	....	....	....	....	....	....	....	....	....	....	....	....	....	....
	Binghamton	AHL	19	2	8	10	6	....	....	....	....	....	....	....	....	....	4	0	0	0	10	....	....	....	....
2014-15	Binghamton	AHL	58	6	27	33	57	....	....	....	....	....	....	....	....	....	....	....	....	....	....	....	....	....	....
	NHL Totals		**2**	**2**	**0**	**2**	**2**	**0**	**0**	**0**	**2**	**100.0**		**0**	**0.0**	**12:11**	....	....	....	....	....	....	....	....	....

• Missed majority of 2010-11 due to recurring wrist injury. Traded to **Anaheim** by **Pittsburgh** for Harry Zolnierczyk, June 24, 2013. Traded to **Ottawa** by **Anaheim** for Andre Petersson, March 5, 2014. Signed as a free agent by **Arizona**, July 2, 2015.

GRANT, Derek

(GRANT, DAIR-ihk) **CGY**

Center. Shoots left. 6'3", 206 lbs. Born, Abbotsford, BC, April 20, 1990. Ottawa's 5th choice, 119th overall, in 2008 Entry Draft.

Season	Club	League	GP	G	A	Pts	PIM	PP	SH	GW	S	S%	+/-	TF	F%	Min	GP	G	A	Pts	PIM	PP	SH	GW	Min
2006-07	Abbotsford Pilots	PIJHL	47	31	20	51	42	....	....	....	....	....	....	....	....	....	11	6	5	11	20	....	....	....	....
2007-08	Langley Chiefs	BCHL	57	24	39	63	44	....	....	....	....	....	....	....	....	....	12	5	5	10	15	....	....	....	....
2008-09	Langley Chiefs	BCHL	35	25	35	60	22	....	....	....	....	....	....	....	....	....	4	2	1	3	2	....	....	....	....
2009-10	Michigan State	CCHA	38	12	18	30	10	....	....	....	....	....	....	....	....	....	....	....	....	....	....	....	....	....	....
2010-11	Michigan State	CCHA	38	8	25	33	44	....	....	....	....	....	....	....	....	....	....	....	....	....	....	....	....	....	....
	Binghamton	AHL	14	1	5	6	0	....	....	....	....	....	....	....	....	....	7	1	1	2	2	....	....	....	....
2011-12	Binghamton	AHL	60	8	15	23	26	....	....	....	....	....	....	....	....	....	....	....	....	....	....	....	....	....	....
2012-13	Binghamton	AHL	63	19	9	28	37	....	....	....	....	....	....	....	....	....	3	0	0	0	6	....	....	....	....
	Ottawa	**NHL**	**5**	**0**	**0**	**0**	**0**	**0**	**0**	**0**	**5**	**0.0**	**–1**	**31**	**54.8**	**8:40**	....	....	....	....	....	....	....	....	....
2013-14	**Ottawa**	**NHL**	**20**	**0**	**2**	**2**	**4**	**0**	**0**	**0**	**31**	**0.0**	**–3**	**150**	**52.7**	**9:34**	....	....	....	....	....	....	....	....	....
	Binghamton	AHL	46	12	10	22	30	....	....	....	....	....	....	....	....	....	4	0	1	1	2	....	....	....	....
2014-15	Binghamton	AHL	73	21	17	38	45	....	....	....	....	....	....	....	....	....	....	....	....	....	....	....	....	....	....
	NHL Totals		**25**	**0**	**2**	**2**	**4**	**0**	**0**	**0**	**36**	**0.0**		**181**	**53.0**	**9:23**	....	....	....	....	....	....	....	....	....

Signed as a free agent by **Calgary**, July 1, 2015.

GRANT, Triston

(GRANT, TRIHS-tuhn)

Left wing. Shoots left. 6'2", 215 lbs. Born, Neepawa, MB, February 2, 1984. Philadelphia's 10th choice, 286th overall, in 2004 Entry Draft.

Season	Club	League	GP	G	A	Pts	PIM	PP	SH	GW	S	S%	+/-	TF	F%	Min	GP	G	A	Pts	PIM	PP	SH	GW	Min
2000-01	Neepawa Natives	MJHL	STATISTICS NOT AVAILABLE																						
	Lethbridge	WHL	23	2	0	2	75	....	....	....	....	....	....	....	....	....	5	0	0	0	11	....	....	....	....
2001-02	Lethbridge	WHL	36	8	1	9	110	....	....	....	....	....	....	....	....	....	....	....	....	....	....	....	....	....	....
	Vancouver Giants	WHL	21	2	4	6	53	....	....	....	....	....	....	....	....	....	....	....	....	....	....	....	....	....	....
2002-03	Vancouver Giants	WHL	72	10	10	20	200	....	....	....	....	....	....	....	....	....	4	0	0	0	10	....	....	....	....
2003-04	Vancouver Giants	WHL	69	10	8	18	267	....	....	....	....	....	....	....	....	....	11	1	1	2	33	....	....	....	....
2004-05	Vancouver Giants	WHL	70	20	12	32	193	....	....	....	....	....	....	....	....	....	6	1	0	1	8	....	....	....	....
2005-06	Philadelphia	AHL	64	2	3	5	190	....	....	....	....	....	....	....	....	....	....	....	....	....	....	....	....	....	....
2006-07	**Philadelphia**	**NHL**	**8**	**0**	**1**	**1**	**10**	**0**	**0**	**0**	**3**	**0.0**	**–1**	**0**	**0.0**	**4:32**	....	....	....	....	....	....	....	....	....
	Philadelphia	AHL	61	5	6	11	199	....	....	....	....	....	....	....	....	....	....	....	....	....	....	....	....	....	....
2007-08	Philadelphia	AHL	72	10	11	21	181	....	....	....	....	....	....	....	....	....	12	0	2	2	34	....	....	....	....
2008-09	Milwaukee	AHL	55	3	8	11	153	....	....	....	....	....	....	....	....	....	11	1	1	2	12	....	....	....	....
2009-10	**Nashville**	**NHL**	**3**	**0**	**0**	**0**	**9**	**0**	**0**	**0**	**2**	**0.0**	**–1**	**0**	**0.0**	**7:14**	....	....	....	....	....	....	....	....	....
	Milwaukee	AHL	74	12	13	25	236	....	....	....	....	....	....	....	....	....	5	0	2	2	16	....	....	....	....
2010-11	Rochester	AHL	56	7	6	13	144	....	....	....	....	....	....	....	....	....	....	....	....	....	....	....	....	....	....
2011-12	Oklahoma City	AHL	53	11	4	15	163	....	....	....	....	....	....	....	....	....	7	0	0	0	29	....	....	....	....
2012-13	Grand Rapids	AHL	75	4	6	10	196	....	....	....	....	....	....	....	....	....	24	2	2	4	26	....	....	....	....
2013-14	Grand Rapids	AHL	51	6	10	16	103	....	....	....	....	....	....	....	....	....	4	0	0	0	4	....	....	....	....
2014-15	Milwaukee	AHL	73	13	13	26	123	....	....	....	....	....	....	....	....	....	....	....	....	....	....	....	....	....	....
	NHL Totals		**11**	**0**	**1**	**1**	**19**	**0**	**0**	**0**	**5**	**0.0**		**0**	**0.0**	**5:16**	....	....	....	....	....	....	....	....	....

Traded to **Nashville** by **Philadelphia** with Philadelphia's 7th round choice (later traded to St. Louis – St. Louis selected Maxwell Tardy) in 2009 Entry Draft for Janne Niskala, June 24, 2008. Signed as a free agent by **Florida**, July 2, 2010. Signed as a free agent by **Grand Rapids** (AHL), July 9, 2012. Signed as a free agent by **Milwaukee** (AHL), July 21, 2014.

GRAOVAC, Tyler

(GRAW-vak, TIGH-luhr) **MIN**

Center. Shoots left. 6'5", 200 lbs. Born, Brampton, ON, April 27, 1993. Minnesota's 6th choice, 191st overall, in 2011 Entry Draft.

Season	Club	League	GP	G	A	Pts	PIM	PP	SH	GW	S	S%	+/-	TF	F%	Min	GP	G	A	Pts	PIM	PP	SH	GW	Min
2008-09	Mississauga Reps	GTHL	26	13	18	31	12	....	....	....	....	....	....	....	....	....	....	....	....	....	....	....	....	....	....
2009-10	Ottawa 67's	OHL	52	2	7	9	17	....	....	....	....	....	....	....	....	....	12	0	0	0	2	....	....	....	....
2010-11	Ottawa 67's	OHL	66	10	11	21	10	....	....	....	....	....	....	....	....	....	....	....	....	....	....	....	....	....	....
2011-12	Ottawa 67's	OHL	50	8	19	27	31	....	....	....	....	....	....	....	....	....	18	4	6	10	12	....	....	....	....
2012-13	Ottawa 67's	OHL	30	21	14	35	8	....	....	....	....	....	....	....	....	....	....	....	....	....	....	....	....	....	....
	Belleville Bulls	OHL	30	17	21	38	10	....	....	....	....	....	....	....	....	....	15	6	16	22	17	....	....	....	....
2013-14	Iowa Wild	AHL	64	13	12	25	29	....	....	....	....	....	....	....	....	....	....	....	....	....	....	....	....	....	....
2014-15	**Minnesota**	**NHL**	**3**	**0**	**0**	**0**	**0**	**0**	**0**	**0**	**4**	**0.0**	**0**	**22**	**27.3**	**9:13**	....	....	....	....	....	....	....	....	....
	Iowa Wild	AHL	73	21	25	46	26	....	....	....	....	....	....	....	....	....	....	....	....	....	....	....	....	....	....
	NHL Totals		**3**	**0**	**0**	**0**	**0**	**0**	**0**	**0**	**4**	**0.0**		**22**	**27.3**	**9:13**	....	....	....	....	....	....	....	....	....

Canadian Major Junior Sportsman of the Year (2013)

GREEN, Mike

(GREEN, MIGHK) **DET**

Defense. Shoots right. 6'1", 207 lbs. Born, Calgary, AB, October 12, 1985. Washington's 3rd choice, 29th overall, in 2004 Entry Draft.

Season	Club	League	GP	G	A	Pts	PIM	PP	SH	GW	S	S%	+/-	TF	F%	Min	GP	G	A	Pts	PIM	PP	SH	GW	Min
2000-01	Cgy. North Stars	AMHL	36	4	23	27	34	....	....	....	....	....	....	....	....	....	....	....	....	....	....	....	....	....	....
	Saskatoon Blades	WHL	5	0	2	2	0	....	....	....	....	....	....	....	....	....	....	....	....	....	....	....	....	....	....
2001-02	Saskatoon Blades	WHL	62	3	20	23	57	....	....	....	....	....	....	....	....	....	7	0	1	1	2	....	....	....	....
2002-03	Saskatoon Blades	WHL	72	6	36	42	70	....	....	....	....	....	....	....	....	....	6	0	2	2	6	....	....	....	....
2003-04	Saskatoon Blades	WHL	59	14	25	39	92	....	....	....	....	....	....	....	....	....	....	....	....	....	....	....	....	....	....
2004-05	Saskatoon Blades	WHL	67	14	52	66	105	....	....	....	....	....	....	....	....	....	4	0	0	0	6	....	....	....	....
2005-06	**Washington**	**NHL**	**22**	**1**	**2**	**3**	**18**	**0**	**0**	**0**	**13**	**7.7**	**–8**	**0**	**0.0**	**14:54**	....	....	....	....	....	....	....	....	....
	Hershey Bears	AHL	56	9	34	43	79	....	....	....	....	....	....	....	....	....	21	3	15	18	30	....	....	....	....
2006-07	**Washington**	**NHL**	**70**	**2**	**10**	**12**	**36**	**0**	**0**	**0**	**68**	**2.9**	**–10**	**0**	**0.0**	**15:29**	....	....	....	....	....	....	....	....	....
2007-08	**Washington**	**NHL**	**82**	**18**	**38**	**56**	**62**	**8**	**0**	**4**	**234**	**7.7**	**6**	**1**	**0.0**	**23:38**	**7**	**3**	**4**	**7**	**15**	**2**	**0**	**0**	**26:59**
2008-09	**Washington**	**NHL**	**68**	**31**	**42**	**73**	**68**	**18**	**1**	**4**	**243**	**12.8**	**24**	**0**	**0.0**	**25:46**	**14**	**1**	**8**	**9**	**12**	**1**	**0**	**0**	**24:59**
2009-10	**Washington**	**NHL**	**75**	**19**	**57**	**76**	**54**	**10**	**0**	**4**	**205**	**9.3**	**39**	**0**	**0.0**	**25:29**	**7**	**0**	**3**	**3**	**12**	**0**	**0**	**0**	**26:01**
2010-11	**Washington**	**NHL**	**49**	**8**	**16**	**24**	**48**	**5**	**0**	**1**	**115**	**7.0**	**6**	**0**	**0.0**	**25:12**	**8**	**1**	**5**	**6**	**8**	**1**	**0**	**0**	**21:27**
2011-12	**Washington**	**NHL**	**32**	**3**	**4**	**7**	**12**	**3**	**0**	**1**	**64**	**4.7**	**5**	**0**	**0.0**	**21:03**	**14**	**2**	**2**	**4**	**10**	**1**	**0**	**1**	**23:45**
2012-13	**Washington**	**NHL**	**35**	**12**	**14**	**26**	**20**	**4**	**0**	**2**	**96**	**12.5**	**–3**	**0**	**0.0**	**24:51**	**7**	**2**	**2**	**4**	**4**	**1**	**0**	**1**	**25:32**

			Regular Season														Playoffs								
Season	Club	League	GP	G	A	Pts	PIM	PP	SH	GW	S	S%	+/-	TF	F%	Min	GP	G	A	Pts	PIM	PP	SH	GW	Min
2013-14	**Washington**	**NHL**	**70**	**9**	**29**	**38**	**64**	**3**	**0**	**2**	**172**	**5.2**	**–16**	**0**	**0.0**	**22:44**	....	....	....	....	....	....	....	....	....
2014-15	**Washington**	**NHL**	**72**	**10**	**35**	**45**	**34**	**1**	**0**	**2**	**159**	**6.3**	**15**	**0**	**0.0**	**19:06**	**14**	**0**	**2**	**2**	**14**	**0**	**0**	**0**	**18:24**
	NHL Totals		**575**	**113**	**247**	**360**	**416**	**52**	**1**	**20**	**1369**	**8.3**		**1**	**0.0**	**22:11**	**71**	**9**	**26**	**35**	**75**	**6**	**0**	**2**	**23:24**

WHL East First All-Star Team (2005) • AHL All-Rookie Team (2006) • NHL First All-Star Team (2009, 2010)
Played in NHL All-Star Game (2011)
Signed as a free agent by **Detroit**, July 1, 2015.

GREENE, Andy

(GREEN, AN-dee) **N.J.**

Defense. Shoots left. 5'11", 190 lbs. Born, Trenton, MI, October 30, 1982.

Season	Club	League	GP	G	A	Pts	PIM	PP	SH	GW	S	S%	+/-	TF	F%	Min	GP	G	A	Pts	PIM	PP	SH	GW	Min
2002-03	Miami U.	CCHA	41	4	19	23	64	....	....	....	....	....	....	....	....	....	....	....	....	....	....	....	....	....	....
2003-04	Miami U.	CCHA	41	7	19	26	78	....	....	....	....	....	....	....	....	....	....	....	....	....	....	....	....	....	....
2004-05	Miami U.	CCHA	38	7	27	34	66	....	....	....	....	....	....	....	....	....	....	....	....	....	....	....	....	....	....
2005-06	Miami U.	CCHA	39	9	22	31	48	....	....	....	....	....	....	....	....	....	....	....	....	....	....	....	....	....	....
2006-07	**New Jersey**	**NHL**	**23**	**1**	**5**	**6**	**6**	**1**	**0**	**0**	**23**	**4.3**	**–1**	**0**	**0.0**	**14:15**	**11**	**2**	**1**	**3**	**2**	**0**	**0**	**1**	**17:04**
	Lowell Devils	AHL	52	5	16	21	28	....	....	....	....	....	....	....	....	....	....	....	....	....	....	....	....	....	....
2007-08	**New Jersey**	**NHL**	**59**	**2**	**8**	**10**	**22**	**2**	**0**	**0**	**50**	**4.0**	**0**	**0**	**0.0**	**19:30**	**2**	**0**	**0**	**0**	**0**	**0**	**0**	**0**	**15:11**
2008-09	**New Jersey**	**NHL**	**49**	**2**	**7**	**9**	**22**	**0**	**0**	**0**	**38**	**5.3**	**3**	**0**	**0.0**	**16:17**	**3**	**0**	**1**	**1**	**0**	**0**	**0**	**0**	**15:18**
2009-10	**New Jersey**	**NHL**	**78**	**6**	**31**	**37**	**14**	**4**	**0**	**4**	**86**	**7.0**	**9**	**0**	**0.0**	**23:32**	**5**	**1**	**1**	**2**	**6**	**1**	**0**	**0**	**19:42**
2010-11	**New Jersey**	**NHL**	**82**	**4**	**19**	**23**	**22**	**1**	**0**	**1**	**91**	**4.4**	**–23**	**0**	**0.0**	**22:22**	....	....	....	....	....	....	....	....	....
2011-12	**New Jersey**	**NHL**	**56**	**1**	**15**	**16**	**16**	**0**	**0**	**0**	**53**	**1.9**	**3**	**0**	**0.0**	**19:30**	**24**	**0**	**1**	**1**	**8**	**0**	**0**	**0**	**22:02**
2012-13	**New Jersey**	**NHL**	**48**	**4**	**12**	**16**	**20**	**2**	**1**	**1**	**63**	**6.3**	**12**	**0**	**0.0**	**23:02**	....	....	....	....	....	....	....	....	....
2013-14	**New Jersey**	**NHL**	**82**	**8**	**24**	**32**	**32**	**3**	**0**	**3**	**134**	**6.0**	**3**	**0**	**0.0**	**24:35**	....	....	....	....	....	....	....	....	....
2014-15	**New Jersey**	**NHL**	**82**	**3**	**19**	**22**	**20**	**0**	**0**	**1**	**83**	**3.6**	**1**	**0**	**0.0**	**23:33**	....	....	....	....	....	....	....	....	....
	NHL Totals		**559**	**31**	**140**	**171**	**174**	**13**	**1**	**10**	**621**	**5.0**		**0**	**0.0**	**21:38**	**45**	**3**	**4**	**7**	**16**	**1**	**0**	**1**	**19:48**

CCHA All-Rookie Team (2003) • CCHA First All-Star Team (2004, 2005, 2006) • NCAA West Second All-American Team (2005) • NCAA West First All-American Team (2006)
Signed as a free agent by **New Jersey**, April 4, 2006.

GREENE, Matt

(GREEN, MAT) **L.A.**

Defense. Shoots right. 6'3", 233 lbs. Born, Grand Ledge, MI, May 13, 1983. Edmonton's 4th choice, 44th overall, in 2002 Entry Draft.

Season	Club	League	GP	G	A	Pts	PIM	PP	SH	GW	S	S%	+/-	TF	F%	Min	GP	G	A	Pts	PIM	PP	SH	GW	Min
2000-01	USNTDP	U-18	34	0	9	9	8	....	....	....	....	....	....	....	....	....	....	....	....	....	....	....	....	....	....
	USNTDP	USHL	20	0	1	1	51	....	....	....	....	....	....	....	....	....	....	....	....	....	....	....	....	....	....
2001-02	Green Bay	USHL	55	4	20	24	150	....	....	....	....	....	....	....	....	....	7	0	1	1	31	....	....	....	....
2002-03	North Dakota	WCHA	39	0	4	4	*135	....	....	....	....	....	....	....	....	....	....	....	....	....	....	....	....	....	....
2003-04	North Dakota	WCHA	40	1	16	17	86	....	....	....	....	....	....	....	....	....	....	....	....	....	....	....	....	....	....
2004-05	North Dakota	WCHA	43	2	8	10	*126	....	....	....	....	....	....	....	....	....	....	....	....	....	....	....	....	....	....
2005-06	**Edmonton**	**NHL**	**27**	**0**	**2**	**2**	**43**	**0**	**0**	**0**	**10**	**0.0**	**–6**	**0**	**0.0**	**11:13**	**18**	**0**	**1**	**1**	**34**	**0**	**0**	**0**	**10:03**
	Iowa Stars	AHL	26	2	5	7	47	....	....	....	....	....	....	....	....	....	....	....	....	....	....	....	....	....	....
2006-07	**Edmonton**	**NHL**	**78**	**1**	**9**	**10**	**109**	**0**	**0**	**0**	**52**	**1.9**	**–22**	**0**	**0.0**	**17:36**	....	....	....	....	....	....	....	....	....
2007-08	**Edmonton**	**NHL**	**46**	**0**	**1**	**1**	**53**	**0**	**0**	**0**	**28**	**0.0**	**–3**	**0**	**0.0**	**16:42**	....	....	....	....	....	....	....	....	....
	Springfield	AHL	1	0	0	0	0	....	....	....	....	....	....	....	....	....	....	....	....	....	....	....	....	....	....
2008-09	**Los Angeles**	**NHL**	**82**	**2**	**12**	**14**	**111**	**0**	**0**	**0**	**76**	**2.6**	**1**	**1**	**100.0**	**19:44**	....	....	....	....	....	....	....	....	....
2009-10	**Los Angeles**	**NHL**	**75**	**2**	**7**	**9**	**83**	**0**	**0**	**1**	**57**	**3.5**	**4**	**0**	**0.0**	**17:29**	**6**	**0**	**1**	**1**	**0**	**0**	**0**	**0**	**18:45**
2010-11	**Los Angeles**	**NHL**	**71**	**2**	**9**	**11**	**70**	**0**	**0**	**1**	**50**	**4.0**	**3**	**0**	**0.0**	**16:59**	**6**	**0**	**0**	**0**	**14**	**0**	**0**	**0**	**16:44**
2011-12♦	**Los Angeles**	**NHL**	**82**	**4**	**11**	**15**	**58**	**0**	**0**	**2**	**76**	**5.3**	**4**	**0**	**0.0**	**16:40**	**20**	**2**	**4**	**6**	**12**	**0**	**1**	**1**	**16:06**
2012-13	**Los Angeles**	**NHL**	**5**	**0**	**1**	**1**	**8**	**0**	**0**	**0**	**3**	**0.0**	**–1**	**0**	**0.0**	**15:17**	**9**	**0**	**2**	**2**	**6**	**0**	**0**	**0**	**15:29**
2013-14♦	**Los Angeles**	**NHL**	**38**	**2**	**4**	**6**	**47**	**0**	**0**	**0**	**38**	**5.3**	**6**	**1**	**0.0**	**15:53**	**20**	**0**	**4**	**4**	**16**	**0**	**0**	**0**	**14:28**
2014-15	**Los Angeles**	**NHL**	**82**	**3**	**6**	**9**	**54**	**0**	**0**	**0**	**69**	**4.3**	**1**	**0**	**0.0**	**15:48**	....	....	....	....	....	....	....	....	....
	NHL Totals		**586**	**16**	**62**	**78**	**636**	**0**	**0**	**4**	**459**	**3.5**		**2**	**50.0**	**16:56**	**79**	**2**	**12**	**14**	**82**	**0**	**1**	**1**	**14:29**

USHL Second All-Star Team (2002)

Traded to **Los Angeles** by **Edmonton** with Jarret Stoll for Lubomir Visnovsky, June 29, 2008. • Missed majority of 2012-13 due to back injury vs. Chicago, January 19, 2013. • Missed majority of 2013-14 due to upper-body injury vs. Nashville, November 2, 2013 and as a healthy reserve.

GREENING, Colin

(GREEN-ihng, KAW-lihn) **OTT**

Center/Left wing. Shoots left. 6'3", 215 lbs. Born, St. John's, NL, March 9, 1986. Ottawa's 8th choice, 204th overall, in 2005 Entry Draft.

Season	Club	League	GP	G	A	Pts	PIM	PP	SH	GW	S	S%	+/-	TF	F%	Min	GP	G	A	Pts	PIM	PP	SH	GW	Min
2002-03	St. John's	NFAHA	60	24	34	58	48	....	....	....	....	....	....	....	....	....	....	....	....	....	....	....	....	....	....
2003-04	Upper Canada	High-ON	53	30	43	73	40	....	....	....	....	....	....	....	....	....	....	....	....	....	....	....	....	....	....
2004-05	Upper Canada	High-ON	35	24	22	46	24	....	....	....	....	....	....	....	....	....	....	....	....	....	....	....	....	....	....
2005-06	Nanaimo Clippers	BCHL	56	27	35	62	46	....	....	....	....	....	....	....	....	....	5	3	0	3	2	....	....	....	....
2006-07	Cornell Big Red	ECAC	31	11	8	19	26	....	....	....	....	....	....	....	....	....	....	....	....	....	....	....	....	....	....
2007-08	Cornell Big Red	ECAC	36	14	19	33	41	....	....	....	....	....	....	....	....	....	....	....	....	....	....	....	....	....	....
2008-09	Cornell Big Red	ECAC	36	15	16	31	28	....	....	....	....	....	....	....	....	....	....	....	....	....	....	....	....	....	....
2009-10	Cornell Big Red	ECAC	34	15	20	35	31	....	....	....	....	....	....	....	....	....	....	....	....	....	....	....	....	....	....
2010-11	**Ottawa**	**NHL**	**24**	**6**	**7**	**13**	**10**	**0**	**0**	**2**	**57**	**10.5**	**2**	**24**	**45.8**	**15:05**	....	....	....	....	....	....	....	....	....
	Binghamton	AHL	59	15	25	40	41	....	....	....	....	....	....	....	....	....	23	1	4	5	13	....	....	....	....
2011-12	**Ottawa**	**NHL**	**82**	**17**	**20**	**37**	**46**	**4**	**0**	**0**	**184**	**9.2**	**–4**	**62**	**41.9**	**15:35**	**7**	**0**	**1**	**1**	**0**	**0**	**0**	**0**	**13:59**
2012-13	Aalborg Pirates	Denmark	17	13	12	25	12	....	....	....	....	....	....	....	....	....	....	....	....	....	....	....	....	....	....
	Ottawa	**NHL**	**47**	**8**	**11**	**19**	**11**	**2**	**0**	**2**	**80**	**10.0**	**5**	**47**	**46.8**	**14:44**	**10**	**3**	**1**	**4**	**2**	**0**	**0**	**1**	**15:57**
2013-14	**Ottawa**	**NHL**	**76**	**6**	**11**	**17**	**41**	**2**	**0**	**1**	**108**	**5.6**	**–15**	**59**	**37.3**	**13:45**	....	....	....	....	....	....	....	....	....
2014-15	**Ottawa**	**NHL**	**26**	**1**	**0**	**1**	**29**	**0**	**0**	**0**	**39**	**2.6**	**–5**	**9**	**66.7**	**9:49**	....	....	....	....	....	....	....	....	....
	Binghamton	AHL	12	5	2	7	13	....	....	....	....	....	....	....	....	....	....	....	....	....	....	....	....	....	....
	NHL Totals		**255**	**38**	**49**	**87**	**137**	**8**	**0**	**5**	**468**	**8.1**		**201**	**43.3**	**14:15**	**17**	**3**	**2**	**5**	**2**	**0**	**0**	**1**	**15:08**

ECAC Second All-Star Team (2008, 2009, 2010)
Signed as a free agent by **Aalborg** (Denmark), October 21, 2012. • Missed majority of 2014-15 as a healthy reserve.

GRIFFITH, Seth

(GRIH-fihth, SEHTH) **BOS**

Center. Shoots right. 5'9", 192 lbs. Born, Wallaceburg, ON, January 4, 1993. Boston's 3rd choice, 131st overall, in 2012 Entry Draft.

Season	Club	League	GP	G	A	Pts	PIM	PP	SH	GW	S	S%	+/-	TF	F%	Min	GP	G	A	Pts	PIM	PP	SH	GW	Min
2008-09	Chatham-Kent	Minor-ON	52	42	45	87	112	....	....	....	....	....	....	....	....	....	....	....	....	....	....	....	....	....	....
	Chatham	ON-Jr.B	1	0	0	0	0	....	....	....	....	....	....	....	....	....	....	....	....	....	....	....	....	....	....
2009-10	St. Mary's Lincolns	ON-Jr.B	49	43	35	78	56	....	....	....	....	....	....	....	....	....	5	6	3	9	4	....	....	....	....
	London Knights	OHL	17	2	1	3	2	....	....	....	....	....	....	....	....	....	10	4	3	7	2	....	....	....	....
2010-11	London Knights	OHL	68	22	40	62	28	....	....	....	....	....	....	....	....	....	6	3	4	7	6	....	....	....	....
2011-12	London Knights	OHL	68	45	40	85	49	....	....	....	....	....	....	....	....	....	19	10	13	23	12	....	....	....	....
2012-13	London Knights	OHL	54	33	48	81	52	....	....	....	....	....	....	....	....	....	21	9	16	25	14	....	....	....	....
2013-14	Providence Bruins	AHL	69	20	30	50	28	....	....	....	....	....	....	....	....	....	12	4	7	11	8	....	....	....	....
2014-15	**Boston**	**NHL**	**30**	**6**	**4**	**10**	**6**	**1**	**0**	**1**	**33**	**18.2**	**–2**	**9**	**33.3**	**13:27**	....	....	....	....	....	....	....	....	....
	Providence Bruins	AHL	39	12	19	31	12	....	....	....	....	....	....	....	....	....	5	2	3	5	0	....	....	....	....
	NHL Totals		**30**	**6**	**4**	**10**	**6**	**1**	**0**	**1**	**33**	**18.2**		**9**	**33.3**	**13:27**	....	....	....	....	....	....	....	....	....

OHL Second All-Star Team (2012) • OHL First All-Star Team (2013)

GRIGORENKO, Mikhail

(grih-gohr-EHN-koh, mih-khigh-IHL) **COL**

Center. Shoots left. 6'3", 209 lbs. Born, Khabarovsk, Russia, May 16, 1994. Buffalo's 1st choice, 12th overall, in 2012 Entry Draft.

Season	Club	League	GP	G	A	Pts	PIM	PP	SH	GW	S	S%	+/-	TF	F%	Min	GP	G	A	Pts	PIM	PP	SH	GW	Min
2010-11	CSKA Jr.	Russia-Jr.	43	17	18	35	22	....	....	....	....	....	....	....	....	....	10	1	4	5	4	....	....	....	....
2011-12	Quebec Remparts	QMJHL	59	40	45	85	12	....	....	....	....	....	....	....	....	....	11	3	7	10	4	....	....	....	....
2012-13	Quebec Remparts	QMJHL	33	30	24	54	8	....	....	....	....	....	....	....	....	....	11	5	9	14	0	....	....	....	....
	Buffalo	**NHL**	**25**	**1**	**4**	**5**	**0**	**0**	**0**	**0**	**31**	**3.2**	**–1**	**149**	**38.3**	**10:14**	....	....	....	....	....	....	....	....	....
	Rochester	AHL	....	....	....	....	....	....	....	....	....	....	....	....	....	....	2	0	0	0	0	....	....	....	....
2013-14	**Buffalo**	**NHL**	**18**	**2**	**1**	**3**	**2**	**0**	**0**	**0**	**20**	**10.0**	**–3**	**103**	**51.5**	**11:26**	....	....	....	....	....	....	....	....	....
	Quebec Remparts	QMJHL	23	15	24	39	6	....	....	....	....	....	....	....	....	....	5	1	8	9	6	....	....	....	....
	Rochester	AHL	9	0	4	4	0	....	....	....	....	....	....	....	....	....	5	0	0	0	2	....	....	....	....

			Regular Season														Playoffs								
Season	Club	League	GP	G	A	Pts	PIM	PP	SH	GW	S	S%	+/-	TF	F%	Min	GP	G	A	Pts	PIM	PP	SH	GW	Min
2014-15	**Buffalo**	**NHL**	**25**	**3**	**3**	**6**	**2**	**1**	**0**	**0**	**35**	**8.6**	**−10**	**331**	**46.2**	**15:10**	....	....	....	....	....	....	....	....	....
	Rochester	AHL	43	14	22	36	27	....	....	....	....	....	....	....	....	....	....	....	....	....	....	....	....	....	....
	NHL Totals		**68**	**6**	**8**	**14**	**4**	**1**	**0**	**0**	**86**	**7.0**		**583**	**45.1**	**12:22**	....	....	....	....	....	....	....	....	....

QMJHL All-Rookie Team (2012) • QMJHL First All-Star Team (2012) • Canadian Major Junior Rookie of the Year (2012)

Traded to **Colorado** by **Buffalo** with Nikita Zadorov, JT Compher and Buffalo's 2nd round choice (later traded to San Jose – San Jose selected Jeremy Roy) in 2015 Entry Draft for Ryan O'Reilly and Jamie McGinn, June 26, 2015.

GRIMALDI, Rocco

(grih-MAL-dee, RAW-koh) **FLA**

Center. Shoots right. 5'6", 180 lbs. Born, Anaheim, CA, February 8, 1993. Florida's 2nd choice, 33rd overall, in 2011 Entry Draft.

2008-09	Det. Lit. Caesars	T1EHL	32	11	9	20	22	....	....	....	....	....	....	....	....	....	7	1	5	6	0	....	....	....	....
	Det. Lit. Caesars	Other	19	19	15	34	....	....	....	....	....	....	....	....	....	....	....	....	....	....	....	....	....	....	....
2009-10	USNTDP	USHL	32	11	9	20	22	....	....	....	....	....	....	....	....	....	....	....	....	....	....	....	....	....	....
	USNTDP	U-17	16	7	18	25	20	....	....	....	....	....	....	....	....	....	....	....	....	....	....	....	....	....	....
	USNTDP	U-18	14	3	15	18	12	....	....	....	....	....	....	....	....	....	....	....	....	....	....	....	....	....	....
2010-11	USNTDP	USHL	23	12	13	25	18	....	....	....	....	....	....	....	....	....	....	....	....	....	....	....	....	....	....
	USNTDP	U-18	35	27	21	48	47	....	....	....	....	....	....	....	....	....	....	....	....	....	....	....	....	....	....
2011-12	North Dakota	WCHA	4	1	1	2	2	....	....	....	....	....	....	....	....	....	....	....	....	....	....	....	....	....	....
2012-13	North Dakota	WCHA	40	13	23	36	18	....	....	....	....	....	....	....	....	....	....	....	....	....	....	....	....	....	....
2013-14	North Dakota	NCHC	42	17	22	39	48	....	....	....	....	....	....	....	....	....	....	....	....	....	....	....	....	....	....
2014-15	**Florida**	**NHL**	**7**	**1**	**0**	**1**	**4**	**0**	**0**	**0**	**18**	**5.6**	**1**	**14**	**42.9**	**12:37**	....	....	....	....	....	....	....	....	....
	San Antonio	AHL	64	14	28	42	22	....	....	....	....	....	....	....	....	....	3	1	0	1	4	....	....	....	....
	NHL Totals		**7**	**1**	**0**	**1**	**4**	**0**	**0**	**0**	**18**	**5.6**		**14**	**42.9**	**12:37**	....	....	....	....	....	....	....	....	....

WCHA All-Rookie Team (2013)

• Missed majority of 2011-12 due to training camp knee injury and resulting surgery.

GROSSMANN, Nicklas

(GROHS-man, NIHK-luhs) **ARI**

Defense. Shoots left. 6'4", 230 lbs. Born, Stockholm, Sweden, January 22, 1985. Dallas' 4th choice, 56th overall, in 2004 Entry Draft.

2002-03	Sodertalje SK Jr.	Swe-Jr.	34	1	1	2	32	....	....	....	....	....	....	....	....	....	....	....	....	....	....	....	....	....	....
2003-04	Sodertalje SK Jr.	Swe-Jr.	33	1	2	3	32	....	....	....	....	....	....	....	....	....	2	0	0	0	0	....	....	....	....
	Sodertalje SK	Sweden	1	0	0	0	0	....	....	....	....	....	....	....	....	....	....	....	....	....	....	....	....	....	....
2004-05	Sodertalje SK Jr.	Swe-Jr.	12	3	6	9	8	....	....	....	....	....	....	....	....	....	1	0	0	0	0	....	....	....	....
	Sodertalje SK	Sweden	31	0	2	2	14	....	....	....	....	....	....	....	....	....	9	0	0	0	0	....	....	....	....
2005-06	Iowa Stars	AHL	61	2	3	5	49	....	....	....	....	....	....	....	....	....	7	0	1	1	4	....	....	....	....
2006-07	**Dallas**	**NHL**	**8**	**0**	**0**	**0**	**4**	**0**	**0**	**0**	**8**	**0.0**	**−1**	**0**	**0.0**	**12:49**	....	....	....	....	....	....	....	....	....
	Iowa Stars	AHL	67	2	8	10	40	....	....	....	....	....	....	....	....	....	8	0	0	0	10	....	....	....	....
2007-08	**Dallas**	**NHL**	**62**	**0**	**7**	**7**	**22**	**0**	**0**	**0**	**34**	**0.0**	**10**	**0**	**0.0**	**15:33**	**18**	**1**	**1**	**2**	**6**	**0**	**0**	**0**	**18:37**
	Iowa Stars	AHL	10	0	0	0	10	....	....	....	....	....	....	....	....	....	....	....	....	....	....	....	....	....	....
2008-09	**Dallas**	**NHL**	**81**	**2**	**10**	**12**	**51**	**0**	**0**	**1**	**60**	**3.3**	**−8**	**0**	**0.0**	**17:39**	....	....	....	....	....	....	....	....	....
2009-10	**Dallas**	**NHL**	**71**	**0**	**7**	**7**	**32**	**0**	**0**	**0**	**58**	**0.0**	**−3**	**1**	**0.0**	**19:11**	....	....	....	....	....	....	....	....	....
2010-11	**Dallas**	**NHL**	**59**	**1**	**9**	**10**	**35**	**0**	**0**	**0**	**38**	**2.6**	**7**	**0**	**0.0**	**18:12**	....	....	....	....	....	....	....	....	....
2011-12	**Dallas**	**NHL**	**52**	**0**	**5**	**5**	**26**	**0**	**0**	**0**	**38**	**0.0**	**0**	**0**	**0.0**	**18:59**	....	....	....	....	....	....	....	....	....
	Philadelphia	**NHL**	**22**	**0**	**6**	**6**	**10**	**0**	**0**	**0**	**18**	**0.0**	**5**	**0**	**0.0**	**18:25**	**9**	**0**	**1**	**1**	**8**	**0**	**0**	**0**	**18:55**
2012-13	Sodertalje SK	Sweden-2	4	0	1	1	4	....	....	....	....	....	....	....	....	....	....	....	....	....	....	....	....	....	....
	Philadelphia	**NHL**	**30**	**1**	**3**	**4**	**21**	**0**	**0**	**0**	**21**	**4.8**	**−1**	**0**	**0.0**	**18:20**	....	....	....	....	....	....	....	....	....
2013-14	**Philadelphia**	**NHL**	**78**	**1**	**13**	**14**	**55**	**0**	**0**	**0**	**71**	**1.4**	**−6**	**0**	**0.0**	**19:07**	**4**	**0**	**0**	**0**	**2**	**0**	**0**	**0**	**16:24**
2014-15	**Philadelphia**	**NHL**	**68**	**5**	**9**	**14**	**32**	**0**	**0**	**0**	**43**	**11.6**	**8**	**0**	**0.0**	**17:39**	....	....	....	....	....	....	....	....	....
	NHL Totals		**531**	**10**	**69**	**79**	**288**	**0**	**0**	**1**	**389**	**2.6**		**1**	**0.0**	**18:01**	**31**	**1**	**2**	**3**	**16**	**0**	**0**	**0**	**18:25**

Traded to **Philadelphia** by **Dallas** for Los Angeles' 2nd round choice (previously acquired, Dallas selected Devin Shore) in 2012 Entry Draft and Minnesota's 3rd round choice (previously acquired, later traded to Pittsburgh – Pittsburgh selected Jake Guentzel) in 2013 Entry Draft, February 16, 2012. Signed as a free agent by **Sodertalje** (Sweden-2), November 14, 2012. Traded to **Arizona** by **Philadelphia** with Chris Pronger for Sam Gagner and future considerations, June 27, 2015.

GRYBA, Eric

(GREE-buh, AIR-ihk) **EDM**

Defense. Shoots right. 6'4", 225 lbs. Born, Saskatoon, SK, April 14, 1988. Ottawa's 2nd choice, 68th overall, in 2006 Entry Draft.

2003-04	Sask. Contacts	SMHL	39	1	10	11	89	....	....	....	....	....	....	....	....	....	10	4	8	12	20	....	....	....	....
2004-05	Sask. Contacts	SMHL	32	11	29	40	83	....	....	....	....	....	....	....	....	....	11	5	7	12	22	....	....	....	....
2005-06	Green Bay	USHL	56	3	12	15	*205	....	....	....	....	....	....	....	....	....	3	1	1	2	27	....	....	....	....
2006-07	Boston University	H-East	38	1	3	4	76	....	....	....	....	....	....	....	....	....	....	....	....	....	....	....	....	....	....
2007-08	Boston University	H-East	32	1	1	2	54	....	....	....	....	....	....	....	....	....	....	....	....	....	....	....	....	....	....
2008-09	Boston University	H-East	45	0	6	6	106	....	....	....	....	....	....	....	....	....	....	....	....	....	....	....	....	....	....
2009-10	Boston University	H-East	38	4	6	10	*118	....	....	....	....	....	....	....	....	....	....	....	....	....	....	....	....	....	....
	Binghamton	AHL	6	1	0	1	2	....	....	....	....	....	....	....	....	....	....	....	....	....	....	....	....	....	....
2010-11	Binghamton	AHL	66	3	4	7	133	....	....	....	....	....	....	....	....	....	10	0	1	1	26	....	....	....	....
2011-12	Binghamton	AHL	73	5	15	20	95	....	....	....	....	....	....	....	....	....	....	....	....	....	....	....	....	....	....
2012-13	Binghamton	AHL	38	5	6	11	75	....	....	....	....	....	....	....	....	....	....	....	....	....	....	....	....	....	....
	Ottawa	**NHL**	**33**	**2**	**4**	**6**	**26**	**0**	**0**	**0**	**51**	**3.9**	**−3**	**0**	**0.0**	**20:17**	**4**	**0**	**0**	**0**	**17**	**0**	**0**	**0**	**12:12**
2013-14	**Ottawa**	**NHL**	**57**	**2**	**9**	**11**	**64**	**0**	**0**	**0**	**57**	**3.5**	**9**	**0**	**0.0**	**17:31**	....	....	....	....	....	....	....	....	....
2014-15	**Ottawa**	**NHL**	**75**	**0**	**12**	**12**	**97**	**0**	**0**	**0**	**64**	**0.0**	**11**	**0**	**0.0**	**15:39**	**6**	**0**	**0**	**0**	**14**	**0**	**0**	**0**	**16:07**
	NHL Totals		**165**	**4**	**25**	**29**	**187**	**0**	**0**	**0**	**172**	**2.3**		**0**	**0.0**	**17:13**	**10**	**0**	**0**	**0**	**31**	**0**	**0**	**0**	**14:33**

Traded to **Edmonton** by **Ottawa** for Travis Ewanyk and Pittsburgh's 4th round choice (previously acquired, Ottawa selected Christian Wolanin) in 2015 Entry Draft, June 27, 2015.

GUDAS, Radko

(GOO-duhs, RAHD-koh) **PHI**

Defense. Shoots right. 6', 204 lbs. Born, Prague, Czech., June 5, 1990. Tampa Bay's 3rd choice, 66th overall, in 2010 Entry Draft.

2004-05	HC Kladno U17	CzR-U17	46	1	5	6	70	....	....	....	....	....	....	....	....	....	7	0	0	0	10	....	....	....	....
2005-06	HC Kladno U17	CzR-U17	46	12	14	26	178	....	....	....	....	....	....	....	....	....	5	1	2	3	8	....	....	....	....
2006-07	HC Kladno U17	CzR-U17	16	6	7	13	34	....	....	....	....	....	....	....	....	....	7	4	1	5	14	....	....	....	....
	Kladno Jr.	CzRep-Jr.	15	0	1	1	18	....	....	....	....	....	....	....	....	....	1	0	0	0	0	....	....	....	....
	Beroun	CzRep-2	9	0	1	1	6	....	....	....	....	....	....	....	....	....	....	....	....	....	....	....	....	....	....
2007-08	Beroun	CzRep-2	43	1	5	6	90	....	....	....	....	....	....	....	....	....	....	....	....	....	....	....	....	....	....
	Kladno	CzRep	....	....	....	....	....	....	....	....	....	....	....	....	....	....	1	0	0	0	0	....	....	....	....
2008-09	Kladno Jr.	CzRep-Jr.	2	0	1	1	0	....	....	....	....	....	....	....	....	....	....	....	....	....	....	....	....	....	....
	Beroun	CzRep-2	32	1	6	7	110	....	....	....	....	....	....	....	....	....	....	....	....	....	....	....	....	....	....
	Kladno	CzRep	14	0	1	1	10	....	....	....	....	....	....	....	....	....	....	....	....	....	....	....	....	....	....
2009-10	Everett Silvertips	WHL	65	7	30	37	151	....	....	....	....	....	....	....	....	....	3	0	2	2	4	....	....	....	....
2010-11	Norfolk Admirals	AHL	76	4	13	17	165	....	....	....	....	....	....	....	....	....	6	0	0	0	7	....	....	....	....
2011-12	Norfolk Admirals	AHL	73	7	13	20	195	....	....	....	....	....	....	....	....	....	16	0	3	3	14	....	....	....	....
2012-13	Syracuse Crunch	AHL	57	4	16	20	207	....	....	....	....	....	....	....	....	....	12	2	1	3	34	....	....	....	....
	Tampa Bay	**NHL**	**22**	**2**	**3**	**5**	**38**	**0**	**0**	**1**	**31**	**6.5**	**3**	**0**	**0.0**	**17:00**	....	....	....	....	....	....	....	....	....
2013-14	**Tampa Bay**	**NHL**	**73**	**3**	**19**	**22**	**152**	**1**	**0**	**1**	**114**	**2.6**	**2**	**0**	**0.0**	**19:08**	**3**	**0**	**1**	**1**	**9**	**0**	**0**	**0**	**19:07**
	Czech Republic	Olympics	3	0	0	0	0	....	....	....	....	....	....	....	....	....	....	....	....	....	....	....	....	....	....
2014-15	**Tampa Bay**	**NHL**	**31**	**2**	**3**	**5**	**34**	**0**	**0**	**1**	**63**	**3.2**	**−5**	**0**	**0.0**	**17:00**	....	....	....	....	....	....	....	....	....
	NHL Totals		**126**	**7**	**25**	**32**	**224**	**1**	**0**	**3**	**208**	**3.4**		**0**	**0.0**	**18:14**	**3**	**0**	**1**	**1**	**9**	**0**	**0**	**0**	**19:07**

WHL West Second All-Star Team (2010)

Traded to **Philadelphia** by **Tampa Bay** with Tampa Bay's 1st (later traded to Columbus – Columbus selected Gabriel Carlsson) and 3rd (Matej Tomek) round choices in 2015 Entry Draft for Braydon Coburn, March 2, 2015. • Missed majority of 2014-15 due to knee injury vs. Toronto, December 29, 2014.

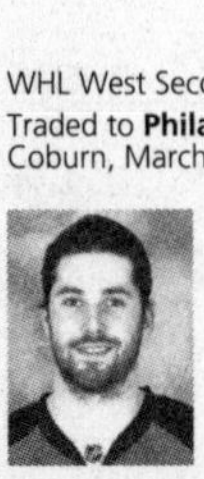

GUDBRANSON, Erik

(guhd-BRAN-suhn, AIR-ihk) **FLA**

Defense. Shoots right. 6'5", 216 lbs. Born, Ottawa, ON, January 7, 1992. Florida's 1st choice, 3rd overall, in 2010 Entry Draft.

2007-08	Ottawa Jr. 67's	Minor-ON	70	15	40	55	118	....	....	....	....	....	....	....	....	....	....	....	....	....	....	....	....	....	....
2008-09	Kingston	OHL	63	3	19	22	69	....	....	....	....	....	....	....	....	....	....	....	....	....	....	....	....	....	....
2009-10	Kingston	OHL	41	2	21	23	68	....	....	....	....	....	....	....	....	....	7	1	2	3	6	....	....	....	....
2010-11	Kingston	OHL	44	12	22	34	105	....	....	....	....	....	....	....	....	....	5	1	3	4	10	....	....	....	....
2011-12	**Florida**	**NHL**	**72**	**2**	**6**	**8**	**78**	**0**	**0**	**0**	**76**	**2.6**	**−19**	**0**	**0.0**	**14:12**	**7**	**0**	**0**	**0**	**8**	**0**	**0**	**0**	**17:07**

			Regular Season														Playoffs								
Season	Club	League	GP	G	A	Pts	PIM	PP	SH	GW	S	S%	+/-	TF	F%	Min	GP	G	A	Pts	PIM	PP	SH	GW	Min
2012-13	San Antonio	AHL	2	0	0	0	2	....	....	....	....	....	....	....	....	....	....	....	....	....	....	....	....	....	....
	Florida	**NHL**	**32**	**0**	**4**	**4**	**47**	**0**	**0**	**0**	**49**	**0.0**	**-22**	**0**	**0.0**	**18:45**	....	....	....	....	....	....	....	....	....
2013-14	**Florida**	**NHL**	**65**	**3**	**6**	**9**	**114**	**0**	**0**	**0**	**92**	**3.3**	**-7**	**0**	**0.0**	**17:59**	....	....	....	....	....	....	....	....	....
2014-15	**Florida**	**NHL**	**76**	**4**	**9**	**13**	**58**	**0**	**0**	**0**	**110**	**3.6**	**-4**	**0**	**0.0**	**18:37**	....	....	....	....	....	....	....	....	....
	NHL Totals		**245**	**9**	**25**	**34**	**297**	**0**	**0**	**0**	**327**	**2.8**		**0**	**0.0**	**17:10**	**7**	**0**	**0**	**0**	**8**	**0**	**0**	**0**	**17:07**

GUENIN, Nate

(GEH-nihn, NAYT) **COL**

Defense. Shoots right. 6'3", 207 lbs. Born, Alquippa, PA, December 10, 1982. NY Rangers' 3rd choice, 127th overall, in 2002 Entry Draft.

99-2000	Pittsburgh	AAHA	40	3	10	13	122	....	....	....	....	....	....	....	....	....	....	....	....	....	....	....	....	....	....
2000-01	Green Bay	USHL	54	2	11	13	70	....	....	....	....	....	....	....	....	....	4	1	1	2	6	....	....	....	....
2001-02	Green Bay	USHL	56	4	11	15	150	....	....	....	....	....	....	....	....	....	7	3	3	6	10	....	....	....	....
2002-03	Ohio State	CCHA	42	2	9	11	75	....	....	....	....	....	....	....	....	....	....	....	....	....	....	....	....	....	....
2003-04	Ohio State	CCHA	29	2	15	17	92	....	....	....	....	....	....	....	....	....	....	....	....	....	....	....	....	....	....
2004-05	Ohio State	CCHA	41	2	12	14	136	....	....	....	....	....	....	....	....	....	....	....	....	....	....	....	....	....	....
2005-06	Ohio State	CCHA	39	0	11	11	87	....	....	....	....	....	....	....	....	....	....	....	....	....	....	....	....	....	....
2006-07	**Philadelphia**	**NHL**	**9**	**0**	**2**	**2**	**4**	**0**	**0**	**0**	**0**	**0.0**	**0**	**0**	**0.0**	**8:40**	....	....	....	....	....	....	....	....	....
	Philadelphia	AHL	68	3	9	12	92	....	....	....	....	....	....	....	....	....	....	....	....	....	....	....	....	....	....
2007-08	**Philadelphia**	**NHL**	**2**	**0**	**0**	**0**	**2**	**0**	**0**	**0**	**0**	**0.0**	**2**	**0**	**0.0**	**9:57**	....	....	....	....	....	....	....	....	....
	Philadelphia	AHL	77	4	13	17	146	....	....	....	....	....	....	....	....	....	12	0	1	1	18	....	....	....	....
2008-09	**Philadelphia**	**NHL**	**1**	**0**	**0**	**0**	**0**	**0**	**0**	**0**	**0**	**0.0**	**0**	**0**	**0.0**	**13:25**	....	....	....	....	....	....	....	....	....
	Philadelphia	AHL	62	0	14	14	95	....	....	....	....	....	....	....	....	....	4	0	0	0	10	....	....	....	....
2009-10	**Pittsburgh**	**NHL**	**2**	**0**	**0**	**0**	**0**	**0**	**0**	**0**	**1**	**0.0**	**-2**	**0**	**0.0**	**13:32**	....	....	....	....	....	....	....	....	....
	Wilkes-Barre	AHL	41	3	2	5	63	....	....	....	....	....	....	....	....	....	....	....	....	....	....	....	....	....	....
	Peoria Rivermen	AHL	27	2	11	13	35	....	....	....	....	....	....	....	....	....	....	....	....	....	....	....	....	....	....
2010-11	**Columbus**	**NHL**	**3**	**0**	**0**	**0**	**2**	**0**	**0**	**0**	**2**	**0.0**	**-3**	**0**	**0.0**	**14:48**	....	....	....	....	....	....	....	....	....
	Springfield	AHL	30	0	5	5	21	....	....	....	....	....	....	....	....	....	....	....	....	....	....	....	....	....	....
	Syracuse Crunch	AHL	43	2	10	12	44	....	....	....	....	....	....	....	....	....	....	....	....	....	....	....	....	....	....
2011-12	**Anaheim**	**NHL**	**15**	**2**	**0**	**2**	**6**	**0**	**0**	**1**	**5**	**40.0**	**6**	**0**	**0.0**	**11:09**	....	....	....	....	....	....	....	....	....
	Syracuse Crunch	AHL	27	0	5	5	16	....	....	....	....	....	....	....	....	....	4	0	0	0	14	....	....	....	....
2012-13	Norfolk Admirals	AHL	66	4	20	24	38	....	....	....	....	....	....	....	....	....	....	....	....	....	....	....	....	....	....
2013-14	**Colorado**	**NHL**	**68**	**1**	**8**	**9**	**46**	**0**	**0**	**0**	**52**	**1.9**	**3**	**0**	**0.0**	**17:17**	**7**	**0**	**1**	**1**	**4**	**0**	**0**	**0**	**16:00**
2014-15	**Colorado**	**NHL**	**76**	**2**	**13**	**15**	**32**	**0**	**0**	**0**	**38**	**5.3**	**-1**	**0**	**0.0**	**16:51**	....	....	....	....	....	....	....	....	....
	NHL Totals		**176**	**5**	**23**	**28**	**92**	**0**	**0**	**1**	**98**	**5.1**		**0**	**0.0**	**15:56**	**7**	**0**	**1**	**1**	**4**	**0**	**0**	**0**	**16:00**

USHL All-Rookie Team (2001) • CCHA Second All-Star Team (2005)

Signed as a free agent by **Philadelphia**, August 16, 2006. Signed as a free agent by **Pittsburgh**, July 3, 2009. Traded to **St. Louis** by **Pittsburgh** for Steve Wagner, February 11, 2010. Signed as a free agent by **Columbus**, July 2, 2010. Traded to **Anaheim** by **Columbus** for Trevor Smith, January 4, 2011. Signed as a free agent by **Colorado**, July 5, 2013.

GUNNARSSON, Carl

(GUHN-nuhr-suhn, KARL) **ST.L.**

Defense. Shoots left. 6'2", 196 lbs. Born, Orebro, Sweden, November 9, 1986. Toronto's 6th choice, 194th overall, in 2007 Entry Draft.

2003-04	HC Orebro 90	Sweden-2	43	0	4	4	16	....	....	....	....	....	....	....	....	....	....	....	....	....	....	....	....	....	....
2004-05	Linkoping U18	Swe-U18	1	0	1	1	2	....	....	....	....	....	....	....	....	....	....	....	....	....	....	....	....	....	....
	Linkopings HC Jr.	Swe-Jr.	22	2	5	7	24	....	....	....	....	....	....	....	....	....	....	....	....	....	....	....	....	....	....
2005-06	Linkopings HC Jr.	Swe-Jr.	30	7	6	13	26	....	....	....	....	....	....	....	....	....	4	1	0	1	4	....	....	....	....
	IFK Arboga IK	Sweden-2	12	1	5	6	8	....	....	....	....	....	....	....	....	....	....	....	....	....	....	....	....	....	....
	Linkopings HC	Sweden	14	0	0	0	0	....	....	....	....	....	....	....	....	....	....	....	....	....	....	....	....	....	....
2006-07	Linkopings HC Jr.	Swe-Jr.	6	0	5	5	6	....	....	....	....	....	....	....	....	....	....	....	....	....	....	....	....	....	....
	VIK Vasteras HK	Sweden-2	15	2	3	5	14	....	....	....	....	....	....	....	....	....	....	....	....	....	....	....	....	....	....
	Linkopings HC	Sweden	30	2	2	4	8	....	....	....	....	....	....	....	....	....	15	0	4	4	4	....	....	....	....
2007-08	Linkopings HC	Sweden	53	2	7	9	26	....	....	....	....	....	....	....	....	....	16	0	4	4	10	....	....	....	....
2008-09	Linkopings HC	Sweden	53	6	10	16	26	....	....	....	....	....	....	....	....	....	7	0	1	1	2	....	....	....	....
2009-10	**Toronto**	**NHL**	**43**	**3**	**12**	**15**	**10**	**0**	**0**	**0**	**45**	**6.7**	**8**	**1**	**0.0**	**21:26**	....	....	....	....	....	....	....	....	....
	Toronto Marlies	AHL	12	0	2	2	2	....	....	....	....	....	....	....	....	....	....	....	....	....	....	....	....	....	....
2010-11	**Toronto**	**NHL**	**68**	**4**	**16**	**20**	**14**	**1**	**0**	**1**	**69**	**5.8**	**-2**	**0**	**0.0**	**18:15**	....	....	....	....	....	....	....	....	....
2011-12	**Toronto**	**NHL**	**76**	**4**	**15**	**19**	**20**	**0**	**0**	**0**	**89**	**4.5**	**-9**	**1**	**0.0**	**21:42**	....	....	....	....	....	....	....	....	....
2012-13	Orebro HK	Sweden-2	10	0	4	4	2	....	....	....	....	....	....	....	....	....	....	....	....	....	....	....	....	....	....
	Toronto	**NHL**	**37**	**1**	**14**	**15**	**14**	**0**	**0**	**0**	**28**	**3.6**	**5**	**0**	**0.0**	**21:17**	**7**	**0**	**1**	**1**	**0**	**0**	**0**	**0**	**22:05**
2013-14	**Toronto**	**NHL**	**80**	**3**	**14**	**17**	**34**	**0**	**0**	**1**	**48**	**6.3**	**12**	**0**	**0.0**	**19:25**	....	....	....	....	....	....	....	....	....
2014-15	**St. Louis**	**NHL**	**61**	**2**	**10**	**12**	**2**	**0**	**0**	**0**	**54**	**3.7**	**10**	**0**	**0.0**	**18:04**	**6**	**0**	**0**	**0**	**0**	**0**	**0**	**0**	**17:51**
	NHL Totals		**365**	**17**	**81**	**98**	**94**	**1**	**0**	**2**	**333**	**5.1**		**2**	**0.0**	**19:52**	**13**	**0**	**1**	**1**	**0**	**0**	**0**	**0**	**20:08**

Signed as a free agent by **Orebro** (Sweden-2), November 12, 2012. Traded to **St. Louis** by **Toronto** with Calgary's 4th round choice (previously acquired, St. Louis selected Ville Husso) in 2014 Entry Draft for Roman Polak, June 28, 2014.

GUSTAFSSON, Erik

(GOOS-tahf-suhn, AIR-ihk)

Defense. Shoots left. 5'10", 180 lbs. Born, Kvissleby, Sweden, December 15, 1988.

2004-05	Timra IK U18	Swe-U18	14	4	2	6	12	....	....	....	....	....	....	....	....	....	3	0	0	0	0	....	....	....	....
2005-06	Timra IK U18	Swe-U18	8	2	1	3	8	....	....	....	....	....	....	....	....	....	....	....	....	....	....	....	....	....	....
	Timra IK Jr.	Swe-Jr.	38	3	4	7	26	....	....	....	....	....	....	....	....	....	1	0	0	0	0	....	....	....	....
2006-07	Timra IK Jr.	Swe-Jr.	41	7	13	20	93	....	....	....	....	....	....	....	....	....	3	0	0	0	14	....	....	....	....
2007-08	Northern Mich.	CCHA	44	0	27	27	12	....	....	....	....	....	....	....	....	....	....	....	....	....	....	....	....	....	....
2008-09	Northern Mich.	CCHA	40	4	30	34	10	....	....	....	....	....	....	....	....	....	....	....	....	....	....	....	....	....	....
2009-10	Northern Mich.	CCHA	39	3	29	32	26	....	....	....	....	....	....	....	....	....	....	....	....	....	....	....	....	....	....
	Adirondack	AHL	5	2	5	7	0	....	....	....	....	....	....	....	....	....	....	....	....	....	....	....	....	....	....
2010-11	**Philadelphia**	**NHL**	**3**	**0**	**0**	**0**	**4**	**0**	**0**	**0**	**2**	**0.0**	**-1**	**0**	**0.0**	**10:57**	....	....	....	....	....	....	....	....	....
	Adirondack	AHL	72	5	44	49	14	....	....	....	....	....	....	....	....	....	....	....	....	....	....	....	....	....	....
2011-12	**Philadelphia**	**NHL**	**30**	**1**	**4**	**5**	**2**	**0**	**0**	**0**	**18**	**5.6**	**12**	**0**	**0.0**	**16:48**	**7**	**1**	**1**	**2**	**0**	**0**	**0**	**0**	**15:13**
	Adirondack	AHL	28	1	16	17	14	....	....	....	....	....	....	....	....	....	....	....	....	....	....	....	....	....	....
2012-13	Adirondack	AHL	39	5	17	22	37	....	....	....	....	....	....	....	....	....	....	....	....	....	....	....	....	....	....
	Philadelphia	**NHL**	**27**	**3**	**5**	**8**	**2**	**0**	**0**	**1**	**36**	**8.3**	**-1**	**1**	**0.0**	**20:09**	....	....	....	....	....	....	....	....	....
2013-14	**Philadelphia**	**NHL**	**31**	**2**	**8**	**10**	**6**	**0**	**0**	**0**	**30**	**6.7**	**7**	**0**	**0.0**	**17:31**	**2**	**1**	**0**	**1**	**2**	**0**	**0**	**1**	**17:10**
2014-15	Omsk	KHL	56	6	16	22	18	....	....	....	....	....	....	....	....	....	12	0	3	3	6	....	....	....	....
	NHL Totals		**91**	**6**	**17**	**23**	**14**	**0**	**0**	**1**	**86**	**7.0**		**1**	**0.0**	**17:51**	**9**	**2**	**1**	**3**	**4**	**0**	**0**	**1**	**15:39**

CCHA All-Rookie Team (2008) • CCHA First All-Star Team (2009, 2010) • NCAA West Second All-American Team (2009, 2010) • AHL All-Rookie Team (2011)

Signed as a free agent by **Philadelphia**, March 31, 2010. • Missed majority of 2013-14 as a healthy reserve. Signed as a free agent by **Omsk** (KHL), May 16, 2014.

HAGELIN, Carl

(HAG-eh-lihn, KARL) **ANA**

Left wing. Shoots left. 5'11", 186 lbs. Born, Sodertalje, Sweden, August 23, 1988. NY Rangers' 4th choice, 168th overall, in 2007 Entry Draft.

2004-05	Sodertalje SK U18	Swe-U18	14	10	7	17	16	....	....	....	....	....	....	....	....	....	2	0	2	2	0	....	....	....	....
2005-06	Sodertalje SK U18	Swe-U18	7	4	8	12	2	....	....	....	....	....	....	....	....	....	....	....	....	....	....	....	....	....	....
	Sodertalje SK Jr.	Swe-Jr.	41	20	20	40	42	....	....	....	....	....	....	....	....	....	4	1	2	3	22	....	....	....	....
2006-07	Sodertalje SK Jr.	Swe-Jr.	40	24	31	55	42	....	....	....	....	....	....	....	....	....	3	1	5	6	20	....	....	....	....
2007-08	U. of Michigan	CCHA	41	11	11	22	28	....	....	....	....	....	....	....	....	....	....	....	....	....	....	....	....	....	....
2008-09	U. of Michigan	CCHA	41	13	18	31	32	....	....	....	....	....	....	....	....	....	....	....	....	....	....	....	....	....	....
2009-10	U. of Michigan	CCHA	45	19	*31	*50	34	....	....	....	....	....	....	....	....	....	....	....	....	....	....	....	....	....	....
2010-11	U. of Michigan	CCHA	44	18	31	49	39	....	....	....	....	....	....	....	....	....	....	....	....	....	....	....	....	....	....
	Connecticut	AHL	....	....	....	....	....	....	....	....	....	....	....	....	....	....	5	1	1	2	4	....	....	....	....
2011-12	**NY Rangers**	**NHL**	**64**	**14**	**24**	**38**	**24**	**0**	**2**	**2**	**131**	**10.7**	**21**	**6**	**16.7**	**15:03**	**17**	**0**	**3**	**3**	**17**	**0**	**0**	**0**	**16:45**
	Connecticut	AHL	17	7	6	13	6	....	....	....	....	....	....	....	....	....	....	....	....	....	....	....	....	....	....
2012-13	Sodertalje SK	Sweden-2	8	5	6	11	0	....	....	....	....	....	....	....	....	....	....	....	....	....	....	....	....	....	....
	NY Rangers	**NHL**	**48**	**10**	**14**	**24**	**18**	**1**	**0**	**1**	**132**	**7.6**	**10**	**17**	**41.2**	**17:18**	**12**	**3**	**3**	**6**	**0**	**0**	**0**	**0**	**18:06**

			Regular Season														Playoffs								
Season	Club	League	GP	G	A	Pts	PIM	PP	SH	GW	S	S%	+/-	TF	F%	Min	GP	G	A	Pts	PIM	PP	SH	GW	Min
2013-14	NY Rangers	NHL	72	17	16	33	44	0	1	5	144	11.8	8	5	0.0	15:32	25	7	5	12	16	0	*2	1	15:59
	Sweden	Olympics	6	2	0	2	0	....	....	....	....	....	....	....	....	....	....	....	....	....	....	....	....	....	....
2014-15	NY Rangers	NHL	82	17	18	35	46	1	0	4	185	9.2	18	17	35.3	15:14	19	2	3	5	6	0	0	1	16:38
	NHL Totals		266	58	72	130	132	2	3	12	592	9.8		45	31.1	15:39	73	12	14	26	39	0	2	2	16:41

CCHA First All-Star Team (2011) • NCAA West Second All-American Team (2011)

Signed as a free agent by **Sodertalje** (Sweden-2), September 28, 2012. Traded to **Anaheim** by **NY Rangers** with NY Rangers' 2nd (Julius Naatinen) and 6th (Garrett Metcalf) round choices in 2015 Entry Draft for Emerson Etem and Florida's 2nd round choice (previously acquired, NY Rangers selected Ryan Gropp) in 2015 Entry Draft, June 27, 2015.

HAINSEY, Ron

(HAYN-zee, RAWN) **CAR**

Defense. Shoots left. 6'3", 210 lbs. Born, Bolton, CT, March 24, 1981. Montreal's 1st choice, 13th overall, in 2000 Entry Draft.

1997-98	USNTDP	U-17	18	2	7	9	28	....	....	....	....	....	....	....	....	....	....	....	....	....	....	....	....	....	....
	USNTDP	USHL	3	0	0	0	0	....	....	....	....	....	....	....	....	....	....	....	....	....	....	....	....	....	....
	USNTDP	NAHL	40	4	7	11	16	....	....	....	....	....	....	....	....	....	5	0	1	1	0	....	....	....	....
1998-99	USNTDP	USHL	48	5	12	17	45	....	....	....	....	....	....	....	....	....	....	....	....	....	....	....	....	....	....
99-2000	U. Mass Lowell	H-East	30	3	8	11	20	....	....	....	....	....	....	....	....	....	....	....	....	....	....	....	....	....	....
2000-01	U. Mass Lowell	H-East	33	10	26	36	51	....	....	....	....	....	....	....	....	....	....	....	....	....	....	....	....	....	....
	Quebec Citadelles	AHL	4	1	0	1	0	....	....	....	....	....	....	....	....	....	1	0	0	0	0	....	....	....	....
2001-02	Quebec Citadelles	AHL	63	7	24	31	26	....	....	....	....	....	....	....	....	....	3	0	0	0	0	....	....	....	....
2002-03	Montreal	NHL	21	0	0	0	2	0	0	0	12	0.0	–1	0	0.0	12:25	....	....	....	....	....	....	....	....	....
	Hamilton	AHL	33	2	11	13	26	....	....	....	....	....	....	....	....	....	23	1	10	11	20	....	....	....	....
2003-04	Montreal	NHL	11	1	1	2	4	0	0	0	11	9.1	3	0	0.0	13:15	....	....	....	....	....	....	....	....	....
	Hamilton	AHL	54	7	24	31	35	....	....	....	....	....	....	....	....	....	10	0	5	5	6	....	....	....	....
2004-05	Hamilton	AHL	68	9	14	23	45	....	....	....	....	....	....	....	....	....	4	1	1	2	0	....	....	....	....
2005-06	Hamilton	AHL	22	3	14	17	19	....	....	....	....	....	....	....	....	....	....	....	....	....	....	....	....	....	....
	Columbus	NHL	55	2	15	17	43	1	0	0	81	2.5	13	1	0.0	17:47	....	....	....	....	....	....	....	....	....
2006-07	Columbus	NHL	80	9	25	34	69	7	0	0	136	6.6	–19	2	50.0	22:53	....	....	....	....	....	....	....	....	....
2007-08	Columbus	NHL	78	8	24	32	25	8	0	0	161	5.0	–7	0	0.0	22:34	....	....	....	....	....	....	....	....	....
2008-09	Atlanta	NHL	81	6	33	39	32	4	0	0	148	4.1	–16	0	0.0	22:22	....	....	....	....	....	....	....	....	....
2009-10	Atlanta	NHL	80	5	21	26	39	0	0	0	121	4.1	–6	0	0.0	22:08	....	....	....	....	....	....	....	....	....
2010-11	Atlanta	NHL	82	3	16	19	24	0	0	2	83	3.6	3	0	0.0	18:05	....	....	....	....	....	....	....	....	....
2011-12	Winnipeg	NHL	56	0	10	10	23	0	0	0	57	0.0	9	0	0.0	21:06	....	....	....	....	....	....	....	....	....
2012-13	Winnipeg	NHL	47	0	13	13	10	0	0	0	52	0.0	–8	0	0.0	22:52	....	....	....	....	....	....	....	....	....
2013-14	Carolina	NHL	82	4	11	15	45	0	0	1	72	5.6	–9	0	0.0	21:26	....	....	....	....	....	....	....	....	....
2014-15	Carolina	NHL	81	2	8	10	16	0	0	0	83	2.4	–14	1	100.0	21:06	....	....	....	....	....	....	....	....	....
	NHL Totals		754	40	177	217	332	20	0	3	1017	3.9		4	50.0	20:55	....	....	....	....	....	....	....	....	....

Hockey East First All-Star Team (2001) • NCAA East Second All-American Team (2001) • AHL All-Rookie Team (2002)

Claimed on waivers by **Columbus** from **Montreal**, November 29, 2005. Signed as a free agent by **Atlanta**, July 2, 2008. • Transferred to **Winnipeg** after **Atlanta** franchise relocated, June 21, 2011. Signed as a free agent by **Carolina**, September 12, 2013.

HALEY, Micheal

(HAY-lee, MIGH-kuhl) **S.J.**

Center. Shoots left. 5'10", 205 lbs. Born, Guelph, ON, March 30, 1986.

2002-03	Sarnia Sting	OHL	43	3	3	6	32	....	....	....	....	....	....	....	....	....	6	0	0	0	2	....	....	....	....
2003-04	Sarnia Sting	OHL	51	8	8	16	69	....	....	....	....	....	....	....	....	....	....	....	....	....	....	....	....	....	....
2004-05	Sarnia Sting	OHL	61	14	16	30	122	....	....	....	....	....	....	....	....	....	....	....	....	....	....	....	....	....	....
2005-06	Sarnia Sting	OHL	23	2	6	8	83	....	....	....	....	....	....	....	....	....	....	....	....	....	....	....	....	....	....
	St. Michael's	OHL	30	12	0	12	78	....	....	....	....	....	....	....	....	....	4	0	1	1	11	....	....	....	....
2006-07	St. Michael's	OHL	68	30	24	54	174	....	....	....	....	....	....	....	....	....	....	....	....	....	....	....	....	....	....
	South Carolina	ECHL	7	5	1	6	13	....	....	....	....	....	....	....	....	....	....	....	....	....	....	....	....	....	....
2007-08	Bridgeport	AHL	36	2	2	4	75	....	....	....	....	....	....	....	....	....	....	....	....	....	....	....	....	....	....
	Utah Grizzlies	ECHL	28	11	8	19	115	....	....	....	....	....	....	....	....	....	14	7	6	13	49	....	....	....	....
2008-09	Bridgeport	AHL	45	5	3	8	99	....	....	....	....	....	....	....	....	....	5	1	0	1	10	....	....	....	....
2009-10	NY Islanders	NHL	2	0	0	0	9	0	0	0	0	0.0	–3	5	20.0	7:37	....	....	....	....	....	....	....	....	....
	Bridgeport	AHL	65	6	8	14	196	....	....	....	....	....	....	....	....	....	3	0	0	0	4	....	....	....	....
2010-11	NY Islanders	NHL	27	2	1	3	85	0	0	0	13	15.4	–4	20	35.0	8:02	....	....	....	....	....	....	....	....	....
	Bridgeport	AHL	50	12	10	22	144	....	....	....	....	....	....	....	....	....	....	....	....	....	....	....	....	....	....
2011-12	NY Islanders	NHL	14	0	0	0	57	0	0	0	13	0.0	–1	2	50.0	7:57	....	....	....	....	....	....	....	....	....
	Bridgeport	AHL	51	15	10	25	125	....	....	....	....	....	....	....	....	....	3	0	0	0	2	....	....	....	....
2012-13	Connecticut	AHL	69	10	13	23	170	....	....	....	....	....	....	....	....	....	....	....	....	....	....	....	....	....	....
	NY Rangers	NHL	9	0	0	0	12	0	0	0	4	0.0	–1	3	66.7	6:38	2	0	0	0	0	0	0	0	6:02
2013-14	Hartford	AHL	53	7	11	18	131	....	....	....	....	....	....	....	....	....	....	....	....	....	....	....	....	....	....
2014-15	San Jose	NHL	4	0	0	0	11	0	0	0	1	0.0	–1	2	100.0	7:31	....	....	....	....	....	....	....	....	....
	Worcester Sharks	AHL	68	18	13	31	106	....	....	....	....	....	....	....	....	....	4	2	1	3	2	....	....	....	....
	NHL Totals		56	2	1	3	174	0	0	0	31	6.5		32	40.6	7:44	2	0	0	0	0	0	0	0	6:02

Signed as a free agent by **NY Islanders**, May 19, 2008. Signed as a free agent by **NY Rangers**, July 1, 2012. Signed as a free agent by **San Jose**, July 10, 2014.

HALISCHUK, Matt

(ha-LIHS-chuhk, MAT) **WPG**

Right wing. Shoots right. 5'11", 187 lbs. Born, Toronto, ON, June 1, 1988. New Jersey's 4th choice, 117th overall, in 2007 Entry Draft.

2003-04	Tor. Jr. Canadiens	GTHL	53	37	48	85	27	....	....	....	....	....	....	....	....	....	....	....	....	....	....	....	....	....	....
2004-05	St. Michael's	OHL	30	3	3	6	4	....	....	....	....	....	....	....	....	....	....	....	....	....	....	....	....	....	....
	St. Mike's B's	ON-Jr.A	17	5	11	16	8	....	....	....	....	....	....	....	....	....	32	10	15	25	4	....	....	....	....
2005-06	St. Michael's	OHL	61	13	18	31	16	....	....	....	....	....	....	....	....	....	4	1	1	2	0	....	....	....	....
2006-07	Kitchener Rangers	OHL	67	33	33	66	20	....	....	....	....	....	....	....	....	....	9	4	1	5	10	....	....	....	....
2007-08	Kitchener Rangers	OHL	40	13	46	59	16	....	....	....	....	....	....	....	....	....	20	*16	16	32	0	....	....	....	....
2008-09	New Jersey	NHL	1	0	1	1	0	0	0	0	0	0.0	–1	0	0.0	9:47	....	....	....	....	....	....	....	....	....
	Lowell Devils	AHL	47	14	15	29	10	....	....	....	....	....	....	....	....	....	....	....	....	....	....	....	....	....	....
2009-10	New Jersey	NHL	20	1	1	2	2	0	0	0	22	4.5	–4	4	25.0	11:18	....	....	....	....	....	....	....	....	....
	Lowell Devils	AHL	32	11	11	22	2	....	....	....	....	....	....	....	....	....	1	0	0	0	0	....	....	....	....
2010-11	Nashville	NHL	27	4	8	12	2	0	0	1	29	13.8	5	4	0.0	10:08	12	2	0	2	0	0	0	1	11:45
	Milwaukee	AHL	37	11	12	23	12	....	....	....	....	....	....	....	....	....	1	1	1	2	0	....	....	....	....
2011-12	Nashville	NHL	73	15	13	28	27	0	0	2	96	15.6	9	30	36.7	11:15	5	0	1	1	4	0	0	0	7:01
2012-13	Nashville	NHL	36	5	6	11	10	0	0	1	51	9.8	1	6	33.3	11:57	....	....	....	....	....	....	....	....	....
	Milwaukee	AHL	2	2	1	3	0	....	....	....	....	....	....	....	....	....	....	....	....	....	....	....	....	....	....
2013-14	Winnipeg	NHL	46	5	5	10	6	0	0	1	56	8.9	–3	4	50.0	11:20	....	....	....	....	....	....	....	....	....
2014-15	Winnipeg	NHL	47	3	5	8	6	0	0	1	59	5.1	5	1	100.0	9:45	1	0	0	0	0	0	0	0	9:18
	NHL Totals		250	33	39	72	53	0	0	6	313	10.5		49	34.7	10:58	18	2	1	3	4	0	0	1	10:18

OHL First All-Star Team (2008) • George Parsons Trophy (Memorial Cup - Most Sportsmanlike Player) (2008)

Traded to **Nashville** by **New Jersey** with New Jersey's 2nd round choice (Magnus Hellberg) in 2011 Entry Draft for Jason Arnott, June 19, 2010. Signed as a free agent by **Winnipeg**, July 11, 2013.

HALL, Adam

(HAWL, A-duhm)

Right wing. Shoots right. 6'2", 212 lbs. Born, Kalamazoo, MI, August 14, 1980. Nashville's 3rd choice, 52nd overall, in 1999 Entry Draft.

1996-97	Bramalea Blues	ON-Jr.A	43	9	14	23	92	....	....	....	....	....	....	....	....	....	....	....	....	....	....	....	....	....	....
1997-98	USNTDP	U-18	29	18	9	27	19	....	....	....	....	....	....	....	....	....	....	....	....	....	....	....	....	....	....
	USNTDP	USHL	21	9	11	20	20	....	....	....	....	....	....	....	....	....	....	....	....	....	....	....	....	....	....
	USNTDP	NAHL	15	12	1	13	20	....	....	....	....	....	....	....	....	....	6	3	2	5	4	....	....	....	....
1998-99	Michigan State	CCHA	36	16	7	23	74	....	....	....	....	....	....	....	....	....	....	....	....	....	....	....	....	....	....
99-2000	Michigan State	CCHA	40	*26	13	39	38	....	....	....	....	....	....	....	....	....	....	....	....	....	....	....	....	....	....
2000-01	Michigan State	CCHA	42	18	12	30	42	....	....	....	....	....	....	....	....	....	....	....	....	....	....	....	....	....	....
2001-02	Michigan State	CCHA	41	19	15	34	36	....	....	....	....	....	....	....	....	....	....	....	....	....	....	....	....	....	....
	Nashville	NHL	1	0	1	1	0	0	0	0	2	0.0	0	0	0.0	14:04	....	....	....	....	....	....	....	....	....
	Milwaukee	AHL	6	2	2	4	4	....	....	....	....	....	....	....	....	....	....	....	....	....	....	....	....	....	....
2002-03	Nashville	NHL	79	16	12	28	31	8	0	2	146	11.0	–8	17	52.9	14:09	....	....	....	....	....	....	....	....	....
	Milwaukee	AHL	1	0	0	0	2	....	....	....	....	....	....	....	....	....	....	....	....	....	....	....	....	....	....
2003-04	Nashville	NHL	79	13	14	27	37	6	0	1	151	8.6	–8	348	56.3	16:14	6	2	1	3	2	0	0	1	18:29
2004-05	KalPa Kuopio	Finland-2	36	23	17	40	28	....	....	....	....	....	....	....	....	....	9	2	3	5	4	....	....	....	....

			Regular Season														Playoffs								
Season	Club	League	GP	G	A	Pts	PIM	PP	SH	GW	S	S%	+/-	TF	F%	Min	GP	G	A	Pts	PIM	PP	SH	GW	Min
2005-06	Nashville	NHL	75	14	15	29	40	10	0	5	122	11.5	0	470	48.9	16:47	5	1	0	1	0	1	0	1	12:10
2006-07	NY Rangers	NHL	49	4	8	12	18	3	0	0	61	6.6	–13	59	45.8	12:27									
	Minnesota	NHL	23	2	3	5	8	0	0	0	42	4.8	2	11	72.7	12:13	3	0	0	0	7	0	0	0	10:06
2007-08	Pittsburgh	NHL	46	2	4	6	24	0	0	0	39	5.1	–2	290	50.3	11:52	17	3	1	4	8	0	0	1	10:59
2008-09	Tampa Bay	NHL	74	5	5	10	29	1	0	0	90	5.6	–9	338	50.0	11:12									
2009-10	Norfolk Admirals	AHL	79	16	25	41	47																		
2010-11	Tampa Bay	NHL	82	7	11	18	32	0	0	1	167	4.2	–12	655	55.0	14:51	18	1	4	5	8	0	0	0	13:53
2011-12	Tampa Bay	NHL	57	2	5	7	17	0	0	1	63	3.2	–11	464	59.5	11:52									
2012-13	Ravensburg	German-2	17	11	4	15	39																		
	Tampa Bay	NHL	20	0	4	4	23	0	0	0	16	0.0	3	165	56.4	10:18									
	Carolina	NHL	6	0	0	0	0	0	0	0	3	0.0	–2	8	25.0	10:31									
	Philadelphia	NHL	11	0	0	0	0	0	0	0	15	0.0	–1	78	59.0	10:59									
2013-14	Philadelphia	NHL	80	4	5	9	23	0	2	0	61	6.6	–15	527	59.6	9:50	7	0	1	1	7	0	0	0	10:01
2014-15	HC Ambri-Piotta	Swiss	55	13	18	31	38										6	2	3	5	0				
	NHL Totals		682	69	87	156	282	28	2	10	978	7.1		3430	54.7	13:13	56	7	7	14	32	1	0	3	12:39

CCHA Second All-Star Team (2000)

Signed as a free agent by **Kuopio** (Finland-2), October 11, 2004. Traded to **NY Rangers** by **Nashville** for Dominic Moore, July 19, 2006. Traded to **Minnesota** by **NY Rangers** for Pascal Dupuis, February 9, 2007. Signed as a free agent by **Pittsburgh**, October 1, 2007. Signed as a free agent by **Tampa Bay**, July 1, 2008. Signed as a free agent by **Ravensburg** (German-2), October 11, 2012. Claimed on waivers by **Carolina** from **Tampa Bay**, March 16, 2013. Traded to **Tampa Bay** by **Carolina** with Carolina's 7th round choice (Joel Vermin) in 2013 Entry Draft for Marc-Andre Bergeron, April 2, 2013. Claimed on waivers by **Philadelphia** from **Tampa Bay**, April 3, 2013. Signed as a free agent by **Ambri-Piotta** (Swiss), August 3, 2014.

HALL, Taylor (HAWL, TAY-luhr) EDM

Left wing. Shoots left. 6'1", 201 lbs. Born, Calgary, AB, November 14, 1991. Edmonton's 1st choice, 1st overall, in 2010 Entry Draft.

Season	Club	League	GP	G	A	Pts	PIM	PP	SH	GW	S	S%	+/-	TF	F%	Min	GP	G	A	Pts	PIM	PP	SH	GW	Min
2006-07	King. Jr. Front.	Minor-ON	29	44	41	85	10																		
2007-08	Windsor Spitfires	OHL	63	45	39	84	22										5	2	3	5	2				
2008-09	Windsor Spitfires	OHL	63	38	52	90	60										20	*16	20	*36	12				
2009-10	Windsor Spitfires	OHL	57	40	*66	*106	56										19	17	18	*35	32				
2010-11	Edmonton	NHL	65	22	20	42	27	8	0	4	186	11.8	–9	105	40.0	18:13									
2011-12	Edmonton	NHL	61	27	26	53	36	13	0	7	207	13.0	–3	57	40.4	18:13									
2012-13	Oklahoma City	AHL	26	14	20	34	33																		
	Edmonton	NHL	45	16	34	50	33	4	0	4	154	10.4	5	53	54.7	18:37									
2013-14	Edmonton	NHL	75	27	53	80	44	7	0	1	250	10.8	–15	81	45.7	20:01									
2014-15	Edmonton	NHL	53	14	24	38	40	3	0	0	158	8.9	–1	98	45.9	19:13									
	NHL Totals		299	106	157	263	180	35	0	16	955	11.1		394	44.7	18:54									

Canadian Major Junior All-Rookie Team (2008) • Canadian Major Junior Rookie of the Year (2008) • OHL First All-Star Team (2009, 2010) • OHL Playoff MVP (2009) • Canadian Major Junior Second All-Star Team (2010) • Memorial Cup All-Star Team (2009, 2010) • Ed Chynoweth Trophy (Memorial Cup - Leading Scorer) (2010) • Stafford Smythe Memorial Trophy (Memorial Cup - MVP) (2009, 2010)

HALMO, Mike (HAL-moh, MIGHK) NYI

Left wing. Shoots left. 5'10", 209 lbs. Born, Waterloo, ON, May 11, 1991.

Season	Club	League	GP	G	A	Pts	PIM	PP	SH	GW	S	S%	+/-	TF	F%	Min	GP	G	A	Pts	PIM	PP	SH	GW	Min
2008-09	Owen Sound	OHL	62	5	3	8	90										4	0	1	1	2				
2009-10	Owen Sound	OHL	60	11	18	29	121																		
2010-11	Owen Sound	OHL	59	20	23	43	121										22	5	10	15	36				
2011-12	Owen Sound	OHL	66	40	45	85	162																		
	Bridgeport	AHL	5	1	0	1	5																		
2012-13	Bridgeport	AHL	46	5	9	14	46																		
2013-14	NY Islanders	NHL	20	1	0	1	32	0	0	0	25	4.0	–1	20	20.0	9:30									
	Bridgeport	AHL	56	18	20	38	137																		
2014-15	Bridgeport	AHL	33	10	8	18	83																		
	NHL Totals		20	1	0	1	32	0	0	0	25	4.0		20	20.0	9:30									

Signed as a free agent by **NY Islanders**, March 10, 2012. • Missed majority of 2014-15 due to injury at Wilkes-Barre (AHL), December 12, 2014.

HAMHUIS, Dan (HAM-HOOS, DAN) VAN

Defense. Shoots left. 6'1", 209 lbs. Born, Smithers, BC, December 13, 1982. Nashville's 1st choice, 12th overall, in 2001 Entry Draft.

Season	Club	League	GP	G	A	Pts	PIM	PP	SH	GW	S	S%	+/-	TF	F%	Min	GP	G	A	Pts	PIM	PP	SH	GW	Min
1997-98	Smithers A's	Minor-BC	59	59	72	131	59																		
1998-99	Prince George	WHL	56	1	3	4	45										7	1	2	3	8				
99-2000	Prince George	WHL	70	10	23	33	140										13	2	3	5	35				
2000-01	Prince George	WHL	62	13	47	60	125										6	2	3	5	15				
2001-02	Prince George	WHL	59	10	50	60	135										7	0	5	5	16				
2002-03	Milwaukee	AHL	68	6	21	27	81										6	0	3	3	2				
2003-04	Nashville	NHL	80	7	19	26	57	2	0	4	115	6.1	–12	0	0.0	22:08	6	0	2	2	6	0	0	0	20:29
2004-05	Milwaukee	AHL	76	13	38	51	85										7	0	2	2	10				
2005-06	Nashville	NHL	82	7	31	38	70	4	1	1	135	5.2	11	0	0.0	22:34	5	0	2	2	2	0	0	0	19:41
2006-07	Nashville	NHL	81	6	14	20	66	0	0	1	84	7.1	8	1	0.0	21:20	5	0	1	1	2	0	0	0	21:36
2007-08	Nashville	NHL	80	4	23	27	66	1	0	1	127	3.1	–4	0	0.0	22:44	6	1	1	2	6	1	0	0	22:47
2008-09	Nashville	NHL	82	3	23	26	67	1	1	1	135	2.2	–4	0	0.0	22:50									
2009-10	Nashville	NHL	78	5	19	24	49	0	0	0	115	4.3	4	0	0.0	21:15	6	0	2	2	2	0	0	0	22:25
2010-11	Vancouver	NHL	64	6	17	23	34	2	0	1	109	5.5	29	0	0.0	22:41	19	1	5	6	6	1	0	0	24:50
2011-12	Vancouver	NHL	82	4	33	37	46	1	0	0	140	2.9	29	0	0.0	23:26	5	0	3	3	6	0	0	0	24:23
2012-13	Vancouver	NHL	47	4	20	24	12	0	1	0	61	6.6	9	0	0.0	23:23	4	1	1	2	8	0	0	0	25:14
2013-14	Vancouver	NHL	79	5	17	22	26	0	0	0	150	3.3	13	0	0.0	23:57									
	Canada	Olympics	5	0	0	0	0																		
2014-15	Vancouver	NHL	59	1	22	23	44	1	0	0	82	1.2	0	0	0.0	21:32	6	0	1	1	16	0	0	0	19:40
	NHL Totals		814	52	238	290	537	12	3	9	1253	4.2		1	0.0	22:31	62	3	18	21	54	2	0	0	22:48

WHL West First All-Star Team (2001, 2002) • WHL Player of the Year (2002) • Canadian Major Junior First All-Star Team (2002) • Canadian Major Junior Defenseman of the Year (2002) • AHL Second All-Star Team (2005)

Traded to **Philadelphia** by **Nashville** for Ryan Parent and future considerations, June 19, 2010. Traded to **Pittsburgh** by **Philadelphia** for Pittsburgh's 3rd round choice (later traded to Phoenix – Phoenix selected Harrison Ruopp) in 2011 Entry Draft, June 25, 2010. Signed as a free agent by **Vancouver**, July 1, 2010.

HAMILTON, Curtis (HAM-ihl-tuhn, KUHR-tihs)

Left wing. Shoots left. 6'2", 212 lbs. Born, Tacoma, WA, December 4, 1991. Edmonton's 4th choice, 48th overall, in 2010 Entry Draft.

Season	Club	League	GP	G	A	Pts	PIM	PP	SH	GW	S	S%	+/-	TF	F%	Min	GP	G	A	Pts	PIM	PP	SH	GW	Min
2006-07	Okan. Rockets	BCMML	37	26	27	53	68																		
	Saskatoon Blades	WHL	2	0	0	0	0																		
2007-08	Saskatoon Blades	WHL	68	14	13	27	43																		
2008-09	Saskatoon Blades	WHL	58	20	28	48	24										7	1	1	2	2				
2009-10	Saskatoon Blades	WHL	26	7	9	16	6										5	2	1	3	6				
2010-11	Saskatoon Blades	WHL	62	26	56	82	22										10	4	7	11	4				
2011-12	Oklahoma City	AHL	41	5	6	11	8										2	0	0	0	2				
2012-13	Oklahoma City	AHL	61	5	4	9	10										1	0	0	0	0				
2013-14	Oklahoma City	AHL	43	8	8	16	23										3	1	0	1	2				
2014-15	Edmonton	NHL	1	0	0	0	5	0	0	0	0	0.0	0	0	0.0	8:01									
	Oklahoma City	AHL	63	12	20	32	38										10	1	1	2	6				
	NHL Totals		1	0	0	0	5	0	0	0	0	0.0		0	0.0	8:01									

HAMILTON, Dougie (HAM-ihl-tuhn, DUH-gee) CGY

Defense. Shoots right. 6'5", 220 lbs. Born, Toronto, ON, June 17, 1993. Boston's 1st choice, 9th overall, in 2011 Entry Draft.

Season	Club	League	GP	G	A	Pts	PIM	PP	SH	GW	S	S%	+/-	TF	F%	Min	GP	G	A	Pts	PIM	PP	SH	GW	Min
2008-09	St. Cath. Falcons	Minor-ON	67	20	33	53	26																		
2009-10	Niagara Ice Dogs	OHL	64	3	13	16	36										5	0	1	1	4				
2010-11	Niagara Ice Dogs	OHL	67	12	46	58	77										14	4	12	16	16				
2011-12	Niagara Ice Dogs	OHL	50	17	55	72	47										20	5	18	23	16				
2012-13	Boston	NHL	42	5	11	16	14	2	0	0	83	6.0	4	0	0.0	17:08	7	0	3	3	0	0	0	0	15:47

Season	Club	League	Regular Season														Playoffs								
			GP	G	A	Pts	PIM	PP	SH	GW	S	S%	+/-	TF	F%	Min	GP	G	A	Pts	PIM	PP	SH	GW	Min
2013-14	**Boston**	**NHL**	**64**	**7**	**18**	**25**	**40**	**2**	**0**	**1**	**114**	**6.1**	**22**	**0**	**0.0**	**19:06**	**12**	**2**	**5**	**7**	**14**	**1**	**0**	**1**	**19:07**
2014-15	**Boston**	**NHL**	**72**	**10**	**32**	**42**	**41**	**5**	**0**	**2**	**188**	**5.3**	**–3**	**0**	**0.0**	**21:20**	....	....	....	....	....	....	....	....	....
	NHL Totals		**178**	**22**	**61**	**83**	**95**	**9**	**0**	**3**	**385**	**5.7**		**0**	**0.0**	**19:32**	**19**	**2**	**8**	**10**	**14**	**1**	**0**	**1**	**17:53**

OHL Second All-Star Team (2011) • Canadian Major Junior Scholastic Player of the Year (2011) • OHL First All-Star Team (2012) • Canadian Major Junior Defenseman of the Year (2012)

Traded to **Calgary** by **Boston** for Calgary's 1st (Zachary Senyshyn) and 2nd (Jakob Forsbacks-Karlsson) round choices in 2015 Entry Draft and Washington's 2nd round choice (previously acquired, Boston selected Jeremy Lauzon) in 2015 Entry Draft, June 26, 2015.

HAMILTON, Freddie

(HAM-ihl-tuhn, FREH-dee) **COL**

Center. Shoots right. 6'1", 195 lbs. Born, Toronto, ON, January 1, 1992. San Jose's 4th choice, 129th overall, in 2010 Entry Draft.

Season	Club	League	GP	G	A	Pts	PIM	PP	SH	GW	S	S%	+/-	TF	F%	Min	GP	G	A	Pts	PIM	PP	SH	GW	Min
2007-08	Tor. Marlboros	GTHL	51	39	42	81	4	....	....	....	....	....	....	....	....	....	....	....	....	....	....	....	....	....	....
2008-09	Niagara Ice Dogs	OHL	65	10	18	28	8	....	....	....	....	....	....	....	....	....	12	2	2	4	4	....	....	....	....
2009-10	Niagara Ice Dogs	OHL	64	25	30	55	12	....	....	....	....	....	....	....	....	....	5	1	1	2	6	....	....	....	....
2010-11	Niagara Ice Dogs	OHL	68	38	45	83	20	....	....	....	....	....	....	....	....	....	14	4	10	14	4	....	....	....	....
2011-12	Niagara Ice Dogs	OHL	61	35	51	86	31	....	....	....	....	....	....	....	....	....	20	7	17	24	9	....	....	....	....
2012-13	Worcester Sharks	AHL	76	13	13	26	16	....	....	....	....	....	....	....	....	....	....	....	....	....	....	....	....	....	....
2013-14	**San Jose**	**NHL**	**11**	**0**	**0**	**0**	**2**	**0**	**0**	**0**	**13**	**0.0**	**–5**	**36**	**38.9**	**10:19**	....	....	....	....	....	....	....	....	....
	Worcester Sharks	AHL	64	22	21	43	6	....	....	....	....	....	....	....	....	....	....	....	....	....	....	....	....	....	....
2014-15	**San Jose**	**NHL**	**1**	**0**	**0**	**0**	**0**	**0**	**0**	**0**	**0**	**0.0**	**–1**	**2**	**50.0**	**8:27**	....	....	....	....	....	....	....	....	....
	Worcester Sharks	AHL	52	9	21	30	12	....	....	....	....	....	....	....	....	....	....	....	....	....	....	....	....	....	....
	Colorado	**NHL**	**17**	**1**	**0**	**1**	**0**	**0**	**0**	**1**	**11**	**9.1**	**–1**	**59**	**39.0**	**7:32**	....	....	....	....	....	....	....	....	....
	Lake Erie	AHL	5	2	2	4	0	....	....	....	....	....	....	....	....	....	....	....	....	....	....	....	....	....	....
	NHL Totals		**29**	**1**	**0**	**1**	**2**	**0**	**0**	**1**	**24**	**4.2**		**97**	**39.2**	**8:37**	....	....	....	....	....	....	....	....	....

Traded to **Colorado** by **San Jose** for Karl Stollery, March 2, 2015.

HAMILTON, Ryan

(HAM-ihl-tuhn, RIGH-uhn) **EDM**

Left wing. Shoots left. 6'2", 219 lbs. Born, Oshawa, ON, April 15, 1985.

Season	Club	League	GP	G	A	Pts	PIM	PP	SH	GW	S	S%	+/-	TF	F%	Min	GP	G	A	Pts	PIM	PP	SH	GW	Min
2002-03	Couchiching	ON-Jr.A	11	5	8	13	2	....	....	....	....	....	....	....	....	....	....	....	....	....	....	....	....	....	....
	Peterborough	ON-Jr.A	27	3	10	13	43	....	....	....	....	....	....	....	....	....	....	....	....	....	....	....	....	....	....
	Trenton Sting	ON-Jr.A	17	3	8	11	24	....	....	....	....	....	....	....	....	....	....	....	....	....	....	....	....	....	....
	Barrie Colts	OHL	24	3	2	5	10	....	....	....	....	....	....	....	....	....	6	1	0	1	0	....	....	....	....
2003-04	Kingston	ON-Jr.A	14	1	5	6	23	....	....	....	....	....	....	....	....	....	....	....	....	....	....	....	....	....	....
	Barrie Colts	OHL	46	17	10	27	21	....	....	....	....	....	....	....	....	....	7	0	1	1	8	....	....	....	....
2004-05	Barrie Colts	OHL	37	13	11	24	6	....	....	....	....	....	....	....	....	....	6	2	0	2	2	....	....	....	....
2005-06	Barrie Colts	OHL	63	46	26	72	58	....	....	....	....	....	....	....	....	....	14	8	9	17	11	....	....	....	....
	Houston Aeros	AHL	....	....	....	....	....	....	....	....	....	....	....	....	....	....	1	0	0	0	0	....	....	....	....
2006-07	Houston Aeros	AHL	62	7	9	16	36	....	....	....	....	....	....	....	....	....	....	....	....	....	....	....	....	....	....
2007-08	Houston Aeros	AHL	72	20	19	39	38	....	....	....	....	....	....	....	....	....	2	1	0	1	0	....	....	....	....
2008-09	Houston Aeros	AHL	29	8	4	12	24	....	....	....	....	....	....	....	....	....	....	....	....	....	....	....	....	....	....
	Toronto Marlies	AHL	36	7	6	13	33	....	....	....	....	....	....	....	....	....	6	1	2	3	4	....	....	....	....
2009-10	Toronto Marlies	AHL	47	16	9	25	37	....	....	....	....	....	....	....	....	....	....	....	....	....	....	....	....	....	....
2010-11	Toronto Marlies	AHL	45	16	13	29	21	....	....	....	....	....	....	....	....	....	....	....	....	....	....	....	....	....	....
2011-12	**Toronto**	**NHL**	**2**	**0**	**1**	**1**	**2**	**0**	**0**	**0**	**1**	**0.0**	**–1**	**0**	**0.0**	**13:08**	....	....	....	....	....	....	....	....	....
	Toronto Marlies	AHL	74	25	26	51	36	....	....	....	....	....	....	....	....	....	17	2	3	5	6	....	....	....	....
2012-13	Toronto Marlies	AHL	56	30	18	48	31	....	....	....	....	....	....	....	....	....	4	1	1	2	0	....	....	....	....
	Toronto	**NHL**	**10**	**0**	**2**	**2**	**0**	**0**	**0**	**0**	**6**	**0.0**	**1**	**18**	**22.2**	**10:51**	**2**	**0**	**1**	**1**	**0**	**0**	**0**	**0**	**8:08**
2013-14	**Edmonton**	**NHL**	**2**	**0**	**0**	**0**	**0**	**0**	**0**	**0**	**0**	**0.0**	**–2**	**0**	**0.0**	**10:02**	....	....	....	....	....	....	....	....	....
	Oklahoma City	AHL	30	7	9	16	26	....	....	....	....	....	....	....	....	....	....	....	....	....	....	....	....	....	....
2014-15	**Edmonton**	**NHL**	**16**	**1**	**1**	**2**	**6**	**1**	**0**	**0**	**12**	**8.3**	**–8**	**4**	**25.0**	**13:13**	....	....	....	....	....	....	....	....	....
	Oklahoma City	AHL	43	18	19	37	15	....	....	....	....	....	....	....	....	....	10	5	0	5	2	....	....	....	....
	NHL Totals		**30**	**1**	**4**	**5**	**8**	**1**	**0**	**0**	**19**	**5.3**		**22**	**22.7**	**12:12**	**2**	**0**	**1**	**1**	**0**	**0**	**0**	**0**	**8:08**

Signed as a free agent by **Minnesota**, July 5, 2006. Traded to **Toronto** by **Minnesota** for Robbie Earl, January 21, 2009. Signed as a free agent by **Edmointon**, July 5, 2013. • Missed majority of 2013-14 due to knee and sholder injuries and as a healthy reserve.

HAMONIC, Travis

(HA-mohn-ihk, TRA-vihs) **NYI**

Defense. Shoots right. 6'2", 217 lbs. Born, St. Malo, MB, August 16, 1990. NY Islanders' 4th choice, 53rd overall, in 2008 Entry Draft.

Season	Club	League	GP	G	A	Pts	PIM	PP	SH	GW	S	S%	+/-	TF	F%	Min	GP	G	A	Pts	PIM	PP	SH	GW	Min
2006-07	Winnipeg Saints	MJHL	....	2	13	15	....	....	....	....	....	....	....	....	....	....	....	....	....	....	....	....	....	....	....
	Moose Jaw	WHL	22	0	3	3	30	....	....	....	....	....	....	....	....	....	....	....	....	....	....	....	....	....	....
2007-08	Moose Jaw	WHL	61	5	17	22	101	....	....	....	....	....	....	....	....	....	6	0	1	1	6	....	....	....	....
2008-09	Moose Jaw	WHL	57	13	27	40	126	....	....	....	....	....	....	....	....	....	....	....	....	....	....	....	....	....	....
2009-10	Moose Jaw	WHL	31	10	29	39	48	....	....	....	....	....	....	....	....	....	....	....	....	....	....	....	....	....	....
	Brandon	WHL	10	1	4	5	17	....	....	....	....	....	....	....	....	....	15	4	7	11	23	....	....	....	....
2010-11	**NY Islanders**	**NHL**	**62**	**5**	**21**	**26**	**103**	**1**	**0**	**0**	**118**	**4.2**	**4**	**0**	**0.0**	**21:34**	....	....	....	....	....	....	....	....	....
	Bridgeport	AHL	19	2	5	7	45	....	....	....	....	....	....	....	....	....	....	....	....	....	....	....	....	....	....
2011-12	**NY Islanders**	**NHL**	**73**	**2**	**22**	**24**	**73**	**1**	**0**	**0**	**124**	**1.6**	**6**	**0**	**0.0**	**22:26**	....	....	....	....	....	....	....	....	....
2012-13	Bridgeport	AHL	21	4	6	10	37	....	....	....	....	....	....	....	....	....	....	....	....	....	....	....	....	....	....
	NY Islanders	**NHL**	**48**	**3**	**7**	**10**	**28**	**1**	**0**	**1**	**83**	**3.6**	**–8**	**0**	**0.0**	**22:48**	**6**	**0**	**1**	**1**	**23**	**0**	**0**	**0**	**24:59**
2013-14	**NY Islanders**	**NHL**	**69**	**3**	**15**	**18**	**68**	**2**	**0**	**0**	**134**	**2.2**	**2**	**0**	**0.0**	**25:01**	....	....	....	....	....	....	....	....	....
2014-15	**NY Islanders**	**NHL**	**71**	**5**	**28**	**33**	**85**	**1**	**0**	**0**	**132**	**3.8**	**15**	**0**	**0.0**	**21:47**	....	....	....	....	....	....	....	....	....
	NHL Totals		**323**	**18**	**93**	**111**	**357**	**6**	**0**	**1**	**591**	**3.0**		**0**	**0.0**	**22:44**	**6**	**0**	**1**	**1**	**23**	**0**	**0**	**0**	**24:59**

WHL East Second All-Star Team (2010) • Memorial Cup All-Star Team (2010)

HANNAN, Scott

(HAN-nan, SKAWT)

Defense. Shoots left. 6'1", 215 lbs. Born, Richmond, BC, January 23, 1979. San Jose's 2nd choice, 23rd overall, in 1997 Entry Draft.

Season	Club	League	GP	G	A	Pts	PIM	PP	SH	GW	S	S%	+/-	TF	F%	Min	GP	G	A	Pts	PIM	PP	SH	GW	Min
1994-95	Surrey Wolves	Minor-BC	70	54	54	108	200	....	....	....	....	....	....	....	....	....	....	....	....	....	....	....	....	....	....
	Tacoma Rockets	WHL	2	0	0	0	0	....	....	....	....	....	....	....	....	....	....	....	....	....	....	....	....	....	....
1995-96	Kelowna Rockets	WHL	69	4	5	9	76	....	....	....	....	....	....	....	....	....	6	0	1	1	4	....	....	....	....
1996-97	Kelowna Rockets	WHL	70	17	26	43	84	....	....	....	....	....	....	....	....	....	6	0	0	0	8	....	....	....	....
1997-98	Kelowna Rockets	WHL	47	10	30	40	70	....	....	....	....	....	....	....	....	....	7	2	7	9	14	....	....	....	....
1998-99	**San Jose**	**NHL**	**5**	**0**	**2**	**2**	**6**	**0**	**0**	**0**	**4**	**0.0**	**0**	**0**	**0.0**	**7:15**	....	....	....	....	....	....	....	....	....
	Kelowna Rockets	WHL	47	15	30	45	92	....	....	....	....	....	....	....	....	....	6	1	2	3	14	....	....	....	....
	Kentucky	AHL	2	0	0	0	2	....	....	....	....	....	....	....	....	....	12	0	2	2	10	....	....	....	....
99-2000	**San Jose**	**NHL**	**30**	**1**	**2**	**3**	**10**	**0**	**0**	**0**	**28**	**3.6**	**7**	**1**	**0.0**	**17:09**	**1**	**0**	**1**	**1**	**0**	**0**	**0**	**0**	**18:14**
	Kentucky	AHL	41	5	12	17	40	....	....	....	....	....	....	....	....	....	....	....	....	....	....	....	....	....	....
2000-01	**San Jose**	**NHL**	**75**	**3**	**14**	**17**	**51**	**0**	**0**	**1**	**96**	**3.1**	**10**	**0**	**0.0**	**19:02**	**6**	**0**	**1**	**1**	**6**	**0**	**0**	**0**	**25:10**
2001-02	**San Jose**	**NHL**	**75**	**2**	**12**	**14**	**57**	**0**	**0**	**1**	**68**	**2.9**	**10**	**1**	**100.0**	**20:19**	**12**	**0**	**2**	**2**	**12**	**0**	**0**	**0**	**20:46**
2002-03	**San Jose**	**NHL**	**81**	**3**	**19**	**22**	**61**	**1**	**0**	**0**	**103**	**2.9**	**0**	**3**	**33.3**	**24:16**	....	....	....	....	....	....	....	....	....
2003-04	**San Jose**	**NHL**	**82**	**6**	**15**	**21**	**48**	**0**	**0**	**0**	**114**	**5.3**	**10**	**0**	**0.0**	**23:41**	**17**	**1**	**5**	**6**	**22**	**1**	**0**	**1**	**26:38**
2004-05			DID NOT PLAY																						
2005-06	**San Jose**	**NHL**	**81**	**6**	**18**	**24**	**58**	**2**	**0**	**1**	**104**	**5.8**	**7**	**0**	**0.0**	**24:34**	**11**	**0**	**1**	**1**	**6**	**0**	**0**	**0**	**25:16**
2006-07	**San Jose**	**NHL**	**79**	**4**	**20**	**24**	**38**	**0**	**1**	**1**	**79**	**5.1**	**1**	**0**	**0.0**	**22:49**	**11**	**0**	**2**	**2**	**33**	**0**	**0**	**0**	**21:42**
2007-08	**Colorado**	**NHL**	**82**	**2**	**19**	**21**	**55**	**0**	**0**	**0**	**79**	**2.5**	**–5**	**1**	**100.0**	**22:41**	**9**	**0**	**1**	**1**	**4**	**0**	**0**	**0**	**19:15**
2008-09	**Colorado**	**NHL**	**81**	**1**	**9**	**10**	**26**	**0**	**0**	**0**	**70**	**1.4**	**–21**	**1**	**0.0**	**22:22**	....	....	....	....	....	....	....	....	....
2009-10	**Colorado**	**NHL**	**81**	**2**	**14**	**16**	**40**	**0**	**0**	**0**	**53**	**3.8**	**2**	**2**	**100.0**	**21:56**	**6**	**0**	**0**	**0**	**4**	**0**	**0**	**0**	**22:33**
2010-11	**Colorado**	**NHL**	**23**	**0**	**6**	**6**	**6**	**0**	**0**	**0**	**21**	**0.0**	**1**	**0**	**0.0**	**18:38**	....	....	....	....	....	....	....	....	....
	Washington	**NHL**	**55**	**1**	**4**	**5**	**28**	**0**	**0**	**0**	**35**	**2.9**	**3**	**0**	**0.0**	**20:16**	**9**	**0**	**1**	**1**	**2**	**0**	**0**	**0**	**23:37**
2011-12	**Calgary**	**NHL**	**78**	**2**	**10**	**12**	**38**	**0**	**0**	**0**	**49**	**4.1**	**–10**	**1**	**100.0**	**20:21**	....	....	....	....	....	....	....	....	....
2012-13	**Nashville**	**NHL**	**29**	**0**	**1**	**1**	**20**	**0**	**0**	**0**	**20**	**0.0**	**–11**	**0**	**0.0**	**19:30**	....	....	....	....	....	....	....	....	....
	San Jose	**NHL**	**4**	**0**	**0**	**0**	**2**	**0**	**0**	**0**	**5**	**0.0**	**–3**	**0**	**0.0**	**18:17**	**11**	**0**	**4**	**4**	**4**	**0**	**0**	**0**	**17:18**
2013-14	**San Jose**	**NHL**	**56**	**3**	**9**	**12**	**55**	**0**	**0**	**0**	**52**	**5.8**	**1**	**0**	**0.0**	**17:46**	**7**	**0**	**2**	**2**	**0**	**0**	**0**	**0**	**17:40**
2014-15	**San Jose**	**NHL**	**58**	**2**	**5**	**7**	**26**	**0**	**0**	**0**	**53**	**3.8**	**0**	**0**	**0.0**	**16:19**	....	....	....	....	....	....	....	....	....
	NHL Totals		**1055**	**38**	**179**	**217**	**625**	**3**	**1**	**4**	**1033**	**3.7**		**10**	**60.0**	**21:12**	**100**	**1**	**20**	**21**	**93**	**1**	**0**	**1**	**22:14**

WHL West First All-Star Team (1999)

Signed as a free agent by **Colorado**, July 1, 2007. Traded to **Washington** by **Colorado** for Tomas Fleischmann, November 30, 2010. Signed as a free agent by **Calgary**, August 13, 2011. Signed as a free agent by **Nashville**, August 17, 2012. Traded to **San Jose** by **Nashville** for San Jose's 6th round choice (Tommy Veilleux) in 2013 Entry Draft, April 3, 2013.

HANOWSKI, Ben

(ha-NOW-skee, BEHN)

Wing. Shoots left. 6'2", 210 lbs. Born, Little Falls, MN, October 18, 1990. Pittsburgh's 3rd choice, 63rd overall, in 2009 Entry Draft.

Season	Club	League	GP	G	A	Pts	PIM	PP	SH	GW	S	S%	+/-	TF	F%	Min	Playoffs GP	G	A	Pts	PIM	PP	SH	GW	Min
2005-06	Little Falls Flyers	High-MN	31	35	29	64	....	....	....	....	....	....	....	....	....	....	....	....	....	....	....	....	....	....	....
2006-07	Little Falls Flyers	High-MN	29	40	71	111	....	....	....	....	....	....	....	....	....	....	....	....	....	....	....	....	....	....	....
2007-08	Little Falls Flyers	High-MN	26	48	47	95	....	....	....	....	....	....	....	....	....	....	....	....	....	....	....	....	....	....	....
	Team North	UMHSEL	....	17	16	33	....	....	....	....	....	....	....	....	....	....	....	....	....	....	....	....	....	....	....
2008-09	Little Falls Flyers	High-MN	31	73	62	135	16	....	....	....	....	....	....	....	....	....	....	....	....	....	....	....	....	....	....
	Team North	UMHSEL	19	14	8	22	....	....	....	....	....	....	....	....	....	....	....	....	....	....	....	....	....	....	....
2009-10	St. Cloud State	WCHA	43	9	10	19	19	....	....	....	....	....	....	....	....	....	....	....	....	....	....	....	....	....	....
2010-11	St. Cloud State	WCHA	37	13	7	20	18	....	....	....	....	....	....	....	....	....	....	....	....	....	....	....	....	....	....
2011-12	St. Cloud State	WCHA	39	23	20	43	25	....	....	....	....	....	....	....	....	....	....	....	....	....	....	....	....	....	....
2012-13	St. Cloud State	WCHA	37	17	14	31	18	....	....	....	....	....	....	....	....	....	....	....	....	....	....	....	....	....	....
	Calgary	**NHL**	**5**	**1**	**0**	**1**	**0**	**0**	**0**	**0**	**4**	**25.0**	**0**	**2**	**0.0**	**13:18**	....	....	....	....	....	....	....	....	....
2013-14	**Calgary**	**NHL**	**11**	**0**	**2**	**2**	**2**	**0**	**0**	**0**	**10**	**0.0**	**–2**	**1**	**100.0**	**7:15**	....	....	....	....	....	....	....	....	....
	Abbotsford Heat	AHL	55	13	18	31	18	....	....	....	....	....	....	....	....	....	4	0	1	1	2	....	....	....	....
2014-15	Adirondack	AHL	56	16	9	25	21	....	....	....	....	....	....	....	....	....	....	....	....	....	....	....	....	....	....
	NHL Totals		**16**	**1**	**2**	**3**	**2**	**0**	**0**	**0**	**14**	**7.1**		**3**	**33.3**	**9:08**	....	....	....	....	....	....	....	....	....

Traded to **Calgary** by **Pittsburgh** with Kenny Agostino and Pittsburgh's 1st round choice (Morgan Klimchuk) in 2013 Entry Draft for Jarome Iginla, March 28, 2013.

HANSEN, Jannik

(HAHN-suhn, YAH-nihk) **VAN**

Right wing. Shoots right. 6'1", 195 lbs. Born, Herlev, Denmark, March 15, 1986. Vancouver's 7th choice, 287th overall, in 2004 Entry Draft.

Season	Club	League	GP	G	A	Pts	PIM	PP	SH	GW	S	S%	+/-	TF	F%	Min	Playoffs GP	G	A	Pts	PIM	PP	SH	GW	Min
2002-03	Rodovre	Denmark	15	0	0	0	0	....	....	....	....	....	....	....	....	....	....	....	....	....	....	....	....	....	....
	Malmo U18	Swe-U18	12	8	7	15	2	....	....	....	....	....	....	....	....	....	3	2	0	2	0	....	....	....	....
	Denmark	WJ18-B	5	2	5	7	14	....	....	....	....	....	....	....	....	....	....	....	....	....	....	....	....	....	....
2003-04	Rodovre	Denmark	35	12	7	19	48	....	....	....	....	....	....	....	....	....	....	....	....	....	....	....	....	....	....
	Denmark	WJC-B	3	0	1	1	12	....	....	....	....	....	....	....	....	....	....	....	....	....	....	....	....	....	....
	Denmark	WJ18-B	6	3	4	7	32	....	....	....	....	....	....	....	....	....	....	....	....	....	....	....	....	....	....
2004-05	Rodovre	Denmark	32	17	17	34	40	....	....	....	....	....	....	....	....	....	5	3	1	4	24	....	....	....	....
	Denmark	Oly-Q	3	0	1	1	4	....	....	....	....	....	....	....	....	....	....	....	....	....	....	....	....	....	....
2005-06	Portland	WHL	64	24	40	64	67	....	....	....	....	....	....	....	....	....	12	7	6	13	16	....	....	....	....
2006-07	Manitoba Moose	AHL	72	12	22	34	38	....	....	....	....	....	....	....	....	....	6	0	0	0	2	....	....	....	....
	Vancouver	**NHL**	....	....	....	....	....	....	....	....	....	....	....	....	....	....	**10**	**0**	**1**	**1**	**4**	**0**	**0**	**0**	**12:41**
2007-08	**Vancouver**	**NHL**	**5**	**0**	**0**	**0**	**2**	**0**	**0**	**0**	**3**	**0.0**	**0**	**1**	**100.0**	**11:34**	....	....	....	....	....	....	....	....	....
	Manitoba Moose	AHL	50	21	22	43	22	....	....	....	....	....	....	....	....	....	6	2	2	4	0	....	....	....	....
2008-09	**Vancouver**	**NHL**	**55**	**6**	**15**	**21**	**37**	**0**	**0**	**1**	**64**	**9.4**	**5**	**12**	**16.7**	**12:31**	**2**	**0**	**0**	**0**	**0**	**0**	**0**	**0**	**10:16**
	Manitoba Moose	AHL	2	1	0	1	2	....	....	....	....	....	....	....	....	....	....	....	....	....	....	....	....	....	....
2009-10	**Vancouver**	**NHL**	**47**	**9**	**6**	**15**	**18**	**0**	**1**	**3**	**67**	**13.4**	**–5**	**14**	**42.9**	**12:20**	**12**	**1**	**2**	**3**	**4**	**0**	**0**	**0**	**10:05**
	Manitoba Moose	AHL	5	0	2	2	5	....	....	....	....	....	....	....	....	....	....	....	....	....	....	....	....	....	....
2010-11	**Vancouver**	**NHL**	**82**	**9**	**20**	**29**	**32**	**0**	**0**	**2**	**113**	**8.0**	**13**	**19**	**42.1**	**14:43**	**25**	**3**	**6**	**9**	**18**	**0**	**0**	**0**	**15:50**
2011-12	**Vancouver**	**NHL**	**82**	**16**	**23**	**39**	**34**	**0**	**1**	**1**	**137**	**11.7**	**18**	**29**	**41.4**	**14:54**	**5**	**1**	**0**	**1**	**14**	**0**	**0**	**0**	**16:26**
2012-13	Tappara Tampere	Finland	20	7	10	17	43	....	....	....	....	....	....	....	....	....	....	....	....	....	....	....	....	....	....
	Vancouver	**NHL**	**47**	**10**	**17**	**27**	**8**	**1**	**0**	**2**	**99**	**10.1**	**12**	**31**	**9.7**	**17:33**	**4**	**0**	**0**	**0**	**2**	**0**	**0**	**0**	**18:12**
2013-14	**Vancouver**	**NHL**	**71**	**11**	**9**	**20**	**43**	**0**	**1**	**3**	**112**	**9.8**	**–9**	**29**	**41.4**	**15:40**	....	....	....	....	....	....	....	....	....
2014-15	**Vancouver**	**NHL**	**81**	**16**	**17**	**33**	**27**	**0**	**1**	**2**	**145**	**11.0**	**–6**	**6**	**16.7**	**13:58**	**6**	**2**	**2**	**4**	**0**	**0**	**0**	**0**	**16:27**
	NHL Totals		**470**	**77**	**107**	**184**	**201**	**1**	**4**	**14**	**740**	**10.4**		**141**	**31.9**	**14:31**	**64**	**7**	**11**	**18**	**42**	**0**	**0**	**0**	**14:20**

Signed as a free agent by **Tappara Tampere** (Finland), October 30, 2012.

HANZAL, Martin

(HAHN-zuhl, MAHR-tihn) **ARI**

Center. Shoots left. 6'6", 230 lbs. Born, Pisek, Czech., February 20, 1987. Phoenix's 1st choice, 17th overall, in 2005 Entry Draft.

Season	Club	League	GP	G	A	Pts	PIM	PP	SH	GW	S	S%	+/-	TF	F%	Min	Playoffs GP	G	A	Pts	PIM	PP	SH	GW	Min
2002-03	C. Budejovice U17	CzR-U17	47	24	30	54	28	....	....	....	....	....	....	....	....	....	7	1	3	4	25	....	....	....	....
2003-04	C. Budejovice U17	CzR-U17	2	0	2	2	2	....	....	....	....	....	....	....	....	....	2	1	0	1	4	....	....	....	....
	C. Budejovice Jr.	CzRep-Jr.	53	15	7	22	32	....	....	....	....	....	....	....	....	....	....	....	....	....	....	....	....	....	....
2004-05	C. Budejovice Jr.	CzRep-Jr.	37	22	22	44	80	....	....	....	....	....	....	....	....	....	2	1	2	3	2	....	....	....	....
	C. Budejovice	CzRep-2	15	1	2	3	2	....	....	....	....	....	....	....	....	....	6	0	0	0	6	....	....	....	....
2005-06	C. Budejovice Jr.	CzRep-Jr.	7	3	5	8	20	....	....	....	....	....	....	....	....	....	....	....	....	....	....	....	....	....	....
	C. Budejovice	CzRep	19	0	1	1	10	....	....	....	....	....	....	....	....	....	....	....	....	....	....	....	....	....	....
	BK Mlada Boleslav	CzRep-2	5	2	0	2	0	....	....	....	....	....	....	....	....	....	....	....	....	....	....	....	....	....	....
	Omaha Lancers	USHL	19	4	15	19	30	....	....	....	....	....	....	....	....	....	5	1	0	1	4	....	....	....	....
2006-07	Red Deer Rebels	WHL	60	26	59	85	94	....	....	....	....	....	....	....	....	....	6	2	7	9	19	....	....	....	....
2007-08	**Phoenix**	**NHL**	**72**	**8**	**27**	**35**	**28**	**1**	**1**	**3**	**111**	**7.2**	**–7**	**1019**	**46.1**	**16:45**	....	....	....	....	....	....	....	....	....
2008-09	**Phoenix**	**NHL**	**74**	**11**	**20**	**31**	**40**	**0**	**2**	**2**	**97**	**11.3**	**–4**	**1078**	**48.3**	**16:21**	....	....	....	....	....	....	....	....	....
2009-10	**Phoenix**	**NHL**	**81**	**11**	**22**	**33**	**104**	**2**	**0**	**0**	**147**	**7.5**	**0**	**1104**	**50.6**	**18:29**	**7**	**0**	**3**	**3**	**10**	**0**	**0**	**0**	**18:58**
2010-11	**Phoenix**	**NHL**	**61**	**16**	**10**	**26**	**54**	**7**	**0**	**5**	**149**	**10.7**	**4**	**1029**	**50.3**	**19:30**	**4**	**1**	**2**	**3**	**8**	**1**	**0**	**0**	**19:50**
2011-12	**Phoenix**	**NHL**	**64**	**8**	**26**	**34**	**63**	**3**	**0**	**2**	**145**	**5.5**	**12**	**1097**	**52.1**	**18:27**	**12**	**3**	**3**	**6**	**29**	**0**	**0**	**2**	**16:35**
2012-13	C. Budejovice	CzRep	18	8	11	19	73	....	....	....	....	....	....	....	....	....	....	....	....	....	....	....	....	....	....
	Phoenix	**NHL**	**39**	**11**	**12**	**23**	**24**	**4**	**0**	**2**	**93**	**11.8**	**2**	**637**	**46.8**	**18:32**	....	....	....	....	....	....	....	....	....
2013-14	**Phoenix**	**NHL**	**65**	**15**	**25**	**40**	**73**	**5**	**0**	**2**	**169**	**8.9**	**–9**	**1099**	**54.5**	**18:41**	....	....	....	....	....	....	....	....	....
	Czech Republic	Olympics	4	0	1	1	4	....	....	....	....	....	....	....	....	....	....	....	....	....	....	....	....	....	....
2014-15	**Arizona**	**NHL**	**37**	**8**	**16**	**24**	**31**	**1**	**0**	**3**	**85**	**9.4**	**–1**	**612**	**56.5**	**17:44**	....	....	....	....	....	....	....	....	....
	NHL Totals		**493**	**88**	**158**	**246**	**417**	**23**	**3**	**19**	**996**	**8.8**		**7675**	**50.6**	**18:00**	**23**	**4**	**8**	**12**	**47**	**1**	**0**	**2**	**17:52**

WHL East Second All-Star Team (2007)

Signed as a free agent by **Ceske Budejovice** (CzRep), October 28, 2012.

HARRINGTON, Scott

(HAIR-ihng-tuhn, SKAWT) **TOR**

Defense. Shoots left. 6'2", 201 lbs. Born, Kingston, ON, March 10, 1993. Pittsburgh's 2nd choice, 54th overall, in 2011 Entry Draft.

Season	Club	League	GP	G	A	Pts	PIM	PP	SH	GW	S	S%	+/-	TF	F%	Min	Playoffs GP	G	A	Pts	PIM	PP	SH	GW	Min
2008-09	King. Jr. Front.	Minor-ON	66	19	48	67	46	....	....	....	....	....	....	....	....	....	....	....	....	....	....	....	....	....	....
	Kingston	ON-Jr.A	2	1	0	1	2	....	....	....	....	....	....	....	....	....	18	1	6	7	6	....	....	....	....
2009-10	London Knights	OHL	55	1	13	14	20	....	....	....	....	....	....	....	....	....	12	0	2	2	4	....	....	....	....
2010-11	London Knights	OHL	67	6	16	22	51	....	....	....	....	....	....	....	....	....	6	0	1	1	0	....	....	....	....
2011-12	London Knights	OHL	44	3	23	26	32	....	....	....	....	....	....	....	....	....	19	1	6	7	6	....	....	....	....
2012-13	Wilkes-Barre	AHL	....	....	....	....	....	....	....	....	....	....	....	....	....	....	2	1	0	1	0	....	....	....	....
	London Knights	OHL	50	3	16	19	26	....	....	....	....	....	....	....	....	....	17	0	4	4	14	....	....	....	....
2013-14	Wilkes-Barre	AHL	76	5	19	24	55	....	....	....	....	....	....	....	....	....	16	0	1	1	12	....	....	....	....
2014-15	**Pittsburgh**	**NHL**	**10**	**0**	**0**	**0**	**4**	**0**	**0**	**0**	**9**	**0.0**	**–10**	**0**	**0.0**	**15:48**	....	....	....	....	....	....	....	....	....
	Wilkes-Barre	AHL	48	2	10	12	20	....	....	....	....	....	....	....	....	....	8	0	1	1	0	....	....	....	....
	NHL Totals		**10**	**0**	**0**	**0**	**4**	**0**	**0**	**0**	**9**	**0.0**		**0**	**0.0**	**15:48**	....	....	....	....	....	....	....	....	....

OHL All-Rookie Team (2010) • OHL First All-Star Team (2012, 2013)

Traded to **Toronto** by **Pittsburgh** with Nick Spaling, Kasperi Kapanen, New Jersey's 3rd round choice (previously acquired) in 2016 Entry Draft and future considerations for Phil Kessel, Tyler Biggs, Tim Erixon and future considerations, July 1, 2015.

HARRISON, Jay

(HAIR-ih-suhn, JAY) **WPG**

Defense. Shoots left. 6'4", 220 lbs. Born, Oshawa, ON, November 3, 1982. Toronto's 4th choice, 82nd overall, in 2001 Entry Draft.

Season	Club	League	GP	G	A	Pts	PIM	PP	SH	GW	S	S%	+/-	TF	F%	Min	Playoffs GP	G	A	Pts	PIM	PP	SH	GW	Min
1997-98	Oshawa	ON-Jr.A	42	1	11	12	143	....	....	....	....	....	....	....	....	....	....	....	....	....	....	....	....	....	....
1998-99	Brampton	OHL	63	1	14	15	108	....	....	....	....	....	....	....	....	....	....	....	....	....	....	....	....	....	....
99-2000	Brampton	OHL	68	2	18	20	139	....	....	....	....	....	....	....	....	....	6	0	2	2	15	....	....	....	....
2000-01	Brampton	OHL	53	4	15	19	112	....	....	....	....	....	....	....	....	....	9	1	1	2	17	....	....	....	....
2001-02	Brampton	OHL	61	12	31	43	116	....	....	....	....	....	....	....	....	....	....	....	....	....	....	....	....	....	....
	St. John's	AHL	7	0	1	1	2	....	....	....	....	....	....	....	....	....	10	0	0	0	4	....	....	....	....
	Memphis	CHL	....	....	....	....	....	....	....	....	....	....	....	....	....	....	1	0	0	0	2	....	....	....	....
2002-03	St. John's	AHL	72	2	8	10	72	....	....	....	....	....	....	....	....	....	....	....	....	....	....	....	....	....	....
2003-04	St. John's	AHL	70	4	5	9	141	....	....	....	....	....	....	....	....	....	....	....	....	....	....	....	....	....	....
2004-05	St. John's	AHL	60	0	4	4	108	....	....	....	....	....	....	....	....	....	4	0	1	1	14	....	....	....	....
2005-06	**Toronto**	**NHL**	**8**	**0**	**1**	**1**	**2**	**0**	**0**	**0**	**7**	**0.0**	**5**	**0**	**0.0**	**18:50**	....	....	....	....	....	....	....	....	....
	Toronto Marlies	AHL	57	9	20	29	100	....	....	....	....	....	....	....	....	....	5	1	3	4	8	....	....	....	....

			Regular Season														Playoffs								
Season	Club	League	GP	G	A	Pts	PIM	PP	SH	GW	S	S%	+/-	TF	F%	Min	GP	G	A	Pts	PIM	PP	SH	GW	Min
2006-07	Toronto	NHL	5	0	0	0	6	0	0	0	3	0.0	–5	0	0.0	8:22									
	Toronto Marlies	AHL	41	4	14	18	68																		
2007-08	Toronto Marlies	AHL	69	13	14	27	73										18	2	10	12	35				
2008-09	EV Zug	Swiss	41	6	9	15	96										7	1	2	3	33				
	Toronto	NHL	7	0	1	1	10	0	0	0	6	0.0	–2	0	0.0	17:16									
2009-10	Carolina	NHL	38	1	5	6	50	0	0	0	30	3.3	–8	0	0.0	14:43									
	Albany River Rats	AHL	32	2	12	14	22										8	0	3	3	23				
2010-11	Carolina	NHL	72	3	7	10	72	0	0	0	49	6.1	5	0	0.0	15:16									
2011-12	Carolina	NHL	72	9	14	23	60	2	0	2	128	7.0	–10	0	0.0	20:33									
2012-13	Carolina	NHL	47	3	7	10	51	0	0	2	54	5.6	–10	0	0.0	19:54									
2013-14	Carolina	NHL	68	4	11	15	44	1	0	1	103	3.9	–1	0	0.0	16:38									
2014-15	Carolina	NHL	20	1	3	4	42	0	0	0	23	4.3	–5	0	0.0	16:30									
	Winnipeg	NHL	35	2	3	5	23	1	0	0	27	7.4	4	0	0.0	15:36									
	NHL Totals		372	23	52	75	360	4	0	5	430	5.3		0	0.0	17:11									

OHL All-Rookie Team (1999)

Signed as a free agent by **Zug** (Swiss), June 16, 2008. Signed as a free agent by **Toronto**, March 27, 2009. Signed as a free agent by **Carolina**, July 9, 2009. Traded to **Winnipeg** by **Carolina** for Ottawa's 6th round choice (previously acquired, Carolina selected David Cotton) in 2015 Entry Draft, December 18, 2014.

HARROLD, Peter

(HAIR-ohld, PEE-tuhr) **ST.L.**

Defense. Shoots right. 5'11", 180 lbs. Born, Kirtland Hills, OH, June 8, 1983.

2003-04	Boston College	H-East	40	2	12	14	12																		
2004-05	Boston College	H-East	35	4	10	14	22																		
2005-06	Boston College	H-East	42	7	23	30	32																		
2006-07	Los Angeles	NHL	12	0	2	2	8	0	0	0	11	0.0	0	1	0.0	15:12									
	Manchester	AHL	62	7	27	34	43										16	3	8	11	18				
2007-08	Los Angeles	NHL	25	2	3	5	2	0	0	0	16	12.5	3	2	50.0	16:23									
	Manchester	AHL	49	7	36	43	25										4	0	1	1	4				
2008-09	Los Angeles	NHL	69	4	8	12	28	1	0	1	95	4.2	–13	16	37.5	13:10									
2009-10	Los Angeles	NHL	39	1	2	3	8	0	0	0	23	4.3	–2	14	14.3	9:15	2	0	0	0	0	0	0	0	11:58
2010-11	Los Angeles	NHL	19	1	3	4	4	0	0	0	12	8.3	3	0	0.0	12:15									
2011-12	New Jersey	NHL	11	0	2	2	0	0	0	0	11	0.0	0	0	0.0	14:36	17	0	4	4	6	0	0	0	15:31
	Albany Devils	AHL	61	5	21	26	36																		
2012-13	New Jersey	NHL	23	2	3	5	6	1	0	0	36	5.6	–8	0	0.0	17:38									
2013-14	New Jersey	NHL	33	0	4	4	14	0	0	0	32	0.0	–2	0	0.0	18:40									
2014-15	New Jersey	NHL	43	3	2	5	4	0	0	0	31	9.7	–10	0	0.0	15:15									
	Albany Devils	AHL	13	1	1	2	10																		
	NHL Totals		274	13	29	42	74	2	0	1	267	4.9		33	27.3	14:21	19	0	4	4	6	0	0	0	15:09

Hockey East First All-Star Team (2006) • NCAA East First All-American Team (2006)

Signed as a free agent by **Los Angeles**, April 12, 2006. • Missed majority of 2009-10 and 2010-11 as a healthy reserve. Signed as a free agent by **New Jersey**, August 22, 2011. • Missed majority of 2012-13 as a healthy reserve. • Missed majority of 2013-14 due to foot injury at NY Rangers, December 7, 2013 and as a healthy reserve. Signed as a free agent by **St. Louis**, July 3, 2015.

HARTIKAINEN, Teemu

(har-tih-KIGH-nehn, TEE-moo) **TOR**

Center. Shoots left. 6'1", 215 lbs. Born, Kuopio, Finland, May 3, 1990. Edmonton's 4th choice, 163rd overall, in 2008 Entry Draft.

2006-07	KalPa Kuopio U18	Fin-U18	19	24	13	37	51																		
	KalPa Kuopio Jr.	Fin-Jr.	11	2	1	3	0										3	0	0	0	4				
2007-08	KalPa Kuopio U18	Fin-U18	7	9	6	15	6																		
	KalPa Kuopio Jr.	Fin-Jr.	37	10	7	17	24										11	1	4	5	6				
	KalPa Kuopio	Finland	1	0	0	0	0																		
2008-09	Suomi U20	Finland-2	3	0	2	2	8																		
	KalPa Kuopio	Finland	51	17	6	23	12										12	3	0	3	0				
2009-10	KalPa Kuopio	Finland	53	15	18	33	22										13	6	1	7	28				
	Suomi U20	Finland-2	1	0	0	0	0																		
2010-11	Edmonton	NHL	12	3	2	5	4	1	0	0	21	14.3	–3	18	33.3	17:25									
	Oklahoma City	AHL	66	17	25	42	27										6	0	1	1	4				
2011-12	Edmonton	NHL	17	2	3	5	6	0	0	1	24	8.3	1	12	33.3	13:01									
	Oklahoma City	AHL	51	14	18	32	19										14	4	4	8	4				
2012-13	Oklahoma City	AHL	47	14	23	37	23										17	7	8	15	6				
	Edmonton	NHL	23	1	2	3	6	1	0	0	21	4.8	–8	4	25.0	10:34									
2013-14	Ufa	KHL	47	14	16	30	32										18	2	6	8	10				
2014-15	Ufa	KHL	60	15	25	40	26										5	2	2	4	2				
	NHL Totals		52	6	7	13	16	2	0	1	66	9.1		34	32.4	12:57									

Signed as a free agent by **Ufa** (KHL), June 11, 2013. Traded to **Toronto** by **Edmonton** with Cameron Abney for Mark Fraser, January 31, 2014.

HARTMAN, Ryan

(HAHRT-man, RIGH-uhn) **CHI**

Right wing. Shoots right. 5'11", 191 lbs. Born, Hilton Head Island, SC, September 20, 1994. Chicago's 1st choice, 30th overall, in 2013 Entry Draft.

2009-10	Chicago Mission	T1EHL	38	25	19	44	64																		
	Chicago Mission	Other	25	21	30	51	....																		
2010-11	USNTDP	USHL	35	12	8	20	59										2	1	0	1	17				
	USNTDP	U-17	17	9	5	14	12																		
	USNTDP	U-18	2	0	0	0	4																		
2011-12	USNTDP	USHL	24	7	9	16	46																		
	USNTDP	U-18	35	9	16	25	90																		
2012-13	Plymouth Whalers	OHL	56	23	37	60	120										9	4	2	6	16				
2013-14	Plymouth Whalers	OHL	52	26	28	54	91										5	0	4	4	8				
	Rockford IceHogs	AHL	9	3	4	7	8																		
2014-15	Chicago	NHL	5	0	0	0	2	0	0	0	8	0.0	–1	0	0.0	8:17									
	Rockford IceHogs	AHL	69	13	24	37	120										8	2	1	3	8				
	NHL Totals		5	0	0	0	2	0	0	0	8	0.0		0	0.0	8:17									

HARTNELL, Scott

(HAHRT-nuhl, SKAWT) **CBJ**

Left wing. Shoots left. 6'2", 210 lbs. Born, Regina, SK, April 18, 1982. Nashville's 1st choice, 6th overall, in 2000 Entry Draft.

1997-98	Lloydminster	AJHL	56	9	25	34	82										4	2	1	3	8				
	Prince Albert	WHL	1	0	1	1	2																		
1998-99	Prince Albert	WHL	65	10	34	44	104										14	0	5	5	22				
99-2000	Prince Albert	WHL	62	27	55	82	124										6	3	2	5	6				
2000-01	Nashville	NHL	75	2	14	16	48	0	0	0	92	2.2	–8	3	33.3	10:54									
2001-02	Nashville	NHL	75	14	27	41	111	3	0	4	162	8.6	5	12	25.0	16:58									
2002-03	Nashville	NHL	82	12	22	34	101	2	0	2	221	5.4	–3	23	30.4	15:17									
2003-04	Nashville	NHL	59	18	15	33	87	5	0	3	154	11.7	–5	48	37.5	16:16	6	1	2	3	2	0	0	0	15:37
2004-05	Valerengen	Norway	28	17	12	29	103										11	12	7	19	24				
2005-06	Nashville	NHL	81	25	23	48	101	10	2	8	211	11.8	8	58	37.9	16:05	5	1	0	1	4	0	0	0	12:12
2006-07	Nashville	NHL	64	22	17	39	96	10	0	2	150	14.7	19	134	47.0	15:43	5	1	1	2	28	1	0	0	14:23
2007-08	Philadelphia	NHL	80	24	19	43	159	10	1	6	176	13.6	2	32	40.6	16:11	17	3	4	7	20	0	0	0	15:28
2008-09	Philadelphia	NHL	82	30	30	60	143	6	1	5	210	14.3	14	36	50.0	17:48	6	1	1	2	23	1	0	0	18:36
2009-10	Philadelphia	NHL	81	14	30	44	155	8	0	4	171	8.2	–6	5	20.0	15:43	23	8	9	17	25	3	0	0	16:14
2010-11	Philadelphia	NHL	82	24	25	49	142	4	0	4	177	13.6	14	10	50.0	16:36	11	1	3	4	23	0	0	0	16:18
2011-12	Philadelphia	NHL	82	37	30	67	136	16	0	6	232	15.9	19	63	31.8	17:47	11	3	5	8	15	3	0	1	17:29
2012-13	Philadelphia	NHL	32	8	3	11	70	4	0	1	74	10.8	–5	4	75.0	15:52									

								Regular Season									Playoffs								
Season	Club	League	GP	G	A	Pts	PIM	PP	SH	GW	S	S%	+/-	TF	F%	Min	GP	G	A	Pts	PIM	PP	SH	GW	Min
2013-14	**Philadelphia**	**NHL**	**78**	**20**	**32**	**52**	**103**	**9**	**0**	**3**	**207**	**9.7**	**11**	**18**	**22.2**	**16:53**	**7**	**0**	**3**	**3**	**6**	**0**	**0**	**0**	**16:52**
2014-15	**Columbus**	**NHL**	**77**	**28**	**32**	**60**	**100**	**8**	**0**	**2**	**204**	**13.7**	**1**	**14**	**50.0**	**17:18**	....	....	....	....	....	....	....	....	....
	NHL Totals		**1030**	**278**	**319**	**597**	**1552**	**95**	**4**	**50**	**2441**	**11.4**		**460**	**40.2**	**16:08**	**91**	**19**	**28**	**47**	**146**	**8**	**0**	**1**	**16:05**

Played in NHL All-Star Game (2012)

Signed as a free agent by **Oslo** (Norway), October 21, 2004. Traded to **Philadelphia** by **Nashville** with Kimmo Timmonen for Nashville's 1st round choice (previously acquired, Nashville selected Jonathon Blum) in 2007 Entry Draft, June 18, 2007. Traded to **Columbus** by **Philadelphia** for RJ Umberger and Columbus' 4th round choice (later traded to Los Angeles – Los Angeles selected Austin Wagner) in 2015 Entry Draft, June 23, 2014.

HAULA, Erik
(HAWL-la, AIR-ihk) **MIN**

Left wing. Shoots left. 5'11", 192 lbs. Born, Pori, Finland, March 23, 1991. Minnesota's 7th choice, 182nd overall, in 2009 Entry Draft.

2006-07	Assat Pori U18	Fin-U18	29	19	24	43	24	....	....	....	....	....	....	....	....	....	6	1	3	4	4	....	....	....	....
2007-08	Assat Pori U18	Fin-U18	3	1	1	2	0	....	....	....	....	....	....	....	....	....	2	4	2	6	14	....	....	....	....
	Assat Pori Jr.	Fin-Jr.	40	7	15	22	26	....	....	....	....	....	....	....	....	....	12	2	0	2	4	....	....	....	....
2008-09	Shat.-St. Mary's	High-MN	53	26	58	84	46	....	....	....	....	....	....	....	....	....	....	....	....	....	....	....	....	....	....
2009-10	Omaha Lancers	USHL	56	28	44	72	59	....	....	....	....	....	....	....	....	....	8	2	9	11	2	....	....	....	....
2010-11	U. of Minnesota	WCHA	34	6	18	24	22	....	....	....	....	....	....	....	....	....	....	....	....	....	....	....	....	....	....
2011-12	U. of Minnesota	WCHA	43	20	29	49	30	....	....	....	....	....	....	....	....	....	....	....	....	....	....	....	....	....	....
2012-13	U. of Minnesota	WCHA	37	16	35	51	14	....	....	....	....	....	....	....	....	....	....	....	....	....	....	....	....	....	....
	Houston Aeros	AHL	6	0	2	2	2	....	....	....	....	....	....	....	....	....	5	1	1	2	4	....	....	....	....
2013-14	**Minnesota**	**NHL**	**46**	**6**	**9**	**15**	**29**	**0**	**1**	**1**	**56**	**10.7**	**14**	**348**	**46.3**	**10:09**	**13**	**4**	**3**	**7**	**0**	**0**	**0**	**1**	**14:12**
	Iowa Wild	AHL	31	14	13	27	14	....	....	....	....	....	....	....	....	....	....	....	....	....	....	....	....	....	....
2014-15	**Minnesota**	**NHL**	**72**	**7**	**7**	**14**	**32**	**1**	**0**	**1**	**92**	**7.6**	**–7**	**573**	**45.4**	**12:09**	**2**	**1**	**0**	**1**	**0**	**0**	**0**	**0**	**11:00**
	NHL Totals		**118**	**13**	**16**	**29**	**61**	**1**	**1**	**2**	**148**	**8.8**		**921**	**45.7**	**11:22**	**15**	**5**	**3**	**8**	**0**	**0**	**0**	**1**	**13:47**

USHL All-Rookie Team (2010) • USHL Second All-Star Team (2010) • WCHA Second All-Star Team (2013)

HAVLAT, Martin
(HAV-lat, MAHR-tihn)

Left wing. Shoots left. 6'2", 210 lbs. Born, Mlada Boleslav, Czech., April 19, 1981. Ottawa's 1st choice, 26th overall, in 1999 Entry Draft.

1997-98	Ytong Brno Jr.	CzRep-Jr.	32	38	29	67	....	....	....	....	....	....	....	....	....	....	....	....	....	....	....	....	....	....	....
1998-99	HC Trinec Jr.	CzRep-Jr.	31	28	23	51	....	....	....	....	....	....	....	....	....	....	....	....	....	....	....	....	....	....	....
	Trinec	CzRep	24	2	3	5	4	....	....	....	....	....	....	....	....	....	8	0	0	0	....	....	....	....	....
99-2000	HC Ocelari Trinec	CzRep	46	13	29	42	42	....	....	....	....	....	....	....	....	....	4	0	2	2	8	....	....	....	....
2000-01	**Ottawa**	**NHL**	**73**	**19**	**23**	**42**	**20**	**7**	**0**	**5**	**133**	**14.3**	**8**	**40**	**30.0**	**13:47**	**4**	**0**	**0**	**0**	**2**	**0**	**0**	**0**	**14:04**
2001-02	**Ottawa**	**NHL**	**72**	**22**	**28**	**50**	**66**	**9**	**0**	**6**	**145**	**15.2**	**–7**	**15**	**40.0**	**14:46**	**12**	**2**	**5**	**7**	**14**	**2**	**0**	**2**	**16:19**
	Czech Republic	Olympics	4	3	1	4	27	....	....	....	....	....	....	....	....	....	....	....	....	....	....	....	....	....	....
2002-03	**Ottawa**	**NHL**	**67**	**24**	**35**	**59**	**30**	**9**	**0**	**4**	**179**	**13.4**	**20**	**7**	**14.3**	**16:27**	**18**	**5**	**6**	**11**	**14**	**1**	**0**	**2**	**16:27**
2003-04	HC Sparta Praha	CzRep	5	1	3	4	8	....	....	....	....	....	....	....	....	....	....	....	....	....	....	....	....	....	....
	Ottawa	**NHL**	**68**	**31**	**37**	**68**	**46**	**13**	**0**	**7**	**175**	**17.7**	**12**	**11**	**36.4**	**16:44**	**7**	**0**	**3**	**3**	**2**	**0**	**0**	**0**	**16:10**
2004-05	Znojmo	CzRep	12	10	4	14	16	....	....	....	....	....	....	....	....	....	....	....	....	....	....	....	....	....	....
	Dynamo Moscow	Russia	10	2	0	2	14	....	....	....	....	....	....	....	....	....	....	....	....	....	....	....	....	....	....
	HC Sparta Praha	CzRep	9	5	4	9	37	....	....	....	....	....	....	....	....	....	5	0	0	0	20	....	....	....	....
2005-06	**Ottawa**	**NHL**	**18**	**9**	**7**	**16**	**4**	**2**	**1**	**1**	**57**	**15.8**	**6**	**25**	**36.0**	**18:11**	**10**	**7**	**6**	**13**	**4**	**3**	**0**	**1**	**17:13**
2006-07	**Chicago**	**NHL**	**56**	**25**	**32**	**57**	**28**	**5**	**0**	**1**	**176**	**14.2**	**15**	**12**	**33.3**	**21:24**	....	....	....	....	....	....	....	....	....
2007-08	**Chicago**	**NHL**	**35**	**10**	**17**	**27**	**22**	**3**	**0**	**2**	**87**	**11.5**	**4**	**3**	**0.0**	**18:35**	....	....	....	....	....	....	....	....	....
2008-09	**Chicago**	**NHL**	**81**	**29**	**48**	**77**	**30**	**5**	**0**	**5**	**249**	**11.6**	**29**	**8**	**25.0**	**17:25**	**16**	**5**	**10**	**15**	**8**	**0**	**0**	**1**	**15:34**
2009-10	**Minnesota**	**NHL**	**73**	**18**	**36**	**54**	**34**	**4**	**0**	**3**	**169**	**10.7**	**–19**	**12**	**50.0**	**17:56**	....	....	....	....	....	....	....	....	....
	Czech Republic	Olympics	5	0	2	2	0	....	....	....	....	....	....	....	....	....	....	....	....	....	....	....	....	....	....
2010-11	**Minnesota**	**NHL**	**78**	**22**	**40**	**62**	**52**	**3**	**0**	**4**	**229**	**9.6**	**–10**	**10**	**30.0**	**18:21**	....	....	....	....	....	....	....	....	....
2011-12	**San Jose**	**NHL**	**39**	**7**	**20**	**27**	**22**	**4**	**0**	**1**	**96**	**7.3**	**10**	**7**	**0.0**	**17:37**	**5**	**2**	**1**	**3**	**8**	**1**	**0**	**1**	**19:01**
2012-13	**San Jose**	**NHL**	**40**	**8**	**10**	**18**	**30**	**1**	**0**	**1**	**89**	**9.0**	**7**	**6**	**16.7**	**15:51**	**2**	**0**	**0**	**0**	**0**	**0**	**0**	**0**	**4:04**
2013-14	**San Jose**	**NHL**	**48**	**12**	**10**	**22**	**10**	**1**	**0**	**2**	**72**	**16.7**	**14**	**4**	**0.0**	**14:43**	**1**	**0**	**0**	**0**	**0**	**0**	**0**	**0**	**11:49**
2014-15	**New Jersey**	**NHL**	**40**	**5**	**9**	**14**	**10**	**3**	**0**	**1**	**49**	**10.2**	**–11**	**0**	**0.0**	**14:48**	....	....	....	....	....	....	....	....	....
	NHL Totals		**788**	**241**	**352**	**593**	**404**	**69**	**1**	**43**	**1905**	**12.7**		**160**	**30.0**	**16:49**	**75**	**21**	**31**	**52**	**52**	**7**	**0**	**7**	**15:58**

NHL All-Rookie Team (2001)

Played in NHL All-Star Game (2007, 2011)

Signed as a free agent by **Znojmo** (CzRep), September 24, 2004. Signed as a free agent by **Dynamo Moscow** (Russia), November 10, 2004. Signed as a free agent by **Sparta Praha** (CzRep), January 31, 2005. • Missed majority of 2005-06 due to shoulder injury vs. Montreal, November 29, 2005. Traded to **Chicago** by **Ottawa** with Bryan Smolinski for Tom Preissing, Josh Hennessy, Michal Barinka and Chicago's 2nd round choice (Patrick Wiercioch) in 2008 Entry Draft, July 10, 2006. • Missed majority of 2007-08 due to shoulder (October 4, 2007 at Minnesota) and groin (December 22, 2007 at Ottawa) injuries. Signed as a free agent by **Minnesota**, July 1, 2009. Traded to **San Jose** by **Minnesota** for Dany Heatley, July 3, 2011. • Missed majority of 2011-12 due to lower-body injury vs. Edmonton, December 17, 2011. Signed as a free agent by **New Jersey**, July 1, 2014. • Missed majority of 2014-15 due to recurring lower-body injury and as a healthy reserve.

HAYES, Eriah
(HAYZ, ee-RIGH-uh)

Right wing. Shoots right. 6'4", 210 lbs. Born, La Crescent, MN, July 7, 1988.

2007-08	Topeka	NAHL	53	30	26	56	61	....	....	....	....	....	....	....	....	....	12	5	5	10	6	....	....	....	....
2008-09	Waterloo	USHL	59	27	18	45	81	....	....	....	....	....	....	....	....	....	3	1	0	1	4	....	....	....	....
2009-10	Minnesota State	WCHA	38	8	6	14	59	....	....	....	....	....	....	....	....	....	....	....	....	....	....	....	....	....	....
2010-11	Minnesota State	WCHA	38	11	11	22	52	....	....	....	....	....	....	....	....	....	....	....	....	....	....	....	....	....	....
2011-12	Minnesota State	WCHA	36	13	11	24	83	....	....	....	....	....	....	....	....	....	....	....	....	....	....	....	....	....	....
2012-13	Minnesota State	WCHA	41	20	16	36	51	....	....	....	....	....	....	....	....	....	....	....	....	....	....	....	....	....	....
	Worcester Sharks	AHL	7	3	1	4	4	....	....	....	....	....	....	....	....	....	....	....	....	....	....	....	....	....	....
2013-14	**San Jose**	**NHL**	**15**	**1**	**0**	**1**	**2**	**0**	**0**	**0**	**17**	**5.9**	**–2**	**21**	**42.9**	**7:50**	....	....	....	....	....	....	....	....	....
	Worcester Sharks	AHL	59	12	9	21	43	....	....	....	....	....	....	....	....	....	....	....	....	....	....	....	....	....	....
2014-15	**San Jose**	**NHL**	**4**	**0**	**0**	**0**	**2**	**0**	**0**	**0**	**10**	**0.0**	**–2**	**1**	**100.0**	**9:58**	....	....	....	....	....	....	....	....	....
	Worcester Sharks	AHL	59	8	17	25	40	....	....	....	....	....	....	....	....	....	4	1	2	3	0	....	....	....	....
	NHL Totals		**19**	**1**	**0**	**1**	**4**	**0**	**0**	**0**	**27**	**3.7**		**22**	**45.5**	**8:17**	....	....	....	....	....	....	....	....	....

Signed as a free agent by **San Jose**, April 5, 2013. Signed as a free agent by **Chicago** (AHL), August 13, 2015.

HAYES, Jimmy
(HAYZ, JIH-mee) **BOS**

Right wing. Shoots right. 6'6", 221 lbs. Born, Boston, MA, November 21, 1989. Toronto's 2nd choice, 60th overall, in 2008 Entry Draft.

2006-07	USNTDP	U-17	42	17	14	31	37	....	....	....	....	....	....	....	....	....	....	....	....	....	....	....	....	....	....
	USNTDP	NAHL	14	6	8	14	4	....	....	....	....	....	....	....	....	....	....	....	....	....	....	....	....	....	....
2007-08	USNTDP	U-18	18	2	5	7	6	....	....	....	....	....	....	....	....	....	....	....	....	....	....	....	....	....	....
	USNTDP	NAHL	19	2	8	10	6	....	....	....	....	....	....	....	....	....	....	....	....	....	....	....	....	....	....
	Lincoln Stars	USHL	21	4	11	15	18	....	....	....	....	....	....	....	....	....	8	4	5	9	8	....	....	....	....
2008-09	Boston College	H-East	36	8	5	13	22	....	....	....	....	....	....	....	....	....	....	....	....	....	....	....	....	....	....
2009-10	Boston College	H-East	42	13	22	35	14	....	....	....	....	....	....	....	....	....	....	....	....	....	....	....	....	....	....
2010-11	Boston College	H-East	39	21	12	33	24	....	....	....	....	....	....	....	....	....	....	....	....	....	....	....	....	....	....
	Rockford IceHogs	AHL	7	0	0	0	2	....	....	....	....	....	....	....	....	....	....	....	....	....	....	....	....	....	....
2011-12	**Chicago**	**NHL**	**31**	**5**	**4**	**9**	**16**	**1**	**0**	**0**	**41**	**12.2**	**–3**	**10**	**50.0**	**10:15**	**2**	**0**	**0**	**0**	**15**	**0**	**0**	**0**	**10:08**
	Rockford IceHogs	AHL	33	7	16	23	11	....	....	....	....	....	....	....	....	....	....	....	....	....	....	....	....	....	....
2012-13	Rockford IceHogs	AHL	67	25	20	45	23	....	....	....	....	....	....	....	....	....	....	....	....	....	....	....	....	....	....
	Chicago	**NHL**	**10**	**1**	**3**	**4**	**0**	**0**	**0**	**0**	**13**	**7.7**	**0**	**7**	**57.1**	**14:20**	....	....	....	....	....	....	....	....	....
2013-14	**Chicago**	**NHL**	**2**	**0**	**0**	**0**	**0**	**0**	**0**	**0**	**1**	**0.0**	**1**	**0**	**0.0**	**11:51**	....	....	....	....	....	....	....	....	....
	Rockford IceHogs	AHL	13	4	4	8	2	....	....	....	....	....	....	....	....	....	....	....	....	....	....	....	....	....	....
	Florida	**NHL**	**53**	**11**	**7**	**18**	**18**	**3**	**0**	**0**	**71**	**15.5**	**–6**	**30**	**36.7**	**10:56**	....	....	....	....	....	....	....	....	....
2014-15	**Florida**	**NHL**	**72**	**19**	**16**	**35**	**20**	**4**	**0**	**3**	**166**	**11.4**	**–4**	**9**	**44.4**	**15:09**	....	....	....	....	....	....	....	....	....
	NHL Totals		**168**	**36**	**30**	**66**	**54**	**8**	**0**	**3**	**292**	**12.3**		**56**	**42.9**	**12:49**	**2**	**0**	**0**	**0**	**15**	**0**	**0**	**0**	**10:08**

Traded to **Chicago** by **Toronto** for Calgary's 2nd round choice (previously acquired, Toronto selected Brad Ross) in 2010 Entry Draft, June 25, 2010. Traded to **Florida** by **Chicago** with Dylan Olsen for Kris Versteeg and Phillipe Lefebvre, November 14, 2013. Traded to **Boston** by **Florida** for Reilly Smith and Marc Savard, July 1, 2015.

HAYES, Kevin
(HAYZ, KEH-vihn) **NYR**

Right wing. Shoots left. 6'5", 225 lbs. Born, Boston, MA, May 8, 1992. Chicago's 1st choice, 24th overall, in 2010 Entry Draft.

Season	Club	League	GP	G	A	Pts	PIM	PP	SH	GW	S	S%	+/-	TF	F%	Min	GP	G	A	Pts	PIM	PP	SH	GW	Min
			Regular Season														Playoffs								
2007-08	Nobles	High-MA	29	8	5	13	2	....	....	....	....	....	....	....	....	....	....	....	....	....	....	....	....	....	....
2008-09	Nobles	High-MA	23	28	27	55	15	....	....	....	....	....	....	....	....	....	....	....	....	....	....	....	....	....	....
2009-10	Cape Cod	Minor-MA	25	21	30	51	....	....	....	....	....	....	....	....	....	....	....	....	....	....	....	....	....	....	....
	Nobles	High-MA	29	25	44	69	8	....	....	....	....	....	....	....	....	....	....	....	....	....	....	....	....	....	....
	USNTDP	U-18	2	2	0	2	0	....	....	....	....	....	....	....	....	....	....	....	....	....	....	....	....	....	....
2010-11	Boston College	H-East	31	4	10	14	8	....	....	....	....	....	....	....	....	....	....	....	....	....	....	....	....	....	....
2011-12	Boston College	H-East	44	7	21	28	10	....	....	....	....	....	....	....	....	....	....	....	....	....	....	....	....	....	....
2012-13	Boston College	H-East	27	6	19	25	14	....	....	....	....	....	....	....	....	....	....	....	....	....	....	....	....	....	....
2013-14	Boston College	H-East	40	27	38	65	16	....	....	....	....	....	....	....	....	....	....	....	....	....	....	....	....	....	....
2014-15	**NY Rangers**	**NHL**	**79**	**17**	**28**	**45**	**22**	**1**	**1**	**1**	**111**	**15.3**	**15**	**681**	**36.3**	**13:02**	**19**	**2**	**5**	**7**	**2**	**1**	**0**	**1**	**14:13**
	NHL Totals		**79**	**17**	**28**	**45**	**22**	**1**	**1**	**1**	**111**	**15.3**		**681**	**36.3**	**13:02**	**19**	**2**	**5**	**7**	**2**	**1**	**0**	**1**	**14:13**

Hockey East First All-Star Team (2014) • NCAA East First All-American Team (2014)

Signed as a a free agent by **NY Rangers**, August 20, 2014.

HEATLEY, Dany
(HEET-lee, DA-nee)

Left wing. Shoots left. 6'3", 212 lbs. Born, Freiburg, West Germany, January 21, 1981. Atlanta's 1st choice, 2nd overall, in 2000 Entry Draft.

Season	Club	League	GP	G	A	Pts	PIM	PP	SH	GW	S	S%	+/-	TF	F%	Min	GP	G	A	Pts	PIM	PP	SH	GW	Min
1996-97	Calgary Blazers	AMHL	25	30	42	72	26	....	....	....	....	....	....	....	....	....	....	....	....	....	....	....	....	....	....
1997-98	Calgary Buffaloes	AMHL	36	39	52	*91	34	....	....	....	....	....	....	....	....	....	10	10	12	*22	30	....	....	....	....
1998-99	Calgary Canucks	AJHL	60	*70	56	*126	91	....	....	....	....	....	....	....	....	....	13	*22	13	*35	6	....	....	....	....
99-2000	U. of Wisconsin	WCHA	38	28	28	56	32	....	....	....	....	....	....	....	....	....	....	....	....	....	....	....	....	....	....
2000-01	U. of Wisconsin	WCHA	39	24	33	57	74	....	....	....	....	....	....	....	....	....	....	....	....	....	....	....	....	....	....
2001-02	**Atlanta**	**NHL**	**82**	**26**	**41**	**67**	**56**	**7**	**0**	**4**	**202**	**12.9**	**-19**	**116**	**32.8**	**19:53**	....	....	....	....	....	....	....	....	....
2002-03	**Atlanta**	**NHL**	**77**	**41**	**48**	**89**	**58**	**19**	**1**	**6**	**252**	**16.3**	**-8**	**49**	**36.7**	**21:57**	....	....	....	....	....	....	....	....	....
2003-04	**Atlanta**	**NHL**	**31**	**13**	**12**	**25**	**18**	**5**	**0**	**3**	**83**	**15.7**	**-8**	**41**	**24.4**	**19:53**	....	....	....	....	....	....	....	....	....
2004-05	SC Bern	Swiss	16	14	10	24	58	....	....	....	....	....	....	....	....	....	....	....	....	....	....	....	....	....	....
	Ak Bars Kazan	Russia	11	3	1	4	22	....	....	....	....	....	....	....	....	....	4	2	1	3	4	....	....	....	....
2005-06	**Ottawa**	**NHL**	**82**	**50**	**53**	**103**	**86**	**23**	**2**	**7**	**300**	**16.7**	**29**	**166**	**53.6**	**21:09**	**10**	**3**	**9**	**12**	**11**	**3**	**0**	**1**	**18:56**
	Canada	Olympics	6	2	1	3	8	....	....	....	....	....	....	....	....	....	....	....	....	....	....	....	....	....	....
2006-07	**Ottawa**	**NHL**	**82**	**50**	**55**	**105**	**74**	**17**	**3**	***10**	**310**	**16.1**	**31**	**60**	**38.3**	**21:02**	**20**	**7**	***15**	***22**	**14**	**2**	**0**	**2**	**21:18**
2007-08	**Ottawa**	**NHL**	**71**	**41**	**41**	**82**	**76**	**13**	**0**	**8**	**224**	**18.3**	**33**	**26**	**57.7**	**21:44**	**4**	**0**	**1**	**1**	**6**	**0**	**0**	**0**	**21:41**
2008-09	**Ottawa**	**NHL**	**82**	**39**	**33**	**72**	**88**	**15**	**0**	**6**	**258**	**15.1**	**-11**	**30**	**46.7**	**20:07**	....	....	....	....	....	....	....	....	....
2009-10	**San Jose**	**NHL**	**82**	**39**	**43**	**82**	**54**	**18**	**1**	**9**	**280**	**13.9**	**14**	**35**	**40.0**	**20:14**	**14**	**2**	**11**	**13**	**16**	**1**	**0**	**0**	**20:41**
	Canada	Olympics	7	4	3	7	4	....	....	....	....	....	....	....	....	....	....	....	....	....	....	....	....	....	....
2010-11	**San Jose**	**NHL**	**80**	**26**	**38**	**64**	**56**	**11**	**1**	**5**	**217**	**12.0**	**8**	**20**	**45.0**	**19:39**	**18**	**3**	**6**	**9**	**12**	**0**	**0**	**0**	**18:56**
2011-12	**Minnesota**	**NHL**	**82**	**24**	**29**	**53**	**28**	**8**	**0**	**3**	**238**	**10.1**	**2**	**67**	**53.7**	**20:57**	....	....	....	....	....	....	....	....	....
2012-13	**Minnesota**	**NHL**	**36**	**11**	**10**	**21**	**8**	**3**	**0**	**1**	**83**	**13.3**	**-12**	**31**	**38.7**	**18:32**	....	....	....	....	....	....	....	....	....
2013-14	**Minnesota**	**NHL**	**76**	**12**	**16**	**28**	**18**	**4**	**0**	**2**	**110**	**10.9**	**-18**	**17**	**41.2**	**14:49**	**11**	**1**	**5**	**6**	**4**	**0**	**0**	**0**	**11:33**
2014-15	**Anaheim**	**NHL**	**6**	**0**	**0**	**0**	**0**	**0**	**0**	**0**	**8**	**0.0**	**-3**	**0**	**0.0**	**12:08**	....	....	....	....	....	....	....	....	....
	Norfolk Admirals	AHL	25	2	5	7	8	....	....	....	....	....	....	....	....	....	....	....	....	....	....	....	....	....	....
	San Antonio	AHL	18	6	7	13	8	....	....	....	....	....	....	....	....	....	3	0	0	0	0	....	....	....	....
	NHL Totals		**869**	**372**	**419**	**791**	**620**	**143**	**8**	**64**	**2565**	**14.5**		**658**	**43.3**	**20:02**	**77**	**16**	**47**	**63**	**63**	**6**	**0**	**3**	**18:57**

WCHA First All-Star Team (2000) • WCHA Rookie of the Year (2000) • NCAA West Second All-American Team (2000) • WCHA Second All-Star Team (2001) • NCAA West First All-American Team (2001) • NHL All-Rookie Team (2002) • Calder Memorial Trophy (2002) • NHL Second All-Star Team (2006) • NHL First All-Star Team (2007)

Played in NHL All-Star Game (2003, 2007, 2009)

• Missed majority of 2003-04 due to automobile accident, September 29, 2003. Signed as a free agent by **Bern** (Swiss), October 13, 2004. Signed as a free agent by **Kazan** (Russia), February 9, 2005. Traded to **Ottawa** by **Atlanta** for Marian Hossa and Greg de Vries, August 23, 2005. Traded to **San Jose** by **Ottawa** with Ottawa's 5th round choice (Isaac MacLeod) in 2010 Entry Draft for Milan Michalek, Jonathan Cheechoo and San Jose's 2nd round choice (later traded to NY Islanders, later traded to Chicago – Chicago selected Kent Simpson) in 2010 Entry Draft, September 12, 2009. Traded to **Minnesota** by **San Jose** for Martin Havlat, July 3, 2011. Signed as a free agent by **Anaheim**, July 9, 2014. Traded to **Florida** by **Anaheim** with Anaheim's 3rd round choice (Thomas Schemitsch) in 2015 Entry Draft for Tomas Fleischmann, February 28, 2015.

HEDMAN, Victor
(HEHD-muhn, VIHK-tohr) **T.B.**

Defense. Shoots left. 6'6", 233 lbs. Born, Ornskoldsvik, Sweden, December 18, 1990. Tampa Bay's 1st choice, 2nd overall, in 2009 Entry Draft.

Season	Club	League	GP	G	A	Pts	PIM	PP	SH	GW	S	S%	+/-	TF	F%	Min	GP	G	A	Pts	PIM	PP	SH	GW	Min
2005-06	MODO U18	Swe-U18	8	3	3	6	14	....	....	....	....	....	....	....	....	....	2	0	0	0	0	....	....	....	....
	MODO Jr.	Swe-Jr.	10	0	1	1	8	....	....	....	....	....	....	....	....	....	....	....	....	....	....	....	....	....	....
2006-07	MODO U18	Swe-U18	3	3	0	3	29	....	....	....	....	....	....	....	....	....	....	....	....	....	....	....	....	....	....
	MODO Jr.	Swe-Jr.	34	13	12	25	30	....	....	....	....	....	....	....	....	....	5	1	1	2	44	....	....	....	....
2007-08	MODO Jr.	Swe-Jr.	6	2	1	3	26	....	....	....	....	....	....	....	....	....	3	2	0	2	4	....	....	....	....
	MODO	Sweden	39	2	2	4	44	....	....	....	....	....	....	....	....	....	5	1	0	1	4	....	....	....	....
2008-09	MODO Jr.	Swe-Jr.	2	0	2	2	10	....	....	....	....	....	....	....	....	....	5	0	1	1	2	....	....	....	....
	MODO	Sweden	43	7	14	21	52	....	....	....	....	....	....	....	....	....	....	....	....	....	....	....	....	....	....
2009-10	**Tampa Bay**	**NHL**	**74**	**4**	**16**	**20**	**79**	**0**	**0**	**0**	**90**	**4.4**	**-3**	**0**	**0.0**	**20:51**	....	....	....	....	....	....	....	....	....
2010-11	**Tampa Bay**	**NHL**	**79**	**3**	**23**	**26**	**70**	**0**	**0**	**0**	**101**	**3.0**	**3**	**0**	**0.0**	**21:01**	**18**	**0**	**6**	**6**	**8**	**0**	**0**	**0**	**22:16**
2011-12	**Tampa Bay**	**NHL**	**61**	**5**	**18**	**23**	**65**	**0**	**0**	**0**	**82**	**6.1**	**-9**	**0**	**0.0**	**23:06**	....	....	....	....	....	....	....	....	....
2012-13	Barys Astana	KHL	26	1	21	22	70	....	....	....	....	....	....	....	....	....	....	....	....	....	....	....	....	....	....
	Tampa Bay	**NHL**	**44**	**4**	**16**	**20**	**31**	**0**	**0**	**0**	**76**	**5.3**	**1**	**0**	**0.0**	**22:40**	....	....	....	....	....	....	....	....	....
2013-14	**Tampa Bay**	**NHL**	**75**	**13**	**42**	**55**	**53**	**3**	**0**	**2**	**170**	**7.6**	**5**	**0**	**0.0**	**22:26**	**4**	**1**	**2**	**3**	**2**	**0**	**0**	**0**	**24:29**
2014-15	**Tampa Bay**	**NHL**	**59**	**10**	**28**	**38**	**40**	**3**	**0**	**2**	**115**	**8.7**	**12**	**0**	**0.0**	**22:41**	**26**	**1**	**13**	**14**	**6**	**1**	**0**	**0**	**23:58**
	NHL Totals		**392**	**39**	**143**	**182**	**338**	**6**	**0**	**4**	**634**	**6.2**		**0**	**0.0**	**22:01**	**48**	**2**	**21**	**23**	**16**	**1**	**0**	**0**	**23:22**

Signed as a free agent by **Astana** (KHL), September 25, 2012.

HEJDA, Jan
(HAY-dah, YAHN)

Defense. Shoots left. 6'4", 237 lbs. Born, Prague, Czech., June 18, 1978. Buffalo's 4th choice, 106th overall, in 2003 Entry Draft.

Season	Club	League	GP	G	A	Pts	PIM	PP	SH	GW	S	S%	+/-	TF	F%	Min	GP	G	A	Pts	PIM	PP	SH	GW	Min
1997-98	HC Slavia Praha	CzRep	44	2	5	7	51	....	....	....	....	....	....	....	....	....	5	0	0	0	6	....	....	....	....
1998-99	HC Slavia Praha	CzRep	34	1	2	3	38	....	....	....	....	....	....	....	....	....	....	....	....	....	....	....	....	....	....
99-2000	HC Slavia Praha	CzRep	26	1	2	3	14	....	....	....	....	....	....	....	....	....	....	....	....	....	....	....	....	....	....
	HC Femax Havirov	CzRep	7	0	2	2	6	....	....	....	....	....	....	....	....	....	....	....	....	....	....	....	....	....	....
	Liberec	CzRep-2	1	0	0	0	4	....	....	....	....	....	....	....	....	....	....	....	....	....	....	....	....	....	....
2000-01	HC Slavia Praha	CzRep	38	2	6	8	70	....	....	....	....	....	....	....	....	....	11	3	0	3	12	....	....	....	....
	SK Kadan	CzRep-2	8	1	0	1	6	....	....	....	....	....	....	....	....	....	....	....	....	....	....	....	....	....	....
2001-02	HC Slavia Praha	CzRep	42	9	8	17	52	....	....	....	....	....	....	....	....	....	9	1	1	2	14	....	....	....	....
2002-03	HC Slavia Praha	CzRep	52	6	11	17	44	....	....	....	....	....	....	....	....	....	17	5	8	13	12	....	....	....	....
2003-04	CSKA Moscow	Russia	60	1	5	6	26	....	....	....	....	....	....	....	....	....	....	....	....	....	....	....	....	....	....
2004-05	CSKA Moscow	Russia	60	2	11	13	59	....	....	....	....	....	....	....	....	....	....	....	....	....	....	....	....	....	....
2005-06	Mytischi	Russia	50	3	12	15	56	....	....	....	....	....	....	....	....	....	9	2	3	5	24	....	....	....	....
2006-07	**Edmonton**	**NHL**	**39**	**1**	**8**	**9**	**20**	**0**	**0**	**1**	**33**	**3.0**	**-6**	**0**	**0.0**	**20:23**	....	....	....	....	....	....	....	....	....
	Hamilton	AHL	5	0	3	3	21	....	....	....	....	....	....	....	....	....	....	....	....	....	....	....	....	....	....
2007-08	**Columbus**	**NHL**	**81**	**0**	**13**	**13**	**61**	**0**	**0**	**0**	**71**	**0.0**	**20**	**0**	**0.0**	**21:08**	....	....	....	....	....	....	....	....	....
2008-09	**Columbus**	**NHL**	**82**	**3**	**18**	**21**	**38**	**0**	**0**	**1**	**66**	**4.5**	**23**	**1**	**0.0**	**22:23**	**3**	**0**	**0**	**0**	**2**	**0**	**0**	**0**	**16:53**
2009-10	**Columbus**	**NHL**	**62**	**3**	**10**	**13**	**36**	**1**	**0**	**0**	**63**	**4.8**	**-14**	**2**	**50.0**	**20:39**	....	....	....	....	....	....	....	....	....
	Czech Republic	Olympics	5	0	0	0	4	....	....	....	....	....	....	....	....	....	....	....	....	....	....	....	....	....	....
2010-11	**Columbus**	**NHL**	**77**	**5**	**15**	**20**	**28**	**0**	**0**	**0**	**79**	**6.3**	**-6**	**1**	**100.0**	**21:07**	....	....	....	....	....	....	....	....	....
2011-12	**Colorado**	**NHL**	**81**	**5**	**14**	**19**	**24**	**0**	**0**	**1**	**78**	**6.4**	**-17**	**1**	**100.0**	**20:41**	....	....	....	....	....	....	....	....	....
2012-13	**Colorado**	**NHL**	**46**	**1**	**9**	**10**	**28**	**0**	**0**	**1**	**50**	**2.0**	**-3**	**1**	**0.0**	**19:42**	....	....	....	....	....	....	....	....	....
2013-14	**Colorado**	**NHL**	**78**	**6**	**11**	**17**	**40**	**0**	**0**	**0**	**75**	**8.0**	**8**	**0**	**0.0**	**22:20**	**7**	**0**	**0**	**0**	**6**	**0**	**0**	**0**	**21:38**
2014-15	**Colorado**	**NHL**	**81**	**1**	**12**	**13**	**42**	**0**	**0**	**0**	**84**	**1.2**	**-12**	**0**	**0.0**	**20:39**	....	....	....	....	....	....	....	....	....
	NHL Totals		**627**	**25**	**110**	**135**	**317**	**1**	**0**	**4**	**599**	**4.2**		**6**	**50.0**	**21:07**	**10**	**0**	**0**	**0**	**8**	**0**	**0**	**0**	**20:13**

Traded to **Edmonton** by **Buffalo** for Edmonton's 7th round choice (Nick Eno) in 2007 Entry Draft, July 10, 2006. Signed as a free agent by **Columbus**, July 5, 2007. Signed as a free agent by **Colorado**, July 1, 2011.

			Regular Season															Playoffs								
Season	Club	League	GP	G	A	Pts	PIM	PP	SH	GW	S	S%	+/-	TF	F%	Min	GP	G	A	Pts	PIM	PP	SH	GW	Min

HELGESON, Seth (HEHL-guh-suhn, SEHTH) N.J.

Defense. Shoots left. 6'4", 215 lbs. Born, Faribault, MN, October 8, 1990. New Jersey's 4th choice, 114th overall, in 2009 Entry Draft.

Season	Club	League	GP	G	A	Pts	PIM	PP	SH	GW	S	S%	+/-	TF	F%	Min	GP	G	A	Pts	PIM	PP	SH	GW	Min
2006-07	Faribault Falcons	High-MN	27	19	17	36	....	....	....	....	....	....	....	....	....	....	....	....	....	....	....	....	....	....	....
2007-08	Sioux City	USHL	58	3	8	11	41	....	....	....	....	....	....	....	....	....	4	0	1	1	2	....	....	....	....
2008-09	Sioux City	USHL	58	4	12	16	64	....	....	....	....	....	....	....	....	....	....	....	....	....	....	....	....	....	....
2009-10	U. of Minnesota	WCHA	31	1	0	1	24	....	....	....	....	....	....	....	....	....	....	....	....	....	....	....	....	....	....
2010-11	U. of Minnesota	WCHA	36	1	6	7	66	....	....	....	....	....	....	....	....	....	....	....	....	....	....	....	....	....	....
2011-12	U. of Minnesota	WCHA	43	5	9	14	70	....	....	....	....	....	....	....	....	....	....	....	....	....	....	....	....	....	....
2012-13	U. of Minnesota	WCHA	40	0	5	5	62	....	....	....	....	....	....	....	....	....	....	....	....	....	....	....	....	....	....
2013-14	Albany Devils	AHL	75	1	9	10	100	....	....	....	....	....	....	....	....	....	4	0	0	0	2	....	....	....	....
2014-15	**New Jersey**	**NHL**	**22**	**0**	**2**	**2**	**18**	**0**	**0**	**0**	**11**	**0.0**	**4**	**0**	**0.0**	**13:28**	....	....	....	....	....	....	....	....	....
	Albany Devils	AHL	49	2	10	12	58	....	....	....	....	....	....	....	....	....	....	....	....	....	....	....	....	....	....
	NHL Totals		**22**	**0**	**2**	**2**	**18**	**0**	**0**	**0**	**11**	**0.0**		**0**	**0.0**	**13:28**	....	....	....	....	....	....	....	....	....

HELM, Darren (HEHLM, DAIR-ehn) DET

Center/Left wing. Shoots left. 6', 196 lbs. Born, Winnipeg, MB, January 21, 1987. Detroit's 5th choice, 132nd overall, in 2005 Entry Draft.

Season	Club	League	GP	G	A	Pts	PIM	PP	SH	GW	S	S%	+/-	TF	F%	Min	GP	G	A	Pts	PIM	PP	SH	GW	Min
2003-04	Selkirk Fishermen	MJBHL	34	39	32	71	34	....	....	....	....	....	....	....	....	....	....	....	....	....	....	....	....	....	....
2004-05	Medicine Hat	WHL	72	10	14	24	27	....	....	....	....	....	....	....	....	....	13	2	6	8	10	....	....	....	....
2005-06	Medicine Hat	WHL	70	41	38	79	37	....	....	....	....	....	....	....	....	....	13	5	4	9	2	....	....	....	....
2006-07	Medicine Hat	WHL	59	25	39	64	53	....	....	....	....	....	....	....	....	....	23	10	12	22	14	....	....	....	....
2007-08 •	**Detroit**	**NHL**	**7**	**0**	**0**	**0**	**2**	**0**	**0**	**0**	**7**	**0.0**	**–2**	**23**	**21.7**	**7:00**	**18**	**2**	**2**	**4**	**2**	**0**	**0**	**0**	**7:30**
	Grand Rapids	AHL	67	16	15	31	30	....	....	....	....	....	....	....	....	....	....	....	....	....	....	....	....	....	....
2008-09	**Detroit**	**NHL**	**16**	**0**	**1**	**1**	**4**	**0**	**0**	**0**	**29**	**0.0**	**–7**	**132**	**56.1**	**12:26**	**23**	**4**	**1**	**5**	**4**	**0**	**0**	**1**	**12:06**
	Grand Rapids	AHL	55	13	24	37	24	....	....	....	....	....	....	....	....	....	....	....	....	....	....	....	....	....	....
2009-10	**Detroit**	**NHL**	**75**	**11**	**13**	**24**	**18**	**0**	**3**	**3**	**165**	**6.7**	**–2**	**875**	**51.1**	**14:30**	**12**	**1**	**0**	**1**	**4**	**0**	**0**	**0**	**13:56**
2010-11	**Detroit**	**NHL**	**82**	**12**	**20**	**32**	**16**	**0**	**2**	**2**	**177**	**6.8**	**9**	**938**	**52.6**	**13:18**	**11**	**3**	**3**	**6**	**8**	**0**	**0**	**1**	**13:28**
2011-12	**Detroit**	**NHL**	**68**	**9**	**17**	**26**	**12**	**0**	**0**	**2**	**124**	**7.3**	**5**	**777**	**51.9**	**14:31**	**1**	**0**	**0**	**0**	**0**	**0**	**0**	**0**	**3:08**
2012-13	**Detroit**	**NHL**	**1**	**0**	**0**	**0**	**2**	**0**	**0**	**0**	**1**	**0.0**	**0**	**14**	**42.9**	**12:27**	....	....	....	....	....	....	....	....	....
2013-14	**Detroit**	**NHL**	**42**	**12**	**8**	**20**	**14**	**1**	**2**	**3**	**83**	**14.5**	**2**	**548**	**49.1**	**15:10**	**5**	**0**	**1**	**1**	**0**	**0**	**0**	**0**	**15:12**
	Grand Rapids	AHL	2	0	0	0	0	....	....	....	....	....	....	....	....	....	....	....	....	....	....	....	....	....	....
2014-15	**Detroit**	**NHL**	**75**	**15**	**18**	**33**	**12**	**3**	**2**	**1**	**160**	**9.4**	**7**	**421**	**53.0**	**15:50**	**7**	**0**	**3**	**3**	**4**	**0**	**0**	**0**	**19:17**
	NHL Totals		**366**	**59**	**77**	**136**	**80**	**4**	**9**	**11**	**746**	**7.9**		**3728**	**51.5**	**14:21**	**77**	**10**	**10**	**20**	**22**	**0**	**0**	**2**	**12:15**

WHL East First All-Star Team (2006) • WHL East Second All-Star Team (2007) • Memorial Cup All-Star Team (2007)

• Missed majority of 2012-13 due to recurring back injury.

HEMSKY, Ales (HEHM-skee, ahl-EHSH) DAL

Right wing. Shoots right. 6', 185 lbs. Born, Pardubice, Czech., August 13, 1983. Edmonton's 1st choice, 13th overall, in 2001 Entry Draft.

Season	Club	League	GP	G	A	Pts	PIM	PP	SH	GW	S	S%	+/-	TF	F%	Min	GP	G	A	Pts	PIM	PP	SH	GW	Min
99-2000	HC Pardubice Jr.	CzRep-Jr.	45	20	36	56	54	....	....	....	....	....	....	....	....	....	7	4	14	18	36	....	....	....	....
	Pardubice	CzRep	4	0	1	1	0	....	....	....	....	....	....	....	....	....	....	....	....	....	....	....	....	....	....
2000-01	Hull Olympiques	QMJHL	68	36	64	100	67	....	....	....	....	....	....	....	....	....	5	2	3	5	2	....	....	....	....
2001-02	Hull Olympiques	QMJHL	53	27	70	97	86	....	....	....	....	....	....	....	....	....	10	6	10	16	6	....	....	....	....
2002-03	**Edmonton**	**NHL**	**59**	**6**	**24**	**30**	**14**	**0**	**0**	**1**	**50**	**12.0**	**5**	**3**	**33.3**	**12:04**	**6**	**0**	**0**	**0**	**0**	**0**	**0**	**0**	**12:46**
2003-04	**Edmonton**	**NHL**	**71**	**12**	**22**	**34**	**14**	**4**	**0**	**3**	**87**	**13.8**	**–7**	**3**	**33.3**	**14:26**	....	....	....	....	....	....	....	....	....
2004-05	Pardubice	CzRep	47	13	18	31	28	....	....	....	....	....	....	....	....	....	16	4	*10	*14	26	....	....	....	....
2005-06	**Edmonton**	**NHL**	**81**	**19**	**58**	**77**	**64**	**7**	**1**	**4**	**178**	**10.7**	**–5**	**7**	**42.9**	**16:59**	**24**	**6**	**11**	**17**	**14**	**4**	**0**	**2**	**16:06**
	Czech Republic	Olympics	8	1	2	3	2	....	....	....	....	....	....	....	....	....	....	....	....	....	....	....	....	....	....
2006-07	**Edmonton**	**NHL**	**64**	**13**	**40**	**53**	**40**	**5**	**0**	**1**	**122**	**10.7**	**–7**	**10**	**30.0**	**16:59**	....	....	....	....	....	....	....	....	....
2007-08	**Edmonton**	**NHL**	**74**	**20**	**51**	**71**	**34**	**8**	**0**	**2**	**184**	**10.9**	**–9**	**5**	**20.0**	**18:35**	....	....	....	....	....	....	....	....	....
2008-09	**Edmonton**	**NHL**	**72**	**23**	**43**	**66**	**32**	**4**	**0**	**2**	**185**	**12.4**	**1**	**4**	**0.0**	**18:39**	....	....	....	....	....	....	....	....	....
2009-10	**Edmonton**	**NHL**	**22**	**7**	**15**	**22**	**8**	**3**	**0**	**0**	**57**	**12.3**	**7**	**1**	**100.0**	**17:56**	....	....	....	....	....	....	....	....	....
2010-11	**Edmonton**	**NHL**	**47**	**14**	**28**	**42**	**18**	**1**	**1**	**1**	**100**	**14.0**	**3**	**7**	**14.3**	**18:17**	....	....	....	....	....	....	....	....	....
2011-12	**Edmonton**	**NHL**	**69**	**10**	**26**	**36**	**43**	**1**	**0**	**1**	**137**	**7.3**	**–13**	**6**	**33.3**	**17:36**	....	....	....	....	....	....	....	....	....
2012-13	Pardubice	CzRep	27	14	18	32	52	....	....	....	....	....	....	....	....	....	....	....	....	....	....	....	....	....	....
	Edmonton	**NHL**	**38**	**9**	**11**	**20**	**16**	**5**	**0**	**1**	**82**	**11.0**	**–6**	**24**	**50.0**	**15:42**	....	....	....	....	....	....	....	....	....
2013-14	**Edmonton**	**NHL**	**55**	**9**	**17**	**26**	**20**	**2**	**0**	**1**	**94**	**9.6**	**–13**	**4**	**25.0**	**16:05**	....	....	....	....	....	....	....	....	....
	Czech Republic	Olympics	5	3	1	4	0	....	....	....	....	....	....	....	....	....	....	....	....	....	....	....	....	....	....
	Ottawa	**NHL**	**20**	**4**	**13**	**17**	**4**	**0**	**0**	**0**	**44**	**9.1**	**–2**	**0**	**0.0**	**15:38**	....	....	....	....	....	....	....	....	....
2014-15	**Dallas**	**NHL**	**76**	**11**	**21**	**32**	**16**	**1**	**0**	**1**	**140**	**7.9**	**–8**	**0**	**0.0**	**13:38**	....	....	....	....	....	....	....	....	....
	NHL Totals		**748**	**157**	**369**	**526**	**323**	**41**	**2**	**18**	**1460**	**10.8**		**74**	**35.1**	**16:20**	**30**	**6**	**11**	**17**	**14**	**4**	**0**	**2**	**15:26**

QMJHL Second All-Star Team (2002)

Signed as a free agent by **Pardubice** (CzRep), September 18, 2004. • Missed majority of 2009-10 due to shoulder injury vs. Los Angeles, November 25, 2009. Signed as a free agent by **Pardubice** (CzRep), September 17, 2012. Traded to **Ottawa** by **Edmonton** for Ottawa's 5th round choice (Liam Coughlin) in 2014 Entry Draft and Ottawa's 3rd round choice (later traded to NY Rangers – NY Rangers selected Sergey Zobrovskiy) in 2015 Entry Draft, July 1, 2014.

HENDERSON, Kevin (HEHN-duhr-SOHN, KEH-vihn)

Left wing. Shoots left. 6'3", 210 lbs. Born, Toronto, ON, December 3, 1986.

Season	Club	League	GP	G	A	Pts	PIM	PP	SH	GW	S	S%	+/-	TF	F%	Min	GP	G	A	Pts	PIM	PP	SH	GW	Min
2003-04	Thornhill Islanders	ON-Jr.A	47	11	23	34	44	....	....	....	....	....	....	....	....	....	....	....	....	....	....	....	....	....	....
2004-05	Kitchener Rangers	OHL	47	5	8	13	46	....	....	....	....	....	....	....	....	....	15	0	3	3	8	....	....	....	....
	Thornhill	ON-Jr.A	11	5	9	14	33	....	....	....	....	....	....	....	....	....	....	....	....	....	....	....	....	....	....
2005-06	Kitchener Rangers	OHL	63	6	11	17	66	....	....	....	....	....	....	....	....	....	2	1	0	1	0	....	....	....	....
2006-07	Kitchener Rangers	OHL	56	33	15	48	69	....	....	....	....	....	....	....	....	....	9	4	6	10	13	....	....	....	....
2007-08	New Brunswick	AUAA	27	5	10	15	22	....	....	....	....	....	....	....	....	....	....	....	....	....	....	....	....	....	....
2008-09	New Brunswick	AUAA	28	19	31	50	28	....	....	....	....	....	....	....	....	....	....	....	....	....	....	....	....	....	....
2009-10	Worcester Sharks	AHL	64	2	13	15	45	....	....	....	....	....	....	....	....	....	11	0	1	1	4	....	....	....	....
2010-11	Worcester Sharks	AHL	73	8	13	21	45	....	....	....	....	....	....	....	....	....	....	....	....	....	....	....	....	....	....
2011-12	Milwaukee	AHL	30	4	7	11	12	....	....	....	....	....	....	....	....	....	3	0	0	0	2	....	....	....	....
	Cincinnati	ECHL	2	0	0	0	4	....	....	....	....	....	....	....	....	....	....	....	....	....	....	....	....	....	....
2012-13	Milwaukee	AHL	67	17	12	29	24	....	....	....	....	....	....	....	....	....	3	1	0	1	2	....	....	....	....
	Nashville	**NHL**	**4**	**1**	**0**	**1**	**0**	**0**	**0**	**0**	**3**	**33.3**	**–1**	**0**	**0.0**	**14:42**	....	....	....	....	....	....	....	....	....
2013-14	Milwaukee	AHL	50	7	7	14	14	....	....	....	....	....	....	....	....	....	....	....	....	....	....	....	....	....	....
	Texas Stars	AHL	15	5	4	9	8	....	....	....	....	....	....	....	....	....	21	1	5	6	16	....	....	....	....
2014-15	Texas Stars	AHL	56	7	5	12	27	....	....	....	....	....	....	....	....	....	2	0	0	0	0	....	....	....	....
	NHL Totals		**4**	**1**	**0**	**1**	**0**	**0**	**0**	**0**	**3**	**33.3**		**0**	**0.0**	**14:42**	....	....	....	....	....	....	....	....	....

Signed as a free agent by **San Jose**, April 22, 2009. Signed as a free agent by **Nashville**, July 1, 2012.

HENDRICKS, Matt (HEHN-drihks, MAT) EDM

Center. Shoots left. 6', 211 lbs. Born, Blaine, MN, June 17, 1981. Nashville's 5th choice, 131st overall, in 2000 Entry Draft.

Season	Club	League	GP	G	A	Pts	PIM	PP	SH	GW	S	S%	+/-	TF	F%	Min	GP	G	A	Pts	PIM	PP	SH	GW	Min
1998-99	Blaine Bengals	High-MN	22	23	34	57	42	....	....	....	....	....	....	....	....	....	....	....	....	....	....	....	....	....	....
99-2000	Blaine Bengals	High-MN	21	23	30	53	28	....	....	....	....	....	....	....	....	....	....	....	....	....	....	....	....	....	....
2000-01	St. Cloud State	WCHA	37	3	9	12	23	....	....	....	....	....	....	....	....	....	....	....	....	....	....	....	....	....	....
2001-02	St. Cloud State	WCHA	42	19	20	39	74	....	....	....	....	....	....	....	....	....	....	....	....	....	....	....	....	....	....
2002-03	St. Cloud State	WCHA	37	18	18	36	64	....	....	....	....	....	....	....	....	....	....	....	....	....	....	....	....	....	....
2003-04	St. Cloud State	WCHA	37	14	11	25	32	....	....	....	....	....	....	....	....	....	....	....	....	....	....	....	....	....	....
	Milwaukee	AHL	1	0	0	0	2	....	....	....	....	....	....	....	....	....	....	....	....	....	....	....	....	....	....
2004-05	Lowell	AHL	15	1	2	3	10	....	....	....	....	....	....	....	....	....	....	....	....	....	....	....	....	....	....
	Florida Everblades	ECHL	54	24	26	50	94	....	....	....	....	....	....	....	....	....	4	0	0	0	4	....	....	....	....
2005-06	Rochester	AHL	56	13	14	27	84	....	....	....	....	....	....	....	....	....	....	....	....	....	....	....	....	....	....
2006-07	Hershey Bears	AHL	65	18	26	44	105	....	....	....	....	....	....	....	....	....	19	8	4	12	18	....	....	....	....
2007-08	Providence Bruins	AHL	67	22	30	52	121	....	....	....	....	....	....	....	....	....	10	0	3	3	6	....	....	....	....
2008-09	**Colorado**	**NHL**	**4**	**0**	**0**	**0**	**13**	**0**	**0**	**0**	**5**	**0.0**	**1**	**1**	**0.0**	**8:30**	....	....	....	....	....	....	....	....	....
	Lake Erie	AHL	43	14	15	29	71	....	....	....	....	....	....	....	....	....	....	....	....	....	....	....	....	....	....
2009-10	**Colorado**	**NHL**	**56**	**9**	**7**	**16**	**74**	**0**	**1**	**1**	**63**	**14.3**	**1**	**83**	**39.8**	**9:16**	**6**	**0**	**0**	**0**	**0**	**0**	**0**	**0**	**9:52**
2010-11	**Washington**	**NHL**	**77**	**9**	**16**	**25**	**110**	**1**	**0**	**3**	**113**	**8.0**	**–2**	**98**	**53.1**	**11:28**	**7**	**0**	**0**	**0**	**4**	**0**	**0**	**0**	**9:08**
2011-12	**Washington**	**NHL**	**78**	**4**	**5**	**9**	**95**	**0**	**0**	**0**	**97**	**4.1**	**–6**	**265**	**53.6**	**12:07**	**14**	**1**	**1**	**2**	**6**	**0**	**0**	**0**	**16:05**

			Regular Season														Playoffs								
Season	Club	League	GP	G	A	Pts	PIM	PP	SH	GW	S	S%	+/-	TF	F%	Min	GP	G	A	Pts	PIM	PP	SH	GW	Min
2012-13	Washington	NHL	48	5	3	8	73	0	0	1	54	9.3	–6	259	56.8	11:43	7	0	0	0	0	0	0	0	10:32
2013-14	Nashville	NHL	44	2	2	4	54	0	0	0	53	3.8	–5	26	53.9	11:33	....	....	....	....	....	....	....	....	....
	Edmonton	NHL	33	3	0	3	58	0	1	1	49	6.1	–6	37	54.1	14:19	....	....	....	....	....	....	....	....	....
2014-15	Edmonton	NHL	71	8	8	16	76	0	1	0	103	7.8	–14	198	49.5	13:09	....	....	....	....	....	....	....	....	....
	NHL Totals		411	40	41	81	553	1	3	6	537	7.4		967	52.3	11:49	34	1	1	2	10	0	0	0	12:25

Signed as a free agent by **Boston**, July 9, 2007. Traded to **Colorado** by **Boston** for Johnny Boychuk, June 24, 2008. Signed as a free agent by **Washington**, September 27, 2010. Signed as a free agent by **Nashville**, July 5, 2013. Traded to **Edmonton** by **Nashville** for Devan Dubnyk, January 15, 2014.

HENRIQUE, Adam (HEHN-reek, A-duhm) N.J.

Center. Shoots left. 6', 195 lbs. Born, Brantford, ON, February 6, 1990. New Jersey's 4th choice, 82nd overall, in 2008 Entry Draft.

Season	Club	League	GP	G	A	Pts	PIM	PP	SH	GW	S	S%	+/-	TF	F%	Min	GP	G	A	Pts	PIM	PP	SH	GW	Min
2006-07	Windsor Spitfires	OHL	62	23	21	44	20	....	....	....	....	....	....	....	....	....	....	....	....	....	....	....	....	....	....
2007-08	Windsor Spitfires	OHL	66	20	24	44	28	....	....	....	....	....	....	....	....	....	5	2	3	5	4	....	....	....	....
2008-09	Windsor Spitfires	OHL	56	30	33	63	47	....	....	....	....	....	....	....	....	....	20	8	9	17	19	....	....	....	....
2009-10	Windsor Spitfires	OHL	54	38	39	77	57	....	....	....	....	....	....	....	....	....	19	*20	5	25	12	....	....	....	....
2010-11	New Jersey	NHL	1	0	0	0	0	0	0	0	3	0.0	1	1	0.0	13:21	....	....	....	....	....	....	....	....	....
	Albany Devils	AHL	73	25	25	50	26	....	....	....	....	....	....	....	....	....	....	....	....	....	....	....	....	....	....
2011-12	New Jersey	NHL	74	16	35	51	7	0	*4	3	130	12.3	8	1026	48.8	18:10	24	5	8	13	11	0	0	*3	17:15
	Albany Devils	AHL	3	0	1	1	2	....	....	....	....	....	....	....	....	....	....	....	....	....	....	....	....	....	....
2012-13	Albany Devils	AHL	16	5	3	8	12	....	....	....	....	....	....	....	....	....	....	....	....	....	....	....	....	....	....
	New Jersey	NHL	42	11	5	16	16	3	2	2	78	14.1	–3	680	49.0	18:19	....	....	....	....	....	....	....	....	....
2013-14	New Jersey	NHL	77	25	18	43	20	7	3	4	137	18.2	3	918	44.3	18:03	....	....	....	....	....	....	....	....	....
2014-15	New Jersey	NHL	75	16	27	43	34	5	0	3	127	12.6	–6	519	52.0	17:45	....	....	....	....	....	....	....	....	....
	NHL Totals		269	68	85	153	77	15	9	12	475	14.3		3144	48.1	18:01	24	5	8	13	11	0	0	3	17:15

OHL Playoff MVP (2010) • NHL All-Rookie Team (2012)

HENSICK, T.J. (HEHN-sihk, TEE-JAY) CAR

Center. Shoots right. 5'9", 170 lbs. Born, Howell, MI, December 10, 1985. Colorado's 5th choice, 88th overall, in 2005 Entry Draft.

Season	Club	League	GP	G	A	Pts	PIM	PP	SH	GW	S	S%	+/-	TF	F%	Min	GP	G	A	Pts	PIM	PP	SH	GW	Min
2001-02	USNTDP	U-17	17	10	5	15	....	....	....	....	....	....	....	....	....	....	....	....	....	....	....	....	....	....	....
	USNTDP	NAHL	46	15	25	40	10	....	....	....	....	....	....	....	....	....	....	....	....	....	....	....	....	....	....
2002-03	USNTDP	U-18	48	24	24	48	11	....	....	....	....	....	....	....	....	....	....	....	....	....	....	....	....	....	....
	USNTDP	NAHL	10	6	7	13	0	....	....	....	....	....	....	....	....	....	....	....	....	....	....	....	....	....	....
2003-04	U. of Michigan	CCHA	43	12	*34	46	38	....	....	....	....	....	....	....	....	....	....	....	....	....	....	....	....	....	....
2004-05	U. of Michigan	CCHA	39	23	32	55	24	....	....	....	....	....	....	....	....	....	....	....	....	....	....	....	....	....	....
2005-06	U. of Michigan	CCHA	41	17	35	52	44	....	....	....	....	....	....	....	....	....	....	....	....	....	....	....	....	....	....
2006-07	U. of Michigan	CCHA	41	23	*46	*69	38	....	....	....	....	....	....	....	....	....	....	....	....	....	....	....	....	....	....
2007-08	Colorado	NHL	31	6	5	11	2	4	0	1	52	11.5	–4	256	42.2	11:59	2	0	1	1	0	0	0	0	15:29
	Lake Erie	AHL	50	12	33	45	18	....	....	....	....	....	....	....	....	....	....	....	....	....	....	....	....	....	....
2008-09	Colorado	NHL	61	4	17	21	14	1	0	0	116	3.4	–7	510	47.3	12:54	....	....	....	....	....	....	....	....	....
	Lake Erie	AHL	12	7	9	16	2	....	....	....	....	....	....	....	....	....	....	....	....	....	....	....	....	....	....
2009-10	Colorado	NHL	7	1	2	3	0	0	0	0	13	7.7	0	14	42.9	9:27	....	....	....	....	....	....	....	....	....
	Lake Erie	AHL	58	20	50	70	25	....	....	....	....	....	....	....	....	....	....	....	....	....	....	....	....	....	....
2010-11	St. Louis	NHL	13	1	2	3	2	0	0	0	12	8.3	–5	29	37.9	9:05	....	....	....	....	....	....	....	....	....
	Peoria Rivermen	AHL	59	21	48	69	27	....	....	....	....	....	....	....	....	....	4	2	1	3	2	....	....	....	....
2011-12	Peoria Rivermen	AHL	66	21	49	70	20	....	....	....	....	....	....	....	....	....	....	....	....	....	....	....	....	....	....
2012-13	Peoria Rivermen	AHL	76	19	48	67	50	....	....	....	....	....	....	....	....	....	....	....	....	....	....	....	....	....	....
2013-14	MODO	Sweden	31	4	11	15	2	....	....	....	....	....	....	....	....	....	....	....	....	....	....	....	....	....	....
	Hartford	AHL	42	11	23	34	0	....	....	....	....	....	....	....	....	....	....	....	....	....	....	....	....	....	....
2014-15	Hamilton	AHL	75	19	41	60	10	....	....	....	....	....	....	....	....	....	....	....	....	....	....	....	....	....	....
	NHL Totals		112	12	26	38	18	5	0	1	193	6.2		809	45.2	11:59	2	0	1	1	0	0	0	0	15:29

CCHA All-Rookie Team (2004) • CCHA First All-Star Team (2004, 2005, 2007) • CCHA Rookie of the Year (2004) • NCAA West First All-American Team (2005, 2007) • CCHA Second All-Star Team (2006) • AHL Second All-Star Team (2012)

Traded to **St. Louis** by **Colorado** for Julian Talbot, June 17, 2010. Signed as a free agent by **MODO** (Sweden), June 13, 2013. Signed as a free agent by **Hartford** (AHL), January 11, 2014. Signed as a free agent by **Hamilton** (AHL), July 3, 2014. Signed as a free agent by **Carolina**, July 1, 2015.

HERTL, Tomas (HUHR-tuhl, TAW-muhsh) S.J.

Center. Shoots left. 6'2", 210 lbs. Born, Prague, Czech Rep., November 12, 1993. San Jose's 1st choice, 17th overall, in 2012 Entry Draft.

Season	Club	League	GP	G	A	Pts	PIM	PP	SH	GW	S	S%	+/-	TF	F%	Min	GP	G	A	Pts	PIM	PP	SH	GW	Min
2007-08	Slavia U17	CzR-U17	22	7	6	13	4	....	....	....	....	....	....	....	....	....	5	1	0	1	2	....	....	....	....
2008-09	Slavia U17	CzR-U17	35	16	15	31	12	....	....	....	....	....	....	....	....	....	8	5	2	7	4	....	....	....	....
2009-10	Slavia U18	CzR-U18	7	13	10	23	8	....	....	....	....	....	....	....	....	....	5	5	6	11	31	....	....	....	....
	Slavia Jr.	CzRep-Jr.	42	12	26	38	12	....	....	....	....	....	....	....	....	....	4	1	0	1	2	....	....	....	....
2010-11	Slavia U18	CzR-U18	4	2	6	8	0	....	....	....	....	....	....	....	....	....	....	....	....	....	....	....	....	....	....
	Slavia Jr.	CzRep-Jr.	33	14	27	41	49	....	....	....	....	....	....	....	....	....	4	4	2	6	0	....	....	....	....
	HC Slavia Praha	CzRep	1	0	0	0	0	....	....	....	....	....	....	....	....	....	....	....	....	....	....	....	....	....	....
2011-12	HC Slavia Praha	CzRep	50	15	13	28	28	....	....	....	....	....	....	....	....	....	....	....	....	....	....	....	....	....	....
	Usti nad Labem	CzRep-2	....	....	....	....	....	....	....	....	....	....	....	....	....	....	3	2	0	2	2	....	....	....	....
2012-13	HC Slavia Praha	CzRep	43	18	12	30	16	....	....	....	....	....	....	....	....	....	11	3	5	8	0	....	....	....	....
2013-14	San Jose	NHL	37	15	10	25	4	3	0	3	98	15.3	11	51	56.9	15:20	7	2	3	5	2	0	0	0	13:35
2014-15	San Jose	NHL	82	13	18	31	16	3	0	4	145	9.0	–5	83	45.8	14:33	....	....	....	....	....	....	....	....	....
	Worcester Sharks	AHL	2	0	2	2	0	....	....	....	....	....	....	....	....	....	....	....	....	....	....	....	....	....	....
	NHL Totals		119	28	28	56	20	6	0	7	243	11.5		134	50.0	14:48	7	2	3	5	2	0	0	0	13:35

• Missed majority of 2013-14 due to knee injury at Los Angeles, December 19, 2013 .

HICKEY, Thomas (HIH-kee, TAW-muhs) NYI

Defense. Shoots left. 6', 190 lbs. Born, Calgary, AB, February 8, 1989. Los Angeles' 1st choice, 4th overall, in 2007 Entry Draft.

Season	Club	League	GP	G	A	Pts	PIM	PP	SH	GW	S	S%	+/-	TF	F%	Min	GP	G	A	Pts	PIM	PP	SH	GW	Min
2003-04	Calgary Royals	CBHL	32	13	25	38	51	....	....	....	....	....	....	....	....	....	....	....	....	....	....	....	....	....	....
2004-05	Calgary Royals	AMHL	33	9	13	22	36	....	....	....	....	....	....	....	....	....	....	....	....	....	....	....	....	....	....
	Seattle	WHL	5	2	1	3	6	....	....	....	....	....	....	....	....	....	....	....	....	....	....	....	....	....	....
2005-06	Seattle	WHL	69	1	27	28	53	....	....	....	....	....	....	....	....	....	7	1	3	4	10	....	....	....	....
2006-07	Seattle	WHL	68	9	41	50	70	....	....	....	....	....	....	....	....	....	11	3	4	7	4	....	....	....	....
2007-08	Seattle	WHL	63	11	34	45	49	....	....	....	....	....	....	....	....	....	9	1	9	10	4	....	....	....	....
2008-09	Seattle	WHL	57	16	35	51	30	....	....	....	....	....	....	....	....	....	5	2	1	3	4	....	....	....	....
	Manchester	AHL	7	1	6	7	2	....	....	....	....	....	....	....	....	....	....	....	....	....	....	....	....	....	....
2009-10	Manchester	AHL	19	1	5	6	12	....	....	....	....	....	....	....	....	....	4	0	3	3	0	....	....	....	....
2010-11	Manchester	AHL	77	6	18	24	38	....	....	....	....	....	....	....	....	....	7	0	2	2	0	....	....	....	....
2011-12	Manchester	AHL	76	3	23	26	36	....	....	....	....	....	....	....	....	....	4	0	4	4	2	....	....	....	....
2012-13	Manchester	AHL	33	3	9	12	12	....	....	....	....	....	....	....	....	....	....	....	....	....	....	....	....	....	....
	NY Islanders	NHL	39	1	3	4	8	0	0	1	40	2.5	9	0	0.0	16:52	2	0	0	0	2	0	0	0	18:17
2013-14	NY Islanders	NHL	82	4	18	22	34	0	0	0	96	4.2	5	0	0.0	18:52	....	....	....	....	....	....	....	....	....
2014-15	NY Islanders	NHL	81	2	20	22	26	0	0	1	82	2.4	–12	2	50.0	18:56	7	0	1	1	2	0	0	0	21:25
	NHL Totals		202	7	41	48	68	0	0	2	218	3.2		2	50.0	18:30	9	0	1	1	4	0	0	0	20:43

WHL West Second All-Star Team (2007) • WHL West First All-Star Team (2008, 2009)

• Missed majority of 2009-10 due to shoulder injury vs. Providence (AHL), November 22, 2009. Claimed on waivers by **NY Islanders** from **Los Angeles**, January 15, 2013.

HIGGINS, Chris (HIH-gihns, KRIHS) VAN

Left wing. Shoots left. 6', 205 lbs. Born, Smithtown, NY, June 2, 1983. Montreal's 1st choice, 14th overall, in 2002 Entry Draft.

Season	Club	League	GP	G	A	Pts	PIM	PP	SH	GW	S	S%	+/-	TF	F%	Min	GP	G	A	Pts	PIM	PP	SH	GW	Min
99-2000	Avon Old Farms	High-CT	27	19	20	39	10	....	....	....	....	....	....	....	....	....	....	....	....	....	....	....	....	....	....
2000-01	Avon Old Farms	High-CT	24	22	14	36	29	....	....	....	....	....	....	....	....	....	....	....	....	....	....	....	....	....	....
2001-02	Yale	ECAC	27	14	17	31	32	....	....	....	....	....	....	....	....	....	....	....	....	....	....	....	....	....	....
2002-03	Yale	ECAC	28	20	21	41	41	....	....	....	....	....	....	....	....	....	....	....	....	....	....	....	....	....	....
2003-04	Montreal	NHL	2	0	0	0	0	0	0	0	0	0.0	0	9	22.2	6:18	....	....	....	....	....	....	....	....	....
	Hamilton	AHL	67	21	27	48	18	....	....	....	....	....	....	....	....	....	10	3	2	5	0	....	....	....	....
2004-05	Hamilton	AHL	76	28	23	51	33	....	....	....	....	....	....	....	....	....	4	3	3	6	4	....	....	....	....
2005-06	Montreal	NHL	80	23	15	38	26	7	3	3	148	15.5	–1	45	51.1	14:25	6	1	3	4	0	0	0	0	17:04

Season	Club	League	GP	G	A	Pts	PIM	PP	SH	GW	S	S%	+/-	TF	F%	Min	GP	G	A	Pts	PIM	PP	SH	GW	Min
			Regular Season														Playoffs								
2006-07	**Montreal**	**NHL**	**61**	**22**	**16**	**38**	**26**	**8**	**3**	**3**	**159**	**13.8**	**-11**	**53**	**34.0**	**17:54**	....	....	....	....	....	....	....	....	....
2007-08	**Montreal**	**NHL**	**82**	**27**	**25**	**52**	**22**	**12**	**0**	**5**	**241**	**11.2**	**0**	**62**	**35.5**	**17:57**	**12**	**3**	**2**	**5**	**2**	**0**	**0**	**0**	**18:27**
2008-09	**Montreal**	**NHL**	**57**	**12**	**11**	**23**	**22**	**2**	**2**	**1**	**151**	**7.9**	**-1**	**57**	**50.9**	**17:00**	**4**	**2**	**0**	**2**	**2**	**0**	**0**	**0**	**17:35**
2009-10	**NY Rangers**	**NHL**	**55**	**6**	**8**	**14**	**32**	**0**	**0**	**1**	**137**	**4.4**	**-9**	**63**	**41.3**	**17:55**	....	....	....	....	....	....	....	....	....
	Calgary	**NHL**	**12**	**2**	**1**	**3**	**0**	**0**	**0**	**0**	**28**	**7.1**	**0**	**7**	**28.6**	**15:52**	....	....	....	....	....	....	....	....	....
2010-11	**Florida**	**NHL**	**48**	**11**	**12**	**23**	**10**	**0**	**0**	**0**	**126**	**8.7**	**5**	**65**	**46.2**	**16:39**	....	....	....	....	....	....	....	....	....
	Vancouver	**NHL**	**14**	**2**	**3**	**5**	**6**	**1**	**0**	**0**	**34**	**5.9**	**0**	**20**	**55.0**	**15:07**	**25**	**4**	**4**	**8**	**2**	**1**	**0**	**3**	**17:08**
2011-12	**Vancouver**	**NHL**	**71**	**18**	**25**	**43**	**16**	**1**	**1**	**4**	**165**	**10.9**	**11**	**30**	**40.0**	**16:19**	**5**	**0**	**0**	**0**	**2**	**0**	**0**	**0**	**15:34**
2012-13	**Vancouver**	**NHL**	**41**	**10**	**5**	**15**	**10**	**0**	**0**	**1**	**77**	**13.0**	**-4**	**91**	**36.3**	**16:25**	**4**	**0**	**0**	**0**	**0**	**0**	**0**	**0**	**16:41**
2013-14	**Vancouver**	**NHL**	**78**	**17**	**22**	**39**	**30**	**2**	**0**	**4**	**216**	**7.9**	**-14**	**38**	**44.7**	**19:10**	....	....	....	....	....	....	....	....	....
2014-15	**Vancouver**	**NHL**	**77**	**12**	**24**	**36**	**16**	**3**	**0**	**1**	**171**	**7.0**	**8**	**9**	**33.3**	**15:47**	**6**	**1**	**1**	**2**	**2**	**1**	**0**	**1**	**16:36**
	NHL Totals		**678**	**162**	**167**	**329**	**216**	**36**	**9**	**23**	**1653**	**9.8**		**549**	**41.5**	**16:51**	**62**	**11**	**10**	**21**	**10**	**2**	**0**	**4**	**17:12**

ECAC All-Rookie Team (2002) • ECAC Second All-Star Team (2002) • ECAC Rookie of the Year (2002) • ECAC First All-Star Team (2003) • ECAC Player of the Year (2003) (co-winner - David LeNeveu) • NCAA East First All-American Team (2003)

Traded to **NY Rangers** by **Montreal** with Ryan McDonagh and Pavel Valentenko for Scott Gomez, Tom Pyatt and Michael Busto, June 30, 2009. Traded to **Calgary** by **NY Rangers** with Ales Kotalik for Olli Jokinen and Brandon Prust, February 2, 2010. Signed as a free agent by **Florida**, July 2, 2010. Traded to **Vancouver** by **Florida** for Evan Oberg and Vancouver's 3rd round choice (later traded back to Vancouver – Vancouver selected Cole Cassels) in 2013 Entry Draft, February 28, 2011.

HILLEN, Jack

(HIHL-uhn, JAK)

Defense. Shoots left. 5'10", 190 lbs. Born, Minnetonka, MN, January 24, 1986.

Season	Club	League	GP	G	A	Pts	PIM	PP	SH	GW	S	S%	+/-	TF	F%	Min	GP	G	A	Pts	PIM	PP	SH	GW	Min
2003-04	Tri-City Storm	USHL	21	2	2	4	16	....	....	....	....	....	....	....	....	....	8	0	1	1	4	....	....	....	....
2004-05	Colorado College	WCHA	30	2	9	11	20	....	....	....	....	....	....	....	....	....	....	....	....	....	....	....	....	....	....
2005-06	Colorado College	WCHA	42	4	9	13	48	....	....	....	....	....	....	....	....	....	....	....	....	....	....	....	....	....	....
2006-07	Colorado College	WCHA	38	7	8	15	38	....	....	....	....	....	....	....	....	....	....	....	....	....	....	....	....	....	....
2007-08	Colorado College	WCHA	41	6	*31	37	60	....	....	....	....	....	....	....	....	....	....	....	....	....	....	....	....	....	....
	NY Islanders	**NHL**	**2**	**0**	**1**	**1**	**4**	**0**	**0**	**0**	**3**	**0.0**	**1**	**0**	**0.0**	**15:32**	....	....	....	....	....	....	....	....	....
2008-09	**NY Islanders**	**NHL**	**40**	**1**	**5**	**6**	**16**	**0**	**0**	**0**	**47**	**2.1**	**-9**	**0**	**0.0**	**15:13**	....	....	....	....	....	....	....	....	....
	Bridgeport	AHL	33	4	13	17	31	....	....	....	....	....	....	....	....	....	5	0	2	2	2	....	....	....	....
2009-10	**NY Islanders**	**NHL**	**69**	**3**	**18**	**21**	**44**	**1**	**0**	**0**	**78**	**3.8**	**-5**	**1**	**100.0**	**20:42**	....	....	....	....	....	....	....	....	....
2010-11	**NY Islanders**	**NHL**	**64**	**4**	**18**	**22**	**45**	**0**	**0**	**1**	**81**	**4.9**	**-5**	**0**	**0.0**	**18:49**	....	....	....	....	....	....	....	....	....
2011-12	**Nashville**	**NHL**	**55**	**2**	**4**	**6**	**20**	**0**	**0**	**0**	**51**	**3.9**	**6**	**0**	**0.0**	**14:04**	**2**	**0**	**0**	**0**	**2**	**0**	**0**	**0**	**7:54**
2012-13	**Washington**	**NHL**	**23**	**3**	**6**	**9**	**14**	**0**	**0**	**1**	**28**	**10.7**	**9**	**0**	**0.0**	**17:37**	**7**	**0**	**1**	**1**	**6**	**0**	**0**	**0**	**16:37**
2013-14	**Washington**	**NHL**	**13**	**0**	**1**	**1**	**4**	**0**	**0**	**0**	**12**	**0.0**	**-4**	**0**	**0.0**	**18:16**	....	....	....	....	....	....	....	....	....
	Hershey Bears	AHL	2	0	2	2	0	....	....	....	....	....	....	....	....	....	....	....	....	....	....	....	....	....	....
2014-15	**Washington**	**NHL**	**35**	**0**	**5**	**5**	**10**	**0**	**0**	**0**	**20**	**0.0**	**1**	**0**	**0.0**	**12:22**	....	....	....	....	....	....	....	....	....
	Carolina	**NHL**	**3**	**0**	**0**	**0**	**0**	**0**	**0**	**0**	**4**	**0.0**	**-2**	**0**	**0.0**	**18:36**	....	....	....	....	....	....	....	....	....
	NHL Totals		**304**	**13**	**58**	**71**	**157**	**1**	**0**	**2**	**324**	**4.0**		**1**	**100.0**	**17:02**	**9**	**0**	**1**	**1**	**8**	**0**	**0**	**0**	**14:41**

WCHA First All-Star Team (2008) • NCAA West First All-American Team (2008)

Signed as a free agent by **NY Islanders**, April 1, 2008. Signed as a free agent by **Nashville**, August 8, 2011. Signed as a free agent by **Washington**, July 3, 2012. • Missed majority of 2012-13 due to upper-body injury at Tampa Bay, January 19, 2013. • Missed majority of 2013-14 due to leg injury vs. Calgary, October 3, 2013. Traded to **Carolina** by **Washington** with Arizona's 4th round choice (previously acquired, Carolina selected Callum Booth) in 2015 Entry Draft for Tim Gleason, February 26, 2015. • Missed majority of 2014-15 due to head injury vs. Philadelphia, March 6, 2015 and as a healthy reserve.

HISHON, Joey

(HIHS-hawn, JOH-ee) **COL**

Center. Shoots left. 5'10", 170 lbs. Born, Stratford, ON, October 20, 1991. Colorado's 1st choice, 17th overall, in 2010 Entry Draft.

Season	Club	League	GP	G	A	Pts	PIM	PP	SH	GW	S	S%	+/-	TF	F%	Min	GP	G	A	Pts	PIM	PP	SH	GW	Min
2006-07	Stratford Warriors	Minor-ON	50	44	42	86	114	....	....	....	....	....	....	....	....	....	....	....	....	....	....	....	....	....	....
2007-08	Owen Sound	OHL	63	20	27	47	38	....	....	....	....	....	....	....	....	....	....	....	....	....	....	....	....	....	....
2008-09	Owen Sound	OHL	65	37	44	81	34	....	....	....	....	....	....	....	....	....	4	4	3	7	6	....	....	....	....
2009-10	Owen Sound	OHL	36	16	24	40	26	....	....	....	....	....	....	....	....	....	....	....	....	....	....	....	....	....	....
2010-11	Owen Sound	OHL	50	37	50	87	64	....	....	....	....	....	....	....	....	....	22	5	*19	*24	32	....	....	....	....
2011-12			DID NOT PLAY – INJURED																						
2012-13	Lake Erie	AHL	9	1	5	6	2	....	....	....	....	....	....	....	....	....	....	....	....	....	....	....	....	....	....
2013-14	Lake Erie	AHL	50	10	14	24	16	....	....	....	....	....	....	....	....	....	....	....	....	....	....	....	....	....	....
	Colorado	**NHL**	....	....	....	....	....	....	....	....	....	....	....	....	....	....	**3**	**0**	**1**	**1**	**2**	**0**	**0**	**0**	**6:12**
2014-15	**Colorado**	**NHL**	**13**	**1**	**1**	**2**	**0**	**0**	**0**	**1**	**19**	**5.3**	**-1**	**78**	**44.9**	**10:07**	....	....	....	....	....	....	....	....	....
	Lake Erie	AHL	53	16	20	36	34	....	....	....	....	....	....	....	....	....	....	....	....	....	....	....	....	....	....
	NHL Totals		**13**	**1**	**1**	**2**	**0**	**0**	**0**	**1**	**19**	**5.3**		**78**	**44.9**	**10:07**	**3**	**0**	**1**	**1**	**2**	**0**	**0**	**0**	**6:12**

OHL First All-Star Team (2011)

• Missed 2011-12 and majority of 2012-13 due to head injury in 2011 Memorial Cup.

HJALMARSSON, Niklas

(JAHL-muhr-suhn, NIHK-luhs) **CHI**

Defense. Shoots left. 6'3", 197 lbs. Born, Eksjo, Sweden, June 6, 1987. Chicago's 5th choice, 108th overall, in 2005 Entry Draft.

Season	Club	League	GP	G	A	Pts	PIM	PP	SH	GW	S	S%	+/-	TF	F%	Min	GP	G	A	Pts	PIM	PP	SH	GW	Min
2003-04	HV 71 Jr.	Swe-Jr.	15	1	3	4	14	....	....	....	....	....	....	....	....	....	2	0	0	0	8	....	....	....	....
2004-05	HV 71 U18	Swe-U18	3	0	2	2	4	....	....	....	....	....	....	....	....	....	....	....	....	....	....	....	....	....	....
	HV 71 Jr.	Swe-Jr.	31	4	11	15	87	....	....	....	....	....	....	....	....	....	....	....	....	....	....	....	....	....	....
	HV 71 Jonkoping	Sweden	14	0	0	0	0	....	....	....	....	....	....	....	....	....	....	....	....	....	....	....	....	....	....
2005-06	HV 71 Jr.	Swe-Jr.	7	3	2	5	12	....	....	....	....	....	....	....	....	....	....	....	....	....	....	....	....	....	....
	HV 71 Jonkoping	Sweden	4	1	2	3	0	....	....	....	....	....	....	....	....	....	12	0	1	1	4	....	....	....	....
2006-07	HV 71 Jonkoping	Sweden	37	2	0	2	24	....	....	....	....	....	....	....	....	....	14	1	1	2	0	....	....	....	....
	HV 71 Jr.	Swe-Jr.	7	0	2	2	14	....	....	....	....	....	....	....	....	....	....	....	....	....	....	....	....	....	....
	IK Oskarshamn	Sweden-2	8	1	2	3	6	....	....	....	....	....	....	....	....	....	....	....	....	....	....	....	....	....	....
2007-08	**Chicago**	**NHL**	**13**	**0**	**1**	**1**	**13**	**0**	**0**	**0**	**5**	**0.0**	**-2**	**0**	**0.0**	**13:37**	....	....	....	....	....	....	....	....	....
	Rockford IceHogs	AHL	47	4	9	13	31	....	....	....	....	....	....	....	....	....	12	0	4	4	8	....	....	....	....
2008-09	**Chicago**	**NHL**	**21**	**1**	**2**	**3**	**0**	**0**	**0**	**0**	**15**	**6.7**	**4**	**0**	**0.0**	**14:59**	**17**	**0**	**1**	**1**	**6**	**0**	**0**	**0**	**16:37**
	Rockford IceHogs	AHL	52	2	16	18	53	....	....	....	....	....	....	....	....	....	....	....	....	....	....	....	....	....	....
2009-10♦	**Chicago**	**NHL**	**77**	**2**	**15**	**17**	**20**	**0**	**0**	**1**	**62**	**3.2**	**9**	**0**	**0.0**	**19:40**	**22**	**1**	**7**	**8**	**6**	**0**	**0**	**0**	**21:01**
2010-11	**Chicago**	**NHL**	**80**	**3**	**7**	**10**	**39**	**0**	**0**	**0**	**64**	**4.7**	**13**	**0**	**0.0**	**18:29**	**7**	**0**	**2**	**2**	**2**	**0**	**0**	**0**	**18:55**
2011-12	**Chicago**	**NHL**	**69**	**1**	**14**	**15**	**14**	**0**	**0**	**0**	**65**	**1.5**	**9**	**0**	**0.0**	**20:11**	**6**	**0**	**1**	**1**	**4**	**0**	**0**	**0**	**18:10**
2012-13	HC Bolzano Foxes	Italy	18	6	16	22	8	....	....	....	....	....	....	....	....	....	....	....	....	....	....	....	....	....	....
	♦ Chicago	**NHL**	**46**	**2**	**8**	**10**	**22**	**0**	**0**	**0**	**43**	**4.7**	**15**	**0**	**0.0**	**20:54**	**23**	**0**	**5**	**5**	**4**	**0**	**0**	**0**	**23:15**
2013-14	**Chicago**	**NHL**	**81**	**4**	**22**	**26**	**34**	**0**	**1**	**1**	**98**	**4.1**	**11**	**0**	**0.0**	**21:17**	**19**	**0**	**4**	**4**	**14**	**0**	**0**	**0**	**22:58**
	Sweden	Olympics	6	0	0	0	0	....	....	....	....	....	....	....	....	....	....	....	....	....	....	....	....	....	....
2014-15♦	**Chicago**	**NHL**	**82**	**3**	**16**	**19**	**44**	**0**	**0**	**1**	**97**	**3.1**	**25**	**0**	**0.0**	**21:53**	**23**	**1**	**5**	**6**	**8**	**0**	**0**	**0**	**26:02**
	NHL Totals		**469**	**16**	**85**	**101**	**186**	**0**	**1**	**3**	**449**	**3.6**		**0**	**0.0**	**19:57**	**117**	**2**	**25**	**27**	**44**	**0**	**0**	**0**	**21:51**

Signed as a free agent by **Bolzano** (Italy), November 8, 2012.

HODGMAN, Justin

(HAWDG-muhn, JUHS-tihn)

Center. Shoots right. 6'1", 203 lbs. Born, Brampton, ON, June 27, 1988.

Season	Club	League	GP	G	A	Pts	PIM	PP	SH	GW	S	S%	+/-	TF	F%	Min	GP	G	A	Pts	PIM	PP	SH	GW	Min
2003-04	Brampton	Minor-ON	30	19	29	48	34	....	....	....	....	....	....	....	....	....	....	....	....	....	....	....	....	....	....
2004-05	Huntsville	ON-Jr.A	44	10	10	20	36	....	....	....	....	....	....	....	....	....	....	....	....	....	....	....	....	....	....
2005-06	Erie Otters	OHL	57	7	13	20	55	....	....	....	....	....	....	....	....	....	....	....	....	....	....	....	....	....	....
2006-07	Erie Otters	OHL	67	19	32	51	63	....	....	....	....	....	....	....	....	....	....	....	....	....	....	....	....	....	....
2007-08	Erie Otters	OHL	64	37	43	80	75	....	....	....	....	....	....	....	....	....	....	....	....	....	....	....	....	....	....
	Fort Wayne	IHL	11	4	4	8	7	....	....	....	....	....	....	....	....	....	13	7	7	14	12	....	....	....	....
2008-09	Erie Otters	OHL	66	24	42	66	71	....	....	....	....	....	....	....	....	....	5	0	1	1	4	....	....	....	....
	Fort Wayne	IHL	6	2	3	5	20	....	....	....	....	....	....	....	....	....	11	7	5	12	16	....	....	....	....
2009-10	Toledo Walleye	ECHL	33	9	12	21	35	....	....	....	....	....	....	....	....	....	....	....	....	....	....	....	....	....	....
	Toronto Marlies	AHL	38	7	5	12	23	....	....	....	....	....	....	....	....	....	....	....	....	....	....	....	....	....	....
	Fort Wayne	IHL	3	1	2	3	0	....	....	....	....	....	....	....	....	....	10	4	12	16	8	....	....	....	....
2010-11	Toronto Marlies	AHL	42	12	17	29	44	....	....	....	....	....	....	....	....	....	....	....	....	....	....	....	....	....	....
	Reading Royals	ECHL	3	0	1	1	4	....	....	....	....	....	....	....	....	....	....	....	....	....	....	....	....	....	....
2011-12	Pelicans Lahti	Finland	59	14	39	53	123	....	....	....	....	....	....	....	....	....	17	3	8	11	42	....	....	....	....
2012-13	Magnitogorsk	KHL	51	11	20	31	46	....	....	....	....	....	....	....	....	....	7	1	1	2	18	....	....	....	....

			Regular Season														Playoffs								
Season	Club	League	GP	G	A	Pts	PIM	PP	SH	GW	S	S%	+/-	TF	F%	Min	GP	G	A	Pts	PIM	PP	SH	GW	Min
2013-14	Magnitogorsk	KHL	18	3	6	9	12																		
	Nizhny Novgorod	KHL	14	1	6	7	6																		
	Vladivostok	KHL	17	7	3	10	12										5	1	3	4	2				
2014-15	**Arizona**	**NHL**	**5**	**1**	**0**	**1**	**2**	**1**	**0**	**0**	**3**	**33.3**	**–2**	**46**	**54.4**	**11:24**									
	Portland Pirates	AHL	62	11	24	35	55																		
	NHL Totals		**5**	**1**	**0**	**1**	**2**	**1**	**0**	**0**	**3**	**33.3**		**46**	**54.3**	**11:24**									

Signed as a free agent by **Arizona**, July 1, 2014.

HODGSON, Cody

(HAWD-suhn, KOH-dee) **NSH**

Center. Shoots right. 6', 192 lbs. Born, Toronto, ON, February 18, 1990. Vancouver's 1st choice, 10th overall, in 2008 Entry Draft.

Season	Club	League	GP	G	A	Pts	PIM	PP	SH	GW	S	S%	+/-	TF	F%	Min	GP	G	A	Pts	PIM	PP	SH	GW	Min
2005-06	Markham Waxers	Minor-ON	30	27	24	51	22										15	13	14	27	8				
2006-07	Brampton	OHL	63	23	23	46	24										4	1	3	4	0				
2007-08	Brampton	OHL	68	40	45	85	36										5	5	0	5	2				
2008-09	Brampton	OHL	53	43	49	92	33										21	11	20	31	18				
	Manitoba Moose	AHL															11	2	4	6	4				
2009-10	Brampton	OHL	13	8	12	20	9										11	3	7	10	4				
2010-11	**Vancouver**	**NHL**	**8**	**1**	**1**	**2**	**0**	**0**	**0**	**0**	**9**	**11.1**	**1**	**42**	**38.1**	**7:44**	**12**	**0**	**1**	**1**	**2**	**0**	**0**	**0**	**6:45**
	Manitoba Moose	AHL	52	17	13	30	14																		
2011-12	**Vancouver**	**NHL**	**63**	**16**	**17**	**33**	**8**	**5**	**0**	**2**	**103**	**15.5**	**8**	**414**	**42.8**	**12:44**									
	Buffalo	**NHL**	**20**	**3**	**5**	**8**	**2**	**2**	**0**	**1**	**51**	**5.9**	**–7**	**296**	**51.4**	**17:16**									
2012-13	Rochester	AHL	19	5	14	19	10																		
	Buffalo	**NHL**	**48**	**15**	**19**	**34**	**20**	**3**	**1**	**1**	**114**	**13.2**	**–4**	**812**	**46.8**	**18:24**									
2013-14	**Buffalo**	**NHL**	**72**	**20**	**24**	**44**	**20**	**9**	**0**	**0**	**182**	**11.0**	**–26**	**969**	**46.8**	**18:09**									
2014-15	**Buffalo**	**NHL**	**78**	**6**	**7**	**13**	**12**	**0**	**0**	**0**	**127**	**4.7**	**–28**	**377**	**45.9**	**12:51**									
	NHL Totals		**289**	**61**	**73**	**134**	**62**	**19**	**1**	**4**	**586**	**10.4**		**2910**	**46.4**	**15:14**	**12**	**0**	**1**	**1**	**2**	**0**	**0**	**0**	**6:46**

OHL First All-Star Team (2009) • OHL Player of the Year (2009) • Canadian Major Junior First All-Star Team (2009) • Canadian Major Junior Player of the Year (2009)

Traded to **Buffalo** by **Vancouver** for Zack Kassian, February 27, 2012. Signed as a free agent by **Nashville**, July 1, 2015.

HOFFMAN, Mike

(HAWF-muhn, MIGHK) **OTT**

Center/Left wing. Shoots left. 6'1", 183 lbs. Born, Kitchener, ON, November 24, 1989. Ottawa's 5th choice, 130th overall, in 2009 Entry Draft.

Season	Club	League	GP	G	A	Pts	PIM	PP	SH	GW	S	S%	+/-	TF	F%	Min	GP	G	A	Pts	PIM	PP	SH	GW	Min
2006-07	Kitchener	ON-Jr.B	47	28	29	57	70										6	3	5	8	6				
	Kitchener Rangers	OHL	2	0	0	0	2										4	0	0	0	0				
2007-08	Gatineau	QMJHL	19	5	7	12	16																		
	Drummondville	QMJHL	43	19	17	36	77																		
2008-09	Drummondville	QMJHL	62	52	42	94	86										19	21	13	34	26				
2009-10	Saint John	QMJHL	56	46	39	85	38										21	11	13	24	23				
2010-11	Binghamton	AHL	74	7	18	25	16										19	1	8	9	16				
	Elmira Jackals	ECHL	4	0	3	3	0																		
2011-12	**Ottawa**	**NHL**	**1**	**0**	**0**	**0**	**0**	**0**	**0**	**0**	**0**	**0.0**	**–1**	**0**	**0.0**	**9:01**									
	Binghamton	AHL	76	21	28	49	44																		
2012-13	Binghamton	AHL	41	13	15	28	38																		
	Ottawa	**NHL**	**3**	**0**	**0**	**0**	**2**	**0**	**0**	**0**	**6**	**0.0**	**–1**	**2**	**100.0**	**12:19**									
2013-14	**Ottawa**	**NHL**	**25**	**3**	**3**	**6**	**2**	**1**	**0**	**0**	**61**	**4.9**	**–2**	**9**	**66.7**	**13:11**									
	Binghamton	AHL	51	30	37	67	32																		
2014-15	**Ottawa**	**NHL**	**79**	**27**	**21**	**48**	**14**	**1**	**0**	**4**	**199**	**13.6**	**16**	**14**	**50.0**	**14:33**	**6**	**1**	**2**	**3**	**2**	**0**	**0**	**1**	**13:01**
	NHL Totals		**108**	**30**	**24**	**54**	**18**	**2**	**0**	**4**	**266**	**11.3**		**25**	**60.0**	**14:07**	**6**	**1**	**2**	**3**	**2**	**0**	**0**	**1**	**13:01**

QMJHL First All-Star Team (2009, 2010) • QMJHL Player of the Year (2010) • Canadian Major Junior Second All-Star Team (2010) • AHL First All-Star Team (2014)

HOGGAN, Jeff

(HOH-guhn, JEHF)

Left wing. Shoots left. 6'1", 193 lbs. Born, Hope, BC, February 1, 1978.

Season	Club	League	GP	G	A	Pts	PIM	PP	SH	GW	S	S%	+/-	TF	F%	Min	GP	G	A	Pts	PIM	PP	SH	GW	Min
1998-99	Powell River Kings	BCHL	STATISTICS NOT AVAILABLE																						
99-2000	Nebraska-Omaha	CCHA	34	16	9	25	82																		
2000-01	Nebraska-Omaha	CCHA	42	12	17	29	78																		
2001-02	Nebraska-Omaha	CCHA	41	24	21	45	92																		
	Houston Aeros	AHL															4	0	0	0	2				
2002-03	Houston Aeros	AHL	65	6	5	11	45										14	1	2	3	23				
2003-04	Houston Aeros	AHL	77	21	15	36	88										2	0	1	1	4				
2004-05	Worcester IceCats	AHL	47	16	9	25	55																		
2005-06	**St. Louis**	**NHL**	**52**	**2**	**6**	**8**	**34**	**0**	**0**	**0**	**60**	**3.3**	**–16**	**4**	**25.0**	**8:47**									
2006-07	**Boston**	**NHL**	**46**	**0**	**2**	**2**	**33**	**0**	**0**	**0**	**53**	**0.0**	**–8**	**3**	**33.3**	**7:04**									
	Providence Bruins	AHL	22	4	7	11	27										13	4	3	7	17				
2007-08	**Boston**	**NHL**	**1**	**0**	**0**	**0**	**0**	**0**	**0**	**0**	**0**	**0.0**	**0**	**0**	**0.0**	**7:57**									
	Providence Bruins	AHL	71	29	31	60	59										5	3	4	7	4				
2008-09	**Phoenix**	**NHL**	**4**	**0**	**1**	**1**	**7**	**0**	**0**	**0**	**7**	**0.0**	**–1**	**2**	**0.0**	**12:00**									
	San Antonio	AHL	60	22	13	35	64																		
2009-10	**Phoenix**	**NHL**	**4**	**0**	**0**	**0**	**2**	**0**	**0**	**0**	**5**	**0.0**	**–1**	**2**	**0.0**	**7:07**									
	San Antonio	AHL	70	13	20	33	44																		
2010-11	Wolfsburg	Germany	38	11	10	21	63										2	0	0	0	2				
2011-12	Hannover Scorp.	Germany	43	14	14	28	14																		
2012-13	Grand Rapids	AHL	76	20	25	45	31										24	5	7	12	14				
2013-14	Grand Rapids	AHL	59	14	17	31	31										10	4	1	5	12				
2014-15	Grand Rapids	AHL	76	14	17	31	39										16	2	7	9	26				
	NHL Totals		**107**	**2**	**9**	**11**	**76**	**0**	**0**	**0**	**125**	**1.6**		**11**	**18.2**	**8:06**									

CCHA First All-Star Team (2002) • NCAA West Second All-American Team (2002) • Fred T. Hunt Memorial Award (AHL – Sportsmanship) (2015)

Signed to a PTO (professional tryout) contract by **Houston** (AHL), April 4, 2002. Signed as a free agent by **Minnesota**, August 20, 2002. Signed as a free agent by **Worcester** (AHL), October 11, 2004. Signed as a free agent by **St. Louis**, August 2, 2005. Signed as a free agent by **Boston**, July 21, 2006. Signed as a free agent by **Phoenix**, July 15, 2008. Signed as a free agent by **Wolfsburg** (Germany), July 29, 2010. Signed as a free agent by **Hannover** (Germany), June 14, 2011. Signed as a free agent by **Grand Rapids** (AHL), September 28, 2012.

HOLDEN, Nick

(HOHL-dehn, NIHK) **COL**

Defense. Shoots left. 6'4", 210 lbs. Born, St. Albert, AB, May 15, 1987.

Season	Club	League	GP	G	A	Pts	PIM	PP	SH	GW	S	S%	+/-	TF	F%	Min	GP	G	A	Pts	PIM	PP	SH	GW	Min
2003-04			STATISTICS NOT AVAILABLE																						
	St. Albert Raiders	AMHL	2	0	0	0	0																		
2004-05	St. Albert Raiders	AMHL	35	7	15	22	24																		
	Camrose Kodiaks	AJHL	4	0	0	0	0																		
2005-06	Camrose Kodiaks	AJHL	29	5	8	13	27																		
	Sherwood Park	AJHL	28	2	15	17	19																		
2006-07	Chilliwack Bruins	WHL	67	8	23	31	62										5	1	1	2	6				
2007-08	Chilliwack Bruins	WHL	70	22	38	60	54										4	1	3	4	0				
	Syracuse Crunch	AHL	1	0	0	0	2																		
2008-09	Syracuse Crunch	AHL	61	4	18	22	46																		
2009-10	Syracuse Crunch	AHL	68	6	17	23	52																		
2010-11	**Columbus**	**NHL**	**5**	**0**	**0**	**0**	**0**	**0**	**0**	**0**	**6**	**0.0**	**0**	**0**	**0.0**	**17:11**									
	Springfield	AHL	67	4	21	25	63																		
2011-12	Springfield	AHL	25	3	6	9	14																		
2012-13	Springfield	AHL	73	9	30	39	58										8	0	3	3	6				
	Columbus	**NHL**	**2**	**0**	**0**	**0**	**0**	**0**	**0**	**0**	**2**	**0.0**	**1**	**0**	**0.0**	**8:35**									
2013-14	**Colorado**	**NHL**	**54**	**10**	**15**	**25**	**22**	**2**	**0**	**2**	**66**	**15.2**	**12**	**0**	**0.0**	**18:41**	**7**	**3**	**1**	**4**	**8**	**2**	**0**	**0**	**22:09**
2014-15	**Colorado**	**NHL**	**78**	**5**	**9**	**14**	**28**	**2**	**0**	**2**	**94**	**5.3**	**–11**	**0**	**0.0**	**19:48**									
	NHL Totals		**139**	**15**	**24**	**39**	**50**	**4**	**0**	**4**	**168**	**8.9**		**0**	**0.0**	**19:07**	**7**	**3**	**1**	**4**	**8**	**2**	**0**	**0**	**22:09**

Signed as a free agent by **Columbus**, March 28, 2008. • Missed majority of 2011-12 due to shoulder injury vs. Portland (AHL), January 13, 2012. Signed as a free agent by **Colorado**, July 6, 2013.

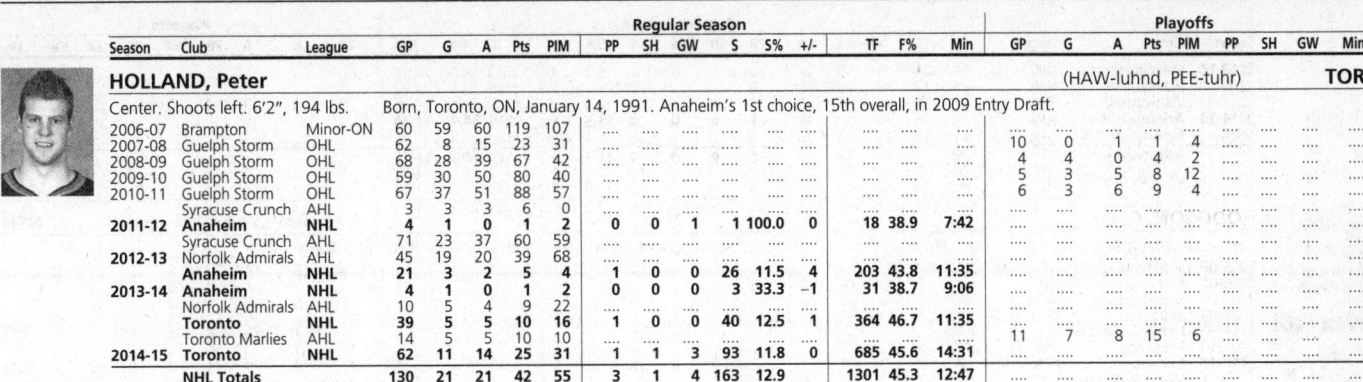

HOLLAND, Peter
(HAW-luhnd, PEE-tuhr) **TOR**

Center. Shoots left. 6'2", 194 lbs. Born, Toronto, ON, January 14, 1991. Anaheim's 1st choice, 15th overall, in 2009 Entry Draft.

			Regular Season														Playoffs								
Season	Club	League	GP	G	A	Pts	PIM	PP	SH	GW	S	S%	+/-	TF	F%	Min	GP	G	A	Pts	PIM	PP	SH	GW	Min
2006-07	Brampton	Minor-ON	60	59	60	119	107																		
2007-08	Guelph Storm	OHL	62	8	15	23	31										10	0	1	1	4				
2008-09	Guelph Storm	OHL	68	28	39	67	42										4	4	0	4	2				
2009-10	Guelph Storm	OHL	59	30	50	80	40										5	3	5	8	12				
2010-11	Guelph Storm	OHL	67	37	51	88	57										6	3	6	9	4				
	Syracuse Crunch	AHL	3	3	3	6	0																		
2011-12	**Anaheim**	**NHL**	4	1	0	1	2	0	0	1	1	100.0	0	18	38.9	7:42									
	Syracuse Crunch	AHL	71	23	37	60	59																		
2012-13	Norfolk Admirals	AHL	45	19	20	39	68																		
	Anaheim	**NHL**	21	3	2	5	4	1	0	0	26	11.5	4	203	43.8	11:35									
2013-14	**Anaheim**	**NHL**	4	1	0	1	2	0	0	0	3	33.3	–1	31	38.7	9:06									
	Norfolk Admirals	AHL	10	5	4	9	22																		
	Toronto	**NHL**	39	5	5	10	16	1	0	0	40	12.5	1	364	46.7	11:35									
	Toronto Marlies	AHL	14	5	5	10	10										11	7	8	15	6				
2014-15	**Toronto**	**NHL**	62	11	14	25	31	1	1	3	93	11.8	0	685	45.6	14:31									
	NHL Totals		130	21	21	42	55	3	1	4	163	12.9		1301	45.3	12:47									

Traded to **Toronto** by **Anaheim** with Brad Staubitz for Jesse Blacker, Toronto's 2nd round choice (Marcus Pettersson) in 2014 Entry Draft and Anaheim's 7th round choice (previously acquired, Anaheim selected Ondrej Kase) in 2014 Entry Draft, November 16, 2013.

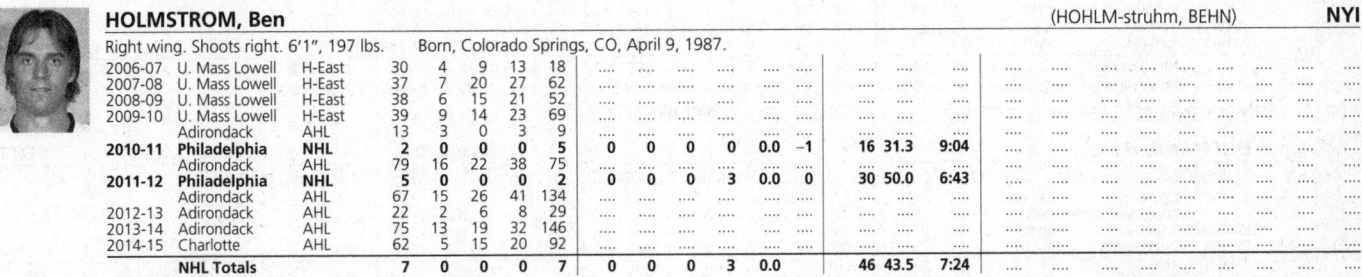

HOLMSTROM, Ben
(HOHLM-struhm, BEHN) **NYI**

Right wing. Shoots right. 6'1", 197 lbs. Born, Colorado Springs, CO, April 9, 1987.

Season	Club	League	GP	G	A	Pts	PIM	PP	SH	GW	S	S%	+/-	TF	F%	Min	GP	G	A	Pts	PIM	PP	SH	GW	Min
2006-07	U. Mass Lowell	H-East	30	4	9	13	18																		
2007-08	U. Mass Lowell	H-East	37	7	20	27	62																		
2008-09	U. Mass Lowell	H-East	38	6	15	21	52																		
2009-10	U. Mass Lowell	H-East	39	9	14	23	69																		
	Adirondack	AHL	13	3	0	3	9																		
2010-11	**Philadelphia**	**NHL**	2	0	0	0	5	0	0	0	0	0.0	–1	16	31.3	9:04									
	Adirondack	AHL	79	16	22	38	75																		
2011-12	**Philadelphia**	**NHL**	5	0	0	0	2	0	0	0	3	0.0	0	30	50.0	6:43									
	Adirondack	AHL	67	15	26	41	134																		
2012-13	Adirondack	AHL	22	2	6	8	29																		
2013-14	Adirondack	AHL	75	13	19	32	146																		
2014-15	Charlotte	AHL	62	5	15	20	92																		
	NHL Totals		7	0	0	0	7	0	0	0	3	0.0		46	43.5	7:24									

Signed as a free agent by **Philadelphia**, March 17, 2010. • Missed majority of 2012-13 due to knee injury vs. Syracuse (AHL), December 8, 2012. Signed as a free agent by **Carolina**, July 4, 2014. Signed as a free agent by **NY Islanders**, July 2, 2015.

HOLZER, Korbinian
(HOHL-zuhr, kohr-BIHN-EE-uhn) **ANA**

Defense. Shoots right. 6'3", 205 lbs. Born, Munich, West Germany, February 16, 1988. Toronto's 4th choice, 111th overall, in 2006 Entry Draft.

Season	Club	League	GP	G	A	Pts	PIM	PP	SH	GW	S	S%	+/-	TF	F%	Min	GP	G	A	Pts	PIM	PP	SH	GW	Min
2004-05	EC Bad Tolz Jr.	Ger-Jr.	34	7	11	18	66										5	0	2	2	2				
2005-06	EC Bad Tolz Jr.	Ger-Jr.	2	1	1	2	6																		
	Tolzer Lowen	German-2	46	3	3	6	94																		
2006-07	Regensburg	German-2	42	2	6	8	68										4	0	0	0	2				
2007-08	Dusseldorf	Germany	35	2	5	7	66										13	0	2	2	20				
2008-09	Dusseldorf	Germany	38	4	5	9	89										16	0	1	1	18				
2009-10	Dusseldorf	Germany	52	6	16	22	96										3	0	0	0	4				
	Germany	Olympics	4	0	0	0	2																		
2010-11	**Toronto**	**NHL**	2	0	0	0	2	0	0	0	1	0.0	–1	0	0.0	13:01									
	Toronto Marlies	AHL	73	3	10	13	88																		
2011-12	Toronto Marlies	AHL	67	1	19	20	68										17	1	4	5	39				
2012-13	Toronto Marlies	AHL	46	1	10	11	46										8	0	1	1	24				
	Toronto	**NHL**	22	2	1	3	28	0	0	1	16	12.5	–12	0	0.0	18:30									
2013-14	Toronto Marlies	AHL	72	5	18	23	104										10	2	5	7	4				
2014-15	**Toronto**	**NHL**	34	0	6	6	25	0	0	0	32	0.0	3	0	0.0	17:06									
	Toronto Marlies	AHL	9	0	2	2	10																		
	NHL Totals		58	2	7	9	55	0	0	1	49	4.1		0	0.0	17:30									

Traded to **Anaheim** by **Toronto** for Eric Brewer and Anaheim's 5th round choice in 2016 Entry Draft, March 2, 2015.

HORAK, Roman
(HOH-rak, ROH-muhn)

Center. Shoots left. 6', 170 lbs. Born, Ceske Budejovice, Czech., May 21, 1991. NY Rangers' 4th choice, 127th overall, in 2009 Entry Draft.

Season	Club	League	GP	G	A	Pts	PIM	PP	SH	GW	S	S%	+/-	TF	F%	Min	GP	G	A	Pts	PIM	PP	SH	GW	Min
2004-05	C. Budejovice U17	CzR-U17	2	0	0	0	0																		
2005-06	C. Budejovice U17	CzR-U17	34	5	3	8	10										3	0	0	0	4				
2006-07	C. Budejovice U17	CzR-U17	24	22	16	38	38										2	1	0	1	4				
	C. Budejovice Jr.	CzRep-Jr.	16	1	4	5	6										1	0	0	0	0				
2007-08	C. Budejovice U17	CzR-U17	2	3	2	5	0																		
	C. Budejovice Jr.	CzRep-Jr.	34	17	11	28	14										3	0	1	1	0				
	C. Budejovice	CzRep	1	0	0	0	0																		
2008-09	C. Budejovice Jr.	CzRep-Jr.	31	16	17	33	14										2	0	0	0	0				
	C. Budejovice	CzRep	17	1	0	1	0																		
2009-10	Chilliwack Bruins	WHL	66	21	26	47	39										6	2	4	6	4				
2010-11	Chilliwack Bruins	WHL	64	26	52	78	60										5	1	2	3	0				
2011-12	**Calgary**	**NHL**	61	3	8	11	14	0	0	1	53	5.7	3	441	41.5	10:12									
	Abbotsford Heat	AHL	14	2	2	4	6										8	0	3	3	2				
2012-13	Abbotsford Heat	AHL	59	16	14	30	24																		
	Calgary	**NHL**	20	2	5	7	2	0	0	0	28	7.1	–5	205	45.4	14:32									
2013-14	**Calgary**	**NHL**	1	0	0	0	0	0	0	0	0	0.0	0	1	0.0	4:04									
	Abbotsford Heat	AHL	13	2	5	7	6																		
	Edmonton	**NHL**	2	1	0	1	0	0	0	0	2	50.0	–1	5	80.0	12:06									
	Oklahoma City	AHL	53	21	27	48	16										3	1	0	1	0				
2014-15	Podolsk	KHL	53	18	13	31	26																		
	NHL Totals		84	6	13	19	16	0	0	1	83	7.2		652	42.9	11:12									

Traded to **Calgary** by **NY Rangers** with NY Rangers' 2nd round choice (Markus Granlund) in 2011 Entry Draft and Pittsburgh's 2nd round choice (previously acquired, Calgary selected Tyler Wotherspoon) in 2011 Entry Draft for Tim Erixon and Calgary's 5th round choice (Shane McColgan) in 2011 Entry Draft, June 1, 2011. Traded to **Edmonton** by **Calgary** with Laurent Brossoit for Olivier Roy and Ladislav Smid, November 8, 2013. Signed as a free agent by **Vityaz Podolsk** (KHL), May 12, 2014.

HORCOFF, Shawn
(hohr-KAWF, SHAWN) **ANA**

Center. Shoots left. 6'1", 210 lbs. Born, Trail, BC, September 17, 1978. Edmonton's 3rd choice, 99th overall, in 1998 Entry Draft.

Season	Club	League	GP	G	A	Pts	PIM	PP	SH	GW	S	S%	+/-	TF	F%	Min	GP	G	A	Pts	PIM	PP	SH	GW	Min
1994-95	Trail Smokies	RMJHL	47	50	46	96	26																		
1995-96	Chilliwack Chiefs	BCHL	58	49	96	*145	44										9	5	19	24	12				
1996-97	Michigan State	CCHA	40	10	13	23	20																		
1997-98	Michigan State	CCHA	34	14	13	27	50																		
1998-99	Michigan State	CCHA	39	12	25	37	70																		
99-2000	Michigan State	CCHA	42	14	*51	*65	50																		
2000-01	**Edmonton**	**NHL**	49	9	7	16	10	0	0	2	42	21.4	8	122	41.8	9:14	5	0	0	0	0	0	0	0	6:31
	Hamilton	AHL	24	10	18	28	19																		
2001-02	**Edmonton**	**NHL**	61	8	14	22	18	0	0	0	57	14.0	3	454	46.3	11:20									
	Hamilton	AHL	2	1	2	3	6																		
2002-03	**Edmonton**	**NHL**	78	12	21	33	55	2	0	3	98	12.2	10	301	42.9	13:30	6	3	1	4	6	0	0	1	15:27
2003-04	**Edmonton**	**NHL**	80	15	25	40	73	0	2	3	110	13.6	0	1378	50.7	17:31									
2004-05	Mora IK	Sweden	50	19	27	46	117																		
2005-06	**Edmonton**	**NHL**	79	22	51	73	85	3	3	5	167	13.2	0	1421	52.7	19:59	24	7	12	19	12	1	1	2	21:37
2006-07	**Edmonton**	**NHL**	80	16	35	51	56	5	0	5	168	9.5	–22	1422	50.6	20:50									

			Regular Season														Playoffs								
Season	Club	League	GP	G	A	Pts	PIM	PP	SH	GW	S	S%	+/-	TF	F%	Min	GP	G	A	Pts	PIM	PP	SH	GW	Min
2007-08	Edmonton	NHL	53	21	29	50	30	6	0	2	115	18.3	1	963	50.6	22:13	....	....	....	....	....	....	....	....	....
2008-09	Edmonton	NHL	80	17	36	53	39	8	0	2	178	9.6	7	1756	53.9	21:22	....	....	....	....	....	....	....	....	....
2009-10	Edmonton	NHL	77	13	23	36	51	4	0	1	123	10.6	–29	1337	46.5	19:26	....	....	....	....	....	....	....	....	....
2010-11	Edmonton	NHL	47	9	18	27	46	5	0	1	78	11.5	–1	813	48.3	18:41	....	....	....	....	....	....	....	....	....
2011-12	Edmonton	NHL	81	13	21	34	24	5	0	0	123	10.6	–23	1475	49.4	19:35	....	....	....	....	....	....	....	....	....
2012-13	Edmonton	NHL	31	7	5	12	24	3	0	1	41	17.1	8	500	49.0	16:51	....	....	....	....	....	....	....	....	....
2013-14	Dallas	NHL	77	7	13	20	52	4	1	0	68	10.3	1	417	50.1	12:52	6	1	5	6	5	0	0	0	14:13
2014-15	Dallas	NHL	76	11	18	29	27	4	0	1	82	13.4	9	472	50.2	13:01	....	....	....	....	....	....	....	....	....
	NHL Totals		949	180	316	496	590	49	6	26	1450	12.4		12831	50.1	17:04	41	11	18	29	23	1	1	3	17:47

CCHA First All-Star Team (2000) • CCHA Player of the Year (2000) • NCAA West First All-American Team (2000)

Played in NHL All-Star Game (2008)

Signed as a free agent by **Mora** (Sweden), September 6, 2004. Traded to **Dallas** by **Edmonton** for Phillip Larsen and Dallas' 7th round choice in 2016 Entry Draft, July 5, 2013. Signed as a free agent by **Anaheim**, July 3, 2015.

HORNQVIST, Patric (HOHRN-kwihst, PAT-rihk) PIT

Right wing. Shoots right. 5'11", 189 lbs. Born, Sollentuna, Sweden, January 1, 1987. Nashville's 7th choice, 230th overall, in 2005 Entry Draft.

Season	Club	League	GP	G	A	Pts	PIM	PP	SH	GW	S	S%	+/-	TF	F%	Min	GP	G	A	Pts	PIM	PP	SH	GW	Min
2003-04	Vasby Jr.	Swe-Jr.	10	7	10	17	30	....	....	....	....	....	....	....	....	....	....	....	....	....	....	....	....	....	....
	Vasby	Sweden-3	32	8	5	13	26	....	....	....	....	....	....	....	....	....	....	....	....	....	....	....	....	....	....
2004-05	Vasby	Sweden-3	28	12	12	24	36	....	....	....	....	....	....	....	....	....	....	....	....	....	....	....	....	....	....
	Djurgarden Jr.	Swe-Jr.	5	3	0	3	2	....	....	....	....	....	....	....	....	....	....	....	....	....	....	....	....	....	....
2005-06	Djurgarden Jr.	Swe-Jr.	4	2	1	3	2	....	....	....	....	....	....	....	....	....	4	1	2	3	2	....	....	....	....
	Djurgarden	Sweden	47	5	2	7	36	....	....	....	....	....	....	....	....	....	....	....	....	....	....	....	....	....	....
2006-07	Djurgarden	Sweden	49	23	11	34	38	....	....	....	....	....	....	....	....	....	....	....	....	....	....	....	....	....	....
	Djurgarden Jr.	Swe-Jr.	....	....	....	....	....	....	....	....	....	....	....	....	....	....	7	2	5	7	14	....	....	....	....
2007-08	Djurgarden	Sweden	53	18	12	30	58	....	....	....	....	....	....	....	....	....	5	0	1	1	6	....	....	....	....
2008-09	Nashville	NHL	28	2	5	7	16	0	0	0	54	3.7	–3	5	20.0	11:24	....	....	....	....	....	....	....	....	....
	Milwaukee	AHL	49	17	18	35	44	....	....	....	....	....	....	....	....	....	11	4	4	8	6	....	....	....	....
2009-10	Nashville	NHL	80	30	21	51	40	10	0	8	275	10.9	18	18	27.8	15:41	2	0	1	1	4	0	0	0	13:10
	Sweden	Olympics	4	1	0	1	4	....	....	....	....	....	....	....	....	....	....	....	....	....	....	....	....	....	....
2010-11	Nashville	NHL	79	21	27	48	47	6	0	5	265	7.9	11	45	48.9	15:44	12	2	1	3	6	1	0	0	15:16
2011-12	Nashville	NHL	76	27	16	43	28	8	0	3	230	11.7	9	9	66.7	15:20	10	1	3	4	2	1	0	0	15:25
2012-13	Martigny	Swiss-2	9	7	7	14	8	....	....	....	....	....	....	....	....	....	....	....	....	....	....	....	....	....	....
	Djurgarden	Sweden-2	10	2	3	5	6	....	....	....	....	....	....	....	....	....	....	....	....	....	....	....	....	....	....
	Nashville	NHL	24	4	10	14	14	4	0	1	87	4.6	–1	2	50.0	16:14	....	....	....	....	....	....	....	....	....
2013-14	Nashville	NHL	76	22	31	53	28	7	0	6	248	8.9	1	6	0.0	16:52	....	....	....	....	....	....	....	....	....
2014-15	Pittsburgh	NHL	64	25	26	51	38	6	0	4	220	11.4	12	7	28.6	17:39	5	2	1	3	2	0	0	0	18:44
	NHL Totals		427	131	136	267	211	41	0	27	1379	9.5		92	40.2	15:53	29	5	6	11	14	2	0	0	15:46

Signed as a free agent by **Martigny** (Swiss-2), October 2, 2012. Signed as a free agent by **Djurgarden** (Sweden-2), November 12, 2012. Traded to **Pittsburgh** by **Nashville** with Nick Spaling for James Neal, June 27, 2014.

HORTON, Nathan (HOHR-tuhn, NAY-thuhn) TOR

Right wing. Shoots right. 6'2", 229 lbs. Born, Welland, ON, May 29, 1985. Florida's 1st choice, 3rd overall, in 2003 Entry Draft.

Season	Club	League	GP	G	A	Pts	PIM	PP	SH	GW	S	S%	+/-	TF	F%	Min	GP	G	A	Pts	PIM	PP	SH	GW	Min
2000-01	Thorold	ON-Jr.B	41	16	31	47	75	....	....	....	....	....	....	....	....	....	....	....	....	....	....	....	....	....	....
2001-02	Oshawa Generals	OHL	64	31	36	67	84	....	....	....	....	....	....	....	....	....	5	1	2	3	10	....	....	....	....
2002-03	Oshawa Generals	OHL	54	33	35	68	111	....	....	....	....	....	....	....	....	....	13	9	6	15	10	....	....	....	....
2003-04	Florida	NHL	55	14	8	22	57	6	1	0	81	17.3	–5	270	41.9	13:20	....	....	....	....	....	....	....	....	....
2004-05	San Antonio	AHL	21	5	4	9	21	....	....	....	....	....	....	....	....	....	....	....	....	....	....	....	....	....	....
2005-06	Florida	NHL	71	28	19	47	89	3	0	1	162	17.3	8	24	45.8	16:53	....	....	....	....	....	....	....	....	....
2006-07	Florida	NHL	82	31	31	62	61	7	1	3	217	14.3	15	31	48.4	18:04	....	....	....	....	....	....	....	....	....
2007-08	Florida	NHL	82	27	35	62	85	9	0	3	212	12.7	15	73	39.7	18:44	....	....	....	....	....	....	....	....	....
2008-09	Florida	NHL	67	22	23	45	48	5	1	5	131	16.8	–5	863	43.7	17:51	....	....	....	....	....	....	....	....	....
2009-10	Florida	NHL	65	20	37	57	42	7	2	4	159	12.6	–1	85	56.5	20:53	....	....	....	....	....	....	....	....	....
2010-11 ♦	Boston	NHL	80	26	27	53	85	6	0	2	188	13.8	29	19	42.1	16:17	21	8	9	17	35	1	0	3	16:54
2011-12	Boston	NHL	46	17	15	32	54	6	0	3	90	18.9	0	3	66.7	15:56	....	....	....	....	....	....	....	....	....
2012-13	Boston	NHL	43	13	9	22	22	0	0	1	114	11.4	1	10	50.0	16:51	22	7	12	19	14	2	0	3	18:29
2013-14	Columbus	NHL	36	5	14	19	24	2	0	2	48	10.4	–3	1	100.0	15:27	....	....	....	....	....	....	....	....	....
2014-15			DID NOT PLAY – INJURED														....	....	....	....	....	....	....	....	....
	NHL Totals		627	203	218	421	567	51	5	24	1402	14.5		1379	44.2	17:16	43	15	21	36	49	3	0	6	17:43

OHL All-Rookie Team (2002)

Signed as a free agent by **San Antonio** (AHL), October 28, 2004. Traded to **Boston** by **Florida** with Gregory Campbell for Dennis Wideman, Boston's 1st round choice (later traded to Los Angeles – Los Angeles selected Derek Forbort) in 2010 Entry Draft and Boston's 3rd round choice (Kyle Rau) in 2011 Entry Draft, June 22, 2010. Signed as a free agent by **Columbus**, July 5, 2013. • Missed majority of 2013-14 due to shoulder surgery, July 17, 2013. Traded to **Toronto** by **Columbus** for David Clarkson, February 26, 2015. • Missed 2014-15 due to recurring back injury.

HORVAT, Bo (HOHR-vat, BOH) VAN

Center. Shoots left. 6', 206 lbs. Born, Rodney, ON, April 5, 1995. Vancouver's 1st choice, 9th overall, in 2013 Entry Draft.

Season	Club	League	GP	G	A	Pts	PIM	PP	SH	GW	S	S%	+/-	TF	F%	Min	GP	G	A	Pts	PIM	PP	SH	GW	Min
2010-11	Elgin-Mid. Chiefs	Minor-ON	30	30	31	61	12	....	....	....	....	....	....	....	....	....	12	5	7	12	4	....	....	....	....
	Elgin-Middlesex	Other	32	14	38	52	8	....	....	....	....	....	....	....	....	....	....	....	....	....	....	....	....	....	....
	St. Thomas Stars	ON-Jr.B	5	1	3	4	0	....	....	....	....	....	....	....	....	....	7	3	3	6	0	....	....	....	....
2011-12	London Knights	OHL	64	11	19	30	8	....	....	....	....	....	....	....	....	....	18	1	3	4	0	....	....	....	....
2012-13	London Knights	OHL	67	33	28	61	29	....	....	....	....	....	....	....	....	....	21	*16	7	23	10	....	....	....	....
2013-14	London Knights	OHL	54	30	44	74	36	....	....	....	....	....	....	....	....	....	9	5	6	11	4	....	....	....	....
2014-15	Vancouver	NHL	68	13	12	25	16	0	1	1	93	14.0	–8	848	51.4	12:16	6	1	3	4	2	0	0	0	12:40
	Utica Comets	AHL	5	0	0	0	4	....	....	....	....	....	....	....	....	....	....	....	....	....	....	....	....	....	....
	NHL Totals		68	13	12	25	16	0	1	1	93	14.0		848	51.4	12:16	6	1	3	4	2	0	0	0	12:40

OHL Playoff MVP (2013) • George Parsons Trophy (Memorial Cup – Most Sportsmanlike Player) (2013)

HOSSA, Marian (HOH-sa, MAIR-ee-uhn) CHI

Right wing. Shoots left. 6'1", 207 lbs. Born, Stara Lubovna, Czech., January 12, 1979. Ottawa's 1st choice, 12th overall, in 1997 Entry Draft.

Season	Club	League	GP	G	A	Pts	PIM	PP	SH	GW	S	S%	+/-	TF	F%	Min	GP	G	A	Pts	PIM	PP	SH	GW	Min
1995-96	Dukla Trencin Jr.	Slovak-Jr.	53	42	49	91	26	....	....	....	....	....	....	....	....	....	....	....	....	....	....	....	....	....	....
1996-97	Dukla Trencin	Slovakia	46	25	19	44	33	....	....	....	....	....	....	....	....	....	7	5	5	10	....	....	....	....	....
1997-98	Portland	WHL	53	45	40	85	50	....	....	....	....	....	....	....	....	....	16	13	6	19	6	....	....	....	....
	Ottawa	NHL	7	0	1	1	0	0	0	0	10	0.0	–1	....	....	....	....	....	....	....	....	....	....	....	....
1998-99	Ottawa	NHL	60	15	15	30	37	1	0	2	124	12.1	18	4	25.0	13:59	4	0	2	2	4	0	0	0	16:46
99-2000	Ottawa	NHL	78	29	27	56	32	5	0	4	240	12.1	5	7	57.1	17:12	6	0	0	0	2	0	0	0	15:22
2000-01	Ottawa	NHL	81	32	43	75	44	11	2	7	249	12.9	19	14	42.9	18:01	4	1	1	2	4	0	0	0	19:02
2001-02	Dukla Trencin	Slovakia	8	3	4	7	16	....	....	....	....	....	....	....	....	....	....	....	....	....	....	....	....	....	....
	Ottawa	NHL	80	31	35	66	50	9	1	4	278	11.2	11	12	33.3	18:29	12	4	6	10	2	1	0	0	19:04
	Slovakia	Olympics	2	4	2	6	0	....	....	....	....	....	....	....	....	....	....	....	....	....	....	....	....	....	....
2002-03	Ottawa	NHL	80	45	35	80	34	14	0	10	229	19.7	8	19	36.8	18:31	18	5	11	16	6	3	0	1	18:41
2003-04	Ottawa	NHL	81	36	46	82	46	14	1	5	233	15.5	4	25	40.0	18:37	7	3	1	4	0	1	0	2	21:24
2004-05	Dukla Trencin	Slovakia	25	22	20	42	38	....	....	....	....	....	....	....	....	....	5	4	5	9	14	....	....	....	....
	Mora IK	Sweden	24	18	14	32	22	....	....	....	....	....	....	....	....	....	....	....	....	....	....	....	....	....	....
2005-06	Atlanta	NHL	80	39	53	92	67	14	*7	7	341	11.4	17	15	26.7	21:41	....	....	....	....	....	....	....	....	....
	Slovakia	Olympics	6	5	5	10	4	....	....	....	....	....	....	....	....	....	....	....	....	....	....	....	....	....	....
2006-07	Atlanta	NHL	82	43	57	100	49	17	3	5	340	12.6	18	18	22.2	21:41	4	0	1	1	6	0	0	0	18:55
2007-08	Atlanta	NHL	60	26	30	56	30	8	2	4	229	11.4	–14	14	28.6	21:55	....	....	....	....	....	....	....	....	....
	Pittsburgh	NHL	12	3	7	10	6	0	0	0	35	8.6	0	1	0.0	18:34	20	12	14	26	12	5	0	2	21:00
2008-09	Detroit	NHL	74	40	31	71	63	10	0	8	307	13.0	27	19	21.1	17:48	23	6	9	15	10	2	1	1	18:38
2009-10 ♦	Chicago	NHL	57	24	27	51	18	2	5	2	199	12.1	24	1	0.0	18:44	22	3	12	15	25	0	0	1	18:25
	Slovakia	Olympics	7	3	6	9	6	....	....	....	....	....	....	....	....	....	....	....	....	....	....	....	....	....	....
2010-11	Chicago	NHL	65	25	32	57	32	8	2	2	205	12.2	9	4	75.0	19:42	7	2	4	6	2	1	0	1	18:35
2011-12	Chicago	NHL	81	29	48	77	20	9	2	4	248	11.7	18	9	33.3	19:58	3	0	0	0	0	0	0	0	17:21
2012-13 ♦	Chicago	NHL	40	17	14	31	16	4	1	6	116	14.7	20	3	33.3	18:02	22	7	9	16	2	3	0	2	19:57

Season	Club	League	GP	G	A	Pts	PIM	PP	SH	GW	S	S%	+/-	TF	F%	Min	GP	G	A	Pts	PIM	PP	SH	GW	Min
			Regular Season														Playoffs								
2013-14	Chicago	NHL	72	30	30	60	20	4	3	4	241	12.4	28	3	33.3	18:16	19	2	12	14	8	1	0	0	20:25
	Slovakia	Olympics	4	2	1	3	4	....	....	....	....	....	....	....	....	....	....	....	....	....	....	....	....	....	....
2014-15♦	Chicago	NHL	82	22	39	61	32	6	1	2	247	8.9	17	7	57.1	18:33	23	4	13	17	10	1	1	2	19:52
	NHL Totals		1172	486	570	1056	596	136	30	76	3871	12.6		175	34.3	18:53	194	49	95	144	93	18	2	12	19:18

WHL West First All-Star Team (1998) • WHL Rookie of the Year (1998) • Canadian Major Junior First All-Star Team (1998) • Memorial Cup All-Star Team (1998) • NHL All-Rookie Team (1999) • NHL Second All-Star Team (2009)

Played in NHL All-Star Game (2001, 2003, 2007, 2008, 2012)

Signed as a free agent by **Trencin** (Slovakia), September 16, 2004. Signed as a free agent by **Mora** (Sweden), November 11, 2004. Signed as a free agent by **Trencin** (Slovakia), January 31, 2005. Traded to **Atlanta** by **Ottawa** with Greg de Vries for Dany Heatley, August 23, 2005. Traded to **Pittsburgh** by **Atlanta** with Pascal Dupuis for Colby Armstrong, Erik Christensen, Angelo Esposito and Pittsburgh's 1st round choice (Daulton Leveille) in 2008 Entry Draft, February 26, 2008. Signed as a free agent by **Detroit**, July 2, 2008. Signed as a free agent by **Chicago**, July 1, 2009.

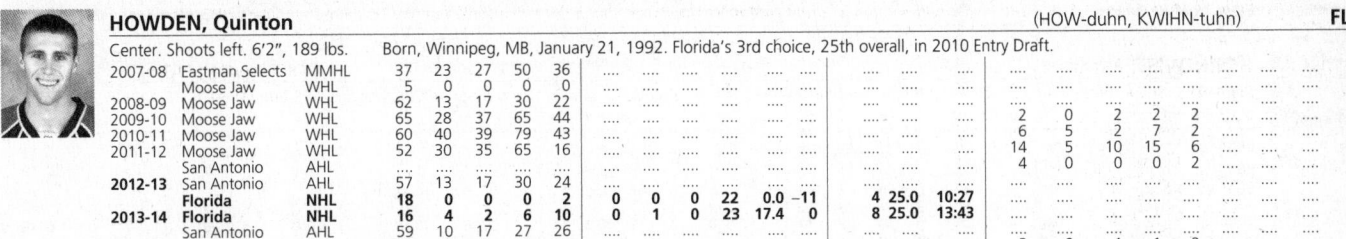

HOWDEN, Quinton

(HOW-duhn, KWIHN-tuhn) **FLA**

Center. Shoots left. 6'2", 189 lbs. Born, Winnipeg, MB, January 21, 1992. Florida's 3rd choice, 25th overall, in 2010 Entry Draft.

Season	Club	League	GP	G	A	Pts	PIM	PP	SH	GW	S	S%	+/-	TF	F%	Min	GP	G	A	Pts	PIM	PP	SH	GW	Min
2007-08	Eastman Selects	MMHL	37	23	27	50	36	....	....	....	....	....	....	....	....	....	....	....	....	....	....	....	....	....	....
	Moose Jaw	WHL	5	0	0	0	0	....	....	....	....	....	....	....	....	....	....	....	....	....	....	....	....	....	....
2008-09	Moose Jaw	WHL	62	13	17	30	22	....	....	....	....	....	....	....	....	....	....	....	....	....	....	....	....	....	....
2009-10	Moose Jaw	WHL	65	28	37	65	44	....	....	....	....	....	....	....	....	....	2	0	2	2	2	....	....	....	....
2010-11	Moose Jaw	WHL	60	40	39	79	43	....	....	....	....	....	....	....	....	....	6	5	2	7	2	....	....	....	....
2011-12	Moose Jaw	WHL	52	30	35	65	16	....	....	....	....	....	....	....	....	....	14	5	10	15	6	....	....	....	....
	San Antonio	AHL	....	....	....	....	....	....	....	....	....	....	....	....	....	....	4	0	0	0	2	....	....	....	....
2012-13	San Antonio	AHL	57	13	17	30	24	....	....	....	....	....	....	....	....	....	....	....	....	....	....	....	....	....	....
	Florida	NHL	18	0	0	0	2	0	0	0	22	0.0	-11	4	25.0	10:27	....	....	....	....	....	....	....	....	....
2013-14	Florida	NHL	16	4	2	6	10	0	1	0	23	17.4	0	8	25.0	13:43	....	....	....	....	....	....	....	....	....
	San Antonio	AHL	59	10	17	27	26	....	....	....	....	....	....	....	....	....	....	....	....	....	....	....	....	....	....
2014-15	San Antonio	AHL	33	3	15	18	16	....	....	....	....	....	....	....	....	....	3	0	1	1	2	....	....	....	....
	NHL Totals		34	4	2	6	12	0	1	0	45	8.9		12	25.0	11:59	....	....	....	....	....	....	....	....	....

WHL East Second All-Star Team (2011)

• Missed majority of 2014-15 due to recurring upper-body injury.

HRABARENKA, Raman

(h'rab-ah-REHN-kah, rah-MAHN) **N.J.**

Defense. Shoots right. 6'5", 235 lbs. Born, Mogilev, Belarus, August 24, 1992.

Season	Club	League	GP	G	A	Pts	PIM	PP	SH	GW	S	S%	+/-	TF	F%	Min	GP	G	A	Pts	PIM	PP	SH	GW	Min
2009-10	Phi. Revolution	EJHL	32	4	5	9	59	....	....	....	....	....	....	....	....	....	....	....	....	....	....	....	....	....	....
2010-11	Cape Breton	QMJHL	50	2	7	9	68	....	....	....	....	....	....	....	....	....	4	0	0	0	8	....	....	....	....
2011-12	Cape Breton	QMJHL	30	1	5	6	26	....	....	....	....	....	....	....	....	....	....	....	....	....	....	....	....	....	....
	Drummondville	QMJHL	27	3	11	14	29	....	....	....	....	....	....	....	....	....	4	2	1	3	6	....	....	....	....
2012-13	Albany Devils	AHL	34	1	4	5	18	....	....	....	....	....	....	....	....	....	....	....	....	....	....	....	....	....	....
2013-14	Albany Devils	AHL	48	6	15	21	26	....	....	....	....	....	....	....	....	....	....	....	....	....	....	....	....	....	....
	Elmira Jackals	ECHL	5	0	2	2	4	....	....	....	....	....	....	....	....	....	....	....	....	....	....	....	....	....	....
2014-15	New Jersey	NHL	1	0	0	0	0	0	0	0	0	0.0	1	0	0.0	11:55	....	....	....	....	....	....	....	....	....
	Albany Devils	AHL	47	9	18	27	26	....	....	....	....	....	....	....	....	....	....	....	....	....	....	....	....	....	....
	NHL Totals		1	0	0	0	0	0	0	0	0	0.0		0	0.0	11:55	....	....	....	....	....	....	....	....	....

Signed as a free agent by **Albany** (AHL), October 7, 2012. • Missed majority of 2012-13 as a healthy reserve. Signed as a free agent by **New Jersey**, July 12, 2013.

HUBERDEAU, Jonathan

(hoo-BAIR-doh, JAWN-ah-thuhn) **FLA**

Center. Shoots left. 6'1", 188 lbs. Born, Saint-Jerome, QC, June 4, 1993. Florida's 1st choice, 3rd overall, in 2011 Entry Draft.

Season	Club	League	GP	G	A	Pts	PIM	PP	SH	GW	S	S%	+/-	TF	F%	Min	GP	G	A	Pts	PIM	PP	SH	GW	Min
2008-09	Saint-Eustache	QAAA	43	20	30	50	60	....	....	....	....	....	....	....	....	....	8	2	7	9	18	....	....	....	....
2009-10	Saint John	QMJHL	61	15	20	35	43	....	....	....	....	....	....	....	....	....	21	11	7	18	22	....	....	....	....
2010-11	Saint John	QMJHL	67	43	62	105	88	....	....	....	....	....	....	....	....	....	19	*16	14	30	16	....	....	....	....
2011-12	Saint John	QMJHL	37	30	42	72	50	....	....	....	....	....	....	....	....	....	15	10	11	21	18	....	....	....	....
2012-13	Saint John	QMJHL	30	16	29	45	48	....	....	....	....	....	....	....	....	....	....	....	....	....	....	....	....	....	....
	Florida	NHL	48	14	17	31	18	2	0	1	112	12.5	-15	33	33.3	16:56	....	....	....	....	....	....	....	....	....
2013-14	Florida	NHL	69	9	19	28	37	2	0	1	108	8.3	-5	11	45.5	15:40	....	....	....	....	....	....	....	....	....
2014-15	Florida	NHL	79	15	39	54	38	0	0	0	169	8.9	10	8	25.0	16:45	....	....	....	....	....	....	....	....	....
	NHL Totals		196	38	75	113	93	4	0	2	389	9.8		52	34.6	16:25	....	....	....	....	....	....	....	....	....

QMJHL First All-Star Team (2011) • Memorial Cup All-Star Team (2011) • Stafford Smythe Memorial Trophy (Memorial Cup – MVP) (2011) • QMJHL Second All-Star Team (2012) • NHL All-Rookie Team (2013) • Calder Memorial Trophy (2013)

HUDLER, Jiri

(HOOD-luhr, YIH-ree) **CGY**

Center. Shoots left. 5'10", 186 lbs. Born, Olomouc, Czech., January 4, 1984. Detroit's 1st choice, 58th overall, in 2002 Entry Draft.

Season	Club	League	GP	G	A	Pts	PIM	PP	SH	GW	S	S%	+/-	TF	F%	Min	GP	G	A	Pts	PIM	PP	SH	GW	Min
1998-99	HC Vsetin U17	CzR-U17	46	57	57	114	....	....	....	....	....	....	....	....	....	....	....	....	....	....	....	....	....	....	....
99-2000	HC Vsetin Jr.	CzRep-Jr.	53	29	31	60	75	....	....	....	....	....	....	....	....	....	....	....	....	....	....	....	....	....	....
	Vsetin	CzRep	2	0	1	1	0	....	....	....	....	....	....	....	....	....	....	....	....	....	....	....	....	....	....
2000-01	HC Vsetin Jr.	CzRep-Jr.	16	8	14	22	16	....	....	....	....	....	....	....	....	....	....	....	....	....	....	....	....	....	....
	HC Slovnaft Vsetin	CzRep	22	1	4	5	10	....	....	....	....	....	....	....	....	....	....	....	....	....	....	....	....	....	....
	HC Femax Havirov	CzRep	15	5	1	6	12	....	....	....	....	....	....	....	....	....	....	....	....	....	....	....	....	....	....
2001-02	HC Vsetin	CzRep	46	15	31	46	54	....	....	....	....	....	....	....	....	....	....	....	....	....	....	....	....	....	....
	Liberec	CzRep-2	13	9	7	16	10	....	....	....	....	....	....	....	....	....	....	....	....	....	....	....	....	....	....
	HC Olomouc	CzRep-3	1	0	2	2	4	....	....	....	....	....	....	....	....	....	....	....	....	....	....	....	....	....	....
2002-03	HC Vsetin	CzRep	30	19	27	46	22	....	....	....	....	....	....	....	....	....	....	....	....	....	....	....	....	....	....
	Ak Bars Kazan	Russia	11	1	5	6	12	....	....	....	....	....	....	....	....	....	1	0	0	0	0	....	....	....	....
2003-04	Detroit	NHL	12	1	2	3	10	1	0	0	8	12.5	-1	50	30.0	8:10	....	....	....	....	....	....	....	....	....
	Grand Rapids	AHL	57	17	32	49	46	....	....	....	....	....	....	....	....	....	4	1	5	6	2	....	....	....	....
2004-05	Grand Rapids	AHL	52	12	22	34	10	....	....	....	....	....	....	....	....	....	....	....	....	....	....	....	....	....	....
	HC Vsetin	CzRep	7	5	2	7	10	....	....	....	....	....	....	....	....	....	....	....	....	....	....	....	....	....	....
2005-06	Detroit	NHL	4	0	0	0	2	0	0	0	3	0.0	0	0	0.0	7:13	....	....	....	....	....	....	....	....	....
	Grand Rapids	AHL	76	36	61	97	56	....	....	....	....	....	....	....	....	....	16	6	16	22	20	....	....	....	....
2006-07	Detroit	NHL	76	15	10	25	36	3	0	4	107	14.0	16	20	30.0	10:02	6	0	2	2	4	0	0	0	9:09
2007-08♦	Detroit	NHL	81	13	29	42	26	3	0	2	131	9.9	11	26	38.5	13:10	22	5	9	14	14	2	0	2	11:36
2008-09	Detroit	NHL	82	23	34	57	16	6	0	2	155	14.8	7	29	44.8	13:39	23	4	8	12	6	2	0	1	13:28
2009-10	Dynamo Moscow	KHL	54	19	35	54	18	....	....	....	....	....	....	....	....	....	4	0	1	1	4	....	....	....	....
2010-11	Detroit	NHL	73	10	27	37	28	3	0	2	105	9.5	-7	70	44.3	13:40	10	1	2	3	6	0	0	0	11:57
2011-12	Detroit	NHL	81	25	25	50	42	2	0	2	127	19.7	10	7	28.6	15:40	5	2	0	2	4	1	0	0	16:53
2012-13	HC Lev Praha	KHL	4	0	1	1	2	....	....	....	....	....	....	....	....	....	....	....	....	....	....	....	....	....	....
	HC Ocelari Trinec	CzRep	4	3	2	5	4	....	....	....	....	....	....	....	....	....	....	....	....	....	....	....	....	....	....
	Calgary	NHL	42	10	17	27	22	5	0	0	56	17.9	-13	31	32.3	17:10	....	....	....	....	....	....	....	....	....
2013-14	Calgary	NHL	75	17	37	54	16	2	0	1	109	15.6	4	22	18.2	18:51	....	....	....	....	....	....	....	....	....
2014-15	Calgary	NHL	78	31	45	76	14	6	0	5	158	19.6	17	46	45.7	18:01	11	4	4	8	2	3	0	1	16:22
	NHL Totals		604	145	226	371	212	31	0	18	959	15.1		301	37.2	14:42	77	16	25	41	36	8	0	4	13:02

AHL Second All-Star Team (2006) • Lady Byng Memorial Trophy (2015)

Signed as a free agent by **Vsetin** (CzRep), December 2, 2004. Signed as a free agent by **Dynamo Moscow** (KHL), July 10, 2009. Signed as a free agent by **Detroit**, May 24, 2010. Signed as a free agent by **Calgary**, July 2, 2012. Signed as a free agent by **Lev Praha** (KHL), September 20, 2012. Signed as a free agent by **Trinec** (CzRep), December 19, 2012.

HUNT, Brad

(HUHNT, BRAD) **EDM**

Defense. Shoots left. 5'9", 187 lbs. Born, Ridge Meadows, BC, August 24, 1988.

Season	Club	League	GP	G	A	Pts	PIM	PP	SH	GW	S	S%	+/-	TF	F%	Min	GP	G	A	Pts	PIM	PP	SH	GW	Min
2005-06	Ridge Meadow	PIJHL	STATISTICS NOT AVAILABLE																						
	Burnaby Express	BCHL	3	0	0	0	0	....	....	....	....	....	....	....	....	....	2	0	0	0	0	....	....	....	....
2006-07	Burnaby Express	BCHL	60	4	34	38	65	....	....	....	....	....	....	....	....	....	14	2	6	8	16	....	....	....	....
2007-08	Burnaby Express	BCHL	60	16	39	55	53	....	....	....	....	....	....	....	....	....	5	1	6	7	4	....	....	....	....
2008-09	Bemidji State	CHA	37	9	23	32	24	....	....	....	....	....	....	....	....	....	....	....	....	....	....	....	....	....	....
2009-10	Bemidji State	CHA	37	7	26	33	35	....	....	....	....	....	....	....	....	....	....	....	....	....	....	....	....	....	....
2010-11	Bemidji State	WCHA	38	3	18	21	33	....	....	....	....	....	....	....	....	....	....	....	....	....	....	....	....	....	....

Season	Club	League	GP	G	A	Pts	PIM	PP	SH	GW	S	S%	+/-	TF	F%	Min	GP	G	A	Pts	PIM	PP	SH	GW	Min
			Regular Season														Playoffs								
2011-12	Bemidji State	WCHA	38	5	21	26	8	....	....	....	....	....	....	....	....	....	....	....	....	....	....	....	....	....	....
	Chicago Wolves	AHL	14	1	4	5	8	....	....	....	....	....	....	....	....	....	5	1	3	4	0	....	....	....	....
2012-13	Chicago Wolves	AHL	65	4	29	33	22	....	....	....	....	....	....	....	....	....	....	....	....	....	....	....	....	....	....
2013-14	**Edmonton**	**NHL**	**3**	**0**	**0**	**0**	**0**	**0**	**0**	**0**	**1**	**0.0**	**–3**	**0**	**0.0**	**12:36**	....	....	....	....	....	....	....	....	....
	Oklahoma City	AHL	66	11	39	50	34	....	....	....	....	....	....	....	....	....	3	1	0	1	4	....	....	....	....
2014-15	**Edmonton**	**NHL**	**11**	**1**	**2**	**3**	**0**	**1**	**0**	**0**	**20**	**5.0**	**–6**	**0**	**0.0**	**19:29**	....	....	....	....	....	....	....	....	....
	Oklahoma City	AHL	62	19	32	51	18	....	....	....	....	....	....	....	....	....	10	3	7	10	6	....	....	....	....
	NHL Totals		**14**	**1**	**2**	**3**	**0**	**1**	**0**	**0**	**21**	**4.8**		**0**	**0.0**	**18:01**	....	....	....	....	....	....	....	....	....

AHL Second All-Star Team (2014) • AHL First All-Star Team (2015)

Signed as a free agent by **Edmonton**, July 6, 2013.

HUNWICK, Matt

(HUHN-wihk, MAT) **TOR**

Defense. Shoots left. 5'11", 190 lbs. Born, Warren, MI, May 21, 1985. Boston's 6th choice, 224th overall, in 2004 Entry Draft.

Season	Club	League	GP	G	A	Pts	PIM	PP	SH	GW	S	S%	+/-	TF	F%	Min	GP	G	A	Pts	PIM	PP	SH	GW	Min
2001-02	USNTDP	U-17	14	3	4	7	6	....	....	....	....	....	....	....	....	....	....	....	....	....	....	....	....	....	....
	USNTDP	NAHL	29	2	1	3	30	....	....	....	....	....	....	....	....	....	....	....	....	....	....	....	....	....	....
2002-03	USNTDP	U-18	40	6	16	22	40	....	....	....	....	....	....	....	....	....	....	....	....	....	....	....	....	....	....
	USNTDP	NAHL	8	2	2	4	23	....	....	....	....	....	....	....	....	....	....	....	....	....	....	....	....	....	....
2003-04	U. of Michigan	CCHA	41	1	14	15	62	....	....	....	....	....	....	....	....	....	....	....	....	....	....	....	....	....	....
2004-05	U. of Michigan	CCHA	40	6	19	25	60	....	....	....	....	....	....	....	....	....	....	....	....	....	....	....	....	....	....
2005-06	U. of Michigan	CCHA	41	11	19	30	70	....	....	....	....	....	....	....	....	....	....	....	....	....	....	....	....	....	....
2006-07	U. of Michigan	CCHA	41	6	21	27	64	....	....	....	....	....	....	....	....	....	....	....	....	....	....	....	....	....	....
2007-08	**Boston**	**NHL**	**13**	**0**	**1**	**1**	**4**	**0**	**0**	**0**	**6**	**0.0**	**–1**	**0**	**0.0**	**10:36**	....	....	....	....	....	....	....	....	....
	Providence Bruins	AHL	55	2	21	23	49	....	....	....	....	....	....	....	....	....	10	0	5	5	8	....	....	....	....
2008-09	**Boston**	**NHL**	**53**	**6**	**21**	**27**	**31**	**0**	**0**	**1**	**58**	**10.3**	**15**	**0**	**0.0**	**16:59**	**1**	**0**	**0**	**0**	**0**	**0**	**0**	**0**	**15:59**
	Providence Bruins	AHL	3	0	3	3	0	....	....	....	....	....	....	....	....	....	....	....	....	....	....	....	....	....	....
2009-10	**Boston**	**NHL**	**76**	**6**	**8**	**14**	**32**	**1**	**1**	**1**	**60**	**10.0**	**–16**	**1**	**0.0**	**17:58**	**13**	**0**	**6**	**6**	**2**	**0**	**0**	**0**	**21:57**
2010-11	**Boston**	**NHL**	**22**	**1**	**2**	**3**	**9**	**0**	**0**	**0**	**26**	**3.8**	**4**	**0**	**0.0**	**16:13**	....	....	....	....	....	....	....	....	....
	Colorado	**NHL**	**51**	**0**	**10**	**10**	**16**	**0**	**0**	**0**	**74**	**0.0**	**–19**	**0**	**0.0**	**19:30**	....	....	....	....	....	....	....	....	....
2011-12	**Colorado**	**NHL**	**33**	**3**	**3**	**6**	**8**	**0**	**0**	**0**	**40**	**7.5**	**–3**	**1**	**0.0**	**18:04**	....	....	....	....	....	....	....	....	....
2012-13	**Colorado**	**NHL**	**43**	**0**	**6**	**6**	**16**	**0**	**0**	**0**	**57**	**0.0**	**4**	**0**	**0.0**	**21:31**	....	....	....	....	....	....	....	....	....
2013-14	**Colorado**	**NHL**	**1**	**0**	**0**	**0**	**0**	**0**	**0**	**0**	**1**	**0.0**	**0**	**0**	**0.0**	**17:27**	....	....	....	....	....	....	....	....	....
	Lake Erie	AHL	52	10	21	31	33	....	....	....	....	....	....	....	....	....	....	....	....	....	....	....	....	....	....
2014-15	**NY Rangers**	**NHL**	**55**	**2**	**9**	**11**	**16**	**0**	**0**	**1**	**72**	**2.8**	**17**	**0**	**0.0**	**15:49**	**6**	**0**	**0**	**0**	**0**	**0**	**0**	**0**	**11:47**
	NHL Totals		**347**	**18**	**60**	**78**	**132**	**1**	**1**	**3**	**394**	**4.6**		**2**	**0.0**	**17:46**	**20**	**0**	**6**	**6**	**2**	**0**	**0**	**0**	**18:36**

CCHA All-Rookie Team (2004) • CCHA Second All-Star Team (2005, 2006) • CCHA First All-Star Team (2007) • NCAA West Second All-American Team (2007)

Traded to **Colorado** by **Boston** for Colby Cohen, November 29, 2010. • Missed majority of 2011-12 as a healthy reserve. Signed as a free agent by **NY Rangers**, July 1, 2014. Signed as a free agent by **Toronto**, July 1, 2015.

HUSKINS, Kent

(HUHS-kihnz, KEHNT)

Defense. Shoots left. 6'4", 210 lbs. Born, Ottawa, ON, May 4, 1979. Chicago's 3rd choice, 156th overall, in 1998 Entry Draft.

Season	Club	League	GP	G	A	Pts	PIM	PP	SH	GW	S	S%	+/-	TF	F%	Min	GP	G	A	Pts	PIM	PP	SH	GW	Min
1995-96	Kanata Valley	ON-Jr.A	49	6	21	27	18	....	....	....	....	....	....	....	....	....	5	0	1	1	10	....	....	....	....
1996-97	Kanata Valley	ON-Jr.A	53	11	36	47	89	....	....	....	....	....	....	....	....	....	14	4	4	8	18	....	....	....	....
1997-98	Clarkson Knights	ECAC	35	2	8	10	46	....	....	....	....	....	....	....	....	....	....	....	....	....	....	....	....	....	....
1998-99	Clarkson Knights	ECAC	37	5	11	16	28	....	....	....	....	....	....	....	....	....	....	....	....	....	....	....	....	....	....
99-2000	Clarkson Knights	ECAC	28	2	16	18	30	....	....	....	....	....	....	....	....	....	....	....	....	....	....	....	....	....	....
2000-01	Clarkson Knights	ECAC	35	6	28	34	22	....	....	....	....	....	....	....	....	....	....	....	....	....	....	....	....	....	....
2001-02	Norfolk Admirals	AHL	65	4	11	15	44	....	....	....	....	....	....	....	....	....	4	0	1	1	0	....	....	....	....
2002-03	Norfolk Admirals	AHL	80	5	22	27	48	....	....	....	....	....	....	....	....	....	9	2	2	4	4	....	....	....	....
2003-04	San Antonio	AHL	79	5	14	19	42	....	....	....	....	....	....	....	....	....	....	....	....	....	....	....	....	....	....
2004-05	Manitoba Moose	AHL	65	5	11	16	41	....	....	....	....	....	....	....	....	....	14	0	2	2	12	....	....	....	....
2005-06	Portland Pirates	AHL	80	8	23	31	64	....	....	....	....	....	....	....	....	....	18	3	6	9	14	....	....	....	....
2006-07 ♦	**Anaheim**	**NHL**	**33**	**0**	**3**	**3**	**14**	**0**	**0**	**0**	**16**	**0.0**	**–3**	**0**	**0.0**	**14:04**	**21**	**0**	**1**	**1**	**11**	**0**	**0**	**0**	**11:45**
	Portland Pirates	AHL	39	3	12	15	23	....	....	....	....	....	....	....	....	....	....	....	....	....	....	....	....	....	....
2007-08	**Anaheim**	**NHL**	**76**	**4**	**15**	**19**	**59**	**1**	**0**	**2**	**46**	**8.7**	**23**	**0**	**0.0**	**16:05**	**6**	**0**	**1**	**1**	**2**	**0**	**0**	**0**	**14:35**
2008-09	**Anaheim**	**NHL**	**33**	**2**	**4**	**6**	**27**	**0**	**0**	**0**	**20**	**10.0**	**6**	**1**	**0.0**	**18:47**	....	....	....	....	....	....	....	....	....
2009-10	**San Jose**	**NHL**	**82**	**3**	**19**	**22**	**47**	**0**	**0**	**0**	**47**	**6.4**	**6**	**0**	**0.0**	**17:29**	**15**	**0**	**0**	**0**	**6**	**0**	**0**	**0**	**12:48**
2010-11	**San Jose**	**NHL**	**50**	**2**	**8**	**10**	**12**	**0**	**0**	**0**	**38**	**5.3**	**8**	**0**	**0.0**	**16:37**	**5**	**0**	**1**	**1**	**2**	**0**	**0**	**0**	**18:48**
2011-12	**St. Louis**	**NHL**	**25**	**2**	**5**	**7**	**10**	**0**	**0**	**0**	**16**	**12.5**	**9**	**0**	**0.0**	**15:28**	**1**	**0**	**0**	**0**	**2**	**0**	**0**	**0**	**24:29**
2012-13	Norfolk Admirals	AHL	2	0	1	1	2	....	....	....	....	....	....	....	....	....	....	....	....	....	....	....	....	....	....
	Detroit	**NHL**	**11**	**0**	**0**	**0**	**4**	**0**	**0**	**0**	**2**	**0.0**	**–3**	**0**	**0.0**	**15:21**	....	....	....	....	....	....	....	....	....
	Philadelphia	**NHL**	**8**	**0**	**1**	**1**	**0**	**0**	**0**	**0**	**2**	**0.0**	**0**	**0**	**0.0**	**16:06**	....	....	....	....	....	....	....	....	....
2013-14	Utica Comets	AHL	65	3	7	10	31	....	....	....	....	....	....	....	....	....	....	....	....	....	....	....	....	....	....
2014-15	Utica Comets	AHL	50	1	5	6	8	....	....	....	....	....	....	....	....	....	20	1	2	3	6	....	....	....	....
	NHL Totals		**318**	**13**	**55**	**68**	**173**	**1**	**0**	**2**	**187**	**7.0**		**1**	**0.0**	**16:32**	**48**	**0**	**3**	**3**	**23**	**0**	**0**	**0**	**13:26**

ECAC First All-Star Team (2000, 2001) • NCAA East First All-American Team (2001)

Signed as a free agent by **Florida**, August 14, 2003. Signed as a free agent by **Manitoba** (AHL), September 16, 2004. Signed as a free agent by **Anaheim**, August 30, 2005. Traded to **San Jose** by **Anaheim** with Travis Moen for Timo Pielmeier, Nick Bonino and San Jose's 4th round choice (Andrew O'Brien) iun 2012 Entry Draft, March 4, 2009. Signed as a free agent by **St. Louis**, July 2, 2011. • Missed majority of 2011-12 due to ankle injury at Calgary, October 28, 2011. Signed as a free agent by **Norfolk** (AHL), January 17, 2013. Signed as a free agent by **Detroit**, January 22, 2013. Traded to **Philadelphia** by **Detroit** for future considerations, March 30, 2013. Signed as a free agent by **Utica** (AHL), November 4, 2013.

IGINLA, Jarome

(ih-GIHN-lah, jah-ROHM) **COL**

Right wing. Shoots right. 6'1", 210 lbs. Born, Edmonton, AB, July 1, 1977. Dallas' 1st choice, 11th overall, in 1995 Entry Draft.

Season	Club	League	GP	G	A	Pts	PIM	PP	SH	GW	S	S%	+/-	TF	F%	Min	GP	G	A	Pts	PIM	PP	SH	GW	Min
1991-92	St. Albert Raiders	AMHL	36	26	30	56	22	....	....	....	....	....	....	....	....	....	....	....	....	....	....	....	....	....	....
1992-93	St. Albert Raiders	AMHL	36	34	53	*87	20	....	....	....	....	....	....	....	....	....	....	....	....	....	....	....	....	....	....
1993-94	Kamloops Blazers	WHL	48	6	23	29	33	....	....	....	....	....	....	....	....	....	19	3	6	9	10	....	....	....	....
1994-95	Kamloops Blazers	WHL	72	33	38	71	111	....	....	....	....	....	....	....	....	....	21	7	11	18	34	....	....	....	....
1995-96	Kamloops Blazers	WHL	63	63	73	136	120	....	....	....	....	....	....	....	....	....	16	16	13	29	44	....	....	....	....
	Calgary	**NHL**	....	....	....	....	....	....	....	....	....	....	....	....	....	....	**2**	**1**	**1**	**2**	**0**	**0**	**0**	**0**	....
1996-97	**Calgary**	**NHL**	**82**	**21**	**29**	**50**	**37**	**8**	**1**	**3**	**169**	**12.4**	**–4**	....	....	....	....	....	....	....	....	....	....	....	....
1997-98	**Calgary**	**NHL**	**70**	**13**	**19**	**32**	**29**	**0**	**2**	**1**	**154**	**8.4**	**–10**	....	....	....	....	....	....	....	....	....	....	....	....
1998-99	**Calgary**	**NHL**	**82**	**28**	**23**	**51**	**58**	**7**	**0**	**4**	**211**	**13.3**	**1**	**111**	**51.4**	**16:30**	....	....	....	....	....	....	....	....	....
99-2000	**Calgary**	**NHL**	**77**	**29**	**34**	**63**	**26**	**12**	**0**	**4**	**256**	**11.3**	**0**	**278**	**52.9**	**18:24**	....	....	....	....	....	....	....	....	....
2000-01	**Calgary**	**NHL**	**77**	**31**	**40**	**71**	**62**	**10**	**0**	**4**	**229**	**13.5**	**–2**	**638**	**51.7**	**19:58**	....	....	....	....	....	....	....	....	....
2001-02	**Calgary**	**NHL**	**82**	***52**	**44**	***96**	**77**	**16**	**1**	**7**	**311**	**16.7**	**27**	**308**	**55.2**	**22:22**	....	....	....	....	....	....	....	....	....
	Canada	Olympics	6	3	1	4	0	....	....	....	....	....	....	....	....	....	....	....	....	....	....	....	....	....	....
2002-03	**Calgary**	**NHL**	**75**	**35**	**32**	**67**	**49**	**11**	**3**	**6**	**316**	**11.1**	**–10**	**90**	**43.3**	**21:26**	....	....	....	....	....	....	....	....	....
2003-04	**Calgary**	**NHL**	**81**	***41**	**32**	**73**	**84**	**8**	**4**	***10**	**265**	**15.5**	**21**	**305**	**54.4**	**21:18**	**26**	***13**	**9**	**22**	**45**	**4**	***2**	**3**	**23:18**
2004-05			DID NOT PLAY																						
2005-06	**Calgary**	**NHL**	**82**	**35**	**32**	**67**	**86**	**17**	**1**	**6**	**293**	**11.9**	**5**	**541**	**54.2**	**21:42**	**7**	**5**	**3**	**8**	**11**	**1**	**1**	**1**	**24:14**
	Canada	Olympics	6	2	1	3	4	....	....	....	....	....	....	....	....	....	....	....	....	....	....	....	....	....	....
2006-07	**Calgary**	**NHL**	**70**	**39**	**55**	**94**	**40**	**13**	**1**	**7**	**264**	**14.8**	**12**	**406**	**53.0**	**22:04**	**6**	**2**	**2**	**4**	**12**	**0**	**0**	**1**	**23:45**
2007-08	**Calgary**	**NHL**	**82**	**50**	**48**	**98**	**83**	**15**	**0**	**9**	**338**	**14.8**	**27**	**445**	**55.1**	**21:26**	**7**	**4**	**5**	**9**	**2**	**3**	**0**	**0**	**22:43**
2008-09	**Calgary**	**NHL**	**82**	**35**	**54**	**89**	**37**	**10**	**0**	**4**	**289**	**12.1**	**–2**	**501**	**52.5**	**21:37**	**6**	**3**	**1**	**4**	**0**	**2**	**0**	**0**	**20:56**
2009-10	**Calgary**	**NHL**	**82**	**32**	**37**	**69**	**58**	**10**	**0**	**5**	**257**	**12.5**	**–2**	**323**	**47.1**	**20:36**	....	....	....	....	....	....	....	....	....
	Canada	Olympics	7	*5	2	7	0	....	....	....	....	....	....	....	....	....	....	....	....	....	....	....	....	....	....
2010-11	**Calgary**	**NHL**	**82**	**43**	**43**	**86**	**40**	**14**	**0**	**6**	**289**	**14.9**	**0**	**420**	**54.1**	**20:56**	....	....	....	....	....	....	....	....	....
2011-12	**Calgary**	**NHL**	**82**	**32**	**35**	**67**	**43**	**8**	**0**	**5**	**251**	**12.7**	**–10**	**426**	**50.2**	**20:36**	....	....	....	....	....	....	....	....	....
2012-13	**Calgary**	**NHL**	**31**	**9**	**13**	**22**	**22**	**2**	**0**	**2**	**100**	**9.0**	**–7**	**237**	**50.2**	**19:18**	....	....	....	....	....	....	....	....	....
	Pittsburgh	**NHL**	**13**	**5**	**6**	**11**	**9**	**4**	**0**	**1**	**34**	**14.7**	**2**	**10**	**40.0**	**17:40**	**15**	**4**	**8**	**12**	**16**	**2**	**0**	**0**	**15:45**

			Regular Season														Playoffs								
Season	Club	League	GP	G	A	Pts	PIM	PP	SH	GW	S	S%	+/-	TF	F%	Min	GP	G	A	Pts	PIM	PP	SH	GW	Min
2013-14	**Boston**	**NHL**	**78**	**30**	**31**	**61**	**47**	**4**	**0**	**8**	**209**	**14.4**	**34**	**37**	**21.6**	**18:13**	**12**	**5**	**2**	**7**	**12**	**2**	**0**	**2**	**18:28**
2014-15	**Colorado**	**NHL**	**82**	**29**	**30**	**59**	**42**	**8**	**0**	**2**	**189**	**15.3**	**0**	**128**	**44.5**	**18:08**	....	....	....	....	....	....	....	....	....
	NHL Totals		**1392**	**589**	**637**	**1226**	**929**	**177**	**13**	**94**	**4424**	**13.3**		**5204**	**52.0**	**20:17**	**81**	**37**	**31**	**68**	**98**	**14**	**3**	**7**	**21:01**

George Parsons Trophy (Memorial Cup - Most Sportsmanlike Player) (1995) • WHL West First All-Star Team (1996) • WHL Player of the Year (1996) • Canadian Major Junior First All-Star Team (1996) • NHL All-Rookie Team (1997) • NHL First All-Star Team (2002, 2008, 2009) • Maurice "Rocket" Richard Trophy (2002) • Art Ross Trophy (2002) • Lester B. Pearson Award (2002) • NHL Second All-Star Team (2004) • NHL Foundation Player Award (2004) • King Clancy Memorial Trophy (2004) • Maurice "Rocket" Richard Trophy (2004) (tied with Ilya Kovalchuk and Rick Nash) • Mark Messier NHL Leadership Award (2009)

Played in NHL All-Star Game (2002, 2003, 2004, 2008, 2009, 2012)

Traded to **Calgary** by **Dallas** with Corey Millen for Joe Nieuwendyk, December 19, 1995. Traded to **Pittsburgh** by **Calgary** for Kenny Agostino, Ben Hanowski and Pittsburgh's 1st round choice (Morgan Klimchuk) in 2013 Entry Draft, March 28, 2013. Signed as a free agent by **Boston**, July 5, 2013. Signed as a free agent by **Colorado**, July 1, 2014.

IRWIN, Matt

(UHR-wihn, MAT) **BOS**

Defense. Shoots left. 6'2", 210 lbs. Born, Brentwood Bay, BC, November 29, 1987.

Season	Club	League	GP	G	A	Pts	PIM	PP	SH	GW	S	S%	+/-	TF	F%	Min	GP	G	A	Pts	PIM	PP	SH	GW	Min
2004-05	Saanich Braves	VIJHL	STATISTICS NOT AVAILABLE																						
	Nanaimo Clippers	BCHL	3	0	0	0	2	....	....	....	....	....	....	....	....	....	....	....	....	....	....	....	....	....	....
2005-06	Nanaimo Clippers	BCHL	56	3	6	9	41	....	....	....	....	....	....	....	....	....	5	0	1	1	4	....	....	....	....
2006-07	Nanaimo Clippers	BCHL	60	22	27	49	67	....	....	....	....	....	....	....	....	....	24	10	4	14	18	....	....	....	....
2007-08	Nanaimo Clippers	BCHL	59	16	37	53	40	....	....	....	....	....	....	....	....	....	14	6	7	13	22	....	....	....	....
2008-09	Massachusetts	H-East	31	7	11	18	8	....	....	....	....	....	....	....	....	....	....	....	....	....	....	....	....	....	....
2009-10	Massachusetts	H-East	36	7	17	24	16	....	....	....	....	....	....	....	....	....	....	....	....	....	....	....	....	....	....
	Worcester Sharks	AHL	3	0	0	0	2	....	....	....	....	....	....	....	....	....	1	0	0	0	0	....	....	....	....
2010-11	Worcester Sharks	AHL	72	10	21	31	43	....	....	....	....	....	....	....	....	....	....	....	....	....	....	....	....	....	....
2011-12	Worcester Sharks	AHL	71	11	31	42	48	....	....	....	....	....	....	....	....	....	....	....	....	....	....	....	....	....	....
2012-13	Worcester Sharks	AHL	35	1	14	15	26	....	....	....	....	....	....	....	....	....	....	....	....	....	....	....	....	....	....
	San Jose	**NHL**	**38**	**6**	**6**	**12**	**10**	**4**	**0**	**0**	**79**	**7.6**	**–1**	**0**	**0.0**	**19:06**	**11**	**0**	**1**	**1**	**4**	**0**	**0**	**0**	**17:47**
2013-14	**San Jose**	**NHL**	**62**	**2**	**17**	**19**	**35**	**1**	**0**	**0**	**147**	**1.4**	**5**	**1**	**0.0**	**18:49**	**2**	**1**	**0**	**1**	**0**	**0**	**0**	**0**	**19:48**
2014-15	**San Jose**	**NHL**	**53**	**8**	**11**	**19**	**18**	**1**	**0**	**1**	**93**	**8.6**	**3**	**0**	**0.0**	**17:01**	....	....	....	....	....	....	....	....	....
	NHL Totals		**153**	**16**	**34**	**50**	**63**	**6**	**0**	**1**	**319**	**5.0**		**1**	**0.0**	**18:16**	**13**	**1**	**1**	**2**	**4**	**0**	**0**	**0**	**18:06**

Signed as a free agent by **San Jose**, March 23, 2010. Signed as a free agent by **Boston**, July 10, 2015.

JACKMAN, Barret

(JAK-man, BAIR-reht) **NSH**

Defense. Shoots left. 6', 203 lbs. Born, Trail, BC, March 5, 1981. St. Louis' 1st choice, 17th overall, in 1999 Entry Draft.

Season	Club	League	GP	G	A	Pts	PIM	PP	SH	GW	S	S%	+/-	TF	F%	Min	GP	G	A	Pts	PIM	PP	SH	GW	Min
1996-97	Beaver Valley	VIJHL	32	22	25	47	180	....	....	....	....	....	....	....	....	....	....	....	....	....	....	....	....	....	....
1997-98	Regina Pats	WHL	68	2	11	13	224	....	....	....	....	....	....	....	....	....	9	0	3	3	32	....	....	....	....
1998-99	Regina Pats	WHL	70	8	36	44	259	....	....	....	....	....	....	....	....	....	....	....	....	....	....	....	....	....	....
99-2000	Regina Pats	WHL	53	9	37	46	175	....	....	....	....	....	....	....	....	....	6	1	1	2	19	....	....	....	....
	Worcester IceCats	AHL	....	....	....	....	....	....	....	....	....	....	....	....	....	....	2	0	0	0	13	....	....	....	....
2000-01	Regina Pats	WHL	43	9	27	36	138	....	....	....	....	....	....	....	....	....	6	0	3	3	8	....	....	....	....
2001-02	**St. Louis**	**NHL**	**1**	**0**	**0**	**0**	**0**	**0**	**0**	**0**	**1**	**0.0**	**0**	**0**	**0.0**	**18:56**	**1**	**0**	**0**	**0**	**2**	**0**	**0**	**0**	**18:24**
	Worcester IceCats	AHL	75	2	12	14	266	....	....	....	....	....	....	....	....	....	3	0	1	1	4	....	....	....	....
2002-03	**St. Louis**	**NHL**	**82**	**3**	**16**	**19**	**190**	**0**	**0**	**0**	**66**	**4.5**	**23**	**0**	**0.0**	**20:03**	**7**	**0**	**0**	**0**	**14**	**0**	**0**	**0**	**21:59**
2003-04	**St. Louis**	**NHL**	**15**	**1**	**2**	**3**	**41**	**0**	**0**	**0**	**11**	**9.1**	**–1**	**0**	**0.0**	**18:16**	....	....	....	....	....	....	....	....	....
2004-05	Missouri	UHL	28	3	17	20	61	....	....	....	....	....	....	....	....	....	3	0	0	0	4	....	....	....	....
2005-06	**St. Louis**	**NHL**	**63**	**4**	**6**	**10**	**156**	**0**	**0**	**2**	**56**	**7.1**	**–6**	**0**	**0.0**	**18:46**	....	....	....	....	....	....	....	....	....
2006-07	**St. Louis**	**NHL**	**70**	**3**	**24**	**27**	**82**	**1**	**0**	**1**	**86**	**3.5**	**20**	**0**	**0.0**	**21:30**	....	....	....	....	....	....	....	....	....
	Peoria Rivermen	AHL	1	0	0	0	0	....	....	....	....	....	....	....	....	....	....	....	....	....	....	....	....	....	....
2007-08	**St. Louis**	**NHL**	**78**	**2**	**14**	**16**	**93**	**1**	**0**	**0**	**80**	**2.5**	**–12**	**0**	**0.0**	**22:24**	....	....	....	....	....	....	....	....	....
2008-09	**St. Louis**	**NHL**	**82**	**4**	**17**	**21**	**86**	**1**	**1**	**0**	**89**	**4.5**	**–17**	**0**	**0.0**	**23:26**	**4**	**0**	**1**	**1**	**5**	**0**	**0**	**0**	**25:18**
2009-10	**St. Louis**	**NHL**	**66**	**2**	**15**	**17**	**81**	**0**	**1**	**0**	**73**	**2.7**	**3**	**1**	**0.0**	**22:41**	....	....	....	....	....	....	....	....	....
2010-11	**St. Louis**	**NHL**	**60**	**0**	**13**	**13**	**57**	**0**	**0**	**0**	**65**	**0.0**	**3**	**0**	**0.0**	**20:48**	....	....	....	....	....	....	....	....	....
2011-12	**St. Louis**	**NHL**	**81**	**1**	**12**	**13**	**57**	**0**	**0**	**0**	**82**	**1.2**	**20**	**0**	**0.0**	**20:41**	**9**	**0**	**1**	**1**	**21**	**0**	**0**	**0**	**18:54**
2012-13	**St. Louis**	**NHL**	**46**	**3**	**9**	**12**	**39**	**0**	**0**	**0**	**39**	**7.7**	**6**	**0**	**0.0**	**19:19**	**6**	**1**	**1**	**2**	**10**	**0**	**0**	**1**	**20:12**
2013-14	**St. Louis**	**NHL**	**79**	**3**	**12**	**15**	**97**	**0**	**0**	**1**	**83**	**3.6**	**11**	**1**	**0.0**	**17:56**	**6**	**1**	**2**	**3**	**6**	**0**	**0**	**1**	**19:55**
2014-15	**St. Louis**	**NHL**	**80**	**2**	**13**	**15**	**47**	**0**	**0**	**1**	**86**	**2.3**	**3**	**0**	**0.0**	**16:49**	**6**	**0**	**0**	**0**	**4**	**0**	**0**	**0**	**13:00**
	NHL Totals		**803**	**28**	**153**	**181**	**1026**	**3**	**2**	**5**	**817**	**3.4**		**2**	**0.0**	**20:23**	**39**	**2**	**5**	**7**	**62**	**0**	**0**	**2**	**19:33**

WHL East Second All-Star Team (2000) • AHL All-Rookie Team (2002) • NHL All-Rookie Team (2003) • Calder Memorial Trophy (2003)

• Missed majority of 2003-04 due to shoulder injury vs. Vancouver, October 22, 2003. Signed as a free agent by **Missouri** (UHL), February 3, 2005. Signed as a free agent by **Nashville**, July 1, 2015.

JACKMAN, Tim

(JAK-man, TIHM) **ANA**

Right wing. Shoots right. 6'2", 225 lbs. Born, Minot, ND, November 14, 1981. Columbus' 2nd choice, 38th overall, in 2001 Entry Draft.

Season	Club	League	GP	G	A	Pts	PIM	PP	SH	GW	S	S%	+/-	TF	F%	Min	GP	G	A	Pts	PIM	PP	SH	GW	Min
1998-99	Park Center	High-MN	22	22	22	44	....	....	....	....	....	....	....	....	....	....	....	....	....	....	....	....	....	....	....
99-2000	Park Center	High-MN	19	34	22	56	....	....	....	....	....	....	....	....	....	....	....	....	....	....	....	....	....	....	....
	Twin Cities	USHL	25	11	9	20	58	....	....	....	....	....	....	....	....	....	13	8	5	13	12	....	....	....	....
2000-01	Minnesota State	WCHA	37	11	14	25	92	....	....	....	....	....	....	....	....	....	....	....	....	....	....	....	....	....	....
2001-02	Minnesota State	WCHA	36	14	14	28	86	....	....	....	....	....	....	....	....	....	....	....	....	....	....	....	....	....	....
2002-03	Syracuse Crunch	AHL	77	9	7	16	48	....	....	....	....	....	....	....	....	....	....	....	....	....	....	....	....	....	....
2003-04	**Columbus**	**NHL**	**19**	**1**	**2**	**3**	**16**	**0**	**0**	**0**	**18**	**5.6**	**–7**	**1**	**100.0**	**9:56**	....	....	....	....	....	....	....	....	....
	Syracuse Crunch	AHL	64	23	13	36	61	....	....	....	....	....	....	....	....	....	7	2	3	5	12	....	....	....	....
2004-05	Syracuse Crunch	AHL	73	14	21	35	98	....	....	....	....	....	....	....	....	....	....	....	....	....	....	....	....	....	....
2005-06	**Phoenix**	**NHL**	**8**	**0**	**0**	**0**	**21**	**0**	**0**	**0**	**4**	**0.0**	**1**	**1**	**0.0**	**7:13**	....	....	....	....	....	....	....	....	....
	San Antonio	AHL	50	7	13	20	127	....	....	....	....	....	....	....	....	....	....	....	....	....	....	....	....	....	....
	Manchester	AHL	18	2	3	5	33	....	....	....	....	....	....	....	....	....	7	0	3	3	20	....	....	....	....
2006-07	**Los Angeles**	**NHL**	**5**	**0**	**0**	**0**	**10**	**0**	**0**	**0**	**3**	**0.0**	**–1**	**0**	**0.0**	**6:36**	....	....	....	....	....	....	....	....	....
	Manchester	AHL	69	19	14	33	143	....	....	....	....	....	....	....	....	....	16	3	3	6	26	....	....	....	....
2007-08	**NY Islanders**	**NHL**	**36**	**1**	**3**	**4**	**57**	**0**	**0**	**0**	**36**	**2.8**	**–3**	**2**	**100.0**	**6:37**	....	....	....	....	....	....	....	....	....
	Bridgeport	AHL	44	15	21	36	67	....	....	....	....	....	....	....	....	....	....	....	....	....	....	....	....	....	....
2008-09	**NY Islanders**	**NHL**	**69**	**5**	**7**	**12**	**155**	**0**	**1**	**0**	**99**	**5.1**	**–17**	**22**	**31.8**	**11:45**	....	....	....	....	....	....	....	....	....
	Bridgeport	AHL	12	6	1	7	35	....	....	....	....	....	....	....	....	....	....	....	....	....	....	....	....	....	....
2009-10	**NY Islanders**	**NHL**	**54**	**4**	**5**	**9**	**98**	**0**	**0**	**0**	**51**	**7.8**	**–4**	**7**	**42.9**	**9:39**	....	....	....	....	....	....	....	....	....
2010-11	**Calgary**	**NHL**	**82**	**10**	**13**	**23**	**86**	**1**	**0**	**1**	**131**	**7.6**	**4**	**16**	**37.5**	**9:49**	....	....	....	....	....	....	....	....	....
2011-12	**Calgary**	**NHL**	**75**	**1**	**6**	**7**	**94**	**0**	**0**	**0**	**103**	**1.0**	**–21**	**34**	**44.1**	**9:07**	....	....	....	....	....	....	....	....	....
2012-13	**Calgary**	**NHL**	**42**	**1**	**4**	**5**	**76**	**0**	**0**	**0**	**42**	**2.4**	**–9**	**24**	**45.8**	**7:36**	....	....	....	....	....	....	....	....	....
2013-14	**Calgary**	**NHL**	**10**	**1**	**0**	**1**	**41**	**0**	**0**	**0**	**9**	**11.1**	**–1**	**1**	**0.0**	**6:23**	....	....	....	....	....	....	....	....	....
	Anaheim	**NHL**	**26**	**3**	**1**	**4**	**62**	**0**	**0**	**0**	**37**	**8.1**	**–2**	**2**	**100.0**	**7:23**	....	....	....	....	....	....	....	....	....
2014-15	**Anaheim**	**NHL**	**55**	**5**	**2**	**7**	**86**	**0**	**0**	**1**	**55**	**9.1**	**–4**	**14**	**71.4**	**8:23**	**9**	**0**	**0**	**0**	**12**	**0**	**0**	**0**	**6:33**
	NHL Totals		**481**	**32**	**43**	**75**	**802**	**1**	**1**	**2**	**588**	**5.4**		**124**	**46.0**	**9:06**	**9**	**0**	**0**	**0**	**12**	**0**	**0**	**0**	**6:33**

Traded to **Phoenix** by **Columbus** with Geoff Sanderson for Cale Hulse, Mike Rupp and Jason Chimera, October 8, 2005. Traded to **Los Angeles** by **Phoenix** for Yanick Lehoux, March 9, 2006. Signed as a free agent by **NY Islanders**, July 5, 2007. Signed as a free agent by **Calgary**, July 2, 2010. Traded to **Anaheim** by **Calgary** for Anaheim's 6th round choice (Adam Ollas Mattsson) in 2014 Entry Draft, November 21, 2013. • Missed majority of 2013-14 as a healthy reserve.

JAGR, Jaromir

(YAH-guhr, YAIR-oh-MEER) **FLA**

Right wing. Shoots left. 6'3", 230 lbs. Born, Kladno, Czech., February 15, 1972. Pittsburgh's 1st choice, 5th overall, in 1990 Entry Draft.

Season	Club	League	GP	G	A	Pts	PIM	PP	SH	GW	S	S%	+/-	TF	F%	Min	GP	G	A	Pts	PIM	PP	SH	GW	Min
1984-85	Kladno Jr.	Czech-Jr.	34	24	17	41	....	....	....	....	....	....	....	....	....	....	....	....	....	....	....	....	....	....	....
1985-86	Kladno Jr.	Czech-Jr.	36	41	29	70	....	....	....	....	....	....	....	....	....	....	....	....	....	....	....	....	....	....	....
1986-87	Kladno Jr.	Czech-Jr.	30	35	35	70	....	....	....	....	....	....	....	....	....	....	....	....	....	....	....	....	....	....	....
1987-88	Kladno Jr.	Czech-Jr.	35	57	27	84	....	....	....	....	....	....	....	....	....	....	....	....	....	....	....	....	....	....	....
1988-89	Kladno	Czech	29	3	3	6	4	....	....	....	....	....	....	....	....	....	10	5	7	12	0	....	....	....	....
1989-90	Poldi Kladno	Czech	42	22	28	50	....	....	....	....	....	....	....	....	....	....	9	*8	2	10	....	....	....	....	....
1990-91 ♦	**Pittsburgh**	**NHL**	**80**	**27**	**30**	**57**	**42**	**7**	**0**	**4**	**136**	**19.9**	**–4**	....	....	....	**24**	**3**	**10**	**13**	**6**	**1**	**0**	**1**	....
1991-92 ♦	**Pittsburgh**	**NHL**	**70**	**32**	**37**	**69**	**34**	**4**	**0**	**4**	**194**	**16.5**	**12**	....	....	....	**21**	**11**	**13**	**24**	**6**	**2**	**0**	**4**	....
1992-93	**Pittsburgh**	**NHL**	**81**	**34**	**60**	**94**	**61**	**10**	**1**	**9**	**242**	**14.0**	**30**	....	....	....	**12**	**5**	**4**	**9**	**23**	**1**	**0**	**1**	....
1993-94	**Pittsburgh**	**NHL**	**80**	**32**	**67**	**99**	**61**	**9**	**0**	**6**	**298**	**10.7**	**15**	....	....	....	**6**	**2**	**4**	**6**	**16**	**0**	**0**	**1**	....

Season	Club	League	Regular Season														Playoffs								
			GP	G	A	Pts	PIM	PP	SH	GW	S	S%	+/-	TF	F%	Min	GP	G	A	Pts	PIM	PP	SH	GW	Min
1994-95	HC Kladno	CzRep	11	8	14	22	10																		
	HC Bolzano	Euroliga	5	8	8	16	4																		
	HC Bolzano	Italy	1	0	0	0	0																		
	Schalke	German-2	1	1	10	11	0																		
	Pittsburgh	NHL	48	32	38	*70	37	8	3	7	192	16.7	23				12	10	5	15	6	2	1	1	
1995-96	Pittsburgh	NHL	82	62	87	149	96	20	1	*12	403	15.4	31				18	11	12	23	18	5	1	1	
1996-97	Pittsburgh	NHL	63	47	48	95	40	11	2	6	234	20.1	22				5	4	4	8	4	2	0	0	
1997-98	Pittsburgh	NHL	77	35	*67	*102	64	7	0	8	262	13.4	17				6	4	5	9	2	1	0	0	
	Czech Republic	Olympics	6	1	4	5	2																		
1998-99	Pittsburgh	NHL	81	44	*83	*127	66	10	1	7	343	12.8	17	4	50.0	25:51	9	5	7	12	16	1	0	1	25:32
99-2000	Pittsburgh	NHL	63	42	54	*96	50	10	0	5	290	14.5	25	9	22.2	23:12	11	8	8	16	6	2	0	*4	24:32
2000-01	Pittsburgh	NHL	81	52	*69	*121	42	14	1	10	317	16.4	19	2	0.0	23:19	16	2	10	12	18	2	0	0	22:15
2001-02	Washington	NHL	69	31	48	79	30	10	0	3	197	15.7	0	2	50.0	21:43									
	Czech Republic	Olympics	4	2	3	5	4																		
2002-03	Washington	NHL	75	36	41	77	38	13	2	9	290	12.4	5	5	20.0	21:18	6	2	5	7	2	1	0	0	25:13
2003-04	Washington	NHL	46	16	29	45	26	6	0	1	159	10.1	–4	1	0.0	21:05									
	NY Rangers	NHL	31	15	14	29	12	4	0	2	98	15.3	–1	0	0.0	20:45									
2004-05	HC Rabat Kladno	CzRep	17	11	17	28	16																		
	Avangard Omsk	Russia	32	16	22	38	63										11	4	*10	*14	22				
2005-06	NY Rangers	NHL	82	54	69	123	72	24	0	9	368	14.7	34	6	16.7	22:05	3	0	1	1	2	0	0	0	13:47
	Czech Republic	Olympics	8	2	5	7	6																		
2006-07	NY Rangers	NHL	82	30	66	96	78	7	0	5	324	9.3	26	6	16.7	21:46	10	5	6	11	12	2	0	0	22:07
2007-08	NY Rangers	NHL	82	25	46	71	58	7	0	5	249	10.0	8	3	33.3	20:28	10	5	10	15	12	2	0	1	19:54
2008-09	Omsk	KHL	55	25	28	53	62										9	4	5	9	4				
2009-10	Omsk	KHL	51	22	20	42	50										3	1	1	2	0				
	Czech Republic	Olympics	5	2	1	3	6																		
2010-11	Omsk	KHL	49	19	31	50	48										14	2	7	9	8				
2011-12	Philadelphia	NHL	73	19	35	54	30	8	0	2	170	11.2	5	1	0.0	16:20	11	1	7	8	2	0	0	1	15:00
2012-13	Rytiri Kladno	CzRep	34	24	33	57	28																		
	Dallas	NHL	34	14	12	26	20	6	0	2	87	16.1	–5	1	0.0	18:18									
	Boston	NHL	11	2	7	9	2	0	0	2	28	7.1	3	0	0.0	18:27	22	0	10	10	8	0	0	0	17:55
2013-14	New Jersey	NHL	82	24	43	67	46	5	0	6	231	10.4	16	2	0.0	19:10									
	Czech Republic	Olympics	5	2	1	3	2																		
2014-15	New Jersey	NHL	57	11	18	29	42	2	0	3	119	9.2	–10	0	0.0	17:41									
	Florida	NHL	20	6	12	18	6	2	0	2	50	12.0	7	1	100.0	17:15									
	NHL Totals		1550	722	1080	1802	1053	204	11	129	5281	13.7		43	23.3	21:01	202	78	121	199	159	24	2	16	20:42

NHL All-Rookie Team (1991) • NHL First All-Star Team (1995, 1996, 1998, 1999, 2000, 2001, 2006) • Art Ross Trophy (1995, 1998, 1999, 2000, 2001) • NHL Second All-Star Team (1997) • Lester B. Pearson Award (1999, 2000, 2006) • Hart Memorial Trophy (1999)

Played in NHL All-Star Game (1992, 1993, 1996, 1998, 1999, 2000, 2002, 2003, 2004)

Traded to **Washington** by **Pittsburgh** with Frantisek Kucera for Kris Beech, Michal Sivek, Ross Lupaschuk and future considerations, July 11, 2001. Traded to **NY Rangers** by **Washington** for Anson Carter, January 23, 2004. Signed as a free agent by **Kladno** (CzRep), September 17, 2004. Signed as a free agent by **Omsk** (Russia), November 7, 2004. Signed as a free agent by **Omsk** (KHL), July 4, 2008. Signed as a free agent by **Philadelphia**, July 1, 2011. Signed as a free agent by **Dallas**, July 3, 2012. Signed as a free agent by **Kladno** (CzRep), September 16, 2012. Traded to **Boston** by **Dallas** for Lane MacDermid, Cody Payne and Boston's 1st round choice (Jason Dickinson) in 2013 Entry Draft, April 2, 2013. Signed as a free agent by **New Jersey**, July 23, 2013. Traded to **Florida** by **New Jersey** for Florida's 2nd round choice (later traded to Anaheim, later traded to NY Rangers – NY Rangers selected Ryan Gropp) in 2015 Entry Draft and future considerations, February 26, 2015.

JANSSEN, Cam

(JAN-suhn, KAM)

Right wing. Shoots right. 6', 215 lbs. Born, St. Louis, MO, April 15, 1984. New Jersey's 6th choice, 117th overall, in 2002 Entry Draft.

Season	Club	League	Regular Season														Playoffs								
			GP	G	A	Pts	PIM	PP	SH	GW	S	S%	+/-	TF	F%	Min	GP	G	A	Pts	PIM	PP	SH	GW	Min
2000-01	St. Louis Jr. Blues	CSJHL	45	1	2	3	244																		
2001-02	Windsor Spitfires	OHL	64	5	17	22	*268										10	0	0	0	13				
2002-03	Windsor Spitfires	OHL	50	1	12	13	211										7	0	1	1	22				
2003-04	Windsor Spitfires	OHL	35	4	9	13	144																		
	Guelph Storm	OHL	29	7	4	11	125										22	3	3	6	49				
2004-05	Albany River Rats	AHL	70	1	3	4	337																		
2005-06	New Jersey	NHL	47	0	0	0	91	0	0	0	10	0.0	–3	2	100.0	4:44	9	0	0	0	26	0	0	0	3:43
	Albany River Rats	AHL	26	1	3	4	117																		
2006-07	New Jersey	NHL	48	1	0	1	114	0	0	0	9	11.1	–2	1	100.0	4:06									
	Lowell Devils	AHL	9	0	1	1	29																		
2007-08	St. Louis	NHL	12	0	1	1	18	0	0	0	9	0.0	–1	0	0.0	7:07									
	Lowell Devils	AHL	3	0	0	0	4																		
2008-09	St. Louis	NHL	56	1	3	4	131	0	0	0	22	4.5	–5	2	0.0	5:01	1	0	0	0	0	0	0	0	3:59
2009-10	St. Louis	NHL	43	0	0	0	190	0	0	0	11	0.0	–3	1	0.0	4:43									
2010-11	St. Louis	NHL	54	1	3	4	131	0	0	0	16	6.3	–6	0	0.0	4:53									
2011-12	New Jersey	NHL	48	0	1	1	75	0	0	0	17	0.0	–8	5	40.0	4:41									
2012-13	Albany Devils	AHL	36	1	4	5	65																		
	New Jersey	NHL	4	0	0	0	2	0	0	0	0	0.0	–1	0	0.0	3:58									
2013-14	New Jersey	NHL	24	3	0	3	22	0	0	0	11	27.3	3	0	0.0	4:55									
	Albany Devils	AHL	27	0	3	3	24																		
2014-15	Albany Devils	AHL	34	1	1	2	81																		
	NHL Totals		336	6	8	14	774	0	0	0	105	5.7		11	45.5	4:47	10	0	0	0	26	0	0	0	3:45

Traded to **St. Louis** by **New Jersey** for Bryce Salvador, February 26, 2008. Signed as a free agent by **New Jersey**, July 14, 2011. • Missed majority of 2014-15 due to various injuries and as a healthy reserve. Signed as a free agent by **Nottingham** (Britain), August 15, 2015.

JARNKROK, Calle

(YAHRN-krohk, KAHL-leh) **NSH**

Center. Shoots right. 5'11", 156 lbs. Born, Gavle, Sweden, September 25, 1991. Detroit's 2nd choice, 51st overall, in 2010 Entry Draft.

Season	Club	League	Regular Season														Playoffs								
			GP	G	A	Pts	PIM	PP	SH	GW	S	S%	+/-	TF	F%	Min	GP	G	A	Pts	PIM	PP	SH	GW	Min
2007-08	Brynas U18	Swe-U18	13	4	4	8	4										5	0	1	1	0				
	Brynas IF Gavle Jr.	Swe-Jr.	2	0	0	0	2																		
2008-09	Brynas U18	Swe-U18	7	5	7	12	12										2	0	1	1	2				
	Brynas IF Gavle Jr.	Swe-Jr.	41	8	18	26	37										7	4	3	7	2				
2009-10	Brynas IF Gavle Jr.	Swe-Jr.	19	11	20	31	30										2	0	1	1	0				
	Brynas IF Gavle	Sweden	33	4	6	10	2										5	1	1	2	0				
2010-11	Brynas IF Gavle	Sweden	49	11	16	27	4										3	3	0	3	2				
2011-12	Brynas IF Gavle	Sweden	50	16	23	39	22										16	4	12	16	12				
2012-13	Brynas IF Gavle	Sweden	53	13	29	42	12										4	0	0	0	6				
	Grand Rapids	AHL	9	0	3	3	0																		
2013-14	Grand Rapids	AHL	57	13	23	36	14																		
	Nashville	NHL	12	2	7	9	4	0	0	0	13	15.4	7	147	39.5	14:04									
	Milwaukee	AHL	6	5	4	9	0										3	1	1	2	2				
2014-15	Nashville	NHL	74	7	11	18	18	0	0	1	95	7.4	2	641	46.2	12:51	6	0	2	2	0	0	0	0	16:29
	NHL Totals		86	9	18	27	22	0	0	1	108	8.3		788	44.9	13:01	6	0	2	2	0	0	0	0	16:29

Traded to **Nashville** by **Detroit** with Patrick Eaves and Detroit's 2nd round choice (later traded to San Jose – San Jose selected Julius Bergman) in 2014 Entry Draft for David Legwand, March 5, 2014.

JASKIN, Dmitrij

(YASH-kihn, dih-MEE-tree) **ST.L.**

Right wing. Shoots left. 6'2", 196 lbs. Born, Omsk, Russia, March 23, 1993. St. Louis' 2nd choice, 41st overall, in 2011 Entry Draft.

Season	Club	League	Regular Season														Playoffs								
			GP	G	A	Pts	PIM	PP	SH	GW	S	S%	+/-	TF	F%	Min	GP	G	A	Pts	PIM	PP	SH	GW	Min
2006-07	HC Vsetin U17	CzR-U17	4	1	0	1	0																		
2007-08	HC Vsetin U17	CzR-U17	40	15	25	40	72										2	2	0	2	6				
2008-09	Slavia U17	CzR-U17	46	28	19	47	34										9	6	2	8	8				
2009-10	Slavia U18	CzR-U18	12	15	12	27	36										2	1	3	4	4				
	Slavia Jr.	CzRep-Jr.	40	13	10	23	67										7	2	5	7	26				
2010-11	Slavia Jr.	CzRep-Jr.	1	0	0	0	0										2	2	3	5	2				
	HC Slavia Praha	CzRep	33	3	7	10	16										17	2	1	3	31				
2011-12	HC Slavia Praha	CzRep	37	4	2	6	18																		
	Beroun	CzRep-2	10	2	6	8	16																		
	Slavia Jr.	CzRep-Jr.	10	6	11	17	12										2	1	3	4	14				
2012-13	Moncton Wildcats	QMJHL	51	46	53	99	73										5	1	2	3	16				
	St. Louis	NHL	2	0	0	0	0	0	0	0	2	0.0	–1	0	0.0	7:30									
2013-14	St. Louis	NHL	18	1	1	2	8	0	0	0	18	5.6	–3	2	50.0	10:37									
	Chicago Wolves	AHL	42	15	14	29	28										9	4	5	9	10				

			Regular Season														Playoffs								
Season	Club	League	GP	G	A	Pts	PIM	PP	SH	GW	S	S%	+/-	TF	F%	Min	GP	G	A	Pts	PIM	PP	SH	GW	Min
2014-15	**St. Louis**	**NHL**	**54**	**13**	**5**	**18**	**16**	**3**	**0**	**4**	**108**	**12.0**	**7**	**7**	**42.9**	**13:28**	**6**	**0**	**1**	**1**	**2**	**0**	**0**	**0**	**12:56**
	Chicago Wolves	AHL	18	4	11	15	31	....	....	....	....	....	....	....	....	....	....	....	....	....	....	....	....	....	....
	NHL Totals		**74**	**14**	**6**	**20**	**24**	**3**	**0**	**4**	**128**	**10.9**		**9**	**44.4**	**12:37**	**6**	**0**	**1**	**1**	**2**	**0**	**0**	**0**	**12:56**

QMJHL First All-Star Team (2013)

JEFFREY, Dustin

(JEHF-ree, DUHS-tihn) **ARI**

Center. Shoots left. 6'1", 205 lbs. Born, Sarnia, ON, February 27, 1988. Pittsburgh's 8th choice, 171st overall, in 2007 Entry Draft.

Season	Club	League	GP	G	A	Pts	PIM	PP	SH	GW	S	S%	+/-	TF	F%	Min	GP	G	A	Pts	PIM	PP	SH	GW	Min
2003-04	Lambton Jr. Sting	Minor-ON	40	44	23	67	22	....	....	....	....	....	....	....	....	....	....	....	....	....	....	....	....	....	....
2004-05	Mississauga	OHL	53	10	15	25	20	....	....	....	....	....	....	....	....	....	....	....	....	....	....	....	....	....	....
2005-06	Mississauga	OHL	30	6	9	15	26	....	....	....	....	....	....	....	....	....	....	....	....	....	....	....	....	....	....
	Sault Ste. Marie	OHL	39	12	11	23	10	....	....	....	....	....	....	....	....	....	4	1	2	3	2	....	....	....	....
2006-07	Sault Ste. Marie	OHL	68	34	58	92	40	....	....	....	....	....	....	....	....	....	13	6	12	18	11	....	....	....	....
2007-08	Sault Ste. Marie	OHL	56	38	59	97	30	....	....	....	....	....	....	....	....	....	14	3	8	11	12	....	....	....	....
	Wilkes-Barre	AHL	....	....	....	....	....	....	....	....	....	....	....	....	....	....	15	2	1	3	4	....	....	....	....
2008-09	**Pittsburgh**	**NHL**	**14**	**1**	**2**	**3**	**0**	**0**	**0**	**0**	**18**	**5.6**	**4**	**103**	**41.8**	**10:47**	....	....	....	....	....	....	....	....	....
	Wilkes-Barre	AHL	63	11	26	37	31	....	....	....	....	....	....	....	....	....	12	5	5	10	8	....	....	....	....
2009-10	**Pittsburgh**	**NHL**	**1**	**0**	**0**	**0**	**0**	**0**	**0**	**0**	**0**	**0.0**	**0**	**0**	**0.0**	**8:35**	....	....	....	....	....	....	....	....	....
	Wilkes-Barre	AHL	77	24	47	71	16	....	....	....	....	....	....	....	....	....	4	0	1	1	6	....	....	....	....
2010-11	**Pittsburgh**	**NHL**	**25**	**7**	**5**	**12**	**4**	**1**	**0**	**1**	**39**	**17.9**	**5**	**247**	**44.1**	**12:58**	....	....	....	....	....	....	....	....	....
	Wilkes-Barre	AHL	40	17	28	45	8	....	....	....	....	....	....	....	....	....	....	....	....	....	....	....	....	....	....
2011-12	**Pittsburgh**	**NHL**	**26**	**4**	**2**	**6**	**2**	**0**	**1**	**0**	**33**	**12.1**	**–4**	**225**	**48.4**	**12:06**	....	....	....	....	....	....	....	....	....
	Wilkes-Barre	AHL	2	0	1	1	0	....	....	....	....	....	....	....	....	....	....	....	....	....	....	....	....	....	....
2012-13	Zagreb	Austria	20	11	12	23	20	....	....	....	....	....	....	....	....	....	....	....	....	....	....	....	....	....	....
	Pittsburgh	**NHL**	**24**	**3**	**3**	**6**	**2**	**0**	**0**	**0**	**26**	**11.5**	**1**	**200**	**47.0**	**11:31**	....	....	....	....	....	....	....	....	....
2013-14	**Pittsburgh**	**NHL**	**10**	**0**	**1**	**1**	**2**	**0**	**0**	**0**	**9**	**0.0**	**–2**	**13**	**61.5**	**10:50**	....	....	....	....	....	....	....	....	....
	Dallas	**NHL**	**24**	**2**	**1**	**3**	**0**	**0**	**0**	**0**	**21**	**9.5**	**–2**	**102**	**46.1**	**9:03**	....	....	....	....	....	....	....	....	....
	Texas Stars	AHL	21	4	6	10	2	....	....	....	....	....	....	....	....	....	19	7	5	12	2	....	....	....	....
2014-15	Utica Comets	AHL	49	17	24	41	18	....	....	....	....	....	....	....	....	....	....	....	....	....	....	....	....	....	....
	Bridgeport	AHL	20	8	15	23	4	....	....	....	....	....	....	....	....	....	....	....	....	....	....	....	....	....	....
	NHL Totals		**124**	**17**	**14**	**31**	**10**	**1**	**1**	**1**	**146**	**11.6**		**890**	**46.1**	**11:18**	....	....	....	....	....	....	....	....	....

• Missed majority of 2011-12 due to recurring knee injury and as a healthy reserve. Signed as a free agent by **Zagreb** (Austria), October 10, 2012. Claimed on waivers by **Dallas** from **Pittsburgh**, November 17, 2013. Signed as a free agent by **Vancouver**, July 2, 2014. Traded to **NY Islanders** by **Vancouver** for Cory Conacher, March 2, 2015. Signed as a free agent by **Arizona**, July, 2015.

JENNER, Boone

(JEH-nuhr, BOON) **CBJ**

Center. Shoots left. 6'2", 208 lbs. Born, Dorchester, ON, June 15, 1993. Columbus' 1st choice, 37th overall, in 2011 Entry Draft.

Season	Club	League	GP	G	A	Pts	PIM	PP	SH	GW	S	S%	+/-	TF	F%	Min	GP	G	A	Pts	PIM	PP	SH	GW	Min
2008-09	Elgin-Mid. Chiefs	Minor-ON	54	49	54	103	72	....	....	....	....	....	....	....	....	....	15	10	19	29	22	....	....	....	....
	St. Thomas Stars	ON-Jr.B	4	0	0	0	16	....	....	....	....	....	....	....	....	....	....	....	....	....	....	....	....	....	....
2009-10	Oshawa Generals	OHL	65	19	30	49	91	....	....	....	....	....	....	....	....	....	....	....	....	....	....	....	....	....	....
2010-11	Oshawa Generals	OHL	63	25	41	66	57	....	....	....	....	....	....	....	....	....	10	7	5	12	14	....	....	....	....
2011-12	Oshawa Generals	OHL	43	22	27	49	59	....	....	....	....	....	....	....	....	....	6	4	7	11	10	....	....	....	....
	Springfield	AHL	5	1	0	1	2	....	....	....	....	....	....	....	....	....	....	....	....	....	....	....	....	....	....
2012-13	Oshawa Generals	OHL	56	45	37	82	58	....	....	....	....	....	....	....	....	....	9	2	6	8	8	....	....	....	....
	Springfield	AHL	5	3	1	4	0	....	....	....	....	....	....	....	....	....	8	2	3	5	8	....	....	....	....
2013-14	**Columbus**	**NHL**	**72**	**16**	**13**	**29**	**45**	**4**	**0**	**5**	**127**	**12.6**	**6**	**30**	**46.7**	**14:05**	**6**	**3**	**2**	**5**	**4**	**2**	**0**	**0**	**17:15**
2014-15	**Columbus**	**NHL**	**31**	**9**	**8**	**17**	**12**	**2**	**0**	**2**	**83**	**10.8**	**–5**	**306**	**49.4**	**18:16**	....	....	....	....	....	....	....	....	....
	NHL Totals		**103**	**25**	**21**	**46**	**57**	**6**	**0**	**7**	**210**	**11.9**		**336**	**49.1**	**15:20**	**6**	**3**	**2**	**5**	**4**	**2**	**0**	**0**	**17:15**

OHL All-Rookie Team (2010)

• Missed majority of 2014-15 due to hand injury in practice, September 28, 2014 and recurring back injury.

JENSEN, Nicklas

(YEHN-suhn, NIHK-luhs) **VAN**

Left wing. Shoots left. 6'3", 202 lbs. Born, Herning, Denmark, March 6, 1993. Vancouver's 1st choice, 29th overall, in 2011 Entry Draft.

Season	Club	League	GP	G	A	Pts	PIM	PP	SH	GW	S	S%	+/-	TF	F%	Min	GP	G	A	Pts	PIM	PP	SH	GW	Min
2008-09	Herning IK Jr.	Den-Jr.	28	28	15	43	30	....	....	....	....	....	....	....	....	....	....	....	....	....	....	....	....	....	....
	Herning IK II	Den-2	4	3	0	3	0	....	....	....	....	....	....	....	....	....	....	....	....	....	....	....	....	....	....
2009-10	Herning Blue Fox	Denmark	34	12	14	26	28	....	....	....	....	....	....	....	....	....	10	6	4	10	8	....	....	....	....
2010-11	Oshawa Generals	OHL	61	29	29	58	42	....	....	....	....	....	....	....	....	....	10	7	4	11	2	....	....	....	....
2011-12	Oshawa Generals	OHL	57	25	33	58	29	....	....	....	....	....	....	....	....	....	6	1	4	5	0	....	....	....	....
	Chicago Wolves	AHL	6	4	0	4	6	....	....	....	....	....	....	....	....	....	2	2	0	2	0	....	....	....	....
2012-13	AIK Solna	Sweden	50	17	6	23	16	....	....	....	....	....	....	....	....	....	....	....	....	....	....	....	....	....	....
	Chicago Wolves	AHL	20	2	2	4	8	....	....	....	....	....	....	....	....	....	....	....	....	....	....	....	....	....	....
	Vancouver	**NHL**	**2**	**0**	**0**	**0**	**0**	**0**	**0**	**0**	**0**	**0.0**	**–1**	**0**	**0.0**	**13:51**	....	....	....	....	....	....	....	....	....
2013-14	**Vancouver**	**NHL**	**17**	**3**	**3**	**6**	**10**	**0**	**0**	**1**	**30**	**10.0**	**–1**	**1**	**0.0**	**15:38**	....	....	....	....	....	....	....	....	....
	Utica Comets	AHL	54	15	6	21	26	....	....	....	....	....	....	....	....	....	....	....	....	....	....	....	....	....	....
2014-15	**Vancouver**	**NHL**	**5**	**0**	**0**	**0**	**0**	**0**	**0**	**0**	**7**	**0.0**	**–1**	**0**	**0.0**	**9:33**	....	....	....	....	....	....	....	....	....
	Utica Comets	AHL	59	14	14	28	39	....	....	....	....	....	....	....	....	....	18	4	1	5	10	....	....	....	....
	NHL Totals		**24**	**3**	**3**	**6**	**10**	**0**	**0**	**1**	**37**	**8.1**		**1**	**0.0**	**14:13**	....	....	....	....	....	....	....	....	....

JOENSUU, Jesse

(YOH-ehn-soo, JEH-see)

Left wing. Shoots left. 6'4", 213 lbs. Born, Pori, Finland, October 5, 1987. NY Islanders' 2nd choice, 60th overall, in 2006 Entry Draft.

Season	Club	League	GP	G	A	Pts	PIM	PP	SH	GW	S	S%	+/-	TF	F%	Min	GP	G	A	Pts	PIM	PP	SH	GW	Min
2002-03	Assat Pori U18	Fin-U18	26	8	10	18	53	....	....	....	....	....	....	....	....	....	3	1	2	3	0	....	....	....	....
	Assat Pori Jr.	Fin-Jr.	3	0	1	1	2	....	....	....	....	....	....	....	....	....	....	....	....	....	....	....	....	....	....
2003-04	Assat Pori U18	Fin-U18	6	7	2	9	8	....	....	....	....	....	....	....	....	....	....	....	....	....	....	....	....	....	....
	Assat Pori Jr.	Fin-Jr.	28	7	9	16	18	....	....	....	....	....	....	....	....	....	3	0	1	1	2	....	....	....	....
	Assat Pori	Finland	6	0	0	0	0	....	....	....	....	....	....	....	....	....	....	....	....	....	....	....	....	....	....
2004-05	Assat Pori Jr.	Fin-Jr.	17	7	13	20	20	....	....	....	....	....	....	....	....	....	2	1	1	2	2	....	....	....	....
	Assat Pori	Finland	39	1	1	2	4	....	....	....	....	....	....	....	....	....	....	....	....	....	....	....	....	....	....
2005-06	Assat Pori	Finland	51	4	8	12	57	....	....	....	....	....	....	....	....	....	14	0	2	2	12	....	....	....	....
	Suomi U20	Finland-2	2	1	0	1	12	....	....	....	....	....	....	....	....	....	....	....	....	....	....	....	....	....	....
2006-07	Assat Pori Jr.	Fin-Jr.	5	2	1	3	6	....	....	....	....	....	....	....	....	....	....	....	....	....	....	....	....	....	....
	Suomi U20	Finland-2	2	0	2	2	6	....	....	....	....	....	....	....	....	....	....	....	....	....	....	....	....	....	....
	Assat Pori	Finland	52	9	17	26	74	....	....	....	....	....	....	....	....	....	....	....	....	....	....	....	....	....	....
2007-08	Assat Pori	Finland	56	17	18	35	89	....	....	....	....	....	....	....	....	....	....	....	....	....	....	....	....	....	....
	Bridgeport	AHL	1	0	0	0	0	....	....	....	....	....	....	....	....	....	....	....	....	....	....	....	....	....	....
2008-09	**NY Islanders**	**NHL**	**7**	**1**	**2**	**3**	**4**	**0**	**0**	**0**	**9**	**11.1**	**–1**	**0**	**0.0**	**12:06**	....	....	....	....	....	....	....	....	....
	Bridgeport	AHL	71	20	19	39	58	....	....	....	....	....	....	....	....	....	5	2	1	3	4	....	....	....	....
2009-10	**NY Islanders**	**NHL**	**11**	**1**	**0**	**1**	**4**	**0**	**0**	**0**	**13**	**7.7**	**4**	**1**	**0.0**	**11:09**	....	....	....	....	....	....	....	....	....
	Bridgeport	AHL	70	14	34	48	66	....	....	....	....	....	....	....	....	....	5	0	2	2	6	....	....	....	....
2010-11	**NY Islanders**	**NHL**	**42**	**6**	**3**	**9**	**33**	**0**	**0**	**2**	**41**	**14.6**	**–6**	**9**	**55.6**	**11:35**	....	....	....	....	....	....	....	....	....
	Bridgeport	AHL	35	8	16	24	31	....	....	....	....	....	....	....	....	....	....	....	....	....	....	....	....	....	....
2011-12	HV 71 Jonkoping	Sweden	50	13	16	29	58	....	....	....	....	....	....	....	....	....	6	2	1	3	37	....	....	....	....
2012-13	Assat Pori	Finland	24	11	14	25	83	....	....	....	....	....	....	....	....	....	....	....	....	....	....	....	....	....	....
	NY Islanders	**NHL**	**7**	**0**	**2**	**2**	**6**	**0**	**0**	**0**	**15**	**0.0**	**2**	**0**	**0.0**	**10:08**	**1**	**0**	**0**	**0**	**0**	**0**	**0**	**0**	**8:26**
2013-14	**Edmonton**	**NHL**	**42**	**3**	**2**	**5**	**16**	**1**	**0**	**1**	**41**	**7.3**	**–16**	**5**	**0.0**	**9:19**	....	....	....	....	....	....	....	....	....
2014-15	**Edmonton**	**NHL**	**20**	**2**	**2**	**4**	**14**	**0**	**1**	**0**	**18**	**11.1**	**–8**	**0**	**0.0**	**10:38**	....	....	....	....	....	....	....	....	....
	SC Bern	Swiss	15	2	5	7	30	....	....	....	....	....	....	....	....	....	8	2	1	3	8	....	....	....	....
	NHL Totals		**129**	**13**	**11**	**24**	**77**	**1**	**1**	**3**	**137**	**9.5**		**15**	**33.3**	**10:37**	**1**	**0**	**0**	**0**	**0**	**0**	**0**	**0**	**8:26**

Signed as a free agent by **Jonkoping** (Sweden), July 1, 2011. Signed as a free agent by **Assat Pori** (Finland), September 18, 2012. • Missed majority of 2012-13 due to sports hernia surgery and as a healthy reserve. Signed as a free agent by **Edmonton**, July 5, 2013. • Re-assigned to **Bern** (Swiss) by **Edmonton**, December 12, 2014. • Missed majority of 2014-15 as a healthy reserve.

JOHANSEN, Ryan
(joh-HAN-suhn, RIGH-uhn) **CBJ**

Center. Shoots right. 6'3", 223 lbs. Born, Port Moody, BC, July 31, 1992. Columbus' 1st choice, 4th overall, in 2010 Entry Draft.

Season	Club	League	GP	G	A	Pts	PIM	PP	SH	GW	S	S%	+/-	TF	F%	Min	GP	G	A	Pts	PIM	PP	SH	GW	Min
			Regular Season														Playoffs								
2007-08	Van. NE Chiefs	BCMML	41	18	30	48	26																		
2008-09	Penticton Vees	BCHL	47	5	12	17	21										10	4	3	7	2				
2009-10	Portland	WHL	71	25	44	69	53										13	6	12	18	18				
2010-11	Portland	WHL	63	40	52	92	64										21	13	15	*28	6				
2011-12	**Columbus**	**NHL**	**67**	**9**	**12**	**21**	**24**	**3**	**0**	**3**	**99**	**9.1**	**-2**	**215**	**45.1**	**12:44**									
2012-13	Springfield	AHL	40	17	16	33	20										5	0	1	1	2				
	Columbus	**NHL**	**40**	**5**	**7**	**12**	**12**	**0**	**0**	**2**	**84**	**6.0**	**-7**	**529**	**51.4**	**16:05**									
2013-14	**Columbus**	**NHL**	**82**	**33**	**30**	**63**	**43**	**7**	**0**	**5**	**237**	**13.9**	**3**	**1311**	**52.8**	**17:39**	**6**	**2**	**4**	**6**	**4**	**2**	**0**	**0**	**19:03**
2014-15	**Columbus**	**NHL**	**82**	**26**	**45**	**71**	**40**	**7**	**2**	**0**	**202**	**12.9**	**-6**	**1638**	**52.0**	**19:30**									
	NHL Totals		**271**	**73**	**94**	**167**	**119**	**17**	**2**	**10**	**622**	**11.7**		**3693**	**51.8**	**16:46**	**6**	**2**	**4**	**6**	**4**	**2**	**0**	**0**	**19:03**

WHL West First All-Star Team (2011)
Played in NHL All-Star Game (2015)

JOHANSSON, Marcus
(yoh-HAHN-suhn, MAHR-kuhs) **WSH**

Center/Wing. Shoots left. 6'1", 205 lbs. Born, Landskrona, Sweden, October 6, 1990. Washington's 1st choice, 24th overall, in 2009 Entry Draft.

Season	Club	League	GP	G	A	Pts	PIM	PP	SH	GW	S	S%	+/-	TF	F%	Min	GP	G	A	Pts	PIM	PP	SH	GW	Min
2005-06	Malmo U18	Swe-U18	12	0	7	7	0										6	0	4	4	0				
2006-07	Farjestad U18	Swe-U18	12	5	9	14	8										8	7	3	10	2				
2007-08	Farjestad U18	Swe-U18	24	12	26	38	16										8	4	8	12	0				
	Skare BK	Sweden-3	19	2	10	12	10																		
	Farjestad	Sweden															3	0	0	0	0				
2008-09	Farjestad U18	Swe-U18	2	2	0	2	0																		
	Skare BK Karlstad	Sweden-3	5	5	5	10	0																		
	Farjestad	Sweden	45	5	5	10	10										6	0	0	0	0				
2009-10	Farjestad	Sweden	42	10	10	20	10										7	0	5	5	2				
2010-11	**Washington**	**NHL**	**69**	**13**	**14**	**27**	**10**	**2**	**1**	**2**	**102**	**12.7**	**2**	**669**	**40.5**	**14:43**	**9**	**2**	**4**	**6**	**0**	**0**	**0**	**0**	**18:22**
	Hershey Bears	AHL	2	0	0	0	0																		
2011-12	**Washington**	**NHL**	**80**	**14**	**32**	**46**	**8**	**1**	**0**	**3**	**90**	**15.6**	**-5**	**710**	**43.2**	**16:48**	**14**	**1**	**2**	**3**	**0**	**0**	**0**	**0**	**19:35**
2012-13	Bofors	Sweden-2	16	8	10	18	8																		
	Washington	**NHL**	**34**	**6**	**16**	**22**	**4**	**3**	**0**	**1**	**40**	**15.0**	**3**	**87**	**46.0**	**16:35**	**7**	**1**	**1**	**2**	**0**	**0**	**0**	**1**	**16:59**
2013-14	**Washington**	**NHL**	**80**	**8**	**36**	**44**	**4**	**6**	**0**	**1**	**107**	**7.5**	**-21**	**274**	**34.7**	**17:32**									
	Sweden	Olympics	5	0	1	1	4																		
2014-15	**Washington**	**NHL**	**82**	**20**	**27**	**47**	**10**	**3**	**0**	**1**	**138**	**14.5**	**6**	**16**	**43.8**	**16:29**	**14**	**1**	**3**	**4**	**2**	**0**	**0**	**0**	**17:38**
	NHL Totals		**345**	**61**	**125**	**186**	**36**	**15**	**1**	**8**	**477**	**12.8**		**1756**	**41.0**	**16:27**	**44**	**5**	**10**	**15**	**2**	**0**	**0**	**1**	**18:18**

Signed as a free agent by **Karlskoga Bofors** (Sweden-2), October 30, 2012.

JOHNSON, Aaron
(JAWN-suhn, AIR-ruhn)

Defense. Shoots left. 6'2", 211 lbs. Born, Port Hawkesbury, NS, April 30, 1983. Columbus' 4th choice, 85th overall, in 2001 Entry Draft.

Season	Club	League	GP	G	A	Pts	PIM	PP	SH	GW	S	S%	+/-	TF	F%	Min	GP	G	A	Pts	PIM	PP	SH	GW	Min
1998-99	Cape Breton	NSAHA	56	28	42	70	98																		
99-2000	Rimouski Oceanic	QMJHL	63	1	14	15	57										8	0	0	0	0				
2000-01	Rimouski Oceanic	QMJHL	64	12	41	53	128										11	2	4	6	35				
2001-02	Rimouski Oceanic	QMJHL	68	17	49	66	172										7	1	2	3	12				
2002-03	Rimouski Oceanic	QMJHL	25	4	20	24	41																		
	Quebec Remparts	QMJHL	32	6	31	37	41										11	4	4	8	25				
2003-04	**Columbus**	**NHL**	**29**	**2**	**6**	**8**	**32**	**0**	**0**	**1**	**33**	**6.1**	**-2**	**0**	**0.0**	**15:02**									
	Syracuse Crunch	AHL	49	6	15	21	83										7	2	3	5	27				
2004-05	Syracuse Crunch	AHL	77	6	17	23	140																		
2005-06	**Columbus**	**NHL**	**26**	**2**	**6**	**8**	**23**	**1**	**0**	**1**	**28**	**7.1**	**9**	**0**	**0.0**	**14:12**									
	Syracuse Crunch	AHL	49	5	24	29	122										6	1	3	4	19				
2006-07	**Columbus**	**NHL**	**61**	**3**	**7**	**10**	**38**	**0**	**0**	**0**	**52**	**5.8**	**-9**	**0**	**0.0**	**12:44**									
2007-08	**NY Islanders**	**NHL**	**30**	**0**	**2**	**2**	**30**	**0**	**0**	**0**	**16**	**0.0**	**2**	**0**	**0.0**	**13:52**									
	Bridgeport	AHL	2	0	0	0	0																		
2008-09	**Chicago**	**NHL**	**38**	**3**	**5**	**8**	**33**	**0**	**0**	**1**	**27**	**11.1**	**19**	**0**	**0.0**	**14:09**									
	Rockford IceHogs	AHL	2	0	1	1	4																		
2009-10	**Calgary**	**NHL**	**22**	**1**	**2**	**3**	**19**	**0**	**0**	**0**	**13**	**7.7**	**0**	**0**	**0.0**	**12:11**									
	Edmonton	**NHL**	**19**	**3**	**4**	**7**	**16**	**1**	**0**	**0**	**23**	**13.0**	**-6**	**0**	**0.0**	**19:40**									
2010-11	Milwaukee	AHL	72	9	26	35	70										13	1	2	3	16				
2011-12	**Columbus**	**NHL**	**56**	**3**	**13**	**16**	**26**	**1**	**0**	**0**	**63**	**4.8**	**-12**	**0**	**0.0**	**16:30**									
2012-13	Providence Bruins	AHL	2	0	1	1	2																		
	Boston	**NHL**	**10**	**0**	**0**	**0**	**10**	**0**	**0**	**0**	**8**	**0.0**	**0**	**0**	**0.0**	**14:52**									
2013-14	Hartford	AHL	75	4	36	40	70																		
2014-15	Binghamton	AHL	73	6	29	35	76																		
	NHL Totals		**291**	**17**	**45**	**62**	**227**	**3**	**0**	**3**	**263**	**6.5**		**0**	**0.0**	**14:36**									

Signed as a free agent by **NY Islanders**, July 12, 2007. • Missed majority of 2007-08 due to knee injury and as a healthy reserve. Signed as a free agent by **Chicago**, July 15, 2008. Traded to **Calgary** by **Chicago** for Kyle Greentree, October 7, 2009. Traded to **Edmonton** by **Calgary** with Calgary's 3rd round choice (Travis Ewanyk) in 2011 Entry Draft for Steve Staios, March 3, 2010. Signed as a free agent by **Nashville**, August 31, 2010. Signed as a free agent by **Columbus**, July 5, 2011. Signed as a free agent by **Boston**, July 18. 2012. • Missed majority of 2012-13 as a healthy reserve. Signed as a free agent by **NY Rangers**, July 5, 2013. Signed as a free agent by **Ottawa**, July 3, 2014.

JOHNSON, Erik
(JAWN-suhn, AIR-ihk) **COL**

Defense. Shoots right. 6'4", 232 lbs. Born, Bloomington, MN, March 21, 1988. St. Louis' 1st choice, 1st overall, in 2006 Entry Draft.

Season	Club	League	GP	G	A	Pts	PIM	PP	SH	GW	S	S%	+/-	TF	F%	Min	GP	G	A	Pts	PIM	PP	SH	GW	Min
2003-04	Holy Angels	High-MN	31	13	21	34	....																		
2004-05	USNTDP	U-17	26	5	9	14	14																		
	USNTDP	NAHL	31	6	6	12	12																		
2005-06	USNTDP	U-18	36	12	22	34	78																		
	USNTDP	NAHL	11	4	11	15	10																		
2006-07	U. of Minnesota	WCHA	41	4	20	24	50																		
2007-08	**St. Louis**	**NHL**	**69**	**5**	**28**	**33**	**28**	**4**	**0**	**3**	**105**	**4.8**	**-9**	**1**	**0.0**	**18:11**									
	Peoria Rivermen	AHL	1	0	0	0	2																		
2008-09	**St. Louis**	**NHL**	DID NOT PLAY – INJURED																						
2009-10	**St. Louis**	**NHL**	**79**	**10**	**29**	**39**	**79**	**6**	**0**	**2**	**186**	**5.4**	**1**	**0**	**0.0**	**21:27**									
	United States	Olympics	6	1	0	1	4																		
2010-11	**St. Louis**	**NHL**	**55**	**5**	**14**	**19**	**37**	**1**	**1**	**2**	**108**	**4.6**	**-8**	**0**	**0.0**	**22:08**									
	Colorado	**NHL**	**22**	**3**	**7**	**10**	**19**	**2**	**0**	**0**	**53**	**5.7**	**-5**	**0**	**0.0**	**24:33**									
2011-12	**Colorado**	**NHL**	**73**	**4**	**22**	**26**	**26**	**1**	**0**	**1**	**155**	**2.6**	**-7**	**0**	**0.0**	**20:50**									
2012-13	**Colorado**	**NHL**	**31**	**0**	**4**	**4**	**18**	**0**	**0**	**0**	**64**	**0.0**	**-3**	**0**	**0.0**	**20:45**									
2013-14	**Colorado**	**NHL**	**80**	**9**	**30**	**39**	**61**	**2**	**0**	**2**	**157**	**5.7**	**5**	**0**	**0.0**	**23:00**	**7**	**1**	**1**	**2**	**2**	**0**	**0**	**0**	**26:13**
2014-15	**Colorado**	**NHL**	**47**	**12**	**11**	**23**	**33**	**3**	**0**	**2**	**115**	**10.4**	**2**	**0**	**0.0**	**24:25**									
	NHL Totals		**456**	**48**	**145**	**193**	**301**	**19**	**1**	**12**	**943**	**5.1**		**1**	**0.0**	**21:37**	**7**	**1**	**1**	**2**	**2**	**0**	**0**	**0**	**26:13**

WCHA All-Rookie Team (2007)

• Missed 2008-09 due to off-ice knee injury, September 16, 2008. Traded to **Colorado** by **St. Louis** with Jay McClement and St. Louis' 1st round choice (Duncan Siemens) in 2011 Entry Draft for Kevin Shattenkirk, Chris Stewart and Colorado's 2nd round choice (Ty Rattie) in 2011 Entry Draft, February 18, 2011.

JOHNSON, Jack
(JAWN-suhn, JAK) **CBJ**

Defense. Shoots left. 6'1", 238 lbs. Born, Indianapolis, IN, January 13, 1987. Carolina's 1st choice, 3rd overall, in 2005 Entry Draft.

Season	Club	League	GP	G	A	Pts	PIM	PP	SH	GW	S	S%	+/-	TF	F%	Min	GP	G	A	Pts	PIM	PP	SH	GW	Min
2002-03	Shat.-St. Mary's	High-MN	48	15	27	42	....																		
2003-04	USNTDP	U-17	31	12	9	21	78																		
	USNTDP	NAHL	29	3	12	15	93																		
2004-05	USNTDP	U-18	26	5	9	14	86																		
	USNTDP	NAHL	12	7	10	17	57																		
2005-06	U. of Michigan	CCHA	38	10	22	32	*149																		
2006-07	U. of Michigan	CCHA	36	16	23	39	87																		
	Los Angeles	**NHL**	**5**	**0**	**0**	**0**	**18**	**0**	**0**	**0**	**5**	**0.0**	**-5**	**0**	**0.0**	**21:23**									

			Regular Season														Playoffs								
Season	Club	League	GP	G	A	Pts	PIM	PP	SH	GW	S	S%	+/-	TF	F%	Min	GP	G	A	Pts	PIM	PP	SH	GW	Min
2007-08	Los Angeles	NHL	74	3	8	11	76	0	0	0	81	3.7	-19	5	60.0	21:42	....	....	....	....	....	....	....	....	....
2008-09	Los Angeles	NHL	41	6	5	11	46	3	0	0	50	12.0	-18	0	0.0	20:17	....	....	....	....	....	....	....	....	....
2009-10	Los Angeles	NHL	80	8	28	36	48	3	0	0	130	6.2	-15	0	0.0	22:37	6	0	7	7	6	0	0	0	23:42
	United States	Olympics	6	0	1	1	2	....	....	....	....	....	....	....	....	....	....	....	....	....	....	....	....	....	....
2010-11	Los Angeles	NHL	82	5	37	42	44	3	0	0	153	3.3	-21	0	0.0	23:12	6	1	4	5	0	1	0	1	22:48
2011-12	Los Angeles	NHL	61	8	16	24	24	5	0	4	120	6.7	-12	0	0.0	22:31	....	....	....	....	....	....	....	....	....
	Columbus	NHL	21	4	10	14	15	0	0	1	56	7.1	5	0	0.0	27:25	....	....	....	....	....	....	....	....	....
2012-13	Columbus	NHL	44	5	14	19	12	3	0	1	96	5.2	-5	0	0.0	25:58	....	....	....	....	....	....	....	....	....
2013-14	Columbus	NHL	82	5	28	33	48	4	0	0	147	3.4	-7	1	0.0	24:41	6	3	4	7	4	1	0	0	29:21
2014-15	Columbus	NHL	79	8	32	40	44	3	0	1	141	5.7	-13	0	0.0	24:10	....	....	....	....	....	....	....	....	....
	NHL Totals		569	52	178	230	375	24	0	7	979	5.3		6	50.0	23:20	18	4	15	19	10	2	0	1	25:17

CCHA All-Rookie Team (2006) • CCHA First All-Star Team (2007) • NCAA West First All-American Team (2007)

Traded to **Los Angeles** by **Carolina** with Oleg Tverdovsky for Eric Belanger and Tim Gleason, September 29, 2006. Traded to **Columbus** by **Los Angeles** with Los Angeles' 1st round choice (Marko Dano) in 2013 Entry Draft for Jeff Carter, February 23, 2012.

JOHNSON, Justin

(JAWN-suhn, JUHS-tihn)

Right wing. Shoots right. 6'1", 220 lbs. Born, Seattle, WA, May 5, 1981.

1998-99	E. Anchorage	High-AK	20	16	28	44	....	....	....	....	....	....	....	....	....	....	....	....	....	....	....	....	....	....	....
99-2000	E. Anchorage	High-AK	18	20	26	46	....	....	....	....	....	....	....	....	....	....	....	....	....	....	....	....	....	....	....
2000-01	Danville Wings	NAHL	41	17	19	36	65	....	....	....	....	....	....	....	....	....	....	....	....	....	....	....	....	....	....
2001-02	Omaha Lancers	USHL	46	7	8	15	36	....	....	....	....	....	....	....	....	....	10	2	1	3	11	....	....	....	....
2002-03	Alaska Anchorage	WCHA	33	3	5	8	12	....	....	....	....	....	....	....	....	....	....	....	....	....	....	....	....	....	....
2003-04	Alaska Anchorage	WCHA	38	2	10	12	31	....	....	....	....	....	....	....	....	....	....	....	....	....	....	....	....	....	....
2004-05	Alaska Anchorage	WCHA	36	4	4	8	55	....	....	....	....	....	....	....	....	....	....	....	....	....	....	....	....	....	....
2005-06	Alaska Anchorage	WCHA	36	4	3	7	49	....	....	....	....	....	....	....	....	....	....	....	....	....	....	....	....	....	....
	Alaska Aces	ECHL	4	0	1	1	9	....	....	....	....	....	....	....	....	....	....	....	....	....	....	....	....	....	....
2006-07	Alaska Aces	ECHL	4	0	0	0	7	....	....	....	....	....	....	....	....	....	....	....	....	....	....	....	....	....	....
	Idaho Steelheads	ECHL	12	0	1	1	27	....	....	....	....	....	....	....	....	....	....	....	....	....	....	....	....	....	....
2007-08	Utah Grizzlies	ECHL	57	8	3	11	118	....	....	....	....	....	....	....	....	....	6	0	0	0	12	....	....	....	....
2008-09	Utah Grizzlies	ECHL	16	1	0	1	51	....	....	....	....	....	....	....	....	....	....	....	....	....	....	....	....	....	....
	Cincinnati	ECHL	42	12	10	22	208	....	....	....	....	....	....	....	....	....	13	2	4	6	26	....	....	....	....
2009-10	Alaska Aces	ECHL	54	3	4	7	249	....	....	....	....	....	....	....	....	....	....	....	....	....	....	....	....	....	....
2010-11	Manchester	AHL	47	3	5	8	186	....	....	....	....	....	....	....	....	....	4	0	0	0	4	....	....	....	....
2011-12	Manchester	AHL	44	1	2	3	187	....	....	....	....	....	....	....	....	....	1	0	0	0	2	....	....	....	....
2012-13	Manchester	AHL	12	0	0	0	19	....	....	....	....	....	....	....	....	....	....	....	....	....	....	....	....	....	....
2013-14	Bridgeport	AHL	50	1	4	5	195	....	....	....	....	....	....	....	....	....	....	....	....	....	....	....	....	....	....
	NY Islanders	NHL	2	0	0	0	7	0	0	0	0	0.0	-1	0	0.0	6:29	....	....	....	....	....	....	....	....	....
2014-15	Alaska Aces	ECHL	45	3	2	5	147	....	....	....	....	....	....	....	....	....	....	....	....	....	....	....	....	....	....
	NHL Totals		2	0	0	0	7	0	0	0	0	0.0		0	0.0	6:29									

• Missed majority of 2012-13 due to various injuries and as a healthy reserve. Signed as a free agent by **Bridgeport** (AHL), October 3, 2013. Signed as a free agent by **NY Islanders**, March 3, 2014. Signed as a free agent by **Toronto** (AHL), July 3, 2015.

JOHNSON, Tyler

(JAWN-suhn, TIGH-luhr) **T.B.**

Center. Shoots right. 5'9", 182 lbs. Born, Spokane, WA, July 29, 1990.

2007-08	Spokane Chiefs	WHL	69	13	22	35	34	....	....	....	....	....	....	....	....	....	21	5	3	8	24	....	....	....	....
2008-09	Spokane Chiefs	WHL	62	26	35	61	52	....	....	....	....	....	....	....	....	....	12	5	3	8	8	....	....	....	....
2009-10	Spokane Chiefs	WHL	64	36	35	71	32	....	....	....	....	....	....	....	....	....	7	3	5	8	0	....	....	....	....
2010-11	Spokane Chiefs	WHL	71	*53	62	115	48	....	....	....	....	....	....	....	....	....	14	7	7	14	9	....	....	....	....
2011-12	Norfolk Admirals	AHL	75	31	37	68	28	....	....	....	....	....	....	....	....	....	14	6	8	14	6	....	....	....	....
2012-13	Syracuse Crunch	AHL	62	*37	28	65	34	....	....	....	....	....	....	....	....	....	18	10	11	21	18	....	....	....	....
	Tampa Bay	NHL	14	3	3	6	4	0	0	0	11	27.3	3	121	59.5	13:04	....	....	....	....	....	....	....	....	....
2013-14	Tampa Bay	NHL	82	24	26	50	26	5	*5	4	181	13.3	23	1275	48.2	18:47	4	1	1	2	0	0	0	0	20:59
2014-15	Tampa Bay	NHL	77	29	43	72	24	8	0	6	203	14.3	33	1103	48.7	17:14	26	13	10	23	24	2	1	4	18:31
	NHL Totals		173	56	72	128	54	13	5	10	395	14.2		2499	48.9	17:38	30	14	11	25	24	2	1	4	18:50

WHL West First All-Star Team (2011) • AHL All-Rookie Team (2012) • Willie Marshall Award (AHL – Top Goal-scorer) (2013) • Les Cunningham Award (AHL – MVP) (2013) • NHL All-Rookie Team (2014)

Signed as a free agent by **Tampa Bay**, March 7, 2011.

JOKINEN, Jussi

(YOH-kih-nihn, YEW-see) **FLA**

Center. Shoots left. 5'11", 198 lbs. Born, Kalajoki, Finland, April 1, 1983. Dallas' 7th choice, 192nd overall, in 2001 Entry Draft.

99-2000	Karpat Oulu U18	Fin-U18	15	6	25	31	14	....	....	....	....	....	....	....	....	....	6	2	3	5	0	....	....	....	....
	Karpat Oulu Jr.	Fin-Jr.	28	4	7	11	14	....	....	....	....	....	....	....	....	....	....	....	....	....	....	....	....	....	....
2000-01	Karpat Oulu U18	Fin-U18	1	2	1	3	0	....	....	....	....	....	....	....	....	....	....	....	....	....	....	....	....	....	....
	Karpat Oulu Jr.	Fin-Jr.	41	18	31	49	69	....	....	....	....	....	....	....	....	....	6	2	1	3	0	....	....	....	....
2001-02	Karpat Oulu Jr.	Fin-Jr.	2	4	1	5	2	....	....	....	....	....	....	....	....	....	1	1	1	2	0	....	....	....	....
	Karpat Oulu	Finland	54	10	6	16	38	....	....	....	....	....	....	....	....	....	4	1	0	1	0	....	....	....	....
2002-03	Karpat Oulu	Finland	51	14	23	37	10	....	....	....	....	....	....	....	....	....	15	2	1	3	33	....	....	....	....
2003-04	Karpat Oulu	Finland	55	15	23	38	20	....	....	....	....	....	....	....	....	....	15	3	4	7	6	....	....	....	....
2004-05	Karpat Oulu	Finland	56	23	24	47	24	....	....	....	....	....	....	....	....	....	12	3	4	7	2	....	....	....	....
2005-06	Dallas	NHL	81	17	38	55	30	8	0	2	107	15.9	2	23	30.4	13:34	5	2	1	3	0	1	0	0	13:40
	Finland	Olympics	8	1	3	4	2	....	....	....	....	....	....	....	....	....	....	....	....	....	....	....	....	....	....
2006-07	Dallas	NHL	82	14	34	48	18	6	0	1	121	11.6	8	278	52.2	13:54	4	0	1	1	0	0	0	0	13:22
2007-08	Dallas	NHL	52	14	14	28	14	5	0	2	93	15.1	2	295	53.2	12:44	....	....	....	....	....	....	....	....	....
	Tampa Bay	NHL	20	2	12	14	4	1	0	0	38	5.3	-16	46	45.7	18:57	....	....	....	....	....	....	....	....	....
2008-09	Tampa Bay	NHL	46	6	10	16	16	2	0	0	64	9.4	-8	510	52.2	15:38	....	....	....	....	....	....	....	....	....
	Carolina	NHL	25	1	10	11	12	0	0	1	37	2.7	-2	163	58.3	14:43	18	7	4	11	2	2	0	*3	15:35
2009-10	Carolina	NHL	81	30	35	65	36	10	0	6	160	18.8	3	265	51.3	16:49	....	....	....	....	....	....	....	....	....
2010-11	Carolina	NHL	70	19	33	52	24	8	0	1	136	14.0	3	320	52.8	17:13	....	....	....	....	....	....	....	....	....
2011-12	Carolina	NHL	79	12	34	46	54	3	2	3	118	10.2	-2	833	55.1	17:40	....	....	....	....	....	....	....	....	....
2012-13	Karpat Oulu	Finland	21	7	14	21	10	....	....	....	....	....	....	....	....	....	....	....	....	....	....	....	....	....	....
	Carolina	NHL	33	6	5	11	18	2	0	3	61	9.8	-8	283	59.4	15:35	....	....	....	....	....	....	....	....	....
	Pittsburgh	NHL	10	7	4	11	6	1	0	0	13	53.8	3	149	55.0	14:55	8	0	3	3	4	0	0	0	11:01
2013-14	Pittsburgh	NHL	81	21	36	57	18	6	0	4	172	12.2	12	299	53.5	15:42	13	7	3	10	10	1	0	3	15:43
	Finland	Olympics	6	2	3	5	0	....	....	....	....	....	....	....	....	....	....	....	....	....	....	....	....	....	....
2014-15	Florida	NHL	81	8	36	44	34	2	0	0	134	6.0	-2	250	50.4	16:44	....	....	....	....	....	....	....	....	....
	NHL Totals		741	157	301	458	284	54	2	23	1254	12.5		3714	53.6	15:41	48	16	12	28	16	4	0	6	14:28

Traded to **Tampa Bay** by **Dallas** with Jeff Halpern, Mike Smith and Dallas' 4th round choice (later traded to Minnesota, later traded to Edmonton – Edmonton selected Kyle Bigos) in 2009 Entry Draft for Brad Richards and Johan Holmqvist, February 26, 2008. Traded to **Carolina** by **Tampa Bay** for Wade Brookbank, Josef Melichar and future considerations, February 7, 2009. Signed as a free agent by **Oulu** (Finland), September 17, 2012. Traded to **Pittsburgh** by **Carolina** for future considerations, April 3, 2013. Signed as a free agent by **Florida**, July 1, 2014.

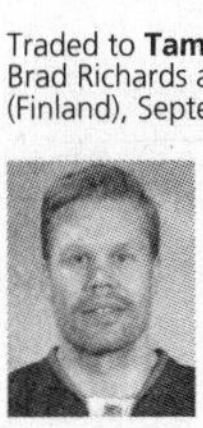

JOKINEN, Olli

(YOH-kih-nihn, OH-lee) **ST.L.**

Center. Shoots left. 6'2", 210 lbs. Born, Kuopio, Finland, December 5, 1978. Los Angeles' 1st choice, 3rd overall, in 1997 Entry Draft.

1994-95	KalPa Kuopio U18	Fin-U18	30	22	28	50	92	....	....	....	....	....	....	....	....	....	....	....	....	....	....	....	....	....	....
	KalPa Kuopio Jr.	Fin-Jr.	6	0	1	1	6	....	....	....	....	....	....	....	....	....	....	....	....	....	....	....	....	....	....
1995-96	KalPa Kuopio U18	Fin-U18	9	9	13	22	4	....	....	....	....	....	....	....	....	....	....	....	....	....	....	....	....	....	....
	KalPa Kuopio Jr.	Fin-Jr.	25	20	14	34	47	....	....	....	....	....	....	....	....	....	7	4	4	8	20	....	....	....	....
	KalPa Kuopio	Finland	15	1	1	2	2	....	....	....	....	....	....	....	....	....	....	....	....	....	....	....	....	....	....
1996-97	HIFK Helsinki Jr.	Fin-Jr.	2	1	0	1	6	....	....	....	....	....	....	....	....	....	....	....	....	....	....	....	....	....	....
	HIFK Helsinki	Finland	50	14	27	41	88	....	....	....	....	....	....	....	....	....	....	....	....	....	....	....	....	....	....
1997-98	Los Angeles	NHL	8	0	0	0	6	0	0	0	12	0.0	-5	....	....	....	....	....	....	....	....	....	....	....	....
	HIFK Helsinki	Finland	30	11	28	39	32	....	....	....	....	....	....	....	....	....	9	7	2	9	2	....	....	....	....
1998-99	Los Angeles	NHL	66	9	12	21	44	3	1	1	87	10.3	-10	779	43.9	14:42	....	....	....	....	....	....	....	....	....
	Springfield	AHL	9	3	6	9	6	....	....	....	....	....	....	....	....	....	....	....	....	....	....	....	....	....	....
99-2000	NY Islanders	NHL	82	11	10	21	80	1	2	3	138	8.0	0	841	46.1	16:15	....	....	....	....	....	....	....	....	....
2000-01	Florida	NHL	78	6	10	16	106	0	0	0	121	5.0	-22	638	42.3	13:23	....	....	....	....	....	....	....	....	....

			Regular Season														Playoffs								
Season	Club	League	GP	G	A	Pts	PIM	PP	SH	GW	S	S%	+/-	TF	F%	Min	GP	G	A	Pts	PIM	PP	SH	GW	Min
2001-02	**Florida**	**NHL**	**80**	**9**	**20**	**29**	**98**	**3**	**1**	**0**	**153**	**5.9**	**–16**	**1222**	**45.2**	**18:05**	....	....	....	....	....	....	....	....	....
	Finland	Olympics	4	2	1	3	0	....	....	....	....	....	....	....	....	....	....	....	....	....	....	....	....	....	....
2002-03	**Florida**	**NHL**	**81**	**36**	**29**	**65**	**79**	**13**	**3**	**6**	**240**	**15.0**	**–17**	**1925**	**46.7**	**22:02**	....	....	....	....	....	....	....	....	....
2003-04	**Florida**	**NHL**	**82**	**26**	**32**	**58**	**81**	**8**	**2**	**8**	**280**	**9.3**	**–16**	**1986**	**47.1**	**22:35**	....	....	....	....	....	....	....	....	....
2004-05	Kloten Flyers	Swiss	8	6	1	7	14	....	....	....	....	....	....	....	....	....	....	....	....	....	....	....	....	....	....
	Sodertalje SK	Sweden	23	13	9	22	52	....	....	....	....	....	....	....	....	....	....	....	....	....	....	....	....	....	....
	HIFK Helsinki	Finland	14	9	8	17	10	....	....	....	....	....	....	....	....	....	5	2	0	2	24	....	....	....	....
2005-06	**Florida**	**NHL**	**82**	**38**	**51**	**89**	**88**	**14**	**1**	**9**	**351**	**10.8**	**14**	**955**	**46.9**	**20:29**	....	....	....	....	....	....	....	....	....
	Finland	Olympics	8	6	2	8	2	....	....	....	....	....	....	....	....	....	....	....	....	....	....	....	....	....	....
2006-07	**Florida**	**NHL**	**82**	**39**	**52**	**91**	**78**	**9**	**1**	**8**	**351**	**11.1**	**18**	**1074**	**44.3**	**20:32**	....	....	....	....	....	....	....	....	....
2007-08	**Florida**	**NHL**	**82**	**34**	**37**	**71**	**67**	**18**	**0**	**5**	**341**	**10.0**	**–19**	**938**	**43.1**	**19:54**	....	....	....	....	....	....	....	....	....
2008-09	**Phoenix**	**NHL**	**57**	**21**	**21**	**42**	**49**	**6**	**2**	**2**	**169**	**12.4**	**–5**	**737**	**42.2**	**18:10**	....	....	....	....	....	....	....	....	....
	Calgary	**NHL**	**19**	**8**	**7**	**15**	**18**	**3**	**0**	**1**	**67**	**11.9**	**–7**	**215**	**47.4**	**21:03**	**6**	**2**	**3**	**5**	**4**	**0**	**0**	**0**	**19:24**
2009-10	**Calgary**	**NHL**	**56**	**11**	**24**	**35**	**53**	**2**	**0**	**2**	**162**	**6.8**	**2**	**739**	**49.3**	**18:30**	....	....	....	....	....	....	....	....	....
	NY Rangers	**NHL**	**26**	**4**	**11**	**15**	**22**	**1**	**0**	**1**	**74**	**5.4**	**1**	**234**	**49.6**	**16:29**	....	....	....	....	....	....	....	....	....
	Finland	Olympics	6	3	1	4	2	....	....	....	....	....	....	....	....	....	....	....	....	....	....	....	....	....	....
2010-11	**Calgary**	**NHL**	**79**	**17**	**37**	**54**	**44**	**5**	**0**	**1**	**208**	**8.2**	**–17**	**1165**	**47.4**	**17:47**	....	....	....	....	....	....	....	....	....
2011-12	**Calgary**	**NHL**	**82**	**23**	**38**	**61**	**54**	**9**	**0**	**5**	**223**	**10.3**	**–12**	**1333**	**46.5**	**18:58**	....	....	....	....	....	....	....	....	....
2012-13	**Winnipeg**	**NHL**	**45**	**7**	**7**	**14**	**14**	**0**	**0**	**0**	**85**	**8.2**	**–19**	**630**	**47.6**	**17:08**	....	....	....	....	....	....	....	....	....
2013-14	**Winnipeg**	**NHL**	**82**	**18**	**25**	**43**	**62**	**2**	**0**	**1**	**171**	**10.5**	**–8**	**1330**	**46.0**	**17:01**	....	....	....	....	....	....	....	....	....
	Finland	Olympics	6	2	2	4	2	....	....	....	....	....	....	....	....	....	....	....	....	....	....	....	....	....	....
2014-15	**Nashville**	**NHL**	**48**	**3**	**3**	**6**	**26**	**0**	**0**	**0**	**83**	**3.6**	**2**	**187**	**39.6**	**13:31**	....	....	....	....	....	....	....	....	....
	Toronto	**NHL**	**6**	**0**	**1**	**1**	**2**	**0**	**0**	**0**	**10**	**0.0**	**1**	**108**	**44.4**	**14:18**	....	....	....	....	....	....	....	....	....
	St. Louis	**NHL**	**8**	**1**	**2**	**3**	**0**	**0**	**0**	**1**	**17**	**5.9**	**3**	**35**	**34.3**	**11:00**	....	....	....	....	....	....	....	....	....
	NHL Totals		**1231**	**321**	**429**	**750**	**1071**	**97**	**13**	**54**	**3343**	**9.6**		**17071**	**45.8**	**18:13**	**6**	**2**	**3**	**5**	**4**	**0**	**0**	**0**	**19:24**

Played in NHL All-Star Game (2003)

Traded to **NY Islanders** by **Los Angeles** with Josh Green, Mathieu Biron and Los Angeles' 1st round choice (Taylor Pyatt) in 1999 Entry Draft for Ziggy Palffy, Bryan Smolinski, Marcel Cousineau and New Jersey's 4th round choice (previously acquired, Los Angeles selected Daniel Johansson) in 1999 Entry Draft, June 20, 1999. Traded to **Florida** by **NY Islanders** with Roberto Luongo for Mark Parrish and Oleg Kvasha, June 24, 2000. Signed as a free agent by **Kloten** (Swiss), September 15, 2004. Signed as a free agent by **Sodertalje** (Sweden), November, 2004. Signed as a free agent by **HIFK Helsinki** (Finland), January 30, 2005.Traded to **Phoenix** by **Florida** for Keith Ballard, Nick Boynton and Ottawa's 2nd round choice (previously acquired, later traded back to Phoenix - Phoenix selected Jared Staal) in 2008 Entry Draft, June 20, 2008. Traded to **Calgary** by **Phoenix** with Phoenix's 3rd round choice (later traded to Florida – Florida selected Josh Birkholz) in 2009 Entry Draft for Matthew Lombardi, Brandon Prust and Calgary's 1st round choice (Brandon Gormley) in 2010 Entry Draft, March 4, 2009. Traded to **NY Rangers** by **Calgary** with Brandon Prust for Chris Higgins and Ales Kotalik, February 2, 2010. Signed as a free agent by **Calgary**, July 1, 2010. Signed as a free agent by **Winnipeg**, July 2, 2012. Signed as a free agent by **Nashville**, July 2, 2014. Traded to **Toronto** by **Nashville** with Brendan Leipsic and Nashville's 1st round choice (later traded to Philadelphia – Philadelphia selected Travis Konecny) in 2015 Entry Draft for Cody Franson and Mike Santorelli, February 15, 2015. Traded to **St. Louis** by **Toronto** for Joakim Lindstrom and future considerations, March 2, 2015.

JOKIPAKKA, Jyrki

(yoh-kih-PA-ka, YUHR-kee) **DAL**

Defense. Shoots left. 6'3", 205 lbs. Born, Tampere, Finland, August 20, 1991. Dallas' 6th choice, 195th overall, in 2011 Entry Draft.

Season	Club	League	GP	G	A	Pts	PIM	PP	SH	GW	S	S%	+/-	TF	F%	Min	GP	G	A	Pts	PIM	PP	SH	GW	Min
2007-08	Ilves Tampere U17	Fin-U17	24	6	15	21	26	....	....	....	....	....	....	....	....	....	2	1	1	2	0	....	....	....	....
2008-09	Ilves Tampere U18	Fin-U18	33	4	7	11	12	....	....	....	....	....	....	....	....	....	....	....	....	....	....	....	....	....	....
	Ilves Tampere Jr.	Fin-Jr.	4	0	0	0	2	....	....	....	....	....	....	....	....	....	....	....	....	....	....	....	....	....	....
2009-10	Ilves Tampere Jr.	Fin-Jr.	38	3	12	15	77	....	....	....	....	....	....	....	....	....	5	1	0	1	2	....	....	....	....
2010-11	Suomi U20	Finland-2	6	0	3	3	2	....	....	....	....	....	....	....	....	....	....	....	....	....	....	....	....	....	....
	Ilves Tampere Jr.	Fin-Jr.	3	0	0	0	6	....	....	....	....	....	....	....	....	....	2	0	0	0	2	....	....	....	....
	LeKi Lempaala	Finland-2	1	0	0	0	0	....	....	....	....	....	....	....	....	....	....	....	....	....	....	....	....	....	....
	Ilves Tampere	Finland	48	1	8	9	18	....	....	....	....	....	....	....	....	....	5	0	0	0	2	....	....	....	....
2011-12	Ilves Tampere Jr.	Fin-Jr.	1	0	1	1	2	....	....	....	....	....	....	....	....	....	....	....	....	....	....	....	....	....	....
	LeKi Lempaala	Finland-2	3	1	0	1	0	....	....	....	....	....	....	....	....	....	....	....	....	....	....	....	....	....	....
	Ilves Tampere	Finland	52	9	8	17	18	....	....	....	....	....	....	....	....	....	....	....	....	....	....	....	....	....	....
	Ilves Tampere	Finland-Q	....	....	....	....	....	....	....	....	....	....	....	....	....	....	5	0	2	2	2	....	....	....	....
2012-13	Ilves Tampere	Finland	59	5	13	18	20	....	....	....	....	....	....	....	....	....	....	....	....	....	....	....	....	....	....
	Ilves Tampere	Finland-Q	....	....	....	....	....	....	....	....	....	....	....	....	....	....	5	0	0	0	0	....	....	....	....
2013-14	Texas Stars	AHL	68	5	16	21	32	....	....	....	....	....	....	....	....	....	21	0	5	5	8	....	....	....	....
2014-15	**Dallas**	**NHL**	**51**	**0**	**10**	**10**	**8**	**0**	**0**	**0**	**40**	**0.0**	**–2**	**0**	**0.0**	**16:31**	....	....	....	....	....	....	....	....	....
	Texas Stars	AHL	19	3	2	5	4	....	....	....	....	....	....	....	....	....	....	....	....	....	....	....	....	....	....
	NHL Totals		**51**	**0**	**10**	**10**	**8**	**0**	**0**	**0**	**40**	**0.0**		**0**	**0.0**	**16:31**	....	....	....	....	....	....	....	....	....

JONES, Blair

(JOHNZ, BLAYR) **VAN**

Center. Shoots right. 6'2", 216 lbs. Born, Central Butte, SK, September 27, 1986. Tampa Bay's 5th choice, 102nd overall, in 2005 Entry Draft.

Season	Club	League	GP	G	A	Pts	PIM	PP	SH	GW	S	S%	+/-	TF	F%	Min	GP	G	A	Pts	PIM	PP	SH	GW	Min
2002-03	Bethune	SBHL	STATISTICS NOT AVAILABLE																						
	Red Deer Rebels	WHL	37	3	4	7	17	....	....	....	....	....	....	....	....	....	10	1	0	1	0	....	....	....	....
2003-04	Red Deer Rebels	WHL	72	9	22	31	55	....	....	....	....	....	....	....	....	....	19	1	5	6	24	....	....	....	....
2004-05	Red Deer Rebels	WHL	39	7	18	25	48	....	....	....	....	....	....	....	....	....	....	....	....	....	....	....	....	....	....
	Moose Jaw	WHL	29	7	18	25	30	....	....	....	....	....	....	....	....	....	5	2	5	7	8	....	....	....	....
2005-06	Moose Jaw	WHL	72	35	50	85	85	....	....	....	....	....	....	....	....	....	22	9	12	21	45	....	....	....	....
2006-07	**Tampa Bay**	**NHL**	**20**	**1**	**2**	**3**	**2**	**0**	**0**	**0**	**6**	**16.7**	**0**	**65**	**41.5**	**5:46**	....	....	....	....	....	....	....	....	....
	Springfield	AHL	45	5	16	21	36	....	....	....	....	....	....	....	....	....	....	....	....	....	....	....	....	....	....
2007-08	**Tampa Bay**	**NHL**	**4**	**0**	**0**	**0**	**0**	**0**	**0**	**0**	**1**	**0.0**	**0**	**8**	**12.5**	**1:55**	....	....	....	....	....	....	....	....	....
	Norfolk Admirals	AHL	75	14	28	42	50	....	....	....	....	....	....	....	....	....	....	....	....	....	....	....	....	....	....
2008-09	Norfolk Admirals	AHL	80	20	34	54	61	....	....	....	....	....	....	....	....	....	....	....	....	....	....	....	....	....	....
2009-10	**Tampa Bay**	**NHL**	**14**	**0**	**0**	**0**	**10**	**0**	**0**	**0**	**26**	**0.0**	**–5**	**28**	**53.6**	**12:50**	....	....	....	....	....	....	....	....	....
	Norfolk Admirals	AHL	63	9	21	30	27	....	....	....	....	....	....	....	....	....	....	....	....	....	....	....	....	....	....
2010-11	**Tampa Bay**	**NHL**	**18**	**1**	**2**	**3**	**2**	**0**	**0**	**0**	**20**	**5.0**	**–2**	**86**	**53.5**	**8:01**	**7**	**0**	**0**	**0**	**2**	**0**	**0**	**0**	**6:24**
	Norfolk Admirals	AHL	56	24	31	55	75	....	....	....	....	....	....	....	....	....	4	1	0	1	8	....	....	....	....
2011-12	**Tampa Bay**	**NHL**	**22**	**2**	**2**	**4**	**10**	**0**	**0**	**0**	**21**	**9.5**	**–3**	**67**	**40.3**	**8:26**	....	....	....	....	....	....	....	....	....
	Norfolk Admirals	AHL	5	2	2	4	16	....	....	....	....	....	....	....	....	....	....	....	....	....	....	....	....	....	....
	Calgary	**NHL**	**21**	**1**	**3**	**4**	**8**	**0**	**0**	**1**	**37**	**2.7**	**2**	**235**	**43.0**	**14:25**	....	....	....	....	....	....	....	....	....
2012-13	Abbotsford Heat	AHL	21	3	4	7	23	....	....	....	....	....	....	....	....	....	....	....	....	....	....	....	....	....	....
	Calgary	**NHL**	**15**	**0**	**1**	**1**	**10**	**0**	**0**	**0**	**22**	**0.0**	**–6**	**109**	**53.2**	**10:45**	....	....	....	....	....	....	....	....	....
2013-14	**Calgary**	**NHL**	**14**	**2**	**0**	**2**	**21**	**0**	**1**	**0**	**14**	**14.3**	**0**	**76**	**47.4**	**11:23**	....	....	....	....	....	....	....	....	....
	Abbotsford Heat	AHL	38	17	21	38	47	....	....	....	....	....	....	....	....	....	4	0	1	1	6	....	....	....	....
2014-15	**Philadelphia**	**NHL**	**4**	**0**	**0**	**0**	**2**	**0**	**0**	**0**	**0**	**0.0**	**–4**	**10**	**50.0**	**6:55**	....	....	....	....	....	....	....	....	....
	Lehigh Valley	AHL	33	9	12	21	46	....	....	....	....	....	....	....	....	....	....	....	....	....	....	....	....	....	....
	NHL Totals		**132**	**7**	**10**	**17**	**65**	**0**	**1**	**1**	**147**	**4.8**		**684**	**46.2**	**9:43**	**7**	**0**	**0**	**0**	**2**	**0**	**0**	**0**	**6:24**

WHL East Second All-Star Team (2006)

Traded to **Calgary** by **Tampa Bay** for Brendan Mikkelson, January 6, 2012. Signed as a free agent by **Philadelphia**, July 3, 2014. • Missed majority of 2014-15 due to lower-body injury vs. Albany (AHL), January 16, 2015. Signed as a free agent by **Vancouver**, July 3, 2015.

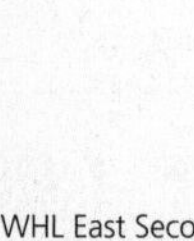

JONES, David

(JOHNZ, DAY-vihd) **CGY**

Right wing. Shoots right. 6'2", 210 lbs. Born, Guelph, ON, August 10, 1984. Colorado's 8th choice, 288th overall, in 2003 Entry Draft.

Season	Club	League	GP	G	A	Pts	PIM	PP	SH	GW	S	S%	+/-	TF	F%	Min	GP	G	A	Pts	PIM	PP	SH	GW	Min
2000-01	Port Coquitlam	PIJHL	40	18	11	29	33	....	....	....	....	....	....	....	....	....	....	....	....	....	....	....	....	....	....
2001-02	Coquitlam	BCHL	59	19	32	51	62	....	....	....	....	....	....	....	....	....	....	....	....	....	....	....	....	....	....
2002-03	Coquitlam	BCHL	35	9	19	28	55	....	....	....	....	....	....	....	....	....	7	2	6	8	8	....	....	....	....
2003-04	Coquitlam	BCHL	53	33	60	93	78	....	....	....	....	....	....	....	....	....	7	3	6	9	4	....	....	....	....
2004-05	Dartmouth	ECAC	34	9	5	14	26	....	....	....	....	....	....	....	....	....	....	....	....	....	....	....	....	....	....
2005-06	Dartmouth	ECAC	33	17	17	34	38	....	....	....	....	....	....	....	....	....	....	....	....	....	....	....	....	....	....
2006-07	Dartmouth	ECAC	33	18	26	*44	22	....	....	....	....	....	....	....	....	....	....	....	....	....	....	....	....	....	....
2007-08	**Colorado**	**NHL**	**27**	**2**	**4**	**6**	**8**	**1**	**0**	**0**	**37**	**5.4**	**–5**	**8**	**37.5**	**11:22**	**10**	**0**	**1**	**1**	**6**	**0**	**0**	**0**	**11:50**
	Lake Erie	AHL	45	14	16	30	16	....	....	....	....	....	....	....	....	....	....	....	....	....	....	....	....	....	....
2008-09	**Colorado**	**NHL**	**40**	**8**	**5**	**13**	**8**	**1**	**0**	**1**	**47**	**17.0**	**–8**	**8**	**50.0**	**12:44**	....	....	....	....	....	....	....	....	....
2009-10	**Colorado**	**NHL**	**23**	**10**	**6**	**16**	**2**	**1**	**2**	**3**	**39**	**25.6**	**1**	**7**	**28.6**	**17:56**	....	....	....	....	....	....	....	....	....
2010-11	**Colorado**	**NHL**	**77**	**27**	**18**	**45**	**28**	**6**	**0**	**4**	**153**	**17.6**	**–2**	**21**	**47.6**	**17:41**	....	....	....	....	....	....	....	....	....
2011-12	**Colorado**	**NHL**	**72**	**20**	**17**	**37**	**32**	**3**	**1**	**5**	**136**	**14.7**	**–8**	**34**	**47.1**	**15:45**	....	....	....	....	....	....	....	....	....
2012-13	**Colorado**	**NHL**	**33**	**3**	**6**	**9**	**6**	**1**	**0**	**2**	**62**	**4.8**	**–11**	**21**	**28.6**	**16:49**	....	....	....	....	....	....	....	....	....

Season	Club	League	GP	G	A	Pts	PIM	PP	SH	GW	S	S%	+/-	TF	F%	Min	GP	G	A	Pts	PIM	PP	SH	GW	Min
			Regular Season														Playoffs								
2013-14	Calgary	NHL	48	9	8	17	10	2	0	1	104	8.7	1	73	52.1	15:28	....	....	....	....	....	....	....	....	....
2014-15	Calgary	NHL	67	14	16	30	18	2	0	1	114	12.3	–3	31	48.4	14:20	11	2	3	5	2	0	0	0	14:01
	NHL Totals		387	93	80	173	112	17	3	17	692	13.4		203	46.3	15:27	21	2	4	6	8	0	0	0	12:59

ECAC Second All-Star Team (2006) • ECAC First All-Star Tearm (2007) • NCAA East First All-American Team (2007)

• Missed majority of 2008-09 due to shoulder injury vs. San Jose, January 27, 2009. • Missed majority of 2009-10 due to knee injury vs. Minnesota, November 28, 2009. Traded to **Calgary** by **Colorado** with Shane O'Brien for Alex Tanguay and Cory Sarich. June 27, 2013.

JONES, Ryan

(JOHNZ, RIGH-uhn)

Right wing. Shoots left. 6'1", 208 lbs. Born, Chatham, ON, June 14, 1984. Minnesota's 5th choice, 111th overall, in 2004 Entry Draft.

Season	Club	League	GP	G	A	Pts	PIM	PP	SH	GW	S	S%	+/-	TF	F%	Min	GP	G	A	Pts	PIM	PP	SH	GW	Min
2002-03	Chatham	ON-Jr.B	38	12	11	23	42	....	....	....	....	....	....	....	....	....	....	....	....	....	....	....	....	....	....
2003-04	Chatham	ON-Jr.B	46	39	30	69	64	....	....	....	....	....	....	....	....	....	17	17	9	26	25	....	....	....	....
2004-05	Miami U.	CCHA	38	8	7	15	79	....	....	....	....	....	....	....	....	....	....	....	....	....	....	....	....	....	....
2005-06	Miami U.	CCHA	39	22	13	35	72	....	....	....	....	....	....	....	....	....	....	....	....	....	....	....	....	....	....
2006-07	Miami U.	CCHA	42	29	19	48	88	....	....	....	....	....	....	....	....	....	....	....	....	....	....	....	....	....	....
2007-08	Miami U.	CCHA	42	31	18	49	83	....	....	....	....	....	....	....	....	....	....	....	....	....	....	....	....	....	....
	Houston Aeros	AHL	4	0	0	0	2	....	....	....	....	....	....	....	....	....	4	1	1	2	2	....	....	....	....
2008-09	**Nashville**	**NHL**	**46**	**7**	**10**	**17**	**22**	**2**	**0**	**1**	**63**	**11.1**	**1**	**10**	**10.0**	**11:26**	....	....	....	....	....	....	....	....	....
	Milwaukee	AHL	25	13	9	22	30	....	....	....	....	....	....	....	....	....	11	4	3	7	10	....	....	....	....
2009-10	**Nashville**	**NHL**	**41**	**7**	**4**	**11**	**18**	**2**	**0**	**0**	**53**	**13.2**	**3**	**1**	**0.0**	**10:43**	....	....	....	....	....	....	....	....	....
	Milwaukee	AHL	15	4	1	5	15	....	....	....	....	....	....	....	....	....	....	....	....	....	....	....	....	....	....
	Edmonton	**NHL**	**8**	**1**	**0**	**1**	**8**	**0**	**0**	**0**	**9**	**11.1**	**–3**	**0**	**0.0**	**10:21**	....	....	....	....	....	....	....	....	....
2010-11	**Edmonton**	**NHL**	**81**	**18**	**7**	**25**	**34**	**2**	**1**	**2**	**126**	**14.3**	**–5**	**29**	**34.5**	**13:50**	....	....	....	....	....	....	....	....	....
2011-12	**Edmonton**	**NHL**	**79**	**17**	**16**	**33**	**42**	**3**	**2**	**2**	**137**	**12.4**	**–7**	**15**	**20.0**	**15:26**	....	....	....	....	....	....	....	....	....
2012-13	**Edmonton**	**NHL**	**27**	**2**	**5**	**7**	**17**	**0**	**0**	**0**	**38**	**5.3**	**0**	**9**	**22.2**	**12:59**	....	....	....	....	....	....	....	....	....
2013-14	**Edmonton**	**NHL**	**52**	**2**	**4**	**6**	**40**	**0**	**0**	**1**	**59**	**3.4**	**0**	**6**	**33.3**	**9:50**	....	....	....	....	....	....	....	....	....
	Oklahoma City	AHL	4	2	0	2	2	....	....	....	....	....	....	....	....	....	....	....	....	....	....	....	....	....	....
2014-15	Utica Comets	AHL	5	0	1	1	9	....	....	....	....	....	....	....	....	....	....	....	....	....	....	....	....	....	....
	Kolner Haie	Germany	30	12	5	17	20	....	....	....	....	....	....	....	....	....	....	....	....	....	....	....	....	....	....
	NHL Totals		**334**	**54**	**46**	**100**	**181**	**9**	**3**	**6**	**485**	**11.1**		**70**	**25.7**	**12:43**	....	....	....	....	....	....	....	....	....

CCHA Second All-Star Team (2006, 2007) • CCHA First All-Star Team (2008) • NCAA West First All-American Team (2008)

Traded to **Nashville** by **Minnesota** with Minnesota's 2nd round choice (Charles-Olivier Roussel) in 2009 Entry Draft for Marek Zidlicky, July 1, 2008. Claimed on waivers by **Edmonton** from **Nashville**, March 3, 2010. Signed to a PTO (professional tryout) contract by **Utica** (AHL), October 9, 2014. Signed as a free agent by **Koln** (Germany), November 17, 2014.

JONES, Seth

(JOHNZ, SEHTH) **NSH**

Defense. Shoots right. 6'4", 205 lbs. Born, Arlington, TX, October 3, 1994. Nashville's 1st choice, 4th overall, in 2013 Entry Draft.

Season	Club	League	GP	G	A	Pts	PIM	PP	SH	GW	S	S%	+/-	TF	F%	Min	GP	G	A	Pts	PIM	PP	SH	GW	Min
2009-10	Dallas Stars	T1EHL	42	5	13	18	20	....	....	....	....	....	....	....	....	....	....	....	....	....	....	....	....	....	....
2010-11	USNTDP	USHL	28	1	13	14	20	....	....	....	....	....	....	....	....	....	....	....	....	....	....	....	....	....	....
	USNTDP	U-17	17	3	7	10	8	....	....	....	....	....	....	....	....	....	....	....	....	....	....	....	....	....	....
	USNTDP	U-18	12	0	7	7	4	....	....	....	....	....	....	....	....	....	....	....	....	....	....	....	....	....	....
2011-12	USNTDP	USHL	20	4	8	12	6	....	....	....	....	....	....	....	....	....	....	....	....	....	....	....	....	....	....
	USNTDP	U-18	32	4	15	19	12	....	....	....	....	....	....	....	....	....	....	....	....	....	....	....	....	....	....
2012-13	Portland	WHL	61	14	42	56	33	....	....	....	....	....	....	....	....	....	21	5	10	15	4	....	....	....	....
2013-14	**Nashville**	**NHL**	**77**	**6**	**19**	**25**	**24**	**2**	**0**	**2**	**100**	**6.0**	**–23**	**0**	**0.0**	**19:37**	....	....	....	....	....	....	....	....	....
2014-15	**Nashville**	**NHL**	**82**	**8**	**19**	**27**	**20**	**2**	**1**	**0**	**123**	**6.5**	**3**	**0**	**0.0**	**19:53**	**6**	**0**	**4**	**4**	**6**	**0**	**0**	**0**	**28:02**
	NHL Totals		**159**	**14**	**38**	**52**	**44**	**4**	**1**	**2**	**223**	**6.3**		**0**	**0.0**	**19:45**	**6**	**0**	**4**	**4**	**6**	**0**	**0**	**0**	**28:02**

WHL West First All-Star Team (2013) • WHL Rookie of the Year (2013) • Canadian Major Junior Top Prospect of the Year (2013)

JOORIS, Josh

(JUHR-his, JAWSH) **CGY**

Right wing. Shoots right. 6'1", 190 lbs. Born, Burlington, ON, July 14, 1990.

Season	Club	League	GP	G	A	Pts	PIM	PP	SH	GW	S	S%	+/-	TF	F%	Min	GP	G	A	Pts	PIM	PP	SH	GW	Min
2008-09	Burlington	ON-Jr.A	42	8	26	34	36	....	....	....	....	....	....	....	....	....	8	1	7	8	12	....	....	....	....
2009-10	Burlington	ON-Jr.A	50	26	*90	*116	42	....	....	....	....	....	....	....	....	....	12	5	10	15	10	....	....	....	....
2010-11	Union College	ECAC	40	9	23	32	18	....	....	....	....	....	....	....	....	....	....	....	....	....	....	....	....	....	....
2011-12	Union College	ECAC	38	8	20	28	30	....	....	....	....	....	....	....	....	....	....	....	....	....	....	....	....	....	....
2012-13	Union College	ECAC	39	12	16	28	46	....	....	....	....	....	....	....	....	....	....	....	....	....	....	....	....	....	....
2013-14	Abbotsford Heat	AHL	73	11	16	27	67	....	....	....	....	....	....	....	....	....	1	0	0	0	2	....	....	....	....
2014-15	**Calgary**	**NHL**	**60**	**12**	**12**	**24**	**16**	**4**	**0**	**4**	**89**	**13.5**	**1**	**567**	**48.7**	**14:30**	**9**	**0**	**0**	**0**	**4**	**0**	**0**	**0**	**11:20**
	Adirondack	AHL	2	0	0	0	0	....	....	....	....	....	....	....	....	....	....	....	....	....	....	....	....	....	....
	NHL Totals		**60**	**12**	**12**	**24**	**16**	**4**	**0**	**4**	**89**	**13.5**		**567**	**48.7**	**14:30**	**9**	**0**	**0**	**0**	**4**	**0**	**0**	**0**	**11:20**

Signed as a free agent by **Calgary**, July 30, 2013.

JORDAN, Michal

(yohr-DAHN, MIH-kahl) **CAR**

Defense. Shoots left. 6'1", 195 lbs. Born, Zlin, Czech., July 17, 1990. Carolina's 3rd choice, 105th overall, in 2008 Entry Draft.

Season	Club	League	GP	G	A	Pts	PIM	PP	SH	GW	S	S%	+/-	TF	F%	Min	GP	G	A	Pts	PIM	PP	SH	GW	Min
2005-06	HC Zlin U17	CzR-U17	43	7	15	22	12	....	....	....	....	....	....	....	....	....	5	0	1	1	2	....	....	....	....
2006-07	HC Zlin U17	CzR-U17	1	0	0	0	4	....	....	....	....	....	....	....	....	....	....	....	....	....	....	....	....	....	....
	HC Zlin Jr.	CzRep-Jr.	40	7	11	18	20	....	....	....	....	....	....	....	....	....	12	1	5	6	12	....	....	....	....
2007-08	Windsor Spitfires	OHL	22	1	5	6	12	....	....	....	....	....	....	....	....	....	....	....	....	....	....	....	....	....	....
	Plymouth Whalers	OHL	39	5	17	22	32	....	....	....	....	....	....	....	....	....	4	0	3	3	6	....	....	....	....
2008-09	Plymouth Whalers	OHL	58	12	30	42	39	....	....	....	....	....	....	....	....	....	11	0	3	3	12	....	....	....	....
2009-10	Plymouth Whalers	OHL	41	13	19	32	18	....	....	....	....	....	....	....	....	....	9	0	5	5	8	....	....	....	....
2010-11	Charlotte	AHL	67	4	14	18	35	....	....	....	....	....	....	....	....	....	16	0	2	2	0	....	....	....	....
2011-12	Charlotte	AHL	76	4	18	22	43	....	....	....	....	....	....	....	....	....	....	....	....	....	....	....	....	....	....
2012-13	Charlotte	AHL	54	6	10	16	22	....	....	....	....	....	....	....	....	....	1	0	1	1	0	....	....	....	....
	Carolina	**NHL**	**5**	**0**	**0**	**0**	**2**	**0**	**0**	**0**	**2**	**0.0**	**–2**	**0**	**0.0**	**10:41**	....	....	....	....	....	....	....	....	....
2013-14	Charlotte	AHL	70	4	21	25	20	....	....	....	....	....	....	....	....	....	....	....	....	....	....	....	....	....	....
2014-15	**Carolina**	**NHL**	**38**	**2**	**4**	**6**	**4**	**2**	**0**	**0**	**44**	**4.5**	**–7**	**0**	**0.0**	**15:57**	....	....	....	....	....	....	....	....	....
	Charlotte	AHL	30	2	9	11	4	....	....	....	....	....	....	....	....	....	....	....	....	....	....	....	....	....	....
	NHL Totals		**43**	**2**	**4**	**6**	**6**	**2**	**0**	**0**	**46**	**4.3**		**0**	**0.0**	**15:20**	....	....	....	....	....	....	....	....	....

JOSEFSON, Jacob

(JOH-sehf-suhn, YA-kuhb) **N.J.**

Center. Shoots left. 6', 190 lbs. Born, Stockholm, Sweden, March 2, 1991. New Jersey's 1st choice, 20th overall, in 2009 Entry Draft.

Season	Club	League	GP	G	A	Pts	PIM	PP	SH	GW	S	S%	+/-	TF	F%	Min	GP	G	A	Pts	PIM	PP	SH	GW	Min
2005-06	Djurgarden U18	Swe-U18	5	1	1	2	0	....	....	....	....	....	....	....	....	....	....	....	....	....	....	....	....	....	....
2006-07	Djurgarden U18	Swe-U18	25	14	17	31	22	....	....	....	....	....	....	....	....	....	3	0	0	0	0	....	....	....	....
2007-08	Djurgarden U18	Swe-U18	4	1	2	3	12	....	....	....	....	....	....	....	....	....	6	0	6	6	4	....	....	....	....
	Djurgarden Jr.	Swe-Jr.	34	14	17	31	22	....	....	....	....	....	....	....	....	....	7	2	3	5	8	....	....	....	....
	Djurgarden	Sweden	1	0	0	0	0	....	....	....	....	....	....	....	....	....	....	....	....	....	....	....	....	....	....
2008-09	Djurgarden Jr.	Swe-Jr.	5	1	2	3	8	....	....	....	....	....	....	....	....	....	6	1	3	4	4	....	....	....	....
	Djurgarden	Sweden	50	5	11	16	14	....	....	....	....	....	....	....	....	....	....	....	....	....	....	....	....	....	....
	Djurgarden U18	Swe-U18	....	....	....	....	....	....	....	....	....	....	....	....	....	....	1	0	0	0	0	....	....	....	....
2009-10	Djurgarden	Sweden	43	8	12	20	20	....	....	....	....	....	....	....	....	....	14	3	2	5	4	....	....	....	....
2010-11	**New Jersey**	**NHL**	**28**	**3**	**7**	**10**	**6**	**0**	**0**	**1**	**31**	**9.7**	**5**	**202**	**47.0**	**13:14**	....	....	....	....	....	....	....	....	....
	Albany Devils	AHL	18	3	9	12	4	....	....	....	....	....	....	....	....	....	....	....	....	....	....	....	....	....	....
2011-12	**New Jersey**	**NHL**	**41**	**2**	**7**	**9**	**6**	**0**	**0**	**0**	**37**	**5.4**	**10**	**354**	**51.1**	**12:06**	**6**	**0**	**1**	**1**	**0**	**0**	**0**	**0**	**13:41**
	Albany Devils	AHL	4	2	1	3	2	....	....	....	....	....	....	....	....	....	....	....	....	....	....	....	....	....	....
2012-13	Albany Devils	AHL	38	10	15	25	29	....	....	....	....	....	....	....	....	....	....	....	....	....	....	....	....	....	....
	New Jersey	**NHL**	**22**	**1**	**2**	**3**	**2**	**0**	**0**	**0**	**20**	**5.0**	**–10**	**236**	**48.3**	**12:59**	....	....	....	....	....	....	....	....	....
2013-14	**New Jersey**	**NHL**	**27**	**1**	**2**	**3**	**4**	**0**	**1**	**0**	**21**	**4.8**	**0**	**168**	**49.4**	**10:08**	....	....	....	....	....	....	....	....	....
2014-15	**New Jersey**	**NHL**	**62**	**6**	**5**	**11**	**24**	**0**	**3**	**1**	**61**	**9.8**	**0**	**586**	**49.3**	**12:26**	....	....	....	....	....	....	....	....	....
	NHL Totals		**180**	**13**	**23**	**36**	**42**	**0**	**4**	**2**	**170**	**7.6**		**1546**	**49.3**	**12:12**	**6**	**0**	**1**	**1**	**0**	**0**	**0**	**0**	**13:41**

• Missed majority of 2013-14 as a healthy reserve.

JOSI, Roman (YOH-see, ROH-man) NSH

Defense. Shoots left. 6'1", 192 lbs. Born, Bern, Switzerland, June 1, 1990. Nashville's 3rd choice, 38th overall, in 2008 Entry Draft.

			Regular Season														Playoffs								
Season	Club	League	GP	G	A	Pts	PIM	PP	SH	GW	S	S%	+/-	TF	F%	Min	GP	G	A	Pts	PIM	PP	SH	GW	Min
2005-06	SC Bern Future Jr.	Swiss-Jr.	5	0	0	0	0																		
2006-07	SC Bern Future Jr.	Swiss-Jr.	33	14	16	30	28										14	1	3	4	2				
	Switzerland U20	Swiss-2	5	1	1	2	2																		
	SC Bern	Swiss	3	0	1	1	0																		
2007-08	Switzerland U20	Swiss-2	2	0	1	1	0																		
	HC Neuchatel	Swiss-2	3	2	0	2	4																		
	SC Bern	Swiss	35	2	6	8	10										6	0	0	0	0				
2008-09	SC Bern	Swiss	42	7	17	24	16										6	0	0	0	2				
2009-10	SC Bern	Swiss	26	9	12	21	12										15	6	7	13	8				
2010-11	Milwaukee	AHL	69	6	34	40	22										13	1	6	7	8				
2011-12	**Nashville**	**NHL**	52	5	11	16	14	1	0	0	64	7.8	1	0	0.0	18:23	10	0	0	0	10	0	0	0	18:48
	Milwaukee	AHL	5	1	3	4	0																		
2012-13	SC Bern	Swiss	26	6	11	17	14																		
	Nashville	**NHL**	48	5	13	18	8	1	0	1	96	5.2	–7	0	0.0	23:32									
2013-14	**Nashville**	**NHL**	72	13	27	40	18	3	0	2	168	7.7	–2	0	0.0	26:25									
	Switzerland	Olympics	4	0	0	0	0																		
2014-15	**Nashville**	**NHL**	81	15	40	55	26	3	0	4	201	7.5	15	1	0.0	26:28	6	1	0	1	0	0	0	0	31:37
	NHL Totals		253	38	91	129	66	8	0	7	529	7.2		1	0.0	24:14	16	1	0	1	10	0	0	0	23:36

Signed as a free agent by **Bern** (Swiss), September 20, 2012.

JOUDREY, Andrew (JOO-dree, AN-droo)

Center. Shoots left. 5'10", 185 lbs. Born, Halifax, NS, July 15, 1984. Washington's 5th choice, 249th overall, in 2003 Entry Draft.

Season	Club	League	GP	G	A	Pts	PIM	PP	SH	GW	S	S%	+/-	TF	F%	Min	GP	G	A	Pts	PIM	PP	SH	GW	Min
2000-01	Dartmouth	NSMHL	82	51	70	121	....																		
2001-02	Notre Dame	SJHL	57	24	38	62	14																		
2002-03	Notre Dame	SJHL	53	27	51	78	16																		
2003-04	U. of Wisconsin	WCHA	42	7	15	22	2																		
2004-05	U. of Wisconsin	WCHA	41	7	17	24	18																		
2005-06	U. of Wisconsin	WCHA	37	8	10	18	14																		
2006-07	U. of Wisconsin	WCHA	40	9	20	29	18																		
	Hershey Bears	AHL	5	2	1	3	0										10	0	2	2	0				
2007-08	Hershey Bears	AHL	61	11	14	25	22										5	0	1	1	0				
2008-09	Hershey Bears	AHL	69	7	20	27	22										22	1	3	4	6				
2009-10	Hershey Bears	AHL	78	15	19	34	11										21	1	2	3	4				
2010-11	Hershey Bears	AHL	66	7	7	14	20										6	0	1	1	0				
2011-12	**Columbus**	**NHL**	1	0	0	0	0	0	0	0	1	0.0	0	1	100.0	9:16									
	Springfield	AHL	73	14	11	25	18																		
2012-13	Springfield	AHL	73	9	13	22	26										6	1	2	3	2				
2013-14	Springfield	AHL	67	12	20	32	38										2	1	1	2	0				
2014-15	Adler Mannheim	Germany	52	11	18	29	22										15	5	3	8	18				
	NHL Totals		1	0	0	0	0	0	0	0	1	0.0		1	100.0	9:16									

Signed as a free agent by **Columbus**, July 1, 2011. Signed as a free agent by **Mannheim** (Germany), June 19, 2014.

JUNLAND, Jonas (YUHN-land, YOH-nuhs) ST.L.

Defense. Shoots left. 6'2", 200 lbs. Born, Linkoping, Sweden, November 15, 1987. St. Louis' 4th choice, 64th overall, in 2006 Entry Draft.

Season	Club	League	GP	G	A	Pts	PIM	PP	SH	GW	S	S%	+/-	TF	F%	Min	GP	G	A	Pts	PIM	PP	SH	GW	Min
2002-03	Linkoping U18	Swe-U18	7	0	0	0	6																		
2003-04	Linkoping U18	Swe-U18	4	0	0	0	4																		
	Linkopings HC Jr.	Swe-Jr.	19	1	0	1	12																		
2004-05	Linkoping U18	Swe-U18	11	6	5	11	35																		
	Linkopings HC Jr.	Swe-Jr.	32	3	5	8	96																		
2005-06	Linkopings HC Jr.	Swe-Jr.	32	17	23	40	44																		
	Linkoping U18	Swe-U18	1	5	0	5	2																		
	Linkopings HC	Sweden	4	0	0	0	0																		
2006-07	Linkopings HC Jr.	Swe-Jr.	9	6	7	13	26																		
	IK Oskarshamn	Sweden-2	4	0	3	3	4																		
	Linkopings HC	Sweden	41	1	4	5	22										15	0	5	5	20				
2007-08	Linkopings HC	Sweden	52	3	17	20	42										16	4	3	7	18				
2008-09	**St. Louis**	**NHL**	1	0	0	0	2	0	0	0	0	0.0	0	0	0.0	12:28									
	Peoria Rivermen	AHL	70	13	18	31	52										5	0	1	1	6				
2009-10	**St. Louis**	**NHL**	3	0	2	2	0	0	0	0	7	0.0	–3	0	0.0	17:11									
	Peoria Rivermen	AHL	74	14	30	44	49																		
2010-11	Farjestad	Sweden	41	5	17	22	18										14	3	3	6	12				
2011-12	Barys Astana	KHL	46	4	11	15	30										7	1	1	2	6				
2012-13	Barys Astana	KHL	3	0	0	0	10																		
	Pelicans Lahti	Finland	6	1	1	2	6																		
2013-14	Linkopings HC	Sweden	44	6	7	13	46										10	2	2	4	8				
2014-15	Linkopings HC	Sweden	55	9	22	31	32										11	2	7	9	4				
	NHL Totals		4	0	2	2	2	0	0	0	7	0.0		0	0.0	16:00									

Signed as a free agent by **Farjestad** (Sweden), May 1, 2010. Signed as a free agent by **Astana** (KHL), April 27, 2011. Signed as a free agent by **Lahti** (Finland), October 4, 2012. Signed as a free agent by **Linkoping** (Sweden), April 24, 2013

JURCO, Tomas (YUHR-koh, TAW-mahsh) DET

Right wing. Shoots left. 6'1", 203 lbs. Born, Kosice, Czech., December 28, 1992. Detroit's 1st choice, 35th overall, in 2011 Entry Draft.

Season	Club	League	GP	G	A	Pts	PIM	PP	SH	GW	S	S%	+/-	TF	F%	Min	GP	G	A	Pts	PIM	PP	SH	GW	Min
2007-08	HC Kosice U18	Svk-U18	57	28	24	52	30																		
2008-09	HC Kosice U18	Svk-U18	5	8	5	13	2																		
	HC Kosice Jr.	Slovak-Jr.	48	19	30	49	20										3	5	0	5	0				
2009-10	Saint John	QMJHL	64	26	25	51	24										21	7	10	17	8				
2010-11	Saint John	QMJHL	60	31	25	56	17										19	6	12	18	8				
2011-12	Saint John	QMJHL	48	30	38	68	37										16	13	16	29	12				
2012-13	Grand Rapids	AHL	74	14	14	28	22										24	8	6	14	21				
2013-14	**Detroit**	**NHL**	36	8	7	15	14	2	0	0	77	10.4	0	0	0.0	13:28	3	0	0	0	0	0	0	0	12:52
	Grand Rapids	AHL	32	13	19	32	14										8	5	2	7	11				
	Slovakia	Olympics	4	1	0	1	2																		
2014-15	**Detroit**	**NHL**	63	3	15	18	14	1	0	0	92	3.3	6	2	0.0	11:31	7	1	1	2	2	1	0	0	8:32
	NHL Totals		99	11	22	33	28	3	0	0	169	6.5		2	0.0	12:13	10	1	1	2	2	1	0	0	9:50

KADRI, Nazem (KAH-dree, NA-zihm) TOR

Center. Shoots left. 6', 188 lbs. Born, London, ON, October 6, 1990. Toronto's 1st choice, 7th overall, in 2009 Entry Draft.

Season	Club	League	GP	G	A	Pts	PIM	PP	SH	GW	S	S%	+/-	TF	F%	Min	GP	G	A	Pts	PIM	PP	SH	GW	Min
2005-06	Lon. Jr. Knights	Minor-ON	62	49	43	92	82																		
2006-07	Kitchener Rangers	OHL	62	7	15	22	30										9	0	2	2	4				
2007-08	Kitchener Rangers	OHL	68	25	40	65	57										20	9	17	26	26				
2008-09	London Knights	OHL	56	25	53	78	31										14	9	12	21	22				
2009-10	London Knights	OHL	56	35	58	93	105										12	9	18	27	26				
	Toronto	**NHL**	1	0	0	0	0	0	0	0	0	0.0	–1	13	15.4	17:26									
2010-11	**Toronto**	**NHL**	29	3	9	12	8	0	0	0	51	5.9	–3	121	40.5	15:47									
	Toronto Marlies	AHL	44	17	24	41	62																		
2011-12	**Toronto**	**NHL**	21	5	2	7	8	1	0	1	28	17.9	2	15	26.7	14:10									
	Toronto Marlies	AHL	48	18	22	40	39										11	3	7	10	6				
2012-13	Toronto Marlies	AHL	27	8	18	26	26																		
	Toronto	**NHL**	48	18	26	44	23	5	0	1	107	16.8	15	565	44.3	16:03	7	1	3	4	10	0	0	0	13:35

Season	Club	League	GP	G	A	Pts	PIM	PP	SH	GW	S	S%	+/-	TF	F%	Min	GP	G	A	Pts	PIM	PP	SH	GW	Min
					Regular Season															Playoffs					
2013-14	**Toronto**	**NHL**	**78**	**20**	**30**	**50**	**67**	**7**	**0**	**2**	**148**	**13.5**	**−11**	**1127**	**45.3**	**17:23**	....	....	....	....	....	....	....	....	....
2014-15	**Toronto**	**NHL**	**73**	**18**	**21**	**39**	**28**	**3**	**1**	**1**	**176**	**10.2**	**−7**	**1144**	**46.2**	**17:36**	....	....	....	....	....	....	....	....	....
	NHL Totals		**250**	**64**	**88**	**152**	**134**	**16**	**1**	**5**	**510**	**12.5**		**2985**	**45.0**	**16:44**	**7**	**1**	**3**	**4**	**10**	**0**	**0**	**0**	**13:35**

OHL Second All-Star Team (2010)

KALETA, Patrick

(ka-LEH-tuh, PAT-rihk)

Right wing. Shoots right. 6'1", 198 lbs. Born, Buffalo, NY, June 8, 1986. Buffalo's 5th choice, 176th overall, in 2004 Entry Draft.

Season	Club	League	GP	G	A	Pts	PIM	PP	SH	GW	S	S%	+/-	TF	F%	Min	GP	G	A	Pts	PIM	PP	SH	GW	Min
2002-03	Peterborough	OHL	67	7	9	16	67	....	....	....	....	....	....	....	....	....	7	0	0	0	6	....	....	....	....
2003-04	Peterborough	OHL	67	14	14	28	124	....	....	....	....	....	....	....	....	....	....	....	....	....	....	....	....	....	....
2004-05	Peterborough	OHL	62	24	28	52	146	....	....	....	....	....	....	....	....	....	14	3	3	6	30	....	....	....	....
2005-06	Peterborough	OHL	68	16	35	51	121	....	....	....	....	....	....	....	....	....	19	8	10	18	43	....	....	....	....
2006-07	**Buffalo**	**NHL**	**7**	**0**	**2**	**2**	**21**	**0**	**0**	**0**	**6**	**0.0**	**3**	**0**	**0.0**	**6:49**	....	....	....	....	....	....	....	....	....
	Rochester	AHL	58	5	10	15	133	....	....	....	....	....	....	....	....	....	5	0	0	0	12	....	....	....	....
2007-08	**Buffalo**	**NHL**	**40**	**3**	**2**	**5**	**41**	**0**	**0**	**0**	**26**	**11.5**	**1**	**6**	**16.7**	**6:19**	....	....	....	....	....	....	....	....	....
	Rochester	AHL	29	1	3	4	109	....	....	....	....	....	....	....	....	....	....	....	....	....	....	....	....	....	....
2008-09	**Buffalo**	**NHL**	**51**	**4**	**5**	**9**	**89**	**0**	**0**	**0**	**35**	**11.4**	**1**	**5**	**20.0**	**8:55**	....	....	....	....	....	....	....	....	....
2009-10	**Buffalo**	**NHL**	**55**	**10**	**5**	**15**	**89**	**0**	**2**	**4**	**64**	**15.6**	**2**	**2**	**0.0**	**10:09**	**6**	**1**	**1**	**2**	**22**	**0**	**0**	**0**	**10:04**
2010-11	**Buffalo**	**NHL**	**51**	**4**	**5**	**9**	**78**	**0**	**1**	**0**	**65**	**6.2**	**−4**	**12**	**41.7**	**10:11**	**6**	**1**	**2**	**3**	**6**	**0**	**0**	**1**	**10:58**
2011-12	**Buffalo**	**NHL**	**63**	**5**	**5**	**10**	**116**	**0**	**0**	**1**	**69**	**7.2**	**−5**	**19**	**52.6**	**13:09**	....	....	....	....	....	....	....	....	....
2012-13	**Buffalo**	**NHL**	**34**	**1**	**0**	**1**	**67**	**0**	**0**	**0**	**34**	**2.9**	**−4**	**11**	**45.5**	**10:48**	....	....	....	....	....	....	....	....	....
2013-14	**Buffalo**	**NHL**	**5**	**0**	**0**	**0**	**5**	**0**	**0**	**0**	**0**	**0.0**	**−1**	**1**	**100.0**	**8:21**	....	....	....	....	....	....	....	....	....
	Rochester	AHL	7	1	3	4	2	....	....	....	....	....	....	....	....	....	....	....	....	....	....	....	....	....	....
2014-15	**Buffalo**	**NHL**	**42**	**0**	**3**	**3**	**36**	**0**	**0**	**0**	**25**	**0.0**	**−11**	**8**	**37.5**	**8:52**	....	....	....	....	....	....	....	....	....
	NHL Totals		**348**	**27**	**27**	**54**	**542**	**0**	**3**	**5**	**324**	**8.3**		**64**	**40.6**	**9:54**	**12**	**2**	**3**	**5**	**28**	**0**	**0**	**1**	**10:31**

• Missed majority of 2013-14 due to leg injury vs. Lake Erie (AHL), November 29, 2013.

KAMPFER, Steven

(KAMP-fuhr, STEE-vehn) **FLA**

Defense. Shoots right. 5'11", 197 lbs. Born, Ann Arbor, MI, September 24, 1988. Anaheim's 5th choice, 93rd overall, in 2007 Entry Draft.

Season	Club	League	GP	G	A	Pts	PIM	PP	SH	GW	S	S%	+/-	TF	F%	Min	GP	G	A	Pts	PIM	PP	SH	GW	Min
2004-05	Sioux City	USHL	47	6	13	19	91	....	....	....	....	....	....	....	....	....	13	2	5	7	12	....	....	....	....
2005-06	Sioux City	USHL	56	6	10	16	99	....	....	....	....	....	....	....	....	....	....	....	....	....	....	....	....	....	....
2006-07	U. of Michigan	CCHA	35	1	3	4	24	....	....	....	....	....	....	....	....	....	....	....	....	....	....	....	....	....	....
2007-08	U. of Michigan	CCHA	42	2	15	17	36	....	....	....	....	....	....	....	....	....	....	....	....	....	....	....	....	....	....
2008-09	U. of Michigan	CCHA	25	1	12	13	24	....	....	....	....	....	....	....	....	....	....	....	....	....	....	....	....	....	....
2009-10	U. of Michigan	CCHA	45	3	23	26	50	....	....	....	....	....	....	....	....	....	....	....	....	....	....	....	....	....	....
	Providence Bruins	AHL	6	1	2	3	4	....	....	....	....	....	....	....	....	....	....	....	....	....	....	....	....	....	....
2010-11	**Boston**	**NHL**	**38**	**5**	**5**	**10**	**12**	**0**	**0**	**1**	**57**	**8.8**	**9**	**0**	**0.0**	**17:44**	....	....	....	....	....	....	....	....	....
	Providence Bruins	AHL	22	3	13	16	12	....	....	....	....	....	....	....	....	....	....	....	....	....	....	....	....	....	....
2011-12	**Boston**	**NHL**	**10**	**0**	**2**	**2**	**4**	**0**	**0**	**0**	**8**	**0.0**	**6**	**0**	**0.0**	**10:30**	....	....	....	....	....	....	....	....	....
	Providence Bruins	AHL	12	1	3	4	8	....	....	....	....	....	....	....	....	....	....	....	....	....	....	....	....	....	....
	Minnesota	**NHL**	**13**	**2**	**1**	**3**	**2**	**0**	**0**	**0**	**12**	**16.7**	**−7**	**0**	**0.0**	**18:17**	....	....	....	....	....	....	....	....	....
	Houston Aeros	AHL	12	1	3	4	8	....	....	....	....	....	....	....	....	....	4	0	0	0	2	....	....	....	....
2012-13	Houston Aeros	AHL	55	4	17	21	28	....	....	....	....	....	....	....	....	....	5	1	1	2	9	....	....	....	....
2013-14	Iowa Wild	AHL	69	6	20	26	48	....	....	....	....	....	....	....	....	....	....	....	....	....	....	....	....	....	....
2014-15	**Florida**	**NHL**	**25**	**2**	**2**	**4**	**12**	**0**	**0**	**1**	**28**	**7.1**	**−4**	**0**	**0.0**	**17:12**	....	....	....	....	....	....	....	....	....
	San Antonio	AHL	42	8	11	19	49	....	....	....	....	....	....	....	....	....	....	....	....	....	....	....	....	....	....
	NHL Totals		**86**	**9**	**10**	**19**	**30**	**0**	**0**	**2**	**105**	**8.6**		**0**	**0.0**	**16:49**	....	....	....	....	....	....	....	....	....

Traded to **Boston** by **Anaheim** for Boston's 4th round choice (later traded to Carolina - Carolina selected Justin Shugg) in 2010 Entry Draft, March 2, 2010. Traded to **Minnesota** by **Boston** for Greg Zanon, February 27, 2012. Signed as a free agent by **NY Rangers**, July 1, 2014. Traded to **Florida** by **NY Rangers** with Andrew Yogan for Joey Crabb, October 6, 2014.

KANE, Evander

(KAYN, ee-VAN-duhr) **BUF**

Left wing. Shoots left. 6'2", 195 lbs. Born, Vancouver, BC, August 2, 1991. Atlanta's 1st choice, 4th overall, in 2009 Entry Draft.

Season	Club	League	GP	G	A	Pts	PIM	PP	SH	GW	S	S%	+/-	TF	F%	Min	GP	G	A	Pts	PIM	PP	SH	GW	Min
2006-07	Greater Van.	BCMML	30	22	32	54	150	....	....	....	....	....	....	....	....	....	....	....	....	....	....	....	....	....	....
	Vancouver Giants	WHL	8	1	0	1	11	....	....	....	....	....	....	....	....	....	5	0	0	0	0	....	....	....	....
2007-08	Vancouver Giants	WHL	65	24	17	41	66	....	....	....	....	....	....	....	....	....	10	1	2	3	8	....	....	....	....
2008-09	Vancouver Giants	WHL	61	48	48	96	89	....	....	....	....	....	....	....	....	....	17	7	8	15	45	....	....	....	....
2009-10	**Atlanta**	**NHL**	**66**	**14**	**12**	**26**	**62**	**0**	**1**	**3**	**127**	**11.0**	**2**	**26**	**53.9**	**14:00**	....	....	....	....	....	....	....	....	....
2010-11	**Atlanta**	**NHL**	**73**	**19**	**24**	**43**	**68**	**4**	**0**	**2**	**234**	**8.1**	**−12**	**64**	**40.6**	**17:52**	....	....	....	....	....	....	....	....	....
2011-12	**Winnipeg**	**NHL**	**74**	**30**	**27**	**57**	**53**	**6**	**0**	**4**	**287**	**10.5**	**11**	**44**	**34.1**	**17:31**	....	....	....	....	....	....	....	....	....
2012-13	Dynamo Minsk	KHL	12	1	1	2	47	....	....	....	....	....	....	....	....	....	....	....	....	....	....	....	....	....	....
	Winnipeg	**NHL**	**48**	**17**	**16**	**33**	**80**	**2**	**0**	**4**	**190**	**8.9**	**−3**	**33**	**39.4**	**20:27**	....	....	....	....	....	....	....	....	....
2013-14	**Winnipeg**	**NHL**	**63**	**19**	**22**	**41**	**66**	**1**	**2**	**4**	**250**	**7.6**	**−7**	**105**	**42.9**	**20:17**	....	....	....	....	....	....	....	....	....
2014-15	**Winnipeg**	**NHL**	**37**	**10**	**12**	**22**	**56**	**4**	**1**	**1**	**126**	**7.9**	**−1**	**67**	**44.8**	**19:19**	....	....	....	....	....	....	....	....	....
	NHL Totals		**361**	**109**	**113**	**222**	**385**	**17**	**4**	**18**	**1214**	**9.0**		**339**	**42.2**	**18:00**	....	....	....	....	....	....	....	....	....

WHL West First All-Star Team (2009)

• Transferred to **Winnipeg** after **Atlanta** franchise relocated, June 21, 2011. Signed as a free agent by **Minsk** (KHL), September 28, 2012. Traded to **Buffalo** by **Winnipeg** with Zach Bogosian and Jason Kasdorf for Tyler Myers, Drew Stafford, Joel Armia, Brendan Lemieux and St. Louis' 1st round choice (previously acquired, Winnipeg selected Jack Roslovic) in 2015 Entry Draft, February 11, 2015. • Missed majority of 2014-15 due to recurring shoulder injury and follow-up surgery, February 7, 2015.

KANE, Patrick

(KAYN, PAT-rihk) **CHI**

Right wing. Shoots left. 5'11", 177 lbs. Born, Buffalo, NY, November 19, 1988. Chicago's 1st choice, 1st overall, in 2007 Entry Draft.

Season	Club	League	GP	G	A	Pts	PIM	PP	SH	GW	S	S%	+/-	TF	F%	Min	GP	G	A	Pts	PIM	PP	SH	GW	Min
2003-04	Det. Honeybaked	MWEHL	70	83	77	160	....	....	....	....	....	....	....	....	....	....	....	....	....	....	....	....	....	....	....
2004-05	USNTDP	U-17	23	16	17	33	8	....	....	....	....	....	....	....	....	....	....	....	....	....	....	....	....	....	....
	USNTDP	NAHL	40	16	21	37	8	....	....	....	....	....	....	....	....	....	9	7	8	15	2	....	....	....	....
2005-06	USNTDP	U-18	43	35	33	68	10	....	....	....	....	....	....	....	....	....	....	....	....	....	....	....	....	....	....
	USNTDP	NAHL	15	17	17	34	12	....	....	....	....	....	....	....	....	....	....	....	....	....	....	....	....	....	....
2006-07	London Knights	OHL	58	62	83	*145	52	....	....	....	....	....	....	....	....	....	16	10	21	*31	16	....	....	....	....
2007-08	**Chicago**	**NHL**	**82**	**21**	**51**	**72**	**52**	**7**	**0**	**4**	**191**	**11.0**	**−5**	**26**	**61.5**	**18:22**	....	....	....	....	....	....	....	....	....
2008-09	**Chicago**	**NHL**	**80**	**25**	**45**	**70**	**42**	**13**	**0**	**4**	**254**	**9.8**	**−2**	**31**	**41.9**	**18:40**	**16**	**9**	**5**	**14**	**12**	**2**	**0**	**0**	**16:36**
2009-10♦	**Chicago**	**NHL**	**82**	**30**	**58**	**88**	**20**	**9**	**0**	**6**	**261**	**11.5**	**16**	**22**	**40.9**	**19:12**	**22**	**10**	**18**	**28**	**6**	**1**	**1**	**1**	**18:55**
	United States	Olympics	6	3	2	5	2	....	....	....	....	....	....	....	....	....	....	....	....	....	....	....	....	....	....
2010-11	**Chicago**	**NHL**	**73**	**27**	**46**	**73**	**28**	**5**	**0**	**2**	**216**	**12.5**	**7**	**14**	**14.3**	**19:17**	**7**	**1**	**5**	**6**	**2**	**1**	**0**	**0**	**21:50**
2011-12	**Chicago**	**NHL**	**82**	**23**	**43**	**66**	**40**	**4**	**0**	**5**	**253**	**9.1**	**7**	**569**	**42.2**	**20:12**	**6**	**0**	**4**	**4**	**10**	**0**	**0**	**0**	**21:58**
2012-13	EHC Biel-Bienne	Swiss	20	13	10	23	6	....	....	....	....	....	....	....	....	....	....	....	....	....	....	....	....	....	....
	♦ Chicago	**NHL**	**47**	**23**	**32**	**55**	**8**	**8**	**0**	**3**	**138**	**16.7**	**11**	**10**	**20.0**	**20:03**	**23**	**9**	**10**	**19**	**8**	**0**	**0**	**2**	**20:56**
2013-14	**Chicago**	**NHL**	**69**	**29**	**40**	**69**	**22**	**10**	**0**	**6**	**227**	**12.8**	**7**	**8**	**50.0**	**19:37**	**19**	**8**	**12**	**20**	**8**	**1**	**0**	***4**	**21:23**
	United States	Olympics	6	0	4	4	6	....	....	....	....	....	....	....	....	....	....	....	....	....	....	....	....	....	....
2014-15♦	**Chicago**	**NHL**	**61**	**27**	**37**	**64**	**10**	**6**	**0**	**5**	**186**	**14.5**	**10**	**7**	**42.9**	**19:51**	**23**	**11**	**12**	**23**	**0**	**2**	**0**	**3**	**20:24**
	NHL Totals		**576**	**205**	**352**	**557**	**222**	**62**	**0**	**35**	**1726**	**11.9**		**687**	**42.1**	**19:21**	**116**	**48**	**66**	**114**	**46**	**7**	**1**	**10**	**20:01**

OHL All-Rookie Team (2007) • OHL First All-Star Team (2007) • OHL Rookie of the Year (2007) • Canadian Major Junior First All-Star Team (2007) • Canadian Major Junior Rookie of the Year (2007) • NHL All-Rookie Team (2008) • Calder Memorial Trophy (2008) • NHL First All-Star Team (2010) • Conn Smythe Trophy (2013)

Played in NHL All-Star Game (2009, 2011, 2012, 2015)

Signed as a free agent by **Biel-Bienne** (Swiss), October 23, 2012.

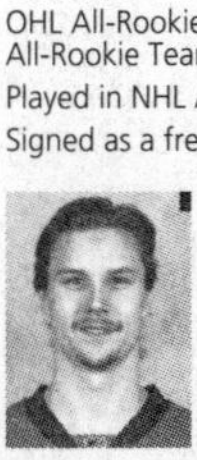

KARLSSON, Erik

(KAHRL-suhn, AIR-ihk) **OTT**

Defense. Shoots right. 6', 184 lbs. Born, Landsbro, Sweden, May 31, 1990. Ottawa's 1st choice, 15th overall, in 2008 Entry Draft.

Season	Club	League	GP	G	A	Pts	PIM	PP	SH	GW	S	S%	+/-	TF	F%	Min	GP	G	A	Pts	PIM	PP	SH	GW	Min
2006-07	Sodertalje SK U18	Swe-U18	2	0	1	1	33	....	....	....	....	....	....	....	....	....	....	....	....	....	....	....	....	....	....
	Sodertalje SK Jr.	Swe-Jr.	10	2	8	10	8	....	....	....	....	....	....	....	....	....	....	....	....	....	....	....	....	....	....
2007-08	Frolunda U18	Swe-U18	3	1	2	3	2	....	....	....	....	....	....	....	....	....	2	0	1	1	10	....	....	....	....
	Frolunda Jr.	Swe-Jr.	38	13	24	37	68	....	....	....	....	....	....	....	....	....	5	1	0	1	4	....	....	....	....
	Frolunda	Sweden	7	1	0	1	0	....	....	....	....	....	....	....	....	....	6	0	0	0	0	....	....	....	....

			Regular Season														Playoffs								
Season	Club	League	GP	G	A	Pts	PIM	PP	SH	GW	S	S%	+/-	TF	F%	Min	GP	G	A	Pts	PIM	PP	SH	GW	Min
2008-09	Frolunda Jr.	Swe-Jr.	1	0	2	2	2	....	....	....	....	....	....	....	....	....	....	....	....	....	....	....	....	....	....
	Boras HC	Sweden-2	7	0	1	1	14	....	....	....	....	....	....	....	....	....	....	....	....	....	....	....	....	....	....
	Frolunda	Sweden	45	5	5	10	10	....	....	....	....	....	....	....	....	....	11	1	2	3	24	....	....	....	....
2009-10	Ottawa	NHL	60	5	21	26	24	1	0	0	112	4.5	–5	0	0.0	20:07	6	1	5	6	4	1	0	0	25:52
	Binghamton	AHL	12	0	11	11	22	....	....	....	....	....	....	....	....	....	....	....	....	....	....	....	....	....	....
2010-11	Ottawa	NHL	75	13	32	45	50	4	0	4	182	7.1	–30	0	0.0	23:31	....	....	....	....	....	....	....	....	....
2011-12	Ottawa	NHL	81	19	59	78	42	3	0	5	261	7.3	16	1	0.0	25:19	7	1	0	1	4	1	0	0	25:22
2012-13	Jokerit Helsinki	Finland	30	9	25	34	24	....	....	....	....	....	....	....	....	....	....	....	....	....	....	....	....	....	....
	Ottawa	NHL	17	6	8	14	8	2	1	2	79	7.6	8	0	0.0	27:09	10	1	7	8	6	0	0	0	26:44
2013-14	Ottawa	NHL	82	20	54	74	36	5	0	1	257	7.8	–15	0	0.0	27:04	....	....	....	....	....	....	....	....	....
	Sweden	Olympics	6	4	4	8	0	....	....	....	....	....	....	....	....	....	....	....	....	....	....	....	....	....	....
2014-15	Ottawa	NHL	82	21	45	66	42	6	0	3	292	7.2	7	0	0.0	27:15	6	1	3	4	2	1	0	0	28:58
	NHL Totals		397	84	219	303	202	21	1	15	1183	7.1		1	0.0	25:02	29	4	15	19	16	3	0	0	26:41

NHL First All-Star Team (2012, 2015) • James Norris Memorial Trophy (2012, 2015) • Olympic All-Star Team (2014) • Best Defenceman – Olympics (2014)
Played in NHL All-Star Game (2011, 2012)
Signed as a free agent by **Jokerit Helsinki** (Finland), September 26, 2012. • Missed majority of 2012-13 due to Achilles injury at Pittsburgh, February 13, 2013.

KARLSSON, Melker (KAHRL-suhn, MEHL-kuhr) S.J.

Center. Shoots right. 6', 180 lbs. Born, Lycksele, Sweden, July 18, 1990.

			Regular Season														Playoffs								
Season	Club	League	GP	G	A	Pts	PIM	PP	SH	GW	S	S%	+/-	TF	F%	Min	GP	G	A	Pts	PIM	PP	SH	GW	Min
2006-07	Skelleftea U18	Swe-U18	14	5	4	9	20	....	....	....	....	....	....	....	....	....	....	....	....	....	....	....	....	....	....
	Skelleftea Jr.	Swe-Jr.	1	0	0	0	0	....	....	....	....	....	....	....	....	....	....	....	....	....	....	....	....	....	....
2007-08	Skelleftea U18	Swe-U18	30	21	13	34	14	....	....	....	....	....	....	....	....	....	....	....	....	....	....	....	....	....	....
	Skelleftea Jr.	Swe-Jr.	9	4	2	6	0	....	....	....	....	....	....	....	....	....	2	1	0	1	0	....	....	....	....
2008-09	Skelleftea AIK Jr.	Swe-Jr.	34	10	14	24	58	....	....	....	....	....	....	....	....	....	6	1	3	4	2	....	....	....	....
	Skelleftea AIK	Sweden	4	0	0	0	0	....	....	....	....	....	....	....	....	....	1	0	0	0	0	....	....	....	....
2009-10	Skelleftea AIK Jr.	Swe-Jr.	27	14	21	35	10	....	....	....	....	....	....	....	....	....	2	1	1	2	0	....	....	....	....
	Skelleftea AIK	Sweden	36	2	0	2	8	....	....	....	....	....	....	....	....	....	8	0	2	2	0	....	....	....	....
2010-11	Skelleftea AIK Jr.	Swe-Jr.	5	3	1	4	0	....	....	....	....	....	....	....	....	....	....	....	....	....	....	....	....	....	....
	Orebro HK	Sweden-2	10	2	4	6	12	....	....	....	....	....	....	....	....	....	....	....	....	....	....	....	....	....	....
	Skelleftea AIK	Sweden	40	4	2	6	2	....	....	....	....	....	....	....	....	....	16	1	3	4	2	....	....	....	....
2011-12	Skelleftea AIK	Sweden	44	3	2	5	8	....	....	....	....	....	....	....	....	....	19	2	2	4	4	....	....	....	....
2012-13	Skelleftea AIK	Sweden	44	13	15	28	14	....	....	....	....	....	....	....	....	....	13	2	8	10	10	....	....	....	....
2013-14	Skelleftea AIK	Sweden	48	9	16	25	14	....	....	....	....	....	....	....	....	....	14	4	8	12	12	....	....	....	....
2014-15	San Jose	NHL	53	13	11	24	20	1	0	2	100	13.0	–3	33	39.4	15:26	....	....	....	....	....	....	....	....	....
	Worcester Sharks	AHL	20	5	5	10	6	....	....	....	....	....	....	....	....	....	....	....	....	....	....	....	....	....	....
	NHL Totals		53	13	11	24	20	1	0	2	100	13.0		33	39.4	15:26	....	....	....	....	....	....	....	....	....

Signed as a free agent by **San Jose**, May 30, 2014.

KARLSSON, William (KAHRL-suhn, WIHL-yuhm) CBJ

Center. Shoots left. 6'1", 179 lbs. Born, Marsta, Sweden, January 8, 1993. Anaheim's 3rd choice, 53rd overall, in 2011 Entry Draft.

			Regular Season														Playoffs								
Season	Club	League	GP	G	A	Pts	PIM	PP	SH	GW	S	S%	+/-	TF	F%	Min	GP	G	A	Pts	PIM	PP	SH	GW	Min
2007-08	Arlanda U18	Swe-U18	5	2	7	9	4	....	....	....	....	....	....	....	....	....	....	....	....	....	....	....	....	....	....
2008-09	Arlanda U18	Swe-U18	33	10	18	28	16	....	....	....	....	....	....	....	....	....	....	....	....	....	....	....	....	....	....
2009-10	Vasteras U18	Swe-U18	39	23	21	44	62	....	....	....	....	....	....	....	....	....	....	....	....	....	....	....	....	....	....
	Vasteras Jr.	Swe-Jr.	6	0	1	1	2	....	....	....	....	....	....	....	....	....	2	0	1	1	0	....	....	....	....
2010-11	Vasteras U18	Swe-U18	11	5	9	14	10	....	....	....	....	....	....	....	....	....	6	7	8	15	2	....	....	....	....
	Vasteras Jr.	Swe-Jr.	38	20	34	54	45	....	....	....	....	....	....	....	....	....	....	....	....	....	....	....	....	....	....
	VIK Vasteras HK	Sweden-2	14	1	3	4	2	....	....	....	....	....	....	....	....	....	....	....	....	....	....	....	....	....	....
2011-12	VIK Vasteras HK	Sweden-2	52	13	34	47	6	....	....	....	....	....	....	....	....	....	....	....	....	....	....	....	....	....	....
	Vasteras Jr.	Swe-Jr.	....	....	....	....	....	....	....	....	....	....	....	....	....	....	5	2	2	4	2	....	....	....	....
2012-13	HV 71 Jonkoping	Sweden	50	4	24	28	12	....	....	....	....	....	....	....	....	....	5	0	2	2	0	....	....	....	....
	HV 71 Jr.	Swe-Jr.	....	....	....	....	....	....	....	....	....	....	....	....	....	....	2	2	2	4	2	....	....	....	....
2013-14	HV 71 Jonkoping	Sweden	55	15	22	37	14	....	....	....	....	....	....	....	....	....	8	3	4	7	8	....	....	....	....
	Norfolk Admirals	AHL	9	2	7	9	6	....	....	....	....	....	....	....	....	....	8	1	2	3	2	....	....	....	....
2014-15	Anaheim	NHL	18	2	1	3	2	0	0	1	24	8.3	1	164	48.8	12:09	....	....	....	....	....	....	....	....	....
	Norfolk Admirals	AHL	37	8	16	24	2	....	....	....	....	....	....	....	....	....	....	....	....	....	....	....	....	....	....
	Columbus	NHL	3	1	1	2	0	0	0	0	5	20.0	2	33	39.4	12:46	....	....	....	....	....	....	....	....	....
	Springfield	AHL	15	0	0	0	0	....	....	....	....	....	....	....	....	....	....	....	....	....	....	....	....	....	....
	NHL Totals		21	3	2	5	2	0	0	1	29	10.3		197	47.2	12:14	....	....	....	....	....	....	....	....	....

Traded to **Columbus** by **Anaheim** with Rene Bourque and Anaheim's 2nd round choice (Kevin Stenlund) in 2015 Entry Draft for James Wisniewski and Detroit's 3rd round choice (previously acquired, Anaheim selected Brent Gates) in 2015 Entry Draft, March 2, 2015.

KASSIAN, Matt (KA-see-uhn, MAT)

Left wing. Shoots left. 6'4", 240 lbs. Born, Edmonton, AB, October 28, 1986. Minnesota's 2nd choice, 57th overall, in 2005 Entry Draft.

			Regular Season														Playoffs								
Season	Club	League	GP	G	A	Pts	PIM	PP	SH	GW	S	S%	+/-	TF	F%	Min	GP	G	A	Pts	PIM	PP	SH	GW	Min
2002-03	Sherwood Park	AJHL	33	5	7	12	38	....	....	....	....	....	....	....	....	....	....	....	....	....	....	....	....	....	....
2003-04	Vancouver Giants	WHL	37	1	0	1	42	....	....	....	....	....	....	....	....	....	3	0	0	0	4	....	....	....	....
2004-05	Vancouver Giants	WHL	41	0	3	3	89	....	....	....	....	....	....	....	....	....	....	....	....	....	....	....	....	....	....
	Kamloops Blazers	WHL	28	3	0	3	83	....	....	....	....	....	....	....	....	....	6	1	2	3	14	....	....	....	....
2005-06	Kamloops Blazers	WHL	67	5	6	11	147	....	....	....	....	....	....	....	....	....	....	....	....	....	....	....	....	....	....
2006-07	Kamloops Blazers	WHL	72	8	10	18	162	....	....	....	....	....	....	....	....	....	4	0	1	1	0	....	....	....	....
2007-08	Houston Aeros	AHL	19	0	0	0	48	....	....	....	....	....	....	....	....	....	....	....	....	....	....	....	....	....	....
	Texas Wildcatters	ECHL	47	6	4	10	90	....	....	....	....	....	....	....	....	....	....	....	....	....	....	....	....	....	....
2008-09	Houston Aeros	AHL	56	1	2	3	130	....	....	....	....	....	....	....	....	....	4	0	0	0	10	....	....	....	....
2009-10	Houston Aeros	AHL	59	2	4	6	149	....	....	....	....	....	....	....	....	....	....	....	....	....	....	....	....	....	....
2010-11	Minnesota	NHL	4	0	0	0	12	0	0	0	1	0.0	–1	0	0.0	5:29	....	....	....	....	....	....	....	....	....
	Houston Aeros	AHL	60	4	4	8	132	....	....	....	....	....	....	....	....	....	8	0	0	0	2	....	....	....	....
2011-12	Minnesota	NHL	24	2	0	2	55	0	0	0	13	15.4	–2	0	0.0	5:33	....	....	....	....	....	....	....	....	....
	Houston Aeros	AHL	26	2	2	4	34	....	....	....	....	....	....	....	....	....	....	....	....	....	....	....	....	....	....
2012-13	Houston Aeros	AHL	9	1	0	1	12	....	....	....	....	....	....	....	....	....	....	....	....	....	....	....	....	....	....
	Ottawa	NHL	15	1	0	1	47	0	0	0	6	16.7	0	0	0.0	6:23	5	0	2	2	17	0	0	0	8:51
2013-14	Ottawa	NHL	33	1	1	2	63	0	0	0	12	8.3	–1	0	0.0	4:26	....	....	....	....	....	....	....	....	....
2014-15	Portland Pirates	AHL	2	0	0	0	0	....	....	....	....	....	....	....	....	....	....	....	....	....	....	....	....	....	....
	NHL Totals		76	4	1	5	177	0	0	0	32	12.5		0	0.0	5:14	5	0	2	2	17	0	0	0	8:51

Traded to **Ottawa** by **Minnesota** for Ottawa's 6th round choice (Pontus Sjalin) in 2014 Entry Draft, March 12, 2013. • Missed majority of 2012-13 and 2013-14 as a healthy reserve. Signed to a PTO (professional tryout) contract by **Portland** (AHL), October 9, 2014. • Released by **Portland** (AHL), October 21, 2014.

KASSIAN, Zack (KA-see-uhn, ZAK) MTL

Right wing. Shoots right. 6'3", 214 lbs. Born, Windsor, ON, January 24, 1991. Buffalo's 1st choice, 13th overall, in 2009 Entry Draft.

			Regular Season														Playoffs								
Season	Club	League	GP	G	A	Pts	PIM	PP	SH	GW	S	S%	+/-	TF	F%	Min	GP	G	A	Pts	PIM	PP	SH	GW	Min
2006-07	Wind. Jr. Spitfires	Minor-ON	57	32	48	80	136	....	....	....	....	....	....	....	....	....	....	....	....	....	....	....	....	....	....
	Leamington Flyers	ON-Jr.B	2	0	0	0	6	....	....	....	....	....	....	....	....	....	....	....	....	....	....	....	....	....	....
2007-08	Peterborough	OHL	58	9	12	21	74	....	....	....	....	....	....	....	....	....	5	1	0	1	2	....	....	....	....
2008-09	Peterborough	OHL	61	24	39	63	136	....	....	....	....	....	....	....	....	....	4	0	2	2	8	....	....	....	....
2009-10	Peterborough	OHL	33	8	19	27	58	....	....	....	....	....	....	....	....	....	....	....	....	....	....	....	....	....	....
	Windsor Spitfires	OHL	5	4	0	4	23	....	....	....	....	....	....	....	....	....	19	7	9	16	38	....	....	....	....
2010-11	Windsor Spitfires	OHL	56	26	51	77	67	....	....	....	....	....	....	....	....	....	16	6	10	16	37	....	....	....	....
	Portland Pirates	AHL	....	....	....	....	....	....	....	....	....	....	....	....	....	....	3	0	0	0	2	....	....	....	....
2011-12	Buffalo	NHL	27	3	4	7	20	0	0	0	36	8.3	–1	14	50.0	11:56	....	....	....	....	....	....	....	....	....
	Rochester	AHL	30	15	11	26	31	....	....	....	....	....	....	....	....	....	....	....	....	....	....	....	....	....	....
	Vancouver	NHL	17	1	2	3	31	0	0	0	18	5.6	–1	9	44.4	10:17	4	0	0	0	2	0	0	0	4:51
2012-13	Chicago Wolves	AHL	29	8	13	21	61	....	....	....	....	....	....	....	....	....	....	....	....	....	....	....	....	....	....
	Vancouver	NHL	39	7	4	11	51	2	0	1	49	14.3	–7	14	42.9	13:29	4	0	0	0	4	0	0	0	12:05
2013-14	Vancouver	NHL	73	14	15	29	124	1	0	2	91	15.4	–4	21	28.6	12:56	....	....	....	....	....	....	....	....	....
2014-15	Vancouver	NHL	42	10	6	16	81	1	0	3	55	18.2	–5	6	0.0	12:37	....	....	....	....	....	....	....	....	....
	NHL Totals		198	35	31	66	307	4	0	6	249	14.1		64	35.9	12:37	8	0	0	0	6	0	0	0	8:28

Traded to **Vancouver** by **Buffalo** for Cody Hodgson, February 27, 2012. Traded to **Montreal** by **Vancouver** with Vancouver's 5th round choice in 2016 Entry Draft for Brandon Prust, July 1, 2015.

KEARNS, Bracken (KUHNRZ, BRAK-en) NYI

Center. Shoots right. 6', 195 lbs. Born, Vancouver, BC, May 12, 1981.

			Regular Season														Playoffs								
Season	Club	League	GP	G	A	Pts	PIM	PP	SH	GW	S	S%	+/-	TF	F%	Min	GP	G	A	Pts	PIM	PP	SH	GW	Min
2001-02	U. of Calgary	CWUAA	26	0	8	8	2	....	....	....	....	....	....	....	....	....	....	....	....	....	....	....	....	....	....
2002-03	U. of Calgary	CWUAA	29	8	9	17	14	....	....	....	....	....	....	....	....	....	....	....	....	....	....	....	....	....	....
2003-04	U. of Calgary	CWUAA	38	11	12	23	22	....	....	....	....	....	....	....	....	....	....	....	....	....	....	....	....	....	....
2004-05	U. of Calgary	CWUAA	43	12	23	35	18	....	....	....	....	....	....	....	....	....	....	....	....	....	....	....	....	....	....
2005-06	Cleveland Barons	AHL	1	0	1	1	0	....	....	....	....	....	....	....	....	....	....	....	....	....	....	....	....	....	....
	Toledo Storm	ECHL	71	33	36	69	66	....	....	....	....	....	....	....	....	....	13	7	6	13	6	....	....	....	....
2006-07	Milwaukee	AHL	79	11	15	26	59	....	....	....	....	....	....	....	....	....	4	0	0	0	8	....	....	....	....
2007-08	Norfolk Admirals	AHL	53	9	16	25	40	....	....	....	....	....	....	....	....	....	....	....	....	....	....	....	....	....	....
	Reading Royals	ECHL	17	5	13	18	17	....	....	....	....	....	....	....	....	....	....	....	....	....	....	....	....	....	....
2008-09	Norfolk Admirals	AHL	53	12	10	22	63	....	....	....	....	....	....	....	....	....	....	....	....	....	....	....	....	....	....
2009-10	Rockford IceHogs	AHL	80	15	36	51	99	....	....	....	....	....	....	....	....	....	4	0	2	2	2	....	....	....	....
2010-11	San Antonio	AHL	72	20	23	43	104	....	....	....	....	....	....	....	....	....	....	....	....	....	....	....	....	....	....
2011-12	**Florida**	**NHL**	**5**	**0**	**0**	**0**	**10**	**0**	**0**	**0**	**0**	**0.0**	**0**	**2**	**50.0**	**7:14**	....	....	....	....	....	....	....	....	....
	San Antonio	AHL	69	22	30	52	58	....	....	....	....	....	....	....	....	....	10	2	5	7	4	....	....	....	....
2012-13	Worcester Sharks	AHL	66	21	25	46	73	....	....	....	....	....	....	....	....	....	....	....	....	....	....	....	....	....	....
	San Jose	**NHL**	**1**	**0**	**0**	**0**	**0**	**0**	**0**	**0**	**0**	**0.0**	**0**	**0**	**0.0**	**12:04**	**7**	**0**	**0**	**0**	**2**	**0**	**0**	**0**	**7:37**
2013-14	**San Jose**	**NHL**	**25**	**3**	**2**	**5**	**6**	**1**	**0**	**0**	**37**	**8.1**	**–2**	**71**	**42.3**	**13:12**	....	....	....	....	....	....	....	....	....
	Worcester Sharks	AHL	45	6	19	25	72	....	....	....	....	....	....	....	....	....	....	....	....	....	....	....	....	....	....
2014-15	Blues Espoo	Finland	45	10	10	20	38	....	....	....	....	....	....	....	....	....	4	0	0	0	0	....	....	....	....
	NHL Totals		**31**	**3**	**2**	**5**	**16**	**1**	**0**	**0**	**37**	**8.1**		**73**	**42.5**	**12:12**	**7**	**0**	**0**	**0**	**2**	**0**	**0**	**0**	**7:37**

Signed as a free agent by **Phoenix**, July 27, 2010. Signed as a free agent by **Florida**, July 14, 2011. Signed as a free agent by **San Jose**, July 2, 2012. Signed as a free agent by **Espoo** (Finland), October 23, 2014. Signed as a free agent by **NY Islanders**, July 2, 2015.

KEITH, Duncan (KEETH, DUHN-kuhn) CHI

Defense. Shoots left. 6'1", 192 lbs. Born, Winnipeg, MB, July 16, 1983. Chicago's 2nd choice, 54th overall, in 2002 Entry Draft.

Season	Club	League	GP	G	A	Pts	PIM	PP	SH	GW	S	S%	+/-	TF	F%	Min	GP	G	A	Pts	PIM	PP	SH	GW	Min
1998-99	Penticton	Minor-BC	44	51	57	108	45	....	....	....	....	....	....	....	....	....	....	....	....	....	....	....	....	....	....
99-2000	Penticton	BCHL	59	9	27	36	37	....	....	....	....	....	....	....	....	....	....	....	....	....	....	....	....	....	....
2000-01	Penticton	BCHL	60	18	64	82	61	....	....	....	....	....	....	....	....	....	9	4	6	10	18	....	....	....	....
2001-02	Michigan State	CCHA	41	3	12	15	18	....	....	....	....	....	....	....	....	....	....	....	....	....	....	....	....	....	....
2002-03	Michigan State	CCHA	15	3	6	9	8	....	....	....	....	....	....	....	....	....	....	....	....	....	....	....	....	....	....
	Kelowna Rockets	WHL	37	11	35	46	60	....	....	....	....	....	....	....	....	....	19	3	11	14	12	....	....	....	....
2003-04	Norfolk Admirals	AHL	75	7	18	25	44	....	....	....	....	....	....	....	....	....	8	1	1	2	6	....	....	....	....
2004-05	Norfolk Admirals	AHL	79	9	17	26	78	....	....	....	....	....	....	....	....	....	6	0	0	0	14	....	....	....	....
2005-06	**Chicago**	**NHL**	**81**	**9**	**12**	**21**	**79**	**1**	**1**	**0**	**134**	**6.7**	**–11**	**0**	**0.0**	**23:26**	....	....	....	....	....	....	....	....	....
2006-07	**Chicago**	**NHL**	**82**	**2**	**29**	**31**	**76**	**0**	**0**	**0**	**122**	**1.6**	**0**	**0**	**0.0**	**23:36**	....	....	....	....	....	....	....	....	....
2007-08	**Chicago**	**NHL**	**82**	**12**	**20**	**32**	**56**	**1**	**1**	**0**	**148**	**8.1**	**30**	**0**	**0.0**	**25:34**	....	....	....	....	....	....	....	....	....
2008-09	**Chicago**	**NHL**	**77**	**8**	**36**	**44**	**60**	**2**	**1**	**1**	**173**	**4.6**	**33**	**0**	**0.0**	**25:34**	**17**	**0**	**6**	**6**	**10**	**0**	**0**	**0**	**24:39**
2009-10♦	**Chicago**	**NHL**	**82**	**14**	**55**	**69**	**51**	**3**	**1**	**1**	**213**	**6.6**	**21**	**0**	**0.0**	**26:36**	**22**	**2**	**15**	**17**	**10**	**0**	**0**	**0**	**28:11**
	Canada	Olympics	7	0	6	6	2	....	....	....	....	....	....	....	....	....	....	....	....	....	....	....	....	....	....
2010-11	**Chicago**	**NHL**	**82**	**7**	**38**	**45**	**22**	**3**	**1**	**1**	**173**	**4.0**	**–1**	**0**	**0.0**	**26:53**	**7**	**4**	**2**	**6**	**6**	**1**	**0**	**1**	**26:55**
2011-12	**Chicago**	**NHL**	**74**	**4**	**36**	**40**	**42**	**1**	**0**	**1**	**162**	**2.5**	**15**	**0**	**0.0**	**26:54**	**6**	**0**	**1**	**1**	**2**	**0**	**0**	**0**	**30:16**
2012-13♦	**Chicago**	**NHL**	**47**	**3**	**24**	**27**	**31**	**2**	**0**	**0**	**91**	**3.3**	**16**	**0**	**0.0**	**24:07**	**22**	**2**	**11**	**13**	**18**	**0**	**0**	**0**	**27:37**
2013-14	**Chicago**	**NHL**	**79**	**6**	**55**	**61**	**28**	**3**	**0**	**3**	**198**	**3.0**	**22**	**0**	**0.0**	**24:39**	**19**	**4**	**7**	**11**	**8**	**0**	**0**	**1**	**27:49**
	Canada	Olympics	6	0	1	1	4	....	....	....	....	....	....	....	....	....	....	....	....	....	....	....	....	....	....
2014-15♦	**Chicago**	**NHL**	**80**	**10**	**35**	**45**	**20**	**3**	**0**	**2**	**171**	**5.8**	**12**	**0**	**0.0**	**25:34**	**23**	**3**	**18**	**21**	**4**	**0**	**0**	**3**	**31:07**
	NHL Totals		**766**	**75**	**340**	**415**	**465**	**19**	**5**	**9**	**1585**	**4.7**		**0**	**0.0**	**25:19**	**116**	**15**	**60**	**75**	**58**	**1**	**0**	**5**	**28:07**

NHL First All-Star Team (2010, 2014) • James Norris Memorial Trophy (2010, 2014) • Conn Smythe Trophy (2015)
Played in NHL All-Star Game (2008, 2011, 2015)

• Left **Michigan State University** (CCHA) and signed as a free agent by **Kelowna** (WHL), December 27, 2002.

KELLY, Chris (KEHL-lee, KRIHS) BOS

Center/Left wing. Shoots left. 6', 198 lbs. Born, Toronto, ON, November 11, 1980. Ottawa's 4th choice, 94th overall, in 1999 Entry Draft.

Season	Club	League	GP	G	A	Pts	PIM	PP	SH	GW	S	S%	+/-	TF	F%	Min	GP	G	A	Pts	PIM	PP	SH	GW	Min
1995-96	Toronto Marlies	MTHL	42	25	45	70	25	....	....	....	....	....	....	....	....	....	....	....	....	....	....	....	....	....	....
1996-97	Vaughan Vipers	ON-Jr.A	5	0	0	0	5	....	....	....	....	....	....	....	....	....	....	....	....	....	....	....	....	....	....
	Aurora Tigers	ON-Jr.A	49	14	20	34	11	....	....	....	....	....	....	....	....	....	....	....	....	....	....	....	....	....	....
1997-98	London Knights	OHL	54	15	14	29	4	....	....	....	....	....	....	....	....	....	16	4	5	9	12	....	....	....	....
1998-99	London Knights	OHL	68	36	41	77	60	....	....	....	....	....	....	....	....	....	25	9	17	26	22	....	....	....	....
99-2000	London Knights	OHL	63	29	43	72	57	....	....	....	....	....	....	....	....	....	....	....	....	....	....	....	....	....	....
2000-01	London Knights	OHL	31	21	34	55	46	....	....	....	....	....	....	....	....	....	....	....	....	....	....	....	....	....	....
	Sudbury Wolves	OHL	19	5	16	21	17	....	....	....	....	....	....	....	....	....	12	11	5	16	14	....	....	....	....
2001-02	Grand Rapids	AHL	31	3	3	6	20	....	....	....	....	....	....	....	....	....	5	1	1	2	5	....	....	....	....
	Muskegon Fury	UHL	4	1	2	3	0	....	....	....	....	....	....	....	....	....	....	....	....	....	....	....	....	....	....
2002-03	Binghamton	AHL	77	17	14	31	73	....	....	....	....	....	....	....	....	....	14	2	3	5	8	....	....	....	....
2003-04	**Ottawa**	**NHL**	**4**	**0**	**0**	**0**	**0**	**0**	**0**	**0**	**4**	**0.0**	**–2**	**5**	**40.0**	**9:29**	....	....	....	....	....	....	....	....	....
	Binghamton	AHL	54	15	19	34	40	....	....	....	....	....	....	....	....	....	2	0	0	0	4	....	....	....	....
2004-05	Binghamton	AHL	77	24	36	60	57	....	....	....	....	....	....	....	....	....	6	1	2	3	11	....	....	....	....
2005-06	**Ottawa**	**NHL**	**82**	**10**	**20**	**30**	**76**	**1**	**0**	**2**	**112**	**8.9**	**21**	**808**	**45.8**	**12:20**	**10**	**0**	**0**	**0**	**2**	**0**	**0**	**0**	**11:49**
2006-07	**Ottawa**	**NHL**	**82**	**15**	**23**	**38**	**40**	**1**	**2**	**0**	**131**	**11.5**	**28**	**564**	**49.8**	**15:18**	**20**	**3**	**4**	**7**	**4**	**0**	**0**	**0**	**15:28**
2007-08	**Ottawa**	**NHL**	**75**	**11**	**19**	**30**	**30**	**0**	**1**	**1**	**124**	**8.9**	**3**	**162**	**53.1**	**16:36**	....	....	....	....	....	....	....	....	....
2008-09	**Ottawa**	**NHL**	**82**	**12**	**11**	**23**	**38**	**0**	**1**	**1**	**118**	**10.2**	**–10**	**494**	**47.4**	**15:36**	....	....	....	....	....	....	....	....	....
2009-10	**Ottawa**	**NHL**	**81**	**15**	**17**	**32**	**38**	**0**	**0**	**3**	**112**	**13.4**	**–7**	**894**	**45.6**	**14:58**	**6**	**1**	**5**	**6**	**2**	**1**	**0**	**0**	**18:46**
2010-11	**Ottawa**	**NHL**	**57**	**12**	**11**	**23**	**27**	**0**	**1**	**2**	**89**	**13.5**	**–12**	**726**	**50.1**	**15:39**	....	....	....	....	....	....	....	....	....
	♦ Boston	**NHL**	**24**	**2**	**3**	**5**	**6**	**0**	**0**	**0**	**24**	**8.3**	**–1**	**190**	**53.7**	**14:52**	**25**	**5**	**8**	**13**	**6**	**0**	**0**	**0**	**15:28**
2011-12	**Boston**	**NHL**	**82**	**20**	**19**	**39**	**41**	**1**	**2**	**6**	**122**	**16.4**	**33**	**809**	**51.8**	**14:44**	**7**	**1**	**2**	**3**	**4**	**0**	**0**	**1**	**16:05**
2012-13	Martigny	Swiss-2	8	4	5	9	8	....	....	....	....	....	....	....	....	....	....	....	....	....	....	....	....	....	....
	Boston	**NHL**	**34**	**3**	**6**	**9**	**16**	**1**	**0**	**0**	**40**	**7.5**	**–8**	**373**	**57.9**	**14:58**	**22**	**2**	**1**	**3**	**19**	**0**	**0**	**0**	**15:40**
2013-14	**Boston**	**NHL**	**57**	**9**	**9**	**18**	**32**	**0**	**1**	**0**	**69**	**13.0**	**2**	**579**	**48.9**	**14:42**	....	....	....	....	....	....	....	....	....
2014-15	**Boston**	**NHL**	**80**	**7**	**21**	**28**	**48**	**0**	**1**	**2**	**112**	**6.3**	**6**	**539**	**48.6**	**15:08**	....	....	....	....	....	....	....	....	....
	NHL Totals		**740**	**116**	**159**	**275**	**392**	**4**	**9**	**17**	**1057**	**11.0**		**6143**	**49.3**	**14:56**	**90**	**12**	**20**	**32**	**37**	**1**	**0**	**1**	**15:23**

Traded to **Boston** by **Ottawa** for Boston's 2nd round choice (Shane Prince) in 2011 Entry Draft, February 15, 2011. Signed as a free agent by **Martigny** (Swiss-2), October 31, 2012.

KENINS, Ronalds (CHEHN-ihsh, RAWN-uhlds) VAN

Left wing. Shoots left. 6', 201 lbs. Born, Riga, Latvia, February 28, 1991.

Season	Club	League	GP	G	A	Pts	PIM	PP	SH	GW	S	S%	+/-	TF	F%	Min	GP	G	A	Pts	PIM	PP	SH	GW	Min
2008-09	GC Kusnacht Jr.	Swiss-Jr.	6	6	6	12	6	....	....	....	....	....	....	....	....	....	....	....	....	....	....	....	....	....	....
	GCK Lions Zurich	Swiss-2	42	2	8	10	24	....	....	....	....	....	....	....	....	....	....	....	....	....	....	....	....	....	....
2009-10	GCK Zurich Jr.	Swiss-Jr.	30	13	18	31	38	....	....	....	....	....	....	....	....	....	9	0	4	4	10	....	....	....	....
	GCK Lions Zurich	Swiss-2	4	1	3	4	4	....	....	....	....	....	....	....	....	....	....	....	....	....	....	....	....	....	....
2010-11	GCK Zurich Jr.	Swiss-Jr.	18	7	14	21	45	....	....	....	....	....	....	....	....	....	11	7	13	20	24	....	....	....	....
	GCK Lions Zurich	Swiss-2	11	1	2	3	8	....	....	....	....	....	....	....	....	....	....	....	....	....	....	....	....	....	....
2011-12	ZSC Lions Zurich	Swiss	47	6	12	18	48	....	....	....	....	....	....	....	....	....	15	0	4	4	6	....	....	....	....
2012-13	ZSC Lions Zurich	Swiss	45	3	14	17	12	....	....	....	....	....	....	....	....	....	12	4	4	8	10	....	....	....	....
2013-14	ZSC Lions Zurich	Swiss	39	8	17	25	40	....	....	....	....	....	....	....	....	....	18	4	0	4	6	....	....	....	....
	Latvia	Olympics	5	0	0	0	0	....	....	....	....	....	....	....	....	....	....	....	....	....	....	....	....	....	....
2014-15	**Vancouver**	**NHL**	**30**	**4**	**8**	**12**	**8**	**0**	**0**	**0**	**38**	**10.5**	**–2**	**0**	**0.0**	**12:16**	**5**	**1**	**1**	**2**	**4**	**0**	**0**	**0**	**10:52**
	Utica Comets	AHL	36	5	7	12	23	....	....	....	....	....	....	....	....	....	....	....	....	....	....	....	....	....	....
	NHL Totals		**30**	**4**	**8**	**12**	**8**	**0**	**0**	**0**	**38**	**10.5**		**0**	**0.0**	**12:16**	**5**	**1**	**1**	**2**	**4**	**0**	**0**	**0**	**10:52**

Signed as a free agent by **Vancouver**, July 30, 2013.

KENNEDY, Tim

(KEH-nuh-dee, TIHM)

Left wing. Shoots left. 5'10", 175 lbs. Born, Buffalo, NY, April 30, 1986. Washington's 6th choice, 181st overall, in 2005 Entry Draft.

			Regular Season														Playoffs								
Season	Club	League	GP	G	A	Pts	PIM	PP	SH	GW	S	S%	+/-	TF	F%	Min	GP	G	A	Pts	PIM	PP	SH	GW	Min
2003-04	Sioux City	USHL	56	9	10	19	42	....	....	....	....	....	....	....	....	....	7	2	2	4	6	....	....	....	....
2004-05	Sioux City	USHL	54	30	31	61	112	....	....	....	....	....	....	....	....	....	13	*6	*11	*17	18	....	....	....	....
2005-06	Michigan State	CCHA	29	4	15	19	31	....	....	....	....	....	....	....	....	....	....	....	....	....	....	....	....	....	....
2006-07	Michigan State	CCHA	42	18	25	43	49	....	....	....	....	....	....	....	....	....	....	....	....	....	....	....	....	....	....
2007-08	Michigan State	CCHA	42	20	23	43	50	....	....	....	....	....	....	....	....	....	....	....	....	....	....	....	....	....	....
2008-09	**Buffalo**	**NHL**	**1**	**0**	**0**	**0**	**0**	**0**	**0**	**0**	**1**	**0.0**	**0**	**1**	**0.0**	**11:04**	....	....	....	....	....	....	....	....	....
	Portland Pirates	AHL	73	18	49	67	51	....	....	....	....	....	....	....	....	....	5	0	1	1	2	....	....	....	....
2009-10	**Buffalo**	**NHL**	**78**	**10**	**16**	**26**	**50**	**1**	**0**	**3**	**98**	**10.2**	**-3**	**397**	**33.5**	**12:57**	**6**	**1**	**2**	**3**	**4**	**0**	**0**	**0**	**14:25**
2010-11	Connecticut	AHL	53	12	30	42	44	....	....	....	....	....	....	....	....	....	....	....	....	....	....	....	....	....	....
	Florida	**NHL**	**6**	**0**	**1**	**1**	**0**	**0**	**0**	**0**	**2**	**0.0**	**0**	**30**	**40.0**	**10:23**	....	....	....	....	....	....	....	....	....
	Rochester	AHL	14	0	7	7	8	....	....	....	....	....	....	....	....	....	....	....	....	....	....	....	....	....	....
2011-12	**Florida**	**NHL**	**27**	**1**	**1**	**2**	**4**	**0**	**0**	**1**	**22**	**4.5**	**-11**	**141**	**45.4**	**11:08**	....	....	....	....	....	....	....	....	....
	San Antonio	AHL	18	3	6	9	18	....	....	....	....	....	....	....	....	....	....	....	....	....	....	....	....	....	....
	Worcester Sharks	AHL	35	10	21	31	26	....	....	....	....	....	....	....	....	....	....	....	....	....	....	....	....	....	....
2012-13	Worcester Sharks	AHL	37	13	24	37	14	....	....	....	....	....	....	....	....	....	....	....	....	....	....	....	....	....	....
	San Jose	**NHL**	**13**	**2**	**0**	**2**	**2**	**0**	**0**	**1**	**24**	**8.3**	**-3**	**10**	**30.0**	**13:35**	**3**	**0**	**0**	**0**	**2**	**0**	**0**	**0**	**8:45**
2013-14	**Phoenix**	**NHL**	**37**	**2**	**6**	**8**	**4**	**0**	**0**	**0**	**42**	**4.8**	**0**	**49**	**36.7**	**11:46**	....	....	....	....	....	....	....	....	....
	Portland Pirates	AHL	30	4	11	15	14	....	....	....	....	....	....	....	....	....	....	....	....	....	....	....	....	....	....
2014-15	Hershey Bears	AHL	75	11	48	59	56	....	....	....	....	....	....	....	....	....	10	3	5	8	10	....	....	....	....
	NHL Totals		**162**	**15**	**24**	**39**	**60**	**1**	**0**	**5**	**189**	**7.9**		**628**	**36.6**	**12:19**	**9**	**1**	**2**	**3**	**6**	**0**	**0**	**0**	**12:32**

USHL Second All-Star Team (2005) • NCAA Championship All-Tournament Team (2007) • CCHA Second All-Star Team (2008) • AHL All-Rookie Team (2009)

Traded to **Buffalo** by **Washington** for Buffalo's 6th round choice (Mathieu Perreault) in 2006 Entry Draft, July 30, 2005. Signed as a free agent by **NY Rangers**, August 30, 2010. Traded to **Florida** by **NY Rangers** with NY Rangers' 3rd round choice (Logan Shaw) in 2011 Entry Draft for Bryan McCabe, February 26, 2011. Traded to **San Jose** by **Florida** for Sean Sullivan, January 26, 2012. Signed as a free agent by **Phoenix**, July 11, 2013. Signed as a free agent by **Washington**, July 4, 2014.

KENNEDY, Tyler

(KEH-nuh-dee, TIGH-luhr)

Center. Shoots right. 5'11", 185 lbs. Born, Sault Ste. Marie, ON, July 15, 1986. Pittsburgh's 6th choice, 99th overall, in 2004 Entry Draft.

			Regular Season														Playoffs								
Season	Club	League	GP	G	A	Pts	PIM	PP	SH	GW	S	S%	+/-	TF	F%	Min	GP	G	A	Pts	PIM	PP	SH	GW	Min
2002-03	Sault Ste. Marie	OHL	61	5	10	15	28	....	....	....	....	....	....	....	....	....	4	0	0	0	0	....	....	....	....
2003-04	Sault Ste. Marie	OHL	63	16	26	42	28	....	....	....	....	....	....	....	....	....	....	....	....	....	....	....	....	....	....
2004-05	Sault Ste. Marie	OHL	61	21	36	57	37	....	....	....	....	....	....	....	....	....	4	1	3	4	4	....	....	....	....
2005-06	Sault Ste. Marie	OHL	64	22	48	70	60	....	....	....	....	....	....	....	....	....	4	1	2	3	2	....	....	....	....
2006-07	Wilkes-Barre	AHL	40	12	25	37	20	....	....	....	....	....	....	....	....	....	....	....	....	....	....	....	....	....	....
2007-08	**Pittsburgh**	**NHL**	**55**	**10**	**9**	**19**	**35**	**1**	**0**	**4**	**104**	**9.6**	**2**	**8**	**25.0**	**12:13**	**20**	**0**	**4**	**4**	**13**	**0**	**0**	**0**	**10:18**
	Wilkes-Barre	AHL	10	5	4	9	10	....	....	....	....	....	....	....	....	....	....	....	....	....	....	....	....	....	....
2008-09♦	**Pittsburgh**	**NHL**	**67**	**15**	**20**	**35**	**30**	**0**	**0**	**3**	**171**	**8.8**	**15**	**78**	**53.9**	**13:46**	**24**	**5**	**4**	**9**	**4**	**0**	**0**	**3**	**13:40**
2009-10	**Pittsburgh**	**NHL**	**64**	**13**	**12**	**25**	**31**	**1**	**0**	**4**	**175**	**7.4**	**10**	**64**	**42.2**	**12:35**	**10**	**0**	**0**	**0**	**2**	**0**	**0**	**0**	**11:57**
2010-11	**Pittsburgh**	**NHL**	**80**	**21**	**24**	**45**	**37**	**7**	**0**	**2**	**234**	**9.0**	**1**	**60**	**45.0**	**14:32**	**7**	**2**	**1**	**3**	**2**	**1**	**0**	**1**	**17:32**
2011-12	**Pittsburgh**	**NHL**	**60**	**11**	**22**	**33**	**29**	**0**	**0**	**1**	**195**	**5.6**	**10**	**89**	**47.2**	**14:22**	**6**	**3**	**3**	**6**	**2**	**0**	**0**	**1**	**14:22**
2012-13	**Pittsburgh**	**NHL**	**46**	**6**	**5**	**11**	**19**	**1**	**0**	**1**	**100**	**6.0**	**-6**	**29**	**44.8**	**12:28**	**9**	**2**	**3**	**5**	**2**	**0**	**0**	**1**	**12:33**
2013-14	**San Jose**	**NHL**	**67**	**4**	**13**	**17**	**34**	**0**	**0**	**1**	**143**	**2.8**	**-10**	**136**	**41.9**	**12:43**	....	....	....	....	....	....	....	....	....
2014-15	**San Jose**	**NHL**	**25**	**4**	**5**	**9**	**8**	**0**	**0**	**2**	**48**	**8.3**	**1**	**18**	**44.4**	**11:03**	....	....	....	....	....	....	....	....	....
	Worcester Sharks	AHL	3	2	1	3	0	....	....	....	....	....	....	....	....	....	....	....	....	....	....	....	....	....	....
	NY Islanders	**NHL**	**13**	**2**	**3**	**5**	**2**	**0**	**0**	**0**	**31**	**6.5**	**-3**	**10**	**50.0**	**11:23**	**3**	**0**	**0**	**0**	**2**	**0**	**0**	**0**	**10:33**
	NHL Totals		**477**	**86**	**113**	**199**	**225**	**10**	**0**	**18**	**1201**	**7.2**		**492**	**45.3**	**13:09**	**79**	**12**	**15**	**27**	**27**	**1**	**0**	**6**	**12:45**

Traded to **San Jose** by **Pittsburgh** for San Jose's 2nd round choice (later traded to Columbus – Columbus selected Dillon Heatherington) in 2013 Entry Draft, June 30, 2013. Traded to **NY Islanders** by **San Jose** for Tampa Bay's 7th round choice (previously acquired, later traded to Vancouver – Vancouver selected Tate Olson) in 2015 Entry Draft, March 2, 2015.

KESLER, Ryan

(KEHZ-luhr, RIGH-uhn) **ANA**

Center. Shoots right. 6'2", 202 lbs. Born, Livonia, MI, August 31, 1984. Vancouver's 1st choice, 23rd overall, in 2003 Entry Draft.

			Regular Season														Playoffs								
Season	Club	League	GP	G	A	Pts	PIM	PP	SH	GW	S	S%	+/-	TF	F%	Min	GP	G	A	Pts	PIM	PP	SH	GW	Min
99-2000	Det. Honeybaked	MWEHL	72	44	73	117	....	....	....	....	....	....	....	....	....	....	....	....	....	....	....	....	....	....	....
2000-01	USNTDP	U-18	26	8	20	28	24	....	....	....	....	....	....	....	....	....	....	....	....	....	....	....	....	....	....
	USNTDP	NAHL	56	7	21	28	40	....	....	....	....	....	....	....	....	....	....	....	....	....	....	....	....	....	....
2001-02	USNTDP	U-18	46	11	33	44	23	....	....	....	....	....	....	....	....	....	....	....	....	....	....	....	....	....	....
	USNTDP	USHL	13	5	5	10	10	....	....	....	....	....	....	....	....	....	....	....	....	....	....	....	....	....	....
	USNTDP	NAHL	10	5	6	11	4	....	....	....	....	....	....	....	....	....	....	....	....	....	....	....	....	....	....
2002-03	Ohio State	CCHA	40	11	20	31	44	....	....	....	....	....	....	....	....	....	....	....	....	....	....	....	....	....	....
2003-04	**Vancouver**	**NHL**	**28**	**2**	**3**	**5**	**16**	**0**	**0**	**0**	**23**	**8.7**	**-2**	**194**	**40.2**	**10:42**	....	....	....	....	....	....	....	....	....
	Manitoba Moose	AHL	33	3	8	11	29	....	....	....	....	....	....	....	....	....	....	....	....	....	....	....	....	....	....
2004-05	Manitoba Moose	AHL	78	30	27	57	105	....	....	....	....	....	....	....	....	....	14	4	5	9	8	....	....	....	....
2005-06	**Vancouver**	**NHL**	**82**	**10**	**13**	**23**	**79**	**1**	**0**	**2**	**119**	**8.4**	**1**	**984**	**46.8**	**14:03**	....	....	....	....	....	....	....	....	....
2006-07	**Vancouver**	**NHL**	**48**	**6**	**10**	**16**	**40**	**0**	**0**	**0**	**88**	**6.8**	**1**	**690**	**46.1**	**16:26**	**1**	**0**	**0**	**0**	**0**	**0**	**0**	**0**	**27:51**
2007-08	**Vancouver**	**NHL**	**80**	**21**	**16**	**37**	**79**	**4**	**2**	**2**	**177**	**11.9**	**1**	**1358**	**53.0**	**19:03**	....	....	....	....	....	....	....	....	....
2008-09	**Vancouver**	**NHL**	**82**	**26**	**33**	**59**	**61**	**10**	**2**	**2**	**179**	**14.5**	**8**	**976**	**54.0**	**19:28**	**10**	**2**	**2**	**4**	**14**	**1**	**0**	**0**	**20:29**
2009-10	**Vancouver**	**NHL**	**82**	**25**	**50**	**75**	**104**	**12**	**1**	**5**	**214**	**11.7**	**1**	**1401**	**55.1**	**19:38**	**12**	**1**	**9**	**10**	**4**	**0**	**0**	**0**	**21:19**
	United States	Olympics	6	2	0	2	2	....	....	....	....	....	....	....	....	....	....	....	....	....	....	....	....	....	....
2010-11	**Vancouver**	**NHL**	**82**	**41**	**32**	**73**	**66**	**15**	**3**	**7**	**260**	**15.8**	**24**	**1496**	**57.4**	**20:30**	**25**	**7**	**12**	**19**	**47**	**4**	**0**	**2**	**22:34**
2011-12	**Vancouver**	**NHL**	**77**	**22**	**27**	**49**	**56**	**8**	**1**	**1**	**222**	**9.9**	**11**	**1351**	**53.6**	**20:06**	**5**	**0**	**3**	**3**	**6**	**0**	**0**	**0**	**22:04**
2012-13	**Vancouver**	**NHL**	**17**	**4**	**9**	**13**	**12**	**2**	**0**	**1**	**36**	**11.1**	**-5**	**303**	**57.4**	**18:57**	**4**	**2**	**0**	**2**	**0**	**1**	**0**	**0**	**23:06**
2013-14	**Vancouver**	**NHL**	**77**	**25**	**18**	**43**	**81**	**9**	**1**	**5**	**239**	**10.5**	**-15**	**1406**	**52.6**	**21:49**	....	....	....	....	....	....	....	....	....
	United States	Olympics	6	1	3	4	0	....	....	....	....	....	....	....	....	....	....	....	....	....	....	....	....	....	....
2014-15	**Anaheim**	**NHL**	**81**	**20**	**27**	**47**	**75**	**5**	**1**	**4**	**205**	**9.8**	**-5**	**1664**	**56.3**	**19:31**	**16**	**7**	**6**	**13**	**24**	**1**	**0**	**1**	**20:29**
	NHL Totals		**736**	**202**	**238**	**440**	**669**	**66**	**11**	**29**	**1762**	**11.5**		**11823**	**53.4**	**18:43**	**73**	**19**	**32**	**51**	**95**	**7**	**0**	**3**	**21:41**

Frank J. Selke Trophy (2011)

Played in NHL All-Star Game (2011)

• Missed majority of 2012-13 due to recurring shoulder injury and foot injuriy vs. Dallas, February 15, 2013. Traded to **Anaheim** by **Vancouver** with Vancouver's 3rd round choice (Deven Sideroff) in 2015 Entry Draft for Nick Bonino, Luca Sbisa and Anaheim's 1st (Jared McCann) and 3rd (later traded to NY Rangers – NY Rangers selected Keegan Iverson) round choices in 2014 Entry Draft, June 27, 2014.

KESSEL, Phil

(KEH-suhl, FIHL) **PIT**

Right wing. Shoots right. 6', 202 lbs. Born, Madison, WI, October 2, 1987. Boston's 1st choice, 5th overall, in 2006 Entry Draft.

			Regular Season														Playoffs								
Season	Club	League	GP	G	A	Pts	PIM	PP	SH	GW	S	S%	+/-	TF	F%	Min	GP	G	A	Pts	PIM	PP	SH	GW	Min
2003-04	USNTDP	U-17	32	31	18	49	8	....	....	....	....	....	....	....	....	....	....	....	....	....	....	....	....	....	....
	USNTDP	NAHL	30	21	12	33	18	....	....	....	....	....	....	....	....	....	....	....	....	....	....	....	....	....	....
2004-05	USNTDP	U-18	31	41	32	73	16	....	....	....	....	....	....	....	....	....	....	....	....	....	....	....	....	....	....
	USNTDP	NAHL	14	11	14	25	21	....	....	....	....	....	....	....	....	....	....	....	....	....	....	....	....	....	....
2005-06	U. of Minnesota	WCHA	39	18	33	51	28	....	....	....	....	....	....	....	....	....	....	....	....	....	....	....	....	....	....
2006-07	**Boston**	**NHL**	**70**	**11**	**18**	**29**	**12**	**1**	**0**	**0**	**170**	**6.5**	**-12**	**373**	**40.8**	**14:04**	....	....	....	....	....	....	....	....	....
	Providence Bruins	AHL	2	1	0	1	2	....	....	....	....	....	....	....	....	....	....	....	....	....	....	....	....	....	....
2007-08	**Boston**	**NHL**	**82**	**19**	**18**	**37**	**28**	**5**	**0**	**3**	**213**	**8.9**	**-6**	**326**	**42.3**	**15:14**	**4**	**3**	**1**	**4**	**2**	**1**	**0**	**0**	**14:31**
2008-09	**Boston**	**NHL**	**70**	**36**	**24**	**60**	**16**	**8**	**0**	**6**	**232**	**15.5**	**23**	**87**	**48.3**	**16:34**	**11**	**6**	**5**	**11**	**4**	**0**	**0**	**0**	**15:55**
2009-10	**Toronto**	**NHL**	**70**	**30**	**25**	**55**	**21**	**8**	**0**	**5**	**297**	**10.1**	**-8**	**122**	**48.4**	**19:33**	....	....	....	....	....	....	....	....	....
	United States	Olympics	6	1	1	2	0	....	....	....	....	....	....	....	....	....	....	....	....	....	....	....	....	....	....
2010-11	**Toronto**	**NHL**	**82**	**32**	**32**	**64**	**24**	**12**	**1**	**6**	**325**	**9.8**	**-20**	**59**	**40.7**	**19:39**	....	....	....	....	....	....	....	....	....
2011-12	**Toronto**	**NHL**	**82**	**37**	**45**	**82**	**20**	**10**	**0**	**6**	**295**	**12.5**	**-10**	**28**	**32.1**	**20:03**	....	....	....	....	....	....	....	....	....
2012-13	**Toronto**	**NHL**	**48**	**20**	**32**	**52**	**18**	**6**	**0**	**4**	**161**	**12.4**	**-3**	**8**	**62.5**	**19:49**	**7**	**4**	**2**	**6**	**2**	**1**	**0**	**2**	**18:29**
2013-14	**Toronto**	**NHL**	**82**	**37**	**43**	**80**	**27**	**8**	**0**	**6**	**305**	**12.1**	**-5**	**14**	**14.3**	**20:40**	....	....	....	....	....	....	....	....	....
	United States	Olympics	6	5	3	8	4	....	....	....	....	....	....	....	....	....	....	....	....	....	....	....	....	....	....
2014-15	**Toronto**	**NHL**	**82**	**25**	**36**	**61**	**30**	**8**	**0**	**4**	**280**	**8.9**	**-34**	**5**	**40.0**	**18:48**	....	....	....	....	....	....	....	....	....
	NHL Totals		**668**	**247**	**273**	**520**	**196**	**66**	**1**	**40**	**2278**	**10.8**		**1022**	**42.4**	**18:16**	**22**	**13**	**8**	**21**	**8**	**2**	**0**	**2**	**16:29**

WCHA All-Rookie Team (2006) • WCHA Rookie of the Year (2006) • Bill Masterton Memorial Trophy (2007) • Olympic All-Star Team (2014) • Olympics – Best Forward (2014)

Played in NHL All-Star Game (2011, 2012, 2015)

Traded to **Toronto** by **Boston** for Toronto's 1st (Tyler Seguin) and 2nd (Jared Knight) round choices in 2010 Entry Draft and Toronto's 1st round choice (Dougie Hamilton) in 2011 Entry Draft, September 18, 2009. Traded to **Pittsburgh** by **Toronto** with Tim Erixon, Tyler Biggs and future considerations for Nick Spaling, Kasperi Kapanen, Scott Harrington, New Jersey's 3rd round choice (previously acquired) in 2016 Entry Draft and future considerations, July 1, 2015.

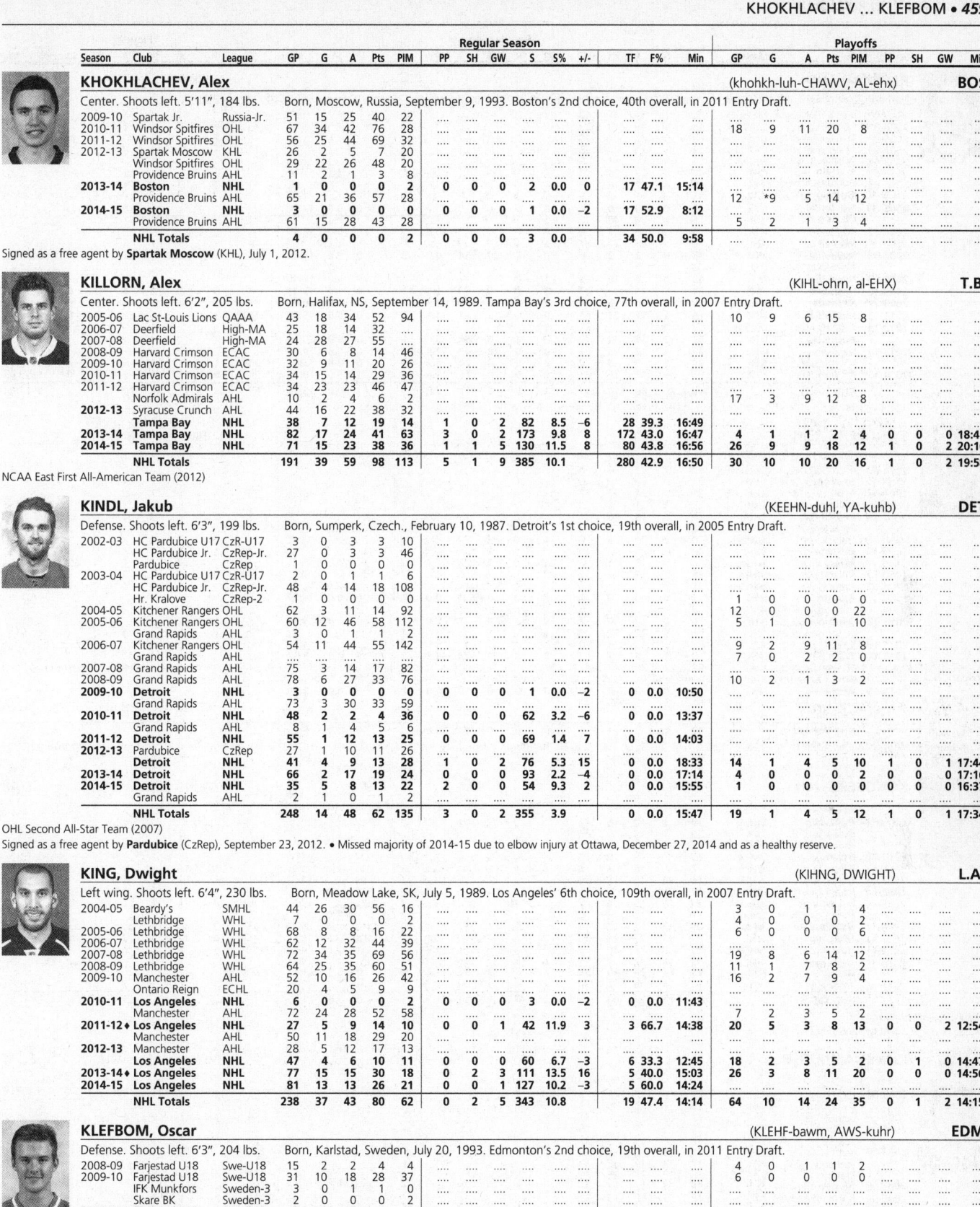

KHOKHLACHEV, Alex

(khohkh-luh-CHAWV, AL-ehx) **BOS**

Center. Shoots left. 5'11", 184 lbs. Born, Moscow, Russia, September 9, 1993. Boston's 2nd choice, 40th overall, in 2011 Entry Draft.

			Regular Season														Playoffs								
Season	Club	League	GP	G	A	Pts	PIM	PP	SH	GW	S	S%	+/-	TF	F%	Min	GP	G	A	Pts	PIM	PP	SH	GW	Min
2009-10	Spartak Jr.	Russia-Jr.	51	15	25	40	22	....	....	....	....	....	....	....	....	....	....	....	....	....	....	....	....	....	....
2010-11	Windsor Spitfires	OHL	67	34	42	76	28	....	....	....	....	....	....	....	....	....	18	9	11	20	8	....	....	....	....
2011-12	Windsor Spitfires	OHL	56	25	44	69	32	....	....	....	....	....	....	....	....	....	....	....	....	....	....	....	....	....	....
2012-13	Spartak Moscow	KHL	26	2	5	7	20	....	....	....	....	....	....	....	....	....	....	....	....	....	....	....	....	....	....
	Windsor Spitfires	OHL	29	22	26	48	20	....	....	....	....	....	....	....	....	....	....	....	....	....	....	....	....	....	....
	Providence Bruins	AHL	11	2	1	3	8	....	....	....	....	....	....	....	....	....	....	....	....	....	....	....	....	....	....
2013-14	**Boston**	**NHL**	**1**	**0**	**0**	**0**	**2**	**0**	**0**	**0**	**2**	**0.0**	**0**	**17**	**47.1**	**15:14**	....	....	....	....	....	....	....	....	....
	Providence Bruins	AHL	65	21	36	57	28	....	....	....	....	....	....	....	....	....	12	*9	5	14	12	....	....	....	....
2014-15	**Boston**	**NHL**	**3**	**0**	**0**	**0**	**0**	**0**	**0**	**0**	**1**	**0.0**	**-2**	**17**	**52.9**	**8:12**	....	....	....	....	....	....	....	....	....
	Providence Bruins	AHL	61	15	28	43	28	....	....	....	....	....	....	....	....	....	5	2	1	3	4	....	....	....	....
	NHL Totals		**4**	**0**	**0**	**0**	**2**	**0**	**0**	**0**	**3**	**0.0**		**34**	**50.0**	**9:58**	....	....	....	....	....	....	....	....	....

Signed as a free agent by **Spartak Moscow** (KHL), July 1, 2012.

KILLORN, Alex

(KIHL-ohrn, al-EHX) **T.B.**

Center. Shoots left. 6'2", 205 lbs. Born, Halifax, NS, September 14, 1989. Tampa Bay's 3rd choice, 77th overall, in 2007 Entry Draft.

Season	Club	League	GP	G	A	Pts	PIM	PP	SH	GW	S	S%	+/-	TF	F%	Min	GP	G	A	Pts	PIM	PP	SH	GW	Min
2005-06	Lac St-Louis Lions	QAAA	43	18	34	52	94	....	....	....	....	....	....	....	....	....	10	9	6	15	8	....	....	....	....
2006-07	Deerfield	High-MA	25	18	14	32	....	....	....	....	....	....	....	....	....	....	....	....	....	....	....	....	....	....	....
2007-08	Deerfield	High-MA	24	28	27	55	....	....	....	....	....	....	....	....	....	....	....	....	....	....	....	....	....	....	....
2008-09	Harvard Crimson	ECAC	30	6	8	14	46	....	....	....	....	....	....	....	....	....	....	....	....	....	....	....	....	....	....
2009-10	Harvard Crimson	ECAC	32	9	11	20	26	....	....	....	....	....	....	....	....	....	....	....	....	....	....	....	....	....	....
2010-11	Harvard Crimson	ECAC	34	15	14	29	36	....	....	....	....	....	....	....	....	....	....	....	....	....	....	....	....	....	....
2011-12	Harvard Crimson	ECAC	34	23	23	46	47	....	....	....	....	....	....	....	....	....	....	....	....	....	....	....	....	....	....
	Norfolk Admirals	AHL	10	2	4	6	2	....	....	....	....	....	....	....	....	....	17	3	9	12	8	....	....	....	....
2012-13	Syracuse Crunch	AHL	44	16	22	38	32	....	....	....	....	....	....	....	....	....	....	....	....	....	....	....	....	....	....
	Tampa Bay	**NHL**	**38**	**7**	**12**	**19**	**14**	**1**	**0**	**2**	**82**	**8.5**	**-6**	**28**	**39.3**	**16:49**	....	....	....	....	....	....	....	....	....
2013-14	**Tampa Bay**	**NHL**	**82**	**17**	**24**	**41**	**63**	**3**	**0**	**2**	**173**	**9.8**	**8**	**172**	**43.0**	**16:47**	**4**	**1**	**1**	**2**	**4**	**0**	**0**	**0**	**18:41**
2014-15	**Tampa Bay**	**NHL**	**71**	**15**	**23**	**38**	**36**	**1**	**1**	**5**	**130**	**11.5**	**8**	**80**	**43.8**	**16:56**	**26**	**9**	**9**	**18**	**12**	**1**	**0**	**2**	**20:10**
	NHL Totals		**191**	**39**	**59**	**98**	**113**	**5**	**1**	**9**	**385**	**10.1**		**280**	**42.9**	**16:50**	**30**	**10**	**10**	**20**	**16**	**1**	**0**	**2**	**19:58**

NCAA East First All-American Team (2012)

KINDL, Jakub

(KEEHN-duhl, YA-kuhb) **DET**

Defense. Shoots left. 6'3", 199 lbs. Born, Sumperk, Czech., February 10, 1987. Detroit's 1st choice, 19th overall, in 2005 Entry Draft.

Season	Club	League	GP	G	A	Pts	PIM	PP	SH	GW	S	S%	+/-	TF	F%	Min	GP	G	A	Pts	PIM	PP	SH	GW	Min
2002-03	HC Pardubice U17	CzR-U17	3	0	3	3	10	....	....	....	....	....	....	....	....	....	....	....	....	....	....	....	....	....	....
	HC Pardubice Jr.	CzRep-Jr.	27	0	3	3	46	....	....	....	....	....	....	....	....	....	....	....	....	....	....	....	....	....	....
	Pardubice	CzRep	1	0	0	0	0	....	....	....	....	....	....	....	....	....	....	....	....	....	....	....	....	....	....
2003-04	HC Pardubice U17	CzR-U17	2	0	1	1	6	....	....	....	....	....	....	....	....	....	....	....	....	....	....	....	....	....	....
	HC Pardubice Jr.	CzRep-Jr.	48	4	14	18	108	....	....	....	....	....	....	....	....	....	....	....	....	....	....	....	....	....	....
	Hr. Kralove	CzRep-2	1	0	0	0	0	....	....	....	....	....	....	....	....	....	1	0	0	0	0	....	....	....	....
2004-05	Kitchener Rangers	OHL	62	3	11	14	92	....	....	....	....	....	....	....	....	....	12	0	0	0	22	....	....	....	....
2005-06	Kitchener Rangers	OHL	60	12	46	58	112	....	....	....	....	....	....	....	....	....	5	1	0	1	10	....	....	....	....
	Grand Rapids	AHL	3	0	1	1	2	....	....	....	....	....	....	....	....	....	....	....	....	....	....	....	....	....	....
2006-07	Kitchener Rangers	OHL	54	11	44	55	142	....	....	....	....	....	....	....	....	....	9	2	9	11	8	....	....	....	....
	Grand Rapids	AHL	....	....	....	....	....	....	....	....	....	....	....	....	....	....	7	0	2	2	0	....	....	....	....
2007-08	Grand Rapids	AHL	75	3	14	17	82	....	....	....	....	....	....	....	....	....	....	....	....	....	....	....	....	....	....
2008-09	Grand Rapids	AHL	78	6	27	33	76	....	....	....	....	....	....	....	....	....	10	2	1	3	2	....	....	....	....
2009-10	**Detroit**	**NHL**	**3**	**0**	**0**	**0**	**0**	**0**	**0**	**0**	**1**	**0.0**	**-2**	**0**	**0.0**	**10:50**	....	....	....	....	....	....	....	....	....
	Grand Rapids	AHL	73	3	30	33	59	....	....	....	....	....	....	....	....	....	....	....	....	....	....	....	....	....	....
2010-11	**Detroit**	**NHL**	**48**	**2**	**2**	**4**	**36**	**0**	**0**	**0**	**62**	**3.2**	**-6**	**0**	**0.0**	**13:37**	....	....	....	....	....	....	....	....	....
	Grand Rapids	AHL	8	1	4	5	6	....	....	....	....	....	....	....	....	....	....	....	....	....	....	....	....	....	....
2011-12	**Detroit**	**NHL**	**55**	**1**	**12**	**13**	**25**	**0**	**0**	**0**	**69**	**1.4**	**7**	**0**	**0.0**	**14:03**	....	....	....	....	....	....	....	....	....
2012-13	Pardubice	CzRep	27	1	10	11	26	....	....	....	....	....	....	....	....	....	....	....	....	....	....	....	....	....	....
	Detroit	**NHL**	**41**	**4**	**9**	**13**	**28**	**1**	**0**	**2**	**76**	**5.3**	**15**	**0**	**0.0**	**18:33**	**14**	**1**	**4**	**5**	**10**	**1**	**0**	**1**	**17:44**
2013-14	**Detroit**	**NHL**	**66**	**2**	**17**	**19**	**24**	**0**	**0**	**0**	**93**	**2.2**	**-4**	**0**	**0.0**	**17:14**	**4**	**0**	**0**	**0**	**2**	**0**	**0**	**0**	**17:16**
2014-15	**Detroit**	**NHL**	**35**	**5**	**8**	**13**	**22**	**2**	**0**	**0**	**54**	**9.3**	**2**	**0**	**0.0**	**15:55**	**1**	**0**	**0**	**0**	**0**	**0**	**0**	**0**	**16:37**
	Grand Rapids	AHL	2	1	0	1	2	....	....	....	....	....	....	....	....	....	....	....	....	....	....	....	....	....	....
	NHL Totals		**248**	**14**	**48**	**62**	**135**	**3**	**0**	**2**	**355**	**3.9**		**0**	**0.0**	**15:47**	**19**	**1**	**4**	**5**	**12**	**1**	**0**	**1**	**17:34**

OHL Second All-Star Team (2007)

Signed as a free agent by **Pardubice** (CzRep), September 23, 2012. • Missed majority of 2014-15 due to elbow injury at Ottawa, December 27, 2014 and as a healthy reserve.

KING, Dwight

(KIHNG, DWIGHT) **L.A.**

Left wing. Shoots left. 6'4", 230 lbs. Born, Meadow Lake, SK, July 5, 1989. Los Angeles' 6th choice, 109th overall, in 2007 Entry Draft.

Season	Club	League	GP	G	A	Pts	PIM	PP	SH	GW	S	S%	+/-	TF	F%	Min	GP	G	A	Pts	PIM	PP	SH	GW	Min
2004-05	Beardy's	SMHL	44	26	30	56	16	....	....	....	....	....	....	....	....	....	3	0	1	1	4	....	....	....	....
	Lethbridge	WHL	7	0	0	0	2	....	....	....	....	....	....	....	....	....	4	0	0	0	2	....	....	....	....
2005-06	Lethbridge	WHL	68	8	8	16	22	....	....	....	....	....	....	....	....	....	6	0	0	0	6	....	....	....	....
2006-07	Lethbridge	WHL	62	12	32	44	39	....	....	....	....	....	....	....	....	....	....	....	....	....	....	....	....	....	....
2007-08	Lethbridge	WHL	72	34	35	69	56	....	....	....	....	....	....	....	....	....	19	8	6	14	12	....	....	....	....
2008-09	Lethbridge	WHL	64	25	35	60	51	....	....	....	....	....	....	....	....	....	11	1	7	8	2	....	....	....	....
2009-10	Manchester	AHL	52	10	16	26	42	....	....	....	....	....	....	....	....	....	16	2	7	9	4	....	....	....	....
	Ontario Reign	ECHL	20	4	5	9	9	....	....	....	....	....	....	....	....	....	....	....	....	....	....	....	....	....	....
2010-11	**Los Angeles**	**NHL**	**6**	**0**	**0**	**0**	**2**	**0**	**0**	**0**	**3**	**0.0**	**-2**	**0**	**0.0**	**11:43**	....	....	....	....	....	....	....	....	....
	Manchester	AHL	72	24	28	52	58	....	....	....	....	....	....	....	....	....	7	2	3	5	2	....	....	....	....
2011-12♦	**Los Angeles**	**NHL**	**27**	**5**	**9**	**14**	**10**	**0**	**0**	**1**	**42**	**11.9**	**3**	**3**	**66.7**	**14:38**	**20**	**5**	**3**	**8**	**13**	**0**	**0**	**2**	**12:54**
	Manchester	AHL	50	11	18	29	20	....	....	....	....	....	....	....	....	....	....	....	....	....	....	....	....	....	....
2012-13	Manchester	AHL	28	5	12	17	13	....	....	....	....	....	....	....	....	....	....	....	....	....	....	....	....	....	....
	Los Angeles	**NHL**	**47**	**4**	**6**	**10**	**11**	**0**	**0**	**0**	**60**	**6.7**	**-3**	**6**	**33.3**	**12:45**	**18**	**2**	**3**	**5**	**2**	**0**	**1**	**0**	**14:47**
2013-14♦	**Los Angeles**	**NHL**	**77**	**15**	**15**	**30**	**18**	**0**	**2**	**3**	**111**	**13.5**	**16**	**5**	**40.0**	**15:03**	**26**	**3**	**8**	**11**	**20**	**0**	**0**	**0**	**14:56**
2014-15	**Los Angeles**	**NHL**	**81**	**13**	**13**	**26**	**21**	**0**	**0**	**1**	**127**	**10.2**	**-3**	**5**	**60.0**	**14:24**	....	....	....	....	....	....	....	....	....
	NHL Totals		**238**	**37**	**43**	**80**	**62**	**0**	**2**	**5**	**343**	**10.8**		**19**	**47.4**	**14:14**	**64**	**10**	**14**	**24**	**35**	**0**	**1**	**2**	**14:15**

KLEFBOM, Oscar

(KLEHF-bawm, AWS-kuhr) **EDM**

Defense. Shoots left. 6'3", 204 lbs. Born, Karlstad, Sweden, July 20, 1993. Edmonton's 2nd choice, 19th overall, in 2011 Entry Draft.

Season	Club	League	GP	G	A	Pts	PIM	PP	SH	GW	S	S%	+/-	TF	F%	Min	GP	G	A	Pts	PIM	PP	SH	GW	Min
2008-09	Farjestad U18	Swe-U18	15	2	2	4	4	....	....	....	....	....	....	....	....	....	4	0	1	1	2	....	....	....	....
2009-10	Farjestad U18	Swe-U18	31	10	18	28	37	....	....	....	....	....	....	....	....	....	6	0	0	0	0	....	....	....	....
	IFK Munkfors	Sweden-3	3	0	1	1	0	....	....	....	....	....	....	....	....	....	....	....	....	....	....	....	....	....	....
	Skare BK	Sweden-3	2	0	0	0	2	....	....	....	....	....	....	....	....	....	....	....	....	....	....	....	....	....	....
2010-11	Farjestad U18	Swe-U18	8	3	3	6	2	....	....	....	....	....	....	....	....	....	....	....	....	....	....	....	....	....	....
	Skare BK	Sweden-3	12	0	1	1	0	....	....	....	....	....	....	....	....	....	....	....	....	....	....	....	....	....	....
	Farjestad	Sweden	23	1	1	2	2	....	....	....	....	....	....	....	....	....	....	....	....	....	....	....	....	....	....
2011-12	Farjestad Jr.	Swe-Jr.	15	1	3	4	0	....	....	....	....	....	....	....	....	....	....	....	....	....	....	....	....	....	....
	Farjestad	Sweden	33	2	0	2	4	....	....	....	....	....	....	....	....	....	11	0	1	1	2	....	....	....	....
2012-13	Farjestad	Sweden	11	0	3	3	2	....	....	....	....	....	....	....	....	....	....	....	....	....	....	....	....	....	....
2013-14	**Edmonton**	**NHL**	**17**	**1**	**2**	**3**	**0**	**0**	**0**	**0**	**14**	**7.1**	**-6**	**0**	**0.0**	**15:48**	....	....	....	....	....	....	....	....	....
	Oklahoma City	AHL	48	1	9	10	10	....	....	....	....	....	....	....	....	....	2	0	1	1	4	....	....	....	....
2014-15	**Edmonton**	**NHL**	**60**	**2**	**18**	**20**	**4**	**0**	**0**	**0**	**98**	**2.0**	**-21**	**0**	**0.0**	**22:00**	....	....	....	....	....	....	....	....	....
	Oklahoma City	AHL	9	1	7	8	4	....	....	....	....	....	....	....	....	....	....	....	....	....	....	....	....	....	....
	NHL Totals		**77**	**3**	**20**	**23**	**4**	**0**	**0**	**0**	**112**	**2.7**		**0**	**0.0**	**20:38**	....	....	....	....	....	....	....	....	....

KLEIN, Kevin (KLIGHN, KEH-vihn) NYR

Defense. Shoots right. 6'1", 199 lbs. Born, Kitchener, ON, December 13, 1984. Nashville's 3rd choice, 37th overall, in 2003 Entry Draft.

			Regular Season														Playoffs								
Season	Club	League	GP	G	A	Pts	PIM	PP	SH	GW	S	S%	+/-	TF	F%	Min	GP	G	A	Pts	PIM	PP	SH	GW	Min
99-2000	Kitchener Midget	Minor-ON	54	12	29	41	40	....	....	....	....	....	....	....	....	....	....	....	....	....	....	....	....	....	....
2000-01	St. Michael's	OHL	58	3	16	19	21	....	....	....	....	....	....	....	....	....	18	0	5	5	17	....	....	....	....
2001-02	St. Michael's	OHL	68	5	22	27	35	....	....	....	....	....	....	....	....	....	15	2	7	9	12	....	....	....	....
2002-03	St. Michael's	OHL	67	11	33	44	88	....	....	....	....	....	....	....	....	....	17	1	9	10	8	....	....	....	....
2003-04	St. Michael's	OHL	5	0	1	1	2	....	....	....	....	....	....	....	....	....	....	....	....	....	....	....	....	....	....
	Guelph Storm	OHL	46	6	23	29	40	....	....	....	....	....	....	....	....	....	22	10	11	21	12	....	....	....	....
2004-05	Milwaukee	AHL	65	4	12	16	22	....	....	....	....	....	....	....	....	....	7	0	0	0	11	....	....	....	....
	Rockford IceHogs	UHL	3	2	1	3	0	....	....	....	....	....	....	....	....	....	....	....	....	....	....	....	....	....	....
2005-06	**Nashville**	**NHL**	**2**	**0**	**0**	**0**	**0**	**0**	**0**	**0**	**0**	**0.0**	**–1**	**0**	**0.0**	**13:40**	....	....	....	....	....	....	....	....	....
	Milwaukee	AHL	76	10	33	43	31	....	....	....	....	....	....	....	....	....	21	3	7	10	31	....	....	....	....
2006-07	**Nashville**	**NHL**	**3**	**1**	**0**	**1**	**0**	**0**	**0**	**0**	**2**	**50.0**	**3**	**0**	**0.0**	**16:37**	....	....	....	....	....	....	....	....	....
	Milwaukee	AHL	70	5	15	20	67	....	....	....	....	....	....	....	....	....	4	1	0	1	0	....	....	....	....
2007-08	**Nashville**	**NHL**	**13**	**0**	**2**	**2**	**6**	**0**	**0**	**0**	**14**	**0.0**	**–3**	**0**	**0.0**	**14:24**	....	....	....	....	....	....	....	....	....
	Milwaukee	AHL	9	0	3	3	2	....	....	....	....	....	....	....	....	....	....	....	....	....	....	....	....	....	....
2008-09	**Nashville**	**NHL**	**63**	**4**	**8**	**12**	**19**	**1**	**0**	**0**	**41**	**9.8**	**–2**	**0**	**0.0**	**12:40**	....	....	....	....	....	....	....	....	....
2009-10	**Nashville**	**NHL**	**81**	**1**	**10**	**11**	**27**	**0**	**0**	**0**	**67**	**1.5**	**–13**	**0**	**0.0**	**19:55**	**6**	**0**	**2**	**2**	**4**	**0**	**0**	**0**	**17:43**
2010-11	**Nashville**	**NHL**	**81**	**2**	**16**	**18**	**24**	**0**	**0**	**0**	**99**	**2.0**	**9**	**0**	**0.0**	**20:48**	**12**	**1**	**2**	**3**	**6**	**0**	**0**	**0**	**20:14**
2011-12	**Nashville**	**NHL**	**66**	**4**	**17**	**21**	**4**	**0**	**0**	**2**	**91**	**4.4**	**–8**	**0**	**0.0**	**19:56**	**10**	**2**	**2**	**4**	**2**	**0**	**0**	**1**	**19:31**
2012-13	Herlev Eagles	Denmark	8	1	2	3	29	....	....	....	....	....	....	....	....	....	....	....	....	....	....	....	....	....	....
	Nashville	**NHL**	**47**	**3**	**11**	**14**	**9**	**0**	**0**	**0**	**54**	**5.6**	**–1**	**0**	**0.0**	**20:25**	....	....	....	....	....	....	....	....	....
2013-14	**Nashville**	**NHL**	**47**	**1**	**2**	**3**	**21**	**0**	**0**	**0**	**49**	**2.0**	**–11**	**0**	**0.0**	**18:48**	....	....	....	....	....	....	....	....	....
	NY Rangers	**NHL**	**30**	**1**	**5**	**6**	**0**	**0**	**0**	**0**	**24**	**4.2**	**4**	**0**	**0.0**	**15:01**	**25**	**1**	**3**	**4**	**6**	**0**	**0**	**0**	**13:17**
2014-15	**NY Rangers**	**NHL**	**65**	**9**	**17**	**26**	**25**	**0**	**0**	**4**	**76**	**11.8**	**24**	**1**	**0.0**	**18:29**	**14**	**0**	**4**	**4**	**2**	**0**	**0**	**0**	**19:05**
	NHL Totals		**498**	**26**	**88**	**114**	**135**	**1**	**0**	**6**	**517**	**5.0**		**1**	**0.0**	**18:25**	**67**	**4**	**13**	**17**	**20**	**0**	**0**	**1**	**17:04**

Signed as a free agent by **Herlev** (Denmark), November 14, 2012. Traded to **NY Rangers** by **Nashville** for Michael Del Zotto, January 22, 2014.

KLINGBERG, Carl (KLIHNG-buhrg, KAHRL)

Left wing. Shoots right. 6'3", 205 lbs. Born, Goteborg, Sweden, January 28, 1991. Atlanta's 2nd choice, 34th overall, in 2009 Entry Draft.

Season	Club	League	GP	G	A	Pts	PIM	PP	SH	GW	S	S%	+/-	TF	F%	Min	GP	G	A	Pts	PIM	PP	SH	GW	Min
2006-07	Frolunda U18	Swe-U18	7	3	1	4	0	....	....	....	....	....	....	....	....	....	....	....	....	....	....	....	....	....	....
	Frolunda Jr.	Swe-Jr.	2	0	0	0	0	....	....	....	....	....	....	....	....	....	....	....	....	....	....	....	....	....	....
2007-08	Frolunda U18	Swe-U18	31	19	24	43	22	....	....	....	....	....	....	....	....	....	5	2	1	3	8	....	....	....	....
2008-09	Frolunda U18	Swe-U18	3	4	1	5	0	....	....	....	....	....	....	....	....	....	5	2	2	4	2	....	....	....	....
	Frolunda Jr.	Swe-Jr.	35	13	13	26	34	....	....	....	....	....	....	....	....	....	2	0	0	0	4	....	....	....	....
	Boras HC	Sweden-2	8	4	2	6	2	....	....	....	....	....	....	....	....	....	....	....	....	....	....	....	....	....	....
	Frolunda	Sweden	10	2	1	3	0	....	....	....	....	....	....	....	....	....	....	....	....	....	....	....	....	....	....
2009-10	Frolunda	Sweden	42	6	7	13	16	....	....	....	....	....	....	....	....	....	7	0	0	0	2	....	....	....	....
	Boras HC	Sweden-2	4	0	5	5	2	....	....	....	....	....	....	....	....	....	....	....	....	....	....	....	....	....	....
2010-11	Frolunda	Sweden	38	2	1	3	12	....	....	....	....	....	....	....	....	....	....	....	....	....	....	....	....	....	....
	Timra IK	Sweden	11	3	2	5	2	....	....	....	....	....	....	....	....	....	....	....	....	....	....	....	....	....	....
	Atlanta	**NHL**	**1**	**0**	**0**	**0**	**0**	**0**	**0**	**0**	**0**	**0.0**	**0**	**0**	**0.0**	**10:22**	....	....	....	....	....	....	....	....	....
	Chicago Wolves	AHL	8	1	0	1	6	....	....	....	....	....	....	....	....	....	....	....	....	....	....	....	....	....	....
2011-12	**Winnipeg**	**NHL**	**6**	**0**	**0**	**0**	**4**	**0**	**0**	**0**	**7**	**0.0**	**–1**	**0**	**0.0**	**5:30**	....	....	....	....	....	....	....	....	....
	St. John's IceCaps	AHL	66	15	22	37	39	....	....	....	....	....	....	....	....	....	12	1	1	2	0	....	....	....	....
2012-13	St. John's IceCaps	AHL	66	11	12	23	40	....	....	....	....	....	....	....	....	....	....	....	....	....	....	....	....	....	....
2013-14	**Winnipeg**	**NHL**	**3**	**1**	**0**	**1**	**0**	**0**	**0**	**0**	**3**	**33.3**	**2**	**0**	**0.0**	**8:52**	....	....	....	....	....	....	....	....	....
	St. John's IceCaps	AHL	65	22	20	42	42	....	....	....	....	....	....	....	....	....	21	3	5	8	14	....	....	....	....
	Nizhny Novgorod	KHL	....	....	....	....	....	....	....	....	....	....	....	....	....	....	....	....	....	....	....	....	....	....	....
2014-15	**Winnipeg**	**NHL**	**2**	**0**	**0**	**0**	**0**	**0**	**0**	**0**	**0**	**0.0**	**–1**	**0**	**0.0**	**3:19**	....	....	....	....	....	....	....	....	....
	St. John's IceCaps	AHL	51	15	15	30	41	....	....	....	....	....	....	....	....	....	....	....	....	....	....	....	....	....	....
	Hartford	AHL	13	2	9	11	4	....	....	....	....	....	....	....	....	....	13	4	3	7	6	....	....	....	....
	NHL Totals		**12**	**1**	**0**	**1**	**4**	**0**	**0**	**0**	**10**	**10.0**		**0**	**0.0**	**6:23**	....	....	....	....	....	....	....	....	....

• Transferred to **Winnipeg** after **Atlanta** franchise relocated, June 21, 2011. Traded to **NY Rangers** by **Winnipeg** for Lee Stempniak, March 1, 2015. Signed as a free agent by **Nizhny Novgorod** (KHL), June 21, 2015.

KLINGBERG, John (KLIHNG-buhrg, JAWN) DAL

Defense. Shoots right. 6'2", 180 lbs. Born, Lerum, Sweden, August 14, 1992. Dallas' 5th choice, 131st overall, in 2010 Entry Draft.

Season	Club	League	GP	G	A	Pts	PIM	PP	SH	GW	S	S%	+/-	TF	F%	Min	GP	G	A	Pts	PIM	PP	SH	GW	Min
2008-09	Frolunda U18	Swe-U18	30	3	12	15	12	....	....	....	....	....	....	....	....	....	3	0	0	0	0	....	....	....	....
2009-10	Frolunda U18	Swe-U18	20	3	13	16	22	....	....	....	....	....	....	....	....	....	7	2	9	11	10	....	....	....	....
	Frolunda Jr.	Swe-Jr.	27	0	5	5	32	....	....	....	....	....	....	....	....	....	5	1	0	1	6	....	....	....	....
2010-11	Frolunda	Sweden	26	0	5	5	10	....	....	....	....	....	....	....	....	....	....	....	....	....	....	....	....	....	....
	Boras HC	Sweden-2	7	1	0	1	2	....	....	....	....	....	....	....	....	....	....	....	....	....	....	....	....	....	....
	Frolunda Jr.	Swe-Jr.	13	3	14	17	29	....	....	....	....	....	....	....	....	....	7	1	10	11	6	....	....	....	....
2011-12	Jokerit Helsinki	Finland	20	1	2	3	8	....	....	....	....	....	....	....	....	....	....	....	....	....	....	....	....	....	....
	Skelleftea AIK	Sweden	16	1	3	4	6	....	....	....	....	....	....	....	....	....	16	0	4	4	14	....	....	....	....
2012-13	Skelleftea AIK Jr.	Swe-Jr.	1	0	0	0	0	....	....	....	....	....	....	....	....	....	....	....	....	....	....	....	....	....	....
	Skelleftea AIK	Sweden	25	1	12	13	6	....	....	....	....	....	....	....	....	....	13	1	3	4	8	....	....	....	....
	Texas Stars	AHL	....	....	....	....	....	....	....	....	....	....	....	....	....	....	1	0	0	0	0	....	....	....	....
2013-14	Frolunda	Sweden	50	11	17	28	12	....	....	....	....	....	....	....	....	....	7	0	4	4	2	....	....	....	....
	Texas Stars	AHL	3	0	1	1	4	....	....	....	....	....	....	....	....	....	....	....	....	....	....	....	....	....	....
2014-15	**Dallas**	**NHL**	**65**	**11**	**29**	**40**	**32**	**2**	**0**	**3**	**98**	**11.2**	**5**	**0**	**0.0**	**21:50**	....	....	....	....	....	....	....	....	....
	Texas Stars	AHL	10	4	8	12	6	....	....	....	....	....	....	....	....	....	....	....	....	....	....	....	....	....	....
	NHL Totals		**65**	**11**	**29**	**40**	**32**	**2**	**0**	**3**	**98**	**11.2**		**0**	**0.0**	**21:50**	....	....	....	....	....	....	....	....	....

NHL All-Rookie Team (2015)

Signed as a free agent by **Frolunda** (Sweden), May 20, 2013.

KLINKHAMMER, Rob (KLIHNK-ham-uhr, RAWB) EDM

Left wing. Shoots left. 6'3", 220 lbs. Born, Lethbridge, AB, August 12, 1986.

Season	Club	League	GP	G	A	Pts	PIM	PP	SH	GW	S	S%	+/-	TF	F%	Min	GP	G	A	Pts	PIM	PP	SH	GW	Min
2003-04	Lethbridge	AMHL	29	20	22	42	8	....	....	....	....	....	....	....	....	....	....	....	....	....	....	....	....	....	....
	Lethbridge	WHL	25	2	3	5	12	....	....	....	....	....	....	....	....	....	....	....	....	....	....	....	....	....	....
2004-05	Lethbridge	WHL	72	14	12	26	81	....	....	....	....	....	....	....	....	....	5	0	1	1	4	....	....	....	....
2005-06	Lethbridge	WHL	35	5	7	12	15	....	....	....	....	....	....	....	....	....	....	....	....	....	....	....	....	....	....
	Seattle	WHL	32	3	5	8	37	....	....	....	....	....	....	....	....	....	7	0	1	1	6	....	....	....	....
2006-07	Seattle	WHL	1	0	0	0	9	....	....	....	....	....	....	....	....	....	....	....	....	....	....	....	....	....	....
	Portland	WHL	37	23	19	42	70	....	....	....	....	....	....	....	....	....	....	....	....	....	....	....	....	....	....
	Brandon	WHL	28	10	21	31	29	....	....	....	....	....	....	....	....	....	11	4	4	8	22	....	....	....	....
2007-08	Norfolk Admirals	AHL	66	12	12	24	41	....	....	....	....	....	....	....	....	....	....	....	....	....	....	....	....	....	....
2008-09	Rockford IceHogs	AHL	76	15	18	33	32	....	....	....	....	....	....	....	....	....	4	0	1	1	0	....	....	....	....
2009-10	Rockford IceHogs	AHL	72	10	13	23	38	....	....	....	....	....	....	....	....	....	4	1	1	2	7	....	....	....	....
2010-11	**Chicago**	**NHL**	**1**	**0**	**0**	**0**	**0**	**0**	**0**	**0**	**1**	**0.0**	**1**	**0**	**0.0**	**11:36**	....	....	....	....	....	....	....	....	....
	Rockford IceHogs	AHL	76	17	29	46	63	....	....	....	....	....	....	....	....	....	....	....	....	....	....	....	....	....	....
2011-12	Rockford IceHogs	AHL	18	2	4	6	6	....	....	....	....	....	....	....	....	....	....	....	....	....	....	....	....	....	....
	Ottawa	**NHL**	**15**	**0**	**2**	**2**	**2**	**0**	**0**	**0**	**26**	**0.0**	**0**	**3**	**66.7**	**11:27**	....	....	....	....	....	....	....	....	....
	Binghamton	AHL	35	12	23	35	30	....	....	....	....	....	....	....	....	....	....	....	....	....	....	....	....	....	....
2012-13	Portland Pirates	AHL	53	14	30	44	36	....	....	....	....	....	....	....	....	....	....	....	....	....	....	....	....	....	....
	Phoenix	**NHL**	**22**	**5**	**6**	**11**	**10**	**1**	**0**	**1**	**34**	**14.7**	**7**	**2**	**100.0**	**12:14**	....	....	....	....	....	....	....	....	....
2013-14	**Phoenix**	**NHL**	**72**	**11**	**9**	**20**	**19**	**1**	**0**	**1**	**103**	**10.7**	**6**	**6**	**16.7**	**11:22**	....	....	....	....	....	....	....	....	....
2014-15	**Arizona**	**NHL**	**19**	**3**	**0**	**3**	**4**	**0**	**0**	**0**	**23**	**13.0**	**3**	**1**	**0.0**	**11:33**	....	....	....	....	....	....	....	....	....
	Pittsburgh	**NHL**	**10**	**1**	**2**	**3**	**0**	**0**	**0**	**0**	**10**	**10.0**	**0**	**1**	**100.0**	**11:08**	....	....	....	....	....	....	....	....	....
	Edmonton	**NHL**	**40**	**1**	**2**	**3**	**23**	**0**	**0**	**0**	**31**	**3.2**	**–7**	**35**	**25.7**	**11:05**	....	....	....	....	....	....	....	....	....
	NHL Totals		**179**	**21**	**21**	**42**	**58**	**2**	**0**	**2**	**228**	**9.2**		**48**	**31.3**	**11:25**	....	....	....	....	....	....	....	....	....

Signed as a free agent by **Tampa Bay**, July 24, 2007. Signed as a free agent by **Chicago**, June 8, 2009. Traded to **Ottawa** by **Chicago** for Ottawa's 7th round choice (later traded to Calgary – Calgary selected John Gilmour) in 2013 Entry Draft, December 2, 2011. Signed as a free agent by **Phoenix**, July 3, 2012. Traded to **Pittsburgh** by **Arizona** with future considerations for Philip Samuelsson, December 5, 2014. Traded to **Edmonton** by **Pittsburgh** with Pittsburgh's 1st round choice (later traded to NY Islanders – NY Islanders selected Mathew Barzal) in 2015 Entry Draft for David Perron, January 2, 2015.

KNIGHT, Corban

(NIGHT, KOHR-buhn) **FLA**

Center. Shoots right. 6'2", 195 lbs. Born, Oliver, BC, September 10, 1990. Florida's 5th choice, 135th overall, in 2009 Entry Draft.

			Regular Season														Playoffs								
Season	Club	League	GP	G	A	Pts	PIM	PP	SH	GW	S	S%	+/-	TF	F%	Min	GP	G	A	Pts	PIM	PP	SH	GW	Min
2006-07	UFA Bisons	AMHL	36	6	18	24	44										8	2	4	6	16				
2007-08	UFA Bisons	AMHL	36	29	36	65	64										6	5	4	9	10				
	Okotoks Oilers	AJHL	4	1	0	1	0										7	0	0	0	0				
2008-09	Okotoks Oilers	AJHL	61	34	38	72	55										9	10	2	12	12				
2009-10	North Dakota	WCHA	37	6	7	13	35																		
2010-11	North Dakota	WCHA	44	14	30	44	34																		
2011-12	North Dakota	WCHA	39	16	24	40	36																		
2012-13	North Dakota	WCHA	41	16	33	49	40																		
2013-14	**Calgary**	**NHL**	**7**	**1**	**0**	**1**	**0**	**0**	**0**	**0**	**4**	**25.0**	**–1**	**51**	**47.1**	**7:56**									
	Abbotsford Heat	AHL	70	18	27	45	50										2	0	1	1	2				
2014-15	**Calgary**	**NHL**	**2**	**0**	**0**	**0**	**0**	**0**	**0**	**0**	**2**	**0.0**	**0**	**11**	**81.8**	**6:24**									
	Adirondack	AHL	22	8	4	12	12																		
	San Antonio	AHL	36	8	16	24	8										3	1	0	1	0				
	NHL Totals		**9**	**1**	**0**	**1**	**0**	**0**	**0**	**0**	**6**	**16.7**		**62**	**53.2**	**7:36**									

WCHA Second All-Star Team (2013) • NCAA West Second All-American Team (2013)

Traded to **Calgary** by **Florida** for Calgary's 4th round choice (Michael Downing) in 2013 Entry Draft, June 18, 2013. Traded to **Florida** by **Calgary** for Drew Shore, January 9, 2015.

KOEKKOEK, Slater

(KOO-KOO, SLAY-tuhr) **T.B.**

Defense. Shoots left. 6'2", 184 lbs. Born, Winchester, ON, February 18, 1994. Tampa Bay's 1st choice, 10th overall, in 2012 Entry Draft.

Season	Club	League	GP	G	A	Pts	PIM	PP	SH	GW	S	S%	+/-	TF	F%	Min	GP	G	A	Pts	PIM	PP	SH	GW	Min
2008-09	Notre Dame	Minor-SK	47	20	39	59	40																		
2009-10	Notre Dame	SMHL	44	16	27	43	91										13	3	4	7	6				
2010-11	Peterborough	OHL	65	7	16	23	67																		
2011-12	Peterborough	OHL	26	5	13	18	17																		
2012-13	Peterborough	OHL	40	6	22	28	28																		
	Windsor Spitfires	OHL	2	0	1	1	0																		
2013-14	Windsor Spitfires	OHL	62	15	38	53	51																		
2014-15	**Tampa Bay**	**NHL**	**3**	**0**	**0**	**0**	**2**	**0**	**0**	**0**	**6**	**0.0**	**0**	**0**	**0.0**	**16:35**									
	Syracuse Crunch	AHL	72	5	21	26	44										3	0	1	1	6				
	NHL Totals		**3**	**0**	**0**	**0**	**2**	**0**	**0**	**0**	**6**	**0.0**		**0**	**0.0**	**16:35**									

OHL First All-Star Team (2014)

• Missed majority of 2011-12 due to shoulder injury vs. Windsor (OHL), November 27, 2011.

KOIVU, Mikko

(KOI-voo, MEE-koh) **MIN**

Center. Shoots left. 6'3", 222 lbs. Born, Turku, Finland, March 12, 1983. Minnesota's 1st choice, 6th overall, in 2001 Entry Draft.

Season	Club	League	GP	G	A	Pts	PIM	PP	SH	GW	S	S%	+/-	TF	F%	Min	GP	G	A	Pts	PIM	PP	SH	GW	Min
99-2000	TPS Turku U18	Fin-U18	11	4	9	13	18																		
	TPS Turku Jr.	Fin-Jr.	30	4	8	12	22										13	1	4	5	8				
2000-01	TPS Turku U18	Fin-U18															7	2	10	12	2				
	TPS Turku Jr.	Fin-Jr.	26	9	36	45	26										3	1	1	2	6				
	TPS Turku	Finland	21	0	1	1	2																		
2001-02	TPS Turku Jr.	Fin-Jr.	2	0	1	1	12																		
	TPS Turku	Finland	48	4	3	7	34										8	0	3	3	4				
2002-03	TPS Turku	Finland	37	7	13	20	20										7	2	2	4	6				
2003-04	TPS Turku	Finland	45	6	24	30	36										13	1	7	8	8				
2004-05	Houston Aeros	AHL	67	20	28	48	47										5	1	0	1	2				
2005-06	**Minnesota**	**NHL**	**64**	**6**	**15**	**21**	**40**	**3**	**0**	**0**	**96**	**6.3**	**–9**	**724**	**47.4**	**13:17**									
	Finland	Olympics	8	0	0	0	6																		
2006-07	**Minnesota**	**NHL**	**82**	**20**	**34**	**54**	**58**	**9**	**2**	**2**	**162**	**12.3**	**6**	**1165**	**50.9**	**17:29**	**5**	**1**	**0**	**1**	**4**	**0**	**0**	**0**	**17:43**
2007-08	**Minnesota**	**NHL**	**57**	**11**	**31**	**42**	**42**	**2**	**0**	**2**	**144**	**7.6**	**13**	**1032**	**52.5**	**20:53**	**6**	**4**	**1**	**5**	**4**	**0**	**1**	**0**	**21:56**
2008-09	**Minnesota**	**NHL**	**79**	**20**	**47**	**67**	**66**	**5**	**4**	**3**	**236**	**8.5**	**2**	**1625**	**52.7**	**21:29**									
2009-10	**Minnesota**	**NHL**	**80**	**22**	**49**	**71**	**50**	**8**	**1**	**2**	**246**	**8.9**	**–2**	**1518**	**56.9**	**20:45**									
	Finland	Olympics	6	0	4	4	2																		
2010-11	**Minnesota**	**NHL**	**71**	**17**	**45**	**62**	**50**	**7**	**1**	**3**	**191**	**8.9**	**4**	**1293**	**52.8**	**19:29**									
2011-12	**Minnesota**	**NHL**	**55**	**12**	**32**	**44**	**28**	**2**	**1**	**2**	**129**	**9.3**	**10**	**1123**	**52.3**	**21:21**									
2012-13	TPS Turku	Finland	10	5	5	10	16																		
	Minnesota	**NHL**	**48**	**11**	**26**	**37**	**26**	**0**	**0**	**3**	**127**	**8.7**	**2**	**971**	**54.0**	**21:06**	**5**	**0**	**0**	**0**	**8**	**0**	**0**	**0**	**20:30**
2013-14	**Minnesota**	**NHL**	**65**	**11**	**43**	**54**	**24**	**2**	**0**	**4**	**147**	**7.5**	**0**	**1311**	**54.8**	**20:56**	**13**	**1**	**6**	**7**	**10**	**0**	**0**	**0**	**20:32**
2014-15	**Minnesota**	**NHL**	**80**	**14**	**34**	**48**	**38**	**4**	**0**	**4**	**179**	**7.8**	**2**	**1791**	**55.2**	**19:16**	**10**	**1**	**3**	**4**	**2**	**1**	**0**	**0**	**18:13**
	NHL Totals		**681**	**144**	**356**	**500**	**422**	**42**	**9**	**25**	**1657**	**8.7**		**12553**	**53.4**	**19:32**	**39**	**7**	**10**	**17**	**28**	**1**	**1**	**0**	**19:47**

Signed as a free agent by **TPS Turku** (Finland), October 22, 2012.

KOMAROV, Leo

(koh-mah-RAWV, L'YAY-oh) **TOR**

Center. Shoots left. 5'11", 198 lbs. Born, Narva, USSR, January 23, 1987. Toronto's 7th choice, 180th overall, in 2006 Entry Draft.

Season	Club	League	GP	G	A	Pts	PIM	PP	SH	GW	S	S%	+/-	TF	F%	Min	GP	G	A	Pts	PIM	PP	SH	GW	Min
2003-04	Sport Vaasa U18	Fin-U18	30	9	15	24	8																		
2004-05	Assat Pori U18	Fin-U18	9	4	5	9	62																		
	Assat Pori Jr.	Fin-Jr.	38	8	6	13	59										2	0	0	0	2				
2005-06	Suomi U20	Finland-2	5	0	3	3	4																		
	Assat Pori Jr.	Fin-Jr.	10	5	6	11	59										2	2	1	3	10				
	Assat Pori	Finland	44	3	3	6	106										14	1	3	4	22				
2006-07	Suomi U20	Finland-2	1	1	0	1	0																		
	Pelicans Lahti	Finland	49	3	9	12	108										6	1	0	1	6				
2007-08	Pelicans Lahti Jr.	Fin-Jr.	2	0	3	3	0																		
	Pelicans Lahti	Finland	53	4	10	14	76										6	1	1	2	8				
2008-09	Pelicans Lahti	Finland	56	8	16	24	144										10	0	1	1	16				
2009-10	Dynamo Moscow	KHL	47	5	11	16	44										4	0	1	1	16				
2010-11	Dynamo Moscow	KHL	52	14	12	26	70										6	4	2	6	2				
2011-12	Dynamo Moscow	KHL	46	11	13	24	58										20	5	2	7	49				
2012-13	Toronto Marlies	AHL	14	6	3	9	22																		
	Dynamo Moscow	KHL	13	2	8	10	42																		
	Toronto	**NHL**	**42**	**4**	**5**	**9**	**18**	**0**	**0**	**3**	**51**	**7.8**	**–1**	**57**	**50.9**	**13:56**	**7**	**0**	**0**	**0**	**17**	**0**	**0**	**0**	**9:13**
2013-14	Dynamo Moscow	KHL	52	12	22	34	42										7	3	1	4	22				
	Finland	Olympics	6	0	0	0	0																		
2014-15	**Toronto**	**NHL**	**62**	**8**	**18**	**26**	**18**	**0**	**1**	**1**	**84**	**9.5**	**0**	**192**	**49.5**	**14:42**									
	NHL Totals		**104**	**12**	**23**	**35**	**36**	**0**	**1**	**4**	**135**	**8.9**		**249**	**49.8**	**14:23**	**7**	**0**	**0**	**0**	**17**	**0**	**0**	**0**	**9:13**

Signed as a free agent by **Dynamo Moscow** (KHL), June 10, 2013. Signed as a free agent by **Toronto**, July 1, 2014.

KOPECKY, Tomas

(koh-PEHTS-kee, TAW-mahsh)

Center. Shoots left. 6'3", 210 lbs. Born, Ilava, Czech., February 5, 1982. Detroit's 2nd choice, 38th overall, in 2000 Entry Draft.

Season	Club	League	GP	G	A	Pts	PIM	PP	SH	GW	S	S%	+/-	TF	F%	Min	GP	G	A	Pts	PIM	PP	SH	GW	Min
1997-98	Dukla Trencin Jr.	Slovak-Jr.	41	19	22	41																			
1998-99	Dukla Trencin Jr.	Slovak-Jr.	44	13	16	29	18																		
99-2000	Dukla Trencin Jr.	Slovak-Jr.	14	8	9	17	36																		
	Dukla Trencin	Slovakia	52	3	4	7	24										5	0	0	0	0				
2000-01	Lethbridge	WHL	49	22	28	50	52										5	1	1	2	6				
	Cincinnati	AHL	1	0	0	0	0																		
2001-02	Lethbridge	WHL	60	34	42	76	94										4	2	1	3	15				
	Cincinnati	AHL	2	1	1	2	6										2	0	0	0	0				
2002-03	Grand Rapids	AHL	70	17	21	38	32										14	0	0	0	6				
2003-04	Grand Rapids	AHL	48	6	6	12	28										1	0	0	0	2				
2004-05	Grand Rapids	AHL	48	8	8	16	35																		
2005-06	**Detroit**	**NHL**	**1**	**0**	**0**	**0**	**2**	**0**	**0**	**0**	**1**	**0.0**	**1**	**0**	**0.0**	**9:41**									
	Grand Rapids	AHL	77	32	37	69	108										16	3	4	7	25				
2006-07	**Detroit**	**NHL**	**26**	**1**	**0**	**1**	**22**	**0**	**0**	**0**	**27**	**3.7**	**–2**	**5**	**40.0**	**7:15**	**4**	**0**	**0**	**0**	**6**	**0**	**0**	**0**	**3:38**
2007-08♦	**Detroit**	**NHL**	**77**	**5**	**7**	**12**	**43**	**0**	**0**	**1**	**87**	**5.7**	**2**	**109**	**40.4**	**9:37**									

			Regular Season														Playoffs								
Season	Club	League	GP	G	A	Pts	PIM	PP	SH	GW	S	S%	+/-	TF	F%	Min	GP	G	A	Pts	PIM	PP	SH	GW	Min
2008-09	**Detroit**	**NHL**	**79**	**6**	**13**	**19**	**46**	**1**	**1**	**2**	**110**	**5.5**	**–7**	**79**	**45.6**	**10:25**	**8**	**0**	**1**	**1**	**7**	**0**	**0**	**0**	**9:32**
2009-10♦	**Chicago**	**NHL**	**74**	**10**	**11**	**21**	**28**	**1**	**0**	**2**	**95**	**10.5**	**0**	**118**	**44.1**	**9:29**	**17**	**4**	**2**	**6**	**8**	**1**	**0**	**1**	**13:35**
	Slovakia	Olympics	7	1	0	1	2	....	....	....	....	....	....	....	....	....	....	....	....	....	....	....	....	....	....
2010-11	**Chicago**	**NHL**	**81**	**15**	**27**	**42**	**60**	**3**	**0**	**2**	**178**	**8.4**	**–13**	**284**	**42.3**	**15:19**	**1**	**0**	**0**	**0**	**0**	**0**	**0**	**0**	**2:22**
2011-12	**Florida**	**NHL**	**80**	**10**	**22**	**32**	**32**	**2**	**0**	**2**	**143**	**7.0**	**–8**	**266**	**52.6**	**17:16**	**7**	**1**	**0**	**1**	**4**	**0**	**1**	**0**	**15:23**
2012-13	Dukla Trencin	Slovakia	5	2	2	4	0	....	....	....	....	....	....	....	....	....	....	....	....	....	....	....	....	....	....
	Florida	**NHL**	**47**	**15**	**12**	**27**	**28**	**4**	**1**	**0**	**92**	**16.3**	**–8**	**86**	**48.8**	**17:41**	....	....	....	....	....	....	....	....	....
2013-14	**Florida**	**NHL**	**49**	**4**	**8**	**12**	**18**	**0**	**1**	**0**	**95**	**4.2**	**0**	**29**	**27.6**	**15:53**	....	....	....	....	....	....	....	....	....
	Slovakia	Olympics	2	0	0	0	0	....	....	....	....	....	....	....	....	....	....	....	....	....	....	....	....	....	....
2014-15	**Florida**	**NHL**	**64**	**2**	**6**	**8**	**28**	**0**	**0**	**1**	**106**	**1.9**	**–19**	**4**	**75.0**	**12:54**	....	....	....	....	....	....	....	....	....
	NHL Totals		**578**	**68**	**106**	**174**	**307**	**11**	**3**	**10**	**934**	**7.3**		**980**	**45.6**	**13:01**	**37**	**5**	**3**	**8**	**25**	**1**	**1**	**1**	**11:40**

• Missed majority of 2006-07 due to broken collarbone vs. Chicago, December 14, 2006. Signed as a free agent by **Chicago**, July 1, 2009. Traded to **Florida** by **Chicago** for Florida's 7th round choice (later traded to Buffalo – Buffalo selected Judd Peterson) in 2012 Entry Draft June 27, 2011. Signed as a free agent by **Trencin** (Slovokia), October 13, 2012.

KOPITAR, Anze

(KOH-pih-tahr, AHN-zheh) **L.A.**

Center. Shoots left. 6'3", 228 lbs. Born, Jesenice, Yugoslavia, August 24, 1987. Los Angeles' 1st choice, 11th overall, in 2005 Entry Draft.

Season	Club	League	GP	G	A	Pts	PIM	PP	SH	GW	S	S%	+/-	TF	F%	Min	GP	G	A	Pts	PIM	PP	SH	GW	Min
2002-03	Jesenice U18	Sloven-U18	14	38	38	76	10	....	....	....	....	....	....	....	....	....	....	....	....	....	....	....	....	....	....
	Jesenice Jr.	Sloven-Jr.	20	15	12	27	8	....	....	....	....	....	....	....	....	....	....	....	....	....	....	....	....	....	....
	Kranjska Gora	Slovenia	11	4	4	8	4	....	....	....	....	....	....	....	....	....	....	....	....	....	....	....	....	....	....
2003-04	Jesenice Jr.	Sloven-Jr.	25	32	28	60	16	....	....	....	....	....	....	....	....	....	....	....	....	....	....	....	....	....	....
	Kranjska Gora	Slovenia	21	14	11	25	10	....	....	....	....	....	....	....	....	....	4	1	1	2	0	....	....	....	....
2004-05	Sodertalje SK U18	Swe-U18	1	1	2	3	0	....	....	....	....	....	....	....	....	....	1	0	0	0	2	....	....	....	....
	Sodertalje SK Jr.	Swe-Jr.	30	28	21	49	26	....	....	....	....	....	....	....	....	....	2	1	1	2	0	....	....	....	....
	Sodertalje SK	Sweden	5	0	0	0	0	....	....	....	....	....	....	....	....	....	10	0	0	0	0	....	....	....	....
	Slovenia	Oly-Q	3	1	1	2	2	....	....	....	....	....	....	....	....	....	....	....	....	....	....	....	....	....	....
2005-06	Sodertalje SK	Sweden	47	8	12	20	28	....	....	....	....	....	....	....	....	....	....	....	....	....	....	....	....	....	....
	Sodertalje SK	Sweden-Q	10	7	4	11	6	....	....	....	....	....	....	....	....	....	....	....	....	....	....	....	....	....	....
2006-07	**Los Angeles**	**NHL**	**72**	**20**	**41**	**61**	**24**	**7**	**2**	**1**	**193**	**10.4**	**–12**	**1204**	**46.1**	**20:32**	....	....	....	....	....	....	....	....	....
2007-08	**Los Angeles**	**NHL**	**82**	**32**	**45**	**77**	**22**	**12**	**2**	**3**	**201**	**15.9**	**–15**	**1150**	**49.2**	**20:41**	....	....	....	....	....	....	....	....	....
2008-09	**Los Angeles**	**NHL**	**82**	**27**	**39**	**66**	**32**	**7**	**1**	**3**	**234**	**11.5**	**–17**	**1355**	**49.5**	**20:27**	....	....	....	....	....	....	....	....	....
2009-10	**Los Angeles**	**NHL**	**82**	**34**	**47**	**81**	**16**	**14**	**1**	**2**	**259**	**13.1**	**6**	**1211**	**49.7**	**21:47**	**6**	**2**	**3**	**5**	**2**	**1**	**0**	**1**	**21:13**
2010-11	**Los Angeles**	**NHL**	**75**	**25**	**48**	**73**	**20**	**6**	**1**	**6**	**233**	**10.7**	**25**	**1160**	**49.9**	**21:35**	....	....	....	....	....	....	....	....	....
2011-12♦	**Los Angeles**	**NHL**	**82**	**25**	**51**	**76**	**20**	**8**	**2**	**2**	**230**	**10.9**	**12**	**1418**	**53.8**	**21:20**	**20**	***8**	***12**	***20**	**9**	**0**	***2**	**1**	**22:03**
2012-13	Mora IK	Sweden-2	31	10	24	34	14	....	....	....	....	....	....	....	....	....	....	....	....	....	....	....	....	....	....
	Los Angeles	**NHL**	**47**	**10**	**32**	**42**	**16**	**0**	**0**	**1**	**98**	**10.2**	**14**	**888**	**53.3**	**20:29**	**18**	**3**	**6**	**9**	**12**	**1**	**0**	**1**	**21:15**
2013-14♦	**Los Angeles**	**NHL**	**82**	**29**	**41**	**70**	**24**	**10**	**0**	**9**	**200**	**14.5**	**34**	**1451**	**53.3**	**20:53**	**26**	**5**	***21**	***26**	**14**	**1**	**0**	**1**	**21:13**
	Slovenia	Olympics	5	2	1	3	4	....	....	....	....	....	....	....	....	....	....	....	....	....	....	....	....	....	....
2014-15	**Los Angeles**	**NHL**	**79**	**16**	**48**	**64**	**10**	**6**	**0**	**4**	**134**	**11.9**	**–2**	**1430**	**52.6**	**19:23**	....	....	....	....	....	....	....	....	....
	NHL Totals		**683**	**218**	**392**	**610**	**184**	**70**	**9**	**31**	**1782**	**12.2**		**11267**	**50.9**	**20:49**	**70**	**18**	**42**	**60**	**37**	**3**	**2**	**4**	**21:28**

Played in NHL All-Star Game (2008, 2011, 2015)

Signed as a free agent by **Mora** (Sweden-2), September 19, 2012.

KORPIKOSKI, Lauri

(kohr-pih-KAWS-kee, LOW-ree) **EDM**

Left wing. Shoots left. 6'1", 205 lbs. Born, Turku, Finland, July 28, 1986. NY Rangers' 2nd choice, 19th overall, in 2004 Entry Draft.

Season	Club	League	GP	G	A	Pts	PIM	PP	SH	GW	S	S%	+/-	TF	F%	Min	GP	G	A	Pts	PIM	PP	SH	GW	Min
2002-03	TPS Turku U18	Fin-U18	21	7	4	11	10	....	....	....	....	....	....	....	....	....	....	....	....	....	....	....	....	....	....
2003-04	TPS Turku U18	Fin-U18	....	....	....	....	....	....	....	....	....	....	....	....	....	....	4	5	3	8	16	....	....	....	....
	TPS Turku Jr.	Fin-Jr.	36	12	8	20	20	....	....	....	....	....	....	....	....	....	4	0	2	2	4	....	....	....	....
2004-05	TPS Turku Jr.	Fin-Jr.	3	3	0	3	0	....	....	....	....	....	....	....	....	....	....	....	....	....	....	....	....	....	....
	TPS Turku	Finland	41	0	6	6	12	....	....	....	....	....	....	....	....	....	6	1	0	1	0	....	....	....	....
2005-06	TPS Turku Jr.	Fin-Jr.	1	1	0	1	2	....	....	....	....	....	....	....	....	....	....	....	....	....	....	....	....	....	....
	Suomi U20	Finland-2	3	1	3	4	0	....	....	....	....	....	....	....	....	....	....	....	....	....	....	....	....	....	....
	TPS Turku	Finland	51	3	4	7	16	....	....	....	....	....	....	....	....	....	2	0	1	1	0	....	....	....	....
	Hartford	AHL	5	2	1	3	0	....	....	....	....	....	....	....	....	....	11	1	0	1	2	....	....	....	....
2006-07	Hartford	AHL	78	11	27	38	23	....	....	....	....	....	....	....	....	....	7	0	0	0	0	....	....	....	....
2007-08	Hartford	AHL	79	23	27	50	71	....	....	....	....	....	....	....	....	....	5	1	1	2	0	....	....	....	....
	NY Rangers	**NHL**	....	....	....	....	....	....	....	....	....	....	....	....	....	....	**1**	**1**	**0**	**1**	**0**	**0**	**0**	**0**	**7:14**
2008-09	**NY Rangers**	**NHL**	**68**	**6**	**8**	**14**	**14**	**0**	**0**	**1**	**63**	**9.5**	**–10**	**220**	**40.0**	**10:55**	**7**	**0**	**2**	**2**	**0**	**0**	**0**	**0**	**13:10**
	Hartford	AHL	4	4	2	6	0	....	....	....	....	....	....	....	....	....	....	....	....	....	....	....	....	....	....
2009-10	**Phoenix**	**NHL**	**71**	**5**	**6**	**11**	**16**	**0**	**0**	**1**	**68**	**7.4**	**–10**	**49**	**28.6**	**12:18**	**7**	**1**	**0**	**1**	**2**	**0**	**1**	**0**	**16:16**
2010-11	**Phoenix**	**NHL**	**79**	**19**	**21**	**40**	**20**	**0**	**2**	**4**	**103**	**18.4**	**17**	**244**	**43.9**	**15:32**	**4**	**0**	**1**	**1**	**2**	**0**	**0**	**0**	**16:33**
2011-12	**Phoenix**	**NHL**	**82**	**17**	**20**	**37**	**14**	**0**	**3**	**3**	**146**	**11.6**	**3**	**87**	**26.4**	**17:08**	**11**	**0**	**0**	**0**	**2**	**0**	**0**	**0**	**18:16**
2012-13	TPS Turku	Finland	11	6	11	17	10	....	....	....	....	....	....	....	....	....	....	....	....	....	....	....	....	....	....
	Phoenix	**NHL**	**36**	**6**	**5**	**11**	**12**	**1**	**0**	**0**	**83**	**7.2**	**–3**	**16**	**37.5**	**17:07**	....	....	....	....	....	....	....	....	....
2013-14	**Phoenix**	**NHL**	**64**	**9**	**16**	**25**	**24**	**1**	**0**	**0**	**109**	**8.3**	**–7**	**17**	**29.4**	**16:05**	....	....	....	....	....	....	....	....	....
	Finland	Olympics	6	2	2	4	2	....	....	....	....	....	....	....	....	....	....	....	....	....	....	....	....	....	....
2014-15	**Arizona**	**NHL**	**69**	**6**	**15**	**21**	**12**	**5**	**0**	**1**	**82**	**7.3**	**–27**	**33**	**33.3**	**15:15**	....	....	....	....	....	....	....	....	....
	NHL Totals		**469**	**68**	**91**	**159**	**112**	**7**	**5**	**10**	**654**	**10.4**		**666**	**38.1**	**14:49**	**30**	**2**	**3**	**5**	**6**	**0**	**1**	**0**	**16:01**

Traded to **Phoenix** by **NY Rangers** for Enver Lisin, July 13, 2009. Signed as a free agent by **TPS Turku** (Finland), October 2, 2012. Traded to **Edmonton** by **Arizona** for Boyd Gordon, June 30, 2015.

KOSTKA, Mike

(KOHST-kuh, MIGHK) **OTT**

Defense. Shoots right. 6'1", 210 lbs. Born, Etobicoke, ON, November 28, 1985.

Season	Club	League	GP	G	A	Pts	PIM	PP	SH	GW	S	S%	+/-	TF	F%	Min	GP	G	A	Pts	PIM	PP	SH	GW	Min
2001-02	Ajax Axemen	ON-Jr.A	19	1	4	5	8	....	....	....	....	....	....	....	....	....	....	....	....	....	....	....	....	....	....
2002-03	Ajax Axemen	ON-Jr.A	39	4	11	15	32	....	....	....	....	....	....	....	....	....	....	....	....	....	....	....	....	....	....
2003-04	Aurora Tigers	ON-Jr.A	42	9	27	36	4	....	....	....	....	....	....	....	....	....	....	....	....	....	....	....	....	....	....
2004-05	Massachusetts	H-East	32	1	5	6	14	....	....	....	....	....	....	....	....	....	....	....	....	....	....	....	....	....	....
2005-06	Massachusetts	H-East	36	2	6	8	20	....	....	....	....	....	....	....	....	....	....	....	....	....	....	....	....	....	....
2006-07	Massachusetts	H-East	39	3	15	18	20	....	....	....	....	....	....	....	....	....	....	....	....	....	....	....	....	....	....
2007-08	Massachusetts	H-East	36	9	12	21	20	....	....	....	....	....	....	....	....	....	....	....	....	....	....	....	....	....	....
	Rochester	AHL	1	0	0	0	2	....	....	....	....	....	....	....	....	....	....	....	....	....	....	....	....	....	....
2008-09	Portland Pirates	AHL	80	4	26	30	33	....	....	....	....	....	....	....	....	....	4	1	0	1	6	....	....	....	....
2009-10	Portland Pirates	AHL	76	2	25	27	37	....	....	....	....	....	....	....	....	....	4	0	0	0	0	....	....	....	....
2010-11	Rochester	AHL	80	16	38	54	46	....	....	....	....	....	....	....	....	....	....	....	....	....	....	....	....	....	....
2011-12	San Antonio	AHL	18	2	4	6	14	....	....	....	....	....	....	....	....	....	....	....	....	....	....	....	....	....	....
	Norfolk Admirals	AHL	52	7	25	32	43	....	....	....	....	....	....	....	....	....	18	6	6	12	8	....	....	....	....
2012-13	Toronto Marlies	AHL	34	6	28	34	38	....	....	....	....	....	....	....	....	....	....	....	....	....	....	....	....	....	....
	Toronto	**NHL**	**35**	**0**	**8**	**8**	**27**	**0**	**0**	**0**	**49**	**0.0**	**–7**	**0**	**0.0**	**22:05**	**1**	**0**	**0**	**0**	**0**	**0**	**0**	**0**	**22:22**
2013-14	**Chicago**	**NHL**	**9**	**2**	**1**	**3**	**8**	**0**	**0**	**1**	**18**	**11.1**	**3**	**0**	**0.0**	**14:26**	....	....	....	....	....	....	....	....	....
	Tampa Bay	**NHL**	**19**	**2**	**6**	**8**	**0**	**0**	**0**	**0**	**31**	**6.5**	**7**	**0**	**0.0**	**15:54**	**3**	**0**	**2**	**2**	**0**	**0**	**0**	**0**	**16:56**
2014-15	**NY Rangers**	**NHL**	**7**	**0**	**1**	**1**	**0**	**0**	**0**	**0**	**7**	**0.0**	**1**	**0**	**0.0**	**15:23**	....	....	....	....	....	....	....	....	....
	Hartford	AHL	63	5	25	30	35	....	....	....	....	....	....	....	....	....	15	1	4	5	6	....	....	....	....
	NHL Totals		**70**	**4**	**16**	**20**	**35**	**0**	**0**	**1**	**105**	**3.8**		**0**	**0.0**	**18:45**	**4**	**0**	**2**	**2**	**0**	**0**	**0**	**0**	**18:17**

Hockey East Second All-Star Team (2008)

Signed as a free agent by **Buffalo**, March 25, 2008. Signed as a free agent by **Rochester** (AHL), August 25, 2010. Signed as a free agent by **Florida**, June 30, 2011. Traded to **Tampa Bay** by **Florida** with Evan Oberg for James Wright and Mike Vernace, December 2, 2011. Signed as a free agent by **Toronto**, July 1, 2012. Signed as a free agent by **Chicago**, July 19, 2013. Claimed on waivers by **Tampa Bay** from **Chicago**, February 23, 2014. • Missed majority of 2013-14 due to lower-body injury vs. Toronto, October 19, 2013 and as a healthy reserve. Signed as a free agent by **NY Rangers**, July 1, 2014. Signed as a free agent by **Ottawa**, July 1, 2015.

KOSTOPOULOS, Tom

(kaw-STAWP-oh-lihs, TAWM)

Right wing. Shoots right. 6', 197 lbs. Born, Mississauga, ON, January 24, 1979. Pittsburgh's 9th choice, 204th overall, in 1999 Entry Draft.

Season	Club	League	GP	G	A	Pts	PIM	PP	SH	GW	S	S%	+/-	TF	F%	Min	GP	G	A	Pts	PIM	PP	SH	GW	Min
1995-96	Brampton	ON-Jr.A	24	9	9	18	28	....	....	....	....	....	....	....	....	....	....	....	....	....	....	....	....	....	....
1996-97	London Knights	OHL	64	13	12	25	67	....	....	....	....	....	....	....	....	....	....	....	....	....	....	....	....	....	....
1997-98	London Knights	OHL	66	24	26	50	108	....	....	....	....	....	....	....	....	....	16	6	4	10	26	....	....	....	....
1998-99	London Knights	OHL	66	27	60	87	114	....	....	....	....	....	....	....	....	....	25	19	16	35	32	....	....	....	....
99-2000	Wilkes-Barre	AHL	76	26	32	58	121	....	....	....	....	....	....	....	....	....	....	....	....	....	....	....	....	....	....
2000-01	Wilkes-Barre	AHL	80	16	36	52	120	....	....	....	....	....	....	....	....	....	21	3	9	12	6	....	....	....	....

			Regular Season														Playoffs								
Season	Club	League	GP	G	A	Pts	PIM	PP	SH	GW	S	S%	+/-	TF	F%	Min	GP	G	A	Pts	PIM	PP	SH	GW	Min
2001-02	**Pittsburgh**	**NHL**	**11**	**1**	**2**	**3**	**9**	**0**	**0**	**0**	**8**	**12.5**	**–1**	**0**	**0.0**	**12:03**	....	....	....	....	....	....	....	....	....
	Wilkes-Barre	AHL	70	27	26	53	112	....	....	....	....	....	....	....	....	....	....	....	....	....	....	....	....	....	....
2002-03	**Pittsburgh**	**NHL**	**8**	**0**	**1**	**1**	**0**	**0**	**0**	**0**	**6**	**0.0**	**–4**	**2**	**0.0**	**4:33**	....	....	....	....	....	....	....	....	....
	Wilkes-Barre	AHL	71	21	42	63	131	....	....	....	....	....	....	....	....	....	6	1	2	3	7	....	....	....	....
2003-04	**Pittsburgh**	**NHL**	**60**	**9**	**13**	**22**	**67**	**2**	**1**	**1**	**101**	**8.9**	**–14**	**10**	**30.0**	**14:26**	....	....	....	....	....	....	....	....	....
	Wilkes-Barre	AHL	21	7	13	20	43	....	....	....	....	....	....	....	....	....	24	7	16	23	32	....	....	....	....
2004-05	Manchester	AHL	64	25	46	71	99	....	....	....	....	....	....	....	....	....	6	0	7	7	10	....	....	....	....
2005-06	**Los Angeles**	**NHL**	**76**	**8**	**14**	**22**	**100**	**0**	**0**	**1**	**74**	**10.8**	**–8**	**30**	**36.7**	**12:56**	....	....	....	....	....	....	....	....	....
2006-07	**Los Angeles**	**NHL**	**76**	**7**	**15**	**22**	**73**	**0**	**0**	**0**	**90**	**7.8**	**–2**	**62**	**29.0**	**11:34**	....	....	....	....	....	....	....	....	....
2007-08	**Montreal**	**NHL**	**67**	**7**	**6**	**13**	**113**	**0**	**3**	**1**	**98**	**7.1**	**–3**	**28**	**28.6**	**11:16**	**12**	**3**	**1**	**4**	**6**	**0**	**0**	**1**	**13:35**
2008-09	**Montreal**	**NHL**	**78**	**8**	**14**	**22**	**106**	**0**	**1**	**0**	**121**	**6.6**	**–1**	**16**	**31.3**	**14:09**	**4**	**0**	**1**	**1**	**4**	**0**	**0**	**0**	**14:01**
2009-10	**Carolina**	**NHL**	**82**	**8**	**13**	**21**	**106**	**0**	**2**	**0**	**103**	**7.8**	**4**	**21**	**47.6**	**12:31**	....	....	....	....	....	....	....	....	....
2010-11	**Carolina**	**NHL**	**17**	**1**	**3**	**4**	**30**	**0**	**0**	**0**	**13**	**7.7**	**–1**	**14**	**28.6**	**11:17**	....	....	....	....	....	....	....	....	....
	Calgary	**NHL**	**59**	**7**	**7**	**14**	**44**	**2**	**0**	**0**	**66**	**10.6**	**–3**	**53**	**26.4**	**12:38**	....	....	....	....	....	....	....	....	....
2011-12	**Calgary**	**NHL**	**81**	**4**	**8**	**12**	**57**	**1**	**1**	**1**	**91**	**4.4**	**–15**	**84**	**29.8**	**12:19**	....	....	....	....	....	....	....	....	....
2012-13	Wilkes-Barre	AHL	17	3	4	7	43	....	....	....	....	....	....	....	....	....	....	....	....	....	....	....	....	....	....
	New Jersey	**NHL**	**15**	**1**	**0**	**1**	**18**	**0**	**0**	**0**	**13**	**7.7**	**0**	**5**	**60.0**	**9:06**	....	....	....	....	....	....	....	....	....
2013-14	Wilkes-Barre	AHL	71	22	25	47	72	....	....	....	....	....	....	....	....	....	17	4	6	10	20	....	....	....	....
2014-15	Wilkes-Barre	AHL	72	16	28	44	62	....	....	....	....	....	....	....	....	....	8	3	2	5	12	....	....	....	....
	NHL Totals		**630**	**61**	**96**	**157**	**723**	**5**	**8**	**4**	**784**	**7.8**		**325**	**31.1**	**12:28**	**16**	**3**	**2**	**5**	**10**	**0**	**0**	**1**	**13:41**

Signed as a free agent by **Manchester** (AHL), July 12, 2004. Signed as a free agent by **Los Angeles**, August 1, 2005. Signed as a free agent by **Montreal**, July 4, 2007. Signed as a free agent by **Carolina**, July 14, 2009. Traded to **Calgary** by **Carolina** with Anton Babchuk for Ian White and Brett Sutter, November 17, 2010. Signed as a free agent by **Wilkes-Barre** (AHL), January 23, 2013. Signed as a free agent by **Pittsburgh**, March 5, 2013. Claimed on waivers by **New Jersey** from **Pittsburgh**, March 6, 2013. Signed as a free agent by **Wilkes-Barre** (AHL), September 3, 2013.

KOZUN, Brandon

(KOH-zuhn, BRAN-duhn)

Right wing. Shoots right. 5'8", 167 lbs. Born, Los Angeles, CA, March 8, 1990. Los Angeles' 8th choice, 179th overall, in 2009 Entry Draft.

Season	Club	League	GP	G	A	Pts	PIM	PP	SH	GW	S	S%	+/-	TF	F%	Min	GP	G	A	Pts	PIM	PP	SH	GW	Min
2006-07	Calgary Royals	AJHL	39	20	22	42	38	....	....	....	....	....	....	....	....	....	4	2	1	3	2	....	....	....	....
	Calgary Hitmen	WHL	11	1	1	2	4	....	....	....	....	....	....	....	....	....	....	....	....	....	....	....	....	....	....
2007-08	Calgary Hitmen	WHL	69	19	34	53	46	....	....	....	....	....	....	....	....	....	16	4	14	18	6	....	....	....	....
2008-09	Calgary Hitmen	WHL	72	40	68	108	58	....	....	....	....	....	....	....	....	....	18	7	12	19	8	....	....	....	....
2009-10	Calgary Hitmen	WHL	65	32	*75	*107	50	....	....	....	....	....	....	....	....	....	23	8	*22	*30	12	....	....	....	....
2010-11	Manchester	AHL	73	23	25	48	48	....	....	....	....	....	....	....	....	....	7	1	3	4	2	....	....	....	....
2011-12	Manchester	AHL	74	20	26	46	58	....	....	....	....	....	....	....	....	....	3	1	1	2	2	....	....	....	....
2012-13	Manchester	AHL	74	26	30	56	52	....	....	....	....	....	....	....	....	....	4	0	2	2	0	....	....	....	....
2013-14	Manchester	AHL	43	10	19	29	38	....	....	....	....	....	....	....	....	....	....	....	....	....	....	....	....	....	....
	Toronto Marlies	AHL	32	7	10	17	32	....	....	....	....	....	....	....	....	....	14	4	2	6	8	....	....	....	....
2014-15	**Toronto**	**NHL**	**20**	**2**	**2**	**4**	**6**	**0**	**0**	**0**	**8**	**25.0**	**–3**	**2**	**50.0**	**7:55**	....	....	....	....	....	....	....	....	....
	Toronto Marlies	AHL	23	5	6	11	16	....	....	....	....	....	....	....	....	....	....	....	....	....	....	....	....	....	....
	NHL Totals		**20**	**2**	**2**	**4**	**6**	**0**	**0**	**0**	**8**	**25.0**		**2**	**50.0**	**7:55**	....	....	....	....	....	....	....	....	....

WHL East First All-Star Team (2009, 2010) • Canadian Major Junior First All-Star Team (2010

Traded to **Toronto** by **Los Angeles** for Andrew Crescenzi, January 22, 2014. • Missed majority of 2014-15 due to ankle injury vs. Detroit, October 17, 2014 and as a healthy reserve. Signed as a free agent by **Jokerit Helsinki** (Finland), June 18, 2015.

KREIDER, Chris

(KRIGH-duhr, KRIHS) **NYR**

Center. Shoots left. 6'3", 226 lbs. Born, Boxford, MA, April 30, 1991. NY Rangers' 1st choice, 19th overall, in 2009 Entry Draft.

Season	Club	League	GP	G	A	Pts	PIM	PP	SH	GW	S	S%	+/-	TF	F%	Min	GP	G	A	Pts	PIM	PP	SH	GW	Min
2005-06	Masconomet	High-MA	19	5	10	15	....	....	....	....	....	....	....	....	....	....	....	....	....	....	....	....	....	....	....
2006-07	Masconomet	High-MA	20	28	13	41	....	....	....	....	....	....	....	....	....	....	....	....	....	....	....	....	....	....	....
2007-08	Andover	High-MA	24	26	15	41	....	....	....	....	....	....	....	....	....	....	....	....	....	....	....	....	....	....	....
2008-09	Andover	High-MA	26	33	23	56	10	....	....	....	....	....	....	....	....	....	....	....	....	....	....	....	....	....	....
	Valley Jr. Warriors	Minor-MA	5	4	2	6	....	....	....	....	....	....	....	....	....	....	....	....	....	....	....	....	....	....	....
2009-10	Boston College	H-East	38	15	8	23	26	....	....	....	....	....	....	....	....	....	....	....	....	....	....	....	....	....	....
2010-11	Boston College	H-East	32	11	13	24	37	....	....	....	....	....	....	....	....	....	....	....	....	....	....	....	....	....	....
2011-12	Boston College	H-East	44	23	22	45	66	....	....	....	....	....	....	....	....	....	....	....	....	....	....	....	....	....	....
	NY Rangers	**NHL**	....	....	....	....	....	....	....	....	....	....	....	....	....	....	**18**	**5**	**2**	**7**	**6**	**2**	**0**	**2**	**13:09**
2012-13	Connecticut	AHL	48	12	11	23	73	....	....	....	....	....	....	....	....	....	....	....	....	....	....	....	....	....	....
	NY Rangers	**NHL**	**23**	**2**	**1**	**3**	**6**	**0**	**0**	**0**	**19**	**10.5**	**–1**	**1**	**0.0**	**10:07**	**8**	**1**	**1**	**2**	**0**	**0**	**0**	**1**	**9:42**
2013-14	**NY Rangers**	**NHL**	**66**	**17**	**20**	**37**	**72**	**6**	**0**	**0**	**136**	**12.5**	**14**	**19**	**42.1**	**15:44**	**15**	**5**	**8**	**13**	**14**	**3**	**0**	**1**	**16:49**
	Hartford	AHL	6	2	2	4	16	....	....	....	....	....	....	....	....	....	....	....	....	....	....	....	....	....	....
2014-15	**NY Rangers**	**NHL**	**80**	**21**	**25**	**46**	**88**	**7**	**0**	**5**	**180**	**11.7**	**24**	**21**	**42.9**	**15:43**	**19**	**7**	**2**	**9**	**14**	**2**	**0**	**2**	**17:15**
	NHL Totals		**169**	**40**	**46**	**86**	**166**	**13**	**0**	**5**	**335**	**11.9**		**41**	**41.5**	**14:57**	**60**	**18**	**13**	**31**	**34**	**7**	**0**	**6**	**14:54**

Hockey East All-Rookie Team (2010) • Hockey East Second All-Star Team (2012)

KREJCI, David

(KRAY-chee, DAY-vihd) **BOS**

Center. Shoots right. 6', 188 lbs. Born, Sternberk, Czech., April 28, 1986. Boston's 1st choice, 63rd overall, in 2004 Entry Draft.

Season	Club	League	GP	G	A	Pts	PIM	PP	SH	GW	S	S%	+/-	TF	F%	Min	GP	G	A	Pts	PIM	PP	SH	GW	Min
2000-01	HC Olomouc U17	CzR-U17	26	2	6	8	4	....	....	....	....	....	....	....	....	....	3	1	1	2	0	....	....	....	....
2001-02	HC Trinec U17	CzR-U17	48	32	27	59	30	....	....	....	....	....	....	....	....	....	6	2	4	6	2	....	....	....	....
2002-03	HC Trinec U17	CzR-U17	22	12	24	36	42	....	....	....	....	....	....	....	....	....	....	....	....	....	....	....	....	....	....
	HC Trinec Jr.	CzRep-Jr.	12	4	5	9	2	....	....	....	....	....	....	....	....	....	12	5	5	10	8	....	....	....	....
2003-04	HC Kladno Jr.	CzRep-Jr.	50	23	37	60	37	....	....	....	....	....	....	....	....	....	7	3	6	9	4	....	....	....	....
2004-05	Gatineau	QMJHL	62	22	41	63	31	....	....	....	....	....	....	....	....	....	10	2	7	9	10	....	....	....	....
2005-06	Gatineau	QMJHL	55	27	54	81	54	....	....	....	....	....	....	....	....	....	17	10	22	32	24	....	....	....	....
2006-07	**Boston**	**NHL**	**6**	**0**	**0**	**0**	**2**	**0**	**0**	**0**	**2**	**0.0**	**–3**	**14**	**28.6**	**4:24**	....	....	....	....	....	....	....	....	....
	Providence Bruins	AHL	69	31	43	74	47	....	....	....	....	....	....	....	....	....	13	3	13	16	22	....	....	....	....
2007-08	**Boston**	**NHL**	**56**	**6**	**21**	**27**	**20**	**1**	**1**	**0**	**73**	**8.2**	**–3**	**635**	**48.2**	**14:55**	**7**	**1**	**4**	**5**	**2**	**1**	**0**	**0**	**19:09**
	Providence Bruins	AHL	25	7	21	28	19	....	....	....	....	....	....	....	....	....	....	....	....	....	....	....	....	....	....
2008-09	**Boston**	**NHL**	**82**	**22**	**51**	**73**	**26**	**5**	**2**	**6**	**146**	**15.1**	***37**	**1048**	**50.3**	**16:52**	**11**	**2**	**6**	**8**	**2**	**0**	**0**	**1**	**17:18**
2009-10	**Boston**	**NHL**	**79**	**17**	**35**	**52**	**26**	**6**	**0**	**3**	**156**	**10.9**	**8**	**1104**	**50.7**	**18:15**	**9**	**4**	**4**	**8**	**2**	**2**	**0**	**0**	**19:06**
	Czech Republic	Olympics	5	2	1	3	6	....	....	....	....	....	....	....	....	....	....	....	....	....	....	....	....	....	....
2010-11♦	**Boston**	**NHL**	**75**	**13**	**49**	**62**	**28**	**1**	**0**	**2**	**157**	**8.3**	**23**	**1149**	**48.7**	**18:51**	**25**	***12**	**11**	***23**	**10**	**2**	**0**	**4**	**20:07**
2011-12	**Boston**	**NHL**	**79**	**23**	**39**	**62**	**36**	**2**	**0**	**2**	**145**	**15.9**	**–5**	**1045**	**52.1**	**18:25**	**7**	**1**	**2**	**3**	**4**	**1**	**0**	**0**	**21:29**
2012-13	Pardubice	CzRep	24	16	11	27	22	....	....	....	....	....	....	....	....	....	....	....	....	....	....	....	....	....	....
	Boston	**NHL**	**47**	**10**	**23**	**33**	**20**	**0**	**0**	**5**	**93**	**10.8**	**1**	**654**	**55.2**	**18:30**	**22**	**9**	***17**	***26**	**14**	**1**	**0**	**2**	**22:15**
2013-14	**Boston**	**NHL**	**80**	**19**	**50**	**69**	**28**	**3**	**0**	**6**	**169**	**11.2**	**39**	**1208**	**51.2**	**19:07**	**12**	**0**	**4**	**4**	**4**	**1**	**0**	**0**	**20:52**
	Czech Republic	Olympics	5	1	2	3	0	....	....	....	....	....	....	....	....	....	....	....	....	....	....	....	....	....	....
2014-15	**Boston**	**NHL**	**47**	**7**	**24**	**31**	**22**	**1**	**1**	**1**	**70**	**10.0**	**7**	**594**	**53.2**	**18:10**	....	....	....	....	....	....	....	....	....
	NHL Totals		**551**	**117**	**292**	**409**	**208**	**19**	**4**	**25**	**1011**	**11.6**		**7451**	**50.9**	**17:48**	**93**	**29**	**48**	**77**	**38**	**7**	**0**	**7**	**20:19**

Signed as a free agent by **Pardubice** (CzRep), October 3, 2012.

KRONWALL, Niklas

(KRAWN-wahl, NIHK-luhs) **DET**

Defense. Shoots left. 6', 190 lbs. Born, Stockholm, Sweden, January 12, 1981. Detroit's 1st choice, 29th overall, in 2000 Entry Draft.

Season	Club	League	GP	G	A	Pts	PIM	PP	SH	GW	S	S%	+/-	TF	F%	Min	GP	G	A	Pts	PIM	PP	SH	GW	Min
1996-97	Djurgarden Jr.	Swe-Jr.	1	0	0	0	0	....	....	....	....	....	....	....	....	....	....	....	....	....	....	....	....	....	....
1997-98	Djurgarden Jr.	Swe-Jr.	27	4	3	7	71	....	....	....	....	....	....	....	....	....	2	0	0	0	2	....	....	....	....
1998-99	Huddinge IK	Sweden-2	14	0	1	1	10	....	....	....	....	....	....	....	....	....	....	....	....	....	....	....	....	....	....
	Huddinge IK Jr.	Swe-Jr.	2	0	0	0	6	....	....	....	....	....	....	....	....	....	....	....	....	....	....	....	....	....	....
99-2000	Djurgarden	Sweden	37	1	4	5	16	....	....	....	....	....	....	....	....	....	8	0	0	0	8	....	....	....	....
2000-01	Djurgarden	Sweden	31	1	9	10	32	....	....	....	....	....	....	....	....	....	15	0	1	1	8	....	....	....	....
2001-02	Djurgarden	Sweden	48	5	7	12	34	....	....	....	....	....	....	....	....	....	5	0	0	0	0	....	....	....	....
2002-03	Djurgarden	Sweden	50	5	13	18	46	....	....	....	....	....	....	....	....	....	12	3	2	5	18	....	....	....	....
2003-04	**Detroit**	**NHL**	**20**	**1**	**4**	**5**	**16**	**0**	**0**	**1**	**18**	**5.6**	**5**	**0**	**0.0**	**13:51**	....	....	....	....	....	....	....	....	....
	Grand Rapids	AHL	25	2	11	13	20	....	....	....	....	....	....	....	....	....	....	....	....	....	....	....	....	....	....
2004-05	Grand Rapids	AHL	76	13	40	53	53	....	....	....	....	....	....	....	....	....	....	....	....	....	....	....	....	....	....
2005-06	**Detroit**	**NHL**	**27**	**1**	**8**	**9**	**28**	**1**	**0**	**0**	**28**	**3.6**	**11**	**0**	**0.0**	**20:31**	**6**	**0**	**3**	**3**	**2**	**0**	**0**	**0**	**22:43**
	Grand Rapids	AHL	1	0	0	0	0	....	....	....	....	....	....	....	....	....	....	....	....	....	....	....	....	....	....
	Sweden	Olympics	2	1	1	2	8	....	....	....	....	....	....	....	....	....	....	....	....	....	....	....	....	....	....
2006-07	**Detroit**	**NHL**	**68**	**1**	**21**	**22**	**54**	**1**	**0**	**0**	**104**	**1.0**	**0**	**0**	**0.0**	**20:39**	....	....	....	....	....	....	....	....	....

			Regular Season														Playoffs								
Season	Club	League	GP	G	A	Pts	PIM	PP	SH	GW	S	S%	+/-	TF	F%	Min	GP	G	A	Pts	PIM	PP	SH	GW	Min
2007-08♦	Detroit	NHL	65	7	28	35	44	0	0	0	108	6.5	25	0	0.0	21:06	22	0	15	15	18	0	0	0	23:20
2008-09	Detroit	NHL	80	6	45	51	50	4	0	1	121	5.0	2	1	100.0	22:54	23	2	7	9	33	2	0	0	23:24
2009-10	Detroit	NHL	48	7	15	22	32	3	0	0	68	10.3	5	0	0.0	21:55	12	0	5	5	12	0	0	0	23:15
	Sweden	Olympics	4	0	0	0	2	....	....	....	....	....	....	....	....	....	....	....	....	....	....	....	....	....	....
2010-11	Detroit	NHL	77	11	26	37	36	5	0	3	131	8.4	5	0	0.0	22:52	11	2	4	6	4	1	0	0	23:04
2011-12	Detroit	NHL	82	15	21	36	38	7	0	4	141	10.6	–2	0	0.0	22:52	5	0	2	2	4	0	0	0	22:32
2012-13	Detroit	NHL	48	5	24	29	44	2	0	2	67	7.5	–5	0	0.0	24:22	14	0	2	2	4	0	0	0	25:21
2013-14	Detroit	NHL	79	8	41	49	44	5	0	0	110	7.3	0	0	0.0	24:19	5	1	1	2	0	1	0	0	25:58
	Sweden	Olympics	6	0	2	2	4	....	....	....	....	....	....	....	....	....	....	....	....	....	....	....	....	....	....
2014-15	Detroit	NHL	80	9	35	44	40	3	0	1	101	8.9	–4	1	100.0	23:50	6	0	2	2	4	0	0	0	23:35
	NHL Totals		674	71	268	339	426	31	0	12	997	7.1		2	100.0	22:26	104	5	41	46	81	4	0	0	23:39

AHL First All-Star Team (2005) • Eddie Shore Award (AHL – Outstanding Defenseman) (2005)
• Missed majority of 2005-06 due to pre-season knee injury vs. Colorado, September 27, 2005..

KRUG, Torey (KROOG, TOHR-ee) BOS

Defense. Shoots left. 5'9", 181 lbs. Born, Livonia, MI, April 12, 1991.

Season	Club	League	GP	G	A	Pts	PIM	PP	SH	GW	S	S%	+/-	TF	F%	Min	GP	G	A	Pts	PIM	PP	SH	GW	Min
2008-09	Indiana Ice	USHL	59	10	37	47	50	....	....	....	....	....	....	....	....	....	13	1	6	7	13	....	....	....	....
2009-10	Michigan State	CCHA	38	3	18	21	67	....	....	....	....	....	....	....	....	....	....	....	....	....	....	....	....	....	....
2010-11	Michigan State	CCHA	38	11	17	28	59	....	....	....	....	....	....	....	....	....	....	....	....	....	....	....	....	....	....
2011-12	Michigan State	CCHA	38	12	22	34	51	....	....	....	....	....	....	....	....	....	....	....	....	....	....	....	....	....	....
	Boston	NHL	2	0	1	1	0	0	0	0	3	0.0	0	0	0.0	17:08	....	....	....	....	....	....	....	....	....
2012-13	Providence Bruins	AHL	63	13	32	45	37	....	....	....	....	....	....	....	....	....	7	0	3	3	2	....	....	....	....
	Boston	NHL	1	0	1	1	0	0	0	0	0	0.0	–1	0	0.0	15:47	15	4	2	6	0	3	0	0	15:49
2013-14	Boston	NHL	79	14	26	40	28	6	0	2	183	7.7	18	2	50.0	17:31	12	2	8	10	6	1	0	0	19:37
2014-15	Boston	NHL	78	12	27	39	20	2	0	0	205	5.9	13	0	0.0	19:36	....	....	....	....	....	....	....	....	....
	NHL Totals		160	26	55	81	48	8	0	2	391	6.6		2	50.0	18:31	27	6	10	16	6	4	0	0	17:31

CCHA All-Rookie Team (2010) • CCHA First All-Star Team (2011, 2012) • CCHA Player of the Year (2012) • NCAA West First All-American Team (2012) • NHL All-Rookie Team (2014)
Signed as a free agent by **Boston**, March 25, 2012.

KRUGER, Marcus (KROO-guhr, MAHR-kuhs) CHI

Center. Shoots left. 6', 186 lbs. Born, Stockholm, Sweden, May 27, 1990. Chicago's 5th choice, 149th overall, in 2009 Entry Draft.

Season	Club	League	GP	G	A	Pts	PIM	PP	SH	GW	S	S%	+/-	TF	F%	Min	GP	G	A	Pts	PIM	PP	SH	GW	Min
2006-07	Djurgarden U18	Swe-U18	23	5	14	19	10	....	....	....	....	....	....	....	....	....	3	2	1	3	2	....	....	....	....
2007-08	Djurgarden U18	Swe-U18	22	11	20	31	22	....	....	....	....	....	....	....	....	....	7	3	8	11	6	....	....	....	....
	Djurgarden Jr.	Swe-Jr.	22	3	13	16	16	....	....	....	....	....	....	....	....	....	7	5	3	8	0	....	....	....	....
2008-09	Djurgarden Jr.	Swe-Jr.	34	9	30	39	24	....	....	....	....	....	....	....	....	....	6	1	5	6	2	....	....	....	....
	Djurgarden	Sweden	15	2	2	4	2	....	....	....	....	....	....	....	....	....	....	....	....	....	....	....	....	....	....
2009-10	Djurgarden	Sweden	38	11	20	31	14	....	....	....	....	....	....	....	....	....	16	3	7	10	6	....	....	....	....
2010-11	Djurgarden	Sweden	52	6	29	35	52	....	....	....	....	....	....	....	....	....	3	0	1	1	0	....	....	....	....
	Chicago	NHL	7	0	0	0	4	0	0	0	7	0.0	–4	39	35.9	11:58	5	0	1	1	0	0	0	0	11:51
2011-12	Chicago	NHL	71	9	17	26	22	0	0	1	89	10.1	11	619	45.9	15:24	6	0	0	0	0	0	0	0	17:48
2012-13	Rockford IceHogs	AHL	34	8	14	22	24	....	....	....	....	....	....	....	....	....	....	....	....	....	....	....	....	....	....
	♦ Chicago	NHL	47	4	9	13	24	0	0	2	50	8.0	3	493	46.3	14:10	23	3	2	5	2	0	0	1	13:48
2013-14	Chicago	NHL	81	8	20	28	36	0	0	2	96	8.3	6	773	56.7	13:52	19	1	3	4	6	0	0	0	15:39
	Sweden	Olympics	6	0	0	0	4	....	....	....	....	....	....	....	....	....	....	....	....	....	....	....	....	....	....
2014-15♦	Chicago	NHL	81	7	10	17	32	0	0	1	126	5.6	–5	670	53.3	13:05	23	2	2	4	4	0	0	1	15:06
	NHL Totals		287	28	56	84	118	0	0	6	368	7.6		2594	50.9	14:02	76	6	8	14	12	0	0	2	14:51

KUCHEROV, Nikita (KOO-chuhr-awv, nih-KEE-tuh) T.B.

Left wing. Shoots left. 5'11", 171 lbs. Born, Maikop, Russia, June 17, 1993. Tampa Bay's 2nd choice, 58th overall, in 2011 Entry Draft.

Season	Club	League	GP	G	A	Pts	PIM	PP	SH	GW	S	S%	+/-	TF	F%	Min	GP	G	A	Pts	PIM	PP	SH	GW	Min
2009-10	CSKA Jr.	Russia-Jr.	53	29	25	54	40	....	....	....	....	....	....	....	....	....	5	0	2	2	2	....	....	....	....
2010-11	CSKA Jr.	Russia-Jr.	41	27	31	58	81	....	....	....	....	....	....	....	....	....	10	5	8	13	16	....	....	....	....
	CSKA Moscow	KHL	8	0	2	2	0	....	....	....	....	....	....	....	....	....	....	....	....	....	....	....	....	....	....
2011-12	CSKA Jr.	Russia-Jr.	23	24	19	43	40	....	....	....	....	....	....	....	....	....	7	3	1	4	0	....	....	....	....
	CSKA Moscow	KHL	18	1	4	5	4	....	....	....	....	....	....	....	....	....	....	....	....	....	....	....	....	....	....
2012-13	Quebec Remparts	QMJHL	6	3	7	10	2	....	....	....	....	....	....	....	....	....	....	....	....	....	....	....	....	....	....
	Rouyn-Noranda	QMJHL	27	26	27	53	12	....	....	....	....	....	....	....	....	....	14	9	15	24	10	....	....	....	....
2013-14	Tampa Bay	NHL	52	9	9	18	14	3	0	3	102	8.8	3	1	100.0	13:07	2	1	0	1	0	0	0	0	11:37
	Syracuse Crunch	AHL	17	13	11	24	10	....	....	....	....	....	....	....	....	....	....	....	....	....	....	....	....	....	....
2014-15	Tampa Bay	NHL	82	29	36	65	37	2	0	2	191	15.2	38	2	0.0	14:57	26	10	12	22	14	3	0	3	16:59
	NHL Totals		134	38	45	83	51	5	0	5	293	13.0		3	33.3	14:14	28	11	12	23	14	3	0	3	16:36

KULAK, Brett (koo-LAK, BREHT) CGY

Defense. Shoots left. 6'2", 190 lbs. Born, Edmonton, AB, January 6, 1994. Calgary's 4th choice, 105th overall, in 2012 Entry Draft.

Season	Club	League	GP	G	A	Pts	PIM	PP	SH	GW	S	S%	+/-	TF	F%	Min	GP	G	A	Pts	PIM	PP	SH	GW	Min
2008-09	PAC Spruce Grove	AMBHL	33	2	19	21	28	....	....	....	....	....	....	....	....	....	....	....	....	....	....	....	....	....	....
2009-10	PAC Spruce Grove	Minor-AB	32	4	34	38	42	....	....	....	....	....	....	....	....	....	10	2	8	10	14	....	....	....	....
2010-11	St. Albert Raiders	AMHL	31	9	18	27	71	....	....	....	....	....	....	....	....	....	5	1	1	2	0	....	....	....	....
	Vancouver Giants	WHL	3	0	0	0	0	....	....	....	....	....	....	....	....	....	....	....	....	....	....	....	....	....	....
2011-12	Vancouver Giants	WHL	72	9	15	24	22	....	....	....	....	....	....	....	....	....	6	0	4	4	2	....	....	....	....
2012-13	Vancouver Giants	WHL	72	12	32	44	34	....	....	....	....	....	....	....	....	....	....	....	....	....	....	....	....	....	....
	Abbotsford Heat	AHL	4	0	0	0	0	....	....	....	....	....	....	....	....	....	....	....	....	....	....	....	....	....	....
2013-14	Vancouver Giants	WHL	69	14	46	60	51	....	....	....	....	....	....	....	....	....	4	1	2	3	7	....	....	....	....
	Abbotsford Heat	AHL	6	1	2	3	2	....	....	....	....	....	....	....	....	....	4	0	0	0	2	....	....	....	....
2014-15	Calgary	NHL	1	0	0	0	2	0	0	0	0	0.0	0	0	0.0	19:31	....	....	....	....	....	....	....	....	....
	Adirondack	AHL	26	4	9	13	27	....	....	....	....	....	....	....	....	....	....	....	....	....	....	....	....	....	....
	Colorado Eagles	ECHL	39	9	21	30	15	....	....	....	....	....	....	....	....	....	....	....	....	....	....	....	....	....	....
	NHL Totals		1	0	0	0	2	0	0	0	0	0.0		0	0.0	19:31	....	....	....	....	....	....	....	....	....

KULEMIN, Nikolay (KOOL-ay-mihn, NIH-koh-ligh) NYI

Left wing. Shoots left. 6'1", 226 lbs. Born, Magnitogorsk, USSR, July 14, 1986. Toronto's 2nd choice, 44th overall, in 2006 Entry Draft.

Season	Club	League	GP	G	A	Pts	PIM	PP	SH	GW	S	S%	+/-	TF	F%	Min	GP	G	A	Pts	PIM	PP	SH	GW	Min
2003-04	Magnitogorsk 2	Russia-3	43	8	18	26	91	....	....	....	....	....	....	....	....	....	....	....	....	....	....	....	....	....	....
2004-05	Magnitogorsk 2	Russia-3	43	9	13	22	44	....	....	....	....	....	....	....	....	....	....	....	....	....	....	....	....	....	....
2005-06	Magnitogorsk 2	Russia-3	4	3	1	4	6	....	....	....	....	....	....	....	....	....	....	....	....	....	....	....	....	....	....
	Magnitogorsk	Russia	31	5	7	12	8	....	....	....	....	....	....	....	....	....	11	2	4	6	6	....	....	....	....
2006-07	Magnitogorsk	Russia	54	27	12	39	42	....	....	....	....	....	....	....	....	....	15	10	1	11	10	....	....	....	....
2007-08	Magnitogorsk	Russia	57	21	12	33	63	....	....	....	....	....	....	....	....	....	11	2	2	4	29	....	....	....	....
2008-09	Toronto	NHL	73	15	16	31	18	2	0	1	129	11.6	–8	66	53.0	13:48	....	....	....	....	....	....	....	....	....
	Toronto Marlies	AHL	5	0	0	0	0	....	....	....	....	....	....	....	....	....	....	....	....	....	....	....	....	....	....
2009-10	Toronto	NHL	78	16	20	36	16	0	1	3	145	11.0	0	66	40.9	16:22	....	....	....	....	....	....	....	....	....
2010-11	Toronto	NHL	82	30	27	57	26	5	1	5	173	17.3	7	111	54.1	17:19	....	....	....	....	....	....	....	....	....
2011-12	Toronto	NHL	70	7	21	28	6	1	0	1	107	6.5	2	78	41.0	15:13	....	....	....	....	....	....	....	....	....
2012-13	Magnitogorsk	KHL	36	14	24	38	26	....	....	....	....	....	....	....	....	....	....	....	....	....	....	....	....	....	....
	Toronto	NHL	48	7	16	23	22	0	0	0	72	9.7	–5	20	50.0	16:44	7	0	1	1	0	0	0	0	18:11
2013-14	Toronto	NHL	70	9	11	20	24	0	0	4	81	11.1	–4	108	35.2	16:13	....	....	....	....	....	....	....	....	....
2014-15	NY Islanders	NHL	82	15	16	31	21	0	3	0	115	13.0	7	24	29.2	14:52	7	1	1	2	2	0	0	1	15:42
	NHL Totals		503	99	127	226	133	8	5	14	822	12.0		473	44.2	15:46	14	1	2	3	2	0	0	1	16:57

Signed as a free agent by **Magnitogorsk** (KHL), September 15, 2012. Signed as a free agent by **NY Islanders**, July 2, 2014.

KULIKOV, Dmitry

(kool-YIH-kawf, dih-MEE-tree) **FLA**

Defense. Shoots left. 6'1", 204 lbs. Born, Lipetsk, USSR, October 29, 1990. Florida's 1st choice, 14th overall, in 2009 Entry Draft.

			Regular Season															Playoffs							
Season	Club	League	GP	G	A	Pts	PIM	PP	SH	GW	S	S%	+/-	TF	F%	Min	GP	G	A	Pts	PIM	PP	SH	GW	Min
2007-08	Yaroslavl 2	Russia-3	STATISTICS NOT AVAILABLE																						
2008-09	Drummondville	QMJHL	57	12	50	62	46										19	2	18	20	16				
2009-10	**Florida**	**NHL**	**68**	**3**	**13**	**16**	**32**	**1**	**0**	**0**	**87**	**3.4**	**–5**	**0**	**0.0**	**17:56**									
2010-11	**Florida**	**NHL**	**72**	**6**	**20**	**26**	**45**	**1**	**0**	**1**	**83**	**7.2**	**–5**	**0**	**0.0**	**19:57**									
2011-12	**Florida**	**NHL**	**58**	**4**	**24**	**28**	**36**	**2**	**0**	**1**	**104**	**3.8**	**–5**	**0**	**0.0**	**21:51**	**7**	**0**	**1**	**1**	**4**	**0**	**0**	**0**	**21:16**
2012-13	Yaroslavl	KHL	22	3	4	7	28																		
	Florida	**NHL**	**34**	**3**	**7**	**10**	**22**	**2**	**0**	**2**	**52**	**5.8**	**–5**	**0**	**0.0**	**20:59**									
2013-14	**Florida**	**NHL**	**81**	**8**	**11**	**19**	**66**	**2**	**1**	**0**	**127**	**6.3**	**–26**	**0**	**0.0**	**21:42**									
2014-15	**Florida**	**NHL**	**73**	**3**	**19**	**22**	**48**	**1**	**0**	**0**	**83**	**3.6**	**0**	**0**	**0.0**	**21:19**									
	NHL Totals		**386**	**27**	**94**	**121**	**249**	**9**	**1**	**4**	**536**	**5.0**		**0**	**0.0**	**20:36**	**7**	**0**	**1**	**1**	**4**	**0**	**0**	**0**	**21:16**

QMJHL All-Rookie Team (2009) • QMJHL First All-Star Team (2009) • QMJHL Rookie of the Year (2009) • Canadian Major Junior Second All-Star Team (2009) • Canadian Major Junior All-Rookie Team (2009)

Signed as a free agent by **Yaroslavl** (KHL), September 25, 2012.

KUNITZ, Chris

(KOO-nihtz, KRIHS) **PIT**

Left wing. Shoots left. 6', 195 lbs. Born, Regina, SK, September 26, 1979.

			Regular Season															Playoffs							
Season	Club	League	GP	G	A	Pts	PIM	PP	SH	GW	S	S%	+/-	TF	F%	Min	GP	G	A	Pts	PIM	PP	SH	GW	Min
1996-97	Yorkton Mallers	SMHL	64	38	38	76	233																		
1997-98	Melville	SJHL	STATISTICS NOT AVAILABLE																						
1998-99	Melville	SJHL	63	57	32	89	222																		
99-2000	Ferris State	CCHA	38	20	9	29	70																		
2000-01	Ferris State	CCHA	37	16	13	29	81																		
2001-02	Ferris State	CCHA	35	*28	10	38	68																		
2002-03	Ferris State	CCHA	42	*35	*44	*79	56																		
2003-04	**Anaheim**	**NHL**	**21**	**0**	**6**	**6**	**12**	**0**	**0**	**0**	**31**	**0.0**	**1**	**7**	**14.3**	**9:07**									
	Cincinnati	AHL	59	19	25	44	101										9	3	2	5	24				
2004-05	Cincinnati	AHL	54	22	17	39	71										12	1	7	8	20				
2005-06	**Atlanta**	**NHL**	**2**	**0**	**0**	**0**	**2**	**0**	**0**	**0**	**0**	**0.0**	**–3**	**0**	**0.0**	**5:43**									
	Anaheim	**NHL**	**67**	**19**	**22**	**41**	**69**	**5**	**1**	**2**	**149**	**12.8**	**19**	**15**	**46.7**	**14:08**	**16**	**3**	**5**	**8**	**8**	**0**	**0**	**0**	**12:30**
	Portland Pirates	AHL	5	0	4	4	12																		
2006-07♦	**Anaheim**	**NHL**	**81**	**25**	**35**	**60**	**81**	**11**	**0**	**5**	**180**	**13.9**	**23**	**13**	**30.8**	**17:03**	**13**	**1**	**5**	**6**	**19**	**0**	**0**	**0**	**17:47**
2007-08	**Anaheim**	**NHL**	**82**	**21**	**29**	**50**	**80**	**7**	**1**	**6**	**196**	**10.7**	**8**	**49**	**32.7**	**16:54**	**6**	**0**	**2**	**2**	**8**	**0**	**0**	**0**	**18:30**
2008-09	**Anaheim**	**NHL**	**62**	**16**	**19**	**35**	**55**	**3**	**0**	**2**	**139**	**11.5**	**9**	**22**	**45.5**	**16:29**									
	♦ Pittsburgh	**NHL**	**20**	**7**	**11**	**18**	**16**	**3**	**0**	**1**	**39**	**17.9**	**3**	**5**	**60.0**	**16:17**	**24**	**1**	**13**	**14**	**19**	**0**	**0**	**0**	**16:55**
2009-10	**Pittsburgh**	**NHL**	**50**	**13**	**19**	**32**	**39**	**2**	**1**	**0**	**131**	**9.9**	**3**	**15**	**40.0**	**16:26**	**13**	**4**	**7**	**11**	**8**	**1**	**0**	**0**	**17:26**
2010-11	**Pittsburgh**	**NHL**	**66**	**23**	**25**	**48**	**47**	**7**	**1**	**2**	**133**	**17.3**	**18**	**8**	**50.0**	**18:17**	**6**	**1**	**0**	**1**	**6**	**0**	**0**	**0**	**17:22**
2011-12	**Pittsburgh**	**NHL**	**82**	**26**	**35**	**61**	**49**	**6**	**0**	**3**	**230**	**11.3**	**16**	**38**	**52.6**	**18:19**	**6**	**2**	**4**	**6**	**8**	**2**	**0**	**0**	**19:03**
2012-13	**Pittsburgh**	**NHL**	**48**	**22**	**30**	**52**	**39**	**9**	**0**	**5**	**113**	**19.5**	**30**	**9**	**44.4**	**18:01**	**15**	**5**	**5**	**10**	**6**	**3**	**0**	**1**	**18:19**
2013-14	**Pittsburgh**	**NHL**	**78**	**35**	**33**	**68**	**66**	**13**	**0**	**8**	**218**	**16.1**	**25**	**4**	**75.0**	**19:09**	**13**	**3**	**5**	**8**	**16**	**2**	**0**	**0**	**19:01**
	Canada	Olympics	6	1	0	1	6																		
2014-15	**Pittsburgh**	**NHL**	**74**	**17**	**23**	**40**	**56**	**9**	**1**	**5**	**170**	**10.0**	**2**	**13**	**53.9**	**17:53**	**5**	**1**	**2**	**3**	**8**	**1**	**0**	**1**	**18:11**
	NHL Totals		**733**	**224**	**287**	**511**	**611**	**75**	**5**	**39**	**1729**	**13.0**		**198**	**42.9**	**17:01**	**117**	**21**	**48**	**69**	**106**	**9**	**0**	**2**	**17:09**

CCHA First All-Star Team (2002, 2003) • CCHA Player of the Year (2003) • NCAA West First All-American Team (2003) • NHL First All-Star Team (2013)

Signed as a free agent by **Anaheim**, April 1, 2003. Claimed on waivers by **Atlanta** from **Anaheim**, October 4, 2005. Claimed on waivers by **Anaheim** from **Atlanta**, October 18, 2005. Traded to **Pittsburgh** by **Anaheim** with Eric Tangradi for Ryan Whitney, February 26, 2009.

KUNYK, Cody

(KOO-nihk, KOH-dee)

Center. Shoots left. 5'11", 195 lbs. Born, Sherwood Park, AB, May 20, 1990.

			Regular Season															Playoffs							
Season	Club	League	GP	G	A	Pts	PIM	PP	SH	GW	S	S%	+/-	TF	F%	Min	GP	G	A	Pts	PIM	PP	SH	GW	Min
2003-04	Sherwood Park	AMBHL	31	16	20	36	19																		
2004-05	Sherwood Park	AMBHL	39	16	15	31	46																		
2005-06	Sherwood Park	Minor-AB	32	21	37	58	26																		
2006-07	Sherwood Park	AMHL	35	16	16	32	58										8	0	6	6	22				
2007-08	Sherwood Park	AJHL	51	13	11	24	34																		
2008-09	Sherwood Park	AJHL	61	25	33	58	61										10	3	5	8	2				
2009-10	Sherwood Park	AJHL	51	44	43	87	33										3	0	1	1	2				
2010-11	Alaska	CCHA	38	12	18	30	28																		
2011-12	Alaska	CCHA	36	15	17	32	18																		
2012-13	Alaska	CCHA	37	11	17	28	22																		
2013-14	Alaska	WCHA	37	*22	21	43	22																		
	Tampa Bay	**NHL**	**1**	**0**	**0**	**0**	**0**	**0**	**0**	**0**	**2**	**0.0**	**0**	**5**	**20.0**	**10:12**									
2014-15	Syracuse Crunch	AHL	69	10	16	26	38										2	0	0	0	0				
	NHL Totals		**1**	**0**	**0**	**0**	**0**	**0**	**0**	**0**	**2**	**0.0**		**5**	**20.0**	**10:12**									

CCHA Second All-Star Team (2012) • WCHA First All-Star Team (2014) • WCHA Player of the Year (2014) • NCAA West Second All-American Team (2014)

Signed as a free agent by **Tampa Bay**, March 20, 2014.

KUZNETSOV, Evgeny

(kooz-neht-SAWF, ehv-GEH-nee) **WSH**

Center. Shoots left. 6', 172 lbs. Born, Chelyabinsk, Russia, May 19, 1992. Washington's 1st choice, 26th overall, in 2010 Entry Draft.

			Regular Season															Playoffs							
Season	Club	League	GP	G	A	Pts	PIM	PP	SH	GW	S	S%	+/-	TF	F%	Min	GP	G	A	Pts	PIM	PP	SH	GW	Min
2007-08	Chelyabinsk 2	Russia-3	2	0	0	0	0																		
2008-09	Chelyabinsk 2	Russia-3	22	5	11	16	40																		
2009-10	Chelyabinsk Jr.	Russia-Jr.	9	4	12	16	8										2	1	2	3	4				
	Chelyabinsk	KHL	35	2	6	8	10										4	1	0	1	0				
2010-11	Chelyabinsk	KHL	44	17	15	32	30																		
	Chelyabinsk Jr.	Russia-Jr.	8	10	5	15	4										5	0	2	2	10				
2011-12	Chelyabinsk	KHL	49	19	22	41	30										12	7	2	9	10				
2012-13	Chelyabinsk	KHL	51	19	25	44	42										25	5	6	11	28				
2013-14	Chelyabinsk	KHL	31	8	13	21	12																		
	Washington	**NHL**	**17**	**3**	**6**	**9**	**6**	**0**	**1**	**0**	**22**	**13.6**	**–2**	**27**	**18.5**	**13:28**									
2014-15	**Washington**	**NHL**	**80**	**11**	**26**	**37**	**24**	**4**	**0**	**1**	**127**	**8.7**	**10**	**681**	**44.6**	**13:20**	**14**	**5**	**2**	**7**	**8**	**0**	**0**	**1**	**16:37**
	NHL Totals		**97**	**14**	**32**	**46**	**30**	**4**	**1**	**1**	**149**	**9.4**		**708**	**43.6**	**13:21**	**14**	**5**	**2**	**7**	**8**	**0**	**0**	**1**	**16:37**

LABRIE, Pierre-Cedric

(la-BREE, pee-AIR-SEH-DRIHK)

Left wing. Shoots left. 6'3", 226 lbs. Born, Baie Comeau, QC, June 12, 1986.

			Regular Season															Playoffs							
Season	Club	League	GP	G	A	Pts	PIM	PP	SH	GW	S	S%	+/-	TF	F%	Min	GP	G	A	Pts	PIM	PP	SH	GW	Min
2002-03	Jonquiere Elites	QAAA	42	7	12	19	70										3	2	1	2	2				
2003-04	Coaticook	QJHL	46	13	12	25	96																		
	Quebec Remparts	QMJHL	1	0	0	0	0																		
2004-05	Coaticook	QJHL	15	3	4	7	59																		
2005-06	Restigouche	MJrHL	54	43	43	86	153										4	3	2	5	16				
	Baie-Comeau	QMJHL															4	2	2	4	6				
2006-07	Baie-Comeau	QMJHL	68	35	28	63	113										11	8	6	14	35				
2007-08	Manitoba Moose	AHL	67	7	11	18	108										3	0	0	0	2				
2008-09	Manitoba Moose	AHL	63	6	9	15	79										14	0	1	1	37				
2009-10	Manitoba Moose	AHL	45	5	1	6	69																		
	Peoria Rivermen	AHL	16	0	1	1	16																		
2010-11	Norfolk Admirals	AHL	64	7	19	26	148										6	0	1	1	4				
2011-12	Norfolk Admirals	AHL	56	14	21	35	107										18	5	4	9	34				
	Tampa Bay	**NHL**	**14**	**0**	**2**	**2**	**15**	**0**	**0**	**0**	**5**	**0.0**	**–2**	**5**	**60.0**	**5:54**									
2012-13	Syracuse Crunch	AHL	39	11	7	18	83																		
	Tampa Bay	**NHL**	**19**	**2**	**1**	**3**	**30**	**0**	**0**	**0**	**16**	**12.5**	**2**	**4**	**50.0**	**8:33**									

Season	Club	League	GP	G	A	Pts	PIM	PP	SH	GW	S	S%	+/-	TF	F%	Min	GP	G	A	Pts	PIM	PP	SH	GW	Min
			Regular Season														Playoffs								
2013-14	Tampa Bay	NHL	13	0	0	0	20	0	0	0	2	0.0	–4	2	100.0	6:53	....	....	....	....	....	....	....	....	....
	Syracuse Crunch	AHL	38	2	4	6	112	....	....	....	....	....	....	....	....	....	....	....	....	....	....	....	....	....	....
2014-15	Rockford IceHogs	AHL	60	9	7	16	113	....	....	....	....	....	....	....	....	....	8	0	1	1	28	....	....	....	....
	NHL Totals		46	2	3	5	65	0	0	0	23	8.7		11	63.6	7:16	....	....	....	....	....	....	....	....	....

Signed as a free agent by **Vancouver**, July 3, 2007. Traded to **St. Louis** by **Vancouver** for Yan Stastny, March 3, 2010. Signed as a free agent by **Norfolk** (AHL), December 8, 2010. Signed as a free agent by **Tampa Bay**, December 29, 2011. Signed as a free agent by **Chicago**, July 1, 2014.

LADD, Andrew (LAD, AN-droo) WPG

Left wing. Shoots left. 6'3", 205 lbs. Born, Maple Ridge, BC, December 12, 1985. Carolina's 1st choice, 4th overall, in 2004 Entry Draft.

Season	Club	League	GP	G	A	Pts	PIM	PP	SH	GW	S	S%	+/-	TF	F%	Min	GP	G	A	Pts	PIM	PP	SH	GW	Min
2000-01	Port Coquitlam	Minor-BC	50	50	41	91	80	....	....	....	....	....	....	....	....	....	....	....	....	....	....	....	....	....	....
	Okanagan Chiefs	Minor-BC	6	4	8	12	10	....	....	....	....	....	....	....	....	....	....	....	....	....	....	....	....	....	....
2001-02	Port Coquitlam	Minor-BC	50	50	41	91	49	....	....	....	....	....	....	....	....	....	....	....	....	....	....	....	....	....	....
	Vancouver Giants	WHL	1	0	0	0	0	....	....	....	....	....	....	....	....	....	....	....	....	....	....	....	....	....	....
2002-03	Coquitlam	BCHL	58	15	40	55	61	....	....	....	....	....	....	....	....	....	....	....	....	....	....	....	....	....	....
2003-04	Calgary Hitmen	WHL	71	30	45	75	119	....	....	....	....	....	....	....	....	....	7	1	6	7	10	....	....	....	....
2004-05	Calgary Hitmen	WHL	65	19	26	45	167	....	....	....	....	....	....	....	....	....	12	7	4	11	18	....	....	....	....
2005-06♦	Carolina	NHL	29	6	5	11	4	3	0	0	43	14.0	0	0	0.0	11:10	17	2	3	5	4	0	0	1	9:27
	Lowell	AHL	25	11	8	19	28	....	....	....	....	....	....	....	....	....	....	....	....	....	....	....	....	....	....
2006-07	Carolina	NHL	65	11	10	21	46	2	0	3	109	10.1	1	1	0.0	11:12	....	....	....	....	....	....	....	....	....
2007-08	Carolina	NHL	43	9	9	18	31	0	0	1	76	11.8	9	5	60.0	11:45	....	....	....	....	....	....	....	....	....
	Albany River Rats	AHL	2	1	0	1	4	....	....	....	....	....	....	....	....	....	....	....	....	....	....	....	....	....	....
	Chicago	NHL	20	5	7	12	4	1	0	0	55	9.1	4	3	33.3	14:58	....	....	....	....	....	....	....	....	....
2008-09	Chicago	NHL	82	15	34	49	28	0	0	2	195	7.7	26	42	23.8	14:24	17	3	1	4	12	0	0	1	12:55
2009-10♦	Chicago	NHL	82	17	21	38	67	0	0	1	148	11.5	2	12	41.7	13:42	19	3	3	6	12	0	0	0	12:48
2010-11	Atlanta	NHL	81	29	30	59	39	9	2	2	195	14.9	–10	44	34.1	20:04	....	....	....	....	....	....	....	....	....
2011-12	Winnipeg	NHL	82	28	22	50	64	4	0	6	265	10.6	–8	59	54.2	19:34	....	....	....	....	....	....	....	....	....
2012-13	Winnipeg	NHL	48	18	28	46	22	3	0	4	121	14.9	10	54	53.7	19:41	....	....	....	....	....	....	....	....	....
2013-14	Winnipeg	NHL	78	23	31	54	57	4	0	2	189	12.2	8	62	38.7	19:44	....	....	....	....	....	....	....	....	....
2014-15	Winnipeg	NHL	81	24	38	62	72	9	0	6	224	10.7	9	20	35.0	20:04	4	0	1	1	4	0	0	0	20:29
	NHL Totals		691	185	235	420	434	35	2	27	1620	11.4		302	41.7	16:38	57	8	8	16	32	0	0	2	12:22

Traded to **Chicago** by **Carolina** for Tuomo Ruutu, February 26, 2008. Traded to **Atlanta** by **Chicago** for Ivan Vishnevskiy and Atlanta/Winnipeg's 2nd round choice (Adam Clendening) in 2011 Entry Draft, July 1, 2010. • Transferred to **Winnipeg** after **Atlanta** franchise relocated, June 21, 2011.

LAICH, Brooks (LIGHK, BRUKS) WSH

Center. Shoots left. 6'2", 210 lbs. Born, Wawota, SK, June 23, 1983. Ottawa's 7th choice, 193rd overall, in 2001 Entry Draft.

Season	Club	League	GP	G	A	Pts	PIM	PP	SH	GW	S	S%	+/-	TF	F%	Min	GP	G	A	Pts	PIM	PP	SH	GW	Min
99-2000	Tisdale Trojans	SMHL	57	51	52	103	....	....	....	....	....	....	....	....	....	....	....	....	....	....	....	....	....	....	....
2000-01	Moose Jaw	WHL	71	9	21	30	28	....	....	....	....	....	....	....	....	....	4	0	0	0	5	....	....	....	....
2001-02	Moose Jaw	WHL	28	6	14	20	12	....	....	....	....	....	....	....	....	....	....	....	....	....	....	....	....	....	....
	Seattle	WHL	47	22	36	58	42	....	....	....	....	....	....	....	....	....	11	5	3	8	11	....	....	....	....
2002-03	Seattle	WHL	60	41	53	94	65	....	....	....	....	....	....	....	....	....	15	5	14	19	24	....	....	....	....
2003-04	Ottawa	NHL	1	0	0	0	2	0	0	0	1	0.0	0	7	42.9	9:34	....	....	....	....	....	....	....	....	....
	Binghamton	AHL	44	15	18	33	16	....	....	....	....	....	....	....	....	....	....	....	....	....	....	....	....	....	....
	Washington	NHL	4	0	1	1	0	0	0	0	2	0.0	–1	49	51.0	10:50	....	....	....	....	....	....	....	....	....
	Portland Pirates	AHL	22	1	3	4	12	....	....	....	....	....	....	....	....	....	6	0	0	0	0	....	....	....	....
2004-05	Portland Pirates	AHL	68	16	10	26	33	....	....	....	....	....	....	....	....	....	....	....	....	....	....	....	....	....	....
2005-06	Washington	NHL	73	7	14	21	26	1	0	1	118	5.9	–9	666	49.7	11:13	....	....	....	....	....	....	....	....	....
	Hershey Bears	AHL	10	7	6	13	8	....	....	....	....	....	....	....	....	....	21	8	7	15	29	....	....	....	....
2006-07	Washington	NHL	73	8	10	18	29	2	3	0	119	6.7	–2	563	51.9	13:36	....	....	....	....	....	....	....	....	....
2007-08	Washington	NHL	82	21	16	37	35	8	2	4	122	17.2	–3	596	47.2	14:03	7	1	5	6	4	0	0	0	18:37
2008-09	Washington	NHL	82	23	30	53	31	9	1	3	185	12.4	–1	511	51.1	17:17	14	3	4	7	10	2	0	0	17:27
2009-10	Washington	NHL	78	25	34	59	34	12	1	4	222	11.3	16	337	45.1	18:17	7	2	1	3	4	0	0	1	19:57
2010-11	Washington	NHL	82	16	32	48	46	4	1	3	207	7.7	14	524	51.3	18:25	9	1	6	7	2	0	0	0	21:54
2011-12	Washington	NHL	82	16	25	41	34	5	1	5	191	8.4	–8	1394	47.6	18:30	14	2	5	7	6	0	0	0	20:13
2012-13	Kloten Flyers	Swiss	19	6	12	18	28	....	....	....	....	....	....	....	....	....	....	....	....	....	....	....	....	....	....
	Washington	NHL	9	1	3	4	6	0	0	0	10	10.0	2	81	50.6	16:32	....	....	....	....	....	....	....	....	....
2013-14	Washington	NHL	51	8	7	15	16	1	1	1	75	10.7	–7	460	44.1	17:15	....	....	....	....	....	....	....	....	....
2014-15	Washington	NHL	66	7	13	20	24	0	0	2	106	6.6	–2	198	43.9	14:43	14	1	1	2	0	0	0	0	11:56
	NHL Totals		683	132	185	317	283	42	10	23	1358	9.7		5386	48.4	15:56	65	10	22	32	26	2	0	1	17:52

WHL West First All-Star Team (2003)

Traded to **Washington** by **Ottawa** with Ottawa's 2nd round choice (later traded to Colorado - Colorado selected Chris Durand) in 2005 Entry Draft for Peter Bondra, February 18, 2004. Signed as a free agent by **Kloten** (Swiss), September 28, 2012. • Missed majority of 2012-13 due to recurring groin injury and lower-body injury vs. NY Islanders, April 4, 2013.

LAIN, Kellan (LANE, KEHL-uhn)

Left wing. Shoots left. 6'6", 210 lbs. Born, Oakville, ON, August 11, 1989.

Season	Club	League	GP	G	A	Pts	PIM	PP	SH	GW	S	S%	+/-	TF	F%	Min	GP	G	A	Pts	PIM	PP	SH	GW	Min
2007-08	Orleans Blues	ON-Jr.A	31	9	13	22	51	....	....	....	....	....	....	....	....	....	21	11	4	15	60	....	....	....	....
2008-09	Oakville Blades	ON-Jr.A	47	19	23	42	74	....	....	....	....	....	....	....	....	....	18	10	6	16	22	....	....	....	....
2009-10	Oakville Blades	ON-Jr.A	16	8	9	17	16	....	....	....	....	....	....	....	....	....	17	5	17	22	22	....	....	....	....
2010-11	Lake Superior	CCHA	38	4	4	8	40	....	....	....	....	....	....	....	....	....	....	....	....	....	....	....	....	....	....
2011-12	Lake Superior	CCHA	38	9	6	15	59	....	....	....	....	....	....	....	....	....	....	....	....	....	....	....	....	....	....
2012-13	Lake Superior	CCHA	32	8	8	16	*111	....	....	....	....	....	....	....	....	....	....	....	....	....	....	....	....	....	....
	Chicago Wolves	AHL	13	0	0	0	6	....	....	....	....	....	....	....	....	....	....	....	....	....	....	....	....	....	....
2013-14	Vancouver	NHL	9	1	0	1	21	0	0	0	7	14.3	1	37	48.7	5:13	....	....	....	....	....	....	....	....	....
	Utica Comets	AHL	63	7	12	19	129	....	....	....	....	....	....	....	....	....	....	....	....	....	....	....	....	....	....
2014-15	Utica Comets	AHL	10	0	1	1	20	....	....	....	....	....	....	....	....	....	....	....	....	....	....	....	....	....	....
	Oklahoma City	AHL	2	0	0	0	4	....	....	....	....	....	....	....	....	....	....	....	....	....	....	....	....	....	....
	NHL Totals		9	1	0	1	21	0	0	0	7	14.3		37	48.6	5:13	....	....	....	....	....	....	....	....	....

Signed as a free agent by **Vancouver**, July 19, 2013. Traded to **Edmonton** by **Vancouver** for Will Acton, November 20, 2014.

LANDER, Anton (LAN-duhr, AN-tawn) EDM

Center. Shoots left. 6', 194 lbs. Born, Sundsvall, Sweden, April 24, 1991. Edmonton's 2nd choice, 40th overall, in 2009 Entry Draft.

Season	Club	League	GP	G	A	Pts	PIM	PP	SH	GW	S	S%	+/-	TF	F%	Min	GP	G	A	Pts	PIM	PP	SH	GW	Min
2005-06	Timra IK U18	Swe-U18	14	1	6	7	14	....	....	....	....	....	....	....	....	....	....	....	....	....	....	....	....	....	....
2006-07	Timra IK U18	Swe-U18	12	6	10	16	14	....	....	....	....	....	....	....	....	....	2	1	2	3	0	....	....	....	....
	Timra IK Jr.	Swe-Jr.	10	2	1	3	10	....	....	....	....	....	....	....	....	....	....	....	....	....	....	....	....	....	....
2007-08	Timra IK U18	Swe-U18	4	6	4	10	8	....	....	....	....	....	....	....	....	....	....	....	....	....	....	....	....	....	....
	Timra IK Jr.	Swe-Jr.	18	5	14	19	39	....	....	....	....	....	....	....	....	....	....	....	....	....	....	....	....	....	....
	Timra IK	Sweden	32	1	2	3	4	....	....	....	....	....	....	....	....	....	10	0	0	0	0	....	....	....	....
2008-09	Timra IK Jr.	Swe-Jr.	8	5	1	6	8	....	....	....	....	....	....	....	....	....	....	....	....	....	....	....	....	....	....
	Timra IK	Sweden	47	4	6	10	12	....	....	....	....	....	....	....	....	....	7	0	0	0	4	....	....	....	....
2009-10	Timra IK	Sweden	49	7	9	16	14	....	....	....	....	....	....	....	....	....	5	0	2	2	2	....	....	....	....
2010-11	Timra IK	Sweden	49	11	15	26	38	....	....	....	....	....	....	....	....	....	....	....	....	....	....	....	....	....	....
	Timra IK Jr.	Swe-Jr.	....	....	....	....	....	....	....	....	....	....	....	....	....	....	2	1	2	3	0	....	....	....	....
2011-12	Edmonton	NHL	56	2	4	6	12	0	1	0	54	3.7	–8	344	43.3	10:37	....	....	....	....	....	....	....	....	....
	Oklahoma City	AHL	14	1	4	5	10	....	....	....	....	....	....	....	....	....	14	2	2	4	4	....	....	....	....
2012-13	Oklahoma City	AHL	47	9	11	20	22	....	....	....	....	....	....	....	....	....	8	5	3	8	4	....	....	....	....
	Edmonton	NHL	11	0	1	1	2	0	0	0	11	0.0	–4	55	49.1	11:02	....	....	....	....	....	....	....	....	....
2013-14	Edmonton	NHL	27	0	1	1	4	0	0	0	18	0.0	–10	160	44.4	13:38	....	....	....	....	....	....	....	....	....
	Oklahoma City	AHL	46	18	34	52	30	....	....	....	....	....	....	....	....	....	3	1	1	2	0	....	....	....	....
2014-15	Edmonton	NHL	38	6	14	20	14	4	0	2	61	9.8	–12	451	50.1	15:01	....	....	....	....	....	....	....	....	....
	Oklahoma City	AHL	29	9	22	31	20	....	....	....	....	....	....	....	....	....	....	....	....	....	....	....	....	....	....
	NHL Totals		132	8	20	28	32	4	1	2	144	5.6		1010	46.8	12:32	....	....	....	....	....	....	....	....	....

LANDESKOG, Gabriel
(LAND-ehs-kawg, GAY-bree-ehl) **COL**

Left wing. Shoots left. 6'1", 210 lbs. Born, Stockholm, Sweden, November 23, 1992. Colorado's 1st choice, 2nd overall, in 2011 Entry Draft.

			Regular Season														Playoffs								
Season	Club	League	GP	G	A	Pts	PIM	PP	SH	GW	S	S%	+/-	TF	F%	Min	GP	G	A	Pts	PIM	PP	SH	GW	Min
2007-08	Djurgarden U18	Swe-U18	23	12	10	22	4	....	....	....	....	....	....	....	....	....	2	0	0	0	0	....	....	....	....
	Djurgarden Jr.	Swe-Jr.	1	0	0	0	0	....	....	....	....	....	....	....	....	....	....	....	....	....	....	....	....	....	....
2008-09	Djurgarden U18	Swe-U18	8	5	7	12	41	....	....	....	....	....	....	....	....	....	2	0	0	0	0	....	....	....	....
	Djurgarden Jr.	Swe-Jr.	31	7	14	21	63	....	....	....	....	....	....	....	....	....	6	1	0	1	8	....	....	....	....
	Djurgarden	Sweden	3	0	1	1	2	....	....	....	....	....	....	....	....	....	....	....	....	....	....	....	....	....	....
2009-10	Kitchener Rangers	OHL	61	24	22	46	51	....	....	....	....	....	....	....	....	....	20	8	15	23	18	....	....	....	....
2010-11	Kitchener Rangers	OHL	53	36	30	66	61	....	....	....	....	....	....	....	....	....	7	6	4	10	4	....	....	....	....
2011-12	**Colorado**	**NHL**	**82**	**22**	**30**	**52**	**51**	**6**	**0**	**5**	**270**	**8.1**	**20**	**36**	**22.2**	**18:37**	....	....	....	....	....	....	....	....	....
2012-13	Djurgarden	Sweden-2	17	6	8	14	32	....	....	....	....	....	....	....	....	....	....	....	....	....	....	....	....	....	....
	Colorado	**NHL**	**36**	**9**	**8**	**17**	**22**	**0**	**3**	**1**	**109**	**8.3**	**-4**	**18**	**33.3**	**19:20**	....	....	....	....	....	....	....	....	....
2013-14	**Colorado**	**NHL**	**81**	**26**	**39**	**65**	**71**	**5**	**0**	**4**	**222**	**11.7**	**21**	**18**	**72.2**	**18:41**	**7**	**3**	**1**	**4**	**8**	**0**	**0**	**1**	**21:12**
	Sweden	Olympics	6	0	1	1	4	....	....	....	....	....	....	....	....	....	....	....	....	....	....	....	....	....	....
2014-15	**Colorado**	**NHL**	**82**	**23**	**36**	**59**	**79**	**8**	**0**	**2**	**214**	**10.7**	**-2**	**45**	**35.6**	**18:30**	....	....	....	....	....	....	....	....	....
	NHL Totals		**281**	**80**	**113**	**193**	**223**	**19**	**3**	**12**	**815**	**9.8**		**117**	**36.8**	**18:41**	**7**	**3**	**1**	**4**	**8**	**0**	**0**	**1**	**21:12**

OHL All-Rookie Team (2010) • NHL All-Rookie Team (2012) • Calder Memorial Trophy (2012)

Signed as a free agent by **Djurgarden** (Sweden-2), October 3, 2012.

LAPIERRE, Maxim
(la-PEE-air, max-EEM)

Center. Shoots right. 6'2", 215 lbs. Born, St. Leonard, QC, March 29, 1985. Montreal's 3rd choice, 61st overall, in 2003 Entry Draft.

Season	Club	League	GP	G	A	Pts	PIM	PP	SH	GW	S	S%	+/-	TF	F%	Min	GP	G	A	Pts	PIM	PP	SH	GW	Min
2000-01	Cap-d-Madeleine	QAAA	42	14	27	41	44	....	....	....	....	....	....	....	....	....	10	3	5	8	16	....	....	....	....
2001-02	Cap-d-Madeleine	QAAA	32	16	24	40	102	....	....	....	....	....	....	....	....	....	15	7	10	17	20	....	....	....	....
	Montreal Rocket	QMJHL	9	2	0	2	2	....	....	....	....	....	....	....	....	....	....	....	....	....	....	....	....	....	....
2002-03	Montreal Rocket	QMJHL	72	22	21	43	55	....	....	....	....	....	....	....	....	....	7	1	3	4	6	....	....	....	....
2003-04	P.E.I. Rocket	QMJHL	67	25	36	61	138	....	....	....	....	....	....	....	....	....	11	7	2	9	14	....	....	....	....
2004-05	P.E.I. Rocket	QMJHL	69	25	27	52	139	....	....	....	....	....	....	....	....	....	....	....	....	....	....	....	....	....	....
2005-06	**Montreal**	**NHL**	**1**	**0**	**0**	**0**	**0**	**0**	**0**	**0**	**0**	**0.0**	**-1**	**2**	**50.0**	**3:04**	....	....	....	....	....	....	....	....	....
	Hamilton	AHL	73	13	23	36	214	....	....	....	....	....	....	....	....	....	....	....	....	....	....	....	....	....	....
2006-07	**Montreal**	**NHL**	**46**	**6**	**6**	**12**	**24**	**0**	**1**	**2**	**82**	**7.3**	**-7**	**425**	**45.2**	**11:25**	....	....	....	....	....	....	....	....	....
	Hamilton	AHL	37	11	13	24	59	....	....	....	....	....	....	....	....	....	22	6	6	12	41	....	....	....	....
2007-08	**Montreal**	**NHL**	**53**	**7**	**11**	**18**	**60**	**0**	**0**	**0**	**68**	**10.3**	**5**	**527**	**49.2**	**13:10**	**12**	**0**	**3**	**3**	**6**	**0**	**0**	**0**	**11:38**
	Hamilton	AHL	19	7	7	14	63	....	....	....	....	....	....	....	....	....	....	....	....	....	....	....	....	....	....
2008-09	**Montreal**	**NHL**	**79**	**15**	**13**	**28**	**76**	**1**	**2**	**2**	**165**	**9.1**	**9**	**987**	**53.2**	**14:48**	**4**	**0**	**0**	**0**	**26**	**0**	**0**	**0**	**14:56**
2009-10	**Montreal**	**NHL**	**76**	**7**	**7**	**14**	**61**	**0**	**0**	**1**	**101**	**6.9**	**-14**	**425**	**48.9**	**12:16**	**19**	**3**	**1**	**4**	**20**	**0**	**0**	**1**	**12:20**
2010-11	**Montreal**	**NHL**	**38**	**5**	**3**	**8**	**63**	**0**	**0**	**0**	**78**	**6.4**	**-7**	**50**	**58.0**	**11:42**	....	....	....	....	....	....	....	....	....
	Anaheim	**NHL**	**21**	**0**	**3**	**3**	**9**	**0**	**0**	**0**	**28**	**0.0**	**-6**	**133**	**53.4**	**11:35**	....	....	....	....	....	....	....	....	....
	Vancouver	**NHL**	**19**	**1**	**0**	**1**	**8**	**0**	**0**	**0**	**23**	**4.3**	**-1**	**157**	**46.5**	**11:32**	**25**	**3**	**2**	**5**	***66**	**0**	**0**	**1**	**13:34**
2011-12	**Vancouver**	**NHL**	**82**	**9**	**10**	**19**	**130**	**0**	**0**	**0**	**103**	**8.7**	**-3**	**482**	**52.1**	**11:14**	**5**	**0**	**1**	**1**	**16**	**0**	**0**	**0**	**10:20**
2012-13	**Vancouver**	**NHL**	**48**	**4**	**6**	**10**	**45**	**0**	**0**	**1**	**54**	**7.4**	**-6**	**542**	**50.6**	**12:36**	**4**	**0**	**0**	**0**	**6**	**0**	**0**	**0**	**9:30**
2013-14	**St. Louis**	**NHL**	**71**	**9**	**6**	**15**	**78**	**0**	**0**	**1**	**78**	**11.5**	**-3**	**593**	**50.8**	**11:10**	**6**	**1**	**1**	**2**	**4**	**0**	**0**	**0**	**16:27**
2014-15	**St. Louis**	**NHL**	**45**	**2**	**7**	**9**	**16**	**0**	**0**	**0**	**43**	**4.7**	**-2**	**244**	**54.9**	**10:21**	....	....	....	....	....	....	....	....	....
	Pittsburgh	**NHL**	**35**	**0**	**2**	**2**	**16**	**0**	**0**	**0**	**43**	**0.0**	**-13**	**338**	**50.6**	**11:10**	**5**	**0**	**0**	**0**	**0**	**0**	**0**	**0**	**13:59**
	NHL Totals		**614**	**65**	**74**	**139**	**586**	**1**	**3**	**7**	**866**	**7.5**		**4905**	**50.7**	**12:04**	**80**	**7**	**8**	**15**	**144**	**0**	**0**	**2**	**12:53**

Traded to **Anaheim** by **Montreal** for Brett Festerling and Anaheim's 5th round choice (later traded back to Anaheim – Anaheim selected Brian Cooper) in 2012 Entry Draft, December 31, 2010. Traded to **Vancouver** by **Anaheim** with MacGregor Sharp for Joel Perrault and Vancouver's 3rd round choice (Frederik Andersen) in 2012 Entry Draft, February 28, 2011. Signed as a free agent by **St. Louis**, July 5, 2013. Traded to **Pittsburgh** by **St. Louis** for Marcel Goc, January 27, 2015.

LARSEN, Philip
(LAHR-suhn, FIHL-ihp)

Defense. Shoots right. 6', 182 lbs. Born, Esbjerg, Denmark, December 7, 1989. Dallas' 3rd choice, 149th overall, in 2008 Entry Draft.

Season	Club	League	GP	G	A	Pts	PIM	PP	SH	GW	S	S%	+/-	TF	F%	Min	GP	G	A	Pts	PIM	PP	SH	GW	Min
2004-05	Esbjerg IK Jr.	Den-Jr.	10	1	0	1	2	....	....	....	....	....	....	....	....	....	....	....	....	....	....	....	....	....	....
2005-06	Rogle Jr.	Swe-Jr.	32	1	4	5	24	....	....	....	....	....	....	....	....	....	....	....	....	....	....	....	....	....	....
	Rogle	Sweden-2	13	0	0	0	0	....	....	....	....	....	....	....	....	....	....	....	....	....	....	....	....	....	....
2006-07	Frolunda U18	Swe-U18	3	1	2	3	2	....	....	....	....	....	....	....	....	....	4	2	1	3	8	....	....	....	....
	Frolunda Jr.	Swe-Jr.	37	3	15	18	50	....	....	....	....	....	....	....	....	....	8	0	1	1	6	....	....	....	....
	Frolunda	Sweden	5	0	0	0	0	....	....	....	....	....	....	....	....	....	....	....	....	....	....	....	....	....	....
2007-08	Frolunda Jr.	Swe-Jr.	8	1	4	5	12	....	....	....	....	....	....	....	....	....	7	0	4	4	6	....	....	....	....
	Boras HC	Sweden-2	24	5	5	10	32	....	....	....	....	....	....	....	....	....	....	....	....	....	....	....	....	....	....
	Frolunda	Sweden	16	0	0	0	2	....	....	....	....	....	....	....	....	....	....	....	....	....	....	....	....	....	....
2008-09	Frolunda Jr.	Swe-Jr.	1	1	0	1	0	....	....	....	....	....	....	....	....	....	....	....	....	....	....	....	....	....	....
	Frolunda	Sweden	53	2	15	17	18	....	....	....	....	....	....	....	....	....	11	2	1	3	4	....	....	....	....
2009-10	Frolunda	Sweden	42	1	9	10	20	....	....	....	....	....	....	....	....	....	7	0	0	0	4	....	....	....	....
	Dallas	**NHL**	**2**	**0**	**1**	**1**	**0**	**0**	**0**	**0**	**1**	**0.0**	**1**	**0**	**0.0**	**12:27**	....	....	....	....	....	....	....	....	....
2010-11	**Dallas**	**NHL**	**6**	**0**	**2**	**2**	**0**	**0**	**0**	**0**	**11**	**0.0**	**1**	**0**	**0.0**	**13:26**	....	....	....	....	....	....	....	....	....
	Texas Stars	AHL	54	4	18	22	12	....	....	....	....	....	....	....	....	....	6	2	3	5	4	....	....	....	....
2011-12	**Dallas**	**NHL**	**55**	**3**	**8**	**11**	**16**	**1**	**0**	**0**	**69**	**4.3**	**11**	**0**	**0.0**	**17:57**	....	....	....	....	....	....	....	....	....
	Texas Stars	AHL	12	1	9	10	6	....	....	....	....	....	....	....	....	....	....	....	....	....	....	....	....	....	....
2012-13	Lukko Rauma	Finland	27	5	10	15	24	....	....	....	....	....	....	....	....	....	....	....	....	....	....	....	....	....	....
	Dallas	**NHL**	**32**	**2**	**3**	**5**	**18**	**1**	**0**	**0**	**30**	**6.7**	**-10**	**0**	**0.0**	**14:53**	....	....	....	....	....	....	....	....	....
2013-14	**Edmonton**	**NHL**	**30**	**3**	**9**	**12**	**8**	**1**	**0**	**0**	**47**	**6.4**	**-4**	**0**	**0.0**	**17:10**	....	....	....	....	....	....	....	....	....
	Oklahoma City	AHL	7	1	6	7	4	....	....	....	....	....	....	....	....	....	....	....	....	....	....	....	....	....	....
2014-15	Khanty-Mansiisk	KHL	56	6	19	25	34	....	....	....	....	....	....	....	....	....	....	....	....	....	....	....	....	....	....
	NHL Totals		**125**	**8**	**23**	**31**	**42**	**3**	**0**	**0**	**158**	**5.1**		**0**	**0.0**	**16:40**									

Signed as a free agent by **Rauma** (Finland), September 27, 2012. Traded to **Edmonton** by **Dallas** with Dallas' 7th round choice in 2016 Entry Draft for Shawn Horcoff, July 5, 2013. • Missed majority of 2013-14 due to back injuries. Signed as a free agent by **Khanty-Mansiisk** (KHL), May 28, 2014. Signed as a free agent by **Jokerit Helsinki** (Finland), May 25, 2015.

LARSSON, Adam
(LAHR-suhn, A-duhm) **N.J.**

Defense. Shoots right. 6'3", 210 lbs. Born, Skelleftea, Sweden, November 12, 1992. New Jersey's 1st choice, 4th overall, in 2011 Entry Draft.

Season	Club	League	GP	G	A	Pts	PIM	PP	SH	GW	S	S%	+/-	TF	F%	Min	GP	G	A	Pts	PIM	PP	SH	GW	Min
2007-08	Skelleftea U18	Swe-U18	24	5	15	20	30	....	....	....	....	....	....	....	....	....	....	....	....	....	....	....	....	....	....
	Skelleftea Jr.	Swe-Jr.	3	0	5	5	6	....	....	....	....	....	....	....	....	....	....	....	....	....	....	....	....	....	....
2008-09	Skelleftea AIK U18	Swe-U18	7	3	8	11	6	....	....	....	....	....	....	....	....	....	8	0	6	6	6	....	....	....	....
	Skelleftea AIK Jr.	Swe-Jr.	26	2	7	9	28	....	....	....	....	....	....	....	....	....	5	0	4	4	2	....	....	....	....
	Skelleftea AIK	Sweden	1	0	0	0	0	....	....	....	....	....	....	....	....	....	....	....	....	....	....	....	....	....	....
2009-10	Skelleftea AIK Jr.	Swe-Jr.	1	1	0	1	2	....	....	....	....	....	....	....	....	....	....	....	....	....	....	....	....	....	....
	Skelleftea AIK	Sweden	49	4	13	17	18	....	....	....	....	....	....	....	....	....	11	0	1	1	31	....	....	....	....
2010-11	Skelleftea AIK	Sweden	37	1	8	9	41	....	....	....	....	....	....	....	....	....	17	0	4	4	12	....	....	....	....
2011-12	**New Jersey**	**NHL**	**65**	**2**	**16**	**18**	**20**	**0**	**0**	**0**	**68**	**2.9**	**-7**	**0**	**0.0**	**20:37**	**5**	**1**	**0**	**1**	**4**	**0**	**0**	**0**	**16:25**
2012-13	Albany Devils	AHL	33	4	15	19	24	....	....	....	....	....	....	....	....	....	....	....	....	....	....	....	....	....	....
	New Jersey	**NHL**	**37**	**0**	**6**	**6**	**12**	**0**	**0**	**0**	**30**	**0.0**	**4**	**0**	**0.0**	**18:06**	....	....	....	....	....	....	....	....	....
2013-14	**New Jersey**	**NHL**	**26**	**1**	**2**	**3**	**12**	**0**	**0**	**1**	**20**	**5.0**	**-1**	**0**	**0.0**	**17:47**	....	....	....	....	....	....	....	....	....
	Albany Devils	AHL	33	3	16	19	16	....	....	....	....	....	....	....	....	....	4	0	0	0	2	....	....	....	....
2014-15	**New Jersey**	**NHL**	**64**	**3**	**21**	**24**	**34**	**0**	**0**	**1**	**91**	**3.3**	**2**	**0**	**0.0**	**20:58**	....	....	....	....	....	....	....	....	....
	Albany Devils	AHL	1	0	2	2	0	....	....	....	....	....	....	....	....	....	....	....	....	....	....	....	....	....	....
	NHL Totals		**192**	**6**	**45**	**51**	**78**	**0**	**0**	**2**	**209**	**2.9**		**0**	**0.0**	**19:52**	**5**	**1**	**0**	**1**	**4**	**0**	**0**	**0**	**16:25**

LARSSON, Johan
(LAHR-suhn, YOH-han) **BUF**

Left wing. Shoots left. 5'11", 206 lbs. Born, Lau, Sweden, July 25, 1992. Minnesota's 3rd choice, 56th overall, in 2010 Entry Draft.

Season	Club	League	GP	G	A	Pts	PIM	PP	SH	GW	S	S%	+/-	TF	F%	Min	GP	G	A	Pts	PIM	PP	SH	GW	Min
2005-06	Sudrets	Sweden-4	2	0	2	2	2	....	....	....	....	....	....	....	....	....	....	....	....	....	....	....	....	....	....
2006-07	Sudrets	Sweden-4	29	13	7	20	40	....	....	....	....	....	....	....	....	....	....	....	....	....	....	....	....	....	....
2007-08	Sudrets	Sweden-4	25	11	11	22	71	....	....	....	....	....	....	....	....	....	....	....	....	....	....	....	....	....	....
2008-09	Brynas U18	Swe-U18	11	6	4	10	76	....	....	....	....	....	....	....	....	....	3	0	3	3	2	....	....	....	....
	Brynas IF Gavle Jr.	Swe-Jr.	33	4	5	9	55	....	....	....	....	....	....	....	....	....	5	0	0	0	2	....	....	....	....
2009-10	Brynas U18	Swe-U18	4	1	1	2	2	....	....	....	....	....	....	....	....	....	4	4	4	8	6	....	....	....	....
	Brynas IF Gavle Jr.	Swe-Jr.	40	15	19	34	80	....	....	....	....	....	....	....	....	....	5	1	1	2	2	....	....	....	....

			Regular Season														Playoffs								
Season	Club	League	GP	G	A	Pts	PIM	PP	SH	GW	S	S%	+/-	TF	F%	Min	GP	G	A	Pts	PIM	PP	SH	GW	Min
2010-11	Brynas IF Gavle	Sweden	43	4	4	8	18	....	....	....	....	....	....	....	....	....	5	0	2	2	4	....	....	....	....
	Brynas IF Gavle Jr.	Swe-Jr.	10	6	9	15	8	....	....	....	....	....	....	....	....	....	1	0	0	0	0	....	....	....	....
2011-12	Brynas IF Gavle	Sweden	49	12	24	36	34	....	....	....	....	....	....	....	....	....	16	2	7	9	16	....	....	....	....
2012-13	Houston Aeros	AHL	62	15	22	37	38	....	....	....	....	....	....	....	....	....	....	....	....	....	....	....	....	....	....
	Minnesota	NHL	1	0	0	0	0	0	0	0	2	0.0	0	0	0.0	14:02	....	....	....	....	....	....	....	....	....
	Rochester	AHL	7	1	3	4	2	....	....	....	....	....	....	....	....	....	3	0	3	3	6	....	....	....	....
2013-14	Buffalo	NHL	28	0	4	4	19	0	0	0	21	0.0	0	285	47.4	13:27	....	....	....	....	....	....	....	....	....
	Rochester	AHL	51	15	26	41	75	....	....	....	....	....	....	....	....	....	5	1	2	3	4	....	....	....	....
2014-15	Buffalo	NHL	39	6	10	16	12	1	0	0	50	12.0	0	341	44.0	14:31	....	....	....	....	....	....	....	....	....
	Rochester	AHL	44	15	25	40	38	....	....	....	....	....	....	....	....	....	....	....	....	....	....	....	....	....	....
	NHL Totals		68	6	14	20	31	1	0	0	73	8.2		626	45.5	14:04	....	....	....	....	....	....	....	....	....

Traded to **Buffalo** by **Minnesota** with Matt Hackett, Minnesota's 1st round choice (Nikita Zadorov) in 2013 Entry Draft and Minnesota's 2nd round choice (Vaclav Karabacek) in 2014 Entry Draft for Jason Pominville and Buffalo's 4th round choice (later traded to Edmonton – Edmonton selected William Lagesson) in 2014 Entry Draft, April 3, 2013.

LASHOFF, Brian (LASH-awf, BRIGH-uhn) DET

Defense. Shoots left. 6'3", 221 lbs. Born, Albany, NY, July 16, 1990.

Season	Club	League	GP	G	A	Pts	PIM	PP	SH	GW	S	S%	+/-	TF	F%	Min	GP	G	A	Pts	PIM	PP	SH	GW	Min
2006-07	Barrie Colts	OHL	47	2	10	12	20	....	....	....	....	....	....	....	....	....	5	0	1	1	2	....	....	....	....
2007-08	Barrie Colts	OHL	50	5	15	20	44	....	....	....	....	....	....	....	....	....	8	0	1	1	4	....	....	....	....
2008-09	Barrie Colts	OHL	25	1	12	13	19	....	....	....	....	....	....	....	....	....	....	....	....	....	....	....	....	....	....
	Kingston	OHL	35	6	13	19	32	....	....	....	....	....	....	....	....	....	....	....	....	....	....	....	....	....	....
	Grand Rapids	AHL	6	1	4	5	0	....	....	....	....	....	....	....	....	....	8	1	4	5	2	....	....	....	....
2009-10	Kingston	OHL	58	6	21	27	71	....	....	....	....	....	....	....	....	....	7	0	0	0	12	....	....	....	....
	Grand Rapids	AHL	6	0	2	2	2	....	....	....	....	....	....	....	....	....	....	....	....	....	....	....	....	....	....
2010-11	Grand Rapids	AHL	37	0	3	3	25	....	....	....	....	....	....	....	....	....	....	....	....	....	....	....	....	....	....
	Toledo Walleye	ECHL	3	0	1	1	0	....	....	....	....	....	....	....	....	....	....	....	....	....	....	....	....	....	....
2011-12	Grand Rapids	AHL	76	8	11	19	41	....	....	....	....	....	....	....	....	....	....	....	....	....	....	....	....	....	....
2012-13	Grand Rapids	AHL	37	2	4	6	23	....	....	....	....	....	....	....	....	....	18	0	1	1	10	....	....	....	....
	Detroit	NHL	31	1	4	5	15	0	0	0	26	3.8	–10	0	0.0	17:47	3	0	0	0	0	0	0	0	18:00
2013-14	Detroit	NHL	75	1	5	6	36	0	0	0	38	2.6	–2	0	0.0	14:26	5	0	0	0	0	0	0	0	13:59
2014-15	Detroit	NHL	11	0	2	2	6	0	0	0	7	0.0	4	0	0.0	13:17	....	....	....	....	....	....	....	....	....
	Grand Rapids	AHL	32	1	6	7	12	....	....	....	....	....	....	....	....	....	16	0	3	3	8	....	....	....	....
	NHL Totals		117	2	11	13	57	0	0	0	71	2.8		0	0.0	15:13	8	0	0	0	0	0	0	0	15:29

Signed as a free agent by **Detroit**, October 1, 2008.

LASHOFF, Matt (LASH-awf, MAT)

Defense. Shoots left. 6'2", 204 lbs. Born, East Greenbush, NY, September 29, 1986. Boston's 1st choice, 22nd overall, in 2005 Entry Draft.

Season	Club	League	GP	G	A	Pts	PIM	PP	SH	GW	S	S%	+/-	TF	F%	Min	GP	G	A	Pts	PIM	PP	SH	GW	Min
2002-03	USNTDP	U-17	16	1	3	4	14	....	....	....	....	....	....	....	....	....	....	....	....	....	....	....	....	....	....
	USNTDP	NAHL	46	2	5	7	53	....	....	....	....	....	....	....	....	....	....	....	....	....	....	....	....	....	....
2003-04	Kitchener Rangers	OHL	62	5	19	24	94	....	....	....	....	....	....	....	....	....	5	0	1	1	0	....	....	....	....
2004-05	Kitchener Rangers	OHL	44	4	18	22	44	....	....	....	....	....	....	....	....	....	13	0	3	3	18	....	....	....	....
2005-06	Kitchener Rangers	OHL	56	7	40	47	146	....	....	....	....	....	....	....	....	....	5	1	1	2	12	....	....	....	....
	Providence Bruins	AHL	7	1	1	2	6	....	....	....	....	....	....	....	....	....	6	0	0	0	6	....	....	....	....
2006-07	Boston	NHL	12	0	2	2	12	0	0	0	8	0.0	–6	0	0.0	14:55	....	....	....	....	....	....	....	....	....
	Providence Bruins	AHL	64	11	26	37	60	....	....	....	....	....	....	....	....	....	....	....	....	....	....	....	....	....	....
2007-08	Boston	NHL	18	1	4	5	0	1	0	0	11	9.1	–2	0	0.0	13:35	....	....	....	....	....	....	....	....	....
	Providence Bruins	AHL	60	9	27	36	79	....	....	....	....	....	....	....	....	....	9	0	4	4	6	....	....	....	....
2008-09	Boston	NHL	16	0	1	1	10	0	0	0	6	0.0	1	0	0.0	13:07	....	....	....	....	....	....	....	....	....
	Providence Bruins	AHL	33	5	16	21	36	....	....	....	....	....	....	....	....	....	....	....	....	....	....	....	....	....	....
	Tampa Bay	NHL	12	0	7	7	10	0	0	0	19	0.0	–7	0	0.0	23:46	....	....	....	....	....	....	....	....	....
	Norfolk Admirals	AHL	2	0	0	0	2	....	....	....	....	....	....	....	....	....	....	....	....	....	....	....	....	....	....
2009-10	Tampa Bay	NHL	5	0	0	0	21	0	0	0	2	0.0	–2	0	0.0	8:53	....	....	....	....	....	....	....	....	....
	Norfolk Admirals	AHL	68	8	16	24	105	....	....	....	....	....	....	....	....	....	....	....	....	....	....	....	....	....	....
2010-11	Toronto	NHL	11	0	1	1	6	0	0	0	8	0.0	1	0	0.0	13:50	....	....	....	....	....	....	....	....	....
	Toronto Marlies	AHL	69	7	21	28	137	....	....	....	....	....	....	....	....	....	....	....	....	....	....	....	....	....	....
2011-12	Toronto Marlies	AHL	9	1	4	5	12	....	....	....	....	....	....	....	....	....	8	0	4	4	8	....	....	....	....
2012-13	ZSC Lions Zurich	Swiss	49	1	9	10	43	....	....	....	....	....	....	....	....	....	12	0	1	1	14	....	....	....	....
2013-14	Leksands IF	Sweden	40	0	6	6	58	....	....	....	....	....	....	....	....	....	3	0	0	0	4	....	....	....	....
2014-15	Novokuznetsk	KHL	23	0	2	2	14	....	....	....	....	....	....	....	....	....	....	....	....	....	....	....	....	....	....
	Bridgeport	AHL	11	1	3	4	22	....	....	....	....	....	....	....	....	....	....	....	....	....	....	....	....	....	....
	Portland Pirates	AHL	14	0	0	0	17	....	....	....	....	....	....	....	....	....	....	....	....	....	....	....	....	....	....
	NHL Totals		74	1	15	16	59	1	0	0	54	1.9		0	0.0	15:04	....	....	....	....	....	....	....	....	....

AHL All-Rookie Team (2007)

Traded to **Tampa Bay** by **Boston** with Martins Karsums for Mark Recchi and Tampa Bay's 2nd round choice (later traded to Florida – Florida selected Alexander Petrovic) in 2010 Entry Draft, March 4, 2009. Traded to **Toronto** by **Tampa Bay** for Alex Berry and Stefano Giliati, August 27, 2010. • Missed majority of 2011-12 due to knee injury at Lake Erie (AHL), October 30. 2011. Signed as a free agent by **Zurich** (Swiss), August 3, 2012. Signed as a free agent by **Leksand** (Sweden), October 9, 2013. Signed as a free agent by **Novokuznetsk** (KHL), June 25, 2014. Signed as a free agent by **Bridgeport** (AHL), January 12, 2015. Signed as a free agent by **Portland** (AHL), March 2, 2015.

LATTA, Michael (LA-tuh, MIGH-kuhl) WSH

Center. Shoots right. 6', 209 lbs. Born, Kitchener, ON, May 25, 1991. Nashville's 5th choice, 72nd overall, in 2009 Entry Draft.

Season	Club	League	GP	G	A	Pts	PIM	PP	SH	GW	S	S%	+/-	TF	F%	Min	GP	G	A	Pts	PIM	PP	SH	GW	Min
2006-07	Waterloo Wolves	Minor-ON	73	52	66	118	213	....	....	....	....	....	....	....	....	....	....	....	....	....	....	....	....	....	....
2007-08	Ottawa 67's	OHL	50	14	14	28	78	....	....	....	....	....	....	....	....	....	4	0	1	1	2	....	....	....	....
2008-09	Ottawa 67's	OHL	23	8	13	21	32	....	....	....	....	....	....	....	....	....	....	....	....	....	....	....	....	....	....
	Guelph Storm	OHL	42	14	22	36	60	....	....	....	....	....	....	....	....	....	4	0	2	2	12	....	....	....	....
2009-10	Guelph Storm	OHL	58	33	40	73	157	....	....	....	....	....	....	....	....	....	5	2	7	9	14	....	....	....	....
	Milwaukee	AHL	....	....	....	....	....	....	....	....	....	....	....	....	....	....	1	0	0	0	0	....	....	....	....
2010-11	Guelph Storm	OHL	68	34	55	89	158	....	....	....	....	....	....	....	....	....	6	5	5	10	11	....	....	....	....
	Milwaukee	AHL	4	0	1	1	2	....	....	....	....	....	....	....	....	....	7	0	0	0	12	....	....	....	....
2011-12	Milwaukee	AHL	51	14	13	27	100	....	....	....	....	....	....	....	....	....	3	0	1	1	2	....	....	....	....
2012-13	Milwaukee	AHL	67	9	26	35	184	....	....	....	....	....	....	....	....	....	....	....	....	....	....	....	....	....	....
	Hershey Bears	AHL	9	1	2	3	14	....	....	....	....	....	....	....	....	....	5	2	1	3	6	....	....	....	....
2013-14	Washington	NHL	17	1	3	4	12	0	0	0	6	16.7	0	115	52.2	7:43	....	....	....	....	....	....	....	....	....
	Hershey Bears	AHL	52	14	20	34	134	....	....	....	....	....	....	....	....	....	....	....	....	....	....	....	....	....	....
2014-15	Washington	NHL	53	0	6	6	68	0	0	0	24	0.0	4	335	47.8	8:23	4	0	0	0	2	0	0	0	6:56
	NHL Totals		70	1	9	10	80	0	0	0	30	3.3		450	48.9	8:13	4	0	0	0	2	0	0	0	6:56

Traded to **Washington** by **Nashville** with Martin Erat for Filip Forsberg, April 3, 2013.

LAUGHTON, Scott (LAW-tuhn, SKAWT) PHI

Center. Shoots left. 6'1", 190 lbs. Born, Oakville, ON, May 30, 1994. Philadelphia's 1st choice, 20th overall, in 2012 Entry Draft.

Season	Club	League	GP	G	A	Pts	PIM	PP	SH	GW	S	S%	+/-	TF	F%	Min	GP	G	A	Pts	PIM	PP	SH	GW	Min
2009-10	Tor. Marlboros	GTHL	76	55	40	95	109	....	....	....	....	....	....	....	....	....	....	....	....	....	....	....	....	....	....
	St. Michael's	ON-Jr.A	2	0	0	0	4	....	....	....	....	....	....	....	....	....	....	....	....	....	....	....	....	....	....
2010-11	Oshawa Generals	OHL	63	12	11	23	58	....	....	....	....	....	....	....	....	....	10	1	1	2	11	....	....	....	....
2011-12	Oshawa Generals	OHL	64	21	32	53	101	....	....	....	....	....	....	....	....	....	6	2	3	5	17	....	....	....	....
2012-13	Oshawa Generals	OHL	49	23	33	56	72	....	....	....	....	....	....	....	....	....	7	7	6	13	11	....	....	....	....
	Philadelphia	NHL	5	0	0	0	0	0	0	0	10	0.0	0	43	44.2	11:31	....	....	....	....	....	....	....	....	....
	Adirondack	AHL	6	1	2	3	0	....	....	....	....	....	....	....	....	....	....	....	....	....	....	....	....	....	....
2013-14	Oshawa Generals	OHL	54	40	47	87	72	....	....	....	....	....	....	....	....	....	9	4	7	11	17	....	....	....	....
2014-15	Philadelphia	NHL	31	2	4	6	17	0	0	0	51	3.9	–1	283	47.4	12:43	....	....	....	....	....	....	....	....	....
	Lehigh Valley	AHL	39	14	13	27	31	....	....	....	....	....	....	....	....	....	....	....	....	....	....	....	....	....	....
	NHL Totals		36	2	4	6	17	0	0	0	61	3.3		326	46.9	12:33	....	....	....	....	....	....	....	....	....

OHL First All-Star Team (2014)

					Regular Season												Playoffs							
Season	Club	League	GP	G	A	Pts	PIM	PP	SH	GW	S	S%	+/-	TF	F%	Min	GP	G	A	Pts	PIM	PP	SH	GW	Min

LAURIDSEN, Oliver — (LAW-rihd-suhn, AW-lih-vuhr)

Defense. Shoots left. 6'6", 220 lbs.   Born, Gentofte, Denmark, March 24, 1989. Philadelphia's 6th choice, 196th overall, in 2009 Entry Draft.

Season	Club	League	GP	G	A	Pts	PIM	PP	SH	GW	S	S%	+/-	TF	F%	Min	GP	G	A	Pts	PIM	PP	SH	GW	Min
2004-05	IC Gentofte Jr.	Den-Jr.	24	4	12	16	22	....	....	....	....	....	....				....								
	IC Gentofte	Den-2	8	0	1	1	0	....	....	....	....	....	....				....								
2005-06	Rogle Jr.	Swe-Jr.	28	1	1	2	32	....	....	....	....	....	....				....								
2006-07	Linkopings HC Jr.	Swe-Jr.	34	0	2	2	95	....	....	....	....	....	....				5	0	0	0	8				
2007-08	Linkoping U18	Swe-U18	2	1	3	4	0	....	....	....	....	....	....				....								
	Tranas AIF	Sweden-3	1	0	0	0	0	....	....	....	....	....	....				....								
	Linkopings HC Jr.	Swe-Jr.	35	5	6	11	159	....	....	....	....	....	....				1	0	1	1	0				
2008-09	St. Cloud State	WCHA	28	0	1	1	38	....	....	....	....	....	....				....								
2009-10	St. Cloud State	WCHA	43	6	6	12	54	....	....	....	....	....	....				....								
2010-11	St. Cloud State	WCHA	37	1	8	9	51	....	....	....	....	....	....				....								
	Adirondack	AHL	2	0	0	0	30	....	....	....	....	....	....				....								
2011-12	Adirondack	AHL	65	3	4	7	85	....	....	....	....	....	....				....								
2012-13	Adirondack	AHL	59	1	5	6	77	....	....	....	....	....	....				....								
	Philadelphia	**NHL**	15	2	1	3	34	0	0	2	14	14.3	0	0	0.0	15:08	....								
2013-14	Adirondack	AHL	63	1	10	11	167	....	....	....	....	....	....				....								
2014-15	**Philadelphia**	**NHL**	1	0	0	0	10	0	0	0	2	0.0	-1	0	0.0	10:26	....								
	Lehigh Valley	AHL	75	4	6	10	152	....	....	....	....	....	....				....								
	NHL Totals		16	2	1	3	44	0	0	2	16	12.5		0	0.0	14:50	....								

LAZAR, Curtis — (lah-ZAHR, KUHR-tihs)   **OTT**

Center/Right wing. Shoots right. 6', 210 lbs.   Born, Salmon Arm, BC, February 2, 1995. Ottawa's 1st choice, 17th overall, in 2013 Entry Draft.

Season	Club	League	GP	G	A	Pts	PIM	PP	SH	GW	S	S%	+/-	TF	F%	Min	GP	G	A	Pts	PIM	PP	SH	GW	Min
2009-10	PoE Academy	High-BC	51	57	58	115	....	....	....	....	....	....	....				....								
2010-11	Okanagan H.A.	CSSHL	6	4	5	9	4	....	....	....	....	....	....				1	0	0	0	0				
	Okanagan H.A.	High-BC	39	22	27	49	67	....	....	....	....	....	....				4	1	0	1	0				
	Edmonton	WHL	6	0	1	1	0	....	....	....	....	....	....				20	8	11	19	4				
2011-12	Edmonton	WHL	63	20	11	31	56	....	....	....	....	....	....				22	9	2	11	20				
2012-13	Edmonton	WHL	72	38	23	61	47	....	....	....	....	....	....				21	10	12	22	12				
2013-14	Edmonton	WHL	58	41	35	76	30	....	....	....	....	....	....				....								
2014-15	**Ottawa**	**NHL**	67	6	9	15	14	0	0	0	92	6.5	1	273	47.3	12:54	6	0	0	0	2	0	0	0	13:52
	NHL Totals		67	6	9	15	14	0	0	0	92	6.5		273	47.3	12:54	6	0	0	0	2	0	0	0	13:52

WHL East First All-Star Team (2014) • George Parsons Trophy (Memorial Cup – Most Sportsmanlike Player) (2014)

LeBLANC, Drew — (luh-BLAWNK, DROO)

Center. Shoots left. 6', 194 lbs.   Born, Hermantown, MN, June 29, 1989.

Season	Club	League	GP	G	A	Pts	PIM	PP	SH	GW	S	S%	+/-	TF	F%	Min	GP	G	A	Pts	PIM	PP	SH	GW	Min
2004-05	Hermantown	High-MN	....	....	....	26	....	....	....	....	....	....	....				....								
2005-06	Hermantown	High-MN	....	....	....	83	....	....	....	....	....	....	....				....								
2006-07	Hermantown	High-MN	....	....	....	90	....	....	....	....	....	....	....				....								
	Chicago Steel	USHL	14	0	5	5	20	....	....	....	....	....	....				5	0	2	2	4				
2007-08	Chicago Steel	USHL	58	19	35	54	36	....	....	....	....	....	....				7	3	1	4	4				
2008-09	St. Cloud State	WCHA	38	8	7	15	18	....	....	....	....	....	....				....								
2009-10	St. Cloud State	WCHA	43	6	25	31	10	....	....	....	....	....	....				....								
2010-11	St. Cloud State	WCHA	38	13	26	39	18	....	....	....	....	....	....				....								
2011-12	St. Cloud State	WCHA	10	2	10	12	4	....	....	....	....	....	....				....								
2012-13	St. Cloud State	WCHA	42	13	*37	50	14	....	....	....	....	....	....				....								
	Chicago	**NHL**	2	0	0	0	0	0	0	0	3	0.0	-3	18	50.0	13:20	....								
2013-14	Rockford IceHogs	AHL	76	7	15	22	18	....	....	....	....	....	....				....								
2014-15	Rockford IceHogs	AHL	41	4	2	6	8	....	....	....	....	....	....				....								
	NHL Totals		2	0	0	0	0	0	0	0	3	0.0		18	50.0	13:20	....								

WCHA First All-Star Team (2013) • WCHA Player of the Year (2013) • NCAA West First All-American Team (2013) • Hobey Baker Memorial Award (Top U.S. Collegiate Player) (2013)
• Missed majority of 2011-12 due to leg injury vs. University of Wisconsin (WCHA), November 5, 2011. Signed as a free agent by **Chicago**, April 12, 2013.

LEBLANC, Louis — (luh-BLAWNK, LOU-ee)   **NYI**

Center. Shoots right. 6', 184 lbs.   Born, Pointe-Claire, QC, January 26, 1991. Montreal's 1st choice, 18th overall, in 2009 Entry Draft.

Season	Club	League	GP	G	A	Pts	PIM	PP	SH	GW	S	S%	+/-	TF	F%	Min	GP	G	A	Pts	PIM	PP	SH	GW	Min
2006-07	Lac St-Louis Lions	QAAA	40	31	18	49	72	....	....	....	....	....	....				22	14	7	21	10				
2007-08	Lac St-Louis Lions	QAAA	43	54	37	91	152	....	....	....	....	....	....				14	8	14	22	76				
2008-09	Omaha Lancers	USHL	60	28	31	59	78	....	....	....	....	....	....				3	2	1	3	2				
2009-10	Harvard Crimson	ECAC	31	11	12	23	50	....	....	....	....	....	....				....								
2010-11	Montreal	QMJHL	51	26	32	58	100	....	....	....	....	....	....				10	6	3	9	16				
2011-12	**Montreal**	**NHL**	42	5	5	10	28	0	0	0	58	8.6	3	64	43.8	11:12	....								
	Hamilton	AHL	31	11	11	22	30	....	....	....	....	....	....				....								
2012-13	Hamilton	AHL	62	10	8	18	53	....	....	....	....	....	....				....								
2013-14	**Montreal**	**NHL**	8	0	0	0	4	0	0	0	7	0.0	1	4	50.0	9:52	....								
	Hamilton	AHL	70	13	15	28	63	....	....	....	....	....	....				....								
2014-15	Norfolk Admirals	AHL	71	14	15	29	38	....	....	....	....	....	....				....								
	NHL Totals		50	5	5	10	32	0	0	0	65	7.7		68	44.1	10:59	....								

USHL All-Rookie Team (2009) • USHL Rookie of the Year (2009) • ECAC All-Rookie Team (2010)
Traded to **Anaheim** by **Montreal** for future consideratins, June 14, 2014. Signed as a free agent by **NY Islanders**, July 17, 2015.

LEBLANC, Peter — (luh-BLAWNK, PEE-tuhr)

Center. Shoots left. 5'10", 175 lbs.   Born, Hamilton, ON, February 3, 1988. Chicago's 9th choice, 186th overall, in 2006 Entry Draft.

Season	Club	League	GP	G	A	Pts	PIM	PP	SH	GW	S	S%	+/-	TF	F%	Min	GP	G	A	Pts	PIM	PP	SH	GW	Min
2004-05	Hamilton	ON-Jr.A	49	14	22	36	....	....	....	....	....	....	....				....								
2005-06	Hamilton	ON-Jr.A	21	10	12	22	25	....	....	....	....	....	....				14	8	8	16	8				
2006-07	New Hampshire	H-East	39	1	4	5	4	....	....	....	....	....	....				....								
2007-08	New Hampshire	H-East	37	5	10	15	37	....	....	....	....	....	....				....								
2008-09	New Hampshire	H-East	38	14	16	30	8	....	....	....	....	....	....				....								
2009-10	New Hampshire	H-East	39	14	21	35	24	....	....	....	....	....	....				....								
2010-11	Rockford IceHogs	AHL	57	12	18	30	12	....	....	....	....	....	....				....								
	Toledo Walleye	ECHL	22	8	14	22	6	....	....	....	....	....	....				....								
2011-12	Rockford IceHogs	AHL	72	24	20	44	14	....	....	....	....	....	....				....								
2012-13	Rockford IceHogs	AHL	34	4	8	12	15	....	....	....	....	....	....				....								
	Hershey Bears	AHL	33	8	10	18	4	....	....	....	....	....	....				5	0	8	8	0				
2013-14	**Washington**	**NHL**	1	0	0	0	0	0	0	0	0	0.0	0	0	0.0	9:26	....								
	Hershey Bears	AHL	65	12	16	28	16	....	....	....	....	....	....				....								
2014-15	Rogle	Sweden-2	50	6	12	18	16	....	....	....	....	....	....				....								
	NHL Totals		1	0	0	0	0	0	0	0	0	0.0		0	0.0	9:26	....								

OPJHL Rookie of the Year (2005)
• Missed majority of 2005-06 due to mononucleosis. Signed as a free agent by **Rockford** (AHL), July 29, 2010. Traded to **Washington** by **Chicago** for Mathieu Beaudoin, January 31, 2013. Signed as a free agent by **Rogle** (Sweden-2), June 12, 2014.

LECAVALIER, Vincent — (luh-KAV-uhl-YAY, VIHN-sihnt)   **PHI**

Center. Shoots left. 6'4", 215 lbs.   Born, Ile Bizard, QC, April 21, 1980. Tampa Bay's 1st choice, 1st overall, in 1998 Entry Draft.

Season	Club	League	GP	G	A	Pts	PIM	PP	SH	GW	S	S%	+/-	TF	F%	Min	GP	G	A	Pts	PIM	PP	SH	GW	Min
1995-96	Notre Dame	SMHL	22	52	52	104	....	....	....	....	....	....	....				....								
1996-97	Rimouski Oceanic	QMJHL	64	42	60	102	36	....	....	....	....	....	....				4	4	3	7	2				
1997-98	Rimouski Oceanic	QMJHL	58	44	71	115	117	....	....	....	....	....	....				18	*15	*26	*41	46				
1998-99	**Tampa Bay**	**NHL**	82	13	15	28	23	2	0	2	125	10.4	-19	953	40.3	13:40	....								
99-2000	**Tampa Bay**	**NHL**	80	25	42	67	43	6	0	3	166	15.1	-25	1288	44.4	19:18	....								
2000-01	**Tampa Bay**	**NHL**	68	23	28	51	66	7	0	3	165	13.9	-26	1278	44.9	19:57	....								
2001-02	**Tampa Bay**	**NHL**	76	20	17	37	61	5	0	3	164	12.2	-18	931	41.5	17:09	....								
2002-03	**Tampa Bay**	**NHL**	80	33	45	78	39	11	2	3	274	12.0	0	1200	43.9	19:33	11	3	3	6	22	1	0	1	22:36
2003-04♦	**Tampa Bay**	**NHL**	81	32	34	66	52	5	2	6	242	13.2	24	1119	41.4	18:04	23	9	7	16	25	2	0	0	19:39

Season	Club	League	GP	G	A	Pts	PIM	PP	SH	GW	S	S%	+/-	TF	F%	Min	GP	G	A	Pts	PIM	PP	SH	GW	Min
								Regular Season									Playoffs								
2004-05	Ak Bars Kazan	Russia	30	7	9	16	78	....	....	....	....	....	....	....	....	....	4	1	0	1	6	....	....	....	....
2005-06	Tampa Bay	NHL	80	35	40	75	90	13	2	7	309	11.3	0	1366	51.2	20:08	5	1	3	4	7	1	0	0	22:17
	Canada	Olympics	6	0	3	3	16	....	....	....	....	....	....	....	....	....	....	....	....	....	....	....	....	....	....
2006-07	Tampa Bay	NHL	82	*52	56	108	44	16	5	7	339	15.3	2	1653	46.6	22:36	6	5	2	7	10	1	0	1	26:29
2007-08	Tampa Bay	NHL	81	40	52	92	89	10	1	7	318	12.6	–17	1671	48.8	22:57	....	....	....	....	....	....	....	....	....
2008-09	Tampa Bay	NHL	77	29	38	67	54	10	1	6	291	10.0	–9	1395	50.9	20:15	....	....	....	....	....	....	....	....	....
2009-10	Tampa Bay	NHL	82	24	46	70	63	5	0	3	295	8.1	–16	1449	53.2	19:47	....	....	....	....	....	....	....	....	....
2010-11	Tampa Bay	NHL	65	25	29	54	43	12	0	5	210	11.9	–5	1161	50.9	18:27	18	6	13	19	16	3	0	3	19:51
2011-12	Tampa Bay	NHL	64	22	27	49	50	5	0	5	182	12.1	–2	1162	47.9	18:56	....	....	....	....	....	....	....	....	....
2012-13	Tampa Bay	NHL	39	10	22	32	29	5	0	0	86	11.6	–5	742	54.5	17:53	....	....	....	....	....	....	....	....	....
2013-14	Philadelphia	NHL	69	20	17	37	44	8	0	3	132	15.2	–16	448	44.6	15:11	7	1	1	2	2	1	0	0	10:41
2014-15	Philadelphia	NHL	57	8	12	20	36	1	0	0	103	7.8	–7	191	49.7	12:39	....	....	....	....	....	....	....	....	....
	NHL Totals		1163	411	520	931	826	121	13	63	3401	12.1		18007	47.3	18:41	70	25	29	54	82	9	0	5	20:03

QMJHL All-Rookie Team (1997) • QMJHL Offensive Rookie of the Year (1997) • Canadian Major Junior Rookie of the Year (1997) • QMJHL First All-Star Team (1998) • Canadian Major Junior First All-Star Team (1998) • NHL Second All-Star Team (2007) • Maurice "Rocket" Richard Trophy (2007) • King Clancy Memorial Trophy (2008) • NHL Foundation Player Award (2008)

Played in NHL All-Star Game (2003, 2007, 2008, 2009)

Signed as a free agent by **Kazan** (Russia), November 4, 2004. Signed as a free agent by **Philadelphia**, July 6, 2013.

LEDDY, Nick

(LEH-dee, NIHK) **NYI**

Defense. Shoots left. 6', 191 lbs. Born, Eden Prairie, MN, March 20, 1991. Minnesota's 1st choice, 16th overall, in 2009 Entry Draft.

Season	Club	League	GP	G	A	Pts	PIM	PP	SH	GW	S	S%	+/-	TF	F%	Min	GP	G	A	Pts	PIM	PP	SH	GW	Min
2006-07	Eden Prairie	High-MN	28	2	16	18	10	....	....	....	....	....	....	....	....	....	....	....	....	....	....	....	....	....	....
2007-08	Eden Prairie	High-MN	27	6	22	28	14	....	....	....	....	....	....	....	....	....	....	....	....	....	....	....	....	....	....
	USNTDP	U-18	4	0	2	2	....	....	....	....	....	....	....	....	....	....	....	....	....	....	....	....	....	....	....
2008-09	Eden Prairie	High-MN	31	12	33	45	26	....	....	....	....	....	....	....	....	....	....	....	....	....	....	....	....	....	....
	Team Southwest	UMHSEL	24	9	11	20	....	....	....	....	....	....	....	....	....	....	....	....	....	....	....	....	....	....	....
2009-10	U. of Minnesota	WCHA	30	3	8	11	4	....	....	....	....	....	....	....	....	....	....	....	....	....	....	....	....	....	....
2010-11	Chicago	NHL	46	4	3	7	4	0	0	0	37	10.8	–3	0	0.0	14:19	7	0	0	0	0	0	0	0	14:36
	Rockford IceHogs	AHL	22	2	8	10	2	....	....	....	....	....	....	....	....	....	....	....	....	....	....	....	....	....	....
2011-12	Chicago	NHL	82	3	34	37	10	0	0	0	94	3.2	–12	0	0.0	22:05	6	1	2	3	0	0	0	0	20:02
2012-13	Rockford IceHogs	AHL	31	3	13	16	12	....	....	....	....	....	....	....	....	....	....	....	....	....	....	....	....	....	....
	♦ Chicago	NHL	48	6	12	18	10	2	0	2	65	9.2	15	0	0.0	17:25	23	0	2	2	4	0	0	0	14:21
2013-14	Chicago	NHL	82	7	24	31	10	4	0	1	123	5.7	10	0	0.0	16:22	18	1	4	5	6	1	0	0	15:50
2014-15	NY Islanders	NHL	78	10	27	37	14	1	0	1	120	8.3	18	0	0.0	20:22	7	0	5	5	0	0	0	0	24:40
	NHL Totals		336	30	100	130	48	7	0	4	439	6.8		0	0.0	18:34	61	2	13	15	10	1	0	0	16:33

Traded to **Chicago** by **Minnesota** with Kim Johnsson for Cam Barker, February 12, 2010. Traded to **NY Islanders** by **Chicago** with Kent Simpson for T.J. Brennan, Ville Pokka and Anders Nilsson, October 4, 2014.

LEE, Anders

(LEE, AN-duhrz) **NYI**

Center. Shoots left. 6'2", 227 lbs. Born, Edina, MN, July 3, 1990. NY Islanders' 7th choice, 152nd overall, in 2009 Entry Draft.

Season	Club	League	GP	G	A	Pts	PIM	PP	SH	GW	S	S%	+/-	TF	F%	Min	GP	G	A	Pts	PIM	PP	SH	GW	Min
2006-07	Saint Thomas	High-MN	31	24	17	41	....	....	....	....	....	....	....	....	....	....	....	....	....	....	....	....	....	....	....
2007-08	Edina Hornets	High-MN	31	32	22	54	....	....	....	....	....	....	....	....	....	....	....	....	....	....	....	....	....	....	....
2008-09	Edina Hornets	High-MN	31	25	59	84	30	....	....	....	....	....	....	....	....	....	....	....	....	....	....	....	....	....	....
	Team Southwest	UMHSEL	18	12	17	29	....	....	....	....	....	....	....	....	....	....	....	....	....	....	....	....	....	....	....
2009-10	Green Bay	USHL	59	35	31	66	54	....	....	....	....	....	....	....	....	....	12	*10	*12	*22	13	....	....	....	....
2010-11	U. of Notre Dame	CCHA	44	24	20	44	16	....	....	....	....	....	....	....	....	....	....	....	....	....	....	....	....	....	....
2011-12	U. of Notre Dame	CCHA	40	17	17	34	24	....	....	....	....	....	....	....	....	....	....	....	....	....	....	....	....	....	....
2012-13	U. of Notre Dame	CCHA	41	*20	18	38	37	....	....	....	....	....	....	....	....	....	....	....	....	....	....	....	....	....	....
	NY Islanders	NHL	2	1	1	2	0	0	0	0	2	50.0	–3	2	0.0	8:12	....	....	....	....	....	....	....	....	....
2013-14	NY Islanders	NHL	22	9	5	14	14	2	0	0	68	13.2	3	6	16.7	15:43	....	....	....	....	....	....	....	....	....
	Bridgeport	AHL	54	22	19	41	83	....	....	....	....	....	....	....	....	....	....	....	....	....	....	....	....	....	....
2014-15	NY Islanders	NHL	76	25	16	41	33	5	0	6	197	12.7	9	1	100.0	14:24	5	0	1	1	7	0	0	0	14:45
	Bridgeport	AHL	5	3	2	5	2	....	....	....	....	....	....	....	....	....	....	....	....	....	....	....	....	....	....
	NHL Totals		100	35	22	57	47	7	0	6	267	13.1		9	22.2	14:34	5	0	1	1	7	0	0	0	14:45

USHL All-Rookie Team (2010) • USHL First All-Star Team (2010) • USHL Rookie of the Year (2010) • CCHA All-Rookie Team (2011) • CCHA Second All-Star Team (2011) • CCHA First All-Star Team (2013) • NCAA West Second All-American Team (2013)

LEGWAND, David

(LEHG-wawnd, DAY-vihd) **BUF**

Center. Shoots left. 6'2", 205 lbs. Born, Detroit, MI, August 17, 1980. Nashville's 1st choice, 2nd overall, in 1998 Entry Draft.

Season	Club	League	GP	G	A	Pts	PIM	PP	SH	GW	S	S%	+/-	TF	F%	Min	GP	G	A	Pts	PIM	PP	SH	GW	Min
1996-97	Det. Compuware	MNHL	44	21	41	62	58	....	....	....	....	....	....	....	....	....	....	....	....	....	....	....	....	....	....
1997-98	Plymouth Whalers	OHL	59	54	51	105	56	....	....	....	....	....	....	....	....	....	15	8	12	20	24	....	....	....	....
1998-99	Plymouth Whalers	OHL	55	31	49	80	65	....	....	....	....	....	....	....	....	....	11	3	8	11	8	....	....	....	....
	Nashville	NHL	1	0	0	0	0	0	0	0	2	0.0	0	9	55.6	12:50	....	....	....	....	....	....	....	....	....
99-2000	Nashville	NHL	71	13	15	28	30	4	0	2	111	11.7	–6	637	41.6	14:43	....	....	....	....	....	....	....	....	....
2000-01	Nashville	NHL	81	13	28	41	38	3	0	3	172	7.6	1	888	40.3	15:14	....	....	....	....	....	....	....	....	....
2001-02	Nashville	NHL	63	11	19	30	54	1	1	1	121	9.1	1	843	40.5	16:25	....	....	....	....	....	....	....	....	....
2002-03	Nashville	NHL	64	17	31	48	34	3	1	4	167	10.2	–2	1095	46.6	19:14	....	....	....	....	....	....	....	....	....
2003-04	Nashville	NHL	82	18	29	47	46	5	1	5	165	10.9	9	1109	45.1	17:17	6	1	0	1	8	0	1	0	15:41
2004-05	EHC Basel	Swiss-2	3	6	2	8	2	....	....	....	....	....	....	....	....	....	19	16	23	39	20	....	....	....	....
2005-06	Nashville	NHL	44	7	19	26	34	0	0	5	109	6.4	3	580	44.7	16:50	5	0	1	1	8	0	0	0	17:21
	Milwaukee	AHL	3	0	0	0	0	....	....	....	....	....	....	....	....	....	....	....	....	....	....	....	....	....	....
2006-07	Nashville	NHL	78	27	36	63	44	3	1	7	153	17.6	23	1108	45.3	18:22	5	0	3	3	2	0	0	0	22:23
2007-08	Nashville	NHL	65	15	29	44	38	4	0	1	144	10.4	–4	700	43.6	18:01	3	1	0	1	2	0	0	0	18:15
2008-09	Nashville	NHL	73	20	22	42	32	1	3	1	175	11.4	–3	1023	49.8	19:27	....	....	....	....	....	....	....	....	....
2009-10	Nashville	NHL	82	11	27	38	24	0	1	3	151	7.3	–5	1124	47.9	18:42	6	2	5	7	8	0	0	1	19:16
2010-11	Nashville	NHL	64	17	24	41	24	0	2	3	130	13.1	13	837	47.2	18:48	12	6	3	9	8	1	*2	0	22:06
2011-12	Nashville	NHL	78	19	34	53	26	5	0	2	140	13.6	3	1109	46.2	18:31	10	3	3	6	10	1	0	2	18:40
2012-13	Nashville	NHL	48	12	13	25	20	2	0	2	78	15.4	–6	721	50.2	18:26	....	....	....	....	....	....	....	....	....
2013-14	Nashville	NHL	62	10	30	40	30	4	0	2	107	9.3	–8	888	51.1	17:13	....	....	....	....	....	....	....	....	....
	Detroit	NHL	21	4	7	11	31	2	0	2	39	10.3	–9	268	48.9	16:16	5	0	0	0	0	0	0	0	13:59
2014-15	Ottawa	NHL	80	9	18	27	32	6	0	0	91	9.9	1	968	46.6	13:54	3	0	0	0	0	0	0	0	9:52
	NHL Totals		1057	223	381	604	537	43	10	43	2055	10.9		13907	46.0	17:20	55	13	15	28	46	2	3	3	18:27

OHL All-Rookie Team (1998) • OHL First All-Star Team (1998) • OHL Rookie of the Year (1998) • OHL Player of the Year (1998) • Canadian Major Junior Rookie of the Year (1998)

Signed as a free agent by **Basel** (Swiss-2), January 27, 2005. Traded to **Detroit** by **Nashville** for Patrick Eaves, Calle Jarnkrok and Detroit's 2nd round choice (later traded to San Jose – San Jose selected Julius Bergman) in 2014 Entry Draft, March 5, 2014. Signed as a free agent by **Ottawa**, July 4, 2014. Traded to **Buffalo** by **Ottawa** with Robin Lehner for NY Islanders' 1st round choice (previously acquired, Ottawa selected Colin White) in 2015 Entry Draft, June 26, 2015.

LEHTERA, Jori

(LEH-tuhr-a, YOHR-ee) **ST.L.**

Center. Shoots left. 6'2", 191 lbs. Born, Helsinki, Finland, December 23, 1987. St. Louis' 4th choice, 65th overall, in 2008 Entry Draft.

Season	Club	League	GP	G	A	Pts	PIM	PP	SH	GW	S	S%	+/-	TF	F%	Min	GP	G	A	Pts	PIM	PP	SH	GW	Min
2003-04	Jokerit U18	Fin-U18	19	0	6	6	2	....	....	....	....	....	....	....	....	....	5	3	1	4	0	....	....	....	....
2004-05	Jokerit U18	Fin-U18	30	13	37	50	24	....	....	....	....	....	....	....	....	....	7	6	5	11	2	....	....	....	....
2005-06	Suomi U20	Finland-2	2	0	0	0	0	....	....	....	....	....	....	....	....	....	....	....	....	....	....	....	....	....	....
	Jokerit Helsinki Jr.	Fin-Jr.	39	14	33	47	16	....	....	....	....	....	....	....	....	....	4	1	4	5	0	....	....	....	....
2006-07	Suomi U20	Finland-2	10	4	7	11	10	....	....	....	....	....	....	....	....	....	....	....	....	....	....	....	....	....	....
	Jokerit Helsinki Jr.	Fin-Jr.	24	18	48	66	20	....	....	....	....	....	....	....	....	....	5	1	7	8	2	....	....	....	....
	Jokerit Helsinki	Finland	28	6	6	12	14	....	....	....	....	....	....	....	....	....	....	....	....	....	....	....	....	....	....
2007-08	Tappara Tampere	Finland	54	13	29	42	32	....	....	....	....	....	....	....	....	....	11	4	2	6	8	....	....	....	....
2008-09	Tappara Tampere	Finland	58	9	38	47	34	....	....	....	....	....	....	....	....	....	3	4	5	9	4	....	....	....	....
	Peoria Rivermen	AHL	7	0	1	1	2	....	....	....	....	....	....	....	....	....	7	1	1	2	10	....	....	....	....
2009-10	Tappara Tampere	Finland	57	19	*50	*69	58	....	....	....	....	....	....	....	....	....	9	1	9	10	8	....	....	....	....
2010-11	Yaroslavl	KHL	53	16	21	37	38	....	....	....	....	....	....	....	....	....	18	0	3	3	14	....	....	....	....
2011-12	Sibir Novosibirsk	KHL	25	10	16	26	10	....	....	....	....	....	....	....	....	....	....	....	....	....	....	....	....	....	....
2012-13	Sibir Novosibirsk	KHL	52	17	29	46	46	....	....	....	....	....	....	....	....	....	3	0	2	2	0	....	....	....	....

			Regular Season														Playoffs								
Season	Club	League	GP	G	A	Pts	PIM	PP	SH	GW	S	S%	+/-	TF	F%	Min	GP	G	A	Pts	PIM	PP	SH	GW	Min
2013-14	Novosibirsk	KHL	48	12	32	44	22	....	....	....	....	....	....	....	....	....	10	0	6	6	2	....	....	....	....
	Finland	Olympics	6	1	3	4	0	....	....	....	....	....	....	....	....	....	....	....	....	....	....	....	....	....	....
2014-15	**St. Louis**	**NHL**	**75**	**14**	**30**	**44**	**48**	**2**	**1**	**2**	**103**	**13.6**	**21**	**1061**	**51.2**	**16:13**	**5**	**0**	**2**	**2**	**0**	**0**	**0**	**0**	**14:53**
	NHL Totals		**75**	**14**	**30**	**44**	**48**	**2**	**1**	**2**	**103**	**13.6**		**1061**	**51.2**	**16:13**	**5**	**0**	**2**	**2**	**0**	**0**	**0**	**0**	**14:53**

LEIVO, Josh

(LEE-voh, JAWSH) **TOR**

Left wing. Shoots right. 6'1", 173 lbs. Born, Innisfil, ON, May 26, 1993. Toronto's 3rd choice, 86th overall, in 2011 Entry Draft.

Season	Club	League	GP	G	A	Pts	PIM	PP	SH	GW	S	S%	+/-	TF	F%	Min	GP	G	A	Pts	PIM	PP	SH	GW	Min
2008-09	Barrie Colts MM	Minor-ON	71	31	35	66	65	....	....	....	....	....	....	....	....	....	....	....	....	....	....	....	....	....	....
2009-10	Barrie Colts Mid.	Minor-ON	52	27	41	68	59	....	....	....	....	....	....	....	....	....	....	....	....	....	....	....	....	....	....
2010-11	Sudbury Wolves	OHL	64	13	17	30	37	....	....	....	....	....	....	....	....	....	8	6	7	13	4	....	....	....	....
2011-12	Sudbury Wolves	OHL	66	32	41	73	61	....	....	....	....	....	....	....	....	....	4	2	1	3	6	....	....	....	....
	Toronto Marlies	AHL	1	0	0	0	0	....	....	....	....	....	....	....	....	....	....	....	....	....	....	....	....	....	....
2012-13	Sudbury Wolves	OHL	34	19	25	44	34	....	....	....	....	....	....	....	....	....	....	....	....	....	....	....	....	....	....
	Kitchener Rangers	OHL	29	10	19	29	18	....	....	....	....	....	....	....	....	....	10	3	9	12	8	....	....	....	....
	Toronto Marlies	AHL	4	0	2	2	2	....	....	....	....	....	....	....	....	....	3	0	1	1	0	....	....	....	....
2013-14	**Toronto**	**NHL**	**7**	**1**	**1**	**2**	**0**	**0**	**0**	**0**	**4**	**25.0**	**0**	**1**	**0.0**	**9:52**	....	....	....	....	....	....	....	....	....
	Toronto Marlies	AHL	59	23	19	42	27	....	....	....	....	....	....	....	....	....	12	3	5	8	2	....	....	....	....
2014-15	**Toronto**	**NHL**	**9**	**1**	**0**	**1**	**4**	**0**	**0**	**0**	**10**	**10.0**	**-1**	**2**	**0.0**	**7:39**	....	....	....	....	....	....	....	....	....
	Toronto Marlies	AHL	51	11	21	32	44	....	....	....	....	....	....	....	....	....	5	1	5	6	0	....	....	....	....
	NHL Totals		**16**	**2**	**1**	**3**	**4**	**0**	**0**	**0**	**14**	**14.3**		**3**	**0.0**	**8:37**	....	....	....	....	....	....	....	....	....

LEOPOLD, Jordan

(LEE-oh-pohld, JOHR-dahn)

Defense. Shoots left. 6'1", 206 lbs. Born, Golden Valley, MN, August 3, 1980. Anaheim's 1st choice, 44th overall, in 1999 Entry Draft.

Season	Club	League	GP	G	A	Pts	PIM	PP	SH	GW	S	S%	+/-	TF	F%	Min	GP	G	A	Pts	PIM	PP	SH	GW	Min
1995-96	Armstrong	High-MN	19	11	14	25	30	....	....	....	....	....	....	....	....	....	....	....	....	....	....	....	....	....	....
1996-97	Armstrong	High-MN	30	24	36	60	....	....	....	....	....	....	....	....	....	....	....	....	....	....	....	....	....	....	....
1997-98	USNTDP	U-18	25	7	3	10	2	....	....	....	....	....	....	....	....	....	....	....	....	....	....	....	....	....	....
	USNTDP	USHL	19	2	4	6	6	....	....	....	....	....	....	....	....	....	....	....	....	....	....	....	....	....	....
	USNTDP	NAHL	16	2	5	7	8	....	....	....	....	....	....	....	....	....	....	....	....	....	....	....	....	....	....
1998-99	U. of Minnesota	WCHA	39	7	16	23	20	....	....	....	....	....	....	....	....	....	....	....	....	....	....	....	....	....	....
99-2000	U. of Minnesota	WCHA	39	6	18	24	20	....	....	....	....	....	....	....	....	....	....	....	....	....	....	....	....	....	....
2000-01	U. of Minnesota	WCHA	42	12	37	49	38	....	....	....	....	....	....	....	....	....	....	....	....	....	....	....	....	....	....
2001-02	U. of Minnesota	WCHA	44	20	28	48	28	....	....	....	....	....	....	....	....	....	....	....	....	....	....	....	....	....	....
2002-03	**Calgary**	**NHL**	**58**	**4**	**10**	**14**	**12**	**3**	**0**	**0**	**78**	**5.1**	**-15**	**0**	**0.0**	**20:36**	....	....	....	....	....	....	....	....	....
	Saint John Flames	AHL	3	1	2	3	0	....	....	....	....	....	....	....	....	....	....	....	....	....	....	....	....	....	....
2003-04	**Calgary**	**NHL**	**82**	**9**	**24**	**33**	**24**	**6**	**0**	**1**	**138**	**6.5**	**8**	**0**	**0.0**	**22:14**	**26**	**0**	**10**	**10**	**6**	**0**	**0**	**0**	**25:41**
2004-05			DID NOT PLAY																						
2005-06	**Calgary**	**NHL**	**74**	**2**	**18**	**20**	**68**	**2**	**0**	**1**	**87**	**2.3**	**6**	**0**	**0.0**	**22:20**	**7**	**0**	**1**	**1**	**4**	**0**	**0**	**0**	**19:13**
	United States	Olympics	6	1	0	1	4	....	....	....	....	....	....	....	....	....	....	....	....	....	....	....	....	....	....
2006-07	**Colorado**	**NHL**	**15**	**2**	**3**	**5**	**14**	**1**	**1**	**0**	**19**	**10.5**	**-4**	**0**	**0.0**	**19:47**	....	....	....	....	....	....	....	....	....
2007-08	**Colorado**	**NHL**	**43**	**5**	**8**	**13**	**20**	**2**	**0**	**1**	**35**	**14.3**	**5**	**0**	**0.0**	**15:59**	**7**	**0**	**3**	**3**	**0**	**0**	**0**	**0**	**17:00**
2008-09	**Colorado**	**NHL**	**64**	**6**	**14**	**20**	**18**	**1**	**0**	**1**	**82**	**7.3**	**-10**	**0**	**0.0**	**18:10**	....	....	....	....	....	....	....	....	....
	Calgary	**NHL**	**19**	**1**	**3**	**4**	**6**	**0**	**0**	**0**	**25**	**4.0**	**-5**	**0**	**0.0**	**20:58**	**6**	**0**	**1**	**1**	**8**	**0**	**0**	**0**	**23:10**
2009-10	**Florida**	**NHL**	**61**	**7**	**11**	**18**	**22**	**1**	**0**	**1**	**69**	**10.1**	**-7**	**0**	**0.0**	**22:25**	....	....	....	....	....	....	....	....	....
	Pittsburgh	**NHL**	**20**	**4**	**4**	**8**	**6**	**0**	**0**	**2**	**26**	**15.4**	**5**	**0**	**0.0**	**20:27**	**8**	**0**	**0**	**0**	**2**	**0**	**0**	**0**	**16:31**
2010-11	**Buffalo**	**NHL**	**71**	**13**	**22**	**35**	**36**	**5**	**0**	**1**	**134**	**9.7**	**-11**	**0**	**0.0**	**23:20**	**5**	**0**	**1**	**1**	**4**	**0**	**0**	**0**	**20:57**
2011-12	**Buffalo**	**NHL**	**79**	**10**	**14**	**24**	**28**	**1**	**0**	**0**	**110**	**9.1**	**4**	**0**	**0.0**	**22:22**	....	....	....	....	....	....	....	....	....
2012-13	**Buffalo**	**NHL**	**24**	**2**	**6**	**8**	**14**	**0**	**0**	**0**	**38**	**5.3**	**-6**	**0**	**0.0**	**21:08**	....	....	....	....	....	....	....	....	....
	St. Louis	**NHL**	**15**	**0**	**2**	**2**	**0**	**0**	**0**	**0**	**22**	**0.0**	**-2**	**0**	**0.0**	**18:22**	**6**	**0**	**0**	**0**	**0**	**0**	**0**	**0**	**16:33**
2013-14	**St. Louis**	**NHL**	**27**	**1**	**5**	**6**	**6**	**0**	**0**	**0**	**40**	**2.5**	**1**	**0**	**0.0**	**15:36**	**6**	**0**	**1**	**1**	**2**	**0**	**0**	**0**	**16:40**
2014-15	**St. Louis**	**NHL**	**7**	**0**	**0**	**0**	**2**	**0**	**0**	**0**	**1**	**0.0**	**0**	**0**	**0.0**	**13:04**	....	....	....	....	....	....	....	....	....
	Columbus	**NHL**	**18**	**1**	**2**	**3**	**9**	**1**	**0**	**0**	**21**	**4.8**	**-7**	**0**	**0.0**	**17:15**	....	....	....	....	....	....	....	....	....
	Minnesota	**NHL**	**18**	**0**	**1**	**1**	**8**	**0**	**0**	**0**	**17**	**0.0**	**1**	**0**	**0.0**	**13:19**	**9**	**0**	**0**	**0**	**0**	**0**	**0**	**0**	**12:00**
	NHL Totals		**695**	**67**	**147**	**214**	**293**	**23**	**1**	**8**	**942**	**7.1**		**0**	**0.0**	**20:31**	**80**	**0**	**17**	**17**	**26**	**0**	**0**	**0**	**20:03**

WCHA All-Rookie Team (1999) • WCHA Second All-Star Team (2000) • WCHA First All-Star Team (2001, 2002) • NCAA West First All-American Team (2001) • Hobey Baker Memorial Award (Top U.S. Collegiate Player) (2002)

Traded to **Calgary** by **Anaheim** for Andrei Nazarov and Calgary's 2nd round choice (later traded to Phoenix, later traded back to Calgary – Calgary selected Andrei Taratukhin) in 2001 Entry Draft, September 26, 2000. Traded to **Colorado** by **Calgary** with Calgary's 2nd round choice (Codey Burki) in 2006 Entry Draft and Calgary's 2nd round choice (Trevor Cann) in 2007 Entry Draft for Alex Tanguay, June 24, 2006. • Missed majority of 2006-07 due to off-season hernia surgery, groin injury and wrist injury vs. Calgary, February 15, 2007. Traded to **Calgary** by **Colorado** for Ryan Wilson, Lawrence Nycholat and Montreal's 2nd round choice (previously acquired, Colorado selected Stefan Elliott) in 2009 Entry Draft, March 4, 2009. Traded to **Florida** by **Calgary** with Phoenix's 3rd round choice (previously acquired, Florida selected Josh Birkholz) in 2009 Entry Draft for Jay Bouwmeester, June 27, 2009. Traded to **Pittsburgh** by **Florida** for Pittsburgh's 2nd round choice (Connor Brickley) in 2010 Entry Draft, March 1, 2010. Signed as a free agent by **Buffalo**, July 1, 2010. Traded to **St. Louis** by **Buffalo** for St. Louis' 2nd (Justin Bailey) and 5th (Anthony Florentino) round choices in 2013 Entry Draft, March 30, 2013. • Missed majority of 2013-14 due to hand (November 7, 2013 vs. Calgary) and ankle (February 8, 2014 vs. Winnipeg) injuries. Traded to **Columbus** by **St. Louis** for a 5th round choice in 2016 Entry Draft, November 15, 2014. Traded to **Minnesota** by **Columbus** for Justin Falk and Minnesota's 5th round choice (Veeti Vainio) in 2015 Entry Draft, March 2, 2015.

LERG, Bryan

(LEHRG, BRIGH-uhn) **S.J.**

Center. Shoots left. 5'10", 175 lbs. Born, Livonia, MI, January 20, 1986.

Season	Club	League	GP	G	A	Pts	PIM	PP	SH	GW	S	S%	+/-	TF	F%	Min	GP	G	A	Pts	PIM	PP	SH	GW	Min
2002-03	USNTDP	U-17	19	11	6	17	5	....	....	....	....	....	....	....	....	....	....	....	....	....	....	....	....	....	....
	USNTDP	NAHL	46	10	12	22	32	....	....	....	....	....	....	....	....	....	....	....	....	....	....	....	....	....	....
2003-04	USNTDP	U-18	46	22	25	47	....	....	....	....	....	....	....	....	....	....	....	....	....	....	....	....	....	....	....
	USNTDP	NAHL	11	5	7	12	10	....	....	....	....	....	....	....	....	....	....	....	....	....	....	....	....	....	....
2004-05	Michigan State	CCHA	41	10	5	15	14	....	....	....	....	....	....	....	....	....	....	....	....	....	....	....	....	....	....
2005-06	Michigan State	CCHA	45	15	23	38	26	....	....	....	....	....	....	....	....	....	....	....	....	....	....	....	....	....	....
2006-07	Michigan State	CCHA	41	23	13	36	21	....	....	....	....	....	....	....	....	....	....	....	....	....	....	....	....	....	....
2007-08	Michigan State	CCHA	42	20	19	39	18	....	....	....	....	....	....	....	....	....	....	....	....	....	....	....	....	....	....
	Springfield	AHL	4	0	2	2	2	....	....	....	....	....	....	....	....	....	....	....	....	....	....	....	....	....	....
2008-09	Springfield	AHL	42	9	8	17	24	....	....	....	....	....	....	....	....	....	....	....	....	....	....	....	....	....	....
	Stockton Thunder	ECHL	7	2	8	10	4	....	....	....	....	....	....	....	....	....	....	....	....	....	....	....	....	....	....
2009-10	Springfield	AHL	36	4	3	7	11	....	....	....	....	....	....	....	....	....	....	....	....	....	....	....	....	....	....
2010-11	Geneve	Swiss	1	0	0	0	0	....	....	....	....	....	....	....	....	....	....	....	....	....	....	....	....	....	....
	Wilkes-Barre	AHL	65	15	17	32	21	....	....	....	....	....	....	....	....	....	9	1	2	3	4	....	....	....	....
2011-12	Wilkes-Barre	AHL	70	27	26	53	32	....	....	....	....	....	....	....	....	....	12	0	2	2	4	....	....	....	....
2012-13	Lake Erie	AHL	28	9	7	16	6	....	....	....	....	....	....	....	....	....	....	....	....	....	....	....	....	....	....
2013-14	Lake Erie	AHL	35	12	15	27	4	....	....	....	....	....	....	....	....	....	....	....	....	....	....	....	....	....	....
2014-15	**San Jose**	**NHL**	**2**	**1**	**0**	**1**	**0**	**0**	**0**	**1**	**8**	**12.5**	**-1**	**4**	**100.0**	**12:36**	....	....	....	....	....	....	....	....	....
	Worcester Sharks	AHL	68	13	28	41	10	....	....	....	....	....	....	....	....	....	4	0	1	1	0	....	....	....	....
	NHL Totals		**2**	**1**	**0**	**1**	**0**	**0**	**0**	**1**	**8**	**12.5**		**4**	**100.0**	**12:36**	....	....	....	....	....	....	....	....	....

Signed as a free agent by **Edmonton**, April 2, 2008. Signed as a free agent by **Geneve** (Swiss), September 3, 2010. Signed as a free agent by **Wilkes-Barre** (AHL), December 8, 2010. Signed as a free agent by **Colorado**, July 13, 2012. Signed as a free agent by **San Jose**, July 10, 2014.

LESSIO, Lucas

(LEH-see-oh, LOO-kuhs) **ARI**

Left wing. Shoots left. 6'1", 212 lbs. Born, Maple, ON, January 23, 1993. Phoenix's 3rd choice, 56th overall, in 2011 Entry Draft.

Season	Club	League	GP	G	A	Pts	PIM	PP	SH	GW	S	S%	+/-	TF	F%	Min	GP	G	A	Pts	PIM	PP	SH	GW	Min
2008-09	Tor. Marlboros	GTHL	72	53	60	113	126	....	....	....	....	....	....	....	....	....	....	....	....	....	....	....	....	....	....
2009-10	St. Michael's	ON-Jr.A	41	30	42	72	87	....	....	....	....	....	....	....	....	....	5	0	3	3	10	....	....	....	....
2010-11	Oshawa Generals	OHL	66	27	27	54	66	....	....	....	....	....	....	....	....	....	10	5	4	9	6	....	....	....	....
2011-12	Oshawa Generals	OHL	66	34	28	62	71	....	....	....	....	....	....	....	....	....	6	3	2	5	6	....	....	....	....
2012-13	Oshawa Generals	OHL	35	19	15	34	38	....	....	....	....	....	....	....	....	....	9	1	2	3	20	....	....	....	....
	Portland Pirates	AHL	5	1	1	2	4	....	....	....	....	....	....	....	....	....	3	0	2	2	0	....	....	....	....
2013-14	**Phoenix**	**NHL**	**3**	**0**	**0**	**0**	**2**	**0**	**0**	**0**	**4**	**0.0**	**-2**	**0**	**0.0**	**11:32**	....	....	....	....	....	....	....	....	....
	Portland Pirates	AHL	69	29	25	54	63	....	....	....	....	....	....	....	....	....	....	....	....	....	....	....	....	....	....
2014-15	**Arizona**	**NHL**	**26**	**2**	**3**	**5**	**8**	**0**	**0**	**0**	**44**	**4.5**	**-10**	**2**	**0.0**	**12:45**	....	....	....	....	....	....	....	....	....
	Portland Pirates	AHL	49	15	16	31	26	....	....	....	....	....	....	....	....	....	5	0	3	3	0	....	....	....	....
	NHL Totals		**29**	**2**	**3**	**5**	**10**	**0**	**0**	**0**	**48**	**4.2**		**2**	**0.0**	**12:38**	....	....	....	....	....	....	....	....	....

OHL All-Rookie Team (2011)

LETANG, Kris (leh-TANG, KRIHS) PIT

Defense. Shoots right. 6', 201 lbs. Born, Montreal, QC, April 24, 1987. Pittsburgh's 3rd choice, 62nd overall, in 2005 Entry Draft.

			Regular Season														Playoffs								
Season	Club	League	GP	G	A	Pts	PIM	PP	SH	GW	S	S%	+/-	TF	F%	Min	GP	G	A	Pts	PIM	PP	SH	GW	Min
2002-03	Antoine-Girouard	QAAA	42	2	10	12	34	....	....	....	....	....	....	....	....	....	14	1	8	9	10	....	....	....	....
2003-04	Antoine-Girouard	QAAA	39	12	43	55	94	....	....	....	....	....	....	....	....	....	13	7	9	16	38	....	....	....	....
2004-05	Val-d'Or Foreurs	QMJHL	70	13	19	32	79	....	....	....	....	....	....	....	....	....	....	....	....	....	....	....	....	....	....
2005-06	Val-d'Or Foreurs	QMJHL	60	25	43	68	156	....	....	....	....	....	....	....	....	....	5	1	5	6	20	....	....	....	....
2006-07	**Pittsburgh**	**NHL**	**7**	**2**	**0**	**2**	**4**	**2**	**0**	**0**	**8**	**25.0**	**–3**	**0**	**0.0**	**11:33**	....	....	....	....	....	....	....	....	....
	Val-d'Or Foreurs	QMJHL	40	14	38	52	74	....	....	....	....	....	....	....	....	....	19	12	19	31	48	....	....	....	....
	Wilkes-Barre	AHL	....	....	....	....	....	....	....	....	....	....	....	....	....	....	1	0	1	1	2	....	....	....	....
2007-08	**Pittsburgh**	**NHL**	**63**	**6**	**11**	**17**	**23**	**1**	**0**	**3**	**68**	**8.8**	**–1**	**0**	**0.0**	**18:10**	**16**	**0**	**2**	**2**	**12**	**0**	**0**	**0**	**17:07**
	Wilkes-Barre	AHL	10	1	6	7	4	....	....	....	....	....	....	....	....	....	....	....	....	....	....	....	....	....	....
2008-09♦	**Pittsburgh**	**NHL**	**74**	**10**	**23**	**33**	**24**	**4**	**1**	**3**	**138**	**7.2**	**–7**	**1**	**0.0**	**21:09**	**23**	**4**	**9**	**13**	**26**	**2**	**0**	**1**	**19:18**
2009-10	**Pittsburgh**	**NHL**	**73**	**3**	**24**	**27**	**51**	**0**	**0**	**0**	**174**	**1.7**	**1**	**0**	**0.0**	**21:34**	**13**	**5**	**2**	**7**	**6**	**4**	**0**	**1**	**23:15**
2010-11	**Pittsburgh**	**NHL**	**82**	**8**	**42**	**50**	**101**	**4**	**0**	**2**	**236**	**3.4**	**15**	**1**	**100.0**	**24:02**	**7**	**0**	**4**	**4**	**10**	**0**	**0**	**0**	**26:32**
2011-12	**Pittsburgh**	**NHL**	**51**	**10**	**32**	**42**	**34**	**4**	**1**	**3**	**142**	**7.0**	**21**	**0**	**0.0**	**24:50**	**6**	**1**	**4**	**5**	**21**	**1**	**0**	**0**	**23:01**
2012-13	**Pittsburgh**	**NHL**	**35**	**5**	**33**	**38**	**8**	**1**	**0**	**1**	**95**	**5.3**	**16**	**0**	**0.0**	**25:38**	**15**	**3**	**13**	**16**	**8**	**2**	**0**	**1**	**27:38**
2013-14	**Pittsburgh**	**NHL**	**37**	**11**	**11**	**22**	**16**	**6**	**0**	**1**	**108**	**10.2**	**–8**	**0**	**0.0**	**24:14**	**13**	**2**	**4**	**6**	**14**	**0**	**0**	**1**	**24:10**
2014-15	**Pittsburgh**	**NHL**	**69**	**11**	**43**	**54**	**79**	**2**	**1**	**1**	**197**	**5.6**	**12**	**1**	**0.0**	**25:29**	....	....	....	....	....	....	....	....	....
	NHL Totals		**491**	**66**	**219**	**285**	**340**	**24**	**3**	**14**	**1166**	**5.7**		**3**	**33.3**	**22:43**	**93**	**15**	**38**	**53**	**97**	**9**	**0**	**4**	**22:17**

QMJHL All-Rookie Team (2005) • Canadian Major Junior All-Rookie Team (2005) • QMJHL First All-Star Team (2006, 2007) • Canadian Major Junior Second All-Star Team (2006, 2007) • NHL Second All-Star Team (2013)

Played in NHL All-Star Game (2011, 2012)

• Missed majority of 2013-14 due to pre-season knee injury and heart ailment, February 7, 2014.

LETESTU, Mark (luh-TEHS- too, MAHRK) EDM

Center. Shoots right. 5'10", 199 lbs. Born, Elk Point, AB, February 4, 1985.

			Regular Season														Playoffs								
Season	Club	League	GP	G	A	Pts	PIM	PP	SH	GW	S	S%	+/-	TF	F%	Min	GP	G	A	Pts	PIM	PP	SH	GW	Min
2003-04	Bonnyville	AJHL	58	22	27	49	24	....	....	....	....	....	....	....	....	....	....	....	....	....	....	....	....	....	....
2004-05	Bonnyville	AJHL	63	39	47	86	32	....	....	....	....	....	....	....	....	....	....	....	....	....	....	....	....	....	....
2005-06	Bonnyville	AJHL	58	50	55	105	59	....	....	....	....	....	....	....	....	....	....	....	....	....	....	....	....	....	....
2006-07	Western Mich.	CCHA	37	24	22	46	14	....	....	....	....	....	....	....	....	....	....	....	....	....	....	....	....	....	....
2007-08	Wilkes-Barre	AHL	52	6	12	18	28	....	....	....	....	....	....	....	....	....	13	0	3	3	0	....	....	....	....
	Wheeling Nailers	ECHL	6	1	2	3	4	....	....	....	....	....	....	....	....	....	....	....	....	....	....	....	....	....	....
2008-09	Wilkes-Barre	AHL	73	24	37	61	6	....	....	....	....	....	....	....	....	....	12	2	8	10	4	....	....	....	....
2009-10	**Pittsburgh**	**NHL**	**10**	**1**	**0**	**1**	**2**	**0**	**0**	**0**	**9**	**11.1**	**–2**	**74**	**55.4**	**9:38**	**4**	**0**	**1**	**1**	**0**	**0**	**0**	**0**	**9:39**
	Wilkes-Barre	AHL	63	21	34	55	21	....	....	....	....	....	....	....	....	....	4	0	3	3	0	....	....	....	....
2010-11	**Pittsburgh**	**NHL**	**64**	**14**	**13**	**27**	**13**	**4**	**0**	**3**	**128**	**10.9**	**4**	**734**	**55.5**	**14:15**	**7**	**0**	**1**	**1**	**0**	**0**	**0**	**0**	**15:29**
2011-12	**Pittsburgh**	**NHL**	**11**	**0**	**1**	**1**	**2**	**0**	**0**	**0**	**9**	**0.0**	**–6**	**132**	**55.3**	**12:50**	....	....	....	....	....	....	....	....	....
	Columbus	**NHL**	**51**	**11**	**13**	**24**	**6**	**4**	**0**	**0**	**105**	**10.5**	**–3**	**590**	**51.2**	**16:15**	....	....	....	....	....	....	....	....	....
2012-13	Almtuna	Sweden-2	7	4	0	4	2	....	....	....	....	....	....	....	....	....	....	....	....	....	....	....	....	....	....
	Columbus	**NHL**	**46**	**13**	**14**	**27**	**10**	**3**	**2**	**2**	**92**	**14.1**	**7**	**487**	**50.1**	**16:31**	....	....	....	....	....	....	....	....	....
2013-14	**Columbus**	**NHL**	**82**	**12**	**22**	**34**	**20**	**5**	**1**	**1**	**122**	**9.8**	**1**	**730**	**51.2**	**14:41**	**6**	**1**	**1**	**2**	**0**	**1**	**0**	**0**	**16:51**
2014-15	**Columbus**	**NHL**	**54**	**7**	**6**	**13**	**0**	**0**	**1**	**1**	**63**	**11.1**	**–9**	**603**	**52.9**	**13:20**	....	....	....	....	....	....	....	....	....
	NHL Totals		**318**	**58**	**69**	**127**	**53**	**16**	**4**	**7**	**528**	**11.0**		**3350**	**52.5**	**14:40**	**17**	**1**	**3**	**4**	**0**	**1**	**0**	**0**	**14:36**

Signed as a free agent by **Pittsburgh**, March 22, 2007. Traded to **Columbus** by **Pittsburgh** for Columbus's 4th round choice (Matia Marcantuoni) in 2012 Entry Draft, November 8, 2011. Signed as a free agent by **Almtuna** (Sweden-2), December 3, 2012. Signed as a free agent by **Edmonton**, July 1, 2015.

LETOURNEAU-LEBLOND, Pierre-Luc (leh-TOOR-noh-leh-BLAWN)

Left wing. Shoots left. 6'1", 214 lbs. Born, Levis, QC, June 4, 1985. New Jersey's 4th choice, 216th overall, in 2004 Entry Draft.

			Regular Season														Playoffs								
Season	Club	League	GP	G	A	Pts	PIM	PP	SH	GW	S	S%	+/-	TF	F%	Min	GP	G	A	Pts	PIM	PP	SH	GW	Min
2003-04	Baie-Comeau	QMJHL	62	2	3	5	198	....	....	....	....	....	....	....	....	....	4	0	0	0	6	....	....	....	....
2004-05	Baie-Comeau	QMJHL	67	1	6	7	229	....	....	....	....	....	....	....	....	....	6	0	1	1	10	....	....	....	....
2005-06	Albany River Rats	AHL	27	1	1	2	130	....	....	....	....	....	....	....	....	....	....	....	....	....	....	....	....	....	....
	Adirondack	UHL	31	3	6	9	165	....	....	....	....	....	....	....	....	....	6	0	1	1	29	....	....	....	....
2006-07	Trenton Titans	ECHL	52	4	9	13	183	....	....	....	....	....	....	....	....	....	4	0	0	0	15	....	....	....	....
2007-08	Lowell Devils	AHL	36	3	3	6	98	....	....	....	....	....	....	....	....	....	....	....	....	....	....	....	....	....	....
	Trenton Devils	ECHL	6	0	1	1	46	....	....	....	....	....	....	....	....	....	....	....	....	....	....	....	....	....	....
2008-09	**New Jersey**	**NHL**	**8**	**0**	**1**	**1**	**22**	**0**	**0**	**0**	**3**	**0.0**	**3**	**0**	**0.0**	**4:51**	....	....	....	....	....	....	....	....	....
	Lowell Devils	AHL	60	5	5	10	216	....	....	....	....	....	....	....	....	....	....	....	....	....	....	....	....	....	....
2009-10	**New Jersey**	**NHL**	**27**	**0**	**2**	**2**	**48**	**0**	**0**	**0**	**9**	**0.0**	**–4**	**2**	**50.0**	**5:31**	**5**	**0**	**0**	**0**	**10**	**0**	**0**	**0**	**4:34**
	Lowell Devils	AHL	5	0	2	2	18	....	....	....	....	....	....	....	....	....	....	....	....	....	....	....	....	....	....
2010-11	**New Jersey**	**NHL**	**2**	**0**	**0**	**0**	**21**	**0**	**0**	**0**	**0**	**0.0**	**–2**	**0**	**0.0**	**3:28**	....	....	....	....	....	....	....	....	....
	Albany Devils	AHL	64	8	5	13	*334	....	....	....	....	....	....	....	....	....	....	....	....	....	....	....	....	....	....
2011-12	**Calgary**	**NHL**	**3**	**0**	**0**	**0**	**10**	**0**	**0**	**0**	**3**	**0.0**	**1**	**0**	**0.0**	**4:51**	....	....	....	....	....	....	....	....	....
	Abbotsford Heat	AHL	50	1	5	6	167	....	....	....	....	....	....	....	....	....	5	0	0	0	18	....	....	....	....
2012-13	Norfolk Admirals	AHL	33	3	5	8	98	....	....	....	....	....	....	....	....	....	....	....	....	....	....	....	....	....	....
2013-14	Wilkes-Barre	AHL	66	2	4	6	259	....	....	....	....	....	....	....	....	....	2	0	0	0	12	....	....	....	....
	Pittsburgh	**NHL**	**1**	**0**	**0**	**0**	**0**	**0**	**0**	**0**	**1**	**0.0**	**0**	**0**	**0.0**	**4:34**	....	....	....	....	....	....	....	....	....
2014-15	Wilkes-Barre	AHL	55	2	4	6	241	....	....	....	....	....	....	....	....	....	4	0	0	0	7	....	....	....	....
	NHL Totals		**41**	**0**	**3**	**3**	**101**	**0**	**0**	**0**	**16**	**0.0**		**2**	**50.0**	**5:13**	**5**	**0**	**0**	**0**	**10**	**0**	**0**	**0**	**4:34**

• Missed majority of 2009-10 due to recurring upper-body injury and as a healthy reserve. Traded to **Calgary** by **New Jersey** for Calgary's 5th round choice (Graham Black) in 2012 Entry Draft, July 12, 2011. Signed as a free agent by **Anaheim**, January 15, 2013. Signed as a free agent by **Wilkes-Barre** (AHL), August 20, 2013. Signed as a free agent by **Pittsburgh**, November 7, 2013.

LEWIS, Trevor (LOO-ihs, TREH-vuhr) L.A.

Center. Shoots right. 6'1", 197 lbs. Born, Salt Lake City, UT, January 8, 1987. Los Angeles' 2nd choice, 17th overall, in 2006 Entry Draft.

			Regular Season														Playoffs								
Season	Club	League	GP	G	A	Pts	PIM	PP	SH	GW	S	S%	+/-	TF	F%	Min	GP	G	A	Pts	PIM	PP	SH	GW	Min
2004-05	Des Moines	USHL	52	10	12	22	70	....	....	....	....	....	....	....	....	....	....	....	....	....	....	....	....	....	....
2005-06	Des Moines	USHL	56	35	40	75	69	....	....	....	....	....	....	....	....	....	11	3	*13	*16	16	....	....	....	....
2006-07	Owen Sound	OHL	62	29	44	73	51	....	....	....	....	....	....	....	....	....	4	1	2	3	0	....	....	....	....
	Manchester	AHL	8	4	2	6	2	....	....	....	....	....	....	....	....	....	2	0	0	0	0	....	....	....	....
2007-08	Manchester	AHL	76	12	16	28	43	....	....	....	....	....	....	....	....	....	4	0	0	0	2	....	....	....	....
2008-09	**Los Angeles**	**NHL**	**6**	**1**	**2**	**3**	**0**	**0**	**0**	**0**	**10**	**10.0**	**0**	**4**	**25.0**	**11:36**	....	....	....	....	....	....	....	....	....
	Manchester	AHL	75	20	31	51	30	....	....	....	....	....	....	....	....	....	....	....	....	....	....	....	....	....	....
2009-10	**Los Angeles**	**NHL**	**5**	**0**	**0**	**0**	**0**	**0**	**0**	**0**	**4**	**0.0**	**–3**	**5**	**0.0**	**9:08**	....	....	....	....	....	....	....	....	....
	Manchester	AHL	23	5	2	7	6	....	....	....	....	....	....	....	....	....	16	5	4	9	10	....	....	....	....
2010-11	**Los Angeles**	**NHL**	**72**	**3**	**10**	**13**	**6**	**0**	**0**	**2**	**105**	**2.9**	**–11**	**385**	**39.2**	**11:29**	**6**	**1**	**3**	**4**	**2**	**1**	**0**	**0**	**16:39**
2011-12♦	**Los Angeles**	**NHL**	**72**	**3**	**4**	**7**	**26**	**0**	**0**	**1**	**103**	**2.9**	**–3**	**199**	**43.7**	**13:14**	**20**	**3**	**6**	**9**	**2**	**1**	**0**	**0**	**14:54**
2012-13	Utah Grizzlies	ECHL	6	3	6	9	4	....	....	....	....	....	....	....	....	....	....	....	....	....	....	....	....	....	....
	Los Angeles	**NHL**	**48**	**5**	**9**	**14**	**19**	**0**	**1**	**2**	**92**	**5.4**	**5**	**64**	**48.4**	**15:12**	**18**	**1**	**2**	**3**	**2**	**1**	**0**	**1**	**16:25**
2013-14♦	**Los Angeles**	**NHL**	**73**	**6**	**5**	**11**	**6**	**0**	**1**	**2**	**111**	**5.4**	**–1**	**262**	**48.5**	**13:15**	**26**	**4**	**1**	**5**	**6**	**0**	**0**	**1**	**12:39**
2014-15	**Los Angeles**	**NHL**	**73**	**9**	**16**	**25**	**14**	**0**	**1**	**2**	**143**	**6.3**	**8**	**177**	**42.9**	**14:06**	....	....	....	....	....	....	....	....	....
	NHL Totals		**349**	**27**	**46**	**73**	**71**	**0**	**3**	**9**	**568**	**4.8**		**1096**	**43.2**	**13:15**	**70**	**9**	**12**	**21**	**12**	**3**	**0**	**2**	**14:36**

USHL Player of the Year (2006)

• Missed majority of 2009-10 due to lower-body injury and as a healthy reserve.

LILES, John-Michael (LIGH-uhls, JAWN-MIGHK-uhl) CAR

Defense. Shoots left. 5'10", 185 lbs. Born, Indianapolis, IN, November 25, 1980. Colorado's 8th choice, 159th overall, in 2000 Entry Draft.

			Regular Season														Playoffs								
Season	Club	League	GP	G	A	Pts	PIM	PP	SH	GW	S	S%	+/-	TF	F%	Min	GP	G	A	Pts	PIM	PP	SH	GW	Min
1997-98	USNTDP	U-17	15	0	6	6	4	....	....	....	....	....	....	....	....	....	....	....	....	....	....	....	....	....	....
	USNTDP	USHL	5	0	1	1	0	....	....	....	....	....	....	....	....	....	....	....	....	....	....	....	....	....	....
	USNTDP	NAHL	42	4	7	11	40	....	....	....	....	....	....	....	....	....	5	2	0	2	0	....	....	....	....
1998-99	USNTDP	USHL	46	4	14	18	47	....	....	....	....	....	....	....	....	....	....	....	....	....	....	....	....	....	....
	USNTDP	NAHL	13	2	5	7	6	....	....	....	....	....	....	....	....	....	....	....	....	....	....	....	....	....	....
99-2000	Michigan State	CCHA	40	8	20	28	26	....	....	....	....	....	....	....	....	....	....	....	....	....	....	....	....	....	....
2000-01	Michigan State	CCHA	42	7	18	25	28	....	....	....	....	....	....	....	....	....	....	....	....	....	....	....	....	....	....
2001-02	Michigan State	CCHA	41	13	22	35	18	....	....	....	....	....	....	....	....	....	....	....	....	....	....	....	....	....	....

			Regular Season														Playoffs								
Season	Club	League	GP	G	A	Pts	PIM	PP	SH	GW	S	S%	+/-	TF	F%	Min	GP	G	A	Pts	PIM	PP	SH	GW	Min
2002-03	Michigan State	CCHA	39	16	34	50	46	....	....	....	....	....	....	....	....	....	....	....	....	....	....	....	....	....	....
	Hershey Bears	AHL	5	0	1	1	4	....	....	....	....	....	....	....	....	....	5	0	0	0	2	....	....	....	....
2003-04	**Colorado**	**NHL**	**79**	**10**	**24**	**34**	**28**	**2**	**0**	**1**	**115**	**8.7**	**7**	**0**	**0.0**	**16:14**	**11**	**0**	**1**	**1**	**4**	**0**	**0**	**0**	**16:41**
2004-05	Iserlohn Roosters	Germany	17	5	6	11	24	....	....	....	....	....	....	....	....	....	....	....	....	....	....	....	....	....	....
2005-06	**Colorado**	**NHL**	**82**	**14**	**35**	**49**	**44**	**6**	**0**	**1**	**154**	**9.1**	**5**	**1**	**100.0**	**18:31**	**9**	**1**	**2**	**3**	**6**	**1**	**0**	**0**	**17:35**
	United States	Olympics	6	0	2	2	2	....	....	....	....	....	....	....	....	....	....	....	....	....	....	....	....	....	....
2006-07	**Colorado**	**NHL**	**71**	**14**	**30**	**44**	**24**	**8**	**0**	**3**	**128**	**10.9**	**0**	**0**	**0.0**	**17:46**	....	....	....	....	....	....	....	....	....
2007-08	**Colorado**	**NHL**	**81**	**6**	**26**	**32**	**26**	**5**	**0**	**1**	**163**	**3.7**	**2**	**0**	**0.0**	**19:40**	**10**	**2**	**3**	**5**	**2**	**1**	**0**	**0**	**19:08**
2008-09	**Colorado**	**NHL**	**75**	**12**	**27**	**39**	**31**	**6**	**0**	**1**	**146**	**8.2**	**–19**	**0**	**0.0**	**21:33**	....	....	....	....	....	....	....	....	....
2009-10	**Colorado**	**NHL**	**59**	**6**	**25**	**31**	**30**	**3**	**0**	**2**	**96**	**6.3**	**–2**	**0**	**0.0**	**18:28**	**6**	**1**	**1**	**2**	**4**	**1**	**0**	**0**	**19:01**
2010-11	**Colorado**	**NHL**	**76**	**6**	**40**	**46**	**35**	**3**	**0**	**0**	**163**	**3.7**	**–9**	**0**	**0.0**	**22:01**	....	....	....	....	....	....	....	....	....
2011-12	**Toronto**	**NHL**	**66**	**7**	**20**	**27**	**20**	**4**	**0**	**0**	**106**	**6.6**	**–14**	**0**	**0.0**	**21:21**	....	....	....	....	....	....	....	....	....
2012-13	**Toronto**	**NHL**	**32**	**2**	**9**	**11**	**4**	**0**	**0**	**0**	**47**	**4.3**	**–1**	**1**	**0.0**	**18:46**	**4**	**0**	**0**	**0**	**2**	**0**	**0**	**0**	**15:25**
2013-14	**Toronto**	**NHL**	**6**	**0**	**0**	**0**	**0**	**0**	**0**	**0**	**5**	**0.0**	**–2**	**1**	**100.0**	**17:04**	....	....	....	....	....	....	....	....	....
	Toronto Marlies	AHL	16	3	10	13	14	....	....	....	....	....	....	....	....	....	....	....	....	....	....	....	....	....	....
	Carolina	**NHL**	**35**	**2**	**7**	**9**	**8**	**1**	**0**	**0**	**51**	**3.9**	**7**	**0**	**0.0**	**20:06**	....	....	....	....	....	....	....	....	....
2014-15	**Carolina**	**NHL**	**57**	**2**	**20**	**22**	**14**	**0**	**0**	**0**	**90**	**2.2**	**–9**	**0**	**0.0**	**19:09**	....	....	....	....	....	....	....	....	....
	NHL Totals		**719**	**81**	**263**	**344**	**264**	**38**	**0**	**9**	**1264**	**6.4**		**3**	**66.7**	**19:23**	**40**	**4**	**7**	**11**	**18**	**3**	**0**	**0**	**17:43**

CCHA Second All-Star Team (2001) • CCHA First All-Star Team (2002, 2003) • NCAA West Second All-American Team (2002) • NCAA West First All-American Team (2003) • NHL All-Rookie Team (2004)

Signed as a free agent by **Iserlohn** (Germany), December 29, 2004. Traded to **Toronto** by **Colorado** for Boston's 2nd round choice (previously acquired, later traded to Washington, later traded to Dallas – Dallas selected Mike Winther) in 2012 Entry Draft, June 24, 2011. Traded to **Carolina** by **Toronto** with Dennis Robertson for Tim Gleason, January 1, 2014.

LINDBERG, Oscar

(LIHND-buhrg, AWS-kuhr) **NYR**

Center. Shoots left. 6'1", 195 lbs. Born, Skelleftea, Sweden, October 29, 1991. Phoenix's 4th choice, 57th overall, in 2010 Entry Draft.

Season	Club	League	GP	G	A	Pts	PIM	PP	SH	GW	S	S%	+/-	TF	F%	Min	GP	G	A	Pts	PIM	PP	SH	GW	Min
2007-08	Skelleftea U18	Swe-U18	31	19	29	48	36	....	....	....	....	....	....	....	....	....	....	....	....	....	....	....	....	....	....
	Skelleftea Jr.	Swe-Jr.	1	0	0	0	2	....	....	....	....	....	....	....	....	....	2	0	1	1	0	....	....	....	....
2008-09	Skelleftea AIK U18	Swe-U18	6	8	10	18	14	....	....	....	....	....	....	....	....	....	7	4	5	9	8	....	....	....	....
	Skelleftea AIK Jr.	Swe-Jr.	38	14	19	33	54	....	....	....	....	....	....	....	....	....	5	0	1	1	4	....	....	....	....
2009-10	Skelleftea AIK Jr.	Swe-Jr.	30	14	23	37	44	....	....	....	....	....	....	....	....	....	1	1	1	2	12	....	....	....	....
	Skelleftea AIK	Sweden	36	1	1	2	35	....	....	....	....	....	....	....	....	....	10	2	0	2	2	....	....	....	....
2010-11	Skelleftea AIK Jr.	Swe-Jr.	9	8	4	12	8	....	....	....	....	....	....	....	....	....	....	....	....	....	....	....	....	....	....
	Skelleftea AIK	Sweden	41	5	9	14	31	....	....	....	....	....	....	....	....	....	18	3	4	7	4	....	....	....	....
2011-12	Skelleftea AIK Jr.	Swe-Jr.	2	1	3	4	2	....	....	....	....	....	....	....	....	....	....	....	....	....	....	....	....	....	....
	Sundsvall	Sweden-2	5	1	1	2	2	....	....	....	....	....	....	....	....	....	....	....	....	....	....	....	....	....	....
	Skelleftea AIK	Sweden	46	5	5	10	18	....	....	....	....	....	....	....	....	....	18	1	3	4	10	....	....	....	....
2012-13	Skelleftea AIK	Sweden	55	17	25	42	54	....	....	....	....	....	....	....	....	....	13	4	8	*12	16	....	....	....	....
2013-14	Hartford	AHL	75	18	26	44	58	....	....	....	....	....	....	....	....	....	....	....	....	....	....	....	....	....	....
2014-15	**NY Rangers**	**NHL**	**1**	**0**	**0**	**0**	**0**	**0**	**0**	**0**	**2**	**0.0**	**0**	**5**	**40.0**	**8:18**	....	....	....	....	....	....	....	....	....
	Hartford	AHL	75	28	28	56	68	....	....	....	....	....	....	....	....	....	15	3	13	16	6	....	....	....	....
	NHL Totals		**1**	**0**	**0**	**0**	**0**	**0**	**0**	**0**	**2**	**0.0**		**5**	**40.0**	**8:18**	....	....	....	....	....	....	....	....	....

Traded to **NY Rangers** by **Phoenix** for Ethan Werek, May 8, 2011.

LINDBLAD, Matt

(LIHN-blad, MAT) **NYR**

Left wing. Shoots left. 5'11", 193 lbs. Born, Winnetka, IL, March 23, 1990.

Season	Club	League	GP	G	A	Pts	PIM	PP	SH	GW	S	S%	+/-	TF	F%	Min	GP	G	A	Pts	PIM	PP	SH	GW	Min
2008-09	Chicago Steel	USHL	51	5	20	25	17	....	....	....	....	....	....	....	....	....	....	....	....	....	....	....	....	....	....
2009-10	Sioux Falls	USHL	57	24	46	70	20	....	....	....	....	....	....	....	....	....	3	1	2	3	2	....	....	....	....
2010-11	Dartmouth	ECAC	33	13	15	28	4	....	....	....	....	....	....	....	....	....	....	....	....	....	....	....	....	....	....
2011-12	Dartmouth	ECAC	26	6	18	24	2	....	....	....	....	....	....	....	....	....	....	....	....	....	....	....	....	....	....
2012-13	Dartmouth	ECAC	30	10	18	28	2	....	....	....	....	....	....	....	....	....	....	....	....	....	....	....	....	....	....
	Providence Bruins	AHL	4	1	4	5	0	....	....	....	....	....	....	....	....	....	....	....	....	....	....	....	....	....	....
2013-14	**Boston**	**NHL**	**2**	**0**	**0**	**0**	**0**	**0**	**0**	**0**	**0**	**0.0**	**0**	**2**	**100.0**	**11:46**	....	....	....	....	....	....	....	....	....
	Providence Bruins	AHL	55	8	16	24	8	....	....	....	....	....	....	....	....	....	12	3	4	7	10	....	....	....	....
2014-15	**Boston**	**NHL**	**2**	**0**	**0**	**0**	**0**	**0**	**0**	**0**	**3**	**0.0**	**0**	**5**	**0.0**	**7:46**	....	....	....	....	....	....	....	....	....
	Providence Bruins	AHL	47	9	13	22	6	....	....	....	....	....	....	....	....	....	3	0	0	0	0	....	....	....	....
	NHL Totals		**4**	**0**	**0**	**0**	**0**	**0**	**0**	**0**	**3**	**0.0**		**7**	**28.6**	**9:46**	....	....	....	....	....	....	....	....	....

Signed as a free agent by **Boston**, April 5, 2013. Signed as a free agent by **NY Rangers**, July 1, 2015.

LINDBOHM, Petteri

(LIHND-bawm, PEH-tuh-ree) **ST.L.**

Defense. Shoots left. 6'3", 198 lbs. Born, Helsinki, Finland, September 23, 1993. St. Louis' 7th choice, 176th overall, in 2012 Entry Draft.

Season	Club	League	GP	G	A	Pts	PIM	PP	SH	GW	S	S%	+/-	TF	F%	Min	GP	G	A	Pts	PIM	PP	SH	GW	Min
2009-10	K-Vantaa U18	Fin-U18	31	1	3	4	34	....	....	....	....	....	....	....	....	....	6	0	0	0	24	....	....	....	....
2010-11	Blues Espoo U18	Fin-U18	7	2	6	8	10	....	....	....	....	....	....	....	....	....	2	0	2	2	2	....	....	....	....
	Blues Espoo Jr.	Fin-Jr.	41	1	8	9	56	....	....	....	....	....	....	....	....	....	13	0	3	3	12	....	....	....	....
2011-12	Jokerit Helsinki Jr.	Fin-Jr.	41	3	7	10	98	....	....	....	....	....	....	....	....	....	12	0	3	3	12	....	....	....	....
	Kiekko-Vantaa	Finland-2	5	0	3	3	8	....	....	....	....	....	....	....	....	....	....	....	....	....	....	....	....	....	....
2012-13	Jokerit Helsinki Jr.	Fin-Jr.	2	0	1	1	2	....	....	....	....	....	....	....	....	....	....	....	....	....	....	....	....	....	....
	Kiekko-Vantaa	Finland-2	6	3	0	3	4	....	....	....	....	....	....	....	....	....	....	....	....	....	....	....	....	....	....
	Jokerit Helsinki	Finland	35	0	4	4	61	....	....	....	....	....	....	....	....	....	....	....	....	....	....	....	....	....	....
2013-14	Assat Pori	Finland	19	1	4	5	8	....	....	....	....	....	....	....	....	....	....	....	....	....	....	....	....	....	....
	Jokerit Helsinki Jr.	Fin-Jr.	3	0	0	0	4	....	....	....	....	....	....	....	....	....	....	....	....	....	....	....	....	....	....
	Kiekko-Vantaa	Finland-2	13	1	1	2	12	....	....	....	....	....	....	....	....	....	....	....	....	....	....	....	....	....	....
	Jokerit Helsinki	Finland	18	0	1	1	18	....	....	....	....	....	....	....	....	....	....	....	....	....	....	....	....	....	....
2014-15	**St. Louis**	**NHL**	**23**	**2**	**1**	**3**	**26**	**0**	**0**	**0**	**32**	**6.3**	**–1**	**0**	**0.0**	**15:34**	....	....	....	....	....	....	....	....	....
	Chicago Wolves	AHL	53	6	12	18	62	....	....	....	....	....	....	....	....	....	5	0	1	1	10	....	....	....	....
	NHL Totals		**23**	**2**	**1**	**3**	**26**	**0**	**0**	**0**	**32**	**6.3**		**0**	**0.0**	**15:34**	....	....	....	....	....	....	....	....	....

LINDHOLM, Elias

(LIHND-hohlm, uh-LIGH-uhs) **CAR**

Center. Shoots right. 6'1", 192 lbs. Born, Boden , Sweden, December 2, 1994. Carolina's 1st choice, 5th overall, in 2013 Entry Draft.

Season	Club	League	GP	G	A	Pts	PIM	PP	SH	GW	S	S%	+/-	TF	F%	Min	GP	G	A	Pts	PIM	PP	SH	GW	Min
2009-10	Brynas U18	Swe-U18	9	4	6	10	0	....	....	....	....	....	....	....	....	....	....	....	....	....	....	....	....	....	....
2010-11	Brynas U18	Swe-U18	40	17	44	61	32	....	....	....	....	....	....	....	....	....	4	3	3	6	29	....	....	....	....
	Brynas IF Gavle Jr.	Swe-Jr.	2	0	0	0	0	....	....	....	....	....	....	....	....	....	2	0	1	1	0	....	....	....	....
2011-12	Brynas U18	Swe-U18	4	1	6	7	0	....	....	....	....	....	....	....	....	....	3	1	2	3	0	....	....	....	....
	Brynas IF Gavle Jr.	Swe-Jr.	36	14	35	49	45	....	....	....	....	....	....	....	....	....	2	1	1	2	16	....	....	....	....
	Brynas IF Gavle	Sweden	12	0	0	0	0	....	....	....	....	....	....	....	....	....	2	0	0	0	0	....	....	....	....
2012-13	Brynas IF Gavle	Sweden	48	11	19	30	2	....	....	....	....	....	....	....	....	....	4	0	0	0	4	....	....	....	....
2013-14	**Carolina**	**NHL**	**58**	**9**	**12**	**21**	**4**	**4**	**0**	**2**	**70**	**12.9**	**–14**	**229**	**46.3**	**14:32**	....	....	....	....	....	....	....	....	....
	Sweden	Olympics	6	2	7	9	6	....	....	....	....	....	....	....	....	....	....	....	....	....	....	....	....	....	....
2014-15	**Carolina**	**NHL**	**81**	**17**	**22**	**39**	**14**	**4**	**0**	**4**	**170**	**10.0**	**–23**	**220**	**52.3**	**16:25**	....	....	....	....	....	....	....	....	....
	NHL Totals		**139**	**26**	**34**	**60**	**18**	**8**	**0**	**6**	**240**	**10.8**		**449**	**49.2**	**15:38**	....	....	....	....	....	....	....	....	....

LINDHOLM, Hampus

(LIHND-hohlm, HAM-puhs) **ANA**

Defense. Shoots left. 6'3", 197 lbs. Born, Helsingborg, Sweden, January 20, 1994. Anaheim's 1st choice, 6th overall, in 2012 Entry Draft.

Season	Club	League	GP	G	A	Pts	PIM	PP	SH	GW	S	S%	+/-	TF	F%	Min	GP	G	A	Pts	PIM	PP	SH	GW	Min
2008-09	Jonstorps IF U18	Swe-U18	1	0	0	0	0	....	....	....	....	....	....	....	....	....	....	....	....	....	....	....	....	....	....
2009-10	Jonstorps IF U18	Swe-U18	15	3	4	7	8	....	....	....	....	....	....	....	....	....	....	....	....	....	....	....	....	....	....
	Jonstorps IF Jr.	Swe-Jr.	3	1	2	3	0	....	....	....	....	....	....	....	....	....	....	....	....	....	....	....	....	....	....
2010-11	Rogle U18	Swe-U18	11	2	3	5	10	....	....	....	....	....	....	....	....	....	3	0	2	2	0	....	....	....	....
	Rogle Jr.	Swe-Jr.	39	0	4	4	34	....	....	....	....	....	....	....	....	....	3	0	0	0	0	....	....	....	....
2011-12	Rogle U18	Swe-U18	1	1	3	4	2	....	....	....	....	....	....	....	....	....	....	....	....	....	....	....	....	....	....
	Rogle Jr.	Swe-Jr.	28	5	12	17	16	....	....	....	....	....	....	....	....	....	....	....	....	....	....	....	....	....	....
	Rogle	Sweden-2	36	2	7	9	18	....	....	....	....	....	....	....	....	....	....	....	....	....	....	....	....	....	....
2012-13	Norfolk Admirals	AHL	44	1	10	11	16	....	....	....	....	....	....	....	....	....	....	....	....	....	....	....	....	....	....

			Regular Season														Playoffs								
Season	Club	League	GP	G	A	Pts	PIM	PP	SH	GW	S	S%	+/-	TF	F%	Min	GP	G	A	Pts	PIM	PP	SH	GW	Min
2013-14	**Anaheim**	**NHL**	78	6	24	30	36	1	0	1	116	5.2	29	1	0.0	19:26	11	0	2	2	0	0	0	0	18:10
2014-15	**Anaheim**	**NHL**	78	7	27	34	32	0	0	1	107	6.5	25	5	0.0	21:46	16	2	8	10	10	0	0	0	23:15
	NHL Totals		156	13	51	64	68	1	0	2	223	5.8		6	0.0	20:36	27	2	10	12	10	0	0	0	21:11

NHL All-Rookie Team (2014)

LINDSTROM, Joakim

(LIHND-struhm, YOH-ah-kihm)

Center. Shoots left. 6', 187 lbs. Born, Skelleftea, Sweden, December 5, 1983. Columbus' 2nd choice, 41st overall, in 2002 Entry Draft.

99-2000	MoDo U18	Swe-U18	17	6	*14	20	32	....	....	....	....	....	....	....	....	....	....	....	....	....	....	....	....	....	....
	Malmo Jr.	Swe-Jr.	10	4	4	8	2	....	....	....	....	....	....	....	....	....	....	....	....	....	....	....	....	....	....
2000-01	Malmo Jr.	Swe-Jr.	12	7	14	21	46	....	....	....	....	....	....	....	....	....	4	2	3	5	24	....	....	....	....
	MoDo	Sweden	10	2	3	5	2	....	....	....	....	....	....	....	....	....	7	0	1	1	0	....	....	....	....
2001-02	Malmo Jr.	Swe-Jr.	10	9	6	15	67	....	....	....	....	....	....	....	....	....	....	....	....	....	....	....	....	....	....
	IF Troja-Ljungby	Sweden-2	3	0	0	0	12	....	....	....	....	....	....	....	....	....	....	....	....	....	....	....	....	....	....
	MODO	Sweden	42	4	3	7	20	....	....	....	....	....	....	....	....	....	14	3	5	8	8	....	....	....	....
2002-03	MODO	Sweden	29	4	2	6	14	....	....	....	....	....	....	....	....	....	6	1	1	2	2	....	....	....	....
	Malmo Jr.	Swe-Jr.	2	5	1	6	8	....	....	....	....	....	....	....	....	....	....	....	....	....	....	....	....	....	....
	Ornskoldsviks SK	Sweden-2	2	1	1	2	4	....	....	....	....	....	....	....	....	....	....	....	....	....	....	....	....	....	....
2003-04	MODO	Sweden	15	0	2	2	0	....	....	....	....	....	....	....	....	....	....	....	....	....	....	....	....	....	....
	Sundsvall	Sweden-2	2	0	5	5	0	....	....	....	....	....	....	....	....	....	....	....	....	....	....	....	....	....	....
2004-05	MODO Jr.	Swe-Jr.	2	4	1	5	0	....	....	....	....	....	....	....	....	....	....	....	....	....	....	....	....	....	....
	MODO	Sweden	37	2	3	5	24	....	....	....	....	....	....	....	....	....	....	....	....	....	....	....	....	....	....
	Syracuse Crunch	AHL	13	4	4	8	0	....	....	....	....	....	....	....	....	....	....	....	....	....	....	....	....	....	....
2005-06	**Columbus**	**NHL**	3	0	0	0	0	0	0	0	4	0.0	0	0	0.0	5:11	....	....	....	....	....	....	....	....	....
	Syracuse Crunch	AHL	64	14	29	43	52	....	....	....	....	....	....	....	....	....	6	1	1	2	0	....	....	....	....
2006-07	**Columbus**	**NHL**	9	1	0	1	4	0	0	0	9	11.1	−3	0	0.0	8:28	....	....	....	....	....	....	....	....	....
	Syracuse Crunch	AHL	50	22	26	48	34	....	....	....	....	....	....	....	....	....	....	....	....	....	....	....	....	....	....
2007-08	**Columbus**	**NHL**	25	3	4	7	14	2	0	1	25	12.0	0	7	28.6	9:26	....	....	....	....	....	....	....	....	....
	Syracuse Crunch	AHL	49	25	35	60	68	....	....	....	....	....	....	....	....	....	13	4	3	7	6	....	....	....	....
2008-09	Iowa Chops	AHL	21	7	14	21	33	....	....	....	....	....	....	....	....	....	....	....	....	....	....	....	....	....	....
	Phoenix	**NHL**	44	9	11	20	28	3	0	2	77	11.7	−6	14	35.7	14:52	....	....	....	....	....	....	....	....	....
2009-10	Nizhny Novgorod	KHL	55	10	20	30	62	....	....	....	....	....	....	....	....	....	....	....	....	....	....	....	....	....	....
2010-11	Skelleftea AIK	Sweden	54	28	32	*60	134	....	....	....	....	....	....	....	....	....	18	4	7	11	16	....	....	....	....
2011-12	**Colorado**	**NHL**	16	2	3	5	0	1	0	0	22	9.1	−9	5	40.0	13:55	....	....	....	....	....	....	....	....	....
	Skelleftea AIK	Sweden	21	7	13	20	45	....	....	....	....	....	....	....	....	....	19	5	12	17	22	....	....	....	....
2012-13	Skelleftea AIK	Sweden	53	18	36	54	56	....	....	....	....	....	....	....	....	....	13	4	7	11	4	....	....	....	....
2013-14	Skelleftea AIK	Sweden	55	23	40	63	72	....	....	....	....	....	....	....	....	....	14	6	12	*18	10	....	....	....	....
2014-15	**St. Louis**	**NHL**	34	3	3	6	8	2	0	0	41	7.3	−8	22	31.8	11:05	....	....	....	....	....	....	....	....	....
	Toronto	**NHL**	19	1	3	4	4	0	0	0	20	5.0	−7	1	0.0	10:30	....	....	....	....	....	....	....	....	....
	NHL Totals		150	19	24	43	58	8	0	3	198	9.6		49	32.7	11:52	....	....	....	....	....	....	....	....	....

Traded to **Anaheim** by **Columbus** for Anaheim's 4th round choice (Mathieu Corbeil-Theriault) in 2010 Entry Draft, July 14, 2008. Claimed on waivers by **Chicago** from **Anaheim**, October 3, 2008. Claimed on waivers by **Anaheim** from **Chicago**, October 7, 2008. Traded to **Phoenix** by **Anaheim** for Logan Stephenson, December 3, 2008. Signed as a free agent by **Nizhny Novgorod** (KHL). June 30, 2009. Signed as a free agent by **Skelleftea** (Sweden), May 18, 2010. Signed as a free agent by **Colorado**, June 16, 2011. Signed as a free agent by **Skelleftea** (Sweden), December 2, 2011. Signed as a free agent by **St. Louis**, May 27, 2014. Traded to **Toronto** by **St. Louis** with future considerations for Olli Jokinen, March 2, 2015. Signed as a free agent by **St. Petersburg** (KHL), May 1, 2015.

LITTLE, Bryan

(LIH-tuhl, BRIGH-uhn) **WPG**

Center. Shoots right. 5'11", 185 lbs. Born, Edmonton, AB, November 12, 1987. Atlanta's 1st choice, 12th overall, in 2006 Entry Draft.

2003-04	Barrie Colts	OHL	64	34	24	58	18	....	....	....	....	....	....	....	....	....	12	5	5	10	7	....	....	....	....
2004-05	Barrie Colts	OHL	62	36	32	68	34	....	....	....	....	....	....	....	....	....	4	5	1	6	2	....	....	....	....
2005-06	Barrie Colts	OHL	64	42	67	109	99	....	....	....	....	....	....	....	....	....	14	8	15	23	19	....	....	....	....
2006-07	Barrie Colts	OHL	57	41	66	107	77	....	....	....	....	....	....	....	....	....	8	4	5	9	8	....	....	....	....
	Chicago Wolves	AHL	....	....	....	....	....	....	....	....	....	....	....	....	....	....	2	0	0	0	0	....	....	....	....
2007-08	**Atlanta**	**NHL**	48	6	10	16	18	2	0	1	76	7.9	−2	505	45.2	15:37	....	....	....	....	....	....	....	....	....
	Chicago Wolves	AHL	34	9	16	25	10	....	....	....	....	....	....	....	....	....	24	8	5	13	10	....	....	....	....
2008-09	**Atlanta**	**NHL**	79	31	20	51	24	12	0	4	172	18.0	−5	214	43.5	16:55	....	....	....	....	....	....	....	....	....
2009-10	**Atlanta**	**NHL**	79	13	21	34	20	3	0	1	165	7.9	−6	154	44.2	15:45	....	....	....	....	....	....	....	....	....
2010-11	**Atlanta**	**NHL**	76	18	30	48	33	2	2	1	158	11.4	11	1331	46.3	18:27	....	....	....	....	....	....	....	....	....
2011-12	**Winnipeg**	**NHL**	74	24	22	46	26	6	0	6	162	14.8	−11	1479	49.6	20:13	....	....	....	....	....	....	....	....	....
2012-13	**Winnipeg**	**NHL**	48	7	25	32	4	2	0	2	84	8.3	8	842	51.2	19:48	....	....	....	....	....	....	....	....	....
2013-14	**Winnipeg**	**NHL**	82	23	41	64	58	8	2	1	170	13.5	8	1653	47.5	20:00	....	....	....	....	....	....	....	....	....
2014-15	**Winnipeg**	**NHL**	70	24	28	52	24	9	1	3	148	16.2	8	1551	49.1	19:55	4	2	1	3	0	1	0	0	19:16
	NHL Totals		556	146	197	343	207	44	5	19	1135	12.9		7729	48.1	18:22	4	2	1	3	0	1	0	0	19:16

OHL Second All-Star Team (2007)

• Transferred to **Winnipeg** after **Atlanta** franchise relocated, June 21, 2011.

LOKTIONOV, Andrei

(lawk-too-OH-nawf, ahn-DRAY)

Center. Shoots left. 5'11", 190 lbs. Born, Voskresensk, USSR, May 30, 1990. Los Angeles' 7th choice, 123rd overall, in 2008 Entry Draft.

2005-06	Spartak 2	Russia-3	4	1	1	2	2	....	....	....	....	....	....	....	....	....	....	....	....	....	....	....	....	....	....
2006-07	Yaroslavl 2	Russia-3	31	7	21	28	26	....	....	....	....	....	....	....	....	....	....	....	....	....	....	....	....	....	....
2007-08	Yaroslavl 2	Russia-3	STATISTICS NOT AVAILABLE																						
	Yaroslavl	Russia	5	0	1	1	0	....	....	....	....	....	....	....	....	....	1	0	0	0	0	....	....	....	....
2008-09	Windsor Spitfires	OHL	51	24	42	66	16	....	....	....	....	....	....	....	....	....	20	11	22	33	2	....	....	....	....
2009-10	**Los Angeles**	**NHL**	1	0	0	0	0	0	0	0	1	0.0	0	8	12.5	11:52	....	....	....	....	....	....	....	....	....
	Manchester	AHL	29	9	15	24	12	....	....	....	....	....	....	....	....	....	16	1	8	9	2	....	....	....	....
2010-11	**Los Angeles**	**NHL**	19	4	3	7	2	0	0	2	26	15.4	2	55	41.8	14:46	....	....	....	....	....	....	....	....	....
	Manchester	AHL	34	8	23	31	6	....	....	....	....	....	....	....	....	....	....	....	....	....	....	....	....	....	....
2011-12	**Los Angeles**	**NHL**	39	3	4	7	2	1	0	0	60	5.0	−4	149	43.0	12:32	2	0	0	0	0	0	0	0	4:09
	Manchester	AHL	32	5	15	20	10	....	....	....	....	....	....	....	....	....	....	....	....	....	....	....	....	....	....
2012-13	Manchester	AHL	37	7	15	22	6	....	....	....	....	....	....	....	....	....	....	....	....	....	....	....	....	....	....
	Albany Devils	AHL	3	0	0	0	0	....	....	....	....	....	....	....	....	....	....	....	....	....	....	....	....	....	....
	New Jersey	**NHL**	28	8	4	12	4	1	0	0	47	17.0	−2	206	38.8	14:15	....	....	....	....	....	....	....	....	....
2013-14	**New Jersey**	**NHL**	48	4	8	12	12	0	0	1	44	9.1	2	315	42.9	12:19	....	....	....	....	....	....	....	....	....
	Carolina	**NHL**	20	3	7	10	2	2	0	1	34	8.8	−4	54	35.2	14:36	....	....	....	....	....	....	....	....	....
2014-15	Yaroslavl	KHL	26	9	6	15	10	....	....	....	....	....	....	....	....	....	6	0	1	1	2	....	....	....	....
	NHL Totals		155	22	26	48	22	4	0	4	212	10.4		787	40.9	13:19	2	0	0	0	0	0	0	0	4:09

• Missed majority of 2009-10 due to shoulder injury at Edmonton, November 26, 2009. Traded to **New Jersey** by **Los Angeles** for New Jersey's 5th round choice (later traded to Florida, later traded to Buffalo – Buffalo selected Gustav Possler) in 2013 Entry Draft, February 6, 2013. Traded to **Carolina** by **New Jersey** with future considerations for Tuomo Ruutu, March 5, 2014. Signed as a free agent by **Yaroslavl** (KHL), November 28, 2014.

LOVEJOY, Ben

(LUHV-joi, BEHN) **PIT**

Defense. Shoots right. 6'2", 205 lbs. Born, Concord, NH, February 20, 1984.

2002-03	Boston College	H-East	22	0	6	6	6	....	....	....	....	....	....	....	....	....	....	....	....	....	....	....	....	....	....
2003-04	Dartmouth	ECAC	DID NOT PLAY – TRANSFERRED COLLEGES																						
2004-05	Dartmouth	ECAC	32	2	11	13	28	....	....	....	....	....	....	....	....	....	....	....	....	....	....	....	....	....	....
2005-06	Dartmouth	ECAC	32	2	16	18	24	....	....	....	....	....	....	....	....	....	....	....	....	....	....	....	....	....	....
2006-07	Dartmouth	ECAC	32	7	16	23	28	....	....	....	....	....	....	....	....	....	....	....	....	....	....	....	....	....	....
	Norfolk Admirals	AHL	5	0	0	0	6	....	....	....	....	....	....	....	....	....	....	....	....	....	....	....	....	....	....
2007-08	Wilkes-Barre	AHL	72	2	18	20	63	....	....	....	....	....	....	....	....	....	23	2	8	10	18	....	....	....	....
2008-09	**Pittsburgh**	**NHL**	2	0	0	0	0	0	0	0	1	0.0	0	0	0.0	11:53	....	....	....	....	....	....	....	....	....
	Wilkes-Barre	AHL	76	7	24	31	84	....	....	....	....	....	....	....	....	....	12	1	1	2	14	....	....	....	....
2009-10	**Pittsburgh**	**NHL**	12	0	3	3	2	0	0	0	14	0.0	8	0	0.0	16:37	....	....	....	....	....	....	....	....	....
	Wilkes-Barre	AHL	65	9	20	29	92	....	....	....	....	....	....	....	....	....	2	0	2	2	2	....	....	....	....
2010-11	**Pittsburgh**	**NHL**	47	3	14	17	48	0	0	0	60	5.0	11	0	0.0	15:00	7	0	2	2	4	0	0	0	10:54
2011-12	**Pittsburgh**	**NHL**	34	1	4	5	13	0	0	0	48	2.1	3	0	0.0	13:15	2	0	0	0	0	0	0	0	10:33
2012-13	**Pittsburgh**	**NHL**	3	0	0	0	0	0	0	0	7	0.0	−2	0	0.0	13:36	....	....	....	....	....	....	....	....	....
	Anaheim	**NHL**	32	0	10	10	29	0	0	0	51	0.0	6	0	0.0	18:13	7	0	2	2	0	0	0	0	21:05

			Regular Season														Playoffs								
Season	Club	League	GP	G	A	Pts	PIM	PP	SH	GW	S	S%	+/-	TF	F%	Min	GP	G	A	Pts	PIM	PP	SH	GW	Min
2013-14	Anaheim	NHL	78	5	13	18	39	0	0	2	107	4.7	21	0	0.0	19:24	13	2	0	2	8	0	0	1	19:38
2014-15	Anaheim	NHL	40	1	10	11	17	0	0	0	50	2.0	3	0	0.0	18:33	....	....	....	....	....	....	....	....	....
	Pittsburgh	NHL	20	1	2	3	8	0	0	0	36	2.8	–7	0	0.0	21:13	5	0	2	2	0	0	0	0	22:55
	NHL Totals		**268**	**11**	**56**	**67**	**156**	**0**	**0**	**2**	**374**	**2.9**		**0**	**0.0**	**17:28**	**34**	**2**	**6**	**8**	**12**	**0**	**0**	**1**	**18:05**

AHL Second All-Star Team (2009)

Signed as a free agent by **Wilkes-Barre** (AHL), June 14, 2007. Signed as a free agent by **Pittsburgh**, July 7, 2008. • Missed majority of 2011-12 due to broken wrist, knee surgery and as a healthy reserve. Traded to **Anaheim** by **Pittsburgh** for Anaheim's 5th round choice (Anthony Angello) in 2014 Entry Draft, February 6, 2013. Traded to **Pittsburgh** by **Anaheim** for Simon Despres, March 2, 2015.

LOWE, Keegan
(LOH, KEE-guhn) **CAR**

Defense. Shoots left. 6'2", 195 lbs. Born, Greenwich, CT, March 29, 1993. Carolina's 3rd choice, 73rd overall, in 2011 Entry Draft.

Season	Club	League	GP	G	A	Pts	PIM	PP	SH	GW	S	S%	+/-	TF	F%	Min	GP	G	A	Pts	PIM	PP	SH	GW	Min
2008-09	Shattuck U16	High-MN	55	7	26	33	77	....	....	....	....	....	....	....	....	....	....	....	....	....	....	....	....	....	....
2009-10	Edmonton	WHL	69	2	12	14	60	....	....	....	....	....	....	....	....	....	....	....	....	....	....	....	....	....	....
2010-11	Edmonton	WHL	71	2	22	24	123	....	....	....	....	....	....	....	....	....	4	1	0	1	4	....	....	....	....
2011-12	Edmonton	WHL	72	3	20	23	139	....	....	....	....	....	....	....	....	....	20	3	4	7	44	....	....	....	....
2012-13	Edmonton	WHL	64	15	16	31	148	....	....	....	....	....	....	....	....	....	22	1	7	8	28	....	....	....	....
2013-14	Charlotte	AHL	63	2	10	12	86	....	....	....	....	....	....	....	....	....	....	....	....	....	....	....	....	....	....
2014-15	**Carolina**	**NHL**	**2**	**0**	**0**	**0**	**10**	**0**	**0**	**0**	**0**	**0.0**	**–2**	**0**	**0.0**	**13:51**	....	....	....	....	....	....	....	....	....
	Charlotte	AHL	58	2	9	11	106	....	....	....	....	....	....	....	....	....	....	....	....	....	....	....	....	....	....
	NHL Totals		**2**	**0**	**0**	**0**	**10**	**0**	**0**	**0**	**0**	**0.0**		**0**	**0.0**	**13:51**	....	....	....	....	....	....	....	....	....

WHL East Second All-Star Team (2013)

LOWRY, Adam
(LOW-ree, A-duhm) **WPG**

Center. Shoots left. 6'5", 210 lbs. Born, St. Louis, MO, March 29, 1993. Winnipeg's 2nd choice, 67th overall, in 2011 Entry Draft.

Season	Club	League	GP	G	A	Pts	PIM	PP	SH	GW	S	S%	+/-	TF	F%	Min	GP	G	A	Pts	PIM	PP	SH	GW	Min
2007-08	Calgary Bisons	AMBHL	33	27	21	48	56	....	....	....	....	....	....	....	....	....	12	4	6	10	10	....	....	....	....
	Cgy. Blackhawks	Minor-AB	1	0	1	1	0	....	....	....	....	....	....	....	....	....	....	....	....	....	....	....	....	....	....
2008-09	Calgary Rangers	Minor-AB	29	29	25	54	51	....	....	....	....	....	....	....	....	....	....	....	....	....	....	....	....	....	....
2009-10	Swift Current	WHL	61	15	19	34	57	....	....	....	....	....	....	....	....	....	3	0	1	1	6	....	....	....	....
2010-11	Swift Current	WHL	66	18	27	45	84	....	....	....	....	....	....	....	....	....	....	....	....	....	....	....	....	....	....
2011-12	Swift Current	WHL	36	12	25	37	90	....	....	....	....	....	....	....	....	....	....	....	....	....	....	....	....	....	....
2012-13	Swift Current	WHL	72	45	43	88	102	....	....	....	....	....	....	....	....	....	5	3	2	5	4	....	....	....	....
	St. John's IceCaps	AHL	9	0	1	1	4	....	....	....	....	....	....	....	....	....	....	....	....	....	....	....	....	....	....
2013-14	St. John's IceCaps	AHL	64	17	16	33	49	....	....	....	....	....	....	....	....	....	17	2	3	5	16	....	....	....	....
2014-15	**Winnipeg**	**NHL**	**80**	**11**	**12**	**23**	**46**	**0**	**1**	**2**	**104**	**10.6**	**1**	**851**	**47.2**	**13:45**	**4**	**1**	**2**	**3**	**2**	**0**	**0**	**0**	**14:46**
	NHL Totals		**80**	**11**	**12**	**23**	**46**	**0**	**1**	**2**	**104**	**10.6**		**851**	**47.2**	**13:45**	**4**	**1**	**2**	**3**	**2**	**0**	**0**	**0**	**14:46**

WHL East First All-Star Team (2013) • WHL Player of the Year (2013)

LUCIC, Milan
(LOO-cheech, MEE-lahn) **L.A.**

Left wing. Shoots left. 6'3", 228 lbs. Born, Vancouver, BC, June 7, 1988. Boston's 3rd choice, 50th overall, in 2006 Entry Draft.

Season	Club	League	GP	G	A	Pts	PIM	PP	SH	GW	S	S%	+/-	TF	F%	Min	GP	G	A	Pts	PIM	PP	SH	GW	Min
2004-05	Coquitlam	BCHL	50	9	14	23	100	....	....	....	....	....	....	....	....	....	....	....	....	....	....	....	....	....	....
	Vancouver Giants	WHL	1	0	0	0	2	....	....	....	....	....	....	....	....	....	2	0	0	0	0	....	....	....	....
2005-06	Vancouver Giants	WHL	62	9	10	19	149	....	....	....	....	....	....	....	....	....	18	3	4	7	23	....	....	....	....
2006-07	Vancouver Giants	WHL	70	30	38	68	147	....	....	....	....	....	....	....	....	....	22	7	12	19	26	....	....	....	....
2007-08	**Boston**	**NHL**	**77**	**8**	**19**	**27**	**89**	**1**	**0**	**4**	**88**	**9.1**	**–2**	**8**	**50.0**	**12:07**	**7**	**2**	**0**	**2**	**4**	**0**	**0**	**0**	**16:24**
2008-09	**Boston**	**NHL**	**72**	**17**	**25**	**42**	**136**	**2**	**0**	**3**	**97**	**17.5**	**17**	**10**	**60.0**	**14:57**	**10**	**3**	**6**	**9**	**43**	**0**	**0**	**0**	**15:14**
2009-10	**Boston**	**NHL**	**50**	**9**	**11**	**20**	**44**	**0**	**0**	**2**	**72**	**12.5**	**–7**	**14**	**21.4**	**14:21**	**13**	**5**	**4**	**9**	**19**	**2**	**0**	**1**	**16:27**
2010-11 ♦	**Boston**	**NHL**	**79**	**30**	**32**	**62**	**121**	**5**	**0**	**7**	**173**	**17.3**	**28**	**54**	**38.9**	**16:35**	**25**	**5**	**7**	**12**	**63**	**1**	**0**	**0**	**17:54**
2011-12	**Boston**	**NHL**	**81**	**26**	**35**	**61**	**135**	**7**	**0**	**1**	**149**	**17.4**	**7**	**30**	**46.7**	**17:02**	**7**	**0**	**3**	**3**	**8**	**1**	**0**	**0**	**20:17**
2012-13	**Boston**	**NHL**	**46**	**7**	**20**	**27**	**75**	**0**	**0**	**0**	**79**	**8.9**	**8**	**35**	**48.6**	**16:55**	**22**	**7**	**12**	**19**	**14**	**0**	**0**	**0**	**20:57**
2013-14	**Boston**	**NHL**	**80**	**24**	**35**	**59**	**91**	**3**	**0**	**5**	**153**	**15.7**	**30**	**131**	**46.6**	**17:23**	**12**	**4**	**3**	**7**	**4**	**0**	**0**	**1**	**18:27**
2014-15	**Boston**	**NHL**	**81**	**18**	**26**	**44**	**81**	**2**	**0**	**4**	**141**	**12.8**	**13**	**76**	**44.7**	**16:21**	....	....	....	....	....	....	....	....	....
	NHL Totals		**566**	**139**	**203**	**342**	**772**	**20**	**0**	**26**	**952**	**14.6**		**358**	**44.7**	**15:44**	**96**	**26**	**35**	**61**	**155**	**3**	**0**	**2**	**18:15**

Memorial Cup All-Star Team (2007) • Stafford Smythe Memorial Trophy (Memorial Cup - MVP) (2007)

Traded to **Los Angeles** by **Boston** for Martin Jones, Colin Miller and Los Angeles' 1st round choice (Jakub Zboril) in 2015 Entry Draft, June 26, 2015.

LUPUL, Joffrey
(LOO-puhl, JAWF-ree) **TOR**

Left wing. Shoots right. 6'1", 206 lbs. Born, Fort Saskatchewan, AB, September 23, 1983. Anaheim's 1st choice, 7th overall, in 2002 Entry Draft.

Season	Club	League	GP	G	A	Pts	PIM	PP	SH	GW	S	S%	+/-	TF	F%	Min	GP	G	A	Pts	PIM	PP	SH	GW	Min
1998-99	Ft. Saskatchewan	Minor-AB	36	40	50	90	40	....	....	....	....	....	....	....	....	....	....	....	....	....	....	....	....	....	....
99-2000	Ft. Saskatchewan	AMHL	34	43	30	*73	47	....	....	....	....	....	....	....	....	....	4	0	1	1	2	....	....	....	....
2000-01	Medicine Hat	WHL	69	30	26	56	39	....	....	....	....	....	....	....	....	....	22	3	6	9	2	....	....	....	....
2001-02	Medicine Hat	WHL	72	*56	50	106	95	....	....	....	....	....	....	....	....	....	....	....	....	....	....	....	....	....	....
2002-03	Medicine Hat	WHL	50	41	37	78	82	....	....	....	....	....	....	....	....	....	11	4	11	15	20	....	....	....	....
2003-04	**Anaheim**	**NHL**	**75**	**13**	**21**	**34**	**28**	**4**	**0**	**2**	**137**	**9.5**	**–6**	**11**	**9.1**	**13:37**	....	....	....	....	....	....	....	....	....
	Cincinnati	AHL	3	3	2	5	2	....	....	....	....	....	....	....	....	....	....	....	....	....	....	....	....	....	....
2004-05	Cincinnati	AHL	65	30	26	56	58	....	....	....	....	....	....	....	....	....	12	3	9	12	27	....	....	....	....
2005-06	**Anaheim**	**NHL**	**81**	**28**	**25**	**53**	**48**	**12**	**2**	**2**	**296**	**9.5**	**–13**	**101**	**37.6**	**16:38**	**16**	**9**	**2**	**11**	**31**	**1**	**0**	**1**	**16:43**
2006-07	**Edmonton**	**NHL**	**81**	**16**	**12**	**28**	**45**	**5**	**0**	**1**	**172**	**9.3**	**–29**	**14**	**35.7**	**15:36**	....	....	....	....	....	....	....	....	....
2007-08	**Philadelphia**	**NHL**	**56**	**20**	**26**	**46**	**35**	**7**	**0**	**3**	**176**	**11.4**	**2**	**4**	**75.0**	**18:13**	**17**	**4**	**6**	**10**	**2**	**2**	**0**	**1**	**16:13**
2008-09	**Philadelphia**	**NHL**	**79**	**25**	**25**	**50**	**58**	**6**	**0**	**4**	**194**	**12.9**	**1**	**21**	**47.6**	**15:41**	**6**	**1**	**1**	**2**	**2**	**0**	**0**	**0**	**17:07**
2009-10	**Anaheim**	**NHL**	**23**	**10**	**4**	**14**	**18**	**0**	**0**	**0**	**66**	**15.2**	**3**	**5**	**20.0**	**15:58**	....	....	....	....	....	....	....	....	....
2010-11	**Anaheim**	**NHL**	**26**	**5**	**8**	**13**	**14**	**2**	**0**	**1**	**54**	**9.3**	**–4**	**14**	**50.0**	**13:13**	....	....	....	....	....	....	....	....	....
	Syracuse Crunch	AHL	3	1	3	4	0	....	....	....	....	....	....	....	....	....	....	....	....	....	....	....	....	....	....
	Toronto	**NHL**	**28**	**9**	**9**	**18**	**19**	**2**	**0**	**1**	**75**	**12.0**	**–7**	**18**	**27.8**	**17:51**	....	....	....	....	....	....	....	....	....
2011-12	**Toronto**	**NHL**	**66**	**25**	**42**	**67**	**48**	**8**	**0**	**3**	**191**	**13.1**	**1**	**58**	**36.2**	**18:37**	....	....	....	....	....	....	....	....	....
2012-13	Avtomobilist	KHL	9	1	3	4	4	....	....	....	....	....	....	....	....	....	....	....	....	....	....	....	....	....	....
	Toronto	**NHL**	**16**	**11**	**7**	**18**	**12**	**3**	**0**	**3**	**42**	**26.2**	**8**	**8**	**37.5**	**16:07**	**7**	**3**	**1**	**4**	**4**	**1**	**0**	**0**	**18:59**
2013-14	**Toronto**	**NHL**	**69**	**22**	**22**	**44**	**44**	**6**	**0**	**1**	**191**	**11.5**	**–15**	**55**	**43.6**	**18:27**	....	....	....	....	....	....	....	....	....
2014-15	**Toronto**	**NHL**	**55**	**10**	**11**	**21**	**26**	**2**	**0**	**1**	**97**	**10.3**	**–10**	**6**	**66.7**	**15:29**	....	....	....	....	....	....	....	....	....
	NHL Totals		**655**	**194**	**212**	**406**	**395**	**57**	**2**	**22**	**1691**	**11.5**		**315**	**38.7**	**16:21**	**46**	**17**	**10**	**27**	**39**	**4**	**0**	**2**	**16:56**

WHL East First All-Star Team (2002) • Canadian Major Junior First All-Star Team (2002)

Played in NHL All-Star Game (2012)

Traded to **Edmonton** by **Anaheim** with Ladislav Smid, Anaheim's 1st round choice (later traded to Phoenix - Phoenix selected Nick Ross) in 2007 Entry Draft and Anaheim's 1st (Jordan Eberle) and 2nd (later traded to NY Islanders - NY Islanders selected Travis Hamonic) round choices in 2008 Entry Draft for Chris Pronger, July 3, 2006. Traded to **Philadelphia** by **Edmonton** with Jason Smith for Joni Pitkanen, Geoff Sanderson and Philadelphia's 3rd round choice (Cameron Abney) in 2009 Entry Draft, July 1, 2007. Traded to **Anaheim** by **Philadelphia** with Luca Sbisa, Philadelphia's 1st round choice in 2009 (later traded to Columbus - Columbus selected John Moore) and 2010 (Emerson Etem) Entry Drafts and future considerations for Chris Pronger and Ryan Dingle, June 26, 2009. • Missed majority of 2009-10 due to back injury, December 16, 2009. Traded to **Toronto** by **Anaheim** with Jake Gardiner and Anaheim's 4th round choice (later traded to San Jose – San Jose selected Fredrik Bergvik) in 2013 Entry Draft for Francois Beauchemin, February 9, 2011. Signed as a free agent by **Avtomobilist Yekaterinburg** (KHL), October 30, 2012. • Missed majority of 2012-13 due to arm (January 23, 2013 at Pittsburgh) and head (April 4, 2013 vs. Philadelphia) injuries.

MAATTA, Olli
(MA-TA, OH-lee) **PIT**

Defense. Shoots left. 6'2", 206 lbs. Born, Jyvaskyla, Finland, August 22, 1994. Pittsburgh's 2nd choice, 22nd overall, in 2012 Entry Draft.

Season	Club	League	GP	G	A	Pts	PIM	PP	SH	GW	S	S%	+/-	TF	F%	Min	GP	G	A	Pts	PIM	PP	SH	GW	Min
2009-10	JyP Jyvaskyla U18	Fin-U18	2	0	0	0	2	....	....	....	....	....	....	....	....	....	....	....	....	....	....	....	....	....	....
	JyP Jyvaskyla Jr.	Fin-Jr.	1	0	1	1	0	....	....	....	....	....	....	....	....	....	....	....	....	....	....	....	....	....	....
2010-11	Suomi U20	Finland-2	2	0	2	2	2	....	....	....	....	....	....	....	....	....	....	....	....	....	....	....	....	....	....
	JyP Jyvaskyla U18	Fin-U18	1	0	0	0	0	....	....	....	....	....	....	....	....	....	....	....	....	....	....	....	....	....	....
	D Team Jyvaskyla	Finland-2	23	1	5	6	6	....	....	....	....	....	....	....	....	....	....	....	....	....	....	....	....	....	....
	JyP Jyvaskyla Jr.	Fin-Jr.	19	2	6	8	8	....	....	....	....	....	....	....	....	....	12	1	4	5	6	....	....	....	....
2011-12	London Knights	OHL	58	5	27	32	25	....	....	....	....	....	....	....	....	....	19	6	17	23	2	....	....	....	....
2012-13	London Knights	OHL	57	8	30	38	30	....	....	....	....	....	....	....	....	....	21	4	10	14	8	....	....	....	....
	Wilkes-Barre	AHL	....	....	....	....	....	....	....	....	....	....	....	....	....	....	3	0	0	0	0	....	....	....	....

Season	Club	League	GP	G	A	Pts	PIM	PP	SH	GW	S	S%	+/-	TF	F%	Min	GP	G	A	Pts	PIM	PP	SH	GW	Min
		Regular Season															Playoffs								
2013-14	Pittsburgh	NHL	78	9	20	29	14	3	1	1	119	7.6	8	0	0.0	18:30	13	0	4	4	0	0	0	0	18:05
	Finland	Olympics	6	3	2	5	0	....	....	....	....	....	....	....	....	....	....	....	....	....	....	....	....	....	....
2014-15	Pittsburgh	NHL	20	1	8	9	10	0	0	0	27	3.7	1	0	0.0	20:43	....	....	....	....	....	....	....	....	....
	NHL Totals		98	10	28	38	24	3	1	1	146	6.8		0	0.0	18:57	13	0	4	4	0	0	0	0	18:05

OHL All-Rookie Team (2012)

• Missed majority of 2014-15 due to shoulder injury vs. Ottawa, December 6, 2014.

MacARTHUR, Clarke

(muh-KAR-thuhr, KLAHRK) **OTT**

Left wing. Shoots left. 6', 190 lbs. Born, Lloydminster, AB, April 6, 1985. Buffalo's 3rd choice, 74th overall, in 2003 Entry Draft.

Season	Club	League	GP	G	A	Pts	PIM	PP	SH	GW	S	S%	+/-	TF	F%	Min	GP	G	A	Pts	PIM	PP	SH	GW	Min
99-2000	Lloydminster	CABHL	24	19	45	64	51	....	....	....	....	....	....	....	....	....	5	9	6	15	4	....	....	....	....
2000-01	Strathcona	AMBHL	38	36	63	99	44	....	....	....	....	....	....	....	....	....	8	6	2	8	10	....	....	....	....
2001-02	Drayton Valley	AJHL	61	22	40	62	33	....	....	....	....	....	....	....	....	....	16	5	8	13	34	....	....	....	....
2002-03	Medicine Hat	WHL	70	23	52	75	104	....	....	....	....	....	....	....	....	....	11	3	6	9	8	....	....	....	....
2003-04	Medicine Hat	WHL	62	35	40	75	93	....	....	....	....	....	....	....	....	....	20	8	10	18	16	....	....	....	....
2004-05	Medicine Hat	WHL	58	30	44	74	100	....	....	....	....	....	....	....	....	....	13	3	8	11	18	....	....	....	....
	Rochester	AHL	....	....	....	....	....	....	....	....	....	....	....	....	....	....	3	0	1	1	0	....	....	....	....
2005-06	Rochester	AHL	69	21	32	53	71	....	....	....	....	....	....	....	....	....	....	....	....	....	....	....	....	....	....
2006-07	Buffalo	NHL	19	3	4	7	4	0	0	0	16	18.8	4	50	46.0	8:54	....	....	....	....	....	....	....	....	....
	Rochester	AHL	51	21	42	63	57	....	....	....	....	....	....	....	....	....	6	2	4	6	4	....	....	....	....
2007-08	Buffalo	NHL	37	8	7	15	20	0	0	1	51	15.7	3	14	28.6	14:34	....	....	....	....	....	....	....	....	....
	Rochester	AHL	43	14	28	42	26	....	....	....	....	....	....	....	....	....	....	....	....	....	....	....	....	....	....
2008-09	Buffalo	NHL	71	17	14	31	56	5	0	0	108	15.7	–4	218	34.9	13:50	....	....	....	....	....	....	....	....	....
2009-10	Buffalo	NHL	60	13	13	26	47	3	0	3	99	13.1	–14	143	43.4	14:22	....	....	....	....	....	....	....	....	....
	Atlanta	NHL	21	3	6	9	2	1	1	0	30	10.0	–2	10	50.0	15:37	....	....	....	....	....	....	....	....	....
2010-11	Toronto	NHL	82	21	41	62	37	6	0	3	154	13.6	–3	16	56.3	17:07	....	....	....	....	....	....	....	....	....
2011-12	Toronto	NHL	73	20	23	43	37	3	0	4	148	13.5	3	11	45.5	15:51	....	....	....	....	....	....	....	....	....
2012-13	Crimmitschau	German-2	9	4	7	11	16	....	....	....	....	....	....	....	....	....	....	....	....	....	....	....	....	....	....
	Toronto	NHL	40	8	12	20	26	2	0	1	62	12.9	3	6	83.3	14:55	5	2	1	3	2	0	0	1	12:21
2013-14	Ottawa	NHL	79	24	31	55	78	8	1	5	159	15.1	12	32	46.9	17:38	....	....	....	....	....	....	....	....	....
2014-15	Ottawa	NHL	62	16	20	36	36	6	0	5	140	11.4	–6	22	36.4	17:00	6	2	0	2	18	0	0	0	15:59
	NHL Totals		544	133	171	304	343	34	2	22	967	13.8		522	40.6	15:36	11	4	1	5	20	0	0	1	14:20

Memorial Cup All-Star Team (2004) • WHL East First All-Star Team (2005)

Traded to **Atlanta** by **Buffalo** for Atlanta's 3rd (Jerome Gauthier-Leduc) and 4th (Steven Shipley) round choices in 2010 Entry Draft, March 3, 2010. Signed as a free agent by **Toronto**, August 28, 2010. Signed as a free agent by **Crimmitschau** (German-2), October 23, 2012. Signed as a free agent by **Ottawa**, July 5, 2013.

MacDONALD, Andrew

(MAK-DAWN-uhld, AN-droo) **PHI**

Defense. Shoots left. 6'1", 204 lbs. Born, Judique, NS, September 7, 1986. NY Islanders' 10th choice, 160th overall, in 2006 Entry Draft.

Season	Club	League	GP	G	A	Pts	PIM	PP	SH	GW	S	S%	+/-	TF	F%	Min	GP	G	A	Pts	PIM	PP	SH	GW	Min
2003-04	Truro Bearcats	MJrHL	50	8	20	28	43	....	....	....	....	....	....	....	....	....	10	0	0	0	....	....	....	....	....
2004-05	Truro Bearcats	MJrHL	56	11	22	33	60	....	....	....	....	....	....	....	....	....	17	6	7	13	....	....	....	....	....
2005-06	Moncton Wildcats	QMJHL	68	6	40	46	62	....	....	....	....	....	....	....	....	....	21	2	11	13	10	....	....	....	....
2006-07	Moncton Wildcats	QMJHL	65	14	44	58	81	....	....	....	....	....	....	....	....	....	7	1	5	6	4	....	....	....	....
	Bridgeport	AHL	3	0	0	0	0	....	....	....	....	....	....	....	....	....	....	....	....	....	....	....	....	....	....
2007-08	Bridgeport	AHL	21	2	3	5	10	....	....	....	....	....	....	....	....	....	....	....	....	....	....	....	....	....	....
	Utah Grizzlies	ECHL	37	1	11	12	39	....	....	....	....	....	....	....	....	....	15	3	9	12	12	....	....	....	....
2008-09	NY Islanders	NHL	3	0	0	0	2	0	0	0	1	0.0	2	0	0.0	10:10	....	....	....	....	....	....	....	....	....
	Bridgeport	AHL	69	9	24	33	46	....	....	....	....	....	....	....	....	....	5	1	1	2	4	....	....	....	....
2009-10	NY Islanders	NHL	46	1	6	7	20	0	0	0	43	2.3	4	1	0.0	20:05	....	....	....	....	....	....	....	....	....
	Bridgeport	AHL	21	2	6	8	29	....	....	....	....	....	....	....	....	....	5	3	1	4	10	....	....	....	....
2010-11	NY Islanders	NHL	60	4	23	27	37	1	0	1	72	5.6	9	0	0.0	23:25	....	....	....	....	....	....	....	....	....
2011-12	NY Islanders	NHL	75	5	14	19	26	1	0	0	71	7.0	–5	0	0.0	23:22	....	....	....	....	....	....	....	....	....
2012-13	Karlovy Vary	CzRep	21	1	4	5	10	....	....	....	....	....	....	....	....	....	....	....	....	....	....	....	....	....	....
	HC Banik Sokolov	CzRep-3	1	0	0	0	0	....	....	....	....	....	....	....	....	....	....	....	....	....	....	....	....	....	....
	NY Islanders	NHL	48	3	9	12	20	1	0	1	45	6.7	–2	0	0.0	23:31	4	0	0	0	4	0	0	0	23:26
2013-14	NY Islanders	NHL	63	4	20	24	34	2	0	2	72	5.6	–19	0	0.0	25:25	....	....	....	....	....	....	....	....	....
	Philadelphia	NHL	19	0	4	4	16	0	0	0	20	0.0	–3	0	0.0	22:00	7	1	1	2	8	0	0	0	22:37
2014-15	Philadelphia	NHL	58	2	10	12	41	1	0	0	62	3.2	–5	0	0.0	20:01	....	....	....	....	....	....	....	....	....
	NHL Totals		372	19	86	105	196	6	0	4	386	4.9		1	0.0	22:38	11	1	1	2	12	0	0	0	22:55

QMJHL First All-Star Team (2007)

Signed as a free agent by **Karlovy Vary** (CzRep), October 9, 2012. Traded to **Philadelphia** by **NY Islanders** for Matt Mangene, Philadelphia's 3rd round choice (Ilya Sorokin) in 2014 Entry Draft and Philadelphia's 2nd round choice in (later traded to Boston – Boston selected Brandon Carlo) 2015 Entry Draft, March 4, 2014.

MACENAUER, Maxime

(MAY-sehn-owr, mahx-EEM)

Center. Shoots left. 6', 205 lbs. Born, Laval, QC, January 4, 1989. Anaheim's 3rd choice, 63rd overall, in 2007 Entry Draft.

Season	Club	League	GP	G	A	Pts	PIM	PP	SH	GW	S	S%	+/-	TF	F%	Min	GP	G	A	Pts	PIM	PP	SH	GW	Min
2004-05	Ecole Montpetit	QAAA	37	17	22	39	56	....	....	....	....	....	....	....	....	....	3	0	0	0	0	....	....	....	....
2005-06	Rimouski Oceanic	QMJHL	41	8	14	22	30	....	....	....	....	....	....	....	....	....	....	....	....	....	....	....	....	....	....
2006-07	Rouyn-Noranda	QMJHL	14	1	3	4	10	....	....	....	....	....	....	....	....	....	....	....	....	....	....	....	....	....	....
2007-08	Rouyn-Noranda	QMJHL	67	23	37	60	53	....	....	....	....	....	....	....	....	....	17	6	10	16	8	....	....	....	....
2008-09	Rouyn-Noranda	QMJHL	35	15	9	24	34	....	....	....	....	....	....	....	....	....	....	....	....	....	....	....	....	....	....
	Shawinigan	QMJHL	19	7	9	16	18	....	....	....	....	....	....	....	....	....	21	5	9	14	20	....	....	....	....
2009-10	Bakersfield	ECHL	45	5	16	21	49	....	....	....	....	....	....	....	....	....	6	1	0	1	0	....	....	....	....
2010-11	Syracuse Crunch	AHL	79	13	19	32	65	....	....	....	....	....	....	....	....	....	....	....	....	....	....	....	....	....	....
2011-12	Anaheim	NHL	29	1	3	4	18	0	0	1	14	7.1	–4	227	49.8	10:49	....	....	....	....	....	....	....	....	....
	Syracuse Crunch	AHL	13	4	2	6	2	....	....	....	....	....	....	....	....	....	....	....	....	....	....	....	....	....	....
	St. John's IceCaps	AHL	9	0	1	1	2	....	....	....	....	....	....	....	....	....	10	1	0	1	0	....	....	....	....
2012-13	St. John's IceCaps	AHL	68	11	11	22	57	....	....	....	....	....	....	....	....	....	....	....	....	....	....	....	....	....	....
2013-14	Hamilton	AHL	74	9	15	24	56	....	....	....	....	....	....	....	....	....	....	....	....	....	....	....	....	....	....
2014-15	Hamilton	AHL	47	6	4	10	28	....	....	....	....	....	....	....	....	....	....	....	....	....	....	....	....	....	....
	NHL Totals		29	1	3	4	18	0	0	1	14	7.1		227	49.8	10:49	....	....	....	....	....	....	....	....	....

Traded to **Winnipeg** by **Anaheim** for Riley Holzapfel, February 13, 2012. Signed to a PTO (professional tryout) contract by **Hamilton** (AHL), October 4, 2013.

MacINTYRE, Steve

(MAK-ihn-tighr, STEEV)

Left wing. Shoots left. 6'5", 250 lbs. Born, Brock, SK, August 8, 1980.

Season	Club	League	GP	G	A	Pts	PIM	PP	SH	GW	S	S%	+/-	TF	F%	Min	GP	G	A	Pts	PIM	PP	SH	GW	Min
2002-03	St. Jean Mission	QSPHL	10	1	1	2	68	....	....	....	....	....	....	....	....	....	....	....	....	....	....	....	....	....	....
	Muskegon Fury	UHL	54	2	1	3	279	....	....	....	....	....	....	....	....	....	5	0	0	0	24	....	....	....	....
2003-04	Hartford	AHL	3	0	0	0	0	....	....	....	....	....	....	....	....	....	....	....	....	....	....	....	....	....	....
	Charlotte	ECHL	61	1	4	5	217	....	....	....	....	....	....	....	....	....	....	....	....	....	....	....	....	....	....
	Jacksonville	WHA2	6	0	2	2	18	....	....	....	....	....	....	....	....	....	5	0	1	1	17	....	....	....	....
2004-05	Hartford	AHL	27	1	1	2	207	....	....	....	....	....	....	....	....	....	....	....	....	....	....	....	....	....	....
	Charlotte	ECHL	46	1	4	5	214	....	....	....	....	....	....	....	....	....	11	0	4	4	17	....	....	....	....
2005-06	Charlotte	ECHL	61	3	2	5	238	....	....	....	....	....	....	....	....	....	1	0	0	0	4	....	....	....	....
2006-07	Quad City	UHL	46	2	1	3	168	....	....	....	....	....	....	....	....	....	5	0	0	0	6	....	....	....	....
2007-08	Providence Bruins	AHL	62	2	3	5	213	....	....	....	....	....	....	....	....	....	5	0	0	0	9	....	....	....	....
2008-09	Edmonton	NHL	22	2	0	2	40	0	0	1	6	33.3	–2	0	0.0	3:55	....	....	....	....	....	....	....	....	....
2009-10	Edmonton	NHL	4	0	0	0	7	0	0	0	0	0.0	0	0	0.0	1:35	....	....	....	....	....	....	....	....	....
	Florida	NHL	18	0	1	1	17	0	0	0	3	0.0	–3	0	0.0	3:10	....	....	....	....	....	....	....	....	....
	Rochester	AHL	34	0	2	2	86	....	....	....	....	....	....	....	....	....	6	0	0	0	23	....	....	....	....
2010-11	Edmonton	NHL	34	0	1	1	93	0	0	0	6	0.0	–1	0	0.0	3:32	....	....	....	....	....	....	....	....	....
2011-12	Pittsburgh	NHL	12	0	0	0	6	0	0	0	0	0.0	0	0	0.0	3:11	....	....	....	....	....	....	....	....	....
	Wilkes-Barre	AHL	24	1	0	1	59	....	....	....	....	....	....	....	....	....	....	....	....	....	....	....	....	....	....
2012-13	Wilkes-Barre	AHL	29	0	0	0	70	....	....	....	....	....	....	....	....	....	....	....	....	....	....	....	....	....	....
	Pittsburgh	NHL	1	0	0	0	12	0	0	0	0	0.0	0	0	0.0	4:31	....	....	....	....	....	....	....	....	....
2013-14	Oklahoma City	AHL	11	0	0	0	34	....	....	....	....	....	....	....	....	....	....	....	....	....	....	....	....	....	....

			Regular Season														Playoffs								
Season	Club	League	GP	G	A	Pts	PIM	PP	SH	GW	S	S%	+/-	TF	F%	Min	GP	G	A	Pts	PIM	PP	SH	GW	Min
2014-15	Utah Grizzlies	ECHL	21	0	3	3	16	....	....	....	....	....	....	....	....	....	....	....	....	....	....	....	....	....	....
	Norfolk Admirals	AHL	18	0	0	0	28	....	....	....	....	....	....	....	....	....	....	....	....	....	....	....	....	....	....
	NHL Totals		**91**	**2**	**2**	**4**	**175**	**0**	**0**	**1**	**15**	**13.3**		**0**	**0.0**	**3:26**	....	....	....	....	....	....	....	....	....

Signed as a free agent by **NY Rangers**, August 15, 2005. Signed as a free agent by **Quad City** (UHL), August 24, 2006. Signed as a free agent by **Florida**, July 3, 2008. Claimed on waivers by **Edmonton** from **Florida**, September 30, 2008. • Missed majority of 2008-09 due to facial injury and as a healthy reserve. Claimed on waivers by **Florida** from **Edmonton**, November 10, 2009. Signed as a free agent by **Edmonton**, July 2, 2010. • Missed majority of 2010-11 as a healthy reserve. Signed as a free agent by **Pittsburgh**, July 12, 2011. • Missed majority of 2011-12 and 2012-13 as a healthy reserve. Claimed on waivers by **Edmonton** from **Los Angeles**, September 23, 2013. • Missed majority of 2013-14 due to knee injury at Texas (AHL), September 27, 2013.

MacKENZIE, Derek

(muh-KEHN-zee, DAIR-ihk) **FLA**

Center. Shoots left. 5'11", 181 lbs. Born, Sudbury, ON, June 11, 1981. Atlanta's 6th choice, 128th overall, in 1999 Entry Draft.

1996-97	Rayside-Balfour	NOJHA	40	23	32	55	40	....	....	....	....	....	....	....	....	....	....	....	....	....	....	....	....	....	....
1997-98	Sudbury Wolves	OHL	59	9	11	20	26	....	....	....	....	....	....	....	....	....	10	0	1	1	0	....	....	....	....
1998-99	Sudbury Wolves	OHL	68	22	65	87	74	....	....	....	....	....	....	....	....	....	4	2	4	6	2	....	....	....	....
99-2000	Sudbury Wolves	OHL	68	24	33	57	110	....	....	....	....	....	....	....	....	....	12	5	9	14	16	....	....	....	....
2000-01	Sudbury Wolves	OHL	62	40	49	89	89	....	....	....	....	....	....	....	....	....	12	6	8	14	16	....	....	....	....
2001-02	**Atlanta**	**NHL**	**1**	**0**	**0**	**0**	**2**	**0**	**0**	**0**	**1**	**0.0**	**–1**	**16**	**56.3**	**13:51**	....	....	....	....	....	....	....	....	....
	Chicago Wolves	AHL	68	13	12	25	80	....	....	....	....	....	....	....	....	....	25	4	2	6	20	....	....	....	....
2002-03	Chicago Wolves	AHL	80	14	18	32	97	....	....	....	....	....	....	....	....	....	9	0	0	0	4	....	....	....	....
2003-04	**Atlanta**	**NHL**	**12**	**0**	**1**	**1**	**10**	**0**	**0**	**0**	**7**	**0.0**	**0**	**63**	**46.0**	**6:38**	....	....	....	....	....	....	....	....	....
	Chicago Wolves	AHL	63	19	16	35	67	....	....	....	....	....	....	....	....	....	10	7	1	8	13	....	....	....	....
2004-05	Chicago Wolves	AHL	78	13	20	33	87	....	....	....	....	....	....	....	....	....	18	5	6	11	33	....	....	....	....
2005-06	**Atlanta**	**NHL**	**11**	**0**	**1**	**1**	**8**	**0**	**0**	**0**	**11**	**0.0**	**0**	**59**	**55.9**	**6:33**	....	....	....	....	....	....	....	....	....
	Chicago Wolves	AHL	36	10	12	22	48	....	....	....	....	....	....	....	....	....	....	....	....	....	....	....	....	....	....
2006-07	**Atlanta**	**NHL**	**4**	**0**	**0**	**0**	**0**	**0**	**0**	**0**	**3**	**0.0**	**1**	**16**	**56.3**	**5:00**	....	....	....	....	....	....	....	....	....
	Chicago Wolves	AHL	52	14	23	37	62	....	....	....	....	....	....	....	....	....	....	....	....	....	....	....	....	....	....
2007-08	**Columbus**	**NHL**	**17**	**2**	**0**	**2**	**8**	**0**	**0**	**0**	**19**	**10.5**	**–2**	**73**	**34.3**	**7:47**	....	....	....	....	....	....	....	....	....
	Syracuse Crunch	AHL	62	25	24	49	46	....	....	....	....	....	....	....	....	....	13	6	8	14	22	....	....	....	....
2008-09	**Columbus**	**NHL**	**1**	**0**	**0**	**0**	**2**	**0**	**0**	**0**	**1**	**0.0**	**–1**	**4**	**50.0**	**7:15**	....	....	....	....	....	....	....	....	....
	Syracuse Crunch	AHL	64	22	30	52	50	....	....	....	....	....	....	....	....	....	....	....	....	....	....	....	....	....	....
2009-10	**Columbus**	**NHL**	**18**	**1**	**3**	**4**	**0**	**0**	**0**	**0**	**14**	**7.1**	**3**	**104**	**54.8**	**8:42**	....	....	....	....	....	....	....	....	....
	Syracuse Crunch	AHL	47	17	30	47	30	....	....	....	....	....	....	....	....	....	....	....	....	....	....	....	....	....	....
2010-11	**Columbus**	**NHL**	**63**	**9**	**14**	**23**	**22**	**0**	**1**	**1**	**76**	**11.8**	**14**	**473**	**52.0**	**10:51**	....	....	....	....	....	....	....	....	....
2011-12	**Columbus**	**NHL**	**66**	**7**	**7**	**14**	**40**	**1**	**2**	**2**	**61**	**11.5**	**4**	**429**	**54.6**	**10:30**	....	....	....	....	....	....	....	....	....
2012-13	**Columbus**	**NHL**	**43**	**3**	**5**	**8**	**36**	**0**	**0**	**0**	**33**	**9.1**	**1**	**323**	**59.4**	**10:20**	....	....	....	....	....	....	....	....	....
2013-14	**Columbus**	**NHL**	**71**	**9**	**9**	**18**	**47**	**0**	**2**	**0**	**70**	**12.9**	**0**	**497**	**51.5**	**11:16**	**6**	**1**	**0**	**1**	**2**	**0**	**1**	**0**	**13:49**
2014-15	**Florida**	**NHL**	**82**	**5**	**6**	**11**	**45**	**1**	**0**	**0**	**72**	**6.9**	**–17**	**1022**	**53.1**	**12:27**	....	....	....	....	....	....	....	....	....
	NHL Totals		**389**	**36**	**46**	**82**	**220**	**2**	**5**	**3**	**368**	**9.8**		**3079**	**53.1**	**10:36**	**6**	**1**	**0**	**1**	**2**	**0**	**1**	**0**	**13:49**

Signed as a free agent by **Columbus**, July 11, 2007. Signed as a free agent by **Florida**, July 1, 2014.

MacKINNON, Nathan

(muh-KIH-nuhn, NAY-thuhn) **COL**

Center. Shoots right. 6', 195 lbs. Born, Halifax, NS, September 1, 1995. Colorado's 1st choice, 1st overall, in 2013 Entry Draft.

2009-10	Shattuck Bantam	High-MN	58	54	47	101	56	....	....	....	....	....	....	....	....	....	....	....	....	....	....	....	....	....	....
2010-11	Shattuck Midget	High-MN	40	45	48	93	72	....	....	....	....	....	....	....	....	....	....	....	....	....	....	....	....	....	....
2011-12	Halifax	QMJHL	58	31	47	78	45	....	....	....	....	....	....	....	....	....	17	13	15	28	12	....	....	....	....
2012-13	Halifax	QMJHL	44	32	43	75	45	....	....	....	....	....	....	....	....	....	17	11	22	33	12	....	....	....	....
2013-14	**Colorado**	**NHL**	**82**	**24**	**39**	**63**	**26**	**8**	**0**	**5**	**241**	**10.0**	**20**	**452**	**42.9**	**17:21**	**7**	**2**	**8**	**10**	**4**	**0**	**0**	**1**	**20:34**
2014-15	**Colorado**	**NHL**	**64**	**14**	**24**	**38**	**34**	**3**	**0**	**2**	**192**	**7.3**	**–7**	**428**	**47.0**	**17:03**	....	....	....	....	....	....	....	....	....
	NHL Totals		**146**	**38**	**63**	**101**	**60**	**11**	**0**	**7**	**433**	**8.8**		**880**	**44.9**	**17:13**	**7**	**2**	**8**	**10**	**4**	**0**	**0**	**1**	**20:34**

QMJHL Second All-Star Team (2013) • Memorial Cup All-Star Team (2013) • Ed Chynoweth Trophy (Memorial Cup - Leading Scorer) (2013) • Stafford Smythe Memorial Trophy (Memorial Cup - MVP) (2013) • NHL All-Rookie Team (2014) • Calder Memorial Trophy (2014)

MacWILLIAM, Andrew

(MAK-WIHL-yuhm, AN-droo) **WPG**

Defense. Shoots left. 6'2", 230 lbs. Born, Calgary, AB, March 25, 1990. Toronto's 8th choice, 188th overall, in 2008 Entry Draft.

2006-07	Calgary Royals	AMHL	35	5	13	18	125	....	....	....	....	....	....	....	....	....	....	....	....	....	....	....	....	....	....
	Camrose Kodiaks	AJHL	2	0	0	0	0	....	....	....	....	....	....	....	....	....	1	0	0	0	0	....	....	....	....
2007-08	Camrose Kodiaks	AJHL	54	0	13	13	130	....	....	....	....	....	....	....	....	....	18	0	5	5	49	....	....	....	....
2008-09	Camrose Kodiaks	AJHL	57	8	21	29	220	....	....	....	....	....	....	....	....	....	11	0	4	4	39	....	....	....	....
2009-10	North Dakota	WCHA	43	0	3	3	87	....	....	....	....	....	....	....	....	....	....	....	....	....	....	....	....	....	....
2010-11	North Dakota	WCHA	37	0	8	8	49	....	....	....	....	....	....	....	....	....	....	....	....	....	....	....	....	....	....
2011-12	North Dakota	WCHA	42	2	5	7	75	....	....	....	....	....	....	....	....	....	....	....	....	....	....	....	....	....	....
2012-13	North Dakota	WCHA	41	2	11	13	*116	....	....	....	....	....	....	....	....	....	....	....	....	....	....	....	....	....	....
	Toronto Marlies	AHL	2	0	0	0	0	....	....	....	....	....	....	....	....	....	....	....	....	....	....	....	....	....	....
2013-14	Toronto Marlies	AHL	57	0	9	9	96	....	....	....	....	....	....	....	....	....	9	0	1	1	8	....	....	....	....
2014-15	**Toronto**	**NHL**	**12**	**0**	**2**	**2**	**12**	**0**	**0**	**0**	**5**	**0.0**	**–6**	**1**	**0.0**	**15:24**	....	....	....	....	....	....	....	....	....
	Toronto Marlies	AHL	58	3	4	7	47	....	....	....	....	....	....	....	....	....	4	0	1	1	6	....	....	....	....
	NHL Totals		**12**	**0**	**2**	**2**	**12**	**0**	**0**	**0**	**5**	**0.0**		**1**	**0.0**	**15:24**	....	....	....	....	....	....	....	....	....

Signed as a free agent by **Winnipeg**, July 3, 2015.

MALHOTRA, Manny

(mal-HOH-truh, MAN-ee)

Center. Shoots left. 6'2", 220 lbs. Born, Mississauga, ON, May 18, 1980. NY Rangers' 1st choice, 7th overall, in 1998 Entry Draft.

1995-96	Mississauga Reps	MTHL	54	27	44	71	62	....	....	....	....	....	....	....	....	....	....	....	....	....	....	....	....	....	....
1996-97	Guelph Storm	OHL	61	16	28	44	26	....	....	....	....	....	....	....	....	....	18	7	7	14	11	....	....	....	....
1997-98	Guelph Storm	OHL	57	16	35	51	29	....	....	....	....	....	....	....	....	....	12	7	6	13	8	....	....	....	....
1998-99	**NY Rangers**	**NHL**	**73**	**8**	**8**	**16**	**13**	**1**	**0**	**2**	**61**	**13.1**	**–2**	**588**	**43.9**	**8:36**	....	....	....	....	....	....	....	....	....
99-2000	**NY Rangers**	**NHL**	**27**	**0**	**0**	**0**	**4**	**0**	**0**	**0**	**18**	**0.0**	**–6**	**132**	**44.7**	**6:42**	....	....	....	....	....	....	....	....	....
	Guelph Storm	OHL	5	2	2	4	4	....	....	....	....	....	....	....	....	....	6	0	2	2	4	....	....	....	....
	Hartford	AHL	12	1	5	6	2	....	....	....	....	....	....	....	....	....	23	1	2	3	10	....	....	....	....
2000-01	**NY Rangers**	**NHL**	**50**	**4**	**8**	**12**	**31**	**0**	**0**	**2**	**46**	**8.7**	**–10**	**248**	**44.4**	**9:03**	....	....	....	....	....	....	....	....	....
	Hartford	AHL	28	5	6	11	69	....	....	....	....	....	....	....	....	....	5	0	0	0	0	....	....	....	....
2001-02	**NY Rangers**	**NHL**	**56**	**7**	**6**	**13**	**42**	**0**	**1**	**1**	**41**	**17.1**	**–1**	**310**	**42.9**	**10:14**	....	....	....	....	....	....	....	....	....
	Dallas	**NHL**	**16**	**1**	**0**	**1**	**5**	**0**	**0**	**0**	**19**	**5.3**	**–3**	**121**	**48.8**	**10:37**	....	....	....	....	....	....	....	....	....
2002-03	**Dallas**	**NHL**	**59**	**3**	**7**	**10**	**42**	**0**	**0**	**1**	**62**	**4.8**	**–2**	**447**	**47.0**	**9:22**	**5**	**1**	**0**	**1**	**0**	**0**	**0**	**0**	**8:13**
2003-04	**Dallas**	**NHL**	**9**	**0**	**0**	**0**	**4**	**0**	**0**	**0**	**4**	**0.0**	**–2**	**13**	**61.5**	**7:48**	....	....	....	....	....	....	....	....	....
	Columbus	**NHL**	**56**	**12**	**13**	**25**	**24**	**1**	**0**	**2**	**103**	**11.7**	**–5**	**840**	**53.8**	**14:47**	....	....	....	....	....	....	....	....	....
2004-05	Ljubljana	Slovenia	13	6	7	13	20	....	....	....	....	....	....	....	....	....	....	....	....	....	....	....	....	....	....
	Ljubljana	Interliga	13	7	7	14	16	....	....	....	....	....	....	....	....	....	....	....	....	....	....	....	....	....	....
	HV 71 Jonkoping	Sweden	20	5	2	7	16	....	....	....	....	....	....	....	....	....	....	....	....	....	....	....	....	....	....
2005-06	**Columbus**	**NHL**	**58**	**10**	**21**	**31**	**41**	**1**	**1**	**0**	**102**	**9.8**	**1**	**827**	**56.4**	**16:21**	....	....	....	....	....	....	....	....	....
2006-07	**Columbus**	**NHL**	**82**	**9**	**16**	**25**	**76**	**2**	**0**	**3**	**109**	**8.3**	**–8**	**1127**	**55.1**	**14:48**	....	....	....	....	....	....	....	....	....
2007-08	**Columbus**	**NHL**	**71**	**11**	**18**	**29**	**34**	**2**	**0**	**2**	**112**	**9.8**	**–3**	**1158**	**59.0**	**16:28**	....	....	....	....	....	....	....	....	....
2008-09	**Columbus**	**NHL**	**77**	**11**	**24**	**35**	**28**	**0**	**0**	**3**	**116**	**9.5**	**9**	**1380**	**58.0**	**18:01**	**4**	**0**	**0**	**0**	**0**	**0**	**0**	**0**	**17:54**
2009-10	**San Jose**	**NHL**	**71**	**14**	**19**	**33**	**41**	**2**	**0**	**4**	**111**	**12.6**	**17**	**664**	**62.5**	**15:37**	**15**	**1**	**0**	**1**	**0**	**1**	**0**	**0**	**16:55**
2010-11	**Vancouver**	**NHL**	**72**	**11**	**19**	**30**	**22**	**3**	**1**	**2**	**111**	**9.9**	**9**	**1261**	**61.7**	**16:10**	**6**	**0**	**0**	**0**	**0**	**0**	**0**	**0**	**11:50**
2011-12	**Vancouver**	**NHL**	**78**	**7**	**11**	**18**	**14**	**0**	**0**	**2**	**60**	**11.7**	**–11**	**916**	**58.5**	**12:21**	**5**	**0**	**0**	**0**	**0**	**0**	**0**	**0**	**9:41**
2012-13	**Vancouver**	**NHL**	**9**	**0**	**0**	**0**	**0**	**0**	**0**	**0**	**2**	**0.0**	**–3**	**98**	**65.3**	**11:08**	....	....	....	....	....	....	....	....	....
2013-14	**Carolina**	**NHL**	**69**	**7**	**6**	**13**	**18**	**0**	**0**	**1**	**53**	**13.2**	**0**	**952**	**59.5**	**11:36**	....	....	....	....	....	....	....	....	....
	Charlotte	AHL	8	0	0	0	17	....	....	....	....	....	....	....	....	....	....	....	....	....	....	....	....	....	....
2014-15	**Montreal**	**NHL**	**58**	**1**	**3**	**4**	**12**	**0**	**0**	**1**	**46**	**2.2**	**–6**	**906**	**59.3**	**10:51**	....	....	....	....	....	....	....	....	....
	NHL Totals		**991**	**116**	**179**	**295**	**451**	**12**	**3**	**26**	**1176**	**9.9**		**11988**	**56.4**	**13:03**	**35**	**2**	**0**	**2**	**0**	**1**	**0**	**0**	**13:53**

Memorial Cup All-Star Team (1998) • George Parsons Trophy (Memorial Cup - Most Sportsmanlike Player) (1998)

Traded to **Dallas** by **NY Rangers** with Barrett Heisten for Martin Rucinsky and Roman Lyashenko, March 12, 2002. Claimed on waivers by **Columbus** from **Dallas**, November 21, 2003. Signed as a free agent by **Ljubljana** (Slovenia), October 8, 2004. Signed as a free agent by **Jonkoping** (Sweden), December 20, 2004. Signed as a free agent by **San Jose**, September 23, 2009. Signed as a free agent by **Vancouver**, July 1, 2010. • Missed majority of 2012-13 due to recurring eye injury. Signed as a free agent by **Carolina**, October 31, 2013. Signed as a free agent by **Montreal**, July 1, 2014.

MALKIN, Evgeni

(MAHL-kihn, ehv-GEH-nee) **PIT**

Center. Shoots left. 6'3", 195 lbs. Born, Magnitogorsk, USSR, July 31, 1986. Pittsburgh's 1st choice, 2nd overall, in 2004 Entry Draft.

Season	Club	League	GP	G	A	Pts	PIM	PP	SH	GW	S	S%	+/-	TF	F%	Min	Playoffs GP	G	A	Pts	PIM	PP	SH	GW	Min
2002-03	Magnitogorsk 2	Russia-3	STATISTICS NOT AVAILABLE																						
2003-04	Magnitogorsk 2	Russia-3	2	1	0	1	8																		
	Magnitogorsk	Russia	34	3	9	12	12																		
2004-05	Magnitogorsk 2	Russia-3	2	1	1	2	2																		
	Magnitogorsk	Russia	52	12	20	32	24										5	0	4	4	0				
2005-06	Magnitogorsk	Russia	46	21	26	47	46										11	5	10	15	41				
	Russia	Olympics	7	2	4	6	31																		
2006-07	**Pittsburgh**	**NHL**	**78**	**33**	**52**	**85**	**80**	**16**	**0**	**6**	**242**	**13.6**	**2**	**728**	**43.3**	**19:10**	**5**	**0**	**4**	**4**	**8**	**0**	**0**	**0**	**19:34**
2007-08	**Pittsburgh**	**NHL**	**82**	**47**	**59**	**106**	**78**	**17**	**0**	**5**	**272**	**17.3**	**16**	**890**	**39.3**	**21:19**	**20**	**10**	**12**	**22**	**24**	**5**	**1**	**3**	**20:48**
2008-09 ♦	**Pittsburgh**	**NHL**	**82**	**35**	***78**	***113**	**80**	**14**	**2**	**4**	**290**	**12.1**	**17**	**668**	**42.4**	**22:31**	**24**	**14**	***22**	***36**	**51**	***7**	**0**	***3**	**20:57**
2009-10	**Pittsburgh**	**NHL**	**67**	**28**	**49**	**77**	**100**	**13**	**2**	**7**	**268**	**10.4**	**−6**	**498**	**40.0**	**20:51**	**13**	**5**	**6**	**11**	**6**	**4**	**0**	**1**	**21:54**
	Russia	Olympics	4	3	3	6	0																		
2010-11	**Pittsburgh**	**NHL**	**43**	**15**	**22**	**37**	**18**	**5**	**0**	**3**	**182**	**8.2**	**−4**	**200**	**38.5**	**19:49**									
2011-12	**Pittsburgh**	**NHL**	**75**	**50**	**59**	***109**	**70**	**12**	**0**	**9**	**339**	**14.7**	**18**	**1210**	**47.5**	**21:01**	**6**	**3**	**5**	**8**	**6**	**1**	**0**	**0**	**22:15**
2012-13	Magnitogorsk	KHL	37	23	42	65	58																		
	Pittsburgh	**NHL**	**31**	**9**	**24**	**33**	**36**	**4**	**0**	**3**	**99**	**9.1**	**5**	**413**	**47.2**	**19:42**	**15**	**4**	**12**	**16**	**26**	**0**	**0**	**1**	**20:29**
2013-14	**Pittsburgh**	**NHL**	**60**	**23**	**49**	**72**	**62**	**7**	**0**	**3**	**191**	**12.0**	**10**	**621**	**48.8**	**20:04**	**13**	**6**	**8**	**14**	**8**	**1**	**0**	**1**	**21:00**
	Russia	Olympics	5	1	2	3	2																		
2014-15	**Pittsburgh**	**NHL**	**69**	**28**	**42**	**70**	**60**	**9**	**0**	**4**	**212**	**13.2**	**−2**	**755**	**42.7**	**18:58**	**5**	**0**	**0**	**0**	**0**	**0**	**0**	**0**	**19:19**
	NHL Totals		**587**	**268**	**434**	**702**	**584**	**97**	**4**	**44**	**2095**	**12.8**		**5983**	**43.8**	**20:31**	**101**	**42**	**69**	**111**	**129**	**18**	**1**	**9**	**20:55**

NHL All-Rookie Team (2007) • Calder Memorial Trophy (2007) • NHL First All-Star Team (2008, 2009, 2012) • Art Ross Trophy (2009, 2012) • Conn Smythe Trophy (2009) • Ted Lindsay Award (2012) • Hart Memorial Trophy (2012)

Played in NHL All-Star Game (2008, 2009, 2012)

Signed as a free agent by **Magnitogorsk** (KHL), September 16, 2012.

MALONE, Brad

(ma-LOHN, BRAD) **CAR**

Center/Left wing. Shoots left. 6'2", 207 lbs. Born, Miramichi, NB, May 20, 1989. Colorado's 5th choice, 105th overall, in 2007 Entry Draft.

Season	Club	League	GP	G	A	Pts	PIM	PP	SH	GW	S	S%	+/-	TF	F%	Min	Playoffs GP	G	A	Pts	PIM	PP	SH	GW	Min
2005-06	Cushing	High-MA	36	9	33	42	....																		
2006-07	Sioux Falls	USHL	57	14	19	33	134										8	3	1	4	24				
2007-08	North Dakota	WCHA	34	1	2	3	44																		
2008-09	North Dakota	WCHA	41	5	12	17	75																		
2009-10	North Dakota	WCHA	43	11	14	25	*102																		
2010-11	North Dakota	WCHA	43	16	24	40	*108																		
	Lake Erie	AHL	....	....	....	....	....										3	0	1	1	2				
2011-12	**Colorado**	**NHL**	**9**	**0**	**2**	**2**	**0**	**0**	**0**	**0**	**6**	**0.0**	**1**	**8**	**12.5**	**10:03**									
	Lake Erie	AHL	67	11	25	36	89																		
2012-13	Lake Erie	AHL	63	10	14	24	99																		
	Colorado	**NHL**	**13**	**1**	**1**	**2**	**16**	**0**	**0**	**0**	**10**	**10.0**	**−7**	**46**	**47.8**	**8:47**									
2013-14	**Colorado**	**NHL**	**32**	**3**	**2**	**5**	**23**	**0**	**0**	**0**	**16**	**18.8**	**−4**	**96**	**46.9**	**6:46**	**6**	**0**	**0**	**0**	**2**	**0**	**0**	**0**	**5:53**
	Lake Erie	AHL	35	8	7	15	75																		
2014-15	**Carolina**	**NHL**	**65**	**7**	**8**	**15**	**74**	**0**	**0**	**2**	**65**	**10.8**	**−8**	**49**	**61.2**	**10:09**									
	NHL Totals		**119**	**11**	**13**	**24**	**113**	**0**	**0**	**2**	**97**	**11.3**		**199**	**49.2**	**9:05**	**6**	**0**	**0**	**0**	**2**	**0**	**0**	**0**	**5:53**

Signed as a free agent by **Carolina**, July 1, 2014.

MALONE, Ryan

(ma-LOHN, RIGH-uhn)

Left wing. Shoots left. 6'4", 224 lbs. Born, Pittsburgh, PA, December 1, 1979. Pittsburgh's 5th choice, 115th overall, in 1999 Entry Draft.

Season	Club	League	GP	G	A	Pts	PIM	PP	SH	GW	S	S%	+/-	TF	F%	Min	Playoffs GP	G	A	Pts	PIM	PP	SH	GW	Min
1997-98	Shat.-St. Mary's	High-MN	50	41	44	85	69																		
1998-99	Omaha Lancers	USHL	51	14	22	36	81										12	2	4	6	23				
99-2000	St. Cloud State	WCHA	38	9	21	30	68																		
2000-01	St. Cloud State	WCHA	36	7	18	25	52																		
2001-02	St. Cloud State	WCHA	41	24	25	49	76																		
2002-03	St. Cloud State	WCHA	27	16	20	36	85																		
	Wilkes-Barre	AHL	3	0	1	1	2																		
2003-04	**Pittsburgh**	**NHL**	**81**	**22**	**21**	**43**	**64**	**5**	**3**	**4**	**139**	**15.8**	**−23**	**230**	**27.4**	**18:54**									
2004-05	Blues Espoo	Finland	9	2	1	3	36																		
	SV Renon	Italy	10	6	2	8	20										6	4	4	8	36				
	HC Ambri-Piotta	Swiss	....	....	....	....	....										1	0	0	0	2				
2005-06	**Pittsburgh**	**NHL**	**77**	**22**	**22**	**44**	**63**	**10**	**5**	**1**	**153**	**14.4**	**−22**	**728**	**39.6**	**18:06**									
2006-07	**Pittsburgh**	**NHL**	**64**	**16**	**15**	**31**	**71**	**1**	**1**	**0**	**125**	**12.8**	**4**	**109**	**44.0**	**16:15**	**5**	**0**	**0**	**0**	**0**	**0**	**0**	**0**	**13:48**
2007-08	**Pittsburgh**	**NHL**	**77**	**27**	**24**	**51**	**103**	**11**	**2**	**6**	**159**	**17.0**	**14**	**38**	**31.6**	**19:05**	**20**	**6**	**10**	**16**	**25**	**3**	**0**	**2**	**18:43**
2008-09	**Tampa Bay**	**NHL**	**70**	**26**	**19**	**45**	**98**	**7**	**0**	**3**	**124**	**21.0**	**4**	**47**	**29.8**	**17:45**									
2009-10	**Tampa Bay**	**NHL**	**69**	**21**	**26**	**47**	**68**	**7**	**0**	**7**	**172**	**12.2**	**−8**	**97**	**39.2**	**18:46**									
	United States	Olympics	6	3	2	5	6																		
2010-11	**Tampa Bay**	**NHL**	**54**	**14**	**24**	**38**	**51**	**9**	**0**	**1**	**149**	**9.4**	**−3**	**143**	**39.2**	**16:02**	**18**	**3**	**3**	**6**	**24**	**1**	**0**	**1**	**15:35**
2011-12	**Tampa Bay**	**NHL**	**68**	**20**	**28**	**48**	**82**	**5**	**1**	**2**	**144**	**13.9**	**−11**	**79**	**36.7**	**17:41**									
2012-13	**Tampa Bay**	**NHL**	**24**	**6**	**2**	**8**	**22**	**2**	**0**	**1**	**37**	**16.2**	**−3**	**23**	**39.1**	**15:44**									
2013-14	**Tampa Bay**	**NHL**	**57**	**5**	**10**	**15**	**67**	**0**	**0**	**0**	**95**	**5.3**	**−7**	**7**	**28.6**	**11:47**									
2014-15	**NY Rangers**	**NHL**	**6**	**0**	**0**	**0**	**4**	**0**	**0**	**0**	**6**	**0.0**	**−4**	**1**	**100.0**	**10:02**									
	Hartford	AHL	24	4	6	10	29																		
	NHL Totals		**647**	**179**	**191**	**370**	**693**	**57**	**12**	**25**	**1303**	**13.7**		**1502**	**37.3**	**17:14**	**43**	**9**	**13**	**22**	**49**	**4**	**0**	**3**	**16:50**

NHL All-Rookie Team (2004)

Signed as a free agent by **Espoo** (Finland), September 29, 2004. Signed as a free agent by **Renon** (Italy), January 3, 2005. Signed as a free agent by **Ambri-Piotta** (Swiss), February 25, 2005. Traded to **Tampa Bay** by **Pittsburgh** with Gary Roberts for Tampa Bay's 3rd round choice (Ben Hanowski) in 2009 Entry Draft, June 28, 2008. • Missed majority of 2012-13 due to lower-body and shoulder injuries. Signed as a free agent by **NY Rangers**, September 11, 2014.

MANCARI, Mark

(man-KAIR-ee, MAHRK)

Right wing. Shoots right. 6'3", 225 lbs. Born, London, ON, July 11, 1985. Buffalo's 6th choice, 207th overall, in 2004 Entry Draft.

Season	Club	League	GP	G	A	Pts	PIM	PP	SH	GW	S	S%	+/-	TF	F%	Min	Playoffs GP	G	A	Pts	PIM	PP	SH	GW	Min
2001-02	Ottawa 67's	OHL	34	3	3	6	10										2	0	1	1	0				
2002-03	Ottawa 67's	OHL	61	8	11	19	20										11	2	1	3	2				
2003-04	Ottawa 67's	OHL	67	29	36	65	56										7	5	3	8	11				
2004-05	Ottawa 67's	OHL	64	36	32	68	86										21	*14	10	24	24				
2005-06	Rochester	AHL	71	18	24	42	80																		
2006-07	**Buffalo**	**NHL**	**3**	**0**	**1**	**1**	**2**	**0**	**0**	**0**	**1**	**0.0**	**−1**	**0**	**0.0**	**6:12**									
	Rochester	AHL	64	23	34	57	49										6	1	5	6	6				
2007-08	Rochester	AHL	80	21	36	57	78																		
2008-09	**Buffalo**	**NHL**	**7**	**1**	**1**	**2**	**4**	**0**	**0**	**0**	**21**	**4.8**	**−4**	**7**	**57.1**	**13:16**									
	Portland Pirates	AHL	73	29	38	67	61										5	1	2	3	2				
2009-10	**Buffalo**	**NHL**	**6**	**1**	**1**	**2**	**4**	**0**	**0**	**0**	**19**	**5.3**	**3**	**3**	**0.0**	**14:04**									
	Portland Pirates	AHL	74	28	46	74	55										4	1	1	2	2				
2010-11	**Buffalo**	**NHL**	**20**	**1**	**7**	**8**	**12**	**1**	**0**	**0**	**43**	**2.3**	**−1**	**6**	**50.0**	**12:19**	**1**	**0**	**0**	**0**	**0**	**0**	**0**	**0**	**9:50**
	Portland Pirates	AHL	56	32	32	64	57										9	6	6	12	0				
2011-12	**Vancouver**	**NHL**	**6**	**0**	**0**	**0**	**0**	**0**	**0**	**0**	**5**	**0.0**	**0**	**2**	**0.0**	**8:19**									
	Chicago Wolves	AHL	69	30	28	58	40										5	0	7	7	6				
2012-13	Rochester	AHL	76	22	39	61	68										3	0	2	2	12				
2013-14	Chicago Wolves	AHL	44	9	22	31	22																		
	San Antonio	AHL	11	0	2	2	2																		
2014-15	San Antonio	AHL	74	13	33	46	41										3	0	1	1	2				
	NHL Totals		**42**	**3**	**10**	**13**	**22**	**1**	**0**	**0**	**89**	**3.4**		**18**	**38.9**	**11:43**	**1**	**0**	**0**	**0**	**0**	**0**	**0**	**0**	**9:50**

AHL First All-Star Team (2011)

Signed as a free agent by **Vancouver**, July 1, 2011. Signed as a free agent by **Buffalo**, July 6, 2012. Signed as a free agent by **St. Louis**, July 5, 2013. Traded to **Florida** by **St. Lous** for Eric Selleck. March 2, 2014.

			Regular Season														Playoffs								
Season	Club	League	GP	G	A	Pts	PIM	PP	SH	GW	S	S%	+/-	TF	F%	Min	GP	G	A	Pts	PIM	PP	SH	GW	Min

MANNING, Brandon

(MAN-nihng, BRAN-duhn) **PHI**

Defense. Shoots left. 6'1", 205 lbs. Born, Prince George, BC, June 4, 1990.

2007-08	Prince George	BCHL	58	7	19	26	107	....	....	....	....	....	....	....	....	....	4	0	3	3	6	....	....	....	....
	Chilliwack Bruins	WHL	6	0	0	0	8	....	....	....	....	....	....	....	....	....	4	0	0	0	4	....	....	....	....
2008-09	Chilliwack Bruins	WHL	72	11	18	29	140	....	....	....	....	....	....	....	....	....	....	....	....	....	....	....	....	....	....
2009-10	Chilliwack Bruins	WHL	69	13	41	54	138	....	....	....	....	....	....	....	....	....	6	0	6	6	10	....	....	....	....
2010-11	Chilliwack Bruins	WHL	53	21	32	53	129	....	....	....	....	....	....	....	....	....	5	1	0	1	8	....	....	....	....
2011-12	**Philadelphia**	**NHL**	**4**	**0**	**0**	**0**	**0**	**0**	**0**	**0**	**6**	**0.0**	**1**	**0**	**0.0**	**13:44**	....	....	....	....	....	....	....	....	....
	Adirondack	AHL	46	6	13	19	81	....	....	....	....	....	....	....	....	....	....	....	....	....	....	....	....	....	....
2012-13	Adirondack	AHL	65	6	15	21	135	....	....	....	....	....	....	....	....	....	....	....	....	....	....	....	....	....	....
	Philadelphia	**NHL**	**6**	**0**	**2**	**2**	**0**	**0**	**0**	**0**	**5**	**0.0**	**4**	**0**	**0.0**	**14:48**	....	....	....	....	....	....	....	....	....
2013-14	Adirondack	AHL	73	8	23	31	231	....	....	....	....	....	....	....	....	....	....	....	....	....	....	....	....	....	....
2014-15	**Philadelphia**	**NHL**	**11**	**0**	**3**	**3**	**7**	**0**	**0**	**0**	**10**	**0.0**	**3**	**0**	**0.0**	**17:10**	....	....	....	....	....	....	....	....	....
	Lehigh Valley	AHL	60	11	32	43	150	....	....	....	....	....	....	....	....	....	....	....	....	....	....	....	....	....	....
	NHL Totals		**21**	**0**	**5**	**5**	**7**	**0**	**0**	**0**	**21**	**0.0**		**0**	**0.0**	**15:50**	....	....	....	....	....	....	....	....	....

Signed as a free agent by **Philadelphia**, November 23, 2010.

MANSON, Josh

(MAN-suhn, JAWSH) **ANA**

Defense. Shoots right. 6'3", 217 lbs. Born, Prince Albert, SK, October 7, 1991. Anaheim's 7th choice, 160th overall, in 2011 Entry Draft.

2008-09	Prince Albert	SMHL	40	19	16	35	64	....	....	....	....	....	....	....	....	....	3	1	0	1	4	....	....	....	....
	Flin Flon Bombers	SJHL	2	0	0	0	0	....	....	....	....	....	....	....	....	....	....	....	....	....	....	....	....	....	....
2009-10	Salmon Arm	BCHL	54	10	14	24	75	....	....	....	....	....	....	....	....	....	6	1	0	1	15	....	....	....	....
2010-11	Salmon Arm	BCHL	57	12	35	47	80	....	....	....	....	....	....	....	....	....	14	2	7	9	15	....	....	....	....
2011-12	Northeastern	H-East	33	0	4	4	48	....	....	....	....	....	....	....	....	....	....	....	....	....	....	....	....	....	....
2012-13	Northeastern	H-East	33	3	4	7	45	....	....	....	....	....	....	....	....	....	....	....	....	....	....	....	....	....	....
2013-14	Northeastern	H-East	33	3	7	10	65	....	....	....	....	....	....	....	....	....	....	....	....	....	....	....	....	....	....
	Norfolk Admirals	AHL	9	1	0	1	26	....	....	....	....	....	....	....	....	....	10	1	0	1	6	....	....	....	....
2014-15	**Anaheim**	**NHL**	**28**	**0**	**3**	**3**	**31**	**0**	**0**	**0**	**26**	**0.0**	**1**	**0**	**0.0**	**18:26**	....	....	....	....	....	....	....	....	....
	Norfolk Admirals	AHL	36	3	9	12	47	....	....	....	....	....	....	....	....	....	....	....	....	....	....	....	....	....	....
	NHL Totals		**28**	**0**	**3**	**3**	**31**	**0**	**0**	**0**	**26**	**0.0**		**0**	**0.0**	**18:26**	....	....	....	....	....	....	....	....	....

Hockey East Second All-Star Team (2014)

MARCHAND, Brad

(mahr-SHAND, BRAD) **BOS**

Left wing. Shoots left. 5'9", 183 lbs. Born, Halifax, NS, May 11, 1988. Boston's 4th choice, 71st overall, in 2006 Entry Draft.

2003-04	Dartmouth	NSMHL	60	47	47	94	104	....	....	....	....	....	....	....	....	....	....	....	....	....	....	....	....	....	....
2004-05	Moncton Wildcats	QMJHL	61	9	20	29	52	....	....	....	....	....	....	....	....	....	11	1	0	1	7	....	....	....	....
2005-06	Moncton Wildcats	QMJHL	68	29	37	66	83	....	....	....	....	....	....	....	....	....	20	5	14	19	34	....	....	....	....
2006-07	Val-d'Or Foreurs	QMJHL	57	33	47	80	108	....	....	....	....	....	....	....	....	....	20	*16	*24	*40	36	....	....	....	....
2007-08	Val-d'Or Foreurs	QMJHL	33	21	23	44	36	....	....	....	....	....	....	....	....	....	....	....	....	....	....	....	....	....	....
	Halifax	QMJHL	26	10	19	29	40	....	....	....	....	....	....	....	....	....	14	3	16	19	18	....	....	....	....
2008-09	Providence Bruins	AHL	79	18	41	59	67	....	....	....	....	....	....	....	....	....	16	7	8	15	26	....	....	....	....
2009-10	**Boston**	**NHL**	**20**	**0**	**1**	**1**	**20**	**0**	**0**	**0**	**32**	**0.0**	**–3**	**11**	**27.3**	**11:58**	....	....	....	....	....	....	....	....	....
	Providence Bruins	AHL	34	13	19	32	51	....	....	....	....	....	....	....	....	....	....	....	....	....	....	....	....	....	....
2010-11 ♦	**Boston**	**NHL**	**77**	**21**	**20**	**41**	**51**	**2**	**5**	**2**	**149**	**14.1**	**25**	**25**	**32.0**	**13:59**	**25**	**11**	**8**	**19**	**40**	**0**	**1**	**1**	**16:46**
2011-12	**Boston**	**NHL**	**76**	**28**	**27**	**55**	**87**	**5**	**1**	**3**	**167**	**16.8**	**31**	**9**	**55.6**	**17:37**	**7**	**1**	**1**	**2**	**2**	**0**	**0**	**0**	**18:04**
2012-13	**Boston**	**NHL**	**45**	**18**	**18**	**36**	**27**	**4**	**2**	**5**	**91**	**19.8**	**23**	**12**	**50.0**	**16:58**	**22**	**4**	**9**	**13**	**21**	**0**	**0**	**1**	**19:35**
2013-14	**Boston**	**NHL**	**82**	**25**	**28**	**53**	**64**	**1**	***5**	**5**	**149**	**16.8**	**36**	**23**	**26.1**	**15:57**	**12**	**0**	**5**	**5**	**18**	**0**	**0**	**0**	**17:38**
2014-15	**Boston**	**NHL**	**77**	**24**	**18**	**42**	**95**	**2**	**2**	**5**	**180**	**13.3**	**5**	**33**	**39.4**	**16:54**	....	....	....	....	....	....	....	....	....
	NHL Totals		**377**	**116**	**112**	**228**	**344**	**14**	**15**	**20**	**768**	**15.1**		**113**	**36.3**	**15:59**	**66**	**16**	**23**	**39**	**81**	**0**	**1**	**2**	**18:00**

MARCHENKO, Alexey

(MAHR-chehn-koh, al-EHX-ay) **DET**

Defense. Shoots right. 6'3", 210 lbs. Born, Moscow, Russia, January 2, 1992. Detroit's 9th choice, 205th overall, in 2011 Entry Draft.

2009-10	CSKA Jr.	Russia-Jr.	43	11	23	34	59	....	....	....	....	....	....	....	....	....	2	0	0	0	4	....	....	....	....
	CSKA Moscow	KHL	10	0	0	0	0	....	....	....	....	....	....	....	....	....	....	....	....	....	....	....	....	....	....
2010-11	CSKA Jr.	Russia-Jr.	36	5	33	38	28	....	....	....	....	....	....	....	....	....	15	3	8	11	31	....	....	....	....
	CSKA Moscow	KHL	22	0	2	2	4	....	....	....	....	....	....	....	....	....	....	....	....	....	....	....	....	....	....
2011-12	CSKA Jr.	Russia-Jr.	5	2	4	6	10	....	....	....	....	....	....	....	....	....	19	4	14	18	18	....	....	....	....
	CSKA Moscow	KHL	6	0	0	0	2	....	....	....	....	....	....	....	....	....	5	0	1	1	4	....	....	....	....
2012-13	CSKA Moscow	KHL	44	4	5	9	6	....	....	....	....	....	....	....	....	....	7	0	0	0	0	....	....	....	....
2013-14	**Detroit**	**NHL**	**1**	**0**	**0**	**0**	**2**	**0**	**0**	**0**	**0**	**0.0**	**2**	**0**	**0.0**	**13:21**	....	....	....	....	....	....	....	....	....
	Grand Rapids	AHL	49	3	15	18	14	....	....	....	....	....	....	....	....	....	....	....	....	....	....	....	....	....	....
2014-15	**Detroit**	**NHL**	**13**	**1**	**1**	**2**	**2**	**0**	**0**	**0**	**7**	**14.3**	**1**	**0**	**0.0**	**15:26**	**3**	**0**	**0**	**0**	**0**	**0**	**0**	**0**	**16:52**
	Grand Rapids	AHL	51	3	17	20	26	....	....	....	....	....	....	....	....	....	11	0	4	4	2	....	....	....	....
	NHL Totals		**14**	**1**	**1**	**2**	**4**	**0**	**0**	**0**	**7**	**14.3**		**0**	**0.0**	**15:17**	**3**	**0**	**0**	**0**	**0**	**0**	**0**	**0**	**16:52**

MARCHESSAULT, Jon

(mahr-SHUH-sohn, JAWN) **T.B.**

Center. Shoots right. 5'9", 175 lbs. Born, Cap-Rouge, QC, December 27, 1990.

2007-08	Quebec Remparts	QMJHL	56	10	10	20	18	....	....	....	....	....	....	....	....	....	11	1	0	1	6	....	....	....	....
2008-09	Quebec Remparts	QMJHL	62	18	35	53	75	....	....	....	....	....	....	....	....	....	14	2	4	6	10	....	....	....	....
2009-10	Quebec Remparts	QMJHL	68	30	41	71	54	....	....	....	....	....	....	....	....	....	9	3	11	14	14	....	....	....	....
2010-11	Quebec Remparts	QMJHL	68	40	55	95	41	....	....	....	....	....	....	....	....	....	18	11	22	33	12	....	....	....	....
2011-12	Connecticut	AHL	76	24	40	64	50	....	....	....	....	....	....	....	....	....	9	4	0	4	26	....	....	....	....
2012-13	Springfield	AHL	74	21	46	67	65	....	....	....	....	....	....	....	....	....	8	0	3	3	8	....	....	....	....
	Columbus	**NHL**	**2**	**0**	**0**	**0**	**0**	**0**	**0**	**0**	**0**	**0.0**	**–1**	**0**	**0.0**	**10:57**	....	....	....	....	....	....	....	....	....
2013-14	Springfield	AHL	56	14	27	41	51	....	....	....	....	....	....	....	....	....	....	....	....	....	....	....	....	....	....
	Syracuse Crunch	AHL	21	9	6	15	8	....	....	....	....	....	....	....	....	....	....	....	....	....	....	....	....	....	....
2014-15	**Tampa Bay**	**NHL**	**2**	**1**	**0**	**1**	**0**	**0**	**0**	**0**	**3**	**33.3**	**1**	**3**	**33.3**	**11:57**	**2**	**0**	**0**	**0**	**0**	**0**	**0**	**0**	**11:28**
	Syracuse Crunch	AHL	68	24	43	67	38	....	....	....	....	....	....	....	....	....	3	0	0	0	0	....	....	....	....
	NHL Totals		**4**	**1**	**0**	**1**	**0**	**0**	**0**	**0**	**3**	**33.3**		**3**	**33.3**	**11:27**	**2**	**0**	**0**	**0**	**0**	**0**	**0**	**0**	**11:28**

QMJHL First All-Star Team (2011) • AHL First All-Star Team (2013)

Signed as a free agent by **Columbus**, July 1, 2012. Traded to **Tampa Bay** by **Columbus** with Dalton Smith for Matt Taormina and Dana Tyrell, March 5, 2014.

MARINCIN, Martin

(mah-RIHN-chihn, MAHR-tihn) **TOR**

Defense. Shoots left. 6'4", 203 lbs. Born, Kosice, Czech., February 18, 1992. Edmonton's 3rd choice, 46th overall, in 2010 Entry Draft.

2006-07	HC Kosice U18	Svk-U18	16	0	3	3	6	....	....	....	....	....	....	....	....	....	....	....	....	....	....	....	....	....	....
2007-08	HC Kosice U18	Svk-U18	59	3	29	32	36	....	....	....	....	....	....	....	....	....	....	....	....	....	....	....	....	....	....
2008-09	HC Kosice U18	Svk-U18	5	4	4	8	35	....	....	....	....	....	....	....	....	....	....	....	....	....	....	....	....	....	....
	HC Kosice Jr.	Slovak-Jr.	46	11	15	26	50	....	....	....	....	....	....	....	....	....	3	0	0	0	0	....	....	....	....
2009-10	Slovakia U20	Slovakia	35	2	4	6	71	....	....	....	....	....	....	....	....	....	....	....	....	....	....	....	....	....	....
	HC Kosice Jr.	Slovak-Jr.	....	....	....	....	....	....	....	....	....	....	....	....	....	....	2	0	0	0	0	....	....	....	....
2010-11	Prince George	WHL	67	14	42	56	65	....	....	....	....	....	....	....	....	....	4	1	4	5	6	....	....	....	....
	Oklahoma City	AHL	1	0	0	0	2	....	....	....	....	....	....	....	....	....	....	....	....	....	....	....	....	....	....
2011-12	Prince George	WHL	30	4	13	17	25	....	....	....	....	....	....	....	....	....	....	....	....	....	....	....	....	....	....
	Regina Pats	WHL	28	7	16	23	10	....	....	....	....	....	....	....	....	....	5	2	0	2	6	....	....	....	....
	Oklahoma City	AHL	6	0	1	1	2	....	....	....	....	....	....	....	....	....	....	....	....	....	....	....	....	....	....
2012-13	Oklahoma City	AHL	69	7	23	30	40	....	....	....	....	....	....	....	....	....	17	1	6	7	2	....	....	....	....
2013-14	**Edmonton**	**NHL**	**44**	**0**	**6**	**6**	**16**	**0**	**0**	**0**	**28**	**0.0**	**–2**	**0**	**0.0**	**19:10**	....	....	....	....	....	....	....	....	....
	Oklahoma City	AHL	24	3	4	7	4	....	....	....	....	....	....	....	....	....	....	....	....	....	....	....	....	....	....
	Slovakia	Olympics	4	0	0	0	4	....	....	....	....	....	....	....	....	....	....	....	....	....	....	....	....	....	....

Season	Club	League	GP	G	A	Pts	PIM	PP	SH	GW	S	S%	+/-	TF	F%	Min	GP	G	A	Pts	PIM	PP	SH	GW	Min
								Regular Season												Playoffs				

Season	Club	League	GP	G	A	Pts	PIM	PP	SH	GW	S	S%	+/-	TF	F%	Min	GP	G	A	Pts	PIM	PP	SH	GW	Min
2014-15	Edmonton	NHL	41	1	4	5	16	0	0	0	38	2.6	−4		1100.0	18:39	....	....	....	....	....	....	....	....	....
	Oklahoma City	AHL	28	0	7	7	20										8	0	2	2	6	....	....	....	....
	NHL Totals		85	1	10	11	32	0	0	0	66	1.5			1100.0	18:55	....								

Traded to **Toronto** by **Edmonton** for Brad Ross and Pittsburgh's 4th round choice (previously acquired, later traded to Ottawa – Ottawa selected Christian Wolanin) in 2015 Entry Draft, June 27, 2015.

MARKOV, Andrei   (MAHR-kahf, AHN-dray)   MTL

Defense. Shoots left. 6', 197 lbs.   Born, Voskresensk, USSR, December 20, 1978. Montreal's 6th choice, 162nd overall, in 1998 Entry Draft.

Season	Club	League	GP	G	A	Pts	PIM	PP	SH	GW	S	S%	+/-	TF	F%	Min	GP	G	A	Pts	PIM	PP	SH	GW	Min
1995-96	Voskresensk	CIS	38	0	0	0	14										....	....	....	....	....				
1996-97	Voskresensk	Russia	43	8	4	12	32										2	1	1	2	0	....	....		
1997-98	Voskresensk	Russia	43	10	5	15	83										....	....	....	....	....				
1998-99	Dynamo Moscow	Russia	38	10	11	21	32										16	3	6	9	6	....	....		
	Dynamo Moscow	EuroHL	12	7	5	12	12										6	2	2	4	4				
99-2000	Dynamo Moscow	Russia	29	11	12	23	28										17	4	3	7	8				
2000-01	**Montreal**	NHL	63	6	17	23	18	2	0	0	82	7.3	−6	2	50.0	16:53	....	....	....	....	....				
	Quebec Citadelles	AHL	14	0	5	5	4										7	1	1	2	2				
2001-02	**Montreal**	NHL	56	5	19	24	24	2	0	1	73	6.8	−1	0	0.0	17:15	12	1	3	4	8	0	0	1	15:53
	Quebec Citadelles	AHL	12	4	6	10	7										....	....	....	....	....				
2002-03	**Montreal**	NHL	79	13	24	37	34	3	0	2	159	8.2	13	1	0.0	23:17	....	....	....	....	....				
2003-04	**Montreal**	NHL	69	6	22	28	20	2	0	0	105	5.7	−2	2	50.0	21:29	11	1	4	5	8	0	0	1	22:52
2004-05	Dynamo Moscow	Russia	42	7	16	23	76										10	2	0	2	22				
2005-06	**Montreal**	NHL	67	10	36	46	74	6	1	1	88	11.4	13	1	0.0	23:33	6	0	1	1	4	0	0	0	25:29
	Russia	Olympics	8	1	2	3	6										....	....	....	....	....				
2006-07	**Montreal**	NHL	77	6	43	49	56	5	0	2	128	4.7	2	1	0.0	24:29	....	....	....	....	....				
2007-08	**Montreal**	NHL	82	16	42	58	63	10	1	2	145	11.0	1	0	0.0	24:58	12	1	3	4	8	0	0	0	24:54
2008-09	**Montreal**	NHL	78	12	52	64	36	7	0	3	165	7.3	−2	0	0.0	24:38	....	....	....	....	....				
2009-10	**Montreal**	NHL	45	6	28	34	32	4	0	1	85	7.1	11	0	0.0	23:48	8	0	4	4	0	0	0	0	23:47
	Russia	Olympics	4	0	2	2	0										....	....	....	....	....				
2010-11	**Montreal**	NHL	7	1	2	3	4	0	0	1	20	5.0	2	0	0.0	22:55	....	....	....	....	....				
2011-12	**Montreal**	NHL	13	0	3	3	4	0	0	0	17	0.0	−4	0	0.0	18:00	....	....	....	....	....				
2012-13	Vityaz Chekhov	KHL	21	1	7	8	16										....	....	....	....	....				
	Montreal	NHL	48	10	20	30	14	8	0	4	79	12.7	−9	0	0.0	24:08	5	0	1	1	0	0	0	0	23:54
2013-14	**Montreal**	NHL	81	7	36	43	34	2	1	1	131	5.3	12	0	0.0	25:14	17	1	9	10	10	0	0	0	26:00
	Russia	Olympics	5	0	2	2	0										....	....	....	....	....				
2014-15	**Montreal**	NHL	81	10	40	50	38	4	0	1	135	7.4	22	0	0.0	24:55	12	1	1	2	8	0	0	0	24:04
	NHL Totals		846	108	384	492	451	55	3	19	1412	7.6		7	28.6	23:01	83	5	26	31	46	0	0	2	23:18

Played in NHL All-Star Game (2008, 2009)

Signed as a free agent by **Dynamo Moscow** (Russia), June 19, 2004. • Missed majority of 2010-11 and 2011-12 due to knee injury vs. Carolina, November 13, 2010. Signed as a free agent by **Chekhov** (KHL), October 3, 2012.

MARLEAU, Patrick   (mahr-LOH, PAT-rihk)   S.J.

Center. Shoots left. 6'2", 220 lbs.   Born, Swift Current, SK, September 15, 1979. San Jose's 1st choice, 2nd overall, in 1997 Entry Draft.

Season	Club	League	GP	G	A	Pts	PIM	PP	SH	GW	S	S%	+/-	TF	F%	Min	GP	G	A	Pts	PIM	PP	SH	GW	Min
1993-94	Swift Current	SMHL	53	72	95	167	....										....	....	....	....	....				
1994-95	Swift Current	SMHL	31	30	22	52	18										....	....	....	....	....				
1995-96	Seattle	WHL	72	32	42	74	22										5	3	4	7	4				
1996-97	Seattle	WHL	71	51	74	125	37										15	7	16	23	12				
1997-98	San Jose	NHL	74	13	19	32	14	1	0	2	90	14.4	5			15:11	5	0	1	1	0	0	0	0	
1998-99	San Jose	NHL	81	21	24	45	24	4	0	4	134	15.7	10	1121	43.4	15:11	6	2	1	3	4	2	0	0	11:08
99-2000	San Jose	NHL	81	17	23	40	36	3	0	3	161	10.6	−9	851	42.0	14:11	5	1	1	2	2	1	0	0	11:51
2000-01	San Jose	NHL	81	25	27	52	22	5	0	4	146	17.1	7	1088	44.8	16:17	6	2	0	2	4	0	0	0	14:50
2001-02	San Jose	NHL	79	21	23	44	40	3	0	5	121	17.4	9	897	47.3	14:04	12	6	5	11	6	1	0	3	15:50
2002-03	San Jose	NHL	82	28	29	57	33	8	1	3	172	16.3	−10	1403	47.3	18:31	....	....	....	....	....				
2003-04	San Jose	NHL	80	28	29	57	24	9	2	5	220	12.7	−5	1014	41.6	18:12	17	8	4	12	6	4	1	2	19:16
2004-05				DID NOT PLAY																					
2005-06	San Jose	NHL	82	34	52	86	26	20	1	4	260	13.1	−12	1216	46.8	19:56	11	9	5	14	8	4	0	2	21:07
2006-07	San Jose	NHL	77	32	46	78	33	14	0	9	180	17.8	9	693	50.5	18:34	11	3	3	6	2	1	0	1	18:59
2007-08	San Jose	NHL	78	19	29	48	33	7	0	2	185	10.3	−19	605	52.4	18:14	13	4	4	8	2	0	*2	0	23:04
2008-09	San Jose	NHL	76	38	33	71	18	11	5	10	251	15.1	16	591	52.5	21:21	6	2	1	3	2	1	0	2	20:29
2009-10	San Jose	NHL	82	44	39	83	22	12	4	6	274	16.1	21	615	51.4	21:13	14	8	5	13	8	3	1	2	22:07
	Canada	Olympics	7	2	3	5	0										....	....	....	....	....				
2010-11	San Jose	NHL	82	37	36	73	16	11	2	9	279	13.3	−3	549	52.5	20:47	18	7	6	13	9	3	0	1	22:21
2011-12	San Jose	NHL	82	30	34	64	26	10	0	8	251	12.0	10	467	52.0	20:29	5	0	0	0	4	0	0	0	20:21
2012-13	San Jose	NHL	48	17	14	31	24	6	1	3	150	11.3	−2	150	47.3	19:07	11	5	3	8	2	1	0	1	21:18
2013-14	San Jose	NHL	82	33	37	70	18	11	2	4	285	11.6	0	308	52.9	20:31	7	3	4	7	2	0	0	1	20:07
	Canada	Olympics	6	0	4	4	2										....	....	....	....	....				
2014-15	San Jose	NHL	82	19	38	57	12	7	0	4	233	8.2	−17	356	48.0	19:35	....	....	....	....	....				
	NHL Totals		1329	456	532	988	421	142	16	87	3392	13.4		11924	47.3	18:30	147	60	43	103	67	21	4	15	19:37

WHL West First All-Star Team (1997)

Played in NHL All-Star Game (2004, 2007, 2009)

MAROON, Patrick   (ma-ROON, PAT-rihk)   ANA

Left wing. Shoots left. 6'3", 230 lbs.   Born, St Louis, MO, April 23, 1988. Philadelphia's 6th choice, 161st overall, in 2007 Entry Draft.

Season	Club	League	GP	G	A	Pts	PIM	PP	SH	GW	S	S%	+/-	TF	F%	Min	GP	G	A	Pts	PIM	PP	SH	GW	Min
2005-06	Texarkana Bandits	NAHL	57	23	37	60	61										8	3	1	4	22	....	....		
2006-07	St. Louis Bandits	NAHL	57	40	55	*95	152										12	*10	*13	*23	12	....	....		
2007-08	London Knights	OHL	64	35	55	90	57										5	0	1	1	10	....	....		
	Philadelphia	AHL	1	0	0	0	0										....	....	....	....	....				
2008-09	Philadelphia	AHL	80	23	31	54	62										4	1	2	3	13				
2009-10	Adirondack	AHL	67	11	33	44	125										....	....	....	....	....				
2010-11	Adirondack	AHL	9	5	3	8	30										....	....	....	....	....				
	Syracuse Crunch	AHL	57	21	27	48	68										....	....	....	....	....				
2011-12	**Anaheim**	NHL	2	0	0	0	2	0	0	0	1	0.0	0	0	0.0	12:33	....	....	....	....	....				
	Syracuse Crunch	AHL	75	32	42	74	120										4	0	4	4	4				
2012-13	Norfolk Admirals	AHL	64	26	24	50	139										....	....	....	....	....				
	Anaheim	NHL	13	2	1	3	10	0	0	0	21	9.5	−1	14	28.6	9:47	....	....	....	....	....				
2013-14	**Anaheim**	NHL	62	11	18	29	101	1	0	3	93	11.8	11	15	46.7	12:19	13	2	5	7	38	1	0	0	13:04
2014-15	**Anaheim**	NHL	71	9	25	34	82	1	0	1	120	7.5	−5	21	33.3	14:17	16	7	4	11	6	3	0	1	17:56
	NHL Totals		148	22	44	66	195	2	0	4	235	9.4		50	36.0	13:02	29	9	9	18	44	4	0	1	15:45

Traded to **Anaheim** by **Philadelphia** with David Laliberte for Danny Syvret and Rob Bordson, November 21, 2010.

MARSHALL, Kevin   (MAR-shuhl, KEH-vihn)

Defense. Shoots left. 6'1", 191 lbs.   Born, Boucherville, QC, March 10, 1989. Philadelphia's 2nd choice, 41st overall, in 2007 Entry Draft.

Season	Club	League	GP	G	A	Pts	PIM	PP	SH	GW	S	S%	+/-	TF	F%	Min	GP	G	A	Pts	PIM	PP	SH	GW	Min
2004-05	C.C. Lemoyne	QAAA	39	2	9	11	88										5	0	1	1	16				
2005-06	Lewiston	QMJHL	60	1	10	11	112										6	0	1	1	14				
2006-07	Lewiston	QMJHL	70	5	27	32	141										17	0	7	7	38				
2007-08	Lewiston	QMJHL	66	11	24	35	143										6	1	1	2	12				
2008-09	Quebec Remparts	QMJHL	61	9	29	38	125										17	1	10	11	32				
2009-10	Adirondack	AHL	75	2	7	9	80										....	....	....	....	....				
2010-11	Adirondack	AHL	78	1	14	14	120										....	....	....	....	....				
2011-12	**Philadelphia**	NHL	10	0	0	0	8	0	0	0	6	0.0	−1	0	0.0	8:46	....	....	....	....	....				
	Adirondack	AHL	32	2	3	5	55										....	....	....	....	....				
	Hershey Bears	AHL	31	0	1	1	61										5	0	2	2	0				
2012-13	Hershey Bears	AHL	52	1	4	5	77										....	....	....	....	....				
	Toronto Marlies	AHL	15	1	5	6	10										9	0	2	2	10				

			Regular Season														Playoffs								
Season	Club	League	GP	G	A	Pts	PIM	PP	SH	GW	S	S%	+/-	TF	F%	Min	GP	G	A	Pts	PIM	PP	SH	GW	Min
2013-14	Toronto Marlies	AHL	59	1	9	10	109	....	....	....	....	....	....	....	....	....	12	0	3	3	12	....	....	....	....
2014-15	Toronto Marlies	AHL	44	1	6	7	36	....	....	....	....	....	....	....	....	....	....	....	....	....	....	....	....	....	....
	NHL Totals		**10**	**0**	**0**	**0**	**8**	**0**	**0**	**0**	**6**	**0.0**		**0**	**0.0**	**8:46**	....	....	....	....	....	....	....	....	....

QMJHL Second All-Star Team (2008)

Traded to **Washington** by **Philadelphia** for Matthew Ford, February 2, 2012. Traded to **Toronto** by **Washington** for Nicolas Deschamps, March 14, 2013. Signed as a free agent by **Rogle** (Sweden), August 6, 2015.

MARTIN, Matt
(MAHR-tihn, MAT) **NYI**

Left wing. Shoots left. 6'3", 215 lbs. Born, Windsor, ON, May 8, 1989. NY Islanders' 11th choice, 148th overall, in 2008 Entry Draft.

2005-06	Blenheim Blast	ON-Jr.C	40	11	12	23	102	....	....	....	....	....	....	....	....	....	....	....	....	....	....	....	....	....	....
2006-07	Sarnia Blast	ON-Jr.B	9	2	5	7	16	....	....	....	....	....	....	....	....	....	....	....	....	....	....	....	....	....	....
	Sarnia Sting	OHL	39	3	3	6	52	....	....	....	....	....	....	....	....	....	4	0	0	0	0	....	....	....	....
2007-08	Sarnia Sting	OHL	66	25	13	38	155	....	....	....	....	....	....	....	....	....	9	3	3	6	16	....	....	....	....
2008-09	Sarnia Sting	OHL	61	35	30	65	142	....	....	....	....	....	....	....	....	....	5	3	0	3	10	....	....	....	....
2009-10	**NY Islanders**	**NHL**	**5**	**0**	**2**	**2**	**26**	**0**	**0**	**0**	**10**	**0.0**	**–1**	**0**	**0.0**	**13:14**	....	....	....	....	....	....	....	....	....
	Bridgeport	AHL	76	12	19	31	113	....	....	....	....	....	....	....	....	....	5	1	2	3	4	....	....	....	....
2010-11	**NY Islanders**	**NHL**	**68**	**5**	**9**	**14**	**147**	**0**	**0**	**1**	**60**	**8.3**	**–13**	**27**	**37.0**	**10:57**	....	....	....	....	....	....	....	....	....
	Bridgeport	AHL	7	1	2	3	11	....	....	....	....	....	....	....	....	....	....	....	....	....	....	....	....	....	....
2011-12	**NY Islanders**	**NHL**	**80**	**7**	**7**	**14**	**121**	**0**	**0**	**1**	**130**	**5.4**	**–17**	**23**	**43.5**	**12:09**	....	....	....	....	....	....	....	....	....
2012-13	**NY Islanders**	**NHL**	**48**	**4**	**7**	**11**	**63**	**1**	**0**	**1**	**67**	**6.0**	**–2**	**18**	**33.3**	**11:54**	**6**	**1**	**0**	**1**	**14**	**0**	**0**	**0**	**12:10**
2013-14	**NY Islanders**	**NHL**	**79**	**8**	**6**	**14**	**90**	**0**	**0**	**3**	**120**	**6.7**	**–11**	**9**	**33.3**	**11:54**	....	....	....	....	....	....	....	....	....
2014-15	**NY Islanders**	**NHL**	**78**	**8**	**6**	**14**	**114**	**0**	**0**	**2**	**90**	**8.9**	**–4**	**10**	**50.0**	**11:16**	**7**	**0**	**1**	**1**	**12**	**0**	**0**	**0**	**11:55**
	NHL Totals		**358**	**32**	**37**	**69**	**561**	**1**	**0**	**8**	**477**	**6.7**		**87**	**39.1**	**11:40**	**13**	**1**	**1**	**2**	**26**	**0**	**0**	**0**	**12:02**

MARTIN, Paul
(MAHR-tihn, PAWL) **S.J.**

Defense. Shoots left. 6'1", 200 lbs. Born, Minneapolis, MN, March 5, 1981. New Jersey's 5th choice, 62nd overall, in 2000 Entry Draft.

1998-99	Elk River Elks	High-MN	24	9	11	20	....	....	....	....	....	....	....	....	....	....	....	....	....	....	....	....	....	....	....
99-2000	Elk River Elks	High-MN	24	15	35	50	26	....	....	....	....	....	....	....	....	....	....	....	....	....	....	....	....	....	....
2000-01	U. of Minnesota	WCHA	38	3	17	20	8	....	....	....	....	....	....	....	....	....	....	....	....	....	....	....	....	....	....
2001-02	U. of Minnesota	WCHA	44	8	30	38	22	....	....	....	....	....	....	....	....	....	....	....	....	....	....	....	....	....	....
2002-03	U. of Minnesota	WCHA	45	9	30	39	32	....	....	....	....	....	....	....	....	....	....	....	....	....	....	....	....	....	....
2003-04	**New Jersey**	**NHL**	**70**	**6**	**18**	**24**	**4**	**2**	**0**	**2**	**82**	**7.3**	**12**	**0**	**0.0**	**20:08**	**5**	**1**	**1**	**2**	**4**	**1**	**0**	**0**	**23:40**
2004-05	Fribourg	Swiss	11	3	4	7	2	....	....	....	....	....	....	....	....	....	....	....	....	....	....	....	....	....	....
2005-06	**New Jersey**	**NHL**	**80**	**5**	**32**	**37**	**32**	**3**	**0**	**0**	**97**	**5.2**	**1**	**0**	**0.0**	**23:37**	**9**	**0**	**3**	**3**	**4**	**0**	**0**	**0**	**24:17**
2006-07	**New Jersey**	**NHL**	**82**	**3**	**23**	**26**	**18**	**1**	**0**	**0**	**84**	**3.6**	**–9**	**0**	**0.0**	**25:13**	**11**	**0**	**4**	**4**	**6**	**0**	**0**	**0**	**25:09**
2007-08	**New Jersey**	**NHL**	**73**	**5**	**27**	**32**	**22**	**2**	**0**	**2**	**93**	**5.4**	**20**	**0**	**0.0**	**23:53**	**5**	**1**	**2**	**3**	**2**	**1**	**0**	**0**	**25:35**
2008-09	**New Jersey**	**NHL**	**73**	**5**	**28**	**33**	**36**	**2**	**0**	**1**	**107**	**4.7**	**21**	**0**	**0.0**	**24:22**	**7**	**0**	**4**	**4**	**2**	**0**	**0**	**0**	**26:20**
2009-10	**New Jersey**	**NHL**	**22**	**2**	**9**	**11**	**2**	**1**	**0**	**0**	**21**	**9.5**	**10**	**0**	**0.0**	**22:30**	**5**	**0**	**0**	**0**	**0**	**0**	**0**	**0**	**22:24**
2010-11	**Pittsburgh**	**NHL**	**77**	**3**	**21**	**24**	**16**	**2**	**0**	**1**	**104**	**2.9**	**9**	**0**	**0.0**	**23:22**	**7**	**0**	**2**	**2**	**2**	**0**	**0**	**0**	**24:42**
2011-12	**Pittsburgh**	**NHL**	**73**	**2**	**25**	**27**	**18**	**0**	**0**	**0**	**93**	**2.2**	**9**	**0**	**0.0**	**23:00**	**3**	**1**	**0**	**1**	**0**	**0**	**0**	**0**	**22:08**
2012-13	**Pittsburgh**	**NHL**	**34**	**6**	**17**	**23**	**16**	**2**	**0**	**1**	**38**	**15.8**	**14**	**0**	**0.0**	**25:20**	**15**	**2**	**9**	**11**	**4**	**1**	**0**	**0**	**26:38**
2013-14	**Pittsburgh**	**NHL**	**39**	**3**	**12**	**15**	**10**	**1**	**0**	**2**	**54**	**5.6**	**–4**	**0**	**0.0**	**24:34**	**13**	**0**	**8**	**8**	**6**	**0**	**0**	**0**	**27:20**
	United States	Olympics	4	0	0	0	0	....	....	....	....	....	....	....	....	....	....	....	....	....	....	....	....	....	....
2014-15	**Pittsburgh**	**NHL**	**74**	**3**	**17**	**20**	**20**	**0**	**0**	**0**	**61**	**4.9**	**17**	**0**	**0.0**	**22:47**	**5**	**0**	**2**	**2**	**2**	**0**	**0**	**0**	**24:36**
	NHL Totals		**697**	**43**	**229**	**272**	**194**	**16**	**0**	**9**	**834**	**5.2**		**0**	**0.0**	**23:29**	**85**	**5**	**35**	**40**	**32**	**3**	**0**	**0**	**25:21**

Minnesota High School Player of the Year (1999) • WCHA All-Rookie Team (2001) • WCHA Second All-Star Team (2002, 2003) • NCAA West Second All-American Team (2003) • NCAA Championship All-Tournament Team (2003)

Signed as a free agent by **Fribourg** (Swiss), November 4, 2004. • Missed majority of 2009-10 due to arm injury at Pittsburgh, October 24, 2009. Signed as a free agent by **Pittsburgh**, July 1, 2010. • Missed majority of 2013-14 due to leg (November 25, 2013 vs. Ottawa) and hand (February 19, 2014 vs. Czech Republic (Olympics) injuries. Signed as a free agent by **San Jose**, July 1, 2015.

MARTINEZ, Alec
(mar-TEE-nehz, AL-ehk) **L.A.**

Defense. Shoots left. 6'1", 205 lbs. Born, Rochester Hills, MI, July 26, 1987. Los Angeles' 5th choice, 95th overall, in 2007 Entry Draft.

2004-05	Cedar Rapids	USHL	58	10	11	21	30	....	....	....	....	....	....	....	....	....	11	1	2	3	8	....	....	....	....
2005-06	Miami U.	CCHA	39	3	8	11	31	....	....	....	....	....	....	....	....	....	....	....	....	....	....	....	....	....	....
2006-07	Miami U.	CCHA	42	9	15	24	40	....	....	....	....	....	....	....	....	....	....	....	....	....	....	....	....	....	....
2007-08	Miami U.	CCHA	42	9	23	32	42	....	....	....	....	....	....	....	....	....	....	....	....	....	....	....	....	....	....
2008-09	Manchester	AHL	72	8	15	23	42	....	....	....	....	....	....	....	....	....	....	....	....	....	....	....	....	....	....
2009-10	**Los Angeles**	**NHL**	**4**	**0**	**0**	**0**	**2**	**0**	**0**	**0**	**6**	**0.0**	**–2**	**0**	**0.0**	**15:25**	....	....	....	....	....	....	....	....	....
	Manchester	AHL	55	7	23	30	26	....	....	....	....	....	....	....	....	....	16	0	3	3	10	....	....	....	....
2010-11	**Los Angeles**	**NHL**	**60**	**5**	**11**	**16**	**18**	**1**	**0**	**0**	**74**	**6.8**	**11**	**0**	**0.0**	**15:17**	**6**	**0**	**1**	**1**	**2**	**0**	**0**	**0**	**13:29**
	Manchester	AHL	20	5	11	16	14	....	....	....	....	....	....	....	....	....	....	....	....	....	....	....	....	....	....
2011-12 ♦	**Los Angeles**	**NHL**	**51**	**6**	**6**	**12**	**8**	**3**	**0**	**0**	**78**	**7.7**	**–1**	**1**	**0.0**	**14:43**	**20**	**1**	**2**	**3**	**8**	**0**	**0**	**1**	**14:28**
2012-13	TPS Turku	Finland	11	1	1	2	8	....	....	....	....	....	....	....	....	....	....	....	....	....	....	....	....	....	....
	Allen Americans	CHL	3	1	1	2	0	....	....	....	....	....	....	....	....	....	....	....	....	....	....	....	....	....	....
	Los Angeles	**NHL**	**27**	**1**	**4**	**5**	**10**	**0**	**0**	**0**	**30**	**3.3**	**–2**	**0**	**0.0**	**16:01**	**7**	**0**	**2**	**2**	**8**	**0**	**0**	**0**	**13:14**
2013-14 ♦	**Los Angeles**	**NHL**	**61**	**11**	**11**	**22**	**14**	**3**	**0**	**2**	**79**	**13.9**	**17**	**0**	**0.0**	**15:41**	**26**	**5**	**5**	**10**	**12**	**2**	**0**	**3**	**16:37**
2014-15	**Los Angeles**	**NHL**	**56**	**6**	**16**	**22**	**10**	**1**	**0**	**1**	**103**	**5.8**	**9**	**0**	**0.0**	**19:56**	....	....	....	....	....	....	....	....	....
	NHL Totals		**259**	**29**	**48**	**77**	**62**	**8**	**0**	**3**	**370**	**7.8**		**1**	**0.0**	**16:21**	**59**	**6**	**10**	**16**	**30**	**2**	**0**	**4**	**15:10**

CCHA First All-Star Team (2008) • NCAA West Second All-American Team (2008)

Signed as a free agent by **TPS Turku** (Finland), October 5, 2012. Signed as a free agent by **Allen** (CHL), December 31, 2012.

MARTINOOK, Jordan
(mahr-TIHN-ook, JOHR-dahn) **ARI**

Left wing. Shoots left. 6', 202 lbs. Born, Leduc, AB, July 25, 1992. Phoenix's 2nd choice, 58th overall, in 2012 Entry Draft.

2006-07	Leduc Oil Kings	AMBHL	30	19	14	33	32	....	....	....	....	....	....	....	....	....	....	....	....	....	....	....	....	....	....
2007-08	Leduc Oil Kings	Minor-AB	STATISTICS NOT AVAILABLE																						
	Leduc Oil Kings	AMHL	3	1	0	1	0	....	....	....	....	....	....	....	....	....	....	....	....	....	....	....	....	....	....
2008-09	Leduc Oil Kings	AMHL	33	7	13	20	38	....	....	....	....	....	....	....	....	....	....	....	....	....	....	....	....	....	....
	Drayton Valley	AJHL	2	0	0	0	0	....	....	....	....	....	....	....	....	....	....	....	....	....	....	....	....	....	....
2009-10	Drayton Valley	AJHL	59	21	19	40	48	....	....	....	....	....	....	....	....	....	....	....	....	....	....	....	....	....	....
2010-11	Vancouver Giants	WHL	72	11	17	28	67	....	....	....	....	....	....	....	....	....	4	1	0	1	8	....	....	....	....
2011-12	Vancouver Giants	WHL	72	40	24	64	80	....	....	....	....	....	....	....	....	....	6	3	6	9	2	....	....	....	....
2012-13	Portland Pirates	AHL	53	9	10	19	30	....	....	....	....	....	....	....	....	....	3	0	1	1	0	....	....	....	....
2013-14	Portland Pirates	AHL	67	14	16	30	48	....	....	....	....	....	....	....	....	....	....	....	....	....	....	....	....	....	....
2014-15	**Arizona**	**NHL**	**8**	**0**	**1**	**1**	**0**	**0**	**0**	**0**	**8**	**0.0**	**–3**	**1**	**100.0**	**11:42**	....	....	....	....	....	....	....	....	....
	Portland Pirates	AHL	62	15	28	43	41	....	....	....	....	....	....	....	....	....	....	....	....	....	....	....	....	....	....
	NHL Totals		**8**	**0**	**1**	**1**	**0**	**0**	**0**	**0**	**8**	**0.0**		**1**	**100.0**	**11:42**	....	....	....	....	....	....	....	....	....

MASHINTER, Brandon
(ma-SHIHN-tuhr, BRAN-duhn) **CHI**

Left wing. Shoots left. 6'4", 212 lbs. Born, Bradford, ON, September 20, 1988.

2004-05	Tor. T-Birds	ON-Jr.A	49	3	6	9	19	....	....	....	....	....	....	....	....	....	....	....	....	....	....	....	....	....	....
	Sarnia Sting	OHL	8	0	0	0	9	....	....	....	....	....	....	....	....	....	....	....	....	....	....	....	....	....	....
2005-06	Sarnia Sting	OHL	65	6	1	7	65	....	....	....	....	....	....	....	....	....	....	....	....	....	....	....	....	....	....
2006-07	Sarnia Sting	OHL	55	7	8	15	49	....	....	....	....	....	....	....	....	....	4	0	2	2	0	....	....	....	....
2007-08	Kitchener Rangers	OHL	62	10	10	20	84	....	....	....	....	....	....	....	....	....	20	2	2	4	16	....	....	....	....
2008-09	Kitchener Rangers	OHL	21	14	12	26	24	....	....	....	....	....	....	....	....	....	....	....	....	....	....	....	....	....	....
	Belleville Bulls	OHL	31	20	12	32	32	....	....	....	....	....	....	....	....	....	17	8	3	11	13	....	....	....	....
2009-10	Worcester Sharks	AHL	79	22	15	37	117	....	....	....	....	....	....	....	....	....	11	1	5	6	6	....	....	....	....
2010-11	**San Jose**	**NHL**	**13**	**0**	**0**	**0**	**17**	**0**	**0**	**0**	**5**	**0.0**	**–2**	**0**	**0.0**	**6:23**	....	....	....	....	....	....	....	....	....
	Worcester Sharks	AHL	62	14	19	33	96	....	....	....	....	....	....	....	....	....	....	....	....	....	....	....	....	....	....
2011-12	Worcester Sharks	AHL	65	16	17	33	67	....	....	....	....	....	....	....	....	....	....	....	....	....	....	....	....	....	....
2012-13	Worcester Sharks	AHL	30	2	3	5	44	....	....	....	....	....	....	....	....	....	....	....	....	....	....	....	....	....	....
	NY Rangers	**NHL**	**4**	**0**	**0**	**0**	**0**	**0**	**0**	**0**	**2**	**0.0**	**–2**	**1**	**100.0**	**5:55**	....	....	....	....	....	....	....	....	....
	Connecticut	AHL	35	10	9	19	52	....	....	....	....	....	....	....	....	....	....	....	....	....	....	....	....	....	....

			Regular Season														Playoffs								
Season	Club	League	GP	G	A	Pts	PIM	PP	SH	GW	S	S%	+/-	TF	F%	Min	GP	G	A	Pts	PIM	PP	SH	GW	Min
2013-14	NY Rangers	NHL	6	0	0	0	10	0	0	0	3	0.0	−1	0	0.0	4:34	....	....	....	....	....	....	....	....	....
	Hartford	AHL	11	1	6	7	15	....	....	....	....	....	....	....	....	....	....	....	....	....	....	....	....	....	....
	Rockford IceHogs	AHL	47	14	14	28	79	....	....	....	....	....	....	....	....	....	....	....	....	....	....	....	....	....	....
2014-15	Rockford IceHogs	AHL	69	17	15	32	57	....	....	....	....	....	....	....	....	....	8	3	3	6	4	....	....	....	....
	NHL Totals		23	0	0	0	27	0	0	0	10	0.0		1	100.0	5:50	....	....	....	....	....	....	....	....	....

Signed as a free agent by **San Jose**, March 3, 2009. Traded to **NY Rangers** by **San Jose** for Tommy Grant and NY Rangers' 6th round choice (later traded to Chicago – Chicago selected Ivan Nalimov) in 2014 Entry Draft, January 16, 2013. Traded to **Chicago** by **NY Rangers** for Kyle Beach, December 6, 2013.

MATTEAU, Stefan

(mah-TOH, steh-FAN) **N.J.**

Left wing. Shoots left. 6'2", 220 lbs. Born, Chicago, IL, February 23, 1994. New Jersey's 1st choice, 29th overall, in 2012 Entry Draft.

2009-10	Notre Dame	SMHL	40	15	22	37	67	....	....	....	....	....	....	....	....	....	13	4	8	12	6	....	....	....	....
2010-11	USNTDP	USHL	28	4	5	9	47	....	....	....	....	....	....	....	....	....	2	0	0	0	2	....	....	....	....
	USNTDP	U-17	17	3	6	9	18	....	....	....	....	....	....	....	....	....	....	....	....	....	....	....	....	....	....
2011-12	USNTDP	USHL	18	6	4	10	93	....	....	....	....	....	....	....	....	....	....	....	....	....	....	....	....	....	....
	USNTDP	U-18	28	9	13	22	73	....	....	....	....	....	....	....	....	....	....	....	....	....	....	....	....	....	....
2012-13	Blainville-Bois.	QMJHL	35	18	10	28	70	....	....	....	....	....	....	....	....	....	11	3	6	9	16	....	....	....	....
	New Jersey	NHL	17	1	2	3	6	0	0	0	22	4.5	−1	4	0.0	9:11	....	....	....	....	....	....	....	....	....
2013-14	Albany Devils	AHL	67	13	13	26	66	....	....	....	....	....	....	....	....	....	4	1	0	1	4	....	....	....	....
2014-15	Albany Devils	AHL	61	12	15	27	40	....	....	....	....	....	....	....	....	....	....	....	....	....	....	....	....	....	....
	New Jersey	NHL	7	1	0	1	4	0	0	0	8	12.5	0	0	0.0	11:52	....	....	....	....	....	....	....	....	....
	NHL Totals		24	2	2	4	10	0	0	0	30	6.7		4	0.0	9:58	....	....	....	....	....	....	....	....	....

MATTHIAS, Shawn

(muh-TIGH-uhs, SHAWN) **TOR**

Center. Shoots left. 6'4", 223 lbs. Born, Mississauga, ON, February 19, 1988. Detroit's 2nd choice, 47th overall, in 2006 Entry Draft.

2004-05	Belleville Bulls	OHL	37	1	1	2	15	....	....	....	....	....	....	....	....	....	3	0	0	0	0	....	....	....	....
2005-06	Belleville Bulls	OHL	67	13	21	34	42	....	....	....	....	....	....	....	....	....	6	3	0	3	2	....	....	....	....
2006-07	Belleville Bulls	OHL	64	38	35	73	61	....	....	....	....	....	....	....	....	....	15	13	5	18	10	....	....	....	....
2007-08	Florida	NHL	4	2	0	2	2	1	0	0	5	40.0	−2	38	44.7	13:08	....	....	....	....	....	....	....	....	....
	Belleville Bulls	OHL	53	32	47	79	50	....	....	....	....	....	....	....	....	....	1	1	0	1	0	....	....	....	....
2008-09	Florida	NHL	16	0	2	2	2	0	0	0	11	0.0	−3	91	50.6	9:10	....	....	....	....	....	....	....	....	....
	Rochester	AHL	61	10	10	20	16	....	....	....	....	....	....	....	....	....	....	....	....	....	....	....	....	....	....
2009-10	Florida	NHL	55	7	9	16	10	0	0	2	67	10.4	−3	313	38.0	10:48	....	....	....	....	....	....	....	....	....
	Rochester	AHL	27	6	7	13	12	....	....	....	....	....	....	....	....	....	7	2	5	7	7	....	....	....	....
2010-11	Florida	NHL	51	6	10	16	16	0	0	0	90	6.7	0	370	50.8	11:50	....	....	....	....	....	....	....	....	....
2011-12	Florida	NHL	79	10	14	24	49	1	0	1	133	7.5	−2	597	49.4	13:49	7	0	1	1	6	0	0	0	11:08
2012-13	EHC Linz	Austria	4	1	2	3	0	....	....	....	....	....	....	....	....	....	....	....	....	....	....	....	....	....	....
	Florida	NHL	48	14	7	21	16	2	1	1	106	13.2	−8	347	44.1	15:11	....	....	....	....	....	....	....	....	....
2013-14	Florida	NHL	59	9	7	16	14	0	0	0	88	10.2	0	209	38.3	12:14	....	....	....	....	....	....	....	....	....
	Vancouver	NHL	18	3	4	7	12	0	0	0	39	7.7	−3	224	46.0	15:35	....	....	....	....	....	....	....	....	....
2014-15	Vancouver	NHL	78	18	9	27	16	1	0	0	132	13.6	−3	187	44.9	13:06	6	1	1	2	10	0	0	0	12:12
	NHL Totals		408	69	62	131	137	5	1	4	671	10.3		2376	45.7	12:51	13	1	2	3	16	0	0	0	11:38

Traded to **Florida** by **Detroit** with Detroit's 2nd round choice (later traded to Nashville - Nashville selected Nick Spaling) in 2007 Entry Draft for Todd Bertuzzi, February 27, 2007. Signed as a free agent by **Linz** (Austria), December 3, 2012. Traded to **Vancouver** by **Florida** with Jacob Markstrom for Roberto Luongo and Steven Anthony, March 4, 2014. Signed as a free agent by **Toronto**, July 6, 2015.

MAYFIELD, Scott

(MAY-feeld, SKAWT) **NYI**

Defense. Shoots right. 6'5", 218 lbs. Born, St. Louis, MO, October 14, 1992. NY Islanders' 2nd choice, 34th overall, in 2011 Entry Draft.

2008-09	St.L. AAA Blues	Minor-MO	62	10	20	30	84	....	....	....	....	....	....	....	....	....	....	....	....	....	....	....	....	....	....
2009-10	Youngstown	USHL	59	10	12	22	145	....	....	....	....	....	....	....	....	....	....	....	....	....	....	....	....	....	....
2010-11	Youngstown	USHL	52	7	9	16	159	....	....	....	....	....	....	....	....	....	....	....	....	....	....	....	....	....	....
2011-12	U. of Denver	WCHA	42	3	9	12	76	....	....	....	....	....	....	....	....	....	....	....	....	....	....	....	....	....	....
2012-13	U. of Denver	WCHA	39	4	13	17	112	....	....	....	....	....	....	....	....	....	....	....	....	....	....	....	....	....	....
	Bridgeport	AHL	6	0	0	0	2	....	....	....	....	....	....	....	....	....	....	....	....	....	....	....	....	....	....
2013-14	NY Islanders	NHL	5	0	0	0	7	0	0	0	7	0.0	−3	0	0.0	17:22	....	....	....	....	....	....	....	....	....
	Bridgeport	AHL	71	3	15	18	129	....	....	....	....	....	....	....	....	....	....	....	....	....	....	....	....	....	....
2014-15	NY Islanders	NHL	....	....	....	....	....	....	....	....	....	....	....	....	....	....	2	0	0	0	0	0	0	0	12:25
	Bridgeport	AHL	69	1	13	14	173	....	....	....	....	....	....	....	....	....	....	....	....	....	....	....	....	....	....
	NHL Totals		5	0	0	0	7	0	0	0	7	0.0		0	0.0	17:22	2	0	0	0	0	0	0	0	12:25

McBAIN, Jamie

(muhk-BAYN, JAY-mee) **L.A.**

Defense. Shoots right. 6'1", 181 lbs. Born, Edina, MN, February 25, 1988. Carolina's 1st choice, 63rd overall, in 2006 Entry Draft.

2003-04	Shat.-St. Mary's	High-MN	73	6	27	33	....	....	....	....	....	....	....	....	....	....	....	....	....	....	....	....	....	....	....
2004-05	USNTDP	U-17	14	1	6	7	16	....	....	....	....	....	....	....	....	....	....	....	....	....	....	....	....	....	....
	USNTDP	NAHL	38	2	7	9	22	....	....	....	....	....	....	....	....	....	10	0	3	3	4	....	....	....	....
2005-06	USNTDP	U-18	41	9	16	25	35	....	....	....	....	....	....	....	....	....	....	....	....	....	....	....	....	....	....
	USNTDP	NAHL	14	0	5	5	6	....	....	....	....	....	....	....	....	....	....	....	....	....	....	....	....	....	....
2006-07	U. of Wisconsin	WCHA	36	3	15	18	36	....	....	....	....	....	....	....	....	....	....	....	....	....	....	....	....	....	....
2007-08	U. of Wisconsin	WCHA	35	5	19	24	18	....	....	....	....	....	....	....	....	....	....	....	....	....	....	....	....	....	....
2008-09	U. of Wisconsin	WCHA	40	7	30	37	30	....	....	....	....	....	....	....	....	....	....	....	....	....	....	....	....	....	....
	Albany River Rats	AHL	10	1	1	2	2	....	....	....	....	....	....	....	....	....	....	....	....	....	....	....	....	....	....
2009-10	Carolina	NHL	14	3	7	10	0	1	0	1	29	10.3	6	0	0.0	25:47	....	....	....	....	....	....	....	....	....
	Albany River Rats	AHL	68	7	33	40	10	....	....	....	....	....	....	....	....	....	8	4	2	6	8	....	....	....	....
2010-11	Carolina	NHL	76	7	23	30	32	1	0	2	95	7.4	−8	0	0.0	19:06	....	....	....	....	....	....	....	....	....
2011-12	Carolina	NHL	76	8	19	27	4	5	0	1	127	6.3	−7	0	0.0	19:48	....	....	....	....	....	....	....	....	....
2012-13	Pelicans Lahti	Finland	7	0	1	1	6	....	....	....	....	....	....	....	....	....	....	....	....	....	....	....	....	....	....
	Carolina	NHL	40	1	7	8	12	0	0	0	46	2.2	0	0	0.0	18:25	....	....	....	....	....	....	....	....	....
2013-14	Buffalo	NHL	69	6	11	17	14	2	0	0	98	6.1	−13	0	0.0	20:10	....	....	....	....	....	....	....	....	....
2014-15	Los Angeles	NHL	26	3	6	9	4	1	0	0	18	16.7	4	0	0.0	12:41	....	....	....	....	....	....	....	....	....
	Manchester	AHL	5	1	2	3	2	....	....	....	....	....	....	....	....	....	....	....	....	....	....	....	....	....	....
	NHL Totals		301	28	73	101	66	10	0	4	413	6.8		0	0.0	19:11	....	....	....	....	....	....	....	....	....

WCHA All-Rookie Team (2007) • WCHA First All-Star Team (2009) • WCHA Player of the Year (2009) • NCAA West First All-American Team (2009)

Signed as a free agent by **Lahti** (Finland), November 2, 2012. Traded to **Buffalo** by **Carolina** with Carolina's 2nd round choice (J.T. Compher) in 2013 Entry Draft for Andrej Sekera, June 30, 2013. Signed as a free agent by **Los Angeles**, November 11, 2014.

McCABE, Jake

(muh-KAYB, JAYK) **BUF**

Defense. Shoots left. 6', 215 lbs. Born, Eau Claire, WI, October 12, 1993. Buffalo's 3rd choice, 44th overall, in 2012 Entry Draft.

2008-09	Eau Claire Mem.	High-WI	23	2	20	22	16	....	....	....	....	....	....	....	....	....	....	....	....	....	....	....	....	....	....
	Team Wisconsin	UMHSEL	22	3	7	10	....	....	....	....	....	....	....	....	....	....	....	....	....	....	....	....	....	....	....
2009-10	USNTDP	USHL	35	0	5	5	34	....	....	....	....	....	....	....	....	....	....	....	....	....	....	....	....	....	....
	USNTDP	U-17	16	0	3	3	16	....	....	....	....	....	....	....	....	....	....	....	....	....	....	....	....	....	....
	USNTDP	U-18	1	0	0	0	2	....	....	....	....	....	....	....	....	....	....	....	....	....	....	....	....	....	....
2010-11	USNTDP	USHL	19	2	4	6	4	....	....	....	....	....	....	....	....	....	....	....	....	....	....	....	....	....	....
	USNTDP	U-18	27	2	8	10	10	....	....	....	....	....	....	....	....	....	....	....	....	....	....	....	....	....	....
2011-12	U. of Wisconsin	WCHA	26	3	9	12	12	....	....	....	....	....	....	....	....	....	....	....	....	....	....	....	....	....	....
2012-13	U. of Wisconsin	WCHA	38	3	18	21	50	....	....	....	....	....	....	....	....	....	....	....	....	....	....	....	....	....	....
2013-14	U. of Wisconsin	Big Ten	36	8	17	25	53	....	....	....	....	....	....	....	....	....	....	....	....	....	....	....	....	....	....
	Buffalo	NHL	7	0	1	1	15	0	0	0	1	0.0	−3	0	0.0	15:13	....	....	....	....	....	....	....	....	....
2014-15	Buffalo	NHL	2	0	0	0	0	0	0	0	2	0.0	0	0	0.0	11:08	....	....	....	....	....	....	....	....	....
	Rochester	AHL	57	5	24	29	50	....	....	....	....	....	....	....	....	....	....	....	....	....	....	....	....	....	....
	NHL Totals		9	0	1	1	15	0	0	0	3	0.0		0	0.0	14:18	....	....	....	....	....	....	....	....	....

Big Ten First All-Star Team (2014) • NCAA West First All-American Team (2014)

McCARTHY, John

(muh-KAHR-thee, JAWN) **S.J.**

Left wing. Shoots left. 6'1", 195 lbs. Born, Boston, MA, August 9, 1986. San Jose's 5th choice, 202nd overall, in 2006 Entry Draft.

Season	Club	League	GP	G	A	Pts	PIM	PP	SH	GW	S	S%	+/-	TF	F%	Min	Playoffs GP	G	A	Pts	PIM	PP	SH	GW	Min
2004-05	Des Moines	USHL	60	8	10	18	32																		
2005-06	Boston University	H-East	32	2	2	4	12																		
2006-07	Boston University	H-East	39	2	3	5	18																		
2007-08	Boston University	H-East	38	4	3	7	24																		
2008-09	Boston University	H-East	45	6	23	29	24																		
2009-10	**San Jose**	**NHL**	**4**	**0**	**0**	**0**	**0**	0	0	0	3	0.0	-3	0	0.0	9:08									
	Worcester Sharks	AHL	74	15	27	42	39										11	2	3	5	10				
2010-11	**San Jose**	**NHL**	**37**	**2**	**2**	**4**	**8**	0	0	0	41	4.9	-8	36	36.1	8:45									
	Worcester Sharks	AHL	25	7	5	12	13																		
2011-12	**San Jose**	**NHL**	**10**	**0**	**0**	**0**	**10**	0	0	0	14	0.0	-2	43	41.9	9:26									
	Worcester Sharks	AHL	65	20	27	47	41																		
2012-13	Worcester Sharks	AHL	65	9	16	25	12																		
2013-14	**San Jose**	**NHL**	**36**	**1**	**1**	**2**	**4**	0	0	0	49	2.0	-11	133	53.4	11:03									
	Worcester Sharks	AHL	13	3	4	7	9																		
2014-15	Chicago Wolves	AHL	25	5	3	8	11																		
	Worcester Sharks	AHL	35	9	9	18	8																		
	NHL Totals		**87**	**3**	**3**	**6**	**22**	0	0	0	107	2.8		212	48.1	9:48									

Signed as a free agent by **St. Louis**, July 4, 2014. Signed as a free agent by **San Jose**, July 2, 2015.

McCLEMENT, Jay

(muh-KLEHM-ehnt, JAY) **CAR**

Center. Shoots left. 6'1", 205 lbs. Born, Kingston, ON, March 2, 1983. St. Louis' 1st choice, 57th overall, in 2001 Entry Draft.

Season	Club	League	GP	G	A	Pts	PIM	PP	SH	GW	S	S%	+/-	TF	F%	Min	Playoffs GP	G	A	Pts	PIM	PP	SH	GW	Min
1997-98	Kingston	ON-Jr.A	48	3	8	11	15																		
1998-99	Kingston	ON-Jr.A	51	25	28	53	34																		
99-2000	Brampton	OHL	63	13	16	29	34										6	0	4	4	8				
2000-01	Brampton	OHL	66	30	19	49	61										9	4	2	6	10				
2001-02	Brampton	OHL	61	26	29	55	43																		
2002-03	Brampton	OHL	45	22	27	49	37										11	3	4	7	11				
	Worcester IceCats	AHL															1	0	0	0	0				
2003-04	Worcester IceCats	AHL	69	12	13	25	20										10	0	3	3	0				
2004-05	Worcester IceCats	AHL	79	17	34	51	45																		
2005-06	**St. Louis**	**NHL**	**67**	**6**	**21**	**27**	**30**	1	0	2	76	7.9	-23	691	46.9	13:56									
	Peoria Rivermen	AHL	11	4	5	9	4										4	0	2	2	2				
2006-07	**St. Louis**	**NHL**	**81**	**8**	**28**	**36**	**55**	0	0	0	104	7.7	3	839	52.7	13:53									
2007-08	**St. Louis**	**NHL**	**81**	**9**	**13**	**22**	**26**	0	0	2	110	8.2	-17	700	52.3	13:55									
2008-09	**St. Louis**	**NHL**	**82**	**12**	**14**	**26**	**29**	0	3	3	137	8.8	-10	1451	52.1	16:36	**4**	**0**	**0**	**0**	**4**	**0**	**0**	**0**	**16:28**
2009-10	**St. Louis**	**NHL**	**82**	**11**	**18**	**29**	**22**	0	0	3	109	10.1	0	1412	49.7	16:44									
2010-11	**St. Louis**	**NHL**	**56**	**6**	**10**	**16**	**18**	1	0	1	89	6.7	-13	831	51.4	17:08									
	Colorado	**NHL**	**24**	**1**	**3**	**4**	**12**	0	0	0	38	2.6	-8	321	52.3	15:39									
2011-12	**Colorado**	**NHL**	**80**	**10**	**7**	**17**	**31**	0	1	1	95	10.5	-8	873	51.3	13:45									
2012-13	**Toronto**	**NHL**	**48**	**8**	**9**	**17**	**11**	0	1	0	48	16.7	0	393	51.7	15:15	**7**	**0**	**0**	**0**	**0**	**0**	**0**	**0**	**14:44**
2013-14	**Toronto**	**NHL**	**81**	**4**	**6**	**10**	**32**	0	0	1	67	6.0	-8	1260	53.7	14:46									
2014-15	**Carolina**	**NHL**	**82**	**7**	**14**	**21**	**17**	0	0	2	68	10.3	-7	990	55.5	13:35									
	NHL Totals		**764**	**82**	**143**	**225**	**283**	2	4	15	941	8.7		9761	51.8	14:55	**11**	**0**	**0**	**0**	**4**	**0**	**0**	**0**	**15:22**

Traded to **Colorado** by **St. Louis** with Erik Johnson and St. Louis' 1st round choice (Duncan Siemens) in 2011 Entry Draft for Kevin Shattenkirk, Chris Stewart and Colorado's 2nd round choice (Ty Rattie) in 2011 Entry Draft, February 18, 2011. Signed as a free agent by **Toronto**, July 1, 2012. Signed as a free agent by **Carolina**, July 2, 2014.

McCORMICK, Cody

(muh-KOHR-mihk, KOH-dee) **BUF**

Center/Right wing. Shoots right. 6'2", 224 lbs. Born, London, ON, April 18, 1983. Colorado's 5th choice, 144th overall, in 2001 Entry Draft.

Season	Club	League	GP	G	A	Pts	PIM	PP	SH	GW	S	S%	+/-	TF	F%	Min	Playoffs GP	G	A	Pts	PIM	PP	SH	GW	Min
1998-99	Elgin-Middlesex	MHAO	58	22	40	62	81																		
99-2000	Belleville Bulls	OHL	45	3	4	7	42										9	1	0	1	10				
2000-01	Belleville Bulls	OHL	66	7	16	23	135										10	1	1	2	23				
2001-02	Belleville Bulls	OHL	63	10	17	27	118										11	2	4	6	24				
2002-03	Belleville Bulls	OHL	61	36	33	69	166										7	4	7	11	11				
2003-04	**Colorado**	**NHL**	**44**	**2**	**3**	**5**	**73**	0	0	1	33	6.1	-4	110	32.7	8:07									
	Hershey Bears	AHL	32	3	6	9	60																		
2004-05	Hershey Bears	AHL	40	5	6	11	68																		
2005-06	**Colorado**	**NHL**	**45**	**4**	**4**	**8**	**29**	0	0	1	43	9.3	1	16	25.0	7:42									
	Lowell	AHL	13	1	6	7	34																		
2006-07	**Colorado**	**NHL**	**6**	**0**	**1**	**1**	**6**	0	0	0	6	0.0	1	3	33.3	6:44									
	Albany River Rats	AHL	42	8	8	16	64										5	1	0	1	4				
2007-08	**Colorado**	**NHL**	**40**	**2**	**2**	**4**	**50**	0	0	1	45	4.4	5	17	35.3	10:58	**4**	**0**	**1**	**1**	**7**	**0**	**0**	**0**	**11:53**
	Lake Erie	AHL	13	2	4	6	16																		
2008-09	**Colorado**	**NHL**	**55**	**1**	**11**	**12**	**92**	0	0	0	66	1.5	-5	107	35.5	9:36									
2009-10	Portland Pirates	AHL	66	17	12	29	168										3	0	0	0	9				
	Buffalo	**NHL**															**3**	**0**	**2**	**2**	**14**	**0**	**0**	**0**	**10:41**
2010-11	**Buffalo**	**NHL**	**81**	**8**	**12**	**20**	**142**	0	0	1	104	7.7	2	316	41.8	10:57	**7**	**1**	**0**	**1**	**2**	**0**	**0**	**0**	**8:11**
2011-12	**Buffalo**	**NHL**	**50**	**1**	**3**	**4**	**56**	0	0	0	43	2.3	-7	17	47.1	7:50									
2012-13	**Buffalo**	**NHL**	**8**	**0**	**0**	**0**	**10**	0	0	0	6	0.0	-2	25	48.0	6:27									
	Rochester	AHL	25	6	5	11	42										3	1	0	1	26				
2013-14	**Buffalo**	**NHL**	**29**	**1**	**4**	**5**	**45**	0	0	0	20	5.0	-8	153	43.8	8:29									
	Minnesota	**NHL**	**14**	**1**	**1**	**2**	**7**	0	0	0	6	16.7	2	45	48.9	9:47	**13**	**1**	**0**	**1**	**14**	**0**	**0**	**0**	**8:16**
2014-15	**Buffalo**	**NHL**	**33**	**1**	**3**	**4**	**40**	0	1	0	31	3.2	-9	294	50.0	11:43									
	NHL Totals		**405**	**21**	**44**	**65**	**550**	0	1	4	403	5.2		1103	42.9	9:25	**27**	**2**	**3**	**5**	**37**	**0**	**0**	**0**	**9:03**

OHL First All-Star Team (2003)

Signed as a free agent by **Buffalo**, August 1, 2009. • Missed majority of 2012-13 due to recurring upper-body and head injuries. Traded to **Minnesota** by **Buffalo** with Matt Moulson for Torrey Mitchell, Winnipeg's 2nd round choice (previously acquired, later traded to Washington – Washington selected Vitek Vanecek) in 2014 Entry Draft and Minnesota's 2nd round choice in 2016 Entry Draft, March 5, 2014. Signed as a free agent by **Buffalo**, July 1, 2014. • Missed majority of 2014-15 after blood clot in leg was discovered, January 11, 2015.

McDONAGH, Ryan

(muhk-DUHN-uh, RIGH-uhn) **NYR**

Defense. Shoots left. 6'1", 216 lbs. Born, St.Paul, MN, June 13, 1989. Montreal's 1st choice, 12th overall, in 2007 Entry Draft.

Season	Club	League	GP	G	A	Pts	PIM	PP	SH	GW	S	S%	+/-	TF	F%	Min	Playoffs GP	G	A	Pts	PIM	PP	SH	GW	Min
2004-05	Cretin-Derham	High-MN	28	12	18	30																			
2005-06	Cretin-Derham	High-MN	25	12	33	45																			
2006-07	Cretin-Derham	High-MN	26	14	26	40																			
2007-08	U. of Wisconsin	WCHA	40	5	7	12	42																		
2008-09	U. of Wisconsin	WCHA	36	5	11	16	59																		
2009-10	U. of Wisconsin	WCHA	43	4	14	18	73																		
2010-11	**NY Rangers**	**NHL**	**40**	**1**	**8**	**9**	**14**	0	0	1	27	3.7	16	0	0.0	18:44	**5**	**0**	**0**	**0**	**4**	**0**	**0**	**0**	**22:49**
	Connecticut	AHL	38	1	7	8	12																		
2011-12	**NY Rangers**	**NHL**	**82**	**7**	**25**	**32**	**44**	0	0	1	123	5.7	25	2	50.0	24:44	**20**	**0**	**4**	**4**	**11**	**0**	**0**	**0**	**26:49**
2012-13	Barys Astana	KHL	10	0	3	3	6																		
	NY Rangers	**NHL**	**47**	**4**	**15**	**19**	**22**	0	0	1	83	4.8	13	1	0.0	24:21	**12**	**1**	**3**	**4**	**6**	**0**	**0**	**0**	**25:53**
2013-14	**NY Rangers**	**NHL**	**77**	**14**	**29**	**43**	**36**	2	3	4	177	7.9	11	0	0.0	24:49	**25**	**4**	**13**	**17**	**8**	**2**	**0**	**0**	**26:49**
	United States	Olympics	6	1	1	2	0																		
2014-15	**NY Rangers**	**NHL**	**71**	**8**	**25**	**33**	**26**	3	0	2	148	5.4	23	0	0.0	23:08	**19**	**3**	**6**	**9**	**8**	**2**	**0**	**2**	**23:31**
	NHL Totals		**317**	**34**	**102**	**136**	**142**	5	3	9	558	6.1		3	33.3	23:35	**81**	**8**	**26**	**34**	**37**	**4**	**0**	**2**	**25:39**

WCHA All-Rookie Team (2008) • WCHA Second All-Star Team (2010)

Traded to **NY Rangers** by **Montreal** with Chris Higgins and Pavel Valentenko for Scott Gomez, Tom Pyatt and Michael Busto, June 30, 2009. Signed as a free agent by **Astana** (KHL), October 9, 2012.

McDONALD, Colin
(muhk-DAWN-uhld, KAW-lihn) **PHI**

Right wing. Shoots right. 6'2", 214 lbs. Born, Wethersfield, CT, September 30, 1984. Edmonton's 2nd choice, 51st overall, in 2003 Entry Draft.

			Regular Season														Playoffs								
Season	Club	League	GP	G	A	Pts	PIM	PP	SH	GW	S	S%	+/-	TF	F%	Min	GP	G	A	Pts	PIM	PP	SH	GW	Min
2001-02	N.E. Jr. Coyotes	EJHL	39	16	20	36	50	....	....	....	....	....	....	....	....	....	....	....	....	....	....	....	....	....	....
2002-03	N.E. Jr. Coyotes	EJHL	44	28	40	*68	59	....	....	....	....	....	....	....	....	....	....	....	....	....	....	....	....	....	....
2003-04	Providence	H-East	37	10	6	16	47	....	....	....	....	....	....	....	....	....	....	....	....	....	....	....	....	....	....
2004-05	Providence	H-East	26	11	5	16	14	....	....	....	....	....	....	....	....	....	....	....	....	....	....	....	....	....	....
2005-06	Providence	H-East	36	9	19	28	29	....	....	....	....	....	....	....	....	....	....	....	....	....	....	....	....	....	....
2006-07	Providence	H-East	36	13	4	17	30	....	....	....	....	....	....	....	....	....	....	....	....	....	....	....	....	....	....
2007-08	Springfield	AHL	73	12	11	23	46	....	....	....	....	....	....	....	....	....	....	....	....	....	....	....	....	....	....
2008-09	Springfield	AHL	77	10	12	22	65	....	....	....	....	....	....	....	....	....	....	....	....	....	....	....	....	....	....
	Stockton Thunder	ECHL	3	0	2	2	0	....	....	....	....	....	....	....	....	....	....	....	....	....	....	....	....	....	....
2009-10	**Edmonton**	**NHL**	**2**	**1**	**0**	**1**	**0**	**0**	**0**	**0**	**3**	**33.3**	**1**	**0**	**0.0**	**6:42**	....	....	....	....	....	....	....	....	....
	Springfield	AHL	76	12	11	23	38	....	....	....	....	....	....	....	....	....	....	....	....	....	....	....	....	....	....
2010-11	Oklahoma City	AHL	80	*42	16	58	63	....	....	....	....	....	....	....	....	....	6	1	1	2	6	....	....	....	....
2011-12	**Pittsburgh**	**NHL**	**5**	**0**	**0**	**0**	**0**	**0**	**0**	**0**	**6**	**0.0**	**0**	**0**	**0.0**	**8:28**	....	....	....	....	....	....	....	....	....
	Wilkes-Barre	AHL	68	14	35	49	41	....	....	....	....	....	....	....	....	....	12	6	7	13	2	....	....	....	....
2012-13	Bridgeport	AHL	35	6	21	27	32	....	....	....	....	....	....	....	....	....	....	....	....	....	....	....	....	....	....
	NY Islanders	**NHL**	**45**	**7**	**10**	**17**	**32**	**1**	**0**	**0**	**82**	**8.5**	**–1**	**8**	**50.0**	**11:22**	**6**	**2**	**1**	**3**	**2**	**0**	**0**	**0**	**11:57**
2013-14	**NY Islanders**	**NHL**	**70**	**8**	**10**	**18**	**34**	**0**	**0**	**0**	**96**	**8.3**	**–22**	**15**	**46.7**	**12:23**	....	....	....	....	....	....	....	....	....
2014-15	**NY Islanders**	**NHL**	**18**	**2**	**6**	**8**	**0**	**0**	**0**	**0**	**29**	**6.9**	**–3**	**4**	**50.0**	**10:30**	**2**	**0**	**0**	**0**	**2**	**0**	**0**	**0**	**11:45**
	Bridgeport	AHL	40	14	21	35	28	....	....	....	....	....	....	....	....	....	....	....	....	....	....	....	....	....	....
	NHL Totals		**140**	**18**	**26**	**44**	**66**	**1**	**0**	**0**	**216**	**8.3**		**27**	**48.1**	**11:36**	**8**	**2**	**1**	**3**	**4**	**0**	**0**	**0**	**11:54**

Hockey East All-Rookie Team (2004) • Willie Marshall Award (AHL – Top Goal-scorer) (2011)

Signed as a free agent by **Oklahoma City** (AHL). July 9, 2010. Signed as a free agent by **Pittsburgh**, July 1, 2011. Signed as a free agent by **NY Islanders**, July 2, 2012. Signed as a free agent by **Philadelphia**, July 3, 2015.

McGINN, Jamie
(muh-GIHN, JAY-mee) **BUF**

Left wing. Shoots left. 6'1", 210 lbs. Born, Fergus, ON, August 5, 1988. San Jose's 2nd choice, 36th overall, in 2006 Entry Draft.

Season	Club	League	GP	G	A	Pts	PIM	PP	SH	GW	S	S%	+/-	TF	F%	Min	GP	G	A	Pts	PIM	PP	SH	GW	Min
2003-04	Tor. Jr. Canadiens	GTHL	31	....	....	48	....	....	....	....	....	....	....	....	....	....	18	14	18	32	....	....	....	....	....
2004-05	Ottawa 67's	OHL	59	10	12	22	35	....	....	....	....	....	....	....	....	....	18	4	7	11	0	....	....	....	....
2005-06	Ottawa 67's	OHL	65	26	31	57	113	....	....	....	....	....	....	....	....	....	6	2	2	4	4	....	....	....	....
2006-07	Ottawa 67's	OHL	68	46	43	89	49	....	....	....	....	....	....	....	....	....	5	5	1	6	2	....	....	....	....
	Worcester Sharks	AHL	4	1	1	2	4	....	....	....	....	....	....	....	....	....	6	0	0	0	8	....	....	....	....
2007-08	Ottawa 67's	OHL	51	29	29	58	54	....	....	....	....	....	....	....	....	....	4	2	2	4	4	....	....	....	....
	Worcester Sharks	AHL	8	0	2	2	0	....	....	....	....	....	....	....	....	....	....	....	....	....	....	....	....	....	....
2008-09	**San Jose**	**NHL**	**35**	**4**	**2**	**6**	**2**	**1**	**0**	**1**	**27**	**14.8**	**–6**	**7**	**85.7**	**8:55**	....	....	....	....	....	....	....	....	....
	Worcester Sharks	AHL	47	19	11	30	52	....	....	....	....	....	....	....	....	....	6	4	0	4	19	....	....	....	....
2009-10	**San Jose**	**NHL**	**59**	**10**	**3**	**13**	**38**	**0**	**0**	**2**	**76**	**13.2**	**–3**	**16**	**43.8**	**10:00**	**15**	**0**	**0**	**0**	**8**	**0**	**0**	**0**	**7:45**
	Worcester Sharks	AHL	27	7	14	21	15	....	....	....	....	....	....	....	....	....	....	....	....	....	....	....	....	....	....
2010-11	**San Jose**	**NHL**	**49**	**1**	**5**	**6**	**33**	**0**	**0**	**0**	**63**	**1.6**	**–6**	**11**	**72.7**	**11:35**	**7**	**0**	**1**	**1**	**30**	**0**	**0**	**0**	**6:33**
	Worcester Sharks	AHL	30	9	11	20	27	....	....	....	....	....	....	....	....	....	....	....	....	....	....	....	....	....	....
2011-12	**San Jose**	**NHL**	**61**	**12**	**12**	**24**	**26**	**3**	**0**	**0**	**104**	**11.5**	**1**	**3**	**66.7**	**12:33**	....	....	....	....	....	....	....	....	....
	Colorado	**NHL**	**17**	**8**	**5**	**13**	**11**	**3**	**0**	**2**	**55**	**14.5**	**–4**	**4**	**100.0**	**16:40**	....	....	....	....	....	....	....	....	....
2012-13	**Colorado**	**NHL**	**47**	**11**	**11**	**22**	**26**	**3**	**0**	**2**	**128**	**8.6**	**–13**	**6**	**50.0**	**17:17**	....	....	....	....	....	....	....	....	....
2013-14	**Colorado**	**NHL**	**79**	**19**	**19**	**38**	**30**	**5**	**0**	**3**	**167**	**11.4**	**–3**	**2**	**50.0**	**15:47**	**7**	**2**	**3**	**5**	**2**	**0**	**0**	**0**	**17:18**
2014-15	**Colorado**	**NHL**	**19**	**4**	**2**	**6**	**6**	**1**	**0**	**0**	**36**	**11.1**	**–9**	**1**	**100.0**	**14:46**	....	....	....	....	....	....	....	....	....
	NHL Totals		**366**	**69**	**59**	**128**	**172**	**16**	**0**	**10**	**656**	**10.5**		**50**	**64.0**	**13:16**	**29**	**2**	**4**	**6**	**40**	**0**	**0**	**0**	**9:46**

Traded to **Colorado** by **San Jose** with Michael Sgarbossa and Mike Connolly for T.J. Galiardi, Daniel Winnik and Anaheim's 7th round choice (previously acquired, San Jose selected Emil Galimov) in 2013 Entry Draft, February 27, 2012. • Missed majority of 2014-15 due to back injury at New Jersey, November 15, 2014. Traded to **Buffalo** by **Colorado** with Ryan O'Reilly for Nikita Zadorov, Mikhail Grigorenko, JT Compher and Buffalo's 2nd round choice (later traded to San Jose – San Jose selected Jeremy Roy) in 2015 Entry Draft, June 26, 2015.

McGINN, Tye
(muhk-GIHN, TIGH) **T.B.**

Left wing. Shoots left. 6'2", 205 lbs. Born, Fergus, ON, July 29, 1990. Philadelphia's 2nd choice, 119th overall, in 2010 Entry Draft.

Season	Club	League	GP	G	A	Pts	PIM	PP	SH	GW	S	S%	+/-	TF	F%	Min	GP	G	A	Pts	PIM	PP	SH	GW	Min
2006-07	Waterloo Wolves	Minor-ON	62	41	55	96	42	....	....	....	....	....	....	....	....	....	....	....	....	....	....	....	....	....	....
2007-08	Ottawa 67's	OHL	59	3	8	11	25	....	....	....	....	....	....	....	....	....	4	0	0	0	2	....	....	....	....
2008-09	Listowel Cyclones	ON-Jr.B	14	10	18	28	10	....	....	....	....	....	....	....	....	....	....	....	....	....	....	....	....	....	....
	Gatineau	QMJHL	48	8	22	30	25	....	....	....	....	....	....	....	....	....	10	7	6	13	19	....	....	....	....
2009-10	Gatineau	QMJHL	50	27	35	62	50	....	....	....	....	....	....	....	....	....	10	2	5	7	12	....	....	....	....
2010-11	Gatineau	QMJHL	42	31	33	64	39	....	....	....	....	....	....	....	....	....	14	5	8	13	17	....	....	....	....
2011-12	Adirondack	AHL	63	12	6	18	45	....	....	....	....	....	....	....	....	....	....	....	....	....	....	....	....	....	....
2012-13	Adirondack	AHL	46	14	12	26	54	....	....	....	....	....	....	....	....	....	....	....	....	....	....	....	....	....	....
	Philadelphia	**NHL**	**18**	**3**	**2**	**5**	**19**	**0**	**0**	**1**	**33**	**9.1**	**0**	**0**	**0.0**	**12:43**	....	....	....	....	....	....	....	....	....
2013-14	**Philadelphia**	**NHL**	**18**	**4**	**1**	**5**	**4**	**0**	**0**	**0**	**16**	**25.0**	**–1**	**0**	**0.0**	**11:11**	....	....	....	....	....	....	....	....	....
	Adirondack	AHL	54	20	15	35	62	....	....	....	....	....	....	....	....	....	....	....	....	....	....	....	....	....	....
2014-15	**San Jose**	**NHL**	**33**	**1**	**4**	**5**	**11**	**0**	**0**	**0**	**35**	**2.9**	**1**	**1**	**100.0**	**10:20**	....	....	....	....	....	....	....	....	....
	Arizona	**NHL**	**18**	**1**	**1**	**2**	**10**	**0**	**0**	**0**	**25**	**4.0**	**–1**	**1**	**0.0**	**9:40**	....	....	....	....	....	....	....	....	....
	NHL Totals		**87**	**9**	**8**	**17**	**44**	**0**	**0**	**1**	**109**	**8.3**		**2**	**50.0**	**10:52**	....	....	....	....	....	....	....	....	....

Traded to **San Jose** by **Philadelphia** for San Jose's 3rd round choice (Felix Sandstrom) in 2015 Entry Draft, July 2, 2014. Claimed on waivers by **Arizona** from **San Jose**, March 2, 2015. Signed as a free agent by **Tampa Bay**, July 21, 2015.

McGRATTAN, Brian
(muh-GRA-tuhn, BRIGH-uhn) **ANA**

Right wing. Shoots right. 6'4", 235 lbs. Born, Hamilton, ON, September 2, 1981. Los Angeles' 5th choice, 104th overall, in 1999 Entry Draft.

Season	Club	League	GP	G	A	Pts	PIM	PP	SH	GW	S	S%	+/-	TF	F%	Min	GP	G	A	Pts	PIM	PP	SH	GW	Min
1997-98	Guelph Fire	ON-Jr.B	15	4	3	7	94	....	....	....	....	....	....	....	....	....	....	....	....	....	....	....	....	....	....
	Guelph Storm	OHL	25	3	2	5	11	....	....	....	....	....	....	....	....	....	....	....	....	....	....	....	....	....	....
1998-99	Guelph Storm	OHL	6	1	3	4	15	....	....	....	....	....	....	....	....	....	....	....	....	....	....	....	....	....	....
	Sudbury Wolves	OHL	53	7	10	17	153	....	....	....	....	....	....	....	....	....	4	0	0	0	8	....	....	....	....
99-2000	Sudbury Wolves	OHL	25	2	8	10	79	....	....	....	....	....	....	....	....	....	....	....	....	....	....	....	....	....	....
	Mississauga	OHL	42	9	13	22	166	....	....	....	....	....	....	....	....	....	....	....	....	....	....	....	....	....	....
2000-01	Mississauga	OHL	31	20	9	29	83	....	....	....	....	....	....	....	....	....	....	....	....	....	....	....	....	....	....
2001-02	Mississauga	OHL	7	2	3	5	16	....	....	....	....	....	....	....	....	....	....	....	....	....	....	....	....	....	....
	Owen Sound	OHL	2	0	0	0	0	....	....	....	....	....	....	....	....	....	....	....	....	....	....	....	....	....	....
	Oshawa Generals	OHL	25	10	5	15	72	....	....	....	....	....	....	....	....	....	....	....	....	....	....	....	....	....	....
	Sault Ste. Marie	OHL	26	8	7	15	71	....	....	....	....	....	....	....	....	....	6	2	0	2	20	....	....	....	....
2002-03	Binghamton	AHL	59	9	10	19	173	....	....	....	....	....	....	....	....	....	1	0	0	0	0	....	....	....	....
2003-04	Binghamton	AHL	66	9	11	20	327	....	....	....	....	....	....	....	....	....	1	0	0	0	0	....	....	....	....
2004-05	Binghamton	AHL	71	7	1	8	*551	....	....	....	....	....	....	....	....	....	6	0	2	2	28	....	....	....	....
2005-06	**Ottawa**	**NHL**	**60**	**2**	**3**	**5**	**141**	**0**	**0**	**0**	**36**	**5.6**	**0**	**0**	**0.0**	**4:14**	....	....	....	....	....	....	....	....	....
2006-07	**Ottawa**	**NHL**	**45**	**0**	**2**	**2**	**100**	**0**	**0**	**0**	**22**	**0.0**	**–1**	**1**	**100.0**	**3:51**	....	....	....	....	....	....	....	....	....
2007-08	**Ottawa**	**NHL**	**38**	**0**	**3**	**3**	**46**	**0**	**0**	**0**	**11**	**0.0**	**0**	**0**	**0.0**	**2:52**	....	....	....	....	....	....	....	....	....
2008-09	**Phoenix**	**NHL**	**5**	**0**	**0**	**0**	**22**	**0**	**0**	**0**	**2**	**0.0**	**–2**	**0**	**0.0**	**5:31**	....	....	....	....	....	....	....	....	....
	San Antonio	AHL	1	0	0	0	2	....	....	....	....	....	....	....	....	....	....	....	....	....	....	....	....	....	....
2009-10	**Calgary**	**NHL**	**34**	**1**	**3**	**4**	**86**	**0**	**0**	**0**	**19**	**5.3**	**3**	**0**	**0.0**	**3:26**	....	....	....	....	....	....	....	....	....
2010-11	Providence Bruins	AHL	39	4	1	5	97	....	....	....	....	....	....	....	....	....	....	....	....	....	....	....	....	....	....
	Syracuse Crunch	AHL	20	6	4	10	56	....	....	....	....	....	....	....	....	....	....	....	....	....	....	....	....	....	....
2011-12	**Nashville**	**NHL**	**30**	**0**	**2**	**2**	**61**	**0**	**0**	**0**	**10**	**0.0**	**–1**	**0**	**0.0**	**5:19**	....	....	....	....	....	....	....	....	....
2012-13	**Nashville**	**NHL**	**2**	**0**	**0**	**0**	**0**	**0**	**0**	**0**	**0**	**0.0**	**0**	**0**	**0.0**	**6:17**	....	....	....	....	....	....	....	....	....
	Milwaukee	AHL	6	0	0	0	4	....	....	....	....	....	....	....	....	....	....	....	....	....	....	....	....	....	....
	Calgary	**NHL**	**19**	**3**	**0**	**3**	**49**	**0**	**0**	**1**	**18**	**16.7**	**–4**	**1**	**0.0**	**7:11**	....	....	....	....	....	....	....	....	....
2013-14	**Calgary**	**NHL**	**76**	**4**	**4**	**8**	**100**	**0**	**0**	**0**	**79**	**5.1**	**–4**	**3**	**66.7**	**6:43**	....	....	....	....	....	....	....	....	....

						Regular Season														Playoffs					
Season	Club	League	GP	G	A	Pts	PIM	PP	SH	GW	S	S%	+/-	TF	F%	Min	GP	G	A	Pts	PIM	PP	SH	GW	Min
2014-15	**Calgary**	**NHL**	**8**	**0**	**0**	**0**	**4**	**0**	**0**	**0**	**10**	**0.0**	**–2**	**0**	**0.0**	**6:38**	....	....	....	....	....	....	....	....	....
	Adirondack	AHL	16	1	5	6	25	....	....	....	....	....	....	....	....	....	....	....	....	....	....	....	....	....	....
	NHL Totals		**317**	**10**	**17**	**27**	**609**	**0**	**0**	**1**	**207**	**4.8**		**5**	**60.0**	**4:54**	....	....	....	....	....	....	....	....	....

• Missed majority of 2000-01 due to knee injury vs. Kingston (OHL), January 1, 2001. Signed as a free agent by **Ottawa**, June 2, 2002. • Missed majority of 2007-08 as a healthy reserve. Traded to **Phoenix** by **Ottawa** for Boston's 5th round choice (previously acquired, Ottawa selected Jeff Costello) in 2009 Entry Draft, June 25, 2008. Signed as a free agent by **Calgary**, July 11, 2009. • Missed majority of 2009-10 as a healthy reserve. Signed as a free agent by **Boston**, October 11, 2010. Traded to **Anaheim** by **Boston** with Sean Zimmerman for David Laliberte and Stefan Chaput, February 27, 2011. Claimed on waivers by **Nashville** from **Anaheim**, October 11, 2011. • Missed majority of 2011-12 due to upper-body injury vs. St. Louis, February 4, 2012 and as a healthy reserve. Traded to **Calgary** by **Nashville** for Joe Piskula, February 28, 2013. • Missed majority of 2014-15 as a healthy reserve. Signed as a free agent by **Anaheim**, July 10, 2015.

McILRATH, Dylan

(MAK-ihl-rayth, DIH-luhn) **NYR**

Defense. Shoots right. 6'5", 230 lbs. Born, Winnipeg, MB, April 20, 1992. NY Rangers' 1st choice, 10th overall, in 2010 Entry Draft.

Season	Club	League	GP	G	A	Pts	PIM	PP	SH	GW	S	S%	+/-	TF	F%	Min	GP	G	A	Pts	PIM	PP	SH	GW	Min
2007-08	Wpg. Warriors	Minor-MB	34	5	17	22	68	....	....	....	....	....	....	....	....	....	....	....	....	....	....	....	....	....	....
2008-09	Moose Jaw	WHL	53	1	3	4	102	....	....	....	....	....	....	....	....	....	....	....	....	....	....	....	....	....	....
2009-10	Moose Jaw	WHL	65	7	17	24	169	....	....	....	....	....	....	....	....	....	7	0	1	1	21	....	....	....	....
2010-11	Moose Jaw	WHL	62	5	18	23	153	....	....	....	....	....	....	....	....	....	6	0	0	0	15	....	....	....	....
	Connecticut	AHL	2	0	0	0	7	....	....	....	....	....	....	....	....	....	....	....	....	....	....	....	....	....	....
2011-12	Moose Jaw	WHL	52	3	20	23	127	....	....	....	....	....	....	....	....	....	14	0	6	6	12	....	....	....	....
	Connecticut	AHL	....	....	....	....	....	....	....	....	....	....	....	....	....	....	5	0	0	0	9	....	....	....	....
2012-13	Connecticut	AHL	45	0	5	5	125	....	....	....	....	....	....	....	....	....	....	....	....	....	....	....	....	....	....
2013-14	**NY Rangers**	**NHL**	**2**	**0**	**0**	**0**	**7**	**0**	**0**	**0**	**0**	**0.0**	**–1**	**0**	**0.0**	**7:02**	....	....	....	....	....	....	....	....	....
	Hartford	AHL	62	6	11	17	165	....	....	....	....	....	....	....	....	....	....	....	....	....	....	....	....	....	....
2014-15	**NY Rangers**	**NHL**	**1**	**0**	**0**	**0**	**9**	**0**	**0**	**0**	**0**	**0.0**	**0**	**0**	**0.0**	**8:02**	....	....	....	....	....	....	....	....	....
	Hartford	AHL	73	6	11	17	165	....	....	....	....	....	....	....	....	....	15	0	2	2	23	....	....	....	....
	NHL Totals		**3**	**0**	**0**	**0**	**16**	**0**	**0**	**0**	**0**	**0.0**		**0**	**0.0**	**7:22**	....	....	....	....	....	....	....	....	....

McIVER, Nathan

(muh-KEE-vuhr, NAY-thuhn)

Defense. Shoots left. 6'2", 205 lbs. Born, Summerside, PE, January 6, 1985. Vancouver's 9th choice, 254th overall, in 2003 Entry Draft.

Season	Club	League	GP	G	A	Pts	PIM	PP	SH	GW	S	S%	+/-	TF	F%	Min	GP	G	A	Pts	PIM	PP	SH	GW	Min
2001-02	Summerside	MJrHL	47	4	4	8	91	....	....	....	....	....	....	....	....	....	5	0	0	0	9	....	....	....	....
2002-03	St. Michael's	OHL	68	5	10	15	121	....	....	....	....	....	....	....	....	....	19	0	4	4	41	....	....	....	....
2003-04	St. Michael's	OHL	57	4	11	15	183	....	....	....	....	....	....	....	....	....	16	0	1	1	22	....	....	....	....
2004-05	St. Michael's	OHL	67	4	22	26	160	....	....	....	....	....	....	....	....	....	3	0	1	1	13	....	....	....	....
2005-06	Manitoba Moose	AHL	66	1	6	7	155	....	....	....	....	....	....	....	....	....	12	0	0	0	28	....	....	....	....
2006-07	**Vancouver**	**NHL**	**1**	**0**	**0**	**0**	**7**	**0**	**0**	**0**	**0**	**0.0**	**–3**	**0**	**0.0**	**11:20**	....	....	....	....	....	....	....	....	....
	Manitoba Moose	AHL	63	1	2	3	139	....	....	....	....	....	....	....	....	....	2	0	0	0	0	....	....	....	....
2007-08	**Vancouver**	**NHL**	**17**	**0**	**0**	**0**	**52**	**0**	**0**	**0**	**9**	**0.0**	**–8**	**0**	**0.0**	**10:28**	....	....	....	....	....	....	....	....	....
	Manitoba Moose	AHL	43	3	3	6	108	....	....	....	....	....	....	....	....	....	6	0	1	1	11	....	....	....	....
2008-09	**Anaheim**	**NHL**	**18**	**0**	**1**	**1**	**36**	**0**	**0**	**0**	**5**	**0.0**	**2**	**0**	**0.0**	**9:24**	....	....	....	....	....	....	....	....	....
	Manitoba Moose	AHL	28	0	2	2	59	....	....	....	....	....	....	....	....	....	10	0	0	0	10	....	....	....	....
2009-10	Manitoba Moose	AHL	44	1	4	5	109	....	....	....	....	....	....	....	....	....	....	....	....	....	....	....	....	....	....
2010-11	Providence Bruins	AHL	60	0	3	3	176	....	....	....	....	....	....	....	....	....	....	....	....	....	....	....	....	....	....
2011-12	Providence Bruins	AHL	41	1	0	1	68	....	....	....	....	....	....	....	....	....	....	....	....	....	....	....	....	....	....
2012-13	Bridgeport	AHL	62	1	4	5	287	....	....	....	....	....	....	....	....	....	....	....	....	....	....	....	....	....	....
2013-14	Hamilton	AHL	40	0	3	3	111	....	....	....	....	....	....	....	....	....	....	....	....	....	....	....	....	....	....
2014-15	Norfolk Admirals	AHL	61	2	1	3	174	....	....	....	....	....	....	....	....	....	....	....	....	....	....	....	....	....	....
	NHL Totals		**36**	**0**	**1**	**1**	**95**	**0**	**0**	**0**	**14**	**0.0**		**0**	**0.0**	**9:57**	....	....	....	....	....	....	....	....	....

Claimed on waivers by **Anaheim** from **Vancouver**, October 4, 2008. Traded to **Vancouver** by **Anaheim** for Mike Brown, February 4, 2009. Signed as a free agent by **Boston**, July 5, 2010. Signed as a free agent by **NY Islanders**, July 25, 2012. Signed as a free agent by **Hamilton** (AHL), October 3, 2013. Signed as a free agent by **Norfolk** (AHL), October 9, 2014.

McKEGG, Greg

(muh-KEHG, GREHG) **FLA**

Center. Shoots left. 6', 191 lbs. Born, St.Thomas, ON, June 17, 1992. Toronto's 2nd choice, 62nd overall, in 2010 Entry Draft.

Season	Club	League	GP	G	A	Pts	PIM	PP	SH	GW	S	S%	+/-	TF	F%	Min	GP	G	A	Pts	PIM	PP	SH	GW	Min
2007-08	Elgin-Mid. Chiefs	Minor-ON	64	73	53	126	....	....	....	....	....	....	....	....	....	....	....	....	....	....	....	....	....	....	....
	St. Thomas Stars	ON-Jr.B	3	4	1	5	2	....	....	....	....	....	....	....	....	....	....	....	....	....	....	....	....	....	....
2008-09	Erie Otters	OHL	64	8	10	18	22	....	....	....	....	....	....	....	....	....	5	2	1	3	4	....	....	....	....
2009-10	Erie Otters	OHL	67	37	48	85	32	....	....	....	....	....	....	....	....	....	4	2	1	3	0	....	....	....	....
2010-11	Erie Otters	OHL	66	49	43	92	35	....	....	....	....	....	....	....	....	....	7	4	1	5	12	....	....	....	....
	Toronto Marlies	AHL	2	1	0	1	0	....	....	....	....	....	....	....	....	....	....	....	....	....	....	....	....	....	....
2011-12	Erie Otters	OHL	35	12	22	34	32	....	....	....	....	....	....	....	....	....	....	....	....	....	....	....	....	....	....
	London Knights	OHL	30	19	22	41	22	....	....	....	....	....	....	....	....	....	15	4	7	11	2	....	....	....	....
2012-13	Toronto Marlies	AHL	61	8	15	23	22	....	....	....	....	....	....	....	....	....	9	3	3	6	10	....	....	....	....
2013-14	**Toronto**	**NHL**	**1**	**0**	**0**	**0**	**0**	**0**	**0**	**0**	**1**	**0.0**	**0**	**6**	**16.7**	**3:43**	....	....	....	....	....	....	....	....	....
	Toronto Marlies	AHL	65	19	28	47	31	....	....	....	....	....	....	....	....	....	14	3	3	6	10	....	....	....	....
2014-15	**Toronto**	**NHL**	**3**	**0**	**0**	**0**	**0**	**0**	**0**	**0**	**1**	**0.0**	**0**	**33**	**51.5**	**9:11**	....	....	....	....	....	....	....	....	....
	Toronto Marlies	AHL	62	22	15	37	39	....	....	....	....	....	....	....	....	....	5	2	0	2	12	....	....	....	....
	NHL Totals		**4**	**0**	**0**	**0**	**0**	**0**	**0**	**0**	**2**	**0.0**		**39**	**46.2**	**7:49**	....	....	....	....	....	....	....	....	....

Traded to **Florida** by **Toronto** for Zach Hyman and future considerations, June 19, 2015.

McKENZIE, Curtis

(muh-KEHN-zee, KUHR-tihs) **DAL**

Left wing. Shoots left. 6'2", 210 lbs. Born, Golden, BC, February 22, 1991. Dallas' 5th choice, 159th overall, in 2009 Entry Draft.

Season	Club	League	GP	G	A	Pts	PIM	PP	SH	GW	S	S%	+/-	TF	F%	Min	GP	G	A	Pts	PIM	PP	SH	GW	Min
2007-08	Penticton Vees	BCHL	49	3	7	10	81	....	....	....	....	....	....	....	....	....	7	0	1	1	9	....	....	....	....
2008-09	Penticton Vees	BCHL	53	30	34	64	90	....	....	....	....	....	....	....	....	....	10	3	7	10	81	....	....	....	....
2009-10	Miami U.	CCHA	42	6	21	27	88	....	....	....	....	....	....	....	....	....	....	....	....	....	....	....	....	....	....
2010-11	Miami U.	CCHA	37	7	5	12	57	....	....	....	....	....	....	....	....	....	....	....	....	....	....	....	....	....	....
2011-12	Miami U.	CCHA	40	5	12	17	60	....	....	....	....	....	....	....	....	....	....	....	....	....	....	....	....	....	....
2012-13	Miami U.	CCHA	39	11	13	24	80	....	....	....	....	....	....	....	....	....	....	....	....	....	....	....	....	....	....
	Texas Stars	AHL	5	0	1	1	14	....	....	....	....	....	....	....	....	....	2	0	0	0	0	....	....	....	....
2013-14	Texas Stars	AHL	75	27	38	65	92	....	....	....	....	....	....	....	....	....	21	3	11	14	21	....	....	....	....
2014-15	**Dallas**	**NHL**	**36**	**4**	**1**	**5**	**48**	**0**	**0**	**0**	**41**	**9.8**	**–8**	**8**	**37.5**	**11:32**	....	....	....	....	....	....	....	....	....
	Texas Stars	AHL	31	6	15	21	46	....	....	....	....	....	....	....	....	....	3	1	1	2	18	....	....	....	....
	NHL Totals		**36**	**4**	**1**	**5**	**48**	**0**	**0**	**0**	**41**	**9.8**		**8**	**37.5**	**11:32**	....	....	....	....	....	....	....	....	....

AHL All-Rookie Team (2014) • Dudley "Red" Garrett Memorial Award (AHL) (2014)

McLAREN, Frazer

(muh-KLAIR-uhn, FRAY-zuhr)

Left wing. Shoots left. 6'5", 230 lbs. Born, Winnipeg, MB, October 29, 1987. San Jose's 8th choice, 203rd overall, in 2007 Entry Draft.

Season	Club	League	GP	G	A	Pts	PIM	PP	SH	GW	S	S%	+/-	TF	F%	Min	GP	G	A	Pts	PIM	PP	SH	GW	Min
2002-03	Kelvin	High-MB	56	27	24	51	136	....	....	....	....	....	....	....	....	....	....	....	....	....	....	....	....	....	....
2003-04	Portland	WHL	50	0	3	3	44	....	....	....	....	....	....	....	....	....	1	0	0	0	0	....	....	....	....
2004-05	Portland	WHL	71	6	5	11	124	....	....	....	....	....	....	....	....	....	7	0	0	0	10	....	....	....	....
2005-06	Portland	WHL	70	12	6	18	194	....	....	....	....	....	....	....	....	....	12	0	2	2	27	....	....	....	....
2006-07	Portland	WHL	61	19	12	31	186	....	....	....	....	....	....	....	....	....	....	....	....	....	....	....	....	....	....
2007-08	Portland	WHL	18	4	3	7	45	....	....	....	....	....	....	....	....	....	....	....	....	....	....	....	....	....	....
	Moose Jaw	WHL	48	15	18	33	119	....	....	....	....	....	....	....	....	....	6	1	1	2	8	....	....	....	....
	Worcester Sharks	AHL	4	0	1	1	17	....	....	....	....	....	....	....	....	....	....	....	....	....	....	....	....	....	....
2008-09	Worcester Sharks	AHL	75	7	1	8	181	....	....	....	....	....	....	....	....	....	12	1	4	5	*50	....	....	....	....
2009-10	**San Jose**	**NHL**	**23**	**1**	**5**	**6**	**54**	**0**	**0**	**0**	**13**	**7.7**	**6**	**0**	**0.0**	**6:02**	....	....	....	....	....	....	....	....	....
	Worcester Sharks	AHL	52	4	11	15	148	....	....	....	....	....	....	....	....	....	11	0	0	0	37	....	....	....	....
2010-11	**San Jose**	**NHL**	**9**	**0**	**0**	**0**	**22**	**0**	**0**	**0**	**1**	**0.0**	**–1**	**0**	**0.0**	**4:15**	....	....	....	....	....	....	....	....	....
	Worcester Sharks	AHL	40	2	2	4	71	....	....	....	....	....	....	....	....	....	....	....	....	....	....	....	....	....	....
2011-12	**San Jose**	**NHL**	**7**	**0**	**0**	**0**	**9**	**0**	**0**	**0**	**2**	**0.0**	**0**	**5**	**0.0**	**4:53**	....	....	....	....	....	....	....	....	....
	Worcester Sharks	AHL	20	0	1	1	73	....	....	....	....	....	....	....	....	....	....	....	....	....	....	....	....	....	....
2012-13	Worcester Sharks	AHL	26	0	1	1	87	....	....	....	....	....	....	....	....	....	....	....	....	....	....	....	....	....	....
	San Jose	**NHL**	**1**	**0**	**0**	**0**	**0**	**0**	**0**	**0**	**0**	**0.0**	**0**	**0**	**0.0**	**6:54**	....	....	....	....	....	....	....	....	....
	Toronto	**NHL**	**35**	**3**	**2**	**5**	**102**	**0**	**0**	**2**	**20**	**15.0**	**0**	**11**	**36.4**	**5:09**	**1**	**0**	**0**	**0**	**2**	**0**	**0**	**0**	**7:46**

			Regular Season														Playoffs								
Season	Club	League	GP	G	A	Pts	PIM	PP	SH	GW	S	S%	+/-	TF	F%	Min	GP	G	A	Pts	PIM	PP	SH	GW	Min
2013-14	**Toronto**	**NHL**	**27**	**0**	**0**	**0**	**77**	**0**	**0**	**0**	**4**	**0.0**	**–2**	**1**	**100.0**	**4:00**	....	....	....	....	....	....	....	....	....
	Toronto Marlies	AHL	6	0	0	0	39	....	....	....	....	....	....	....	....	....	7	1	1	2	16	....	....	....	....
2014-15	Toronto Marlies	AHL	22	0	1	1	62	....	....	....	....	....	....	....	....	....	....	....	....	....	....	....	....	....	....
	NHL Totals		**102**	**4**	**7**	**11**	**264**	**0**	**0**	**2**	**40**	**10.0**		**12**	**41.7**	**4:58**	**1**	**0**	**0**	**0**	**2**	**0**	**0**	**0**	**7:46**

• Missed majority of 2011-12 recovering from off-season hip surgery and as a healthy reserve. Claimed on waivers by **Toronto** from **San Jose**, January 31, 2013. • Missed majority of 2013-14 due to hand (September 14, 2013 during scrimmage) and shoulder (January 14, 2014 at Boston) injuries and as a healthy reserve. • Missed majority of 2014-15 as a healthy reserve.

McLEOD, Cody

(muh-KLOWD, KOH-dee) **COL**

Left wing. Shoots left. 6'2", 210 lbs. Born, Binscarth, MB, June 26, 1984.

Season	Club	League	GP	G	A	Pts	PIM	PP	SH	GW	S	S%	+/-	TF	F%	Min	GP	G	A	Pts	PIM	PP	SH	GW	Min
2001-02	Portland	WHL	47	10	3	13	86	....	....	....	....	....	....	....	....	....	5	0	0	0	0	....	....	....	....
2002-03	Portland	WHL	71	15	18	33	153	....	....	....	....	....	....	....	....	....	7	1	1	2	13	....	....	....	....
2003-04	Portland	WHL	69	13	18	31	227	....	....	....	....	....	....	....	....	....	5	2	2	4	6	....	....	....	....
2004-05	Portland	WHL	70	31	29	60	195	....	....	....	....	....	....	....	....	....	7	0	3	3	8	....	....	....	....
	Adirondack	UHL	1	0	0	0	0	....	....	....	....	....	....	....	....	....	5	0	0	0	11	....	....	....	....
2005-06	Lowell	AHL	33	4	5	9	87	....	....	....	....	....	....	....	....	....	....	....	....	....	....	....	....	....	....
	San Diego Gulls	ECHL	16	4	5	9	48	....	....	....	....	....	....	....	....	....	2	2	1	3	14	....	....	....	....
2006-07	Albany River Rats	AHL	73	11	8	19	180	....	....	....	....	....	....	....	....	....	5	0	0	0	4	....	....	....	....
2007-08	**Colorado**	**NHL**	**49**	**4**	**5**	**9**	**120**	**0**	**0**	**0**	**60**	**6.7**	**–6**	**3**	**0.0**	**10:07**	**10**	**1**	**1**	**2**	**26**	**0**	**0**	**0**	**12:23**
	Lake Erie	AHL	27	6	7	13	101	....	....	....	....	....	....	....	....	....	....	....	....	....	....	....	....	....	....
2008-09	**Colorado**	**NHL**	**79**	**15**	**5**	**20**	**162**	**0**	**0**	**3**	**118**	**12.7**	**–11**	**5**	**40.0**	**11:35**	....	....	....	....	....	....	....	....	....
2009-10	**Colorado**	**NHL**	**74**	**7**	**11**	**18**	**138**	**0**	**0**	**1**	**117**	**6.0**	**–13**	**13**	**30.8**	**12:56**	**6**	**0**	**0**	**0**	**5**	**0**	**0**	**0**	**11:03**
2010-11	**Colorado**	**NHL**	**71**	**5**	**3**	**8**	**189**	**2**	**0**	**0**	**73**	**6.8**	**–7**	**8**	**37.5**	**9:47**	....	....	....	....	....	....	....	....	....
2011-12	**Colorado**	**NHL**	**75**	**6**	**5**	**11**	**164**	**0**	**0**	**0**	**62**	**9.7**	**0**	**3**	**66.7**	**7:12**	....	....	....	....	....	....	....	....	....
2012-13	**Colorado**	**NHL**	**48**	**8**	**4**	**12**	**83**	**0**	**0**	**0**	**79**	**10.1**	**4**	**17**	**41.2**	**13:05**	....	....	....	....	....	....	....	....	....
2013-14	**Colorado**	**NHL**	**71**	**5**	**8**	**13**	**122**	**0**	**1**	**0**	**76**	**6.6**	**2**	**10**	**20.0**	**10:20**	**7**	**1**	**0**	**1**	**22**	**0**	**1**	**0**	**10:50**
2014-15	**Colorado**	**NHL**	**82**	**7**	**5**	**12**	**191**	**0**	**1**	**2**	**94**	**7.4**	**–2**	**9**	**11.1**	**11:11**	....	....	....	....	....	....	....	....	....
	NHL Totals		**549**	**57**	**46**	**103**	**1169**	**2**	**2**	**6**	**679**	**8.4**		**68**	**30.9**	**10:43**	**23**	**2**	**1**	**3**	**53**	**0**	**1**	**0**	**11:34**

Signed as a free agent by **Colorado**, July 6, 2006.

McMILLAN, Brandon

(muhk-MIHL-uhn, BRAN-duhn)

Left wing. Shoots left. 5'11", 190 lbs. Born, Richmond, BC, March 22, 1990. Anaheim's 7th choice, 85th overall, in 2008 Entry Draft.

Season	Club	League	GP	G	A	Pts	PIM	PP	SH	GW	S	S%	+/-	TF	F%	Min	GP	G	A	Pts	PIM	PP	SH	GW	Min
2006-07	Kelowna Rockets	WHL	55	2	10	12	27	....	....	....	....	....	....	....	....	....	....	....	....	....	....	....	....	....	....
2007-08	Kelowna Rockets	WHL	71	15	26	41	56	....	....	....	....	....	....	....	....	....	7	0	0	0	6	....	....	....	....
2008-09	Kelowna Rockets	WHL	70	14	35	49	75	....	....	....	....	....	....	....	....	....	22	0	5	5	20	....	....	....	....
2009-10	Kelowna Rockets	WHL	55	25	42	67	63	....	....	....	....	....	....	....	....	....	12	5	10	15	14	....	....	....	....
2010-11	**Anaheim**	**NHL**	**60**	**11**	**10**	**21**	**18**	**2**	**2**	**2**	**77**	**14.3**	**–5**	**293**	**38.9**	**14:04**	**6**	**1**	**1**	**2**	**0**	**0**	**0**	**0**	**13:08**
	Syracuse Crunch	AHL	16	4	2	6	10	....	....	....	....	....	....	....	....	....	....	....	....	....	....	....	....	....	....
2011-12	**Anaheim**	**NHL**	**25**	**0**	**4**	**4**	**20**	**0**	**0**	**0**	**26**	**0.0**	**–10**	**67**	**34.3**	**11:13**	....	....	....	....	....	....	....	....	....
	Syracuse Crunch	AHL	55	12	18	30	36	....	....	....	....	....	....	....	....	....	4	1	1	2	4	....	....	....	....
2012-13	Norfolk Admirals	AHL	41	8	5	13	42	....	....	....	....	....	....	....	....	....	....	....	....	....	....	....	....	....	....
	Anaheim	**NHL**	**6**	**0**	**1**	**1**	**2**	**0**	**0**	**0**	**2**	**0.0**	**–1**	**26**	**46.2**	**8:45**	....	....	....	....	....	....	....	....	....
	Portland Pirates	AHL	2	0	0	0	2	....	....	....	....	....	....	....	....	....	3	0	0	0	6	....	....	....	....
2013-14	**Phoenix**	**NHL**	**22**	**2**	**4**	**6**	**4**	**0**	**0**	**0**	**35**	**5.7**	**0**	**14**	**50.0**	**12:35**	....	....	....	....	....	....	....	....	....
	Portland Pirates	AHL	46	11	15	26	76	....	....	....	....	....	....	....	....	....	....	....	....	....	....	....	....	....	....
2014-15	**Arizona**	**NHL**	**50**	**1**	**2**	**3**	**16**	**0**	**0**	**0**	**44**	**2.3**	**–18**	**21**	**42.9**	**10:23**	....	....	....	....	....	....	....	....	....
	Vancouver	**NHL**	**8**	**0**	**1**	**1**	**0**	**0**	**0**	**0**	**7**	**0.0**	**–1**	**2**	**50.0**	**11:02**	**2**	**1**	**0**	**1**	**4**	**0**	**0**	**0**	**8:51**
	NHL Totals		**171**	**14**	**22**	**36**	**60**	**2**	**2**	**2**	**191**	**7.3**		**423**	**39.2**	**12:03**	**8**	**2**	**1**	**3**	**4**	**0**	**0**	**0**	**12:04**

Traded to **Phoenix** by **Anaheim** for Matthew Lombardi, April 3, 2013. Claimed on waivers by **Vancouver** from **Arizona**, February 12, 2015.

McMILLAN, Carson

(muhk-MIHL-lihn, KAHR-suhn)

Right wing. Shoots right. 6'1", 196 lbs. Born, Brandon, MB, September 10, 1988. Minnesota's 5th choice, 200th overall, in 2007 Entry Draft.

Season	Club	League	GP	G	A	Pts	PIM	PP	SH	GW	S	S%	+/-	TF	F%	Min	GP	G	A	Pts	PIM	PP	SH	GW	Min
2003-04	Crocus Plains	High-MB	STATISTICS NOT AVAILABLE																						
	Brandon	MMHL	4	0	0	0	0	....	....	....	....	....	....	....	....	....	....	....	....	....	....	....	....	....	....
2004-05	Brandon	MMHL	40	17	19	36	34	....	....	....	....	....	....	....	....	....	5	3	4	7	8	....	....	....	....
	Winkler Flyers	MJHL	4	1	1	2	2	....	....	....	....	....	....	....	....	....	....	....	....	....	....	....	....	....	....
2005-06	Calgary Hitmen	WHL	59	3	2	5	42	....	....	....	....	....	....	....	....	....	13	0	0	0	2	....	....	....	....
2006-07	Calgary Hitmen	WHL	72	7	15	22	76	....	....	....	....	....	....	....	....	....	18	2	0	2	17	....	....	....	....
2007-08	Calgary Hitmen	WHL	72	16	26	42	87	....	....	....	....	....	....	....	....	....	16	1	0	1	22	....	....	....	....
2008-09	Calgary Hitmen	WHL	68	31	41	72	93	....	....	....	....	....	....	....	....	....	18	3	8	11	18	....	....	....	....
2009-10	Houston Aeros	AHL	56	4	4	8	70	....	....	....	....	....	....	....	....	....	....	....	....	....	....	....	....	....	....
2010-11	**Minnesota**	**NHL**	**4**	**1**	**1**	**2**	**0**	**0**	**0**	**0**	**5**	**20.0**	**1**	**23**	**39.1**	**9:20**	....	....	....	....	....	....	....	....	....
	Houston Aeros	AHL	78	12	10	22	80	....	....	....	....	....	....	....	....	....	21	3	2	5	14	....	....	....	....
2011-12	**Minnesota**	**NHL**	**11**	**1**	**2**	**3**	**11**	**0**	**0**	**1**	**8**	**12.5**	**1**	**14**	**35.7**	**11:04**	....	....	....	....	....	....	....	....	....
	Houston Aeros	AHL	51	4	8	12	43	....	....	....	....	....	....	....	....	....	4	0	2	2	2	....	....	....	....
2012-13	Houston Aeros	AHL	64	9	9	18	31	....	....	....	....	....	....	....	....	....	4	0	0	0	2	....	....	....	....
2013-14	**Minnesota**	**NHL**	**1**	**0**	**0**	**0**	**0**	**0**	**0**	**0**	**0**	**0.0**	**0**	**0**	**0.0**	**8:06**	....	....	....	....	....	....	....	....	....
	Iowa Wild	AHL	68	12	16	28	36	....	....	....	....	....	....	....	....	....	....	....	....	....	....	....	....	....	....
2014-15	Toronto Marlies	AHL	13	0	1	1	8	....	....	....	....	....	....	....	....	....	....	....	....	....	....	....	....	....	....
	Orlando	ECHL	22	5	9	14	12	....	....	....	....	....	....	....	....	....	....	....	....	....	....	....	....	....	....
	Bridgeport	AHL	21	4	2	6	4	....	....	....	....	....	....	....	....	....	....	....	....	....	....	....	....	....	....
	NHL Totals		**16**	**2**	**3**	**5**	**11**	**0**	**0**	**1**	**13**	**15.4**		**37**	**37.8**	**10:27**	....	....	....	....	....	....	....	....	....

Signed as a free agent by **Toronto** (AHL), October 20, 2014. Signed to a PTO (professional tryout) contract by **Bridgeport** AHL), February 20, 2015.

McNABB, Brayden

(muhk-NAB, BRAY-duhn) **L.A.**

Defense. Shoots left. 6'4", 209 lbs. Born, Davidson, SK, January 21, 1991. Buffalo's 2nd choice, 66th overall, in 2009 Entry Draft.

Season	Club	League	GP	G	A	Pts	PIM	PP	SH	GW	S	S%	+/-	TF	F%	Min	GP	G	A	Pts	PIM	PP	SH	GW	Min
2006-07	Notre Dame	SMHL	41	5	13	18	72	....	....	....	....	....	....	....	....	....	....	....	....	....	....	....	....	....	....
	Kootenay Ice	WHL	3	0	0	0	0	....	....	....	....	....	....	....	....	....	....	....	....	....	....	....	....	....	....
2007-08	Kootenay Ice	WHL	65	2	9	11	63	....	....	....	....	....	....	....	....	....	10	0	1	1	10	....	....	....	....
2008-09	Kootenay Ice	WHL	67	10	26	36	140	....	....	....	....	....	....	....	....	....	4	0	5	5	2	....	....	....	....
2009-10	Kootenay Ice	WHL	64	17	40	57	121	....	....	....	....	....	....	....	....	....	6	0	4	4	18	....	....	....	....
2010-11	Kootenay Ice	WHL	59	21	51	72	95	....	....	....	....	....	....	....	....	....	19	3	*24	27	37	....	....	....	....
2011-12	**Buffalo**	**NHL**	**25**	**1**	**7**	**8**	**15**	**1**	**0**	**0**	**23**	**4.3**	**–1**	**0**	**0.0**	**17:50**	....	....	....	....	....	....	....	....	....
	Rochester	AHL	45	5	25	30	31	....	....	....	....	....	....	....	....	....	3	0	1	1	0	....	....	....	....
2012-13	Rochester	AHL	62	5	31	36	50	....	....	....	....	....	....	....	....	....	....	....	....	....	....	....	....	....	....
2013-14	**Buffalo**	**NHL**	**12**	**0**	**0**	**0**	**6**	**0**	**0**	**0**	**10**	**0.0**	**1**	**0**	**0.0**	**17:14**	....	....	....	....	....	....	....	....	....
	Rochester	AHL	38	7	22	29	45	....	....	....	....	....	....	....	....	....	....	....	....	....	....	....	....	....	....
	Manchester	AHL	14	3	4	7	18	....	....	....	....	....	....	....	....	....	4	0	1	1	2	....	....	....	....
2014-15	**Los Angeles**	**NHL**	**71**	**2**	**22**	**24**	**52**	**0**	**0**	**1**	**74**	**2.7**	**11**	**1**	**100.0**	**15:54**	....	....	....	....	....	....	....	....	....
	NHL Totals		**108**	**3**	**29**	**32**	**73**	**1**	**0**	**1**	**107**	**2.8**		**1**	**100.0**	**16:30**	....	....	....	....	....	....	....	....	....

WHL East First All-Star Team (2010, 2011)

Traded to **Los Angeles** by **Buffalo** with Jonathan Parker and Los Angeles' 2nd round choice (previously acquired, Los Angeles selected Alex Lintuniemi) in 2014 Entry Draft and Los Angeles' 2nd round choice (previously acquired, Los Angeles selected Erik Cernak) in 2015 Entry Draft for Nicolas Deslauriers and Hudson Fasching, March 5, 2014.

McQUAID, Adam

(muh-KWAYD, A-duhm) **BOS**

Defense. Shoots right. 6'5", 209 lbs. Born, Charlottetown, PE, October 12, 1986. Columbus' 2nd choice, 55th overall, in 2005 Entry Draft.

Season	Club	League	GP	G	A	Pts	PIM	PP	SH	GW	S	S%	+/-	TF	F%	Min	GP	G	A	Pts	PIM	PP	SH	GW	Min
2003-04	Sudbury Wolves	OHL	47	3	6	9	25	....	....	....	....	....	....	....	....	....	7	0	1	1	2	....	....	....	....
2004-05	Sudbury Wolves	OHL	66	3	16	19	98	....	....	....	....	....	....	....	....	....	8	0	2	2	10	....	....	....	....
2005-06	Sudbury Wolves	OHL	68	3	14	17	107	....	....	....	....	....	....	....	....	....	10	0	1	1	16	....	....	....	....
2006-07	Sudbury Wolves	OHL	65	9	22	31	110	....	....	....	....	....	....	....	....	....	21	1	5	6	24	....	....	....	....
2007-08	Providence Bruins	AHL	68	1	8	9	73	....	....	....	....	....	....	....	....	....	10	0	0	0	9	....	....	....	....
2008-09	Providence Bruins	AHL	78	4	11	15	141	....	....	....	....	....	....	....	....	....	16	0	3	3	26	....	....	....	....
2009-10	**Boston**	**NHL**	**19**	**1**	**0**	**1**	**21**	**0**	**0**	**1**	**10**	**10.0**	**–5**	**0**	**0.0**	**10:44**	**9**	**0**	**0**	**0**	**6**	**0**	**0**	**0**	**10:12**
	Providence Bruins	AHL	32	3	7	10	66	....	....	....	....	....	....	....	....	....	....	....	....	....	....	....	....	....	....

Season	Club	League	GP	G	A	Pts	PIM	PP	SH	GW	S	S%	+/-	TF	F%	Min	GP	G	A	Pts	PIM	PP	SH	GW	Min
			Regular Season														Playoffs								
2010-11♦	Boston	NHL	67	3	12	15	96	0	0	0	46	6.5	30	0	0.0	14:52	23	0	4	4	14	0	0	0	13:01
2011-12	Boston	NHL	72	2	8	10	99	0	0	0	63	3.2	16	0	0.0	14:57	....	....	....	....	....	....	....	....	....
2012-13	Boston	NHL	32	1	3	4	60	0	0	0	26	3.8	0	0	0.0	14:18	22	2	2	4	10	0	0	1	14:47
2013-14	Boston	NHL	30	1	5	6	69	0	0	0	25	4.0	12	0	0.0	16:03	....	....	....	....	....	....	....	....	....
2014-15	Boston	NHL	63	1	6	7	85	0	0	0	60	1.7	−2	1	0.0	18:26	....	....	....	....	....	....	....	....	....
	NHL Totals		**283**	**9**	**34**	**43**	**430**	**0**	**0**	**1**	**230**	**3.9**		**1**	**0.0**	**15:28**	**54**	**2**	**6**	**8**	**30**	**0**	**0**	**1**	**13:16**

Traded to **Boston** by **Columbus** for Boston's 5th round choice (later traded to Dallas – Dallas selected Jamie Benn) in 2007 Entry Draft, May 16, 2007.

McRAE, Philip

(muh-KRAY, FIHL-ihp) **ST.L.**

Center. Shoots left. 6'2", 200 lbs. Born, Minneapolis, MN, March 15, 1990. St. Louis' 2nd choice, 33rd overall, in 2008 Entry Draft.

Season	Club	League	GP	G	A	Pts	PIM	PP	SH	GW	S	S%	+/-	TF	F%	Min	GP	G	A	Pts	PIM	PP	SH	GW	Min
2005-06	USNTDP	U-17	15	1	1	2	0	....	....	....	....	....	....	....	....	....	....	....	....	....	....	....	....	....	....
	USNTDP	NAHL	33	8	8	16	9	....	....	....	....	....	....	....	....	....	10	1	2	3	2	....	....	....	....
2006-07	London Knights	OHL	63	2	8	10	27	....	....	....	....	....	....	....	....	....	16	0	0	0	6	....	....	....	....
2007-08	London Knights	OHL	66	18	28	46	61	....	....	....	....	....	....	....	....	....	4	0	0	0	7	....	....	....	....
2008-09	London Knights	OHL	59	29	31	60	54	....	....	....	....	....	....	....	....	....	14	5	5	10	12	....	....	....	....
2009-10	London Knights	OHL	33	11	26	37	43	....	....	....	....	....	....	....	....	....	....	....	....	....	....	....	....	....	....
	Plymouth Whalers	OHL	19	5	9	14	21	....	....	....	....	....	....	....	....	....	9	6	9	15	11	....	....	....	....
2010-11	**St. Louis**	**NHL**	**15**	**1**	**2**	**3**	**2**	**0**	**0**	**0**	**13**	**7.7**	**−10**	**64**	**53.1**	**9:02**	....	....	....	....	....	....	....	....	....
	Peoria Rivermen	AHL	46	12	14	26	23	....	....	....	....	....	....	....	....	....	....	....	....	....	....	....	....	....	....
2011-12	Peoria Rivermen	AHL	71	23	16	39	26	....	....	....	....	....	....	....	....	....	....	....	....	....	....	....	....	....	....
2012-13	Peoria Rivermen	AHL	45	7	11	18	19	....	....	....	....	....	....	....	....	....	....	....	....	....	....	....	....	....	....
2013-14	Tappara Tampere	Finland	8	0	1	1	2	....	....	....	....	....	....	....	....	....	....	....	....	....	....	....	....	....	....
	Blues Espoo	Finland	45	8	12	20	12	....	....	....	....	....	....	....	....	....	7	3	1	4	2	....	....	....	....
2014-15	Chicago Wolves	AHL	67	15	18	33	21	....	....	....	....	....	....	....	....	....	....	....	....	....	....	....	....	....	....
	NHL Totals		**15**	**1**	**2**	**3**	**2**	**0**	**0**	**0**	**13**	**7.7**		**64**	**53.1**	**9:02**	....	....	....	....	....	....	....	....	....

Signed as a free agent by **Tappara Tampere** (Finland), July 12, 2013. Signed as a free agent by **Espoo** (Finland), October 17, 2013.

MEECH, Derek

(MEECH, DAIR-ihk)

Defense. Shoots left. 5'11", 205 lbs. Born, Winnipeg, MB, April 21, 1984. Detroit's 7th choice, 229th overall, in 2002 Entry Draft.

Season	Club	League	GP	G	A	Pts	PIM	PP	SH	GW	S	S%	+/-	TF	F%	Min	GP	G	A	Pts	PIM	PP	SH	GW	Min
99-2000	Wpg. Warriors	MMMHL	36	15	40	55	24	....	....	....	....	....	....	....	....	....	....	....	....	....	....	....	....	....	....
	Red Deer Rebels	WHL	5	1	0	1	2	....	....	....	....	....	....	....	....	....	....	....	....	....	....	....	....	....	....
2000-01	Red Deer Rebels	WHL	60	2	7	9	40	....	....	....	....	....	....	....	....	....	22	0	0	0	9	....	....	....	....
2001-02	Red Deer Rebels	WHL	71	8	19	27	33	....	....	....	....	....	....	....	....	....	13	1	1	2	6	....	....	....	....
2002-03	Red Deer Rebels	WHL	65	6	16	22	53	....	....	....	....	....	....	....	....	....	12	1	1	2	12	....	....	....	....
2003-04	Red Deer Rebels	WHL	62	10	28	38	40	....	....	....	....	....	....	....	....	....	19	4	7	11	10	....	....	....	....
2004-05	Grand Rapids	AHL	78	6	8	14	40	....	....	....	....	....	....	....	....	....	....	....	....	....	....	....	....	....	....
2005-06	Grand Rapids	AHL	79	4	16	20	85	....	....	....	....	....	....	....	....	....	16	0	2	2	4	....	....	....	....
2006-07	**Detroit**	**NHL**	**4**	**0**	**0**	**0**	**2**	**0**	**0**	**0**	**3**	**0.0**	**1**	**0**	**0.0**	**5:47**	....	....	....	....	....	....	....	....	....
	Grand Rapids	AHL	67	6	23	29	40	....	....	....	....	....	....	....	....	....	7	0	1	1	4	....	....	....	....
2007-08	**Detroit**	**NHL**	**32**	**0**	**3**	**3**	**6**	**0**	**0**	**0**	**44**	**0.0**	**−5**	**0**	**0.0**	**12:08**	....	....	....	....	....	....	....	....	....
	Grand Rapids	AHL	6	1	1	2	0	....	....	....	....	....	....	....	....	....	....	....	....	....	....	....	....	....	....
2008-09	**Detroit**	**NHL**	**41**	**2**	**5**	**7**	**12**	**0**	**0**	**0**	**44**	**4.5**	**−12**	**2**	**0.0**	**10:03**	**2**	**0**	**0**	**0**	**0**	**0**	**0**	**0**	**4:04**
2009-10	**Detroit**	**NHL**	**49**	**2**	**4**	**6**	**19**	**1**	**0**	**2**	**57**	**3.5**	**−12**	**2**	**0.0**	**11:55**	....	....	....	....	....	....	....	....	....
2010-11	Grand Rapids	AHL	74	10	27	37	81	....	....	....	....	....	....	....	....	....	....	....	....	....	....	....	....	....	....
2011-12	**Winnipeg**	**NHL**	**2**	**0**	**0**	**0**	**4**	**0**	**0**	**0**	**2**	**0.0**	**1**	**0**	**0.0**	**11:27**	....	....	....	....	....	....	....	....	....
	St. John's IceCaps	AHL	6	0	2	2	0	....	....	....	....	....	....	....	....	....	15	4	5	9	2	....	....	....	....
2012-13	St. John's IceCaps	AHL	46	3	20	23	38	....	....	....	....	....	....	....	....	....	....	....	....	....	....	....	....	....	....
	Winnipeg	**NHL**	**16**	**0**	**1**	**1**	**2**	**0**	**0**	**0**	**5**	**0.0**	**0**	**0**	**0.0**	**14:42**	....	....	....	....	....	....	....	....	....
2013-14	Dynamo Minsk	KHL	23	0	5	5	14	....	....	....	....	....	....	....	....	....	....	....	....	....	....	....	....	....	....
	Texas Stars	AHL	36	2	15	17	22	....	....	....	....	....	....	....	....	....	21	3	8	11	8	....	....	....	....
2014-15	Texas Stars	AHL	63	10	25	35	32	....	....	....	....	....	....	....	....	....	2	0	0	0	4	....	....	....	....
	NHL Totals		**144**	**4**	**13**	**17**	**45**	**1**	**0**	**2**	**155**	**2.6**		**2**	**0.0**	**11:34**	**2**	**0**	**0**	**0**	**0**	**0**	**0**	**0**	**4:04**

WHL East Second All-Star Team (2004)

• Missed majority of 2007-08 as a healthy reserve. Signed as a free agent by **Winnipeg**, July 2, 2011. • Missed majority of 2011-12 due to recurring lower-body injury.and as a healthy reserve. Signed as a free agent by **Minsk** (KHL), July 14, 2013. Signed as a free agent by **Texas** (AHL), January 6, 2014. Signed as a free agent by **Malmo** (Sweden-2), May 6, 2015.

MEGNA, Jayson

(MEHG-na, JAY-suhn) **NYR**

Right wing. Shoots right. 6'1", 195 lbs. Born, Fort Lauderdale, FL, February 1, 1990.

Season	Club	League	GP	G	A	Pts	PIM	PP	SH	GW	S	S%	+/-	TF	F%	Min	GP	G	A	Pts	PIM	PP	SH	GW	Min
2009-10	Cedar Rapids	USHL	56	11	15	26	62	....	....	....	....	....	....	....	....	....	5	0	0	0	6	....	....	....	....
2010-11	Cedar Rapids	USHL	60	30	28	58	45	....	....	....	....	....	....	....	....	....	8	4	3	7	4	....	....	....	....
2011-12	Nebraska-Omaha	WCHA	38	13	18	31	27	....	....	....	....	....	....	....	....	....	....	....	....	....	....	....	....	....	....
2012-13	Wilkes-Barre	AHL	56	5	7	12	28	....	....	....	....	....	....	....	....	....	12	2	3	5	0	....	....	....	....
2013-14	**Pittsburgh**	**NHL**	**36**	**5**	**4**	**9**	**6**	**0**	**0**	**2**	**36**	**13.9**	**1**	**10**	**20.0**	**10:29**	**2**	**0**	**0**	**0**	**0**	**0**	**0**	**0**	**9:10**
	Wilkes-Barre	AHL	25	9	6	15	4	....	....	....	....	....	....	....	....	....	13	1	2	3	4	....	....	....	....
2014-15	**Pittsburgh**	**NHL**	**12**	**0**	**1**	**1**	**14**	**0**	**0**	**0**	**13**	**0.0**	**−2**	**0**	**0.0**	**11:02**	....	....	....	....	....	....	....	....	....
	Wilkes-Barre	AHL	63	26	13	39	40	....	....	....	....	....	....	....	....	....	8	1	4	5	2	....	....	....	....
	NHL Totals		**48**	**5**	**5**	**10**	**20**	**0**	**0**	**2**	**49**	**10.2**		**10**	**20.0**	**10:37**	**2**	**0**	**0**	**0**	**0**	**0**	**0**	**0**	**9:10**

USHL First All-Star Team (2011)

Signed as a free agent by **Pittsburgh**, August 1, 2012. Signed as a free agent by **NY Rangers**, July 1, 2015.

MELCHIORI, Julian

(mehl-KEE-awr-ee, JOO-lee-ehn) **WPG**

Defense. Shoots left. 6'5", 214 lbs. Born, Richmond Hill, ON, December 6, 1991. Atlanta's 2nd choice, 87th overall, in 2010 Entry Draft.

Season	Club	League	GP	G	A	Pts	PIM	PP	SH	GW	S	S%	+/-	TF	F%	Min	GP	G	A	Pts	PIM	PP	SH	GW	Min
2007-08	Tor. Marlboros	GTHL	43	2	13	15	36	....	....	....	....	....	....	....	....	....	....	....	....	....	....	....	....	....	....
2008-09	Newmarket	ON-Jr.A	48	2	20	22	34	....	....	....	....	....	....	....	....	....	9	1	2	3	14	....	....	....	....
2009-10	Newmarket	ON-Jr.A	39	7	16	23	16	....	....	....	....	....	....	....	....	....	20	2	9	11	10	....	....	....	....
2010-11	Kitchener Rangers	OHL	63	1	18	19	55	....	....	....	....	....	....	....	....	....	3	0	0	0	0	....	....	....	....
2011-12	Kitchener Rangers	OHL	35	2	17	19	42	....	....	....	....	....	....	....	....	....	....	....	....	....	....	....	....	....	....
	Oshawa Generals	OHL	26	0	17	17	22	....	....	....	....	....	....	....	....	....	6	2	1	3	2	....	....	....	....
	St. John's IceCaps	AHL	1	0	0	0	0	....	....	....	....	....	....	....	....	....	....	....	....	....	....	....	....	....	....
2012-13	St. John's IceCaps	AHL	52	1	7	8	39	....	....	....	....	....	....	....	....	....	....	....	....	....	....	....	....	....	....
2013-14	**Winnipeg**	**NHL**	**1**	**0**	**0**	**0**	**0**	**0**	**0**	**0**	**0**	**0.0**	**−1**	**0**	**0.0**	**8:41**	....	....	....	....	....	....	....	....	....
	St. John's IceCaps	AHL	50	1	10	11	32	....	....	....	....	....	....	....	....	....	....	....	....	....	....	....	....	....	....
2014-15	St. John's IceCaps	AHL	70	1	5	6	54	....	....	....	....	....	....	....	....	....	....	....	....	....	....	....	....	....	....
	NHL Totals		**1**	**0**	**0**	**0**	**0**	**0**	**0**	**0**	**0**	**0.0**		**0**	**0.0**	**8:41**	....	....	....	....	....	....	....	....	....

• Transferred to **Winnipeg** after **Atlanta** franchise relocated, June 21, 2011.

MERRILL, Jon

(MAIR-ihl, JAWN) **N.J.**

Defense. Shoots left. 6'3", 205 lbs. Born, Oklahoma City, OK, February 3, 1992. New Jersey's 1st choice, 38th overall, in 2010 Entry Draft.

Season	Club	League	GP	G	A	Pts	PIM	PP	SH	GW	S	S%	+/-	TF	F%	Min	GP	G	A	Pts	PIM	PP	SH	GW	Min
2007-08	Det. Caesars	MWEHL	25	2	9	11	26	....	....	....	....	....	....	....	....	....	....	....	....	....	....	....	....	....	....
	Little Caesars	Minor-MI	....	7	21	28	....	....	....	....	....	....	....	....	....	....	....	....	....	....	....	....	....	....	....
2008-09	USNTDP	NAHL	26	2	2	4	14	....	....	....	....	....	....	....	....	....	....	....	....	....	....	....	....	....	....
	USNTDP	U-17	8	0	1	1	6	....	....	....	....	....	....	....	....	....	....	....	....	....	....	....	....	....	....
	USNTDP	U-18	9	1	2	3	4	....	....	....	....	....	....	....	....	....	....	....	....	....	....	....	....	....	....
2009-10	USNTDP	USHL	22	1	8	9	12	....	....	....	....	....	....	....	....	....	....	....	....	....	....	....	....	....	....
	USNTDP	U-18	34	4	19	23	6	....	....	....	....	....	....	....	....	....	....	....	....	....	....	....	....	....	....
2010-11	U. of Michigan	CCHA	42	7	18	25	16	....	....	....	....	....	....	....	....	....	....	....	....	....	....	....	....	....	....
2011-12	U. of Michigan	CCHA	19	2	9	11	15	....	....	....	....	....	....	....	....	....	....	....	....	....	....	....	....	....	....
2012-13	U. of Michigan	CCHA	21	2	9	11	26	....	....	....	....	....	....	....	....	....	....	....	....	....	....	....	....	....	....
	Albany Devils	AHL	12	1	7	8	4	....	....	....	....	....	....	....	....	....	....	....	....	....	....	....	....	....	....

			Regular Season														Playoffs								
Season	Club	League	GP	G	A	Pts	PIM	PP	SH	GW	S	S%	+/-	TF	F%	Min	GP	G	A	Pts	PIM	PP	SH	GW	Min
2013-14	**New Jersey**	**NHL**	52	2	9	11	12	0	0	2	45	4.4	–3	0	0.0	19:14									
	Albany Devils	AHL	15	2	8	10	0										4	1	1	2	10				
2014-15	**New Jersey**	**NHL**	66	2	12	14	24	2	0	0	47	4.3	–14	0	0.0	20:33									
	NHL Totals		118	4	21	25	36	2	0	2	92	4.3		0	0.0	19:58									

CCHA All-Rookie Team (2011) • CCHA Second All-Star Team (2011) • NCAA Championship All-Tournament Team (2011)

MESZAROS, Andrej

(MEHT-zahr-ohsh, AWN-dray)

Defense. Shoots left. 6'2", 223 lbs. Born, Povazska Bystrica, Czech., October 13, 1985. Ottawa's 1st choice, 23rd overall, in 2004 Entry Draft.

2002-03	Dukla Trencin Jr.	Slovak-Jr.	33	6	10	16	12																		
	Dukla Trencin	Slovakia	23	0	1	1	4																		
2003-04	Dukla Trencin	Slovakia	44	3	3	6	8										14	3	1	4	2				
	Dukla Trencin Jr.	Slovak-Jr.	5	2	2	4	0																		
2004-05	Vancouver Giants	WHL	59	11	30	41	94										6	1	3	4	14				
2005-06	**Ottawa**	**NHL**	82	10	29	39	61	5	0	2	137	7.3	34	1	0.0	18:11	10	1	0	1	18	0	0	0	17:50
	Slovakia	Olympics	6	0	2	2	4																		
2006-07	**Ottawa**	**NHL**	82	7	28	35	102	0	0	1	147	4.8	–15	0	0.0	21:41	20	1	6	7	12	0	0	0	20:29
2007-08	**Ottawa**	**NHL**	82	9	27	36	50	6	1	1	160	5.6	5	1	0.0	21:02	4	0	1	1	6	0	0	0	18:59
2008-09	**Tampa Bay**	**NHL**	52	2	14	16	36	1	0	1	87	2.3	–4	1	0.0	24:11									
2009-10	**Tampa Bay**	**NHL**	81	6	11	17	50	2	0	1	145	4.1	–14	0	0.0	20:11									
	Slovakia	Olympics	7	0	0	0	4																		
2010-11	**Philadelphia**	**NHL**	81	8	24	32	42	3	0	2	144	5.6	30	0	0.0	21:07	11	2	4	6	8	0	0	0	26:01
2011-12	**Philadelphia**	**NHL**	62	7	18	25	38	2	0	2	114	6.1	6	0	0.0	20:40	1	0	0	0	0	0	0	0	19:26
2012-13	**Philadelphia**	**NHL**	11	0	2	2	2	0	0	0	18	0.0	–9	0	0.0	18:28									
2013-14	**Philadelphia**	**NHL**	38	5	12	17	34	0	0	0	62	8.1	1	0	0.0	17:22									
	Slovakia	Olympics	4	0	0	0	6																		
	Boston	**NHL**	14	2	3	5	6	1	0	0	22	9.1	4	0	0.0	18:54	4	0	2	2	2	0	0	0	17:34
2014-15	**Buffalo**	**NHL**	60	7	7	14	36	1	0	1	67	10.4	–13	0	0.0	17:55									
	NHL Totals		645	63	175	238	457	21	1	11	1103	5.7		3	0.0	20:17	50	4	13	17	46	0	0	0	20:48

WHL West Second All-Star Team (2005) • NHL All-Rookie Team (2006)

Traded to **Tampa Bay** by **Ottawa** for Filip Kuba, Alexandre Picard and San Jose's 1st round choice (previously acquired, later traded to NY Islanders, later traded to Columbus, later traded to Anaheim – Anaheim selected Kyle Palmieri) in 2009 Entry Draft, August 29, 2008. Traded to **Philadelphia** by **Tampa Bay** for Philadelphia's 2nd round choice (Nikita Kucharev) in 2011 Entry Draft, July 1, 2010. • Missed majority of 2012-13 due to shoulder injury vs. NY Rangers, January 24, 2013. Traded to **Boston** by **Philadelphia** for Boston's 3rd round choice (Mark Friedman) in 2014 Entry Draft, March 5, 2014. Signed as a free agent by **Buffalo**, July 1, 2014.

METHOT, Marc

(meh-THAWT, MAHRK) **OTT**

Defense. Shoots left. 6'3", 228 lbs. Born, Ottawa, ON, June 21, 1985. Columbus' 7th choice, 168th overall, in 2003 Entry Draft.

2001-02	Kanata Valley	ON-Jr.A	50	3	10	13	22										11	0	1	1	24				
2002-03	London Knights	OHL	68	2	13	15	46										14	2	4	6	6				
2003-04	London Knights	OHL	63	2	9	11	66										15	0	3	3	18				
2004-05	London Knights	OHL	67	4	12	16	88										18	2	1	3	32				
2005-06	Syracuse Crunch	AHL	70	2	11	13	75										5	0	0	0	8				
2006-07	**Columbus**	**NHL**	20	0	4	4	12	0	0	0	11	0.0	5	0	0.0	14:38									
	Syracuse Crunch	AHL	59	1	15	16	58																		
2007-08	**Columbus**	**NHL**	9	0	0	0	8	0	0	0	9	0.0	–1	0	0.0	14:14									
	Syracuse Crunch	AHL	66	7	6	13	130										13	0	6	6	14				
2008-09	**Columbus**	**NHL**	66	4	13	17	55	0	0	0	58	6.9	7	0	0.0	17:57	4	0	0	0	2	0	0	0	16:15
2009-10	**Columbus**	**NHL**	60	2	6	8	51	0	0	0	42	4.8	–8	0	0.0	19:31									
2010-11	**Columbus**	**NHL**	74	0	15	15	58	0	0	0	58	0.0	2	0	0.0	19:53									
2011-12	**Columbus**	**NHL**	46	1	6	7	24	0	0	0	42	2.4	–11	0	0.0	20:03									
2012-13	**Ottawa**	**NHL**	47	2	9	11	31	0	0	0	53	3.8	2	0	0.0	22:14	10	1	4	5	6	0	0	1	22:44
2013-14	**Ottawa**	**NHL**	75	6	17	23	28	0	0	1	117	5.1	0	0	0.0	21:45									
2014-15	**Ottawa**	**NHL**	45	1	10	11	18	0	0	0	49	2.0	22	1	0.0	22:40	6	0	0	0	6	0	0	0	23:48
	Binghamton	AHL	1	0	0	0	0																		
	NHL Totals		442	16	80	96	285	0	0	1	439	3.6		1	0.0	20:04	20	1	4	5	14	0	0	1	21:46

Traded to **Ottawa** by **Columbus** for Nick Foligno, July 1, 2012.

MICHALEK, Milan

(mih-KHAL-ihk, MEE-lan) **OTT**

Right wing. Shoots left. 6'2", 215 lbs. Born, Jindrichuv Hradec, Czech., December 7, 1984. San Jose's 1st choice, 6th overall, in 2003 Entry Draft.

99-2000	C. Budejovice Jr.	CzRep-Jr.	48	16	26	42	42										6	3	1	4	4				
2000-01	C. Budejovice Jr.	CzRep-Jr.	30	10	13	23	30										4	1	3	4	2				
	C. Budejovice	CzRep	5	0	0	0	0																		
2001-02	C. Budejovice	CzRep	47	6	11	17	12																		
	C. Budejovice Jr.	CzRep-Jr.	5	3	2	5	4										7	5	4	9	14				
2002-03	C. Budejovice	CzRep	46	3	5	8	14										4	1	0	1	2				
	Kladno	CzRep-2															6	2	2	4	16				
2003-04	**San Jose**	**NHL**	2	1	0	1	4	0	0	0	1	100.0	1	0	0.0	9:05									
	Cleveland Barons	AHL	7	2	2	4	4																		
2004-05			DID NOT PLAY																						
2005-06	**San Jose**	**NHL**	81	17	18	35	45	4	0	2	159	10.7	1	4	0.0	15:46	9	1	4	5	8	1	0	0	15:11
2006-07	**San Jose**	**NHL**	78	26	40	66	36	11	0	9	191	13.6	17	11	18.2	16:46	11	4	2	6	4	0	0	1	18:50
2007-08	**San Jose**	**NHL**	79	24	31	55	47	5	1	8	233	10.3	19	10	60.0	18:05	13	4	0	4	4	1	0	1	17:34
2008-09	**San Jose**	**NHL**	77	23	34	57	52	6	0	6	179	12.8	11	30	46.7	18:27	6	1	0	1	2	1	0	0	19:22
2009-10	**Ottawa**	**NHL**	66	22	12	34	18	8	2	3	163	13.5	–12	8	50.0	18:15	1	0	0	0	0	0	0	0	12:08
	Czech Republic	Olympics	5	2	0	2	0																		
2010-11	**Ottawa**	**NHL**	66	18	15	33	49	1	4	0	167	10.8	–12	13	30.8	18:04									
2011-12	**Ottawa**	**NHL**	77	35	25	60	32	10	1	3	212	16.5	4	6	16.7	19:33	7	1	1	2	4	0	0	0	21:54
2012-13	C. Budejovice	CzRep	21	13	11	24	26																		
	Ottawa	**NHL**	23	4	10	14	17	0	0	0	58	6.9	8	4	50.0	18:11	10	3	2	5	2	0	1	0	17:51
2013-14	**Ottawa**	**NHL**	82	17	22	39	41	4	0	1	169	10.1	–25	14	42.9	17:35									
	Czech Republic	Olympics	5	0	0	0	0																		
2014-15	**Ottawa**	**NHL**	66	13	21	34	33	5	1	1	130	10.0	3	23	47.8	16:22	6	1	0	1	4	0	0	0	16:44
	NHL Totals		697	200	228	428	374	54	9	33	1662	12.0		123	40.7	17:38	63	15	9	24	28	3	1	2	17:59

Played in NHL All-Star Game (2012)

• Missed majority of 2003-04 due to knee injury vs. Calgary, October 11, 2003. Traded to **Ottawa** by **San Jose** with Jonathan Cheechoo and San Jose's 2nd round choice (later traded to NY Islanders, later traded to Chicago - Chicago selected Kent Simpson) in 2010 Entry Draft for Dany Heatley and Ottawa's 5th round choice (Isaac MacLeod) in 2010 Entry Draft, September 12, 2009. Signed as a free agent by **Ceske Budejovice** (CzRep), October 28, 2012.

MICHALEK, Zbynek

(mih-KHAL-ihk, z'BIGH-nehk) **ARI**

Defense. Shoots right. 6'2", 210 lbs. Born, Jindrichuv Hradec, Czech., December 23, 1982.

99-2000	Karlovy Vary Jr.	CzRep-Jr.	40	2	10	12	20																		
2000-01	Shawinigan	QMJHL	69	10	29	39	52										3	0	0	0	0				
2001-02	Shawinigan	QMJHL	68	16	35	51	54										12	8	9	17	17				
2002-03	Houston Aeros	AHL	62	4	10	14	26										23	1	1	2	6				
2003-04	**Minnesota**	**NHL**	22	1	1	2	4	0	0	0	17	5.9	–7	0	0.0	14:13									
	Houston Aeros	AHL	55	5	16	21	32										2	1	0	1	0				
2004-05	Houston Aeros	AHL	76	7	17	24	48										5	1	2	3	4				
2005-06	**Phoenix**	**NHL**	82	9	15	24	62	5	0	2	105	8.6	4	0	0.0	22:50									
2006-07	**Phoenix**	**NHL**	82	4	24	28	34	3	0	0	144	2.8	–20	1	100.0	23:40									
2007-08	**Phoenix**	**NHL**	75	4	13	17	34	0	0	2	92	4.3	9	0	0.0	21:36									
2008-09	**Phoenix**	**NHL**	82	6	21	27	28	0	0	0	106	5.7	–13	0	0.0	22:43									
2009-10	**Phoenix**	**NHL**	72	3	14	17	30	2	0	1	104	2.9	5	0	0.0	22:39	7	0	2	2	2	0	0	0	20:28
	Czech Republic	Olympics	5	0	0	0	2																		
2010-11	**Pittsburgh**	**NHL**	73	5	14	19	30	1	0	2	104	4.8	0	0	0.0	21:50	7	0	1	1	0	0	0	0	27:20
2011-12	**Pittsburgh**	**NHL**	62	2	11	13	24	0	0	0	77	2.6	0	0	0.0	21:39	6	0	1	1	0	0	0	0	21:08
2012-13	**Phoenix**	**NHL**	34	0	2	2	14	0	0	0	42	0.0	4	0	0.0	21:18									

			Regular Season														Playoffs								
Season	Club	League	GP	G	A	Pts	PIM	PP	SH	GW	S	S%	+/-	TF	F%	Min	GP	G	A	Pts	PIM	PP	SH	GW	Min
2013-14	**Phoenix**	**NHL**	**59**	**2**	**8**	**10**	**24**	**0**	**0**	**1**	**78**	**2.6**	**6**	**0**	**0.0**	**20:59**									
	Czech Republic	Olympics	5	0	1	1	2																		
2014-15	**Arizona**	**NHL**	**53**	**2**	**6**	**8**	**12**	**0**	**0**	**0**	**67**	**3.0**	**–6**	**0**	**0.0**	**21:05**									
	St. Louis	**NHL**	**15**	**2**	**2**	**4**	**6**	**0**	**0**	**0**	**19**	**10.5**	**3**	**0**	**0.0**	**19:37**	**6**	**0**	**0**	**0**	**4**	**0**	**0**	**0**	**16:21**
	NHL Totals		**711**	**40**	**131**	**171**	**302**	**11**	**0**	**8**	**955**	**4.2**		**110**	**0.0**	**21:52**	**26**	**0**	**4**	**4**	**6**	**0**	**0**	**0**	**21:31**

Signed as a free agent by **Minnesota**, September 29, 2001. Traded to **Phoenix** by **Minnesota** for Erik Westrum and Dustin Wood, August 26, 2005. Signed as a free agent by **Pittsburgh**, July 1, 2010. Traded to **Phoenix** by **Pittsburgh** for Harrison Ruopp, Marc Cheverie and Philadelphia's 3rd round choice (previously acquired, Pittsburgh selected Oskar Sundqvist) in 2012 Entry Draft, June 22, 2012. Traded to **St. Louis** by **Arizona** with future considerations for Maxim Letunov. March 2. 2015. Signed as a free agent by **Arizona**, July 1, 2015.

MIELE, Andy
(MEE-lee, AN-dee) **DET**

Left wing. Shoots left. 5'7", 169 lbs. Born, Grosse Pointe Woods, MI, April 15, 1988.

Season	Club	League	GP	G	A	Pts	PIM	PP	SH	GW	S	S%	+/-	TF	F%	Min	GP	G	A	Pts	PIM	PP	SH	GW	Min
2005-06	Cedar Rapids	USHL	52	10	17	27	41										8	0	4	4	4				
2006-07	Cedar Rapids	USHL	13	7	8	15	15																		
	Chicago Steel	USHL	45	13	29	42	70										4	2	4	6	14				
2007-08	Chicago Steel	USHL	29	30	11	41	78																		
	Miami U.	CCHA	18	6	8	14	4																		
2008-09	Miami U.	CCHA	41	15	16	31	34																		
2009-10	Miami U.	CCHA	43	15	29	44	61																		
2010-11	Miami U.	CCHA	39	24	*47	*71	35																		
2011-12	**Phoenix**	**NHL**	**7**	**0**	**0**	**0**	**6**	**0**	**0**	**0**	**4**	**0.0**	**–3**	**28**	**25.0**	**8:56**									
	Portland Pirates	AHL	69	16	38	54	43																		
2012-13	Portland Pirates	AHL	70	19	34	53	72										3	1	2	3	15				
	Phoenix	**NHL**	**1**	**0**	**0**	**0**	**0**	**0**	**0**	**0**	**0**	**0.0**	**1**	**3**	**66.7**	**9:02**									
2013-14	**Phoenix**	**NHL**	**7**	**0**	**2**	**2**	**5**	**0**	**0**	**0**	**6**	**0.0**	**4**	**42**	**35.7**	**9:21**									
	Portland Pirates	AHL	70	27	45	72	66																		
2014-15	Grand Rapids	AHL	71	26	44	70	42										16	3	11	14	20				
	NHL Totals		**15**	**0**	**2**	**2**	**11**	**0**	**0**	**0**	**10**	**0.0**		**73**	**32.9**	**9:08**									

CCHA Second All-Star Team (2010) • CCHA First All-Star Team (2011) • CCHA Player of the Year (2011) • NCAA West First All-American Team (2011) • Hobey Baker Memorial Award (Top U.S. Collegiate Player) (2011) • AHL Second All-Star Team (2014) • AHL First All-Star Team (2015)

Signed as a free agent by **Phoenix**, April 2, 2011. Signed as a free agent by **Detroit**, July 3, 2014.

MILLER, Andrew
(MIH-luhr, AN-droo) **EDM**

Center. Shoots right. 5'10", 181 lbs. Born, Bloomfield Hills, MI, September 18, 1988.

Season	Club	League	GP	G	A	Pts	PIM	PP	SH	GW	S	S%	+/-	TF	F%	Min	GP	G	A	Pts	PIM	PP	SH	GW	Min
2007-08	Chicago Steel	USHL	59	14	27	41	28										7	2	4	6	4				
2008-09	Chicago Steel	USHL	58	32	50	82	76																		
2009-10	Yale	ECAC	34	5	29	34	12																		
2010-11	Yale	ECAC	36	12	33	45	18																		
2011-12	Yale	ECAC	34	7	29	36	8																		
2012-13	Yale	ECAC	37	18	23	41	15																		
2013-14	Oklahoma City	AHL	52	8	26	34	14										3	0	0	0	4				
2014-15	**Edmonton**	**NHL**	**9**	**1**	**5**	**6**	**0**	**0**	**0**	**0**	**14**	**7.1**	**–2**	**2**	**50.0**	**13:45**									
	Oklahoma City	AHL	63	27	33	60	16										10	3	3	6	8				
	NHL Totals		**9**	**1**	**5**	**6**	**0**	**0**	**0**	**0**	**14**	**7.1**		**2**	**50.0**	**13:45**									

USHL Player of the Year (2009) • ECAC First All-Star Team (2011, 2013) • NCAA East Second All-American Team (2013) • NCAA Championship All-Tournament Team (2013) • NCAA Championship Tournament MVP (2013)

Signed as a free agent by **Edmonton**, April 17, 2013.

MILLER, Drew
(MIH-luhr, DROO) **DET**

Left wing. Shoots left. 6'2", 178 lbs. Born, Dover, NJ, February 17, 1984. Anaheim's 6th choice, 186th overall, in 2003 Entry Draft.

Season	Club	League	GP	G	A	Pts	PIM	PP	SH	GW	S	S%	+/-	TF	F%	Min	GP	G	A	Pts	PIM	PP	SH	GW	Min
2000-01	Capital Centre	NAHL	37	4	3	7	22																		
2001-02	Capital Centre	NAHL	54	18	16	34	56																		
2002-03	Capital Centre	NAHL	11	10	9	19																			
	River City Lancers	USHL	49	14	11	25	22										11	5	4	9	6				
2003-04	Michigan State	CCHA	41	4	6	10	39																		
2004-05	Michigan State	CCHA	40	17	16	33	20																		
2005-06	Michigan State	CCHA	44	18	25	43	30																		
	Portland Pirates	AHL															1	0	0	0	0				
2006-07	Portland Pirates	AHL	79	16	20	36	51																		
	♦ **Anaheim**	**NHL**															**3**	**0**	**0**	**0**	**2**	**0**	**0**	**0**	**7:00**
2007-08	**Anaheim**	**NHL**	**26**	**2**	**3**	**5**	**6**	**0**	**0**	**0**	**30**	**6.7**	**–1**	**9**	**33.3**	**11:11**									
	Portland Pirates	AHL	31	16	20	36	12										16	1	7	8	12				
2008-09	**Anaheim**	**NHL**	**27**	**4**	**6**	**10**	**17**	**0**	**0**	**0**	**45**	**8.9**	**0**	**14**	**21.4**	**12:59**	**13**	**2**	**1**	**3**	**2**	**0**	**0**	**1**	**16:09**
	Iowa Chops	AHL	53	23	15	38	10																		
2009-10	**Tampa Bay**	**NHL**	**14**	**0**	**0**	**0**	**2**	**0**	**0**	**0**	**10**	**0.0**	**–3**	**2**	**0.0**	**12:14**									
	Detroit	**NHL**	**66**	**10**	**9**	**19**	**10**	**1**	**1**	**3**	**93**	**10.8**	**5**	**41**	**34.2**	**12:42**	**12**	**1**	**1**	**2**	**4**	**0**	**0**	**0**	**12:35**
2010-11	**Detroit**	**NHL**	**67**	**10**	**8**	**18**	**13**	**0**	**1**	**2**	**85**	**11.8**	**–2**	**17**	**23.5**	**11:45**	**9**	**1**	**1**	**2**	**4**	**0**	**0**	**0**	**10:17**
2011-12	**Detroit**	**NHL**	**80**	**14**	**11**	**25**	**20**	**0**	**0**	**4**	**131**	**10.7**	**6**	**25**	**20.0**	**12:52**	**5**	**0**	**1**	**1**	**2**	**0**	**0**	**0**	**11:32**
2012-13	Braehead Clan	Britain	23	15	15	30	7																		
	Detroit	**NHL**	**44**	**4**	**4**	**8**	**2**	**1**	**0**	**2**	**54**	**7.4**	**–8**	**4**	**25.0**	**13:49**	**6**	**1**	**1**	**2**	**2**	**0**	**0**	**1**	**13:13**
2013-14	**Detroit**	**NHL**	**82**	**7**	**8**	**15**	**21**	**0**	**0**	**1**	**117**	**6.0**	**–11**	**23**	**39.1**	**14:08**	**5**	**0**	**1**	**1**	**0**	**0**	**0**	**0**	**14:33**
2014-15	**Detroit**	**NHL**	**82**	**5**	**8**	**13**	**25**	**0**	**1**	**0**	**98**	**5.1**	**–3**	**19**	**31.6**	**13:26**	**7**	**1**	**1**	**2**	**2**	**0**	**0**	**0**	**16:44**
	NHL Totals		**488**	**56**	**57**	**113**	**116**	**2**	**3**	**12**	**663**	**8.4**		**154**	**29.2**	**12:59**	**60**	**6**	**7**	**13**	**18**	**0**	**0**	**2**	**13:21**

Traded to **Tampa Bay** by **Anaheim** with Anaheim's 3rd round choice (Adam Janosik) in 2010 Entry Draft for Evgeny Artyukhin, August 13, 2009. Claimed on waivers by **Detroit** from **Tampa Bay**, November 11, 2009. Signed as a free agent by **Braehead** (Britain), October 8, 2012.

MILLER, J.T.
(MIH-luhr, JAY-TEE) **NYR**

Center. Shoots left. 6'1", 205 lbs. Born, East Palestine, OH, March 14, 1993. NY Rangers' 1st choice, 15th overall, in 2011 Entry Draft.

Season	Club	League	GP	G	A	Pts	PIM	PP	SH	GW	S	S%	+/-	TF	F%	Min	GP	G	A	Pts	PIM	PP	SH	GW	Min
2008-09	Pit. Hornets	T1EHL	45	21	21	42	76																		
2009-10	USNTDP	USHL	29	5	7	12	32																		
	USNTDP	U-17	17	10	9	19	47																		
	USNTDP	U-18	1	0	0	0	0																		
2010-11	USNTDP	USHL	21	3	12	15	48																		
	USNTDP	U-18	35	12	23	35	38																		
2011-12	Plymouth Whalers	OHL	61	25	37	62	61										13	2	8	10	18				
	Connecticut	AHL															8	0	1	1	2				
2012-13	Connecticut	AHL	42	8	15	23	29																		
	NY Rangers	**NHL**	**26**	**2**	**2**	**4**	**8**	**1**	**0**	**0**	**43**	**4.7**	**–7**	**118**	**53.4**	**13:31**									
2013-14	**NY Rangers**	**NHL**	**30**	**3**	**3**	**6**	**18**	**0**	**0**	**0**	**46**	**6.5**	**–6**	**51**	**51.0**	**11:27**	**4**	**0**	**2**	**2**	**2**	**0**	**0**	**0**	**9:16**
	Hartford	AHL	41	15	27	42	47																		
2014-15	**NY Rangers**	**NHL**	**58**	**10**	**13**	**23**	**23**	**2**	**0**	**3**	**92**	**10.9**	**5**	**205**	**45.4**	**12:42**	**19**	**1**	**7**	**8**	**2**	**0**	**0**	**0**	**14:39**
	Hartford	AHL	18	6	9	15	12																		
	NHL Totals		**114**	**15**	**18**	**33**	**49**	**3**	**0**	**3**	**181**	**8.3**		**374**	**48.7**	**12:34**	**23**	**1**	**9**	**10**	**4**	**0**	**0**	**0**	**13:43**

MILLER, Kevan
(MIH-luhr, KEH-vuhn) **BOS**

Defense. Shoots right. 6'2", 210 lbs. Born, Los Angeles, CA, November 15, 1987.

Season	Club	League	GP	G	A	Pts	PIM	PP	SH	GW	S	S%	+/-	TF	F%	Min	GP	G	A	Pts	PIM	PP	SH	GW	Min
2007-08	U. of Vermont	H-East	39	2	5	7	12																		
2008-09	U. of Vermont	H-East	39	1	7	8	30																		
2009-10	U. of Vermont	H-East	39	1	10	11	26																		
2010-11	U. of Vermont	H-East	27	1	3	4	29																		
	Providence Bruins	AHL	6	0	0	0	9																		
2011-12	Providence Bruins	AHL	65	3	21	24	98																		
2012-13	Providence Bruins	AHL	64	2	14	16	71										9	0	5	5	10				

			Regular Season														Playoffs								
Season	Club	League	GP	G	A	Pts	PIM	PP	SH	GW	S	S%	+/-	TF	F%	Min	GP	G	A	Pts	PIM	PP	SH	GW	Min
2013-14	**Boston**	**NHL**	**47**	**1**	**5**	**6**	**38**	**0**	**0**	**1**	**41**	**2.4**	**20**	**0**	**0.0**	**17:28**	**11**	**0**	**2**	**2**	**8**	**0**	**0**	**0**	**19:26**
	Providence Bruins	AHL	19	2	3	5	39	....	....	....	....	....	....	....	....	....	....	....	....	....	....	....	....	....	....
2014-15	**Boston**	**NHL**	**41**	**2**	**5**	**7**	**15**	**0**	**0**	**1**	**37**	**5.4**	**20**	**0**	**0.0**	**18:02**	....	....	....	....	....	....	....	....	....
	NHL Totals		**88**	**3**	**10**	**13**	**53**	**0**	**0**	**2**	**78**	**3.8**		**0**	**0.0**	**17:44**	**11**	**0**	**2**	**2**	**8**	**0**	**0**	**0**	**19:26**

Signed as a free agent by **Providence** (AHL), March 18, 2011. Signed as a free agent by **Boston**, October 21, 2011.

MILLS, Brad
(MIHLS, BRAD)

Right wing. Shoots right. 6', 195 lbs. Born, Terrace, BC, May 3, 1983.

Season	Club	League	GP	G	A	Pts	PIM	PP	SH	GW	S	S%	+/-	TF	F%	Min	GP	G	A	Pts	PIM	PP	SH	GW	Min
2002-03	Fort McMurray	AJHL	62	20	47	67	73	....	....	....	....	....	....	....	....	....	....	....	....	....	....	....	....	....	....
2003-04	Yale	ECAC	27	4	7	11	18	....	....	....	....	....	....	....	....	....	....	....	....	....	....	....	....	....	....
2004-05	Yale	ECAC	27	12	14	26	30	....	....	....	....	....	....	....	....	....	....	....	....	....	....	....	....	....	....
2005-06	Yale	ECAC	22	8	8	16	65	....	....	....	....	....	....	....	....	....	....	....	....	....	....	....	....	....	....
2006-07	Yale	ECAC	20	2	6	8	39	....	....	....	....	....	....	....	....	....	....	....	....	....	....	....	....	....	....
	Lowell Devils	AHL	8	0	1	1	4	....	....	....	....	....	....	....	....	....	....	....	....	....	....	....	....	....	....
2007-08	Lowell Devils	AHL	16	1	2	3	44	....	....	....	....	....	....	....	....	....	....	....	....	....	....	....	....	....	....
	Trenton Devils	ECHL	26	9	7	16	67	....	....	....	....	....	....	....	....	....	....	....	....	....	....	....	....	....	....
2008-09	Lowell Devils	AHL	75	5	16	21	108	....	....	....	....	....	....	....	....	....	....	....	....	....	....	....	....	....	....
2009-10	Lowell Devils	AHL	51	12	7	19	67	....	....	....	....	....	....	....	....	....	2	1	2	3	4	....	....	....	....
2010-11	**New Jersey**	**NHL**	**4**	**1**	**0**	**1**	**5**	**0**	**0**	**0**	**6**	**16.7**	**1**	**17**	**41.2**	**8:16**	....	....	....	....	....	....	....	....	....
	Albany Devils	AHL	53	15	9	24	102	....	....	....	....	....	....	....	....	....	....	....	....	....	....	....	....	....	....
2011-12	**New Jersey**	**NHL**	**27**	**0**	**1**	**1**	**32**	**0**	**0**	**0**	**18**	**0.0**	**–10**	**126**	**61.1**	**7:11**	....	....	....	....	....	....	....	....	....
	Albany Devils	AHL	49	6	16	22	90	....	....	....	....	....	....	....	....	....	....	....	....	....	....	....	....	....	....
2012-13	Utah Grizzlies	ECHL	27	15	20	35	116	....	....	....	....	....	....	....	....	....	....	....	....	....	....	....	....	....	....
	Rockford IceHogs	AHL	33	7	9	16	60	....	....	....	....	....	....	....	....	....	....	....	....	....	....	....	....	....	....
2013-14	**Chicago**	**NHL**	**3**	**0**	**0**	**0**	**0**	**0**	**0**	**0**	**2**	**0.0**	**–1**	**14**	**57.1**	**10:20**	....	....	....	....	....	....	....	....	....
	Rockford IceHogs	AHL	28	8	6	14	49	....	....	....	....	....	....	....	....	....	....	....	....	....	....	....	....	....	....
2014-15	Binghamton	AHL	34	4	10	14	79	....	....	....	....	....	....	....	....	....	....	....	....	....	....	....	....	....	....
	NHL Totals		**34**	**1**	**1**	**2**	**37**	**0**	**0**	**0**	**26**	**3.8**		**157**	**58.6**	**7:35**	....	....	....	....	....	....	....	....	....

Signed as a free agent by **Lowell** (AHL), March 16, 2007. Signed as a free agent by **New Jersey**, June 1, 2009. Signed as a free agent by **Utah** (ECHL), October 3, 2012. Signed as a free agent by **Chicago**, October 25, 2013. • Missed majority of 2013-14 due to lower-body injury vs. Ottawa, October 29, 2013. Signed to a PTO (professional tryout) contract by **Binghamton** (AHL) ,October 8, 2014. • Missed majority of 2014-15 as a healthy reserve and due to a 20-game suspension for violating terms of the AHL/PHPA Program for Performance Enhancing Substances, October 28, 2014. Signed as a free agent by **Ottawa**, January 27, 2015.

MITCHELL, John
(MIH-chuhl, JAWN) **COL**

Center. Shoots left. 6'1", 204 lbs. Born, Oakville, ON, January 22, 1985. Toronto's 4th choice, 158th overall, in 2003 Entry Draft.

Season	Club	League	GP	G	A	Pts	PIM	PP	SH	GW	S	S%	+/-	TF	F%	Min	GP	G	A	Pts	PIM	PP	SH	GW	Min
2000-01	Waterloo Siskens	ON-Jr.A	47	15	29	44	33	....	....	....	....	....	....	....	....	....	....	....	....	....	....	....	....	....	....
2001-02	Plymouth Whalers	OHL	62	9	9	18	23	....	....	....	....	....	....	....	....	....	6	1	0	1	4	....	....	....	....
2002-03	Plymouth Whalers	OHL	68	18	37	55	31	....	....	....	....	....	....	....	....	....	18	2	10	12	8	....	....	....	....
2003-04	Plymouth Whalers	OHL	65	28	54	82	45	....	....	....	....	....	....	....	....	....	9	6	6	12	6	....	....	....	....
2004-05	Plymouth Whalers	OHL	63	25	50	75	59	....	....	....	....	....	....	....	....	....	4	1	1	2	0	....	....	....	....
	St. John's	AHL	2	0	0	0	0	....	....	....	....	....	....	....	....	....	....	....	....	....	....	....	....	....	....
2005-06	Toronto Marlies	AHL	51	5	12	17	22	....	....	....	....	....	....	....	....	....	2	0	0	0	0	....	....	....	....
2006-07	Toronto Marlies	AHL	73	16	20	36	46	....	....	....	....	....	....	....	....	....	....	....	....	....	....	....	....	....	....
2007-08	Toronto Marlies	AHL	79	20	31	51	56	....	....	....	....	....	....	....	....	....	19	8	4	12	12	....	....	....	....
2008-09	**Toronto**	**NHL**	**76**	**12**	**17**	**29**	**33**	**2**	**0**	**0**	**98**	**12.2**	**–16**	**669**	**48.7**	**13:48**	....	....	....	....	....	....	....	....	....
2009-10	**Toronto**	**NHL**	**60**	**6**	**17**	**23**	**31**	**1**	**0**	**1**	**90**	**6.7**	**–7**	**477**	**51.2**	**15:49**	....	....	....	....	....	....	....	....	....
2010-11	**Toronto**	**NHL**	**23**	**2**	**1**	**3**	**12**	**1**	**0**	**1**	**28**	**7.1**	**–7**	**149**	**55.7**	**12:31**	....	....	....	....	....	....	....	....	....
	Toronto Marlies	AHL	10	1	4	5	2	....	....	....	....	....	....	....	....	....	....	....	....	....	....	....	....	....	....
	Connecticut	AHL	14	7	5	12	10	....	....	....	....	....	....	....	....	....	6	3	3	6	0	....	....	....	....
2011-12	**NY Rangers**	**NHL**	**63**	**5**	**11**	**16**	**8**	**0**	**0**	**0**	**64**	**7.8**	**10**	**199**	**51.8**	**10:10**	**18**	**0**	**1**	**1**	**2**	**0**	**0**	**0**	**7:05**
	Connecticut	AHL	17	7	7	14	20	....	....	....	....	....	....	....	....	....	....	....	....	....	....	....	....	....	....
2012-13	**Colorado**	**NHL**	**47**	**10**	**10**	**20**	**18**	**1**	**0**	**1**	**72**	**13.9**	**5**	**344**	**49.7**	**16:45**	....	....	....	....	....	....	....	....	....
2013-14	**Colorado**	**NHL**	**75**	**11**	**21**	**32**	**36**	**3**	**0**	**2**	**107**	**10.3**	**13**	**748**	**50.0**	**16:16**	....	....	....	....	....	....	....	....	....
2014-15	**Colorado**	**NHL**	**68**	**11**	**15**	**26**	**32**	**3**	**1**	**1**	**105**	**10.5**	**–9**	**735**	**50.9**	**15:51**	....	....	....	....	....	....	....	....	....
	NHL Totals		**412**	**57**	**92**	**149**	**170**	**11**	**1**	**6**	**564**	**10.1**		**3321**	**50.4**	**14:36**	**18**	**0**	**1**	**1**	**2**	**0**	**0**	**0**	**7:05**

Traded to **NY Rangers** by **Toronto** for NY Rangers' 7th round choice (Viktor Loov) in 2012 Entry Draft, February 28, 2011. Signed as a free agent by **Colorado**, July 1, 2012.

MITCHELL, Torrey
(MIH-chuhl, TOH-ree) **MTL**

Center. Shoots right. 5'11", 189 lbs. Born, Montreal, QC, January 30, 1985. San Jose's 3rd choice, 126th overall, in 2004 Entry Draft.

Season	Club	League	GP	G	A	Pts	PIM	PP	SH	GW	S	S%	+/-	TF	F%	Min	GP	G	A	Pts	PIM	PP	SH	GW	Min
2001-02	C.C. Lemoyne	QAAA	41	15	41	56	54	....	....	....	....	....	....	....	....	....	19	13	14	27	18	....	....	....	....
2002-03	Hotchkiss School	High-CT	26	19	30	49	33	....	....	....	....	....	....	....	....	....	....	....	....	....	....	....	....	....	....
2003-04	Hotchkiss School	High-CT	25	25	37	62	42	....	....	....	....	....	....	....	....	....	....	....	....	....	....	....	....	....	....
2004-05	U. of Vermont	ECAC	38	11	19	30	74	....	....	....	....	....	....	....	....	....	....	....	....	....	....	....	....	....	....
2005-06	U. of Vermont	H-East	38	12	28	40	34	....	....	....	....	....	....	....	....	....	....	....	....	....	....	....	....	....	....
2006-07	U. of Vermont	H-East	39	12	23	35	46	....	....	....	....	....	....	....	....	....	....	....	....	....	....	....	....	....	....
	Worcester Sharks	AHL	11	2	5	7	27	....	....	....	....	....	....	....	....	....	6	1	1	2	15	....	....	....	....
2007-08	**San Jose**	**NHL**	**82**	**10**	**10**	**20**	**50**	**1**	**2**	**0**	**110**	**9.1**	**–3**	**692**	**49.4**	**14:19**	**13**	**1**	**2**	**3**	**10**	**1**	**0**	**0**	**14:00**
2008-09	Worcester Sharks	AHL	2	1	0	1	0	....	....	....	....	....	....	....	....	....	....	....	....	....	....	....	....	....	....
	San Jose	**NHL**	....	....	....	....	....	....	....	....	....	....	....	....	....	....	**4**	**0**	**0**	**0**	**2**	**0**	**0**	**0**	**9:38**
2009-10	**San Jose**	**NHL**	**56**	**2**	**9**	**11**	**27**	**0**	**0**	**0**	**59**	**3.4**	**6**	**205**	**43.4**	**11:26**	**15**	**0**	**2**	**2**	**2**	**0**	**0**	**0**	**13:05**
	Worcester Sharks	AHL	5	1	2	3	10	....	....	....	....	....	....	....	....	....	....	....	....	....	....	....	....	....	....
2010-11	**San Jose**	**NHL**	**66**	**9**	**14**	**23**	**46**	**0**	**0**	**1**	**116**	**7.8**	**10**	**203**	**48.8**	**13:21**	**18**	**1**	**4**	**5**	**10**	**0**	**0**	**0**	**15:02**
2011-12	**San Jose**	**NHL**	**76**	**9**	**10**	**19**	**29**	**0**	**0**	**0**	**100**	**9.0**	**–6**	**83**	**43.4**	**12:26**	**5**	**0**	**1**	**1**	**6**	**0**	**0**	**0**	**13:02**
2012-13	San Francisco	ECHL	2	1	0	1	0	....	....	....	....	....	....	....	....	....	....	....	....	....	....	....	....	....	....
	Minnesota	**NHL**	**45**	**4**	**4**	**8**	**21**	**0**	**0**	**1**	**39**	**10.3**	**–8**	**42**	**50.0**	**10:30**	**5**	**1**	**0**	**1**	**0**	**0**	**0**	**0**	**11:24**
2013-14	**Minnesota**	**NHL**	**58**	**1**	**8**	**9**	**21**	**0**	**0**	**0**	**47**	**2.1**	**–3**	**24**	**37.5**	**10:08**	....	....	....	....	....	....	....	....	....
	Buffalo	**NHL**	**9**	**1**	**0**	**1**	**4**	**0**	**0**	**0**	**9**	**11.1**	**0**	**7**	**42.9**	**15:39**	....	....	....	....	....	....	....	....	....
2014-15	**Buffalo**	**NHL**	**51**	**6**	**7**	**13**	**26**	**0**	**0**	**2**	**45**	**13.3**	**–6**	**661**	**47.2**	**15:20**	....	....	....	....	....	....	....	....	....
	Montreal	**NHL**	**14**	**0**	**1**	**1**	**8**	**0**	**0**	**0**	**10**	**0.0**	**–2**	**153**	**56.9**	**10:03**	**12**	**1**	**4**	**5**	**6**	**0**	**0**	**0**	**12:31**
	NHL Totals		**457**	**42**	**63**	**105**	**232**	**1**	**2**	**4**	**535**	**7.9**		**2070**	**48.2**	**12:37**	**72**	**4**	**13**	**17**	**36**	**1**	**0**	**0**	**13:20**

ECAC All-Rookie Team (2005)

• Missed majority of 2008-09 due to training camp leg injury, September 18, 2008. Signed as a free agent by **Minnesota**, July 1, 2012. Traded to **Buffalo** by **Minnesota** with Winnipeg's 2nd round choice (previously acquired, later traded to Washington – Washington selected Vitek Vanecek) in 2014 Entry Draft and Minnesota's 2nd round choice in 2016 Entry Draft for Matt Moulson and Cody McCormick, March 5, 2014. Traded to **Montreal** by **Buffalo** for Jack Nevins and a 7th round choice in 2016 Entry Draft, March 2, 2015.

MITCHELL, Willie
(MIH-chuhl, WIH-lee) **FLA**

Defense. Shoots left. 6'3", 210 lbs. Born, Port McNeill, BC, April 23, 1977. New Jersey's 12th choice, 199th overall, in 1996 Entry Draft.

Season	Club	League	GP	G	A	Pts	PIM	PP	SH	GW	S	S%	+/-	TF	F%	Min	GP	G	A	Pts	PIM	PP	SH	GW	Min
1993-94	Notre Dame	SMHL	31	4	11	15	81	....	....	....	....	....	....	....	....	....	....	....	....	....	....	....	....	....	....
1994-95	Kelowna Spartans	BCHL	42	3	8	11	71	....	....	....	....	....	....	....	....	....	....	....	....	....	....	....	....	....	....
1995-96	Melfort Mustangs	SJHL	19	2	6	8	....	....	....	....	....	....	....	....	....	....	14	0	2	2	12	....	....	....	....
1996-97	Melfort Mustangs	SJHL	64	14	42	56	227	....	....	....	....	....	....	....	....	....	4	0	1	1	23	....	....	....	....
1997-98	Clarkson Knights	ECAC	34	9	17	26	105	....	....	....	....	....	....	....	....	....	....	....	....	....	....	....	....	....	....
1998-99	Clarkson Knights	ECAC	34	10	19	29	40	....	....	....	....	....	....	....	....	....	....	....	....	....	....	....	....	....	....
	Albany River Rats	AHL	6	1	3	4	29	....	....	....	....	....	....	....	....	....	....	....	....	....	....	....	....	....	....
99-2000	**New Jersey**	**NHL**	**2**	**0**	**0**	**0**	**0**	**0**	**0**	**0**	**2**	**0.0**	**1**	**0**	**0.0**	**16:04**	....	....	....	....	....	....	....	....	....
	Albany River Rats	AHL	63	5	14	19	71	....	....	....	....	....	....	....	....	....	5	1	2	3	4	....	....	....	....
2000-01	**New Jersey**	**NHL**	**16**	**0**	**2**	**2**	**29**	**0**	**0**	**0**	**14**	**0.0**	**0**	**0**	**0.0**	**14:52**	....	....	....	....	....	....	....	....	....
	Albany River Rats	AHL	41	3	13	16	94	....	....	....	....	....	....	....	....	....	....	....	....	....	....	....	....	....	....
	Minnesota	**NHL**	**17**	**1**	**7**	**8**	**11**	**0**	**0**	**0**	**16**	**6.3**	**4**	**0**	**0.0**	**20:49**	....	....	....	....	....	....	....	....	....
2001-02	**Minnesota**	**NHL**	**68**	**3**	**10**	**13**	**68**	**0**	**0**	**1**	**67**	**4.5**	**–16**	**0**	**0.0**	**21:25**	....	....	....	....	....	....	....	....	....
2002-03	**Minnesota**	**NHL**	**69**	**2**	**12**	**14**	**84**	**0**	**1**	**1**	**67**	**3.0**	**13**	**0**	**0.0**	**21:28**	**18**	**1**	**3**	**4**	**14**	**0**	**0**	**0**	**24:48**
2003-04	**Minnesota**	**NHL**	**70**	**1**	**13**	**14**	**83**	**0**	**0**	**0**	**58**	**1.7**	**12**	**2**	**50.0**	**22:36**	....	....	....	....	....	....	....	....	....
2004-05			DID NOT PLAY																						
2005-06	**Minnesota**	**NHL**	**64**	**2**	**6**	**8**	**87**	**0**	**0**	**0**	**48**	**4.2**	**15**	**0**	**0.0**	**20:52**	....	....	....	....	....	....	....	....	....
	Dallas	**NHL**	**16**	**0**	**2**	**2**	**26**	**0**	**0**	**0**	**10**	**0.0**	**4**	**0**	**0.0**	**20:46**	**5**	**0**	**0**	**0**	**2**	**0**	**0**	**0**	**23:21**

			Regular Season														Playoffs								
Season	Club	League	GP	G	A	Pts	PIM	PP	SH	GW	S	S%	+/-	TF	F%	Min	GP	G	A	Pts	PIM	PP	SH	GW	Min
2006-07	**Vancouver**	**NHL**	**62**	**1**	**10**	**11**	**45**	**0**	**0**	**0**	**54**	**1.9**	**1**	**0**	**0.0**	**22:13**	**12**	**0**	**1**	**1**	**12**	**0**	**0**	**0**	**27:14**
2007-08	**Vancouver**	**NHL**	**72**	**2**	**10**	**12**	**81**	**0**	**0**	**1**	**65**	**3.1**	**6**	**0**	**0.0**	**23:12**	....	....	....	....	....	....	....	....	....
2008-09	**Vancouver**	**NHL**	**82**	**3**	**20**	**23**	**59**	**0**	**0**	**1**	**88**	**3.4**	**29**	**1**	**0.0**	**22:55**	**10**	**0**	**2**	**2**	**22**	**0**	**0**	**0**	**24:13**
2009-10	**Vancouver**	**NHL**	**48**	**4**	**8**	**12**	**48**	**0**	**0**	**1**	**47**	**8.5**	**13**	**0**	**0.0**	**22:37**	....	....	....	....	....	....	....	....	....
2010-11	**Los Angeles**	**NHL**	**57**	**5**	**5**	**10**	**21**	**0**	**1**	**1**	**59**	**8.5**	**4**	**0**	**0.0**	**21:49**	**6**	**1**	**1**	**2**	**4**	**0**	**0**	**0**	**24:17**
2011-12♦	**Los Angeles**	**NHL**	**76**	**5**	**19**	**24**	**44**	**0**	**0**	**2**	**104**	**4.8**	**20**	**1**	**0.0**	**22:14**	**20**	**1**	**2**	**3**	**16**	**1**	**0**	**0**	**25:19**
2012-13	**Los Angeles**	**NHL**	DID NOT PLAY – INJURED																						
2013-14♦	**Los Angeles**	**NHL**	**76**	**1**	**11**	**12**	**58**	**0**	**0**	**0**	**73**	**1.4**	**14**	**0**	**0.0**	**20:20**	**18**	**1**	**3**	**4**	**20**	**1**	**0**	**0**	**22:20**
2014-15	**Florida**	**NHL**	**66**	**3**	**5**	**8**	**25**	**0**	**0**	**0**	**78**	**3.8**	**1**	**0**	**0.0**	**21:41**	....	....	....	....	....	....	....	....	....
	NHL Totals		**861**	**33**	**140**	**173**	**769**	**0**	**2**	**8**	**850**	**3.9**		**4**	**25.0**	**21:45**	**89**	**4**	**12**	**16**	**90**	**2**	**0**	**0**	**24:34**

SJHL First All-Star Team (1997) • SJHL Top Defenseman Award (1997) • ECAC Second All-Star Team (1998) • ECAC Rookie of the Year (1998) (co-winner - Erik Cole) • ECAC First All-Star Team (1999) • NCAA East Second All-American Team (1999)

Traded to **Minnesota** by **New Jersey** for Sean O'Donnell, March 4, 2001. Traded to **Dallas** by **Minnesota** with Minnesota's 2nd round choice (Nico Saccheti) in 2007 Entry Draft for Martin Skoula and Shawn Belle, March 9, 2006. Signed as a free agent by **Vancouver**, July 1, 2006. Signed as a free agent by **Los Angeles**, August 25, 2010. • Missed 2012-13 due to recurring knee injury and resulting surgery, January 18, 2013. Signed as a free agent by **Florida**, July 1, 2014.

MOEN, Travis (MOH-ehn, TRA-vihs) DAL

Left wing. Shoots left. 6'2", 210 lbs. Born, Stewart Valley, SK, April 6, 1982. Calgary's 6th choice, 155th overall, in 2000 Entry Draft.

Season	Club	League	GP	G	A	Pts	PIM	PP	SH	GW	S	S%	+/-	TF	F%	Min	GP	G	A	Pts	PIM	PP	SH	GW	Min
1998-99	Swift Current	SMHL	STATISTICS NOT AVAILABLE																						
	Kelowna Rockets	WHL	4	0	0	0	0	....	....	....	....	....	....	....	....	....	....	....	....	....	....	....	....	....	....
99-2000	Kelowna Rockets	WHL	66	9	6	15	96	....	....	....	....	....	....	....	....	....	5	1	1	2	2	....	....	....	....
2000-01	Kelowna Rockets	WHL	40	8	8	16	106	....	....	....	....	....	....	....	....	....	....	....	....	....	....	....	....	....	....
2001-02	Kelowna Rockets	WHL	71	10	17	27	197	....	....	....	....	....	....	....	....	....	13	1	0	1	28	....	....	....	....
2002-03	Norfolk Admirals	AHL	42	1	2	3	62	....	....	....	....	....	....	....	....	....	9	0	0	0	20	....	....	....	....
2003-04	**Chicago**	**NHL**	**82**	**4**	**2**	**6**	**142**	**0**	**0**	**2**	**51**	**7.8**	**–17**	**19**	**15.8**	**10:57**	....	....	....	....	....	....	....	....	....
2004-05	Norfolk Admirals	AHL	79	8	12	20	187	....	....	....	....	....	....	....	....	....	6	0	1	1	6	....	....	....	....
2005-06	**Anaheim**	**NHL**	**39**	**4**	**1**	**5**	**72**	**0**	**0**	**0**	**28**	**14.3**	**–3**	**8**	**12.5**	**11:03**	**9**	**1**	**0**	**1**	**10**	**0**	**0**	**0**	**8:25**
2006-07♦	**Anaheim**	**NHL**	**82**	**11**	**10**	**21**	**101**	**0**	**0**	**0**	**124**	**8.9**	**–4**	**10**	**30.0**	**14:48**	**21**	**7**	**5**	**12**	**22**	**0**	**0**	**3**	**17:19**
2007-08	**Anaheim**	**NHL**	**77**	**3**	**5**	**8**	**81**	**0**	**1**	**1**	**98**	**3.1**	**–10**	**25**	**32.0**	**15:50**	**6**	**1**	**1**	**2**	**2**	**0**	**0**	**0**	**14:09**
2008-09	**Anaheim**	**NHL**	**63**	**4**	**7**	**11**	**77**	**0**	**2**	**1**	**77**	**5.2**	**–17**	**7**	**28.6**	**14:53**	....	....	....	....	....	....	....	....	....
	San Jose	**NHL**	**19**	**3**	**2**	**5**	**14**	**0**	**1**	**1**	**24**	**12.5**	**–1**	**11**	**18.2**	**15:21**	**6**	**0**	**0**	**0**	**2**	**0**	**0**	**0**	**12:54**
2009-10	**Montreal**	**NHL**	**81**	**8**	**11**	**19**	**57**	**1**	**2**	**0**	**107**	**7.5**	**–2**	**12**	**25.0**	**15:00**	**19**	**2**	**1**	**3**	**4**	**0**	**1**	**1**	**13:15**
2010-11	**Montreal**	**NHL**	**79**	**6**	**10**	**16**	**96**	**0**	**1**	**0**	**99**	**6.1**	**–4**	**22**	**36.4**	**13:11**	**7**	**0**	**1**	**1**	**2**	**0**	**0**	**0**	**16:33**
2011-12	**Montreal**	**NHL**	**48**	**9**	**7**	**16**	**41**	**0**	**1**	**0**	**45**	**20.0**	**–3**	**12**	**41.7**	**15:43**	....	....	....	....	....	....	....	....	....
2012-13	**Montreal**	**NHL**	**45**	**2**	**4**	**6**	**32**	**0**	**0**	**0**	**32**	**6.3**	**–4**	**10**	**40.0**	**11:39**	**5**	**0**	**0**	**0**	**17**	**0**	**0**	**0**	**12:53**
2013-14	**Montreal**	**NHL**	**65**	**2**	**10**	**12**	**49**	**0**	**0**	**0**	**56**	**3.6**	**2**	**8**	**87.5**	**11:32**	**4**	**0**	**0**	**0**	**0**	**0**	**0**	**0**	**10:28**
2014-15	**Montreal**	**NHL**	**10**	**0**	**0**	**0**	**4**	**0**	**0**	**0**	**9**	**0.0**	**0**	**2**	**0.0**	**10:30**	....	....	....	....	....	....	....	....	....
	Dallas	**NHL**	**34**	**3**	**6**	**9**	**14**	**0**	**0**	**0**	**25**	**12.0**	**0**	**2**	**0.0**	**9:03**	....	....	....	....	....	....	....	....	....
	NHL Totals		**724**	**59**	**75**	**134**	**780**	**1**	**8**	**5**	**775**	**7.6**		**148**	**31.1**	**13:23**	**77**	**11**	**8**	**19**	**59**	**0**	**1**	**4**	**13:58**

Signed as a free agent by **Chicago**, October 21, 2002. Traded to **Anaheim** by **Chicago** for Michael Holmqvist, July 30, 2005. • Missed majority of 2005-06 due to knee and shoulder injuries and as a healthy reserve. Traded to **San Jose** by **Anaheim** with Kent Huskins for Timo Pielmeier, Nick Bonino and San Jose's 4th round choice (Andrew O'Brien) in 2012 Entry Draft, March 4, 2009. Signed as a free agent by **Montreal**, July 10, 2009. Traded to **Dallas** by **Montreal** for Sergei Gonchar, November 11, 2014.

MOLLER, Oscar (MOH-luhr, AH-skuhr)

Center. Shoots right. 5'10", 189 lbs. Born, Stockholm, Sweden, January 22, 1989. Los Angeles' 2nd choice, 52nd overall, in 2007 Entry Draft.

Season	Club	League	GP	G	A	Pts	PIM	PP	SH	GW	S	S%	+/-	TF	F%	Min	GP	G	A	Pts	PIM	PP	SH	GW	Min
2003-04	Spanga U18	Swe-U18	32	28	12	40	68	....	....	....	....	....	....	....	....	....	....	....	....	....	....	....	....	....	....
2004-05	Spanga U18	Swe-U18	24	28	16	44	52	....	....	....	....	....	....	....	....	....	....	....	....	....	....	....	....	....	....
	Spanga Jr.	Swe-Jr.	4	6	1	7	6	....	....	....	....	....	....	....	....	....	....	....	....	....	....	....	....	....	....
	Spanga	Sweden-4	6	6	4	10	0	....	....	....	....	....	....	....	....	....	....	....	....	....	....	....	....	....	....
2005-06	Djurgarden U18	Swe-U18	8	8	5	13	6	....	....	....	....	....	....	....	....	....	2	1	0	1	0	....	....	....	....
	Djurgarden Jr.	Swe-Jr.	25	8	5	13	41	....	....	....	....	....	....	....	....	....	4	2	0	2	0	....	....	....	....
2006-07	Chilliwack Bruins	WHL	68	32	37	69	50	....	....	....	....	....	....	....	....	....	5	0	3	3	6	....	....	....	....
2007-08	Chilliwack Bruins	WHL	63	39	43	82	42	....	....	....	....	....	....	....	....	....	4	2	1	3	4	....	....	....	....
	Manchester	AHL	....	....	....	....	....	....	....	....	....	....	....	....	....	....	2	0	1	1	0	....	....	....	....
2008-09	**Los Angeles**	**NHL**	**40**	**7**	**8**	**15**	**16**	**5**	**0**	**0**	**81**	**8.6**	**–3**	**86**	**43.0**	**13:22**	....	....	....	....	....	....	....	....	....
	Manchester	AHL	8	2	3	5	6	....	....	....	....	....	....	....	....	....	....	....	....	....	....	....	....	....	....
2009-10	**Los Angeles**	**NHL**	**34**	**4**	**3**	**7**	**4**	**1**	**0**	**0**	**42**	**9.5**	**–6**	**104**	**30.8**	**8:35**	....	....	....	....	....	....	....	....	....
	Manchester	AHL	43	15	18	33	20	....	....	....	....	....	....	....	....	....	16	2	5	7	0	....	....	....	....
2010-11	**Los Angeles**	**NHL**	**13**	**1**	**3**	**4**	**2**	**0**	**0**	**0**	**27**	**3.7**	**–1**	**5**	**80.0**	**14:36**	**1**	**0**	**0**	**0**	**0**	**0**	**0**	**0**	**10:37**
	Manchester	AHL	59	23	27	50	34	....	....	....	....	....	....	....	....	....	....	....	....	....	....	....	....	....	....
2011-12	Skelleftea AIK	Sweden	54	14	17	31	6	....	....	....	....	....	....	....	....	....	19	7	8	15	8	....	....	....	....
2012-13	Skelleftea AIK	Sweden	28	18	8	26	2	....	....	....	....	....	....	....	....	....	13	5	5	10	2	....	....	....	....
2013-14	Skelleftea AIK	Sweden	48	27	18	45	14	....	....	....	....	....	....	....	....	....	14	5	*13	*18	2	....	....	....	....
2014-15	Ak Bars Kazan	KHL	54	14	18	32	6	....	....	....	....	....	....	....	....	....	20	9	3	12	4	....	....	....	....
	NHL Totals		**87**	**12**	**14**	**26**	**22**	**6**	**0**	**0**	**150**	**8.0**		**195**	**37.4**	**11:41**	**1**	**0**	**0**	**0**	**0**	**0**	**0**	**0**	**10:37**

WHL West First All-Star Team (2008)

Signed as a free agent by **Skelleftea** (Sweden), May 17, 2011. Signed as a free agent by **Kazan** (KHL), July 2, 2014.

MONAHAN, Sean (MAWN-ah-han, SHAWN) CGY

Center. Shoots left. 6'2", 185 lbs. Born, Brampton, ON, October 12, 1994. Calgary's 1st choice, 6th overall, in 2013 Entry Draft.

Season	Club	League	GP	G	A	Pts	PIM	PP	SH	GW	S	S%	+/-	TF	F%	Min	GP	G	A	Pts	PIM	PP	SH	GW	Min
2009-10	Miss. Rebels	GTHL	47	46	44	90	48	....	....	....	....	....	....	....	....	....	....	....	....	....	....	....	....	....	....
2010-11	Ottawa 67's	OHL	65	20	27	47	32	....	....	....	....	....	....	....	....	....	4	2	2	4	0	....	....	....	....
2011-12	Ottawa 67's	OHL	62	33	45	78	38	....	....	....	....	....	....	....	....	....	18	8	7	15	12	....	....	....	....
2012-13	Ottawa 67's	OHL	58	31	47	78	24	....	....	....	....	....	....	....	....	....	....	....	....	....	....	....	....	....	....
2013-14	**Calgary**	**NHL**	**75**	**22**	**12**	**34**	**8**	**3**	**0**	**2**	**140**	**15.7**	**–20**	**1036**	**46.0**	**15:59**	....	....	....	....	....	....	....	....	....
2014-15	**Calgary**	**NHL**	**81**	**31**	**31**	**62**	**12**	**10**	**1**	**8**	**191**	**16.2**	**8**	**1830**	**49.3**	**19:37**	**11**	**3**	**3**	**6**	**2**	**1**	**0**	**0**	**19:47**
	NHL Totals		**156**	**53**	**43**	**96**	**20**	**13**	**1**	**10**	**331**	**16.0**		**2866**	**48.1**	**17:52**	**11**	**3**	**3**	**6**	**2**	**1**	**0**	**0**	**19:47**

OHL Second All-Star Team (2012)

MOORE, Dominic (MOOR, DOHM-ihn-ihk) NYR

Center. Shoots left. 6', 192 lbs. Born, Sarnia, ON, August 3, 1980. NY Rangers' 2nd choice, 95th overall, in 2000 Entry Draft.

Season	Club	League	GP	G	A	Pts	PIM	PP	SH	GW	S	S%	+/-	TF	F%	Min	GP	G	A	Pts	PIM	PP	SH	GW	Min
1996-97	Thornhill Rattlers	ON-Jr.A	29	4	6	10	48	....	....	....	....	....	....	....	....	....	1	0	1	1	0	....	....	....	....
1997-98	Aurora Tigers	ON-Jr.A	51	10	15	25	16	....	....	....	....	....	....	....	....	....	....	....	....	....	....	....	....	....	....
1998-99	Aurora Tigers	ON-Jr.A	51	34	53	87	70	....	....	....	....	....	....	....	....	....	....	....	....	....	....	....	....	....	....
99-2000	Harvard Crimson	ECAC	30	12	12	24	28	....	....	....	....	....	....	....	....	....	....	....	....	....	....	....	....	....	....
2000-01	Harvard Crimson	ECAC	32	15	28	43	40	....	....	....	....	....	....	....	....	....	....	....	....	....	....	....	....	....	....
2001-02	Harvard Crimson	ECAC	32	13	16	29	37	....	....	....	....	....	....	....	....	....	....	....	....	....	....	....	....	....	....
2002-03	Harvard Crimson	ECAC	34	*24	27	*51	30	....	....	....	....	....	....	....	....	....	....	....	....	....	....	....	....	....	....
2003-04	**NY Rangers**	**NHL**	**5**	**0**	**3**	**3**	**0**	**0**	**0**	**0**	**3**	**0.0**	**0**	**36**	**30.6**	**9:18**	....	....	....	....	....	....	....	....	....
	Hartford	AHL	70	14	25	39	60	....	....	....	....	....	....	....	....	....	16	3	3	6	8	....	....	....	....
2004-05	Hartford	AHL	78	19	31	50	78	....	....	....	....	....	....	....	....	....	6	1	1	2	4	....	....	....	....
2005-06	**NY Rangers**	**NHL**	**82**	**9**	**9**	**18**	**28**	**2**	**0**	**1**	**139**	**6.5**	**4**	**814**	**46.3**	**12:28**	**4**	**0**	**0**	**0**	**2**	**0**	**0**	**0**	**11:21**
2006-07	**Pittsburgh**	**NHL**	**59**	**6**	**9**	**15**	**46**	**0**	**0**	**0**	**100**	**6.0**	**1**	**678**	**51.6**	**13:04**	....	....	....	....	....	....	....	....	....
	Minnesota	**NHL**	**10**	**2**	**0**	**2**	**10**	**0**	**0**	**1**	**11**	**18.2**	**3**	**66**	**62.1**	**10:12**	....	....	....	....	....	....	....	....	....
2007-08	**Minnesota**	**NHL**	**30**	**1**	**2**	**3**	**10**	**0**	**0**	**0**	**28**	**3.6**	**–11**	**311**	**52.4**	**11:57**	....	....	....	....	....	....	....	....	....
	Toronto	**NHL**	**38**	**4**	**10**	**14**	**14**	**1**	**0**	**0**	**72**	**5.6**	**7**	**393**	**50.6**	**14:21**	....	....	....	....	....	....	....	....	....
2008-09	**Toronto**	**NHL**	**63**	**12**	**29**	**41**	**69**	**4**	**1**	**1**	**132**	**9.1**	**–1**	**1007**	**54.8**	**17:18**	....	....	....	....	....	....	....	....	....
	Buffalo	**NHL**	**18**	**1**	**3**	**4**	**23**	**0**	**0**	**0**	**33**	**3.0**	**–1**	**237**	**51.1**	**15:12**	....	....	....	....	....	....	....	....	....
2009-10	**Florida**	**NHL**	**48**	**8**	**9**	**17**	**35**	**2**	**1**	**0**	**81**	**9.9**	**–7**	**462**	**55.8**	**14:55**	....	....	....	....	....	....	....	....	....
	Montreal	**NHL**	**21**	**2**	**9**	**11**	**8**	**0**	**1**	**0**	**38**	**5.3**	**4**	**201**	**53.2**	**14:40**	**19**	**4**	**1**	**5**	**6**	**0**	**0**	**1**	**14:34**
2010-11	**Tampa Bay**	**NHL**	**77**	**18**	**14**	**32**	**52**	**6**	**0**	**3**	**175**	**10.3**	**–12**	**892**	**53.3**	**15:36**	**18**	**3**	**8**	**11**	**18**	**1**	**0**	**0**	**17:46**
2011-12	**Tampa Bay**	**NHL**	**56**	**4**	**15**	**19**	**48**	**0**	**1**	**1**	**74**	**5.4**	**–10**	**573**	**55.7**	**16:17**	....	....	....	....	....	....	....	....	....
	San Jose	**NHL**	**23**	**0**	**6**	**6**	**6**	**0**	**0**	**0**	**29**	**0.0**	**–8**	**189**	**52.9**	**13:43**	**3**	**0**	**0**	**0**	**5**	**0**	**0**	**0**	**15:08**

			Regular Season														Playoffs								
Season	Club	League	GP	G	A	Pts	PIM	PP	SH	GW	S	S%	+/-	TF	F%	Min	GP	G	A	Pts	PIM	PP	SH	GW	Min
2012-13			Did not play																						
2013-14	**NY Rangers**	**NHL**	**73**	**6**	**12**	**18**	**18**	**0**	**1**	**1**	**96**	**6.3**	**0**	**648**	**54.6**	**11:43**	**25**	**3**	**5**	**8**	**24**	**0**	**0**	**2**	**13:28**
2014-15	**NY Rangers**	**NHL**	**82**	**10**	**17**	**27**	**28**	**0**	**2**	**3**	**116**	**8.6**	**5**	**1074**	**54.5**	**13:49**	**19**	**1**	**2**	**3**	**12**	**0**	**0**	**1**	**14:49**
	NHL Totals		**685**	**83**	**147**	**230**	**395**	**15**	**7**	**11**	**1127**	**7.4**		**7581**	**52.9**	**14:05**	**88**	**11**	**16**	**27**	**67**	**1**	**0**	**4**	**14:50**

ECAC All-Rookie Team (2000) • ECAC Second All-Star Team (2001) • ECAC First All-Star Team (2003) • NCAA East First All-American Team (2003) • Bill Masterton Memorial Trophy (2014)

Traded to **Nashville** by **NY Rangers** for Adam Hall, July 19, 2006. Traded to **Pittsburgh** by **Nashville** with Libor Pivko for Pittsburgh's 3rd round choice (Ryan Thang) in 2007 Entry Draft, July 19, 2006. Traded to **Minnesota** by **Pittsburgh** for Minnesota's 3rd round choice (Casey Pierro-Zabotel) in 2007 Entry Draft, February 27, 2007. Claimed on waivers by **Toronto** from **Minnesota**, January 11, 2008. Traded to **Buffalo** by **Toronto** for Carolina's 2nd round choice (previously acquired, Toronto selected Jesse Blacker) in 2009 Entry Draft, March 4, 2009. Signed as a free agent by **Florida**, October 5, 2009. Traded to **Montreal** by **Florida** for Montreal's 2nd round choice (later traded to San Jose – San Jose selected Matthew Nieto) in 2011 Entry Draft, February 11, 2010. Signed as a free agent by **Tampa Bay**, July 30, 2010. Traded to **San Jose** by **Tampa Bay** with Tampa Bay's 7th round choice (later traded to Chicago – Chicago selected Brandon Whitney) in 2012 Entry Draft for Minnesota's 2nd round choice (previously acquired, later traded to Nashville – Nashville selected Pontius Aberg) in 2012 Entry Draft, February 16, 2012. • Missed 2012-13 due to personal reasons. Signed as a free agent by **NY Rangers**, July 5, 2013.

MOORE, John

(MOOR, JAWN) **N.J.**

Defense. Shoots left. 6'3", 200 lbs. Born, Winnetka, IL, November 19, 1990. Columbus' 1st choice, 21st overall, in 2009 Entry Draft.

			Regular Season														Playoffs								
Season	Club	League	GP	G	A	Pts	PIM	PP	SH	GW	S	S%	+/-	TF	F%	Min	GP	G	A	Pts	PIM	PP	SH	GW	Min
2006-07	Chicago Mission	MWEHL	31	1	12	13	26	....	....	....	....	....	....	....	....	....	....	....	....	....	....	....	....	....	....
	Chicago Mission	Other	30	13	37	50	14	....	....	....	....	....	....	....	....	....	....	....	....	....	....	....	....	....	....
2007-08	Chicago Steel	USHL	56	4	11	15	26	....	....	....	....	....	....	....	....	....	7	0	2	2	2	....	....	....	....
2008-09	Chicago Steel	USHL	57	14	25	39	50	....	....	....	....	....	....	....	....	....	....	....	....	....	....	....	....	....	....
2009-10	Kitchener Rangers	OHL	61	10	37	47	53	....	....	....	....	....	....	....	....	....	20	4	12	16	2	....	....	....	....
2010-11	**Columbus**	**NHL**	**2**	**0**	**0**	**0**	**0**	**0**	**0**	**0**	**0**	**0.0**	**0**	**0**	**0.0**	**11:28**	....	....	....	....	....	....	....	....	....
	Springfield	AHL	73	5	19	24	23	....	....	....	....	....	....	....	....	....	....	....	....	....	....	....	....	....	....
2011-12	**Columbus**	**NHL**	**67**	**2**	**5**	**7**	**8**	**0**	**0**	**0**	**64**	**3.1**	**–23**	**0**	**0.0**	**15:49**	....	....	....	....	....	....	....	....	....
	Springfield	AHL	5	1	1	2	2	....	....	....	....	....	....	....	....	....	....	....	....	....	....	....	....	....	....
2012-13	Springfield	AHL	24	3	6	9	10	....	....	....	....	....	....	....	....	....	....	....	....	....	....	....	....	....	....
	Columbus	**NHL**	**17**	**0**	**1**	**1**	**2**	**0**	**0**	**0**	**14**	**0.0**	**–5**	**0**	**0.0**	**14:31**	....	....	....	....	....	....	....	....	....
	NY Rangers	**NHL**	**13**	**1**	**5**	**6**	**5**	**0**	**0**	**0**	**15**	**6.7**	**9**	**0**	**0.0**	**11:46**	**12**	**0**	**1**	**1**	**2**	**0**	**0**	**0**	**17:08**
2013-14	**NY Rangers**	**NHL**	**74**	**4**	**11**	**15**	**25**	**0**	**0**	**2**	**115**	**3.5**	**7**	**0**	**0.0**	**15:20**	**21**	**0**	**2**	**2**	**16**	**0**	**0**	**0**	**14:32**
2014-15	**NY Rangers**	**NHL**	**38**	**1**	**5**	**6**	**19**	**0**	**0**	**0**	**56**	**1.8**	**7**	**0**	**0.0**	**15:06**	....	....	....	....	....	....	....	....	....
	Arizona	**NHL**	**19**	**1**	**4**	**5**	**11**	**0**	**0**	**0**	**21**	**4.8**	**–11**	**0**	**0.0**	**18:43**	....	....	....	....	....	....	....	....	....
	NHL Totals		**230**	**9**	**31**	**40**	**70**	**0**	**0**	**2**	**285**	**3.2**		**0**	**0.0**	**15:25**	**33**	**0**	**3**	**3**	**18**	**0**	**0**	**0**	**15:29**

USHL First All-Star Team (2009) • USHL Defenseman of the Year (2009)

Traded to **NY Rangers** by **Columbus** with Derek Dorsett, Derick Brassard and Columbus' 6th round choice (later traded to Minnesota – Minnesota selected Chase Lang) in 2014 Entry Draft for Marian Gaborik, Blake Parlett and Steven Delisle, April 3, 2013. Traded to **Arizona** by **NY Rangers** with Anthony Duclair, Tampa Bay's 2nd round choice (previously acquired, later traded to Calgary – Calgary selected Oliver Kylington) in 2015 Entry Draft and future considerations for Keith Yandle, Chris Summers and a 4th round choice in 2016 Entry Draft, March 1, 2015. Signed as a free agent by **New Jersey**, July 1, 2015.

MOORE, Mike

(MOOR, MIGHK) **WSH**

Defense. Shoots left. 6'1", 210 lbs. Born, Calgary, AB, December 12, 1984.

			Regular Season														Playoffs								
Season	Club	League	GP	G	A	Pts	PIM	PP	SH	GW	S	S%	+/-	TF	F%	Min	GP	G	A	Pts	PIM	PP	SH	GW	Min
2002-03	South Surrey	BCHL	55	3	10	13	187	....	....	....	....	....	....	....	....	....	....	....	....	....	....	....	....	....	....
2003-04	Surrey Eagles	BCHL	52	6	21	27	148	....	....	....	....	....	....	....	....	....	10	0	2	2	6	....	....	....	....
2004-05	Princeton	ECAC	25	3	7	10	22	....	....	....	....	....	....	....	....	....	....	....	....	....	....	....	....	....	....
2005-06	Princeton	ECAC	30	0	4	4	42	....	....	....	....	....	....	....	....	....	....	....	....	....	....	....	....	....	....
2006-07	Princeton	ECAC	32	4	10	14	50	....	....	....	....	....	....	....	....	....	....	....	....	....	....	....	....	....	....
2007-08	Princeton	ECAC	34	7	17	24	40	....	....	....	....	....	....	....	....	....	....	....	....	....	....	....	....	....	....
	Worcester Sharks	AHL	3	0	0	0	16	....	....	....	....	....	....	....	....	....	....	....	....	....	....	....	....	....	....
2008-09	Worcester Sharks	AHL	76	5	13	18	132	....	....	....	....	....	....	....	....	....	12	0	1	1	17	....	....	....	....
2009-10	Worcester Sharks	AHL	64	3	19	22	82	....	....	....	....	....	....	....	....	....	11	0	0	0	14	....	....	....	....
2010-11	**San Jose**	**NHL**	**6**	**1**	**0**	**1**	**7**	**0**	**0**	**0**	**5**	**20.0**	**–1**	**0**	**0.0**	**10:07**	....	....	....	....	....	....	....	....	....
	Worcester Sharks	AHL	49	2	10	12	50	....	....	....	....	....	....	....	....	....	....	....	....	....	....	....	....	....	....
2011-12	Worcester Sharks	AHL	61	4	16	20	85	....	....	....	....	....	....	....	....	....	....	....	....	....	....	....	....	....	....
2012-13	Milwaukee	AHL	50	5	11	16	42	....	....	....	....	....	....	....	....	....	4	1	0	1	2	....	....	....	....
2013-14	Providence Bruins	AHL	75	7	14	21	106	....	....	....	....	....	....	....	....	....	12	0	2	2	22	....	....	....	....
2014-15	Hershey Bears	AHL	41	3	11	14	47	....	....	....	....	....	....	....	....	....	9	0	1	1	10	....	....	....	....
	NHL Totals		**6**	**1**	**0**	**1**	**7**	**0**	**0**	**0**	**5**	**20.0**		**0**	**0.0**	**10:07**	....	....	....	....	....	....	....	....	....

ECAC First All-Star Team (2008) • NCAA East First All-American Team (2008)

Signed as a free agent by **San Jose**, April 8, 2008. Signed as a free agent by **Nashville**, July 3, 2012. Signed as a free agent by **Boston**, July 5, 2013. Signed as a free agent by **Washington**, July 1, 2014.

MORIN, Jeremy

(moh-REHN, JAIR-eh-mee) **CHI**

Right wing. Shoots right. 6'1", 189 lbs. Born, Auburn, NY, April 16, 1991. Atlanta's 3rd choice, 45th overall, in 2009 Entry Draft.

			Regular Season														Playoffs								
Season	Club	League	GP	G	A	Pts	PIM	PP	SH	GW	S	S%	+/-	TF	F%	Min	GP	G	A	Pts	PIM	PP	SH	GW	Min
2006-07	Rochester	EJHL	45	26	28	54	80	....	....	....	....	....	....	....	....	....	....	....	....	....	....	....	....	....	....
2007-08	USNTDP	NAHL	30	17	17	34	26	....	....	....	....	....	....	....	....	....	....	....	....	....	....	....	....	....	....
	USNTDP	U-17	7	11	1	12	4	....	....	....	....	....	....	....	....	....	....	....	....	....	....	....	....	....	....
	USNTDP	U-18	28	20	14	34	36	....	....	....	....	....	....	....	....	....	....	....	....	....	....	....	....	....	....
2008-09	USNTDP	NAHL	14	12	15	27	28	....	....	....	....	....	....	....	....	....	....	....	....	....	....	....	....	....	....
	USNTDP	U-18	41	21	11	32	79	....	....	....	....	....	....	....	....	....	....	....	....	....	....	....	....	....	....
2009-10	Kitchener Rangers	OHL	58	47	36	83	76	....	....	....	....	....	....	....	....	....	20	12	9	21	32	....	....	....	....
2010-11	**Chicago**	**NHL**	**9**	**2**	**1**	**3**	**9**	**0**	**0**	**0**	**13**	**15.4**	**2**	**0**	**0.0**	**12:06**	....	....	....	....	....	....	....	....	....
	Rockford IceHogs	AHL	22	8	4	12	34	....	....	....	....	....	....	....	....	....	....	....	....	....	....	....	....	....	....
2011-12	**Chicago**	**NHL**	**3**	**0**	**0**	**0**	**0**	**0**	**0**	**0**	**2**	**0.0**	**–1**	**0**	**0.0**	**8:52**	....	....	....	....	....	....	....	....	....
	Rockford IceHogs	AHL	69	18	22	40	121	....	....	....	....	....	....	....	....	....	....	....	....	....	....	....	....	....	....
2012-13	Rockford IceHogs	AHL	67	30	28	58	86	....	....	....	....	....	....	....	....	....	....	....	....	....	....	....	....	....	....
	Chicago	**NHL**	**3**	**1**	**1**	**2**	**0**	**0**	**0**	**0**	**7**	**14.3**	**1**	**4**	**0.0**	**13:01**	....	....	....	....	....	....	....	....	....
2013-14	**Chicago**	**NHL**	**24**	**5**	**6**	**11**	**32**	**0**	**0**	**0**	**46**	**10.9**	**5**	**6**	**66.7**	**9:10**	**2**	**0**	**0**	**0**	**2**	**0**	**0**	**0**	**6:26**
	Rockford IceHogs	AHL	47	24	23	47	58	....	....	....	....	....	....	....	....	....	....	....	....	....	....	....	....	....	....
2014-15	**Chicago**	**NHL**	**15**	**0**	**0**	**0**	**15**	**0**	**0**	**0**	**28**	**0.0**	**0**	**1**	**100.0**	**7:44**	....	....	....	....	....	....	....	....	....
	Rockford IceHogs	AHL	3	1	0	1	2	....	....	....	....	....	....	....	....	....	....	....	....	....	....	....	....	....	....
	Columbus	**NHL**	**28**	**2**	**4**	**6**	**13**	**0**	**0**	**0**	**45**	**4.4**	**1**	**4**	**25.0**	**11:31**	....	....	....	....	....	....	....	....	....
	NHL Totals		**82**	**10**	**12**	**22**	**69**	**0**	**0**	**0**	**141**	**7.1**		**15**	**40.0**	**10:10**	**2**	**0**	**0**	**0**	**2**	**0**	**0**	**0**	**6:26**

OHL Second All-Star Team (2010)

Traded to **Chicago** by **Atlanta** with Marty Reasoner, Joey Crabb and New Jersey's 1st (previously acquired, Chicago selected Kevin Hayes) and 2nd (previously acquired, Chicago selected Justin Holl) round choices in 2010 Entry Draft for Dustin Byfuglien, Brent Sopel, Ben Eager and Akim Aliu, June 24, 2010. • Missed majority of 2010-11 due to recurring upper-body injury. Traded to **Columbus** by **Chicago** for Tim Erixon, December 14, 2014. Traded to **Chicago** by **Columbus** with Artem Anisimov, Corey Tropp, Marko Dano and Columbus' 4th round choice in 2016 Entry Draft for Brandon Saad, Michael Paliotta and Alex Broadhurst, June 30, 2015.

MORIN, Travis

(moh-REHN, TRA-vihs) **DAL**

Center. Shoots left. 6'1", 190 lbs. Born, Minneapolis, MN, January 9, 1984. Washington's 13th choice, 263rd overall, in 2004 Entry Draft.

			Regular Season														Playoffs								
Season	Club	League	GP	G	A	Pts	PIM	PP	SH	GW	S	S%	+/-	TF	F%	Min	GP	G	A	Pts	PIM	PP	SH	GW	Min
2001-02	Chicago Steel	USHL	20	5	8	13	....	....	....	....	....	....	....	....	....	....	4	0	0	0	2	....	....	....	....
2002-03	Chicago Steel	USHL	60	21	26	47	46	....	....	....	....	....	....	....	....	....	....	....	....	....	....	....	....	....	....
2003-04	Minnesota State	WCHA	38	9	12	21	14	....	....	....	....	....	....	....	....	....	....	....	....	....	....	....	....	....	....
2004-05	Minnesota State	WCHA	36	12	19	31	20	....	....	....	....	....	....	....	....	....	....	....	....	....	....	....	....	....	....
2005-06	Minnesota State	WCHA	39	20	22	42	16	....	....	....	....	....	....	....	....	....	....	....	....	....	....	....	....	....	....
2006-07	Minnesota State	WCHA	38	17	22	39	34	....	....	....	....	....	....	....	....	....	....	....	....	....	....	....	....	....	....
	South Carolina	ECHL	8	2	1	3	0	....	....	....	....	....	....	....	....	....	....	....	....	....	....	....	....	....	....
2007-08	Hershey Bears	AHL	4	0	0	0	0	....	....	....	....	....	....	....	....	....	....	....	....	....	....	....	....	....	....
	South Carolina	ECHL	68	34	50	84	30	....	....	....	....	....	....	....	....	....	20	*10	7	17	18	....	....	....	....
2008-09	Hershey Bears	AHL	1	0	1	1	0	....	....	....	....	....	....	....	....	....	....	....	....	....	....	....	....	....	....
	South Carolina	ECHL	71	26	*62	88	46	....	....	....	....	....	....	....	....	....	19	4	*18	22	12	....	....	....	....
2009-10	Texas Stars	AHL	80	21	31	52	30	....	....	....	....	....	....	....	....	....	24	4	12	16	6	....	....	....	....
2010-11	**Dallas**	**NHL**	**3**	**0**	**0**	**0**	**0**	**0**	**0**	**0**	**2**	**0.0**	**0**	**14**	**57.1**	**8:52**	....	....	....	....	....	....	....	....	....
	Texas Stars	AHL	64	21	24	45	30	....	....	....	....	....	....	....	....	....	6	3	4	7	0	....	....	....	....
2011-12	Texas Stars	AHL	76	13	53	66	46	....	....	....	....	....	....	....	....	....	....	....	....	....	....	....	....	....	....
2012-13	Texas Stars	AHL	59	12	32	44	14	....	....	....	....	....	....	....	....	....	7	0	3	3	4	....	....	....	....
2013-14	**Dallas**	**NHL**	**4**	**0**	**1**	**1**	**0**	**0**	**0**	**0**	**4**	**0.0**	**2**	**38**	**50.0**	**10:20**	....	....	....	....	....	....	....	....	....
	Texas Stars	AHL	66	32	*56	*88	52	....	....	....	....	....	....	....	....	....	21	*9	*13	*22	12	....	....	....	....

			Regular Season														Playoffs								
Season	Club	League	GP	G	A	Pts	PIM	PP	SH	GW	S	S%	+/-	TF	F%	Min	GP	G	A	Pts	PIM	PP	SH	GW	Min
2014-15	**Dallas**	**NHL**	**6**	**0**	**0**	**0**	**0**	**0**	**0**	**0**	**10**	**0.0**	**1**	**60**	**46.7**	**12:06**	....	....	....	....	....	....	....	....	....
	Texas Stars	AHL	63	22	41	63	40	....	....	....	....	....	....	....	....	....	3	0	0	0	0	....	....	....	....
	NHL Totals		**13**	**0**	**1**	**1**	**0**	**0**	**0**	**0**	**16**	**0.0**		**112**	**49.1**	**10:48**	....	....	....	....	....	....	....	....	....

WCHA Second All-Star Team (2007) • ECHL First All-Star Team (2009) • AHL First All-Star Team (2014) • John P. Sollenberger Trophy (AHL - Top Scorer) (2014) • Les Cunningham Award (AHL – MVP) (2014)

Signed as a free agent by **Texas** (AHL), October 21, 2009. Signed as a free agent by **Dallas**, July 12, 2010.

MORMINA, Joey

(mohr-MEE-nah, JOH-ee)

Defense. Shoots left. 6'6", 220 lbs. Born, Montreal, QC, June 29, 1982. Philadelphia's 6th choice, 193rd overall, in 2002 Entry Draft.

Season	Club	League	GP	G	A	Pts	PIM	PP	SH	GW	S	S%	+/-	TF	F%	Min	GP	G	A	Pts	PIM	PP	SH	GW	Min
2000-01	Holderness	High-NH	29	15	15	30	....	....	....	....	....	....	....	....	....	....	....	....	....	....	....	....	....	....	....
2001-02	Colgate	ECAC	34	2	13	15	28	....	....	....	....	....	....	....	....	....	....	....	....	....	....	....	....	....	....
2002-03	Colgate	ECAC	40	4	9	13	52	....	....	....	....	....	....	....	....	....	....	....	....	....	....	....	....	....	....
2003-04	Colgate	ECAC	28	2	10	12	26	....	....	....	....	....	....	....	....	....	....	....	....	....	....	....	....	....	....
2004-05	Colgate	ECAC	39	8	8	16	50	....	....	....	....	....	....	....	....	....	....	....	....	....	....	....	....	....	....
2005-06	Manchester	AHL	61	0	13	13	70	....	....	....	....	....	....	....	....	....	7	0	0	0	4	....	....	....	....
2006-07	Manchester	AHL	62	2	9	11	108	....	....	....	....	....	....	....	....	....	1	0	0	0	2	....	....	....	....
2007-08	**Carolina**	**NHL**	**1**	**0**	**0**	**0**	**0**	**0**	**0**	**0**	**1**	**0.0**	**0**	**0**	**0.0**	**7:45**	....	....	....	....	....	....	....	....	....
	Albany River Rats	AHL	77	4	9	13	96	....	....	....	....	....	....	....	....	....	7	0	0	0	4	....	....	....	....
2008-09	Wilkes-Barre	AHL	70	2	9	11	71	....	....	....	....	....	....	....	....	....	12	0	0	0	12	....	....	....	....
2009-10	Adirondack	AHL	77	5	18	23	102	....	....	....	....	....	....	....	....	....	....	....	....	....	....	....	....	....	....
2010-11	Wilkes-Barre	AHL	50	2	9	11	44	....	....	....	....	....	....	....	....	....	12	0	0	0	16	....	....	....	....
2011-12	Wilkes-Barre	AHL	59	6	15	21	70	....	....	....	....	....	....	....	....	....	12	1	1	2	10	....	....	....	....
2012-13	Wilkes-Barre	AHL	54	3	7	10	60	....	....	....	....	....	....	....	....	....	15	1	7	8	36	....	....	....	....
2013-14	Syracuse Crunch	AHL	56	3	10	13	86	....	....	....	....	....	....	....	....	....	....	....	....	....	....	....	....	....	....
2014-15	Syracuse Crunch	AHL	54	4	15	19	70	....	....	....	....	....	....	....	....	....	3	0	0	0	0	....	....	....	....
	NHL Totals		**1**	**0**	**0**	**0**	**0**	**0**	**0**	**0**	**1**	**0.0**		**0**	**0.0**	**7:45**	....	....	....	....	....	....	....	....	....

Signed as a free agent by **Los Angeles**, August 24, 2005. Signed as a free agent by **Carolina**, July 2, 2007. Signed as a free agent by **Pittsburgh**, July 10, 2008. Signed as a free agent by **Philadelphia**, July 23, 2009. Signed as a free agent by **Wilkes-Barre** (AHL), December 8, 2010. Signed as a free agent by **Syracuse** (AHL), July 3, 2013.

MORROW, Brenden

(MOHR-roh, BREHN-duhn)

Left wing. Shoots left. 6', 205 lbs. Born, Carlyle, SK, January 16, 1979. Dallas' 1st choice, 25th overall, in 1997 Entry Draft.

Season	Club	League	GP	G	A	Pts	PIM	PP	SH	GW	S	S%	+/-	TF	F%	Min	GP	G	A	Pts	PIM	PP	SH	GW	Min
1994-95	Estevan	SMBHL	60	117	72	189	45	....	....	....	....	....	....	....	....	....	....	....	....	....	....	....	....	....	....
1995-96	Portland	WHL	65	13	12	25	61	....	....	....	....	....	....	....	....	....	7	0	0	0	8	....	....	....	....
1996-97	Portland	WHL	71	39	49	88	149	....	....	....	....	....	....	....	....	....	6	2	1	3	4	....	....	....	....
1997-98	Portland	WHL	68	34	52	86	184	....	....	....	....	....	....	....	....	....	16	10	8	18	65	....	....	....	....
1998-99	Portland	WHL	61	41	44	85	248	....	....	....	....	....	....	....	....	....	4	0	4	4	18	....	....	....	....
99-2000	**Dallas**	**NHL**	**64**	**14**	**19**	**33**	**81**	**3**	**0**	**3**	**113**	**12.4**	**8**	**25**	**48.0**	**15:51**	**21**	**2**	**4**	**6**	**22**	**1**	**0**	**0**	**15:04**
	Michigan	IHL	9	2	0	2	18	....	....	....	....	....	....	....	....	....	....	....	....	....	....	....	....	....	....
2000-01	**Dallas**	**NHL**	**82**	**20**	**24**	**44**	**128**	**7**	**0**	**6**	**121**	**16.5**	**18**	**22**	**45.5**	**15:29**	**10**	**0**	**3**	**3**	**12**	**0**	**0**	**0**	**17:00**
2001-02	**Dallas**	**NHL**	**72**	**17**	**18**	**35**	**109**	**4**	**0**	**3**	**102**	**16.7**	**12**	**39**	**41.0**	**16:52**	....	....	....	....	....	....	....	....	....
2002-03	**Dallas**	**NHL**	**71**	**21**	**22**	**43**	**134**	**2**	**3**	**4**	**105**	**20.0**	**20**	**29**	**27.6**	**15:43**	**12**	**3**	**5**	**8**	**16**	**2**	**0**	**0**	**21:03**
2003-04	**Dallas**	**NHL**	**81**	**25**	**24**	**49**	**121**	**9**	**0**	**3**	**132**	**18.9**	**10**	**38**	**47.4**	**19:24**	**5**	**0**	**1**	**1**	**4**	**0**	**0**	**0**	**21:29**
2004-05	Oklahoma City	CHL	19	8	14	22	31	....	....	....	....	....	....	....	....	....	....	....	....	....	....	....	....	....	....
2005-06	**Dallas**	**NHL**	**81**	**23**	**42**	**65**	**183**	**8**	**1**	**4**	**146**	**15.8**	**30**	**32**	**37.5**	**19:15**	**5**	**1**	**5**	**6**	**6**	**0**	**0**	**0**	**21:57**
2006-07	**Dallas**	**NHL**	**40**	**16**	**15**	**31**	**33**	**8**	**0**	**3**	**101**	**15.8**	**–2**	**51**	**39.2**	**18:16**	**7**	**2**	**1**	**3**	**18**	**2**	**0**	**1**	**21:54**
2007-08	**Dallas**	**NHL**	**82**	**32**	**42**	**74**	**105**	**12**	**2**	**7**	**207**	**15.5**	**23**	**41**	**39.0**	**20:00**	**18**	**9**	**6**	**15**	**22**	**4**	**0**	**2**	**23:17**
2008-09	**Dallas**	**NHL**	**18**	**5**	**10**	**15**	**49**	**2**	**0**	**0**	**52**	**9.6**	**–4**	**9**	**33.3**	**21:21**	....	....	....	....	....	....	....	....	....
2009-10	**Dallas**	**NHL**	**76**	**20**	**26**	**46**	**69**	**9**	**1**	**2**	**155**	**12.9**	**–3**	**31**	**29.0**	**19:10**	....	....	....	....	....	....	....	....	....
	Canada	Olympics	7	2	1	3	2	....	....	....	....	....	....	....	....	....	....	....	....	....	....	....	....	....	....
2010-11	**Dallas**	**NHL**	**82**	**33**	**23**	**56**	**76**	**9**	**1**	**5**	**209**	**15.8**	**–3**	**11**	**9.1**	**19:14**	....	....	....	....	....	....	....	....	....
2011-12	**Dallas**	**NHL**	**57**	**11**	**15**	**26**	**97**	**5**	**0**	**2**	**88**	**12.5**	**1**	**27**	**40.7**	**17:02**	....	....	....	....	....	....	....	....	....
2012-13	**Dallas**	**NHL**	**29**	**6**	**5**	**11**	**18**	**1**	**0**	**1**	**31**	**19.4**	**–8**	**23**	**56.5**	**14:55**	....	....	....	....	....	....	....	....	....
	Pittsburgh	**NHL**	**15**	**6**	**8**	**14**	**19**	**1**	**0**	**1**	**24**	**25.0**	**5**	**1**	**0.0**	**14:44**	**14**	**2**	**2**	**4**	**8**	**0**	**0**	**1**	**13:47**
2013-14	**St. Louis**	**NHL**	**71**	**13**	**12**	**25**	**76**	**4**	**0**	**3**	**56**	**23.2**	**1**	**29**	**31.0**	**11:54**	**2**	**0**	**0**	**0**	**0**	**0**	**0**	**0**	**12:35**
2014-15	**Tampa Bay**	**NHL**	**70**	**3**	**5**	**8**	**64**	**0**	**0**	**0**	**28**	**10.7**	**–1**	**0**	**0.0**	**9:20**	**24**	**0**	**0**	**0**	**22**	**0**	**0**	**0**	**8:40**
	NHL Totals		**991**	**265**	**310**	**575**	**1362**	**84**	**8**	**47**	**1670**	**15.9**		**408**	**38.7**	**16:48**	**118**	**19**	**27**	**46**	**130**	**9**	**0**	**4**	**16:34**

WHL West First All-Star Team (1999)

Signed as a free agent by **Oklahoma City** (CHL), October 19, 2004. • Missed majority of 2006-07 due to groin (November 22, 2006 vs. Nashville) and wrist (December 26, 2006 at Chicago) injuries. • Missed majority of 2008-09 due to knee injury vs. Chicago, November 20, 2008. Traded to **Pittsburgh** by **Dallas** with Minnesota's 3rd round choice (previously acquired, Pittsburgh selected Jake Guentzel) in 2013 Entry Draft for Joe Morrow and Pittsburgh's 5th round choice (Matej Paulovic) in 2013 Entry Draft, March 24, 2013. Signed as a free agent by **St. Louis**, September 23, 2013. Signed as a free agent by **Tampa Bay**, July 11, 2014.

MORROW, Joe

(MOH-row, JOH) **BOS**

Defense. Shoots left. 6'1", 204 lbs. Born, Edmonton, AB, December 9, 1992. Pittsburgh's 1st choice, 23rd overall, in 2011 Entry Draft.

Season	Club	League	GP	G	A	Pts	PIM	PP	SH	GW	S	S%	+/-	TF	F%	Min	GP	G	A	Pts	PIM	PP	SH	GW	Min
2006-07	Strathcona	AMBHL	32	16	16	32	75	....	....	....	....	....	....	....	....	....	4	2	3	5	8	....	....	....	....
2007-08	Sherwood Park	Minor-AB	24	7	11	18	57	....	....	....	....	....	....	....	....	....	....	....	....	....	....	....	....	....	....
	Portland	WHL	1	0	0	0	0	....	....	....	....	....	....	....	....	....	....	....	....	....	....	....	....	....	....
2008-09	Portland	WHL	41	0	7	7	26	....	....	....	....	....	....	....	....	....	....	....	....	....	....	....	....	....	....
2009-10	Portland	WHL	63	7	24	31	59	....	....	....	....	....	....	....	....	....	13	0	2	2	6	....	....	....	....
2010-11	Portland	WHL	60	9	40	49	67	....	....	....	....	....	....	....	....	....	21	6	14	20	27	....	....	....	....
2011-12	Portland	WHL	62	17	47	64	99	....	....	....	....	....	....	....	....	....	22	4	13	17	35	....	....	....	....
2012-13	Wilkes-Barre	AHL	57	4	11	15	35	....	....	....	....	....	....	....	....	....	....	....	....	....	....	....	....	....	....
	Texas Stars	AHL	9	1	3	4	4	....	....	....	....	....	....	....	....	....	8	2	1	3	8	....	....	....	....
2013-14	Providence Bruins	AHL	56	6	23	29	28	....	....	....	....	....	....	....	....	....	10	2	5	7	8	....	....	....	....
2014-15	**Boston**	**NHL**	**15**	**1**	**0**	**1**	**4**	**0**	**0**	**0**	**20**	**5.0**	**3**	**0**	**0.0**	**16:41**	....	....	....	....	....	....	....	....	....
	Providence Bruins	AHL	33	3	9	12	14	....	....	....	....	....	....	....	....	....	5	0	0	0	6	....	....	....	....
	NHL Totals		**15**	**1**	**0**	**1**	**4**	**0**	**0**	**0**	**20**	**5.0**		**0**	**0.0**	**16:41**	....	....	....	....	....	....	....	....	....

WHL West First All-Star Team (2012)

Traded to **Dallas** by **Pittsburgh** with Pittsburgh's 5th round choce (Matej Paulovic) in 2013 Entry Draft for Brenden Morrow and Minnesota's 3rd round choice (previously acquired, Philadelphia selected Jake Guentzel) in 2013 Entry Draft, March 24, 2013. Traded to **Boston** by **Dallas** with Loui Eriksson, Reilly Smith and Matt Fraser for Tyler Seguin, Rich Peverley and Ryan Button, July 4, 2013.

MOSER, Simon

(MOH-zuhr, SIGH-muhn)

Left wing. Shoots left. 6'2", 215 lbs. Born, Bern, Switz., March 10, 1989.

Season	Club	League	GP	G	A	Pts	PIM	PP	SH	GW	S	S%	+/-	TF	F%	Min	GP	G	A	Pts	PIM	PP	SH	GW	Min
2007-08	HC Martigny	Swiss-2	42	7	5	12	72	....	....	....	....	....	....	....	....	....	....	....	....	....	....	....	....	....	....
	Langnau	Swiss	4	1	0	1	0	....	....	....	....	....	....	....	....	....	5	1	0	1	0	....	....	....	....
2008-09	Langnau	Swiss	47	7	6	13	37	....	....	....	....	....	....	....	....	....	7	2	1	3	0	....	....	....	....
2009-10	Langnau	Swiss	50	9	9	18	28	....	....	....	....	....	....	....	....	....	11	5	3	8	6	....	....	....	....
2010-11	Langnau	Swiss	46	11	12	23	20	....	....	....	....	....	....	....	....	....	4	2	0	2	2	....	....	....	....
2011-12	Langnau	Swiss	50	18	16	34	50	....	....	....	....	....	....	....	....	....	4	1	0	1	0	....	....	....	....
2012-13	Langnau	Swiss	35	10	11	21	44	....	....	....	....	....	....	....	....	....	12	5	4	9	6	....	....	....	....
2013-14	**Nashville**	**NHL**	**6**	**1**	**1**	**2**	**2**	**0**	**0**	**0**	**7**	**14.3**	**0**	**0**	**0.0**	**10:08**	....	....	....	....	....	....	....	....	....
	Milwaukee	AHL	48	8	18	26	8	....	....	....	....	....	....	....	....	....	3	0	0	0	0	....	....	....	....
2014-15	SC Bern	Swiss	28	5	2	7	18	....	....	....	....	....	....	....	....	....	11	0	1	1	4	....	....	....	....
	NHL Totals		**6**	**1**	**1**	**2**	**2**	**0**	**0**	**0**	**7**	**14.3**		**0**	**0.0**	**10:08**	....	....	....	....	....	....	....	....	....

Signed as a free agent by **Nashville**, September 30, 2013. Signed as a free agent by **Bern** (Swiss), July 31, 2014.

MOSS, Dave

(MAWS, DAYV)

Right wing. Shoots right. 6'4", 210 lbs. Born, Livonia, MI, December 28, 1981. Calgary's 9th choice, 220th overall, in 2001 Entry Draft.

			Regular Season														Playoffs								
Season	Club	League	GP	G	A	Pts	PIM	PP	SH	GW	S	S%	+/-	TF	F%	Min	GP	G	A	Pts	PIM	PP	SH	GW	Min
99-2000	Catholic Central	High-MI	28	18	20	28	20	....	....	....	....	....	....	....	....	....	....	....	....	....	....	....	....	....	....
2000-01	St. Louis Jr. Blues	CSJHL	9	2	2	4	2	....	....	....	....	....	....	....	....	....	....	....	....	....	....	....	....	....	....
	Cedar Rapids	USHL	51	20	18	38	14	....	....	....	....	....	....	....	....	....	4	0	1	1	2	....	....	....	....
2001-02	U. of Michigan	CCHA	43	4	9	13	10	....	....	....	....	....	....	....	....	....	....	....	....	....	....	....	....	....	....
2002-03	U. of Michigan	CCHA	43	14	17	31	37	....	....	....	....	....	....	....	....	....	....	....	....	....	....	....	....	....	....
2003-04	U. of Michigan	CCHA	38	8	12	20	18	....	....	....	....	....	....	....	....	....	....	....	....	....	....	....	....	....	....
2004-05	U. of Michigan	CCHA	38	10	20	30	26	....	....	....	....	....	....	....	....	....	....	....	....	....	....	....	....	....	....
2005-06	Omaha	AHL	63	21	27	48	28	....	....	....	....	....	....	....	....	....	....	....	....	....	....	....	....	....	....
2006-07	**Calgary**	**NHL**	41	10	8	18	12	3	0	1	70	14.3	5	11	36.4	11:13	6	0	1	1	0	0	0	0	10:30
	Omaha	AHL	28	9	12	21	22	....	....	....	....	....	....	....	....	....	....	....	....	....	....	....	....	....	....
2007-08	**Calgary**	**NHL**	41	4	7	11	10	0	0	0	60	6.7	-4	17	41.2	12:24	5	1	1	2	4	0	0	0	10:20
2008-09	**Calgary**	**NHL**	81	20	19	39	22	8	0	4	194	10.3	-5	46	50.0	13:36	6	3	0	3	0	0	0	1	12:50
2009-10	**Calgary**	**NHL**	64	8	9	17	20	3	0	2	133	6.0	-9	43	34.9	13:43	....	....	....	....	....	....	....	....	....
2010-11	**Calgary**	**NHL**	58	17	13	30	18	5	0	3	127	13.4	9	364	43.1	13:41	....	....	....	....	....	....	....	....	....
2011-12	**Calgary**	**NHL**	32	2	7	9	12	0	0	0	82	2.4	-3	220	42.3	14:01	....	....	....	....	....	....	....	....	....
2012-13	**Phoenix**	**NHL**	45	5	15	20	21	1	1	0	82	6.1	3	31	29.0	15:33	....	....	....	....	....	....	....	....	....
2013-14	**Phoenix**	**NHL**	79	8	14	22	18	0	0	1	151	5.3	-1	51	41.2	14:39	....	....	....	....	....	....	....	....	....
2014-15	**Arizona**	**NHL**	60	4	8	12	24	1	0	0	96	4.2	-18	13	46.2	12:55	....	....	....	....	....	....	....	....	....
	NHL Totals		501	78	100	178	157	21	1	11	995	7.8		796	42.1	13:37	17	4	2	6	4	0	0	1	11:16

Signed as a free agent by **Phoenix**, July 1. 2012. • Missed majority of 2011-12 due to ankle injury at Colorado, November 6, 2011.

MOUILLIERAT, Kael

(MOOL-uhr-aht, KAYL) **PIT**

Center. Shoots left. 6', 188 lbs. Born, Edmonton, AB, September 7, 1987.

			Regular Season														Playoffs								
Season	Club	League	GP	G	A	Pts	PIM	PP	SH	GW	S	S%	+/-	TF	F%	Min	GP	G	A	Pts	PIM	PP	SH	GW	Min
2001-02	K of C Squires	AMBHL	36	18	26	44	26	....	....	....	....	....	....	....	....	....	5	1	2	3	0	....	....	....	....
2002-03	K of C Pats	AMHL	34	4	11	15	66	....	....	....	....	....	....	....	....	....	....	....	....	....	....	....	....	....	....
2003-04	K of C Pats	AMHL	36	24	27	51	40	....	....	....	....	....	....	....	....	....	....	....	....	....	....	....	....	....	....
2004-05	Drayton Valley	AJHL	62	30	28	58	105	....	....	....	....	....	....	....	....	....	....	....	....	....	....	....	....	....	....
2005-06	Drayton Valley	AJHL	51	31	40	71	190	....	....	....	....	....	....	....	....	....	....	....	....	....	....	....	....	....	....
2006-07	Minnesota State	WCHA	37	8	7	15	52	....	....	....	....	....	....	....	....	....	....	....	....	....	....	....	....	....	....
2007-08	Minnesota State	WCHA	39	11	11	22	30	....	....	....	....	....	....	....	....	....	....	....	....	....	....	....	....	....	....
2008-09	Minnesota State	WCHA	30	17	13	30	48	....	....	....	....	....	....	....	....	....	....	....	....	....	....	....	....	....	....
2009-10	Minnesota State	WCHA	38	13	12	25	64	....	....	....	....	....	....	....	....	....	....	....	....	....	....	....	....	....	....
	Idaho Steelheads	ECHL	9	2	0	2	8	....	....	....	....	....	....	....	....	....	....	....	....	....	....	....	....	....	....
2010-11	Texas Stars	AHL	6	0	2	2	2	....	....	....	....	....	....	....	....	....	....	....	....	....	....	....	....	....	....
	Idaho Steelheads	ECHL	62	25	38	63	108	....	....	....	....	....	....	....	....	....	8	0	3	3	12	....	....	....	....
2011-12	Idaho Steelheads	ECHL	27	14	13	27	42	....	....	....	....	....	....	....	....	....	....	....	....	....	....	....	....	....	....
	Bridgeport	AHL	44	8	15	23	47	....	....	....	....	....	....	....	....	....	2	0	0	0	2	....	....	....	....
2012-13	Idaho Steelheads	ECHL	19	14	13	27	29	....	....	....	....	....	....	....	....	....	....	....	....	....	....	....	....	....	....
	St. John's IceCaps	AHL	50	11	31	42	32	....	....	....	....	....	....	....	....	....	....	....	....	....	....	....	....	....	....
2013-14	St. John's IceCaps	AHL	60	20	33	53	48	....	....	....	....	....	....	....	....	....	21	7	6	13	18	....	....	....	....
2014-15	**NY Islanders**	**NHL**	6	1	1	2	8	0	0	0	1	100.0	-3	34	47.1	8:41	....	....	....	....	....	....	....	....	....
	Bridgeport	AHL	69	24	26	50	110	....	....	....	....	....	....	....	....	....	....	....	....	....	....	....	....	....	....
	NHL Totals		6	1	1	2	8	0	0	0	1	100.0		34	47.1	8:41	....	....	....	....	....	....	....	....	....

Signed as a free agent by **NY Islanders**, July 1, 2014. Signed as a free agent by **Pittsburgh**, July 1, 2015.

MOULSON, Matt

(MOHL-suhn, MAT) **BUF**

Left wing. Shoots left. 6'1", 200 lbs. Born, North York, ON, November 1, 1983. Pittsburgh's 11th choice, 263rd overall, in 2003 Entry Draft.

			Regular Season														Playoffs								
Season	Club	League	GP	G	A	Pts	PIM	PP	SH	GW	S	S%	+/-	TF	F%	Min	GP	G	A	Pts	PIM	PP	SH	GW	Min
2001-02	Guelph	ON-Jr.B	42	56	46	102	80	....	....	....	....	....	....	....	....	....	....	....	....	....	....	....	....	....	....
2002-03	Cornell Big Red	ECAC	33	13	10	23	22	....	....	....	....	....	....	....	....	....	....	....	....	....	....	....	....	....	....
2003-04	Cornell Big Red	ECAC	32	18	17	35	37	....	....	....	....	....	....	....	....	....	....	....	....	....	....	....	....	....	....
2004-05	Cornell Big Red	ECAC	34	22	20	42	33	....	....	....	....	....	....	....	....	....	....	....	....	....	....	....	....	....	....
2005-06	Cornell Big Red	ECAC	35	18	20	38	14	....	....	....	....	....	....	....	....	....	....	....	....	....	....	....	....	....	....
2006-07	Manchester	AHL	77	25	32	57	23	....	....	....	....	....	....	....	....	....	16	2	3	5	8	....	....	....	....
2007-08	**Los Angeles**	**NHL**	22	5	4	9	4	0	0	0	35	14.3	2	4	25.0	12:05	....	....	....	....	....	....	....	....	....
	Manchester	AHL	57	28	28	56	29	....	....	....	....	....	....	....	....	....	4	2	0	2	4	....	....	....	....
2008-09	**Los Angeles**	**NHL**	7	1	0	1	2	0	0	1	6	16.7	-4	0	0.0	14:30	....	....	....	....	....	....	....	....	....
	Manchester	AHL	54	21	26	47	35	....	....	....	....	....	....	....	....	....	....	....	....	....	....	....	....	....	....
2009-10	**NY Islanders**	**NHL**	82	30	18	48	16	8	0	5	208	14.4	-1	4	75.0	16:38	....	....	....	....	....	....	....	....	....
2010-11	**NY Islanders**	**NHL**	82	31	22	53	24	9	0	3	237	13.1	-10	9	55.6	18:52	....	....	....	....	....	....	....	....	....
2011-12	**NY Islanders**	**NHL**	82	36	33	69	6	14	0	5	219	16.4	1	4	50.0	19:18	....	....	....	....	....	....	....	....	....
2012-13	**NY Islanders**	**NHL**	47	15	29	44	4	8	0	0	154	9.7	-3	1	100.0	19:09	6	2	1	3	10	1	0	0	17:23
2013-14	**NY Islanders**	**NHL**	11	6	3	9	6	5	0	0	28	21.4	3	3	0.0	17:39	....	....	....	....	....	....	....	....	....
	Buffalo	**NHL**	44	11	18	29	20	3	0	2	105	10.5	-8	4	25.0	18:44	....	....	....	....	....	....	....	....	....
	Minnesota	**NHL**	20	6	7	13	8	1	0	3	43	14.0	7	2	50.0	16:27	10	1	2	3	4	0	0	0	15:00
2014-15	**Buffalo**	**NHL**	77	13	28	41	4	3	0	2	156	8.3	-11	22	59.1	17:41	....	....	....	....	....	....	....	....	....
	NHL Totals		474	154	162	316	94	51	0	21	1191	12.9		53	50.9	17:52	16	3	3	6	14	1	0	0	15:54

ECAC First All-Star Team (2005) • NCAA East Second All-American Team (2005) • ECAC Second All-Star Team (2006)

Signed as a free agent by **Los Angeles**, September 1, 2006. Signed as a free agent by **NY Islanders**, July 6, 2009. Traded to **Buffalo** by **NY Islanders** with NY Islanders' 1st (later traded to Ottawa – Ottawa selected Colin White) in 2015 Entry Draft and 2nd (Brendan Guhle) round choices in 2015 Entry Draft for Thomas Vanek, October 27, 2013. Traded to **Minnesota** by **Buffalo** with Cody McCormick for Torrey Mitchell, Winnipeg's 2nd round choice (previously acquired, later traded to Washington – Washington selected Vitek Vanecek) in 2014 Entry Draft and Minnesota's 2nd round choice in 2016 Entry Draft, March 5, 2014. Signed as a free agent by **Buffalo**, July 1, 2014.

MUELLER, Chris

(MEW-luhr, KRIHS) **ANA**

Center. Shoots right. 5'11", 210 lbs. Born, West Seneca, NY, March 6, 1986.

			Regular Season														Playoffs								
Season	Club	League	GP	G	A	Pts	PIM	PP	SH	GW	S	S%	+/-	TF	F%	Min	GP	G	A	Pts	PIM	PP	SH	GW	Min
2004-05	Michigan State	CCHA	41	2	16	18	32	....	....	....	....	....	....	....	....	....	....	....	....	....	....	....	....	....	....
2005-06	Michigan State	CCHA	41	11	16	27	47	....	....	....	....	....	....	....	....	....	....	....	....	....	....	....	....	....	....
2006-07	Michigan State	CCHA	42	16	16	32	30	....	....	....	....	....	....	....	....	....	....	....	....	....	....	....	....	....	....
2007-08	Michigan State	CCHA	42	13	14	27	32	....	....	....	....	....	....	....	....	....	....	....	....	....	....	....	....	....	....
	Grand Rapids	AHL	2	0	0	0	0	....	....	....	....	....	....	....	....	....	....	....	....	....	....	....	....	....	....
2008-09	Lake Erie	AHL	59	5	11	16	23	....	....	....	....	....	....	....	....	....	....	....	....	....	....	....	....	....	....
	Johnstown Chiefs	ECHL	3	3	3	6	2	....	....	....	....	....	....	....	....	....	....	....	....	....	....	....	....	....	....
2009-10	Milwaukee	AHL	67	13	14	27	37	....	....	....	....	....	....	....	....	....	7	3	2	5	4	....	....	....	....
	Cincinnati	ECHL	5	4	1	5	0	....	....	....	....	....	....	....	....	....	....	....	....	....	....	....	....	....	....
2010-11	Milwaukee	AHL	67	24	26	50	34	....	....	....	....	....	....	....	....	....	13	4	7	11	13	....	....	....	....
	Nashville	**NHL**	15	0	3	3	2	0	0	0	7	0.0	0	89	48.3	8:38	....	....	....	....	....	....	....	....	....
2011-12	**Nashville**	**NHL**	4	0	0	0	0	0	0	0	4	0.0	-1	27	55.6	9:09	....	....	....	....	....	....	....	....	....
	Milwaukee	AHL	73	32	28	60	30	....	....	....	....	....	....	....	....	....	3	1	0	1	0	....	....	....	....
2012-13	Milwaukee	AHL	55	18	18	36	35	....	....	....	....	....	....	....	....	....	2	0	0	0	2	....	....	....	....
	Nashville	**NHL**	18	2	3	5	6	0	0	1	22	9.1	-4	185	49.7	10:42	....	....	....	....	....	....	....	....	....
2013-14	**Dallas**	**NHL**	9	0	0	0	0	0	0	0	8	0.0	-2	54	53.7	9:15	4	0	0	0	2	0	0	0	6:28
	Texas Stars	AHL	60	25	32	57	29	....	....	....	....	....	....	....	....	....	19	6	5	11	12	....	....	....	....
2014-15	**NY Rangers**	**NHL**	7	1	1	2	0	1	0	0	10	10.0	-1	64	59.4	10:27	....	....	....	....	....	....	....	....	....
	Hartford	AHL	64	14	26	40	26	....	....	....	....	....	....	....	....	....	15	5	4	9	6	....	....	....	....
	NHL Totals		53	3	7	10	8	1	0	1	51	5.9		419	51.8	9:43	4	0	0	0	2	0	0	0	6:28

Signed to an ATO (amateur tryout) contract by **Grand Rapids** (AHL), April 9, 2008. Signed as a free agent by **Lake Erie** (AHL), October 8, 2008. Signed as a free agent by **Milwaukee** (AHL), October 13, 2009. Signed as a free agent by **Nashville**, December 27, 2010. Signed as a free agent by **Dallas**, July 8, 2013. Signed as a free agent by **NY Rangers**, July 1, 2014. Signed as a free agent by **Anaheim**, July 1, 2015.

MUELLER, Mirco

(MEW-luhr, MIHR-koh) **S.J.**

Defense. Shoots left. 6'3", 205 lbs. Born, Winterthur, Switz., March 21, 1995. San Jose's 1st choice, 18th overall, in 2013 Entry Draft.

Season	Club	League	GP	G	A	Pts	PIM	PP	SH	GW	S	S%	+/-	TF	F%	Min	Playoffs GP	G	A	Pts	PIM	PP	SH	GW	Min
2009-10	Winterthur U17	Swiss-U17	12	0	4	4	0	....	....	....	....	....	....	....	....	....	....	....	....	....	....	....	....	....	....
2010-11	Kloten Flyers U17	Swiss-U17	32	12	19	31	14	....	....	....	....	....	....	....	....	....	10	0	6	6	12	....	....	....	....
	Kloten Flyers Jr.	Swiss-Jr.	1	0	0	0	0	....	....	....	....	....	....	....	....	....	....	....	....	....	....	....	....	....	....
2011-12	Kloten Flyers U17	Swiss-U17	4	1	3	4	0	....	....	....	....	....	....	....	....	....	....	....	....	....	....	....	....	....	....
	Kloten Flyers Jr.	Swiss-Jr.	26	3	3	6	8	....	....	....	....	....	....	....	....	....	4	1	2	3	2	....	....	....	....
	Kloten Flyers	Swiss	7	1	0	1	0	....	....	....	....	....	....	....	....	....	....	....	....	....	....	....	....	....	....
2012-13	Everett Silvertips	WHL	63	6	25	31	57	....	....	....	....	....	....	....	....	....	6	0	1	1	6	....	....	....	....
2013-14	Everett Silvertips	WHL	60	5	22	27	31	....	....	....	....	....	....	....	....	....	5	1	1	2	4	....	....	....	....
	Worcester Sharks	AHL	9	0	2	2	2	....	....	....	....	....	....	....	....	....	....	....	....	....	....	....	....	....	....
2014-15	**San Jose**	**NHL**	**39**	**1**	**3**	**4**	**10**	**0**	**0**	**0**	**31**	**3.2**	**–8**	**0**	**0.0**	**16:58**	....	....	....	....	....	....	....	....	....
	Worcester Sharks	AHL	3	1	0	1	4	....	....	....	....	....	....	....	....	....	....	....	....	....	....	....	....	....	....
	NHL Totals		**39**	**1**	**3**	**4**	**10**	**0**	**0**	**0**	**31**	**3.2**		**0**	**0.0**	**16:58**	....	....	....	....	....	....	....	....	....

MUELLER, Peter

(MEW-luhr, PEE-tuhr)

Center. Shoots right. 6'2", 204 lbs. Born, Bloomington, MN, April 14, 1988. Phoenix's 1st choice, 8th overall, in 2006 Entry Draft.

Season	Club	League	GP	G	A	Pts	PIM	PP	SH	GW	S	S%	+/-	TF	F%	Min	Playoffs GP	G	A	Pts	PIM	PP	SH	GW	Min
2003-04	USNTDP	U-17	17	4	9	13	25	....	....	....	....	....	....	....	....	....	....	....	....	....	....	....	....	....	....
	USNTDP	NAHL	43	10	16	26	26	....	....	....	....	....	....	....	....	....	7	3	2	5	4	....	....	....	....
2004-05	USNTDP	U-18	43	27	27	64	75	....	....	....	....	....	....	....	....	....	....	....	....	....	....	....	....	....	....
	USNTDP	NAHL	14	11	13	24	16	....	....	....	....	....	....	....	....	....	....	....	....	....	....	....	....	....	....
2005-06	Everett Silvertips	WHL	52	26	32	58	44	....	....	....	....	....	....	....	....	....	15	7	6	13	10	....	....	....	....
2006-07	Everett Silvertips	WHL	51	21	57	78	45	....	....	....	....	....	....	....	....	....	12	7	9	16	12	....	....	....	....
2007-08	**Phoenix**	**NHL**	**81**	**22**	**32**	**54**	**32**	**7**	**0**	**3**	**201**	**10.9**	**–13**	**251**	**41.8**	**17:16**	....	....	....	....	....	....	....	....	....
2008-09	**Phoenix**	**NHL**	**72**	**13**	**23**	**36**	**24**	**5**	**0**	**4**	**138**	**9.4**	**–7**	**92**	**44.6**	**16:05**	....	....	....	....	....	....	....	....	....
2009-10	**Phoenix**	**NHL**	**54**	**4**	**13**	**17**	**8**	**1**	**0**	**1**	**89**	**4.5**	**–5**	**42**	**42.9**	**12:55**	....	....	....	....	....	....	....	....	....
	Colorado	**NHL**	**15**	**9**	**11**	**20**	**8**	**3**	**0**	**1**	**35**	**25.7**	**4**	**2**	**0.0**	**17:50**	....	....	....	....	....	....	....	....	....
2010-11			DID NOT PLAY – INJURED																						
2011-12	**Colorado**	**NHL**	**32**	**7**	**9**	**16**	**8**	**1**	**0**	**1**	**82**	**8.5**	**–3**	**10**	**60.0**	**14:39**	....	....	....	....	....	....	....	....	....
2012-13	**Florida**	**NHL**	**43**	**8**	**9**	**17**	**18**	**2**	**0**	**0**	**131**	**6.1**	**–11**	**104**	**44.2**	**16:16**	....	....	....	....	....	....	....	....	....
2013-14	Kloten Flyers	Swiss	49	*24	22	46	12	....	....	....	....	....	....	....	....	....	10	2	1	3	4	....	....	....	....
2014-15	Kloten Flyers	Swiss	39	10	8	18	12	....	....	....	....	....	....	....	....	....	....	....	....	....	....	....	....	....	....
	NHL Totals		**297**	**63**	**97**	**160**	**98**	**19**	**0**	**10**	**676**	**9.3**		**501**	**43.1**	**15:47**	....	....	....	....	....	....	....	....	....

WHL Rookie ot the Year (2006) • WHL West First All-Star Team (2007) • Canadian Major Junior Second All-Star Team (2007)

Traded to **Colorado** by **Phoenix** with Kevin Porter for Wojtek Wolski, March 3, 2010. • Missed 2010-11 and majority of 2011-12 due to head injury vs. San Jose, April 14, 2010. Signed as a free agent by **Florida**, July 12, 2012. Signed as a free agent by **Kloten** (Swiss), September 6, 2013.

MURPHY, Connor

(MUHR-fee, KAW-nuhr) **ARI**

Defense. Shoots right. 6'3", 205 lbs. Born, Dublin, OH, March 26, 1993. Phoenix's 1st choice, 20th overall, in 2011 Entry Draft.

Season	Club	League	GP	G	A	Pts	PIM	PP	SH	GW	S	S%	+/-	TF	F%	Min	Playoffs GP	G	A	Pts	PIM	PP	SH	GW	Min
2008-09	Ohio Blue Jackets	Ind.	35	7	11	18	....	....	....	....	....	....	....	....	....	....	....	....	....	....	....	....	....	....	....
2009-10	USNTDP	USHL	2	0	0	0	2	....	....	....	....	....	....	....	....	....	....	....	....	....	....	....	....	....	....
	USNTDP	U-17	6	1	0	1	2	....	....	....	....	....	....	....	....	....	....	....	....	....	....	....	....	....	....
2010-11	USNTDP	USHL	9	3	1	4	6	....	....	....	....	....	....	....	....	....	....	....	....	....	....	....	....	....	....
	USNTDP	U-18	13	3	3	6	0	....	....	....	....	....	....	....	....	....	....	....	....	....	....	....	....	....	....
2011-12	Sarnia Sting	OHL	35	8	18	26	26	....	....	....	....	....	....	....	....	....	6	1	2	3	6	....	....	....	....
2012-13	Sarnia Sting	OHL	33	6	12	18	32	....	....	....	....	....	....	....	....	....	....	....	....	....	....	....	....	....	....
2013-14	**Phoenix**	**NHL**	**30**	**1**	**7**	**8**	**10**	**0**	**0**	**1**	**30**	**3.3**	**5**	**0**	**0.0**	**17:59**	....	....	....	....	....	....	....	....	....
	Portland Pirates	AHL	36	0	13	13	48	....	....	....	....	....	....	....	....	....	....	....	....	....	....	....	....	....	....
2014-15	**Arizona**	**NHL**	**73**	**4**	**3**	**7**	**42**	**0**	**0**	**0**	**72**	**5.6**	**–27**	**1**	**0.0**	**16:48**	....	....	....	....	....	....	....	....	....
	NHL Totals		**103**	**5**	**10**	**15**	**52**	**0**	**0**	**1**	**102**	**4.9**		**1**	**0.0**	**17:09**	....	....	....	....	....	....	....	....	....

• Missed majority of 2009-10 and 2010-11 due to recurring back injury.

MURPHY, Ryan

(MUHR-fee, RIGH-uhn) **CAR**

Defense. Shoots right. 5'11", 185 lbs. Born, Aurora, ON, March 31, 1993. Carolina's 1st choice, 12th overall, in 2011 Entry Draft.

Season	Club	League	GP	G	A	Pts	PIM	PP	SH	GW	S	S%	+/-	TF	F%	Min	Playoffs GP	G	A	Pts	PIM	PP	SH	GW	Min
2008-09	York Simcoe	Minor-ON	73	30	65	95	52	....	....	....	....	....	....	....	....	....	....	....	....	....	....	....	....	....	....
	Villanova Knights	ON-Jr.A	4	4	2	6	0	....	....	....	....	....	....	....	....	....	....	....	....	....	....	....	....	....	....
2009-10	Kitchener Rangers	OHL	62	6	33	39	22	....	....	....	....	....	....	....	....	....	20	5	12	17	16	....	....	....	....
2010-11	Kitchener Rangers	OHL	63	26	53	79	36	....	....	....	....	....	....	....	....	....	7	2	9	11	8	....	....	....	....
2011-12	Kitchener Rangers	OHL	49	11	43	54	30	....	....	....	....	....	....	....	....	....	16	2	20	22	12	....	....	....	....
2012-13	Kitchener Rangers	OHL	54	10	38	48	34	....	....	....	....	....	....	....	....	....	10	3	4	7	8	....	....	....	....
	Carolina	**NHL**	**4**	**0**	**0**	**0**	**2**	**0**	**0**	**0**	**7**	**0.0**	**–4**	**0**	**0.0**	**21:04**	....	....	....	....	....	....	....	....	....
	Charlotte	AHL	3	0	2	2	0	....	....	....	....	....	....	....	....	....	5	0	2	2	2	....	....	....	....
2013-14	**Carolina**	**NHL**	**48**	**2**	**10**	**12**	**10**	**1**	**0**	**0**	**81**	**2.5**	**–9**	**0**	**0.0**	**18:17**	....	....	....	....	....	....	....	....	....
	Charlotte	AHL	22	3	19	22	8	....	....	....	....	....	....	....	....	....	....	....	....	....	....	....	....	....	....
2014-15	**Carolina**	**NHL**	**37**	**4**	**9**	**13**	**8**	**3**	**0**	**1**	**61**	**6.6**	**–11**	**0**	**0.0**	**18:17**	....	....	....	....	....	....	....	....	....
	Charlotte	AHL	25	0	17	17	10	....	....	....	....	....	....	....	....	....	....	....	....	....	....	....	....	....	....
	NHL Totals		**89**	**6**	**19**	**25**	**20**	**4**	**0**	**1**	**149**	**4.0**		**0**	**0.0**	**18:25**	....	....	....	....	....	....	....	....	....

OHL All-Rookie Team (2010) • OHL First All-Star Team (2011) • OHL Second All-Star Team (2012, 2013)

MURRAY, Andrew

(MUHR-ree, AN-droo)

Center. Shoots left. 6'2", 210 lbs. Born, Selkirk, MB, November 6, 1981. Columbus' 11th choice, 242nd overall, in 2001 Entry Draft.

Season	Club	League	GP	G	A	Pts	PIM	PP	SH	GW	S	S%	+/-	TF	F%	Min	Playoffs GP	G	A	Pts	PIM	PP	SH	GW	Min
99-2000	Selkirk Steelers	MJHL	63	29	48	77	....	....	....	....	....	....	....	....	....	....	....	....	....	....	....	....	....	....	....
2000-01	Selkirk Steelers	MJHL	64	46	56	102	72	....	....	....	....	....	....	....	....	....	5	3	0	3	6	....	....	....	....
2001-02	Bemidji State	CHA	35	15	15	30	22	....	....	....	....	....	....	....	....	....	....	....	....	....	....	....	....	....	....
2002-03	Bemidji State	CHA	36	9	18	27	38	....	....	....	....	....	....	....	....	....	....	....	....	....	....	....	....	....	....
2003-04	Bemidji State	CHA	25	6	14	20	41	....	....	....	....	....	....	....	....	....	....	....	....	....	....	....	....	....	....
2004-05	Bemidji State	CHA	32	16	22	38	30	....	....	....	....	....	....	....	....	....	....	....	....	....	....	....	....	....	....
2005-06	Syracuse Crunch	AHL	77	13	16	29	73	....	....	....	....	....	....	....	....	....	6	0	1	1	17	....	....	....	....
2006-07	Syracuse Crunch	AHL	72	10	12	22	62	....	....	....	....	....	....	....	....	....	....	....	....	....	....	....	....	....	....
2007-08	**Columbus**	**NHL**	**39**	**6**	**4**	**10**	**12**	**0**	**0**	**0**	**45**	**13.3**	**0**	**32**	**46.9**	**11:42**	....	....	....	....	....	....	....	....	....
	Syracuse Crunch	AHL	34	13	2	15	15	....	....	....	....	....	....	....	....	....	....	....	....	....	....	....	....	....	....
2008-09	**Columbus**	**NHL**	**67**	**8**	**3**	**11**	**10**	**1**	**0**	**3**	**89**	**9.0**	**–6**	**85**	**45.9**	**11:16**	....	....	....	....	....	....	....	....	....
2009-10	**Columbus**	**NHL**	**46**	**5**	**2**	**7**	**6**	**0**	**0**	**0**	**73**	**6.8**	**–6**	**118**	**41.5**	**10:22**	....	....	....	....	....	....	....	....	....
2010-11	**Columbus**	**NHL**	**29**	**4**	**4**	**8**	**4**	**0**	**0**	**1**	**48**	**8.3**	**2**	**41**	**46.3**	**11:23**	....	....	....	....	....	....	....	....	....
2011-12	**San Jose**	**NHL**	**39**	**1**	**3**	**4**	**4**	**0**	**0**	**0**	**33**	**3.0**	**3**	**15**	**33.3**	**7:42**	....	....	....	....	....	....	....	....	....
	Worcester Sharks	AHL	10	2	1	3	0	....	....	....	....	....	....	....	....	....	....	....	....	....	....	....	....	....	....
2012-13	Peoria Rivermen	AHL	51	14	17	31	18	....	....	....	....	....	....	....	....	....	....	....	....	....	....	....	....	....	....
	St. Louis	**NHL**	**1**	**0**	**0**	**0**	**0**	**0**	**0**	**0**	**2**	**0.0**	**0**	**0**	**0.0**	**7:49**	....	....	....	....	....	....	....	....	....
2013-14	Zagreb	KHL	54	3	3	6	28	....	....	....	....	....	....	....	....	....	3	0	1	1	0	....	....	....	....
2014-15	Zagreb	KHL	51	3	4	7	14	....	....	....	....	....	....	....	....	....	....	....	....	....	....	....	....	....	....
	NHL Totals		**221**	**24**	**16**	**40**	**36**	**1**	**0**	**4**	**290**	**8.3**		**291**	**43.6**	**10:32**	....	....	....	....	....	....	....	....	....

CHA All-Rookie Team (2002)

• Missed majority of 2010-11 due to recurring lower-body injury. Signed as a free agent by **San Jose**, July 19, 2011. Traded to **Detroit** by **San Jose** with San Jose's 7th round choice (Alexander Kadeykin) in 2014 Entry Draft for Brad Stuart, June 10, 2012. Signed as a free agent by **St. Louis**, July 6, 2012. Signed as a free agent by **Zagreb** (KHL), July 29, 2013.

			Regular Season														Playoffs								
Season	Club	League	GP	G	A	Pts	PIM	PP	SH	GW	S	S%	+/-	TF	F%	Min	GP	G	A	Pts	PIM	PP	SH	GW	Min

MURRAY, Ryan (MUHR-ee, RIGH-uhn) CBJ

Defense. Shoots left. 6'1", 208 lbs. Born, Regina, SK, September 27, 1993. Columbus' 1st choice, 2nd overall, in 2012 Entry Draft.

Season	Club	League	GP	G	A	Pts	PIM	PP	SH	GW	S	S%	+/-	TF	F%	Min	GP	G	A	Pts	PIM	PP	SH	GW	Min
2007-08	Balgonie	SMBHL	25	11	31	42	26																		
	Balgonie	Minor-SK	10	2	5	7																			
2008-09	Moose Jaw	SMHL	41	12	26	38	12										5	1	6	7	6				
	Everett Silvertips	WHL															5	0	1	1	2				
2009-10	Everett Silvertips	WHL	52	5	22	27	31										7	2	5	7	2				
2010-11	Everett Silvertips	WHL	70	6	40	46	45										4	1	2	3	4				
2011-12	Everett Silvertips	WHL	46	9	22	31	31										4	3	2	5	0				
2012-13	Everett Silvertips	WHL	23	2	15	17	14																		
2013-14	**Columbus**	**NHL**	**66**	**4**	**17**	**21**	**10**	**3**	**0**	**0**	**62**	**6.5**	**4**	**0**	**0.0**	**19:52**	**5**	**0**	**1**	**1**	**0**	**0**	**0**	**0**	**22:44**
2014-15	**Columbus**	**NHL**	**12**	**1**	**2**	**3**	**8**	**1**	**0**	**0**	**8**	**12.5**	**1**	**0**	**0.0**	**18:55**									
	NHL Totals		**78**	**5**	**19**	**24**	**18**	**4**	**0**	**0**	**70**	**7.1**		**0**	**0.0**	**19:43**	**5**	**0**	**1**	**1**	**0**	**0**	**0**	**0**	**22:44**

WHL West Second All-Star Team (2011, 2012)

• Missed majority of 2012-13 due to shoulder surgery, January 20, 2013. • Missed majority of 2014-15 due to recurring knee injury and ankle injury vs. St. Louis, February 6, 2015.

MUSIL, David (moo-SIHL, DAY-vihd) EDM

Defense. Shoots left. 6'4", 207 lbs. Born, Calgary, AB, AB, April 9, 1993. Edmonton's 3rd choice, 31st overall, in 2011 Entry Draft.

Season	Club	League	GP	G	A	Pts	PIM	PP	SH	GW	S	S%	+/-	TF	F%	Min	GP	G	A	Pts	PIM	PP	SH	GW	Min
2005-06	Jihlava U17	CzR-U17	5	0	0	0	0																		
2006-07	Jihlava U17	CzR-U17	36	7	23	30	42																		
	Trebic U17	CzR-U17	14	1	3	4	26																		
2007-08	Jihlava U17	CzR-U17	42	8	27	35	98										3	0	1	1	6				
	Jihlava Jr.	CzRep-Jr.	9	0	5	5	6																		
2008-09	Jihlava U17	CzR-U17	9	3	3	6	46																		
	Jihlava Jr.	CzRep-Jr.	27	9	12	21	46										8	3	3	6	10				
	HC Dukla Jihlava	CzRep-2	14	0	1	1	4										4	0	0	0	4				
2009-10	Vancouver Giants	WHL	71	7	25	32	67										16	2	2	4	8				
2010-11	Vancouver Giants	WHL	62	6	19	25	83										4	0	1	1	2				
2011-12	Vancouver Giants	WHL	59	6	21	27	104																		
2012-13	Vancouver Giants	WHL	14	2	6	8	18																		
	Edmonton	WHL	48	7	16	23	56										22	0	6	6	26				
2013-14	Oklahoma City	AHL	61	2	10	12	54										2	0	1	1	0				
	Bakersfield	ECHL	3	1	0	1	2																		
2014-15	**Edmonton**	**NHL**	**4**	**0**	**2**	**2**	**2**	**0**	**0**	**0**	**3**	**0.0**	**-2**	**0**	**0.0**	**19:48**									
	Oklahoma City	AHL	65	2	9	11	35										6	0	0	0	6				
	NHL Totals		**4**	**0**	**2**	**2**	**2**	**0**	**0**	**0**	**3**	**0.0**		**0**	**0.0**	**19:48**									

MUZZIN, Jake (MUH-zihn, JAYK) L.A.

Defense. Shoots left. 6'3", 216 lbs. Born, Woodstock, ON, February 21, 1989. Pittsburgh's 7th choice, 141st overall, in 2007 Entry Draft.

Season	Club	League	GP	G	A	Pts	PIM	PP	SH	GW	S	S%	+/-	TF	F%	Min	GP	G	A	Pts	PIM	PP	SH	GW	Min
2004-05	Brantford 99ers	Minor-ON	57	20	23	43	78																		
2005-06	Sault Ste. Marie	OHL	DID NOT PLAY – INJURED																						
2006-07	Soo Thunderbirds	NOJHL	4	0	3	3	2																		
	Sault Ste. Marie	OHL	37	1	3	4	10										13	0	4	4	6				
2007-08	Sault Ste. Marie	OHL	67	6	12	18	53										10	1	3	4	4				
2008-09	Sault Ste. Marie	OHL	62	6	23	29	57																		
2009-10	Sault Ste. Marie	OHL	64	15	52	67	76										5	0	1	1	2				
	Manchester	AHL	1	0	1	1	0										13	1	3	4	6				
2010-11	**Los Angeles**	**NHL**	**11**	**0**	**1**	**1**	**0**	**0**	**0**	**0**	**8**	**0.0**	**-2**	**0**	**0.0**	**13:43**									
	Manchester	AHL	45	3	15	18	39										7	3	1	4	2				
2011-12	Manchester	AHL	71	7	24	31	40										3	0	1	1	2				
2012-13	Manchester	AHL	29	2	9	11	24																		
	Los Angeles	**NHL**	**45**	**7**	**9**	**16**	**35**	**3**	**0**	**1**	**77**	**9.1**	**16**	**0**	**0.0**	**17:54**	**17**	**0**	**3**	**3**	**6**	**0**	**0**	**0**	**15:50**
2013-14♦	**Los Angeles**	**NHL**	**76**	**5**	**19**	**24**	**58**	**1**	**0**	**0**	**175**	**2.9**	**8**	**0**	**0.0**	**19:02**	**26**	**6**	**6**	**12**	**8**	**3**	**0**	**1**	**23:24**
2014-15	**Los Angeles**	**NHL**	**76**	**10**	**31**	**41**	**22**	**4**	**0**	**3**	**173**	**5.8**	**-4**	**0**	**0.0**	**22:42**									
	NHL Totals		**208**	**22**	**60**	**82**	**115**	**8**	**0**	**4**	**433**	**5.1**		**0**	**0.0**	**19:51**	**43**	**6**	**9**	**15**	**14**	**3**	**0**	**1**	**20:24**

OHL First All-Star Team (2010) • Canadian Major Junior First All-Star Team (2010)

• Missed 2005-06 due to off-season back surgery. Signed as a free agent by **Los Angeles**, January 4, 2010.

MYERS, Tyler (MIGH-uhrz, TIGH-luhr) WPG

Defense. Shoots right. 6'8", 219 lbs. Born, Houston, TX, February 1, 1990. Buffalo's 1st choice, 12th overall, in 2008 Entry Draft.

Season	Club	League	GP	G	A	Pts	PIM	PP	SH	GW	S	S%	+/-	TF	F%	Min	GP	G	A	Pts	PIM	PP	SH	GW	Min
2005-06	Notre Dame	SMHL	34	4	6	10	78																		
	Kelowna Rockets	WHL	9	0	1	1	2										8	1	0	1	2				
2006-07	Kelowna Rockets	WHL	59	2	13	15	78																		
2007-08	Kelowna Rockets	WHL	65	6	13	19	97										7	1	2	3	12				
2008-09	Kelowna Rockets	WHL	58	9	33	42	105										22	5	15	20	29				
2009-10	**Buffalo**	**NHL**	**82**	**11**	**37**	**48**	**32**	**3**	**0**	**1**	**104**	**10.6**	**13**	**0**	**0.0**	**23:44**	**6**	**1**	**0**	**1**	**4**	**0**	**0**	**0**	**25:54**
2010-11	**Buffalo**	**NHL**	**80**	**10**	**27**	**37**	**40**	**3**	**0**	**5**	**122**	**8.2**	**0**	**0**	**0.0**	**22:27**	**7**	**1**	**5**	**6**	**16**	**0**	**0**	**0**	**23:52**
2011-12	**Buffalo**	**NHL**	**55**	**8**	**15**	**23**	**33**	**3**	**0**	**1**	**84**	**9.5**	**5**	**0**	**0.0**	**22:29**									
2012-13	Klagenfurter AC	Austria	17	3	7	10	37																		
	Buffalo	**NHL**	**39**	**3**	**5**	**8**	**32**	**1**	**0**	**2**	**48**	**6.3**	**-8**	**0**	**0.0**	**21:19**									
2013-14	**Buffalo**	**NHL**	**62**	**9**	**13**	**22**	**58**	**3**	**0**	**0**	**99**	**9.1**	**-26**	**0**	**0.0**	**21:54**									
2014-15	**Buffalo**	**NHL**	**47**	**4**	**9**	**13**	**61**	**1**	**0**	**0**	**72**	**5.6**	**-15**	**0**	**0.0**	**25:04**									
	Winnipeg	**NHL**	**24**	**3**	**12**	**15**	**16**	**1**	**0**	**0**	**52**	**5.8**	**9**	**0**	**0.0**	**23:49**	**4**	**1**	**0**	**1**	**2**	**1**	**0**	**0**	**24:23**
	NHL Totals		**389**	**48**	**118**	**166**	**272**	**15**	**0**	**9**	**581**	**8.3**		**0**	**0.0**	**22:56**	**17**	**3**	**5**	**8**	**22**	**1**	**0**	**0**	**24:42**

WHL West Second All-Star Team (2009) • NHL All-Rookie Team (2010) • Calder Memorial Trophy (2010)

Signed as a free agent by **Klagenfurt** (Austria), October 15, 2012. Traded to **Winnipeg** by **Buffalo** with Drew Stafford, Joel Armia, Brendan Lemieux and St. Louis' 1st round choice (previously acquired, Winnipeg selected Jack Roslovic) in 2015 Entry Draft for Evander Kane, Zach Bogosian and Jason Kasdorf, February 11, 2015.

NAMESTNIKOV, Vladislav (nah-MEHST-nih-kawv, vla-dih-SLAHV) T.B.

Center. Shoots left. 6', 179 lbs. Born, Zhukovsky, Russia, November 22, 1992. Tampa Bay's 1st choice, 27th overall, in 2011 Entry Draft.

Season	Club	League	GP	G	A	Pts	PIM	PP	SH	GW	S	S%	+/-	TF	F%	Min	GP	G	A	Pts	PIM	PP	SH	GW	Min
2009-10	Khimik	Russia-2	33	12	9	21	18										2	1	0	1	2				
2010-11	London Knights	OHL	68	30	39	69	49										6	1	4	5	6				
2011-12	London Knights	OHL	63	22	49	71	50										19	4	14	18	20				
2012-13	Syracuse Crunch	AHL	44	7	14	21	32										18	2	5	7	10				
2013-14	**Tampa Bay**	**NHL**	**4**	**0**	**0**	**0**	**4**	**0**	**0**	**0**	**4**	**0.0**	**-1**	**26**	**46.2**	**9:28**									
	Syracuse Crunch	AHL	56	19	29	48	40																		
2014-15	**Tampa Bay**	**NHL**	**43**	**9**	**7**	**16**	**13**	**1**	**0**	**3**	**46**	**19.6**	**1**	**155**	**45.2**	**12:00**	**12**	**0**	**1**	**1**	**4**	**0**	**0**	**0**	**7:52**
	Syracuse Crunch	AHL	34	14	21	35	12																		
	NHL Totals		**47**	**9**	**7**	**16**	**17**	**1**	**0**	**3**	**50**	**18.0**		**181**	**45.3**	**11:47**	**12**	**0**	**1**	**1**	**4**	**0**	**0**	**0**	**7:52**

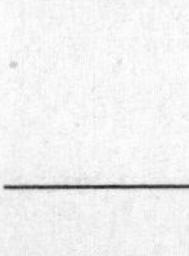

NASH, Rick (NASH, RIHK) NYR

Left wing. Shoots left. 6'4", 220 lbs. Born, Brampton, ON, June 16, 1984. Columbus' 1st choice, 1st overall, in 2002 Entry Draft.

Season	Club	League	GP	G	A	Pts	PIM	PP	SH	GW	S	S%	+/-	TF	F%	Min	GP	G	A	Pts	PIM	PP	SH	GW	Min
99-2000	Tor. Marlboros	GTHL	34	61	54	115	34																		
2000-01	London Knights	OHL	58	31	35	66	56										4	3	3	6	8				
2001-02	London Knights	OHL	54	32	40	72	88										12	10	9	19	21				
2002-03	**Columbus**	**NHL**	**74**	**17**	**22**	**39**	**78**	**6**	**0**	**2**	**154**	**11.0**	**-27**	**14**	**35.7**	**13:57**									
2003-04	**Columbus**	**NHL**	**80**	***41**	**16**	**57**	**87**	***19**	**0**	**7**	**269**	**15.2**	**-35**	**21**	**28.6**	**17:38**									
2004-05	HC Davos	Swiss	44	26	20	46	83										15	9	2	11	26				
2005-06	**Columbus**	**NHL**	**54**	**31**	**23**	**54**	**51**	**11**	**0**	**4**	**170**	**18.2**	**5**	**38**	**50.0**	**18:16**									
	Canada	Olympics	6	0	1	1	10																		
2006-07	**Columbus**	**NHL**	**75**	**27**	**30**	**57**	**73**	**9**	**1**	**5**	**228**	**11.8**	**-8**	**143**	**42.7**	**19:12**									
2007-08	**Columbus**	**NHL**	**80**	**38**	**31**	**69**	**95**	**10**	**4**	**6**	**329**	**11.6**	**2**	**44**	**31.8**	**20:29**									

			Regular Season														Playoffs								
Season	Club	League	GP	G	A	Pts	PIM	PP	SH	GW	S	S%	+/-	TF	F%	Min	GP	G	A	Pts	PIM	PP	SH	GW	Min
2008-09	Columbus	NHL	78	40	39	79	52	6	5	5	263	15.2	11	18	27.8	21:10	4	1	2	3	2	0	0	0	20:52
2009-10	Columbus	NHL	76	33	34	67	58	10	2	6	254	13.0	–2	22	50.0	20:56	....	....	....	....	....	....	....	....	....
	Canada	Olympics	7	2	3	5	0	....	....	....	....	....	....	....	....	....	....	....	....	....	....	....	....	....	....
2010-11	Columbus	NHL	75	32	34	66	34	6	0	7	305	10.5	2	24	29.2	18:56	....	....	....	....	....	....	....	....	....
2011-12	Columbus	NHL	82	30	29	59	40	6	2	2	306	9.8	–19	19	31.6	19:05	....	....	....	....	....	....	....	....	....
2012-13	HC Davos	Swiss	17	12	6	18	8	....	....	....	....	....	....	....	....	....	....	....	....	....	....	....	....	....	....
	NY Rangers	NHL	44	21	21	42	26	3	1	3	176	11.9	16	12	41.7	19:58	12	1	4	5	0	0	0	0	20:28
2013-14	NY Rangers	NHL	65	26	13	39	36	4	2	9	258	10.1	10	2	100.0	17:01	25	3	7	10	8	1	0	1	17:25
	Canada	Olympics	6	0	1	1	2	....	....	....	....	....	....	....	....	....	....	....	....	....	....	....	....	....	....
2014-15	NY Rangers	NHL	79	42	27	69	36	6	4	8	304	13.8	29	4	50.0	17:27	19	5	9	14	4	2	0	0	18:30
	NHL Totals		862	378	319	697	666	96	21	64	3016	12.5		361	39.6	18:40	60	10	22	32	14	3	0	1	18:36

OHL All-Rookie Team (2001) • OHL Rookie of the Year (2001) • CHL All-Rookie Team (2001) • NHL All-Rookie Team (2003) • Maurice "Rocket" Richard Trophy (2004) (tied with Jarome Iginla and Ilya Kovalchuk) • NHL Foundation Player Award (2009)

Played in NHL All-Star Game (2004, 2007, 2008, 2009, 2011, 2015)

Signed as a free agent by **Davos** (Swiss), August 3, 2004. Traded to **NY Rangers** by **Columbus** with Steven Delisle and Columbus' 3rd round choice (Pavel Buchnevich) in 2013 Entry Draft for Brandon Dubinsky, Artem Anisimov, Tim Erixon and NY Rangers' 1st round choice (Kerby Rychel) in 2013 Entry Draft, July 23, 2012. Signed as a free agent by **Davos** (Swiss), September 18, 2012.

NASH, Riley (NASH, RIGH-lee) CAR

Center. Shoots right. 6'1", 200 lbs. Born, Consort, AB, May 9, 1989. Edmonton's 3rd choice, 21st overall, in 2007 Entry Draft.

Season	Club	League	GP	G	A	Pts	PIM	PP	SH	GW	S	S%	+/-	TF	F%	Min	GP	G	A	Pts	PIM	PP	SH	GW	Min
2005-06	Thompson Blazers	BCMML	31	29	31	60	100	....	....	....	....	....	....	....	....	....	....	....	....	....	....	....	....	....	....
	Salmon Arm	BCHL	1	0	0	0	0	....	....	....	....	....	....	....	....	....	5	1	2	3	0	....	....	....	....
2006-07	Salmon Arm	BCHL	55	38	46	84	87	....	....	....	....	....	....	....	....	....	11	4	7	11	31	....	....	....	....
2007-08	Cornell Big Red	ECAC	36	12	20	32	28	....	....	....	....	....	....	....	....	....	....	....	....	....	....	....	....	....	....
2008-09	Cornell Big Red	ECAC	36	13	22	35	34	....	....	....	....	....	....	....	....	....	....	....	....	....	....	....	....	....	....
2009-10	Cornell Big Red	ECAC	30	12	23	35	39	....	....	....	....	....	....	....	....	....	....	....	....	....	....	....	....	....	....
2010-11	Charlotte	AHL	79	14	18	32	26	....	....	....	....	....	....	....	....	....	16	1	3	4	16	....	....	....	....
2011-12	Carolina	NHL	5	0	1	1	2	0	0	0	2	0.0	1	35	31.4	10:34	....	....	....	....	....	....	....	....	....
	Charlotte	AHL	58	8	12	20	26	....	....	....	....	....	....	....	....	....	....	....	....	....	....	....	....	....	....
2012-13	Charlotte	AHL	51	13	24	37	20	....	....	....	....	....	....	....	....	....	5	1	2	3	0	....	....	....	....
	Carolina	NHL	32	4	5	9	8	0	0	0	36	11.1	–4	289	44.3	12:48	....	....	....	....	....	....	....	....	....
2013-14	Carolina	NHL	73	10	14	24	29	1	0	3	86	11.6	0	666	46.0	12:40	....	....	....	....	....	....	....	....	....
2014-15	Carolina	NHL	68	8	17	25	12	1	0	0	94	8.5	–10	958	50.9	16:19	....	....	....	....	....	....	....	....	....
	NHL Totals		178	22	37	59	51	2	0	3	218	10.1		1948	47.9	14:02	....	....	....	....	....	....	....	....	....

ECAC All-Rookie Team (2008) • ECAC Rookie of the Year (2008) • ECAC First All-Star Team (2009)

Traded to **Carolina** by **Edmonton** for Ottawa's 2nd round choice (previously acquired, Edmonton selected Martin Marincin) in 2010 Entry Draft, June 25, 2010.

NEAL, James (NEEL, JAYMS) NSH

Left wing. Shoots left. 6'2", 208 lbs. Born, Whitby, ON, September 3, 1987. Dallas' 2nd choice, 33rd overall, in 2005 Entry Draft.

Season	Club	League	GP	G	A	Pts	PIM	PP	SH	GW	S	S%	+/-	TF	F%	Min	GP	G	A	Pts	PIM	PP	SH	GW	Min
2003-04	Bowmanville	ON-Jr.A	43	28	27	55	....	....	....	....	....	....	....	....	....	....	....	....	....	....	....	....	....	....	....
	Plymouth Whalers	OHL	9	2	4	6	0	....	....	....	....	....	....	....	....	....	....	....	....	....	....	....	....	....	....
2004-05	Plymouth Whalers	OHL	67	18	26	44	32	....	....	....	....	....	....	....	....	....	4	1	1	2	6	....	....	....	....
2005-06	Plymouth Whalers	OHL	66	21	37	58	109	....	....	....	....	....	....	....	....	....	13	9	7	16	33	....	....	....	....
2006-07	Plymouth Whalers	OHL	45	27	38	65	94	....	....	....	....	....	....	....	....	....	20	13	12	25	54	....	....	....	....
2007-08	Iowa Stars	AHL	62	18	19	37	63	....	....	....	....	....	....	....	....	....	....	....	....	....	....	....	....	....	....
2008-09	Dallas	NHL	77	24	13	37	51	9	0	2	171	14.0	–11	31	35.5	15:52	....	....	....	....	....	....	....	....	....
	Manitoba Moose	AHL	5	4	1	5	2	....	....	....	....	....	....	....	....	....	....	....	....	....	....	....	....	....	....
2009-10	Dallas	NHL	78	27	28	55	64	2	1	4	200	13.5	–5	60	31.7	18:12	....	....	....	....	....	....	....	....	....
2010-11	Dallas	NHL	59	21	18	39	60	5	0	3	160	13.1	8	17	41.2	17:42	....	....	....	....	....	....	....	....	....
	Pittsburgh	NHL	20	1	5	6	6	0	0	0	52	1.9	–1	6	16.7	16:54	7	1	1	2	6	0	0	1	17:25
2011-12	Pittsburgh	NHL	80	40	41	81	87	*18	0	4	329	12.2	6	15	26.7	19:08	5	2	4	6	12	1	0	0	19:50
2012-13	Pittsburgh	NHL	40	21	15	36	26	9	0	6	136	15.4	5	6	16.7	17:28	13	6	4	10	8	2	0	1	17:43
2013-14	Pittsburgh	NHL	59	27	34	61	55	11	0	4	238	11.3	15	18	27.8	18:27	13	2	2	4	24	0	0	0	18:26
2014-15	Nashville	NHL	67	23	14	37	57	3	0	6	221	10.4	12	17	41.2	18:05	6	4	1	5	8	1	0	0	20:37
	NHL Totals		480	184	168	352	406	57	1	29	1507	12.2		170	32.4	17:49	44	15	12	27	58	4	0	2	18:31

OHL First All-Star Team (2007) • Canadian Major Junior Second All-Star Team (2007) • NHL First All-Star Team (2012)

Played in NHL All-Star Game (2012)

Traded to **Pittsburgh** by **Dallas** with Matt Niskanen for Alex Goligoski, February 21, 2011. Traded to **Nashville** by **Pittsburgh** for Patric Hornqvist and Nick Spaling, June 27, 2014.

NEIL, Chris (NEEL, KRIHS) OTT

Right wing. Shoots right. 6'1", 215 lbs. Born, Markdale, ON, June 18, 1979. Ottawa's 7th choice, 161st overall, in 1998 Entry Draft.

Season	Club	League	GP	G	A	Pts	PIM	PP	SH	GW	S	S%	+/-	TF	F%	Min	GP	G	A	Pts	PIM	PP	SH	GW	Min
1995-96	Orangeville	ON-Jr.B	43	15	15	30	50	....	....	....	....	....	....	....	....	....	....	....	....	....	....	....	....	....	....
1996-97	North Bay	OHL	65	13	16	29	150	....	....	....	....	....	....	....	....	....	....	....	....	....	....	....	....	....	....
1997-98	North Bay	OHL	59	26	29	55	231	....	....	....	....	....	....	....	....	....	....	....	....	....	....	....	....	....	....
1998-99	North Bay	OHL	66	26	46	72	215	....	....	....	....	....	....	....	....	....	4	1	0	1	15	....	....	....	....
99-2000	Mobile Mysticks	ECHL	4	0	2	2	39	....	....	....	....	....	....	....	....	....	....	....	....	....	....	....	....	....	....
	Grand Rapids	IHL	51	9	10	19	301	....	....	....	....	....	....	....	....	....	8	0	2	2	24	....	....	....	....
2000-01	Grand Rapids	IHL	78	15	21	36	354	....	....	....	....	....	....	....	....	....	10	2	2	4	22	....	....	....	....
2001-02	Ottawa	NHL	72	10	7	17	231	1	0	0	56	17.9	5	0	0.0	8:22	12	0	0	0	12	0	0	0	7:12
2002-03	Ottawa	NHL	68	6	4	10	147	0	0	0	62	9.7	8	5	60.0	7:40	15	1	0	1	24	0	0	0	7:57
2003-04	Ottawa	NHL	82	8	8	16	194	0	0	1	76	10.5	13	14	42.9	8:51	7	0	1	1	19	0	0	0	6:45
2004-05	Binghamton	AHL	22	4	6	10	132	....	....	....	....	....	....	....	....	....	6	1	1	2	26	....	....	....	....
2005-06	Ottawa	NHL	79	16	17	33	204	8	0	0	126	12.7	9	9	22.2	12:18	10	1	0	1	14	0	0	0	6:58
2006-07	Ottawa	NHL	82	12	16	28	177	3	0	3	139	8.6	6	13	38.5	13:08	20	2	2	4	20	0	0	0	10:40
2007-08	Ottawa	NHL	68	6	14	20	199	0	0	1	78	7.7	–3	0	0.0	12:46	4	0	1	1	22	0	0	0	11:17
2008-09	Ottawa	NHL	60	3	7	10	146	0	0	0	59	5.1	–13	6	16.7	10:58	....	....	....	....	....	....	....	....	....
2009-10	Ottawa	NHL	68	10	12	22	175	1	0	2	100	10.0	–1	4	50.0	11:59	6	3	1	4	20	0	0	0	14:11
2010-11	Ottawa	NHL	80	6	10	16	210	0	0	2	105	5.7	–14	6	50.0	12:46	....	....	....	....	....	....	....	....	....
2011-12	Ottawa	NHL	72	13	15	28	178	2	0	0	127	10.2	–10	2	0.0	12:48	7	2	1	3	22	1	0	1	13:35
2012-13	Ottawa	NHL	48	4	8	12	144	0	0	3	87	4.6	0	6	50.0	13:52	10	0	4	4	*39	0	0	0	12:42
2013-14	Ottawa	NHL	76	8	6	14	211	0	0	0	99	8.1	–10	3	33.3	11:48	....	....	....	....	....	....	....	....	....
2014-15	Ottawa	NHL	38	4	3	7	78	1	0	0	23	17.4	5	5	60.0	9:44	2	0	0	0	0	0	0	0	7:15
	NHL Totals		893	106	127	233	2294	16	0	12	1137	9.3		73	39.7	11:19	93	9	10	19	192	1	0	1	9:42

Signed as a free agent by **Binghamton** (AHL), March 2, 2005. • Missed majority of 2014-15 due to lower-body (December 11, 2014 vs. Los Angeles) and thumb (February 14, 2015 vs. Edmonton) injuries.

NELSON, Brock (NEHL-suhn, BRAWK) NYI

Center. Shoots left. 6'3", 196 lbs. Born, Warroad, MN, October 15, 1991. NY Islanders' 2nd choice, 30th overall, in 2010 Entry Draft.

Season	Club	League	GP	G	A	Pts	PIM	PP	SH	GW	S	S%	+/-	TF	F%	Min	GP	G	A	Pts	PIM	PP	SH	GW	Min
2007-08	Warroad Warriors	High-MN	31	14	9	23	....	....	....	....	....	....	....	....	....	....	....	....	....	....	....	....	....	....	....
2008-09	Warroad Warriors	High-MN	31	45	36	81	....	....	....	....	....	....	....	....	....	....	....	....	....	....	....	....	....	....	....
2009-10	Team Great Plains	UMHSEL	24	5	10	15	....	....	....	....	....	....	....	....	....	....	....	....	....	....	....	....	....	....	....
	Warroad Warriors	High-MN	25	39	34	73	38	....	....	....	....	....	....	....	....	....	6	14	8	22	8	....	....	....	....
2010-11	North Dakota	WCHA	42	8	13	21	27	....	....	....	....	....	....	....	....	....	....	....	....	....	....	....	....	....	....
2011-12	North Dakota	WCHA	42	28	19	47	4	....	....	....	....	....	....	....	....	....	....	....	....	....	....	....	....	....	....
	Bridgeport	AHL	4	0	0	0	0	....	....	....	....	....	....	....	....	....	2	0	0	0	0	....	....	....	....
2012-13	Bridgeport	AHL	66	25	27	52	34	....	....	....	....	....	....	....	....	....	....	....	....	....	....	....	....	....	....
	NY Islanders	NHL	....	....	....	....	....	....	....	....	....	....	....	....	....	....	1	0	0	0	0	0	0	0	7:44
2013-14	NY Islanders	NHL	72	14	12	26	12	3	0	1	132	10.6	–10	451	42.4	14:16	....	....	....	....	....	....	....	....	....
	Bridgeport	AHL	1	0	1	1	2	....	....	....	....	....	....	....	....	....	....	....	....	....	....	....	....	....	....
2014-15	NY Islanders	NHL	82	20	22	42	24	10	0	3	190	10.5	6	799	44.3	15:53	6	2	0	2	2	0	0	0	14:20
	NHL Totals		154	34	34	68	36	13	0	4	322	10.6		1250	43.6	15:08	7	2	0	2	2	0	0	0	13:24

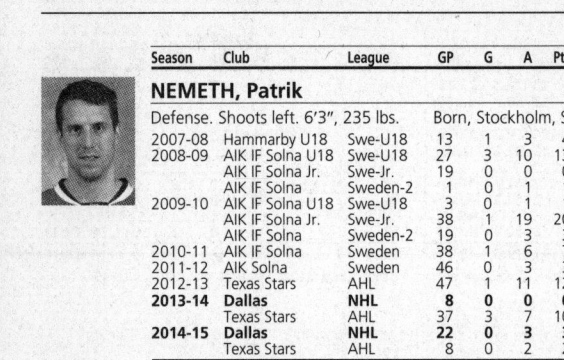

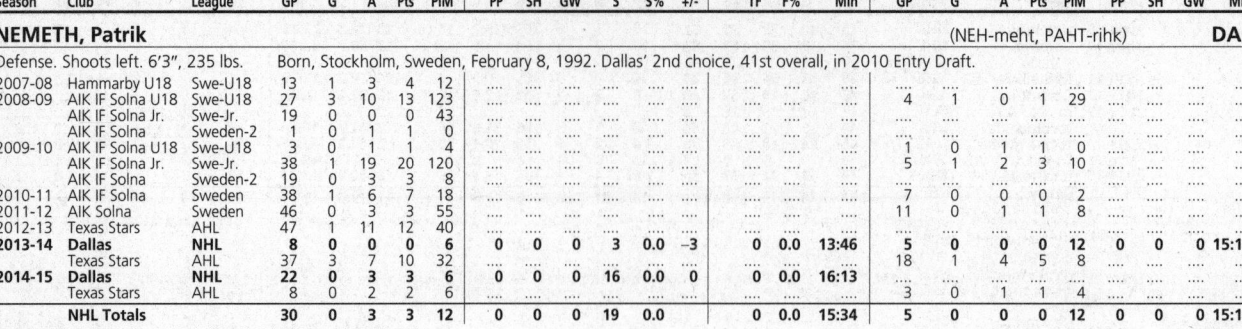

NEMETH, Patrik
(NEH-meht, PAHT-rihk) **DAL**

Defense. Shoots left. 6'3", 235 lbs. Born, Stockholm, Sweden, February 8, 1992. Dallas' 2nd choice, 41st overall, in 2010 Entry Draft.

			Regular Season														Playoffs								
Season	Club	League	GP	G	A	Pts	PIM	PP	SH	GW	S	S%	+/-	TF	F%	Min	GP	G	A	Pts	PIM	PP	SH	GW	Min
2007-08	Hammarby U18	Swe-U18	13	1	3	4	12	....	....	....	....	....	....	....	....	....	....	....	....	....	....	....	....	....	....
2008-09	AIK IF Solna U18	Swe-U18	27	3	10	13	123	....	....	....	....	....	....	....	....	....	4	1	0	1	29	....	....	....	....
	AIK IF Solna Jr.	Swe-Jr.	19	0	0	0	43	....	....	....	....	....	....	....	....	....	....	....	....	....	....	....	....	....	....
	AIK IF Solna	Sweden-2	1	0	1	1	0	....	....	....	....	....	....	....	....	....	....	....	....	....	....	....	....	....	....
2009-10	AIK IF Solna U18	Swe-U18	3	0	1	1	4	....	....	....	....	....	....	....	....	....	1	0	1	1	0	....	....	....	....
	AIK IF Solna Jr.	Swe-Jr.	38	1	19	20	120	....	....	....	....	....	....	....	....	....	5	1	2	3	10	....	....	....	....
	AIK IF Solna	Sweden-2	19	0	3	3	8	....	....	....	....	....	....	....	....	....	....	....	....	....	....	....	....	....	....
2010-11	AIK IF Solna	Sweden	38	1	6	7	18	....	....	....	....	....	....	....	....	....	7	0	0	0	2	....	....	....	....
2011-12	AIK Solna	Sweden	46	0	3	3	55	....	....	....	....	....	....	....	....	....	11	0	1	1	8	....	....	....	....
2012-13	Texas Stars	AHL	47	1	11	12	40	....	....	....	....	....	....	....	....	....	....	....	....	....	....	....	....	....	....
2013-14	**Dallas**	**NHL**	**8**	**0**	**0**	**0**	**6**	**0**	**0**	**0**	**3**	**0.0**	**–3**	**0**	**0.0**	**13:46**	**5**	**0**	**0**	**0**	**12**	**0**	**0**	**0**	**15:16**
	Texas Stars	AHL	37	3	7	10	32	....	....	....	....	....	....	....	....	....	18	1	4	5	8	....	....	....	....
2014-15	**Dallas**	**NHL**	**22**	**0**	**3**	**3**	**6**	**0**	**0**	**0**	**16**	**0.0**	**0**	**0**	**0.0**	**16:13**	....	....	....	....	....	....	....	....	....
	Texas Stars	AHL	8	0	2	2	6	....	....	....	....	....	....	....	....	....	3	0	1	1	4	....	....	....	....
	NHL Totals		**30**	**0**	**3**	**3**	**12**	**0**	**0**	**0**	**19**	**0.0**		**0**	**0.0**	**15:34**	**5**	**0**	**0**	**0**	**12**	**0**	**0**	**0**	**15:16**

• Missed majority of 2014-15 due to arm injury vs. Philadelphia, October 18, 2014.

NEMISZ, Greg
(NEH-mihtz, GREHG)

Center. Shoots right. 6'3", 197 lbs. Born, Courtice, ON, June 5, 1990. Calgary's 1st choice, 25th overall, in 2008 Entry Draft.

			Regular Season														Playoffs								
Season	Club	League	GP	G	A	Pts	PIM	PP	SH	GW	S	S%	+/-	TF	F%	Min	GP	G	A	Pts	PIM	PP	SH	GW	Min
2005-06	Clarington Toros	Minor-ON	32	29	24	53	24	....	....	....	....	....	....	....	....	....	....	....	....	....	....	....	....	....	....
2006-07	Windsor Spitfires	OHL	62	11	23	34	23	....	....	....	....	....	....	....	....	....	....	....	....	....	....	....	....	....	....
2007-08	Windsor Spitfires	OHL	68	34	33	67	52	....	....	....	....	....	....	....	....	....	5	2	1	3	8	....	....	....	....
2008-09	Windsor Spitfires	OHL	65	36	41	77	48	....	....	....	....	....	....	....	....	....	20	8	12	20	22	....	....	....	....
2009-10	Windsor Spitfires	OHL	51	34	36	70	50	....	....	....	....	....	....	....	....	....	15	2	10	12	12	....	....	....	....
2010-11	**Calgary**	**NHL**	**6**	**0**	**1**	**1**	**0**	**0**	**0**	**0**	**5**	**0.0**	**–1**	**3**	**33.3**	**5:06**	....	....	....	....	....	....	....	....	....
	Abbotsford Heat	AHL	68	14	19	33	28	....	....	....	....	....	....	....	....	....	....	....	....	....	....	....	....	....	....
2011-12	**Calgary**	**NHL**	**9**	**0**	**0**	**0**	**0**	**0**	**0**	**0**	**2**	**0.0**	**1**	**48**	**39.6**	**7:43**	....	....	....	....	....	....	....	....	....
	Abbotsford Heat	AHL	51	13	16	29	29	....	....	....	....	....	....	....	....	....	8	2	4	6	4	....	....	....	....
2012-13	Abbotsford Heat	AHL	55	3	7	10	34	....	....	....	....	....	....	....	....	....	....	....	....	....	....	....	....	....	....
2013-14	Abbotsford Heat	AHL	32	5	4	9	9	....	....	....	....	....	....	....	....	....	....	....	....	....	....	....	....	....	....
	Charlotte	AHL	14	3	8	11	4	....	....	....	....	....	....	....	....	....	....	....	....	....	....	....	....	....	....
2014-15	Charlotte	AHL	21	8	6	14	6	....	....	....	....	....	....	....	....	....	....	....	....	....	....	....	....	....	....
	NHL Totals		**15**	**0**	**1**	**1**	**0**	**0**	**0**	**0**	**7**	**0.0**		**51**	**39.2**	**6:40**	....	....	....	....	....	....	....	....	....

OHL Second All-Star Team (2009)

Traded to **Carolina** by **Calgary** for Kevin Westgarth, December 30. 2013. • Officially announced his retirement, July 15, 2015.

NESS, Aaron
(NEHS, AIR-uhn) **WSH**

Defense. Shoots left. 5'10", 187 lbs. Born, Roseau, MN, May 18, 1990. NY Islanders' 3rd choice, 40th overall, in 2008 Entry Draft.

			Regular Season														Playoffs								
Season	Club	League	GP	G	A	Pts	PIM	PP	SH	GW	S	S%	+/-	TF	F%	Min	GP	G	A	Pts	PIM	PP	SH	GW	Min
2005-06	Roseau Rams	High-MN	30	3	18	21	8	....	....	....	....	....	....	....	....	....	....	....	....	....	....	....	....	....	....
2006-07	Roseau Rams	High-MN	31	13	38	51	12	....	....	....	....	....	....	....	....	....	....	....	....	....	....	....	....	....	....
	Team Great Plains	UMWEHL	11	0	8	8	....	....	....	....	....	....	....	....	....	....	....	....	....	....	....	....	....	....	....
2007-08	Roseau Rams	High-MN	31	28	44	72	16	....	....	....	....	....	....	....	....	....	....	....	....	....	....	....	....	....	....
	Team Great Plains	UMWEHL	11	2	11	13	....	....	....	....	....	....	....	....	....	....	....	....	....	....	....	....	....	....	....
2008-09	U. of Minnesota	WCHA	37	2	15	17	16	....	....	....	....	....	....	....	....	....	....	....	....	....	....	....	....	....	....
2009-10	U. of Minnesota	WCHA	39	2	10	12	24	....	....	....	....	....	....	....	....	....	....	....	....	....	....	....	....	....	....
2010-11	U. of Minnesota	WCHA	35	2	12	14	41	....	....	....	....	....	....	....	....	....	....	....	....	....	....	....	....	....	....
	Bridgeport	AHL	13	1	3	4	4	....	....	....	....	....	....	....	....	....	....	....	....	....	....	....	....	....	....
2011-12	**NY Islanders**	**NHL**	**9**	**0**	**0**	**0**	**2**	**0**	**0**	**0**	**6**	**0.0**	**0**	**0**	**0.0**	**16:56**	....	....	....	....	....	....	....	....	....
	Bridgeport	AHL	69	5	22	27	36	....	....	....	....	....	....	....	....	....	3	0	0	0	4	....	....	....	....
2012-13	Bridgeport	AHL	76	3	24	27	30	....	....	....	....	....	....	....	....	....	....	....	....	....	....	....	....	....	....
2013-14	**NY Islanders**	**NHL**	**20**	**1**	**2**	**3**	**10**	**0**	**0**	**0**	**23**	**4.3**	**–13**	**0**	**0.0**	**14:48**	....	....	....	....	....	....	....	....	....
	Bridgeport	AHL	48	6	14	20	47	....	....	....	....	....	....	....	....	....	....	....	....	....	....	....	....	....	....
2014-15	Bridgeport	AHL	74	8	37	45	62	....	....	....	....	....	....	....	....	....	....	....	....	....	....	....	....	....	....
	NHL Totals		**29**	**1**	**2**	**3**	**12**	**0**	**0**	**0**	**29**	**3.4**		**0**	**0.0**	**15:28**	....	....	....	....	....	....	....	....	....

Signed as a free agent by **Washington**, July 1, 2015.

NESTEROV, Nikita
(NEHS-tehr-awf, nih-KEE-tuh) **T.B.**

Defense. Shoots left. 6', 191 lbs. Born, Chelyabinsk, Russia, March 28, 1993. Tampa Bay's 3rd choice, 148th overall, in 2011 Entry Draft.

			Regular Season														Playoffs								
Season	Club	League	GP	G	A	Pts	PIM	PP	SH	GW	S	S%	+/-	TF	F%	Min	GP	G	A	Pts	PIM	PP	SH	GW	Min
2009-10	Chelyabinsk Jr.	Russia-Jr.	9	5	2	7	8	....	....	....	....	....	....	....	....	....	4	0	0	0	6	....	....	....	....
2010-11	Chelyabinsk Jr.	Russia-Jr.	46	5	14	19	72	....	....	....	....	....	....	....	....	....	5	0	0	0	6	....	....	....	....
2011-12	Chelyabinsk Jr.	Russia-Jr.	41	11	20	31	66	....	....	....	....	....	....	....	....	....	4	0	5	5	6	....	....	....	....
	Chelyabinsk	KHL	10	0	1	1	4	....	....	....	....	....	....	....	....	....	3	0	0	0	0	....	....	....	....
2012-13	Chelyabinsk Jr.	Russia-Jr.	2	0	1	1	2	....	....	....	....	....	....	....	....	....	4	2	1	3	0	....	....	....	....
	Chelyabinsk	KHL	35	0	0	0	14	....	....	....	....	....	....	....	....	....	19	0	4	4	6	....	....	....	....
2013-14	Syracuse Crunch	AHL	54	4	12	16	39	....	....	....	....	....	....	....	....	....	....	....	....	....	....	....	....	....	....
2014-15	**Tampa Bay**	**NHL**	**27**	**2**	**5**	**7**	**16**	**1**	**0**	**0**	**44**	**4.5**	**6**	**0**	**0.0**	**16:03**	**17**	**1**	**5**	**6**	**8**	**0**	**0**	**0**	**10:46**
	Syracuse Crunch	AHL	32	3	11	14	26	....	....	....	....	....	....	....	....	....	....	....	....	....	....	....	....	....	....
	NHL Totals		**27**	**2**	**5**	**7**	**16**	**1**	**0**	**0**	**44**	**4.5**		**0**	**0.0**	**16:03**	**17**	**1**	**5**	**6**	**8**	**0**	**0**	**0**	**10:46**

NESTRASIL, Andrej
(NEHS-tra-shihl, ahn-DRAY) **CAR**

Right wing. Shoots left. 6'2", 210 lbs. Born, Prague, Czech., February 22, 1991. Detroit's 3rd choice, 75th overall, in 2009 Entry Draft.

			Regular Season														Playoffs								
Season	Club	League	GP	G	A	Pts	PIM	PP	SH	GW	S	S%	+/-	TF	F%	Min	GP	G	A	Pts	PIM	PP	SH	GW	Min
2004-05	Slavia U17	CzR-U17	3	0	1	1	2	....	....	....	....	....	....	....	....	....	....	....	....	....	....	....	....	....	....
2005-06	Slavia U17	CzR-U17	41	6	12	18	18	....	....	....	....	....	....	....	....	....	....	....	....	....	....	....	....	....	....
2006-07	Slavia U17	CzR-U17	43	24	37	61	75	....	....	....	....	....	....	....	....	....	5	2	2	4	6	....	....	....	....
2007-08	Slavia U17	CzR-U17	....	....	....	....	....	....	....	....	....	....	....	....	....	....	2	1	0	1	2	....	....	....	....
	Slavia Jr.	CzRep-Jr.	40	12	16	28	58	....	....	....	....	....	....	....	....	....	5	1	2	3	4	....	....	....	....
2008-09	Victoriaville Tigres	QMJHL	66	22	35	57	67	....	....	....	....	....	....	....	....	....	4	2	1	3	10	....	....	....	....
2009-10	Victoriaville Tigres	QMJHL	50	16	35	51	40	....	....	....	....	....	....	....	....	....	16	2	4	6	10	....	....	....	....
2010-11	P.E.I. Rocket	QMJHL	58	19	51	70	40	....	....	....	....	....	....	....	....	....	5	1	5	6	2	....	....	....	....
2011-12	Grand Rapids	AHL	25	3	1	4	6	....	....	....	....	....	....	....	....	....	....	....	....	....	....	....	....	....	....
	Toledo Walleye	ECHL	51	7	22	29	20	....	....	....	....	....	....	....	....	....	....	....	....	....	....	....	....	....	....
2012-13	Toledo Walleye	ECHL	40	11	30	41	26	....	....	....	....	....	....	....	....	....	4	1	2	3	0	....	....	....	....
	Grand Rapids	AHL	25	3	3	6	2	....	....	....	....	....	....	....	....	....	1	0	0	0	0	....	....	....	....
2013-14	Grand Rapids	AHL	70	16	20	36	24	....	....	....	....	....	....	....	....	....	10	4	2	6	4	....	....	....	....
2014-15	**Detroit**	**NHL**	**13**	**0**	**2**	**2**	**4**	**0**	**0**	**0**	**16**	**0.0**	**–3**	**2**	**100.0**	**11:04**	....	....	....	....	....	....	....	....	....
	Carolina	**NHL**	**41**	**7**	**11**	**18**	**4**	**2**	**0**	**0**	**66**	**10.6**	**2**	**92**	**57.6**	**14:05**	....	....	....	....	....	....	....	....	....
	Charlotte	AHL	3	0	0	0	17	....	....	....	....	....	....	....	....	....	....	....	....	....	....	....	....	....	....
	NHL Totals		**54**	**7**	**13**	**20**	**8**	**2**	**0**	**0**	**82**	**8.5**		**94**	**58.5**	**13:21**	....	....	....	....	....	....	....	....	....

Claimed on waivers by **Carolina** from **Detroit**, November 20, 2014.

NEWBURY, Kris
(new-BUHR-ee, KRIHS)

Center. Shoots left. 5'11", 205 lbs. Born, Brampton, ON, February 19, 1982. San Jose's 4th choice, 139th overall, in 2002 Entry Draft.

			Regular Season														Playoffs								
Season	Club	League	GP	G	A	Pts	PIM	PP	SH	GW	S	S%	+/-	TF	F%	Min	GP	G	A	Pts	PIM	PP	SH	GW	Min
1996-97	Brampton	ON-Jr.A	28	9	4	13	36	....	....	....	....	....	....	....	....	....	....	....	....	....	....	....	....	....	....
1997-98	Brampton	ON-Jr.A	46	11	21	32	161	....	....	....	....	....	....	....	....	....	....	....	....	....	....	....	....	....	....
1998-99	Belleville Bulls	OHL	51	6	8	14	89	....	....	....	....	....	....	....	....	....	21	4	6	10	0	....	....	....	....
99-2000	Belleville Bulls	OHL	34	6	18	24	72	....	....	....	....	....	....	....	....	....	....	....	....	....	....	....	....	....	....
	Sarnia Sting	OHL	27	6	8	14	44	....	....	....	....	....	....	....	....	....	7	0	3	3	16	....	....	....	....
2000-01	Sarnia Sting	OHL	64	28	30	58	126	....	....	....	....	....	....	....	....	....	4	1	3	4	20	....	....	....	....
2001-02	Sarnia Sting	OHL	66	42	62	104	141	....	....	....	....	....	....	....	....	....	5	1	3	4	15	....	....	....	....
2002-03	Sarnia Sting	OHL	64	34	58	92	149	....	....	....	....	....	....	....	....	....	6	4	4	8	16	....	....	....	....

			Regular Season														Playoffs								
Season	Club	League	GP	G	A	Pts	PIM	PP	SH	GW	S	S%	+/-	TF	F%	Min	GP	G	A	Pts	PIM	PP	SH	GW	Min
2003-04	St. John's	AHL	72	5	15	20	153																		
2004-05	St. John's	AHL	55	4	9	13	103										5	0	0	0	36				
	Pensacola	ECHL	6	2	4	6	20																		
2005-06	Toronto Marlies	AHL	74	22	37	59	215										5	0	1	1	12				
2006-07	Toronto	NHL	15	2	2	4	26	0	0	0	30	6.7	4	20	45.0	7:42									
	Toronto Marlies	AHL	37	12	24	36	87																		
2007-08	Toronto	NHL	28	1	1	2	32	0	0	0	14	7.1	–7	55	40.0	4:22									
	Toronto Marlies	AHL	54	16	27	43	101										19	4	9	13	*73				
2008-09	Toronto	NHL	1	0	0	0	2	0	0	0	0	0.0	0	3	33.3	4:55									
	Toronto Marlies	AHL	33	6	23	29	72																		
2009-10	Detroit	NHL	4	1	0	1	4	0	0	0	3	33.3	1	18	38.9	8:41									
	Grand Rapids	AHL	52	11	22	33	144																		
	Hartford	AHL	18	4	14	18	61																		
2010-11	NY Rangers	NHL	11	0	1	1	35	0	0	0	6	0.0	–1	56	60.7	7:38									
	Connecticut	AHL	69	17	44	61	139										6	2	2	4	2				
2011-12	NY Rangers	NHL	7	0	0	0	24	0	0	0	2	0.0	–1	17	35.3	5:53									
	Connecticut	AHL	65	25	39	64	130										9	1	3	4	20				
2012-13	Connecticut	AHL	70	20	42	62	127																		
	NY Rangers	NHL	6	0	1	1	9	0	0	0	4	0.0	1	32	50.0	7:53	3	0	0	0	2	0	0	0	6:10
2013-14	Philadelphia	NHL	4	0	1	1	7	0	0	0	1	0.0	0	14	42.9	5:02									
	Adirondack	AHL	46	14	22	36	182																		
	Hershey Bears	AHL	17	4	9	13	25																		
2014-15	Hershey Bears	AHL	68	18	30	48	171										10	0	4	4	16				
	NHL Totals		76	4	6	10	139	0	0	0	60	6.7		215	47.0	6:11	3	0	0	0	2	0	0	0	6:10

OHL Second All-Star Team (2002)

Signed as a free agent by **St. John's** (AHL), October 2, 2003. Signed as a free agent by **Toronto**, July 17, 2006. Signed as a free agent by **Detroit**, July 7, 2009. Traded to **NY Rangers** by **Detroit** for Jordan Owens, March 3, 2010. Traded to **Philadelphia** by **NY Rangers** for Danny Syvret, July 1, 2013. Signed as a free agent by **Washington**, July 4, 2014.

NICHUSHKIN, Valeri

(nih-CHOOSH-kihn, val-AIR-ee) **DAL**

Right wing. Shoots left. 6'4", 210 lbs. Born, Chelyabinsk, Russia, March 4, 1995. Dallas' 1st choice, 10th overall, in 2013 Entry Draft.

Season	Club	League	GP	G	A	Pts	PIM	PP	SH	GW	S	S%	+/-	TF	F%	Min	GP	G	A	Pts	PIM	PP	SH	GW	Min
2011-12	Chelyabinsk Jr.	Russia-Jr.	38	4	6	10	6																		
2012-13	Chelyabinsk Jr.	Russia-Jr.	9	4	4	8	0																		
	Chelmet	Russia-2	15	8	2	10	4																		
	Chelyabinsk	KHL	18	4	2	6	0										25	6	3	9	0				
2013-14	Dallas	NHL	79	14	20	34	8	2	0	2	128	10.9	20	1	0.0	14:58	6	1	1	2	2	0	0	0	13:28
	Russia	Olympics	5	1	0	1	0																		
2014-15	Dallas	NHL	8	0	1	1	2	0	0	0	6	0.0	–5	0	0.0	13:46									
	Texas Stars	AHL	5	0	4	4	12																		
	NHL Totals		87	14	21	35	10	2	0	2	134	10.4		1	0.0	14:52	6	1	1	2	2	0	0	0	13:28

• Missed majority of 2014-15 due to recurring hip and groin injuries.

NIEDERREITER, Nino

(nee-duhr-RIGH-tuhr, NEE-noh) **MIN**

Right wing. Shoots left. 6'2", 209 lbs. Born, Chur, Switzerland, September 8, 1992. NY Islanders' 1st choice, 5th overall, in 2010 Entry Draft.

Season	Club	League	GP	G	A	Pts	PIM	PP	SH	GW	S	S%	+/-	TF	F%	Min	GP	G	A	Pts	PIM	PP	SH	GW	Min
2006-07	HC Davos U18	Swiss-U18	32	43	19	62	38																		
	HC Davos Jr.	Swiss-Jr.															1	0	0	0	4				
2007-08	HC Davos U18	Swiss-U18	32	39	26	65	62										5	6	3	9	4				
	HC Davos Jr.	Swiss-Jr.	8	7	3	10	4										3	0	1	1	8				
2008-09	HC Davos U18	Swiss-U18	6	6	6	12	6																		
	HC Davos Jr.	Swiss-Jr.	30	20	14	34	44										8	5	6	11	12				
	HC Davos	Swiss															3	0	1	1	0				
2009-10	Portland	WHL	65	36	24	60	68										13	8	8	16	16				
2010-11	NY Islanders	NHL	9	1	1	2	8	0	0	0	12	8.3	–1	0	0.0	13:36									
	Portland	WHL	55	41	29	70	67										21	9	18	27	30				
2011-12	NY Islanders	NHL	55	1	0	1	12	0	0	0	74	1.4	–29	2	0.0	10:07									
	Bridgeport	AHL	6	3	1	4	4																		
2012-13	Bridgeport	AHL	74	28	22	50	38																		
2013-14	Minnesota	NHL	81	14	22	36	44	2	0	1	143	9.8	12	26	26.9	14:06	13	3	3	6	8	0	0	2	14:40
	Switzerland	Olympics	4	0	0	0	2																		
2014-15	Minnesota	NHL	80	24	13	37	28	6	1	5	149	16.1	2	7	28.6	14:33	10	4	1	5	10	0	0	1	15:06
	NHL Totals		225	40	36	76	92	8	1	6	378	10.6		35	25.7	13:16	23	7	4	11	18	0	0	3	14:51

WHL West Second All-Star Team (2010)

Traded to **Minnesota** by **NY Islanders** for Cal Clutterbuck and New Jersey's 3rd round choice (previously acquired, Minnesota selected Eamon McAdam) in 2013 Entry Draft, June 30, 2013.

NIELSEN, Frans

(NEEL-sehn, FRAHNZ) **NYI**

Center. Shoots left. 6'1", 190 lbs. Born, Herning, Denmark, April 24, 1984. NY Islanders' 2nd choice, 87th overall, in 2002 Entry Draft.

Season	Club	League	GP	G	A	Pts	PIM	PP	SH	GW	S	S%	+/-	TF	F%	Min	GP	G	A	Pts	PIM	PP	SH	GW	Min
99-2000	Herning IK Jr.	Den-Jr.	36	18	16	34	6																		
	Denmark	WJ18-B	5	3	4	7	0																		
2000-01	Herning IK	Denmark	38	18	19	37	6																		
	Denmark	WJ18-B	3	2	1	3	0																		
2001-02	Malmo	Sweden	20	0	1	1	0																		
	Malmo Jr.	Swe-Jr.	29	15	27	42	8										7	3	7	10	2				
2002-03	Malmo	Sweden	47	3	6	9	10																		
	Malmo Jr.	Swe-Jr.	2	1	3	4	0																		
	Denmark	WJC-B	5	3	7	10	0																		
	Denmark	WC-A	6	0	0	0	4																		
2003-04	Malmo	Sweden	50	9	7	16	28																		
	Malmo	Sweden-Q	10	3	5	8	2																		
2004-05	Malmo	Sweden	49	8	7	15	6																		
	Malmo	Sweden-Q	10	7	2	9	0																		
	Denmark	Oly-Q	3	2	3	5	0																		
2005-06	Timra IK	Sweden	50	5	13	18	22																		
2006-07	NY Islanders	NHL	15	1	1	2	0	0	0	1	16	6.3	–2	53	45.3	5:13									
	Bridgeport	AHL	54	20	24	44	10																		
2007-08	NY Islanders	NHL	16	2	1	3	0	0	0	0	17	11.8	1	111	48.7	8:42									
	Bridgeport	AHL	48	10	28	38	18																		
2008-09	NY Islanders	NHL	59	9	24	33	18	3	1	2	101	8.9	–4	758	47.2	16:32									
2009-10	NY Islanders	NHL	76	12	26	38	6	0	1	1	136	8.8	4	1165	50.0	17:13									
2010-11	NY Islanders	NHL	71	13	31	44	38	0	*7	1	156	8.3	13	965	46.2	17:46									
2011-12	NY Islanders	NHL	82	17	30	47	6	5	0	1	133	12.8	–3	1156	45.2	17:27									
2012-13	Lukko Rauma	Finland	27	4	20	24	10																		
	NY Islanders	NHL	48	6	23	29	12	2	1	1	93	6.5	–3	558	48.0	18:01	6	0	2	2	0	0	0	0	18:00
2013-14	NY Islanders	NHL	80	25	33	58	8	5	2	0	167	15.0	–11	1084	49.3	18:20									
2014-15	NY Islanders	NHL	78	14	29	43	12	4	1	4	157	8.9	8	1050	48.2	16:35	7	1	1	2	0	0	0	0	16:11
	NHL Totals		525	99	198	297	100	19	13	11	976	10.1		6900	47.8	16:48	13	1	3	4	0	0	0	0	17:01

Signed as a free agent by **Rauma** (Finland), September 26, 2012.

NIETO, Matt

(NEE-eh-toh, MAT) **S.J.**

Left wing. Shoots left. 5'11", 190 lbs. Born, Long Beach, CA, November 5, 1992. San Jose's 1st choice, 47th overall, in 2011 Entry Draft.

Season	Club	League	GP	G	A	Pts	PIM	PP	SH	GW	S	S%	+/-	TF	F%	Min	GP	G	A	Pts	PIM	PP	SH	GW	Min
2007-08	Salisbury School	High-CT	23	8	10	18																			
2008-09	USNTDP	NAHL	38	11	24	35	14																		
	USNTDP	U-17	14	9	9	18	8																		
	USNTDP	U-18	13	6	8	14	14																		
2009-10	USNTDP	USHL	24	15	14	29	19																		
	USNTDP	U-18	30	13	12	25	12																		
2010-11	Boston University	H-East	39	10	13	23	16																		

			Regular Season														Playoffs								
Season	Club	League	GP	G	A	Pts	PIM	PP	SH	GW	S	S%	+/-	TF	F%	Min	GP	G	A	Pts	PIM	PP	SH	GW	Min
2011-12	Boston University	H-East	37	16	26	42	26	....	....	....	....	....	....	....	....	....	....	....	....	....	....	....	....	....	....
2012-13	Boston University	H-East	39	18	19	37	24	....	....	....	....	....	....	....	....	....	....	....	....	....	....	....	....	....	....
2013-14	**San Jose**	**NHL**	**66**	**10**	**14**	**24**	**16**	**1**	**0**	**2**	**124**	**8.1**	**–4**	**11**	**27.3**	**14:05**	**7**	**2**	**3**	**5**	**0**	**0**	**0**	**0**	**14:20**
	Worcester Sharks	AHL	2	2	3	5	0	....	....	....	....	....	....	....	....	....	....	....	....	....	....	....	....	....	....
2014-15	**San Jose**	**NHL**	**72**	**10**	**17**	**27**	**20**	**1**	**0**	**1**	**135**	**7.4**	**–12**	**1**	**0.0**	**15:15**	....	....	....	....	....	....	....	....	....
	NHL Totals		**138**	**20**	**31**	**51**	**36**	**2**	**0**	**3**	**259**	**7.7**		**12**	**25.0**	**14:42**	**7**	**2**	**3**	**5**	**0**	**0**	**0**	**0**	**14:20**

NIKITIN, Nikita

(nih-KEE-tihn, nih-KEE-tuh) **EDM**

Defense. Shoots left. 6'4", 223 lbs. Born, Omsk, USSR, June 16, 1986. St. Louis' 5th choice, 136th overall, in 2004 Entry Draft.

Season	Club	League	GP	G	A	Pts	PIM	PP	SH	GW	S	S%	+/-	TF	F%	Min	GP	G	A	Pts	PIM	PP	SH	GW	Min
2002-03	Omsk 2	Russia-3	34	3	7	10	4	....	....	....	....	....	....	....	....	....	....	....	....	....	....	....	....	....	....
2003-04	Omsk 2	Russia-3	34	3	8	11	22	....	....	....	....	....	....	....	....	....	....	....	....	....	....	....	....	....	....
2004-05	Avangard Omsk	Russia	12	0	0	0	2	....	....	....	....	....	....	....	....	....	3	0	0	0	0	....	....	....	....
	Omsk 2	Russia-3	31	3	8	11	20	....	....	....	....	....	....	....	....	....	....	....	....	....	....	....	....	....	....
2005-06	Avangard Omsk	Russia	43	1	2	3	22	....	....	....	....	....	....	....	....	....	13	1	2	3	6	....	....	....	....
	Omsk 2	Russia-3	1	0	0	0	0	....	....	....	....	....	....	....	....	....	....	....	....	....	....	....	....	....	....
2006-07	Avangard Omsk	Russia	54	1	15	16	99	....	....	....	....	....	....	....	....	....	9	0	4	4	35	....	....	....	....
2007-08	Avangard Omsk	Russia	57	3	11	14	48	....	....	....	....	....	....	....	....	....	4	0	1	1	2	....	....	....	....
2008-09	Omsk	KHL	53	4	11	15	28	....	....	....	....	....	....	....	....	....	9	1	2	3	8	....	....	....	....
2009-10	Omsk	KHL	43	4	9	13	14	....	....	....	....	....	....	....	....	....	3	0	0	0	0	....	....	....	....
2010-11	**St. Louis**	**NHL**	**41**	**1**	**8**	**9**	**10**	**0**	**0**	**0**	**46**	**2.2**	**1**	**0**	**0.0**	**16:24**	....	....	....	....	....	....	....	....	....
	Peoria Rivermen	AHL	22	3	11	14	12	....	....	....	....	....	....	....	....	....	....	....	....	....	....	....	....	....	....
2011-12	**St. Louis**	**NHL**	**7**	**0**	**0**	**0**	**4**	**0**	**0**	**0**	**10**	**0.0**	**–5**	**0**	**0.0**	**20:15**	....	....	....	....	....	....	....	....	....
	Columbus	**NHL**	**54**	**7**	**25**	**32**	**14**	**3**	**0**	**3**	**93**	**7.5**	**–5**	**0**	**0.0**	**23:35**	....	....	....	....	....	....	....	....	....
2012-13	Omsk	KHL	33	2	12	14	8	....	....	....	....	....	....	....	....	....	....	....	....	....	....	....	....	....	....
	Columbus	**NHL**	**38**	**3**	**6**	**9**	**17**	**1**	**0**	**0**	**60**	**5.0**	**2**	**0**	**0.0**	**21:12**	....	....	....	....	....	....	....	....	....
2013-14	**Columbus**	**NHL**	**66**	**2**	**13**	**15**	**20**	**0**	**0**	**1**	**95**	**2.1**	**9**	**0**	**0.0**	**17:07**	**5**	**0**	**0**	**0**	**0**	**0**	**0**	**0**	**16:21**
	Russia	Olympics	5	0	1	1	0	....	....	....	....	....	....	....	....	....	....	....	....	....	....	....	....	....	....
2014-15	**Edmonton**	**NHL**	**42**	**4**	**6**	**10**	**12**	**2**	**0**	**1**	**80**	**5.0**	**–12**	**0**	**0.0**	**19:38**	....	....	....	....	....	....	....	....	....
	NHL Totals		**248**	**17**	**58**	**75**	**77**	**6**	**0**	**5**	**384**	**4.4**		**0**	**0.0**	**19:33**	**5**	**0**	**0**	**0**	**0**	**0**	**0**	**0**	**16:21**

Traded to **Columbus** by **St. Louis** for Kris Russell, November 11, 2011. Signed as a free agent by **Omsk** (KHL), September 24, 2012. Traded to **Edmonton** by **Columbus** for Columbus' 5th round choice (previously acquired, Columbus selected Tyler Bird) in 2014 Entry Draft, June 25, 2014.

NISKANEN, Matt

(NIHS-kah-nehn, MAT) **WSH**

Defense. Shoots right. 6', 209 lbs. Born, Virginia, MN, December 6, 1986. Dallas' 1st choice, 28th overall, in 2005 Entry Draft.

Season	Club	League	GP	G	A	Pts	PIM	PP	SH	GW	S	S%	+/-	TF	F%	Min	GP	G	A	Pts	PIM	PP	SH	GW	Min
2003-04	Virginia	High-MN	....	24	37	61	....	....	....	....	....	....	....	....	....	....	....	....	....	....	....	....	....	....	....
2004-05	Virginia	High-MN	29	27	38	65	34	....	....	....	....	....	....	....	....	....	....	....	....	....	....	....	....	....	....
2005-06	U. Minn-Duluth	WCHA	38	1	13	14	40	....	....	....	....	....	....	....	....	....	....	....	....	....	....	....	....	....	....
2006-07	U. Minn-Duluth	WCHA	39	9	22	31	42	....	....	....	....	....	....	....	....	....	....	....	....	....	....	....	....	....	....
	Iowa Stars	AHL	13	0	3	3	6	....	....	....	....	....	....	....	....	....	12	2	5	7	10	....	....	....	....
2007-08	**Dallas**	**NHL**	**78**	**7**	**19**	**26**	**36**	**2**	**0**	**0**	**99**	**7.1**	**22**	**0**	**0.0**	**20:30**	**16**	**0**	**3**	**3**	**10**	**0**	**0**	**0**	**16:23**
2008-09	**Dallas**	**NHL**	**80**	**6**	**29**	**35**	**52**	**2**	**0**	**0**	**111**	**5.4**	**–11**	**0**	**0.0**	**19:58**	....	....	....	....	....	....	....	....	....
2009-10	**Dallas**	**NHL**	**74**	**3**	**12**	**15**	**18**	**0**	**0**	**2**	**110**	**2.7**	**–15**	**0**	**0.0**	**18:16**	....	....	....	....	....	....	....	....	....
2010-11	**Dallas**	**NHL**	**45**	**0**	**6**	**6**	**30**	**0**	**0**	**0**	**51**	**0.0**	**–1**	**0**	**0.0**	**15:44**	....	....	....	....	....	....	....	....	....
	Pittsburgh	**NHL**	**18**	**1**	**3**	**4**	**20**	**0**	**0**	**0**	**26**	**3.8**	**–2**	**0**	**0.0**	**18:31**	**7**	**0**	**1**	**1**	**0**	**0**	**0**	**0**	**12:58**
2011-12	**Pittsburgh**	**NHL**	**75**	**4**	**17**	**21**	**47**	**3**	**0**	**0**	**118**	**3.4**	**9**	**0**	**0.0**	**17:56**	**4**	**1**	**2**	**3**	**6**	**1**	**0**	**0**	**18:31**
2012-13	**Pittsburgh**	**NHL**	**40**	**4**	**10**	**14**	**12**	**0**	**0**	**2**	**67**	**6.0**	**4**	**0**	**0.0**	**20:21**	**15**	**0**	**2**	**2**	**11**	**0**	**0**	**0**	**18:55**
2013-14	**Pittsburgh**	**NHL**	**81**	**10**	**36**	**46**	**51**	**3**	**0**	**6**	**162**	**6.2**	**33**	**0**	**0.0**	**21:18**	**13**	**2**	**7**	**9**	**8**	**2**	**0**	**0**	**19:54**
2014-15	**Washington**	**NHL**	**82**	**4**	**27**	**31**	**47**	**2**	**0**	**0**	**117**	**3.4**	**7**	**0**	**0.0**	**22:21**	**14**	**0**	**4**	**4**	**0**	**0**	**0**	**0**	**23:47**
	NHL Totals		**573**	**39**	**159**	**198**	**313**	**12**	**0**	**10**	**861**	**4.5**		**0**	**0.0**	**19:44**	**69**	**3**	**19**	**22**	**35**	**3**	**0**	**0**	**18:53**

WCHA First All-Star Team (2007)

Traded to **Pittsburgh** by **Dallas** with James Neal for Alex Goligoski, February 21, 2011. Signed as a free agent by **Washington**, July 1, 2014.

NOESEN, Stefan

(NAY-sehn, STEH-fan) **ANA**

Right wing. Shoots right. 6'2", 205 lbs. Born, Plano, TX, February 12, 1993. Ottawa's 2nd choice, 21st overall, in 2011 Entry Draft.

Season	Club	League	GP	G	A	Pts	PIM	PP	SH	GW	S	S%	+/-	TF	F%	Min	GP	G	A	Pts	PIM	PP	SH	GW	Min
2006-07	Dallas Ice Jets	Minor-TX	52	78	60	138	78	....	....	....	....	....	....	....	....	....	....	....	....	....	....	....	....	....	....
2007-08	Det. Compuware	MWEHL	31	31	14	45	54	....	....	....	....	....	....	....	....	....	....	....	....	....	....	....	....	....	....
	Det. Compuware	Other	4	3	2	5	4	....	....	....	....	....	....	....	....	....	....	....	....	....	....	....	....	....	....
2008-09	Det. Compuware	T1EHL	28	14	9	23	67	....	....	....	....	....	....	....	....	....	5	4	5	9	0	....	....	....	....
	Det. Compuware	Other	20	6	10	16	....	....	....	....	....	....	....	....	....	....	....	....	....	....	....	....	....	....	....
2009-10	Plymouth Whalers	OHL	33	3	5	8	4	....	....	....	....	....	....	....	....	....	....	....	....	....	....	....	....	....	....
2010-11	Plymouth Whalers	OHL	68	33	44	77	80	....	....	....	....	....	....	....	....	....	11	6	5	11	16	....	....	....	....
2011-12	Plymouth Whalers	OHL	63	38	44	82	74	....	....	....	....	....	....	....	....	....	7	7	8	15	4	....	....	....	....
2012-13	Plymouth Whalers	OHL	51	25	28	53	43	....	....	....	....	....	....	....	....	....	15	7	12	19	24	....	....	....	....
2013-14	Norfolk Admirals	AHL	2	0	0	0	4	....	....	....	....	....	....	....	....	....	4	0	4	4	4	....	....	....	....
2014-15	**Anaheim**	**NHL**	**1**	**0**	**0**	**0**	**0**	**0**	**0**	**0**	**0**	**0.0**	**0**	**0**	**0.0**	**6:54**	....	....	....	....	....	....	....	....	....
	Norfolk Admirals	AHL	27	7	9	16	27	....	....	....	....	....	....	....	....	....	....	....	....	....	....	....	....	....	....
	NHL Totals		**1**	**0**	**0**	**0**	**0**	**0**	**0**	**0**	**0**	**0.0**		**0**	**0.0**	**6:54**	....	....	....	....	....	....	....	....	....

Traded to **Anaheim** by **Ottawa** wirh Jakob Silfverberg and Ottawa's 1st round choice (Nicholas Ritchie) in 2014 Entry Draft for Bobby Ryan, July 5, 2013. • Missed majority of 2013-14 due to knee injury in practice, October 14, 2013. • Missed majority of 2014-15 due to ankle injury vs. Manchester (AHL), October 18, 2014.

NOLAN, Jordan

(NOH-luhn, JOHR-dahn) **L.A.**

Center. Shoots left. 6'3", 226 lbs. Born, Garden River First Nation, ON, June 23, 1989. Los Angeles' 9th choice, 186th overall, in 2009 Entry Draft.

Season	Club	League	GP	G	A	Pts	PIM	PP	SH	GW	S	S%	+/-	TF	F%	Min	GP	G	A	Pts	PIM	PP	SH	GW	Min
2005-06	Erie Otters	OHL	33	3	4	7	20	....	....	....	....	....	....	....	....	....	....	....	....	....	....	....	....	....	....
2006-07	Windsor Spitfires	OHL	60	11	16	27	100	....	....	....	....	....	....	....	....	....	....	....	....	....	....	....	....	....	....
2007-08	Windsor Spitfires	OHL	62	13	14	27	69	....	....	....	....	....	....	....	....	....	5	3	0	3	2	....	....	....	....
2008-09	Sault Ste. Marie	OHL	64	16	27	43	158	....	....	....	....	....	....	....	....	....	....	....	....	....	....	....	....	....	....
2009-10	Sault Ste. Marie	OHL	49	23	25	48	88	....	....	....	....	....	....	....	....	....	5	1	1	2	4	....	....	....	....
	Ontario Reign	ECHL	3	1	1	2	4	....	....	....	....	....	....	....	....	....	....	....	....	....	....	....	....	....	....
2010-11	Manchester	AHL	75	5	12	17	115	....	....	....	....	....	....	....	....	....	7	0	2	2	4	....	....	....	....
2011-12♦	**Los Angeles**	**NHL**	**26**	**2**	**2**	**4**	**28**	**0**	**0**	**1**	**19**	**10.5**	**2**	**1**	**100.0**	**9:21**	**20**	**1**	**1**	**2**	**21**	**0**	**0**	**0**	**7:17**
	Manchester	AHL	40	9	13	22	119	....	....	....	....	....	....	....	....	....	....	....	....	....	....	....	....	....	....
2012-13	Manchester	AHL	21	2	4	6	21	....	....	....	....	....	....	....	....	....	....	....	....	....	....	....	....	....	....
	Los Angeles	**NHL**	**44**	**2**	**4**	**6**	**46**	**0**	**0**	**0**	**23**	**8.7**	**–5**	**8**	**0.0**	**8:28**	**7**	**0**	**0**	**0**	**4**	**0**	**0**	**0**	**8:53**
2013-14♦	**Los Angeles**	**NHL**	**64**	**6**	**4**	**10**	**54**	**0**	**0**	**1**	**58**	**10.3**	**–1**	**4**	**25.0**	**9:00**	**3**	**0**	**0**	**0**	**2**	**0**	**0**	**0**	**8:09**
2014-15	**Los Angeles**	**NHL**	**60**	**6**	**3**	**9**	**54**	**0**	**0**	**1**	**44**	**13.6**	**–6**	**6**	**16.7**	**9:58**	....	....	....	....	....	....	....	....	....
	NHL Totals		**194**	**16**	**13**	**29**	**182**	**0**	**0**	**3**	**144**	**11.1**		**19**	**15.8**	**9:14**	**30**	**1**	**1**	**2**	**27**	**0**	**0**	**0**	**7:45**

NORDSTROM, Joakim

(NOHRD-struhm, JOH-keem) **CHI**

Center. Shoots left. 6'1", 189 lbs. Born, Tyreso, Sweden, February 25, 1992. Chicago's 6th choice, 90th overall, in 2010 Entry Draft.

Season	Club	League	GP	G	A	Pts	PIM	PP	SH	GW	S	S%	+/-	TF	F%	Min	GP	G	A	Pts	PIM	PP	SH	GW	Min
2008-09	AIK IF Solna U18	Swe-U18	35	8	16	24	32	....	....	....	....	....	....	....	....	....	7	2	2	4	2	....	....	....	....
	AIK IF Solna Jr.	Swe-Jr.	4	2	0	2	2	....	....	....	....	....	....	....	....	....	....	....	....	....	....	....	....	....	....
2009-10	AIK IF Solna U18	Swe-U18	2	1	1	2	0	....	....	....	....	....	....	....	....	....	3	1	2	3	4	....	....	....	....
	AIK IF Solna Jr.	Swe-Jr.	28	6	9	15	53	....	....	....	....	....	....	....	....	....	....	....	....	....	....	....	....	....	....
	AIK IF Solna	Sweden-2	2	0	0	0	0	....	....	....	....	....	....	....	....	....	....	....	....	....	....	....	....	....	....
2010-11	AIK IF Solna Jr.	Swe-Jr.	25	9	11	20	36	....	....	....	....	....	....	....	....	....	....	....	....	....	....	....	....	....	....
	Almtuna	Sweden-2	12	0	1	1	4	....	....	....	....	....	....	....	....	....	....	....	....	....	....	....	....	....	....
	AIK IF Solna	Sweden	11	0	1	1	0	....	....	....	....	....	....	....	....	....	1	0	0	0	0	....	....	....	....
2011-12	AIK Solna	Sweden	47	3	3	6	4	....	....	....	....	....	....	....	....	....	10	1	2	3	2	....	....	....	....
2012-13	AIK Solna	Sweden	43	5	4	9	29	....	....	....	....	....	....	....	....	....	....	....	....	....	....	....	....	....	....
	Rockford IceHogs	AHL	11	0	3	3	12	....	....	....	....	....	....	....	....	....	....	....	....	....	....	....	....	....	....
2013-14	**Chicago**	**NHL**	**16**	**1**	**2**	**3**	**2**	**0**	**0**	**0**	**26**	**3.8**	**–2**	**27**	**37.0**	**11:41**	**7**	**0**	**0**	**0**	**0**	**0**	**0**	**0**	**8:30**
	Rockford IceHogs	AHL	58	17	16	33	21	....	....	....	....	....	....	....	....	....	....	....	....	....	....	....	....	....	....

Season	Club	League	GP	G	A	Pts	PIM	PP	SH	GW	S	S%	+/-	TF	F%	Min	GP	G	A	Pts	PIM	PP	SH	GW	Min
			Regular Season														Playoffs								
2014-15♦	**Chicago**	**NHL**	**38**	**0**	**3**	**3**	**4**	**0**	**0**	**0**	**42**	**0.0**	**–5**	**10**	**20.0**	**10:58**	**3**	**0**	**0**	**0**	**0**	**0**	**0**	**0**	**13:14**
	Rockford IceHogs	AHL	23	9	7	16	19	....	....	....	....	....	....	....	....	....	....	....	....	....	....	....	....	....	....
	NHL Totals		**54**	**1**	**5**	**6**	**6**	**0**	**0**	**0**	**68**	**1.5**		**37**	**32.4**	**11:11**	**10**	**0**	**0**	**0**	**0**	**0**	**0**	**0**	**9:56**

NOREAU, Maxim

(NOHR-oh, max-EEM) **COL**

Defense. Shoots right. 6', 194 lbs. Born, Montreal, QC, May 24, 1987.

Season	Club	League	GP	G	A	Pts	PIM	PP	SH	GW	S	S%	+/-	TF	F%	Min	GP	G	A	Pts	PIM	PP	SH	GW	Min
2003-04	West Island Lions	QAAA	41	12	20	32	82	....	....	....	....	....	....	....	....	....	9	0	7	7	38	....	....	....	....
2004-05	Victoriaville Tigres	QMJHL	65	5	8	13	47	....	....	....	....	....	....	....	....	....	7	0	0	0	8	....	....	....	....
2005-06	Victoriaville Tigres	QMJHL	69	22	43	65	116	....	....	....	....	....	....	....	....	....	5	2	4	6	7	....	....	....	....
2006-07	Victoriaville Tigres	QMJHL	69	17	53	70	106	....	....	....	....	....	....	....	....	....	6	2	1	3	8	....	....	....	....
2007-08	Houston Aeros	AHL	50	8	8	16	48	....	....	....	....	....	....	....	....	....	5	0	0	0	4	....	....	....	....
	Texas Wildcatters	ECHL	2	0	3	3	0	....	....	....	....	....	....	....	....	....	....	....	....	....	....	....	....	....	....
2008-09	Houston Aeros	AHL	77	14	25	39	49	....	....	....	....	....	....	....	....	....	20	4	7	11	2	....	....	....	....
2009-10	**Minnesota**	**NHL**	**1**	**0**	**0**	**0**	**0**	**0**	**0**	**0**	**0**	**0.0**	**0**	**0**	**0.0**	**7:01**	....	....	....	....	....	....	....	....	....
	Houston Aeros	AHL	76	18	34	52	60	....	....	....	....	....	....	....	....	....	....	....	....	....	....	....	....	....	....
2010-11	**Minnesota**	**NHL**	**5**	**0**	**0**	**0**	**0**	**0**	**0**	**0**	**8**	**0.0**	**–1**	**0**	**0.0**	**14:17**	....	....	....	....	....	....	....	....	....
	Houston Aeros	AHL	76	10	44	54	58	....	....	....	....	....	....	....	....	....	24	2	10	12	23	....	....	....	....
2011-12	HC Ambri-Piotta	Swiss	44	7	23	30	22	....	....	....	....	....	....	....	....	....	13	1	8	9	8	....	....	....	....
2012-13	HC Ambri-Piotta	Swiss	45	10	25	35	38	....	....	....	....	....	....	....	....	....	5	1	3	4	2	....	....	....	....
2013-14	HC Ambri-Piotta	Swiss	35	8	16	24	28	....	....	....	....	....	....	....	....	....	4	0	0	0	2	....	....	....	....
2014-15	Lake Erie	AHL	39	8	22	30	29	....	....	....	....	....	....	....	....	....	....	....	....	....	....	....	....	....	....
	NHL Totals		**6**	**0**	**0**	**0**	**0**	**0**	**0**	**0**	**8**	**0.0**		**0**	**0.0**	**13:04**	....	....	....	....	....	....	....	....	....

AHL Second All-Star Team (2010) • AHL First All-Star Team (2011)

Signed as a free agent by **Minnesota**, May 22, 2008. Traded to **New Jersey** by **Minnesota** for David McIntyre, June 16, 2011. Signed as a free agent by **Ambri-Piotta** (Swiss), July 31, 2011. Signed as a free agent by **Colorado**, July 7, 2014. • Missed majority of 2014-15 due to recurring shoulder injury.

NUGENT-HOPKINS, Ryan

(NOO-jehnt-HAWP-kihnz, RIGH-uhn) **EDM**

Center. Shoots left. 6'1", 180 lbs. Born, Burnaby, BC, April 12, 1993. Edmonton's 1st choice, 1st overall, in 2011 Entry Draft.

Season	Club	League	GP	G	A	Pts	PIM	PP	SH	GW	S	S%	+/-	TF	F%	Min	GP	G	A	Pts	PIM	PP	SH	GW	Min
2006-07	Burnaby W.C.	Minor-BC	65	43	43	86	34	....	....	....	....	....	....	....	....	....	....	....	....	....	....	....	....	....	....
2007-08	Burnaby W.C.	Minor-BC	66	119	95	214	84	....	....	....	....	....	....	....	....	....	....	....	....	....	....	....	....	....	....
2008-09	Van. NW Giants	BCMML	36	*40	*47	*87	78	....	....	....	....	....	....	....	....	....	5	*5	*5	*10	4	....	....	....	....
	Red Deer Rebels	WHL	5	2	4	6	0	....	....	....	....	....	....	....	....	....	....	....	....	....	....	....	....	....	....
2009-10	Red Deer Rebels	WHL	67	24	41	65	28	....	....	....	....	....	....	....	....	....	4	0	2	2	0	....	....	....	....
2010-11	Red Deer Rebels	WHL	69	31	*75	106	51	....	....	....	....	....	....	....	....	....	9	4	7	11	6	....	....	....	....
2011-12	**Edmonton**	**NHL**	**62**	**18**	**34**	**52**	**16**	**3**	**0**	**2**	**134**	**13.4**	**–2**	**605**	**37.5**	**17:36**	....	....	....	....	....	....	....	....	....
2012-13	Oklahoma City	AHL	19	8	12	20	6	....	....	....	....	....	....	....	....	....	....	....	....	....	....	....	....	....	....
	Edmonton	**NHL**	**40**	**4**	**20**	**24**	**8**	**2**	**0**	**0**	**78**	**5.1**	**3**	**551**	**41.0**	**18:52**	....	....	....	....	....	....	....	....	....
2013-14	**Edmonton**	**NHL**	**80**	**19**	**37**	**56**	**26**	**6**	**0**	**4**	**178**	**10.7**	**–12**	**1280**	**42.4**	**20:24**	....	....	....	....	....	....	....	....	....
2014-15	**Edmonton**	**NHL**	**76**	**24**	**32**	**56**	**25**	**2**	**0**	**2**	**189**	**12.7**	**–12**	**1356**	**45.7**	**20:38**	....	....	....	....	....	....	....	....	....
	NHL Totals		**258**	**65**	**123**	**188**	**75**	**13**	**0**	**8**	**579**	**11.2**		**3792**	**42.6**	**19:34**	....	....	....	....	....	....	....	....	....

WHL Rookie of the Year (2010) • Canadian Major Junior All-Rookie Team (2010) • WHL East First All-Star Team (2011) • NHL All-Rookie Team (2012
Played in NHL All-Star Game (2015)

NURSE, Darnell

(NUHRS, dahr-NEHL) **EDM**

Defense. Shoots left. 6'4", 205 lbs. Born, Hamilton, ON, February 4, 1995. Edmonton's 1st choice, 7th overall, in 2013 Entry Draft.

Season	Club	League	GP	G	A	Pts	PIM	PP	SH	GW	S	S%	+/-	TF	F%	Min	GP	G	A	Pts	PIM	PP	SH	GW	Min
2010-11	Don Mills Flyers	GTHL	38	11	18	29	72	....	....	....	....	....	....	....	....	....	....	....	....	....	....	....	....	....	....
	St. Michael's	ON-Jr.A	2	0	0	0	4	....	....	....	....	....	....	....	....	....	....	....	....	....	....	....	....	....	....
2011-12	Sault Ste. Marie	OHL	53	1	9	10	61	....	....	....	....	....	....	....	....	....	....	....	....	....	....	....	....	....	....
2012-13	Sault Ste. Marie	OHL	68	12	29	41	116	....	....	....	....	....	....	....	....	....	6	1	3	4	6	....	....	....	....
2013-14	Sault Ste. Marie	OHL	64	13	37	50	91	....	....	....	....	....	....	....	....	....	9	3	5	8	12	....	....	....	....
	Oklahoma City	AHL	4	0	1	1	0	....	....	....	....	....	....	....	....	....	3	0	1	1	7	....	....	....	....
2014-15	**Edmonton**	**NHL**	**2**	**0**	**0**	**0**	**0**	**0**	**0**	**0**	**2**	**0.0**	**–2**	**0**	**0.0**	**17:00**	....	....	....	....	....	....	....	....	....
	Sault Ste. Marie	OHL	36	10	23	33	58	....	....	....	....	....	....	....	....	....	14	3	5	8	26	....	....	....	....
	Oklahoma City	AHL	....	....	....	....	....	....	....	....	....	....	....	....	....	....	4	0	4	4	4	....	....	....	....
	NHL Totals		**2**	**0**	**0**	**0**	**0**	**0**	**0**	**0**	**2**	**0.0**		**0**	**0.0**	**17:00**	....	....	....	....	....	....	....	....	....

OHL Second All-Star Team (2015)

• Missed majority of 2014-15 due to leg injury vs. Saginaw (OHL), February 13, 2015.

NYQUIST, Gustav

(NEW-kwihst, GUHS-tav) **DET**

Right wing. Shoots left. 5'11", 185 lbs. Born, Halmstad, Sweden, September 1, 1989. Detroit's 3rd choice, 121st overall, in 2008 Entry Draft.

Season	Club	League	GP	G	A	Pts	PIM	PP	SH	GW	S	S%	+/-	TF	F%	Min	GP	G	A	Pts	PIM	PP	SH	GW	Min
2005-06	Malmo U18	Swe-U18	14	9	3	12	10	....	....	....	....	....	....	....	....	....	6	1	3	4	0	....	....	....	....
2006-07	Malmo Jr.	Swe-Jr.	42	21	23	44	57	....	....	....	....	....	....	....	....	....	4	2	2	4	6	....	....	....	....
2007-08	Malmo Jr.	Swe-Jr.	24	11	20	31	20	....	....	....	....	....	....	....	....	....	7	5	5	10	6	....	....	....	....
2008-09	U. of Maine	H-East	38	13	19	32	28	....	....	....	....	....	....	....	....	....	....	....	....	....	....	....	....	....	....
2009-10	U. of Maine	H-East	39	19	*42	*61	20	....	....	....	....	....	....	....	....	....	....	....	....	....	....	....	....	....	....
2010-11	U. of Maine	H-East	36	18	*33	51	20	....	....	....	....	....	....	....	....	....	....	....	....	....	....	....	....	....	....
	Grand Rapids	AHL	8	1	3	4	2	....	....	....	....	....	....	....	....	....	....	....	....	....	....	....	....	....	....
2011-12	**Detroit**	**NHL**	**18**	**1**	**6**	**7**	**2**	**0**	**0**	**0**	**19**	**5.3**	**2**	**0**	**0.0**	**10:36**	**4**	**0**	**0**	**0**	**0**	**0**	**0**	**0**	**8:52**
	Grand Rapids	AHL	56	22	36	58	18	....	....	....	....	....	....	....	....	....	....	....	....	....	....	....	....	....	....
2012-13	Grand Rapids	AHL	58	23	37	60	34	....	....	....	....	....	....	....	....	....	10	2	5	7	19	....	....	....	....
	Detroit	**NHL**	**22**	**3**	**3**	**6**	**6**	**0**	**0**	**0**	**46**	**6.5**	**0**	**4**	**25.0**	**13:02**	**14**	**2**	**3**	**5**	**2**	**1**	**0**	**1**	**12:36**
2013-14	**Detroit**	**NHL**	**57**	**28**	**20**	**48**	**10**	**6**	**0**	**6**	**153**	**18.3**	**16**	**9**	**55.6**	**16:51**	**5**	**0**	**0**	**0**	**0**	**0**	**0**	**0**	**15:23**
	Grand Rapids	AHL	15	7	14	21	6	....	....	....	....	....	....	....	....	....	....	....	....	....	....	....	....	....	....
	Sweden	Olympics	6	0	0	0	0	....	....	....	....	....	....	....	....	....	....	....	....	....	....	....	....	....	....
2014-15	**Detroit**	**NHL**	**82**	**27**	**27**	**54**	**26**	**14**	**0**	**4**	**195**	**13.8**	**–11**	**9**	**11.1**	**16:39**	**7**	**1**	**1**	**2**	**2**	**0**	**0**	**0**	**15:39**
	NHL Totals		**179**	**59**	**56**	**115**	**44**	**20**	**0**	**10**	**413**	**14.3**		**22**	**31.8**	**15:40**	**30**	**3**	**4**	**7**	**4**	**1**	**0**	**1**	**13:17**

Hockey East All-Rookie Team (2009) • Hockey East First All-Star Team (2010, 2011) • NCAA East First All-American Team (2010) • NCAA East Second All-American Team (2011) • AHL All-Rookie Team (2012) • AHL First All-Star Team (2013)

NYSTROM, Eric

(NIGH-stuhm, AIR-ihk) **NSH**

Left wing. Shoots left. 6'1", 195 lbs. Born, Syosset, NY, February 14, 1983. Calgary's 1st choice, 10th overall, in 2002 Entry Draft.

Season	Club	League	GP	G	A	Pts	PIM	PP	SH	GW	S	S%	+/-	TF	F%	Min	GP	G	A	Pts	PIM	PP	SH	GW	Min
99-2000	USNTDP	NAHL	55	7	16	23	57	....	....	....	....	....	....	....	....	....	3	0	0	0	0	....	....	....	....
2000-01	USNTDP	U-18	43	10	12	22	52	....	....	....	....	....	....	....	....	....	....	....	....	....	....	....	....	....	....
	USNTDP	USHL	23	5	5	10	50	....	....	....	....	....	....	....	....	....	....	....	....	....	....	....	....	....	....
2001-02	U. of Michigan	CCHA	40	18	13	31	42	....	....	....	....	....	....	....	....	....	....	....	....	....	....	....	....	....	....
2002-03	U. of Michigan	CCHA	39	15	11	26	24	....	....	....	....	....	....	....	....	....	....	....	....	....	....	....	....	....	....
2003-04	U. of Michigan	CCHA	43	10	12	22	50	....	....	....	....	....	....	....	....	....	....	....	....	....	....	....	....	....	....
2004-05	U. of Michigan	CCHA	38	13	19	32	33	....	....	....	....	....	....	....	....	....	....	....	....	....	....	....	....	....	....
2005-06	**Calgary**	**NHL**	**2**	**0**	**0**	**0**	**0**	**0**	**0**	**0**	**0**	**0.0**	**–1**	**5**	**60.0**	**12:01**	....	....	....	....	....	....	....	....	....
	Omaha	AHL	78	15	18	33	37	....	....	....	....	....	....	....	....	....	....	....	....	....	....	....	....	....	....
2006-07	Omaha	AHL	12	2	0	2	0	....	....	....	....	....	....	....	....	....	5	0	0	0	2	....	....	....	....
2007-08	**Calgary**	**NHL**	**44**	**3**	**7**	**10**	**48**	**0**	**0**	**0**	**42**	**7.1**	**–5**	**14**	**50.0**	**11:30**	**7**	**0**	**0**	**0**	**2**	**0**	**0**	**0**	**7:39**
	Quad City Flames	AHL	18	4	3	7	15	....	....	....	....	....	....	....	....	....	....	....	....	....	....	....	....	....	....
2008-09	**Calgary**	**NHL**	**76**	**5**	**5**	**10**	**89**	**0**	**1**	**3**	**83**	**6.0**	**–7**	**29**	**37.9**	**9:16**	**6**	**2**	**2**	**4**	**0**	**0**	**0**	**1**	**10:57**
2009-10	**Calgary**	**NHL**	**82**	**11**	**8**	**19**	**54**	**0**	**0**	**2**	**91**	**12.1**	**0**	**279**	**45.5**	**13:11**	....	....	....	....	....	....	....	....	....
2010-11	**Minnesota**	**NHL**	**82**	**4**	**8**	**12**	**30**	**1**	**0**	**0**	**83**	**4.8**	**–16**	**131**	**34.4**	**13:19**	....	....	....	....	....	....	....	....	....
2011-12	Houston Aeros	AHL	1	0	0	0	0	....	....	....	....	....	....	....	....	....	....	....	....	....	....	....	....	....	....
	Dallas	**NHL**	**74**	**16**	**5**	**21**	**24**	**0**	**0**	**1**	**102**	**15.7**	**–10**	**29**	**48.3**	**13:45**	....	....	....	....	....	....	....	....	....
2012-13	Stavanger Oilers	Norway	6	4	10	14	6	....	....	....	....	....	....	....	....	....	....	....	....	....	....	....	....	....	....
	Dallas	**NHL**	**48**	**7**	**4**	**11**	**61**	**0**	**1**	**3**	**49**	**14.3**	**–3**	**26**	**57.7**	**14:21**	....	....	....	....	....	....	....	....	....

			Regular Season														Playoffs								
Season	Club	League	GP	G	A	Pts	PIM	PP	SH	GW	S	S%	+/-	TF	F%	Min	GP	G	A	Pts	PIM	PP	SH	GW	Min
2013-14	**Nashville**	**NHL**	**79**	**15**	**6**	**21**	**60**	**0**	**1**	**1**	**120**	**12.5**	**–25**	**10**	**20.0**	**14:52**	....	....	....	....	....	....	....	....	....
2014-15	**Nashville**	**NHL**	**60**	**7**	**5**	**12**	**15**	**0**	**1**	**1**	**60**	**11.7**	**0**	**12**	**33.3**	**13:12**	....	....	....	....	....	....	....	....	....
	NHL Totals		**547**	**68**	**48**	**116**	**381**	**1**	**4**	**11**	**630**	**10.8**		**535**	**42.6**	**12:56**	**13**	**2**	**2**	**4**	**2**	**0**	**0**	**1**	**9:10**

CCHA All-Rookie Team (2002)

• Missed majority of 2006-07 due to pre-season shoulder injury. Signed as a free agent by **Minnesota**, July 1, 2010. Traded to **Dallas** by **Minnesota** for future considerations, October 12, 2011. Signed as a free agent by **Stavanger** (Norway), November 30, 2012. Signed as a free agent by **Nashville**, July 5, 2013.

OBERG, Evan

(OH-buhrg, EH-vuhn)

Defense. Shoots left. 6', 165 lbs. Born, Forestburg, AB, February 16, 1988.

Season	Club	League	GP	G	A	Pts	PIM	PP	SH	GW	S	S%	+/-	TF	F%	Min	GP	G	A	Pts	PIM	PP	SH	GW	Min
2005-06	Camrose Kodiaks	AJHL	44	4	9	13	56	....	....	....	....	....	....	....	....	....	14	1	1	2	14	....	....	....	....
2006-07	Camrose Kodiaks	AJHL	52	9	14	23	86	....	....	....	....	....	....	....	....	....	16	3	11	14	24	....	....	....	....
2007-08	U. Minn-Duluth	WCHA	24	1	2	3	10	....	....	....	....	....	....	....	....	....	....	....	....	....	....	....	....	....	....
2008-09	U. Minn-Duluth	WCHA	43	7	20	27	50	....	....	....	....	....	....	....	....	....	....	....	....	....	....	....	....	....	....
2009-10	**Vancouver**	**NHL**	**2**	**0**	**0**	**0**	**0**	**0**	**0**	**0**	**0**	**0.0**	**0**	**0**	**0.0**	**6:17**	....	....	....	....	....	....	....	....	....
	Manitoba Moose	AHL	70	3	23	26	64	....	....	....	....	....	....	....	....	....	5	1	1	2	4	....	....	....	....
2010-11	**Vancouver**	**NHL**	**2**	**0**	**0**	**0**	**0**	**0**	**0**	**0**	**1**	**0.0**	**0**	**0**	**0.0**	**9:50**	....	....	....	....	....	....	....	....	....
	Manitoba Moose	AHL	38	6	5	11	28	....	....	....	....	....	....	....	....	....	....	....	....	....	....	....	....	....	....
	Rochester	AHL	5	1	1	2	0	....	....	....	....	....	....	....	....	....	....	....	....	....	....	....	....	....	....
2011-12	San Antonio	AHL	12	0	2	2	14	....	....	....	....	....	....	....	....	....	....	....	....	....	....	....	....	....	....
	Tampa Bay	**NHL**	**3**	**0**	**0**	**0**	**0**	**0**	**0**	**0**	**3**	**0.0**	**2**	**0**	**0.0**	**9:50**	....	....	....	....	....	....	....	....	....
	Norfolk Admirals	AHL	42	7	16	23	32	....	....	....	....	....	....	....	....	....	18	2	8	10	14	....	....	....	....
2012-13	Syracuse Crunch	AHL	56	0	9	9	20	....	....	....	....	....	....	....	....	....	4	0	0	0	6	....	....	....	....
2013-14	Chicago Wolves	AHL	60	6	19	25	62	....	....	....	....	....	....	....	....	....	7	0	0	0	2	....	....	....	....
2014-15	Portland Pirates	AHL	48	7	11	18	47	....	....	....	....	....	....	....	....	....	....	....	....	....	....	....	....	....	....
	NHL Totals		**7**	**0**	**0**	**0**	**0**	**0**	**0**	**0**	**4**	**0.0**		**0**	**0.0**	**8:49**	....	....	....	....	....	....	....	....	....

Signed as a free agent by **Vancouver**, April 10, 2009. Traded to **Florida** by **Vancouver** with Vancouver's 3rd round choice (later traded back to Vancouver – Vancouver selected Cole Cassels) in 2013 Entry Draft for Chris Higgins, February 28, 2011. Traded to **Tampa Bay** by **Florida** with Mike Kostka for James Wright and Mike Vernace, December 2, 2011. Signed as a free agent by **Chicago** (AHL), August 19, 2013. Signed as a free agent by **Portland** (AHL), July 31, 2014.

O'BRIEN, Jim

(oh-BRIGH-uhn, JIHM) **N.J.**

Center. Shoots right. 6'2", 200 lbs. Born, Maplewood, MN, January 29, 1989. Ottawa's 1st choice, 29th overall, in 2007 Entry Draft.

Season	Club	League	GP	G	A	Pts	PIM	PP	SH	GW	S	S%	+/-	TF	F%	Min	GP	G	A	Pts	PIM	PP	SH	GW	Min
2003-04	Det. Caesars	MWEHL	68	19	24	43	72	....	....	....	....	....	....	....	....	....	....	....	....	....	....	....	....	....	....
2004-05	USNTDP	U-17	13	6	6	12	10	....	....	....	....	....	....	....	....	....	....	....	....	....	....	....	....	....	....
	USNTDP	NAHL	40	10	12	22	41	....	....	....	....	....	....	....	....	....	1	0	0	0	0	....	....	....	....
2005-06	USNTDP	U-18	38	11	14	25	62	....	....	....	....	....	....	....	....	....	....	....	....	....	....	....	....	....	....
	USNTDP	NAHL	13	6	10	16	14	....	....	....	....	....	....	....	....	....	....	....	....	....	....	....	....	....	....
2006-07	U. of Minnesota	WCHA	43	7	8	15	51	....	....	....	....	....	....	....	....	....	....	....	....	....	....	....	....	....	....
2007-08	Seattle	WHL	70	21	34	55	66	....	....	....	....	....	....	....	....	....	12	2	6	8	14	....	....	....	....
2008-09	Seattle	WHL	63	27	35	62	55	....	....	....	....	....	....	....	....	....	5	1	0	1	10	....	....	....	....
	Binghamton	AHL	6	0	1	1	0	....	....	....	....	....	....	....	....	....	....	....	....	....	....	....	....	....	....
2009-10	Binghamton	AHL	76	8	9	17	49	....	....	....	....	....	....	....	....	....	....	....	....	....	....	....	....	....	....
2010-11	**Ottawa**	**NHL**	**6**	**0**	**0**	**0**	**2**	**0**	**0**	**0**	**11**	**0.0**	**–3**	**16**	**50.0**	**9:40**	....	....	....	....	....	....	....	....	....
	Binghamton	AHL	74	24	32	56	67	....	....	....	....	....	....	....	....	....	23	3	4	7	12	....	....	....	....
2011-12	**Ottawa**	**NHL**	**28**	**3**	**3**	**6**	**4**	**0**	**0**	**1**	**37**	**8.1**	**6**	**256**	**47.3**	**11:45**	**7**	**0**	**1**	**1**	**0**	**0**	**0**	**0**	**8:38**
	Binghamton	AHL	27	7	7	14	10	....	....	....	....	....	....	....	....	....	....	....	....	....	....	....	....	....	....
2012-13	**Ottawa**	**NHL**	**29**	**5**	**1**	**6**	**8**	**1**	**0**	**0**	**38**	**13.2**	**–2**	**219**	**45.7**	**11:25**	....	....	....	....	....	....	....	....	....
2013-14	Binghamton	AHL	51	11	18	29	46	....	....	....	....	....	....	....	....	....	2	1	1	2	2	....	....	....	....
2014-15	Novokuznetsk	KHL	22	2	10	12	30	....	....	....	....	....	....	....	....	....	....	....	....	....	....	....	....	....	....
	Hershey Bears	AHL	32	10	19	29	26	....	....	....	....	....	....	....	....	....	10	3	1	4	8	....	....	....	....
	NHL Totals		**63**	**8**	**4**	**12**	**14**	**1**	**0**	**1**	**86**	**9.3**		**491**	**46.6**	**11:24**	**7**	**0**	**1**	**1**	**0**	**0**	**0**	**0**	**8:38**

Signed as a free agent by **Novokuznetsk** (KHL), September, 2014. Signed as a free agent by **Hershey**, (AHL), December 26, 2014. Signed as a free agent by **New Jersey**, July 1, 2015.

O'BRIEN, Liam

(oh-BRIGH-uhn, LEE-uhm) **WSH**

Left wing. Shoots left. 6'1", 205 lbs. Born, Halifax, NS, July 29, 1994.

Season	Club	League	GP	G	A	Pts	PIM	PP	SH	GW	S	S%	+/-	TF	F%	Min	GP	G	A	Pts	PIM	PP	SH	GW	Min
2010-11	Rimouski Oceanic	QMJHL	61	2	8	10	45	....	....	....	....	....	....	....	....	....	5	0	0	0	6	....	....	....	....
2011-12	Rimouski Oceanic	QMJHL	40	7	9	16	67	....	....	....	....	....	....	....	....	....	....	....	....	....	....	....	....	....	....
	Rouyn-Noranda	QMJHL	27	3	7	10	69	....	....	....	....	....	....	....	....	....	4	1	0	1	11	....	....	....	....
2012-13	Rouyn-Noranda	QMJHL	65	10	14	24	164	....	....	....	....	....	....	....	....	....	12	2	1	3	17	....	....	....	....
2013-14	Rouyn-Noranda	QMJHL	68	20	15	35	148	....	....	....	....	....	....	....	....	....	9	1	3	4	12	....	....	....	....
2014-15	**Washington**	**NHL**	**13**	**1**	**1**	**2**	**23**	**0**	**0**	**0**	**16**	**6.3**	**4**	**2**	**50.0**	**7:33**	....	....	....	....	....	....	....	....	....
	Hershey Bears	AHL	45	4	4	8	121	....	....	....	....	....	....	....	....	....	10	3	3	6	14	....	....	....	....
	NHL Totals		**13**	**1**	**1**	**2**	**23**	**0**	**0**	**0**	**16**	**6.3**		**2**	**50.0**	**7:33**	....	....	....	....	....	....	....	....	....

Signed as a free agent by **Washington**, October 6, 2014.

O'BRIEN, Shane

(oh-BRIGH-uhn, SHAYN) **ANA**

Defense. Shoots left. 6'3", 230 lbs. Born, Port Hope, ON, August 9, 1983. Anaheim's 8th choice, 250th overall, in 2003 Entry Draft.

Season	Club	League	GP	G	A	Pts	PIM	PP	SH	GW	S	S%	+/-	TF	F%	Min	GP	G	A	Pts	PIM	PP	SH	GW	Min
99-2000	Port Hope	ON-Jr.A	47	6	27	33	110	....	....	....	....	....	....	....	....	....	....	....	....	....	....	....	....	....	....
2000-01	Kingston	OHL	61	2	12	14	89	....	....	....	....	....	....	....	....	....	4	0	1	1	6	....	....	....	....
2001-02	Kingston	OHL	67	10	23	33	132	....	....	....	....	....	....	....	....	....	1	0	0	0	2	....	....	....	....
2002-03	Kingston	OHL	28	8	15	23	100	....	....	....	....	....	....	....	....	....	....	....	....	....	....	....	....	....	....
	St. Michael's	OHL	34	8	11	19	108	....	....	....	....	....	....	....	....	....	19	4	10	14	*79	....	....	....	....
2003-04	Cincinnati	AHL	60	2	8	10	163	....	....	....	....	....	....	....	....	....	9	0	2	2	20	....	....	....	....
2004-05	Cincinnati	AHL	77	5	20	25	319	....	....	....	....	....	....	....	....	....	12	1	3	4	57	....	....	....	....
2005-06	Portland Pirates	AHL	77	8	33	41	287	....	....	....	....	....	....	....	....	....	19	6	16	22	*81	....	....	....	....
2006-07	**Anaheim**	**NHL**	**62**	**2**	**12**	**14**	**140**	**1**	**0**	**2**	**55**	**3.6**	**5**	**0**	**0.0**	**14:04**	....	....	....	....	....	....	....	....	....
	Tampa Bay	**NHL**	**18**	**0**	**2**	**2**	**36**	**0**	**0**	**0**	**17**	**0.0**	**–8**	**0**	**0.0**	**18:08**	**6**	**0**	**0**	**0**	**12**	**0**	**0**	**0**	**17:12**
2007-08	**Tampa Bay**	**NHL**	**77**	**4**	**17**	**21**	**154**	**0**	**0**	**1**	**69**	**5.8**	**–2**	**0**	**0.0**	**21:13**	....	....	....	....	....	....	....	....	....
2008-09	**Tampa Bay**	**NHL**	**1**	**0**	**0**	**0**	**0**	**0**	**0**	**0**	**0**	**0.0**	**–1**	**0**	**0.0**	**14:04**	....	....	....	....	....	....	....	....	....
	Vancouver	**NHL**	**76**	**0**	**10**	**10**	**196**	**0**	**0**	**0**	**39**	**0.0**	**6**	**0**	**0.0**	**14:56**	**10**	**1**	**1**	**2**	**24**	**0**	**0**	**0**	**12:06**
2009-10	**Vancouver**	**NHL**	**65**	**2**	**6**	**8**	**79**	**0**	**0**	**0**	**37**	**5.4**	**15**	**0**	**0.0**	**17:01**	**12**	**1**	**2**	**3**	**25**	**0**	**0**	**0**	**17:44**
2010-11	**Nashville**	**NHL**	**80**	**2**	**7**	**9**	**83**	**0**	**0**	**0**	**50**	**4.0**	**1**	**0**	**0.0**	**17:07**	**12**	**0**	**0**	**0**	**18**	**0**	**0**	**0**	**16:47**
2011-12	**Colorado**	**NHL**	**76**	**3**	**17**	**20**	**105**	**1**	**0**	**0**	**114**	**2.6**	**2**	**0**	**0.0**	**19:13**	....	....	....	....	....	....	....	....	....
2012-13	**Colorado**	**NHL**	**28**	**0**	**4**	**4**	**60**	**0**	**0**	**0**	**28**	**0.0**	**0**	**0**	**0.0**	**15:30**	....	....	....	....	....	....	....	....	....
2013-14	**Calgary**	**NHL**	**45**	**0**	**3**	**3**	**58**	**0**	**0**	**0**	**16**	**0.0**	**–8**	**0**	**0.0**	**11:16**	....	....	....	....	....	....	....	....	....
	Abbotsford Heat	AHL	31	3	5	8	58	....	....	....	....	....	....	....	....	....	4	1	0	1	18	....	....	....	....
2014-15	**Florida**	**NHL**	**9**	**0**	**1**	**1**	**5**	**0**	**0**	**0**	**4**	**0.0**	**–4**	**0**	**0.0**	**13:29**	....	....	....	....	....	....	....	....	....
	San Antonio	AHL	51	11	19	30	127	....	....	....	....	....	....	....	....	....	2	0	1	1	17	....	....	....	....
	NHL Totals		**537**	**13**	**79**	**92**	**916**	**2**	**0**	**3**	**429**	**3.0**		**0**	**0.0**	**16:43**	**40**	**2**	**3**	**5**	**79**	**0**	**0**	**0**	**15:58**

Traded to **Tampa Bay** by **Anaheim** with Colorado's 3rd round choice (previously acquired, Tampa Bay selected Luca Cunti) in 2007 Entry Draft for Gerald Coleman and Tampa Bay's 1st round choice (later traded to Minnesota - Minnesota selected Colton Gillies) in 2007 Entry Draft, February 24, 2007. Traded to **Vancouver** by **Tampa Bay** with Michel Ouellet for Lukas Krajicek and Juraj Simek, October 6, 2008. Traded to **Nashville** by **Vancouver** with Dan Gendur for Ryan Parent and Jonas Andersson, October 5, 2010. Signed as a free agent by **Colorado**, July 13, 2011. Traded to **Calgary** by **Colorado** with David Jones for Alex Tanguay and Cory Sarich. June 27, 2013. Signed as a free agent by **Florida**, October 7, 2014. Signed as a free agent by **Anaheim**, July 16, 2015.

O'DELL, Eric

(OH-DEHL, AIR-ihk) **OTT**

Center. Shoots right. 6'1", 181 lbs. Born, Ottawa, ON, June 21, 1990. Anaheim's 3rd choice, 39th overall, in 2008 Entry Draft.

Season	Club	League	GP	G	A	Pts	PIM	PP	SH	GW	S	S%	+/-	TF	F%	Min	GP	G	A	Pts	PIM	PP	SH	GW	Min
2006-07	Ottawa West	ON-Jr.B	40	28	20	48	45	....	....	....	....	....	....	....	....	....	....	....	....	....	....	....	....	....	....
	Ottawa Jr. Sens	ON-Jr.A	2	1	0	1	0	....	....	....	....	....	....	....	....	....	....	....	....	....	....	....	....	....	....
2007-08	Cumberland	ON-Jr.A	34	23	33	56	12	....	....	....	....	....	....	....	....	....	....	....	....	....	....	....	....	....	....
	Sudbury Wolves	OHL	26	14	18	32	19	....	....	....	....	....	....	....	....	....	....	....	....	....	....	....	....	....	....
2008-09	Sudbury Wolves	OHL	65	33	30	63	55	....	....	....	....	....	....	....	....	....	6	0	4	4	4	....	....	....	....
2009-10	Sudbury Wolves	OHL	68	33	35	68	63	....	....	....	....	....	....	....	....	....	4	0	2	2	7	....	....	....	....
	Chicago Wolves	AHL	3	0	0	0	0	....	....	....	....	....	....	....	....	....	....	....	....	....	....	....	....	....	....
2010-11	Sudbury Wolves	OHL	39	20	24	44	34	....	....	....	....	....	....	....	....	....	8	7	5	12	15	....	....	....	....

			Regular Season														Playoffs								
Season	Club	League	GP	G	A	Pts	PIM	PP	SH	GW	S	S%	+/-	TF	F%	Min	GP	G	A	Pts	PIM	PP	SH	GW	Min
2011-12	St. John's IceCaps	AHL	39	12	10	22	27	....	....	....	....	....	....	....	....	....	3	0	0	0	2	....	....	....	....
2012-13	St. John's IceCaps	AHL	59	29	26	55	26	....	....	....	....	....	....	....	....	....	....	....	....	....	....	....	....	....	....
2013-14	**Winnipeg**	**NHL**	**30**	**3**	**4**	**7**	**10**	**0**	**0**	**1**	**17**	**17.6**	**–2**	**156**	**50.0**	**9:41**	....	....	....	....	....	....	....	....	....
	St. John's IceCaps	AHL	42	17	25	42	35	....	....	....	....	....	....	....	....	....	21	*9	5	14	20	....	....	....	....
2014-15	**Winnipeg**	**NHL**	**11**	**0**	**1**	**1**	**19**	**0**	**0**	**0**	**6**	**0.0**	**0**	**41**	**43.9**	**7:26**	....	....	....	....	....	....	....	....	....
	St. John's IceCaps	AHL	37	14	15	29	34	....	....	....	....	....	....	....	....	....	....	....	....	....	....	....	....	....	....
	NHL Totals		**41**	**3**	**5**	**8**	**29**	**0**	**0**	**1**	**23**	**13.0**		**197**	**48.7**	**9:05**	....	....	....	....	....	....	....	....	....

Traded to **Atlanta** by **Anaheim** for Erik Christensen, March 4, 2009. • Transferred to **Winnipeg** after **Atlanta** franchise relocated, June 21, 2011. Signed as a free agent by **Ottawa**, July 1, 2015.

ODUYA, Johnny
(oh-DOO-yuh, JAW-nee) **DAL**

Defense. Shoots left. 6', 190 lbs. Born, Stockholm, Sweden, October 1, 1981. Washington's 6th choice, 221st overall, in 2001 Entry Draft.

Season	Club	League	GP	G	A	Pts	PIM	PP	SH	GW	S	S%	+/-	TF	F%	Min	GP	G	A	Pts	PIM	PP	SH	GW	Min
1996-97	Hammarby Jr.	Swe-Jr.	13	0	0	0	....	....	....	....	....	....	....	....	....	....	....	....	....	....	....	....	....	....	....
1997-98	Hammarby Jr.	Swe-Jr.	26	3	11	14	70	....	....	....	....	....	....	....	....	....	....	....	....	....	....	....	....	....	....
1998-99	Hammarby Jr.	Swe-Jr.	38	14	31	45	45	....	....	....	....	....	....	....	....	....	....	....	....	....	....	....	....	....	....
99-2000	Hammarby Jr.	Swe-Jr.	32	3	18	21	48	....	....	....	....	....	....	....	....	....	6	1	2	3	4	....	....	....	....
	Hammarby	Sweden-2	1	0	0	0	0	....	....	....	....	....	....	....	....	....	1	0	0	0	0	....	....	....	....
2000-01	Moncton Wildcats	QMJHL	44	11	38	49	147	....	....	....	....	....	....	....	....	....	....	....	....	....	....	....	....	....	....
	Victoriaville Tigres	QMJHL	24	3	16	19	112	....	....	....	....	....	....	....	....	....	13	4	9	13	10	....	....	....	....
2001-02	Hammarby	Sweden-2	46	11	14	25	66	....	....	....	....	....	....	....	....	....	2	1	0	1	4	....	....	....	....
2002-03	Hammarby	Sweden-2	48	15	25	40	200	....	....	....	....	....	....	....	....	....	....	....	....	....	....	....	....	....	....
2003-04	Djurgarden	Sweden	42	4	4	8	*173	....	....	....	....	....	....	....	....	....	4	0	0	0	6	....	....	....	....
2004-05	Djurgarden	Sweden	49	2	4	6	139	....	....	....	....	....	....	....	....	....	12	0	2	2	39	....	....	....	....
2005-06	Frolunda	Sweden	47	8	11	19	95	....	....	....	....	....	....	....	....	....	17	1	2	3	16	....	....	....	....
2006-07	**New Jersey**	**NHL**	**76**	**2**	**9**	**11**	**61**	**0**	**0**	**0**	**55**	**3.6**	**–5**	**0**	**0.0**	**18:31**	**6**	**0**	**1**	**1**	**6**	**0**	**0**	**0**	**12:59**
2007-08	**New Jersey**	**NHL**	**75**	**6**	**20**	**26**	**46**	**2**	**0**	**0**	**63**	**9.5**	**27**	**0**	**0.0**	**19:02**	**5**	**0**	**1**	**1**	**6**	**0**	**0**	**0**	**20:40**
2008-09	**New Jersey**	**NHL**	**82**	**7**	**22**	**29**	**30**	**1**	**1**	**4**	**108**	**6.5**	**21**	**0**	**0.0**	**20:52**	**7**	**0**	**0**	**0**	**2**	**0**	**0**	**0**	**20:19**
2009-10	**New Jersey**	**NHL**	**40**	**2**	**2**	**4**	**18**	**0**	**0**	**0**	**44**	**4.5**	**2**	**0**	**0.0**	**21:11**	....	....	....	....	....	....	....	....	....
	Atlanta	**NHL**	**27**	**1**	**8**	**9**	**12**	**0**	**0**	**0**	**24**	**4.2**	**6**	**0**	**0.0**	**21:22**	....	....	....	....	....	....	....	....	....
	Sweden	Olympics	4	0	0	0	12	....	....	....	....	....	....	....	....	....	....	....	....	....	....	....	....	....	....
2010-11	**Atlanta**	**NHL**	**82**	**2**	**15**	**17**	**22**	**0**	**0**	**0**	**90**	**2.2**	**–15**	**0**	**0.0**	**20:43**	....	....	....	....	....	....	....	....	....
2011-12	**Winnipeg**	**NHL**	**63**	**2**	**11**	**13**	**33**	**0**	**0**	**1**	**52**	**3.8**	**–9**	**0**	**0.0**	**19:20**	....	....	....	....	....	....	....	....	....
	Chicago	**NHL**	**18**	**1**	**4**	**5**	**0**	**0**	**0**	**0**	**30**	**3.3**	**3**	**0**	**0.0**	**24:25**	**6**	**0**	**3**	**3**	**0**	**0**	**0**	**0**	**23:14**
2012-13	Flying Farangs	Thailand	STATISTICS NOT AVAILABLE																						
	♦ Chicago	**NHL**	**48**	**3**	**9**	**12**	**10**	**0**	**0**	**0**	**52**	**5.8**	**12**	**0**	**0.0**	**20:31**	**23**	**3**	**5**	**8**	**16**	**0**	**0**	**1**	**22:45**
2013-14	**Chicago**	**NHL**	**77**	**3**	**13**	**16**	**38**	**0**	**0**	**1**	**83**	**3.6**	**11**	**1**	**100.0**	**20:06**	**19**	**2**	**5**	**7**	**8**	**0**	**0**	**0**	**21:54**
	Sweden	Olympics	6	0	1	1	0	....	....	....	....	....	....	....	....	....	....	....	....	....	....	....	....	....	....
2014-15♦	**Chicago**	**NHL**	**76**	**2**	**8**	**10**	**26**	**0**	**0**	**0**	**76**	**2.6**	**5**	**0**	**0.0**	**20:17**	**23**	**0**	**5**	**5**	**6**	**0**	**0**	**0**	**24:45**
	NHL Totals		**664**	**31**	**121**	**152**	**296**	**3**	**1**	**6**	**677**	**4.6**		**1**	**100.0**	**20:11**	**89**	**5**	**20**	**25**	**44**	**0**	**0**	**1**	**22:09**

Signed as a free agent by **New Jersey**, July 24, 2006. Traded to **Atlanta** by **New Jersey** with Niclas Bergfors, Patrice Cormier and New Jersey's 1st (later traded to Chicago - Chicago selected Kevin Hayes) and 2nd (later traded to Chicago - Chicago selected Justin Holl) round choices in 2010 Entry Draft for Ilya Kovalchuk, Anssi Salmela and Atlanta's 2nd round choice (Jonathon Merrill) in 2010 Entry Draft, February 4, 2010. • Transferred to **Winnipeg** after **Atlanta** franchise relocated, June 21, 2011. Signed as a free agent by **Flying Farangs Bangkok** (Thailand), October 31, 2012. Traded to **Chicago** by **Winnipeg** for Chicago's 2nd (later traded to Washington – Washington selected Zachary Sanford) and 3rd (J.C. Lipon) round choices in 2013 Entry Draft, February 27, 2012. Signed as a free agent by **Dallas**, July 15, 2014.

OESTERLE, Jordan
(OH-stuhr-lee, JOHR-duhn) **EDM**

Defense. Shoots left. 6', 182 lbs. Born, Dearborn Heights, MI, June 25, 1992.

Season	Club	League	GP	G	A	Pts	PIM	PP	SH	GW	S	S%	+/-	TF	F%	Min	GP	G	A	Pts	PIM	PP	SH	GW	Min
2008-09	Detroit Belle Tire	T1EHL	31	5	15	20	10	....	....	....	....	....	....	....	....	....	....	....	....	....	....	....	....	....	....
	Detroit Belle Tire	Other	3	0	2	2	15	....	....	....	....	....	....	....	....	....	....	....	....	....	....	....	....	....	....
2009-10	Detroit Belle Tire	T1EHL	47	5	25	30	42	....	....	....	....	....	....	....	....	....	4	0	1	1	0	....	....	....	....
	Detroit Belle Tire	Other	6	1	3	4	4	....	....	....	....	....	....	....	....	....	....	....	....	....	....	....	....	....	....
2010-11	Sioux Falls	USHL	54	2	13	15	16	....	....	....	....	....	....	....	....	....	10	2	3	5	0	....	....	....	....
2011-12	Western Mich.	CCHA	41	2	6	8	8	....	....	....	....	....	....	....	....	....	....	....	....	....	....	....	....	....	....
2012-13	Western Mich.	CCHA	38	3	6	9	14	....	....	....	....	....	....	....	....	....	....	....	....	....	....	....	....	....	....
2013-14	Western Mich.	NCHC	34	2	15	17	27	....	....	....	....	....	....	....	....	....	....	....	....	....	....	....	....	....	....
	Oklahoma City	AHL	4	1	0	1	2	....	....	....	....	....	....	....	....	....	1	0	0	0	0	....	....	....	....
2014-15	**Edmonton**	**NHL**	**6**	**0**	**1**	**1**	**0**	**0**	**0**	**0**	**7**	**0.0**	**–4**	**0**	**0.0**	**14:42**	....	....	....	....	....	....	....	....	....
	Oklahoma City	AHL	65	8	17	25	8	....	....	....	....	....	....	....	....	....	10	1	3	4	8	....	....	....	....
	NHL Totals		**6**	**0**	**1**	**1**	**0**	**0**	**0**	**0**	**7**	**0.0**		**0**	**0.0**	**14:42**	....	....	....	....	....	....	....	....	....

Signed as a free agent by **Edmonton**, April 3, 2014.

OKPOSO, Kyle
(OH-poh-soh, KIGHL) **NYI**

Right wing. Shoots right. 6', 216 lbs. Born, St. Paul, MN, April 16, 1988. NY Islanders' 1st choice, 7th overall, in 2006 Entry Draft.

Season	Club	League	GP	G	A	Pts	PIM	PP	SH	GW	S	S%	+/-	TF	F%	Min	GP	G	A	Pts	PIM	PP	SH	GW	Min
2004-05	Shat.-St. Mary's	High-MN	65	47	45	92	72	....	....	....	....	....	....	....	....	....	....	....	....	....	....	....	....	....	....
2005-06	Des Moines	USHL	50	27	31	58	56	....	....	....	....	....	....	....	....	....	11	5	11	*16	8	....	....	....	....
2006-07	U. of Minnesota	WCHA	40	19	21	40	34	....	....	....	....	....	....	....	....	....	....	....	....	....	....	....	....	....	....
2007-08	U. of Minnesota	WCHA	18	7	4	11	6	....	....	....	....	....	....	....	....	....	....	....	....	....	....	....	....	....	....
	NY Islanders	**NHL**	**9**	**2**	**3**	**5**	**2**	**1**	**0**	**1**	**15**	**13.3**	**3**	**0**	**0.0**	**16:28**	....	....	....	....	....	....	....	....	....
	Bridgeport	AHL	35	9	19	28	12	....	....	....	....	....	....	....	....	....	....	....	....	....	....	....	....	....	....
2008-09	**NY Islanders**	**NHL**	**65**	**18**	**21**	**39**	**36**	**9**	**0**	**3**	**165**	**10.9**	**–6**	**15**	**33.3**	**18:01**	....	....	....	....	....	....	....	....	....
	Bridgeport	AHL	....	....	....	....	....	....	....	....	....	....	....	....	....	....	2	1	0	1	2	....	....	....	....
2009-10	**NY Islanders**	**NHL**	**80**	**19**	**33**	**52**	**34**	**4**	**0**	**4**	**249**	**7.6**	**–22**	**69**	**47.8**	**20:32**	....	....	....	....	....	....	....	....	....
2010-11	**NY Islanders**	**NHL**	**38**	**5**	**15**	**20**	**40**	**0**	**0**	**2**	**72**	**6.9**	**3**	**87**	**41.4**	**16:35**	....	....	....	....	....	....	....	....	....
2011-12	**NY Islanders**	**NHL**	**79**	**24**	**21**	**45**	**46**	**3**	**0**	**2**	**152**	**15.8**	**–15**	**142**	**47.9**	**17:04**	....	....	....	....	....	....	....	....	....
2012-13	**NY Islanders**	**NHL**	**48**	**4**	**20**	**24**	**38**	**0**	**0**	**0**	**101**	**4.0**	**–2**	**186**	**55.9**	**16:57**	**6**	**3**	**1**	**4**	**5**	**0**	**1**	**1**	**19:13**
2013-14	**NY Islanders**	**NHL**	**71**	**27**	**42**	**69**	**51**	**5**	**0**	**4**	**195**	**13.8**	**–9**	**204**	**47.6**	**20:26**	....	....	....	....	....	....	....	....	....
2014-15	**NY Islanders**	**NHL**	**60**	**18**	**33**	**51**	**12**	**6**	**0**	**2**	**195**	**9.2**	**–8**	**161**	**49.7**	**19:33**	**7**	**2**	**1**	**3**	**2**	**0**	**0**	**0**	**18:31**
	NHL Totals		**450**	**117**	**188**	**305**	**259**	**28**	**0**	**18**	**1144**	**10.2**		**864**	**49.0**	**18:37**	**13**	**5**	**2**	**7**	**7**	**0**	**1**	**1**	**18:50**

USHL All-Rookie Team (2006) • USHL First All-Star Team (2006) • USHL Rookie of the Year (2006) • WCHA All-Rookie Team (2007) • WCHA Second All-Star Team (2007)

• Missed majority of 2010-11 due to training camp shoulder injury.

OLEKSIAK, Jamie
(oh-LEHK-see-ak, JAY-mih) **DAL**

Defense. Shoots left. 6'7", 250 lbs. Born, Toronto, ON, December 21, 1992. Dallas' 1st choice, 14th overall, in 2011 Entry Draft.

Season	Club	League	GP	G	A	Pts	PIM	PP	SH	GW	S	S%	+/-	TF	F%	Min	GP	G	A	Pts	PIM	PP	SH	GW	Min
2007-08	Tor. Young Nats	GTHL	51	1	10	11	46	....	....	....	....	....	....	....	....	....	....	....	....	....	....	....	....	....	....
2008-09	Det. Lit. Caesars	T1EHL	30	3	7	10	31	....	....	....	....	....	....	....	....	....	....	....	....	....	....	....	....	....	....
	Chicago Steel	USHL	29	0	4	4	47	....	....	....	....	....	....	....	....	....	....	....	....	....	....	....	....	....	....
2009-10	Chicago Steel	USHL	29	0	10	10	43	....	....	....	....	....	....	....	....	....	....	....	....	....	....	....	....	....	....
	Sioux Falls	USHL	24	2	2	4	32	....	....	....	....	....	....	....	....	....	3	0	1	1	2	....	....	....	....
2010-11	Northeastern	H-East	38	4	9	13	57	....	....	....	....	....	....	....	....	....	....	....	....	....	....	....	....	....	....
2011-12	Saginaw Spirit	OHL	31	6	5	11	24	....	....	....	....	....	....	....	....	....	....	....	....	....	....	....	....	....	....
	Niagara Ice Dogs	OHL	28	6	15	21	23	....	....	....	....	....	....	....	....	....	20	0	4	4	6	....	....	....	....
2012-13	Texas Stars	AHL	59	6	27	33	29	....	....	....	....	....	....	....	....	....	9	0	1	1	6	....	....	....	....
	Dallas	**NHL**	**16**	**0**	**2**	**2**	**14**	**0**	**0**	**0**	**11**	**0.0**	**–5**	**0**	**0.0**	**14:50**	....	....	....	....	....	....	....	....	....
2013-14	**Dallas**	**NHL**	**7**	**0**	**0**	**0**	**2**	**0**	**0**	**0**	**5**	**0.0**	**–3**	**0**	**0.0**	**17:47**	....	....	....	....	....	....	....	....	....
	Texas Stars	AHL	69	5	18	23	31	....	....	....	....	....	....	....	....	....	21	0	5	5	8	....	....	....	....
2014-15	**Dallas**	**NHL**	**36**	**1**	**7**	**8**	**8**	**0**	**0**	**0**	**36**	**2.8**	**0**	**0**	**0.0**	**13:24**	....	....	....	....	....	....	....	....	....
	Texas Stars	AHL	35	4	12	16	12	....	....	....	....	....	....	....	....	....	3	0	0	0	0	....	....	....	....
	NHL Totals		**59**	**1**	**9**	**10**	**24**	**0**	**0**	**0**	**52**	**1.9**		**0**	**0.0**	**14:19**	....	....	....	....	....	....	....	....	....

OLEKSY, Steve
(oh-LEHK-see, STEEV) **PIT**

Defense. Shoots right. 6', 190 lbs. Born, Chesterfield, MI, February 4, 1986.

			Regular Season														Playoffs								
Season	Club	League	GP	G	A	Pts	PIM	PP	SH	GW	S	S%	+/-	TF	F%	Min	GP	G	A	Pts	PIM	PP	SH	GW	Min
2005-06	Traverse City	NAHL	57	11	19	30	140	....	....	....	....	....	....	....	....	....	....	....	....	....	....	....	....	....	....
2006-07	Lake Superior	CCHA	39	2	2	4	24	....	....	....	....	....	....	....	....	....	....	....	....	....	....	....	....	....	....
2007-08	Lake Superior	CCHA	36	1	6	7	36	....	....	....	....	....	....	....	....	....	....	....	....	....	....	....	....	....	....
2008-09	Lake Superior	CCHA	38	0	9	9	50	....	....	....	....	....	....	....	....	....	....	....	....	....	....	....	....	....	....
	Las Vegas	ECHL	2	0	0	0	0	....	....	....	....	....	....	....	....	....	....	....	....	....	....	....	....	....	....
2009-10	Toledo Walleye	ECHL	3	0	0	0	2	....	....	....	....	....	....	....	....	....	....	....	....	....	....	....	....	....	....
	Port Huron	IHL	28	1	1	2	35	....	....	....	....	....	....	....	....	....	....	....	....	....	....	....	....	....	....
	Idaho Steelheads	ECHL	33	1	8	9	72	....	....	....	....	....	....	....	....	....	8	0	0	0	25	....	....	....	....
2010-11	Idaho Steelheads	ECHL	55	7	14	21	134	....	....	....	....	....	....	....	....	....	....	....	....	....	....	....	....	....	....
	Lake Erie	AHL	17	0	4	4	39	....	....	....	....	....	....	....	....	....	3	0	1	1	2	....	....	....	....
2011-12	Idaho Steelheads	ECHL	14	1	7	8	47	....	....	....	....	....	....	....	....	....	....	....	....	....	....	....	....	....	....
	Bridgeport	AHL	50	1	14	15	98	....	....	....	....	....	....	....	....	....	3	0	0	0	2	....	....	....	....
2012-13	Hershey Bears	AHL	55	2	12	14	151	....	....	....	....	....	....	....	....	....	....	....	....	....	....	....	....	....	....
	Washington	**NHL**	**28**	**1**	**8**	**9**	**33**	**0**	**0**	**0**	**25**	**4.0**	**9**	**0**	**0.0**	**17:16**	**7**	**0**	**1**	**1**	**4**	**0**	**0**	**0**	**15:09**
2013-14	**Washington**	**NHL**	**33**	**2**	**8**	**10**	**53**	**0**	**0**	**1**	**27**	**7.4**	**7**	**0**	**0.0**	**15:16**	....	....	....	....	....	....	....	....	....
	Hershey Bears	AHL	30	0	6	6	39	....	....	....	....	....	....	....	....	....	....	....	....	....	....	....	....	....	....
2014-15	**Washington**	**NHL**	**1**	**0**	**0**	**0**	**0**	**0**	**0**	**0**	**1**	**0.0**	**–1**	**0**	**0.0**	**12:11**	....	....	....	....	....	....	....	....	....
	Hershey Bears	AHL	68	4	11	15	147	....	....	....	....	....	....	....	....	....	8	0	3	3	8	....	....	....	....
	NHL Totals		**62**	**3**	**16**	**19**	**86**	**0**	**0**	**1**	**53**	**5.7**		**0**	**0.0**	**16:07**	**7**	**0**	**1**	**1**	**4**	**0**	**0**	**0**	**15:09**

Signed as a free agent by **Hershey** (AHL), July 2, 2012. Signed as a free agent by **Washington**, March 4, 2013. Signed as a free agent by **Pittsburgh**, July 1, 2015.

OLESZ, Rostislav
(OH-lehsh, RAHS-tih-slav)

Left wing. Shoots left. 6'2", 215 lbs. Born, Bilovec, Czech., October 10, 1985. Florida's 1st choice, 7th overall, in 2004 Entry Draft.

Season	Club	League	GP	G	A	Pts	PIM	PP	SH	GW	S	S%	+/-	TF	F%	Min	GP	G	A	Pts	PIM	PP	SH	GW	Min
2000-01	HC Vitkovice Jr.	CzRep-Jr.	15	10	3	13	14	....	....	....	....	....	....	....	....	....	....	....	....	....	....	....	....	....	....
	HC Vitkovice	CzRep	3	0	1	1	0	....	....	....	....	....	....	....	....	....	....	....	....	....	....	....	....	....	....
2001-02	HC Vitkovice	CzRep	11	1	2	3	0	....	....	....	....	....	....	....	....	....	....	....	....	....	....	....	....	....	....
	HC Vitkovice Jr.	CzRep-Jr.	34	19	20	39	81	....	....	....	....	....	....	....	....	....	2	0	0	0	2	....	....	....	....
2002-03	HC Vitkovice Jr.	CzRep-Jr.	7	1	1	2	12	....	....	....	....	....	....	....	....	....	....	....	....	....	....	....	....	....	....
	HC Vitkovice	CzRep	40	6	3	9	41	....	....	....	....	....	....	....	....	....	5	0	0	0	2	....	....	....	....
	HC Slezan Opava	CzRep-2	1	0	0	0	0	....	....	....	....	....	....	....	....	....	....	....	....	....	....	....	....	....	....
2003-04	HC Vitkovice Jr.	CzRep-Jr.	3	2	0	2	0	....	....	....	....	....	....	....	....	....	....	....	....	....	....	....	....	....	....
	HC Vitkovice	CzRep	35	1	11	12	10	....	....	....	....	....	....	....	....	....	6	2	1	3	4	....	....	....	....
	HC Dukla Jihlava	CzRep-2	2	1	0	1	0	....	....	....	....	....	....	....	....	....	1	0	0	0	0	....	....	....	....
2004-05	HC Sparta Praha	CzRep	47	6	7	13	12	....	....	....	....	....	....	....	....	....	5	0	2	2	0	....	....	....	....
	Sparta Jr.	CzRep-Jr.	....	....	....	....	....	....	....	....	....	....	....	....	....	....	1	0	1	1	0	....	....	....	....
2005-06	**Florida**	**NHL**	**59**	**8**	**13**	**21**	**24**	**0**	**1**	**3**	**105**	**7.6**	**–4**	**10**	**30.0**	**14:52**	....	....	....	....	....	....	....	....	....
	Czech Republic	Olympics	8	0	0	0	2	....	....	....	....	....	....	....	....	....	....	....	....	....	....	....	....	....	....
2006-07	**Florida**	**NHL**	**75**	**11**	**19**	**30**	**28**	**2**	**0**	**2**	**164**	**6.7**	**2**	**12**	**58.3**	**15:30**	....	....	....	....	....	....	....	....	....
	Rochester	AHL	4	1	2	3	4	....	....	....	....	....	....	....	....	....	....	....	....	....	....	....	....	....	....
2007-08	**Florida**	**NHL**	**56**	**14**	**12**	**26**	**16**	**5**	**0**	**2**	**139**	**10.1**	**3**	**10**	**70.0**	**17:04**	....	....	....	....	....	....	....	....	....
2008-09	**Florida**	**NHL**	**37**	**4**	**5**	**9**	**8**	**0**	**0**	**0**	**69**	**5.8**	**–5**	**5**	**20.0**	**13:12**	....	....	....	....	....	....	....	....	....
2009-10	**Florida**	**NHL**	**78**	**14**	**15**	**29**	**28**	**3**	**0**	**3**	**178**	**7.9**	**–4**	**9**	**22.2**	**15:24**	....	....	....	....	....	....	....	....	....
2010-11	**Florida**	**NHL**	**44**	**6**	**11**	**17**	**8**	**1**	**0**	**1**	**71**	**8.5**	**–1**	**10**	**20.0**	**13:53**	....	....	....	....	....	....	....	....	....
2011-12	**Chicago**	**NHL**	**6**	**0**	**0**	**0**	**6**	**0**	**0**	**0**	**6**	**0.0**	**–1**	**2**	**0.0**	**9:06**	....	....	....	....	....	....	....	....	....
	Rockford IceHogs	AHL	50	17	24	41	32	....	....	....	....	....	....	....	....	....	....	....	....	....	....	....	....	....	....
2012-13	Rockford IceHogs	AHL	14	7	12	19	4	....	....	....	....	....	....	....	....	....	....	....	....	....	....	....	....	....	....
2013-14	**New Jersey**	**NHL**	**10**	**0**	**2**	**2**	**0**	**0**	**0**	**0**	**9**	**0.0**	**–1**	**3**	**33.3**	**11:25**	....	....	....	....	....	....	....	....	....
	Albany Devils	AHL	5	1	3	4	4	....	....	....	....	....	....	....	....	....	....	....	....	....	....	....	....	....	....
	SC Bern	Swiss	29	11	5	16	14	....	....	....	....	....	....	....	....	....	....	....	....	....	....	....	....	....	....
2014-15	Vitkovice	CzRep	39	12	10	22	32	....	....	....	....	....	....	....	....	....	4	0	2	2	18	....	....	....	....
	NHL Totals		**365**	**57**	**77**	**134**	**118**	**11**	**1**	**11**	**741**	**7.7**		**61**	**37.7**	**14:58**	....	....	....	....	....	....	....	....	....

• Missed majority of 2008-09 due to groin injury and resulting sports hernia surgery. Traded to **Chicago** by **Florida** for Brian Campbell, June 25, 2011. • Missed majority of 2012-13 due to knee surgery, January 19, 2013. Signed as a free agent by **New Jersey**, July 5, 2013. Signed as a free agent by **Bern** (Swiss), November 20. 2013. Signed as a free agent by **Vitkovice** (CzRep), September 11, 2014.

OLSEN, Dylan
(OHL-suhn, DIH-luhn) **FLA**

Defense. Shoots left. 6'2", 223 lbs. Born, Salt Lake City, UT, January 3, 1991. Chicago's 1st choice, 28th overall, in 2009 Entry Draft.

Season	Club	League	GP	G	A	Pts	PIM	PP	SH	GW	S	S%	+/-	TF	F%	Min	GP	G	A	Pts	PIM	PP	SH	GW	Min
2006-07	Calgary Blazers	SAMHL	53	19	41	60	119	....	....	....	....	....	....	....	....	....	....	....	....	....	....	....	....	....	....
	Camrose Kodiaks	AJHL	2	1	0	1	0	....	....	....	....	....	....	....	....	....	....	....	....	....	....	....	....	....	....
2007-08	Camrose Kodiaks	AJHL	49	8	16	24	45	....	....	....	....	....	....	....	....	....	16	1	5	6	6	....	....	....	....
2008-09	Camrose Kodiaks	AJHL	53	10	19	29	123	....	....	....	....	....	....	....	....	....	10	1	6	7	12	....	....	....	....
2009-10	U. Minn-Duluth	WCHA	36	1	10	11	49	....	....	....	....	....	....	....	....	....	....	....	....	....	....	....	....	....	....
2010-11	U. Minn-Duluth	WCHA	17	1	12	13	8	....	....	....	....	....	....	....	....	....	....	....	....	....	....	....	....	....	....
	Rockford IceHogs	AHL	42	0	4	4	10	....	....	....	....	....	....	....	....	....	....	....	....	....	....	....	....	....	....
2011-12	**Chicago**	**NHL**	**28**	**0**	**1**	**1**	**6**	**0**	**0**	**0**	**16**	**0.0**	**–5**	**0**	**0.0**	**13:02**	**1**	**0**	**0**	**0**	**0**	**0**	**0**	**0**	**4:56**
	Rockford IceHogs	AHL	44	4	3	7	44	....	....	....	....	....	....	....	....	....	....	....	....	....	....	....	....	....	....
2012-13	Rockford IceHogs	AHL	50	2	9	11	27	....	....	....	....	....	....	....	....	....	....	....	....	....	....	....	....	....	....
2013-14	Rockford IceHogs	AHL	16	0	8	8	8	....	....	....	....	....	....	....	....	....	....	....	....	....	....	....	....	....	....
	Florida	**NHL**	**44**	**3**	**9**	**12**	**8**	**0**	**0**	**0**	**60**	**5.0**	**–3**	**0**	**0.0**	**15:26**	....	....	....	....	....	....	....	....	....
	San Antonio	AHL	4	1	1	2	2	....	....	....	....	....	....	....	....	....	....	....	....	....	....	....	....	....	....
2014-15	**Florida**	**NHL**	**44**	**2**	**6**	**8**	**20**	**0**	**0**	**0**	**44**	**4.5**	**–7**	**0**	**0.0**	**15:54**	....	....	....	....	....	....	....	....	....
	San Antonio	AHL	12	1	2	3	22	....	....	....	....	....	....	....	....	....	2	1	0	1	2	....	....	....	....
	NHL Totals		**116**	**5**	**16**	**21**	**34**	**0**	**0**	**0**	**120**	**4.2**		**0**	**0.0**	**15:02**	**1**	**0**	**0**	**0**	**0**	**0**	**0**	**0**	**4:56**

Traded to **Florida** by **Chicago** with Jimmy Hayes for Kris Versteeg and Phillipe Lefebvre, November 14, 2013.

O'REILLY, Cal
(oh-RIGH-lee, KAL) **BUF**

Center. Shoots left. 6', 188 lbs. Born, Toronto, ON, September 30, 1986. Nashville's 4th choice, 150th overall, in 2005 Entry Draft.

Season	Club	League	GP	G	A	Pts	PIM	PP	SH	GW	S	S%	+/-	TF	F%	Min	GP	G	A	Pts	PIM	PP	SH	GW	Min
2002-03	St. Mary's Lincolns	ON-Jr.B	46	11	19	30	2	....	....	....	....	....	....	....	....	....	....	....	....	....	....	....	....	....	....
2003-04	Windsor Spitfires	OHL	61	3	18	21	2	....	....	....	....	....	....	....	....	....	3	0	1	1	0	....	....	....	....
2004-05	Windsor Spitfires	OHL	68	24	50	74	16	....	....	....	....	....	....	....	....	....	11	4	5	9	4	....	....	....	....
2005-06	Windsor Spitfires	OHL	68	18	81	99	8	....	....	....	....	....	....	....	....	....	7	3	8	11	0	....	....	....	....
	Milwaukee	AHL	2	0	0	0	0	....	....	....	....	....	....	....	....	....	10	0	1	1	0	....	....	....	....
2006-07	Milwaukee	AHL	78	18	47	65	20	....	....	....	....	....	....	....	....	....	4	1	2	3	0	....	....	....	....
2007-08	Milwaukee	AHL	80	16	63	79	22	....	....	....	....	....	....	....	....	....	6	1	2	3	0	....	....	....	....
2008-09	**Nashville**	**NHL**	**11**	**3**	**2**	**5**	**2**	**0**	**0**	**0**	**6**	**50.0**	**2**	**88**	**39.8**	**12:36**	....	....	....	....	....	....	....	....	....
	Milwaukee	AHL	67	13	56	69	20	....	....	....	....	....	....	....	....	....	11	2	6	8	0	....	....	....	....
2009-10	**Nashville**	**NHL**	**31**	**2**	**9**	**11**	**4**	**1**	**0**	**0**	**23**	**8.7**	**1**	**281**	**47.3**	**13:38**	....	....	....	....	....	....	....	....	....
	Milwaukee	AHL	35	9	31	40	8	....	....	....	....	....	....	....	....	....	....	....	....	....	....	....	....	....	....
2010-11	**Nashville**	**NHL**	**38**	**6**	**12**	**18**	**2**	**1**	**0**	**1**	**44**	**13.6**	**4**	**497**	**46.5**	**16:54**	....	....	....	....	....	....	....	....	....
2011-12	**Nashville**	**NHL**	**5**	**0**	**1**	**1**	**2**	**0**	**0**	**0**	**1**	**0.0**	**–2**	**44**	**45.5**	**14:06**	....	....	....	....	....	....	....	....	....
	Phoenix	**NHL**	**22**	**2**	**3**	**5**	**2**	**1**	**0**	**0**	**13**	**15.4**	**–5**	**170**	**44.7**	**12:37**	....	....	....	....	....	....	....	....	....
	Portland Pirates	AHL	5	1	1	2	0	....	....	....	....	....	....	....	....	....	....	....	....	....	....	....	....	....	....
	Pittsburgh	**NHL**	**6**	**0**	**1**	**1**	**0**	**0**	**0**	**0**	**3**	**0.0**	**–4**	**54**	**44.4**	**12:11**	....	....	....	....	....	....	....	....	....
	Wilkes-Barre	AHL	21	0	10	10	8	....	....	....	....	....	....	....	....	....	12	5	4	9	0	....	....	....	....
2012-13	Magnitogorsk	KHL	32	3	16	19	30	....	....	....	....	....	....	....	....	....	7	2	2	4	2	....	....	....	....
2013-14	Magnitogorsk	KHL	14	0	1	1	2	....	....	....	....	....	....	....	....	....	....	....	....	....	....	....	....	....	....
	Yuzhny Ural Orsk	Russia-2	3	1	3	4	0	....	....	....	....	....	....	....	....	....	....	....	....	....	....	....	....	....	....
	Utica Comets	AHL	52	7	38	45	6	....	....	....	....	....	....	....	....	....	....	....	....	....	....	....	....	....	....
2014-15	Utica Comets	AHL	76	10	51	61	10	....	....	....	....	....	....	....	....	....	23	2	17	19	4	....	....	....	....
	NHL Totals		**113**	**13**	**28**	**41**	**12**	**3**	**0**	**1**	**90**	**14.4**		**1134**	**45.8**	**14:23**	....	....	....	....	....	....	....	....	....

• Missed majority of 2010-11 due to recurring leg injury. Traded to **Phoenix** by **Nashville** for Phoenix's 4th round choice (Mikko Vainonen) in 2012 Entry Draft, October 28, 2011. Claimed on waivers by **Pittsburgh** from **Phoenix**, February 1, 2012. Signed as a free agent by **Magnitogorsk** (KHL), July 18, 2012. Signed as a free agent by **Utica** (AHL), November 19, 2013. Signed as a free agent by **Vancouver**, July 3, 2014. Signed as a free agent by **Buffalo**, July 3, 2015.

O'REILLY, Ryan

(oh-RIGH-lee, RIGH-uhn) **BUF**

Center. Shoots left. 6', 200 lbs. Born, Clinton, ON, February 7, 1991. Colorado's 2nd choice, 33rd overall, in 2009 Entry Draft.

			Regular Season														Playoffs								
Season	Club	League	GP	G	A	Pts	PIM	PP	SH	GW	S	S%	+/-	TF	F%	Min	GP	G	A	Pts	PIM	PP	SH	GW	Min
2006-07	Tor. Jr. Canadiens	GTHL	50	31	43	74																			
	Tor. Canadiens	ON-Jr.A	1	1	0	1	0																		
2007-08	Erie Otters	OHL	61	19	33	52	14																		
2008-09	Erie Otters	OHL	68	16	50	66	26										5	0	5	5	2				
2009-10	**Colorado**	**NHL**	**81**	**8**	**18**	**26**	**18**	**0**	**2**	**2**	**135**	**5.9**	**4**	**1014**	**47.8**	**16:46**	**6**	**1**	**0**	**1**	**2**	**0**	**0**	**1**	**17:05**
2010-11	**Colorado**	**NHL**	**74**	**13**	**13**	**26**	**16**	**2**	**1**	**0**	**119**	**10.9**	**–7**	**1025**	**51.8**	**16:03**									
2011-12	**Colorado**	**NHL**	**81**	**18**	**37**	**55**	**12**	**4**	**0**	**3**	**189**	**9.5**	**–1**	**1443**	**52.8**	**19:32**									
2012-13	Magnitogorsk	KHL	12	5	5	10	2																		
	Colorado	**NHL**	**29**	**6**	**14**	**20**	**4**	**3**	**0**	**0**	**66**	**9.1**	**–3**	**456**	**52.9**	**18:30**									
2013-14	**Colorado**	**NHL**	**80**	**28**	**36**	**64**	**2**	**9**	**0**	**6**	**201**	**13.9**	**–1**	**371**	**51.8**	**19:49**	**7**	**2**	**4**	**6**	**0**	**0**	**0**	**0**	**22:21**
2014-15	**Colorado**	**NHL**	**82**	**17**	**38**	**55**	**12**	**2**	**1**	**1**	**171**	**9.9**	**–5**	**1334**	**53.5**	**19:43**									
	NHL Totals		**427**	**90**	**156**	**246**	**64**	**20**	**4**	**12**	**881**	**10.2**		**5643**	**51.8**	**18:26**	**13**	**3**	**4**	**7**	**2**	**0**	**0**	**1**	**19:55**

Lady Byng Memorial Trophy (2014)

Signed as a free agent by **Magnitogorsk** (KHL), December 7, 2012. Traded to **Buffalo** by **Colorado** with Jamie McGinn for Nikita Zadorov, Mikhail Grigorenko, JT Compher and Buffalo's 2nd round choice (later traded to San Jose – San Jose selected Jeremy Roy) in 2015 Entry Draft, June 26, 2015.

ORLOV, Dmitry

(ohr-LAWF, dih-MEE-tree) **WSH**

Defense. Shoots left. 6', 210 lbs. Born, Novokuznetsk, USSR, July 23, 1991. Washington's 2nd choice, 55th overall, in 2009 Entry Draft.

Season	Club	League	GP	G	A	Pts	PIM	PP	SH	GW	S	S%	+/-	TF	F%	Min	GP	G	A	Pts	PIM	PP	SH	GW	Min
2007-08	Novokuznetsk	Russia	6	0	0	0	0																		
2008-09	Novokuznetsk 2	Russia-3	STATISTICS NOT AVAILABLE																						
	Novokuznetsk	KHL	16	1	0	1	4																		
2009-10	Novokuznetsk	KHL	41	4	3	7	49																		
	Novokuznetsk Jr.	Russia-Jr.	7	7	6	13	6										17	9	10	19	26				
2010-11	Novokuznetsk	KHL	45	2	11	13	43																		
	Novokuznetsk Jr.	Russia-Jr.	1	0	0	0	0																		
	Hershey Bears	AHL	19	2	7	9	12										6	0	1	1	4				
2011-12	**Washington**	**NHL**	**60**	**3**	**16**	**19**	**18**	**0**	**0**	**1**	**51**	**5.9**	**1**	**1**	**0.0**	**16:52**									
	Hershey Bears	AHL	15	4	5	9	12																		
2012-13	Hershey Bears	AHL	31	3	14	17	20										4	1	2	3	4				
	Washington	**NHL**	**5**	**0**	**1**	**1**	**0**	**0**	**0**	**0**	**1**	**0.0**	**5**	**0**	**0.0**	**14:57**									
2013-14	**Washington**	**NHL**	**54**	**3**	**8**	**11**	**19**	**0**	**0**	**0**	**59**	**5.1**	**–1**	**0**	**0.0**	**19:36**									
	Hershey Bears	AHL	11	3	6	9	4																		
2014-15	Hershey Bears	AHL	3	0	3	3	4																		
	NHL Totals		**119**	**6**	**25**	**31**	**37**	**0**	**0**	**1**	**111**	**5.4**		**1**	**0.0**	**18:02**									

• Missed majority of 2014-15 due to wrist injury vs. USA in 2014 WC-A, May 12, 2014.

ORPIK, Brooks

(OHR-pihk, BRUKS) **WSH**

Defense. Shoots left. 6'2", 219 lbs. Born, San Francisco, CA, September 26, 1980. Pittsburgh's 1st choice, 18th overall, in 2000 Entry Draft.

Season	Club	League	GP	G	A	Pts	PIM	PP	SH	GW	S	S%	+/-	TF	F%	Min	GP	G	A	Pts	PIM	PP	SH	GW	Min
1996-97	Thayer Academy	High-MA	20	4	1	5																			
1997-98	Thayer Academy	High-MA	22	0	7	7																			
1998-99	Boston College	H-East	41	1	10	11	*96																		
99-2000	Boston College	H-East	38	1	9	10	102																		
2000-01	Boston College	H-East	40	0	20	20	*124																		
2001-02	Wilkes-Barre	AHL	78	2	18	20	99																		
2002-03	**Pittsburgh**	**NHL**	**6**	**0**	**0**	**0**	**2**	**0**	**0**	**0**	**2**	**0.0**	**–5**	**0**	**0.0**	**18:19**									
	Wilkes-Barre	AHL	71	4	14	18	105										6	0	0	0	14				
2003-04	**Pittsburgh**	**NHL**	**79**	**1**	**9**	**10**	**127**	**0**	**0**	**0**	**56**	**1.8**	**–36**	**0**	**0.0**	**18:25**									
	Wilkes-Barre	AHL	3	0	0	0	2										24	0	4	4	53				
2005-06	**Pittsburgh**	**NHL**	**64**	**2**	**7**	**9**	**124**	**0**	**0**	**0**	**32**	**6.3**	**–3**	**0**	**0.0**	**18:50**									
2006-07	**Pittsburgh**	**NHL**	**70**	**0**	**6**	**6**	**82**	**0**	**0**	**0**	**59**	**0.0**	**4**	**0**	**0.0**	**16:37**	**5**	**0**	**0**	**0**	**8**	**0**	**0**	**0**	**15:43**
2007-08	**Pittsburgh**	**NHL**	**78**	**1**	**10**	**11**	**57**	**0**	**0**	**0**	**50**	**2.0**	**11**	**0**	**0.0**	**16:58**	**20**	**0**	**2**	**2**	**18**	**0**	**0**	**0**	**20:47**
2008-09 ♦	**Pittsburgh**	**NHL**	**79**	**2**	**17**	**19**	**73**	**1**	**0**	**0**	**39**	**5.1**	**10**	**0**	**0.0**	**20:20**	**24**	**0**	**4**	**4**	**22**	**0**	**0**	**0**	**20:04**
2009-10	**Pittsburgh**	**NHL**	**73**	**2**	**23**	**25**	**64**	**0**	**0**	**0**	**61**	**3.3**	**6**	**0**	**0.0**	**20:06**	**13**	**0**	**2**	**2**	**12**	**0**	**0**	**0**	**21:40**
	United States	Olympics	6	0	0	0	0																		
2010-11	**Pittsburgh**	**NHL**	**63**	**1**	**12**	**13**	**66**	**0**	**0**	**0**	**56**	**1.8**	**12**	**1**	**100.0**	**20:53**	**7**	**0**	**3**	**3**	**14**	**0**	**0**	**0**	**24:11**
2011-12	**Pittsburgh**	**NHL**	**73**	**2**	**16**	**18**	**61**	**0**	**0**	**0**	**44**	**4.5**	**19**	**0**	**0.0**	**22:33**	**6**	**0**	**0**	**0**	**4**	**0**	**0**	**0**	**22:17**
2012-13	**Pittsburgh**	**NHL**	**46**	**0**	**8**	**8**	**32**	**0**	**0**	**0**	**32**	**0.0**	**17**	**0**	**0.0**	**22:17**	**12**	**1**	**1**	**2**	**10**	**0**	**0**	**1**	**25:08**
2013-14	**Pittsburgh**	**NHL**	**72**	**2**	**11**	**13**	**46**	**0**	**0**	**0**	**50**	**4.0**	**–3**	**0**	**0.0**	**21:12**	**5**	**1**	**1**	**2**	**0**	**0**	**0**	**0**	**19:55**
	United States	Olympics	6	0	0	0	2																		
2014-15	**Washington**	**NHL**	**78**	**0**	**19**	**19**	**66**	**0**	**0**	**0**	**66**	**0.0**	**5**	**0**	**0.0**	**21:48**	**14**	**0**	**2**	**2**	**8**	**0**	**0**	**0**	**22:17**
	NHL Totals		**781**	**13**	**138**	**151**	**800**	**1**	**0**	**0**	**547**	**2.4**		**1**	**100.0**	**19:54**	**106**	**2**	**15**	**17**	**96**	**0**	**0**	**1**	**21:27**

Signed as a free agent by **Washington**, July 1, 2014.

ORR, Colton

(OHR, KOHL-tuhn)

Right wing. Shoots right. 6'3", 222 lbs. Born, Winnipeg, MB, March 3, 1982.

Season	Club	League	GP	G	A	Pts	PIM	PP	SH	GW	S	S%	+/-	TF	F%	Min	GP	G	A	Pts	PIM	PP	SH	GW	Min
1998-99	St. Boniface	MJHL	STATISTICS NOT AVAILABLE																						
	Swift Current	WHL	2	0	0	0	0																		
99-2000	Swift Current	WHL	61	3	2	5	130										12	1	0	1	25				
2000-01	Swift Current	WHL	19	0	4	4	67																		
	Kamloops Blazers	WHL	41	8	1	9	179										3	0	0	0	20				
2001-02	Kamloops Blazers	WHL	1	0	0	0	7										2	0	0	0	2				
2002-03	Kamloops Blazers	WHL	3	2	0	2	17																		
	Regina Pats	WHL	37	6	2	8	170										3	0	0	0	19				
	Providence Bruins	AHL	1	0	0	0	7																		
2003-04	**Boston**	**NHL**	**1**	**0**	**0**	**0**	**0**	**0**	**0**	**0**	**0**	**0.0**	**–1**	**0**	**0.0**	**2:13**									
	Providence Bruins	AHL	64	1	4	5	257										2	0	0	0	9				
2004-05	Providence Bruins	AHL	61	1	6	7	279										17	1	0	1	44				
2005-06	**Boston**	**NHL**	**20**	**0**	**0**	**0**	**27**	**0**	**0**	**0**	**1**	**0.0**	**0**	**0**	**0.0**	**1:49**									
	NY Rangers	**NHL**	**15**	**0**	**1**	**1**	**44**	**0**	**0**	**0**	**0**	**0.0**	**1**	**0**	**0.0**	**4:19**	**1**	**0**	**0**	**0**	**2**	**0**	**0**	**0**	**4:17**
2006-07	**NY Rangers**	**NHL**	**53**	**2**	**1**	**3**	**126**	**0**	**0**	**1**	**23**	**8.7**	**–2**	**0**	**0.0**	**5:20**	**4**	**0**	**0**	**0**	**12**	**0**	**0**	**0**	**4:57**
2007-08	**NY Rangers**	**NHL**	**74**	**1**	**1**	**2**	**159**	**0**	**0**	**1**	**24**	**4.2**	**–13**	**2**	**50.0**	**7:49**	**2**	**0**	**0**	**0**	**0**	**0**	**0**	**0**	**4:26**
2008-09	**NY Rangers**	**NHL**	**82**	**1**	**4**	**5**	**193**	**0**	**0**	**0**	**40**	**2.5**	**–15**	**16**	**25.0**	**6:29**	**5**	**0**	**0**	**0**	**16**	**0**	**0**	**0**	**3:50**
2009-10	**Toronto**	**NHL**	**82**	**4**	**2**	**6**	**239**	**0**	**0**	**1**	**43**	**9.3**	**–4**	**2**	**50.0**	**6:52**									
2010-11	**Toronto**	**NHL**	**46**	**2**	**0**	**2**	**128**	**0**	**0**	**1**	**14**	**14.3**	**–1**	**1**	**0.0**	**5:04**									
2011-12	**Toronto**	**NHL**	**5**	**1**	**0**	**1**	**5**	**0**	**0**	**0**	**3**	**33.3**	**1**	**1**	**0.0**	**4:29**									
	Toronto Marlies	AHL	26	1	0	1	46										8	0	0	0	9				
2012-13	**Toronto**	**NHL**	**44**	**1**	**3**	**4**	***155**	**0**	**0**	**0**	**13**	**7.7**	**4**	**1**	**0.0**	**6:23**	**7**	**0**	**0**	**0**	**18**	**0**	**0**	**0**	**6:31**
2013-14	**Toronto**	**NHL**	**54**	**0**	**0**	**0**	**110**	**0**	**0**	**0**	**12**	**0.0**	**–3**	**2**	**50.0**	**5:23**									
2014-15	**Toronto**	**NHL**	**1**	**0**	**0**	**0**	**0**	**0**	**0**	**0**	**0**	**0.0**	**0**	**0**	**0.0**	**6:06**									
	Toronto Marlies	AHL	14	0	0	0	4																		
	NHL Totals		**477**	**12**	**12**	**24**	**1186**	**0**	**0**	**4**	**173**	**6.9**		**25**	**28.0**	**6:04**	**19**	**0**	**0**	**0**	**48**	**0**	**0**	**0**	**5:09**

Signed as a free agent by **Boston**, September 19, 2001. • Missed majority of 2001-02 due to wrist injury vs. Red Deer (WHL), October 20, 2001. Claimed on waivers by **NY Rangers** from **Boston**, November 29, 2005. Signed as a free agent by **Toronto**, July 1, 2009. • Missed majority of 2011-12 and 2014-15 as a healthy reserve.

			Regular Season														Playoffs								
Season	Club	League	GP	G	A	Pts	PIM	PP	SH	GW	S	S%	+/-	TF	F%	Min	GP	G	A	Pts	PIM	PP	SH	GW	Min

OSHIE, T.J.
(OH-shee, TEE-JAY) **WSH**

Center. Shoots right. 5'11", 189 lbs. Born, Mt. Vernon, WA, December 23, 1986. St. Louis' 1st choice, 24th overall, in 2005 Entry Draft.

Season	Club	League	GP	G	A	Pts	PIM	PP	SH	GW	S	S%	+/-	TF	F%	Min	GP	G	A	Pts	PIM	PP	SH	GW	Min
2004-05	Warroad Warriors	High-MN	31	37	62	99	22	....	....	....	....	....	....	....	....	....	....	....	....	....	....	....	....	....	....
	Sioux Falls	USHL	11	3	2	5	6	....	....	....	....	....	....	....	....	....	....	....	....	....	....	....	....	....	....
2005-06	North Dakota	WCHA	44	24	21	45	33	....	....	....	....	....	....	....	....	....	....	....	....	....	....	....	....	....	....
2006-07	North Dakota	WCHA	43	17	*35	52	30	....	....	....	....	....	....	....	....	....	....	....	....	....	....	....	....	....	....
2007-08	North Dakota	WCHA	42	18	27	45	57	....	....	....	....	....	....	....	....	....	....	....	....	....	....	....	....	....	....
2008-09	**St. Louis**	**NHL**	**57**	**14**	**25**	**39**	**30**	**6**	**1**	**1**	**101**	**13.9**	**16**	**109**	**43.1**	**16:35**	**4**	**0**	**0**	**0**	**2**	**0**	**0**	**0**	**19:01**
2009-10	**St. Louis**	**NHL**	**76**	**18**	**30**	**48**	**36**	**1**	**1**	**3**	**158**	**11.4**	**–1**	**153**	**41.8**	**18:19**	....	....	....	....	....	....	....	....	....
2010-11	**St. Louis**	**NHL**	**49**	**12**	**22**	**34**	**15**	**3**	**1**	**3**	**103**	**11.7**	**10**	**227**	**44.1**	**19:11**	....	....	....	....	....	....	....	....	....
2011-12	**St. Louis**	**NHL**	**80**	**19**	**35**	**54**	**50**	**3**	**1**	**3**	**188**	**10.1**	**15**	**53**	**45.3**	**19:32**	**9**	**0**	**3**	**3**	**6**	**0**	**0**	**0**	**18:49**
2012-13	**St. Louis**	**NHL**	**30**	**7**	**13**	**20**	**15**	**2**	**1**	**1**	**65**	**10.8**	**–5**	**13**	**38.5**	**19:06**	**6**	**2**	**0**	**2**	**2**	**1**	**0**	**0**	**18:31**
2013-14	**St. Louis**	**NHL**	**79**	**21**	**39**	**60**	**42**	**5**	**2**	**5**	**152**	**13.8**	**19**	**66**	**42.4**	**18:59**	**5**	**2**	**0**	**2**	**2**	**0**	**0**	**0**	**24:22**
	United States	Olympics	6	1	3	4	4	....	....	....	....	....	....	....	....	....	....	....	....	....	....	....	....	....	....
2014-15	**St. Louis**	**NHL**	**72**	**19**	**36**	**55**	**51**	**3**	**0**	**4**	**162**	**11.7**	**17**	**13**	**23.1**	**18:50**	**6**	**1**	**1**	**2**	**0**	**0**	**0**	**0**	**19:08**
	NHL Totals		**443**	**110**	**200**	**310**	**239**	**23**	**7**	**20**	**929**	**11.8**		**634**	**42.7**	**18:40**	**30**	**5**	**4**	**9**	**12**	**1**	**0**	**0**	**19:46**

WCHA All-Rookie Team (2006) • WCHA First All-Star Team (2008) • NCAA West First All-American Team (2008)

Traded to **Washington** by **St. Louis** for Troy Brouwer, Pheonix Copley and Washington's 3rd round choice in 2016 Entry Draft, July 2, 2015.

OTT, Steve
(AWT, STEEV) **ST.L.**

Center. Shoots left. 6', 189 lbs. Born, Summerside, PE, August 19, 1982. Dallas' 1st choice, 25th overall, in 2000 Entry Draft.

Season	Club	League	GP	G	A	Pts	PIM	PP	SH	GW	S	S%	+/-	TF	F%	Min	GP	G	A	Pts	PIM	PP	SH	GW	Min
1998-99	Leamington Flyers	ON-Jr.B	48	14	30	44	110	....	....	....	....	....	....	....	....	....	....	....	....	....	....	....	....	....	....
99-2000	Windsor Spitfires	OHL	66	23	39	62	131	....	....	....	....	....	....	....	....	....	12	3	5	8	21	....	....	....	....
2000-01	Windsor Spitfires	OHL	55	50	37	87	164	....	....	....	....	....	....	....	....	....	9	3	8	11	27	....	....	....	....
2001-02	Windsor Spitfires	OHL	53	43	45	88	178	....	....	....	....	....	....	....	....	....	14	6	10	16	49	....	....	....	....
2002-03	**Dallas**	**NHL**	**26**	**3**	**4**	**7**	**31**	**0**	**0**	**0**	**25**	**12.0**	**6**	**4**	**50.0**	**8:46**	**1**	**0**	**0**	**0**	**0**	**0**	**0**	**0**	**6:57**
	Utah Grizzlies	AHL	40	9	11	20	98	....	....	....	....	....	....	....	....	....	....	....	....	....	....	....	....	....	....
2003-04	**Dallas**	**NHL**	**73**	**2**	**10**	**12**	**152**	**0**	**0**	**1**	**74**	**2.7**	**–2**	**59**	**49.2**	**10:14**	**4**	**1**	**0**	**1**	**0**	**0**	**0**	**1**	**6:55**
2004-05	Hamilton	AHL	67	18	21	39	279	....	....	....	....	....	....	....	....	....	4	0	0	0	20	....	....	....	....
2005-06	**Dallas**	**NHL**	**82**	**5**	**17**	**22**	**178**	**0**	**0**	**1**	**89**	**5.6**	**1**	**535**	**49.2**	**11:54**	**5**	**0**	**1**	**1**	**2**	**0**	**0**	**0**	**7:41**
2006-07	**Dallas**	**NHL**	**19**	**0**	**4**	**4**	**35**	**0**	**0**	**0**	**17**	**0.0**	**–4**	**39**	**59.0**	**9:11**	**6**	**0**	**0**	**0**	**8**	**0**	**0**	**0**	**6:43**
	Iowa Stars	AHL	3	0	0	0	8	....	....	....	....	....	....	....	....	....	....	....	....	....	....	....	....	....	....
2007-08	**Dallas**	**NHL**	**73**	**11**	**11**	**22**	**147**	**0**	**1**	**2**	**89**	**12.4**	**2**	**311**	**58.8**	**14:28**	**18**	**2**	**1**	**3**	**22**	**1**	**0**	**1**	**13:46**
2008-09	**Dallas**	**NHL**	**64**	**19**	**27**	**46**	**135**	**5**	**0**	**0**	**132**	**14.4**	**3**	**172**	**46.5**	**17:35**	....	....	....	....	....	....	....	....	....
2009-10	**Dallas**	**NHL**	**73**	**22**	**14**	**36**	**153**	**8**	**1**	**2**	**146**	**15.1**	**–14**	**352**	**56.8**	**16:28**	....	....	....	....	....	....	....	....	....
2010-11	**Dallas**	**NHL**	**82**	**12**	**20**	**32**	**183**	**3**	**2**	**4**	**120**	**10.0**	**–9**	**1138**	**56.6**	**17:09**	....	....	....	....	....	....	....	....	....
2011-12	**Dallas**	**NHL**	**74**	**11**	**28**	**39**	**156**	**4**	**0**	**2**	**108**	**10.2**	**5**	**1011**	**55.5**	**18:21**	....	....	....	....	....	....	....	....	....
2012-13	**Buffalo**	**NHL**	**48**	**9**	**15**	**24**	**93**	**2**	**0**	**3**	**73**	**12.3**	**3**	**535**	**55.7**	**18:33**	....	....	....	....	....	....	....	....	....
2013-14	**Buffalo**	**NHL**	**59**	**9**	**11**	**20**	**55**	**6**	**0**	**1**	**99**	**9.1**	**–26**	**701**	**52.1**	**19:42**	....	....	....	....	....	....	....	....	....
	St. Louis	**NHL**	**23**	**0**	**3**	**3**	**37**	**0**	**0**	**0**	**28**	**0.0**	**–12**	**216**	**59.7**	**14:27**	**6**	**0**	**2**	**2**	**14**	**0**	**0**	**0**	**19:05**
2014-15	**St. Louis**	**NHL**	**78**	**3**	**9**	**12**	**86**	**0**	**0**	**0**	**49**	**6.1**	**–8**	**284**	**56.3**	**11:38**	**6**	**0**	**0**	**0**	**26**	**0**	**0**	**0**	**11:15**
	NHL Totals		**774**	**106**	**173**	**279**	**1441**	**28**	**4**	**16**	**1049**	**10.1**		**5357**	**54.8**	**14:57**	**46**	**3**	**4**	**7**	**72**	**1**	**0**	**2**	**11:48**

Canadian Major Junior Second All-Star Team (2001) • OHL Second All-Star Team (2002)

• Missed majority of 2006-07 due to ankle injury vs. Los Angeles, October 28, 2006. Traded to **Buffalo** by **Dallas** with Adam Pardy for Derek Roy, July 2, 2012. Traded to **St. Louis** by **Buffalo** with Ryan Miller for Jaroslav Halak, Chris Stewart, William Carrier, St. Louis' 1st round choice (later traded to Winnipeg – Winnipeg selected Jack Roslovic) in 2015 Entry Draft and St. Louis' 3rd round choce in 2016 Entry Draft, February 28, 2014.

OUELLET, Xavier
(OO-leht, ehx-AV-ee-ay) **DET**

Defense. Shoots left. 6'1", 200 lbs. Born, Bayonne, France, July 29, 1993. Detroit's 2nd choice, 48th overall, in 2011 Entry Draft.

Season	Club	League	GP	G	A	Pts	PIM	PP	SH	GW	S	S%	+/-	TF	F%	Min	GP	G	A	Pts	PIM	PP	SH	GW	Min
2008-09	Esther-Blondin	QAAA	41	2	9	11	49	....	....	....	....	....	....	....	....	....	14	1	3	4	24	....	....	....	....
2009-10	Montreal	QMJHL	43	2	14	16	22	....	....	....	....	....	....	....	....	....	7	0	3	3	12	....	....	....	....
2010-11	Montreal	QMJHL	67	8	35	43	44	....	....	....	....	....	....	....	....	....	10	0	8	8	6	....	....	....	....
2011-12	Blainville-Bois.	QMJHL	63	21	39	60	67	....	....	....	....	....	....	....	....	....	11	3	7	10	14	....	....	....	....
2012-13	Blainville-Bois.	QMJHL	50	10	31	41	44	....	....	....	....	....	....	....	....	....	15	7	9	16	22	....	....	....	....
2013-14	**Detroit**	**NHL**	**4**	**0**	**0**	**0**	**2**	**0**	**0**	**0**	**4**	**0.0**	**0**	**0**	**0.0**	**14:34**	**1**	**0**	**0**	**0**	**0**	**0**	**0**	**0**	**9:20**
	Grand Rapids	AHL	70	4	13	17	22	....	....	....	....	....	....	....	....	....	8	0	0	0	4	....	....	....	....
2014-15	**Detroit**	**NHL**	**21**	**2**	**1**	**3**	**2**	**0**	**0**	**0**	**27**	**7.4**	**4**	**0**	**0.0**	**16:23**	....	....	....	....	....	....	....	....	....
	Grand Rapids	AHL	52	1	15	16	24	....	....	....	....	....	....	....	....	....	16	1	5	6	8	....	....	....	....
	NHL Totals		**25**	**2**	**1**	**3**	**4**	**0**	**0**	**0**	**31**	**6.5**		**0**	**0.0**	**16:06**	**1**	**0**	**0**	**0**	**0**	**0**	**0**	**0**	**9:20**

QMJHL All-Rookie Team (2010) • QMJHL First All-Star Team (2012, 2013)

OVECHKIN, Alex
(oh-VEHCH-kihn, AL-ehx) **WSH**

Left wing. Shoots right. 6'3", 230 lbs. Born, Moscow, USSR, September 17, 1985. Washington's 1st choice, 1st overall, in 2004 Entry Draft.

Season	Club	League	GP	G	A	Pts	PIM	PP	SH	GW	S	S%	+/-	TF	F%	Min	GP	G	A	Pts	PIM	PP	SH	GW	Min
2001-02	Dyn'o Moscow 2	Russia-3	19	18	8	26	20	....	....	....	....	....	....	....	....	....	....	....	....	....	....	....	....	....	....
	Dynamo Moscow	Russia	22	2	2	4	4	....	....	....	....	....	....	....	....	....	3	0	0	0	0	....	....	....	....
2002-03	Dynamo Moscow	Russia	40	8	7	15	28	....	....	....	....	....	....	....	....	....	5	0	0	0	2	....	....	....	....
2003-04	Dynamo Moscow	Russia	53	13	11	24	40	....	....	....	....	....	....	....	....	....	3	0	0	0	2	....	....	....	....
2004-05	Dynamo Moscow	Russia	37	13	13	26	32	....	....	....	....	....	....	....	....	....	10	2	4	6	31	....	....	....	....
2005-06	**Washington**	**NHL**	**81**	**52**	**54**	**106**	**52**	**21**	**3**	**5**	**425**	**12.2**	**2**	**16**	**12.5**	**21:37**	....	....	....	....	....	....	....	....	....
	Russia	Olympics	8	5	0	5	8	....	....	....	....	....	....	....	....	....	....	....	....	....	....	....	....	....	....
2006-07	**Washington**	**NHL**	**82**	**46**	**46**	**92**	**52**	**16**	**0**	**8**	**392**	**11.7**	**–19**	**17**	**47.1**	**21:23**	....	....	....	....	....	....	....	....	....
2007-08	**Washington**	**NHL**	**82**	***65**	**47**	***112**	**40**	***22**	**0**	***11**	**446**	**14.6**	**28**	**18**	**38.9**	**23:06**	**7**	**4**	**5**	**9**	**0**	**1**	**0**	**2**	**24:03**
2008-09	**Washington**	**NHL**	**79**	***56**	**54**	**110**	**72**	**19**	**1**	**10**	**528**	**10.6**	**8**	**32**	**25.0**	**23:00**	**14**	**11**	**10**	**21**	**8**	**3**	**0**	**1**	**23:21**
2009-10	**Washington**	**NHL**	**72**	**50**	**59**	**109**	**89**	**13**	**0**	**7**	**368**	**13.6**	**45**	**22**	**45.5**	**21:48**	**7**	**5**	**5**	**10**	**0**	**1**	**0**	**0**	**23:06**
	Russia	Olympics	4	2	2	4	2	....	....	....	....	....	....	....	....	....	....	....	....	....	....	....	....	....	....
2010-11	**Washington**	**NHL**	**79**	**32**	**53**	**85**	**41**	**7**	**0**	***11**	**367**	**8.7**	**24**	**18**	**33.3**	**21:22**	**9**	**5**	**5**	**10**	**10**	**1**	**0**	**1**	**23:30**
2011-12	**Washington**	**NHL**	**78**	**38**	**27**	**65**	**26**	**13**	**0**	**3**	**303**	**12.5**	**–8**	**15**	**40.0**	**19:48**	**14**	**5**	**4**	**9**	**8**	**2**	**0**	**1**	**19:51**
2012-13	Dynamo Moscow	KHL	31	19	21	40	14	....	....	....	....	....	....	....	....	....	....	....	....	....	....	....	....	....	....
	Washington	**NHL**	**48**	***32**	**24**	**56**	**36**	***16**	**0**	**4**	**220**	**14.5**	**2**	**1**	**0.0**	**20:53**	**7**	**1**	**1**	**2**	**4**	**1**	**0**	**0**	**20:44**
2013-14	**Washington**	**NHL**	**78**	***51**	**28**	**79**	**48**	***24**	**0**	**10**	**386**	**13.2**	**–35**	**3**	**66.7**	**20:33**	....	....	....	....	....	....	....	....	....
	Russia	Olympics	5	1	1	2	0	....	....	....	....	....	....	....	....	....	....	....	....	....	....	....	....	....	....
2014-15	**Washington**	**NHL**	**81**	***53**	**28**	**81**	**58**	**25**	**0**	**11**	**395**	**13.4**	**10**	**5**	**40.0**	**20:20**	**14**	**5**	**4**	**9**	**6**	**1**	**0**	**0**	**19:57**
	NHL Totals		**760**	**475**	**420**	**895**	**514**	**176**	**4**	**80**	**3830**	**12.4**		**147**	**34.7**	**21:24**	**72**	**36**	**34**	**70**	**36**	**10**	**0**	**5**	**21:49**

Olympic All-Star Team (2006) • NHL All-Rookie Team (2006) • NHL First All-Star Team (2006, 2007, 2008, 2009, 2010, 2013, 2015) • Calder Memorial Trophy (2006) • Maurice "Rocket" Richard Trophy (2008, 2009, 2013, 2014, 2015) • Art Ross Trophy (2008) • Lester B. Pearson Award (2008, 2009) • Hart Memorial Trophy (2008, 2009, 2013) • Ted Lindsay Award (2010) • NHL Second All-Star Team (2011, 2013, 2014)

Played in NHL All-Star Game (2007, 2008, 2009, 2011, 2015)

Signed as a free agent by **Dynamo Moscow** (KHL), September 19, 2012. • In 2012-13 Ovechkin was voted to the NHL First All-Star Team as a Right wing and voted to the NHL Second All-Star Team as a Left wing.

PAAJARVI, Magnus
(pe-ya-YAR-vee, MAG-nuhs) **ST.L.**

Left wing. Shoots left. 6'3", 208 lbs. Born, Norrkoping, Sweden, April 12, 1991. Edmonton's 1st choice, 10th overall, in 2009 Entry Draft.

Season	Club	League	GP	G	A	Pts	PIM	PP	SH	GW	S	S%	+/-	TF	F%	Min	GP	G	A	Pts	PIM	PP	SH	GW	Min
2005-06	Malmo U18	Swe-U18	13	2	3	5	4	....	....	....	....	....	....	....	....	....	1	0	0	0	0	....	....	....	....
	Malmo Jr.	Swe-Jr.	2	0	0	0	0	....	....	....	....	....	....	....	....	....	....	....	....	....	....	....	....	....	....
2006-07	Malmo U18	Swe-U18	3	3	3	6	0	....	....	....	....	....	....	....	....	....	....	....	....	....	....	....	....	....	....
	Malmo Jr.	Swe-Jr.	20	4	2	6	6	....	....	....	....	....	....	....	....	....	4	0	1	1	0	....	....	....	....
2007-08	Timra IK U18	Swe-U18	5	1	6	7	4	....	....	....	....	....	....	....	....	....	....	....	....	....	....	....	....	....	....
	Timra IK Jr.	Swe-Jr.	18	7	15	22	6	....	....	....	....	....	....	....	....	....	....	....	....	....	....	....	....	....	....
	Timra IK	Sweden	35	1	2	3	2	....	....	....	....	....	....	....	....	....	11	0	0	0	2	....	....	....	....
2008-09	Timra IK Jr.	Swe-Jr.	1	0	0	0	0	....	....	....	....	....	....	....	....	....	....	....	....	....	....	....	....	....	....
	Timra IK	Sweden	50	7	10	17	4	....	....	....	....	....	....	....	....	....	7	1	0	1	0	....	....	....	....
2009-10	Timra IK	Sweden	49	12	17	29	6	....	....	....	....	....	....	....	....	....	5	0	1	1	2	....	....	....	....
2010-11	**Edmonton**	**NHL**	**80**	**15**	**19**	**34**	**16**	**3**	**0**	**0**	**180**	**8.3**	**–13**	**5**	**20.0**	**15:23**	....	....	....	....	....	....	....	....	....

Season	Club	League	GP	G	A	Pts	PIM	PP	SH	GW	S	S%	+/-	TF	F%	Min	GP	G	A	Pts	PIM	PP	SH	GW	Min
			Regular Season														Playoffs								
2011-12	**Edmonton**	**NHL**	**41**	**2**	**6**	**8**	**4**	**0**	**0**	**0**	**79**	**2.5**	**-7**	**7**	**28.6**	**13:11**	....	....	....	....	....	....	....	....	....
	Oklahoma City	AHL	34	7	18	25	4	....	....	....	....	....	....	....	....	....	14	2	9	11	2	....	....	....	....
2012-13	Oklahoma City	AHL	38	4	16	20	10	....	....	....	....	....	....	....	....	....	....	....	....	....	....	....	....	....	....
	Edmonton	**NHL**	**42**	**9**	**7**	**16**	**14**	**2**	**1**	**2**	**75**	**12.0**	**-1**	**12**	**33.3**	**14:08**	....	....	....	....	....	....	....	....	....
2013-14	**St. Louis**	**NHL**	**55**	**6**	**6**	**12**	**6**	**0**	**0**	**1**	**60**	**10.0**	**-6**	**6**	**33.3**	**10:15**	....	....	....	....	....	....	....	....	....
2014-15	**St. Louis**	**NHL**	**10**	**0**	**1**	**1**	**6**	**0**	**0**	**0**	**9**	**0.0**	**-2**	**1**	**100.0**	**9:48**	....	....	....	....	....	....	....	....	....
	Chicago Wolves	AHL	36	11	18	29	6	....	....	....	....	....	....	....	....	....	5	3	1	4	0	....	....	....	....
	NHL Totals		**228**	**32**	**39**	**71**	**46**	**5**	**1**	**3**	**403**	**7.9**		**31**	**32.3**	**13:16**	....	....	....	....	....	....	....	....	....

Traded to **St. Louis** by **Edmonton** with Edmonton's 2nd round choice (Ivan Barbashev) in 2014 Entry Draft and Edmonton's 4th round choice Adam Musil) in 2015 Entry Draft for David Perron and St. Louis' 3rd round choice (later forfeited to San Jose as a result of Edmonton's hiring of Todd McLellan as head coach – San Jose selected Mike Robinson) in 2015 Entry Draft, July 10, 2014.

PACIORETTY, Max

(pahk-OHR-eht-tee, MAX) **MTL**

Left wing. Shoots left. 6'2", 214 lbs. Born, New Canaan, CT, November 20, 1988. Montreal's 2nd choice, 22nd overall, in 2007 Entry Draft.

Season	Club	League	GP	G	A	Pts	PIM	PP	SH	GW	S	S%	+/-	TF	F%	Min	GP	G	A	Pts	PIM	PP	SH	GW	Min
2004-05	Taft Rhinos	High-CT	23	5	14	19	....	....	....	....	....	....	....	....	....	....	....	....	....	....	....	....	....	....	....
2005-06	Taft Rhinos	High-CT	26	7	26	33	....	....	....	....	....	....	....	....	....	....	....	....	....	....	....	....	....	....	....
2006-07	Sioux City	USHL	60	21	42	63	119	....	....	....	....	....	....	....	....	....	7	4	6	10	10	....	....	....	....
2007-08	U. of Michigan	CCHA	37	15	24	39	59	....	....	....	....	....	....	....	....	....	....	....	....	....	....	....	....	....	....
2008-09	**Montreal**	**NHL**	**34**	**3**	**8**	**11**	**27**	**1**	**0**	**0**	**57**	**5.3**	**-3**	**2**	**50.0**	**12:37**	....	....	....	....	....	....	....	....	....
	Hamilton	AHL	37	6	23	29	43	....	....	....	....	....	....	....	....	....	....	....	....	....	....	....	....	....	....
2009-10	**Montreal**	**NHL**	**52**	**3**	**11**	**14**	**20**	**0**	**0**	**0**	**74**	**4.1**	**-5**	**7**	**14.3**	**12:43**	....	....	....	....	....	....	....	....	....
	Hamilton	AHL	18	2	9	11	10	....	....	....	....	....	....	....	....	....	5	1	0	1	2	....	....	....	....
2010-11	**Montreal**	**NHL**	**37**	**14**	**10**	**24**	**39**	**7**	**0**	**2**	**112**	**12.5**	**-1**	**1**	**0.0**	**15:54**	....	....	....	....	....	....	....	....	....
	Hamilton	AHL	27	17	15	32	20	....	....	....	....	....	....	....	....	....	....	....	....	....	....	....	....	....	....
2011-12	**Montreal**	**NHL**	**79**	**33**	**32**	**65**	**56**	**4**	**0**	**5**	**286**	**11.5**	**2**	**5**	**20.0**	**18:16**	....	....	....	....	....	....	....	....	....
2012-13	HC Ambri-Piotta	Swiss	5	1	0	1	4	....	....	....	....	....	....	....	....	....	....	....	....	....	....	....	....	....	....
	Montreal	**NHL**	**44**	**15**	**24**	**39**	**28**	**4**	**0**	**0**	**163**	**9.2**	**8**	**7**	**28.6**	**16:31**	**4**	**0**	**0**	**0**	**4**	**0**	**0**	**0**	**17:16**
2013-14	**Montreal**	**NHL**	**73**	**39**	**21**	**60**	**35**	**10**	**1**	***11**	**270**	**14.4**	**8**	**10**	**60.0**	**18:29**	**17**	**5**	**6**	**11**	**8**	**1**	**0**	**2**	**19:19**
	United States	Olympics	5	0	1	1	4	....	....	....	....	....	....	....	....	....	....	....	....	....	....	....	....	....	....
2014-15	**Montreal**	**NHL**	**80**	**37**	**30**	**67**	**32**	**7**	**3**	**10**	**302**	**12.3**	**38**	**9**	**22.2**	**19:24**	**11**	**5**	**2**	**7**	**16**	**1**	**1**	**0**	**19:51**
	NHL Totals		**399**	**144**	**136**	**280**	**237**	**33**	**4**	**28**	**1264**	**11.4**		**41**	**31.7**	**16:55**	**32**	**10**	**8**	**18**	**28**	**2**	**1**	**2**	**19:15**

USHL All-Rookie Team (2007) • USHL Rookie of the Year (2007) • CCHA All-Rookie Team (2008) • CCHA Rookie of the Year (2008) • Bill Masterton Memorial Trophy (2012)

Signed as a free agent by **Ambri-Piotta** (Swiss), September 24, 2012.

PAETSCH, Nathan

(PASH, NAY-thuhn)

Defense. Shoots left. 6', 195 lbs. Born, Humboldt, SK, March 30, 1983. Buffalo's 8th choice, 202nd overall, in 2003 Entry Draft.

Season	Club	League	GP	G	A	Pts	PIM	PP	SH	GW	S	S%	+/-	TF	F%	Min	GP	G	A	Pts	PIM	PP	SH	GW	Min
1998-99	Tisdale Trojans	SMHL	74	20	55	75	120	....	....	....	....	....	....	....	....	....	....	....	....	....	....	....	....	....	....
	Moose Jaw	WHL	2	0	0	0	0	....	....	....	....	....	....	....	....	....	1	0	0	0	0	....	....	....	....
99-2000	Moose Jaw	WHL	68	9	35	44	49	....	....	....	....	....	....	....	....	....	4	0	1	1	0	....	....	....	....
2000-01	Moose Jaw	WHL	70	8	54	62	118	....	....	....	....	....	....	....	....	....	4	1	2	3	6	....	....	....	....
2001-02	Moose Jaw	WHL	59	16	36	52	86	....	....	....	....	....	....	....	....	....	12	0	4	4	16	....	....	....	....
2002-03	Moose Jaw	WHL	59	15	39	54	81	....	....	....	....	....	....	....	....	....	13	3	10	13	6	....	....	....	....
2003-04	Rochester	AHL	54	5	5	10	49	....	....	....	....	....	....	....	....	....	16	1	1	2	28	....	....	....	....
2004-05	Rochester	AHL	80	4	19	23	150	....	....	....	....	....	....	....	....	....	9	1	1	2	16	....	....	....	....
2005-06	**Buffalo**	**NHL**	**1**	**0**	**1**	**1**	**0**	**0**	**0**	**0**	**0**	**0.0**	**-1**	**0**	**0.0**	**15:38**	**1**	**0**	**0**	**0**	**0**	**0**	**0**	**0**	**12:06**
	Rochester	AHL	72	11	39	50	90	....	....	....	....	....	....	....	....	....	....	....	....	....	....	....	....	....	....
2006-07	**Buffalo**	**NHL**	**63**	**2**	**22**	**24**	**50**	**0**	**0**	**0**	**62**	**3.2**	**10**	**0**	**0.0**	**15:15**	....	....	....	....	....	....	....	....	....
2007-08	**Buffalo**	**NHL**	**59**	**2**	**7**	**9**	**27**	**0**	**0**	**0**	**49**	**4.1**	**3**	**0**	**0.0**	**13:38**	....	....	....	....	....	....	....	....	....
2008-09	**Buffalo**	**NHL**	**23**	**2**	**4**	**6**	**25**	**0**	**0**	**0**	**21**	**9.5**	**3**	**0**	**0.0**	**12:11**	....	....	....	....	....	....	....	....	....
2009-10	**Buffalo**	**NHL**	**11**	**1**	**1**	**2**	**6**	**0**	**0**	**0**	**9**	**11.1**	**2**	**0**	**0.0**	**9:39**	....	....	....	....	....	....	....	....	....
	Columbus	**NHL**	**10**	**0**	**0**	**0**	**6**	**0**	**0**	**0**	**8**	**0.0**	**-5**	**0**	**0.0**	**11:14**	....	....	....	....	....	....	....	....	....
2010-11	Rochester	AHL	9	1	2	3	2	....	....	....	....	....	....	....	....	....	....	....	....	....	....	....	....	....	....
	Syracuse Crunch	AHL	34	8	9	17	12	....	....	....	....	....	....	....	....	....	....	....	....	....	....	....	....	....	....
2011-12	Wolfsburg	Germany	52	7	18	25	46	....	....	....	....	....	....	....	....	....	2	0	0	0	0	....	....	....	....
2012-13	Grand Rapids	AHL	70	4	27	31	32	....	....	....	....	....	....	....	....	....	24	0	11	11	21	....	....	....	....
2013-14	Grand Rapids	AHL	68	4	27	31	40	....	....	....	....	....	....	....	....	....	10	0	5	5	4	....	....	....	....
2014-15	Grand Rapids	AHL	75	8	30	38	42	....	....	....	....	....	....	....	....	....	16	0	4	4	2	....	....	....	....
	NHL Totals		**167**	**7**	**35**	**42**	**114**	**0**	**0**	**0**	**149**	**4.7**		**0**	**0.0**	**13:39**	**1**	**0**	**0**	**0**	**0**	**0**	**0**	**0**	**12:06**

• Re-entered NHL Entry Draft. Originally Washington's 1st choice, 58th overall, in 2001 Entry Draft.

WHL East Second All-Star Team (2003)

• Missed majority of 2008-09 as a healthy reserve. Traded to **Columbus** by **Buffalo** with Vancouver's 2nd round choice (previously acquired, Columbus selected Petr Straka) in 2010 Entry Draft for Raffi Torres, March 3, 2010. • Missed majority of 2009-10 as a healthy reserve. Signed as a free agent by **Florida**, July 7, 2010. Traded to **Vancouver** by **Florida** for Sean Zimmerman, October 7, 2010. Signed as a free agent by **Wolfsburg** (Germany), June 22, 2011. Signed as a free agent by **Grand Rapids** (AHL), July 9, 2012.

PAGEAU, Jean-Gabriel

(pah-ZHOH, ZHAWN-ga-BREE-ehl) **OTT**

Center. Shoots right. 5'9", 180 lbs. Born, Ottawa, ON, November 11, 1992. Ottawa's 5th choice, 96th overall, in 2011 Entry Draft.

Season	Club	League	GP	G	A	Pts	PIM	PP	SH	GW	S	S%	+/-	TF	F%	Min	GP	G	A	Pts	PIM	PP	SH	GW	Min
2008-09	Gatineau	QAAA	37	15	16	31	6	....	....	....	....	....	....	....	....	....	....	....	....	....	....	....	....	....	....
2009-10	Gatineau	QMJHL	62	16	15	31	20	....	....	....	....	....	....	....	....	....	4	1	0	1	0	....	....	....	....
2010-11	Gatineau	QMJHL	67	32	47	79	22	....	....	....	....	....	....	....	....	....	24	13	16	29	20	....	....	....	....
2011-12	Gatineau	QMJHL	23	23	16	39	12	....	....	....	....	....	....	....	....	....	....	....	....	....	....	....	....	....	....
	Chicoutimi	QMJHL	23	9	17	26	13	....	....	....	....	....	....	....	....	....	16	4	10	14	6	....	....	....	....
2012-13	Binghamton	AHL	69	7	22	29	33	....	....	....	....	....	....	....	....	....	....	....	....	....	....	....	....	....	....
	Ottawa	**NHL**	**9**	**2**	**2**	**4**	**0**	**0**	**0**	**2**	**14**	**14.3**	**3**	**82**	**48.8**	**11:30**	**10**	**4**	**2**	**6**	**8**	**1**	**0**	**1**	**12:52**
2013-14	**Ottawa**	**NHL**	**28**	**2**	**0**	**2**	**12**	**0**	**0**	**0**	**31**	**6.5**	**-5**	**246**	**48.0**	**10:15**	....	....	....	....	....	....	....	....	....
	Binghamton	AHL	46	20	24	44	23	....	....	....	....	....	....	....	....	....	4	1	0	1	2	....	....	....	....
2014-15	**Ottawa**	**NHL**	**50**	**10**	**9**	**19**	**9**	**0**	**2**	**2**	**97**	**10.3**	**4**	**681**	**49.2**	**14:11**	**6**	**0**	**0**	**0**	**0**	**0**	**0**	**0**	**15:34**
	Binghamton	AHL	27	11	10	21	27	....	....	....	....	....	....	....	....	....	....	....	....	....	....	....	....	....	....
	NHL Totals		**87**	**14**	**11**	**25**	**21**	**0**	**2**	**4**	**142**	**9.9**		**1009**	**48.9**	**12:38**	**16**	**4**	**2**	**6**	**8**	**1**	**0**	**1**	**13:53**

PAILLE, Daniel

(PIGH-yay, DAN-yehl)

Left wing. Shoots left. 6'1", 200 lbs. Born, Welland, ON, April 15, 1984. Buffalo's 2nd choice, 20th overall, in 2002 Entry Draft.

Season	Club	League	GP	G	A	Pts	PIM	PP	SH	GW	S	S%	+/-	TF	F%	Min	GP	G	A	Pts	PIM	PP	SH	GW	Min
99-2000	Welland Cougars	ON-Jr.B	42	14	17	31	19	....	....	....	....	....	....	....	....	....	16	16	16	32	....	....	....	....	....
2000-01	Guelph Storm	OHL	64	22	31	53	57	....	....	....	....	....	....	....	....	....	4	2	0	2	2	....	....	....	....
2001-02	Guelph Storm	OHL	62	27	30	57	54	....	....	....	....	....	....	....	....	....	9	5	2	7	9	....	....	....	....
2002-03	Guelph Storm	OHL	54	30	27	57	28	....	....	....	....	....	....	....	....	....	11	8	6	14	6	....	....	....	....
2003-04	Guelph Storm	OHL	59	37	43	80	63	....	....	....	....	....	....	....	....	....	22	9	9	18	14	....	....	....	....
2004-05	Rochester	AHL	79	14	15	29	54	....	....	....	....	....	....	....	....	....	9	2	2	4	6	....	....	....	....
2005-06	**Buffalo**	**NHL**	**14**	**1**	**2**	**3**	**2**	**0**	**0**	**0**	**15**	**6.7**	**5**	**4**	**25.0**	**10:24**	....	....	....	....	....	....	....	....	....
	Rochester	AHL	45	14	13	27	29	....	....	....	....	....	....	....	....	....	....	....	....	....	....	....	....	....	....
2006-07	**Buffalo**	**NHL**	**29**	**3**	**8**	**11**	**18**	**0**	**0**	**0**	**45**	**6.7**	**5**	**6**	**33.3**	**12:47**	**1**	**0**	**0**	**0**	**0**	**0**	**0**	**0**	**4:52**
	Rochester	AHL	29	7	14	21	12	....	....	....	....	....	....	....	....	....	....	....	....	....	....	....	....	....	....
2007-08	**Buffalo**	**NHL**	**77**	**19**	**16**	**35**	**14**	**0**	**3**	**2**	**110**	**17.3**	**9**	**41**	**36.6**	**13:16**	....	....	....	....	....	....	....	....	....
2008-09	**Buffalo**	**NHL**	**73**	**12**	**15**	**27**	**20**	**0**	**0**	**2**	**80**	**15.0**	**0**	**17**	**17.7**	**11:54**	....	....	....	....	....	....	....	....	....
2009-10	**Buffalo**	**NHL**	**2**	**0**	**1**	**1**	**0**	**0**	**0**	**0**	**2**	**0.0**	**1**	**0**	**0.0**	**10:22**	....	....	....	....	....	....	....	....	....
	Boston	**NHL**	**74**	**10**	**9**	**19**	**12**	**0**	**1**	**0**	**118**	**8.5**	**-4**	**13**	**30.8**	**13:49**	**13**	**0**	**2**	**2**	**2**	**0**	**0**	**0**	**16:01**
2010-11 ♦	**Boston**	**NHL**	**43**	**6**	**7**	**13**	**28**	**0**	**1**	**0**	**48**	**12.5**	**3**	**0**	**0.0**	**11:18**	**25**	**3**	**3**	**6**	**4**	**0**	**1**	**0**	**8:43**
2011-12	**Boston**	**NHL**	**69**	**9**	**6**	**15**	**15**	**0**	**2**	**1**	**86**	**10.5**	**-5**	**7**	**28.6**	**11:30**	**7**	**1**	**0**	**1**	**2**	**0**	**0**	**0**	**9:39**
2012-13	Ilves Tampere	Finland	9	2	4	6	6	....	....	....	....	....	....	....	....	....	....	....	....	....	....	....	....	....	....
	Boston	**NHL**	**46**	**10**	**7**	**17**	**8**	**0**	**2**	**1**	**70**	**14.3**	**3**	**10**	**20.0**	**12:41**	**22**	**4**	**5**	**9**	**0**	**0**	**1**	**3**	**12:32**
2013-14	**Boston**	**NHL**	**72**	**9**	**9**	**18**	**6**	**0**	**1**	**1**	**71**	**12.7**	**9**	**17**	**64.7**	**10:58**	**7**	**1**	**0**	**1**	**2**	**0**	**0**	**0**	**11:31**
2014-15	**Boston**	**NHL**	**71**	**6**	**7**	**13**	**12**	**0**	**1**	**1**	**66**	**9.1**	**-9**	**7**	**28.6**	**11:31**	....	....	....	....	....	....	....	....	....
	NHL Totals		**570**	**85**	**87**	**172**	**135**	**0**	**11**	**8**	**711**	**12.0**		**122**	**34.4**	**12:08**	**75**	**9**	**10**	**19**	**10**	**0**	**2**	**3**	**11:24**

Traded to **Boston** by **Buffalo** for Boston's 3rd round choice (Kevin Sundher) in 2010 Entry Draft, October 20, 2009. Signed as a free agent by **Ilves Tampere** (Finland), December 2, 2012.

PAKARINEN, Iiro
(pa-ka-REE-nehn, YEE-roh) **EDM**

Right wing. Shoots right. 6'1", 198 lbs. Born, Suonenjoki, Finland, August 25, 1991. Florida's 10th choice, 184th overall, in 2011 Entry Draft.

			Regular Season														Playoffs								
Season	Club	League	GP	G	A	Pts	PIM	PP	SH	GW	S	S%	+/-	TF	F%	Min	GP	G	A	Pts	PIM	PP	SH	GW	Min
2006-07	KalPa Kuopio U18	Fin-U18	2	1	1	2	0																		
2007-08	KalPa Kuopio U18	Fin-U18	20	14	14	28	59										2	0	0	0	4				
	KalPa Kuopio Jr.	Fin-Jr.	1	0	0	0	0																		
2008-09	KalPa Kuopio Jr.	Fin-Jr.	37	11	10	21	44										5	1	0	1	2				
2009-10	Suomi U20	Finland-2	6	1	2	3	6																		
	KalPa Kuopio Jr.	Fin-Jr.	11	8	4	12	10																		
	KalPa Kuopio	Finland	38	3	5	8	37										12	3	0	3	8				
2010-11	Suomi U20	Finland-2	3	0	0	0	0																		
	KalPa Kuopio Jr.	Fin-Jr.	4	3	2	5	6																		
	KalPa Kuopio	Finland	47	7	3	10	34										7	1	0	1	37				
2011-12	KalPa Kuopio	Finland	54	10	3	13	47										7	2	2	4	0				
2012-13	HIFK Helsinki	Finland	33	5	7	12	6										6	3	0	3	4				
2013-14	HIFK Helsinki	Finland	60	20	10	30	32										2	0	0	0	2				
2014-15	**Edmonton**	**NHL**	**17**	**1**	**2**	**3**	**2**	**0**	**0**	**0**	**34**	**2.9**	**–4**	**1**	**100.0**	**10:08**									
	Oklahoma City	AHL	39	17	11	28	20																		
	NHL Totals		**17**	**1**	**2**	**3**	**2**	**0**	**0**	**0**	**34**	**2.9**		**1**	**100.0**	**10:08**									

Signed as a free agent by **Edmonton**, June 16, 2014.

PALAT, Ondrej
(PAL-at, AWN-dray) **T.B.**

Left wing. Shoots left. 6', 180 lbs. Born, Frydek-Mistek, Czech., March 28, 1991. Tampa Bay's 6th choice, 208th overall, in 2011 Entry Draft.

Season	Club	League	GP	G	A	Pts	PIM	PP	SH	GW	S	S%	+/-	TF	F%	Min	GP	G	A	Pts	PIM	PP	SH	GW	Min
2005-06	HC Vitkovice U17	CzR-U17	22	2	7	9	4										1	0	0	0	0				
2006-07	HC Vitkovice U17	CzR-U17	33	32	24	56	18										9	3	6	9	4				
	HC Vitkovice Jr.	CzRep-Jr.	13	5	2	7	12										3	0	0	0	0				
2007-08	HC Vitkovice U17	CzR-U17	4	2	3	5	0										2	1	1	2	2				
	HC Vitkovice Jr.	CzRep-Jr.	42	19	18	37	28										2	1	0	1	2				
2008-09	HC Vitkovice Jr.	CzRep-Jr.	42	23	33	56	14										10	8	6	14	12				
2009-10	Drummondville	QMJHL	59	17	23	40	24										7	1	1	2	0				
2010-11	Drummondville	QMJHL	61	39	57	96	24										10	4	7	11	6				
2011-12	Norfolk Admirals	AHL	61	9	21	30	10										18	4	5	9	6				
2012-13	Syracuse Crunch	AHL	56	13	39	52	35										18	7	*19	*26	12				
	Tampa Bay	**NHL**	**14**	**2**	**2**	**4**	**0**	**0**	**0**	**1**	**16**	**12.5**	**5**	**6**	**0.0**	**11:44**									
2013-14	**Tampa Bay**	**NHL**	**81**	**23**	**36**	**59**	**20**	**3**	**2**	**3**	**165**	**13.9**	**32**	**37**	**13.5**	**18:02**	**3**	**2**	**1**	**3**	**0**	**1**	**1**	**0**	**18:02**
	Czech Republic	Olympics	4	0	0	0	0																		
2014-15	**Tampa Bay**	**NHL**	**75**	**16**	**47**	**63**	**24**	**3**	**1**	**5**	**139**	**11.5**	**31**	**35**	**28.6**	**17:26**	**26**	**8**	**8**	**16**	**12**	**4**	**0**	**0**	**19:10**
	NHL Totals		**170**	**41**	**85**	**126**	**44**	**6**	**3**	**9**	**320**	**12.8**		**78**	**19.2**	**17:15**	**29**	**10**	**9**	**19**	**12**	**5**	**1**	**0**	**19:03**

NHL All-Rookie Team (2014)

PALIOTTA, Michael
(pal-ee-AW-tuh, MIGH-kuhl) **CBJ**

Defense. Shoots right. 6'3", 207 lbs. Born, Westport, CT, April 6, 1993. Chicago's 5th choice, 70th overall, in 2011 Entry Draft.

Season	Club	League	GP	G	A	Pts	PIM	PP	SH	GW	S	S%	+/-	TF	F%	Min	GP	G	A	Pts	PIM	PP	SH	GW	Min
2008-09	Choate-Rosemary	High-CT	24	1	14	15	....																		
2009-10	USNTDP	USHL	32	1	6	7	43																		
	USNTDP	U-17	18	1	6	7	10																		
2010-11	USNTDP	USHL	24	0	5	5	35																		
	USNTDP	U-18	36	1	9	10	42																		
2011-12	U. of Vermont	H-East	30	4	6	10	44																		
2012-13	U. of Vermont	H-East	35	1	9	10	50																		
2013-14	U. of Vermont	H-East	38	5	22	27	51																		
2014-15	U. of Vermont	H-East	41	9	27	36	40																		
	Chicago	**NHL**	**1**	**0**	**1**	**1**	**0**	**0**	**0**	**0**	**2**	**0.0**	**0**	**0**	**0.0**	**12:45**									
	NHL Totals		**1**	**0**	**1**	**1**	**0**	**0**	**0**	**0**	**2**	**0.0**		**0**	**0.0**	**12:45**									

Hockey East Second All-Star Team (2015) • NCAA East Second All-American Team (2015)

Traded to **Columbus** by **Chicago** with Brandon Saad and Alex Broadhurst for Artem Anisimov, Jeremy Morin, Corey Tropp, Marko Dano and Columbus' 4th round choice in 2016 Entry Draft, June 30, 2015.

PALMIERI, Kyle
(pawl-mee-AIR-ee, KIGHL) **N.J.**

Right wing. Shoots right. 5'11", 195 lbs. Born, Smithtown, NY, February 1, 1991. Anaheim's 2nd choice, 26th overall, in 2009 Entry Draft.

Season	Club	League	GP	G	A	Pts	PIM	PP	SH	GW	S	S%	+/-	TF	F%	Min	GP	G	A	Pts	PIM	PP	SH	GW	Min
2007-08	USNTDP	NAHL	32	15	10	25	43																		
	USNTDP	U-17	7	5	0	5	8																		
	USNTDP	U-18	27	9	9	18	20																		
2008-09	USNTDP	NAHL	5	1	1	2	2																		
	USNTDP	U-18	28	14	14	28	49																		
2009-10	U. of Notre Dame	CCHA	33	9	8	17	36																		
2010-11	**Anaheim**	**NHL**	**10**	**1**	**0**	**1**	**0**	**0**	**0**	**0**	**10**	**10.0**	**–1**	**0**	**0.0**	**8:41**	**1**	**0**	**0**	**0**	**0**	**0**	**0**	**0**	**10:07**
	Syracuse Crunch	AHL	62	29	22	51	56																		
2011-12	**Anaheim**	**NHL**	**18**	**4**	**3**	**7**	**6**	**0**	**0**	**0**	**34**	**11.8**	**3**	**2**	**100.0**	**11:31**									
	Syracuse Crunch	AHL	51	33	25	58	53										4	1	1	2	0				
2012-13	Norfolk Admirals	AHL	33	13	12	25	54																		
	Anaheim	**NHL**	**42**	**10**	**11**	**21**	**9**	**2**	**0**	**5**	**92**	**10.9**	**2**	**12**	**8.3**	**12:20**	**7**	**3**	**2**	**5**	**4**	**0**	**0**	**0**	**10:34**
2013-14	**Anaheim**	**NHL**	**71**	**14**	**17**	**31**	**38**	**0**	**0**	**4**	**147**	**9.5**	**9**	**23**	**39.1**	**11:57**	**9**	**3**	**0**	**3**	**14**	**0**	**0**	**0**	**10:12**
2014-15	**Anaheim**	**NHL**	**57**	**14**	**15**	**29**	**37**	**5**	**0**	**4**	**112**	**12.5**	**–2**	**12**	**50.0**	**14:06**	**16**	**1**	**3**	**4**	**4**	**0**	**0**	**1**	**13:12**
	Norfolk Admirals	AHL	2	0	0	0	4																		
	NHL Totals		**198**	**43**	**46**	**89**	**90**	**7**	**0**	**13**	**395**	**10.9**		**49**	**36.7**	**12:26**	**33**	**7**	**5**	**12**	**22**	**0**	**0**	**1**	**11:44**

AHL First All-Star Team (2012)

Traded to **New Jersey** by **Anaheim** for Florida's 2nd round choice (previously acquired, later traded to NY Rangers – NY Rangers selected Ryan Gropp) in 2015 Entry Draft and New Jersey's 3rd round choice in 2016 Entry Draft, June 27, 2015.

PALUSHAJ, Aaron
(puh-LOO-shigh, AIR-ruhn) **PHI**

Right wing. Shoots right. 6', 188 lbs. Born, Livonia, MI, September 7, 1989. St. Louis' 5th choice, 44th overall, in 2007 Entry Draft.

Season	Club	League	GP	G	A	Pts	PIM	PP	SH	GW	S	S%	+/-	TF	F%	Min	GP	G	A	Pts	PIM	PP	SH	GW	Min
2005-06	Des Moines	USHL	58	10	23	33	53										11	2	4	6	15				
2006-07	Des Moines	USHL	56	22	45	67	62										8	6	5	11	6				
2007-08	U. of Michigan	CCHA	43	10	*34	44	22																		
2008-09	U. of Michigan	CCHA	39	13	*37	*50	26																		
	Peoria Rivermen	AHL	4	2	0	2	4										4	0	1	1	2				
2009-10	Peoria Rivermen	AHL	44	5	17	22	22																		
	Hamilton	AHL	18	3	7	10	8										19	2	10	12	28				
2010-11	**Montreal**	**NHL**	**3**	**0**	**0**	**0**	**2**	**0**	**0**	**0**	**3**	**0.0**	**1**	**1**	**0.0**	**8:31**									
	Hamilton	AHL	68	22	35	57	42										19	7	12	19	14				
2011-12	**Montreal**	**NHL**	**38**	**1**	**4**	**5**	**8**	**0**	**0**	**0**	**37**	**2.7**	**1**	**4**	**0.0**	**7:34**									
	Hamilton	AHL	35	15	20	35	35																		
2012-13	Hamilton	AHL	21	7	3	10	18																		
	Colorado	**NHL**	**25**	**2**	**7**	**9**	**8**	**0**	**0**	**0**	**29**	**6.9**	**–2**	**8**	**25.0**	**11:19**									
2013-14	**Carolina**	**NHL**	**2**	**0**	**0**	**0**	**0**	**0**	**0**	**0**	**2**	**0.0**	**–1**	**1**	**0.0**	**9:20**									
	Charlotte	AHL	68	22	36	58	80																		
2014-15	Zagreb	KHL	25	3	9	12	26																		
	Avtomobilist	KHL	28	4	5	9	22										5	0	0	0	0				
	NHL Totals		**68**	**3**	**11**	**14**	**18**	**0**	**0**	**0**	**71**	**4.2**		**14**	**14.3**	**9:02**									

CCHA First All-Star Team (2009) • NCAA West First All-American Team (2009)

Traded to **Montreal** by **St. Louis** for Matt D'Agostini, March 2, 2010. Claimed on waivers by **Colorado** from **Montreal**, February 5, 2013. Signed as a free agent by **Carolina**, July 11, 2013. Signed as a free agent by **Zagreb** (KHL), September 15, 2014. Signed as a free agent by **Avtomobilist Yekaterinburg** (KHL), November 21, 2014. Signed as a free agent by **Philadelphia**, May 21, 2015.

			Regular Season														Playoffs								
Season	Club	League	GP	G	A	Pts	PIM	PP	SH	GW	S	S%	+/-	TF	F%	Min	GP	G	A	Pts	PIM	PP	SH	GW	Min

PANIK, Richard — (PAH-nihk, RIH-chuhrd) — TOR

Right wing. Shoots left. 6'1", 208 lbs.   Born, Martin, Czech., February 7, 1991. Tampa Bay's 3rd choice, 52nd overall, in 2009 Entry Draft.

Season	Club	League	GP	G	A	Pts	PIM	PP	SH	GW	S	S%	+/-	TF	F%	Min	GP	G	A	Pts	PIM	PP	SH	GW	Min
2005-06	MHC Martin U18	Svk-U18	40	11	13	24	20	....	....	....	....	....	....				4	4	2	6	4	....	....	....	
2006-07	HC Trinec U17	CzR-U17	12	10	6	16	48	....	....	....	....	....	....				3	1	4	5	8	....	....	....	
	HC Trinec Jr.	CzRep-Jr.	27	16	9	25	30	....	....	....	....	....	....				4	1	4	5	6	....	....	....	
2007-08	HC Trinec Jr.	CzRep-Jr.	39	35	27	62	70	....	....	....	....	....	....				8	8	4	12	52	....	....	....	
	HC Ocelari Trinec	CzRep	6	0	0	0	0	....	....	....	....	....	....				....	....	....	....	....	....	....	....	
2008-09	HC Trinec Jr.	CzRep-Jr.	16	10	9	19	36	....	....	....	....	....	....				8	6	1	7	41	....	....	....	
	HC Havirov	CzRep-2	3	2	1	3	0	....	....	....	....	....	....				....	....	....	....	....	....	....	....	
	HC Ocelari Trinec	CzRep	15	1	1	2	4	....	....	....	....	....	....				4	0	0	0	0	....	....	....	
2009-10	Windsor Spitfires	OHL	33	9	9	18	19	....	....	....	....	....	....				....	....	....	....	....	....	....	....	
	Belleville Bulls	OHL	27	12	11	23	36	....	....	....	....	....	....				....	....	....	....	....	....	....	....	
	Norfolk Admirals	AHL	5	0	1	1	0	....	....	....	....	....	....				....	....	....	....	....	....	....	....	
2010-11	Belleville Bulls	OHL	27	14	17	31	33	....	....	....	....	....	....				....	....	....	....	....	....	....	....	
	Guelph Storm	OHL	24	13	12	25	42	....	....	....	....	....	....				6	1	2	3	10	....	....	....	
2011-12	Norfolk Admirals	AHL	64	19	22	41	62	....	....	....	....	....	....				18	5	1	6	23	....	....	....	
2012-13	Syracuse Crunch	AHL	51	22	19	41	81	....	....	....	....	....	....				16	9	5	14	59	....	....	....	
	Tampa Bay	**NHL**	25	5	4	9	4	1	0	1	34	14.7	-2	3	33.3	11:20	....	....	....	....	....	....	....	....	
2013-14	**Tampa Bay**	**NHL**	50	3	10	13	21	0	0	0	56	5.4	-9	8	37.5	12:42	2	0	0	0	4	0	0	0	15:03
	Syracuse Crunch	AHL	13	3	8	11	8	....	....	....	....	....	....				....	....	....	....	....	....	....	....	
	Slovakia	Olympics	4	0	0	0	0	....	....	....	....	....	....				....	....	....	....	....	....	....	....	
2014-15	**Toronto**	**NHL**	76	11	6	17	49	2	0	1	87	12.6	-8	7	28.6	11:39	....	....	....	....	....	....	....	....	
	NHL Totals		151	19	20	39	74	3	0	2	177	10.7		18	33.3	11:56	2	0	0	0	4	0	0	0	15:03

Claimed on waivers by **Toronto** from **Tampa Bay**, October 8, 2014.

PAQUETTE, Cedric — (pah-KEHT, SEH-drihk) — T.B.

Center. Shoots left. 6'1", 198 lbs.   Born, Gaspe, QC, August 13, 1993. Tampa Bay's 6th choice, 101st overall, in 2012 Entry Draft.

Season	Club	League	GP	G	A	Pts	PIM	PP	SH	GW	S	S%	+/-	TF	F%	Min	GP	G	A	Pts	PIM	PP	SH	GW	Min
2008-09	Ecole Notre Dame	QAAA	45	12	6	18	34	....	....	....	....	....	....				4	0	0	0	4	....	....	....	
2009-10	Ecole Notre Dame	QAAA	32	10	18	28	83	....	....	....	....	....	....				8	5	2	7	24	....	....	....	
2010-11	Ecole Notre Dame	QAAA	34	28	27	55	102	....	....	....	....	....	....				17	5	11	16	36	....	....	....	
2011-12	Blainville-Bois.	QMJHL	63	31	17	48	88	....	....	....	....	....	....				11	7	10	17	22	....	....	....	
2012-13	Blainville-Bois.	QMJHL	63	27	56	83	103	....	....	....	....	....	....				15	7	5	12	33	....	....	....	
	Syracuse Crunch	AHL	....	....	....	....	....	....	....	....	....	....	....				3	0	0	0	0	....	....	....	
2013-14	**Tampa Bay**	**NHL**	2	0	1	1	0	0	0	0	1	0.0	1	29	55.2	14:33	4	0	2	2	16	0	0	0	10:34
	Syracuse Crunch	AHL	70	20	24	44	153	....	....	....	....	....	....				....	....	....	....	....	....	....	....	
2014-15	**Tampa Bay**	**NHL**	64	12	7	19	51	0	2	3	91	13.2	4	235	47.7	13:37	24	3	0	3	28	0	1	1	12:48
	Syracuse Crunch	AHL	5	4	3	7	7	....	....	....	....	....	....				....	....	....	....	....	....	....	....	
	NHL Totals		66	12	8	20	51	0	2	3	92	13.0		264	48.5	13:38	28	3	2	5	44	0	1	1	12:29

PARDY, Adam — (PAHR-dee, A-duhm) — WPG

Defense. Shoots left. 6'4", 220 lbs.   Born, Bonavista, NL, March 29, 1984. Calgary's 6th choice, 173rd overall, in 2004 Entry Draft.

Season	Club	League	GP	G	A	Pts	PIM	PP	SH	GW	S	S%	+/-	TF	F%	Min	GP	G	A	Pts	PIM	PP	SH	GW	Min
2002-03	Yarmouth	MJrHL	1	0	0	0	2	....	....	....	....	....	....				....	....	....	....	....	....	....	....	
	Antigonish	MJrHL	31	5	16	21	42	....	....	....	....	....	....				....	....	....	....	....	....	....	....	
	Cape Breton	QMJHL	7	0	1	1	2	....	....	....	....	....	....				2	0	0	0	0	....	....	....	
2003-04	Cape Breton	QMJHL	68	4	12	16	137	....	....	....	....	....	....				5	0	1	1	8	....	....	....	
2004-05	Cape Breton	QMJHL	69	12	27	39	163	....	....	....	....	....	....				5	2	2	4	8	....	....	....	
2005-06	Omaha	AHL	24	0	0	0	18	....	....	....	....	....	....				....	....	....	....	....	....	....	....	
	Las Vegas	ECHL	41	1	11	12	55	....	....	....	....	....	....				10	2	1	3	12	....	....	....	
2006-07	Omaha	AHL	70	2	6	8	60	....	....	....	....	....	....				6	1	1	2	0	....	....	....	
2007-08	Quad City Flames	AHL	65	5	13	18	67	....	....	....	....	....	....				....	....	....	....	....	....	....	....	
2008-09	**Calgary**	**NHL**	60	1	9	10	69	0	0	0	38	2.6	3	0	0.0	15:00	6	0	0	0	0	0	0	0	14:51
2009-10	**Calgary**	**NHL**	57	2	7	9	48	0	0	0	40	5.0	-3	0	0.0	15:51	....	....	....	....	....	....	....	....	
2010-11	**Calgary**	**NHL**	30	1	6	7	24	0	0	0	36	2.8	3	0	0.0	14:41	....	....	....	....	....	....	....	....	
2011-12	**Dallas**	**NHL**	36	0	3	3	16	0	0	0	29	0.0	-5	0	0.0	16:28	....	....	....	....	....	....	....	....	
	Texas Stars	AHL	2	0	4	4	2	....	....	....	....	....	....				....	....	....	....	....	....	....	....	
2012-13	Rochester	AHL	21	2	7	9	22	....	....	....	....	....	....				....	....	....	....	....	....	....	....	
	Buffalo	**NHL**	17	0	4	4	14	0	0	0	6	0.0	4	0	0.0	16:30	....	....	....	....	....	....	....	....	
2013-14	**Winnipeg**	**NHL**	60	0	6	6	38	0	0	0	47	0.0	4	0	0.0	14:25	....	....	....	....	....	....	....	....	
	St. John's IceCaps	AHL	3	0	0	0	9	....	....	....	....	....	....				....	....	....	....	....	....	....	....	
2014-15	**Winnipeg**	**NHL**	55	0	9	9	40	0	0	0	29	0.0	9	0	0.0	15:01	2	1	0	1	2	0	0	0	18:16
	NHL Totals		315	4	44	48	249	0	0	0	225	1.8		0	0.0	15:16	8	1	2	3	7	0	0	0	15:43

• Missed majority of 2010-11 due to shoulder (October 10, 2010 vs. Los Angeles) and upper-body (February 7, 2011 vs. Chicago) injuries. Signed as a free agent by **Dallas**, July 1, 2011. Traded to **Buffalo** by **Dallas** with Steve Ott for Derek Roy, July 2, 2012. Signed as a free agent by **Winnipeg**, July 6, 2013.

PARENT, Ryan — (PAIR-ehnt, RIGH-uhn)

Defense. Shoots left. 6'3", 198 lbs.   Born, Prince Albert, SK, March 17, 1987. Nashville's 1st choice, 18th overall, in 2005 Entry Draft.

Season	Club	League	GP	G	A	Pts	PIM	PP	SH	GW	S	S%	+/-	TF	F%	Min	GP	G	A	Pts	PIM	PP	SH	GW	Min
2002-03	Waterloo Siskins	ON-Jr.B	41	2	8	10	35	....	....	....	....	....	....				....	....	....	....	....	....	....	....	
2003-04	Guelph Storm	OHL	58	1	5	6	18	....	....	....	....	....	....				22	0	0	0	2	....	....	....	
2004-05	Guelph Storm	OHL	66	2	17	19	36	....	....	....	....	....	....				4	0	1	1	4	....	....	....	
2005-06	Guelph Storm	OHL	60	4	17	21	122	....	....	....	....	....	....				15	1	4	5	24	....	....	....	
	Milwaukee	AHL	....	....	....	....	....	....	....	....	....	....	....				10	0	0	0	4	....	....	....	
2006-07	**Philadelphia**	**NHL**	1	0	0	0	0	0	0	0	1	0.0	0	0	0.0	14:10	....	....	....	....	....	....	....	....	
	Philadelphia	AHL	6	1	0	1	4	....	....	....	....	....	....				....	....	....	....	....	....	....	....	
	Guelph Storm	OHL	43	3	7	10	86	....	....	....	....	....	....				4	0	1	1	14	....	....	....	
2007-08	**Philadelphia**	**NHL**	22	0	0	0	6	0	0	0	9	0.0	-4	0	0.0	14:59	4	0	1	1	0	0	0	0	16:36
	Philadelphia	AHL	53	1	7	8	42	....	....	....	....	....	....				....	....	....	....	....	....	....	....	
2008-09	**Philadelphia**	**NHL**	31	0	4	4	10	0	0	0	9	0.0	3	0	0.0	18:12	6	0	0	0	0	0	0	0	18:52
	Philadelphia	AHL	15	0	1	1	18	....	....	....	....	....	....				....	....	....	....	....	....	....	....	
2009-10	**Philadelphia**	**NHL**	48	1	2	3	20	0	0	0	27	3.7	-14	0	0.0	14:46	17	1	0	1	2	0	0	0	7:28
2010-11	**Vancouver**	**NHL**	4	0	0	0	0	0	0	0	3	0.0	-3	0	0.0	13:54	....	....	....	....	....	....	....	....	
	Manitoba Moose	AHL	39	1	1	2	56	....	....	....	....	....	....				....	....	....	....	....	....	....	....	
2011-12	Chicago Wolves	AHL	22	1	5	6	31	....	....	....	....	....	....				5	0	1	1	10	....	....	....	
2012-13	Norfolk Admirals	AHL	56	0	5	5	52	....	....	....	....	....	....				....	....	....	....	....	....	....	....	
2013-14	Norfolk Admirals	AHL	26	0	3	3	26	....	....	....	....	....	....				5	0	0	0	4	....	....	....	
2014-15	Ontario Reign	ECHL	6	0	1	1	2	....	....	....	....	....	....				....	....	....	....	....	....	....	....	
	St. John's IceCaps	AHL	22	0	2	2	16	....	....	....	....	....	....				....	....	....	....	....	....	....	....	
	Wilkes-Barre	AHL						....	....	....	....	....	....				....	....	....	....	....	....	....	....	
	NHL Totals		106	1	6	7	36	0	0	0	49	2.0		0	0.0	15:47	27	1	1	2	8	0	0	0	11:21

OHL Second All-Star Team (2006, 2007).

Traded to **Philadelphia** by **Nashville** with Scottie Upshall and Nashville's 1st (later traded back to Nashville - Nashville selected Jonathon Blum) and 3rd (later traded to Washington - Washington selected Phil Desimone) round choices in 2007 Entry Draft for Peter Forsberg, February 15, 2007. Traded to **Nashville** by **Philadelphia** with future considerations for Dan Hamhuis, June 19, 2010. Traded to **Vancouver** by **Nashville** with Jonas Andersson for Shane O'Brien and Dan Gendur, October 5, 2010. • Missed majority of 2011-12 due to various injuries. Signed to a PTO (professional tryout) contract by **Norfolk** (AHL), October 24, 2012. • Missed majority of 2013-14 as a healthy reserve. Signed to a PTO (professional tryout) contract by **St. John's** (AHL), December 18, 2014. . Signed to a PTO (professional tryout) contract by **Wilkes-Barre** (AHL), April 19, 2015.

PARENTEAU, Pierre-Alexandre — (pair-ehn-TOH, PEE-AIR-al-EHX-ahn-druh) — TOR

Left wing. Shoots right. 6', 193 lbs.   Born, Hull, QC, March 24, 1983. Anaheim's 11th choice, 264th overall, in 2001 Entry Draft.

Season	Club	League	GP	G	A	Pts	PIM	PP	SH	GW	S	S%	+/-	TF	F%	Min	GP	G	A	Pts	PIM	PP	SH	GW	Min
99-2000	C.C. Lemoyne	QAAA	40	25	40	65	18	....	....	....	....	....	....				16	4	9	13	8	....	....	....	
2000-01	Moncton Wildcats	QMJHL	45	10	19	29	38	....	....	....	....	....	....				....	....	....	....	....	....	....	....	
	Chicoutimi	QMJHL	28	10	13	23	14	....	....	....	....	....	....				7	4	7	11	2	....	....	....	
2001-02	Chicoutimi	QMJHL	68	51	67	118	120	....	....	....	....	....	....				4	3	1	4	10	....	....	....	
2002-03	Chicoutimi	QMJHL	31	20	35	55	56	....	....	....	....	....	....				....	....	....	....	....	....	....	....	
	Sherbrooke	QMJHL	28	13	35	48	84	....	....	....	....	....	....				12	8	11	19	6	....	....	....	
2003-04	Cincinnati	AHL	66	14	16	30	20	....	....	....	....	....	....				7	1	2	3	6	....	....	....	

			Regular Season														Playoffs								
Season	Club	League	GP	G	A	Pts	PIM	PP	SH	GW	S	S%	+/-	TF	F%	Min	GP	G	A	Pts	PIM	PP	SH	GW	Min
2004-05	Cincinnati	AHL	76	17	24	41	58	....	....	....	....	....	....	....	....	....	9	2	0	2	8	....	....	....	....
2005-06	Portland Pirates	AHL	56	22	27	49	42	....	....	....	....	....	....	....	....	....	19	5	17	22	24	....	....	....	....
	Augusta Lynx	ECHL	2	0	1	1	0	....	....	....	....	....	....	....	....	....	....	....	....	....	....	....	....	....	....
2006-07	Portland Pirates	AHL	28	15	13	28	35	....	....	....	....	....	....	....	....	....	....	....	....	....	....	....	....	....	....
	Chicago	NHL	5	0	1	1	2	0	0	0	7	0.0	-1	2	50.0	11:05	....	....	....	....	....	....	....	....	....
	Norfolk Admirals	AHL	40	15	36	51	12	....	....	....	....	....	....	....	....	....	6	2	1	3	2	....	....	....	....
2007-08	Hartford	AHL	75	34	47	81	81	....	....	....	....	....	....	....	....	....	5	3	2	5	13	....	....	....	....
2008-09	Hartford	AHL	74	29	49	78	142	....	....	....	....	....	....	....	....	....	....	....	....	....	....	....	....	....	....
2009-10	NY Rangers	NHL	22	3	5	8	4	1	0	0	38	7.9	-2	12	33.3	13:42	....	....	....	....	....	....	....	....	....
	Hartford	AHL	35	20	25	45	63	....	....	....	....	....	....	....	....	....	....	....	....	....	....	....	....	....	....
2010-11	NY Islanders	NHL	81	20	33	53	46	9	0	2	161	12.4	-8	30	36.7	18:13	....	....	....	....	....	....	....	....	....
2011-12	NY Islanders	NHL	80	18	49	67	89	6	0	2	167	10.8	-8	26	38.5	18:39	....	....	....	....	....	....	....	....	....
2012-13	Colorado	NHL	48	18	25	43	38	6	0	1	105	17.1	-11	13	7.7	19:09	....	....	....	....	....	....	....	....	....
2013-14	Colorado	NHL	55	14	19	33	30	1	0	1	110	12.7	3	14	14.3	16:57	7	1	2	3	2	0	0	0	17:53
2014-15	Montreal	NHL	56	8	14	22	30	3	0	1	97	8.2	0	26	38.5	14:59	8	1	1	2	2	0	0	1	14:22
	NHL Totals		347	81	146	227	239	26	0	7	685	11.8		123	31.7	17:20	15	2	3	5	4	0	0	1	16:01

AHL Second All-Star Team (2008) • AHL First All-Star Team (2009)

Traded to **Chicago** by **Anaheim** with Bruno St. Jacques for Sebastien Caron, Matt Keith and Chris Durno, December 28, 2006. Traded to **NY Rangers** by **Chicago** for future considerations, October 11, 2007. Signed as a free agent by **NY Islanders**, July 2, 2010. Signed as a free agent by **Colorado**, July 1, 2012. Traded to **Montreal** by **Colorado** with Colorado's 5th round choice (Matthew Bradley) in 2015 Entry Draft for Daniel Briere, June 30, 2014. Signed as a free agent by **Toronto**, July 1, 2015.

PARISE, Zach (pah-REE-say, ZAK) MIN

Left wing. Shoots left. 5'11", 197 lbs. Born, Minneapolis, MN, July 28, 1984. New Jersey's 1st choice, 17th overall, in 2003 Entry Draft.

Season	Club	League	GP	G	A	Pts	PIM	PP	SH	GW	S	S%	+/-	TF	F%	Min	GP	G	A	Pts	PIM	PP	SH	GW	Min
2000-01	Shat.-St. Mary's	High-MN	58	69	93	162	....	....	....	....	....	....	....	....	....	....	....	....	....	....	....	....	....	....	....
2001-02	Shat.-St. Mary's	High-MN	67	77	101	178	58	....	....	....	....	....	....	....	....	....	....	....	....	....	....	....	....	....	....
	USNTDP	U-18	12	7	7	14	6	....	....	....	....	....	....	....	....	....	....	....	....	....	....	....	....	....	....
2002-03	North Dakota	WCHA	39	26	35	61	34	....	....	....	....	....	....	....	....	....	....	....	....	....	....	....	....	....	....
2003-04	North Dakota	WCHA	37	23	32	55	24	....	....	....	....	....	....	....	....	....	....	....	....	....	....	....	....	....	....
2004-05	Albany River Rats	AHL	73	18	40	58	56	....	....	....	....	....	....	....	....	....	....	....	....	....	....	....	....	....	....
2005-06	New Jersey	NHL	81	14	18	32	28	2	0	5	133	10.5	-1	162	42.6	13:08	9	1	2	3	2	0	0	0	15:03
2006-07	New Jersey	NHL	82	31	31	62	30	9	0	7	247	12.6	-3	52	44.2	17:32	11	7	3	10	8	2	0	1	19:08
2007-08	New Jersey	NHL	81	32	33	65	25	10	1	8	266	12.0	13	104	48.1	18:04	5	1	4	5	2	1	0	0	18:29
2008-09	New Jersey	NHL	82	45	49	94	24	14	0	8	364	12.4	30	121	44.6	18:45	7	3	3	6	2	1	0	1	19:02
2009-10	New Jersey	NHL	81	38	44	82	32	9	1	5	347	11.0	24	48	37.5	19:46	5	1	3	4	0	0	1	0	20:44
	United States	Olympics	6	4	4	8	0	....	....	....	....	....	....	....	....	....	....	....	....	....	....	....	....	....	....
2010-11	New Jersey	NHL	13	3	3	6	6	0	0	1	49	6.1	-1	11	36.4	19:51	....	....	....	....	....	....	....	....	....
2011-12	New Jersey	NHL	82	31	38	69	32	7	3	3	293	10.6	-5	63	47.6	21:29	24	*8	7	15	4	3	0	1	20:53
2012-13	Minnesota	NHL	48	18	20	38	16	7	0	4	182	9.9	2	9	33.3	20:40	5	1	0	1	2	0	0	0	21:24
2013-14	Minnesota	NHL	67	29	27	56	30	14	1	5	245	11.8	10	24	41.7	20:26	13	4	10	14	6	2	0	1	20:29
	United States	Olympics	6	1	0	1	0	....	....	....	....	....	....	....	....	....	....	....	....	....	....	....	....	....	....
2014-15	Minnesota	NHL	74	33	29	62	41	11	0	3	259	12.7	21	12	16.7	19:11	10	4	6	10	4	1	1	0	18:53
	NHL Totals		691	274	292	566	264	83	6	49	2385	11.5		606	43.4	18:41	89	30	38	68	30	10	2	4	19:32

WCHA All-Rookie Team (2003) • WCHA First All-Star Team (2004) • NCAA West First All-American Team (2004) • NHL Second All-Star Team (2009) • Olympic All-Star Team (2010)

Played in NHL All-Star Game (2009)

• Missed majority of 2010-11 due to knee injury at Los Angeles, October 30, 2010. Signed as a free agent by **Minnesota**, July 4, 2012.

PASTRNAK, David (PAS-tuhr-nak, DAY-vihd) BOS

Left wing. Shoots right. 6', 167 lbs. Born, Havirov, Czech Republic, May 25, 1996. Boston's 1st choice, 25th overall, in 2014 Entry Draft.

Season	Club	League	GP	G	A	Pts	PIM	PP	SH	GW	S	S%	+/-	TF	F%	Min	GP	G	A	Pts	PIM	PP	SH	GW	Min
2010-11	HC Havirov U18	CzR-U18	16	7	12	19	4	....	....	....	....	....	....	....	....	....	1	0	0	0	0	....	....	....	....
2011-12	HC Havirov U18	CzR-U18	17	18	22	40	28	....	....	....	....	....	....	....	....	....	....	....	....	....	....	....	....	....	....
	HC Trinec U18	CzR-U18	31	33	14	47	6	....	....	....	....	....	....	....	....	....	....	....	....	....	....	....	....	....	....
	AZ Havirov Jr.	CzRep-Jr.	3	0	1	1	2	....	....	....	....	....	....	....	....	....	....	....	....	....	....	....	....	....	....
	AZ Havirov	CzRep-3	2	0	0	0	0	....	....	....	....	....	....	....	....	....	4	0	0	0	0	....	....	....	....
2012-13	Sodertalje SK U18	Swe-U18	7	6	8	14	4	....	....	....	....	....	....	....	....	....	....	....	....	....	....	....	....	....	....
	Sodertalje SK Jr.	Swe-Jr.	36	12	17	29	67	....	....	....	....	....	....	....	....	....	4	2	2	4	10	....	....	....	....
	Sodertalje SK	Sweden-2	16	2	1	3	0	....	....	....	....	....	....	....	....	....	....	....	....	....	....	....	....	....	....
2013-14	Sodertalje SK Jr.	Swe-Jr.	1	1	1	2	0	....	....	....	....	....	....	....	....	....	2	0	0	0	0	....	....	....	....
	Sodertalje SK	Sweden-2	36	8	16	24	24	....	....	....	....	....	....	....	....	....	....	....	....	....	....	....	....	....	....
2014-15	Boston	NHL	46	10	17	27	8	2	0	3	93	10.8	12	17	29.4	13:58	....	....	....	....	....	....	....	....	....
	Providence Bruins	AHL	25	11	17	28	12	....	....	....	....	....	....	....	....	....	3	0	0	0	0	....	....	....	....
	NHL Totals		46	10	17	27	8	2	0	3	93	10.8		17	29.4	13:58	....	....	....	....	....	....	....	....	....

PATERYN, Greg (PA-tuhr-ihn, GREHG) MTL

Defense. Shoots right. 6'2", 222 lbs. Born, Sterling Heights, MI, June 20, 1990. Toronto's 4th choice, 128th overall, in 2008 Entry Draft.

Season	Club	League	GP	G	A	Pts	PIM	PP	SH	GW	S	S%	+/-	TF	F%	Min	GP	G	A	Pts	PIM	PP	SH	GW	Min
2004-05	Brother Rice	High-MI	29	2	8	10	42	....	....	....	....	....	....	....	....	....	....	....	....	....	....	....	....	....	....
2005-06	Brother Rice	High-MI	24	0	8	8	34	....	....	....	....	....	....	....	....	....	....	....	....	....	....	....	....	....	....
2006-07	Brother Rice	High-MI	27	9	19	28	44	....	....	....	....	....	....	....	....	....	....	....	....	....	....	....	....	....	....
2007-08	Ohio	USHL	60	3	24	27	145	....	....	....	....	....	....	....	....	....	....	....	....	....	....	....	....	....	....
2008-09	U. of Michigan	CCHA	28	0	5	5	32	....	....	....	....	....	....	....	....	....	....	....	....	....	....	....	....	....	....
2009-10	U. of Michigan	CCHA	33	1	5	6	18	....	....	....	....	....	....	....	....	....	....	....	....	....	....	....	....	....	....
2010-11	U. of Michigan	CCHA	40	3	14	17	28	....	....	....	....	....	....	....	....	....	....	....	....	....	....	....	....	....	....
2011-12	U. of Michigan	CCHA	41	2	13	15	65	....	....	....	....	....	....	....	....	....	....	....	....	....	....	....	....	....	....
2012-13	Hamilton	AHL	39	7	5	12	27	....	....	....	....	....	....	....	....	....	....	....	....	....	....	....	....	....	....
	Montreal	NHL	3	0	0	0	0	0	0	0	0	0.0	0	0	0.0	9:36	....	....	....	....	....	....	....	....	....
2013-14	Hamilton	AHL	68	15	19	34	67	....	....	....	....	....	....	....	....	....	....	....	....	....	....	....	....	....	....
2014-15	Montreal	NHL	17	0	0	0	6	0	0	0	10	0.0	0	0	0.0	12:39	7	0	3	3	0	0	0	0	10:58
	Hamilton	AHL	53	3	12	15	56	....	....	....	....	....	....	....	....	....	....	....	....	....	....	....	....	....	....
	NHL Totals		20	0	0	0	6	0	0	0	10	0.0		0	0.0	12:12	7	0	3	3	0	0	0	0	10:58

Traded to **Montreal** by **Toronto** with Toronto's 2nd round choice (later traded to Chicago, later traded back to Toronto, later traded to Boston - Boston selected Jared Knight) in 2010 Entry Draft for Mikhail Grabovski, July 3, 2008.

PAVELSKI, Joe (pah-VEHL-skee, JOH) S.J.

Center. Shoots right. 5'11", 190 lbs. Born, Plover, WI, July 11, 1984. San Jose's 7th choice, 205th overall, in 2003 Entry Draft.

Season	Club	League	GP	G	A	Pts	PIM	PP	SH	GW	S	S%	+/-	TF	F%	Min	GP	G	A	Pts	PIM	PP	SH	GW	Min
2001-02	Stevens Point High	High-WI	STATISTICS NOT AVAILABLE																						
2002-03	Waterloo	USHL	60	36	33	69	32	....	....	....	....	....	....	....	....	....	7	5	7	12	8	....	....	....	....
2003-04	Waterloo	USHL	54	21	31	52	58	....	....	....	....	....	....	....	....	....	12	6	6	12	10	....	....	....	....
2004-05	U. of Wisconsin	WCHA	41	16	29	45	26	....	....	....	....	....	....	....	....	....	....	....	....	....	....	....	....	....	....
2005-06	U. of Wisconsin	WCHA	43	23	33	56	34	....	....	....	....	....	....	....	....	....	....	....	....	....	....	....	....	....	....
2006-07	San Jose	NHL	46	14	14	28	18	5	0	3	111	12.6	4	389	48.6	15:02	6	1	0	1	0	0	0	0	10:27
	Worcester Sharks	AHL	16	8	18	26	8	....	....	....	....	....	....	....	....	....	....	....	....	....	....	....	....	....	....
2007-08	San Jose	NHL	82	19	21	40	28	8	1	4	207	9.2	1	501	53.5	14:07	13	5	4	9	0	2	0	3	22:03
2008-09	San Jose	NHL	80	25	34	59	46	8	3	3	266	9.4	5	1274	56.3	18:58	6	0	1	1	9	0	0	0	19:21
2009-10	San Jose	NHL	67	25	26	51	26	3	1	5	228	11.0	1	821	58.1	19:29	15	9	8	17	6	5	0	3	21:32
	United States	Olympics	6	0	3	3	4	....	....	....	....	....	....	....	....	....	....	....	....	....	....	....	....	....	....
2010-11	San Jose	NHL	74	20	46	66	24	11	1	5	282	7.1	10	1020	54.3	19:39	18	5	5	10	10	1	0	1	21:08
2011-12	San Jose	NHL	82	31	30	61	31	8	1	2	269	11.5	18	864	58.7	20:37	5	0	0	0	5	0	0	0	21:00
2012-13	Dynamo Minsk	KHL	17	7	8	15	10	....	....	....	....	....	....	....	....	....	....	....	....	....	....	....	....	....	....
	San Jose	NHL	48	16	15	31	10	5	0	5	130	12.3	2	660	51.8	18:55	11	4	8	12	0	3	0	0	21:13

			Regular Season														Playoffs								
Season	Club	League	GP	G	A	Pts	PIM	PP	SH	GW	S	S%	+/-	TF	F%	Min	GP	G	A	Pts	PIM	PP	SH	GW	Min
2013-14	**San Jose**	**NHL**	**82**	**41**	**38**	**79**	**32**	**16**	**1**	**3**	**225**	**18.2**	**23**	**1206**	**56.0**	**19:51**	**7**	**2**	**4**	**6**	**2**	**1**	**0**	**0**	**20:33**
	United States	Olympics	6	1	4	5	0	....	....	....	....	....	....	....	....	....	....	....	....	....	....	....	....	....	....
2014-15	**San Jose**	**NHL**	**82**	**37**	**33**	**70**	**29**	**19**	**0**	**5**	**261**	**14.2**	**12**	**1147**	**56.0**	**20:08**	....	....	....	....	....	....	....	....	....
	NHL Totals		**643**	**228**	**257**	**485**	**244**	**83**	**8**	**35**	**1979**	**11.5**		**7882**	**55.5**	**18:40**	**81**	**26**	**30**	**56**	**32**	**12**	**0**	**7**	**20:23**

USHL All-Rookie Team (2003) • USHL First All-Star Team (2003) • USHL Rookie of the Year (2003) • WCHA All-Rookie Team (2005) • WCHA Second All-Star Team (2006) • NCAA West Second All-American Team (2006) • NHL Second All-Star Team (2014)

Signed as a free agent by **Minsk** (KHL), October 5, 2012.

PAYERL, Adam

(PAIR-uhl, A-duhm)

Center. Shoots right. 6'3", 218 lbs. Born, Kitchener, ON, March 4, 1991.

Season	Club	League	GP	G	A	Pts	PIM	PP	SH	GW	S	S%	+/-	TF	F%	Min	GP	G	A	Pts	PIM	PP	SH	GW	Min
2007-08	Barrie Colts	OHL	47	4	3	7	20	....	....	....	....	....	....	....	....	....	1	0	0	0	0	....	....	....	....
2008-09	Barrie Colts	OHL	68	7	10	17	59	....	....	....	....	....	....	....	....	....	5	0	1	1	8	....	....	....	....
2009-10	Belleville Bulls	OHL	67	17	26	43	39	....	....	....	....	....	....	....	....	....	....	....	....	....	....	....	....	....	....
2010-11	Belleville Bulls	OHL	63	10	19	29	79	....	....	....	....	....	....	....	....	....	4	0	0	0	0	....	....	....	....
2011-12	Belleville Bulls	OHL	61	22	25	47	106	....	....	....	....	....	....	....	....	....	6	1	2	3	9	....	....	....	....
	Wilkes-Barre	AHL	2	0	1	1	2	....	....	....	....	....	....	....	....	....	....	....	....	....	....	....	....	....	....
2012-13	Wilkes-Barre	AHL	44	3	7	10	53	....	....	....	....	....	....	....	....	....	15	2	1	3	13	....	....	....	....
	Wheeling Nailers	ECHL	4	1	0	1	15	....	....	....	....	....	....	....	....	....	....	....	....	....	....	....	....	....	....
2013-14	**Pittsburgh**	**NHL**	**2**	**0**	**0**	**0**	**2**	**0**	**0**	**0**	**4**	**0.0**	**–1**	**0**	**0.0**	**9:09**	....	....	....	....	....	....	....	....	....
	Wilkes-Barre	AHL	43	5	6	11	39	....	....	....	....	....	....	....	....	....	13	1	1	2	10	....	....	....	....
2014-15	Wilkes-Barre	AHL	41	2	7	9	76	....	....	....	....	....	....	....	....	....	....	....	....	....	....	....	....	....	....
	NHL Totals		**2**	**0**	**0**	**0**	**2**	**0**	**0**	**0**	**4**	**0.0**		**0**	**0.0**	**9:09**	....	....	....	....	....	....	....	....	....

Signed as a free agent by **Pittsburgh**, March 1, 2012.

PEARSON, Tanner

(PEER-suhn, TA-nuhr) **L.A.**

Left wing. Shoots left. 6'1", 205 lbs. Born, Kitchener, ON, August 10, 1992. Los Angeles' 1st choice, 30th overall, in 2012 Entry Draft.

Season	Club	League	GP	G	A	Pts	PIM	PP	SH	GW	S	S%	+/-	TF	F%	Min	GP	G	A	Pts	PIM	PP	SH	GW	Min
2007-08	Kit. Jr. Rangers	Minor-ON	STATISTICS NOT AVAILABLE																						
	Kitchener	ON-Jr.B	1	0	0	0	2	....	....	....	....	....	....	....	....	....	....	....	....	....	....	....	....	....	....
2008-09	Waterloo Siskins	ON-Jr.B	52	15	33	48	28	....	....	....	....	....	....	....	....	....	14	5	4	9	16	....	....	....	....
2009-10	Waterloo Siskins	ON-Jr.B	51	29	41	70	78	....	....	....	....	....	....	....	....	....	11	5	11	16	20	....	....	....	....
2010-11	Barrie Colts	OHL	66	15	27	42	35	....	....	....	....	....	....	....	....	....	....	....	....	....	....	....	....	....	....
2011-12	Barrie Colts	OHL	60	37	54	91	37	....	....	....	....	....	....	....	....	....	....	....	....	....	....	....	....	....	....
2012-13	Manchester	AHL	64	19	28	47	14	....	....	....	....	....	....	....	....	....	4	0	1	1	4	....	....	....	....
	Los Angeles	**NHL**	....	....	....	....	....	....	....	....	....	....	....	....	....	....	**1**	**0**	**0**	**0**	**0**	**0**	**0**	**0**	**5:44**
2013-14♦	**Los Angeles**	**NHL**	**25**	**3**	**4**	**7**	**8**	**1**	**0**	**1**	**31**	**9.7**	**2**	**2**	**50.0**	**10:49**	**24**	**4**	**8**	**12**	**8**	**0**	**0**	**0**	**12:17**
	Manchester	AHL	41	17	15	32	18	....	....	....	....	....	....	....	....	....	....	....	....	....	....	....	....	....	....
2014-15	**Los Angeles**	**NHL**	**42**	**12**	**4**	**16**	**14**	**1**	**0**	**3**	**68**	**17.6**	**14**	**8**	**62.5**	**13:18**	....	....	....	....	....	....	....	....	....
	NHL Totals		**67**	**15**	**8**	**23**	**22**	**2**	**0**	**4**	**99**	**15.2**		**10**	**60.0**	**12:22**	**25**	**4**	**8**	**12**	**8**	**0**	**0**	**0**	**12:01**

OHL Second All-Star Team (2012)

PELECH, Matt

(PEH-lihk, MAT)

Right wing. Shoots right. 6'4", 230 lbs. Born, Toronto, ON, September 4, 1987. Calgary's 1st choice, 26th overall, in 2005 Entry Draft.

Season	Club	League	GP	G	A	Pts	PIM	PP	SH	GW	S	S%	+/-	TF	F%	Min	GP	G	A	Pts	PIM	PP	SH	GW	Min
2002-03	Vaughan Kings	GTHL	44	3	13	16	113	....	....	....	....	....	....	....	....	....	....	....	....	....	....	....	....	....	....
2003-04	Sarnia Sting	OHL	62	4	6	10	39	....	....	....	....	....	....	....	....	....	5	0	1	1	12	....	....	....	....
2004-05	Sarnia Sting	OHL	31	1	5	6	74	....	....	....	....	....	....	....	....	....	....	....	....	....	....	....	....	....	....
2005-06	Sarnia Sting	OHL	18	0	2	2	59	....	....	....	....	....	....	....	....	....	....	....	....	....	....	....	....	....	....
	London Knights	OHL	34	1	7	8	80	....	....	....	....	....	....	....	....	....	19	0	0	0	48	....	....	....	....
2006-07	Belleville Bulls	OHL	58	5	30	35	171	....	....	....	....	....	....	....	....	....	12	0	3	3	22	....	....	....	....
2007-08	Quad City Flames	AHL	77	3	6	9	141	....	....	....	....	....	....	....	....	....	....	....	....	....	....	....	....	....	....
2008-09	**Calgary**	**NHL**	**5**	**0**	**3**	**3**	**9**	**0**	**0**	**0**	**4**	**0.0**	**1**	**0**	**0.0**	**13:16**	....	....	....	....	....	....	....	....	....
	Quad City Flames	AHL	59	3	6	9	130	....	....	....	....	....	....	....	....	....	....	....	....	....	....	....	....	....	....
2009-10	Abbotsford Heat	AHL	42	2	8	10	125	....	....	....	....	....	....	....	....	....	13	0	4	4	31	....	....	....	....
2010-11	Abbotsford Heat	AHL	59	3	2	5	198	....	....	....	....	....	....	....	....	....	....	....	....	....	....	....	....	....	....
2011-12	Worcester Sharks	AHL	59	1	7	8	168	....	....	....	....	....	....	....	....	....	....	....	....	....	....	....	....	....	....
2012-13	Worcester Sharks	AHL	58	3	4	7	238	....	....	....	....	....	....	....	....	....	....	....	....	....	....	....	....	....	....
	San Jose	**NHL**	**2**	**0**	**0**	**0**	**7**	**0**	**0**	**0**	**0**	**0.0**	**0**	**0**	**0.0**	**9:03**	....	....	....	....	....	....	....	....	....
2013-14	**San Jose**	**NHL**	**6**	**1**	**0**	**1**	**22**	**0**	**0**	**1**	**3**	**33.3**	**1**	**0**	**0.0**	**3:56**	....	....	....	....	....	....	....	....	....
	Worcester Sharks	AHL	32	3	1	4	73	....	....	....	....	....	....	....	....	....	....	....	....	....	....	....	....	....	....
2014-15	Utah Grizzlies	ECHL	15	2	9	11	44	....	....	....	....	....	....	....	....	....	11	1	4	5	53	....	....	....	....
	Rochester	AHL	39	0	2	2	80	....	....	....	....	....	....	....	....	....	....	....	....	....	....	....	....	....	....
	NHL Totals		**13**	**1**	**3**	**4**	**38**	**0**	**0**	**1**	**7**	**14.3**		**0**	**0.0**	**8:19**	....	....	....	....	....	....	....	....	....

Signed as a free agent by **San Jose**, July 6, 2011. • Missed majority of 2013-14 due to hand injury at Providence (AHL), January 3, 2014. Signed to a PTO (professional tryout) contract by **Rochester** (AHL), December 16, 2014.

PELLETIER, Pascal

(PEHL-tyay, pas-KAL)

Left wing. Shoots right. 5'11", 191 lbs. Born, Labrador City, NL, June 16, 1983.

Season	Club	League	GP	G	A	Pts	PIM	PP	SH	GW	S	S%	+/-	TF	F%	Min	GP	G	A	Pts	PIM	PP	SH	GW	Min
99-2000	Ste-Foy	QAAA	42	19	23	42	44	....	....	....	....	....	....	....	....	....	14	9	6	15	42	....	....	....	....
2000-01	Baie-Comeau	QMJHL	70	15	44	59	176	....	....	....	....	....	....	....	....	....	11	2	11	13	6	....	....	....	....
2001-02	Baie-Comeau	QMJHL	56	12	25	37	115	....	....	....	....	....	....	....	....	....	5	3	4	7	0	....	....	....	....
2002-03	Baie-Comeau	QMJHL	67	46	55	101	113	....	....	....	....	....	....	....	....	....	12	5	7	12	14	....	....	....	....
2003-04	Shawinigan	QMJHL	64	39	52	91	85	....	....	....	....	....	....	....	....	....	11	3	9	12	20	....	....	....	....
2004-05	Louisiana	ECHL	61	10	28	38	75	....	....	....	....	....	....	....	....	....	....	....	....	....	....	....	....	....	....
	Gwinnett	ECHL	6	0	1	1	2	....	....	....	....	....	....	....	....	....	5	0	2	2	2	....	....	....	....
2005-06	Providence Bruins	AHL	53	20	26	46	42	....	....	....	....	....	....	....	....	....	6	2	4	6	23	....	....	....	....
	Gwinnett	ECHL	21	18	12	30	18	....	....	....	....	....	....	....	....	....	....	....	....	....	....	....	....	....	....
2006-07	Providence Bruins	AHL	80	14	35	49	60	....	....	....	....	....	....	....	....	....	13	5	4	9	16	....	....	....	....
2007-08	**Boston**	**NHL**	**6**	**0**	**0**	**0**	**0**	**0**	**0**	**0**	**8**	**0.0**	**–2**	**1**	**100.0**	**11:04**	....	....	....	....	....	....	....	....	....
	Providence Bruins	AHL	73	37	38	75	66	....	....	....	....	....	....	....	....	....	10	6	6	12	4	....	....	....	....
2008-09	**Chicago**	**NHL**	**7**	**0**	**0**	**0**	**0**	**0**	**0**	**0**	**7**	**0.0**	**–4**	**33**	**39.4**	**9:08**	....	....	....	....	....	....	....	....	....
	Rockford IceHogs	AHL	71	29	26	55	45	....	....	....	....	....	....	....	....	....	4	1	0	1	6	....	....	....	....
2009-10	Syracuse Crunch	AHL	25	3	13	16	23	....	....	....	....	....	....	....	....	....	....	....	....	....	....	....	....	....	....
	Peoria Rivermen	AHL	55	14	28	42	41	....	....	....	....	....	....	....	....	....	....	....	....	....	....	....	....	....	....
2010-11	Langnau	Swiss	47	17	21	38	95	....	....	....	....	....	....	....	....	....	4	1	1	2	29	....	....	....	....
2011-12	Langnau	Swiss	43	14	22	36	71	....	....	....	....	....	....	....	....	....	4	2	6	8	2	....	....	....	....
2012-13	Langnau	Swiss	46	19	16	35	76	....	....	....	....	....	....	....	....	....	12	6	2	8	6	....	....	....	....
	Langnau	Swiss-Q	....	....	....	....	....	....	....	....	....	....	....	....	....	....	6	3	6	9	4	....	....	....	....
2013-14	**Vancouver**	**NHL**	**3**	**0**	**0**	**0**	**0**	**0**	**0**	**0**	**1**	**0.0**	**0**	**4**	**25.0**	**8:57**	....	....	....	....	....	....	....	....	....
	Utica Comets	AHL	69	22	40	62	64	....	....	....	....	....	....	....	....	....	....	....	....	....	....	....	....	....	....
2014-15	Zagreb	KHL	57	16	23	39	44	....	....	....	....	....	....	....	....	....	....	....	....	....	....	....	....	....	....
	NHL Totals		**16**	**0**	**0**	**0**	**0**	**0**	**0**	**0**	**16**	**0.0**		**38**	**39.5**	**9:49**	....	....	....	....	....	....	....	....	....

AHL First All-Star Team (2008)

Signed as a free agent by **Boston**, August 7, 2006. Traded to **Chicago** by **Boston** for Martin St. Pierre, July 24, 2008. Signed as a free agent by **Columbus**, July 6, 2009. Traded to **St. Louis** by **Columbus** for Tomas Kana and Brendan Bell, December 8, 2009. Signed as a free agent by **Langnau** (Swiss), May 20, 2010. Signed as a free agent by **Vancouver**, July 9, 2013. Signed as a free agent by **Zagreb** (KHL), June 25, 2014.

PELLEY, Rod

(PEHL-lee, RAWD) **N.J.**

Center. Shoots left. 5'11", 200 lbs. Born, Kitimat, BC, September 1, 1984.

Season	Club	League	GP	G	A	Pts	PIM	PP	SH	GW	S	S%	+/-	TF	F%	Min	GP	G	A	Pts	PIM	PP	SH	GW	Min
2002-03	Ohio State	CCHA	43	8	3	11	26	....	....	....	....	....	....	....	....	....	....	....	....	....	....	....	....	....	....
2003-04	Ohio State	CCHA	42	10	12	22	38	....	....	....	....	....	....	....	....	....	....	....	....	....	....	....	....	....	....
2004-05	Ohio State	CCHA	41	22	19	41	54	....	....	....	....	....	....	....	....	....	....	....	....	....	....	....	....	....	....
2005-06	Ohio State	CCHA	39	7	7	14	42	....	....	....	....	....	....	....	....	....	....	....	....	....	....	....	....	....	....
2006-07	**New Jersey**	**NHL**	**9**	**0**	**0**	**0**	**0**	**0**	**0**	**0**	**8**	**0.0**	**–3**	**98**	**40.8**	**11:00**	....	....	....	....	....	....	....	....	....
	Lowell Devils	AHL	65	17	12	29	35	....	....	....	....	....	....	....	....	....	....	....	....	....	....	....	....	....	....

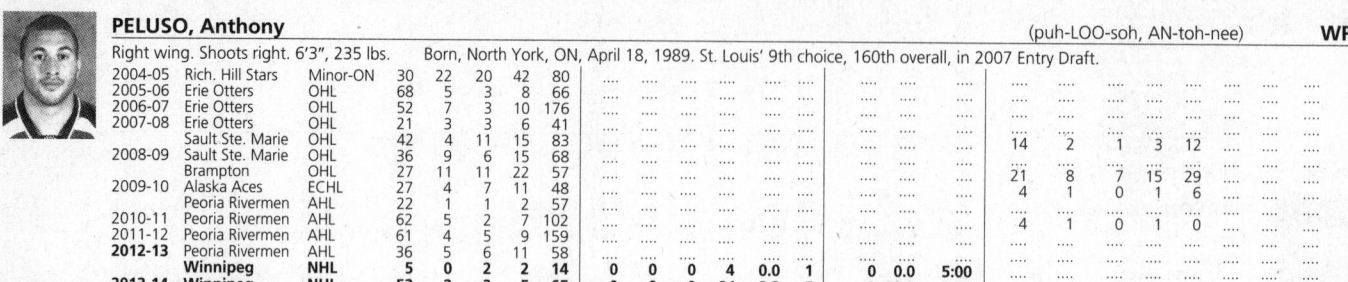

			Regular Season														Playoffs								
Season	Club	League	GP	G	A	Pts	PIM	PP	SH	GW	S	S%	+/-	TF	F%	Min	GP	G	A	Pts	PIM	PP	SH	GW	Min
2007-08	New Jersey	NHL	58	2	4	6	19	0	0	1	59	3.4	–3	321	46.7	9:19	....	....	....	....	....	....	....	....	....
	Lowell Devils	AHL	11	2	1	3	18	....	....	....	....	....	....	....	....	....	....	....	....	....	....	....	....	....	....
2008-09	Lowell Devils	AHL	75	15	23	38	78	....	....	....	....	....	....	....	....	....	....	....	....	....	....	....	....	....	....
2009-10	New Jersey	NHL	63	2	8	10	40	0	0	0	74	2.7	–4	198	49.5	7:52	3	0	0	0	2	0	0	0	9:12
2010-11	New Jersey	NHL	74	3	7	10	27	1	0	0	88	3.4	–9	320	52.8	11:48	....	....	....	....	....	....	....	....	....
2011-12	New Jersey	NHL	7	0	0	0	7	0	0	0	3	0.0	0	10	30.0	6:12	....	....	....	....	....	....	....	....	....
	Anaheim	NHL	45	2	1	3	9	0	0	0	41	4.9	–3	244	50.0	8:00	....	....	....	....	....	....	....	....	....
2012-13	Norfolk Admirals	AHL	60	3	7	10	34	....	....	....	....	....	....	....	....	....	....	....	....	....	....	....	....	....	....
2013-14	Albany Devils	AHL	74	13	7	20	55	....	....	....	....	....	....	....	....	....	4	0	0	0	2	....	....	....	....
2014-15	Albany Devils	AHL	70	7	6	13	65	....	....	....	....	....	....	....	....	....	....	....	....	....	....	....	....	....	....
	NHL Totals		256	9	20	29	102	1	0	1	273	3.3		1191	48.9	9:25	3	0	0	0	2	0	0	0	9:12

CCHA Second All-Star Team (2005)

Signed as a free agent by **New Jersey**, July 17, 2006. Traded to **Anaheim** by **New Jersey** with Mark Fraser and New Jersey's 7th round choice (Jaycob Megna) in 2012 Entry Draft for Kurtis Foster and Timo Pielmeier, December 12, 2011. Signed as a free agent by **New Jersey**, July 8, 2013.

PELUSO, Anthony

(puh-LOO-soh, AN-toh-nee) **WPG**

Right wing. Shoots right. 6'3", 235 lbs. Born, North York, ON, April 18, 1989. St. Louis' 9th choice, 160th overall, in 2007 Entry Draft.

Season	Club	League	GP	G	A	Pts	PIM	PP	SH	GW	S	S%	+/-	TF	F%	Min	GP	G	A	Pts	PIM	PP	SH	GW	Min
2004-05	Rich. Hill Stars	Minor-ON	30	22	20	42	80	....	....	....	....	....	....	....	....	....	....	....	....	....	....	....	....	....	....
2005-06	Erie Otters	OHL	68	5	3	8	66	....	....	....	....	....	....	....	....	....	....	....	....	....	....	....	....	....	....
2006-07	Erie Otters	OHL	52	7	3	10	176	....	....	....	....	....	....	....	....	....	....	....	....	....	....	....	....	....	....
2007-08	Erie Otters	OHL	21	3	3	6	41	....	....	....	....	....	....	....	....	....	....	....	....	....	....	....	....	....	....
	Sault Ste. Marie	OHL	42	4	11	15	83	....	....	....	....	....	....	....	....	....	14	2	1	3	12	....	....	....	....
2008-09	Sault Ste. Marie	OHL	36	9	6	15	68	....	....	....	....	....	....	....	....	....	....	....	....	....	....	....	....	....	....
	Brampton	OHL	27	11	11	22	57	....	....	....	....	....	....	....	....	....	21	8	7	15	29	....	....	....	....
2009-10	Alaska Aces	ECHL	27	4	7	11	48	....	....	....	....	....	....	....	....	....	4	1	0	1	6	....	....	....	....
	Peoria Rivermen	AHL	22	1	1	2	57	....	....	....	....	....	....	....	....	....	....	....	....	....	....	....	....	....	....
2010-11	Peoria Rivermen	AHL	62	5	2	7	102	....	....	....	....	....	....	....	....	....	4	1	0	1	0	....	....	....	....
2011-12	Peoria Rivermen	AHL	61	4	5	9	159	....	....	....	....	....	....	....	....	....	....	....	....	....	....	....	....	....	....
2012-13	Peoria Rivermen	AHL	36	5	6	11	58	....	....	....	....	....	....	....	....	....	....	....	....	....	....	....	....	....	....
	Winnipeg	NHL	5	0	2	2	14	0	0	0	4	0.0	1	0	0.0	5:00	....	....	....	....	....	....	....	....	....
2013-14	Winnipeg	NHL	53	2	3	5	65	0	0	0	24	8.3	–5	3	33.3	5:46	....	....	....	....	....	....	....	....	....
2014-15	Winnipeg	NHL	49	1	1	2	86	0	0	0	23	4.3	–3	1	0.0	5:53	....	....	....	....	....	....	....	....	....
	NHL Totals		107	3	6	9	165	0	0	0	51	5.9		4	25.0	5:47	....	....	....	....	....	....	....	....	....

Signed as a free agent by **Winnipeg**, July 24, 2013.

PENNER, Dustin

(PEH-nuhr, DUHS-tihn)

Left wing. Shoots left. 6'4", 247 lbs. Born, Winkler, MB, September 28, 1982.

Season	Club	League	GP	G	A	Pts	PIM	PP	SH	GW	S	S%	+/-	TF	F%	Min	GP	G	A	Pts	PIM	PP	SH	GW	Min
2001-02	MSU - Bottineau	NJCAA	23	20	12	32	30	....	....	....	....	....	....	....	....	....	....	....	....	....	....	....	....	....	....
2002-03	U. of Maine	H-East	DID NOT PLAY – FRESHMAN																						
2003-04	U. of Maine	H-East	43	11	12	23	52	....	....	....	....	....	....	....	....	....	....	....	....	....	....	....	....	....	....
2004-05	Cincinnati	AHL	77	10	18	28	82	....	....	....	....	....	....	....	....	....	9	2	3	5	13	....	....	....	....
2005-06	Anaheim	NHL	19	4	3	7	14	2	0	1	46	8.7	3	1	0.0	11:58	13	3	6	9	12	0	0	0	13:16
	Portland Pirates	AHL	57	39	45	84	68	....	....	....	....	....	....	....	....	....	5	4	3	7	0	....	....	....	....
2006-07♦	Anaheim	NHL	82	29	16	45	58	9	0	5	204	14.2	–2	58	46.6	13:59	21	3	5	8	2	0	0	2	14:05
2007-08	Edmonton	NHL	82	23	24	47	45	13	0	4	201	11.4	–12	189	55.0	17:12	....	....	....	....	....	....	....	....	....
2008-09	Edmonton	NHL	78	17	20	37	61	5	0	5	137	12.4	7	114	47.4	15:23	....	....	....	....	....	....	....	....	....
2009-10	Edmonton	NHL	82	32	31	63	38	9	0	1	203	15.8	6	421	47.7	18:23	....	....	....	....	....	....	....	....	....
2010-11	Edmonton	NHL	62	21	18	39	45	6	1	3	137	15.3	–12	294	43.2	18:28	....	....	....	....	....	....	....	....	....
	Los Angeles	NHL	19	2	4	6	2	0	0	0	36	5.6	0	12	33.3	17:01	6	1	1	2	4	0	0	0	14:32
2011-12♦	Los Angeles	NHL	65	7	10	17	43	1	0	0	119	5.9	–7	32	43.8	14:19	20	3	8	11	32	0	0	2	13:14
2012-13	Los Angeles	NHL	33	2	12	14	18	0	0	0	61	3.3	–2	5	40.0	12:42	18	3	2	5	8	0	0	1	14:32
2013-14	Anaheim	NHL	49	13	19	32	28	5	0	2	100	13.0	22	41	29.3	15:16	....	....	....	....	....	....	....	....	....
	Washington	NHL	18	1	2	3	2	0	0	0	19	5.3	3	6	50.0	12:18	....	....	....	....	....	....	....	....	....
2014-15			DID NOT PLAY																						
	NHL Totals		589	151	159	310	354	50	1	21	1263	12.0		1173	46.7	15:45	78	13	22	35	58	0	0	5	13:52

NCAA Championship All-Tournament Team (2004) • AHL Second All-Star Team (2006)

Signed as a free agent by **Anaheim**, May 12, 2004. Signed as a free agent by **Edmonton**, August 2, 2007. Traded to **Los Angeles** by **Edmonton** for Colten Teubert, Los Angeles' 1st round choice (Oscar Klefborn) in 2011 Entry Draft and Los Angeles' 3rd round choice (Daniil Zharkov) in 2012 Entry Draft, February 28, 2011. Signed as a free agent by **Anaheim**, July 16, 2013. Traded to **Washington** by **Anaheim** for Anaheim's 4th round choice (previously acquired, later traded to Dallas – Dallas selected Brent Moran) in 2014 Entry Draft, March 4, 2014. • Missed 2014-15 due to recurring upper-body injury.

PERCY, Stuart

(PUHR-see, STEW-uhrt) **TOR**

Defense. Shoots left. 6'1", 187 lbs. Born, Oakville, ON, May 18, 1993. Toronto's 2nd choice, 25th overall, in 2011 Entry Draft.

Season	Club	League	GP	G	A	Pts	PIM	PP	SH	GW	S	S%	+/-	TF	F%	Min	GP	G	A	Pts	PIM	PP	SH	GW	Min
2008-09	Tor. Marlboros	GTHL	79	13	44	57	42	....	....	....	....	....	....	....	....	....	....	....	....	....	....	....	....	....	....
2009-10	St. Michael's	OHL	52	3	15	18	40	....	....	....	....	....	....	....	....	....	16	0	1	1	12	....	....	....	....
2010-11	St. Michael's	OHL	64	4	30	34	50	....	....	....	....	....	....	....	....	....	20	2	10	12	14	....	....	....	....
2011-12	St. Michael's	OHL	34	5	20	25	41	....	....	....	....	....	....	....	....	....	6	1	1	2	4	....	....	....	....
	Toronto Marlies	AHL	1	0	1	1	0	....	....	....	....	....	....	....	....	....	3	0	0	0	0	....	....	....	....
2012-13	Mississauga	OHL	68	13	32	45	44	....	....	....	....	....	....	....	....	....	6	0	2	2	4	....	....	....	....
	Toronto Marlies	AHL	4	1	2	3	2	....	....	....	....	....	....	....	....	....	....	....	....	....	....	....	....	....	....
2013-14	Toronto Marlies	AHL	71	4	21	25	30	....	....	....	....	....	....	....	....	....	14	0	2	2	4	....	....	....	....
2014-15	Toronto	NHL	9	0	3	3	2	0	0	0	13	0.0	–4	0	0.0	18:05	....	....	....	....	....	....	....	....	....
	Toronto Marlies	AHL	43	1	10	11	14	....	....	....	....	....	....	....	....	....	4	0	2	2	2	....	....	....	....
	NHL Totals		9	0	3	3	2	0	0	0	13	0.0		0	0.0	18:05	....	....	....	....	....	....	....	....	....

Memorial Cup All-Star Team (2011)

PERREAULT, Mathieu

(pair-OH, MA-tyew) **WPG**

Center. Shoots left. 5'10", 185 lbs. Born, Drummondville, QC, January 5, 1988. Washington's 10th choice, 177th overall, in 2006 Entry Draft.

Season	Club	League	GP	G	A	Pts	PIM	PP	SH	GW	S	S%	+/-	TF	F%	Min	GP	G	A	Pts	PIM	PP	SH	GW	Min
2004-05	Magog	QAAA	41	25	47	72	68	....	....	....	....	....	....	....	....	....	9	5	10	15	12	....	....	....	....
2005-06	Acadie-Bathurst	QMJHL	62	18	34	52	42	....	....	....	....	....	....	....	....	....	17	10	11	21	8	....	....	....	....
2006-07	Acadie-Bathurst	QMJHL	67	41	78	119	66	....	....	....	....	....	....	....	....	....	12	6	8	14	8	....	....	....	....
2007-08	Acadie-Bathurst	QMJHL	65	34	*80	*114	61	....	....	....	....	....	....	....	....	....	12	3	19	22	6	....	....	....	....
	Hershey Bears	AHL	....	....	....	....	....	....	....	....	....	....	....	....	....	....	3	0	0	0	0	....	....	....	....
2008-09	Hershey Bears	AHL	77	11	39	50	36	....	....	....	....	....	....	....	....	....	21	2	6	8	8	....	....	....	....
2009-10	Washington	NHL	21	4	5	9	6	1	0	0	27	14.8	4	210	45.2	11:21	....	....	....	....	....	....	....	....	....
	Hershey Bears	AHL	56	16	34	50	34	....	....	....	....	....	....	....	....	....	21	7	12	19	18	....	....	....	....
2010-11	Washington	NHL	35	7	7	14	20	1	0	1	41	17.1	–3	305	45.6	11:53	....	....	....	....	....	....	....	....	....
	Hershey Bears	AHL	34	11	24	35	38	....	....	....	....	....	....	....	....	....	6	3	3	6	6	....	....	....	....
2011-12	Washington	NHL	64	16	14	30	24	2	0	4	60	26.7	9	451	50.8	12:02	4	0	0	0	0	0	0	0	10:43
2012-13	HIFK Helsinki	Finland	7	1	6	7	6	....	....	....	....	....	....	....	....	....	....	....	....	....	....	....	....	....	....
	Washington	NHL	39	6	11	17	20	2	0	1	47	12.8	7	325	51.7	11:40	7	1	3	4	0	0	0	0	13:38
2013-14	Anaheim	NHL	69	18	25	43	36	4	0	1	120	15.0	13	830	52.7	13:52	11	2	3	5	18	2	0	1	12:36
2014-15	Winnipeg	NHL	62	18	23	41	38	5	0	2	129	14.0	7	438	51.6	16:15	3	0	2	2	0	0	0	0	17:03
	NHL Totals		290	69	85	154	144	15	0	9	424	16.3		2559	50.6	13:15	25	3	8	11	18	2	0	1	13:07

QMJHL First All-Star Team (2007) • QMJHL Player of the Year (2007) • QMJHL Second All-Star Team (2008) • Canadian Major Junior Second All-Star Team (2007, 2008)

Signed as a free agent by **HIFK Helsinki** (Finland), November 24, 2012. Traded to **Anaheim** by **Washington** for John Mitchell and Anaheim's 4th round choice (later traded back to Anaheim, later traded to Dallas – Dallas selected Brent Moran) in 2014 Entry Draft, September 29, 2013. Signed as a free agent by **Winnipeg**, July 1, 2014.

PERRON, David

(peh-RAWN, DAY-vihd) **PIT**

Left wing. Shoots right. 6', 198 lbs. Born, Sherbrooke, QC, May 28, 1988. St. Louis' 3rd choice, 26th overall, in 2007 Entry Draft.

			Regular Season														Playoffs								
Season	Club	League	GP	G	A	Pts	PIM	PP	SH	GW	S	S%	+/-	TF	F%	Min	GP	G	A	Pts	PIM	PP	SH	GW	Min
2005-06	St-Jerome	QJHL	51	24	45	69	92	....	....	....	....	....	....	....	....	....	8	4	5	9	8	....	....	....	....
2006-07	Lewiston	QMJHL	70	39	44	83	75	....	....	....	....	....	....	....	....	....	17	12	16	28	22	....	....	....	....
2007-08	**St. Louis**	**NHL**	**62**	**13**	**14**	**27**	**38**	**3**	**0**	**1**	**68**	**19.1**	**16**	**14**	**35.7**	**12:33**	....	....	....	....	....	....	....	....	....
2008-09	**St. Louis**	**NHL**	**81**	**15**	**35**	**50**	**50**	**4**	**0**	**3**	**161**	**9.3**	**13**	**6**	**16.7**	**14:32**	**4**	**1**	**1**	**2**	**4**	**0**	**0**	**0**	**17:12**
2009-10	**St. Louis**	**NHL**	**82**	**20**	**27**	**47**	**60**	**5**	**1**	**2**	**166**	**12.0**	**-10**	**21**	**38.1**	**16:09**	....	....	....	....	....	....	....	....	....
2010-11	**St. Louis**	**NHL**	**10**	**5**	**2**	**7**	**12**	**0**	**0**	**0**	**29**	**17.2**	**7**	**0**	**0.0**	**18:25**	....	....	....	....	....	....	....	....	....
2011-12	**St. Louis**	**NHL**	**57**	**21**	**21**	**42**	**28**	**5**	**1**	**4**	**114**	**18.4**	**19**	**10**	**20.0**	**18:17**	**9**	**1**	**4**	**5**	**10**	**0**	**0**	**1**	**17:06**
2012-13	**St. Louis**	**NHL**	**48**	**10**	**15**	**25**	**44**	**2**	**0**	**2**	**84**	**11.9**	**0**	**22**	**36.4**	**18:00**	**6**	**0**	**2**	**2**	**6**	**0**	**0**	**0**	**17:11**
2013-14	**Edmonton**	**NHL**	**78**	**28**	**29**	**57**	**90**	**8**	**1**	**2**	**220**	**12.7**	**-16**	**39**	**33.3**	**19:08**	....	....	....	....	....	....	....	....	....
2014-15	**Edmonton**	**NHL**	**38**	**5**	**14**	**19**	**20**	**0**	**0**	**1**	**74**	**6.8**	**-17**	**9**	**33.3**	**17:00**	....	....	....	....	....	....	....	....	....
	Pittsburgh	**NHL**	**43**	**12**	**10**	**22**	**42**	**3**	**0**	**1**	**122**	**9.8**	**-8**	**3**	**0.0**	**17:37**	**5**	**0**	**1**	**1**	**4**	**0**	**0**	**0**	**17:17**
	NHL Totals		**499**	**129**	**167**	**296**	**384**	**30**	**3**	**16**	**1038**	**12.4**		**124**	**32.3**	**16:34**	**24**	**2**	**8**	**10**	**24**	**0**	**0**	**1**	**17:11**

• Missed majority of 2010-11 due to head injury vs. San Jose, November 4, 2010. Traded to **Edmonton** by **St. Louis** with St. Louis' 3rd round choice (later forfeited to San Jose as a result of Edmonton's hiring of Todd McLellan as head coach – San Jose selected Mike Robinson) in 2015 Entry Draft for Magnus Paajarvi, Edmonton's 2nd round choice (Ivan Barbashev) in 2014 Entry Draft and Edmonton's 4th round choice (Adam Musil) in 2015 Entry Draft, July 10, 2013. Traded to **Pittsburgh** by **Edmonton** for Rob Klinkhammer and Pittsburgh's 1st round choice (later traded to NY Islanders – NY Islanders selected Matthew Barzal) in 2015 Entry Draft, January 2, 2015.

PERRY, Corey

(PAIR-ee, KOH-ree) **ANA**

Right wing. Shoots right. 6'3", 212 lbs. Born, Peterborough, ON, May 16, 1985. Anaheim's 2nd choice, 28th overall, in 2003 Entry Draft.

Season	Club	League	GP	G	A	Pts	PIM	PP	SH	GW	S	S%	+/-	TF	F%	Min	GP	G	A	Pts	PIM	PP	SH	GW	Min
2000-01	Peterborough	Minor-ON	64	69	46	115	20	....	....	....	....	....	....	....	....	....	3	3	0	3	0	....	....	....	....
2001-02	London Knights	OHL	67	28	31	59	56	....	....	....	....	....	....	....	....	....	12	2	3	5	30	....	....	....	....
2002-03	London Knights	OHL	67	25	53	78	145	....	....	....	....	....	....	....	....	....	14	7	16	23	27	....	....	....	....
2003-04	London Knights	OHL	66	40	*73	113	98	....	....	....	....	....	....	....	....	....	15	7	15	22	20	....	....	....	....
	Cincinnati	AHL	....	....	....	....	....	....	....	....	....	....	....	....	....	....	3	1	1	2	4	....	....	....	....
2004-05	London Knights	OHL	60	*47	*83	*130	117	....	....	....	....	....	....	....	....	....	18	11	*27	*38	46	....	....	....	....
2005-06	**Anaheim**	**NHL**	**56**	**13**	**12**	**25**	**50**	**4**	**0**	**2**	**98**	**13.3**	**1**	**11**	**27.3**	**11:34**	**11**	**0**	**3**	**3**	**16**	**0**	**0**	**0**	**9:33**
	Portland Pirates	AHL	19	16	18	34	32	....	....	....	....	....	....	....	....	....	1	1	0	1	0	....	....	....	....
2006-07 ♦	**Anaheim**	**NHL**	**82**	**17**	**27**	**44**	**55**	**4**	**0**	**3**	**194**	**8.8**	**12**	**21**	**42.9**	**12:28**	**21**	**6**	**9**	**15**	**37**	**1**	**0**	**1**	**16:30**
2007-08	**Anaheim**	**NHL**	**70**	**29**	**25**	**54**	**108**	**11**	**0**	**4**	**200**	**14.5**	**12**	**16**	**18.8**	**17:57**	**3**	**2**	**1**	**3**	**8**	**0**	**0**	**0**	**14:55**
2008-09	**Anaheim**	**NHL**	**78**	**32**	**40**	**72**	**109**	**10**	**0**	**8**	**283**	**11.3**	**10**	**31**	**29.0**	**18:36**	**13**	**8**	**6**	**14**	**36**	**2**	**0**	**1**	**22:00**
2009-10	**Anaheim**	**NHL**	**82**	**27**	**49**	**76**	**111**	**6**	**1**	**2**	**270**	**10.0**	**0**	**28**	**21.4**	**21:04**	....	....	....	....	....	....	....	....	....
	Canada	Olympics	7	4	1	5	2	....	....	....	....	....	....	....	....	....	....	....	....	....	....	....	....	....	....
2010-11	**Anaheim**	**NHL**	**82**	***50**	**48**	**98**	**104**	**14**	**4**	***11**	**290**	**17.2**	**9**	**22**	**40.9**	**22:19**	**6**	**2**	**6**	**8**	**4**	**1**	**1**	**1**	**25:15**
2011-12	**Anaheim**	**NHL**	**80**	**37**	**23**	**60**	**127**	**14**	**1**	**6**	**277**	**13.4**	**-7**	**48**	**39.6**	**21:23**	....	....	....	....	....	....	....	....	....
2012-13	**Anaheim**	**NHL**	**44**	**15**	**21**	**36**	**72**	**5**	**0**	**5**	**128**	**11.7**	**10**	**29**	**20.7**	**19:04**	**7**	**0**	**2**	**2**	**4**	**0**	**0**	**0**	**20:20**
2013-14	**Anaheim**	**NHL**	**81**	**43**	**39**	**82**	**65**	**8**	**0**	**9**	**280**	**15.4**	**32**	**25**	**36.0**	**19:29**	**13**	**4**	**7**	**11**	**19**	**2**	**0**	**0**	**19:41**
	Canada	Olympics	6	0	1	1	2	....	....	....	....	....	....	....	....	....	....	....	....	....	....	....	....	....	....
2014-15	**Anaheim**	**NHL**	**67**	**33**	**22**	**55**	**67**	**4**	**0**	**3**	**193**	**17.1**	**13**	**12**	**25.0**	**18:06**	**16**	**10**	**8**	**18**	**14**	**2**	**0**	**2**	**19:54**
	NHL Totals		**722**	**296**	**306**	**602**	**868**	**80**	**6**	**53**	**2213**	**13.4**		**243**	**31.3**	**18:23**	**90**	**32**	**42**	**74**	**138**	**8**	**1**	**5**	**18:20**

OHL First All-Star Team (2004, 2005) • Canadian Major Junior Second All-Star Team (2004) • Canadian Major Junior First All-Star Team (2005) • OHL Playoff MVP (2005) • Memorial Cup All-Star Team (2005) • Stafford Smythe Memorial Trophy (Memorial Cup - MVP) (2005) • NHL First All-Star Team (2011, 2014) • Maurice "Rocket" Richard Trophy (2011) • Hart Memorial Trophy (2011)

Played in NHL All-Star Game (2008, 2011, 2012)

PESONEN, Harri

(pih-SOH-nihn, HAHR-ree)

Right wing. Shoots left. 6', 195 lbs. Born, Muurame, Finland, August 6, 1988.

Season	Club	League	GP	G	A	Pts	PIM	PP	SH	GW	S	S%	+/-	TF	F%	Min	GP	G	A	Pts	PIM	PP	SH	GW	Min
2004-05	JYP Jyvaskyla U18	Fin-U18	19	6	3	9	6	....	....	....	....	....	....	....	....	....	....	....	....	....	....	....	....	....	....
2005-06	JYP Jyvaskyla U18	Fin-U18	33	16	17	33	55	....	....	....	....	....	....	....	....	....	....	....	....	....	....	....	....	....	....
2006-07	JyP Jyvaskyla Jr.	Fin-Jr.	46	11	25	36	14	....	....	....	....	....	....	....	....	....	3	2	0	2	2	....	....	....	....
2007-08	Suomi U20	Finland-2	7	1	2	3	2	....	....	....	....	....	....	....	....	....	....	....	....	....	....	....	....	....	....
	JyP Jyvaskyla Jr.	Fin-Jr.	37	21	24	45	63	....	....	....	....	....	....	....	....	....	9	4	13	17	33	....	....	....	....
	JYP Jyvaskyla	Finland	3	0	0	0	0	....	....	....	....	....	....	....	....	....	....	....	....	....	....	....	....	....	....
2008-09	JYP Jr.	Finland-Jr.	1	0	0	0	2	....	....	....	....	....	....	....	....	....	....	....	....	....	....	....	....	....	....
	D Team Jyvaskyla	Finland-2	10	10	6	16	10	....	....	....	....	....	....	....	....	....	....	....	....	....	....	....	....	....	....
	JYP Jyvaskyla	Finland	47	4	3	7	12	....	....	....	....	....	....	....	....	....	15	4	1	5	8	....	....	....	....
2009-10	JYP Jyvaskyla	Finland	25	4	2	6	35	....	....	....	....	....	....	....	....	....	....	....	....	....	....	....	....	....	....
	D Team Jyvaskyla	Finland-2	18	4	3	7	33	....	....	....	....	....	....	....	....	....	11	1	3	4	8	....	....	....	....
2010-11	D Team Jyvaskyla	Finland-2	2	0	3	3	4	....	....	....	....	....	....	....	....	....	....	....	....	....	....	....	....	....	....
	JYP Jyvaskyla	Finland	54	11	15	26	26	....	....	....	....	....	....	....	....	....	10	4	6	10	6	....	....	....	....
2011-12	JYP Jyvaskyla	Finland	60	21	14	35	52	....	....	....	....	....	....	....	....	....	14	6	5	11	37	....	....	....	....
2012-13	Albany Devils	AHL	64	14	17	31	24	....	....	....	....	....	....	....	....	....	....	....	....	....	....	....	....	....	....
	New Jersey	**NHL**	**4**	**0**	**0**	**0**	**2**	**0**	**0**	**0**	**3**	**0.0**	**-1**	**0**	**0.0**	**9:11**	....	....	....	....	....	....	....	....	....
2013-14	Albany Devils	AHL	75	15	21	36	52	....	....	....	....	....	....	....	....	....	4	0	1	1	0	....	....	....	....
2014-15	Lausanne HC	Swiss	48	10	19	29	49	....	....	....	....	....	....	....	....	....	7	1	3	4	2	....	....	....	....
	NHL Totals		**4**	**0**	**0**	**0**	**2**	**0**	**0**	**0**	**3**	**0.0**		**0**	**0.0**	**9:11**	....	....	....	....	....	....	....	....	....

Signed as a free agent by **New Jersey**, June 15, 2012. Signed as a free agent by **Lausanne** (Swiss), May 20, 2014.

PETERSSON, Andre

(PEH-tuhr-suhn, AHN-dray)

Right wing. Shoots right. 5'9", 172 lbs. Born, Olofstrom, Sweden, September 11, 1990. Ottawa's 4th choice, 109th overall, in 2008 Entry Draft.

Season	Club	League	GP	G	A	Pts	PIM	PP	SH	GW	S	S%	+/-	TF	F%	Min	GP	G	A	Pts	PIM	PP	SH	GW	Min
2005-06	Tingsryds AIF U18	Swe-U18	9	5	3	8	0	....	....	....	....	....	....	....	....	....	....	....	....	....	....	....	....	....	....
2006-07	HV 71 U18	Swe-U18	10	14	10	24	6	....	....	....	....	....	....	....	....	....	2	1	2	3	0	....	....	....	....
	HV 71 Jr.	Swe-Jr.	6	1	1	2	8	....	....	....	....	....	....	....	....	....	....	....	....	....	....	....	....	....	....
2007-08	HV 71 U18	Swe-U18	4	4	5	9	4	....	....	....	....	....	....	....	....	....	....	....	....	....	....	....	....	....	....
	HV 71 Jr.	Swe-Jr.	36	16	22	38	34	....	....	....	....	....	....	....	....	....	3	0	0	0	2	....	....	....	....
2008-09	HV 71 Jonkoping	Sweden	10	0	1	1	0	....	....	....	....	....	....	....	....	....	....	....	....	....	....	....	....	....	....
	HV 71 Jr.	Swe-Jr.	36	24	31	55	28	....	....	....	....	....	....	....	....	....	7	7	4	11	8	....	....	....	....
2009-10	HV 71 Jonkoping	Sweden	37	10	5	15	14	....	....	....	....	....	....	....	....	....	6	0	1	1	2	....	....	....	....
	Boras HC	Sweden-2	1	1	0	1	0	....	....	....	....	....	....	....	....	....	....	....	....	....	....	....	....	....	....
2010-11	HV 71 Jonkoping	Sweden	31	8	4	12	18	....	....	....	....	....	....	....	....	....	....	....	....	....	....	....	....	....	....
2011-12	**Ottawa**	**NHL**	**1**	**0**	**0**	**0**	**0**	**0**	**0**	**0**	**0**	**0.0**	**0**	**0**	**0.0**	**5:02**	....	....	....	....	....	....	....	....	....
	Binghamton	AHL	60	23	21	44	20	....	....	....	....	....	....	....	....	....	....	....	....	....	....	....	....	....	....
2012-13	Binghamton	AHL	17	2	3	5	16	....	....	....	....	....	....	....	....	....	....	....	....	....	....	....	....	....	....
2013-14	Binghamton	AHL	47	17	23	40	28	....	....	....	....	....	....	....	....	....	....	....	....	....	....	....	....	....	....
	Norfolk Admirals	AHL	18	6	10	16	8	....	....	....	....	....	....	....	....	....	10	3	3	6	2	....	....	....	....
2014-15	HK Sochi	KHL	54	20	18	38	32	....	....	....	....	....	....	....	....	....	4	1	0	1	2	....	....	....	....
	NHL Totals		**1**	**0**	**0**	**0**	**0**	**0**	**0**	**0**	**0**	**0.0**		**0**	**0.0**	**5:02**	....	....	....	....	....	....	....	....	....

• Missed majority of 2012-13 due to hip injury vs. Adirondack (AHL), November 30, 2012. Traded to **Anaheim** by **Ottawa** for Alex Grant, March 5, 2014. Signed as a free agent by **Sochi** (KHL), June 16, 2014.

PETRECKI, Nicholas

(peh-TREH-kee, NIH-koh-las)

Defense. Shoots left. 6'3", 230 lbs. Born, Schenectady, NY, July 11, 1989. San Jose's 2nd choice, 28th overall, in 2007 Entry Draft.

Season	Club	League	GP	G	A	Pts	PIM	PP	SH	GW	S	S%	+/-	TF	F%	Min	GP	G	A	Pts	PIM	PP	SH	GW	Min
2004-05	Capital District	EmJHL	53	5	18	23	159	....	....	....	....	....	....	....	....	....	....	....	....	....	....	....	....	....	....
2005-06	Omaha Lancers	USHL	53	0	3	3	110	....	....	....	....	....	....	....	....	....	5	0	0	0	0	....	....	....	....
2006-07	Omaha Lancers	USHL	54	11	14	25	177	....	....	....	....	....	....	....	....	....	5	0	0	0	10	....	....	....	....
2007-08	Boston College	H-East	42	5	7	12	*102	....	....	....	....	....	....	....	....	....	....	....	....	....	....	....	....	....	....
2008-09	Boston College	H-East	35	0	7	7	*161	....	....	....	....	....	....	....	....	....	....	....	....	....	....	....	....	....	....
2009-10	Worcester Sharks	AHL	65	2	12	14	106	....	....	....	....	....	....	....	....	....	....	....	....	....	....	....	....	....	....
2010-11	Worcester Sharks	AHL	67	3	11	14	129	....	....	....	....	....	....	....	....	....	....	....	....	....	....	....	....	....	....
2011-12	Worcester Sharks	AHL	68	1	8	9	107	....	....	....	....	....	....	....	....	....	....	....	....	....	....	....	....	....	....
2012-13	Worcester Sharks	AHL	41	1	5	6	135	....	....	....	....	....	....	....	....	....	....	....	....	....	....	....	....	....	....
	San Jose	**NHL**	**1**	**0**	**0**	**0**	**0**	**0**	**0**	**0**	**0**	**0.0**	**0**	**0**	**0.0**	**11:58**	....	....	....	....	....	....	....	....	....

			Regular Season														Playoffs								
Season	Club	League	GP	G	A	Pts	PIM	PP	SH	GW	S	S%	+/-	TF	F%	Min	GP	G	A	Pts	PIM	PP	SH	GW	Min
2013-14	Worcester Sharks	AHL	35	1	2	3	54	....	....	....	....	....	....	....	....	....	....	....	....	....	....	....	....	....	....
	Rochester	AHL	14	0	1	1	28	....	....	....	....	....	....	....	....	....	5	0	0	0	2	....	....	....	....
2014-15	Rochester	AHL	19	0	2	2	56	....	....	....	....	....	....	....	....	....	....	....	....	....	....	....	....	....	....
	NHL Totals		**1**	**0**	**0**	**0**	**0**	**0**	**0**	**0**	**0**	**0.0**		**0**	**0.0**	**11:58**	....	....	....	....	....	....	....	....	....

USHL Second All-Star Team (2007) • Yanick Dupre Memorial Award (AHL – Man of the Year) (2012)

PETROVIC, Alex

(peh-TROH-vihk, AL-ehx) **FLA**

Defense. Shoots right. 6'4", 206 lbs. Born, Edmonton, AB, March 3, 1992. Florida's 5th choice, 36th overall, in 2010 Entry Draft.

Season	Club	League	GP	G	A	Pts	PIM	PP	SH	GW	S	S%	+/-	TF	F%	Min	GP	G	A	Pts	PIM	PP	SH	GW	Min
2007-08	Edmonton MLAC	AMHL	31	3	8	11	80	....	....	....	....	....	....	....	....	....	....	....	....	....	....	....	....	....	....
	Red Deer Rebels	WHL	10	1	0	1	2	....	....	....	....	....	....	....	....	....	....	....	....	....	....	....	....	....	....
2008-09	Red Deer Rebels	WHL	66	1	12	13	70	....	....	....	....	....	....	....	....	....	....	....	....	....	....	....	....	....	....
2009-10	Red Deer Rebels	WHL	57	8	19	27	87	....	....	....	....	....	....	....	....	....	4	0	0	0	4	....	....	....	....
2010-11	Red Deer Rebels	WHL	69	7	50	57	140	....	....	....	....	....	....	....	....	....	9	0	6	6	23	....	....	....	....
2011-12	Red Deer Rebels	WHL	68	12	36	48	141	....	....	....	....	....	....	....	....	....	....	....	....	....	....	....	....	....	....
	San Antonio	AHL	5	0	1	1	0	....	....	....	....	....	....	....	....	....	9	2	4	6	14	....	....	....	....
2012-13	San Antonio	AHL	55	4	13	17	102	....	....	....	....	....	....	....	....	....	....	....	....	....	....	....	....	....	....
	Florida	**NHL**	**6**	**0**	**0**	**0**	**25**	**0**	**0**	**0**	**5**	**0.0**	**–8**	**0**	**0.0**	**18:47**	....	....	....	....	....	....	....	....	....
2013-14	**Florida**	**NHL**	**7**	**0**	**1**	**1**	**8**	**0**	**0**	**0**	**4**	**0.0**	**3**	**0**	**0.0**	**12:14**	....	....	....	....	....	....	....	....	....
	San Antonio	AHL	43	2	11	13	79	....	....	....	....	....	....	....	....	....	....	....	....	....	....	....	....	....	....
2014-15	**Florida**	**NHL**	**33**	**0**	**3**	**3**	**34**	**0**	**0**	**0**	**29**	**0.0**	**–4**	**0**	**0.0**	**16:16**	....	....	....	....	....	....	....	....	....
	San Antonio	AHL	41	3	17	20	59	....	....	....	....	....	....	....	....	....	3	0	1	1	0	....	....	....	....
	NHL Totals		**46**	**0**	**4**	**4**	**67**	**0**	**0**	**0**	**38**	**0.0**		**0**	**0.0**	**15:59**	....	....	....	....	....	....	....	....	....

WHL East Second All-Star Team (2011) • WHL East First All-Star Team (2012) • WHL Defenseman of the Year (2012)

PETRY, Jeff

(PEH-tree, JEHF) **MTL**

Defense. Shoots right. 6'3", 198 lbs. Born, Ann Arbor, MI, December 9, 1987. Edmonton's 1st choice, 45th overall, in 2006 Entry Draft.

Season	Club	League	GP	G	A	Pts	PIM	PP	SH	GW	S	S%	+/-	TF	F%	Min	GP	G	A	Pts	PIM	PP	SH	GW	Min
2004-05	St. Mary's Prep	High-MI	23	2	8	10	....	....	....	....	....	....	....	....	....	....	6	2	5	7	....	....	....	....	....
2005-06	Det. Caesers	MWEHL	33	7	21	28	24	....	....	....	....	....	....	....	....	....	....	....	....	....	....	....	....	....	....
	Des Moines	USHL	48	1	14	15	68	....	....	....	....	....	....	....	....	....	11	2	5	7	8	....	....	....	....
2006-07	Des Moines	USHL	55	18	27	45	71	....	....	....	....	....	....	....	....	....	8	0	6	6	10	....	....	....	....
2007-08	Michigan State	CCHA	42	3	21	24	28	....	....	....	....	....	....	....	....	....	....	....	....	....	....	....	....	....	....
2008-09	Michigan State	CCHA	38	2	12	14	32	....	....	....	....	....	....	....	....	....	....	....	....	....	....	....	....	....	....
2009-10	Michigan State	CCHA	38	4	25	29	26	....	....	....	....	....	....	....	....	....	....	....	....	....	....	....	....	....	....
	Springfield	AHL	8	0	3	3	2	....	....	....	....	....	....	....	....	....	....	....	....	....	....	....	....	....	....
2010-11	**Edmonton**	**NHL**	**35**	**1**	**4**	**5**	**10**	**0**	**0**	**0**	**41**	**2.4**	**–12**	**0**	**0.0**	**20:22**	....	....	....	....	....	....	....	....	....
	Oklahoma City	AHL	41	7	17	24	18	....	....	....	....	....	....	....	....	....	6	0	1	1	4	....	....	....	....
2011-12	**Edmonton**	**NHL**	**73**	**2**	**23**	**25**	**26**	**1**	**0**	**0**	**111**	**1.8**	**–7**	**0**	**0.0**	**21:46**	....	....	....	....	....	....	....	....	....
	Oklahoma City	AHL	2	0	1	1	2	....	....	....	....	....	....	....	....	....	....	....	....	....	....	....	....	....	....
2012-13	**Edmonton**	**NHL**	**48**	**3**	**9**	**12**	**29**	**0**	**1**	**0**	**66**	**4.5**	**1**	**1**	**0.0**	**21:55**	....	....	....	....	....	....	....	....	....
2013-14	**Edmonton**	**NHL**	**80**	**7**	**10**	**17**	**42**	**1**	**0**	**0**	**96**	**7.3**	**–22**	**0**	**0.0**	**21:35**	....	....	....	....	....	....	....	....	....
2014-15	**Edmonton**	**NHL**	**59**	**4**	**11**	**15**	**32**	**1**	**0**	**1**	**103**	**3.9**	**–25**	**0**	**0.0**	**20:57**	....	....	....	....	....	....	....	....	....
	Montreal	**NHL**	**19**	**3**	**4**	**7**	**10**	**0**	**0**	**0**	**23**	**13.0**	**–3**	**0**	**0.0**	**22:11**	**12**	**2**	**1**	**3**	**4**	**1**	**0**	**0**	**22:17**
	NHL Totals		**314**	**20**	**61**	**81**	**149**	**3**	**1**	**1**	**440**	**4.5**		**1**	**0.0**	**21:27**	**12**	**2**	**1**	**3**	**4**	**1**	**0**	**0**	**22:17**

USHL First All-Star Team (2007) • USHL Defenseman of the Year (2007) • CCHA All-Rookie Team (2008) • CCHA Second All-Star Team (2010) • NCAA West Second All-American Team (2010)

Traded to **Montreal** by **Edmonton** for Montreal's 2nd (later traded to NY Rangers, later traded to Washington – Washington selected Jonas Siegenthaler) and 4th (Caleb Jones) round choices in 2015 Entry Draft, March 2, 2015.

PHANEUF, Dion

(fah-NUF, DEE-awn) **TOR**

Defense. Shoots left. 6'3", 214 lbs. Born, Edmonton, AB, April 10, 1985. Calgary's 1st choice, 9th overall, in 2003 Entry Draft.

Season	Club	League	GP	G	A	Pts	PIM	PP	SH	GW	S	S%	+/-	TF	F%	Min	GP	G	A	Pts	PIM	PP	SH	GW	Min
2000-01	Southgate	AMBHL	35	15	50	65	208	....	....	....	....	....	....	....	....	....	4	3	4	7	15	....	....	....	....
2001-02	Red Deer Rebels	WHL	67	5	12	17	170	....	....	....	....	....	....	....	....	....	21	0	2	2	14	....	....	....	....
2002-03	Red Deer Rebels	WHL	71	16	14	30	185	....	....	....	....	....	....	....	....	....	23	7	7	14	34	....	....	....	....
2003-04	Red Deer Rebels	WHL	62	19	24	43	126	....	....	....	....	....	....	....	....	....	19	2	9	11	30	....	....	....	....
2004-05	Red Deer Rebels	WHL	55	24	32	56	73	....	....	....	....	....	....	....	....	....	7	1	4	5	12	....	....	....	....
2005-06	**Calgary**	**NHL**	**82**	**20**	**29**	**49**	**93**	**16**	**0**	**7**	**242**	**8.3**	**5**	**0**	**0.0**	**21:44**	**7**	**1**	**0**	**1**	**7**	**1**	**0**	**0**	**18:37**
2006-07	**Calgary**	**NHL**	**79**	**17**	**33**	**50**	**98**	**13**	**0**	**4**	**230**	**7.4**	**10**	**0**	**0.0**	**25:40**	**6**	**1**	**0**	**1**	**7**	**1**	**0**	**0**	**26:24**
2007-08	**Calgary**	**NHL**	**82**	**17**	**43**	**60**	**182**	**10**	**1**	**4**	**263**	**6.5**	**12**	**0**	**0.0**	**26:25**	**7**	**3**	**4**	**7**	**4**	**1**	**0**	**0**	**27:07**
2008-09	**Calgary**	**NHL**	**80**	**11**	**36**	**47**	**100**	**4**	**0**	**4**	**277**	**4.0**	**–11**	**0**	**0.0**	**26:32**	**5**	**0**	**3**	**3**	**4**	**0**	**0**	**0**	**24:48**
2009-10	**Calgary**	**NHL**	**55**	**10**	**12**	**22**	**49**	**5**	**0**	**2**	**138**	**7.2**	**3**	**0**	**0.0**	**23:14**	....	....	....	....	....	....	....	....	....
	Toronto	**NHL**	**26**	**2**	**8**	**10**	**34**	**0**	**0**	**1**	**87**	**2.3**	**–2**	**0**	**0.0**	**26:22**	....	....	....	....	....	....	....	....	....
2010-11	**Toronto**	**NHL**	**66**	**8**	**22**	**30**	**88**	**3**	**0**	**1**	**190**	**4.2**	**–2**	**0**	**0.0**	**25:18**	....	....	....	....	....	....	....	....	....
2011-12	**Toronto**	**NHL**	**82**	**12**	**32**	**44**	**92**	**7**	**0**	**1**	**202**	**5.9**	**–10**	**0**	**0.0**	**25:17**	....	....	....	....	....	....	....	....	....
2012-13	**Toronto**	**NHL**	**48**	**9**	**19**	**28**	**65**	**3**	**0**	**1**	**88**	**10.2**	**–4**	**0**	**0.0**	**25:11**	**7**	**1**	**2**	**3**	**6**	**0**	**0**	**0**	**25:22**
2013-14	**Toronto**	**NHL**	**80**	**8**	**23**	**31**	**144**	**2**	**0**	**0**	**145**	**5.5**	**2**	**1**	**0.0**	**23:34**	....	....	....	....	....	....	....	....	....
2014-15	**Toronto**	**NHL**	**70**	**3**	**26**	**29**	**108**	**2**	**0**	**1**	**138**	**2.2**	**–11**	**0**	**0.0**	**23:43**	....	....	....	....	....	....	....	....	....
	NHL Totals		**750**	**117**	**283**	**400**	**1053**	**65**	**1**	**26**	**2000**	**5.9**		**1**	**0.0**	**24:45**	**32**	**6**	**9**	**15**	**28**	**3**	**0**	**0**	**24:23**

WHL East First All-Star Team (2004, 2005) • WHL Defenseman of the Year (2004, 2005) • Canadian Major Junior First All-Star Team (2004, 2005) • NHL All-Rookie Team (2006) • NHL First All-Star Team (2008)

Played in NHL All-Star Game (2007, 2008, 2012)

Traded to **Toronto** by **Calgary** with Fredrik Sjostrom and Keith Aulie for Matt Stajan, Niklas Hagman, Jamal Mayers and Ian White, January 31, 2010.

PHILLIPS, Chris

(FIHL-ihps, KRIHS) **OTT**

Defense. Shoots left. 6'3", 219 lbs. Born, Calgary, AB, March 9, 1978. Ottawa's 1st choice, 1st overall, in 1996 Entry Draft.

Season	Club	League	GP	G	A	Pts	PIM	PP	SH	GW	S	S%	+/-	TF	F%	Min	GP	G	A	Pts	PIM	PP	SH	GW	Min
1993-94	Fort McMurray	AJHL	56	6	16	22	72	....	....	....	....	....	....	....	....	....	10	0	3	3	16	....	....	....	....
1994-95	Fort McMurray	AJHL	48	16	32	48	127	....	....	....	....	....	....	....	....	....	11	4	2	6	10	....	....	....	....
1995-96	Prince Albert	WHL	61	10	30	40	97	....	....	....	....	....	....	....	....	....	18	2	12	14	30	....	....	....	....
1996-97	Prince Albert	WHL	32	3	23	26	58	....	....	....	....	....	....	....	....	....	....	....	....	....	....	....	....	....	....
	Lethbridge	WHL	26	4	18	22	28	....	....	....	....	....	....	....	....	....	19	4	*21	25	20	....	....	....	....
1997-98	**Ottawa**	**NHL**	**72**	**5**	**11**	**16**	**38**	**2**	**0**	**2**	**107**	**4.7**	**2**	....	....	....	**11**	**0**	**2**	**2**	**2**	**0**	**0**	**0**	....
1998-99	**Ottawa**	**NHL**	**34**	**3**	**3**	**6**	**32**	**2**	**0**	**0**	**51**	**5.9**	**–5**	**0**	**0.0**	**18:06**	**3**	**0**	**0**	**0**	**0**	**0**	**0**	**0**	**13:50**
99-2000	**Ottawa**	**NHL**	**65**	**5**	**14**	**19**	**39**	**0**	**0**	**1**	**96**	**5.2**	**12**	**0**	**0.0**	**16:50**	**6**	**0**	**1**	**1**	**4**	**0**	**0**	**0**	**18:17**
2000-01	**Ottawa**	**NHL**	**73**	**2**	**12**	**14**	**31**	**2**	**0**	**0**	**77**	**2.6**	**8**	**1**	**0.0**	**21:28**	**1**	**1**	**0**	**1**	**0**	**0**	**0**	**0**	**20:52**
2001-02	**Ottawa**	**NHL**	**63**	**6**	**16**	**22**	**29**	**1**	**0**	**1**	**103**	**5.8**	**5**	**0**	**0.0**	**19:31**	**12**	**0**	**0**	**0**	**12**	**0**	**0**	**0**	**21:44**
2002-03	**Ottawa**	**NHL**	**78**	**3**	**16**	**19**	**71**	**2**	**0**	**1**	**97**	**3.1**	**7**	**0**	**0.0**	**20:13**	**18**	**2**	**4**	**6**	**12**	**0**	**0**	**1**	**21:36**
2003-04	**Ottawa**	**NHL**	**82**	**7**	**16**	**23**	**46**	**0**	**0**	**1**	**93**	**7.5**	**15**	**1**	**100.0**	**20:50**	**7**	**1**	**0**	**1**	**12**	**1**	**0**	**0**	**20:26**
2004-05	Brynas IF Gavle	Sweden	27	5	3	8	45	....	....	....	....	....	....	....	....	....	....	....	....	....	....	....	....	....	....
	Brynas IF Gavle	Sweden-Q	9	1	2	3	2	....	....	....	....	....	....	....	....	....	....	....	....	....	....	....	....	....	....
2005-06	**Ottawa**	**NHL**	**69**	**1**	**18**	**19**	**90**	**0**	**0**	**0**	**79**	**1.3**	**19**	**0**	**0.0**	**20:52**	**9**	**2**	**0**	**2**	**6**	**0**	**0**	**0**	**21:41**
2006-07	**Ottawa**	**NHL**	**82**	**8**	**18**	**26**	**80**	**0**	**1**	**3**	**94**	**8.5**	**36**	**2**	**0.0**	**22:22**	**20**	**0**	**0**	**0**	**24**	**0**	**0**	**0**	**23:11**
2007-08	**Ottawa**	**NHL**	**81**	**5**	**13**	**18**	**56**	**1**	**0**	**1**	**80**	**6.3**	**15**	**1**	**0.0**	**22:29**	**4**	**0**	**0**	**0**	**4**	**0**	**0**	**0**	**22:00**
2008-09	**Ottawa**	**NHL**	**82**	**6**	**16**	**22**	**66**	**0**	**1**	**0**	**88**	**6.8**	**–14**	**0**	**0.0**	**21:52**	....	....	....	....	....	....	....	....	....
2009-10	**Ottawa**	**NHL**	**82**	**8**	**16**	**24**	**45**	**1**	**1**	**2**	**82**	**9.8**	**8**	**0**	**0.0**	**22:21**	**6**	**0**	**0**	**0**	**4**	**0**	**0**	**0**	**24:57**
2010-11	**Ottawa**	**NHL**	**82**	**1**	**8**	**9**	**32**	**1**	**0**	**0**	**81**	**1.2**	**–35**	**0**	**0.0**	**21:31**	....	....	....	....	....	....	....	....	....
2011-12	**Ottawa**	**NHL**	**80**	**5**	**14**	**19**	**16**	**4**	**0**	**1**	**85**	**5.9**	**12**	**0**	**0.0**	**19:07**	**7**	**0**	**1**	**1**	**4**	**0**	**0**	**0**	**21:34**
2012-13	**Ottawa**	**NHL**	**48**	**5**	**9**	**14**	**43**	**1**	**0**	**0**	**89**	**5.6**	**–5**	**0**	**0.0**	**21:03**	**10**	**0**	**1**	**1**	**21**	**0**	**0**	**0**	**21:08**
2013-14	**Ottawa**	**NHL**	**70**	**1**	**14**	**15**	**30**	**1**	**0**	**0**	**90**	**1.1**	**–12**	**0**	**0.0**	**19:14**	....	....	....	....	....	....	....	....	....
2014-15	**Ottawa**	**NHL**	**36**	**0**	**3**	**3**	**12**	**0**	**0**	**0**	**29**	**0.0**	**0**	**0**	**0.0**	**20:54**	....	....	....	....	....	....	....	....	....
	NHL Totals		**1179**	**71**	**217**	**288**	**756**	**17**	**3**	**13**	**1421**	**5.0**		**5**	**20.0**	**20:42**	**114**	**6**	**9**	**15**	**105**	**1**	**0**	**1**	**21:35**

WHL Rookie of the Year (1996) • WHL East First All-Star Team (1997) • Canadian Major Junior First All-Star Team (1997) • Memorial Cup All-Star Team (1997)

• Missed majority of 1998-99 due to ankle injury vs. Buffalo, December 30, 1998. Signed as a free agent by **Gavle** (Sweden), November 2, 2004. • Missed majority of 2014-15 due to recurring back injury.

PIETRANGELO, Alex
(puh-TRAN-geh-loh, AL-ehx) **ST.L.**

Defense. Shoots right. 6'3", 201 lbs. Born, King City, ON, January 18, 1990. St. Louis' 1st choice, 4th overall, in 2008 Entry Draft.

Season	Club	League	GP	G	A	Pts	PIM	PP	SH	GW	S	S%	+/-	TF	F%	Min	GP	G	A	Pts	PIM	PP	SH	GW	Min
			Regular Season														Playoffs								
2005-06	Tor. Jr. Canadiens	GTHL	44	13	31	44	33	....	....	....	....	....	....	....	....	....	....	....	....	....	....	....	....	....	....
2006-07	Mississauga	OHL	59	7	45	52	45	....	....	....	....	....	....	....	....	....	4	0	0	0	8	....	....	....	....
2007-08	Niagara Ice Dogs	OHL	60	13	40	53	94	....	....	....	....	....	....	....	....	....	6	5	4	9	4	....	....	....	....
2008-09	Niagara Ice Dogs	OHL	36	8	21	29	32	....	....	....	....	....	....	....	....	....	12	1	5	6	20	....	....	....	....
	St. Louis	**NHL**	**8**	**0**	**1**	**1**	**2**	**0**	**0**	**0**	**7**	**0.0**	**0**	**0**	**0.0**	**16:31**	....	....	....	....	....	....	....	....	....
	Peoria Rivermen	AHL	1	0	0	0	4	....	....	....	....	....	....	....	....	....	7	0	3	3	2	....	....	....	....
2009-10	**St. Louis**	**NHL**	**9**	**1**	**1**	**2**	**6**	**0**	**0**	**0**	**7**	**14.3**	**–9**	**0**	**0.0**	**16:34**	....	....	....	....	....	....	....	....	....
	Barrie Colts	OHL	25	9	20	29	27	....	....	....	....	....	....	....	....	....	17	2	12	14	8	....	....	....	....
2010-11	**St. Louis**	**NHL**	**79**	**11**	**32**	**43**	**19**	**4**	**0**	**1**	**161**	**6.8**	**18**	**0**	**0.0**	**22:00**	....	....	....	....	....	....	....	....	....
2011-12	**St. Louis**	**NHL**	**81**	**12**	**39**	**51**	**36**	**6**	**0**	**6**	**202**	**5.9**	**16**	**0**	**0.0**	**24:44**	**8**	**0**	**5**	**5**	**0**	**0**	**0**	**0**	**25:26**
2012-13	**St. Louis**	**NHL**	**47**	**5**	**19**	**24**	**10**	**2**	**0**	**0**	**93**	**5.4**	**0**	**0**	**0.0**	**25:07**	**6**	**1**	**1**	**2**	**2**	**0**	**0**	**0**	**26:34**
2013-14	**St. Louis**	**NHL**	**81**	**8**	**43**	**51**	**32**	**2**	**0**	**1**	**164**	**4.9**	**20**	**0**	**0.0**	**25:22**	**6**	**1**	**2**	**3**	**0**	**0**	**0**	**0**	**30:15**
	Canada	Olympics	6	0	1	1	0	....	....	....	....	....	....	....	....	....	....	....	....	....	....	....	....	....	....
2014-15	**St. Louis**	**NHL**	**81**	**7**	**39**	**46**	**28**	**1**	**0**	**2**	**195**	**3.6**	**–2**	**0**	**0.0**	**25:25**	**6**	**0**	**2**	**2**	**0**	**0**	**0**	**0**	**26:48**
	NHL Totals		**386**	**44**	**174**	**218**	**133**	**15**	**0**	**10**	**829**	**5.3**		**0**	**0.0**	**24:08**	**26**	**2**	**10**	**12**	**2**	**0**	**0**	**0**	**27:07**

NHL Second All-Star Team (2012, 2014)

• Missed majority of 2009-10 as a healthy reserve.

PINIZZOTTO, Steve
(pih-nih-ZAW-toh, STEEV)

Center. Shoots right. 6'1", 205 lbs. Born, Mississauga, ON, April 26, 1984.

Season	Club	League	GP	G	A	Pts	PIM	PP	SH	GW	S	S%	+/-	TF	F%	Min	GP	G	A	Pts	PIM	PP	SH	GW	Min
2001-02	Oakville Blades	ON-Jr.A	34	10	16	26	40	....	....	....	....	....	....	....	....	....	....	....	....	....	....	....	....	....	....
2002-03	Oakville Blades	ON-Jr.A	44	16	24	40	152	....	....	....	....	....	....	....	....	....	2	0	0	0	2	....	....	....	....
2003-04	Oakville Blades	ON-Jr.A	39	17	34	51	177	....	....	....	....	....	....	....	....	....	....	....	....	....	....	....	....	....	....
2004-05	Oakville Blades	ON-Jr.A	48	33	62	95	86	....	....	....	....	....	....	....	....	....	....	....	....	....	....	....	....	....	....
2005-06	RIT Tigers	NCAA	20	7	6	13	32	....	....	....	....	....	....	....	....	....	....	....	....	....	....	....	....	....	....
2006-07	RIT Tigers	AH	34	13	31	44	76	....	....	....	....	....	....	....	....	....	....	....	....	....	....	....	....	....	....
	Hershey Bears	AHL	5	0	0	0	4	....	....	....	....	....	....	....	....	....	....	....	....	....	....	....	....	....	....
2007-08	Hershey Bears	AHL	23	0	4	4	12	....	....	....	....	....	....	....	....	....	5	0	0	0	13	....	....	....	....
	South Carolina	ECHL	40	15	17	32	58	....	....	....	....	....	....	....	....	....	10	1	2	3	34	....	....	....	....
2008-09	Hershey Bears	AHL	45	4	7	11	61	....	....	....	....	....	....	....	....	....	21	3	2	5	28	....	....	....	....
	South Carolina	ECHL	11	4	6	10	19	....	....	....	....	....	....	....	....	....	....	....	....	....	....	....	....	....	....
2009-10	Hershey Bears	AHL	69	13	28	41	124	....	....	....	....	....	....	....	....	....	21	5	3	8	33	....	....	....	....
2010-11	Hershey Bears	AHL	68	17	25	42	178	....	....	....	....	....	....	....	....	....	6	2	2	4	6	....	....	....	....
2011-12			DID NOT PLAY – INJURED																						
2012-13	Chicago Wolves	AHL	24	4	8	12	29	....	....	....	....	....	....	....	....	....	....	....	....	....	....	....	....	....	....
	Vancouver	**NHL**	**12**	**0**	**0**	**0**	**29**	**0**	**0**	**0**	**9**	**0.0**	**–6**	**0**	**0.0**	**10:00**	**1**	**0**	**0**	**0**	**0**	**0**	**0**	**0**	**3:57**
2013-14	San Antonio	AHL	21	6	1	7	67	....	....	....	....	....	....	....	....	....	....	....	....	....	....	....	....	....	....
	Edmonton	**NHL**	**6**	**0**	**2**	**2**	**15**	**0**	**0**	**0**	**2**	**0.0**	**–1**	**0**	**0.0**	**9:39**	....	....	....	....	....	....	....	....	....
	Oklahoma City	AHL	30	6	12	18	116	....	....	....	....	....	....	....	....	....	1	0	0	0	14	....	....	....	....
2014-15	**Edmonton**	**NHL**	**18**	**2**	**2**	**4**	**30**	**0**	**0**	**0**	**15**	**13.3**	**1**	**0**	**0.0**	**7:56**	....	....	....	....	....	....	....	....	....
	Oklahoma City	AHL	25	1	10	11	117	....	....	....	....	....	....	....	....	....	....	....	....	....	....	....	....	....	....
	NHL Totals		**36**	**2**	**4**	**6**	**74**	**0**	**0**	**0**	**26**	**7.7**		**0**	**0.0**	**8:54**	**1**	**0**	**0**	**0**	**0**	**0**	**0**	**0**	**3:57**

Signed as a free agent by **Washington**, March 16, 2007. Signed as a free agent by **Vancouver**, July 3, 2011. • Missed 2011-12 due to pre-season shoulder injury vs. San Jose, September 25, 2011. • Missed majority of 2012-13 due to recurring groin injury and as a healthy reserve. Signed as a free agent by **Florida**, August 5, 2013. Traded to **Edmonton** by **Florida** for Ryan Martindale, January 17, 2014. Signed as a free agent by **Munchen** (Germany), May 26, 2015.

PIRRI, Brandon
(PIHR-ee, BRAN-duhn) **FLA**

Center. Shoots left. 6', 183 lbs. Born, Toronto, ON, April 10, 1991. Chicago's 2nd choice, 59th overall, in 2009 Entry Draft.

Season	Club	League	GP	G	A	Pts	PIM	PP	SH	GW	S	S%	+/-	TF	F%	Min	GP	G	A	Pts	PIM	PP	SH	GW	Min
2006-07	Tor. Young Nats	GTHL	44	54	72	128	18	....	....	....	....	....	....	....	....	....	....	....	....	....	....	....	....	....	....
2007-08	Streetsville Derbys	ON-Jr.A	40	18	32	50	42	....	....	....	....	....	....	....	....	....	....	....	....	....	....	....	....	....	....
2008-09	Streetsville Derbys	ON-Jr.A	18	21	28	49	24	....	....	....	....	....	....	....	....	....	....	....	....	....	....	....	....	....	....
	Georgetown	ON-Jr.A	26	25	20	45	22	....	....	....	....	....	....	....	....	....	14	8	13	21	10	....	....	....	....
2009-10	RPI Engineers	ECAC	39	11	*32	43	67	....	....	....	....	....	....	....	....	....	....	....	....	....	....	....	....	....	....
2010-11	**Chicago**	**NHL**	**1**	**0**	**0**	**0**	**0**	**0**	**0**	**0**	**1**	**0.0**	**–1**	**6**	**33.3**	**8:56**	....	....	....	....	....	....	....	....	....
	Rockford IceHogs	AHL	70	12	31	43	50	....	....	....	....	....	....	....	....	....	....	....	....	....	....	....	....	....	....
2011-12	**Chicago**	**NHL**	**5**	**0**	**2**	**2**	**0**	**0**	**0**	**0**	**5**	**0.0**	**2**	**54**	**48.2**	**13:31**	....	....	....	....	....	....	....	....	....
	Rockford IceHogs	AHL	66	23	33	56	36	....	....	....	....	....	....	....	....	....	....	....	....	....	....	....	....	....	....
2012-13	Rockford IceHogs	AHL	76	22	*53	*75	72	....	....	....	....	....	....	....	....	....	....	....	....	....	....	....	....	....	....
	Chicago	**NHL**	**1**	**0**	**0**	**0**	**0**	**0**	**0**	**0**	**2**	**0.0**	**0**	**14**	**42.9**	**17:55**	....	....	....	....	....	....	....	....	....
2013-14	**Chicago**	**NHL**	**28**	**6**	**5**	**11**	**6**	**1**	**0**	**0**	**34**	**17.6**	**6**	**247**	**42.9**	**12:15**	....	....	....	....	....	....	....	....	....
	Rockford IceHogs	AHL	26	11	15	26	10	....	....	....	....	....	....	....	....	....	....	....	....	....	....	....	....	....	....
	Florida	**NHL**	**21**	**7**	**7**	**14**	**2**	**2**	**0**	**0**	**46**	**15.2**	**0**	**207**	**47.3**	**13:56**	....	....	....	....	....	....	....	....	....
2014-15	**Florida**	**NHL**	**49**	**22**	**2**	**24**	**14**	**7**	**0**	**4**	**143**	**15.4**	**6**	**175**	**49.1**	**14:46**	....	....	....	....	....	....	....	....	....
	NHL Totals		**105**	**35**	**16**	**51**	**22**	**10**	**0**	**4**	**231**	**15.2**		**703**	**46.1**	**13:51**	....	....	....	....	....	....	....	....	....

ECAC All-Rookie Team (2010) • John P. Sollenberger Trophy (AHL - Top Scorer) (2013)

Traded to **Florida** by **Chicago** for Florida's 3rd round choice (later traded to Nashville – Nashville selected Justin Kirkland) in 2014 Entry Draft and Florida's 5th round choice in 2016 Entry Draft, March 2, 2014.

PISKULA, Joe
(pihs-KOO-luh, JOH) **ANA**

Defense. Shoots left. 6'3", 212 lbs. Born, Antigo, WI, July 5, 1984.

Season	Club	League	GP	G	A	Pts	PIM	PP	SH	GW	S	S%	+/-	TF	F%	Min	GP	G	A	Pts	PIM	PP	SH	GW	Min
2002-03	Chicago Steel	USHL	13	0	0	0	18	....	....	....	....	....	....	....	....	....	....	....	....	....	....	....	....	....	....
	Des Moines	USHL	32	2	6	8	18	....	....	....	....	....	....	....	....	....	4	0	1	1	4	....	....	....	....
2003-04	Des Moines	USHL	58	2	4	6	68	....	....	....	....	....	....	....	....	....	3	0	1	1	0	....	....	....	....
2004-05	U. of Wisconsin	WCHA	40	0	6	6	24	....	....	....	....	....	....	....	....	....	....	....	....	....	....	....	....	....	....
2005-06	U. of Wisconsin	WCHA	34	2	9	11	22	....	....	....	....	....	....	....	....	....	....	....	....	....	....	....	....	....	....
2006-07	U. of Wisconsin	WCHA	38	1	4	5	34	....	....	....	....	....	....	....	....	....	....	....	....	....	....	....	....	....	....
	Los Angeles	**NHL**	**5**	**0**	**0**	**0**	**6**	**0**	**0**	**0**	**4**	**0.0**	**–3**	**0**	**0.0**	**9:59**	....	....	....	....	....	....	....	....	....
2007-08	Manchester	AHL	55	0	7	7	57	....	....	....	....	....	....	....	....	....	4	0	0	0	4	....	....	....	....
2008-09	Manchester	AHL	67	0	12	12	40	....	....	....	....	....	....	....	....	....	....	....	....	....	....	....	....	....	....
2009-10	Manchester	AHL	72	2	10	12	51	....	....	....	....	....	....	....	....	....	16	2	2	4	12	....	....	....	....
2010-11	Abbotsford Heat	AHL	71	1	11	12	73	....	....	....	....	....	....	....	....	....	....	....	....	....	....	....	....	....	....
2011-12	**Calgary**	**NHL**	**5**	**0**	**0**	**0**	**2**	**0**	**0**	**0**	**2**	**0.0**	**–5**	**0**	**0.0**	**10:54**	....	....	....	....	....	....	....	....	....
	Abbotsford Heat	AHL	59	3	15	18	48	....	....	....	....	....	....	....	....	....	6	0	1	1	0	....	....	....	....
2012-13	Abbotsford Heat	AHL	46	2	8	10	51	....	....	....	....	....	....	....	....	....	....	....	....	....	....	....	....	....	....
	Milwaukee	AHL	23	1	3	4	15	....	....	....	....	....	....	....	....	....	4	0	0	0	0	....	....	....	....
2013-14	**Nashville**	**NHL**	**2**	**0**	**0**	**0**	**0**	**0**	**0**	**0**	**2**	**0.0**	**1**	**0**	**0.0**	**12:11**	....	....	....	....	....	....	....	....	....
	Milwaukee	AHL	73	3	20	23	56	....	....	....	....	....	....	....	....	....	3	0	1	1	4	....	....	....	....
2014-15	**Nashville**	**NHL**	**1**	**0**	**0**	**0**	**2**	**0**	**0**	**0**	**0**	**0.0**	**–1**	**0**	**0.0**	**16:27**	....	....	....	....	....	....	....	....	....
	Milwaukee	AHL	67	1	16	17	30	....	....	....	....	....	....	....	....	....	....	....	....	....	....	....	....	....	....
	NHL Totals		**13**	**0**	**0**	**0**	**10**	**0**	**0**	**0**	**8**	**0.0**		**0**	**0.0**	**11:10**	....	....	....	....	....	....	....	....	....

Signed as a free agent by **Los Angeles**, March 21, 2007. Signed as a free agent by **Abbotsford** (AHL), October 6, 2010. Signed as a free agent by **Calgary**, July 1, 2011. Traded to **Nashville** by **Calgary** for Brian McGrattan, February 28, 2013. Signed as a free agent by **Anaheim**, July 1, 2015.

PITLICK, Tyler
(PIHT-lihk, TIGH-luhr) **EDM**

Center. Shoots right. 6'2", 195 lbs. Born, Minneapolis, MN, November 1, 1991. Edmonton's 2nd choice, 31st overall, in 2010 Entry Draft.

Season	Club	League	GP	G	A	Pts	PIM	PP	SH	GW	S	S%	+/-	TF	F%	Min	GP	G	A	Pts	PIM	PP	SH	GW	Min
2007-08	Centennial	High-MN	....	25	34	59	....	....	....	....	....	....	....	....	....	....	....	....	....	....	....	....	....	....	....
2008-09	Centennial	High-MN	25	31	33	64	....	....	....	....	....	....	....	....	....	....	....	....	....	....	....	....	....	....	....
2009-10	Minnesota State	WCHA	38	11	8	19	27	....	....	....	....	....	....	....	....	....	....	....	....	....	....	....	....	....	....
2010-11	Medicine Hat	WHL	56	27	35	62	31	....	....	....	....	....	....	....	....	....	....	....	....	....	....	....	....	....	....
2011-12	Oklahoma City	AHL	62	7	16	23	28	....	....	....	....	....	....	....	....	....	13	2	5	7	2	....	....	....	....
2012-13	Oklahoma City	AHL	44	3	7	10	10	....	....	....	....	....	....	....	....	....	16	2	4	6	8	....	....	....	....

			Regular Season														Playoffs								
Season	Club	League	GP	G	A	Pts	PIM	PP	SH	GW	S	S%	+/-	TF	F%	Min	GP	G	A	Pts	PIM	PP	SH	GW	Min
2013-14	Edmonton	NHL	10	1	0	1	0	0	0	0	9	11.1	–2	3	33.3	8:58	....	....	....	....	....	....	....	....	....
	Oklahoma City	AHL	39	8	14	22	10	....	....	....	....	....	....	....	....	....	2	0	0	0	0	....	....	....	....
2014-15	Edmonton	NHL	17	2	0	2	4	0	0	1	18	11.1	–3	9	55.6	12:27	....	....	....	....	....	....	....	....	....
	Oklahoma City	AHL	14	3	6	9	8	....	....	....	....	....	....	....	....	....	....	....	....	....	....	....	....	....	....
	NHL Totals		27	3	0	3	4	0	0	1	27	11.1		12	50.0	11:09	....	....	....	....	....	....	....	....	....

• Missed majority of 2014-15 due to spleen injury at Calgary, December 31, 2014.

PLEKANEC, Tomas

(pleh-KA-nehts, TAW-muhs) **MTL**

Left wing. Shoots left. 5'11", 198 lbs. Born, Kladno, Czech., October 31, 1982. Montreal's 4th choice, 71st overall, in 2001 Entry Draft.

Season	Club	League	GP	G	A	Pts	PIM	PP	SH	GW	S	S%	+/-	TF	F%	Min	GP	G	A	Pts	PIM	PP	SH	GW	Min
1996-97	Kladno U17	CzR-U17	13	1	3	4	....	....	....	....	....	....	....	....	....	....	....	....	....	....	....	....	....	....	....
1997-98	HC Kladno U17	CzR-U17	45	38	26	64	....	....	....	....	....	....	....	....	....	....	....	....	....	....	....	....	....	....	....
1998-99	HC Kladno Jr.	CzRep-Jr.	53	22	20	42	....	....	....	....	....	....	....	....	....	....	....	....	....	....	....	....	....	....	....
99-2000	HC Kladno Jr.	CzRep-Jr.	43	14	16	30	....	....	....	....	....	....	....	....	....	....	....	....	....	....	....	....	....	....	....
	Kralupy	CzRep-3	6	2	2	4	2	....	....	....	....	....	....	....	....	....	....	....	....	....	....	....	....	....	....
	HC CKD Slany	CzRep-3	3	0	1	1	6	....	....	....	....	....	....	....	....	....	....	....	....	....	....	....	....	....	....
2000-01	Kladno	CzRep	47	9	9	18	24	....	....	....	....	....	....	....	....	....	....	....	....	....	....	....	....	....	....
	HC Kladno Jr.	CzRep-Jr.	9	6	4	10	4	....	....	....	....	....	....	....	....	....	....	....	....	....	....	....	....	....	....
2001-02	Kladno	CzRep	48	7	16	23	28	....	....	....	....	....	....	....	....	....	....	....	....	....	....	....	....	....	....
	BK Mlada Boleslav	CzRep-3	6	6	3	9	14	....	....	....	....	....	....	....	....	....	....	....	....	....	....	....	....	....	....
	Kladno	CzRep-Q	5	0	1	1	0	....	....	....	....	....	....	....	....	....	....	....	....	....	....	....	....	....	....
2002-03	Hamilton	AHL	77	19	27	46	74	....	....	....	....	....	....	....	....	....	13	3	2	5	8	....	....	....	....
2003-04	Montreal	NHL	2	0	0	0	0	0	0	0	0	0.0	0	11	45.5	9:02	....	....	....	....	....	....	....	....	....
	Hamilton	AHL	74	23	43	66	90	....	....	....	....	....	....	....	....	....	10	2	5	7	6	....	....	....	....
2004-05	Hamilton	AHL	80	29	35	64	68	....	....	....	....	....	....	....	....	....	4	2	4	6	6	....	....	....	....
2005-06	Montreal	NHL	67	9	20	29	32	1	0	0	99	9.1	4	708	50.3	13:15	6	0	4	4	6	0	0	0	18:00
	Hamilton	AHL	2	0	0	0	2	....	....	....	....	....	....	....	....	....	....	....	....	....	....	....	....	....	....
2006-07	Montreal	NHL	81	20	27	47	36	5	2	1	150	13.3	10	1159	48.3	15:59	....	....	....	....	....	....	....	....	....
2007-08	Montreal	NHL	81	29	40	69	42	12	2	6	186	15.6	15	1381	49.5	18:05	12	4	5	9	2	2	0	0	18:02
2008-09	Montreal	NHL	80	20	19	39	54	6	3	2	202	9.9	–9	1351	50.6	17:15	3	0	0	0	4	0	0	0	13:36
2009-10	Montreal	NHL	82	25	45	70	50	3	1	4	216	11.6	5	1615	49.0	19:58	19	4	7	11	20	1	0	1	19:57
	Czech Republic	Olympics	5	2	1	3	2	....	....	....	....	....	....	....	....	....	....	....	....	....	....	....	....	....	....
2010-11	Montreal	NHL	77	22	35	57	60	3	1	4	227	9.7	8	1577	50.0	20:15	7	2	3	5	2	0	1	0	23:20
2011-12	Montreal	NHL	81	17	35	52	56	5	3	2	220	7.7	–15	1678	49.1	20:45	....	....	....	....	....	....	....	....	....
2012-13	Rytiri Kladno	CzRep	32	21	25	46	38	....	....	....	....	....	....	....	....	....	....	....	....	....	....	....	....	....	....
	Montreal	NHL	47	14	19	33	24	4	0	2	133	10.5	3	961	50.6	19:13	5	0	4	4	2	0	0	0	20:53
2013-14	Montreal	NHL	81	20	23	43	38	3	3	5	199	10.1	11	1713	48.0	19:47	17	4	5	9	8	0	0	1	20:19
	Czech Republic	Olympics	5	1	3	4	0	....	....	....	....	....	....	....	....	....	....	....	....	....	....	....	....	....	....
2014-15	Montreal	NHL	82	26	34	60	46	7	3	5	248	10.5	8	1557	49.9	19:09	12	1	3	4	6	0	0	0	20:23
	NHL Totals		761	202	297	499	438	49	18	31	1880	10.7		13711	49.4	18:24	81	15	31	46	50	3	1	2	19:47

Signed as a free agent by **Kladno** (CzRep), September 16, 2012.

POIRIER, Emile

(p'wah-REE-ay, eh-MEEL) **CGY**

Left wing. Shoots left. 6'2", 200 lbs. Born, Montreal, QC, December 14, 1994. Calgary's 2nd choice, 22nd overall, in 2013 Entry Draft.

Season	Club	League	GP	G	A	Pts	PIM	PP	SH	GW	S	S%	+/-	TF	F%	Min	GP	G	A	Pts	PIM	PP	SH	GW	Min
2010-11	Laval-Montreal	QAAA	42	27	24	51	30	....	....	....	....	....	....	....	....	....	5	1	2	3	4	....	....	....	....
2011-12	Gatineau	QMJHL	67	15	25	40	53	....	....	....	....	....	....	....	....	....	4	1	0	1	8	....	....	....	....
2012-13	Gatineau	QMJHL	65	32	38	70	101	....	....	....	....	....	....	....	....	....	10	6	4	10	14	....	....	....	....
2013-14	Gatineau	QMJHL	63	43	44	87	129	....	....	....	....	....	....	....	....	....	9	7	3	10	26	....	....	....	....
	Abbotsford Heat	AHL	2	2	2	4	0	....	....	....	....	....	....	....	....	....	3	1	0	1	2	....	....	....	....
2014-15	Calgary	NHL	6	0	1	1	0	0	0	0	2	0.0	1	1	0.0	7:59	....	....	....	....	....	....	....	....	....
	Adirondack	AHL	55	19	23	42	50	....	....	....	....	....	....	....	....	....	....	....	....	....	....	....	....	....	....
	NHL Totals		6	0	1	1	0	0	0	0	2	0.0		1	0.0	7:59	....	....	....	....	....	....	....	....	....

POLAK, Roman

(POH-lahk, ROH-muhn) **TOR**

Defense. Shoots right. 6', 236 lbs. Born, Ostrava, Czech., April 28, 1986. St. Louis' 6th choice, 180th overall, in 2004 Entry Draft.

Season	Club	League	GP	G	A	Pts	PIM	PP	SH	GW	S	S%	+/-	TF	F%	Min	GP	G	A	Pts	PIM	PP	SH	GW	Min
2001-02	HC Ostrava Jr.	CzRep-Jr.	46	4	9	13	84	....	....	....	....	....	....	....	....	....	....	....	....	....	....	....	....	....	....
2002-03	HC Ostrava Jr.	CzRep-Jr.	32	3	12	15	34	....	....	....	....	....	....	....	....	....	....	....	....	....	....	....	....	....	....
2003-04	HC Vitkovice Jr.	CzRep-Jr.	52	4	8	12	48	....	....	....	....	....	....	....	....	....	....	....	....	....	....	....	....	....	....
2004-05	Kootenay Ice	WHL	65	5	18	23	85	....	....	....	....	....	....	....	....	....	9	0	0	0	6	....	....	....	....
2005-06	HC Vitkovice Jr.	CzRep-Jr.	1	0	0	0	4	....	....	....	....	....	....	....	....	....	....	....	....	....	....	....	....	....	....
	Vitkovice	CzRep	37	0	1	1	16	....	....	....	....	....	....	....	....	....	6	0	0	0	6	....	....	....	....
2006-07	St. Louis	NHL	19	0	0	0	6	0	0	0	13	0.0	–3	0	0.0	13:38	....	....	....	....	....	....	....	....	....
	Peoria Rivermen	AHL	53	4	8	12	66	....	....	....	....	....	....	....	....	....	....	....	....	....	....	....	....	....	....
2007-08	St. Louis	NHL	6	0	1	1	0	0	0	0	2	0.0	1	0	0.0	11:32	....	....	....	....	....	....	....	....	....
	Peoria Rivermen	AHL	34	0	7	7	33	....	....	....	....	....	....	....	....	....	....	....	....	....	....	....	....	....	....
2008-09	St. Louis	NHL	69	1	14	15	45	0	0	1	73	1.4	–15	1	0.0	21:32	4	0	0	0	0	0	0	0	21:49
2009-10	St. Louis	NHL	78	4	17	21	59	0	0	1	73	5.5	7	0	0.0	19:59	....	....	....	....	....	....	....	....	....
	Czech Republic	Olympics	5	0	0	0	4	....	....	....	....	....	....	....	....	....	....	....	....	....	....	....	....	....	....
2010-11	St. Louis	NHL	55	3	9	12	33	0	0	1	54	5.6	–4	1	0.0	19:57	....	....	....	....	....	....	....	....	....
2011-12	St. Louis	NHL	77	0	11	11	57	0	0	0	88	0.0	6	0	0.0	18:52	9	0	0	0	19	0	0	0	20:41
2012-13	Vitkovice	CzRep	22	2	6	8	79	....	....	....	....	....	....	....	....	....	....	....	....	....	....	....	....	....	....
	St. Louis	NHL	48	1	5	6	48	0	0	1	39	2.6	–2	0	0.0	18:25	6	0	1	1	2	0	0	0	20:09
2013-14	St. Louis	NHL	72	4	9	13	71	0	0	0	83	4.8	3	0	0.0	17:20	6	0	1	1	4	0	0	0	18:38
2014-15	Toronto	NHL	56	5	4	9	48	0	0	1	61	8.2	–22	1	100.0	21:05	....	....	....	....	....	....	....	....	....
	NHL Totals		480	18	70	88	367	0	0	5	486	3.7		3	33.3	19:15	25	0	2	2	25	0	0	0	20:15

Signed as a free agent by **Vitkovice** (CzRep), September 20, 2012. Traded to **Toronto** by **St. Louis** for Carl Gunnarsson and Calgary's 4th round choice (previously acquired, St. Louis selected Ville Husso) in 2014 Entry Draft, June 28, 2014.

POMINVILLE, Jason

(paw-MIHN-vihl, JAY-suhn) **MIN**

Right wing. Shoots right. 6', 185 lbs. Born, Repentigny, QC, November 30, 1982. Buffalo's 4th choice, 55th overall, in 2001 Entry Draft.

Season	Club	League	GP	G	A	Pts	PIM	PP	SH	GW	S	S%	+/-	TF	F%	Min	GP	G	A	Pts	PIM	PP	SH	GW	Min
1997-98	Cap-d-Madeleine	QAAA	13	3	7	10	....	....	....	....	....	....	....	....	....	....	....	....	....	....	....	....	....	....	....
1998-99	Cap-d-Madeleine	QAAA	41	18	38	56	16	....	....	....	....	....	....	....	....	....	7	2	7	9	0	....	....	....	....
	Shawinigan	QMJHL	2	0	0	0	0	....	....	....	....	....	....	....	....	....	....	....	....	....	....	....	....	....	....
99-2000	Shawinigan	QMJHL	60	4	17	21	12	....	....	....	....	....	....	....	....	....	13	2	3	5	0	....	....	....	....
2000-01	Shawinigan	QMJHL	71	46	67	113	24	....	....	....	....	....	....	....	....	....	10	6	6	12	0	....	....	....	....
2001-02	Shawinigan	QMJHL	66	57	64	121	32	....	....	....	....	....	....	....	....	....	2	0	0	0	0	....	....	....	....
2002-03	Rochester	AHL	73	13	21	34	16	....	....	....	....	....	....	....	....	....	3	1	1	2	0	....	....	....	....
2003-04	Buffalo	NHL	1	0	0	0	0	0	0	0	3	0.0	0	0	0.0	14:22	....	....	....	....	....	....	....	....	....
	Rochester	AHL	66	34	30	64	30	....	....	....	....	....	....	....	....	....	16	9	10	19	6	....	....	....	....
2004-05	Rochester	AHL	78	30	38	68	43	....	....	....	....	....	....	....	....	....	....	....	....	....	....	....	....	....	....
2005-06	Buffalo	NHL	57	18	12	30	22	10	2	2	124	14.5	–4	5	20.0	14:07	18	5	5	10	8	0	1	1	12:11
	Rochester	AHL	18	19	7	26	11	....	....	....	....	....	....	....	....	....	....	....	....	....	....	....	....	....	....
2006-07	Buffalo	NHL	82	34	34	68	30	2	2	5	212	16.0	25	14	42.9	17:25	16	4	6	10	0	0	0	0	17:54
2007-08	Buffalo	NHL	82	27	53	80	20	2	1	1	232	11.6	16	67	37.3	19:58	....	....	....	....	....	....	....	....	....
2008-09	Buffalo	NHL	82	20	46	66	18	6	1	2	239	8.4	–4	67	37.3	19:46	....	....	....	....	....	....	....	....	....
2009-10	Buffalo	NHL	82	24	38	62	22	8	0	2	252	9.5	13	120	35.0	18:45	6	2	2	4	2	0	0	1	20:17
2010-11	Buffalo	NHL	73	22	30	52	15	5	1	2	215	10.2	1	155	43.2	18:09	5	1	3	4	2	0	0	1	15:51
2011-12	Buffalo	NHL	82	30	43	73	12	8	2	5	235	12.8	–7	375	47.7	19:41	....	....	....	....	....	....	....	....	....
2012-13	Adler Mannheim	Germany	7	5	7	12	0	....	....	....	....	....	....	....	....	....	....	....	....	....	....	....	....	....	....
	Buffalo	NHL	37	10	15	25	8	1	1	1	94	10.6	1	86	46.5	20:54	....	....	....	....	....	....	....	....	....
	Minnesota	NHL	10	4	5	9	0	1	0	1	24	16.7	0	19	57.9	17:31	2	0	0	0	0	0	0	0	13:32

			Regular Season														Playoffs								
Season	Club	League	GP	G	A	Pts	PIM	PP	SH	GW	S	S%	+/-	TF	F%	Min	GP	G	A	Pts	PIM	PP	SH	GW	Min
2013-14	Minnesota	NHL	82	30	30	60	16	7	0	5	226	13.3	3	159	54.7	18:35	13	2	7	9	0	0	0	0	18:16
2014-15	Minnesota	NHL	82	18	36	54	8	3	0	4	252	7.1	9	87	44.8	18:17	10	3	3	6	0	2	0	1	17:29
	NHL Totals		752	237	342	579	171	53	10	30	2108	11.2		1154	45.2	18:33	70	17	26	43	12	2	1	4	16:22

QMJHL First All-Star Team (2002)

Played in NHL All-Star Game (2012)

Signed as a free agent by **Mannheim** (Germany), December 4, 2012. Traded to **Minnesota** by **Buffalo** with Buffalo's 4th round choice (later traded to Edmonton – Edmonton selected William Lagesson) in 2014 Entry Draft for Matt Hackett, Johan Larsson, Minnesota's 1st round choice (Nikita Zadorov) in 2013 Entry Draft and Minnesota's 2nd round choice (Vaclav Karabacek) in 2014 Entry Draft, April 3, 2013.

PORTER, Chris (POHR-tuhr, KRIHS) PHI

Center. Shoots left. 6'1", 206 lbs. Born, Toronto, ON, May 29, 1984. Chicago's 10th choice, 282nd overall, in 2003 Entry Draft.

Season	Club	League	GP	G	A	Pts	PIM	PP	SH	GW	S	S%	+/-	TF	F%	Min	GP	G	A	Pts	PIM	PP	SH	GW	Min
2001-02	Shat.-St. Mary's	High-MN	75	10	25	35	32	....	....	....	....	....	....	....	....	....	....	....	....	....	....	....	....	....	....
2002-03	Lincoln Stars	USHL	59	13	22	35	74	....	....	....	....	....	....	....	....	....	10	4	3	7	10	....	....	....	....
2003-04	North Dakota	WCHA	41	10	15	25	46	....	....	....	....	....	....	....	....	....	....	....	....	....	....	....	....	....	....
2004-05	North Dakota	WCHA	45	12	3	15	36	....	....	....	....	....	....	....	....	....	....	....	....	....	....	....	....	....	....
2005-06	North Dakota	WCHA	46	7	16	23	40	....	....	....	....	....	....	....	....	....	....	....	....	....	....	....	....	....	....
2006-07	North Dakota	WCHA	43	13	17	30	38	....	....	....	....	....	....	....	....	....	....	....	....	....	....	....	....	....	....
2007-08	Peoria Rivermen	AHL	80	12	25	37	72	....	....	....	....	....	....	....	....	....	....	....	....	....	....	....	....	....	....
2008-09	**St. Louis**	**NHL**	**6**	**1**	**1**	**2**	**0**	**0**	**0**	**0**	**7**	**14.3**	**–1**	**3**	**33.3**	**10:32**	....	....	....	....	....	....	....	....	....
	Peoria Rivermen	AHL	74	7	16	23	72	....	....	....	....	....	....	....	....	....	7	1	1	2	0	....	....	....	....
2009-10	Peoria Rivermen	AHL	80	13	18	31	53	....	....	....	....	....	....	....	....	....	....	....	....	....	....	....	....	....	....
2010-11	**St. Louis**	**NHL**	**45**	**3**	**4**	**7**	**16**	**0**	**0**	**1**	**55**	**5.5**	**–4**	**22**	**54.6**	**10:23**	....	....	....	....	....	....	....	....	....
	Peoria Rivermen	AHL	36	9	11	20	63	....	....	....	....	....	....	....	....	....	....	....	....	....	....	....	....	....	....
2011-12	**St. Louis**	**NHL**	**47**	**4**	**3**	**7**	**11**	**0**	**0**	**1**	**61**	**6.6**	**–1**	**19**	**42.1**	**10:24**	....	....	....	....	....	....	....	....	....
	Peoria Rivermen	AHL	2	0	1	1	2	....	....	....	....	....	....	....	....	....	....	....	....	....	....	....	....	....	....
2012-13	Peoria Rivermen	AHL	12	7	3	10	11	....	....	....	....	....	....	....	....	....	....	....	....	....	....	....	....	....	....
	St. Louis	**NHL**	**29**	**2**	**6**	**8**	**0**	**0**	**0**	**2**	**46**	**4.3**	**5**	**58**	**43.1**	**11:38**	**6**	**1**	**0**	**1**	**0**	**0**	**0**	**0**	**9:14**
2013-14	**St. Louis**	**NHL**	**22**	**0**	**1**	**1**	**0**	**0**	**0**	**0**	**24**	**0.0**	**–3**	**10**	**30.0**	**10:23**	**6**	**1**	**2**	**3**	**0**	**0**	**0**	**0**	**12:14**
	Chicago Wolves	AHL	38	7	11	18	37	....	....	....	....	....	....	....	....	....	....	....	....	....	....	....	....	....	....
2014-15	**St. Louis**	**NHL**	**24**	**1**	**1**	**2**	**6**	**0**	**0**	**1**	**24**	**4.2**	**–3**	**9**	**44.4**	**9:33**	**3**	**0**	**1**	**1**	**0**	**0**	**0**	**0**	**8:11**
	NHL Totals		**173**	**11**	**16**	**27**	**33**	**0**	**0**	**5**	**217**	**5.1**		**121**	**43.8**	**10:29**	**15**	**2**	**3**	**5**	**0**	**0**	**0**	**0**	**10:13**

Signed as a free agent by **St. Louis**, August 21, 2007. • Missed majority of 2014-15 due to lower-body injury vs. Coloradro, December 29, 2014 and as a healthy reserve. Signed as a free agent by **Philadelphia**, August 8, 2015.

PORTER, Kevin (POHR-tuhr, KEH-vihn) PIT

Center. Shoots left. 6', 190 lbs. Born, Detroit, MI, March 12, 1986. Phoenix's 5th choice, 119th overall, in 2004 Entry Draft.

Season	Club	League	GP	G	A	Pts	PIM	PP	SH	GW	S	S%	+/-	TF	F%	Min	GP	G	A	Pts	PIM	PP	SH	GW	Min
2002-03	USNTDP	U-17	19	9	11	20	8	....	....	....	....	....	....	....	....	....	....	....	....	....	....	....	....	....	....
	USNTDP	U-18	13	1	2	3	2	....	....	....	....	....	....	....	....	....	....	....	....	....	....	....	....	....	....
	USNTDP	NAHL	40	19	9	28	17	....	....	....	....	....	....	....	....	....	....	....	....	....	....	....	....	....	....
2003-04	USNTDP	U-18	44	5	21	26	26	....	....	....	....	....	....	....	....	....	....	....	....	....	....	....	....	....	....
	USNTDP	NAHL	11	3	8	11	4	....	....	....	....	....	....	....	....	....	....	....	....	....	....	....	....	....	....
2004-05	U. of Michigan	CCHA	39	11	13	24	51	....	....	....	....	....	....	....	....	....	....	....	....	....	....	....	....	....	....
2005-06	U. of Michigan	CCHA	39	17	21	38	30	....	....	....	....	....	....	....	....	....	....	....	....	....	....	....	....	....	....
2006-07	U. of Michigan	CCHA	41	24	34	58	16	....	....	....	....	....	....	....	....	....	....	....	....	....	....	....	....	....	....
2007-08	U. of Michigan	CCHA	43	*33	30	*63	18	....	....	....	....	....	....	....	....	....	....	....	....	....	....	....	....	....	....
	San Antonio	AHL	....	....	....	....	....	....	....	....	....	....	....	....	....	....	7	0	4	4	0	....	....	....	....
2008-09	**Phoenix**	**NHL**	**34**	**5**	**5**	**10**	**4**	**1**	**0**	**2**	**39**	**12.8**	**–2**	**95**	**29.5**	**13:38**	....	....	....	....	....	....	....	....	....
	San Antonio	AHL	42	13	22	35	14	....	....	....	....	....	....	....	....	....	....	....	....	....	....	....	....	....	....
2009-10	**Phoenix**	**NHL**	**4**	**0**	**0**	**0**	**0**	**0**	**0**	**0**	**3**	**0.0**	**1**	**15**	**33.3**	**7:22**	....	....	....	....	....	....	....	....	....
	San Antonio	AHL	52	15	25	40	31	....	....	....	....	....	....	....	....	....	....	....	....	....	....	....	....	....	....
	Colorado	**NHL**	**16**	**2**	**1**	**3**	**0**	**0**	**1**	**0**	**18**	**11.1**	**–4**	**27**	**48.2**	**13:13**	**4**	**0**	**0**	**0**	**0**	**0**	**0**	**0**	**10:38**
	Lake Erie	AHL	4	1	0	1	2	....	....	....	....	....	....	....	....	....	....	....	....	....	....	....	....	....	....
2010-11	**Colorado**	**NHL**	**74**	**14**	**11**	**25**	**27**	**1**	**0**	**3**	**102**	**13.7**	**–11**	**58**	**32.8**	**13:49**	....	....	....	....	....	....	....	....	....
2011-12	**Colorado**	**NHL**	**35**	**4**	**3**	**7**	**17**	**0**	**0**	**0**	**32**	**12.5**	**–2**	**46**	**30.4**	**9:11**	....	....	....	....	....	....	....	....	....
2012-13	Rochester	AHL	48	15	29	44	38	....	....	....	....	....	....	....	....	....	....	....	....	....	....	....	....	....	....
	Buffalo	**NHL**	**31**	**4**	**5**	**9**	**10**	**0**	**1**	**0**	**37**	**10.8**	**–1**	**271**	**40.2**	**15:14**	....	....	....	....	....	....	....	....	....
2013-14	**Buffalo**	**NHL**	**12**	**0**	**1**	**1**	**2**	**0**	**0**	**0**	**3**	**0.0**	**–5**	**53**	**34.0**	**11:38**	....	....	....	....	....	....	....	....	....
	Rochester	AHL	50	19	17	36	24	....	....	....	....	....	....	....	....	....	5	0	3	3	0	....	....	....	....
2014-15	Grand Rapids	AHL	76	16	23	39	25	....	....	....	....	....	....	....	....	....	16	1	3	4	14	....	....	....	....
	NHL Totals		**206**	**29**	**26**	**55**	**60**	**2**	**2**	**5**	**234**	**12.4**		**565**	**36.5**	**12:55**	**4**	**0**	**0**	**0**	**0**	**0**	**0**	**0**	**10:38**

CCHA Second All-Star Team (2007) • CCHA First All-Star Team (2008) • CCHA Player of the Year (2008) • NCAA West First All-American Team (2008)

Traded to **Colorado** by **Phoenix** with Peter Mueller for Wojtek Wolski, March 3, 2010. Signed as a free agent by **Buffalo**, July 6, 2012. • Missed majority of 2011-12 as a healthy reserve. Signed as a free agent by **Detroit**, July 3, 2014. Signed as a free agent by **Pittsburgh**, July 1, 2015.

POSTMA, Paul (POHST-muh, PAWL) WPG

Defense. Shoots right. 6'3", 195 lbs. Born, Red Deer, AB, February 22, 1989. Atlanta's 4th choice, 205th overall, in 2007 Entry Draft.

Season	Club	League	GP	G	A	Pts	PIM	PP	SH	GW	S	S%	+/-	TF	F%	Min	GP	G	A	Pts	PIM	PP	SH	GW	Min
2004-05	Red Deer	AMHL	36	6	5	11	24	....	....	....	....	....	....	....	....	....	....	....	....	....	....	....	....	....	....
	Swift Current	WHL	4	0	0	0	0	....	....	....	....	....	....	....	....	....	....	....	....	....	....	....	....	....	....
2005-06	Swift Current	WHL	58	2	9	11	6	....	....	....	....	....	....	....	....	....	4	0	0	0	0	....	....	....	....
2006-07	Swift Current	WHL	70	5	19	24	42	....	....	....	....	....	....	....	....	....	6	0	1	1	0	....	....	....	....
2007-08	Swift Current	WHL	2	0	0	0	2	....	....	....	....	....	....	....	....	....	....	....	....	....	....	....	....	....	....
	Calgary Hitmen	WHL	66	14	28	42	30	....	....	....	....	....	....	....	....	....	16	6	4	10	4	....	....	....	....
2008-09	Calgary Hitmen	WHL	70	23	61	84	28	....	....	....	....	....	....	....	....	....	18	5	8	13	10	....	....	....	....
2009-10	Chicago Wolves	AHL	63	15	14	29	24	....	....	....	....	....	....	....	....	....	7	0	2	2	0	....	....	....	....
2010-11	**Atlanta**	**NHL**	**1**	**0**	**0**	**0**	**0**	**0**	**0**	**0**	**1**	**0.0**	**0**	**0**	**0.0**	**9:55**	....	....	....	....	....	....	....	....	....
	Chicago Wolves	AHL	69	12	33	45	20	....	....	....	....	....	....	....	....	....	....	....	....	....	....	....	....	....	....
2011-12	**Winnipeg**	**NHL**	**3**	**0**	**0**	**0**	**0**	**0**	**0**	**0**	**3**	**0.0**	**0**	**0**	**0.0**	**8:31**	....	....	....	....	....	....	....	....	....
	St. John's IceCaps	AHL	56	13	31	44	32	....	....	....	....	....	....	....	....	....	15	1	9	10	14	....	....	....	....
2012-13	St. John's IceCaps	AHL	27	7	11	18	16	....	....	....	....	....	....	....	....	....	....	....	....	....	....	....	....	....	....
	Winnipeg	**NHL**	**34**	**4**	**5**	**9**	**6**	**2**	**0**	**0**	**32**	**12.5**	**–5**	**0**	**0.0**	**15:02**	....	....	....	....	....	....	....	....	....
2013-14	**Winnipeg**	**NHL**	**20**	**1**	**2**	**3**	**8**	**0**	**0**	**1**	**19**	**5.3**	**1**	**0**	**0.0**	**16:08**	....	....	....	....	....	....	....	....	....
	St. John's IceCaps	AHL	4	1	5	6	4	....	....	....	....	....	....	....	....	....	....	....	....	....	....	....	....	....	....
2014-15	**Winnipeg**	**NHL**	**42**	**2**	**4**	**6**	**16**	**2**	**0**	**0**	**40**	**5.0**	**1**	**0**	**0.0**	**14:08**	....	....	....	....	....	....	....	....	....
	NHL Totals		**100**	**7**	**11**	**18**	**30**	**4**	**0**	**1**	**95**	**7.4**		**0**	**0.0**	**14:37**	....	....	....	....	....	....	....	....	....

WHL East First All-Star Team (2009) • Canadian Major Junior Second All-Star Team (2009) • AHL First All-Star Team (2012)

• Transferred to **Winnipeg** after **Atlanta** franchise relocated, June 21, 2011. • Missed majority of 2013-14 due to blood clot in his leg. • Missed majority of 2014-15 due to lower-body injury at Tampa Bay, March 14, 2015 and as a healthy reserve.

POTTER, Corey (PAW-tuhr, KOHR-ee)

Defense. Shoots right. 6'3", 204 lbs. Born, Lansing, MI, January 5, 1984. NY Rangers' 4th choice, 122nd overall, in 2003 Entry Draft.

Season	Club	League	GP	G	A	Pts	PIM	PP	SH	GW	S	S%	+/-	TF	F%	Min	GP	G	A	Pts	PIM	PP	SH	GW	Min
99-2000	Det. Honeybaked	MWEHL	58	10	38	48	....	....	....	....	....	....	....	....	....	....	....	....	....	....	....	....	....	....	....
2000-01	USNTDP	U-17	13	0	0	0	6	....	....	....	....	....	....	....	....	....	....	....	....	....	....	....	....	....	....
	USNTDP	NAHL	53	4	4	8	20	....	....	....	....	....	....	....	....	....	....	....	....	....	....	....	....	....	....
2001-02	USNTDP	U-18	38	4	6	10	49	....	....	....	....	....	....	....	....	....	....	....	....	....	....	....	....	....	....
	USNTDP	USHL	13	2	2	4	12	....	....	....	....	....	....	....	....	....	....	....	....	....	....	....	....	....	....
	USNTDP	NAHL	10	0	3	3	4	....	....	....	....	....	....	....	....	....	....	....	....	....	....	....	....	....	....
2002-03	Michigan State	CCHA	35	4	4	8	30	....	....	....	....	....	....	....	....	....	....	....	....	....	....	....	....	....	....
2003-04	Michigan State	CCHA	38	0	8	8	63	....	....	....	....	....	....	....	....	....	....	....	....	....	....	....	....	....	....
2004-05	Michigan State	CCHA	32	0	6	6	73	....	....	....	....	....	....	....	....	....	....	....	....	....	....	....	....	....	....
2005-06	Michigan State	CCHA	45	4	18	22	117	....	....	....	....	....	....	....	....	....	....	....	....	....	....	....	....	....	....
2006-07	Hartford	AHL	30	2	8	10	21	....	....	....	....	....	....	....	....	....	7	1	4	5	12	....	....	....	....
	Charlotte	ECHL	43	6	13	19	56	....	....	....	....	....	....	....	....	....	....	....	....	....	....	....	....	....	....
2007-08	Hartford	AHL	80	5	27	32	102	....	....	....	....	....	....	....	....	....	5	0	1	1	14	....	....	....	....

			Regular Season														Playoffs								
Season	Club	League	GP	G	A	Pts	PIM	PP	SH	GW	S	S%	+/-	TF	F%	Min	GP	G	A	Pts	PIM	PP	SH	GW	Min
2008-09	**NY Rangers**	**NHL**	**5**	**1**	**1**	**2**	**0**	**0**	**0**	**0**	**4**	**25.0**	**–1**	**0**	**0.0**	**13:15**	....	....	....	....	....	....	....	....	....
	Hartford	AHL	67	10	22	32	82	....	....	....	....	....	....	....	....	....	6	1	3	4	23	....	....	....	....
2009-10	**NY Rangers**	**NHL**	**3**	**0**	**0**	**0**	**2**	**0**	**0**	**0**	**2**	**0.0**	**0**	**0**	**0.0**	**12:07**	....	....	....	....	....	....	....	....	....
	Hartford	AHL	69	4	24	28	54	....	....	....	....	....	....	....	....	....	....	....	....	....	....	....	....	....	....
2010-11	**Pittsburgh**	**NHL**	**1**	**0**	**0**	**0**	**0**	**0**	**0**	**0**	**1**	**0.0**	**0**	**0**	**0.0**	**16:43**	....	....	....	....	....	....	....	....	....
	Wilkes-Barre	AHL	75	7	30	37	52	....	....	....	....	....	....	....	....	....	12	2	7	9	10	....	....	....	....
2011-12	**Edmonton**	**NHL**	**62**	**4**	**17**	**21**	**24**	**1**	**0**	**0**	**98**	**4.1**	**–16**	**0**	**0.0**	**19:57**	....	....	....	....	....	....	....	....	....
2012-13	Vienna Capitals	Austria	17	1	3	4	10	....	....	....	....	....	....	....	....	....	....	....	....	....	....	....	....	....	....
	Edmonton	**NHL**	**33**	**3**	**1**	**4**	**6**	**0**	**0**	**0**	**36**	**8.3**	**8**	**0**	**0.0**	**17:27**	....	....	....	....	....	....	....	....	....
2013-14	**Edmonton**	**NHL**	**16**	**0**	**5**	**5**	**21**	**0**	**0**	**0**	**16**	**0.0**	**0**	**0**	**0.0**	**13:47**	....	....	....	....	....	....	....	....	....
	Oklahoma City	AHL	6	0	1	1	4	....	....	....	....	....	....	....	....	....	....	....	....	....	....	....	....	....	....
	Boston	**NHL**	**3**	**0**	**0**	**0**	**0**	**0**	**0**	**0**	**1**	**0.0**	**–1**	**0**	**0.0**	**13:45**	**1**	**0**	**0**	**0**	**0**	**0**	**0**	**0**	**16:57**
2014-15	**Calgary**	**NHL**	**6**	**0**	**0**	**0**	**0**	**0**	**0**	**0**	**2**	**0.0**	**–1**	**0**	**0.0**	**9:40**	**2**	**0**	**0**	**0**	**0**	**0**	**0**	**0**	**4:45**
	Adirondack	AHL	25	0	10	10	18	....	....	....	....	....	....	....	....	....	....	....	....	....	....	....	....	....	....
	NHL Totals		**129**	**8**	**24**	**32**	**53**	**1**	**0**	**0**	**160**	**5.0**		**0**	**0.0**	**17:27**	**3**	**0**	**0**	**0**	**0**	**0**	**0**	**0**	**8:49**

Signed as a free agent by **Pittsburgh**, July 16, 2010. Signed as a free agent by **Edmonton**, July 1, 2011. Signed as a free agent by **Vienna** (Austria), October 2, 2012. Claimed on waivers by **Boston** from **Edmonton**, March 5, 2014. • Missed majority of 2013-14 due to back and groin injuries and as a healthy reserve. Signed as a free agent by **Calgary**, September 5, 2014. • Missed majority of 2014 -15 as a healthy reserve.

POTULNY, Ryan

(poh-TUHL-nee, RIGH-uhn)

Center. Shoots left. 6', 190 lbs. Born, Grand Forks, ND, September 5, 1984. Philadelphia's 6th choice, 87th overall, in 2003 Entry Draft.

2001-02	Lincoln Stars	USHL	60	23	34	57	65	....	....	....	....	....	....	....	....	....	4	0	1	1	2	....	....	....	....
2002-03	Lincoln Stars	USHL	54	35	*43	*78	18	....	....	....	....	....	....	....	....	....	10	6	*11	*17	8	....	....	....	....
2003-04	U. of Minnesota	WCHA	15	6	8	14	10	....	....	....	....	....	....	....	....	....	....	....	....	....	....	....	....	....	....
2004-05	U. of Minnesota	WCHA	44	24	17	41	20	....	....	....	....	....	....	....	....	....	....	....	....	....	....	....	....	....	....
2005-06	U. of Minnesota	WCHA	41	*38	25	*63	31	....	....	....	....	....	....	....	....	....	....	....	....	....	....	....	....	....	....
	Philadelphia	**NHL**	**2**	**0**	**1**	**1**	**0**	**0**	**0**	**0**	**0**	**0.0**	**1**	**9**	**44.4**	**6:09**	....	....	....	....	....	....	....	....	....
2006-07	**Philadelphia**	**NHL**	**35**	**7**	**5**	**12**	**22**	**0**	**0**	**2**	**56**	**12.5**	**1**	**278**	**43.5**	**11:00**	....	....	....	....	....	....	....	....	....
	Philadelphia	AHL	30	12	14	26	34	....	....	....	....	....	....	....	....	....	....	....	....	....	....	....	....	....	....
2007-08	**Philadelphia**	**NHL**	**7**	**0**	**1**	**1**	**4**	**0**	**0**	**0**	**5**	**0.0**	**0**	**32**	**43.8**	**6:30**	....	....	....	....	....	....	....	....	....
	Philadelphia	AHL	58	21	26	47	51	....	....	....	....	....	....	....	....	....	12	3	5	8	10	....	....	....	....
2008-09	**Edmonton**	**NHL**	**8**	**0**	**3**	**3**	**0**	**0**	**0**	**0**	**9**	**0.0**	**2**	**10**	**10.0**	**10:29**	....	....	....	....	....	....	....	....	....
	Springfield	AHL	70	38	24	62	48	....	....	....	....	....	....	....	....	....	....	....	....	....	....	....	....	....	....
2009-10	**Edmonton**	**NHL**	**64**	**15**	**17**	**32**	**28**	**7**	**1**	**2**	**152**	**9.9**	**–21**	**820**	**47.4**	**16:17**	....	....	....	....	....	....	....	....	....
	Springfield	AHL	14	3	5	8	8	....	....	....	....	....	....	....	....	....	....	....	....	....	....	....	....	....	....
2010-11	**Chicago**	**NHL**	**3**	**0**	**0**	**0**	**0**	**0**	**0**	**0**	**2**	**0.0**	**–1**	**26**	**38.5**	**10:07**	....	....	....	....	....	....	....	....	....
	Rockford IceHogs	AHL	58	18	23	41	30	....	....	....	....	....	....	....	....	....	....	....	....	....	....	....	....	....	....
	Ottawa	**NHL**	**7**	**0**	**0**	**0**	**0**	**0**	**0**	**0**	**5**	**0.0**	**0**	**0**	**0.0**	**6:57**	....	....	....	....	....	....	....	....	....
	Binghamton	AHL	13	3	5	8	4	....	....	....	....	....	....	....	....	....	23	*14	12	*26	12	....	....	....	....
2011-12	Hershey Bears	AHL	61	33	32	65	32	....	....	....	....	....	....	....	....	....	5	2	2	4	0	....	....	....	....
2012-13	Hershey Bears	AHL	66	19	22	41	30	....	....	....	....	....	....	....	....	....	5	0	2	2	2	....	....	....	....
2013-14	Hershey Bears	AHL	38	3	7	10	10	....	....	....	....	....	....	....	....	....	....	....	....	....	....	....	....	....	....
2014-15	Hartford	AHL	25	2	3	5	10	....	....	....	....	....	....	....	....	....	7	0	0	0	0	....	....	....	....
	NHL Totals		**126**	**22**	**27**	**49**	**54**	**7**	**1**	**4**	**229**	**9.6**		**1175**	**45.9**	**13:05**	....	....	....	....	....	....	....	....	....

USHL First All-Star Team (2003) • USHL Player of the Year (2003) • WCHA First All-Star Team (2006) • NCAA West First All-American Team (2006)

• Missed majority of 2003-04 due to knee injury vs. North Dakota (WCHA), November 7, 2003. Traded to **Edmonton** by **Philadelphia** for Danny Syvret, June 6, 2008. Signed as a free agent by **Chicago**, September 9, 2010. Traded to **Ottawa** by **Chicago** with Chicago's 2nd round choice (later traded to Detroit – Detroit selected Xavier Ouellet) in 2011 Entry Draft for Chris Campoli and future considerations, February 28, 2011. Signed as a free agent by **Washington**, July 1, 2011. Signed as a free agent by **Hershey** (AHL), December 27, 2013. Signed as a free agent by **Hartford** (AHL), August 6, 2014. Signed as a free agent by **Lahti** (Finland), June 11, 2015.

POULIOT, Benoit

(POO-lee-oh, BEHN-wah) **EDM**

Left wing. Shoots Left. 6'3", 197 lbs. Born, Alfred, ON, September 29, 1986. Minnesota's 1st choice, 4th overall, in 2005 Entry Draft.

2002-03	Clarence Beavers	ON-Jr.B	38	13	17	30	86	....	....	....	....	....	....	....	....	....	5	0	2	2	8	....	....	....	....
	Hawkesbury	ON-Jr.A	1	1	0	1	0	....	....	....	....	....	....	....	....	....	....	....	....	....	....	....	....	....	....
2003-04	Hawkesbury	ON-Jr.A	45	21	21	42	85	....	....	....	....	....	....	....	....	....	6	3	7	10	10	....	....	....	....
	Sudbury Wolves	OHL	4	2	2	4	0	....	....	....	....	....	....	....	....	....	4	2	1	3	0	....	....	....	....
2004-05	Sudbury Wolves	OHL	67	29	38	67	102	....	....	....	....	....	....	....	....	....	12	6	8	14	20	....	....	....	....
2005-06	Sudbury Wolves	OHL	51	35	30	65	141	....	....	....	....	....	....	....	....	....	8	8	3	11	16	....	....	....	....
	Houston Aeros	AHL	....	....	....	....	....	....	....	....	....	....	....	....	....	....	2	0	0	0	2	....	....	....	....
2006-07	**Minnesota**	**NHL**	**3**	**0**	**0**	**0**	**0**	**0**	**0**	**0**	**1**	**0.0**	**–1**	**2**	**0.0**	**6:58**	....	....	....	....	....	....	....	....	....
	Houston Aeros	AHL	67	19	17	36	109	....	....	....	....	....	....	....	....	....	....	....	....	....	....	....	....	....	....
2007-08	**Minnesota**	**NHL**	**11**	**2**	**1**	**3**	**0**	**0**	**0**	**0**	**10**	**20.0**	**–1**	**65**	**40.0**	**8:49**	**1**	**0**	**0**	**0**	**0**	**0**	**0**	**0**	**10:16**
	Houston Aeros	AHL	46	10	14	24	67	....	....	....	....	....	....	....	....	....	3	0	0	0	2	....	....	....	....
2008-09	**Minnesota**	**NHL**	**37**	**5**	**6**	**11**	**18**	**2**	**0**	**1**	**34**	**14.7**	**1**	**217**	**42.9**	**11:51**	....	....	....	....	....	....	....	....	....
	Houston Aeros	AHL	30	9	15	24	20	....	....	....	....	....	....	....	....	....	20	1	7	8	28	....	....	....	....
2009-10	**Minnesota**	**NHL**	**14**	**2**	**2**	**4**	**12**	**0**	**0**	**0**	**19**	**10.5**	**0**	**8**	**50.0**	**11:56**	....	....	....	....	....	....	....	....	....
	Montreal	**NHL**	**39**	**15**	**9**	**24**	**31**	**4**	**0**	**3**	**92**	**16.3**	**8**	**3**	**33.3**	**16:44**	**18**	**0**	**2**	**2**	**6**	**0**	**0**	**0**	**11:45**
	Hamilton	AHL	3	1	2	3	4	....	....	....	....	....	....	....	....	....	....	....	....	....	....	....	....	....	....
2010-11	**Montreal**	**NHL**	**79**	**13**	**17**	**30**	**87**	**1**	**0**	**4**	**129**	**10.1**	**2**	**22**	**45.5**	**11:32**	**3**	**0**	**0**	**0**	**7**	**0**	**0**	**0**	**6:12**
2011-12	**Boston**	**NHL**	**74**	**16**	**16**	**32**	**38**	**1**	**0**	**5**	**107**	**15.0**	**18**	**18**	**44.4**	**12:13**	**7**	**1**	**1**	**2**	**6**	**0**	**0**	**0**	**12:40**
2012-13	**Tampa Bay**	**NHL**	**34**	**8**	**12**	**20**	**15**	**0**	**0**	**1**	**60**	**13.3**	**8**	**31**	**32.3**	**13:14**	....	....	....	....	....	....	....	....	....
2013-14	**NY Rangers**	**NHL**	**80**	**15**	**21**	**36**	**56**	**7**	**0**	**4**	**141**	**10.6**	**10**	**39**	**51.3**	**13:26**	**25**	**5**	**5**	**10**	**26**	**1**	**0**	**1**	**15:42**
2014-15	**Edmonton**	**NHL**	**58**	**19**	**15**	**34**	**28**	**4**	**1**	**3**	**105**	**18.1**	**–1**	**34**	**38.2**	**16:37**	....	....	....	....	....	....	....	....	....
	NHL Totals		**429**	**95**	**99**	**194**	**285**	**19**	**1**	**21**	**698**	**13.6**		**439**	**42.1**	**13:14**	**54**	**6**	**8**	**14**	**45**	**1**	**0**	**1**	**13:22**

OHL All-Rookie Team (2005) • OHL First All-Star Team (2005) • OHL Rookie of the Year (2005) • Canadian Major Junior All-Rookie Team (2005) • Canadian Major Junior Rookie of the Year (2005)

Traded to **Montreal** by **Minnesota** for Guillaume Latendresse, November 23, 2009. Signed as a free agent by **Boston**, July 1, 2011. Traded to **Tampa Bay** by **Boston** for Michel Ouellet and Tampa Bay's 5th round choice (Seth Griffith) in 2012 Entry Draft, June 23, 2012. Signed as a free agent by **NY Rangers**, July 5, 2013. Signed as a free agent by **Edmonton**, July 1, 2014.

POULIOT, Derrick

(POO-lee-oh, DAIR-ihk) **PIT**

Defense. Shoots left. 5'11", 195 lbs. Born, Estevan, SK, January 16, 1994. Pittsburgh's 1st choice, 8th overall, in 2012 Entry Draft.

2008-09	Weyburn Wings	Minor-SK	26	25	38	63	24	....	....	....	....	....	....	....	....	....	5	5	1	6	....	....	....	....	....
	Moose Jaw	SMHL	5	1	1	2	0	....	....	....	....	....	....	....	....	....	....	....	....	....	....	....	....	....	....
2009-10	Moose Jaw	SMHL	43	14	29	43	38	....	....	....	....	....	....	....	....	....	4	0	2	2	4	....	....	....	....
	Portland	WHL	7	0	1	1	0	....	....	....	....	....	....	....	....	....	....	....	....	....	....	....	....	....	....
2010-11	Portland	WHL	66	5	25	30	38	....	....	....	....	....	....	....	....	....	21	1	3	4	16	....	....	....	....
2011-12	Portland	WHL	72	11	48	59	79	....	....	....	....	....	....	....	....	....	22	3	14	17	18	....	....	....	....
2012-13	Portland	WHL	44	9	36	45	60	....	....	....	....	....	....	....	....	....	21	4	16	20	12	....	....	....	....
	Wilkes-Barre	AHL	....	....	....	....	....	....	....	....	....	....	....	....	....	....	1	0	0	0	0	....	....	....	....
2013-14	Portland	WHL	58	17	53	70	74	....	....	....	....	....	....	....	....	....	21	5	*27	32	13	....	....	....	....
2014-15	**Pittsburgh**	**NHL**	**34**	**2**	**5**	**7**	**4**	**1**	**0**	**2**	**56**	**3.6**	**–11**	**0**	**0.0**	**17:33**	....	....	....	....	....	....	....	....	....
	Wilkes-Barre	AHL	31	7	17	24	20	....	....	....	....	....	....	....	....	....	6	1	2	3	2	....	....	....	....
	NHL Totals		**34**	**2**	**5**	**7**	**4**	**1**	**0**	**2**	**56**	**3.6**		**0**	**0.0**	**17:33**	....	....	....	....	....	....	....	....	....

Memorial Cup All-Star Team (2013) • WHL West First All-Star Team (2014) • WHL Defenseman of the Year (2014) • Canadian Major Junior Defenseman of the Year (2014)

POWE, Darroll

(POW, DAIR-ohl)

Left wing. Shoots left. 5'11", 212 lbs. Born, Saskatoon, SK, June 22, 1985.

2001-02	Kanata Valley	ON-Jr.A	48	6	7	13	102	....	....	....	....	....	....	....	....	....	4	2	1	3	....	....	....	....	....
2002-03	Kanata Valley	ON-Jr.A	46	21	20	41	126	....	....	....	....	....	....	....	....	....	4	0	1	1	10	....	....	....	....
2003-04	Princeton	ECAC	29	4	5	9	28	....	....	....	....	....	....	....	....	....	....	....	....	....	....	....	....	....	....
2004-05	Princeton	ECAC	30	5	2	7	41	....	....	....	....	....	....	....	....	....	....	....	....	....	....	....	....	....	....
2005-06	Princeton	ECAC	27	6	10	16	48	....	....	....	....	....	....	....	....	....	....	....	....	....	....	....	....	....	....
2006-07	Princeton	ECAC	34	13	15	28	63	....	....	....	....	....	....	....	....	....	....	....	....	....	....	....	....	....	....
	Philadelphia	AHL	11	2	2	4	20	....	....	....	....	....	....	....	....	....	....	....	....	....	....	....	....	....	....
2007-08	Philadelphia	AHL	76	9	14	23	133	....	....	....	....	....	....	....	....	....	10	1	0	1	6	....	....	....	....

			Regular Season														Playoffs								
Season	Club	League	GP	G	A	Pts	PIM	PP	SH	GW	S	S%	+/-	TF	F%	Min	GP	G	A	Pts	PIM	PP	SH	GW	Min
2008-09	**Philadelphia**	**NHL**	**60**	**6**	**5**	**11**	**35**	**0**	**0**	**0**	**72**	**8.3**	**–8**	**263**	**48.7**	**10:32**	**6**	**1**	**2**	**3**	**7**	**0**	**0**	**0**	**14:02**
	Philadelphia	AHL	8	4	3	7	20																		
2009-10	**Philadelphia**	**NHL**	**63**	**9**	**6**	**15**	**54**	**0**	**0**	**0**	**103**	**8.7**	**0**	**210**	**45.2**	**12:05**	**23**	**0**	**1**	**1**	**6**	**0**	**0**	**0**	**12:33**
2010-11	**Philadelphia**	**NHL**	**81**	**7**	**10**	**17**	**41**	**0**	**2**	**2**	**87**	**8.0**	**–6**	**134**	**49.3**	**12:17**	**11**	**0**	**1**	**1**	**4**	**0**	**0**	**0**	**12:10**
2011-12	**Minnesota**	**NHL**	**82**	**6**	**7**	**13**	**57**	**0**	**0**	**1**	**109**	**5.5**	**–20**	**105**	**43.8**	**13:59**									
2012-13	**Minnesota**	**NHL**	**8**	**0**	**0**	**0**	**9**	**0**	**0**	**0**	**5**	**0.0**	**1**	**4**	**75.0**	**10:13**									
	NY Rangers	**NHL**	**34**	**0**	**0**	**0**	**18**	**0**	**0**	**0**	**18**	**0.0**	**–2**	**100**	**53.0**	**8:43**	**3**	**0**	**0**	**0**	**0**	**0**	**0**	**0**	**6:25**
2013-14	**NY Rangers**	**NHL**	**1**	**0**	**0**	**0**	**0**	**0**	**0**	**0**	**0**	**0.0**	**–2**	**1**	**100.0**	**8:33**									
	Hartford	AHL	73	13	11	24	106																		
2014-15	Lehigh Valley	AHL	43	5	9	14	49																		
	NHL Totals		**329**	**28**	**28**	**56**	**214**	**0**	**2**	**3**	**394**	**7.1**		**817**	**48.0**	**11:55**	**43**	**1**	**4**	**5**	**17**	**0**	**0**	**0**	**12:14**

Signed as a free agent by **Philadelphia**, April 17, 2008. Traded to **Minnesota** by **Philadelphia** for Minnesota's 3rd round choice (later traded to Dallas, later traded to Pittsburgh – Pittsburgh selected Jake Guentzel) in 2013 Entry Draft, June 27, 2011. Traded to **NY Rangers** by **Minnesota** with Nick Palmieri for Mke Rupp, February 4, 2013. Signed as a free agent by **Lehigh Valley** (AHL), August 13, 2014.

PRINCE, Shane

(PRIHNS, SHAYN) **OTT**

Center. Shoots left. 5'11", 185 lbs. Born, Rochester, NY, November 16, 1992. Ottawa's 4th choice, 61st overall, in 2011 Entry Draft.

Season	Club	League	GP	G	A	Pts	PIM	PP	SH	GW	S	S%	+/-	TF	F%	Min	GP	G	A	Pts	PIM	PP	SH	GW	Min
2007-08	Maksymum	EmJHL	34	15	31	46	10																		
	Maksymum	Other	10	3	4	7	4																		
	Rochester	EJHL	11	3	3	6	4																		
2008-09	Kitchener Rangers	OHL	63	3	9	12	34																		
2009-10	Kitchener Rangers	OHL	39	8	9	17	32																		
	Ottawa 67's	OHL	26	7	6	13	13										12	2	2	4	4				
2010-11	Ottawa 67's	OHL	59	25	63	88	18										3	1	0	1	0				
2011-12	Ottawa 67's	OHL	57	43	47	90	12										18	7	9	16	6				
2012-13	Binghamton	AHL	65	18	17	35	24										3	1	0	1	0				
2013-14	Binghamton	AHL	69	21	27	48	53										4	1	1	2	0				
2014-15	**Ottawa**	**NHL**	**2**	**0**	**1**	**1**	**0**	**0**	**0**	**0**	**2**	**0.0**	**1**	**0**	**0.0**	**10:29**									
	Binghamton	AHL	72	28	37	65	31																		
	NHL Totals		**2**	**0**	**1**	**1**	**0**	**0**	**0**	**0**	**2**	**0.0**		**0**	**0.0**	**10:29**									

AHL Second All-Star Team (2015)

PROSSER, Nate

(PRAW-suhr, NAYT) **MIN**

Defense. Shoots right. 6'2", 203 lbs. Born, Elk River, MN, May 7, 1986.

Season	Club	League	GP	G	A	Pts	PIM	PP	SH	GW	S	S%	+/-	TF	F%	Min	GP	G	A	Pts	PIM	PP	SH	GW	Min
2006-07	Colorado College	WCHA	21	0	3	3	8																		
2007-08	Colorado College	WCHA	39	3	17	20	51																		
2008-09	Colorado College	WCHA	38	5	8	13	61																		
2009-10	**Minnesota**	**NHL**	**3**	**0**	**1**	**1**	**8**	**0**	**0**	**0**	**4**	**0.0**	**2**	**0**	**0.0**	**19:37**									
	Colorado College	WCHA	39	4	24	28	58																		
2010-11	**Minnesota**	**NHL**	**2**	**0**	**0**	**0**	**0**	**0**	**0**	**0**	**1**	**0.0**	**0**	**0**	**0.0**	**14:48**									
	Houston Aeros	AHL	73	8	19	27	31										24	2	2	4	16				
2011-12	**Minnesota**	**NHL**	**51**	**1**	**11**	**12**	**57**	**0**	**0**	**0**	**32**	**3.1**	**–17**	**0**	**0.0**	**19:15**									
	Houston Aeros	AHL	23	0	4	4	10										2	1	0	1	2				
2012-13	**Minnesota**	**NHL**	**17**	**0**	**0**	**0**	**4**	**0**	**0**	**0**	**5**	**0.0**	**4**	**0**	**0.0**	**11:15**									
2013-14	**Minnesota**	**NHL**	**53**	**2**	**6**	**8**	**58**	**0**	**0**	**2**	**30**	**6.7**	**2**	**0**	**0.0**	**14:32**	**10**	**0**	**0**	**0**	**12**	**0**	**0**	**0**	**12:31**
2014-15	**Minnesota**	**NHL**	**63**	**2**	**5**	**7**	**32**	**0**	**0**	**1**	**38**	**5.3**	**–1**	**0**	**0.0**	**12:48**	**1**	**0**	**0**	**0**	**2**	**0**	**0**	**0**	**4:02**
	NHL Totals		**189**	**5**	**23**	**28**	**159**	**0**	**0**	**3**	**110**	**4.5**		**0**	**0.0**	**15:01**	**11**	**0**	**0**	**0**	**14**	**0**	**0**	**0**	**11:45**

WCHA Second All-Star Team (2010)

Signed as a free agent by **Minnesota**, March 18, 2010. • Missed majority of 2012-13 as a healthy reserve. Signed as a free agent by **St. Louis**, July 21, 2014. Claimed on waivers by **Minnesota** from **St. Louis**, October 2, 2014.

PROUT, Dalton

(PROWT, DAHL-tuhn) **CBJ**

Defense. Shoots right. 6'3", 222 lbs. Born, LaSalle, ON, March 13, 1990. Columbus' 7th choice, 154th overall, in 2010 Entry Draft.

Season	Club	League	GP	G	A	Pts	PIM	PP	SH	GW	S	S%	+/-	TF	F%	Min	GP	G	A	Pts	PIM	PP	SH	GW	Min
2005-06	Wind. Jr. Spitfires	Minor-ON	58	11	19	30	78																		
2006-07	Sarnia Sting	OHL	49	1	2	3	36										4	0	0	0	0				
2007-08	Sarnia Sting	OHL	32	0	2	2	43																		
	Barrie Colts	OHL	25	0	3	3	39										8	0	2	2	16				
2008-09	Barrie Colts	OHL	65	0	6	6	98										5	0	1	1	10				
2009-10	Barrie Colts	OHL	63	7	14	21	121										17	1	6	7	20				
2010-11	Barrie Colts	OHL	23	7	14	21	55																		
	Saginaw Spirit	OHL	29	2	8	10	44										12	2	0	2	27				
2011-12	**Columbus**	**NHL**	**5**	**0**	**0**	**0**	**0**	**0**	**0**	**0**	**2**	**0.0**	**1**	**0**	**0.0**	**11:48**									
	Springfield	AHL	62	4	9	13	54																		
2012-13	Springfield	AHL	40	1	8	9	73										6	0	1	1	14				
	Columbus	**NHL**	**28**	**1**	**6**	**7**	**25**	**0**	**0**	**0**	**16**	**6.3**	**15**	**0**	**0.0**	**18:32**									
2013-14	**Columbus**	**NHL**	**49**	**2**	**4**	**6**	**37**	**0**	**0**	**0**	**56**	**3.6**	**–7**	**1**	**0.0**	**17:12**	**2**	**0**	**0**	**0**	**2**	**0**	**0**	**0**	**13:12**
	Springfield	AHL	15	0	3	3	11																		
2014-15	**Columbus**	**NHL**	**63**	**0**	**8**	**8**	**85**	**0**	**0**	**0**	**64**	**0.0**	**–14**	**0**	**0.0**	**18:25**									
	NHL Totals		**145**	**3**	**18**	**21**	**147**	**0**	**0**	**0**	**138**	**2.2**		**1**	**0.0**	**17:48**	**2**	**0**	**0**	**0**	**2**	**0**	**0**	**0**	**13:12**

PRUST, Brandon

(PROOST, BRAN-duhn) **VAN**

Left wing. Shoots left. 6', 194 lbs. Born, London, ON, March 16, 1984. Calgary's 2nd choice, 70th overall, in 2004 Entry Draft.

Season	Club	League	GP	G	A	Pts	PIM	PP	SH	GW	S	S%	+/-	TF	F%	Min	GP	G	A	Pts	PIM	PP	SH	GW	Min
2001-02	London Nationals	ON-Jr.B	52	17	35	52	38																		
2002-03	London Knights	OHL	65	12	17	29	94										14	2	1	3	21				
2003-04	London Knights	OHL	64	19	33	52	269										15	7	13	20	33				
2004-05	London Knights	OHL	48	10	20	30	174										15	3	5	8	*71				
2005-06	Omaha	AHL	79	12	14	26	294																		
2006-07	**Calgary**	**NHL**	**10**	**0**	**0**	**0**	**25**	**0**	**0**	**0**	**1**	**0.0**	**1**	**0**	**0.0**	**6:03**									
	Omaha	AHL	63	17	10	27	211										6	0	3	3	20				
2007-08	Quad City Flames	AHL	79	10	27	37	248																		
2008-09	**Calgary**	**NHL**	**25**	**1**	**1**	**2**	**79**	**0**	**0**	**1**	**15**	**6.7**	**–4**	**15**	**53.3**	**6:21**									
	Phoenix	**NHL**	**11**	**0**	**1**	**1**	**29**	**0**	**0**	**0**	**8**	**0.0**	**–4**	**16**	**56.3**	**9:59**									
2009-10	**Calgary**	**NHL**	**43**	**1**	**4**	**5**	**98**	**0**	**0**	**1**	**23**	**4.3**	**6**	**29**	**37.9**	**6:33**									
	NY Rangers	**NHL**	**26**	**4**	**5**	**9**	**65**	**0**	**0**	**2**	**21**	**19.0**	**3**	**2**	**100.0**	**9:20**									
2010-11	**NY Rangers**	**NHL**	**82**	**13**	**16**	**29**	**160**	**0**	**5**	**1**	**87**	**14.9**	**2**	**9**	**44.4**	**13:49**	**5**	**0**	**1**	**1**	**4**	**0**	**0**	**0**	**16:24**
2011-12	**NY Rangers**	**NHL**	**82**	**5**	**12**	**17**	**156**	**0**	**2**	**2**	**68**	**7.4**	**–1**	**5**	**60.0**	**11:57**	**19**	**1**	**1**	**2**	**31**	**0**	**0**	**0**	**12:47**
2012-13	**Montreal**	**NHL**	**38**	**5**	**9**	**14**	**110**	**0**	**0**	**1**	**39**	**12.8**	**11**	**55**	**45.5**	**13:38**	**4**	**0**	**1**	**1**	**14**	**0**	**0**	**0**	**15:27**
2013-14	**Montreal**	**NHL**	**52**	**6**	**7**	**13**	**121**	**0**	**0**	**3**	**49**	**12.2**	**–1**	**125**	**52.0**	**12:49**	**13**	**0**	**2**	**2**	**32**	**0**	**0**	**0**	**12:13**
2014-15	**Montreal**	**NHL**	**82**	**4**	**14**	**18**	**134**	**0**	**0**	**0**	**78**	**5.1**	**6**	**31**	**51.6**	**12:58**	**12**	**1**	**3**	**4**	**35**	**0**	**0**	**0**	**13:47**
	NHL Totals		**451**	**39**	**69**	**108**	**977**	**0**	**7**	**11**	**389**	**10.0**		**287**	**49.8**	**11:34**	**53**	**2**	**8**	**10**	**116**	**0**	**0**	**0**	**13:25**

Traded to **Phoenix** by **Calgary** with Matthew Lombardi and Calgary's 1st round choice (Brandon Gormley) in 2010 Entry Draft for Olli Jokinen and Phoenix's 3rd round choice (later traded to Florida – Florida selected Josh Birkholz) in 2009 Entry Draft, March 4, 2009. Traded to **Calgary** by **Phoenix** for Jim Vandermeer, June 27, 2009. Traded to **NY Rangers** by **Calgary** with Olli Jokinen for Chris Higgins and Ales Kotalik, February 2, 2010. Signed as a free agent by **Montreal**, July 1, 2012. Traded to **Vancouver** by **Montreal** for Zack Kassian and Vancouver's 5th round choice in 2016 Entry Draft, July 1, 2015.

PUEMPEL, Matt

(PUHM-puhl, MAT) **OTT**

Left wing. Shoots left. 6'2", 209 lbs. Born, Windsor, ON, January 24, 1993. Ottawa's 3rd choice, 24th overall, in 2011 Entry Draft.

Season	Club	League	GP	G	A	Pts	PIM	PP	SH	GW	S	S%	+/-	TF	F%	Min	GP	G	A	Pts	PIM	PP	SH	GW	Min
2008-09	Sun County	Minor-ON	76	88	56	144																			
	Leamington Flyers	ON-Jr.B	1	2	0	2	0																		
2009-10	Peterborough	OHL	59	33	31	64	43										4	1	1	2	6				
2010-11	Peterborough	OHL	55	34	35	69	49																		
2011-12	Peterborough	OHL	30	17	16	33	31																		
	Binghamton	AHL	9	1	0	1	2																		

			Regular Season														Playoffs								
Season	Club	League	GP	G	A	Pts	PIM	PP	SH	GW	S	S%	+/-	TF	F%	Min	GP	G	A	Pts	PIM	PP	SH	GW	Min
2012-13	Kitchener Rangers	OHL	51	35	12	47	43	....	....	....	....	....	....	....	....	....	10	3	4	7	10	....	....	....	....
	Binghamton	AHL	2	0	0	0	0	....	....	....	....	....	....	....	....	....	3	2	0	2	0	....	....	....	....
2013-14	Binghamton	AHL	74	30	18	48	94	....	....	....	....	....	....	....	....	....	1	0	0	0	0	....	....	....	....
2014-15	**Ottawa**	**NHL**	**13**	**2**	**1**	**3**	**8**	**0**	**0**	**0**	**14**	**14.3**	**6**	**1**	**0.0**	**8:02**	....	....	....	....	....	....	....	....	....
	Binghamton	AHL	51	12	20	32	31	....	....	....	....	....	....	....	....	....	....	....	....	....	....	....	....	....	....
	NHL Totals		**13**	**2**	**1**	**3**	**8**	**0**	**0**	**0**	**14**	**14.3**		**1**	**0.0**	**8:02**	....	....	....	....	....	....	....	....	....

OHL All-Rookie Team (2010) • OHL Rookie of the Year (2010) • Canadian Major Junior All-Rookie Team (2010) • Canadian Major Junior Rookie of the Year (2010)

PULKKINEN, Teemu

(PUHL-kih-nuhn, TEE-moo) **DET**

Left wing. Shoots right. 5'11", 183 lbs. Born, Vantaa, Finland, January 2, 1992. Detroit's 4th choice, 111th overall, in 2010 Entry Draft.

2007-08	Jokerit U18	Fin-U18	32	36	24	60	8	....	....	....	....	....	....	....	....	....	6	11	6	17	6	....	....	....	....
2008-09	Suomi U20	Finland-2	1	0	0	0	0	....	....	....	....	....	....	....	....	....	....	....	....	....	....	....	....	....	....
	Jokerit U18	Fin-U18	9	16	19	35	4	....	....	....	....	....	....	....	....	....	....	....	....	....	....	....	....	....	....
	Jokerit Helsinki Jr.	Fin-Jr.	24	15	13	28	12	....	....	....	....	....	....	....	....	....	....	....	....	....	....	....	....	....	....
	Jokerit Helsinki	Finland	3	0	0	0	6	....	....	....	....	....	....	....	....	....	....	....	....	....	....	....	....	....	....
2009-10	Jokerit Helsinki Jr.	Fin-Jr.	17	20	21	41	41	....	....	....	....	....	....	....	....	....	4	3	3	6	0	....	....	....	....
	Jokerit Helsinki	Finland	12	1	2	3	6	....	....	....	....	....	....	....	....	....	....	....	....	....	....	....	....	....	....
2010-11	Suomi U20	Finland-2	1	1	0	1	0	....	....	....	....	....	....	....	....	....	....	....	....	....	....	....	....	....	....
	Jokerit Helsinki	Finland	55	18	36	54	32	....	....	....	....	....	....	....	....	....	3	0	1	1	0	....	....	....	....
2011-12	Jokerit Helsinki	Finland	56	16	21	37	41	....	....	....	....	....	....	....	....	....	4	0	1	1	2	....	....	....	....
2012-13	Jokerit Helsinki	Finland	59	14	20	34	49	....	....	....	....	....	....	....	....	....	6	2	3	5	22	....	....	....	....
	Grand Rapids	AHL	2	0	1	1	2	....	....	....	....	....	....	....	....	....	14	3	2	5	10	....	....	....	....
2013-14	**Detroit**	**NHL**	**3**	**0**	**0**	**0**	**2**	**0**	**0**	**0**	**4**	**0.0**	**0**	**0**	**0.0**	**7:28**	....	....	....	....	....	....	....	....	....
	Grand Rapids	AHL	71	31	28	59	34	....	....	....	....	....	....	....	....	....	10	5	6	11	10	....	....	....	....
2014-15	**Detroit**	**NHL**	**31**	**5**	**3**	**8**	**10**	**1**	**0**	**2**	**67**	**7.5**	**5**	**0**	**0.0**	**11:29**	....	....	....	....	....	....	....	....	....
	Grand Rapids	AHL	46	*34	27	61	30	....	....	....	....	....	....	....	....	....	16	14	4	18	22	....	....	....	....
	NHL Totals		**34**	**5**	**3**	**8**	**12**	**1**	**0**	**2**	**71**	**7.0**		**0**	**0.0**	**11:07**	....	....	....	....	....	....	....	....	....

AHL All-Rookie Team (2014) • AHL First All-Star Team (2015) • Willie Marshall Award (AHL – Top Goal-scorer) (2015)

PURCELL, Teddy

(PUHR-sihl, TEH-dee) **EDM**

Right wing. Shoots right. 6'3", 203 lbs. Born, St. Johns, NL, September 8, 1985.

2003-04	Notre Dame	SJHL	51	21	25	46	8	....	....	....	....	....	....	....	....	....	....	....	....	....	....	....	....	....	....
2004-05	Cedar Rapids	USHL	58	20	47	67	22	....	....	....	....	....	....	....	....	....	11	5	9	14	4	....	....	....	....
2005-06	Cedar Rapids	USHL	55	19	*52	71	14	....	....	....	....	....	....	....	....	....	8	3	8	11	4	....	....	....	....
2006-07	U. of Maine	H-East	40	16	27	43	34	....	....	....	....	....	....	....	....	....	....	....	....	....	....	....	....	....	....
2007-08	**Los Angeles**	**NHL**	**10**	**1**	**2**	**3**	**0**	**0**	**0**	**0**	**10**	**10.0**	**2**	**0**	**0.0**	**11:59**	....	....	....	....	....	....	....	....	....
	Manchester	AHL	67	25	58	83	34	....	....	....	....	....	....	....	....	....	4	0	3	3	0	....	....	....	....
2008-09	**Los Angeles**	**NHL**	**40**	**4**	**12**	**16**	**4**	**2**	**0**	**1**	**68**	**5.9**	**–4**	**29**	**17.2**	**13:31**	....	....	....	....	....	....	....	....	....
	Manchester	AHL	38	16	22	38	12	....	....	....	....	....	....	....	....	....	....	....	....	....	....	....	....	....	....
2009-10	**Los Angeles**	**NHL**	**41**	**3**	**3**	**6**	**4**	**1**	**0**	**1**	**55**	**5.5**	**–1**	**3**	**33.3**	**11:22**	....	....	....	....	....	....	....	....	....
	Tampa Bay	**NHL**	**19**	**3**	**6**	**9**	**6**	**1**	**0**	**0**	**46**	**6.5**	**–8**	**1**	**100.0**	**16:05**	....	....	....	....	....	....	....	....	....
2010-11	**Tampa Bay**	**NHL**	**81**	**17**	**34**	**51**	**10**	**3**	**0**	**1**	**196**	**8.7**	**5**	**37**	**32.4**	**14:06**	**18**	**6**	**11**	**17**	**2**	**1**	**0**	**1**	**13:42**
2011-12	**Tampa Bay**	**NHL**	**81**	**24**	**41**	**65**	**16**	**8**	**0**	**3**	**152**	**15.8**	**9**	**17**	**17.7**	**16:08**	....	....	....	....	....	....	....	....	....
2012-13	**Tampa Bay**	**NHL**	**48**	**11**	**25**	**36**	**12**	**3**	**0**	**2**	**94**	**11.7**	**–1**	**6**	**33.3**	**16:45**	....	....	....	....	....	....	....	....	....
2013-14	**Tampa Bay**	**NHL**	**81**	**12**	**30**	**42**	**14**	**3**	**0**	**4**	**157**	**7.6**	**–3**	**16**	**25.0**	**16:28**	**4**	**1**	**0**	**1**	**0**	**1**	**0**	**0**	**15:32**
2014-15	**Edmonton**	**NHL**	**82**	**12**	**22**	**34**	**24**	**5**	**0**	**0**	**146**	**8.2**	**–33**	**7**	**57.1**	**17:10**	....	....	....	....	....	....	....	....	....
	NHL Totals		**483**	**87**	**175**	**262**	**90**	**26**	**0**	**12**	**924**	**9.4**		**116**	**27.6**	**15:22**	**22**	**7**	**11**	**18**	**2**	**2**	**0**	**1**	**14:02**

AHL All-Rookie Team (2008) • AHL First All-Star Team (2008) • Dudley "Red" Garrett Memorial Award (AHL) (AHL - Top Rookie) (2008)

Signed as a free agent by **Los Angeles**, April 27, 2007. Traded to **Tampa Bay** by **Los Angeles** with Florida's 3rd round choice (previously acquired, Tampa Bay selected Brock Beukeboom) in 2010 Entry Draft for Jeff Halpern, March 3, 2010. Traded to **Edmonton** by **Tampa Bay** for Sam Gagner, June 29, 2014.

PYATT, Tom

(PIGH-at, TAWM)

Center. Shoots left. 5'11", 188 lbs. Born, Thunder Bay, ON, February 14, 1987. NY Rangers' 6th choice, 107th overall, in 2005 Entry Draft.

2003-04	Saginaw Spirit	OHL	67	9	9	18	21	....	....	....	....	....	....	....	....	....	....	....	....	....	....	....	....	....	....
2004-05	Saginaw Spirit	OHL	57	18	30	48	14	....	....	....	....	....	....	....	....	....	....	....	....	....	....	....	....	....	....
2005-06	Saginaw Spirit	OHL	58	24	29	53	29	....	....	....	....	....	....	....	....	....	4	1	2	3	4	....	....	....	....
2006-07	Saginaw Spirit	OHL	58	43	38	81	18	....	....	....	....	....	....	....	....	....	6	3	5	8	0	....	....	....	....
	Hartford	AHL	1	0	0	0	0	....	....	....	....	....	....	....	....	....	....	....	....	....	....	....	....	....	....
2007-08	Hartford	AHL	41	4	7	11	6	....	....	....	....	....	....	....	....	....	3	0	0	0	0	....	....	....	....
	Charlotte	ECHL	16	6	9	15	8	....	....	....	....	....	....	....	....	....	3	0	0	0	0	....	....	....	....
2008-09	Hartford	AHL	73	15	22	37	22	....	....	....	....	....	....	....	....	....	4	0	0	0	2	....	....	....	....
2009-10	**Montreal**	**NHL**	**40**	**2**	**3**	**5**	**10**	**0**	**0**	**0**	**48**	**4.2**	**–5**	**50**	**42.0**	**11:04**	**18**	**2**	**2**	**4**	**2**	**0**	**0**	**1**	**13:03**
	Hamilton	AHL	41	13	22	35	8	....	....	....	....	....	....	....	....	....	....	....	....	....	....	....	....	....	....
2010-11	**Montreal**	**NHL**	**61**	**2**	**5**	**7**	**9**	**0**	**0**	**0**	**65**	**3.1**	**–1**	**110**	**50.0**	**10:38**	**7**	**0**	**0**	**0**	**0**	**0**	**0**	**0**	**9:54**
2011-12	**Tampa Bay**	**NHL**	**74**	**12**	**7**	**19**	**8**	**1**	**0**	**1**	**95**	**12.6**	**–19**	**281**	**45.6**	**14:48**	....	....	....	....	....	....	....	....	....
2012-13	**Tampa Bay**	**NHL**	**43**	**8**	**8**	**16**	**12**	**0**	**0**	**1**	**60**	**13.3**	**5**	**290**	**50.0**	**13:35**	....	....	....	....	....	....	....	....	....
2013-14	**Tampa Bay**	**NHL**	**27**	**3**	**4**	**7**	**4**	**0**	**0**	**1**	**27**	**11.1**	**–2**	**193**	**52.3**	**11:28**	**1**	**0**	**0**	**0**	**0**	**0**	**0**	**0**	**7:54**
2014-15	Geneve	Swiss	50	11	22	33	10	....	....	....	....	....	....	....	....	....	11	2	8	10	0	....	....	....	....
	NHL Totals		**245**	**27**	**27**	**54**	**43**	**1**	**0**	**3**	**295**	**9.2**		**924**	**48.7**	**12:34**	**26**	**2**	**2**	**4**	**2**	**0**	**0**	**1**	**12:00**

Traded to **Montreal** by **NY Rangers** with Scott Gomez and Michael Busto for Chris Higgins, Ryan McDonagh and Pavel Valentenko, June 30, 2009. Signed as a free agent by **Tampa Bay**, July 6, 2011. • Missed majority of 2013-14 due to collar bone injury at Buffalo, October 8, 2013 and as a healthy reserve. Signed as a free agent by **Geneve** (Swiss), August 4, 2014.

PYSYK, Mark

(PEHS-ihk, MAHRK) **BUF**

Defense. Shoots right. 6'1", 192 lbs. Born, Edmonton, AB, January 11, 1992. Buffalo's 1st choice, 23rd overall, in 2010 Entry Draft.

2007-08	Sherwood Park	AMHL	34	10	10	20	60	....	....	....	....	....	....	....	....	....	2	1	0	1	16	....	....	....	....
	Edmonton	WHL	14	1	2	3	8	....	....	....	....	....	....	....	....	....	....	....	....	....	....	....	....	....	....
2008-09	Edmonton	WHL	61	5	15	20	27	....	....	....	....	....	....	....	....	....	4	0	0	0	2	....	....	....	....
2009-10	Edmonton	WHL	48	7	17	24	47	....	....	....	....	....	....	....	....	....	....	....	....	....	....	....	....	....	....
2010-11	Edmonton	WHL	63	6	34	40	88	....	....	....	....	....	....	....	....	....	4	0	0	0	6	....	....	....	....
2011-12	Edmonton	WHL	57	6	32	38	83	....	....	....	....	....	....	....	....	....	20	3	8	11	16	....	....	....	....
2012-13	Rochester	AHL	57	4	14	18	20	....	....	....	....	....	....	....	....	....	3	0	0	0	2	....	....	....	....
	Buffalo	**NHL**	**19**	**1**	**4**	**5**	**0**	**1**	**0**	**0**	**21**	**4.8**	**–7**	**0**	**0.0**	**16:17**	....	....	....	....	....	....	....	....	....
2013-14	**Buffalo**	**NHL**	**44**	**1**	**6**	**7**	**16**	**0**	**0**	**1**	**51**	**2.0**	**–11**	**0**	**0.0**	**19:37**	....	....	....	....	....	....	....	....	....
	Rochester	AHL	31	1	11	12	28	....	....	....	....	....	....	....	....	....	5	0	0	0	14	....	....	....	....
2014-15	**Buffalo**	**NHL**	**7**	**2**	**1**	**3**	**2**	**0**	**0**	**1**	**4**	**50.0**	**4**	**0**	**0.0**	**18:11**	....	....	....	....	....	....	....	....	....
	Rochester	AHL	54	3	14	17	32	....	....	....	....	....	....	....	....	....	....	....	....	....	....	....	....	....	....
	NHL Totals		**70**	**4**	**11**	**15**	**18**	**1**	**0**	**2**	**76**	**5.3**		**0**	**0.0**	**18:34**	....	....	....	....	....	....	....	....	....

WHL East Second All-Star Team (2012)

QUINCEY, Kyle

(KWIHN-see, KIGHL) **DET**

Defense. Shoots left. 6'2", 216 lbs. Born, Kitchener, ON, August 12, 1985. Detroit's 2nd choice, 132nd overall, in 2003 Entry Draft.

2001-02	Mississauga	ON-Jr.A	27	5	14	19	31	....	....	....	....	....	....	....	....	....	....	....	....	....	....	....	....	....	....
2002-03	London Knights	OHL	66	6	12	18	77	....	....	....	....	....	....	....	....	....	14	3	4	7	11	....	....	....	....
2003-04	London Knights	OHL	3	0	2	2	4	....	....	....	....	....	....	....	....	....	....	....	....	....	....	....	....	....	....
	Mississauga	OHL	61	14	23	37	135	....	....	....	....	....	....	....	....	....	24	3	13	16	32	....	....	....	....
2004-05	Mississauga	OHL	59	15	31	46	111	....	....	....	....	....	....	....	....	....	5	0	3	3	4	....	....	....	....
2005-06	**Detroit**	**NHL**	**1**	**0**	**0**	**0**	**0**	**0**	**0**	**0**	**1**	**0.0**	**0**	**0**	**0.0**	**11:37**	....	....	....	....	....	....	....	....	....
	Grand Rapids	AHL	70	7	26	33	107	....	....	....	....	....	....	....	....	....	16	0	1	1	27	....	....	....	....
2006-07	**Detroit**	**NHL**	**6**	**1**	**0**	**1**	**0**	**0**	**0**	**0**	**7**	**14.3**	**0**	**0**	**0.0**	**11:26**	**13**	**0**	**0**	**0**	**2**	**0**	**0**	**0**	**8:11**
	Grand Rapids	AHL	65	4	18	22	126	....	....	....	....	....	....	....	....	....	2	0	0	0	0	....	....	....	....
2007-08	**Detroit**	**NHL**	**6**	**0**	**0**	**0**	**4**	**0**	**0**	**0**	**5**	**0.0**	**–3**	**0**	**0.0**	**13:58**	....	....	....	....	....	....	....	....	....
	Grand Rapids	AHL	66	5	15	20	149	....	....	....	....	....	....	....	....	....	....	....	....	....	....	....	....	....	....
2008-09	**Los Angeles**	**NHL**	**72**	**4**	**34**	**38**	**63**	**2**	**0**	**2**	**150**	**2.7**	**–5**	**0**	**0.0**	**20:59**	....	....	....	....	....	....	....	....	....

Season	Club	League	GP	G	A	Pts	PIM	PP	SH	GW	S	S%	+/-	TF	F%	Min	GP	G	A	Pts	PIM	PP	SH	GW	Min
						Regular Season														Playoffs					
2009-10	Colorado	NHL	79	6	23	29	76	1	0	0	139	4.3	9	1	0.0	23:37	6	0	0	0	8	0	0	0	22:06
2010-11	Colorado	NHL	21	0	1	1	18	0	0	0	39	0.0	-5	0	0.0	19:35	….	….	….	….	….	….	….	….	….
2011-12	Colorado	NHL	54	5	18	23	60	3	0	1	131	3.8	-1	1	0.0	22:21	….	….	….	….	….	….	….	….	….
	Detroit	NHL	18	2	1	3	29	1	0	0	37	5.4	0	0	0.0	20:22	5	0	2	2	6	0	0	0	16:29
2012-13	Denver	CHL	12	2	9	11	6									
	Detroit	NHL	36	1	2	3	18	0	0	0	36	2.8	7	0	0.0	19:13	14	0	2	2	12	0	0	0	19:02
2013-14	Detroit	NHL	82	4	9	13	88	0	0	1	106	3.8	-5	0	0.0	20:48	5	0	0	0	2	0	0	0	21:25
2014-15	Detroit	NHL	73	3	15	18	77	0	0	0	90	3.3	10	0	0.0	19:29	7	0	3	3	4	0	0	0	19:39
	NHL Totals		448	26	103	129	433	7	0	4	741	3.5		2	0.0	20:52	50	0	7	7	34	0	0	0	16:39

OHL Second All-Star Team (2005)

Claimed on waivers by **Los Angeles** from **Detroit**, October 13, 2008. Traded to **Colorado** by **Los Angeles** with Tom Preissing and Los Angeles' 5th round choice (Luke Walker) in 2010 Entry Draft for Ryan Smyth, July 3, 2009. • Missed majority of 2010-11 due to shoulder injury at Atlanta, December 10, 2010. Traded to **Tampa Bay** by **Colorado** for Steve Downie, February 21, 2012. Traded to **Detroit** by **Tampa Bay** for Sebastien Piche and Detroit's 1st round choice (Andrei Vasilevski) in 2012 Entry Draft, February 21, 2012. Signed as a free agent by **Denver** (CHL), October 12, 2012.

RACINE, Jonathan

(RAY-seen, JAWN-ah-thuhn) **FLA**

Defense. Shoots left. 6'2", 194 lbs.   Born, Montreal, QC, May 28, 1993. Florida's 6th choice, 87th overall, in 2011 Entry Draft.

Season	Club	League	GP	G	A	Pts	PIM	PP	SH	GW	S	S%	+/-	TF	F%	Min	GP	G	A	Pts	PIM	PP	SH	GW	Min
2008-09	Saint-Eustache	QAAA	45	5	7	12	74										8	0	2	2	12	….	….	….	….
2009-10	Shawinigan	QMJHL	55	0	4	4	43										6	0	0	0	0	….	….	….	….
2010-11	Shawinigan	QMJHL	68	2	5	7	86										12	0	1	1	22	….	….	….	….
2011-12	Shawinigan	QMJHL	61	3	10	13	107										11	1	5	6	22	….	….	….	….
2012-13	Moncton Wildcats	QMJHL	61	8	13	21	138										5	0	0	0	7	….	….	….	….
	San Antonio	AHL	8	0	0	0	4									
2013-14	**Florida**	**NHL**	1	0	0	0	2	0	0	0	0	0.0	-1	0	0.0	15:35	….	….	….	….	….	….	….	….	….
	San Antonio	AHL	51	0	6	6	91									
2014-15	San Antonio	AHL	70	0	7	7	149										3	0	1	1	4	….	….	….	….
	NHL Totals		1	0	0	0	2	0	0	0	0	0.0		0	0.0	15:35	….	….	….	….	….	….	….	….	….

RAFFL, Michael

(RA-fuhl, mi-KHIGH-ehl) **PHI**

Left wing. Shoots left. 6', 200 lbs.   Born, Villach, Austria, December 1, 1988.

Season	Club	League	GP	G	A	Pts	PIM	PP	SH	GW	S	S%	+/-	TF	F%	Min	GP	G	A	Pts	PIM	PP	SH	GW	Min
2005-06	EC VSV Villach Jr.	Austria-Jr.	26	11	27	38	91										4	6	6	12	10	….	….	….	….
	EC VSV Villach	Austria	5	0	0	0	0										3	0	0	0	0	….	….	….	….
2006-07	EC VSV Villach Jr.	Austria-Jr.	21	23	24	47	82														
	EC VSV Villach	Austria	43	4	2	6	22										4	0	0	0	0	….	….	….	….
2007-08	EC VSV Villach Jr.	Austria-Jr.	6	5	7	12	28														
	EC VSV Villach	Austria	40	3	6	9	24										5	2	0	2	2	….	….	….	….
2008-09	EC VSV Villach	Austria	49	9	10	19	77										6	0	2	2	12	….	….	….	….
2009-10	EC VSV Villach	Austria	42	25	18	43	54										5	1	0	1	14	….	….	….	….
2010-11	EC VSV Villach	Austria	50	26	29	55	62										8	5	4	9	20	….	….	….	….
2011-12	Leksands IF	Sweden-2	45	10	14	24	26														
2012-13	Leksands IF	Sweden-2	59	27	25	52	44														
2013-14	**Philadelphia**	**NHL**	68	9	13	22	28	0	0	3	101	8.9	2	93	55.9	12:59	7	0	1	1	0	0	0	0	12:35
	Adirondack	AHL	2	1	2	3	0									
	Austria	Olympics	4	1	2	3	4									
2014-15	**Philadelphia**	**NHL**	67	21	7	28	34	2	1	2	134	15.7	6	97	45.4	14:12	….	….	….	….	….	….	….	….	….
	NHL Totals		135	30	20	50	62	2	1	5	235	12.8		190	50.5	13:35	7	0	1	1	0	0	0	0	12:35

Signed as a free agent by **Philadelphia**, May 31, 2013.

RAKELL, Rickard

(ra-KEHL, REE-kahrd) **ANA**

Right wing. Shoots right. 6'1", 192 lbs.   Born, Sundbyberg, Sweden, May 5, 1993. Anaheim's 1st choice, 30th overall, in 2011 Entry Draft.

Season	Club	League	GP	G	A	Pts	PIM	PP	SH	GW	S	S%	+/-	TF	F%	Min	GP	G	A	Pts	PIM	PP	SH	GW	Min
2007-08	Spanga Hockey	Sweden-4	24	4	3	7	12														
2008-09	AIK IF Solna U18	Swe-U18	16	2	3	5	22														
2009-10	AIK IF Solna U18	Swe-U18	30	25	16	41	18										3	2	2	4	0	….	….	….	….
	AIK IF Solna Jr.	Swe-Jr.	8	3	1	4	2										2	1	0	1	0	….	….	….	….
2010-11	Plymouth Whalers	OHL	49	20	25	45	12										1	0	0	0	0	….	….	….	….
2011-12	Plymouth Whalers	OHL	60	28	34	62	12										13	2	10	12	0	….	….	….	….
2012-13	Plymouth Whalers	OHL	40	21	23	44	12										15	6	9	15	10	….	….	….	….
	Anaheim	**NHL**	4	0	0	0	0	0	0	0	3	0.0	-2	21	47.6	8:57	….	….	….	….	….	….	….	….	….
2013-14	**Anaheim**	**NHL**	18	0	4	4	2	0	0	0	22	0.0	-3	194	49.0	11:43	4	1	1	2	0	1	0	0	10:58
	Norfolk Admirals	AHL	46	14	23	37	12										1	1	0	1	0	….	….	….	….
2014-15	**Anaheim**	**NHL**	71	9	22	31	10	2	0	1	105	8.6	6	665	46.6	12:34	16	1	0	1	2	0	0	1	11:32
	Norfolk Admirals	AHL	2	1	3	4	0									
	NHL Totals		93	9	26	35	12	2	0	1	130	6.9		880	47.2	12:15	20	2	1	3	2	1	0	1	11:25

RALLO, Greg

(RA-loh, GREHG)

Center. Shoots right. 6', 195 lbs.   Born, Gurnee, IL, August 26, 1981.

Season	Club	League	GP	G	A	Pts	PIM	PP	SH	GW	S	S%	+/-	TF	F%	Min	GP	G	A	Pts	PIM	PP	SH	GW	Min
2002-03	Ferris State	CCHA	41	15	14	29	46														
2003-04	Ferris State	CCHA	38	7	11	18	42														
2004-05	Ferris State	CCHA	33	7	15	22	22														
2005-06	Ferris State	CCHA	40	17	22	39	30														
	Idaho Steelheads	ECHL	7	2	2	4	2										7	2	1	3	4	….	….	….	….
2006-07	Idaho Steelheads	ECHL	37	13	18	31	43										14	8	3	11	12	….	….	….	….
	Iowa Stars	AHL	28	3	2	5	25										2	1	0	1	2	….	….	….	….
2007-08	Idaho Steelheads	ECHL	39	17	19	36	47														
	Albany River Rats	AHL	5	0	0	0	0									
	Rockford IceHogs	AHL	2	0	0	0	0									
	Manitoba Moose	AHL	13	4	5	9	2										3	0	0	0	9	….	….	….	….
2008-09	Manitoba Moose	AHL	55	4	5	9	17										20	2	2	4	9	….	….	….	….
2009-10	Texas Stars	AHL	69	19	25	44	25										24	3	1	7	10	….	….	….	….
2010-11	Texas Stars	AHL	78	26	28	54	46										6	1	1	2	8	….	….	….	….
2011-12	**Florida**	**NHL**	1	0	0	0	0	0	0	0	1	0.0	0	0	0.0	3:31	….	….	….	….	….	….	….	….	….
	San Antonio	AHL	72	22	20	42	18										4	0	2	2	0	….	….	….	….
2012-13	San Antonio	AHL	66	23	17	40	36														
	Florida	**NHL**	10	1	0	1	2	1	0	0	10	10.0	-5	3	33.3	9:33	….	….	….	….	….	….	….	….	….
2013-14	San Antonio	AHL	69	10	24	34	26										3	0	1	1	4	….	….	….	….
2014-15	Texas Stars	AHL	72	27	22	49	38														
	NHL Totals		11	1	0	1	2	1	0	0	11	9.1		3	33.3	9:00	….	….	….	….	….	….	….	….	….

Signed as a free agent by **Florida**, July 2, 2011. Signed as a free agent by **Texas** (AHL), August 1, 2014.

RAMAGE, John

(RAM-ihj, JAWN) **CBJ**

Defense. Shoots right. 6', 200 lbs.   Born, Mississauga, ON, February 7, 1991. Calgary's 3rd choice, 103rd overall, in 2010 Entry Draft.

Season	Club	League	GP	G	A	Pts	PIM	PP	SH	GW	S	S%	+/-	TF	F%	Min	GP	G	A	Pts	PIM	PP	SH	GW	Min
2007-08	St. Louis Bandits	NAHL	45	4	5	9	75										11	0	2	2	2	….	….	….	….
	USNTDP	U-17	3	0	0	0	0									
2008-09	USNTDP	NAHL	14	1	4	5	12									
	USNTDP	U-18	40	1	4	5	32									
2009-10	U. of Wisconsin	WCHA	41	0	12	12	51									
2010-11	U. of Wisconsin	WCHA	37	1	10	11	59									
2011-12	U. of Wisconsin	WCHA	37	3	7	10	62									
2012-13	U. of Wisconsin	WCHA	42	8	12	20	65									
2013-14	Abbotsford Heat	AHL	50	0	1	1	46									
	Alaska Aces	ECHL	6	1	0	1	6										20	4	9	13	20	….	….	….	….

			Regular Season														Playoffs								
Season	Club	League	GP	G	A	Pts	PIM	PP	SH	GW	S	S%	+/-	TF	F%	Min	GP	G	A	Pts	PIM	PP	SH	GW	Min
2014-15	**Calgary**	**NHL**	**1**	**0**	**0**	**0**	**0**	**0**	**0**	**0**	**4**	**0.0**	**–1**	**0**	**0.0**	**18:10**	....	....	....	....	....	....	....	....	....
	Adirondack	AHL	57	3	12	15	81	....	....	....	....	....	....	....	....	....	....	....	....	....	....	....	....	....	....
	NHL Totals		**1**	**0**	**0**	**0**	**0**	**0**	**0**	**0**	**4**	**0.0**		**0**	**0.0**	**18:10**	....	....	....	....	....	....	....	....	....

Signed as a free agent by **Columbus**, July 3, 2015.

RANFORD, Brendan

(RAN-fohrd, BREHN-duhn) **DAL**

Left wing. Shoots left. 5'10", 190 lbs. Born, Edmonton, AB, May 3, 1992. Philadelphia's 6th choice, 209th overall, in 2010 Entry Draft.

Season	Club	League	GP	G	A	Pts	PIM	PP	SH	GW	S	S%	+/-	TF	F%	Min	GP	G	A	Pts	PIM	PP	SH	GW	Min
2007-08	Gregg Distributors	AMHL	35	*33	46	*79	58	....	....	....	....	....	....	....	....	....	12	10	5	15	6	....	....	....	....
	Kamloops Blazers	WHL	3	0	0	0	0	....	....	....	....	....	....	....	....	....	....	....	....	....	....	....	....	....	....
2008-09	Kamloops Blazers	WHL	66	13	14	27	46	....	....	....	....	....	....	....	....	....	4	0	3	3	2	....	....	....	....
2009-10	Kamloops Blazers	WHL	72	29	36	65	83	....	....	....	....	....	....	....	....	....	4	2	3	5	4	....	....	....	....
2010-11	Kamloops Blazers	WHL	68	33	53	86	68	....	....	....	....	....	....	....	....	....	....	....	....	....	....	....	....	....	....
2011-12	Kamloops Blazers	WHL	69	40	52	92	73	....	....	....	....	....	....	....	....	....	11	5	9	14	8	....	....	....	....
2012-13	Kamloops Blazers	WHL	70	22	65	87	28	....	....	....	....	....	....	....	....	....	15	5	15	20	0	....	....	....	....
2013-14	Texas Stars	AHL	65	12	21	33	14	....	....	....	....	....	....	....	....	....	21	8	8	16	12	....	....	....	....
2014-15	**Dallas**	**NHL**	**1**	**0**	**0**	**0**	**0**	**0**	**0**	**0**	**0**	**0.0**	**0**	**0**	**0.0**	**9:19**	....	....	....	....	....	....	....	....	....
	Texas Stars	AHL	73	18	33	51	22	....	....	....	....	....	....	....	....	....	3	0	1	1	0	....	....	....	....
	NHL Totals		**1**	**0**	**0**	**0**	**0**	**0**	**0**	**0**	**0**	**0.0**		**0**	**0.0**	**9:19**	....	....	....	....	....	....	....	....	....

WHL West Second All-Star Team (2011)

Signed as a free agent by **Texas** (AHL), May 24, 2013. Signed as a free agent by **Dallas**, July 3, 2014.

RANGER, Paul

(RAIN-juhr, PAWL)

Defense. Shoots left. 6'3", 210 lbs. Born, Whitby, ON, September 12, 1984. Tampa Bay's 7th choice, 183rd overall, in 2002 Entry Draft.

Season	Club	League	GP	G	A	Pts	PIM	PP	SH	GW	S	S%	+/-	TF	F%	Min	GP	G	A	Pts	PIM	PP	SH	GW	Min
2000-01	Oshawa Generals	OHL	32	0	1	1	2	....	....	....	....	....	....	....	....	....	....	....	....	....	....	....	....	....	....
2001-02	Oshawa Generals	OHL	62	0	9	9	49	....	....	....	....	....	....	....	....	....	5	0	0	0	4	....	....	....	....
2002-03	Oshawa Generals	OHL	68	10	28	38	70	....	....	....	....	....	....	....	....	....	13	0	3	3	10	....	....	....	....
2003-04	Oshawa Generals	OHL	62	12	31	43	72	....	....	....	....	....	....	....	....	....	7	0	1	1	10	....	....	....	....
2004-05	Springfield	AHL	69	3	8	11	46	....	....	....	....	....	....	....	....	....	....	....	....	....	....	....	....	....	....
2005-06	**Tampa Bay**	**NHL**	**76**	**1**	**17**	**18**	**58**	**0**	**0**	**1**	**73**	**1.4**	**5**	**0**	**0.0**	**17:07**	**5**	**2**	**4**	**6**	**0**	**1**	**0**	**0**	**21:43**
	Springfield	AHL	1	1	2	3	0	....	....	....	....	....	....	....	....	....	....	....	....	....	....	....	....	....	....
2006-07	**Tampa Bay**	**NHL**	**72**	**4**	**24**	**28**	**42**	**0**	**0**	**2**	**90**	**4.4**	**5**	**0**	**0.0**	**20:19**	**6**	**0**	**1**	**1**	**4**	**0**	**0**	**0**	**21:22**
2007-08	**Tampa Bay**	**NHL**	**72**	**10**	**21**	**31**	**56**	**0**	**1**	**0**	**105**	**9.5**	**–13**	**0**	**0.0**	**25:13**	....	....	....	....	....	....	....	....	....
2008-09	**Tampa Bay**	**NHL**	**42**	**2**	**11**	**13**	**56**	**0**	**0**	**0**	**69**	**2.9**	**–5**	**0**	**0.0**	**24:30**	....	....	....	....	....	....	....	....	....
2009-10	**Tampa Bay**	**NHL**	**8**	**1**	**1**	**2**	**6**	**0**	**0**	**0**	**11**	**9.1**	**–2**	**0**	**0.0**	**20:19**	....	....	....	....	....	....	....	....	....
2010-11			OUT OF HOCKEY – RETIRED																						
2011-12			OUT OF HOCKEY – RETIRED																						
2012-13	Toronto Marlies	AHL	51	8	17	25	54	....	....	....	....	....	....	....	....	....	9	2	2	4	14	....	....	....	....
2013-14	**Toronto**	**NHL**	**53**	**6**	**8**	**14**	**36**	**0**	**1**	**0**	**59**	**10.2**	**–1**	**0**	**0.0**	**17:25**	....	....	....	....	....	....	....	....	....
2014-15	Geneve	Swiss	23	1	3	4	16	....	....	....	....	....	....	....	....	....	....	....	....	....	....	....	....	....	....
	Kloten Flyers	Swiss	4	1	1	2	2	....	....	....	....	....	....	....	....	....	....	....	....	....	....	....	....	....	....
	NHL Totals		**323**	**24**	**82**	**106**	**254**	**0**	**2**	**3**	**407**	**5.9**		**0**	**0.0**	**20:44**	**11**	**2**	**5**	**7**	**4**	**1**	**0**	**0**	**21:31**

• Missed majority of 2009-10 and all of 2010-11 and 2011-12 for personal reasons. Signed as a free agent by **Toronto** (AHL), August 21, 2012. Signed as a free agent by **Toronto**, July 24, 2013. Signed as a free agent by **Geneve** (Swiss), July 15, 2014. • Loaned to **Kloten** (Swiss) by **Geneve** (Swiss), January 14, 2015.

RASK, Victor

(RASK, VIHK-tohr) **CAR**

Center. Shoots left. 6'2", 200 lbs. Born, Leksand, Sweden, March 1, 1993. Carolina's 2nd choice, 42nd overall, in 2011 Entry Draft.

Season	Club	League	GP	G	A	Pts	PIM	PP	SH	GW	S	S%	+/-	TF	F%	Min	GP	G	A	Pts	PIM	PP	SH	GW	Min
2007-08	Leksands IF U18	Swe-U18	8	0	2	2	2	....	....	....	....	....	....	....	....	....	2	0	0	0	0	....	....	....	....
2008-09	Leksands IF U18	Swe-U18	26	9	6	15	8	....	....	....	....	....	....	....	....	....	....	....	....	....	....	....	....	....	....
2009-10	Leksands IF U18	Swe-U18	10	6	3	9	4	....	....	....	....	....	....	....	....	....	4	4	3	7	2	....	....	....	....
	Leksands IF Jr.	Swe-Jr.	39	22	19	41	35	....	....	....	....	....	....	....	....	....	5	3	2	5	2	....	....	....	....
	Leksands IF	Sweden-2	8	0	0	0	0	....	....	....	....	....	....	....	....	....	....	....	....	....	....	....	....	....	....
2010-11	Leksands IF U18	Swe-U18	4	4	4	8	0	....	....	....	....	....	....	....	....	....	6	3	2	5	6	....	....	....	....
	Leksands IF Jr.	Swe-Jr.	13	3	9	12	2	....	....	....	....	....	....	....	....	....	....	....	....	....	....	....	....	....	....
	Leksands IF	Sweden-2	37	5	6	11	8	....	....	....	....	....	....	....	....	....	....	....	....	....	....	....	....	....	....
2011-12	Calgary Hitmen	WHL	64	33	30	63	21	....	....	....	....	....	....	....	....	....	....	....	....	....	....	....	....	....	....
2012-13	Calgary Hitmen	WHL	37	14	27	41	16	....	....	....	....	....	....	....	....	....	17	6	10	16	10	....	....	....	....
	Charlotte	AHL	10	1	4	5	0	....	....	....	....	....	....	....	....	....	....	....	....	....	....	....	....	....	....
2013-14	Charlotte	AHL	76	16	23	39	20	....	....	....	....	....	....	....	....	....	....	....	....	....	....	....	....	....	....
2014-15	**Carolina**	**NHL**	**80**	**11**	**22**	**33**	**16**	**2**	**0**	**2**	**172**	**6.4**	**–14**	**918**	**51.0**	**16:20**	....	....	....	....	....	....	....	....	....
	NHL Totals		**80**	**11**	**22**	**33**	**16**	**2**	**0**	**2**	**172**	**6.4**		**918**	**51.0**	**16:20**	....	....	....	....	....	....	....	....	....

RATTIE, Ty

(RA-tee, TIGH) **ST.L.**

Right wing. Shoots right. 6', 178 lbs. Born, Calgary, AB, February 5, 1993. St. Louis' 1st choice, 32nd overall, in 2011 Entry Draft.

Season	Club	League	GP	G	A	Pts	PIM	PP	SH	GW	S	S%	+/-	TF	F%	Min	GP	G	A	Pts	PIM	PP	SH	GW	Min
2007-08	Airdrie Xtreme	AMBHL	33	*75	56	*131	24	....	....	....	....	....	....	....	....	....	10	12	*11	*23	16	....	....	....	....
2008-09	UFA Bisons	AMHL	34	29	25	54	12	....	....	....	....	....	....	....	....	....	3	1	4	5	2	....	....	....	....
	Portland	WHL	10	1	0	1	0	....	....	....	....	....	....	....	....	....	....	....	....	....	....	....	....	....	....
	Brooks Bandits	AJHL	2	0	0	0	0	....	....	....	....	....	....	....	....	....	2	0	1	1	0	....	....	....	....
2009-10	Portland	WHL	61	17	20	37	38	....	....	....	....	....	....	....	....	....	13	2	2	4	12	....	....	....	....
2010-11	Portland	WHL	67	28	51	79	55	....	....	....	....	....	....	....	....	....	21	9	13	22	22	....	....	....	....
2011-12	Portland	WHL	69	57	64	121	54	....	....	....	....	....	....	....	....	....	21	19	14	33	12	....	....	....	....
2012-13	Portland	WHL	62	48	62	110	27	....	....	....	....	....	....	....	....	....	21	*20	16	*36	17	....	....	....	....
2013-14	**St. Louis**	**NHL**	**2**	**0**	**0**	**0**	**0**	**0**	**0**	**0**	**4**	**0.0**	**–2**	**0**	**0.0**	**11:03**	....	....	....	....	....	....	....	....	....
	Chicago Wolves	AHL	72	31	17	48	37	....	....	....	....	....	....	....	....	....	9	1	2	3	4	....	....	....	....
2014-15	**St. Louis**	**NHL**	**11**	**0**	**2**	**2**	**2**	**0**	**0**	**0**	**8**	**0.0**	**0**	**0**	**0.0**	**9:06**	....	....	....	....	....	....	....	....	....
	Chicago Wolves	AHL	59	21	21	42	12	....	....	....	....	....	....	....	....	....	3	0	0	0	2	....	....	....	....
	NHL Totals		**13**	**0**	**2**	**2**	**2**	**0**	**0**	**0**	**12**	**0.0**		**0**	**0.0**	**9:24**	....	....	....	....	....	....	....	....	....

WHL West First All-Star Team (2012) • WHL West Second All-Star Team (2013) • Memorial Cup All-Star Team (2013)

RAYMOND, Mason

(RAY-muhnd, MAY-sohn) **CGY**

Left wing. Shoots left. 6', 185 lbs. Born, Cochrane, AB, September 17, 1985. Vancouver's 2nd choice, 51st overall, in 2005 Entry Draft.

Season	Club	League	GP	G	A	Pts	PIM	PP	SH	GW	S	S%	+/-	TF	F%	Min	GP	G	A	Pts	PIM	PP	SH	GW	Min
2003-04	Camrose Kodiaks	AJHL	....	27	35	62	....	....	....	....	....	....	....	....	....	....	....	....	....	....	....	....	....	....	....
2004-05	Camrose Kodiaks	AJHL	55	*41	41	82	80	....	....	....	....	....	....	....	....	....	15	8	*12	20	....	....	....	....	....
2005-06	U. Minn-Duluth	WCHA	40	11	17	28	30	....	....	....	....	....	....	....	....	....	....	....	....	....	....	....	....	....	....
2006-07	U. Minn-Duluth	WCHA	39	14	32	46	45	....	....	....	....	....	....	....	....	....	....	....	....	....	....	....	....	....	....
	Manitoba Moose	AHL	11	2	2	4	6	....	....	....	....	....	....	....	....	....	13	0	1	1	0	....	....	....	....
2007-08	**Vancouver**	**NHL**	**49**	**9**	**12**	**21**	**2**	**1**	**0**	**0**	**80**	**11.3**	**1**	**63**	**38.1**	**12:31**	....	....	....	....	....	....	....	....	....
	Manitoba Moose	AHL	20	7	10	17	6	....	....	....	....	....	....	....	....	....	....	....	....	....	....	....	....	....	....
2008-09	**Vancouver**	**NHL**	**72**	**11**	**12**	**23**	**24**	**4**	**0**	**0**	**145**	**7.6**	**2**	**50**	**34.0**	**13:43**	**10**	**2**	**1**	**3**	**2**	**0**	**0**	**0**	**15:12**
2009-10	**Vancouver**	**NHL**	**82**	**25**	**28**	**53**	**48**	**8**	**0**	**4**	**217**	**11.5**	**0**	**23**	**34.8**	**17:20**	**12**	**3**	**1**	**4**	**6**	**0**	**0**	**1**	**17:36**
2010-11	**Vancouver**	**NHL**	**70**	**15**	**24**	**39**	**10**	**2**	**1**	**5**	**197**	**7.6**	**8**	**65**	**40.0**	**15:48**	**24**	**2**	**6**	**8**	**6**	**0**	**0**	**0**	**17:29**
2011-12	**Vancouver**	**NHL**	**55**	**10**	**10**	**20**	**18**	**1**	**1**	**2**	**125**	**8.0**	**4**	**25**	**28.0**	**15:35**	**5**	**0**	**1**	**1**	**0**	**0**	**0**	**0**	**12:34**
2012-13	Orebro HK	Sweden-2	2	0	1	1	2	....	....	....	....	....	....	....	....	....	....	....	....	....	....	....	....	....	....
	Vancouver	**NHL**	**46**	**10**	**12**	**22**	**16**	**4**	**0**	**1**	**79**	**12.7**	**2**	**50**	**34.0**	**15:49**	**4**	**1**	**1**	**2**	**0**	**0**	**0**	**0**	**16:49**
2013-14	**Toronto**	**NHL**	**82**	**19**	**26**	**45**	**22**	**6**	**1**	**4**	**178**	**10.7**	**–6**	**16**	**43.8**	**17:21**	....	....	....	....	....	....	....	....	....
2014-15	**Calgary**	**NHL**	**57**	**12**	**11**	**23**	**8**	**0**	**0**	**1**	**123**	**9.8**	**–8**	**3**	**0.0**	**14:49**	**8**	**0**	**2**	**2**	**0**	**0**	**0**	**0**	**9:41**
	NHL Totals		**513**	**111**	**135**	**246**	**148**	**26**	**3**	**17**	**1144**	**9.7**		**295**	**35.9**	**15:33**	**63**	**8**	**12**	**20**	**14**	**0**	**0**	**1**	**15:43**

AJHL MVP (2005) • WCHA All-Rookie Team (2006) • WCHA First All-Star Team (2007)

Signed as a free agent by **Orebro** (Sweden-2), December 26, 2012. Signed as a free agent by **Toronto**, September 23, 2013. Signed as a free agent by **Calgary**, July 1, 2014.

READ, Matt
(REED, MAT) **PHI**

Right wing. Shoots right. 5'10", 185 lbs. Born, Ilderton, ON, June 14, 1986.

Season	Club	League	GP	G	A	Pts	PIM	PP	SH	GW	S	S%	+/-	TF	F%	Min	GP	G	A	Pts	PIM	PP	SH	GW	Min
			Regular Season														Playoffs								
2005-06	Milton Icehawks	ON-Jr.A	48	34	34	68	52	....	....	....	....	....	....	....	....	....	11	6	13	19	6	....	....	....	....
2006-07	Des Moines	USHL	58	28	34	62	110	....	....	....	....	....	....	....	....	....	8	2	0	2	6	....	....	....	....
2007-08	Bemidji State	CHA	36	9	18	27	37	....	....	....	....	....	....	....	....	....	....	....	....	....	....	....	....	....	....
2008-09	Bemidji State	CHA	37	15	25	40	50	....	....	....	....	....	....	....	....	....	....	....	....	....	....	....	....	....	....
2009-10	Bemidji State	CHA	37	19	22	41	32	....	....	....	....	....	....	....	....	....	....	....	....	....	....	....	....	....	....
2010-11	Bemidji State	WCHA	37	22	13	35	34	....	....	....	....	....	....	....	....	....	....	....	....	....	....	....	....	....	....
	Adirondack	AHL	11	7	6	13	6	....	....	....	....	....	....	....	....	....	....	....	....	....	....	....	....	....	....
2011-12	**Philadelphia**	**NHL**	**79**	**24**	**23**	**47**	**12**	**4**	**2**	**6**	**155**	**15.5**	**13**	**346**	**41.0**	**17:04**	**11**	**3**	**2**	**5**	**4**	**1**	**0**	**1**	**15:14**
2012-13	Sodertalje SK	Sweden-2	20	6	18	24	12	....	....	....	....	....	....	....	....	....	....	....	....	....	....	....	....	....	....
	Philadelphia	**NHL**	**42**	**11**	**13**	**24**	**2**	**1**	**0**	**2**	**72**	**15.3**	**1**	**48**	**29.2**	**18:01**	....	....	....	....	....	....	....	....	....
2013-14	**Philadelphia**	**NHL**	**75**	**22**	**18**	**40**	**16**	**0**	**4**	**3**	**151**	**14.6**	**–4**	**28**	**42.9**	**18:48**	**7**	**1**	**2**	**3**	**4**	**0**	**0**	**0**	**19:04**
2014-15	**Philadelphia**	**NHL**	**80**	**8**	**22**	**30**	**14**	**2**	**0**	**2**	**142**	**5.6**	**–4**	**21**	**52.4**	**17:34**	....	....	....	....	....	....	....	....	....
	NHL Totals		**276**	**65**	**76**	**141**	**44**	**7**	**6**	**13**	**520**	**12.5**		**443**	**40.4**	**17:50**	**18**	**4**	**4**	**8**	**8**	**1**	**0**	**1**	**16:43**

CHA All-Rookie Team (2008) • CHA Rookie of the Year (2008) • CHA First All-Star Team (2009) • NCAA West Second All-American Team (2010)

Signed as a free agent by **Philadelphia**, March 24, 2011. Signed as a free agent by **Sodertalje** (Sweden-2), September 30. 2012.

REAVES, Ryan
(REEVZ, RIGH-uhn) **ST.L.**

Right wing. Shoots right. 6'1", 224 lbs. Born, Winnipeg, MB, January 20, 1987. St. Louis' 4th choice, 156th overall, in 2005 Entry Draft.

Season	Club	League	GP	G	A	Pts	PIM	PP	SH	GW	S	S%	+/-	TF	F%	Min	GP	G	A	Pts	PIM	PP	SH	GW	Min
2004-05	Brandon	WHL	64	7	9	16	79	....	....	....	....	....	....	....	....	....	23	2	4	6	43	....	....	....	....
2005-06	Brandon	WHL	68	14	14	28	91	....	....	....	....	....	....	....	....	....	6	0	1	1	8	....	....	....	....
2006-07	Brandon	WHL	69	15	20	35	76	....	....	....	....	....	....	....	....	....	11	1	4	5	19	....	....	....	....
2007-08	Peoria Rivermen	AHL	31	4	3	7	46	....	....	....	....	....	....	....	....	....	....	....	....	....	....	....	....	....	....
	Alaska Aces	ECHL	9	2	0	2	42	....	....	....	....	....	....	....	....	....	2	0	0	0	22	....	....	....	....
2008-09	Peoria Rivermen	AHL	57	8	9	17	130	....	....	....	....	....	....	....	....	....	4	0	0	0	2	....	....	....	....
2009-10	Peoria Rivermen	AHL	76	4	7	11	167	....	....	....	....	....	....	....	....	....	....	....	....	....	....	....	....	....	....
2010-11	**St. Louis**	**NHL**	**28**	**2**	**2**	**4**	**78**	**0**	**0**	**1**	**16**	**12.5**	**–1**	**2**	**0.0**	**6:48**	....	....	....	....	....	....	....	....	....
	Peoria Rivermen	AHL	50	4	6	10	146	....	....	....	....	....	....	....	....	....	....	....	....	....	....	....	....	....	....
2011-12	**St. Louis**	**NHL**	**60**	**3**	**1**	**4**	**124**	**0**	**0**	**1**	**32**	**9.4**	**0**	**2**	**50.0**	**6:32**	**2**	**0**	**0**	**0**	**0**	**0**	**0**	**0**	**7:47**
2012-13	Orlando	ECHL	13	6	3	9	34	....	....	....	....	....	....	....	....	....	....	....	....	....	....	....	....	....	....
	St. Louis	**NHL**	**43**	**4**	**2**	**6**	**79**	**0**	**0**	**1**	**24**	**16.7**	**3**	**3**	**100.0**	**7:27**	**6**	**0**	**0**	**0**	**2**	**0**	**0**	**0**	**7:30**
2013-14	**St. Louis**	**NHL**	**63**	**2**	**6**	**8**	**126**	**0**	**0**	**0**	**25**	**8.0**	**–1**	**8**	**75.0**	**8:31**	**6**	**0**	**0**	**0**	**6**	**0**	**0**	**0**	**6:08**
2014-15	**St. Louis**	**NHL**	**81**	**6**	**6**	**12**	**116**	**0**	**0**	**1**	**55**	**10.9**	**–3**	**0**	**0.0**	**8:31**	**6**	**1**	**0**	**1**	**0**	**0**	**0**	**0**	**8:43**
	NHL Totals		**275**	**17**	**17**	**34**	**523**	**0**	**0**	**4**	**152**	**11.2**		**15**	**66.7**	**7:45**	**20**	**1**	**0**	**1**	**8**	**0**	**0**	**0**	**7:29**

Signed as a free agent by **Orlando** (ECHL), December 8, 2012.

RECHLICZ, Joel
(REHK-lihj, JOHL)

Right wing. Shoots right. 6'4", 220 lbs. Born, Brookfield, WI, June 14, 1987.

Season	Club	League	GP	G	A	Pts	PIM	PP	SH	GW	S	S%	+/-	TF	F%	Min	GP	G	A	Pts	PIM	PP	SH	GW	Min
2004-05	Santa Fe	NAHL	3	0	1	1	29	....	....	....	....	....	....	....	....	....	....	....	....	....	....	....	....	....	....
2005-06	Des Moines	USHL	2	0	0	0	4	....	....	....	....	....	....	....	....	....	....	....	....	....	....	....	....	....	....
	Indiana Ice	USHL	2	0	0	0	16	....	....	....	....	....	....	....	....	....	....	....	....	....	....	....	....	....	....
	Gatineau	QMJHL	3	0	0	0	17	....	....	....	....	....	....	....	....	....	....	....	....	....	....	....	....	....	....
2006-07	Chicoutimi	QMJHL	55	0	1	1	159	....	....	....	....	....	....	....	....	....	1	0	0	0	2	....	....	....	....
	Chicago Hounds	UHL	2	0	0	0	9	....	....	....	....	....	....	....	....	....	....	....	....	....	....	....	....	....	....
2007-08	Albany River Rats	AHL	25	0	1	1	106	....	....	....	....	....	....	....	....	....	....	....	....	....	....	....	....	....	....
	Kalamazoo Wings	IHL	25	1	0	1	100	....	....	....	....	....	....	....	....	....	....	....	....	....	....	....	....	....	....
2008-09	**NY Islanders**	**NHL**	**17**	**0**	**1**	**1**	**68**	**0**	**0**	**0**	**7**	**0.0**	**–1**	**0**	**0.0**	**4:52**	....	....	....	....	....	....	....	....	....
	Bridgeport	AHL	4	0	0	0	12	....	....	....	....	....	....	....	....	....	....	....	....	....	....	....	....	....	....
	Utah Grizzlies	ECHL	45	0	1	1	110	....	....	....	....	....	....	....	....	....	....	....	....	....	....	....	....	....	....
2009-10	**NY Islanders**	**NHL**	**6**	**0**	**0**	**0**	**27**	**0**	**0**	**0**	**1**	**0.0**	**–2**	**0**	**0.0**	**2:41**	....	....	....	....	....	....	....	....	....
	Bridgeport	AHL	21	0	0	0	128	....	....	....	....	....	....	....	....	....	....	....	....	....	....	....	....	....	....
2010-11	Hershey Bears	AHL	28	1	0	1	132	....	....	....	....	....	....	....	....	....	....	....	....	....	....	....	....	....	....
2011-12	Hershey Bears	AHL	44	1	1	2	267	....	....	....	....	....	....	....	....	....	....	....	....	....	....	....	....	....	....
	Washington	**NHL**	**3**	**0**	**0**	**0**	**10**	**0**	**0**	**0**	**0**	**0.0**	**0**	**0**	**0.0**	**1:59**	....	....	....	....	....	....	....	....	....
2012-13	Portland Pirates	AHL	36	0	0	0	149	....	....	....	....	....	....	....	....	....	....	....	....	....	....	....	....	....	....
	Hershey Bears	AHL	4	0	0	0	5	....	....	....	....	....	....	....	....	....	....	....	....	....	....	....	....	....	....
2013-14	Hershey Bears	AHL	25	1	1	2	87	....	....	....	....	....	....	....	....	....	....	....	....	....	....	....	....	....	....
2014-15	Iowa Wild	AHL	20	1	0	1	60	....	....	....	....	....	....	....	....	....	....	....	....	....	....	....	....	....	....
	NHL Totals		**26**	**0**	**1**	**1**	**105**	**0**	**0**	**0**	**8**	**0.0**		**0**	**0.0**	**4:02**	....	....	....	....	....	....	....	....	....

Signed as a free agent by **NY Islanders**, May 6, 2008. • Missed majority of 2009-10 as a healthy reserve. Signed as a free agent by **Hershey** (AHL), July 29, 2010. Signed as a free agent by **Washington**, January 30, 2012. Signed as a free agent by **Phoenix**, July 11, 2012. Traded to **Washington** by **Phoenix** for Matt Clackson, April 2, 2013. Signed as a free agent by **Minnesota**, July 2, 2014. • Missed majority of 2013-14 and 2014-15 as a healthy reserve.

REDMOND, Zach
(REHD-muhnd, ZAK) **COL**

Defense. Shoots right. 6'2", 205 lbs. Born, Traverse City, MI, July 26, 1988. Atlanta's 7th choice, 184th overall, in 2008 Entry Draft.

Season	Club	League	GP	G	A	Pts	PIM	PP	SH	GW	S	S%	+/-	TF	F%	Min	GP	G	A	Pts	PIM	PP	SH	GW	Min
2005-06	Sioux Falls	USHL	48	4	7	11	57	....	....	....	....	....	....	....	....	....	11	1	2	3	4	....	....	....	....
2006-07	Sioux Falls	USHL	60	8	31	39	37	....	....	....	....	....	....	....	....	....	8	3	7	10	8	....	....	....	....
2007-08	Ferris State	CCHA	37	6	13	19	33	....	....	....	....	....	....	....	....	....	....	....	....	....	....	....	....	....	....
2008-09	Ferris State	CCHA	38	3	21	24	48	....	....	....	....	....	....	....	....	....	....	....	....	....	....	....	....	....	....
2009-10	Ferris State	CCHA	40	6	21	27	46	....	....	....	....	....	....	....	....	....	....	....	....	....	....	....	....	....	....
2010-11	Ferris State	CCHA	26	7	13	20	20	....	....	....	....	....	....	....	....	....	....	....	....	....	....	....	....	....	....
	Chicago Wolves	AHL	3	0	0	0	4	....	....	....	....	....	....	....	....	....	....	....	....	....	....	....	....	....	....
2011-12	St. John's IceCaps	AHL	72	8	23	31	33	....	....	....	....	....	....	....	....	....	10	1	2	3	10	....	....	....	....
2012-13	St. John's IceCaps	AHL	38	8	11	19	34	....	....	....	....	....	....	....	....	....	....	....	....	....	....	....	....	....	....
	Winnipeg	**NHL**	**8**	**1**	**3**	**4**	**12**	**0**	**1**	**0**	**13**	**7.7**	**0**	**0**	**0.0**	**19:35**	....	....	....	....	....	....	....	....	....
2013-14	**Winnipeg**	**NHL**	**10**	**1**	**2**	**3**	**0**	**0**	**0**	**0**	**10**	**10.0**	**1**	**0**	**0.0**	**15:20**	....	....	....	....	....	....	....	....	....
	St. John's IceCaps	AHL	40	6	19	25	26	....	....	....	....	....	....	....	....	....	21	2	12	14	16	....	....	....	....
2014-15	**Colorado**	**NHL**	**59**	**5**	**15**	**20**	**24**	**1**	**0**	**1**	**93**	**5.4**	**–1**	**0**	**0.0**	**17:09**	....	....	....	....	....	....	....	....	....
	NHL Totals		**77**	**7**	**20**	**27**	**36**	**1**	**1**	**1**	**116**	**6.0**		**0**	**0.0**	**17:10**	....	....	....	....	....	....	....	....	....

CCHA Second All-Star Team (2010) • CCHA First All-Star Team (2011) • NCAA West Second All-American Team (2011)

• Transferred to **Winnipeg** after **Atlanta** franchise relocated, June 21, 2011. Signed as a free agent by **Colorado**, July 1, 2014.

REESE, Dylan
(REES, DIH-luhn) **ARI**

Defense. Shoots right. 6'1", 205 lbs. Born, Pittsburgh, PA, August 29, 1984. NY Rangers' 9th choice, 209th overall, in 2003 Entry Draft.

Season	Club	League	GP	G	A	Pts	PIM	PP	SH	GW	S	S%	+/-	TF	F%	Min	GP	G	A	Pts	PIM	PP	SH	GW	Min
2000-01	Pittsburgh	MWEHL	66	14	42	66	....	....	....	....	....	....	....	....	....	....	....	....	....	....	....	....	....	....	....
2001-02	Pittsburgh Forge	NAHL	48	7	16	23	70	....	....	....	....	....	....	....	....	....	7	0	2	2	4	....	....	....	....
2002-03	Pittsburgh Forge	NAHL	56	11	30	41	98	....	....	....	....	....	....	....	....	....	5	2	3	5	6	....	....	....	....
2003-04	Harvard Crimson	ECAC	21	1	4	5	18	....	....	....	....	....	....	....	....	....	....	....	....	....	....	....	....	....	....
2004-05	Harvard Crimson	ECAC	34	7	12	19	44	....	....	....	....	....	....	....	....	....	....	....	....	....	....	....	....	....	....
2005-06	Harvard Crimson	ECAC	33	4	15	19	36	....	....	....	....	....	....	....	....	....	....	....	....	....	....	....	....	....	....
2006-07	Harvard Crimson	ECAC	33	9	9	18	26	....	....	....	....	....	....	....	....	....	....	....	....	....	....	....	....	....	....
	Hartford	AHL	10	0	4	4	12	....	....	....	....	....	....	....	....	....	2	0	0	0	2	....	....	....	....
2007-08	San Antonio	AHL	59	1	6	7	49	....	....	....	....	....	....	....	....	....	3	1	1	2	4	....	....	....	....
2008-09	San Antonio	AHL	75	1	27	28	64	....	....	....	....	....	....	....	....	....	....	....	....	....	....	....	....	....	....
2009-10	Syracuse Crunch	AHL	51	4	18	22	31	....	....	....	....	....	....	....	....	....	....	....	....	....	....	....	....	....	....
	NY Islanders	**NHL**	**19**	**2**	**2**	**4**	**14**	**0**	**0**	**1**	**16**	**12.5**	**4**	**0**	**0.0**	**15:02**	....	....	....	....	....	....	....	....	....
	Bridgeport	AHL	1	1	1	2	0	....	....	....	....	....	....	....	....	....	5	1	3	4	0	....	....	....	....
2010-11	**NY Islanders**	**NHL**	**27**	**0**	**6**	**6**	**15**	**0**	**0**	**0**	**23**	**0.0**	**–12**	**0**	**0.0**	**14:49**	....	....	....	....	....	....	....	....	....
	Bridgeport	AHL	37	4	14	18	30	....	....	....	....	....	....	....	....	....	....	....	....	....	....	....	....	....	....
2011-12	**NY Islanders**	**NHL**	**28**	**1**	**6**	**7**	**11**	**0**	**0**	**0**	**26**	**3.8**	**0**	**0**	**0.0**	**17:05**	....	....	....	....	....	....	....	....	....
	Bridgeport	AHL	27	2	13	15	12	....	....	....	....	....	....	....	....	....	....	....	....	....	....	....	....	....	....
2012-13	**Pittsburgh**	**NHL**	**3**	**0**	**0**	**0**	**0**	**0**	**0**	**0**	**1**	**0.0**	**0**	**0**	**0.0**	**15:16**	....	....	....	....	....	....	....	....	....
	Wilkes-Barre	AHL	66	8	17	25	34	....	....	....	....	....	....	....	....	....	5	0	1	1	2	....	....	....	....

			Regular Season														Playoffs								
Season	Club	League	GP	G	A	Pts	PIM	PP	SH	GW	S	S%	+/-	TF	F%	Min	GP	G	A	Pts	PIM	PP	SH	GW	Min
2013-14	Amur Khabarovsk	KHL	45	2	5	7	20	....	....	....	....	....	....	....	....	....	2	0	0	0	0	....	....	....	....
2014-15	Arizona	NHL	1	0	0	0	0	0	0	0	3	0.0	-1	0	0.0	19:58	....	....	....	....	....	....	....	....	....
	Portland Pirates	AHL	72	10	30	40	42	....	....	....	....	....	....	....	....	....	5	0	2	2	2	....	....	....	....
	NHL Totals		78	3	14	17	40	0	0	1	69	4.3		0	0.0	15:46	....	....	....	....	....	....	....	....	....

ECAC Second All-Star Team (2006, 2007)

Signed as a free agent by **San Antonio** (AHL), September 5, 2007. Signed as a free agent by **Columbus**, September 29, 2009. Traded to **NY Islanders** by **Columbus** for Greg Moore, March 1, 2010. Signed as a free agent by **Pittsburgh**, July 1, 2012. Signed as a free agent by **Khabarovsk** (KHL), June 15, 2013. Signed as a free agent by **Arizona**, July 1, 2014.

REGEHR, Robyn
(reh-GEER, RAW-bihn)

Defense. Shoots left. 6'3", 222 lbs. Born, Recife, Brazil, April 19, 1980. Colorado's 3rd choice, 19th overall, in 1998 Entry Draft.

Season	Club	League	GP	G	A	Pts	PIM	PP	SH	GW	S	S%	+/-	TF	F%	Min	GP	G	A	Pts	PIM	PP	SH	GW	Min
1995-96	Prince Albert	SMHL	59	8	24	32	157	....	....	....	....	....	....	....	....	....	....	....	....	....	....	....	....	....	....
1996-97	Kamloops Blazers	WHL	64	4	19	23	67	....	....	....	....	....	....	....	....	....	5	0	1	1	18	....	....	....	....
1997-98	Kamloops Blazers	WHL	65	4	10	14	120	....	....	....	....	....	....	....	....	....	5	0	3	3	8	....	....	....	....
1998-99	Kamloops Blazers	WHL	54	12	20	32	130	....	....	....	....	....	....	....	....	....	12	1	4	5	21	....	....	....	....
99-2000	Calgary	NHL	57	5	7	12	46	2	0	0	64	7.8	-2	0	0.0	18:24	....	....	....	....	....	....	....	....	....
	Saint John Flames	AHL	5	0	0	0	0	....	....	....	....	....	....	....	....	....	....	....	....	....	....	....	....	....	....
2000-01	Calgary	NHL	71	1	3	4	70	0	0	0	62	1.6	-7	1	0.0	19:43	....	....	....	....	....	....	....	....	....
2001-02	Calgary	NHL	77	2	6	8	93	0	0	0	82	2.4	-24	0	0.0	20:54	....	....	....	....	....	....	....	....	....
2002-03	Calgary	NHL	76	0	12	12	87	0	0	0	109	0.0	-9	1	100.0	22:45	....	....	....	....	....	....	....	....	....
2003-04	Calgary	NHL	82	4	14	18	74	2	0	1	106	3.8	14	2	50.0	22:21	26	2	7	9	20	0	0	0	26:27
2004-05		DID NOT PLAY																							
2005-06	Calgary	NHL	68	6	20	26	67	5	0	2	89	6.7	6	1	100.0	23:08	7	1	3	4	6	1	0	0	22:22
	Canada	Olympics	6	0	1	1	2	....	....	....	....	....	....	....	....	....	....	....	....	....	....	....	....	....	....
2006-07	Calgary	NHL	78	2	19	21	75	0	0	0	66	3.0	27	1	0.0	21:55	1	0	0	0	0	0	0	0	11:15
2007-08	Calgary	NHL	82	5	15	20	79	1	1	0	93	5.4	11	0	0.0	21:20	7	0	2	2	2	0	0	0	21:50
2008-09	Calgary	NHL	75	0	8	8	73	0	0	0	79	0.0	10	0	0.0	21:09	....	....	....	....	....	....	....	....	....
2009-10	Calgary	NHL	81	2	15	17	80	0	0	0	78	2.6	2	1	0.0	21:38	....	....	....	....	....	....	....	....	....
2010-11	Calgary	NHL	79	2	15	17	58	1	0	0	72	2.8	2	0	0.0	21:29	....	....	....	....	....	....	....	....	....
2011-12	Buffalo	NHL	76	1	4	5	56	0	0	0	49	2.0	-12	0	0.0	18:38	....	....	....	....	....	....	....	....	....
2012-13	Buffalo	NHL	29	0	2	2	21	0	0	0	15	0.0	-4	0	0.0	18:39	....	....	....	....	....	....	....	....	....
	Los Angeles	NHL	12	0	2	2	2	0	0	0	12	0.0	0	0	0.0	21:16	18	0	1	1	6	0	0	0	21:14
2013-14♦	Los Angeles	NHL	79	3	11	14	46	0	0	1	73	4.1	6	0	0.0	18:57	8	0	2	2	7	0	0	0	17:12
2014-15	Los Angeles	NHL	67	3	10	13	45	0	0	0	63	4.8	10	0	0.0	20:20	....	....	....	....	....	....	....	....	....
	NHL Totals		1089	36	163	199	972	11	1	4	1112	3.2		7	42.9	20:54	67	3	15	18	41	1	0	0	22:48

WHL West First All-Star Team (1999)

Traded to **Calgary** by **Colorado** with Rene Corbet, Wade Belak and Colorado's 2nd round compensatory choice (Jarret Stoll) in 2000 Entry Draft for Theoren Fleury and Chris Dingman, February 28, 1999. Traded to **Buffalo** by **Calgary** with Ales Kotalik and Calgary's 2nd round choice (Jake McCabe) in 2012 Entry Draft for Chris Butler and Paul Byron, June 25, 2011. Traded to **Los Angeles** by **Buffalo** for Los Angeles' 2nd round choice (later traded back to Los Angeles – Los Angeles selected Alex Lintuniemi) in 2014 Entry Draft and Los Angeles' 2nd round choice (later traded back to Los Angeles – Los Angeles selected Erik Cernak) in 2015 Entry Draft, April 1, 2013.

REGIN, Peter
(REE-gihn, PEE-tuhr)

Center. Shoots left. 6'2", 190 lbs. Born, Herning, Denmark, April 16, 1986. Ottawa's 4th choice, 87th overall, in 2004 Entry Draft.

Season	Club	League	GP	G	A	Pts	PIM	PP	SH	GW	S	S%	+/-	TF	F%	Min	GP	G	A	Pts	PIM	PP	SH	GW	Min
2002-03	Herning IK	Denmark	24	0	1	1	4	....	....	....	....	....	....	....	....	....	10	1	3	4	4	....	....	....	....
	Denmark	WJC-B	5	2	0	2	0	....	....	....	....	....	....	....	....	....	....	....	....	....	....	....	....	....	....
	Denmark	WJ18-B	5	0	2	2	6	....	....	....	....	....	....	....	....	....	....	....	....	....	....	....	....	....	....
2003-04	Herning IK	Denmark	33	9	11	20	14	....	....	....	....	....	....	....	....	....	....	....	....	....	....	....	....	....	....
	Denmark	WJC-B	5	1	2	3	2	....	....	....	....	....	....	....	....	....	....	....	....	....	....	....	....	....	....
	Denmark	WJ18-B	6	5	4	9	0	....	....	....	....	....	....	....	....	....	....	....	....	....	....	....	....	....	....
2004-05	Herning Blue Fox	Denmark	36	19	27	46	43	....	....	....	....	....	....	....	....	....	16	5	8	13	2	....	....	....	....
	Denmark	Oly-Q	3	1	1	2	2	....	....	....	....	....	....	....	....	....	....	....	....	....	....	....	....	....	....
2005-06	Timra IK	Sweden	44	4	7	11	14	....	....	....	....	....	....	....	....	....	....	....	....	....	....	....	....	....	....
2006-07	Timra IK	Sweden	51	9	7	16	16	....	....	....	....	....	....	....	....	....	7	2	2	4	2	....	....	....	....
2007-08	Timra IK	Sweden	55	12	19	31	36	....	....	....	....	....	....	....	....	....	11	2	7	9	2	....	....	....	....
2008-09	Ottawa	NHL	11	1	1	2	2	0	0	1	7	14.3	0	77	53.3	10:32	....	....	....	....	....	....	....	....	....
	Binghamton	AHL	56	18	29	47	36	....	....	....	....	....	....	....	....	....	....	....	....	....	....	....	....	....	....
2009-10	Ottawa	NHL	75	13	16	29	20	1	0	1	135	9.6	10	538	44.6	12:54	6	3	1	4	6	0	0	0	18:06
2010-11	Ottawa	NHL	55	3	14	17	12	0	0	1	87	3.4	-4	316	41.8	13:23	....	....	....	....	....	....	....	....	....
2011-12	Ottawa	NHL	10	2	2	4	2	0	0	0	15	13.3	3	59	49.2	14:06	....	....	....	....	....	....	....	....	....
2012-13	SC Langenthal	Swiss-2	4	2	3	5	2	....	....	....	....	....	....	....	....	....	....	....	....	....	....	....	....	....	....
	Ottawa	NHL	27	0	3	3	8	0	0	0	37	0.0	-4	210	43.8	11:31	....	....	....	....	....	....	....	....	....
2013-14	NY Islanders	NHL	44	2	5	7	18	0	0	0	53	3.8	-10	311	41.5	11:51	....	....	....	....	....	....	....	....	....
	Chicago	NHL	17	2	2	4	2	0	0	0	16	12.5	5	85	55.3	10:24	5	0	0	0	0	0	0	0	11:35
2014-15	Chicago	NHL	4	0	1	1	0	0	0	0	3	0.0	1	2	50.0	8:20	....	....	....	....	....	....	....	....	....
	Rockford IceHogs	AHL	69	10	31	41	30	....	....	....	....	....	....	....	....	....	8	1	4	5	2	....	....	....	....
	NHL Totals		243	23	44	67	64	1	0	3	353	6.5		1598	44.5	12:21	11	3	1	4	6	0	0	0	15:08

• Missed majority of 2011-12 due to recurring shoulder injury and resulting surgery, January 30, 2012. Signed as a free agent by **Langenthal** (Swiss-2), October 18, 2012. Signed as a free agent by **NY Islanders**, July 5, 2013. Traded to **Chicago** by **NY Islanders** with Pierre-Marc Bouchard for Chicago's 4th round choice (later traded to Washington, later traded to NY Rangers – NY Rangers selected Igor Shesterkin) in 2014 Entry Draft, February 6, 2014. Signed as a free agent by **Jokerit Helsinki** (Finland), May 11, 2015.

REINHART, Griffin
(RIGHN-hart, GRIHF-uhn) **EDM**

Defense. Shoots left. 6'4", 202 lbs. Born, North Vancouver, BC, January 24, 1994. NY Islanders' 1st choice, 4th overall, in 2012 Entry Draft.

Season	Club	League	GP	G	A	Pts	PIM	PP	SH	GW	S	S%	+/-	TF	F%	Min	GP	G	A	Pts	PIM	PP	SH	GW	Min
2008-09	Hollyburn Huskies	Minor-BC	STATISTICS NOT AVAILABLE																						
	Van. NW Giants	BCMML	3	1	3	4	0	....	....	....	....	....	....	....	....	....	2	0	0	0	0	....	....	....	....
2009-10	Van. NW Giants	BCMML	32	9	25	34	24	....	....	....	....	....	....	....	....	....	5	3	5	8	14	....	....	....	....
	Edmonton	WHL	2	0	0	0	0	....	....	....	....	....	....	....	....	....	....	....	....	....	....	....	....	....	....
2010-11	Edmonton	WHL	45	6	19	25	36	....	....	....	....	....	....	....	....	....	4	0	0	0	6	....	....	....	....
2011-12	Edmonton	WHL	58	12	24	36	38	....	....	....	....	....	....	....	....	....	20	2	6	8	20	....	....	....	....
2012-13	Edmonton	WHL	59	8	21	29	35	....	....	....	....	....	....	....	....	....	12	3	4	7	12	....	....	....	....
2013-14	Edmonton	WHL	45	4	17	21	55	....	....	....	....	....	....	....	....	....	21	4	9	13	18	....	....	....	....
2014-15	NY Islanders	NHL	8	0	1	1	6	0	0	0	4	0.0	1	0	0.0	14:10	1	0	0	0	0	0	0	0	12:42
	Bridgeport	AHL	59	7	15	22	64	....	....	....	....	....	....	....	....	....	....	....	....	....	....	....	....	....	....
	NHL Totals		8	0	1	1	6	0	0	0	4	0.0		0	0.0	14:10	1	0	0	0	0	0	0	0	12:42

WHL East Second All-Star Team (2014)

Traded to **Edmonton** by **NY Islanders** for Pittsburgh's 1st round choice (previously acquired, NY Islanders selected Matthew Barzal) in 2015 Entry Draft and Edmonton's 2nd round choice (later traded to Tampa Bay – Tampa Bay selected Mitchell Stephens) in 2015 Entry Draft, June 26, 2015.

REINHART, Max
(RIGHN-hart, MAX) **NSH**

Center. Shoots left. 6'1", 190 lbs. Born, West Vancouver, BC, February 4, 1992. Calgary's 1st choice, 64th overall, in 2010 Entry Draft.

Season	Club	League	GP	G	A	Pts	PIM	PP	SH	GW	S	S%	+/-	TF	F%	Min	GP	G	A	Pts	PIM	PP	SH	GW	Min
2007-08	Van. NW Giants	BCMML	40	17	8	25	28	....	....	....	....	....	....	....	....	....	2	0	1	1	0	....	....	....	....
	Langley Chiefs	BCHL	1	0	0	0	2	....	....	....	....	....	....	....	....	....	....	....	....	....	....	....	....	....	....
2008-09	Kootenay Ice	WHL	62	11	16	27	21	....	....	....	....	....	....	....	....	....	4	1	0	1	2	....	....	....	....
2009-10	Kootenay Ice	WHL	72	21	30	51	38	....	....	....	....	....	....	....	....	....	6	1	1	2	6	....	....	....	....
2010-11	Kootenay Ice	WHL	71	34	45	79	41	....	....	....	....	....	....	....	....	....	19	15	12	27	12	....	....	....	....
2011-12	Kootenay Ice	WHL	61	28	50	78	40	....	....	....	....	....	....	....	....	....	3	0	2	2	6	....	....	....	....
	Abbotsford Heat	AHL	1	2	0	2	0	....	....	....	....	....	....	....	....	....	4	1	1	2	0	....	....	....	....
2012-13	Abbotsford Heat	AHL	67	7	14	21	32	....	....	....	....	....	....	....	....	....	....	....	....	....	....	....	....	....	....
	Calgary	NHL	11	1	2	3	4	0	0	0	26	3.8	-3	91	37.4	14:25	....	....	....	....	....	....	....	....	....
2013-14	Calgary	NHL	8	0	2	2	2	0	0	0	7	0.0	1	9	22.2	10:42	....	....	....	....	....	....	....	....	....
	Abbotsford Heat	AHL	66	21	42	63	47	....	....	....	....	....	....	....	....	....	4	1	3	4	4	....	....	....	....
2014-15	Calgary	NHL	4	0	0	0	0	0	0	0	3	0.0	-3	29	20.7	8:05	....	....	....	....	....	....	....	....	....
	Adirondack	AHL	69	15	24	39	38	....	....	....	....	....	....	....	....	....	....	....	....	....	....	....	....	....	....
	NHL Totals		23	1	4	5	6	0	0	0	36	2.8		129	32.6	12:01	....	....	....	....	....	....	....	....	....

WHL East Second All-Star Team (2012)

Traded to **Nashville** by **Calgary** for future considerations, July 1, 2015.

REINHART, Sam
(RIGHN-hahrt, SAM) **BUF**

Center. Shoots right. 6'1", 187 lbs. Born, North Vancouver, BC, November 6, 1995. Buffalo's 1st choice, 2nd overall, in 2014 Entry Draft.

Season	Club	League	GP	G	A	Pts	PIM	PP	SH	GW	S	S%	+/-	TF	F%	Min	GP	G	A	Pts	PIM	PP	SH	GW	Min
			Regular Season														Playoffs								
2009-10	Hollyburn Huskies	Minor-BC	STATISTICS NOT AVAILABLE																						
	Van. NW Giants	BCMML	5	2	0	2	0	....	....	....	....	....	....	....	....	....	5	0	1	1	2	....	....	....	....
2010-11	Van. NW Giants	BCMML	34	38	40	78	6	....	....	....	....	....	....	....	....	....	5	5	4	9	....	....	....	....	....
	Kootenay Ice	WHL	4	2	0	2	0	....	....	....	....	....	....	....	....	....	7	0	0	0	0	....	....	....	....
2011-12	Kootenay Ice	WHL	67	28	34	62	2	....	....	....	....	....	....	....	....	....	4	1	1	2	0	....	....	....	....
2012-13	Kootenay Ice	WHL	72	35	50	85	22	....	....	....	....	....	....	....	....	....	5	0	1	1	4	....	....	....	....
2013-14	Kootenay Ice	WHL	60	36	69	105	11	....	....	....	....	....	....	....	....	....	13	6	17	23	2	....	....	....	....
2014-15	**Buffalo**	**NHL**	**9**	**0**	**1**	**1**	**2**	**0**	**0**	**0**	**3**	**0.0**	**-1**	**86**	**24.4**	**10:22**	....	....	....	....	....	....	....	....	....
	Kootenay Ice	WHL	47	19	46	65	20	....	....	....	....	....	....	....	....	....	7	6	3	9	8	....	....	....	....
	Rochester	AHL	3	0	3	3	0	....	....	....	....	....	....	....	....	....	....	....	....	....	....	....	....	....	....
	NHL Totals		**9**	**0**	**1**	**1**	**2**	**0**	**0**	**0**	**3**	**0.0**		**86**	**24.4**	**10:22**	....	....	....	....	....	....	....	....	....

WHL East Second All-Star Team (2013, 2015) • WHL East First All-Star Team (2014)

RENDULIC, Borna
(REHN-dew-LIHCH, BOHR-na) **COL**

Right wing. Shoots right. 6'2", 200 lbs. Born, Zagreb, Croatia, March 25, 1992.

Season	Club	League	GP	G	A	Pts	PIM	PP	SH	GW	S	S%	+/-	TF	F%	Min	GP	G	A	Pts	PIM	PP	SH	GW	Min
2010-11	Assat Pori Jr.	Fin-Jr.	31	4	14	18	36	....	....	....	....	....	....	....	....	....	....	....	....	....	....	....	....	....	....
	Medvescak Zagreb	Austria	12	1	1	2	2	....	....	....	....	....	....	....	....	....	....	....	....	....	....	....	....	....	....
	Zagreb 2	Croatia	....	....	....	....	....	....	....	....	....	....	....	....	....	....	4	1	5	6	2	....	....	....	....
2011-12	Assat Pori Jr.	Fin-Jr.	34	21	28	49	41	....	....	....	....	....	....	....	....	....	5	4	8	12	27	....	....	....	....
	Assat Pori	Finland	3	0	0	0	0	....	....	....	....	....	....	....	....	....	....	....	....	....	....	....	....	....	....
	SaPKo Savonlinna	Finland-2	7	2	3	5	14	....	....	....	....	....	....	....	....	....	....	....	....	....	....	....	....	....	....
2012-13	HPK Jr.	Fin-Jr.	1	0	0	0	0	....	....	....	....	....	....	....	....	....	....	....	....	....	....	....	....	....	....
	Peliitat Heinola	Finland-2	5	2	2	4	0	....	....	....	....	....	....	....	....	....	....	....	....	....	....	....	....	....	....
	HPK Hameenlinna	Finland	37	8	4	12	6	....	....	....	....	....	....	....	....	....	5	0	1	1	0	....	....	....	....
2013-14	HPK Hameenlinna	Finland	57	11	21	32	34	....	....	....	....	....	....	....	....	....	6	3	0	3	2	....	....	....	....
2014-15	**Colorado**	**NHL**	**11**	**1**	**1**	**2**	**6**	**0**	**0**	**0**	**6**	**16.7**	**1**	**0**	**0.0**	**9:24**	....	....	....	....	....	....	....	....	....
	Lake Erie	AHL	26	4	4	8	12	....	....	....	....	....	....	....	....	....	....	....	....	....	....	....	....	....	....
	NHL Totals		**11**	**1**	**1**	**2**	**6**	**0**	**0**	**0**	**6**	**16.7**		**0**	**0.0**	**9:24**	....	....	....	....	....	....	....	....	....

Signed as a free agent by **Colorado**, May 19, 2014. • Missed majority of 2014-15 due to leg injury vs. Florida, January 15, 2015.

REPIK, Michal
(REH-pihk, MEE-khahl)

Right wing. Shoots right. 5'10", 180 lbs. Born, Vlasim, Czech., December 31, 1988. Florida's 2nd choice, 40th overall, in 2007 Entry Draft.

Season	Club	League	GP	G	A	Pts	PIM	PP	SH	GW	S	S%	+/-	TF	F%	Min	GP	G	A	Pts	PIM	PP	SH	GW	Min
2002-03	Sparta U17	CzR-U17	18	7	10	17	6	....	....	....	....	....	....	....	....	....	2	0	0	0	0	....	....	....	....
2003-04	Sparta U17	CzR-U17	33	25	17	42	42	....	....	....	....	....	....	....	....	....	3	0	0	0	0	....	....	....	....
	Sparta Jr.	CzRep-Jr.	23	12	5	17	10	....	....	....	....	....	....	....	....	....	....	....	....	....	....	....	....	....	....
2004-05	Sparta U17	CzR-U17	2	2	3	5	6	....	....	....	....	....	....	....	....	....	....	....	....	....	....	....	....	....	....
	Sparta Jr.	CzRep-Jr.	45	26	31	57	24	....	....	....	....	....	....	....	....	....	8	2	4	6	10	....	....	....	....
2005-06	Vancouver Giants	WHL	69	24	28	52	55	....	....	....	....	....	....	....	....	....	14	3	3	6	19	....	....	....	....
2006-07	Vancouver Giants	WHL	56	24	31	55	56	....	....	....	....	....	....	....	....	....	22	10	*16	*26	24	....	....	....	....
2007-08	Vancouver Giants	WHL	51	27	34	61	62	....	....	....	....	....	....	....	....	....	10	5	6	11	18	....	....	....	....
2008-09	**Florida**	**NHL**	**5**	**2**	**0**	**2**	**2**	**0**	**0**	**0**	**7**	**28.6**	**1**	**1**	**100.0**	**7:32**	....	....	....	....	....	....	....	....	....
	Rochester	AHL	75	19	30	49	58	....	....	....	....	....	....	....	....	....	....	....	....	....	....	....	....	....	....
2009-10	**Florida**	**NHL**	**19**	**3**	**2**	**5**	**6**	**0**	**0**	**0**	**23**	**13.0**	**1**	**1**	**100.0**	**8:35**	....	....	....	....	....	....	....	....	....
	Rochester	AHL	60	22	31	53	57	....	....	....	....	....	....	....	....	....	7	1	1	2	4	....	....	....	....
2010-11	**Florida**	**NHL**	**31**	**2**	**6**	**8**	**22**	**0**	**0**	**0**	**54**	**3.7**	**-6**	**7**	**42.9**	**12:47**	....	....	....	....	....	....	....	....	....
	Rochester	AHL	53	11	34	45	38	....	....	....	....	....	....	....	....	....	....	....	....	....	....	....	....	....	....
2011-12	**Florida**	**NHL**	**17**	**2**	**3**	**5**	**6**	**1**	**0**	**0**	**35**	**5.7**	**-3**	**5**	**60.0**	**10:22**	....	....	....	....	....	....	....	....	....
	San Antonio	AHL	55	14	21	35	51	....	....	....	....	....	....	....	....	....	4	1	3	4	6	....	....	....	....
2012-13	HC Lev Praha	KHL	47	4	6	10	32	....	....	....	....	....	....	....	....	....	4	1	2	3	8	....	....	....	....
2013-14	HC Lev Praha	KHL	51	8	4	12	32	....	....	....	....	....	....	....	....	....	22	4	6	10	22	....	....	....	....
2014-15	Pelicans Lahti	Finland	48	9	22	31	18	....	....	....	....	....	....	....	....	....	....	....	....	....	....	....	....	....	....
	EV Zug	Swiss	4	2	1	3	0	....	....	....	....	....	....	....	....	....	3	0	2	2	0	....	....	....	....
	NHL Totals		**72**	**9**	**11**	**20**	**36**	**1**	**0**	**0**	**119**	**7.6**		**14**	**57.1**	**10:44**	....	....	....	....	....	....	....	....	....

Memorial Cup All-Star Team (2007) • Ed Chynoweth Trophy (Memorial Cup - Leading Scorer) (2007)

Signed as a free agent by **Lev Praha** (KHL), June 20, 2012. Signed as a free agent by **Lahti** (Finland), July 28, 2014. Signed as a free agent by **Zug** (Swiss), February 13, 2015. Signed as a free agent by **Liberec** (CzRep), April 22, 2015.

RIBEIRO, Mike
(rih-BAIR-roh, MIGHK) **NSH**

Center. Shoots left. 6', 177 lbs. Born, Montreal, QC, February 10, 1980. Montreal's 2nd choice, 45th overall, in 1998 Entry Draft.

Season	Club	League	GP	G	A	Pts	PIM	PP	SH	GW	S	S%	+/-	TF	F%	Min	GP	G	A	Pts	PIM	PP	SH	GW	Min
1995-96	Mtl-Bourassa	QAAA	43	13	26	39	18	....	....	....	....	....	....	....	....	....	....	....	....	....	....	....	....	....	....
1996-97	Mtl-Bourassa	QAAA	43	32	57	89	48	....	....	....	....	....	....	....	....	....	16	15	23	38	14	....	....	....	....
1997-98	Rouyn-Noranda	QMJHL	67	40	*85	125	55	....	....	....	....	....	....	....	....	....	6	3	1	4	0	....	....	....	....
1998-99	Rouyn-Noranda	QMJHL	69	*67	*100	*167	137	....	....	....	....	....	....	....	....	....	11	5	11	16	12	....	....	....	....
	Fredericton	AHL	....	....	....	....	....	....	....	....	....	....	....	....	....	....	5	0	1	1	2	....	....	....	....
99-2000	**Montreal**	**NHL**	**19**	**1**	**1**	**2**	**2**	**1**	**0**	**0**	**18**	**5.6**	**-6**	**95**	**34.7**	**10:40**	....	....	....	....	....	....	....	....	....
	Quebec Citadelles	AHL	3	0	0	0	2	....	....	....	....	....	....	....	....	....	....	....	....	....	....	....	....	....	....
	Rouyn-Noranda	QMJHL	2	1	3	4	0	....	....	....	....	....	....	....	....	....	....	....	....	....	....	....	....	....	....
	Quebec Remparts	QMJHL	21	17	28	45	30	....	....	....	....	....	....	....	....	....	11	3	20	23	38	....	....	....	....
2000-01	**Montreal**	**NHL**	**2**	**0**	**0**	**0**	**2**	**0**	**0**	**0**	**3**	**0.0**	**0**	**11**	**18.2**	**10:38**	....	....	....	....	....	....	....	....	....
	Quebec Citadelles	AHL	74	26	40	66	44	....	....	....	....	....	....	....	....	....	9	1	5	6	23	....	....	....	....
2001-02	**Montreal**	**NHL**	**43**	**8**	**10**	**18**	**12**	**3**	**0**	**0**	**48**	**16.7**	**-11**	**141**	**44.0**	**13:55**	....	....	....	....	....	....	....	....	....
	Quebec Citadelles	AHL	23	9	14	23	36	....	....	....	....	....	....	....	....	....	3	0	3	3	0	....	....	....	....
2002-03	**Montreal**	**NHL**	**52**	**5**	**12**	**17**	**6**	**2**	**0**	**0**	**57**	**8.8**	**-3**	**358**	**50.3**	**11:07**	....	....	....	....	....	....	....	....	....
	Hamilton	AHL	3	0	1	1	0	....	....	....	....	....	....	....	....	....	....	....	....	....	....	....	....	....	....
2003-04	**Montreal**	**NHL**	**81**	**20**	**45**	**65**	**34**	**7**	**0**	**5**	**103**	**19.4**	**15**	**913**	**44.8**	**17:05**	**11**	**2**	**1**	**3**	**18**	**0**	**0**	**0**	**16:31**
2004-05	Blues Espoo	Finland	17	8	9	17	4	....	....	....	....	....	....	....	....	....	....	....	....	....	....	....	....	....	....
2005-06	**Montreal**	**NHL**	**79**	**16**	**35**	**51**	**36**	**8**	**0**	**2**	**130**	**12.3**	**-6**	**843**	**44.7**	**16:35**	**6**	**0**	**2**	**2**	**0**	**0**	**0**	**0**	**18:22**
2006-07	**Dallas**	**NHL**	**81**	**18**	**41**	**59**	**22**	**6**	**0**	**3**	**111**	**16.2**	**3**	**678**	**46.6**	**14:56**	**7**	**0**	**3**	**3**	**4**	**0**	**0**	**0**	**18:28**
2007-08	**Dallas**	**NHL**	**76**	**27**	**56**	**83**	**46**	**7**	**0**	**5**	**107**	**25.2**	**21**	**883**	**45.0**	**18:26**	**18**	**3**	**14**	**17**	**16**	**0**	**0**	**0**	**21:45**
2008-09	**Dallas**	**NHL**	**82**	**22**	**56**	**78**	**52**	**7**	**0**	**1**	**163**	**13.5**	**-4**	**1240**	**45.5**	**20:57**	....	....	....	....	....	....	....	....	....
2009-10	**Dallas**	**NHL**	**66**	**19**	**34**	**53**	**38**	**8**	**2**	**0**	**155**	**12.3**	**-5**	**1102**	**44.8**	**19:32**	....	....	....	....	....	....	....	....	....
2010-11	**Dallas**	**NHL**	**82**	**19**	**52**	**71**	**28**	**7**	**0**	**4**	**161**	**11.8**	**-4**	**1213**	**46.6**	**19:58**	....	....	....	....	....	....	....	....	....
2011-12	**Dallas**	**NHL**	**74**	**18**	**45**	**63**	**66**	**2**	**0**	**5**	**142**	**12.7**	**5**	**808**	**42.2**	**20:03**	....	....	....	....	....	....	....	....	....
2012-13	**Washington**	**NHL**	**48**	**13**	**36**	**49**	**53**	**6**	**0**	**1**	**63**	**20.6**	**-4**	**505**	**44.8**	**17:50**	**7**	**1**	**1**	**2**	**10**	**0**	**0**	**1**	**18:33**
2013-14	**Phoenix**	**NHL**	**80**	**16**	**31**	**47**	**52**	**4**	**0**	**3**	**110**	**14.5**	**-13**	**903**	**43.3**	**18:00**	....	....	....	....	....	....	....	....	....
2014-15	**Nashville**	**NHL**	**82**	**15**	**47**	**62**	**52**	**1**	**0**	**3**	**96**	**15.6**	**11**	**1348**	**43.2**	**18:45**	**6**	**1**	**4**	**5**	**4**	**0**	**0**	**0**	**23:22**
	NHL Totals		**947**	**217**	**501**	**718**	**501**	**69**	**2**	**32**	**1467**	**14.8**		**11041**	**44.7**	**17:36**	**55**	**7**	**25**	**32**	**52**	**0**	**0**	**1**	**19:41**

QMJHL Second All-Star Team (1998) • QMJHL First All-Star Team (1999) • Canadian Major Junior First All-Star Team (1999)

Played in NHL All-Star Game (2008)

Signed as a free agent by **Espoo** (Finland), January 17, 2005. Traded to **Dallas** by **Montreal** with Montreal's 6th round choice (Matthew Tassone) in 2008 Entry Draft for Janne Niinimaa and Dallas' 5th round choice (Andrew Conboy) in 2007 Entry Draft, September 30, 2006. Traded to **Washington** by **Dallas** for Cody Eakin and Boston's 2nd round choice (previously acquired, Dallas selected Mike Winther) in 2012 Entry Draft, June 22, 2012. Signed as a free agent by **Phoenix**, July 5, 2013. Signed as a free agent by **Nashville**, July 15, 2014.

RICHARDS, Brad
(RIH-chuhrds, BRAD) **DET**

Center. Shoots left. 6', 196 lbs. Born, Murray Harbour, PE, May 2, 1980. Tampa Bay's 2nd choice, 64th overall, in 1998 Entry Draft.

Season	Club	League	GP	G	A	Pts	PIM	PP	SH	GW	S	S%	+/-	TF	F%	Min	GP	G	A	Pts	PIM	PP	SH	GW	Min
1996-97	Notre Dame	SJHL	63	39	48	87	73	....	....	....	....	....	....	....	....	....	....	....	....	....	....	....	....	....	....
1997-98	Rimouski Oceanic	QMJHL	68	33	82	115	44	....	....	....	....	....	....	....	....	....	19	8	24	32	2	....	....	....	....
1998-99	Rimouski Oceanic	QMJHL	59	39	92	131	55	....	....	....	....	....	....	....	....	....	11	9	12	21	6	....	....	....	....
99-2000	Rimouski Oceanic	QMJHL	63	*71	*115	*186	69	....	....	....	....	....	....	....	....	....	12	13	*24	*37	16	....	....	....	....
2000-01	**Tampa Bay**	**NHL**	**82**	**21**	**41**	**62**	**14**	**7**	**0**	**3**	**179**	**11.7**	**-10**	**955**	**41.4**	**16:54**	....	....	....	....	....	....	....	....	....
2001-02	**Tampa Bay**	**NHL**	**82**	**20**	**42**	**62**	**13**	**5**	**0**	**0**	**251**	**8.0**	**-18**	**911**	**41.2**	**19:48**	....	....	....	....	....	....	....	....	....

			Regular Season														Playoffs								
Season	Club	League	GP	G	A	Pts	PIM	PP	SH	GW	S	S%	+/-	TF	F%	Min	GP	G	A	Pts	PIM	PP	SH	GW	Min
2002-03	Tampa Bay	NHL	80	17	57	74	24	4	0	2	277	6.1	3	1007	47.5	19:56	11	0	5	5	12	0	0	0	22:21
2003-04♦	Tampa Bay	NHL	82	26	53	79	12	5	1	6	244	10.7	13	1167	46.7	20:26	23	12	14	*26	4	*7	0	*7	23:28
2004-05	Ak Bars Kazan	Russia	6	2	5	7	16	....	....	....	....	....	....	....	....	....	....	....	....	....	....	....	....	....	....
2005-06	Tampa Bay	NHL	82	23	68	91	32	7	4	0	282	8.2	0	1288	50.2	22:45	5	3	5	8	6	0	0	0	24:11
	Canada	Olympics	6	2	2	4	6	....	....	....	....	....	....	....	....	....	....	....	....	....	....	....	....	....	....
2006-07	Tampa Bay	NHL	82	25	45	70	23	12	1	3	272	9.2	–19	1580	51.4	24:07	6	3	5	8	6	2	0	0	25:39
2007-08	Tampa Bay	NHL	62	18	33	51	15	9	1	4	228	7.9	–25	944	48.1	24:17	....	....	....	....	....	....	....	....	....
	Dallas	NHL	12	2	9	11	0	0	1	0	21	9.5	–2	130	56.2	19:15	18	3	12	15	8	0	0	0	21:06
2008-09	Dallas	NHL	56	16	32	48	6	5	0	2	180	8.9	–4	911	50.6	20:29	....	....	....	....	....	....	....	....	....
2009-10	Dallas	NHL	80	24	67	91	14	13	0	2	284	8.5	–12	1140	51.5	20:52	....	....	....	....	....	....	....	....	....
2010-11	Dallas	NHL	72	28	49	77	24	7	0	3	272	10.3	1	990	50.6	21:43	....	....	....	....	....	....	....	....	....
2011-12	NY Rangers	NHL	82	25	41	66	22	7	0	9	229	10.9	–1	1316	51.8	20:16	20	6	9	15	8	2	0	0	22:12
2012-13	NY Rangers	NHL	46	11	23	34	14	3	0	1	110	10.0	8	773	50.6	18:49	10	1	0	1	2	0	0	0	14:43
2013-14	NY Rangers	NHL	82	20	31	51	18	5	0	2	259	7.7	–8	1029	49.8	18:41	25	5	7	12	4	2	0	2	17:01
2014-15♦	Chicago	NHL	76	12	25	37	12	2	0	3	199	6.0	3	825	48.4	14:53	23	3	11	14	8	1	0	0	16:44
	NHL Totals		1058	288	616	904	243	91	8	40	3287	8.8		14966	48.9	20:15	141	36	68	104	58	14	0	9	20:09

QMJHL First All-Star Team (2000) • Canadian Major Junior First All-Star Team (2000) • Canadian Major Junior Player of the Year (2000) • Memorial Cup All-Star Team (2000) • Stafford Smythe Memorial Trophy (Memorial Cup - MVP) (2000) • NHL All-Rookie Team (2001) • Lady Byng Memorial Trophy (2004) • Conn Smythe Trophy (2004)

Played in NHL All-Star Game (2011)

Signed as a free agent by **Kazan** (Russia), November 8, 2004. Traded to **Dallas** by **Tampa Bay** with Johan Holmqvist for Jussi Jokinen, Jeff Halpern, Mike Smith and Dallas' 4th round choice (later traded to Minnesota, later traded to Edmonton – Edmonton selected Kyle Bigos) in 2009 Entry Draft, February 26, 2008. Signed as a free agent by **NY Rangers**, July 2, 2011. Signed as a free agent by **Chicago**, July 1, 2014. Signed as a free agent by **Detroit**, July 1, 2015.

RICHARDS, Mike

(RIH-chuhrds, MIGHK)

Center. Shoots left. 5'11", 196 lbs. Born, Kenora, ON, February 11, 1985. Philadelphia's 2nd choice, 24th overall, in 2003 Entry Draft.

Season	Club	League	GP	G	A	Pts	PIM	PP	SH	GW	S	S%	+/-	TF	F%	Min	GP	G	A	Pts	PIM	PP	SH	GW	Min
2000-01	Kenora Stars	NOHA	85	76	73	149	20	....	....	....	....	....	....	....	....	....	....	....	....	....	....	....	....	....	....
2001-02	Kitchener Rangers	OHL	65	20	38	58	52	....	....	....	....	....	....	....	....	....	4	0	1	1	6	....	....	....	....
2002-03	Kitchener Rangers	OHL	67	37	50	87	99	....	....	....	....	....	....	....	....	....	21	9	18	27	24	....	....	....	....
2003-04	Kitchener Rangers	OHL	58	36	53	89	82	....	....	....	....	....	....	....	....	....	1	0	0	0	0	....	....	....	....
2004-05	Kitchener Rangers	OHL	43	22	36	58	75	....	....	....	....	....	....	....	....	....	15	11	17	28	36	....	....	....	....
	Philadelphia	AHL	....	....	....	....	....	....	....	....	....	....	....	....	....	....	14	7	8	15	28	....	....	....	....
2005-06	Philadelphia	NHL	79	11	23	34	65	1	3	1	168	6.5	6	914	45.7	15:23	6	0	1	1	0	0	0	0	15:41
2006-07	Philadelphia	NHL	59	10	22	32	52	1	4	3	130	7.7	–12	978	47.8	17:50	....	....	....	....	....	....	....	....	....
2007-08	Philadelphia	NHL	73	28	47	75	76	8	5	6	212	13.2	14	1381	50.5	21:31	17	7	7	14	10	1	*2	0	20:55
2008-09	Philadelphia	NHL	79	30	50	80	63	8	*7	4	238	12.6	22	1660	49.0	21:44	6	1	4	5	6	1	0	0	22:58
2009-10	Philadelphia	NHL	82	31	31	62	79	13	1	3	237	13.1	–2	1373	50.7	20:24	23	7	16	23	18	2	1	1	21:45
	Canada	Olympics	7	2	3	5	0	....	....	....	....	....	....	....	....	....	....	....	....	....	....	....	....	....	....
2010-11	Philadelphia	NHL	81	23	43	66	62	5	3	4	184	12.5	11	1216	49.8	18:53	11	1	6	7	15	1	0	0	19:19
2011-12♦	Los Angeles	NHL	74	18	26	44	71	3	*4	1	171	10.5	3	1067	50.5	18:53	20	4	11	15	17	2	0	1	19:31
2012-13	Los Angeles	NHL	48	12	20	32	42	6	0	3	82	14.6	–8	441	49.0	16:21	15	3	9	12	8	1	0	0	19:09
2013-14♦	Los Angeles	NHL	82	11	30	41	28	4	1	3	157	7.0	–6	907	53.9	16:59	26	3	7	10	17	0	0	1	15:33
2014-15	Los Angeles	NHL	53	5	11	16	39	1	0	1	63	7.9	–10	593	48.7	13:22	....	....	....	....	....	....	....	....	....
	Manchester	AHL	16	3	11	14	4	....	....	....	....	....	....	....	....	....	....	....	....	....	....	....	....	....	....
	NHL Totals		710	179	303	482	577	50	28	29	1642	10.9		10530	49.7	18:22	124	26	61	87	91	8	3	3	19:13

Memorial Cup All-Star Team (2003) • OHL Second All-Star Team (2005) • Canadian Major Junior Second All-Star Team (2005)

Played in NHL All-Star Game (2008)

Traded to **Los Angeles** by **Philadelphia** with Rob Bordson for Brayden Schenn, Wayne Simmonds and Los Angeles' 2nd round choice (later traded to Dallas – Dallas selected Devin Shore) in 2012 Entry Draft, June 23, 2011.

RICHARDSON, Brad

(RIH-chuhrd-suhn, BRAD) **ARI**

Center. Shoots left. 6', 197 lbs. Born, Belleville, ON, February 4, 1985. Colorado's 4th choice, 163rd overall, in 2003 Entry Draft.

Season	Club	League	GP	G	A	Pts	PIM	PP	SH	GW	S	S%	+/-	TF	F%	Min	GP	G	A	Pts	PIM	PP	SH	GW	Min
2001-02	Owen Sound	OHL	58	12	21	33	20	....	....	....	....	....	....	....	....	....	....	....	....	....	....	....	....	....	....
2002-03	Owen Sound	OHL	67	27	40	67	54	....	....	....	....	....	....	....	....	....	4	1	1	2	10	....	....	....	....
2003-04	Owen Sound	OHL	15	7	9	16	4	....	....	....	....	....	....	....	....	....	....	....	....	....	....	....	....	....	....
2004-05	Owen Sound	OHL	68	41	56	97	60	....	....	....	....	....	....	....	....	....	8	6	4	10	8	....	....	....	....
2005-06	Colorado	NHL	41	3	10	13	12	1	0	0	51	5.9	0	305	41.0	10:44	9	1	0	1	6	0	0	0	11:41
	Lowell	AHL	29	4	13	17	20	....	....	....	....	....	....	....	....	....	....	....	....	....	....	....	....	....	....
2006-07	Colorado	NHL	73	14	8	22	28	0	3	3	129	10.9	4	358	40.8	13:10	....	....	....	....	....	....	....	....	....
	Albany River Rats	AHL	3	0	1	1	2	....	....	....	....	....	....	....	....	....	....	....	....	....	....	....	....	....	....
2007-08	Colorado	NHL	22	2	3	5	8	0	0	0	32	6.3	–3	60	43.3	13:29	....	....	....	....	....	....	....	....	....
	Lake Erie	AHL	38	14	26	40	18	....	....	....	....	....	....	....	....	....	....	....	....	....	....	....	....	....	....
2008-09	Los Angeles	NHL	31	0	5	5	11	0	0	0	37	0.0	–6	95	54.7	10:48	....	....	....	....	....	....	....	....	....
	Manchester	AHL	3	1	2	3	0	....	....	....	....	....	....	....	....	....	....	....	....	....	....	....	....	....	....
2009-10	Los Angeles	NHL	81	11	16	27	37	0	1	4	148	7.4	1	391	48.1	12:51	6	1	1	2	2	0	0	1	14:41
2010-11	Los Angeles	NHL	68	7	12	19	47	0	1	1	103	6.8	–13	181	50.8	11:46	6	2	3	5	2	0	0	0	15:37
2011-12♦	Los Angeles	NHL	59	5	3	8	30	0	1	0	98	5.1	–6	56	58.9	12:52	13	1	0	1	4	0	0	0	8:35
2012-13	Los Angeles	NHL	16	1	5	6	10	0	0	0	27	3.7	2	56	48.2	10:54	11	0	1	1	0	0	0	0	10:46
2013-14	Vancouver	NHL	73	11	12	23	39	1	2	2	85	12.9	1	966	55.2	14:54	....	....	....	....	....	....	....	....	....
2014-15	Vancouver	NHL	45	8	13	21	34	0	1	1	66	12.1	0	578	47.8	14:28	5	0	0	0	15	0	0	0	12:37
	NHL Totals		509	62	87	149	256	2	9	11	776	8.0		3046	49.2	12:52	50	5	5	10	29	0	0	1	11:36

Traded to **Los Angeles** by **Colorado** for Detroit's 2nd round choice (previously acquired, Colorado selected Peter Delmas) in 2008 Entry Draft, June 21, 2008. • Missed majority of 2012-13 as a healthy reserve. Signed as a free agent by **Vancouver**, July 5, 2013. Signed as a free agent by **Arizona**, July 1, 2015.

RIEDER, Tobias

(REE-duhr, TOH-bee-uhs) **ARI**

Right wing. Shoots left. 5'11", 190 lbs. Born, Landshut, Germany, January 10, 1993. Edmonton's 7th choice, 114th overall, in 2011 Entry Draft.

Season	Club	League	GP	G	A	Pts	PIM	PP	SH	GW	S	S%	+/-	TF	F%	Min	GP	G	A	Pts	PIM	PP	SH	GW	Min
2008-09	EV Landshut Jr.	Ger-Jr.	36	27	24	51	18	....	....	....	....	....	....	....	....	....	9	6	8	14	10	....	....	....	....
2009-10	EV Landshut Jr.	Ger-Jr.	5	6	3	9	25	....	....	....	....	....	....	....	....	....	4	5	1	6	2	....	....	....	....
	Landshut Cann.	German-2	45	10	13	23	28	....	....	....	....	....	....	....	....	....	6	0	0	0	0	....	....	....	....
2010-11	Kitchener Rangers	OHL	65	23	26	49	35	....	....	....	....	....	....	....	....	....	7	0	2	2	4	....	....	....	....
2011-12	Kitchener Rangers	OHL	60	42	43	85	25	....	....	....	....	....	....	....	....	....	16	13	14	27	4	....	....	....	....
2012-13	Kitchener Rangers	OHL	52	27	29	56	12	....	....	....	....	....	....	....	....	....	9	2	10	12	4	....	....	....	....
2013-14	Portland Pirates	AHL	64	28	20	48	10	....	....	....	....	....	....	....	....	....	....	....	....	....	....	....	....	....	....
2014-15	Arizona	NHL	72	13	8	21	14	0	3	1	189	6.9	–19	5	20.0	16:54	....	....	....	....	....	....	....	....	....
	Portland Pirates	AHL	9	4	1	5	0	....	....	....	....	....	....	....	....	....	....	....	....	....	....	....	....	....	....
	NHL Totals		72	13	8	21	14	0	3	1	189	6.9		5	20.0	16:54									

Traded to **Phoenix** by **Edmonton** for Kale Kessy, March 30, 2013.

RIELLY, Morgan

(RIGH-lee, MOHR-guhn) **TOR**

Defense. Shoots left. 6'1", 205 lbs. Born, Vancouver, BC, March 9, 1994. Toronto's 1st choice, 5th overall, in 2012 Entry Draft.

Season	Club	League	GP	G	A	Pts	PIM	PP	SH	GW	S	S%	+/-	TF	F%	Min	GP	G	A	Pts	PIM	PP	SH	GW	Min
2008-09	Notre Dame	Minor-SK	43	41	43	84	10	....	....	....	....	....	....	....	....	....	....	....	....	....	....	....	....	....	....
2009-10	Notre Dame	SMHL	43	18	37	55	20	....	....	....	....	....	....	....	....	....	13	7	2	9	0	....	....	....	....
2010-11	Moose Jaw	WHL	65	6	22	28	21	....	....	....	....	....	....	....	....	....	6	0	6	6	0	....	....	....	....
2011-12	Moose Jaw	WHL	18	3	15	18	2	....	....	....	....	....	....	....	....	....	5	0	3	3	0	....	....	....	....
2012-13	Moose Jaw	WHL	60	12	42	54	19	....	....	....	....	....	....	....	....	....	....	....	....	....	....	....	....	....	....
	Toronto Marlies	AHL	14	1	2	3	0	....	....	....	....	....	....	....	....	....	8	1	0	1	0	....	....	....	....
2013-14	Toronto	NHL	73	2	25	27	12	1	0	0	96	2.1	–13	0	0.0	17:38	....	....	....	....	....	....	....	....	....
2014-15	Toronto	NHL	81	8	21	29	14	1	0	0	148	5.4	–16	0	0.0	20:20	....	....	....	....	....	....	....	....	....
	NHL Totals		154	10	46	56	26	2	0	0	244	4.1		0	0.0	19:03	....	....	....	....	....	....	....	....	....

WHL East First All-Star Team (2013)

• Missed majority of 2011-12 due to knee injury vs. Calgary (WHL), November 6, 2011.

RINALDO, Zac

(rih-NAL-doh, ZAK) **BOS**

Center. Shoots left. 5'11", 169 lbs. Born, Mississauga, ON, June 15, 1990. Philadelphia's 4th choice, 178th overall, in 2008 Entry Draft.

			Regular Season														Playoffs								
Season	Club	League	GP	G	A	Pts	PIM	PP	SH	GW	S	S%	+/-	TF	F%	Min	GP	G	A	Pts	PIM	PP	SH	GW	Min
2006-07	Hamilton	ON-Jr.A	44	16	16	32	193	....	....	....	....	....	....	....	....	....	16	4	4	8	48	....	....	....	....
	St. Michael's	OHL	6	0	0	0	2	....	....	....	....	....	....	....	....	....	....	....	....	....	....	....	....	....	....
2007-08	St. Michael's	OHL	63	7	7	14	191	....	....	....	....	....	....	....	....	....	4	0	0	0	9	....	....	....	....
2008-09	St. Michael's	OHL	34	6	7	13	*112	....	....	....	....	....	....	....	....	....	....	....	....	....	....	....	....	....	....
	London Knights	OHL	22	4	13	17	*89	....	....	....	....	....	....	....	....	....	8	1	1	2	26	....	....	....	....
2009-10	London Knights	OHL	34	8	7	15	*148	....	....	....	....	....	....	....	....	....	....	....	....	....	....	....	....	....	....
	Barrie Colts	OHL	26	2	8	10	*107	....	....	....	....	....	....	....	....	....	4	2	0	2	11	....	....	....	....
2010-11	Adirondack	AHL	60	3	6	9	331	....	....	....	....	....	....	....	....	....	....	....	....	....	....	....	....	....	....
	Philadelphia	**NHL**	....	....	....	....	....	....	....	....	....	....	....	....	....	....	**2**	**0**	**0**	**0**	**12**	**0**	**0**	**0**	**2:53**
2011-12	**Philadelphia**	**NHL**	**66**	**2**	**7**	**9**	**232**	**0**	**0**	**0**	**54**	**3.7**	**–1**	**9**	**66.7**	**7:29**	**5**	**0**	**0**	**0**	**48**	**0**	**0**	**0**	**5:41**
	Adirondack	AHL	4	1	1	2	11	....	....	....	....	....	....	....	....	....	....	....	....	....	....	....	....	....	....
2012-13	Adirondack	AHL	31	2	3	5	92	....	....	....	....	....	....	....	....	....	....	....	....	....	....	....	....	....	....
	Philadelphia	**NHL**	**32**	**3**	**2**	**5**	**85**	**0**	**0**	**0**	**15**	**20.0**	**–7**	**2**	**50.0**	**8:23**	....	....	....	....	....	....	....	....	....
2013-14	**Philadelphia**	**NHL**	**67**	**2**	**2**	**4**	**153**	**0**	**0**	**1**	**54**	**3.7**	**–13**	**3**	**66.7**	**7:42**	**7**	**0**	**0**	**0**	**4**	**0**	**0**	**0**	**6:51**
2014-15	**Philadelphia**	**NHL**	**58**	**1**	**5**	**6**	**102**	**0**	**0**	**0**	**45**	**2.2**	**–9**	**3**	**33.3**	**8:55**	....	....	....	....	....	....	....	....	....
	NHL Totals		**223**	**8**	**16**	**24**	**572**	**0**	**0**	**1**	**168**	**4.8**		**17**	**58.8**	**8:03**	**14**	**0**	**0**	**0**	**64**	**0**	**0**	**0**	**5:52**

Traded to **Boston** by **Philadelphia** for Boston's 3rd round choice in 2017 Entry Draft, June 29, 2015.

RISSANEN, Rasmus

(RIH-sa-nehn, RAS-mus) **CAR**

Defense. Shoots left. 6'3", 217 lbs. Born, Kuopio, Finland, July 13, 1991. Carolina's 5th choice, 178th overall, in 2009 Entry Draft.

2006-07	KalPa Kuopio U18	Fin-U18	9	1	1	2	28	....	....	....	....	....	....	....	....	....	3	0	1	1	8	....	....	....	....
2007-08	KalPa Kuopio U18	Fin-U18	29	7	9	16	99	....	....	....	....	....	....	....	....	....	2	0	0	0	8	....	....	....	....
	KalPa Kuopio Jr.	Fin-Jr.	5	0	0	0	10	....	....	....	....	....	....	....	....	....	....	....	....	....	....	....	....	....	....
2008-09	KalPa Kuopio Jr.	Fin-Jr.	29	1	8	9	56	....	....	....	....	....	....	....	....	....	4	0	1	1	6	....	....	....	....
2009-10	Everett Silvertips	WHL	71	4	11	15	103	....	....	....	....	....	....	....	....	....	7	0	1	1	8	....	....	....	....
2010-11	Everett Silvertips	WHL	68	1	11	12	89	....	....	....	....	....	....	....	....	....	4	2	0	2	8	....	....	....	....
	Charlotte	AHL	1	0	0	0	0	....	....	....	....	....	....	....	....	....	....	....	....	....	....	....	....	....	....
2011-12	Charlotte	AHL	64	3	3	6	57	....	....	....	....	....	....	....	....	....	....	....	....	....	....	....	....	....	....
2012-13	Charlotte	AHL	61	0	9	9	84	....	....	....	....	....	....	....	....	....	5	0	0	0	10	....	....	....	....
2013-14	Charlotte	AHL	62	3	7	10	91	....	....	....	....	....	....	....	....	....	....	....	....	....	....	....	....	....	....
2014-15	**Carolina**	**NHL**	**6**	**0**	**0**	**0**	**4**	**0**	**0**	**0**	**3**	**0.0**	**–5**	**0**	**0.0**	**14:59**	....	....	....	....	....	....	....	....	....
	Charlotte	AHL	52	1	10	11	69	....	....	....	....	....	....	....	....	....	....	....	....	....	....	....	....	....	....
	NHL Totals		**6**	**0**	**0**	**0**	**4**	**0**	**0**	**0**	**3**	**0.0**		**0**	**0.0**	**14:59**	....	....	....	....	....	....	....	....	....

RISTOLAINEN, Rasmus

(rihs-toh-LIGH-nehn, RAZ-muhs) **BUF**

Defense. Shoots right. 6'4", 207 lbs. Born, Turku, Finland, October 27, 1994. Buffalo's 1st choice, 8th overall, in 2013 Entry Draft.

2009-10	TPS Turku U18	Fin-U18	32	3	7	10	28	....	....	....	....	....	....	....	....	....	3	1	0	1	4	....	....	....	....
	TPS Turku Jr.	Fin-Jr.	5	1	1	2	0	....	....	....	....	....	....	....	....	....	....	....	....	....	....	....	....	....	....
2010-11	TPS Turku U18	Fin-U18	2	1	2	3	0	....	....	....	....	....	....	....	....	....	13	5	3	8	8	....	....	....	....
	TPS Turku Jr.	Fin-Jr.	27	0	12	12	30	....	....	....	....	....	....	....	....	....	....	....	....	....	....	....	....	....	....
	TPS Turku	Finland	1	0	0	0	0	....	....	....	....	....	....	....	....	....	....	....	....	....	....	....	....	....	....
2011-12	TPS Turku Jr.	Fin-Jr.	8	0	4	4	6	....	....	....	....	....	....	....	....	....	....	....	....	....	....	....	....	....	....
	TPS Turku	Finland	40	3	5	8	78	....	....	....	....	....	....	....	....	....	2	0	0	0	0	....	....	....	....
2012-13	TPS Turku	Finland	52	3	12	15	32	....	....	....	....	....	....	....	....	....	....	....	....	....	....	....	....	....	....
	TPS Turku Jr.	Fin-Jr.	....	....	....	....	....	....	....	....	....	....	....	....	....	....	5	2	1	3	2	....	....	....	....
2013-14	**Buffalo**	**NHL**	**34**	**2**	**2**	**4**	**6**	**0**	**0**	**0**	**52**	**3.8**	**–15**	**1**	**0.0**	**19:07**	....	....	....	....	....	....	....	....	....
	Rochester	AHL	34	6	14	20	22	....	....	....	....	....	....	....	....	....	5	0	2	2	2	....	....	....	....
2014-15	**Buffalo**	**NHL**	**78**	**8**	**12**	**20**	**26**	**4**	**0**	**0**	**121**	**6.6**	**–32**	**1**	**100.0**	**20:37**	....	....	....	....	....	....	....	....	....
	NHL Totals		**112**	**10**	**14**	**24**	**32**	**4**	**0**	**0**	**173**	**5.8**		**2**	**50.0**	**20:10**	....	....	....	....	....	....	....	....	....

RITCHIE, Brett

(RIH-chee, BREHT) **DAL**

Right wing. Shoots right. 6'3", 220 lbs. Born, Orangeville, ON, July 1, 1993. Dallas' 2nd choice, 44th overall, in 2011 Entry Draft.

2008-09	Tor. Marlboros	GTHL	71	36	33	69	67	....	....	....	....	....	....	....	....	....	....	....	....	....	....	....	....	....	....
2009-10	Sarnia Sting	OHL	65	13	16	29	35	....	....	....	....	....	....	....	....	....	....	....	....	....	....	....	....	....	....
2010-11	Sarnia Sting	OHL	49	21	20	41	47	....	....	....	....	....	....	....	....	....	....	....	....	....	....	....	....	....	....
2011-12	Sarnia Sting	OHL	23	8	7	15	30	....	....	....	....	....	....	....	....	....	....	....	....	....	....	....	....	....	....
	Niagara Ice Dogs	OHL	30	16	14	30	24	....	....	....	....	....	....	....	....	....	20	3	8	11	14	....	....	....	....
2012-13	Niagara Ice Dogs	OHL	53	41	35	76	40	....	....	....	....	....	....	....	....	....	4	1	3	4	9	....	....	....	....
	Texas Stars	AHL	5	3	1	4	0	....	....	....	....	....	....	....	....	....	9	2	0	2	2	....	....	....	....
2013-14	Texas Stars	AHL	68	22	26	48	53	....	....	....	....	....	....	....	....	....	13	7	4	11	10	....	....	....	....
2014-15	**Dallas**	**NHL**	**31**	**6**	**3**	**9**	**12**	**0**	**0**	**1**	**78**	**7.7**	**–1**	**4**	**25.0**	**13:59**	....	....	....	....	....	....	....	....	....
	Texas Stars	AHL	33	14	7	21	40	....	....	....	....	....	....	....	....	....	3	1	1	2	2	....	....	....	....
	NHL Totals		**31**	**6**	**3**	**9**	**12**	**0**	**0**	**1**	**78**	**7.7**		**4**	**25.0**	**13:59**	....	....	....	....	....	....	....	....	....

OHL Second All-Star Team (2013)

ROBAK, Colby

(ROH-bak, KOHL-bee)

Defense. Shoots left. 6'3", 194 lbs. Born, Dauphin, MB, April 24, 1990. Florida's 2nd choice, 46th overall, in 2008 Entry Draft.

2005-06	Parkland Rangers	MMHL	40	14	20	34	14	....	....	....	....	....	....	....	....	....	....	....	....	....	....	....	....	....	....
2006-07	Brandon	WHL	39	2	3	5	12	....	....	....	....	....	....	....	....	....	1	0	0	0	0	....	....	....	....
2007-08	Brandon	WHL	71	6	24	30	25	....	....	....	....	....	....	....	....	....	6	0	2	2	8	....	....	....	....
2008-09	Brandon	WHL	65	13	29	42	41	....	....	....	....	....	....	....	....	....	12	6	8	14	4	....	....	....	....
2009-10	Brandon	WHL	71	16	50	66	9	....	....	....	....	....	....	....	....	....	15	3	9	12	2	....	....	....	....
2010-11	Rochester	AHL	76	7	17	24	22	....	....	....	....	....	....	....	....	....	....	....	....	....	....	....	....	....	....
2011-12	**Florida**	**NHL**	**3**	**0**	**0**	**0**	**0**	**0**	**0**	**0**	**1**	**0.0**	**1**	**0**	**0.0**	**12:34**	....	....	....	....	....	....	....	....	....
	San Antonio	AHL	73	9	30	39	30	....	....	....	....	....	....	....	....	....	8	1	4	5	4	....	....	....	....
2012-13	San Antonio	AHL	63	5	18	23	50	....	....	....	....	....	....	....	....	....	....	....	....	....	....	....	....	....	....
	Florida	**NHL**	**16**	**0**	**1**	**1**	**17**	**0**	**0**	**0**	**15**	**0.0**	**–1**	**0**	**0.0**	**15:11**	....	....	....	....	....	....	....	....	....
2013-14	**Florida**	**NHL**	**16**	**0**	**2**	**2**	**6**	**0**	**0**	**0**	**15**	**0.0**	**–4**	**0**	**0.0**	**18:34**	....	....	....	....	....	....	....	....	....
	San Antonio	AHL	56	8	13	21	24	....	....	....	....	....	....	....	....	....	....	....	....	....	....	....	....	....	....
2014-15	**Florida**	**NHL**	**7**	**0**	**0**	**0**	**2**	**0**	**0**	**0**	**6**	**0.0**	**–1**	**0**	**0.0**	**12:58**	....	....	....	....	....	....	....	....	....
	Anaheim	**NHL**	**5**	**0**	**1**	**1**	**0**	**0**	**0**	**0**	**2**	**0.0**	**3**	**0**	**0.0**	**15:15**	....	....	....	....	....	....	....	....	....
	Norfolk Admirals	AHL	29	1	5	6	18	....	....	....	....	....	....	....	....	....	....	....	....	....	....	....	....	....	....
	NHL Totals		**47**	**0**	**4**	**4**	**25**	**0**	**0**	**0**	**39**	**0.0**		**0**	**0.0**	**15:51**	....	....	....	....	....	....	....	....	....

WHL East Second All-Star Team (2010)

Traded to **Anaheim** by **Florida** for Jesse Blacker and future considerations, December 4, 2014.

ROBIDAS, Stephane

(ROH-bih-dah, STEH-fan) **TOR**

Defense. Shoots right. 5'11", 190 lbs. Born, Sherbrooke, QC, March 3, 1977. Montreal's 7th choice, 164th overall, in 1995 Entry Draft.

1992-93	Magog	QAAA	41	3	12	15	16	....	....	....	....	....	....	....	....	....	5	1	1	2	2	....	....	....	....
1993-94	Shawinigan	QMJHL	67	3	19	22	33	....	....	....	....	....	....	....	....	....	1	0	0	0	0	....	....	....	....
1994-95	Shawinigan	QMJHL	71	13	56	69	44	....	....	....	....	....	....	....	....	....	15	7	12	19	4	....	....	....	....
1995-96	Shawinigan	QMJHL	67	23	56	79	53	....	....	....	....	....	....	....	....	....	6	1	5	6	10	....	....	....	....
1996-97	Shawinigan	QMJHL	67	24	51	75	59	....	....	....	....	....	....	....	....	....	7	4	6	10	14	....	....	....	....
1997-98	Fredericton	AHL	79	10	21	31	50	....	....	....	....	....	....	....	....	....	4	0	2	2	0	....	....	....	....
1998-99	Fredericton	AHL	79	8	33	41	59	....	....	....	....	....	....	....	....	....	15	1	5	6	10	....	....	....	....
99-2000	**Montreal**	**NHL**	**1**	**0**	**0**	**0**	**0**	**0**	**0**	**0**	**0**	**0.0**	**0**	**0**	**0.0**	**15:54**	....	....	....	....	....	....	....	....	....
	Quebec Citadelles	AHL	76	14	31	45	36	....	....	....	....	....	....	....	....	....	3	0	1	1	0	....	....	....	....
2000-01	**Montreal**	**NHL**	**65**	**6**	**6**	**12**	**14**	**1**	**0**	**0**	**77**	**7.8**	**0**	**1**	**100.0**	**20:44**	....	....	....	....	....	....	....	....	....
2001-02	**Montreal**	**NHL**	**56**	**1**	**10**	**11**	**14**	**1**	**0**	**0**	**68**	**1.5**	**–25**	**3**	**33.3**	**18:58**	**2**	**0**	**0**	**0**	**4**	**0**	**0**	**0**	**13:07**
2002-03	**Dallas**	**NHL**	**76**	**3**	**7**	**10**	**35**	**0**	**0**	**1**	**47**	**6.4**	**15**	**1**	**100.0**	**12:54**	**12**	**0**	**1**	**1**	**20**	**0**	**0**	**0**	**13:54**

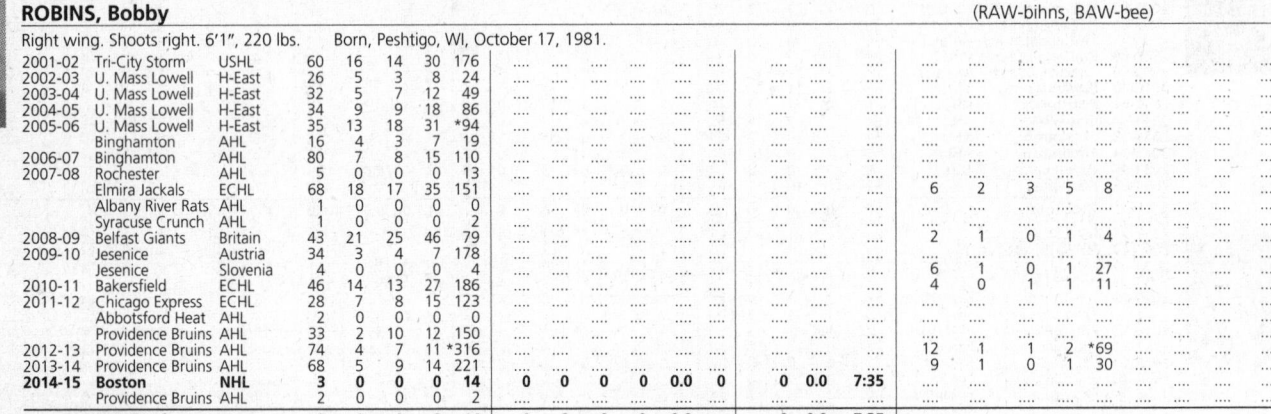

			Regular Season														Playoffs								
Season	Club	League	GP	G	A	Pts	PIM	PP	SH	GW	S	S%	+/-	TF	F%	Min	GP	G	A	Pts	PIM	PP	SH	GW	Min
2003-04	**Dallas**	**NHL**	**14**	**1**	**0**	**1**	**8**	**1**	**0**	**0**	**8**	**12.5**	**−2**	**1**	**100.0**	**12:57**	....	....	....	....	....	....	....	....	....
	Chicago	**NHL**	**45**	**2**	**10**	**12**	**33**	**0**	**1**	**1**	**55**	**3.6**	**6**	**0**	**0.0**	**20:56**	....	....	....	....	....	....	....	....	....
2004-05	Frankfurt Lions	Germany	51	15	32	47	64	....	....	....	....	....	....	....	....	....	6	1	2	3	6	....	....	....	....
2005-06	**Dallas**	**NHL**	**75**	**5**	**15**	**20**	**67**	**1**	**1**	**0**	**95**	**5.3**	**15**	**0**	**0.0**	**16:59**	**5**	**0**	**2**	**2**	**4**	**0**	**0**	**0**	**16:42**
2006-07	**Dallas**	**NHL**	**75**	**0**	**17**	**17**	**86**	**0**	**0**	**0**	**106**	**0.0**	**−1**	**0**	**0.0**	**18:04**	**7**	**0**	**1**	**1**	**2**	**0**	**0**	**0**	**19:02**
2007-08	**Dallas**	**NHL**	**82**	**9**	**17**	**26**	**85**	**7**	**0**	**2**	**153**	**5.9**	**0**	**0**	**0.0**	**20:39**	**18**	**3**	**8**	**11**	**12**	**3**	**0**	**0**	**25:31**
2008-09	**Dallas**	**NHL**	**72**	**3**	**23**	**26**	**76**	**1**	**0**	**0**	**158**	**1.9**	**10**	**1**	**100.0**	**24:32**	....	....	....	....	....	....	....	....	....
2009-10	**Dallas**	**NHL**	**82**	**10**	**31**	**41**	**70**	**7**	**0**	**1**	**199**	**5.0**	**−10**	**0**	**0.0**	**24:29**	....	....	....	....	....	....	....	....	....
2010-11	**Dallas**	**NHL**	**81**	**5**	**25**	**30**	**67**	**1**	**0**	**1**	**106**	**4.7**	**−7**	**0**	**0.0**	**24:32**	....	....	....	....	....	....	....	....	....
2011-12	**Dallas**	**NHL**	**75**	**5**	**17**	**22**	**48**	**2**	**0**	**1**	**75**	**6.7**	**−5**	**0**	**0.0**	**22:46**	....	....	....	....	....	....	....	....	....
2012-13	HIFK Helsinki	Finland	15	2	3	5	22	....	....	....	....	....	....	....	....	....	....	....	....	....	....	....	....	....	....
	Dallas	**NHL**	**48**	**1**	**12**	**13**	**56**	**0**	**0**	**0**	**46**	**2.2**	**2**	**0**	**0.0**	**22:14**	....	....	....	....	....	....	....	....	....
2013-14	**Dallas**	**NHL**	**24**	**4**	**1**	**5**	**12**	**1**	**0**	**0**	**35**	**11.4**	**7**	**0**	**0.0**	**19:55**	....	....	....	....	....	....	....	....	....
	Anaheim	**NHL**	**14**	**1**	**4**	**5**	**8**	**0**	**0**	**1**	**21**	**4.8**	**3**	**0**	**0.0**	**20:37**	**3**	**0**	**0**	**0**	**2**	**0**	**0**	**0**	**15:52**
2014-15	**Toronto**	**NHL**	**52**	**1**	**6**	**7**	**34**	**0**	**0**	**0**	**34**	**2.9**	**8**	**0**	**0.0**	**17:04**	....	....	....	....	....	....	....	....	....
	NHL Totals		**937**	**57**	**201**	**258**	**713**	**23**	**2**	**8**	**1283**	**4.4**		**7**	**71.4**	**20:19**	**47**	**3**	**12**	**15**	**44**	**3**	**0**	**0**	**19:30**

QMJHL First All-Star Team (1996, 1997)

Played in NHL All-Star Game (2009)

Claimed by **Atlanta** from **Montreal** in Waiver Draft, October 4, 2002. Traded to **Dallas** by **Atlanta** for future considerations, October 4, 2002. Traded to **Chicago** by **Dallas** with Dallas' 2nd round choice (Jakub Sindel) in 2004 Entry Draft for Jon Klemm and NY Rangers' 4th round choice (previously acquired, Dallas selected Fredrik Naslund) in 2004 Entry Draft, November 17, 2003. Signed as a free agent by **Frankfurt** (Germany), September 17, 2004. Signed as a free agent by **Dallas**, August 6, 2005. Signed as a free agent by **HIFK Helsinki** (Finland), October 8, 2012. Traded to **Anaheim** by **Dallas** for Anaheim's 4th round choice (later traded back to Anaheim, later traded to Dallas – Dallas selected Brent Moran) in 2014 Entry Draft, March 4, 2014. • Misssed majority of 2013-14 due to leg injury vs. Chicago, November 29, 2013. Signed as a free agent by **Toronto**, July 1, 2014.

ROBINS, Bobby

(RAW-bihns, BAW-bee)

Right wing. Shoots right. 6'1", 220 lbs. Born, Peshtigo, WI, October 17, 1981.

2001-02	Tri-City Storm	USHL	60	16	14	30	176	....	....	....	....	....	....	....	....	....	....	....	....	....	....	....	....	....	....
2002-03	U. Mass Lowell	H-East	26	5	3	8	24	....	....	....	....	....	....	....	....	....	....	....	....	....	....	....	....	....	....
2003-04	U. Mass Lowell	H-East	32	5	7	12	49	....	....	....	....	....	....	....	....	....	....	....	....	....	....	....	....	....	....
2004-05	U. Mass Lowell	H-East	34	9	9	18	86	....	....	....	....	....	....	....	....	....	....	....	....	....	....	....	....	....	....
2005-06	U. Mass Lowell	H-East	35	13	18	31	*94	....	....	....	....	....	....	....	....	....	....	....	....	....	....	....	....	....	....
	Binghamton	AHL	16	4	3	7	19	....	....	....	....	....	....	....	....	....	....	....	....	....	....	....	....	....	....
2006-07	Binghamton	AHL	80	7	8	15	110	....	....	....	....	....	....	....	....	....	....	....	....	....	....	....	....	....	....
2007-08	Rochester	AHL	5	0	0	0	13	....	....	....	....	....	....	....	....	....	....	....	....	....	....	....	....	....	....
	Elmira Jackals	ECHL	68	18	17	35	151	....	....	....	....	....	....	....	....	....	6	2	3	5	8	....	....	....	....
	Albany River Rats	AHL	1	0	0	0	0	....	....	....	....	....	....	....	....	....	....	....	....	....	....	....	....	....	....
	Syracuse Crunch	AHL	1	0	0	0	2	....	....	....	....	....	....	....	....	....	....	....	....	....	....	....	....	....	....
2008-09	Belfast Giants	Britain	43	21	25	46	79	....	....	....	....	....	....	....	....	....	2	1	0	1	4	....	....	....	....
2009-10	Jesenice	Austria	34	3	4	7	178	....	....	....	....	....	....	....	....	....	....	....	....	....	....	....	....	....	....
	Jesenice	Slovenia	4	0	0	0	4	....	....	....	....	....	....	....	....	....	6	1	0	1	27	....	....	....	....
2010-11	Bakersfield	ECHL	46	14	13	27	186	....	....	....	....	....	....	....	....	....	4	0	1	1	11	....	....	....	....
2011-12	Chicago Express	ECHL	28	7	8	15	123	....	....	....	....	....	....	....	....	....	....	....	....	....	....	....	....	....	....
	Abbotsford Heat	AHL	2	0	0	0	0	....	....	....	....	....	....	....	....	....	....	....	....	....	....	....	....	....	....
	Providence Bruins	AHL	33	2	10	12	150	....	....	....	....	....	....	....	....	....	....	....	....	....	....	....	....	....	....
2012-13	Providence Bruins	AHL	74	4	7	11	*316	....	....	....	....	....	....	....	....	....	12	1	1	2	*69	....	....	....	....
2013-14	Providence Bruins	AHL	68	5	9	14	221	....	....	....	....	....	....	....	....	....	9	1	0	1	30	....	....	....	....
2014-15	**Boston**	**NHL**	**3**	**0**	**0**	**0**	**14**	**0**	**0**	**0**	**0**	**0.0**	**0**	**0**	**0.0**	**7:35**	....	....	....	....	....	....	....	....	....
	Providence Bruins	AHL	2	0	0	0	2	....	....	....	....	....	....	....	....	....	....	....	....	....	....	....	....	....	....
	NHL Totals		**3**	**0**	**0**	**0**	**14**	**0**	**0**	**0**	**0**	**0.0**		**0**	**0.0**	**7:35**	....	....	....	....	....	....	....	....	....

Signed as a free agent by **Ottawa**, July 13, 2006. Signed to PTO (professional tryout) contract by **Abbotsford** (AHL), December 20, 2011. Signed to PTO (professional tryout) contract by **Providence** (AHL), December 28, 2011. Signed as a free agent by **Boston**, July 6, 2013. • Missed majority of 2014-15 due to head injury vs. Philadelphia, October 8, 2014.

ROSEHILL, Jay

(ROHZ-hihl, JAY)

Left wing. Shoots left. 6'3", 215 lbs. Born, Olds, AB, July 16, 1985. Tampa Bay's 6th choice, 227th overall, in 2003 Entry Draft.

2002-03	Olds Grizzlys	AJHL	59	1	4	5	219	....	....	....	....	....	....	....	....	....	....	....	....	....	....	....	....	....	....
2003-04	Olds Grizzlys	AJHL	42	4	12	16	172	....	....	....	....	....	....	....	....	....	14	2	2	4	....	....	....	....	....
2004-05	U. Minn-Duluth	WCHA	34	0	5	5	103	....	....	....	....	....	....	....	....	....	....	....	....	....	....	....	....	....	....
2005-06	Springfield	AHL	45	1	2	3	68	....	....	....	....	....	....	....	....	....	....	....	....	....	....	....	....	....	....
	Johnstown Chiefs	ECHL	5	0	0	0	13	....	....	....	....	....	....	....	....	....	5	0	0	0	4	....	....	....	....
2006-07	Springfield	AHL	64	0	6	6	85	....	....	....	....	....	....	....	....	....	....	....	....	....	....	....	....	....	....
	Johnstown Chiefs	ECHL	1	0	0	0	2	....	....	....	....	....	....	....	....	....	....	....	....	....	....	....	....	....	....
2007-08	Norfolk Admirals	AHL	66	3	4	7	194	....	....	....	....	....	....	....	....	....	....	....	....	....	....	....	....	....	....
	Mississippi	ECHL	2	0	0	0	6	....	....	....	....	....	....	....	....	....	....	....	....	....	....	....	....	....	....
2008-09	Norfolk Admirals	AHL	57	5	7	12	221	....	....	....	....	....	....	....	....	....	....	....	....	....	....	....	....	....	....
	Toronto Marlies	AHL	13	2	1	3	54	....	....	....	....	....	....	....	....	....	6	0	0	0	4	....	....	....	....
2009-10	**Toronto**	**NHL**	**15**	**1**	**1**	**2**	**67**	**0**	**0**	**0**	**6**	**16.7**	**−2**	**3**	**33.3**	**6:14**	....	....	....	....	....	....	....	....	....
	Toronto Marlies	AHL	46	1	2	3	172	....	....	....	....	....	....	....	....	....	....	....	....	....	....	....	....	....	....
2010-11	**Toronto**	**NHL**	**26**	**1**	**2**	**3**	**71**	**0**	**0**	**0**	**12**	**8.3**	**−6**	**0**	**0.0**	**5:12**	....	....	....	....	....	....	....	....	....
	Toronto Marlies	AHL	32	7	6	13	114	....	....	....	....	....	....	....	....	....	....	....	....	....	....	....	....	....	....
2011-12	**Toronto**	**NHL**	**31**	**0**	**0**	**0**	**60**	**0**	**0**	**0**	**15**	**0.0**	**−4**	**4**	**25.0**	**5:55**	....	....	....	....	....	....	....	....	....
	Toronto Marlies	AHL	4	0	0	0	20	....	....	....	....	....	....	....	....	....	13	0	0	0	44	....	....	....	....
2012-13	Norfolk Admirals	AHL	33	4	4	8	90	....	....	....	....	....	....	....	....	....	....	....	....	....	....	....	....	....	....
	Philadelphia	**NHL**	**11**	**1**	**0**	**1**	**64**	**0**	**0**	**1**	**7**	**14.3**	**−4**	**0**	**0.0**	**6:48**	....	....	....	....	....	....	....	....	....
2013-14	**Philadelphia**	**NHL**	**34**	**2**	**0**	**2**	**90**	**0**	**0**	**0**	**14**	**14.3**	**−8**	**1**	**0.0**	**4:57**	....	....	....	....	....	....	....	....	....
2014-15	Lehigh Valley	AHL	65	5	7	12	219	....	....	....	....	....	....	....	....	....	....	....	....	....	....	....	....	....	....
	NHL Totals		**117**	**5**	**3**	**8**	**352**	**0**	**0**	**1**	**54**	**9.3**		**8**	**25.0**	**5:36**	....	....	....	....	....	....	....	....	....

Signed as a free agent by **Toronto**, July 6 2009. • Missed majority of 2011-12 as a healthy reserve. Signed to a PTO (professional tryout) contract by **Norfolk** (AHL), October 3, 2012. Signed as a free agent by **Anaheim**, January 17, 2013. Traded to **Philadelphia** by **Anaheim** for Harry Zolnierczyk, April 1, 2013. • Missed majority of 2013-14 as a healthy reserve.

ROUSSEL, Antoine

(roo-SEHL, an-TWAHN) **DAL**

Left wing. Shoots left. 6', 200 lbs. Born, Roubaix, France, November 21, 1989.

2006-07	C.C. Lemoyne	QAAA	12	4	10	14	18	....	....	....	....	....	....	....	....	....	....	....	....	....	....	....	....	....	....
	Chicoutimi	QMJHL	56	7	13	20	55	....	....	....	....	....	....	....	....	....	4	0	0	0	14	....	....	....	....
2007-08	Chicoutimi	QMJHL	70	13	24	37	121	....	....	....	....	....	....	....	....	....	5	0	4	4	29	....	....	....	....
2008-09	Chicoutimi	QMJHL	58	15	20	35	110	....	....	....	....	....	....	....	....	....	4	0	2	2	15	....	....	....	....
2009-10	Chicoutimi	QMJHL	68	24	23	47	131	....	....	....	....	....	....	....	....	....	7	4	5	9	10	....	....	....	....
2010-11	Providence Bruins	AHL	42	1	7	8	88	....	....	....	....	....	....	....	....	....	....	....	....	....	....	....	....	....	....
	Reading Royals	ECHL	5	0	1	1	7	....	....	....	....	....	....	....	....	....	8	0	3	3	14	....	....	....	....
2011-12	Chicago Wolves	AHL	61	4	5	9	177	....	....	....	....	....	....	....	....	....	2	0	0	0	6	....	....	....	....
2012-13	Texas Stars	AHL	43	8	11	19	107	....	....	....	....	....	....	....	....	....	....	....	....	....	....	....	....	....	....
	Dallas	**NHL**	**39**	**7**	**7**	**14**	**85**	**0**	**0**	**0**	**46**	**15.2**	**3**	**55**	**54.6**	**9:24**	....	....	....	....	....	....	....	....	....
2013-14	**Dallas**	**NHL**	**81**	**14**	**15**	**29**	**209**	**0**	**0**	**2**	**113**	**12.4**	**−1**	**44**	**43.2**	**13:20**	**6**	**0**	**3**	**3**	**27**	**0**	**0**	**0**	**13:26**
2014-15	**Dallas**	**NHL**	**80**	**13**	**12**	**25**	**148**	**0**	**0**	**1**	**113**	**11.5**	**−20**	**17**	**17.7**	**14:31**	....	....	....	....	....	....	....	....	....
	NHL Totals		**200**	**34**	**34**	**68**	**442**	**0**	**0**	**3**	**272**	**12.5**		**116**	**44.8**	**13:02**	**6**	**0**	**3**	**3**	**27**	**0**	**0**	**0**	**13:26**

Signed as a free agent by **Chicago** (AHL), October 2, 2011. Signed as a free agent by **Dallas**, July 2, 2012.

ROY, Derek

(ROI, DAIR-ihk)

Center. Shoots left. 5'9", 184 lbs. Born, Ottawa, ON, May 4, 1983. Buffalo's 2nd choice, 32nd overall, in 2001 Entry Draft.

1998-99	Ontario East	Minor-ON	34	61	31	92	42	....	....	....	....	....	....	....	....	....	....	....	....	....	....	....	....	....	....
99-2000	Kitchener Rangers	OHL	66	34	53	87	44	....	....	....	....	....	....	....	....	....	5	4	1	5	6	....	....	....	....
2000-01	Kitchener Rangers	OHL	65	42	39	81	114	....	....	....	....	....	....	....	....	....	....	....	....	....	....	....	....	....	....
2001-02	Kitchener Rangers	OHL	62	43	46	89	92	....	....	....	....	....	....	....	....	....	4	1	2	3	2	....	....	....	....
2002-03	Kitchener Rangers	OHL	49	28	50	78	73	....	....	....	....	....	....	....	....	....	21	9	*23	32	14	....	....	....	....
2003-04	**Buffalo**	**NHL**	**49**	**9**	**10**	**19**	**12**	**1**	**0**	**4**	**71**	**12.7**	**−8**	**715**	**47.4**	**15:19**	....	....	....	....	....	....	....	....	....
	Rochester	AHL	26	10	16	26	20	....	....	....	....	....	....	....	....	....	16	6	8	14	18	....	....	....	....

			Regular Season														Playoffs								
Season	Club	League	GP	G	A	Pts	PIM	PP	SH	GW	S	S%	+/-	TF	F%	Min	GP	G	A	Pts	PIM	PP	SH	GW	Min
2004-05	Rochester	AHL	67	16	45	61	60	....	....	....	....	....	....	....	....	....	9	6	5	11	6	....	....	....	....
2005-06	**Buffalo**	**NHL**	**70**	**18**	**28**	**46**	**57**	**5**	**1**	**1**	**151**	**11.9**	**1**	**807**	**48.0**	**17:02**	**18**	**5**	**10**	**15**	**16**	**1**	**1**	**0**	**17:03**
	Rochester	AHL	8	7	13	20	10	....	....	....	....	....	....	....	....	....	....	....	....	....	....	....	....	....	....
2006-07	**Buffalo**	**NHL**	**75**	**21**	**42**	**63**	**60**	**6**	**1**	**3**	**130**	**16.2**	**37**	**1129**	**48.5**	**18:28**	**16**	**2**	**5**	**7**	**14**	**0**	**0**	**0**	**18:03**
2007-08	**Buffalo**	**NHL**	**78**	**32**	**49**	**81**	**46**	**6**	**3**	**4**	**218**	**14.7**	**13**	**1393**	**51.2**	**20:58**	....	....	....	....	....	....	....	....	....
2008-09	**Buffalo**	**NHL**	**82**	**28**	**42**	**70**	**38**	**9**	**1**	**9**	**221**	**12.7**	**–5**	**1469**	**50.7**	**21:12**	....	....	....	....	....	....	....	....	....
2009-10	**Buffalo**	**NHL**	**80**	**26**	**43**	**69**	**48**	**10**	**1**	**6**	**215**	**12.1**	**9**	**1225**	**50.4**	**19:23**	**6**	**0**	**2**	**2**	**4**	**0**	**0**	**0**	**22:59**
2010-11	**Buffalo**	**NHL**	**35**	**10**	**25**	**35**	**16**	**2**	**0**	**1**	**89**	**11.2**	**–1**	**528**	**46.4**	**19:32**	**1**	**0**	**1**	**1**	**0**	**0**	**0**	**0**	**20:01**
2011-12	**Buffalo**	**NHL**	**80**	**17**	**27**	**44**	**54**	**6**	**1**	**2**	**176**	**9.7**	**–7**	**1329**	**50.6**	**19:19**	....	....	....	....	....	....	....	....	....
2012-13	**Dallas**	**NHL**	**30**	**4**	**18**	**22**	**4**	**1**	**0**	**1**	**65**	**6.2**	**3**	**520**	**46.7**	**18:58**	....	....	....	....	....	....	....	....	....
	Vancouver	**NHL**	**12**	**3**	**3**	**6**	**2**	**1**	**0**	**0**	**20**	**15.0**	**1**	**127**	**40.9**	**17:39**	**4**	**0**	**1**	**1**	**2**	**0**	**0**	**0**	**17:15**
2013-14	**St. Louis**	**NHL**	**75**	**9**	**28**	**37**	**30**	**4**	**0**	**2**	**114**	**7.9**	**–1**	**466**	**47.0**	**13:37**	**4**	**0**	**1**	**1**	**0**	**0**	**0**	**0**	**12:09**
2014-15	**Nashville**	**NHL**	**26**	**1**	**9**	**10**	**2**	**0**	**0**	**0**	**35**	**2.9**	**0**	**244**	**48.0**	**13:31**	....	....	....	....	....	....	....	....	....
	Edmonton	**NHL**	**46**	**11**	**11**	**22**	**22**	**4**	**0**	**2**	**78**	**14.1**	**–13**	**665**	**43.6**	**16:54**	....	....	....	....	....	....	....	....	....
	NHL Totals		**738**	**189**	**335**	**524**	**391**	**55**	**8**	**35**	**1583**	**11.9**		**10617**	**48.9**	**18:10**	**49**	**7**	**20**	**27**	**36**	**1**	**1**	**0**	**17:47**

OHL All-Rookie Team (2000) • OHL Rookie of the Year (2000) • CHL All-Rookie Team (2000) • CHL Plus/Minus Award (2000) • CHL Most Sportsmanlike Player (2000) • OHL Playoff MVP (2003) • Memorial Cup All-Star Team (2003) • Stafford Smythe Memorial Trophy (Memorial Cup - MVP) (2003)

• Missed majority of 2010-11 due to leg injury vs. Florida, December 23, 2010. Traded to **Dallas** by **Buffalo** for Steve Ott and Adam Pardy, July 2, 2012. Traded to **Vancouver** by **Dallas** for Kevin Connauton and Vancouver 2nd round choice (Philippe Desrosiers) in 2013 Entry Draft, April 2, 2013. Signed as a free agent by **St. Louis**, July 6, 2013. Signed as a free agent by **Nashville**, July 15, 2014. Traded to **Edmonton** by **Nashville** for Mark Arcobello, December 29, 2014.

ROZSIVAL, Michal

(roh-ZIH-vahl, MEE-khahl)

Defense. Shoots right. 6'1", 212 lbs. Born, Vlasim, Czech., September 3, 1978. Pittsburgh's 5th choice, 105th overall, in 1996 Entry Draft.

Season	Club	League	GP	G	A	Pts	PIM	PP	SH	GW	S	S%	+/-	TF	F%	Min	GP	G	A	Pts	PIM	PP	SH	GW	Min
1994-95	Jihlava Jr.	CzRep-Jr.	31	8	13	21	....	....	....	....	....	....	....	....	....	....	....	....	....	....	....	....	....	....	....
1995-96	HC Dukla Jihlava	CzRep	36	3	4	7	....	....	....	....	....	....	....	....	....	....	....	....	....	....	....	....	....	....	....
1996-97	Swift Current	WHL	63	8	31	39	69	....	....	....	....	....	....	....	....	....	10	0	6	6	15	....	....	....	....
1997-98	Swift Current	WHL	71	14	55	69	122	....	....	....	....	....	....	....	....	....	12	0	5	5	33	....	....	....	....
1998-99	Syracuse Crunch	AHL	49	3	22	25	72	....	....	....	....	....	....	....	....	....	....	....	....	....	....	....	....	....	....
99-2000	**Pittsburgh**	**NHL**	**75**	**4**	**17**	**21**	**48**	**1**	**0**	**1**	**73**	**5.5**	**11**	**1**	**0.0**	**19:01**	**2**	**0**	**0**	**0**	**4**	**0**	**0**	**0**	**30:56**
2000-01	**Pittsburgh**	**NHL**	**30**	**1**	**4**	**5**	**26**	**0**	**0**	**0**	**17**	**5.9**	**3**	**1**	**100.0**	**17:06**	....	....	....	....	....	....	....	....	....
	Wilkes-Barre	AHL	29	8	8	16	32	....	....	....	....	....	....	....	....	....	21	3	*19	22	23	....	....	....	....
2001-02	**Pittsburgh**	**NHL**	**79**	**9**	**20**	**29**	**47**	**4**	**0**	**4**	**89**	**10.1**	**–6**	**0**	**0.0**	**20:01**	....	....	....	....	....	....	....	....	....
2002-03	**Pittsburgh**	**NHL**	**53**	**4**	**6**	**10**	**40**	**1**	**0**	**0**	**61**	**6.6**	**–5**	**0**	**0.0**	**20:25**	....	....	....	....	....	....	....	....	....
2003-04	Wilkes-Barre	AHL	1	0	0	0	2	....	....	....	....	....	....	....	....	....	....	....	....	....	....	....	....	....	....
2004-05	HC Ocelari Trinec	CzRep	35	1	10	11	40	....	....	....	....	....	....	....	....	....	....	....	....	....	....	....	....	....	....
	Pardubice	CzRep	16	1	3	4	30	....	....	....	....	....	....	....	....	....	16	1	2	3	34	....	....	....	....
2005-06	**NY Rangers**	**NHL**	**82**	**5**	**25**	**30**	**90**	**3**	**0**	**3**	**115**	**4.3**	***35**	**1**	**0.0**	**22:27**	**4**	**0**	**1**	**1**	**8**	**0**	**0**	**0**	**24:31**
2006-07	**NY Rangers**	**NHL**	**80**	**10**	**30**	**40**	**52**	**7**	**0**	**3**	**104**	**9.6**	**10**	**3**	**0.0**	**23:46**	**10**	**3**	**4**	**7**	**10**	**2**	**0**	**1**	**24:45**
2007-08	**NY Rangers**	**NHL**	**80**	**13**	**25**	**38**	**80**	**6**	**2**	**0**	**127**	**10.2**	**0**	**0**	**0.0**	**24:33**	**10**	**1**	**5**	**6**	**10**	**0**	**0**	**0**	**25:05**
2008-09	**NY Rangers**	**NHL**	**76**	**8**	**22**	**30**	**52**	**3**	**0**	**2**	**120**	**6.7**	**–7**	**0**	**0.0**	**22:31**	**7**	**0**	**0**	**0**	**4**	**0**	**0**	**0**	**22:41**
2009-10	**NY Rangers**	**NHL**	**82**	**3**	**20**	**23**	**78**	**1**	**0**	**1**	**80**	**3.8**	**3**	**1**	**100.0**	**21:26**	....	....	....	....	....	....	....	....	....
2010-11	**NY Rangers**	**NHL**	**32**	**3**	**12**	**15**	**22**	**0**	**0**	**1**	**24**	**12.5**	**3**	**0**	**0.0**	**22:03**	....	....	....	....	....	....	....	....	....
	Phoenix	**NHL**	**33**	**3**	**3**	**6**	**20**	**2**	**0**	**2**	**31**	**9.7**	**3**	**0**	**0.0**	**19:59**	**4**	**0**	**0**	**0**	**2**	**0**	**0**	**0**	**19:54**
2011-12	**Phoenix**	**NHL**	**54**	**1**	**12**	**13**	**34**	**0**	**0**	**0**	**49**	**2.0**	**8**	**0**	**0.0**	**19:20**	**15**	**0**	**0**	**0**	**2**	**0**	**0**	**0**	**21:48**
2012-13♦	**Chicago**	**NHL**	**27**	**0**	**12**	**12**	**14**	**0**	**0**	**0**	**13**	**0.0**	**18**	**2**	**0.0**	**18:07**	**23**	**0**	**4**	**4**	**16**	**0**	**0**	**0**	**19:16**
2013-14	**Chicago**	**NHL**	**42**	**1**	**7**	**8**	**32**	**0**	**0**	**0**	**39**	**2.6**	**7**	**0**	**0.0**	**16:39**	**17**	**1**	**5**	**6**	**8**	**0**	**0**	**0**	**17:37**
	Czech Republic	Olympics	5	0	0	0	0	....	....	....	....	....	....	....	....	....	....	....	....	....	....	....	....	....	....
2014-15♦	**Chicago**	**NHL**	**65**	**1**	**12**	**13**	**22**	**0**	**0**	**0**	**56**	**1.8**	**0**	**0**	**0.0**	**17:01**	**10**	**0**	**1**	**1**	**6**	**0**	**0**	**0**	**17:26**
	NHL Totals		**890**	**66**	**227**	**293**	**657**	**28**	**2**	**17**	**998**	**6.6**		**9**	**22.2**	**20:46**	**102**	**5**	**20**	**25**	**70**	**2**	**0**	**1**	**20:59**

WHL East First All-Star Team (1998)

• Missed majority of 2003-04 due to training camp knee injury, September 18, 2003. Signed as a free agent by **Trinec** (CzRep), September 17, 2004. Signed as a free agent by **Pardubice** (CzRep), January, 2005. Signed as a free agent by **NY Rangers**, August 29, 2005. Traded to **Phoenix** by **NY Rangers** for Wojtek Wolski, January 10, 2011. Signed as a free agent by **Chicago**, September 11, 2012.

RUHWEDEL, Chad

(ROO-WEE-dehl, CHAD) **BUF**

Defense. Shoots right. 5'11", 181 lbs. Born, San Diego, CA, May 7, 1990.

Season	Club	League	GP	G	A	Pts	PIM	PP	SH	GW	S	S%	+/-	TF	F%	Min	GP	G	A	Pts	PIM	PP	SH	GW	Min
2008-09	Sioux Falls	USHL	55	0	11	11	30	....	....	....	....	....	....	....	....	....	4	0	1	1	4	....	....	....	....
2009-10	Sioux Falls	USHL	59	5	17	22	55	....	....	....	....	....	....	....	....	....	3	0	1	1	2	....	....	....	....
2010-11	U. Mass Lowell	H-East	32	2	13	15	10	....	....	....	....	....	....	....	....	....	....	....	....	....	....	....	....	....	....
2011-12	U. Mass Lowell	H-East	37	6	19	25	26	....	....	....	....	....	....	....	....	....	....	....	....	....	....	....	....	....	....
2012-13	U. Mass Lowell	H-East	41	7	16	23	20	....	....	....	....	....	....	....	....	....	....	....	....	....	....	....	....	....	....
	Buffalo	**NHL**	**7**	**0**	**0**	**0**	**0**	**0**	**0**	**0**	**8**	**0.0**	**0**	**0**	**0.0**	**14:12**	....	....	....	....	....	....	....	....	....
2013-14	**Buffalo**	**NHL**	**21**	**0**	**1**	**1**	**2**	**0**	**0**	**0**	**35**	**0.0**	**–3**	**0**	**0.0**	**17:53**	....	....	....	....	....	....	....	....	....
	Rochester	AHL	47	4	24	28	22	....	....	....	....	....	....	....	....	....	5	2	3	5	4	....	....	....	....
2014-15	**Buffalo**	**NHL**	**4**	**0**	**1**	**1**	**0**	**0**	**0**	**0**	**4**	**0.0**	**3**	**0**	**0.0**	**12:28**	....	....	....	....	....	....	....	....	....
	Rochester	AHL	72	10	26	36	22	....	....	....	....	....	....	....	....	....	....	....	....	....	....	....	....	....	....
	NHL Totals		**32**	**0**	**2**	**2**	**2**	**0**	**0**	**0**	**47**	**0.0**		**0**	**0.0**	**16:24**	....	....	....	....	....	....	....	....	....

Hockey East First All-Star Team (2013) • NCAA East First All-American Team (2013)

Signed as a free agent by **Buffalo**, April 13, 2013.

RUNDBLAD, David

(RUHND-blahd, DAY-vihd) **CHI**

Defense. Shoots right. 6'2", 187 lbs. Born, Lycksele, Sweden, October 8, 1990. St. Louis' 1st choice, 17th overall, in 2009 Entry Draft.

Season	Club	League	GP	G	A	Pts	PIM	PP	SH	GW	S	S%	+/-	TF	F%	Min	GP	G	A	Pts	PIM	PP	SH	GW	Min
2004-05	Lycksele SK	Sweden-4	1	0	0	0	0	....	....	....	....	....	....	....	....	....	....	....	....	....	....	....	....	....	....
2005-06	Lycksele SK	Sweden-4	11	5	2	7	2	....	....	....	....	....	....	....	....	....	....	....	....	....	....	....	....	....	....
2006-07	Skelleftea U18	Swe-U18	4	1	1	2	0	....	....	....	....	....	....	....	....	....	....	....	....	....	....	....	....	....	....
	Skelleftea Jr.	Swe-Jr.	14	3	4	7	12	....	....	....	....	....	....	....	....	....	2	0	0	0	2	....	....	....	....
2007-08	Skelleftea U18	Swe-U18	4	3	2	5	29	....	....	....	....	....	....	....	....	....	....	....	....	....	....	....	....	....	....
	Skelleftea Jr.	Swe-Jr.	35	11	15	26	44	....	....	....	....	....	....	....	....	....	2	1	3	4	6	....	....	....	....
	Skelleftea AIK HK	Sweden	6	0	0	0	2	....	....	....	....	....	....	....	....	....	....	....	....	....	....	....	....	....	....
2008-09	Skelleftea AIK Jr.	Swe-Jr.	10	8	7	15	2	....	....	....	....	....	....	....	....	....	....	....	....	....	....	....	....	....	....
	Skelleftea AIK	Sweden	45	0	10	10	8	....	....	....	....	....	....	....	....	....	10	1	1	2	2	....	....	....	....
2009-10	Skelleftea AIK Jr.	Swe-Jr.	3	2	2	4	4	....	....	....	....	....	....	....	....	....	....	....	....	....	....	....	....	....	....
	Skelleftea AIK	Sweden	47	1	12	13	14	....	....	....	....	....	....	....	....	....	12	0	1	1	2	....	....	....	....
2010-11	Skelleftea AIK	Sweden	55	11	*39	50	14	....	....	....	....	....	....	....	....	....	18	3	7	10	20	....	....	....	....
2011-12	**Ottawa**	**NHL**	**24**	**1**	**3**	**4**	**6**	**0**	**0**	**0**	**26**	**3.8**	**–11**	**0**	**0.0**	**15:14**	....	....	....	....	....	....	....	....	....
	Phoenix	**NHL**	**6**	**0**	**3**	**3**	**0**	**0**	**0**	**0**	**8**	**0.0**	**–1**	**0**	**0.0**	**14:07**	....	....	....	....	....	....	....	....	....
	Portland Pirates	AHL	30	7	9	16	27	....	....	....	....	....	....	....	....	....	....	....	....	....	....	....	....	....	....
2012-13	Portland Pirates	AHL	50	9	30	39	26	....	....	....	....	....	....	....	....	....	3	1	0	1	0	....	....	....	....
	Phoenix	**NHL**	**8**	**0**	**1**	**1**	**0**	**0**	**0**	**0**	**9**	**0.0**	**–5**	**0**	**0.0**	**13:44**	....	....	....	....	....	....	....	....	....
2013-14	**Phoenix**	**NHL**	**12**	**0**	**1**	**1**	**6**	**0**	**0**	**0**	**17**	**0.0**	**–3**	**0**	**0.0**	**16:01**	....	....	....	....	....	....	....	....	....
	Portland Pirates	AHL	6	0	4	4	0	....	....	....	....	....	....	....	....	....	....	....	....	....	....	....	....	....	....
	Chicago	**NHL**	**5**	**0**	**0**	**0**	**0**	**0**	**0**	**0**	**4**	**0.0**	**–1**	**0**	**0.0**	**8:20**	....	....	....	....	....	....	....	....	....
2014-15♦	**Chicago**	**NHL**	**49**	**3**	**11**	**14**	**12**	**0**	**0**	**1**	**58**	**5.2**	**17**	**0**	**0.0**	**12:48**	**5**	**0**	**0**	**0**	**0**	**0**	**0**	**0**	**7:29**
	NHL Totals		**104**	**4**	**19**	**23**	**24**	**0**	**0**	**1**	**122**	**3.3**		**0**	**0.0**	**13:40**	**5**	**0**	**0**	**0**	**0**	**0**	**0**	**0**	**7:29**

Traded to **Ottawa** by **St. Louis** for Ottawa's 1st round choice (Vladimir Tarasenko) in 2010 Entry Draft, June 25, 2010. Traded to **Phoenix** by **Ottawa** with Ottawa's 2nd round choice (later traded to Columbus, later traded to Philadelphia – Philadelphia selected Anthony Stolarz) in 2012 Entry Draft for Kyle Turris, December 17, 2011. Traded to **Chicago** by **Phoenix** with Mathieu Brisebois for Chicago's 2nd round choice (Christian Dvorak) in 2014 Entry Draft, March 4, 2014. • Missed majority of 2013-14 as a healthy reserve.

RUSSELL, Kris

(RUH-sehl, KRIHS) **CGY**

Defense. Shoots left. 5'10", 173 lbs. Born, Caroline, AB, May 2, 1987. Columbus' 3rd choice, 67th overall, in 2005 Entry Draft.

			Regular Season														Playoffs								
Season	Club	League	GP	G	A	Pts	PIM	PP	SH	GW	S	S%	+/-	TF	F%	Min	GP	G	A	Pts	PIM	PP	SH	GW	Min
2003-04	Medicine Hat	WHL	55	4	15	19	30	....	....	....	....	....	....	....	....	....	20	3	2	5	4	....	....	....	....
2004-05	Medicine Hat	WHL	72	26	35	61	37	....	....	....	....	....	....	....	....	....	10	2	1	3	4	....	....	....	....
2005-06	Medicine Hat	WHL	55	14	33	47	18	....	....	....	....	....	....	....	....	....	13	4	8	12	11	....	....	....	....
2006-07	Medicine Hat	WHL	59	32	37	69	56	....	....	....	....	....	....	....	....	....	23	4	15	19	24	....	....	....	....
2007-08	**Columbus**	**NHL**	**67**	**2**	**8**	**10**	**14**	**1**	**0**	**1**	**90**	**2.2**	**-12**	**0**	**0.0**	**14:47**	....	....	....	....	....	....	....	....	....
2008-09	**Columbus**	**NHL**	**66**	**2**	**19**	**21**	**28**	**1**	**0**	**1**	**86**	**2.3**	**-10**	**0**	**0.0**	**16:07**	**4**	**1**	**1**	**2**	**2**	**0**	**0**	**0**	**16:40**
	Syracuse Crunch	AHL	14	3	5	8	0	....	....	....	....	....	....	....	....	....	....	....	....	....	....	....	....	....	....
2009-10	**Columbus**	**NHL**	**70**	**7**	**15**	**22**	**32**	**0**	**0**	**1**	**108**	**6.5**	**3**	**0**	**0.0**	**18:35**	....	....	....	....	....	....	....	....	....
2010-11	**Columbus**	**NHL**	**73**	**5**	**18**	**23**	**37**	**1**	**0**	**0**	**88**	**5.7**	**-9**	**0**	**0.0**	**17:31**	....	....	....	....	....	....	....	....	....
2011-12	**Columbus**	**NHL**	**12**	**2**	**1**	**3**	**13**	**0**	**0**	**0**	**20**	**10.0**	**-1**	**0**	**0.0**	**17:34**	....	....	....	....	....	....	....	....	....
	St. Louis	**NHL**	**43**	**4**	**5**	**9**	**12**	**0**	**0**	**1**	**36**	**11.1**	**13**	**0**	**0.0**	**16:51**	**9**	**0**	**3**	**3**	**5**	**0**	**0**	**0**	**19:27**
2012-13	TPS Turku	Finland	15	2	12	14	8	....	....	....	....	....	....	....	....	....	....	....	....	....	....	....	....	....	....
	St. Louis	**NHL**	**33**	**1**	**6**	**7**	**9**	**1**	**0**	**0**	**41**	**2.4**	**6**	**0**	**0.0**	**16:03**	....	....	....	....	....	....	....	....	....
2013-14	**Calgary**	**NHL**	**68**	**7**	**22**	**29**	**15**	**4**	**0**	**1**	**109**	**6.4**	**-11**	**0**	**0.0**	**23:08**	....	....	....	....	....	....	....	....	....
2014-15	**Calgary**	**NHL**	**79**	**4**	**30**	**34**	**17**	**1**	**0**	**0**	**111**	**3.6**	**18**	**0**	**0.0**	**23:57**	**11**	**2**	**5**	**7**	**7**	**1**	**0**	**1**	**26:45**
	NHL Totals		**511**	**34**	**124**	**158**	**177**	**9**	**0**	**5**	**689**	**4.9**		**0**	**0.0**	**18:43**	**24**	**3**	**9**	**12**	**14**	**1**	**0**	**1**	**22:20**

WHL East Second All-Star Team (2005) • WHL East First All-Star Team (2006, 2007) • WHL Defenseman of the Year (2006, 2007) • Canadian Major Junior Second All-Star Team (2006) • Canadian Major Junior Sportsman of the Year (2006) • WHL Player of the Year (2007) • Canadian Major Junior First All-Star Team (2007) • Canadian Major Junior Defenseman of the Year (2007)

Traded to **St. Louis** by **Columbus** for Nikita Nikitin, November 11, 2011. Signed as a free agent by **TPS Turku** (Finland), September 26, 2012. Traded to **Calgary** by **St. Louis** for Calgary's 5th round choice (Jaedon Descheneau) in 2014 Entry Draft, July 5, 2013.

RUST, Bryan

(RUHST, BRIGH-uhn) **PIT**

Right wing. Shoots right. 5'11", 192 lbs. Born, Pontiac, MI, May 11, 1992. Pittsburgh's 2nd choice, 80th overall, in 2010 Entry Draft.

Season	Club	League	GP	G	A	Pts	PIM	PP	SH	GW	S	S%	+/-	TF	F%	Min	GP	G	A	Pts	PIM	PP	SH	GW	Min
2007-08	Det. Honeybaked	MWEHL	31	17	28	45	6	....	....	....	....	....	....	....	....	....	....	....	....	....	....	....	....	....	....
	Det. Honeybaked	Minor-MI	37	27	20	47	....	....	....	....	....	....	....	....	....	....	....	....	....	....	....	....	....	....	....
2008-09	USNTDP	NAHL	42	6	9	15	18	....	....	....	....	....	....	....	....	....	9	0	2	2	4	....	....	....	....
	USNTDP	U-17	16	3	2	5	4	....	....	....	....	....	....	....	....	....	....	....	....	....	....	....	....	....	....
2009-10	USNTDP	USHL	27	10	13	23	6	....	....	....	....	....	....	....	....	....	....	....	....	....	....	....	....	....	....
	USNTDP	U-17	1	0	0	0	0	....	....	....	....	....	....	....	....	....	....	....	....	....	....	....	....	....	....
	USNTDP	U-18	38	16	13	29	18	....	....	....	....	....	....	....	....	....	....	....	....	....	....	....	....	....	....
2010-11	U. of Notre Dame	CCHA	40	6	13	19	4	....	....	....	....	....	....	....	....	....	....	....	....	....	....	....	....	....	....
2011-12	U. of Notre Dame	CCHA	40	5	6	11	14	....	....	....	....	....	....	....	....	....	....	....	....	....	....	....	....	....	....
2012-13	U. of Notre Dame	CCHA	41	15	19	34	4	....	....	....	....	....	....	....	....	....	....	....	....	....	....	....	....	....	....
2013-14	U. of Notre Dame	H-East	40	17	16	33	12	....	....	....	....	....	....	....	....	....	....	....	....	....	....	....	....	....	....
	Wilkes-Barre	AHL	2	0	0	0	0	....	....	....	....	....	....	....	....	....	1	0	0	0	0	....	....	....	....
2014-15	**Pittsburgh**	**NHL**	**14**	**1**	**1**	**2**	**4**	**0**	**0**	**0**	**34**	**2.9**	**-3**	**0**	**0.0**	**12:02**	....	....	....	....	....	....	....	....	....
	Wilkes-Barre	AHL	45	13	14	27	14	....	....	....	....	....	....	....	....	....	3	2	0	2	0	....	....	....	....
	NHL Totals		**14**	**1**	**1**	**2**	**4**	**0**	**0**	**0**	**34**	**2.9**		**0**	**0.0**	**12:02**	....	....	....	....	....	....	....	....	....

RUUTU, Tuomo

(ROO-too, TOO-oh-moh) **N.J.**

Left wing. Shoots left. 6', 205 lbs. Born, Vantaa, Finland, February 16, 1983. Chicago's 1st choice, 9th overall, in 2001 Entry Draft.

Season	Club	League	GP	G	A	Pts	PIM	PP	SH	GW	S	S%	+/-	TF	F%	Min	GP	G	A	Pts	PIM	PP	SH	GW	Min
1998-99	HIFK Helsinki U18	Fin-U18	25	9	11	20	88	....	....	....	....	....	....	....	....	....	2	1	1	2	2	....	....	....	....
99-2000	HIFK Helsinki U18	Fin-U18	5	0	3	3	12	....	....	....	....	....	....	....	....	....	3	1	2	3	2	....	....	....	....
	HIFK Helsinki Jr.	Fin-Jr.	35	11	16	27	32	....	....	....	....	....	....	....	....	....	3	0	1	1	4	....	....	....	....
	HIFK Helsinki	Finland	1	0	0	0	2	....	....	....	....	....	....	....	....	....	....	....	....	....	....	....	....	....	....
2000-01	Jokerit Helsinki Jr.	Fin-Jr.	2	1	0	1	0	....	....	....	....	....	....	....	....	....	....	....	....	....	....	....	....	....	....
	Jokerit Helsinki	Finland	47	11	11	22	94	....	....	....	....	....	....	....	....	....	5	0	0	0	4	....	....	....	....
2001-02	Jokerit Helsinki	Finland	51	7	16	23	69	....	....	....	....	....	....	....	....	....	10	0	6	6	29	....	....	....	....
2002-03	HIFK Helsinki	Finland	30	12	15	27	24	....	....	....	....	....	....	....	....	....	....	....	....	....	....	....	....	....	....
2003-04	**Chicago**	**NHL**	**82**	**23**	**21**	**44**	**58**	**10**	**0**	**3**	**174**	**13.2**	**-31**	**317**	**46.4**	**16:24**	....	....	....	....	....	....	....	....	....
2004-05			DID NOT PLAY																						
2005-06	**Chicago**	**NHL**	**15**	**2**	**3**	**5**	**31**	**1**	**0**	**0**	**30**	**6.7**	**-7**	**90**	**46.7**	**14:43**	....	....	....	....	....	....	....	....	....
2006-07	**Chicago**	**NHL**	**71**	**17**	**21**	**38**	**95**	**1**	**0**	**1**	**115**	**14.8**	**4**	**347**	**42.7**	**17:21**	....	....	....	....	....	....	....	....	....
2007-08	**Chicago**	**NHL**	**60**	**6**	**15**	**21**	**75**	**1**	**0**	**1**	**71**	**8.5**	**3**	**49**	**53.1**	**15:35**	....	....	....	....	....	....	....	....	....
	Carolina	**NHL**	**17**	**4**	**7**	**11**	**16**	**3**	**0**	**0**	**29**	**13.8**	**1**	**17**	**11.8**	**17:01**	....	....	....	....	....	....	....	....	....
2008-09	**Carolina**	**NHL**	**79**	**26**	**28**	**54**	**79**	**10**	**0**	**4**	**190**	**13.7**	**0**	**37**	**51.4**	**18:19**	**16**	**1**	**3**	**4**	**8**	**0**	**0**	**0**	**14:16**
2009-10	**Carolina**	**NHL**	**54**	**14**	**21**	**35**	**50**	**5**	**0**	**1**	**122**	**11.5**	**-4**	**47**	**40.4**	**16:23**	....	....	....	....	....	....	....	....	....
	Finland	Olympics	6	1	0	1	2	....	....	....	....	....	....	....	....	....	....	....	....	....	....	....	....	....	....
2010-11	**Carolina**	**NHL**	**82**	**19**	**38**	**57**	**54**	**7**	**0**	**1**	**148**	**12.8**	**1**	**643**	**41.2**	**16:50**	....	....	....	....	....	....	....	....	....
2011-12	**Carolina**	**NHL**	**72**	**18**	**16**	**34**	**50**	**3**	**0**	**2**	**156**	**11.5**	**-3**	**124**	**35.5**	**16:28**	....	....	....	....	....	....	....	....	....
2012-13	**Carolina**	**NHL**	**17**	**4**	**5**	**9**	**8**	**0**	**0**	**0**	**30**	**13.3**	**-6**	**8**	**12.5**	**15:14**	....	....	....	....	....	....	....	....	....
2013-14	**Carolina**	**NHL**	**57**	**5**	**11**	**16**	**34**	**2**	**0**	**1**	**79**	**6.3**	**-19**	**31**	**35.5**	**14:15**	....	....	....	....	....	....	....	....	....
	Finland	Olympics	6	1	4	5	2	....	....	....	....	....	....	....	....	....	....	....	....	....	....	....	....	....	....
	New Jersey	**NHL**	**19**	**3**	**5**	**8**	**10**	**1**	**0**	**1**	**26**	**11.5**	**1**	**6**	**50.0**	**15:32**	....	....	....	....	....	....	....	....	....
2014-15	**New Jersey**	**NHL**	**77**	**7**	**6**	**13**	**28**	**0**	**0**	**0**	**74**	**9.5**	**-3**	**9**	**44.4**	**10:52**	....	....	....	....	....	....	....	....	....
	NHL Totals		**702**	**148**	**197**	**345**	**588**	**44**	**0**	**15**	**1244**	**11.9**		**1725**	**42.4**	**15:50**	**16**	**1**	**3**	**4**	**8**	**0**	**0**	**0**	**14:16**

• Missed majority of 2005-06 due to back (October 15, 2005 at San Jose) and ankle (January 8, 2006 vs. Nashville) injuries. Traded to **Carolina** by **Chicago** for Andrew Ladd, February 26, 2008. • Missed majority of 2012-13 due to recurring hip injury and resulting surgery, January 18, 2013. Traded to **New Jersey** by **Carolina** for Andrei Loktionov and future considerations, March 5, 2014.

RYAN, Bobby

(RIGH-uhn, BAW-bee) **OTT**

Left wing. Shoots right. 6'2", 208 lbs. Born, Cherry Hill, NJ, March 17, 1987. Anaheim's 1st choice, 2nd overall, in 2005 Entry Draft.

Season	Club	League	GP	G	A	Pts	PIM	PP	SH	GW	S	S%	+/-	TF	F%	Min	GP	G	A	Pts	PIM	PP	SH	GW	Min
2003-04	Owen Sound	OHL	65	22	17	39	52	....	....	....	....	....	....	....	....	....	7	1	2	3	2	....	....	....	....
2004-05	Owen Sound	OHL	62	37	52	89	51	....	....	....	....	....	....	....	....	....	8	2	7	9	8	....	....	....	....
2005-06	Owen Sound	OHL	59	31	64	95	44	....	....	....	....	....	....	....	....	....	11	5	7	12	14	....	....	....	....
	Portland Pirates	AHL	....	....	....	....	....	....	....	....	....	....	....	....	....	....	19	1	7	8	22	....	....	....	....
2006-07	Owen Sound	OHL	63	43	59	102	63	....	....	....	....	....	....	....	....	....	4	1	1	2	2	....	....	....	....
	Portland Pirates	AHL	8	3	6	9	6	....	....	....	....	....	....	....	....	....	....	....	....	....	....	....	....	....	....
2007-08	**Anaheim**	**NHL**	**23**	**5**	**5**	**10**	**6**	**3**	**0**	**0**	**37**	**13.5**	**-1**	**1**	**100.0**	**11:16**	**2**	**0**	**0**	**0**	**2**	**0**	**0**	**0**	**11:09**
	Portland Pirates	AHL	48	21	28	49	38	....	....	....	....	....	....	....	....	....	16	8	12	20	18	....	....	....	....
2008-09	**Anaheim**	**NHL**	**64**	**31**	**26**	**57**	**33**	**12**	**0**	**3**	**174**	**17.8**	**13**	**13**	**46.2**	**15:26**	**13**	**5**	**2**	**7**	**0**	**2**	**0**	**1**	**19:41**
	Iowa Chops	AHL	14	9	10	19	19	....	....	....	....	....	....	....	....	....	....	....	....	....	....	....	....	....	....
2009-10	**Anaheim**	**NHL**	**81**	**35**	**29**	**64**	**81**	**11**	**0**	**3**	**258**	**13.6**	**9**	**93**	**44.1**	**18:29**	....	....	....	....	....	....	....	....	....
	United States	Olympics	6	1	1	2	2	....	....	....	....	....	....	....	....	....	....	....	....	....	....	....	....	....	....
2010-11	**Anaheim**	**NHL**	**82**	**34**	**37**	**71**	**61**	**5**	**1**	**5**	**270**	**12.6**	**15**	**219**	**39.7**	**20:11**	**4**	**3**	**1**	**4**	**2**	**0**	**0**	**0**	**20:29**
2011-12	**Anaheim**	**NHL**	**82**	**31**	**26**	**57**	**53**	**3**	**2**	**3**	**204**	**15.2**	**1**	**69**	**29.0**	**18:21**	....	....	....	....	....	....	....	....	....
2012-13	Mora IK	Sweden-2	11	10	3	13	8	....	....	....	....	....	....	....	....	....	....	....	....	....	....	....	....	....	....
	Anaheim	**NHL**	**46**	**11**	**19**	**30**	**17**	**2**	**0**	**1**	**101**	**10.9**	**3**	**81**	**30.9**	**16:35**	**7**	**2**	**2**	**4**	**0**	**0**	**0**	**0**	**16:17**
2013-14	**Ottawa**	**NHL**	**70**	**23**	**25**	**48**	**45**	**6**	**0**	**2**	**190**	**12.1**	**7**	**13**	**61.5**	**16:52**	....	....	....	....	....	....	....	....	....
2014-15	**Ottawa**	**NHL**	**78**	**18**	**36**	**54**	**24**	**4**	**0**	**5**	**221**	**8.1**	**5**	**11**	**36.4**	**17:28**	**6**	**2**	**0**	**2**	**0**	**1**	**0**	**0**	**15:18**
	NHL Totals		**526**	**188**	**203**	**391**	**320**	**46**	**3**	**22**	**1455**	**12.9**		**500**	**38.4**	**17:31**	**32**	**12**	**5**	**17**	**4**	**3**	**0**	**1**	**17:41**

OHL First All-Star Team (2005) • AHL All-Rookie Team (2008) • NHL All-Rookie Team (2009)

Played in NHL All-Star Game (2015)

Signed as a free agent by **Mora** (Sweden-2), November 21, 2012. Traded to **Ottawa** by **Anaheim** for Jakob Silfverberg, Stefan Noesen and Ottawa's 1st round choice (Nicholas Ritchie) in 2014 Entry Draft, July 5, 2013.

RYCHEL, Kerby

(RIGH-kuhl, KUHR-bee) **CBJ**

Left wing. Shoots left. 6'1", 205 lbs. Born, Torrance, CA, October 7, 1994. Columbus' 2nd choice, 19th overall, in 2013 Entry Draft.

			Regular Season														Playoffs								
Season	Club	League	GP	G	A	Pts	PIM	PP	SH	GW	S	S%	+/-	TF	F%	Min	GP	G	A	Pts	PIM	PP	SH	GW	Min
2008-09	Sun County	Minor-ON	26	11	17	28	24	....	....	....	....	....	....	....	....	....	12	8	5	13	2	....	....	....	....
2009-10	Detroit Belle Tire	T1EHL	29	13	10	23	29	....	....	....	....	....	....	....	....	....	....	....	....	....	....	....	....	....	....
	Detroit Belle Tire	Other	26	17	9	26	29	....	....	....	....	....	....	....	....	....	....	....	....	....	....	....	....	....	....
2010-11	St. Michael's	OHL	30	2	6	8	47	....	....	....	....	....	....	....	....	....	....	....	....	....	....	....	....	....	....
	Windsor Spitfires	OHL	32	5	8	13	26	....	....	....	....	....	....	....	....	....	18	2	4	6	14	....	....	....	....
2011-12	Windsor Spitfires	OHL	68	41	33	74	54	....	....	....	....	....	....	....	....	....	4	2	0	2	5	....	....	....	....
2012-13	Windsor Spitfires	OHL	68	40	47	87	94	....	....	....	....	....	....	....	....	....	....	....	....	....	....	....	....	....	....
2013-14	Windsor Spitfires	OHL	27	16	23	39	15	....	....	....	....	....	....	....	....	....	....	....	....	....	....	....	....	....	....
	Guelph Storm	OHL	31	18	33	51	28	....	....	....	....	....	....	....	....	....	20	11	*21	*32	23	....	....	....	....
2014-15	**Columbus**	**NHL**	**5**	**0**	**3**	**3**	**2**	**0**	**0**	**0**	**4**	**0.0**	**3**	**0**	**0.0**	**10:42**	....	....	....	....	....	....	....	....	....
	Springfield	AHL	51	12	21	33	43	....	....	....	....	....	....	....	....	....	....	....	....	....	....	....	....	....	....
	NHL Totals		**5**	**0**	**3**	**3**	**2**	**0**	**0**	**0**	**4**	**0.0**		**0**	**0.0**	**10:42**	....	....	....	....	....	....	....	....	....

Memorial Cup All-Star Team (2014)

RYDER, Michael

(RIGH-duhr, MIGH-kuhl)

Right wing. Shoots right. 6'1", 200 lbs. Born, St. John's, NL, March 31, 1980. Montreal's 9th choice, 216th overall, in 1998 Entry Draft.

			Regular Season														Playoffs								
Season	Club	League	GP	G	A	Pts	PIM	PP	SH	GW	S	S%	+/-	TF	F%	Min	GP	G	A	Pts	PIM	PP	SH	GW	Min
1996-97	Bonavista Saints	NFAHA	23	31	17	48	....	....	....	....	....	....	....	....	....	....	....	....	....	....	....	....	....	....	....
1997-98	Hull Olympiques	QMJHL	69	34	28	62	41	....	....	....	....	....	....	....	....	....	10	4	2	6	4	....	....	....	....
1998-99	Hull Olympiques	QMJHL	69	44	43	87	65	....	....	....	....	....	....	....	....	....	23	*20	16	36	39	....	....	....	....
99-2000	Hull Olympiques	QMJHL	63	50	58	108	50	....	....	....	....	....	....	....	....	....	15	11	17	28	28	....	....	....	....
2000-01	Tallahassee	ECHL	5	4	5	9	6	....	....	....	....	....	....	....	....	....	....	....	....	....	....	....	....	....	....
	Quebec Citadelles	AHL	61	6	9	15	14	....	....	....	....	....	....	....	....	....	....	....	....	....	....	....	....	....	....
2001-02	Mississippi	ECHL	20	14	13	27	2	....	....	....	....	....	....	....	....	....	....	....	....	....	....	....	....	....	....
	Quebec Citadelles	AHL	50	11	17	28	9	....	....	....	....	....	....	....	....	....	3	0	1	1	2	....	....	....	....
2002-03	Hamilton	AHL	69	34	33	67	43	....	....	....	....	....	....	....	....	....	23	11	6	17	8	....	....	....	....
2003-04	**Montreal**	**NHL**	**81**	**25**	**38**	**63**	**26**	**10**	**0**	**4**	**215**	**11.6**	**10**	**25**	**24.0**	**16:00**	**11**	**1**	**2**	**3**	**4**	**0**	**0**	**0**	**16:52**
2004-05	Leksands IF	Sweden-2	42	34	27	61	32	....	....	....	....	....	....	....	....	....	....	....	....	....	....	....	....	....	....
2005-06	**Montreal**	**NHL**	**81**	**30**	**25**	**55**	**40**	**18**	**0**	**6**	**243**	**12.3**	**–5**	**17**	**52.9**	**16:10**	**6**	**2**	**3**	**5**	**0**	**1**	**0**	**1**	**16:09**
2006-07	**Montreal**	**NHL**	**82**	**30**	**28**	**58**	**60**	**17**	**2**	**3**	**221**	**13.6**	**–25**	**28**	**42.9**	**16:17**	....	....	....	....	....	....	....	....	....
2007-08	**Montreal**	**NHL**	**70**	**14**	**17**	**31**	**30**	**1**	**0**	**2**	**134**	**10.4**	**–4**	**19**	**26.3**	**13:15**	**4**	**0**	**0**	**0**	**2**	**0**	**0**	**0**	**10:46**
2008-09	**Boston**	**NHL**	**74**	**27**	**26**	**53**	**26**	**10**	**0**	**7**	**185**	**14.6**	**28**	**15**	**46.7**	**14:55**	**11**	**5**	**8**	**13**	**8**	**1**	**0**	**1**	**15:45**
2009-10	**Boston**	**NHL**	**82**	**18**	**15**	**33**	**35**	**7**	**0**	**1**	**191**	**9.4**	**3**	**15**	**13.3**	**15:18**	**13**	**4**	**1**	**5**	**2**	**1**	**0**	**0**	**15:47**
2010-11♦	**Boston**	**NHL**	**79**	**18**	**23**	**41**	**26**	**8**	**0**	**6**	**165**	**10.9**	**–1**	**8**	**62.5**	**14:29**	**25**	**8**	**9**	**17**	**8**	**2**	**0**	**2**	**14:34**
2011-12	**Dallas**	**NHL**	**82**	**35**	**27**	**62**	**46**	**7**	**0**	**6**	**211**	**16.6**	**17**	**71**	**47.9**	**17:23**	....	....	....	....	....	....	....	....	....
2012-13	**Dallas**	**NHL**	**19**	**6**	**8**	**14**	**8**	**2**	**0**	**2**	**42**	**14.3**	**4**	**6**	**33.3**	**16:22**	....	....	....	....	....	....	....	....	....
	Montreal	**NHL**	**27**	**10**	**11**	**21**	**8**	**6**	**0**	**3**	**59**	**16.9**	**–2**	**3**	**33.3**	**15:49**	**5**	**1**	**1**	**2**	**2**	**0**	**0**	**0**	**14:51**
2013-14	**New Jersey**	**NHL**	**82**	**18**	**16**	**34**	**18**	**4**	**1**	**2**	**166**	**10.8**	**–6**	**12**	**33.3**	**15:47**	....	....	....	....	....	....	....	....	....
2014-15	**New Jersey**	**NHL**	**47**	**6**	**13**	**19**	**30**	**0**	**0**	**0**	**89**	**6.7**	**–1**	**6**	**33.3**	**14:29**	....	....	....	....	....	....	....	....	....
	NHL Totals		**806**	**237**	**247**	**484**	**353**	**90**	**3**	**42**	**1921**	**12.3**		**225**	**39.6**	**15:31**	**75**	**21**	**24**	**45**	**26**	**5**	**0**	**4**	**15:14**

NHL All-Rookie Team (2004)

Signed as a free agent by **Leksands** (Sweden-2), September 19, 2004. Signed as a free agent by **Boston**, July 1, 2008. Signed as a free agent by **Dallas**, July 1, 2011. Traded to **Montreal** by **Dallas** for Erik Cole and Dallas' 3rd round choice (Connor Crisp) in 2013 Entry Draft, February 26, 2013. Signed as a free agent by **New Jersey**, July 5, 2013.

SAAD, Brandon

(SAHD, BRAN-duhn) **CBJ**

Left wing. Shoots left. 6'1", 202 lbs. Born, Pittsburgh, PA, October 27, 1992. Chicago's 4th choice, 43rd overall, in 2011 Entry Draft.

			Regular Season														Playoffs								
Season	Club	League	GP	G	A	Pts	PIM	PP	SH	GW	S	S%	+/-	TF	F%	Min	GP	G	A	Pts	PIM	PP	SH	GW	Min
2007-08	Pittsburgh	MWEHL	26	11	19	30	16	....	....	....	....	....	....	....	....	....	....	....	....	....	....	....	....	....	....
2008-09	Mahoning Valley	NAHL	47	29	18	47	48	....	....	....	....	....	....	....	....	....	7	5	1	6	10	....	....	....	....
	USNTDP	U-17	7	6	5	11	2	....	....	....	....	....	....	....	....	....	....	....	....	....	....	....	....	....	....
2009-10	USNTDP	USHL	24	12	14	26	18	....	....	....	....	....	....	....	....	....	....	....	....	....	....	....	....	....	....
	USNTDP	U-18	39	17	15	32	16	....	....	....	....	....	....	....	....	....	....	....	....	....	....	....	....	....	....
2010-11	Saginaw Spirit	OHL	59	27	28	55	47	....	....	....	....	....	....	....	....	....	12	3	9	12	10	....	....	....	....
2011-12	Saginaw Spirit	OHL	44	34	42	76	38	....	....	....	....	....	....	....	....	....	12	8	9	17	4	....	....	....	....
	Chicago	**NHL**	**2**	**0**	**0**	**0**	**0**	**0**	**0**	**0**	**3**	**0.0**	**0**	**0**	**0.0**	**14:01**	**2**	**0**	**1**	**1**	**0**	**0**	**0**	**0**	**12:21**
2012-13	Rockford IceHogs	AHL	31	8	12	20	10	....	....	....	....	....	....	....	....	....	....	....	....	....	....	....	....	....	....
	♦ Chicago	**NHL**	**46**	**10**	**17**	**27**	**12**	**0**	**1**	**2**	**98**	**10.2**	**17**	**46**	**37.0**	**16:28**	**23**	**1**	**5**	**6**	**4**	**0**	**0**	**0**	**16:24**
2013-14	**Chicago**	**NHL**	**78**	**19**	**28**	**47**	**20**	**3**	**0**	**2**	**159**	**11.9**	**20**	**122**	**41.0**	**16:17**	**19**	**6**	**10**	**16**	**6**	**1**	**0**	**1**	**17:31**
2014-15♦	**Chicago**	**NHL**	**82**	**23**	**29**	**52**	**12**	**2**	**0**	**6**	**203**	**11.3**	**7**	**88**	**43.2**	**17:15**	**23**	**8**	**3**	**11**	**6**	**0**	**1**	**2**	**20:16**
	NHL Totals		**208**	**52**	**74**	**126**	**44**	**5**	**1**	**10**	**463**	**11.2**		**256**	**41.0**	**16:41**	**67**	**15**	**19**	**34**	**16**	**1**	**1**	**3**	**17:55**

OHL First All-Star Team (2012) • NHL All-Rookie Team (2013)

Traded to **Columbus** by **Chicago** with Michael Paliotta and Alex Broadhurst for Artem Anisimov, Jeremy Morin, Corey Tropp, Marko Dano and Columbus' 4th round choice in 2016 Entry Draft, June 30, 2015.

ST. DENIS, Frederic

(SAINT-deh-nee, FREHD-uhr-ihk)

Defense. Shoots left. 5'11", 192 lbs. Born, Greenfield Park, QC, January 23, 1986.

			Regular Season														Playoffs								
Season	Club	League	GP	G	A	Pts	PIM	PP	SH	GW	S	S%	+/-	TF	F%	Min	GP	G	A	Pts	PIM	PP	SH	GW	Min
2001-02	C.C. Lemoyne	QAAA	42	4	6	10	4	....	....	....	....	....	....	....	....	....	19	2	5	7	4	....	....	....	....
2002-03	C.C. Lemoyne	QAAA	31	8	15	23	6	....	....	....	....	....	....	....	....	....	15	2	8	10	4	....	....	....	....
	Drummondville	QMJHL	14	0	0	0	0	....	....	....	....	....	....	....	....	....	....	....	....	....	....	....	....	....	....
2003-04	Drummondville	QMJHL	67	7	10	17	30	....	....	....	....	....	....	....	....	....	5	0	1	1	2	....	....	....	....
2004-05	Drummondville	QMJHL	70	11	22	33	36	....	....	....	....	....	....	....	....	....	6	2	3	5	0	....	....	....	....
2005-06	Drummondville	QMJHL	69	17	50	67	74	....	....	....	....	....	....	....	....	....	....	....	....	....	....	....	....	....	....
2006-07	Drummondville	QMJHL	65	9	29	38	59	....	....	....	....	....	....	....	....	....	12	1	7	8	8	....	....	....	....
2007-08	U. Quebec T-R	OUAA	28	4	14	18	4	....	....	....	....	....	....	....	....	....	....	....	....	....	....	....	....	....	....
2008-09	Hamilton	AHL	7	1	1	2	6	....	....	....	....	....	....	....	....	....	....	....	....	....	....	....	....	....	....
	Cincinnati	ECHL	41	1	22	23	22	....	....	....	....	....	....	....	....	....	15	0	5	5	14	....	....	....	....
2009-10	Hamilton	AHL	59	3	14	17	38	....	....	....	....	....	....	....	....	....	19	0	1	1	20	....	....	....	....
2010-11	Hamilton	AHL	76	5	18	23	34	....	....	....	....	....	....	....	....	....	20	1	9	10	12	....	....	....	....
2011-12	**Montreal**	**NHL**	**17**	**1**	**2**	**3**	**10**	**0**	**0**	**0**	**11**	**9.1**	**3**	**0**	**0.0**	**14:31**	....	....	....	....	....	....	....	....	....
	Hamilton	AHL	58	3	25	28	18	....	....	....	....	....	....	....	....	....	....	....	....	....	....	....	....	....	....
2012-13	Hamilton	AHL	63	7	11	18	24	....	....	....	....	....	....	....	....	....	....	....	....	....	....	....	....	....	....
2013-14	Springfield	AHL	60	9	17	26	32	....	....	....	....	....	....	....	....	....	5	0	2	2	0	....	....	....	....
2014-15	**Columbus**	**NHL**	**4**	**0**	**1**	**1**	**0**	**0**	**0**	**0**	**2**	**0.0**	**–1**	**0**	**0.0**	**13:18**	....	....	....	....	....	....	....	....	....
	Springfield	AHL	59	3	17	20	32	....	....	....	....	....	....	....	....	....	....	....	....	....	....	....	....	....	....
	NHL Totals		**21**	**1**	**3**	**4**	**10**	**0**	**0**	**0**	**13**	**7.7**		**0**	**0.0**	**14:17**	....	....	....	....	....	....	....	....	....

QMJHL Second All-Star Team (2006)

Signed as a free agent by **Hamilton** (AHL), September 27, 2008. Signed as a free agent by **Montreal**. July 1, 2010. Signed as a free agent by **Columbus**, July 7, 2013. Signed as a free agent by **Munchen** (Germany), August 11, 2015.

ST. LOUIS, Martin

(SAINT loo-EE, mahr-TEHN)

Right wing. Shoots left. 5'8", 180 lbs. Born, Laval, QC, June 18, 1975.

			Regular Season														Playoffs								
Season	Club	League	GP	G	A	Pts	PIM	PP	SH	GW	S	S%	+/-	TF	F%	Min	GP	G	A	Pts	PIM	PP	SH	GW	Min
1991-92	Laval-Laurentides	QAAA	42	29	*74	*103	38	....	....	....	....	....	....	....	....	....	12	7	15	22	16	....	....	....	....
1992-93	Hawkesbury	ON-Jr.A	31	37	50	87	70	....	....	....	....	....	....	....	....	....	....	....	....	....	....	....	....	....	....
1993-94	U. of Vermont	ECAC	33	15	36	51	24	....	....	....	....	....	....	....	....	....	....	....	....	....	....	....	....	....	....
1994-95	U. of Vermont	ECAC	35	23	48	71	36	....	....	....	....	....	....	....	....	....	....	....	....	....	....	....	....	....	....
1995-96	U. of Vermont	ECAC	35	29	56	85	38	....	....	....	....	....	....	....	....	....	....	....	....	....	....	....	....	....	....
1996-97	U. of Vermont	ECAC	36	24	*36	60	65	....	....	....	....	....	....	....	....	....	....	....	....	....	....	....	....	....	....
1997-98	Cleveland	IHL	56	16	34	50	24	....	....	....	....	....	....	....	....	....	....	....	....	....	....	....	....	....	....
	Saint John Flames	AHL	25	15	11	26	20	....	....	....	....	....	....	....	....	....	20	5	15	20	16	....	....	....	....
1998-99	**Calgary**	**NHL**	**13**	**1**	**1**	**2**	**10**	**0**	**0**	**0**	**14**	**7.1**	**–2**	**0**	**0.0**	**8:15**	....	....	....	....	....	....	....	....	....
	Saint John Flames	AHL	53	28	34	62	30	....	....	....	....	....	....	....	....	....	7	4	4	8	2	....	....	....	....
99-2000	**Calgary**	**NHL**	**56**	**3**	**15**	**18**	**22**	**0**	**0**	**1**	**73**	**4.1**	**–5**	**3**	**0.0**	**14:41**	....	....	....	....	....	....	....	....	....
	Saint John Flames	AHL	17	15	11	26	14	....	....	....	....	....	....	....	....	....	....	....	....	....	....	....	....	....	....

								Regular Season									Playoffs								
Season	Club	League	GP	G	A	Pts	PIM	PP	SH	GW	S	S%	+/-	TF	F%	Min	GP	G	A	Pts	PIM	PP	SH	GW	Min
2000-01	**Tampa Bay**	**NHL**	**78**	**18**	**22**	**40**	**12**	**3**	**3**	**4**	**141**	**12.8**	**–4**	**48**	**41.7**	**15:14**	....	....	....	....	....	....	....	....	....
2001-02	**Tampa Bay**	**NHL**	**53**	**16**	**19**	**35**	**20**	**6**	**1**	**2**	**105**	**15.2**	**4**	**33**	**39.4**	**18:41**	....	....	....	....	....	....	....	....	....
2002-03	**Tampa Bay**	**NHL**	**82**	**33**	**37**	**70**	**32**	**12**	**3**	**5**	**201**	**16.4**	**10**	**37**	**37.8**	**19:43**	**11**	**7**	**5**	**12**	**0**	**1**	***2**	**3**	**22:21**
2003-04♦	**Tampa Bay**	**NHL**	**82**	**38**	***56**	***94**	**24**	**8**	***8**	**7**	**212**	**17.9**	***35**	**24**	**33.3**	**20:35**	**23**	**9**	***15**	**24**	**14**	**3**	**1**	**3**	**22:52**
2004-05	Lausanne HC	Swiss	23	9	16	25	16	....	....	....	....	....	....	....	....	....	....	....	....	....	....	....	....	....	....
2005-06	**Tampa Bay**	**NHL**	**80**	**31**	**30**	**61**	**38**	**9**	**3**	**7**	**221**	**14.0**	**–3**	**13**	**23.1**	**20:59**	**5**	**4**	**0**	**4**	**2**	**1**	**0**	**1**	**22:53**
	Canada	Olympics	6	2	1	3	0	....	....	....	....	....	....	....	....	....	....	....	....	....	....	....	....	....	....
2006-07	**Tampa Bay**	**NHL**	**82**	**43**	**59**	**102**	**28**	**14**	**5**	**7**	**273**	**15.8**	**7**	**20**	**35.0**	**24:09**	**6**	**3**	**5**	**8**	**8**	**1**	**0**	**0**	**28:07**
2007-08	**Tampa Bay**	**NHL**	**82**	**25**	**58**	**83**	**26**	**10**	**2**	**5**	**241**	**10.4**	**–23**	**12**	**25.0**	**24:17**	....	....	....	....	....	....	....	....	....
2008-09	**Tampa Bay**	**NHL**	**82**	**30**	**50**	**80**	**14**	**7**	**2**	**3**	**262**	**11.5**	**4**	**30**	**46.7**	**21:17**	....	....	....	....	....	....	....	....	....
2009-10	**Tampa Bay**	**NHL**	**82**	**29**	**65**	**94**	**12**	**7**	**1**	**7**	**242**	**12.0**	**–8**	**157**	**45.2**	**21:49**	....	....	....	....	....	....	....	....	....
2010-11	**Tampa Bay**	**NHL**	**82**	**31**	**68**	**99**	**12**	**4**	**0**	**7**	**254**	**12.2**	**0**	**131**	**38.2**	**20:59**	**18**	**10**	**10**	**20**	**4**	**4**	**0**	**1**	**21:11**
2011-12	**Tampa Bay**	**NHL**	**77**	**25**	**49**	**74**	**16**	**4**	**0**	**3**	**185**	**13.5**	**–3**	**41**	**43.9**	**22:38**	....	....	....	....	....	....	....	....	....
2012-13	**Tampa Bay**	**NHL**	**48**	**17**	***43**	***60**	**14**	**3**	**0**	**2**	**112**	**15.2**	**0**	**28**	**42.9**	**21:59**	....	....	....	....	....	....	....	....	....
2013-14	**Tampa Bay**	**NHL**	**62**	**29**	**32**	**61**	**6**	**9**	**0**	**5**	**167**	**17.4**	**12**	**160**	**41.9**	**21:41**	....	....	....	....	....	....	....	....	....
	NY Rangers	**NHL**	**19**	**1**	**7**	**8**	**4**	**0**	**1**	**0**	**37**	**2.7**	**1**	**7**	**14.3**	**18:30**	**25**	**8**	**7**	**15**	**2**	**2**	**0**	**3**	**19:16**
	Canada	Olympics	5	0	0	0	2	....	....	....	....	....	....	....	....	....	....	....	....	....	....	....	....	....	....
2014-15	**NY Rangers**	**NHL**	**74**	**21**	**31**	**52**	**20**	**5**	**0**	**1**	**144**	**14.6**	**12**	**110**	**46.4**	**17:34**	**19**	**1**	**6**	**7**	**4**	**1**	**0**	**0**	**16:30**
	NHL Totals		**1134**	**391**	**642**	**1033**	**310**	**101**	**29**	**66**	**2884**	**13.6**		**854**	**41.2**	**20:23**	**107**	**42**	**48**	**90**	**34**	**13**	**3**	**11**	**20:51**

ECAC First All-Star Team (1995, 1996, 1997) • ECAC Player of the Year (1995) • NCAA East First All-American Team (1995, 1996, 1997) • NCAA Championship All-Tournament Team (1996) • NHL First All-Star Team (2004) • Art Ross Trophy (2004, 2013) • Lester B. Pearson Award (2004) • Hart Memorial Trophy (2004) • NHL Second All-Star Team (2007, 2010, 2011, 2013) • Lady Byng Memorial Trophy (2010, 2011, 2013)

Played in NHL All-Star Game (2003, 2004, 2007, 2008, 2009, 2011)

Signed as a free agent by **Calgary**, February 19, 1998. Signed as a free agent by **Tampa Bay**, July 31, 2000. Signed as a free agent by **Lausanne** (Swiss), November 4, 2004. Traded to **NY Rangers** by **Tampa Bay** for Ryan Callahan, NY Rangers' 1st round choice (later traded to NY Islanders – NY Islanders selected Joshua Ho-Sang) in 2014 Entry Draft and NY Rangers' 1st (later traded to NY Islanders – NY Islanders selected Anthony Beauvillier) and 7th (previously acquired, later traded to Edmonton – Edmonton selected Ziyat Paigin) round choices in 2015 Entry Draft, March 5, 2014. • Officially announced his retirement, July 2, 2015.

SALOMAKI, Miikka

(sa-loh-MYA-kee, MEEKA) **NSH**

Right wing. Shoots left. 5'11", 198 lbs. Born, Raahe, Finland, March 9, 1993. Nashville's 2nd choice, 52nd overall, in 2011 Entry Draft.

2008-09	Laser HT U18	Fin-U18	23	13	30	43	71	....	....	....	....	....	....	....	....	....	....	....	....	....	....	....	....	....	....
2009-10	Karpat Oulu U18	Fin-U18	3	4	2	6	4	....	....	....	....	....	....	....	....	....	....	....	....	....	....	....	....	....	....
	Karpat Oulu Jr.	Fin-Jr.	37	18	25	43	93	....	....	....	....	....	....	....	....	....	....	....	....	....	....	....	....	....	....
2010-11	Suomi U20	Finland-2	3	1	1	2	27	....	....	....	....	....	....	....	....	....	....	....	....	....	....	....	....	....	....
	Karpat Oulu	Finland	40	4	6	10	53	....	....	....	....	....	....	....	....	....	3	0	1	1	27	....	....	....	....
	Karpat Oulu U18	Fin-U18	....	....	....	....	....	....	....	....	....	....	....	....	....	....	2	0	1	1	2	....	....	....	....
2011-12	Karpat Oulu	Finland	40	12	9	21	56	....	....	....	....	....	....	....	....	....	7	1	0	1	56	....	....	....	....
2012-13	Karpat Oulu	Finland	42	9	10	19	44	....	....	....	....	....	....	....	....	....	3	2	0	2	14	....	....	....	....
2013-14	Milwaukee	AHL	75	20	30	50	83	....	....	....	....	....	....	....	....	....	3	0	0	0	6	....	....	....	....
2014-15	**Nashville**	**NHL**	**1**	**1**	**0**	**1**	**0**	**0**	**0**	**0**	**4**	**25.0**	**1**	**0**	**0.0**	**10:49**	....	....	....	....	....	....	....	....	....
	Milwaukee	AHL	38	7	11	18	30	....	....	....	....	....	....	....	....	....	....	....	....	....	....	....	....	....	....
	NHL Totals		**1**	**1**	**0**	**1**	**0**	**0**	**0**	**0**	**4**	**25.0**		**0**	**0.0**	**10:49**	....	....	....	....	....	....	....	....	....

• Missed majority of 2014-15 as a healthy reserve.

SALVADOR, Bryce

(SAL-vuh-dohr, BRIGHS)

Defense. Shoots left. 6'4", 215 lbs. Born, Brandon, MB, February 11, 1976. Tampa Bay's 6th choice, 138th overall, in 1994 Entry Draft.

1991-92	Brandon	MAHA	52	6	23	29	38	....	....	....	....	....	....	....	....	....	....	....	....	....	....	....	....	....	....
1992-93	Lethbridge	WHL	64	1	4	5	29	....	....	....	....	....	....	....	....	....	4	0	0	0	0	....	....	....	....
1993-94	Lethbridge	WHL	61	4	14	18	36	....	....	....	....	....	....	....	....	....	9	0	1	1	2	....	....	....	....
1994-95	Lethbridge	WHL	67	1	9	10	88	....	....	....	....	....	....	....	....	....	....	....	....	....	....	....	....	....	....
1995-96	Lethbridge	WHL	56	4	12	16	75	....	....	....	....	....	....	....	....	....	3	0	1	1	2	....	....	....	....
1996-97	Lethbridge	WHL	63	8	32	40	81	....	....	....	....	....	....	....	....	....	19	0	7	7	14	....	....	....	....
1997-98	Worcester IceCats	AHL	46	2	8	10	74	....	....	....	....	....	....	....	....	....	11	0	1	1	45	....	....	....	....
1998-99	Worcester IceCats	AHL	69	5	13	18	129	....	....	....	....	....	....	....	....	....	4	0	1	1	2	....	....	....	....
99-2000	Worcester IceCats	AHL	55	0	13	13	53	....	....	....	....	....	....	....	....	....	9	0	1	1	2	....	....	....	....
2000-01	**St. Louis**	**NHL**	**75**	**2**	**8**	**10**	**69**	**0**	**0**	**1**	**60**	**3.3**	**–4**	**1**	**0.0**	**16:38**	**14**	**2**	**0**	**2**	**18**	**0**	**0**	**1**	**14:41**
2001-02	**St. Louis**	**NHL**	**66**	**5**	**7**	**12**	**78**	**1**	**0**	**2**	**37**	**13.5**	**3**	**0**	**0.0**	**16:55**	**10**	**0**	**1**	**1**	**4**	**0**	**0**	**0**	**12:34**
2002-03	**St. Louis**	**NHL**	**71**	**2**	**8**	**10**	**95**	**1**	**0**	**0**	**73**	**2.7**	**7**	**0**	**0.0**	**18:57**	**7**	**0**	**0**	**0**	**2**	**0**	**0**	**0**	**17:17**
2003-04	**St. Louis**	**NHL**	**69**	**3**	**5**	**8**	**47**	**0**	**0**	**1**	**60**	**5.0**	**–4**	**0**	**0.0**	**17:29**	**5**	**0**	**0**	**0**	**2**	**0**	**0**	**0**	**14:31**
	Worcester IceCats	AHL	2	0	1	1	0	....	....	....	....	....	....	....	....	....	....	....	....	....	....	....	....	....	....
2004-05	Missouri	UHL	7	0	0	0	16	....	....	....	....	....	....	....	....	....	3	0	0	0	0	....	....	....	....
2005-06	**St. Louis**	**NHL**	**46**	**1**	**4**	**5**	**26**	**0**	**0**	**0**	**23**	**4.3**	**–24**	**1**	**0.0**	**19:48**	....	....	....	....	....	....	....	....	....
2006-07	**St. Louis**	**NHL**	**64**	**2**	**5**	**7**	**55**	**0**	**0**	**0**	**40**	**5.0**	**–5**	**0**	**0.0**	**19:44**	....	....	....	....	....	....	....	....	....
2007-08	**St. Louis**	**NHL**	**56**	**1**	**10**	**11**	**43**	**0**	**0**	**1**	**29**	**3.4**	**12**	**1**	**0.0**	**19:38**	....	....	....	....	....	....	....	....	....
	New Jersey	**NHL**	**8**	**0**	**0**	**0**	**11**	**0**	**0**	**0**	**0**	**0.0**	**0**	**0**	**0.0**	**20:54**	**5**	**1**	**0**	**1**	**2**	**0**	**0**	**0**	**17:55**
2008-09	**New Jersey**	**NHL**	**76**	**3**	**13**	**16**	**78**	**0**	**0**	**2**	**68**	**4.4**	**–1**	**1**	**100.0**	**19:29**	**4**	**0**	**0**	**0**	**4**	**0**	**0**	**0**	**15:29**
2009-10	**New Jersey**	**NHL**	**79**	**4**	**10**	**14**	**57**	**0**	**0**	**2**	**47**	**8.5**	**8**	**0**	**0.0**	**18:52**	**5**	**0**	**0**	**0**	**6**	**0**	**0**	**0**	**16:04**
2010-11			DID NOT PLAY – INJURED																						
2011-12	**New Jersey**	**NHL**	**82**	**0**	**9**	**9**	**66**	**0**	**0**	**0**	**52**	**0.0**	**18**	**0**	**0.0**	**20:13**	**24**	**4**	**10**	**14**	**26**	**0**	**1**	**1**	**22:25**
2012-13	**New Jersey**	**NHL**	**39**	**0**	**2**	**2**	**22**	**0**	**0**	**0**	**29**	**0.0**	**–12**	**0**	**0.0**	**21:20**	....	....	....	....	....	....	....	....	....
2013-14	**New Jersey**	**NHL**	**40**	**1**	**3**	**4**	**29**	**0**	**0**	**0**	**24**	**4.2**	**–2**	**0**	**0.0**	**20:18**	....	....	....	....	....	....	....	....	....
2014-15	**New Jersey**	**NHL**	**15**	**0**	**2**	**2**	**20**	**0**	**0**	**0**	**13**	**0.0**	**–5**	**0**	**0.0**	**18:30**	....	....	....	....	....	....	....	....	....
	NHL Totals		**786**	**24**	**86**	**110**	**696**	**2**	**0**	**9**	**555**	**4.3**		**4**	**25.0**	**18:58**	**74**	**7**	**11**	**18**	**64**	**0**	**1**	**2**	**17:30**

Signed as a free agent by **St. Louis**, December 16, 1996. Signed as a free agent by **Missouri** (UHL), March 11, 2005. Traded to **New Jersey** by **St. Louis** for Cam Janssen, February 26, 2008. • Missed 2010-11 due to pre-season head injury vs. Philadelphia, September 28, 2010. • Missed majority of 2013-14 due to foot (October 22, 2013 at Columbus) and lower-body (March 29, 2014 vs. NY Islanders) injuries. • Missed majority of 2014-15 due to lower-body injury at Boston, November 10, 2014.

SAMSON, Jerome

(SAM-sohn, jeh-ROHM)

Right wing. Shoots right. 6', 195 lbs. Born, Greenfield Park, QC, September 4, 1987.

2002-03			STATISTICS NOT AVAILABLE																						
	Antoine-Girouard	QAAA	5	2	2	4	6	....	....	....	....	....	....	....	....	....	8	2	3	5	2	....	....	....	....
2003-04	Antoine-Girouard	QAAA	42	18	31	49	30	....	....	....	....	....	....	....	....	....	13	3	14	17	4	....	....	....	....
2004-05	Moncton Wildcats	QMJHL	63	6	11	17	22	....	....	....	....	....	....	....	....	....	12	1	4	5	8	....	....	....	....
2005-06	Moncton Wildcats	QMJHL	62	20	32	52	46	....	....	....	....	....	....	....	....	....	21	6	12	18	15	....	....	....	....
2006-07	Moncton Wildcats	QMJHL	38	19	33	52	20	....	....	....	....	....	....	....	....	....	....	....	....	....	....	....	....	....	....
	Val-d'Or Foreurs	QMJHL	33	25	22	47	16	....	....	....	....	....	....	....	....	....	20	14	12	26	10	....	....	....	....
2007-08	Albany River Rats	AHL	65	21	18	39	38	....	....	....	....	....	....	....	....	....	7	1	1	2	2	....	....	....	....
2008-09	Albany River Rats	AHL	70	22	32	54	56	....	....	....	....	....	....	....	....	....	....	....	....	....	....	....	....	....	....
2009-10	**Carolina**	**NHL**	**7**	**0**	**2**	**2**	**10**	**0**	**0**	**0**	**17**	**0.0**	**–1**	**1**	**0.0**	**8:27**	....	....	....	....	....	....	....	....	....
	Albany River Rats	AHL	74	37	41	78	66	....	....	....	....	....	....	....	....	....	8	6	3	9	8	....	....	....	....
2010-11	**Carolina**	**NHL**	**23**	**0**	**2**	**2**	**0**	**0**	**0**	**0**	**28**	**0.0**	**0**	**3**	**66.7**	**6:51**	....	....	....	....	....	....	....	....	....
	Charlotte	AHL	53	26	28	54	44	....	....	....	....	....	....	....	....	....	....	....	....	....	....	....	....	....	....
2011-12	**Carolina**	**NHL**	**16**	**2**	**3**	**5**	**8**	**1**	**0**	**0**	**31**	**6.5**	**–3**	**0**	**0.0**	**12:17**	....	....	....	....	....	....	....	....	....
	Charlotte	AHL	57	20	17	37	26	....	....	....	....	....	....	....	....	....	....	....	....	....	....	....	....	....	....
2012-13	Charlotte	AHL	37	7	11	18	27	....	....	....	....	....	....	....	....	....	....	....	....	....	....	....	....	....	....
2013-14	St. John's IceCaps	AHL	68	27	29	56	49	....	....	....	....	....	....	....	....	....	17	3	3	6	4	....	....	....	....
2014-15	Syracuse Crunch	AHL	26	1	7	8	14	....	....	....	....	....	....	....	....	....	....	....	....	....	....	....	....	....	....
	EHC Biel-Bienne	Swiss	12	5	4	9	40	....	....	....	....	....	....	....	....	....	6	1	0	1	0	....	....	....	....
	NHL Totals		**46**	**2**	**7**	**9**	**18**	**1**	**0**	**0**	**76**	**2.6**		**4**	**50.0**	**8:59**	....	....	....	....	....	....	....	....	....

AHL First All-Star Team (2010)

Signed as a free agent by **Carolina**, July 2, 2007. Signed as a free agent by **Winnipeg**, July 6, 2013. Signed as a free agent by **Tampa Bay**, July 10, 2014. Signed as a free agent by **Biel-Bienne** (Swiss), January 6, 2015.

SAMUELSSON, Henrik (SAM-yuhl-suhn, HEHN-rihk) ARI

Center/Right wing. Shoots right. 6'3", 219 lbs. Born, Pittsburgh, PA, February 7, 1994. Phoenix's 1st choice, 27th overall, in 2012 Entry Draft.

Season	Club	League	GP	G	A	Pts	PIM	PP	SH	GW	S	S%	+/-	TF	F%	Min	Playoffs GP	G	A	Pts	PIM	PP	SH	GW	Min
2009-10	P.F. Chang's	T1EHL	37	12	23	35	73	....	....	....	....	....	....	....	....	....	....	....	....	....	....	....	....	....	....
	P.F. Chang's	Other	11	15	13	28	....	....	....	....	....	....	....	....	....	....	....	....	....	....	....	....	....	....	....
	P.F. Chang's U18	T1EHL	8	2	6	8	25	....	....	....	....	....	....	....	....	....	....	....	....	....	....	....	....	....	....
2010-11	USNTDP	USHL	27	4	7	11	78	....	....	....	....	....	....	....	....	....	....	....	....	....	....	....	....	....	....
	USNTDP	U-17	17	8	10	18	24	....	....	....	....	....	....	....	....	....	....	....	....	....	....	....	....	....	....
	USNTDP	U-18	10	3	3	6	10	....	....	....	....	....	....	....	....	....	....	....	....	....	....	....	....	....	....
2011-12	MODO U18	Swe-U18	3	4	1	5	8	....	....	....	....	....	....	....	....	....	....	....	....	....	....	....	....	....	....
	MODO Jr.	Swe-Jr.	16	4	5	9	22	....	....	....	....	....	....	....	....	....	....	....	....	....	....	....	....	....	....
	MODO	Sweden	15	0	2	2	12	....	....	....	....	....	....	....	....	....	....	....	....	....	....	....	....	....	....
	Edmonton	WHL	28	7	16	23	42	....	....	....	....	....	....	....	....	....	17	4	10	14	20	....	....	....	....
2012-13	Edmonton	WHL	69	33	47	80	97	....	....	....	....	....	....	....	....	....	22	11	8	19	*43	....	....	....	....
2013-14	Edmonton	WHL	65	35	60	95	97	....	....	....	....	....	....	....	....	....	21	8	15	23	*51	....	....	....	....
2014-15	**Arizona**	**NHL**	**3**	**0**	**0**	**0**	**2**	**0**	**0**	**0**	**4**	**0.0**	**–2**	**2**	**100.0**	**13:16**	....	....	....	....	....	....	....	....	....
	Portland Pirates	AHL	68	18	22	40	56	....	....	....	....	....	....	....	....	....	5	2	3	5	13	....	....	....	....
	NHL Totals		**3**	**0**	**0**	**0**	**2**	**0**	**0**	**0**	**4**	**0.0**		**2**	**100.0**	**13:16**	....	....	....	....	....	....	....	....	....

Memorial Cup All-Star Team (2012, 2014) • Ed Chynoweth Trophy (Memorial Cup - Leading Scorer) (2014)

SAMUELSSON, Philip (SAM-yuhl-suhn, FIHL-ihp) ARI

Defense. Shoots left. 6'2", 194 lbs. Born, Leksand, Sweden, July 26, 1991. Pittsburgh's 2nd choice, 61st overall, in 2009 Entry Draft.

Season	Club	League	GP	G	A	Pts	PIM	PP	SH	GW	S	S%	+/-	TF	F%	Min	Playoffs GP	G	A	Pts	PIM	PP	SH	GW	Min
2006-07	P.F. Chang's	Minor-AZ	54	9	31	40	70	....	....	....	....	....	....	....	....	....	....	....	....	....	....	....	....	....	....
2007-08	P.F. Chang's	Minor-AZ	41	8	25	33	48	....	....	....	....	....	....	....	....	....	....	....	....	....	....	....	....	....	....
2008-09	Chicago Steel	USHL	54	0	22	22	60	....	....	....	....	....	....	....	....	....	....	....	....	....	....	....	....	....	....
	USNTDP	U-18	4	0	0	0	6	....	....	....	....	....	....	....	....	....	....	....	....	....	....	....	....	....	....
2010-11	Boston College	H-East	39	4	12	16	72	....	....	....	....	....	....	....	....	....	....	....	....	....	....	....	....	....	....
2011-12	Wilkes-Barre	AHL	46	1	8	9	26	....	....	....	....	....	....	....	....	....	10	0	1	1	18	....	....	....	....
	Wheeling Nailers	ECHL	5	0	1	1	11	....	....	....	....	....	....	....	....	....	3	1	0	1	0	....	....	....	....
2012-13	Wilkes-Barre	AHL	65	2	8	10	70	....	....	....	....	....	....	....	....	....	15	0	2	2	8	....	....	....	....
2013-14	**Pittsburgh**	**NHL**	**5**	**0**	**0**	**0**	**0**	**0**	**0**	**0**	**5**	**0.0**	**–1**	**0**	**0.0**	**15:34**	....	....	....	....	....	....	....	....	....
	Wilkes-Barre	AHL	64	3	19	22	66	....	....	....	....	....	....	....	....	....	8	0	1	1	8	....	....	....	....
2014-15	Wilkes-Barre	AHL	22	0	4	4	20	....	....	....	....	....	....	....	....	....	....	....	....	....	....	....	....	....	....
	Arizona	**NHL**	**4**	**0**	**0**	**0**	**0**	**0**	**0**	**0**	**4**	**0.0**	**–3**	**0**	**0.0**	**16:53**	....	....	....	....	....	....	....	....	....
	Portland Pirates	AHL	51	5	15	20	31	....	....	....	....	....	....	....	....	....	5	1	2	3	4	....	....	....	....
	NHL Totals		**9**	**0**	**0**	**0**	**0**	**0**	**0**	**0**	**9**	**0.0**		**0**	**0.0**	**16:09**	....	....	....	....	....	....	....	....	....

Traded to **Arizona** by **Pittsburgh** for Rob Klinkhammer and future considerations, December 5, 2014.

SANGUINETTI, Bobby (san-GIH-neh-tee, BAW-bee) BUF

Defense. Shoots right. 6'3", 190 lbs. Born, Trenton, NJ, February 29, 1988. NY Rangers' 1st choice, 21st overall, in 2006 Entry Draft.

Season	Club	League	GP	G	A	Pts	PIM	PP	SH	GW	S	S%	+/-	TF	F%	Min	Playoffs GP	G	A	Pts	PIM	PP	SH	GW	Min
2003-04	Lawrenceville	High-NJ	26	4	17	21	....	....	....	....	....	....	....	....	....	....	....	....	....	....	....	....	....	....	....
2004-05	Owen Sound	OHL	67	4	20	24	12	....	....	....	....	....	....	....	....	....	5	0	2	2	0	....	....	....	....
2005-06	Owen Sound	OHL	68	14	51	65	44	....	....	....	....	....	....	....	....	....	11	5	10	15	4	....	....	....	....
2006-07	Owen Sound	OHL	67	23	30	53	48	....	....	....	....	....	....	....	....	....	4	3	3	6	2	....	....	....	....
	Hartford	AHL	5	0	3	3	2	....	....	....	....	....	....	....	....	....	7	0	1	1	2	....	....	....	....
2007-08	Brampton	OHL	61	29	41	70	38	....	....	....	....	....	....	....	....	....	5	1	3	4	10	....	....	....	....
	Hartford	AHL	6	0	1	1	2	....	....	....	....	....	....	....	....	....	5	0	0	0	2	....	....	....	....
2008-09	Hartford	AHL	78	6	36	42	42	....	....	....	....	....	....	....	....	....	6	1	4	5	6	....	....	....	....
2009-10	**NY Rangers**	**NHL**	**5**	**0**	**0**	**0**	**4**	**0**	**0**	**0**	**5**	**0.0**	**0**	**0**	**0.0**	**11:32**	....	....	....	....	....	....	....	....	....
	Hartford	AHL	61	9	29	38	22	....	....	....	....	....	....	....	....	....	....	....	....	....	....	....	....	....	....
2010-11	Charlotte	AHL	31	3	12	15	6	....	....	....	....	....	....	....	....	....	10	0	2	2	6	....	....	....	....
2011-12	**Carolina**	**NHL**	**3**	**0**	**0**	**0**	**0**	**0**	**0**	**0**	**5**	**0.0**	**0**	**0**	**0.0**	**11:56**	....	....	....	....	....	....	....	....	....
	Charlotte	AHL	60	10	40	50	20	....	....	....	....	....	....	....	....	....	....	....	....	....	....	....	....	....	....
2012-13	Charlotte	AHL	36	6	15	21	16	....	....	....	....	....	....	....	....	....	....	....	....	....	....	....	....	....	....
	Carolina	**NHL**	**37**	**2**	**4**	**6**	**4**	**0**	**0**	**1**	**48**	**4.2**	**–6**	**1**	**0.0**	**14:45**	....	....	....	....	....	....	....	....	....
2013-14	Mytischi	KHL	15	2	5	7	2	....	....	....	....	....	....	....	....	....	....	....	....	....	....	....	....	....	....
2014-15	Utica Comets	AHL	61	16	24	40	16	....	....	....	....	....	....	....	....	....	23	3	11	14	6	....	....	....	....
	NHL Totals		**45**	**2**	**4**	**6**	**8**	**0**	**0**	**1**	**58**	**3.4**		**1**	**0.0**	**14:12**	....	....	....	....	....	....	....	....	....

OHL Second All-Star Team (2008) • AHL Second All-Star Team (2015)

Traded to **Carolina** by **NY Rangers** for Carolina's 6th round choice (Jesper Fasth) in 2010 Entry Draft and Washington's 2nd round choice (previously acquired, later traded to Calgary – Calgary selected Tyler Wotherspoon) in 2011 Entry Draft, June 25, 2010. • Missed majority of 2010-11 due to hip injury vs. Adirondack (AHL), November 19, 2010. Signed as a free agent by **Mytischi** (KHL), July 11, 2013. Signed as a free agent by **Vancouver**, July 1, 2014. Signed as a free agent by **Buffalo**, July 2, 2015.

SANTORELLI, Mike (san-toh-REHL-ee, MIGHK)

Center. Shoots right. 6', 189 lbs. Born, Vancouver, BC, December 14, 1985. Nashville's 6th choice, 178th overall, in 2004 Entry Draft.

Season	Club	League	GP	G	A	Pts	PIM	PP	SH	GW	S	S%	+/-	TF	F%	Min	Playoffs GP	G	A	Pts	PIM	PP	SH	GW	Min
2003-04	Vernon Vipers	BCHL	60	43	53	96	26	....	....	....	....	....	....	....	....	....	5	0	2	2	0	....	....	....	....
2004-05	Northern Mich.	CCHA	40	16	14	30	22	....	....	....	....	....	....	....	....	....	....	....	....	....	....	....	....	....	....
2005-06	Northern Mich.	CCHA	40	15	18	33	24	....	....	....	....	....	....	....	....	....	....	....	....	....	....	....	....	....	....
2006-07	Northern Mich.	CCHA	41	*30	17	47	28	....	....	....	....	....	....	....	....	....	....	....	....	....	....	....	....	....	....
2007-08	Milwaukee	AHL	80	21	21	42	60	....	....	....	....	....	....	....	....	....	6	0	0	0	2	....	....	....	....
2008-09	**Nashville**	**NHL**	**7**	**0**	**0**	**0**	**2**	**0**	**0**	**0**	**11**	**0.0**	**–5**	**47**	**44.7**	**12:15**	....	....	....	....	....	....	....	....	....
	Milwaukee	AHL	70	27	43	70	36	....	....	....	....	....	....	....	....	....	11	6	5	11	6	....	....	....	....
2009-10	**Nashville**	**NHL**	**25**	**2**	**1**	**3**	**8**	**0**	**0**	**0**	**36**	**5.6**	**–8**	**105**	**45.7**	**10:57**	....	....	....	....	....	....	....	....	....
	Milwaukee	AHL	57	26	33	59	20	....	....	....	....	....	....	....	....	....	7	3	4	7	2	....	....	....	....
2010-11	**Florida**	**NHL**	**82**	**20**	**21**	**41**	**20**	**5**	**1**	**1**	**193**	**10.4**	**–17**	**1032**	**50.2**	**16:41**	....	....	....	....	....	....	....	....	....
2011-12	**Florida**	**NHL**	**60**	**9**	**2**	**11**	**18**	**2**	**0**	**1**	**117**	**7.7**	**–10**	**389**	**45.2**	**12:24**	....	....	....	....	....	....	....	....	....
2012-13	Tingsryds AIF	Sweden-2	4	0	1	1	0	....	....	....	....	....	....	....	....	....	....	....	....	....	....	....	....	....	....
	Florida	**NHL**	**24**	**2**	**1**	**3**	**2**	**0**	**0**	**0**	**21**	**9.5**	**–7**	**52**	**57.7**	**11:06**	....	....	....	....	....	....	....	....	....
	San Antonio	AHL	7	2	3	5	0	....	....	....	....	....	....	....	....	....	....	....	....	....	....	....	....	....	....
	Winnipeg	**NHL**	**10**	**0**	**1**	**1**	**0**	**0**	**0**	**0**	**14**	**0.0**	**–5**	**42**	**61.9**	**13:43**	....	....	....	....	....	....	....	....	....
2013-14	**Vancouver**	**NHL**	**49**	**10**	**18**	**28**	**6**	**0**	**0**	**3**	**91**	**11.0**	**9**	**419**	**51.3**	**18:34**	....	....	....	....	....	....	....	....	....
2014-15	**Toronto**	**NHL**	**57**	**11**	**18**	**29**	**8**	**0**	**1**	**1**	**102**	**10.8**	**7**	**166**	**46.4**	**14:57**	....	....	....	....	....	....	....	....	....
	Nashville	**NHL**	**22**	**1**	**3**	**4**	**6**	**0**	**0**	**1**	**43**	**2.3**	**–7**	**20**	**45.0**	**12:55**	**4**	**1**	**0**	**1**	**0**	**0**	**0**	**0**	**13:20**
	NHL Totals		**336**	**55**	**65**	**120**	**70**	**7**	**2**	**7**	**628**	**8.8**		**2272**	**49.3**	**14:39**	**4**	**1**	**0**	**1**	**0**	**0**	**0**	**0**	**13:20**

CCHA All-Rookie Team (2005) • CCHA First All-Star Team (2007) • NCAA West Second All-American Team (2007)

Traded to **Florida** by **Nashville** for Florida's 4th round choice (Josh Shalla) in 2011 Entry Draft, August 5, 2010. Signed as a free agent by **Tingsryds** (Sweden-2), October 15, 2012. Claimed on waivers by **Winnipeg** from **Florida**, April 3, 2013. Signed as a free agent by **Vancouver**, July 6, 2013. Signed as a free agent by **Toronto**, July 3, 2014. Traded to **Nashville** by **Toronto** with Cody Franson for Olli Jokinen, Brendan Leipsic and Nashville's 1st round choice (later traded to Philadelphia – Philadelphia selected Travis Konecny) in 2015 Entry Draft, February 15, 2015.

SAUVE, Yann (soh-VAY, YAHN)

Defense. Shoots left. 6'3", 213 lbs. Born, Montreal, QC, February 18, 1990. Vancouver's 2nd choice, 41st overall, in 2008 Entry Draft.

Season	Club	League	GP	G	A	Pts	PIM	PP	SH	GW	S	S%	+/-	TF	F%	Min	Playoffs GP	G	A	Pts	PIM	PP	SH	GW	Min
2005-06	Chateauguay	QAAA	42	14	15	29	63	....	....	....	....	....	....	....	....	....	19	2	12	14	44	....	....	....	....
2006-07	Saint John	QMJHL	60	2	13	15	75	....	....	....	....	....	....	....	....	....	....	....	....	....	....	....	....	....	....
2007-08	Saint John	QMJHL	69	6	15	21	92	....	....	....	....	....	....	....	....	....	14	1	2	3	23	....	....	....	....
2008-09	Saint John	QMJHL	61	5	25	30	64	....	....	....	....	....	....	....	....	....	4	0	2	2	8	....	....	....	....
2009-10	Saint John	QMJHL	61	7	29	36	65	....	....	....	....	....	....	....	....	....	21	5	10	15	36	....	....	....	....
2010-11	**Vancouver**	**NHL**	**5**	**0**	**0**	**0**	**0**	**0**	**0**	**0**	**6**	**0.0**	**–2**	**0**	**0.0**	**13:00**	....	....	....	....	....	....	....	....	....
	Manitoba Moose	AHL	39	3	11	14	24	....	....	....	....	....	....	....	....	....	13	0	1	1	4	....	....	....	....
	Victoria	ECHL	8	0	2	2	4	....	....	....	....	....	....	....	....	....	....	....	....	....	....	....	....	....	....
2011-12	Chicago Wolves	AHL	73	3	6	9	78	....	....	....	....	....	....	....	....	....	3	0	1	1	2	....	....	....	....
2012-13	Chicago Wolves	AHL	17	0	2	2	10	....	....	....	....	....	....	....	....	....	....	....	....	....	....	....	....	....	....
	Kalamazoo Wings	ECHL	32	10	9	19	40	....	....	....	....	....	....	....	....	....	....	....	....	....	....	....	....	....	....
2013-14	**Vancouver**	**NHL**	**3**	**0**	**0**	**0**	**0**	**0**	**0**	**0**	**1**	**0.0**	**–2**	**0**	**0.0**	**12:17**	....	....	....	....	....	....	....	....	....
	Utica Comets	AHL	67	1	13	14	63	....	....	....	....	....	....	....	....	....	....	....	....	....	....	....	....	....	....

			Regular Season														Playoffs								
Season	Club	League	GP	G	A	Pts	PIM	PP	SH	GW	S	S%	+/-	TF	F%	Min	GP	G	A	Pts	PIM	PP	SH	GW	Min
2014-15	St. John's IceCaps	AHL	4	1	0	1	0	....	....	....	....	....	....	....	....	....	....	....	....	....	....	....	....	....	....
	Springfield	AHL	17	0	2	2	12	....	....	....	....	....	....	....	....	....	....	....	....	....	....	....	....	....	....
	Orlando	ECHL	13	2	2	4	19	....	....	....	....	....	....	....	....	....	4	0	2	2	4	....	....	....	....
	Providence Bruins	AHL	4	0	1	1	2	....	....	....	....	....	....	....	....	....	....	....	....	....	....	....	....	....	....
	NHL Totals		**8**	**0**	**0**	**0**	**0**	**0**	**0**	**0**	**7**	**0.0**		**0**	**0.0**	**12:44**	....	....	....	....	....	....	....	....	....

Signed to a PTO (professional tryout) contract by **St. John's** (AHL), December 29, 2014. Signed to a PTO (professional tryout) contract by **Springfield** (AHL), February 4, 2015. Signed to a PTO (professional tryout) contract by **Providence** (AHL), March 25, 2015. Signed as a free agent by **Portland** (AHL), July 16, 2015.

SAVARD, David

(suh-VAHRD, DAY-vihd) **CBJ**

Defense. Shoots right. 6'2", 219 lbs. Born, St. Hyacinthe, QC, October 22, 1990. Columbus' 3rd choice, 94th overall, in 2009 Entry Draft.

Season	Club	League	GP	G	A	Pts	PIM	PP	SH	GW	S	S%	+/-	TF	F%	Min	GP	G	A	Pts	PIM	PP	SH	GW	Min
2006-07	Sem. St-Francois	QAAA	44	10	16	26	52	....	....	....	....	....	....	....	....	....	18	1	12	13	10	....	....	....	....
2007-08	Baie-Comeau	QMJHL	35	1	6	7	22	....	....	....	....	....	....	....	....	....	....	....	....	....	....	....	....	....	....
	Moncton Wildcats	QMJHL	32	0	5	5	18	....	....	....	....	....	....	....	....	....	....	....	....	....	....	....	....	....	....
2008-09	Moncton Wildcats	QMJHL	68	9	35	44	33	....	....	....	....	....	....	....	....	....	10	5	5	10	10	....	....	....	....
2009-10	Moncton Wildcats	QMJHL	64	13	*64	77	36	....	....	....	....	....	....	....	....	....	21	1	14	15	8	....	....	....	....
2010-11	Springfield	AHL	72	11	32	43	18	....	....	....	....	....	....	....	....	....	....	....	....	....	....	....	....	....	....
2011-12	**Columbus**	**NHL**	**31**	**2**	**8**	**10**	**16**	**1**	**0**	**0**	**34**	**5.9**	**0**	**0**	**0.0**	**16:34**	....	....	....	....	....	....	....	....	....
	Springfield	AHL	44	4	18	22	72	....	....	....	....	....	....	....	....	....	....	....	....	....	....	....	....	....	....
2012-13	Springfield	AHL	60	5	26	31	40	....	....	....	....	....	....	....	....	....	8	2	3	5	8	....	....	....	....
	Columbus	**NHL**	**4**	**0**	**0**	**0**	**0**	**0**	**0**	**0**	**1**	**0.0**	**–3**	**0**	**0.0**	**13:12**	....	....	....	....	....	....	....	....	....
2013-14	**Columbus**	**NHL**	**70**	**5**	**10**	**15**	**28**	**1**	**0**	**1**	**63**	**7.9**	**2**	**1**	**100.0**	**17:50**	**6**	**0**	**4**	**4**	**4**	**0**	**0**	**0**	**23:20**
2014-15	**Columbus**	**NHL**	**82**	**11**	**25**	**36**	**71**	**3**	**0**	**3**	**112**	**9.8**	**0**	**1**	**100.0**	**22:57**	....	....	....	....	....	....	....	....	....
	NHL Totals		**187**	**18**	**43**	**61**	**115**	**5**	**0**	**4**	**210**	**8.6**		**2**	**100.0**	**19:46**	**6**	**0**	**4**	**4**	**4**	**0**	**0**	**0**	**23:20**

QMJHL First All-Star Team (2010) • Canadian Major Junior First All-Star Team (2010) • Canadian Major Junior Defenseman of the Year (2010)

SBISA, Luca

(S'BEE-za, LOO-ka) **VAN**

Defense. Shoots left. 6'2", 198 lbs. Born, Ozieri, Italy, January 30, 1990. Philadelphia's 1st choice, 19th overall, in 2008 Entry Draft.

Season	Club	League	GP	G	A	Pts	PIM	PP	SH	GW	S	S%	+/-	TF	F%	Min	GP	G	A	Pts	PIM	PP	SH	GW	Min
2005-06	EV Zug Jr.	Swiss-Jr.	18	0	3	3	18	....	....	....	....	....	....	....	....	....	....	....	....	....	....	....	....	....	....
2006-07	EV Zug Jr.	Swiss-Jr.	STATISTICS NOT AVAILABLE																						
	EHC Seewen	Swiss-3	6	1	2	3	4	....	....	....	....	....	....	....	....	....	....	....	....	....	....	....	....	....	....
	EV Zug	Swiss	7	0	0	0	0	....	....	....	....	....	....	....	....	....	1	0	0	0	0	....	....	....	....
2007-08	Lethbridge	WHL	62	6	27	33	63	....	....	....	....	....	....	....	....	....	19	3	12	15	17	....	....	....	....
2008-09	**Philadelphia**	**NHL**	**39**	**0**	**7**	**7**	**36**	**0**	**0**	**0**	**38**	**0.0**	**–6**	**0**	**0.0**	**17:29**	**1**	**0**	**0**	**0**	**2**	**0**	**0**	**0**	**5:37**
	Lethbridge	WHL	18	4	11	15	19	....	....	....	....	....	....	....	....	....	11	2	1	3	12	....	....	....	....
	Philadelphia	AHL	2	1	1	2	2	....	....	....	....	....	....	....	....	....	....	....	....	....	....	....	....	....	....
2009-10	**Anaheim**	**NHL**	**8**	**0**	**0**	**0**	**6**	**0**	**0**	**0**	**3**	**0.0**	**–1**	**0**	**0.0**	**12:38**	....	....	....	....	....	....	....	....	....
	Lethbridge	WHL	17	1	12	13	18	....	....	....	....	....	....	....	....	....	....	....	....	....	....	....	....	....	....
	Portland	WHL	12	3	2	5	11	....	....	....	....	....	....	....	....	....	13	2	2	4	26	....	....	....	....
	Switzerland	Olympics	5	0	0	0	0	....	....	....	....	....	....	....	....	....	....	....	....	....	....	....	....	....	....
2010-11	**Anaheim**	**NHL**	**68**	**2**	**9**	**11**	**43**	**1**	**0**	**0**	**76**	**2.6**	**–11**	**0**	**0.0**	**16:48**	**6**	**0**	**1**	**1**	**8**	**0**	**0**	**0**	**16:29**
	Syracuse Crunch	AHL	8	2	7	9	4	....	....	....	....	....	....	....	....	....	....	....	....	....	....	....	....	....	....
2011-12	**Anaheim**	**NHL**	**80**	**5**	**19**	**24**	**66**	**0**	**0**	**0**	**88**	**5.7**	**–5**	**0**	**0.0**	**17:56**	....	....	....	....	....	....	....	....	....
2012-13	HC Lugano	Swiss	30	5	7	12	14	....	....	....	....	....	....	....	....	....	....	....	....	....	....	....	....	....	....
	Anaheim	**NHL**	**41**	**1**	**7**	**8**	**23**	**0**	**0**	**1**	**39**	**2.6**	**0**	**0**	**0.0**	**19:50**	**5**	**0**	**0**	**0**	**4**	**0**	**0**	**0**	**21:26**
2013-14	**Anaheim**	**NHL**	**30**	**1**	**5**	**6**	**43**	**0**	**0**	**0**	**30**	**3.3**	**0**	**0**	**0.0**	**17:03**	**2**	**0**	**1**	**1**	**5**	**0**	**0**	**0**	**14:20**
	Norfolk Admirals	AHL	4	0	2	2	0	....	....	....	....	....	....	....	....	....	....	....	....	....	....	....	....	....	....
2014-15	**Vancouver**	**NHL**	**76**	**3**	**8**	**11**	**46**	**0**	**0**	**2**	**79**	**3.8**	**–8**	**0**	**0.0**	**18:47**	**6**	**1**	**1**	**2**	**7**	**0**	**0**	**0**	**17:27**
	NHL Totals		**342**	**12**	**55**	**67**	**263**	**1**	**0**	**3**	**353**	**3.4**		**0**	**0.0**	**17:52**	**20**	**1**	**3**	**4**	**26**	**0**	**0**	**0**	**17:15**

Traded to **Anaheim** by **Philadelphia** with Joffrey Lupul, Philadelphia's 1st round choices in 2009 (later traded to Columbus - Columbus selected John Moore) and 2010 (Emerson Etem) Entry Drafts and future considerations for Chris Pronger and Ryan Dingle, June 26, 2009. Signed as a free agent by **Lugano** (Swiss), September 19, 2012. • Missed majority of 2013-14 due to hand injury vs. Tampa Bay, November 22, 2013 and as a healthy reserve. Traded to **Vancouver** by **Anaheim** with Nick Bonino and Anaheim's 1st (Jared McCann) and 3rd (later traded to NY Rangers – NY Rangers selected Keegan Iverson) round choices in 2014 Entry Draft for Ryan Kesler and Vancouver's 3rd round choice (Deven Sideroff) in 2015 Entry Draft, June 27, 2014.

SCANDELLA, Marco

(skan-DEHL-a, MAHR-koh) **MIN**

Defense. Shoots left. 6'2", 207 lbs. Born, Montreal, QC, February 23, 1990. Minnesota's 2nd choice, 55th overall, in 2008 Entry Draft.

Season	Club	League	GP	G	A	Pts	PIM	PP	SH	GW	S	S%	+/-	TF	F%	Min	GP	G	A	Pts	PIM	PP	SH	GW	Min
2005-06	Ecole Montpetit	QAAA	42	3	4	7	40	....	....	....	....	....	....	....	....	....	3	0	0	0	2	....	....	....	....
2006-07	Mtl. Predateurs	QAAA	42	7	13	20	66	....	....	....	....	....	....	....	....	....	3	0	1	1	10	....	....	....	....
2007-08	Val-d'Or Foreurs	QMJHL	65	4	10	14	35	....	....	....	....	....	....	....	....	....	4	0	1	1	4	....	....	....	....
2008-09	Val-d'Or Foreurs	QMJHL	58	10	27	37	64	....	....	....	....	....	....	....	....	....	....	....	....	....	....	....	....	....	....
	Houston Aeros	AHL	2	0	0	0	0	....	....	....	....	....	....	....	....	....	6	0	0	0	2	....	....	....	....
2009-10	Val-d'Or Foreurs	QMJHL	31	9	22	31	41	....	....	....	....	....	....	....	....	....	6	2	4	6	4	....	....	....	....
	Houston Aeros	AHL	7	0	1	1	7	....	....	....	....	....	....	....	....	....	....	....	....	....	....	....	....	....	....
2010-11	**Minnesota**	**NHL**	**20**	**0**	**2**	**2**	**2**	**0**	**0**	**0**	**13**	**0.0**	**–9**	**0**	**0.0**	**14:58**	....	....	....	....	....	....	....	....	....
	Houston Aeros	AHL	33	3	16	19	17	....	....	....	....	....	....	....	....	....	20	2	6	8	8	....	....	....	....
2011-12	**Minnesota**	**NHL**	**63**	**3**	**9**	**12**	**19**	**1**	**0**	**1**	**77**	**3.9**	**–22**	**0**	**0.0**	**21:47**	....	....	....	....	....	....	....	....	....
	Houston Aeros	AHL	9	2	3	5	4	....	....	....	....	....	....	....	....	....	....	....	....	....	....	....	....	....	....
2012-13	Houston Aeros	AHL	45	2	15	17	23	....	....	....	....	....	....	....	....	....	2	1	0	1	2	....	....	....	....
	Minnesota	**NHL**	**6**	**1**	**0**	**1**	**4**	**0**	**0**	**0**	**7**	**14.3**	**–1**	**0**	**0.0**	**14:26**	**5**	**1**	**1**	**2**	**0**	**0**	**0**	**0**	**18:01**
2013-14	**Minnesota**	**NHL**	**76**	**3**	**14**	**17**	**20**	**0**	**0**	**1**	**80**	**3.8**	**10**	**0**	**0.0**	**18:49**	**13**	**2**	**1**	**3**	**0**	**0**	**1**	**0**	**21:28**
2014-15	**Minnesota**	**NHL**	**64**	**11**	**12**	**23**	**56**	**1**	**0**	**4**	**112**	**9.8**	**8**	**0**	**0.0**	**21:43**	**10**	**2**	**1**	**3**	**0**	**0**	**0**	**0**	**20:44**
	NHL Totals		**229**	**18**	**37**	**55**	**101**	**2**	**0**	**6**	**289**	**6.2**		**0**	**0.0**	**20:00**	**28**	**5**	**3**	**8**	**0**	**0**	**1**	**0**	**20:35**

SCEVIOUR, Colton

(SEE-vee-yuhr, KOHL-tuhn) **DAL**

Center/Right wing. Shoots right. 6', 200 lbs. Born, Red Deer, AB, April 20, 1989. Dallas' 3rd choice, 112th overall, in 2007 Entry Draft.

Season	Club	League	GP	G	A	Pts	PIM	PP	SH	GW	S	S%	+/-	TF	F%	Min	GP	G	A	Pts	PIM	PP	SH	GW	Min
2004-05	Red Deer	AMHL	36	15	22	37	32	....	....	....	....	....	....	....	....	....	....	....	....	....	....	....	....	....	....
	Portland	WHL	6	1	0	1	6	....	....	....	....	....	....	....	....	....	4	0	0	0	0	....	....	....	....
2005-06	Portland	WHL	58	3	6	9	25	....	....	....	....	....	....	....	....	....	12	0	1	1	4	....	....	....	....
2006-07	Portland	WHL	49	12	26	38	38	....	....	....	....	....	....	....	....	....	....	....	....	....	....	....	....	....	....
2007-08	Portland	WHL	17	2	8	10	9	....	....	....	....	....	....	....	....	....	....	....	....	....	....	....	....	....	....
	Lethbridge	WHL	52	31	23	54	36	....	....	....	....	....	....	....	....	....	19	3	10	13	15	....	....	....	....
2008-09	Lethbridge	WHL	69	29	51	80	48	....	....	....	....	....	....	....	....	....	11	4	3	7	12	....	....	....	....
2009-10	Texas Stars	AHL	80	9	22	31	19	....	....	....	....	....	....	....	....	....	24	1	7	8	12	....	....	....	....
2010-11	**Dallas**	**NHL**	**1**	**0**	**0**	**0**	**0**	**0**	**0**	**0**	**0**	**0.0**	**–1**	**0**	**0.0**	**5:09**	....	....	....	....	....	....	....	....	....
	Texas Stars	AHL	77	16	25	41	17	....	....	....	....	....	....	....	....	....	6	1	0	1	0	....	....	....	....
2011-12	Texas Stars	AHL	75	21	32	53	25	....	....	....	....	....	....	....	....	....	....	....	....	....	....	....	....	....	....
2012-13	Texas Stars	AHL	62	21	31	52	20	....	....	....	....	....	....	....	....	....	9	1	3	4	4	....	....	....	....
	Dallas	**NHL**	**1**	**0**	**1**	**1**	**0**	**0**	**0**	**0**	**0**	**0.0**	**–1**	**3**	**33.3**	**4:51**	....	....	....	....	....	....	....	....	....
2013-14	**Dallas**	**NHL**	**26**	**8**	**4**	**12**	**4**	**2**	**0**	**2**	**69**	**11.6**	**–3**	**43**	**39.5**	**14:53**	**6**	**1**	**2**	**3**	**0**	**0**	**0**	**0**	**15:02**
	Texas Stars	AHL	54	32	31	63	31	....	....	....	....	....	....	....	....	....	....	....	....	....	....	....	....	....	....
2014-15	**Dallas**	**NHL**	**71**	**9**	**17**	**26**	**13**	**0**	**0**	**2**	**113**	**8.0**	**1**	**71**	**42.3**	**12:43**	....	....	....	....	....	....	....	....	....
	NHL Totals		**99**	**17**	**22**	**39**	**17**	**2**	**0**	**4**	**182**	**9.3**		**117**	**41.0**	**13:08**	**6**	**1**	**2**	**3**	**0**	**0**	**0**	**0**	**15:02**

AHL First All-Star Team (2014)

SCHALLER, Tim

(SHAL-uhr, TIHM) **BUF**

Left wing. Shoots left. 6'2", 206 lbs. Born, Merrimack, NH, November 16, 1990.

Season	Club	League	GP	G	A	Pts	PIM	PP	SH	GW	S	S%	+/-	TF	F%	Min	GP	G	A	Pts	PIM	PP	SH	GW	Min
2007-08	N.E. Jr. Huskies	EJHL	44	8	25	33	29	....	....	....	....	....	....	....	....	....	....	....	....	....	....	....	....	....	....
2008-09	Islanders H.C.	EJHL	45	16	23	39	54	....	....	....	....	....	....	....	....	....	2	0	1	1	0	....	....	....	....
2009-10	Providence	H-East	33	2	3	5	40	....	....	....	....	....	....	....	....	....	....	....	....	....	....	....	....	....	....
2010-11	Providence	H-East	34	5	14	19	36	....	....	....	....	....	....	....	....	....	....	....	....	....	....	....	....	....	....
2011-12	Providence	H-East	26	14	7	21	24	....	....	....	....	....	....	....	....	....	....	....	....	....	....	....	....	....	....
2012-13	Providence	H-East	38	8	15	23	61	....	....	....	....	....	....	....	....	....	....	....	....	....	....	....	....	....	....
2013-14	Rochester	AHL	72	11	7	18	36	....	....	....	....	....	....	....	....	....	5	0	1	1	2	....	....	....	....

			Regular Season														Playoffs								
Season	Club	League	GP	G	A	Pts	PIM	PP	SH	GW	S	S%	+/-	TF	F%	Min	GP	G	A	Pts	PIM	PP	SH	GW	Min
2014-15	Buffalo	NHL	18	1	1	2	2	0	0	0	19	5.3	−5	186	39.8	11:21	....	....	....	....	....	....	....	....	....
	Rochester	AHL	65	15	28	43	116	....	....	....	....	....	....	....	....	....	....	....	....	....	....	....	....	....	....
	NHL Totals		18	1	1	2	2	0	0	0	19	5.3		186	39.8	11:21	....	....	....	....	....	....	....	....	....

Signed as a free agent by **Buffalo**, April 2, 2013.

SCHEIFELE, Mark
(SHIHF-lee, MAHRK) **WPG**

Center. Shoots right. 6'2", 195 lbs. Born, Kitchener, ON, March 15, 1993. Winnipeg's 1st choice, 7th overall, in 2011 Entry Draft.

Season	Club	League	GP	G	A	Pts	PIM	PP	SH	GW	S	S%	+/-	TF	F%	Min	GP	G	A	Pts	PIM	PP	SH	GW	Min
2008-09	Kit. Jr. Rangers	Minor-ON	31	20	19	39	16	....	....	....	....	....	....	....	....	....	....	....	....	....	....	....	....	....	....
	Kit. Jr. Rangers	Other	18	20	20	40	14	....	....	....	....	....	....	....	....	....	....	....	....	....	....	....	....	....	....
2009-10	Kitchener	ON-Jr.B	51	18	37	55	20	....	....	....	....	....	....	....	....	....	5	0	3	3	6	....	....	....	....
2010-11	Barrie Colts	OHL	66	22	53	75	35	....	....	....	....	....	....	....	....	....	....	....	....	....	....	....	....	....	....
2011-12	**Winnipeg**	**NHL**	**7**	**1**	**0**	**1**	**0**	**1**	**0**	**0**	**5**	**20.0**	**0**	**51**	**35.3**	**10:57**	....	....	....	....	....	....	....	....	....
	Barrie Colts	OHL	47	23	40	63	36	....	....	....	....	....	....	....	....	....	13	5	7	12	12	....	....	....	....
	St. John's IceCaps	AHL	....	....	....	....	....	....	....	....	....	....	....	....	....	....	10	0	1	1	2	....	....	....	....
2012-13	Barrie Colts	OHL	45	39	40	79	30	....	....	....	....	....	....	....	....	....	21	15	*26	*41	14	....	....	....	....
	Winnipeg	**NHL**	**4**	**0**	**0**	**0**	**0**	**0**	**0**	**0**	**6**	**0.0**	**0**	**14**	**71.4**	**11:32**	....	....	....	....	....	....	....	....	....
2013-14	**Winnipeg**	**NHL**	**63**	**13**	**21**	**34**	**14**	**1**	**0**	**2**	**100**	**13.0**	**9**	**785**	**42.2**	**16:21**	....	....	....	....	....	....	....	....	....
2014-15	**Winnipeg**	**NHL**	**82**	**15**	**34**	**49**	**24**	**3**	**0**	**2**	**170**	**8.8**	**11**	**1148**	**42.9**	**18:35**	**4**	**0**	**1**	**1**	**4**	**0**	**0**	**0**	**17:40**
	NHL Totals		**156**	**29**	**55**	**84**	**38**	**5**	**0**	**4**	**281**	**10.3**		**1998**	**42.6**	**17:10**	**4**	**0**	**1**	**1**	**4**	**0**	**0**	**0**	**17:40**

SCHENN, Brayden
(SHEHN, BRAY-duhn) **PHI**

Center. Shoots left. 6'1", 195 lbs. Born, Saskatoon, SK, August 22, 1991. Los Angeles' 1st choice, 5th overall, in 2009 Entry Draft.

Season	Club	League	GP	G	A	Pts	PIM	PP	SH	GW	S	S%	+/-	TF	F%	Min	GP	G	A	Pts	PIM	PP	SH	GW	Min
2006-07	Sask. Contacts	SMHL	41	27	43	70	63	....	....	....	....	....	....	....	....	....	....	....	....	....	....	....	....	....	....
2007-08	Brandon	WHL	66	28	43	71	48	....	....	....	....	....	....	....	....	....	6	2	1	3	14	....	....	....	....
2008-09	Brandon	WHL	70	32	56	88	82	....	....	....	....	....	....	....	....	....	12	8	10	18	12	....	....	....	....
2009-10	Brandon	WHL	59	34	65	99	55	....	....	....	....	....	....	....	....	....	15	8	11	19	2	....	....	....	....
	Los Angeles	**NHL**	**1**	**0**	**0**	**0**	**0**	**0**	**0**	**0**	**0**	**0.0**	**−1**	**14**	**28.6**	**12:31**	....	....	....	....	....	....	....	....	....
2010-11	**Los Angeles**	**NHL**	**8**	**0**	**2**	**2**	**0**	**0**	**0**	**0**	**11**	**0.0**	**−1**	**51**	**33.3**	**11:15**	....	....	....	....	....	....	....	....	....
	Brandon	WHL	2	1	3	4	2	....	....	....	....	....	....	....	....	....	....	....	....	....	....	....	....	....	....
	Saskatoon Blades	WHL	27	21	32	53	23	....	....	....	....	....	....	....	....	....	10	6	5	11	14	....	....	....	....
	Manchester	AHL	7	3	4	7	4	....	....	....	....	....	....	....	....	....	5	1	3	4	0	....	....	....	....
2011-12	**Philadelphia**	**NHL**	**54**	**12**	**6**	**18**	**34**	**4**	**0**	**3**	**97**	**12.4**	**−7**	**436**	**46.1**	**14:07**	**11**	**3**	**6**	**9**	**8**	**2**	**0**	**0**	**14:16**
	Adirondack	AHL	7	6	6	12	4	....	....	....	....	....	....	....	....	....	....	....	....	....	....	....	....	....	....
2012-13	Adirondack	AHL	33	13	20	33	15	....	....	....	....	....	....	....	....	....	....	....	....	....	....	....	....	....	....
	Philadelphia	**NHL**	**47**	**8**	**18**	**26**	**24**	**2**	**0**	**0**	**79**	**10.1**	**−8**	**453**	**45.5**	**15:32**	....	....	....	....	....	....	....	....	....
2013-14	**Philadelphia**	**NHL**	**82**	**20**	**21**	**41**	**54**	**4**	**0**	**6**	**178**	**11.2**	**0**	**685**	**43.2**	**15:45**	**7**	**0**	**3**	**3**	**8**	**0**	**0**	**0**	**14:12**
2014-15	**Philadelphia**	**NHL**	**82**	**18**	**29**	**47**	**34**	**7**	**0**	**6**	**156**	**11.5**	**−5**	**184**	**46.7**	**17:05**	....	....	....	....	....	....	....	....	....
	NHL Totals		**274**	**58**	**76**	**134**	**146**	**17**	**0**	**15**	**521**	**11.1**		**1823**	**44.4**	**15:39**	**18**	**3**	**9**	**12**	**16**	**2**	**0**	**0**	**14:15**

WHL Rookie of the Year (2008) • Canadian Major Junior All-Rookie Team (2008) • WHL East Second All-Star Team (2009, 2011) • WHL East First All-Star Team (2010)

Traded to **Philadelphia** by **Los Angeles** with Wayne Simmonds and Los Angeles' 2nd round choice (Devin Shore) in 2012 Entry Draft for Mike Richards and the righjts to Rob Bordson, June 23, 2011.

SCHENN, Luke
(SHEHN, LEWK) **PHI**

Defense. Shoots right. 6'2", 225 lbs. Born, Saskatoon, SK, November 2, 1989. Toronto's 1st choice, 5th overall, in 2008 Entry Draft.

Season	Club	League	GP	G	A	Pts	PIM	PP	SH	GW	S	S%	+/-	TF	F%	Min	GP	G	A	Pts	PIM	PP	SH	GW	Min
2004-05	Sask. Contacts	SMHL	41	5	22	27	69	....	....	....	....	....	....	....	....	....	....	....	....	....	....	....	....	....	....
2005-06	Kelowna Rockets	WHL	60	3	8	11	86	....	....	....	....	....	....	....	....	....	12	0	0	0	14	....	....	....	....
2006-07	Kelowna Rockets	WHL	72	2	27	29	139	....	....	....	....	....	....	....	....	....	....	....	....	....	....	....	....	....	....
2007-08	Kelowna Rockets	WHL	57	7	21	28	100	....	....	....	....	....	....	....	....	....	7	2	2	4	6	....	....	....	....
2008-09	**Toronto**	**NHL**	**70**	**2**	**12**	**14**	**71**	**1**	**0**	**0**	**102**	**2.0**	**−12**	**0**	**0.0**	**21:32**	....	....	....	....	....	....	....	....	....
2009-10	**Toronto**	**NHL**	**79**	**5**	**12**	**17**	**50**	**0**	**0**	**1**	**101**	**5.0**	**2**	**0**	**0.0**	**16:53**	....	....	....	....	....	....	....	....	....
2010-11	**Toronto**	**NHL**	**82**	**5**	**17**	**22**	**34**	**0**	**0**	**0**	**128**	**3.9**	**−7**	**0**	**0.0**	**22:22**	....	....	....	....	....	....	....	....	....
2011-12	**Toronto**	**NHL**	**79**	**2**	**20**	**22**	**62**	**0**	**0**	**0**	**81**	**2.5**	**−6**	**0**	**0.0**	**16:02**	....	....	....	....	....	....	....	....	....
2012-13	**Philadelphia**	**NHL**	**47**	**3**	**8**	**11**	**34**	**0**	**0**	**0**	**81**	**3.7**	**3**	**0**	**0.0**	**21:52**	....	....	....	....	....	....	....	....	....
2013-14	**Philadelphia**	**NHL**	**79**	**4**	**8**	**12**	**58**	**0**	**0**	**0**	**78**	**5.1**	**0**	**0**	**0.0**	**16:32**	**7**	**1**	**0**	**1**	**0**	**0**	**0**	**1**	**17:22**
2014-15	**Philadelphia**	**NHL**	**58**	**3**	**11**	**14**	**18**	**0**	**0**	**0**	**67**	**4.5**	**−2**	**0**	**0.0**	**18:04**	....	....	....	....	....	....	....	....	....
	NHL Totals		**494**	**24**	**88**	**112**	**327**	**1**	**0**	**1**	**638**	**3.8**		**0**	**0.0**	**18:52**	**7**	**1**	**0**	**1**	**0**	**0**	**0**	**1**	**17:22**

WHL West Second All-Star Team (2008) • NHL All-Rookie Team (2009)

Traded to **Philadelphia** by **Toronto** for James van Riemsdyk, June 23, 2012.

SCHILLING, Cameron
(SHIHL-ihng, KAM-r'uhn) **CHI**

Defense. Shoots left. 6'2", 182 lbs. Born, Carmel, IN, October 7, 1988.

Season	Club	League	GP	G	A	Pts	PIM	PP	SH	GW	S	S%	+/-	TF	F%	Min	GP	G	A	Pts	PIM	PP	SH	GW	Min
2007-08	Indiana Ice	USHL	55	2	8	10	91	....	....	....	....	....	....	....	....	....	4	0	0	0	2	....	....	....	....
2008-09	Miami U.	CCHA	25	0	7	7	43	....	....	....	....	....	....	....	....	....	....	....	....	....	....	....	....	....	....
2009-10	Miami U.	CCHA	42	4	15	19	58	....	....	....	....	....	....	....	....	....	....	....	....	....	....	....	....	....	....
2010-11	Miami U.	CCHA	38	3	14	17	34	....	....	....	....	....	....	....	....	....	....	....	....	....	....	....	....	....	....
2011-12	Miami U.	CCHA	39	1	13	14	20	....	....	....	....	....	....	....	....	....	....	....	....	....	....	....	....	....	....
	Hershey Bears	AHL	7	0	0	0	14	....	....	....	....	....	....	....	....	....	4	2	0	2	4	....	....	....	....
2012-13	Hershey Bears	AHL	70	7	9	16	61	....	....	....	....	....	....	....	....	....	5	0	1	1	4	....	....	....	....
	Washington	**NHL**	**1**	**0**	**0**	**0**	**0**	**0**	**0**	**0**	**0**	**0.0**	**−1**	**0**	**0.0**	**11:58**	....	....	....	....	....	....	....	....	....
2013-14	**Washington**	**NHL**	**1**	**0**	**0**	**0**	**0**	**0**	**0**	**0**	**2**	**0.0**	**−2**	**0**	**0.0**	**17:45**	....	....	....	....	....	....	....	....	....
	Hershey Bears	AHL	70	3	13	16	89	....	....	....	....	....	....	....	....	....	....	....	....	....	....	....	....	....	....
2014-15	**Washington**	**NHL**	**4**	**0**	**0**	**0**	**4**	**0**	**0**	**0**	**2**	**0.0**	**1**	**0**	**0.0**	**11:23**	....	....	....	....	....	....	....	....	....
	Hershey Bears	AHL	63	3	15	18	63	....	....	....	....	....	....	....	....	....	10	3	5	8	2	....	....	....	....
	NHL Totals		**6**	**0**	**0**	**0**	**4**	**0**	**0**	**0**	**4**	**0.0**		**0**	**0.0**	**12:32**	....	....	....	....	....	....	....	....	....

Signed as a free agent by **Washington**, March 27, 2012. Signed as a free agent by **Chicago**, July 2, 2015.

SCHLEMKO, David
(SHLEHM-koh, DAY-vihd)

Defense. Shoots left. 6'1", 190 lbs. Born, Edmonton, AB, May 7, 1987.

Season	Club	League	GP	G	A	Pts	PIM	PP	SH	GW	S	S%	+/-	TF	F%	Min	GP	G	A	Pts	PIM	PP	SH	GW	Min
2004-05	Medicine Hat	WHL	65	5	24	29	23	....	....	....	....	....	....	....	....	....	13	0	3	3	10	....	....	....	....
2005-06	Medicine Hat	WHL	69	9	35	44	44	....	....	....	....	....	....	....	....	....	13	2	5	7	15	....	....	....	....
2006-07	Medicine Hat	WHL	64	8	50	58	78	....	....	....	....	....	....	....	....	....	23	3	13	16	12	....	....	....	....
2007-08	San Antonio	AHL	1	0	0	0	4	....	....	....	....	....	....	....	....	....	....	....	....	....	....	....	....	....	....
	Arizona Sundogs	CHL	58	10	29	39	24	....	....	....	....	....	....	....	....	....	14	3	5	8	6	....	....	....	....
2008-09	**Phoenix**	**NHL**	**3**	**0**	**1**	**1**	**0**	**0**	**0**	**0**	**3**	**0.0**	**−2**	**0**	**0.0**	**19:16**	....	....	....	....	....	....	....	....	....
	San Antonio	AHL	68	7	22	29	20	....	....	....	....	....	....	....	....	....	....	....	....	....	....	....	....	....	....
2009-10	**Phoenix**	**NHL**	**17**	**1**	**4**	**5**	**8**	**0**	**0**	**0**	**19**	**5.3**	**1**	**0**	**0.0**	**17:49**	....	....	....	....	....	....	....	....	....
	San Antonio	AHL	55	5	26	31	30	....	....	....	....	....	....	....	....	....	....	....	....	....	....	....	....	....	....
2010-11	**Phoenix**	**NHL**	**43**	**4**	**10**	**14**	**24**	**0**	**0**	**0**	**47**	**8.5**	**8**	**0**	**0.0**	**16:02**	**4**	**1**	**0**	**1**	**4**	**1**	**0**	**0**	**15:54**
	San Antonio	AHL	3	0	0	0	2	....	....	....	....	....	....	....	....	....	....	....	....	....	....	....	....	....	....
2011-12	**Phoenix**	**NHL**	**46**	**1**	**10**	**11**	**10**	**0**	**0**	**0**	**58**	**1.7**	**7**	**0**	**0.0**	**18:21**	**5**	**0**	**0**	**0**	**0**	**0**	**0**	**0**	**16:13**
2012-13	Arizona Sundogs	CHL	14	3	7	10	4	....	....	....	....	....	....	....	....	....	....	....	....	....	....	....	....	....	....
	Phoenix	**NHL**	**30**	**1**	**5**	**6**	**12**	**0**	**0**	**0**	**35**	**2.9**	**8**	**0**	**0.0**	**17:13**	....	....	....	....	....	....	....	....	....
2013-14	**Phoenix**	**NHL**	**48**	**1**	**8**	**9**	**18**	**0**	**0**	**0**	**61**	**1.6**	**2**	**0**	**0.0**	**16:24**	....	....	....	....	....	....	....	....	....
2014-15	**Arizona**	**NHL**	**20**	**1**	**3**	**4**	**4**	**0**	**0**	**0**	**24**	**4.2**	**−5**	**0**	**0.0**	**18:07**	....	....	....	....	....	....	....	....	....
	Portland Pirates	AHL	2	1	3	4	0	....	....	....	....	....	....	....	....	....	....	....	....	....	....	....	....	....	....
	Dallas	**NHL**	**5**	**0**	**0**	**0**	**0**	**0**	**0**	**0**	**6**	**0.0**	**0**	**0**	**0.0**	**14:25**	....	....	....	....	....	....	....	....	....
	Calgary	**NHL**	**19**	**0**	**0**	**0**	**8**	**0**	**0**	**0**	**15**	**0.0**	**6**	**0**	**0.0**	**12:39**	**11**	**0**	**1**	**1**	**2**	**0**	**0**	**0**	**14:06**
	NHL Totals		**231**	**9**	**41**	**50**	**84**	**0**	**0**	**0**	**268**	**3.4**		**0**	**0.0**	**16:46**	**20**	**1**	**1**	**2**	**6**	**1**	**0**	**0**	**14:59**

WHL East Second All-Star Team (2007)

Signed as a free agent by **Phoenix**, July 19, 2007. Signed as a free agent by **Arizona** (CHL), October 2, 2012. Claimed on waivers by **Dallas** from **Arizona**, January 3, 2015. Claimed on waivers by **Calgary** from **Dallas**, March 1, 2015.

SCHMIDT, Nate

(SHMIHT, NAYT) **WSH**

Defense. Shoots left. 6', 194 lbs. Born, St. Cloud, MN, July 16, 1991.

			Regular Season														Playoffs								
Season	Club	League	GP	G	A	Pts	PIM	PP	SH	GW	S	S%	+/-	TF	F%	Min	GP	G	A	Pts	PIM	PP	SH	GW	Min
2009-10	Fargo Force	USHL	57	14	23	37	81	....	....	....	....	....	....	....	....	....	13	0	6	6	2	....	....	....	....
2010-11	U. of Minnesota	WCHA	13	0	1	1	6	....	....	....	....	....	....	....	....	....	....	....	....	....	....	....	....	....	....
2011-12	U. of Minnesota	WCHA	43	3	38	41	14	....	....	....	....	....	....	....	....	....	....	....	....	....	....	....	....	....	....
2012-13	U. of Minnesota	WCHA	40	9	23	32	16	....	....	....	....	....	....	....	....	....	....	....	....	....	....	....	....	....	....
	Hershey Bears	AHL	8	1	3	4	2	....	....	....	....	....	....	....	....	....	5	0	2	2	0	....	....	....	....
2013-14	**Washington**	**NHL**	**29**	**2**	**4**	**6**	**6**	**0**	**0**	**0**	**41**	**4.9**	**4**	**0**	**0.0**	**18:42**	....	....	....	....	....	....	....	....	....
	Hershey Bears	AHL	38	2	11	13	12	....	....	....	....	....	....	....	....	....	....	....	....	....	....	....	....	....	....
2014-15	**Washington**	**NHL**	**39**	**1**	**3**	**4**	**10**	**0**	**0**	**0**	**40**	**2.5**	**–2**	**0**	**0.0**	**13:53**	....	....	....	....	....	....	....	....	....
	Hershey Bears	AHL	19	3	6	9	6	....	....	....	....	....	....	....	....	....	8	4	5	9	0	....	....	....	....
	NHL Totals		**68**	**3**	**7**	**10**	**16**	**0**	**0**	**0**	**81**	**3.7**		**0**	**0.0**	**15:56**	....	....	....	....	....	....	....	....	....

WCHA Second All-Star Team (2012) • WCHA First All-Star Team (2013) • NCAA West Second All-American Team (2013)

Signed as a free agent by **Washington**, April 3, 2013.

SCHROEDER, Jordan

(SHRAY-duhr, JOHR-dahn) **MIN**

Center. Shoots right. 5'8", 175 lbs. Born, Prior Lake, MN, September 29, 1990. Vancouver's 1st choice, 22nd overall, in 2009 Entry Draft.

Season	Club	League	GP	G	A	Pts	PIM	PP	SH	GW	S	S%	+/-	TF	F%	Min	GP	G	A	Pts	PIM	PP	SH	GW	Min
2005-06	Saint Thomas	High-MN	31	27	35	62	....	....	....	....	....	....	....	....	....	....	....	....	....	....	....	....	....	....	....
	Team Southeast	UMHSEL	....	7	14	21	....	....	....	....	....	....	....	....	....	....	....	....	....	....	....	....	....	....	....
2006-07	USNTDP	NAHL	31	12	11	23	10	....	....	....	....	....	....	....	....	....	....	....	....	....	....	....	....	....	....
	USNTDP	U-17	8	2	8	10	2	....	....	....	....	....	....	....	....	....	....	....	....	....	....	....	....	....	....
	USNTDP	U-18	17	6	13	19	4	....	....	....	....	....	....	....	....	....	....	....	....	....	....	....	....	....	....
2007-08	USNTDP	NAHL	14	1	8	9	4	....	....	....	....	....	....	....	....	....	....	....	....	....	....	....	....	....	....
	USNTDP	U-18	41	21	23	44	12	....	....	....	....	....	....	....	....	....	....	....	....	....	....	....	....	....	....
2008-09	U. of Minnesota	WCHA	35	13	32	45	29	....	....	....	....	....	....	....	....	....	....	....	....	....	....	....	....	....	....
2009-10	U. of Minnesota	WCHA	37	9	19	28	14	....	....	....	....	....	....	....	....	....	....	....	....	....	....	....	....	....	....
	Manitoba Moose	AHL	11	4	5	9	0	....	....	....	....	....	....	....	....	....	6	3	3	6	4	....	....	....	....
2010-11	Manitoba Moose	AHL	61	10	18	28	10	....	....	....	....	....	....	....	....	....	14	1	5	6	2	....	....	....	....
2011-12	Chicago Wolves	AHL	76	21	23	44	18	....	....	....	....	....	....	....	....	....	5	1	1	2	0	....	....	....	....
2012-13	Chicago Wolves	AHL	42	12	21	33	14	....	....	....	....	....	....	....	....	....	....	....	....	....	....	....	....	....	....
	Vancouver	**NHL**	**31**	**3**	**6**	**9**	**4**	**1**	**0**	**2**	**28**	**10.7**	**0**	**321**	**43.6**	**13:43**	....	....	....	....	....	....	....	....	....
2013-14	**Vancouver**	**NHL**	**25**	**3**	**3**	**6**	**2**	**0**	**0**	**0**	**25**	**12.0**	**–7**	**244**	**45.9**	**12:01**	....	....	....	....	....	....	....	....	....
	Utica Comets	AHL	2	0	1	1	2	....	....	....	....	....	....	....	....	....	....	....	....	....	....	....	....	....	....
2014-15	**Minnesota**	**NHL**	**25**	**3**	**5**	**8**	**2**	**0**	**0**	**0**	**48**	**6.3**	**9**	**0**	**0.0**	**10:51**	**3**	**0**	**0**	**0**	**0**	**0**	**0**	**0**	**11:14**
	Iowa Wild	AHL	35	10	18	28	10	....	....	....	....	....	....	....	....	....	....	....	....	....	....	....	....	....	....
	NHL Totals		**81**	**9**	**14**	**23**	**8**	**1**	**0**	**2**	**101**	**8.9**		**565**	**44.6**	**12:18**	**3**	**0**	**0**	**0**	**0**	**0**	**0**	**0**	**11:14**

WCHA All-Rookie Team (2009) • WCHA Second All-Star Team (2009) • WCHA Rookie of the Year (2009)

• Missed majority of 2013-14 due to ankle inury at Pittsburgh, October 19. 2013. Signed as a free agent by **Minnesota**, July 14, 2014.

SCHULTZ, Jeff

(SHUHLTZ, JEHF) **L.A.**

Defense. Shoots left. 6'6", 222 lbs. Born, Calgary, AB, February 25, 1986. Washington's 2nd choice, 27th overall, in 2004 Entry Draft.

Season	Club	League	GP	G	A	Pts	PIM	PP	SH	GW	S	S%	+/-	TF	F%	Min	GP	G	A	Pts	PIM	PP	SH	GW	Min
2000-01	Calgary Hawks	CBHL	27	7	8	15	20	....	....	....	....	....	....	....	....	....	....	....	....	....	....	....	....	....	....
2001-02	Calgary Rangers	CBHL	27	5	18	23	42	....	....	....	....	....	....	....	....	....	....	....	....	....	....	....	....	....	....
2002-03	Calgary Hitmen	WHL	50	2	1	3	4	....	....	....	....	....	....	....	....	....	4	0	0	0	0	....	....	....	....
2003-04	Calgary Hitmen	WHL	72	11	24	35	33	....	....	....	....	....	....	....	....	....	7	1	1	2	0	....	....	....	....
2004-05	Calgary Hitmen	WHL	72	2	27	29	31	....	....	....	....	....	....	....	....	....	12	2	1	3	6	....	....	....	....
2005-06	Calgary Hitmen	WHL	68	7	33	40	36	....	....	....	....	....	....	....	....	....	13	4	6	10	6	....	....	....	....
	Hershey Bears	AHL	....	....	....	....	....	....	....	....	....	....	....	....	....	....	7	1	3	4	4	....	....	....	....
2006-07	**Washington**	**NHL**	**38**	**0**	**3**	**3**	**16**	**0**	**0**	**0**	**22**	**0.0**	**5**	**0**	**0.0**	**18:13**	....	....	....	....	....	....	....	....	....
	Hershey Bears	AHL	44	2	10	12	39	....	....	....	....	....	....	....	....	....	19	0	1	1	18	....	....	....	....
2007-08	**Washington**	**NHL**	**72**	**5**	**13**	**18**	**28**	**0**	**0**	**0**	**36**	**13.9**	**12**	**1**	**100.0**	**18:05**	**2**	**0**	**0**	**0**	**2**	**0**	**0**	**0**	**10:25**
	Hershey Bears	AHL	1	0	0	0	0	....	....	....	....	....	....	....	....	....	....	....	....	....	....	....	....	....	....
2008-09	**Washington**	**NHL**	**64**	**1**	**11**	**12**	**21**	**0**	**1**	**0**	**40**	**2.5**	**13**	**0**	**0.0**	**19:46**	**1**	**0**	**0**	**0**	**0**	**0**	**0**	**0**	**12:26**
2009-10	**Washington**	**NHL**	**73**	**3**	**20**	**23**	**32**	**0**	**0**	**0**	**43**	**7.0**	**50**	**0**	**0.0**	**19:52**	**7**	**0**	**1**	**1**	**4**	**0**	**0**	**0**	**19:43**
2010-11	**Washington**	**NHL**	**72**	**1**	**9**	**10**	**12**	**0**	**0**	**1**	**34**	**2.9**	**6**	**0**	**0.0**	**19:47**	**9**	**0**	**0**	**0**	**6**	**0**	**0**	**0**	**20:45**
2011-12	**Washington**	**NHL**	**54**	**1**	**5**	**6**	**12**	**0**	**0**	**0**	**22**	**4.5**	**–2**	**0**	**0.0**	**15:18**	**10**	**0**	**0**	**0**	**2**	**0**	**0**	**0**	**15:35**
2012-13	**Washington**	**NHL**	**26**	**0**	**3**	**3**	**12**	**0**	**0**	**0**	**12**	**0.0**	**–6**	**0**	**0.0**	**14:15**	....	....	....	....	....	....	....	....	....
2013-14	Manchester	AHL	67	2	11	13	32	....	....	....	....	....	....	....	....	....	2	0	0	0	2	....	....	....	....
	♦ **Los Angeles**	**NHL**	....	....	....	....	....	....	....	....	....	....	....	....	....	....	**7**	**0**	**0**	**0**	**0**	**0**	**0**	**0**	**18:51**
2014-15	**Los Angeles**	**NHL**	**9**	**0**	**1**	**1**	**4**	**0**	**0**	**0**	**7**	**0.0**	**1**	**0**	**0.0**	**16:45**	....	....	....	....	....	....	....	....	....
	Manchester	AHL	52	3	13	16	30	....	....	....	....	....	....	....	....	....	14	0	3	3	10	....	....	....	....
	NHL Totals		**408**	**11**	**65**	**76**	**137**	**0**	**1**	**1**	**216**	**5.1**		**1**	**100.0**	**18:20**	**36**	**0**	**1**	**1**	**14**	**0**	**0**	**0**	**17:57**

WHL East Second All-Star Team (2006)

• Missed majority of 2012-13 as a healthy reserve. Signed as a free agent by **Los Angeles**, July 5, 2013.

SCHULTZ, Justin

(SHUHLTZ, JUHS-tihn) **EDM**

Defense. Shoots right. 6'2", 188 lbs. Born, Kelowna, BC, July 6, 1990. Anaheim's 4th choice, 43rd overall, in 2008 Entry Draft.

Season	Club	League	GP	G	A	Pts	PIM	PP	SH	GW	S	S%	+/-	TF	F%	Min	GP	G	A	Pts	PIM	PP	SH	GW	Min
2006-07	Westside Warriors	Minor-BC	....	29	29	58	29	....	....	....	....	....	....	....	....	....	....	....	....	....	....	....	....	....	....
2007-08	Westside Warriors	BCHL	57	9	31	40	28	....	....	....	....	....	....	....	....	....	11	3	5	8	4	....	....	....	....
2008-09	Westside Warriors	BCHL	49	15	35	50	29	....	....	....	....	....	....	....	....	....	6	1	2	3	2	....	....	....	....
2009-10	U. of Wisconsin	WCHA	43	6	16	22	12	....	....	....	....	....	....	....	....	....	....	....	....	....	....	....	....	....	....
2010-11	U. of Wisconsin	WCHA	41	18	29	47	28	....	....	....	....	....	....	....	....	....	....	....	....	....	....	....	....	....	....
2011-12	U. of Wisconsin	WCHA	37	16	28	44	12	....	....	....	....	....	....	....	....	....	....	....	....	....	....	....	....	....	....
2012-13	Oklahoma City	AHL	34	18	30	48	6	....	....	....	....	....	....	....	....	....	....	....	....	....	....	....	....	....	....
	Edmonton	**NHL**	**48**	**8**	**19**	**27**	**8**	**4**	**0**	**3**	**85**	**9.4**	**–17**	**1**	**0.0**	**21:27**	....	....	....	....	....	....	....	....	....
2013-14	**Edmonton**	**NHL**	**74**	**11**	**22**	**33**	**16**	**1**	**0**	**3**	**109**	**10.1**	**–22**	**1**	**0.0**	**23:21**	....	....	....	....	....	....	....	....	....
2014-15	**Edmonton**	**NHL**	**81**	**6**	**25**	**31**	**12**	**0**	**0**	**1**	**122**	**4.9**	**–17**	**1**	**100.0**	**22:37**	....	....	....	....	....	....	....	....	....
	NHL Totals		**203**	**25**	**66**	**91**	**36**	**5**	**0**	**7**	**316**	**7.9**		**3**	**33.3**	**22:36**	....	....	....	....	....	....	....	....	....

WCHA All-Rookie Team (2010) • WCHA First All-Star Team (2011, 2012) • NCAA West First All-American Team (2011, 2012) • AHL All-Rookie Team (2013) • AHL First All-Star Team (2013) • Eddie Shore Award (AHL - Outstanding Defenseman) (2013) • NHL All-Rookie Team (2013)

Signed as a free agent by **Edmonton**, July 1, 2012.

SCHULTZ, Nick

(SHUHLTZ, NIHK) **PHI**

Defense. Shoots left. 6'1", 203 lbs. Born, Strasbourg, SK, August 25, 1982. Minnesota's 2nd choice, 33rd overall, in 2000 Entry Draft.

Season	Club	League	GP	G	A	Pts	PIM	PP	SH	GW	S	S%	+/-	TF	F%	Min	GP	G	A	Pts	PIM	PP	SH	GW	Min
1997-98	Yorkton Mallers	SMHL	59	10	30	40	74	....	....	....	....	....	....	....	....	....	....	....	....	....	....	....	....	....	....
1998-99	Prince Albert	WHL	58	5	18	23	37	....	....	....	....	....	....	....	....	....	14	0	7	7	0	....	....	....	....
99-2000	Prince Albert	WHL	72	11	33	44	38	....	....	....	....	....	....	....	....	....	6	0	3	3	2	....	....	....	....
2000-01	Prince Albert	WHL	59	17	30	47	120	....	....	....	....	....	....	....	....	....	....	....	....	....	....	....	....	....	....
	Cleveland	IHL	4	1	1	2	2	....	....	....	....	....	....	....	....	....	3	0	1	1	0	....	....	....	....
2001-02	**Minnesota**	**NHL**	**52**	**4**	**6**	**10**	**14**	**1**	**0**	**1**	**47**	**8.5**	**0**	**0**	**0.0**	**16:08**	....	....	....	....	....	....	....	....	....
	Houston Aeros	AHL	....	....	....	....	....	....	....	....	....	....	....	....	....	....	14	1	5	6	2	....	....	....	....
2002-03	**Minnesota**	**NHL**	**75**	**3**	**7**	**10**	**23**	**0**	**0**	**1**	**70**	**4.3**	**11**	**0**	**0.0**	**18:28**	**18**	**0**	**1**	**1**	**10**	**0**	**0**	**0**	**19:39**
2003-04	**Minnesota**	**NHL**	**79**	**6**	**10**	**16**	**16**	**1**	**0**	**0**	**72**	**8.3**	**12**	**0**	**0.0**	**20:19**	....	....	....	....	....	....	....	....	....
2004-05	Kassel Huskies	Germany	46	7	15	22	26	....	....	....	....	....	....	....	....	....	7	0	4	4	6	....	....	....	....
2005-06	**Minnesota**	**NHL**	**79**	**2**	**12**	**14**	**43**	**0**	**0**	**0**	**45**	**4.4**	**2**	**0**	**0.0**	**17:58**	....	....	....	....	....	....	....	....	....
2006-07	**Minnesota**	**NHL**	**82**	**2**	**10**	**12**	**42**	**0**	**0**	**1**	**69**	**2.9**	**0**	**0**	**0.0**	**20:13**	**5**	**0**	**1**	**1**	**0**	**0**	**0**	**0**	**18:06**
2007-08	**Minnesota**	**NHL**	**81**	**2**	**13**	**15**	**42**	**0**	**0**	**0**	**52**	**3.8**	**9**	**0**	**0.0**	**20:10**	**1**	**0**	**0**	**0**	**0**	**0**	**0**	**0**	**16:11**
2008-09	**Minnesota**	**NHL**	**79**	**2**	**9**	**11**	**31**	**0**	**0**	**0**	**48**	**4.2**	**–4**	**1**	**0.0**	**20:33**	....	....	....	....	....	....	....	....	....
2009-10	**Minnesota**	**NHL**	**80**	**1**	**19**	**20**	**43**	**1**	**0**	**0**	**83**	**1.2**	**–8**	**0**	**0.0**	**20:58**	....	....	....	....	....	....	....	....	....
2010-11	**Minnesota**	**NHL**	**74**	**3**	**14**	**17**	**38**	**0**	**0**	**0**	**46**	**6.5**	**–4**	**1**	**100.0**	**20:13**	....	....	....	....	....	....	....	....	....
2011-12	**Minnesota**	**NHL**	**62**	**1**	**2**	**3**	**30**	**1**	**0**	**0**	**38**	**2.6**	**–10**	**0**	**0.0**	**19:36**	....	....	....	....	....	....	....	....	....
	Edmonton	**NHL**	**20**	**0**	**4**	**4**	**10**	**0**	**0**	**0**	**13**	**0.0**	**–2**	**0**	**0.0**	**20:04**	....	....	....	....	....	....	....	....	....
2012-13	**Edmonton**	**NHL**	**48**	**1**	**8**	**9**	**24**	**0**	**0**	**0**	**33**	**3.0**	**–13**	**2**	**0.0**	**18:38**	....	....	....	....	....	....	....	....	....

			Regular Season														Playoffs								
Season	Club	League	GP	G	A	Pts	PIM	PP	SH	GW	S	S%	+/-	TF	F%	Min	GP	G	A	Pts	PIM	PP	SH	GW	Min
2013-14	**Edmonton**	**NHL**	**60**	**0**	**4**	**4**	**24**	**0**	**0**	**0**	**27**	**0.0**	**-11**	**0**	**0.0**	**16:58**	....	....	....	....	....	....	....	....	....
	Columbus	**NHL**	**9**	**0**	**1**	**1**	**4**	**0**	**0**	**0**	**8**	**0.0**	**-2**	**0**	**0.0**	**11:54**	**2**	**0**	**0**	**0**	**0**	**0**	**0**	**0**	**9:44**
2014-15	**Philadelphia**	**NHL**	**80**	**2**	**13**	**15**	**47**	**0**	**0**	**1**	**69**	**2.9**	**2**	**0**	**0.0**	**19:03**	....	....	....	....	....	....	....	....	....
	NHL Totals		**960**	**29**	**132**	**161**	**431**	**4**	**0**	**4**	**720**	**4.0**		**4**	**25.0**	**19:16**	**26**	**0**	**2**	**2**	**10**	**0**	**0**	**0**	**18:27**

Signed as a free agent by **Kassel** (Germany), September 24, 2004. Traded to **Edmonton** by **Minnesota** for Tom Gilbert, February 27, 2012. Traded to **Columbus** by **Edmonton** for Columbus's 5th round choice (later traded back to Columbus – Columbus selected Tyler Bird) in 2014 Entry Draft. March 5, 2014. Signed as a free agent by **Philadelphia**, July 2, 2014.

SCHWARTZ, Jaden

(SHWOHRTZ, JAY-duhn) **ST.L.**

Center. Shoots left. 5'10", 190 lbs. Born, Melfort, SK, June 25, 1992. St. Louis' 1st choice, 14th overall, in 2010 Entry Draft.

Season	Club	League	GP	G	A	Pts	PIM	PP	SH	GW	S	S%	+/-	TF	F%	Min	GP	G	A	Pts	PIM	PP	SH	GW	Min
2008-09	Notre Dame	SJHL	46	34	42	76	15	....	....	....	....	....	....	....	....	....	....	....	....	....	....	....	....	....	....
2009-10	Tri-City Storm	USHL	60	33	50	*83	18	....	....	....	....	....	....	....	....	....	3	3	0	3	0	....	....	....	....
2010-11	Colorado College	WCHA	30	17	30	47	22	....	....	....	....	....	....	....	....	....	....	....	....	....	....	....	....	....	....
2011-12	Colorado College	WCHA	30	15	26	41	18	....	....	....	....	....	....	....	....	....	....	....	....	....	....	....	....	....	....
	St. Louis	**NHL**	**7**	**2**	**1**	**3**	**0**	**1**	**0**	**1**	**6**	**33.3**	**1**	**2**	**50.0**	**11:41**	....	....	....	....	....	....	....	....	....
2012-13	Peoria Rivermen	AHL	33	9	10	19	14	....	....	....	....	....	....	....	....	....	....	....	....	....	....	....	....	....	....
	St. Louis	**NHL**	**45**	**7**	**6**	**13**	**4**	**0**	**0**	**1**	**50**	**14.0**	**-4**	**27**	**55.6**	**12:28**	**6**	**0**	**1**	**1**	**2**	**0**	**0**	**0**	**16:06**
2013-14	**St. Louis**	**NHL**	**80**	**25**	**31**	**56**	**27**	**5**	**3**	**1**	**188**	**13.3**	**28**	**78**	**56.4**	**17:32**	**6**	**1**	**2**	**3**	**0**	**0**	**0**	**0**	**22:10**
2014-15	**St. Louis**	**NHL**	**75**	**28**	**35**	**63**	**16**	**8**	**0**	**4**	**184**	**15.2**	**13**	**146**	**46.6**	**18:15**	**6**	**1**	**2**	**3**	**0**	**0**	**0**	**0**	**18:01**
	NHL Totals		**207**	**62**	**73**	**135**	**47**	**14**	**3**	**7**	**428**	**14.5**		**253**	**50.6**	**16:29**	**18**	**2**	**5**	**7**	**2**	**0**	**0**	**0**	**18:45**

USHL First All-Star Team (2010) • WCHA All-Rookie Team (2011) • WCHA Second All-Star Team (2012) • NCAA West First All-American Team (2012)

SCOTT, John

(SKAWT, JAWN) **ARI**

Left wing. Shoots left. 6'8", 259 lbs. Born, St. Catharines, ON, September 26, 1982.

Season	Club	League	GP	G	A	Pts	PIM	PP	SH	GW	S	S%	+/-	TF	F%	Min	GP	G	A	Pts	PIM	PP	SH	GW	Min
2002-03	Michigan Tech	WCHA	31	1	3	4	64	....	....	....	....	....	....	....	....	....	....	....	....	....	....	....	....	....	....
2003-04	Michigan Tech	WCHA	35	1	3	4	100	....	....	....	....	....	....	....	....	....	....	....	....	....	....	....	....	....	....
2004-05	Michigan Tech	WCHA	36	2	4	6	101	....	....	....	....	....	....	....	....	....	....	....	....	....	....	....	....	....	....
2005-06	Michigan Tech	WCHA	24	3	2	5	87	....	....	....	....	....	....	....	....	....	....	....	....	....	....	....	....	....	....
2006-07	Houston Aeros	AHL	65	1	5	6	107	....	....	....	....	....	....	....	....	....	....	....	....	....	....	....	....	....	....
2007-08	Houston Aeros	AHL	64	3	0	3	184	....	....	....	....	....	....	....	....	....	5	0	0	0	13	....	....	....	....
2008-09	**Minnesota**	**NHL**	**20**	**0**	**1**	**1**	**21**	**0**	**0**	**0**	**6**	**0.0**	**-1**	**0**	**0.0**	**9:14**	....	....	....	....	....	....	....	....	....
	Houston Aeros	AHL	44	2	2	4	111	....	....	....	....	....	....	....	....	....	....	....	....	....	....	....	....	....	....
2009-10	**Minnesota**	**NHL**	**51**	**1**	**1**	**2**	**90**	**0**	**0**	**0**	**22**	**4.5**	**-3**	**0**	**0.0**	**8:36**	....	....	....	....	....	....	....	....	....
2010-11	**Chicago**	**NHL**	**40**	**0**	**1**	**1**	**72**	**0**	**0**	**0**	**15**	**0.0**	**0**	**3**	**0.0**	**6:15**	**4**	**0**	**0**	**0**	**22**	**0**	**0**	**0**	**6:37**
2011-12	**Chicago**	**NHL**	**29**	**0**	**1**	**1**	**48**	**0**	**0**	**0**	**8**	**0.0**	**0**	**0**	**0.0**	**6:56**	....	....	....	....	....	....	....	....	....
	NY Rangers	**NHL**	**6**	**0**	**0**	**0**	**5**	**0**	**0**	**0**	**1**	**0.0**	**-1**	**0**	**0.0**	**5:33**	....	....	....	....	....	....	....	....	....
2012-13	**Buffalo**	**NHL**	**34**	**0**	**0**	**0**	**69**	**0**	**0**	**0**	**15**	**0.0**	**-1**	**0**	**0.0**	**5:27**	....	....	....	....	....	....	....	....	....
2013-14	**Buffalo**	**NHL**	**56**	**1**	**0**	**1**	**125**	**0**	**0**	**0**	**16**	**6.3**	**-12**	**0**	**0.0**	**6:45**	....	....	....	....	....	....	....	....	....
2014-15	**San Jose**	**NHL**	**38**	**3**	**1**	**4**	**87**	**0**	**0**	**0**	**19**	**15.8**	**0**	**0**	**0.0**	**7:27**	....	....	....	....	....	....	....	....	....
	NHL Totals		**274**	**5**	**5**	**10**	**517**	**0**	**0**	**0**	**102**	**4.9**		**3**	**0.0**	**7:08**	**4**	**0**	**0**	**0**	**22**	**0**	**0**	**0**	**6:38**

Signed as a free agent by **Houston** (AHL), September 26, 2006. Signed as a free agent by **Minnesota**, December 31, 2006. Signed as a free agent by **Chicago**, July 2, 2010. • Missed majority of 2010-11 and 2011-12 as a healthy reserve. Traded to **NY Rangers** by **Chicago** for NY Rangers' 5th round choice (Travis Brown) in 2012 Entry Draft, February 27, 2012. Signed as a free agent by **Buffalo**, July 1, 2012. Signed as a free agent by **San Jose**, July 2, 2014. • Missed majority of 2014-15 as a healthy reserve. Signed as a free agent by **Arizona**, July 10, 2015.

SCUDERI, Rob

(SKUD-uh-ree, RAWB) **PIT**

Defense. Shoots left. 6'1", 212 lbs. Born, Syosset, NY, December 30, 1978. Pittsburgh's 5th choice, 134th overall, in 1998 Entry Draft.

Season	Club	League	GP	G	A	Pts	PIM	PP	SH	GW	S	S%	+/-	TF	F%	Min	GP	G	A	Pts	PIM	PP	SH	GW	Min
1995-96	NY Apple Core	MtJHL	76	18	60	78	....	....	....	....	....	....	....	....	....	....	....	....	....	....	....	....	....	....	....
1996-97	NY Apple Core	MtJHL	82	42	70	112	64	....	....	....	....	....	....	....	....	....	....	....	....	....	....	....	....	....	....
1997-98	Boston College	H-East	42	0	24	24	12	....	....	....	....	....	....	....	....	....	....	....	....	....	....	....	....	....	....
1998-99	Boston College	H-East	41	2	8	10	20	....	....	....	....	....	....	....	....	....	....	....	....	....	....	....	....	....	....
99-2000	Boston College	H-East	42	1	12	13	22	....	....	....	....	....	....	....	....	....	....	....	....	....	....	....	....	....	....
2000-01	Boston College	H-East	43	4	19	23	42	....	....	....	....	....	....	....	....	....	....	....	....	....	....	....	....	....	....
2001-02	Wilkes-Barre	AHL	75	1	22	23	66	....	....	....	....	....	....	....	....	....	....	....	....	....	....	....	....	....	....
2002-03	Wilkes-Barre	AHL	74	4	17	21	44	....	....	....	....	....	....	....	....	....	6	0	1	1	4	....	....	....	....
2003-04	**Pittsburgh**	**NHL**	**13**	**1**	**2**	**3**	**4**	**0**	**0**	**0**	**4**	**25.0**	**2**	**0**	**0.0**	**20:06**	....	....	....	....	....	....	....	....	....
	Wilkes-Barre	AHL	64	1	15	16	54	....	....	....	....	....	....	....	....	....	24	0	3	3	14	....	....	....	....
2004-05	Wilkes-Barre	AHL	79	2	18	20	34	....	....	....	....	....	....	....	....	....	11	2	1	3	2	....	....	....	....
2005-06	**Pittsburgh**	**NHL**	**57**	**0**	**4**	**4**	**36**	**0**	**0**	**0**	**28**	**0.0**	**-18**	**0**	**0.0**	**20:15**	....	....	....	....	....	....	....	....	....
	Wilkes-Barre	AHL	13	0	8	8	8	....	....	....	....	....	....	....	....	....	....	....	....	....	....	....	....	....	....
2006-07	**Pittsburgh**	**NHL**	**78**	**1**	**10**	**11**	**28**	**0**	**0**	**0**	**31**	**3.2**	**3**	**0**	**0.0**	**18:49**	**5**	**0**	**0**	**0**	**2**	**0**	**0**	**0**	**17:14**
2007-08	**Pittsburgh**	**NHL**	**71**	**0**	**5**	**5**	**26**	**0**	**0**	**0**	**28**	**0.0**	**3**	**0**	**0.0**	**18:45**	**20**	**0**	**3**	**3**	**2**	**0**	**0**	**0**	**19:02**
2008-09♦	**Pittsburgh**	**NHL**	**81**	**1**	**15**	**16**	**18**	**0**	**0**	**0**	**51**	**2.0**	**23**	**0**	**0.0**	**19:10**	**24**	**1**	**4**	**5**	**6**	**0**	**0**	**0**	**20:30**
2009-10	**Los Angeles**	**NHL**	**73**	**0**	**11**	**11**	**21**	**0**	**0**	**0**	**38**	**0.0**	**16**	**0**	**0.0**	**19:16**	**6**	**0**	**0**	**0**	**6**	**0**	**0**	**0**	**20:40**
2010-11	**Los Angeles**	**NHL**	**82**	**2**	**13**	**15**	**16**	**0**	**0**	**1**	**46**	**4.3**	**1**	**0**	**0.0**	**20:17**	**6**	**0**	**2**	**2**	**0**	**0**	**0**	**0**	**20:49**
2011-12♦	**Los Angeles**	**NHL**	**82**	**1**	**8**	**9**	**16**	**0**	**0**	**0**	**63**	**1.6**	**-7**	**0**	**0.0**	**20:37**	**20**	**0**	**1**	**1**	**4**	**0**	**0**	**0**	**21:44**
2012-13	**Los Angeles**	**NHL**	**48**	**1**	**11**	**12**	**4**	**0**	**0**	**0**	**33**	**3.0**	**-6**	**1**	**0.0**	**21:47**	**18**	**0**	**3**	**3**	**0**	**0**	**0**	**0**	**23:18**
2013-14	**Pittsburgh**	**NHL**	**53**	**0**	**4**	**4**	**2**	**0**	**0**	**0**	**28**	**0.0**	**-8**	**0**	**0.0**	**18:55**	**13**	**0**	**0**	**0**	**6**	**0**	**0**	**0**	**17:45**
2014-15	**Pittsburgh**	**NHL**	**82**	**1**	**9**	**10**	**17**	**0**	**0**	**0**	**52**	**1.9**	**9**	**0**	**0.0**	**19:09**	**5**	**0**	**0**	**0**	**0**	**0**	**0**	**0**	**22:00**
	NHL Totals		**720**	**8**	**92**	**100**	**188**	**0**	**0**	**1**	**402**	**2.0**		**1**	**0.0**	**19:39**	**117**	**1**	**13**	**14**	**26**	**0**	**0**	**0**	**20:32**

NCAA Championship All-Tournament Team (2001)

Signed as a free agent by **Los Angeles** July 2, 2009. Signed as a free agent by **Pittsburgh**, July 5, 2013.

SEABROOK, Brent

(SEE-bruk, BREHNT) **CHI**

Defense. Shoots right. 6'3", 220 lbs. Born, Richmond, BC, April 20, 1985. Chicago's 1st choice, 14th overall, in 2003 Entry Draft.

Season	Club	League	GP	G	A	Pts	PIM	PP	SH	GW	S	S%	+/-	TF	F%	Min	GP	G	A	Pts	PIM	PP	SH	GW	Min
2000-01	Delta Ice Hawks	PIJHL	54	16	26	42	55	....	....	....	....	....	....	....	....	....	....	....	....	....	....	....	....	....	....
	Lethbridge	WHL	4	0	0	0	0	....	....	....	....	....	....	....	....	....	....	....	....	....	....	....	....	....	....
2001-02	Lethbridge	WHL	67	6	33	39	70	....	....	....	....	....	....	....	....	....	4	1	1	2	2	....	....	....	....
2002-03	Lethbridge	WHL	69	9	33	42	113	....	....	....	....	....	....	....	....	....	....	....	....	....	....	....	....	....	....
2003-04	Lethbridge	WHL	61	12	29	41	107	....	....	....	....	....	....	....	....	....	....	....	....	....	....	....	....	....	....
2004-05	Lethbridge	WHL	63	12	42	54	107	....	....	....	....	....	....	....	....	....	5	1	2	3	10	....	....	....	....
	Norfolk Admirals	AHL	3	0	0	0	2	....	....	....	....	....	....	....	....	....	6	0	1	1	6	....	....	....	....
2005-06	**Chicago**	**NHL**	**69**	**5**	**27**	**32**	**60**	**1**	**0**	**2**	**114**	**4.4**	**5**	**0**	**0.0**	**20:02**	....	....	....	....	....	....	....	....	....
2006-07	**Chicago**	**NHL**	**81**	**4**	**20**	**24**	**104**	**0**	**0**	**0**	**144**	**2.8**	**-6**	**2**	**50.0**	**20:46**	....	....	....	....	....	....	....	....	....
2007-08	**Chicago**	**NHL**	**82**	**9**	**23**	**32**	**90**	**4**	**0**	**2**	**152**	**5.9**	**13**	**1**	**0.0**	**21:30**	....	....	....	....	....	....	....	....	....
2008-09	**Chicago**	**NHL**	**82**	**8**	**18**	**26**	**62**	**3**	**1**	**1**	**132**	**6.1**	**23**	**0**	**0.0**	**23:19**	**17**	**1**	**11**	**12**	**14**	**1**	**0**	**0**	**26:00**
2009-10♦	**Chicago**	**NHL**	**78**	**4**	**26**	**30**	**59**	**0**	**0**	**2**	**129**	**3.1**	**20**	**0**	**0.0**	**23:13**	**22**	**4**	**7**	**11**	**14**	**1**	**0**	**0**	**24:11**
	Canada	Olympics	7	0	1	1	2	....	....	....	....	....	....	....	....	....	....	....	....	....	....	....	....	....	....
2010-11	**Chicago**	**NHL**	**82**	**9**	**39**	**48**	**47**	**5**	**0**	**1**	**135**	**6.7**	**0**	**0**	**0.0**	**24:23**	**5**	**0**	**1**	**1**	**6**	**0**	**0**	**0**	**22:57**
2011-12	**Chicago**	**NHL**	**78**	**9**	**25**	**34**	**22**	**2**	**0**	**3**	**156**	**5.8**	**21**	**0**	**0.0**	**24:43**	**6**	**1**	**2**	**3**	**0**	**0**	**0**	**0**	**30:01**
2012-13♦	**Chicago**	**NHL**	**47**	**8**	**12**	**20**	**23**	**3**	**0**	**1**	**65**	**12.3**	**12**	**0**	**0.0**	**22:00**	**23**	**3**	**1**	**4**	**4**	**0**	**0**	**2**	**23:05**
2013-14	**Chicago**	**NHL**	**82**	**7**	**34**	**41**	**22**	**3**	**1**	**0**	**149**	**4.7**	**23**	**0**	**0.0**	**22:16**	**16**	**3**	**12**	**15**	**21**	**0**	**0**	**0**	**23:22**
2014-15♦	**Chicago**	**NHL**	**82**	**8**	**23**	**31**	**27**	**4**	**0**	**2**	**181**	**4.4**	**-3**	**0**	**0.0**	**22:11**	**23**	**7**	**4**	**11**	**10**	**1**	**0**	**1**	**26:17**
	NHL Totals		**763**	**71**	**247**	**318**	**516**	**25**	**2**	**14**	**1357**	**5.2**		**3**	**33.3**	**22:29**	**112**	**19**	**38**	**57**	**69**	**5**	**0**	**3**	**24:48**

WHL East Second All-Star Team (2005)

Played in NHL All-Star Game (2015)

SEDIN, Daniel

(suh-DEEN, DAN-yehl) **VAN**

Left wing. Shoots left. 6'1", 187 lbs. Born, Ornskoldsvik, Sweden, September 26, 1980. Vancouver's 1st choice, 2nd overall, in 1999 Entry Draft.

			Regular Season														Playoffs								
Season	Club	League	GP	G	A	Pts	PIM	PP	SH	GW	S	S%	+/-	TF	F%	Min	GP	G	A	Pts	PIM	PP	SH	GW	Min
1997-98	Malmo Jr.	Swe-Jr.	4	3	3	6	4	....	....	....	....	....	....	....	....	....	....	....	....	....	....	....	....	....	....
	MoDo Jr.	Swe-Jr.	26	26	14	40	....	....	....	....	....	....	....	....	....	....	....	....	....	....	....	....	....	....	....
	MoDo	Sweden	45	4	8	12	26	....	....	....	....	....	....	....	....	....	9	0	0	0	2	....	....	....	....
1998-99	MoDo	Sweden	50	21	21	42	20	....	....	....	....	....	....	....	....	....	13	4	8	12	14	....	....	....	....
99-2000	MoDo	Sweden	50	19	26	45	28	....	....	....	....	....	....	....	....	....	13	*8	6	14	18	....	....	....	....
	MoDo	EuroHL	4	3	3	6	0	....	....	....	....	....	....	....	....	....	2	0	0	0	0	....	....	....	....
2000-01	Vancouver	NHL	75	20	14	34	24	10	0	3	127	15.7	–3	10	60.0	13:00	4	1	2	3	0	0	0	0	16:15
2001-02	Vancouver	NHL	79	9	23	32	32	4	0	2	117	7.7	1	18	33.3	12:22	6	0	1	1	0	0	0	0	10:44
2002-03	Vancouver	NHL	79	14	17	31	34	4	0	2	134	10.4	8	24	45.8	12:26	14	1	5	6	8	1	0	1	12:23
2003-04	Vancouver	NHL	82	18	36	54	18	1	0	3	153	11.8	18	71	47.9	13:33	7	1	2	3	0	1	0	0	16:03
2004-05	MODO	Sweden	49	13	20	33	40	....	....	....	....	....	....	....	....	....	6	0	3	3	6	....	....	....	....
2005-06	Vancouver	NHL	82	22	49	71	34	11	0	4	204	10.8	7	49	42.9	16:40	....	....	....	....	....	....	....	....	....
	Sweden	Olympics	8	1	3	4	2	....	....	....	....	....	....	....	....	....	....	....	....	....	....	....	....	....	....
2006-07	Vancouver	NHL	81	36	48	84	36	16	0	8	236	15.3	19	44	22.7	18:04	12	2	3	5	4	0	0	0	21:31
2007-08	Vancouver	NHL	82	29	45	74	50	12	0	7	247	11.7	6	38	44.7	19:03	....	....	....	....	....	....	....	....	....
2008-09	Vancouver	NHL	82	31	51	82	36	9	0	7	285	10.9	24	35	40.0	18:48	10	4	6	10	8	2	0	0	18:37
2009-10	Vancouver	NHL	63	29	56	85	28	8	0	8	225	12.9	36	33	33.3	19:08	12	5	9	14	12	1	0	2	19:46
	Sweden	Olympics	4	1	2	3	0	....	....	....	....	....	....	....	....	....	....	....	....	....	....	....	....	....	....
2010-11	Vancouver	NHL	82	41	63	*104	32	*18	0	10	266	15.4	30	17	23.5	18:33	25	9	11	20	32	*5	0	2	20:12
2011-12	Vancouver	NHL	72	30	37	67	40	10	0	6	229	13.1	14	19	31.6	18:49	2	0	2	2	0	0	0	0	20:07
2012-13	Vancouver	NHL	47	12	28	40	18	3	0	3	138	8.7	12	7	42.9	19:01	4	0	3	3	14	0	0	0	20:43
2013-14	Vancouver	NHL	73	16	31	47	38	5	0	4	224	7.1	0	27	29.6	20:36	....	....	....	....	....	....	....	....	....
	Sweden	Olympics	6	1	4	5	4	....	....	....	....	....	....	....	....	....	....	....	....	....	....	....	....	....	....
2014-15	Vancouver	NHL	82	20	56	76	18	4	0	5	226	8.8	5	5	40.0	18:21	6	2	2	4	0	0	0	1	18:22
	NHL Totals		1061	327	554	881	438	115	0	72	2811	11.6		397	38.5	16:56	102	25	46	71	78	10	0	6	18:00

NHL Second All-Star Team (2010) • NHL First All-Star Team (2011) • Art Ross Trophy (2011) • Ted Lindsay Award (2011)
Played in NHL All-Star Game (2011, 2012)
Signed as a free agent by **MODO** (Sweden), September 18, 2004.

SEDIN, Henrik

(suh-DEEN, HEHN-rihk) **VAN**

Center. Shoots left. 6'2", 188 lbs. Born, Ornskoldsvik, Sweden, September 26, 1980. Vancouver's 2nd choice, 3rd overall, in 1999 Entry Draft.

			Regular Season														Playoffs								
Season	Club	League	GP	G	A	Pts	PIM	PP	SH	GW	S	S%	+/-	TF	F%	Min	GP	G	A	Pts	PIM	PP	SH	GW	Min
1997-98	Malmo Jr.	Swe-Jr.	8	4	7	11	6	....	....	....	....	....	....	....	....	....	....	....	....	....	....	....	....	....	....
	MoDo Jr.	Swe-Jr.	26	14	22	36	....	....	....	....	....	....	....	....	....	....	....	....	....	....	....	....	....	....	....
	MoDo	Sweden	39	1	4	5	8	....	....	....	....	....	....	....	....	....	7	0	0	0	0	....	....	....	....
1998-99	MoDo	Sweden	49	12	22	34	32	....	....	....	....	....	....	....	....	....	13	2	8	10	6	....	....	....	....
99-2000	MoDo	Sweden	50	9	38	47	22	....	....	....	....	....	....	....	....	....	13	5	9	14	2	....	....	....	....
2000-01	Vancouver	NHL	82	9	20	29	38	2	0	1	98	9.2	–2	1020	44.1	13:31	4	0	4	4	0	0	0	0	16:31
2001-02	Vancouver	NHL	82	16	20	36	36	3	0	1	78	20.5	9	785	47.4	12:48	6	3	0	3	0	0	0	1	11:55
2002-03	Vancouver	NHL	78	8	31	39	38	4	1	1	81	9.9	9	995	48.2	13:58	14	3	2	5	8	1	0	0	13:01
2003-04	Vancouver	NHL	76	11	31	42	32	2	0	2	99	11.1	23	961	50.0	14:02	7	2	2	4	2	2	0	0	16:02
2004-05	MODO	Sweden	44	14	22	36	50	....	....	....	....	....	....	....	....	....	6	1	3	4	6	....	....	....	....
2005-06	Vancouver	NHL	82	18	57	75	56	5	1	0	113	15.9	11	1238	50.7	16:54	....	....	....	....	....	....	....	....	....
	Sweden	Olympics	8	3	1	4	2	....	....	....	....	....	....	....	....	....	....	....	....	....	....	....	....	....	....
2006-07	Vancouver	NHL	82	10	71	81	66	1	0	2	134	7.5	19	1220	52.5	18:26	12	2	2	4	14	1	0	1	22:12
2007-08	Vancouver	NHL	82	15	61	76	56	4	1	2	141	10.6	6	1369	47.0	19:31	....	....	....	....	....	....	....	....	....
2008-09	Vancouver	NHL	82	22	60	82	48	4	0	8	143	15.4	22	1364	49.6	19:31	10	4	6	10	2	1	0	0	20:07
2009-10	Vancouver	NHL	82	29	*83	*112	48	4	2	5	166	17.5	35	1527	49.5	19:41	12	3	11	14	6	0	0	1	20:38
	Sweden	Olympics	4	0	2	2	2	....	....	....	....	....	....	....	....	....	....	....	....	....	....	....	....	....	....
2010-11	Vancouver	NHL	82	19	*75	94	40	8	0	4	157	12.1	26	1387	52.0	19:16	25	3	*19	22	16	2	0	1	20:56
2011-12	Vancouver	NHL	82	14	*67	81	52	8	0	6	113	12.4	23	1302	50.1	19:05	5	2	3	5	4	2	0	0	21:21
2012-13	Vancouver	NHL	48	11	34	45	24	1	1	1	70	15.7	19	891	49.4	19:21	4	0	3	3	4	0	0	0	20:45
2013-14	Vancouver	NHL	70	11	39	50	42	4	0	1	97	11.3	3	1097	52.3	20:40	....	....	....	....	....	....	....	....	....
2014-15	Vancouver	NHL	82	18	55	73	22	5	0	0	101	17.8	11	1565	45.0	18:37	6	1	3	4	2	1	0	0	18:50
	NHL Totals		1092	211	704	915	598	55	6	34	1591	13.3		16721	49.1	17:28	105	23	55	78	58	10	0	4	18:48

NHL First All-Star Team (2010, 2011) • Art Ross Trophy (2010) • Hart Memorial Trophy (2010)
Played in NHL All-Star Game (2008, 2011, 2012)
Signed as a free agent by **MODO** (Sweden), September 18, 2004.

SEGAL, Brandon

(SEE-guhl, BRAN-duhn)

Right wing. Shoots right. 6'2", 215 lbs. Born, Richmond, BC, July 12, 1983. Nashville's 2nd choice, 102nd overall, in 2002 Entry Draft.

			Regular Season														Playoffs								
Season	Club	League	GP	G	A	Pts	PIM	PP	SH	GW	S	S%	+/-	TF	F%	Min	GP	G	A	Pts	PIM	PP	SH	GW	Min
99-2000	Calgary Hitmen	WHL	44	2	6	8	76	....	....	....	....	....	....	....	....	....	13	1	1	2	13	....	....	....	....
	Delta Ice Hawks	PIJHL	....	....	....	....	....	....	....	....	....	....	....	....	....	....	3	0	1	1	2	....	....	....	....
2000-01	Calgary Hitmen	WHL	72	16	11	27	103	....	....	....	....	....	....	....	....	....	12	1	1	2	17	....	....	....	....
2001-02	Calgary Hitmen	WHL	71	43	40	83	122	....	....	....	....	....	....	....	....	....	7	1	4	5	16	....	....	....	....
2002-03	Calgary Hitmen	WHL	71	31	27	58	104	....	....	....	....	....	....	....	....	....	5	2	2	4	4	....	....	....	....
2003-04	Calgary Hitmen	WHL	28	18	12	30	29	....	....	....	....	....	....	....	....	....	....	....	....	....	....	....	....	....	....
	Milwaukee	AHL	44	11	10	21	54	....	....	....	....	....	....	....	....	....	13	2	1	3	21	....	....	....	....
2004-05	Milwaukee	AHL	59	7	8	15	45	....	....	....	....	....	....	....	....	....	3	1	0	1	11	....	....	....	....
	Rockford IceHogs	UHL	10	5	4	9	27	....	....	....	....	....	....	....	....	....	11	11	5	16	10	....	....	....	....
2005-06	Milwaukee	AHL	79	18	15	33	126	....	....	....	....	....	....	....	....	....	21	1	2	3	16	....	....	....	....
2006-07	Milwaukee	AHL	77	20	9	29	84	....	....	....	....	....	....	....	....	....	4	1	0	1	2	....	....	....	....
2007-08	Portland Pirates	AHL	54	5	9	14	46	....	....	....	....	....	....	....	....	....	....	....	....	....	....	....	....	....	....
	Norfolk Admirals	AHL	22	7	6	13	25	....	....	....	....	....	....	....	....	....	....	....	....	....	....	....	....	....	....
2008-09	Tampa Bay	NHL	2	0	0	0	0	0	0	0	2	0.0	0	0	0.0	13:48	....	....	....	....	....	....	....	....	....
	Norfolk Admirals	AHL	69	26	26	52	95	....	....	....	....	....	....	....	....	....	....	....	....	....	....	....	....	....	....
2009-10	Los Angeles	NHL	25	1	1	2	20	0	0	0	24	4.2	0	3	0.0	6:47	....	....	....	....	....	....	....	....	....
	Manchester	AHL	21	6	8	14	34	....	....	....	....	....	....	....	....	....	....	....	....	....	....	....	....	....	....
	Dallas	NHL	19	5	5	10	18	0	0	2	31	16.1	3	0	0.0	11:20	....	....	....	....	....	....	....	....	....
2010-11	Dallas	NHL	46	5	5	10	41	0	0	1	40	12.5	0	4	50.0	8:17	....	....	....	....	....	....	....	....	....
	Texas Stars	AHL	30	7	10	17	38	....	....	....	....	....	....	....	....	....	....	....	....	....	....	....	....	....	....
2011-12	Rockford IceHogs	AHL	53	13	12	25	63	....	....	....	....	....	....	....	....	....	....	....	....	....	....	....	....	....	....
	Tampa Bay	NHL	10	0	0	0	4	0	0	0	8	0.0	–2	4	25.0	6:35	....	....	....	....	....	....	....	....	....
	Norfolk Admirals	AHL	8	5	6	11	6	....	....	....	....	....	....	....	....	....	18	5	4	9	17	....	....	....	....
2012-13	Connecticut	AHL	73	24	20	44	82	....	....	....	....	....	....	....	....	....	....	....	....	....	....	....	....	....	....
	NY Rangers	NHL	1	0	0	0	2	0	0	0	0	0.0	0	0	0.0	5:21	....	....	....	....	....	....	....	....	....
2013-14	Hershey Bears	AHL	63	17	27	44	64	....	....	....	....	....	....	....	....	....	....	....	....	....	....	....	....	....	....
2014-15	Zagreb	KHL	54	10	15	25	52	....	....	....	....	....	....	....	....	....	....	....	....	....	....	....	....	....	....
	NHL Totals		103	11	11	22	85	0	0	3	105	10.5		11	27.3	8:24	....	....	....	....	....	....	....	....	....

Traded to **Anaheim** by **Nashville** for future considerations, June 25, 2007. Traded to **Tampa Bay** by **Anaheim** with Anaheim's 7th round choice (David Carle) in 2008 Entry Draft for Jay Leach, February 26, 2008. Signed as a free agent by **Los Angeles**, July 13, 2009. Claimed on waivers by **Dallas** from **Los Angeles**, February 11, 2010. Signed as a free agent by **Chicago**, September 1, 2011. Traded to **Tampa Bay** by **Chicago** for future considerations, February 21, 2012. Signed as a free agent by **NY Rangers**, July 11, 2012. Signed as a free agent by **Washington**, August 20, 2013. Signed as a free agent by **Zagreb** (KHL), July 8, 2014.

SEGUIN, Tyler

(SAY-gihn, TIGH-luhr) **DAL**

Center. Shoots right. 6'1", 200 lbs. Born, Brampton, ON, January 31, 1992. Boston's 1st choice, 2nd overall, in 2010 Entry Draft.

			Regular Season														Playoffs								
Season	Club	League	GP	G	A	Pts	PIM	PP	SH	GW	S	S%	+/-	TF	F%	Min	GP	G	A	Pts	PIM	PP	SH	GW	Min
2007-08	Tor. Young Nats	GTHL	51	39	47	86	56	....	....	....	....	....	....	....	....	....	....	....	....	....	....	....	....	....	....
2008-09	Plymouth Whalers	OHL	61	21	46	67	28	....	....	....	....	....	....	....	....	....	11	5	11	16	8	....	....	....	....
2009-10	Plymouth Whalers	OHL	63	48	58	*106	54	....	....	....	....	....	....	....	....	....	9	5	5	10	8	....	....	....	....
2010-11 ♦	Boston	NHL	74	11	11	22	18	1	0	0	131	8.4	–4	303	49.5	12:13	13	3	4	7	2	0	0	0	10:35
2011-12	Boston	NHL	81	29	38	67	30	5	0	7	242	12.0	34	106	43.4	16:56	7	2	1	3	0	0	0	1	18:14
2012-13	EHC Biel-Bienne	Swiss	29	25	15	40	24	....	....	....	....	....	....	....	....	....	....	....	....	....	....	....	....	....	....
	Boston	NHL	48	16	16	32	16	4	0	2	161	9.9	23	45	48.9	17:01	22	1	7	8	4	0	0	0	16:03

Season	Club	League	GP	G	A	Pts	PIM	PP	SH	GW	S	S%	+/-	TF	F%	Min	GP	G	A	Pts	PIM	PP	SH	GW	Min
			Regular Season														Playoffs								
2013-14	Dallas	NHL	80	37	47	84	18	11	0	8	294	12.6	16	677	41.5	19:21	6	1	2	3	0	0	0	0	19:57
2014-15	Dallas	NHL	71	37	40	77	20	13	0	5	280	13.2	−1	511	53.8	19:33	....	....	....	....	....	....	....	....	....
	NHL Totals		354	130	152	282	102	34	0	22	1108	11.7		1642	47.1	17:02	48	7	14	21	6	0	0	1	15:23

OHL First All-Star Team (2010) • OHL Player of the Year (2010) • Canadian Major Junior First All-Star Team (2010)

Played in NHL All-Star Game (2012, 2015)

Signed as a free agent by **Biel-Bienne** (Swiss), September 20, 2012. Traded to **Dallas** by **Boston** with Rich Peverley and Ryan Button for Loui Eriksson, Joe Morrow, Reilly Smith and Matt Fraser, July 4, 2013.

SEIDENBERG, Dennis (SIGH-dehn-buhrg, DEH-nihs) BOS

Defense. Shoots left. 6'1", 210 lbs. Born, Schwenningen, West Germany, July 18, 1981. Philadelphia's 6th choice, 172nd overall, in 2001 Entry Draft.

Season	Club	League	GP	G	A	Pts	PIM	PP	SH	GW	S	S%	+/-	TF	F%	Min	GP	G	A	Pts	PIM	PP	SH	GW	Min
99-2000	Mannheim Jr.	Ger-Jr.	52	12	28	40	28	....	....	....	....	....	....	....	....	....	....	....	....	....	....	....	....	....	....
	Adler Mannheim	Germany	3	0	0	0	0	....	....	....	....	....	....	....	....	....	....	....	....	....	....	....	....	....	....
2000-01	Mannheim Jr.	Ger-Jr.	9	3	8	11	20	....	....	....	....	....	....	....	....	....	....	....	....	....	....	....	....	....	....
	Adler Mannheim	Germany	55	2	5	7	6	....	....	....	....	....	....	....	....	....	12	0	1	1	10	....	....	....	....
2001-02	Adler Mannheim	Germany	55	7	13	20	56	....	....	....	....	....	....	....	....	....	8	0	0	0	2	....	....	....	....
2002-03	**Philadelphia**	**NHL**	**58**	**4**	**9**	**13**	**20**	1	0	0	123	3.3	8	1	0.0	16:50	....	....	....	....	....	....	....	....	....
	Philadelphia	AHL	19	5	6	11	17	....	....	....	....	....	....	....	....	....	....	....	....	....	....	....	....	....	....
2003-04	**Philadelphia**	**NHL**	**5**	**0**	**0**	**0**	**2**	0	0	0	14	0.0	−4	0	0.0	17:20	3	0	0	0	0	0	0	0	7:36
	Philadelphia	AHL	33	7	12	19	31	....	....	....	....	....	....	....	....	....	9	2	2	4	4	....	....	....	....
2004-05	Philadelphia	AHL	79	13	28	41	47	....	....	....	....	....	....	....	....	....	18	2	8	10	19	....	....	....	....
2005-06	**Philadelphia**	**NHL**	**29**	**2**	**5**	**7**	**4**	1	0	0	34	5.9	−4	1	0.0	14:22	....	....	....	....	....	....	....	....	....
	Phoenix	**NHL**	**34**	**1**	**10**	**11**	**14**	1	0	0	49	2.0	−9	0	0.0	19:13	....	....	....	....	....	....	....	....	....
	Germany	Olympics	5	0	0	0	6	....	....	....	....	....	....	....	....	....	....	....	....	....	....	....	....	....	....
2006-07	**Phoenix**	**NHL**	**32**	**1**	**1**	**2**	**16**	0	0	0	36	2.8	−4	0	0.0	14:43	....	....	....	....	....	....	....	....	....
	Carolina	**NHL**	**20**	**1**	**5**	**6**	**2**	0	0	0	47	2.1	−12	0	0.0	18:29	....	....	....	....	....	....	....	....	....
2007-08	**Carolina**	**NHL**	**47**	**0**	**15**	**15**	**18**	0	0	0	80	0.0	6	1	100.0	18:50	....	....	....	....	....	....	....	....	....
2008-09	**Carolina**	**NHL**	**70**	**5**	**25**	**30**	**37**	2	0	1	129	3.9	−9	0	0.0	22:20	16	1	5	6	16	0	0	0	22:25
2009-10	**Florida**	**NHL**	**62**	**2**	**21**	**23**	**33**	1	0	0	116	1.7	−3	1	0.0	22:55	....	....	....	....	....	....	....	....	....
	Boston	**NHL**	**17**	**2**	**7**	**9**	**6**	1	0	1	37	5.4	9	0	0.0	22:57	....	....	....	....	....	....	....	....	....
	Germany	Olympics	4	1	0	1	2	....	....	....	....	....	....	....	....	....	....	....	....	....	....	....	....	....	....
2010-11•	**Boston**	**NHL**	**81**	**7**	**25**	**32**	**41**	1	0	2	166	4.2	3	0	0.0	23:33	25	1	10	11	31	0	0	0	27:37
2011-12	**Boston**	**NHL**	**80**	**5**	**18**	**23**	**39**	0	0	2	174	2.9	15	0	0.0	24:02	7	1	2	3	2	0	0	0	26:43
2012-13	Adler Mannheim	Germany	26	2	18	20	20	....	....	....	....	....	....	....	....	....	....	....	....	....	....	....	....	....	....
	Boston	**NHL**	**46**	**4**	**13**	**17**	**10**	0	0	2	83	4.8	18	0	0.0	23:48	18	0	1	1	4	0	0	0	25:59
2013-14	**Boston**	**NHL**	**34**	**1**	**9**	**10**	**10**	0	0	0	53	1.9	11	0	0.0	21:50	....	....	....	....	....	....	....	....	....
2014-15	**Boston**	**NHL**	**82**	**3**	**11**	**14**	**34**	0	0	0	103	2.9	−1	0	0.0	22:06	....	....	....	....	....	....	....	....	....
	NHL Totals		**697**	**38**	**174**	**212**	**286**	8	0	8	1244	3.1		4	25.0	21:07	69	3	18	21	53	0	0	0	25:02

• Missed majority of 2003-04 due to leg injury vs. Edmonton, January 10, 2004. Traded to **Phoenix** by **Philadelphia** with Philadelphia's 4th round choice (later traded to NY Islanders - NY Islanders selected Tomas Marcinko) in 2006 Entry Draft for Petr Nedved and Phoenix's 4th round choice (Joonas Lehtivuori) in 2006 Entry Draft, January 20, 2006. Traded to **Carolina** by **Phoenix** for Kevyn Adams, January 8, 2007. Signed as a free agent by **Florida**, September 14, 2009. Traded to **Boston** by **Florida** with Matt Bartkowski for Byron Bitz, Craig Weller and Tampa Bay's 2nd round choice (previously acquired, Florida selected Alexander Petrovic) in 2010 Entry Draft, March 3, 2010. Signed as a free agent by **Mannheim** (Germany), September 21, 2012. • Missed majority of 2013-14 due to knee (December 27, 2013 vs. Ottawa) and lower-body (January 17, 2014 at Chicago) injuries.

SEKAC, Jiri (SEH-katch, YIH-ree) ANA

Left wing. Shoots left. 6'2", 182 lbs. Born, Kladno, Czech., June 10, 1992.

Season	Club	League	GP	G	A	Pts	PIM	PP	SH	GW	S	S%	+/-	TF	F%	Min	GP	G	A	Pts	PIM	PP	SH	GW	Min
2007-08	HC Kladno U17	CzR-U17	45	6	9	15	6	....	....	....	....	....	....	....	....	....	3	2	1	3	0	....	....	....	....
2008-09	HC Kladno U17	CzR-U17	46	38	49	87	48	....	....	....	....	....	....	....	....	....	5	3	3	6	6	....	....	....	....
2009-10	Peterborough	OHL	8	0	0	0	0	....	....	....	....	....	....	....	....	....	....	....	....	....	....	....	....	....	....
	Youngstown	USHL	38	2	9	11	35	....	....	....	....	....	....	....	....	....	....	....	....	....	....	....	....	....	....
2010-11	Youngstown	USHL	58	18	27	45	27	....	....	....	....	....	....	....	....	....	....	....	....	....	....	....	....	....	....
2011-12	Poprad Jr.	Russia-Jr.	6	8	2	10	22	....	....	....	....	....	....	....	....	....	....	....	....	....	....	....	....	....	....
	Lev Poprad	KHL	36	2	8	10	4	....	....	....	....	....	....	....	....	....	....	....	....	....	....	....	....	....	....
2012-13	HC Sparta Praha	CzRep	21	4	6	10	8	....	....	....	....	....	....	....	....	....	....	....	....	....	....	....	....	....	....
	HC Lev Praha	KHL	26	0	1	1	8	....	....	....	....	....	....	....	....	....	3	0	0	0	0	....	....	....	....
2013-14	HC Lev Praha	KHL	47	11	17	28	18	....	....	....	....	....	....	....	....	....	21	1	7	8	24	....	....	....	....
2014-15	**Montreal**	**NHL**	**50**	**7**	**9**	**16**	**18**	2	0	0	56	12.5	−2	1	0.0	13:49	....	....	....	....	....	....	....	....	....
	Anaheim	**NHL**	**19**	**2**	**5**	**7**	**4**	0	0	0	29	6.9	2	1	0.0	12:57	7	0	0	0	2	0	0	0	11:23
	NHL Totals		**69**	**9**	**14**	**23**	**22**	2	0	0	85	10.6		2	0.0	13:34	7	0	0	0	2	0	0	0	11:23

Signed as a free agent by **Montreal**, July 1, 2014. Traded to **Anaheim** by **Montreal** for Devante Smith-Pelly, February 24, 2015.

SEKERA, Andrej (seh-KAIR-ah, AWN-dray) EDM

Defense. Shoots left. 6', 201 lbs. Born, Bojnice, Czech., June 8, 1986. Buffalo's 3rd choice, 71st overall, in 2004 Entry Draft.

Season	Club	League	GP	G	A	Pts	PIM	PP	SH	GW	S	S%	+/-	TF	F%	Min	GP	G	A	Pts	PIM	PP	SH	GW	Min
2001-02	Dukla Trencin Jr.	Slovak-Jr.	52	5	10	15	10	....	....	....	....	....	....	....	....	....	....	....	....	....	....	....	....	....	....
2002-03	Dukla Trencin Jr.	Slovak-Jr.	48	9	15	24	20	....	....	....	....	....	....	....	....	....	....	....	....	....	....	....	....	....	....
2003-04	Dukla Trencin Jr.	Slovak-Jr.	42	5	12	17	40	....	....	....	....	....	....	....	....	....	2	0	1	1	4	....	....	....	....
	Dukla Trencin	Slovakia	3	0	0	0	2	....	....	....	....	....	....	....	....	....	....	....	....	....	....	....	....	....	....
	Dukla Trencin U18	Svk-U18	5	0	0	0	0	....	....	....	....	....	....	....	....	....	....	....	....	....	....	....	....	....	....
2004-05	Owen Sound	OHL	51	7	21	28	18	....	....	....	....	....	....	....	....	....	6	0	4	4	4	....	....	....	....
2005-06	Owen Sound	OHL	51	21	34	55	54	....	....	....	....	....	....	....	....	....	11	5	8	13	9	....	....	....	....
2006-07	**Buffalo**	**NHL**	**2**	**0**	**0**	**0**	**2**	0	0	0	0	0.0	1	0	0.0	7:31	....	....	....	....	....	....	....	....	....
	Rochester	AHL	54	3	16	19	28	....	....	....	....	....	....	....	....	....	....	....	....	....	....	....	....	....	....
2007-08	**Buffalo**	**NHL**	**37**	**2**	**6**	**8**	**16**	0	0	1	28	7.1	5	0	0.0	19:37	....	....	....	....	....	....	....	....	....
	Rochester	AHL	40	2	15	17	22	....	....	....	....	....	....	....	....	....	....	....	....	....	....	....	....	....	....
2008-09	**Buffalo**	**NHL**	**69**	**3**	**16**	**19**	**22**	1	0	1	84	3.6	−11	1	0.0	20:42	....	....	....	....	....	....	....	....	....
2009-10	**Buffalo**	**NHL**	**49**	**4**	**7**	**11**	**6**	0	0	0	59	6.8	−1	1	0.0	17:27	6	0	0	0	7	0	0	0	13:55
	Slovakia	Olympics	7	1	0	1	0	....	....	....	....	....	....	....	....	....	....	....	....	....	....	....	....	....	....
2010-11	**Buffalo**	**NHL**	**76**	**3**	**26**	**29**	**34**	0	0	0	88	3.4	11	0	0.0	21:06	2	1	0	1	4	0	0	0	16:18
2011-12	**Buffalo**	**NHL**	**69**	**3**	**10**	**13**	**18**	1	0	0	88	3.4	3	1	0.0	19:36	....	....	....	....	....	....	....	....	....
2012-13	Bratislava	KHL	25	3	9	12	8	....	....	....	....	....	....	....	....	....	....	....	....	....	....	....	....	....	....
	Buffalo	**NHL**	**37**	**2**	**10**	**12**	**4**	0	0	0	33	6.1	−2	0	0.0	21:12	....	....	....	....	....	....	....	....	....
2013-14	**Carolina**	**NHL**	**74**	**11**	**33**	**44**	**20**	4	1	1	142	7.7	4	0	0.0	23:41	....	....	....	....	....	....	....	....	....
	Slovakia	Olympics	4	0	2	2	0	....	....	....	....	....	....	....	....	....	....	....	....	....	....	....	....	....	....
2014-15	**Carolina**	**NHL**	**57**	**2**	**17**	**19**	**8**	1	0	0	77	2.6	−7	0	0.0	22:46	....	....	....	....	....	....	....	....	....
	Los Angeles	**NHL**	**16**	**1**	**3**	**4**	**6**	0	0	0	23	4.3	4	0	0.0	19:13	....	....	....	....	....	....	....	....	....
	NHL Totals		**486**	**31**	**128**	**159**	**136**	7	1	3	622	5.0		3	0.0	20:50	8	1	0	1	11	0	0	0	14:31

OHL All-Rookie Team (2005) • OHL First All-Star Team (2006)

Signed as a free agent by **Bratislava** (KHL), September 27, 2012. Traded to **Carolina** by **Buffalo** for Jamie McBain and Carolina's 2nd round choice (J.T. Compher) in 2013 Entry Draft, June 30, 2013. Traded to **Los Angeles** by **Carolina** for Roland McKeown and Los Angeles' 1st round choice in 2016 Entry Draft, February 25, 2015. Signed as a free agent by **Edmonton**, July 1, 2015.

SELLECK, Eric (SEHL-ehk, AIR-ihk) ARI

Left wing. Shoots left. 6'2", 208 lbs. Born, Spencerville, ON, October 20, 1987.

Season	Club	League	GP	G	A	Pts	PIM	PP	SH	GW	S	S%	+/-	TF	F%	Min	GP	G	A	Pts	PIM	PP	SH	GW	Min
2006-07	Pembroke	ON-Jr.A	53	23	24	47	137	....	....	....	....	....	....	....	....	....	15	4	8	12	29	....	....	....	....
2007-08	Pembroke	ON-Jr.A	49	43	38	81	120	....	....	....	....	....	....	....	....	....	14	8	21	29	28	....	....	....	....
2008-09	Oswego State	NCAA-3	26	13	13	26	45	....	....	....	....	....	....	....	....	....	....	....	....	....	....	....	....	....	....
2009-10	Oswego State	NCAA-3	28	21	33	54	48	....	....	....	....	....	....	....	....	....	....	....	....	....	....	....	....	....	....
2010-11	Rochester	AHL	67	5	11	16	214	....	....	....	....	....	....	....	....	....	....	....	....	....	....	....	....	....	....
2011-12	San Antonio	AHL	71	5	4	9	204	....	....	....	....	....	....	....	....	....	9	0	0	0	4	....	....	....	....
2012-13	San Antonio	AHL	60	5	11	16	181	....	....	....	....	....	....	....	....	....	....	....	....	....	....	....	....	....	....
	Florida	**NHL**	**2**	**0**	**1**	**1**	**17**	0	0	0	2	0.0	2	0	0.0	7:55	....	....	....	....	....	....	....	....	....

			Regular Season														Playoffs								
Season	Club	League	GP	G	A	Pts	PIM	PP	SH	GW	S	S%	+/-	TF	F%	Min	GP	G	A	Pts	PIM	PP	SH	GW	Min
2013-14	San Antonio	AHL	42	3	4	7	93	....	....	....	....	....	....	....	....	....	....	....	....	....	....	....	....	....	....
	Chicago Wolves	AHL	18	3	2	5	70	....	....	....	....	....	....	....	....	....	9	0	1	1	17	....	....	....	....
2014-15	Portland Pirates	AHL	74	8	15	23	185	....	....	....	....	....	....	....	....	....	5	1	1	2	8	....	....	....	....
	NHL Totals		**2**	**0**	**1**	**1**	**17**	**0**	**0**	**0**	**2**	**0.0**		**0**	**0.0**	**7:55**	....	....	....	....	....	....	....	....	....

SUNYAC (NCAA-3) Rookie of the Year (2009) • SUNYAC (NCAA-3) Player of the Year (2010) • NCAA-3 East All-American Team (2010)

Signed as a free agent by **Florida**, April 21, 2010. Traded to **St. Louis** by **Florida** for Mark Mancari, March 2, 2014. Signed as a free agent by **Arizona**, July 3, 2015.

SEMIN, Alexander (SEH-min, al-EHX-AN-duhr) MTL

Left wing. Shoots right. 6'2", 209 lbs. Born, Krasnoyarsk, USSR, March 3, 1984. Washington's 2nd choice, 13th overall, in 2002 Entry Draft.

Season	Club	League	GP	G	A	Pts	PIM	PP	SH	GW	S	S%	+/-	TF	F%	Min	GP	G	A	Pts	PIM	PP	SH	GW	Min
2001-02	Chelyabinsk	Russia-2	46	13	8	21	52	....	....	....	....	....	....	....	....	....	2	2	0	2	0	....	....	....	....
2002-03	Lada Togliatti	Russia	47	10	7	17	36	....	....	....	....	....	....	....	....	....	10	*5	3	8	10	....	....	....	....
2003-04	**Washington**	**NHL**	**52**	**10**	**12**	**22**	**36**	**4**	**0**	**2**	**92**	**10.9**	**-2**	**6**	**50.0**	**12:37**	....	....	....	....	....	....	....	....	....
	Portland Pirates	AHL	4	3	1	4	6	....	....	....	....	....	....	....	....	....	7	4	7	11	19	....	....	....	....
2004-05	Lada Togliatti	Russia	50	19	11	30	56	....	....	....	....	....	....	....	....	....	10	1	1	2	0	....	....	....	....
2005-06	Lada Togliatti	Russia	16	5	4	9	52	....	....	....	....	....	....	....	....	....	....	....	....	....	....	....	....	....	....
	Mytischi	Russia	26	3	7	10	24	....	....	....	....	....	....	....	....	....	8	3	2	5	6	....	....	....	....
2006-07	**Washington**	**NHL**	**77**	**38**	**35**	**73**	**90**	**17**	**0**	**6**	**243**	**15.6**	**-7**	**44**	**27.3**	**18:24**	....	....	....	....	....	....	....	....	....
2007-08	**Washington**	**NHL**	**63**	**26**	**16**	**42**	**54**	**10**	**0**	**2**	**185**	**14.1**	**-18**	**11**	**36.4**	**16:55**	**7**	**3**	**5**	**8**	**8**	**2**	**0**	**1**	**19:45**
2008-09	**Washington**	**NHL**	**62**	**34**	**45**	**79**	**77**	**8**	**0**	**8**	**223**	**15.2**	**25**	**24**	**50.0**	**19:14**	**14**	**5**	**9**	**14**	**16**	**1**	**0**	**1**	**19:58**
2009-10	**Washington**	**NHL**	**73**	**40**	**44**	**84**	**66**	**8**	**2**	**5**	**278**	**14.4**	**36**	**16**	**37.5**	**19:07**	**7**	**0**	**2**	**2**	**4**	**0**	**0**	**0**	**19:21**
	Russia	Olympics	4	0	2	2	4	....	....	....	....	....	....	....	....	....	....	....	....	....	....	....	....	....	....
2010-11	**Washington**	**NHL**	**65**	**28**	**26**	**54**	**71**	**6**	**1**	**4**	**196**	**14.3**	**22**	**13**	**30.8**	**18:04**	**9**	**4**	**2**	**6**	**8**	**0**	**0**	**1**	**18:36**
2011-12	**Washington**	**NHL**	**77**	**21**	**33**	**54**	**56**	**2**	**0**	**1**	**183**	**11.5**	**9**	**11**	**9.1**	**16:47**	**14**	**3**	**1**	**4**	**10**	**2**	**0**	**1**	**17:28**
2012-13	Sokol Krasnoyarsk	Russia-2	4	2	2	4	8	....	....	....	....	....	....	....	....	....	....	....	....	....	....	....	....	....	....
	Nizhny Novgorod	KHL	20	7	10	17	10	....	....	....	....	....	....	....	....	....	....	....	....	....	....	....	....	....	....
	Carolina	**NHL**	**44**	**13**	**31**	**44**	**46**	**4**	**0**	**1**	**150**	**8.7**	**14**	**21**	**23.8**	**20:57**	....	....	....	....	....	....	....	....	....
2013-14	**Carolina**	**NHL**	**65**	**22**	**20**	**42**	**42**	**6**	**1**	**3**	**210**	**10.5**	**1**	**10**	**10.0**	**19:55**	....	....	....	....	....	....	....	....	....
2014-15	**Carolina**	**NHL**	**57**	**6**	**13**	**19**	**32**	**0**	**0**	**0**	**93**	**6.5**	**-10**	**9**	**33.3**	**15:55**	....	....	....	....	....	....	....	....	....
	NHL Totals		**635**	**238**	**275**	**513**	**570**	**65**	**4**	**32**	**1853**	**12.8**		**165**	**30.9**	**17:49**	**51**	**15**	**19**	**34**	**46**	**5**	**0**	**4**	**18:56**

Signed as a free agent by **Togliatti** (Russia), September 25, 2004. • Suspended by **Washington** for failing to report to **Portland** (AHL), September 28, 2004. Signed as a free agent by **Mytischi** (Russia), November 22, 2005. Signed as a free agent by **Carolina**, July 26, 2012. Signed as a free agent by **Krasnoyarsk** (Russia-2), September 25, 2012. Signed as a free agent by **Nizhny Novgorod** (KHL), October 12, 2012. Signed as a fee agent by **Montreal**, July 24, 2015.

SESTITO, Tim (sehs-TEE-toh, TIHM)

Center. Shoots left. 5'11", 195 lbs. Born, Rome, NY, August 28, 1984.

Season	Club	League	GP	G	A	Pts	PIM	PP	SH	GW	S	S%	+/-	TF	F%	Min	GP	G	A	Pts	PIM	PP	SH	GW	Min
2001-02	Plymouth Whalers	OHL	51	10	11	21	40	....	....	....	....	....	....	....	....	....	6	0	0	0	0	....	....	....	....
2002-03	Plymouth Whalers	OHL	61	11	7	18	49	....	....	....	....	....	....	....	....	....	18	2	3	5	4	....	....	....	....
2003-04	Plymouth Whalers	OHL	57	10	20	30	68	....	....	....	....	....	....	....	....	....	9	4	1	5	14	....	....	....	....
2004-05	Plymouth Whalers	OHL	67	14	18	32	93	....	....	....	....	....	....	....	....	....	4	0	0	0	14	....	....	....	....
	Bridgeport	AHL	9	2	1	3	12	....	....	....	....	....	....	....	....	....	....	....	....	....	....	....	....	....	....
2005-06	Greenville	ECHL	72	21	23	44	127	....	....	....	....	....	....	....	....	....	6	2	2	4	24	....	....	....	....
2006-07	Wilkes-Barre	AHL	4	0	0	0	6	....	....	....	....	....	....	....	....	....	....	....	....	....	....	....	....	....	....
	Stockton Thunder	ECHL	66	13	13	26	132	....	....	....	....	....	....	....	....	....	6	2	1	3	6	....	....	....	....
2007-08	Springfield	AHL	77	7	10	17	175	....	....	....	....	....	....	....	....	....	....	....	....	....	....	....	....	....	....
2008-09	**Edmonton**	**NHL**	**1**	**0**	**0**	**0**	**0**	**0**	**0**	**0**	**1**	**0.0**	**0**	**2**	**50.0**	**5:53**	....	....	....	....	....	....	....	....	....
	Springfield	AHL	51	5	3	8	77	....	....	....	....	....	....	....	....	....	....	....	....	....	....	....	....	....	....
2009-10	**New Jersey**	**NHL**	**9**	**0**	**1**	**1**	**2**	**0**	**0**	**0**	**7**	**0.0**	**-2**	**64**	**53.1**	**12:16**	....	....	....	....	....	....	....	....	....
	Lowell Devils	AHL	66	18	17	35	38	....	....	....	....	....	....	....	....	....	5	0	0	0	8	....	....	....	....
2010-11	**New Jersey**	**NHL**	**36**	**0**	**2**	**2**	**9**	**0**	**0**	**0**	**22**	**0.0**	**-5**	**253**	**45.9**	**10:49**	....	....	....	....	....	....	....	....	....
	Albany Devils	AHL	23	5	8	13	28	....	....	....	....	....	....	....	....	....	....	....	....	....	....	....	....	....	....
2011-12	**New Jersey**	**NHL**	**18**	**0**	**0**	**0**	**7**	**0**	**0**	**0**	**6**	**0.0**	**-5**	**75**	**41.3**	**8:15**	**1**	**0**	**0**	**0**	**0**	**0**	**0**	**0**	**6:51**
	Albany Devils	AHL	45	9	10	19	127	....	....	....	....	....	....	....	....	....	....	....	....	....	....	....	....	....	....
2012-13	Albany Devils	AHL	67	7	16	23	106	....	....	....	....	....	....	....	....	....	....	....	....	....	....	....	....	....	....
	New Jersey	**NHL**	**6**	**0**	**0**	**0**	**2**	**0**	**0**	**0**	**4**	**0.0**	**1**	**26**	**53.9**	**7:52**	....	....	....	....	....	....	....	....	....
2013-14	**New Jersey**	**NHL**	**16**	**0**	**3**	**3**	**2**	**0**	**0**	**0**	**13**	**0.0**	**1**	**47**	**42.6**	**9:06**	....	....	....	....	....	....	....	....	....
	Albany Devils	AHL	51	13	14	27	79	....	....	....	....	....	....	....	....	....	4	0	0	0	6	....	....	....	....
2014-15	**New Jersey**	**NHL**	**15**	**0**	**2**	**2**	**33**	**0**	**0**	**0**	**10**	**0.0**	**-1**	**106**	**45.3**	**9:53**	....	....	....	....	....	....	....	....	....
	Albany Devils	AHL	58	10	15	25	79	....	....	....	....	....	....	....	....	....	....	....	....	....	....	....	....	....	....
	NHL Totals		**101**	**0**	**8**	**8**	**55**	**0**	**0**	**0**	**63**	**0.0**		**573**	**46.1**	**9:51**	**1**	**0**	**0**	**0**	**0**	**0**	**0**	**0**	**6:51**

Signed as a free agent by **Edmonton**, August 28, 2006. Traded to **New Jersey** by **Edmonton** for future considerations, July 9, 2009.

SESTITO, Tom (sehs-TEE-toh, TAWM)

Left wing. Shoots left. 6'5", 228 lbs. Born, Rome, NY, September 28, 1987. Columbus' 3rd choice, 85th overall, in 2006 Entry Draft.

Season	Club	League	GP	G	A	Pts	PIM	PP	SH	GW	S	S%	+/-	TF	F%	Min	GP	G	A	Pts	PIM	PP	SH	GW	Min
2003-04	Syracuse Jr. Stars	EmJHL	31	13	16	29	137	....	....	....	....	....	....	....	....	....	6	5	6	11	32	....	....	....	....
2004-05	Plymouth Whalers	OHL	35	1	3	4	88	....	....	....	....	....	....	....	....	....	....	....	....	....	....	....	....	....	....
2005-06	Plymouth Whalers	OHL	57	10	10	20	176	....	....	....	....	....	....	....	....	....	13	5	2	7	29	....	....	....	....
2006-07	Plymouth Whalers	OHL	60	42	22	64	135	....	....	....	....	....	....	....	....	....	19	11	6	17	57	....	....	....	....
2007-08	**Columbus**	**NHL**	**1**	**0**	**0**	**0**	**17**	**0**	**0**	**0**	**0**	**0.0**	**0**	**0**	**0.0**	**4:36**	....	....	....	....	....	....	....	....	....
	Syracuse Crunch	AHL	66	7	16	23	202	....	....	....	....	....	....	....	....	....	9	3	0	3	57	....	....	....	....
2008-09	Syracuse Crunch	AHL	52	8	12	20	168	....	....	....	....	....	....	....	....	....	....	....	....	....	....	....	....	....	....
2009-10	**Columbus**	**NHL**	**3**	**0**	**0**	**0**	**7**	**0**	**0**	**0**	**0**	**0.0**	**0**	**0**	**0.0**	**5:34**	....	....	....	....	....	....	....	....	....
	Syracuse Crunch	AHL	36	10	7	17	138	....	....	....	....	....	....	....	....	....	....	....	....	....	....	....	....	....	....
2010-11	**Columbus**	**NHL**	**9**	**2**	**2**	**4**	**40**	**1**	**0**	**0**	**7**	**28.6**	**-4**	**1**	**100.0**	**9:32**	....	....	....	....	....	....	....	....	....
	Springfield	AHL	46	11	21	32	192	....	....	....	....	....	....	....	....	....	....	....	....	....	....	....	....	....	....
	Adirondack	AHL	11	2	1	3	45	....	....	....	....	....	....	....	....	....	....	....	....	....	....	....	....	....	....
2011-12	**Philadelphia**	**NHL**	**14**	**0**	**1**	**1**	**83**	**0**	**0**	**0**	**4**	**0.0**	**-3**	**4**	**50.0**	**6:54**	....	....	....	....	....	....	....	....	....
	Adirondack	AHL	34	9	8	17	120	....	....	....	....	....	....	....	....	....	....	....	....	....	....	....	....	....	....
2012-13	Sheffield Steelers	Britain	17	8	11	19	69	....	....	....	....	....	....	....	....	....	....	....	....	....	....	....	....	....	....
	Philadelphia	**NHL**	**7**	**2**	**0**	**2**	**12**	**0**	**0**	**1**	**3**	**66.7**	**1**	**1**	**100.0**	**5:46**	....	....	....	....	....	....	....	....	....
	Adirondack	AHL	1	0	0	0	2	....	....	....	....	....	....	....	....	....	....	....	....	....	....	....	....	....	....
	Vancouver	**NHL**	**23**	**1**	**0**	**1**	**53**	**0**	**0**	**0**	**11**	**9.1**	**-3**	**1**	**0.0**	**6:38**	**1**	**0**	**0**	**0**	**2**	**0**	**0**	**0**	**5:51**
2013-14	**Vancouver**	**NHL**	**77**	**5**	**4**	**9**	***213**	**1**	**0**	**0**	**31**	**16.1**	**-14**	**11**	**27.3**	**6:27**	....	....	....	....	....	....	....	....	....
2014-15	**Vancouver**	**NHL**	**3**	**0**	**1**	**1**	**7**	**0**	**0**	**0**	**1**	**0.0**	**1**	**0**	**0.0**	**6:14**	....	....	....	....	....	....	....	....	....
	Utica Comets	AHL	10	1	0	1	20	....	....	....	....	....	....	....	....	....	....	....	....	....	....	....	....	....	....
	NHL Totals		**137**	**10**	**8**	**18**	**432**	**2**	**0**	**1**	**57**	**17.5**		**18**	**38.9**	**6:40**	**1**	**0**	**0**	**0**	**2**	**0**	**0**	**0**	**5:51**

Traded to **Philadelphia** by **Columbus** for Michael Chaput and Greg Moore, February 28, 2011. Signed as a free agent by **Sheffield** (Britain), October 8, 2012. Claimed on waivers by **Vancouver** from **Philadelphia**, March 1, 2013. • Missed majority of 2014-15 due to leg injury vs. Nashville, November 2, 2014 and as a healthy reserve.

SETOGUCHI, Devin (SEHT-oh-GOO-chee, DEH-vihn)

Right wing. Shoots right. 6'", 205 lbs. Born, Taber, AB, January 1, 1987. San Jose's 1st choice, 8th overall, in 2005 Entry Draft.

Season	Club	League	GP	G	A	Pts	PIM	PP	SH	GW	S	S%	+/-	TF	F%	Min	GP	G	A	Pts	PIM	PP	SH	GW	Min
2003-04	Saskatoon Blades	WHL	66	13	18	31	53	....	....	....	....	....	....	....	....	....	....	....	....	....	....	....	....	....	....
2004-05	Saskatoon Blades	WHL	69	33	31	64	34	....	....	....	....	....	....	....	....	....	4	0	1	1	0	....	....	....	....
2005-06	Saskatoon Blades	WHL	65	36	47	83	69	....	....	....	....	....	....	....	....	....	10	8	4	12	8	....	....	....	....
2006-07	Prince George	WHL	55	36	29	65	55	....	....	....	....	....	....	....	....	....	15	*11	10	21	24	....	....	....	....
2007-08	**San Jose**	**NHL**	**44**	**11**	**6**	**17**	**8**	**3**	**0**	**2**	**105**	**10.5**	**6**	**17**	**64.7**	**14:15**	**9**	**1**	**1**	**2**	**2**	**0**	**0**	**0**	**10:25**
	Worcester Sharks	AHL	23	8	11	19	25	....	....	....	....	....	....	....	....	....	....	....	....	....	....	....	....	....	....
2008-09	**San Jose**	**NHL**	**81**	**31**	**34**	**65**	**25**	**11**	**0**	**3**	**246**	**12.6**	**16**	**21**	**28.6**	**16:13**	**6**	**1**	**2**	**3**	**2**	**0**	**0**	**0**	**16:21**
2009-10	**San Jose**	**NHL**	**70**	**20**	**16**	**36**	**19**	**8**	**0**	**4**	**165**	**12.1**	**0**	**10**	**30.0**	**15:18**	**15**	**5**	**4**	**9**	**6**	**1**	**0**	**1**	**18:25**
2010-11	**San Jose**	**NHL**	**72**	**22**	**19**	**41**	**37**	**4**	**0**	**5**	**199**	**11.1**	**-2**	**11**	**45.5**	**15:12**	**18**	**7**	**3**	**10**	**12**	**3**	**0**	**2**	**17:26**
2011-12	**Minnesota**	**NHL**	**69**	**19**	**17**	**36**	**28**	**7**	**0**	**2**	**174**	**10.9**	**-17**	**11**	**27.3**	**17:36**	....	....	....	....	....	....	....	....	....
2012-13	Ontario Reign	ECHL	10	4	9	13	2	....	....	....	....	....	....	....	....	....	....	....	....	....	....	....	....	....	....
	Minnesota	**NHL**	**48**	**13**	**14**	**27**	**20**	**5**	**0**	**3**	**97**	**13.4**	**5**	**17**	**41.2**	**14:26**	**5**	**1**	**0**	**1**	**0**	**0**	**0**	**0**	**16:04**
2013-14	**Winnipeg**	**NHL**	**75**	**11**	**16**	**27**	**22**	**2**	**0**	**3**	**129**	**8.5**	**-7**	**20**	**25.0**	**15:03**	....	....	....	....	....	....	....	....	....

Season	Club	League	GP	G	A	Pts	PIM	PP	SH	GW	S	S%	+/-	TF	F%	Min	GP	G	A	Pts	PIM	PP	SH	GW	Min
			Regular Season														Playoffs								
2014-15	Calgary	NHL	12	0	0	0	4	0	0	0	12	0.0	-7	2	50.0	12:09	....	....	....	....	....	....	....	....	....
	Adirondack	AHL	19	3	7	10	4	....	....	....	....	....	....	....	....	....	....	....	....	....	....	....	....	....	....
	NHL Totals		471	127	122	249	163	40	0	22	1127	11.3		109	37.6	15:28	53	15	10	25	22	4	0	3	16:16

WHL East Second All-Star Team (2006)

Traded to **Minnesota** by **San Jose** with Charlie Coyle and San Jose's 1st round choice (Zack Phillips) in 2011 Entry Draft for Brent Burns and Minnesota's 2nd round choice (later traded to Tampa Bay – later traded to Nashville – Nashville selected Pontius Aberg) in 2012 Entry Draft, June 24, 2011. Signed as a free agent by **Ontario** (ECHL), October 30, 2012. Traded to **Winnipeg** by **Minnesota** for Winnipeg's 2nd round choice (later traded to Buffalo, later traded to Washington – Washington selected Vitak Vanecek) in 2014 Entry Draft, July 5, 2013. Signed as a free agent by **Calgary**, August 23, 2014. • Missed majority of 2014-15 due to upper-body injury at Florida, November 8, 2014.

SEVERSON, Damon (seh-VUHR-suhn, DAY-muhn) N.J.

Defense. Shoots right. 6'2", 205 lbs. Born, Brandon, MB, August 7, 1994. New Jersey's 2nd choice, 60th overall, in 2012 Entry Draft.

Season	Club	League	GP	G	A	Pts	PIM	PP	SH	GW	S	S%	+/-	TF	F%	Min	GP	G	A	Pts	PIM	PP	SH	GW	Min
2009-10	Yorkton Harvest	SMHL	44	9	25	34	53	....	....	....	....	....	....	....	....	....	4	1	1	2	18	....	....	....	....
	Melville	SJHL	1	0	1	1	2	....	....	....	....	....	....	....	....	....	....	....	....	....	....	....	....	....	....
	Kelowna Rockets	WHL	5	0	0	0	0	....	....	....	....	....	....	....	....	....	....	....	....	....	....	....	....	....	....
2010-11	Kelowna Rockets	WHL	64	4	13	17	53	....	....	....	....	....	....	....	....	....	10	2	0	2	13	....	....	....	....
2011-12	Kelowna Rockets	WHL	56	7	30	37	80	....	....	....	....	....	....	....	....	....	4	2	0	2	2	....	....	....	....
2012-13	Kelowna Rockets	WHL	71	10	42	52	74	....	....	....	....	....	....	....	....	....	11	1	9	10	18	....	....	....	....
	Albany Devils	AHL	2	0	2	2	0	....	....	....	....	....	....	....	....	....	....	....	....	....	....	....	....	....	....
2013-14	Kelowna Rockets	WHL	64	15	46	61	63	....	....	....	....	....	....	....	....	....	14	4	14	18	18	....	....	....	....
2014-15	**New Jersey**	**NHL**	51	5	12	17	22	0	0	0	93	5.4	-13	1	0.0	21:58	....	....	....	....	....	....	....	....	....
	NHL Totals		51	5	12	17	22	0	0	0	93	5.4		1	0.0	21:58	....	....	....	....	....	....	....	....	....

WHL West Second All-Star Team (2014)

SGARBOSSA, Michael (s'gahr-BOH-suh, MIGH-kuhl) ANA

Center. Shoots left. 5'11", 180 lbs. Born, Campbellville, ON, July 25, 1992.

Season	Club	League	GP	G	A	Pts	PIM	PP	SH	GW	S	S%	+/-	TF	F%	Min	GP	G	A	Pts	PIM	PP	SH	GW	Min
2008-09	Barrie Colts	OHL	67	10	33	43	43	....	....	....	....	....	....	....	....	....	5	3	3	6	10	....	....	....	....
2009-10	Barrie Colts	OHL	19	7	13	20	14	....	....	....	....	....	....	....	....	....	....	....	....	....	....	....	....	....	....
	Saginaw Spirit	OHL	48	13	19	32	49	....	....	....	....	....	....	....	....	....	6	0	2	2	4	....	....	....	....
2010-11	Saginaw Spirit	OHL	26	7	13	20	24	....	....	....	....	....	....	....	....	....	....	....	....	....	....	....	....	....	....
	Sudbury Wolves	OHL	37	29	33	62	53	....	....	....	....	....	....	....	....	....	8	5	9	14	16	....	....	....	....
2011-12	Sudbury Wolves	OHL	66	47	55	*102	68	....	....	....	....	....	....	....	....	....	4	2	1	3	6	....	....	....	....
2012-13	Lake Erie	AHL	57	19	25	44	71	....	....	....	....	....	....	....	....	....	....	....	....	....	....	....	....	....	....
	Colorado	**NHL**	6	0	0	0	4	0	0	0	6	0.0	-3	25	36.0	10:22	....	....	....	....	....	....	....	....	....
2013-14	Lake Erie	AHL	49	5	15	20	56	....	....	....	....	....	....	....	....	....	....	....	....	....	....	....	....	....	....
2014-15	**Colorado**	**NHL**	3	0	1	1	10	0	0	0	2	0.0	0	20	45.0	7:06	....	....	....	....	....	....	....	....	....
	Lake Erie	AHL	40	4	19	23	35	....	....	....	....	....	....	....	....	....	....	....	....	....	....	....	....	....	....
	Norfolk Admirals	AHL	20	6	9	15	29	....	....	....	....	....	....	....	....	....	....	....	....	....	....	....	....	....	....
	NHL Totals		9	0	1	1	14	0	0	0	8	0.0		45	40.0	9:16	....	....	....	....	....	....	....	....	....

OHL First All-Star Team (2012)

Signed as a free agent by **San Jose**, September 20, 2010. Traded to **Colorado** by **San Jose** with Jamie McGinn and Mike Connolly for T.J. Galiardi, Daniel Winnik and Anaheim's 7th round choice (previously acquired, San Jose selected Emil Galimov) in 2013 Entry Draft, February 27, 2012. Traded to **Anaheim** by **Colorado** for Mat Clark, March 2, 2015.

SHARP, Patrick (SHAHRP, PAT-rihk) DAL

Left wing. Shoots right. 6'1", 199 lbs. Born, Winnipeg, MB, December 27, 1981. Philadelphia's 2nd choice, 95th overall, in 2001 Entry Draft.

Season	Club	League	GP	G	A	Pts	PIM	PP	SH	GW	S	S%	+/-	TF	F%	Min	GP	G	A	Pts	PIM	PP	SH	GW	Min
1997-98	Kanata Valley	ON-Jr.A	54	11	23	34	22	....	....	....	....	....	....	....	....	....	7	0	5	5	0	....	....	....	....
1998-99	Thunder Bay	USHL	55	19	24	43	48	....	....	....	....	....	....	....	....	....	3	1	1	2	0	....	....	....	....
99-2000	Thunder Bay	USHL	56	20	35	55	41	....	....	....	....	....	....	....	....	....	....	....	....	....	....	....	....	....	....
2000-01	U. of Vermont	ECAC	34	12	15	27	36	....	....	....	....	....	....	....	....	....	....	....	....	....	....	....	....	....	....
2001-02	U. of Vermont	ECAC	31	13	13	26	50	....	....	....	....	....	....	....	....	....	....	....	....	....	....	....	....	....	....
2002-03	**Philadelphia**	**NHL**	3	0	0	0	2	0	0	0	3	0.0	0	7	42.9	5:59	....	....	....	....	....	....	....	....	....
	Philadelphia	AHL	53	14	19	33	39	....	....	....	....	....	....	....	....	....	....	....	....	....	....	....	....	....	....
2003-04	**Philadelphia**	**NHL**	41	5	2	7	55	0	0	1	44	11.4	-3	272	46.7	9:56	12	1	0	1	2	0	0	0	6:12
	Philadelphia	AHL	35	15	14	29	45	....	....	....	....	....	....	....	....	....	1	2	0	2	0	....	....	....	....
2004-05	Philadelphia	AHL	75	23	29	52	80	....	....	....	....	....	....	....	....	....	21	8	13	*21	20	....	....	....	....
2005-06	**Philadelphia**	**NHL**	22	5	3	8	10	1	0	3	33	15.2	4	38	52.6	7:43	....	....	....	....	....	....	....	....	....
	Chicago	**NHL**	50	9	14	23	36	0	1	2	111	8.1	1	664	48.0	16:19	....	....	....	....	....	....	....	....	....
2006-07	**Chicago**	**NHL**	80	20	15	35	74	5	3	1	160	12.5	-15	1008	46.5	17:04	....	....	....	....	....	....	....	....	....
2007-08	**Chicago**	**NHL**	80	36	26	62	55	9	*7	7	209	17.2	23	594	51.4	18:47	....	....	....	....	....	....	....	....	....
2008-09	**Chicago**	**NHL**	61	26	18	44	41	9	0	4	184	14.1	6	566	45.8	17:57	17	7	4	11	6	3	0	2	16:17
2009-10♦	**Chicago**	**NHL**	82	25	41	66	28	4	2	4	266	9.4	24	466	51.7	18:07	22	11	11	22	16	3	1	1	17:52
2010-11	**Chicago**	**NHL**	74	34	37	71	38	12	2	6	268	12.7	-1	508	48.0	19:25	7	3	2	5	2	3	0	0	18:55
2011-12	**Chicago**	**NHL**	74	33	36	69	38	7	1	8	282	11.7	28	291	47.8	19:54	6	1	0	1	4	0	0	0	20:18
2012-13♦	**Chicago**	**NHL**	28	6	14	20	14	1	0	1	88	6.8	8	62	64.5	18:50	23	*10	6	16	8	2	0	2	18:15
2013-14	**Chicago**	**NHL**	82	34	44	78	40	10	0	3	313	10.9	13	152	54.6	18:53	19	5	5	10	6	1	0	0	18:35
	Canada	Olympics	5	1	0	1	4	....	....	....	....	....	....	....	....	....	....	....	....	....	....	....	....	....	....
2014-15♦	**Chicago**	**NHL**	68	16	27	43	33	8	0	2	230	7.0	-8	108	49.1	16:49	23	5	10	15	8	1	0	0	15:35
	NHL Totals		745	249	277	526	464	66	16	42	2191	11.4		4736	48.6	17:26	129	43	38	81	52	13	1	5	16:31

Played in NHL All-Star Game (2011)

Traded to **Chicago** by **Philadelphia** with Eric Meloche for Matt Ellison and Chicago's 3rd round choice (later traded to Montreal - Montreal selected Ryan White) in 2006 Entry Draft, December 5, 2005. Traded to **Dallas** by **Chicago** with Stephen Johns for Trevor Daley and Ryan Garbutt, July 12, 2015.

SHATTENKIRK, Kevin (SHAH-tehn-kuhrk, KEH-vihn) ST.L.

Defense. Shoots right. 5'11", 207 lbs. Born, New Rochelle, NY, January 29, 1989. Colorado's 1st choice, 14th overall, in 2007 Entry Draft.

Season	Club	League	GP	G	A	Pts	PIM	PP	SH	GW	S	S%	+/-	TF	F%	Min	GP	G	A	Pts	PIM	PP	SH	GW	Min
2004-05	Brunswick Bruins	High-CT	22	10	18	28	....	....	....	....	....	....	....	....	....	....	....	....	....	....	....	....	....	....	....
2005-06	USNTDP	U-17	13	4	4	8	4	....	....	....	....	....	....	....	....	....	....	....	....	....	....	....	....	....	....
	USNTDP	NAHL	28	6	9	15	17	....	....	....	....	....	....	....	....	....	12	3	7	10	10	....	....	....	....
2006-07	USNTDP	U-18	43	8	19	27	36	....	....	....	....	....	....	....	....	....	....	....	....	....	....	....	....	....	....
	USNTDP	NAHL	14	5	8	13	26	....	....	....	....	....	....	....	....	....	....	....	....	....	....	....	....	....	....
2007-08	Boston University	H-East	40	4	17	21	38	....	....	....	....	....	....	....	....	....	....	....	....	....	....	....	....	....	....
2008-09	Boston University	H-East	43	7	21	28	40	....	....	....	....	....	....	....	....	....	....	....	....	....	....	....	....	....	....
2009-10	Boston University	H-East	38	7	22	29	38	....	....	....	....	....	....	....	....	....	....	....	....	....	....	....	....	....	....
	Lake Erie	AHL	3	0	2	2	0	....	....	....	....	....	....	....	....	....	....	....	....	....	....	....	....	....	....
2010-11	**Colorado**	**NHL**	46	7	19	26	20	2	0	1	67	10.4	-11	0	0.0	19:50	....	....	....	....	....	....	....	....	....
	Lake Erie	AHL	10	0	0	0	10	....	....	....	....	....	....	....	....	....	....	....	....	....	....	....	....	....	....
	St. Louis	**NHL**	26	2	15	17	16	1	0	1	41	4.9	7	0	0.0	19:51	....	....	....	....	....	....	....	....	....
2011-12	**St. Louis**	**NHL**	81	9	34	43	60	5	0	2	178	5.1	20	4	25.0	21:36	9	1	1	2	6	0	0	0	21:26
2012-13	TPS Turku	Finland	12	2	4	6	22	....	....	....	....	....	....	....	....	....	....	....	....	....	....	....	....	....	....
	St. Louis	**NHL**	48	5	18	23	20	2	0	0	84	6.0	2	0	0.0	21:18	6	0	2	2	6	0	0	0	18:38
2013-14	**St. Louis**	**NHL**	81	10	35	45	38	7	0	5	188	5.3	1	0	0.0	20:34	6	1	4	5	2	0	0	0	25:39
	United States	Olympics	6	0	3	3	0	....	....	....	....	....	....	....	....	....	....	....	....	....	....	....	....	....	....
2014-15	**St. Louis**	**NHL**	56	8	36	44	52	4	0	1	135	5.9	19	0	0.0	22:34	6	0	8	8	2	0	0	0	22:55
	NHL Totals		338	41	157	198	206	21	0	10	693	5.9		4	25.0	21:06	27	2	15	17	16	0	0	0	22:05

Hockey East All-Rookie Team (2008) • Hockey East Second All-Star Team (2009) • NCAA East Second All-American Team (2009)

Played in NHL All-Star Game (2015)

Traded to **St. Louis** by **Colorado** with Chris Stewart and Colorado's 2nd round choice (Ty Rattie) in 2011 Entry Draft for Erik Johnson, Jay McClement and St. Louis' 1st round choice (Duncan Siemens) in 2011 Entry Draft, February 18, 2011. Signed as a free agent by **TPS Turku** (Finland), November 24, 2012.

SHAW, Andrew (SHAW, AN-droo) CHI

Center. Shoots right. 5'11", 179 lbs. Born, Belleville, ON, July 20, 1991. Chicago's 8th choice, 139th overall, in 2011 Entry Draft.

			Regular Season														Playoffs								
Season	Club	League	GP	G	A	Pts	PIM	PP	SH	GW	S	S%	+/-	TF	F%	Min	GP	G	A	Pts	PIM	PP	SH	GW	Min
2006-07	Quinte Red Devils	Minor-ON	32	24	27	51	88	....	....	....	....	....	....	....	....	....	3	1	2	3	....	....	....	....	....
	Quinte Red Devils	Other	18	14	18	32	....	....	....	....	....	....	....	....	....	....	....	....	....	....	....	....	....	....	....
2007-08	Quinte Red Devils	Minor-ON	STATISTICS NOT AVAILABLE																						
2008-09	Niagara Ice Dogs	OHL	56	8	9	17	97	....	....	....	....	....	....	....	....	....	12	2	1	3	22	....	....	....	....
2009-10	Niagara Ice Dogs	OHL	68	11	25	36	129	....	....	....	....	....	....	....	....	....	5	0	0	0	4	....	....	....	....
2010-11	Owen Sound	OHL	66	22	32	54	135	....	....	....	....	....	....	....	....	....	20	10	7	17	*53	....	....	....	....
2011-12	**Chicago**	**NHL**	**37**	**12**	**11**	**23**	**50**	**0**	**0**	**2**	**74**	**16.2**	**-1**	**88**	**46.6**	**15:12**	**3**	**0**	**0**	**0**	**15**	**0**	**0**	**0**	**13:55**
	Rockford IceHogs	AHL	38	12	11	23	99	....	....	....	....	....	....	....	....	....	....	....	....	....	....	....	....	....	....
2012-13	Rockford IceHogs	AHL	28	8	6	14	84	....	....	....	....	....	....	....	....	....	....	....	....	....	....	....	....	....	....
	♦ Chicago	**NHL**	**48**	**9**	**6**	**15**	**38**	**2**	**0**	**2**	**64**	**14.1**	**6**	**457**	**44.0**	**15:03**	**23**	**5**	**4**	**9**	**35**	**1**	**0**	**2**	**14:49**
2013-14	**Chicago**	**NHL**	**80**	**20**	**19**	**39**	**76**	**5**	**0**	**2**	**149**	**13.4**	**12**	**684**	**43.3**	**15:41**	**12**	**2**	**6**	**8**	**12**	**1**	**0**	**0**	**17:06**
2014-15♦	**Chicago**	**NHL**	**79**	**15**	**11**	**26**	**67**	**5**	**0**	**2**	**146**	**10.3**	**-8**	**712**	**50.1**	**14:57**	**23**	**5**	**7**	**12**	**36**	**2**	**0**	**0**	**15:33**
	NHL Totals		**244**	**56**	**47**	**103**	**231**	**12**	**0**	**8**	**433**	**12.9**		**1941**	**46.1**	**15:15**	**61**	**12**	**17**	**29**	**98**	**4**	**0**	**2**	**15:30**

Memorial Cup All-Star Team (2011) • Ed Chynoweth Trophy (Memorial Cup – Leading Scorer) (2011)

SHEAHAN, Riley (SHEE-huhn, RIGH-lee) DET

Center. Shoots left. 6'3", 222 lbs. Born, St. Catharines, ON, December 7, 1991. Detroit's 1st choice, 21st overall, in 2010 Entry Draft.

			Regular Season														Playoffs								
Season	Club	League	GP	G	A	Pts	PIM	PP	SH	GW	S	S%	+/-	TF	F%	Min	GP	G	A	Pts	PIM	PP	SH	GW	Min
2007-08	St. Catharines	ON-Jr.B	45	22	39	61	39	....	....	....	....	....	....	....	....	....	16	5	10	15	14	....	....	....	....
2008-09	St. Catharines	ON-Jr.B	40	27	46	73	55	....	....	....	....	....	....	....	....	....	11	8	5	13	30	....	....	....	....
2009-10	U. of Notre Dame	CCHA	37	6	11	17	22	....	....	....	....	....	....	....	....	....	....	....	....	....	....	....	....	....	....
2010-11	U. of Notre Dame	CCHA	40	5	17	22	28	....	....	....	....	....	....	....	....	....	....	....	....	....	....	....	....	....	....
2011-12	U. of Notre Dame	CCHA	37	9	16	25	24	....	....	....	....	....	....	....	....	....	....	....	....	....	....	....	....	....	....
	Detroit	**NHL**	**1**	**0**	**0**	**0**	**4**	**0**	**0**	**0**	**3**	**0.0**	**0**	**0**	**0.0**	**6:03**	....	....	....	....	....	....	....	....	....
	Grand Rapids	AHL	7	1	1	2	0	....	....	....	....	....	....	....	....	....	....	....	....	....	....	....	....	....	....
2012-13	Grand Rapids	AHL	72	16	20	36	33	....	....	....	....	....	....	....	....	....	24	3	13	16	10	....	....	....	....
	Detroit	**NHL**	**1**	**0**	**0**	**0**	**0**	**0**	**0**	**0**	**1**	**0.0**	**0**	**1**	**0.0**	**6:47**	....	....	....	....	....	....	....	....	....
2013-14	**Detroit**	**NHL**	**42**	**9**	**15**	**24**	**6**	**2**	**0**	**1**	**59**	**15.3**	**8**	**512**	**49.0**	**14:27**	**5**	**0**	**0**	**0**	**0**	**0**	**0**	**0**	**14:24**
	Grand Rapids	AHL	31	8	10	18	12	....	....	....	....	....	....	....	....	....	8	1	4	5	0	....	....	....	....
2014-15	**Detroit**	**NHL**	**79**	**13**	**23**	**36**	**16**	**5**	**0**	**0**	**123**	**10.6**	**-3**	**970**	**49.9**	**15:39**	**7**	**2**	**1**	**3**	**2**	**2**	**0**	**1**	**14:08**
	NHL Totals		**123**	**22**	**38**	**60**	**26**	**7**	**0**	**1**	**186**	**11.8**		**1483**	**49.6**	**15:05**	**12**	**2**	**1**	**3**	**2**	**2**	**0**	**1**	**14:15**

SHEPPARD, James (sheh-PUHRD, JAYMZ)

Center. Shoots left. 6'1", 215 lbs. Born, Halifax, NS, April 25, 1988. Minnesota's 1st choice, 9th overall, in 2006 Entry Draft.

			Regular Season														Playoffs								
Season	Club	League	GP	G	A	Pts	PIM	PP	SH	GW	S	S%	+/-	TF	F%	Min	GP	G	A	Pts	PIM	PP	SH	GW	Min
2003-04	Dartmouth	NSMHL	61	38	54	92	46	....	....	....	....	....	....	....	....	....	....	....	....	....	....	....	....	....	....
2004-05	Cape Breton	QMJHL	65	14	31	45	40	....	....	....	....	....	....	....	....	....	5	1	3	4	2	....	....	....	....
2005-06	Cape Breton	QMJHL	66	30	54	84	78	....	....	....	....	....	....	....	....	....	9	2	5	7	12	....	....	....	....
2006-07	Cape Breton	QMJHL	56	33	63	96	62	....	....	....	....	....	....	....	....	....	16	8	12	20	14	....	....	....	....
2007-08	**Minnesota**	**NHL**	**78**	**4**	**15**	**19**	**29**	**0**	**0**	**1**	**57**	**7.0**	**0**	**655**	**41.5**	**10:37**	**6**	**0**	**1**	**1**	**4**	**0**	**0**	**0**	**10:37**
2008-09	**Minnesota**	**NHL**	**82**	**5**	**19**	**24**	**41**	**0**	**0**	**1**	**88**	**5.7**	**-14**	**870**	**41.5**	**15:11**	....	....	....	....	....	....	....	....	....
2009-10	**Minnesota**	**NHL**	**64**	**2**	**4**	**6**	**38**	**0**	**0**	**0**	**64**	**3.1**	**-14**	**343**	**45.2**	**11:59**	....	....	....	....	....	....	....	....	....
2010-11			DID NOT PLAY – INJURED																						
2011-12	Worcester Sharks	AHL	4	0	0	0	2	....	....	....	....	....	....	....	....	....	....	....	....	....	....	....	....	....	....
2012-13	Worcester Sharks	AHL	34	8	15	23	52	....	....	....	....	....	....	....	....	....	....	....	....	....	....	....	....	....	....
	San Jose	**NHL**	**32**	**1**	**3**	**4**	**12**	**0**	**0**	**1**	**40**	**2.5**	**-9**	**6**	**33.3**	**11:45**	**11**	**0**	**0**	**0**	**4**	**0**	**0**	**0**	**10:28**
2013-14	**San Jose**	**NHL**	**67**	**4**	**16**	**20**	**35**	**0**	**0**	**0**	**84**	**4.8**	**3**	**233**	**45.1**	**12:10**	**7**	**2**	**4**	**6**	**6**	**0**	**0**	**0**	**12:19**
2014-15	**San Jose**	**NHL**	**57**	**5**	**11**	**16**	**28**	**0**	**0**	**0**	**68**	**7.4**	**-3**	**534**	**50.0**	**13:43**	....	....	....	....	....	....	....	....	....
	Worcester Sharks	AHL	2	0	1	1	0	....	....	....	....	....	....	....	....	....	....	....	....	....	....	....	....	....	....
	NY Rangers	**NHL**	**14**	**2**	**0**	**2**	**9**	**0**	**0**	**1**	**11**	**18.2**	**-1**	**21**	**52.4**	**11:22**	**13**	**1**	**1**	**2**	**8**	**0**	**0**	**1**	**8:55**
	NHL Totals		**394**	**23**	**68**	**91**	**192**	**0**	**0**	**4**	**412**	**5.6**		**2662**	**44.1**	**12:37**	**37**	**3**	**6**	**9**	**22**	**0**	**0**	**1**	**10:18**

QMJHL Second All-Star Team (2007)

• Missed 2010-11 and majority of 2011-12 due to off-season knee injury, September 4, 2010. Traded to **San Jose** by **Minnesota** for San Jose's 3rd round choice (Kurtis Gabriel) in 2013 Entry Draft, August 7, 2011. Traded to **NY Rangers** by **San Jose** for a 4th round choice in 2016 Entry Draft, March 1, 2015.

SHINNIMIN, Brendan (SHIHN-ih-mihm, BREHN-duhn) ARI

Center. Shoots left. 5'10", 185 lbs. Born, Winnipeg, MB, January 7, 1991.

			Regular Season														Playoffs								
Season	Club	League	GP	G	A	Pts	PIM	PP	SH	GW	S	S%	+/-	TF	F%	Min	GP	G	A	Pts	PIM	PP	SH	GW	Min
2007-08	Selkirk Steelers	MJHL	51	7	19	26	38	....	....	....	....	....	....	....	....	....	....	....	....	....	....	....	....	....	....
	Tri-City	WHL	4	0	0	0	0	....	....	....	....	....	....	....	....	....	....	....	....	....	....	....	....	....	....
2008-09	Tri-City	WHL	64	12	13	25	69	....	....	....	....	....	....	....	....	....	11	0	5	5	16	....	....	....	....
2009-10	Tri-City	WHL	70	27	55	82	82	....	....	....	....	....	....	....	....	....	22	8	17	25	29	....	....	....	....
2010-11	Tri-City	WHL	60	34	62	96	84	....	....	....	....	....	....	....	....	....	10	4	7	11	16	....	....	....	....
2011-12	Tri-City	WHL	69	58	76	*134	82	....	....	....	....	....	....	....	....	....	15	7	16	23	28	....	....	....	....
2012-13	Portland Pirates	AHL	74	12	21	33	77	....	....	....	....	....	....	....	....	....	1	0	1	1	0	....	....	....	....
2013-14	Portland Pirates	AHL	52	13	15	28	31	....	....	....	....	....	....	....	....	....	....	....	....	....	....	....	....	....	....
2014-15	**Arizona**	**NHL**	**12**	**0**	**1**	**1**	**8**	**0**	**0**	**0**	**10**	**0.0**	**-1**	**101**	**41.6**	**11:02**	....	....	....	....	....	....	....	....	....
	Portland Pirates	AHL	64	22	25	47	80	....	....	....	....	....	....	....	....	....	5	2	4	6	8	....	....	....	....
	NHL Totals		**12**	**0**	**1**	**1**	**8**	**0**	**0**	**0**	**10**	**0.0**		**101**	**41.6**	**11:02**	....	....	....	....	....	....	....	....	....

WHL West Second All-Star Team (2011) • WHL West First All-Star Team (2012) • WHL Player of the Year (2012) • Canadian Major Junior Player of the Year (2012)

Signed as a free agent by **Phoenix**, March 2, 2012.

SHORE, Drew (SHOHR, DROO) CGY

Center. Shoots right. 6'3", 205 lbs. Born, Denver, CO, January 29, 1991. Florida's 2nd choice, 44th overall, in 2009 Entry Draft.

			Regular Season														Playoffs								
Season	Club	League	GP	G	A	Pts	PIM	PP	SH	GW	S	S%	+/-	TF	F%	Min	GP	G	A	Pts	PIM	PP	SH	GW	Min
2006-07	Det. Honeybaked	MWEHL	31	9	25	34	20	....	....	....	....	....	....	....	....	....	....	....	....	....	....	....	....	....	....
	Det. Honeybaked	Other	34	17	23	40	....	....	....	....	....	....	....	....	....	....	....	....	....	....	....	....	....	....	....
2007-08	USNTDP	NAHL	35	9	16	25	12	....	....	....	....	....	....	....	....	....	3	0	1	1	0	....	....	....	....
	USNTDP	U-17	16	4	8	12	6	....	....	....	....	....	....	....	....	....	....	....	....	....	....	....	....	....	....
2008-09	USNTDP	NAHL	15	7	7	14	16	....	....	....	....	....	....	....	....	....	....	....	....	....	....	....	....	....	....
	USNTDP	U-18	47	10	25	35	30	....	....	....	....	....	....	....	....	....	....	....	....	....	....	....	....	....	....
2009-10	U. of Denver	WCHA	41	5	14	19	18	....	....	....	....	....	....	....	....	....	....	....	....	....	....	....	....	....	....
2010-11	U. of Denver	WCHA	40	23	23	46	38	....	....	....	....	....	....	....	....	....	....	....	....	....	....	....	....	....	....
2011-12	U. of Denver	WCHA	42	22	31	53	45	....	....	....	....	....	....	....	....	....	....	....	....	....	....	....	....	....	....
	San Antonio	AHL	8	1	2	3	4	....	....	....	....	....	....	....	....	....	9	2	0	2	2	....	....	....	....
2012-13	San Antonio	AHL	41	10	20	30	18	....	....	....	....	....	....	....	....	....	....	....	....	....	....	....	....	....	....
	Florida	**NHL**	**43**	**3**	**10**	**13**	**14**	**1**	**1**	**1**	**96**	**3.1**	**-10**	**443**	**47.9**	**15:48**	....	....	....	....	....	....	....	....	....
2013-14	**Florida**	**NHL**	**24**	**5**	**2**	**7**	**8**	**1**	**1**	**1**	**23**	**21.7**	**-1**	**208**	**41.4**	**12:00**	....	....	....	....	....	....	....	....	....
	San Antonio	AHL	50	6	26	32	25	....	....	....	....	....	....	....	....	....	....	....	....	....	....	....	....	....	....
2014-15	**Calgary**	**NHL**	**11**	**1**	**2**	**3**	**0**	**0**	**0**	**0**	**13**	**7.7**	**-5**	**59**	**49.2**	**10:40**	**1**	**0**	**0**	**0**	**2**	**0**	**0**	**0**	**14:17**
	San Antonio	AHL	35	9	21	30	16	....	....	....	....	....	....	....	....	....	....	....	....	....	....	....	....	....	....
	Adirondack	AHL	12	3	4	7	8	....	....	....	....	....	....	....	....	....	....	....	....	....	....	....	....	....	....
	NHL Totals		**78**	**9**	**14**	**23**	**22**	**2**	**2**	**2**	**132**	**6.8**		**710**	**46.1**	**13:55**	**1**	**0**	**0**	**0**	**2**	**0**	**0**	**0**	**14:17**

WCHA Second All-Star Team (2011, 2012

Traded to **Calgary** by **Florida** for Corban Knight, January 9, 2015.

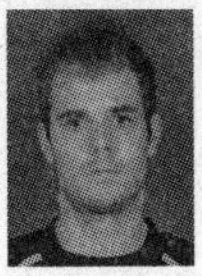

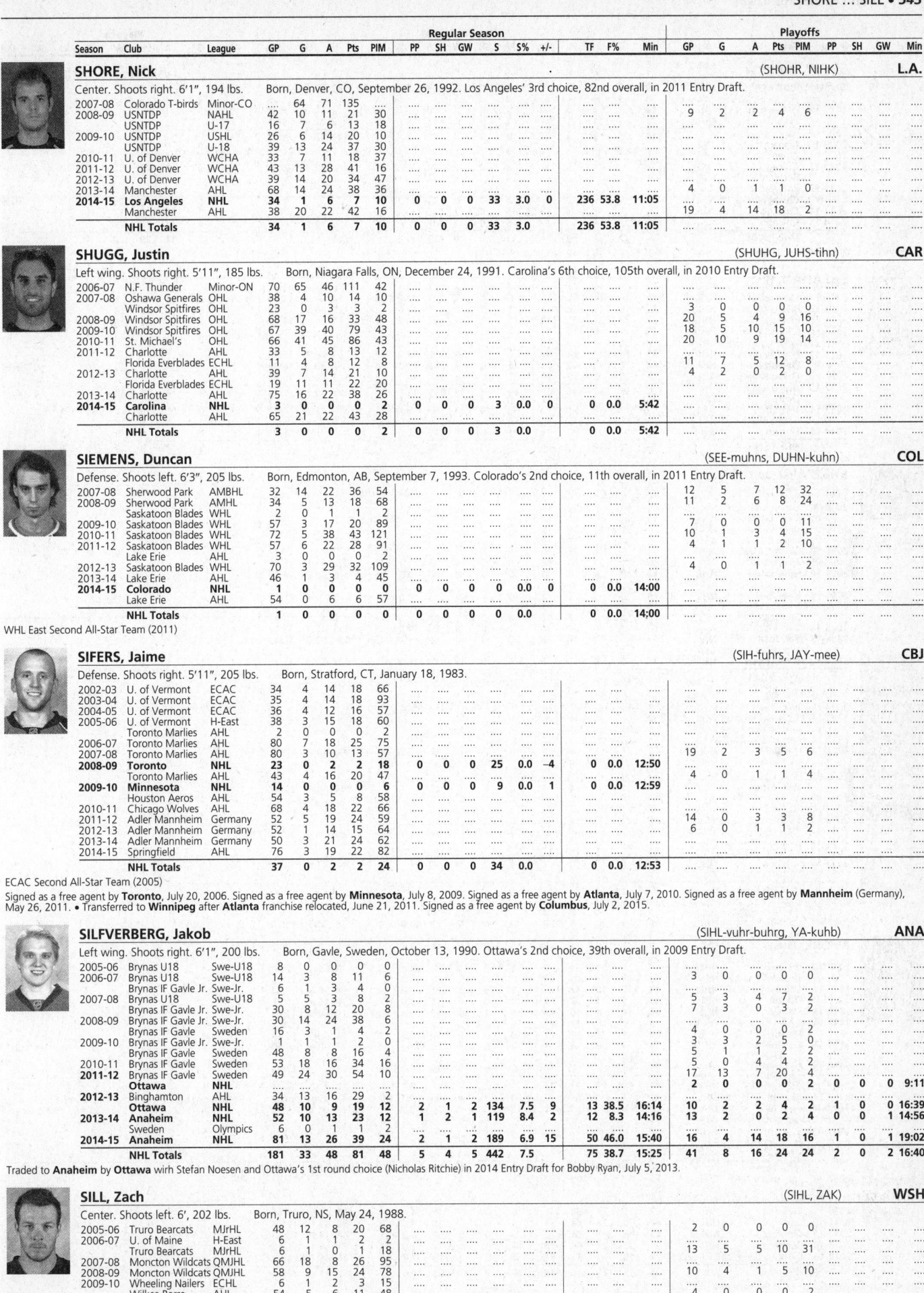

SHORE, Nick — (SHOHR, NIHK) — L.A.

Center. Shoots right. 6'1", 194 lbs. Born, Denver, CO, September 26, 1992. Los Angeles' 3rd choice, 82nd overall, in 2011 Entry Draft.

Season	Club	League	GP	G	A	Pts	PIM	PP	SH	GW	S	S%	+/-	TF	F%	Min	GP	G	A	Pts	PIM	PP	SH	GW	Min
			Regular Season														Playoffs								
2007-08	Colorado T-birds	Minor-CO		64	71	135																			
2008-09	USNTDP	NAHL	42	10	11	21	30										9	2	2	4	6				
	USNTDP	U-17	16	7	6	13	18																		
2009-10	USNTDP	USHL	26	6	14	20	10																		
	USNTDP	U-18	39	13	24	37	30																		
2010-11	U. of Denver	WCHA	33	7	11	18	37																		
2011-12	U. of Denver	WCHA	43	13	28	41	16																		
2012-13	U. of Denver	WCHA	39	14	20	34	47																		
2013-14	Manchester	AHL	68	14	24	38	36										4	0	1	1	0				
2014-15	**Los Angeles**	**NHL**	**34**	**1**	**6**	**7**	**10**	**0**	**0**	**0**	**33**	**3.0**	**0**	**236**	**53.8**	**11:05**									
	Manchester	AHL	38	20	22	42	16										19	4	14	18	2				
	NHL Totals		**34**	**1**	**6**	**7**	**10**	**0**	**0**	**0**	**33**	**3.0**		**236**	**53.8**	**11:05**									

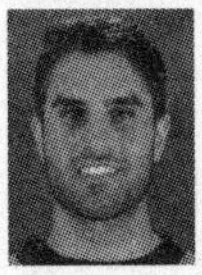

SHUGG, Justin — (SHUHG, JUHS-tihn) — CAR

Left wing. Shoots right. 5'11", 185 lbs. Born, Niagara Falls, ON, December 24, 1991. Carolina's 6th choice, 105th overall, in 2010 Entry Draft.

Season	Club	League	GP	G	A	Pts	PIM	PP	SH	GW	S	S%	+/-	TF	F%	Min	GP	G	A	Pts	PIM	PP	SH	GW	Min
2006-07	N.F. Thunder	Minor-ON	70	65	46	111	42																		
2007-08	Oshawa Generals	OHL	38	4	10	14	10																		
	Windsor Spitfires	OHL	23	0	3	3	2										3	0	0	0	0				
2008-09	Windsor Spitfires	OHL	68	17	16	33	48										20	5	4	9	16				
2009-10	Windsor Spitfires	OHL	67	39	40	79	43										18	5	10	15	10				
2010-11	St. Michael's	OHL	66	41	45	86	43										20	10	9	19	14				
2011-12	Charlotte	AHL	33	5	8	13	12																		
	Florida Everblades	ECHL	11	4	8	12	8										11	7	5	12	8				
2012-13	Charlotte	AHL	39	7	14	21	10										4	2	0	2	0				
	Florida Everblades	ECHL	19	11	11	22	20																		
2013-14	Charlotte	AHL	75	16	22	38	26																		
2014-15	**Carolina**	**NHL**	**3**	**0**	**0**	**0**	**2**	**0**	**0**	**0**	**3**	**0.0**	**0**	**0**	**0.0**	**5:42**									
	Charlotte	AHL	65	21	22	43	28																		
	NHL Totals		**3**	**0**	**0**	**0**	**2**	**0**	**0**	**0**	**3**	**0.0**		**0**	**0.0**	**5:42**									

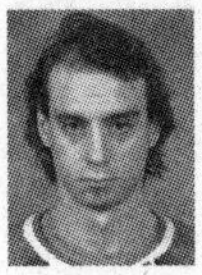

SIEMENS, Duncan — (SEE-muhns, DUHN-kuhn) — COL

Defense. Shoots left. 6'3", 205 lbs. Born, Edmonton, AB, September 7, 1993. Colorado's 2nd choice, 11th overall, in 2011 Entry Draft.

Season	Club	League	GP	G	A	Pts	PIM	PP	SH	GW	S	S%	+/-	TF	F%	Min	GP	G	A	Pts	PIM	PP	SH	GW	Min
2007-08	Sherwood Park	AMBHL	32	14	22	36	54										12	5	7	12	32				
2008-09	Sherwood Park	AMHL	34	5	13	18	68										11	2	6	8	24				
	Saskatoon Blades	WHL	2	0	1	1	2																		
2009-10	Saskatoon Blades	WHL	57	3	17	20	89										7	0	0	0	11				
2010-11	Saskatoon Blades	WHL	72	5	38	43	121										10	1	3	4	15				
2011-12	Saskatoon Blades	WHL	57	6	22	28	91										4	1	1	2	10				
	Lake Erie	AHL	3	0	0	0	2																		
2012-13	Saskatoon Blades	WHL	70	3	29	32	109										4	0	1	1	2				
2013-14	Lake Erie	AHL	46	1	3	4	45																		
2014-15	**Colorado**	**NHL**	**1**	**0**	**0**	**0**	**0**	**0**	**0**	**0**	**0**	**0.0**	**0**	**0**	**0.0**	**14:00**									
	Lake Erie	AHL	54	0	6	6	57																		
	NHL Totals		**1**	**0**	**0**	**0**	**0**	**0**	**0**	**0**	**0**	**0.0**		**0**	**0.0**	**14:00**									

WHL East Second All-Star Team (2011)

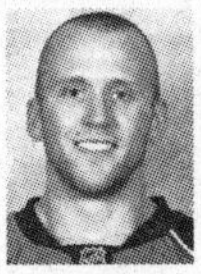

SIFERS, Jaime — (SIH-fuhrs, JAY-mee) — CBJ

Defense. Shoots right. 5'11", 205 lbs. Born, Stratford, CT, January 18, 1983.

Season	Club	League	GP	G	A	Pts	PIM	PP	SH	GW	S	S%	+/-	TF	F%	Min	GP	G	A	Pts	PIM	PP	SH	GW	Min
2002-03	U. of Vermont	ECAC	34	4	14	18	66																		
2003-04	U. of Vermont	ECAC	35	4	14	18	93																		
2004-05	U. of Vermont	ECAC	36	4	12	16	57																		
2005-06	U. of Vermont	H-East	38	3	15	18	60																		
	Toronto Marlies	AHL	2	0	0	0	2																		
2006-07	Toronto Marlies	AHL	80	7	18	25	75																		
2007-08	Toronto Marlies	AHL	80	3	10	13	57										19	2	3	5	6				
2008-09	**Toronto**	**NHL**	**23**	**0**	**2**	**2**	**18**	**0**	**0**	**0**	**25**	**0.0**	**–4**	**0**	**0.0**	**12:50**									
	Toronto Marlies	AHL	43	4	16	20	47										4	0	1	1	4				
2009-10	**Minnesota**	**NHL**	**14**	**0**	**0**	**0**	**6**	**0**	**0**	**0**	**9**	**0.0**	**1**	**0**	**0.0**	**12:59**									
	Houston Aeros	AHL	54	3	5	8	58																		
2010-11	Chicago Wolves	AHL	68	4	18	22	66																		
2011-12	Adler Mannheim	Germany	52	5	19	24	59										14	0	3	3	8				
2012-13	Adler Mannheim	Germany	52	1	14	15	64										6	0	1	1	2				
2013-14	Adler Mannheim	Germany	50	3	21	24	62																		
2014-15	Springfield	AHL	76	3	19	22	82																		
	NHL Totals		**37**	**0**	**2**	**2**	**24**	**0**	**0**	**0**	**34**	**0.0**		**0**	**0.0**	**12:53**									

ECAC Second All-Star Team (2005)

Signed as a free agent by **Toronto**, July 20, 2006. Signed as a free agent by **Minnesota**, July 8, 2009. Signed as a free agent by **Atlanta**, July 7, 2010. Signed as a free agent by **Mannheim** (Germany), May 26, 2011. • Transferred to **Winnipeg** after **Atlanta** franchise relocated, June 21, 2011. Signed as a free agent by **Columbus**, July 2, 2015.

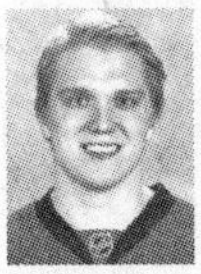

SILFVERBERG, Jakob — (SIHL-vuhr-buhrg, YA-kuhb) — ANA

Left wing. Shoots right. 6'1", 200 lbs. Born, Gavle, Sweden, October 13, 1990. Ottawa's 2nd choice, 39th overall, in 2009 Entry Draft.

Season	Club	League	GP	G	A	Pts	PIM	PP	SH	GW	S	S%	+/-	TF	F%	Min	GP	G	A	Pts	PIM	PP	SH	GW	Min
2005-06	Brynas U18	Swe-U18	8	0	0	0	0																		
2006-07	Brynas U18	Swe-U18	14	3	8	11	6										3	0	0	0	0				
	Brynas IF Gavle Jr.	Swe-Jr.	6	1	3	4	0																		
2007-08	Brynas U18	Swe-U18	5	5	3	8	2										5	3	4	7	2				
	Brynas IF Gavle Jr.	Swe-Jr.	30	8	12	20	8										7	3	0	3	2				
2008-09	Brynas IF Gavle Jr.	Swe-Jr.	30	14	24	38	6																		
	Brynas IF Gavle	Sweden	16	3	1	4	2										4	0	0	0	2				
2009-10	Brynas IF Gavle Jr.	Swe-Jr.	1	1	1	2	0										3	3	2	5	0				
	Brynas IF Gavle	Sweden	48	8	8	16	4										5	1	1	2	2				
2010-11	Brynas IF Gavle	Sweden	53	18	16	34	16										5	0	4	4	2				
2011-12	Brynas IF Gavle	Sweden	49	24	30	54	10										17	13	7	20	4				
	Ottawa	**NHL**															**2**	**0**	**0**	**0**	**2**	**0**	**0**	**0**	**9:11**
2012-13	Binghamton	AHL	34	13	16	29	2																		
	Ottawa	**NHL**	**48**	**10**	**9**	**19**	**12**	**2**	**1**	**2**	**134**	**7.5**	**9**	**13**	**38.5**	**16:14**	**10**	**2**	**2**	**4**	**2**	**1**	**0**	**0**	**16:39**
2013-14	**Anaheim**	**NHL**	**52**	**10**	**13**	**23**	**12**	**1**	**2**	**1**	**119**	**8.4**	**2**	**12**	**8.3**	**14:16**	**13**	**2**	**0**	**2**	**4**	**0**	**0**	**1**	**14:56**
	Sweden	Olympics	6	0	1	1	2																		
2014-15	**Anaheim**	**NHL**	**81**	**13**	**26**	**39**	**24**	**2**	**1**	**2**	**189**	**6.9**	**15**	**50**	**46.0**	**15:40**	**16**	**4**	**14**	**18**	**16**	**1**	**0**	**1**	**19:02**
	NHL Totals		**181**	**33**	**48**	**81**	**48**	**5**	**4**	**5**	**442**	**7.5**		**75**	**38.7**	**15:25**	**41**	**8**	**16**	**24**	**24**	**2**	**0**	**2**	**16:40**

Traded to **Anaheim** by **Ottawa** wirh Stefan Noesen and Ottawa's 1st round choice (Nicholas Ritchie) in 2014 Entry Draft for Bobby Ryan, July 5, 2013.

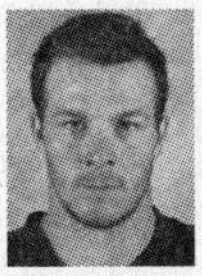

SILL, Zach — (SIHL, ZAK) — WSH

Center. Shoots left. 6', 202 lbs. Born, Truro, NS, May 24, 1988.

Season	Club	League	GP	G	A	Pts	PIM	PP	SH	GW	S	S%	+/-	TF	F%	Min	GP	G	A	Pts	PIM	PP	SH	GW	Min
2005-06	Truro Bearcats	MJrHL	48	12	8	20	68										2	0	0	0	0				
2006-07	U. of Maine	H-East	6	1	1	2	2																		
	Truro Bearcats	MJrHL	6	1	0	1	18										13	5	5	10	31				
2007-08	Moncton Wildcats	QMJHL	66	18	8	26	95																		
2008-09	Moncton Wildcats	QMJHL	58	9	15	24	78										10	4	1	5	10				
2009-10	Wheeling Nailers	ECHL	6	1	2	3	15																		
	Wilkes-Barre	AHL	54	5	6	11	48										4	0	0	0	2				
2010-11	Wilkes-Barre	AHL	80	11	19	30	85										12	1	2	3	6				

			Regular Season														Playoffs								
Season	Club	League	GP	G	A	Pts	PIM	PP	SH	GW	S	S%	+/-	TF	F%	Min	GP	G	A	Pts	PIM	PP	SH	GW	Min
2011-12	Wilkes-Barre	AHL	68	10	7	17	40	....	....	....	....	....	....	....	....	....	12	3	1	4	0	....	....	....	....
2012-13	Wilkes-Barre	AHL	57	4	5	9	108	....	....	....	....	....	....	....	....	....	15	2	2	4	6	....	....	....	....
2013-14	**Pittsburgh**	**NHL**	**20**	**0**	**0**	**0**	**12**	**0**	**0**	**0**	**14**	**0.0**	**–4**	**90**	**37.8**	**10:48**	....	....	....	....	....	....	....	....	....
	Wilkes-Barre	AHL	18	3	3	6	34	....	....	....	....	....	....	....	....	....	17	1	2	3	18	....	....	....	....
2014-15	**Pittsburgh**	**NHL**	**42**	**1**	**2**	**3**	**60**	**0**	**0**	**0**	**26**	**3.8**	**–3**	**1**	**0.0**	**8:18**	....	....	....	....	....	....	....	....	....
	Toronto	**NHL**	**21**	**0**	**1**	**1**	**24**	**0**	**0**	**0**	**17**	**0.0**	**–2**	**92**	**50.0**	**8:34**	....	....	....	....	....	....	....	....	....
	NHL Totals		**83**	**1**	**3**	**4**	**96**	**0**	**0**	**0**	**57**	**1.8**		**183**	**43.7**	**8:58**	....	....	....	....	....	....	....	....	....

Signed as a free agent by **Pittsburgh**, May 16, 2011. • Missed majority of 2013-14 due to wrist injury at Norfolk (AHL), January 25, 2014. Traded to **Toronto** by **Pittsburgh** with Pittsburgh's 4th round choice (later traded to Edmonton, later traded to Ottawa – Ottawa selected Christian Wolanin) in 2015 Entry Draft and Pittsburgh's 2nd round choice in 2016 Entry Draft for Daniel Winnik, February 25, 2015. Signed as a free agent by **Washington**, July 16, 2015.

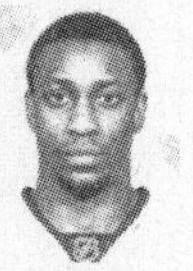

SIMMONDS, Wayne

(SIH-muhnds, WAYN) **PHI**

Right wing. Shoots right. 6'2", 185 lbs. Born, Scarborough, ON, August 26, 1988. Los Angeles' 3rd choice, 61st overall, in 2007 Entry Draft.

2004-05	Tor. Jr. Canadiens	GTHL	67	32	40	72	97	....	....	....	....	....	....	....	....	....	....	....	....	....	....	....	....	....	....
2005-06	Brockville Braves	ON-Jr.A	49	24	19	43	127	....	....	....	....	....	....	....	....	....	7	4	2	6	12	....	....	....	....
2006-07	Owen Sound	OHL	66	23	26	49	112	....	....	....	....	....	....	....	....	....	4	1	1	2	4	....	....	....	....
2007-08	Owen Sound	OHL	29	17	22	39	43	....	....	....	....	....	....	....	....	....	....	....	....	....	....	....	....	....	....
	Sault Ste. Marie	OHL	31	16	20	36	68	....	....	....	....	....	....	....	....	....	14	5	9	14	22	....	....	....	....
2008-09	**Los Angeles**	**NHL**	**82**	**9**	**14**	**23**	**73**	**2**	**0**	**2**	**127**	**7.1**	**–8**	**25**	**36.0**	**13:50**	....	....	....	....	....	....	....	....	....
2009-10	**Los Angeles**	**NHL**	**78**	**16**	**24**	**40**	**116**	**0**	**0**	**2**	**127**	**12.6**	**22**	**10**	**30.0**	**14:29**	**6**	**2**	**1**	**3**	**9**	**0**	**0**	**0**	**14:21**
2010-11	**Los Angeles**	**NHL**	**80**	**14**	**16**	**30**	**75**	**1**	**0**	**3**	**117**	**12.0**	**–2**	**19**	**36.8**	**13:27**	**6**	**1**	**2**	**3**	**20**	**0**	**0**	**0**	**14:44**
2011-12	**Philadelphia**	**NHL**	**82**	**28**	**21**	**49**	**114**	**11**	**0**	**4**	**197**	**14.2**	**–1**	**17**	**41.2**	**15:55**	**11**	**1**	**5**	**6**	**38**	**1**	**0**	**0**	**14:52**
2012-13	Crimmitschau	German-2	9	4	10	14	35	....	....	....	....	....	....	....	....	....	....	....	....	....	....	....	....	....	....
	Liberec	CzRep	6	4	2	6	16	....	....	....	....	....	....	....	....	....	....	....	....	....	....	....	....	....	....
	Philadelphia	**NHL**	**45**	**15**	**17**	**32**	**82**	**6**	**0**	**4**	**110**	**13.6**	**–7**	**3**	**66.7**	**15:38**	....	....	....	....	....	....	....	....	....
2013-14	**Philadelphia**	**NHL**	**82**	**29**	**31**	**60**	**106**	**15**	**0**	**4**	**209**	**13.9**	**–4**	**2**	**50.0**	**16:46**	**7**	**4**	**1**	**5**	**20**	**3**	**0**	**0**	**15:23**
2014-15	**Philadelphia**	**NHL**	**75**	**28**	**22**	**50**	**66**	**14**	**0**	**6**	**188**	**14.9**	**–5**	**5**	**80.0**	**16:48**	....	....	....	....	....	....	....	....	....
	NHL Totals		**524**	**139**	**145**	**284**	**632**	**49**	**0**	**25**	**1075**	**12.9**		**81**	**40.7**	**15:14**	**30**	**8**	**9**	**17**	**87**	**4**	**0**	**0**	**14:52**

Traded to **Philadelphia** by **Los Angeles** with Brayden Schenn and Los Angeles' 2nd round choice (later traded to Dallas – Dallas selected Devin Shore) in 2012 Entry Draft for Mike Richards and Rob Bordson, June 23, 2011. Signed as a free agent by **Crimmitschau** (German-2), September 24, 2012. Signed as a free agent by **Liberec** (CzRep), October 23, 2012.

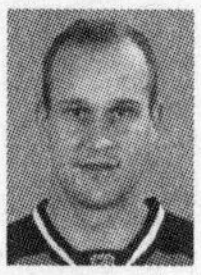

SISLO, Mike

(SIHS-loh, MIGHK) **N.J.**

Right wing. Shoots right. 5'11", 195 lbs. Born, Superior, WI, January 20, 1988.

2005-06	Green Bay	USHL	57	3	3	6	36	....	....	....	....	....	....	....	....	....	3	0	0	0	5	....	....	....	....
2006-07	Green Bay	USHL	60	23	26	49	28	....	....	....	....	....	....	....	....	....	4	3	1	4	2	....	....	....	....
2007-08	New Hampshire	H-East	38	3	5	8	12	....	....	....	....	....	....	....	....	....	....	....	....	....	....	....	....	....	....
2008-09	New Hampshire	H-East	38	19	12	31	12	....	....	....	....	....	....	....	....	....	....	....	....	....	....	....	....	....	....
2009-10	New Hampshire	H-East	39	14	15	29	20	....	....	....	....	....	....	....	....	....	....	....	....	....	....	....	....	....	....
2010-11	New Hampshire	H-East	39	15	*33	48	38	....	....	....	....	....	....	....	....	....	....	....	....	....	....	....	....	....	....
	Albany Devils	AHL	3	0	0	0	0	....	....	....	....	....	....	....	....	....	....	....	....	....	....	....	....	....	....
2011-12	Albany Devils	AHL	59	9	18	27	20	....	....	....	....	....	....	....	....	....	....	....	....	....	....	....	....	....	....
2012-13	Albany Devils	AHL	61	13	13	26	46	....	....	....	....	....	....	....	....	....	....	....	....	....	....	....	....	....	....
2013-14	**New Jersey**	**NHL**	**14**	**0**	**0**	**0**	**0**	**0**	**0**	**0**	**20**	**0.0**	**–1**	**6**	**83.3**	**8:51**	....	....	....	....	....	....	....	....	....
	Albany Devils	AHL	59	23	18	41	26	....	....	....	....	....	....	....	....	....	4	1	1	2	0	....	....	....	....
2014-15	**New Jersey**	**NHL**	**10**	**0**	**1**	**1**	**2**	**0**	**0**	**0**	**13**	**0.0**	**–2**	**0**	**0.0**	**12:13**	....	....	....	....	....	....	....	....	....
	Albany Devils	AHL	65	20	20	40	53	....	....	....	....	....	....	....	....	....	....	....	....	....	....	....	....	....	....
	NHL Totals		**24**	**0**	**1**	**1**	**2**	**0**	**0**	**0**	**33**	**0.0**		**6**	**83.3**	**10:15**	....	....	....	....	....	....	....	....	....

Signed as a free agent by **New Jersey**, April 6, 2011.

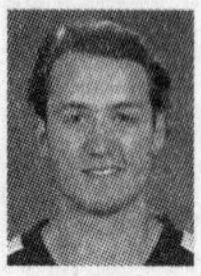

SISSONS, Colton

(SIH-suhnz, KOHL-tuhn) **NSH**

Center. Shoots right. 6'1", 187 lbs. Born, North Vancouver, BC, November 5, 1993. Nashville's 2nd choice, 50th overall, in 2012 Entry Draft.

2008-09	Van. NW Giants	BCMML	39	30	24	54	44	....	....	....	....	....	....	....	....	....	....	....	....	....	....	....	....	....	....
2009-10	Westside Warriors	BCHL	58	6	16	22	29	....	....	....	....	....	....	....	....	....	11	1	1	2	4	....	....	....	....
2010-11	Kelowna Rockets	WHL	63	17	24	41	46	....	....	....	....	....	....	....	....	....	10	3	3	6	6	....	....	....	....
2011-12	Kelowna Rockets	WHL	58	26	15	41	62	....	....	....	....	....	....	....	....	....	4	1	1	2	2	....	....	....	....
2012-13	Kelowna Rockets	WHL	61	28	39	67	54	....	....	....	....	....	....	....	....	....	....	....	....	....	....	....	....	....	....
2013-14	**Nashville**	**NHL**	**17**	**1**	**3**	**4**	**4**	**0**	**0**	**0**	**13**	**7.7**	**0**	**144**	**48.6**	**10:37**	....	....	....	....	....	....	....	....	....
	Milwaukee	AHL	62	25	19	44	8	....	....	....	....	....	....	....	....	....	3	0	1	1	2	....	....	....	....
2014-15	Milwaukee	AHL	76	25	17	42	27	....	....	....	....	....	....	....	....	....	....	....	....	....	....	....	....	....	....
	NHL Totals		**17**	**1**	**3**	**4**	**4**	**0**	**0**	**0**	**13**	**7.7**		**144**	**48.6**	**10:37**	....	....	....	....	....	....	....	....	....

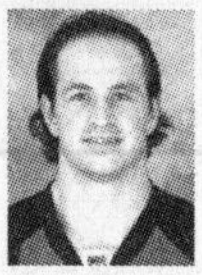

SKILLE, Jack

(SKIH-lee, JAK)

Right wing. Shoots right. 6'1", 219 lbs. Born, Madison, WI, May 19, 1987. Chicago's 1st choice, 7th overall, in 2005 Entry Draft.

2003-04	USNTDP	NAHL	28	11	9	20	31	....	....	....	....	....	....	....	....	....	....	....	....	....	....	....	....	....	....
	USNTDP	U-17	33	14	10	24	30	....	....	....	....	....	....	....	....	....	....	....	....	....	....	....	....	....	....
2004-05	USNTDP	NAHL	16	6	11	17	20	....	....	....	....	....	....	....	....	....	....	....	....	....	....	....	....	....	....
	USNTDP	U-18	26	9	11	20	36	....	....	....	....	....	....	....	....	....	....	....	....	....	....	....	....	....	....
2005-06	U. of Wisconsin	WCHA	41	13	8	21	37	....	....	....	....	....	....	....	....	....	....	....	....	....	....	....	....	....	....
2006-07	U. of Wisconsin	WCHA	26	8	10	18	12	....	....	....	....	....	....	....	....	....	....	....	....	....	....	....	....	....	....
	Norfolk Admirals	AHL	9	4	4	8	0	....	....	....	....	....	....	....	....	....	3	0	0	0	2	....	....	....	....
2007-08	**Chicago**	**NHL**	**16**	**3**	**2**	**5**	**0**	**0**	**0**	**0**	**23**	**13.0**	**1**	**4**	**50.0**	**11:59**	....	....	....	....	....	....	....	....	....
	Rockford IceHogs	AHL	59	16	18	34	44	....	....	....	....	....	....	....	....	....	12	2	1	3	6	....	....	....	....
2008-09	**Chicago**	**NHL**	**8**	**1**	**0**	**1**	**5**	**0**	**0**	**0**	**14**	**7.1**	**–3**	**0**	**0.0**	**9:26**	....	....	....	....	....	....	....	....	....
	Rockford IceHogs	AHL	58	20	25	45	56	....	....	....	....	....	....	....	....	....	....	....	....	....	....	....	....	....	....
2009-10	**Chicago**	**NHL**	**6**	**1**	**1**	**2**	**0**	**0**	**0**	**0**	**9**	**11.1**	**–3**	**0**	**0.0**	**7:40**	....	....	....	....	....	....	....	....	....
	Rockford IceHogs	AHL	63	23	26	49	50	....	....	....	....	....	....	....	....	....	4	0	0	0	0	....	....	....	....
2010-11	**Chicago**	**NHL**	**49**	**7**	**10**	**17**	**25**	**1**	**0**	**1**	**121**	**5.8**	**3**	**4**	**50.0**	**10:44**	....	....	....	....	....	....	....	....	....
	Florida	**NHL**	**13**	**1**	**1**	**2**	**4**	**0**	**0**	**0**	**33**	**3.0**	**–12**	**6**	**16.7**	**16:25**	....	....	....	....	....	....	....	....	....
2011-12	**Florida**	**NHL**	**46**	**4**	**6**	**10**	**28**	**0**	**1**	**1**	**76**	**5.3**	**–9**	**16**	**50.0**	**11:58**	....	....	....	....	....	....	....	....	....
2012-13	Rosenborg Elite	Norway	9	6	6	12	20	....	....	....	....	....	....	....	....	....	....	....	....	....	....	....	....	....	....
	Florida	**NHL**	**40**	**3**	**9**	**12**	**11**	**0**	**0**	**0**	**69**	**4.3**	**–9**	**16**	**50.0**	**13:19**	....	....	....	....	....	....	....	....	....
2013-14	**Columbus**	**NHL**	**16**	**4**	**0**	**4**	**6**	**0**	**0**	**1**	**23**	**17.4**	**2**	**1**	**100.0**	**8:40**	**6**	**0**	**1**	**1**	**0**	**0**	**0**	**0**	**11:01**
	Springfield	AHL	22	13	11	24	9	....	....	....	....	....	....	....	....	....	....	....	....	....	....	....	....	....	....
2014-15	**Columbus**	**NHL**	**45**	**6**	**2**	**8**	**16**	**0**	**0**	**0**	**95**	**6.3**	**–18**	**8**	**37.5**	**12:31**	....	....	....	....	....	....	....	....	....
	NHL Totals		**239**	**30**	**31**	**61**	**95**	**1**	**1**	**3**	**463**	**6.5**		**55**	**45.5**	**11:52**	**6**	**0**	**1**	**1**	**0**	**0**	**0**	**0**	**11:01**

Traded to **Florida** by **Chicago** with Hugh Jessiman and David Pacan for Michael Frolik and Alexander Salak, February 9, 2011. Signed as a free agent by **Rosenborg** (Norway), October 11, 2012. Signed as a free agent by **Columbus**, July 7, 2013. • Missed majority of 2013-14 due to upper-body injury at Colorado, December 31, 2013. Signed as a free agent by **NY Islanders**, July 1, 2014. Claimed on waivers by **Columbus** from **NY Islanders**, October 5, 2014.

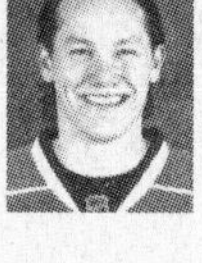

SKINNER, Jeff

(SKIH-nuhr, JEHF) **CAR**

Center. Shoots left. 5'11", 200 lbs. Born, Markham, ON, May 16, 1992. Carolina's 1st choice, 7th overall, in 2010 Entry Draft.

2007-08	Tor. Young Nats	GTHL	56	65	44	109	163	....	....	....	....	....	....	....	....	....	....	....	....	....	....	....	....	....	....
2008-09	Kitchener Rangers	OHL	63	27	24	51	34	....	....	....	....	....	....	....	....	....	....	....	....	....	....	....	....	....	....
2009-10	Kitchener Rangers	OHL	64	50	40	90	72	....	....	....	....	....	....	....	....	....	20	*20	13	33	14	....	....	....	....
2010-11	**Carolina**	**NHL**	**82**	**31**	**32**	**63**	**46**	**6**	**0**	**2**	**215**	**14.4**	**3**	**157**	**36.9**	**16:44**	....	....	....	....	....	....	....	....	....
2011-12	**Carolina**	**NHL**	**64**	**20**	**24**	**44**	**56**	**4**	**0**	**5**	**210**	**9.5**	**–8**	**159**	**42.1**	**18:37**	....	....	....	....	....	....	....	....	....
2012-13	**Carolina**	**NHL**	**42**	**13**	**11**	**24**	**26**	**5**	**0**	**0**	**159**	**8.2**	**–21**	**44**	**47.7**	**18:28**	....	....	....	....	....	....	....	....	....
2013-14	**Carolina**	**NHL**	**71**	**33**	**21**	**54**	**22**	**11**	**0**	**6**	**274**	**12.0**	**–14**	**51**	**45.1**	**17:12**	....	....	....	....	....	....	....	....	....
2014-15	**Carolina**	**NHL**	**77**	**18**	**13**	**31**	**18**	**4**	**0**	**2**	**235**	**7.7**	**–24**	**46**	**45.7**	**16:03**	....	....	....	....	....	....	....	....	....
	NHL Totals		**336**	**115**	**101**	**216**	**168**	**30**	**0**	**15**	**1093**	**10.5**		**457**	**41.6**	**17:15**	....	....	....	....	....	....	....	....	....

NHL All-Rookie Team (2011) • Calder Memorial Trophy (2011)
Played in NHL All-Star Game (2011)

SLATER, Jim
(SLAY-tuhr, JIHM)

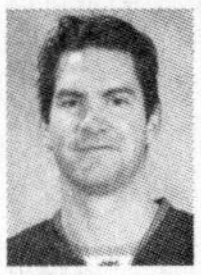

Center. Shoots left. 6', 200 lbs. Born, Lapeer, MI, December 9, 1982. Atlanta's 2nd choice, 30th overall, in 2002 Entry Draft.

			Regular Season														Playoffs								
Season	Club	League	GP	G	A	Pts	PIM	PP	SH	GW	S	S%	+/-	TF	F%	Min	GP	G	A	Pts	PIM	PP	SH	GW	Min
1998-99	USNTDP	U-18	3	0	1	1	0	....	....	....	....	....	....	....	....	....	....	....	....	....	....	....	....	....	....
	Cleveland Barons	NAHL	50	13	20	33	58	....	....	....	....	....	....	....	....	....	2	0	0	0	2	....	....	....	....
99-2000	Cleveland Barons	NAHL	56	35	50	85	129	....	....	....	....	....	....	....	....	....	3	1	3	4	4	....	....	....	....
2000-01	Cleveland Barons	NAHL	48	27	37	64	122	....	....	....	....	....	....	....	....	....	6	6	6	12	6	....	....	....	....
2001-02	Michigan State	CCHA	37	11	21	32	50	....	....	....	....	....	....	....	....	....	....	....	....	....	....	....	....	....	....
2002-03	Michigan State	CCHA	37	18	26	44	26	....	....	....	....	....	....	....	....	....	....	....	....	....	....	....	....	....	....
2003-04	Michigan State	CCHA	42	19	29	*48	38	....	....	....	....	....	....	....	....	....	....	....	....	....	....	....	....	....	....
2004-05	Michigan State	CCHA	41	16	32	48	30	....	....	....	....	....	....	....	....	....	....	....	....	....	....	....	....	....	....
2005-06	**Atlanta**	**NHL**	**71**	**10**	**10**	**20**	**46**	**1**	**0**	**0**	**108**	**9.3**	**1**	**287**	**56.5**	**10:06**	....	....	....	....	....	....	....	....	....
	Chicago Wolves	AHL	4	0	2	2	2	....	....	....	....	....	....	....	....	....	....	....	....	....	....	....	....	....	....
2006-07	**Atlanta**	**NHL**	**74**	**5**	**14**	**19**	**62**	**0**	**0**	**2**	**90**	**5.6**	**8**	**373**	**54.4**	**10:14**	**4**	**0**	**0**	**0**	**2**	**0**	**0**	**0**	**5:10**
2007-08	**Atlanta**	**NHL**	**69**	**8**	**5**	**13**	**41**	**0**	**2**	**0**	**95**	**8.4**	**–10**	**367**	**52.0**	**10:24**	....	....	....	....	....	....	....	....	....
	Chicago Wolves	AHL	3	0	0	0	0	....	....	....	....	....	....	....	....	....	....	....	....	....	....	....	....	....	....
2008-09	**Atlanta**	**NHL**	**60**	**8**	**10**	**18**	**52**	**0**	**2**	**0**	**94**	**8.5**	**0**	**462**	**53.0**	**11:15**	....	....	....	....	....	....	....	....	....
2009-10	**Atlanta**	**NHL**	**61**	**11**	**7**	**18**	**60**	**1**	**0**	**2**	**107**	**10.3**	**1**	**431**	**58.9**	**12:12**	....	....	....	....	....	....	....	....	....
2010-11	**Atlanta**	**NHL**	**36**	**5**	**7**	**12**	**19**	**0**	**0**	**1**	**53**	**9.4**	**4**	**301**	**61.5**	**10:35**	....	....	....	....	....	....	....	....	....
2011-12	**Winnipeg**	**NHL**	**78**	**13**	**8**	**21**	**42**	**0**	**1**	**1**	**118**	**11.0**	**–9**	**1165**	**54.4**	**14:46**	....	....	....	....	....	....	....	....	....
2012-13	**Winnipeg**	**NHL**	**26**	**1**	**1**	**2**	**19**	**0**	**0**	**0**	**22**	**4.5**	**–3**	**267**	**54.3**	**10:27**	....	....	....	....	....	....	....	....	....
2013-14	**Winnipeg**	**NHL**	**27**	**1**	**1**	**2**	**8**	**0**	**0**	**0**	**24**	**4.2**	**–5**	**281**	**58.0**	**10:38**	....	....	....	....	....	....	....	....	....
2014-15	**Winnipeg**	**NHL**	**82**	**5**	**8**	**13**	**58**	**0**	**0**	**1**	**51**	**9.8**	**–4**	**751**	**59.7**	**9:13**	**4**	**0**	**0**	**0**	**0**	**0**	**0**	**0**	**9:33**
	NHL Totals		**584**	**67**	**71**	**138**	**407**	**2**	**5**	**7**	**762**	**8.8**		**4685**	**56.1**	**11:03**	**8**	**0**	**0**	**0**	**2**	**0**	**0**	**0**	**7:22**

CCHA All-Rookie Team (2002) • CCHA First All-Star Team (2003, 2004) • NCAA West Second All-American Team (2004)

• Missed majority of 2010-11 due to head injury at New Jersey, December 31, 2010. • Transferred to **Winnipeg** after **Atlanta** franchise relocated, June 21, 2011. • Missed majority of 2013-14 due to sports hernia surgery, October 20, 2013.

SMID, Ladislav
(SHMIHD, LA-dih-slahv) **CGY**

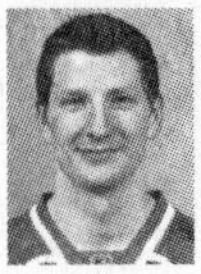

Defense. Shoots left. 6'3", 209 lbs. Born, Frydlant V Cechach, Czech., February 1, 1986. Anaheim's 1st choice, 9th overall, in 2004 Entry Draft.

Season	Club	League	GP	G	A	Pts	PIM	PP	SH	GW	S	S%	+/-	TF	F%	Min	GP	G	A	Pts	PIM	PP	SH	GW	Min
2001-02	HC Liberec Jr.	CzRep-Jr.	43	6	10	16	87	....	....	....	....	....	....	....	....	....	....	....	....	....	....	....	....	....	....
2002-03	HC Liberec Jr.	CzRep-Jr.	32	1	14	15	12	....	....	....	....	....	....	....	....	....	8	2	1	3	31	....	....	....	....
	Liberec	CzRep	4	0	0	0	0	....	....	....	....	....	....	....	....	....	....	....	....	....	....	....	....	....	....
2003-04	HC Liberec Jr.	CzRep-Jr.	14	4	10	14	38	....	....	....	....	....	....	....	....	....	2	1	0	1	6	....	....	....	....
	Liberec	CzRep	45	1	1	2	51	....	....	....	....	....	....	....	....	....	....	....	....	....	....	....	....	....	....
	Beroun	CzRep-2	....	....	....	....	....	....	....	....	....	....	....	....	....	....	3	1	1	2	4	....	....	....	....
2004-05	HC Liberec Jr.	CzRep-Jr.	3	0	1	1	4	....	....	....	....	....	....	....	....	....	....	....	....	....	....	....	....	....	....
	Liberec	CzRep	39	1	3	4	14	....	....	....	....	....	....	....	....	....	12	0	0	0	6	....	....	....	....
2005-06	Portland Pirates	AHL	71	3	25	28	48	....	....	....	....	....	....	....	....	....	16	0	1	1	16	....	....	....	....
2006-07	**Edmonton**	**NHL**	**77**	**3**	**7**	**10**	**37**	**0**	**0**	**0**	**53**	**5.7**	**–16**	**0**	**0.0**	**19:14**	....	....	....	....	....	....	....	....	....
2007-08	**Edmonton**	**NHL**	**65**	**0**	**4**	**4**	**58**	**0**	**0**	**0**	**45**	**0.0**	**–15**	**0**	**0.0**	**17:52**	....	....	....	....	....	....	....	....	....
	Springfield	AHL	8	1	4	5	15	....	....	....	....	....	....	....	....	....	....	....	....	....	....	....	....	....	....
2008-09	**Edmonton**	**NHL**	**60**	**0**	**11**	**11**	**57**	**0**	**0**	**0**	**33**	**0.0**	**–6**	**0**	**0.0**	**14:57**	....	....	....	....	....	....	....	....	....
2009-10	**Edmonton**	**NHL**	**51**	**1**	**8**	**9**	**39**	**0**	**0**	**0**	**36**	**2.8**	**5**	**0**	**0.0**	**19:11**	....	....	....	....	....	....	....	....	....
2010-11	**Edmonton**	**NHL**	**78**	**0**	**10**	**10**	**85**	**0**	**0**	**0**	**48**	**0.0**	**–10**	**0**	**0.0**	**20:17**	....	....	....	....	....	....	....	....	....
2011-12	**Edmonton**	**NHL**	**78**	**5**	**10**	**15**	**44**	**0**	**0**	**0**	**47**	**10.6**	**4**	**0**	**0.0**	**20:54**	....	....	....	....	....	....	....	....	....
2012-13	Liberec	CzRep	22	2	12	14	22	....	....	....	....	....	....	....	....	....	....	....	....	....	....	....	....	....	....
	Edmonton	**NHL**	**48**	**1**	**3**	**4**	**55**	**0**	**0**	**0**	**30**	**3.3**	**–1**	**0**	**0.0**	**20:19**	....	....	....	....	....	....	....	....	....
2013-14	**Edmonton**	**NHL**	**17**	**1**	**1**	**2**	**16**	**0**	**0**	**0**	**6**	**16.7**	**–6**	**0**	**0.0**	**17:54**	....	....	....	....	....	....	....	....	....
	Czech Republic	Olympics	5	0	0	0	2	....	....	....	....	....	....	....	....	....	....	....	....	....	....	....	....	....	....
	Calgary	**NHL**	**56**	**1**	**5**	**6**	**62**	**0**	**0**	**0**	**35**	**2.9**	**–4**	**0**	**0.0**	**18:12**	....	....	....	....	....	....	....	....	....
2014-15	**Calgary**	**NHL**	**31**	**0**	**1**	**1**	**13**	**0**	**0**	**0**	**21**	**0.0**	**–12**	**0**	**0.0**	**13:58**	....	....	....	....	....	....	....	....	....
	NHL Totals		**561**	**12**	**60**	**72**	**466**	**0**	**0**	**0**	**354**	**3.4**		**0**	**0.0**	**18:39**	....	....	....	....	....	....	....	....	....

Traded to **Edmonton** by **Anaheim** with Joffrey Lupul, Anaheim's 1st round choice (later traded to Phoenix - Phoenix selected Nick Ross) in 2007 Entry Draft and Anaheim's 1st (Jordan Eberle) and 2nd (later traded to NY Islanders - NY Islanders selected Travis Hamonic) round choices in 2008 Entry Draft for Chris Pronger, July 3, 2006. Signed as a free agent by **Liberec** (CzRep), September 21, 2012. Traded to **Calgary** by **Edmonton** with Olivier Roy for Laurent Brossoit and Roman Horak, November 8, 2013. • Missed majority of 2014-15 due to neck injury at Los Angeles, January 19, 2015.

SMITH, Ben
(SMIHTH, BEHN) **S.J.**

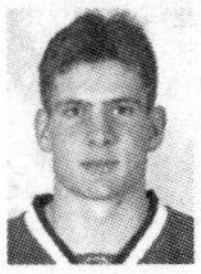

Right wing. Shoots right. 5'11", 200 lbs. Born, Winston-Salem, NC, July 11, 1988. Chicago's 5th choice, 169th overall, in 2008 Entry Draft.

Season	Club	League	GP	G	A	Pts	PIM	PP	SH	GW	S	S%	+/-	TF	F%	Min	GP	G	A	Pts	PIM	PP	SH	GW	Min
2006-07	Boston College	H-East	42	10	8	18	10	....	....	....	....	....	....	....	....	....	....	....	....	....	....	....	....	....	....
2007-08	Boston College	H-East	44	25	25	50	12	....	....	....	....	....	....	....	....	....	....	....	....	....	....	....	....	....	....
2008-09	Boston College	H-East	37	6	11	17	6	....	....	....	....	....	....	....	....	....	....	....	....	....	....	....	....	....	....
2009-10	Boston College	H-East	42	16	21	37	8	....	....	....	....	....	....	....	....	....	....	....	....	....	....	....	....	....	....
	Rockford IceHogs	AHL	....	....	....	....	....	....	....	....	....	....	....	....	....	....	3	1	0	1	0	....	....	....	....
2010-11	**Chicago**	**NHL**	**6**	**1**	**0**	**1**	**0**	**0**	**0**	**0**	**6**	**16.7**	**1**	**8**	**75.0**	**13:47**	**7**	**3**	**0**	**3**	**0**	**0**	**0**	**1**	**14:50**
	Rockford IceHogs	AHL	63	19	12	31	16	....	....	....	....	....	....	....	....	....	....	....	....	....	....	....	....	....	....
2011-12	**Chicago**	**NHL**	**13**	**2**	**0**	**2**	**0**	**0**	**0**	**0**	**18**	**11.1**	**–5**	**14**	**50.0**	**9:49**	....	....	....	....	....	....	....	....	....
	Rockford IceHogs	AHL	38	15	16	31	10	....	....	....	....	....	....	....	....	....	....	....	....	....	....	....	....	....	....
2012-13	Rockford IceHogs	AHL	54	27	20	47	13	....	....	....	....	....	....	....	....	....	....	....	....	....	....	....	....	....	....
	♦ **Chicago**	**NHL**	**1**	**1**	**0**	**1**	**0**	**0**	**0**	**0**	**1**	**100.0**	**1**	**2**	**0.0**	**18:21**	**1**	**0**	**0**	**0**	**0**	**0**	**0**	**0**	**10:23**
2013-14	**Chicago**	**NHL**	**75**	**14**	**12**	**26**	**2**	**1**	**0**	**2**	**90**	**15.6**	**3**	**394**	**50.8**	**12:44**	**19**	**4**	**2**	**6**	**2**	**0**	**0**	**0**	**15:14**
2014-15	**Chicago**	**NHL**	**61**	**5**	**4**	**9**	**2**	**0**	**0**	**0**	**77**	**6.5**	**–1**	**452**	**51.1**	**13:35**	....	....	....	....	....	....	....	....	....
	San Jose	**NHL**	**19**	**2**	**3**	**5**	**0**	**0**	**0**	**1**	**15**	**13.3**	**3**	**142**	**55.6**	**11:20**	....	....	....	....	....	....	....	....	....
	NHL Totals		**175**	**25**	**19**	**44**	**4**	**1**	**0**	**3**	**207**	**12.1**		**1012**	**51.7**	**12:44**	**27**	**7**	**2**	**9**	**2**	**0**	**0**	**1**	**14:57**

NCAA Championship All-Tournament Team (2008, 2010) • NCAA Championship Tournament MVP (2010)

Traded to **San Jose** by **Chicago** with future considerations for Andrew Desjardins, March 2, 2015.

SMITH, Brendan
(SMIHTH, BREHN-duhn) **DET**

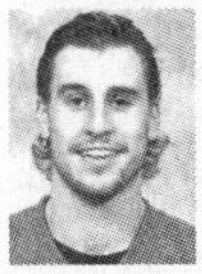

Defense. Shoots left. 6'2", 198 lbs. Born, Toronto, ON, February 8, 1989. Detroit's 1st choice, 27th overall, in 2007 Entry Draft.

Season	Club	League	GP	G	A	Pts	PIM	PP	SH	GW	S	S%	+/-	TF	F%	Min	GP	G	A	Pts	PIM	PP	SH	GW	Min
2004-05	Tor. Marlboros	GTHL	66	22	63	85	120	....	....	....	....	....	....	....	....	....	....	....	....	....	....	....	....	....	....
2005-06	St. Michael's	ON-Jr.A	39	5	21	26	55	....	....	....	....	....	....	....	....	....	17	1	5	6	44	....	....	....	....
2006-07	St. Michael's	ON-Jr.A	39	12	24	36	90	....	....	....	....	....	....	....	....	....	16	6	14	20	30	....	....	....	....
2007-08	U. of Wisconsin	WCHA	22	2	10	12	26	....	....	....	....	....	....	....	....	....	....	....	....	....	....	....	....	....	....
2008-09	U. of Wisconsin	WCHA	31	9	14	23	75	....	....	....	....	....	....	....	....	....	....	....	....	....	....	....	....	....	....
2009-10	U. of Wisconsin	WCHA	42	15	37	52	76	....	....	....	....	....	....	....	....	....	....	....	....	....	....	....	....	....	....
2010-11	Grand Rapids	AHL	63	12	20	32	124	....	....	....	....	....	....	....	....	....	....	....	....	....	....	....	....	....	....
2011-12	**Detroit**	**NHL**	**14**	**1**	**6**	**7**	**13**	**0**	**0**	**0**	**13**	**7.7**	**3**	**0**	**0.0**	**15:38**	....	....	....	....	....	....	....	....	....
	Grand Rapids	AHL	57	10	24	34	90	....	....	....	....	....	....	....	....	....	....	....	....	....	....	....	....	....	....
2012-13	Grand Rapids	AHL	32	5	15	20	49	....	....	....	....	....	....	....	....	....	....	....	....	....	....	....	....	....	....
	Detroit	**NHL**	**34**	**0**	**8**	**8**	**36**	**0**	**0**	**0**	**33**	**0.0**	**1**	**0**	**0.0**	**18:24**	**14**	**2**	**3**	**5**	**10**	**0**	**0**	**1**	**19:08**
2013-14	**Detroit**	**NHL**	**71**	**5**	**14**	**19**	**68**	**1**	**0**	**0**	**90**	**5.6**	**–2**	**0**	**0.0**	**18:23**	**5**	**0**	**0**	**0**	**8**	**0**	**0**	**0**	**19:37**
2014-15	**Detroit**	**NHL**	**76**	**4**	**9**	**13**	**68**	**0**	**0**	**1**	**88**	**4.5**	**–2**	**0**	**0.0**	**17:53**	**5**	**0**	**0**	**0**	**6**	**0**	**0**	**0**	**16:05**
	NHL Totals		**195**	**10**	**37**	**47**	**185**	**1**	**0**	**1**	**224**	**4.5**		**0**	**0.0**	**18:00**	**24**	**2**	**3**	**5**	**24**	**0**	**0**	**1**	**18:36**

WCHA First All-Star Team (2010) • NCAA West First All-American Team (2010) • NCAA Championship All-Tournament Team (2010) • AHL All-Rookie Team (2011)

SMITH, Colin
(SMIHTH, KAW-lihn) **COL**

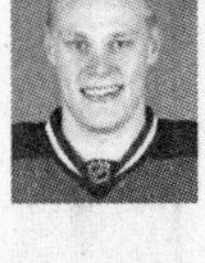

Center. Shoots right. 5'10", 175 lbs. Born, Edmonton, AB, June 20, 1993. Colorado's 5th choice, 192nd overall, in 2012 Entry Draft.

Season	Club	League	GP	G	A	Pts	PIM	PP	SH	GW	S	S%	+/-	TF	F%	Min	GP	G	A	Pts	PIM	PP	SH	GW	Min
2006-07	CAC Lehigh	AMBHL	30	24	37	61	8	....	....	....	....	....	....	....	....	....	....	....	....	....	....	....	....	....	....
2007-08	CAC Lehigh	AMBHL	33	36	*70	106	28	....	....	....	....	....	....	....	....	....	2	2	1	3	0	....	....	....	....
2008-09	CAC Gregg's Dist.	AMHL	34	23	32	55	10	....	....	....	....	....	....	....	....	....	5	3	4	7	2	....	....	....	....
	Kamloops Blazers	WHL	8	0	4	4	4	....	....	....	....	....	....	....	....	....	4	1	0	1	0	....	....	....	....
2009-10	Kamloops Blazers	WHL	48	5	21	26	46	....	....	....	....	....	....	....	....	....	4	2	2	4	2	....	....	....	....
2010-11	Kamloops Blazers	WHL	72	21	29	50	61	....	....	....	....	....	....	....	....	....	....	....	....	....	....	....	....	....	....
2011-12	Kamloops Blazers	WHL	72	35	50	85	51	....	....	....	....	....	....	....	....	....	11	3	7	10	12	....	....	....	....

Season	Club	League	GP	G	A	Pts	PIM	PP	SH	GW	S	S%	+/-	TF	F%	Min	GP	G	A	Pts	PIM	PP	SH	GW	Min
2012-13	Kamloops Blazers	WHL	72	41	65	106	72	....	....	....	....	....	....	....	....	....	12	2	12	14	2	....	....	....	....
2013-14	Lake Erie	AHL	76	8	26	34	66	....	....	....	....	....	....	....	....	....									
2014-15	**Colorado**	**NHL**	**1**	**0**	**0**	**0**	**0**	0	0	0	1	0.0	0	10	40.0	6:06									
	Lake Erie	AHL	53	12	19	31	22	....	....	....	....	....	....	....	....	....									
	NHL Totals		**1**	**0**	**0**	**0**	**0**	0	0	0	1	0.0		10	40.0	6:06									

WHL West First All-Star Team (2013)

SMITH, Craig
(SMIHTH, KRAYG)   **NSH**

Center. Shoots right. 6'1", 202 lbs.   Born, Madison, WI, September 5, 1989. Nashville's 6th choice, 98th overall, in 2009 Entry Draft.

Season	Club	League	GP	G	A	Pts	PIM	PP	SH	GW	S	S%	+/-	TF	F%	Min	GP	G	A	Pts	PIM	PP	SH	GW	Min
2004-05	Madison Lancers	High-WI	20	16	24	40	....																		
2005-06	Madison Lancers	High-WI	20	35	26	61	....																		
2006-07	Waterloo	USHL	45	8	10	18	28										4	0	1	1	8				
2007-08	Waterloo	USHL	58	13	10	23	90										11	2	3	5	8				
2008-09	Waterloo	USHL	54	28	48	76	108										3	1	3	4	26				
2009-10	U. of Wisconsin	WCHA	41	8	25	33	72																		
2010-11	U. of Wisconsin	WCHA	41	19	24	43	87																		
2011-12	**Nashville**	**NHL**	**72**	**14**	**22**	**36**	**30**	6	0	1	172	8.1	-9	393	44.0	14:11	2	0	1	1	0	0	0	0	8:25
2012-13	KalPa Kuopio	Finland	8	4	4	8	20																		
	Nashville	**NHL**	**44**	**4**	**8**	**12**	**20**	2	0	0	83	4.8	-11	200	39.5	13:51									
	Milwaukee	AHL	4	1	4	5	0																		
2013-14	**Nashville**	**NHL**	**79**	**24**	**28**	**52**	**22**	7	0	4	215	11.2	16	19	15.8	16:24									
2014-15	**Nashville**	**NHL**	**82**	**23**	**21**	**44**	**44**	6	0	4	252	9.1	11	30	40.0	15:44	6	2	3	5	0	0	0	1	20:34
	NHL Totals		**277**	**65**	**79**	**144**	**116**	21	0	9	722	9.0		642	41.6	15:14	8	2	4	6	0	0	0	1	17:31

USHL First All-Star Team (2009) • WCHA All-Rookie Team (2010)
Signed as a free agent by Kuopio (Finland), October 2, 2012.

SMITH, Derek
(SMIHTH, DAIR-ihk)   **ARI**

Defense. Shoots left. 6'1", 197 lbs.   Born, Belleville, ON, October 13, 1984.

Season	Club	League	GP	G	A	Pts	PIM	PP	SH	GW	S	S%	+/-	TF	F%	Min	GP	G	A	Pts	PIM	PP	SH	GW	Min
2000-01	Quinte Red Devils	Minor-ON	STATISTICS NOT AVAILABLE																					
	Wellington Dukes	ON-Jr.A	12	1	1	2	4																		
2001-02	Wellington Dukes	ON-Jr.A	46	5	15	20	26																		
2002-03	Wellington Dukes	ON-Jr.A	21	6	10	16	26																		
2003-04	Wellington Dukes	ON-Jr.A	44	8	26	34	34																		
2004-05	Lake Superior	CCHA	38	1	4	5	28																		
2005-06	Lake Superior	CCHA	36	2	8	10	18																		
2006-07	Lake Superior	CCHA	43	10	20	30	10																		
2007-08	Binghamton	AHL	52	2	11	13	18																		
	Elmira Jackals	ECHL	1	0	1	1	0																		
2008-09	Binghamton	AHL	75	7	17	24	49																		
2009-10	**Ottawa**	**NHL**	**2**	**0**	**0**	**0**	**0**	0	0	0	4	0.0	-4	0	0.0	12:20									
	Binghamton	AHL	74	14	37	51	24																		
2010-11	**Ottawa**	**NHL**	**9**	**0**	**1**	**1**	**0**	0	0	0	13	0.0	3	0	0.0	15:19									
	Binghamton	AHL	71	10	44	54	21										6	1	1	2	6				
2011-12	**Calgary**	**NHL**	**47**	**2**	**9**	**11**	**12**	0	0	1	44	4.5	-1	0	0.0	15:56									
2012-13	**Calgary**	**NHL**	**22**	**0**	**1**	**1**	**0**	0	0	0	18	0.0	-5	0	0.0	12:15									
2013-14	**Calgary**	**NHL**	**14**	**0**	**1**	**1**	**2**	0	0	0	12	0.0	-10	3	66.7	9:32									
	Abbotsford Heat	AHL	32	7	17	24	22										1	0	0	0	0				
2014-15	ZSC Lions Zurich	Swiss	25	3	2	5	4										5	0	1	1	6				
	NHL Totals		**94**	**2**	**12**	**14**	**24**	0	0	1	91	2.2		3	66.7	13:59									

Signed as a free agent by Ottawa, April 12, 2007. Signed as a free agent by Calgary, July 13, 2011. • Missed majority of 2012-13 due to upper-body injury and as a healthy reserve. Signed as a free agent by Zurich (Swiss), July 28, 2014. Signed as a free agent by Arizona, July 3, 2015.

SMITH, Reilly
(SMIHTH, RIGH-lee)   **FLA**

Right wing. Shoots left. 6', 185 lbs.   Born, Toronto, ON, April 1, 1991. Dallas' 3rd choice, 69th overall, in 2009 Entry Draft.

Season	Club	League	GP	G	A	Pts	PIM	PP	SH	GW	S	S%	+/-	TF	F%	Min	GP	G	A	Pts	PIM	PP	SH	GW	Min
2007-08	Tor. Young Nats	GTHL	70	80	77	157	56																		
	St. Michael's	ON-Jr.A	13	2	7	9	22										1	0	0	0	2				
2008-09	St. Michael's	ON-Jr.A	49	27	48	75	44										6	9	6	15	10				
2009-10	Miami U.	CCHA	44	8	12	20	24																		
2010-11	Miami U.	CCHA	38	28	26	54	18																		
2011-12	Miami U.	CCHA	39	30	18	48	22																		
	Dallas	**NHL**	**3**	**0**	**0**	**0**	**2**	0	0	0	2	0.0	-3	1	100.0	8:24									
2012-13	Texas Stars	AHL	45	14	21	35	20										7	0	4	4	0				
	Dallas	**NHL**	**37**	**3**	**6**	**9**	**8**	0	0	0	34	8.8	0	4	75.0	10:55									
2013-14	**Boston**	**NHL**	**82**	**20**	**31**	**51**	**14**	6	0	3	146	13.7	28	2	0.0	14:42	12	4	1	5	0	2	0	2	15:46
2014-15	**Boston**	**NHL**	**81**	**13**	**27**	**40**	**20**	1	0	0	143	9.1	7	8	25.0	15:24									
	NHL Totals		**203**	**36**	**64**	**100**	**44**	7	0	3	325	11.1		15	40.0	14:12	12	4	1	5	0	2	0	2	15:46

CCHA First All-Star Team (2011, 2012) • NCAA West First All-American Team (2012)
Traded to **Boston** by Dallas with Loui Eriksson, Joe Morrow and Matt Fraser for Tyler Seguin, Rich Peverley and Ryan Button, July 4, 2013. Traded to **Florida** by Boston with Marc Savard for Jimmy Hayes, July 1, 2015.

SMITH, Trevor
(SMIHTH, TREH-vuhr)

Center. Shoots left. 6'1", 195 lbs.   Born, Ottawa, ON, February 8, 1985.

Season	Club	League	GP	G	A	Pts	PIM	PP	SH	GW	S	S%	+/-	TF	F%	Min	GP	G	A	Pts	PIM	PP	SH	GW	Min
2003-04	Quesnel	BCHL	44	28	19	47	50																		
2004-05	Omaha Lancers	USHL	60	29	39	68	78										5	3	1	4	2				
2005-06	New Hampshire	H-East	39	10	10	20	34																		
2006-07	New Hampshire	H-East	39	21	22	43	39																		
	Bridgeport	AHL	8	1	2	3	2																		
2007-08	Bridgeport	AHL	53	20	17	37	16																		
	Utah Grizzlies	ECHL	22	11	14	25	28																		
2008-09	**NY Islanders**	**NHL**	**7**	**1**	**0**	**1**	**0**	0	0	0	7	14.3	-3	9	66.7	11:48									
	Bridgeport	AHL	76	30	32	62	40										5	1	3	4	0				
2009-10	Bridgeport	AHL	77	21	26	47	73										5	1	2	3	2				
2010-11	Syracuse Crunch	AHL	35	12	15	27	16																		
	Springfield	AHL	33	8	8	16	10																		
2011-12	**Tampa Bay**	**NHL**	**16**	**2**	**3**	**5**	**4**	0	0	0	17	11.8	2	83	41.0	12:28									
	Norfolk Admirals	AHL	64	26	43	69	70										18	5	11	16	20				
2012-13	Wilkes-Barre	AHL	75	23	31	54	64										15	5	8	13	9				
	Pittsburgh	**NHL**	**1**	**0**	**0**	**0**	**0**	0	0	0	0	0.0	0	0	0.0	10:24									
2013-14	**Toronto**	**NHL**	**28**	**4**	**5**	**9**	**4**	0	0	2	24	16.7	-3	258	44.6	10:22									
	Toronto Marlies	AHL	24	10	16	26	10										14	3	8	11	2				
2014-15	**Toronto**	**NHL**	**54**	**2**	**3**	**5**	**12**	0	0	0	46	4.3	-9	561	52.2	11:04									
	Toronto Marlies	AHL	8	2	3	5	12																		
	NHL Totals		**106**	**9**	**11**	**20**	**20**	0	0	2	94	9.6		911	49.2	11:08									

NCAA East Second All-American Team (2007)
Signed as a free agent by **NY Islanders**, April 2, 2007. Signed as a free agent by **Anaheim**, July 2, 2010. Traded to **Columbus** by **Anaheim** for Nate Guenin, January 4, 2011. Signed as a free agent by **Tampa Bay**, July 5, 2011. Signed as a free agent by **Pittsburgh**, July 1, 2012. Signed as a free agent by **Toronto**, July 5, 2013.

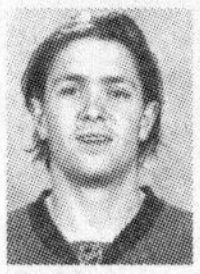

SMITH, Zack
(SMIHTH, ZAK) **OTT**

Center. Shoots left. 6'2", 209 lbs. Born, Medicine Hat, AB, April 5, 1988. Ottawa's 3rd choice, 79th overall, in 2008 Entry Draft.

			Regular Season														Playoffs								
Season	Club	League	GP	G	A	Pts	PIM	PP	SH	GW	S	S%	+/-	TF	F%	Min	GP	G	A	Pts	PIM	PP	SH	GW	Min
2004-05	Swift Current	SMHL	43	15	27	42	83	....	....	....	....	....	....	....	....	....	....	....	....	....	....	....	....	....	....
	Swift Current	WHL	14	1	1	2	0	....	....	....	....	....	....	....	....	....	....	....	....	....	....	....	....	....	....
2005-06	Swift Current	WHL	64	2	5	7	78	....	....	....	....	....	....	....	....	....	3	0	0	0	9	....	....	....	....
2006-07	Swift Current	WHL	71	16	15	31	130	....	....	....	....	....	....	....	....	....	6	0	2	2	11	....	....	....	....
2007-08	Swift Current	WHL	72	22	47	69	136	....	....	....	....	....	....	....	....	....	12	5	5	10	29	....	....	....	....
	Manitoba Moose	AHL	....	....	....	....	....	....	....	....	....	....	....	....	....	....	6	0	1	1	0	....	....	....	....
2008-09	**Ottawa**	**NHL**	**1**	**0**	**0**	**0**	**0**	**0**	**0**	**0**	**0**	**0.0**	**0**	**1**	**0.0**	**7:01**	....	....	....	....	....	....	....	....	....
	Binghamton	AHL	79	24	24	48	132	....	....	....	....	....	....	....	....	....	....	....	....	....	....	....	....	....	....
2009-10	**Ottawa**	**NHL**	**15**	**2**	**1**	**3**	**14**	**0**	**1**	**0**	**11**	**18.2**	**1**	**61**	**47.5**	**9:03**	**6**	**0**	**0**	**0**	**5**	**0**	**0**	**0**	**7:25**
	Binghamton	AHL	68	14	27	41	100	....	....	....	....	....	....	....	....	....	....	....	....	....	....	....	....	....	....
2010-11	**Ottawa**	**NHL**	**55**	**4**	**5**	**9**	**120**	**0**	**0**	**0**	**78**	**5.1**	**–11**	**388**	**53.9**	**12:36**	....	....	....	....	....	....	....	....	....
	Binghamton	AHL	22	7	5	12	32	....	....	....	....	....	....	....	....	....	23	8	12	20	36	....	....	....	....
2011-12	**Ottawa**	**NHL**	**81**	**14**	**12**	**26**	**98**	**1**	**2**	**3**	**134**	**10.4**	**4**	**990**	**48.9**	**14:04**	**7**	**0**	**1**	**1**	**10**	**0**	**0**	**0**	**13:22**
2012-13	Frederikshavn	Denmark	7	4	6	10	18	....	....	....	....	....	....	....	....	....	....	....	....	....	....	....	....	....	....
	Ottawa	**NHL**	**48**	**4**	**11**	**15**	**56**	**0**	**0**	**0**	**94**	**4.3**	**–9**	**731**	**51.9**	**15:09**	**10**	**1**	**1**	**2**	**31**	**0**	**0**	**0**	**13:17**
2013-14	**Ottawa**	**NHL**	**82**	**13**	**9**	**22**	**111**	**0**	**1**	**4**	**154**	**8.4**	**–9**	**1291**	**52.7**	**15:32**	....	....	....	....	....	....	....	....	....
2014-15	**Ottawa**	**NHL**	**37**	**2**	**1**	**3**	**18**	**0**	**0**	**0**	**38**	**5.3**	**–8**	**231**	**44.6**	**12:02**	**3**	**0**	**0**	**0**	**0**	**0**	**0**	**0**	**9:53**
	Binghamton	AHL	2	1	1	2	2	....	....	....	....	....	....	....	....	....	....	....	....	....	....	....	....	....	....
	NHL Totals		**319**	**39**	**39**	**78**	**417**	**1**	**4**	**7**	**509**	**7.7**		**3693**	**51.0**	**13:52**	**26**	**1**	**2**	**3**	**46**	**0**	**0**	**0**	**11:33**

Signed as a free agent by **Frederikshavn** (Denmark), November 26, 2012. • Missed majority of 2014-15 due to wrist injury at Boston, December 13, 2014.

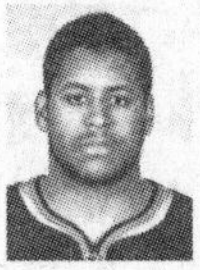

SMITH-PELLY, Devante
(SMIHTH-PEH-lee, deh-VAHN-tay) **MTL**

Right wing. Shoots right. 6', 220 lbs. Born, Scarborough, ON, June 14, 1992. Anaheim's 3rd choice, 42nd overall, in 2010 Entry Draft.

Season	Club	League	GP	G	A	Pts	PIM	PP	SH	GW	S	S%	+/-	TF	F%	Min	GP	G	A	Pts	PIM	PP	SH	GW	Min
2007-08	Tor. Jr. Canadiens	GTHL	85	38	39	77	159	....	....	....	....	....	....	....	....	....	....	....	....	....	....	....	....	....	....
2008-09	St. Michael's	OHL	57	13	12	25	24	....	....	....	....	....	....	....	....	....	11	2	3	5	4	....	....	....	....
2009-10	St. Michael's	OHL	60	29	33	62	35	....	....	....	....	....	....	....	....	....	16	8	6	14	20	....	....	....	....
2010-11	St. Michael's	OHL	67	36	30	66	50	....	....	....	....	....	....	....	....	....	20	*15	6	21	16	....	....	....	....
2011-12	**Anaheim**	**NHL**	**49**	**7**	**6**	**13**	**16**	**1**	**1**	**1**	**66**	**10.6**	**–7**	**21**	**28.6**	**12:03**	....	....	....	....	....	....	....	....	....
	Syracuse Crunch	AHL	4	0	1	1	2	....	....	....	....	....	....	....	....	....	....	....	....	....	....	....	....	....	....
2012-13	Norfolk Admirals	AHL	65	14	18	32	65	....	....	....	....	....	....	....	....	....	....	....	....	....	....	....	....	....	....
	Anaheim	**NHL**	**7**	**0**	**0**	**0**	**0**	**0**	**0**	**0**	**5**	**0.0**	**–4**	**0**	**0.0**	**9:00**	....	....	....	....	....	....	....	....	....
2013-14	**Anaheim**	**NHL**	**19**	**2**	**8**	**10**	**2**	**0**	**0**	**0**	**23**	**8.7**	**5**	**4**	**0.0**	**12:39**	**12**	**5**	**0**	**5**	**24**	**2**	**0**	**1**	**14:42**
	Norfolk Admirals	AHL	55	27	16	43	29	....	....	....	....	....	....	....	....	....	....	....	....	....	....	....	....	....	....
2014-15	**Anaheim**	**NHL**	**54**	**5**	**12**	**17**	**12**	**0**	**1**	**1**	**76**	**6.6**	**1**	**82**	**28.1**	**14:39**	....	....	....	....	....	....	....	....	....
	Montreal	**NHL**	**20**	**1**	**2**	**3**	**12**	**0**	**0**	**0**	**28**	**3.6**	**–2**	**1**	**0.0**	**13:18**	**12**	**1**	**2**	**3**	**2**	**0**	**0**	**0**	**12:19**
	NHL Totals		**149**	**15**	**28**	**43**	**42**	**1**	**2**	**2**	**198**	**7.6**		**108**	**26.9**	**13:05**	**24**	**6**	**2**	**8**	**26**	**2**	**0**	**1**	**13:30**

Memorial Cup All-Star Team (2011)

Traded to **Montreal** by **Anaheim** for Jiri Sekac, February 24, 2014.,

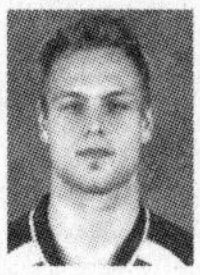

SOBOTKA, Vladimir
(suh-BOHT-kah, vla-DIH-meer)

Center. Shoots left. 5'10", 197 lbs. Born, Trebic, Czech., July 2, 1987. Boston's 5th choice, 106th overall, in 2005 Entry Draft.

Season	Club	League	GP	G	A	Pts	PIM	PP	SH	GW	S	S%	+/-	TF	F%	Min	GP	G	A	Pts	PIM	PP	SH	GW	Min
2002-03	Slavia U17	CzR-U17	46	16	24	40	48	....	....	....	....	....	....	....	....	....	8	1	1	2	29	....	....	....	....
2003-04	Slavia U17	CzR-U17	35	24	41	65	109	....	....	....	....	....	....	....	....	....	7	7	12	19	8	....	....	....	....
	Slavia Jr.	CzRep-Jr.	18	6	6	12	16	....	....	....	....	....	....	....	....	....	....	....	....	....	....	....	....	....	....
	HC Slavia Praha	CzRep	1	0	0	0	0	....	....	....	....	....	....	....	....	....	....	....	....	....	....	....	....	....	....
2004-05	Slavia Jr.	CzRep-Jr.	27	12	21	33	93	....	....	....	....	....	....	....	....	....	....	....	....	....	....	....	....	....	....
	HC Slavia Praha	CzRep	18	0	1	1	8	....	....	....	....	....	....	....	....	....	....	....	....	....	....	....	....	....	....
	Havl. Brod	CzRep-3	7	3	0	3	31	....	....	....	....	....	....	....	....	....	7	1	5	6	0	....	....	....	....
2005-06	Slavia Jr.	CzRep-Jr.	8	10	4	14	42	....	....	....	....	....	....	....	....	....	....	....	....	....	....	....	....	....	....
	HC Slavia Praha	CzRep	33	1	9	10	28	....	....	....	....	....	....	....	....	....	11	2	3	5	10	....	....	....	....
2006-07	HC Slavia Praha	CzRep	33	7	6	13	38	....	....	....	....	....	....	....	....	....	....	....	....	....	....	....	....	....	....
2007-08	**Boston**	**NHL**	**48**	**1**	**6**	**7**	**24**	**0**	**0**	**1**	**40**	**2.5**	**1**	**247**	**48.6**	**8:50**	**6**	**2**	**0**	**2**	**0**	**0**	**0**	**0**	**8:37**
	Providence Bruins	AHL	18	10	10	20	37	....	....	....	....	....	....	....	....	....	6	0	4	4	0	....	....	....	....
2008-09	**Boston**	**NHL**	**25**	**1**	**4**	**5**	**10**	**0**	**0**	**0**	**19**	**5.3**	**–10**	**52**	**57.7**	**10:33**	....	....	....	....	....	....	....	....	....
	Providence Bruins	AHL	44	20	24	44	83	....	....	....	....	....	....	....	....	....	14	2	11	13	43	....	....	....	....
2009-10	**Boston**	**NHL**	**61**	**4**	**6**	**10**	**30**	**0**	**0**	**0**	**67**	**6.0**	**–7**	**361**	**54.3**	**11:06**	**13**	**0**	**2**	**2**	**15**	**0**	**0**	**0**	**13:20**
	Providence Bruins	AHL	6	4	6	10	4	....	....	....	....	....	....	....	....	....	....	....	....	....	....	....	....	....	....
2010-11	**St. Louis**	**NHL**	**65**	**7**	**22**	**29**	**69**	**1**	**1**	**0**	**75**	**9.3**	**–4**	**419**	**51.6**	**16:11**	....	....	....	....	....	....	....	....	....
2011-12	**St. Louis**	**NHL**	**73**	**5**	**15**	**20**	**42**	**0**	**1**	**1**	**117**	**4.3**	**12**	**501**	**56.1**	**15:51**	**9**	**1**	**1**	**2**	**15**	**0**	**0**	**1**	**13:09**
2012-13	HC Slavia Praha	CzRep	27	10	15	25	8	....	....	....	....	....	....	....	....	....	....	....	....	....	....	....	....	....	....
	St. Louis	**NHL**	**48**	**8**	**11**	**19**	**35**	**1**	**0**	**2**	**69**	**11.6**	**–4**	**506**	**56.5**	**15:27**	**6**	**0**	**3**	**3**	**0**	**0**	**0**	**0**	**16:37**
2013-14	**St. Louis**	**NHL**	**61**	**9**	**24**	**33**	**72**	**1**	**0**	**1**	**102**	**8.8**	**14**	**813**	**61.9**	**16:45**	**6**	**0**	**3**	**3**	**4**	**0**	**0**	**0**	**21:12**
2014-15	Omsk	KHL	53	10	28	38	51	....	....	....	....	....	....	....	....	....	4	1	1	2	0	....	....	....	....
	NHL Totals		**381**	**35**	**88**	**123**	**282**	**3**	**2**	**5**	**489**	**7.2**		**2899**	**56.3**	**14:00**	**40**	**3**	**9**	**12**	**34**	**0**	**0**	**1**	**14:15**

Traded to **St. Louis** by **Boston** for David Warsofsky, June 26, 2010. Signed as a free agent by **Slavia Praha** (CzRep), September 15, 2012. Signed as a free agent by **Omsk** (KHL), July 10, 2014.

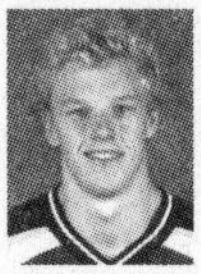

SODERBERG, Carl
(SOH-dehr-buhrg, KAHRL) **COL**

Center. Shoots left. 6'3", 216 lbs. Born, Malmo, Sweden, October 12, 1985. St. Louis' 2nd choice, 49th overall, in 2004 Entry Draft.

Season	Club	League	GP	G	A	Pts	PIM	PP	SH	GW	S	S%	+/-	TF	F%	Min	GP	G	A	Pts	PIM	PP	SH	GW	Min
2000-01	Skane	Other	8	1	2	3	2	....	....	....	....	....	....	....	....	....	....	....	....	....	....	....	....	....	....
	Malmo U18	Swe-U18	3	1	1	2	0	....	....	....	....	....	....	....	....	....	....	....	....	....	....	....	....	....	....
2001-02	Malmo U18	Swe-U18	13	9	20	29	18	....	....	....	....	....	....	....	....	....	....	....	....	....	....	....	....	....	....
	Malmo Jr.	Swe-Jr.	4	0	2	2	2	....	....	....	....	....	....	....	....	....	7	0	2	2	4	....	....	....	....
2002-03	Malmo U18	Swe-U18	4	6	3	9	25	....	....	....	....	....	....	....	....	....	....	....	....	....	....	....	....	....	....
	Malmo Jr.	Swe-Jr.	28	17	18	35	22	....	....	....	....	....	....	....	....	....	6	2	4	6	8	....	....	....	....
2003-04	Malmo U18	Swe-U18	27	23	25	48	30	....	....	....	....	....	....	....	....	....	6	1	2	3	10	....	....	....	....
	Malmo	Sweden	24	1	1	2	8	....	....	....	....	....	....	....	....	....	....	....	....	....	....	....	....	....	....
	Malmo	Sweden-Q	8	1	1	2	4	....	....	....	....	....	....	....	....	....	....	....	....	....	....	....	....	....	....
2004-05	Morrums GoIS IK	Sweden-2	14	5	6	11	8	....	....	....	....	....	....	....	....	....	....	....	....	....	....	....	....	....	....
	Malmo Jr.	Swe-Jr.	12	13	6	19	43	....	....	....	....	....	....	....	....	....	3	2	1	3	12	....	....	....	....
	Malmo	Sweden	38	0	5	5	8	....	....	....	....	....	....	....	....	....	....	....	....	....	....	....	....	....	....
	Malmo	Sweden-Q	7	0	0	0	0	....	....	....	....	....	....	....	....	....	....	....	....	....	....	....	....	....	....
2005-06	Malmo	Sweden-2	49	20	27	47	47	....	....	....	....	....	....	....	....	....	....	....	....	....	....	....	....	....	....
2006-07	Malmo	Sweden	31	12	18	30	14	....	....	....	....	....	....	....	....	....	....	....	....	....	....	....	....	....	....
2007-08	Malmo	Sweden-2	42	22	36	58	18	....	....	....	....	....	....	....	....	....	....	....	....	....	....	....	....	....	....
2008-09	Malmo	Sweden-2	45	18	41	59	26	....	....	....	....	....	....	....	....	....	....	....	....	....	....	....	....	....	....
2009-10	Malmo	Sweden-2	51	20	31	51	53	....	....	....	....	....	....	....	....	....	5	0	1	1	0	....	....	....	....
2010-11	Malmo	Sweden-2	52	12	34	46	18	....	....	....	....	....	....	....	....	....	....	....	....	....	....	....	....	....	....
2011-12	Linkopings HC	Sweden	42	14	21	35	20	....	....	....	....	....	....	....	....	....	....	....	....	....	....	....	....	....	....
2012-13	Linkopings HC	Sweden	54	*31	29	60	48	....	....	....	....	....	....	....	....	....	6	1	1	2	27	....	....	....	....
	Boston	**NHL**	**6**	**0**	**2**	**2**	**6**	**0**	**0**	**0**	**6**	**0.0**	**–2**	**13**	**53.9**	**14:44**	**2**	**0**	**0**	**0**	**0**	**0**	**0**	**0**	**12:15**
2013-14	**Boston**	**NHL**	**73**	**16**	**32**	**48**	**36**	**5**	**0**	**3**	**129**	**12.4**	**4**	**328**	**42.4**	**14:16**	**12**	**1**	**5**	**6**	**2**	**0**	**0**	**0**	**15:41**
2014-15	**Boston**	**NHL**	**82**	**13**	**31**	**44**	**26**	**5**	**0**	**3**	**163**	**8.0**	**10**	**766**	**48.2**	**16:49**	....	....	....	....	....	....	....	....	....
	NHL Totals		**161**	**29**	**65**	**94**	**68**	**10**	**0**	**6**	**298**	**9.7**		**1107**	**46.5**	**15:35**	**14**	**1**	**5**	**6**	**2**	**0**	**0**	**0**	**15:12**

Traded to **Boston** by **St. Louis** for Hannu Toivonen, July 23, 2007.Traded to **Colorado** by **Boston** for Boston's 6th round choice (previously acquired) in 2016 Entry Draft, June 25, 2015.

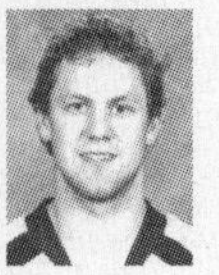

SPALING, Nick (SPAHL-ihng, NIHK) TOR

Center. Shoots left. 6'1", 201 lbs. Born, Palmerston, ON, September 19, 1988. Nashville's 3rd choice, 58th overall, in 2007 Entry Draft.

			Regular Season														Playoffs								
Season	Club	League	GP	G	A	Pts	PIM	PP	SH	GW	S	S%	+/-	TF	F%	Min	GP	G	A	Pts	PIM	PP	SH	GW	Min
2004-05	Listowel Cyclones	ON-Jr.B	61	25	27	52	58	....	....	....	....	....	....	....	....	....	....	....	....	....	....	....	....	....	....
2005-06	Kitchener Rangers	OHL	62	10	15	25	22	....	....	....	....	....	....	....	....	....	5	0	3	3	0	....	....	....	....
2006-07	Kitchener Rangers	OHL	61	23	36	59	41	....	....	....	....	....	....	....	....	....	9	2	3	5	4	....	....	....	....
2007-08	Kitchener Rangers	OHL	56	38	34	72	18	....	....	....	....	....	....	....	....	....	20	14	16	30	9	....	....	....	....
2008-09	Milwaukee	AHL	79	12	23	35	28	....	....	....	....	....	....	....	....	....	11	0	3	3	8	....	....	....	....
2009-10	**Nashville**	**NHL**	**28**	**0**	**3**	**3**	**0**	**0**	**0**	**0**	**26**	**0.0**	**3**	**95**	**41.1**	**11:03**	**6**	**0**	**0**	**0**	**0**	**0**	**0**	**0**	**8:24**
	Milwaukee	AHL	48	7	10	17	21	....	....	....	....	....	....	....	....	....	....	....	....	....	....	....	....	....	....
2010-11	**Nashville**	**NHL**	**74**	**8**	**6**	**14**	**20**	**1**	**0**	**2**	**75**	**10.7**	**-10**	**497**	**50.9**	**13:56**	**12**	**2**	**4**	**6**	**0**	**0**	**0**	**1**	**15:19**
	Milwaukee	AHL	4	1	1	2	2	....	....	....	....	....	....	....	....	....	....	....	....	....	....	....	....	....	....
2011-12	**Nashville**	**NHL**	**77**	**10**	**12**	**22**	**18**	**0**	**0**	**3**	**107**	**9.3**	**-7**	**894**	**50.1**	**15:43**	**10**	**0**	**3**	**3**	**0**	**0**	**0**	**0**	**15:49**
2012-13	**Nashville**	**NHL**	**47**	**9**	**4**	**13**	**18**	**1**	**0**	**2**	**57**	**15.8**	**-10**	**482**	**46.3**	**15:52**	....	....	....	....	....	....	....	....	....
2013-14	**Nashville**	**NHL**	**71**	**13**	**19**	**32**	**14**	**3**	**1**	**1**	**85**	**15.3**	**2**	**167**	**52.7**	**16:01**	....	....	....	....	....	....	....	....	....
2014-15	**Pittsburgh**	**NHL**	**82**	**9**	**18**	**27**	**26**	**1**	**0**	**0**	**90**	**10.0**	**-2**	**174**	**48.3**	**15:14**	**5**	**1**	**1**	**2**	**4**	**0**	**0**	**0**	**13:40**
	NHL Totals		**379**	**49**	**62**	**111**	**96**	**6**	**1**	**8**	**440**	**11.1**		**2309**	**49.2**	**15:00**	**33**	**3**	**8**	**11**	**4**	**0**	**0**	**1**	**13:58**

Traded to **Pittsburgh** by **Nashville** with Patric Hornqvist for James Neal, June 27, 2014. Traded to **Toronto** by **Pittsburgh** with Kasperi Kapanen, Scott Harrington, New Jersey's 3rd round choice (previously acquired) in 2016 Entry Draft and future considerations for Phil Kessel, Tim Erixon, Tyler Biggs and future considerations, July 1, 2015.

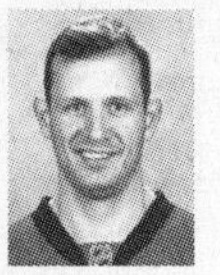

SPEZZA, Jason (SPEHT-zuh, JAY-suhn) DAL

Center. Shoots right. 6'3", 220 lbs. Born, Mississauga, ON, June 13, 1983. Ottawa's 1st choice, 2nd overall, in 2001 Entry Draft.

			Regular Season														Playoffs								
Season	Club	League	GP	G	A	Pts	PIM	PP	SH	GW	S	S%	+/-	TF	F%	Min	GP	G	A	Pts	PIM	PP	SH	GW	Min
1997-98	Toronto Marlies	MTHL	54	53	61	114	42	....	....	....	....	....	....	....	....	....	....	....	....	....	....	....	....	....	....
1998-99	Brampton	OHL	67	22	49	71	18	....	....	....	....	....	....	....	....	....	....	....	....	....	....	....	....	....	....
99-2000	Mississauga	OHL	52	24	37	61	33	....	....	....	....	....	....	....	....	....	....	....	....	....	....	....	....	....	....
2000-01	Mississauga	OHL	15	7	23	30	11	....	....	....	....	....	....	....	....	....	....	....	....	....	....	....	....	....	....
	Windsor Spitfires	OHL	41	36	50	86	32	....	....	....	....	....	....	....	....	....	9	4	5	9	10	....	....	....	....
2001-02	Windsor Spitfires	OHL	27	19	26	45	16	....	....	....	....	....	....	....	....	....	....	....	....	....	....	....	....	....	....
	Belleville Bulls	OHL	26	23	37	60	26	....	....	....	....	....	....	....	....	....	11	5	6	11	18	....	....	....	....
	Grand Rapids	AHL	....	....	....	....	....	....	....	....	....	....	....	....	....	....	3	1	0	1	2	....	....	....	....
2002-03	**Ottawa**	**NHL**	**33**	**7**	**14**	**21**	**8**	**3**	**0**	**0**	**65**	**10.8**	**-3**	**330**	**45.8**	**12:40**	**3**	**1**	**1**	**2**	**0**	**1**	**0**	**0**	**11:34**
	Binghamton	AHL	43	22	32	54	71	....	....	....	....	....	....	....	....	....	2	1	2	3	4	....	....	....	....
2003-04	**Ottawa**	**NHL**	**78**	**22**	**33**	**55**	**71**	**5**	**0**	**3**	**142**	**15.5**	**22**	**956**	**47.7**	**14:38**	**3**	**0**	**0**	**0**	**2**	**0**	**0**	**0**	**9:44**
2004-05	Binghamton	AHL	80	32	*85	*117	50	....	....	....	....	....	....	....	....	....	6	1	3	4	6	....	....	....	....
2005-06	**Ottawa**	**NHL**	**68**	**19**	**71**	**90**	**33**	**7**	**0**	**5**	**156**	**12.2**	**23**	**1220**	**52.6**	**19:00**	**10**	**5**	**9**	**14**	**2**	**3**	**0**	**1**	**17:59**
2006-07	**Ottawa**	**NHL**	**67**	**34**	**53**	**87**	**45**	**13**	**1**	**5**	**162**	**21.0**	**19**	**1261**	**53.0**	**19:17**	**20**	**7**	***15**	***22**	**10**	**3**	**0**	**0**	**20:58**
2007-08	**Ottawa**	**NHL**	**76**	**34**	**58**	**92**	**66**	**11**	**0**	**6**	**210**	**16.2**	**26**	**1445**	**50.5**	**20:40**	**4**	**0**	**1**	**1**	**0**	**0**	**0**	**0**	**19:45**
2008-09	**Ottawa**	**NHL**	**82**	**32**	**41**	**73**	**79**	**13**	**1**	**3**	**246**	**13.0**	**-14**	**1477**	**53.3**	**19:41**	....	....	....	....	....	....	....	....	....
2009-10	**Ottawa**	**NHL**	**60**	**23**	**34**	**57**	**20**	**11**	**0**	**5**	**165**	**13.9**	**0**	**1018**	**50.5**	**19:04**	**6**	**1**	**6**	**7**	**4**	**1**	**0**	**0**	**22:46**
2010-11	**Ottawa**	**NHL**	**62**	**21**	**36**	**57**	**28**	**7**	**0**	**2**	**188**	**11.2**	**-7**	**1210**	**56.3**	**20:12**	....	....	....	....	....	....	....	....	....
2011-12	**Ottawa**	**NHL**	**80**	**34**	**50**	**84**	**36**	**10**	**0**	**2**	**232**	**14.7**	**11**	**1700**	**53.5**	**19:55**	**7**	**3**	**2**	**5**	**8**	**0**	**0**	**1**	**20:59**
2012-13	Rapperswil	Swiss	28	9	21	30	12	....	....	....	....	....	....	....	....	....	....	....	....	....	....	....	....	....	....
	Ottawa	**NHL**	**5**	**2**	**3**	**5**	**2**	**1**	**0**	**0**	**12**	**16.7**	**3**	**119**	**57.1**	**19:11**	**3**	**0**	**1**	**1**	**0**	**0**	**0**	**0**	**18:27**
2013-14	**Ottawa**	**NHL**	**75**	**23**	**43**	**66**	**46**	**9**	**0**	**5**	**223**	**10.3**	**-26**	**1436**	**54.0**	**18:13**	....	....	....	....	....	....	....	....	....
2014-15	**Dallas**	**NHL**	**82**	**17**	**45**	**62**	**28**	**4**	**0**	**1**	**204**	**8.3**	**-7**	**1262**	**54.0**	**17:13**	....	....	....	....	....	....	....	....	....
	NHL Totals		**768**	**268**	**481**	**749**	**462**	**94**	**2**	**37**	**2005**	**13.4**		**13434**	**52.6**	**18:29**	**56**	**17**	**35**	**52**	**26**	**8**	**0**	**2**	**19:18**

OHL All-Rookie Team (1999) • AHL All-Rookie Team (2003) • AHL First All-Star Team (2005) • John P. Sollenberger Trophy (AHL - Top Scorer) (2005) • Les Cunningham Award (AHL – MVP) (2005)

Played in NHL All-Star Game (2008, 2012)

Signed as a free agent by **Rapperswil** (Swiss), September 19, 2012. Traded to **Dallas** by **Ottawa** with Ludwig Karlsson for Alex Chiasson. Alexander Guptill, Nicholas Paul and Dallas' 2nd round choice (later traded to New Jersey – New Jersey selected Mackenzie Blackwood) in 2015 Entry Draft, July 1, 2014.

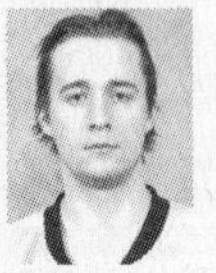

SPOONER, Ryan (SPOO-nuhr, RIGH-uhn) BOS

Center. Shoots left. 5'11", 181 lbs. Born, Ottawa, ON, January 30, 1992. Boston's 3rd choice, 45th overall, in 2010 Entry Draft.

			Regular Season														Playoffs								
Season	Club	League	GP	G	A	Pts	PIM	PP	SH	GW	S	S%	+/-	TF	F%	Min	GP	G	A	Pts	PIM	PP	SH	GW	Min
2007-08	Ott. Jr. Senators	Minor-ON	53	52	45	97	16	....	....	....	....	....	....	....	....	....	....	....	....	....	....	....	....	....	....
2008-09	Peterborough	OHL	62	30	28	58	8	....	....	....	....	....	....	....	....	....	4	0	1	1	0	....	....	....	....
2009-10	Peterborough	OHL	47	19	35	54	12	....	....	....	....	....	....	....	....	....	3	0	1	1	2	....	....	....	....
2010-11	Peterborough	OHL	14	10	9	19	2	....	....	....	....	....	....	....	....	....	....	....	....	....	....	....	....	....	....
	Kingston	OHL	50	25	37	62	6	....	....	....	....	....	....	....	....	....	5	4	2	6	2	....	....	....	....
	Providence Bruins	AHL	3	2	1	3	0	....	....	....	....	....	....	....	....	....	....	....	....	....	....	....	....	....	....
2011-12	Kingston	OHL	27	14	18	32	8	....	....	....	....	....	....	....	....	....	....	....	....	....	....	....	....	....	....
	Sarnia Sting	OHL	30	15	19	34	8	....	....	....	....	....	....	....	....	....	6	1	2	3	8	....	....	....	....
	Providence Bruins	AHL	5	1	3	4	0	....	....	....	....	....	....	....	....	....	....	....	....	....	....	....	....	....	....
2012-13	Providence Bruins	AHL	59	17	40	57	14	....	....	....	....	....	....	....	....	....	12	2	3	5	4	....	....	....	....
	Boston	**NHL**	**4**	**0**	**0**	**0**	**0**	**0**	**0**	**0**	**4**	**0.0**	**0**	**24**	**45.8**	**9:07**	....	....	....	....	....	....	....	....	....
2013-14	**Boston**	**NHL**	**23**	**0**	**11**	**11**	**6**	**0**	**0**	**0**	**42**	**0.0**	**0**	**145**	**40.7**	**12:49**	....	....	....	....	....	....	....	....	....
	Providence Bruins	AHL	49	11	35	46	8	....	....	....	....	....	....	....	....	....	12	6	9	15	2	....	....	....	....
2014-15	**Boston**	**NHL**	**29**	**8**	**10**	**18**	**2**	**3**	**0**	**1**	**73**	**11.0**	**2**	**220**	**45.5**	**14:32**	....	....	....	....	....	....	....	....	....
	Providence Bruins	AHL	34	8	18	26	10	....	....	....	....	....	....	....	....	....	5	0	4	4	0	....	....	....	....
	NHL Totals		**56**	**8**	**21**	**29**	**8**	**3**	**0**	**1**	**119**	**6.7**		**389**	**43.7**	**13:26**	....	....	....	....	....	....	....	....	....

AHL All-Rookie Team (2013)

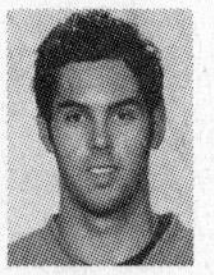

SPROUL, Ryan (SPROHL, RIGH-uhn) DET

Defense. Shoots right. 6'4", 206 lbs. Born, Mississauga, ON, January 13, 1993. Detroit's 3rd choice, 55th overall, in 2011 Entry Draft.

			Regular Season														Playoffs								
Season	Club	League	GP	G	A	Pts	PIM	PP	SH	GW	S	S%	+/-	TF	F%	Min	GP	G	A	Pts	PIM	PP	SH	GW	Min
2008-09	Vaughan Kings	GTHL	31	2	7	9	14	....	....	....	....	....	....	....	....	....	....	....	....	....	....	....	....	....	....
2009-10	Bramalea Blues	ON-Jr.A	6	0	1	1	6	....	....	....	....	....	....	....	....	....	....	....	....	....	....	....	....	....	....
	Vaughan Vipers	ON-Jr.A	8	1	1	2	0	....	....	....	....	....	....	....	....	....	2	0	0	0	0	....	....	....	....
2010-11	Vaughan Vipers	ON-Jr.A	3	1	2	3	4	....	....	....	....	....	....	....	....	....	....	....	....	....	....	....	....	....	....
	Sault Ste. Marie	OHL	61	14	19	33	36	....	....	....	....	....	....	....	....	....	....	....	....	....	....	....	....	....	....
2011-12	Sault Ste. Marie	OHL	61	23	31	54	53	....	....	....	....	....	....	....	....	....	....	....	....	....	....	....	....	....	....
2012-13	Sault Ste. Marie	OHL	50	20	46	66	45	....	....	....	....	....	....	....	....	....	6	2	3	5	0	....	....	....	....
	Grand Rapids	AHL	2	0	0	0	2	....	....	....	....	....	....	....	....	....	....	....	....	....	....	....	....	....	....
2013-14	**Detroit**	**NHL**	**1**	**0**	**0**	**0**	**0**	**0**	**0**	**0**	**3**	**0.0**	**0**	**0**	**0.0**	**18:25**	....	....	....	....	....	....	....	....	....
	Grand Rapids	AHL	72	11	21	32	49	....	....	....	....	....	....	....	....	....	10	2	3	5	4	....	....	....	....
2014-15	Grand Rapids	AHL	66	5	19	24	26	....	....	....	....	....	....	....	....	....	5	0	0	0	0	....	....	....	....
	NHL Totals		**1**	**0**	**0**	**0**	**0**	**0**	**0**	**0**	**3**	**0.0**		**0**	**0.0**	**18:25**	....	....	....	....	....	....	....	....	....

OHL First All-Star Team (2013) • Canadian Major Junior Defenseman of the Year (2013) • AHL All-Rookie Team (2014)

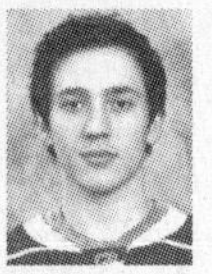

SPURGEON, Jared (SPUHR-juhn, JAIR-uhd) MIN

Defense. Shoots right. 5'9", 176 lbs. Born, Edmonton, AB, November 29, 1989. NY Islanders' 12th choice, 156th overall, in 2008 Entry Draft.

			Regular Season														Playoffs								
Season	Club	League	GP	G	A	Pts	PIM	PP	SH	GW	S	S%	+/-	TF	F%	Min	GP	G	A	Pts	PIM	PP	SH	GW	Min
2004-05	K of C Pats	AMHL	26	9	21	30	16	....	....	....	....	....	....	....	....	....	....	....	....	....	....	....	....	....	....
2005-06	Spokane Chiefs	WHL	46	3	9	12	28	....	....	....	....	....	....	....	....	....	....	....	....	....	....	....	....	....	....
2006-07	Spokane Chiefs	WHL	38	4	15	19	16	....	....	....	....	....	....	....	....	....	....	....	....	....	....	....	....	....	....
2007-08	Spokane Chiefs	WHL	69	12	31	43	19	....	....	....	....	....	....	....	....	....	21	0	5	5	16	....	....	....	....
2008-09	Spokane Chiefs	WHL	59	10	35	45	37	....	....	....	....	....	....	....	....	....	12	2	3	5	10	....	....	....	....
2009-10	Spokane Chiefs	WHL	54	8	43	51	18	....	....	....	....	....	....	....	....	....	7	0	4	4	2	....	....	....	....
2010-11	**Minnesota**	**NHL**	**53**	**4**	**8**	**12**	**2**	**2**	**0**	**1**	**38**	**10.5**	**-1**	**0**	**0.0**	**15:04**	....	....	....	....	....	....	....	....	....
	Houston Aeros	AHL	23	2	7	9	10	....	....	....	....	....	....	....	....	....	23	1	10	11	10	....	....	....	....
2011-12	**Minnesota**	**NHL**	**70**	**3**	**20**	**23**	**6**	**2**	**0**	**1**	**92**	**3.3**	**-4**	**0**	**0.0**	**21:36**	....	....	....	....	....	....	....	....	....
2012-13	Langnau	Swiss	12	3	4	7	6	....	....	....	....	....	....	....	....	....	....	....	....	....	....	....	....	....	....
	Minnesota	**NHL**	**39**	**5**	**10**	**15**	**4**	**4**	**0**	**2**	**67**	**7.5**	**1**	**0**	**0.0**	**21:33**	**5**	**0**	**0**	**0**	**2**	**0**	**0**	**0**	**21:15**
2013-14	**Minnesota**	**NHL**	**67**	**5**	**21**	**26**	**16**	**2**	**0**	**1**	**91**	**5.5**	**15**	**0**	**0.0**	**22:38**	**13**	**3**	**3**	**6**	**2**	**1**	**0**	**0**	**24:04**
2014-15	**Minnesota**	**NHL**	**66**	**9**	**16**	**25**	**6**	**3**	**0**	**2**	**128**	**7.0**	**3**	**0**	**0.0**	**22:37**	**10**	**1**	**3**	**4**	**4**	**1**	**0**	**0**	**21:20**
	NHL Totals		**295**	**26**	**75**	**101**	**34**	**13**	**0**	**7**	**416**	**6.3**		**0**	**0.0**	**20:53**	**28**	**4**	**6**	**10**	**8**	**2**	**0**	**0**	**22:35**

Signed as a free agent by **Minnesota**, September 23, 2010. Signed as a free agent by **Langnau** (Swiss), September 21, 2012.

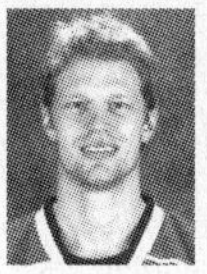

STAAL, Eric

(STAWL, AIR-ihk) **CAR**

Center. Shoots left. 6'4", 205 lbs. Born, Thunder Bay, ON, October 29, 1984. Carolina's 1st choice, 2nd overall, in 2003 Entry Draft.

			Regular Season														Playoffs								
Season	Club	League	GP	G	A	Pts	PIM	PP	SH	GW	S	S%	+/-	TF	F%	Min	GP	G	A	Pts	PIM	PP	SH	GW	Min
99-2000	Thunder Bay	Other	7	4	8	12	0	....	....	....	....	....	....	....	....	....	....	....	....	....	....	....	....	....	....
2000-01	Peterborough	OHL	63	19	30	49	23	....	....	....	....	....	....	....	....	....	7	2	5	7	4	....	....	....	....
2001-02	Peterborough	OHL	56	23	39	62	40	....	....	....	....	....	....	....	....	....	6	3	6	9	10	....	....	....	....
2002-03	Peterborough	OHL	66	39	59	98	36	....	....	....	....	....	....	....	....	....	7	9	5	14	6	....	....	....	....
2003-04	**Carolina**	**NHL**	**81**	**11**	**20**	**31**	**40**	**2**	**1**	**3**	**164**	**6.7**	**–6**	**669**	**43.1**	**16:40**	....	....	....	....	....	....	....	....	....
2004-05	Lowell	AHL	77	26	51	77	88	....	....	....	....	....	....	....	....	....	11	2	8	10	12	....	....	....	....
2005-06♦	**Carolina**	**NHL**	**82**	**45**	**55**	**100**	**81**	**19**	**4**	**4**	**279**	**16.1**	**–8**	**1309**	**42.6**	**19:39**	**25**	**9**	***19**	***28**	**8**	***7**	**0**	**1**	**19:48**
2006-07	**Carolina**	**NHL**	**82**	**30**	**40**	**70**	**68**	**12**	**1**	**1**	**288**	**10.4**	**–6**	**1238**	**45.2**	**20:08**	....	....	....	....	....	....	....	....	....
2007-08	**Carolina**	**NHL**	**82**	**38**	**44**	**82**	**50**	**14**	**0**	**7**	**310**	**12.3**	**–2**	**1708**	**44.9**	**21:38**	....	....	....	....	....	....	....	....	....
2008-09	**Carolina**	**NHL**	**82**	**40**	**35**	**75**	**50**	**14**	**1**	**8**	**372**	**10.8**	**15**	**1586**	**45.3**	**21:03**	**18**	**10**	**5**	**15**	**4**	**3**	**0**	**1**	**21:31**
2009-10	**Carolina**	**NHL**	**70**	**29**	**41**	**70**	**68**	**13**	**0**	**5**	**277**	**10.5**	**4**	**1162**	**41.8**	**20:43**	....	....	....	....	....	....	....	....	....
	Canada	Olympics	7	1	5	6	6	....	....	....	....	....	....	....	....	....	....	....	....	....	....	....	....	....	....
2010-11	**Carolina**	**NHL**	**81**	**33**	**43**	**76**	**72**	**12**	**3**	**8**	**296**	**11.1**	**–10**	**1751**	**48.0**	**21:56**	....	....	....	....	....	....	....	....	....
2011-12	**Carolina**	**NHL**	**82**	**24**	**46**	**70**	**48**	**7**	**3**	**3**	**262**	**9.2**	**–20**	**1681**	**52.5**	**21:33**	....	....	....	....	....	....	....	....	....
2012-13	**Carolina**	**NHL**	**48**	**18**	**35**	**53**	**54**	**3**	**1**	**4**	**152**	**11.8**	**5**	**1014**	**52.0**	**21:00**	....	....	....	....	....	....	....	....	....
2013-14	**Carolina**	**NHL**	**79**	**21**	**40**	**61**	**74**	**1**	**2**	**0**	**230**	**9.1**	**–13**	**1430**	**52.7**	**20:17**	....	....	....	....	....	....	....	....	....
2014-15	**Carolina**	**NHL**	**77**	**23**	**31**	**54**	**41**	**1**	**0**	**4**	**244**	**9.4**	**–13**	**669**	**51.3**	**18:51**	....	....	....	....	....	....	....	....	....
	NHL Totals		**846**	**312**	**430**	**742**	**646**	**104**	**16**	**47**	**2874**	**10.9**		**14217**	**47.3**	**20:17**	**43**	**19**	**24**	**43**	**12**	**10**	**0**	**2**	**20:31**

OHL Second All-Star Team (2003) • Canadian Major Junior First All-Star Team (2003) • NHL Second All-Star Team (2006)
Played in NHL All-Star Game (2007, 2008, 2009, 2011)

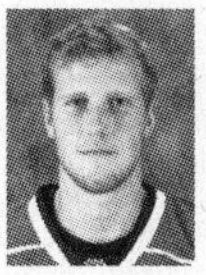

STAAL, Jared

(STAWL, JAIR-uhd)

Right wing. Shoots right. 6'4", 210 lbs. Born, Thunder Bay, ON, August 21, 1990. Phoenix's 3rd choice, 49th overall, in 2008 Entry Draft.

			Regular Season														Playoffs								
Season	Club	League	GP	G	A	Pts	PIM	PP	SH	GW	S	S%	+/-	TF	F%	Min	GP	G	A	Pts	PIM	PP	SH	GW	Min
2005-06	Thunder Bay	Minor-ON	64	24	25	49	72	....	....	....	....	....	....	....	....	....	....	....	....	....	....	....	....	....	....
2006-07	Sudbury Wolves	OHL	63	2	1	3	18	....	....	....	....	....	....	....	....	....	21	1	0	1	2	....	....	....	....
2007-08	Sudbury Wolves	OHL	60	21	28	49	44	....	....	....	....	....	....	....	....	....	....	....	....	....	....	....	....	....	....
2008-09	Sudbury Wolves	OHL	67	19	33	52	38	....	....	....	....	....	....	....	....	....	6	0	1	1	2	....	....	....	....
	San Antonio	AHL	5	0	0	0	0	....	....	....	....	....	....	....	....	....	....	....	....	....	....	....	....	....	....
2009-10	Sudbury Wolves	OHL	59	12	37	49	57	....	....	....	....	....	....	....	....	....	3	0	0	0	4	....	....	....	....
	San Antonio	AHL	5	0	1	1	2	....	....	....	....	....	....	....	....	....	....	....	....	....	....	....	....	....	....
2010-11	Charlotte	AHL	13	1	1	2	2	....	....	....	....	....	....	....	....	....	....	....	....	....	....	....	....	....	....
	Florida Everblades	ECHL	33	6	5	11	6	....	....	....	....	....	....	....	....	....	....	....	....	....	....	....	....	....	....
2011-12	Charlotte	AHL	37	3	3	6	18	....	....	....	....	....	....	....	....	....	....	....	....	....	....	....	....	....	....
	Providence Bruins	AHL	7	0	2	2	2	....	....	....	....	....	....	....	....	....	....	....	....	....	....	....	....	....	....
2012-13	Charlotte	AHL	52	4	3	7	25	....	....	....	....	....	....	....	....	....	3	0	0	0	0	....	....	....	....
	Carolina	**NHL**	**2**	**0**	**0**	**0**	**2**	**0**	**0**	**0**	**3**	**0.0**	**–2**	**0**	**0.0**	**13:23**	....	....	....	....	....	....	....	....	....
2013-14	Charlotte	AHL	50	2	5	7	23	....	....	....	....	....	....	....	....	....	....	....	....	....	....	....	....	....	....
2014-15	Charlotte	AHL	63	7	4	11	27	....	....	....	....	....	....	....	....	....	....	....	....	....	....	....	....	....	....
	NHL Totals		**2**	**0**	**0**	**0**	**2**	**0**	**0**	**0**	**3**	**0.0**		**0**	**0.0**	**13:23**	....	....	....	....	....	....	....	....	....

Traded to **Carolina** by **Phoenix** for Nashville's 5th round choice (previously acquired, Phoenix selected Louis Domingue) in 2010 Entry Draft, May 13, 2010.

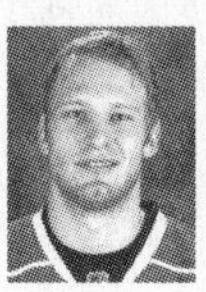

STAAL, Jordan

(STAWL, JOHR-dahn) **CAR**

Center. Shoots left. 6'4", 220 lbs. Born, Thunder Bay, ON, September 10, 1988. Pittsburgh's 1st choice, 2nd overall, in 2006 Entry Draft.

			Regular Season														Playoffs								
Season	Club	League	GP	G	A	Pts	PIM	PP	SH	GW	S	S%	+/-	TF	F%	Min	GP	G	A	Pts	PIM	PP	SH	GW	Min
2004-05	Peterborough	OHL	66	9	19	28	29	....	....	....	....	....	....	....	....	....	14	5	5	10	16	....	....	....	....
2005-06	Peterborough	OHL	68	28	40	68	69	....	....	....	....	....	....	....	....	....	19	10	6	16	16	....	....	....	....
2006-07	**Pittsburgh**	**NHL**	**81**	**29**	**13**	**42**	**24**	**4**	***7**	**4**	**131**	**22.1**	**16**	**383**	**37.1**	**14:56**	**5**	**3**	**0**	**3**	**2**	**0**	**0**	**0**	**16:00**
2007-08	**Pittsburgh**	**NHL**	**82**	**12**	**16**	**28**	**55**	**3**	**0**	**4**	**183**	**6.6**	**–5**	**1202**	**42.2**	**18:16**	**20**	**6**	**1**	**7**	**14**	**1**	**0**	**1**	**18:16**
2008-09♦	**Pittsburgh**	**NHL**	**82**	**22**	**27**	**49**	**37**	**2**	**1**	**3**	**166**	**13.3**	**5**	**1206**	**47.0**	**19:51**	**24**	**4**	**5**	**9**	**8**	**0**	**1**	**0**	**19:13**
2009-10	**Pittsburgh**	**NHL**	**82**	**21**	**28**	**49**	**57**	**1**	**2**	**1**	**195**	**10.8**	**19**	**1324**	**48.3**	**19:24**	**11**	**3**	**2**	**5**	**6**	**2**	**0**	**0**	**18:14**
2010-11	**Pittsburgh**	**NHL**	**42**	**11**	**19**	**30**	**24**	**3**	**0**	**4**	**91**	**12.1**	**7**	**801**	**46.9**	**21:21**	**7**	**1**	**2**	**3**	**2**	**0**	**0**	**0**	**21:28**
2011-12	**Pittsburgh**	**NHL**	**62**	**25**	**25**	**50**	**34**	**5**	**3**	**0**	**149**	**16.8**	**11**	**1158**	**51.0**	**20:03**	**6**	**6**	**3**	**9**	**2**	**1**	**0**	**1**	**19:49**
2012-13	**Carolina**	**NHL**	**48**	**10**	**21**	**31**	**32**	**1**	**0**	**1**	**114**	**8.8**	**–18**	**914**	**50.1**	**20:06**	....	....	....	....	....	....	....	....	....
2013-14	**Carolina**	**NHL**	**82**	**15**	**25**	**40**	**34**	**2**	**1**	**2**	**165**	**9.1**	**2**	**1477**	**54.4**	**18:57**	....	....	....	....	....	....	....	....	....
2014-15	**Carolina**	**NHL**	**46**	**6**	**18**	**24**	**14**	**1**	**0**	**1**	**92**	**6.5**	**–6**	**885**	**56.4**	**18:33**	....	....	....	....	....	....	....	....	....
	NHL Totals		**607**	**151**	**192**	**343**	**311**	**22**	**14**	**20**	**1286**	**11.7**		**9350**	**49.0**	**18:51**	**73**	**23**	**13**	**36**	**34**	**4**	**1**	**2**	**18:51**

NHL All-Rookie Team (2007)
Traded to **Carolina** by **Pittsburgh** for Brandon Sutter, Brian Dumoulin and Carolina's 1st round choice (Derrick Pouliot) in 2012 Entry Draft, June 22, 2012.

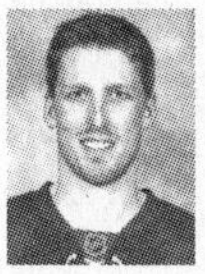

STAAL, Marc

(STAWL, MAHRK) **NYR**

Defense. Shoots left. 6'4", 207 lbs. Born, Thunder Bay, ON, January 13, 1987. NY Rangers' 1st choice, 12th overall, in 2005 Entry Draft.

			Regular Season														Playoffs								
Season	Club	League	GP	G	A	Pts	PIM	PP	SH	GW	S	S%	+/-	TF	F%	Min	GP	G	A	Pts	PIM	PP	SH	GW	Min
2003-04	Sudbury Wolves	OHL	61	1	13	14	34	....	....	....	....	....	....	....	....	....	7	1	2	3	2	....	....	....	....
2004-05	Sudbury Wolves	OHL	65	6	20	26	53	....	....	....	....	....	....	....	....	....	12	0	4	4	15	....	....	....	....
2005-06	Sudbury Wolves	OHL	57	11	38	49	60	....	....	....	....	....	....	....	....	....	10	0	8	8	8	....	....	....	....
	Hartford	AHL	....	....	....	....	....	....	....	....	....	....	....	....	....	....	12	0	2	2	8	....	....	....	....
2006-07	Sudbury Wolves	OHL	53	5	29	34	68	....	....	....	....	....	....	....	....	....	21	5	15	20	22	....	....	....	....
2007-08	**NY Rangers**	**NHL**	**80**	**2**	**8**	**10**	**42**	**0**	**0**	**0**	**78**	**2.6**	**2**	**0**	**0.0**	**18:48**	**10**	**1**	**2**	**3**	**8**	**0**	**0**	**1**	**22:21**
2008-09	**NY Rangers**	**NHL**	**82**	**3**	**12**	**15**	**64**	**0**	**0**	**1**	**96**	**3.1**	**–7**	**0**	**0.0**	**21:08**	**7**	**1**	**0**	**1**	**0**	**0**	**0**	**0**	**21:33**
2009-10	**NY Rangers**	**NHL**	**82**	**8**	**19**	**27**	**44**	**0**	**0**	**2**	**78**	**10.3**	**11**	**0**	**0.0**	**23:08**	....	....	....	....	....	....	....	....	....
2010-11	**NY Rangers**	**NHL**	**77**	**7**	**22**	**29**	**50**	**4**	**2**	**2**	**116**	**6.0**	**8**	**0**	**0.0**	**25:44**	**5**	**0**	**1**	**1**	**0**	**0**	**0**	**0**	**28:01**
2011-12	**NY Rangers**	**NHL**	**46**	**2**	**3**	**5**	**16**	**1**	**0**	**0**	**61**	**3.3**	**–7**	**0**	**0.0**	**19:54**	**20**	**3**	**3**	**6**	**12**	**2**	**0**	**1**	**25:18**
2012-13	**NY Rangers**	**NHL**	**21**	**2**	**9**	**11**	**14**	**1**	**0**	**0**	**20**	**10.0**	**4**	**0**	**0.0**	**24:27**	**1**	**0**	**0**	**0**	**0**	**0**	**0**	**0**	**17:17**
2013-14	**NY Rangers**	**NHL**	**72**	**3**	**11**	**14**	**24**	**1**	**0**	**0**	**92**	**3.3**	**–1**	**1**	**100.0**	**20:32**	**25**	**1**	**4**	**5**	**6**	**0**	**0**	**0**	**21:49**
2014-15	**NY Rangers**	**NHL**	**80**	**5**	**15**	**20**	**42**	**0**	**0**	**0**	**97**	**5.2**	**18**	**2**	**50.0**	**21:08**	**19**	**0**	**1**	**1**	**10**	**0**	**0**	**0**	**20:41**
	NHL Totals		**540**	**32**	**99**	**131**	**296**	**7**	**2**	**5**	**638**	**5.0**		**3**	**66.7**	**21:41**	**87**	**6**	**11**	**17**	**36**	**2**	**0**	**2**	**22:43**

OHL First All-Star Team (2006, 2007) • Canadian Major Junior First All-Star Team (2006, 2007) • OHL Playoff MVP (2007)
Played in NHL All-Star Game (2011)
• Missed majority of 2012-13 due to eye injury vs. Philadelphia, March 5, 2013.

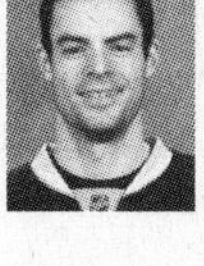

STAFFORD, Drew

(STA-fuhrd, DROO) **WPG**

Right wing. Shoots right. 6'2", 214 lbs. Born, Milwaukee, WI, October 30, 1985. Buffalo's 1st choice, 13th overall, in 2004 Entry Draft.

			Regular Season														Playoffs								
Season	Club	League	GP	G	A	Pts	PIM	PP	SH	GW	S	S%	+/-	TF	F%	Min	GP	G	A	Pts	PIM	PP	SH	GW	Min
2001-02	Shat.-St. Mary's	High-MN	45	35	53	88	30	....	....	....	....	....	....	....	....	....	....	....	....	....	....	....	....	....	....
2002-03	Shat.-St. Mary's	High-MN	65	49	67	116	....	....	....	....	....	....	....	....	....	....	....	....	....	....	....	....	....	....	....
2003-04	North Dakota	WCHA	36	11	21	32	30	....	....	....	....	....	....	....	....	....	....	....	....	....	....	....	....	....	....
2004-05	North Dakota	WCHA	42	13	25	38	34	....	....	....	....	....	....	....	....	....	....	....	....	....	....	....	....	....	....
2005-06	North Dakota	WCHA	42	24	24	48	63	....	....	....	....	....	....	....	....	....	....	....	....	....	....	....	....	....	....
2006-07	**Buffalo**	**NHL**	**41**	**13**	**14**	**27**	**33**	**3**	**0**	**3**	**67**	**19.4**	**5**	**13**	**46.2**	**13:08**	**10**	**2**	**2**	**4**	**4**	**0**	**0**	**0**	**11:52**
	Rochester	AHL	34	22	22	44	30	....	....	....	....	....	....	....	....	....	....	....	....	....	....	....	....	....	....
2007-08	**Buffalo**	**NHL**	**64**	**16**	**22**	**38**	**51**	**1**	**0**	**5**	**103**	**15.5**	**3**	**21**	**38.1**	**13:32**	....	....	....	....	....	....	....	....	....
2008-09	**Buffalo**	**NHL**	**79**	**20**	**25**	**45**	**29**	**9**	**0**	**0**	**183**	**10.9**	**3**	**20**	**20.0**	**15:38**	....	....	....	....	....	....	....	....	....
2009-10	**Buffalo**	**NHL**	**71**	**14**	**20**	**34**	**35**	**5**	**0**	**1**	**181**	**7.7**	**4**	**86**	**47.7**	**14:28**	**3**	**0**	**0**	**0**	**0**	**0**	**0**	**0**	**14:06**
2010-11	**Buffalo**	**NHL**	**62**	**31**	**21**	**52**	**34**	**11**	**0**	**4**	**179**	**17.3**	**13**	**56**	**30.4**	**16:32**	**7**	**1**	**2**	**3**	**2**	**1**	**0**	**0**	**20:01**
2011-12	**Buffalo**	**NHL**	**80**	**20**	**30**	**50**	**46**	**3**	**1**	**4**	**226**	**8.8**	**5**	**86**	**52.3**	**17:39**	....	....	....	....	....	....	....	....	....
2012-13	**Buffalo**	**NHL**	**46**	**6**	**12**	**18**	**21**	**0**	**0**	**0**	**121**	**5.0**	**–16**	**84**	**44.1**	**17:01**	....	....	....	....	....	....	....	....	....
2013-14	**Buffalo**	**NHL**	**70**	**16**	**18**	**34**	**39**	**2**	**1**	**1**	**185**	**8.6**	**–19**	**197**	**53.8**	**18:38**	....	....	....	....	....	....	....	....	....
2014-15	**Buffalo**	**NHL**	**50**	**9**	**15**	**24**	**39**	**2**	**0**	**1**	**91**	**9.9**	**–18**	**160**	**50.0**	**15:59**	....	....	....	....	....	....	....	....	....
	Winnipeg	**NHL**	**26**	**9**	**10**	**19**	**8**	**2**	**0**	**0**	**56**	**16.1**	**6**	**14**	**42.9**	**17:30**	**4**	**1**	**1**	**2**	**0**	**0**	**0**	**0**	**17:19**
	NHL Totals		**589**	**154**	**187**	**341**	**335**	**38**	**2**	**19**	**1392**	**11.1**		**737**	**47.5**	**16:02**	**24**	**4**	**5**	**9**	**6**	**1**	**0**	**0**	**15:26**

Traded to **Winnipeg** by **Buffalo** with Tyler Myers, Joel Armia, Brendan Lemieux and St. Louis' 1st round choice (previously acquired, Winnipeg selected Jack Roslovic) in 2015 Entry Draft for Evander Kane, Zach Bogosian and Jason Kasdorf, February 11, 2015.

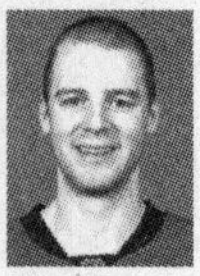

STAJAN, Matt
(STAY-juhn, MAT) **CGY**

Center. Shoots left. 6'1", 192 lbs. Born, Mississauga, ON, December 19, 1983. Toronto's 2nd choice, 57th overall, in 2002 Entry Draft.

			Regular Season														Playoffs								
Season	Club	League	GP	G	A	Pts	PIM	PP	SH	GW	S	S%	+/-	TF	F%	Min	GP	G	A	Pts	PIM	PP	SH	GW	Min
99-2000	Miss. Senators	GTHL	STATISTICS NOT AVAILABLE																						
2000-01	Belleville Bulls	OHL	57	9	18	27	27										7	1	6	7	5				
2001-02	Belleville Bulls	OHL	68	33	52	85	50										11	3	8	11	14				
2002-03	Belleville Bulls	OHL	57	34	60	94	75										7	5	8	13	16				
	St. John's	AHL	1	0	1	1	0																		
	Toronto	NHL	1	1	0	1	0	0	0	0	1	100.0	1	12	33.3	11:00									
2003-04	Toronto	NHL	69	14	13	27	22	0	0	0	63	22.2	7	450	38.9	11:00	3	0	0	0	2	0	0	0	11:13
2004-05	St. John's	AHL	80	23	43	66	43										5	2	2	4	6				
2005-06	Toronto	NHL	80	15	12	27	50	3	4	5	83	18.1	5	373	44.5	11:38									
2006-07	Toronto	NHL	82	10	29	39	44	1	1	1	132	7.6	3	985	46.1	16:09									
2007-08	Toronto	NHL	82	16	17	33	47	2	1	3	127	12.6	–11	1293	47.6	18:54									
2008-09	Toronto	NHL	76	15	40	55	54	5	1	1	114	13.2	–4	1177	51.4	16:56									
2009-10	Toronto	NHL	55	16	25	41	30	7	0	2	99	16.2	–3	926	51.6	18:47									
	Calgary	NHL	27	3	13	16	2	0	0	2	33	9.1	–3	408	52.0	19:11									
2010-11	Calgary	NHL	76	6	25	31	32	0	1	0	81	7.4	1	845	51.6	14:14									
2011-12	Calgary	NHL	61	8	10	18	29	0	0	1	77	10.4	–3	639	51.8	13:01									
2012-13	Calgary	NHL	43	5	18	23	26	0	0	1	44	11.4	7	770	46.2	17:10									
2013-14	Calgary	NHL	63	14	19	33	42	0	1	2	70	20.0	–13	1096	48.1	18:22									
2014-15	Calgary	NHL	59	7	10	17	28	0	0	0	46	15.2	7	602	50.3	12:00	11	1	3	4	21	0	0	1	16:07
	NHL Totals		774	130	231	361	406	18	9	18	970	13.4		9576	48.7	15:22	14	1	3	4	23	0	0	1	15:04

• Scored a goal in his first NHL game (April 5, 2003 vs. Ottawa).

Traded to **Calgary** by **Toronto** with Niklas Hagman, Jamal Mayers and Ian White for Dion Phaneuf, Fredrik Sjostrom and Keith Aulie, January 31, 2010.

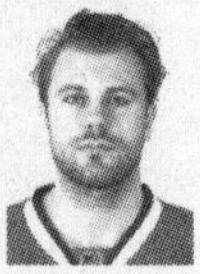

STALBERG, Viktor
(STAHL-buhrg, VIHK-tuhr) **NYR**

Left wing. Shoots left. 6'3", 206 lbs. Born, Stockholm, Sweden, January 17, 1986. Toronto's 5th choice, 161st overall, in 2006 Entry Draft.

Season	Club	League	GP	G	A	Pts	PIM	PP	SH	GW	S	S%	+/-	TF	F%	Min	GP	G	A	Pts	PIM	PP	SH	GW	Min
2003-04	Molndal U18	Swe-U18	13	14	13	27																			
	Molndal Jr.	Swe-Jr.	18	25	10	35																			
	Molndal	Sweden-4		11	9	20																			
2004-05	Molndal Jr.	Swe-Jr.	11	16	7	23																			
	Molndal	Sweden-3	29	6	9	15	54																		
2005-06	Frolunda Jr.	Swe-Jr.	41	27	26	53	89										7	6	5	11	6				
2006-07	U. of Vermont	H-East	39	7	8	15	53																		
2007-08	U. of Vermont	H-East	39	10	13	23	34																		
2008-09	U. of Vermont	H-East	39	24	22	46	32																		
	Toronto Marlies	AHL															2	0	1	1	0				
2009-10	Toronto	NHL	40	9	5	14	30	0	0	0	117	7.7	–13	9	33.3	14:37									
	Toronto Marlies	AHL	39	12	21	33	36																		
2010-11	Chicago	NHL	77	12	12	24	43	0	0	3	135	8.9	2	9	55.6	10:42	7	1	0	1	5	0	0	0	12:17
2011-12	Chicago	NHL	79	22	21	43	34	0	0	6	215	10.2	6	11	45.5	14:04	6	0	2	2	8	0	0	0	14:54
2012-13	Frolunda	Sweden	11	7	5	12	10																		
	Mytischi	KHL	14	3	7	10	4																		
	♦ Chicago	NHL	47	9	14	23	25	0	0	1	113	8.0	16	1	0.0	14:07	19	0	3	3	6	0	0	0	10:35
2013-14	Nashville	NHL	70	8	10	18	32	0	0	1	114	7.0	–14	3	33.3	12:35									
2014-15	Nashville	NHL	25	2	8	10	18	0	0	1	27	7.4	0	1	100.0	11:53	6	1	2	3	0	0	0	0	14:08
	Milwaukee	AHL	20	11	6	17	14																		
	NHL Totals		338	62	70	132	182	0	0	12	721	8.6		34	44.1	12:54	38	2	7	9	19	0	0	0	12:09

Hockey East First All-Star Team (2009) • NCAA East First All-American Team (2009)

Traded to **Chicago** by **Toronto** with Chris Didomenico and Phillipe Paradis for Kris Versteeg and Bill Sweatt, June 30, 2010. Signed as a free agent by **Frolunda** (Sweden), October 11, 2012. Signed as a free agent by **Mytischi** (KHL), November 20, 2012. Signed as a free agent by **Nashville**, July 5, 2013. Signed as a free agent by **NY Rangers**, July 1, 2015.

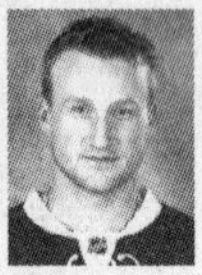

STAMKOS, Steven
(STAM-kohs, STEE-vehn) **T.B.**

Center. Shoots right. 6', 190 lbs. Born, Markham, ON, February 7, 1990. Tampa Bay's 1st choice, 1st overall, in 2008 Entry Draft.

Season	Club	League	GP	G	A	Pts	PIM	PP	SH	GW	S	S%	+/-	TF	F%	Min	GP	G	A	Pts	PIM	PP	SH	GW	Min
2005-06	Markham Waxers	Minor-ON	66	105	92	197	87																		
2006-07	Sarnia Sting	OHL	63	42	50	92	56										4	3	3	6	0				
2007-08	Sarnia Sting	OHL	61	58	47	105	88										9	11	0	11	20				
2008-09	Tampa Bay	NHL	79	23	23	46	39	9	0	1	181	12.7	–13	557	45.4	14:56									
2009-10	Tampa Bay	NHL	82	*51	44	95	38	24	1	5	297	17.2	–2	1004	47.9	20:33									
2010-11	Tampa Bay	NHL	82	45	46	91	74	17	0	8	272	16.5	3	927	46.5	20:12	18	6	7	13	6	3	0	1	19:43
2011-12	Tampa Bay	NHL	82	*60	37	97	66	12	0	*12	303	19.8	7	1227	45.5	22:01									
2012-13	Tampa Bay	NHL	48	29	28	57	32	10	0	2	157	18.5	–4	819	49.6	22:01									
2013-14	Tampa Bay	NHL	37	25	15	40	18	9	1	5	124	20.2	9	529	49.2	20:15	4	2	2	4	6	0	0	0	21:50
2014-15	Tampa Bay	NHL	82	43	29	72	49	13	0	6	268	16.0	2	943	49.7	19:22	26	7	11	18	20	2	0	1	18:33
	NHL Totals		492	276	222	498	316	94	2	39	1602	17.2		6006	47.6	19:46	48	15	20	35	32	5	0	2	19:16

OHL Second All-Star Team (2008) • Canadian Major Junior First All-Star Team (2008) • Maurice "Rocket" Richard Trophy (2010) (tied with Sidney Crosby) • NHL Second All-Star Team (2011, 2012) • Maurice "Rocket" Richard Trophy (2012)

Played in NHL All-Star Game (2011, 2012, 2015)

• Missed majority of 2013-14 due to leg injury at Boston, November 11, 2013.

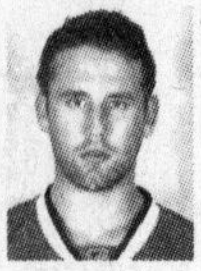

STANTON, Ryan
(STAN-tuhn, RIGH-uhn)

Defense. Shoots left. 6'2", 196 lbs. Born, St. Albert, AB, July 20, 1989.

Season	Club	League	GP	G	A	Pts	PIM	PP	SH	GW	S	S%	+/-	TF	F%	Min	GP	G	A	Pts	PIM	PP	SH	GW	Min
2004-05	St. Albert	Minor-AB	32	4	10	14	77																		
	St. Albert Raiders	AMHL	8	0	0	0	2																		
2005-06	St. Albert Raiders	AMHL	35	3	15	18	64																		
	Moose Jaw	WHL	2	0	0	0	2																		
2006-07	Moose Jaw	WHL	54	0	8	8	75																		
2007-08	Moose Jaw	WHL	58	4	16	20	68										6	0	0	0	2				
2008-09	Moose Jaw	WHL	69	5	29	34	111																		
2009-10	Moose Jaw	WHL	59	10	30	40	81										7	0	6	6	4				
	Rockford IceHogs	AHL	2	0	1	1	0										2	0	0	0	0				
2010-11	Rockford IceHogs	AHL	73	3	14	17	76																		
2011-12	Rockford IceHogs	AHL	76	3	14	17	130																		
2012-13	Rockford IceHogs	AHL	73	3	22	25	126																		
	Chicago	NHL	1	0	0	0	2	0	0	0	1	0.0	1	0	0.0	17:05									
2013-14	Vancouver	NHL	64	1	15	16	32	0	0	0	65	1.5	5	1	100.0	14:43									
2014-15	Vancouver	NHL	54	3	8	11	35	0	0	0	59	5.1	9	0	0.0	16:00									
	NHL Totals		119	4	23	27	69	0	0	0	125	3.2		1	100.0	15:19									

Signed as a free agent by **Chicago**, March 12, 2010. Claimed on waivers by **Vancouver** from **Chicago**, September 30, 2013.

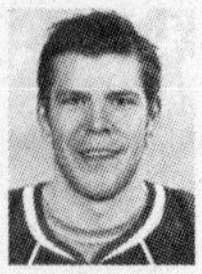

STASTNY, Paul
(STAS-nee, PAWL) **ST.L.**

Center. Shoots left. 6', 205 lbs. Born, Quebec City, QC, December 27, 1985. Colorado's 2nd choice, 44th overall, in 2005 Entry Draft.

Season	Club	League	GP	G	A	Pts	PIM	PP	SH	GW	S	S%	+/-	TF	F%	Min	GP	G	A	Pts	PIM	PP	SH	GW	Min
2002-03	River City Lancers	USHL	57	10	20	30	39										8	0	1	1	2				
2003-04	River City Lancers	USHL	56	30	*47	77	46										3	1	2	3	0				
2004-05	U. of Denver	WCHA	42	17	28	45	30																		
2005-06	U. of Denver	WCHA	39	19	34	53	79																		
2006-07	Colorado	NHL	82	28	50	78	42	11	0	6	185	15.1	4	1226	48.5	18:10									
2007-08	Colorado	NHL	66	24	47	71	24	3	0	4	138	17.4	22	1101	51.0	21:05	9	2	1	3	6	0	0	1	19:56
2008-09	Colorado	NHL	45	11	25	36	22	7	0	2	118	9.3	–9	850	51.8	21:14									
2009-10	Colorado	NHL	81	20	59	79	50	9	0	2	199	10.1	2	1703	50.0	21:24	6	1	4	5	4	1	0	0	20:23
	United States	Olympics	6	1	2	3	0																		
2010-11	Colorado	NHL	74	22	35	57	56	4	1	3	181	12.2	–7	1524	53.2	19:44									
2011-12	Colorado	NHL	79	21	32	53	34	7	0	2	190	11.1	–8	1424	55.4	18:50									

			Regular Season														Playoffs								
Season	Club	League	GP	G	A	Pts	PIM	PP	SH	GW	S	S%	+/-	TF	F%	Min	GP	G	A	Pts	PIM	PP	SH	GW	Min
2012-13	EHC Munchen	Germany	13	7	11	18	20																		
	Colorado	**NHL**	**40**	**9**	**15**	**24**	**14**	**2**	**0**	**1**	**87**	**10.3**	**–7**	**781**	**52.4**	**19:21**									
2013-14	**Colorado**	**NHL**	**71**	**25**	**35**	**60**	**22**	**4**	**0**	**4**	**150**	**16.7**	**9**	**1210**	**54.1**	**18:24**	**7**	**5**	**5**	**10**	**4**	**1**	**1**	**1**	**22:13**
	United States	Olympics	6	2	0	2	0																		
2014-15	**St. Louis**	**NHL**	**74**	**16**	**30**	**46**	**40**	**7**	**0**	**7**	**143**	**11.2**	**5**	**1158**	**57.9**	**17:38**	**6**	**1**	**0**	**1**	**4**	**0**	**0**	**0**	**17:28**
	NHL Totals		**612**	**176**	**328**	**504**	**304**	**54**	**1**	**31**	**1391**	**12.7**		**10977**	**52.7**	**19:27**	**28**	**9**	**10**	**19**	**18**	**2**	**1**	**2**	**20:04**

WCHA All-Rookie Team (2005) • WCHA Rookie of the Year (2005) • NCAA Championship All-Tournament Team (2005) • WCHA First All-Star Team (2006) • NCAA West Second All-American Team (2006) • NHL All-Rookie Team (2007)

Played in NHL All-Star Game (2011)

Signed as a free agent by **Munchen** (Germany), November 16, 2012. Signed as a free agent by **St. Louis**, July 1, 2014.

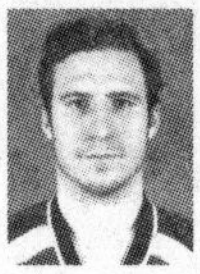

STEEN, Alexander (STEEN, al-ehx-AN-duhr) ST.L.

Center. Shoots left. 5'11", 212 lbs. Born, Winnipeg, MB, March 1, 1984. Toronto's 1st choice, 24th overall, in 2002 Entry Draft.

Season	Club	League	GP	G	A	Pts	PIM	PP	SH	GW	S	S%	+/-	TF	F%	Min	GP	G	A	Pts	PIM	PP	SH	GW	Min
99-2000	V.Frolunda Jr.	Swe-Jr.	8	5	7	12	0																		
	V.Frolunda U18	Swe-U18	14	3	5	8	16																		
2000-01	V.Frolunda Jr.	Swe-Jr.	23	11	12	23	15										3	1	0	1	2				
	V.Frolunda U18	Swe-U18	6	3	3	6	9																		
2001-02	V.Frolunda Jr.	Swe-Jr.	23	21	17	38	47										2	1	1	2	2				
	V.Frolunda	Sweden	26	0	3	3	14										10	1	2	3	0				
2002-03	V.Frolunda	Sweden	45	5	10	15	18										16	2	3	5	4				
	V.Frolunda Jr.	Swe-Jr.	2	0	2	2	0																		
2003-04	V.Frolunda	Sweden	48	10	14	24	50										10	4	6	10	14				
2004-05	MODO	Sweden	50	9	8	17	26										6	1	0	1	4				
2005-06	**Toronto**	**NHL**	**75**	**18**	**27**	**45**	**42**	**9**	**1**	**3**	**176**	**10.2**	**–9**	**29**	**24.1**	**17:37**									
2006-07	**Toronto**	**NHL**	**82**	**15**	**20**	**35**	**26**	**4**	**0**	**5**	**192**	**7.8**	**5**	**44**	**34.1**	**15:42**									
2007-08	**Toronto**	**NHL**	**76**	**15**	**27**	**42**	**32**	**2**	**1**	**2**	**169**	**8.9**	**0**	**179**	**33.0**	**18:05**									
2008-09	**Toronto**	**NHL**	**20**	**2**	**2**	**4**	**6**	**1**	**0**	**0**	**31**	**6.5**	**–4**	**82**	**52.4**	**15:38**									
	St. Louis	**NHL**	**61**	**6**	**18**	**24**	**24**	**2**	**1**	**0**	**117**	**5.1**	**–6**	**154**	**41.6**	**16:34**	**4**	**0**	**1**	**1**	**0**	**0**	**0**	**0**	**17:47**
2009-10	**St. Louis**	**NHL**	**68**	**24**	**23**	**47**	**30**	**7**	**2**	**4**	**189**	**12.7**	**6**	**73**	**41.1**	**16:17**									
2010-11	**St. Louis**	**NHL**	**72**	**20**	**31**	**51**	**26**	**1**	**2**	**5**	**218**	**9.2**	**–3**	**106**	**38.7**	**19:33**									
2011-12	**St. Louis**	**NHL**	**43**	**15**	**13**	**28**	**28**	**3**	**0**	**3**	**134**	**11.2**	**24**	**95**	**55.8**	**19:08**	**9**	**1**	**2**	**3**	**6**	**1**	**0**	**1**	**20:54**
2012-13	MODO	Sweden	20	8	15	23	28																		
	St. Louis	**NHL**	**40**	**8**	**19**	**27**	**14**	**3**	**0**	**3**	**129**	**6.2**	**5**	**204**	**46.1**	**19:00**	**6**	**3**	**0**	**3**	**6**	**1**	**1**	**1**	**20:56**
2013-14	**St. Louis**	**NHL**	**68**	**33**	**29**	**62**	**46**	**7**	**1**	**9**	**211**	**15.6**	**17**	**541**	**49.0**	**20:17**	**6**	**1**	**2**	**3**	**6**	**0**	**0**	**1**	**25:24**
	Sweden	Olympics	6	1	3	4	4																		
2014-15	**St. Louis**	**NHL**	**74**	**24**	**40**	**64**	**33**	**8**	**0**	**5**	**223**	**10.8**	**8**	**433**	**50.4**	**19:59**	**6**	**1**	**3**	**4**	**2**	**0**	**1**	**0**	**19:35**
	NHL Totals		**679**	**180**	**249**	**429**	**307**	**47**	**8**	**39**	**1789**	**10.1**		**1940**	**45.8**	**18:03**	**31**	**6**	**8**	**14**	**20**	**2**	**2**	**3**	**21:07**

Traded to **St. Louis** by **Toronto** with Carlo Colaiacovo for Lee Stempniak, November 24, 2008. Signed as a free agent by **MODO** (Sweden), September 25, 2012.

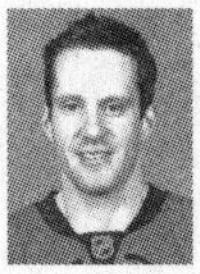

STEMPNIAK, Lee (STEHMP-nee-ak, LEE)

Right wing. Shoots right. 5'11", 196 lbs. Born, Buffalo, NY, February 4, 1983. St. Louis' 7th choice, 148th overall, in 2003 Entry Draft.

Season	Club	League	GP	G	A	Pts	PIM	PP	SH	GW	S	S%	+/-	TF	F%	Min	GP	G	A	Pts	PIM	PP	SH	GW	Min
2000-01	Buffalo Lightning	ON-Jr.A	48	34	51	86	36																		
2001-02	Dartmouth	ECAC	32	12	9	21	8																		
2002-03	Dartmouth	ECAC	34	21	28	49	32																		
2003-04	Dartmouth	ECAC	34	16	22	38	42																		
2004-05	Dartmouth	ECAC	35	14	*29	43	34																		
2005-06	**St. Louis**	**NHL**	**57**	**14**	**13**	**27**	**22**	**5**	**0**	**2**	**100**	**14.0**	**–10**	**7**	**42.9**	**14:22**									
	Peoria Rivermen	AHL	26	8	7	15	32										3	0	3	3	2				
2006-07	**St. Louis**	**NHL**	**82**	**27**	**25**	**52**	**33**	**8**	**0**	**4**	**166**	**16.3**	**–2**	**7**	**14.3**	**14:43**									
2007-08	**St. Louis**	**NHL**	**80**	**13**	**25**	**38**	**40**	**3**	**0**	**2**	**162**	**8.0**	**0**	**11**	**36.4**	**15:53**									
2008-09	**St. Louis**	**NHL**	**14**	**3**	**10**	**13**	**2**	**0**	**0**	**1**	**43**	**7.0**	**–3**	**1**	**0.0**	**19:28**									
	Toronto	**NHL**	**61**	**11**	**20**	**31**	**31**	**3**	**0**	**0**	**128**	**8.6**	**–9**	**12**	**33.3**	**15:52**									
2009-10	**Toronto**	**NHL**	**62**	**14**	**16**	**30**	**18**	**5**	**1**	**1**	**164**	**8.5**	**–10**	**25**	**36.0**	**17:53**									
	Phoenix	**NHL**	**18**	**14**	**4**	**18**	**8**	**4**	**0**	**1**	**48**	**29.2**	**10**	**14**	**57.1**	**15:22**	**7**	**0**	**2**	**2**	**0**	**0**	**0**	**0**	**14:28**
2010-11	**Phoenix**	**NHL**	**82**	**19**	**19**	**38**	**19**	**2**	**0**	**0**	**199**	**9.5**	**4**	**45**	**40.0**	**15:15**	**4**	**0**	**0**	**0**	**0**	**0**	**0**	**0**	**12:13**
2011-12	**Calgary**	**NHL**	**61**	**14**	**14**	**28**	**16**	**2**	**0**	**2**	**130**	**10.8**	**–2**	**26**	**26.9**	**16:14**									
2012-13	**Calgary**	**NHL**	**47**	**9**	**23**	**32**	**12**	**4**	**0**	**2**	**113**	**8.0**	**2**	**23**	**13.0**	**17:54**									
2013-14	**Calgary**	**NHL**	**52**	**8**	**15**	**23**	**28**	**0**	**2**	**0**	**144**	**5.6**	**–21**	**28**	**32.1**	**19:24**									
	Pittsburgh	**NHL**	**21**	**4**	**7**	**11**	**4**	**0**	**0**	**1**	**34**	**11.8**	**5**	**5**	**20.0**	**16:08**	**13**	**2**	**1**	**3**	**6**	**0**	**0**	**0**	**15:03**
2014-15	**NY Rangers**	**NHL**	**53**	**9**	**9**	**18**	**18**	**0**	**0**	**1**	**86**	**10.5**	**7**	**25**	**44.0**	**12:26**									
	Winnipeg	**NHL**	**18**	**6**	**4**	**10**	**2**	**0**	**0**	**2**	**29**	**20.7**	**1**	**7**	**14.3**	**13:33**	**4**	**1**	**0**	**1**	**0**	**0**	**0**	**0**	**12:45**
	NHL Totals		**708**	**165**	**204**	**369**	**253**	**36**	**3**	**19**	**1546**	**10.7**		**236**	**33.5**	**15:54**	**28**	**3**	**3**	**6**	**6**	**0**	**0**	**0**	**14:10**

ECAC All-Rookie Team (2002) • ECAC First All-Star Team (2004, 2005) • NCAA East First All-American Team (2004) • NCAA East Second All-American Team (2005)

Traded to **Toronto** by **St. Louis** for Alexander Steen and Carlo Colaiacovo, November 24, 2008. Traded to **Phoenix** by **Toronto** for Matt Jones and Phoenix's 4th (later traded to Washington – Washington selected Philipp Grubauer) and 7th (later traded to Edmonton – Edmonton selected Kellen Jones) round choices in 2010 Entry Draft, March 3, 2010. Traded to **Calgary** by **Phoenix** for Daymond Langkow, August 29, 2011. Traded to **Pittsburgh** by **Calgary** for Pittsburgh's 3rd round choice (later traded to Chicago – Chicago selected Matt Iacopelli) in 2014 Entry Draft, March 5, 2014. Signed as a free agent by **NY Rangers**, July 19, 2014. Traded to **Winnipeg** by **NY Rangers** for Carl Klingberg, March 1, 2015.

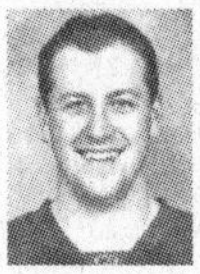

STEPAN, Derek (STEH-pan, DAIR-ihk) NYR

Center. Shoots right. 6', 196 lbs. Born, Hastings, MN, June 18, 1990. NY Rangers' 2nd choice, 51st overall, in 2008 Entry Draft.

Season	Club	League	GP	G	A	Pts	PIM	PP	SH	GW	S	S%	+/-	TF	F%	Min	GP	G	A	Pts	PIM	PP	SH	GW	Min
2006-07	Shat.-St. Mary's	High-MN	63	38	32	70	22																		
2007-08	Shat.-St. Mary's	High-MN	60	44	67	111	22																		
2008-09	U. of Wisconsin	WCHA	40	9	24	33	6																		
2009-10	U. of Wisconsin	WCHA	41	12	*42	*54	8																		
2010-11	**NY Rangers**	**NHL**	**82**	**21**	**24**	**45**	**20**	**3**	**0**	**3**	**166**	**12.7**	**8**	**719**	**38.5**	**16:27**	**5**	**0**	**0**	**0**	**2**	**0**	**0**	**0**	**20:29**
2011-12	**NY Rangers**	**NHL**	**82**	**17**	**34**	**51**	**22**	**4**	**0**	**4**	**169**	**10.1**	**14**	**867**	**44.5**	**18:57**	**20**	**1**	**8**	**9**	**4**	**1**	**0**	**0**	**19:07**
2012-13	KalPa Kuopio	Finland	12	2	2	4	0																		
	NY Rangers	**NHL**	**48**	**18**	**26**	**44**	**12**	**4**	**1**	**6**	**108**	**16.7**	**25**	**977**	**45.9**	**20:55**	**12**	**4**	**1**	**5**	**2**	**0**	**0**	**2**	**22:30**
2013-14	**NY Rangers**	**NHL**	**82**	**17**	**40**	**57**	**18**	**5**	**0**	**2**	**199**	**8.5**	**12**	**1512**	**45.2**	**18:03**	**24**	**5**	**10**	**15**	**2**	**2**	**0**	**0**	**19:47**
	United States	Olympics	1	0	0	0	0																		
2014-15	**NY Rangers**	**NHL**	**68**	**16**	**39**	**55**	**22**	**3**	**2**	**3**	**155**	**10.3**	**26**	**1232**	**44.1**	**18:11**	**19**	**5**	**7**	**12**	**10**	**2**	**0**	**1**	**19:31**
	NHL Totals		**362**	**89**	**163**	**252**	**94**	**19**	**3**	**18**	**797**	**11.2**		**5307**	**44.0**	**18:18**	**80**	**15**	**26**	**41**	**20**	**5**	**0**	**3**	**20:00**

Signed as a free agent by **Kuopio** (Finland), November 11, 2012.

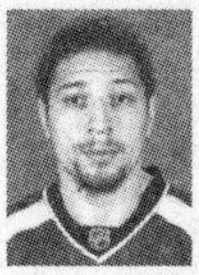

STEWART, Chris (STEW-ahrt, KRIHS) ANA

Right wing. Shoots right. 6'2", 231 lbs. Born, Toronto, ON, October 30, 1987. Colorado's 1st choice, 18th overall, in 2006 Entry Draft.

Season	Club	League	GP	G	A	Pts	PIM	PP	SH	GW	S	S%	+/-	TF	F%	Min	GP	G	A	Pts	PIM	PP	SH	GW	Min
2004-05	Kingston	OHL	64	18	12	30	45																		
2005-06	Kingston	OHL	62	37	50	87	118										6	2	0	2	13				
2006-07	Kingston	OHL	61	36	46	82	108										5	4	2	6	6				
	Albany River Rats	AHL	5	1	2	3	2										1	0	0	0	0				
2007-08	Lake Erie	AHL	77	25	19	44	93																		
2008-09	**Colorado**	**NHL**	**53**	**11**	**8**	**19**	**54**	**1**	**1**	**1**	**98**	**11.2**	**–18**	**21**	**33.3**	**12:20**									
	Lake Erie	AHL	19	5	6	11	23																		
2009-10	**Colorado**	**NHL**	**77**	**28**	**36**	**64**	**73**	**3**	**0**	**5**	**221**	**12.7**	**4**	**8**	**37.5**	**16:42**	**6**	**3**	**0**	**3**	**4**	**0**	**0**	**1**	**18:00**
	Lake Erie	AHL	2	0	0	0	2																		
2010-11	**Colorado**	**NHL**	**36**	**13**	**17**	**30**	**38**	**5**	**0**	**3**	**95**	**13.7**	**–10**	**6**	**33.3**	**16:56**									
	St. Louis	**NHL**	**26**	**15**	**8**	**23**	**15**	**7**	**0**	**2**	**67**	**22.4**	**4**	**26**	**42.3**	**18:16**									
2011-12	**St. Louis**	**NHL**	**79**	**15**	**15**	**30**	**109**	**2**	**0**	**1**	**166**	**9.0**	**1**	**13**	**23.1**	**15:26**	**7**	**2**	**0**	**2**	**12**	**0**	**0**	**0**	**10:47**
2012-13	Crimmitschau	German-2	15	6	14	20	24																		
	Liberec	CzRep	5	0	1	1	2																		
	St. Louis	**NHL**	**48**	**18**	**18**	**36**	**40**	**6**	**0**	**3**	**97**	**18.6**	**0**	**27**	**29.6**	**15:49**	**6**	**0**	**1**	**1**	**0**	**0**	**0**	**0**	**16:32**
2013-14	**St. Louis**	**NHL**	**58**	**15**	**11**	**26**	**112**	**3**	**0**	**3**	**107**	**14.0**	**2**	**25**	**32.0**	**13:42**									
	Buffalo	**NHL**	**5**	**0**	**0**	**0**	**6**	**0**	**0**	**0**	**3**	**0.0**	**–2**	**10**	**40.0**	**13:36**									

			Regular Season														Playoffs								
Season	Club	League	GP	G	A	Pts	PIM	PP	SH	GW	S	S%	+/-	TF	F%	Min	GP	G	A	Pts	PIM	PP	SH	GW	Min
2014-15	**Buffalo**	**NHL**	**61**	**11**	**14**	**25**	**63**	**5**	**0**	**0**	**116**	**9.5**	**–30**	**37**	**27.0**	**16:00**	....	....	....	....	....	....	....	....	....
	Minnesota	**NHL**	**20**	**3**	**8**	**11**	**25**	**0**	**0**	**0**	**39**	**7.7**	**4**	**4**	**0.0**	**15:31**	**8**	**0**	**2**	**2**	**2**	**0**	**0**	**0**	**15:59**
	NHL Totals		**463**	**129**	**135**	**264**	**535**	**32**	**1**	**18**	**1009**	**12.8**		**177**	**31.6**	**15:27**	**27**	**5**	**3**	**8**	**18**	**0**	**0**	**1**	**15:12**

Traded to **St. Louis** by **Colorado** with Kevin Shattenkirk and Colorado's 2nd round choice (Ty Rattie) in 2011 Entry Draft for Erik Johnson, Jay McClement and St. Louis' 1st round choice (Duncan Siemens) in 2011 Entry Draft, February 18, 2011. Signed as a free agent by **Crimmitschau** (German-2), September 24, 2012. Signed as a free agent by **Liberec** (CzRep), October 23, 2012. Traded to **Buffalo** by **St. Louis** with Jaroslav Halak, William Carrier, St. Louis' 1st round choice (later traded to Winnipeg – Winnipeg selected Jack Roslovic) in 2015 Entry Draft and St. Louis' 3rd round choice in 2016 Entry Draft for Ryan Miller and Steve Ott, February 28, 2014. Traded to **Minnesota** by **Buffalo** for a 2nd round choice in 2017 Entry Draft, March 2, 2015. Signed as a free agent by **Anaheim**, July 12, 2015.

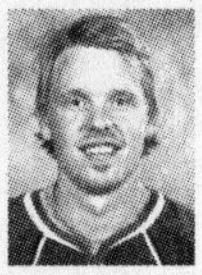

STOA, Ryan

(STOH-ah, RIGH-uhn)

Center. Shoots left. 6'3", 200 lbs. Born, Bloomington, MN, April 13, 1987. Colorado's 1st choice, 34th overall, in 2005 Entry Draft.

2003-04	USNTDP	U-17	18	9	8	17	....	....	....	....	....	....	....	....	....	....	....	....	....	....	....	....	....	....	....
	USNTDP	NAHL	42	10	12	22	26	....	....	....	....	....	....	....	....	....	7	7	1	8	2	....	....	....	....
2004-05	USNTDP	U-18	23	4	11	15	16	....	....	....	....	....	....	....	....	....	....	....	....	....	....	....	....	....	....
	USNTDP	NAHL	15	10	13	23	20	....	....	....	....	....	....	....	....	....	....	....	....	....	....	....	....	....	....
2005-06	U. of Minnesota	WCHA	41	10	15	25	43	....	....	....	....	....	....	....	....	....	....	....	....	....	....	....	....	....	....
2006-07	U. of Minnesota	WCHA	41	12	12	24	44	....	....	....	....	....	....	....	....	....	....	....	....	....	....	....	....	....	....
2007-08	U. of Minnesota	WCHA	2	1	1	2	2	....	....	....	....	....	....	....	....	....	....	....	....	....	....	....	....	....	....
2008-09	U. of Minnesota	WCHA	36	24	22	46	76	....	....	....	....	....	....	....	....	....	....	....	....	....	....	....	....	....	....
2009-10	**Colorado**	**NHL**	**12**	**2**	**1**	**3**	**0**	**0**	**0**	**0**	**26**	**7.7**	**–3**	**0**	**0.0**	**11:04**	**1**	**0**	**0**	**0**	**2**	**0**	**0**	**0**	**8:45**
	Lake Erie	AHL	54	23	17	40	42	....	....	....	....	....	....	....	....	....	....	....	....	....	....	....	....	....	....
2010-11	**Colorado**	**NHL**	**25**	**2**	**2**	**4**	**20**	**0**	**0**	**1**	**45**	**4.4**	**–4**	**5**	**40.0**	**13:21**	....	....	....	....	....	....	....	....	....
	Lake Erie	AHL	48	16	17	33	55	....	....	....	....	....	....	....	....	....	7	1	0	1	4	....	....	....	....
2011-12	Lake Erie	AHL	75	16	20	36	65	....	....	....	....	....	....	....	....	....	....	....	....	....	....	....	....	....	....
2012-13	Hershey Bears	AHL	46	11	8	19	43	....	....	....	....	....	....	....	....	....	4	1	0	1	0	....	....	....	....
2013-14	**Washington**	**NHL**	**3**	**0**	**0**	**0**	**0**	**0**	**0**	**0**	**2**	**0.0**	**–1**	**9**	**0.0**	**9:05**	....	....	....	....	....	....	....	....	....
	Hershey Bears	AHL	67	16	24	40	51	....	....	....	....	....	....	....	....	....	....	....	....	....	....	....	....	....	....
2014-15	Novokuznetsk	KHL	60	15	15	30	40	....	....	....	....	....	....	....	....	....	....	....	....	....	....	....	....	....	....
	NHL Totals		**40**	**4**	**3**	**7**	**20**	**0**	**0**	**1**	**73**	**5.5**		**14**	**14.3**	**12:20**	**1**	**0**	**0**	**0**	**2**	**0**	**0**	**0**	**8:45**

WCHA First All-Star Team (2009) • NCAA West First All-American Team (2009)

• Missed remainder of 2007-08 due to knee injury vs. University of Michigan (CCHA), October 13, 2007. Signed as a free agent by **Washington**, July 7, 2012. Signed as a free agent by **Novokuznetsk** (KHL). June 26, 2014.

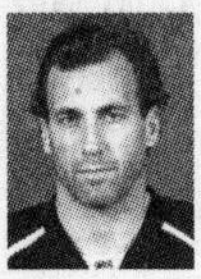

STOLL, Jarret

(STOHL, JAIR-iht) **NYR**

Center. Shoots right. 6'1", 213 lbs. Born, Melville, SK, June 24, 1982. Edmonton's 3rd choice, 36th overall, in 2002 Entry Draft.

1997-98	Saskatoon Blazers	SMHL	44	45	44	*89	78	....	....	....	....	....	....	....	....	....	....	....	....	....	....	....	....	....	....
	Edmonton Ice	WHL	8	2	3	5	4	....	....	....	....	....	....	....	....	....	....	....	....	....	....	....	....	....	....
1998-99	Kootenay Ice	WHL	57	13	21	34	38	....	....	....	....	....	....	....	....	....	4	0	0	0	2	....	....	....	....
99-2000	Kootenay Ice	WHL	71	37	38	75	64	....	....	....	....	....	....	....	....	....	20	7	9	16	24	....	....	....	....
2000-01	Kootenay Ice	WHL	62	40	66	106	105	....	....	....	....	....	....	....	....	....	11	5	9	14	22	....	....	....	....
2001-02	Kootenay Ice	WHL	47	32	34	66	64	....	....	....	....	....	....	....	....	....	22	6	14	20	35	....	....	....	....
2002-03	**Edmonton**	**NHL**	**4**	**0**	**1**	**1**	**0**	**0**	**0**	**0**	**5**	**0.0**	**–3**	**30**	**63.3**	**7:44**	....	....	....	....	....	....	....	....	....
	Hamilton	AHL	76	21	33	54	86	....	....	....	....	....	....	....	....	....	23	5	8	13	25	....	....	....	....
2003-04	**Edmonton**	**NHL**	**68**	**10**	**11**	**21**	**42**	**1**	**1**	**2**	**107**	**9.3**	**8**	**1019**	**54.1**	**13:54**	....	....	....	....	....	....	....	....	....
2004-05	Edmonton	AHL	66	21	17	38	92	....	....	....	....	....	....	....	....	....	....	....	....	....	....	....	....	....	....
2005-06	**Edmonton**	**NHL**	**82**	**22**	**46**	**68**	**74**	**11**	**1**	**4**	**243**	**9.1**	**4**	**1348**	**56.8**	**18:23**	**24**	**4**	**6**	**10**	**24**	**2**	**0**	**1**	**17:06**
2006-07	**Edmonton**	**NHL**	**51**	**13**	**26**	**39**	**48**	**6**	**1**	**2**	**115**	**11.3**	**2**	**901**	**55.6**	**18:12**	....	....	....	....	....	....	....	....	....
2007-08	**Edmonton**	**NHL**	**81**	**14**	**22**	**36**	**74**	**8**	**3**	**1**	**187**	**7.5**	**–23**	**1229**	**55.1**	**17:56**	....	....	....	....	....	....	....	....	....
2008-09	**Los Angeles**	**NHL**	**74**	**18**	**23**	**41**	**68**	**10**	**0**	**1**	**155**	**11.6**	**–7**	**1047**	**57.2**	**17:05**	....	....	....	....	....	....	....	....	....
2009-10	**Los Angeles**	**NHL**	**73**	**16**	**31**	**47**	**40**	**4**	**0**	**4**	**164**	**9.8**	**13**	**1105**	**56.0**	**17:25**	**6**	**1**	**0**	**1**	**4**	**1**	**0**	**0**	**15:51**
2010-11	**Los Angeles**	**NHL**	**82**	**20**	**23**	**43**	**42**	**4**	**1**	**5**	**187**	**10.7**	**–6**	**1310**	**57.5**	**17:10**	**5**	**0**	**3**	**3**	**0**	**0**	**0**	**0**	**18:44**
2011-12♦	**Los Angeles**	**NHL**	**78**	**6**	**15**	**21**	**60**	**1**	**0**	**0**	**133**	**4.5**	**2**	**1204**	**55.0**	**16:41**	**20**	**2**	**3**	**5**	**18**	**1**	**0**	**2**	**17:06**
2012-13	**Los Angeles**	**NHL**	**48**	**7**	**11**	**18**	**28**	**1**	**1**	**3**	**73**	**9.6**	**1**	**746**	**56.0**	**16:31**	**12**	**0**	**1**	**1**	**4**	**0**	**0**	**0**	**16:01**
2013-14♦	**Los Angeles**	**NHL**	**78**	**8**	**19**	**27**	**48**	**1**	**0**	**0**	**109**	**7.3**	**9**	**1239**	**54.7**	**15:52**	**26**	**3**	**3**	**6**	**18**	**1**	**0**	**0**	**17:03**
2014-15	**Los Angeles**	**NHL**	**73**	**6**	**11**	**17**	**58**	**3**	**0**	**2**	**83**	**7.2**	**3**	**1161**	**51.0**	**15:29**	....	....	....	....	....	....	....	....	....
	NHL Totals		**792**	**140**	**239**	**379**	**582**	**50**	**8**	**24**	**1561**	**9.0**		**12339**	**55.4**	**16:45**	**93**	**10**	**16**	**26**	**68**	**5**	**0**	**3**	**16:57**

• Re-entered NHL Entry Draft. Originally Calgary's 3rd choice, 46th overall, in 2000 Entry Draft.

WHL East First All-Star Team (2001) • Canadian Major Junior First All-Star Team (2001) • WHL West First All-Star Team (2002)

Traded to **Los Angeles** by **Edmonton** with Matt Greene for Lubomir Visnovsky, June 29, 2008. Signed as a free agent by **NY Rangers**, August 10, 2015.

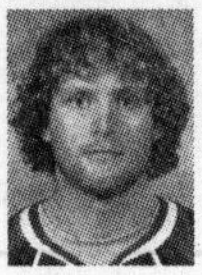

STOLLERY, Karl

(STAW-luh-ree, KAHRL) **S.J.**

Defense. Shoots left. 5'11", 180 lbs. Born, Camrose, AB, November 21, 1987.

2004-05	Camrose AA	Minor-AB	STATISTICS NOT AVAILABLE																						
	Camrose Kodiaks	AJHL	4	0	0	0	0	....	....	....	....	....	....	....	....	....	....	....	....	....	....	....	....	....	....
2005-06	Camrose Kodiaks	AJHL	42	1	5	6	40	....	....	....	....	....	....	....	....	....	11	1	2	3	6	....	....	....	....
2006-07	Camrose Kodiaks	AJHL	59	11	24	35	57	....	....	....	....	....	....	....	....	....	17	2	7	9	26	....	....	....	....
2007-08	Camrose Kodiaks	AJHL	52	3	24	27	40	....	....	....	....	....	....	....	....	....	18	5	10	15	18	....	....	....	....
2008-09	Merrimack	H-East	34	5	11	16	26	....	....	....	....	....	....	....	....	....	....	....	....	....	....	....	....	....	....
2009-10	Merrimack	H-East	35	4	15	19	42	....	....	....	....	....	....	....	....	....	....	....	....	....	....	....	....	....	....
2010-11	Merrimack	H-East	39	6	21	27	48	....	....	....	....	....	....	....	....	....	....	....	....	....	....	....	....	....	....
2011-12	Merrimack	H-East	37	7	14	21	58	....	....	....	....	....	....	....	....	....	....	....	....	....	....	....	....	....	....
	Lake Erie	AHL	9	2	5	7	4	....	....	....	....	....	....	....	....	....	....	....	....	....	....	....	....	....	....
2012-13	Lake Erie	AHL	72	5	29	34	62	....	....	....	....	....	....	....	....	....	....	....	....	....	....	....	....	....	....
2013-14	**Colorado**	**NHL**	**2**	**0**	**0**	**0**	**2**	**0**	**0**	**0**	**1**	**0.0**	**1**	**0**	**0.0**	**6:31**	....	....	....	....	....	....	....	....	....
	Lake Erie	AHL	68	7	23	30	42	....	....	....	....	....	....	....	....	....	....	....	....	....	....	....	....	....	....
2014-15	**Colorado**	**NHL**	**5**	**0**	**0**	**0**	**2**	**0**	**0**	**0**	**3**	**0.0**	**3**	**0**	**0.0**	**11:25**	....	....	....	....	....	....	....	....	....
	Lake Erie	AHL	46	5	9	14	55	....	....	....	....	....	....	....	....	....	....	....	....	....	....	....	....	....	....
	San Jose	**NHL**	**5**	**0**	**0**	**0**	**4**	**0**	**0**	**0**	**6**	**0.0**	**–4**	**0**	**0.0**	**18:02**	....	....	....	....	....	....	....	....	....
	Worcester Sharks	AHL	14	2	4	6	8	....	....	....	....	....	....	....	....	....	4	1	1	2	6	....	....	....	....
	NHL Totals		**12**	**0**	**0**	**0**	**8**	**0**	**0**	**0**	**10**	**0.0**		**0**	**0.0**	**13:22**	....	....	....	....	....	....	....	....	....

Hockey East All-Rookie Team (2009) • Hockey East Second All-Star Team (2012)

Signed to a ATO (amateur tryout) contract by **Lake Erie** (AHL), March 23, 2012. Signed as a free agent by **Colorado**, May 2, 2013. Traded to **San Jose** by **Colorado** for Freddie Hamilton, March 2, 2015.

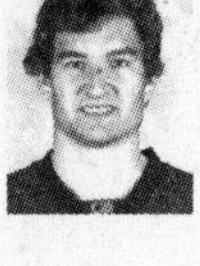

STONE, Mark

(STOHN, MAHRK) **OTT**

Right wing. Shoots right. 6'2", 204 lbs. Born, Winnipeg, MB, May 13, 1992. Ottawa's 3rd choice, 178th overall, in 2010 Entry Draft.

2007-08	Wpg. Thrashers	MMHL	40	22	31	53	28	....	....	....	....	....	....	....	....	....	9	7	7	14	2	....	....	....	....
2008-09	Brandon	WHL	56	17	22	39	27	....	....	....	....	....	....	....	....	....	12	1	3	4	4	....	....	....	....
2009-10	Brandon	WHL	39	11	17	28	25	....	....	....	....	....	....	....	....	....	15	1	3	4	4	....	....	....	....
2010-11	Brandon	WHL	71	37	69	106	28	....	....	....	....	....	....	....	....	....	6	1	9	10	4	....	....	....	....
2011-12	Brandon	WHL	66	41	*82	123	22	....	....	....	....	....	....	....	....	....	8	2	4	6	6	....	....	....	....
	Ottawa	**NHL**	....	....	....	....	....	....	....	....	....	....	....	....	....	....	**1**	**0**	**1**	**1**	**0**	**0**	**0**	**0**	**8:43**
2012-13	Binghamton	AHL	54	15	23	38	14	....	....	....	....	....	....	....	....	....	3	1	2	3	0	....	....	....	....
	Ottawa	**NHL**	**4**	**0**	**0**	**0**	**2**	**0**	**0**	**0**	**3**	**0.0**	**–1**	**1**	**100.0**	**10:00**	**1**	**0**	**0**	**0**	**0**	**0**	**0**	**0**	**11:23**
2013-14	**Ottawa**	**NHL**	**19**	**4**	**4**	**8**	**4**	**1**	**0**	**0**	**36**	**11.1**	**5**	**1**	**100.0**	**14:29**	....	....	....	....	....	....	....	....	....
	Binghamton	AHL	37	15	26	41	6	....	....	....	....	....	....	....	....	....	4	1	3	4	0	....	....	....	....
2014-15	**Ottawa**	**NHL**	**80**	**26**	**38**	**64**	**14**	**5**	**1**	**6**	**157**	**16.6**	**21**	**18**	**38.9**	**17:01**	**6**	**0**	**4**	**4**	**2**	**0**	**0**	**0**	**19:10**
	NHL Totals		**103**	**30**	**42**	**72**	**20**	**6**	**1**	**6**	**196**	**15.3**		**20**	**45.0**	**16:17**	**8**	**0**	**5**	**5**	**2**	**0**	**0**	**0**	**16:53**

WHL East First All-Star Team (2011, 2012) • Canadian Major Junior Sportsman of the Year (2012) • NHL All-Rookie Team (2015)

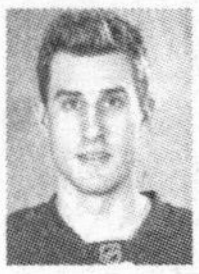

STONE, Michael (STOHN, MIGH-kuhl) ARI

Defense. Shoots right. 6'3", 210 lbs. Born, Winnipeg, MB, June 7, 1990. Phoenix's 4th choice, 69th overall, in 2008 Entry Draft.

Season	Club	League	Regular Season GP	G	A	Pts	PIM	PP	SH	GW	S	S%	+/-	TF	F%	Min	Playoffs GP	G	A	Pts	PIM	PP	SH	GW	Min
2005-06	Wpg. Thrashers	MMHL	40	14	18	32	14																		
2006-07	Calgary Hitmen	WHL	55	2	18	20	32										17	0	3	3	14				
2007-08	Calgary Hitmen	WHL	71	10	25	35	28										14	3	4	7	10				
2008-09	Calgary Hitmen	WHL	69	19	42	61	87										18	2	11	13	16				
2009-10	Calgary Hitmen	WHL	69	21	44	65	91										23	5	15	20	26				
2010-11	San Antonio	AHL	70	2	11	13	27																		
2011-12	**Phoenix**	**NHL**	**13**	**1**	**2**	**3**	**2**	**0**	**0**	**0**	**13**	**7.7**	**7**	**0**	**0.0**	**13:53**	**2**	**0**	**0**	**0**	**0**	**0**	**0**	**0**	**11:19**
	Portland Pirates	AHL	51	9	13	22	24																		
2012-13	Portland Pirates	AHL	36	6	22	28	20										1	0	1	1	4				
	Phoenix	**NHL**	**40**	**5**	**4**	**9**	**16**	**1**	**0**	**0**	**50**	**10.0**	**2**	**0**	**0.0**	**16:41**									
2013-14	**Phoenix**	**NHL**	**70**	**8**	**13**	**21**	**38**	**2**	**0**	**1**	**105**	**7.6**	**–10**	**0**	**0.0**	**18:12**									
2014-15	**Arizona**	**NHL**	**81**	**3**	**15**	**18**	**60**	**0**	**0**	**0**	**144**	**2.1**	**–24**	**1**	**100.0**	**20:52**									
	NHL Totals		**204**	**17**	**34**	**51**	**116**	**3**	**0**	**1**	**312**	**5.4**		**1**	**100.0**	**18:41**	**2**	**0**	**0**	**0**	**0**	**0**	**0**	**0**	**11:19**

WHL East Second All-Star Team (2009) • WHL East First All-Star Team (2010)

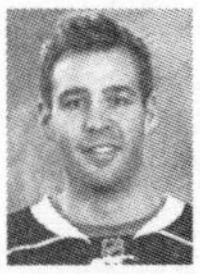

STONER, Clayton (STOH-nuhr, KLAY-tuhn) ANA

Defense. Shoots left. 6'4", 216 lbs. Born, Port McNeill, BC, February 19, 1985. Minnesota's 4th choice, 79th overall, in 2004 Entry Draft.

Season	Club	League	Regular Season GP	G	A	Pts	PIM	PP	SH	GW	S	S%	+/-	TF	F%	Min	Playoffs GP	G	A	Pts	PIM	PP	SH	GW	Min
2000-01	Campbell River	VIJHL	47	4	16	20	57																		
2001-02	Campbell River	VIJHL	42	12	35	47	199																		
2002-03	Tri-City	WHL	58	4	12	16	85																		
2003-04	Tri-City	WHL	71	7	24	31	109										11	1	1	2	8				
2004-05	Tri-City	WHL	60	12	34	46	81										4	0	3	3	2				
2005-06	Houston Aeros	AHL	73	6	18	24	92										3	1	1	2	7				
2006-07	Houston Aeros	AHL	65	1	6	7	104																		
2007-08	Houston Aeros	AHL	56	3	12	15	78																		
2008-09	Houston Aeros	AHL	63	2	22	24	81										20	1	4	5	27				
2009-10	**Minnesota**	**NHL**	**8**	**0**	**2**	**2**	**12**	**0**	**0**	**0**	**5**	**0.0**	**1**	**0**	**0.0**	**13:19**									
	Houston Aeros	AHL	26	3	7	10	52																		
2010-11	**Minnesota**	**NHL**	**57**	**2**	**7**	**9**	**96**	**0**	**0**	**1**	**40**	**5.0**	**5**	**0**	**0.0**	**16:52**									
2011-12	**Minnesota**	**NHL**	**51**	**1**	**4**	**5**	**62**	**0**	**0**	**0**	**47**	**2.1**	**3**	**0**	**0.0**	**17:36**									
2012-13	B. Bystrica	Slovakia	8	1	4	5	16																		
	Minnesota	**NHL**	**48**	**0**	**10**	**10**	**42**	**0**	**0**	**0**	**40**	**0.0**	**0**	**0**	**0.0**	**18:13**	**1**	**0**	**1**	**1**	**0**	**0**	**0**	**0**	**8:18**
2013-14	**Minnesota**	**NHL**	**63**	**1**	**4**	**5**	**84**	**0**	**0**	**0**	**48**	**2.1**	**–6**	**0**	**0.0**	**13:20**	**13**	**1**	**2**	**3**	**26**	**0**	**0**	**0**	**12:17**
2014-15	**Anaheim**	**NHL**	**69**	**1**	**7**	**8**	**68**	**0**	**0**	**1**	**68**	**1.5**	**–2**	**0**	**0.0**	**17:39**	**16**	**1**	**0**	**1**	**10**	**0**	**0**	**0**	**18:14**
	NHL Totals		**296**	**5**	**34**	**39**	**364**	**0**	**0**	**2**	**248**	**2.0**		**0**	**0.0**	**16:32**	**30**	**2**	**3**	**5**	**36**	**0**	**0**	**0**	**15:19**

WHL West Second All-Star Team (2005)
• Missed majority of 2009-10 due to groin injury. Signed as a free agent by **Banska Bystrica** (Slovakia), November 29, 2012. Signed as a free agent by **Anaheim**, July 1, 2014.

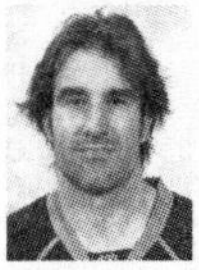

STORTINI, Zack (stohr-TEE-nee, ZAK) OTT

Right wing. Shoots right. 6'4", 215 lbs. Born, Elliot Lake, ON, September 11, 1985. Edmonton's 5th choice, 94th overall, in 2003 Entry Draft.

Season	Club	League	Regular Season GP	G	A	Pts	PIM	PP	SH	GW	S	S%	+/-	TF	F%	Min	Playoffs GP	G	A	Pts	PIM	PP	SH	GW	Min
2000-01	Newmarket	ON-Jr.A	34	3	10	13	68																		
2001-02	Sudbury Wolves	OHL	65	8	6	14	187										5	1	0	1	24				
2002-03	Sudbury Wolves	OHL	62	13	16	29	222																		
2003-04	Sudbury Wolves	OHL	62	21	16	37	151										7	1	1	2	14				
	Toronto	AHL	2	0	0	0	7										3	0	0	0	4				
2004-05	Sudbury Wolves	OHL	58	13	27	40	186										12	2	5	7	27				
2005-06	Iowa Stars	AHL	27	2	1	3	108																		
	Milwaukee	AHL	37	0	7	7	153										17	2	0	2	19				
2006-07	**Edmonton**	**NHL**	**29**	**1**	**0**	**1**	**105**	**0**	**0**	**0**	**17**	**5.9**	**–7**	**3**	**100.0**	**7:09**									
	Hamilton	AHL	47	9	6	15	195										22	3	0	3	*56				
2007-08	**Edmonton**	**NHL**	**66**	**3**	**9**	**12**	**201**	**0**	**0**	**0**	**38**	**7.9**	**3**	**7**	**42.9**	**8:10**									
	Springfield	AHL	4	3	2	5	21																		
2008-09	**Edmonton**	**NHL**	**52**	**6**	**5**	**11**	**181**	**0**	**0**	**0**	**23**	**26.1**	**–3**	**11**	**63.6**	**7:17**									
2009-10	**Edmonton**	**NHL**	**77**	**4**	**9**	**13**	**155**	**1**	**0**	**1**	**46**	**8.7**	**3**	**183**	**47.5**	**9:17**									
2010-11	**Edmonton**	**NHL**	**32**	**0**	**4**	**4**	**76**	**0**	**0**	**0**	**16**	**0.0**	**–2**	**33**	**42.4**	**7:06**									
	Oklahoma City	AHL	29	1	2	3	53										5	1	0	1	6				
2011-12	**Nashville**	**NHL**	**1**	**0**	**0**	**0**	**7**	**0**	**0**	**0**	**1**	**0.0**	**0**	**0**	**0.0**	**4:53**									
	Milwaukee	AHL	74	9	6	15	146										3	0	1	1	2				
2012-13	Hamilton	AHL	73	2	4	6	241																		
2013-14	Norfolk Admirals	AHL	73	4	5	9	*299										9	0	2	2	4				
2014-15	Lehigh Valley	AHL	76	13	12	25	184																		
	NHL Totals		**257**	**14**	**27**	**41**	**725**	**1**	**0**	**1**	**141**	**9.9**		**237**	**48.1**	**8:04**									

Signed as a free agent by **Nashville**, July 5, 2011. Signed as a free agent by **Hamilton** (AHL), September 21, 2012. Signed as a free agent by **Anaheim**, July 8, 2013. Signed as a free agent by **Philadelphia**, July 2, 2014. Signed as a free agent by **Ottawa**, July 1, 2015.

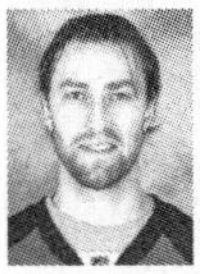

STRACHAN, Tyson (STRAWN, TIGH-suhn) MIN

Defense. Shoots right. 6'3", 215 lbs. Born, Melfort, SK, October 30, 1984. Carolina's 6th choice, 137th overall, in 2003 Entry Draft.

Season	Club	League	Regular Season GP	G	A	Pts	PIM	PP	SH	GW	S	S%	+/-	TF	F%	Min	Playoffs GP	G	A	Pts	PIM	PP	SH	GW	Min
2001-02	Tisdale Trojans	SMHL	42	5	18	23	70																		
	Melville	SJHL	2	0	0	0	0																		
2002-03	Vernon Vipers	BCHL	56	6	22	28	99																		
2003-04	Ohio State	CCHA	30	2	5	7	8																		
2004-05	Ohio State	CCHA	31	1	4	5	32																		
2005-06	Ohio State	CCHA	23	3	2	5	37																		
2006-07	Ohio State	CCHA	35	7	11	18	55																		
	Albany River Rats	AHL	1	0	0	0	0																		
2007-08	Peoria Rivermen	AHL	34	1	2	3	61																		
	Las Vegas	ECHL	25	2	7	9	68										16	0	4	4	12				
2008-09	**St. Louis**	**NHL**	**30**	**0**	**3**	**3**	**39**	**0**	**0**	**0**	**21**	**0.0**	**8**	**0**	**0.0**	**13:26**									
	Peoria Rivermen	AHL	29	2	3	5	67										3	0	0	0	11				
2009-10	**St. Louis**	**NHL**	**8**	**0**	**2**	**2**	**4**	**0**	**0**	**0**	**7**	**0.0**	**3**	**0**	**0.0**	**14:02**									
	Peoria Rivermen	AHL	65	5	21	26	75																		
2010-11	**St. Louis**	**NHL**	**29**	**0**	**1**	**1**	**39**	**0**	**0**	**0**	**28**	**0.0**	**–10**	**0**	**0.0**	**12:08**									
	Peoria Rivermen	AHL	13	0	8	8	4										1	0	0	0	2				
2011-12	**Florida**	**NHL**	**15**	**1**	**2**	**3**	**5**	**0**	**0**	**0**	**14**	**7.1**	**1**	**0**	**0.0**	**14:21**	**2**	**0**	**1**	**1**	**0**	**0**	**0**	**0**	**13:30**
	San Antonio	AHL	50	3	14	17	41										7	1	3	4	0				
2012-13	San Antonio	AHL	24	1	8	9	22																		
	Florida	**NHL**	**38**	**0**	**4**	**4**	**40**	**0**	**0**	**0**	**42**	**0.0**	**–13**	**0**	**0.0**	**18:58**									
2013-14	**Washington**	**NHL**	**18**	**0**	**2**	**2**	**28**	**0**	**0**	**0**	**7**	**0.0**	**–2**	**0**	**0.0**	**17:20**									
	Hershey Bears	AHL	60	4	15	19	56																		
2014-15	**Buffalo**	**NHL**	**46**	**0**	**5**	**5**	**44**	**0**	**0**	**0**	**38**	**0.0**	**–30**	**0**	**0.0**	**18:59**									
	NHL Totals		**184**	**1**	**19**	**20**	**199**	**0**	**0**	**0**	**157**	**0.6**		**0**	**0.0**	**16:14**	**2**	**0**	**1**	**1**	**0**	**0**	**0**	**0**	**13:30**

Signed as a free agent by **St. Louis**, October 9, 2008. Signed as a free agent by **Florida**, July 12, 2011. Signed as a free agent by **Washington**, July 8, 2013. Signed as a free agent by **Buffalo**, July 3, 2014. Signed as a free agent by **Minnesota**, July 2, 2015.

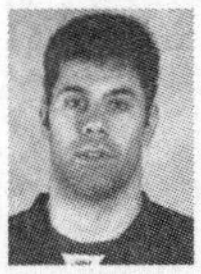

STRAIT, Brian (STRAYT, BRIGH-uhn) NYI

Defense. Shoots left. 6'1", 209 lbs. Born, Boston, MA, January 4, 1988. Pittsburgh's 3rd choice, 65th overall, in 2006 Entry Draft.

Season	Club	League	Regular Season GP	G	A	Pts	PIM	PP	SH	GW	S	S%	+/-	TF	F%	Min	Playoffs GP	G	A	Pts	PIM	PP	SH	GW	Min
2003-04	NMH School	High-MA	30	5	15	20	....																		
2004-05	USNTDP	U-17	18	1	5	6	8																		
	USNTDP	NAHL	42	4	8	12	42										10	0	2	2	2				
2005-06	USNTDP	U-18	40	2	7	9	31																		
	USNTDP	NAHL	15	0	5	5	41																		
2006-07	Boston University	H-East	36	3	3	6	47																		

Season	Club	League	GP	G	A	Pts	PIM	PP	SH	GW	S	S%	+/-	TF	F%	Min	GP	G	A	Pts	PIM	PP	SH	GW	Min
			Regular Season														Playoffs								
2007-08	Boston University	H-East	37	0	10	10	20	....	....	....	....	....	....	....	....	....	....	....	....	....	....	....	....	....	....
2008-09	Boston University	H-East	38	2	5	7	67	....	....	....	....	....	....	....	....	....	....	....	....	....	....	....	....	....	....
2009-10	Wilkes-Barre	AHL	78	2	12	14	73	....	....	....	....	....	....	....	....	....	4	0	1	1	0	....	....	....	....
2010-11	**Pittsburgh**	**NHL**	**3**	**0**	**0**	**0**	**0**	**0**	**0**	**0**	**0**	**0.0**	**-1**	**0**	**0.0**	**13:32**	....	....	....	....	....	....	....	....	....
	Wilkes-Barre	AHL	75	2	8	10	49	....	....	....	....	....	....	....	....	....	12	1	3	4	10	....	....	....	....
2011-12	**Pittsburgh**	**NHL**	**9**	**0**	**1**	**1**	**4**	**0**	**0**	**0**	**4**	**0.0**	**-2**	**0**	**0.0**	**12:53**	**3**	**0**	**0**	**0**	**0**	**0**	**0**	**0**	**9:35**
	Wilkes-Barre	AHL	41	4	12	16	26	....	....	....	....	....	....	....	....	....	2	0	1	1	0	....	....	....	....
2012-13	Wilkes-Barre	AHL	26	0	0	0	34	....	....	....	....	....	....	....	....	....	....	....	....	....	....	....	....	....	....
	NY Islanders	**NHL**	**19**	**0**	**4**	**4**	**10**	**0**	**0**	**0**	**13**	**0.0**	**4**	**0**	**0.0**	**17:09**	**6**	**1**	**0**	**1**	**12**	**0**	**0**	**0**	**20:35**
2013-14	**NY Islanders**	**NHL**	**47**	**3**	**6**	**9**	**14**	**0**	**0**	**0**	**40**	**7.5**	**-14**	**0**	**0.0**	**17:57**	....	....	....	....	....	....	....	....	....
2014-15	**NY Islanders**	**NHL**	**52**	**2**	**5**	**7**	**32**	**0**	**0**	**0**	**59**	**3.4**	**-1**	**1**	**0.0**	**18:22**	**7**	**0**	**0**	**0**	**4**	**0**	**0**	**0**	**18:50**
	NHL Totals		**130**	**5**	**16**	**21**	**60**	**0**	**0**	**0**	**116**	**4.3**		**1**	**0.0**	**17:33**	**16**	**1**	**0**	**1**	**16**	**0**	**0**	**0**	**17:45**

Claimed on waivers by **NY Islanders** from **Pittsburgh**, January 18, 2013. • Missed majority of 2012-13 due to ankle injury vs. Philadelphia, February 18, 2013.

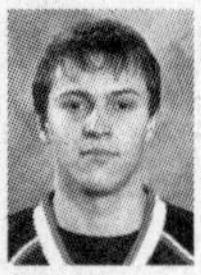

STRAKA, Petr
(STRAH-kuh, PEH-tuhr) **PHI**

Right wing. Shoots left. 6'1", 185 lbs. Born, Plzen, Czech., June 15, 1992. Columbus' 3rd choice, 55th overall, in 2010 Entry Draft.

Season	Club	League	GP	G	A	Pts	PIM	PP	SH	GW	S	S%	+/-	TF	F%	Min	GP	G	A	Pts	PIM	PP	SH	GW	Min
2006-07	HC Plzen U17	CzR-U17	22	5	6	11	14	....	....	....	....	....	....	....	....	....	7	0	0	0	0	....	....	....	....
2007-08	HC Plzen U17	CzR-U17	46	40	34	74	42	....	....	....	....	....	....	....	....	....	8	5	9	14	4	....	....	....	....
2008-09	HC Plzen U17	CzR-U17	1	1	2	3	4	....	....	....	....	....	....	....	....	....	1	0	2	2	2	....	....	....	....
	HC Plzen Jr.	CzRep-Jr.	27	13	10	23	6	....	....	....	....	....	....	....	....	....	5	3	1	4	2	....	....	....	....
2009-10	Rimouski Oceanic	QMJHL	62	28	36	64	54	....	....	....	....	....	....	....	....	....	12	5	9	14	10	....	....	....	....
2010-11	Rimouski Oceanic	QMJHL	41	10	15	25	33	....	....	....	....	....	....	....	....	....	5	2	2	4	0	....	....	....	....
2011-12	Rimouski Oceanic	QMJHL	54	18	19	37	41	....	....	....	....	....	....	....	....	....	21	10	12	22	6	....	....	....	....
2012-13	Baie-Comeau	QMJHL	55	41	41	82	34	....	....	....	....	....	....	....	....	....	19	11	14	25	12	....	....	....	....
2013-14	Adirondack	AHL	60	9	18	27	22	....	....	....	....	....	....	....	....	....	....	....	....	....	....	....	....	....	....
2014-15	**Philadelphia**	**NHL**	**3**	**0**	**2**	**2**	**0**	**0**	**0**	**0**	**2**	**0.0**	**1**	**0**	**0.0**	**9:27**	....	....	....	....	....	....	....	....	....
	Lehigh Valley	AHL	68	14	10	24	26	....	....	....	....	....	....	....	....	....	....	....	....	....	....	....	....	....	....
	NHL Totals		**3**	**0**	**2**	**2**	**0**	**0**	**0**	**0**	**2**	**0.0**		**0**	**0.0**	**9:27**	....	....	....	....	....	....	....	....	....

QMJHL All-Rookie Team (2010) • Canadian Major Junior All-Rookie Team (2010)
Signed as a free agent by **Philadelphia**, April 24, 2013.

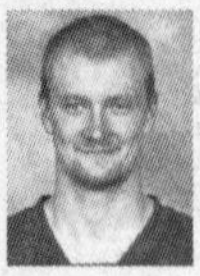

STRALMAN, Anton
(STROHL-muhn, AN-tawn) **T.B.**

Defense. Shoots right. 5'11", 190 lbs. Born, Tibro, Sweden, August 1, 1986. Toronto's 5th choice, 216th overall, in 2005 Entry Draft.

Season	Club	League	GP	G	A	Pts	PIM	PP	SH	GW	S	S%	+/-	TF	F%	Min	GP	G	A	Pts	PIM	PP	SH	GW	Min
2002-03	Skovde IK Jr.	Swe-Jr.	46	20	9	29	38	....	....	....	....	....	....	....	....	....	....	....	....	....	....	....	....	....	....
2003-04	Skovde IK	Sweden-3	27	4	8	12	18	....	....	....	....	....	....	....	....	....	....	....	....	....	....	....	....	....	....
2004-05	Skovde IK	Sweden-2	50	10	11	21	40	....	....	....	....	....	....	....	....	....	....	....	....	....	....	....	....	....	....
2005-06	Timra IK	Sweden	45	1	4	5	28	....	....	....	....	....	....	....	....	....	....	....	....	....	....	....	....	....	....
	Timra IK Jr.	Swe-Jr.	....	....	....	....	....	....	....	....	....	....	....	....	....	....	3	0	0	0	4	....	....	....	....
2006-07	Timra IK	Sweden	53	10	11	21	34	....	....	....	....	....	....	....	....	....	7	1	3	4	10	....	....	....	....
2007-08	**Toronto**	**NHL**	**50**	**3**	**6**	**9**	**18**	**0**	**0**	**0**	**40**	**7.5**	**-10**	**0**	**0.0**	**12:49**	....	....	....	....	....	....	....	....	....
	Toronto Marlies	AHL	21	0	11	11	22	....	....	....	....	....	....	....	....	....	....	....	....	....	....	....	....	....	....
2008-09	**Toronto**	**NHL**	**38**	**1**	**12**	**13**	**20**	**0**	**0**	**1**	**43**	**2.3**	**-2**	**1**	**100.0**	**15:34**	....	....	....	....	....	....	....	....	....
	Toronto Marlies	AHL	36	7	9	16	24	....	....	....	....	....	....	....	....	....	6	1	2	3	0	....	....	....	....
2009-10	**Columbus**	**NHL**	**73**	**6**	**28**	**34**	**37**	**4**	**0**	**0**	**121**	**5.0**	**-17**	**0**	**0.0**	**20:29**	....	....	....	....	....	....	....	....	....
2010-11	**Columbus**	**NHL**	**51**	**1**	**17**	**18**	**22**	**1**	**0**	**1**	**80**	**1.3**	**-11**	**0**	**0.0**	**19:44**	....	....	....	....	....	....	....	....	....
2011-12	**NY Rangers**	**NHL**	**53**	**2**	**16**	**18**	**20**	**0**	**0**	**0**	**55**	**3.6**	**9**	**0**	**0.0**	**17:06**	**20**	**3**	**3**	**6**	**4**	**2**	**0**	**0**	**16:56**
2012-13	**NY Rangers**	**NHL**	**48**	**4**	**3**	**7**	**16**	**0**	**0**	**0**	**66**	**6.1**	**14**	**1**	**0.0**	**18:03**	**10**	**0**	**0**	**0**	**0**	**0**	**0**	**0**	**21:06**
2013-14	**NY Rangers**	**NHL**	**81**	**1**	**12**	**13**	**26**	**0**	**0**	**0**	**104**	**1.0**	**9**	**0**	**0.0**	**19:25**	**25**	**0**	**5**	**5**	**4**	**0**	**0**	**0**	**21:03**
2014-15	**Tampa Bay**	**NHL**	**82**	**9**	**30**	**39**	**26**	**2**	**0**	**0**	**138**	**6.5**	**22**	**0**	**0.0**	**21:57**	**26**	**1**	**8**	**9**	**8**	**0**	**0**	**0**	**22:31**
	NHL Totals		**476**	**27**	**124**	**151**	**185**	**7**	**0**	**2**	**647**	**4.2**		**2**	**50.0**	**18:39**	**81**	**4**	**16**	**20**	**16**	**2**	**0**	**0**	**20:31**

Traded to **Calgary** by **Toronto** with Colin Stuart and Toronto's 7th round choice (Matt DeBlouw) in 2012 Entry Draft for Wayne Primeau and Calgary's 2nd round choice (later traded to Chicago – Chicago selected Brandon Saad) in 2011 Entry Draft, July 27, 2009. Traded to **Columbus** by **Calgary** for Columbus' 3rd round choice (Max Reinhart) in 2010 Entry Draft, September 29, 2009. Signed as a free agent by **NY Rangers**, November 5, 2011. Signed as a free agent by **Tampa Bay**, July 1, 2014.

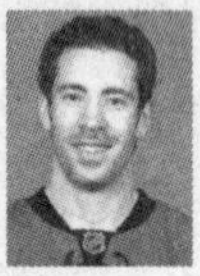

STREET, Ben
(STREET, BEHN) **COL**

Center. Shoots left. 5'11", 185 lbs. Born, Coquitlam, BC, February 13, 1987.

Season	Club	League	GP	G	A	Pts	PIM	PP	SH	GW	S	S%	+/-	TF	F%	Min	GP	G	A	Pts	PIM	PP	SH	GW	Min
2003-04	Salmon Arm	BCHL	54	13	21	34	14	....	....	....	....	....	....	....	....	....	13	1	9	10	0	....	....	....	....
2004-05	Salmon Arm	BCHL	56	29	39	68	21	....	....	....	....	....	....	....	....	....	11	7	8	15	0	....	....	....	....
2005-06	U. of Wisconsin	WCHA	43	10	5	15	0	....	....	....	....	....	....	....	....	....	....	....	....	....	....	....	....	....	....
2006-07	U. of Wisconsin	WCHA	41	10	7	17	16	....	....	....	....	....	....	....	....	....	....	....	....	....	....	....	....	....	....
2007-08	U. of Wisconsin	WCHA	40	13	17	30	36	....	....	....	....	....	....	....	....	....	....	....	....	....	....	....	....	....	....
2008-09	U. of Wisconsin	WCHA	4	1	0	1	8	....	....	....	....	....	....	....	....	....	....	....	....	....	....	....	....	....	....
2009-10	U. of Wisconsin	WCHA	43	14	16	30	30	....	....	....	....	....	....	....	....	....	....	....	....	....	....	....	....	....	....
2010-11	Wilkes-Barre	AHL	36	12	11	23	8	....	....	....	....	....	....	....	....	....	8	0	1	1	0	....	....	....	....
	Wheeling Nailers	ECHL	38	24	27	51	10	....	....	....	....	....	....	....	....	....	....	....	....	....	....	....	....	....	....
2011-12	Wilkes-Barre	AHL	71	27	30	57	24	....	....	....	....	....	....	....	....	....	12	1	2	3	2	....	....	....	....
2012-13	Abbotsford Heat	AHL	69	15	22	37	22	....	....	....	....	....	....	....	....	....	....	....	....	....	....	....	....	....	....
	Calgary	**NHL**	**6**	**0**	**1**	**1**	**0**	**0**	**0**	**0**	**13**	**0.0**	**-1**	**51**	**47.1**	**13:37**	....	....	....	....	....	....	....	....	....
2013-14	**Calgary**	**NHL**	**13**	**0**	**1**	**1**	**4**	**0**	**0**	**0**	**17**	**0.0**	**-2**	**137**	**46.0**	**10:36**	....	....	....	....	....	....	....	....	....
	Abbotsford Heat	AHL	58	28	32	60	24	....	....	....	....	....	....	....	....	....	4	0	1	1	2	....	....	....	....
2014-15	**Colorado**	**NHL**	**3**	**0**	**0**	**0**	**0**	**0**	**0**	**0**	**4**	**0.0**	**0**	**32**	**53.1**	**11:36**	....	....	....	....	....	....	....	....	....
	Lake Erie	AHL	44	9	30	39	10	....	....	....	....	....	....	....	....	....	....	....	....	....	....	....	....	....	....
	NHL Totals		**22**	**0**	**2**	**2**	**4**	**0**	**0**	**0**	**34**	**0.0**		**220**	**47.3**	**11:33**	....	....	....	....	....	....	....	....	....

Signed as a free agent by **Calgary**, July 2, 2012. Signed as a free agent by **Colorado**, July 1, 2014.

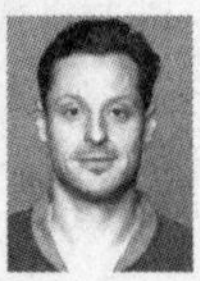

STREIT, Mark
(STRIGHT, MAHRK) **PHI**

Defense. Shoots left. 5'11", 191 lbs. Born, Bern, Switz., December 11, 1977. Montreal's 8th choice, 262nd overall, in 2004 Entry Draft.

Season	Club	League	GP	G	A	Pts	PIM	PP	SH	GW	S	S%	+/-	TF	F%	Min	GP	G	A	Pts	PIM	PP	SH	GW	Min
1995-96	Fribourg	Swiss	34	2	2	4	6	....	....	....	....	....	....	....	....	....	4	0	0	0	2	....	....	....	....
1996-97	HC Davos	Swiss	46	2	9	11	18	....	....	....	....	....	....	....	....	....	6	0	0	0	0	....	....	....	....
1997-98	HC Ambri-Piotta	Swiss	2	0	0	0	0	....	....	....	....	....	....	....	....	....	....	....	....	....	....	....	....	....	....
	HC Davos	Swiss	38	4	10	14	14	....	....	....	....	....	....	....	....	....	18	1	5	6	20	....	....	....	....
1998-99	HC Davos	Swiss	44	7	18	25	42	....	....	....	....	....	....	....	....	....	6	3	3	6	8	....	....	....	....
99-2000	Springfield	AHL	43	3	12	15	18	....	....	....	....	....	....	....	....	....	5	0	0	0	2	....	....	....	....
	Utah Grizzlies	IHL	1	0	1	1	2	....	....	....	....	....	....	....	....	....	....	....	....	....	....	....	....	....	....
	Tallahassee	ECHL	14	0	5	5	16	....	....	....	....	....	....	....	....	....	....	....	....	....	....	....	....	....	....
2000-01	ZSC Lions Zurich	Swiss	44	5	11	16	48	....	....	....	....	....	....	....	....	....	16	2	5	7	37	....	....	....	....
2001-02	ZSC Lions Zurich	Swiss	28	6	17	23	36	....	....	....	....	....	....	....	....	....	16	0	6	6	14	....	....	....	....
	Switzerland	Olympics	4	1	1	2	0	....	....	....	....	....	....	....	....	....	....	....	....	....	....	....	....	....	....
2002-03	ZSC Lions Zurich	Swiss	37	4	19	23	62	....	....	....	....	....	....	....	....	....	12	1	7	8	2	....	....	....	....
2003-04	ZSC Lions Zurich	Swiss	48	12	24	36	78	....	....	....	....	....	....	....	....	....	13	5	2	7	14	....	....	....	....
2004-05	ZSC Lions Zurich	Swiss	44	14	29	43	46	....	....	....	....	....	....	....	....	....	15	4	11	15	20	....	....	....	....
2005-06	**Montreal**	**NHL**	**48**	**2**	**9**	**11**	**28**	**2**	**0**	**0**	**52**	**3.8**	**-6**	**1**	**0.0**	**14:36**	**1**	**0**	**0**	**0**	**0**	**0**	**0**	**0**	**3:29**
	Switzerland	Olympics	6	2	1	3	6	....	....	....	....	....	....	....	....	....	....	....	....	....	....	....	....	....	....
2006-07	**Montreal**	**NHL**	**76**	**10**	**26**	**36**	**14**	**2**	**1**	**1**	**102**	**9.8**	**-5**	**12**	**33.3**	**14:01**	....	....	....	....	....	....	....	....	....
2007-08	**Montreal**	**NHL**	**81**	**13**	**49**	**62**	**28**	**7**	**0**	**3**	**165**	**7.9**	**-6**	**1**	**0.0**	**17:31**	**11**	**1**	**3**	**4**	**8**	**0**	**0**	**0**	**14:48**
2008-09	**NY Islanders**	**NHL**	**74**	**16**	**40**	**56**	**62**	**10**	**1**	**1**	**150**	**10.7**	**5**	**0**	**0.0**	**25:13**	....	....	....	....	....	....	....	....	....
2009-10	**NY Islanders**	**NHL**	**82**	**11**	**38**	**49**	**48**	**9**	**0**	**2**	**187**	**5.9**	**0**	**1**	**0.0**	**25:42**	....	....	....	....	....	....	....	....	....
	Switzerland	Olympics	5	0	3	3	0	....	....	....	....	....	....	....	....	....	....	....	....	....	....	....	....	....	....
2010-11		DID NOT PLAY – INJURED																							
2011-12	**NY Islanders**	**NHL**	**82**	**7**	**40**	**47**	**46**	**3**	**0**	**1**	**149**	**4.7**	**-27**	**1**	**0.0**	**23:23**	....	....	....	....	....	....	....	....	....
2012-13	SC Bern	Swiss	32	7	19	26	30	....	....	....	....	....	....	....	....	....	....	....	....	....	....	....	....	....	....
	NY Islanders	**NHL**	**48**	**6**	**21**	**27**	**22**	**3**	**0**	**1**	**83**	**7.2**	**-14**	**0**	**0.0**	**23:21**	**6**	**2**	**3**	**5**	**4**	**1**	**0**	**0**	**20:18**

| | | | | | Regular Season | | | | | | | | | | | | Playoffs | | | | | | | |
Season	Club	League	GP	G	A	Pts	PIM	PP	SH	GW	S	S%	+/-	TF	F%	Min	GP	G	A	Pts	PIM	PP	SH	GW	Min
2013-14	Philadelphia	NHL	82	10	34	44	44	4	0	2	121	8.3	3	0	0.0	20:39	7	1	2	3	0	0	0	0	19:59
	Switzerland	Olympics	4	0	1	1	2																		
2014-15	Philadelphia	NHL	81	9	43	52	36	4	0	0	144	6.3	-8	0	0.0	22:22									
	NHL Totals		654	84	300	384	328	44	2	11	1153	7.3		16	25.0	20:57	25	4	8	12	12	1	0	0	17:07

Played in NHL All-Star Game (2009)

Signed as a free agent by **NY Islanders**, July 1, 2008. • Missed 2010-11 due to shoulder injury in training camp, September 25, 2010. Signed as a free agent by **Bern** (Swiss), September 15, 2012. Traded to **Philadelphia** by **NY Islanders** for Shane Harper and Philadelphia's 4th round choice (Devon Toews) in 2014 Entry Draft, June 12, 2013.

STROME, Ryan

(STROHM, RIGH-uhn) **NYI**

Center. Shoots right. 6'1", 196 lbs. Born, Mississauga, ON, July 11, 1993. NY Islanders' 1st choice, 5th overall, in 2011 Entry Draft.

2008-09	Tor. Marlboros	GTHL	76	41	63	104	86																		
2009-10	Barrie Colts	OHL	34	5	9	14	35																		
	Niagara Ice Dogs	OHL	27	3	10	13	26										5	3	0	3	0				
2010-11	Niagara Ice Dogs	OHL	65	33	73	106	82										14	6	6	12	19				
2011-12	Niagara Ice Dogs	OHL	46	30	38	68	47										20	7	16	23	31				
2012-13	Niagara Ice Dogs	OHL	53	34	60	94	59										5	2	1	3	8				
	Bridgeport	AHL	10	2	5	7	4																		
2013-14	**NY Islanders**	**NHL**	37	7	11	18	8	4	0	1	89	7.9	-1	374	44.1	15:11									
	Bridgeport	AHL	37	13	36	49	41																		
2014-15	**NY Islanders**	**NHL**	81	17	33	50	47	1	1	2	179	9.5	23	319	46.7	15:24	7	2	2	4	2	0	0	1	17:33
	NHL Totals		118	24	44	68	55	5	1	3	268	9.0		693	45.3	15:20	7	2	2	4	2	0	0	1	17:33

OHL Second All-Star Team (2011) • AHL All-Rookie Team (2014)

STUART, Brad

(STEW-ahrt, BRAD) **COL**

Defense. Shoots left. 6'2", 215 lbs. Born, Rocky Mountain House, AB, November 6, 1979. San Jose's 1st choice, 3rd overall, in 1998 Entry Draft.

1995-96	Red Deer	AMHL	35	12	25	37	83																		
	Regina Pats	WHL	3	0	0	0	0																		
1996-97	Regina Pats	WHL	57	7	36	43	58										5	0	4	4	14				
1997-98	Regina Pats	WHL	72	20	45	65	82										9	3	4	7	10				
1998-99	Regina Pats	WHL	29	10	19	29	43																		
	Calgary Hitmen	WHL	30	11	22	33	26										21	8	15	23	59				
99-2000	San Jose	NHL	82	10	26	36	32	5	1	3	133	7.5	3	0	0.0	20:24	12	1	0	1	6	1	0	0	16:30
2000-01	San Jose	NHL	77	5	18	23	56	1	0	2	119	4.2	10	0	0.0	20:06	5	1	0	1	0	0	0	0	20:19
2001-02	San Jose	NHL	82	6	23	29	39	2	0	2	96	6.3	13	0	0.0	21:41	12	0	3	3	8	0	0	0	19:42
2002-03	San Jose	NHL	36	4	10	14	46	2	0	1	63	6.3	-6	0	0.0	20:53									
2003-04	San Jose	NHL	77	9	30	39	34	5	0	0	129	7.0	9	0	0.0	22:09	17	1	5	6	13	0	0	0	23:23
2004-05			DID NOT PLAY																					
2005-06	San Jose	NHL	23	2	10	12	14	1	0	0	41	4.9	-2	0	0.0	23:15									
	Boston	NHL	55	10	21	31	38	6	0	2	122	8.2	-6	0	0.0	25:40									
2006-07	Boston	NHL	48	7	10	17	26	1	0	0	74	9.5	-22	0	0.0	22:55									
	Calgary	NHL	27	0	5	5	18	0	0	0	35	0.0	12	0	0.0	22:48	6	0	1	1	6	0	0	0	25:16
2007-08	Los Angeles	NHL	63	5	16	21	67	2	0	1	111	4.5	-16	4	0.0	21:13									
	♦ Detroit	NHL	9	1	1	2	2	0	0	0	21	4.8	6	0	0.0	20:46	21	1	6	7	14	0	0	1	21:40
2008-09	Detroit	NHL	67	2	13	15	26	1	0	0	105	1.9	-3	0	0.0	20:13	23	3	6	9	12	1	0	0	24:09
2009-10	Detroit	NHL	82	4	16	20	22	1	0	2	153	2.6	-12	2	50.0	23:10	12	2	4	6	8	0	0	0	22:04
2010-11	Detroit	NHL	67	3	17	20	40	1	0	0	81	3.7	4	0	0.0	21:32	11	0	2	2	8	0	0	0	21:33
2011-12	Detroit	NHL	81	6	15	21	29	1	1	2	96	6.3	16	0	0.0	21:03	5	0	1	1	0	0	0	0	19:22
2012-13	San Jose	NHL	48	0	6	6	25	0	0	0	39	0.0	4	0	0.0	20:27	11	1	2	3	0	0	0	0	19:09
2013-14	San Jose	NHL	61	3	8	11	35	0	0	3	64	4.7	4	0	0.0	19:10	7	0	0	0	0	0	0	0	19:48
2014-15	Colorado	NHL	65	3	10	13	16	0	0	0	64	4.7	-4	1100	0.0	20:21									
	NHL Totals		1050	80	255	335	565	29	2	21	1546	5.2		7	28.6	21:27	142	10	30	40	77	2	0	1	21:26

WHL East Second All-Star Team (1998) • WHL East First All-Star Team (1999) • Canadian Major Junior First All-Star Team (1999) • Canadian Major Junior Defenseman of the Year (1999) • NHL All-Rookie Team (2000)

• Missed majority of 2002-03 due to ankle (January 4, 2003 vs. Los Angeles) and head (February 21, 2003 vs. Columbus) injuries. Traded to **Boston** by **San Jose** with Marco Sturm and Wayne Primeau for Joe Thornton, November 30, 2005. Traded to **Calgary** by **Boston** with Wayne Primeau and Washington's 4th round choice (previously acquired, Calgary selected T.J. Brodie) in 2008 Entry Draft for Andrew Ference and Chuck Kobasew, February 10, 2007. Signed as a free agent by **Los Angeles**, July 3, 2007. Traded to **Detroit** by **Los Angeles** for Detroit's 2nd round choice (later traded to Colorado – Colorado selected Peter Delmas) in 2008 Entry Draft and Detroit's 4th round choice (later traded to Atlanta – Atlanta selected Ben Chiarot) in 2009 Entry Draft, February 26, 2008. Traded to **San Jose** by **Detroit** for Andrew Murray and San Jose's 7th round choice (Alexander Kadeykin) in 2014 Entry Draft, June 10, 2012. Traded to **Colorado** by **San Jose** for a 2nd round choice in 2016 Entry Draft and a 6th round choice in 2017 Entry Draft, July 1, 2014.

STUART, Colin

(STEW-ahrt, KAW-lihn)

Left wing. Shoots left. 6'2", 205 lbs. Born, Rochester, MN, July 8, 1982. Atlanta's 5th choice, 135th overall, in 2001 Entry Draft.

1998-99	Roch. Lourdes	High-MN	23	22	32	54																			
99-2000	Lincoln Stars	USHL	53	18	19	37	38										9	1	3	4	2				
2000-01	Colorado College	WCHA	41	2	7	9	26																		
2001-02	Colorado College	WCHA	43	13	9	22	34																		
2002-03	Colorado College	WCHA	42	13	11	24	56																		
2003-04	Colorado College	WCHA	30	10	12	22	38																		
2004-05	Chicago Wolves	AHL	39	3	2	5	12																		
	Gwinnett	ECHL	5	1	3	4	4																		
2005-06	Chicago Wolves	AHL	78	13	14	27	65										15	2	5	7	10				
2006-07	Chicago Wolves	AHL	67	18	11	29	75																		
2007-08	**Atlanta**	**NHL**	18	3	2	5	6	0	1	1	19	15.8	2	7	57.1	12:20									
	Chicago Wolves	AHL	58	8	8	16	45										24	3	6	18					
2008-09	**Atlanta**	**NHL**	33	5	3	8	18	0	3	0	54	9.3	3	12	41.7	12:29									
	Chicago Wolves	AHL	42	9	6	15	38										3	0	0	0	6				
2009-10	Abbotsford Heat	AHL	67	17	19	36	36																		
2010-11	**Buffalo**	**NHL**	3	0	0	0	2	0	0	0	5	0.0	1	2	50.0	13:09									
	Portland Pirates	AHL	72	16	28	44	53										12	3	4	7	8				
2011-12	**Buffalo**	**NHL**	2	0	0	0	0	0	0	0	0	0.0	-3	0	0.0	6:12									
	Rochester	AHL	51	13	19	32	32										3	0	0	0	4				
2012-13	Iserlohn Roosters	Germany	45	9	12	21	35																		
2013-14	Utica Comets	AHL	54	17	8	25	38																		
2014-15	Providence Bruins	AHL	44	17	9	26	22										5	1	2	3	4				
	NHL Totals		56	8	5	13	26	0	4	1	78	10.3		21	47.6	12:15									

Traded to **Toronto** by **Atlanta** with Garnet Exelby for Pavel Kubina and Tim Stapleton, July 1, 2009. Traded to **Calgary** by **Toronto** with Anton Stralman and Toronto's 7th round choice (Matt DeBlouw) in 2012 Entry Draft for Wayne Primeau and Calgary's 2nd round choice (later traded to Chicago – Chicago selected Brandon Saad) in 2011 Entry Draft, July 27, 2009. Signed as a free agent by **Buffalo**, August 26, 2010. Signed as a free agent by **Iserlohn** (Germany), September 18, 2012. Signed as a free agent by **Vancouver**, July 25, 2013. Signed as a free agent by **Providence** (AHL), December 19, 2014.

STUART, Mark

(STEW-uhrt, MAHRK) **WPG**

Defense. Shoots left. 6'2", 213 lbs. Born, Rochester, MN, April 27, 1984. Boston's 1st choice, 21st overall, in 2003 Entry Draft.

99-2000	Roch. Lourdes	High-MN	28	19	22	41																				
2000-01	USNTDP	U-17	12	1	5	6	6																		
	USNTDP	NAHL	52	2	11	13	114																		
2001-02	USNTDP	U-18	40	9	9	18																				
	USNTDP	USHL	12	0	1	1	25																		
	USNTDP	NAHL	9	0	1	1	18																		
2002-03	Colorado College	WCHA	38	3	17	20	81																		
2003-04	Colorado College	WCHA	37	4	11	15	100																		
2004-05	Colorado College	WCHA	43	5	14	19	94																		
2005-06	**Boston**	**NHL**	17	1	1	2	10	0	0	0	9	11.1	-1	0	0.0	17:46									
	Providence Bruins	AHL	60	4	3	7	76										6	0	0	0	25				
2006-07	**Boston**	**NHL**	15	0	1	1	14	0	0	0	4	0.0	7	0	0.0	10:23									
	Providence Bruins	AHL	49	4	16	20	62										3	0	1	1	9				

Season	Club	League	GP	G	A	Pts	PIM	PP	SH	GW	S	S%	+/-	TF	F%	Min	GP	G	A	Pts	PIM	PP	SH	GW	Min
			Regular Season														Playoffs								
2007-08	Boston	NHL	82	4	4	8	81	0	0	1	60	6.7	2	0	0.0	15:22	7	0	1	1	8	0	0	0	16:00
2008-09	Boston	NHL	82	5	12	17	76	0	0	1	61	8.2	20	0	0.0	15:25	11	0	1	1	7	0	0	0	17:57
2009-10	Boston	NHL	56	2	5	7	80	0	0	0	53	3.8	1	0	0.0	17:01	4	0	0	0	6	0	0	0	14:39
2010-11	Boston	NHL	31	1	4	5	23	0	0	1	20	5.0	8	1	100.0	16:15									
	Atlanta	NHL	23	1	0	1	24	0	0	0	21	4.8	–8	0	0.0	14:51									
2011-12	Winnipeg	NHL	80	3	11	14	98	0	1	1	60	5.0	–4	0	0.0	17:12									
2012-13	Florida Everblades	ECHL	9	2	1	3	12																		
	Winnipeg	NHL	42	2	2	4	53	0	0	0	40	5.0	5	0	0.0	16:42									
2013-14	Winnipeg	NHL	69	2	11	13	101	0	0	0	73	2.7	11	0	0.0	18:38									
2014-15	Winnipeg	NHL	70	2	12	14	69	0	0	1	51	3.9	5	1	0.0	19:13	4	1	1	2	2	0	0	0	17:46
	NHL Totals		567	23	63	86	629	0	1	5	452	5.1		2	50.0	16:44	26	1	3	4	23	0	0	0	16:53

WCHA All-Rookie Team (2003) • WCHA Second All-Star Team (2005) • NCAA West First All-American Team (2005)

Traded to **Atlanta** by **Boston** with Blake Wheeler for Rich Peverley and Boris Valabik, February 18, 2011. • Transferred to **Winnipeg** after **Atlanta** franchise relocated, June 21, 2011. Signed as a free agent by **Florida** (ECHL), December 11, 2012.

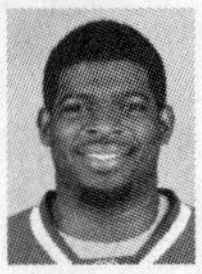

SUBBAN, P.K. (soo-BAN, PEE-KAY) MTL

Defense. Shoots right. 6', 214 lbs. Born, Toronto, ON, May 13, 1989. Montreal's 3rd choice, 43rd overall, in 2007 Entry Draft.

Season	Club	League	GP	G	A	Pts	PIM	PP	SH	GW	S	S%	+/-	TF	F%	Min	GP	G	A	Pts	PIM	PP	SH	GW	Min
2004-05	Markham	GTHL	67	15	28	43	179																		
2005-06	Belleville Bulls	OHL	52	5	7	12	70										3	0	0	0	2				
2006-07	Belleville Bulls	OHL	68	15	41	56	89										15	5	8	13	26				
2007-08	Belleville Bulls	OHL	58	8	38	46	100										21	8	15	23	28				
2008-09	Belleville Bulls	OHL	56	14	62	76	94										17	3	12	15	22				
2009-10	Montreal	NHL	2	0	2	2	2	0	0	0	4	0.0	1	0	0.0	20:06	14	1	7	8	6	0	0	0	20:44
	Hamilton	AHL	77	18	35	53	82										7	3	7	10	6				
2010-11	Montreal	NHL	77	14	24	38	124	9	0	3	197	7.1	–8	0	0.0	22:16	7	2	2	4	2	2	0	0	28:33
2011-12	Montreal	NHL	81	7	29	36	119	5	0	0	205	3.4	9	0	0.0	24:18									
2012-13	Montreal	NHL	42	11	27	38	57	7	0	0	126	8.7	12	0	0.0	23:15	5	2	2	4	31	1	0	0	23:56
2013-14	Montreal	NHL	82	10	43	53	81	4	0	1	204	4.9	–4	0	0.0	24:37	17	5	9	14	24	*4	0	1	27:26
	Canada	Olympics	1	0	0	0	0																		
2014-15	Montreal	NHL	82	15	45	60	74	8	0	5	170	8.8	21	0	0.0	26:12	12	1	7	8	31	0	0	0	26:45
	NHL Totals		366	57	170	227	457	33	0	9	906	6.3		0	0.0	24:14	55	11	27	38	94	7	0	1	25:24

OHL First All-Star Team (2009) • AHL All-Rookie Team (2010) • AHL First All-Star Team (2010) • NHL All-Rookie Team (2011) • NHL First All-Star Team (2013, 2015) • James Norris Memorial Trophy (2013)

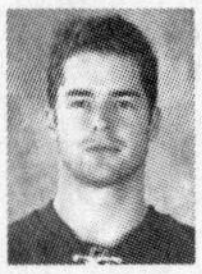

SUMMERS, Chris (SUHM-mehrs, KRIHS) NYR

Defense. Shoots left. 6'2", 209 lbs. Born, Ann Arbor, MI, February 5, 1988. Phoenix's 2nd choice, 29th overall, in 2006 Entry Draft.

Season	Club	League	GP	G	A	Pts	PIM	PP	SH	GW	S	S%	+/-	TF	F%	Min	GP	G	A	Pts	PIM	PP	SH	GW	Min
2004-05	USNTDP	U-17	13	2	2	4	10																		
	USNTDP	NAHL	31	2	5	7	20										7	1	0	1	0				
2005-06	USNTDP	U-18	42	4	9	13	67																		
	USNTDP	NAHL	17	2	2	4	20																		
2006-07	U. of Michigan	CCHA	41	6	8	14	58																		
2007-08	U. of Michigan	CCHA	41	2	11	13	65																		
2008-09	U. of Michigan	CCHA	41	4	13	17	40																		
2009-10	U. of Michigan	CCHA	40	4	12	16	28																		
	San Antonio	AHL	6	1	0	1	0																		
2010-11	Phoenix	NHL	2	0	0	0	4	0	0	0	0	0.0	–3	0	0.0	13:52									
	San Antonio	AHL	75	1	9	10	54																		
2011-12	Phoenix	NHL	21	0	3	3	11	0	0	0	10	0.0	–4	0	0.0	12:27									
	Portland Pirates	AHL	28	0	2	2	37																		
2012-13	Portland Pirates	AHL	60	2	10	12	53										3	0	0	0	0				
	Phoenix	NHL	6	0	0	0	9	0	0	0	5	0.0	–3	0	0.0	12:39									
2013-14	Phoenix	NHL	18	2	1	3	15	0	0	0	17	11.8	0	0	0.0	14:55									
	Portland Pirates	AHL	48	2	7	9	47																		
2014-15	Arizona	NHL	17	0	3	3	8	0	0	0	13	0.0	–12	0	0.0	13:43									
	Portland Pirates	AHL	8	0	1	1	6																		
	NY Rangers	NHL	3	0	0	0	0	0	0	0	2	0.0	0	0	0.0	17:15									
	Hartford	AHL	13	0	1	1	17																		
	NHL Totals		67	2	7	9	47	0	0	0	47	4.3		0	0.0	13:43									

Traded to **NY Rangers** by **Arizona** with Keith Yandle and a 4th round choice in 2016 Entry Draft for John Moore, Anthony Duclair, Tampa Bay's 2nd round choice (previously acquired, later traded to Calgary – Calgary selected Oliver Kylington) in 2015 Entry Draft and future considerations, March 1, 2015.

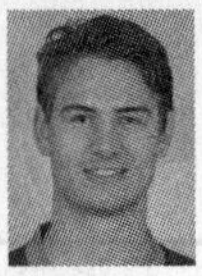

SUNDSTROM, Johan (SOOND-struhm, YOH-han) NYI

Center. Shoots right. 6'3", 201 lbs. Born, Gothenburg, Sweden, September 21, 1992. NY Islanders' 3rd choice, 50th overall, in 2011 Entry Draft.

Season	Club	League	GP	G	A	Pts	PIM	PP	SH	GW	S	S%	+/-	TF	F%	Min	GP	G	A	Pts	PIM	PP	SH	GW	Min
2008-09	Frolunda U18	Swe-U18	22	6	7	13	4										7	0	2	2	0				
2009-10	Frolunda U18	Swe-U18	5	6	4	10	6										1	0	0	0	0				
	Frolunda Jr.	Swe-Jr.	37	13	17	30	14										1	0	0	0	0				
	Frolunda	Sweden	1	0	0	0	0																		
2010-11	Frolunda Jr.	Swe-Jr.	15	10	9	19	4										7	8	7	15	2				
	Boras HC	Sweden-2	1	0	0	0	0																		
	Frolunda	Sweden	41	1	0	1	10																		
2011-12	Frolunda	Sweden	49	6	5	11	8										6	0	0	0	2				
2012-13	Bridgeport	AHL	59	11	21	32	30																		
2013-14	NY Islanders	NHL	11	0	1	1	6	0	0	0	13	0.0	0	11	36.4	8:40									
	Bridgeport	AHL	40	8	10	18	41																		
2014-15	Bridgeport	AHL	72	7	12	19	81																		
	NHL Totals		11	0	1	1	6	0	0	0	13	0.0		11	36.4	8:40									

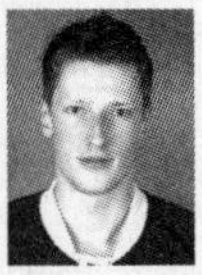

SUSTR, Andrej (SHOO-stuhr, an-DRAY) T.B.

Defense. Shoots right. 6'7", 220 lbs. Born, Plzen, Czech., November 29, 1990.

Season	Club	League	GP	G	A	Pts	PIM	PP	SH	GW	S	S%	+/-	TF	F%	Min	GP	G	A	Pts	PIM	PP	SH	GW	Min
2006-07	Jihlava U17	CzR-U17	37	5	15	20	56																		
	Jihlava Jr.	CzRep-Jr.	5	0	0	0	4																		
2007-08	HC Plzen Jr.	CzRep-Jr.	41	2	8	10	44										5	1	0	1	4				
2008-09	HC Plzen Jr.	CzRep-Jr.	13	1	4	5	14																		
	HC Rokycany	CzRep-3	2	0	0	0	2																		
	Kenai River	NAHL	36	1	7	8	58										2	0	0	0	2				
2009-10	Youngstown	USHL	50	1	18	19	95																		
2010-11	Nebraska-Omaha	WCHA	39	2	7	9	38																		
2011-12	Nebraska-Omaha	WCHA	33	4	13	17	26																		
2012-13	Nebraska-Omaha	WCHA	39	9	16	25	53																		
	Tampa Bay	NHL	2	0	0	0	0	0	0	0	2	0.0	1	0	0.0	10:43									
	Syracuse Crunch	AHL	8	2	1	3	8										18	2	5	7	25				
2013-14	Tampa Bay	NHL	43	1	7	8	16	0	0	0	39	2.6	3	0	0.0	15:48	3	0	0	0	2	0	0	0	18:26
	Syracuse Crunch	AHL	12	1	3	4	2																		
2014-15	Tampa Bay	NHL	72	0	13	13	34	0	0	0	55	0.0	10	0	0.0	17:42	26	1	1	2	18	0	0	0	15:14
	NHL Totals		117	1	20	21	50	0	0	0	96	1.0		0	0.0	16:53	29	1	1	2	20	0	0	0	15:34

Signed as a free agent by **Tampa Bay** March 21, 2013.

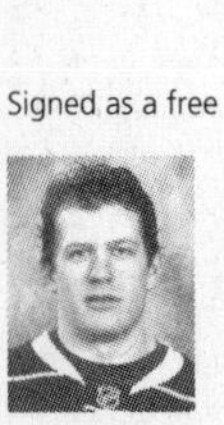

SUTER, Ryan (SOO-tuhr, RIGH-uhn) MIN

Defense. Shoots left. 6'1", 200 lbs. Born, Madison, WI, January 21, 1985. Nashville's 1st choice, 7th overall, in 2003 Entry Draft.

Season	Club	League	GP	G	A	Pts	PIM	PP	SH	GW	S	S%	+/-	TF	F%	Min	GP	G	A	Pts	PIM	PP	SH	GW	Min
2000-01	Culver Academy	High-IN	26	13	32	45	....																		
2001-02	USNTDP	U-17	8	2	11	13	21																		
	USNTDP	U-18	27	4	10	14	6																		
	USNTDP	NAHL	35	2	10	12	75																		
2002-03	USNTDP	NAHL	9	2	5	7	12																		
	USNTDP	U-18	42	7	17	24	124																		

			Regular Season														Playoffs								
Season	Club	League	GP	G	A	Pts	PIM	PP	SH	GW	S	S%	+/-	TF	F%	Min	GP	G	A	Pts	PIM	PP	SH	GW	Min
2003-04	U. of Wisconsin	WCHA	39	3	16	19	93	....	....	....	....	....	....	....	....	....	....	....	....	....	....	....	....	....	....
2004-05	Milwaukee	AHL	63	7	16	23	70	....	....	....	....	....	....	....	....	....	7	1	5	6	16	....	....	....	....
2005-06	Nashville	NHL	71	1	15	16	66	0	0	0	84	1.2	7	0	0.0	17:21	....	....	....	....	....	....	....	....	....
2006-07	Nashville	NHL	82	8	16	24	54	1	0	0	87	9.2	10	0	0.0	20:09	5	1	0	1	8	0	0	0	23:19
2007-08	Nashville	NHL	76	7	24	31	71	1	0	1	138	5.1	3	0	0.0	20:35	6	1	1	2	4	0	0	0	21:12
2008-09	Nashville	NHL	82	7	38	45	73	3	0	3	143	4.9	-16	0	0.0	24:16	....	....	....	....	....	....	....	....	....
2009-10	Nashville	NHL	82	4	33	37	48	2	0	1	125	3.2	4	1	0.0	23:59	6	0	0	0	0	0	0	0	24:09
	United States	Olympics	6	0	4	4	2	....	....	....	....	....	....	....	....	....	....	....	....	....	....	....	....	....	....
2010-11	Nashville	NHL	70	4	35	39	54	1	0	1	115	3.5	20	1	0.0	25:12	12	1	5	6	6	0	0	0	28:51
2011-12	Nashville	NHL	79	7	39	46	30	3	1	1	134	5.2	15	1	0.0	26:30	10	1	3	4	4	1	0	0	28:50
2012-13	Minnesota	NHL	48	4	28	32	24	3	0	1	91	4.4	2	0	0.0	27:17	5	0	0	0	4	0	0	0	31:37
2013-14	Minnesota	NHL	82	8	35	43	34	3	0	0	150	5.3	15	1	100.0	29:25	13	1	6	7	4	1	0	0	29:13
	United States	Olympics	6	0	3	3	4	....	....	....	....	....	....	....	....	....	....	....	....	....	....	....	....	....	....
2014-15	Minnesota	NHL	77	2	36	38	48	1	0	1	150	1.3	7	0	0.0	29:04	10	0	3	3	0	0	0	0	26:59
	NHL Totals		749	52	299	351	502	18	1	9	1217	4.3		4	25.0	24:20	67	5	18	23	30	2	0	0	27:20

WCHA All-Rookie Team (2004) • NHL First All-Star Team (2013)
Played in NHL All-Star Game (2012, 2015)
Signed as a free agent by **Minnesota**, July 4, 2012.

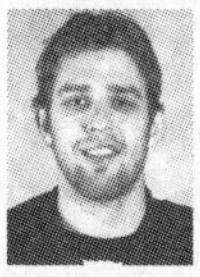

SUTTER, Brandon (SUH-tuhr, BRAN-duhn) VAN

Center/Right wing. Shoots right. 6'3", 190 lbs. Born, Huntington, NY, February 14, 1989. Carolina's 1st choice, 11th overall, in 2007 Entry Draft.

Season	Club	League	GP	G	A	Pts	PIM	PP	SH	GW	S	S%	+/-	TF	F%	Min	GP	G	A	Pts	PIM	PP	SH	GW	Min
2003-04	Red Deer Chiefs	AMBHL	35	25	34	59	28	....	....	....	....	....	....	....	....	....	11	5	4	9	....	....	....	....	....
2004-05	Red Deer	AMHL	34	4	16	20	28	....	....	....	....	....	....	....	....	....	....	....	....	....	....	....	....	....	....
	Red Deer Rebels	WHL	7	0	2	2	8	....	....	....	....	....	....	....	....	....	7	1	4	5	2	....	....	....	....
2005-06	Red Deer Rebels	WHL	68	22	24	46	36	....	....	....	....	....	....	....	....	....	....	....	....	....	....	....	....	....	....
2006-07	Red Deer Rebels	WHL	71	20	37	57	54	....	....	....	....	....	....	....	....	....	7	0	3	3	14	....	....	....	....
2007-08	Red Deer Rebels	WHL	59	26	23	49	38	....	....	....	....	....	....	....	....	....	....	....	....	....	....	....	....	....	....
	Albany River Rats	AHL	7	1	1	2	2	....	....	....	....	....	....	....	....	....	7	0	2	2	4	....	....	....	....
2008-09	Carolina	NHL	50	1	5	6	16	0	0	0	57	1.8	-1	332	38.6	8:50	....	....	....	....	....	....	....	....	....
	Albany River Rats	AHL	22	4	8	12	6	....	....	....	....	....	....	....	....	....	....	....	....	....	....	....	....	....	....
2009-10	Carolina	NHL	72	21	19	40	2	5	0	3	168	12.5	-1	997	49.1	16:33	....	....	....	....	....	....	....	....	....
	Albany River Rats	AHL	7	1	3	4	2	....	....	....	....	....	....	....	....	....	....	....	....	....	....	....	....	....	....
2010-11	Carolina	NHL	82	14	15	29	25	1	0	3	145	9.7	13	1349	44.3	16:51	....	....	....	....	....	....	....	....	....
2011-12	Carolina	NHL	82	17	15	32	21	2	3	0	171	9.9	-3	1295	50.5	17:24	....	....	....	....	....	....	....	....	....
2012-13	Pittsburgh	NHL	48	11	8	19	4	3	0	5	82	13.4	3	761	50.2	16:24	15	2	1	3	0	0	0	0	16:18
2013-14	Pittsburgh	NHL	81	13	13	26	12	2	3	1	144	9.0	-9	1150	47.7	15:46	13	5	2	7	2	0	1	1	15:53
2014-15	Pittsburgh	NHL	80	21	12	33	14	3	4	4	180	11.7	6	1359	50.6	17:19	5	1	1	2	2	1	0	0	15:57
	NHL Totals		495	98	87	185	94	16	10	16	947	10.3		7243	48.2	15:57	33	8	4	12	4	1	1	1	16:05

Traded to **Pittsburgh** by **Carolina** with Brian Dumoulin and Carolina's 1st round choice (Derrick Pouliot) in 2012 Entry Draft for Jordan Staal, June 22, 2012. Traded to **Vancouver** by **Pittsburgh** with Pittsburgh's 3rd round compensatory choice in 2016 Entry Draft for Nick Bonino, Adam Clendening and Anaheim's 2nd round choice (previously acquired) in 2016 Entry Draft, July 28, 2015.

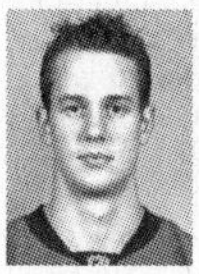

SUTTER, Brett (SUH-tuhr, BREHT) MIN

Left wing. Shoots left. 6', 200 lbs. Born, Viking, AB, June 2, 1987. Calgary's 7th choice, 179th overall, in 2005 Entry Draft.

Season	Club	League	GP	G	A	Pts	PIM	PP	SH	GW	S	S%	+/-	TF	F%	Min	GP	G	A	Pts	PIM	PP	SH	GW	Min
2003-04	Kootenay Ice	WHL	44	5	7	12	26	....	....	....	....	....	....	....	....	....	4	0	0	0	4	....	....	....	....
2004-05	Kootenay Ice	WHL	70	8	11	19	70	....	....	....	....	....	....	....	....	....	16	1	2	3	16	....	....	....	....
2005-06	Kootenay Ice	WHL	16	8	7	15	21	....	....	....	....	....	....	....	....	....	....	....	....	....	....	....	....	....	....
	Red Deer Rebels	WHL	57	9	26	35	80	....	....	....	....	....	....	....	....	....	....	....	....	....	....	....	....	....	....
2006-07	Red Deer Rebels	WHL	67	28	29	57	77	....	....	....	....	....	....	....	....	....	7	3	4	7	11	....	....	....	....
2007-08	Quad City Flames	AHL	75	4	6	10	63	....	....	....	....	....	....	....	....	....	....	....	....	....	....	....	....	....	....
2008-09	Calgary	NHL	4	1	0	1	2	0	0	0	6	16.7	-2	1	0.0	8:04	....	....	....	....	....	....	....	....	....
	Quad City Flames	AHL	71	10	15	25	50	....	....	....	....	....	....	....	....	....	....	....	....	....	....	....	....	....	....
2009-10	Calgary	NHL	10	0	0	0	5	0	0	0	9	0.0	-1	5	20.0	9:40	....	....	....	....	....	....	....	....	....
	Abbotsford Heat	AHL	66	9	15	24	69	....	....	....	....	....	....	....	....	....	13	4	7	11	20	....	....	....	....
2010-11	Calgary	NHL	4	0	1	1	5	0	0	0	3	0.0	-1	23	52.2	10:07	....	....	....	....	....	....	....	....	....
	Charlotte	AHL	60	9	12	21	84	....	....	....	....	....	....	....	....	....	16	4	10	14	15	....	....	....	....
	Carolina	NHL	1	0	0	0	0	0	0	0	0	0.0	0	3	33.3	4:09	....	....	....	....	....	....	....	....	....
2011-12	Carolina	NHL	15	0	3	3	11	0	0	0	11	0.0	-1	21	66.7	7:34	....	....	....	....	....	....	....	....	....
	Charlotte	AHL	63	13	16	29	58	....	....	....	....	....	....	....	....	....	....	....	....	....	....	....	....	....	....
2012-13	Charlotte	AHL	70	19	29	48	62	....	....	....	....	....	....	....	....	....	5	0	0	0	0	....	....	....	....
	Carolina	NHL	3	0	0	0	4	0	0	0	2	0.0	-1	14	57.1	8:21	....	....	....	....	....	....	....	....	....
2013-14	Carolina	NHL	17	1	1	2	9	0	0	1	16	6.3	-4	73	50.7	7:34	....	....	....	....	....	....	....	....	....
	Charlotte	AHL	62	15	29	44	69	....	....	....	....	....	....	....	....	....	....	....	....	....	....	....	....	....	....
2014-15	Minnesota	NHL	6	0	3	3	4	0	0	0	6	0.0	1	0	0.0	9:19	....	....	....	....	....	....	....	....	....
	Iowa Wild	AHL	71	12	17	29	37	....	....	....	....	....	....	....	....	....	....	....	....	....	....	....	....	....	....
	NHL Totals		60	2	8	10	40	0	0	1	53	3.8		140	52.1	8:17	....	....	....	....	....	....	....	....	....

Traded to **Carolina** by **Calgary** with Ian White for Anton Babchuk and Tom Kostopoulos, November 17, 2010. Signed as a free agent by **Minnesota**, July 1, 2014.

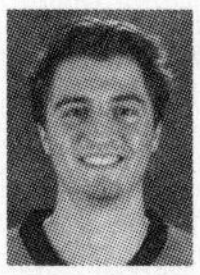

SUTTER, Brody (SUH-tuhr, BROH-dee) CAR

Center. Shoots right. 6'5", 203 lbs. Born, Viking, AB, September 26, 1991. Carolina's 6th choice, 193rd overall, in 2011 Entry Draft.

Season	Club	League	GP	G	A	Pts	PIM	PP	SH	GW	S	S%	+/-	TF	F%	Min	GP	G	A	Pts	PIM	PP	SH	GW	Min
2007-08	Calgary Buffaloes	AMHL	32	8	11	19	24	....	....	....	....	....	....	....	....	....	12	4	6	10	4	....	....	....	....
2008-09	Saskatoon Blades	WHL	18	0	2	2	4	....	....	....	....	....	....	....	....	....	....	....	....	....	....	....	....	....	....
	Lethbridge	WHL	30	4	3	7	7	....	....	....	....	....	....	....	....	....	10	0	0	0	2	....	....	....	....
2009-10	Lethbridge	WHL	72	5	9	14	42	....	....	....	....	....	....	....	....	....	....	....	....	....	....	....	....	....	....
2010-11	Lethbridge	WHL	46	18	24	42	35	....	....	....	....	....	....	....	....	....	....	....	....	....	....	....	....	....	....
2011-12	Lethbridge	WHL	65	30	30	60	49	....	....	....	....	....	....	....	....	....	....	....	....	....	....	....	....	....	....
	Charlotte	AHL	4	1	0	1	0	....	....	....	....	....	....	....	....	....	....	....	....	....	....	....	....	....	....
2012-13	Florida Everblades	ECHL	37	8	8	16	13	....	....	....	....	....	....	....	....	....	....	....	....	....	....	....	....	....	....
	Charlotte	AHL	23	3	2	5	13	....	....	....	....	....	....	....	....	....	5	2	3	5	2	....	....	....	....
2013-14	Charlotte	AHL	69	8	20	28	29	....	....	....	....	....	....	....	....	....	....	....	....	....	....	....	....	....	....
2014-15	Carolina	NHL	4	0	0	0	0	0	0	0	0	0.0	-2	14	50.0	7:26	....	....	....	....	....	....	....	....	....
	Charlotte	AHL	45	12	13	25	17	....	....	....	....	....	....	....	....	....	....	....	....	....	....	....	....	....	....
	NHL Totals		4	0	0	0	0	0	0	0	0	0.0		14	50.0	7:26	....	....	....	....	....	....	....	....	....

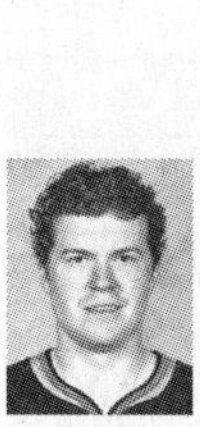

SYVRET, Danny (SIHV-reht, DA-nee)

Defense. Shoots left. 5'11", 203 lbs. Born, Millgrove, ON, June 13, 1985. Edmonton's 3rd choice, 81st overall, in 2005 Entry Draft.

Season	Club	League	GP	G	A	Pts	PIM	PP	SH	GW	S	S%	+/-	TF	F%	Min	GP	G	A	Pts	PIM	PP	SH	GW	Min
2001-02	Cambridge	ON-Jr.B	43	6	41	47	23	....	....	....	....	....	....	....	....	....	....	....	....	....	....	....	....	....	....
	London Knights	OHL	1	0	0	0	0	....	....	....	....	....	....	....	....	....	....	....	....	....	....	....	....	....	....
2002-03	London Knights	OHL	68	8	14	22	31	....	....	....	....	....	....	....	....	....	14	1	6	7	11	....	....	....	....
2003-04	London Knights	OHL	68	3	28	31	32	....	....	....	....	....	....	....	....	....	15	1	6	7	4	....	....	....	....
2004-05	London Knights	OHL	62	23	46	69	33	....	....	....	....	....	....	....	....	....	18	5	15	20	4	....	....	....	....
2005-06	Edmonton	NHL	10	0	0	0	6	0	0	0	8	0.0	-1	0	0.0	12:19	....	....	....	....	....	....	....	....	....
	Hamilton	AHL	62	0	20	20	38	....	....	....	....	....	....	....	....	....	....	....	....	....	....	....	....	....	....
2006-07	Edmonton	NHL	16	0	1	1	6	0	0	0	15	0.0	-10	0	0.0	18:28	....	....	....	....	....	....	....	....	....
	Grand Rapids	AHL	57	4	16	20	16	....	....	....	....	....	....	....	....	....	....	....	....	....	....	....	....	....	....
2007-08	Springfield	AHL	36	1	7	8	14	....	....	....	....	....	....	....	....	....	....	....	....	....	....	....	....	....	....
	Hershey Bears	AHL	27	1	11	12	29	....	....	....	....	....	....	....	....	....	5	0	0	0	0	....	....	....	....
2008-09	Philadelphia	NHL	2	0	0	0	0	0	0	0	0	0.0	-1	0	0.0	9:26	....	....	....	....	....	....	....	....	....
	Philadelphia	AHL	76	12	45	57	44	....	....	....	....	....	....	....	....	....	4	0	1	1	0	....	....	....	....
2009-10	Philadelphia	NHL	21	2	2	4	12	0	0	0	14	14.3	1	0	0.0	12:29	....	....	....	....	....	....	....	....	....
	Adirondack	AHL	15	5	8	13	6	....	....	....	....	....	....	....	....	....	....	....	....	....	....	....	....	....	....
2010-11	Anaheim	NHL	6	1	1	2	4	0	0	0	8	12.5	-3	0	0.0	16:27	....	....	....	....	....	....	....	....	....
	Syracuse Crunch	AHL	8	0	4	4	11	....	....	....	....	....	....	....	....	....	....	....	....	....	....	....	....	....	....
	Philadelphia	NHL	4	0	0	0	2	0	0	0	3	0.0	0	0	0.0	12:58	10	0	0	0	0	0	0	0	6:49
	Adirondack	AHL	51	10	26	36	27	....	....	....	....	....	....	....	....	....	....	....	....	....	....	....	....	....	....
2011-12	Peoria Rivermen	AHL	75	7	35	42	24	....	....	....	....	....	....	....	....	....	....	....	....	....	....	....	....	....	....

			Regular Season														Playoffs								
Season	Club	League	GP	G	A	Pts	PIM	PP	SH	GW	S	S%	+/-	TF	F%	Min	GP	G	A	Pts	PIM	PP	SH	GW	Min
2012-13	Adirondack	AHL	76	6	34	40	34	....	....	....	....	....	....	....	....	....	....	....	....	....	....	....	....	....	....
2013-14	Hartford	AHL	76	9	38	47	34	....	....	....	....	....	....	....	....	....	....	....	....	....	....	....	....	....	....
2014-15	Iowa Wild	AHL	58	4	14	18	24	....	....	....	....	....	....	....	....	....	....	....	....	....	....	....	....	....	....
	Wilkes-Barre	AHL	17	2	3	5	8	....	....	....	....	....	....	....	....	....	2	1	0	1	2	....	....	....	....
	NHL Totals		**59**	**3**	**4**	**7**	**30**	**0**	**0**	**0**	**48**	**6.3**		**0**	**0.0**	**14:24**	**10**	**0**	**0**	**0**	**0**	**0**	**0**	**0**	**6:49**

OHL First All-Star Team (2005) • Canadian Major Junior Defenseman of the Year (2005) • Canadian Major Junior First All-Star Team (2005) • Memorial Cup All-Star Team.. (2005) • AHL First All-Star Team (2009)

Traded to **Philadelphia** by **Edmonton** for Ryan Potulny, June 6, 2008. • Missed majority of 2009-10 due to recurring upper-body injury and as a healthy reserve. Signed as a free agent by **Anaheim**, July 21, 2010. Traded to **Philadelphia** by **Anaheim** with Rob Bordson for Patrick Maroon and David Laliberte, November 21, 2010. Signed as a free agent by **St. Louis**, August 8, 2011. Signed as a free agent by **Philadelphia**, July 3, 2012. Traded to **NY Rangers** by **Philadelphia** for Kris Newbury, July 1, 2013. Signed as a free agent by **Hartford** (AHL), October 3, 2013. Signed to a PTO (professional tryout) contract by **Iowa** (AHL), October 17, 2014. Signed to a PTO (professional tryout) contract by **Wilkes-Barre** (AHL), March 9, 2015.

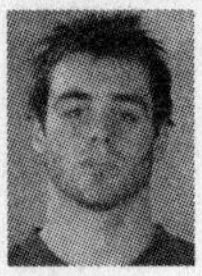

SZWARZ, Jordan (SWAWRZ, JOHR-dahn) ARI

Right wing. Shoots right. 5'11", 196 lbs. Born, Burlington, ON, May 14, 1991. Phoenix's 4th choice, 97th overall, in 2009 Entry Draft.

2006-07	Burlington Eagles	Minor-ON	66	56	54	110	88	....	....	....	....	....	....	....	....	....	....	....	....	....	....	....	....	....	....
2007-08	Saginaw Spirit	OHL	65	12	21	33	56	....	....	....	....	....	....	....	....	....	4	0	0	0	2	....	....	....	....
2008-09	Saginaw Spirit	OHL	67	17	34	51	76	....	....	....	....	....	....	....	....	....	8	1	5	6	10	....	....	....	....
2009-10	Saginaw Spirit	OHL	65	26	28	54	82	....	....	....	....	....	....	....	....	....	6	1	2	3	0	....	....	....	....
	San Antonio	AHL	1	0	0	0	0	....	....	....	....	....	....	....	....	....	....	....	....	....	....	....	....	....	....
2010-11	Saginaw Spirit	OHL	65	27	39	66	90	....	....	....	....	....	....	....	....	....	12	4	9	13	8	....	....	....	....
2011-12	Portland Pirates	AHL	58	7	13	20	28	....	....	....	....	....	....	....	....	....	....	....	....	....	....	....	....	....	....
2012-13	Portland Pirates	AHL	60	11	22	33	31	....	....	....	....	....	....	....	....	....	....	....	....	....	....	....	....	....	....
2013-14	**Phoenix**	**NHL**	**26**	**3**	**0**	**3**	**19**	**0**	**0**	**1**	**25**	**12.0**	**–6**	**3**	**33.3**	**8:39**	....	....	....	....	....	....	....	....	....
	Portland Pirates	AHL	27	8	6	14	55	....	....	....	....	....	....	....	....	....	....	....	....	....	....	....	....	....	....
2014-15	**Arizona**	**NHL**	**9**	**1**	**0**	**1**	**2**	**0**	**0**	**0**	**8**	**12.5**	**–2**	**0**	**0.0**	**13:28**	....	....	....	....	....	....	....	....	....
	Portland Pirates	AHL	45	9	13	22	65	....	....	....	....	....	....	....	....	....	5	1	2	3	8	....	....	....	....
	NHL Totals		**35**	**4**	**0**	**4**	**21**	**0**	**0**	**1**	**33**	**12.1**		**3**	**33.3**	**9:53**	....	....	....	....	....	....	....	....	....

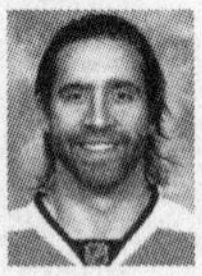

TALBOT, Max (TAL-buht, max) BOS

Center. Shoots left. 5'11", 190 lbs. Born, Lemoyne, QC, February 11, 1984. Pittsburgh's 9th choice, 234th overall, in 2002 Entry Draft.

99-2000	Antoine-Girouard	QAAA	42	19	21	40	32	....	....	....	....	....	....	....	....	....	7	3	6	9	0	....	....	....	....
2000-01	Rouyn-Noranda	QMJHL	40	9	15	24	78	....	....	....	....	....	....	....	....	....	....	....	....	....	....	....	....	....	....
	Hull Olympiques	QMJHL	24	6	7	13	60	....	....	....	....	....	....	....	....	....	5	1	0	1	2	....	....	....	....
2001-02	Hull Olympiques	QMJHL	65	24	36	60	174	....	....	....	....	....	....	....	....	....	12	4	6	10	51	....	....	....	....
2002-03	Hull Olympiques	QMJHL	69	46	58	104	130	....	....	....	....	....	....	....	....	....	20	14	*30	*44	33	....	....	....	....
2003-04	Gatineau	QMJHL	51	25	73	98	41	....	....	....	....	....	....	....	....	....	15	*11	*16	*27	0	....	....	....	....
2004-05	Wilkes-Barre	AHL	75	7	12	19	62	....	....	....	....	....	....	....	....	....	11	0	1	1	22	....	....	....	....
2005-06	**Pittsburgh**	**NHL**	**48**	**5**	**3**	**8**	**59**	**0**	**2**	**1**	**45**	**11.1**	**–12**	**473**	**42.9**	**10:58**	....	....	....	....	....	....	....	....	....
	Wilkes-Barre	AHL	42	12	20	32	80	....	....	....	....	....	....	....	....	....	11	3	6	9	16	....	....	....	....
2006-07	**Pittsburgh**	**NHL**	**75**	**13**	**11**	**24**	**53**	**0**	**4**	**4**	**88**	**14.8**	**–2**	**903**	**44.4**	**13:54**	**5**	**0**	**1**	**1**	**7**	**0**	**0**	**0**	**15:51**
	Wilkes-Barre	AHL	5	4	0	4	2	....	....	....	....	....	....	....	....	....	....	....	....	....	....	....	....	....	....
2007-08	**Pittsburgh**	**NHL**	**63**	**12**	**14**	**26**	**53**	**0**	**2**	**1**	**80**	**15.0**	**8**	**513**	**45.0**	**15:28**	**17**	**3**	**6**	**9**	**36**	**0**	**0**	**1**	**14:27**
2008-09 ♦	**Pittsburgh**	**NHL**	**75**	**12**	**10**	**22**	**63**	**0**	**2**	**1**	**102**	**11.8**	**–9**	**542**	**51.1**	**14:08**	**24**	**8**	**5**	**13**	**19**	**0**	**0**	**2**	**15:14**
2009-10	**Pittsburgh**	**NHL**	**45**	**2**	**5**	**7**	**30**	**0**	**0**	**0**	**49**	**4.1**	**–9**	**165**	**41.2**	**12:13**	**13**	**2**	**4**	**6**	**11**	**0**	**1**	**1**	**14:15**
2010-11	**Pittsburgh**	**NHL**	**82**	**8**	**13**	**21**	**66**	**0**	**2**	**2**	**117**	**6.8**	**–3**	**874**	**48.6**	**15:04**	**7**	**1**	**3**	**4**	**14**	**0**	**0**	**0**	**16:53**
2011-12	**Philadelphia**	**NHL**	**81**	**19**	**15**	**34**	**59**	**1**	**2**	**2**	**115**	**16.5**	**5**	**640**	**44.4**	**16:00**	**11**	**4**	**2**	**6**	**10**	**1**	***2**	**0**	**17:02**
2012-13	Ilves Tampere	Finland	12	3	3	6	34	....	....	....	....	....	....	....	....	....	....	....	....	....	....	....	....	....	....
	Philadelphia	**NHL**	**35**	**5**	**5**	**10**	**23**	**0**	**1**	**0**	**41**	**12.2**	**2**	**192**	**47.9**	**15:26**	....	....	....	....	....	....	....	....	....
2013-14	**Philadelphia**	**NHL**	**11**	**1**	**1**	**2**	**2**	**0**	**0**	**0**	**14**	**7.1**	**1**	**26**	**61.5**	**15:08**	....	....	....	....	....	....	....	....	....
	Colorado	**NHL**	**70**	**7**	**18**	**25**	**43**	**0**	**1**	**1**	**110**	**6.4**	**4**	**199**	**42.2**	**16:19**	**7**	**0**	**0**	**0**	**4**	**0**	**0**	**0**	**17:08**
2014-15	**Colorado**	**NHL**	**63**	**5**	**10**	**15**	**27**	**0**	**0**	**1**	**73**	**6.8**	**2**	**147**	**49.0**	**14:00**	....	....	....	....	....	....	....	....	....
	Boston	**NHL**	**18**	**0**	**3**	**3**	**2**	**0**	**0**	**0**	**24**	**0.0**	**–3**	**11**	**36.4**	**12:13**	....	....	....	....	....	....	....	....	....
	NHL Totals		**666**	**89**	**108**	**197**	**480**	**1**	**16**	**13**	**858**	**10.4**		**4685**	**46.0**	**14:28**	**84**	**18**	**21**	**39**	**101**	**1**	**3**	**4**	**15:29**

QMJHL Second All-Star Team (2003, 2004)

Signed as a free agent by **Philadelphia**, July 1, 2011. Signed as a free agent by **Ilves Tampere** (Finland), November 7, 2012. Traded to **Colorado** by **Philadelphia** for Steve Downie, October 31, 2013. Traded to **Boston** by **Colorado** with Paul Carey for Jordan Caron and a 6th round choice in 2016 Entry Draft, March 2, 2015.

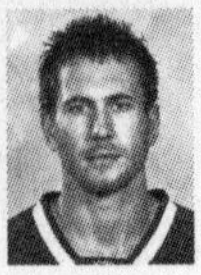

TAMBELLINI, Jeff (tam-buh-LEE-nee, JEHF) T.B.

Left wing. Shoots left. 5'11", 186 lbs. Born, Calgary, AB, April 13, 1984. Los Angeles' 3rd choice, 27th overall, in 2003 Entry Draft.

99-2000	Port Coquitlam	PIJHL	41	30	34	64	....	....	....	....	....	....	....	....	....	....	....	....	....	....	....	....	....	....	....
2000-01	Chilliwack Chiefs	BCHL	54	21	30	51	13	....	....	....	....	....	....	....	....	....	....	....	....	....	....	....	....	....	....
2001-02	Chilliwack Chiefs	BCHL	34	46	71	117	23	....	....	....	....	....	....	....	....	....	29	27	27	54	....	....	....	....	....
2002-03	U. of Michigan	CCHA	43	26	19	45	24	....	....	....	....	....	....	....	....	....	....	....	....	....	....	....	....	....	....
2003-04	U. of Michigan	CCHA	39	15	12	27	18	....	....	....	....	....	....	....	....	....	....	....	....	....	....	....	....	....	....
2004-05	U. of Michigan	CCHA	42	*24	33	*57	32	....	....	....	....	....	....	....	....	....	....	....	....	....	....	....	....	....	....
2005-06	**Los Angeles**	**NHL**	**4**	**0**	**0**	**0**	**2**	**0**	**0**	**0**	**6**	**0.0**	**–1**	**1**	**0.0**	**9:23**	....	....	....	....	....	....	....	....	....
	Manchester	AHL	56	25	31	56	26	....	....	....	....	....	....	....	....	....	....	....	....	....	....	....	....	....	....
	NY Islanders	**NHL**	**21**	**1**	**3**	**4**	**8**	**0**	**0**	**0**	**11**	**9.1**	**2**	**3**	**33.3**	**9:54**	....	....	....	....	....	....	....	....	....
	Bridgeport	AHL	....	....	....	....	....	....	....	....	....	....	....	....	....	....	7	1	2	3	2	....	....	....	....
2006-07	**NY Islanders**	**NHL**	**23**	**2**	**7**	**9**	**6**	**0**	**0**	**0**	**20**	**10.0**	**6**	**1**	**0.0**	**7:14**	....	....	....	....	....	....	....	....	....
	Bridgeport	AHL	50	30	29	59	46	....	....	....	....	....	....	....	....	....	....	....	....	....	....	....	....	....	....
2007-08	**NY Islanders**	**NHL**	**31**	**1**	**3**	**4**	**8**	**0**	**0**	**0**	**43**	**2.3**	**–9**	**0**	**0.0**	**10:25**	....	....	....	....	....	....	....	....	....
	Bridgeport	AHL	57	38	38	76	38	....	....	....	....	....	....	....	....	....	....	....	....	....	....	....	....	....	....
2008-09	**NY Islanders**	**NHL**	**65**	**7**	**8**	**15**	**32**	**0**	**0**	**0**	**98**	**7.1**	**–20**	**5**	**60.0**	**13:07**	....	....	....	....	....	....	....	....	....
	Bridgeport	AHL	6	3	0	3	2	....	....	....	....	....	....	....	....	....	....	....	....	....	....	....	....	....	....
2009-10	**NY Islanders**	**NHL**	**36**	**7**	**7**	**14**	**14**	**3**	**0**	**0**	**55**	**12.7**	**–8**	**4**	**0.0**	**11:28**	....	....	....	....	....	....	....	....	....
2010-11	**Vancouver**	**NHL**	**62**	**9**	**8**	**17**	**18**	**1**	**0**	**0**	**114**	**7.9**	**10**	**35**	**54.3**	**11:47**	**6**	**0**	**0**	**0**	**2**	**0**	**0**	**0**	**7:12**
	Manitoba Moose	AHL	7	5	2	7	0	....	....	....	....	....	....	....	....	....	....	....	....	....	....	....	....	....	....
2011-12	ZSC Lions Zurich	Swiss	50	23	22	45	14	....	....	....	....	....	....	....	....	....	15	4	8	12	4	....	....	....	....
2012-13	ZSC Lions Zurich	Swiss	27	5	7	12	14	....	....	....	....	....	....	....	....	....	....	....	....	....	....	....	....	....	....
2013-14	MODO	Sweden	45	13	7	20	32	....	....	....	....	....	....	....	....	....	....	....	....	....	....	....	....	....	....
2014-15	Vaxjo Lakers HC	Sweden	20	6	3	9	2	....	....	....	....	....	....	....	....	....	18	5	8	13	2	....	....	....	....
	Fribourg	Swiss	30	5	8	13	10	....	....	....	....	....	....	....	....	....	....	....	....	....	....	....	....	....	....
	NHL Totals		**242**	**27**	**36**	**63**	**88**	**4**	**0**	**0**	**347**	**7.8**		**49**	**46.9**	**11:17**	**6**	**0**	**0**	**0**	**2**	**0**	**0**	**0**	**7:12**

CCHA All-Rookie Team (2003) • CCHA Second All-Star Team (2003) • CCHA Rookie of the Year (2003) • CCHA First All-Star Team (2005) • NCAA West Second All-American Team (2005)

Traded to **NY Islanders** by **Los Angeles** with Denis Grebeshkov for Mark Parrish and Brent Sopel, March 8, 2006. • Missed majority of 2009-10 as a healthy reserve. Signed as a free agent by **Vancouver**, July 1, 2010. Signed as a free agent by **Zurich** (Swiss), July 6, 2011. Signed as a free agent by **MODO** (Sweden), March 25, 2013. Signed as a free agent by **Fribourg Gotteron** (Swiss), April 24, 2014. Signed as a free agent by **Vaxjo** (Sweden), January 23, 2015. Signed as a free agent by **Tampa Bay**, July 5, 2015.

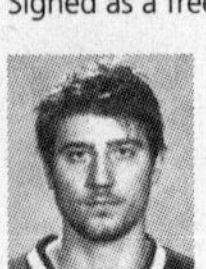

TANEV, Chris (TA-nehv, KRIHS) VAN

Defense. Shoots right. 6'2", 185 lbs. Born, Toronto, ON, December 20, 1989.

2006-07	Durham Fury	ON-Jr.A	40	0	9	9	8	....	....	....	....	....	....	....	....	....	4	0	3	3	6	....	....	....	....
2007-08	Durham Fury	ON-Jr.A	19	1	6	7	12	....	....	....	....	....	....	....	....	....	....	....	....	....	....	....	....	....	....
	Stouffville Spirit	ON-Jr.A	4	0	0	0	0	....	....	....	....	....	....	....	....	....	....	....	....	....	....	....	....	....	....
	Markham Waxers	ON-Jr.A	26	1	9	10	12	....	....	....	....	....	....	....	....	....	23	1	2	3	4	....	....	....	....
2008-09	Markham Waxers	ON-Jr.A	50	4	37	41	33	....	....	....	....	....	....	....	....	....	14	1	5	6	8	....	....	....	....
2009-10	RIT Tigers	AH	41	10	18	28	4	....	....	....	....	....	....	....	....	....	....	....	....	....	....	....	....	....	....
2010-11	**Vancouver**	**NHL**	**29**	**0**	**1**	**1**	**0**	**0**	**0**	**0**	**15**	**0.0**	**0**	**0**	**0.0**	**13:47**	**5**	**0**	**0**	**0**	**0**	**0**	**0**	**0**	**14:40**
	Manitoba Moose	AHL	39	1	8	9	16	....	....	....	....	....	....	....	....	....	14	1	2	3	4	....	....	....	....
2011-12	**Vancouver**	**NHL**	**25**	**0**	**2**	**2**	**2**	**0**	**0**	**0**	**15**	**0.0**	**10**	**0**	**0.0**	**16:43**	**5**	**0**	**0**	**0**	**0**	**0**	**0**	**0**	**15:11**
	Chicago Wolves	AHL	34	0	14	14	6	....	....	....	....	....	....	....	....	....	....	....	....	....	....	....	....	....	....
2012-13	Chicago Wolves	AHL	29	2	10	12	6	....	....	....	....	....	....	....	....	....	....	....	....	....	....	....	....	....	....
	Vancouver	**NHL**	**38**	**2**	**5**	**7**	**10**	**0**	**0**	**1**	**20**	**10.0**	**4**	**0**	**0.0**	**17:17**	....	....	....	....	....	....	....	....	....

Season	Club	League	GP	G	A	Pts	PIM	PP	SH	GW	S	S%	+/-	TF	F%	Min	Playoffs GP	G	A	Pts	PIM	PP	SH	GW	Min
			Regular Season														Playoffs								
2013-14	Vancouver	NHL	64	6	11	17	8	0	1	2	65	9.2	12	0	0.0	20:44	....	....	....	....	....	....	....	....	....
2014-15	Vancouver	NHL	70	2	18	20	12	0	0	1	53	3.8	8	0	0.0	21:05	6	0	3	3	0	0	0	0	22:00
	NHL Totals		226	10	37	47	32	0	1	4	168	6.0		0	0.0	18:56	16	0	3	3	0	0	0	0	17:35

Signed as a free agent by **Vancouver**, May 31, 2010.

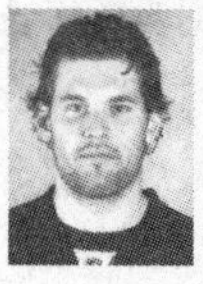

TANGRADI, Eric

(tan-GRAY-dee, AIR-ihk) **DET**

Left wing. Shoots left. 6'4", 221 lbs. Born, Philadelphia, PA, February 10, 1989. Anaheim's 2nd choice, 42nd overall, in 2007 Entry Draft.

Season	Club	League	GP	G	A	Pts	PIM	PP	SH	GW	S	S%	+/-	TF	F%	Min	Playoffs GP	G	A	Pts	PIM	PP	SH	GW	Min
2005-06	Wyoming Prep	High-PA	38	21	23	44	120	....	....	....	....	....	....	....	....	....	....	....	....	....	....	....	....	....	....
2006-07	Belleville Bulls	OHL	65	5	15	20	32	....	....	....	....	....	....	....	....	....	15	8	9	17	14	....	....	....	....
2007-08	Belleville Bulls	OHL	56	24	36	60	41	....	....	....	....	....	....	....	....	....	21	7	11	18	20	....	....	....	....
2008-09	Belleville Bulls	OHL	55	38	50	88	61	....	....	....	....	....	....	....	....	....	16	8	13	21	12	....	....	....	....
2009-10	**Pittsburgh**	**NHL**	**1**	**0**	**0**	**0**	**0**	**0**	**0**	**0**	**3**	**0.0**	**0**	**0**	**0.0**	**13:49**	....	....	....	....	....	....	....	....	....
	Wilkes-Barre	AHL	65	17	22	39	31	....	....	....	....	....	....	....	....	....	4	1	1	2	6	....	....	....	....
2010-11	**Pittsburgh**	**NHL**	**15**	**1**	**2**	**3**	**10**	**0**	**0**	**0**	**18**	**5.6**	**–4**	**3**	**33.3**	**11:12**	**1**	**0**	**0**	**0**	**0**	**0**	**0**	**0**	**15:12**
	Wilkes-Barre	AHL	42	18	15	33	86	....	....	....	....	....	....	....	....	....	....	....	....	....	....	....	....	....	....
2011-12	**Pittsburgh**	**NHL**	**24**	**0**	**2**	**2**	**16**	**0**	**0**	**0**	**20**	**0.0**	**–4**	**2**	**0.0**	**8:56**	**2**	**0**	**1**	**1**	**0**	**0**	**0**	**0**	**8:07**
	Wilkes-Barre	AHL	37	15	16	31	40	....	....	....	....	....	....	....	....	....	10	4	5	9	14	....	....	....	....
2012-13	Wilkes-Barre	AHL	34	10	8	18	57	....	....	....	....	....	....	....	....	....	....	....	....	....	....	....	....	....	....
	Pittsburgh	**NHL**	**5**	**0**	**0**	**0**	**0**	**0**	**0**	**0**	**4**	**0.0**	**2**	**0**	**0.0**	**8:32**	....	....	....	....	....	....	....	....	....
	Winnipeg	**NHL**	**36**	**1**	**3**	**4**	**22**	**0**	**0**	**0**	**44**	**2.3**	**–4**	**2**	**0.0**	**10:18**	....	....	....	....	....	....	....	....	....
2013-14	**Winnipeg**	**NHL**	**55**	**3**	**3**	**6**	**21**	**0**	**0**	**0**	**52**	**5.8**	**–6**	**3**	**100.0**	**8:39**	....	....	....	....	....	....	....	....	....
2014-15	**Montreal**	**NHL**	**7**	**0**	**0**	**0**	**17**	**0**	**0**	**0**	**5**	**0.0**	**–3**	**1**	**100.0**	**7:44**	....	....	....	....	....	....	....	....	....
	Hamilton	AHL	48	14	17	31	56	....	....	....	....	....	....	....	....	....	....	....	....	....	....	....	....	....	....
	NHL Totals		**143**	**5**	**10**	**15**	**86**	**0**	**0**	**0**	**146**	**3.4**		**11**	**45.5**	**9:22**	**3**	**0**	**1**	**1**	**0**	**0**	**0**	**0**	**10:29**

Traded to **Pittsburgh** by **Anaheim** with Chris Kunitz for Ryan Whitney, February 26, 2009. Traded to **Winnipeg** by **Pittsburgh** for Winnipeg's 6th round choice (Dane Birks) in 2013 Entry Draft, February 13, 2013. Traded to **Montreal** by **Winnipeg** for Peter Budaj and Patrick Holland, October 5, 2014. Signed as a free agent by **Detroit**, July 8, 2015.

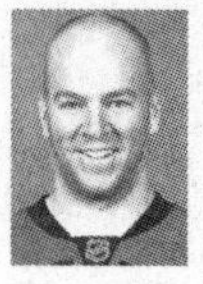

TANGUAY, Alex

(TAHNG-ay, AL-ehx) **COL**

Left wing. Shoots left. 6'1", 194 lbs. Born, Ste-Justine, QC, November 21, 1979. Colorado's 1st choice, 12th overall, in 1998 Entry Draft.

Season	Club	League	GP	G	A	Pts	PIM	PP	SH	GW	S	S%	+/-	TF	F%	Min	Playoffs GP	G	A	Pts	PIM	PP	SH	GW	Min
1994-95	Cap-d-Madeleine	QAAA	1	0	1	1	0	....	....	....	....	....	....	....	....	....	....	....	....	....	....	....	....	....	....
1995-96	Cap-d-Madeleine	QAAA	44	29	34	63	64	....	....	....	....	....	....	....	....	....	5	2	4	6	14	....	....	....	....
1996-97	Halifax	QMJHL	70	27	41	68	50	....	....	....	....	....	....	....	....	....	12	4	8	12	8	....	....	....	....
1997-98	Halifax	QMJHL	51	47	38	85	32	....	....	....	....	....	....	....	....	....	5	7	6	13	4	....	....	....	....
1998-99	Halifax	QMJHL	31	27	34	61	30	....	....	....	....	....	....	....	....	....	5	1	2	3	2	....	....	....	....
	Hershey Bears	AHL	5	1	2	3	2	....	....	....	....	....	....	....	....	....	5	0	2	2	0	....	....	....	....
99-2000	**Colorado**	**NHL**	**76**	**17**	**34**	**51**	**22**	**5**	**0**	**3**	**74**	**23.0**	**6**	**11**	**45.5**	**15:38**	**17**	**2**	**1**	**3**	**2**	**1**	**0**	**1**	**10:49**
2000-01♦	**Colorado**	**NHL**	**82**	**27**	**50**	**77**	**37**	**7**	**1**	**3**	**135**	**20.0**	**35**	**30**	**43.3**	**17:51**	**23**	**6**	**15**	**21**	**8**	**1**	**0**	**2**	**19:18**
2001-02	**Colorado**	**NHL**	**70**	**13**	**35**	**48**	**36**	**7**	**0**	**2**	**90**	**14.4**	**8**	**37**	**40.5**	**18:20**	**19**	**5**	**8**	**13**	**0**	**3**	**0**	**0**	**17:25**
2002-03	**Colorado**	**NHL**	**82**	**26**	**41**	**67**	**36**	**3**	**0**	**5**	**142**	**18.3**	**34**	**123**	**39.0**	**17:48**	**7**	**1**	**2**	**3**	**4**	**0**	**0**	**1**	**19:06**
2003-04	**Colorado**	**NHL**	**69**	**25**	**54**	**79**	**42**	**7**	**0**	**5**	**117**	**21.4**	**30**	**71**	**40.9**	**18:21**	**8**	**2**	**2**	**4**	**2**	**1**	**0**	**1**	**15:46**
2004-05	HC Lugano	Swiss	6	3	3	6	4	....	....	....	....	....	....	....	....	....	....	....	....	....	....	....	....	....	....
2005-06	**Colorado**	**NHL**	**71**	**29**	**49**	**78**	**46**	**8**	**0**	**4**	**125**	**23.2**	**8**	**20**	**30.0**	**18:22**	**9**	**2**	**4**	**6**	**12**	**0**	**0**	**1**	**18:20**
2006-07	**Calgary**	**NHL**	**81**	**22**	**59**	**81**	**44**	**5**	**0**	**0**	**107**	**20.6**	**12**	**24**	**25.0**	**17:40**	**6**	**1**	**3**	**4**	**8**	**1**	**0**	**0**	**17:56**
2007-08	**Calgary**	**NHL**	**78**	**18**	**40**	**58**	**48**	**3**	**2**	**3**	**121**	**14.9**	**11**	**20**	**35.0**	**18:46**	**7**	**0**	**4**	**4**	**4**	**0**	**0**	**0**	**18:15**
2008-09	**Montreal**	**NHL**	**50**	**16**	**25**	**41**	**34**	**5**	**0**	**3**	**76**	**21.1**	**13**	**9**	**33.3**	**16:05**	**2**	**0**	**1**	**1**	**2**	**0**	**0**	**0**	**15:29**
2009-10	**Tampa Bay**	**NHL**	**80**	**10**	**27**	**37**	**32**	**5**	**0**	**2**	**91**	**11.0**	**–2**	**25**	**44.0**	**15:47**	....	....	....	....	....	....	....	....	....
2010-11	**Calgary**	**NHL**	**79**	**22**	**47**	**69**	**24**	**3**	**0**	**2**	**120**	**18.3**	**0**	**107**	**39.3**	**19:46**	....	....	....	....	....	....	....	....	....
2011-12	**Calgary**	**NHL**	**64**	**13**	**36**	**49**	**28**	**1**	**1**	**3**	**84**	**15.5**	**7**	**67**	**37.3**	**19:03**	....	....	....	....	....	....	....	....	....
2012-13	**Calgary**	**NHL**	**40**	**11**	**16**	**27**	**22**	**2**	**1**	**1**	**44**	**25.0**	**–13**	**173**	**39.3**	**19:22**	....	....	....	....	....	....	....	....	....
2013-14	**Colorado**	**NHL**	**16**	**4**	**7**	**11**	**4**	**0**	**1**	**2**	**24**	**16.7**	**7**	**3**	**33.3**	**17:17**	....	....	....	....	....	....	....	....	....
2014-15	**Colorado**	**NHL**	**80**	**22**	**33**	**55**	**40**	**2**	**1**	**4**	**104**	**21.2**	**–1**	**28**	**42.9**	**18:10**	....	....	....	....	....	....	....	....	....
	NHL Totals		**1018**	**275**	**553**	**828**	**495**	**61**	**7**	**42**	**1454**	**18.9**		**748**	**38.9**	**17:53**	**98**	**19**	**40**	**59**	**42**	**7**	**0**	**6**	**16:50**

QMJHL All-Rookie Team (1997)

Played in NHL All-Star Game (2004)

Signed as a free agent by **Lugano** (Swiss), October 7, 2004. Traded to **Calgary** by **Colorado** for Jordan Leopold, Calgary's 2nd round choice (Codey Burki) in 2006 Entry Draft and Calgary's 2nd round choice (Trevor Cann) in 2007 Entry Draft, June 24, 2006. Traded to **Montreal** by **Calgary** with Calgary's 5th round choice (Maxim Trunev) in 2008 Entry Draft for Montreal's 1st round choice (Greg Nemisz) in 2008 Entry Draft and Montreal's 2nd round choice (later traded to Colorado – Colorado selected Stefan Elliott) in 2009 Entry Draft, June 20, 2008. Signed as a free agent by **Tampa Bay**, September 1, 2009. Signed as a free agent by **Calgary**, July 1, 2010. Traded to **Colorado** by **Calgary** with Cory Sarich for David Jones and Shane O'Brien, June 27, 2013. • Missed majority of 2013-14 due to knee injury vs. Montreal, November 2, 2013.

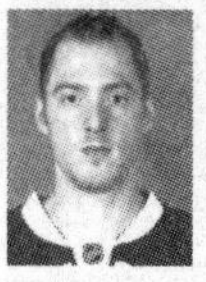

TAORMINA, Matt

(tah'ohr-MEE-nah, MAT) **T.B.**

Defense. Shoots left. 5'10", 182 lbs. Born, Warren, MI, October 20, 1986.

Season	Club	League	GP	G	A	Pts	PIM	PP	SH	GW	S	S%	+/-	TF	F%	Min	Playoffs GP	G	A	Pts	PIM	PP	SH	GW	Min
2004-05	Texarkana Bandits	NAHL	52	14	30	44	44	....	....	....	....	....	....	....	....	....	9	3	3	6	6	....	....	....	....
2005-06	Providence	H-East	36	1	10	11	16	....	....	....	....	....	....	....	....	....	....	....	....	....	....	....	....	....	....
2006-07	Providence	H-East	35	5	2	7	6	....	....	....	....	....	....	....	....	....	....	....	....	....	....	....	....	....	....
2007-08	Providence	H-East	36	9	18	27	12	....	....	....	....	....	....	....	....	....	....	....	....	....	....	....	....	....	....
2008-09	Providence	H-East	34	5	15	20	16	....	....	....	....	....	....	....	....	....	....	....	....	....	....	....	....	....	....
	Binghamton	AHL	11	2	3	5	4	....	....	....	....	....	....	....	....	....	....	....	....	....	....	....	....	....	....
2009-10	Lowell Devils	AHL	75	10	40	50	45	....	....	....	....	....	....	....	....	....	5	1	3	4	4	....	....	....	....
2010-11	**New Jersey**	**NHL**	**17**	**3**	**2**	**5**	**2**	**1**	**0**	**0**	**38**	**7.9**	**–2**	**0**	**0.0**	**20:40**	....	....	....	....	....	....	....	....	....
2011-12	**New Jersey**	**NHL**	**30**	**1**	**6**	**7**	**4**	**0**	**0**	**0**	**33**	**3.0**	**6**	**0**	**0.0**	**16:32**	....	....	....	....	....	....	....	....	....
	Albany Devils	AHL	33	6	10	16	12	....	....	....	....	....	....	....	....	....	....	....	....	....	....	....	....	....	....
2012-13	Syracuse Crunch	AHL	55	4	20	24	21	....	....	....	....	....	....	....	....	....	18	2	10	12	4	....	....	....	....
	Tampa Bay	**NHL**	**2**	**0**	**0**	**0**	**0**	**0**	**0**	**0**	**0**	**0.0**	**–1**	**0**	**0.0**	**16:39**	....	....	....	....	....	....	....	....	....
2013-14	**Tampa Bay**	**NHL**	**7**	**0**	**0**	**0**	**0**	**0**	**0**	**0**	**6**	**0.0**	**0**	**0**	**0.0**	**13:24**	....	....	....	....	....	....	....	....	....
	Syracuse Crunch	AHL	41	6	12	18	20	....	....	....	....	....	....	....	....	....	....	....	....	....	....	....	....	....	....
	Springfield	AHL	17	3	5	8	2	....	....	....	....	....	....	....	....	....	4	0	1	1	0	....	....	....	....
2014-15	Worcester Sharks	AHL	76	11	27	38	24	....	....	....	....	....	....	....	....	....	4	1	0	1	0	....	....	....	....
	NHL Totals		**56**	**4**	**8**	**12**	**6**	**1**	**0**	**0**	**77**	**5.2**		**0**	**0.0**	**17:24**	....	....	....	....	....	....	....	....	....

Signed as a free agent by **Binghamton** (AHL), March 10, 2009. Signed as a free agent by **Lowell** (AHL), August 14, 2009. Signed as a free agent by **New Jersey**, February 26, 2010. • Missed majority of 2010-11 due to ankle injury at Boston, November 15, 2010. Signed as a free agent by **Tampa Bay**, July 6, 2012. Traded to **Columbus** by **Tampa Bay** with Dana Tyrell for Jon Marchessault and Dalton Smith, March 5, 2014. Signed as a free agent by **Worcester** (AHL). September 26, 2014. Signed as a free agent by **Tampa Bay**, July 1, 2015.

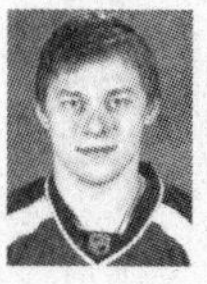

TARASENKO, Vladimir

(ta-rah-SEHN-koh, vla-DIH-meer) **ST.L.**

Right wing. Shoots left. 6', 219 lbs. Born, Yaroslavl, USSR, December 13, 1991. St. Louis' 2nd choice, 16th overall, in 2010 Entry Draft.

Season	Club	League	GP	G	A	Pts	PIM	PP	SH	GW	S	S%	+/-	TF	F%	Min	Playoffs GP	G	A	Pts	PIM	PP	SH	GW	Min
2007-08	Sibir Novosibirsk 2	Russia-3	17	6	4	10	2	....	....	....	....	....	....	....	....	....	....	....	....	....	....	....	....	....	....
2008-09	Sibir Novosibirsk 2	Russia-3	STATISTICS NOT AVAILABLE																						
	Sibir Novosibirsk	KHL	38	7	3	10	2	....	....	....	....	....	....	....	....	....	....	....	....	....	....	....	....	....	....
2009-10	Novosibirsk Jr.	Russia-Jr.	1	1	0	1	0	....	....	....	....	....	....	....	....	....	....	....	....	....	....	....	....	....	....
	Sibir Novosibirsk	KHL	42	13	11	24	18	....	....	....	....	....	....	....	....	....	....	....	....	....	....	....	....	....	....
2010-11	Sibir Novosibirsk	KHL	42	9	10	19	8	....	....	....	....	....	....	....	....	....	3	0	0	0	0	....	....	....	....
	Novosibirsk Jr.	Russia-Jr.	3	2	2	4	2	....	....	....	....	....	....	....	....	....	....	....	....	....	....	....	....	....	....
2011-12	Sibir Novosibirsk	KHL	39	18	20	38	15	....	....	....	....	....	....	....	....	....	....	....	....	....	....	....	....	....	....
	St. Petersburg	KHL	15	5	4	9	0	....	....	....	....	....	....	....	....	....	15	10	6	16	6	....	....	....	....
2012-13	St. Petersburg	KHL	31	14	18	32	8	....	....	....	....	....	....	....	....	....	....	....	....	....	....	....	....	....	....
	St. Louis	**NHL**	**38**	**8**	**11**	**19**	**10**	**3**	**0**	**1**	**75**	**10.7**	**1**	**1**	**100.0**	**13:25**	**1**	**0**	**0**	**0**	**0**	**0**	**0**	**0**	**5:51**
2013-14	**St. Louis**	**NHL**	**64**	**21**	**22**	**43**	**16**	**5**	**0**	**3**	**136**	**15.4**	**20**	**6**	**33.3**	**15:10**	**6**	**4**	**0**	**4**	**0**	**2**	**0**	**0**	**18:58**
	Russia	Olympics	5	0	1	1	0	....	....	....	....	....	....	....	....	....	....	....	....	....	....	....	....	....	....
2014-15	**St. Louis**	**NHL**	**77**	**37**	**36**	**73**	**31**	**8**	**0**	**6**	**264**	**14.0**	**27**	**3**	**0.0**	**17:37**	**6**	**6**	**1**	**7**	**0**	**2**	**0**	**2**	**17:23**
	NHL Totals		**179**	**66**	**69**	**135**	**57**	**16**	**0**	**10**	**475**	**13.9**		**10**	**30.0**	**15:51**	**13**	**10**	**1**	**11**	**0**	**4**	**0**	**2**	**17:13**

NHL Second All-Star Team (2015)

Played in NHL All-Star Game (2015)

Signed as a free agent by **St. Petersburg** (KHL), September 24, 2012.

						Regular Season													Playoffs							
Season	Club	League	GP	G	A	Pts	PIM	PP	SH	GW	S	S%	+/-	TF	F%	Min	GP	G	A	Pts	PIM	PP	SH	GW	Min

TARASOV, Daniil (TAIR-ah-sawv, DAN-ihl) **S.J.**

Right wing. Shoots right. 6', 185 lbs.   Born, Moscow, USSR, June 20, 1991.

Season	Club	League	GP	G	A	Pts	PIM	PP	SH	GW	S	S%	+/-	TF	F%	Min	GP	G	A	Pts	PIM	PP	SH	GW	Min
2010-11	Indiana Ice	USHL	57	37	38	75	46	....	....	....	....	....	....	....	....	....	5	2	4	6	6				
2011-12	Indiana Ice	USHL	60	47	41	88	86	....	....	....	....	....	....	....	....	....	6	5	5	10	8				
2012-13	Worcester Sharks	AHL	43	14	14	28	20	....	....	....	....	....	....	....	....	....									
	San Francisco	ECHL	17	3	11	14	5	....	....	....	....	....	....	....	....	....									
2013-14	Worcester Sharks	AHL	47	14	17	31	40	....	....	....	....	....	....	....	....	....									
2014-15	**San Jose**	**NHL**	**5**	**0**	**1**	**1**	**0**	0	0	0	5	0.0	2		1100.0	7:34									
	Worcester Sharks	AHL	54	16	17	33	27	....	....	....	....	....	....	....	....	....	4	0	3	3	2				
	NHL Totals		**5**	**0**	**1**	**1**	**0**	0	0	0	5	0.0			1100.0	7:34									

USHL All-Rookie Team (2011) • USHL Second All-Star Team (2011) • USHL First All-Star Team (2012)
Signed as a free agent by **Worcester** (AHL), June 1, 2012. Signed as a free agent by **San Jose**, April 2, 2013. Signed as a free agent by **Dynamo Moscow**, July 17, 2015.

TARNASKY, Nick (tahr-NAS-kee, NIHK) **NYR**

Center. Shoots left. 6'2", 230 lbs.   Born, Rocky Mtn. House, AB, November 25, 1984. Tampa Bay's 11th choice, 287th overall, in 2003 Entry Draft.

Season	Club	League	GP	G	A	Pts	PIM	PP	SH	GW	S	S%	+/-	TF	F%	Min	GP	G	A	Pts	PIM	PP	SH	GW	Min
99-2000	Leduc Oil Kings	AMBHL	36	21	11	32	59	....	....	....	....	....	....	....	....	....									
2000-01	Leduc Oil Kings	AMHL	35	39	29	68	95	....	....	....	....	....	....	....	....	....									
2001-02	Drayton Valley	AJHL	20	7	4	11	10	....	....	....	....	....	....	....	....	....									
	Vancouver Giants	WHL	10	1	0	1	5	....	....	....	....	....	....	....	....	....									
2002-03	Kelowna Rockets	WHL	39	4	12	16	39	....	....	....	....	....	....	....	....	....									
	Lethbridge	WHL	30	5	8	13	45	....	....	....	....	....	....	....	....	....									
2003-04	Lethbridge	WHL	71	26	23	49	108	....	....	....	....	....	....	....	....	....									
2004-05	Springfield	AHL	80	7	10	17	176	....	....	....	....	....	....	....	....	....									
2005-06	**Tampa Bay**	**NHL**	**12**	**0**	**1**	**1**	**4**	0	0	0	9	0.0	-3		15	40.0	4:40									
	Springfield	AHL	68	14	9	23	100	....	....	....	....	....	....	....	....	....									
2006-07	**Tampa Bay**	**NHL**	**77**	**5**	**4**	**9**	**80**	0	0	1	41	12.2	-6		13	30.8	6:30	6	0	0	0	10	0	0	0	6:13
2007-08	**Tampa Bay**	**NHL**	**80**	**6**	**4**	**10**	**78**	1	0	1	91	6.6	-15		9	44.4	8:15									
2008-09	**Nashville**	**NHL**	**11**	**0**	**1**	**1**	**17**	0	0	0	6	0.0	1		0	0.0	5:38									
	Florida	**NHL**	**34**	**1**	**5**	**6**	**33**	0	0	0	32	3.1	-2		1	0.0	7:52									
2009-10	**Florida**	**NHL**	**31**	**1**	**2**	**3**	**85**	0	0	0	19	5.3	-5		0	0.0	6:49									
	Rochester	AHL	5	3	0	3	7	....	....	....	....	....	....	....	....	....									
2010-11	Florida Everblades	ECHL	3	1	2	3	0	....	....	....	....	....	....	....	....	....									
	Springfield	AHL	66	7	13	20	150	....	....	....	....	....	....	....	....	....									
2011-12	Vityaz Chekhov	KHL	36	5	7	12	173	....	....	....	....	....	....	....	....	....									
2012-13	Rochester	AHL	74	16	10	26	138	....	....	....	....	....	....	....	....	....	3	1	0	1	4				
2013-14	Hamilton	AHL	76	13	9	22	144	....	....	....	....	....	....	....	....	....									
2014-15	Hartford	AHL	26	1	4	5	36	....	....	....	....	....	....	....	....	....									
	NHL Totals		**245**	**13**	**17**	**30**	**297**	1	0	2	198	6.6			38	36.8	7:10	6	0	0	0	10	0	0	0	6:13

Traded to **Nashville** by **Tampa Bay** for Nashville's 6th round choice (Jaroslav Janus) in 2009 Entry Draft, September 29, 2008. Traded to **Florida** by **Nashville** for Wade Belak, November 27, 2008.
Missed majority of 2009-10 due to eye injury in pre-season game at Ottawa, September 16, 2009. Signed as a free agent by **Florida** (ECHL), November 5, 2010. Signed to a PTO (professional tryout) contract by **Springfield** (AHL), November 11, 2010. Signed as a free agent by **Chekhov** (KHL), July 3, 2011. Signed as a free agent by **Buffalo**, July 17, 2012. Signed as a free agent by **Montreal**, July 6, 2013. Signed as a free agent by **NY Rangers**, July 3, 2014.

TATAR, Tomas (TAH-tahr, TAW-mahsh) **DET**

Center. Shoots left. 5'10", 186 lbs.   Born, Ilava, Czech., December 1, 1990. Detroit's 2nd choice, 60th overall, in 2009 Entry Draft.

Season	Club	League	GP	G	A	Pts	PIM	PP	SH	GW	S	S%	+/-	TF	F%	Min	GP	G	A	Pts	PIM	PP	SH	GW	Min
2004-05	Dubnica U18	Svk-U18	1	0	0	0	0	....	....	....	....	....	....	....	....	....									
2005-06	Dubnica U18	Svk-U18	43	11	15	26	18	....	....	....	....	....	....	....	....	....									
2006-07	Dubnica Jr.	Slovak-Jr.	6	3	0	3	2	....	....	....	....	....	....	....	....	....									
	Dukla Trencin U18	Svk-U18	48	33	44	77	42	....	....	....	....	....	....	....	....	....									
2007-08	Dukla Trencin U18	Svk-U18	4	9	4	13	0	....	....	....	....	....	....	....	....	....									
	Dukla Trencin Jr.	Slovak-Jr.	42	41	35	76	32	....	....	....	....	....	....	....	....	....									
2008-09	HC 07 Detva	Slovak-2	1	1	1	2	2	....	....	....	....	....	....	....	....	....									
	HKm Zvolen	Slovakia	48	7	8	15	20	....	....	....	....	....	....	....	....	....	13	5	3	8	4				
2009-10	Grand Rapids	AHL	58	16	16	32	12	....	....	....	....	....	....	....	....	....									
2010-11	**Detroit**	**NHL**	**9**	**1**	**0**	**1**	**0**	0	0	0	6	16.7	0		0	0.0	9:36									
	Grand Rapids	AHL	70	24	33	57	45	....	....	....	....	....	....	....	....	....									
2011-12	Grand Rapids	AHL	76	24	34	58	45	....	....	....	....	....	....	....	....	....									
2012-13	SHK 37 Piestany	Slovakia	8	5	5	10	6	....	....	....	....	....	....	....	....	....									
	Grand Rapids	AHL	61	23	26	49	50	....	....	....	....	....	....	....	....	....	24	*16	5	21	23				
	Detroit	**NHL**	**18**	**4**	**3**	**7**	**4**	1	0	0	32	12.5	2		1100.0		11:22									
2013-14	**Detroit**	**NHL**	**73**	**19**	**20**	**39**	**30**	2	0	3	158	12.0	12		52	50.0	14:21	5	0	0	0	8	0	0	0	15:07
	Slovakia	Olympics	4	1	1	2	2	....	....	....	....	....	....	....	....	....									
2014-15	**Detroit**	**NHL**	**82**	**29**	**27**	**56**	**28**	9	0	7	211	13.7	6		12	50.0	16:13	7	3	1	4	2	1	0	0	15:45
	NHL Totals		**182**	**53**	**50**	**103**	**62**	12	0	10	407	13.0			65	50.8	14:40	12	3	1	4	10	1	0	0	15:29

Jack A. Butterfield Trophy (AHL - Playoff MVP) (2013)
Signed as a free agent by **Piestany** (Slovakia), September 20, 2012.

TAVARES, John (tah-VAHR-ehs, JAWN) **NYI**

Center. Shoots left. 6'1", 209 lbs.   Born, Mississauga, ON, September 20, 1990. NY Islanders' 1st choice, 1st overall, in 2009 Entry Draft.

Season	Club	League	GP	G	A	Pts	PIM	PP	SH	GW	S	S%	+/-	TF	F%	Min	GP	G	A	Pts	PIM	PP	SH	GW	Min
2004-05	Tor. Marlboros	GTHL	72	91	67	158		....	....	....	....	....	....	....	....	....									
	Milton Icehawks	ON-Jr.A	20	13	15	28	10	....	....	....	....	....	....	....	....	....									
2005-06	Oshawa Generals	OHL	65	45	32	77	72	....	....	....	....	....	....	....	....	....									
2006-07	Oshawa Generals	OHL	67	*72	62	134	60	....	....	....	....	....	....	....	....	....	9	7	12	19	6				
2007-08	Oshawa Generals	OHL	59	40	78	118	69	....	....	....	....	....	....	....	....	....	15	3	13	16	20				
2008-09	Oshawa Generals	OHL	32	*26	28	*54	32	....	....	....	....	....	....	....	....	....									
	London Knights	OHL	24	*32	18	*50	22	....	....	....	....	....	....	....	....	....	14	10	11	21	8				
2009-10	**NY Islanders**	**NHL**	**82**	**24**	**30**	**54**	**22**	11	0	2	186	12.9	-15		1129	47.5	18:00									
2010-11	**NY Islanders**	**NHL**	**79**	**29**	**38**	**67**	**53**	9	0	4	243	11.9	-16		1319	52.5	19:15									
2011-12	**NY Islanders**	**NHL**	**82**	**31**	**50**	**81**	**26**	7	0	8	286	10.8	-6		1586	51.3	20:34									
2012-13	SC Bern	Swiss	28	17	25	42	28	....	....	....	....	....	....	....	....	....									
	NY Islanders	**NHL**	**48**	**28**	**19**	**47**	**18**	9	0	5	162	17.3	-2		930	49.4	20:46	6	3	2	5	4	0	0	1	20:34
2013-14	**NY Islanders**	**NHL**	**59**	**24**	**42**	**66**	**40**	8	0	4	188	12.8	-6		1129	49.1	21:15									
	Canada	Olympics	4	0	0	0	0	....	....	....	....	....	....	....	....	....									
2014-15	**NY Islanders**	**NHL**	**82**	**38**	**48**	**86**	**46**	13	0	8	278	13.7	5		1442	52.2	20:40	7	2	4	6	2	0	0	1	19:19
	NHL Totals		**432**	**174**	**227**	**401**	**205**	57	0	31	1343	13.0			7535	50.6	19:59	13	5	6	11	6	0	0	2	19:54

OHL All-Rookie Team (2006) • Canadian Major Junior Rookie of the Year (2006) • OHL First All-Star Team (2007) • OHL Player of the Year (2007) • Canadian Major Junior First All-Star Team (2007, 2009) • Canadian Major Junior Player of the Year (2007) • OHL Second All-Star Team (2009) • NHL All-Rookie Team (2010) • NHL First All-Star Team (2015)
Played in NHL All-Star Game (2012, 2015)
Signed as a free agent by **Bern** (Swiss), September 28, 2012.

TEDENBY, Mattias (TEH-dehn-bew, muh-TIGH-uhs)

Left wing. Shoots left. 5'9", 175 lbs.   Born, Vetlanda, Sweden, February 21, 1990. New Jersey's 1st choice, 24th overall, in 2008 Entry Draft.

Season	Club	League	GP	G	A	Pts	PIM	PP	SH	GW	S	S%	+/-	TF	F%	Min	GP	G	A	Pts	PIM	PP	SH	GW	Min
2005-06	HV 71 U18	Swe-U18	13	8	7	15	24	....	....	....	....	....	....	....	....	....	5	1	0	1	10				
2006-07	HV 71 U18	Swe-U18	2	4	0	4	2	....	....	....	....	....	....	....	....	....	5	7	2	9	14				
	HV 71 Jr.	Swe-Jr.	27	10	10	20	43	....	....	....	....	....	....	....	....	....	4	3	1	4	2				
2007-08	HV 71 U18	Swe-U18	1	1	0	1	0	....	....	....	....	....	....	....	....	....									
	HV 71 Jr.	Swe-Jr.	25	14	16	30	14	....	....	....	....	....	....	....	....	....	2	0	0	0	0				
	HV 71 Jonkoping	Sweden	23	3	3	6	6	....	....	....	....	....	....	....	....	....	5	0	0	0	0				
2008-09	IK Oskarshamn	Sweden-2	13	2	9	11	6	....	....	....	....	....	....	....	....	....									
	HV 71 Jonkoping	Sweden	32	3	1	4	6	....	....	....	....	....	....	....	....	....	18	6	3	9	6				
2009-10	HV 71 Jonkoping	Sweden	44	12	7	19	30	....	....	....	....	....	....	....	....	....	16	2	3	5	4				
2010-11	**New Jersey**	**NHL**	**58**	**8**	**14**	**22**	**14**	2	0	2	87	9.2	3		0	0.0	12:33									
	Albany Devils	AHL	12	3	2	5	6	....	....	....	....	....	....	....	....	....									

			Regular Season														Playoffs								
Season	Club	League	GP	G	A	Pts	PIM	PP	SH	GW	S	S%	+/-	TF	F%	Min	GP	G	A	Pts	PIM	PP	SH	GW	Min
2011-12	**New Jersey**	**NHL**	**43**	**1**	**5**	**6**	**16**	**0**	**0**	**0**	**46**	**2.2**	**–15**	**3**	**33.3**	**10:45**	....	....	....	....	....	....	....	....	....
	Albany Devils	AHL	35	6	14	20	22	....	....	....	....	....	....	....	....	....	....	....	....	....	....	....	....	....	....
2012-13	Albany Devils	AHL	37	10	9	19	12	....	....	....	....	....	....	....	....	....	....	....	....	....	....	....	....	....	....
	New Jersey	**NHL**	**4**	**0**	**1**	**1**	**2**	**0**	**0**	**0**	**2**	**0.0**	**0**	**0**	**0.0**	**9:00**	....	....	....	....	....	....	....	....	....
2013-14	**New Jersey**	**NHL**	**15**	**1**	**0**	**1**	**10**	**0**	**0**	**0**	**9**	**11.1**	**–8**	**2**	**0.0**	**10:01**	....	....	....	....	....	....	....	....	....
	Albany Devils	AHL	42	9	13	22	24	....	....	....	....	....	....	....	....	....	4	1	1	2	0	....	....	....	....
2014-15	HV 71 Jonkoping	Sweden	53	10	9	19	32	....	....	....	....	....	....	....	....	....	6	1	0	1	4	....	....	....	....
	NHL Totals		**120**	**10**	**20**	**30**	**42**	**2**	**0**	**2**	**144**	**6.9**		**5**	**20.0**	**11:28**	....	....	....	....	....	....	....	....	....

Signed as a free agent by **Jonkoping** (Sweden), August 14, 2014.

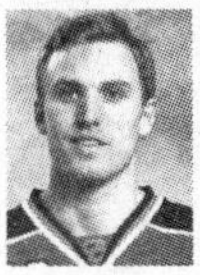

TENNYSON, Matt

(TEHN-ihs-suhn, MAT) **S.J.**

Defense. Shoots right. 6'2", 205 lbs. Born, Pleasanton, CA, April 23, 1990.

2007-08	Texas Tornado	NAHL	58	4	10	14	80	....	....	....	....	....	....	....	....	....	....	....	....	....	....	....	....	....	....
2008-09	Cedar Rapids	USHL	57	4	6	10	51	....	....	....	....	....	....	....	....	....	5	0	0	0	2	....	....	....	....
2009-10	Western Mich.	CCHA	34	2	7	9	30	....	....	....	....	....	....	....	....	....	....	....	....	....	....	....	....	....	....
2010-11	Western Mich.	CCHA	42	9	12	21	38	....	....	....	....	....	....	....	....	....	....	....	....	....	....	....	....	....	....
2011-12	Western Mich.	CCHA	41	11	13	24	28	....	....	....	....	....	....	....	....	....	....	....	....	....	....	....	....	....	....
	Worcester Sharks	AHL	7	1	1	2	0	....	....	....	....	....	....	....	....	....	....	....	....	....	....	....	....	....	....
2012-13	Worcester Sharks	AHL	60	5	22	27	44	....	....	....	....	....	....	....	....	....	....	....	....	....	....	....	....	....	....
	San Jose	**NHL**	**4**	**0**	**2**	**2**	**2**	**0**	**0**	**0**	**8**	**0.0**	**2**	**0**	**0.0**	**15:43**	....	....	....	....	....	....	....	....	....
2013-14	Worcester Sharks	AHL	54	7	14	21	33	....	....	....	....	....	....	....	....	....	....	....	....	....	....	....	....	....	....
2014-15	**San Jose**	**NHL**	**27**	**2**	**6**	**8**	**16**	**1**	**0**	**0**	**37**	**5.4**	**0**	**0**	**0.0**	**17:34**	....	....	....	....	....	....	....	....	....
	Worcester Sharks	AHL	43	4	11	15	30	....	....	....	....	....	....	....	....	....	4	0	0	0	0	....	....	....	....
	NHL Totals		**31**	**2**	**8**	**10**	**18**	**1**	**0**	**0**	**45**	**4.4**		**0**	**0.0**	**17:20**	....	....	....	....	....	....	....	....	....

CCHA Second All-Star Team (2012)

Signed as a free agent by **San Jose**, March 29, 2012.

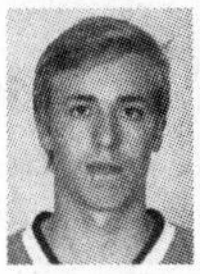

TERAVAINEN, Teuvo

(tair-uh-VIGH-nehn, TAY-voh) **CHI**

Center. Shoots left. 5'11", 178 lbs. Born, Helsinki, Finland, September 11, 1994. Chicago's 1st choice, 18th overall, in 2012 Entry Draft.

2009-10	Jokerit U18	Fin-U18	29	16	14	30	6	....	....	....	....	....	....	....	....	....	4	0	4	4	0	....	....	....	....
2010-11	Jokerit U18	Fin-U18	4	1	3	4	2	....	....	....	....	....	....	....	....	....	1	0	1	1	25	....	....	....	....
	Jokerit Helsinki Jr.	Fin-Jr.	26	3	17	20	8	....	....	....	....	....	....	....	....	....	8	1	4	5	4	....	....	....	....
2011-12	Jokerit Helsinki Jr.	Fin-Jr.	11	12	8	20	4	....	....	....	....	....	....	....	....	....	2	1	1	2	0	....	....	....	....
	Kiekko-Vantaa	Finland-2	3	1	2	3	0	....	....	....	....	....	....	....	....	....	....	....	....	....	....	....	....	....	....
	Jokerit Helsinki	Finland	40	11	7	18	6	....	....	....	....	....	....	....	....	....	9	2	4	6	0	....	....	....	....
2012-13	Kiekko-Vantaa	Finland-2	1	0	1	1	0	....	....	....	....	....	....	....	....	....	....	....	....	....	....	....	....	....	....
	Jokerit Helsinki	Finland	44	13	18	31	6	....	....	....	....	....	....	....	....	....	6	1	1	2	0	....	....	....	....
2013-14	Jokerit Helsinki	Finland	49	9	35	44	12	....	....	....	....	....	....	....	....	....	2	0	0	0	0	....	....	....	....
	Chicago	**NHL**	**3**	**0**	**0**	**0**	**0**	**0**	**0**	**0**	**4**	**0.0**	**0**	**25**	**52.0**	**14:06**	....	....	....	....	....	....	....	....	....
	Rockford IceHogs	AHL	5	2	0	2	2	....	....	....	....	....	....	....	....	....	....	....	....	....	....	....	....	....	....
2014-15♦	**Chicago**	**NHL**	**34**	**4**	**5**	**9**	**2**	**0**	**0**	**1**	**66**	**6.1**	**4**	**62**	**46.8**	**12:47**	**18**	**4**	**6**	**10**	**0**	**1**	**0**	**1**	**13:28**
	Rockford IceHogs	AHL	39	6	19	25	6	....	....	....	....	....	....	....	....	....	....	....	....	....	....	....	....	....	....
	NHL Totals		**37**	**4**	**5**	**9**	**2**	**0**	**0**	**1**	**70**	**5.7**		**87**	**48.3**	**12:53**	**18**	**4**	**6**	**10**	**0**	**1**	**0**	**1**	**13:28**

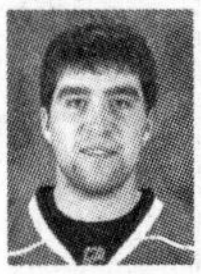

TERRY, Chris

(TAIR-ee, KRIHS) **CAR**

Left wing. Shoots left. 5'10", 195 lbs. Born, Brampton, ON, April 7, 1989. Carolina's 4th choice, 132nd overall, in 2007 Entry Draft.

2003-04	Markham	GTHL	66	39	50	89	....	....	....	....	....	....	....	....	....	....	....	....	....	....	....	....	....	....	....
2004-05	Markham	GTHL	60	42	53	95	113	....	....	....	....	....	....	....	....	....	9	0	9	9	14	....	....	....	....
2005-06	Plymouth Whalers	OHL	64	9	19	28	72	....	....	....	....	....	....	....	....	....	11	3	2	5	4	....	....	....	....
2006-07	Plymouth Whalers	OHL	68	22	44	66	98	....	....	....	....	....	....	....	....	....	20	8	10	18	21	....	....	....	....
2007-08	Plymouth Whalers	OHL	68	44	57	101	107	....	....	....	....	....	....	....	....	....	4	4	3	7	6	....	....	....	....
	Albany River Rats	AHL	1	0	0	0	0	....	....	....	....	....	....	....	....	....	....	....	....	....	....	....	....	....	....
2008-09	Plymouth Whalers	OHL	53	39	55	94	75	....	....	....	....	....	....	....	....	....	11	7	9	16	18	....	....	....	....
2009-10	Albany River Rats	AHL	80	17	30	47	47	....	....	....	....	....	....	....	....	....	8	2	4	6	0	....	....	....	....
2010-11	Charlotte	AHL	80	34	30	64	52	....	....	....	....	....	....	....	....	....	16	6	3	9	14	....	....	....	....
2011-12	Charlotte	AHL	74	16	43	59	67	....	....	....	....	....	....	....	....	....	....	....	....	....	....	....	....	....	....
2012-13	Charlotte	AHL	70	25	35	60	40	....	....	....	....	....	....	....	....	....	5	2	2	4	8	....	....	....	....
	Carolina	**NHL**	**3**	**1**	**0**	**1**	**0**	**0**	**0**	**1**	**1**	**100.0**	**0**	**1**	**100.0**	**9:36**	....	....	....	....	....	....	....	....	....
2013-14	**Carolina**	**NHL**	**10**	**0**	**2**	**2**	**0**	**0**	**0**	**0**	**13**	**0.0**	**–4**	**0**	**0.0**	**12:05**	....	....	....	....	....	....	....	....	....
	Charlotte	AHL	70	28	41	69	62	....	....	....	....	....	....	....	....	....	....	....	....	....	....	....	....	....	....
2014-15	**Carolina**	**NHL**	**57**	**11**	**9**	**20**	**14**	**3**	**0**	**0**	**71**	**15.5**	**–4**	**11**	**54.6**	**12:43**	....	....	....	....	....	....	....	....	....
	Charlotte	AHL	5	1	1	2	4	....	....	....	....	....	....	....	....	....	....	....	....	....	....	....	....	....	....
	NHL Totals		**70**	**12**	**11**	**23**	**14**	**3**	**0**	**1**	**85**	**14.1**		**12**	**58.3**	**12:30**	....	....	....	....	....	....	....	....	....

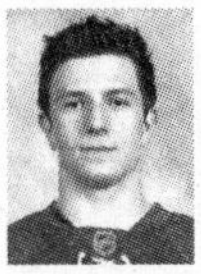

THOMAS, Christian

(TAW-muhs, KRIHS-ch'yehn) **MTL**

Right wing. Shoots right. 5'9", 179 lbs. Born, Toronto, ON, May 26, 1992. NY Rangers' 2nd choice, 40th overall, in 2010 Entry Draft.

2007-08	Tor. Marlboros	GTHL	52	32	34	66	36	....	....	....	....	....	....	....	....	....	....	....	....	....	....	....	....	....	....
2008-09	London Knights	OHL	32	4	7	11	4	....	....	....	....	....	....	....	....	....	....	....	....	....	....	....	....	....	....
	Oshawa Generals	OHL	27	4	10	14	10	....	....	....	....	....	....	....	....	....	....	....	....	....	....	....	....	....	....
2009-10	Oshawa Generals	OHL	64	41	25	66	27	....	....	....	....	....	....	....	....	....	....	....	....	....	....	....	....	....	....
2010-11	Oshawa Generals	OHL	66	54	45	99	38	....	....	....	....	....	....	....	....	....	10	9	10	19	4	....	....	....	....
2011-12	Oshawa Generals	OHL	55	34	33	67	12	....	....	....	....	....	....	....	....	....	6	2	2	4	0	....	....	....	....
	Connecticut	AHL	5	1	1	2	0	....	....	....	....	....	....	....	....	....	6	0	0	0	0	....	....	....	....
2012-13	Connecticut	AHL	73	19	16	35	15	....	....	....	....	....	....	....	....	....	....	....	....	....	....	....	....	....	....
	NY Rangers	**NHL**	**1**	**0**	**0**	**0**	**0**	**0**	**0**	**0**	**2**	**0.0**	**0**	**0**	**0.0**	**12:46**	....	....	....	....	....	....	....	....	....
2013-14	**Montreal**	**NHL**	**2**	**0**	**0**	**0**	**0**	**0**	**0**	**0**	**1**	**0.0**	**–1**	**0**	**0.0**	**7:11**	....	....	....	....	....	....	....	....	....
	Hamilton	AHL	55	11	16	27	22	....	....	....	....	....	....	....	....	....	....	....	....	....	....	....	....	....	....
2014-15	**Montreal**	**NHL**	**18**	**1**	**0**	**1**	**7**	**0**	**0**	**0**	**26**	**3.8**	**–2**	**1**	**0.0**	**9:06**	....	....	....	....	....	....	....	....	....
	Hamilton	AHL	52	11	11	22	18	....	....	....	....	....	....	....	....	....	....	....	....	....	....	....	....	....	....
	NHL Totals		**21**	**1**	**0**	**1**	**7**	**0**	**0**	**0**	**29**	**3.4**		**1**	**0.0**	**9:05**	....	....	....	....	....	....	....	....	....

Traded to **Montreal** by **NY Rangers** for Danny Kristo, July 2, 2013.

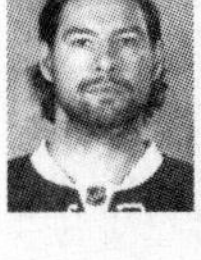

THOMPSON, Nate

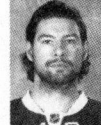

(TAWM-suhn, NAYT) **ANA**

Center. Shoots left. 6', 212 lbs. Born, Anchorage, AK, October 5, 1984. Boston's 8th choice, 183rd overall, in 2003 Entry Draft.

2001-02	Seattle	WHL	69	13	26	39	42	....	....	....	....	....	....	....	....	....	11	1	3	4	13	....	....	....	....
2002-03	Seattle	WHL	61	10	24	34	48	....	....	....	....	....	....	....	....	....	15	5	4	9	6	....	....	....	....
2003-04	Seattle	WHL	65	13	23	36	24	....	....	....	....	....	....	....	....	....	....	....	....	....	....	....	....	....	....
2004-05	Seattle	WHL	58	19	15	34	39	....	....	....	....	....	....	....	....	....	12	1	2	3	2	....	....	....	....
	Providence Bruins	AHL	....	....	....	....	....	....	....	....	....	....	....	....	....	....	11	0	1	1	6	....	....	....	....
2005-06	Providence Bruins	AHL	74	8	10	18	58	....	....	....	....	....	....	....	....	....	3	0	0	0	10	....	....	....	....
2006-07	**Boston**	**NHL**	**4**	**0**	**0**	**0**	**0**	**0**	**0**	**0**	**5**	**0.0**	**0**	**10**	**40.0**	**4:46**	....	....	....	....	....	....	....	....	....
	Providence Bruins	AHL	67	8	15	23	74	....	....	....	....	....	....	....	....	....	13	0	2	2	9	....	....	....	....
2007-08	Providence Bruins	AHL	75	19	20	39	83	....	....	....	....	....	....	....	....	....	10	2	3	5	4	....	....	....	....
2008-09	**NY Islanders**	**NHL**	**43**	**2**	**2**	**4**	**49**	**0**	**1**	**0**	**56**	**3.6**	**–11**	**429**	**50.4**	**12:05**	....	....	....	....	....	....	....	....	....
2009-10	**NY Islanders**	**NHL**	**39**	**1**	**5**	**6**	**39**	**0**	**0**	**0**	**48**	**2.1**	**–14**	**210**	**49.5**	**12:56**	....	....	....	....	....	....	....	....	....
	Tampa Bay	**NHL**	**32**	**1**	**3**	**4**	**17**	**0**	**0**	**0**	**44**	**2.3**	**–3**	**385**	**56.9**	**13:58**	....	....	....	....	....	....	....	....	....
2010-11	**Tampa Bay**	**NHL**	**79**	**10**	**15**	**25**	**29**	**0**	**1**	**2**	**123**	**8.1**	**–6**	**664**	**54.2**	**15:05**	**18**	**1**	**3**	**4**	**4**	**0**	**0**	**0**	**15:37**
2011-12	**Tampa Bay**	**NHL**	**68**	**9**	**6**	**15**	**21**	**0**	**0**	**1**	**85**	**10.6**	**–23**	**592**	**49.5**	**14:49**	....	....	....	....	....	....	....	....	....
2012-13	Alaska Aces	ECHL	24	7	14	21	23	....	....	....	....	....	....	....	....	....	....	....	....	....	....	....	....	....	....
	Tampa Bay	**NHL**	**45**	**7**	**8**	**15**	**17**	**0**	**0**	**0**	**58**	**12.1**	**–2**	**605**	**51.2**	**14:20**	....	....	....	....	....	....	....	....	....

			Regular Season														Playoffs								
Season	Club	League	GP	G	A	Pts	PIM	PP	SH	GW	S	S%	+/-	TF	F%	Min	GP	G	A	Pts	PIM	PP	SH	GW	Min
2013-14	**Tampa Bay**	**NHL**	**81**	**9**	**7**	**16**	**27**	**0**	**2**	**1**	**105**	**8.6**	**3**	**974**	**50.9**	**12:52**	**4**	**0**	**0**	**0**	**0**	**0**	**0**	**0**	**11:36**
2014-15	**Anaheim**	**NHL**	**80**	**5**	**13**	**18**	**39**	**0**	**1**	**3**	**87**	**5.7**	**0**	**1056**	**52.8**	**13:19**	**12**	**2**	**4**	**6**	**6**	**0**	**0**	**0**	**15:28**
	NHL Totals		**471**	**44**	**59**	**103**	**238**	**0**	**5**	**7**	**611**	**7.2**		**4925**	**52.0**	**13:41**	**34**	**3**	**7**	**10**	**10**	**0**	**0**	**0**	**15:06**

Claimed on waivers by **NY Islanders** from **Boston**, October 8, 2008. Claimed on waivers by **Tampa Bay** from **NY Islanders**, January 21, 2010. Signed to a PTO (professional tryout) contract by **Alaska** (ECHL), September 28, 2012. Traded to **Anaheim** by **Tampa Bay** for Anaheim's 4th (Jonne Tammela) and 7th (later traded to Edmonton – Edmonton selected Miroslav Svoboda) round choices in 2015 Entry Draft, June 29, 2014.

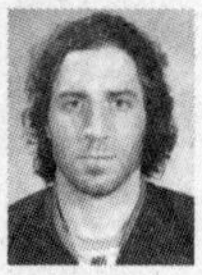

THORBURN, Chris

(THOHR-buhrn, KRIHS) **WPG**

Right wing. Shoots right. 6'3", 230 lbs. Born, Sault Ste. Marie, ON, June 3, 1983. Buffalo's 3rd choice, 50th overall, in 2001 Entry Draft.

Season	Club	League	GP	G	A	Pts	PIM	PP	SH	GW	S	S%	+/-	TF	F%	Min	GP	G	A	Pts	PIM	PP	SH	GW	Min
1998-99	Elliot Lake Vikings	NOJHA	40	21	12	33	28	....	....	....	....	....	....	....	....	....	....	....	....	....	....	....	....	....	....
99-2000	North Bay	OHL	56	12	8	20	33	....	....	....	....	....	....	....	....	....	6	0	2	2	0	....	....	....	....
2000-01	North Bay	OHL	66	22	32	54	64	....	....	....	....	....	....	....	....	....	4	0	1	1	9	....	....	....	....
2001-02	North Bay	OHL	67	15	43	58	112	....	....	....	....	....	....	....	....	....	5	1	2	3	8	....	....	....	....
2002-03	Saginaw Spirit	OHL	37	19	19	38	68	....	....	....	....	....	....	....	....	....	....	....	....	....	....	....	....	....	....
	Plymouth Whalers	OHL	27	11	22	33	56	....	....	....	....	....	....	....	....	....	18	11	9	20	10	....	....	....	....
2003-04	Rochester	AHL	58	6	16	22	77	....	....	....	....	....	....	....	....	....	16	3	2	5	18	....	....	....	....
2004-05	Rochester	AHL	73	12	17	29	185	....	....	....	....	....	....	....	....	....	4	0	1	1	2	....	....	....	....
2005-06	**Buffalo**	**NHL**	**2**	**0**	**1**	**1**	**7**	**0**	**0**	**0**	**1**	**0.0**	**–1**	**1**	**0.0**	**6:52**	....	....	....	....	....	....	....	....	....
	Rochester	AHL	77	23	27	50	134	....	....	....	....	....	....	....	....	....	....	....	....	....	....	....	....	....	....
2006-07	**Pittsburgh**	**NHL**	**39**	**3**	**2**	**5**	**69**	**0**	**0**	**1**	**40**	**7.5**	**1**	**8**	**25.0**	**7:54**	....	....	....	....	....	....	....	....	....
	Wilkes-Barre	AHL	3	0	1	1	2	....	....	....	....	....	....	....	....	....	....	....	....	....	....	....	....	....	....
2007-08	**Atlanta**	**NHL**	**73**	**5**	**13**	**18**	**92**	**0**	**0**	**1**	**72**	**6.9**	**–4**	**20**	**60.0**	**8:56**	....	....	....	....	....	....	....	....	....
2008-09	**Atlanta**	**NHL**	**82**	**7**	**8**	**15**	**104**	**0**	**0**	**1**	**85**	**8.2**	**–10**	**37**	**40.5**	**9:35**	....	....	....	....	....	....	....	....	....
2009-10	**Atlanta**	**NHL**	**76**	**4**	**9**	**13**	**89**	**0**	**3**	**0**	**63**	**6.3**	**6**	**29**	**55.2**	**9:59**	....	....	....	....	....	....	....	....	....
2010-11	**Atlanta**	**NHL**	**82**	**9**	**10**	**19**	**77**	**2**	**0**	**0**	**114**	**7.9**	**–4**	**251**	**49.8**	**13:48**	....	....	....	....	....	....	....	....	....
2011-12	**Winnipeg**	**NHL**	**72**	**4**	**7**	**11**	**83**	**0**	**0**	**0**	**69**	**5.8**	**–6**	**67**	**58.2**	**10:11**	....	....	....	....	....	....	....	....	....
2012-13	**Winnipeg**	**NHL**	**42**	**2**	**2**	**4**	**70**	**0**	**0**	**0**	**13**	**15.4**	**–5**	**46**	**43.5**	**6:19**	....	....	....	....	....	....	....	....	....
2013-14	**Winnipeg**	**NHL**	**55**	**2**	**9**	**11**	**65**	**0**	**0**	**1**	**26**	**7.7**	**0**	**33**	**60.6**	**8:57**	....	....	....	....	....	....	....	....	....
2014-15	**Winnipeg**	**NHL**	**81**	**7**	**7**	**14**	**76**	**0**	**0**	**2**	**67**	**10.4**	**–5**	**56**	**64.3**	**8:05**	**4**	**0**	**0**	**0**	**0**	**0**	**0**	**0**	**7:29**
	NHL Totals		**604**	**43**	**68**	**111**	**732**	**2**	**3**	**6**	**550**	**7.8**		**548**	**52.0**	**9:36**	**4**	**0**	**0**	**0**	**0**	**0**	**0**	**0**	**7:29**

Claimed on waivers by **Pittsburgh** from **Buffalo**, October 3, 2006. Traded to **Atlanta** by **Pittsburgh** for NY Rangers' 3rd round choice (previously acquired, Pittsburgh selected Robert Bortuzzo) in 2007 Entry Draft, June 22, 2007. • Transferred to **Winnipeg** after **Atlanta** franchise relocated, June 21, 2011.

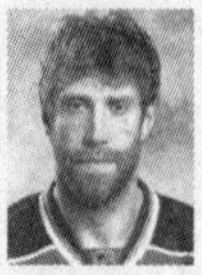

THORNTON, Joe

(THOHRN-tuhn, JOH) **S.J.**

Center. Shoots left. 6'4", 220 lbs. Born, London, ON, July 2, 1979. Boston's 1st choice, 1st overall, in 1997 Entry Draft.

Season	Club	League	GP	G	A	Pts	PIM	PP	SH	GW	S	S%	+/-	TF	F%	Min	GP	G	A	Pts	PIM	PP	SH	GW	Min
1993-94	Elgin-Mid. Chiefs	Minor-ON	67	*83	*85	*168	45	....	....	....	....	....	....	....	....	....	....	....	....	....	....	....	....	....	....
	St. Thomas Stars	ON-Jr.B	6	2	6	8	2	....	....	....	....	....	....	....	....	....	....	....	....	....	....	....	....	....	....
1994-95	St. Thomas Stars	ON-Jr.B	50	40	64	104	53	....	....	....	....	....	....	....	....	....	....	....	....	....	....	....	....	....	....
1995-96	Sault Ste. Marie	OHL	66	30	46	76	53	....	....	....	....	....	....	....	....	....	4	1	1	2	11	....	....	....	....
1996-97	Sault Ste. Marie	OHL	59	41	81	122	123	....	....	....	....	....	....	....	....	....	11	11	8	19	24	....	....	....	....
1997-98	**Boston**	**NHL**	**55**	**3**	**4**	**7**	**19**	**0**	**0**	**1**	**33**	**9.1**	**–6**	....	....	....	**6**	**0**	**0**	**0**	**9**	**0**	**0**	**0**	....
1998-99	**Boston**	**NHL**	**81**	**16**	**25**	**41**	**69**	**7**	**0**	**1**	**128**	**12.5**	**3**	**1073**	**48.7**	**15:21**	**11**	**3**	**6**	**9**	**4**	**2**	**0**	**2**	**19:52**
99-2000	**Boston**	**NHL**	**81**	**23**	**37**	**60**	**82**	**5**	**0**	**3**	**171**	**13.5**	**–5**	**1861**	**49.5**	**21:18**	....	....	....	....	....	....	....	....	....
2000-01	**Boston**	**NHL**	**72**	**37**	**34**	**71**	**107**	**19**	**1**	**5**	**181**	**20.4**	**–4**	**1651**	**52.1**	**21:45**	....	....	....	....	....	....	....	....	....
2001-02	**Boston**	**NHL**	**66**	**22**	**46**	**68**	**127**	**6**	**0**	**5**	**152**	**14.5**	**7**	**1341**	**49.1**	**19:59**	**6**	**2**	**4**	**6**	**10**	**0**	**0**	**0**	**21:09**
2002-03	**Boston**	**NHL**	**77**	**36**	**65**	**101**	**109**	**12**	**2**	**4**	**196**	**18.4**	**12**	**1766**	**49.5**	**22:33**	**5**	**1**	**2**	**3**	**4**	**1**	**0**	**0**	**20:13**
2003-04	**Boston**	**NHL**	**77**	**23**	**50**	**73**	**98**	**4**	**0**	**6**	**187**	**12.3**	**18**	**1671**	**56.3**	**21:38**	**7**	**0**	**0**	**0**	**14**	**0**	**0**	**0**	**21:30**
2004-05	HC Davos	Swiss	40	10	44	54	80	....	....	....	....	....	....	....	....	....	14	4	*20	*24	29	....	....	....	....
2005-06	**Boston**	**NHL**	**23**	**9**	***24**	***33**	**6**	**3**	**0**	**2**	**60**	**15.0**	**0**	**511**	**52.3**	**21:33**	....	....	....	....	....	....	....	....	....
	San Jose	**NHL**	**58**	**20**	***72**	***92**	**55**	**8**	**0**	**4**	**135**	**14.8**	**31**	**1287**	**50.9**	**21:15**	**11**	**2**	**7**	**9**	**12**	**1**	**0**	**1**	**25:09**
	Canada	Olympics	6	1	2	3	0	....	....	....	....	....	....	....	....	....	....	....	....	....	....	....	....	....	....
2006-07	**San Jose**	**NHL**	**82**	**22**	***92**	**114**	**44**	**10**	**0**	**5**	**213**	**10.3**	**24**	**1522**	**51.1**	**20:19**	**11**	**1**	**10**	**11**	**10**	**0**	**0**	**0**	**22:00**
2007-08	**San Jose**	**NHL**	**82**	**29**	***67**	**96**	**59**	**11**	**0**	**5**	**178**	**16.3**	**18**	**1485**	**52.9**	**21:24**	**13**	**2**	**8**	**10**	**2**	**1**	**0**	**1**	**24:42**
2008-09	**San Jose**	**NHL**	**82**	**25**	**61**	**86**	**56**	**11**	**0**	**3**	**139**	**18.0**	**16**	**1295**	**55.4**	**19:28**	**6**	**1**	**4**	**5**	**5**	**1**	**0**	**0**	**19:14**
2009-10	**San Jose**	**NHL**	**79**	**20**	**69**	**89**	**54**	**4**	**1**	**2**	**141**	**14.2**	**17**	**1228**	**53.9**	**19:51**	**15**	**3**	**9**	**12**	**18**	**1**	**0**	**1**	**21:20**
	Canada	Olympics	7	1	1	2	0	....	....	....	....	....	....	....	....	....	....	....	....	....	....	....	....	....	....
2010-11	**San Jose**	**NHL**	**80**	**21**	**49**	**70**	**47**	**9**	**2**	**3**	**149**	**14.1**	**4**	**1240**	**54.4**	**19:52**	**18**	**3**	**14**	**17**	**16**	**0**	**0**	**2**	**22:15**
2011-12	**San Jose**	**NHL**	**82**	**18**	**59**	**77**	**31**	**4**	**0**	**2**	**156**	**11.5**	**17**	**993**	**56.1**	**20:28**	**5**	**2**	**3**	**5**	**2**	**0**	**0**	**0**	**21:54**
2012-13	HC Davos	Swiss	33	12	24	36	43	....	....	....	....	....	....	....	....	....	....	....	....	....	....	....	....	....	....
	San Jose	**NHL**	**48**	**7**	**33**	**40**	**26**	**2**	**0**	**1**	**85**	**8.2**	**6**	**701**	**58.5**	**18:23**	**11**	**2**	**8**	**10**	**2**	**1**	**0**	**0**	**20:17**
2013-14	**San Jose**	**NHL**	**82**	**11**	**65**	**76**	**32**	**2**	**0**	**3**	**122**	**9.0**	**20**	**1099**	**56.1**	**18:56**	**7**	**2**	**1**	**3**	**8**	**1**	**0**	**0**	**19:19**
2014-15	**San Jose**	**NHL**	**78**	**16**	**49**	**65**	**30**	**4**	**0**	**0**	**131**	**12.2**	**–4**	**955**	**58.0**	**18:25**	....	....	....	....	....	....	....	....	....
	NHL Totals		**1285**	**358**	**901**	**1259**	**1051**	**121**	**6**	**55**	**2557**	**14.0**		**21679**	**52.8**	**20:05**	**132**	**24**	**76**	**100**	**116**	**9**	**0**	**7**	**21:45**

OHL All-Rookie Team (1996) • OHL Rookie of the Year (1996) • Canadian Major Junior Rookie of the Year (1996) • OHL Second All-Star Team (1997) • NHL Second All-Star Team (2003, 2008) • NHL First All-Star Team (2006) • Art Ross Trophy (2006) • Hart Memorial Trophy (2006)

Played in NHL All-Star Game (2002, 2003, 2004, 2007, 2008, 2009)

Signed as a free agent by **Davos** (Swiss), July 8, 2004. Traded to **San Jose** by **Boston** for Brad Stuart, Marco Sturm and Wayne Primeau, November 30, 2005. Signed as a free agent by **Davos** (Swiss), September 16, 2012.

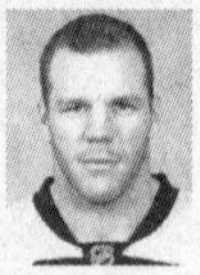

THORNTON, Shawn

(THOHRN-tuhn, SHAWN) **FLA**

Right wing. Shoots right. 6'2", 217 lbs. Born, Oshawa, ON, July 23, 1977. Toronto's 6th choice, 190th overall, in 1997 Entry Draft.

Season	Club	League	GP	G	A	Pts	PIM	PP	SH	GW	S	S%	+/-	TF	F%	Min	GP	G	A	Pts	PIM	PP	SH	GW	Min
1995-96	Peterborough	OHL	63	4	10	14	192	....	....	....	....	....	....	....	....	....	24	3	0	3	25	....	....	....	....
1996-97	Peterborough	OHL	61	19	10	29	204	....	....	....	....	....	....	....	....	....	11	2	4	6	20	....	....	....	....
1997-98	St. John's	AHL	59	0	3	3	225	....	....	....	....	....	....	....	....	....	....	....	....	....	....	....	....	....	....
1998-99	St. John's	AHL	78	8	11	19	354	....	....	....	....	....	....	....	....	....	5	0	0	0	9	....	....	....	....
99-2000	St. John's	AHL	60	4	12	16	316	....	....	....	....	....	....	....	....	....	....	....	....	....	....	....	....	....	....
2000-01	St. John's	AHL	79	5	12	17	320	....	....	....	....	....	....	....	....	....	3	1	2	3	2	....	....	....	....
2001-02	Norfolk Admirals	AHL	70	8	14	22	281	....	....	....	....	....	....	....	....	....	4	0	0	0	4	....	....	....	....
2002-03	**Chicago**	**NHL**	**13**	**1**	**1**	**2**	**31**	**0**	**0**	**0**	**15**	**6.7**	**–4**	**3**	**66.7**	**8:30**	....	....	....	....	....	....	....	....	....
	Norfolk Admirals	AHL	50	11	2	13	213	....	....	....	....	....	....	....	....	....	9	0	2	2	28	....	....	....	....
2003-04	**Chicago**	**NHL**	**8**	**1**	**0**	**1**	**23**	**0**	**0**	**0**	**14**	**7.1**	**2**	**19**	**42.1**	**11:14**	....	....	....	....	....	....	....	....	....
	Norfolk Admirals	AHL	64	6	11	17	259	....	....	....	....	....	....	....	....	....	8	1	1	2	6	....	....	....	....
2004-05	Norfolk Admirals	AHL	71	5	9	14	253	....	....	....	....	....	....	....	....	....	6	0	0	0	8	....	....	....	....
2005-06	**Chicago**	**NHL**	**10**	**0**	**0**	**0**	**16**	**0**	**0**	**0**	**16**	**0.0**	**–5**	**17**	**58.8**	**7:18**	....	....	....	....	....	....	....	....	....
	Norfolk Admirals	AHL	59	10	22	32	192	....	....	....	....	....	....	....	....	....	4	0	0	0	35	....	....	....	....
2006-07 ♦	**Anaheim**	**NHL**	**48**	**2**	**7**	**9**	**88**	**0**	**0**	**0**	**60**	**3.3**	**3**	**8**	**25.0**	**8:26**	**15**	**0**	**0**	**0**	**19**	**0**	**0**	**0**	**3:58**
	Portland Pirates	AHL	15	4	4	8	55	....	....	....	....	....	....	....	....	....	....	....	....	....	....	....	....	....	....
2007-08	**Boston**	**NHL**	**58**	**4**	**3**	**7**	**74**	**0**	**0**	**1**	**65**	**6.2**	**–1**	**7**	**28.6**	**7:24**	**7**	**0**	**0**	**0**	**6**	**0**	**0**	**0**	**8:04**
2008-09	**Boston**	**NHL**	**79**	**6**	**5**	**11**	**123**	**0**	**0**	**2**	**136**	**4.4**	**–2**	**5**	**20.0**	**10:02**	**10**	**1**	**0**	**1**	**6**	**0**	**0**	**0**	**9:07**
2009-10	**Boston**	**NHL**	**74**	**1**	**9**	**10**	**141**	**0**	**0**	**0**	**119**	**0.8**	**–9**	**23**	**47.8**	**9:03**	**12**	**0**	**0**	**0**	**4**	**0**	**0**	**0**	**7:08**
2010-11 ♦	**Boston**	**NHL**	**79**	**10**	**10**	**20**	**122**	**0**	**0**	**2**	**151**	**6.6**	**8**	**31**	**54.8**	**10:05**	**18**	**0**	**1**	**1**	**24**	**0**	**0**	**0**	**6:57**
2011-12	**Boston**	**NHL**	**81**	**5**	**8**	**13**	**154**	**0**	**1**	**0**	**114**	**4.4**	**–7**	**38**	**42.1**	**9:11**	**5**	**0**	**0**	**0**	**0**	**0**	**0**	**0**	**7:30**
2012-13	**Boston**	**NHL**	**45**	**3**	**4**	**7**	**60**	**0**	**0**	**0**	**55**	**5.5**	**1**	**17**	**41.2**	**8:06**	**22**	**0**	**4**	**4**	**18**	**0**	**0**	**0**	**7:21**
2013-14	**Boston**	**NHL**	**64**	**5**	**3**	**8**	**74**	**0**	**0**	**1**	**93**	**5.4**	**3**	**9**	**33.3**	**8:48**	**12**	**0**	**1**	**1**	**4**	**0**	**0**	**0**	**7:22**
2014-15	**Florida**	**NHL**	**46**	**1**	**4**	**5**	**50**	**0**	**0**	**0**	**53**	**1.9**	**–13**	**12**	**25.0**	**9:35**	....	....	....	....	....	....	....	....	....
	NHL Totals		**605**	**39**	**54**	**93**	**956**	**0**	**1**	**6**	**891**	**4.4**		**189**	**43.4**	**9:03**	**101**	**1**	**6**	**7**	**81**	**0**	**0**	**0**	**6:59**

Traded to **Chicago** by **Toronto** for Marty Wilford, September 30, 2001. Signed as a free agent by **Anaheim**, July 14, 2006. Signed as a free agent by **Boston**, July 1, 2007. Signed as a free agent by **Florida**, July 1, 2014.

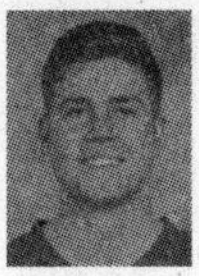

TIERNEY, Chris

(TEER-nee, KRIHS) **S.J.**

Center. Shoots left. 6', 195 lbs. Born, Keswick, ON, July 1, 1994. San Jose's 2nd choice, 55th overall, in 2012 Entry Draft.

			Regular Season														Playoffs								
Season	Club	League	GP	G	A	Pts	PIM	PP	SH	GW	S	S%	+/-	TF	F%	Min	GP	G	A	Pts	PIM	PP	SH	GW	Min
2009-10	York Simcoe	Minor-ON	57	35	55	90	28	....	....	....	....	....	....	....	....	....	....	....	....	....	....	....	....	....	....
	York Simcoe	Other	6	2	1	3	0	....	....	....	....	....	....	....	....	....	....	....	....	....	....	....	....	....	....
2010-11	London Knights	OHL	47	3	8	11	12	....	....	....	....	....	....	....	....	....	4	0	1	1	0	....	....	....	....
2011-12	London Knights	OHL	65	11	23	34	20	....	....	....	....	....	....	....	....	....	19	5	2	7	4	....	....	....	....
2012-13	London Knights	OHL	68	18	39	57	12	....	....	....	....	....	....	....	....	....	21	6	15	21	6	....	....	....	....
2013-14	London Knights	OHL	67	40	49	89	12	....	....	....	....	....	....	....	....	....	9	6	11	17	0	....	....	....	....
2014-15	**San Jose**	**NHL**	**43**	**6**	**15**	**21**	**6**	**1**	**0**	**1**	**48**	**12.5**	**3**	**342**	**43.9**	**12:15**	....	....	....	....	....	....	....	....	....
	Worcester Sharks	AHL	29	8	21	29	10	....	....	....	....	....	....	....	....	....	4	1	2	3	0	....	....	....	....
	NHL Totals		**43**	**6**	**15**	**21**	**6**	**1**	**0**	**1**	**48**	**12.5**		**342**	**43.9**	**12:15**	....	....	....	....	....	....	....	....	....

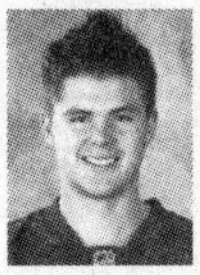

TIKHONOV, Viktor

(TIHK-uh-nawf, VIHK-tohr) **CHI**

Right wing. Shoots right. 6'2", 189 lbs. Born, Riga, Latvia, May 12, 1988. Phoenix's 2nd choice, 28th overall, in 2008 Entry Draft.

Season	Club	League	GP	G	A	Pts	PIM	PP	SH	GW	S	S%	+/-	TF	F%	Min	GP	G	A	Pts	PIM	PP	SH	GW	Min
2004-05	CSKA Moscow 2	Russia-3	STATISTICS NOT AVAILABLE																						
2005-06	CSKA Moscow 2	Russia-3	STATISTICS NOT AVAILABLE																						
	HK Dmitrov	Russia-2	36	6	8	14	10	....	....	....	....	....	....	....	....	....	....	....	....	....	....	....	....	....	....
2006-07	Cherepovets 2	Russia-3	STATISTICS NOT AVAILABLE																						
	Cherepovets	Russia	4	0	0	0	0	....	....	....	....	....	....	....	....	....	....	....	....	....	....	....	....	....	....
2007-08	Cherepovets	Russia	43	7	5	12	43	....	....	....	....	....	....	....	....	....	8	0	1	1	4	....	....	....	....
2008-09	**Phoenix**	**NHL**	**61**	**8**	**8**	**16**	**20**	**1**	**0**	**1**	**71**	**11.3**	**–3**	**60**	**38.3**	**12:08**	....	....	....	....	....	....	....	....	....
	San Antonio	AHL	4	2	1	3	0	....	....	....	....	....	....	....	....	....	....	....	....	....	....	....	....	....	....
2009-10	San Antonio	AHL	18	2	6	8	12	....	....	....	....	....	....	....	....	....	....	....	....	....	....	....	....	....	....
	Cherepovets	KHL	25	14	1	15	12	....	....	....	....	....	....	....	....	....	....	....	....	....	....	....	....	....	....
2010-11	San Antonio	AHL	60	10	23	33	26	....	....	....	....	....	....	....	....	....	....	....	....	....	....	....	....	....	....
2011-12	St. Petersburg	KHL	42	17	13	30	18	....	....	....	....	....	....	....	....	....	10	4	2	6	4	....	....	....	....
2012-13	St. Petersburg	KHL	39	12	15	27	16	....	....	....	....	....	....	....	....	....	15	*10	8	18	20	....	....	....	....
2013-14	St. Petersburg	KHL	52	18	16	34	20	....	....	....	....	....	....	....	....	....	10	2	1	3	2	....	....	....	....
	Russia	Olympics	2	0	1	1	0	....	....	....	....	....	....	....	....	....	....	....	....	....	....	....	....	....	....
2014-15	St. Petersburg	KHL	49	8	16	24	29	....	....	....	....	....	....	....	....	....	15	1	1	2	4	....	....	....	....
	NHL Totals		**61**	**8**	**8**	**16**	**20**	**1**	**0**	**1**	**71**	**11.3**		**60**	**38.3**	**12:08**	....	....	....	....	....	....	....	....	....

• Loaned to **Cherepovets** (KHL) by **Phoenix** (San Antonio) (AHL), November 28, 2009. Signed as a free agent by **St. Petersburg** (KHL), October 11, 2011. Signed as a free agent by **Chicago**, July 1, 2015.

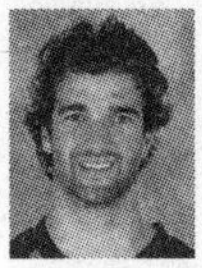

TIMMINS, Scott

(TIHM-mihnz, SKAWT)

Center. Shoots left. 5'11", 190 lbs. Born, Hamilton, ON, September 11, 1989. Florida's 7th choice, 165th overall, in 2009 Entry Draft.

Season	Club	League	GP	G	A	Pts	PIM	PP	SH	GW	S	S%	+/-	TF	F%	Min	GP	G	A	Pts	PIM	PP	SH	GW	Min
2005-06	Burlington	ON-Jr.A	31	8	4	12	8	....	....	....	....	....	....	....	....	....	4	1	1	2	0	....	....	....	....
2006-07	Kitchener Rangers	OHL	42	2	5	7	8	....	....	....	....	....	....	....	....	....	....	....	....	....	....	....	....	....	....
2007-08	Kitchener Rangers	OHL	62	17	12	29	46	....	....	....	....	....	....	....	....	....	20	3	5	8	10	....	....	....	....
2008-09	Kitchener Rangers	OHL	38	25	24	49	28	....	....	....	....	....	....	....	....	....	....	....	....	....	....	....	....	....	....
	Windsor Spitfires	OHL	28	10	14	24	33	....	....	....	....	....	....	....	....	....	20	6	10	16	26	....	....	....	....
2009-10	Windsor Spitfires	OHL	56	30	24	54	47	....	....	....	....	....	....	....	....	....	19	11	11	22	18	....	....	....	....
2010-11	**Florida**	**NHL**	**19**	**1**	**0**	**1**	**8**	**0**	**0**	**0**	**13**	**7.7**	**–8**	**130**	**46.9**	**10:49**	....	....	....	....	....	....	....	....	....
	Rochester	AHL	45	10	12	22	18	....	....	....	....	....	....	....	....	....	....	....	....	....	....	....	....	....	....
2011-12	San Antonio	AHL	70	11	16	27	34	....	....	....	....	....	....	....	....	....	10	1	0	1	8	....	....	....	....
2012-13	San Antonio	AHL	65	11	13	24	58	....	....	....	....	....	....	....	....	....	....	....	....	....	....	....	....	....	....
	Florida	**NHL**	**5**	**0**	**0**	**0**	**4**	**0**	**0**	**0**	**6**	**0.0**	**–2**	**31**	**48.4**	**10:35**	....	....	....	....	....	....	....	....	....
2013-14	Albany Devils	AHL	61	13	26	39	26	....	....	....	....	....	....	....	....	....	4	0	0	0	7	....	....	....	....
2014-15	Albany Devils	AHL	41	10	16	26	8	....	....	....	....	....	....	....	....	....	....	....	....	....	....	....	....	....	....
	NHL Totals		**24**	**1**	**0**	**1**	**12**	**0**	**0**	**0**	**19**	**5.3**		**161**	**47.2**	**10:46**	....	....	....	....	....	....	....	....	....

Traded to **New Jersey** by **Florida** with Florida's 6th round choice (Joey Dudek) in 2014 Entry Draft for Krys Barch and St. Louis' 7th round choice (previously acquired, Florida selected Ryan Bednard) in 2015 Entry Draft, September 28, 2013.

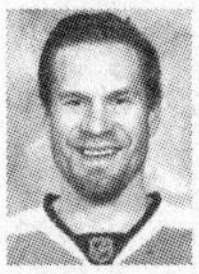

TIMONEN, Kimmo

(TEEM-oh-nehn, KEE-moh)

Defense. Shoots left. 5'10", 194 lbs. Born, Kuopio, Finland, March 18, 1975. Los Angeles' 11th choice, 250th overall, in 1993 Entry Draft.

Season	Club	League	GP	G	A	Pts	PIM	PP	SH	GW	S	S%	+/-	TF	F%	Min	GP	G	A	Pts	PIM	PP	SH	GW	Min
1990-91	KalPa Kuopio Jr.	Fin-Jr.	4	0	1	1	2	....	....	....	....	....	....	....	....	....	....	....	....	....	....	....	....	....	....
1991-92	KalPa Kuopio Jr.	Fin-Jr.	32	7	10	17	4	....	....	....	....	....	....	....	....	....	....	....	....	....	....	....	....	....	....
	KalPa Kuopio	Finland	5	0	0	0	0	....	....	....	....	....	....	....	....	....	....	....	....	....	....	....	....	....	....
1992-93	KalPa Kuopio U18	Fin-U18	3	0	5	5	0	....	....	....	....	....	....	....	....	....	....	....	....	....	....	....	....	....	....
	KalPa Kuopio Jr.	Fin-Jr.	16	9	15	24	10	....	....	....	....	....	....	....	....	....	....	....	....	....	....	....	....	....	....
	KalPa Kuopio	Finland	33	0	2	2	4	....	....	....	....	....	....	....	....	....	....	....	....	....	....	....	....	....	....
1993-94	KalPa Kuopio Jr.	Fin-Jr.	5	4	7	11	0	....	....	....	....	....	....	....	....	....	....	....	....	....	....	....	....	....	....
	KalPa Kuopio	Finland	46	6	7	13	55	....	....	....	....	....	....	....	....	....	....	....	....	....	....	....	....	....	....
1994-95	TPS Turku Jr.	Fin-Jr.	1	0	0	0	0	....	....	....	....	....	....	....	....	....	....	....	....	....	....	....	....	....	....
	TPS Turku	Finland	45	3	4	7	10	....	....	....	....	....	....	....	....	....	13	0	1	1	6	....	....	....	....
1995-96	TPS Turku	Finland	48	3	21	24	22	....	....	....	....	....	....	....	....	....	9	1	2	3	12	....	....	....	....
1996-97	TPS Turku	Finland	50	10	14	24	18	....	....	....	....	....	....	....	....	....	12	2	7	9	6	....	....	....	....
	TPS Turku	EuroHL	6	1	0	1	27	....	....	....	....	....	....	....	....	....	4	0	1	1	0	....	....	....	....
1997-98	HIFK Helsinki	Finland	45	10	15	25	24	....	....	....	....	....	....	....	....	....	9	3	4	7	8	....	....	....	....
	Finland	Olympics	6	0	1	1	2	....	....	....	....	....	....	....	....	....	....	....	....	....	....	....	....	....	....
1998-99	**Nashville**	**NHL**	**50**	**4**	**8**	**12**	**30**	**1**	**0**	**0**	**75**	**5.3**	**–4**	**0**	**0.0**	**19:04**	....	....	....	....	....	....	....	....	....
	Milwaukee	IHL	29	2	13	15	22	....	....	....	....	....	....	....	....	....	....	....	....	....	....	....	....	....	....
99-2000	**Nashville**	**NHL**	**51**	**8**	**25**	**33**	**26**	**2**	**1**	**2**	**97**	**8.2**	**–5**	**0**	**0.0**	**21:06**	....	....	....	....	....	....	....	....	....
2000-01	**Nashville**	**NHL**	**82**	**12**	**13**	**25**	**50**	**6**	**0**	**3**	**151**	**7.9**	**–6**	**2**	**50.0**	**23:11**	....	....	....	....	....	....	....	....	....
2001-02	**Nashville**	**NHL**	**82**	**13**	**29**	**42**	**28**	**9**	**0**	**1**	**154**	**8.4**	**2**	**0**	**0.0**	**24:12**	....	....	....	....	....	....	....	....	....
	Finland	Olympics	4	0	1	1	2	....	....	....	....	....	....	....	....	....	....	....	....	....	....	....	....	....	....
2002-03	**Nashville**	**NHL**	**72**	**6**	**34**	**40**	**46**	**4**	**0**	**0**	**144**	**4.2**	**–3**	**0**	**0.0**	**22:25**	....	....	....	....	....	....	....	....	....
2003-04	**Nashville**	**NHL**	**77**	**12**	**32**	**44**	**52**	**8**	**0**	**1**	**180**	**6.7**	**–7**	**1**	**0.0**	**23:52**	**6**	**0**	**0**	**0**	**10**	**0**	**0**	**0**	**24:16**
2004-05	HC Lugano	Swiss	3	0	1	1	0	....	....	....	....	....	....	....	....	....	....	....	....	....	....	....	....	....	....
	Brynas IF Gavle	Sweden	10	5	3	8	8	....	....	....	....	....	....	....	....	....	....	....	....	....	....	....	....	....	....
	KalPa Kuopio	Finland-2	12	4	13	17	6	....	....	....	....	....	....	....	....	....	8	3	7	10	4	....	....	....	....
2005-06	**Nashville**	**NHL**	**79**	**11**	**39**	**50**	**74**	**8**	**0**	**1**	**156**	**7.1**	**–3**	**5**	**80.0**	**22:26**	**5**	**1**	**3**	**4**	**4**	**0**	**1**	**0**	**24:42**
	Finland	Olympics	8	1	4	5	2	....	....	....	....	....	....	....	....	....	....	....	....	....	....	....	....	....	....
2006-07	**Nashville**	**NHL**	**80**	**13**	**42**	**55**	**42**	**8**	**0**	**2**	**121**	**10.7**	**20**	**1**	**0.0**	**21:51**	**5**	**0**	**2**	**2**	**4**	**0**	**0**	**0**	**24:33**
2007-08	**Philadelphia**	**NHL**	**80**	**8**	**36**	**44**	**50**	**3**	**1**	**1**	**125**	**6.4**	**0**	**0**	**0.0**	**23:35**	**13**	**0**	**6**	**6**	**8**	**0**	**0**	**0**	**24:41**
2008-09	**Philadelphia**	**NHL**	**77**	**3**	**40**	**43**	**54**	**2**	**0**	**0**	**104**	**2.9**	**19**	**2**	**0.0**	**24:31**	**6**	**0**	**1**	**1**	**12**	**0**	**0**	**0**	**26:21**
2009-10	**Philadelphia**	**NHL**	**82**	**6**	**33**	**39**	**50**	**1**	**2**	**1**	**121**	**5.0**	**–2**	**0**	**0.0**	**22:53**	**23**	**1**	**10**	**11**	**20**	**0**	**0**	**0**	**26:38**
	Finland	Olympics	6	2	2	4	2	....	....	....	....	....	....	....	....	....	....	....	....	....	....	....	....	....	....
2010-11	**Philadelphia**	**NHL**	**82**	**6**	**31**	**37**	**36**	**1**	**2**	**0**	**147**	**4.1**	**11**	**1**	**0.0**	**22:28**	**11**	**1**	**5**	**6**	**14**	**0**	**0**	**0**	**24:53**
2011-12	**Philadelphia**	**NHL**	**76**	**4**	**39**	**43**	**46**	**4**	**0**	**0**	**130**	**3.1**	**8**	**1**	**100.0**	**21:14**	**11**	**1**	**3**	**4**	**23**	**1**	**0**	**0**	**20:11**
2012-13	**Philadelphia**	**NHL**	**45**	**5**	**24**	**29**	**36**	**3**	**0**	**1**	**78**	**6.4**	**3**	**0**	**0.0**	**21:46**	....	....	....	....	....	....	....	....	....
2013-14	**Philadelphia**	**NHL**	**77**	**6**	**29**	**35**	**32**	**1**	**0**	**1**	**152**	**3.9**	**5**	**0**	**0.0**	**20:20**	**7**	**0**	**1**	**1**	**4**	**0**	**0**	**0**	**20:01**
	Finland	Olympics	6	0	2	2	2	....	....	....	....	....	....	....	....	....	....	....	....	....	....	....	....	....	....
2014-15 ♦	**Chicago**	**NHL**	**16**	**0**	**0**	**0**	**2**	**0**	**0**	**0**	**10**	**0.0**	**–3**	**0**	**0.0**	**11:59**	**18**	**0**	**0**	**0**	**10**	**0**	**0**	**0**	**8:40**
	NHL Totals		**1108**	**117**	**454**	**571**	**654**	**61**	**6**	**14**	**1945**	**6.0**		**13**	**46.2**	**22:19**	**105**	**4**	**31**	**35**	**109**	**1**	**1**	**0**	**21:40**

Olympic All-Star Team (2006)

Played in NHL All-Star Game (2004, 2007, 2008, 2012)

Traded to **Nashville** by **Los Angeles** with Jan Vopat for future considerations, June 26, 1998. Signed as a free agent by **Lugano** (Swiss), October 31, 2004. Signed as a free agent by **Gavle** (Sweden), November 8, 2004. Signed as a free agent by **Kuopio** (Finland-2), January 3, 2005. Traded to **Philadelphia** by **Nashville** with Scott Hartnell for Nashville's 1st round choice (previously acquired, Nashville selected Jonathon Blum) in 2007 Entry Draft, June 18, 2007. Traded to **Chicago** by **Philadelphia** for Chicago's 2nd round choice (later traded to Toronto – Toronto selected Jeremy Bracco) in 2015 Entry Draft and future considerations, February 27, 2015. • Missed majority of 2014-15 due to blood clots in right leg and both lungs. • Officially announced his retirement, June 16, 2015.

			Regular Season														Playoffs								
Season	Club	League	GP	G	A	Pts	PIM	PP	SH	GW	S	S%	+/-	TF	F%	Min	GP	G	A	Pts	PIM	PP	SH	GW	Min

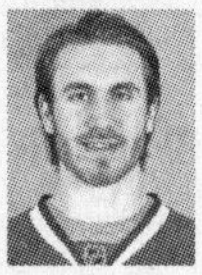

TINORDI, Jarred
(tih-NOHR-dee, JAIR-uhd) **MTL**

Defense. Shoots left. 6'6", 225 lbs. Born, Burnsville, MN, February 20, 1992. Montreal's 1st choice, 22nd overall, in 2010 Entry Draft.

2008-09	USNTDP	NAHL	42	2	13	15	53	....	....	....	....	....	....	....	....	....	9	1	0	1	6	....	....	....	....
	USNTDP	U-17	16	3	1	4	12	....	....	....	....	....	....	....	....	....	....	....	....	....	....	....	....	....	....
	USNTDP	U-18	1	0	1	1	0	....	....	....	....	....	....	....	....	....	....	....	....	....	....	....	....	....	....
2009-10	USNTDP	USHL	26	4	5	9	68	....	....	....	....	....	....	....	....	....	....	....	....	....	....	....	....	....	....
	USNTDP	U-18	39	2	6	8	37	....	....	....	....	....	....	....	....	....	....	....	....	....	....	....	....	....	....
2010-11	London Knights	OHL	63	1	13	14	140	....	....	....	....	....	....	....	....	....	6	0	0	0	17	....	....	....	....
2011-12	London Knights	OHL	48	2	14	16	63	....	....	....	....	....	....	....	....	....	19	3	5	8	27	....	....	....	....
2012-13	**Montreal**	**NHL**	**8**	**0**	**2**	**2**	**2**	**0**	**0**	**0**	**5**	**0.0**	**5**	**0**	**0.0**	**11:43**	**5**	**0**	**1**	**1**	**15**	**0**	**0**	**0**	**13:05**
	Hamilton	AHL	67	2	11	13	71	....	....	....	....	....	....	....	....	....	....	....	....	....	....	....	....	....	....
2013-14	**Montreal**	**NHL**	**22**	**0**	**2**	**2**	**40**	**0**	**0**	**0**	**10**	**0.0**	**-2**	**0**	**0.0**	**14:32**	....	....	....	....	....	....	....	....	....
	Hamilton	AHL	47	3	6	9	70	....	....	....	....	....	....	....	....	....	....	....	....	....	....	....	....	....	....
2014-15	**Montreal**	**NHL**	**13**	**0**	**2**	**2**	**19**	**0**	**0**	**0**	**5**	**0.0**	**-5**	**0**	**0.0**	**12:04**	....	....	....	....	....	....	....	....	....
	Hamilton	AHL	44	1	6	7	36	....	....	....	....	....	....	....	....	....	....	....	....	....	....	....	....	....	....
	NHL Totals		**43**	**0**	**6**	**6**	**61**	**0**	**0**	**0**	**20**	**0.0**		**0**	**0.0**	**13:16**	**5**	**0**	**1**	**1**	**15**	**0**	**0**	**0**	**13:05**

Memorial Cup All-Star Team (2012)

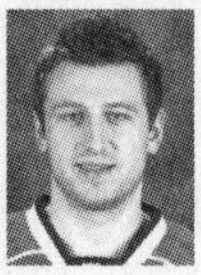

TLUSTY, Jiri
(T'LOO-stee, YIH-ree)

Center. Shoots left. 6', 209 lbs. Born, Slany, Czech., March 16, 1988. Toronto's 1st choice, 13th overall, in 2006 Entry Draft.

2002-03	HC Kladno U17	CzR-U17	48	28	17	45	22	....	....	....	....	....	....	....	....	....	10	5	4	9	12	....	....	....	....
2003-04	HC Kladno U17	CzR-U17	1	0	0	0	2	....	....	....	....	....	....	....	....	....	1	0	0	0	2	....	....	....	....
	HC Kladno Jr.	CzRep-Jr.	51	10	3	13	12	....	....	....	....	....	....	....	....	....	1	0	0	0	0	....	....	....	....
2004-05	HC Kladno Jr.	CzRep-Jr.	42	15	12	27	54	....	....	....	....	....	....	....	....	....	10	2	2	4	8	....	....	....	....
2005-06	HC Kladno Jr.	CzRep-Jr.	6	4	2	6	2	....	....	....	....	....	....	....	....	....	6	7	6	13	6	....	....	....	....
	HC Rabat Kladno	CzRep	44	7	3	10	51	....	....	....	....	....	....	....	....	....	....	....	....	....	....	....	....	....	....
2006-07	Sault Ste. Marie	OHL	37	13	21	34	28	....	....	....	....	....	....	....	....	....	13	9	8	17	14	....	....	....	....
	Toronto Marlies	AHL	6	3	1	4	4	....	....	....	....	....	....	....	....	....	....	....	....	....	....	....	....	....	....
2007-08	**Toronto**	**NHL**	**58**	**10**	**6**	**16**	**14**	**2**	**0**	**2**	**69**	**14.5**	**-12**	**2**	**50.0**	**10:55**	....	....	....	....	....	....	....	....	....
	Toronto Marlies	AHL	14	7	11	18	8	....	....	....	....	....	....	....	....	....	19	2	8	10	8	....	....	....	....
2008-09	**Toronto**	**NHL**	**14**	**0**	**4**	**4**	**0**	**0**	**0**	**0**	**22**	**0.0**	**0**	**3**	**33.3**	**12:42**	....	....	....	....	....	....	....	....	....
	Toronto Marlies	AHL	66	25	41	66	26	....	....	....	....	....	....	....	....	....	6	1	2	3	2	....	....	....	....
2009-10	**Toronto**	**NHL**	**2**	**0**	**0**	**0**	**0**	**0**	**0**	**0**	**2**	**0.0**	**-2**	**0**	**0.0**	**12:13**	....	....	....	....	....	....	....	....	....
	Toronto Marlies	AHL	19	8	7	15	4	....	....	....	....	....	....	....	....	....	....	....	....	....	....	....	....	....	....
	Carolina	**NHL**	**18**	**1**	**5**	**6**	**6**	**0**	**0**	**0**	**15**	**6.7**	**2**	**2**	**100.0**	**12:36**	....	....	....	....	....	....	....	....	....
	Albany River Rats	AHL	20	6	9	15	10	....	....	....	....	....	....	....	....	....	5	0	1	1	0	....	....	....	....
2010-11	**Carolina**	**NHL**	**57**	**6**	**6**	**12**	**14**	**0**	**0**	**0**	**53**	**11.3**	**1**	**15**	**13.3**	**9:52**	....	....	....	....	....	....	....	....	....
	Charlotte	AHL	5	1	1	2	4	....	....	....	....	....	....	....	....	....	....	....	....	....	....	....	....	....	....
2011-12	**Carolina**	**NHL**	**79**	**17**	**19**	**36**	**26**	**2**	**0**	**1**	**136**	**12.5**	**1**	**11**	**27.3**	**14:54**	....	....	....	....	....	....	....	....	....
2012-13	Rytiri Kladno	CzRep	24	12	11	23	12	....	....	....	....	....	....	....	....	....	....	....	....	....	....	....	....	....	....
	Carolina	**NHL**	**48**	**23**	**15**	**38**	**18**	**4**	**0**	**3**	**117**	**19.7**	**15**	**18**	**16.7**	**18:15**	....	....	....	....	....	....	....	....	....
2013-14	**Carolina**	**NHL**	**68**	**16**	**14**	**30**	**22**	**0**	**2**	**5**	**131**	**12.2**	**2**	**15**	**20.0**	**15:10**	....	....	....	....	....	....	....	....	....
2014-15	**Carolina**	**NHL**	**52**	**13**	**10**	**23**	**16**	**6**	**0**	**0**	**97**	**13.4**	**-17**	**15**	**33.3**	**17:12**	....	....	....	....	....	....	....	....	....
	Winnipeg	**NHL**	**20**	**1**	**7**	**8**	**4**	**0**	**0**	**0**	**26**	**3.8**	**-1**	**0**	**0.0**	**12:57**	**4**	**0**	**0**	**0**	**0**	**0**	**0**	**0**	**10:12**
	NHL Totals		**416**	**87**	**86**	**173**	**120**	**14**	**2**	**11**	**668**	**13.0**		**81**	**24.7**	**14:06**	**4**	**0**	**0**	**0**	**0**	**0**	**0**	**0**	**10:12**

Traded to **Carolina** by **Toronto** for Philippe Paradis, December 3, 2009. Signed as a free agent by **Kladno** (CzRep), September 17, 2012. Traded to **Winnipeg** by **Carolina** for Winnipeg's 5th round choice (Spencer Smallman) in 2015 Entry Draft and a 3rd round choice in 2016 Entry Draft, February 25, 2015.

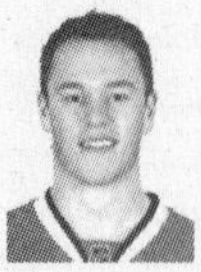

TOEWS, Jonathan
(TAYVZ, JAWN-ah-thuhn) **CHI**

Center. Shoots left. 6'2", 201 lbs. Born, Winnipeg, MB, April 29, 1988. Chicago's 1st choice, 3rd overall, in 2006 Entry Draft.

2004-05	Shat.-St. Mary's	High-MN	64	48	62	110	38	....	....	....	....	....	....	....	....	....	....	....	....	....	....	....	....	....	....
2005-06	North Dakota	WCHA	42	22	17	39	22	....	....	....	....	....	....	....	....	....	....	....	....	....	....	....	....	....	....
2006-07	North Dakota	WCHA	34	18	28	46	10	....	....	....	....	....	....	....	....	....	....	....	....	....	....	....	....	....	....
2007-08	**Chicago**	**NHL**	**64**	**24**	**30**	**54**	**44**	**7**	**0**	**4**	**144**	**16.7**	**11**	**956**	**53.2**	**18:40**	....	....	....	....	....	....	....	....	....
2008-09	**Chicago**	**NHL**	**82**	**34**	**35**	**69**	**51**	**12**	**0**	**7**	**195**	**17.4**	**12**	**1287**	**54.7**	**18:38**	**17**	**7**	**6**	**13**	**26**	**5**	**0**	**2**	**16:14**
2009-10♦	**Chicago**	**NHL**	**76**	**25**	**43**	**68**	**47**	**9**	**1**	**3**	**202**	**12.4**	**22**	**1397**	**57.3**	**20:00**	**22**	**7**	***22**	**29**	**4**	**5**	**0**	**3**	**20:58**
	Canada	Olympics	7	1	*7	8	2	....	....	....	....	....	....	....	....	....	....	....	....	....	....	....	....	....	....
2010-11	**Chicago**	**NHL**	**80**	**32**	**44**	**76**	**26**	**10**	**1**	**8**	**233**	**13.7**	**25**	**1653**	**56.7**	**20:46**	**7**	**1**	**3**	**4**	**2**	**0**	**1**	**0**	**22:31**
2011-12	**Chicago**	**NHL**	**59**	**29**	**28**	**57**	**28**	**5**	**1**	**4**	**185**	**15.7**	**17**	**1137**	**59.4**	**20:51**	**6**	**2**	**2**	**4**	**6**	**0**	**0**	**1**	**22:17**
2012-13♦	**Chicago**	**NHL**	**47**	**23**	**25**	**48**	**27**	**2**	**2**	**5**	**143**	**16.1**	**28**	**933**	**59.9**	**19:21**	**23**	**3**	**11**	**14**	**18**	**1**	**0**	**0**	**21:33**
2013-14	**Chicago**	**NHL**	**76**	**28**	**40**	**68**	**34**	**5**	**3**	**5**	**193**	**14.5**	**26**	**1544**	**57.3**	**20:28**	**19**	**9**	**8**	**17**	**8**	**2**	**1**	***4**	**21:43**
	Canada	Olympics	6	1	2	3	0	....	....	....	....	....	....	....	....	....	....	....	....	....	....	....	....	....	....
2014-15♦	**Chicago**	**NHL**	**81**	**28**	**38**	**66**	**36**	**6**	**2**	**7**	**192**	**14.6**	**30**	**1675**	**56.5**	**19:34**	**23**	**10**	**11**	**21**	**8**	**3**	**1**	**0**	**20:54**
	NHL Totals		**565**	**223**	**283**	**506**	**293**	**56**	**10**	**43**	**1487**	**15.0**		**10582**	**56.9**	**19:48**	**117**	**39**	**63**	**102**	**72**	**16**	**3**	**10**	**20:40**

WCHA Second All-Star Team (2007) • NCAA West First All-American Team (2007) • NHL All-Rookie Team (2008) • Olympic All-Star Team (2010) • Best Forward – Olympics (2010) • Conn Smythe Trophy (2010) • Frank J. Selke Trophy (2013) • NHL Second All-Star Team (2013) • Mark Messier NHL Leadership Award (2015)

Played in NHL All-Star Game (2009, 2011, 2015)

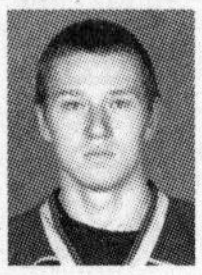

TOFFOLI, Tyler
(TAW-foh-lee, TIGH-luhr) **L.A.**

Center. Shoots right. 6'1", 197 lbs. Born, Scarborough, ON, April 24, 1992. Los Angeles' 2nd choice, 47th overall, in 2010 Entry Draft.

2007-08	Tor. Jr. Canadiens	GTHL	83	68	106	174	72	....	....	....	....	....	....	....	....	....	....	....	....	....	....	....	....	....	....
2008-09	Ottawa 67's	OHL	54	17	29	46	16	....	....	....	....	....	....	....	....	....	7	2	6	8	4	....	....	....	....
2009-10	Ottawa 67's	OHL	65	37	42	79	54	....	....	....	....	....	....	....	....	....	12	7	6	13	10	....	....	....	....
2010-11	Ottawa 67's	OHL	68	*57	51	*108	33	....	....	....	....	....	....	....	....	....	4	3	5	8	4	....	....	....	....
	Manchester	AHL	1	1	0	1	0	....	....	....	....	....	....	....	....	....	5	1	0	1	6	....	....	....	....
2011-12	Ottawa 67's	OHL	65	*52	48	100	22	....	....	....	....	....	....	....	....	....	18	11	7	18	21	....	....	....	....
2012-13	Manchester	AHL	58	28	23	51	18	....	....	....	....	....	....	....	....	....	....	....	....	....	....	....	....	....	....
	Los Angeles	**NHL**	**10**	**2**	**3**	**5**	**2**	**1**	**0**	**0**	**20**	**10.0**	**3**	**0**	**0.0**	**11:59**	**12**	**2**	**4**	**6**	**0**	**1**	**0**	**0**	**10:46**
2013-14♦	**Los Angeles**	**NHL**	**62**	**12**	**17**	**29**	**10**	**1**	**0**	**5**	**124**	**9.7**	**21**	**9**	**22.2**	**12:56**	**26**	**7**	**7**	**14**	**10**	**0**	**0**	**2**	**13:18**
	Manchester	AHL	18	15	8	23	4	....	....	....	....	....	....	....	....	....	....	....	....	....	....	....	....	....	....
2014-15	**Los Angeles**	**NHL**	**76**	**23**	**26**	**49**	**37**	**3**	**5**	**3**	**200**	**11.5**	**25**	**9**	**44.4**	**14:35**	....	....	....	....	....	....	....	....	....
	NHL Totals		**148**	**37**	**46**	**83**	**49**	**5**	**5**	**8**	**344**	**10.8**		**18**	**33.3**	**13:43**	**38**	**9**	**11**	**20**	**10**	**1**	**0**	**2**	**12:30**

OHL First All-Star Team (2011, 2012) • AHL All-Rookie Team (2013) • Dudley "Red" Garrett Memorial Trophy (AHL - Top Rookie) (2013)

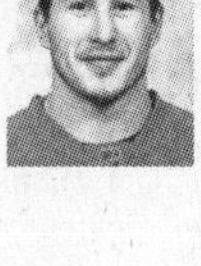

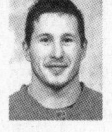

TOOTOO, Jordin
(TOO-TOO, JOHR-dahn) **N.J.**

Right wing. Shoots right. 5'9", 195 lbs. Born, Churchill, MB, February 2, 1983. Nashville's 6th choice, 98th overall, in 2001 Entry Draft.

1997-98	Spruce Grove	AMBHL	34	20	10	30	149	....	....	....	....	....	....	....	....	....	....	....	....	....	....	....	....	....	....
1998-99	OCN Blizzard	MJHL	47	16	21	37	251	....	....	....	....	....	....	....	....	....	....	....	....	....	....	....	....	....	....
99-2000	Brandon	WHL	45	6	10	16	214	....	....	....	....	....	....	....	....	....	....	....	....	....	....	....	....	....	....
2000-01	Brandon	WHL	60	20	28	48	172	....	....	....	....	....	....	....	....	....	6	2	4	6	18	....	....	....	....
2001-02	Brandon	WHL	64	32	39	71	272	....	....	....	....	....	....	....	....	....	16	4	3	7	*58	....	....	....	....
2002-03	Brandon	WHL	51	35	39	74	216	....	....	....	....	....	....	....	....	....	17	6	3	9	49	....	....	....	....
2003-04	**Nashville**	**NHL**	**70**	**4**	**4**	**8**	**137**	**2**	**0**	**0**	**92**	**4.3**	**-6**	**18**	**55.6**	**8:29**	**5**	**0**	**0**	**0**	**4**	**0**	**0**	**0**	**5:09**
2004-05	Milwaukee	AHL	59	10	12	22	266	....	....	....	....	....	....	....	....	....	6	0	0	0	41	....	....	....	....
2005-06	**Nashville**	**NHL**	**34**	**4**	**6**	**10**	**55**	**0**	**0**	**0**	**61**	**6.6**	**9**	**17**	**70.6**	**9:15**	**3**	**0**	**0**	**0**	**0**	**0**	**0**	**0**	**4:04**
	Milwaukee	AHL	41	13	14	27	133	....	....	....	....	....	....	....	....	....	15	9	2	11	35	....	....	....	....
2006-07	**Nashville**	**NHL**	**65**	**3**	**6**	**9**	**116**	**0**	**0**	**0**	**77**	**3.9**	**-11**	**12**	**33.3**	**8:24**	**4**	**0**	**1**	**1**	**21**	**0**	**0**	**0**	**9:32**
2007-08	**Nashville**	**NHL**	**63**	**11**	**7**	**18**	**100**	**0**	**0**	**1**	**98**	**11.2**	**-8**	**4**	**50.0**	**9:54**	**6**	**2**	**0**	**2**	**4**	**0**	**0**	**0**	**12:31**
2008-09	**Nashville**	**NHL**	**72**	**4**	**12**	**16**	**124**	**0**	**0**	**1**	**138**	**2.9**	**-15**	**16**	**56.3**	**12:05**	....	....	....	....	....	....	....	....	....
2009-10	**Nashville**	**NHL**	**51**	**6**	**10**	**16**	**40**	**0**	**0**	**1**	**101**	**5.9**	**2**	**8**	**25.0**	**10:50**	**6**	**0**	**1**	**1**	**2**	**0**	**0**	**0**	**7:58**
2010-11	**Nashville**	**NHL**	**54**	**8**	**10**	**18**	**61**	**0**	**0**	**1**	**85**	**9.4**	**8**	**3**	**66.7**	**11:53**	**12**	**1**	**5**	**6**	**28**	**0**	**0**	**0**	**13:26**
2011-12	**Nashville**	**NHL**	**77**	**6**	**24**	**30**	**92**	**1**	**0**	**1**	**136**	**4.4**	**-5**	**12**	**33.3**	**13:09**	**3**	**0**	**0**	**0**	**4**	**0**	**0**	**0**	**7:46**
2012-13	**Detroit**	**NHL**	**42**	**3**	**5**	**8**	**78**	**0**	**0**	**1**	**45**	**6.7**	**0**	**0**	**0.0**	**9:05**	**1**	**0**	**0**	**0**	**2**	**0**	**0**	**0**	**6:24**

			Regular Season														Playoffs								
Season	Club	League	GP	G	A	Pts	PIM	PP	SH	GW	S	S%	+/-	TF	F%	Min	GP	G	A	Pts	PIM	PP	SH	GW	Min
2013-14	**Detroit**	**NHL**	**11**	**0**	**1**	**1**	**5**	**0**	**0**	**0**	**11**	**0.0**	**–3**	**0**	**0.0**	**6:59**	....	....	....	....	....	....	....	....	....
	Grand Rapids	AHL	51	6	12	18	104	....	....	....	....	....	....	....	....	....	4	0	1	1	4	....	....	....	....
2014-15	**New Jersey**	**NHL**	**68**	**10**	**5**	**15**	**72**	**1**	**0**	**1**	**75**	**13.3**	**1**	**1**	**100.0**	**10:27**	....	....	....	....	....	....	....	....	....
	NHL Totals		**607**	**59**	**90**	**149**	**880**	**4**	**0**	**7**	**919**	**6.4**		**91**	**50.5**	**10:25**	**40**	**3**	**7**	**10**	**65**	**0**	**0**	**0**	**9:45**

WHL East First All-Star Team (2003)

Signed as a free agent by **Detroit**, July 1, 2012. Signed as a free agent by **New Jersey**, October 7, 2014.

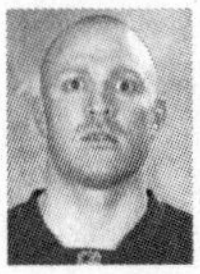

TORRES, Raffi (TOHR-ehz, RA-fee) S.J.

Left wing. Shoots left. 6', 215 lbs. Born, Toronto, ON, October 8, 1981. NY Islanders' 2nd choice, 5th overall, in 2000 Entry Draft.

Season	Club	League	GP	G	A	Pts	PIM	PP	SH	GW	S	S%	+/-	TF	F%	Min	GP	G	A	Pts	PIM	PP	SH	GW	Min
1997-98	Thornhill Rattlers	ON-Jr.A	46	17	16	33	90	....	....	....	....	....	....	....	....	....	....	....	....	....	....	....	....	....	....
1998-99	Brampton	OHL	62	35	27	62	32	....	....	....	....	....	....	....	....	....	....	....	....	....	....	....	....	....	....
99-2000	Brampton	OHL	68	43	48	91	40	....	....	....	....	....	....	....	....	....	6	5	2	7	23	....	....	....	....
2000-01	Brampton	OHL	55	33	37	70	76	....	....	....	....	....	....	....	....	....	8	7	4	11	19	....	....	....	....
2001-02	**NY Islanders**	**NHL**	**14**	**0**	**1**	**1**	**6**	**0**	**0**	**0**	**9**	**0.0**	**2**	**0**	**0.0**	**7:35**	....	....	....	....	....	....	....	....	....
	Bridgeport	AHL	59	20	10	30	45	....	....	....	....	....	....	....	....	....	20	8	9	17	26	....	....	....	....
2002-03	**NY Islanders**	**NHL**	**17**	**0**	**5**	**5**	**10**	**0**	**0**	**0**	**12**	**0.0**	**0**	**4**	**25.0**	**7:40**	....	....	....	....	....	....	....	....	....
	Bridgeport	AHL	49	17	15	32	54	....	....	....	....	....	....	....	....	....	....	....	....	....	....	....	....	....	....
	Hamilton	AHL	11	1	7	8	14	....	....	....	....	....	....	....	....	....	23	6	1	7	29	....	....	....	....
2003-04	**Edmonton**	**NHL**	**80**	**20**	**14**	**34**	**65**	**5**	**0**	**3**	**136**	**14.7**	**12**	**21**	**28.6**	**12:38**	....	....	....	....	....	....	....	....	....
2004-05	Edmonton	AHL	67	21	25	46	165	....	....	....	....	....	....	....	....	....	....	....	....	....	....	....	....	....	....
2005-06	**Edmonton**	**NHL**	**82**	**27**	**14**	**41**	**50**	**6**	**0**	**3**	**164**	**16.5**	**4**	**60**	**41.7**	**13:24**	**22**	**4**	**7**	**11**	**16**	**1**	**0**	**1**	**13:15**
2006-07	**Edmonton**	**NHL**	**82**	**15**	**19**	**34**	**88**	**1**	**0**	**0**	**154**	**9.7**	**–7**	**50**	**44.0**	**14:19**	....	....	....	....	....	....	....	....	....
2007-08	**Edmonton**	**NHL**	**32**	**5**	**6**	**11**	**36**	**1**	**0**	**2**	**87**	**5.7**	**–4**	**20**	**65.0**	**17:01**	....	....	....	....	....	....	....	....	....
2008-09	**Columbus**	**NHL**	**51**	**12**	**8**	**20**	**23**	**2**	**0**	**6**	**74**	**16.2**	**–4**	**19**	**57.9**	**12:06**	**4**	**0**	**2**	**2**	**2**	**0**	**0**	**0**	**12:04**
2009-10	**Columbus**	**NHL**	**60**	**19**	**12**	**31**	**32**	**7**	**0**	**3**	**99**	**19.2**	**–8**	**47**	**36.2**	**13:34**	....	....	....	....	....	....	....	....	....
	Buffalo	**NHL**	**14**	**0**	**5**	**5**	**2**	**0**	**0**	**0**	**21**	**0.0**	**–3**	**3**	**33.3**	**13:21**	**4**	**0**	**2**	**2**	**12**	**0**	**0**	**0**	**12:55**
2010-11	**Vancouver**	**NHL**	**80**	**14**	**15**	**29**	**78**	**3**	**0**	**4**	**115**	**12.2**	**4**	**32**	**31.3**	**12:29**	**23**	**3**	**4**	**7**	**28**	**0**	**0**	**1**	**11:51**
2011-12	**Phoenix**	**NHL**	**79**	**15**	**11**	**26**	**83**	**1**	**0**	**1**	**99**	**15.2**	**2**	**15**	**46.7**	**11:22**	**3**	**1**	**1**	**2**	**2**	**0**	**0**	**0**	**19:16**
2012-13	**Phoenix**	**NHL**	**28**	**5**	**7**	**12**	**13**	**0**	**0**	**0**	**40**	**12.5**	**–1**	**6**	**66.7**	**13:00**	....	....	....	....	....	....	....	....	....
	San Jose	**NHL**	**11**	**2**	**4**	**6**	**4**	**1**	**0**	**0**	**20**	**10.0**	**1**	**7**	**28.6**	**13:57**	**5**	**1**	**0**	**1**	**2**	**0**	**0**	**1**	**17:42**
2013-14	**San Jose**	**NHL**	**5**	**3**	**2**	**5**	**7**	**0**	**0**	**0**	**9**	**33.3**	**4**	**4**	**50.0**	**10:22**	**7**	**2**	**1**	**3**	**18**	**0**	**0**	**1**	**9:10**
2014-15			DID NOT PLAY – INJURED																						
	NHL Totals		**635**	**137**	**123**	**260**	**497**	**27**	**0**	**22**	**1039**	**13.2**		**288**	**42.0**	**12:50**	**68**	**11**	**17**	**28**	**80**	**1**	**0**	**4**	**12:52**

OHL All-Rookie Team (1999) • OHL Second All-Star Team (2000, 2001)

Traded to **Edmonton** by **NY Islanders** with Brad Isbister for Janne Niinimaa and Washington's 2nd round choice (previously acquired, NY Islanders selected Evgeni Tunik) in 2003 Entry Draft, March 11, 2003. • Missed majority of 2007-08 due to knee injury vs. Detroit, December 15, 2007. Traded to **Columbus** by **Edmonton** for Gilbert Brule, July 1, 2008. Traded to **Buffalo** by **Columbus** for Nathan Paetsch and Vancouver's 2nd round choice (previously acquired, Columbus selected Petr Straka) in 2010 Entry Draft, March 3, 2010. Signed as a free agent by **Vancouver**, August 25, 2010. Signed as a free agent by **Phoenix**, July 1, 2011. Traded to **San Jose** by **Phoenix** for Florida's 3rd round choice (previously acquired, later traded to Phoenix – Phoenix selected Pavel Laplante) in 2013 Entry Draft, April 3, 2013. • Missed majority of 2013-14 due to knee surgery, September 26, 2013.

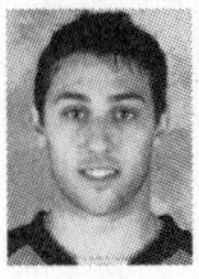

TROCHECK, Vincent (TROH-chehk, VOHN-sihnt) FLA

Center. Shoots right. 5'10", 182 lbs. Born, Pittsburgh, PA, July 11, 1993. Florida's 4th choice, 64th overall, in 2011 Entry Draft.

Season	Club	League	GP	G	A	Pts	PIM	PP	SH	GW	S	S%	+/-	TF	F%	Min	GP	G	A	Pts	PIM	PP	SH	GW	Min
2008-09	Det. Lit. Caesars	T1EHL	44	27	19	46	32	....	....	....	....	....	....	....	....	....	7	1	4	5	0	....	....	....	....
2009-10	Saginaw Spirit	OHL	68	15	28	43	56	....	....	....	....	....	....	....	....	....	6	2	2	4	2	....	....	....	....
2010-11	Saginaw Spirit	OHL	68	26	36	62	60	....	....	....	....	....	....	....	....	....	12	6	5	11	4	....	....	....	....
2011-12	Saginaw Spirit	OHL	65	29	56	85	65	....	....	....	....	....	....	....	....	....	12	5	6	11	10	....	....	....	....
2012-13	Saginaw Spirit	OHL	35	24	26	*50	34	....	....	....	....	....	....	....	....	....	....	....	....	....	....	....	....	....	....
	Plymouth Whalers	OHL	28	26	33	*59	24	....	....	....	....	....	....	....	....	....	15	10	14	24	8	....	....	....	....
2013-14	**Florida**	**NHL**	**20**	**5**	**3**	**8**	**6**	**1**	**1**	**0**	**38**	**13.2**	**–11**	**348**	**47.7**	**18:53**	....	....	....	....	....	....	....	....	....
	San Antonio	AHL	55	16	26	42	32	....	....	....	....	....	....	....	....	....	....	....	....	....	....	....	....	....	....
2014-15	**Florida**	**NHL**	**50**	**7**	**15**	**22**	**24**	**1**	**0**	**0**	**89**	**7.9**	**9**	**481**	**48.7**	**14:00**	....	....	....	....	....	....	....	....	....
	San Antonio	AHL	23	8	11	19	19	....	....	....	....	....	....	....	....	....	3	1	1	2	2	....	....	....	....
	NHL Totals		**70**	**12**	**18**	**30**	**30**	**2**	**1**	**0**	**127**	**9.4**		**829**	**48.3**	**15:24**	....	....	....	....	....	....	....	....	....

OHL First All-Star Team (2013) • OHL Player of the Year (2013)

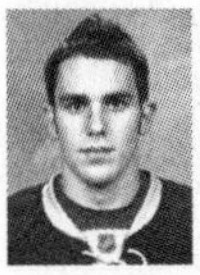

TROPP, Corey (TROHP, KOHR-ee) CHI

Right wing. Shoots right. 6', 185 lbs. Born, Grosse Pointe, MI, July 25, 1989. Buffalo's 3rd choice, 89th overall, in 2007 Entry Draft.

Season	Club	League	GP	G	A	Pts	PIM	PP	SH	GW	S	S%	+/-	TF	F%	Min	GP	G	A	Pts	PIM	PP	SH	GW	Min
2005-06	Sioux Falls	USHL	46	7	8	15	21	....	....	....	....	....	....	....	....	....	14	2	3	5	8	....	....	....	....
2006-07	Sioux Falls	USHL	54	26	36	62	76	....	....	....	....	....	....	....	....	....	8	4	9	*13	0	....	....	....	....
2007-08	Michigan State	CCHA	42	6	11	17	16	....	....	....	....	....	....	....	....	....	....	....	....	....	....	....	....	....	....
2008-09	Michigan State	CCHA	21	3	8	11	45	....	....	....	....	....	....	....	....	....	....	....	....	....	....	....	....	....	....
2009-10	Michigan State	CCHA	37	20	22	42	50	....	....	....	....	....	....	....	....	....	....	....	....	....	....	....	....	....	....
2010-11	Portland Pirates	AHL	76	10	30	40	113	....	....	....	....	....	....	....	....	....	12	2	5	7	12	....	....	....	....
2011-12	**Buffalo**	**NHL**	**34**	**3**	**5**	**8**	**20**	**0**	**0**	**1**	**32**	**9.4**	**0**	**5**	**0.0**	**10:05**	....	....	....	....	....	....	....	....	....
	Rochester	AHL	27	9	13	22	46	....	....	....	....	....	....	....	....	....	3	0	0	0	8	....	....	....	....
2012-13	Rochester	AHL	6	2	2	4	7	....	....	....	....	....	....	....	....	....	....	....	....	....	....	....	....	....	....
2013-14	**Buffalo**	**NHL**	**9**	**0**	**1**	**1**	**0**	**0**	**0**	**0**	**7**	**0.0**	**–8**	**0**	**0.0**	**10:29**	....	....	....	....	....	....	....	....	....
	Columbus	**NHL**	**44**	**2**	**8**	**10**	**37**	**0**	**0**	**0**	**28**	**7.1**	**11**	**1**	**0.0**	**8:37**	**2**	**0**	**0**	**0**	**0**	**0**	**0**	**0**	**6:11**
2014-15	**Columbus**	**NHL**	**61**	**1**	**7**	**8**	**76**	**0**	**0**	**0**	**22**	**4.5**	**–14**	**2**	**50.0**	**8:45**	....	....	....	....	....	....	....	....	....
	NHL Totals		**148**	**6**	**21**	**27**	**133**	**0**	**0**	**1**	**89**	**6.7**		**8**	**12.5**	**9:08**	**2**	**0**	**0**	**0**	**0**	**0**	**0**	**0**	**6:11**

CCHA Second All-Star Team (2010)

Claimed on waivers by **Columbus** from **Buffalo**, November 28, 2013. Traded to **Chicago** by **Columbus** with Artem Anisimov, Jeremy Morin, Marko Dano and Columbus' 4th round choice in 2016 Entry Draft for Brandon Saad, Michael Paliotta and Alex Broadhurst, June 30, 2015.

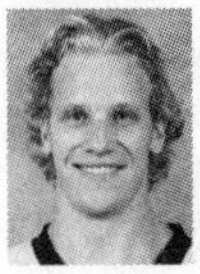

TROTMAN, Zach (TRAWT-muhn, ZAK) BOS

Defense. Shoots right. 6'3", 219 lbs. Born, Novi, MI, August 26, 1990. Boston's 8th choice, 210th overall, in 2010 Entry Draft.

Season	Club	League	GP	G	A	Pts	PIM	PP	SH	GW	S	S%	+/-	TF	F%	Min	GP	G	A	Pts	PIM	PP	SH	GW	Min
2008-09	Wichita Falls	NAHL	47	2	4	6	79	....	....	....	....	....	....	....	....	....	5	0	1	1	8	....	....	....	....
2009-10	Lake Superior	CCHA	36	2	6	8	18	....	....	....	....	....	....	....	....	....	....	....	....	....	....	....	....	....	....
2010-11	Lake Superior	CCHA	38	6	14	20	12	....	....	....	....	....	....	....	....	....	....	....	....	....	....	....	....	....	....
2011-12	Lake Superior	CCHA	40	11	10	21	12	....	....	....	....	....	....	....	....	....	....	....	....	....	....	....	....	....	....
	Providence Bruins	AHL	9	1	2	3	2	....	....	....	....	....	....	....	....	....	....	....	....	....	....	....	....	....	....
2012-13	Providence Bruins	AHL	48	2	14	16	19	....	....	....	....	....	....	....	....	....	4	0	0	0	0	....	....	....	....
2013-14	**Boston**	**NHL**	**2**	**0**	**0**	**0**	**0**	**0**	**0**	**0**	**4**	**0.0**	**0**	**0**	**0.0**	**15:00**	....	....	....	....	....	....	....	....	....
	Providence Bruins	AHL	53	8	16	24	21	....	....	....	....	....	....	....	....	....	8	0	4	4	14	....	....	....	....
2014-15	**Boston**	**NHL**	**27**	**1**	**4**	**5**	**0**	**0**	**0**	**1**	**46**	**2.2**	**–2**	**0**	**0.0**	**16:24**	....	....	....	....	....	....	....	....	....
	Providence Bruins	AHL	40	2	11	13	27	....	....	....	....	....	....	....	....	....	5	1	0	1	2	....	....	....	....
	NHL Totals		**29**	**1**	**4**	**5**	**0**	**0**	**0**	**1**	**50**	**2.0**		**0**	**0.0**	**16:19**	....	....	....	....	....	....	....	....	....

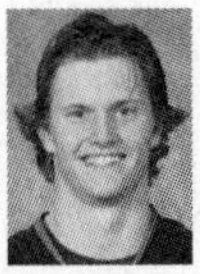

TROUBA, Jacob (TROO-buh, JAY-kuhb) WPG

Defense. Shoots right. 6'2", 187 lbs. Born, Rochester, MI, February 26, 1994. Winnipeg's 1st choice, 9th overall, in 2012 Entry Draft.

Season	Club	League	GP	G	A	Pts	PIM	PP	SH	GW	S	S%	+/-	TF	F%	Min	GP	G	A	Pts	PIM	PP	SH	GW	Min
2009-10	Det. Compuware	T1EHL	38	14	14	28	40	....	....	....	....	....	....	....	....	....	....	....	....	....	....	....	....	....	....
	Det. Compuware	Other	6	3	5	8	12	....	....	....	....	....	....	....	....	....	....	....	....	....	....	....	....	....	....
	Det. Comp. U18	T1EHL	3	3	0	3	2	....	....	....	....	....	....	....	....	....	....	....	....	....	....	....	....	....	....
2010-11	USNTDP	USHL	31	3	4	7	31	....	....	....	....	....	....	....	....	....	....	....	....	....	....	....	....	....	....
	USNTDP	U-17	17	4	12	16	18	....	....	....	....	....	....	....	....	....	....	....	....	....	....	....	....	....	....
	USNTDP	U-18	10	1	2	3	10	....	....	....	....	....	....	....	....	....	....	....	....	....	....	....	....	....	....
2011-12	USNTDP	USHL	22	4	14	18	35	....	....	....	....	....	....	....	....	....	....	....	....	....	....	....	....	....	....
	USNTDP	U-18	32	5	9	14	36	....	....	....	....	....	....	....	....	....	....	....	....	....	....	....	....	....	....
2012-13	U. of Michigan	CCHA	37	12	17	29	88	....	....	....	....	....	....	....	....	....	....	....	....	....	....	....	....	....	....

			Regular Season														Playoffs								
Season	Club	League	GP	G	A	Pts	PIM	PP	SH	GW	S	S%	+/-	TF	F%	Min	GP	G	A	Pts	PIM	PP	SH	GW	Min
2013-14	Winnipeg	NHL	65	10	19	29	43	0	1	1	121	8.3	4	0	0.0	22:26	....	....	....	....	....	....	....	....	....
2014-15	Winnipeg	NHL	65	7	15	22	46	1	0	0	133	5.3	2	1	0.0	23:19	4	0	2	2	2	0	0	0	19:06
	NHL Totals		130	17	34	51	89	1	1	1	254	6.7		1	0.0	22:53	4	0	2	2	2	0	0	0	19:06

CCHA All-Rookie Team (2013) • CCHA First All-Star Team (2013) • NCAA West First All-American Team (2013)

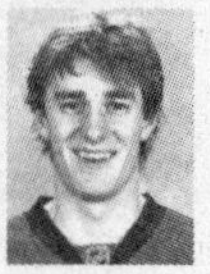

TURRIS, Kyle

(TUH-rihs, KIGHL) **OTT**

Center. Shoots right. 6'1", 190 lbs. Born, New Westminster, BC, August 14, 1989. Phoenix's 1st choice, 3rd overall, in 2007 Entry Draft.

2004-05	Grandview	Minor-BC	30	13	20	33	....	....	....	....	....	....	....	....	....	....	12	3	6	9	....	....	....	....	....
2005-06	Burnaby Express	BCHL	57	36	36	72	32	....	....	....	....	....	....	....	....	....	20	10	13	23	6	....	....	....	....
2006-07	Burnaby Express	BCHL	53	66	55	121	83	....	....	....	....	....	....	....	....	....	14	12	14	26	16	....	....	....	....
2007-08	U. of Wisconsin	WCHA	36	11	24	35	38	....	....	....	....	....	....	....	....	....	....	....	....	....	....	....	....	....	....
	Phoenix	NHL	3	0	1	1	2	0	0	0	11	0.0	–5	42	40.5	19:45	....	....	....	....	....	....	....	....	....
2008-09	Phoenix	NHL	63	8	12	20	21	3	0	3	91	8.8	–15	567	42.9	12:55	....	....	....	....	....	....	....	....	....
	San Antonio	AHL	8	4	3	7	6	....	....	....	....	....	....	....	....	....	....	....	....	....	....	....	....	....	....
2009-10	San Antonio	AHL	76	24	39	63	60	....	....	....	....	....	....	....	....	....	....	....	....	....	....	....	....	....	....
2010-11	Phoenix	NHL	65	11	14	25	16	0	0	1	116	9.5	0	540	50.0	11:16	4	1	2	3	2	0	0	0	13:49
	San Antonio	AHL	2	0	1	1	2	....	....	....	....	....	....	....	....	....	....	....	....	....	....	....	....	....	....
2011-12	Phoenix	NHL	6	0	0	0	4	0	0	0	9	0.0	–2	51	41.2	12:45	....	....	....	....	....	....	....	....	....
	Ottawa	NHL	49	12	17	29	27	1	0	2	133	9.0	12	672	47.2	17:21	7	1	2	3	2	0	0	1	16:37
2012-13	Karpat Oulu	Finland	21	7	12	19	24	....	....	....	....	....	....	....	....	....	....	....	....	....	....	....	....	....	....
	Ottawa	NHL	48	12	17	29	24	3	0	2	118	10.2	6	920	49.0	19:38	10	6	3	9	13	1	1	1	19:58
2013-14	Ottawa	NHL	82	26	32	58	39	6	2	5	215	12.1	22	1429	50.7	18:44	....	....	....	....	....	....	....	....	....
2014-15	Ottawa	NHL	82	24	40	64	36	4	1	6	215	11.2	5	1472	50.1	19:13	6	1	1	2	18	1	0	0	19:50
	NHL Totals		398	93	133	226	169	17	3	19	908	10.2		5693	48.8	16:33	27	9	8	17	35	2	1	2	18:09

WCHA All-Rookie Team (2008)

Traded to **Ottawa** by **Phoenix** for David Rundblad and Ottawa's 2nd round choice (later traded to Columbus, later traded to Philadelphia – Philadelphia selected Anthony Stolarz) in 2012 Entry Draft, December 17, 2011. Signed as a free agent by **Oulu** (Finland), October 6, 2012.

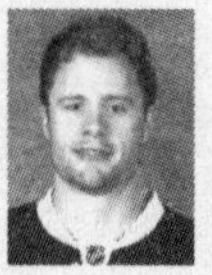

TYRELL, Dana

(TIH-rehl, DAY-nuh)

Center/Right wing. Shoots left. 5'10", 192 lbs. Born, Airdrie, AB, April 23, 1989. Tampa Bay's 1st choice, 47th overall, in 2007 Entry Draft.

2003-04	Airdrie Xtreme	AMBHL	35	21	47	68	28	....	....	....	....	....	....	....	....	....	7	6	4	10	....	....	....	....	....
2004-05	UFA Bisons	AMHL	34	16	23	39	32	....	....	....	....	....	....	....	....	....	16	8	9	*17	....	....	....	....	....
	Prince George	WHL	1	0	0	0	2	....	....	....	....	....	....	....	....	....	....	....	....	....	....	....	....	....	....
2005-06	Prince George	WHL	69	7	11	18	44	....	....	....	....	....	....	....	....	....	5	0	0	0	2	....	....	....	....
2006-07	Prince George	WHL	72	30	26	56	51	....	....	....	....	....	....	....	....	....	15	1	6	7	4	....	....	....	....
2007-08	Prince George	WHL	68	25	40	65	47	....	....	....	....	....	....	....	....	....	....	....	....	....	....	....	....	....	....
	Norfolk Admirals	AHL	11	1	5	6	6	....	....	....	....	....	....	....	....	....	....	....	....	....	....	....	....	....	....
2008-09	Prince George	WHL	30	19	21	40	27	....	....	....	....	....	....	....	....	....	....	....	....	....	....	....	....	....	....
2009-10	Norfolk Admirals	AHL	74	9	27	36	22	....	....	....	....	....	....	....	....	....	....	....	....	....	....	....	....	....	....
2010-11	Tampa Bay	NHL	78	6	9	15	12	0	0	1	73	8.2	–5	11	45.5	12:03	7	0	0	0	2	0	0	0	7:24
2011-12	Tampa Bay	NHL	26	0	5	5	6	0	0	0	23	0.0	–5	3	0.0	10:31	....	....	....	....	....	....	....	....	....
	Norfolk Admirals	AHL	18	4	5	9	8	....	....	....	....	....	....	....	....	....	....	....	....	....	....	....	....	....	....
2012-13	B. Bystrica	Slovakia	4	0	3	3	2	....	....	....	....	....	....	....	....	....	....	....	....	....	....	....	....	....	....
	Tampa Bay	NHL	21	1	3	4	4	0	0	0	19	5.3	–3	15	33.3	10:21	....	....	....	....	....	....	....	....	....
	Syracuse Crunch	AHL	15	5	3	8	11	....	....	....	....	....	....	....	....	....	....	....	....	....	....	....	....	....	....
2013-14	Tampa Bay	NHL	7	0	0	0	4	0	0	0	4	0.0	0	6	33.3	9:14	....	....	....	....	....	....	....	....	....
	Syracuse Crunch	AHL	44	9	12	21	20	....	....	....	....	....	....	....	....	....	....	....	....	....	....	....	....	....	....
	Springfield	AHL	19	6	6	12	0	....	....	....	....	....	....	....	....	....	5	1	2	3	4	....	....	....	....
2014-15	Columbus	NHL	3	0	0	0	0	0	0	0	1	0.0	–1	0	0.0	6:56	....	....	....	....	....	....	....	....	....
	Springfield	AHL	51	13	13	26	34	....	....	....	....	....	....	....	....	....	....	....	....	....	....	....	....	....	....
	NHL Totals		135	7	17	24	26	0	0	1	120	5.8		35	34.3	11:14	7	0	0	0	2	0	0	0	7:25

Signed as a free agent by **Banska Bystrica** (Slovakia), December 4, 2012. Traded to **Columbus** by **Tampa Bay** with Matt Taormina for Jon Marchessault and Dalton Smith, March 5, 2014.

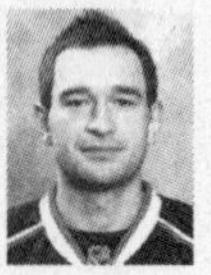

TYUTIN, Fedor

(T'YOO-tihn, FEH-duhr) **CBJ**

Defense. Shoots left. 6'2", 212 lbs. Born, Izhevsk, USSR, July 19, 1983. NY Rangers' 2nd choice, 40th overall, in 2001 Entry Draft.

1998-99	Magnitogorsk 2	Russia-4	7	0	1	1	2	....	....	....	....	....	....	....	....	....	....	....	....	....	....	....	....	....	....
99-2000	Izhstal Izhevsk 2	Russia-3	38	11	8	19	68	....	....	....	....	....	....	....	....	....	....	....	....	....	....	....	....	....	....
	Izhstal Izhevsk	Russia-2	10	0	1	1	12	....	....	....	....	....	....	....	....	....	....	....	....	....	....	....	....	....	....
2000-01	St. Petersburg	Russia	34	2	4	6	20	....	....	....	....	....	....	....	....	....	....	....	....	....	....	....	....	....	....
2001-02	Guelph Storm	OHL	53	19	40	59	54	....	....	....	....	....	....	....	....	....	9	2	8	10	8	....	....	....	....
2002-03	St. Petersburg	Russia	10	1	1	2	16	....	....	....	....	....	....	....	....	....	....	....	....	....	....	....	....	....	....
	Ak Bars Kazan	Russia	10	0	0	0	8	....	....	....	....	....	....	....	....	....	5	0	0	0	4	....	....	....	....
2003-04	NY Rangers	NHL	25	2	5	7	14	0	1	0	33	6.1	–4	1	0.0	20:08	....	....	....	....	....	....	....	....	....
	Hartford	AHL	43	5	9	14	50	....	....	....	....	....	....	....	....	....	16	0	5	5	18	....	....	....	....
2004-05	Hartford	AHL	13	2	1	3	10	....	....	....	....	....	....	....	....	....	....	....	....	....	....	....	....	....	....
	St. Petersburg	Russia	35	5	3	8	24	....	....	....	....	....	....	....	....	....	....	....	....	....	....	....	....	....	....
2005-06	NY Rangers	NHL	77	6	19	25	58	4	0	2	102	5.9	1	1	0.0	20:33	4	0	1	1	0	0	0	0	17:50
	Russia	Olympics	8	0	1	1	4	....	....	....	....	....	....	....	....	....	....	....	....	....	....	....	....	....	....
2006-07	NY Rangers	NHL	66	2	12	14	44	1	1	0	75	2.7	–8	1	0.0	20:02	10	0	5	5	8	0	0	0	19:30
2007-08	NY Rangers	NHL	82	5	15	20	43	1	0	0	131	3.8	5	0	0.0	20:27	10	0	3	3	4	0	0	0	19:52
2008-09	Columbus	NHL	82	9	25	34	81	5	1	0	167	5.4	1	1	100.0	23:31	4	0	0	0	0	0	0	0	23:16
2009-10	Columbus	NHL	80	6	26	32	49	3	0	2	149	4.0	–7	3	33.3	23:31	....	....	....	....	....	....	....	....	....
	Russia	Olympics	4	0	2	2	2	....	....	....	....	....	....	....	....	....	....	....	....	....	....	....	....	....	....
2010-11	Columbus	NHL	80	7	20	27	32	1	0	0	128	5.5	–12	2	50.0	22:42	....	....	....	....	....	....	....	....	....
2011-12	Columbus	NHL	66	5	21	26	49	1	0	0	124	4.0	–21	0	0.0	24:09	....	....	....	....	....	....	....	....	....
2012-13	Mytischi	KHL	17	1	2	3	8	....	....	....	....	....	....	....	....	....	....	....	....	....	....	....	....	....	....
	Columbus	NHL	48	4	18	22	28	0	0	1	56	7.1	9	1	100.0	24:06	....	....	....	....	....	....	....	....	....
2013-14	Columbus	NHL	69	4	22	26	44	1	0	0	87	4.6	6	0	0.0	21:25	4	1	1	2	4	0	1	0	14:56
	Russia	Olympics	5	0	0	0	4	....	....	....	....	....	....	....	....	....	....	....	....	....	....	....	....	....	....
2014-15	Columbus	NHL	67	3	12	15	40	0	0	0	56	5.4	8	0	0.0	19:55	....	....	....	....	....	....	....	....	....
	NHL Totals		742	53	195	248	482	17	3	5	1108	4.8		10	40.0	21:56	32	1	10	11	16	0	1	0	19:18

Signed as a free agent by **St. Petersburg** (Russia), November 11, 2004. Traded to **Columbus** by **NY Rangers** with Christian Backman for Nikolai Zherdev and Dan Fritsche, July 2, 2008. Signed as a free agent by **Mytischi** (KHL), November 12, 2012.

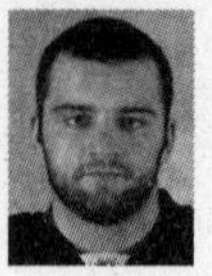

UHER, Dominik

(YEW-air, DOHM-ih-NIHK) **PIT**

Center. Shoots left. 6'1", 202 lbs. Born, Ostrava, Czech., December 31, 1992. Pittsburgh's 3rd choice, 144th overall, in 2011 Entry Draft.

2006-07	HC Trinec U17	CzR-U17	6	1	1	2	2	....	....	....	....	....	....	....	....	....	3	1	0	1	0	....	....	....	....
2007-08	HC Trinec U17	CzR-U17	44	5	11	16	44	....	....	....	....	....	....	....	....	....	5	1	0	1	4	....	....	....	....
2008-09	HC Trinec U17	CzR-U17	38	19	27	46	46	....	....	....	....	....	....	....	....	....	9	5	6	11	6	....	....	....	....
	HC Trinec Jr.	CzRep-Jr.	2	0	1	1	2	....	....	....	....	....	....	....	....	....	....	....	....	....	....	....	....	....	....
2009-10	Spokane Chiefs	WHL	53	4	12	16	45	....	....	....	....	....	....	....	....	....	6	0	0	0	2	....	....	....	....
2010-11	Spokane Chiefs	WHL	65	21	39	60	60	....	....	....	....	....	....	....	....	....	17	2	9	11	18	....	....	....	....
2011-12	Spokane Chiefs	WHL	63	33	35	68	60	....	....	....	....	....	....	....	....	....	13	5	4	9	6	....	....	....	....
2012-13	Wilkes-Barre	AHL	53	4	3	7	61	....	....	....	....	....	....	....	....	....	8	0	3	3	4	....	....	....	....
	Wheeling Nailers	ECHL	3	0	1	1	0	....	....	....	....	....	....	....	....	....	....	....	....	....	....	....	....	....	....
2013-14	Wilkes-Barre	AHL	68	7	17	24	66	....	....	....	....	....	....	....	....	....	12	1	0	1	4	....	....	....	....
2014-15	Pittsburgh	NHL	2	0	0	0	0	0	0	0	0	0.0	–1	0	0.0	6:28	....	....	....	....	....	....	....	....	....
	Wilkes-Barre	AHL	72	13	13	26	60	....	....	....	....	....	....	....	....	....	8	2	2	4	0	....	....	....	....
	NHL Totals		2	0	0	0	0	0	0	0	0	0.0		0	0.0	6:28	....	....	....	....	....	....	....	....	....

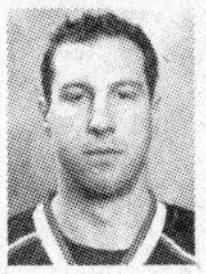

UMBERGER, RJ
(UHM-buhr-guhr, AHR-JAY) **PHI**

Center. Shoots left. 6'2", 214 lbs. Born, Pittsburgh, PA, May 3, 1982. Vancouver's 1st choice, 16th overall, in 2001 Entry Draft.

			Regular Season														Playoffs								
Season	Club	League	GP	G	A	Pts	PIM	PP	SH	GW	S	S%	+/-	TF	F%	Min	GP	G	A	Pts	PIM	PP	SH	GW	Min
1997-98	Plum Mustangs	High-PA	26	*60	*56	*116	....	....	....	....	....	....	....	....	....	....	....	....	....	....	....	....	....	....	....
1998-99	USNTDP	USHL	5	2	2	4	0	....	....	....	....	....	....	....	....	....	....	....	....	....	....	....	....	....	....
	USNTDP	NAHL	50	21	21	42	32	....	....	....	....	....	....	....	....	....	....	....	....	....	....	....	....	....	....
99-2000	USNTDP	U-18	6	1	0	1	2	....	....	....	....	....	....	....	....	....	....	....	....	....	....	....	....	....	....
	USNTDP	USHL	57	33	35	68	20	....	....	....	....	....	....	....	....	....	....	....	....	....	....	....	....	....	....
2000-01	Ohio State	CCHA	32	14	23	37	18	....	....	....	....	....	....	....	....	....	....	....	....	....	....	....	....	....	....
2001-02	Ohio State	CCHA	37	18	21	39	31	....	....	....	....	....	....	....	....	....	....	....	....	....	....	....	....	....	....
2002-03	Ohio State	CCHA	43	26	27	53	16	....	....	....	....	....	....	....	....	....	....	....	....	....	....	....	....	....	....
2003-04			DID NOT PLAY																						
2004-05	Philadelphia	AHL	80	21	44	65	36	....	....	....	....	....	....	....	....	....	21	3	7	10	12	....	....	....	....
2005-06	**Philadelphia**	**NHL**	**73**	**20**	**18**	**38**	**18**	**5**	**0**	**2**	**138**	**14.5**	**9**	**163**	**50.3**	**13:14**	**5**	**1**	**0**	**1**	**2**	**0**	**0**	**0**	**11:15**
	Philadelphia	AHL	8	3	7	10	8	....	....	....	....	....	....	....	....	....	....	....	....	....	....	....	....	....	....
2006-07	**Philadelphia**	**NHL**	**81**	**16**	**12**	**28**	**41**	**2**	**2**	**1**	**134**	**11.9**	**–32**	**535**	**44.5**	**14:32**	....	....	....	....	....	....	....	....	....
2007-08	**Philadelphia**	**NHL**	**74**	**13**	**37**	**50**	**19**	**4**	**0**	**3**	**173**	**7.5**	**0**	**117**	**38.5**	**17:52**	**17**	**10**	**5**	**15**	**10**	**1**	**0**	**2**	**16:51**
2008-09	**Columbus**	**NHL**	**82**	**26**	**20**	**46**	**53**	**9**	**0**	**2**	**234**	**11.1**	**–10**	**841**	**48.0**	**18:46**	**4**	**3**	**0**	**3**	**0**	**2**	**0**	**0**	**16:22**
2009-10	**Columbus**	**NHL**	**82**	**23**	**32**	**55**	**40**	**8**	**1**	**4**	**221**	**10.4**	**–16**	**704**	**52.8**	**19:10**	....	....	....	....	....	....	....	....	....
2010-11	**Columbus**	**NHL**	**82**	**25**	**32**	**57**	**38**	**8**	**3**	**3**	**220**	**11.4**	**3**	**220**	**50.5**	**19:13**	....	....	....	....	....	....	....	....	....
2011-12	**Columbus**	**NHL**	**77**	**20**	**20**	**40**	**27**	**5**	**0**	**3**	**200**	**10.0**	**–10**	**306**	**49.0**	**18:11**	....	....	....	....	....	....	....	....	....
2012-13	**Columbus**	**NHL**	**48**	**8**	**10**	**18**	**16**	**2**	**0**	**0**	**96**	**8.3**	**3**	**108**	**50.0**	**18:29**	....	....	....	....	....	....	....	....	....
2013-14	**Columbus**	**NHL**	**74**	**18**	**16**	**34**	**26**	**8**	**1**	**3**	**136**	**13.2**	**–3**	**40**	**62.5**	**16:11**	**4**	**0**	**1**	**1**	**2**	**0**	**0**	**0**	**12:47**
2014-15	**Philadelphia**	**NHL**	**67**	**9**	**6**	**15**	**19**	**2**	**0**	**0**	**96**	**9.4**	**–9**	**22**	**40.9**	**13:49**	....	....	....	....	....	....	....	....	....
	NHL Totals		**740**	**178**	**203**	**381**	**297**	**53**	**7**	**21**	**1648**	**10.8**		**3056**	**48.8**	**16:59**	**30**	**14**	**6**	**20**	**14**	**3**	**0**	**2**	**15:19**

CCHA All-Rookie Team (2001) • CCHA Rookie of the Year (2001) • CCHA First All-Star Team (2003) • NCAA West Second All-American Team (2003)

• Missed 2003-04 due to contract dispute. Traded to **NY Rangers** by **Vancouver** with Martin Grenier for Martin Rucinsky, March 9, 2004. Signed as a free agent by **Philadelphia**, June 16, 2004. Traded to **Columbus** by **Philadelphia** with Philadelphia's 4th round choice (Drew Olson) in 2008 Entry Draft for Colorado's 1st round choice (previously acquired, Philadelphia selected Luca Sbisa) in 2008 Entry Draft and Columbus' 3rd round choice (Marc-Andre Bourdon) in 2008 Entry Draft, June 20, 2008. Traded to **Philadelphia** by **Columbus** with Columbus' 4th round choice (later traded to Los Angeles – Los Angeles selected Austin Wagner) in 2015 Entry Draft for Scott Hartnell, June 23, 2014.

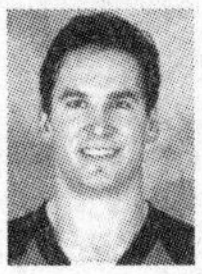

UPSHALL, Scottie
(UHP-shuhl, SKAW-tee)

Left wing. Shoots left. 6', 200 lbs. Born, Fort McMurray, AB, October 7, 1983. Nashville's 1st choice, 6th overall, in 2002 Entry Draft.

Season	Club	League	GP	G	A	Pts	PIM	PP	SH	GW	S	S%	+/-	TF	F%	Min	GP	G	A	Pts	PIM	PP	SH	GW	Min
1998-99	Fort McMurray	AMHL	28	62	40	102	100	....	....	....	....	....	....	....	....	....	....	....	....	....	....	....	....	....	....
99-2000	Fort McMurray	AJHL	52	26	26	52	65	....	....	....	....	....	....	....	....	....	....	....	....	....	....	....	....	....	....
2000-01	Kamloops Blazers	WHL	70	42	45	87	111	....	....	....	....	....	....	....	....	....	4	0	2	2	10	....	....	....	....
2001-02	Kamloops Blazers	WHL	61	32	51	83	139	....	....	....	....	....	....	....	....	....	4	1	2	3	21	....	....	....	....
2002-03	**Nashville**	**NHL**	**8**	**1**	**0**	**1**	**0**	**0**	**0**	**0**	**6**	**16.7**	**2**	**2**	**0.0**	**8:42**	....	....	....	....	....	....	....	....	....
	Kamloops Blazers	WHL	42	25	31	56	111	....	....	....	....	....	....	....	....	....	6	0	2	2	34	....	....	....	....
	Milwaukee	AHL	2	1	0	1	2	....	....	....	....	....	....	....	....	....	6	0	0	0	2	....	....	....	....
2003-04	**Nashville**	**NHL**	**7**	**0**	**1**	**1**	**0**	**0**	**0**	**0**	**6**	**0.0**	**–2**	**8**	**37.5**	**9:11**	....	....	....	....	....	....	....	....	....
	Milwaukee	AHL	31	13	11	24	42	....	....	....	....	....	....	....	....	....	8	3	0	3	4	....	....	....	....
2004-05	Milwaukee	AHL	62	19	27	46	108	....	....	....	....	....	....	....	....	....	5	2	2	4	8	....	....	....	....
2005-06	**Nashville**	**NHL**	**48**	**8**	**16**	**24**	**34**	**1**	**0**	**2**	**72**	**11.1**	**14**	**11**	**45.5**	**10:26**	**2**	**0**	**0**	**0**	**0**	**0**	**0**	**0**	**11:57**
	Milwaukee	AHL	23	17	16	33	44	....	....	....	....	....	....	....	....	....	14	6	10	16	20	....	....	....	....
2006-07	**Nashville**	**NHL**	**14**	**2**	**1**	**3**	**18**	**0**	**0**	**2**	**27**	**7.4**	**–1**	**0**	**0.0**	**10:28**	....	....	....	....	....	....	....	....	....
	Milwaukee	AHL	5	0	1	1	6	....	....	....	....	....	....	....	....	....	....	....	....	....	....	....	....	....	....
	Philadelphia	**NHL**	**18**	**6**	**7**	**13**	**8**	**1**	**1**	**2**	**60**	**10.0**	**4**	**18**	**44.4**	**18:05**	....	....	....	....	....	....	....	....	....
2007-08	**Philadelphia**	**NHL**	**61**	**14**	**16**	**30**	**74**	**3**	**0**	**1**	**128**	**10.9**	**2**	**7**	**28.6**	**13:20**	**17**	**3**	**4**	**7**	***44**	**1**	**0**	**1**	**13:57**
2008-09	**Philadelphia**	**NHL**	**55**	**7**	**14**	**21**	**63**	**2**	**0**	**0**	**126**	**5.6**	**5**	**10**	**10.0**	**13:13**	....	....	....	....	....	....	....	....	....
	Phoenix	**NHL**	**19**	**8**	**5**	**13**	**26**	**3**	**0**	**1**	**66**	**12.1**	**2**	**9**	**44.4**	**18:35**	....	....	....	....	....	....	....	....	....
2009-10	**Phoenix**	**NHL**	**49**	**18**	**14**	**32**	**50**	**2**	**0**	**4**	**119**	**15.1**	**5**	**17**	**41.2**	**15:03**	....	....	....	....	....	....	....	....	....
2010-11	**Phoenix**	**NHL**	**61**	**16**	**11**	**27**	**42**	**2**	**0**	**2**	**144**	**11.1**	**5**	**19**	**21.1**	**13:27**	....	....	....	....	....	....	....	....	....
	Columbus	**NHL**	**21**	**6**	**1**	**7**	**10**	**0**	**0**	**0**	**47**	**12.8**	**–12**	**6**	**66.7**	**15:46**	....	....	....	....	....	....	....	....	....
2011-12	**Florida**	**NHL**	**26**	**2**	**3**	**5**	**29**	**1**	**0**	**1**	**53**	**3.8**	**–3**	**6**	**50.0**	**12:43**	**7**	**1**	**2**	**3**	**4**	**0**	**0**	**0**	**13:22**
2012-13	**Florida**	**NHL**	**27**	**4**	**1**	**5**	**25**	**1**	**0**	**1**	**54**	**7.4**	**–8**	**14**	**64.3**	**13:30**	....	....	....	....	....	....	....	....	....
2013-14	**Florida**	**NHL**	**76**	**15**	**22**	**37**	**73**	**1**	**1**	**3**	**161**	**9.3**	**1**	**71**	**45.1**	**15:55**	....	....	....	....	....	....	....	....	....
2014-15	**Florida**	**NHL**	**63**	**8**	**7**	**15**	**28**	**0**	**0**	**2**	**93**	**8.6**	**–8**	**65**	**52.3**	**12:41**	....	....	....	....	....	....	....	....	....
	NHL Totals		**553**	**115**	**119**	**234**	**480**	**17**	**2**	**21**	**1162**	**9.9**		**263**	**44.1**	**13:44**	**26**	**4**	**6**	**10**	**48**	**1**	**0**	**1**	**13:38**

WHL All-Rookie Team (2001) • WHL Rookie of the Year (2001) • CHL All-Rookie Team (2001) • Canadian Major Junior Rookie of the Year (2001) • WHL West Second All-Star Team (2002)

• Missed majority of 2003-04 due to knee injury vs. Phoenix, December 22, 2003. Traded to **Philadelphia** by **Nashville** with Ryan Parent and Nashville's 1st (later traded back to Nashville – Nashville selected Jonathon Blum) and 3rd (later traded to Washington – Washington selected Phil Desimone) round choices in 2007 Entry Draft for Peter Forsberg, February 15, 2007. Traded to **Phoenix** by **Philadelphia** with Philadelphia's 2nd round choice (Lucas Lessio) in 2011 Entry Draft for Daniel Carcillo, March 4, 2009. Traded to **Columbus** by **Phoenix** with Sami Lepisto for Rostislav Klesla and Dane Byers, February 28, 2011. Signed as a free agent by **Florida**, July 1, 2011.

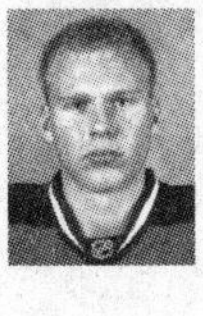

URBOM, Alexander
(OOR-bohm, al-ehx-AN-duhr)

Defense. Shoots left. 6'4", 215 lbs. Born, Stockholm, Sweden, December 20, 1990. New Jersey's 3rd choice, 73rd overall, in 2009 Entry Draft.

Season	Club	League	GP	G	A	Pts	PIM	PP	SH	GW	S	S%	+/-	TF	F%	Min	GP	G	A	Pts	PIM	PP	SH	GW	Min
2005-06	Djurgarden U18	Swe-U18	2	0	0	0	0	....	....	....	....	....	....	....	....	....	....	....	....	....	....	....	....	....	....
2006-07	Djurgarden U18	Swe-U18	31	6	11	17	36	....	....	....	....	....	....	....	....	....	3	0	1	1	2	....	....	....	....
2007-08	Djurgarden U18	Swe-U18	7	2	6	8	6	....	....	....	....	....	....	....	....	....	5	1	0	1	2	....	....	....	....
	Djurgarden Jr.	Swe-Jr.	39	3	8	11	54	....	....	....	....	....	....	....	....	....	7	0	1	1	2	....	....	....	....
2008-09	Djurgarden Jr.	Swe-Jr.	16	5	6	11	45	....	....	....	....	....	....	....	....	....	....	....	....	....	....	....	....	....	....
	Djurgarden	Sweden	28	0	0	0	2	....	....	....	....	....	....	....	....	....	....	....	....	....	....	....	....	....	....
	Djurgarden U18	Swe-U18	....	....	....	....	....	....	....	....	....	....	....	....	....	....	5	1	0	1	2	....	....	....	....
2009-10	Brandon	WHL	66	12	21	33	87	....	....	....	....	....	....	....	....	....	15	4	3	7	17	....	....	....	....
2010-11	**New Jersey**	**NHL**	**8**	**1**	**0**	**1**	**0**	**0**	**0**	**1**	**5**	**20.0**	**–2**	**0**	**0.0**	**12:35**	....	....	....	....	....	....	....	....	....
	Albany Devils	AHL	72	2	21	23	64	....	....	....	....	....	....	....	....	....	....	....	....	....	....	....	....	....	....
2011-12	**New Jersey**	**NHL**	**5**	**1**	**0**	**1**	**9**	**0**	**0**	**0**	**3**	**33.3**	**1**	**0**	**0.0**	**13:36**	....	....	....	....	....	....	....	....	....
	Albany Devils	AHL	50	2	10	12	33	....	....	....	....	....	....	....	....	....	....	....	....	....	....	....	....	....	....
2012-13	Albany Devils	AHL	68	0	8	8	64	....	....	....	....	....	....	....	....	....	....	....	....	....	....	....	....	....	....
	New Jersey	**NHL**	**1**	**0**	**0**	**0**	**0**	**0**	**0**	**0**	**0**	**0.0**	**–1**	**0**	**0.0**	**14:11**	....	....	....	....	....	....	....	....	....
2013-14	**Washington**	**NHL**	**20**	**1**	**1**	**2**	**19**	**0**	**0**	**0**	**16**	**6.3**	**1**	**0**	**0.0**	**14:36**	....	....	....	....	....	....	....	....	....
	Albany Devils	AHL	35	1	10	11	26	....	....	....	....	....	....	....	....	....	3	0	0	0	0	....	....	....	....
2014-15	Cherepovets	KHL	56	1	7	8	34	....	....	....	....	....	....	....	....	....	....	....	....	....	....	....	....	....	....
	NHL Totals		**34**	**3**	**1**	**4**	**28**	**0**	**0**	**1**	**24**	**12.5**		**0**	**0.0**	**13:58**	....	....	....	....	....	....	....	....	....

Claimed on waivers by **Washington** from **New Jersey**, October 4, 2013. Claimed on waivers by **New Jersey** from **Washington**, January 8, 2014. Signed as a free agent by **Cherepovets** (KHL), June 6, 2014.

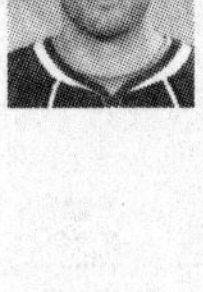

VAN DER GULIK, David
(VAN DUHR-GOO-lihk, DAY-vihd)

Right wing. Shoots left. 5'10", 173 lbs. Born, Abbotsford, BC, April 20, 1983. Calgary's 10th choice, 206th overall, in 2002 Entry Draft.

Season	Club	League	GP	G	A	Pts	PIM	PP	SH	GW	S	S%	+/-	TF	F%	Min	GP	G	A	Pts	PIM	PP	SH	GW	Min
99-2000	Chilliwack Chiefs	BCHL	41	35	46	81	....	....	....	....	....	....	....	....	....	....	....	....	....	....	....	....	....	....	....
2000-01	Chilliwack Chiefs	BCHL	60	42	38	80	....	....	....	....	....	....	....	....	....	....	....	....	....	....	....	....	....	....	....
2001-02	Chilliwack Chiefs	BCHL	56	38	62	100	90	....	....	....	....	....	....	....	....	....	13	8	11	19	....	....	....	....	....
2002-03	Boston University	H-East	40	10	10	20	56	....	....	....	....	....	....	....	....	....	....	....	....	....	....	....	....	....	....
2003-04	Boston University	H-East	35	13	7	20	74	....	....	....	....	....	....	....	....	....	....	....	....	....	....	....	....	....	....
2004-05	Boston University	H-East	41	18	13	31	48	....	....	....	....	....	....	....	....	....	....	....	....	....	....	....	....	....	....
2005-06	Boston University	H-East	25	11	11	22	26	....	....	....	....	....	....	....	....	....	....	....	....	....	....	....	....	....	....
2006-07	Omaha	AHL	80	16	27	43	69	....	....	....	....	....	....	....	....	....	6	0	2	2	4	....	....	....	....
2007-08	Quad City Flames	AHL	80	19	23	42	62	....	....	....	....	....	....	....	....	....	....	....	....	....	....	....	....	....	....
2008-09	**Calgary**	**NHL**	**6**	**0**	**2**	**2**	**0**	**0**	**0**	**0**	**11**	**0.0**	**–1**	**1**	**0.0**	**8:29**	....	....	....	....	....	....	....	....	....
	Quad City Flames	AHL	73	17	19	36	58	....	....	....	....	....	....	....	....	....	....	....	....	....	....	....	....	....	....
2009-10	Abbotsford Heat	AHL	64	16	24	40	58	....	....	....	....	....	....	....	....	....	13	4	2	6	10	....	....	....	....
2010-11	**Colorado**	**NHL**	**6**	**1**	**2**	**3**	**2**	**0**	**0**	**0**	**12**	**8.3**	**4**	**1**	**0.0**	**6:45**	....	....	....	....	....	....	....	....	....
	Lake Erie	AHL	48	15	21	36	36	....	....	....	....	....	....	....	....	....	7	2	2	4	8	....	....	....	....
2011-12	**Colorado**	**NHL**	**25**	**1**	**5**	**6**	**2**	**0**	**0**	**0**	**20**	**5.0**	**3**	**38**	**29.0**	**8:12**	....	....	....	....	....	....	....	....	....
	Lake Erie	AHL	40	12	16	28	36	....	....	....	....	....	....	....	....	....	....	....	....	....	....	....	....	....	....

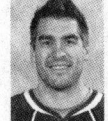

								Regular Season									Playoffs								
Season	Club	League	GP	G	A	Pts	PIM	PP	SH	GW	S	S%	+/-	TF	F%	Min	GP	G	A	Pts	PIM	PP	SH	GW	Min
2012-13	Lake Erie	AHL	60	18	17	35	58	....	....	....	....	....	....	....	....	....	....	....	....	....	....	....	....	....	....
	Colorado	**NHL**	**9**	**0**	**2**	**2**	**6**	**0**	**0**	**0**	**10**	**0.0**	**2**	**8**	**50.0**	**9:26**	....	....	....	....	....	....	....	....	....
2013-14	**Colorado**	**NHL**	**2**	**0**	**0**	**0**	**0**	**0**	**0**	**0**	**3**	**0.0**	**0**	**2**	**50.0**	**5:41**	....	....	....	....	....	....	....	....	....
	Lake Erie	AHL	33	13	9	22	37	....	....	....	....	....	....	....	....	....	....	....	....	....	....	....	....	....	....
2014-15	**Los Angeles**	**NHL**	**1**	**0**	**0**	**0**	**0**	**0**	**0**	**0**	**1**	**0.0**	**0**	**0**	**0.0**	**5:15**	....	....	....	....	....	....	....	....	....
	Manchester	AHL	57	11	14	25	39	....	....	....	....	....	....	....	....	....	14	2	7	9	6	....	....	....	....
	NHL Totals		**49**	**2**	**11**	**13**	**10**	**0**	**0**	**0**	**57**	**3.5**		**50**	**32.0**	**8:07**	....	....	....	....	....	....	....	....	....

Hockey East All-Rookie Team (2003)

Signed as a free agent by **Colorado**, July 2, 2010. • Missed majority of 2013-14 due to an injury and as a healthy reserve. Signed as a free agent by **Los Angeles**, July 1, 2014.

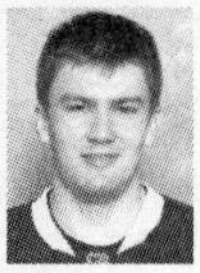

van RIEMSDYK, James (VAN REEMZ-dighk, JAYMZ) TOR

Left wing. Shoots left. 6'3", 200 lbs. Born, Middletown, NJ, May 4, 1989. Philadelphia's 1st choice, 2nd overall, in 2007 Entry Draft.

Season	Club	League	GP	G	A	Pts	PIM	PP	SH	GW	S	S%	+/-	TF	F%	Min	GP	G	A	Pts	PIM	PP	SH	GW	Min
2004-05	Christian Bros.	High-NJ	30	36	24	60	....	....	....	....	....	....	....	....	....	....	....	....	....	....	....	....	....	....	....
2005-06	USNTDP	U-17	11	7	5	12	18	....	....	....	....	....	....	....	....	....	....	....	....	....	....	....	....	....	....
	USNTDP	U-18	14	1	3	4	6	....	....	....	....	....	....	....	....	....	....	....	....	....	....	....	....	....	....
	USNTDP	NAHL	37	18	11	29	26	....	....	....	....	....	....	....	....	....	7	1	0	1	8	....	....	....	....
2006-07	USNTDP	U-18	39	25	28	53	48	....	....	....	....	....	....	....	....	....	....	....	....	....	....	....	....	....	....
	USNTDP	NAHL	12	13	12	25	37	....	....	....	....	....	....	....	....	....	....	....	....	....	....	....	....	....	....
2007-08	New Hampshire	H-East	31	11	23	34	36	....	....	....	....	....	....	....	....	....	....	....	....	....	....	....	....	....	....
2008-09	New Hampshire	H-East	36	17	23	40	47	....	....	....	....	....	....	....	....	....	....	....	....	....	....	....	....	....	....
	Philadelphia	AHL	7	1	1	2	2	....	....	....	....	....	....	....	....	....	4	0	0	0	2	....	....	....	....
2009-10	**Philadelphia**	**NHL**	**78**	**15**	**20**	**35**	**30**	**4**	**0**	**6**	**173**	**8.7**	**–1**	**2**	**0.0**	**12:58**	**21**	**3**	**3**	**6**	**4**	**0**	**0**	**0**	**11:54**
2010-11	**Philadelphia**	**NHL**	**75**	**21**	**19**	**40**	**35**	**3**	**0**	**4**	**173**	**12.1**	**15**	**3**	**0.0**	**14:32**	**11**	**7**	**0**	**7**	**4**	**2**	**0**	**1**	**19:23**
2011-12	**Philadelphia**	**NHL**	**43**	**11**	**13**	**24**	**24**	**2**	**0**	**1**	**121**	**9.1**	**–1**	**5**	**40.0**	**15:10**	**7**	**1**	**1**	**2**	**4**	**0**	**0**	**0**	**13:45**
2012-13	**Toronto**	**NHL**	**48**	**18**	**14**	**32**	**26**	**5**	**0**	**3**	**140**	**12.9**	**–7**	**43**	**55.8**	**19:12**	**7**	**2**	**5**	**7**	**4**	**1**	**0**	**0**	**19:41**
2013-14	**Toronto**	**NHL**	**80**	**30**	**31**	**61**	**50**	**9**	**2**	**3**	**279**	**10.8**	**–9**	**113**	**40.7**	**21:03**	....	....	....	....	....	....	....	....	....
	United States	Olympics	6	1	6	7	2	....	....	....	....	....	....	....	....	....	....	....	....	....	....	....	....	....	....
2014-15	**Toronto**	**NHL**	**82**	**27**	**29**	**56**	**43**	**9**	**1**	**4**	**248**	**10.9**	**–33**	**54**	**38.9**	**19:05**	....	....	....	....	....	....	....	....	....
	NHL Totals		**406**	**122**	**126**	**248**	**208**	**32**	**3**	**21**	**1134**	**10.8**		**220**	**42.3**	**17:03**	**46**	**13**	**9**	**22**	**16**	**3**	**0**	**1**	**15:09**

Hockey East All-Rookie Team (2008) • Hockey East Second All-Star Team (2009)

Traded to **Toronto** by **Philadelphia** for Luke Schenn, June 23, 2012.

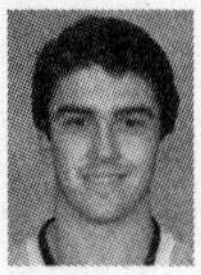

van RIEMSDYK, Trevor (VAN REEMZ-dighk,TREH-vuhr) CHI

Defense. Shoots right. 6'2", 188 lbs. Born, Middletown, NJ, July 24, 1991.

Season	Club	League	GP	G	A	Pts	PIM	PP	SH	GW	S	S%	+/-	TF	F%	Min	GP	G	A	Pts	PIM	PP	SH	GW	Min
2007-08	Christian Bros.	High-NJ	27	9	39	48	12	....	....	....	....	....	....	....	....	....	....	....	....	....	....	....	....	....	....
2008-09	Christian Bros.	High-NJ	29	11	47	58	18	....	....	....	....	....	....	....	....	....	....	....	....	....	....	....	....	....	....
2009-10	N.H. Jr. Monarchs	EJHL	31	8	27	35	4	....	....	....	....	....	....	....	....	....	4	0	3	3	0	....	....	....	....
2010-11	N.H. Jr. Monarchs	EJHL	39	16	22	38	20	....	....	....	....	....	....	....	....	....	6	2	3	5	4	....	....	....	....
2011-12	New Hampshire	H-East	37	4	15	19	24	....	....	....	....	....	....	....	....	....	....	....	....	....	....	....	....	....	....
2012-13	New Hampshire	H-East	39	8	25	33	8	....	....	....	....	....	....	....	....	....	....	....	....	....	....	....	....	....	....
2013-14	New Hampshire	H-East	26	4	19	23	10	....	....	....	....	....	....	....	....	....	....	....	....	....	....	....	....	....	....
2014-15♦	**Chicago**	**NHL**	**18**	**0**	**1**	**1**	**2**	**0**	**0**	**0**	**21**	**0.0**	**0**	**0**	**0.0**	**13:32**	**4**	**0**	**0**	**0**	**0**	**0**	**0**	**0**	**7:02**
	Rockford IceHogs	AHL	8	0	3	3	0	....	....	....	....	....	....	....	....	....	....	....	....	....	....	....	....	....	....
	NHL Totals		**18**	**0**	**1**	**1**	**2**	**0**	**0**	**0**	**21**	**0.0**		**0**	**0.0**	**13:32**	**4**	**0**	**0**	**0**	**0**	**0**	**0**	**0**	**7:02**

Hockey East All-Rookie Team (2012) • Hockey East First All-Star Team (2013) • NCAA East First All-American Team (2013)

Signed as a free agent by **Chicago**, March 24, 2014. • Missed majority of 2014-15 due to knee injury vs. Dallas, November 16, 2014.

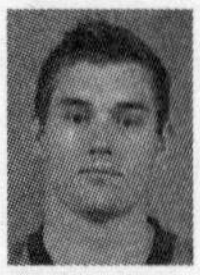

VAN BRABANT, Bryce (VAN-BRAY-behnt, BRIGHS) CGY

Left wing. Shoots left. 6'2", 205 lbs. Born, Morinville, AB, November 12, 1991.

Season	Club	League	GP	G	A	Pts	PIM	PP	SH	GW	S	S%	+/-	TF	F%	Min	GP	G	A	Pts	PIM	PP	SH	GW	Min
2007-08	Ft. Saskatchewan	AMHL	33	11	4	15	65	....	....	....	....	....	....	....	....	....	12	3	4	7	22	....	....	....	....
2008-09	Spruce Grove	AJHL	46	4	7	11	84	....	....	....	....	....	....	....	....	....	4	2	2	4	6	....	....	....	....
2009-10	Spruce Grove	AJHL	51	8	6	14	137	....	....	....	....	....	....	....	....	....	16	1	4	5	16	....	....	....	....
2010-11	Spruce Grove	AJHL	54	10	12	22	163	....	....	....	....	....	....	....	....	....	13	2	3	5	41	....	....	....	....
2011-12	Quinnipiac	ECAC	33	4	3	7	51	....	....	....	....	....	....	....	....	....	....	....	....	....	....	....	....	....	....
2012-13	Quinnipiac	ECAC	42	5	8	13	48	....	....	....	....	....	....	....	....	....	....	....	....	....	....	....	....	....	....
2013-14	Quinnipiac	ECAC	40	15	7	22	*113	....	....	....	....	....	....	....	....	....	....	....	....	....	....	....	....	....	....
	Calgary	**NHL**	**6**	**0**	**0**	**0**	**2**	**0**	**0**	**0**	**4**	**0.0**	**–1**	**0**	**0.0**	**9:09**	....	....	....	....	....	....	....	....	....
2014-15	Adirondack	AHL	52	8	7	15	54	....	....	....	....	....	....	....	....	....	....	....	....	....	....	....	....	....	....
	NHL Totals		**6**	**0**	**0**	**0**	**2**	**0**	**0**	**0**	**4**	**0.0**		**0**	**0.0**	**9:09**	....	....	....	....	....	....	....	....	....

Signed as a free agent by **Calgary**, March 29, 2014.

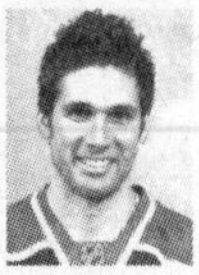

VANDEVELDE, Chris (van-duh-VEHL-dee, KRIHS) PHI

Center. Shoots left. 6'2", 190 lbs. Born, Moorhead, MN, March 15, 1987. Edmonton's 5th choice, 97th overall, in 2005 Entry Draft.

Season	Club	League	GP	G	A	Pts	PIM	PP	SH	GW	S	S%	+/-	TF	F%	Min	GP	G	A	Pts	PIM	PP	SH	GW	Min
2003-04	Moorhead Spuds	High-MN	29	19	24	43	....	....	....	....	....	....	....	....	....	....	....	....	....	....	....	....	....	....	....
2004-05	Moorhead Spuds	High-MN	30	35	32	67	28	....	....	....	....	....	....	....	....	....	....	....	....	....	....	....	....	....	....
	Lincoln Stars	USHL	7	1	4	5	0	....	....	....	....	....	....	....	....	....	4	0	2	2	0	....	....	....	....
2005-06	Lincoln Stars	USHL	56	16	20	36	70	....	....	....	....	....	....	....	....	....	9	1	3	4	10	....	....	....	....
2006-07	North Dakota	WCHA	38	3	6	9	37	....	....	....	....	....	....	....	....	....	....	....	....	....	....	....	....	....	....
2007-08	North Dakota	WCHA	43	15	17	32	38	....	....	....	....	....	....	....	....	....	....	....	....	....	....	....	....	....	....
2008-09	North Dakota	WCHA	43	18	17	35	69	....	....	....	....	....	....	....	....	....	....	....	....	....	....	....	....	....	....
2009-10	North Dakota	WCHA	42	16	25	41	22	....	....	....	....	....	....	....	....	....	....	....	....	....	....	....	....	....	....
2010-11	**Edmonton**	**NHL**	**12**	**0**	**2**	**2**	**12**	**0**	**0**	**0**	**16**	**0.0**	**–6**	**159**	**52.8**	**17:17**	....	....	....	....	....	....	....	....	....
	Oklahoma City	AHL	67	12	4	16	45	....	....	....	....	....	....	....	....	....	6	1	0	1	6	....	....	....	....
2011-12	**Edmonton**	**NHL**	**5**	**1**	**0**	**1**	**2**	**0**	**0**	**0**	**1**	**100.0**	**2**	**40**	**45.0**	**9:52**	....	....	....	....	....	....	....	....	....
	Oklahoma City	AHL	68	7	16	23	33	....	....	....	....	....	....	....	....	....	14	6	0	6	10	....	....	....	....
2012-13	Oklahoma City	AHL	57	7	13	20	27	....	....	....	....	....	....	....	....	....	17	2	2	4	10	....	....	....	....
	Edmonton	**NHL**	**11**	**0**	**0**	**0**	**4**	**0**	**0**	**0**	**7**	**0.0**	**–3**	**44**	**47.7**	**7:03**	....	....	....	....	....	....	....	....	....
2013-14	Adirondack	AHL	41	10	14	24	27	....	....	....	....	....	....	....	....	....	....	....	....	....	....	....	....	....	....
	Philadelphia	**NHL**	**18**	**0**	**1**	**1**	**6**	**0**	**0**	**0**	**8**	**0.0**	**–3**	**40**	**40.0**	**7:44**	....	....	....	....	....	....	....	....	....
2014-15	**Philadelphia**	**NHL**	**72**	**9**	**6**	**15**	**28**	**0**	**0**	**0**	**70**	**12.9**	**–6**	**56**	**37.5**	**11:44**	....	....	....	....	....	....	....	....	....
	Lehigh Valley	AHL	1	2	0	2	0	....	....	....	....	....	....	....	....	....	....	....	....	....	....	....	....	....	....
	NHL Totals		**118**	**10**	**9**	**19**	**52**	**0**	**0**	**0**	**102**	**9.8**		**339**	**47.2**	**11:10**	....	....	....	....	....	....	....	....	....

Signed as a free agent by **Adirondack** (AHL), October 3, 2013. Signed as a free agent by **Philadelphia**, December 12, 2013.

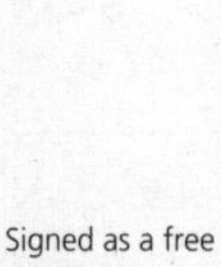

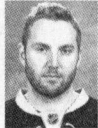

VANEK, Thomas (VAN-ehk, TAW-muhs) MIN

Left wing. Shoots right. 6'2", 217 lbs. Born, Vienna, Austria, January 19, 1984. Buffalo's 1st choice, 5th overall, in 2003 Entry Draft.

Season	Club	League	GP	G	A	Pts	PIM	PP	SH	GW	S	S%	+/-	TF	F%	Min	GP	G	A	Pts	PIM	PP	SH	GW	Min
99-2000	Sioux Falls	USHL	35	15	18	33	12	....	....	....	....	....	....	....	....	....	3	0	1	1	0	....	....	....	....
2000-01	Sioux Falls	USHL	20	19	10	29	15	....	....	....	....	....	....	....	....	....	8	5	4	9	2	....	....	....	....
2001-02	Sioux Falls	USHL	53	46	45	91	54	....	....	....	....	....	....	....	....	....	3	0	0	0	9	....	....	....	....
2002-03	U. of Minnesota	WCHA	45	31	31	62	60	....	....	....	....	....	....	....	....	....	....	....	....	....	....	....	....	....	....
	Austria	WJC-B	5	9	4	13	10	....	....	....	....	....	....	....	....	....	....	....	....	....	....	....	....	....	....
2003-04	U. of Minnesota	WCHA	38	26	25	51	72	....	....	....	....	....	....	....	....	....	....	....	....	....	....	....	....	....	....
2004-05	Rochester	AHL	74	42	26	68	62	....	....	....	....	....	....	....	....	....	5	2	3	5	10	....	....	....	....
	Austria	Oly-Q	3	1	0	1	0	....	....	....	....	....	....	....	....	....	....	....	....	....	....	....	....	....	....
2005-06	**Buffalo**	**NHL**	**81**	**25**	**23**	**48**	**72**	**11**	**0**	**4**	**204**	**12.3**	**–11**	**23**	**21.7**	**14:44**	**10**	**2**	**0**	**2**	**6**	**2**	**0**	**0**	**10:45**
2006-07	**Buffalo**	**NHL**	**82**	**43**	**41**	**84**	**40**	**15**	**0**	**5**	**237**	**18.1**	***47**	**39**	**28.2**	**16:47**	**16**	**6**	**4**	**10**	**10**	**1**	**0**	**2**	**16:27**
2007-08	**Buffalo**	**NHL**	**82**	**36**	**28**	**64**	**64**	**19**	**0**	**9**	**240**	**15.0**	**–5**	**13**	**46.2**	**16:51**	....	....	....	....	....	....	....	....	....
2008-09	**Buffalo**	**NHL**	**73**	**40**	**24**	**64**	**44**	***20**	**2**	**5**	**211**	**19.0**	**–1**	**6**	**16.7**	**17:12**	....	....	....	....	....	....	....	....	....
2009-10	**Buffalo**	**NHL**	**71**	**28**	**25**	**53**	**42**	**10**	**0**	**6**	**182**	**15.4**	**9**	**9**	**22.2**	**16:46**	**3**	**2**	**1**	**3**	**2**	**0**	**0**	**0**	**13:38**
2010-11	**Buffalo**	**NHL**	**80**	**32**	**41**	**73**	**24**	**11**	**0**	**5**	**238**	**13.4**	**2**	**26**	**30.8**	**17:21**	**7**	**5**	**0**	**5**	**0**	**4**	**0**	**0**	**17:10**
2011-12	**Buffalo**	**NHL**	**78**	**26**	**35**	**61**	**52**	**10**	**0**	**5**	**204**	**12.7**	**–6**	**6**	**50.0**	**16:56**	....	....	....	....	....	....	....	....	....

			Regular Season														Playoffs								
Season	Club	League	GP	G	A	Pts	PIM	PP	SH	GW	S	S%	+/-	TF	F%	Min	GP	G	A	Pts	PIM	PP	SH	GW	Min
2012-13	Graz 99ers	Austria	11	5	10	15	4	....	....	....	....	....	....	....	....	....	....	....	....	....	....	....	....	....	....
	Buffalo	**NHL**	**38**	**20**	**21**	**41**	**20**	**9**	**1**	**2**	**119**	**16.8**	**-1**	**12**	**66.7**	**18:24**	....	....	....	....	....	....	....	....	....
2013-14	**Buffalo**	**NHL**	**13**	**4**	**5**	**9**	**4**	**1**	**0**	**0**	**50**	**8.0**	**-5**	**5**	**40.0**	**18:37**	....	....	....	....	....	....	....	....	....
	NY Islanders	**NHL**	**47**	**17**	**27**	**44**	**34**	**5**	**0**	**2**	**137**	**12.4**	**4**	**11**	**100.0**	**20:00**	....	....	....	....	....	....	....	....	....
	Austria	Olympics	4	0	1	1	4	....	....	....	....	....	....	....	....	....	....	....	....	....	....	....	....	....	....
	Montreal	**NHL**	**18**	**6**	**9**	**15**	**8**	**2**	**0**	**2**	**61**	**9.8**	**8**	**40**	**42.5**	**18:11**	**17**	**5**	**5**	**10**	**4**	**3**	**0**	**0**	**14:53**
2014-15	**Minnesota**	**NHL**	**80**	**21**	**31**	**52**	**37**	**5**	**0**	**2**	**171**	**12.3**	**-6**	**20**	**50.0**	**16:13**	**10**	**0**	**4**	**4**	**2**	**0**	**0**	**0**	**14:12**
	NHL Totals		**743**	**298**	**310**	**608**	**441**	**118**	**3**	**47**	**2054**	**14.5**		**200**	**37.0**	**16:58**	**63**	**20**	**14**	**34**	**24**	**10**	**0**	**2**	**14:43**

USHL First All-Star Team (2002) • USHL MVP (2002) • WCHA All-Rookie Team (2003) • WCHA Second All-Star Team (2003, 2004) • WCHA Rookie of the Year (2003) • NCAA Championship All-Tournament Team (2003) • NCAA Championship Tournament MVP (2003) • NCAA West Second All-American Team (2004) • AHL All-Rookie Team (2005) • NHL Second All-Star Team (2007)

Played in NHL All-Star Game (2009)

Signed as a free agent by **Graz** (Austria), October 1, 2012. Traded to **NY Islanders** by **Buffalo** for Matt Moulson and NY Islanders' 1st (later traded to Ottawa – Ottawa selected Colin White) and 2nd (Brendan Guhle) round choices in 2015 Entry Draft, October 27, 2013. Traded to **Montreal** by **NY Islanders** with NY Islanders' 5th round choice (Nikolas Koberstein) in 2014 Entry Draft for Sebastian Collberg and Montreal's 2nd round choice (later traded to Tampa Bay – Tampa Bay selected Johnathan MacLeod) in 2014 Entry Draft, March 5, 2014. Signed as a free agent by **Minnesota**, July 1, 2014.

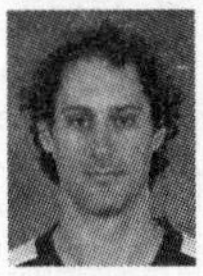

VAN GUILDER, Mark

(VAN GIHL-duhr, MAHRK)

Right wing. Shoots right. 6'1", 186 lbs. Born, Roseville, MN, January 17, 1984.

2002-03	Tri-City Storm	USHL	59	11	8	19	23	....	....	....	....	....	....	....	....	....	3	0	0	0	14	....	....	....	....
2003-04	Tri-City Storm	USHL	60	17	22	39	23	....	....	....	....	....	....	....	....	....	11	3	2	5	18	....	....	....	....
2004-05	U. of Notre Dame	CCHA	38	3	5	8	16	....	....	....	....	....	....	....	....	....	....	....	....	....	....	....	....	....	....
2005-06	U. of Notre Dame	CCHA	36	8	18	26	6	....	....	....	....	....	....	....	....	....	....	....	....	....	....	....	....	....	....
2006-07	U. of Notre Dame	CCHA	42	18	16	34	26	....	....	....	....	....	....	....	....	....	....	....	....	....	....	....	....	....	....
2007-08	U. of Notre Dame	CCHA	47	13	17	30	28	....	....	....	....	....	....	....	....	....	....	....	....	....	....	....	....	....	....
2008-09	Milwaukee	AHL	5	0	0	0	0	....	....	....	....	....	....	....	....	....	....	....	....	....	....	....	....	....	....
	Cincinnati	ECHL	65	26	44	70	18	....	....	....	....	....	....	....	....	....	15	3	4	7	8	....	....	....	....
	Hamilton	AHL	3	0	1	1	0	....	....	....	....	....	....	....	....	....	....	....	....	....	....	....	....	....	....
2009-10	Milwaukee	AHL	28	0	7	7	8	....	....	....	....	....	....	....	....	....	7	0	0	0	2	....	....	....	....
	Cincinnati	ECHL	15	6	5	11	21	....	....	....	....	....	....	....	....	....	14	5	10	15	2	....	....	....	....
2010-11	Milwaukee	AHL	62	10	7	17	10	....	....	....	....	....	....	....	....	....	13	3	3	6	2	....	....	....	....
2011-12	Milwaukee	AHL	70	12	15	27	14	....	....	....	....	....	....	....	....	....	3	1	0	1	0	....	....	....	....
2012-13	Milwaukee	AHL	73	14	18	32	9	....	....	....	....	....	....	....	....	....	4	0	0	0	0	....	....	....	....
2013-14	**Nashville**	**NHL**	**1**	**0**	**0**	**0**	**0**	**0**	**0**	**0**	**0**	**0.0**	**0**	**0**	**0.0**	**8:27**	....	....	....	....	....	....	....	....	....
	Milwaukee	AHL	69	14	15	29	28	....	....	....	....	....	....	....	....	....	3	0	0	0	2	....	....	....	....
2014-15	Milwaukee	AHL	76	11	15	26	22	....	....	....	....	....	....	....	....	....	....	....	....	....	....	....	....	....	....
	NHL Totals		**1**	**0**	**0**	**0**	**0**	**0**	**0**	**0**	**0**	**0.0**		**0**	**0.0**	**8:27**	....	....	....	....	....	....	....	....	....

Signed as a free agent by **Nashville**, May 20, 2013.

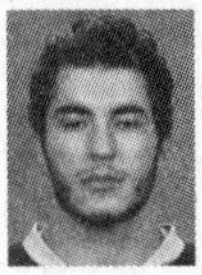

VARONE, Phil

(vah-ROH-nee, FIHL) **BUF**

Center. Shoots left. 5'10", 185 lbs. Born, Vaughan, ON, December 4, 1990. San Jose's 3rd choice, 147th overall, in 2009 Entry Draft.

2005-06	Vaughan M.M.	GTHL	49	34	29	63	....	....	....	....	....	....	....	....	....	....	....	....	....	....	....	....	....	....	....
	Vaughan Midget	GTHL	4	6	1	7	2	....	....	....	....	....	....	....	....	....	....	....	....	....	....	....	....	....	....
2006-07	Kitchener	ON-Jr.B	20	10	11	21	21	....	....	....	....	....	....	....	....	....	....	....	....	....	....	....	....	....	....
	Kitchener Rangers	OHL	13	1	3	4	2	....	....	....	....	....	....	....	....	....	....	....	....	....	....	....	....	....	....
2007-08	Kitchener Rangers	OHL	35	5	20	25	12	....	....	....	....	....	....	....	....	....	....	....	....	....	....	....	....	....	....
	London Knights	OHL	31	10	26	36	14	....	....	....	....	....	....	....	....	....	5	1	1	2	7	....	....	....	....
2008-09	London Knights	OHL	58	19	33	52	32	....	....	....	....	....	....	....	....	....	14	10	9	19	19	....	....	....	....
2009-10	London Knights	OHL	31	9	22	31	17	....	....	....	....	....	....	....	....	....	....	....	....	....	....	....	....	....	....
2010-11	London Knights	OHL	4	1	0	1	2	....	....	....	....	....	....	....	....	....	....	....	....	....	....	....	....	....	....
	Erie Otters	OHL	55	33	48	81	30	....	....	....	....	....	....	....	....	....	7	3	10	13	4	....	....	....	....
2011-12	Rochester	AHL	76	11	41	52	42	....	....	....	....	....	....	....	....	....	3	2	1	3	0	....	....	....	....
2012-13	Rochester	AHL	62	11	24	35	42	....	....	....	....	....	....	....	....	....	3	0	0	0	2	....	....	....	....
2013-14	**Buffalo**	**NHL**	**9**	**1**	**1**	**2**	**4**	**0**	**0**	**0**	**15**	**6.7**	**-3**	**56**	**46.4**	**11:24**	....	....	....	....	....	....	....	....	....
	Rochester	AHL	69	18	43	61	58	....	....	....	....	....	....	....	....	....	5	0	3	3	0	....	....	....	....
2014-15	**Buffalo**	**NHL**	**28**	**3**	**2**	**5**	**10**	**0**	**0**	**0**	**28**	**10.7**	**-14**	**326**	**45.1**	**13:27**	....	....	....	....	....	....	....	....	....
	Rochester	AHL	55	15	29	44	22	....	....	....	....	....	....	....	....	....	....	....	....	....	....	....	....	....	....
	NHL Totals		**37**	**4**	**3**	**7**	**14**	**0**	**0**	**0**	**43**	**9.3**		**382**	**45.3**	**12:57**	....	....	....	....	....	....	....	....	....

Signed as a free agent by **Rochester** (AHL), September 27, 2011. Signed as a free agent by **Buffalo**, March 19. 2012.

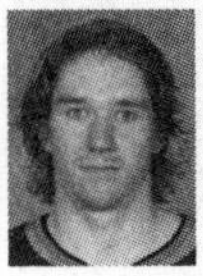

VATANEN, Sami

(VAH-ta-nehn, SA-mee) **ANA**

Defense. Shoots right. 5'10", 183 lbs. Born, Jyvaskyla, Finland, June 3, 1991. Anaheim's 5th choice, 106th overall, in 2009 Entry Draft.

2006-07	JyP Jyvaskyla U18	Fin-U18	....	....	....	....	....	....	....	....	....	....	....	....	....	....	7	1	0	1	2	....	....	....	....
2007-08	JyP Jyvaskyla U18	Fin-U18	35	9	29	38	30	....	....	....	....	....	....	....	....	....	1	0	0	0	0	....	....	....	....
	JyP Jyvaskyla Jr.	Fin-Jr.	....	....	....	....	....	....	....	....	....	....	....	....	....	....	2	0	0	0	0	....	....	....	....
2008-09	JyP Jyvaskyla U18	Fin-U18	2	0	0	0	0	....	....	....	....	....	....	....	....	....	1	1	1	2	14	....	....	....	....
	Suomi U20	Finland-2	2	0	0	0	2	....	....	....	....	....	....	....	....	....	....	....	....	....	....	....	....	....	....
	D Team Jyvaskyla	Finland-2	5	1	1	2	8	....	....	....	....	....	....	....	....	....	....	....	....	....	....	....	....	....	....
	JyP Jyvaskyla Jr.	Fin-Jr.	20	3	7	10	22	....	....	....	....	....	....	....	....	....	....	....	....	....	....	....	....	....	....
2009-10	Suomi U20	Finland-2	1	0	0	0	2	....	....	....	....	....	....	....	....	....	....	....	....	....	....	....	....	....	....
	JYP Jyvaskyla	Finland	55	7	23	30	44	....	....	....	....	....	....	....	....	....	14	3	4	7	6	....	....	....	....
2010-11	Suomi U20	Finland-2	1	0	0	0	0	....	....	....	....	....	....	....	....	....	....	....	....	....	....	....	....	....	....
	JYP Jyvaskyla	Finland	52	11	20	31	30	....	....	....	....	....	....	....	....	....	3	1	1	2	0	....	....	....	....
2011-12	JYP Jyvaskyla	Finland	49	14	28	42	40	....	....	....	....	....	....	....	....	....	4	2	0	2	4	....	....	....	....
2012-13	Norfolk Admirals	AHL	62	9	36	45	44	....	....	....	....	....	....	....	....	....	....	....	....	....	....	....	....	....	....
	Anaheim	**NHL**	**8**	**2**	**0**	**2**	**0**	**1**	**0**	**0**	**6**	**33.3**	**3**	**0**	**0.0**	**15:49**	....	....	....	....	....	....	....	....	....
2013-14	**Anaheim**	**NHL**	**48**	**6**	**15**	**21**	**22**	**2**	**0**	**0**	**73**	**8.2**	**9**	**0**	**0.0**	**17:27**	**5**	**0**	**1**	**1**	**0**	**0**	**0**	**0**	**20:14**
	Norfolk Admirals	AHL	8	2	5	7	4	....	....	....	....	....	....	....	....	....	5	0	3	3	4	....	....	....	....
	Finland	Olympics	6	0	5	5	0	....	....	....	....	....	....	....	....	....	....	....	....	....	....	....	....	....	....
2014-15	**Anaheim**	**NHL**	**67**	**12**	**25**	**37**	**36**	**7**	**1**	**1**	**122**	**9.8**	**5**	**2**	**50.0**	**21:28**	**16**	**3**	**8**	**11**	**8**	**0**	**0**	**0**	**21:14**
	NHL Totals		**123**	**20**	**40**	**60**	**58**	**10**	**1**	**1**	**201**	**10.0**		**2**	**50.0**	**19:32**	**21**	**3**	**9**	**12**	**8**	**0**	**0**	**0**	**21:00**

AHL All-Rookie Team (2013) • AHL First All-Star Team (2013)

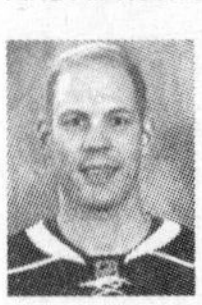

VEILLEUX, Stephane

(VAY-yew, STEH-fan)

Left wing. Shoots left. 6'1", 200 lbs. Born, Beauceville, QC, November 16, 1981. Minnesota's 4th choice, 93rd overall, in 2001 Entry Draft.

1997-98	Beauce-Amiante	Minor-QC	21	20	17	37	....	....	....	....	....	....	....	....	....	....	....	....	....	....	....	....	....	....	....
	Levis	QAAA	14	3	5	8	12	....	....	....	....	....	....	....	....	....	1	0	0	0	0	....	....	....	....
1998-99	Victoriaville Tigres	QMJHL	65	6	13	19	35	....	....	....	....	....	....	....	....	....	6	1	3	4	2	....	....	....	....
99-2000	Victoriaville Tigres	QMJHL	22	1	4	5	17	....	....	....	....	....	....	....	....	....	....	....	....	....	....	....	....	....	....
	Val-d'Or Foreurs	QMJHL	50	14	28	42	100	....	....	....	....	....	....	....	....	....	....	....	....	....	....	....	....	....	....
2000-01	Val-d'Or Foreurs	QMJHL	68	48	67	115	90	....	....	....	....	....	....	....	....	....	21	15	18	33	42	....	....	....	....
2001-02	Houston Aeros	AHL	77	13	22	35	113	....	....	....	....	....	....	....	....	....	14	2	4	6	20	....	....	....	....
2002-03	**Minnesota**	**NHL**	**38**	**3**	**2**	**5**	**23**	**1**	**0**	**0**	**52**	**5.8**	**-6**	**13**	**7.7**	**12:08**	....	....	....	....	....	....	....	....	....
	Houston Aeros	AHL	29	8	4	12	43	....	....	....	....	....	....	....	....	....	23	7	11	18	12	....	....	....	....
2003-04	**Minnesota**	**NHL**	**19**	**2**	**8**	**10**	**20**	**1**	**1**	**1**	**37**	**5.4**	**0**	**10**	**40.0**	**14:20**	....	....	....	....	....	....	....	....	....
	Houston Aeros	AHL	64	13	25	38	66	....	....	....	....	....	....	....	....	....	2	1	1	2	2	....	....	....	....
2004-05	Houston Aeros	AHL	59	15	24	39	35	....	....	....	....	....	....	....	....	....	....	....	....	....	....	....	....	....	....
2005-06	**Minnesota**	**NHL**	**71**	**7**	**9**	**16**	**63**	**0**	**0**	**1**	**87**	**8.0**	**-13**	**33**	**33.3**	**12:58**	....	....	....	....	....	....	....	....	....
2006-07	**Minnesota**	**NHL**	**75**	**7**	**11**	**18**	**47**	**0**	**0**	**1**	**84**	**8.3**	**3**	**32**	**21.9**	**12:17**	**5**	**0**	**0**	**0**	**4**	**0**	**0**	**0**	**12:40**
2007-08	**Minnesota**	**NHL**	**77**	**11**	**7**	**18**	**61**	**0**	**0**	**0**	**136**	**8.1**	**-13**	**45**	**37.8**	**14:32**	**6**	**0**	**0**	**0**	**27**	**0**	**0**	**0**	**15:43**
2008-09	**Minnesota**	**NHL**	**81**	**13**	**10**	**23**	**40**	**0**	**1**	**1**	**146**	**8.9**	**-17**	**22**	**27.3**	**15:48**	....	....	....	....	....	....	....	....	....
2009-10	**Tampa Bay**	**NHL**	**77**	**3**	**6**	**9**	**48**	**0**	**0**	**0**	**94**	**3.2**	**-14**	**25**	**40.0**	**12:17**	....	....	....	....	....	....	....	....	....
2010-11	Blues Espoo	Finland	25	1	6	7	18	....	....	....	....	....	....	....	....	....	....	....	....	....	....	....	....	....	....
	HC Ambri-Piotta	Swiss	7	0	0	0	4	....	....	....	....	....	....	....	....	....	11	0	1	1	31	....	....	....	....
2011-12	**New Jersey**	**NHL**	**1**	**0**	**0**	**0**	**0**	**0**	**0**	**0**	**0**	**0.0**	**0**	**0**	**0.0**	**4:34**	....	....	....	....	....	....	....	....	....
	Albany Devils	AHL	40	11	11	22	53	....	....	....	....	....	....	....	....	....	....	....	....	....	....	....	....	....	....
	Minnesota	**NHL**	**21**	**0**	**2**	**2**	**15**	**0**	**0**	**0**	**16**	**0.0**	**-2**	**10**	**30.0**	**10:04**	....	....	....	....	....	....	....	....	....

			Regular Season														Playoffs								
Season	Club	League	GP	G	A	Pts	PIM	PP	SH	GW	S	S%	+/-	TF	F%	Min	GP	G	A	Pts	PIM	PP	SH	GW	Min
2012-13	Houston Aeros	AHL	33	3	5	8	45	....	....	....	....	....	....	....	....	....	3	0	2	2	6	....	....	....	....
	Minnesota	**NHL**	....	....	....	....	....	....	....	....	....	....	....	....	....	....	**2**	**0**	**0**	**0**	**0**	**0**	**0**	**0**	**7:32**
2013-14	**Minnesota**	**NHL**	**34**	**3**	**0**	**3**	**21**	**0**	**0**	**0**	**26**	**11.5**	**–2**	**2**	**50.0**	**8:26**	**4**	**0**	**0**	**0**	**4**	**0**	**0**	**0**	**7:18**
	Iowa Wild	AHL	34	5	9	14	33	....	....	....	....	....	....	....	....	....	....	....	....	....	....	....	....	....	....
2014-15	**Minnesota**	**NHL**	**12**	**1**	**1**	**2**	**10**	**0**	**0**	**1**	**9**	**11.1**	**0**	**1**	**0.0**	**7:42**	....	....	....	....	....	....	....	....	....
	Iowa Wild	AHL	60	5	15	20	81	....	....	....	....	....	....	....	....	....	....	....	....	....	....	....	....	....	....
	NHL Totals		**506**	**50**	**56**	**106**	**348**	**2**	**2**	**5**	**687**	**7.3**		**193**	**31.1**	**12:53**	**17**	**0**	**0**	**0**	**35**	**0**	**0**	**0**	**11:52**

Signed as a free agent by **Tampa Bay**, July 7, 2009. Signed as a free agent by **Espoo** (Finland), October 15, 2010. Signed as a free agent by **Ambri-Piotta** (Swiss), January 23, 2011. Signed as a free agent by **New Jersey**, July 30, 2011. Traded to **Minnesota** by **New Jersey** with Kurtis Foster, Nick Palmieri, Washington's 2nd round choice (previously acquired, Minnesota selected Raphael Bussieres) in 2012 Entry Draft and New Jersey's 3rd round choice (later traded to NY Islanders – NY Islanders selected Eamon McAdam) in 2013 Entry Draft for Marek Zidlicky, February 24, 2012.

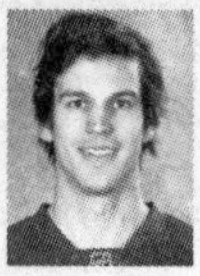

VERMETTE, Antoine

(vuhr-MEHT, AN-twuhn) **ARI**

Center. Shoots left. 6'1", 198 lbs. Born, St-Agapit, QC, July 20, 1982. Ottawa's 3rd choice, 55th overall, in 2000 Entry Draft.

			Regular Season														Playoffs								
Season	Club	League	GP	G	A	Pts	PIM	PP	SH	GW	S	S%	+/-	TF	F%	Min	GP	G	A	Pts	PIM	PP	SH	GW	Min
1997-98	Quebec Select	QAHA	19	11	20	31	36	....	....	....	....	....	....	....	....	....	....	....	....	....	....	....	....	....	....
	Levis	QAAA	8	1	1	2	4	....	....	....	....	....	....	....	....	....	1	0	0	0	0	....	....	....	....
1998-99	Quebec Remparts	QMJHL	57	9	17	26	32	....	....	....	....	....	....	....	....	....	13	0	0	0	2	....	....	....	....
99-2000	Victoriaville Tigres	QMJHL	71	30	41	71	87	....	....	....	....	....	....	....	....	....	6	0	1	1	6	....	....	....	....
2000-01	Victoriaville Tigres	QMJHL	71	57	62	119	102	....	....	....	....	....	....	....	....	....	9	4	6	10	14	....	....	....	....
2001-02	Victoriaville Tigres	QMJHL	4	0	2	2	6	....	....	....	....	....	....	....	....	....	22	10	16	26	10	....	....	....	....
2002-03	Binghamton	AHL	80	34	28	62	57	....	....	....	....	....	....	....	....	....	14	2	9	11	10	....	....	....	....
2003-04	**Ottawa**	**NHL**	**57**	**7**	**7**	**14**	**16**	**0**	**1**	**0**	**63**	**11.1**	**5**	**100**	**44.0**	**11:59**	**4**	**0**	**1**	**1**	**4**	**0**	**0**	**0**	**11:35**
	Binghamton	AHL	3	0	0	0	6	....	....	....	....	....	....	....	....	....	....	....	....	....	....	....	....	....	....
2004-05	Binghamton	AHL	78	28	45	73	36	....	....	....	....	....	....	....	....	....	6	1	4	5	10	....	....	....	....
2005-06	**Ottawa**	**NHL**	**82**	**21**	**12**	**33**	**44**	**1**	**6**	**4**	**123**	**17.1**	**17**	**537**	**57.9**	**12:35**	**10**	**2**	**0**	**2**	**4**	**0**	**0**	**1**	**15:00**
2006-07	**Ottawa**	**NHL**	**77**	**19**	**20**	**39**	**52**	**2**	**3**	**2**	**151**	**12.6**	**–2**	**834**	**53.0**	**15:42**	**20**	**2**	**3**	**5**	**6**	**0**	**0**	**0**	**16:20**
2007-08	**Ottawa**	**NHL**	**81**	**24**	**29**	**53**	**51**	**4**	**3**	**3**	**175**	**13.7**	**3**	**1217**	**56.7**	**17:35**	**4**	**0**	**0**	**0**	**4**	**0**	**0**	**0**	**20:33**
2008-09	**Ottawa**	**NHL**	**62**	**9**	**19**	**28**	**42**	**2**	**0**	**0**	**141**	**6.4**	**–12**	**771**	**58.4**	**18:03**	....	....	....	....	....	....	....	....	....
	Columbus	**NHL**	**17**	**7**	**6**	**13**	**8**	**1**	**1**	**1**	**33**	**21.2**	**5**	**341**	**56.3**	**19:29**	**4**	**0**	**0**	**0**	**10**	**0**	**0**	**0**	**16:47**
2009-10	**Columbus**	**NHL**	**82**	**27**	**38**	**65**	**32**	**6**	**2**	**1**	**156**	**17.3**	**2**	**1573**	**54.2**	**20:09**	....	....	....	....	....	....	....	....	....
2010-11	**Columbus**	**NHL**	**82**	**19**	**28**	**47**	**60**	**3**	**1**	**3**	**183**	**10.4**	**0**	**1540**	**55.6**	**18:49**	....	....	....	....	....	....	....	....	....
2011-12	**Columbus**	**NHL**	**60**	**8**	**19**	**27**	**12**	**2**	**1**	**3**	**106**	**7.5**	**–17**	**804**	**56.3**	**17:14**	....	....	....	....	....	....	....	....	....
	Phoenix	**NHL**	**22**	**3**	**7**	**10**	**16**	**2**	**0**	**1**	**43**	**7.0**	**4**	**336**	**57.1**	**17:07**	**16**	**5**	**5**	**10**	**24**	**3**	**0**	**0**	**18:04**
2012-13	**Phoenix**	**NHL**	**48**	**13**	**8**	**21**	**36**	**3**	**0**	**3**	**91**	**14.3**	**–3**	**839**	**57.5**	**18:15**	....	....	....	....	....	....	....	....	....
2013-14	**Phoenix**	**NHL**	**82**	**24**	**21**	**45**	**44**	**7**	**3**	**4**	**160**	**15.0**	**0**	**1783**	**56.4**	**19:13**	....	....	....	....	....	....	....	....	....
2014-15	**Arizona**	**NHL**	**63**	**13**	**22**	**35**	**34**	**6**	**0**	**1**	**85**	**15.3**	**–23**	**1381**	**56.1**	**18:59**	....	....	....	....	....	....	....	....	....
	♦ Chicago	**NHL**	**19**	**0**	**3**	**3**	**6**	**0**	**0**	**0**	**24**	**0.0**	**–2**	**196**	**50.0**	**14:04**	**20**	**4**	**3**	**7**	**4**	**0**	**0**	**3**	**13:08**
	NHL Totals		**834**	**194**	**239**	**433**	**453**	**39**	**21**	**26**	**1534**	**12.6**		**12252**	**55.8**	**17:10**	**78**	**13**	**12**	**25**	**56**	**3**	**0**	**4**	**15:41**

AHL All-Rookie Team (2003)

• Missed majority of 2001-02 due to neck injury in Team Canada Jr. Selection Camp, June 3, 2001. Traded to **Columbus** by **Ottawa** for Pascal Leclaire and Columbus' 2nd round choice (Robin Lehner) in 2009 Entry Draft, March 4, 2009. Traded to **Phoenix** by **Columbus** for Curtis McElhinney, Ottawa's 2nd round choice (previously acquired, later traded to Philadelphia – Philadelphia selected Anthony Stolarz) in 2012 Entry Draft and Phoenix's 4th round choice (later traded to Philadelphia, later traded to Los Angeles – Los Angeles selected Justin Auger) in 2013 Entry Draft, February 22, 2012. Traded to **Chicago** by **Arizona** for Klas Dahlbeck and Chicago's 1st round choice (Nick Merkley) in 2015 Entry Draft, February 28, 2015. Signed as a free agent by **Arizona**, July 1, 2015.

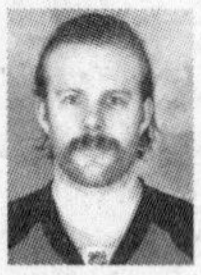

VERSTEEG, Kris

(vuhr-STEEG, KRIHS) **CHI**

Left wing. Shoots right. 5'11", 176 lbs. Born, Lethbridge, AB, May 13, 1986. Boston's 4th choice, 134th overall, in 2004 Entry Draft.

			Regular Season														Playoffs								
Season	Club	League	GP	G	A	Pts	PIM	PP	SH	GW	S	S%	+/-	TF	F%	Min	GP	G	A	Pts	PIM	PP	SH	GW	Min
2002-03	Lethbridge	WHL	57	8	10	18	32	....	....	....	....	....	....	....	....	....	....	....	....	....	....	....	....	....	....
2003-04	Lethbridge	WHL	68	16	33	49	85	....	....	....	....	....	....	....	....	....	....	....	....	....	....	....	....	....	....
2004-05	Lethbridge	WHL	68	22	30	52	68	....	....	....	....	....	....	....	....	....	5	0	1	1	4	....	....	....	....
2005-06	Kamloops Blazers	WHL	14	6	6	12	24	....	....	....	....	....	....	....	....	....	....	....	....	....	....	....	....	....	....
	Red Deer Rebels	WHL	57	10	26	36	103	....	....	....	....	....	....	....	....	....	....	....	....	....	....	....	....	....	....
	Providence Bruins	AHL	13	2	4	6	13	....	....	....	....	....	....	....	....	....	3	0	0	0	6	....	....	....	....
2006-07	Providence Bruins	AHL	43	22	27	49	19	....	....	....	....	....	....	....	....	....	....	....	....	....	....	....	....	....	....
	Norfolk Admirals	AHL	27	4	19	23	20	....	....	....	....	....	....	....	....	....	2	0	0	0	2	....	....	....	....
2007-08	**Chicago**	**NHL**	**13**	**2**	**2**	**4**	**6**	**0**	**0**	**0**	**21**	**9.5**	**–1**	**3**	**66.7**	**15:52**	....	....	....	....	....	....	....	....	....
	Rockford IceHogs	AHL	56	18	31	49	174	....	....	....	....	....	....	....	....	....	12	6	5	11	6	....	....	....	....
2008-09	**Chicago**	**NHL**	**78**	**22**	**31**	**53**	**55**	**6**	**4**	**3**	**139**	**15.8**	**15**	**266**	**46.6**	**17:02**	**17**	**4**	**8**	**12**	**22**	**3**	**0**	**0**	**16:14**
2009-10♦	**Chicago**	**NHL**	**79**	**20**	**24**	**44**	**35**	**4**	**3**	**4**	**184**	**10.9**	**8**	**183**	**42.1**	**15:44**	**22**	**6**	**8**	**14**	**14**	**0**	**0**	**2**	**17:13**
2010-11	**Toronto**	**NHL**	**53**	**14**	**21**	**35**	**29**	**5**	**0**	**0**	**128**	**10.9**	**–13**	**77**	**52.0**	**18:56**	....	....	....	....	....	....	....	....	....
	Philadelphia	**NHL**	**27**	**7**	**4**	**11**	**24**	**1**	**1**	**0**	**52**	**13.5**	**4**	**53**	**43.4**	**15:22**	**11**	**1**	**5**	**6**	**12**	**0**	**0**	**0**	**15:00**
2011-12	**Florida**	**NHL**	**71**	**23**	**31**	**54**	**49**	**8**	**1**	**5**	**181**	**12.7**	**4**	**65**	**32.3**	**19:55**	**7**	**3**	**2**	**5**	**8**	**2**	**0**	**1**	**20:34**
2012-13	**Florida**	**NHL**	**10**	**2**	**2**	**4**	**8**	**0**	**0**	**0**	**20**	**10.0**	**–8**	**5**	**0.0**	**16:53**	....	....	....	....	....	....	....	....	....
2013-14	**Florida**	**NHL**	**18**	**2**	**5**	**7**	**9**	**0**	**0**	**0**	**47**	**4.3**	**–9**	**19**	**47.4**	**15:42**	....	....	....	....	....	....	....	....	....
	Chicago	**NHL**	**63**	**10**	**19**	**29**	**27**	**1**	**0**	**1**	**110**	**9.1**	**9**	**100**	**47.0**	**14:06**	**15**	**1**	**2**	**3**	**4**	**0**	**0**	**0**	**11:56**
2014-15♦	**Chicago**	**NHL**	**61**	**14**	**20**	**34**	**35**	**2**	**0**	**1**	**134**	**10.4**	**11**	**48**	**31.3**	**15:51**	**12**	**1**	**1**	**2**	**6**	**0**	**0**	**0**	**13:21**
	NHL Totals		**473**	**116**	**159**	**275**	**277**	**27**	**9**	**14**	**1016**	**11.4**		**819**	**43.7**	**16:44**	**84**	**16**	**26**	**42**	**66**	**5**	**0**	**3**	**15:31**

NHL All-Rookie Team (2009)

Traded to **Chicago** by **Boston** with future considerations for Brandon Bochenski, February 3, 2007. Traded to **Toronto** by **Chicago** with Bill Sweatt for Viktor Stalberg, Chris Didomenico and Phillipe Paradis, June 30, 2010. Traded to **Philadelphia** by **Toronto** for Philadelphia's 1st (Stuart Percy) and 3rd (Josh Leivo) round choices in 2011 Entry Draft, February 14, 2011. Traded to **Florida** by **Philadelphia** for Florida's 2nd round choice (later traded to Tampa Bay – Tampa Bay selected Brian Hart) in 2012 Entry Draft and San Jose's 3rd round choice (previously acquired, Philadelphia selected Shayne Gostibehere) in 2012 Entry Draft, July 1, 2011. • Missed majority of 2012-13 due to recurring chest injury and knee injury vs. Tampa Bay, March 12, 2013. Traded to **Chicago** by **Florida** with Phillipe Lefebvre for Jimmy Hayes and Dylan Olsen, November 14, 2013.

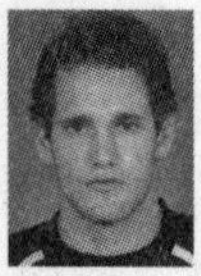

VEY, Linden

(VAY, LIHN-duhn) **VAN**

Right wing. Shoots right. 6', 183 lbs. Born, Wakaw, SK, July 17, 1991. Los Angeles' 5th choice, 96th overall, in 2009 Entry Draft.

			Regular Season														Playoffs								
Season	Club	League	GP	G	A	Pts	PIM	PP	SH	GW	S	S%	+/-	TF	F%	Min	GP	G	A	Pts	PIM	PP	SH	GW	Min
2006-07	Beardy's	SMHL	44	28	44	72	26	....	....	....	....	....	....	....	....	....	....	....	....	....	....	....	....	....	....
	Medicine Hat	WHL	2	0	0	0	2	....	....	....	....	....	....	....	....	....	....	....	....	....	....	....	....	....	....
2007-08	Medicine Hat	WHL	48	8	9	17	21	....	....	....	....	....	....	....	....	....	5	0	1	1	2	....	....	....	....
2008-09	Medicine Hat	WHL	71	24	48	72	20	....	....	....	....	....	....	....	....	....	11	2	5	7	2	....	....	....	....
2009-10	Medicine Hat	WHL	72	24	51	75	34	....	....	....	....	....	....	....	....	....	12	2	6	8	8	....	....	....	....
2010-11	Medicine Hat	WHL	69	46	70	*116	36	....	....	....	....	....	....	....	....	....	15	12	13	25	8	....	....	....	....
2011-12	Manchester	AHL	74	19	24	43	16	....	....	....	....	....	....	....	....	....	4	2	4	6	0	....	....	....	....
2012-13	Manchester	AHL	74	22	45	67	32	....	....	....	....	....	....	....	....	....	4	2	0	2	4	....	....	....	....
2013-14	**Los Angeles**	**NHL**	**18**	**0**	**5**	**5**	**0**	**0**	**0**	**0**	**8**	**0.0**	**0**	**124**	**44.4**	**12:08**	....	....	....	....	....	....	....	....	....
	Manchester	AHL	43	14	34	48	20	....	....	....	....	....	....	....	....	....	4	0	2	2	4	....	....	....	....
2014-15	**Vancouver**	**NHL**	**75**	**10**	**14**	**24**	**18**	**4**	**0**	**2**	**61**	**16.4**	**–3**	**502**	**42.8**	**13:10**	**1**	**0**	**0**	**0**	**0**	**0**	**0**	**0**	**9:59**
	NHL Totals		**93**	**10**	**19**	**29**	**18**	**4**	**0**	**2**	**69**	**14.5**		**626**	**43.1**	**12:58**	**1**	**0**	**0**	**0**	**0**	**0**	**0**	**0**	**9:59**

WHL East First All-Star Team (2011)

Traded to **Vancouver** by **Los Angeles** for Tampa Bay's 2nd round choice (previously acquired, Los Angeles selected Roland McKeown) in 2014 Entry Draft, June 28, 2014.

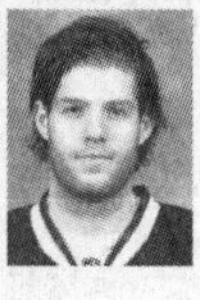

VINCOUR, Tomas

(VIHN-tsoh-oor, TAW-mahsh)

Center. Shoots right. 6'2", 204 lbs. Born, Brno, Czech., November 19, 1990. Dallas' 4th choice, 129th overall, in 2009 Entry Draft.

			Regular Season														Playoffs								
Season	Club	League	GP	G	A	Pts	PIM	PP	SH	GW	S	S%	+/-	TF	F%	Min	GP	G	A	Pts	PIM	PP	SH	GW	Min
2004-05	Brno U17	CzR-U17	42	23	13	36	36	....	....	....	....	....	....	....	....	....	....	....	....	....	....	....	....	....	....
2005-06	Brno U17	CzR-U17	21	13	14	27	77	....	....	....	....	....	....	....	....	....	....	....	....	....	....	....	....	....	....
	Brno Jr.	CzRep-Jr.	28	8	10	18	61	....	....	....	....	....	....	....	....	....	....	....	....	....	....	....	....	....	....
	Brno	CzRep-2	1	0	0	0	0	....	....	....	....	....	....	....	....	....	....	....	....	....	....	....	....	....	....
2006-07	Brno U17	CzR-U17	1	0	0	0	0	....	....	....	....	....	....	....	....	....	2	0	2	2	0	....	....	....	....
	Brno Jr.	CzRep-Jr.	41	15	24	39	58	....	....	....	....	....	....	....	....	....	....	....	....	....	....	....	....	....	....
	Brno	CzRep-2	4	0	1	1	0	....	....	....	....	....	....	....	....	....	....	....	....	....	....	....	....	....	....
2007-08	Edmonton	WHL	65	16	23	39	36	....	....	....	....	....	....	....	....	....	....	....	....	....	....	....	....	....	....
2008-09	Edmonton	WHL	49	17	19	36	23	....	....	....	....	....	....	....	....	....	....	....	....	....	....	....	....	....	....
2009-10	Edmonton	WHL	33	17	9	26	31	....	....	....	....	....	....	....	....	....	....	....	....	....	....	....	....	....	....
	Vancouver Giants	WHL	24	12	10	22	17	....	....	....	....	....	....	....	....	....	15	7	6	13	8	....	....	....	....
2010-11	**Dallas**	**NHL**	**24**	**1**	**1**	**2**	**4**	**0**	**0**	**0**	**26**	**3.8**	**–5**	**4**	**75.0**	**9:26**	....	....	....	....	....	....	....	....	....
	Texas Stars	AHL	44	5	7	12	10	....	....	....	....	....	....	....	....	....	6	0	1	1	4	....	....	....	....

			Regular Season														Playoffs								
Season	Club	League	GP	G	A	Pts	PIM	PP	SH	GW	S	S%	+/-	TF	F%	Min	GP	G	A	Pts	PIM	PP	SH	GW	Min
2011-12	Dallas	NHL	47	4	6	10	2	0	0	1	65	6.2	–2	9	11.1	10:20									
	Texas Stars	AHL	22	12	4	16	8																		
2012-13	Texas Stars	AHL	47	13	15	28	20																		
	Dallas	NHL	15	2	1	3	2	0	0	0	11	18.2	0	5	0.0	8:50									
	Lake Erie	AHL	6	5	6	11	2																		
	Colorado	NHL	2	0	1	1	2	0	0	0	1	0.0	–1	0	0.0	9:04									
2013-14	Ak Bars Kazan	KHL	39	6	5	11	12										3	0	2	2	0				
2014-15	Colorado	NHL	7	0	1	1	2	0	0	0	2	0.0	–1	0	0.0	7:10									
	Lake Erie	AHL	38	10	13	23	10																		
	NHL Totals		95	7	10	17	12	0	0	1	105	6.7		18	22.2	9:36									

Traded to **Colorado** by **Dallas** for Cameron Gaunce, April 2, 2013. Signed as a free agent by **Kazan** (KHL), June 18, 2013.

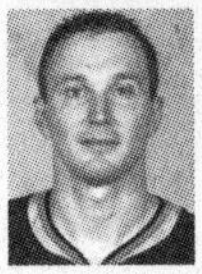

VISNOVSKY, Lubomir

(vihsh-NAWV-skee, LOO-boh-mihr)

Defense. Shoots left. 5'10", 192 lbs. Born, Topolcany, Czech., August 11, 1976. Los Angeles' 4th choice, 118th overall, in 2000 Entry Draft.

Season	Club	League	GP	G	A	Pts	PIM	PP	SH	GW	S	S%	+/-	TF	F%	Min	GP	G	A	Pts	PIM	PP	SH	GW	Min
1994-95	Bratislava	Slovakia	36	11	12	23	10										9	1	3	4	2				
1995-96	Bratislava	Slovakia	35	8	6	14	22										13	1	5	6	2				
1996-97	Bratislava	Slovakia	44	11	12	23											2	0	1	1					
	Bratislava	EuroHL	6	3	1	4	2										2	0	0	0	6				
1997-98	Bratislava	Slovakia	36	7	9	16	16										11	2	4	6	8				
	Bratislava	EuroHL	6	1	0	1	4																		
	Slovakia	Olympics	3	0	0	0	2																		
1998-99	Bratislava	Slovakia	40	9	10	19	31										10	5	5	10	0				
	Bratislava	EuroHL	6	0	3	3	4																		
99-2000	Bratislava	Slovakia	52	21	24	45	38										8	5	3	8	16				
2000-01	Los Angeles	NHL	81	7	32	39	36	3	0	3	105	6.7	16	0	0.0	16:58	8	0	0	0	0	0	0	0	13:57
2001-02	Los Angeles	NHL	72	4	17	21	14	1	0	2	95	4.2	–5	0	0.0	16:15	4	0	1	1	0	0	0	0	8:22
	Slovakia	Olympics	3	1	2	3	0																		
2002-03	Los Angeles	NHL	57	8	16	24	28	1	0	1	85	9.4	2	0	0.0	19:20									
2003-04	Los Angeles	NHL	58	8	21	29	26	5	0	0	114	7.0	8	0	0.0	24:02									
2004-05	Bratislava	Slovakia	43	13	25	38	40										14	2	10	12	10				
2005-06	Los Angeles	NHL	80	17	50	67	50	10	0	3	152	11.2	7	1	100.0	23:16									
	Slovakia	Olympics	6	1	1	2	0																		
2006-07	Los Angeles	NHL	69	18	40	58	26	8	0	0	159	11.3	1	6	33.3	24:27									
2007-08	Los Angeles	NHL	82	8	33	41	34	3	0	1	153	5.2	–18	8	12.5	23:00									
2008-09	Edmonton	NHL	50	8	23	31	30	5	0	1	86	9.3	6	0	0.0	23:01									
2009-10	Edmonton	NHL	57	10	22	32	16	4	0	1	78	12.8	–4	0	0.0	20:45									
	Slovakia	Olympics	7	2	1	3	0																		
	Anaheim	NHL	16	5	8	13	4	1	0	1	53	9.4	–6	0	0.0	26:00									
2010-11	Anaheim	NHL	81	18	50	68	24	5	0	4	152	11.8	18	0	0.0	24:18	6	0	3	3	2	0	0	0	21:21
2011-12	Anaheim	NHL	68	6	21	27	47	1	0	1	112	5.4	7	1	100.0	20:47									
2012-13	Bratislava	KHL	32	6	10	16	22																		
	NY Islanders	NHL	35	3	11	14	20	1	0	0	69	4.3	12	0	0.0	22:48	6	0	2	2	2	0	0	0	22:51
2013-14	NY Islanders	NHL	24	3	8	11	10	2	0	1	34	8.8	–1	0	0.0	20:32									
2014-15	NY Islanders	NHL	53	5	15	20	8	2	0	1	85	5.9	–3	1	0.0	19:32	4	0	2	2	0	0	0	0	16:20
	NHL Totals		883	128	367	495	373	52	0	20	1532	8.4		17	29.4	21:26	28	0	8	8	4	0	0	0	16:59

NHL All-Rookie Team (2001) • NHL Second All-Star Team (2011)

Played in NHL All-Star Game (2007)

Signed as a free agent by **Bratislava** (Slovakia), September 27, 2004. Traded to **Edmonton** by **Los Angeles** for Jarret Stoll and Matt Greene, June 29, 2008. Traded to **Anaheim** by **Edmonton** for Ryan Whitney and Anaheim's 6th round choice (Brandon Davidson) in 2010 Entry Draft, March 3, 2010. Traded to **NY Islanders** by **Anaheim** for NY Islanders' 2nd round choice (Nick Sorensen) in 2013 Entry Draft, June 22, 2012. Signed as a free agent by **Bratislava** (KHL), September 15, 2012. • Missed majority of 2013-14 due to head inury vs. Carolina, October 19, 2013.

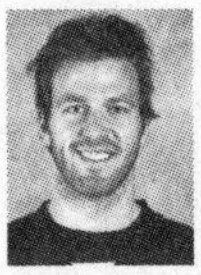

VITALE, Joe

(vih-TA-lee, JOH) **ARI**

Center. Shoots right. 5'11", 205 lbs. Born, St. Louis, MO, August 20, 1985. Pittsburgh's 7th choice, 195th overall, in 2005 Entry Draft.

Season	Club	League	GP	G	A	Pts	PIM	PP	SH	GW	S	S%	+/-	TF	F%	Min	GP	G	A	Pts	PIM	PP	SH	GW	Min
2003-04	St. Louis Jr. Blues	CSJHL	43	21	29	50	42																		
2004-05	Sioux Falls	USHL	53	11	20	31	62																		
2005-06	Northeastern	H-East	31	8	8	16	71																		
2006-07	Northeastern	H-East	35	7	9	16	54																		
2007-08	Northeastern	H-East	37	12	23	35	75																		
2008-09	Northeastern	H-East	40	7	20	27	68																		
	Wilkes-Barre	AHL	5	2	2	4	2										12	0	0	0	12				
2009-10	Wilkes-Barre	AHL	74	6	26	32	70										4	0	2	2	0				
2010-11	Pittsburgh	NHL	9	1	1	2	13	0	0	0	13	7.7	–1	64	56.3	10:34									
	Wilkes-Barre	AHL	60	9	21	30	64										11	3	3	6	18				
2011-12	Pittsburgh	NHL	68	4	10	14	56	0	0	1	70	5.7	–5	723	55.7	11:11	4	0	0	0	12	0	0	0	6:09
2012-13	Pittsburgh	NHL	33	2	3	5	17	0	0	1	26	7.7	–7	257	61.1	9:31	6	0	1	1	6	0	0	0	9:53
2013-14	Pittsburgh	NHL	53	1	13	14	29	0	0	1	42	2.4	–1	320	62.5	10:58	13	0	0	0	4	0	0	0	9:18
2014-15	Arizona	NHL	70	3	6	9	36	0	0	0	55	5.5	–11	733	48.3	11:14									
	NHL Totals		233	11	33	44	151	0	0	3	206	5.3		2097	54.8	10:53	23	0	1	1	22	0	0	0	8:54

Hockey East Second All-Star Team (2008)

Signed as a free agent by **Arizona**, July 1, 2014.

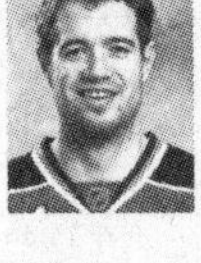

VLASIC, Marc-Edouard

(vih-LASH-ihc, MAHRK-EHD-wahrd) **S.J.**

Defense. Shoots left. 6'1", 205 lbs. Born, Montreal, QC, March 30, 1987. San Jose's 2nd choice, 35th overall, in 2005 Entry Draft.

Season	Club	League	GP	G	A	Pts	PIM	PP	SH	GW	S	S%	+/-	TF	F%	Min	GP	G	A	Pts	PIM	PP	SH	GW	Min
2002-03	West Island Lions	QAAA	41	4	6	10	14										9	0	3	3	0				
2003-04	West Island Lions	QAAA	2	1	1	2	0																		
	Quebec Remparts	QMJHL	41	1	9	10	4										5	0	1	1	0				
2004-05	Quebec Remparts	QMJHL	70	5	25	30	33										13	2	7	9	2				
2005-06	Quebec Remparts	QMJHL	66	16	57	73	57										23	5	24	29	10				
2006-07	San Jose	NHL	81	3	23	26	18	2	0	0	66	4.5	13	0	0.0	22:12	11	0	1	1	2	0	0	0	22:52
2007-08	San Jose	NHL	82	2	12	14	24	1	0	0	72	2.8	–12	0	0.0	21:37	13	0	1	1	0	0	0	0	24:39
	Worcester Sharks	AHL	1	0	2	2	0																		
2008-09	San Jose	NHL	82	6	30	36	42	3	0	1	104	5.8	15	0	0.0	23:54	6	0	1	1	0	0	0	0	20:39
2009-10	San Jose	NHL	64	3	13	16	33	1	0	0	74	4.1	21	0	0.0	22:05	15	0	3	3	4	0	0	0	21:53
2010-11	San Jose	NHL	80	4	14	18	18	0	0	2	116	3.4	14	0	0.0	20:52	18	0	3	3	4	0	0	0	21:45
2011-12	San Jose	NHL	82	4	19	23	40	0	0	1	119	3.4	11	0	0.0	23:09	5	0	0	0	2	0	0	0	20:53
2012-13	San Jose	NHL	48	3	4	7	29	0	0	0	59	5.1	5	0	0.0	20:49	11	1	1	2	6	0	0	0	20:40
2013-14	San Jose	NHL	81	5	19	24	38	0	1	0	138	3.6	31	0	0.0	20:43	5	1	2	3	0	1	0	0	17:00
	Canada	Olympics	6	0	0	0	0																		
2014-15	San Jose	NHL	70	9	14	23	23	0	0	3	98	9.2	12	0	0.0	22:07									
	NHL Totals		670	39	148	187	265	7	1	7	846	4.6		0	0.0	22:00	84	2	12	14	18	1	0	0	21:49

NHL All-Rookie Team (2007)

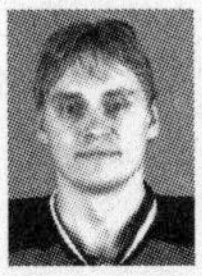

VOLCHENKOV, Anton

(vohl-chen-KAHF, AN-tawn)

Defense. Shoots left. 6'1", 225 lbs. Born, Moscow, USSR, February 25, 1982. Ottawa's 1st choice, 21st overall, in 2000 Entry Draft.

Season	Club	League	GP	G	A	Pts	PIM	PP	SH	GW	S	S%	+/-	TF	F%	Min	GP	G	A	Pts	PIM	PP	SH	GW	Min
99-2000	HK Moscow 2	Russia-3	6	0	1	1	10																		
	HK Moscow	Russia-2	30	2	9	11	36																		
2000-01	Krylja Sovetov	Russia-2	34	3	4	7	56																		
2001-02	Krylja Sovetov 2	Russia-3	1	0	0	0	0																		
	Krylja Sovetov	Russia	47	4	16	20	50										3	0	0	0	29				
2002-03	Ottawa	NHL	57	3	13	16	40	0	0	0	75	4.0	–4	0	0.0	15:30	17	1	1	2	4	0	0	1	13:31
2003-04	Ottawa	NHL	19	1	2	3	8	0	0	0	15	6.7	1	0	0.0	13:04	5	0	0	0	6	0	0	0	11:52
2004-05	Binghamton	AHL	69	10	35	45	62										6	0	3	3	0				
2005-06	Ottawa	NHL	75	4	13	17	53	0	0	0	82	4.9	21	0	0.0	18:03	9	0	4	4	8	0	0	0	13:53
	Russia	Olympics	8	0	0	0	2																		

Season	Club	League	Regular Season GP	G	A	Pts	PIM	PP	SH	GW	S	S%	+/-	TF	F%	Min	Playoffs GP	G	A	Pts	PIM	PP	SH	GW	Min
2006-07	**Ottawa**	**NHL**	**78**	**1**	**18**	**19**	**67**	**0**	**0**	**0**	**85**	**1.2**	**37**	**0**	**0.0**	**21:17**	**20**	**2**	**4**	**6**	**24**	**0**	**0**	**1**	**23:19**
2007-08	**Ottawa**	**NHL**	**67**	**1**	**14**	**15**	**55**	**0**	**0**	**1**	**71**	**1.4**	**14**	**0**	**0.0**	**20:31**	**4**	**0**	**1**	**1**	**2**	**0**	**0**	**0**	**17:11**
2008-09	**Ottawa**	**NHL**	**68**	**2**	**8**	**10**	**36**	**0**	**0**	**1**	**79**	**2.5**	**-10**	**0**	**0.0**	**20:08**	....	....	....	....	....	....	....	....	....
2009-10	**Ottawa**	**NHL**	**64**	**4**	**10**	**14**	**38**	**0**	**0**	**0**	**69**	**5.8**	**2**	**0**	**0.0**	**20:41**	**6**	**0**	**2**	**2**	**4**	**0**	**0**	**0**	**22:30**
	Russia	Olympics	4	0	1	1	2	....	....	....	....	....	....	....	....	....	....	....	....	....	....	....	....	....	....
2010-11	**New Jersey**	**NHL**	**57**	**0**	**8**	**8**	**36**	**0**	**0**	**0**	**65**	**0.0**	**3**	**0**	**0.0**	**18:06**	....	....	....	....	....	....	....	....	....
2011-12	**New Jersey**	**NHL**	**72**	**2**	**9**	**11**	**34**	**0**	**0**	**1**	**63**	**3.2**	**3**	**0**	**0.0**	**17:59**	**24**	**1**	**1**	**2**	**10**	**0**	**0**	**0**	**16:04**
2012-13	Nizhny Novgorod	KHL	11	0	1	1	16	....	....	....	....	....	....	....	....	....	....	....	....	....	....	....	....	....	....
	New Jersey	**NHL**	**37**	**1**	**4**	**5**	**37**	**0**	**0**	**0**	**38**	**2.6**	**-1**	**0**	**0.0**	**16:03**	....	....	....	....	....	....	....	....	....
2013-14	**New Jersey**	**NHL**	**56**	**0**	**8**	**8**	**20**	**0**	**0**	**0**	**42**	**0.0**	**3**	**0**	**0.0**	**16:47**	....	....	....	....	....	....	....	....	....
2014-15	**Nashville**	**NHL**	**46**	**0**	**7**	**7**	**14**	**0**	**0**	**0**	**35**	**0.0**	**4**	**0**	**0.0**	**13:11**	**1**	**0**	**0**	**0**	**2**	**0**	**0**	**0**	**13:51**
	NHL Totals		**696**	**19**	**114**	**133**	**438**	**0**	**0**	**3**	**719**	**2.6**		**0**	**0.0**	**18:13**	**86**	**4**	**13**	**17**	**60**	**0**	**0**	**2**	**17:15**

• Missed majority of 2003-04 due to shoulder injury vs. Boston, December 8, 2003. Signed as a free agent by **New Jersey**, July 1, 2010. Signed as a free agent by **Nizhny Novgorod** (KHL), October 9, 2012. Signed as a free agent by **Nashville**, July 7, 2014.

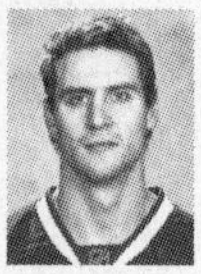

VOLPATTI, Aaron

(vohl-PA-tee, AIR-uhn)

Left wing. Shoots left. 6', 215 lbs. Born, Revelstoke, BC, May 30, 1985.

Season	Club	League	GP	G	A	Pts	PIM	PP	SH	GW	S	S%	+/-	TF	F%	Min	GP	G	A	Pts	PIM	PP	SH	GW	Min
2003-04	Vernon Vipers	BCHL	55	1	4	5	134	....	....	....	....	....	....	....	....	....	....	....	....	....	....	....	....	....	....
2004-05	Vernon Vipers	BCHL	57	6	12	18	106	....	....	....	....	....	....	....	....	....	....	....	....	....	....	....	....	....	....
2005-06	Vernon Vipers	BCHL	25	6	8	14	39	....	....	....	....	....	....	....	....	....	....	....	....	....	....	....	....	....	....
2006-07	Brown U.	ECAC	23	5	2	7	39	....	....	....	....	....	....	....	....	....	....	....	....	....	....	....	....	....	....
2007-08	Brown U.	ECAC	31	4	6	10	28	....	....	....	....	....	....	....	....	....	....	....	....	....	....	....	....	....	....
2008-09	Brown U.	ECAC	32	6	6	12	54	....	....	....	....	....	....	....	....	....	....	....	....	....	....	....	....	....	....
2009-10	Brown U.	ECAC	37	17	15	32	*115	....	....	....	....	....	....	....	....	....	....	....	....	....	....	....	....	....	....
	Manitoba Moose	AHL	8	1	1	2	17	....	....	....	....	....	....	....	....	....	5	1	0	1	21	....	....	....	....
2010-11	**Vancouver**	**NHL**	**15**	**1**	**1**	**2**	**16**	**0**	**0**	**0**	**6**	**16.7**	**-1**	**0**	**0.0**	**6:50**	....	....	....	....	....	....	....	....	....
	Manitoba Moose	AHL	53	2	9	11	74	....	....	....	....	....	....	....	....	....	12	1	2	3	36	....	....	....	....
2011-12	**Vancouver**	**NHL**	**23**	**1**	**0**	**1**	**37**	**0**	**0**	**0**	**17**	**5.9**	**-2**	**4**	**100.0**	**8:58**	....	....	....	....	....	....	....	....	....
2012-13	**Vancouver**	**NHL**	**16**	**1**	**0**	**1**	**28**	**0**	**0**	**0**	**11**	**9.1**	**0**	**2**	**0.0**	**7:19**	....	....	....	....	....	....	....	....	....
	Washington	**NHL**	**17**	**0**	**1**	**1**	**7**	**0**	**0**	**0**	**10**	**0.0**	**-2**	**2**	**50.0**	**9:18**	....	....	....	....	....	....	....	....	....
2013-14	**Washington**	**NHL**	**41**	**2**	**0**	**2**	**49**	**0**	**0**	**0**	**18**	**11.1**	**-3**	**12**	**33.3**	**7:22**	....	....	....	....	....	....	....	....	....
2014-15	**Washington**	**NHL**	**2**	**0**	**0**	**0**	**0**	**0**	**0**	**0**	**1**	**0.0**	**0**	**0**	**0.0**	**9:37**	....	....	....	....	....	....	....	....	....
	Hershey Bears	AHL	5	0	0	0	8	....	....	....	....	....	....	....	....	....	....	....	....	....	....	....	....	....	....
	NHL Totals		**114**	**5**	**2**	**7**	**137**	**0**	**0**	**0**	**63**	**7.9**		**20**	**45.0**	**7:56**	....	....	....	....	....	....	....	....	....

Signed as a free agent by **Vancouver**, March 22, 2010. • Missed majority of 2011-12 due to shoulder injury at Los Angeles, November 10, 2011. Claimed on waivers by **Washington** from **Vancouver**, February 28, 2013. • Missed majority of 2014-15 due to off-season neck surgery and as a healthy reserve.

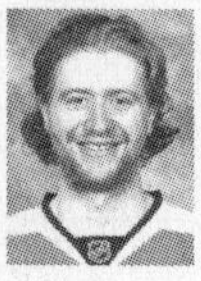

VORACEK, Jakub

(VOHR-rah-chehk, YA-kuhb) **PHI**

Right wing. Shoots left. 6'2", 214 lbs. Born, Kladno, Czech., August 15, 1989. Columbus' 1st choice, 7th overall, in 2007 Entry Draft.

Season	Club	League	GP	G	A	Pts	PIM	PP	SH	GW	S	S%	+/-	TF	F%	Min	GP	G	A	Pts	PIM	PP	SH	GW	Min
2002-03	HC Kladno U17	CzR-U17	2	1	1	2	2	....	....	....	....	....	....	....	....	....	2	1	1	2	0	....	....	....	....
2003-04	HC Kladno U17	CzR-U17	52	30	24	54	26	....	....	....	....	....	....	....	....	....	2	0	0	0	2	....	....	....	....
2004-05	HC Kladno U17	CzR-U17	30	23	39	62	44	....	....	....	....	....	....	....	....	....	7	5	4	9	14	....	....	....	....
	HC Kladno Jr.	CzRep-Jr.	16	5	7	12	6	....	....	....	....	....	....	....	....	....	1	1	0	1	2	....	....	....	....
2005-06	HC Kladno U17	CzR-U17	....	....	....	....	....	....	....	....	....	....	....	....	....	....	2	1	3	4	31	....	....	....	....
	HC Kladno Jr.	CzRep-Jr.	46	21	38	59	54	....	....	....	....	....	....	....	....	....	6	7	4	11	2	....	....	....	....
	HC Rabat Kladno	CzRep	1	0	0	0	0	....	....	....	....	....	....	....	....	....	....	....	....	....	....	....	....	....	....
2006-07	Halifax	QMJHL	59	23	63	86	26	....	....	....	....	....	....	....	....	....	12	7	17	24	6	....	....	....	....
2007-08	Halifax	QMJHL	53	33	68	101	42	....	....	....	....	....	....	....	....	....	15	5	13	18	14	....	....	....	....
2008-09	**Columbus**	**NHL**	**80**	**9**	**29**	**38**	**44**	**0**	**0**	**1**	**101**	**8.9**	**11**	**3**	**0.0**	**12:40**	**4**	**0**	**1**	**1**	**8**	**0**	**0**	**0**	**12:06**
2009-10	**Columbus**	**NHL**	**81**	**16**	**34**	**50**	**26**	**4**	**0**	**1**	**154**	**10.4**	**-7**	**6**	**33.3**	**15:37**	....	....	....	....	....	....	....	....	....
2010-11	**Columbus**	**NHL**	**80**	**14**	**32**	**46**	**26**	**2**	**0**	**2**	**183**	**7.7**	**-3**	**65**	**36.9**	**16:58**	....	....	....	....	....	....	....	....	....
2011-12	**Philadelphia**	**NHL**	**78**	**18**	**31**	**49**	**32**	**0**	**0**	**2**	**190**	**9.5**	**11**	**23**	**30.4**	**16:17**	**11**	**2**	**8**	**10**	**8**	**1**	**0**	**1**	**15:58**
2012-13	HC Lev Praha	KHL	23	7	13	20	22	....	....	....	....	....	....	....	....	....	....	....	....	....	....	....	....	....	....
	Philadelphia	**NHL**	**48**	**22**	**24**	**46**	**35**	**8**	**0**	**3**	**129**	**17.1**	**-7**	**5**	**40.0**	**17:14**	....	....	....	....	....	....	....	....	....
2013-14	**Philadelphia**	**NHL**	**82**	**23**	**39**	**62**	**22**	**8**	**0**	**2**	**235**	**9.8**	**11**	**6**	**66.7**	**17:15**	**7**	**2**	**2**	**4**	**4**	**1**	**0**	**1**	**16:57**
	Czech Republic	Olympics	5	1	1	2	2	....	....	....	....	....	....	....	....	....	....	....	....	....	....	....	....	....	....
2014-15	**Philadelphia**	**NHL**	**82**	**22**	**59**	**81**	**78**	**11**	**0**	**3**	**221**	**10.0**	**1**	**9**	**66.7**	**18:36**	....	....	....	....	....	....	....	....	....
	NHL Totals		**531**	**124**	**248**	**372**	**263**	**33**	**0**	**14**	**1213**	**10.2**		**117**	**38.5**	**16:20**	**22**	**4**	**11**	**15**	**20**	**2**	**0**	**2**	**15:34**

QMJHL All-Rookie Team (2007) • QMJHL Rookie of the Year (2007) • QMJHL Second All-Star Team (2008) • NHL First All-Star Team (2015)

Played in NHL All-Star Game (2015)

Traded to **Philadelphia** by **Columbus** with Columbus' 1st (Sean Couturier) and 3rd (Nick Cousins) round choices in 2011 Entry Draft for Jeff Carter, June 23, 2011. Signed as a free agent by **Lev Praha** (KHL), September 16, 2012.

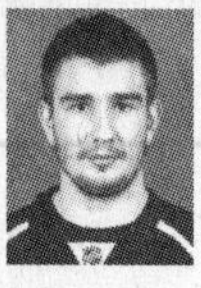

VOYNOV, Slava

(VOY-nawf, SLA-vuh) **L.A.**

Defense. Shoots right. 6', 201 lbs. Born, Chelyabinsk, USSR, January 15, 1990. Los Angeles' 3rd choice, 32nd overall, in 2008 Entry Draft.

Season	Club	League	GP	G	A	Pts	PIM	PP	SH	GW	S	S%	+/-	TF	F%	Min	GP	G	A	Pts	PIM	PP	SH	GW	Min
2005-06	Chelyabinsk 2	Russia-3	2	0	0	0	0	....	....	....	....	....	....	....	....	....	....	....	....	....	....	....	....	....	....
2006-07	Chelyabinsk	Russia	31	0	0	0	12	....	....	....	....	....	....	....	....	....	....	....	....	....	....	....	....	....	....
2007-08	Chelyabinsk 2	Russia-3	2	1	0	1	0	....	....	....	....	....	....	....	....	....	....	....	....	....	....	....	....	....	....
	Chelyabinsk	Russia	36	1	3	4	20	....	....	....	....	....	....	....	....	....	2	0	0	0	0	....	....	....	....
2008-09	Manchester	AHL	61	8	15	23	46	....	....	....	....	....	....	....	....	....	....	....	....	....	....	....	....	....	....
2009-10	Manchester	AHL	79	10	19	29	43	....	....	....	....	....	....	....	....	....	9	1	3	4	0	....	....	....	....
2010-11	Manchester	AHL	76	15	36	51	36	....	....	....	....	....	....	....	....	....	7	2	3	5	6	....	....	....	....
2011-12♦	**Los Angeles**	**NHL**	**54**	**8**	**12**	**20**	**12**	**3**	**0**	**2**	**86**	**9.3**	**12**	**0**	**0.0**	**18:32**	**20**	**1**	**2**	**3**	**4**	**0**	**0**	**0**	**19:32**
	Manchester	AHL	15	2	2	4	4	....	....	....	....	....	....	....	....	....	....	....	....	....	....	....	....	....	....
2012-13	Manchester	AHL	35	7	9	16	22	....	....	....	....	....	....	....	....	....	....	....	....	....	....	....	....	....	....
	Los Angeles	**NHL**	**48**	**6**	**19**	**25**	**14**	**1**	**0**	**2**	**79**	**7.6**	**5**	**2**	**100.0**	**22:18**	**18**	**6**	**7**	**13**	**0**	**0**	**0**	***4**	**21:55**
2013-14♦	**Los Angeles**	**NHL**	**82**	**4**	**30**	**34**	**44**	**1**	**0**	**0**	**143**	**2.8**	**6**	**1**	**100.0**	**22:18**	**26**	**2**	**7**	**9**	**16**	**1**	**0**	**0**	**23:08**
2014-15	**Los Angeles**	**NHL**	**6**	**0**	**2**	**2**	**2**	**0**	**0**	**0**	**5**	**0.0**	**0**	**0**	**0.0**	**23:11**	....	....	....	....	....	....	....	....	....
	NHL Totals		**190**	**18**	**63**	**81**	**72**	**5**	**0**	**4**	**313**	**5.8**		**3**	**100.0**	**21:15**	**64**	**9**	**16**	**25**	**20**	**1**	**0**	**4**	**21:40**

AHL Second All-Star Team (2011)

• Suspended indefinitely by the NHL during the pendancy of a criminal investigation for domestic violence, October 20, 2014.

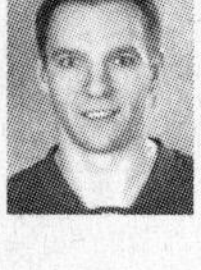

VRBATA, Radim

(vuhr-BA-tuh, RA-dihm) **VAN**

Right wing. Shoots right. 6'1", 194 lbs. Born, Mlada Boleslav, Czech., June 13, 1981. Colorado's 10th choice, 212th overall, in 1999 Entry Draft.

Season	Club	League	GP	G	A	Pts	PIM	PP	SH	GW	S	S%	+/-	TF	F%	Min	GP	G	A	Pts	PIM	PP	SH	GW	Min
1997-98	Ml. Boleslav Jr.	CzRep-Jr.	35	42	31	73	4	....	....	....	....	....	....	....	....	....	....	....	....	....	....	....	....	....	....
1998-99	Hull Olympiques	QMJHL	54	22	38	60	16	....	....	....	....	....	....	....	....	....	23	6	13	19	6	....	....	....	....
99-2000	Hull Olympiques	QMJHL	58	29	45	74	26	....	....	....	....	....	....	....	....	....	15	3	9	12	8	....	....	....	....
2000-01	Shawinigan	QMJHL	55	56	64	120	67	....	....	....	....	....	....	....	....	....	10	4	7	11	4	....	....	....	....
	Hershey Bears	AHL						....	....	....	....	....	....	....	....	....	1	0	1	1	2	....	....	....	....
2001-02	**Colorado**	**NHL**	**52**	**18**	**12**	**30**	**14**	**6**	**0**	**3**	**112**	**16.1**	**7**	**8**	**37.5**	**14:32**	**9**	**0**	**0**	**0**	**0**	**0**	**0**	**0**	**13:05**
	Hershey Bears	AHL	20	8	14	22	8	....	....	....	....	....	....	....	....	....	....	....	....	....	....	....	....	....	....
2002-03	**Colorado**	**NHL**	**66**	**11**	**19**	**30**	**16**	**3**	**0**	**4**	**171**	**6.4**	**0**	**14**	**50.0**	**13:55**	....	....	....	....	....	....	....	....	....
	Carolina	**NHL**	**10**	**5**	**0**	**5**	**2**	**3**	**0**	**0**	**44**	**11.4**	**-7**	**15**	**46.7**	**19:00**	....	....	....	....	....	....	....	....	....
2003-04	**Carolina**	**NHL**	**80**	**12**	**13**	**25**	**24**	**4**	**0**	**2**	**195**	**6.2**	**-10**	**21**	**38.1**	**13:42**	....	....	....	....	....	....	....	....	....
2004-05	Liberec	CzRep	45	18	21	39	91	....	....	....	....	....	....	....	....	....	12	3	2	5	0	....	....	....	....
2005-06	**Carolina**	**NHL**	**16**	**2**	**3**	**5**	**6**	**1**	**0**	**0**	**38**	**5.3**	**0**	**3**	**33.3**	**12:37**	....	....	....	....	....	....	....	....	....
	Chicago	**NHL**	**45**	**13**	**21**	**34**	**16**	**5**	**0**	**0**	**147**	**8.8**	**4**	**6**	**50.0**	**15:43**	....	....	....	....	....	....	....	....	....
2006-07	**Chicago**	**NHL**	**77**	**14**	**27**	**41**	**26**	**5**	**0**	**2**	**215**	**6.5**	**-4**	**12**	**33.3**	**16:53**	....	....	....	....	....	....	....	....	....
2007-08	**Phoenix**	**NHL**	**76**	**27**	**29**	**56**	**14**	**7**	**3**	**5**	**246**	**11.0**	**6**	**19**	**36.8**	**18:12**	....	....	....	....	....	....	....	....	....
2008-09	**Tampa Bay**	**NHL**	**18**	**3**	**3**	**6**	**8**	**1**	**0**	**0**	**41**	**7.3**	**-1**	**3**	**33.3**	**14:13**	....	....	....	....	....	....	....	....	....
	BK Mlada Boleslav	CzRep	11	5	3	8	18	....	....	....	....	....	....	....	....	....	....	....	....	....	....	....	....	....	....
	Liberec	CzRep	7	7	2	9	2	....	....	....	....	....	....	....	....	....	3	0	1	1	2	....	....	....	....
2009-10	**Phoenix**	**NHL**	**82**	**24**	**19**	**43**	**24**	**7**	**0**	**4**	**266**	**9.0**	**6**	**8**	**25.0**	**16:13**	**7**	**2**	**2**	**4**	**4**	**1**	**0**	**1**	**15:42**
2010-11	**Phoenix**	**NHL**	**79**	**19**	**29**	**48**	**20**	**10**	**0**	**2**	**240**	**7.9**	**5**	**7**	**28.6**	**16:22**	**4**	**2**	**3**	**5**	**0**	**1**	**0**	**0**	**19:55**

			Regular Season														Playoffs								
Season	Club	League	GP	G	A	Pts	PIM	PP	SH	GW	S	S%	+/-	TF	F%	Min	GP	G	A	Pts	PIM	PP	SH	GW	Min
2011-12	**Phoenix**	**NHL**	**77**	**35**	**27**	**62**	**24**	**9**	**1**	***12**	**232**	**15.1**	**24**	**67**	**40.3**	**18:39**	**16**	**2**	**3**	**5**	**8**	**1**	**0**	**0**	**17:20**
2012-13	BK Mlada Boleslav	CzRep-2	2	1	1	2	0																		
	Phoenix	**NHL**	**34**	**12**	**16**	**28**	**14**	**2**	**1**	**1**	**106**	**11.3**	**6**	**32**	**31.3**	**18:19**									
2013-14	**Phoenix**	**NHL**	**80**	**20**	**31**	**51**	**22**	**10**	**0**	**2**	**263**	**7.6**	**–6**	**43**	**39.5**	**17:57**									
2014-15	**Vancouver**	**NHL**	**79**	**31**	**32**	**63**	**20**	**12**	**0**	**7**	**267**	**11.6**	**6**	**9**	**55.6**	**16:37**	**6**	**2**	**2**	**4**	**0**	**1**	**0**	**0**	**16:10**
	NHL Totals		**871**	**246**	**281**	**527**	**250**	**85**	**5**	**44**	**2583**	**9.5**		**267**	**39.0**	**16:21**	**42**	**8**	**10**	**18**	**12**	**4**	**0**	**1**	**16:14**

QMJHL First All-Star Team (2001)

Played in NHL All-Star Game (2015)

Traded to **Carolina** by **Colorado** for Bates Battaglia, March 11, 2003. Signed as a free agent by **Liberec** (CzRep), September 4, 2004. Traded to **Chicago** by **Carolina** for Chicago's 4th round choice (later traded to St. Louis - St. Louis selected Cade Fairchild) in 2007 Entry Draft, December 29, 2005. Traded to **Phoenix** by **Chicago** for Kevyn Adams, August 11, 2007. Signed as a free agent by **Tampa Bay**, July 1, 2008. • Assigned to **Mlada Boleslav** (CzRep) by **Tampa Bay**, December 9, 2008. • Loaned to **Liberec** (CzRep) by **Mlada Boleslav** (CzRep), January 29, 2009. Traded to **Phoenix** by **Tampa Bay** for Todd Fedoruk and David Hale, July 21, 2009. Signed as a free agent by **Mlada Boleslav** (CzRep-2), November 1, 2012. Signed as a free agent by **Vancouver**, July 3, 2014.

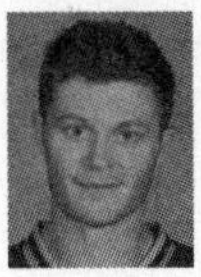

WAGNER, Chris

(WAG-nuhr, KRIHS) **ANA**

Center. Shoots right. 5'11", 201 lbs. Born, Wellesley, MA, May 27, 1991. Anaheim's 4th choice, 122nd overall, in 2010 Entry Draft.

2008-09	South Shore	EJHL	38	20	14	34	72										2	2	0	2	0				
2009-10	South Shore	EJHL	44	34	49	*83	70										4	3	6	9	8				
2010-11	Colgate	ECAC	41	9	10	19	26																		
2011-12	Colgate	ECAC	38	17	34	51	69																		
2012-13	Norfolk Admirals	AHL	70	8	13	21	65																		
2013-14	Norfolk Admirals	AHL	76	14	14	28	68										10	2	3	5	10				
2014-15	**Anaheim**	**NHL**	**9**	**0**	**0**	**0**	**2**	**0**	**0**	**0**	**7**	**0.0**	**–2**	**55**	**60.0**	**8:47**	**2**	**0**	**0**	**0**	**0**	**0**	**0**	**0**	**5:33**
	Norfolk Admirals	AHL	48	15	13	28	65																		
	NHL Totals		**9**	**0**	**0**	**0**	**2**	**0**	**0**	**0**	**7**	**0.0**		**55**	**60.0**	**8:47**	**2**	**0**	**0**	**0**	**0**	**0**	**0**	**0**	**5:33**

ECAC Second All-Star Team (2012)

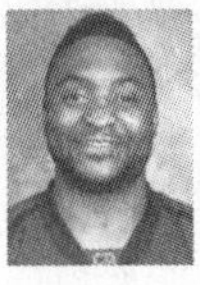

WARD, Joel

(WOHRD, JOHL) **S.J.**

Right wing. Shoots right. 6'1", 226 lbs. Born, Toronto, ON, December 2, 1980.

1997-98	Owen Sound	OHL	47	8	4	12	14										11	1	1	2	5				
1998-99	Owen Sound	OHL	58	19	16	35	23										16	2	4	6	0				
99-2000	Owen Sound	OHL	63	23	20	43	51																		
2000-01	Owen Sound	OHL	67	26	36	62	45										5	2	4	6	4				
	Long Beach	WCHL															8	0	0	0	0				
2001-02	U. of P.E.I.	CIS	22	13	14	27	16																		
2002-03	U. of P.E.I.	CIS	19	11	15	26	24																		
2003-04	U. of P.E.I.	CIS	27	14	24	38	42																		
2004-05	U. of P.E.I.	CIS	28	16	28	44	42																		
2005-06	Houston Aeros	AHL	66	8	14	22	34										8	4	2	6	4				
2006-07	**Minnesota**	**NHL**	**11**	**0**	**1**	**1**	**0**	**0**	**0**	**0**	**12**	**0.0**	**0**	**1**	**0.0**	**7:42**									
	Houston Aeros	AHL	64	9	14	23	45																		
2007-08	Houston Aeros	AHL	79	21	20	41	47										4	0	2	2	0				
2008-09	**Nashville**	**NHL**	**79**	**17**	**18**	**35**	**29**	**3**	**2**	**2**	**133**	**12.8**	**1**	**46**	**43.5**	**16:01**									
2009-10	**Nashville**	**NHL**	**71**	**13**	**21**	**34**	**18**	**3**	**1**	**1**	**134**	**9.7**	**–5**	**81**	**38.3**	**17:33**	**6**	**2**	**2**	**4**	**2**	**0**	**1**	**0**	**19:54**
2010-11	**Nashville**	**NHL**	**80**	**10**	**19**	**29**	**42**	**5**	**0**	**4**	**157**	**6.4**	**–1**	**168**	**48.8**	**17:04**	**12**	**7**	**6**	**13**	**6**	**2**	**0**	**1**	**20:25**
2011-12	**Washington**	**NHL**	**73**	**6**	**12**	**18**	**20**	**0**	**0**	**0**	**79**	**7.6**	**12**	**52**	**55.8**	**12:26**	**14**	**1**	**4**	**5**	**6**	**0**	**0**	**1**	**10:57**
2012-13	**Washington**	**NHL**	**39**	**8**	**12**	**20**	**12**	**1**	**1**	**1**	**52**	**15.4**	**7**	**65**	**58.5**	**15:08**	**7**	**1**	**3**	**4**	**6**	**1**	**0**	**0**	**13:11**
2013-14	**Washington**	**NHL**	**82**	**24**	**25**	**49**	**32**	**6**	**2**	**4**	**133**	**18.0**	**7**	**199**	**45.2**	**16:04**									
2014-15	**Washington**	**NHL**	**82**	**19**	**15**	**34**	**30**	**6**	**0**	**4**	**138**	**13.8**	**–4**	**127**	**47.2**	**16:52**	**14**	**3**	**6**	**9**	**2**	**0**	**0**	**1**	**19:03**
	NHL Totals		**517**	**97**	**123**	**220**	**183**	**24**	**6**	**16**	**838**	**11.6**		**739**	**47.4**	**15:47**	**53**	**14**	**21**	**35**	**22**	**3**	**1**	**3**	**16:32**

Signed as a free agent by **Houston** (AHL), December 4, 2005. Signed as a free agent by **Minnesota**, September 27, 2006. Signed as a free agent by **Nashville**, July 14, 2008. Signed as a free agent by **Washington**, July 1, 2011. Signed as a free agent by **San Jose**, July 3, 2015.

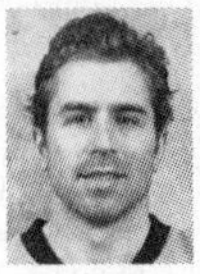

WARSOFSKY, David

(wawr-SAWF-skee, DAY-vihd) **PIT**

Defense. Shoots left. 5'9", 170 lbs. Born, Marshfield, MA, May 30, 1990. St. Louis' 7th choice, 95th overall, in 2008 Entry Draft.

2005-06	Cushing	High-MA		8	26	34																			
2006-07	Cushing	High-MA	29	15	34	49	55																		
2007-08	USNTDP	U-18	41	5	29	34	26																		
	USNTDP	NAHL	15	4	2	6	8																		
2008-09	Boston University	H-East	45	3	20	23	28																		
2009-10	Boston University	H-East	34	12	11	23	48																		
2010-11	Boston University	H-East	34	7	15	22	46																		
	Providence Bruins	AHL	10	0	3	3	6																		
2011-12	Providence Bruins	AHL	66	5	24	29	18																		
2012-13	Providence Bruins	AHL	58	3	13	16	17										12	0	3	3	0				
2013-14	**Boston**	**NHL**	**6**	**1**	**1**	**2**	**0**	**0**	**0**	**0**	**10**	**10.0**	**1**	**0**	**0.0**	**16:10**									
	Providence Bruins	AHL	56	6	26	32	11										12	2	7	9	2				
2014-15	**Boston**	**NHL**	**4**	**0**	**1**	**1**	**0**	**0**	**0**	**0**	**7**	**0.0**	**1**	**0**	**0.0**	**17:46**									
	Providence Bruins	AHL	40	4	11	15	20										5	0	1	1	0				
	NHL Totals		**10**	**1**	**2**	**3**	**0**	**0**	**0**	**0**	**17**	**5.9**		**0**	**0.0**	**16:48**									

Hockey East Second All-Star Team (2011)

Traded to **Boston** by **St. Louis** for Vladimir Sobotka, June 26, 2010. Signed as a free agent by **Pittsburgh**, July 1, 2015.

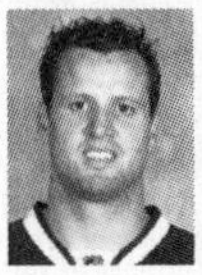

WATHIER, Francis

(waw-TEE-ay, FRAN-sihs)

Left wing. Shoots left. 6'4", 218 lbs. Born, St Isidore, ON, December 7, 1984. Dallas' 8th choice, 185th overall, in 2003 Entry Draft.

2001-02	Hull Olympiques	QMJHL	63	1	3	4	68										12	1	2	3	30				
2002-03	Hull Olympiques	QMJHL	72	9	18	27	143										20	1	6	7	20				
2003-04	Gatineau	QMJHL	51	9	16	25	127										15	0	2	2	23				
2004-05	Gatineau	QMJHL	67	15	20	35	96										10	0	2	2	8				
2005-06	Iowa Stars	AHL	11	0	1	1	26																		
2006-07	Iowa Stars	AHL	57	14	3	17	78										12	0	4	4	25				
	Idaho Steelheads	ECHL	17	4	9	13	31										7	1	1	2	4				
2007-08	Iowa Stars	AHL	19	2	3	5	17																		
2008-09	Iowa Chops	AHL	77	6	10	16	127																		
2009-10	**Dallas**	**NHL**	**5**	**0**	**0**	**0**	**5**	**0**	**0**	**0**	**4**	**0.0**	**0**	**1**	**100.0**	**5:18**									
	Texas Stars	AHL	76	19	21	40	101										24	2	6	8	18				
2010-11	**Dallas**	**NHL**	**3**	**0**	**0**	**0**	**0**	**0**	**0**	**0**	**0**	**0.0**	**–2**	**0**	**0.0**	**3:55**									
	Texas Stars	AHL	68	19	16	35	78										6	0	0	0	4				
2011-12	**Dallas**	**NHL**	**1**	**0**	**0**	**0**	**0**	**0**	**0**	**0**	**0**	**0.0**	**0**	**0**	**0.0**	**5:25**									
	Texas Stars	AHL	75	18	24	42	94																		
2012-13	Texas Stars	AHL	61	4	16	20	77										9	1	0	1	4				
	Dallas	**NHL**	**1**	**0**	**0**	**0**	**0**	**0**	**0**	**0**	**0**	**0.0**	**0**	**2**	**0.0**	**5:40**									
2013-14	Texas Stars	AHL	48	5	4	9	41																		
	Milwaukee	AHL	17	4	7	11	25										3	0	0	0	6				
2014-15	Portland Pirates	AHL	68	5	9	14	53										5	3	0	3	4				
	NHL Totals		**10**	**0**	**0**	**0**	**5**	**0**	**0**	**0**	**4**	**0.0**		**3**	**33.3**	**4:56**									

• Missed majority of 2005-06 and 2007-08 due to shoulder injuries. Signed to a PTO (professional tryout) contract by **Portland** (AHL), October 21, 2014.

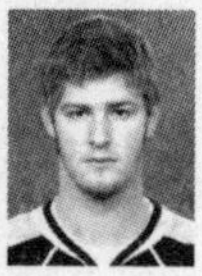

WATSON, Austin

(WAWT-suhn, AW-stuhn) **NSH**

Left wing. Shoots right. 6'4", 193 lbs. Born, Ann Arbor, MI, January 13, 1992. Nashville's 1st choice, 18th overall, in 2010 Entry Draft.

			Regular Season														Playoffs								
Season	Club	League	GP	G	A	Pts	PIM	PP	SH	GW	S	S%	+/-	TF	F%	Min	GP	G	A	Pts	PIM	PP	SH	GW	Min
2007-08	Det. Compuware	Minor-MI	....	45	104	149	....	....	....	....	....	....	....	....	....	....	....	....	....	....	....	....	....	....	....
2008-09	Windsor Spitfires	OHL	63	10	19	29	41	....	....	....	....	....	....	....	....	....	20	0	3	3	15	....	....	....	....
2009-10	Windsor Spitfires	OHL	42	11	23	34	14	....	....	....	....	....	....	....	....	....	....	....	....	....	....	....	....	....	....
	Peterborough	OHL	10	9	11	20	8	....	....	....	....	....	....	....	....	....	4	2	0	2	2	....	....	....	....
2010-11	Peterborough	OHL	68	34	34	68	54	....	....	....	....	....	....	....	....	....	....	....	....	....	....	....	....	....	....
	Milwaukee	AHL	5	0	0	0	0	....	....	....	....	....	....	....	....	....	3	0	0	0	0	....	....	....	....
2011-12	Peterborough	OHL	32	14	19	33	33	....	....	....	....	....	....	....	....	....	....	....	....	....	....	....	....	....	....
	London Knights	OHL	29	11	24	35	14	....	....	....	....	....	....	....	....	....	19	10	7	17	10	....	....	....	....
2012-13	Milwaukee	AHL	72	20	17	37	22	....	....	....	....	....	....	....	....	....	4	1	0	1	0	....	....	....	....
	Nashville	**NHL**	**6**	**1**	**0**	**1**	**0**	**0**	**0**	**0**	**4**	**25.0**	**–2**	**44**	**43.2**	**12:42**	....	....	....	....	....	....	....	....	....
2013-14	Milwaukee	AHL	76	22	24	46	24	....	....	....	....	....	....	....	....	....	3	0	0	0	6	....	....	....	....
2014-15	Milwaukee	AHL	76	26	18	44	34	....	....	....	....	....	....	....	....	....	....	....	....	....	....	....	....	....	....
	NHL Totals		**6**	**1**	**0**	**1**	**0**	**0**	**0**	**0**	**4**	**25.0**		**44**	**43.2**	**12:42**	....	....	....	....	....	....	....	....	....

OHL Playoff MVP (2012) • Memorial Cup All-Star Team (2012)

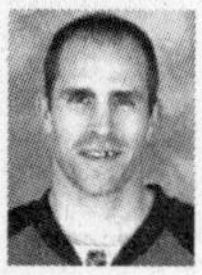

WEAVER, Mike

(WEE-vuhr, MIGHK)

Defense. Shoots right. 5'10", 183 lbs. Born, Bramalea, ON, May 2, 1978.

			Regular Season														Playoffs								
Season	Club	League	GP	G	A	Pts	PIM	PP	SH	GW	S	S%	+/-	TF	F%	Min	GP	G	A	Pts	PIM	PP	SH	GW	Min
1995-96	Bramalea Blues	ON-Jr.A	48	10	39	49	103	....	....	....	....	....	....	....	....	....	....	....	....	....	....	....	....	....	....
1996-97	Michigan State	CCHA	39	0	7	7	46	....	....	....	....	....	....	....	....	....	....	....	....	....	....	....	....	....	....
1997-98	Michigan State	CCHA	44	4	22	26	68	....	....	....	....	....	....	....	....	....	....	....	....	....	....	....	....	....	....
1998-99	Michigan State	CCHA	42	1	6	7	54	....	....	....	....	....	....	....	....	....	....	....	....	....	....	....	....	....	....
99-2000	Michigan State	CCHA	26	0	7	7	20	....	....	....	....	....	....	....	....	....	....	....	....	....	....	....	....	....	....
2000-01	Orlando	IHL	68	0	8	8	34	....	....	....	....	....	....	....	....	....	16	0	2	2	8	....	....	....	....
2001-02	**Atlanta**	**NHL**	**16**	**0**	**1**	**1**	**10**	**0**	**0**	**0**	**9**	**0.0**	**0**	**0**	**0.0**	**13:54**	....	....	....	....	....	....	....	....	....
	Chicago Wolves	AHL	58	2	8	10	67	....	....	....	....	....	....	....	....	....	25	1	3	4	21	....	....	....	....
2002-03	**Atlanta**	**NHL**	**40**	**0**	**5**	**5**	**20**	**0**	**0**	**0**	**21**	**0.0**	**–5**	**0**	**0.0**	**18:38**	....	....	....	....	....	....	....	....	....
	Chicago Wolves	AHL	33	2	2	4	32	....	....	....	....	....	....	....	....	....	9	0	3	3	4	....	....	....	....
2003-04	**Atlanta**	**NHL**	**1**	**0**	**0**	**0**	**0**	**0**	**0**	**0**	**0**	**0.0**	**–1**	**0**	**0.0**	**8:28**	....	....	....	....	....	....	....	....	....
	Chicago Wolves	AHL	78	3	14	17	89	....	....	....	....	....	....	....	....	....	9	2	2	4	20	....	....	....	....
2004-05	Manchester	AHL	79	1	22	23	61	....	....	....	....	....	....	....	....	....	6	0	1	1	0	....	....	....	....
2005-06	**Los Angeles**	**NHL**	**53**	**0**	**9**	**9**	**14**	**0**	**0**	**0**	**21**	**0.0**	**–3**	**0**	**0.0**	**15:03**	....	....	....	....	....	....	....	....	....
2006-07	**Los Angeles**	**NHL**	**39**	**3**	**6**	**9**	**16**	**1**	**0**	**1**	**22**	**13.6**	**–4**	**3**	**66.7**	**15:20**	....	....	....	....	....	....	....	....	....
	Manchester	AHL	7	1	3	4	2	....	....	....	....	....	....	....	....	....	....	....	....	....	....	....	....	....	....
2007-08	**Vancouver**	**NHL**	**55**	**0**	**1**	**1**	**33**	**0**	**0**	**0**	**33**	**0.0**	**1**	**1**	**0.0**	**14:02**	....	....	....	....	....	....	....	....	....
2008-09	**St. Louis**	**NHL**	**58**	**0**	**7**	**7**	**12**	**0**	**0**	**0**	**36**	**0.0**	**–3**	**0**	**0.0**	**17:16**	**4**	**0**	**0**	**0**	**0**	**0**	**0**	**0**	**17:02**
2009-10	**St. Louis**	**NHL**	**77**	**1**	**9**	**10**	**29**	**0**	**0**	**0**	**33**	**3.0**	**10**	**2**	**50.0**	**16:58**	....	....	....	....	....	....	....	....	....
2010-11	**Florida**	**NHL**	**82**	**2**	**11**	**13**	**34**	**0**	**0**	**1**	**53**	**3.8**	**1**	**0**	**0.0**	**20:48**	....	....	....	....	....	....	....	....	....
2011-12	**Florida**	**NHL**	**82**	**0**	**16**	**16**	**14**	**0**	**0**	**0**	**51**	**0.0**	**–2**	**0**	**0.0**	**20:20**	**7**	**1**	**0**	**1**	**0**	**0**	**0**	**0**	**22:21**
2012-13	**Florida**	**NHL**	**27**	**1**	**8**	**9**	**8**	**0**	**0**	**0**	**21**	**4.8**	**–3**	**0**	**0.0**	**20:08**	....	....	....	....	....	....	....	....	....
2013-14	**Florida**	**NHL**	**55**	**0**	**6**	**6**	**23**	**0**	**0**	**0**	**44**	**0.0**	**–9**	**1**	**100.0**	**18:47**	....	....	....	....	....	....	....	....	....
	Montreal	**NHL**	**17**	**1**	**6**	**7**	**8**	**0**	**0**	**0**	**9**	**11.1**	**9**	**0**	**0.0**	**17:30**	**17**	**1**	**3**	**4**	**14**	**0**	**0**	**0**	**15:34**
2014-15	**Montreal**	**NHL**	**31**	**0**	**4**	**4**	**6**	**0**	**0**	**0**	**8**	**0.0**	**0**	**0**	**0.0**	**14:10**	....	....	....	....	....	....	....	....	....
	NHL Totals		**633**	**8**	**89**	**97**	**227**	**1**	**0**	**2**	**361**	**2.2**		**7**	**57.1**	**17:36**	**28**	**2**	**3**	**5**	**14**	**0**	**0**	**0**	**17:28**

OPJHL Defenseman of the Year (1996) • CCHA All-Tournament Team (1997) • CCHA First All-Star Team (1999, 2000) • CCHA Best Defensive Defenseman Award (1999, 2000) • NCAA West Second All-American Team (1999, 2000)

Signed as a free agent by **Atlanta**, June 15, 2000. Signed as a free agent by **Los Angeles**, July 16, 2004. Signed as a free agent by **Pittsburgh**, August 8, 2007. Claimed on waivers by **Vancouver** from **Pittsburgh**, October 2, 2007. Signed as a free agent by **St. Louis**, July 10, 2008. Signed as a free agent by **Florida**, August 3, 2010. Traded to **Montreal** by **Florida** for Montreal's 5th round choice (later traded to NY Islanders – NY Islanders selected Ryan Pilon) in 2015 Entry Draft, March 4, 2014. • Missed majority of 2014-15 as a healthy reserve.

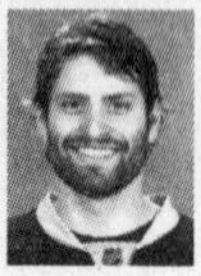

WEBER, Mike

(WEH-buhr, MIGHK) **BUF**

Defense. Shoots left. 6'2", 212 lbs. Born, Pittsburgh, PA, December 16, 1987. Buffalo's 3rd choice, 57th overall, in 2006 Entry Draft.

			Regular Season														Playoffs								
Season	Club	League	GP	G	A	Pts	PIM	PP	SH	GW	S	S%	+/-	TF	F%	Min	GP	G	A	Pts	PIM	PP	SH	GW	Min
2002-03	Jr. Penguins	EmJHL	28	4	11	15	109	....	....	....	....	....	....	....	....	....	3	0	0	0	20	....	....	....	....
2003-04	Windsor Spitfires	OHL	65	0	2	2	49	....	....	....	....	....	....	....	....	....	....	....	....	....	....	....	....	....	....
2004-05	Windsor Spitfires	OHL	68	2	6	8	132	....	....	....	....	....	....	....	....	....	11	0	1	1	18	....	....	....	....
2005-06	Windsor Spitfires	OHL	68	5	21	26	181	....	....	....	....	....	....	....	....	....	7	0	0	0	12	....	....	....	....
2006-07	Windsor Spitfires	OHL	30	3	16	19	86	....	....	....	....	....	....	....	....	....	....	....	....	....	....	....	....	....	....
	Barrie Colts	OHL	30	3	12	15	86	....	....	....	....	....	....	....	....	....	7	0	6	6	10	....	....	....	....
2007-08	**Buffalo**	**NHL**	**16**	**0**	**3**	**3**	**14**	**0**	**0**	**0**	**12**	**0.0**	**12**	**0**	**0.0**	**16:41**	....	....	....	....	....	....	....	....	....
	Rochester	AHL	59	1	13	14	178	....	....	....	....	....	....	....	....	....	....	....	....	....	....	....	....	....	....
2008-09	**Buffalo**	**NHL**	**7**	**0**	**0**	**0**	**19**	**0**	**0**	**0**	**2**	**0.0**	**–3**	**0**	**0.0**	**14:10**	....	....	....	....	....	....	....	....	....
	Portland Pirates	AHL	42	1	7	8	94	....	....	....	....	....	....	....	....	....	....	....	....	....	....	....	....	....	....
2009-10	Portland Pirates	AHL	80	5	16	21	153	....	....	....	....	....	....	....	....	....	4	1	0	1	14	....	....	....	....
2010-11	**Buffalo**	**NHL**	**58**	**4**	**13**	**17**	**69**	**0**	**0**	**0**	**53**	**7.5**	**13**	**0**	**0.0**	**16:54**	**7**	**0**	**1**	**1**	**6**	**0**	**0**	**0**	**15:51**
2011-12	**Buffalo**	**NHL**	**51**	**1**	**4**	**5**	**64**	**0**	**0**	**0**	**51**	**2.0**	**–19**	**0**	**0.0**	**18:35**	....	....	....	....	....	....	....	....	....
2012-13	Lorenskog IK	Norway	5	1	5	6	10	....	....	....	....	....	....	....	....	....	....	....	....	....	....	....	....	....	....
	Buffalo	**NHL**	**42**	**1**	**6**	**7**	**70**	**0**	**0**	**0**	**25**	**4.0**	**3**	**0**	**0.0**	**18:22**	....	....	....	....	....	....	....	....	....
2013-14	**Buffalo**	**NHL**	**68**	**1**	**8**	**9**	**73**	**0**	**0**	**0**	**47**	**2.1**	**–29**	**0**	**0.0**	**17:49**	....	....	....	....	....	....	....	....	....
2014-15	**Buffalo**	**NHL**	**64**	**1**	**6**	**7**	**68**	**0**	**0**	**0**	**41**	**2.4**	**–22**	**0**	**0.0**	**18:45**	....	....	....	....	....	....	....	....	....
	NHL Totals		**306**	**8**	**40**	**48**	**377**	**0**	**0**	**0**	**231**	**3.5**		**0**	**0.0**	**17:54**	**7**	**0**	**1**	**1**	**6**	**0**	**0**	**0**	**15:51**

Signed as a free agent by **Lorenskog** (Norway), November 15, 2012.

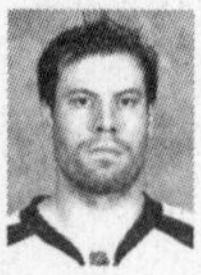

WEBER, Shea

(WEH-buhr, SHAY) **NSH**

Defense. Shoots right. 6'4", 233 lbs. Born, Sicamous, BC, August 14, 1985. Nashville's 4th choice, 49th overall, in 2003 Entry Draft.

			Regular Season														Playoffs								
Season	Club	League	GP	G	A	Pts	PIM	PP	SH	GW	S	S%	+/-	TF	F%	Min	GP	G	A	Pts	PIM	PP	SH	GW	Min
2001-02	Sicamous Eagles	KIJHL	47	9	33	42	87	....	....	....	....	....	....	....	....	....	....	....	....	....	....	....	....	....	....
	Kelowna Rockets	WHL	5	0	0	0	0	....	....	....	....	....	....	....	....	....	....	....	....	....	....	....	....	....	....
2002-03	Kelowna Rockets	WHL	70	2	16	18	167	....	....	....	....	....	....	....	....	....	19	1	4	5	26	....	....	....	....
2003-04	Kelowna Rockets	WHL	60	12	20	32	126	....	....	....	....	....	....	....	....	....	17	3	14	17	16	....	....	....	....
2004-05	Kelowna Rockets	WHL	55	12	29	41	95	....	....	....	....	....	....	....	....	....	18	9	8	17	25	....	....	....	....
2005-06	**Nashville**	**NHL**	**28**	**2**	**8**	**10**	**42**	**2**	**0**	**1**	**46**	**4.3**	**8**	**0**	**0.0**	**17:00**	**4**	**2**	**0**	**2**	**8**	**1**	**0**	**0**	**14:12**
	Milwaukee	AHL	46	12	15	27	49	....	....	....	....	....	....	....	....	....	14	6	5	11	16	....	....	....	....
2006-07	**Nashville**	**NHL**	**79**	**17**	**23**	**40**	**60**	**6**	**0**	**2**	**152**	**11.2**	**13**	**0**	**0.0**	**19:23**	**5**	**0**	**3**	**3**	**2**	**0**	**0**	**0**	**21:41**
2007-08	**Nashville**	**NHL**	**54**	**6**	**14**	**20**	**49**	**5**	**0**	**2**	**152**	**3.9**	**–6**	**0**	**0.0**	**19:30**	**6**	**1**	**3**	**4**	**6**	**0**	**0**	**0**	**19:30**
2008-09	**Nashville**	**NHL**	**81**	**23**	**30**	**53**	**80**	**10**	**1**	**4**	**251**	**9.2**	**1**	**0**	**0.0**	**23:58**	....	....	....	....	....	....	....	....	....
2009-10	**Nashville**	**NHL**	**78**	**16**	**27**	**43**	**36**	**7**	**0**	**3**	**222**	**7.2**	**0**	**0**	**0.0**	**23:10**	**6**	**2**	**1**	**3**	**4**	**0**	**0**	**0**	**24:27**
	Canada	Olympics	7	2	4	6	2	....	....	....	....	....	....	....	....	....	....	....	....	....	....	....	....	....	....
2010-11	**Nashville**	**NHL**	**82**	**16**	**32**	**48**	**56**	**6**	**1**	**3**	**254**	**6.3**	**7**	**0**	**0.0**	**25:19**	**12**	**3**	**2**	**5**	**8**	**2**	**0**	**0**	**27:58**
2011-12	**Nashville**	**NHL**	**78**	**19**	**30**	**49**	**46**	**10**	**2**	**1**	**230**	**8.3**	**21**	**0**	**0.0**	**26:10**	**10**	**2**	**1**	**3**	**9**	**1**	**0**	**0**	**28:27**
2012-13	**Nashville**	**NHL**	**48**	**9**	**19**	**28**	**48**	**3**	**0**	**1**	**124**	**7.3**	**–2**	**0**	**0.0**	**25:55**	....	....	....	....	....	....	....	....	....
2013-14	**Nashville**	**NHL**	**79**	**23**	**33**	**56**	**52**	**12**	**0**	**4**	**195**	**11.8**	**–2**	**0**	**0.0**	**26:54**	....	....	....	....	....	....	....	....	....
	Canada	Olympics	6	3	3	6	0	....	....	....	....	....	....	....	....	....	....	....	....	....	....	....	....	....	....
2014-15	**Nashville**	**NHL**	**78**	**15**	**30**	**45**	**72**	**5**	**1**	**2**	**237**	**6.3**	**15**	**0**	**0.0**	**26:22**	**2**	**0**	**1**	**1**	**2**	**0**	**0**	**0**	**25:49**
	NHL Totals		**685**	**146**	**246**	**392**	**541**	**66**	**5**	**23**	**1863**	**7.8**		**0**	**0.0**	**23:52**	**45**	**10**	**11**	**21**	**39**	**4**	**0**	**0**	**24:28**

WHL West Second All-Star Team (2004) • Memorial Cup All-Star Team (2004) • WHL West First All-Star Team (2005) • Canadian Major Junior Second All-Star Team (2005) • Olympic All-Star Team (2010) • NHL First All-Star Team (2011, 2012) • NHL Second All-Star Team (2014, 2015)

Played in NHL All-Star Game (2009, 2011, 2012, 2015)

			Regular Season															Playoffs								
Season	Club	League	GP	G	A	Pts	PIM	PP	SH	GW	S	S%	+/-	TF	F%	Min	GP	G	A	Pts	PIM	PP	SH	GW	Min

WEBER, Yannick (WEH-buhr, YAH-nihk) **VAN**

Defense. Shoots right. 5'11", 200 lbs.   Born, Morges, Switz., September 23, 1988. Montreal's 5th choice, 73rd overall, in 2007 Entry Draft.

Season	Club	League	GP	G	A	Pts	PIM	PP	SH	GW	S	S%	+/-	TF	F%	Min	GP	G	A	Pts	PIM	PP	SH	GW	Min
2003-04	SC Bern Jr.	Swiss-Jr.	32	2	3	5	39	...	...	...	...	...	...	...	...	...	8	2	0	2	8	...	...	...	...
2004-05	SC Bern Jr.	Swiss-Jr.	37	5	4	9	62	...	...	...	...	...	...	...	...	...	5	0	0	0	22	...	...	...	...
2005-06	SC Bern Future Jr.	Swiss-Jr.	17	1	6	7	46	...	...	...	...	...	...	...	...	...	...	...	...	...	...	...	...	...	...
	SC Langenthal	Swiss-2	28	3	0	3	8	...	...	...	...	...	...	...	...	...	...	...	...	...	...	...	...	...	...
2006-07	SC Bern Future Jr.	Swiss-Jr.	1	0	0	0	2	...	...	...	...	...	...	...	...	...	...	...	...	...	...	...	...	...	...
	Kitchener Rangers	OHL	51	13	28	41	42	...	...	...	...	...	...	...	...	...	9	3	6	9	4	...	...	...	...
2007-08	Kitchener Rangers	OHL	59	20	35	55	79	...	...	...	...	...	...	...	...	...	17	4	13	17	24	...	...	...	...
2008-09	**Montreal**	**NHL**	3	0	1	1	2	0	0	0	6	0.0	-1	0	0.0	15:06	3	1	1	2	0	0	0	0	13:36
	Hamilton	AHL	68	16	28	44	42	...	...	...	...	...	...	...	...	...	2	0	1	1	10	...	...	...	...
2009-10	**Montreal**	**NHL**	5	0	0	0	4	0	0	0	2	0.0	-5	0	0.0	13:53	...	...	...	...	...	...	...	...	...
	Hamilton	AHL	65	7	25	32	58	...	...	...	...	...	...	...	...	...	3	0	0	0	0	...	...	...	...
	Switzerland	Olympics	5	0	0	0	6	...	...	...	...	...	...	...	...	...	...	...	...	...	...	...	...	...	...
2010-11	**Montreal**	**NHL**	41	1	10	11	14	0	0	0	63	1.6	0	0	0.0	16:34	3	2	0	2	0	1	0	0	8:46
	Hamilton	AHL	15	8	4	12	10	...	...	...	...	...	...	...	...	...	...	...	...	...	...	...	...	...	...
2011-12	**Montreal**	**NHL**	60	4	14	18	30	4	0	0	88	4.5	-7	0	0.0	15:37	...	...	...	...	...	...	...	...	...
2012-13	Geneve	Swiss	32	5	16	21	40	...	...	...	...	...	...	...	...	...	...	...	...	...	...	...	...	...	...
	Montreal	**NHL**	6	0	2	2	2	0	0	0	3	0.0	-1	0	0.0	13:45	...	...	...	...	...	...	...	...	...
2013-14	**Vancouver**	**NHL**	49	6	4	10	16	3	0	2	70	8.6	-7	0	0.0	11:55	...	...	...	...	...	...	...	...	...
	Utica Comets	AHL	7	2	5	7	0	...	...	...	...	...	...	...	...	...	...	...	...	...	...	...	...	...	...
	Switzerland	Olympics	4	0	0	0	2	...	...	...	...	...	...	...	...	...	...	...	...	...	...	...	...	...	...
2014-15	**Vancouver**	**NHL**	65	11	10	21	30	5	0	1	117	9.4	4	0	0.0	17:11	6	0	0	0	12	0	0	0	19:10
	NHL Totals		229	22	41	63	98	12	0	3	349	6.3		0	0.0	15:21	12	3	1	4	12	1	0	0	15:11

OHL Second All-Star Team (2008) • AHL All-Rookie Team (2009).
Signed as a free agent by **Geneve** (Swiss), September 18, 2012. Signed as a free agent by **Vancouver**, July 5, 2013.

WEISE, Dale (WEES, DAYL) **MTL**

Right wing. Shoots right. 6'2", 205 lbs.   Born, Winnipeg, MB, August 5, 1988. NY Rangers' 5th choice, 111th overall, in 2008 Entry Draft.

Season	Club	League	GP	G	A	Pts	PIM	PP	SH	GW	S	S%	+/-	TF	F%	Min	GP	G	A	Pts	PIM	PP	SH	GW	Min
2005-06	Swift Current	WHL	53	4	14	18	57	...	...	...	...	...	...	...	...	...	4	0	0	0	2	...	...	...	...
2006-07	Swift Current	WHL	67	18	25	43	94	...	...	...	...	...	...	...	...	...	6	0	1	1	8	...	...	...	...
2007-08	Swift Current	WHL	53	29	22	51	84	...	...	...	...	...	...	...	...	...	12	7	6	13	20	...	...	...	...
2008-09	Hartford	AHL	74	11	12	23	64	...	...	...	...	...	...	...	...	...	6	3	1	4	2	...	...	...	...
2009-10	Hartford	AHL	73	28	22	50	114	...	...	...	...	...	...	...	...	...	...	...	...	...	...	...	...	...	...
2010-11	**NY Rangers**	**NHL**	10	0	0	0	19	0	0	0	9	0.0	-1	0	0.0	6:30	...	...	...	...	...	...	...	...	...
	Connecticut	AHL	47	18	20	38	73	...	...	...	...	...	...	...	...	...	5	2	1	3	8	...	...	...	...
2011-12	**Vancouver**	**NHL**	68	4	4	8	81	0	0	0	48	8.3	-1	4	0.0	8:10	2	0	0	0	0	0	0	0	4:16
2012-13	Trappers Tilburg	Nether.	19	22	26	48	79	...	...	...	...	...	...	...	...	...	...	...	...	...	...	...	...	...	...
	Vancouver	**NHL**	40	3	3	6	43	0	0	2	35	8.6	-7	8	12.5	9:33	4	0	0	0	0	0	0	0	5:38
2013-14	**Vancouver**	**NHL**	44	3	9	12	42	1	0	0	29	10.3	-1	4	0.0	7:46	...	...	...	...	...	...	...	...	...
	Montreal	**NHL**	17	3	1	4	17	0	0	1	12	25.0	4	0	0.0	10:07	16	3	4	7	4	0	0	2	10:14
2014-15	**Montreal**	**NHL**	79	10	19	29	34	0	0	1	91	11.0	21	12	41.7	12:11	12	2	1	3	16	0	0	1	12:31
	NHL Totals		258	23	36	59	236	1	0	4	224	10.3		28	21.4	9:36	34	5	5	10	24	0	0	3	10:09

Claimed on waivers by **Vancouver** from **NY Rangers**, October 4, 2011. Signed as a free agent by **Tilburg** (Netherlands), October 10, 2012. Traded to **Montreal** by **Vancouver** for Raphael Diaz, February 3, 2014.

WEISS, Stephen (WIGHS, STEE-vehn)

Center. Shoots left. 5'11", 190 lbs.   Born, Toronto, ON, April 3, 1983. Florida's 1st choice, 4th overall, in 2001 Entry Draft.

Season	Club	League	GP	G	A	Pts	PIM	PP	SH	GW	S	S%	+/-	TF	F%	Min	GP	G	A	Pts	PIM	PP	SH	GW	Min
1997-98	Tor. Young Nats	MTHL	48	51	58	109	...	...	...	...	...	...	...	...	...	...	...	...	...	...	...	...	...	...	...
1998-99	North York	ON-Jr.A	35	15	22	37	10	...	...	...	...	...	...	...	...	...	...	...	...	...	...	...	...	...	...
99-2000	Plymouth Whalers	OHL	64	24	42	66	35	...	...	...	...	...	...	...	...	...	23	8	18	26	18	...	...	...	...
2000-01	Plymouth Whalers	OHL	62	40	47	87	45	...	...	...	...	...	...	...	...	...	18	7	16	23	10	...	...	...	...
2001-02	**Florida**	**NHL**	7	1	1	2	0	1	0	0	15	6.7	0	107	52.3	16:14	...	...	...	...	...	...	...	...	...
	Plymouth Whalers	OHL	46	25	45	70	69	...	...	...	...	...	...	...	...	...	6	2	7	9	13	...	...	...	...
2002-03	**Florida**	**NHL**	77	6	15	21	17	0	0	2	87	6.9	-13	1065	46.3	14:17	...	...	...	...	...	...	...	...	...
2003-04	**Florida**	**NHL**	50	12	17	29	10	3	0	2	82	14.6	-10	799	44.9	17:42	...	...	...	...	...	...	...	...	...
	San Antonio	AHL	10	6	3	9	14	...	...	...	...	...	...	...	...	...	...	...	...	...	...	...	...	...	...
2004-05	San Antonio	AHL	62	15	23	38	38	...	...	...	...	...	...	...	...	...	...	...	...	...	...	...	...	...	...
	Chicago Wolves	AHL	18	7	9	16	12	...	...	...	...	...	...	...	...	...	18	4	7	9	17	...	...	...	...
2005-06	**Florida**	**NHL**	41	9	12	21	22	5	0	1	74	12.2	-2	514	49.6	15:15	...	...	...	...	...	...	...	...	...
2006-07	**Florida**	**NHL**	74	20	28	48	28	10	0	1	176	11.4	-1	1182	45.9	17:07	...	...	...	...	...	...	...	...	...
2007-08	**Florida**	**NHL**	74	13	29	42	40	4	0	4	132	9.8	14	1198	51.2	17:35	...	...	...	...	...	...	...	...	...
2008-09	**Florida**	**NHL**	78	14	47	61	22	4	1	4	154	9.1	19	1277	50.9	17:48	...	...	...	...	...	...	...	...	...
2009-10	**Florida**	**NHL**	80	28	32	60	40	12	0	2	180	15.6	-17	1551	52.4	20:00	...	...	...	...	...	...	...	...	...
2010-11	**Florida**	**NHL**	76	21	28	49	49	3	2	1	172	12.2	-9	1279	53.9	20:06	...	...	...	...	...	...	...	...	...
2011-12	**Florida**	**NHL**	80	20	37	57	60	5	1	6	149	13.4	5	1469	53.2	20:31	7	3	3	6	3	0	0	0	21:06
2012-13	**Florida**	**NHL**	17	1	3	4	25	1	0	0	19	5.3	-13	276	51.1	18:28	...	...	...	...	...	...	...	...	...
2013-14	**Detroit**	**NHL**	26	2	2	4	12	0	0	1	28	7.1	-4	357	51.5	14:46	...	...	...	...	...	...	...	...	...
2014-15	**Detroit**	**NHL**	52	9	16	25	16	3	0	1	52	17.3	-2	21	47.6	11:21	2	0	0	0	0	0	0	0	10:28
	Grand Rapids	AHL	3	2	0	2	0	...	...	...	...	...	...	...	...	...	...	...	...	...	...	...	...	...	...
	NHL Totals		732	156	267	423	341	51	4	25	1320	11.8		11095	50.4	17:24	9	3	2	5	6	3	0	0	18:44

OHL All-Rookie Team (2000)
• Loaned to **Chicago** (AHL) by **San Antonio** (AHL) for cash, March 8, 2005. • Missed majority of 2012-13 due to recurring wrist injury. Signed as a free agent by **Detroit**, July 5, 2013. • Missed majority of 2013-14 due to groin injury and resulting surgery.

WELLMAN, Casey (WEHL-man, KAY-see)

Center. Shoots right. 6', 173 lbs.   Born, Brentwood, CA, October 18, 1987.

Season	Club	League	GP	G	A	Pts	PIM	PP	SH	GW	S	S%	+/-	TF	F%	Min	GP	G	A	Pts	PIM	PP	SH	GW	Min
2006-07	Cedar Rapids	USHL	50	6	13	19	30	...	...	...	...	...	...	...	...	...	6	1	2	3	0	...	...	...	...
2007-08	Cedar Rapids	USHL	59	22	23	45	30	...	...	...	...	...	...	...	...	...	3	1	1	2	4	...	...	...	...
2008-09	Massachusetts	H-East	39	11	22	33	32	...	...	...	...	...	...	...	...	...	...	...	...	...	...	...	...	...	...
2009-10	**Minnesota**	**NHL**	12	1	3	4	0	0	0	0	18	5.6	-2	32	53.1	12:03	...	...	...	...	...	...	...	...	...
	Massachusetts	H-East	36	23	22	45	38	...	...	...	...	...	...	...	...	...	...	...	...	...	...	...	...	...	...
2010-11	**Minnesota**	**NHL**	15	1	1	2	4	0	0	1	20	5.0	-1	16	50.0	10:39	...	...	...	...	...	...	...	...	...
	Houston Aeros	AHL	42	14	21	35	14	...	...	...	...	...	...	...	...	...	24	6	5	11	6	...	...	...	...
2011-12	**Minnesota**	**NHL**	14	2	5	7	0	0	0	1	25	8.0	-4	9	66.7	12:44	...	...	...	...	...	...	...	...	...
	Houston Aeros	AHL	26	14	11	25	21	...	...	...	...	...	...	...	...	...	...	...	...	...	...	...	...	...	...
	Connecticut	AHL	31	9	13	22	10	...	...	...	...	...	...	...	...	...	9	4	5	9	10	...	...	...	...
2012-13	San Antonio	AHL	37	7	16	23	14	...	...	...	...	...	...	...	...	...	...	...	...	...	...	...	...	...	...
	Hershey Bears	AHL	33	9	21	30	4	...	...	...	...	...	...	...	...	...	5	3	0	3	2	...	...	...	...
2013-14	**Washington**	**NHL**	13	2	1	3	0	0	0	0	15	13.3	3	97	51.6	9:22	...	...	...	...	...	...	...	...	...
	Hershey Bears	AHL	58	18	19	37	12	...	...	...	...	...	...	...	...	...	10	3	3	6	8	...	...	...	...
2014-15	Hershey Bears	AHL	73	25	29	54	28	...	...	...	...	...	...	...	...	...	...	...	...	...	...	...	...	...	...
	NHL Totals		54	6	10	16	4	0	0	2	78	7.7		154	52.6	11:12	...	...	...	...	...	...	...	...	...

Hockey East All-Rookie Team (2009)
Signed as a free agent by **Minnesota**, March 16, 2010. Traded to **NY Rangers** by **Minnesota** for Erik Christensen and NY Rangers' 7th round choice (Alexandre Belanger) in 2013 Entry Draft, February 3, 2012. Traded to **Florida** by **NY Rangers** for Florida's 5th round choice (Richard Nejeezchleb) in 2014 Entry Draft, July 20, 2012. Traded to **Washington** by **Florida** for Zach Hamill, January 31, 2013. Signed as a free agent by **Spartak Moscow** (KHL), June 4, 2015.

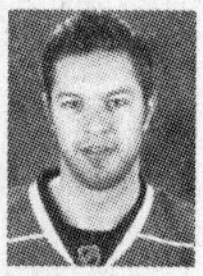

WELSH, Jeremy

(WELSH, JAIR-ih-mee) **ST.L.**

Center. Shoots left. 6'3", 210 lbs. Born, Bayfield, ON, April 30, 1988.

			Regular Season														Playoffs								
Season	Club	League	GP	G	A	Pts	PIM	PP	SH	GW	S	S%	+/-	TF	F%	Min	GP	G	A	Pts	PIM	PP	SH	GW	Min
2007-08	Oakville Blades	ON-Jr.A	48	17	35	52	26	....	....	....	....	....	....	....	....	....	21	6	14	20	8	....	....	....	....
2008-09	Oakville Blades	ON-Jr.A	49	36	47	83	38	....	....	....	....	....	....	....	....	....	28	17	17	34	4	....	....	....	....
2009-10	Union College	ECAC	39	10	9	19	45	....	....	....	....	....	....	....	....	....	....	....	....	....	....	....	....	....	....
2010-11	Union College	ECAC	40	16	21	37	34	....	....	....	....	....	....	....	....	....	....	....	....	....	....	....	....	....	....
2011-12	Union College	ECAC	40	27	17	44	47	....	....	....	....	....	....	....	....	....	....	....	....	....	....	....	....	....	....
	Carolina	**NHL**	**1**	**0**	**0**	**0**	**4**	**0**	**0**	**0**	**2**	**0.0**	**0**	**13**	**30.8**	**16:32**	....	....	....	....	....	....	....	....	....
2012-13	Charlotte	AHL	69	14	12	26	16	....	....	....	....	....	....	....	....	....	5	0	3	3	2	....	....	....	....
	Carolina	**NHL**	**5**	**0**	**1**	**1**	**0**	**0**	**0**	**0**	**4**	**0.0**	**1**	**20**	**75.0**	**5:51**	....	....	....	....	....	....	....	....	....
2013-14	**Vancouver**	**NHL**	**19**	**1**	**0**	**1**	**6**	**0**	**0**	**0**	**13**	**7.7**	**–1**	**90**	**51.1**	**6:51**	....	....	....	....	....	....	....	....	....
	Utica Comets	AHL	49	7	8	15	14	....	....	....	....	....	....	....	....	....	....	....	....	....	....	....	....	....	....
2014-15	Chicago Wolves	AHL	75	20	21	41	32	....	....	....	....	....	....	....	....	....	5	1	1	2	2	....	....	....	....
	NHL Totals		**25**	**1**	**1**	**2**	**10**	**0**	**0**	**0**	**19**	**5.3**		**123**	**52.8**	**7:02**	....	....	....	....	....	....	....	....	....

ECAC Second All-Star Team (2012) • NCAA East Second All-American Team (2012)

Signed as a free agent by **Carolina**, April 5, 2012. Traded to **Vancouver** by **Carolina** with Zac Dalpe for Kellan Tochkin and Vancouver's 4th round choice (Josh Wesley) in 2014 Entry Draft, September 29, 2013. Signed as a free agent by **St. Louis**, July 21, 2014.

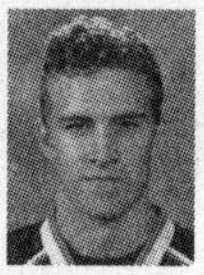

WENNBERG, Alexander

(VEHN-buhrg, al-ehx-AN-duhr) **CBJ**

Center. Shoots left. 6'1", 190 lbs. Born, Stockholm, Sweden, September 22, 1994. Columbus' 1st choice, 14th overall, in 2013 Entry Draft.

			Regular Season														Playoffs								
Season	Club	League	GP	G	A	Pts	PIM	PP	SH	GW	S	S%	+/-	TF	F%	Min	GP	G	A	Pts	PIM	PP	SH	GW	Min
2010-11	Djurgarden U18	Swe-U18	40	11	23	34	6	....	....	....	....	....	....	....	....	....	5	1	2	3	2	....	....	....	....
2011-12	Djurgarden U18	Swe-U18	10	4	2	6	4	....	....	....	....	....	....	....	....	....	2	0	1	1	0	....	....	....	....
	Djurgarden Jr.	Swe-Jr.	42	1	18	19	6	....	....	....	....	....	....	....	....	....	3	0	1	1	0	....	....	....	....
	Djurgarden	Sweden	1	0	0	0	0	....	....	....	....	....	....	....	....	....	....	....	....	....	....	....	....	....	....
2012-13	Djurgarden Jr.	Swe-Jr.	2	1	1	2	0	....	....	....	....	....	....	....	....	....	1	0	1	1	0	....	....	....	....
	Djurgarden	Sweden-2	46	14	18	32	14	....	....	....	....	....	....	....	....	....	3	0	3	3	0	....	....	....	....
2013-14	Frolunda	Sweden	50	16	5	21	8	....	....	....	....	....	....	....	....	....	7	1	0	1	0	....	....	....	....
	Sweden	Olympics	7	3	4	7	2	....	....	....	....	....	....	....	....	....	....	....	....	....	....	....	....	....	....
2014-15	**Columbus**	**NHL**	**68**	**4**	**16**	**20**	**22**	**1**	**0**	**0**	**85**	**4.7**	**–19**	**674**	**42.7**	**15:37**	....	....	....	....	....	....	....	....	....
	Springfield	AHL	6	0	3	3	12	....	....	....	....	....	....	....	....	....	....	....	....	....	....	....	....	....	....
	NHL Totals		**68**	**4**	**16**	**20**	**22**	**1**	**0**	**0**	**85**	**4.7**		**674**	**42.7**	**15:37**	....	....	....	....	....	....	....	....	....

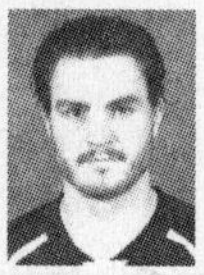

WESTGARTH, Kevin

(WEHST-garth, KEH-vihn)

Right wing. Shoots right. 6'4", 234 lbs. Born, Amherstburg, ON, February 7, 1984.

			Regular Season														Playoffs								
Season	Club	League	GP	G	A	Pts	PIM	PP	SH	GW	S	S%	+/-	TF	F%	Min	GP	G	A	Pts	PIM	PP	SH	GW	Min
2003-04	Princeton	ECAC	25	3	3	6	48	....	....	....	....	....	....	....	....	....	....	....	....	....	....	....	....	....	....
2004-05	Princeton	ECAC	29	4	3	7	36	....	....	....	....	....	....	....	....	....	....	....	....	....	....	....	....	....	....
2005-06	Princeton	ECAC	29	10	13	23	36	....	....	....	....	....	....	....	....	....	....	....	....	....	....	....	....	....	....
2006-07	Princeton	ECAC	33	8	16	24	40	....	....	....	....	....	....	....	....	....	....	....	....	....	....	....	....	....	....
	Manchester	AHL	14	1	2	3	44	....	....	....	....	....	....	....	....	....	....	....	....	....	....	....	....	....	....
2007-08	Manchester	AHL	69	6	6	12	191	....	....	....	....	....	....	....	....	....	4	0	0	0	6	....	....	....	....
2008-09	**Los Angeles**	**NHL**	**9**	**0**	**0**	**0**	**9**	**0**	**0**	**0**	**1**	**0.0**	**1**	**1**	**0.0**	**5:02**	....	....	....	....	....	....	....	....	....
	Manchester	AHL	65	4	6	10	165	....	....	....	....	....	....	....	....	....	....	....	....	....	....	....	....	....	....
2009-10	Manchester	AHL	76	11	14	25	180	....	....	....	....	....	....	....	....	....	6	1	0	1	10	....	....	....	....
2010-11	**Los Angeles**	**NHL**	**56**	**0**	**3**	**3**	**105**	**0**	**0**	**0**	**20**	**0.0**	**–6**	**4**	**50.0**	**5:26**	**6**	**0**	**2**	**2**	**14**	**0**	**0**	**0**	**6:15**
2011-12♦	**Los Angeles**	**NHL**	**25**	**1**	**1**	**2**	**39**	**0**	**0**	**0**	**13**	**7.7**	**–3**	**1**	**0.0**	**5:16**	....	....	....	....	....	....	....	....	....
2012-13	**Carolina**	**NHL**	**31**	**2**	**2**	**4**	**45**	**0**	**0**	**0**	**16**	**12.5**	**1**	**3**	**0.0**	**5:43**	....	....	....	....	....	....	....	....	....
2013-14	**Carolina**	**NHL**	**12**	**0**	**0**	**0**	**4**	**0**	**0**	**0**	**6**	**0.0**	**–2**	**0**	**0.0**	**4:53**	....	....	....	....	....	....	....	....	....
	Calgary	**NHL**	**36**	**4**	**3**	**7**	**64**	**0**	**0**	**1**	**25**	**16.0**	**–2**	**5**	**20.0**	**7:02**	....	....	....	....	....	....	....	....	....
2014-15	Belfast Giants	Britain	39	13	7	20	91	....	....	....	....	....	....	....	....	....	4	0	0	0	4	....	....	....	....
	NHL Totals		**169**	**7**	**9**	**16**	**266**	**0**	**0**	**1**	**81**	**8.6**		**14**	**21.4**	**5:45**	**6**	**0**	**2**	**2**	**14**	**0**	**0**	**0**	**6:15**

Signed as a free agent by **Los Angeles**, March 16, 2007. Traded to **Carolina** by **Los Angeles** for Anthony Stewart, Carolina's 4th round choice (later traded to Edmonton – Edmonton selected Jackson Houck) in 2013 Entry Draft and Carolina's 6th round choice (Jake Marchment) in 2014 Entry Draft, January 13, 2013. Traded to **Calgary** by **Carolina** for Greg Nemisz, December 30. 2013. Signed as a free agent by **Belfast** (Britain), October 30, 2014.

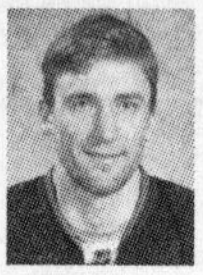

WHEELER, Blake

(WEE-luhr, BLAYK) **WPG**

Right wing. Shoots right. 6'5", 225 lbs. Born, Robbinsdale, MN, August 31, 1986. Phoenix's 1st choice, 5th overall, in 2004 Entry Draft.

			Regular Season														Playoffs								
Season	Club	League	GP	G	A	Pts	PIM	PP	SH	GW	S	S%	+/-	TF	F%	Min	GP	G	A	Pts	PIM	PP	SH	GW	Min
2002-03	Breck Mustangs	High-MN	26	15	27	42	....	....	....	....	....	....	....	....	....	....	....	....	....	....	....	....	....	....	....
2003-04	Team Northwest	UMEHL	24	5	6	11	....	....	....	....	....	....	....	....	....	....	....	....	....	....	....	....	....	....	....
	Breck Mustangs	High-MN	27	39	50	89	34	....	....	....	....	....	....	....	....	....	3	6	5	11	0	....	....	....	....
2004-05	Green Bay	USHL	58	19	28	47	43	....	....	....	....	....	....	....	....	....	....	....	....	....	....	....	....	....	....
2005-06	U. of Minnesota	WCHA	39	9	14	23	41	....	....	....	....	....	....	....	....	....	....	....	....	....	....	....	....	....	....
2006-07	U. of Minnesota	WCHA	44	18	20	38	42	....	....	....	....	....	....	....	....	....	....	....	....	....	....	....	....	....	....
2007-08	U. of Minnesota	WCHA	44	15	20	35	72	....	....	....	....	....	....	....	....	....	....	....	....	....	....	....	....	....	....
2008-09	**Boston**	**NHL**	**81**	**21**	**24**	**45**	**46**	**3**	**2**	**3**	**150**	**14.0**	**36**	**34**	**38.2**	**13:41**	**8**	**0**	**0**	**0**	**0**	**0**	**0**	**0**	**12:08**
2009-10	**Boston**	**NHL**	**82**	**18**	**20**	**38**	**53**	**3**	**1**	**2**	**159**	**11.3**	**–4**	**27**	**48.2**	**15:47**	**13**	**1**	**5**	**6**	**6**	**0**	**0**	**0**	**14:14**
2010-11	**Boston**	**NHL**	**58**	**11**	**16**	**27**	**32**	**0**	**0**	**2**	**101**	**10.9**	**8**	**136**	**38.2**	**15:12**	....	....	....	....	....	....	....	....	....
	Atlanta	**NHL**	**23**	**7**	**10**	**17**	**14**	**0**	**0**	**0**	**78**	**9.0**	**2**	**12**	**0.0**	**18:53**	....	....	....	....	....	....	....	....	....
2011-12	**Winnipeg**	**NHL**	**80**	**17**	**47**	**64**	**55**	**6**	**0**	**3**	**208**	**8.2**	**3**	**10**	**40.0**	**19:05**	....	....	....	....	....	....	....	....	....
2012-13	EHC Munchen	Germany	15	6	14	20	51	....	....	....	....	....	....	....	....	....	....	....	....	....	....	....	....	....	....
	Winnipeg	**NHL**	**48**	**19**	**22**	**41**	**28**	**2**	**0**	**2**	**129**	**14.7**	**–3**	**18**	**22.2**	**18:48**	....	....	....	....	....	....	....	....	....
2013-14	**Winnipeg**	**NHL**	**82**	**28**	**41**	**69**	**63**	**8**	**0**	**4**	**225**	**12.4**	**4**	**40**	**37.5**	**18:41**	....	....	....	....	....	....	....	....	....
	United States	Olympics	6	0	1	1	2	....	....	....	....	....	....	....	....	....	....	....	....	....	....	....	....	....	....
2014-15	**Winnipeg**	**NHL**	**79**	**26**	**35**	**61**	**73**	**2**	**4**	**6**	**244**	**10.7**	**26**	**48**	**45.8**	**19:40**	**4**	**1**	**0**	**1**	**2**	**0**	**0**	**0**	**19:15**
	NHL Totals		**533**	**147**	**215**	**362**	**364**	**24**	**7**	**22**	**1294**	**11.4**		**325**	**37.8**	**17:19**	**25**	**2**	**5**	**7**	**8**	**0**	**0**	**0**	**14:21**

USHL All-Rookie Team (2005)

Signed as a free agent by **Boston**, July 1, 2008. Traded to **Atlanta** by **Boston** with Mark Stuart for Rich Peverley and Boris Valabik, February 18, 2011. • Transferred to **Winnipeg** after **Atlanta** franchise relocated, June 21, 2011. Signed as a free agent by **Munchen** (Germany), October 28, 2012.

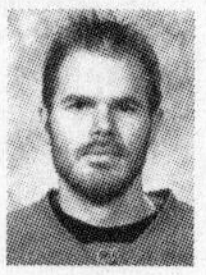

WHITE, Ian

(WIGHT, EE-an)

Defense. Shoots right. 5'10", 191 lbs. Born, Steinbach, MB, June 4, 1984. Toronto's 6th choice, 191st overall, in 2002 Entry Draft.

			Regular Season														Playoffs								
Season	Club	League	GP	G	A	Pts	PIM	PP	SH	GW	S	S%	+/-	TF	F%	Min	GP	G	A	Pts	PIM	PP	SH	GW	Min
99-2000	Eastman Selects	MAHA	32	29	33	62	36	....	....	....	....	....	....	....	....	....	....	....	....	....	....	....	....	....	....
2000-01	Swift Current	WHL	69	12	31	43	24	....	....	....	....	....	....	....	....	....	....	....	....	....	....	....	....	....	....
2001-02	Swift Current	WHL	70	32	47	79	40	....	....	....	....	....	....	....	....	....	12	4	5	9	12	....	....	....	....
2002-03	Swift Current	WHL	64	24	44	68	44	....	....	....	....	....	....	....	....	....	4	0	4	4	0	....	....	....	....
2003-04	Swift Current	WHL	43	9	23	32	32	....	....	....	....	....	....	....	....	....	5	1	3	4	8	....	....	....	....
	St. John's	AHL	8	0	4	4	2	....	....	....	....	....	....	....	....	....	....	....	....	....	....	....	....	....	....
2004-05	St. John's	AHL	78	4	22	26	54	....	....	....	....	....	....	....	....	....	5	0	2	2	2	....	....	....	....
2005-06	**Toronto**	**NHL**	**12**	**1**	**5**	**6**	**10**	**0**	**0**	**0**	**21**	**4.8**	**2**	**0**	**0.0**	**19:07**	....	....	....	....	....	....	....	....	....
	Toronto Marlies	AHL	59	8	30	38	42	....	....	....	....	....	....	....	....	....	5	1	4	5	4	....	....	....	....
2006-07	**Toronto**	**NHL**	**76**	**3**	**23**	**26**	**40**	**1**	**0**	**1**	**138**	**2.2**	**8**	**0**	**0.0**	**18:32**	....	....	....	....	....	....	....	....	....
2007-08	**Toronto**	**NHL**	**81**	**5**	**16**	**21**	**44**	**0**	**0**	**2**	**116**	**4.3**	**–9**	**0**	**0.0**	**18:48**	....	....	....	....	....	....	....	....	....
2008-09	**Toronto**	**NHL**	**71**	**10**	**16**	**26**	**57**	**2**	**0**	**2**	**158**	**6.3**	**6**	**0**	**0.0**	**22:51**	....	....	....	....	....	....	....	....	....
2009-10	**Toronto**	**NHL**	**56**	**9**	**17**	**26**	**39**	**2**	**0**	**1**	**130**	**6.9**	**1**	**0**	**0.0**	**23:47**	....	....	....	....	....	....	....	....	....
	Calgary	**NHL**	**27**	**4**	**8**	**12**	**12**	**1**	**0**	**0**	**43**	**9.3**	**7**	**0**	**0.0**	**20:43**	....	....	....	....	....	....	....	....	....
2010-11	**Calgary**	**NHL**	**16**	**2**	**4**	**6**	**6**	**1**	**0**	**0**	**34**	**5.9**	**–10**	**0**	**0.0**	**21:44**	....	....	....	....	....	....	....	....	....
	Carolina	**NHL**	**39**	**0**	**10**	**10**	**12**	**0**	**0**	**0**	**53**	**0.0**	**4**	**0**	**0.0**	**19:19**	....	....	....	....	....	....	....	....	....
	San Jose	**NHL**	**23**	**2**	**8**	**10**	**8**	**0**	**0**	**0**	**51**	**3.9**	**9**	**0**	**0.0**	**19:56**	**17**	**1**	**8**	**9**	**8**	**1**	**0**	**0**	**20:04**
2011-12	**Detroit**	**NHL**	**77**	**7**	**25**	**32**	**22**	**0**	**0**	**0**	**196**	**3.6**	**23**	**0**	**0.0**	**22:59**	**5**	**1**	**0**	**1**	**0**	**0**	**0**	**0**	**18:34**
2012-13	**Detroit**	**NHL**	**25**	**2**	**2**	**4**	**4**	**0**	**0**	**0**	**27**	**7.4**	**5**	**1**	**100.0**	**19:35**	....	....	....	....	....	....	....	....	....
2013-14	Chelyabinsk	KHL	10	0	1	1	0	....	....	....	....	....	....	....	....	....	....	....	....	....	....	....	....	....	....

Season	Club	League	GP	G	A	Pts	PIM	PP	SH	GW	S	S%	+/-	TF	F%	Min	GP	G	A	Pts	PIM	PP	SH	GW	Min
			Regular Season														Playoffs								
2014-15	Providence Bruins	AHL	8	1	3	4	4	....	....	....	....	....	....	....	....	....	....	....	....	....	....	....	....	....	....
	Milwaukee	AHL	34	3	16	19	13	....	....	....	....	....	....	....	....	....	....	....	....	....	....	....	....	....	....
	NHL Totals		**503**	**45**	**134**	**179**	**254**	**7**	**0**	**6**	**967**	**4.7**		**1**	**100.0**	**20:52**	**22**	**2**	**8**	**10**	**8**	**1**	**0**	**0**	**19:44**

WHL East Second All-Star Team (2002) • WHL East First All-Star Team (2003) • Canadian Major Junior Second All-Star Team (2003)

Traded to **Calgary** by **Toronto** with Matt Stajan, Niklas Hagman and Jamal Mayers for Dion Phaneuf, Fredrik Sjostrom and Keith Aulie, January 31, 2010. Traded to **Carolina** by **Calgary** with Brett Sutter for Anton Babchuk and Tom Kostopoulos, November 17, 2010. Traded to **San Jose** by **Carolina** for San Jose's 2nd round choice (Brock McGinn) in 2012 Entry Draft, February 18, 2011. Signed as a free agent by **Detroit**, July 2, 2011. Signed as a free agent by **Chelyabinsk** (HL), December 20, 2013. Signed to a PTO (professional tryout) contract by **Providence** (AHL), November 21, 2014. Signed to a PTO (professional tryout) contract by **Milwaukee** (AHL), December 17, 2014.

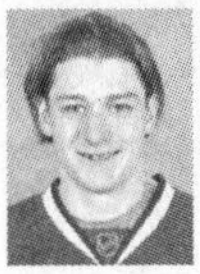

WHITE, Ryan (WIGHT, RIGH-uhn) PHI

Center. Shoots right. 6', 200 lbs. Born, Brandon, MB, March 17, 1988. Montreal's 4th choice, 66th overall, in 2006 Entry Draft.

Season	Club	League	GP	G	A	Pts	PIM	PP	SH	GW	S	S%	+/-	TF	F%	Min	GP	G	A	Pts	PIM	PP	SH	GW	Min
2003-04	Brandon	MMHL	39	21	41	62	90	....	....	....	....	....	....	....	....	....	11	7	7	14	22	....	....	....	....
2004-05	Calgary Hitmen	WHL	63	9	14	23	95	....	....	....	....	....	....	....	....	....	12	2	1	3	26	....	....	....	....
2005-06	Calgary Hitmen	WHL	72	20	33	53	121	....	....	....	....	....	....	....	....	....	13	3	4	7	18	....	....	....	....
2006-07	Calgary Hitmen	WHL	72	34	55	89	97	....	....	....	....	....	....	....	....	....	18	6	8	14	36	....	....	....	....
2007-08	Calgary Hitmen	WHL	68	28	44	72	98	....	....	....	....	....	....	....	....	....	16	6	11	17	8	....	....	....	....
2008-09	Hamilton	AHL	80	11	18	29	68	....	....	....	....	....	....	....	....	....	6	3	1	4	9	....	....	....	....
2009-10	**Montreal**	**NHL**	**16**	**0**	**2**	**2**	**16**	**0**	**0**	**0**	**5**	**0.0**	**-6**	**10**	**70.0**	**11:09**	....	....	....	....	....	....	....	....	....
	Hamilton	AHL	62	17	17	34	173	....	....	....	....	....	....	....	....	....	19	4	5	9	47	....	....	....	....
2010-11	**Montreal**	**NHL**	**27**	**2**	**3**	**5**	**38**	**0**	**0**	**0**	**30**	**6.7**	**5**	**32**	**40.6**	**8:55**	**7**	**0**	**0**	**0**	**2**	**0**	**0**	**0**	**6:35**
	Hamilton	AHL	33	3	9	12	77	....	....	....	....	....	....	....	....	....	13	2	6	8	37	....	....	....	....
2011-12	**Montreal**	**NHL**	**20**	**0**	**3**	**3**	**61**	**0**	**0**	**0**	**12**	**0.0**	**-7**	**59**	**49.2**	**14:31**	....	....	....	....	....	....	....	....	....
	Hamilton	AHL	4	4	1	5	26	....	....	....	....	....	....	....	....	....	....	....	....	....	....	....	....	....	....
2012-13	**Montreal**	**NHL**	**26**	**1**	**0**	**1**	**67**	**0**	**0**	**0**	**16**	**6.3**	**1**	**167**	**54.5**	**9:25**	**3**	**1**	**0**	**1**	**23**	**0**	**0**	**0**	**9:06**
2013-14	**Montreal**	**NHL**	**52**	**2**	**4**	**6**	**50**	**0**	**0**	**1**	**51**	**3.9**	**-8**	**388**	**50.8**	**9:41**	....	....	....	....	....	....	....	....	....
2014-15	**Philadelphia**	**NHL**	**34**	**6**	**6**	**12**	**30**	**0**	**0**	**1**	**45**	**13.3**	**4**	**123**	**52.9**	**11:43**	....	....	....	....	....	....	....	....	....
	Lehigh Valley	AHL	11	1	2	3	39	....	....	....	....	....	....	....	....	....	....	....	....	....	....	....	....	....	....
	NHL Totals		**175**	**11**	**18**	**29**	**262**	**0**	**0**	**2**	**159**	**6.9**		**779**	**51.6**	**10:37**	**10**	**1**	**0**	**1**	**25**	**0**	**0**	**0**	**7:20**

WHL East First All-Star Team (2007) • WHL East Second All-Star Team (2008)

• Missed majority of 2011-12 due to sports hernia injury in training camp. Signed as a free agent by **Philadelphia**, August 7, 2014.

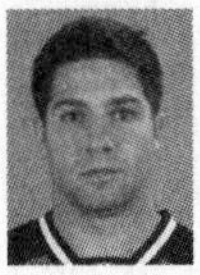

WHITNEY, Joe (WHIHT-nee, JOH) NYI

Right wing. Shoots left. 5'6", 170 lbs. Born, Reading, MA, February 6, 1988.

Season	Club	League	GP	G	A	Pts	PIM	PP	SH	GW	S	S%	+/-	TF	F%	Min	GP	G	A	Pts	PIM	PP	SH	GW	Min
2007-08	Boston College	H-East	41	11	*40	51	50	....	....	....	....	....	....	....	....	....	....	....	....	....	....	....	....	....	....
2008-09	Boston College	H-East	36	7	8	15	36	....	....	....	....	....	....	....	....	....	....	....	....	....	....	....	....	....	....
2009-10	Boston College	H-East	42	17	28	45	61	....	....	....	....	....	....	....	....	....	....	....	....	....	....	....	....	....	....
2010-11	Boston College	H-East	39	5	26	31	60	....	....	....	....	....	....	....	....	....	....	....	....	....	....	....	....	....	....
	Portland Pirates	AHL	1	0	1	1	0	....	....	....	....	....	....	....	....	....	....	....	....	....	....	....	....	....	....
2011-12	Albany Devils	AHL	72	15	29	44	36	....	....	....	....	....	....	....	....	....	....	....	....	....	....	....	....	....	....
2012-13	Albany Devils	AHL	66	26	25	51	32	....	....	....	....	....	....	....	....	....	....	....	....	....	....	....	....	....	....
2013-14	**New Jersey**	**NHL**	**1**	**0**	**0**	**0**	**0**	**0**	**0**	**0**	**0**	**0.0**	**0**	**1**	**0.0**	**8:00**	....	....	....	....	....	....	....	....	....
	Albany Devils	AHL	73	22	31	53	34	....	....	....	....	....	....	....	....	....	4	1	0	1	0	....	....	....	....
2014-15	**New Jersey**	**NHL**	**4**	**1**	**0**	**1**	**0**	**0**	**0**	**0**	**1**	**100.0**	**-1**	**0**	**0.0**	**6:53**	....	....	....	....	....	....	....	....	....
	Albany Devils	AHL	66	23	37	60	64	....	....	....	....	....	....	....	....	....	....	....	....	....	....	....	....	....	....
	NHL Totals		**5**	**1**	**0**	**1**	**0**	**0**	**0**	**0**	**1**	**100.0**		**1**	**0.0**	**7:06**	....	....	....	....	....	....	....	....	....

Hockey East All-Rookie Team (2008) • NCAA Championship All-Tournament Team (2010)

Signed as a free agent by **Albany** (AHL), July 28, 2011. Signed as a free agent by **New Jersey**, May 1, 2013. Signed as a free agent by **NY Islanders**, July 2, 2015.

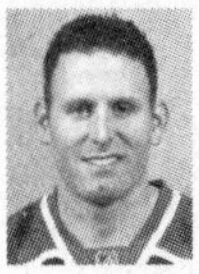

WHITNEY, Ryan (WHIHT-nee, RIGH-uhn)

Defense. Shoots left. 6'3", 206 lbs. Born, Boston, MA, February 19, 1983. Pittsburgh's 1st choice, 5th overall, in 2002 Entry Draft.

Season	Club	League	GP	G	A	Pts	PIM	PP	SH	GW	S	S%	+/-	TF	F%	Min	GP	G	A	Pts	PIM	PP	SH	GW	Min
99-2000	Thayer Academy	High-MA	22	5	33	38	....	....	....	....	....	....	....	....	....	....	....	....	....	....	....	....	....	....	....
2000-01	USNTDP	U-18	40	7	23	30	64	....	....	....	....	....	....	....	....	....	....	....	....	....	....	....	....	....	....
	USNTDP	USHL	20	2	8	10	22	....	....	....	....	....	....	....	....	....	....	....	....	....	....	....	....	....	....
2001-02	Boston University	H-East	35	4	17	21	46	....	....	....	....	....	....	....	....	....	....	....	....	....	....	....	....	....	....
2002-03	Boston University	H-East	34	3	10	13	48	....	....	....	....	....	....	....	....	....	....	....	....	....	....	....	....	....	....
2003-04	Boston University	H-East	38	9	16	25	56	....	....	....	....	....	....	....	....	....	....	....	....	....	....	....	....	....	....
	Wilkes-Barre	AHL	....	....	....	....	....	....	....	....	....	....	....	....	....	....	20	1	9	10	6	....	....	....	....
2004-05	Wilkes-Barre	AHL	80	6	35	41	101	....	....	....	....	....	....	....	....	....	11	2	7	9	12	....	....	....	....
2005-06	**Pittsburgh**	**NHL**	**68**	**6**	**32**	**38**	**85**	**2**	**0**	**1**	**113**	**5.3**	**-7**	**1**	**0.0**	**23:50**	....	....	....	....	....	....	....	....	....
	Wilkes-Barre	AHL	9	5	9	14	6	....	....	....	....	....	....	....	....	....	11	1	4	5	8	....	....	....	....
2006-07	**Pittsburgh**	**NHL**	**81**	**14**	**45**	**59**	**77**	**9**	**0**	**2**	**129**	**10.9**	**9**	**5**	**20.0**	**23:56**	**5**	**1**	**1**	**2**	**6**	**1**	**0**	**0**	**22:51**
2007-08	**Pittsburgh**	**NHL**	**76**	**12**	**28**	**40**	**45**	**7**	**1**	**1**	**119**	**10.1**	**-2**	**0**	**0.0**	**22:27**	**20**	**1**	**5**	**6**	**25**	**1**	**0**	**0**	**20:46**
2008-09	**Pittsburgh**	**NHL**	**28**	**2**	**11**	**13**	**16**	**1**	**0**	**0**	**42**	**4.8**	**-15**	**0**	**0.0**	**24:34**	....	....	....	....	....	....	....	....	....
	Wilkes-Barre	AHL	1	0	1	1	2	....	....	....	....	....	....	....	....	....	....	....	....	....	....	....	....	....	....
	Anaheim	**NHL**	**20**	**0**	**10**	**10**	**12**	**0**	**0**	**0**	**29**	**0.0**	**1**	**0**	**0.0**	**22:53**	**13**	**1**	**5**	**6**	**9**	**1**	**0**	**0**	**21:34**
2009-10	**Anaheim**	**NHL**	**62**	**4**	**24**	**28**	**48**	**3**	**0**	**0**	**107**	**3.7**	**-6**	**1**	**0.0**	**24:34**	....	....	....	....	....	....	....	....	....
	United States	Olympics	6	0	0	0	0	....	....	....	....	....	....	....	....	....	....	....	....	....	....	....	....	....	....
	Edmonton	**NHL**	**19**	**3**	**8**	**11**	**22**	**0**	**0**	**1**	**44**	**6.8**	**7**	**0**	**0.0**	**25:23**	....	....	....	....	....	....	....	....	....
2010-11	**Edmonton**	**NHL**	**35**	**2**	**25**	**27**	**33**	**0**	**0**	**0**	**43**	**4.7**	**13**	**0**	**0.0**	**25:20**	....	....	....	....	....	....	....	....	....
2011-12	**Edmonton**	**NHL**	**51**	**3**	**17**	**20**	**16**	**2**	**0**	**0**	**41**	**7.3**	**-16**	**0**	**0.0**	**20:58**	....	....	....	....	....	....	....	....	....
2012-13	**Edmonton**	**NHL**	**34**	**4**	**9**	**13**	**23**	**0**	**0**	**0**	**30**	**13.3**	**-7**	**0**	**0.0**	**18:29**	....	....	....	....	....	....	....	....	....
2013-14	**Florida**	**NHL**	**7**	**0**	**0**	**0**	**6**	**0**	**0**	**0**	**8**	**0.0**	**-7**	**0**	**0.0**	**16:45**	....	....	....	....	....	....	....	....	....
	San Antonio	AHL	45	7	16	23	52	....	....	....	....	....	....	....	....	....	....	....	....	....	....	....	....	....	....
2014-15	HK Sochi	KHL	42	6	13	19	23	....	....	....	....	....	....	....	....	....	4	0	1	1	0	....	....	....	....
	NHL Totals		**481**	**50**	**209**	**259**	**383**	**24**	**1**	**5**	**705**	**7.1**		**7**	**14.3**	**23:07**	**38**	**3**	**11**	**14**	**40**	**3**	**0**	**0**	**21:19**

Hockey East All-Rookie Team (2002)

Traded to **Anaheim** by **Pittsburgh** for Chris Kunitz and Eric Tangradi, February 26, 2009. Traded to **Edmonton** by **Anaheim** with Anaheim's 6th round choice (Brandon Davidson) in 2010 Entry Draft for Lubomir Visnovsky, March 3, 2010. • Missed majority of 2010-11 due to ankle injury vs. Buffalo, December 28, 2010. Signed as a free agent by **Florida**, September 29, 2013. Signed as a free agent by **Sochi** (KHL), October 16, 2014. Signed as a free agent by **MODO** (Sweden), June 24, 2015.

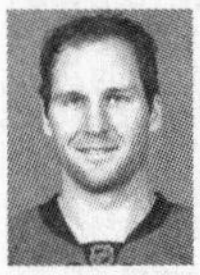

WIDEMAN, Dennis (WIGHD-muhn, DEH-nihs) CGY

Defense. Shoots right. 6', 200 lbs. Born, Kitchener, ON, March 20, 1983. Buffalo's 9th choice, 241st overall, in 2002 Entry Draft.

Season	Club	League	GP	G	A	Pts	PIM	PP	SH	GW	S	S%	+/-	TF	F%	Min	GP	G	A	Pts	PIM	PP	SH	GW	Min
1998-99	Elmira	ON-Jr.B	47	18	30	48	142	....	....	....	....	....	....	....	....	....	....	....	....	....	....	....	....	....	....
99-2000	Sudbury Wolves	OHL	63	10	26	36	64	....	....	....	....	....	....	....	....	....	12	1	2	3	22	....	....	....	....
2000-01	Sudbury Wolves	OHL	25	7	11	18	37	....	....	....	....	....	....	....	....	....	....	....	....	....	....	....	....	....	....
	London Knights	OHL	24	8	8	16	38	....	....	....	....	....	....	....	....	....	5	0	4	4	6	....	....	....	....
2001-02	London Knights	OHL	65	27	42	69	141	....	....	....	....	....	....	....	....	....	12	4	9	13	26	....	....	....	....
2002-03	London Knights	OHL	55	20	27	47	83	....	....	....	....	....	....	....	....	....	14	6	6	12	10	....	....	....	....
2003-04	London Knights	OHL	60	24	41	65	85	....	....	....	....	....	....	....	....	....	15	7	10	17	17	....	....	....	....
2004-05	Worcester IceCats	AHL	79	13	30	43	65	....	....	....	....	....	....	....	....	....	....	....	....	....	....	....	....	....	....
2005-06	**St. Louis**	**NHL**	**67**	**8**	**16**	**24**	**83**	**5**	**1**	**1**	**150**	**5.3**	**-31**	**1**	**0.0**	**21:41**	....	....	....	....	....	....	....	....	....
	Peoria Rivermen	AHL	12	2	4	6	31	....	....	....	....	....	....	....	....	....	....	....	....	....	....	....	....	....	....
2006-07	**St. Louis**	**NHL**	**55**	**5**	**17**	**22**	**44**	**4**	**0**	**1**	**94**	**5.3**	**-7**	**0**	**0.0**	**20:12**	....	....	....	....	....	....	....	....	....
	Boston	**NHL**	**20**	**1**	**2**	**3**	**27**	**0**	**0**	**0**	**28**	**3.6**	**-3**	**1**	**0.0**	**17:20**	....	....	....	....	....	....	....	....	....
2007-08	**Boston**	**NHL**	**81**	**13**	**23**	**36**	**70**	**9**	**0**	**1**	**171**	**7.6**	**11**	**0**	**0.0**	**25:09**	**6**	**0**	**3**	**3**	**0**	**0**	**0**	**0**	**24:21**
2008-09	**Boston**	**NHL**	**79**	**13**	**37**	**50**	**34**	**6**	**1**	**2**	**169**	**7.7**	**32**	**0**	**0.0**	**24:39**	**11**	**0**	**7**	**7**	**4**	**0**	**0**	**0**	**24:42**
2009-10	**Boston**	**NHL**	**76**	**6**	**24**	**30**	**34**	**2**	**0**	**2**	**146**	**4.1**	**-14**	**0**	**0.0**	**23:33**	**13**	**1**	**11**	**12**	**4**	**0**	**0**	**0**	**26:02**
2010-11	**Florida**	**NHL**	**61**	**9**	**24**	**33**	**33**	**8**	**0**	**1**	**135**	**6.7**	**-26**	**1**	**100.0**	**23:58**	....	....	....	....	....	....	....	....	....
	Washington	**NHL**	**14**	**1**	**6**	**7**	**6**	**1**	**0**	**0**	**25**	**4.0**	**7**	**0**	**0.0**	**24:05**	....	....	....	....	....	....	....	....	....
2011-12	**Washington**	**NHL**	**82**	**11**	**35**	**46**	**46**	**4**	**0**	**3**	**175**	**6.3**	**-8**	**0**	**0.0**	**23:54**	**14**	**0**	**3**	**3**	**2**	**0**	**0**	**0**	**20:44**
2012-13	**Calgary**	**NHL**	**46**	**6**	**16**	**22**	**12**	**4**	**0**	**1**	**94**	**6.4**	**-9**	**1**	**0.0**	**25:01**	....	....	....	....	....	....	....	....	....

			Regular Season														Playoffs								
Season	Club	League	GP	G	A	Pts	PIM	PP	SH	GW	S	S%	+/-	TF	F%	Min	GP	G	A	Pts	PIM	PP	SH	GW	Min
2013-14	Calgary	NHL	46	4	17	21	18	2	0	0	102	3.9	−15	0	0.0	22:42	....	....	....	....	....	....	....	....	....
2014-15	Calgary	NHL	80	15	41	56	34	6	0	2	173	8.7	6	0	0.0	24:39	11	0	7	7	12	0	0	0	26:29
	NHL Totals		707	92	258	350	441	51	2	14	1462	6.3		4	25.0	23:30	55	1	31	32	22	0	0	0	24:20

OHL First All-Star Team (2004) • Canadian Major Junior Second All-Star Team (2004)

Played in NHL All-Star Game (2012)

Signed as a free agent by **St. Louis**, June 30, 2004. Traded to **Boston** by **St. Louis** for Brad Boyes, February 27, 2007. Traded to **Florida** by **Boston** with Boston's 1st round choice (later traded to Los Angeles – Los Angeles selected Derek Forbert) in 2010 Entry Draft and Boston's 3rd round choice (Kyle Rau) in 2011 Entry Draft for Nathan Horton and Gregory Campbell, June 22, 2010. Traded to **Washington** by **Florida** for Jake Hauswirth and Washington's 3rd round choice (Jonathan Racine) in 2011 Entry Draft, February 28, 2011. Traded to **Calgary** by **Washington** for Jordan Henry and Calgary's 5th round choice (later traded to Winnipeg – Winnipeg selected Tucker Poolman) in 2013 Entry Draft, June 27, 2012.

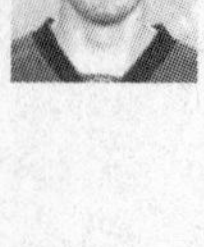

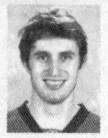

WIERCIOCH, Patrick

(WEER-kawsh, PAT-rihk) **OTT**

Defense. Shoots left. 6'5", 206 lbs. Born, Burnaby, BC, September 12, 1990. Ottawa's 2nd choice, 42nd overall, in 2008 Entry Draft.

Season	Club	League	GP	G	A	Pts	PIM	PP	SH	GW	S	S%	+/-	TF	F%	Min	GP	G	A	Pts	PIM	PP	SH	GW	Min
2006-07	Burnaby Express	BCHL	42	9	16	25	46	....	....	....	....	....	....	....	....	....	14	3	4	7	10	....	....	....	....
2007-08	Omaha Lancers	USHL	40	3	18	21	24	....	....	....	....	....	....	....	....	....	14	2	9	11	22	....	....	....	....
2008-09	U. of Denver	WCHA	36	12	23	35	26	....	....	....	....	....	....	....	....	....	....	....	....	....	....	....	....	....	....
2009-10	U. of Denver	WCHA	39	6	21	27	34	....	....	....	....	....	....	....	....	....	....	....	....	....	....	....	....	....	....
2010-11	Ottawa	NHL	8	0	2	2	4	0	0	0	3	0.0	0	0	0.0	13:54	....	....	....	....	....	....	....	....	....
	Binghamton	AHL	67	4	14	18	25	....	....	....	....	....	....	....	....	....	15	0	1	1	0	....	....	....	....
2011-12	Binghamton	AHL	57	4	16	20	34	....	....	....	....	....	....	....	....	....	....	....	....	....	....	....	....	....	....
2012-13	Binghamton	AHL	32	10	9	19	22	....	....	....	....	....	....	....	....	....	....	....	....	....	....	....	....	....	....
	Ottawa	NHL	42	5	14	19	39	3	0	0	81	6.2	9	0	0.0	15:42	1	0	0	0	0	0	0	0	1:47
2013-14	Ottawa	NHL	53	4	19	23	20	3	0	0	97	4.1	−1	2	0.0	16:22	....	....	....	....	....	....	....	....	....
2014-15	Ottawa	NHL	56	3	10	13	28	1	0	2	79	3.8	3	0	0.0	18:03	6	2	2	4	4	1	0	1	19:18
	NHL Totals		159	12	45	57	91	7	0	2	260	4.6		2	0.0	16:40	7	2	2	4	4	1	0	1	16:47

WCHA All-Rookie Team (2009) • WCHA Second All-Star Team (2009) • WCHA First All-Star Team (2010) • NCAA West First All-American Team (2010)

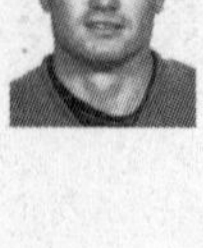

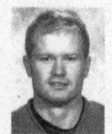

WILLIAMS, Jason

(WIHL-yuhms, JAY-suhn)

Center. Shoots right. 5'11", 192 lbs. Born, London, ON, August 11, 1980.

Season	Club	League	GP	G	A	Pts	PIM	PP	SH	GW	S	S%	+/-	TF	F%	Min	GP	G	A	Pts	PIM	PP	SH	GW	Min
1995-96	Mount Brydges	ON-Jr.D	36	31	28	59	18	....	....	....	....	....	....	....	....	....	....	....	....	....	....	....	....	....	....
1996-97	Peterborough	OHL	60	4	8	12	8	....	....	....	....	....	....	....	....	....	10	1	0	1	2	....	....	....	....
1997-98	Peterborough	OHL	55	8	27	35	31	....	....	....	....	....	....	....	....	....	4	0	1	1	2	....	....	....	....
1998-99	Peterborough	OHL	68	26	48	74	42	....	....	....	....	....	....	....	....	....	5	1	2	3	2	....	....	....	....
99-2000	Peterborough	OHL	66	36	37	75	64	....	....	....	....	....	....	....	....	....	5	2	1	3	2	....	....	....	....
2000-01	Detroit	NHL	5	0	3	3	2	0	0	0	7	0.0	1	56	39.3	12:24	2	0	0	0	0	0	0	0	11:45
	Cincinnati	AHL	76	24	45	69	48	....	....	....	....	....	....	....	....	....	1	0	0	0	2	....	....	....	....
2001-02 ♦	Detroit	NHL	25	8	2	10	4	4	0	0	32	25.0	2	208	47.6	10:50	9	0	0	0	2	0	0	0	6:12
	Cincinnati	AHL	52	23	27	50	27	....	....	....	....	....	....	....	....	....	3	0	1	1	6	....	....	....	....
2002-03	Detroit	NHL	16	3	3	6	2	1	0	0	20	15.0	3	78	51.3	10:43	....	....	....	....	....	....	....	....	....
	Grand Rapids	AHL	45	23	22	45	18	....	....	....	....	....	....	....	....	....	15	1	7	8	16	....	....	....	....
2003-04	Detroit	NHL	49	6	7	13	15	0	0	0	44	13.6	1	315	49.2	9:27	3	0	0	0	2	0	0	0	6:11
2004-05	Assat Pori	Finland	43	26	17	43	52	....	....	....	....	....	....	....	....	....	2	1	1	2	4	....	....	....	....
2005-06	Detroit	NHL	80	21	37	58	26	6	0	4	177	11.9	4	29	55.2	14:55	6	1	1	2	6	0	0	0	18:10
2006-07	Detroit	NHL	58	11	15	26	24	3	0	2	111	9.9	7	11	45.5	14:26	....	....	....	....	....	....	....	....	....
	Chicago	NHL	20	4	2	6	20	2	1	0	38	10.5	−6	193	42.5	18:17	....	....	....	....	....	....	....	....	....
2007-08	Chicago	NHL	43	13	23	36	22	6	0	4	101	12.9	−2	15	60.0	16:35	....	....	....	....	....	....	....	....	....
2008-09	Atlanta	NHL	41	7	11	18	8	4	0	2	79	8.9	−9	381	49.1	16:05	....	....	....	....	....	....	....	....	....
	Columbus	NHL	39	12	17	29	16	3	0	2	74	16.2	5	237	40.9	15:38	4	0	1	1	2	0	0	0	14:12
2009-10	Detroit	NHL	44	6	9	15	8	3	0	1	96	6.3	−7	60	50.0	13:32	3	0	0	0	0	0	0	0	8:12
2010-11	Connecticut	AHL	17	4	5	9	10	....	....	....	....	....	....	....	....	....	....	....	....	....	....	....	....	....	....
	Dallas	NHL	27	2	3	5	6	0	0	1	18	11.1	−2	44	40.9	8:07	....	....	....	....	....	....	....	....	....
2011-12	Pittsburgh	NHL	8	1	1	2	4	0	0	0	4	25.0	1	1	0.0	10:34	....	....	....	....	....	....	....	....	....
	Wilkes-Barre	AHL	59	13	29	42	32	....	....	....	....	....	....	....	....	....	12	3	10	13	2	....	....	....	....
2012-13	HC Ambri-Piotta	Swiss	47	*26	20	46	16	....	....	....	....	....	....	....	....	....	3	0	2	2	0	....	....	....	....
2013-14	HC Ambri-Piotta	Swiss	32	8	10	18	12	....	....	....	....	....	....	....	....	....	2	0	1	1	0	....	....	....	....
2014-15	Oklahoma City	AHL	72	21	32	53	30	....	....	....	....	....	....	....	....	....	10	0	5	5	6	....	....	....	....
	NHL Totals		455	94	133	227	157	32	1	16	801	11.7		1628	46.7	13:43	27	1	2	3	12	0	0	0	10:40

Signed as a free agent by **Detroit**, September 18, 2000. Signed as a free agent by **Pori** (Finland), October 18, 2004. Traded to **Chicago** by **Detroit** for Kyle Calder, February 26, 2007. Signed as a free agent by **Atlanta**, July 14, 2008. Traded to **Columbus** by **Atlanta** for Clay Wilson and San Jose's 6th round choice (previously acquired, later traded to Chicago – Chicago selected David Pacan) in 2009 Entry Draft, January 14, 2009. Signed as a free agent by **Detroit**, August 4, 2009. Signed to a PTO (professional tryout) contract by **Connecticut** (AHL), December 26, 2010. Signed as a free agent by **Dallas**, February 12, 2011. Signed as a free agent by **Pittsburgh**, July 26, 2011. Signed as a free agent by **Ambri-Piotta** (Swiss), May 29, 2012. Signed as a free agent by **Oklahoma City** (AHL), July 25, 2014.

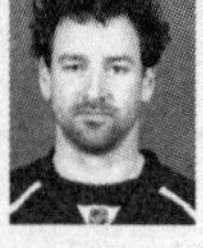

WILLIAMS, Justin

(WIHL-yuhms, JUHS-tihn) **WSH**

Right wing. Shoots right. 6'1", 189 lbs. Born, Cobourg, ON, October 4, 1981. Philadelphia's 1st choice, 28th overall, in 2000 Entry Draft.

Season	Club	League	GP	G	A	Pts	PIM	PP	SH	GW	S	S%	+/-	TF	F%	Min	GP	G	A	Pts	PIM	PP	SH	GW	Min
1997-98	Colborne Colts	ON-Jr.C	36	32	35	67	26	....	....	....	....	....	....	....	....	....	....	....	....	....	....	....	....	....	....
	Cobourg Cougars	ON-Jr.A	17	0	3	3	5	....	....	....	....	....	....	....	....	....	....	....	....	....	....	....	....	....	....
1998-99	Plymouth Whalers	OHL	47	4	8	12	28	....	....	....	....	....	....	....	....	....	7	1	2	3	0	....	....	....	....
99-2000	Plymouth Whalers	OHL	68	37	46	83	46	....	....	....	....	....	....	....	....	....	23	*14	16	*30	10	....	....	....	....
2000-01	Philadelphia	NHL	63	12	13	25	22	0	0	0	99	12.1	6	13	53.9	12:31	....	....	....	....	....	....	....	....	....
2001-02	Philadelphia	NHL	75	17	23	40	32	0	0	1	162	10.5	11	16	25.0	14:27	5	0	0	0	4	0	0	0	16:42
2002-03	Philadelphia	NHL	41	8	16	24	22	0	0	2	105	7.6	15	16	50.0	15:57	12	1	5	6	8	0	0	1	14:11
2003-04	Philadelphia	NHL	47	6	20	26	32	3	0	1	107	5.6	10	38	31.6	15:30	....	....	....	....	....	....	....	....	....
	Carolina	NHL	32	5	13	18	32	1	0	0	96	5.2	2	25	36.0	18:52	....	....	....	....	....	....	....	....	....
2004-05	Lulea HF	Sweden	49	14	18	32	61	....	....	....	....	....	....	....	....	....	4	0	1	1	29	....	....	....	....
2005-06 ♦	Carolina	NHL	82	31	45	76	60	8	4	4	255	12.2	1	17	29.4	21:08	25	7	11	18	34	0	1	1	21:36
2006-07	Carolina	NHL	82	33	34	67	73	12	2	8	258	12.8	−11	24	37.5	20:51	....	....	....	....	....	....	....	....	....
2007-08	Carolina	NHL	37	9	21	30	43	2	0	0	106	8.5	2	13	38.5	19:18	....	....	....	....	....	....	....	....	....
2008-09	Carolina	NHL	32	3	7	10	9	2	0	0	80	3.8	−9	20	30.0	15:08	....	....	....	....	....	....	....	....	....
	Los Angeles	NHL	12	1	3	4	8	1	0	0	28	3.6	1	2	50.0	17:51	....	....	....	....	....	....	....	....	....
2009-10	Los Angeles	NHL	49	10	19	29	39	1	0	1	140	7.1	3	11	36.4	16:23	3	0	1	1	2	0	0	0	11:24
2010-11	Los Angeles	NHL	73	22	35	57	59	5	0	3	213	10.3	14	14	50.0	17:15	6	3	1	4	2	1	0	0	16:44
2011-12 ♦	Los Angeles	NHL	82	22	37	59	44	9	0	2	241	9.1	10	25	44.0	17:09	20	4	11	15	12	1	0	0	18:24
2012-13	Los Angeles	NHL	48	11	22	33	22	1	0	3	142	7.7	15	6	33.3	16:59	18	6	3	9	8	1	0	2	18:36
2013-14 ♦	Los Angeles	NHL	82	19	24	43	48	4	0	1	239	7.9	14	10	20.0	16:57	26	9	16	25	35	2	0	2	16:49
2014-15	Los Angeles	NHL	81	18	23	41	29	4	0	2	174	10.3	8	6	50.0	15:49	....	....	....	....	....	....	....	....	....
	NHL Totals		918	227	355	582	574	53	6	28	2445	9.3		256	37.1	17:04	115	30	48	78	105	5	1	6	17:59

Conn Smythe Trophy (2014)

Played in NHL All-Star Game (2007)

• Missed majority of 2002-03 due to shoulder (November 15, 2002 vs. Carolina) and knee (January 18, 2003 vs. Tampa Bay) injuries. Traded to **Carolina** by **Philadelphia** for Danny Markov, January 20, 2004. Signed as a free agent by **Lulea** (Sweden), September 21, 2004. • Missed majority of 2007-08 due to knee injury at Florida, December 20, 2007. Traded to **Los Angeles** by **Carolina** for Patrick O'Sullivan and Calgary's 2nd round choice (previously acquired, Carolina selected Brian Dumoulin) in 2009 Entry Draft, March 4. 2009. Signed as a free agent by **Washington**, July 1, 2015.

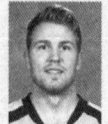

WILSON, Colin

(WIHL-suhn, KAW-lihn) **NSH**

Center. Shoots left. 6'1", 216 lbs. Born, Greenwich, CT, October 20, 1989. Nashville's 1st choice, 7th overall, in 2008 Entry Draft.

Season	Club	League	GP	G	A	Pts	PIM	PP	SH	GW	S	S%	+/-	TF	F%	Min	GP	G	A	Pts	PIM	PP	SH	GW	Min
2005-06	USNTDP	U-17	15	9	7	16	2	....	....	....	....	....	....	....	....	....	....	....	....	....	....	....	....	....	....
	USNTDP	U-18	16	2	4	6	8	....	....	....	....	....	....	....	....	....	....	....	....	....	....	....	....	....	....
	USNTDP	NAHL	34	10	11	21	10	....	....	....	....	....	....	....	....	....	2	0	0	0	2	....	....	....	....
2006-07	USNTDP	U-18	41	19	31	50	32	....	....	....	....	....	....	....	....	....	....	....	....	....	....	....	....	....	....
	USNTDP	NAHL	15	11	13	24	21	....	....	....	....	....	....	....	....	....	....	....	....	....	....	....	....	....	....
2007-08	Boston University	H-East	37	12	23	35	22	....	....	....	....	....	....	....	....	....	....	....	....	....	....	....	....	....	....
2008-09	Boston University	H-East	43	17	*38	*55	52	....	....	....	....	....	....	....	....	....	....	....	....	....	....	....	....	....	....
2009-10	Nashville	NHL	35	8	7	15	7	1	0	3	58	13.8	−2	124	50.0	15:10	6	0	1	1	0	0	0	0	13:43
	Milwaukee	AHL	40	13	21	34	19	....	....	....	....	....	....	....	....	....	....	....	....	....	....	....	....	....	....
2010-11	Nashville	NHL	82	16	18	34	17	2	0	2	101	15.8	9	228	47.4	13:18	3	0	0	0	0	0	0	0	11:37

			Regular Season														Playoffs								
Season	Club	League	GP	G	A	Pts	PIM	PP	SH	GW	S	S%	+/-	TF	F%	Min	GP	G	A	Pts	PIM	PP	SH	GW	Min
2011-12	Nashville	NHL	68	15	20	35	21	5	0	5	114	13.2	5	77	50.7	16:08	4	1	0	1	0	0	0	0	13:25
2012-13	Nashville	NHL	25	7	12	19	4	2	0	1	26	26.9	1	21	38.1	16:34	....	....	....	....	....	....	....	....	....
2013-14	Nashville	NHL	81	11	22	33	21	2	0	3	112	9.8	–1	343	48.4	15:13	....	....	....	....	....	....	....	....	....
2014-15	Nashville	NHL	77	20	22	42	22	3	0	5	172	11.6	19	178	39.9	16:13	6	5	0	5	0	4	0	1	19:44
	NHL Totals		368	77	101	178	92	15	0	19	583	13.2		971	46.8	15:15	19	6	1	7	0	4	0	1	15:13

Hockey East All-Rookie Team (2008) • Hockey East Rookie of the Year (2008) • Hockey East First All-Star Team (2009) • NCAA East First All-American Team (2009) • NCAA Championship All-Tournament Team (2009)

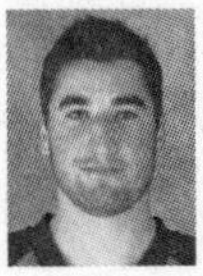

WILSON, Garrett

(WIHL-suhn, GAIR-reht) **FLA**

Left wing. Shoots left. 6'2", 199 lbs. Born, Barrie, ON, March 16, 1991. Florida's 4th choice, 107th overall, in 2009 Entry Draft.

Season	Club	League	GP	G	A	Pts	PIM	PP	SH	GW	S	S%	+/-	TF	F%	Min	GP	G	A	Pts	PIM	PP	SH	GW	Min
2007-08	Tecumseh Chiefs	ON-Jr.B	46	11	26	37	40	....	....	....	....	....	....	....	....	....	14	13	8	21	22	....	....	....	....
	Windsor Spitfires	OHL	7	1	0	1	2	....	....	....	....	....	....	....	....	....	3	0	0	0	0	....	....	....	....
2008-09	Owen Sound	OHL	53	17	18	35	44	....	....	....	....	....	....	....	....	....	4	1	3	4	7	....	....	....	....
2009-10	Owen Sound	OHL	65	36	26	62	80	....	....	....	....	....	....	....	....	....	....	....	....	....	....	....	....	....	....
2010-11	Owen Sound	OHL	66	40	46	86	114	....	....	....	....	....	....	....	....	....	22	11	10	21	28	....	....	....	....
2011-12	Cincinnati	ECHL	63	17	18	35	50	....	....	....	....	....	....	....	....	....	....	....	....	....	....	....	....	....	....
	San Antonio	AHL	11	1	0	1	2	....	....	....	....	....	....	....	....	....	....	....	....	....	....	....	....	....	....
2012-13	Cincinnati	ECHL	38	19	10	29	56	....	....	....	....	....	....	....	....	....	15	4	1	5	17	....	....	....	....
	San Antonio	AHL	26	3	2	5	19	....	....	....	....	....	....	....	....	....	....	....	....	....	....	....	....	....	....
2013-14	**Florida**	**NHL**	**3**	**0**	**0**	**0**	**0**	**0**	**0**	**0**	**4**	**0.0**	**–1**	**0**	**0.0**	**10:20**	....	....	....	....	....	....	....	....	....
	San Antonio	AHL	71	14	16	30	58	....	....	....	....	....	....	....	....	....	....	....	....	....	....	....	....	....	....
2014-15	**Florida**	**NHL**	**2**	**0**	**0**	**0**	**0**	**0**	**0**	**0**	**5**	**0.0**	**–2**	**0**	**0.0**	**8:51**	....	....	....	....	....	....	....	....	....
	San Antonio	AHL	71	23	15	38	80	....	....	....	....	....	....	....	....	....	3	0	2	2	2	....	....	....	....
	NHL Totals		**5**	**0**	**0**	**0**	**0**	**0**	**0**	**0**	**9**	**0.0**		**0**	**0.0**	**9:44**	....	....	....	....	....	....	....	....	....

OHL First All-Star Team (2011)

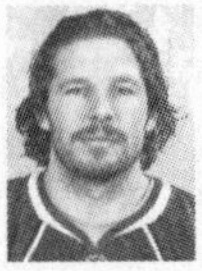

WILSON, Ryan

(WIHL-suhn, RIGH-uhn)

Defense. Shoots left. 6'1", 207 lbs. Born, Windsor, ON, February 3, 1987.

Season	Club	League	GP	G	A	Pts	PIM	PP	SH	GW	S	S%	+/-	TF	F%	Min	GP	G	A	Pts	PIM	PP	SH	GW	Min
2003-04	St. Michael's	OHL	58	3	22	25	88	....	....	....	....	....	....	....	....	....	18	3	7	10	16	....	....	....	....
2004-05	St. Michael's	OHL	68	13	24	37	149	....	....	....	....	....	....	....	....	....	10	4	5	9	12	....	....	....	....
2005-06	St. Michael's	OHL	64	12	49	61	145	....	....	....	....	....	....	....	....	....	4	1	3	4	12	....	....	....	....
2006-07	Sarnia Sting	OHL	68	17	58	75	136	....	....	....	....	....	....	....	....	....	4	1	3	4	14	....	....	....	....
2007-08	Sarnia Sting	OHL	58	7	64	71	84	....	....	....	....	....	....	....	....	....	9	0	7	7	19	....	....	....	....
2008-09	Quad City Flames	AHL	60	4	16	20	56	....	....	....	....	....	....	....	....	....	....	....	....	....	....	....	....	....	....
	Lake Erie	AHL	8	0	2	2	25	....	....	....	....	....	....	....	....	....	....	....	....	....	....	....	....	....	....
2009-10	**Colorado**	**NHL**	**61**	**3**	**18**	**21**	**36**	**0**	**0**	**0**	**46**	**6.5**	**13**	**0**	**0.0**	**16:16**	**4**	**0**	**1**	**1**	**0**	**0**	**0**	**0**	**14:39**
	Lake Erie	AHL	3	0	0	0	17	....	....	....	....	....	....	....	....	....	....	....	....	....	....	....	....	....	....
2010-11	**Colorado**	**NHL**	**67**	**3**	**13**	**16**	**68**	**1**	**0**	**0**	**62**	**4.8**	**–8**	**0**	**0.0**	**19:48**	....	....	....	....	....	....	....	....	....
2011-12	**Colorado**	**NHL**	**59**	**1**	**20**	**21**	**33**	**0**	**0**	**0**	**63**	**1.6**	**11**	**1**	**0.0**	**18:44**	....	....	....	....	....	....	....	....	....
2012-13	**Colorado**	**NHL**	**12**	**0**	**3**	**3**	**8**	**0**	**0**	**0**	**23**	**0.0**	**4**	**0**	**0.0**	**18:30**	....	....	....	....	....	....	....	....	....
2013-14	**Colorado**	**NHL**	**28**	**0**	**6**	**6**	**12**	**0**	**0**	**0**	**23**	**0.0**	**1**	**1**	**0.0**	**14:40**	**4**	**0**	**2**	**2**	**2**	**0**	**0**	**0**	**15:27**
	Lake Erie	AHL	1	0	0	0	0	....	....	....	....	....	....	....	....	....	....	....	....	....	....	....	....	....	....
2014-15	**Colorado**	**NHL**	**3**	**0**	**0**	**0**	**0**	**0**	**0**	**0**	**3**	**0.0**	**–3**	**0**	**0.0**	**11:12**	....	....	....	....	....	....	....	....	....
	NHL Totals		**230**	**7**	**60**	**67**	**157**	**1**	**0**	**0**	**220**	**3.2**		**2**	**0.0**	**17:47**	**8**	**0**	**3**	**3**	**2**	**0**	**0**	**0**	**15:03**

Signed as a free agent by **Calgary**, July 1, 2008. Traded to **Colorado** by **Calgary** with Lawrence Nycholat and Montreal's 2nd round choice (previously acquired, Colorado selected Stefan Elliott) in 2009 Entry Draft for Jordan Leopold, March 4, 2009. • Missed majority of 2012-13 due to ankle injury vs. Edmonton, February 2, 2013. • Missed majority of 2013-14 due to back injury vs. Montreal, November 2, 2013 and as a healthy reserve. • Missed majority of 2014-15 due to shoulder injury vs. Florida, October 21, 2014.

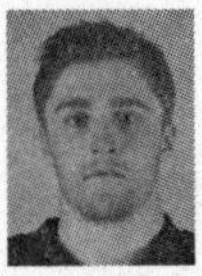

WILSON, Scott

(WIHL-suhn, SKAWT) **PIT**

Center/Left wing. Shoots left. 5'11", 184 lbs. Born, Oakville, ON, April 24, 1992. Pittsburgh's 5th choice, 209th overall, in 2011 Entry Draft.

Season	Club	League	GP	G	A	Pts	PIM	PP	SH	GW	S	S%	+/-	TF	F%	Min	GP	G	A	Pts	PIM	PP	SH	GW	Min
2008-09	Oakville Rangers	Minor-ON	STATISTICS NOT AVAILABLE																						
	Georgetown	ON-Jr.A	6	0	1	1	2	....	....	....	....	....	....	....	....	....	1	0	0	0	0	....	....	....	....
2009-10	Georgetown	ON-Jr.A	56	24	43	67	28	....	....	....	....	....	....	....	....	....	11	9	8	17	2	....	....	....	....
2010-11	Georgetown	ON-Jr.A	42	20	41	61	59	....	....	....	....	....	....	....	....	....	4	1	2	3	8	....	....	....	....
2011-12	U. Mass Lowell	H-East	37	16	22	38	26	....	....	....	....	....	....	....	....	....	....	....	....	....	....	....	....	....	....
2012-13	U. Mass Lowell	H-East	41	16	22	38	32	....	....	....	....	....	....	....	....	....	....	....	....	....	....	....	....	....	....
2013-14	U. Mass Lowell	H-East	31	7	12	19	24	....	....	....	....	....	....	....	....	....	....	....	....	....	....	....	....	....	....
	Wilkes-Barre	AHL	1	0	0	0	0	....	....	....	....	....	....	....	....	....	....	....	....	....	....	....	....	....	....
2014-15	**Pittsburgh**	**NHL**	**1**	**0**	**0**	**0**	**0**	**0**	**0**	**0**	**0**	**0.0**	**0**	**0**	**0.0**	**4:21**	**3**	**0**	**0**	**0**	**0**	**0**	**0**	**0**	**6:44**
	Wilkes-Barre	AHL	55	19	22	41	30	....	....	....	....	....	....	....	....	....	3	2	2	4	0	....	....	....	....
	NHL Totals		**1**	**0**	**0**	**0**	**0**	**0**	**0**	**0**	**0**	**0.0**		**0**	**0.0**	**4:21**	**3**	**0**	**0**	**0**	**0**	**0**	**0**	**0**	**6:44**

Hockey East All-Rookie Team (2012)

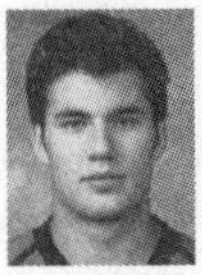

WILSON, Tom

(WIHL-suhn, TAWM) **WSH**

Right wing. Shoots right. 6'4", 210 lbs. Born, Toronto, ON, March 29, 1994. Washington's 2nd choice, 16th overall, in 2012 Entry Draft.

Season	Club	League	GP	G	A	Pts	PIM	PP	SH	GW	S	S%	+/-	TF	F%	Min	GP	G	A	Pts	PIM	PP	SH	GW	Min
2009-10	Tor. Jr. Canadiens	GTHL	73	44	61	105	140	....	....	....	....	....	....	....	....	....	....	....	....	....	....	....	....	....	....
2010-11	Plymouth Whalers	OHL	28	3	3	6	71	....	....	....	....	....	....	....	....	....	....	....	....	....	....	....	....	....	....
2011-12	Plymouth Whalers	OHL	49	9	18	27	141	....	....	....	....	....	....	....	....	....	13	7	6	13	39	....	....	....	....
2012-13	Plymouth Whalers	OHL	48	23	35	58	104	....	....	....	....	....	....	....	....	....	12	9	8	17	41	....	....	....	....
	Hershey Bears	AHL	....	....	....	....	....	....	....	....	....	....	....	....	....	....	3	1	0	1	6	....	....	....	....
	Washington	**NHL**	....	....	....	....	....	....	....	....	....	....	....	....	....	....	**3**	**0**	**0**	**0**	**0**	**0**	**0**	**0**	**6:53**
2013-14	**Washington**	**NHL**	**82**	**3**	**7**	**10**	**151**	**1**	**0**	**0**	**63**	**4.8**	**1**	**3**	**0.0**	**7:56**	....	....	....	....	....	....	....	....	....
2014-15	**Washington**	**NHL**	**67**	**4**	**13**	**17**	**172**	**0**	**0**	**0**	**79**	**5.1**	**–1**	**11**	**18.2**	**10:56**	**13**	**0**	**1**	**1**	**25**	**0**	**0**	**0**	**7:44**
	Hershey Bears	AHL	2	0	0	0	0	....	....	....	....	....	....	....	....	....	....	....	....	....	....	....	....	....	....
	NHL Totals		**149**	**7**	**20**	**27**	**323**	**1**	**0**	**0**	**142**	**4.9**		**14**	**14.3**	**9:17**	**16**	**0**	**1**	**1**	**25**	**0**	**0**	**0**	**7:34**

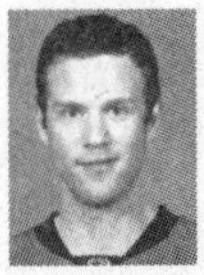

WINCHESTER, Brad

(WIHN-chehs-tuhr, BRAD)

Center/Left wing. Shoots left. 6'5", 230 lbs. Born, Madison, WI, March 1, 1981. Edmonton's 2nd choice, 35th overall, in 2000 Entry Draft.

Season	Club	League	GP	G	A	Pts	PIM	PP	SH	GW	S	S%	+/-	TF	F%	Min	GP	G	A	Pts	PIM	PP	SH	GW	Min
1997-98	USNTDP	U-17	24	8	5	13	64	....	....	....	....	....	....	....	....	....	....	....	....	....	....	....	....	....	....
	USNTDP	USHL	5	2	1	3	6	....	....	....	....	....	....	....	....	....	....	....	....	....	....	....	....	....	....
	USNTDP	NAHL	40	11	17	28	84	....	....	....	....	....	....	....	....	....	5	1	0	1	8	....	....	....	....
1998-99	USNTDP	U-18	6	0	3	3	6	....	....	....	....	....	....	....	....	....	....	....	....	....	....	....	....	....	....
	USNTDP	USHL	48	14	23	37	103	....	....	....	....	....	....	....	....	....	....	....	....	....	....	....	....	....	....
99-2000	U. of Wisconsin	WCHA	33	9	9	18	48	....	....	....	....	....	....	....	....	....	....	....	....	....	....	....	....	....	....
2000-01	U. of Wisconsin	WCHA	41	7	9	16	71	....	....	....	....	....	....	....	....	....	....	....	....	....	....	....	....	....	....
2001-02	U. of Wisconsin	WCHA	38	14	20	34	38	....	....	....	....	....	....	....	....	....	....	....	....	....	....	....	....	....	....
2002-03	U. of Wisconsin	WCHA	38	10	6	16	58	....	....	....	....	....	....	....	....	....	....	....	....	....	....	....	....	....	....
2003-04	Toronto	AHL	65	13	6	19	85	....	....	....	....	....	....	....	....	....	3	0	0	0	2	....	....	....	....
2004-05	Edmonton	AHL	76	22	18	40	143	....	....	....	....	....	....	....	....	....	....	....	....	....	....	....	....	....	....
2005-06	**Edmonton**	**NHL**	**19**	**0**	**1**	**1**	**21**	**0**	**0**	**0**	**19**	**0.0**	**–2**	**2**	**100.0**	**6:05**	**10**	**1**	**2**	**3**	**4**	**0**	**0**	**1**	**9:14**
	Hamilton	AHL	40	26	14	40	118	....	....	....	....	....	....	....	....	....	....	....	....	....	....	....	....	....	....
2006-07	**Edmonton**	**NHL**	**59**	**4**	**5**	**9**	**86**	**0**	**0**	**0**	**66**	**6.1**	**–10**	**3**	**33.3**	**8:04**	....	....	....	....	....	....	....	....	....
2007-08	**Dallas**	**NHL**	**41**	**1**	**2**	**3**	**46**	**0**	**0**	**0**	**36**	**2.8**	**–9**	**2**	**0.0**	**7:34**	**6**	**0**	**0**	**0**	**8**	**0**	**0**	**0**	**6:50**
	Iowa Stars	AHL	1	0	0	0	2	....	....	....	....	....	....	....	....	....	....	....	....	....	....	....	....	....	....
2008-09	**St. Louis**	**NHL**	**64**	**13**	**8**	**21**	**89**	**5**	**0**	**3**	**82**	**15.9**	**–1**	**20**	**45.0**	**12:10**	**4**	**0**	**0**	**0**	**10**	**0**	**0**	**0**	**11:42**
	Peoria Rivermen	AHL	13	4	2	6	46	....	....	....	....	....	....	....	....	....	....	....	....	....	....	....	....	....	....
2009-10	**St. Louis**	**NHL**	**64**	**3**	**5**	**8**	**108**	**1**	**0**	**0**	**69**	**4.3**	**3**	**12**	**25.0**	**9:04**	....	....	....	....	....	....	....	....	....
2010-11	**St. Louis**	**NHL**	**57**	**9**	**5**	**14**	**86**	**3**	**0**	**1**	**67**	**13.4**	**–9**	**7**	**28.6**	**10:29**	....	....	....	....	....	....	....	....	....
	Anaheim	**NHL**	**19**	**1**	**1**	**2**	**28**	**0**	**0**	**0**	**23**	**4.3**	**–9**	**1**	**0.0**	**10:28**	**3**	**0**	**0**	**0**	**4**	**0**	**0**	**0**	**5:24**
2011-12	**San Jose**	**NHL**	**67**	**6**	**4**	**10**	**88**	**0**	**0**	**0**	**72**	**8.3**	**–5**	**33**	**60.6**	**7:48**	**1**	**0**	**0**	**0**	**0**	**0**	**0**	**0**	**6:41**
2012-13	Milwaukee	AHL	37	9	18	27	66	....	....	....	....	....	....	....	....	....	2	0	1	1	2	....	....	....	....
2013-14	Rockford IceHogs	AHL	55	16	14	30	85	....	....	....	....	....	....	....	....	....	....	....	....	....	....	....	....	....	....
	Iowa Wild	AHL	23	3	5	8	64	....	....	....	....	....	....	....	....	....	....	....	....	....	....	....	....	....	....

Season	Club	League	GP	G	A	Pts	PIM	PP	SH	GW	S	S%	+/-	TF	F%	Min	GP	G	A	Pts	PIM	PP	SH	GW	Min
			Regular Season														Playoffs								
2014-15	Norfolk Admirals	AHL	15	4	5	9	39																		
	Oklahoma City	AHL	11	1	0	1	8										10	0	0	0	10				
	NHL Totals		**390**	**37**	**31**	**68**	**552**	**9**	**0**	**4**	**434**	**8.5**		**80**	**46.3**	**9:11**	**24**	**1**	**2**	**3**	**26**	**0**	**0**	**1**	**8:27**

Signed as a free agent by **Dallas**, July 6, 2007. Signed as a free agent by **St. Louis**, July 16, 2008. Traded to **Anaheim** by **St. Louis** for Anaheim's 3rd round choice (Mackenzie MacEachern) in 2012 Entry Draft, February 28, 2011. Signed as a free agent by **San Jose**, October 3, 2011. Signed to a PTO (professional tryout) contract by **Milwaukee** (AHL), January 22, 2013. Signed as a free agent by **Chicago**, August 2, 2013. Traded to **Minnesota** by **Chicago** for Brian Connelly, February 26, 2014. Signed as a free agent by **Norfolk** (AHL), September 11, 2014. Signed as a free agent by **Oklahoma City** (AHL), March 6, 2015.

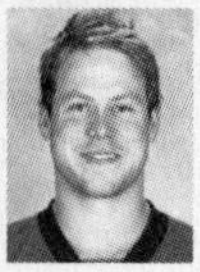

WINCHESTER, Jesse

(WIHN-chehs-tuhr, JEH-see) **COL**

Center. Shoots right. 6'1", 205 lbs. Born, Long Sault, ON, October 4, 1983.

Season	Club	League	GP	G	A	Pts	PIM	PP	SH	GW	S	S%	+/-	TF	F%	Min	GP	G	A	Pts	PIM	PP	SH	GW	Min
2004-05	Colgate	ECAC	28	2	2	4	22																		
2005-06	Colgate	ECAC	37	14	22	36	31																		
2006-07	Colgate	ECAC	37	16	21	37	52																		
2007-08	Colgate	ECAC	40	8	*29	37	51																		
	Ottawa	**NHL**	**1**	**0**	**0**	**0**	**2**	**0**	**0**	**0**	**1**	**0.0**	**0**	**0**	**0.0**	**14:00**									
2008-09	**Ottawa**	**NHL**	**76**	**3**	**15**	**18**	**33**	**0**	**0**	**1**	**115**	**2.6**	**0**	**199**	**56.8**	**10:35**									
2009-10	**Ottawa**	**NHL**	**52**	**2**	**11**	**13**	**22**	**0**	**1**	**0**	**77**	**2.6**	**–1**	**377**	**55.4**	**10:01**	**6**	**0**	**0**	**0**	**0**	**0**	**0**	**0**	**9:38**
	Binghamton	AHL	4	2	2	4	0																		
2010-11	**Ottawa**	**NHL**	**72**	**4**	**9**	**13**	**42**	**0**	**0**	**0**	**118**	**3.4**	**–9**	**545**	**55.6**	**10:50**									
2011-12	**Ottawa**	**NHL**	**32**	**2**	**6**	**8**	**22**	**0**	**1**	**0**	**52**	**3.8**	**2**	**235**	**53.6**	**10:38**	**4**	**0**	**0**	**0**	**0**	**0**	**0**	**0**	**10:53**
2012-13	TuTo Turku	Finland-2	11	3	7	10	58																		
	Jokerit Helsinki	Finland	5	0	3	3	2																		
2013-14	**Florida**	**NHL**	**52**	**9**	**9**	**18**	**38**	**1**	**0**	**2**	**100**	**9.0**	**–2**	**130**	**48.5**	**12:44**									
2014-15	**Colorado**	**NHL**	DID NOT PLAY – INJURED																						
	NHL Totals		**285**	**20**	**50**	**70**	**159**	**1**	**2**	**3**	**463**	**4.3**		**1486**	**54.8**	**10:57**	**10**	**0**	**0**	**0**	**0**	**0**	**0**	**0**	**10:08**

Signed as a free agent by **Ottawa**, March 24, 2008. • Missed majority of 2011-12 due to upper-body injury vs. Buffalo, December 20. 2011. Signed as a free agent by **TuTo Turku** (Finland-2), November 13, 2012. Signed as a free agent by **Jokerit Helsinki** (Finland), January 27, 2013. Signed as a free agent by **Florida**, July 5, 2013. Signed as a free agent by **Colorado**, July 1, 2014. • Missed 2014-15 due to head injury in pre-season game at Calgary, September 30, 2014,

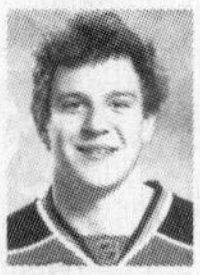

WINGELS, Tommy

(WIHN-guhls, TAW-mee) **S.J.**

Center. Shoots right. 6', 200 lbs. Born, Evanston, IL, April 12, 1988. San Jose's 5th choice, 177th overall, in 2008 Entry Draft.

Season	Club	League	GP	G	A	Pts	PIM	PP	SH	GW	S	S%	+/-	TF	F%	Min	GP	G	A	Pts	PIM	PP	SH	GW	Min
2006-07	Cedar Rapids	USHL	47	10	18	28	52										6	3	0	3	6				
2007-08	Miami U.	CCHA	42	15	14	29	22																		
2008-09	Miami U.	CCHA	41	11	17	28	66																		
2009-10	Miami U.	CCHA	44	17	25	42	49																		
2010-11	**San Jose**	**NHL**	**5**	**0**	**0**	**0**	**0**	**0**	**0**	**0**	**1**	**0.0**	**–1**	**3**	**33.3**	**5:07**									
	Worcester Sharks	AHL	69	17	16	33	69																		
2011-12	**San Jose**	**NHL**	**33**	**3**	**6**	**9**	**18**	**0**	**0**	**0**	**71**	**4.2**	**–1**	**17**	**41.2**	**13:45**	**5**	**0**	**1**	**1**	**7**	**0**	**0**	**0**	**10:30**
	Worcester Sharks	AHL	29	13	8	21	28																		
2012-13	KooKoo Kouvola	Finland-2	18	8	14	22	33																		
	San Jose	**NHL**	**42**	**5**	**8**	**13**	**26**	**0**	**1**	**0**	**69**	**7.2**	**–9**	**16**	**25.0**	**14:14**	**11**	**0**	**2**	**2**	**6**	**0**	**0**	**0**	**13:53**
2013-14	**San Jose**	**NHL**	**77**	**16**	**22**	**38**	**35**	**0**	**2**	**7**	**163**	**9.8**	**11**	**56**	**35.7**	**16:07**	**7**	**0**	**3**	**3**	**4**	**0**	**0**	**0**	**16:47**
2014-15	**San Jose**	**NHL**	**75**	**15**	**21**	**36**	**40**	**4**	**1**	**1**	**158**	**9.5**	**–7**	**154**	**45.5**	**16:28**									
	NHL Totals		**232**	**39**	**57**	**96**	**119**	**4**	**4**	**8**	**462**	**8.4**		**246**	**41.5**	**15:19**	**23**	**0**	**6**	**6**	**17**	**0**	**0**	**0**	**14:02**

NCAA Championship All-Tournament Team (2009) • CCHA Second All-Star Team (2010)

Signed as a free agent by **Kouvola** (Finland-2), October 4, 2012.

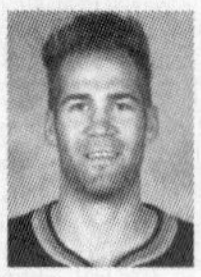

WINNIK, Daniel

(WIHN-ihk, DAN-yehl) **TOR**

Center/Left wing. Shoots left. 6'2", 207 lbs. Born, Toronto, ON, March 6, 1985. Phoenix's 10th choice, 265th overall, in 2004 Entry Draft.

Season	Club	League	GP	G	A	Pts	PIM	PP	SH	GW	S	S%	+/-	TF	F%	Min	GP	G	A	Pts	PIM	PP	SH	GW	Min
2002-03	Wexford Raiders	ON-Jr.A	47	20	33	53	70										18	11	11	22	24				
2003-04	New Hampshire	H-East	38	4	10	14	12																		
2004-05	New Hampshire	H-East	42	18	22	40	26																		
2005-06	New Hampshire	H-East	39	15	26	41	44																		
	San Antonio	AHL	7	1	1	2	8																		
2006-07	San Antonio	AHL	66	9	12	21	34																		
	Phoenix	ECHL	5	0	6	6	9																		
2007-08	**Phoenix**	**NHL**	**79**	**11**	**15**	**26**	**25**	**0**	**0**	**1**	**122**	**9.0**	**–3**	**154**	**42.2**	**14:06**									
2008-09	**Phoenix**	**NHL**	**49**	**3**	**4**	**7**	**63**	**0**	**0**	**0**	**66**	**4.5**	**1**	**138**	**37.0**	**13:04**									
	San Antonio	AHL	5	0	0	0	4																		
2009-10	**Phoenix**	**NHL**	**74**	**4**	**15**	**19**	**12**	**0**	**0**	**1**	**83**	**4.8**	**1**	**110**	**45.5**	**13:09**	**7**	**0**	**0**	**0**	**0**	**0**	**0**	**0**	**12:45**
2010-11	**Colorado**	**NHL**	**80**	**11**	**15**	**26**	**35**	**2**	**2**	**1**	**167**	**6.6**	**–2**	**69**	**36.2**	**16:33**									
2011-12	**Colorado**	**NHL**	**63**	**5**	**13**	**18**	**42**	**0**	**1**	**0**	**155**	**3.2**	**–11**	**47**	**46.8**	**17:42**									
	San Jose	**NHL**	**21**	**3**	**2**	**5**	**10**	**0**	**0**	**1**	**29**	**10.3**	**0**	**19**	**57.9**	**13:40**	**5**	**0**	**1**	**1**	**6**	**0**	**0**	**0**	**12:25**
2012-13	**Anaheim**	**NHL**	**48**	**6**	**13**	**19**	**16**	**0**	**0**	**1**	**95**	**6.3**	**13**	**53**	**30.2**	**16:50**	**7**	**0**	**1**	**1**	**7**	**0**	**0**	**0**	**15:04**
2013-14	**Anaheim**	**NHL**	**76**	**6**	**24**	**30**	**23**	**0**	**2**	**2**	**115**	**5.2**	**6**	**196**	**43.4**	**15:23**	**9**	**0**	**1**	**1**	**2**	**0**	**0**	**0**	**13:37**
2014-15	**Toronto**	**NHL**	**58**	**7**	**18**	**25**	**19**	**0**	**0**	**0**	**70**	**10.0**	**15**	**186**	**48.4**	**16:50**									
	Pittsburgh	**NHL**	**21**	**2**	**7**	**9**	**8**	**0**	**0**	**1**	**27**	**7.4**	**8**	**42**	**40.5**	**16:07**	**5**	**0**	**0**	**0**	**2**	**0**	**0**	**0**	**13:53**
	NHL Totals		**569**	**58**	**126**	**184**	**253**	**2**	**5**	**8**	**929**	**6.2**		**1014**	**42.6**	**15:22**	**33**	**0**	**3**	**3**	**17**	**0**	**0**	**0**	**13:36**

Hockey East Second All-Star Team (2006)

Traded to **Colorado** by **Phoenix** for Colorado's 4th round choice (Rhett Holland) in 2012 Entry Draft, June 28, 2010. Traded to **San Jose** by **Colorado** with T.J. Galiardi and Anaheim's 7th round choice (previously acquired, San Jose selected Emil Galimov) in 2013 Entry Draft for Jamie McGinn, Michael Sgarbossa and Mike Connolly, February 27, 2012. Signed as a free agent by **Anaheim**, July 20, 2012. Signed as a free agent by **Toronto**, July 28, 2014. Traded to **Pittsburgh** by **Toronto** for Zach Sill, Pittsburgh's 4th round choice (later traded to Edmonton, later traded to Ottawa – Ottawa selected Christian Wolanin) in 2015 Entry Draft and Pittsburgh's 2nd round choice (later traded back to Pittsburgh) in 2016 Entry Draft, February 25, 2015. Signed as a free agent by **Toronto**, July 1, 2015.

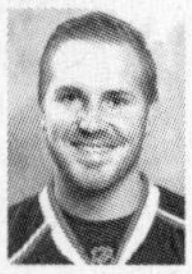

WISNIEWSKI, James

(wihz-NOO-skee, JAYMZ) **CAR**

Defense. Shoots right. 5'11", 203 lbs. Born, Canton, MI, February 21, 1984. Chicago's 5th choice, 156th overall, in 2002 Entry Draft.

Season	Club	League	GP	G	A	Pts	PIM	PP	SH	GW	S	S%	+/-	TF	F%	Min	GP	G	A	Pts	PIM	PP	SH	GW	Min
99-2000	Det. Compuware	NAHL	50	5	11	16	67										5	0	3	3	4				
2000-01	Plymouth Whalers	OHL	53	6	23	29	72										19	3	10	13	34				
2001-02	Plymouth Whalers	OHL	62	11	25	36	100										6	1	2	3	6				
2002-03	Plymouth Whalers	OHL	52	18	34	52	60										18	2	10	12	14				
2003-04	Plymouth Whalers	OHL	50	17	53	70	63										9	3	7	10	8				
2004-05	Norfolk Admirals	AHL	66	7	18	25	110										5	1	3	4	2				
2005-06	**Chicago**	**NHL**	**19**	**2**	**5**	**7**	**36**	**0**	**0**	**0**	**25**	**8.0**	**0**	**1**	**0.0**	**15:52**									
	Norfolk Admirals	AHL	61	7	28	35	67										4	1	2	3	6				
2006-07	**Chicago**	**NHL**	**50**	**2**	**8**	**10**	**39**	**0**	**0**	**0**	**55**	**3.6**	**3**	**1**	**0.0**	**19:00**									
	Norfolk Admirals	AHL	10	0	6	6	8																		
2007-08	**Chicago**	**NHL**	**68**	**7**	**19**	**26**	**103**	**1**	**1**	**0**	**82**	**8.5**	**12**	**0**	**0.0**	**17:00**									
2008-09	**Chicago**	**NHL**	**31**	**2**	**11**	**13**	**14**	**1**	**0**	**0**	**70**	**2.9**	**6**	**0**	**0.0**	**19:15**									
	Rockford IceHogs	AHL	2	3	1	4	0																		
	Anaheim	**NHL**	**17**	**1**	**10**	**11**	**16**	**0**	**0**	**0**	**19**	**5.3**	**3**	**0**	**0.0**	**20:57**	**12**	**1**	**2**	**3**	**10**	**0**	**0**	**0**	**20:22**
2009-10	**Anaheim**	**NHL**	**69**	**3**	**27**	**30**	**56**	**2**	**0**	**0**	**146**	**2.1**	**–5**	**0**	**0.0**	**24:21**									
2010-11	**NY Islanders**	**NHL**	**32**	**3**	**18**	**21**	**18**	**3**	**0**	**0**	**71**	**4.2**	**–18**	**0**	**0.0**	**23:15**									
	Montreal	**NHL**	**43**	**7**	**23**	**30**	**20**	**4**	**0**	**2**	**87**	**8.0**	**4**	**0**	**0.0**	**22:43**	**6**	**0**	**2**	**2**	**7**	**0**	**0**	**0**	**22:23**
2011-12	**Columbus**	**NHL**	**48**	**6**	**21**	**27**	**37**	**2**	**0**	**2**	**99**	**6.1**	**–13**	**1**	**0.0**	**24:48**									
2012-13	**Columbus**	**NHL**	**30**	**5**	**9**	**14**	**15**	**4**	**0**	**0**	**62**	**8.1**	**–1**	**0**	**0.0**	**22:50**									
2013-14	**Columbus**	**NHL**	**75**	**7**	**44**	**51**	**61**	**3**	**0**	**1**	**166**	**4.2**	**0**	**0**	**0.0**	**22:37**	**6**	**0**	**2**	**2**	**10**	**0**	**0**	**0**	**24:45**

			Regular Season														Playoffs								
Season	Club	League	GP	G	A	Pts	PIM	PP	SH	GW	S	S%	+/-	TF	F%	Min	GP	G	A	Pts	PIM	PP	SH	GW	Min
2014-15	**Columbus**	**NHL**	**56**	**8**	**21**	**29**	**34**	**7**	**0**	**2**	**127**	**6.3**	**–10**	**0**	**0.0**	**21:25**	....	....	....	....	....	....	....	....	....
	Anaheim	**NHL**	**13**	**0**	**5**	**5**	**10**	**0**	**0**	**0**	**20**	**0.0**	**–3**	**0**	**0.0**	**20:13**	....	....	....	....	....	....	....	....	....
	NHL Totals		**551**	**53**	**221**	**274**	**459**	**27**	**1**	**7**	**1029**	**5.2**		**3**	**0.0**	**21:24**	**24**	**1**	**6**	**7**	**27**	**0**	**0**	**0**	**21:58**

OHL First All-Star Team (2004) • OHL Defenseman of the Year (2004) • Canadian Major Junior First All-Star Team (2004) • Canadian Major Junior Defenseman of the Year (2004)

Traded to **Anaheim** by **Chicago** with Petri Kontiola for Samuel Pahlsson, Logan Stephenson and future considerations, March 4, 2009. Traded to **NY Islanders** by **Anaheim** for NY Islanders' 3rd round choice (Joseph Cramarossa) in 2011 Entry Draft, July 30, 2010. Traded to **Montreal** by **NY Islanders** for Montreal's 2nd round compensatory choice (Johan Sundstrom) in 2011 Entry Draft, December 28, 2010. Traded to **Columbus** by **Montreal** for Columbus' 5th round choice (Charles Hudson) in 2012 Entry Draft, June 29, 2011. Traded to **Anaheim** by **Columbus** with Detroit's 3rd round choice (previously acquired, Anaheim selected Brent Gates) in 2015 Entry Draft for Rene Bourque, William Karlsson and Anaheim's 2nd round choice (Kevin Stenlund) in 2015 Entry Draft, March 2, 2015. Traded to **Carolina** by **Anaheim** for Anton Khudobin, June 27, 2015.

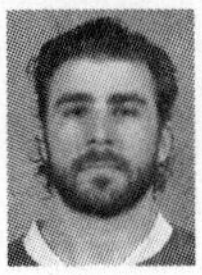

WITKOWSKI, Luke

(wiht-KOW-skee, LEWK) **T.B.**

Defense. Shoots right. 6'2", 200 lbs. Born, Holland, MI, April 14, 1990. Tampa Bay's 6th choice, 160th overall, in 2008 Entry Draft.

2006-07	Team nXi Majors	Minor-MI	59	18	22	40	172	....	....	....	....	....	....	....	....	....	....	....	....	....	....	....	....	....	....
2007-08	Ohio	USHL	58	3	10	13	139	....	....	....	....	....	....	....	....	....	....	....	....	....	....	....	....	....	....
2008-09	Fargo Force	USHL	55	6	16	22	118	....	....	....	....	....	....	....	....	....	10	2	1	3	29	....	....	....	....
2009-10	Western Mich.	CCHA	32	2	4	6	67	....	....	....	....	....	....	....	....	....	....	....	....	....	....	....	....	....	....
2010-11	Western Mich.	CCHA	42	1	8	9	56	....	....	....	....	....	....	....	....	....	....	....	....	....	....	....	....	....	....
2011-12	Western Mich.	CCHA	40	2	11	13	66	....	....	....	....	....	....	....	....	....	....	....	....	....	....	....	....	....	....
2012-13	Western Mich.	CCHA	38	2	8	10	46	....	....	....	....	....	....	....	....	....	....	....	....	....	....	....	....	....	....
	Syracuse Crunch	AHL	3	0	0	0	4	....	....	....	....	....	....	....	....	....	....	....	....	....	....	....	....	....	....
2013-14	Syracuse Crunch	AHL	76	2	10	12	204	....	....	....	....	....	....	....	....	....	....	....	....	....	....	....	....	....	....
2014-15	**Tampa Bay**	**NHL**	**16**	**0**	**0**	**0**	**15**	**0**	**0**	**0**	**10**	**0.0**	**0**	**0**	**0.0**	**15:11**	....	....	....	....	....	....	....	....	....
	Syracuse Crunch	AHL	50	2	6	8	91	....	....	....	....	....	....	....	....	....	3	0	1	1	4	....	....	....	....
	NHL Totals		**16**	**0**	**0**	**0**	**15**	**0**	**0**	**0**	**10**	**0.0**		**0**	**0.0**	**15:11**	....	....	....	....	....	....	....	....	....

CCHA Second All-Star Team (2013)

• Missed majority of 2014-15 as a healthy reserve.

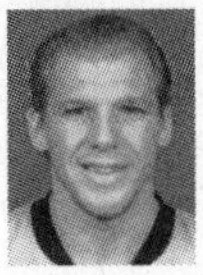

WOLF, David

(WUHLF, DAY-vihd)

Left wing. Shoots left. 6'3", 215 lbs. Born, Dusseldorf, West Germany, September 15, 1989.

2005-06	Mannheim Jr.	Ger-Jr.	33	11	4	15	89	....	....	....	....	....	....	....	....	....	6	3	3	6	4	....	....	....	....
2006-07	Heil./Mann. Jr.	Ger-Jr.	27	14	21	35	99	....	....	....	....	....	....	....	....	....	5	2	1	3	38	....	....	....	....
	Heilbronn	German-3	1	0	0	0	0	....	....	....	....	....	....	....	....	....	....	....	....	....	....	....	....	....	....
2007-08	Crimmitschau Jr.	Ger-Jr.	1	2	3	5	6	....	....	....	....	....	....	....	....	....	....	....	....	....	....	....	....	....	....
	Crimmitschau	German-2	46	7	2	9	40	....	....	....	....	....	....	....	....	....	6	0	1	1	6	....	....	....	....
2008-09	Crimmitschau	German-2	36	2	6	8	120	....	....	....	....	....	....	....	....	....	....	....	....	....	....	....	....	....	....
2009-10	Hannover Scorp.	Germany	54	4	7	11	40	....	....	....	....	....	....	....	....	....	11	3	0	3	12	....	....	....	....
	Bremerhaven	German-2	7	2	2	4	33	....	....	....	....	....	....	....	....	....	....	....	....	....	....	....	....	....	....
2010-11	Hannover Scorp.	Germany	51	2	4	6	97	....	....	....	....	....	....	....	....	....	4	1	1	2	52	....	....	....	....
	Hannover Ind.	German-2	1	0	3	3	4	....	....	....	....	....	....	....	....	....	....	....	....	....	....	....	....	....	....
2011-12	Hamburg Freezers	Germany	46	12	23	35	167	....	....	....	....	....	....	....	....	....	5	0	0	0	2	....	....	....	....
2012-13	Hamburg Freezers	Germany	49	17	19	36	96	....	....	....	....	....	....	....	....	....	6	1	3	4	26	....	....	....	....
2013-14	Hamburg Freezers	Germany	48	14	26	40	*152	....	....	....	....	....	....	....	....	....	10	4	8	12	47	....	....	....	....
2014-15	**Calgary**	**NHL**	**3**	**0**	**0**	**0**	**2**	**0**	**0**	**0**	**1**	**0.0**	**0**	**2**	**50.0**	**9:23**	**1**	**0**	**0**	**0**	**0**	**0**	**0**	**0**	**10:25**
	Adirondack	AHL	59	20	18	38	168	....	....	....	....	....	....	....	....	....	....	....	....	....	....	....	....	....	....
	NHL Totals		**3**	**0**	**0**	**0**	**2**	**0**	**0**	**0**	**1**	**0.0**		**2**	**50.0**	**9:23**	**1**	**0**	**0**	**0**	**0**	**0**	**0**	**0**	**10:25**

Signed as a free agent by **Calgary**, May 13, 2014.

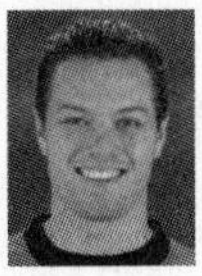

WOODS, Brendan

(WOODZ, BREHN-duhn) **CAR**

Left wing. Shoots left. 6'4", 210 lbs. Born, Humboldt, SK, June 11, 1992. Carolina's 7th choice, 129th overall, in 2012 Entry Draft.

2008-09	Williston North.	High-MA	29	8	11	19	28	....	....	....	....	....	....	....	....	....	....	....	....	....	....	....	....	....	....
2009-10	Chicago Steel	USHL	34	6	4	10	32	....	....	....	....	....	....	....	....	....	....	....	....	....	....	....	....	....	....
2010-11	Muskegon	USHL	57	14	12	26	86	....	....	....	....	....	....	....	....	....	6	1	1	2	14	....	....	....	....
2011-12	U. of Wisconsin	WCHA	34	5	5	10	67	....	....	....	....	....	....	....	....	....	....	....	....	....	....	....	....	....	....
2012-13	U. of Wisconsin	WCHA	41	5	7	12	47	....	....	....	....	....	....	....	....	....	....	....	....	....	....	....	....	....	....
	Charlotte	AHL	2	0	0	0	2	....	....	....	....	....	....	....	....	....	....	....	....	....	....	....	....	....	....
2013-14	Charlotte	AHL	42	5	3	8	40	....	....	....	....	....	....	....	....	....	....	....	....	....	....	....	....	....	....
2014-15	**Carolina**	**NHL**	**2**	**0**	**0**	**0**	**0**	**0**	**0**	**0**	**3**	**0.0**	**–1**	**0**	**0.0**	**6:02**	....	....	....	....	....	....	....	....	....
	Charlotte	AHL	68	13	17	30	101	....	....	....	....	....	....	....	....	....	....	....	....	....	....	....	....	....	....
	NHL Totals		**2**	**0**	**0**	**0**	**0**	**0**	**0**	**0**	**3**	**0.0**		**0**	**0.0**	**6:02**	....	....	....	....	....	....	....	....	....

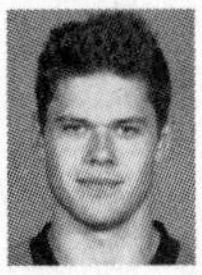

WOTHERSPOON, Tyler

(WUH-thuhr-spoon, TIGH-luhr) **CGY**

Defense. Shoots left. 6'2", 210 lbs. Born, Burnaby, BC, March 12, 1993. Calgary's 3rd choice, 57th overall, in 2011 Entry Draft.

2008-09	Valley West	BCMML	37	11	13	24	85	....	....	....	....	....	....	....	....	....	....	....	....	....	....	....	....	....	....
	Portland	WHL	4	0	0	0	0	....	....	....	....	....	....	....	....	....	....	....	....	....	....	....	....	....	....
2009-10	Portland	WHL	43	1	4	5	21	....	....	....	....	....	....	....	....	....	2	0	0	0	0	....	....	....	....
2010-11	Portland	WHL	64	2	10	12	73	....	....	....	....	....	....	....	....	....	20	3	1	4	10	....	....	....	....
2011-12	Portland	WHL	67	7	21	28	42	....	....	....	....	....	....	....	....	....	22	1	6	7	6	....	....	....	....
2012-13	Portland	WHL	61	7	30	37	30	....	....	....	....	....	....	....	....	....	21	2	8	10	20	....	....	....	....
2013-14	**Calgary**	**NHL**	**14**	**0**	**4**	**4**	**4**	**0**	**0**	**0**	**3**	**0.0**	**–3**	**0**	**0.0**	**13:27**	....	....	....	....	....	....	....	....	....
	Abbotsford Heat	AHL	48	1	8	9	12	....	....	....	....	....	....	....	....	....	....	....	....	....	....	....	....	....	....
2014-15	**Calgary**	**NHL**	**1**	**0**	**0**	**0**	**0**	**0**	**0**	**0**	**1**	**0.0**	**–3**	**0**	**0.0**	**20:19**	**6**	**0**	**0**	**0**	**0**	**0**	**0**	**0**	**6:39**
	Adirondack	AHL	61	2	22	24	20	....	....	....	....	....	....	....	....	....	....	....	....	....	....	....	....	....	....
	NHL Totals		**15**	**0**	**4**	**4**	**4**	**0**	**0**	**0**	**4**	**0.0**		**0**	**0.0**	**13:54**	**6**	**0**	**0**	**0**	**0**	**0**	**0**	**0**	**6:39**

WHL West Second All-Star Team (2013)

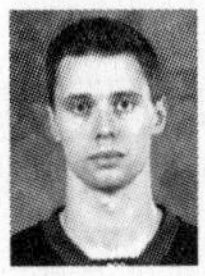

WRIGHT, James

(RIGHT, JAYMZ)

Center. Shoots left. 6'4", 200 lbs. Born, Saskatoon, SK, March 24, 1990. Tampa Bay's 2nd choice, 117th overall, in 2008 Entry Draft.

2005-06	Sask. Contacts	SMHL	41	13	19	32	43	....	....	....	....	....	....	....	....	....	....	....	....	....	....	....	....	....	....
	Vancouver Giants	WHL	2	0	0	0	2	....	....	....	....	....	....	....	....	....	....	....	....	....	....	....	....	....	....
2006-07	Vancouver Giants	WHL	48	5	7	12	31	....	....	....	....	....	....	....	....	....	14	3	1	4	0	....	....	....	....
2007-08	Vancouver Giants	WHL	60	13	23	36	21	....	....	....	....	....	....	....	....	....	6	1	0	1	2	....	....	....	....
2008-09	Vancouver Giants	WHL	71	21	26	47	54	....	....	....	....	....	....	....	....	....	17	3	7	10	13	....	....	....	....
2009-10	**Tampa Bay**	**NHL**	**48**	**2**	**3**	**5**	**18**	**0**	**0**	**0**	**25**	**8.0**	**–9**	**169**	**45.6**	**11:39**	....	....	....	....	....	....	....	....	....
	Vancouver Giants	WHL	21	6	13	19	17	....	....	....	....	....	....	....	....	....	16	7	9	16	4	....	....	....	....
2010-11	**Tampa Bay**	**NHL**	**1**	**0**	**0**	**0**	**0**	**0**	**0**	**0**	**0**	**0.0**	**–2**	**2**	**0.0**	**4:36**	....	....	....	....	....	....	....	....	....
	Norfolk Admirals	AHL	80	16	31	47	64	....	....	....	....	....	....	....	....	....	6	1	0	1	8	....	....	....	....
2011-12	Norfolk Admirals	AHL	22	1	4	5	6	....	....	....	....	....	....	....	....	....	....	....	....	....	....	....	....	....	....
	San Antonio	AHL	54	11	17	28	23	....	....	....	....	....	....	....	....	....	10	3	4	7	2	....	....	....	....
2012-13	San Antonio	AHL	40	5	12	17	31	....	....	....	....	....	....	....	....	....	....	....	....	....	....	....	....	....	....
	Winnipeg	**NHL**	**38**	**2**	**3**	**5**	**31**	**0**	**0**	**0**	**32**	**6.3**	**–5**	**46**	**47.8**	**11:36**	....	....	....	....	....	....	....	....	....
2013-14	**Winnipeg**	**NHL**	**59**	**0**	**2**	**2**	**15**	**0**	**0**	**0**	**41**	**0.0**	**–3**	**269**	**46.8**	**9:35**	....	....	....	....	....	....	....	....	....
2014-15	Zagreb	KHL	53	15	4	19	39	....	....	....	....	....	....	....	....	....	....	....	....	....	....	....	....	....	....
	NHL Totals		**146**	**4**	**8**	**12**	**64**	**0**	**0**	**0**	**98**	**4.1**		**486**	**46.3**	**10:45**	....	....	....	....	....	....	....	....	....

Traded to **Florida** by **Tampa Bay** with Mike Vernace for Mike Kostka and Evan Oberg, December 2, 2011. Claimed on waivers by **Winnipeg** from **Florida**, January 18, 2013. Signed as a free agent by **NY Islanders**, July 2, 2015. Signed as a free agent by **Zagreb** (KHL), September 15, 2014.

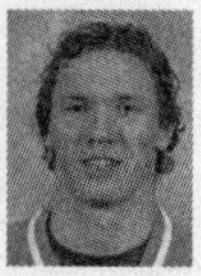

YAKIMOV, Bogdan

(ya-KIH-mawv, bawg-DAHN) **EDM**

Center. Shoots left. 6'5", 232 lbs. Born, Nizhnekamsk, Russia, October 4, 1994. Edmonton's 3rd choice, 83rd overall, in 2013 Entry Draft.

			Regular Season														Playoffs								
Season	Club	League	GP	G	A	Pts	PIM	PP	SH	GW	S	S%	+/-	TF	F%	Min	GP	G	A	Pts	PIM	PP	SH	GW	Min
2011-12	Nizhnekamsk Jr.	Russia-Jr.	46	15	10	25	10	....	....	....	....	....	....	....	....	....	2	2	1	3	0	....	....	....	....
2012-13	Dizel Penza	Russia-2	21	3	6	9	12	....	....	....	....	....	....	....	....	....	....	....	....	....	....	....	....	....	....
	Izhstal Izhevsk	Russia-2	16	5	8	13	4	....	....	....	....	....	....	....	....	....	....	....	....	....	....	....	....	....	....
	Nizhnekamsk Jr.	Russia-Jr.	11	6	7	13	2	....	....	....	....	....	....	....	....	....	....	....	....	....	....	....	....	....	....
2013-14	Nizhnekamsk Jr.	Russia-Jr.	5	4	2	6	0	....	....	....	....	....	....	....	....	....	3	0	2	2	0	....	....	....	....
	Nizhnekamsk	KHL	33	7	5	12	2	....	....	....	....	....	....	....	....	....	2	0	1	1	0	....	....	....	....
2014-15	**Edmonton**	**NHL**	**1**	**0**	**0**	**0**	**0**	**0**	**0**	**0**	**1**	**0.0**	**–1**	**7**	**42.9**	**11:19**	....	....	....	....	....	....	....	....	....
	Oklahoma City	AHL	57	12	16	28	18	....	....	....	....	....	....	....	....	....	....	....	....	....	....	....	....	....	....
	NHL Totals		**1**	**0**	**0**	**0**	**0**	**0**	**0**	**0**	**1**	**0.0**		**7**	**42.9**	**11:19**	....	....	....	....	....	....	....	....	....

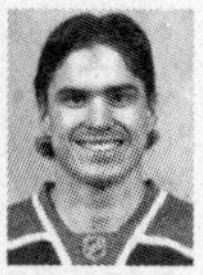

YAKUPOV, Nail

(YA-kuh-pawv, NAY-uhl) **EDM**

Right wing. Shoots left. 5'11", 186 lbs. Born, Nizhnekamsk, Russia, October 6, 1993. Edmonton's 1st choice, 1st overall, in 2012 Entry Draft.

Season	Club	League	GP	G	A	Pts	PIM	PP	SH	GW	S	S%	+/-	TF	F%	Min	GP	G	A	Pts	PIM	PP	SH	GW	Min
2009-10	Nizhnekamsk Jr.	Russia-Jr.	14	4	2	6	26	....	....	....	....	....	....	....	....	....	....	....	....	....	....	....	....	....	....
2010-11	Sarnia Sting	OHL	65	49	52	101	71	....	....	....	....	....	....	....	....	....	....	....	....	....	....	....	....	....	....
2011-12	Sarnia Sting	OHL	42	31	38	69	30	....	....	....	....	....	....	....	....	....	6	2	3	5	4	....	....	....	....
2012-13	Nizhnekamsk	KHL	22	9	9	18	33	....	....	....	....	....	....	....	....	....	....	....	....	....	....	....	....	....	....
	Edmonton	**NHL**	**48**	**17**	**14**	**31**	**24**	**6**	**0**	**2**	**81**	**21.0**	**–4**	**6**	**0.0**	**14:34**	....	....	....	....	....	....	....	....	....
2013-14	**Edmonton**	**NHL**	**63**	**11**	**13**	**24**	**36**	**4**	**0**	**1**	**122**	**9.0**	**–33**	**0**	**0.0**	**14:19**	....	....	....	....	....	....	....	....	....
2014-15	**Edmonton**	**NHL**	**81**	**14**	**19**	**33**	**18**	**5**	**0**	**1**	**191**	**7.3**	**–35**	**1**	**0.0**	**15:27**	....	....	....	....	....	....	....	....	....
	NHL Totals		**192**	**42**	**46**	**88**	**78**	**15**	**0**	**4**	**394**	**10.7**		**7**	**0.0**	**14:51**	....	....	....	....	....	....	....	....	....

OHL All-Rookie Team (2011) • OHL Rookie of the Year (2011) • Canadian Major Junior Rookie of the Year (2011) • Canadian Major Junior Top Prospect of the Year (2012)

Signed as a free agent by **Nizhnekamsk** (KHL), September 20, 2012.

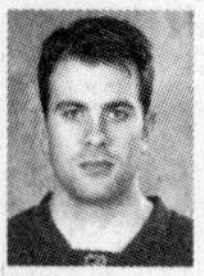

YANDLE, Keith

(Yan-duhl, KEETH) **NYR**

Defense. Shoots left. 6'1", 190 lbs. Born, Boston, MA, September 9, 1986. Phoenix's 3rd choice, 105th overall, in 2005 Entry Draft.

Season	Club	League	GP	G	A	Pts	PIM	PP	SH	GW	S	S%	+/-	TF	F%	Min	GP	G	A	Pts	PIM	PP	SH	GW	Min
2004-05	Cushing	High-MA	34	14	40	54	52	....	....	....	....	....	....	....	....	....	....	....	....	....	....	....	....	....	....
2005-06	Moncton Wildcats	QMJHL	66	25	59	84	109	....	....	....	....	....	....	....	....	....	21	6	14	20	36	....	....	....	....
2006-07	**Phoenix**	**NHL**	**7**	**0**	**2**	**2**	**8**	**0**	**0**	**0**	**10**	**0.0**	**0**	**0**	**0.0**	**20:10**	....	....	....	....	....	....	....	....	....
	San Antonio	AHL	69	6	27	33	97	....	....	....	....	....	....	....	....	....	....	....	....	....	....	....	....	....	....
2007-08	**Phoenix**	**NHL**	**43**	**5**	**7**	**12**	**14**	**4**	**0**	**0**	**72**	**6.9**	**–12**	**0**	**0.0**	**14:04**	....	....	....	....	....	....	....	....	....
	San Antonio	AHL	30	1	14	15	80	....	....	....	....	....	....	....	....	....	5	0	0	0	8	....	....	....	....
2008-09	**Phoenix**	**NHL**	**69**	**4**	**26**	**30**	**37**	**1**	**0**	**0**	**118**	**3.4**	**–4**	**0**	**0.0**	**16:37**	....	....	....	....	....	....	....	....	....
2009-10	**Phoenix**	**NHL**	**82**	**12**	**29**	**41**	**45**	**5**	**0**	**2**	**145**	**8.3**	**16**	**0**	**0.0**	**20:14**	**7**	**2**	**3**	**5**	**4**	**1**	**0**	**0**	**17:12**
2010-11	**Phoenix**	**NHL**	**82**	**11**	**48**	**59**	**68**	**3**	**0**	**0**	**199**	**5.5**	**12**	**0**	**0.0**	**24:23**	**4**	**0**	**5**	**5**	**0**	**0**	**0**	**0**	**25:50**
2011-12	**Phoenix**	**NHL**	**82**	**11**	**32**	**43**	**51**	**0**	**0**	**2**	**196**	**5.6**	**5**	**0**	**0.0**	**22:20**	**16**	**1**	**8**	**9**	**10**	**0**	**0**	**0**	**21:27**
2012-13	**Phoenix**	**NHL**	**48**	**10**	**20**	**30**	**54**	**5**	**0**	**3**	**130**	**7.7**	**4**	**0**	**0.0**	**22:15**	....	....	....	....	....	....	....	....	....
2013-14	**Phoenix**	**NHL**	**82**	**8**	**45**	**53**	**63**	**3**	**0**	**2**	**241**	**3.3**	**–23**	**0**	**0.0**	**24:09**	....	....	....	....	....	....	....	....	....
2014-15	**Arizona**	**NHL**	**63**	**4**	**37**	**41**	**32**	**2**	**0**	**0**	**185**	**2.2**	**–32**	**0**	**0.0**	**23:55**	....	....	....	....	....	....	....	....	....
	NY Rangers	**NHL**	**21**	**2**	**9**	**11**	**8**	**0**	**0**	**2**	**47**	**4.3**	**6**	**0**	**0.0**	**19:56**	**19**	**2**	**9**	**11**	**10**	**0**	**0**	**0**	**18:01**
	NHL Totals		**579**	**67**	**255**	**322**	**380**	**23**	**0**	**11**	**1343**	**5.0**		**0**	**0.0**	**21:20**	**46**	**5**	**25**	**30**	**24**	**1**	**0**	**0**	**19:46**

QMJHL First All-Star Team (2006) • Canadian Major Junior First All-Star Team (2006) • Canadian Major Junior Defenseman of the Year (2006)

Played in NHL All-Star Game (2011, 2012)

Traded to **NY Rangers** by **Arizona** with Chris Summers and a 4th round choice in 2016 Entry Draft for John Moore, Anthony Duclair, Tampa Bay's 2nd round choice (previously acquired, later traded to Calgary – Calgary selected Oliver Kylington) in 2015 Entry Draft and future considerations, March 1, 2015.

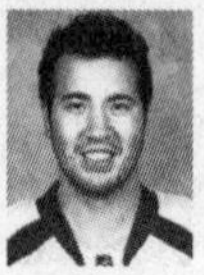

YIP, Brandon

(YIHP, BRAN-duhn)

Right wing. Shoots right. 6'1", 200 lbs. Born, Vancouver, BC, April 25, 1985. Colorado's 7th choice, 239th overall, in 2004 Entry Draft.

Season	Club	League	GP	G	A	Pts	PIM	PP	SH	GW	S	S%	+/-	TF	F%	Min	GP	G	A	Pts	PIM	PP	SH	GW	Min
2003-04	Coquitlam	BCHL	56	31	38	69	87	....	....	....	....	....	....	....	....	....	4	1	2	3	14	....	....	....	....
2004-05	Coquitlam	BCHL	43	20	42	62	92	....	....	....	....	....	....	....	....	....	7	6	1	7	12	....	....	....	....
2005-06	Boston University	H-East	39	9	22	31	59	....	....	....	....	....	....	....	....	....	....	....	....	....	....	....	....	....	....
2006-07	Boston University	H-East	18	5	6	11	29	....	....	....	....	....	....	....	....	....	....	....	....	....	....	....	....	....	....
2007-08	Boston University	H-East	37	11	12	23	28	....	....	....	....	....	....	....	....	....	....	....	....	....	....	....	....	....	....
2008-09	Boston University	H-East	45	20	23	43	118	....	....	....	....	....	....	....	....	....	....	....	....	....	....	....	....	....	....
2009-10	**Colorado**	**NHL**	**32**	**11**	**8**	**19**	**22**	**4**	**0**	**2**	**65**	**16.9**	**5**	**1**	**0.0**	**14:41**	**6**	**2**	**2**	**4**	**6**	**0**	**0**	**0**	**17:51**
	Lake Erie	AHL	6	2	0	2	4	....	....	....	....	....	....	....	....	....	....	....	....	....	....	....	....	....	....
2010-11	**Colorado**	**NHL**	**71**	**12**	**10**	**22**	**54**	**3**	**1**	**1**	**127**	**9.4**	**–22**	**14**	**35.7**	**13:44**	....	....	....	....	....	....	....	....	....
2011-12	**Colorado**	**NHL**	**10**	**0**	**0**	**0**	**8**	**0**	**0**	**0**	**12**	**0.0**	**1**	**2**	**0.0**	**9:55**	....	....	....	....	....	....	....	....	....
	Nashville	**NHL**	**25**	**3**	**4**	**7**	**20**	**0**	**0**	**0**	**29**	**10.3**	**0**	**5**	**40.0**	**10:59**	**10**	**1**	**1**	**2**	**6**	**0**	**0**	**0**	**8:57**
2012-13	**Nashville**	**NHL**	**34**	**3**	**5**	**8**	**26**	**0**	**0**	**0**	**35**	**8.6**	**–3**	**21**	**38.1**	**12:02**	....	....	....	....	....	....	....	....	....
2013-14	**Phoenix**	**NHL**	**2**	**0**	**0**	**0**	**0**	**0**	**0**	**0**	**1**	**0.0**	**0**	**0**	**0.0**	**6:53**	....	....	....	....	....	....	....	....	....
	Portland Pirates	AHL	66	14	20	34	87	....	....	....	....	....	....	....	....	....	....	....	....	....	....	....	....	....	....
2014-15	Norfolk Admirals	AHL	31	3	9	12	8	....	....	....	....	....	....	....	....	....	....	....	....	....	....	....	....	....	....
	Utah Grizzlies	ECHL	7	1	3	4	2	....	....	....	....	....	....	....	....	....	....	....	....	....	....	....	....	....	....
	Adler Mannheim	Germany	6	1	1	2	2	....	....	....	....	....	....	....	....	....	14	0	4	4	38	....	....	....	....
	NHL Totals		**174**	**29**	**27**	**56**	**130**	**7**	**1**	**3**	**269**	**10.8**		**43**	**34.9**	**12:53**	**16**	**3**	**3**	**6**	**12**	**0**	**0**	**0**	**12:17**

Hockey East All-Rookie Team (2006) • Hockey East Rookie of the Year (2006)

• Missed majority of 2009-10 due to hand injury in pre-season game at St. Louis, September 18, 2009. Claimed on waivers by **Nashville** from **Colorado**, January 19, 2012. Signed as a free agent by **Phoenix**, July 19, 2013. Signed as a free agent by **Norfolk** (AHL), September 29, 2014. Signed as a free agent by **Utah** (ECHL), January 15, 2015. Signed as a free agent by **Mannheim** (Germany), February 6, 2015.

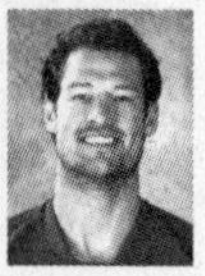

YONKMAN, Nolan

(YAWNK-man, NOH-luhn)

Defense. Shoots right. 6'6", 253 lbs. Born, Punnichy, SK, April 1, 1981. Washington's 5th choice, 37th overall, in 1999 Entry Draft.

Season	Club	League	GP	G	A	Pts	PIM	PP	SH	GW	S	S%	+/-	TF	F%	Min	GP	G	A	Pts	PIM	PP	SH	GW	Min
1996-97	Naicam Vikings	SAHA	64	15	23	38	36	....	....	....	....	....	....	....	....	....	....	....	....	....	....	....	....	....	....
	Kelowna Rockets	WHL	4	0	0	0	0	....	....	....	....	....	....	....	....	....	....	....	....	....	....	....	....	....	....
1997-98	Kelowna Rockets	WHL	65	0	2	2	36	....	....	....	....	....	....	....	....	....	7	0	0	0	2	....	....	....	....
1998-99	Kelowna Rockets	WHL	61	1	6	7	129	....	....	....	....	....	....	....	....	....	6	0	0	0	6	....	....	....	....
99-2000	Kelowna Rockets	WHL	71	5	7	12	153	....	....	....	....	....	....	....	....	....	5	0	0	0	8	....	....	....	....
2000-01	Kelowna Rockets	WHL	7	0	1	1	19	....	....	....	....	....	....	....	....	....	....	....	....	....	....	....	....	....	....
	Brandon	WHL	51	6	10	16	94	....	....	....	....	....	....	....	....	....	6	0	1	1	12	....	....	....	....
2001-02	**Washington**	**NHL**	**11**	**1**	**0**	**1**	**4**	**0**	**0**	**0**	**7**	**14.3**	**3**	**0**	**0.0**	**12:44**	....	....	....	....	....	....	....	....	....
	Portland Pirates	AHL	59	4	3	7	116	....	....	....	....	....	....	....	....	....	....	....	....	....	....	....	....	....	....
2002-03	Portland Pirates	AHL	24	1	4	5	40	....	....	....	....	....	....	....	....	....	3	0	1	1	2	....	....	....	....
2003-04	**Washington**	**NHL**	**1**	**0**	**0**	**0**	**0**	**0**	**0**	**0**	**0**	**0.0**	**0**	**0**	**0.0**	**5:00**	....	....	....	....	....	....	....	....	....
	Portland Pirates	AHL	4	0	0	0	11	....	....	....	....	....	....	....	....	....	....	....	....	....	....	....	....	....	....
2004-05	Portland Pirates	AHL	32	0	3	3	68	....	....	....	....	....	....	....	....	....	....	....	....	....	....	....	....	....	....
2005-06	**Washington**	**NHL**	**38**	**0**	**7**	**7**	**86**	**0**	**0**	**0**	**14**	**0.0**	**1**	**0**	**0.0**	**8:13**	....	....	....	....	....	....	....	....	....
	Hershey Bears	AHL	6	0	0	0	15	....	....	....	....	....	....	....	....	....	....	....	....	....	....	....	....	....	....
2006-07	Milwaukee	AHL	77	3	10	13	113	....	....	....	....	....	....	....	....	....	4	0	0	0	2	....	....	....	....
2007-08	Milwaukee	AHL	69	0	7	7	103	....	....	....	....	....	....	....	....	....	6	0	1	1	18	....	....	....	....
2008-09	Milwaukee	AHL	61	3	7	10	80	....	....	....	....	....	....	....	....	....	11	0	0	0	15	....	....	....	....
2009-10	Milwaukee	AHL	76	2	7	9	170	....	....	....	....	....	....	....	....	....	7	0	1	1	2	....	....	....	....
2010-11	**Phoenix**	**NHL**	**16**	**0**	**1**	**1**	**39**	**0**	**0**	**0**	**8**	**0.0**	**5**	**0**	**0.0**	**12:08**	....	....	....	....	....	....	....	....	....
	San Antonio	AHL	56	1	4	5	104	....	....	....	....	....	....	....	....	....	....	....	....	....	....	....	....	....	....
2011-12	**Florida**	**NHL**	**1**	**0**	**0**	**0**	**0**	**0**	**0**	**0**	**0**	**0.0**	**0**	**0**	**0.0**	**6:19**	....	....	....	....	....	....	....	....	....
	San Antonio	AHL	66	2	11	13	102	....	....	....	....	....	....	....	....	....	10	0	2	2	8	....	....	....	....
2012-13	San Antonio	AHL	71	0	7	7	93	....	....	....	....	....	....	....	....	....	....	....	....	....	....	....	....	....	....
	Florida	**NHL**	**7**	**0**	**0**	**0**	**11**	**0**	**0**	**0**	**4**	**0.0**	**–1**	**0**	**0.0**	**9:46**	....	....	....	....	....	....	....	....	....

Season	Club	League	Regular Season GP	G	A	Pts	PIM	PP	SH	GW	S	S%	+/-	TF	F%	Min	Playoffs GP	G	A	Pts	PIM	PP	SH	GW	Min
2013-14	Anaheim	NHL	2	0	1	1	0	0	0	0	3	0.0	–1	0	0.0	14:54	....	....	....	....	....	....	....	....	....
	Norfolk Admirals	AHL	67	2	5	7	107	....	....	....	....	....	....	....	....	....	8	0	1	1	7	....	....	....	....
2014-15	Adirondack	AHL	65	2	10	12	52	....	....	....	....	....	....	....	....	....	....	....	....	....	....	....	....	....	....
	NHL Totals		76	1	9	10	140	0	0	0	36	2.8		0	0.0	9:57	....	....	....	....	....	....	....	....	....

• Missed majority of 2002-03 due to abdominal injury in training camp, September 25, 2002. • Missed majority of 2003-04 and 2004-05 due to knee injury vs. Worcester (AHL), October 23, 2003. Signed as a free agent by **Nashville**, July 17, 2006. Signed as a free agent by **Phoenix**, July 3, 2010. Signed as a free agent by **Florida**, July 1, 2011. Signed as a free agent by **Anaheim**, July 9, 2013. Signed as a free agent by **Jyvaskyla** (Finland), May 18, 2015.

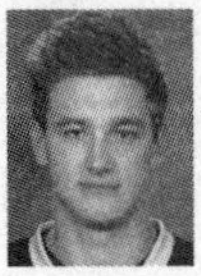

ZADOROV, Nikita (za-DOHR-awv, nih-KEE-tuh) COL

Defense. Shoots left. 6'5", 220 lbs. Born, Moscow, Russia, April 16, 1995. Buffalo's 2nd choice, 16th overall, in 2013 Entry Draft.

Season	Club	League	GP	G	A	Pts	PIM	PP	SH	GW	S	S%	+/-	TF	F%	Min	GP	G	A	Pts	PIM	PP	SH	GW	Min
2011-12	CSKA Jr.	Russia-Jr.	41	2	4	6	63	....	....	....	....	....	....	....	....	....	8	0	0	0	8	....	....	....	....
2012-13	London Knights	OHL	63	6	19	25	54	....	....	....	....	....	....	....	....	....	20	2	4	6	36	....	....	....	....
2013-14	Buffalo	NHL	7	1	0	1	4	0	0	0	4	25.0	–4	0	0.0	17:10	....	....	....	....	....	....	....	....	....
	London Knights	OHL	36	11	19	30	43	....	....	....	....	....	....	....	....	....	9	4	5	9	16	....	....	....	....
2014-15	Buffalo	NHL	60	3	12	15	51	2	0	1	52	5.8	–10	1	100.0	17:42	....	....	....	....	....	....	....	....	....
	NHL Totals		67	4	12	16	55	2	0	1	56	7.1		1	100.0	17:39	....	....	....	....	....	....	....	....	....

OHL All-Rookie Team (2013) • OHL Second All-Star Team (2014)

Traded to **Colorado** by **Buffalo** with Mikhail Grigorenko, JT Compher and Buffalo's 2nd round choice (later traded to San Jose – San Jose selected Jeremy Roy) in 2015 Entry Draft for Ryan O'Reilly and Jamie McGinn, June 26, 2015.

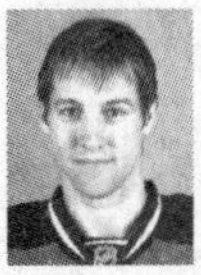

ZAJAC, Travis (ZAY-jak, TRA-vihs) N.J.

Center. Shoots right. 6'3", 205 lbs. Born, Winnipeg, MB, May 13, 1985. New Jersey's 1st choice, 20th overall, in 2004 Entry Draft.

Season	Club	League	GP	G	A	Pts	PIM	PP	SH	GW	S	S%	+/-	TF	F%	Min	GP	G	A	Pts	PIM	PP	SH	GW	Min
2002-03	Salmon Arm	BCHL	59	16	36	52	27	....	....	....	....	....	....	....	....	....	11	2	4	6	6	....	....	....	....
2003-04	Salmon Arm	BCHL	59	43	69	112	110	....	....	....	....	....	....	....	....	....	14	10	13	23	10	....	....	....	....
2004-05	North Dakota	WCHA	45	20	19	39	16	....	....	....	....	....	....	....	....	....	....	....	....	....	....	....	....	....	....
2005-06	North Dakota	WCHA	46	18	29	47	20	....	....	....	....	....	....	....	....	....	....	....	....	....	....	....	....	....	....
	Albany River Rats	AHL	2	0	1	1	2	....	....	....	....	....	....	....	....	....	....	....	....	....	....	....	....	....	....
2006-07	New Jersey	NHL	80	17	25	42	16	6	0	2	134	12.7	1	904	46.9	16:03	11	1	4	5	4	0	0	0	16:22
2007-08	New Jersey	NHL	82	14	20	34	31	5	0	1	155	9.0	–11	1032	51.2	16:44	5	0	1	1	4	0	0	0	13:35
2008-09	New Jersey	NHL	82	20	42	62	29	5	1	2	185	10.8	33	1287	53.1	18:39	7	1	3	4	6	0	0	1	17:51
2009-10	New Jersey	NHL	82	25	42	67	24	6	0	4	210	11.9	22	1373	52.9	20:13	5	1	1	2	2	0	0	0	21:46
2010-11	New Jersey	NHL	82	13	31	44	24	2	1	1	173	7.5	–6	1278	55.3	19:47	....	....	....	....	....	....	....	....	....
2011-12	New Jersey	NHL	15	2	4	6	4	1	0	1	25	8.0	–3	204	57.8	17:22	24	7	7	14	4	1	0	2	20:29
2012-13	New Jersey	NHL	48	7	13	20	22	1	1	1	82	8.5	–5	881	57.4	19:32	....	....	....	....	....	....	....	....	....
2013-14	New Jersey	NHL	80	18	30	48	28	3	0	3	165	10.9	3	1394	54.6	20:19	....	....	....	....	....	....	....	....	....
2014-15	New Jersey	NHL	74	11	14	25	29	4	2	0	112	9.8	–3	1200	53.4	19:04	....	....	....	....	....	....	....	....	....
	NHL Totals		625	127	221	348	207	33	5	15	1241	10.2		9553	53.3	18:43	52	10	16	26	20	1	0	3	18:43

WCHA All-Rookie Team (2005) • NCAA Championship All-Tournament Team (2005)

• Missed majority of 2011-12 due to leg injury during off-ice workout, August 17, 2011.

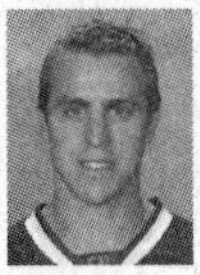

ZALEWSKI, Mike (zuh-LEH-skee, MIGHK) VAN

Left wing. Shoots left. 6'2", 205 lbs. Born, New Hartford, NY, August 18, 1992.

Season	Club	League	GP	G	A	Pts	PIM	PP	SH	GW	S	S%	+/-	TF	F%	Min	GP	G	A	Pts	PIM	PP	SH	GW	Min
2008-09	New Hartford	High-NY	....	44	43	87	....	....	....	....	....	....	....	....	....	....	....	....	....	....	....	....	....	....	....
2009-10	Syracuse Jr. Stars	EJHL	43	16	32	48	28	....	....	....	....	....	....	....	....	....	2	0	1	1	4	....	....	....	....
2010-11	Vernon Vipers	BCHL	46	12	17	29	34	....	....	....	....	....	....	....	....	....	16	5	3	8	4	....	....	....	....
2011-12	Vernon Vipers	BCHL	60	38	37	75	83	....	....	....	....	....	....	....	....	....	....	....	....	....	....	....	....	....	....
2012-13	RPI Engineers	ECAC	36	12	9	21	22	....	....	....	....	....	....	....	....	....	....	....	....	....	....	....	....	....	....
2013-14	RPI Engineers	ECAC	35	9	17	26	53	....	....	....	....	....	....	....	....	....	....	....	....	....	....	....	....	....	....
	Vancouver	NHL	2	0	1	1	0	0	0	0	2	0.0	2	0	0.0	12:08	....	....	....	....	....	....	....	....	....
2014-15	Utica Comets	AHL	55	3	9	12	18	....	....	....	....	....	....	....	....	....	23	1	2	3	14	....	....	....	....
	NHL Totals		2	0	1	1	0	0	0	0	2	0.0		0	0.0	12:08	....	....	....	....	....	....	....	....	....

Signed as a free agent by **Vancouver**, March 14, 2014. Signed as a free agent by **Utica** (AHL), July 8, 2015.

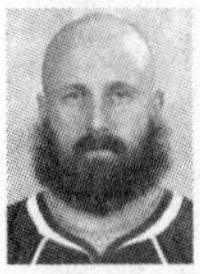

ZANON, Greg (ZA-nuhn, GREHG)

Defense. Shoots left. 5'11", 201 lbs. Born, Burnaby, BC, June 5, 1980. Ottawa's 6th choice, 156th overall, in 2000 Entry Draft.

Season	Club	League	GP	G	A	Pts	PIM	PP	SH	GW	S	S%	+/-	TF	F%	Min	GP	G	A	Pts	PIM	PP	SH	GW	Min
1995-96	Burnaby Beavers	Minor-BC	49	16	27	43	142	....	....	....	....	....	....	....	....	....	....	....	....	....	....	....	....	....	....
1996-97	Victoria Salsa	BCHL	53	4	13	17	124	....	....	....	....	....	....	....	....	....	....	....	....	....	....	....	....	....	....
1997-98	Victoria Salsa	BCHL	59	11	21	32	108	....	....	....	....	....	....	....	....	....	7	0	2	2	10	....	....	....	....
1998-99	South Surrey	BCHL	59	17	54	71	154	....	....	....	....	....	....	....	....	....	....	....	....	....	....	....	....	....	....
99-2000	Nebraska-Omaha	CCHA	42	3	26	29	56	....	....	....	....	....	....	....	....	....	....	....	....	....	....	....	....	....	....
2000-01	Nebraska-Omaha	CCHA	39	12	16	28	64	....	....	....	....	....	....	....	....	....	....	....	....	....	....	....	....	....	....
2001-02	Nebraska-Omaha	CCHA	41	9	16	25	54	....	....	....	....	....	....	....	....	....	....	....	....	....	....	....	....	....	....
2002-03	Nebraska-Omaha	CCHA	32	6	19	25	44	....	....	....	....	....	....	....	....	....	....	....	....	....	....	....	....	....	....
2003-04	Milwaukee	AHL	62	4	12	16	59	....	....	....	....	....	....	....	....	....	22	2	6	8	31	....	....	....	....
2004-05	Milwaukee	AHL	80	2	17	19	59	....	....	....	....	....	....	....	....	....	7	0	1	1	10	....	....	....	....
2005-06	Nashville	NHL	4	0	2	2	6	0	0	0	3	0.0	0	0	0.0	17:19	....	....	....	....	....	....	....	....	....
	Milwaukee	AHL	71	8	27	35	55	....	....	....	....	....	....	....	....	....	21	1	7	8	24	....	....	....	....
2006-07	Nashville	NHL	66	3	5	8	32	0	0	0	43	7.0	16	0	0.0	17:20	5	0	2	2	2	0	0	0	20:44
	Milwaukee	AHL	2	0	2	2	0	....	....	....	....	....	....	....	....	....	....	....	....	....	....	....	....	....	....
2007-08	Nashville	NHL	78	0	5	5	24	0	0	0	38	0.0	–5	0	0.0	18:28	6	0	2	2	4	0	0	0	18:45
2008-09	Nashville	NHL	82	4	7	11	38	0	0	1	54	7.4	8	0	0.0	20:51	....	....	....	....	....	....	....	....	....
2009-10	Minnesota	NHL	81	2	13	15	36	0	0	0	59	3.4	–10	1	0.0	22:22	....	....	....	....	....	....	....	....	....
2010-11	Minnesota	NHL	82	0	7	7	48	0	0	0	55	0.0	–5	0	0.0	21:33	....	....	....	....	....	....	....	....	....
2011-12	Minnesota	NHL	39	2	4	6	14	0	0	1	27	7.4	–1	0	0.0	18:37	....	....	....	....	....	....	....	....	....
	Boston	NHL	17	1	1	2	4	0	0	1	14	7.1	4	0	0.0	15:54	7	0	1	1	0	0	0	0	13:43
2012-13	Colorado	NHL	44	0	6	6	28	0	0	0	40	0.0	–16	0	0.0	19:20	....	....	....	....	....	....	....	....	....
2013-14	San Antonio	AHL	24	0	4	4	34	....	....	....	....	....	....	....	....	....	....	....	....	....	....	....	....	....	....
2014-15	San Antonio	AHL	74	3	23	26	42	....	....	....	....	....	....	....	....	....	3	0	0	0	4	....	....	....	....
	NHL Totals		493	12	50	62	230	0	0	3	333	3.6		1	0.0	19:51	18	0	5	5	6	0	0	0	17:20

CCHA First All-Star Team (2001) • NCAA West Second All-American Team (2001, 2002) • CCHA Second All-Star Team (2002)

Signed as a free agent by **Nashville**, July 9, 2004. Signed as a free agent by **Minnesota**, July 1, 2009. Traded to **Boston** by **Minnesota** for Steven Kampfer, February 27, 2012. Signed as a free agent by **Colorado**, July 1, 2012. Signed to a PTO (professional tryout) contract by **San Antonio** (AHL), October 3, 2013. • Missed majority of 2013-14 due to injury at San Antonio (AHL), October 5, 2013. Signed as a free agent by **Florida**, July 8, 2014.

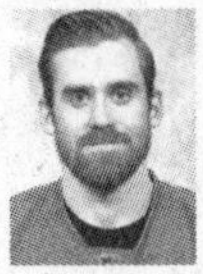

ZETTERBERG, Henrik (ZEH-tuhr-buhrg, HEHN-rihk) DET

Left wing. Shoots left. 6', 195 lbs. Born, Njurunda, Sweden, October 9, 1980. Detroit's 4th choice, 210th overall, in 1999 Entry Draft.

Season	Club	League	GP	G	A	Pts	PIM	PP	SH	GW	S	S%	+/-	TF	F%	Min	GP	G	A	Pts	PIM	PP	SH	GW	Min
1997-98	Timra IK Jr.	Swe-Jr.	18	9	5	14	4	....	....	....	....	....	....	....	....	....	....	....	....	....	....	....	....	....	....
	Timra IK	Sweden-2	16	1	2	3	4	....	....	....	....	....	....	....	....	....	4	0	1	1	0	....	....	....	....
1998-99	Timra IK	Sweden-2	37	15	13	28	2	....	....	....	....	....	....	....	....	....	4	2	1	3	2	....	....	....	....
99-2000	Timra IK	Sweden-2	32	20	14	34	20	....	....	....	....	....	....	....	....	....	10	10	4	14	4	....	....	....	....
2000-01	Timra IK	Sweden	47	15	31	46	24	....	....	....	....	....	....	....	....	....	....	....	....	....	....	....	....	....	....
2001-02	Timra IK	Sweden	48	10	22	32	20	....	....	....	....	....	....	....	....	....	....	....	....	....	....	....	....	....	....
	Sweden	Olympics	4	0	1	1	0	....	....	....	....	....	....	....	....	....	....	....	....	....	....	....	....	....	....
2002-03	Detroit	NHL	79	22	22	44	8	5	1	4	135	16.3	6	401	46.1	16:19	4	1	0	1	0	0	0	0	18:19
2003-04	Detroit	NHL	61	15	28	43	14	7	1	2	137	10.9	15	627	45.6	18:15	12	2	2	4	4	0	0	0	17:17
2004-05	Timra IK	Sweden	50	19	31	*50	24	....	....	....	....	....	....	....	....	....	7	6	2	8	2	....	....	....	....
2005-06	Detroit	NHL	77	39	46	85	30	17	1	9	270	14.4	29	583	50.3	18:57	6	6	0	6	2	4	0	0	21:43
	Sweden	Olympics	8	3	3	6	0	....	....	....	....	....	....	....	....	....	....	....	....	....	....	....	....	....	....
2006-07	Detroit	NHL	63	33	35	68	36	11	1	*10	224	14.7	26	888	52.5	20:50	18	6	8	14	12	3	0	1	22:45
2007-08 ♦	Detroit	NHL	75	43	49	92	34	16	1	7	358	12.0	30	1210	55.0	22:04	22	*13	14	*27	16	4	*2	4	22:36
2008-09	Detroit	NHL	77	31	42	73	36	12	2	5	309	10.0	13	1189	53.3	19:53	23	11	13	24	13	4	0	0	22:10

			Regular Season														Playoffs								
Season	Club	League	GP	G	A	Pts	PIM	PP	SH	GW	S	S%	+/-	TF	F%	Min	GP	G	A	Pts	PIM	PP	SH	GW	Min
2009-10	**Detroit**	**NHL**	**74**	**23**	**47**	**70**	**26**	**3**	**0**	**6**	**309**	**7.4**	**12**	**1098**	**49.5**	**20:04**	**12**	**7**	**8**	**15**	**6**	**2**	**0**	**2**	**20:25**
	Sweden	Olympics	4	1	0	1	2	....	....	....	....	....	....	....	....	....	....	....	....	....	....	....	....	....	....
2010-11	**Detroit**	**NHL**	**80**	**24**	**56**	**80**	**40**	**10**	**0**	**3**	**306**	**7.8**	**−1**	**984**	**52.4**	**19:35**	**7**	**3**	**5**	**8**	**2**	**1**	**0**	**0**	**21:59**
2011-12	**Detroit**	**NHL**	**82**	**22**	**47**	**69**	**47**	**3**	**0**	**4**	**267**	**8.2**	**14**	**1115**	**49.2**	**19:50**	**5**	**2**	**1**	**3**	**4**	**2**	**0**	**0**	**23:05**
2012-13	EV Zug	Swiss	23	16	16	32	20	....	....	....	....	....	....	....	....	....	....	....	....	....	....	....	....	....	....
	Detroit	**NHL**	**46**	**11**	**37**	**48**	**18**	**4**	**2**	**5**	**173**	**6.4**	**2**	**544**	**48.4**	**20:31**	**14**	**4**	**8**	**12**	**8**	**1**	**0**	**1**	**19:59**
2013-14	**Detroit**	**NHL**	**45**	**16**	**32**	**48**	**20**	**3**	**0**	**1**	**151**	**10.6**	**19**	**489**	**53.0**	**20:33**	**2**	**1**	**1**	**2**	**0**	**0**	**0**	**0**	**19:32**
	Sweden	Olympics	1	1	0	1	0	....	....	....	....	....	....	....	....	....	....	....	....	....	....	....	....	....	....
2014-15	**Detroit**	**NHL**	**77**	**17**	**49**	**66**	**32**	**4**	**0**	**3**	**227**	**7.5**	**−6**	**1064**	**50.9**	**19:07**	**7**	**0**	**3**	**3**	**8**	**0**	**0**	**0**	**18:02**
	NHL Totals		**836**	**296**	**490**	**786**	**341**	**95**	**9**	**59**	**2866**	**10.3**		**10192**	**51.0**	**19:36**	**132**	**56**	**63**	**119**	**75**	**21**	**2**	**8**	**21:07**

Swedish Elite League Rookie of the Year (2001) • NHL All-Rookie Team (2003) • NHL Second All-Star Team (2008) • Conn Smythe Trophy (2008) • NHL Foundation Player Award (2013)

Signed as a free agent by **Timra** (Sweden), September 20, 2004. Signed as a free agent by **Zug** (Swiss), October 8, 2012.

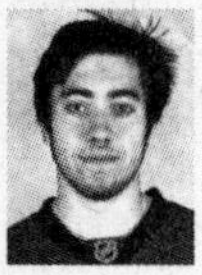

ZIBANEJAD, Mika

(zih-BAN-ih-jad, MEEKA) **OTT**

Center. Shoots right. 6'2", 211 lbs. Born, Huddinge, Sweden, April 18, 1993. Ottawa's 1st choice, 6th overall, in 2011 Entry Draft.

2008-09	AIK IF Solna U18	Swe-U18	11	2	2	4	2	....	....	....	....	....	....	....	....	....	....	....	....	....	....	....	....	....	....
2009-10	Djurgarden U18	Swe-U18	28	14	22	36	18	....	....	....	....	....	....	....	....	....	5	5	4	9	4	....	....	....	....
	Djurgarden Jr.	Swe-Jr.	14	2	2	4	4	....	....	....	....	....	....	....	....	....	....	....	....	....	....	....	....	....	....
2010-11	Djurgarden U18	Swe-U18	2	3	2	5	2	....	....	....	....	....	....	....	....	....	....	....	....	....	....	....	....	....	....
	Djurgarden Jr.	Swe-Jr.	27	12	9	21	12	....	....	....	....	....	....	....	....	....	3	1	2	3	0	....	....	....	....
	Djurgarden	Sweden	26	5	4	9	2	....	....	....	....	....	....	....	....	....	7	1	1	2	2	....	....	....	....
2011-12	**Ottawa**	**NHL**	**9**	**0**	**1**	**1**	**2**	**0**	**0**	**0**	**12**	**0.0**	**−3**	**50**	**44.0**	**12:54**	....	....	....	....	....	....	....	....	....
	Djurgarden	Sweden	26	5	8	13	4	....	....	....	....	....	....	....	....	....	....	....	....	....	....	....	....	....	....
	Djurgarden Jr.	Swe-Jr.	1	0	0	0	2	....	....	....	....	....	....	....	....	....	....	....	....	....	....	....	....	....	....
	Djurgarden	Sweden-Q	10	4	2	6	2	....	....	....	....	....	....	....	....	....	....	....	....	....	....	....	....	....	....
2012-13	**Ottawa**	**NHL**	**42**	**7**	**13**	**20**	**6**	**3**	**0**	**0**	**90**	**7.8**	**9**	**343**	**46.4**	**13:34**	**10**	**1**	**3**	**4**	**0**	**0**	**0**	**0**	**13:36**
2013-14	**Ottawa**	**NHL**	**69**	**16**	**17**	**33**	**18**	**3**	**0**	**0**	**153**	**10.5**	**−15**	**397**	**46.1**	**14:20**	....	....	....	....	....	....	....	....	....
	Binghamton	AHL	6	2	5	7	2	....	....	....	....	....	....	....	....	....	....	....	....	....	....	....	....	....	....
2014-15	**Ottawa**	**NHL**	**80**	**20**	**26**	**46**	**20**	**4**	**0**	**0**	**150**	**13.3**	**0**	**1261**	**48.8**	**16:26**	**6**	**1**	**3**	**4**	**0**	**1**	**0**	**0**	**15:43**
	NHL Totals		**200**	**43**	**57**	**100**	**46**	**10**	**0**	**0**	**405**	**10.6**		**2051**	**47.7**	**14:57**	**16**	**2**	**6**	**8**	**0**	**1**	**0**	**0**	**14:23**

• Re-assigned to **Djurgarden** (Sweden) by **Ottawa**, October 26, 2011.

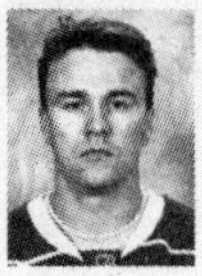

ZIDLICKY, Marek

(zihd-LIH-kee, MAIR-ehk)

Defense. Shoots right. 5'11", 190 lbs. Born, Most, Czech., February 3, 1977. NY Rangers' 6th choice, 176th overall, in 2001 Entry Draft.

1994-95	HC Kladno	CzRep	30	2	2	4	38	....	....	....	....	....	....	....	....	....	11	1	1	2	10	....	....	....	....
1995-96	HC Poldi Kladno	CzRep	37	4	5	9	74	....	....	....	....	....	....	....	....	....	7	1	1	2	8	....	....	....	....
1996-97	HC Poldi Kladno	CzRep	49	5	16	21	60	....	....	....	....	....	....	....	....	....	2	0	0	0	0	....	....	....	....
1997-98	Kladno	CzRep	51	2	13	15	121	....	....	....	....	....	....	....	....	....	....	....	....	....	....	....	....	....	....
1998-99	Kladno	CzRep	50	10	12	22	94	....	....	....	....	....	....	....	....	....	....	....	....	....	....	....	....	....	....
99-2000	HIFK Helsinki	Finland	47	4	16	20	66	....	....	....	....	....	....	....	....	....	9	3	2	5	24	....	....	....	....
	HIFK Helsinki	EuroHL	4	2	2	4	10	....	....	....	....	....	....	....	....	....	1	0	0	0	0	....	....	....	....
2000-01	HIFK Helsinki	Finland	51	12	25	37	146	....	....	....	....	....	....	....	....	....	5	0	1	1	6	....	....	....	....
2001-02	HIFK Helsinki	Finland	56	11	29	40	107	....	....	....	....	....	....	....	....	....	....	....	....	....	....	....	....	....	....
2002-03	HIFK Helsinki	Finland	54	10	37	47	79	....	....	....	....	....	....	....	....	....	4	0	0	0	4	....	....	....	....
2003-04	**Nashville**	**NHL**	**82**	**14**	**39**	**53**	**82**	**9**	**0**	**4**	**143**	**9.8**	**−16**	**0**	**0.0**	**20:02**	**1**	**0**	**0**	**0**	**0**	**0**	**0**	**0**	**2:16**
2004-05	HIFK Helsinki	Finland	49	11	20	31	91	....	....	....	....	....	....	....	....	....	5	0	3	3	14	....	....	....	....
2005-06	**Nashville**	**NHL**	**67**	**12**	**37**	**49**	**82**	**10**	**0**	**1**	**113**	**10.6**	**8**	**0**	**0.0**	**20:04**	**2**	**0**	**1**	**1**	**2**	**0**	**0**	**0**	**15:19**
	Czech Republic	Olympics	7	4	1	5	16	....	....	....	....	....	....	....	....	....	....	....	....	....	....	....	....	....	....
2006-07	**Nashville**	**NHL**	**79**	**4**	**26**	**30**	**72**	**2**	**0**	**1**	**114**	**3.5**	**8**	**0**	**0.0**	**19:43**	**5**	**0**	**2**	**2**	**4**	**0**	**0**	**0**	**19:19**
2007-08	**Nashville**	**NHL**	**79**	**5**	**38**	**43**	**63**	**4**	**0**	**0**	**122**	**4.1**	**−5**	**0**	**0.0**	**20:50**	**6**	**0**	**3**	**3**	**8**	**0**	**0**	**0**	**19:04**
2008-09	**Minnesota**	**NHL**	**76**	**12**	**30**	**42**	**76**	**10**	**0**	**3**	**147**	**8.2**	**−12**	**0**	**0.0**	**22:07**	....	....	....	....	....	....	....	....	....
2009-10	**Minnesota**	**NHL**	**78**	**6**	**37**	**43**	**67**	**4**	**0**	**3**	**116**	**5.2**	**−16**	**0**	**0.0**	**24:10**	....	....	....	....	....	....	....	....	....
	Czech Republic	Olympics	5	0	5	5	2	....	....	....	....	....	....	....	....	....	....	....	....	....	....	....	....	....	....
2010-11	**Minnesota**	**NHL**	**46**	**7**	**17**	**24**	**30**	**3**	**0**	**0**	**53**	**13.2**	**−6**	**0**	**0.0**	**21:46**	....	....	....	....	....	....	....	....	....
2011-12	**Minnesota**	**NHL**	**41**	**0**	**14**	**14**	**24**	**0**	**0**	**0**	**50**	**0.0**	**−6**	**0**	**0.0**	**20:40**	....	....	....	....	....	....	....	....	....
	New Jersey	**NHL**	**22**	**2**	**6**	**8**	**10**	**2**	**0**	**1**	**20**	**10.0**	**0**	**0**	**0.0**	**22:34**	**24**	**1**	**8**	**9**	**22**	**0**	**0**	**0**	**23:47**
2012-13	Rytiri Kladno	CzRep	25	3	22	25	28	....	....	....	....	....	....	....	....	....	....	....	....	....	....	....	....	....	....
	New Jersey	**NHL**	**48**	**4**	**15**	**19**	**38**	**1**	**0**	**0**	**101**	**4.0**	**−12**	**0**	**0.0**	**21:00**	....	....	....	....	....	....	....	....	....
2013-14	**New Jersey**	**NHL**	**81**	**12**	**30**	**42**	**60**	**8**	**0**	**2**	**128**	**9.4**	**−3**	**0**	**0.0**	**21:39**	....	....	....	....	....	....	....	....	....
	Czech Republic	Olympics	4	2	2	4	0	....	....	....	....	....	....	....	....	....	....	....	....	....	....	....	....	....	....
2014-15	**New Jersey**	**NHL**	**63**	**4**	**19**	**23**	**42**	**3**	**0**	**0**	**103**	**3.9**	**−7**	**1**	**0.0**	**21:56**	....	....	....	....	....	....	....	....	....
	Detroit	**NHL**	**21**	**3**	**8**	**11**	**14**	**3**	**0**	**1**	**27**	**11.1**	**−2**	**0**	**0.0**	**18:02**	**6**	**0**	**0**	**0**	**4**	**0**	**0**	**0**	**15:17**
	NHL Totals		**783**	**85**	**316**	**401**	**660**	**59**	**0**	**16**	**1237**	**6.9**		**1**	**0.0**	**21:14**	**44**	**1**	**14**	**15**	**40**	**0**	**0**	**0**	**20:36**

Traded to **Nashville** by **NY Rangers** with Rem Murray and Tomas Kloucek for Mike Dunham, December 12, 2002. Signed as a free agent by **HIFK Helsinki** (Finland), September 17, 2004. Traded to **Minnesota** by **Nashville** for Ryan Jones and Minnesota's 2nd round choice (Charles-Olivier Roussel) in 2009 Entry Draft, July 1, 2008. Traded to **New Jersey** by **Minnesota** for Kurtis Foster, Nick Palmieri, Stepahane Veilleux, Washington's 2nd round choice (previously acquired, later traded to Minnesota – Minnesota selected Raphael Bussieres) in 2012 Entry Draft and New Jersey's 3rd round choice (later traded to NY Islanders – NY Islanders selected Eamon McAdam) in 2012 Entry Draft, February 24 2012. Signed as a free agent by **Kladno** (CzRep), September 9, 2012. Traded to **Detroit** by **New Jersey** for future considerations, March 2, 2015.

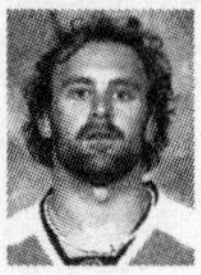

ZOLNIERCZYK, Harry

(ZOHL-nuhr-chuhk, HAIR-ee) **ANA**

Left wing. Shoots left. 6', 185 lbs. Born, Toronto, ON, September 1, 1987.

2005-06	Alberni Valley	BCHL	53	9	13	22	40	....	....	....	....	....	....	....	....	....	6	1	3	4	10	....	....	....	....
2006-07	Alberni Valley	BCHL	47	20	18	38	85	....	....	....	....	....	....	....	....	....	5	3	2	5	10	....	....	....	....
2007-08	Brown U.	ECAC	16	0	3	3	2	....	....	....	....	....	....	....	....	....	....	....	....	....	....	....	....	....	....
2008-09	Brown U.	ECAC	31	1	1	2	30	....	....	....	....	....	....	....	....	....	....	....	....	....	....	....	....	....	....
2009-10	Brown U.	ECAC	37	13	20	33	78	....	....	....	....	....	....	....	....	....	....	....	....	....	....	....	....	....	....
2010-11	Brown U.	ECAC	30	16	15	31	*128	....	....	....	....	....	....	....	....	....	....	....	....	....	....	....	....	....	....
	Adirondack	AHL	16	3	2	5	37	....	....	....	....	....	....	....	....	....	....	....	....	....	....	....	....	....	....
2011-12	**Philadelphia**	**NHL**	**37**	**3**	**3**	**6**	**35**	**0**	**0**	**0**	**49**	**6.1**	**−11**	**28**	**42.9**	**7:42**	....	....	....	....	....	....	....	....	....
	Adirondack	AHL	39	8	13	21	37	....	....	....	....	....	....	....	....	....	....	....	....	....	....	....	....	....	....
2012-13	Adirondack	AHL	52	9	8	17	54	....	....	....	....	....	....	....	....	....	....	....	....	....	....	....	....	....	....
	Philadelphia	**NHL**	**7**	**0**	**1**	**1**	**36**	**0**	**0**	**0**	**4**	**0.0**	**0**	**0**	**0.0**	**7:22**	....	....	....	....	....	....	....	....	....
	Norfolk Admirals	AHL	9	2	0	2	14	....	....	....	....	....	....	....	....	....	....	....	....	....	....	....	....	....	....
2013-14	**Pittsburgh**	**NHL**	**13**	**2**	**0**	**2**	**12**	**0**	**0**	**0**	**12**	**16.7**	**0**	**2**	**100.0**	**10:08**	....	....	....	....	....	....	....	....	....
	Wilkes-Barre	AHL	57	18	18	36	75	....	....	....	....	....	....	....	....	....	17	3	7	10	10	....	....	....	....
2014-15	**NY Islanders**	**NHL**	**2**	**0**	**0**	**0**	**0**	**0**	**0**	**0**	**1**	**0.0**	**−1**	**2**	**0.0**	**11:08**	....	....	....	....	....	....	....	....	....
	Bridgeport	AHL	60	18	26	44	78	....	....	....	....	....	....	....	....	....	....	....	....	....	....	....	....	....	....
	NHL Totals		**59**	**5**	**4**	**9**	**83**	**0**	**0**	**0**	**66**	**7.6**		**32**	**43.8**	**8:19**	....	....	....	....	....	....	....	....	....

Signed as a free agent by **Philadelphia**, March 8, 2011. Traded to **Anaheim** by **Philadelphia** for Jay Rosehill, April 1, 2013. Traded to **Pittsburgh** by **Anaheim** for Alex Grant, June 24, 2013. Signed as a free agent by **NY Islanders**, July 2, 2014. Signed as a free agent by **Anaheim**, July 3, 2015.

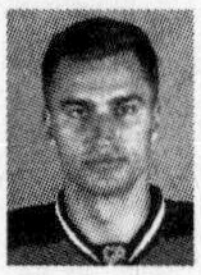

ZUBRUS, Dainius

(ZOO-bruhs, DAYN-ihs)

Left wing. Shoots left. 6'5", 225 lbs. Born, Elektrenai, USSR, June 16, 1978. Philadelphia's 1st choice, 15th overall, in 1996 Entry Draft.

1995-96	Pembroke	ON-Jr.A	28	19	13	32	73	....	....	....	....	....	....	....	....	....	....	....	....	....	....	....	....	....	....
	Caledon	ON-Jr.A	7	3	7	10	2	....	....	....	....	....	....	....	....	....	17	11	12	23	4	....	....	....	....
1996-97	**Philadelphia**	**NHL**	**68**	**8**	**13**	**21**	**22**	**1**	**0**	**2**	**71**	**11.3**	**3**	....	....	....	**19**	**5**	**4**	**9**	**12**	**1**	**0**	**1**	....
1997-98	**Philadelphia**	**NHL**	**69**	**8**	**25**	**33**	**42**	**1**	**0**	**5**	**101**	**7.9**	**29**	....	....	....	**5**	**0**	**1**	**1**	**2**	**0**	**0**	**0**	....
1998-99	**Philadelphia**	**NHL**	**63**	**3**	**5**	**8**	**25**	**0**	**1**	**0**	**49**	**6.1**	**−5**	**29**	**51.7**	**11:00**	....	....	....	....	....	....	....	....	....
	Montreal	**NHL**	**17**	**3**	**5**	**8**	**4**	**0**	**0**	**1**	**31**	**9.7**	**−3**	**2**	**50.0**	**16:53**	....	....	....	....	....	....	....	....	....
99-2000	**Montreal**	**NHL**	**73**	**14**	**28**	**42**	**54**	**3**	**0**	**1**	**139**	**10.1**	**−1**	**212**	**39.2**	**17:37**	....	....	....	....	....	....	....	....	....
2000-01	**Montreal**	**NHL**	**49**	**12**	**12**	**24**	**30**	**3**	**0**	**0**	**70**	**17.1**	**−7**	**190**	**41.1**	**18:30**	....	....	....	....	....	....	....	....	....
	Washington	**NHL**	**12**	**1**	**1**	**2**	**7**	**1**	**0**	**0**	**13**	**7.7**	**−4**	**0**	**0.0**	**13:05**	**6**	**0**	**0**	**0**	**2**	**0**	**0**	**0**	**17:24**
2001-02	**Washington**	**NHL**	**71**	**17**	**26**	**43**	**38**	**4**	**0**	**3**	**138**	**12.3**	**5**	**131**	**37.4**	**18:52**	....	....	....	....	....	....	....	....	....
2002-03	**Washington**	**NHL**	**63**	**13**	**22**	**35**	**43**	**2**	**0**	**0**	**104**	**12.5**	**15**	**565**	**50.3**	**16:26**	**6**	**2**	**2**	**4**	**4**	**1**	**0**	**0**	**21:30**
2003-04	**Washington**	**NHL**	**54**	**12**	**15**	**27**	**38**	**6**	**1**	**2**	**115**	**10.4**	**−16**	**916**	**48.0**	**19:32**	....	....	....	....	....	....	....	....	....

Season	Club	League	GP	G	A	Pts	PIM	PP	SH	GW	S	S%	+/-	TF	F%	Min	GP	G	A	Pts	PIM	PP	SH	GW	Min
																	Regular Season					Playoffs			
2004-05	Lada Togliatti	Russia	42	8	11	19	85	....	....	....	....	....	....	....	....	....	10	3	1	4	22	....	....	....	....
2005-06	Washington	NHL	71	23	34	57	84	13	0	5	181	12.7	3	1118	50.3	20:22	....	....	....	....	....	....	....	....	....
2006-07	Washington	NHL	60	20	32	52	50	9	0	4	127	15.7	−16	1096	49.7	19:51	....	....	....	....	....	....	....	....	....
	Buffalo	NHL	19	4	4	8	12	1	0	0	31	12.9	−3	69	39.1	18:22	15	0	8	8	8	0	0	0	18:38
2007-08	New Jersey	NHL	82	13	25	38	38	4	0	2	128	10.2	2	144	55.6	15:42	5	0	1	1	8	0	0	0	16:18
2008-09	New Jersey	NHL	82	15	25	40	69	1	0	3	130	11.5	6	923	51.3	15:16	7	0	1	1	10	0	0	0	13:57
2009-10	New Jersey	NHL	51	10	17	27	28	1	0	4	86	11.6	4	400	48.5	16:29	5	1	0	1	8	0	0	1	16:25
2010-11	New Jersey	NHL	79	13	17	30	53	1	0	2	115	11.3	−11	449	56.4	17:09	....	....	....	....	....	....	....	....	....
2011-12	New Jersey	NHL	82	17	27	44	34	4	3	2	109	15.6	7	441	43.3	18:41	24	3	7	10	18	1	0	1	18:07
2012-13	New Jersey	NHL	22	2	7	9	12	0	0	0	22	9.1	−3	28	39.3	16:47	....	....	....	....	....	....	....	....	....
2013-14	New Jersey	NHL	82	13	13	26	46	0	0	1	121	10.7	1	424	50.9	17:33	....	....	....	....	....	....	....	....	....
2014-15	New Jersey	NHL	74	4	6	10	42	0	0	0	72	5.6	−9	86	43.0	14:40	....	....	....	....	....	....	....	....	....
	NHL Totals		1243	225	359	584	771	55	5	38	1953	11.5		7223	49.0	17:06	92	11	24	35	72	3	0	3	17:47

Traded to **Montreal** by **Philadelphia** with Philadelphia's 2nd round choice (Matt Carkner) in 1999 Entry Draft and NY Islanders' 6th round choice (previously acquired, Montreal selected Scott Selig) in 2000 Entry Draft for Mark Recchi, March 10, 1999. Traded to **Washington** by **Montreal** with Trevor Linden and New Jersey's 2nd round choice (previously acquired, later traded to Tampa Bay – Tampa Bay selected Andreas Holmqvist) in 2001 Entry Draft for Richard Zednik, Jan Bulis and Washington's 1st round choice (Alexander Perezhogin) in 2001 Entry Draft, March 13, 2001. Signed as a free agent by **Togliatti** (Russia), July 1, 2004. Traded to **Buffalo** by **Washington** with Timo Helbling for Jiri Novotny and Buffalo's 1st round choice (later traded to San Jose - San Jose selected Nicholas Petrecki) in 2007 Entry Draft, February 27, 2007. Signed as a free agent by **New Jersey**, July 3, 2007. • Missed majority of 2012-13 due to wrist injury vs. NY Rangers, February 5, 2013.

ZUCCARELLO, Mats   (zoo-ka-REHL-oh, MATS)   **NYR**

Left wing. Shoots left. 5'7", 179 lbs.   Born, Oslo, Norway, September 1, 1987.

Season	Club	League	GP	G	A	Pts	PIM	PP	SH	GW	S	S%	+/-	TF	F%	Min	GP	G	A	Pts	PIM	PP	SH	GW	Min
2003-04	Frisk-Asker U18	Nor-U18	24	23	14	37	44	....	....	....	....	....	....	....	....	....	2	3	1	4	0	....	....	....	....
	Frisk-Asker Jr.	Nor-Jr.	20	7	14	21	14	....	....	....	....	....	....	....	....	....	3	0	2	2	0	....	....	....	....
2004-05	Frisk-Asker U18	Nor-U18	12	11	18	29	50	....	....	....	....	....	....	....	....	....	....	....	....	....	....	....	....	....	....
	Frisk-Asker Jr.	Nor-Jr.	27	19	17	36	16	....	....	....	....	....	....	....	....	....	5	3	3	6	6	....	....	....	....
	Frisk-Asker IF	Norway	1	0	0	0	0	....	....	....	....	....	....	....	....	....	....	....	....	....	....	....	....	....	....
2005-06	Frisk Asker IF/NTG	Nor-Jr.	2	7	0	7	0	....	....	....	....	....	....	....	....	....	2	2	3	5	0	....	....	....	....
	Frisk-Asker IF	Norway	21	5	3	8	12	....	....	....	....	....	....	....	....	....	4	0	0	0	2	....	....	....	....
2006-07	Frisk Asker IF/NTG	Nor-Jr.	....	....	....	....	....	....	....	....	....	....	....	....	....	....	1	3	4	7	2	....	....	....	....
	Frisk-Asker IF	Norway	43	34	25	59	36	....	....	....	....	....	....	....	....	....	7	4	4	8	2	....	....	....	....
2007-08	Frisk-Asker IF	Norway	33	24	40	64	48	....	....	....	....	....	....	....	....	....	15	12	15	27	24	....	....	....	....
2008-09	MODO	Sweden	35	12	28	40	38	....	....	....	....	....	....	....	....	....	....	....	....	....	....	....	....	....	....
2009-10	MODO	Sweden	55	23	41	*64	62	....	....	....	....	....	....	....	....	....	....	....	....	....	....	....	....	....	....
	Norway	Olympics	4	1	2	3	2	....	....	....	....	....	....	....	....	....	....	....	....	....	....	....	....	....	....
2010-11	NY Rangers	NHL	42	6	17	23	4	0	0	2	74	8.1	3	15	53.3	14:10	1	0	0	0	2	0	0	0	7:34
	Connecticut	AHL	36	13	16	29	16	....	....	....	....	....	....	....	....	....	2	1	1	2	4	....	....	....	....
2011-12	NY Rangers	NHL	10	2	1	3	6	1	0	1	10	20.0	0	0	0.0	10:03	....	....	....	....	....	....	....	....	....
	Connecticut	AHL	37	12	24	36	22	....	....	....	....	....	....	....	....	....	7	2	2	4	10	....	....	....	....
2012-13	Magnitogorsk	KHL	44	11	17	28	30	....	....	....	....	....	....	....	....	....	....	....	....	....	....	....	....	....	....
	NY Rangers	NHL	15	3	5	8	8	0	0	0	27	11.1	10	4	0.0	16:25	12	1	6	7	4	0	0	0	16:22
2013-14	NY Rangers	NHL	77	19	40	59	32	4	1	4	170	11.2	11	8	37.5	17:08	25	5	8	13	20	0	0	0	17:41
	Norway	Olympics	3	0	0	0	2	....	....	....	....	....	....	....	....	....	....	....	....	....	....	....	....	....	....
2014-15	NY Rangers	NHL	78	15	34	49	45	0	0	3	154	9.7	17	37	43.2	17:16	5	0	2	2	0	0	0	0	14:35
	NHL Totals		222	45	97	142	95	5	1	10	435	10.3		64	42.2	16:15	43	6	16	22	26	0	0	0	16:43

Signed as a free agent by **NY Rangers**, May 26, 2010. Signed as a free agent by **Magnitogorsk** (KHL), May 26, 2012. Signed as a free agent by **NY Rangers**, March 28, 2013.

ZUCKER, Jason   (zuh-kuhr, JAY-suhn)   **MIN**

Left wing. Shoots left. 5'11", 188 lbs.   Born, Newport Beach, CA, January 16, 1992. Minnesota's 4th choice, 59th overall, in 2010 Entry Draft.

Season	Club	League	GP	G	A	Pts	PIM	PP	SH	GW	S	S%	+/-	TF	F%	Min	GP	G	A	Pts	PIM	PP	SH	GW	Min
2007-08	Det. Compuware	MWEHL	30	17	21	38	30	....	....	....	....	....	....	....	....	....	....	....	....	....	....	....	....	....	....
	Det. Compuware	Minor-MI	42	29	35	64		....	....	....	....	....	....	....	....	....	....	....	....	....	....	....	....	....	....
2008-09	USNTDP	NAHL	36	11	4	15	55	....	....	....	....	....	....	....	....	....	....	....	....	....	....	....	....	....	....
	USNTDP	U-17	12	8	6	14		....	....	....	....	....	....	....	....	....	....	....	....	....	....	....	....	....	....
	USNTDP	U-18	16	2	6	8	8	....	....	....	....	....	....	....	....	....	....	....	....	....	....	....	....	....	....
2009-10	USNTDP	USHL	22	11	7	18	23	....	....	....	....	....	....	....	....	....	....	....	....	....	....	....	....	....	....
	USNTDP	U-18	38	18	17	35	24	....	....	....	....	....	....	....	....	....	....	....	....	....	....	....	....	....	....
2010-11	U. of Denver	WCHA	40	23	22	45	59	....	....	....	....	....	....	....	....	....	....	....	....	....	....	....	....	....	....
2011-12	U. of Denver	WCHA	38	22	24	46	38	....	....	....	....	....	....	....	....	....	....	....	....	....	....	....	....	....	....
	Minnesota	NHL	6	0	2	2	2	0	0	0	10	0.0	−2	0	0.0	11:02	....	....	....	....	....	....	....	....	....
2012-13	Houston Aeros	AHL	55	24	26	50	43	....	....	....	....	....	....	....	....	....	1	0	0	0	4	....	....	....	....
	Minnesota	NHL	20	4	1	5	8	0	0	0	34	11.8	4	1	0.0	11:16	5	1	1	2	0	0	0	1	13:29
2013-14	Minnesota	NHL	21	4	1	5	2	1	0	1	40	10.0	2	0	0.0	12:59	....	....	....	....	....	....	....	....	....
	Iowa Wild	AHL	22	8	5	13	55	....	....	....	....	....	....	....	....	....	....	....	....	....	....	....	....	....	....
2014-15	Minnesota	NHL	51	21	5	26	18	1	1	3	124	16.9	−9	7	28.6	15:04	10	2	1	3	2	0	0	0	14:11
	NHL Totals		98	29	9	38	30	2	1	4	208	13.9		8	25.0	13:36	15	3	2	5	2	0	0	1	13:57

WCHA All-Rookie Team (2011) • WCHA Second All-Star Team (2011, 2012) • WCHA Rookie of the Year (2011) • NCAA West Second All-American Team (2012) • AHL All-Rookie Team (2013)

NHL Goaltenders

 Jake Allen

 Frederik Andersen

 Craig Anderson

 Niklas Backstrom

 Jonathan Bernier

 Ben Bishop

 Sergei Bobrovsky

 Scott Clemmensen

 Corey Crawford

 Yann Danis

 Scott Darling

 Devan Dubnyk

 Brian Elliott

 Dan Ellis

 Ray Emery

 Jhonas Enroth

 Viktor Fasth

 Marc-Andre Fleury

 John Gibson

 Thomas Greiss

 Philipp Grubauer

 Matt Hackett

 Jaroslav Halak

 Andrew Hammond

 Josh Harding

 Jonas Hiller

 Braden Holtby

 Jimmy Howard

 Michael Hutchinson

 Carter Hutton

 Leland Irving

 Chad Johnson

 Martin Jones

 Anton Khudobin

 Keith Kinkaid

 Darcy Kuemper

 Jason LaBarbera

 Eddie Lack

 Robin Lehner

 Kari Lehtonen

 Anders Lindback

 Henrik Lundqvist

 Roberto Luongo

 Jacob Markstrom

 Steve Mason

 Curtis McElhinney

 Ryan Miller

 Al Montoya

 Petr Mrazek

 Michal Neuvirth

 Antti Niemi

 Joni Ortio

 Ondrej Pavelec

 Justin Peters

 Calvin Pickard

 Kevin Poulin

 Carey Price

Jonathan Quick

Karri Ramo

Tuukka Rask

James Reimer

Pekka Rinne

Cory Schneider

 Ben Scrivens

Mike Smith

Alex Stalock

 Niklas Svedberg

Cam Talbot

 Dustin Tokarski

Semyon Varlamov

 Andrei Vasilevskiy

 Cam Ward

2015-16 Goaltender Register

Note: The 2015-16 Goaltender Register lists all active NHL goaltenders, every goaltender drafted in the 2015 Entry Draft, goaltenders on NHL Reserve Lists and other goaltenders.

Trades and roster changes are current as of August 14, 2015.

To calculate a goaltender's goals-against per game average **(Avg)**, divide goals against **(GA)** by minutes played **(Mins)** and multiply this result by **60**.

Abbreviations: GP – games played; **W** – wins; **L** – losses; **O/T** – overtime losses/ties; **Mins** – minutes played; **GA** – goals against; **SO** – shutouts; **Avg** – goals-against-per-game average; ***** – league-leading total ♦ – member of Stanley Cup-winning team.

NHL Player Register begins on page 344.
Prospect Register begins on page 275.
Retired Player Index begins on page 612.
Retired Goaltender Index begins on page 657.
League Abbreviations are listed on page 670.

AITTOKALLIO, Sami   (ay-toh-KAHL-ee-oh, SAHM-ee)   COL

Goaltender. Catches left. 6'1", 185 lbs.   Born, Tampere, Finland, August 6, 1992.
(Colorado's 5th choice, 107th overall, in 2010 Entry Draft).

					Regular Season							Playoffs			
Season	Club	League	GP	W	L	O/T	Mins	GA	SO	Avg	GP	W	L	Mins	GA	SO	Avg
2008-09	Ilves Tampere U18	Fin-U18	5	5	0	0	305	9	1	1.77							
	Ilves Tampere Jr.	Fin-Jr.	13	7	6	0	731	33	1	2.71							
2009-10	Ilves Tampere	Finland	1	0	0	0	2	0	0	0.00							
	LeKi Lempaala	Finland-2	2	1	1	0	124	7	0	3.38							
	Suomi U20	Finland-2	1	0	1	0	120	8	0	4.00							
	Ilves Tampere U18	Fin-U18	9	6	3	0	542	19	1	2.10							
	Ilves Tampere Jr.	Fin-Jr.	23	13	9	0	1257	67	2	3.20	9	6	3	504	19	0	2.26
2010-11	Ilves Tampere	Finland	16	5	8	0	790	36	1	2.73	2	0	2	117	5	0	2.57
	Suomi U20	Finland-2	4	2	2	0	196	14	0	4.28							
	Ilves Tampere Jr.	Fin-Jr.	6	4	2	0	359	14	1	2.34	3	1	2	174	11	0	3.80
	LeKi Lempaala	Finland-2	6	3	3	0	322	20	0	3.73							
2011-12	Ilves Tampere	Fin-Jr.	11	1	6	3	596	28	0	2.82							
	Ilves Tampere Jr.	Fin-Jr.	6	2	4	0	347	18	0	3.11							
	LeKi Lempaala	Finland-2	7	1	6	0	416	30	0	4.33							
2012-13	Lake Erie Monsters	AHL	27	14	12	1	1540	77	1	3.00							
	Colorado	**NHL**	1	0	0	0	49	2	0	2.45							
2013-14	**Colorado**	**NHL**	1	0	1	0	40	3	0	4.50							
	Lake Erie Monsters	AHL	36	15	15	3	2060	91	4	2.65							
2014-15	Lake Erie Monsters	AHL	16	7	5	1	809	43	0	3.19							
	Fort Wayne	ECHL	4	3	1	0	245	20	0	4.90							
	NHL Totals		2	0	1	0	89	5	0	3.37							

ALLEN, Jake   (AL-luhn, JAYK)   ST.L.

Goaltender. Catches left. 6'2", 195 lbs.   Born, Fredericton, NB, August 7, 1990.
(St. Louis' 3rd choice, 34th overall, in 2008 Entry Draft).

					Regular Season							Playoffs			
Season	Club	League	GP	W	L	O/T	Mins	GA	SO	Avg	GP	W	L	Mins	GA	SO	Avg
2006-07	Fredericton	NBPEI					STATISTICS NOT AVAILABLE										
2007-08	St. John's	QMJHL	30	9	12	0	1507	79	2	3.14	4	2	1	128	8	0	3.74
2008-09	Montreal	QMJHL	53	28	25	0	3023	144	3	2.86	10	4	6	585	35	1	3.59
2009-10	Montreal	QMJHL	23	11	11	0	1241	55	1	2.66							
	Drummondville	QMJHL	22	18	3	0	1271	37	3	1.75	14	9	5	840	34	1	2.43
2010-11	Peoria Rivermen	AHL	47	25	19	3	2805	118	6	2.52	3	0	3	189	12	0	3.80
2011-12	Peoria Rivermen	AHL	38	13	20	2	2148	105	1	2.93							
	St. Louis	**NHL**									1	0	0	1	0	0	0.00
2012-13	Peoria Rivermen	AHL	35	13	19	2	2054	99	2	2.89							
	St. Louis	**NHL**	15	9	4	0	804	33	1	2.46							
2013-14	Chicago Wolves	AHL	*52	*33	16	3	*3138	106	*7	*2.03	9	3	6	511	28	1	3.29
2014-15	**St. Louis**	**NHL**	37	22	7	4	2077	79	4	2.28	6	2	4	328	12	0	2.20
	NHL Totals		52	31	11	4	2881	112	5	2.33	7	2	4	329	12	0	2.19

QMJHL First All-Star Team (2010) • Canadian Major Junior First All-Star Team (2010) • Canadian Major Junior Goaltender of the Year (2010) • NHL All-Rookie Team (2013) • AHL First All-Star Team (2014) • Aldege "Baz" Bastien Award (AHL – Outstanding Goaltender) (2014) • NHL All-Rookie Team (2015)

ALTSHULLER, Daniel   (awl-SHOO-luhr, DAN-yehl)   CAR

Goaltender. Catches left. 6'3", 205 lbs.   Born, Ottawa, ON, July 24, 1994.
(Carolina's 3rd choice, 69th overall, in 2012 Entry Draft).

					Regular Season							Playoffs			
Season	Club	League	GP	W	L	O/T	Mins	GA	SO	Avg	GP	W	L	Mins	GA	SO	Avg
2009-10	Ott. Jr. 67's MM	Minor-ON	24				1080	40	3	1.74							
	Nepean Raiders	ON-Jr.A	1	0	1	0	60	2	0	2.00							
2010-11	Nepean Raiders	ON-Jr.A	43	19	13	10	2515	135	1	3.22							
2011-12	Oshawa Generals	OHL	30	11	16	3	1756	104	0	3.55	5	2	2	279	18	0	3.87
2012-13	Oshawa Generals	OHL	58	*36	18	2	3363	147	3	2.62	9	4	5	541	27	0	3.00
2013-14	Oshawa Generals	OHL	52	31	13	3	2907	124	2	2.56	11	8	3	699	22	*3	*1.89
2014-15	Florida Everblades	ECHL	14	8	3	1	767	41	0	3.21	6	2	3	288	16	1	3.34

OHL All-Rookie Team (2012)

ANDERSEN, Frederik   (AHN-duhr-suhn, FREH-duhr-ihk)   ANA

Goaltender. Catches left. 6'4", 230 lbs.   Born, Herning, Denmark, October 2, 1989.
(Anaheim's 3rd choice, 87th overall, in 2012 Entry Draft).

					Regular Season							Playoffs			
Season	Club	League	GP	W	L	O/T	Mins	GA	SO	Avg	GP	W	L	Mins	GA	SO	Avg
2005-06	Herning IK Jr.	Den-Jr.	29								6						
	Herning IK II	Den-2	3														
2006-07	Herning IK Jr.	Den-Jr.	27														
	Herning IK II	Den-2	18														
2007-08	Herning IK Jr.	Den-Jr.	17														
	Herning IK II	Den-2	9														
2008-09	Herning IK Jr.	Den-Jr.	1														
	Herning Blue Fox	Denmark	22				1249	51	1	2.45							
2009-10	Frederikshavn	Denmark	30				1754	64	6	2.19	10			607	29	0	2.86
2010-11	Frederikshavn	Denmark	35				1953	81		2.49	11			666	26		2.34
2011-12	Frolunda	Sweden	39				2335	65	7	1.67	6			379	17	0	2.69
2012-13	Norfolk Admirals	AHL	47	24	18	1	2685	98	4	2.19							
2013-14	**Anaheim**	**NHL**	28	20	5	0	1569	60	0	2.29	7	3	2	368	19	0	3.10
	Norfolk Admirals	AHL	4	3	1	0	245	8	1	1.96							
2014-15	**Anaheim**	**NHL**	54	35	12	5	3106	123	3	2.38	16	11	5	1050	41	1	2.34
	NHL Totals		82	55	17	5	4675	183	3	2.35	23	14	7	1418	60	1	2.54

• Re-entered NHL Entry Draft. Originally Carolina's 8th choice, 187th overall, in 2010 Entry Draft.

NHL All-Rookie Team (2014)

ANDERSON, Craig   (AN-duhr-suhn, KRAYG)   OTT

Goaltender. Catches left. 6'2", 184 lbs.   Born, Park Ridge, IL, May 21, 1981.
(Chicago's 4th choice, 73rd overall, in 2001 Entry Draft).

					Regular Season							Playoffs			
Season	Club	League	GP	W	L	O/T	Mins	GA	SO	Avg	GP	W	L	Mins	GA	SO	Avg
1997-98	Chicago Jets	MEHL	50				2991	143	2	2.86							
1998-99	Chicago Freeze	NAHL	14	3	0		840	40	0	2.56							
	Guelph Storm	OHL	21	12	5	1	1006	52	1	3.10	3	0	2	114	9	0	4.74
99-2000	Guelph Storm	OHL	38	12	17	2	1955	117	0	3.59	3	0	1	110	5	0	2.73
2000-01	Guelph Storm	OHL	59	30	19	9	3555	156	3	2.63	4	0	4	240	17	0	4.25
2001-02	Norfolk Admirals	AHL	28	9	13	4	1568	77	2	2.95	1	0	1	21	1	0	2.83
2002-03	**Chicago**	**NHL**	6	0	3	2	270	18	0	4.00							
	Norfolk Admirals	AHL	32	15	11	5	1795	58	4	1.94	5	2	3	345	15	0	2.61
2003-04	**Chicago**	**NHL**	21	6	14	0	1205	57	1	2.84							
	Norfolk Admirals	AHL	37	17	20	0	2108	74	3	2.11	5	2	3	327	10	0	1.84
2004-05	Norfolk Admirals	AHL	15	9	4	1	886	27	2	1.83	6	2	4	356	14	0	2.36
2005-06	**Chicago**	**NHL**	29	6	12	4	1554	86	1	3.32							
2006-07	**Florida**	**NHL**	5	1	1	1	217	8	0	2.21							
	Rochester	AHL	34	23	10	1	2060	88	1	2.56	6	2	4	376	18	0	2.87
2007-08	**Florida**	**NHL**	17	8	6	1	935	35	2	2.25							
2008-09	**Florida**	**NHL**	31	15	7	5	1636	74	3	2.71							
2009-10	**Colorado**	**NHL**	71	38	25	7	4235	186	7	2.64	6	2	4	366	16	1	2.62
2010-11	**Colorado**	**NHL**	33	13	15	3	1810	99	0	3.28							
	Ottawa	**NHL**	18	11	5	1	1055	36	2	2.05							
2011-12	**Ottawa**	**NHL**	63	33	22	6	3492	165	3	2.84	7	3	4	419	14	1	2.00
2012-13	**Ottawa**	**NHL**	24	12	9	2	1421	40	3	*1.69	10	5	4	578	29	0	3.01
2013-14	**Ottawa**	**NHL**	53	25	16	8	3000	150	4	3.00							
2014-15	**Ottawa**	**NHL**	35	14	13	2	2093	87	3	2.49	4	2	2	247	4	1	0.97
	NHL Totals		406	182	148	48	22923	1041	29	2.72	27	12	14	1610	63	3	2.35

• Re-entered NHL Entry Draft. Originally Calgary's 3rd choice, 77th overall, in 1999 Entry Draft.

OHL First All-Star Team (2001)

Claimed on waivers by **Boston** from **Chicago**, January 19, 2006. Claimed on waivers by **St. Louis** from **Boston**, January 31, 2006. Claimed on waivers by **Chicago** from **St. Louis**, February 3, 2006. Traded to **Florida** by **Chicago** for Florida's 6th round choice (later traded to Tampa Bay – Tampa Bay selected Luke Witkowski) in 2008 Entry Draft, June 24, 2006. Signed as a free agent by **Colorado**, July 1, 2009. Traded to **Ottawa** by **Colorado** for Brian Elliott, February 18, 2011.

ANDERSON, J.P. (AN-duhr-suhn, JAY-PEE)

Goaltender. Catches right. 5'11", 185 lbs. Born, Toronto, ON, April 27, 1992.

			Regular Season								Playoffs						
Season	Club	League	GP	W	L	O/T	Mins	GA	SO	Avg	GP	W	L	Mins	GA	SO	Avg
2008-09	St. Michael's	OHL	26	12	12	0	1409	69	1	2.94	11	6	5	697	29	0	*2.50
2009-10	St. Michael's	OHL	36	23	10	1	2028	88	1	2.60	10	4	5	519	24	0	2.78
2010-11	St. Michael's	OHL	51	*38	10	1	2897	114	*6	*2.36	*20	*15	5	*1223	43	*4	*2.11
2011-12	St. Michael's	OHL	31	15	11	4	1855	94	0	3.04	....	....	....	....	....	....	....
	Sarnia Sting	OHL	26	12	12	2	1473	74	3	3.01	6	2	3	355	22	0	3.71
2012-13	Sarnia Sting	OHL	53	26	21	5	3031	167	1	3.31	4	0	4	239	24	0	6.02
2013-14	San Francisco Bulls	ECHL	14	1	7	2	672	39	0	3.48	....	....	....	....	....	....	....
	Ontario Reign	ECHL	7	3	2	2	425	18	0	2.54	2	0	2	118	7	0	3.55
2014-15	Worcester Sharks	AHL	16	6	8	1	884	40	1	2.71	....	....	....	....	....	....	....
	Allen Americans	ECHL	10	3	3	2	485	27	0	3.34	....	....	....	....	....	....	....

OHL Second All-Star Team (2011)

Signed as a free agent by **San Jose**, September 20, 2010.

BACHMAN, Richard (BAWK-mahn, RIH-chuhrd) VAN

Goaltender. Catches left. 5'10", 183 lbs. Born, Salt Lake City, UT, July 25, 1987.
(Dallas' 3rd choice, 120th overall, in 2006 Entry Draft).

			Regular Season								Playoffs						
Season	Club	League	GP	W	L	O/T	Mins	GA	SO	Avg	GP	W	L	Mins	GA	SO	Avg
2004-05	Cushing	High-MA	28	....	....	....	1498	53	3	1.89	....	....	....	....	....	....	....
	Junior Bruins	EmJHL	25	....	....	....	....	....	....	....	....	....	....	....	....	....	....
2005-06	Cushing	High-MA	30	....	....	....	1598	60	4	2.25	....	....	....	....	....	....	....
	Junior Bruins	EmJHL	....	31	1	2	....	....	....	1.69	....	....	....	....	....	....	....
2006-07	Chicago Steel	USHL	7	2	5	0	359	29	0	4.85	....	....	....	....	....	....	....
	Cedar Rapids	USHL	26	14	10	2	1565	78	4	2.99	6	4	1	329	7	*2	*1.28
2007-08	Colorado College	WCHA	35	25	9	1	2103	65	4	1.85	....	....	....	....	....	....	....
2008-09	Colorado College	WCHA	35	14	11	10	2073	91	3	2.63	....	....	....	....	....	....	....
2009-10	Texas Stars	AHL	8	4	4	0	446	16	1	2.15	....	....	....	....	....	....	....
	Idaho Steelheads	ECHL	35	22	7	4	2028	77	*4	*2.28	8	6	2	492	13	1	1.59
2010-11	**Dallas**	**NHL**	**1**	**0**	**0**	**0**	**10**	**0**	**0**	**0.00**	....	....	....	....	....	....	....
	Texas Stars	AHL	55	28	19	5	3191	117	6	2.20	6	2	4	394	15	0	2.29
2011-12	**Dallas**	**NHL**	**18**	**8**	**5**	**1**	**933**	**43**	**1**	**2.77**	....	....	....	....	....	....	....
	Texas Stars	AHL	15	7	6	1	844	44	2	3.13	....	....	....	....	....	....	....
2012-13	Texas Stars	AHL	6	5	1	0	363	14	0	2.31	....	....	....	....	....	....	....
	Dallas	**NHL**	**13**	**6**	**5**	**0**	**609**	**33**	**0**	**3.25**	....	....	....	....	....	....	....
2013-14	**Edmonton**	**NHL**	**3**	**0**	**2**	**1**	**139**	**7**	**0**	**3.02**	....	....	....	....	....	....	....
	Oklahoma City	AHL	*52	26	19	6	3074	153	2	2.99	3	0	3	200	9	0	2.70
2014-15	**Edmonton**	**NHL**	**7**	**3**	**2**	**0**	**317**	**15**	**1**	**2.84**	....	....	....	....	....	....	....
	Oklahoma City	AHL	23	14	5	3	1338	53	3	2.38	9	5	4	581	15	0	1.55
	NHL Totals		**42**	**17**	**14**	**2**	**2008**	**98**	**2**	**2.93**	....	....	....	....	....	....	....

WCHA All-Rookie Team (2008) • WCHA First All-Star Team (2008) • WCHA Rookie of the Year (2008) • WCHA Player of the Year (2008) • NCAA West First All-American Team (2008) • NCAA Rookie of the Year (2008)

Signed as a free agent by **Edmonton**, July 6, 2013. Signed as a free agent by **Vancouver**, July 1, 2015.

BACKSTROM, Niklas (BAK-struhm, NIHK-luhs) MIN

Goaltender. Catches left. 6'2", 197 lbs. Born, Helsinki, Finland, February 13, 1978.

			Regular Season								Playoffs						
Season	Club	League	GP	W	L	O/T	Mins	GA	SO	Avg	GP	W	L	Mins	GA	SO	Avg
1994-95	HIFK Helsinki U18	Fin-U18					Statistics Not Available										
1995-96	HIFK Helsinki U18	Fin-U18	12	....	....	....	699	44	....	3.77	4	....	....	203	9	....	2.66
1996-97	HIFK Helsinki Jr.	Fin-Jr.	21	....	....	....	1243	57	....	2.75	....	....	....	....	....	....	....
	PiTa Helsinki	Finland-2	8	....	....	....	390	24	....	3.69	....	....	....	....	....	....	....
	HIFK Helsinki	Finland	2	0	0	0	30	3	0	5.85	....	....	....	....	....	....	....
1997-98	HIFK Helsinki Jr.	Fin-Jr.	14	7	7	0	847	42	....	2.98	....	....	....	....	....	....	....
	Hermes Kokkola	Finland-2	9	4	3	1	468	23	1	2.95	....	....	....	....	....	....	....
1998-99	HIFK Helsinki	Finland	16	9	5	1	923	26	1	*1.69	....	....	....	....	....	....	....
	HIFK Helsinki Jr.	Fin-Jr.	15	7	7	1	898	45	1	3.01	....	....	....	....	....	....	....
99-2000	HIFK Helsinki	Finland	4	0	4	0	155	17	0	6.58	....	....	....	....	....	....	....
	FPS Forssa	Finland-2	22	13	8	1	1320	50	1	2.27	3	1	2	178	8	0	2.69
2000-01	SaiPa	Finland	49	22	24	3	2826	120	2	2.55	....	....	....	....	....	....	....
2001-02	AIK Solna	Sweden	40	....	....	....	2186	111	1	3.05	....	....	....	....	....	....	....
	AIK Solna	Sweden-Q	9	....	....	....	543	20	0	2.21	....	....	....	....	....	....	....
2002-03	Karpat Oulu	Finland	36	16	8	9	2136	77	4	2.16	*15	7	8	*990	33	1	2.00
2003-04	Karpat Oulu	Finland	43	24	8	0	2572	87	7	2.03	*15	*9	6	*927	36	1	2.33
2004-05	Karpat Oulu	Finland	47	27	10	10	2819	102	7	2.17	*12	*10	2	720	15	*3	*1.25
2005-06	Karpat Oulu	Finland	51	*32	9	10	3077	86	*10	*1.68	4	3	1	195	6	0	1.84
	Finland	Olympics					Did Not Play – Spare Goaltender										
2006-07	**Minnesota**	**NHL**	**41**	**23**	**8**	**6**	**2227**	**73**	**5**	***1.97**	**5**	**1**	**4**	**297**	**11**	**0**	**2.22**
2007-08	**Minnesota**	**NHL**	**58**	**33**	**13**	**8**	**3409**	**131**	**4**	**2.31**	**6**	**2**	**4**	**361**	**17**	**0**	**2.83**
2008-09	**Minnesota**	**NHL**	**71**	**37**	**24**	**8**	**4088**	**159**	**8**	**2.33**	....	....	....	....	....	....	....
2009-10	**Minnesota**	**NHL**	**60**	**26**	**23**	**8**	**3489**	**158**	**2**	**2.72**	....	....	....	....	....	....	....
	Finland	Olympics	2	1	0	0	110	2	1	*1.09	....	....	....	....	....	....	....
2010-11	**Minnesota**	**NHL**	**51**	**22**	**23**	**5**	**2978**	**132**	**3**	**2.66**	....	....	....	....	....	....	....
2011-12	**Minnesota**	**NHL**	**46**	**19**	**18**	**7**	**2590**	**105**	**4**	**2.43**	....	....	....	....	....	....	....
2012-13	**Minnesota**	**NHL**	**42**	***24**	**15**	**3**	**2368**	**98**	**2**	**2.48**	....	....	....	....	....	....	....
2013-14	**Minnesota**	**NHL**	**21**	**5**	**11**	**2**	**1094**	**55**	**0**	**3.02**	....	....	....	....	....	....	....
2014-15	**Minnesota**	**NHL**	**19**	**5**	**7**	**3**	**1005**	**51**	**0**	**3.04**	....	....	....	....	....	....	....
	NHL Totals		**409**	**194**	**142**	**50**	**23248**	**962**	**28**	**2.48**	**11**	**3**	**8**	**658**	**28**	**0**	**2.55**

MBNA Roger Crozier Saving Grace Award (2007) • William M. Jennings Trophy (2007) (shared with Manny Fernandez)

Played in NHL All-Star Game (2009)

Signed as a free agent by **Minnesota**, June 1, 2006. • Missed majority of 2013-14 and 2014-15 due to recurring lower-body injuries.

BARTOSAK, Patrik (BAHR-toh-shak, PAT-rihk) L.A.

Goaltender. Catches left. 6'1", 194 lbs. Born, Koprivnice, Czech Rep., March 29, 1993.
(Los Angeles' 4th choice, 146th overall, in 2013 Entry Draft).

			Regular Season								Playoffs						
Season	Club	League	GP	W	L	O/T	Mins	GA	SO	Avg	GP	W	L	Mins	GA	SO	Avg
2007-08	HC Vitkovice U17	CzR-U17	8	....	....	....	484	26	0	3.22	....	....	....	....	....	....	....
2008-09	HC Vitkovice U17	CzR-U17	18	....	....	....	1064	48	1	2.71	4	....	....	229	10	0	2.62
	HC Vitkovice Jr.	CzRep-Jr.	....	....	....	....	....	....	....	....	1	....	....	2	1	0	30.00
2009-10	HC Vitkovice U18	CzR-U18	36	....	....	....	2023	65	3	1.93	2	....	....	130	6	0	2.77
	Frydek-Mistek U18	CzR-U18	7	....	....	....	415	60	0	8.67	....	....	....	....	....	....	....
	HC Vitkovice Jr.	CzRep-Jr.	1	....	....	....	60	1	0	1.00	....	....	....	....	....	....	....
2010-11	HC Vitkovice U18	CzR-U18	13	....	....	....	783	31	1	2.38	4	....	....	243	8	0	1.98
	HC Vitkovice Jr.	CzRep-Jr.	37	....	....	....	2074	95	3	2.75	1	....	....	60	3	0	3.00
2011-12	Red Deer Rebels	WHL	25	14	10	1	1466	67	1	2.74	....	....	....	....	....	....	....
2012-13	Red Deer Rebels	WHL	55	33	14	5	3134	118	5	2.26	9	5	4	548	18	1	1.97
2013-14	Red Deer Rebels	WHL	*65	33	26	5	*3747	175	*8	2.80	....	....	....	....	....	....	....
	Manchester	AHL	4	3	1	0	205	6	1	1.75	....	....	....	....	....	....	....
2014-15	Manchester	AHL	28	13	8	5	1595	57	2	2.14	3	2	1	170	6	0	2.11

WHL East First All-Star Team (2013) • Canadian Major Junior Goaltender of the Year (2013) • WHL East Second All-Star Team (2014)

BEDNARD, Ryan (BEHD-nahrd, RIGH-uhn) FLA

Goaltender. Catches left. 6'4", 179 lbs. Born, Macomb, MI, March 31, 1997.
(Florida's 8th choice, 206th overall, in 2015 Entry Draft).

			Regular Season								Playoffs						
Season	Club	League	GP	W	L	O/T	Mins	GA	SO	Avg	GP	W	L	Mins	GA	SO	Avg
2013-14	Det. Vic. Honda	T1EHL	18	12	6	0	933	28	4	1.62	....	....	....	....	....	....	....
2014-15	Johnstown	NAHL	37	16	16	5	2184	97	1	2.66	....	....	....	....	....	....	....
	Youngstown	USHL	1	0	1	0	59	4	0	4.08	....	....	....	....	....	....	....

• Signed Letter of Intent to attend **Bowling Green State University** (WCHA) in fall of 2016.

BERGVIK, Fredrik (BAIRG-vihk, FREHD-RIHK) S.J.

Goaltender. Catches left. 6'1", 175 lbs. Born, Stockholm, Sweden, February 14, 1995.
(San Jose's 3rd choice, 117th overall, in 2013 Entry Draft).

			Regular Season								Playoffs						
Season	Club	League	GP	W	L	O/T	Mins	GA	SO	Avg	GP	W	L	Mins	GA	SO	Avg
2010-11	Djurgarden U18	Swe-U18	1	....	....	....	60	1	0	1.00	....	....	....	....	....	....	....
2011-12	Frolunda U18	Swe-U18	21	....	....	....	1259	47	4	2.24	....	....	....	....	....	....	....
2012-13	Frolunda U18	Swe-U18	8	5	2	0	465	20	1	2.58	3	1	1	145	11	0	4.55
	Frolunda Jr.	Swe-Jr.	14	12	1	0	834	18	4	1.29	....	....	....	....	....	....	....
2013-14	Frolunda	Sweden	1	0	0	0	34	3	0	5.34	....	....	....	....	....	....	....
	Frolunda Jr.	Swe-Jr.	32	23	9	0	1916	83	3	2.60	3	1	2	178	9	0	3.03
2014-15	Frolunda Jr.	Swe-Jr.	27	17	10	0	1541	60	1	2.34	5	3	2	272	17	0	3.75

BERNIER, Jonathan (BUHRN-yay, JAWN-ah-thuhn) TOR

Goaltender. Catches left. 6', 185 lbs. Born, Laval, QC, August 7, 1988.
(Los Angeles' 1st choice, 11th overall, in 2006 Entry Draft).

			Regular Season								Playoffs						
Season	Club	League	GP	W	L	O/T	Mins	GA	SO	Avg	GP	W	L	Mins	GA	SO	Avg
2003-04	Laval Regents	QAAA	27	16	4	0	1329	62	2	2.80	3	1	2	180	5	0	1.67
2004-05	Lewiston	QMJHL	23	7	12	3	1353	67	0	2.97	1	0	0	20	0	0	0.00
2005-06	Lewiston	QMJHL	54	27	26	0	3241	146	2	2.70	6	2	4	359	17	1	2.84
2006-07	Lewiston	QMJHL	37	26	10	0	2186	94	2	2.58	17	*16	1	1025	40	1	2.34
2007-08	**Los Angeles**	**NHL**	**4**	**1**	**3**	**0**	**238**	**16**	**0**	**4.03**	....	....	....	....	....	....	....
	Lewiston	QMJHL	34	18	15	0	2024	92	0	2.73	6	2	4	348	17	0	2.93
	Manchester	AHL	3	1	1	1	184	5	0	1.63	3	0	3	195	9	0	2.76
2008-09	Manchester	AHL	54	23	24	4	3101	124	5	2.40	....	....	....	....	....	....	....
2009-10	**Los Angeles**	**NHL**	**3**	**3**	**0**	**0**	**185**	**4**	**1**	**1.30**	....	....	....	....	....	....	....
	Manchester	AHL	58	30	21	6	3424	116	*9	2.03	16	10	6	996	30	*3	*1.81
2010-11	**Los Angeles**	**NHL**	**25**	**11**	**8**	**3**	**1378**	**57**	**3**	**2.48**	....	....	....	....	....	....	....
2011-12 ◆	**Los Angeles**	**NHL**	**16**	**5**	**6**	**2**	**890**	**35**	**1**	**2.36**	....	....	....	....	....	....	....
2012-13	Heilbronner Falken	German-2	13	6	7	0	793	34	1	2.57	....	....	....	....	....	....	....
	Los Angeles	**NHL**	**14**	**9**	**3**	**1**	**768**	**24**	**1**	**1.88**	**1**	**0**	**0**	**30**	**0**	**0**	**0.00**
2013-14	**Toronto**	**NHL**	**55**	**26**	**19**	**7**	**3084**	**138**	**1**	**2.68**	....	....	....	....	....	....	....
2014-15	**Toronto**	**NHL**	**58**	**21**	**28**	**7**	**3177**	**152**	**2**	**2.87**	....	....	....	....	....	....	....
	NHL Totals		**175**	**76**	**67**	**20**	**9720**	**426**	**9**	**2.63**	**1**	**0**	**0**	**30**	**0**	**0**	**0.00**

QMJHL Second All-Star Team (2007) • Canadian Major Junior Second All-Star Team (2007) • AHL First All-Star Team (2010) • Aldege "Baz" Bastien Award (AHL – Outstanding Goaltender) (2010)

Signed as a free agent by **Heilbronner** (German-2), October 10, 2012. Traded to **Toronto** by **Los Angeles** for Ben Scrivens, Matt Frattin and Toronto's 2nd round choice (later traded to Columbus, later traded back to Toronto – Toronto selected Travis Dermott) in 2015 Entry Draft, June 23, 2013.

BERRA, Reto (BAIR-uh, REH-toh) COL

Goaltender. Catches left. 6'4", 210 lbs. Born, Bulach, Switz., January 3, 1987.
(St. Louis' 6th choice, 106th overall, in 2006 Entry Draft).

			Regular Season								Playoffs						
Season	Club	League	GP	W	L	O/T	Mins	GA	SO	Avg	GP	W	L	Mins	GA	SO	Avg
2004-05	GCK Zurich Jr.	Swiss-Jr.	22	....	....	....	....	....	....	....	....	....	....	....	....	....	....
	GCK Lions Zurich	Swiss-2	3	....	....	....	180	12	0	4.00	....	....	....	....	....	....	....
	EHC Dubendorf	Swiss-3					Statistics Not Available										
2005-06	GCK Zurich Jr.	Swiss-Jr.	23	....	....	....	....	....	....	....	....	....	....	....	....	....	....
	GCK Lions Zurich	Swiss-2	15	....	....	....	835	51	1	3.56	....	....	....	....	....	....	....
	ZSC Lions Zurich	Swiss	2	0	1	0	90	6	0	3.99	....	....	....	....	....	....	....
2006-07	Switzerland U20	Swiss-2	3	0	3	0	179	13	0	4.69	....	....	....	....	....	....	....
	GCK Lions Zurich	Swiss-2	6	4	2	0	359	18	0	3.01	....	....	....	....	....	....	....
	ZSC Lions Zurich	Swiss	2	1	0	0	78	4	0	3.08	4	0	3	188	9	0	2.87
2007-08	HC Davos	Swiss	16	9	7	0	966	44	0	2.73	....	....	....	....	....	....	....
2008-09	EV Zug	Swiss	6	1	5	0	368	17	0	2.77	....	....	....	....	....	....	....
	SCL Tigers Langnau	Swiss	2	1	1	0	120	9	0	4.50	....	....	....	....	....	....	....
	HC Davos	Swiss	8	3	4	0	445	20	0	2.70	4	3	1	216	5	0	1.39
2009-10	EHC Biel-Bienne	Swiss	40	16	20	0	2319	130	3	3.36	10	3	7	582	33	0	3.40
	EHC Biel-Bienne	Swiss-Q	....	....	....	....	....	....	....	....	7	4	3	419	20	0	2.86
2010-11	EHC Biel-Bienne	Swiss	41	17	24	0	2452	122	3	2.99	....	....	....	....	....	....	....
2011-12	EHC Biel-Bienne	Swiss	49	23	26	0	2865	117	7	2.45	5	1	4	302	18	0	3.57
2012-13	EHC Biel-Bienne	Swiss	49	24	25	0	*2973	149	3	3.01	7	3	4	455	24	0	3.17
2013-14	**Calgary**	**NHL**	**29**	**9**	**17**	**2**	**1648**	**81**	**0**	**2.95**	....	....	....	....	....	....	....
	Abbotsford Heat	AHL	9	4	3	1	473	21	0	2.66	....	....	....	....	....	....	....
	Switzerland	Olympics	1	0	1	0	59	1	0	1.02	....	....	....	....	....	....	....
	Colorado	**NHL**	**2**	**0**	**1**	**1**	**72**	**7**	**0**	**5.83**	....	....	....	....	....	....	....
2014-15	**Colorado**	**NHL**	**19**	**5**	**4**	**1**	**748**	**33**	**1**	**2.65**	....	....	....	....	....	....	....
	Lake Erie Monsters	AHL	5	3	1	1	303	13	0	2.57	....	....	....	....	....	....	....
	NHL Totals		**50**	**14**	**22**	**4**	**2468**	**121**	**1**	**2.94**	....	....	....	....	....	....	....

Traded to **Calgary** by **St. Louis** with Mark Cundari and St. Louis' 1st round choice (Emile Poirier) in 2013 Entry Draft for Jay Bouwmeester, April 1, 2013. Traded to **Colorado** by **Calgary** for Colorado's 2nd round choice (Hunter Smith) in 2014 Entry Draft, March 5, 2014.

BERUBE, Jean-Francois (beh-ROO-bay, ZHAWN-fran-SWUH) L.A.

Goaltender. Catches left. 6'1", 177 lbs. Born, Repentigny, QC, July 13, 1991.
(Los Angeles' 4th choice, 95th overall, in 2009 Entry Draft).

			Regular Season								Playoffs						
Season	Club	League	GP	W	L	O/T	Mins	GA	SO	Avg	GP	W	L	Mins	GA	SO	Avg
2007-08	Laurentides	QAAA	10	0	6	1	511	35	0	4.11	....	....	....	....	....	....	....
	Lachute Stars	QueAA					STATISTICS NOT AVAILABLE										
2008-09	Montreal	QMJHL	20	6	9	0	1059	51	1	2.89	1	0	0	20	1	0	3.00
2009-10	Montreal	QMJHL	45	17	23	0	2394	121	1	3.03	7	3	4	449	18	0	2.40
	Manchester	AHL	3	2	1	0	180	11	0	3.67	....	....	....	....	....	....	....
2010-11	Montreal	QMJHL	50	32	7	8	2935	127	3	2.60	10	6	4	623	29	*2	2.79
2011-12	Ontario Reign	ECHL	37	17	13	4	2091	100	4	2.87	4	1	2	206	11	0	3.20
2012-13	Ontario Reign	ECHL	24	15	6	2	1418	53	1	2.24	10	6	4	608	21	1	2.07
	Manchester	AHL	2	0	2	0	97	7	0	4.32	....	....	....	....	....	....	....
2013-14	Manchester	AHL	48	28	17	2	2790	110	3	2.37	4	1	3	252	7	1	1.67
2014-15	Manchester	AHL	52	37	9	4	3025	110	2	2.18	17	13	3	1019	39	0	2.30

BESKOROWANY, Tyler (behs-koor-WAH-nee, TIGH-luhr)

Goaltender. Catches left. 6'5", 205 lbs. Born, Sudbury, ON, April 28, 1990.
(Dallas' 1st choice, 59th overall, in 2008 Entry Draft).

			Regular Season								Playoffs						
Season	Club	League	GP	W	L	O/T	Mins	GA	SO	Avg	GP	W	L	Mins	GA	SO	Avg
2006-07	Valley East Cobras	GNML	32	....	....	....	1443	80	1	3.33	7	....	....	410	22	2	3.22
2007-08	Owen Sound	OHL	35	12	19	3	2021	136	0	4.04	....	....	....	....	....	....	....
2008-09	Owen Sound	OHL	37	11	12	10	2160	131	1	3.64	1	0	1	27	5	0	11.16
2009-10	Kingston	OHL	62	29	25	4	3461	203	1	3.52	7	3	4	424	23	0	3.26
2010-11	Texas Stars	AHL	18	7	8	1	978	42	1	2.58	1	0	0	20	1	0	3.00
	Idaho Steelheads	ECHL	20	10	5	4	1149	45	1	2.35	....	....	....	....	....	....	....
2011-12	Texas Stars	AHL	33	10	19	0	1769	100	1	3.39	....	....	....	....	....	....	....
2012-13	Idaho Steelheads	ECHL	32	17	12	3	1901	88	2	2.78	6	4	1	319	14	1	2.63
2013-14	St. John's IceCaps	AHL	12	7	2	2	683	25	0	2.20	....	....	....	....	....	....	....
	San Francisco Bulls	ECHL	32	14	13	3	1763	99	0	3.37	....	....	....	....	....	....	....
	Orlando	ECHL	2	2	0	0	120	3	0	1.50	....	....	....	....	....	....	....
2014-15	Dusseldorfer EG	Germany	42	26	15	0	2441	103	0	2.53	12	5	7	730	35	0	2.88

Signed as a free agent by **Springfield** (AHL), June 17, 2015.

BIBEAU, Antoine (Bee-BOH, an-TWAHN) TOR

Goaltender. Catches left. 6'3", 207 lbs. Born, Victoriaville, QC, May 1, 1994.
(Toronto's 4th choice, 172nd overall, in 2013 Entry Draft).

			Regular Season								Playoffs						
Season	Club	League	GP	W	L	O/T	Mins	GA	SO	Avg	GP	W	L	Mins	GA	SO	Avg
2009-10	Trois-Rivieres	QAAA	22	8	4	3	1023	59	0	3.46	2	0	1	79	4	0	3.05
2010-11	Trois-Rivieres	QAAA	29	16	8	2	1521	83	0	3.27	5	2	3	266	21	0	4.74
	Lewiston	QMJHL	3	2	0	0	144	5	0	2.10	....	....	....	....	....	....	....
2011-12	P.E.I. Rocket	QMJHL	29	7	9	1	1183	88	0	4.46	....	....	....	....	....	....	....
2012-13	P.E.I. Rocket	QMJHL	46	28	11	3	2521	118	*5	2.81	6	2	4	374	21	0	3.37
2013-14	Charlottetown	QMJHL	26	8	11	5	1424	78	1	3.29	....	....	....	....	....	....	....
	Val-d'Or Foreurs	QMJHL	22	13	7	1	1267	64	1	3.03	*24	*16	8	*1476	69	1	2.80
2014-15	Toronto Marlies	AHL	31	15	10	5	1809	81	4	2.69	1	0	1	57	3	0	3.13

Memorial Cup All-Star Team (2014) • Hap Emms Memorial Trophy (Memorial Cup - Top Goaltender) (2014)

BINNINGTON, Jordan (BIHN-ihng-tuhn, JOHR-duhn) ST.L.

Goaltender. Catches left. 6'1", 167 lbs. Born, Richmond Hill, ON, July 11, 1993.
(St. Louis' 4th choice, 88th overall, in 2011 Entry Draft).

			Regular Season								Playoffs						
Season	Club	League	GP	W	L	O/T	Mins	GA	SO	Avg	GP	W	L	Mins	GA	SO	Avg
2008-09	Vaughan Kings	GTHL	....	34	15	....	....	....	....	2.18	....	....	....	....	....	....	....
	Dixie Beehives	ON-Jr.A	1	0	1	0	59	3	0	3.04	....	....	....	....	....	....	....
2009-10	Owen Sound	OHL	22	6	10	2	1068	78	0	4.38	....	....	....	....	....	....	....
2010-11	Owen Sound	OHL	46	27	12	5	2596	132	1	3.05	7	4	2	355	19	0	3.21
2011-12	Owen Sound	OHL	39	21	17	1	2304	115	1	2.99	2	0	2	120	10	0	5.00
	Peoria Rivermen	AHL	1	0	1	0	60	3	0	3.02	....	....	....	....	....	....	....
2012-13	Owen Sound	OHL	50	32	12	6	3011	109	*7	2.17	12	6	6	705	33	0	2.81
2013-14	Kalamazoo Wings	ECHL	40	23	13	3	2398	94	1	2.35	3	1	2	223	7	0	1.89
	Chicago Wolves	AHL	1	1	0	0	65	3	0	2.78	....	....	....	....	....	....	....
2014-15	Chicago Wolves	AHL	45	25	15	1	2555	100	3	2.35	5	2	3	333	12	0	2.16

Memorial Cup All-Star Team (2011) • Hap Emms Memorial Trophy (Memorial Cup – Top Goaltender) (2011) • OHL First All-Star Team (2013)

BISHOP, Ben (BIH-shuhp, BEHN) T.B.

Goaltender. Catches left. 6'7", 214 lbs. Born, Denver, CO, November 21, 1986.
(St. Louis' 3rd choice, 85th overall, in 2005 Entry Draft).

			Regular Season								Playoffs						
Season	Club	League	GP	W	L	O/T	Mins	GA	SO	Avg	GP	W	L	Mins	GA	SO	Avg
2003-04	St.L. AAA Blues	MAHL	11	8	1	2	660	19	1	1.73	....	....	....	....	....	....	....
	St.L. AAA Blues	Other	26	15	7	4	1480	62	3	2.51	....	....	....	....	....	....	....
2004-05	Texas Tornado	NAHL	45	*35	8	0	2577	83	5	1.93	*11	*9	2	*660	30	0	2.73
2005-06	University of Maine	H-East	31	21	8	2	1788	68	0	2.28	....	....	....	....	....	....	....
2006-07	University of Maine	H-East	34	21	9	2	1907	68	3	2.14	....	....	....	....	....	....	....
2007-08	University of Maine	H-East	34	13	18	3	1972	80	2	2.43	....	....	....	....	....	....	....
	Peoria Rivermen	AHL	5	2	2	1	302	12	0	2.38	....	....	....	....	....	....	....
2008-09	**St. Louis**	**NHL**	**6**	**1**	**1**	**1**	**245**	**12**	**0**	**2.94**	....	....	....	....	....	....	....
	Peoria Rivermen	AHL	33	15	16	1	1898	89	1	2.81	....	....	....	....	....	....	....
2009-10	Peoria Rivermen	AHL	48	23	18	4	2793	129	0	2.77	....	....	....	....	....	....	....
2010-11	**St. Louis**	**NHL**	**7**	**3**	**4**	**0**	**369**	**17**	**1**	**2.76**	....	....	....	....	....	....	....
	Peoria Rivermen	AHL	35	17	14	2	2043	87	2	2.55	1	0	1	59	2	0	2.04
2011-12	Peoria Rivermen	AHL	38	24	14	0	2258	85	*6	2.26	....	....	....	....	....	....	....
	Ottawa	**NHL**	**10**	**3**	**3**	**2**	**532**	**22**	**0**	**2.48**	....	....	....	....	....	....	....
	Binghamton	AHL	3	2	1	0	179	7	0	2.35	....	....	....	....	....	....	....
2012-13	Binghamton	AHL	13	8	3	2	787	34	0	2.59	....	....	....	....	....	....	....
	Ottawa	**NHL**	**13**	**8**	**5**	**0**	**758**	**31**	**1**	**2.45**	....	....	....	....	....	....	....
	Tampa Bay	**NHL**	**9**	**3**	**4**	**1**	**502**	**25**	**1**	**2.99**	....	....	....	....	....	....	....
2013-14	**Tampa Bay**	**NHL**	**63**	**37**	**14**	**7**	**3586**	**133**	**5**	**2.23**	....	....	....	....	....	....	....
2014-15	**Tampa Bay**	**NHL**	**62**	**40**	**13**	**5**	**3519**	**136**	**4**	**2.32**	**25**	**13**	**11**	**1459**	**53**	**3**	**2.18**
	NHL Totals		**170**	**95**	**44**	**16**	**9511**	**376**	**12**	**2.37**	**25**	**13**	**11**	**1459**	**53**	**3**	**2.18**

Hockey East All-Rookie Team (2006) • Hockey East Second All-Star Team (2008) • AHL Second All-Star Team (2012)

Traded to **Ottawa** by **St. Louis** for Ottawa's 2nd round choice (Thomas Vannelli) in 2013 Entry Draft, February 26. 2012. Traded to **Tampa Bay** by **Ottawa** for Cory Conacher and Philadelphia's 4th round choice (previously acquired, Ottawa selected Tobias Lindberg) in 2013 Entry Draft, April 3, 2013.

BLACKWOOD, Mackenzie (BLAK-wud, muh-KEHN-zee) N.J.

Goaltender. Catches left. 6'4", 215 lbs. Born, Thunder Bay, ON, December 9, 1996.
(New Jersey's 2nd choice, 42nd overall, in 2015 Entry Draft).

			Regular Season								Playoffs						
Season	Club	League	GP	W	L	O/T	Mins	GA	SO	Avg	GP	W	L	Mins	GA	SO	Avg
2011-12	Thunder Bay Kings	Minor-ON	38	15	13	2	1766	121	1	3.08	....	....	....	....	....	....	....
2012-13	Elmira Sugar Kings	ON-Jr.B	24	10	8	2	1309	74	0	3.39	....	....	....	....	....	....	....
2013-14	Barrie Colts	OHL	45	23	15	2	2497	124	1	2.98	10	5	4	552	24	1	2.61
2014-15	Barrie Colts	OHL	51	33	14	2	2953	152	2	3.09	9	5	4	562	27	0	2.88

OHL All-Rookie Team (2014)

BOBROVSKY, Sergei (bawb-RAWF-skee, SAIR-gay) CBJ

Goaltender. Catches left. 6'2", 182 lbs. Born, Novokuznetsk, USSR, September 20, 1988.

			Regular Season								Playoffs						
Season	Club	League	GP	W	L	O/T	Mins	GA	SO	Avg	GP	W	L	Mins	GA	SO	Avg
2006-07	Novokuznetsk	Russia	8	....	....	....	280	13	0	2.78	....	....	....	....	....	....	....
2007-08	Novokuznetsk	Russia	24	....	....	....	1153	57	1	2.97	....	....	....	....	....	....	....
2008-09	Novokuznetsk	KHL	32	....	....	....	1636	69	1	2.53	....	....	....	....	....	....	....
2009-10	Novokuznetsk	KHL	35	....	....	....	1964	89	1	2.72	....	....	....	....	....	....	....
2010-11	**Philadelphia**	**NHL**	**54**	**28**	**13**	**8**	**3017**	**130**	**0**	**2.59**	**6**	**0**	**2**	**186**	**10**	**0**	**3.23**
2011-12	**Philadelphia**	**NHL**	**29**	**14**	**10**	**2**	**1550**	**78**	**0**	**3.02**	**1**	**0**	**0**	**37**	**5**	**0**	**8.11**
2012-13	SKA St. Petersburg	KHL	24	18	3	0	1420	46	4	1.94	....	....	....	....	....	....	....
	Columbus	**NHL**	**38**	**21**	**11**	**6**	**2219**	**74**	**4**	**2.00**	....	....	....	....	....	....	....
2013-14	**Columbus**	**NHL**	**58**	**32**	**20**	**5**	**3299**	**131**	**5**	**2.38**	**6**	**2**	**4**	**378**	**20**	**0**	**3.17**
	Russia	Olympics	3	....	....	....	157	3	....	1.15	....	....	....	....	....	....	....
2014-15	**Columbus**	**NHL**	**51**	**30**	**17**	**3**	**2994**	**134**	**2**	**2.69**	....	....	....	....	....	....	....
	NHL Totals		**230**	**125**	**71**	**24**	**13079**	**547**	**11**	**2.51**	**13**	**2**	**6**	**601**	**35**	**0**	**3.49**

NHL First All-Star Team (2013) • Vezina Trophy (2013)

Signed as a free agent by **Philadelphia**, May 6, 2010. Traded to **Columbus** by **Philadelphia** for Ottawa's 2nd round choice (previously acquired, Philadelphia selected Anthony Stolarz) in 2012 Entry Draft, Vancouver's 4th round choice (previously acquired, Philadelphia selected Taylor Leier) in 2012 Entry Draft and Phoenix's 4th round choice (previously acquired, later traded to Los Angeles – Los Angeles selected Justin Auger) in 2013 Entry Draft, June 22, 2012. Signed as a free agent by **St. Petersburg** (KHL), September 21, 2012.

BOOTH, Callum (BOOTH, KAL-uhm) CAR

Goaltender. Catches left. 6'3", 201 lbs. Born, Montreal, QC, May 21, 1997.
(Carolina's 3rd choice, 93rd overall, in 2015 Entry Draft).

			Regular Season								Playoffs						
Season	Club	League	GP	W	L	O/T	Mins	GA	SO	Avg	GP	W	L	Mins	GA	SO	Avg
2012-13	Salisbury School	High-CT	....	....	....	....	1200	41	....	2.08	....	....	....	....	....	....	....
2013-14	Quebec Remparts	QMJHL	25	11	5	3	1120	50	1	2.68	1	0	1	59	5	0	5.08
2014-15	Quebec Remparts	QMJHL	41	23	13	2	2280	116	2	3.05	4	1	1	169	7	1	2.49

BOUCHARD, Keven (BOO-shahrd, KEH-vuhn) EDM

Goaltender. Catches left. 6'2", 205 lbs. Born, Alma, QC, April 19, 1996.
(Edmonton's 6th choice, 183rd overall, in 2014 Entry Draft).

			Regular Season								Playoffs						
Season	Club	League	GP	W	L	O/T	Mins	GA	SO	Avg	GP	W	L	Mins	GA	SO	Avg
2010-11							STATISTICS NOT AVAILABLE										
	Jonquiere Elites	QAAA	2	0	1	0	77	5	0	3.88	....	....	....	....	....	....	....
2011-12	Jonquiere Elites	QAAA	21	7	9	3	1178	55	2	2.80	3	1	2	151	5	0	1.98
2012-13	Jonquiere Elites	QAAA	25	10	8	5	1356	85	0	3.76	8	4	4	499	23	0	2.76
2013-14	Val-d'Or Foreurs	QMJHL	27	17	6	1	1462	72	2	2.95	1	0	0	14	1	0	4.27
2014-15	Val-d'Or Foreurs	QMJHL	36	15	13	5	1948	125	1	3.85	4	0	2	134	9	0	4.03

BRITTAIN, Sam (brih-TAYN, SAM) FLA

Goaltender. Catches left. 6'3", 229 lbs. Born, Calgary, AB, May 10, 1992.
(Florida's 8th choice, 92nd overall, in 2010 Entry Draft).

			Regular Season								Playoffs						
Season	Club	League	GP	W	L	O/T	Mins	GA	SO	Avg	GP	W	L	Mins	GA	SO	Avg
2008-09	Calgary Buffaloes	AMHL	26	14	9	3	1542	67	....	2.61	15	11	4	901	45	....	3.00
	Canmore Eagles	AJHL	3	1	2	0	179	9	0	3.02	....	....	....	....	....	....	....
2009-10	Canmore Eagles	AJHL	52	23	19	8	3065	167	2	3.27	9	5	4	559	28	0	3.01
2010-11	U. of Denver	WCHA	33	19	9	5	1998	76	1	2.28	....	....	....	....	....	....	....
2011-12	U. of Denver	WCHA	12	8	4	0	736	29	1	2.36	....	....	....	....	....	....	....
2012-13	U. of Denver	WCHA	13	5	7	0	752	37	0	2.95	....	....	....	....	....	....	....
2013-14	U. of Denver	NCHC	*39	19	14	6	*2348	87	*5	2.22	....	....	....	....	....	....	....
2014-15	San Antonio	AHL	7	4	2	1	374	11	1	1.76	....	....	....	....	....	....	....
	Cincinnati	ECHL	27	14	11	1	1547	70	4	2.71	....	....	....	....	....	....	....

WCHA All-Rookie Team (2011) • NCHC First All-Star Team (2014) • NCAA West First All-American Team (2014)

BRODEUR, Martin (broh-DUHR, MAHR-tihn)

Goaltender. Catches left. 6'2", 220 lbs. Born, Montreal, QC, May 6, 1972.
(New Jersey's 1st choice, 20th overall, in 1990 Entry Draft).

			Regular Season								Playoffs						
Season	Club	League	GP	W	L	O/T	Mins	GA	SO	Avg	GP	W	L	Mins	GA	SO	Avg
1988-89	Montreal-Bourassa	QAAA	27	13	12	1	1580	98	0	3.72	4	0	3	210	14	0	3.99
1989-90	St-Hyacinthe Laser	QMJHL	42	23	12	2	2331	156	0	4.02	12	5	7	680	46	0	4.06
1990-91	St-Hyacinthe Laser	QMJHL	52	22	22	4	2946	162	2	3.30	4	0	4	232	16	0	4.14
1991-92	St-Hyacinthe Laser	QMJHL	48	27	14	4	2846	161	2	3.39	5	2	3	317	14	0	2.65
	New Jersey	**NHL**	**4**	**2**	**1**	**0**	**179**	**10**	**0**	**3.35**	**1**	**0**	**1**	**32**	**3**	**0**	**5.63**
1992-93	Utica Devils	AHL	32	14	13	5	1952	131	0	4.03	4	1	3	258	18	0	4.19
1993-94	**New Jersey**	**NHL**	**47**	**27**	**11**	**8**	**2625**	**105**	**3**	**2.40**	**17**	**8**	**9**	**1171**	**38**	**1**	**1.95**
1994-95 ♦	**New Jersey**	**NHL**	**40**	**19**	**11**	**6**	**2184**	**89**	**3**	**2.45**	***20**	***16**	**4**	***1222**	**34**	***3**	***1.67**
1995-96	**New Jersey**	**NHL**	**77**	**34**	**30**	**12**	***4433**	**173**	**6**	**2.34**	....	....	....	....	....	....	....
1996-97	**New Jersey**	**NHL**	**67**	**37**	**14**	**13**	**3838**	**120**	***10**	***1.88**	**10**	**5**	**5**	**659**	**19**	**2**	***1.73**
1997-98	**New Jersey**	**NHL**	**70**	***43**	**17**	**8**	**4128**	**130**	**10**	**1.89**	**6**	**2**	**4**	**366**	**12**	**0**	**1.97**
1998-99	**New Jersey**	**NHL**	***70**	***39**	**21**	**10**	***4239**	**162**	**4**	**2.29**	**7**	**3**	**4**	**425**	**20**	**0**	**2.82**
99-2000 ♦	**New Jersey**	**NHL**	**72**	***43**	**20**	**8**	**4312**	**161**	**6**	**2.24**	***23**	***16**	**7**	***1450**	**39**	**2**	***1.61**
2000-01	**New Jersey**	**NHL**	**72**	***42**	**17**	**11**	**4297**	**166**	**9**	**2.32**	***25**	**15**	**10**	***1505**	**52**	***4**	**2.07**
2001-02	**New Jersey**	**NHL**	***73**	**38**	**26**	**9**	***4347**	**156**	**4**	**2.15**	**6**	**2**	**4**	**381**	**9**	**1**	**1.42**
	Canada	Olympics	5	*4	0	1	300	9	0	*1.80	....	....	....	....	....	....	....
2002-03 ♦	**New Jersey**	**NHL**	**73**	***41**	**23**	**9**	**4374**	**147**	***9**	**2.02**	***24**	***16**	**8**	***1491**	**41**	***7**	**1.65**
2003-04	**New Jersey**	**NHL**	***75**	***38**	**26**	**11**	***4555**	**154**	***11**	**2.03**	**5**	**1**	**4**	**298**	**13**	**0**	**2.62**
2004-05							DID NOT PLAY										
2005-06	**New Jersey**	**NHL**	**73**	***43**	**23**	**7**	**4365**	**187**	**5**	**2.57**	**9**	**5**	**4**	**533**	**20**	**1**	**2.25**
	Canada	Olympics	4	2	2	0	239	8	0	2.01	....	....	....	....	....	....	....
2006-07	**New Jersey**	**NHL**	***78**	***48**	**23**	**7**	***4697**	**171**	***12**	**2.18**	**11**	**5**	**6**	**688**	**28**	**1**	**2.44**
2007-08	**New Jersey**	**NHL**	***77**	**44**	**27**	**6**	***4635**	**168**	**4**	**2.17**	**5**	**1**	**4**	**301**	**16**	**0**	**3.19**
2008-09	**New Jersey**	**NHL**	**31**	**19**	**9**	**3**	**1814**	**73**	**5**	**2.41**	**7**	**3**	**4**	**427**	**17**	**1**	**2.39**
2009-10	**New Jersey**	**NHL**	***77**	***45**	**25**	**6**	***4499**	**168**	***9**	**2.24**	**5**	**1**	**4**	**299**	**15**	**0**	**3.01**
	Canada	Olympics	2	1	1	0	124	6	0	2.90	....	....	....	....	....	....	....
2010-11	**New Jersey**	**NHL**	**56**	**23**	**26**	**3**	**3116**	**127**	**6**	**2.45**	....	....	....	....	....	....	....

2011-12	New Jersey	NHL	59	31	21	4	3392	136	3	2.41	*24	14	9	*1471	52	1	2.12
2012-13	New Jersey	NHL	29	13	9	7	1757	65	2	2.22	....	....	....	....	....	....	....
2013-14	New Jersey	NHL	39	19	14	6	2297	96	3	2.51	....	....	....	....	....	....	....
2014-15	St. Louis	NHL	7	3	3	0	356	17	1	2.87	....	....	....	....	....	....	....
	NHL Totals		*1266	*691	*397	154	*74439	*2781	*125	2.24	205	113	91	12719	428	*24	2.02

QMJHL All-Rookie Team (1990) • QMJHL Second All-Star Team (1992) • NHL All-Rookie Team (1994) • Calder Memorial Trophy (1994) • NHL Second All-Star Team (1997, 1998, 2006, 2008) • William M. Jennings Trophy (1997) (shared with Mike Dunham) • William M. Jennings Trophy (1998, 2004, 2010) • NHL First All-Star Team (2003, 2004, 2007) • William M. Jennings Trophy (2003) (tied with Roman Cechmanek/Robert Esche) • Vezina Trophy (2003, 2004, 2007, 2008)

Played in NHL All-Star Game (1996, 1997, 1998, 1999, 2000, 2001, 2003, 2004, 2007)

• Scored a goal in playoffs vs. Montreal, April 17, 1997. • Missed majority of 2008-09 due to elbow injury vs. Atlanta, November 1, 2008. Signed to a PTO (professional tryout) contract by **St. Louis**, November 26, 2014. Signed as a free agent by **St. Louis**, December 2, 2014. • Officially announced his retirement, January 29, 2015.

BROSSOIT, Laurent (BRAH-sah, LAWR-ehnt) EDM

Goaltender. Catches left. 6'3", 202 lbs. Born, Port Alberni, BC, March 23, 1993.
(Calgary's 5th choice, 164th overall, in 2011 Entry Draft).

			Regular Season								Playoffs						
Season	Club	League	GP	W	L	O/T	Mins	GA	SO	Avg	GP	W	L	Mins	GA	SO	Avg
2008-09	Valley West Hawks	BCMML	STATISTICS NOT AVAILABLE														
	Edmonton	WHL	1	0	0	0	37	5	0	8.11	....	....	....	....	....	....	....
2009-10	Cowichan Valley	BCHL	21	10	8	0	999	61	2	3.66	5	1	3	259	17	0	3.93
	Edmonton	WHL	2	0	1	0	86	4	0	2.79	....	....	....	....	....	....	....
2010-11	Edmonton	WHL	34	13	12	2	1664	92	2	3.32	2	0	2	117	7	0	3.59
2011-12	Edmonton	WHL	61	*42	13	5	3574	147	3	2.47	20	*16	4	1204	41	*2	*2.04
2012-13	Edmonton	WHL	49	33	8	6	2854	107	5	2.25	*22	14	8	*1322	40	*5	1.82
2013-14	Abbotsford Heat	AHL	2	0	1	0	94	9	0	5.72	....	....	....	....	....	....	....
	Alaska Aces	ECHL	3	*2	0	0	126	0	*2	*0.00	....	....	....	....	....	....	....
	Oklahoma City	AHL	8	2	5	0	416	25	0	3.60	....	....	....	....	....	....	....
	Bakersfield	ECHL	35	*24	9	2	2079	74	*6	*2.14	16	10	6	976	37	*3	2.27
2014-15	**Edmonton**	**NHL**	**1**	**0**	**1**	**0**	**60**	**2**	**0**	**2.00**	....	....	....	....	....	....	....
	Oklahoma City	AHL	53	25	22	4	3049	130	4	2.56	2	1	0	87	5	0	3.46
	NHL Totals		**1**	**0**	**1**	**0**	**60**	**2**	**0**	**2.00**	....	....	....	....	....	....	....

WHL East Second All-Star Team (2013)

Traded to **Edmonton** by **Calgary** with Roman Horak for Olivier Roy and Ladislav Smid, November 8, 2013.

BRYZGALOV, Ilya (breez-GAH-lahf, IHL-yah)

Goaltender. Catches left. 6'3", 213 lbs. Born, Togliatti, USSR, June 22, 1980.
(Anaheim's 2nd choice, 44th overall, in 2000 Entry Draft).

			Regular Season								Playoffs						
Season	Club	League	GP	W	L	O/T	Mins	GA	SO	Avg	GP	W	L	Mins	GA	SO	Avg
1996-97	Lada Togliatti 2	Russia-3	5	....	....	....	....	....	....	....	....	....	....	....	....	....	....
1997-98	Lada Togliatti 2	Russia-3	8	....	....	....	....	28	....	....	....	....	....	....	....	....	....
1998-99	Lada Togliatti 2	Russia-4	20	....	....	....	....	43	....	....	....	....	....	....	....	....	....
99-2000	Spartak Moscow	Russia-2	10	....	....	....	500	21	....	2.52	....	....	....	....	....	....	....
	Lada Togliatti 2	Russia-3	2	....	....	....	....	5	....	....	....	....	....	....	....	....	....
	Lada Togliatti	Russia	14	....	....	....	796	18	3	1.36	7	....	....	407	10	1	1.47
2000-01	Lada Togliatti	Russia	34	....	....	....	1992	61	8	1.84	5	....	....	249	8	0	1.93
2001-02	**Anaheim**	**NHL**	**1**	**0**	**0**	**0**	**32**	**1**	**0**	**1.88**	....	....	....	....	....	....	....
	Cincinnati	AHL	45	20	16	4	2399	99	4	2.48	....	....	....	....	....	....	....
	Russia	Olympics	DID NOT PLAY – SPARE GOALTENDER														
2002-03	Cincinnati	AHL	54	12	26	9	3020	142	1	2.82	....	....	....	....	....	....	....
2003-04	**Anaheim**	**NHL**	**1**	**1**	**0**	**0**	**60**	**2**	**0**	**2.00**	....	....	....	....	....	....	....
	Cincinnati	AHL	*64	27	25	10	*3748	145	6	2.32	9	5	4	536	27	1	3.02
2004-05	Cincinnati	AHL	36	17	13	1	2007	87	4	2.60	7	3	3	314	13	0	2.48
2005-06	**Anaheim**	**NHL**	**31**	**13**	**12**	**1**	**1575**	**66**	**1**	**2.51**	**11**	**6**	**4**	**659**	**16**	***3**	***1.46**
	Russia	Olympics	1	0	1	0	60	5	0	5.00	....	....	....	....	....	....	....
2006-07 ♦	**Anaheim**	**NHL**	**27**	**10**	**8**	**6**	**1509**	**62**	**1**	**2.47**	**5**	**3**	**1**	**267**	**10**	**0**	**2.25**
2007-08	**Anaheim**	**NHL**	**9**	**2**	**3**	**1**	**447**	**19**	**0**	**2.55**	....	....	....	....	....	....	....
	Phoenix	**NHL**	**55**	**26**	**22**	**5**	**3167**	**128**	**3**	**2.43**	....	....	....	....	....	....	....
2008-09	**Phoenix**	**NHL**	**65**	**26**	**31**	**6**	**3760**	**187**	**3**	**2.98**	....	....	....	....	....	....	....
2009-10	**Phoenix**	**NHL**	**69**	**42**	**20**	**6**	**4084**	**156**	**8**	**2.29**	**7**	**3**	**4**	**419**	**24**	**0**	**3.44**
	Russia	Olympics	2	0	1	0	101	3	0	1.78	....	....	....	....	....	....	....
2010-11	**Phoenix**	**NHL**	**68**	**36**	**20**	**10**	**4060**	**168**	**7**	**2.48**	**4**	**0**	**4**	**234**	**17**	**0**	**4.36**
2011-12	**Philadelphia**	**NHL**	**59**	**33**	**16**	**7**	**3415**	**141**	**6**	**2.48**	**11**	**5**	**6**	**642**	**37**	**0**	**3.46**
2012-13	CSKA Moscow	KHL	12	6	5	0	647	23	0	2.13	....	....	....	....	....	....	....
	Philadelphia	**NHL**	**40**	**19**	**17**	**3**	**2298**	**107**	**1**	**2.79**	....	....	....	....	....	....	....
2013-14	**Edmonton**	**NHL**	**20**	**5**	**8**	**5**	**1135**	**57**	**1**	**3.01**	....	....	....	....	....	....	....
	Oklahoma City	AHL	2	1	1	0	119	6	0	3.03	....	....	....	....	....	....	....
	Minnesota	**NHL**	**12**	**7**	**1**	**3**	**679**	**24**	**3**	**2.12**	**9**	**3**	**6**	**479**	**21**	**1**	**2.63**
2014-15	**Anaheim**	**NHL**	**8**	**1**	**4**	**1**	**329**	**23**	**0**	**4.19**	....	....	....	....	....	....	....
	Norfolk Admirals	AHL	2	1	1	0	119	5	0	2.53	....	....	....	....	....	....	....
	NHL Totals		**465**	**221**	**162**	**54**	**26550**	**1141**	**34**	**2.58**	**47**	**20**	**25**	**2700**	**125**	**4**	**2.78**

NHL Second All-Star Team (2010)

Claimed on waivers by **Phoenix** from **Anaheim**, November 17, 2007. Traded to **Philadelphia** by **Phoenix** for Matt Clackson, Philadelphia's 3rd round choice (later traded to Pittsburgh – Pittsburgh selected Oskar Sundqvist) in 2012 Entry Draft and future considerations, June 7, 2011. Signed as a free agent by **CSKA Moscow** (KHL), September 19, 2012. Signed as a free agent by **Edmonton**, Novbember 8, 2013. Traded to **Minnesota** by **Edmonton** for Buffalo 4th round choice (previously acquired, Edmonton selected William Lagesson) in 2014 Entry Draft, March 4, 2014. Signed as a free agent by **Anaheim**, December 9, 2014.

BUDAJ, Peter (BOO-digh, PEE-tuhr)

Goaltender. Catches left. 6'1", 192 lbs. Born, Banska Bystrica, Czech., September 18, 1982.
(Colorado's 1st choice, 63rd overall, in 2001 Entry Draft).

			Regular Season								Playoffs						
Season	Club	League	GP	W	L	O/T	Mins	GA	SO	Avg	GP	W	L	Mins	GA	SO	Avg
99-2000	St. Michael's	OHL	34	6	18	1	1676	112	1	4.01	....	....	....	....	....	....	....
2000-01	St. Michael's	OHL	37	17	12	3	1996	95	3	2.86	11	6	4	621	26	1	2.51
2001-02	St. Michael's	OHL	42	26	9	5	2329	89	2	*2.29	12	5	6	621	34	*1	3.29
2002-03	Hershey Bears	AHL	28	10	10	2	1467	65	2	2.66	1	0	0	6	2	0	20.81
2003-04	Hershey Bears	AHL	46	17	20	6	2574	120	3	2.80	....	....	....	....	....	....	....
2004-05	Hershey Bears	AHL	59	29	25	2	3356	148	5	2.65	....	....	....	....	....	....	....
2005-06	**Colorado**	**NHL**	**34**	**14**	**10**	**6**	**1803**	**86**	**2**	**2.86**	....	....	....	....	....	....	....
	Slovakia	Olympics	3	2	1	0	179	6	0	2.01	....	....	....	....	....	....	....
2006-07	**Colorado**	**NHL**	**57**	**31**	**16**	**6**	**3199**	**143**	**3**	**2.68**	....	....	....	....	....	....	....
2007-08	**Colorado**	**NHL**	**35**	**16**	**10**	**4**	**1912**	**82**	**0**	**2.57**	**3**	**0**	**0**	**108**	**6**	**0**	**3.33**
2008-09	**Colorado**	**NHL**	**56**	**20**	**29**	**5**	**3232**	**154**	**2**	**2.86**	....	....	....	....	....	....	....
2009-10	**Colorado**	**NHL**	**15**	**5**	**5**	**2**	**728**	**32**	**1**	**2.64**	**1**	**0**	**0**	**9**	**1**	**0**	**6.67**
	Slovakia	Olympics	DID NOT PLAY – SPARE GOALTENDER														
2010-11	**Colorado**	**NHL**	**45**	**15**	**21**	**4**	**2439**	**130**	**1**	**3.20**	....	....	....	....	....	....	....
2011-12	**Montreal**	**NHL**	**17**	**5**	**7**	**5**	**1037**	**44**	**0**	**2.55**	....	....	....	....	....	....	....
2012-13	**Montreal**	**NHL**	**13**	**8**	**1**	**1**	**656**	**25**	**1**	**2.29**	**2**	**0**	**2**	**63**	**7**	**0**	**6.67**
2013-14	**Montreal**	**NHL**	**24**	**10**	**8**	**3**	**1338**	**56**	**1**	**2.51**	**1**	**0**	**0**	**20**	**3**	**0**	**9.00**
	Slovakia	Olympics	1	0	0	0	27	2	....	4.53	....	....	....	....	....	....	....
2014-15	St. John's IceCaps	AHL	19	0	9	6	913	54	0	3.55	....	....	....	....	....	....	....
	NHL Totals		**296**	**124**	**107**	**36**	**16344**	**752**	**11**	**2.76**	**7**	**0**	**2**	**200**	**17**	**0**	**5.10**

OHL Second All-Star Team (2002)

Signed as a free agent by **Montreal**, July 1, 2011. Traded to **Winnipeg** by **Montreal** with Patrick Holland for Eric Tangradi, October 5, 2014.

BUNZ, Tyler (BUHNZ, TIGH-luhr)

Goaltender. Catches left. 6'21", 205 lbs. Born, Regina, SK, February 11, 1992.
(Edmonton's 7th choice, 121st overall, in 2010 Entry Draft).

			Regular Season								Playoffs						
Season	Club	League	GP	W	L	O/T	Mins	GA	SO	Avg	GP	W	L	Mins	GA	SO	Avg
2007-08	St. Albert	AMHL	24	11	9	4	1503	80	....	3.19	4	2	2	240	16	....	4.00
	Medicine Hat	WHL	1	1	0	0	60	3	0	3.00	....	....	....	....	....	....	....
2008-09	Medicine Hat	WHL	22	9	6	1	1007	58	0	3.46	2	0	1	73	6	0	4.93
2009-10	Medicine Hat	WHL	57	31	19	5	3214	156	2	2.91	12	6	6	720	35	0	2.92
2010-11	Medicine Hat	WHL	56	35	13	8	3350	138	3	2.47	10	4	6	566	28	1	2.97
2011-12	Medicine Hat	WHL	61	39	17	5	3616	155	3	2.57	8	4	4	496	23	1	2.78
2012-13	Oklahoma City	AHL	1	0	0	0	28	5	0	10.56	....	....	....	....	....	....	....
	Stockton Thunder	ECHL	37	16	16	4	2130	119	1	3.35	4	1	1	178	9	0	3.03
2013-14	Oklahoma City	AHL	5	2	1	1	232	14	0	3.63	....	....	....	....	....	....	....
	Bakersfield	ECHL	13	5	2	3	660	28	0	2.55	....	....	....	....	....	....	....
2014-15	**Edmonton**	**NHL**	**1**	**0**	**0**	**0**	**20**	**3**	**0**	**9.00**	....	....	....	....	....	....	....
	Oklahoma City	AHL	2	0	0	0	60	5	0	5.00	....	....	....	....	....	....	....
	Wichita Thunder	ECHL	17	6	10	1	1009	50	2	2.97	....	....	....	....	....	....	....
	NHL Totals		**1**	**0**	**0**	**0**	**20**	**3**	**0**	**9.00**	....	....	....	....	....	....	....

WHL East Second All-Star Team (2011) • WHL East First All-Star Team (2012) • WHL Goaltender of the Year (2012)

CAMPBELL, Jack (KAM-buhl, JAK) DAL

Goaltender. Catches left. 6'3", 195 lbs. Born, Port Huron, MI, January 9, 1992.
(Dallas' 1st choice, 11th overall, in 2010 Entry Draft).

			Regular Season								Playoffs						
Season	Club	League	GP	W	L	O/T	Mins	GA	SO	Avg	GP	W	L	Mins	GA	SO	Avg
2007-08	Det. Honeybaked	MWEHL	12	8	2	2	630	24	2	2.06	....	....	....	....	....	....	....
	Det. Honeybaked	Minor-MI	25	20	4	1	....	....	....	....	....	....	....	....	....	....	....
2008-09	USNTDP	NAHL	21	14	6	1	1262	53	1	2.52	....	....	....	....	....	....	....
	USNTDP	U-17	7	6	0	1	394	7	3	1.07	....	....	....	....	....	....	....
	USNTDP	U-18	7	7	0	0	421	12	2	1.71	....	....	....	....	....	....	....
2009-10	USNTDP	USHL	11	6	3	1	569	21	1	2.21	....	....	....	....	....	....	....
	USNTDP	U-18	25	16	9	0	1469	54	3	2.21	....	....	....	....	....	....	....
2010-11	Windsor Spitfires	OHL	45	24	14	4	2447	155	0	3.80	18	9	9	1124	70	2	3.74
2011-12	Windsor Spitfires	OHL	12	6	3	2	729	38	1	3.13	....	....	....	....	....	....	....
	Sault Ste. Marie	OHL	34	15	12	5	1945	116	1	3.58	....	....	....	....	....	....	....
	Texas Stars	AHL	12	4	7	0	676	34	1	3.02	....	....	....	....	....	....	....
2012-13	Texas Stars	AHL	40	19	13	3	2108	93	2	2.65	....	....	....	....	....	....	....
2013-14	**Dallas**	**NHL**	**1**	**0**	**1**	**0**	**60**	**6**	**0**	**6.00**	....	....	....	....	....	....	....
	Texas Stars	AHL	16	12	2	2	966	24	4	1.49	4	2	1	237	10	0	2.54
2014-15	Texas Stars	AHL	35	14	14	5	1958	99	2	3.03	1	0	1	59	3	0	3.03
	Idaho Steelheads	ECHL	7	5	2	0	417	12	1	1.73	....	....	....	....	....	....	....
	NHL Totals		**1**	**0**	**1**	**0**	**60**	**6**	**0**	**6.00**	....	....	....	....	....	....	....

CANNATA, Joe (ka-NA-tuh, JOH) VAN

Goaltender. Catches left. 6'1", 200 lbs. Born, Wakefield, MA, January 2, 1990.
(Vancouver's 6th choice, 173rd overall, in 2009 Entry Draft).

			Regular Season								Playoffs						
Season	Club	League	GP	W	L	O/T	Mins	GA	SO	Avg	GP	W	L	Mins	GA	SO	Avg
2007-08	USNTDP	NAHL	5	3	1	1	307	12	0	2.35	....	....	....	....	....	....	....
	USNTDP	U-18	28	13	13	2	1474	64	1	2.61	....	....	....	....	....	....	....
2008-09	Merrimack College	H-East	23	7	11	4	1353	53	2	2.35	....	....	....	....	....	....	....
2009-10	Merrimack College	H-East	24	10	13	1	1362	69	2	3.04	....	....	....	....	....	....	....
2010-11	Merrimack College	H-East	*39	25	10	4	2252	93	1	2.48	....	....	....	....	....	....	....
2011-12	Merrimack College	H-East	36	17	12	7	2179	79	2	2.18	....	....	....	....	....	....	....
	Chicago Wolves	AHL	1	1	0	0	60	2	0	2.00	....	....	....	....	....	....	....
2012-13	Kalamazoo Wings	ECHL	7	3	4	0	419	23	0	3.29	....	....	....	....	....	....	....
	Chicago Wolves	AHL	14	6	6	0	747	33	0	2.65	....	....	....	....	....	....	....
2013-14	Utica Comets	AHL	28	11	12	1	1484	70	0	2.83	....	....	....	....	....	....	....
2014-15	Utica Comets	AHL	5	3	2	0	302	10	0	1.99	....	....	....	....	....	....	....
	Ontario Reign	ECHL	21	12	6	2	1249	42	1	2.02	9	4	4	515	20	2	2.33

Hockey East First All-Star Team (2012) • NCAA East Second All-American Team (2012)

CLEMMENSEN, Scott (KLEH-mehn-sehn, SKAWT)

Goaltender. Catches left. 6'2", 200 lbs. Born, Des Moines, IA, July 23, 1977.
(New Jersey's 7th choice, 215th overall, in 1997 Entry Draft).

			Regular Season								Playoffs						
Season	Club	League	GP	W	L	O/T	Mins	GA	SO	Avg	GP	W	L	Mins	GA	SO	Avg
1995-96	Des Moines	USHL	20	10	7	1	1082	62	0	3.44	....	....	....	....	....	....	....
1996-97	Des Moines	USHL	36	22	9	2	2042	111	1	3.26	4	1	2	200	9	1	2.70
1997-98	Boston College	H-East	37	24	9	4	2205	102	*4	2.78	....	....	....	....	....	....	....
1998-99	Boston College	H-East	*42	26	12	4	*2507	120	1	2.87	....	....	....	....	....	....	....
99-2000	Boston College	H-East	29	19	7	0	1610	59	*5	2.20	....	....	....	....	....	....	....
2000-01	Boston College	H-East	*39	*30	7	2	*2312	82	3	2.13	....	....	....	....	....	....	....
2001-02	**New Jersey**	**NHL**	**2**	**0**	**0**	**0**	**20**	**1**	**0**	**3.00**	....	....	....	....	....	....	....
	Albany River Rats	AHL	29	5	19	4	1677	92	0	3.29	....	....	....	....	....	....	....
2002-03	Albany River Rats	AHL	47	12	24	8	2694	119	1	2.65	....	....	....	....	....	....	....
2003-04	**New Jersey**	**NHL**	**4**	**3**	**1**	**0**	**238**	**4**	**2**	**1.01**	....	....	....	....	....	....	....
	Albany River Rats	AHL	22	5	12	4	1309	67	0	3.07	....	....	....	....	....	....	....
2004-05	Albany River Rats	AHL	46	13	25	5	2645	124	2	2.81	....	....	....	....	....	....	....
2005-06	**New Jersey**	**NHL**	**13**	**3**	**4**	**2**	**627**	**35**	**0**	**3.35**	**1**	**0**	**0**	**7**	**0**	**0**	**0.00**
	Albany River Rats	AHL	1	0	1	0	59	5	0	5.05	....	....	....	....	....	....	....
2006-07	**New Jersey**	**NHL**	**6**	**1**	**1**	**2**	**305**	**16**	**0**	**3.15**	....	....	....	....	....	....	....
	Lowell Devils	AHL	1	1	0	0	60	0	1	0.00	....	....	....	....	....	....	....
2007-08	**Toronto**	**NHL**	**3**	**1**	**1**	**0**	**154**	**10**	**0**	**3.90**	....	....	....	....	....	....	....
	Toronto Marlies	AHL	40	23	14	2	2363	96	1	2.44	17	8	9	992	50	0	3.02
2008-09	**New Jersey**	**NHL**	**40**	**25**	**13**	**1**	**2356**	**94**	**2**	**2.39**	....	....	....	....	....	....	....
	Lowell Devils	AHL	12	6	5	1	707	40	0	3.39	....	....	....	....	....	....	....
2009-10	**Florida**	**NHL**	**23**	**9**	**8**	**2**	**1215**	**59**	**1**	**2.91**	....	....	....	....	....	....	....
2010-11	**Florida**	**NHL**	**31**	**8**	**11**	**7**	**1696**	**74**	**1**	**2.62**	....	....	....	....	....	....	....
2011-12	**Florida**	**NHL**	**30**	**14**	**6**	**6**	**1566**	**67**	**1**	**2.57**	**3**	**1**	**2**	**179**	**7**	**0**	**2.35**
	San Antonio	AHL	1	1	0	0	60	1	0	1.00	....	....	....	....	....	....	....
2012-13	**Florida**	**NHL**	**19**	**3**	**7**	**2**	**866**	**53**	**0**	**3.67**	....	....	....	....	....	....	....
2013-14	**Florida**	**NHL**	**17**	**6**	**7**	**1**	**914**	**47**	**0**	**3.09**	....	....	....	....	....	....	....
	San Antonio	AHL	11	4	7	0	652	31	1	2.85	....	....	....	....	....	....	....
2014-15	**New Jersey**	**NHL**	**3**	**0**	**0**	**1**	**102**	**8**	**0**	**4.71**	....	....	....	....	....	....	....
	Albany Devils	AHL	27	12	11	2	1558	58	2	2.23	....	....	....	....	....	....	....
	NHL Totals		**191**	**73**	**59**	**24**	**10059**	**468**	**7**	**2.79**	**4**	**1**	**2**	**186**	**7**	**0**	**2.26**

Hockey East All-Rookie Team (1998) • NCAA Championship All-Tournament Team (2001)

Signed as a free agent by **Toronto**, July 6, 2007. Signed as a free agent by **New Jersey**, July 10, 2008. Signed as a free agent by **Florida**, July 1, 2009. Signed as a free agent by **New Jersey**, July 1, 2014. • Officially announced his retirement, July 2, 2015.

COMRIE, Eric (KAWM-ree, AIR-ihk) WPG

Goaltender. Catches left. 6'1", 175 lbs. Born, Edmonton, AB, July 6, 1995.
(Winnipeg's 3rd choice, 59th overall, in 2013 Entry Draft).

			Regular Season								Playoffs						
Season	Club	League	GP	W	L	O/T	Mins	GA	SO	Avg	GP	W	L	Mins	GA	SO	Avg
2010-11	L.A. Selects	T1EHL	19	16	2	0	966	24	5	1.34	....	....	....	....	....	....	....
	Tri-City Americans	WHL	....	....	....	....	....	....	....	....	1	0	0	20	1	0	3.00
2011-12	Tri-City Americans	WHL	31	19	6	2	1663	74	3	2.67	....	....	....	....	....	....	....
2012-13	Tri-City Americans	WHL	37	20	14	3	2178	95	2	2.62	0	0	0	0	0	0	0.00
2013-14	Tri-City Americans	WHL	60	26	25	9	3523	151	4	2.57	5	1	4	295	17	0	3.46
	St. John's IceCaps	AHL	2	0	2	0	113	12	0	6.35	....	....	....	....	....	....	....
2014-15	Tri-City Americans	WHL	40	20	19	1	2402	115	1	2.87	4	0	4	256	18	0	4.22
	St. John's IceCaps	AHL	3	2	1	0	185	7	0	2.27	....	....	....	....	....	....	....

WHL West Second All-Star Team (2014, 2015)

CONDON, Mike (KAWN-duhn, MIGHK) MTL

Goaltender. Catches left. 6'2", 196 lbs. Born, Needham, MA, April 27, 1990.

			Regular Season								Playoffs						
Season	Club	League	GP	W	L	O/T	Mins	GA	SO	Avg	GP	W	L	Mins	GA	SO	Avg
2008-09	Belmont Hill	High-MA	31	....	....	....	....	....	....	2.12	....	....	....	....	....	....	....
2009-10	Princeton	ECAC	4	0	1	0	123	5	0	2.44	....	....	....	....	....	....	....
2010-11	Princeton	ECAC	11	6	4	1	660	31	1	2.82	....	....	....	....	....	....	....
2011-12	Princeton	ECAC	14	4	6	3	832	40	0	2.88	....	....	....	....	....	....	....
2012-13	Princeton	ECAC	24	8	11	4	1354	56	2	2.48	....	....	....	....	....	....	....
	Ontario Reign	ECHL	4	3	1	0	243	6	1	1.48	....	....	....	....	....	....	....
	Houston Aeros	AHL	5	3	0	0	226	9	0	2.39	....	....	....	....	....	....	....
2013-14	Wheeling Nailers	ECHL	39	23	12	4	2315	84	6	2.18	10	6	4	625	26	2	2.50
2014-15	Hamilton Bulldogs	AHL	48	23	19	0	2857	116	4	2.44	....	....	....	....	....	....	....

Signed to ATO (amateur tryout) contract by **Ontario** (ECHL), March 20, 2013. Signed to a PTO (professional tryout) contract by **Houston** (AHL), April 7, 2013. Signed as a free agent by **Montreal**, May 8, 2013.

COPLEY, Pheonix (KAWP-lee, FEE-nihks) ST.L.

Goaltender. Catches left. 6'4", 196 lbs. Born, North Pole, AK, January 18, 1992.

			Regular Season								Playoffs						
Season	Club	League	GP	W	L	O/T	Mins	GA	SO	Avg	GP	W	L	Mins	GA	SO	Avg
2009-10	So. Cal Titans	NAPHL	10	6	1	1	429	22	1	2.62	....	....	....	....	....	....	....
	So. Cal Titans	Minor-CA	8	4	2	1	442	24	....	2.71	....	....	....	....	....	....	....
2010-11	Corpus Christi	NAHL	42	14	23	4	2376	165	0	4.17	....	....	....	....	....	....	....
2011-12	Tri-City Storm	USHL	25	9	13	0	1451	76	2	3.14	....	....	....	....	....	....	....
	Des Moines	USHL	20	7	11	1	1163	60	0	3.09	....	....	....	....	....	....	....
2012-13	Michigan Tech	WCHA	24	8	15	1	1323	71	3	3.22	....	....	....	....	....	....	....
2013-14	Michigan Tech	WCHA	30	10	13	6	1724	72	1	2.51	....	....	....	....	....	....	....
	South Carolina	ECHL	3	2	1	0	147	8	0	3.26	1	0	1	70	3	0	2.58
2014-15	Hershey Bears	AHL	26	17	4	3	1520	55	3	2.17	5	3	1	229	7	0	1.83

Signed as a free agent by **Washington**, March 20, 2014. Traded to **St. Louis** by **Washington** with Troy Brouwer and Washington's 3rd round choice in 2016 Entry Draft for T.J. Oshie, July 2, 2015.

COREAU, Jared (KOHR-oh, JAIR-uhd) DET

Goaltender. Catches left. 6'6", 235 lbs. Born, Perth, ON, November 5, 1991.

			Regular Season								Playoffs						
Season	Club	League	GP	W	L	O/T	Mins	GA	SO	Avg	GP	W	L	Mins	GA	SO	Avg
2008-09	Peterborough Stars	ON-Jr.A	12	8	1	1	304	23	0	2.16	2	0	0	22	0	0	0.00
2009-10	Lincoln Stars	USHL	38	7	22	4	1988	120	1	3.62	....	....	....	....	....	....	....
2010-11	Northern Mich.	CCHA	15	5	5	2	662	41	0	3.71	....	....	....	....	....	....	....
2011-12	Northern Mich.	CCHA	23	12	7	2	1244	46	1	2.22	....	....	....	....	....	....	....
2012-13	Northern Mich.	CCHA	38	15	19	4	2182	98	1	2.70	....	....	....	....	....	....	....
2013-14	Grand Rapids	AHL	5	0	4	0	205	15	0	4.39	....	....	....	....	....	....	....
	Toledo Walleye	ECHL	21	1	12	6	1146	77	0	4.03	....	....	....	....	....	....	....
2014-15	Grand Rapids	AHL	25	16	8	1	1475	54	3	2.20	1	0	1	58	3	0	3.10
	Toledo Walleye	ECHL	8	5	2	0	439	22	0	3.01	....	....	....	....	....	....	....

Signed as a free agent by **Detroit**, April 3, 2013.

COWLEY, Evan (KOW-lee, EH-vuhn) FLA

Goaltender. Catches left. 6'4", 197 lbs. Born, Cranbrook, BC, July 31, 1995.
(Florida's 3rd choice, 92nd overall, in 2013 Entry Draft).

			Regular Season								Playoffs						
Season	Club	League	GP	W	L	O/T	Mins	GA	SO	Avg	GP	W	L	Mins	GA	SO	Avg
2010-11	Arvada H.A.	Minor-CO	14	5	7	0	573	39	1	3.27	....	....	....	....	....	....	....
	Ralston Valley	High-CO	....	....	....	....	305	14	2	2.34	....	....	....	....	....	....	....
2011-12	Arvada H.A.	Minor-CO	10	4	2	4	493	21	2	1.92	....	....	....	....	....	....	....
	Ralston Valley	High-CO	STATISTICS NOT AVAILABLE														
2012-13	Wichita Falls	NAHL	*50	22	24	4	2897	140	3	2.90	....	....	....	....	....	....	....
	USNTDP	U-18	3	2	1	0	180	7	0	2.33	....	....	....	....	....	....	....
2013-14	U. of Denver	NCHC	5	1	2	0	204	6	0	1.76	....	....	....	....	....	....	....
2014-15	U. of Denver	NCHC	20	9	6	2	1056	38	3	2.16	....	....	....	....	....	....	....

CRAWFORD, Corey (KRAW-fohrd, KOH-ree) CHI

Goaltender. Catches left. 6'2", 216 lbs. Born, Montreal, QC, December 31, 1984.
(Chicago's 2nd choice, 52nd overall, in 2003 Entry Draft).

			Regular Season								Playoffs						
Season	Club	League	GP	W	L	O/T	Mins	GA	SO	Avg	GP	W	L	Mins	GA	SO	Avg
2000-01	Gatineau Intrepide	QAAA	21	17	3	1	1346	43	5	1.92	....	....	....	....	....	....	....
2001-02	Moncton Wildcats	QMJHL	38	9	20	3	1863	116	1	3.74	....	....	....	....	....	....	....
2002-03	Moncton Wildcats	QMJHL	50	24	17	6	2855	130	2	2.73	6	2	3	303	20	0	3.97
2003-04	Moncton Wildcats	QMJHL	54	*35	15	3	3019	132	2	2.62	*20	*13	6	*1170	42	0	2.15
2004-05	Moncton Wildcats	QMJHL	51	28	16	6	2942	121	*5	2.47	12	6	6	725	33	*1	2.73
2005-06	**Chicago**	**NHL**	**2**	**0**	**0**	**1**	**86**	**5**	**0**	**3.49**	....	....	....	....	....	....	....
	Norfolk Admirals	AHL	48	22	23	1	2734	134	1	2.94	1	0	0	17	1	0	3.49
2006-07	Norfolk Admirals	AHL	60	38	20	2	3467	164	1	2.84	6	2	4	363	20	0	3.31
2007-08	**Chicago**	**NHL**	**5**	**1**	**2**	**0**	**224**	**8**	**1**	**2.14**	....	....	....	....	....	....	....
	Rockford IceHogs	AHL	55	29	19	5	3028	143	3	2.83	12	7	5	741	27	0	2.19
2008-09	Rockford IceHogs	AHL	47	22	20	3	2686	116	2	2.59	2	0	2	117	5	0	2.57
	Chicago	**NHL**	....	....	....	....	....	....	....	....	**1**	**0**	**0**	**16**	**1**	**0**	**3.75**
2009-10	**Chicago**	**NHL**	**1**	**0**	**1**	**0**	**59**	**3**	**0**	**3.05**	....	....	....	....	....	....	....
	Rockford IceHogs	AHL	45	24	16	2	2521	112	1	2.67	4	0	4	216	13	0	3.61
2010-11	**Chicago**	**NHL**	**57**	**33**	**18**	**6**	**3337**	**128**	**4**	**2.30**	**7**	**3**	**4**	**435**	**16**	**1**	**2.21**
2011-12	**Chicago**	**NHL**	**57**	**30**	**17**	**7**	**3218**	**146**	**0**	**2.72**	**6**	**2**	**4**	**396**	**17**	**0**	**2.58**
2012-13 ♦	**Chicago**	**NHL**	**30**	**19**	**5**	**5**	**1761**	**57**	**3**	**1.94**	***23**	***16**	**7**	***1504**	**46**	**1**	***1.84**
2013-14	**Chicago**	**NHL**	**59**	**32**	**16**	**10**	**3395**	**128**	**2**	**2.26**	**19**	**11**	**8**	**1234**	**52**	**1**	**2.53**
2014-15 ♦	**Chicago**	**NHL**	**57**	**32**	**20**	**5**	**3333**	**126**	**2**	**2.27**	**20**	**13**	**6**	**1223**	**47**	**2**	**2.31**
	NHL Totals		**268**	**147**	**79**	**34**	**15413**	**601**	**12**	**2.34**	**76**	**45**	**29**	**4808**	**179**	**5**	**2.23**

QMJHL Second All-Star Team (2004, 2005) • NHL All-Rookie Team (2011) • William M. Jennings Trophy (2013) (shared with Ray Emery) • William M. Jennings Trophy (2015) (tied with Carey Price)

CURRY, John (KUH-ree, JAWN)

Goaltender. Catches left. 5'11", 185 lbs. Born, Shorewood, MN, February 27, 1984.

			Regular Season								Playoffs						
Season	Club	League	GP	W	L	O/T	Mins	GA	SO	Avg	GP	W	L	Mins	GA	SO	Avg
2003-04	Boston University	H-East	1	0	0	0	5	0	0	0.00	....	....	....	....	....	....	....
2004-05	Boston University	H-East	33	18	11	3	1950	64	3	1.97	....	....	....	....	....	....	....
2005-06	Boston University	H-East	37	*24	8	4	2166	81	3	2.24	....	....	....	....	....	....	....
2006-07	Boston University	H-East	36	17	10	8	2154	72	*7	2.01	....	....	....	....	....	....	....
2007-08	Wilkes-Barre	AHL	40	24	12	3	2343	87	3	2.23	23	14	9	1358	64	1	2.83
	Las Vegas	ECHL	6	4	1	0	342	16	0	2.81	....	....	....	....	....	....	....
	Wheeling Nailers	ECHL	1	0	1	0	60	4	0	4.00	....	....	....	....	....	....	....
2008-09	**Pittsburgh**	**NHL**	**3**	**2**	**1**	**0**	**150**	**6**	**0**	**2.40**	....	....	....	....	....	....	....
	Wilkes-Barre	AHL	50	33	15	1	2996	119	4	2.38	7	4	3	393	22	0	3.36
2009-10	**Pittsburgh**	**NHL**	**1**	**0**	**1**	**0**	**24**	**5**	**0**	**12.50**	....	....	....	....	....	....	....
	Wilkes-Barre	AHL	46	23	19	2	2657	127	1	2.87	3	0	3	176	9	0	3.07
2010-11	Wilkes-Barre	AHL	41	23	13	0	2239	91	2	2.44	....	....	....	....	....	....	....
2011-12	Hamburg Freezers	Germany	42	22	20	0	2504	114	3	2.73	5	1	4	278	15	0	3.24
2012-13	Orlando	ECHL	32	17	11	2	1776	83	0	2.80	....	....	....	....	....	....	....
	Houston Aeros	AHL	1	0	0	1	65	1	0	0.92	....	....	....	....	....	....	....
2013-14	Iowa Wild	AHL	19	7	9	2	1101	48	1	2.62	....	....	....	....	....	....	....
	Orlando	ECHL	13	10	2	0	767	34	0	2.66	....	....	....	....	....	....	....
	Minnesota	**NHL**	**2**	**1**	**0**	**0**	**80**	**4**	**0**	**3.00**	....	....	....	....	....	....	....
2014-15	**Minnesota**	**NHL**	**2**	**0**	**0**	**1**	**72**	**5**	**0**	**4.17**	....	....	....	....	....	....	....
	Iowa Wild	AHL	41	13	23	2	2274	101	2	2.66	....	....	....	....	....	....	....
	Quad City Mallards	ECHL	1	1	0	0	60	2	0	2.00	....	....	....	....	....	....	....
	NHL Totals		**8**	**3**	**2**	**1**	**326**	**20**	**0**	**3.68**	....	....	....	....	....	....	....

NCAA East Second All-American Team (2006) • NCAA East First All-American Team (2007) • AHL All-Rookie Team (2008) • Harry "Hap" Holmes Memorial Award (AHL – fewest goals against) (2011) (shared with Brad Thiessen)

Signed as a free agent by **Pittsburgh**, July 13, 2007. Signed as a free agent by **Hamburg** (Germany), June 16, 2011. Signed as a free agent by **Orlando** (ECHL), October 12, 2012. Signed as a free agent by **Iowa** (AHL), October 10, 2013. Signed as a free agent by **Minnesota**, February 17, 2014.

DACCORD, Joel (DA-kohrd, JOHL) OTT

Goaltender. Catches left. 6'3", 195 lbs. Born, Boston, MA, August 19, 1996.
(Ottawa's 8th choice, 199th overall, in 2015 Entry Draft).

			Regular Season								Playoffs						
Season	Club	League	GP	W	L	O/T	Mins	GA	SO	Avg	GP	W	L	Mins	GA	SO	Avg
2011-12	North Andover	High-MA	25	....	....	....	1125	....	4	1.53	....	....	....	....	....	....	....
2012-13	Cushing	High-MA	10	....	....	....	526	19	4	1.95	....	....	....	....	....	....	....
2013-14	Cushing	High-MA	....	....	....	....	1442	62	....	2.58	....	....	....	....	....	....	....
2014-15	Boston Jr. Bruins	Minor-MA	11	5	3	0	317	8	2	1.14	....	....	....	....	....	....	....
	Cushing	High-MA	....	....	....	....	1413	47	....	1.80	....	....	....	....	....	....	....

• Signed Letter of Intent to attend **Arizona State University** (NCAA) in fall of 2016.

DANIS, Yann (DA-nihs, YAN) N.J.

Goaltender. Catches left. 6', 185 lbs. Born, Lafontaine, QC, June 21, 1981.

			Regular Season								Playoffs						
Season	**Club**	**League**	**GP**	**W**	**L**	**O/T**	**Mins**	**GA**	**SO**	**Avg**	**GP**	**W**	**L**	**Mins**	**GA**	**SO**	**Avg**
1997-98	St-Jerome	Minor-QC					STATISTICS NOT AVAILABLE										
	Amos Forestiers	QAAA	3	2	0	0	144	2	0	0.83	2	0	1	78	6	0	4.62
99-2000	Cornwall Colts	ON-Jr.A	26	15	5	0	1367	71	0	3.12	13	11	2	786	37	0	2.82
2000-01	Brown U.	ECAC	12	2	8	1	667	40	0	3.60	....	....	....	....	....	....	....
2001-02	Brown U.	ECAC	24	11	10	2	1451	45	3	1.86	....	....	....	....	....	....	....
2002-03	Brown U.	ECAC	*34	15	14	5	*2074	80	5	2.31	....	....	....	....	....	....	....
2003-04	Brown U.	ECAC	30	15	11	4	1821	55	*5	*1.81	....	....	....	....	....	....	....
	Hamilton Bulldogs	AHL	2	2	0	0	120	3	1	1.50	1	0	0	12	0	0	0.00
2004-05	Hamilton Bulldogs	AHL	53	28	17	6	3075	120	5	2.34	4	0	4	237	13	0	3.29
2005-06	**Montreal**	**NHL**	**6**	**3**	**2**	**0**	**312**	**14**	**1**	**2.69**	....	....	....	....	....	....	....
	Hamilton Bulldogs	AHL	39	17	17	3	2242	111	0	2.97	....	....	....	....	....	....	....
2006-07	Hamilton Bulldogs	AHL	44	23	14	5	2540	119	1	2.81	1	1	0	54	1	0	1.12
2007-08	Hamilton Bulldogs	AHL	38	11	19	4	2064	113	0	3.28	....	....	....	....	....	....	....
2008-09	**NY Islanders**	**NHL**	**31**	**10**	**17**	**3**	**1760**	**84**	**2**	**2.86**	....	....	....	....	....	....	....
	Bridgeport	AHL	10	7	3	0	611	23	0	2.26	....	....	....	....	....	....	....
2009-10	**New Jersey**	**NHL**	**12**	**3**	**2**	**1**	**467**	**16**	**0**	**2.06**	....	....	....	....	....	....	....
2010-11	Amur Khabarovsk	KHL	31	....	....	....	1652	84	2	3.05	....	....	....	....	....	....	....
2011-12	**Edmonton**	**NHL**	**1**	**0**	**0**	**0**	**32**	**2**	**0**	**3.75**	....	....	....	....	....	....	....
	Oklahoma City	AHL	43	26	14	2	2545	88	5	2.07	14	8	6	842	33	1	2.35
2012-13	Oklahoma City	AHL	47	26	15	6	2775	120	2	2.59	17	10	7	1019	41	1	2.41
	Edmonton	**NHL**	**3**	**1**	**0**	**0**	**110**	**7**	**0**	**3.82**	....	....	....	....	....	....	....
2013-14	Adirondack	AHL	31	9	11	4	1514	76	2	3.01	....	....	....	....	....	....	....
2014-15	Norfolk Admirals	AHL	11	5	6	0	640	29	2	2.72	....	....	....	....	....	....	....
	Hartford Wolf Pack	AHL	24	12	7	4	1428	56	2	2.35	14	7	7	887	35	0	2.37
	NHL Totals		**53**	**17**	**21**	**4**	**2681**	**123**	**3**	**2.75**	....	....	....	....	....	....	....

ECAC Second All-Star Team (2002, 2003) • ECAC First All-Star Team (2004) • ECAC Goaltender of the Year (2004) • ECAC Player of the Year (2004) • NCAA East First All-American Team (2004) • AHL First All-Star Team (2012) • Baz Bastien Memorial Trophy (AHL –Top Goaltender) (2012)

Signed as a free agent by **Montreal**, March 19, 2004. Signed as a free agent by **NY Islanders**, July 2, 2008. Signed as a free agent by **New Jersey**, July 10, 2009. Signed as a free agent by **Khabarovsk** (KHL), July 27, 2010. Signed as a free agent by **Edmonton**, July 4, 2011. Signed as a free agent by **Philadelphia**, July 5, 2013. Signed to a PTO (professional tryout) contract by **Norfolk** (AHL), November 10, 2014. Signed to a PTO (professional tryout) contract by **Hartford** (AHL), January 1, 2015. Signed as a free agent by **New Jersey**, July 3, 2015.

DANSK, Oscar (DANSK, AWS-kuhr) CBJ

Goaltender. Catches left. 6'3", 192 lbs. Born, Stockholm, Sweden, February 28, 1994.
(Columbus' 2nd choice, 31st overall, in 2012 Entry Draft).

			Regular Season								Playoffs						
Season	**Club**	**League**	**GP**	**W**	**L**	**O/T**	**Mins**	**GA**	**SO**	**Avg**	**GP**	**W**	**L**	**Mins**	**GA**	**SO**	**Avg**
2007-08	Shattuck Bantam	High-MN	39	....	....	....	....	....	....	1.98	....	....	....	....	....	....	....
2008-09	Shattuck Bantam	High-MN	32	....	....	....	....	....	....	1.43	....	....	....	....	....	....	....
2009-10	Shat.-St. Mary's	High-MN	18	13	2	1	....	....	....	1.89	....	....	....	....	....	....	....
2010-11	Brynas U18	Swe-U18	17	....	....	....	1017	30	2	1.77	5	....	....	317	20	0	3.78
	Brynas IF Gavle Jr.	Swe-Jr.	21	....	....	....	1157	52	1	2.70	1	....	....	57	5	0	5.22
2011-12	Brynas U18	Swe-U18	2	....	....	....	121	4	0	1.98	3	....	....	180	3	1	1.00
	Brynas IF Gavle Jr.	Swe-Jr.	28	....	....	....	1511	71	2	2.82	2	....	....	120	7	0	3.49
2012-13	Erie Otters	OHL	43	11	23	6	2393	164	0	4.11	....	....	....	....	....	....	....
2013-14	Erie Otters	OHL	42	29	9	1	2405	96	*6	*2.39	3	0	1	124	14	0	6.79
2014-15	Springfield Falcons	AHL	21	7	7	5	1144	68	0	3.57	....	....	....	....	....	....	....
	Kalamazoo Wings	ECHL	11	1	8	0	530	33	0	3.73	....	....	....	....	....	....	....

DARLING, Scott (DAHR-lihng, SKAWT) CHI

Goaltender. Catches left. 6'6", 232 lbs. Born, Lemont, IL, December 22, 1988.
(Phoenix's 7th choice, 153rd overall, in 2007 Entry Draft).

			Regular Season								Playoffs						
Season	**Club**	**League**	**GP**	**W**	**L**	**O/T**	**Mins**	**GA**	**SO**	**Avg**	**GP**	**W**	**L**	**Mins**	**GA**	**SO**	**Avg**
2005-06	Chicago Y.A.	MWEHL	2	0	2	0	120	10	0	5.00	....	....	....	....	....	....	....
	North Iowa	NAHL	8	2	4	0	405	28	0	4.15	....	....	....	....	....	....	....
2006-07	Capital District	EJHL	22	9	9	3	1243	70	1	3.38	....	....	....	....	....	....	....
	North Iowa	NAHL	1	0	0	0	15	3	0	12.00	....	....	....	....	....	....	....
2007-08	Indiana Ice	USHL	42	27	10	2	2391	121	1	3.04	3	1	2	179	11	0	3.69
2008-09	University of Maine	H-East	27	10	14	3	1566	72	*3	2.76	....	....	....	....	....	....	....
2009-10	University of Maine	H-East	27	15	6	3	1511	78	0	3.10	....	....	....	....	....	....	....
2010-11	Louisiana	SPHL	30	6	22	0	1598	102	0	3.83	....	....	....	....	....	....	....
2011-12	Florida Everblades	ECHL	1	0	1	0	58	5	0	5.14	....	....	....	....	....	....	....
2012-13	Hamilton Bulldogs	AHL	1	0	0	0	25	0	0	0.00	....	....	....	....	....	....	....
	Wheeling Nailers	ECHL	32	13	12	4	1819	85	2	2.80	....	....	....	....	....	....	....
2013-14	Milwaukee	AHL	26	13	6	2	1347	45	6	2.00	....	....	....	....	....	....	....
2014-15 ♦	**Chicago**	**NHL**	**14**	**9**	**4**	**0**	**833**	**27**	**1**	**1.94**	**5**	**3**	**1**	**298**	**11**	**0**	**2.21**
	Rockford IceHogs	AHL	26	14	8	2	1419	52	2	2.20	....	....	....	....	....	....	....
	NHL Totals		**14**	**9**	**4**	**0**	**833**	**27**	**1**	**1.94**	**5**	**3**	**1**	**298**	**11**	**0**	**2.21**

Signed as a free agent by **Hamilton** (AHL), September 26, 2012. Signed as a free agent by **Chicago**, July 1, 2014.

DELL, Aaron (DEHL, AIR-uhn) S.J.

Goaltender. Catches . 6', 210 lbs. Born, Airdrie, AB, May 4, 1989.

			Regular Season								Playoffs						
Season	**Club**	**League**	**GP**	**W**	**L**	**O/T**	**Mins**	**GA**	**SO**	**Avg**	**GP**	**W**	**L**	**Mins**	**GA**	**SO**	**Avg**
2007-08	Calgary Canucks	AJHL	23	5	11	2	1245	65	0	3.13	....	....	....	....	....	....	....
2008-09	Calgary Canucks	AJHL	51	25	17	8	2986	126	3	2.53	4	1	3	253	13	0	3.08
2009-10	North Dakota	WCHA	5	1	3	1	199	6	1	1.81	....	....	....	....	....	....	....
2010-11	North Dakota	WCHA	40	30	7	2	2349	70	6	1.79	....	....	....	....	....	....	....
2011-12	North Dakota	WCHA	33	18	10	2	1800	80	2	2.67	....	....	....	....	....	....	....
2012-13	Allen Americans	CHL	44	22	11	6	2344	90	3	2.30	19	12	7	1097	45	1	2.46
2013-14	Utah Grizzlies	ECHL	29	19	7	3	1735	62	2	2.14	3	1	1	188	6	0	1.92
	Abbotsford Heat	AHL	6	1	2	0	262	10	0	2.29	....	....	....	....	....	....	....
2014-15	Allen Americans	ECHL	12	8	1	2	676	32	1	2.84	....	....	....	....	....	....	....
	Worcester Sharks	AHL	26	15	8	2	1544	53	4	2.06	3	0	3	149	12	0	4.83

WCHA First All-Star Team (2011) • NCAA East Second All-American Team (2011) • CHL All-Rookie Team (2013) • CHL First All-Star Team (2013)

Signed as a free agent by **Allen** (ECHL), October 20, 2012. Signed as a free agent by **Utah** (ECHL), September 9, 2013. • Loaned to **Abbotsford** (AHL) by **Utah** (ECHL), March 8, 2014. Signed as a free agent by **Allen** (ECHL), October 11, 2014. • Loaned to **Worcester** (AHL) by **Allen** (ECHL), November 11, 2014. Signed as a free agent by **San Jose**, March 4, 2015.

DEMKO, Thatcher (DEHM-koh, THA-chur) VAN

Goaltender. Catches left. 6'4", 192 lbs. Born, San Diego, CA, December 8, 1995.
(Vancouver's 3rd choice, 36th overall, in 2014 Entry Draft).

			Regular Season								Playoffs						
Season	**Club**	**League**	**GP**	**W**	**L**	**O/T**	**Mins**	**GA**	**SO**	**Avg**	**GP**	**W**	**L**	**Mins**	**GA**	**SO**	**Avg**
2010-11	San Diego Gulls	Minor-CA	25	12	12	1	....	....	....	2.47	....	....	....	....	....	....	....
2011-12	L.A. Jr. Kings	T1EHL	7	3	0	3	330	14	0	2.29	....	....	....	....	....	....	....
	L.A. Jr. Kings	Minor-CA	3	3	0	0	....	....	....	....	....	....	....	....	....	....	....
	Omaha Lancers	USHL	15	9	3	0	754	36	1	2.87	....	....	....	....	....	....	....
	USNTDP	U-17	3	2	0	0	140	3	0	1.29	....	....	....	....	....	....	....
2012-13	USNTDP	USHL	19	15	3	0	1059	39	1	2.21	....	....	....	....	....	....	....
	USNTDP	U-17	1	1	0	0	60	1	0	1.00	....	....	....	....	....	....	....
	USNTDP	U-18	28	17	6	3	1620	52	5	1.93	....	....	....	....	....	....	....
2013-14	Boston College	H-East	24	16	5	3	1446	54	2	2.24	....	....	....	....	....	....	....
2014-15	Boston College	H-East	35	19	13	3	2107	77	1	2.19	....	....	....	....	....	....	....

DESJARDINS, Cedrick (deh-ZHAHR-dai, SEH-DRIHK) NYR

Goaltender. Catches left. 6', 192 lbs. Born, Edmundston, NB, September 30, 1985.

			Regular Season								Playoffs						
Season	**Club**	**League**	**GP**	**W**	**L**	**O/T**	**Mins**	**GA**	**SO**	**Avg**	**GP**	**W**	**L**	**Mins**	**GA**	**SO**	**Avg**
2001-02	Levis	QAAA	20	13	2	1	1059	50	0	2.83	4	1	2	167	11	0	3.95
2002-03	Coaticook	QJHL					STATISTICS NOT AVAILABLE										
	Rimouski Oceanic	QMJHL	23	1	19	0	1239	109	0	5.28	....	....	....	....	....	....	....
2003-04	Rimouski Oceanic	QMJHL	20	8	11	0	1119	72	0	3.86	1	0	0	14	0	0	0.00
2004-05	Rimouski Oceanic	QMJHL	44	*30	7	4	2439	120	2	2.95	13	*12	1	*767	34	*1	2.66
2005-06	Quebec Remparts	QMJHL	41	28	10	0	2254	111	*5	2.95	*23	14	9	*1413	60	1	2.55
2006-07	Hamilton Bulldogs	AHL	3	0	2	0	142	7	0	2.96	....	....	....	....	....	....	....
	Cincinnati	ECHL	45	24	19	1	2648	112	4	2.54	....	....	....	....	....	....	....
2007-08	Hamilton Bulldogs	AHL	12	4	3	2	572	29	0	3.04	....	....	....	....	....	....	....
	Cincinnati	ECHL	22	16	4	2	1285	41	*5	1.91	16	11	4	947	29	1	*1.83
2008-09	Hamilton Bulldogs	AHL	30	16	12	0	1718	73	4	2.55	....	....	....	....	....	....	....
2009-10	Hamilton Bulldogs	AHL	47	29	9	4	2576	86	6	*2.00	10	6	4	596	26	1	2.62
2010-11	**Tampa Bay**	**NHL**	**2**	**2**	**0**	**0**	**120**	**2**	**0**	**1.00**	....	....	....	....	....	....	....
	Norfolk Admirals	AHL	24	15	6	1	1391	60	1	2.59	....	....	....	....	....	....	....
2011-12	Lake Erie Monsters	AHL	32	16	11	5	1936	68	3	2.11	....	....	....	....	....	....	....
2012-13	Hamilton Bulldogs	AHL	22	7	13	2	1285	63	2	2.94	....	....	....	....	....	....	....
	Tampa Bay	**NHL**	**3**	**0**	**3**	**0**	**160**	**8**	**0**	**3.00**	....	....	....	....	....	....	....
	Syracuse Crunch	AHL	14	8	5	1	851	30	3	2.12	18	13	5	1098	42	3	2.30
2013-14	**Tampa Bay**	**NHL**	**1**	**0**	**1**	**0**	**18**	**2**	**0**	**6.67**	....	....	....	....	....	....	....
	Syracuse Crunch	AHL	35	9	18	4	1984	93	2	2.81	....	....	....	....	....	....	....
2014-15	Hartford Wolf Pack	AHL	15	8	3	1	800	35	1	2.63	....	....	....	....	....	....	....
	NHL Totals		**6**	**2**	**4**	**0**	**298**	**12**	**0**	**2.42**	....	....	....	....	....	....	....

Memorial Cup All-Star Team (2006) • Hap Emms Memorial Trophy (Memorial Cup - Top Goaltender) (2006) • ECHL All-Rookie-Team (2007) • ECHL Playoff MVP (2009) • AHL Second All-Star Team (2010) • Harry ''Hap'' Holmes Memorial Award (AHL – fewest goals against) (2010) (shared with Curtis Sanford)

Signed as a free agent by **Hamilton** (AHL), July 26, 2006. Signed as a free agent by **Montreal**, July 3, 2008. Traded to **Tampa Bay** by **Montreal** for Karri Ramo, August 16, 2010. Signed as a free agent by **Colorado**, July 8, 2011. Signed as a free agent by **Montreal**, July 1, 2012. Traded to **Tampa Bay** by **Montreal** for Dustin Tokarski, February 14, 2013. Signed as a free agent by **NY Rangers**, July 1, 2014.

DESROSIERS, Philippe (duh-ROHZ-ee-yay, fihl-EEP) DAL

Goaltender. Catches left. 6'1", 190 lbs. Born, Saint-Hyacinthe, QC, August 16, 1995.
(Dallas' 4th choice, 54th overall, in 2013 Entry Draft).

			Regular Season								Playoffs						
Season	**Club**	**League**	**GP**	**W**	**L**	**O/T**	**Mins**	**GA**	**SO**	**Avg**	**GP**	**W**	**L**	**Mins**	**GA**	**SO**	**Avg**
2010-11	Antoine-Girouard	QAAA	20	10	9	0	1100	65	2	3.54	3	1	2	139	8	0	3.45
2011-12	Antoine-Girouard	QAAA	23	16	4	3	1320	61	1	2.77	11	6	3	673	29	0	2.58
	Rimouski Oceanic	QMJHL	3	1	2	0	155	9	0	3.48	....	....	....	....	....	....	....
2012-13	Rimouski Oceanic	QMJHL	43	22	8	5	2305	118	1	3.07	4	2	2	239	9	0	2.26
2013-14	Rimouski Oceanic	QMJHL	52	31	14	7	2921	129	5	2.65	11	7	3	640	25	2	2.34
2014-15	Rimouski Oceanic	QMJHL	44	29	9	3	2469	103	5	2.50	9	5	3	411	17	0	2.48

DILLON, Alec (DIHL-luhn, AL-ehk) L.A.

Goaltender. Catches left. 6'4", 168 lbs. Born, Nanaimo, BC, May 5, 1996.
(Los Angeles' 6th choice, 150th overall, in 2014 Entry Draft).

			Regular Season								Playoffs						
Season	**Club**	**League**	**GP**	**W**	**L**	**O/T**	**Mins**	**GA**	**SO**	**Avg**	**GP**	**W**	**L**	**Mins**	**GA**	**SO**	**Avg**
2011-12	S. Island T-birds	BCMML	....	1	10	0	....	....	....	5.81	....	....	....	....	....	....	....
2012-13	Westshore Wolves	VIJHL	24	9	12	0	1257	83	3	3.96	3	1	1	154	10	0	3.90
2013-14	Victoria Grizzlies	BCHL	33	21	7	2	1911	88	1	2.76	9	4	4	540	23	2	2.56
2014-15	Tri-City Storm	USHL	41	23	11	4	2302	87	3	*2.27	....	....	....	....	....	....	....

DOMINGUE, Louis (doh-MIHN-gay, LOO-ee) ARI

Goaltender. Catches right. 6'3", 205 lbs. Born, Mont St. Hilaire, QC, March 6, 1992.
(Phoenix's 5th choice, 138th overall, in 2010 Entry Draft).

			Regular Season								Playoffs						
Season	**Club**	**League**	**GP**	**W**	**L**	**O/T**	**Mins**	**GA**	**SO**	**Avg**	**GP**	**W**	**L**	**Mins**	**GA**	**SO**	**Avg**
2007-08	Lac St-Louis Lions	QAAA	35	22	9	0	1732	90	2	3.12	13	8	4	761	33	1	2.60
2008-09	Moncton Wildcats	QMJHL	12	5	5	0	621	26	0	2.51	....	....	....	....	....	....	....
2009-10	Moncton Wildcats	QMJHL	22	11	9	0	1196	56	1	2.81	....	....	....	....	....	....	....
	Quebec Remparts	QMJHL	19	9	8	0	1017	43	2	2.54	9	3	5	455	33	0	4.35
2010-11	Quebec Remparts	QMJHL	*57	*37	12	3	3033	134	2	2.65	18	11	6	996	41	1	2.47
2011-12	Quebec Remparts	QMJHL	39	23	8	4	2162	94	4	2.61	11	7	4	679	30	0	2.65
2012-13	Portland Pirates	AHL	2	1	0	0	100	4	0	2.40	....	....	....	....	....	....	....
	Gwinnett	ECHL	34	23	9	2	2051	92	3	2.69	10	6	4	619	23	2	2.23
2013-14	Portland Pirates	AHL	36	9	18	2	1783	108	1	3.63	....	....	....	....	....	....	....
	Gwinnett	ECHL	7	1	3	2	388	13	1	2.01	....	....	....	....	....	....	....
2014-15	**Arizona**	**NHL**	**7**	**1**	**2**	**1**	**308**	**14**	**0**	**2.73**	....	....	....	....	....	....	....
	Portland Pirates	AHL	20	11	6	2	1121	50	0	2.68	5	2	2	253	10	1	2.37
	Gwinnett	ECHL	2	1	1	0	119	2	1	1.01	....	....	....	....	....	....	....
	NHL Totals		**7**	**1**	**2**	**1**	**308**	**14**	**0**	**2.73**	....	....	....	....	....	....	....

DRIEDGER, Chris (DREE-guhr, KRIHS) OTT

Goaltender. Catches left. 6'4", 205 lbs. Born, Winnipeg, MB, May 18, 1994.
(Ottawa's 2nd choice, 76th overall, in 2012 Entry Draft).

			Regular Season								Playoffs						
Season	**Club**	**League**	**GP**	**W**	**L**	**O/T**	**Mins**	**GA**	**SO**	**Avg**	**GP**	**W**	**L**	**Mins**	**GA**	**SO**	**Avg**
2009-10	Wpg. Monarchs	Minor-MB	12	....	....	....	....	....	....	1.75	....	....	....	....	....	....	....
2010-11	Tri-City Americans	WHL	22	6	6	1	977	57	0	3.50	....	....	....	....	....	....	....
2011-12	Calgary Hitmen	WHL	44	24	12	3	2294	107	3	2.80	2	0	2	82	9	0	6.59
2012-13	Calgary Hitmen	WHL	54	36	14	4	3199	134	2	2.51	17	11	6	1006	40	1	2.39
2013-14	Calgary Hitmen	WHL	50	28	14	7	2892	127	3	2.64	6	2	3	328	24	1	4.39
	Binghamton	AHL	1	0	0	0	26	2	0	4.58	....	....	....	....	....	....	....
	Elmira Jackals	ECHL	4	1	2	....	199	13	0	3.92	....	....	....	....	....	....	....
2014-15	**Ottawa**	**NHL**	**1**	**0**	**0**	**0**	**23**	**0**	**0**	**0.00**	....	....	....	....	....	....	....
	Binghamton	AHL	8	6	0	0	401	17	0	2.55	....	....	....	....	....	....	....
	Evansville IceMen	ECHL	40	8	27	4	2253	142	2	3.78	....	....	....	....	....	....	....
	NHL Totals		**1**	**0**	**0**	**0**	**23**	**0**	**0**	**0.00**	....	....	....	....	....	....	....

DUBNYK, Devan (DOOB-nihk, DEH-vuhn) MIN

Goaltender. Catches left. 6'5", 210 lbs. Born, Regina, SK, May 4, 1986.
(Edmonton's 1st choice, 14th overall, in 2004 Entry Draft).

			Regular Season								Playoffs						
Season	**Club**	**League**	**GP**	**W**	**L**	**O/T**	**Mins**	**GA**	**SO**	**Avg**	**GP**	**W**	**L**	**Mins**	**GA**	**SO**	**Avg**
2000-01	Calgary Bruins	CBHL	14	....	....	....	815	39	2	3.10	....	....	....	....	....	....	....
2001-02	Calgary Bruins	CBHL	18	7	9	2	1105	68	1	3.69	....	....	....	....	....	....	....
	Kamloops Blazers	WHL	3	1	1	0	143	13	0	5.44	....	....	....	....	....	....	....
2002-03	Kamloops Blazers	WHL	26	12	8	1	1278	66	2	3.10	....	....	....	....	....	....	....
2003-04	Kamloops Blazers	WHL	44	20	18	5	2532	106	6	2.51	4	1	3	245	12	0	2.94
2004-05	Kamloops Blazers	WHL	*65	23	34	7	3699	166	6	2.69	6	2	4	362	22	0	3.65
2005-06	Kamloops Blazers	WHL	54	27	26	1	3207	136	1	2.54	....	....	....	....	....	....	....
2006-07	Wilkes-Barre	AHL	4	2	1	0	204	10	0	2.94	....	....	....	....	....	....	....
	Stockton Thunder	ECHL	43	24	11	7	2529	108	2	2.56	6	2	4	395	18	0	2.73
2007-08	Springfield Falcons	AHL	33	9	17	0	1772	92	0	3.12	....	....	....	....	....	....	....
2008-09	Springfield Falcons	AHL	*62	18	41	2	*3635	180	3	2.97	....	....	....	....	....	....	....
2009-10	**Edmonton**	**NHL**	**19**	**4**	**10**	**2**	**1075**	**64**	**0**	**3.57**	....	....	....	....	....	....	....
	Springfield Falcons	AHL	33	13	17	2	1985	100	0	3.02	....	....	....	....	....	....	....
2010-11	**Edmonton**	**NHL**	**35**	**12**	**13**	**8**	**2061**	**93**	**2**	**2.71**	....	....	....	....	....	....	....
2011-12	**Edmonton**	**NHL**	**47**	**20**	**20**	**3**	**2653**	**118**	**2**	**2.67**	....	....	....	....	....	....	....
2012-13	**Edmonton**	**NHL**	**38**	**14**	**16**	**6**	**2101**	**90**	**2**	**2.57**	....	....	....	....	....	....	....
2013-14	**Edmonton**	**NHL**	**32**	**11**	**17**	**2**	**1678**	**94**	**2**	**3.36**	....	....	....	....	....	....	....
	Nashville	**NHL**	**2**	**0**	**1**	**1**	**124**	**9**	**0**	**4.35**	....	....	....	....	....	....	....
	Hamilton Bulldogs	AHL	8	2	5	0	415	23	0	3.33	....	....	....	....	....	....	....
2014-15	**Arizona**	**NHL**	**19**	**9**	**5**	**2**	**1035**	**47**	**1**	**2.72**	....	....	....	....	....	....	....
	Minnesota	**NHL**	**39**	**27**	**9**	**2**	**2293**	**68**	**5**	**1.78**	**10**	**4**	**6**	**570**	**24**	**1**	**2.53**
	NHL Totals		**231**	**97**	**91**	**26**	**13020**	**583**	**14**	**2.69**	**10**	**4**	**6**	**570**	**24**	**1**	**2.53**

Canadian Major Junior Scholastic Player of the Year (2004) • NHL Second All-Star Team (2015) • Bill Masterton Memorial Trophy (2015)

Traded to **Nashville** by **Edmonton** for Matt Hendricks, January 15, 2014. Traded to **Montreal** by **Nashville** for future considerations, March 5, 2014. Signed as a free agent by **Arizona**, July 1, 2014. Traded to **Minnesota** by **Arizona** for Minnesota's 3rd round choice (Brendan Warren) in 2015 Entry Draft, January 15, 2015.

ELLIOTT, Brian (EHL-lee-awt, BRIGH-uhn) ST.L.

Goaltender. Catches left. 6'2", 209 lbs. Born, Newmarket, ON, April 9, 1985.
(Ottawa's 9th choice, 291st overall, in 2003 Entry Draft).

			Regular Season								Playoffs						
Season	**Club**	**League**	**GP**	**W**	**L**	**O/T**	**Mins**	**GA**	**SO**	**Avg**	**GP**	**W**	**L**	**Mins**	**GA**	**SO**	**Avg**
2002-03	Ajax Axemen	ON-Jr.A	39	....	....	....	2097	135	0	3.86	....	....	....	....	....	....	....
2003-04	U. of Wisconsin	WCHA	6	3	3	0	336	12	0	2.14	....	....	....	....	....	....	....
2004-05	U. of Wisconsin	WCHA	9	6	2	1	467	9	3	1.16	....	....	....	....	....	....	....
2005-06	U. of Wisconsin	WCHA	35	*27	5	3	2128	55	*8	*1.55	....	....	....	....	....	....	....
2006-07	U. of Wisconsin	WCHA	36	15	17	2	2053	72	*5	2.10	....	....	....	....	....	....	....
	Binghamton	AHL	8	3	4	0	425	30	0	4.24	....	....	....	....	....	....	....
2007-08	**Ottawa**	**NHL**	**1**	**1**	**0**	**0**	**60**	**1**	**0**	**1.00**	....	....	....	....	....	....	....
	Binghamton	AHL	44	18	19	1	2394	112	2	2.81	....	....	....	....	....	....	....
2008-09	**Ottawa**	**NHL**	**31**	**16**	**8**	**3**	**1667**	**77**	**1**	**2.77**	....	....	....	....	....	....	....
	Binghamton	AHL	30	18	8	1	1691	65	2	2.31	....	....	....	....	....	....	....
2009-10	**Ottawa**	**NHL**	**55**	**29**	**18**	**4**	**3038**	**130**	**5**	**2.57**	**4**	**1**	**2**	**203**	**14**	**0**	**4.14**
2010-11	**Ottawa**	**NHL**	**43**	**13**	**19**	**8**	**2293**	**122**	**3**	**3.19**	....	....	....	....	....	....	....
	Colorado	**NHL**	**12**	**2**	**8**	**1**	**690**	**44**	**0**	**3.83**	....	....	....	....	....	....	....
2011-12	**St. Louis**	**NHL**	**38**	**23**	**10**	**4**	**2235**	**58**	**9**	***1.56**	**8**	**3**	**4**	**455**	**18**	**0**	**2.37**
2012-13	**St. Louis**	**NHL**	**24**	**14**	**8**	**1**	**1292**	**49**	**3**	**2.28**	**6**	**2**	**4**	**378**	**12**	**0**	**1.90**
	Peoria Rivermen	AHL	2	1	1	0	119	3	1	1.51	....	....	....	....	....	....	....
2013-14	**St. Louis**	**NHL**	**31**	**18**	**6**	**2**	**1624**	**53**	**4**	**1.96**	....	....	....	....	....	....	....
2014-15	**St. Louis**	**NHL**	**46**	**26**	**14**	**3**	**2546**	**96**	**5**	**2.26**	**1**	**0**	**0**	**26**	**1**	**0**	**2.31**
	NHL Totals		**281**	**142**	**91**	**26**	**15445**	**630**	**30**	**2.45**	**19**	**6**	**10**	**1062**	**45**	**0**	**2.54**

WCHA Second All-Star Team (2006, 2007) • NCAA West First All-American Team (2006) • NCAA Championship All-Tournament Team (2006) • William M. Jennings Trophy (2012) (shared with Jaroslav Halak)

Played in NHL All-Star Game (2012, 2015}

Traded to **Colorado** by **Ottawa** for Craig Anderson, February 18, 2011. Signed as a free agent by **St. Louis**, July 1, 2011.

ELLIS, Dan (EHL-ihs, DAN) WSH

Goaltender. Catches left. 6'1", 195 lbs. Born, Saskatoon, SK, June 19, 1980.
(Dallas' 2nd choice, 60th overall, in 2000 Entry Draft).

			Regular Season								Playoffs						
Season	**Club**	**League**	**GP**	**W**	**L**	**O/T**	**Mins**	**GA**	**SO**	**Avg**	**GP**	**W**	**L**	**Mins**	**GA**	**SO**	**Avg**
1998-99	Newmarket	ON-Jr.A	28	24	3	1	1670	63	3	2.25	....	....	....	....	....	....	....
99-2000	Omaha Lancers	USHL	55	*34	16	4	*3274	123	*11	*2.25	4	1	3	238	10	0	2.52
2000-01	Nebraska-Omaha	CCHA	40	21	14	3	2285	95	2	2.49	....	....	....	....	....	....	....
2001-02	Nebraska-Omaha	CCHA	40	20	15	4	2405	97	3	2.42	....	....	....	....	....	....	....
2002-03	Nebraska-Omaha	CCHA	39	11	21	5	2211	117	3	3.18	....	....	....	....	....	....	....
2003-04	**Dallas**	**NHL**	**1**	**1**	**0**	**0**	**60**	**3**	**0**	**3.00**	....	....	....	....	....	....	....
	Utah Grizzlies	AHL	20	5	14	0	1130	55	2	2.92	....	....	....	....	....	....	....
	Idaho Steelheads	ECHL	23	13	8	1	1334	57	2	2.56	*16	*13	3	*966	30	*3	*1.86
2004-05	Hamilton Bulldogs	AHL	31	10	19	0	1774	82	1	2.77	....	....	....	....	....	....	....
2005-06	Iowa Stars	AHL	34	16	13	1	1857	86	2	2.78	....	....	....	....	....	....	....
2006-07	Iowa Stars	AHL	55	30	21	1	3194	148	4	2.78	12	6	6	679	35	0	3.09
2007-08	**Nashville**	**NHL**	**44**	**23**	**10**	**3**	**2229**	**87**	**6**	**2.34**	**6**	**2**	**4**	**357**	**15**	**0**	**2.52**
2008-09	**Nashville**	**NHL**	**35**	**11**	**19**	**4**	**1965**	**96**	**3**	**2.93**	....	....	....	....	....	....	....
2009-10	**Nashville**	**NHL**	**31**	**15**	**13**	**1**	**1715**	**77**	**1**	**2.69**	....	....	....	....	....	....	....
2010-11	**Tampa Bay**	**NHL**	**31**	**13**	**7**	**6**	**1679**	**82**	**2**	**2.93**	....	....	....	....	....	....	....
	Anaheim	**NHL**	**13**	**8**	**3**	**1**	**729**	**29**	**0**	**2.39**	**1**	**0**	**1**	**41**	**4**	**0**	**5.85**
2011-12	**Anaheim**	**NHL**	**10**	**1**	**5**	**0**	**419**	**19**	**0**	**2.72**	....	....	....	....	....	....	....
2012-13	Charlotte Checkers	AHL	18	8	7	2	1026	42	2	2.46	....	....	....	....	....	....	....
	Carolina	**NHL**	**19**	**6**	**8**	**2**	**997**	**52**	**1**	**3.13**	....	....	....	....	....	....	....
2013-14	**Dallas**	**NHL**	**14**	**5**	**6**	**0**	**690**	**35**	**1**	**3.04**	....	....	....	....	....	....	....
	Florida	**NHL**	**6**	**0**	**5**	**0**	**337**	**27**	**0**	**4.81**	....	....	....	....	....	....	....
2014-15	**Florida**	**NHL**	**8**	**4**	**3**	**1**	**486**	**19**	**1**	**2.35**	....	....	....	....	....	....	....
	San Antonio	AHL	37	22	12	3	2191	99	2	2.71	2	0	2	123	5	0	2.44
	NHL Totals		**212**	**87**	**79**	**18**	**11306**	**526**	**15**	**2.79**	**7**	**2**	**5**	**398**	**19**	**0**	**2.86**

USHL First All-Star Team (2000) • USHL Goaltender of the Year (2000) • USHL Player of the Year (2000) • CCHA Second All-Star Team (2002) • ECHL Playoff MVP (2004)

Signed as a free agent by **Nashville**, July 5, 2007. Traded to **Montreal** by **Nashville** with Dustin Boyd and future considerations for Sergei Kostitsyn and future considerations, June 29, 2010. Signed as a free agent by **Tampa Bay**, July 1, 2010. Traded to **Anaheim** by **Tampa Bay** for Curtis McElhinney, February 24, 2011. Signed as a free agent by **Charlotte** (AHL). September 24, 2012. Signed as a free agent by **Carolina**, January 13, 2013. Signed as a free agent by **Dallas**, July 5, 2013. Traded to **Florida** by **Dallas** for Tim Thomas, March 5, 2014. Signed as a free agent by **Washington**, July 4, 2015.

EMERY, Ray (EH-muhr-ee, RAY)

Goaltender. Catches left. 6'2", 196 lbs. Born, Cayuga, ON, September 28, 1982.
(Ottawa's 4th choice, 99th overall, in 2001 Entry Draft).

			Regular Season								Playoffs						
Season	**Club**	**League**	**GP**	**W**	**L**	**O/T**	**Mins**	**GA**	**SO**	**Avg**	**GP**	**W**	**L**	**Mins**	**GA**	**SO**	**Avg**
1998-99	Dunnville Terriers	ON-Jr.C	22	3	19	0	1320	140	0	6.37	....	....	....	....	....	....	....
99-2000	Welland Cougars	ON-Jr.B	23	13	10	1	1323	62	1	2.68	....	....	....	....	....	....	....
	Sault Ste. Marie	OHL	16	9	3	0	716	36	1	3.02	15	8	7	884	33	*3	2.24
2000-01	Sault Ste. Marie	OHL	52	18	29	2	2938	174	1	3.55	....	....	....	....	....	....	....
2001-02	Sault Ste. Marie	OHL	*59	*33	17	9	*3477	158	4	2.73	6	2	4	360	19	*1	3.17
2002-03	**Ottawa**	**NHL**	**3**	**1**	**0**	**0**	**85**	**2**	**0**	**1.41**	....	....	....	....	....	....	....
	Binghamton	AHL	50	27	17	6	2924	118	*7	2.42	14	8	6	848	40	*2	2.83
2003-04	**Ottawa**	**NHL**	**3**	**2**	**0**	**0**	**126**	**5**	**0**	**2.38**	....	....	....	....	....	....	....
	Binghamton	AHL	53	21	23	7	3109	128	3	2.47	2	0	2	120	6	0	3.01
2004-05	Binghamton	AHL	51	28	18	5	2993	132	0	2.65	6	2	4	409	14	0	2.05
2005-06	**Ottawa**	**NHL**	**39**	**23**	**11**	**4**	**2168**	**102**	**3**	**2.82**	**10**	**5**	**5**	**604**	**29**	**0**	**2.88**
2006-07	**Ottawa**	**NHL**	**58**	**33**	**16**	**6**	**3351**	**138**	**5**	**2.47**	***20**	***13**	**7**	***1249**	**47**	***3**	**2.26**
2007-08	**Ottawa**	**NHL**	**31**	**12**	**13**	**4**	**1689**	**88**	**0**	**3.13**	....	....	....	....	....	....	....
	Binghamton	AHL	2	1	1	0	120	6	0	3.00	....	....	....	....	....	....	....
2008-09	Mytischi	KHL	36	....	....	....	2070	73	2	2.12	7	....	....	419	13	1	1.86
2009-10	**Philadelphia**	**NHL**	**29**	**16**	**11**	**1**	**1684**	**74**	**3**	**2.64**	....	....	....	....	....	....	....
	Adirondack	AHL	1	0	1	0	59	2	0	2.03	....	....	....	....	....	....	....
2010-11	**Anaheim**	**NHL**	**10**	**7**	**2**	**0**	**527**	**20**	**0**	**2.28**	**6**	**2**	**3**	**319**	**17**	**0**	**3.20**
	Syracuse Crunch	AHL	5	4	1	0	303	10	0	1.98	....	....	....	....	....	....	....
2011-12	**Chicago**	**NHL**	**34**	**15**	**9**	**4**	**1774**	**83**	**0**	**2.81**	....	....	....	....	....	....	....
2012-13 ♦	**Chicago**	**NHL**	**21**	**17**	**1**	**0**	**1116**	**36**	**3**	**1.94**	....	....	....	....	....	....	....
2013-14	**Philadelphia**	**NHL**	**28**	**9**	**12**	**2**	**1398**	**69**	**2**	**2.96**	**3**	**1**	**2**	**172**	**10**	**0**	**3.49**
2014-15	**Philadelphia**	**NHL**	**31**	**10**	**11**	**7**	**1570**	**80**	**0**	**3.06**	....	....	....	....	....	....	....
	NHL Totals		**287**	**145**	**86**	**28**	**15488**	**697**	**16**	**2.70**	**39**	**21**	**17**	**2344**	**103**	**3**	**2.64**

OHL First All-Star Team (2002) • Canadian Major Junior First All-Star Team (2002) • Canadian Major Junior Goaltender of the Year (2002) • AHL All-Rookie Team (2003) • William M. Jennings Trophy (2013) (shared with Corey Crawford)

Signed as a free agent by **Mytischi** (KHL), July 9, 2008. Signed as a free agent by **Philadelphia** June 10, 2009. Signed as a free agent by **Anaheim**, February 7, 2011. Signed as a free agent by **Chicago**, October 3, 2011. Signed as a free agent by **Philadelphia**, July 5, 2013.

ENROTH, Jhonas (EHN-rawth, YOH-nuhs) L.A.

Goaltender. Catches left. 5'10", 166 lbs. Born, Stockholm, Sweden, June 25, 1988.
(Buffalo's 2nd choice, 46th overall, in 2006 Entry Draft).

			Regular Season								Playoffs						
Season	**Club**	**League**	**GP**	**W**	**L**	**O/T**	**Mins**	**GA**	**SO**	**Avg**	**GP**	**W**	**L**	**Mins**	**GA**	**SO**	**Avg**
2003-04	Huddinge IK U18	Swe-U18	6	....	....	....	324	15	0	2.77	....	....	....	....	....	....	....
2004-05	Huddinge IK Jr.	Swe-Jr.	19	....	....	....	1144	49	3	2.57	3	....	....	186	6	1	1.93
	Huddinge IK U18	Swe-U18	2	....	....	....	125	5	0	2.40	....	....	....	....	....	....	....
	Huddinge IK	Sweden-2	2	....	....	....	51	6	0	6.95	....	....	....	....	....	....	....
2005-06	Sodertalje SK Jr.	Swe-Jr.	39	....	....	....	2378	86	1	2.17	4	....	....	243	9	0	2.22
	Sodertalje SK U18	Swe-U18	2	....	....	....	120	5	0	2.50	....	....	....	....	....	....	....
2006-07	Sodertalje SK Jr.	Swe-Jr.	3	....	....	....	180	4	0	1.33	....	....	....	....	....	....	....
	Sodertalje SK	Sweden-2	33	....	....	....	1938	57	3	1.76	....	....	....	....	....	....	....
2007-08	Sodertalje SK Jr.	Swe-Jr.	1	....	....	....	59	4	0	4.05	....	....	....	....	....	....	....
	Sodertalje SK	Sweden	27	....	....	....	1578	56	2	*2.13	....	....	....	....	....	....	....
2008-09	Portland Pirates	AHL	58	26	23	6	3424	157	3	2.75	5	1	4	264	10	1	2.27
2009-10	**Buffalo**	**NHL**	**1**	**0**	**1**	**0**	**58**	**4**	**0**	**4.14**	....	....	....	....	....	....	....
	Portland Pirates	AHL	48	28	18	1	2781	110	5	2.37	....	....	....	....	....	....	....
2010-11	**Buffalo**	**NHL**	**14**	**9**	**2**	**2**	**769**	**35**	**1**	**2.73**	**1**	**0**	**0**	**17**	**1**	**0**	**3.53**
	Portland Pirates	AHL	41	20	17	2	2393	111	0	2.78	4	1	2	217	10	0	2.77
2011-12	**Buffalo**	**NHL**	**26**	**8**	**11**	**4**	**1399**	**63**	**1**	**2.70**	....	....	....	....	....	....	....
2012-13	Huddinge IK	Sweden-3	2	2	0	0	120	5	0	2.50	....	....	....	....	....	....	....
	Almtuna	Sweden-2	14	....	....	....	....	....	....	2.31	....	....	....	....	....	....	....
	Buffalo	**NHL**	**12**	**4**	**4**	**1**	**623**	**27**	**1**	**2.60**	....	....	....	....	....	....	....
2013-14	**Buffalo**	**NHL**	**28**	**4**	**17**	**5**	**1574**	**74**	**0**	**2.82**	....	....	....	....	....	....	....
	Sweden	Olympics				DID NOT PLAY – SPARE GOALTENDER											
2014-15	**Buffalo**	**NHL**	**37**	**13**	**21**	**2**	**2204**	**120**	**1**	**3.27**	....	....	....	....	....	....	....
	Dallas	**NHL**	**13**	**5**	**5**	**0**	**630**	**25**	**1**	**2.38**	....	....	....	....	....	....	....
	NHL Totals		**131**	**43**	**61**	**14**	**7257**	**348**	**5**	**2.88**	**1**	**0**	**0**	**17**	**1**	**0**	**3.53**

NHL All-Rookie Team (2012)

Signed as a free agent by **Huddinge** (Sweden-3). October 25, 2012. Signed as a free agent by **Almtuna** (Sweden-2), November 5, 2012. Traded to **Dallas** by **Buffalo** for Anders Lindback and future considerations, February 11, 2015. Signed as a free agent by **Los Angeles**, July 1, 2015.

ERIKSSON, Joacim (AIR-ihk-suhn, YOH-a-kihm) VAN

Goaltender. Catches right. 6'1", 189 lbs. Born, Gavle, Sweden, April 9, 1990.
(Philadelphia's 5th choice, 196th overall, in 2008 Entry Draft).

			Regular Season								Playoffs						
Season	**Club**	**League**	**GP**	**W**	**L**	**O/T**	**Mins**	**GA**	**SO**	**Avg**	**GP**	**W**	**L**	**Mins**	**GA**	**SO**	**Avg**
2006-07	Valbo AIF Jr.	Swe-Jr.	18	....	....	....	1072	55	....	3.08	....	....	....	....	....	....	....
	Valbo AIF	Sweden-3	1	....	....	....	34	2	0	3.51	....	....	....	....	....	....	....
2007-08	Brynas U18	Swe-U18	9	....	....	....	545	21	2	2.31	5	....	....	296	7	2	1.42
	Brynas IF Gavle Jr.	Swe-Jr.	16	....	....	....	960	53	0	3.31	7	....	....	426	13	1	1.83
	Valbo HC	Sweden-3	2	....	....	....	123	8	0	3.91	....	....	....	....	....	....	....
2008-09	Brynas IF Gavle Jr.	Swe-Jr.	33	....	....	....	1962	65	6	1.99	7	....	....	468	19	0	2.43
2009-10	Leksands IF Jr.	Swe-Jr.	1	....	....	....	60	0	1	0.00	....	....	....	....	....	....	....
	Leksands IF	Sweden-2	48	....	....	....	2877	115	5	2.40	....	....	....	....	....	....	....
2010-11	Skelleftea AIK Jr.	Swe-Jr.	2	....	....	....	119	7	0	3.54	....	....	....	....	....	....	....
	Skelleftea AIK	Sweden	17	....	....	....	939	40	1	2.56	....	....	....	....	....	....	....
2011-12	Skelleftea AIK	Sweden	33	....	....	....	2016	61	3	1.82	19	....	....	1200	44	1	2.20
2012-13	Skelleftea AIK	Sweden	30	21	9	0	1726	48	5	1.67	10	*10	0	623	11	*3	*1.06
2013-14	**Vancouver**	**NHL**	**1**	**0**	**0**	**0**	**36**	**6**	**0**	**10.00**	....	....	....	....	....	....	....
	Utica Comets	AHL	*52	24	24	2	3009	131	5	2.61	....	....	....	....	....	....	....
2014-15	Utica Comets	AHL	41	22	10	7	2371	100	0	2.53	2	0	0	31	0	0	0.00
	NHL Totals		**1**	**0**	**0**	**0**	**36**	**6**	**0**	**10.00**	....	....	....	....	....	....	....

Signed as a free agent by **Vancouver**, June 17, 2013.

FAGERBLOM, Hugo (FAG-uhr-blawm, HEW-goh) FLA

Goaltender. Catches left. 6'6", 202 lbs. Born, Boras, Sweden, January 9, 1996.
(Florida's 6th choice, 182nd overall, in 2014 Entry Draft).

			Regular Season								Playoffs						
Season	Club	League	GP	W	L	O/T	Mins	GA	SO	Avg	GP	W	L	Mins	GA	SO	Avg
2012-13	Frolunda U18	Swe-U18	21	15	5	0	1193	33	5	1.66	1	0	1	34	2	0	3.54
2013-14	Frolunda U18	Swe-U18	20	15	5	0	1200	45	4	2.25	2	1	1	120	4	0	2.01
2014-15	Boras HC	Sweden-4	3	3	0	0	180	7	0	2.33	....	....	....	....	....	....	....
	Frolunda Jr.	Swe-Jr.	21	12	6	0	1147	49	2	2.56	4	2	1	209	7	0	2.01

FASTH, Viktor (FAWST, VIHK-tohr)

Goaltender. Catches left. 6', 185 lbs. Born, Kalix, Sweden, August 8, 1982.

			Regular Season								Playoffs						
Season	Club	League	GP	W	L	O/T	Mins	GA	SO	Avg	GP	W	L	Mins	GA	SO	Avg
2007-08	Vaxjo Lakers HC	Sweden-2	30	....	....	0	4	....	....	2.26	....	....	....	....	....	....	....
2008-09	Vaxjo Lakers HC	Sweden-2	9	....	....	....	....	....	....	3.04	....	....	....	....	....	....	....
2009-10	Vaxjo Lakers HC	Sweden-2	23	....	....	....	....	....	....	2.15	....	....	....	....	....	....	....
2010-11	AIK IF Solna	Sweden	42	....	....	....	2473	93	2	2.26	8	....	....	472	14	1	1.78
2011-12	AIK Solna	Sweden	46	....	....	....	2683	95	5	2.12	12	....	....	752	35	1	2.79
2012-13	Tingsryds AIF	Sweden-2	12	4	7	0	677	19	1	1.68	....	....	....	....	....	....	....
	Norfolk Admirals	AHL	3	1	2	0	183	6	0	1.96	....	....	....	....	....	....	....
	Anaheim	**NHL**	**25**	**15**	**6**	**2**	**1428**	**52**	**4**	**2.18**	....	....	....	....	....	....	....
2013-14	**Anaheim**	**NHL**	**5**	**2**	**2**	**1**	**305**	**15**	**0**	**2.95**	....	....	....	....	....	....	....
	Norfolk Admirals	AHL	5	3	2	0	275	11	0	2.40	....	....	....	....	....	....	....
	Edmonton	**NHL**	**7**	**3**	**3**	**1**	**396**	**18**	**0**	**2.73**	....	....	....	....	....	....	....
2014-15	**Edmonton**	**NHL**	**26**	**6**	**15**	**3**	**1336**	**76**	**0**	**3.41**	....	....	....	....	....	....	....
	NHL Totals		**63**	**26**	**26**	**7**	**3465**	**161**	**4**	**2.79**	....	....	....	....	....	....	....

Signed as a free agent by **Anaheim**, May 21, 2012. Signed as a free agent by **Tingsryds** (Sweden-2), September 21, 2012. Traded to **Edmonton** by **Anaheim** for Edmonton's 5th round choice (Matthew Berkovitz) in 2014 Entry Draft and Edmonton's 3rd round choice (later traded to Tampa Bay – Tampa Bay selected Dennis Yan) in 2015 Entry Draft, March 4, 2014.

FEDOTOV, Ivan (feh-DOH-tawv, ih-VAHN) PHI

Goaltender. Catches left. 6'6", 191 lbs. Born, St. Petersburg, Russia, November 28, 1996.
(Philadelphia's 9th choice, 188th overall, in 2015 Entry Draft).

			Regular Season								Playoffs						
Season	Club	League	GP	W	L	O/T	Mins	GA	SO	Avg	GP	W	L	Mins	GA	SO	Avg
2013-14	Nizhnekamsk Jr.	Russia-Jr.	24	7	11	0	1273	70	0	3.30	....	....	....	....	....	....	....
2014-15	Nizhnekamsk	KHL	1	0	0	0	20	2	0	6.00	....	....	....	....	....	....	....
	Nizhnekamsk Jr.	Russia-Jr.	41	21	10	0	2305	75	6	1.95	10	6	4	578	29	0	3.01

FLEURY, Marc-Andre (fluh-REE, MAHRK-AWN-dray) PIT

Goaltender. Catches left. 6'2", 180 lbs. Born, Sorel, QC, November 28, 1984.
(Pittsburgh's 1st choice, 1st overall, in 2003 Entry Draft).

			Regular Season								Playoffs						
Season	Club	League	GP	W	L	O/T	Mins	GA	SO	Avg	GP	W	L	Mins	GA	SO	Avg
99-2000	C.C. Lemoyne	QAAA	15	4	9	0	780	36	1	2.77	....	....	....	....	....	....	....
2000-01	Cape Breton	QMJHL	35	12	13	2	1705	115	0	4.05	2	0	1	32	4	0	7.50
2001-02	Cape Breton	QMJHL	55	26	14	8	3043	141	2	2.78	16	9	7	1003	55	0	3.29
2002-03	Cape Breton	QMJHL	51	17	24	6	2889	162	2	3.36	4	0	4	228	17	0	4.47
2003-04	**Pittsburgh**	**NHL**	**21**	**4**	**14**	**2**	**1154**	**70**	**1**	**3.64**	....	....	....	....	....	....	....
	Cape Breton	QMJHL	10	8	1	1	606	20	0	1.98	4	1	3	251	13	0	3.10
	Wilkes-Barre	AHL	....	....	....	....	....	....	....	....	2	0	1	92	6	0	3.90
2004-05	Wilkes-Barre	AHL	54	26	19	4	3029	127	5	2.52	4	0	2	151	11	0	4.36
2005-06	**Pittsburgh**	**NHL**	**50**	**13**	**27**	**6**	**2809**	**152**	**1**	**3.25**	....	....	....	....	....	....	....
	Wilkes-Barre	AHL	12	10	2	0	727	19	0	1.57	5	2	3	311	18	0	3.48
2006-07	**Pittsburgh**	**NHL**	**67**	**40**	**16**	**9**	**3905**	**184**	**5**	**2.83**	**5**	**1**	**4**	**287**	**18**	**0**	**3.76**
2007-08	**Pittsburgh**	**NHL**	**35**	**19**	**10**	**2**	**1857**	**72**	**4**	**2.33**	***20**	***14**	**6**	***1251**	**41**	***3**	**1.97**
	Wilkes-Barre	AHL	5	3	2	0	297	7	0	1.42	....	....	....	....	....	....	....
2008-09 ♦	**Pittsburgh**	**NHL**	**62**	**35**	**18**	**7**	**3641**	**162**	**4**	**2.67**	***24**	***16**	**8**	***1447**	**63**	**0**	**2.61**
2009-10	**Pittsburgh**	**NHL**	**67**	**37**	**21**	**6**	**3798**	**168**	**1**	**2.65**	**13**	**7**	**6**	**798**	**37**	**1**	**2.78**
	Canada	Olympics					DID NOT PLAY – SPARE GOALTENDER										
2010-11	**Pittsburgh**	**NHL**	**65**	**36**	**20**	**5**	**3695**	**143**	**3**	**2.32**	**7**	**3**	**4**	**405**	**17**	**1**	**2.52**
2011-12	**Pittsburgh**	**NHL**	**67**	**42**	**17**	**4**	**3896**	**153**	**3**	**2.36**	**6**	**2**	**4**	**337**	**26**	**0**	**4.63**
2012-13	**Pittsburgh**	**NHL**	**33**	**23**	**8**	**0**	**1858**	**74**	**1**	**2.39**	**5**	**2**	**2**	**290**	**17**	**1**	**3.52**
2013-14	**Pittsburgh**	**NHL**	**64**	**39**	**18**	**5**	**3792**	**150**	**5**	**2.37**	**13**	**7**	**6**	**800**	**32**	***2**	**2.40**
2014-15	**Pittsburgh**	**NHL**	**64**	**34**	**20**	**9**	**3776**	**146**	**10**	**2.32**	**5**	**1**	**4**	**312**	**11**	**0**	**2.12**
	NHL Totals		**595**	**322**	**189**	**55**	**34181**	**1474**	**38**	**2.59**	**98**	**53**	**44**	**5927**	**262**	**8**	**2.65**

QMJHL Second All-Star Team (2003)
Played in NHL All-Star Game (2011, 2015)

FORSBERG, Anton (FOHRZ-buhrg, AN-tawn) CBJ

Goaltender. Catches left. 6'2", 176 lbs. Born, Harnosand, Sweden, November 27, 1992.
(Columbus' 6th choice, 188th overall, in 2011 Entry Draft).

			Regular Season								Playoffs						
Season	Club	League	GP	W	L	O/T	Mins	GA	SO	Avg	GP	W	L	Mins	GA	SO	Avg
2007-08	Harnosand Jr.	Swe-Jr.	9	....	....	....	....	....	....	....	....	....	....	....	....	....	....
	Harnosand	Sweden-3	1	....	....	....	20	2	0	6.00	....	....	....	....	....	....	....
2008-09	MODO U18	Swe-U18	12	....	....	....	619	34	0	3.29	5	....	....	225	11	1	2.93
2009-10	MODO U18	Swe-U18	9	....	....	....	538	26	0	2.90	2	....	....	120	5	0	2.50
	MODO Jr.	Swe-Jr.	21	....	....	....	1183	73	1	3.70	3	....	....	177	7	0	2.37
2010-11	MODO Jr.	Swe-Jr.	33	....	....	....	1942	94	3	2.90	6	....	....	358	17	0	2.85
	AIK Harnosand	Sweden-3	1	....	....	....	59	5	0	5.11	....	....	....	....	....	....	....
2011-12	MODO	Sweden	14	....	....	....	609	32	0	3.15	....	....	....	....	....	....	....
	MODO Jr.	Swe-Jr.	14	....	....	....	847	31	2	2.19	4	....	....	248	14	0	3.39
2012-13	Sodertalje SK	Sweden-2	41	26	14	0	2432	90	3	2.22	....	....	....	....	....	....	....
2013-14	MODO	Sweden	22	11	11	0	1304	53	1	2.44	....	....	....	....	....	....	....
	Springfield Falcons	AHL	4	3	0	0	212	4	0	1.13	2	0	1	59	3	0	3.03
2014-15	**Columbus**	**NHL**	**5**	**0**	**4**	**0**	**256**	**20**	**0**	**4.69**	....	....	....	....	....	....	....
	Springfield Falcons	AHL	30	20	8	1	1764	59	3	2.01	....	....	....	....	....	....	....
	NHL Totals		**5**	**0**	**4**	**0**	**256**	**20**	**0**	**4.69**	....	....	....	....	....	....	....

FUCALE, Zachary (fuh-KAL-ee, za-KAH-ree) MTL

Goaltender. Catches left. 6'1", 187 lbs. Born, Rosemere, QC, May 28, 1995.
(Montreal's 3rd choice, 36th overall, in 2013 Entry Draft).

			Regular Season								Playoffs						
Season	Club	League	GP	W	L	O/T	Mins	GA	SO	Avg	GP	W	L	Mins	GA	SO	Avg
2010-11	Saint-Eustache	QAAA	28	15	5	3	1513	78	3	3.09	10	7	3	664	40	0	3.61
2011-12	Halifax	QMJHL	58	32	18	6	3249	171	2	3.16	17	10	7	1022	49	0	2.88
2012-13	Halifax	QMJHL	55	*45	5	3	3162	124	2	2.35	17	*16	1	*1042	35	*3	*2.02
2013-14	Halifax	QMJHL	50	*36	9	3	2917	110	6	*2.26	15	9	4	797	37	0	2.79
2014-15	Halifax	QMJHL	24	13	9	2	1426	76	2	3.20	....	....	....	....	....	....	....
	Quebec Remparts	QMJHL	17	8	8	0	933	50	1	3.22	20	14	6	1194	51	1	2.56

QMJHL First All-Star Team (2013) • Memorial Cup All-Star Team (2013) • QMJHL Second All-Star Team (2014)

GAYDUCHENKO, Sergei (gay-doo-CHEHN-koh, SAIR-gay) FLA

Goaltender. Catches left. 6'5", 222 lbs. Born, Kiev, USSR, June 6, 1989.
(Florida's 8th choice, 202nd overall, in 2007 Entry Draft).

			Regular Season								Playoffs						
Season	Club	League	GP	W	L	O/T	Mins	GA	SO	Avg	GP	W	L	Mins	GA	SO	Avg
2006-07	Yaroslavl 2	Russia-3	23	....	....	....	1180	57	3	2.90	....	....	....	....	....	....	....
2007-08	Novokuznetsk 2	Russia-3	2	....	....	....	....	5	....	....	....	....	....	....	....	....	....
	Novokuznetsk	Russia	11	....	....	....	533	27	0	3.04	....	....	....	....	....	....	....
2008-09	Yaroslavl 2	Russia-3					STATISTICS NOT AVAILABLE										
	Yaroslavl	KHL	3	....	....	....	185	6	0	1.95	....	....	....	....	....	....	....
2009-10	Yaroslavl	KHL	20	....	....	....	1091	44	0	2.42	....	....	....	....	....	....	....
2010-11	CSKA Moscow	KHL	23	....	....	....	1201	58	1	2.90	....	....	....	....	....	....	....
	CSKA Jr.	Russia-Jr.	7	....	....	....	332	21	1	3.80	15	....	....	872	28	2	1.93
2011-12	CSKA Moscow	KHL	13	2	6	0	623	30	0	2.86	2	0	0	105	7	0	4.01
2012-13	Sibir Novosibirsk	KHL	19	6	9	0	975	39	1	2.40	1	0	0	20	2	0	6.00
2013-14	Novosibirsk	KHL	8	....	....	....	....	....	....	3.42	....	....	....	....	....	....	....
2014-15	Kuban Krasnodar	Russia-2	25	....	....	....	....	2.43	....	....	1	....	....	....	3.87	....	....

GIBSON, Christopher (GIHB-suhn, KRIHS-tuh-fuhr) TOR

Goaltender. Catches left. 6'1", 188 lbs. Born, Karkkila, Finland, December 27, 1992.
(Los Angeles' 1st choice, 49th overall, in 2011 Entry Draft).

			Regular Season								Playoffs						
Season	Club	League	GP	W	L	O/T	Mins	GA	SO	Avg	GP	W	L	Mins	GA	SO	Avg
2008-09	Notre Dame	SMHL	18	16	1	0	1049	46	1	2.63	6	6	0	360	11	1	1.83
2009-10	Chicoutimi	QMJHL	29	8	19	0	1592	93	2	3.50	4	2	1	230	13	0	3.39
2010-11	Chicoutimi	QMJHL	37	14	15	8	2235	90	4	2.42	4	0	4	219	19	0	5.20
2011-12	Chicoutimi	QMJHL	48	27	17	4	2809	139	3	2.97	18	9	9	1116	58	*1	3.12
2012-13	Chicoutimi	QMJHL	41	17	18	4	2279	117	4	3.08	6	2	4	356	23	0	3.87
2013-14	Toronto Marlies	AHL	12	5	6	0	640	26	0	2.44	....	....	....	....	....	....	....
	Orlando	ECHL	20	8	9	2	1178	62	0	3.16	2	1	1	123	4	0	1.94
2014-15	Toronto Marlies	AHL	45	24	17	3	2605	105	2	2.42	4	2	2	231	15	0	3.90

QMJHL First All-Star Team (2011)

Signed as a free agent by **Toronto**, July 21, 2013.

GIBSON, John (GIHB-suhn, JAWN) ANA

Goaltender. Catches left. 6'3", 210 lbs. Born, Pittsburgh, PA, July 14, 1993.
(Anaheim's 2nd choice, 39th overall, in 2011 Entry Draft).

			Regular Season								Playoffs						
Season	Club	League	GP	W	L	O/T	Mins	GA	SO	Avg	GP	W	L	Mins	GA	SO	Avg
2009-10	USNTDP	USHL	18	7	9	0	1023	63	0	3.69	....	....	....	....	....	....	....
	USNTDP	U-17	6	3	1	1	335	16	0	2.87	....	....	....	....	....	....	....
	USNTDP	U-18	2	2	0	0	120	4	0	2.00	....	....	....	....	....	....	....
2010-11	USNTDP	USHL	17	9	4	3	983	39	1	2.38	....	....	....	....	....	....	....
	USNTDP	U-18	23	15	7	0	1255	56	0	2.68	....	....	....	....	....	....	....
2011-12	Kitchener Rangers	OHL	32	21	10	0	1897	87	1	2.75	16	8	7	898	40	1	2.67
2012-13	Kitchener Rangers	OHL	27	17	9	1	1615	65	1	2.41	10	5	5	609	22	1	2.17
	Norfolk Admirals	AHL	1	0	0	0	40	3	0	4.50	....	....	....	....	....	....	....
2013-14	**Anaheim**	**NHL**	**3**	**3**	**0**	**0**	**181**	**4**	**1**	**1.33**	**4**	**2**	**2**	**200**	**9**	**1**	**2.70**
	Norfolk Admirals	AHL	45	21	17	4	2587	101	5	2.34	6	4	2	373	9	1	*1.45
2014-15	**Anaheim**	**NHL**	**23**	**13**	**8**	**0**	**1340**	**58**	**1**	**2.60**	....	....	....	....	....	....	....
	Norfolk Admirals	AHL	11	6	3	2	665	23	1	2.07	....	....	....	....	....	....	....
	NHL Totals		**26**	**16**	**8**	**0**	**1521**	**62**	**2**	**2.45**	**4**	**2**	**2**	**200**	**9**	**1**	**2.70**

OHL Second All-Star Team (2013)

GILLIES, Jon (GIHL-eez, JAWN) CGY

Goaltender. Catches left. 6'5", 216 lbs. Born, Concord, NH, January 22, 1994.
(Calgary's 3rd choice, 75th overall, in 2012 Entry Draft).

			Regular Season								Playoffs						
Season	Club	League	GP	W	L	O/T	Mins	GA	SO	Avg	GP	W	L	Mins	GA	SO	Avg
2009-10	Salisbury School	High-CT	8	....	....	....	313	....	1	1.99	....	....	....	....	....	....	....
	Neponset Valley	Minor-MA					STATISTICS NOT AVAILABLE										
2010-11	Indiana Ice	USHL	25	15	6	2	1447	68	3	2.82	2	0	1	82	3	0	2.20
2011-12	Indiana Ice	USHL	53	31	11	9	2967	137	3	2.77	6	3	3	359	17	0	2.84
2012-13	Providence College	H-East	35	17	12	6	2105	73	5	2.08	....	....	....	....	....	....	....
2013-14	Providence College	H-East	34	19	9	5	2027	73	4	2.16	....	....	....	....	....	....	....
2014-15	Providence College	H-East	*39	24	13	2	*2301	77	*4	*2.01	....	....	....	....	....	....	....

Hockey East All-Rookie Team (2013) • Hockey East First All-Star Team (2013, 2015) • Hockey East Rookie of the Year (2013) • NCAA East Second All-American Team (2013, 2015)

GREISS, Thomas (GRIGHS, TAW-muhs) NYI

Goaltender. Catches left. 6'1", 220 lbs. Born, Fussen, West Germany, January 29, 1986.
(San Jose's 2nd choice, 94th overall, in 2004 Entry Draft).

			Regular Season								Playoffs						
Season	Club	League	GP	W	L	O/T	Mins	GA	SO	Avg	GP	W	L	Mins	GA	SO	Avg
2001-02	EV Fussen Jr.	Ger-Jr.					STATISTICS NOT AVAILABLE										
2002-03	Koln Jr.	Ger-Jr.	25	....	....	....	1613	58	0	2.16	3	1	2	180	8	1	2.67
2003-04	Koln Jr.	Ger-Jr.	24	....	....	....	1286	56	....	2.61	....	....	....	....	....	....	....
	Kolner Haie	Germany	1	....	....	....	20	4	0	12.00	....	....	....	....	....	....	....
2004-05	Kolner Haie	Germany	8	....	....	....	459	16	0	2.09	....	....	....	....	....	....	....
	Regensburg	German-2	1	....	....	....	60	2	0	2.00	2	....	....	56	2	0	2.14
2005-06	Kolner Haie	Germany	27	....	....	....	1560	64	1	2.46	9	....	....	533	27	*1	3.04
	Germany	Olympics	1	0	1	0	60	5	0	5.00	....	....	....	....	....	....	....
2006-07	Worcester Sharks	AHL	43	26	15	2	2555	111	0	2.61	3	0	3	172	12	0	4.18
	Fresno Falcons	ECHL	3	1	2	0	180	7	0	2.34	....	....	....	....	....	....	....
2007-08	**San Jose**	**NHL**	**3**	**0**	**1**	**1**	**129**	**7**	**0**	**3.26**	....	....	....	....	....	....	....
	Worcester Sharks	AHL	41	18	21	2	2424	125	0	3.09	....	....	....	....	....	....	....
2008-09	Worcester Sharks	AHL	57	30	24	2	3346	138	1	2.47	12	6	6	742	30	2	2.43
2009-10	**San Jose**	**NHL**	**16**	**7**	**4**	**1**	**782**	**35**	**0**	**2.69**	**1**	**0**	**0**	**40**	**2**	**0**	**3.00**
	Germany	Olympics	3	0	3	0	179	15	0	5.03	....	....	....	....	....	....	....
2010-11	Brynas IF Gavle	Sweden	32	....	....	....	1850	90	2	2.92	5	....	....	317	18	0	3.40
2011-12	**San Jose**	**NHL**	**19**	**9**	**7**	**1**	**1043**	**40**	**0**	**2.30**	....	....	....	....	....	....	....
2012-13	Hannover Scorp.	Germany	9	3	6	0	535	31	0	3.47	....	....	....	....	....	....	....
	San Jose	**NHL**	**6**	**1**	**4**	**0**	**308**	**13**	**1**	**2.53**	....	....	....	....	....	....	....
	Worcester Sharks	AHL	1	0	1	0	60	5	0	5.04	....	....	....	....	....	....	....
2013-14	**Phoenix**	**NHL**	**25**	**10**	**8**	**5**	**1312**	**50**	**2**	**2.29**	....	....	....	....	....	....	....
2014-15	**Pittsburgh**	**NHL**	**20**	**9**	**6**	**3**	**1159**	**50**	**0**	**2.59**	....	....	....	....	....	....	....
	NHL Totals		**89**	**36**	**30**	**11**	**4733**	**195**	**3**	**2.47**	**1**	**0**	**0**	**40**	**2**	**0**	**3.00**

• Re-assigned to **Gavle** (Sweden) by **San Jose**, October 21, 2010. Signed as a free agent by **Hannover** (Germany), November 20, 2012. Signed as a free agent by **Phoenix**, July 5, 2013. Signed as a free agent by **Pittsburgh**, July 1, 2014. Signed as a free agent by **NY Islanders**, July 1, 2015.

GROSENICK, Troy (GOHS-nihk, TROI) S.J.

Goaltender. Catches left. 6'1", 185 lbs. Born, Brookfield, WI, August 27, 1989.

			Regular Season								Playoffs						
Season	Club	League	GP	W	L	O/T	Mins	GA	SO	Avg	GP	W	L	Mins	GA	SO	Avg
2010-11	Union College	ECAC	3	0	0	1	85	3	0	2.12	....	....	....	....	....	....	....
2011-12	Union College	ECAC	34	22	6	3	1922	53	5	1.65	....	....	....	....	....	....	....
2012-13	Union College	ECAC	34	17	10	5	1929	68	2	2.12	....	....	....	....	....	....	....
2013-14	Worcester Sharks	AHL	35	18	14	0	1966	86	2	2.62	....	....	....	....	....	....	....
2014-15	**San Jose**	**NHL**	**2**	**1**	**1**	**0**	**118**	**3**	**1**	**1.53**	....	....	....	....	....	....	....
	Worcester Sharks	AHL	36	20	13	3	2167	95	1	2.63	2	1	0	88	5	0	3.41
	NHL Totals		**2**	**1**	**1**	**0**	**118**	**3**	**1**	**1.53**	....	....	....	....	....	....	....

ECAC First All-Star Team (2012) • NCAA East First All-American Team (2012)

Signed as a free agent by **San Jose**, April 8, 2013.

GRUBAUER, Philipp (groo-BAHW-uhr, FIHL-ihp) WSH

Goaltender. Catches left. 6'1", 184 lbs. Born, Rosenheim, Germany, November 25, 1991.
(Washington's 3rd choice, 112th overall, in 2010 Entry Draft).

			Regular Season								Playoffs						
Season	Club	League	GP	W	L	O/T	Mins	GA	SO	Avg	GP	W	L	Mins	GA	SO	Avg
2006-07	Rosenheim Jr.	Ger-Jr.	6	....	....	....	354	49	....	8.32	3	....	....	180	12	....	4.00
2007-08	Rosenheim Jr.	Ger-Jr.	23	....	....	....	1288	71	....	3.31	3	....	....	181	8	....	2.65
	Rosenheim	German-3	5	....	....	....	307	14	1	2.74	7	....	....	420	12	....	1.71
2008-09	Belleville Bulls	OHL	17	7	8	0	947	62	1	3.93	1	0	0	56	4	0	4.26
2009-10	Belleville Bulls	OHL	31	10	14	5	1717	90	5	3.14	....	....	....	....	....	....	....
	Windsor Spitfires	OHL	19	13	1	2	1011	40	2	2.37	18	*16	2	1094	49	0	2.69
2010-11	Kingston	OHL	38	22	13	3	2239	135	2	3.62	....	....	....	....	....	....	....
2011-12	South Carolina	ECHL	43	23	13	5	2536	94	1	2.22	....	....	....	....	....	....	....
2012-13	Reading Royals	ECHL	26	19	5	1	1542	59	0	2.30	....	....	....	....	....	....	....
	Hershey Bears	AHL	28	15	9	2	1624	61	2	2.25	5	2	3	301	19	0	3.79
	Washington	**NHL**	**2**	**0**	**1**	**0**	**84**	**5**	**0**	**3.57**	....	....	....	....	....	....	....
2013-14	**Washington**	**NHL**	**17**	**6**	**5**	**5**	**883**	**35**	**0**	**2.38**	....	....	....	....	....	....	....
	Hershey Bears	AHL	28	13	13	2	1685	73	3	2.60	....	....	....	....	....	....	....
2014-15	**Washington**	**NHL**	**1**	**1**	**0**	**0**	**65**	**2**	**0**	**1.85**	**1**	**1**	**0**	**60**	**3**	**0**	**3.00**
	Hershey Bears	AHL	49	27	17	5	2918	112	6	2.30	7	2	4	394	22	0	3.35
	NHL Totals		**20**	**7**	**6**	**5**	**1032**	**42**	**0**	**2.44**	**1**	**1**	**0**	**60**	**3**	**0**	**3.00**

GUDLEVSKIS, Kristers (guhd-LEHV-skihz, KRIHS-tuhrs) T.B.

Goaltender. Catches left. 6'4", 190 lbs. Born, Aizkraukle, Latvia, July 31, 1992.
(Tampa Bay's 3rd choice, 124th overall, in 2013 Entry Draft).

			Regular Season								Playoffs						
Season	Club	League	GP	W	L	O/T	Mins	GA	SO	Avg	GP	W	L	Mins	GA	SO	Avg
2009-10	HK Ogre	Latvia	9	....	....	....	....	....	....	6.12	....	....	....	....	....	....	....
	Ozolnieki-Juniors	Belarus-2	31	....	....	....	....	157	....	....	....	....	....	....	....	....	....
2010-11	HK Riga Jr.	Russia-Jr.	49	....	....	....	2760	101	7	2.20	3	....	....	188	13	0	4.16
2011-12	HK Riga Jr.	Russia-Jr.	40	....	....	....	2285	91	1	2.39	4	....	....	257	15	0	3.50
2012-13	Dynamo Riga	KHL	2	1	1	0	82	3	0	2.18	....	....	....	....	....	....	....
	HK Riga Jr.	Russia-Jr.	56	....	....	....	3190	111	3	2.09	3	....	....	154	19	0	7.42
	Juniors Riga Jr.	Rus.-Jr. B	2	....	....	....	120	6	0	3.00	....	....	....	....	....	....	....
	HK Juniors Riga Jr.	Latvia	....	....	....	....	....	....	....	....	1	....	....	59	1	0	1.02
2013-14	**Tampa Bay**	**NHL**	**1**	**1**	**0**	**0**	**60**	**2**	**0**	**2.00**	**2**	**0**	**1**	**40**	**2**	**0**	**3.00**
	Syracuse Crunch	AHL	34	18	11	4	1901	85	5	2.68	....	....	....	....	....	....	....
	Florida Everblades	ECHL	11	7	4	0	656	20	2	1.83	....	....	....	....	....	....	....
	Latvia	Olympics	2	0	2	0	119	7	0	3.54	....	....	....	....	....	....	....
2014-15	Syracuse Crunch	AHL	46	25	14	4	2673	125	2	2.81	3	0	3	145	12	0	4.96
	NHL Totals		**1**	**1**	**0**	**0**	**60**	**2**	**0**	**2.00**	**2**	**0**	**1**	**40**	**2**	**0**	**3.00**

GUSTAFSSON, Johan (GUHS-tahf-suhn, YOH-han) MIN

Goaltender. Catches left. 6'2", 199 lbs. Born, Koping, Sweden, February 28, 1992.
(Minnesota's 5th choice, 159th overall, in 2010 Entry Draft).

			Regular Season								Playoffs						
Season	Club	League	GP	W	L	O/T	Mins	GA	SO	Avg	GP	W	L	Mins	GA	SO	Avg
2006-07	IFK Arboga IK	Sweden-2	4	....	....	....	201	22	0	6.55	....	....	....	....	....	....	....
2007-08	Kopings HC	Sweden-4					STATISTICS NOT AVAILABLE										
2008-09	Farjestad U18	Swe-U18	27	....	....	....	1581	47	5	1.78	4	....	....	228	14	0	3.68
2009-10	Farjestad U18	Swe-U18	10	....	....	....	600	34	1	3.40	7	....	....	417	22	0	3.16
	Farjestad	Sweden	3	....	....	....	136	9	0	3.96	....	....	....	....	....	....	....
	Skare BK	Sweden-3	26	....	....	....	1553	74	2	2.86	....	....	....	....	....	....	....
2010-11	VIK Vasteras HK Jr.	Swe-Jr.	7	....	....	....	424	20	1	2.83	....	....	....	....	....	....	....
	VIK Vasteras HK	Sweden-2	28	....	....	....	1632	64	2	2.35	....	....	....	....	....	....	....
2011-12	Lulea HF	Sweden	29	....	....	....	1754	51	6	1.74	3	....	....	179	10	0	3.36
2012-13	Lulea HF	Sweden	33	20	13	0	2016	57	4	1.70	*15	8	7	*946	32	0	2.03
2013-14	Iowa Wild	AHL	40	12	20	4	2253	112	1	2.98	....	....	....	....	....	....	....
2014-15	Iowa Wild	AHL	35	8	22	1	1842	107	0	3.48	....	....	....	....	....	....	....
	Alaska Aces	ECHL	5	4	1	0	304	15	0	2.96	....	....	....	....	....	....	....

Signed as a free agent by **Frolunda** (Sweden), May 4, 2015.

GUSTAVSSON, Jonas (GUHS-tahv-suhn, YOH-nuhs)

Goaltender. Catches left. 6'3", 192 lbs. Born, Danderyd, Sweden, October 24, 1984.

			Regular Season								Playoffs						
Season	Club	League	GP	W	L	O/T	Mins	GA	SO	Avg	GP	W	L	Mins	GA	SO	Avg
2000-01	AIK Solna U18	Swe-U18	12	....	....	....	667	42	1	3.78	....	....	....	....	....	....	....
2001-02	AIK Solna U18	Swe-U18	8	....	....	....	439	13	2	1.78	4	....	....	239	12	0	3.01
2002-03	AIK Solna Jr.	Swe-Jr.	21	....	....	....	1261	69	0	3.28	4	....	....	198	9	0	2.72
2003-04	AIK Solna Jr.	Swe-Jr.	9	....	....	....	505	24	0	2.85	....	....	....	....	....	....	....
	AIK Solna	Sweden-2	1	....	....	....	20	1	0	2.95	....	....	....	....	....	....	....
2004-05	AIK Solna Jr.	Swe-Jr.	10	....	....	....	557	32	0	3.45	....	....	....	....	....	....	....
	AIK Solna	Sweden-3	22	....	....	....	1270	32	4	1.51	....	....	....	....	....	....	....
2005-06	AIK Solna Jr.	Swe-Jr.	5	....	....	....	258	14	0	3.26	....	....	....	....	....	....	....
	AIK Solna	Sweden-2	6	....	....	....	351	14	0	2.39	....	....	....	....	....	....	....
2006-07	AIK IF Solna	Sweden-2	23	....	....	....	1269	59	2	2.79	....	....	....	....	....	....	....
2007-08	Skare BK	Sweden-3	6	....	....	....	368	16	0	2.61	....	....	....	....	....	....	....
	Farjestad	Sweden	20	....	....	....	1102	44	2	2.40	10	....	....	517	31	0	3.60
2008-09	Farjestad	Sweden	42	....	....	....	2475	81	3	*1.96	13	....	....	819	14	*5	*1.03
2009-10	**Toronto**	**NHL**	**42**	**16**	**15**	**9**	**2340**	**112**	**1**	**2.87**	....	....	....	....	....	....	....
	Sweden	Olympics	1	1	0	0	60	2	0	2.00	....	....	....	....	....	....	....
2010-11	**Toronto**	**NHL**	**23**	**6**	**13**	**2**	**1242**	**68**	**0**	**3.29**	....	....	....	....	....	....	....
	Toronto Marlies	AHL	5	3	1	1	263	5	0	1.14	....	....	....	....	....	....	....
2011-12	**Toronto**	**NHL**	**42**	**17**	**17**	**4**	**2301**	**112**	**4**	**2.92**	....	....	....	....	....	....	....
2012-13	**Detroit**	**NHL**	**7**	**2**	**2**	**1**	**349**	**17**	**0**	**2.92**	....	....	....	....	....	....	....
	Grand Rapids	AHL	1	1	0	0	60	1	0	1.00	....	....	....	....	....	....	....
2013-14	**Detroit**	**NHL**	**27**	**16**	**5**	**4**	**1551**	**68**	**0**	**2.63**	**2**	**0**	**2**	**133**	**6**	**0**	**2.71**
	Sweden	Olympics					DID NOT PLAY – SPARE GOALTENDER										
2014-15	**Detroit**	**NHL**	**7**	**3**	**3**	**1**	**351**	**15**	**1**	**2.56**	....	....	....	....	....	....	....
	Grand Rapids	AHL	2	1	1	0	119	4	0	2.02	....	....	....	....	....	....	....
	NHL Totals		**148**	**60**	**55**	**21**	**8134**	**392**	**6**	**2.89**	**2**	**0**	**2**	**133**	**6**	**0**	**2.71**

Signed as a free agent by **Toronto**, July 7, 2009. Traded to **Winnipeg** by **Toronto** for future considerations, June 23, 2012. Signed as a free agent by **Detroit**, July 1, 2012. • Missed majority of 2014-15 due to separated shoulder injury vs. NY Rangers, November 5, 2014.

HACKETT, Matt (HA-keht, MA-thew) ANA

Goaltender. Catches left. 6'2", 171 lbs. Born, London, ON, March 7, 1990.
(Minnesota's 2nd choice, 77th overall, in 2009 Entry Draft).

			Regular Season								Playoffs						
Season	Club	League	GP	W	L	O/T	Mins	GA	SO	Avg	GP	W	L	Mins	GA	SO	Avg
2006-07	London Jr. Knights	Minor-ON	38	28	7	3	....	52	20	1.39	6	5	1	....	12	2	2.00
	St. Catharines	ON-Jr.B	16	7	7	0	902	63	0	4.19	....	....	....	....	....	....	....
	Windsor Spitfires	OHL	7	0	7	0	429	36	0	5.04	....	....	....	....	....	....	....
2007-08	Windsor Spitfires	OHL	4	1	1	0	130	10	0	4.61	....	....	....	....	....	....	....
	Plymouth Whalers	OHL	18	6	9	1	978	56	0	3.44	1	0	0	16	0	0	0.00
2008-09	Plymouth Whalers	OHL	55	34	15	3	3036	154	2	3.04	11	6	5	638	32	*1	3.01
2009-10	Plymouth Whalers	OHL	56	33	18	3	3165	138	4	2.62	8	3	4	429	24	0	3.36
2010-11	Houston Aeros	AHL	45	23	16	4	2552	101	2	2.37	*24	*14	10	*1465	61	1	2.50
2011-12	**Minnesota**	**NHL**	**12**	**3**	**6**	**0**	**556**	**22**	**0**	**2.37**	....	....	....	....	....	....	....
	Houston Aeros	AHL	44	20	17	6	2546	101	1	2.38	2	0	2	61	6	0	5.93
2012-13	Houston Aeros	AHL	43	19	20	3	2574	114	0	2.66	....	....	....	....	....	....	....
	Minnesota	**NHL**	**1**	**0**	**1**	**0**	**59**	**5**	**0**	**5.08**	....	....	....	....	....	....	....
	Rochester	AHL	3	3	0	0	185	5	0	1.62	1	0	1	58	2	0	2.08
2013-14	**Buffalo**	**NHL**	**8**	**1**	**6**	**1**	**426**	**22**	**0**	**3.10**	....	....	....	....	....	....	....
	Rochester	AHL	33	13	17	2	1952	100	0	3.07	....	....	....	....	....	....	....
2014-15	**Buffalo**	**NHL**	**5**	**0**	**4**	**1**	**250**	**18**	**0**	**4.32**	....	....	....	....	....	....	....
	Rochester	AHL	16	8	5	3	934	43	0	2.76	....	....	....	....	....	....	....
	NHL Totals		**26**	**4**	**17**	**2**	**1291**	**67**	**0**	**3.11**	....	....	....	....	....	....	....

OHL Second All-Star Team (2010)

Traded to **Buffalo** by **Minnesota** with Johan Larsson, Minnesota's 1st round choice (Nikita Zadorov) in 2013 Entry Draft and Minnesota's 2nd round choice (Vaclav Karabacek) in 2014 Entry Draft for Jason Pominville and Buffalo's 4th round choice (later traded to Edmonton – Edmonton selected William Lagesson) in 2014 Entry Draft, April 3, 2013. Signed as a free agent by **Anaheim**, July 1, 2015.

HALAK, Jaroslav (HA-lak, YAHR-roh-slav) NYI

Goaltender. Catches left. 5'11", 186 lbs. Born, Bratislava, Czech., May 13, 1985.
(Montreal's 11th choice, 271st overall, in 2003 Entry Draft).

			Regular Season								Playoffs						
Season	Club	League	GP	W	L	O/T	Mins	GA	SO	Avg	GP	W	L	Mins	GA	SO	Avg
2001-02	Bratislava Jr.	Slovak-Jr.	22	....	....	....	1257	41	0	1.96	6	6	0	353	7	2	1.19
2002-03	Bratislava Jr.	Slovak-Jr.	20	13	3	3	1200	41	1	2.02	....	....	....	....	....	....	....
2003-04	Bratislava Jr.	Slovak-Jr.	29	....	....	....	1694	51	....	1.81	....	....	....	....	....	....	....
	HK 91 Senica	Slovak-2	21	....	....	....	1240	54	....	2.61	....	....	....	....	....	....	....
	Bratislava	Slovakia	12	....	....	....	650	18	0	1.66	1	....	....	45	6	0	8.00
2004-05	Lewiston	QMJHL	47	24	17	4	2697	125	4	2.78	8	4	4	460	27	0	3.52
2005-06	Hamilton Bulldogs	AHL	13	7	6	0	786	30	3	2.29	....	....	....	....	....	....	....
	Long Beach	ECHL	20	11	4	2	1026	35	2	2.05	4	2	2	252	13	0	3.10
2006-07	**Montreal**	**NHL**	**16**	**10**	**6**	**0**	**912**	**44**	**2**	**2.89**	....	....	....	....	....	....	....
	Hamilton Bulldogs	AHL	28	16	11	0	1618	54	6	*2.00	....	....	....	....	....	....	....
2007-08	**Montreal**	**NHL**	**6**	**2**	**1**	**1**	**285**	**10**	**1**	**2.11**	**2**	**0**	**1**	**77**	**3**	**0**	**2.34**
	Hamilton Bulldogs	AHL	28	15	10	2	1630	57	2	2.10	....	....	....	....	....	....	....
2008-09	**Montreal**	**NHL**	**34**	**18**	**14**	**1**	**1931**	**92**	**1**	**2.86**	**1**	**0**	**0**	**20**	**0**	**0**	**0.00**
2009-10	**Montreal**	**NHL**	**45**	**26**	**13**	**5**	**2630**	**105**	**5**	**2.40**	**18**	**9**	**9**	**1013**	**43**	**0**	**2.55**
	Slovakia	Olympics	7	3	4	0	423	17	1	2.41	....	....	....	....	....	....	....
2010-11	**St. Louis**	**NHL**	**57**	**27**	**21**	**7**	**3294**	**136**	**7**	**2.48**	....	....	....	....	....	....	....
2011-12	**St. Louis**	**NHL**	**46**	**26**	**12**	**7**	**2747**	**90**	**6**	**1.97**	**2**	**1**	**1**	**104**	**3**	**0**	**1.73**
2012-13	Weiswasser	German-2	1	1	0	0	65	1	0	0.92	....	....	....	....	....	....	....
	St. Louis	**NHL**	**16**	**6**	**5**	**1**	**813**	**29**	**3**	**2.14**	....	....	....	....	....	....	....
2013-14	**St. Louis**	**NHL**	**40**	**24**	**9**	**4**	**2238**	**83**	**4**	**2.23**	....	....	....	....	....	....	....
	Slovakia	Olympics	2	....	....	....	94	8	0	5.13	....	....	....	....	....	....	....
	Washington	**NHL**	**12**	**5**	**4**	**3**	**701**	**27**	**1**	**2.31**	....	....	....	....	....	....	....
2014-15	**NY Islanders**	**NHL**	**59**	**38**	**17**	**4**	**3550**	**144**	**6**	**2.43**	**7**	**3**	**4**	**418**	**16**	**0**	**2.30**
	NHL Totals		**331**	**182**	**102**	**33**	**19101**	**760**	**36**	**2.39**	**30**	**13**	**15**	**1632**	**65**	**0**	**2.39**

AHL All-Rookie Team (2007) • William M. Jennings Trophy (2012) (shared with Brian Elliott)

Played in NHL All-Star Game (2015)

Traded to **St. Louis** by **Montreal** for Lars Eller and Ian Schultz, June 17, 2010. Signed as a free agent by **Weiswasser** (German-2), November 21, 2012. Traded to **Buffalo** by **St. Louis** with Chris Stewart, William Carrier, St. Louis' 1st round choice (later traded to Winnipeg – Winnipeg selected Jack Roslovic) in 2015 Entry Draft and St. Louis' 3rd round choice in 2016 Entry Draft for Ryan Miller and Steve Ott, February 28, 2014. Traded to **Washington** by **Buffalo** with Buffalo's 3rd round choice (later traded to NY Rangers – NY Rangers selected Robin Kovacs) in 2015 Entry Draft for Michal Neuvirth and Rostislav Klesla, March 5, 2014. Traded to **NY Islanders** by **Washington** for Chicago's 4th round choice (previously acquired, later traded to NY Rangers – NY Rangers selected Igor Shesterkin) in 2014 Entry Draft, May 1, 2014.

HALVERSON, Brandon (HAL-vuhr-suhn, BRAN-duhn) NYR

Goaltender. Catches left. 6'4", 185 lbs. Born, Traverse City, MI, March 29, 1996.
(NY Rangers' 1st choice, 59th overall, in 2014 Entry Draft).

			Regular Season								Playoffs						
Season	Club	League	GP	W	L	O/T	Mins	GA	SO	Avg	GP	W	L	Mins	GA	SO	Avg
2010-11	Det. Vic. Honda	T1EHL	22	4	10	6	882	61	1	3.11	....	....	....	....	....	....	....
	Det. Vic. Honda	Minor-MI	3	1	2	0	144	9	1	3.00	....	....	....	....	....	....	....
2011-12	Det. L.C. U16	HPHL	20	6	10	2	874	45	1	3.09	....	....	....	....	....	....	....
2012-13	Oak. Grizzlies U18	T1EHL	21	9	9	2	1069	57	0	2.88	4	2	1	209	6	0	1.46
2013-14	Sault Ste. Marie	OHL	19	12	6	1	1136	56	2	2.96	....	....	....	....	....	....	....
2014-15	Sault Ste. Marie	OHL	50	40	5	2	2784	122	6	2.63	14	10	4	796	39	1	2.94

HAMMOND, Andrew (HAM-uhnd, AN-droo) OTT

Goaltender. Catches left. 6'1", 217 lbs. Born, Surrey, BC, February 11, 1988.

			Regular Season								Playoffs						
Season	Club	League	GP	W	L	O/T	Mins	GA	SO	Avg	GP	W	L	Mins	GA	SO	Avg
2006-07	Grandview Steelers	PIJHL	28	17	5	3	1568	60	3	2.30	16	9	7	988	44	1	2.67
	Alberni Valley	BCHL	1	0	1	0	34	4	0	7.03	....	....	....	....	....	....	....
2007-08	Surrey Eagles	BCHL	32	15	14	1	1568	90	2	3.44	....	....	....	....	....	....	....
	Vernon Vipers	BCHL	9	6	3	0	538	22	1	2.45	7	3	3	412	20	0	2.91
2008-09	Vernon Vipers	BCHL	43	27	12	1	2479	95	5	2.30	17	12	5	1082	27	4	1.50
2009-10	Bowling Green	CCHA	19	0	12	2	837	60	0	4.30	....	....	....	....	....	....	....
2010-11	Bowling Green	CCHA	27	6	17	3	1528	68	2	2.67	....	....	....	....	....	....	....
2011-12	Bowling Green	CCHA	44	14	24	5	2615	119	2	2.73	....	....	....	....	....	....	....
2012-13	Bowling Green	CCHA	29	10	15	3	1625	67	3	2.47	....	....	....	....	....	....	....
2013-14	**Ottawa**	**NHL**	**1**	**0**	**0**	**0**	**35**	**0**	**0**	**0.00**	....	....	....	....	....	....	....
	Binghamton	AHL	48	25	19	3	2733	128	1	2.81	4	1	3	265	13	0	2.95
2014-15	**Ottawa**	**NHL**	**24**	**20**	**1**	**2**	**1411**	**42**	**3**	**1.79**	**2**	**0**	**2**	**122**	**7**	**0**	**3.44**
	Binghamton	AHL	25	7	13	2	1369	80	2	3.51	....	....	....	....	....	....	....
	NHL Totals		**25**	**20**	**1**	**2**	**1446**	**42**	**3**	**1.74**	**2**	**0**	**2**	**122**	**7**	**0**	**3.44**

Signed as a free agent by **Ottawa**, March 20, 2013.

HARDING, Josh (HAHR-dihng, JAWSH)

Goaltender. Catches right. 6'2", 194 lbs. Born, Regina, SK, June 18, 1984.
(Minnesota's 2nd choice, 38th overall, in 2002 Entry Draft).

			Regular Season								Playoffs						
Season	Club	League	GP	W	L	O/T	Mins	GA	SO	Avg	GP	W	L	Mins	GA	SO	Avg
2000-01	Reg. Pat Cdns.	SMHL	36	17	13	0	2106	96	2	2.75	3	1	2	170	11	0	3.88
2001-02	Regina Pats	WHL	42	27	13	1	2389	95	*4	2.39	6	2	4	326	16	0	2.95
2002-03	Regina Pats	WHL	57	18	25	13	*3384	155	3	2.75	5	1	4	320	13	0	2.44
2003-04	Regina Pats	WHL	28	12	14	2	1664	67	2	2.42	....	....	....	....	....	....	....
	Brandon	WHL	27	13	11	3	1612	65	5	2.42	11	5	6	660	36	0	3.27
2004-05	Houston Aeros	AHL	42	21	16	3	2388	80	4	2.01	2	0	2	119	8	0	4.03
2005-06	**Minnesota**	**NHL**	**3**	**2**	**1**	**0**	**185**	**8**	**1**	**2.59**	....	....	....	....	....	....	....
	Houston Aeros	AHL	38	29	8	0	2215	99	2	2.68	8	4	4	476	30	0	3.79
2006-07	**Minnesota**	**NHL**	**7**	**3**	**2**	**1**	**361**	**7**	**1**	**1.16**	....	....	....	....	....	....	....
	Houston Aeros	AHL	38	17	16	4	2270	94	1	2.48	....	....	....	....	....	....	....
2007-08	**Minnesota**	**NHL**	**29**	**11**	**15**	**2**	**1571**	**77**	**1**	**2.94**	**1**	**0**	**0**	**20**	**0**	**0**	**0.00**
2008-09	**Minnesota**	**NHL**	**19**	**3**	**9**	**1**	**870**	**32**	**0**	**2.21**	....	....	....	....	....	....	....
2009-10	**Minnesota**	**NHL**	**25**	**9**	**12**	**0**	**1300**	**66**	**1**	**3.05**	....	....	....	....	....	....	....
2010-11	**Minnesota**	**NHL**	DID NOT PLAY – INJURED														
2011-12	**Minnesota**	**NHL**	**34**	**13**	**12**	**4**	**1855**	**81**	**2**	**2.62**	....	....	....	....	....	....	....
2012-13	**Minnesota**	**NHL**	**5**	**1**	**1**	**0**	**185**	**10**	**1**	**3.24**	**5**	**1**	**4**	**245**	**12**	**0**	**2.94**
	Houston Aeros	AHL	2	1	1	0	100	5	0	3.00	....	....	....	....	....	....	....
2013-14	**Minnesota**	**NHL**	**29**	**18**	**7**	**3**	**1668**	**46**	**3**	***1.65**	....	....	....	....	....	....	....
2014-15	Iowa Wild	AHL	2	0	1	1	107	6	0	3.37	....	....	....	....	....	....	....
	NHL Totals		**151**	**60**	**59**	**11**	**7995**	**327**	**10**	**2.45**	**6**	**1**	**4**	**265**	**12**	**0**	**2.72**

WHL East Second All-Star Team (2002) • WHL East First All-Star Team (2003) • WHL Goaltender of the Year (2003) • WHL Player of the Year (2003) • Canadian Major Junior Second All-Star Team (2003) • Bill Masterton Memorial Trophy (2013)

• Missed 2010-11 due to knee injury at St. Louis, September 24, 2010. • Missed majority of 2012-13 after being diagnosed with multiple sclerosis, February 12, 2013. • Missed majority of 2014-15 due to recurring foot injury.

HAWKEY, Hayden (HAW-kee, HAY-duhn) MTL

Goaltender. Catches left. 6'2", 180 lbs. Born, Fremont, CA, March 1, 1995.
(Montreal's 5th choice, 177th overall, in 2014 Entry Draft).

			Regular Season								Playoffs						
Season	Club	League	GP	W	L	O/T	Mins	GA	SO	Avg	GP	W	L	Mins	GA	SO	Avg
2011-12	Col. T-birds U16	T1EHL	20	16	0	3	1060	20	6	1.02	....	....	....	....	....	....	....
	Col. T-birds U18	T1EHL	2	2	0	0	108	3	0	1.50	....	....	....	....	....	....	....
2012-13	Col. T-birds U18	T1EHL	26	18	7	0	1391	50	4	1.94	3	0	1	163	8	0	2.50
2013-14	Omaha Lancers	USHL	33	22	6	3	1901	63	3	*1.99	4	1	3	256	12	0	2.82
2014-15	Omaha Lancers	USHL	15	5	7	2	801	40	1	2.99	....	....	....	....	....	....	....

USHL All-Rookie Team (2014) • USHL First All-Star Team (2014) • USHL Goaltender of the Year (2014)

• Signed Letter of Intent to attend **Providence College** (Hockey East) in fall of 2015.

HELLBERG, Magnus (HEHL-buhrg, MAG-nuhs) NYR

Goaltender. Catches left. 6'6", 199 lbs. Born, Uppsala, Sweden, April 4, 1991.
(Nashville's 1st choice, 38th overall, in 2011 Entry Draft).

			Regular Season								Playoffs						
Season	Club	League	GP	W	L	O/T	Mins	GA	SO	Avg	GP	W	L	Mins	GA	SO	Avg
2007-08	Arlanda U18	Swe-U18	11	....	....	....	....	....	....	....	....	....	....	....	....	....	....
	Arlanda Jr.	Swe-Jr.	1	....	....	....	....	....	....	8.00	....	....	....	....	....	....	....
2008-09	Arlanda U18	Swe-U18	33	....	....	....	1979	103	2	3.12	....	....	....	....	....	....	....
	Wings HC Arlanda	Sweden-3	2	....	....	....	119	7	0	3.52	....	....	....	....	....	....	....
2009-10	Almtuna Jr.	Swe-Jr.	22	....	....	....	1339	44	2	1.97	....	....	....	....	....	....	....
	IF Vallentuna BK	Sweden-3	1	....	....	....	24	3	0	7.57	....	....	....	....	....	....	....
2010-11	IFK Kumla IK	Sweden-3	3	....	....	....	179	6	0	2.01	....	....	....	....	....	....	....
	Almtuna	Sweden-2	31	....	....	....	1790	61	5	2.04	5	....	....	277	15	0	3.24
2011-12	Frolunda	Sweden	17	....	....	....	1016	44	2	2.60	....	....	....	....	....	....	....
	Frolunda Jr.	Swe-Jr.	2	....	....	....	120	8	0	4.00	....	....	....	....	....	....	....
	Orebro HK	Sweden-2	3	....	....	....	180	10	0	3.33	....	....	....	....	....	....	....
2012-13	Milwaukee	AHL	39	22	13	0	2107	75	6	2.14	4	1	3	248	7	1	1.69
	Cincinnati	ECHL	2	1	1	0	119	5	0	2.52	....	....	....	....	....	....	....
2013-14	**Nashville**	**NHL**	**1**	**0**	**0**	**0**	**12**	**1**	**0**	**5.00**	....	....	....	....	....	....	....
	Milwaukee	AHL	21	5	13	1	1168	55	1	2.82	....	....	....	....	....	....	....
	Cincinnati	ECHL	7	5	1	1	394	19	0	2.89	....	....	....	....	....	....	....
2014-15	Milwaukee	AHL	38	15	10	6	2007	78	3	2.33	....	....	....	....	....	....	....
	NHL Totals		**1**	**0**	**0**	**0**	**12**	**1**	**0**	**5.00**	....	....	....	....	....	....	....

Traded to **NY Rangers** by **Nashville** for NY Rangers' 6th round choice in 2017 Entry Draft, July 1, 2015.

HELLEBUYCK, Connor (hehl-ee-BUHK, KAW-nuhr) WPG

Goaltender. Catches left. 6'4", 203 lbs. Born, Commerce, MI, May 19, 1993.
(Winnipeg's 4th choice, 130th overall, in 2012 Entry Draft).

			Regular Season								Playoffs						
Season	Club	League	GP	W	L	O/T	Mins	GA	SO	Avg	GP	W	L	Mins	GA	SO	Avg
2010-11	Walled Lake	High-MI	STATISTICS NOT AVAILABLE														
	Team Michigan	Other	STATISTICS NOT AVAILABLE														
2011-12	Odessa Jackalopes	NAHL	*53	26	21	5	*3085	128	3	2.49	4	1	3	243	14	0	3.46
2012-13	U. Mass Lowell	H-East	24	20	3	0	1397	32	*6	*1.37	....	....	....	....	....	....	....
2013-14	U. Mass Lowell	H-East	29	18	9	2	1748	52	6	*1.79	....	....	....	....	....	....	....
2014-15	St. John's IceCaps	AHL	58	28	22	5	3332	143	6	2.58	....	....	....	....	....	....	....

NAHL Rookie of the Year (2012) • NAHL Goaltender of the Year (2012) • Hockey East All-Rookie Team (2013) • Hockey East Second All-Star Team (2013) • Hockey East First All-Star Team (2014) • NCAA East First All-American Team (2014)

HILL, Adin (HIHL, AY-dihn) ARI

Goaltender. Catches left. 6'4", 198 lbs. Born, Comox, BC, May 11, 1996.
(Arizona's 5th choice, 76th overall, in 2015 Entry Draft).

			Regular Season								Playoffs						
Season	Club	League	GP	W	L	O/T	Mins	GA	SO	Avg	GP	W	L	Mins	GA	SO	Avg
2012-13	Calgary Buffaloes	AMHL	....	9	6	2	927	47	0	3.04	....	0	1	39	5	0	6.15
2013-14	Calgary Canucks	AJHL	19	2	14	1	1041	45	0	3.92	....	....	....	....	....	....	....
	Portland	WHL	4	4	0	0	218	6	0	1.65	....	....	....	....	....	....	....
2014-15	Portland	WHL	46	31	11	1	2604	122	2	2.81	17	10	7	1074	53	1	2.96

HILLER, Jonas (HIHL-uhr, YOH-nuhs) CGY

Goaltender. Catches right. 6'2", 192 lbs. Born, Felben Wellhausen, Switz., February 12, 1982.

			Regular Season								Playoffs						
Season	Club	League	GP	W	L	O/T	Mins	GA	SO	Avg	GP	W	L	Mins	GA	SO	Avg
2000-01	HC Davos	Swiss	1	0	0	0	9	0	0	0.00	....	....	....	....	....	....	....
2001-02	HC Davos	Swiss	DID NOT PLAY														
2002-03	HC Davos	Swiss	DID NOT PLAY														
2003-04	Lausanne HC	Swiss	21	....	....	....	1161	64	1	3.31	....	....	....	....	....	....	....
	Chaux-de-Fonds	Swiss-2	1	0	1	0	60	4	0	4.00	....	....	....	....	....	....	....
	Lausanne HC	Swiss-Q	....	....	....	....	....	....	....	....	4	4	0	251	7	0	1.67
2004-05	HC Davos	Swiss	43	26	12	4	2519	95	*8	2.26	*15	12	3	*932	34	0	*2.19
2005-06	HC Davos	Swiss	*44	23	16	5	*2676	110	3	2.47	15	9	6	900	45	1	3.00
2006-07	HC Davos	Swiss	*44	*28	16	0	*2656	115	3	2.60	*19	*12	7	*1138	39	3	2.05
2007-08	**Anaheim**	**NHL**	**23**	**10**	**7**	**1**	**1223**	**42**	**0**	**2.06**	....	....	....	....	....	....	....
	Portland Pirates	AHL	6	3	2	1	370	13	0	2.11	....	....	....	....	....	....	....
2008-09	**Anaheim**	**NHL**	**46**	**23**	**15**	**1**	**2486**	**99**	**4**	**2.39**	**13**	**7**	**6**	**807**	**30**	***2**	**2.23**
2009-10	**Anaheim**	**NHL**	**59**	**30**	**23**	**4**	**3338**	**152**	**2**	**2.73**	....	....	....	....	....	....	....
	Switzerland	Olympics	5	2	3	0	316	13	0	2.47	....	....	....	....	....	....	....
2010-11	**Anaheim**	**NHL**	**49**	**26**	**16**	**3**	**2672**	**114**	**5**	**2.56**	....	....	....	....	....	....	....
2011-12	**Anaheim**	**NHL**	***73**	**29**	**30**	**12**	***4253**	**182**	**4**	**2.57**	....	....	....	....	....	....	....
2012-13	**Anaheim**	**NHL**	**26**	**15**	**6**	**4**	**1498**	**59**	**1**	**2.36**	**7**	**3**	**4**	**439**	**18**	**1**	**2.46**
2013-14	**Anaheim**	**NHL**	**50**	**29**	**13**	**7**	**2909**	**120**	**5**	**2.48**	**6**	**2**	**2**	**219**	**8**	**0**	**2.19**
	Switzerland	Olympics	3	2	1	0	179	2	2	0.67	....	....	....	....	....	....	....
2014-15	**Calgary**	**NHL**	**52**	**26**	**19**	**4**	**2871**	**113**	**1**	**2.36**	**7**	**3**	**3**	**322**	**14**	**0**	**2.61**
	NHL Totals		**378**	**188**	**129**	**36**	**21250**	**881**	**22**	**2.49**	**33**	**15**	**15**	**1787**	**70**	**3**	**2.35**

Played in NHL All-Star Game (2011)

Signed as a free agent by **Anaheim**, May 25, 2007. Signed as a free agent by **Calgary**, July 1, 2014.

HOFFMAN, Brody (HAWF-muhn, BRO-dee) MIN

Goaltender. Catches left. 6'4", 209 lbs. Born, Swift Current, SK, February 18, 1991.

			Regular Season								Playoffs						
Season	Club	League	GP	W	L	O/T	Mins	GA	SO	Avg	GP	W	L	Mins	GA	SO	Avg
2007-08	Battlefords Stars	SMHL	27	4	17	0	1402	100	0	4.28	....	....	....	....	....	....	....
2008-09	Notre Dame	SMHL	27	18	9	0	1601	77	1	2.88	....	....	....	....	....	....	....
2009-10	Nipawin Hawks	SJHL	....	8	7	3	1204	78	8	3.89	....	....	....	....	....	....	....
2010-11	Nipawin Hawks	SJHL	43	13	24	2	2232	149	1	4.01	....	....	....	....	....	....	....
2011-12	Fort McMurray	AJHL	40	29	7	3	2340	74	*5	1.90	*18	10	7	*1067	51	1	2.87
2012-13	U. of Vermont	H-East	36	11	19	6	2095	100	2	2.86	....	....	....	....	....	....	....
2013-14	U. of Vermont	H-East	20	10	8	1	1166	41	0	2.11	....	....	....	....	....	....	....
2014-15	U. of Vermont	H-East	22	13	6	2	1193	41	1	2.06	....	....	....	....	....	....	....

Signed as a free agent by **Minnesota**, March 30, 2015.

HOGBERG, Marcus (HOHG-buhrg, MAHR-kuhs) OTT

Goaltender. Catches left. 6'5", 220 lbs. Born, Orebro, Sweden, November 25, 1994.
(Ottawa's 2nd choice, 78th overall, in 2013 Entry Draft).

			Regular Season								Playoffs						
Season	Club	League	GP	W	L	O/T	Mins	GA	SO	Avg	GP	W	L	Mins	GA	SO	Avg
2010-11	Linkopings HC U18	Swe-U18	27	....	....	....	1631	53	4	1.95	5	....	....	305	13	0	2.55
	Linkopings HC Jr.	Swe-Jr.	4	....	....	....	163	12	0	4.42	....	....	....	....	....	....	....
2011-12	Linkopings HC U18	Swe-U18	3	....	....	....	179	9	0	3.01	1	....	....	60	2	0	2.00
	Linkopings HC Jr.	Swe-Jr.	35	....	....	....	2055	85	4	2.48	6	....	....	366	10	2	1.64
2012-13	Linkopings HC Jr.	Swe-Jr.	23	13	9	0	1369	55	2	2.41	....	....	....	....	....	....	....
	Linkopings HC	Sweden	3	1	1	0	140	6	0	2.57	....	....	....	....	....	....	....
2013-14	Linkopings HC Jr.	Swe-Jr.	5	4	1	0	304	14	0	2.76	....	....	....	....	....	....	....
	Mora IK	Sweden-2	15	5	8	0	778	38	0	2.93	....	....	....	....	....	....	....
	Linkopings HC	Sweden	4	4	0	0	222	4	0	1.08	11	4	5	569	28	2	2.95
2014-15	Linkopings HC Jr.	Swe-Jr.	1	1	0	0	63	1	0	0.96	....	....	....	....	....	....	....
	Linkopings HC	Sweden	27	12	12	0	1463	56	3	2.30	6	1	4	283	15	0	3.18
	IK Oskarshamn	Sweden-2	2	2	0	0	123	6	0	2.92	....	....	....	....	....	....	....

HOLTBY, Braden (HOHLT-bee, BRAY-duhn) WSH

Goaltender. Catches left. 6'2", 203 lbs. Born, Lloydminster, SK, September 16, 1989.
(Washington's 5th choice, 93rd overall, in 2008 Entry Draft).

			Regular Season								Playoffs						
Season	Club	League	GP	W	L	O/T	Mins	GA	SO	Avg	GP	W	L	Mins	GA	SO	Avg
2005-06	Saskatoon Blazers	SMHL	STATISTICS NOT AVAILABLE														
	Saskatoon Blades	WHL	1	0	1	0	59	4	0	4.07	....	....	....	....	....	....	....
2006-07	Saskatoon Blades	WHL	51	17	29	3	2725	146	0	3.21	....	....	....	....	....	....	....
2007-08	Saskatoon Blades	WHL	*64	25	29	8	3632	172	1	2.84	....	....	....	....	....	....	....
2008-09	Saskatoon Blades	WHL	*61	40	16	4	*3571	156	6	2.62	7	3	4	414	16	0	2.32
2009-10	Hershey Bears	AHL	37	25	8	2	2146	83	2	2.32	3	2	1	200	12	0	3.60
	South Carolina	ECHL	12	7	2	3	712	35	0	2.95	....	....	....	....	....	....	....
2010-11	**Washington**	**NHL**	**14**	**10**	**2**	**2**	**736**	**22**	**2**	**1.79**	....	....	....	....	....	....	....
	Hershey Bears	AHL	30	17	10	2	1785	68	5	2.29	6	2	4	359	18	0	3.01
2011-12	**Washington**	**NHL**	**7**	**4**	**2**	**1**	**361**	**15**	**1**	**2.49**	**14**	**7**	**7**	**922**	**30**	**0**	**1.95**
	Hershey Bears	AHL	40	20	15	2	2322	101	3	2.61	....	....	....	....	....	....	....
2012-13	Hershey Bears	AHL	25	12	12	1	1458	52	4	2.14	....	....	....	....	....	....	....
	Washington	**NHL**	**36**	**23**	**12**	**1**	**2089**	**90**	**4**	**2.58**	**7**	**3**	**4**	**433**	**16**	**1**	**2.22**

2013-14	**Washington**	**NHL**	**48**	**23**	**15**	**4**	**2656**	**126**	**4**	**2.85**	....	....	....	....	....	....	....
2014-15	**Washington**	**NHL**	**73**	**41**	**20**	**10**	**4247**	**157**	**9**	**2.22**	**13**	**6**	**7**	**806**	**23**	**1**	**1.71**
	NHL Totals		**178**	**101**	**51**	**18**	**10089**	**410**	**20**	**2.44**	**34**	**16**	**18**	**2161**	**69**	**2**	**1.92**

WHL East First All-Star Team (2009)

HOUSER, Michael (HOW-zuhr, MIGH-kuhl)

Goaltender. Catches left. 6'1", 185 lbs. Born, Wexford, PA, September 13, 1992.

			Regular Season								Playoffs						
Season	**Club**	**League**	**GP**	**W**	**L**	**O/T**	**Mins**	**GA**	**SO**	**Avg**	**GP**	**W**	**L**	**Mins**	**GA**	**SO**	**Avg**
2008-09	Des Moines	USHL	32	5	18	0	1523	102	0	4.02	....	....	....	....	....	....	....
2009-10	London Knights	OHL	25	17	4	1	1450	75	0	3.10	3	0	0	53	7	0	7.92
2010-11	London Knights	OHL	54	30	19	5	3088	171	1	3.32	6	2	4	332	15	0	2.71
2011-12	London Knights	OHL	62	*46	15	1	*3698	152	6	2.47	19	*16	3	1173	44	1	2.25
2012-13	Cincinnati	ECHL	29	17	10	2	1694	72	2	2.55	17	9	8	1154	43	1	2.24
2013-14	San Antonio	AHL	28	12	13	1	1473	75	1	3.05	....	....	....	....	....	....	....
2014-15	San Antonio	AHL	37	19	9	4	2081	98	2	2.83	1	0	1	64	4	0	3.75

OHL All-Rookie Team (2010) • Canadian Major Junior All-Rookie Team (2010) • OHL First All-Star Team (2012) • Canadian Major Junior Goaltender of the Year (2012) • Memorial Cup All-Star Team (2012)

Signed as a free agent by **Florida**, July 12, 2012.

HOWARD, Jimmy (HOW-uhrd, JIHM-ee) DET

Goaltender. Catches left. 6', 218 lbs. Born, Syracuse, NY, March 26, 1984.
(Detroit's 1st choice, 64th overall, in 2003 Entry Draft).

			Regular Season								Playoffs						
Season	**Club**	**League**	**GP**	**W**	**L**	**O/T**	**Mins**	**GA**	**SO**	**Avg**	**GP**	**W**	**L**	**Mins**	**GA**	**SO**	**Avg**
2000-01	Kanata Valley	ON-Jr.A	25	10	10	2	1350	83	1	3.69	....	....	....	....	....	....	....
2001-02	USNTDP	U-18	19	15	4	1	1170	37	4	1.90	....	....	....	....	....	....	....
	USNTDP	USHL	8	4	3	0	425	14	0	1.98	....	....	....	....	....	....	....
	USNTDP	NAHL	8	3	4	0	381	25	0	3.93	....	....	....	....	....	....	....
2002-03	University of Maine	H-East	21	14	6	0	1151	47	3	2.45	....	....	....	....	....	....	....
2003-04	University of Maine	H-East	23	14	4	3	1364	27	*6	*1.19	....	....	....	....	....	....	....
2004-05	University of Maine	H-East	*39	*19	13	7	*2310	74	*6	1.92	....	....	....	....	....	....	....
2005-06	**Detroit**	**NHL**	**4**	**1**	**2**	**0**	**201**	**10**	**0**	**2.99**	....	....	....	....	....	....	....
	Grand Rapids	AHL	38	27	6	2	2140	92	2	2.58	13	5	7	763	44	0	3.46
2006-07	Grand Rapids	AHL	49	21	21	3	2776	125	6	2.70	7	3	4	434	14	0	*1.93
2007-08	**Detroit**	**NHL**	**4**	**0**	**2**	**0**	**197**	**7**	**0**	**2.13**	....	....	....	....	....	....	....
	Grand Rapids	AHL	54	21	28	2	3097	146	2	2.83	....	....	....	....	....	....	....
2008-09	**Detroit**	**NHL**	**1**	**0**	**1**	**0**	**59**	**4**	**0**	**4.07**	....	....	....	....	....	....	....
	Grand Rapids	AHL	45	21	18	4	2644	112	4	2.54	10	4	6	598	24	0	2.41
2009-10	**Detroit**	**NHL**	**63**	**37**	**15**	**10**	**3740**	**141**	**3**	**2.26**	**12**	**5**	**7**	**720**	**33**	**1**	**2.75**
2010-11	**Detroit**	**NHL**	**63**	**37**	**17**	**5**	**3615**	**168**	**2**	**2.79**	**11**	**7**	**4**	**673**	**28**	**0**	**2.50**
2011-12	**Detroit**	**NHL**	**57**	**35**	**17**	**4**	**3360**	**119**	**6**	**2.13**	**5**	**1**	**4**	**295**	**13**	**0**	**2.64**
2012-13	**Detroit**	**NHL**	**42**	**21**	**13**	**7**	**2446**	**87**	***5**	**2.13**	**14**	**7**	**7**	**859**	**35**	**1**	**2.44**
2013-14	**Detroit**	**NHL**	**51**	**21**	**19**	**11**	**3004**	**133**	**2**	**2.66**	**3**	**1**	**2**	**178**	**6**	**1**	**2.02**
	United States	Olympics	DID NOT PLAY – SPARE GOALTENDER														
2014-15	**Detroit**	**NHL**	**53**	**23**	**13**	**11**	**2971**	**121**	**2**	**2.44**	**1**	**0**	**0**	**20**	**1**	**0**	**3.00**
	NHL Totals		**338**	**175**	**99**	**48**	**19593**	**790**	**20**	**2.42**	**46**	**21**	**24**	**2745**	**116**	**3**	**2.54**

Hockey East All-Rookie Team (2003) • Hockey East Rookie of the Year (2003) • Hockey East First All-Star Team (2004) • NCAA East Second All-American Team (2004) • AHL All-Rookie Team (2006) • NHL All-Rookie Team (2010)

Played in NHL All-Star Game (2012)

HUSKA, Adam (HUHS-kuh, A-duhm) NYR

Goaltender. Catches left. 6'3", 189 lbs. Born, Zvolen, Slovakia, May 12, 1997.
(NY Rangers' 7th choice, 184th overall, in 2015 Entry Draft).

			Regular Season								Playoffs						
Season	**Club**	**League**	**GP**	**W**	**L**	**O/T**	**Mins**	**GA**	**SO**	**Avg**	**GP**	**W**	**L**	**Mins**	**GA**	**SO**	**Avg**
2011-12	HKm Zvolen U18	Svk-U18	3	....	....	....	18	3	0	10.08	....	....	....	....	....	....	....
	HC 07 Detva	Svk-U18	2	....	....	....	60	8	0	7.95	....	....	....	....	....	....	....
2012-13	HKm Zvolen U18	Svk-U18	21	....	....	....	1267	53	1	2.51	2	....	....	90	2	0	1.33
2013-14	Slovakia U18	Slovak-2	14	....	....	....	748	48	0	3.85	....	....	....	....	....	....	....
	HKm Zvolen U18	Svk-U18	27	....	....	....	1461	80	0	3.28	5	....	....	147	11	0	4.49
2014-15	SR 18	Slovak-2	25	....	....	....	1296	79	0	3.66	....	....	....	....	....	....	....
	Green Bay	USHL	5	0	3	1	245	19	0	4.65	....	....	....	....	....	....	....

HUSSO, Ville (HOO-soh, VIHL-ee) ST.L.

Goaltender. Catches left. 6'3", 205 lbs. Born, Helsinki, Finland, February 6, 1995.
(St. Louis' 5th choice, 94th overall, in 2014 Entry Draft).

			Regular Season								Playoffs						
Season	**Club**	**League**	**GP**	**W**	**L**	**O/T**	**Mins**	**GA**	**SO**	**Avg**	**GP**	**W**	**L**	**Mins**	**GA**	**SO**	**Avg**
2010-11	HIFK Helsinki U18	Fin-U18	16	12	3	0	962	37	3	2.31	3	1	2	174	14	0	4.83
2011-12	HIFK Helsinki U18	Fin-U18	15	9	4	0	892	40	2	2.69	1	0	1	60	5	0	5.00
	HIFK Helsinki Jr.	Fin-Jr.	27	14	9	0	1618	65	3	2.41	10	9	1	604	18	0	1.79
2012-13	HIFK Helsinki Jr.	Fin-Jr.	41	....	....	....	2459	108	7	2.63	5	....	....	322	12	0	2.23
2013-14	HIFK Helsinki	Finland	41	20	14	5	2355	78	2	1.99	2	0	2	144	3	0	1.25
	HCK	Finland-2	6	....	....	....	364	13	....	2.14	....	....	....	....	....	....	....
2014-15	HIFK Helsinki	Finland	41	16	11	10	2338	92	3	2.36	3	1	2	159	6	0	2.27

HUTCHINSON, Michael (HUH-chihn-suhn, MIGH-kuhl) WPG

Goaltender. Catches right. 6'3", 192 lbs. Born, Barrie, ON, March 2, 1990.
(Boston's 3rd choice, 77th overall, in 2008 Entry Draft).

			Regular Season								Playoffs						
Season	**Club**	**League**	**GP**	**W**	**L**	**O/T**	**Mins**	**GA**	**SO**	**Avg**	**GP**	**W**	**L**	**Mins**	**GA**	**SO**	**Avg**
2005-06	Markham Majors	GTHL	34	....	....	....	1530	69	9	2.02	....	....	....	....	....	....	....
2006-07	Orangeville	ON-Jr.A	8	1	4	0	289	24	0	4.99	....	....	....	....	....	....	....
	Barrie Colts	OHL	14	8	3	0	768	27	0	2.11	1	1	0	45	1	0	1.33
2007-08	Barrie Colts	OHL	32	12	15	4	1826	92	1	3.02	8	4	4	500	22	1	2.64
2008-09	Barrie Colts	OHL	38	15	20	1	2146	108	5	3.02	3	0	2	112	10	0	5.37
2009-10	London Knights	OHL	46	32	12	2	2667	127	3	2.86	12	7	5	686	47	0	4.11
2010-11	Providence Bruins	AHL	28	13	10	1	1476	77	1	3.13	....	....	....	....	....	....	....
	Reading Royals	ECHL	18	9	5	4	1049	50	1	2.86	....	....	....	....	....	....	....
2011-12	Providence Bruins	AHL	29	13	14	1	1680	66	3	2.36	....	....	....	....	....	....	....
	Reading Royals	ECHL	2	1	1	0	120	7	0	3.50	....	....	....	....	....	....	....
2012-13	Providence Bruins	AHL	30	13	13	3	1749	67	3	2.30	2	0	0	49	1	0	1.22
2013-14	**Winnipeg**	**NHL**	**3**	**2**	**1**	**0**	**183**	**5**	**0**	**1.64**	....	....	....	....	....	....	....
	St. John's IceCaps	AHL	24	17	5	1	1383	53	3	2.30	*21	12	9	*1290	42	*3	1.95
	Ontario Reign	ECHL	28	22	4	2	1671	58	3	2.08	....	....	....	....	....	....	....
2014-15	**Winnipeg**	**NHL**	**38**	**21**	**10**	**5**	**2138**	**85**	**2**	**2.39**	....	....	....	....	....	....	....
	NHL Totals		**41**	**23**	**11**	**5**	**2321**	**90**	**2**	**2.33**	....	....	....	....	....	....	....

Jack A. Butterfield Trophy (AHL - Playoff MVP) (2014)

Signed as a free agent by **Winnipeg**, July 19, 2013.

HUTTON, Carter (HUH-tuhn, KAR-tuhr) NSH

Goaltender. Catches left. 6'1", 195 lbs. Born, Thunder Bay, ON, December 19, 1985.

			Regular Season								Playoffs						
Season	**Club**	**League**	**GP**	**W**	**L**	**O/T**	**Mins**	**GA**	**SO**	**Avg**	**GP**	**W**	**L**	**Mins**	**GA**	**SO**	**Avg**
2005-06	F-Wm. North Stars	ON-Jr.A	36	33	1	0	2053	63	10	1.84	15	12	3	928	36	2	2.33
2006-07	U. Mass Lowell	H-East	19	3	10	5	1097	52	1	2.84	....	....	....	....	....	....	....
2007-08	U. Mass Lowell	H-East	20	7	11	2	1187	49	2	2.48	....	....	....	....	....	....	....
2008-09	U. Mass Lowell	H-East	19	9	8	1	1106	38	*3	2.06	....	....	....	....	....	....	....
2009-10	U. Mass Lowell	H-East	27	13	12	2	1614	55	*4	*2.04	....	....	....	....	....	....	....
	Adirondack	AHL	4	1	2	1	244	11	0	2.71	....	....	....	....	....	....	....
2010-11	Worcester Sharks	AHL	22	11	7	2	1174	59	2	3.01	....	....	....	....	....	....	....
2011-12	Toledo Walleye	ECHL	14	7	7	0	819	43	0	3.15	....	....	....	....	....	....	....
	Rockford IceHogs	AHL	43	22	13	4	2372	93	3	2.35	....	....	....	....	....	....	....
2012-13	Rockford IceHogs	AHL	51	26	22	1	2908	132	2	2.72	....	....	....	....	....	....	....
	Chicago	**NHL**	**1**	**0**	**1**	**0**	**59**	**3**	**0**	**3.05**	....	....	....	....	....	....	....
2013-14	**Nashville**	**NHL**	**40**	**20**	**11**	**4**	**2085**	**91**	**1**	**2.62**	....	....	....	....	....	....	....
2014-15	**Nashville**	**NHL**	**18**	**6**	**7**	**4**	**1010**	**44**	**1**	**2.61**	....	....	....	....	....	....	....
	NHL Totals		**59**	**26**	**19**	**8**	**3154**	**138**	**2**	**2.63**	....	....	....	....	....	....	....

Hockey East Second All-Star Team (2010)

Signed to an ATO (amateur tryout) contract by **Adirondack** (AHL), March 20, 2010. Signed as a free agent by **San Jose**, June 1, 2010. Signed as a free agent by **Chicago**, February 24, 2012. Signed as a free agent by **Nashville**, July 5, 2013.

JARRY, Tristan (JAIR-ee, TRIH-STAN) PIT

Goaltender. Catches left. 6'2", 194 lbs. Born, Surrey, BC, April 29, 1995.
(Pittsburgh's 1st choice, 44th overall, in 2013 Entry Draft).

			Regular Season								Playoffs						
Season	**Club**	**League**	**GP**	**W**	**L**	**O/T**	**Mins**	**GA**	**SO**	**Avg**	**GP**	**W**	**L**	**Mins**	**GA**	**SO**	**Avg**
2009-10	North Delta	Minor-BC	26	....	....	....	....	....	....	1.65	....	....	....	....	....	....	....
2010-11	Greater Van.	BCMML	20	....	....	....	....	....	....	2.31	6	....	....	....	....	....	....
2011-12	Edmonton	WHL	14	8	2	1	718	35	0	2.93	....	....	....	....	....	....	....
2012-13	Edmonton	WHL	27	18	7	0	1495	40	6	*1.61	1	0	0	27	0	0	0.00
2013-14	Edmonton	WHL	63	*44	14	3	3703	138	*8	*2.24	*21	*16	5	*1261	46	*3	2.19
2014-15	Edmonton	WHL	55	23	26	6	3216	147	3	2.74	5	1	4	312	15	0	2.88

WHL East First All-Star Team (2014, 2015)

JOHANSSON, Jonas (yoh-HAHN-suhn, YOH-nuhs) BUF

Goaltender. Catches left. 6'4", 206 lbs. Born, Gavle, Sweden, September 19, 1995.
(Buffalo's 5th choice, 61st overall, in 2014 Entry Draft).

			Regular Season								Playoffs						
Season	**Club**	**League**	**GP**	**W**	**L**	**O/T**	**Mins**	**GA**	**SO**	**Avg**	**GP**	**W**	**L**	**Mins**	**GA**	**SO**	**Avg**
2010-11	Brynas U18	Swe-U18	1	....	....	....	37	1	0	1.63	....	....	....	....	....	....	....
2011-12	Brynas U18	Swe-U18	21	....	....	....	1239	46	2	2.23	3	....	....	178	7	0	2.36
	Brynas IF Gavle Jr.	Swe-Jr.	5	....	....	....	237	13	0	3.29	....	....	....	....	....	....	....
2012-13	Brynas U18	Swe-U18	6	5	1	0	365	14	0	2.30	7	6	1	430	21	0	2.93
	Brynas IF Gavle Jr.	Swe-Jr.	29	14	15	0	1689	84	0	2.98	2	0	2	124	4	0	1.93
2013-14	Brynas IF Gavle Jr.	Swe-Jr.	23	13	9	0	1345	52	1	2.32	7	5	2	433	17	0	2.36
	Brynas IF Gavle	Sweden	4	2	2	0	243	12	0	2.96	....	....	....	....	....	....	....
2014-15	Brynas IF Gavle	Sweden	2	0	2	0	105	11	0	6.30	....	....	....	....	....	....	....
	Brynas IF Gavle Jr.	Swe-Jr.	13	6	6	0	763	46	0	3.62	2	1	1	119	7	0	3.52

JOHNSON, Chad (JAWN-suhn, CHAD) BUF

Goaltender. Catches left. 6'3", 205 lbs. Born, Calgary, AB, June 10, 1986.
(Pittsburgh's 4th choice, 125th overall, in 2006 Entry Draft).

			Regular Season								Playoffs						
Season	**Club**	**League**	**GP**	**W**	**L**	**O/T**	**Mins**	**GA**	**SO**	**Avg**	**GP**	**W**	**L**	**Mins**	**GA**	**SO**	**Avg**
2002-03	Calgary Buffaloes	AMHL	....	8	8	2	1145	62	....	3.25	1	0	1	60	3	0	3.00
2003-04	Brooks Bandits	AJHL	31	6	20	3	1782	117	0	3.94	....	....	....	....	....	....	....
2004-05	Brooks Bandits	AJHL	43	25	16	2	2505	109	2	2.61	119	4	5	493	....	....	....
2005-06	Alaska	CCHA	18	6	7	4	985	42	0	2.56	....	....	....	....	....	....	....
2006-07	Alaska	CCHA	19	5	6	2	1002	52	1	3.11	....	....	....	....	....	....	....
2007-08	Alaska	CCHA	7	0	6	0	357	20	0	3.36	....	....	....	....	....	....	....
2008-09	Alaska	CCHA	35	14	16	5	2062	57	6	*1.66	....	....	....	....	....	....	....
2009-10	**NY Rangers**	**NHL**	**5**	**1**	**2**	**1**	**281**	**11**	**0**	**2.35**	....	....	....	....	....	....	....
	Hartford Wolf Pack	AHL	47	24	18	2	2649	112	3	2.54	....	....	....	....	....	....	....
2010-11	**NY Rangers**	**NHL**	**1**	**0**	**0**	**0**	**20**	**2**	**0**	**6.00**	....	....	....	....	....	....	....
	Connecticut Whale	AHL	40	16	19	3	2271	103	2	2.72	....	....	....	....	....	....	....
2011-12	Connecticut Whale	AHL	49	22	18	6	2775	115	1	2.49	....	....	....	....	....	....	....
2012-13	Portland Pirates	AHL	34	16	15	1	1938	97	2	3.00	3	0	3	204	12	0	3.53
	Phoenix	**NHL**	**4**	**2**	**0**	**2**	**247**	**5**	**1**	**1.21**	....	....	....	....	....	....	....
2013-14	**Boston**	**NHL**	**27**	**17**	**4**	**3**	**1511**	**53**	**2**	**2.10**	....	....	....	....	....	....	....
2014-15	**NY Islanders**	**NHL**	**19**	**8**	**8**	**1**	**1053**	**54**	**0**	**3.08**	....	....	....	....	....	....	....
	NHL Totals		**56**	**28**	**14**	**7**	**3112**	**125**	**3**	**2.41**	....	....	....	....	....	....	....

AJHL South Division First All-Star Team (2005) • CCHA First All-Star Team (2009) • CCHA Rookie of the Year (2009) • NCAA West Second All-American Team (2009)

Traded to **NY Rangers** by **Pittsburgh** for Pittsburgh's 5th round choice (previously acquired, Pittsburgh selected Andy Bathgate) in 2009 Entry Draft, June 27, 2009. Signed as a free agent by **Phoenix**, July 1. 2012. Signed as a free agent by **Boston**, July 5, 2013. Signed as a free agent by **NY Islanders**, July 1, 2014. Traded to **Buffalo** by **NY Islanders** with NY Islanders' 3rd round choice in 2016 Entry Draft for Michael Neuvirth, March 2, 2015.

JONES, Martin (JOHNZ, MAR-tihn) S.J.

Goaltender. Catches left. 6'4", 190 lbs. Born, North Vancouver, BC, January 10, 1990.

			Regular Season								Playoffs						
Season	**Club**	**League**	**GP**	**W**	**L**	**O/T**	**Mins**	**GA**	**SO**	**Avg**	**GP**	**W**	**L**	**Mins**	**GA**	**SO**	**Avg**
2006-07	Calgary Hitmen	WHL	18	9	4	3	1029	52	0	3.03	....	....	....	....	....	....	....
2007-08	Calgary Hitmen	WHL	27	18	8	1	1529	54	1	2.12	5	2	1	250	12	0	2.88
2008-09	Calgary Hitmen	WHL	55	*45	5	4	3295	114	*7	2.08	18	14	4	1095	34	2	1.86
2009-10	Calgary Hitmen	WHL	48	36	11	1	2851	105	*8	*2.21	*23	*16	7	*1401	55	*2	*2.36
2010-11	Manchester	AHL	39	23	12	1	2187	82	4	2.25	4	2	1	213	9	0	2.54
	Ontario Reign	ECHL	1	1	0	0	64	4	0	3.76	....	....	....	....	....	....	....
2011-12	Manchester	AHL	41	18	17	2	2166	94	1	2.60	3	1	1	155	6	0	2.33
2012-13	Manchester	AHL	56	27	25	4	3347	141	5	2.53	4	1	3	277	10	0	2.16
2013-14 ♦	**Los Angeles**	**NHL**	**19**	**12**	**6**	**0**	**1095**	**33**	**4**	**1.81**	**2**	**0**	**0**	**56**	**0**	**0**	**0.00**
	Manchester	AHL	22	16	3	3	1351	48	2	2.13	....	....	....	....	....	....	....
2014-15	**Los Angeles**	**NHL**	**15**	**4**	**5**	**2**	**775**	**29**	**3**	**2.25**	....	....	....	....	....	....	....
	NHL Totals		**34**	**16**	**11**	**2**	**1870**	**62**	**7**	**1.99**	**2**	**0**	**0**	**56**	**0**	**0**	**0.00**

WHL East Second All-Star Team (2009) • WHL East First All-Star Team (2010) • WHL Goaltender of the Year (2010) • Canadian Major Junior Second All-Star Team (2010) • Memorial Cup All-Star Team (2010) • Hap Emms Memorial Trophy (Memorial Cup – Top Goaltender) (2010)

Signed as a free agent by **Los Angeles**, October 2, 2008. Traded to **Boston** by **Los Angeles** with Colin Miller and Los Angeles' 1st round choice (Jakub Zboril) in 2015 Entry Draft for Milan Lucic, June 26, 2015. Traded to **San Jose** by **Boston** for Sean Kuraly and San Jose's 1st round choice in 2016 Entry Draft, June 30, 2015.

JUVONEN, Janne (YOO-voh-nehn, YAH-neh) NSH

Goaltender. Catches left. 6'1", 183 lbs. Born, Kiihtelysvaara, Finland, October 3, 1994.
(Nashville's 10th choice, 203rd overall, in 2013 Entry Draft).

			Regular Season								Playoffs						
Season	Club	League	GP	W	L	O/T	Mins	GA	SO	Avg	GP	W	L	Mins	GA	SO	Avg
2009-10	Jokipojat U18	Fin-U18	19	....	....	....	....	....	....	3.91	....	....	....	....	....	....	....
	Jokipojat Jr.	Fin-Jr.	1	....	....	....	60	3	0	3.02	....	....	....	....	....	....	....
2010-11	Jokipojat U18	Fin-U18	4	....	....	....	240	4	1	1.00	....	....	....	....	....	....	....
	Jokipojat Jr.	Fin-Jr.	27	....	....	....	1575	91	1	3.46	....	....	....	....	....	....	....
2011-12	Pelicans Lahti U18	Fin-U18	15	6	9	0	902	35	3	2.33	....	....	....	....	....	....	....
	Pelicans Lahti Jr.	Fin-Jr.	20	11	9	0	1215	58	1	2.86	....	....	....	....	....	....	....
	Pelicans Lahti	Finland	2	1	1	0	90	4	0	2.66	2	0	2	99	4	0	2.43
2012-13	Pelicans Lahti Jr.	Fin-Jr.	11	....	....	....	646	32	1	2.97	....	....	....	....	....	....	....
	Pelicans Lahti	Finland	4	1	3	0	188	11	0	3.51	....	....	....	....	....	....	....
	Peliitat Heinola	Finland-2	17	....	....	....	961	51	1	3.18	....	....	....	....	....	....	....
2013-14	Pelicans Lahti Jr.	Fin-Jr.	4	....	....	....	240	9	....	2.25	8	....	....	480	10	....	1.25
	Pelicans Lahti	Finland	4	2	1	0	219	12	0	3.29	1	0	0	1	0	0	0.00
	Peliitat Heinola	Finland-2	8	....	....	....	437	33	....	4.53	....	....	....	....	....	....	....
	KooKoo Kouvola	Finland-2	4	....	....	....	241	8	....	1.99	....	....	....	....	....	....	....
2014-15	Pelicans Lahti	Finland	46	12	23	11	2772	116	3	2.51	....	....	....	....	....	....	....

KAHKONEN, Kaapo (kakh-KOH-nihn, KA-poh) MIN

Goaltender. Catches left. 6'2", 219 lbs. Born, Helsinki, Finland, August 16, 1996.
(Minnesota's 3rd choice, 109th overall, in 2014 Entry Draft).

			Regular Season								Playoffs						
Season	Club	League	GP	W	L	O/T	Mins	GA	SO	Avg	GP	W	L	Mins	GA	SO	Avg
2011-12	Blues Espoo U18	Fin-U18	1	1	0	0	60	2	0	2.00	....	....	....	....	....	....	....
2012-13	Blues Espoo U18	Fin-U18	2	....	....	....	120	6	0	3.00	....	....	....	....	....	....	....
	Blues Espoo Jr.	Fin-Jr.	28	....	....	....	1676	68	4	2.43	12	....	....	628	28	2	2.68
2013-14	Blues Espoo Jr.	Fin-Jr.	38	....	....	....	2279	91	....	2.39	10	....	....	599	21	....	2.10
2014-15	TuTo Turku	Finland-2	47	....	....	....	2610	92	....	2.11	13	....	....	801	26	....	1.95

KALLGREN, Erik (KAHL-grehn, AIR-ihk) ARI

Goaltender. Catches left. 6'2", 190 lbs. Born, Stockholm, Sweden, October 14, 1996.
(Arizona's 9th choice, 183rd overall, in 2015 Entry Draft).

			Regular Season								Playoffs						
Season	Club	League	GP	W	L	O/T	Mins	GA	SO	Avg	GP	W	L	Mins	GA	SO	Avg
2012-13	Linkopings HC U18	Swe-U18	17	13	3	0	994	35	4	2.11	....	....	....	....	....	....	....
	Linkopings HC Jr.	Swe-Jr.	2	0	2	0	97	4	0	2.46	....	....	....	....	....	....	....
2013-14	Linkopings HC U18	Swe-U18	25	19	6	0	1507	55	4	2.19	5	3	2	330	11	0	2.00
	Linkopings HC Jr.	Swe-Jr.	2	1	1	0	119	7	0	3.53	1	0	1	47	5	0	6.36
2014-15	Linkopings HC Jr.	Swe-Jr.	34	27	7	0	2052	60	6	1.75	7	5	2	428	18	0	2.52
	IK Oskarshamn	Sweden-2	3	2	1	0	145	6	0	2.49	....	....	....	....	....	....	....

KASDORF, Jason (KAZ-dawrf, JAY-suhn) BUF

Goaltender. Catches left. 6'4", 200 lbs. Born, Winnipeg, MB, May 18, 1992.
(Winnipeg's 6th choice, 157th overall, in 2011 Entry Draft).

			Regular Season								Playoffs						
Season	Club	League	GP	W	L	O/T	Mins	GA	SO	Avg	GP	W	L	Mins	GA	SO	Avg
2008-09	Wpg. Thrashers	MMHL	44	....	....	....	1032	36	4	2.09	....	....	....	....	....	....	....
2009-10	Portage Terriers	MJHL	....	19	10	5	2094	89	2	2.55	....	....	....	....	....	....	....
2010-11	Portage Terriers	MJHL	34	24	10	0	2018	85	2	2.53	16	10	5	930	34	2	2.19
2011-12	Des Moines	USHL	33	10	16	5	1750	100	3	3.43	....	....	....	....	....	....	....
2012-13	RPI Engineers	ECAC	23	14	5	2	1330	36	3	1.62	....	....	....	....	....	....	....
2013-14	RPI Engineers	ECAC	2	1	1	0	103	6	1	3.49	....	....	....	....	....	....	....
2014-15	RPI Engineers	ECAC	33	11	19	2	1816	90	1	2.97	....	....	....	....	....	....	....

ECAC All-Rookie Team (2013) • ECAC Second All-Star Team (2013)

• Missed majority of 2013-14 due to shoulder injury in practice, October 1, 2013. Traded to **Buffalo** by **Winnipeg** with Evander Kane and Zach Bogosian for Tyler Myers, Drew Stafford, Joel Armia, Brendan Lemieux and St. Louis' 1st round choice (previously acquired, Winnipeg selected Jack Roslovic) in 2015 Entry Draft, February 11, 2015.

KHUDOBIN, Anton (hoo-DOH-bihn, AN-tawn) ANA

Goaltender. Catches left. 5'11", 203 lbs. Born, Ust-Kamenogorsk, USSR, May 7, 1986.
(Minnesota's 11th choice, 206th overall, in 2004 Entry Draft).

			Regular Season								Playoffs						
Season	Club	League	GP	W	L	O/T	Mins	GA	SO	Avg	GP	W	L	Mins	GA	SO	Avg
2003-04	Magnitogorsk 2	Russia-3	38	....	....	....	....	80	....	....	....	....	....	....	....	....	....
2004-05	Magnitogorsk	Russia	4	....	....	....	133	0	1	0.00	....	....	....	....	....	....	....
	Magnitogorsk 2	Russia-3	27	....	....	....	....	52	....	....	....	....	....	....	....	....	....
2005-06	Saskatoon Blades	WHL	44	23	13	3	2362	114	4	2.90	10	4	6	685	32	0	2.80
2006-07	Magnitogorsk	Russia	16	....	....	....	618	28	0	2.72	3	....	....	26	1	0	2.30
2007-08	Houston Aeros	AHL	12	2	2	1	482	16	1	1.99	....	....	....	....	....	....	....
	Texas Wildcatters	ECHL	27	20	1	4	1549	51	3	*1.98	9	5	4	547	20	1	2.19
2008-09	Houston Aeros	AHL	10	3	6	1	512	26	0	3.04	17	8	8	890	40	2	2.70
	Florida Everblades	ECHL	33	18	10	1	1706	77	4	2.71	....	....	....	....	....	....	....
2009-10	**Minnesota**	**NHL**	**2**	**2**	**0**	**0**	**69**	**1**	**0**	**0.87**	....	....	....	....	....	....	....
	Houston Aeros	AHL	40	14	19	4	2247	91	4	2.43	....	....	....	....	....	....	....
2010-11	**Minnesota**	**NHL**	**4**	**2**	**1**	**0**	**189**	**5**	**1**	**1.59**	....	....	....	....	....	....	....
	Houston Aeros	AHL	34	19	12	1	1883	81	1	2.58	....	....	....	....	....	....	....
	Providence Bruins	AHL	16	9	4	1	901	36	1	2.40	....	....	....	....	....	....	....
2011-12	**Boston**	**NHL**	**1**	**1**	**0**	**0**	**60**	**1**	**0**	**1.00**	....	....	....	....	....	....	....
	Providence Bruins	AHL	44	21	19	3	2597	113	2	2.61	....	....	....	....	....	....	....
2012-13	Mytischi	KHL	26	6	14	0	1500	74	1	2.96	....	....	....	....	....	....	....
	Boston	**NHL**	**14**	**9**	**4**	**1**	**803**	**31**	**1**	**2.32**	....	....	....	....	....	....	....
2013-14	**Carolina**	**NHL**	**36**	**19**	**14**	**1**	**2084**	**80**	**1**	**2.30**	....	....	....	....	....	....	....
	Charlotte Checkers	AHL	2	1	1	0	119	6	0	3.03	....	....	....	....	....	....	....
2014-15	**Carolina**	**NHL**	**34**	**8**	**17**	**6**	**1920**	**87**	**1**	**2.72**	....	....	....	....	....	....	....
	NHL Totals		**91**	**41**	**36**	**8**	**5125**	**205**	**4**	**2.40**	....	....	....	....	....	....	....

ECHL First All-Star Team (2008) • ECHL Goaltender of the Year (2008)

Traded to **Boston** by **Minnesota** for Jeff Penner and Mikko Lehtonen, February 28, 2011. Signed as a free agent by **Mytischi** (KHL), September 21, 2012. Signed as a free agent by **Carolina**, July 5, 2013. Traded to **Anaheim** by **Carolina** for James Wisniewski, June 27, 2015.

KINKAID, Keith (kihn-KAID, KEETH) N.J.

Goaltender. Catches left. 6'2", 195 lbs. Born, Farmingville, NY, July 4, 1989.

			Regular Season								Playoffs						
Season	Club	League	GP	W	L	O/T	Mins	GA	SO	Avg	GP	W	L	Mins	GA	SO	Avg
2007-08	New York Bobcats	AtJHL	29	20	5	0	1458	58	....	2.39	....	....	....	....	....	....	....
	Des Moines	USHL	15	4	9	2	844	48	0	3.41	....	....	....	....	....	....	....
2008-09	St. Louis Bandits	NAHL	40	*30	5	4	2393	71	*7	*1.78	*12	*10	2	*728	14	*3	*1.15
2009-10	Union College	ECAC	25	12	8	3	1478	61	1	2.48	....	....	....	....	....	....	....
2010-11	Union College	ECAC	*38	25	10	3	*2266	75	3	1.99	....	....	....	....	....	....	....
2011-12	Albany Devils	AHL	42	17	20	3	2347	115	3	2.94	....	....	....	....	....	....	....
2012-13	Albany Devils	AHL	45	21	17	6	2644	120	2	2.72	....	....	....	....	....	....	....
	New Jersey	**NHL**	**1**	**0**	**0**	**0**	**26**	**1**	**0**	**2.31**	....	....	....	....	....	....	....
2013-14	Albany Devils	AHL	43	24	13	5	2519	96	4	2.29	4	1	3	238	9	0	2.26
2014-15	**New Jersey**	**NHL**	**19**	**6**	**5**	**4**	**925**	**40**	**0**	**2.59**	....	....	....	....	....	....	....
	Albany Devils	AHL	13	7	2	3	713	26	1	2.19	....	....	....	....	....	....	....
	NHL Totals		**20**	**6**	**5**	**4**	**951**	**41**	**0**	**2.59**	....	....	....	....	....	....	....

ECAC All-Rookie Team (2010) • ECAC First All-Star Team (2011) • NCAA East First All-American Team (2011)

Signed as a free agent by **New Jersey**, April 18, 2011.

KIVIAHO, Henri (kih-vee-A-hoh, HEHN-ree) DAL

Goaltender. Catches left. 6'1", 185 lbs. Born, Lappeenranta, Finland, February 26, 1994.
(Dallas' 8th choice, 144th overall, in 2012 Entry Draft).

			Regular Season								Playoffs						
Season	Club	League	GP	W	L	O/T	Mins	GA	SO	Avg	GP	W	L	Mins	GA	SO	Avg
2009-10	SaiPa U18	Fin-U18	9	1	5	0	464	59	0	7.64	....	....	....	....	....	....	....
2010-11	SaiPa U18	Fin-U18	8	1	5	0	417	30	0	4.31	....	....	....	....	....	....	....
	SaiPa Jr.	Fin-Jr.	11	4	4	0	503	33	0	3.93	....	....	....	....	....	....	....
2011-12	KalPa Kuopio Jr.	Fin-Jr.	28	16	11	0	1638	76	2	2.78	9	3	6	535	36	0	4.04
2012-13	KalPa Kuopio Jr.	Fin-Jr.	31	....	....	....	1846	82	4	2.66	3	....	....	179	8	0	2.68
2013-14	KalPa Kuopio Jr.	Fin-Jr.	18	....	....	....	1076	62	....	3.44	....	....	....	....	....	....	....
	KalPa Kuopio	Finland	13	1	10	1	739	36	0	2.92	....	....	....	....	....	....	....
2014-15	Idaho Steelheads	ECHL	21	10	6	2	1140	53	0	2.79	....	....	....	....	....	....	....

KORPISALO, Joonas (kohr-pih-SAL-loh, YOH-nuhs) CBJ

Goaltender. Catches left. 6'3", 182 lbs. Born, Pori, Finland, April 28, 1994.
(Columbus' 3rd choice, 62nd overall, in 2012 Entry Draft).

			Regular Season								Playoffs						
Season	Club	League	GP	W	L	O/T	Mins	GA	SO	Avg	GP	W	L	Mins	GA	SO	Avg
2010-11	Jokerit U18	Fin-U18	20	16	4	0	1200	53	0	2.65	8	5	3	460	22	0	2.87
2011-12	Jokerit Helsinki Jr.	Fin-Jr.	38	28	11	0	2295	78	4	2.04	4	3	1	270	8	1	1.77
2012-13	Jokerit Helsinki Jr.	Fin-Jr.	13	....	....	....	787	35	1	2.67	....	....	....	....	....	....	....
	Kiekko-Vantaa	Finland-2	18	....	....	....	997	45	0	2.71	....	....	....	....	....	....	....
	Jokerit Helsinki	Finland	1	0	0	0	15	0	0	0.00	....	....	....	....	....	....	....
2013-14	Jokerit Helsinki Jr.	Fin-Jr.	1	....	....	....	60	1	0	1.00	....	....	....	....	....	....	....
	Jokerit Helsinki	Finland	1	0	1	0	34	3	0	5.32	....	....	....	....	....	....	....
	Kiekko-Vantaa	Finland-2	4	....	....	....	199	11	....	3.31	....	....	....	....	....	....	....
	Ilves Tampere Jr.	Fin-Jr.	2	....	....	....	120	5	0	2.50	....	....	....	....	....	....	....
	Ilves Tampere	Finland	8	3	1	0	337	8	1	1.42	....	....	....	....	....	....	....
	LeKi Lempaala	Finland-2	2	....	....	....	68	7	....	6.13	....	....	....	....	....	....	....
2014-15	Ilves Tampere	Finland	38	14	13	7	2132	83	2	2.34	2	0	2	193	4	0	1.24
	Springfield Falcons	AHL	3	0	2	0	169	9	0	3.20	....	....	....	....	....	....	....

KOSKINEN, Mikko (KAWS-kih-nehn, MEE-koh) NYI

Goaltender. Catches left. 6'6", 205 lbs. Born, Vantaa, Finland, July 18, 1988.
(NY Islanders' 3rd choice, 31st overall, in 2009 Entry Draft).

			Regular Season								Playoffs						
Season	Club	League	GP	W	L	O/T	Mins	GA	SO	Avg	GP	W	L	Mins	GA	SO	Avg
2004-05	Blues-T U18	Fin-U18	21	....	....	....	1138	67	0	3.53	....	....	....	....	....	....	....
2005-06	Blues Espoo U18	Fin-U18	3	....	....	....	142	12	0	5.07	....	....	....	....	....	....	....
2006-07	Kiekko-Vantaa Jr.	Fin-Jr.	27	16	8	0	1567	62	3	2.37	....	....	....	....	....	....	....
2007-08	Blues Espoo Jr.	Fin-Jr.	20	12	4	0	1176	45	2	2.30	2	0	2	81	7	0	5.18
	Blues Espoo	Finland	1	1	0	0	60	0	1	0.00	....	....	....	....	....	....	....
2008-09	Blues Espoo Jr.	Fin-Jr.	9	9	0	0	545	15	2	1.65	....	....	....	....	....	....	....
	Blues Espoo	Finland	33	17	9	7	1921	61	1	1.91	14	6	8	856	37	0	2.59
2009-10	Bridgeport	AHL	2	1	1	0	123	5	0	2.45	3	1	1	147	7	0	2.85
	Utah Grizzlies	ECHL	6	6	0	0	360	15	0	2.50	4	2	1	172	10	0	3.49
2010-11	**NY Islanders**	**NHL**	**4**	**2**	**1**	**0**	**208**	**15**	**0**	**4.33**	....	....	....	....	....	....	....
	Bridgeport	AHL	36	12	21	1	2063	120	0	3.49	....	....	....	....	....	....	....
2011-12	Bridgeport	AHL	3	0	2	0	149	7	0	2.82	....	....	....	....	....	....	....
	KalPa Kuopio	Finland	25	13	5	4	1382	53	5	2.30	6	3	2	323	12	2	2.23
2012-13	KalPa Kuopio	Finland	49	21	15	13	2953	101	7	2.05	5	1	4	295	10	1	2.03
2013-14	Blues Espoo	Finland	2	1	0	1	121	5	0	2.47	....	....	....	....	....	....	....
	Novosibirsk	KHL	41	20	11	0	2362	67	3	1.70	10	4	5	607	20	1	1.98
2014-15	Novosibirsk	KHL	29	16	11	0	1564	58	3	2.22	....	....	....	....	....	....	....
	SKA St. Petersburg	KHL	21	9	8	0	1270	40	1	1.89	22	16	6	1377	37	3	1.61
	NHL Totals		**4**	**2**	**1**	**0**	**208**	**15**	**0**	**4.33**	....	....	....	....	....	....	....

• Re-assigned to **Kuopio** (Finland) by **NY Islanders**, November 15, 2011. • Re-assigned to **Espoo** (Finland) by **NY Islanders**, April 8, 2013. • Re-assigned to **Novosibirsk** (KHL) by **NY Islanders**, September 18, 2013. • Re-assigned to **St. Petersburg** (KHL) by **NY Islanders**, December 5, 2014.

KUEMPER, Darcy (KEHM-puhr, DAHR-see) MIN

Goaltender. Catches left. 6'5", 205 lbs. Born, Saskatoon, SK, May 5, 1990.
(Minnesota's 5th choice, 161st overall, in 2009 Entry Draft).

			Regular Season								Playoffs						
Season	Club	League	GP	W	L	O/T	Mins	GA	SO	Avg	GP	W	L	Mins	GA	SO	Avg
2006-07	Sask. Contacts	SMHL	25	8	14	3	1489	87	1	3.51	4	1	3	200	19	0	5.70
	Spokane Chiefs	WHL	....	....	....	....	....	....	....	....	1	0	0	0	0	0	0.00
2007-08	Saskatoon Blazers	SMHL	26	15	7	4	1578	62	1	2.36	13	7	6	781	34	1	2.61
2008-09	Red Deer Rebels	WHL	55	21	25	8	3167	156	3	2.96	....	....	....	....	....	....	....
2009-10	Houston Aeros	AHL	4	2	1	0	199	8	0	2.41	....	....	....	....	....	....	....
	Red Deer Rebels	WHL	61	28	23	4	3234	147	3	2.73	2	0	2	61	6	0	5.90
2010-11	Red Deer Rebels	WHL	62	*45	12	5	3685	114	*13	*1.86	7	4	3	403	19	0	2.83
2011-12	Houston Aeros	AHL	19	6	6	4	1070	42	1	2.36	....	....	....	....	....	....	....
	Ontario Reign	ECHL	8	7	1	0	484	14	0	1.74	....	....	....	....	....	....	....
2012-13	Houston Aeros	AHL	21	13	8	0	1210	38	4	1.88	2	1	1	119	3	1	1.51
	Orlando	ECHL	3	0	2	1	184	8	0	2.61	....	....	....	....	....	....	....
	Minnesota	**NHL**	**6**	**1**	**2**	**0**	**288**	**10**	**0**	**2.08**	**2**	**0**	**0**	**73**	**4**	**0**	**3.29**
2013-14	**Minnesota**	**NHL**	**26**	**12**	**8**	**4**	**1480**	**60**	**2**	**2.43**	**6**	**3**	**1**	**325**	**11**	**1**	**2.03**
	Iowa Wild	AHL	17	7	10	0	997	41	1	2.47	....	....	....	....	....	....	....
2014-15	**Minnesota**	**NHL**	**31**	**14**	**12**	**2**	**1569**	**68**	**3**	**2.60**	**1**	**0**	**0**	**23**	**0**	**0**	**0.00**
	Iowa Wild	AHL	5	2	3	0	279	15	1	3.22	....	....	....	....	....	....	....
	NHL Totals		**63**	**27**	**22**	**6**	**3337**	**138**	**5**	**2.48**	**9**	**3**	**1**	**421**	**15**	**1**	**2.14**

WHL East Second All-Star Team (2010) • WHL East First All-Star Team (2011) • Canadian Major Junior Goaltender of the Year (2011)

KUPSKY, Jake (KUHP-skee, JAYK) S.J.

Goaltender. Catches right. 6'5", 210 lbs. Born, Waukeshaw, WI, October 27, 1995.
(San Jose's 9th choice, 193rd overall, in 2015 Entry Draft).

			Regular Season								Playoffs						
Season	Club	League	GP	W	L	O/T	Mins	GA	SO	Avg	GP	W	L	Mins	GA	SO	Avg
2010-11	Waukesha Wings	High-WI	4	0	0	0	59	4	0	4.02	....	....	....	....	....	....	....
2011-12	Waukesha Wings	High-WI	10	8	2	0	493	15	2	1.55	1	0	1	50	2	0	2.04
2012-13	Waukesha Wings	High-WI	23	16	6	1	1164	52	3	2.28	3	2	1	158	6	1	1.94
2013-14	Waukesha Wings	High-WI	22	17	4	1	1113	35	8	1.60	3	2	1	153	3	2	1.00
2014-15	Lone Star Brahmas	NAHL	30	19	4	4	1670	60	2	2.16	9	6	3	581	18	0	1.86

• Signed Letter of Intent to attend **Union College** (ECAC) in fall of 2015.

LaBARBERA, Jason (luh-BAHR-buhr-ah, JAY-suhn) PHI

Goaltender. Catches left. 6'3", 232 lbs. Born, Burnaby, BC, January 18, 1980.
(NY Rangers' 3rd choice, 66th overall, in 1998 Entry Draft).

			Regular Season								Playoffs						
Season	Club	League	GP	W	L	O/T	Mins	GA	SO	Avg	GP	W	L	Mins	GA	SO	Avg
1995-96	Prince George	Minor-BC	31	....	....	....	1860	83	0	2.68	....	....	....	....	....	....	....
1996-97	Tri-City Americans	WHL	2	1	0	0	63	4	0	3.81	....	....	....	....	....	....	....
	Portland	WHL	9	5	1	1	443	18	0	2.44	....	....	....	....	....	....	....
1997-98	Portland	WHL	23	18	4	0	1305	72	1	3.31	....	....	....	....	....	....	....
1998-99	Portland	WHL	51	18	23	9	2991	170	4	3.41	4	0	4	252	19	0	4.52
99-2000	Portland	WHL	34	8	24	2	2005	123	1	3.68	....	....	....	....	....	....	....
	Spokane Chiefs	WHL	21	12	6	2	1146	50	0	2.62	9	6	1	435	18	1	2.48
2000-01	**NY Rangers**	**NHL**	**1**	**0**	**0**	**0**	**10**	**0**	**0**	**0.00**	....	....	....	....	....	....	....
	Hartford Wolf Pack	AHL	4	1	1	0	156	12	0	4.61	....	....	....	....	....	....	....
	Charlotte Checkers	ECHL	35	18	10	7	2100	112	1	3.20	2	1	1	143	5	0	2.09
2001-02	Hartford Wolf Pack	AHL	20	7	11	1	1058	55	0	3.12	....	....	....	....	....	....	....
	Charlotte Checkers	ECHL	13	9	3	1	744	29	0	2.34	4	2	2	212	12	0	3.39
2002-03	Hartford Wolf Pack	AHL	46	18	17	6	2452	105	2	2.57	2	0	2	117	6	0	3.07
2003-04	**NY Rangers**	**NHL**	**4**	**1**	**2**	**0**	**198**	**16**	**0**	**4.85**	....	....	....	....	....	....	....
	Hartford Wolf Pack	AHL	59	34	9	9	3393	90	*13	1.59	16	11	5	1043	30	*3	*1.73
2004-05	Hartford Wolf Pack	AHL	53	31	16	2	2937	90	6	1.84	4	1	3	238	9	0	2.27
2005-06	**Los Angeles**	**NHL**	**29**	**11**	**9**	**2**	**1433**	**69**	**1**	**2.89**	....	....	....	....	....	....	....
	Manchester	AHL	3	1	1	1	185	10	0	3.25	....	....	....	....	....	....	....
2006-07	Manchester	AHL	*62	*39	20	1	*3619	133	*7	2.21	13	6	7	824	38	1	2.77
2007-08	**Los Angeles**	**NHL**	**45**	**17**	**23**	**2**	**2421**	**121**	**1**	**3.00**	....	....	....	....	....	....	....
2008-09	**Los Angeles**	**NHL**	**19**	**5**	**8**	**4**	**995**	**47**	**2**	**2.83**	....	....	....	....	....	....	....
	Vancouver	**NHL**	**9**	**3**	**2**	**2**	**451**	**20**	**0**	**2.66**	....	....	....	....	....	....	....
2009-10	**Phoenix**	**NHL**	**17**	**8**	**5**	**1**	**928**	**33**	**0**	**2.13**	....	....	....	....	....	....	....
2010-11	**Phoenix**	**NHL**	**17**	**7**	**6**	**3**	**883**	**48**	**2**	**3.26**	....	....	....	....	....	....	....
2011-12	**Phoenix**	**NHL**	**19**	**3**	**9**	**3**	**1015**	**43**	**0**	**2.54**	....	....	....	....	....	....	....
2012-13	**Phoenix**	**NHL**	**15**	**4**	**6**	**2**	**726**	**32**	**0**	**2.64**	....	....	....	....	....	....	....
2013-14	**Edmonton**	**NHL**	**7**	**1**	**3**	**0**	**348**	**19**	**0**	**3.28**	....	....	....	....	....	....	....
	Oklahoma City	AHL	2	0	1	1	124	4	0	1.93	....	....	....	....	....	....	....
	Rockford IceHogs	AHL	32	15	15	2	1859	91	0	2.94	....	....	....	....	....	....	....
2014-15	**Anaheim**	**NHL**	**5**	**2**	**0**	**1**	**207**	**9**	**0**	**2.61**	....	....	....	....	....	....	....
	Norfolk Admirals	AHL	34	9	16	7	1948	85	3	2.62	....	....	....	....	....	....	....
	NHL Totals		**187**	**62**	**73**	**20**	**9615**	**457**	**6**	**2.85**	....	....	....	....	....	....	....

AHL First All-Star Team (2004, 2007) • Aldege "Baz" Bastien Memorial Award (AHL - Outstanding Goaltender) (2004, 2007) • Les Cunningham Award (AHL - MVP) (2004) • Harry "Hap" Holmes Memorial Trophy (AHL - fewest goals against) (2005) (shared with Steve Valiquette) • Harry "Hap" Holmes Memorial Trophy (AHL - fewest goals against) (2007)

Signed as a free agent by **Los Angeles**, August 2, 2005. Traded to **Vancouver** by **Los Angeles** for Vancouver's 7th round choice (later traded to Atlanta – Atlanta selected Jordan Samuels-Thomas) in 2009 Entry Draft, December 30, 2008. Signed as a free agent by **Phoenix**, July 1, 2009. Signed as a free agent by **Edmonton**, July 5, 2013. Traded to **Chicago** by **Edmonton** for future considerations, December 14, 2013. Signed as a free agent by **Anaheim**, July 1, 2014. Signed as a free agent by **Philadelphia**, July 2, 2015.

LACK, Eddie (LAK, EH-dee) CAR

Goaltender. Catches left. 6'4", 187 lbs. Born, Norrtalje, Sweden, January 5, 1988.

			Regular Season								Playoffs						
Season	Club	League	GP	W	L	O/T	Mins	GA	SO	Avg	GP	W	L	Mins	GA	SO	Avg
2004-05	Djurgarden U18	Swe-U18	9	....	....	....	527	21	1	2.39	3	....	....	140	6	0	2.57
	Djurgarden Jr.	Swe-Jr.	1	....	....	....	60	6	0	6.00	....	....	....	....	....	....	....
2005-06	Djurgarden Jr.	Swe-Jr.	23	....	....	....	1400	49	3	2.10	....	....	....	....	....	....	....
2006-07	Leksands IF Jr.	Swe-Jr.	30	....	....	....	1782	85	0	2.86	....	....	....	....	....	....	....
	Leksands IF	Sweden-2	3	....	....	....	137	7	0	3.06	....	....	....	....	....	....	....
2007-08	Leksands IF Jr.	Swe-Jr.	18	....	....	....	1077	47	4	2.62	3	....	....	179	8	0	2.68
	Leksands IF	Sweden-2	26	....	....	....	1530	50	4	1.96	....	....	....	....	....	....	....
2008-09	Leksands IF Jr.	Swe-Jr.	2	....	....	....	120	4	1	2.00	....	....	....	....	....	....	....
	Leksands IF	Sweden-2	38	....	....	....	2260	78	4	2.07	....	....	....	....	....	....	....
2009-10	Brynas IF Gavle Jr.	Swe-Jr.	6	....	....	....	359	21	0	....	....	....	....	....	....	....	....
	Brynas IF Gavle	Sweden	14	....	....	....	809	36	0	2.67	2	....	....	79	2	0	1.53
2010-11	Manitoba Moose	AHL	53	28	21	4	3135	118	5	2.26	12	6	5	752	25	2	1.99
2011-12	Chicago Wolves	AHL	46	21	20	3	2703	104	4	2.31	5	2	2	304	11	0	2.17
2012-13	Chicago Wolves	AHL	13	7	4	1	760	38	1	3.00	....	....	....	....	....	....	....
2013-14	**Vancouver**	**NHL**	**41**	**16**	**17**	**5**	**2319**	**93**	**4**	**2.41**	....	....	....	....	....	....	....
2014-15	**Vancouver**	**NHL**	**41**	**18**	**13**	**4**	**2324**	**95**	**2**	**2.45**	**4**	**1**	**3**	**198**	**10**	**0**	**3.03**
	NHL Totals		**82**	**34**	**30**	**9**	**4643**	**188**	**6**	**2.43**	**4**	**1**	**3**	**198**	**10**	**0**	**3.03**

AHL All-Rookie Team (2011)

Signed as a free agent by **Vancouver**, April 6, 2010. Traded to **Carolina** by **Vancouver** for Carolina's 3rd round choice (Guillaume Brisebois) in 2015 Entry Draft and Carolina's 7th round choice in 2016 Entry Draft, June 26, 2015.

LAGACE, Maxime (luh-ga-SEE, max-EEM) DAL

Goaltender. Catches left. 6'2", 185 lbs. Born, St-Augustin, QC, January 12, 1993.

			Regular Season								Playoffs						
Season	Club	League	GP	W	L	O/T	Mins	GA	SO	Avg	GP	W	L	Mins	GA	SO	Avg
2008-09	Quebec Typhons	Minor-QC					STATISTICS NOT AVAILABLE										
	St-Francois Blizzard	QAAA	8	1	1	2	346	27	0	4.68	....	....	....	....	....	....	....
2009-10	St-Francois Blizzard	QAAA	22	18	3	1	1256	39	1	1.86	3	1	2	180	10	0	3.33
2010-11	P.E.I. Rocket	QMJHL	18	8	4	0	870	52	1	3.59	....	....	....	....	....	....	....
2011-12	P.E.I. Rocket	QMJHL	56	12	34	5	2912	219	1	4.51	....	....	....	....	....	....	....
2012-13	P.E.I. Rocket	QMJHL	33	13	12	1	1571	106	1	4.05	1	0	0	27	1	0	2.19
2013-14	Cape Breton	QMJHL	8	3	3	1	464	25	0	3.23	....	....	....	....	....	....	....
	Shawinigan	QMJHL	3	1	2	0	180	12	1	4.00	....	....	....	....	....	....	....
	Sherbrooke	QMJHL	15	2	9	3	827	56	0	4.06	....	....	....	....	....	....	....
2014-15	Texas Stars	AHL	1	0	0	0	17	1	0	3.55	....	....	....	....	....	....	....
	Missouri Mavericks	ECHL	15	5	6	3	779	39	1	3.01	....	....	....	....	....	....	....
	Bakersfield	ECHL	13	6	4	1	718	32	1	2.68	....	....	....	....	....	....	....

Signed as a free agent by **Dallas**, July 23, 2012.

LANGHAMER, Marek (lang-HAHM-uhr, MAHR-ehk) ARI

Goaltender. Catches left. 6'2", 192 lbs. Born, Pisek, Czech Rep., July 22, 1994.
(Phoenix's 7th choice, 184th overall, in 2012 Entry Draft).

			Regular Season								Playoffs						
Season	Club	League	GP	W	L	O/T	Mins	GA	SO	Avg	GP	W	L	Mins	GA	SO	Avg
2008-09	HC Pardubice U17	CzR-U17	29	....	....	....	1433	87	0	3.64	6	....	....	352	12	0	2.05
2009-10	HC Pardubice U18	CzR-U18	35	....	....	....	2031	83	4	2.45	6	....	....	327	14	1	2.57
	HC Pardubice Jr.	CzRep-Jr.	2	....	....	....	30	0	0	0.00	....	....	....	....	....	....	....
2010-11	HC Pardubice U18	CzR-U18	17	....	....	....	1028	43	1	2.51	5	....	....	320	12	0	2.25
	HC Pardubice Jr.	CzRep-Jr.	37	....	....	....	2162	113	3	3.14	....	....	....	....	....	....	....
	HC Chrudim	CzRep-2	4	....	....	....	172	5	0	1.74	....	....	....	....	....	....	....
2011-12	HC Pardubice Jr.	CzRep-Jr.	33	....	....	....	1916	105	0	3.29	....	....	....	....	....	....	....
2012-13	Medicine Hat	WHL	30	15	12	1	1450	83	2	3.44	1	0	0	38	5	0	7.83
2013-14	Medicine Hat	WHL	40	23	14	3	2392	103	2	2.58	18	9	9	1071	42	0	2.35
2014-15	Medicine Hat	WHL	50	30	16	3	2904	136	2	2.81	....	....	....	....	....	....	....

LAURIKAINEN, Eetu (lah-ree-KAY-nehn, EE-too) EDM

Goaltender. Catches left. 6', 185 lbs. Born, Jyyaskyla, Finland, February 1, 1993.

			Regular Season								Playoffs						
Season	Club	League	GP	W	L	O/T	Mins	GA	SO	Avg	GP	W	L	Mins	GA	SO	Avg
2011-12	JyP Jyvaskyla Jr.	Fin-Jr.	26	....	....	....	....	....	....	3.15	....	....	....	....	....	....	....
	JYP-Akatemia	Finland-2	6	....	....	....	....	....	....	3.13	....	....	....	....	....	....	....
2012-13	Swift Current	WHL	60	30	23	6	3507	140	1	2.40	....	....	....	....	....	....	....
2013-14	Swift Current	WHL	54	25	20	6	2961	143	4	2.90	6	2	4	359	13	0	2.17
2014-15	Blues Espoo	Finland	37	17	10	9	2201	77	4	2.10	4	0	4	235	13	0	3.32

Signed as a free agent by **Edmonton**, May 12, 2015.

LEGGIO, David (LEH-JEE-oh, DAY-vihd)

Goaltender. Catches left. 6', 180 lbs. Born, Buffalo, NY, July 31, 1984.

			Regular Season								Playoffs						
Season	Club	League	GP	W	L	O/T	Mins	GA	SO	Avg	GP	W	L	Mins	GA	SO	Avg
2003-04	Capital District	EJHL	42	25	10	6	....	....	4	2.80	....	....	....	....	....	....	....
2004-05	Clarkson Knights	ECAC	5	2	1	0	182	9	0	2.97	....	....	....	....	....	....	....
2005-06	Clarkson Knights	ECAC	23	11	9	3	1446	62	1	2.57	....	....	....	....	....	....	....
2006-07	Clarkson Knights	ECAC	37	24	7	5	2167	78	2	2.16	....	....	....	....	....	....	....
2007-08	Clarkson Knights	ECAC	38	22	12	4	2211	81	5	2.20	....	....	....	....	....	....	....
	Binghamton	AHL	1	0	1	0	30	2	0	4.06	....	....	....	....	....	....	....
2008-09	Albany River Rats	AHL	1	0	1	0	60	7	0	7.00	....	....	....	....	....	....	....
	Florida Everblades	ECHL	39	27	7	3	2284	86	4	2.26	11	6	5	734	30	0	2.45
2009-10	TPS Turku	Finland	30	12	13	3	1598	78	1	2.93	7	5	2	419	11	1	1.57
2010-11	Portland Pirates	AHL	36	22	12	0	1993	93	3	2.80	9	5	4	510	27	0	3.18
2011-12	Rochester	AHL	54	28	24	2	3243	142	2	2.63	3	0	3	175	11	0	3.76
2012-13	Rochester	AHL	*64	*38	24	1	*3800	162	4	2.56	2	0	2	125	8	0	3.84
2013-14	Hershey Bears	AHL	45	23	18	3	2688	118	2	2.63	....	....	....	....	....	....	....
2014-15	Bridgeport	AHL	23	7	13	0	1267	83	1	3.93	....	....	....	....	....	....	....
	Portland Pirates	AHL	5	1	2	1	274	11	0	2.41	....	....	....	....	....	....	....

ECAC Second All-Star Team (2008)

Signed as a free agent by **TPS Turku** (Finland), June 4, 2009. Signed as a free agent by **Buffalo**, November 12, 2010. Signed as a free agent by **Washington**, July 8, 2013. Signed as a free agent by **NY Islanders**, July 3, 2014. Traded to **Arizona** by **NY Islanders** for Mark Louis, March 2, 2015.

LEHNER, Robin (LEH-nuhr, RAW-bihn) BUF

Goaltender. Catches left. 6'5", 225 lbs. Born, Goteborg, Sweden, July 24, 1991.
(Ottawa's 3rd choice, 46th overall, in 2009 Entry Draft).

			Regular Season								Playoffs						
Season	Club	League	GP	W	L	O/T	Mins	GA	SO	Avg	GP	W	L	Mins	GA	SO	Avg
2007-08	Frolunda U18	Swe-U18	19	....	....	....	1147	34	6	1.78	4	....	....	243	15	0	3.70
2008-09	Frolunda U18	Swe-U18	2	....	....	....	117	5	0	2.56	7	....	....	438	19	0	2.60
	Frolunda Jr.	Swe-Jr.	22	....	....	....	1318	67	1	3.05	1	....	....	58	3	0	3.08
2009-10	Sault Ste. Marie	OHL	47	27	13	3	2574	120	*5	2.80	5	1	4	279	20	0	4.30
	Binghamton	AHL	2	2	0	0	120	6	0	3.00	....	....	....	....	....	....	....
2010-11	**Ottawa**	**NHL**	**8**	**1**	**4**	**0**	**341**	**20**	**0**	**3.52**	....	....	....	....	....	....	....
	Binghamton	AHL	22	10	8	2	1246	56	3	2.70	19	*14	4	1112	39	*3	2.10
2011-12	**Ottawa**	**NHL**	**5**	**3**	**2**	**0**	**299**	**10**	**1**	**2.01**	....	....	....	....	....	....	....
	Binghamton	AHL	40	13	22	1	2192	119	2	3.26	....	....	....	....	....	....	....
2012-13	Binghamton	AHL	31	18	10	2	1841	65	3	2.12	....	....	....	....	....	....	....
	Ottawa	**NHL**	**12**	**5**	**3**	**4**	**735**	**27**	**0**	**2.20**	**2**	**0**	**1**	**49**	**2**	**0**	**2.45**
2013-14	**Ottawa**	**NHL**	**36**	**12**	**15**	**6**	**1942**	**99**	**1**	**3.06**	....	....	....	....	....	....	....
2014-15	**Ottawa**	**NHL**	**25**	**9**	**12**	**3**	**1471**	**74**	**0**	**3.02**	....	....	....	....	....	....	....
	NHL Totals		**86**	**30**	**36**	**13**	**4788**	**230**	**2**	**2.88**	**2**	**0**	**1**	**49**	**2**	**0**	**2.45**

Jack A. Butterfield Trophy (AHL – Playoff MVP) (2011)

Traded to **Buffalo** by **Ottawa** with David Legwand for NY Islanders' 1st round choice (previously acquired, Ottawa selected Colin White) in 2015 Entry Draft, June 26, 2015.

LEHTONEN, Kari (LEH-tuh-nehn, KAH-ree) DAL

Goaltender. Catches left. 6'4", 210 lbs. Born, Helsinki, Finland, November 16, 1983.
(Atlanta's 1st choice, 2nd overall, in 2002 Entry Draft).

			Regular Season								Playoffs						
Season	Club	League	GP	W	L	O/T	Mins	GA	SO	Avg	GP	W	L	Mins	GA	SO	Avg
1998-99	Jokerit U18	Fin-U18	2								4	2	2	240	7	0	1.75
99-2000	Jokerit Helsinki Jr.	Fin-Jr.	33	21	9	3	1974	86	2	2.61	12	9	3	758	14	4	1.11
2000-01	Jokerit U18	Fin-U18									6						
	Jokerit Helsinki Jr.	Fin-Jr.	31	20	9	1	1799	71	3	2.37	1	0	1	54	4	0	4.44
	Jokerit Helsinki	Finland	4	3	1	0	189	6	0	1.90							
2001-02	Jokerit Helsinki Jr.	Fin-Jr.	6	5	1	0	360	11	1	1.83							
	Jokerit Helsinki	Finland	23	13	5	2	1242	37	4	1.79	11	8	2	623	18	3	1.73
2002-03	Jokerit Helsinki	Finland	45	23	14	6	2634	87	5	1.98	10	6	4	626	17	2	1.63
2003-04	Atlanta	NHL	4	4	0	0	240	5	1	1.25							
	Chicago Wolves	AHL	39	20	14	2	2192	88	3	2.41	10	6	4	663	23	1	2.08
2004-05	Chicago Wolves	AHL	57	38	17	2	3378	128	5	2.27	16	10	6	983	28	2	*1.71
2005-06	Atlanta	NHL	38	20	15	0	2166	106	2	2.94							
	Finland	Olympics	DID NOT PLAY – INJURED														
2006-07	Atlanta	NHL	68	34	24	9	3934	183	4	2.79	2	0	2	118	11	0	5.59
2007-08	Atlanta	NHL	48	17	22	5	2707	131	4	2.90							
	Chicago Wolves	AHL	2	2	0	0	124	4	0	1.93							
2008-09	Atlanta	NHL	46	19	22	3	2624	134	3	3.06							
2009-10	Dallas	NHL	12	6	4	0	663	31	0	2.81							
	Chicago Wolves	AHL	4	1	1	2	247	11	0	2.67							
2010-11	Dallas	NHL	69	34	24	11	4119	175	3	2.55							
2011-12	Dallas	NHL	59	32	22	4	3497	136	4	2.33							
2012-13	Dallas	NHL	36	15	14	3	1986	88	1	2.66							
2013-14	Dallas	NHL	*65	33	20	10	*3804	153	5	2.41	6	2	4	346	19	1	3.29
	Finland	Olympics	2				119	3	0	1.51							
2014-15	Dallas	NHL	65	34	17	10	3698	181	5	2.94							
	NHL Totals		510	248	184	55	29438	1323	32	2.70	8	2	6	464	30	1	3.88

AHL Second All-Star Team (2005)

• Missed majority of 2009-10 due to back injury vs. NY Rangers, October 30, 2008 and resulting surgery, July 20, 2009. Traded to **Dallas** by **Atlanta** for Ivan Vishnevskiy and Dallas' 4th round choice (Ivan Telegin) in 2010 Entry Draft, February 9, 2010.

LEIGHTON, Michael (LAY-tohn, MIGH-kuhl) CHI

Goaltender. Catches left. 6'3", 186 lbs. Born, Petrolia, ON, May 19, 1981.
(Chicago's 5th choice, 165th overall, in 1999 Entry Draft).

			Regular Season								Playoffs						
Season	Club	League	GP	W	L	O/T	Mins	GA	SO	Avg	GP	W	L	Mins	GA	SO	Avg
1997-98	Petrolia Jets	ON-Jr.B	30				1583	87	2	3.30							
1998-99	Windsor Spitfires	OHL	28	4	15	9	1390	112	0	4.83	3	0	1	81	10	0	7.43
99-2000	Windsor Spitfires	OHL	42	17	17	2	2272	118	1	3.12	12	5	6	617	32	0	3.11
2000-01	Windsor Spitfires	OHL	54	32	13	5	3035	138	2	2.73	9	4	5	519	27	1	3.12
2001-02	Norfolk Admirals	AHL	52	27	16	8	3114	111	6	2.14	4	1	2	238	8	0	2.02
2002-03	Chicago	NHL	8	2	3	2	447	21	1	2.82							
	Norfolk Admirals	AHL	36	18	13	5	2184	91	4	2.50	4	3	1	240	7	1	1.75
2003-04	Chicago	NHL	34	6	18	8	1988	99	2	2.99							
	Norfolk Admirals	AHL	18	10	7	1	1081	33	1	1.83	4	2	1	212	2	2	0.57
2004-05	Norfolk Admirals	AHL	41	20	16	3	2319	78	7	2.02							
2005-06	Rochester	AHL	40	15	22	1	2318	124	2	3.21							
2006-07	Portland Pirates	AHL	16	8	6	1	962	37	2	2.31							
	Nashville	NHL	1	0	0	0	20	2	0	6.00							
	Philadelphia	NHL	4	2	2	0	195	12	0	3.69							
	Philadelphia	AHL	5	2	0	2	270	7	0	1.56							
2007-08	Carolina	NHL	3	1	1	0	158	7	0	2.66							
	Albany River Rats	AHL	58	28	25	4	3451	121	*7	2.10	7	3	4	510	10	*2	*1.18
2008-09	Carolina	NHL	19	6	7	2	1029	50	0	2.92							
2009-10	Carolina	NHL	7	1	4	0	350	25	0	4.29							
	Philadelphia	NHL	27	16	5	2	1449	60	1	2.48	14	8	3	757	31	*3	*2.46
2010-11	Philadelphia	NHL	1	1	0	0	60	4	0	4.00	2	0	1	70	4	0	3.43
	Adirondack	AHL	30	14	12	3	1783	66	5	2.22							
2011-12	Adirondack	AHL	*56	28	26	1	3237	139	2	2.58							
2012-13	Philadelphia	NHL	1	0	1	0	59	5	0	5.08							
	Adirondack	AHL	2	1	1	0	119	4	0	2.02							
2013-14	Donetsk	KHL	42	20	16	0	2448	71	6	1.74	8	3	4	467	20	0	2.57
2014-15	Rockford IceHogs	AHL	42	22	13	4	2391	90	5	2.26	8	4	3	440	19	0	2.59
	NHL Totals		105	35	41	14	5755	285	4	2.97	16	8	4	827	35	3	2.54

AHL All-Rookie Team (2002) • AHL First All-Star Team (2008) • Aldege "Baz" Bastien Memorial Award (AHL – Outstanding Goaltender) (2008)

Traded to **Buffalo** by **Chicago** for Milan Bartovic, October 4, 2005. Signed as a free agent by **Anaheim**, July 13, 2006. Claimed on waivers by **Nashville** from **Anaheim**, November 27, 2006. Claimed on waivers by **Philadelphia** from **Nashville**, January 11, 2007. Claimed on waivers by **Montreal** from **Philadelphia**, February 27, 2007. Traded to **Carolina** by **Montreal** for Carolina's 7th round choice (Scott Kishel) in 2007 Entry Draft, June 23, 2007. Claimed on waivers by **Philadelphia** from **Carolina**, December 15, 2009. Traded to **Columbus** by **Philadelphia** with Philadelphia's 3rd round choice (later traded to Toronto – Toronto selected Martins Dzierkals) in 2015 Entry Draft for Steve Mason, April 3, 2013. Signed as a free agent by **Donetsk** (KHL), August 19, 2013. Signed as a free agent by **Chicago**, August 18, 2014.

LIEUWEN, Nathan (l'YEW-uhn, NAY-thun) BUF

Goaltender. Catches left. 6'5", 186 lbs. Born, Abbotsford, BC, August 8, 1991.
(Buffalo's 5th choice, 167th overall, in 2011 Entry Draft).

			Regular Season								Playoffs						
Season	Club	League	GP	W	L	O/T	Mins	GA	SO	Avg	GP	W	L	Mins	GA	SO	Avg
2007-08	Westside Warriors	BCHL	13	9	2	0	710	23	0	1.94	3	0	2	139	10	0	4.32
	Kootenay Ice	WHL	3	1	1	0	184	10	0	3.26							
2008-09	Kootenay Ice	WHL	37	14	12	2	1915	94	3	2.95							
2009-10	Kootenay Ice	WHL	26	10	10	0	1244	64	0	3.09	3	0	1	125	4	0	1.92
2010-11	Kootenay Ice	WHL	55	33	16	4	3098	144	3	2.79	19	*16	3	1178	44	*3	*2.24
2011-12	Kootenay Ice	WHL	57	27	20	8	3340	139	3	2.50	4	0	4	238	14	0	3.53
2012-13	Greenville	ECHL	27	14	10	2	1598	78	1	2.93							
	Rochester	AHL	4	1	2	0	204	9	1	2.65							
2013-14	Buffalo	NHL	7	1	4	0	363	18	0	2.98							
	Rochester	AHL	32	17	11	2	1796	70	2	2.34							
2014-15	Rochester	AHL	16	4	9	0	821	45	0	3.29							
	NHL Totals		7	1	4	0	363	18	0	2.98							

WHL East Second All-Star Team (2012)

LINDBACK, Anders (LIHND-bak, AN-duhrs) ARI

Goaltender. Catches left. 6'6", 210 lbs. Born, Gavle, Sweden, May 3, 1988.
(Nashville's 7th choice, 207th overall, in 2008 Entry Draft).

			Regular Season								Playoffs						
Season	Club	League	GP	W	L	O/T	Mins	GA	SO	Avg	GP	W	L	Mins	GA	SO	Avg
2003-04	Brynas U18	Swe-U18	3				178	13	0	4.38							
2004-05	Brynas U18	Swe-U18	49				2940	108	7	2.20							
2005-06	Brynas U18	Swe-U18	11				666	36	2	3.24							
	Brynas IF Gavle Jr.	Swe-Jr.	5				257	7	2	1.64							
2006-07	Brynas IF Gavle Jr.	Swe-Jr.	36				2143	81	5	2.27	3			180	6	0	2.00
2007-08	Almtuna	Sweden-2	18				1034	53	0	3.07							
2008-09	Brynas IF Gavle Jr.	Swe-Jr.	3				179	7	0	2.35							
	Brynas IF Gavle	Sweden	24				1332	57	1	2.57	3			177	7	0	2.37
2009-10	Timra IK	Sweden	42				2537	104	3	2.46	5			306	15	0	2.94
2010-11	Nashville	NHL	22	11	5	2	1131	49	2	2.60	1	0	0	13	0	0	0.00
	Milwaukee	AHL	4	2	2	0	241	11	0	2.73							
2011-12	Nashville	NHL	16	5	8	0	792	32	0	2.42							
	Milwaukee	AHL	2	1	1	0	119	7	0	3.53							
2012-13	Ilves Tampere	Finland	13	3	6	4	797	31	3	2.33							
	Tampa Bay	NHL	24	10	10	1	1304	63	0	2.90							
2013-14	Tampa Bay	NHL	23	8	12	2	1302	63	1	2.90	4	0	3	215	14	0	3.91
	Syracuse Crunch	AHL	2	1	1	0	117	3	1	1.54							
2014-15	Dallas	NHL	10	2	8	0	517	32	0	3.71							
	Texas Stars	AHL	7	4	2	1	429	12	0	1.68							
	Buffalo	NHL	16	4	8	2	891	41	0	2.76							
	NHL Totals		111	40	51	7	5937	280	3	2.83	5	0	3	228	14	0	3.68

Traded to **Tampa Bay** by **Nashville** with Kyle Wilson and Nashville's 7th round choice (Nikita Gusev) in 2012 Entry Draft for Sebastian Caron, Minnesota's 2nd round choice (previously acquired, Nashville selected Pontus Aberg) in 2012 Entry Draft, Philadelphia's 2nd round choice (previously acquired, Nashville selected Colton Sissons) in 2012 Entry Draft and Tampa Bay's 3rd round choice (Jonathan Diaby) in 2013 Entry Draft, June 15, 2012. Signed as a free agent by **Ilves Tampere** (Finland), October 27, 2012. Signed as a free agent by **Dallas**, July 1, 2014. Traded to **Buffalo** by **Dallas** for Jhonas Enroth, February 11, 2015. Signed as a free agent by **Arizona**, July 1, 2015.

LUNDQVIST, Henrik (LUHND-kvihst, HEHN-rihk) NYR

Goaltender. Catches left. 6'1", 188 lbs. Born, Are, Sweden, March 2, 1982.
(NY Rangers' 7th choice, 205th overall, in 2000 Entry Draft).

			Regular Season								Playoffs						
Season	Club	League	GP	W	L	O/T	Mins	GA	SO	Avg	GP	W	L	Mins	GA	SO	Avg
1998-99	V.Frolunda Jr.	Swe-Jr.	35				2100	95	0	2.73							
99-2000	V.Frolunda Jr.	Swe-Jr.	30				1726	73	0	2.54	5	4	1	300	7	2	1.40
2000-01	V.Frolunda U18	Swe-U18	2				120	5	0	2.50	3	2	1	182	5	0	1.62
	V.Frolunda Jr.	Swe-Jr.	19				1140	50	2	2.64							
	IF Molndal Hockey	Sweden-2	7				420	29	0	4.22							
	V.Frolunda	Sweden	4				190	11	0	3.47							
2001-02	V.Frolunda	Sweden	20				1152	52	2	2.71	8	8	0	489	18	*2	2.21
	V.Frolunda Jr.	Swe-Jr.	1	1	0	0	60	4	0	4.00							
2002-03	V.Frolunda	Sweden	28				1650	40	*6	*1.45	12			739	26	*2	2.11
	V.Frolunda Jr.	Swe-Jr.	1	1	0	0	60	4	0	4.00							
2003-04	V.Frolunda	Sweden	*48				*2897	105	7	2.17	10			610	20	0	1.97
2004-05	Frolunda	Sweden	44	*33	8	3	2642	79	*6	*1.79	*14	*12	2	854	15	*6	*1.05
2005-06	NY Rangers	NHL	53	30	12	9	3112	116	2	2.24	3	0	3	177	13	0	4.41
	Sweden	Olympics	6	5	1	0	360	14	0	2.33							
2006-07	NY Rangers	NHL	70	37	22	8	4109	160	5	2.34	10	6	4	637	22	1	2.07
2007-08	NY Rangers	NHL	72	37	24	10	4305	160	*10	2.23	10	5	5	608	26	1	2.57
2008-09	NY Rangers	NHL	70	38	25	7	4153	168	3	2.43	7	3	4	380	19	1	3.00
2009-10	NY Rangers	NHL	73	35	27	10	4204	167	4	2.38							
	Sweden	Olympics	3	2	1	0	179	4	*2	1.34							
2010-11	NY Rangers	NHL	68	36	27	5	4007	152	*11	2.28	5	1	4	346	13	0	2.25
2011-12	NY Rangers	NHL	62	39	18	5	3754	123	8	1.97	20	10	10	1251	38	*3	1.82
2012-13	NY Rangers	NHL	43	*24	16	3	2575	88	2	2.05	12	5	7	756	27	2	2.14
2013-14	NY Rangers	NHL	63	33	24	5	3655	144	5	2.36	25	13	11	1516	54	1	2.14
	Sweden	Olympics	6	5	1	0	360	9	2	1.50							
2014-15	NY Rangers	NHL	46	30	13	3	2743	103	5	2.25	19	11	8	1166	41	0	2.11
	NHL Totals		620	339	208	65	36617	1381	55	2.26	111	54	56	6837	253	9	2.22

NHL All-Rookie Team (2006) • NHL First All-Star Team (2012) • Vezina Trophy (2012) • NHL Second All-Star Team (2013) • Olympic All-Star Team (2014)

Played in NHL All-Star Game (2009, 2011, 2012)

LUNDSTROM, Niklas (LOOND-struhm, NIHK-luhs) ST.L.

Goaltender. Catches left. 6'1", 194 lbs. Born, Varmdo, Sweden, January 10, 1993.
(St. Louis' 6th choice, 132nd overall, in 2011 Entry Draft).

			Regular Season								Playoffs						
Season	Club	League	GP	W	L	O/T	Mins	GA	SO	Avg	GP	W	L	Mins	GA	SO	Avg
2008-09	AIK IF Solna U18	Swe-U18	8				465	18	0	2.32							
2009-10	AIK IF Solna U18	Swe-U18	16				963	39	3	2.43	2			117	3	0	1.54
	AIK IF Solna Jr.	Swe-Jr.	17				939	46	3	2.94	3			190	7	0	2.22
	AIK IF Solna	Sweden-2	1				34	1	0	1.79							
2010-11	AIK IF Solna U18	Swe-U18	1				60	3	0	3.00	6			388	16	0	2.47
	AIK IF Solna Jr.	Swe-Jr.	22				1260	64	1	3.05							
	AIK IF Solna	Sweden	1				47	5	0	6.34							
	Lindlovens IF	Sweden-3	2				128	5	0	2.35							
2011-12	AIK Solna	Sweden	2				120	3	0	1.50							
	IK Oskarshamn	Sweden-2	3				185	7	0	2.27							
	AIK Solna Jr.	Swe-Jr.	31				1737	73	1	2.52	3			187	8	0	2.57
2012-13	AIK Solna	Sweden	14	3	9	0	754	39	0	3.10							
	AIK Solna Jr.	Swe-Jr.	11	9	1	0	603	15	0	1.49	3	1	2	177	7	0	2.37
2013-14	AIK Solna Jr.	Swe-Jr.	10	9	1	0	606	20	0	1.98							
	AIK Solna	Sweden	2	0	1	0	82	6	0	4.39							
	Sodertalje SK	Sweden-2	24	7	14	0	1302	62	1	2.86							
2014-15	Chicago Wolves	AHL	1	0	0	0	14	0	0	0.00							
	Alaska Aces	ECHL	36	17	16	2	1985	101	0	3.05							

LUONGO, Roberto (loo-WAHN-goh, roh-BUHR-toh) FLA

Goaltender. Catches left. 6'3", 217 lbs. Born, Montreal, QC, April 4, 1979.
(NY Islanders' 1st choice, 4th overall, in 1997 Entry Draft).

			Regular Season								Playoffs						
Season	Club	League	GP	W	L	O/T	Mins	GA	SO	Avg	GP	W	L	Mins	GA	SO	Avg
1994-95	Montreal-Bourassa	QAAA	29	10	16	0	1526	94	2	3.85	4	1	3	240	17	0	4.25
1995-96	Val-d'Or Foreurs	QMJHL	23	6	11	4	1201	74	0	3.70	3	0	1	68	5	0	4.41
1996-97	Val-d'Or Foreurs	QMJHL	60	32	21	2	3305	171	2	3.10	13	8	5	777	44	0	3.40
1997-98	Val-d'Or Foreurs	QMJHL	54	27	20	5	3046	157	*7	3.09	*17	*14	3	*1020	37	*2	*2.18
1998-99	Val-d'Or Foreurs	QMJHL	21	6	10	2	1177	77	1	3.93	....	....	....	....	....	....	....
	Acadie-Bathurst	QMJHL	22	14	7	1	1341	74	0	3.31	*23	*16	6	*1400	64	0	2.74
99-2000	**NY Islanders**	**NHL**	**24**	**7**	**14**	**1**	**1292**	**70**	**1**	**3.25**	....	....	....	....	....	....	....
	Lowell	AHL	26	10	12	4	1517	74	1	2.93	6	3	3	359	18	0	3.01
2000-01	**Florida**	**NHL**	**47**	**12**	**24**	**7**	**2628**	**107**	**5**	**2.44**	....	....	....	....	....	....	....
	Louisville Panthers	AHL	3	1	2	0	178	10	0	3.38	....	....	....	....	....	....	....
2001-02	**Florida**	**NHL**	**58**	**16**	**33**	**4**	**3030**	**140**	**4**	**2.77**	....	....	....	....	....	....	....
2002-03	**Florida**	**NHL**	**65**	**20**	**34**	**7**	**3627**	**164**	**6**	**2.71**	....	....	....	....	....	....	....
2003-04	**Florida**	**NHL**	**72**	**25**	**33**	**14**	**4252**	**172**	**7**	**2.43**	....	....	....	....	....	....	....
2004-05							DID NOT PLAY										
2005-06	**Florida**	**NHL**	***75**	**35**	**30**	**9**	**4305**	**213**	**4**	**2.97**	....	....	....	....	....	....	....
	Canada	Olympics	2	1	1	0	119	3	0	1.51	....	....	....	....	....	....	....
2006-07	**Vancouver**	**NHL**	**76**	**47**	**22**	**6**	**4490**	**171**	**5**	**2.29**	**12**	**5**	**7**	**847**	**25**	**0**	**1.77**
2007-08	**Vancouver**	**NHL**	**73**	**35**	**29**	**9**	**4233**	**168**	**6**	**2.38**	....	....	....	....	....	....	....
2008-09	**Vancouver**	**NHL**	**54**	**33**	**13**	**7**	**3181**	**124**	**9**	**2.34**	**10**	**6**	**4**	**618**	**26**	**1**	**2.52**
2009-10	**Vancouver**	**NHL**	**68**	**40**	**22**	**4**	**3899**	**167**	**4**	**2.57**	**12**	**6**	**6**	**707**	**38**	**0**	**3.22**
	Canada	Olympics	5	5	0	0	308	9	1	1.76	....	....	....	....	....	....	....
2010-11	**Vancouver**	**NHL**	**60**	***38**	**15**	**7**	**3590**	**126**	**4**	**2.11**	***25**	**15**	**10**	**1427**	**61**	***4**	**2.56**
2011-12	**Vancouver**	**NHL**	**55**	**31**	**14**	**8**	**3162**	**127**	**5**	**2.41**	**2**	**0**	**2**	**117**	**7**	**0**	**3.59**
2012-13	**Vancouver**	**NHL**	**20**	**9**	**6**	**3**	**1197**	**51**	**2**	**2.56**	**3**	**0**	**2**	**140**	**6**	**0**	**2.57**
2013-14	**Vancouver**	**NHL**	**42**	**19**	**16**	**6**	**2418**	**96**	**3**	**2.38**	....	....	....	....	....	....	....
	Canada	Olympics	1	1	0	0	60	0	1	0.00	....	....	....	....	....	....	....
	Florida	**NHL**	**14**	**6**	**7**	**1**	**804**	**33**	**1**	**2.46**	....	....	....	....	....	....	....
2014-15	**Florida**	**NHL**	**61**	**28**	**19**	**12**	**3528**	**138**	**2**	**2.35**	....	....	....	....	....	....	....
	NHL Totals		**864**	**401**	**331**	**105**	**49636**	**2067**	**68**	**2.50**	**64**	**32**	**31**	**3856**	**163**	**5**	**2.54**

NHL Second All-Star Team (2004, 2007) • William M. Jennings Trophy (2011) (shared with Cory Schneider)

Played in NHL All-Star Game (2004, 2007, 2009, 2015)

Traded to **Florida** by **NY Islanders** with Olli Jokinen for Mark Parrish and Oleg Kvasha, June 24, 2000. Traded to **Vancouver** by **Florida** with Lukas Krajicek and Florida's 6th round choice (Sergei Shirokov) in 2006 Entry Draft for Todd Bertuzzi, Bryan Allen and Alex Auld, June 23, 2006. Traded to **Florida** by **Vancouver** with Steven Anthony for Jacob Markstrom and Shawn Matthias, March 4, 2014.

MacINTYRE, Drew (MAK-ihn-tighr, DROO) CAR

Goaltender. Catches left. 6'1", 190 lbs. Born, Charlottetown, PE, June 24, 1983.
(Detroit's 2nd choice, 121st overall, in 2001 Entry Draft).

			Regular Season								Playoffs						
Season	Club	League	GP	W	L	O/T	Mins	GA	SO	Avg	GP	W	L	Mins	GA	SO	Avg
1998-99	Trenton Sting	ON-Jr.A	20	....	....	....	1173	71	2	3.63	....	....	....	....	....	....	....
99-2000	Sherbrooke	QMJHL	24	10	7	2	1254	67	0	3.21	....	....	....	....	....	....	....
2000-01	Sherbrooke	QMJHL	48	17	22	3	2552	139	4	3.27	4	0	4	238	19	0	4.78
2001-02	Sherbrooke	QMJHL	55	15	34	3	3028	201	1	3.98	....	....	....	....	....	....	....
2002-03	Sherbrooke	QMJHL	*61	31	24	5	*3515	161	2	2.75	12	5	7	767	52	0	4.07
2003-04	Toledo Storm	ECHL	11	6	4	0	574	25	0	2.61	....	....	....	....	....	....	....
2004-05	Grand Rapids	AHL	24	7	8	0	1049	47	1	2.69	....	....	....	....	....	....	....
	Toledo Storm	ECHL	2	0	1	0	87	6	0	4.12	....	....	....	....	....	....	....
2005-06	Grand Rapids	AHL	13	8	4	0	681	33	0	2.91	5	3	1	260	7	0	1.62
	Toledo Storm	ECHL	33	24	7	2	1981	68	2	*2.06	6	5	1	360	12	0	2.00
2006-07	Manitoba Moose	AHL	41	24	12	2	2290	83	3	2.17	11	4	6	633	21	1	1.99
2007-08	**Vancouver**	**NHL**	**2**	**0**	**1**	**0**	**61**	**3**	**0**	**2.95**	....	....	....	....	....	....	....
	Manitoba Moose	AHL	46	25	18	2	2736	106	2	2.32	1	1	0	31	2	0	3.93
2008-09	Milwaukee	AHL	55	*34	15	4	3180	122	4	2.30	11	7	4	655	18	1	*1.65
2009-10	Chicago Wolves	AHL	41	20	17	2	2246	95	3	2.54	5	1	2	228	11	1	2.90
2010-11	Chicago Wolves	AHL	20	12	5	1	1135	55	0	2.91	....	....	....	....	....	....	....
	Hamilton Bulldogs	AHL	21	12	6	2	1241	39	1	1.89	20	11	9	1289	42	1	1.95
2011-12	**Buffalo**	**NHL**	**2**	**0**	**0**	**0**	**43**	**1**	**0**	**1.40**	....	....	....	....	....	....	....
	Rochester	AHL	23	8	12	2	1375	73	1	3.19	....	....	....	....	....	....	....
2012-13	HC Lev Praha	KHL	2	0	1	0	123	6	0	2.92	....	....	....	....	....	....	....
	Reading Royals	ECHL	10	6	3	1	589	19	0	1.93	....	....	....	....	....	....	....
	Toronto Marlies	AHL	21	13	5	3	1243	38	0	1.83	9	5	4	527	25	1	2.85
2013-14	**Toronto**	**NHL**	**2**	**0**	**1**	**0**	**95**	**4**	**0**	**2.53**	....	....	....	....	....	....	....
	Toronto Marlies	AHL	48	29	15	3	2866	121	1	2.53	14	10	4	837	29	2	2.08
2014-15	Charlotte Checkers	AHL	51	20	26	5	2935	139	0	2.84	....	....	....	....	....	....	....
	NHL Totals		**6**	**0**	**2**	**0**	**199**	**8**	**0**	**2.41**	....	....	....	....	....	....	....

AHL Second All-Star Team (2008, 2009)

• Missed majority of 2003-04 due to thigh injury in practice, December 27, 2003. Traded to **Vancouver** by **Detroit** for future considerations, September 12, 2006. Signed as a free agent by **Nashville**, July 1, 2008. Signed as a free agent by **Atlanta**, July 6, 2009. Traded to **Montreal** by **Atlanta** for Brett Festerling, February 28, 2011. Signed as a free agent by **Buffalo**, July 7, 2011. Signed as a free agent by **Lev Praha** (KHL), June 3, 2012. Signed as a free agent by **Reading** (ECHL), January 3, 2013. Signed to a PTO (professional tryout) contract by **Toronto** (AHL), February 13, 2013. Signed as a free agent by **Toronto**, April 2, 2013. Signed as a free agent by **Carolina**, July 1, 2014.

MADSEN, Merrick (MAD-sehn, MAIR-ihk) PHI

Goaltender. Catches left. 6'5", 190 lbs. Born, Preston, ID, August 22, 1995.
(Philadelphia's 5th choice, 162nd overall, in 2013 Entry Draft).

			Regular Season								Playoffs						
Season	Club	League	GP	W	L	O/T	Mins	GA	SO	Avg	GP	W	L	Mins	GA	SO	Avg
2011-12	Proctor Academy	High-NH	20	....	....	....	748	....	....	4.00	....	....	....	....	....	....	....
2012-13	Proctor Academy	High-NH	26	10	13	3	1171	82	1	3.19	....	....	....	....	....	....	....
2013-14	Minot Minotauros	NAHL	27	10	16	0	1571	72	1	2.75	3	1	2	171	7	....	2.45
2014-15	Harvard Crimson	ECAC	1	0	0	0	43	2	0	2.77	....	....	....	....	....	....	....

• Spent majority of 2014-15 as spare goaltender.

MAGUIRE, Sean (muh-GWIGH-uhr, SHAWN) PIT

Goaltender. Catches left. 6'2", 202 lbs. Born, Edmonton, AB, February 2, 1993.
(Pittsburgh's 7th choice, 113th overall, in 2012 Entry Draft).

			Regular Season								Playoffs						
Season	Club	League	GP	W	L	O/T	Mins	GA	SO	Avg	GP	W	L	Mins	GA	SO	Avg
2009-10	North Island	BCMML	20	....	....	....	....	....	....	....	1	....	....	....	....	....	....
2010-11	Powell River Kings	BCHL	15	10	3	0	841	35	2	2.50	2	0	0	44	1	0	1.36
2011-12	Powell River Kings	BCHL	31	17	12	1	1774	69	3	2.33	15	7	6	808	28	2	2.08
2012-13	Boston University	H-East	21	13	8	0	1230	52	4	2.54	....	....	....	....	....	....	....
2013-14	Boston University	H-East	16	3	12	0	868	42	0	2.90	....	....	....	....	....	....	....
2014-15	Boston University	H-East					DID NOT PLAY – INJURED										

• Missed remainder of 2013-14 and entire 2014-15 due to head injury in practice, March 2, 2014.

MAKAROV, Andrey (mah-KAH-rahv, an-DRAY) BUF

Goaltender. Catches left. 6', 203 lbs. Born, Kazan, Russia, April 20, 1993.

			Regular Season								Playoffs						
Season	Club	League	GP	W	L	O/T	Mins	GA	SO	Avg	GP	W	L	Mins	GA	SO	Avg
2008-09	Lada Togliatti 2	Russia-3	9	....	....	....	....	....	....	3.27	....	....	....	....	....	....	....
2009-10	Ladja Togliatti Jr.	Russia-Jr.	22	....	....	....	1114	....	....	4.04	....	....	....	....	....	....	....
2010-11	Lewiston	QMJHL	27	11	12	2	1390	78	2	3.37	3	....	....	....	....	....	....
2011-12	Saskatoon Blades	WHL	54	29	21	2	3107	156	2	3.01	4	0	4	249	17	0	4.10
2012-13	Saskatoon Blades	WHL	61	*37	17	5	3487	152	7	2.62	4	0	4	196	12	0	3.66
2013-14	Rochester	AHL	10	7	3	0	601	22	0	2.20	5	2	3	299	15	0	3.01
	Fort Wayne	ECHL	31	15	11	4	1850	86	0	2.79	....	....	....	....	....	....	....
2014-15	**Buffalo**	**NHL**	**1**	**0**	**1**	**0**	**60**	**3**	**0**	**3.00**	....	....	....	....	....	....	....
	Rochester	AHL	39	16	18	3	2209	107	3	2.91	....	....	....	....	....	....	....
	NHL Totals		**1**	**0**	**1**	**0**	**60**	**3**	**0**	**3.00**	....	....	....	....	....	....	....

Hap Emms Memorial Trophy (Memorial Cup Tournament – Top Goaltender) (2013)

Signed as a free agent by **Buffalo**, September 14, 2012.

MARKSTROM, Jacob (MAHRK-struhm, JAY-kawb) VAN

Goaltender. Catches left. 6'6", 196 lbs. Born, Gavle, Sweden, January 31, 1990.
(Florida's 1st choice, 31st overall, in 2008 Entry Draft).

			Regular Season								Playoffs						
Season	Club	League	GP	W	L	O/T	Mins	GA	SO	Avg	GP	W	L	Mins	GA	SO	Avg
2006-07	Brynas U18	Swe-U18	13	....	....	....	789	27	0	2.05	3	....	....	193	6	1	1.86
	Brynas IF Gavle Jr.	Swe-Jr.	1	....	....	....	65	3	0	2.77	1	....	....	25	4	0	9.76
2007-08	Brynas U18	Swe-U18	1	....	....	....	60	3	0	3.00	....	....	....	....	....	....	....
	Brynas IF Gavle Jr.	Swe-Jr.	22	....	....	....	1320	44	2	2.00	....	....	....	....	....	....	....
	Brynas IF Gavle	Sweden	7	....	....	....	423	22	0	3.12	....	....	....	....	....	....	....
	Brynas IF Gavle	Sweden-Q	9	....	....	....	505	15	2	1.78	....	....	....	....	....	....	....
2008-09	Brynas IF Gavle	Sweden	35	....	....	....	1992	79	3	2.38	1	....	....	59	2	0	2.02
2009-10	Brynas IF Gavle	Sweden	43	....	....	....	2542	85	*5	*2.01	4	....	....	224	12	0	3.21
	Brynas IF Gavle Jr.	Swe-Jr.	....	....	....	....	....	....	....	....	2	....	....	119	6	0	3.03
2010-11	**Florida**	**NHL**	**1**	**0**	**1**	**0**	**40**	**2**	**0**	**3.00**	....	....	....	....	....	....	....
	Rochester	AHL	37	16	20	1	2174	108	1	2.98	....	....	....	....	....	....	....
2011-12	**Florida**	**NHL**	**7**	**2**	**4**	**1**	**383**	**17**	**0**	**2.66**	....	....	....	....	....	....	....
	San Antonio	AHL	32	17	12	1	1839	71	1	2.32	8	4	4	546	26	0	2.85
2012-13	San Antonio	AHL	33	16	15	2	1972	87	3	2.65	....	....	....	....	....	....	....
	Florida	**NHL**	**23**	**8**	**14**	**1**	**1266**	**68**	**0**	**3.22**	....	....	....	....	....	....	....
2013-14	**Florida**	**NHL**	**12**	**1**	**6**	**3**	**614**	**36**	**0**	**3.52**	....	....	....	....	....	....	....
	San Antonio	AHL	29	12	11	3	1688	72	2	2.56	....	....	....	....	....	....	....
	Vancouver	**NHL**	**4**	**1**	**2**	**0**	**200**	**10**	**0**	**3.00**	....	....	....	....	....	....	....
2014-15	**Vancouver**	**NHL**	**3**	**1**	**1**	**0**	**78**	**4**	**0**	**3.08**	....	....	....	....	....	....	....
	Utica Comets	AHL	32	22	7	2	1880	59	5	1.88	23	12	11	1450	51	2	2.11
	NHL Totals		**50**	**13**	**28**	**5**	**2581**	**137**	**0**	**3.18**	....	....	....	....	....	....	....

AHL Second All-Star Team (2015)

Traded to **Vancouver** by **Florida** with Shawn Matthias for Roberto Luongo and Steven Anthony, March 4, 2014.

MARTIN, Spencer (MAHR-tihn, SPEHN-suhr) COL

Goaltender. Catches left. 6'3", 200 lbs. Born, Oakville, ON, June 8, 1995.
(Colorado's 3rd choice, 63rd overall, in 2013 Entry Draft).

			Regular Season								Playoffs						
Season	Club	League	GP	W	L	O/T	Mins	GA	SO	Avg	GP	W	L	Mins	GA	SO	Avg
2010-11	Tor. Jr. Canadiens	GTHL	50	....	....	....	2250	115	5	2.27	....	....	....	....	....	....	....
2011-12	St. Michael's	OHL	15	2	7	1	753	50	0	3.98	....	....	....	....	....	....	....
2012-13	Mississauga	OHL	46	17	21	4	2504	126	0	3.02	2	0	1	90	9	0	6.01
2013-14	Mississauga	OHL	*64	24	33	5	*3562	210	3	3.54	4	1	3	270	18	0	3.99
2014-15	Mississauga	OHL	31	15	13	1	1713	85	1	2.98	....	....	....	....	....	....	....

MASON, Steve (MAY-sohn, STEEV) PHI

Goaltender. Catches right. 6'4", 210 lbs. Born, Oakville, ON, May 29, 1988.
(Columbus' 2nd choice, 69th overall, in 2006 Entry Draft).

			Regular Season								Playoffs						
Season	Club	League	GP	W	L	O/T	Mins	GA	SO	Avg	GP	W	L	Mins	GA	SO	Avg
2003-04	Oakville Rangers	Minor-ON	27	....	....	....	1209	41	5	1.58	....	....	....	....	....	....	....
2004-05	Grimsby	ON-Jr.C	45	....	....	....	2800	....	6	1.75	....	....	....	....	....	....	....
2005-06	Petrolia Jets	ON-Jr.B	9	6	3	0	522	22	1	2.53	5	3	2	348	9	0	1.55
	London Knights	OHL	12	5	3	0	497	22	0	2.66	4	0	1	150	7	0	2.80
2006-07	London Knights	OHL	*62	*45	13	4	*3733	199	2	3.20	16	9	7	931	54	0	3.48
2007-08	London Knights	OHL	26	19	4	3	1569	73	2	2.79	....	....	....	....	....	....	....
	Kitchener Rangers	OHL	16	13	3	0	961	33	1	2.06	5	5	0	313	10	1	1.92
2008-09	**Columbus**	**NHL**	**61**	**33**	**20**	**7**	**3664**	**140**	***10**	**2.29**	**4**	**0**	**4**	**239**	**17**	**0**	**4.27**
	Syracuse Crunch	AHL	3	2	1	0	184	5	0	1.63	....	....	....	....	....	....	....
2009-10	**Columbus**	**NHL**	**58**	**20**	**26**	**9**	**3201**	**163**	**5**	**3.06**	....	....	....	....	....	....	....
2010-11	**Columbus**	**NHL**	**54**	**24**	**21**	**7**	**3027**	**153**	**3**	**3.03**	....	....	....	....	....	....	....
2011-12	**Columbus**	**NHL**	**46**	**16**	**26**	**3**	**2534**	**143**	**1**	**3.39**	....	....	....	....	....	....	....
2012-13	**Columbus**	**NHL**	**13**	**3**	**6**	**1**	**712**	**35**	**0**	**2.95**	....	....	....	....	....	....	....
	Philadelphia	**NHL**	**7**	**4**	**2**	**0**	**378**	**12**	**0**	**1.90**	....	....	....	....	....	....	....
2013-14	**Philadelphia**	**NHL**	**61**	**33**	**18**	**7**	**3486**	**145**	**4**	**2.50**	**5**	**2**	**2**	**244**	**8**	**0**	**1.97**
2014-15	**Philadelphia**	**NHL**	**51**	**18**	**18**	**11**	**2885**	**108**	**3**	**2.25**	....	....	....	....	....	....	....
	NHL Totals		**351**	**151**	**137**	**45**	**19887**	**899**	**26**	**2.71**	**9**	**2**	**6**	**483**	**25**	**0**	**3.11**

OHL First All-Star Team (2007) • OHL Second All-Star Team (2008) • NHL All-Rookie Team (2009) • NHL Second All-Star Team (2009) • Calder Memorial Trophy (2009)

Traded to **Philadelphia** by **Columbus** for Michael Leighton and Philadelphia's 3rd round choice (later traded to Toronto – Toronto selected Martins Dzierkals) in 2015 Entry Draft, April 3, 2013.

MAZANEC, Marek (muh-ZAN-ehk, MAHR-ehk) NSH

Goaltender. Catches right. 6'4", 187 lbs. Born, Pisek, Czech., July 18, 1991.
(Nashville's 9th choice, 179th overall, in 2012 Entry Draft).

			Regular Season								Playoffs						
Season	**Club**	**League**	**GP**	**W**	**L**	**O/T**	**Mins**	**GA**	**SO**	**Avg**	**GP**	**W**	**L**	**Mins**	**GA**	**SO**	**Avg**
2004-05	IHC Pisek U17	CzR-U17	1	....	....	....	30	7	0	14.00	....	....	....	....	....	....	....
2006-07	HC Plzen U17	CzR-U17	14	....	....	....	666	32	2	2.88	1	....	....	27	1	0	2.22
2007-08	HC Plzen U17	CzR-U17	41	....	....	....	2457	99	5	2.42	8	....	....	492	15	1	1.83
2008-09	HC Plzen Jr.	CzRep-Jr.	27	....	....	....	1577	68	0	2.59	5	....	....	309	9	0	1.75
2009-10	HC Plzen 1929	CzRep	1	....	....	....	20	3	0	9.00	....	....	....	....	....	....	....
	SHC Klatovy	CzRep-3	3	....	....	....	185	10	0	3.24	....	....	....	....	....	....	....
	HC Plzen Jr.	CzRep-Jr.	43	....	....	....	2560	111	3	2.60	2	....	....	120	7	0	3.50
2010-11	HC Plzen Jr.	CzRep-Jr.	30	....	....	....	1683	59	7	2.10	....	....	....	....	....	....	....
	HC Plzen 1929	CzRep	15	....	....	....	860	40	1	2.79	....	....	....	....	....	....	....
	IHC Komterm Pisek	CzRep-2	9	....	....	....	435	17	1	2.34	....	....	....	....	....	....	....
2011-12	HC Plzen Jr.	CzRep-Jr.	1	....	....	....	60	4	0	4.00	....	....	....	....	....	....	....
	HC Plzen 1929	CzRep	19	....	....	....	973	48	1	2.96	5	....	....	222	8	0	2.16
	SHC Klatovy	CzRep-3	17	....	....	....	1033	65	0	3.78	6	....	....	359	19	1	3.18
2012-13	HC Plzen Jr.	CzRep-Jr.	2	....	....	....	120	5	0	2.50	....	....	....	....	....	....	....
	IHC Pisek	CzRep-2	12	....	....	....	706	50	0	4.25	....	....	....	....	....	....	....
	HC Skoda Plzen	CzRep	21	....	....	....	1255	52	1	2.49	*20	....	....	*1241	44	2	2.13
2013-14	**Nashville**	**NHL**	**25**	**8**	**10**	**4**	**1370**	**64**	**2**	**2.80**	....	....	....	....	....	....	....
	Milwaukee	AHL	31	18	10	3	1866	76	0	2.44	3	0	3	178	9	0	3.03
2014-15	**Nashville**	**NHL**	**2**	**0**	**1**	**0**	**106**	**4**	**0**	**2.26**	....	....	....	....	....	....	....
	Milwaukee	AHL	48	18	18	9	2628	121	4	2.76	....	....	....	....	....	....	....
	NHL Totals		**27**	**8**	**11**	**4**	**1476**	**68**	**2**	**2.76**	....	....	....	....	....	....	....

McADAM, Eamon (muhk-A-duhm, AY-muhn) NYI

Goaltender. Catches left. 6'3", 199 lbs. Born, Doylestown, PA, September 24, 1994.
(NY Islanders' 2nd choice, 70th overall, in 2013 Entry Draft).

			Regular Season								Playoffs						
Season	**Club**	**League**	**GP**	**W**	**L**	**O/T**	**Mins**	**GA**	**SO**	**Avg**	**GP**	**W**	**L**	**Mins**	**GA**	**SO**	**Avg**
2010-11	Austin Bruins	NAHL	9	2	4	2	506	28	0	3.32	....	....	....	....	....	....	....
	Waterloo	USHL	4	2	2	0	190	11	0	3.48	....	....	....	....	....	....	....
2011-12	Waterloo	USHL	23	11	7	0	1149	67	0	3.50	....	....	....	....	....	....	....
2012-13	Waterloo	USHL	31	17	9	3	1806	104	2	3.45	....	....	....	....	....	....	....
2013-14	Penn State	Big Ten	10	0	9	0	558	38	0	4.09	....	....	....	....	....	....	....
2014-15	Penn State	Big Ten	12	5	4	1	653	34	0	3.13	....	....	....	....	....	....	....

McCOLLUM, Tom (muh-KAW-luhm, TAWM) DET

Goaltender. Catches left. 6'2", 226 lbs. Born, Amherst, NY, December 7, 1989.
(Detroit's 1st choice, 30th overall, in 2008 Entry Draft).

			Regular Season								Playoffs						
Season	**Club**	**League**	**GP**	**W**	**L**	**O/T**	**Mins**	**GA**	**SO**	**Avg**	**GP**	**W**	**L**	**Mins**	**GA**	**SO**	**Avg**
2005-06	Wheatfield Blades	EmJHL	24	2	19	3	1448	109	1	4.52	....	....	....	....	....	....	....
2006-07	Guelph Storm	OHL	55	26	18	10	3158	126	*5	2.39	4	0	4	233	17	0	4.38
2007-08	Guelph Storm	OHL	51	25	17	6	2978	124	*4	2.50	10	5	5	596	19	1	1.91
2008-09	Guelph Storm	OHL	31	17	10	4	1859	69	*3	2.23	....	....	....	....	....	....	....
	Brampton Battalion	OHL	23	17	6	0	1333	43	*4	1.94	*21	13	8	*1284	62	*1	2.90
2009-10	Grand Rapids	AHL	32	10	16	2	1741	101	0	3.48	....	....	....	....	....	....	....
	Toledo Walleye	ECHL	4	2	1	0	188	14	0	4.48	....	....	....	....	....	....	....
2010-11	**Detroit**	**NHL**	**1**	**0**	**0**	**0**	**15**	**3**	**0**	**12.00**	....	....	....	....	....	....	....
	Grand Rapids	AHL	22	6	12	2	1152	64	1	3.33	....	....	....	....	....	....	....
	Toledo Walleye	ECHL	23	11	9	2	1305	60	3	2.76	....	....	....	....	....	....	....
2011-12	Grand Rapids	AHL	28	11	16	0	1580	92	0	3.49	....	....	....	....	....	....	....
	Toledo Walleye	ECHL	15	6	6	2	870	38	0	2.62	....	....	....	....	....	....	....
2012-13	Grand Rapids	AHL	31	18	11	2	1846	81	2	2.63	....	....	....	....	....	....	....
2013-14	Grand Rapids	AHL	46	24	12	5	2561	98	2	2.30	1	0	0	34	2	0	3.50
2014-15	**Detroit**	**NHL**	**2**	**1**	**0**	**0**	**66**	**1**	**0**	**0.91**	....	....	....	....	....	....	....
	Grand Rapids	AHL	37	19	11	6	2171	87	1	2.40	15	9	6	895	38	0	2.55
	NHL Totals		**3**	**1**	**0**	**0**	**81**	**4**	**0**	**2.96**	....	....	....	....	....	....	....

OHL Second All-Star Team (2009)

McDONALD, Mason (muhk-DAWN-uhld, MAY-suhn) CGY

Goaltender. Catches right. 6'4", 189 lbs. Born, Halifax, NS, April 23, 1996.
(Calgary's 2nd choice, 34th overall, in 2014 Entry Draft).

			Regular Season								Playoffs						
Season	**Club**	**League**	**GP**	**W**	**L**	**O/T**	**Mins**	**GA**	**SO**	**Avg**	**GP**	**W**	**L**	**Mins**	**GA**	**SO**	**Avg**
2010-11	Halifax Hawks	NSBHL	17	10	1	4	925	33	0	2.14	1	1	0	60	1	0	2.10
	Halifax Hawks	Other	....	....	....	....	....	....	....	....	5	3	0	257	9	0	2.10
2011-12	Halifax Titans	NSMHL	20	14	1	0	1162	39	1	2.01	6	5	1	325	11	0	2.03
2012-13	Acadie-Bathurst	QMJHL	26	6	8	3	1004	79	1	4.72	....	....	....	....	....	....	....
2013-14	Acadie-Bathurst	QMJHL	13	3	7	1	655	39	0	3.57	....	....	....	....	....	....	....
	Charlottetown	QMJHL	16	5	8	2	948	53	0	3.35	4	0	4	201	22	0	6.58
2014-15	Charlottetown	QMJHL	56	28	22	4	3194	163	1	3.06	3	1	1	121	8	0	3.98

McELHINNEY, Curtis (MAK-IHL-ehn-ee, KUHR-this) CBJ

Goaltender. Catches left. 6'3", 205 lbs. Born, London, ON, May 23, 1983.
(Calgary's 9th choice, 176th overall, in 2002 Entry Draft).

			Regular Season								Playoffs						
Season	**Club**	**League**	**GP**	**W**	**L**	**O/T**	**Mins**	**GA**	**SO**	**Avg**	**GP**	**W**	**L**	**Mins**	**GA**	**SO**	**Avg**
2000-01	Notre Dame	SJHL					STATISTICS NOT AVAILABLE										
2001-02	Colorado College	WCHA	9	6	0	1	441	15	1	2.04	....	....	....	....	....	....	....
2002-03	Colorado College	WCHA	*37	*25	6	5	*2147	85	*4	2.37	....	....	....	....	....	....	....
2003-04	Colorado College	WCHA	19	10	6	1	1015	41	2	2.42	....	....	....	....	....	....	....
2004-05	Colorado College	WCHA	26	*21	4	1	1550	58	2	2.24	....	....	....	....	....	....	....
2005-06	Omaha	AHL	33	9	14	2	1621	68	3	2.52	....	....	....	....	....	....	....
2006-07	Omaha	AHL	57	35	17	1	3181	113	*7	2.13	5	2	3	311	11	0	2.12
2007-08	**Calgary**	**NHL**	**5**	**0**	**2**	**0**	**150**	**5**	**0**	**2.00**	....	....	....	....	....	....	....
	Quad City Flames	AHL	41	20	18	2	2320	88	3	2.28	....	....	....	....	....	....	....
2008-09	**Calgary**	**NHL**	**14**	**1**	**6**	**1**	**518**	**31**	**0**	**3.59**	**1**	**0**	**0**	**34**	**1**	**0**	**1.76**
2009-10	**Calgary**	**NHL**	**10**	**3**	**4**	**0**	**502**	**27**	**0**	**3.23**	....	....	....	....	....	....	....
	Anaheim	**NHL**	**10**	**5**	**1**	**2**	**521**	**24**	**0**	**2.76**	....	....	....	....	....	....	....
2010-11	**Anaheim**	**NHL**	**21**	**6**	**9**	**1**	**996**	**57**	**2**	**3.43**	....	....	....	....	....	....	....
	Ottawa	**NHL**	**7**	**3**	**4**	**0**	**399**	**17**	**0**	**2.56**	....	....	....	....	....	....	....
2011-12	**Phoenix**	**NHL**	**2**	**1**	**0**	**0**	**72**	**2**	**0**	**1.67**	....	....	....	....	....	....	....
	Portland Pirates	AHL	25	10	13	0	1379	70	0	3.04	....	....	....	....	....	....	....
2012-13	Springfield Falcons	AHL	49	29	16	3	2926	113	*9	2.32	8	3	5	483	25	0	3.10
2013-14	**Columbus**	**NHL**	**28**	**10**	**11**	**1**	**1423**	**64**	**2**	**2.70**	....	....	....	....	....	....	....
2014-15	**Columbus**	**NHL**	**32**	**12**	**14**	**2**	**1710**	**82**	**0**	**2.88**	....	....	....	....	....	....	....
	NHL Totals		**129**	**41**	**51**	**7**	**6291**	**309**	**4**	**2.95**	**1**	**0**	**0**	**34**	**1**	**0**	**1.76**

WCHA First All-Star Team (2003, 2005) • NCAA West Second All-American Team (2003) • NCAA West First All-American Team (2005) • AHL Second All-Star Team (2007, 2013)

Traded to **Anaheim** by **Calgary** for Vesa Toskala, March 3, 2010. Traded to **Tampa Bay** by **Anaheim** for Dan Ellis, February 24, 2011. Claimed on waivers by **Ottawa** from **Tampa Bay**, February 28, 2011. Signed as a free agent by **Phoenix**, July 4, 2011. Traded to **Columbus** by **Phoenix** with Ottawa's 2nd round choice (previously acquired, later traded to Philadelphia – Philadelphia selected Anthony Stolarz) in 2012 Entry Draft and Phoenix's 4th round choice (later traded to Philadelphia, later traded to Los Angeles – Los Angeles selected Justin Auger) in 2013 Entry Draft for Antoine Vermette, February 22, 2012.

McINTYRE, Zane (MAK-ihn-tigh-uhr, ZAYN) BOS

Goaltender. Catches left. 6'2", 205 lbs. Born, Grand Forks, ND, August 20, 1992.
(Boston's 6th choice, 165th overall, in 2010 Entry Draft).

			Regular Season								Playoffs						
Season	**Club**	**League**	**GP**	**W**	**L**	**O/T**	**Mins**	**GA**	**SO**	**Avg**	**GP**	**W**	**L**	**Mins**	**GA**	**SO**	**Avg**
2007-08	Thief River Falls	High-MN	....	14	12	0	....	....	....	2.15	....	....	....	....	....	....	....
2008-09	Thief River Falls	High-MN	27	20	5	2	1354	....	4	1.49	....	....	....	....	....	....	....
2009-10	Team Great Plains	UMHSEL	5	0	4	0	250	32	0	7.68	....	....	....	....	....	....	....
	Thief River Falls	High-MN	25	16	7	1	1281	46	3	1.83	3	2	1	153	5	0	1.67
2010-11	Fargo Force	USHL	23	14	8	0	1318	49	2	2.23	1	0	1	55	3	0	3.25
2011-12	Fargo Force	USHL	46	26	16	4	2758	102	*7	2.22	6	3	3	370	11	0	1.78
2012-13	North Dakota	WCHA	17	9	4	3	1001	41	0	2.46	....	....	....	....	....	....	....
2013-14	North Dakota	NCHC	33	*20	10	3	1930	64	3	*1.99	....	....	....	....	....	....	....
2014-15	North Dakota	NCHC	*42	*29	10	3	*2493	85	1	2.05	....	....	....	....	....	....	....

USHL First All-Star Team (2012)

McKENNA, Mike (mih-KEHN-ah, MIGHK) FLA

Goaltender. Catches right. 6'2", 190 lbs. Born, St. Louis, MO, April 11, 1983.
(Nashville's 4th choice, 172nd overall, in 2002 Entry Draft).

			Regular Season								Playoffs						
Season	**Club**	**League**	**GP**	**W**	**L**	**O/T**	**Mins**	**GA**	**SO**	**Avg**	**GP**	**W**	**L**	**Mins**	**GA**	**SO**	**Avg**
2001-02	St. Lawrence	ECAC	20	7	10	1	1121	59	0	3.16	....	....	....	....	....	....	....
2002-03	St. Lawrence	ECAC	15	1	7	2	618	38	0	3.69	....	....	....	....	....	....	....
2003-04	St. Lawrence	ECAC	27	9	10	3	1475	60	3	2.44	....	....	....	....	....	....	....
2004-05	St. Lawrence	ECAC	35	15	17	2	2022	92	3	2.73	....	....	....	....	....	....	....
2005-06	Norfolk Admirals	AHL	7	4	2	1	388	25	0	3.86	....	....	....	....	....	....	....
	Las Vegas	ECHL	25	19	2	1	1383	49	1	2.13	4	1	1	173	9	0	3.12
2006-07	Milwaukee	AHL	1	0	0	0	11	3	0	15.72	....	....	....	....	....	....	....
	Omaha	AHL	2	0	1	0	96	6	0	3.74	....	....	....	....	....	....	....
	Las Vegas	ECHL	38	27	4	7	2258	83	5	*2.21	6	3	3	358	15	0	2.51
2007-08	Portland Pirates	AHL	41	24	13	1	2269	103	3	2.72	6	2	4	320	18	0	3.38
2008-09	**Tampa Bay**	**NHL**	**15**	**4**	**8**	**1**	**776**	**46**	**1**	**3.56**	....	....	....	....	....	....	....
	Norfolk Admirals	AHL	24	11	10	1	1315	65	1	2.97	....	....	....	....	....	....	....
2009-10	Lowell Devils	AHL	50	24	17	6	2891	119	3	2.47	5	1	4	317	17	0	3.22
2010-11	Albany Devils	AHL	39	14	20	2	2062	124	1	3.61	....	....	....	....	....	....	....
	New Jersey	**NHL**	**2**	**0**	**1**	**0**	**118**	**6**	**0**	**3.05**	....	....	....	....	....	....	....
2011-12	Binghamton	AHL	41	14	22	1	2196	109	0	2.98	....	....	....	....	....	....	....
2012-13	Peoria Rivermen	AHL	39	19	18	1	2307	93	4	2.42	....	....	....	....	....	....	....
2013-14	**Columbus**	**NHL**	**4**	**1**	**1**	**1**	**219**	**11**	**0**	**3.01**	....	....	....	....	....	....	....
	Springfield Falcons	AHL	36	22	10	1	2106	89	3	2.54	5	2	2	245	14	0	3.43
2014-15	**Arizona**	**NHL**	**1**	**0**	**1**	**0**	**60**	**5**	**0**	**5.00**	....	....	....	....	....	....	....
	Portland Pirates	AHL	52	27	18	6	2979	111	7	2.24	2	0	1	41	6	0	8.89
	NHL Totals		**22**	**5**	**11**	**2**	**1173**	**68**	**1**	**3.48**	....	....	....	....	....	....	....

ECHL Second All-Star Team (2007)

Signed as a free agent by **Tampa Bay**, February 3, 2009. Signed as a free agent by **Lowell** (AHL), October 7, 2009. Signed as a free agent by **New Jersey**, February 10, 2010. Signed as a free agent by **Ottawa**, July 8, 2011. Signed as a free agent by **St. Louis**, July 1, 2012. Signed as a free agent by **Columbus**, July 6, 2013. Signed as a free agent by **Arizona**, July 1, 2014. Signed as a free agent by **Florida**, July 1, 2015.

MERZLIKINS, Elvis (muhrz-LEE-kinz, EHL-vihs) CBJ

Goaltender. Catches left. 6'3", 181 lbs. Born, Riga, Latvia, April 13, 1994.
(Columbus' 3rd choice, 76th overall, in 2014 Entry Draft).

			Regular Season								Playoffs						
Season	**Club**	**League**	**GP**	**W**	**L**	**O/T**	**Mins**	**GA**	**SO**	**Avg**	**GP**	**W**	**L**	**Mins**	**GA**	**SO**	**Avg**
2009-10	HC Lugano U17	Swiss-U17	24	....	....	....	....	....	....	....	12	....	....	....	....	....	....
2010-11	HC Lugano U17	Swiss-U17	28	....	....	....	....	....	....	....	5	....	....	....	....	....	....
2011-12	HC Lugano Jr.	Swiss-Jr.	8	....	....	....	....	....	....	3.52	3	....	....	....	....	....	5.07
2012-13	HC Lugano Jr.	Swiss-Jr.	30	....	....	....	....	....	....	2.76	4	....	....	....	....	....	3.84
2013-14	HC Lugano Jr.	Swiss-Jr.	12	....	....	....	....	....	....	2.07	10	....	....	....	....	....	1.68
	HC Lugano	Swiss	22	12	10	0	1269	45	1	2.13	1	0	1	80	1	0	0.75
2014-15	HC Lugano	Swiss	22	14	9	0	1309	57	2	2.61	1	0	1	36	2	0	3.33

METCALF, Garrett (MEHT-caf, GAIR-eht) ANA

Goaltender. Catches left. 6'3", 181 lbs. Born, Salt Lake City, UT, March 5, 1996.
(Anaheim's 7th choice, 179th overall, in 2015 Entry Draft).

			Regular Season								Playoffs						
Season	**Club**	**League**	**GP**	**W**	**L**	**O/T**	**Mins**	**GA**	**SO**	**Avg**	**GP**	**W**	**L**	**Mins**	**GA**	**SO**	**Avg**
2012-13	Col. Rampage U16	T1EHL	13	2	9	1	647	40	0	3.34	2	2	0	102	3	0	1.50
	Om. Lancers U16	NAPHL	1	1	0	0	51	0	1	0.00	....	....	....	....	....	....	....
	Om. Lancers U18	NAPHL	1	0	1	0	51	4	0	4.00	....	....	....	....	....	....	....
2013-14	Col. Rampage U18	T1EHL	14	7	7	0	749	32	2	2.31	....	....	....	....	....	....	....
	Colorado Rampage	Other	1	1	0	0	51	2	0	2.00	....	....	....	....	....	....	....
2014-15	Madison Capitols	USHL	33	10	12	4	1529	83	1	3.26	....	....	....	....	....	....	....

• Signed Letter of Intent to attend **Unversity of Massachusetts Lowell** (Hockey East) in fall of 2016.

MICHALEK, Steve (MIGH-KUHL-ehk, STEEV) MIN

Goaltender. Catches left. 6'3", 205 lbs. Born, Hartford, CT, August 6, 1993.
(Minnesota's 5th choice, 161st overall, in 2011 Entry Draft).

			Regular Season								Playoffs						
Season	**Club**	**League**	**GP**	**W**	**L**	**O/T**	**Mins**	**GA**	**SO**	**Avg**	**GP**	**W**	**L**	**Mins**	**GA**	**SO**	**Avg**
2009-10	Loomis Chaffee	High-CT	35	....	....	....	1121	106	....	....	....	....	....	....	....	....	....
2010-11	Loomis Chaffee	High-CT	23	2	19	2	1203	91	....	3.95	....	....	....	....	....	....	....
	Boston Little Bruins	Minor-MA					STATISTICS NOT AVAILABLE										
2011-12	Harvard Crimson	ECAC	24	7	7	8	1336	71	0	3.19	....	....	....	....	....	....	....
2012-13	Cedar Rapids	USHL	17	7	6	3	992	51	0	3.09	....	....	....	....	....	....	....
2013-14	Harvard Crimson	ECAC	18	5	8	2	970	40	2	2.47	....	....	....	....	....	....	....
2014-15	Harvard Crimson	ECAC	*37	21	13	3	*2232	85	3	2.28	....	....	....	....	....	....	....

ECAC All-Rookie Team (2012)

MILLER, Ryan (MIH-luhr, RIGH-uhn) VAN

Goaltender. Catches left. 6'2", 168 lbs. Born, East Lansing, MI, July 17, 1980.
(Buffalo's 7th choice, 138th overall, in 1999 Entry Draft).

			Regular Season								Playoffs						
Season	Club	League	GP	W	L	O/T	Mins	GA	SO	Avg	GP	W	L	Mins	GA	SO	Avg
1997-98	Soo Indians	NAHL	37	21	14	0	2113	82	3	2.33	2	0	2	158	7	0	2.66
1998-99	Soo Indians	NAHL	47	31	14	1	2711	104	8	2.30	4	2	2	218	10	1	2.76
99-2000	Michigan State	CCHA	26	16	5	3	1525	39	*8	*1.53	....	....	....	....	....	....	....
2000-01	Michigan State	CCHA	40	*31	5	4	2447	54	*10	*1.32	....	....	....	....	....	....	....
2001-02	Michigan State	CCHA	40	26	9	5	2411	71	*8	*1.77	....	....	....	....	....	....	....
2002-03	**Buffalo**	**NHL**	**15**	**6**	**8**	**1**	**912**	**40**	**1**	**2.63**	....	....	....	....	....	....	....
	Rochester	AHL	47	23	18	5	2817	110	2	2.34	3	1	2	190	13	0	4.11
2003-04	**Buffalo**	**NHL**	**3**	**0**	**3**	**0**	**178**	**15**	**0**	**5.06**	....	....	....	....	....	....	....
	Rochester	AHL	60	27	25	7	3579	132	5	2.21	14	7	7	857	26	2	1.82
2004-05	Rochester	AHL	63	*41	17	4	3741	153	8	2.45	9	5	4	547	24	0	2.63
2005-06	**Buffalo**	**NHL**	**48**	**30**	**14**	**3**	**2862**	**124**	**1**	**2.60**	**18**	**11**	**7**	**1123**	**48**	**1**	**2.56**
	Rochester	AHL	2	1	1	0	120	5	0	2.50	....	....	....	....	....	....	....
2006-07	**Buffalo**	**NHL**	**63**	**40**	**16**	**6**	**3692**	**168**	**2**	**2.73**	**16**	**9**	**7**	**1029**	**38**	**0**	**2.22**
2007-08	**Buffalo**	**NHL**	**76**	**36**	**27**	**10**	**4474**	**197**	**3**	**2.64**	....	....	....	....	....	....	....
2008-09	**Buffalo**	**NHL**	**59**	**34**	**18**	**6**	**3443**	**145**	**5**	**2.53**	....	....	....	....	....	....	....
2009-10	**Buffalo**	**NHL**	**69**	**41**	**18**	**8**	**4047**	**150**	**5**	**2.22**	**6**	**2**	**4**	**384**	**15**	**0**	**2.34**
	United States	Olympics	6	5	1	0	355	8	1	1.35	....	....	....	....	....	....	....
2010-11	**Buffalo**	**NHL**	**66**	**34**	**22**	**8**	**3829**	**165**	**5**	**2.59**	**7**	**3**	**4**	**410**	**20**	**2**	**2.93**
2011-12	**Buffalo**	**NHL**	**61**	**31**	**21**	**7**	**3536**	**150**	**6**	**2.55**	....	....	....	....	....	....	....
2012-13	**Buffalo**	**NHL**	**40**	**17**	**17**	**5**	**2302**	**108**	**0**	**2.81**	....	....	....	....	....	....	....
2013-14	**Buffalo**	**NHL**	**40**	**15**	**22**	**3**	**2384**	**108**	**0**	**2.72**	....	....	....	....	....	....	....
	United States	Olympics	1	1	0	0	60	1	0	1.00	....	....	....	....	....	....	....
	St. Louis	**NHL**	**19**	**10**	**8**	**1**	**1117**	**46**	**1**	**2.47**	**6**	**2**	**4**	**422**	**19**	**0**	**2.70**
2014-15	**Vancouver**	**NHL**	**45**	**29**	**15**	**1**	**2542**	**107**	**6**	**2.53**	**3**	**1**	**1**	**156**	**6**	**0**	**2.31**
	NHL Totals		**604**	**323**	**209**	**59**	**35318**	**1523**	**35**	**2.59**	**56**	**28**	**27**	**3524**	**146**	**3**	**2.49**

CCHA Second All-Star Team (2000) • CCHA First All-Star Team (2001, 2002) • CCHA Player of the Year (2001, 2002) • NCAA West First All-American Team (2001, 2002) • Hobey Baker Memorial Award (Top U.S. Collegiate Player) (2001) • AHL First All-Star Team (2005) • Aldege "Baz" Bastien Memorial Award (AHL) – Outstanding Goaltender) (2005) • Olympic All-Star Team (2010) • Olympics – Best Goaltender (2010) • Olympics – MVP (2010) • NHL First All-Star Team (2010) • NHL Foundation Player Award (2010) • Vezina Trophy (2010)

Played in NHL All-Star Game (2007)

Traded to **St. Louis** by **Buffalo** with Steve Ott for Jaroslav Halak, Chris Stewart, William Carrier, St. Louis' 1st round choice (later traded to Winnipeg – Winnipeg selected Jack Roslovic) in 2015 Entry Draft and St. Louis' 3rd round choice in 2016 Entry Draft, February 28, 2014. Signed as a free agent by **Vancouver**, July 1, 2014.

MISSIAEN, Jason (MIHS-ee-ehn, JAY-suhn)

Goaltender. Catches left. 6'8", 206 lbs. Born, Chatham, ON, April 25, 1990.
(Montreal's 3rd choice, 116th overall, in 2008 Entry Draft).

			Regular Season								Playoffs						
Season	Club	League	GP	W	L	O/T	Mins	GA	SO	Avg	GP	W	L	Mins	GA	SO	Avg
2004-05	Dresden Jr. Kings	ON-Jr.C	16	11	4	1	919	47	1	3.07	....	....	....	....	....	....	....
2005-06	Dresden Jr. Kings	ON-Jr.C	26	13	8	2	1560	76	1	2.93	....	....	....	....	....	....	....
	Petrolia Jets	ON-Jr.B	1	0	0	0	14	0	0	0.00	1	0	0	2	0	0	0.00
2006-07	Peterborough	OHL	12	1	7	0	559	48	0	5.15	....	....	....	....	....	....	....
2007-08	Peterborough	OHL	22	8	8	1	1134	62	1	3.28	....	....	....	....	....	....	....
2008-09	Peterborough	OHL	38	12	21	2	2221	141	1	3.81	4	0	4	241	17	0	4.23
2009-10	Peterborough	OHL	59	27	29	3	3358	206	1	3.68	4	0	4	238	11	0	2.77
2010-11	Baie-Comeau	QMJHL	53	10	33	8	3026	168	1	3.33	....	....	....	....	....	....	....
2011-12	Greenville	ECHL	40	22	13	3	2371	107	3	2.71	1	0	1	59	4	0	4.07
2012-13	Connecticut Whale	AHL	25	10	8	2	1348	69	2	3.07	....	....	....	....	....	....	....
	Greenville	ECHL	5	4	1	0	305	14	0	2.75	....	....	....	....	....	....	....
2013-14	Hartford Wolf Pack	AHL	14	2	11	1	783	50	0	3.83	....	....	....	....	....	....	....
	Greenville	ECHL	21	14	6	1	1219	56	1	2.76	12	7	4	706	25	1	2.12
2014-15	Hartford Wolf Pack	AHL	5	1	2	1	236	14	0	3.56	....	....	....	....	....	....	....
	Greenville	ECHL	37	18	15	3	2146	110	2	3.08	....	....	....	....	....	....	....

Signed as a free agent by **NY Rangers**, March 24, 2011.

MONTEMBEAULT, Sam (mawn-tehm-BOH, SAM) FLA

Goaltender. Catches left. 6'3", 180 lbs. Born, Quebec, QC, October 30, 1996.
(Florida's 2nd choice, 77th overall, in 2015 Entry Draft).

			Regular Season								Playoffs						
Season	Club	League	GP	W	L	O/T	Mins	GA	SO	Avg	GP	W	L	Mins	GA	SO	Avg
2012-13	Trois-Rivieres	QAAA	19	11	7	1	1110	47	1	2.54	6	4	2	....	....	....	....
2013-14	Blainville-Bois.	QMJHL	14	9	1	1	714	28	0	2.35	1	1	0	53	3	0	3.40
2014-15	Blainville-Bois.	QMJHL	52	33	11	7	3104	134	3	2.59	6	2	4	354	14	0	2.38

MONTOYA, Al (mawn-TOI-uh, AL) FLA

Goaltender. Catches left. 6'2", 203 lbs. Born, Chicago, IL, February 13, 1985.
(NY Rangers' 1st choice, 6th overall, in 2004 Entry Draft).

			Regular Season								Playoffs						
Season	Club	League	GP	W	L	O/T	Mins	GA	SO	Avg	GP	W	L	Mins	GA	SO	Avg
99-2000	Loyola Academy	High-MN	28	12	13	3	1685	56	1	2.01	....	....	....	....	....	....	....
2000-01	Texas Tornado	NAHL	15	10	3	0	780	38	0	2.92	1	1	0	60	2	0	2.00
	United States	Nat-Tm	2	2	0	0	120	4	0	2.00	....	....	....	....	....	....	....
2001-02	USNTDP	U-17	10	5	5	0	570	24	0	2.53	....	....	....	....	....	....	....
	USNTDP	NAHL	24	6	11	4	1344	79	0	3.53	....	....	....	....	....	....	....
2002-03	U. of Michigan	CCHA	*43	*30	10	3	*2547	99	4	2.33	....	....	....	....	....	....	....
2003-04	U. of Michigan	CCHA	*40	*26	12	2	*2340	87	6	2.23	....	....	....	....	....	....	....
2004-05	U. of Michigan	CCHA	*40	*30	7	3	*2359	99	3	2.52	....	....	....	....	....	....	....
2005-06	Hartford Wolf Pack	AHL	40	23	9	1	2094	91	2	2.61	5	2	1	257	8	1	1.87
	Charlotte Checkers	ECHL	2	1	1	0	123	8	0	3.92	....	....	....	....	....	....	....
2006-07	Hartford Wolf Pack	AHL	48	27	17	0	2556	98	6	2.30	7	3	4	391	20	1	3.07
2007-08	Hartford Wolf Pack	AHL	31	16	8	3	1704	72	0	2.54	....	....	....	....	....	....	....
	San Antonio	AHL	14	8	5	0	789	34	1	2.59	1	0	1	59	4	0	4.04
2008-09	**Phoenix**	**NHL**	**5**	**3**	**1**	**0**	**259**	**9**	**1**	**2.08**	....	....	....	....	....	....	....
	San Antonio	AHL	29	7	17	2	1562	84	0	3.23	....	....	....	....	....	....	....
2009-10	San Antonio	AHL	14	4	7	1	771	34	0	2.65	....	....	....	....	....	....	....
2010-11	**NY Islanders**	**NHL**	**20**	**9**	**5**	**5**	**1154**	**46**	**1**	**2.39**	....	....	....	....	....	....	....
	San Antonio	AHL	21	11	8	0	1130	60	0	3.19	....	....	....	....	....	....	....
2011-12	**NY Islanders**	**NHL**	**31**	**9**	**11**	**5**	**1720**	**89**	**0**	**3.10**	....	....	....	....	....	....	....
2012-13	**Winnipeg**	**NHL**	**7**	**3**	**1**	**0**	**351**	**17**	**1**	**2.91**	....	....	....	....	....	....	....
2013-14	**Winnipeg**	**NHL**	**28**	**13**	**8**	**3**	**1541**	**59**	**2**	**2.30**	....	....	....	....	....	....	....
2014-15	**Florida**	**NHL**	**20**	**6**	**7**	**2**	**977**	**49**	**0**	**3.01**	....	....	....	....	....	....	....
	NHL Totals		**111**	**43**	**33**	**15**	**6002**	**269**	**5**	**2.69**	....	....	....	....	....	....	....

CCHA All-Rookie Team (2003) • NCAA West Second All-American Team (2004)

Traded to **Phoenix** by **NY Rangers** with Marcel Hossa for Josh Gratton, David LeNeveu, Fredrik Sjostrom and Phoenix's 5th round choice (Roman Horak) in 2009 Entry Draft, February 26, 2008. Traded to **NY Islanders** by **Phoenix** for NY Islanders' 6th round choice (Andrew Fritsch) in 2011 Entry Draft, February 9, 2011. Signed as a free agent by **Winnipeg**, July 4, 2012. Signed as a free agent by **Florida**, July 1, 2014.

MORAN, Brent (moh-RAN, BREHNT) DAL

Goaltender. Catches left. 6'4", 180 lbs. Born, Ottawa, ON, July 5, 1996.
(Dallas' 5th choice, 115th overall, in 2014 Entry Draft).

			Regular Season								Playoffs						
Season	Club	League	GP	W	L	O/T	Mins	GA	SO	Avg	GP	W	L	Mins	GA	SO	Avg
2012-13	Niagara Ice Dogs	OHL	19	7	10	0	1042	74	0	4.26	....	....	....	....	....	....	....
2013-14	Niagara Ice Dogs	OHL	40	14	19	4	2294	147	0	3.85	7	3	4	419	20	1	2.86
2014-15	Niagara Ice Dogs	OHL	38	18	18	1	2148	124	1	3.46	2	0	1	40	5	0	7.41

MRAZEK, Petr (M'RAZ-ihk, PEH-tuhr) DET

Goaltender. Catches left. 6'2", 183 lbs. Born, Ostrava, Czech., February 14, 1992.
(Detroit's 5th choice, 141st overall, in 2010 Entry Draft).

			Regular Season								Playoffs						
Season	Club	League	GP	W	L	O/T	Mins	GA	SO	Avg	GP	W	L	Mins	GA	SO	Avg
2006-07	HC Vitkovice U17	CzR-U17	23	....	....	....	1273	51	2	2.40	9	....	....	486	15	1	1.85
2007-08	HC Vitkovice U17	CzR-U17	34	....	....	....	1974	81	4	2.46	3	....	....	179	8	0	2.68
	HC Vitkovice Steel	CzRep	1	....	....	....	24	4	0	10.00	....	....	....	....	....	....	....
2008-09	HC Vitkovice U17	CzR-U17	28	....	....	....	1601	53	5	1.99	4	....	....	193	3	2	0.93
	HC Vitkovice Jr.	CzRep-Jr.	13	....	....	....	795	33	0	2.49	1	....	....	60	1	0	1.00
2009-10	Ottawa 67's	OHL	30	12	9	1	1562	78	2	3.00	8	4	4	451	18	0	2.39
2010-11	Ottawa 67's	OHL	52	33	15	3	3089	146	4	2.84	4	0	3	224	21	0	5.63
2011-12	Ottawa 67's	OHL	50	30	13	6	3016	143	3	2.84	17	9	8	1065	46	0	2.59
2012-13	Grand Rapids	AHL	42	23	16	2	2498	97	1	2.33	*24	*15	9	*1431	55	*4	2.31
	Toledo Walleye	ECHL	3	2	1	0	179	6	0	2.02	....	....	....	....	....	....	....
	Detroit	**NHL**	**2**	**1**	**1**	**0**	**119**	**4**	**0**	**2.02**	....	....	....	....	....	....	....
2013-14	**Detroit**	**NHL**	**9**	**2**	**4**	**0**	**449**	**13**	**2**	**1.74**	....	....	....	....	....	....	....
	Grand Rapids	AHL	32	22	9	1	1830	64	3	2.10	10	5	5	600	28	0	2.80
2014-15	**Detroit**	**NHL**	**29**	**16**	**9**	**2**	**1585**	**63**	**3**	**2.38**	**7**	**3**	**4**	**398**	**14**	**2**	**2.11**
	Grand Rapids	AHL	13	9	2	1	757	26	3	2.06	....	....	....	....	....	....	....
	NHL Totals		**40**	**19**	**14**	**2**	**2153**	**80**	**5**	**2.23**	**7**	**3**	**4**	**398**	**14**	**2**	**2.11**

AHL Second All-Star Team (2014)

MURRAY, Matt (MUHR-ee, MAT) PIT

Goaltender. Catches left. 6'4", 178 lbs. Born, Thunder Bay, ON, May 25, 1994.
(Pittsburgh's 5th choice, 83rd overall, in 2012 Entry Draft).

			Regular Season								Playoffs						
Season	Club	League	GP	W	L	O/T	Mins	GA	SO	Avg	GP	W	L	Mins	GA	SO	Avg
2009-10	Thunder Bay Kings	Minor-ON	40	32	5	0	1975	75	6	1.71	....	....	....	....	....	....	....
2010-11	Sault Ste. Marie	OHL	28	8	11	3	1377	87	1	3.79	....	....	....	....	....	....	....
2011-12	Sault Ste. Marie	OHL	36	13	19	1	1912	130	0	4.08	....	....	....	....	....	....	....
2012-13	Sault Ste. Marie	OHL	53	26	19	4	2910	178	2	3.67	6	2	4	381	17	1	2.67
2013-14	Sault Ste. Marie	OHL	49	32	11	1	2984	128	*6	2.57	9	4	3	547	24	1	2.63
	Wilkes-Barre	AHL	1	0	1	0	60	2	0	2.00	1	0	0	20	0	0	0.00
2014-15	Wilkes-Barre	AHL	40	25	10	3	2321	61	12	1.58	8	4	4	456	18	1	2.37

OHL Second All-Star Team (2014) • AHL All-Rookie Team (2015) • AHL First All-Star Team (2015) • Dudley "Red" Garrett Memorial Trophy (AHL - Top Rookie) (2015) • Harry "Hap" Holmes Memorial Award (AHL – fewest goals against) (2015) (shared with Jeff Zatkoff) • Aldege "Baz" Bastien Award (AHL – Outstanding Goaltender) (2015)

NAGELVOORT, Zach (NA-gehl-voort, ZAK) EDM

Goaltender. Catches left. 6'2", 190 lbs. Born, Ridgewood, NJ, January 30, 1994.
(Edmonton's 3rd choice, 111th overall, in 2014 Entry Draft).

			Regular Season								Playoffs						
Season	Club	League	GP	W	L	O/T	Mins	GA	SO	Avg	GP	W	L	Mins	GA	SO	Avg
2010-11	Det. Comp. U16	T1EHL	17	13	1	2	866	34	1	2.12	....	....	....	....	....	....	....
	Det. Comp. U18	T1EHL	22	11	5	6	1142	38	4	1.80	....	....	....	....	....	....	....
	Det. Comp. U18	Other	10	5	2	3	474	18	1	1.99	....	....	....	....	....	....	....
2011-12	Kalamazoo	NAHL	3	2	1	0	179	8	0	2.68	....	....	....	....	....	....	....
	Traverse City	NAHL	16	8	5	1	850	31	3	2.19	....	....	....	....	....	....	....
2012-13	Soo Eagles	NAHL	18	9	5	1	987	39	0	2.37	....	....	....	....	....	....	....
	Aberdeen Wings	NAHL	10	8	1	1	614	17	1	1.66	....	....	....	....	....	....	....
	Green Bay	USHL	DID NOT PLAY – SPARE GOALTENDER														
2013-14	U. of Michigan	Big Ten	24	11	9	3	1418	52	1	2.20	....	....	....	....	....	....	....
2014-15	U. of Michigan	Big Ten	22	11	9	0	1116	49	1	2.63	....	....	....	....	....	....	....

NALIMOV, Ivan (na-LEE-mawv, ee-VAHN) CHI

Goaltender. Catches left. 6'4", 210 lbs. Born, Novokuznetsk, Russia, March 12, 1994.
(Chicago's 8th choice, 179th overall, in 2014 Entry Draft).

			Regular Season								Playoffs						
Season	Club	League	GP	W	L	O/T	Mins	GA	SO	Avg	GP	W	L	Mins	GA	SO	Avg
2011-12	St. Petersburg Jr.	Russia-Jr.	20	7	6	3	966	36	1	2.24	....	....	....	....	....	....	....
2012-13	St. Petersburg Jr.	Russia-Jr.	47	23	11	10	2772	98	4	2.12	7	3	4	388	21	0	3.25
2013-14	VMF	Russia-2	1	1	0	0	60	1	0	1.00	....	....	....	....	....	....	....
	St. Petersburg Jr.	Russia-Jr.	12	5	7	0	634	30	0	2.84	1	0	0	12	2	0	10.06
2014-15	Vladivostok	KHL	30	10	10	0	1479	68	3	2.76	....	....	....	....	....	....	....

NEDELJKOVIC, Alex (nuh-DEHL-koh-vihch, AL-ehx) CAR

Goaltender. Catches left. 5'11", 190 lbs. Born, Parma, OH, January 7, 1996.
(Carolina's 2nd choice, 37th overall, in 2014 Entry Draft).

			Regular Season								Playoffs						
Season	Club	League	GP	W	L	O/T	Mins	GA	SO	Avg	GP	W	L	Mins	GA	SO	Avg
2012-13	Plymouth Whalers	OHL	26	19	2	2	1371	52	2	2.28	15	9	4	864	39	1	2.71
2013-14	Plymouth Whalers	OHL	61	26	27	7	3436	165	1	2.88	5	1	4	272	20	0	4.41
2014-15	Plymouth Whalers	OHL	55	20	28	7	3206	167	5	3.13	....	....	....	....	....	....	....
	Florida Everblades	ECHL	3	2	1	0	178	10	0	3.38	....	....	....	....	....	....	....

OHL All-Rookie Team (2013) • OHL First All-Star Team (2014)

NEUVIRTH, Michal (NOI-vihrt, MIGHK-ahl) PHI

Goaltender. Catches left. 6', 209 lbs. Born, Usti nad Labem, Czech., March 23, 1988.
(Washington's 3rd choice, 34th overall, in 2006 Entry Draft).

			Regular Season								Playoffs						
Season	Club	League	GP	W	L	O/T	Mins	GA	SO	Avg	GP	W	L	Mins	GA	SO	Avg
2003-04	Sparta U17	CzR-U17	55	....	....	....	3137	96	5	1.84	3	....	....	180	13	0	4.33
2004-05	Sparta U17	CzR-U17	20	....	....	....	1178	49	3	2.50	8	....	....	482	17	0	2.12
	Sparta Jr.	CzRep-Jr.	10	....	....	....	501	20	1	2.40	....	....	....	....	....	....	....
2005-06	Sparta Jr.	CzRep-Jr.	42	....	....	....	2516	82	5	1.96	3	....	....	179	9	0	3.02
2006-07	Plymouth Whalers	OHL	41	26	8	4	2223	86	4	*2.32	*18	*14	4	*1080	44	0	*2.44
2007-08	Plymouth Whalers	OHL	10	5	4	1	600	26	0	2.60	....	....	....	....	....	....	....
	Windsor Spitfires	OHL	8	6	1	1	482	17	0	2.12	....	....	....	....	....	....	....
	Oshawa Generals	OHL	15	6	2	6	844	57	0	4.05	9	7	2	507	21	0	2.49
2008-09	**Washington**	**NHL**	**5**	**2**	**1**	**0**	**220**	**11**	**0**	**3.00**	....	....	....	....	....	....	....
	Hershey Bears	AHL	17	9	5	2	1001	45	1	2.70	*22	*16	6	*1346	43	*4	1.92
	South Carolina	ECHL	13	6	7	0	762	29	2	2.28	....	....	....	....	....	....	....
2009-10	**Washington**	**NHL**	**17**	**9**	**4**	**0**	**872**	**40**	**0**	**2.75**	....	....	....	....	....	....	....
	Hershey Bears	AHL	22	15	6	0	1231	46	1	2.24	*18	*14	4	*1133	39	1	2.07
2010-11	**Washington**	**NHL**	**48**	**27**	**12**	**4**	**2689**	**110**	**4**	**2.45**	**9**	**4**	**5**	**590**	**23**	**1**	**2.34**
2011-12	**Washington**	**NHL**	**38**	**13**	**13**	**5**	**2020**	**95**	**3**	**2.82**	....	....	....	....	....	....	....
2012-13	HC Sparta Praha	CzRep	24	....	....	....	1342	55	1	2.46	....	....	....	....	....	....	....
	Washington	**NHL**	**13**	**4**	**5**	**2**	**723**	**33**	**0**	**2.74**	....	....	....	....	....	....	....
2013-14	**Washington**	**NHL**	**13**	**4**	**6**	**2**	**767**	**36**	**0**	**2.82**	....	....	....	....	....	....	....
	Hershey Bears	AHL	1	1	0	0	60	4	0	4.02	....	....	....	....	....	....	....
	Buffalo	**NHL**	**2**	**0**	**2**	**0**	**117**	**5**	**0**	**2.56**	....	....	....	....	....	....	....
2014-15	**Buffalo**	**NHL**	**27**	**6**	**17**	**3**	**1544**	**77**	**0**	**2.99**	....	....	....	....	....	....	....
	NY Islanders	**NHL**	**5**	**1**	**3**	**1**	**306**	**15**	**0**	**2.94**	**1**	**0**	**0**	**11**	**0**	**0**	**0.00**
	NHL Totals		**168**	**66**	**63**	**17**	**9258**	**422**	**7**	**2.73**	**10**	**4**	**5**	**601**	**23**	**1**	**2.30**

OHL Second All-Star Team (2007) • Jack A. Butterfield Trophy (AHL – Playoff MVP) (2009)

Signed as a free agent by **Sparta Praha** (CzRep), September 20, 2012. Traded to **Buffalo** by **Washington** with Rostislav Klesla for Jaroslav Halak and Buffalo's 3rd round choice (later traded to NY Rangers – NY Rangers selected Robin Kovacs) in 2015 Entry Draft, March 5, 2014. Traded to **NY Islanders** by **Buffalo** for Chad Johnson and NY Islanders' 3rd round choice in 2016 Entry Draft, March 2, 2015. Signed as a free agent by **Philadelphia**, July 1, 2015.

NIEMI, Antti (nee-YEH-mee, AN-tee) DAL

Goaltender. Catches left. 6'2", 210 lbs. Born, Vantaa, Finland, August 29, 1983.

			Regular Season								Playoffs						
Season	Club	League	GP	W	L	O/T	Mins	GA	SO	Avg	GP	W	L	Mins	GA	SO	Avg
2000-01	Kiekko-Vantaa Jr.	Fin-Jr.	4	....	....	....	....	....	....	6.86	....	....	....	....	....	....	....
2001-02	Kiekko-Vantaa	Finland-2	24	....	....	....	....	....	....	....	3	....	....	....	....	....	....
2002-03	Kiekko-Vantaa	Finland-2	....	....	....	....	364	16	0	2.63	....	....	....	....	....	....	....
2003-04	Kiekko-Vantaa	Finland-2	19	....	....	....	1048	47	1	2.52	3	....	....	187	13	0	4.17
	Kiekko-Vantaa Jr.	Fin-Jr.	19	....	....	....	1095	58	2	3.18	....	....	....	....	....	....	....
2004-05	Kiekko-Vantaa	Finland-2	38	....	....	....	2261	95	1	2.52	3	....	....	187	13	0	4.17
2005-06	Pelicans Lahti	Finland	40	12	17	8	2263	103	3	2.73	....	....	....	....	....	....	....
2006-07	Pelicans Lahti	Finland	48	18	21	7	2780	119	3	2.57	6	2	4	371	9	1	1.46
2007-08	Pelicans Lahti	Finland	49	26	14	6	2778	109	4	2.35	6	2	3	327	21	0	3.85
2008-09	**Chicago**	**NHL**	**3**	**1**	**1**	**1**	**141**	**8**	**0**	**3.40**	....	....	....	....	....	....	....
	Rockford IceHogs	AHL	38	18	14	3	2095	85	2	2.43	2	0	2	115	7	0	3.65
2009-10 ♦	**Chicago**	**NHL**	**39**	**26**	**7**	**4**	**2190**	**82**	**7**	**2.25**	***22**	***16**	**6**	***1322**	**58**	**2**	**2.63**
2010-11	**San Jose**	**NHL**	**60**	**35**	**18**	**6**	**3524**	**140**	**6**	**2.38**	**18**	**8**	**9**	**1044**	**56**	**0**	**3.22**
2011-12	**San Jose**	**NHL**	**68**	**34**	**22**	**9**	**3936**	**159**	**6**	**2.42**	**5**	**1**	**4**	**318**	**13**	**0**	**2.45**
2012-13	Pelicans Lahti	Finland	10	3	5	2	597	31	0	3.11	....	....	....	....	....	....	....
	San Jose	**NHL**	**43**	***24**	**12**	**6**	***2581**	**93**	**4**	**2.16**	**11**	**7**	**4**	**673**	**21**	**0**	**1.87**
2013-14	**San Jose**	**NHL**	**64**	**39**	**17**	**7**	**3740**	**149**	**4**	**2.39**	**6**	**3**	**3**	**305**	**19**	**0**	**3.74**
	Finland	Olympics	DID NOT PLAY – SPARE GOALTENDER														
2014-15	**San Jose**	**NHL**	**61**	**31**	**23**	**7**	**3588**	**155**	**5**	**2.59**	....	....	....	....	....	....	....
	NHL Totals		**338**	**190**	**100**	**40**	**19700**	**786**	**32**	**2.39**	**62**	**35**	**26**	**3662**	**167**	**2**	**2.74**

Signed as a free agent by **Chicago**, May 5, 2008. Signed as a free agent by **San Jose**, September 2, 2010. Signed as a free agent by **Lahti** (Finland), October 5, 2012. Traded to **Dallas** by **San Jose** for Dallas' 7th round choice (Jake Kupsky) in 2015 Entry Draft, June 27, 2015.

NILSSON, Anders (NIHL-suhn, AN-duhrz) EDM

Goaltender. Catches left. 6'5", 227 lbs. Born, Lulea, Sweden, March 19, 1990.
(NY Islanders' 4th choice, 62nd overall, in 2009 Entry Draft).

			Regular Season								Playoffs						
Season	Club	League	GP	W	L	O/T	Mins	GA	SO	Avg	GP	W	L	Mins	GA	SO	Avg
2004-05	Lulea HF Jr.	Swe-Jr.	1	....	....	....	24	4	0	9.90	....	....	....	....	....	....	....
2007-08	Lulea HF U18	Swe-U18	11	....	....	....	625	31	0	2.97	....	....	....	....	....	....	....
	Lulea HF Jr.	Swe-Jr.	16	....	....	....	898	31	2	2.07	1	....	....	60	6	0	6.00
2008-09	Lulea HF Jr.	Swe-Jr.	37	....	....	....	2199	75	4	2.05	6	....	....	357	14	1	2.35
	Lulea HF	Sweden	1	....	....	....	28	0	0	0.00	....	....	....	....	....	....	....
	Kalix Ungdoms HC	Sweden-3	1	....	....	....	59	3	0	3.05	....	....	....	....	....	....	....
2009-10	Lulea HF Jr.	Swe-Jr.	4	....	....	....	244	12	0	2.95	....	....	....	....	....	....	....
	Lulea HF	Sweden	27	....	....	....	1383	61	2	2.65	....	....	....	....	....	....	....
2010-11	Lulea HF	Sweden	31	....	....	....	1876	60	6	*1.92	13	....	....	827	27	0	1.96
2011-12	**NY Islanders**	**NHL**	**4**	**1**	**2**	**0**	**218**	**10**	**1**	**2.75**	....	....	....	....	....	....	....
	Bridgeport	AHL	25	15	8	2	1441	58	1	2.42	....	....	....	....	....	....	....
2012-13	Bridgeport	AHL	21	8	11	0	1208	60	1	2.98	....	....	....	....	....	....	....
2013-14	**NY Islanders**	**NHL**	**19**	**8**	**7**	**2**	**1101**	**57**	**0**	**3.11**	....	....	....	....	....	....	....
	Bridgeport	AHL	29	12	14	2	1684	79	2	2.81	....	....	....	....	....	....	....
2014-15	Ak Bars Kazan	KHL	38	20	9	0	2248	64	5	1.71	20	13	7	1207	31	6	1.54
	NHL Totals		**23**	**9**	**9**	**2**	**1319**	**67**	**1**	**3.05**	....	....	....	....	....	....	....

Signed as a free agent by **Kazan** (KHL), May 26, 2014. Traded to **Chicago** by **NY Islanders** with T.J. Brennan and Ville Pokka for Nick Leddy and Kent Simpson, October 4, 2014. Traded to **Edmonton** by **Chicago** for Liam Coughlin, July 6, 2015.

O'CONNOR, Matt (OH-CAW-nuhr, MAT) OTT

Goaltender. Catches left. 6'6", 202 lbs. Born, Sault Ste. Marie, ON, February 14, 1992.

			Regular Season								Playoffs						
Season	Club	League	GP	W	L	O/T	Mins	GA	SO	Avg	GP	W	L	Mins	GA	SO	Avg
2008-09	Upper Canada	ON-Jr.A	27	3	19	1	1428	147	1	6.18	....	....	....	....	....	....	....
2009-10	Upper Canada	ON-Jr.A	23	7	12	2	1325	89	1	4.03	....	....	....	....	....	....	....
	Burlington	ON-Jr.A	5	2	2	0	237	18	0	4.55	4	2	1	164	8	0	2.92
2010-11	Youngstown	USHL	29	10	16	2	1713	98	0	3.43	....	....	....	....	....	....	....
2011-12	Youngstown	USHL	50	28	16	5	2886	146	1	3.04	6	3	3	326	20	0	3.68
2012-13	Boston University	H-East	19	8	8	2	1110	53	0	2.86	....	....	....	....	....	....	....
2013-14	Boston University	H-East	22	7	9	4	1225	59	0	2.89	....	....	....	....	....	....	....
2014-15	Boston University	H-East	35	*25	4	4	2088	76	1	2.18	....	....	....	....	....	....	....

Hockey East Second All-Star Team (2015)

Signed as a free agent by **Ottawa**, May 9, 2015.

OLDHAM, Kristian (OHL-duhm, KRIHS-ch'yehn) T.B.

Goaltender. Catches left. 6'2", 203 lbs. Born, Anchorage, AK, June 25, 1997.
(Tampa Bay's 8th choice, 153rd overall, in 2015 Entry Draft).

			Regular Season								Playoffs						
Season	Club	League	GP	W	L	O/T	Mins	GA	SO	Avg	GP	W	L	Mins	GA	SO	Avg
2012-13	Alaska All-Stars	Minor-AK	5	5	0	0	225	6	2	1.20	....	....	....	....	....	....	....
	Alaska All-Stars	Other	11	7	3	0	468	20	3	2.00	....	....	....	....	....	....	....
	Kenai River	NAHL	1	1	0	0	60	5	0	5.00	....	....	....	....	....	....	....
2013-14	Kenai River	NAHL	23	11	6	4	1288	68	1	3.17	....	....	....	....	....	....	....
2014-15	Omaha Lancers	USHL	33	21	6	4	1853	77	1	2.38	3	0	3	176	8	0	2.73

• Signed Letter of Intent to attend **University of Nebraska Omaha** (NCHC) in fall of 2016.

OLKINUORA, Jussi (ohl-KIHN-oh-rah, YEW-see) WPG

Goaltender. Catches left. 6'2", 201 lbs. Born, Helsinki, Finland, November 4, 1990.

			Regular Season								Playoffs						
Season	Club	League	GP	W	L	O/T	Mins	GA	SO	Avg	GP	W	L	Mins	GA	SO	Avg
2010-11	Sioux Falls	USHL	27	14	13	0	1576	73	1	2.78	....	....	....	....	....	....	....
2011-12	U. of Denver	WCHA	22	9	8	3	1236	45	2	2.18	....	....	....	....	....	....	....
2012-13	U. of Denver	WCHA	24	13	6	5	1428	56	3	2.35	....	....	....	....	....	....	....
	St. John's IceCaps	AHL	1	0	1	0	59	3	0	3.03	....	....	....	....	....	....	....
2013-14	St. John's IceCaps	AHL	10	5	3	1	554	30	1	3.25	....	....	....	....	....	....	....
	Ontario Reign	ECHL	27	14	11	1	1575	79	0	3.01	....	....	....	....	....	....	....
2014-15	St. John's IceCaps	AHL	4	2	1	0	186	13	0	4.20	....	....	....	....	....	....	....
	Ontario Reign	ECHL	43	27	9	6	2560	103	1	2.41	12	7	4	624	24	0	2.31

WCHA All-Rookie Team (2012) • WCHA Second All-Star Team (2013) • NCAA West Second All-American Team (2013)

Signed to an ATO (amateur tryout) contract by **St. John's** (AHL), April 7, 2013. Signed as a free agent by **Winnipeg**, April 24, 2013.

OLSON, Collin (OHL-suhn, KAW-lihn) CAR

Goaltender. Catches left. 6'4", 210 lbs. Born, Burnsville, MN, April 4, 1994.
(Carolina's 8th choice, 159th overall, in 2012 Entry Draft).

			Regular Season								Playoffs						
Season	Club	League	GP	W	L	O/T	Mins	GA	SO	Avg	GP	W	L	Mins	GA	SO	Avg
2009-10	Apple Valley	High-MN	8	3	2	0	258	20	0	3.95	1	0	0	3	0	0	0.00
2010-11	USNTDP	USHL	19	10	8	1	1099	52	3	2.84	1	0	0	20	1	0	3.00
	USNTDP	U-17	10	7	1	0	492	16	0	1.95	....	....	....	....	....	....	....
2011-12	USNTDP	USHL	16	7	6	2	846	36	1	2.55	....	....	....	....	....	....	....
	USNTDP	U-17	1	0	1	0	60	4	0	4.00	....	....	....	....	....	....	....
	USNTDP	U-18	21	12	5	0	1063	40	3	2.26	....	....	....	....	....	....	....
2012-13	Ohio State	CCHA	9	2	3	1	408	21	0	3.09	....	....	....	....	....	....	....
2013-14	Ohio State	Big Ten	2	0	1	0	63	8	0	7.64	....	....	....	....	....	....	....
	USNTDP	USHL	3	2	1	0	140	5	1	2.14	....	....	....	....	....	....	....
	Sioux City	USHL	20	12	3	1	1091	42	1	2.31	2	1	1	137	7	0	3.07
2014-15	Sioux City	USHL	44	27	10	4	2507	116	3	2.78	....	....	....	....	....	....	....

OPILKA, Luke (oh-PIHL-kuh, LOOK) ST.L.

Goaltender. Catches left. 6'1", 192 lbs. Born, Effingham, IL, February 27, 1997.
(St. Louis' 5th choice, 146th overall, in 2015 Entry Draft).

			Regular Season								Playoffs						
Season	Club	League	GP	W	L	O/T	Mins	GA	SO	Avg	GP	W	L	Mins	GA	SO	Avg
2012-13	St.L. AAA Blues	T1EHL	22	18	2	1	1184	34	4	1.55	3	3	0	153	1	2	0.33
2013-14	USNTDP	USHL	18	5	9	1	845	65	0	4.62	....	....	....	....	....	....	....
	USNTDP	U-17	12	9	0	0	587	21	0	2.14	....	....	....	....	....	....	....
2014-15	USNTDP	USHL	15	11	1	2	824	34	1	2.48	....	....	....	....	....	....	....
	USNTDP	U-18	21	14	5	0	1188	59	2	2.98	....	....	....	....	....	....	....

ORTIO, Joni (OHR-tee-oh, YOH-nee) CGY

Goaltender. Catches left. 6'1", 185 lbs. Born, Turku, Finland, April 16, 1991.
(Calgary's 5th choice, 171st overall, in 2009 Entry Draft).

			Regular Season								Playoffs						
Season	Club	League	GP	W	L	O/T	Mins	GA	SO	Avg	GP	W	L	Mins	GA	SO	Avg
2007-08	TuTo Turku U18	Fin-U18	7	1	6	0	392	34	0	5.20	....	....	....	....	....	....	....
	TuTo Turku Jr.	Fin-Jr.	5	1	3	0	302	16	0	3.18	....	....	....	....	....	....	....
2008-09	TPS Turku U18	Fin-U18	1	1	0	0	60	4	0	4.00	....	....	....	....	....	....	....
	TPS Turku Jr.	Fin-Jr.	26	18	8	0	1573	69	1	2.63	12	6	6	716	23	0	1.93
2009-10	Suomi U20	Finland-2	5	3	2	0	312	11	0	2.12	....	....	....	....	....	....	....
	TuTo Turku	Finland-2	9	5	4	0	546	27	0	2.96	....	....	....	....	....	....	....
	TPS Turku Jr.	Fin-Jr.	16	8	6	0	935	45	1	2.89	....	....	....	....	....	....	....
	TPS Turku	Finland	3	1	0	0	108	8	0	4.45	....	....	....	....	....	....	....
2010-11	TPS Turku	Finland	15	2	7	3	730	38	1	3.12	....	....	....	....	....	....	....
	Abbotsford Heat	AHL	1	0	1	0	60	6	0	6.03	....	....	....	....	....	....	....
2011-12	Abbotsford Heat	AHL	9	1	4	0	387	19	0	2.94	....	....	....	....	....	....	....
	TPS Turku	Finland	14	3	6	3	753	33	2	2.63	2	0	1	87	3	0	2.06
2012-13	HIFK Helsinki	Finland	*54	23	20	9	*3120	126	4	2.42	8	3	5	481	20	0	2.49
2013-14	**Calgary**	**NHL**	**9**	**4**	**4**	**0**	**501**	**21**	**0**	**2.51**	....	....	....	....	....	....	....
	Abbotsford Heat	AHL	37	27	8	0	2133	83	2	2.33	4	1	3	250	12	0	2.88
	Alaska Aces	ECHL	4	3	1	0	238	4	2	1.01	....	....	....	....	....	....	....
2014-15	**Calgary**	**NHL**	**6**	**4**	**2**	**0**	**333**	**14**	**1**	**2.52**	....	....	....	....	....	....	....
	Adirondack Flames	AHL	37	21	13	1	2095	94	4	2.69	....	....	....	....	....	....	....
	NHL Totals		**15**	**8**	**6**	**0**	**834**	**35**	**1**	**2.52**	....	....	....	....	....	....	....

AHL All-Rookie Team (2014)

OUELLETTE, Martin (OO-leht, MAHR-tihn) PHI

Goaltender. Catches left. 6'1", 184 lbs. Born, Saint-Jerome, QC, December 30, 1991.
(Columbus' 8th choice, 184th overall, in 2010 Entry Draft).

			Regular Season								Playoffs						
Season	Club	League	GP	W	L	O/T	Mins	GA	SO	Avg	GP	W	L	Mins	GA	SO	Avg
2008-09	Kimball Union	High-NH	16	....	....	....	....	....	....	2.93	....	....	....	....	....	....	....
2009-10	Kimball Union	High-NH	29	21	6	2	1461	45	....	1.61	....	....	....	....	....	....	....
2010-11	University of Maine	H-East	9	3	3	2	490	26	1	3.18	....	....	....	....	....	....	....
2011-12	University of Maine	H-East	9	1	3	0	316	18	0	3.42	....	....	....	....	....	....	....
2012-13	University of Maine	H-East	30	9	12	8	1757	71	2	2.42	....	....	....	....	....	....	....
2013-14	University of Maine	H-East	34	15	15	4	1967	75	4	2.29	....	....	....	....	....	....	....
2014-15	Lehigh Valley	AHL	8	3	2	0	311	15	0	2.90	....	....	....	....	....	....	....
	Reading Royals	ECHL	29	17	10	2	1650	80	1	2.91	....	....	....	....	....	....	....

Signed as a free agent by **Philadelphia**, August 18, 2014.

PAJPACH, Maximilian (PIGH-PAHKH, max-ih-MIHL-y'uhn) COL

Goaltender. Catches left. 6', 207 lbs. Born, Poprad, Slovakia, January 4, 1996.
(Colorado's 6th choice, 174th overall, in 2014 Entry Draft).

			Regular Season								Playoffs						
Season	Club	League	GP	W	L	O/T	Mins	GA	SO	Avg	GP	W	L	Mins	GA	SO	Avg
2010-11	Poprad U18	Svk-U18	1	....	....	....	50	1	0	1.19	....	....	....	....	....	....	....
2011-12	Poprad U18	Svk-U18	34	....	....	....	1760	128	1	4.36	....	....	....	....	....	....	....
2012-13	Poprad U18	Svk-U18	37	....	....	....	2049	105	4	3.07	3	....	....	182	10	0	3.30
	HK SKP Poprad Jr.	Slovak-Jr.	1	....	....	....	19	0	0	0.00	....	....	....	....	....	....	....
2013-14	Slovakia U20	Slovakia	2	....	....	....	93	11	0	7.06	....	....	....	....	....	....	....
	Slovakia U18	Slovak-2	14	....	....	....	736	53	0	4.32	....	....	....	....	....	....	....
	Poprad U18	Svk-U18	....	....	....	....	....	....	....	....	2	....	....	120	4	0	2.00
	HK SKP Poprad Jr.	Slovak-Jr.	2	....	....	....	120	5	0	2.50	3	....	....	185	12	0	3.89
2014-15			DID NOT PLAY – INJURED														

• Missed 2014-15 due to lower-body injury while training with Tappara Tampere Jr. (Fin.-Jr.), September 15, 2014.

PATERSON, Jake (pa-TUHR-suhn, JAYK) DET

Goaltender. Catches left. 6'2", 190 lbs. Born, Mississauga, ON, May 3, 1994.
(Detroit's 2nd choice, 80th overall, in 2012 Entry Draft).

			Regular Season								Playoffs						
Season	Club	League	GP	W	L	O/T	Mins	GA	SO	Avg	GP	W	L	Mins	GA	SO	Avg
2009-10	Toronto Marlboros	GTHL	50	38	7	4	2250	70	15	1.41	....	....	....	....	....	....	....
2010-11	Soo Eagles	NOJHL	13	10	1	2	793	39	2	2.95	15	11	4	916	37	3	2.42
	Saginaw Spirit	OHL	5	3	0	2	303	15	0	2.97	....	....	....	....	....	....	....
2011-12	Saginaw Spirit	OHL	42	18	18	3	2265	129	1	3.42	12	6	6	689	35	0	3.05
2012-13	Saginaw Spirit	OHL	50	25	18	5	2893	170	1	3.53	4	0	4	235	21	0	5.36
2013-14	Saginaw Spirit	OHL	45	24	18	2	2518	143	2	3.41	5	1	4	308	24	0	4.67
2014-15	Saginaw Spirit	OHL	24	12	11	1	1413	82	1	3.48	....	....	....	....	....	....	....
	Kitchener Rangers	OHL	26	14	10	2	1543	61	2	2.37	6	2	4	325	28	0	5.18
	Toledo Walleye	ECHL	2	1	0	0	80	2	0	1.50	....	....	....	....	....	....	....

PAVELEC, Ondrej (pah-vah-LEK, AWN-dray) WPG

Goaltender. Catches left. 6'3", 220 lbs. Born, Kladno, Czech., August 31, 1987.
(Atlanta's 2nd choice, 41st overall, in 2005 Entry Draft).

			Regular Season								Playoffs						
Season	Club	League	GP	W	L	O/T	Mins	GA	SO	Avg	GP	W	L	Mins	GA	SO	Avg
2003-04	HC Kladno U17	CzR-U17	38	....	....	....	2079	77	3	2.22	2	....	....	67	7	0	6.27
2004-05	HC Kladno Jr.	CzRep-Jr.	39	....	....	....	2218	85	7	2.30	10	....	....	587	24	1	2.45
	HK LEV Slany	CzRep-3	1	....	....	....	60	4	0	4.00	....	....	....	....	....	....	....
2005-06	Cape Breton	QMJHL	47	27	18	0	2578	108	3	2.51	9	4	5	507	19	0	*2.25
2006-07	Cape Breton	QMJHL	43	28	11	0	2335	98	1	*2.52	16	11	5	970	37	*2	*2.29
2007-08	**Atlanta**	**NHL**	**7**	**3**	**3**	**0**	**347**	**18**	**0**	**3.11**	....	....	....	....	....	....	....
	Chicago Wolves	AHL	52	33	16	3	3033	140	2	2.77	*24	*16	8	*1438	56	*2	2.34
2008-09	**Atlanta**	**NHL**	**12**	**3**	**7**	**0**	**599**	**36**	**0**	**3.61**	....	....	....	....	....	....	....
	Chicago Wolves	AHL	40	18	20	2	2417	104	3	2.58	....	....	....	....	....	....	....
2009-10	**Atlanta**	**NHL**	**42**	**14**	**18**	**7**	**2317**	**127**	**2**	**3.29**	....	....	....	....	....	....	....
	Czech Republic	Olympics	DID NOT PLAY – SPARE GOALTENDER														
2010-11	**Atlanta**	**NHL**	**58**	**21**	**23**	**9**	**3225**	**147**	**4**	**2.73**	....	....	....	....	....	....	....
	Chicago Wolves	AHL	1	0	1	0	58	3	0	3.10	....	....	....	....	....	....	....
2011-12	**Winnipeg**	**NHL**	**68**	**29**	**28**	**9**	**3932**	**191**	**4**	**2.91**	....	....	....	....	....	....	....
2012-13	Liberec	CzRep	14	4	10	0	772	45	0	3.50	....	....	....	....	....	....	....
	Pelicans Lahti	Finland	6	....	....	....	....	....	....	2.68	....	....	....	....	....	....	....
	Winnipeg	**NHL**	***44**	**21**	**20**	**3**	**2553**	**119**	**0**	**2.80**	....	....	....	....	....	....	....
2013-14	**Winnipeg**	**NHL**	**57**	**22**	**26**	**7**	**3248**	**163**	**1**	**3.01**	....	....	....	....	....	....	....
	Czech Republic	Olympics	4	....	....	....	209	10	0	2.87	....	....	....	....	....	....	....
2014-15	**Winnipeg**	**NHL**	**50**	**22**	**16**	**8**	**2838**	**108**	**5**	**2.28**	**4**	**0**	**4**	**241**	**15**	**0**	**3.73**
	NHL Totals		**338**	**135**	**141**	**43**	**19059**	**909**	**16**	**2.86**	**4**	**0**	**4**	**241**	**15**	**0**	**3.73**

QMJHL All-Rookie Team (2006) • QMJHL First All-Star Team (2006, 2007) • QMJHL Defensive Rookie of the Year (2006)

• Transferred to **Winnipeg** after **Atlanta** franchise relocated, June 21, 2011. Signed as a free agent by **Liberec** (CzRep), September 21, 2012. Signed as a free agent by **Lahti** (Finland), November 26, 2012.

PERRY, Chase (PAIR-ee, CHAYS) DET

Goaltender. Catches left. 6'3", 189 lbs. Born, Grand Forks, ND, February 8, 1996.
(Detroit's 4th choice, 136th overall, in 2014 Entry Draft).

			Regular Season								Playoffs						
Season	Club	League	GP	W	L	O/T	Mins	GA	SO	Avg	GP	W	L	Mins	GA	SO	Avg
2010-11	Andover Huskies	High-MN	16	4	9	0	704	51	2	3.69	....	....	....	....	....	....	....
2011-12	Team Northwest	UMHSEL	1	1	0	0	60	3	0	3.00	....	....	....	....	....	....	....
	Metro Northwest	MEPDL	12	2	1	2	153	20	0	7.83	....	....	....	....	....	....	....
	Andover Huskies	High-MN	25	16	6	2	1219	64	0	2.68	3	2	1	145	11	0	3.87
2012-13	Apple Valley	High-MN	25	10	10	2	1132	60	3	2.70	1	0	1	51	3	0	3.00
	Team Northwest	UMHSEL	18	7	3	3	772	25	0	1.94	3	0	2	103	6	0	3.50
2013-14	Wenatchee Wild	NAHL	35	15	12	6	2048	80	2	2.34	10	5	5	656	20	*3	1.83
2014-15	Colorado College	NCHC	15	1	8	1	695	46	0	3.97	....	....	....	....	....	....	....

PETERS, Justin (PEE-tuhrz, JUHS-tihn) WSH

Goaltender. Catches left. 6'1", 210 lbs. Born, Blyth, ON, August 30, 1986.
(Carolina's 2nd choice, 38th overall, in 2004 Entry Draft).

			Regular Season								Playoffs						
Season	Club	League	GP	W	L	O/T	Mins	GA	SO	Avg	GP	W	L	Mins	GA	SO	Avg
2001-02	Huron-Perth	Minor-ON	17	11	2	4	810	32	1	1.89	13	9	4	285	30	1	2.31
2002-03	St. Michael's	OHL	23	6	10	1	1052	54	0	3.08	7	1	0	126	4	0	1.90
2003-04	St. Michael's	OHL	53	30	16	6	3149	139	4	2.65	18	10	8	1109	37	4	2.00
2004-05	St. Michael's	OHL	58	23	23	5	3150	146	3	2.78	10	4	4	524	25	0	2.86
2005-06	St. Michael's	OHL	20	10	6	3	1174	75	0	3.83	....	....	....	....	....	....	....
	Plymouth Whalers	OHL	35	19	15	1	2073	95	1	2.75	13	6	7	789	42	0	3.19
2006-07	Albany River Rats	AHL	34	10	18	0	1765	96	1	3.26	....	....	....	....	....	....	....
	Florida Everblades	ECHL	1	0	0	1	65	6	0	5.54	....	....	....	....	....	....	....
2007-08	Albany River Rats	AHL	11	7	3	0	645	29	0	2.70	....	....	....	....	....	....	....
	Florida Everblades	ECHL	31	18	10	2	1846	79	1	2.57	....	....	....	....	....	....	....
2008-09	Albany River Rats	AHL	56	19	30	4	3178	153	4	2.89	....	....	....	....	....	....	....
2009-10	**Carolina**	**NHL**	**9**	**6**	**3**	**0**	**488**	**23**	**0**	**2.83**	....	....	....	....	....	....	....
	Albany River Rats	AHL	47	26	18	2	2763	117	1	2.54	8	4	4	509	29	0	3.42
2010-11	**Carolina**	**NHL**	**12**	**3**	**5**	**1**	**648**	**43**	**0**	**3.98**	....	....	....	....	....	....	....
2011-12	**Carolina**	**NHL**	**7**	**2**	**3**	**2**	**387**	**16**	**1**	**2.48**	....	....	....	....	....	....	....
	Charlotte Checkers	AHL	28	10	13	2	1604	74	1	2.77	....	....	....	....	....	....	....
2012-13	Charlotte Checkers	AHL	37	22	12	1	2072	79	6	2.29	....	....	....	....	....	....	....
	Carolina	**NHL**	**19**	**4**	**11**	**1**	**954**	**55**	**1**	**3.46**	....	....	....	....	....	....	....
2013-14	**Carolina**	**NHL**	**21**	**7**	**9**	**4**	**1225**	**51**	**1**	**2.50**	....	....	....	....	....	....	....
	Charlotte Checkers	AHL	6	4	1	1	364	13	0	2.14	....	....	....	....	....	....	....
2014-15	**Washington**	**NHL**	**12**	**3**	**6**	**1**	**647**	**35**	**0**	**3.25**	....	....	....	....	....	....	....
	Hershey Bears	AHL	2	1	1	0	119	3	1	1.51	....	....	....	....	....	....	....
	NHL Totals		**80**	**25**	**37**	**9**	**4349**	**223**	**3**	**3.08**	....	....	....	....	....	....	....

Signed as a free agent by **Washington**, July 1, 2014.

PETERSEN, Cal (PEE-tuhr-suhn, KAL) BUF

Goaltender. Catches right. 6'1", 182 lbs. Born, Waterloo, IA, October 19, 1994.
(Buffalo's 7th choice, 129th overall, in 2013 Entry Draft).

			Regular Season								Playoffs						
Season	Club	League	GP	W	L	O/T	Mins	GA	SO	Avg	GP	W	L	Mins	GA	SO	Avg
2010-11	Chi. Americans	T1EHL	24	13	6	5	1244	53	4	2.30	....	....	....	....	....	....	....
2011-12	Chi. Americans	HPHL	12	3	6	2	680	35	0	3.09	....	....	....	....	....	....	....
	Topeka	NAHL	2	1	0	1	129	4	0	1.86	....	....	....	....	....	....	....
	Waterloo	USHL	5	3	1	0	265	13	0	2.94	....	....	....	....	....	....	....
2012-13	Waterloo	USHL	35	21	11	1	1937	96	3	2.97	4	2	2	211	15	0	4.26
2013-14	Waterloo	USHL	37	*27	7	6	2229	93	2	2.50	*12	*8	4	*800	30	0	2.37
2014-15	U. of Notre Dame	H-East	33	13	16	3	1892	79	*4	2.51	....	....	....	....	....	....	....

USHL All-Rookie Team (2013) • USHL Second All-Star Team (2014) • Hockey East All-Rookie Team (2015)

PHILLIPS, Jamie (FIHL-ihps, JAY-mee) WPG

Goaltender. Catches left. 6'3", 198 lbs. Born, Caledonia, ON, March 24, 1993.
(Winnipeg's 6th choice, 190th overall, in 2012 Entry Draft).

			Regular Season								Playoffs						
Season	Club	League	GP	W	L	O/T	Mins	GA	SO	Avg	GP	W	L	Mins	GA	SO	Avg
2008-09	St. Cath. Falcons	Minor-ON	41	....	....	....	1845	57	1	2.61	....	....	....	....	....	....	....
	Brantford	ON-Jr.B	....	....	....	....	....	....	....	....	1	0	1	60	3	0	3.00
2009-10	Welland	ON-Jr.B	6	0	2	0	202	16	0	4.76	....	....	....	....	....	....	....
	Brantford	ON-Jr.B	3	2	0	0	140	7	0	3.00	....	....	....	....	....	....	....
2010-11	Pembroke	ON-Jr.A	33	25	6	1	1857	66	*6	*2.13	2	2	0	12	3	1	1.50
2011-12	Powell River Kings	BCHL	26	16	6	1	....	....	....	2.01	....	....	....	....	....	....	....
	Tor. Canadiens	ON-Jr.A	11	4	4	0	637	33	1	3.11	10	5	5	581	29	0	2.99
2012-13	Michigan Tech	WCHA	9	2	2	0	324	13	1	2.40	....	....	....	....	....	....	....
2013-14	Michigan Tech	WCHA	13	4	6	1	681	32	0	2.82	....	....	....	....	....	....	....
2014-15	Michigan Tech	WCHA	*41	*28	9	2	2417	70	*6	1.74	....	....	....	....	....	....	....

WCHA First All-Star Team (2015)

PICKARD, Calvin (pih-KARD, KAL-vihn) COL

Goaltender. Catches left. 6'1", 200 lbs. Born, Moncton, NB, April 15, 1992.
(Colorado's 2nd choice, 49th overall, in 2010 Entry Draft).

			Regular Season								Playoffs						
Season	Club	League	GP	W	L	O/T	Mins	GA	SO	Avg	GP	W	L	Mins	GA	SO	Avg
2007-08	Winnipeg Wild	MMHL	40	....	....	....	....	....	....	1.91	....	....	....	....	....	....	....
2008-09	Seattle	WHL	47	23	16	5	2694	137	3	3.05	5	1	4	297	15	0	3.03
2009-10	Seattle	WHL	*62	16	34	12	*3688	190	3	3.09	....	....	....	....	....	....	....
2010-11	Seattle	WHL	*68	27	33	8	*4013	225	1	3.36	....	....	....	....	....	....	....
2011-12	Seattle	WHL	*64	25	37	2	*3630	217	*5	3.59	....	....	....	....	....	....	....
	Lake Erie Monsters	AHL	2	1	0	0	77	4	0	3.12	....	....	....	....	....	....	....
2012-13	Lake Erie Monsters	AHL	47	20	19	5	2749	113	5	2.47	....	....	....	....	....	....	....
2013-14	Lake Erie Monsters	AHL	43	16	18	7	2445	116	2	2.85	....	....	....	....	....	....	....
2014-15	**Colorado**	**NHL**	**16**	**6**	**7**	**3**	**895**	**35**	**0**	**2.35**	....	....	....	....	....	....	....
	Lake Erie Monsters	AHL	50	23	17	9	2943	128	3	2.61	....	....	....	....	....	....	....
	NHL Totals		**16**	**6**	**7**	**3**	**895**	**35**	**0**	**2.35**	....	....	....	....	....	....	....

WHL West First All-Star Team (2010) • WHL West Second All-Star Team (2011)

POULIN, Kevin (POO-lihn, KEH-vihn) NYI

Goaltender. Catches left. 6'2", 199 lbs. Born, Montreal, QC, April 12, 1990.
(NY Islanders' 10th choice, 126th overall, in 2008 Entry Draft).

			Regular Season								Playoffs						
Season	Club	League	GP	W	L	O/T	Mins	GA	SO	Avg	GP	W	L	Mins	GA	SO	Avg
2005-06	C.C. Lemoyne	QAAA	27	13	8	2	1440	71	1	2.96	7	4	3	373	16	1	2.57
2006-07	Victoriaville Tigres	QMJHL	24	10	6	0	1220	68	0	3.34	2	0	0	42	5	0	7.20
2007-08	Victoriaville Tigres	QMJHL	52	18	24	0	2734	168	0	3.69	6	2	4	279	27	0	5.80
2008-09	Victoriaville Tigres	QMJHL	39	18	19	0	2273	120	1	3.17	4	0	4	249	18	0	4.34
2009-10	Victoriaville Tigres	QMJHL	54	*35	16	0	3105	136	*7	2.63	16	10	6	971	46	0	2.84
2010-11	**NY Islanders**	**NHL**	**10**	**4**	**2**	**1**	**491**	**20**	**0**	**2.44**	....	....	....	....	....	....	....
	Bridgeport	AHL	15	10	5	0	903	33	2	2.19	....	....	....	....	....	....	....
2011-12	**NY Islanders**	**NHL**	**6**	**2**	**4**	**0**	**296**	**15**	**0**	**3.04**	....	....	....	....	....	....	....
	Bridgeport	AHL	49	26	18	4	2943	137	3	2.79	3	0	3	194	10	0	3.09
2012-13	Bridgeport	AHL	32	15	14	3	1824	98	1	3.22	....	....	....	....	....	....	....
	NY Islanders	**NHL**	**5**	**1**	**3**	**0**	**258**	**13**	**0**	**3.02**	**2**	**0**	**0**	**52**	**1**	**0**	**1.15**
2013-14	**NY Islanders**	**NHL**	**28**	**11**	**16**	**1**	**1625**	**89**	**0**	**3.29**	....	....	....	....	....	....	....
	Bridgeport	AHL	15	2	12	1	904	40	0	2.65	....	....	....	....	....	....	....
2014-15	**NY Islanders**	**NHL**	**1**	**0**	**0**	**1**	**65**	**3**	**0**	**2.77**	....	....	....	....	....	....	....
	Bridgeport	AHL	45	16	21	7	2612	125	2	2.87	....	....	....	....	....	....	....
	NHL Totals		**50**	**18**	**25**	**3**	**2735**	**140**	**0**	**3.07**	**2**	**0**	**0**	**52**	**1**	**0**	**1.15**

QMJHL Second All-Star Team (2010)

PRICE, Carey (PRIGHS, KAIR-ee) MTL

Goaltender. Catches left. 6'3", 216 lbs. Born, Anahim Lake, BC, August 16, 1987.
(Montreal's 1st choice, 5th overall, in 2005 Entry Draft).

			Regular Season								Playoffs						
Season	Club	League	GP	W	L	O/T	Mins	GA	SO	Avg	GP	W	L	Mins	GA	SO	Avg
2002-03	Williams Lake	Minor-BC	18	....	....	....	1050	48	1	2.70	....	....	....	....	....	....	....
	Tri-City Americans	WHL	1	0	0	0	20	2	0	6.00	....	....	....	....	....	....	....
2003-04	Tri-City Americans	WHL	28	8	9	3	1362	54	1	2.38	8	5	3	470	19	0	2.43
2004-05	Tri-City Americans	WHL	63	24	31	8	3712	145	8	2.34	5	1	4	324	12	0	2.22
2005-06	Tri-City Americans	WHL	55	21	25	6	3072	147	3	2.87	5	1	4	302	12	0	2.39
2006-07	Tri-City Americans	WHL	46	30	13	1	2722	111	3	2.45	6	2	4	348	17	0	2.93
	Hamilton Bulldogs	AHL	2	1	1	0	117	3	0	1.53	*22	*15	6	*1314	45	*2	2.06
2007-08	**Montreal**	**NHL**	**41**	**24**	**12**	**3**	**2413**	**103**	**3**	**2.56**	**11**	**5**	**6**	**648**	**30**	**2**	**2.78**
	Hamilton Bulldogs	AHL	10	6	4	0	581	26	1	2.69	....	....	....	....	....	....	....
2008-09	**Montreal**	**NHL**	**52**	**23**	**16**	**10**	**3036**	**143**	**1**	**2.83**	**4**	**0**	**4**	**219**	**15**	**0**	**4.11**
2009-10	**Montreal**	**NHL**	**41**	**13**	**20**	**5**	**2358**	**109**	**0**	**2.77**	**4**	**0**	**1**	**135**	**8**	**0**	**3.56**
2010-11	**Montreal**	**NHL**	**72**	***38**	**28**	**6**	**4206**	**165**	**8**	**2.35**	**7**	**3**	**4**	**455**	**16**	**1**	**2.11**
2011-12	**Montreal**	**NHL**	**65**	**26**	**28**	**11**	**3944**	**160**	**4**	**2.43**	....	....	....	....	....	....	....
2012-13	**Montreal**	**NHL**	**39**	**21**	**13**	**4**	**2249**	**97**	**3**	**2.59**	**4**	**1**	**2**	**239**	**13**	**0**	**3.26**
2013-14	**Montreal**	**NHL**	**59**	**34**	**20**	**5**	**3464**	**134**	**6**	**2.32**	**12**	**8**	**4**	**739**	**29**	**1**	**2.35**
	Canada	Olympics	5	5	0	0	303	3	2	0.59	....	....	....	....	....	....	....
2014-15	**Montreal**	**NHL**	**66**	**44**	**16**	**6**	**3977**	**130**	**9**	**1.96**	**12**	**6**	**6**	**752**	**28**	**1**	**2.23**
	NHL Totals		**435**	**223**	**153**	**50**	**25647**	**1041**	**34**	**2.44**	**54**	**23**	**27**	**3187**	**139**	**5**	**2.62**

WHL West First All-Star Team (2007) • WHL Goaltender of the Year (2007) • Canadian Major Junior First All-Star Team (2007) • Canadian Major Junior Goaltender of the Year (2007) • Jack A. Butterfield Trophy (AHL - Playoff MVP) (2007) • NHL All-Rookie Team (2008) • Olympics – Best Goaltender (2014) • NHL First All-Star Team (2015) • William M. Jennings Trophy (2015) (tied with Corey Crawford) • Vezina Trophy (2015) • Ted Lindsay Award (2015) • Hart Memorial Trophy (2015)

Played in NHL All-Star Game (2009, 2011, 2012, 2015)

QUICK, Jonathan (KWIHK, JAWN-ah-thuhn) L.A.

Goaltender. Catches left. 6'1", 218 lbs. Born, Milford, CT, January 21, 1986.
(Los Angeles' 4th choice, 72nd overall, in 2005 Entry Draft).

			Regular Season								Playoffs						
Season	Club	League	GP	W	L	O/T	Mins	GA	SO	Avg	GP	W	L	Mins	GA	SO	Avg
2002-03	Avon Old Farms	High-CT	13	8	5	0	780	38	0	2.92	....	....	....	....	....	....	....
2003-04	Avon Old Farms	High-CT	21	20	1	0	1260	26	2	1.71	....	....	....	....	....	....	....
2004-05	Avon Old Farms	High-CT	27	25	2	0	1413	27	9	1.14	....	....	....	....	....	....	....
2005-06	Massachusetts	H-East	17	4	10	1	905	45	0	2.98	....	....	....	....	....	....	....
2006-07	Massachusetts	H-East	37	19	12	5	2224	80	3	2.16	....	....	....	....	....	....	....
2007-08	**Los Angeles**	**NHL**	**3**	**1**	**2**	**0**	**141**	**9**	**0**	**3.83**	....	....	....	....	....	....	....
	Manchester	AHL	19	11	8	0	1085	42	3	2.32	1	0	1	59	1	0	1.02
	Reading Royals	ECHL	38	23	11	3	2257	105	1	2.79	....	....	....	....	....	....	....
2008-09	**Los Angeles**	**NHL**	**44**	**21**	**18**	**2**	**2495**	**103**	**4**	**2.48**	....	....	....	....	....	....	....
	Manchester	AHL	14	6	5	2	827	37	0	2.68	....	....	....	....	....	....	....
2009-10	**Los Angeles**	**NHL**	**72**	**39**	**24**	**7**	**4258**	**180**	**4**	**2.54**	**6**	**2**	**4**	**360**	**21**	**0**	**3.50**
	United States	Olympics				DID NOT PLAY – SPARE GOALTENDER											
2010-11	**Los Angeles**	**NHL**	**61**	**35**	**22**	**3**	**3591**	**134**	**6**	**2.24**	**6**	**2**	**4**	**380**	**20**	**1**	**3.16**
2011-12 ♦	**Los Angeles**	**NHL**	**69**	**35**	**21**	**13**	**4099**	**133**	***10**	**1.95**	**20**	***16**	**4**	**1238**	**29**	***3**	***1.41**
2012-13	**Los Angeles**	**NHL**	**37**	**18**	**13**	**4**	**2134**	**87**	**1**	**2.45**	**18**	**9**	**9**	**1099**	**34**	***3**	**1.86**
2013-14 ♦	**Los Angeles**	**NHL**	**49**	**27**	**17**	**4**	**2904**	**100**	**6**	**2.07**	***26**	***16**	**10**	***1605**	**69**	***2**	**2.58**
	United States	Olympics	5	....	....	....	304	11	0	2.17	....	....	....	....	....	....	....
2014-15	**Los Angeles**	**NHL**	**72**	**36**	**22**	**13**	**4184**	**156**	**6**	**2.24**	....	....	....	....	....	....	....
	NHL Totals		**407**	**212**	**139**	**46**	**23806**	**902**	**37**	**2.27**	**76**	**45**	**31**	**4682**	**173**	**9**	**2.22**

Hockey East Second All-Star Team (2007) • NCAA East Second All-American Team (2007) • NHL Second All-Star Team (2012) • Conn Smythe Trophy (2012) • William M. Jennings Trophy (2014)

Played in NHL All-Star Game (2012)

RAANTA, Antti (RAHN-tah, AN-tee) NYR

Goaltender. Catches left. 6', 187 lbs. Born, Rauma, Finland, May 12, 1989.

			Regular Season								Playoffs						
Season	Club	League	GP	W	L	O/T	Mins	GA	SO	Avg	GP	W	L	Mins	GA	SO	Avg
2007-08	Lukko Rauma Jr.	Fin-Jr.	13	....	....	....	....	....	....	3.23	....	....	....	....	....	....	....
2008-09	Lukko Rauma	Finland	2	....	....	....	....	....	....	2.51	....	....	....	....	....	....	....
2009-10	Lukko Rauma Jr.	Fin-Jr.	15	....	....	....	....	....	....	2.20	4	....	....	....	....	....	1.51
	Lukko Rauma	Finland	15	6	7	1	836	37	2	2.66	....	....	....	....	....	....	....
2010-11	Lukko Rauma	Finland	20	....	....	....	....	....	....	2.37	2	....	....	....	....	....	4.28
2011-12	Assat Pori	Finland	38	....	....	....	....	....	....	2.23	3	....	....	....	....	....	3.07
2012-13	Assat Pori	Finland	45	21	10	11	2595	80	5	*1.85	*16	*12	4	*1039	23	*4	*1.33
2013-14	**Chicago**	**NHL**	**25**	**13**	**5**	**4**	**1397**	**63**	**1**	**2.71**	....	....	....	....	....	....	....
	Rockford IceHogs	AHL	14	7	5	0	677	32	0	2.83	....	....	....	....	....	....	....
2014-15	**Chicago**	**NHL**	**14**	**7**	**4**	**1**	**792**	**25**	**2**	**1.89**	....	....	....	....	....	....	....
	Rockford IceHogs	AHL	11	8	1	1	604	24	2	2.39	....	....	....	....	....	....	....
	NHL Totals		**39**	**20**	**9**	**5**	**2189**	**88**	**3**	**2.41**	....	....	....	....	....	....	....

Signed as a free agent by **Chicago**, June 3, 2013. Traded to **NY Rangers** by **Chicago** for Ryan Haggerty, June 27, 2015.

RAMO, Karri (RAH-moh, KAH-ree) CGY

Goaltender. Catches left. 6'2", 206 lbs. Born, Asikkala, Finland, July 1, 1986.
(Tampa Bay's 7th choice, 191st overall, in 2004 Entry Draft).

			Regular Season								Playoffs						
Season	Club	League	GP	W	L	O/T	Mins	GA	SO	Avg	GP	W	L	Mins	GA	SO	Avg
2002-03	K-Reipas U18	Fin-U18	19	12	3	2	1013	47	0	2.78	4	2	2	182	11	0	3.62
2003-04	Pelicans Lahti U18	Fin-U18	3	3	0	0	180	7	0	2.33	5	2	2	268	10	0	2.24
	Pelicans Lahti Jr.	Fin-Jr.	18	5	9	2	960	53	0	3.31	2	2	0	120	1	1	0.50
	Pelicans Lahti	Finland	3	0	2	0	138	10	0	4.34	....	....	....	....	....	....	....
2004-05	Pelicans Lahti Jr.	Fin-Jr.	21	10	5	6	1269	36	6	1.70	4	1	3	206	16	0	4.66
	Pelicans Lahti	Finland	26	4	12	4	1267	84	1	3.98	....	....	....	....	....	....	....
2005-06	Haukat Jarvenpaa	Finland-2	1	....	....	....	60	5	0	5.00	....	....	....	....	....	....	....
	Suomi U20	Finland-2	3	....	....	....	183	12	0	3.93	....	....	....	....	....	....	....
	HPK Hameenlinna	Finland	24	7	8	7	1359	49	2	2.16	3	2	1	204	5	1	1.46
2006-07	**Tampa Bay**	**NHL**	**2**	**0**	**0**	**0**	**70**	**4**	**0**	**3.43**	....	....	....	....	....	....	....
	Springfield Falcons	AHL	45	15	24	1	2432	127	1	3.13	....	....	....	....	....	....	....
2007-08	**Tampa Bay**	**NHL**	**22**	**7**	**11**	**3**	**1269**	**64**	**0**	**3.03**	....	....	....	....	....	....	....
	Norfolk Admirals	AHL	6	2	4	0	342	19	0	3.33	....	....	....	....	....	....	....
2008-09	**Tampa Bay**	**NHL**	**24**	**4**	**10**	**7**	**1312**	**80**	**0**	**3.66**	....	....	....	....	....	....	....
	Norfolk Admirals	AHL	26	7	14	4	1507	95	0	3.78	....	....	....	....	....	....	....
2009-10	Omsk	KHL	44	....	....	....	2582	91	4	2.11	3	....	....	158	8	0	3.04
2010-11	Omsk	KHL	44	....	....	....	2593	85	5	1.97	14	....	....	891	32	1	2.16
2011-12	Omsk	KHL	45	19	17	0	2667	87	5	1.96	21	14	6	1209	31	3	1.54
2012-13	Omsk	KHL	40	*26	9	0	2401	80	4	2.00	12	5	7	725	24	3	1.99
2013-14	**Calgary**	**NHL**	**40**	**17**	**15**	**4**	**2194**	**97**	**2**	**2.65**	....	....	....	....	....	....	....
2014-15	**Calgary**	**NHL**	**34**	**15**	**9**	**3**	**1732**	**75**	**2**	**2.60**	**7**	**2**	**3**	**336**	**16**	**0**	**2.86**
	NHL Totals		**122**	**43**	**45**	**17**	**6577**	**320**	**4**	**2.92**	**7**	**2**	**3**	**336**	**16**	**0**	**2.86**

Signed as a free agent by **Omsk** (KHL), June 23, 2009. Traded to **Montreal** by **Tampa Bay** for Cedrick Desjardins, August 16, 2010. Traded to **Calgary** by **Montreal** with Mike Cammalleri and Montreal's 5th round choice (Ryan Culkin) in 2012 Entry Draft for Rene Bourque, Patrick Holland and Calgary's 2nd round choice (Zachary Fucale) in 2013 Entry Draft, January 12, 2012.

RASK, Tuukka (RASK, TU-kah) BOS

Goaltender. Catches left. 6'2", 185 lbs. Born, Savonlinna, Finland, March 10, 1987.
(Toronto's 1st choice, 21st overall, in 2005 Entry Draft).

			Regular Season								Playoffs						
Season	Club	League	GP	W	L	O/T	Mins	GA	SO	Avg	GP	W	L	Mins	GA	SO	Avg
2003-04	Ilves Tampere U18	Fin-U18	9	4	3	2	533	25	0	2.81	....	....	....	....	....	....	....
	Ilves Tampere Jr.	Fin-Jr.	30	12	10	7	1767	65	2	2.21	3	1	2	178	6	0	2.02
2004-05	Ilves Tampere Jr.	Fin-Jr.	26	17	3	4	1517	47	2	1.86	10	9	1	619	9	6	0.87
	Ilves Tampere	Finland	4	0	1	1	201	15	0	4.46	....	....	....	....	....	....	....
2005-06	Ilves Tampere Jr.	Fin-Jr.	1	....	....	....	60	2	0	2.00	....	....	....	....	....	....	....
	Suomi U20	Finland-2	3	....	....	....	179	6	0	2.01	....	....	....	....	....	....	....
	Ilves Tampere	Finland	30	12	8	7	1724	60	2	2.09	3	0	3	180	7	0	2.33
2006-07	Suomi U20	Finland-2	1	0	1	0	58	4	0	4.14	....	....	....	....	....	....	....
	Ilves Tampere	Finland	49	18	18	10	2872	114	3	2.38	7	2	5	397	20	0	3.02
2007-08	**Boston**	**NHL**	**4**	**2**	**1**	**1**	**184**	**10**	**0**	**3.26**	....	....	....	....	....	....	....
	Providence Bruins	AHL	45	27	13	2	2570	100	1	2.33	10	6	4	605	22	*2	2.18
2008-09	**Boston**	**NHL**	**1**	**1**	**0**	**0**	**60**	**0**	**1**	**0.00**	....	....	....	....	....	....	....
	Providence Bruins	AHL	57	33	20	4	3340	139	4	2.50	16	9	7	977	36	0	2.21
2009-10	**Boston**	**NHL**	**45**	**22**	**12**	**5**	**2562**	**84**	**5**	***1.97**	**13**	**7**	**6**	**829**	**36**	**0**	**2.61**
2010-11 ♦	**Boston**	**NHL**	**29**	**11**	**14**	**2**	**1594**	**71**	**2**	**2.67**	....	....	....	....	....	....	....
2011-12	**Boston**	**NHL**	**23**	**11**	**8**	**3**	**1289**	**44**	**3**	**2.05**	....	....	....	....	....	....	....
2012-13	HC Skoda Plzen	CzRep	17	....	....	....	993	35	1	2.11	....	....	....	....	....	....	....
	Boston	**NHL**	**36**	**19**	**10**	**5**	**2104**	**70**	***5**	**2.00**	**22**	**14**	**8**	**1466**	**46**	***3**	**1.88**
2013-14	**Boston**	**NHL**	**58**	**36**	**15**	**6**	**3386**	**115**	***7**	**2.04**	**12**	**7**	**5**	**753**	**25**	***2**	***1.99**
	Finland	Olympics	4	3	1	0	243	7	1	1.73	....	....	....	....	....	....	....
2014-15	**Boston**	**NHL**	**70**	**34**	**21**	**13**	**4063**	**156**	**3**	**2.30**	....	....	....	....	....	....	....
	NHL Totals		**266**	**136**	**81**	**35**	**15242**	**550**	**26**	**2.17**	**47**	**28**	**19**	**3048**	**107**	**5**	**2.11**

NHL First All-Star Team (2014) • Vezina Trophy (2014)

Traded to **Boston** by **Toronto** for Andrew Raycroft, June 24, 2006. Signed as a free agent by **Plzen** (CzRep), September 25, 2012.

REIMER, James (RIGH-muhr, JAYMZ) TOR

Goaltender. Catches left. 6'2", 208 lbs. Born, Morweena, MB, March 15, 1988.
(Toronto's 3rd choice, 99th overall, in 2006 Entry Draft).

			Regular Season								Playoffs						
Season	Club	League	GP	W	L	O/T	Mins	GA	SO	Avg	GP	W	L	Mins	GA	SO	Avg
2003-04	Interlake Lightning	MMHL	27	....	....	....	....	....	1	2.85	....	....	....	....	....	....	....
2004-05	Interlake Lightning	MMHL	37	....	....	....	....	....	4	2.11	....	....	....	....	....	....	....
2005-06	Red Deer Rebels	WHL	34	7	18	3	1709	80	0	2.81	....	....	....	....	....	....	....
2006-07	Red Deer Rebels	WHL	60	26	23	7	3339	148	3	2.66	7	3	4	417	27	0	3.88
2007-08	Red Deer Rebels	WHL	30	8	15	4	1668	76	1	2.73	....	....	....	....	....	....	....
2008-09	Toronto Marlies	AHL	3	1	2	0	183	10	0	3.28	....	....	....	....	....	....	....
	Reading Royals	ECHL	22	10	7	3	1236	68	0	3.30	....	....	....	....	....	....	....
	South Carolina	ECHL	6	6	0	0	363	8	2	1.32	8	4	3	497	18	1	2.17
2009-10	Toronto Marlies	AHL	26	14	8	2	1520	57	1	2.25	....	....	....	....	....	....	....
2010-11	**Toronto**	**NHL**	**37**	**20**	**10**	**5**	**2080**	**90**	**3**	**2.60**	....	....	....	....	....	....	....
	Toronto Marlies	AHL	15	9	5	1	858	37	3	2.59	....	....	....	....	....	....	....
2011-12	**Toronto**	**NHL**	**34**	**14**	**14**	**4**	**1879**	**97**	**3**	**3.10**	....	....	....	....	....	....	....
2012-13	**Toronto**	**NHL**	**33**	**19**	**8**	**5**	**1856**	**76**	**4**	**2.46**	**7**	**3**	**4**	**438**	**21**	**0**	**2.88**
2013-14	**Toronto**	**NHL**	**36**	**12**	**16**	**1**	**1785**	**98**	**1**	**3.29**	....	....	....	....	....	....	....
2014-15	**Toronto**	**NHL**	**35**	**9**	**16**	**1**	**1767**	**93**	**0**	**3.16**	....	....	....	....	....	....	....
	NHL Totals		**175**	**74**	**64**	**16**	**9367**	**454**	**11**	**2.91**	**7**	**3**	**4**	**438**	**21**	**0**	**2.88**

ECHL Playoff MVP (2009)

RINNE, Pekka (RIH-neh, PEH-kuh) NSH

Goaltender. Catches left. 6'5", 204 lbs. Born, Kempele, Finland, November 3, 1982.
(Nashville's 10th choice, 258th overall, in 2004 Entry Draft).

			Regular Season								Playoffs						
Season	Club	League	GP	W	L	O/T	Mins	GA	SO	Avg	GP	W	L	Mins	GA	SO	Avg
2000-01	Karpat Oulu Jr.	Fin-Jr.	20	9	4	5	1148	63	0	3.29	....	....	....	....	....	....	....
2001-02	Karpat Oulu Jr.	Fin-Jr.	30	19	7	3	1724	61	3	2.12	3	1	2	184	10	1	3.26
2002-03	Karpat Oulu Jr.	Fin-Jr.	25	14	8	3	1479	48	5	1.95	4	1	3	238	7	0	1.76
	Karpat Oulu	Finland	1	0	1	0	60	7	0	7.00	....	....	....	....	....	....	....
2003-04	Karpat Oulu	Finland	14	5	4	4	824	41	0	2.99	2	1	0	22	0	0	0.00
	Hokki Kajaani	Finland-2	8	5	2	1	463	16	2	2.07	....	....	....	....	....	....	....
2004-05	Karpat Oulu	Finland	10	8	0	1	571	16	0	1.68	....	....	....	....	....	....	....
2005-06	**Nashville**	**NHL**	**2**	**1**	**1**	**0**	**63**	**4**	**0**	**3.81**	....	....	....	....	....	....	....
	Milwaukee	AHL	51	30	18	2	2960	139	2	2.82	14	10	4	734	35	3	2.86
2006-07	Milwaukee	AHL	29	15	7	6	1670	65	3	2.34	4	0	4	247	12	0	2.91
2007-08	**Nashville**	**NHL**	**1**	**0**	**0**	**0**	**29**	**0**	**0**	**0.00**	....	....	....	....	....	....	....
	Milwaukee	AHL	*65	*36	24	3	*3840	158	5	2.47	6	2	4	358	15	1	2.51
2008-09	**Nashville**	**NHL**	**52**	**29**	**15**	**4**	**2999**	**119**	**7**	**2.38**	....	....	....	....	....	....	....
2009-10	**Nashville**	**NHL**	**58**	**32**	**16**	**5**	**3246**	**137**	**7**	**2.53**	**6**	**2**	**4**	**358**	**16**	**0**	**2.68**
2010-11	**Nashville**	**NHL**	**64**	**33**	**22**	**9**	**3789**	**134**	**6**	**2.12**	**12**	**6**	**6**	**748**	**32**	**0**	**2.57**
2011-12	**Nashville**	**NHL**	***73**	***43**	**18**	**8**	**4169**	**166**	**5**	**2.39**	**10**	**5**	**5**	**609**	**21**	**1**	**2.07**
2012-13	Dynamo Minsk	KHL	22	9	11	0	1327	68	1	3.08	....	....	....	....	....	....	....
	Nashville	**NHL**	**43**	**15**	**16**	**8**	**2444**	**99**	***5**	**2.43**	....	....	....	....	....	....	....
2013-14	**Nashville**	**NHL**	**24**	**10**	**10**	**3**	**1367**	**63**	**2**	**2.77**	....	....	....	....	....	....	....
	Milwaukee	AHL	2	2	0	0	121	2	0	0.99	....	....	....	....	....	....	....
2014-15	**Nashville**	**NHL**	**64**	**41**	**17**	**6**	**3851**	**140**	**4**	**2.18**	**6**	**2**	**4**	**425**	**19**	**0**	**2.68**
	NHL Totals		**381**	**204**	**115**	**43**	**21957**	**862**	**36**	**2.36**	**34**	**15**	**19**	**2140**	**88**	**1**	**2.47**

NHL Second All-Star Team (2011)

Signed as a free agent by **Minsk** (KHL), September 25, 2012. • Missed majority of 2013-14 due to hip injury at Minnesota, October 22, 2013.

ROBINSON, Mike (RAW-bihn-suhn, MIGHK) S.J.

Goaltender. Catches left. 6'3", 195 lbs. Born, Bedford, NH, March 27, 1997.
(San Jose's 3rd choice, 86th overall, in 2015 Entry Draft).

			Regular Season								Playoffs						
Season	Club	League	GP	W	L	O/T	Mins	GA	SO	Avg	GP	W	L	Mins	GA	SO	Avg
2013-14	Bos. Jr. Rangers	MtJHL	25	....	....	....	1417	....	....	1.99	....	....	....	....	....	....	....
2014-15	Bos. Jr. Rangers	EHL	8	4	4	0	459	18	0	2.35	....	....	....	....	....	....	....
	Lawrence	High-MA	....	....	....	....	....	....	....	3.52	....	....	....	....	....	....	....

• Signed Letter of Intent to attend **University of New Hampshire** (Hockey East) in fall of 2016.

RUMPEL, Joel (RUHM-puhl, JOHL) S.J.

Goaltender. Catches left. 6'3", 185 lbs. Born, Swift Current, SK, March 14, 1991.

			Regular Season								Playoffs						
Season	Club	League	GP	W	L	O/T	Mins	GA	SO	Avg	GP	W	L	Mins	GA	SO	Avg
2008-09	Swift Current	SMHL	38	18	15	4	2201	108	1	2.94	3	1	1	175	9	0	3.09
2009-10	Penticton Vees	BCHL	24	19	3	0	1308	43	2	1.97	9	5	4	538	22	0	2.45
2010-11	Penticton Vees	BCHL	45	27	12	3	2586	109	1	2.53	1	0	0	20	0	0	0.00
2011-12	U. of Wisconsin	WCHA	26	12	12	2	1525	63	3	2.48	....	....	....	....	....	....	....
2012-13	U. of Wisconsin	WCHA	29	16	9	4	1716	56	4	1.96	....	....	....	....	....	....	....
2013-14	U. of Wisconsin	Big Ten	29	21	6	1	1714	59	2	2.07	....	....	....	....	....	....	....
2014-15	U. of Wisconsin	Big Ten	31	4	23	4	1790	104	1	3.49	....	....	....	....	....	....	....
	Allen Americans	ECHL	4	3	0	1	250	7	0	1.68	7	3	2	367	18	0	2.94

Signed as a free agent by **San Jose**, March 26, 2015.

RUUSU, Markus (ROO-SOO, MAHR-kuhs) DAL

Goaltender. Catches left. 6'2", 174 lbs. Born, Jamsa, Finland, August 23, 1997.
(Dallas' 5th choice, 163rd overall, in 2015 Entry Draft).

			Regular Season								Playoffs						
Season	Club	League	GP	W	L	O/T	Mins	GA	SO	Avg	GP	W	L	Mins	GA	SO	Avg
2013-14	JyP Jyvaskyla U18	Fin-U18	33	....	....	....	1979	121	....	3.67	....	....	....	....	....	....	....
2014-15	JyP Jyvaskyla U18	Fin-U18	34	....	....	....	....	101	....	....	7	....	....	....	13	....	....
	JyP Jyvaskyla Jr.	Fin-Jr.	12	....	....	....	649	32	....	2.96	....	....	....	....	....	....	....

RYNNAS, Jussi (RIH-nuhs, YEW-see)

Goaltender. Catches left. 6'5", 212 lbs. Born, Pori, Finland, May 22, 1987.

			Regular Season								Playoffs						
Season	**Club**	**League**	**GP**	**W**	**L**	**O/T**	**Mins**	**GA**	**SO**	**Avg**	**GP**	**W**	**L**	**Mins**	**GA**	**SO**	**Avg**
2006-07	Assat Pori Jr.	Fin-Jr.	23	....	....	....	....	....	....	4.20	....	....	....	....	....	....	....
2007-08	Assat Pori Jr.	Fin-Jr.	27	....	....	....	....	....	....	2.90	....	....	....	....	....	....	....
2008-09	Assat Pori	Finland	DID NOT PLAY – SPARE GOALTENDER														
	Sport Vaasa	Finland-2	1	....	....	....	....	....	....	6.00	....	....	....	....	....	....	....
	Kiekko-Vantaa	Finland-2	7	....	....	....	....	....	....	3.99	....	....	....	....	....	....	....
2009-10	Assat Pori	Finland	31	14	13	1	1717	71	2	2.48	....	....	....	....	....	....	....
2010-11	Toronto Marlies	AHL	30	10	15	3	1660	75	2	2.71	....	....	....	....	....	....	....
2011-12	**Toronto**	**NHL**	**2**	**0**	**1**	**0**	**99**	**7**	**0**	**4.24**	....	....	....	....	....	....	....
	Toronto Marlies	AHL	22	11	9	1	1272	54	3	2.55	....	....	....	....	....	....	....
	Reading Royals	ECHL	14	8	5	1	767	41	1	3.21	....	....	....	....	....	....	....
2012-13	Toronto Marlies	AHL	21	10	9	1	1231	54	3	2.63	....	....	....	....	....	....	....
	Toronto	**NHL**	**1**	**0**	**0**	**0**	**10**	**0**	**0**	**0.00**	....	....	....	....	....	....	....
2013-14	Karpat Oulu	Finland	40	28	5	7	2382	60	9	*1.51	3	0	3	163	7	0	2.57
2014-15	**Dallas**	**NHL**	**2**	**0**	**1**	**0**	**92**	**7**	**0**	**4.57**	....	....	....	....	....	....	....
	Texas Stars	AHL	39	22	6	8	2202	93	4	2.53	2	0	2	119	6	0	3.02
	NHL Totals		**5**	**0**	**2**	**0**	**201**	**14**	**0**	**4.18**	....	....	....	....	....	....	....

Signed as a free agent by **Toronto**, April 23, 2010. Signed as a free agent by **Oulu** (Finland), July 10, 2013. Signed as a free agent by **Dallas**, July 7, 2014. Signed as a free agent by **Kazan** (KHL), June 15, 2015.

SAMSONOV, Ilya (sam-SAWN-awv, ihl-YAH) WSH

Goaltender. Catches left. 6'3", 203 lbs. Born, Magnitogorsk, Russia, February 22, 1997.
(Washington's 1st choice, 22nd overall, in 2015 Entry Draft).

			Regular Season								Playoffs						
Season	**Club**	**League**	**GP**	**W**	**L**	**O/T**	**Mins**	**GA**	**SO**	**Avg**	**GP**	**W**	**L**	**Mins**	**GA**	**SO**	**Avg**
2014-15	Magnitogorsk	KHL	1	0	0	0	22	2	0	5.50	....	....	....	....	....	....	....
	Magnitogorsk Jr.	Russia-Jr.	18	11	4	0	1039	46	2	2.66	2	1	1	127	6	0	2.83

SANDSTROM, Felix (SAND-struhm, FEH-lihx) PHI

Goaltender. Catches left. 6'2", 196 lbs. Born, Gavle, Sweden, January 12, 1997.
(Philadelphia's 3rd choice, 70th overall, in 2015 Entry Draft).

			Regular Season								Playoffs						
Season	**Club**	**League**	**GP**	**W**	**L**	**O/T**	**Mins**	**GA**	**SO**	**Avg**	**GP**	**W**	**L**	**Mins**	**GA**	**SO**	**Avg**
2011-12	Brynas U18	Swe-U18	1	....	....	....	60	1	0	1.00	....	....	....	....	....	....	....
2012-13	Brynas U18	Swe-U18	28	23	5	0	1706	49	9	1.72	1	0	1	59	4	0	4.10
2013-14	Brynas U18	Swe-U18	26	19	7	0	1568	52	3	1.99	5	3	2	310	10	1	1.94
	Brynas IF Gavle Jr.	Swe-Jr.	6	2	4	0	323	18	0	3.34	....	....	....	....	....	....	....
2014-15	Brynas U18	Swe-U18	4	3	1	0	238	10	1	2.52	4	4	0	244	8	0	1.96
	Brynas IF Gavle Jr.	Swe-Jr.	14	10	4	0	822	36	0	2.63	1	0	1	70	3	0	2.57
	Brynas IF Gavle	Sweden	2	1	0	0	55	1	0	1.09	1	0	0	20	1	0	3.00

SAROS, Juuse (SA-ruhs, YOO-seh) NSH

Goaltender. Catches left. 5'10", 178 lbs. Born, Forssa, Finland, April 19, 1995.
(Nashville's 4th choice, 99th overall, in 2013 Entry Draft).

			Regular Season								Playoffs						
Season	**Club**	**League**	**GP**	**W**	**L**	**O/T**	**Mins**	**GA**	**SO**	**Avg**	**GP**	**W**	**L**	**Mins**	**GA**	**SO**	**Avg**
2011-12	HPK U18	Fin-U18	14	11	3	0	844	19	2	1.35	....	....	....	....	....	....	....
	HPK Jr.	Fin-Jr.	31	20	10	0	1804	76	2	2.53	10	6	4	630	22	0	2.10
2012-13	HPK Jr.	Fin-Jr.	37	24	13	0	2220	69	4	1.86	11	9	2	661	23	0	2.09
2013-14	HPK Hameenlinna	Finland	44	17	16	9	2625	77	7	1.76	6	2	4	367	14	0	2.29
2014-15	HPK Hameenlinna	Finland	47	13	18	16	2834	101	6	2.14	....	....	....	....	....	....	....

SATERI, Harri (SA-teh-ree, HAR-ree) S.J.

Goaltender. Catches left. 6'1", 205 lbs. Born, Toijala, Finland, December 29, 1989.
(San Jose's 3rd choice, 106th overall, in 2008 Entry Draft).

			Regular Season								Playoffs						
Season	**Club**	**League**	**GP**	**W**	**L**	**O/T**	**Mins**	**GA**	**SO**	**Avg**	**GP**	**W**	**L**	**Mins**	**GA**	**SO**	**Avg**
2005-06	HPK U18	Fin-U18	27	....	....	....	1515	66	5	2.61	2	....	....	118	10	0	5.08
	HPK Jr.	Fin-Jr.	1	....	....	....	50	3	0	3.60	....	....	....	....	....	....	....
2006-07	Tappara U18	Fin-U18	2	....	....	....	119	4	0	2.02	....	....	....	....	....	....	....
	Tappara Jr.	Fin-Jr.	23	....	....	....	1346	59	2	2.63	10	....	....	614	31	0	3.03
2007-08	Tappara Jr.	Fin-Jr.	34	13	17	0	2048	102	1	2.99	3	0	3	178	8	0	2.70
2008-09	Suomi U20	Finland-2	4	2	2	0	247	12	0	2.91	....	....	....	....	....	....	....
2009-10	Tappara Tampere	Finland	49	21	22	4	2836	129	2	2.73	9	4	5	572	27	0	2.83
2010-11	Tappara Tampere	Finland	37	9	19	8	2147	106	2	2.96	....	....	....	....	....	....	....
	Worcester Sharks	AHL	7	1	3	1	351	15	0	2.56	....	....	....	....	....	....	....
2011-12	Worcester Sharks	AHL	38	15	20	1	2116	101	2	2.86	....	....	....	....	....	....	....
2012-13	Worcester Sharks	AHL	39	14	21	3	2201	106	1	2.89	....	....	....	....	....	....	....
2013-14	Worcester Sharks	AHL	45	18	24	2	2646	130	1	2.95	....	....	....	....	....	....	....
2014-15	Podolsk	KHL	45	17	21	0	2603	128	3	2.95	....	....	....	....	....	....	....

Signed as a free agent by **Podolsk** (KHL), May 19, 2014.

SCHNEIDER, Cory (SHNIGH-duhr, KOHR-ee) N.J.

Goaltender. Catches left. 6'2", 205 lbs. Born, Marblehead, MA, March 18, 1986.
(Vancouver's 1st choice, 26th overall, in 2004 Entry Draft).

			Regular Season								Playoffs						
Season	**Club**	**League**	**GP**	**W**	**L**	**O/T**	**Mins**	**GA**	**SO**	**Avg**	**GP**	**W**	**L**	**Mins**	**GA**	**SO**	**Avg**
2002-03	Andover	High-MA	23	13	7	2	1385	39	3	1.69	....	....	....	....	....	....	....
2003-04	Andover	High-MA	24	17	5	2	1336	32	6	1.42	....	....	....	....	....	....	....
	USNTDP	U-18	10	9	1	0	559	15	1	1.61	....	....	....	....	....	....	....
	USNTDP	NAHL	2	2	0	0	120	6	0	3.00	....	....	....	....	....	....	....
2004-05	Boston College	H-East	18	13	1	4	1102	35	1	1.90	....	....	....	....	....	....	....
2005-06	Boston College	H-East	*39	*24	13	2	*2362	83	*8	2.11	....	....	....	....	....	....	....
2006-07	Boston College	H-East	*42	*29	12	1	*2517	90	6	2.15	....	....	....	....	....	....	....
2007-08	Manitoba Moose	AHL	36	21	12	2	2054	78	3	2.28	6	1	4	375	12	0	1.92
2008-09	**Vancouver**	**NHL**	**8**	**2**	**4**	**1**	**355**	**20**	**0**	**3.38**	....	....	....	....	....	....	....
	Manitoba Moose	AHL	40	28	10	1	2324	79	5	*2.04	*22	14	7	1315	47	0	2.15
2009-10	**Vancouver**	**NHL**	**2**	**0**	**1**	**0**	**79**	**5**	**0**	**3.80**	....	....	....	....	....	....	....
	Manitoba Moose	AHL	60	35	23	2	*3557	149	4	2.51	6	2	4	366	19	0	3.12
2010-11	**Vancouver**	**NHL**	**25**	**16**	**4**	**2**	**1372**	**51**	**1**	**2.23**	**5**	**0**	**0**	**163**	**7**	**0**	**2.58**
2011-12	**Vancouver**	**NHL**	**33**	**20**	**8**	**1**	**1833**	**60**	**3**	**1.96**	**3**	**1**	**2**	**183**	**4**	**0**	**1.31**
2012-13	HC Ambri-Piotta	Swiss	8	4	4	0	485	26	0	3.22	....	....	....	....	....	....	....
	Vancouver	**NHL**	**30**	**17**	**9**	**4**	**1733**	**61**	***5**	**2.11**	**2**	**0**	**2**	**117**	**9**	**0**	**4.62**
2013-14	**New Jersey**	**NHL**	**45**	**16**	**15**	**12**	**2680**	**88**	**3**	**1.97**	....	....	....	....	....	....	....
2014-15	**New Jersey**	**NHL**	**69**	**26**	**31**	**9**	**3924**	**148**	**5**	**2.26**	....	....	....	....	....	....	....
	NHL Totals		**212**	**97**	**72**	**29**	**11976**	**433**	**17**	**2.17**	**10**	**1**	**4**	**463**	**20**	**0**	**2.59**

Hockey East All-Rookie Team (2005) (co-winners - Kevin Regan and Peter Vetri) • Hockey East Second All-Star Team (2006) • NCAA East First All-American Team (2006) • AHL First All-Star Team (2009) • Harry "Hap" Holmes Memorial Award (AHL – fewest goals against) (2009) (shared with Karl Goehring) • Aldege "Baz" Bastien Memorial Award (AHL – Outstanding Goaltender) (2009) • William M. Jennings Trophy (2011) (shared with Roberto Luongo)

Signed as a free agent by **Ambri-Piotta** (Swiss), November 28, 2012. Traded to **New Jersey** by **Vancouver** for New Jersey's 1st round choice (Bo Horvat) in 2013 Entry Draft, June 30, 2013.

SCRIVENS, Ben (SKRIH-vehnz, BEHN) EDM

Goaltender. Catches left. 6'2", 193 lbs. Born, Spruce Grove, AB, September 11, 1986.

			Regular Season								Playoffs						
Season	**Club**	**League**	**GP**	**W**	**L**	**O/T**	**Mins**	**GA**	**SO**	**Avg**	**GP**	**W**	**L**	**Mins**	**GA**	**SO**	**Avg**
2004-05	Drayton Valley	AJHL	1	0	1	0	59	3	0	3.03	....	....	....	....	....	....	....
	Calgary Canucks	AJHL	16	7	3	3	857	43	1	3.01	....	....	....	....	....	....	....
2005-06	Spruce Grove	AJHL	45	27	12	2	2469	100	3	2.43	13	9	4	777	37	*2	2.86
2006-07	Cornell Big Red	ECAC	12	3	6	2	574	22	1	2.30	....	....	....	....	....	....	....
2007-08	Cornell Big Red	ECAC	35	*19	12	3	1965	66	4	*2.02	....	....	....	....	....	....	....
2008-09	Cornell Big Red	ECAC	36	*22	10	4	2153	65	*7	*1.81	....	....	....	....	....	....	....
2009-10	Cornell Big Red	ECAC	34	*21	9	4	*2018	63	*7	*1.87	....	....	....	....	....	....	....
2010-11	Toronto Marlies	AHL	33	13	12	5	1929	75	2	2.33	....	....	....	....	....	....	....
	Reading Royals	ECHL	13	10	3	0	779	29	0	2.23	3	0	1	107	9	0	5.04
2011-12	**Toronto**	**NHL**	**12**	**4**	**5**	**2**	**672**	**35**	**0**	**3.13**	....	....	....	....	....	....	....
	Toronto Marlies	AHL	39	22	15	1	2293	78	4	*2.04	*17	11	6	*1030	33	*3	1.92
2012-13	Toronto Marlies	AHL	22	14	7	1	1325	49	2	2.22	....	....	....	....	....	....	....
	Toronto	**NHL**	**20**	**7**	**9**	**0**	**1025**	**46**	**2**	**2.69**	....	....	....	....	....	....	....
2013-14	**Los Angeles**	**NHL**	**19**	**7**	**5**	**4**	**975**	**32**	**3**	**1.97**	....	....	....	....	....	....	....
	Edmonton	**NHL**	**21**	**9**	**11**	**0**	**1235**	**62**	**1**	**3.01**	....	....	....	....	....	....	....
2014-15	**Edmonton**	**NHL**	**57**	**15**	**26**	**11**	**3228**	**170**	**1**	**3.16**	....	....	....	....	....	....	....
	NHL Totals		**129**	**42**	**56**	**17**	**7135**	**345**	**7**	**2.90**	....	....	....	....	....	....	....

ECAC Second All-Star Team (2009) • ECAC First All-Star Team (2010) • NCAA East First All-American Team (2010) • Harry "Hap" Holmes Memorial Award (AHL – fewest goals against) (2012)

Signed as a free agent by **Toronto**, April 28, 2010. Traded to **Los Angeles** by **Toronto** with Matt Frattin and Toronto's 2nd round choice (later traded to Columbus, later traded back to Toronto – Toronto selected Travis Dermott) 2015 Entry Draft for Jonathan Bernier, June 23, 2013. Traded to **Edmonton** by **Los Angeles** for Edmonton's 3rd round choice (later traded to Columbus, later traded to Detroit – Detroit selected Dominic Turgeon) in 2014 Entry Draft, January 15, 2014.

SHESTERKIN, Igor (shehs-TUHR-kihn, EE-gohr) NYR

Goaltender. Catches left. 6'1", 187 lbs. Born, Moscow, Russia, December 30, 1995.
(NY Rangers' 4th choice, 118th overall, in 2014 Entry Draft).

			Regular Season								Playoffs						
Season	**Club**	**League**	**GP**	**W**	**L**	**O/T**	**Mins**	**GA**	**SO**	**Avg**	**GP**	**W**	**L**	**Mins**	**GA**	**SO**	**Avg**
2012-13	Spartak Jr.	Russia-Jr.	15	9	1	4	886	31	2	2.10	9	6	3	529	14	3	1.59
2013-14	Spartak Jr.	Russia-Jr.	23	14	5	4	1399	33	5	1.42	19	12	7	1134	33	4	1.75
	Spartak Moscow	KHL	9	1	5	0	428	20	1	2.80	....	....	....	....	....	....	....
2014-15	SKA St. Petersburg	KHL	6	3	0	0	231	9	0	2.33	....	....	....	....	....	....	....
	SKA-Kareliya	Russia-2	8	3	3	0	488	14	1	1.72	....	....	....	....	....	....	....
	St. Petersburg Jr.	Russia-Jr.	3	2	0	0	159	6	0	2.26	13	7	4	778	32	1	2.47

SIMPSON, Kent (SIHMP-suhn, KEHNT)

Goaltender. Catches left. 6'2", 198 lbs. Born, Edmonton, AB, March 26, 1992.
(Chicago's 4th choice, 58th overall, in 2010 Entry Draft).

			Regular Season								Playoffs						
Season	**Club**	**League**	**GP**	**W**	**L**	**O/T**	**Mins**	**GA**	**SO**	**Avg**	**GP**	**W**	**L**	**Mins**	**GA**	**SO**	**Avg**
2007-08	AMC Bulldogs	Minor-AB	....	4	10	6	1126	93	....	4.96	....	....	....	....	....	....	....
	Everett Silvertips	WHL	1	0	0	0	29	1	0	2.07	....	....	....	....	....	....	....
2008-09	Everett Silvertips	WHL	27	8	11	4	1451	93	1	3.85	....	....	....	....	....	....	....
2009-10	Everett Silvertips	WHL	34	22	9	1	1938	73	1	2.26	5	2	3	298	13	1	2.62
2010-11	Everett Silvertips	WHL	53	21	20	9	3132	145	2	2.78	....	....	....	....	....	....	....
2011-12	Everett Silvertips	WHL	60	20	31	7	3481	193	2	3.33	4	0	4	225	15	0	4.00
	Rockford IceHogs	AHL	1	0	0	1	63	3	0	2.85	....	....	....	....	....	....	....
2012-13	Toledo Walleye	ECHL	41	20	14	5	2387	94	2	2.36	3	0	3	193	11	0	3.42
	Rockford IceHogs	AHL	2	1	1	0	98	5	0	3.07	....	....	....	....	....	....	....
2013-14	**Chicago**	**NHL**	**1**	**0**	**0**	**0**	**20**	**2**	**0**	**6.00**	....	....	....	....	....	....	....
	Rockford IceHogs	AHL	31	11	14	1	1615	98	0	3.64	....	....	....	....	....	....	....
2014-15	Colorado Eagles	ECHL	3	1	2	0	178	11	0	3.71	....	....	....	....	....	....	....
	Bridgeport	AHL	4	1	3	0	207	9	0	2.61	....	....	....	....	....	....	....
	Stockton Thunder	ECHL	26	7	17	1	1468	82	0	3.35	....	....	....	....	....	....	....
	NHL Totals		**1**	**0**	**0**	**0**	**20**	**2**	**0**	**6.00**	....	....	....	....	....	....	....

Traded to **NY Islanders** by **Chicago** with Nick Leddy for T.J. Brennan, Ville Pokka and Anders Nilsson, October 4, 2014. • Re-assigned to **Colorado** (ECHL) by **NY Islanders**, October 11, 2014.

SKAPSKI, Mackenzie (SKAP-skee, muh-KEHN-zee) NYR

Goaltender. Catches left. 6'3", 191 lbs. Born, Abbotsford, BC, June 15, 1994.
(NY Rangers' 5th choice, 170th overall, in 2013 Entry Draft).

			Regular Season								Playoffs						
Season	**Club**	**League**	**GP**	**W**	**L**	**O/T**	**Mins**	**GA**	**SO**	**Avg**	**GP**	**W**	**L**	**Mins**	**GA**	**SO**	**Avg**
2009-10	Fraser Valley Bruins	BCMML	STATISTICS NOT AVAILABLE														
2010-11	Ridge Meadow	PIJHL	21	6	11	0	987	75	1	4.56	6	3	3	360	17	0	2.83
	Kootenay Ice	WHL	4	3	1	0	247	13	0	3.16	....	....	....	....	....	....	....
2011-12	Kootenay Ice	WHL	19	9	6	2	1020	53	0	3.12	....	....	....	....	....	....	....
2012-13	Kootenay Ice	WHL	65	34	25	1	3642	169	7	2.78	5	1	4	258	17	0	3.95
2013-14	Kootenay Ice	WHL	53	28	20	4	3018	136	1	2.70	10	3	5	540	34	0	3.78
2014-15	**NY Rangers**	**NHL**	**2**	**2**	**0**	**0**	**119**	**1**	**1**	**0.50**	....	....	....	....	....	....	....
	Hartford Wolf Pack	AHL	28	15	8	3	1522	61	3	2.40	2	0	1	77	7	0	5.43
	Greenville	ECHL	1	0	1	0	57	3	0	3.17	....	....	....	....	....	....	....
	NHL Totals		**2**	**2**	**0**	**0**	**119**	**1**	**1**	**0.50**	....	....	....	....	....	....	....

SMITH, Evan (SMIHTH, EH-vuhn) NSH

Goaltender. Catches left. 6'6", 174 lbs. Born, Parker, CO, February 27, 1997.
(Nashville's 7th choice, 205th overall, in 2015 Entry Draft).

			Regular Season								Playoffs						
Season	**Club**	**League**	**GP**	**W**	**L**	**O/T**	**Mins**	**GA**	**SO**	**Avg**	**GP**	**W**	**L**	**Mins**	**GA**	**SO**	**Avg**
2012-13	Pikes Peak U16	NAPHL	14	7	8	1	743	44	1	3.02	....	....	....	....	....	....	....
2013-14	Pikes Peak U18	NAPHL	13	7	4	1	655	25	1	1.95	....	....	....	....	....	....	....
2014-15	Victoria Royals	WHL	4	1	1	0	157	11	0	4.20	....	....	....	....	....	....	....
	Austin Bruins	NAHL	15	12	1	1	865	25	1	1.73	....	....	....	....	....	....	....

SMITH, Jeremy (SMIHTH, JAIR-eh-mee) BOS

Goaltender. Catches left. 6', 176 lbs. Born, Dearborn, MI, April 13, 1989.
(Nashville's 2nd choice, 54th overall, in 2007 Entry Draft).

			Regular Season								Playoffs						
Season	Club	League	GP	W	L	O/T	Mins	GA	SO	Avg	GP	W	L	Mins	GA	SO	Avg
2005-06	Det. Compuware	MWEHL	13	5	6	0	696	31	0	2.67	....	....	....	....	....	....	....
	Det. Compuware	Other	3	2	1	0	178	8	0	2.70	....	....	....	....	....	....	....
	Plymouth Whalers	OHL	5	0	2	0	111	11	0	5.95	....	....	....	....	....	....	....
2006-07	Plymouth Whalers	OHL	34	23	6	1	1901	82	4	2.59	3	2	0	149	8	0	3.22
2007-08	Plymouth Whalers	OHL	40	23	13	4	2431	116	3	2.86	4	0	4	224	29	0	7.77
2008-09	Plymouth Whalers	OHL	17	3	9	2	901	72	0	4.80	....	....	....	....	....	....	....
	Niagara Ice Dogs	OHL	26	12	9	3	1488	79	1	3.19	12	5	7	724	45	*1	3.73
2009-10	Milwaukee	AHL	1	0	0	0	5	0	0	0.00	....	....	....	....	....	....	....
	Cincinnati	ECHL	42	23	15	2	2468	108	2	2.63	*17	9	8	*988	44	1	2.67
2010-11	Milwaukee	AHL	28	16	8	2	1513	57	2	2.26	13	7	6	843	32	0	2.28
	Cincinnati	ECHL	1	0	0	1	65	3	0	2.78	....	....	....	....	....	....	....
2011-12	Milwaukee	AHL	*56	31	19	2	*3284	119	5	2.17	3	0	3	177	11	0	3.73
2012-13	Milwaukee	AHL	43	19	19	3	2471	114	1	2.77	....	....	....	....	....	....	....
2013-14	Springfield Falcons	AHL	38	21	14	3	2179	101	1	2.78	....	....	....	....	....	....	....
2014-15	Providence Bruins	AHL	39	22	11	5	2278	78	3	2.05	3	1	2	183	6	0	1.96

ECHL Playoff MVP (2010) (co-winner - Robert Mayer)

Signed as a free agent by **Columbus**, July 5, 2013. Signed as a free agent by **Boston**, July 2, 2014.

SMITH, Mike (SMIHTH, MIGHK) ARI

Goaltender. Catches left. 6'4", 215 lbs. Born, Kingston, ON, March 22, 1982.
(Dallas' 5th choice, 161st overall, in 2001 Entry Draft).

			Regular Season								Playoffs						
Season	Club	League	GP	W	L	O/T	Mins	GA	SO	Avg	GP	W	L	Mins	GA	SO	Avg
1998-99	Kingston	ON-Jr.A	16	....	....	....	906	53	0	3.51	....	....	....	....	....	....	....
99-2000	Kingston	OHL	15	4	5	0	666	42	0	3.78	....	....	....	....	....	....	....
2000-01	Kingston	OHL	3	0	0	2	136	8	0	3.53	....	....	....	....	....	....	....
	Sudbury Wolves	OHL	43	22	13	7	2571	108	3	2.52	12	7	5	735	26	2	*2.12
2001-02	Sudbury Wolves	OHL	53	19	28	5	3082	157	3	3.06	5	1	4	302	15	0	2.98
2002-03	Utah Grizzlies	AHL	11	5	5	0	614	33	0	3.23	....	....	....	....	....	....	....
	Lexington	ECHL	27	11	10	4	1553	66	1	2.55	2	0	1	93	8	0	5.14
2003-04	Utah Grizzlies	AHL	21	8	11	0	1186	56	2	2.83	....	....	....	....	....	....	....
2004-05	Houston Aeros	AHL	45	19	17	3	2408	97	5	2.42	3	1	2	181	4	0	1.33
2005-06	Iowa Stars	AHL	50	25	19	6	2998	125	3	2.50	7	3	4	417	19	0	2.74
2006-07	**Dallas**	**NHL**	**23**	**12**	**5**	**2**	**1213**	**45**	**3**	**2.23**	....	....	....	....	....	....	....
2007-08	**Dallas**	**NHL**	**21**	**12**	**9**	**0**	**1172**	**48**	**2**	**2.46**	....	....	....	....	....	....	....
	Tampa Bay	**NHL**	**13**	**3**	**10**	**0**	**774**	**36**	**1**	**2.79**	....	....	....	....	....	....	....
2008-09	**Tampa Bay**	**NHL**	**41**	**14**	**18**	**9**	**2471**	**108**	**2**	**2.62**	....	....	....	....	....	....	....
2009-10	**Tampa Bay**	**NHL**	**42**	**13**	**18**	**7**	**2273**	**117**	**2**	**3.09**	....	....	....	....	....	....	....
2010-11	**Tampa Bay**	**NHL**	**22**	**13**	**6**	**1**	**1202**	**58**	**1**	**2.90**	**3**	**1**	**1**	**120**	**2**	**0**	**1.00**
	Norfolk Admirals	AHL	5	1	4	0	296	9	1	1.83	....	....	....	....	....	....	....
2011-12	**Phoenix**	**NHL**	**67**	**38**	**18**	**10**	**3903**	**144**	**8**	**2.21**	**16**	**9**	**7**	**1027**	**34**	***3**	**1.99**
2012-13	**Phoenix**	**NHL**	**34**	**15**	**12**	**5**	**1956**	**84**	***5**	**2.58**	....	....	....	....	....	....	....
2013-14	**Phoenix**	**NHL**	**62**	**27**	**21**	**10**	**3610**	**159**	**3**	**2.64**	....	....	....	....	....	....	....
	Canada	Olympics				DID NOT PLAY – SPARE GOALTENDER											
2014-15	**Arizona**	**NHL**	**62**	**14**	**42**	**5**	**3556**	**187**	**0**	**3.16**	....	....	....	....	....	....	....
	NHL Totals		**387**	**161**	**159**	**49**	**22130**	**986**	**27**	**2.67**	**19**	**10**	**8**	**1147**	**36**	**3**	**1.88**

NHL All-Rookie Team (2007)

Traded to **Tampa Bay** by **Dallas** with Jussi Jokinen, Jeff Halpern and Dallas' 4th round choice (later traded to Minnesota, later traded to Edmonton – Edmonton selected Kyle Bigos) in 2009 Entry Draft for Brad Richards and Johan Holmqvist, February 26, 2008. Signed as a free agent by **Phoenix**, July 1, 2011.

SODERSTROM, Linus (SOH-duhr-strohm, LEE-nuhs) NYI

Goaltender. Catches left. 6'5", 196 lbs. Born, Stockholm, Sweden, August 23, 1996.
(NY Islanders' 4th choice, 95th overall, in 2014 Entry Draft).

			Regular Season								Playoffs						
Season	Club	League	GP	W	L	O/T	Mins	GA	SO	Avg	GP	W	L	Mins	GA	SO	Avg
2011-12	Djurgarden U18	Swe-U18	3	....	....	....	180	4	0	1.33	....	....	....	....	....	....	....
2012-13	Djurgarden U18	Swe-U18	18	13	5	0	1013	30	5	1.77	9	6	3	556	22	0	2.37
2013-14	Djurgarden Jr.	Swe-Jr.	23	12	11	0	1356	59	0	2.61	1	0	1	60	4	0	4.00
	Djurgarden U18	Swe-U18	....	....	....	....	....	....	....	....	1	0	1	59	3	0	3.03
2014-15	Almtuna	Sweden-2	5	1	4	0	253	11	0	2.61	....	....	....	....	....	....	....
	Sodertalje SK	Sweden-2	4	1	3	0	194	8	0	2.48	....	....	....	....	....	....	....
	Djurgarden Jr.	Swe-Jr.	14	10	4	0	850	41	0	2.89	....	....	....	....	....	....	....

SOROKIN, Ilya (saw-ROH-kihn, IHL-yah) NYI

Goaltender. Catches left. 6'2", 167 lbs. Born, Mezhdurechensk, Russia, August 4, 1995.
(NY Islanders' 3rd choice, 78th overall, in 2014 Entry Draft).

			Regular Season								Playoffs						
Season	Club	League	GP	W	L	O/T	Mins	GA	SO	Avg	GP	W	L	Mins	GA	SO	Avg
2012-13	Novokuznetsk Jr.	Russia-Jr.	27	11	8	3	1423	61	1	2.57	3	0	2	159	9	0	3.40
	Novokuznetsk	KHL	5	1	1	0	151	7	0	2.77	3	1	2	198	10	0	3.03
2013-14	Novokuznetsk Jr.	Russia-Jr.	4	2	1	1	245	11	0	2.69	2	0	2	104	7	0	4.04
	Novokuznetsk	KHL	27	5	12	0	1346	65	0	2.90	1	0	1	60	2	0	2.00
2014-15	Novokuznetsk	KHL	22	4	11	0	978	53	1	3.25	....	....	....	....	....	....	....
	CSKA Moscow	KHL	6	3	2	0	275	6	0	1.31	....	....	....	....	....	....	....
	CSKA Jr.	Russia-Jr.	3	1	1	0	184	4	1	1.31	7	2	4	363	13	1	2.15

SPARKS, Garret (SPARKS, GAIR-eht) TOR

Goaltender. Catches left. 6'2", 200 lbs. Born, Elmhurst, IL, June 28, 1993.
(Toronto's 8th choice, 190th overall, in 2011 Entry Draft).

			Regular Season								Playoffs						
Season	Club	League	GP	W	L	O/T	Mins	GA	SO	Avg	GP	W	L	Mins	GA	SO	Avg
2008-09	Team Illinois	T1EHL	18	9	6	2	854	51	0	3.05	....	....	....	....	....	....	....
2009-10	Chicago Mission	T1EHL	27	19	7	2	1392	51	3	1.98	....	....	....	....	....	....	....
2010-11	Guelph Storm	OHL	19	8	6	1	972	59	0	3.64	....	....	....	....	....	....	....
2011-12	Guelph Storm	OHL	59	27	25	4	3304	171	5	3.11	6	2	4	323	24	0	4.45
2012-13	Guelph Storm	OHL	*60	*36	17	4	*3440	152	*7	2.65	5	1	4	275	14	0	3.05
	Toronto Marlies	AHL	3	2	0	1	189	8	0	2.53	1	0	0	14	1	0	4.23
2013-14	Toronto Marlies	AHL	21	11	6	1	1094	48	0	2.63	....	....	....	....	....	....	....
	Orlando	ECHL	10	4	6	0	552	26	1	2.82	....	....	....	....	....	....	....
2014-15	Toronto Marlies	AHL	2	1	0	0	120	2	1	1.00	....	....	....	....	....	....	....
	Orlando	ECHL	36	21	7	3	1946	76	5	2.34	6	2	4	342	17	0	2.98

STALOCK, Alex (STAY-lahk, AL-ehx) S.J.

Goaltender. Catches left. 6', 190 lbs. Born, St. Paul, MN, July 28, 1987.
(San Jose's 3rd choice, 112th overall, in 2005 Entry Draft).

			Regular Season								Playoffs						
Season	Club	League	GP	W	L	O/T	Mins	GA	SO	Avg	GP	W	L	Mins	GA	SO	Avg
2003-04	South St. Paul	High-MN	31	23	7	1	....	....	....	2.20	....	....	....	....	....	....	....
2004-05	Cedar Rapids	USHL	32	19	9	3	1801	82	1	2.73	9	7	2	582	14	*1	*1.44
2005-06	Cedar Rapids	USHL	44	*28	13	3	2641	112	4	2.54	8	3	5	472	25	0	3.18
2006-07	U. Minn-Duluth	WCHA	23	5	14	3	1364	76	1	3.34	....	....	....	....	....	....	....
2007-08	U. Minn-Duluth	WCHA	36	13	17	6	2170	85	3	2.35	....	....	....	....	....	....	....
2008-09	U. Minn-Duluth	WCHA	*42	21	13	8	*2534	90	*5	*2.13	....	....	....	....	....	....	....
2009-10	Worcester Sharks	AHL	*61	*39	19	2	3534	155	4	2.63	11	6	5	683	26	0	2.28
2010-11	**San Jose**	**NHL**	**1**	**1**	**0**	**0**	**30**	**0**	**0**	**0.00**	....	....	....	....	....	....	....
	Worcester Sharks	AHL	41	19	17	4	2397	105	0	2.63	....	....	....	....	....	....	....
2011-12	Stockton Thunder	ECHL	6	5	1	0	360	17	0	2.83	....	....	....	....	....	....	....
	Worcester Sharks	AHL	2	1	1	0	119	5	0	2.51	....	....	....	....	....	....	....
	Peoria Rivermen	AHL	3	2	0	0	106	2	1	1.13	....	....	....	....	....	....	....
2012-13	Worcester Sharks	AHL	38	17	16	4	2281	99	2	2.60	....	....	....	....	....	....	....
	San Jose	**NHL**	**2**	**0**	**0**	**1**	**42**	**2**	**0**	**2.86**	....	....	....	....	....	....	....
2013-14	**San Jose**	**NHL**	**24**	**12**	**5**	**2**	**1252**	**39**	**2**	**1.87**	**3**	**0**	**1**	**117**	**4**	**0**	**2.05**
2014-15	**San Jose**	**NHL**	**22**	**8**	**9**	**2**	**1237**	**54**	**2**	**2.62**	....	....	....	....	....	....	....
	NHL Totals		**49**	**21**	**14**	**5**	**2561**	**95**	**4**	**2.23**	**3**	**0**	**1**	**117**	**4**	**0**	**2.05**

USHL Playoff MVP (2005) • USHL First All-Star Team (2006) • USHL Goaltender of the Year (2006) • WCHA All-Rookie Team (2007) • WCHA First All-Star Team (2009) • NCAA West First All-American Team (2009) • AHL All-Rookie Team (2010)

• Missed remainder of 2010-11 and majority of 2011-12 due to leg injury vs. Manchester (AHL), February 4, 2011.

STEVENS, Colin (STEE-vehns, KAW-lihn) FLA

Goaltender. Catches left. 6'2", 180 lbs. Born, Niskayuna, NY, June 30, 1993.

			Regular Season								Playoffs						
Season	Club	League	GP	W	L	O/T	Mins	GA	SO	Avg	GP	W	L	Mins	GA	SO	Avg
2009-10	Boston Jr. Bruins	EmJHL	26	23	1	2	....	....	6	1.66	6	4	2	....	....	....	2.66
	USNTDP	USHL	1	0	0	0	40	2	0	3.00	....	....	....	....	....	....	....
	USNTDP	U-18	1	0	1	0	59	7	0	7.19	....	....	....	....	....	....	....
2010-11	Boston Jr. Bruins	EJHL	29	24	3	0	....	....	5	2.41	2	1	1	....	....	....	2.75
2011-12	Union College	ECAC	11	4	2	4	561	21	0	2.25	....	....	....	....	....	....	....
2012-13	Union College	ECAC	12	5	3	0	480	13	3	1.62	....	....	....	....	....	....	....
2013-14	Union College	ECAC	36	28	4	2	2080	71	6	2.05	....	....	....	....	....	....	....
2014-15	Union College	ECAC	31	16	15	0	1742	67	2	2.31	....	....	....	....	....	....	....

Signed as a free agent by **Florida**, March 20, 2015.

STEZKA, Ales (STEHZH-kuh, ah-LEHSH) MIN

Goaltender. Catches left. 6'4", 201 lbs. Born, Liberec, Czech Rep., January 6, 1997.
(Minnesota's 3rd choice, 111th overall, in 2015 Entry Draft).

			Regular Season								Playoffs						
Season	Club	League	GP	W	L	O/T	Mins	GA	SO	Avg	GP	W	L	Mins	GA	SO	Avg
2012-13	HC Liberec U18	CzR-U18	25	....	....	....	1257	65	0	3.10	3	....	....	126	4	0	1.90
	HC Liberec Jr.	CzRep-Jr.	1	....	....	....	60	7	0	7.00	....	....	....	....	....	....	....
2013-14	HC Liberec U18	CzR-U18	24	....	....	....	1347	38	8	1.69	5	....	....	300	9	0	1.80
	HC Liberec Jr.	CzRep-Jr.	2	....	....	....	89	1	0	0.67	....	....	....	....	....	....	....
2014-15	HC Liberec U18	CzR-U18	7	....	....	....	420	10	2	1.42	3	....	....	189	2	2	0.63
	HC Liberec Jr.	CzRep-Jr.	40	....	....	....	2425	112	3	2.77	6	....	....	364	12	0	1.98

STOLARZ, Anthony (STOHL-ahrz, AN-thuh-nee) PHI

Goaltender. Catches left. 6'6", 232 lbs. Born, Edison, NJ, January 20, 1994.
(Philadelphia's 2nd choice, 45th overall, in 2012 Entry Draft).

			Regular Season								Playoffs						
Season	Club	League	GP	W	L	O/T	Mins	GA	SO	Avg	GP	W	L	Mins	GA	SO	Avg
2010-11	Jersey Hitmen	EmJHL	....	12	4	0	884	47	0	3.19	3	1	2	153	8	0	3.13
2011-12	Corpus Christi	NAHL	50	23	22	4	2939	139	3	2.84	....	....	....	....	....	....	....
2012-13	Nebraska-Omaha	WCHA	8	2	5	0	421	18	1	2.56	....	....	....	....	....	....	....
2013-14	London Knights	OHL	35	25	5	2	1927	81	4	2.52	....	....	....	....	....	....	....
2014-15	Lehigh Valley	AHL	31	9	13	4	1592	87	2	3.28	....	....	....	....	....	....	....

SUBBAN, Malcolm (soo-BAN, MAL-kuhm) BOS

Goaltender. Catches left. 6'2", 200 lbs. Born, Toronto, ON, December 21, 1993.
(Boston's 1st choice, 24th overall, in 2012 Entry Draft).

			Regular Season								Playoffs						
Season	Club	League	GP	W	L	O/T	Mins	GA	SO	Avg	GP	W	L	Mins	GA	SO	Avg
2009-10	Mississauga Reps	GTHL	14	....	....	....	....	....	....	1.86	7	....	....	....	....	....	2.00
	Tor. Canadiens	ON-Jr.A	2	0	1	0	71	4	0	3.39	....	....	....	....	....	....	....
	Belleville Bulls	OHL	1	0	0	0	13	0	0	0.00	....	....	....	....	....	....	....
2010-11	Belleville Bulls	OHL	32	10	17	2	1785	94	0	3.16	3	0	3	178	6	0	2.02
2011-12	Belleville Bulls	OHL	39	25	14	0	2258	94	3	2.50	6	2	4	369	18	0	2.93
2012-13	Belleville Bulls	OHL	46	29	11	4	2695	96	5	*2.14	17	11	6	1021	34	*3	*2.00
2013-14	Providence Bruins	AHL	33	15	10	5	1920	74	1	2.31	6	2	2	244	12	0	2.96
2014-15	**Boston**	**NHL**	**1**	**0**	**1**	**0**	**31**	**3**	**0**	**5.81**	....	....	....	....	....	....	....
	Providence Bruins	AHL	35	16	13	4	2017	82	3	2.44	2	1	1	160	3	0	1.12
	NHL Totals		**1**	**0**	**1**	**0**	**31**	**3**	**0**	**5.81**	....	....	....	....	....	....	....

OHL All-Rookie Team (2011)

SVEDBERG, Niklas (SVEHD-buhrg, NIHK-luhs) BOS

Goaltender. Catches left. 6', 176 lbs. Born, Sollentuna, Sweden, September 4, 1989.

			Regular Season								Playoffs						
Season	Club	League	GP	W	L	O/T	Mins	GA	SO	Avg	GP	W	L	Mins	GA	SO	Avg
2007-08	MODO	Sweden	1	0	0	0	8	7.11	....	....	....	....	....	....	....	....	....
2008-09	Huddinge IK	Sweden-2	24	....	....	....	....	....	....	....	....	....	....	....	....	....	....
	MODO	Sweden	3	....	....	....	178	16	0	5.41	....	....	....	....	....	....	....
2009-10	MODO	Sweden	21	....	....	....	1261	82	1	2.59	....	....	....	....	....	....	....
2010-11	Brynas IF Gavle	Sweden	21	....	....	....	1261	48	2	2.28	....	....	....	....	....	....	....
2011-12	Brynas IF Gavle	Sweden	29	....	....	....	1726	71	0	2.47	13	....	....	814	23	4	1.70
2012-13	Providence Bruins	AHL	48	37	8	2	2873	104	4	2.17	12	6	6	675	37	0	3.29
2013-14	**Boston**	**NHL**	**1**	**1**	**0**	**0**	**61**	**2**	**0**	**1.97**	....	....	....	....	....	....	....
	Providence Bruins	AHL	45	25	15	4	2602	114	2	2.63	9	4	4	510	23	1	2.70
2014-15	**Boston**	**NHL**	**18**	**7**	**5**	**1**	**900**	**35**	**2**	**2.33**	....	....	....	....	....	....	....
	Providence Bruins	AHL	4	3	1	0	239	11	0	2.76	....	....	....	....	....	....	....
	NHL Totals		**19**	**8**	**5**	**1**	**961**	**37**	**2**	**2.31**	....	....	....	....	....	....	....

AHL All-Rookie Team (2013) • AHL First All-Star Team (2013) • Aldege "Baz" Bastien Memorial Award (AHL – Outstanding Goaltender) (2013)

Signed as a free agent by **Boston**, May 29, 2012. Signed as a free agent by **Ufa** (KHL), May 10, 2015.

SVOBODA, Miroslav (svoh-BOH-duh, MEER-oh-slav) EDM

Goaltender. Catches left. 6'3", 176 lbs. Born, Vsetin, Czech Rep., March 7, 1995.
(Edmonton's 5th choice, 208th overall, in 2015 Entry Draft).

			Regular Season								Playoffs						
Season	Club	League	GP	W	L	O/T	Mins	GA	SO	Avg	GP	W	L	Mins	GA	SO	Avg
2009-10	HC Vsetin U18	CzR-U18	1	....	....	....	59	1	0	1.02	....	....	....	....	....	....	....
2010-11	HC Vsetin U18	CzR-U18	4	....	....	....	245	9	0	2.20	1	....	....	34	0	0	0.00
2011-12	HC Vsetin U18	CzR-U18	31	....	....	....	1647	84	2	3.06	5	....	....	287	21	0	4.39
2012-13	HC Trinec U18	CzR-U18	28	....	....	....	1621	67	2	2.48	9	....	....	573	20	1	2.09
	HC Trinec Jr.	CzRep-Jr.	4	....	....	....	218	11	0	3.03	....	....	....	....	....	....	....
2013-14	HC Trinec Jr.	CzRep-Jr.	37	....	....	....	2161	79	3	2.19	5	....	....	312	14	0	2.69
	HC Frydek-Mistek	CzRep-3	1	....	....	....	60	1	0	1.00	....	....	....	....	....	....	....
2014-15	HC Trinec Jr.	CzRep-Jr.	33	....	....	....	1986	90	3	2.72	....	....	....	....	....	....	....
	Havirov	CzRep-2	6	....	....	....	340	18	0	3.18	....	....	....	....	....	....	....
	Salith Sumperk	CzRep-2	11	....	....	....	628	38	0	3.63	....	....	....	....	....	....	....
	HC Ocelari Trinec	CzRep	1	....	....	....	60	6	0	6.00	1	....	....	2	0	0	0.00

TALBOT, Cam (TAL-buht, KAM) EDM

Goaltender. Catches left. 6'3", 205 lbs. Born, Caledonia, ON, June 5, 1987.

			Regular Season								Playoffs						
Season	Club	League	GP	W	L	O/T	Mins	GA	SO	Avg	GP	W	L	Mins	GA	SO	Avg
2005-06	Hamilton	ON-Jr.A	35	21	13	1	2046	87	1	2.55	14	8	6	903	52	1	3.46
2006-07	Hamilton	ON-Jr.A	28	19	5	2	1644	57	1	2.08	19	13	6	1243	51	0	2.46
2007-08	AL-Huntsville	CHA	13	1	10	0	583	45	0	4.63	....	....	....	....	....	....	....
2008-09	AL-Huntsville	CHA	24	2	16	3	1320	65	1	2.95	....	....	....	....	....	....	....
2009-10	AL-Huntsville	CHA	*33	12	18	3	*1958	85	1	2.61	....	....	....	....	....	....	....
	Hartford Wolf Pack	AHL	1	0	0	0	19	3	0	9.70	....	....	....	....	....	....	....
2010-11	Connecticut Whale	AHL	22	11	9	2	1308	62	2	2.84	1	0	1	38	2	0	3.13
	Greenville	ECHL	2	1	0	1	122	5	0	2.46	....	....	....	....	....	....	....
2011-12	Connecticut Whale	AHL	33	14	15	1	1865	81	4	2.61	9	5	4	571	20	2	2.10
2012-13	Connecticut Whale	AHL	55	25	28	1	3105	136	2	2.63	....	....	....	....	....	....	....
2013-14	**NY Rangers**	**NHL**	**21**	**12**	**6**	**1**	**1211**	**33**	**3**	**1.64**	**2**	**0**	**1**	**46**	**2**	**0**	**2.61**
	Hartford Wolf Pack	AHL	5	4	0	1	314	13	0	2.49	....	....	....	....	....	....	....
2014-15	**NY Rangers**	**NHL**	**36**	**21**	**9**	**4**	**2095**	**77**	**5**	**2.21**	....	....	....	....	....	....	....
	NHL Totals		**57**	**33**	**15**	**5**	**3306**	**110**	**8**	**2.00**	**2**	**0**	**1**	**46**	**2**	**0**	**2.61**

Signed as a free agent by **NY Rangers**, March 30, 2010. Traded to **Edmonton** by **NY Rangers** with NY Rangers' 7th round choice (Ziyat Paigin) in 2015 Entry Draft for Montreal's 2nd round choice (previously acquired, later traded to Washington – Washington selected Jonas Siegenthaler) in 2015 Entry Draft, Ottawa's 3rd round choice (previously acquired, NY Rangers selected Sergey Zborovskiy) in 2015 Entry Draft and Edmonton's 7th round choice (Adam Huska) in 2015 Entry Draft, June 27, 2015.

THIESSEN, Brad (THEE-suhn, BRAD)

Goaltender. Catches left. 6', 180 lbs. Born, Aldergrove, BC, March 19, 1986.

			Regular Season								Playoffs						
Season	Club	League	GP	W	L	O/T	Mins	GA	SO	Avg	GP	W	L	Mins	GA	SO	Avg
2003-04	Penticton Panthers	BCHL	42	13	17	1	2131	122	2	3.44	....	....	....	....	....	....	....
2004-05	Penticton Vees	BCHL	26	7	18	1	1492	86	1	3.46	....	....	....	....	....	....	....
	Prince George	BCHL	10	5	4	0	561	31	0	3.31	3	1	1	158	9	0	3.42
2005-06	Prince George	BCHL	36	14	17	4	2058	99	5	2.89	....	....	....	....	....	....	....
	Merritt	BCHL	13	8	4	0	754	36	2	2.87	6	3	3	261	16	1	3.68
2006-07	Northeastern	H-East	33	11	17	5	1985	82	4	2.48	....	....	....	....	....	....	....
2007-08	Northeastern	H-East	37	16	17	3	2180	96	2	2.64	....	....	....	....	....	....	....
2008-09	Northeastern	H-East	*41	25	12	4	*2496	88	*3	2.12	....	....	....	....	....	....	....
2009-10	Wilkes-Barre	AHL	30	14	14	1	1763	72	4	2.45	....	....	....	....	....	....	....
	Wheeling Nailers	ECHL	12	8	3	0	674	30	1	2.67	....	....	....	....	....	....	....
2010-11	Wilkes-Barre	AHL	46	*35	8	1	2567	83	7	1.94	12	6	6	720	20	2	*1.67
2011-12	**Pittsburgh**	**NHL**	**5**	**3**	**1**	**0**	**258**	**16**	**0**	**3.72**	....	....	....	....	....	....	....
	Wilkes-Barre	AHL	41	23	15	2	2321	109	2	2.82	12	6	6	756	27	0	2.14
2012-13	Wilkes-Barre	AHL	32	16	12	2	1793	80	4	2.68	12	6	4	654	15	2	*1.38
2013-14	HIFK Helsinki	Finland	8	2	5	1	353	18	1	3.06	....	....	....	....	....	....	....
	Norfolk Admirals	AHL	18	8	6	2	984	37	1	2.26	4	1	3	252	16	0	3.81
2014-15	Adirondack Flames	AHL	34	10	16	7	1908	99	2	3.11	....	....	....	....	....	....	....
	NHL Totals		**5**	**3**	**1**	**0**	**258**	**16**	**0**	**3.72**	....	....	....	....	....	....	....

Hockey East First All-Star Team (2009) • Hockey East Player of the Year (2009) • NCAA East First All-American Team (2009) • AHL First All-Star Team (2011) • Harry "Hap" Holmes Memorial Award (AHL – fewest goals against) (2011) (shared with John Curry) • Aldege "Baz" Bastien Award (AHL – Outstanding Goaltender) (2011) • Harry "Hap" Holmes Memorial Award (AHL – fewest goals against) (2013) (shared with Jeff Zatkoff)

Signed as a free agent by **Pittsburgh**, April 8, 2009. Signed as a free agent by **HIFK Helsinki** (Finland), July 15, 2013. Signed as a free agent by **Norfolk** (AHL), November 28, 2013. Signed as a free agent by **Calgary**, July 3, 2014.

TIRRONEN, Rasmus (tih-ROH-nehn, RAS-muhs) CAR

Goaltender. Catches left. 6'3", 209 lbs. Born, Espoo, Finland, November 9, 1990.

			Regular Season								Playoffs						
Season	Club	League	GP	W	L	O/T	Mins	GA	SO	Avg	GP	W	L	Mins	GA	SO	Avg
2006-07	Blues Espoo U18	Fin-U18	12	....	....	....	....	....	....	3.53	2	....	....	....	....	....	4.67
2007-08	HIFK Helsinki U18	Fin-U18	9	2	4	0	455	31	0	4.09	2	0	1	49	2	0	2.47
2008-09	Blues Espoo Jr.	Fin-Jr.	18	13	5	0	1081	42	0	2.33	1	0	1	60	4	0	4.02
2009-10	Blues Espoo Jr.	Fin-Jr.	2	0	1	0	80	6	0	4.50	....	....	....	....	....	....	....
2010-11	Topeka	NAHL	36	24	9	0	1963	79	4	2.41	10	5	4	585	28	0	2.87
2011-12	Merrimack College	H-East	DID NOT PLAY – FRESHMAN														
2012-13	Merrimack College	H-East	12	3	6	2	702	31	0	2.65	....	....	....	....	....	....	....
2013-14	Merrimack College	H-East	25	7	14	3	1390	59	1	2.55	....	....	....	....	....	....	....
2014-15	Merrimack College	H-East	31	12	14	3	1801	69	2	2.30	....	....	....	....	....	....	....
	Charlotte Checkers	AHL	1	1	0	0	60	3	0	3.00	....	....	....	....	....	....	....

Signed as a free agent by **Carolina**, March 22, 2015.

TOKARSKI, Dustin (toh-KAHR-skee, DUHS-tihn) MTL

Goaltender. Catches left. 6', 204 lbs. Born, Watson, SK, September 16, 1989.
(Tampa Bay's 3rd choice, 122nd overall, in 2008 Entry Draft).

			Regular Season								Playoffs						
Season	Club	League	GP	W	L	O/T	Mins	GA	SO	Avg	GP	W	L	Mins	GA	SO	Avg
2006-07	Spokane Chiefs	WHL	30	13	11	2	1674	78	2	2.80	6	2	4	364	17	0	2.80
2007-08	Spokane Chiefs	WHL	45	30	10	3	2543	87	6	2.05	*21	*16	5	*1352	31	*3	*1.38
2008-09	Spokane Chiefs	WHL	54	34	18	2	3264	107	*7	*1.97	12	7	5	812	23	1	*1.70
2009-10	**Tampa Bay**	**NHL**	**2**	**0**	**0**	**0**	**44**	**3**	**0**	**4.09**	....	....	....	....	....	....	....
	Norfolk Admirals	AHL	55	27	25	3	3319	139	4	2.51	....	....	....	....	....	....	....
2010-11	Norfolk Admirals	AHL	46	21	20	4	2691	119	2	2.65	6	2	4	355	13	1	2.19
2011-12	**Tampa Bay**	**NHL**	**5**	**1**	**3**	**1**	**244**	**14**	**0**	**3.44**	....	....	....	....	....	....	....
	Norfolk Admirals	AHL	45	*32	11	0	2583	96	5	2.23	14	*12	2	866	21	*3	*1.46
2012-13	Syracuse Crunch	AHL	33	18	8	4	1881	77	3	2.46	....	....	....	....	....	....	....
	Hamilton Bulldogs	AHL	15	6	8	0	836	31	3	2.22	....	....	....	....	....	....	....
2013-14	**Montreal**	**NHL**	**3**	**2**	**0**	**0**	**163**	**5**	**1**	**1.84**	**5**	**2**	**3**	**300**	**13**	**0**	**2.60**
	Hamilton Bulldogs	AHL	41	20	16	3	2375	94	1	2.38	....	....	....	....	....	....	....
2014-15	**Montreal**	**NHL**	**17**	**6**	**6**	**4**	**1005**	**46**	**0**	**2.75**	....	....	....	....	....	....	....
	Hamilton Bulldogs	AHL	2	1	1	0	119	5	0	2.52	....	....	....	....	....	....	....
	NHL Totals		**27**	**9**	**9**	**5**	**1456**	**68**	**1**	**2.80**	**5**	**2**	**3**	**300**	**13**	**0**	**2.60**

Memorial Cup All-Star Team (2008) • Hap Emms Memorial Trophy (Memorial Cup - Top Goaltender) (2008) • Stafford Smythe Memorial Trophy (Memorial Cup - MVP) (2008) • WHL West Second All-Star Team (2009)

Traded to **Montreal** by **Tampa Bay** for Cedrick Desjardins, February 14, 2013.

TOMEK, Matej (TOH-mehk, MAH-tay) PHI

Goaltender. Catches . 6'3", 180 lbs. Born, Bratislava, Slovakia, May 24, 1997.
(Philadelphia's 4th choice, 90th overall, in 2015 Entry Draft).

			Regular Season								Playoffs						
Season	Club	League	GP	W	L	O/T	Mins	GA	SO	Avg	GP	W	L	Mins	GA	SO	Avg
2012-13	Bratislava U18	Svk-U18	19	....	....	....	1052	36	3	2.05	4	....	....	212	7	0	1.98
2013-14	Slovakia U18	Slovak-2	14	....	....	....	778	31	1	2.39	....	....	....	....	....	....	....
	Poprad U18	Svk-U18	6	....	....	....	359	14	0	2.34	4	....	....	240	12	1	3.00
	HK SKP Poprad Jr.	Slovak-Jr.	2	....	....	....	120	3	0	1.50	....	....	....	....	....	....	....
2014-15	Topeka	NAHL	33	24	9	0	1938	59	6	1.83	7	4	2	375	20	0	3.20

TOMKINS, Matt (TAWM-kihnz, MAT) CHI

Goaltender. Catches left. 6'3", 194 lbs. Born, Edmonton, AB, June 19, 1994.
(Chicago's 8th choice, 199th overall, in 2012 Entry Draft).

			Regular Season								Playoffs						
Season	Club	League	GP	W	L	O/T	Mins	GA	SO	Avg	GP	W	L	Mins	GA	SO	Avg
2008-09	Leduc Oil Kings	AMBHL	....	8	8	3	1093	75	0	4.12	1	0	1	60	5	0	5.00
2009-10	Sherwood Park	Minor-AB	18	8	5	5	1047	47	0	2.69	8	*8	0	490	17	1	2.08
2010-11	Sherwood Park	AMHL	16	6	8	1	1002	64	0	3.83	6	3	3	333	23	0	4.14
2011-12	Sherwood Park	AJHL	33	18	11	2	1898	108	0	3.41	10	4	6	595	35	1	3.53
2012-13	Sherwood Park	AJHL	44	22	14	6	2533	108	4	2.56	10	5	5	607	33	0	3.26
2013-14	Ohio State	Big Ten	17	6	7	2	929	43	0	2.78	....	....	....	....	....	....	....
2014-15	Ohio State	Big Ten	14	5	7	1	768	42	2	3.28	....	....	....	....	....	....	....

TREMBLAY, Francois (TRAWM-blay, frahn-SWUH)

Goaltender. Catches left. 6'1", 193 lbs. Born, Baie-Comeau, QC, August 29, 1994.
(St. Louis' 6th choice, 146th overall, in 2012 Entry Draft).

			Regular Season								Playoffs						
Season	Club	League	GP	W	L	O/T	Mins	GA	SO	Avg	GP	W	L	Mins	GA	SO	Avg
2009-10	Jonquiere Elites	QAAA	25	12	8	2	1386	72	0	3.12	5	2	3	307	11	1	2.15
2010-11	Val-d'Or Foreurs	QMJHL	26	5	10	4	1261	82	0	3.91	3	0	2	107	11	0	6.20
2011-12	Val-d'Or Foreurs	QMJHL	57	22	28	4	3118	197	2	3.79	4	0	3	209	19	0	5.45
2012-13	Val-d'Or Foreurs	QMJHL	46	22	16	3	2546	145	0	3.42	2	0	0	42	5	0	7.21
2013-14	Val-d'Or Foreurs	QMJHL	23	16	7	0	1349	70	2	3.11	....	....	....	....	....	....	....
	Victoriaville Tigres	QMJHL	25	16	7	1	1422	63	3	2.66	5	1	3	270	21	0	4.66
2014-15	Victoriaville Tigres	QMJHL	6	3	2	1	330	26	0	4.73	....	....	....	....	....	....	....
	Fort Wayne	ECHL	1	1	0	0	60	0	1	0.00	....	....	....	....	....	....	....

TREUTLE, Niklas (TROY-tehl, NIHK-luhs) ARI

Goaltender. Catches left. 6'2", 185 lbs. Born, Nurnberg, Germany, April 29, 1991.

			Regular Season								Playoffs						
Season	Club	League	GP	W	L	O/T	Mins	GA	SO	Avg	GP	W	L	Mins	GA	SO	Avg
2009-10	Nurnberg	Germany	1	0	0	0	26	1	0	2.34	....	....	....	....	....	....	....
	Deggendorf Fire	German-3	31	12	19	0	1771	102	1	3.46	....	....	....	....	....	....	....
2010-11	Hamburg Freezers	Germany	10	4	5	0	539	24	1	2.67	....	....	....	....	....	....	....
	Crimmitschau	German-2	10	2	8	0	591	35	0	3.56	2	0	2	122	8	0	3.95
2011-12	Hamburg Freezers	Germany	12	6	4	0	644	29	1	2.70	1	0	0	20	3	0	9.00
2012-13	Hamburg Freezers	Germany	18	9	8	0	1041	45	1	2.59	6	2	4	374	22	0	3.53
2013-14	Hamburg Freezers	Germany	11	3	8	0	641	35	0	3.28	....	....	....	....	....	....	....
	Riessersee	German-2	6	4	2	0	340	14	1	2.47	....	....	....	....	....	....	....
	EHC Munchen	Germany	8	3	4	0	419	19	0	2.72	....	....	....	....	....	....	....
2014-15	EHC Munchen	Germany	30	20	10	0	1744	60	0	*2.06	....	....	....	....	....	....	....
	Riessersee	German-2	3	3	0	0	18	4	1	1.33	....	....	....	....	....	....	....

Signed as a free agent by **Arizona**, July 29, 2015.

ULLMARK, Linus (UHL-mahrk, LIH-nuhs) BUF

Goaltender. Catches left. 6'3", 220 lbs. Born, Lugnvik, Sweden, July 31, 1993.
(Buffalo's 6th choice, 163rd overall, in 2012 Entry Draft).

			Regular Season								Playoffs						
Season	Club	League	GP	W	L	O/T	Mins	GA	SO	Avg	GP	W	L	Mins	GA	SO	Avg
2008-09	Kramfors U18	Swe-U18	14	....	....	....	824	54	0	3.93	....	....	....	....	....	....	....
2009-10	Kramfors U18	Swe-U18	2	....	....	....	120	11	0	5.50	....	....	....	....	....	....	....
	MODO U18	Swe-U18	8	....	....	....	484	26	1	3.22	2	....	....	120	7	0	3.50
2010-11	MODO U18	Swe-U18	24	....	....	....	1387	51	5	2.20	2	....	....	103	6	0	3.49
	MODO Jr.	Swe-Jr.	1	....	....	....	60	2	0	2.00	....	....	....	....	....	....	....
2011-12	MODO Jr.	Swe-Jr.	25	....	....	....	1521	70	1	2.76	5	....	....	242	9	1	2.24
	MODO	Sweden	3	....	....	....	148	8	0	3.24	....	....	....	....	....	....	....
2012-13	MODO Jr.	Swe-Jr.	23	18	5	0	1352	46	2	2.04	5	4	1	....	1	....	1.39
	Mora IK	Sweden-2	6	4	2	0	343	12	0	2.10	....	....	....	....	....	....	....
	MODO	Sweden	6	3	1	0	320	11	0	2.07	2	1	1	123	3	0	1.47
2013-14	MODO	Sweden	35	17	16	0	2043	71	3	2.08	2	0	2	127	9	0	4.24
2014-15	MODO	Sweden	35	12	20	0	1926	100	1	3.12	....	....	....	....	....	....	....
	MODO	Sweden-Q	....	....	....	....	....	....	....	....	4	4	0	240	2	2	0.50

VAN POTTELBERGHE, Joren (van paw-tehl-BAIRG, YOH-ruhn) DET

Goaltender. Catches left. 6'2", 201 lbs. Born, Zug, Switzerland, June 5, 1997.
(Detroit's 3rd choice, 110th overall, in 2015 Entry Draft).

			Regular Season								Playoffs						
Season	**Club**	**League**	**GP**	**W**	**L**	**O/T**	**Mins**	**GA**	**SO**	**Avg**	**GP**	**W**	**L**	**Mins**	**GA**	**SO**	**Avg**
2011-12	EV Zug U17	Swiss-U17	3	....	....	....	....	....	....	1.64	....	....	....	....	....	....	....
2012-13	EV Zug U17	Swiss-U17	14	....	....	....	....	....	....	2.62	4	....	....	....	....	....	2.71
	EV Zug Jr.	Swiss-Jr.	4	....	....	....	....	....	....	2.17	....	....	....	....	....	....	....
	EV Zug II Jr.	Swiss-Jr.	1	....	....	....	....	....	....	....	....	....	....	....	....	....	....
2013-14	Linkopings HC U18	Swe-U18	15	12	3	0	880	27	3	1.84	....	....	....	....	....	....	....
2014-15	Linkopings HC U18	Swe-U18	26	21	5	0	1577	40	4	1.52	5	2	3	299	12	1	2.41
	Linkopings HC Jr.	Swe-Jr.	5	4	1	0	312	16	0	3.08	....	....	....	....	....	....	....

VANECEK, Vitek (va-NIH-chehk, VIH-tehk) WSH

Goaltender. Catches left. 6'1", 180 lbs. Born, Havlickuv Brod, Czech Rep., January 9, 1996.
(Washington's 2nd choice, 39th overall, in 2014 Entry Draft).

			Regular Season								Playoffs						
Season	**Club**	**League**	**GP**	**W**	**L**	**O/T**	**Mins**	**GA**	**SO**	**Avg**	**GP**	**W**	**L**	**Mins**	**GA**	**SO**	**Avg**
2010-11	Havl. Brod U18	CzR-U18	1	....	....	....	60	6	0	6.00	....	....	....	....	....	....	....
2011-12	Havl. Brod U18	CzR-U18	7	....	....	....	323	22	0	4.09	....	....	....	....	....	....	....
2012-13	Havl. Brod U18	CzR-U18	36	....	....	....	2011	108	1	3.22	....	....	....	....	....	....	....
	Havl. Brod Jr.	CzRep-Jr.	2	....	....	....	....	....	....	2.00	....	....	....	....	....	....	....
2013-14	HC Liberec Jr.	CzRep-Jr.	38	....	....	....	2156	95	2	2.64	4	....	....	213	15	0	4.23
2014-15	HC Liberec Jr.	CzRep-Jr.	4	....	....	....	200	12	1	3.60	....	....	....	....	....	....	....
	Liberec	CzRep	6	....	....	....	359	16	0	2.67	....	....	....	....	....	....	....
	Benatky	CzRep-2	20	....	....	....	1178	44	0	2.24	5	....	....	282	13	0	2.77

VARLAMOV, Semyon (vahr-LA-mawv, sehm-YAWN) COL

Goaltender. Catches left. 6'2", 209 lbs. Born, Kuybyshev, USSR, April 27, 1988.
(Washington's 2nd choice, 23rd overall, in 2006 Entry Draft).

			Regular Season								Playoffs						
Season	**Club**	**League**	**GP**	**W**	**L**	**O/T**	**Mins**	**GA**	**SO**	**Avg**	**GP**	**W**	**L**	**Mins**	**GA**	**SO**	**Avg**
2004-05	Yaroslavl 2	Russia-3	8	....	....	....	369	15	1	2.43	....	....	....	....	....	....	....
2005-06	Yaroslavl 2	Russia-3	33	....	....	....	1782	60	8	2.02	....	....	....	....	....	....	....
2006-07	Yaroslavl 2	Russia-3	2	....	....	....	120	3	0	1.50	....	....	....	....	....	....	....
	Yaroslavl	Russia	33	....	....	....	1936	70	3	2.17	6	....	....	368	18	0	2.94
2007-08	Yaroslavl	Russia	44	....	....	....	2592	106	3	2.45	*16	....	....	*924	25	*5	1.62
2008-09	**Washington**	**NHL**	**6**	**4**	**0**	**1**	**329**	**13**	**0**	**2.37**	**13**	**7**	**6**	**759**	**32**	***2**	**2.53**
	Hershey Bears	AHL	27	19	7	1	1551	62	2	2.40	....	....	....	....	....	....	....
2009-10	**Washington**	**NHL**	**26**	**15**	**4**	**6**	**1527**	**65**	**2**	**2.55**	**6**	**3**	**3**	**349**	**14**	**0**	**2.41**
	Hershey Bears	AHL	3	3	0	0	185	6	0	1.95	....	....	....	....	....	....	....
	Russia	Olympics					DID NOT PLAY – SPARE GOALTENDER										
2010-11	**Washington**	**NHL**	**27**	**11**	**9**	**5**	**1560**	**58**	**2**	**2.23**	....	....	....	....	....	....	....
	Hershey Bears	AHL	3	2	1	0	179	10	0	3.36	....	....	....	....	....	....	....
2011-12	**Colorado**	**NHL**	**53**	**26**	**24**	**3**	**3151**	**136**	**4**	**2.59**	....	....	....	....	....	....	....
2012-13	Yaroslavl	KHL	16	8	4	3	928	27	3	*1.74	....	....	....	....	....	....	....
	Colorado	**NHL**	**35**	**11**	**21**	**3**	**1950**	**98**	**3**	**3.02**	....	....	....	....	....	....	....
2013-14	**Colorado**	**NHL**	**63**	***41**	**14**	**6**	**3640**	**146**	**2**	**2.41**	**7**	**3**	**4**	**432**	**20**	**0**	**2.78**
	Russia	Olympics	3	....	....	....	152	5	....	1.99	....	....	....	....	....	....	....
2014-15	**Colorado**	**NHL**	**57**	**28**	**20**	**8**	**3307**	**141**	**5**	**2.56**	....	....	....	....	....	....	....
	NHL Totals		**267**	**136**	**92**	**32**	**15464**	**657**	**18**	**2.55**	**26**	**13**	**13**	**1540**	**66**	**2**	**2.57**

NHL Second All-Star Team (2014)

Traded to **Colorado** by **Washington** for Colorado's 1st round choice (Filip Forsberg) in 2012 Entry Draft and Boston's 2nd round choice (previously acquired, later traded to Dallas – Dallas selected Mike Winther) in 2012 Entry Draft, July 1, 2011. Signed as a free agent by **Yaroslavl** (KHL), September 27, 2012.

VASILEVSKIY, Andrei (va-sihl-EHV-skee, an-DRAY) T.B.

Goaltender. Catches left. 6'3", 204 lbs. Born, Tyumen, Russia, July 25, 1994.
(Tampa Bay's 2nd choice, 19th overall, in 2012 Entry Draft).

			Regular Season								Playoffs						
Season	**Club**	**League**	**GP**	**W**	**L**	**O/T**	**Mins**	**GA**	**SO**	**Avg**	**GP**	**W**	**L**	**Mins**	**GA**	**SO**	**Avg**
2010-11	Tolpar Ufa Jr.	Russia-Jr.	14	8	2	0	730	22	3	1.81	2	1	1	88	3	0	2.05
2011-12	Tolpar Ufa Jr.	Russia-Jr.	27	15	8	0	1477	55	3	2.23	2	0	2	120	5	0	2.50
2012-13	Ufa	KHL	8	4	1	0	298	11	1	2.22	....	....	....	....	....	....	....
	Tolpar Ufa Jr.	Russia-Jr.	27	17	6	0	1613	52	3	1.93	3	0	2	190	9	0	2.85
2013-14	Ufa	KHL	28	14	8	0	1601	59	3	2.21	18	9	9	1144	38	1	1.99
2014-15	**Tampa Bay**	**NHL**	**16**	**7**	**5**	**1**	**864**	**34**	**1**	**2.36**	**4**	**1**	**1**	**113**	**6**	**0**	**3.19**
	Syracuse Crunch	AHL	25	14	6	5	1469	60	2	2.45	....	....	....	....	....	....	....
	NHL Totals		**16**	**7**	**5**	**1**	**864**	**34**	**1**	**2.36**	**4**	**1**	**1**	**113**	**6**	**0**	**3.19**

VEJMELKA, Karel (vay-MEHL-kuh, KAHR-uhl) NSH

Goaltender. Catches right. 6'3", 202 lbs. Born, Trebic, Czech Rep., May 25, 1996.
(Nashville's 5th choice, 145th overall, in 2015 Entry Draft).

			Regular Season								Playoffs						
Season	**Club**	**League**	**GP**	**W**	**L**	**O/T**	**Mins**	**GA**	**SO**	**Avg**	**GP**	**W**	**L**	**Mins**	**GA**	**SO**	**Avg**
2010-11	Trebic U18	CzR-U18	7	....	....	....	....	....	....	2.18	....	....	....	....	....	....	....
2011-12	Trebic U18	CzR-U18	17	....	....	....	....	....	....	2.87	....	....	....	....	....	....	....
	Trebic Jr.	CzRep-Jr.	2	....	....	....	....	....	....	2.00	....	....	....	....	....	....	....
2012-13	Trebic U18	CzR-U18	1	....	....	....	....	....	....	0.00	....	....	....	....	....	....	....
	Trebic Jr.	CzRep-Jr.	5	....	....	....	....	....	....	2.17	....	....	....	....	....	....	....
	HC Pardubice U18	CzR-U18	17	....	....	....	993	43	3	2.60	1	....	....	60	4	0	4.00
2013-14	HC Pardubice U18	CzR-U18	4	....	....	....	247	10	0	2.43	....	....	....	....	....	....	....
	HC Pardubice Jr.	CzRep-Jr.	36	....	....	....	2053	88	1	2.57	....	....	....	....	....	....	....
2014-15	HC Pardubice Jr.	CzRep-Jr.	37	....	....	....	2222	94	2	2.54	....	....	....	....	....	....	....
	Pardubice	CzRep	7	....	....	....	419	20	0	2.86	6	....	....	338	17	1	3.02
	Trebic	CzRep-2	3	....	....	....	176	4	0	1.36	....	....	....	....	....	....	....

VISENTIN, Mark (vih-SEHN-tihn, MAHRK)

Goaltender. Catches left. 6'2", 201 lbs. Born, Hamilton, ON, August 7, 1992.
(Phoenix's 2nd choice, 27th overall, in 2010 Entry Draft).

			Regular Season								Playoffs						
Season	**Club**	**League**	**GP**	**W**	**L**	**O/T**	**Mins**	**GA**	**SO**	**Avg**	**GP**	**W**	**L**	**Mins**	**GA**	**SO**	**Avg**
2007-08	Halton Hurricanes	Minor-ON	44	....	....	....	1980	98	3	2.22	....	....	....	....	....	....	....
2008-09	Niagara Ice Dogs	OHL	23	5	11	3	1099	78	2	4.26	....	....	....	....	....	....	....
2009-10	Niagara Ice Dogs	OHL	55	24	26	5	3209	160	7	2.99	5	1	4	305	18	0	3.54
2010-11	Niagara Ice Dogs	OHL	46	30	9	6	2714	114	4	2.52	14	9	5	823	35	1	2.55
2011-12	Niagara Ice Dogs	OHL	42	30	9	2	2407	80	*10	*1.99	*20	13	7	*1217	51	0	2.51
2012-13	Portland Pirates	AHL	30	15	12	1	1669	83	2	2.98	....	....	....	....	....	....	....
	Gwinnett	ECHL	1	1	0	0	60	2	0	2.00	....	....	....	....	....	....	....
2013-14	**Phoenix**	**NHL**	**1**	**0**	**1**	**0**	**59**	**3**	**0**	**3.05**	....	....	....	....	....	....	....
	Portland Pirates	AHL	45	14	19	6	2341	127	0	3.25	....	....	....	....	....	....	....
2014-15							DID NOT PLAY – INJURED										
	NHL Totals		**1**	**0**	**1**	**0**	**59**	**3**	**0**	**3.05**	....	....	....	....	....	....	....

OHL First All-Star Team (2011) • OHL Second All-Star Team (2012)

• Missed 2014-15 due to ankle injury at Arizona training camp, September 21, 2014. Signed as a free agent by **Rockford** (AHL), July 8, 2015.

VLADAR, Dan (VLA-duhr, DAN) BOS

Goaltender. Catches left. 6'5", 185 lbs. Born, Prague, Czech Rep., August 20, 1997.
(Boston's 7th choice, 75th overall, in 2015 Entry Draft).

			Regular Season								Playoffs						
Season	**Club**	**League**	**GP**	**W**	**L**	**O/T**	**Mins**	**GA**	**SO**	**Avg**	**GP**	**W**	**L**	**Mins**	**GA**	**SO**	**Avg**
2012-13	HC Kladno U18	CzR-U18	36	....	....	....	2125	107	1	3.02	3	....	....	179	10	0	3.35
	HC KEB Kladno Jr.	CzRep-Jr.	1	....	....	....	60	3	0	3.00	....	....	....	....	....	....	....
2013-14	HC Kladno U18	CzR-U18	31	....	....	....	1829	69	4	2.26	3	....	....	178	10	0	3.37
	HC KEB Kladno Jr.	CzRep-Jr.	6	....	....	....	366	15	1	2.46	....	....	....	....	....	....	....
2014-15	HC KEB Kladno Jr.	CzRep-Jr.	29	....	....	....	1681	78	1	2.78	4	....	....	20	12	0	3.60
	Rytiri Kladno	CzRep-2	8	....	....	....	487	16	1	1.97	....	....	....	....	....	....	....

WARD, Cam (WOHRD, KAM) CAR

Goaltender. Catches left. 6'1", 185 lbs. Born, Saskatoon, SK, February 29, 1984.
(Carolina's 1st choice, 25th overall, in 2002 Entry Draft).

			Regular Season								Playoffs						
Season	**Club**	**League**	**GP**	**W**	**L**	**O/T**	**Mins**	**GA**	**SO**	**Avg**	**GP**	**W**	**L**	**Mins**	**GA**	**SO**	**Avg**
1998-99	Sherwood Park	Minor-AB	24	13	7	4	1403	85	0	3.64	....	....	....	....	....	....	....
99-2000	Sherwood Park	AMHL	20	9	5	1	1194	71	0	3.57	7	4	3	262	22	0	3.57
2000-01	Sherwood Park	AMHL	25	14	6	3	1449	70	0	2.90	....	....	....	....	....	....	....
	Red Deer Rebels	WHL	1	1	0	0	60	0	1	0.00	....	....	....	....	....	....	....
2001-02	Red Deer Rebels	WHL	46	30	11	4	2695	102	1	*2.27	*23	14	9	*1503	52	*2	2.08
2002-03	Red Deer Rebels	WHL	57	*40	13	2	3367	118	5	2.10	*23	14	9	*1407	49	3	2.09
2003-04	Red Deer Rebels	WHL	56	31	16	8	3338	114	4	2.05	19	10	9	1199	37	3	1.85
2004-05	Lowell	AHL	50	27	17	3	2829	94	6	1.99	11	5	6	664	28	2	2.53
2005-06 ♦	**Carolina**	**NHL**	**28**	**14**	**8**	**2**	**1484**	**91**	**0**	**3.68**	***23**	***15**	**8**	***1320**	**47**	**2**	**2.14**
	Lowell	AHL	2	0	2	0	118	5	0	2.54	....	....	....	....	....	....	....
2006-07	**Carolina**	**NHL**	**60**	**30**	**21**	**6**	**3422**	**167**	**2**	**2.93**	....	....	....	....	....	....	....
2007-08	**Carolina**	**NHL**	**69**	**37**	**25**	**5**	**3930**	**180**	**4**	**2.75**	....	....	....	....	....	....	....
2008-09	**Carolina**	**NHL**	**68**	**39**	**23**	**5**	**3928**	**160**	**6**	**2.44**	**18**	**8**	**10**	**1101**	**49**	***2**	**2.67**
2009-10	**Carolina**	**NHL**	**47**	**18**	**23**	**5**	**2651**	**119**	**0**	**2.69**	....	....	....	....	....	....	....
2010-11	**Carolina**	**NHL**	***74**	**37**	**26**	**10**	***4318**	**184**	**4**	**2.56**	....	....	....	....	....	....	....
2011-12	**Carolina**	**NHL**	**68**	**30**	**23**	**13**	**3988**	**182**	**5**	**2.74**	....	....	....	....	....	....	....
2012-13	**Carolina**	**NHL**	**17**	**9**	**6**	**1**	**929**	**44**	**0**	**2.84**	....	....	....	....	....	....	....
2013-14	**Carolina**	**NHL**	**30**	**10**	**12**	**6**	**1645**	**84**	**0**	**3.06**	....	....	....	....	....	....	....
	Charlotte Checkers	AHL	2	1	1	0	119	4	0	2.02	....	....	....	....	....	....	....
2014-15	**Carolina**	**NHL**	**51**	**22**	**24**	**5**	**3026**	**121**	**1**	**2.40**	....	....	....	....	....	....	....
	NHL Totals		**512**	**246**	**191**	**58**	**29321**	**1332**	**22**	**2.73**	**41**	**23**	**18**	**2421**	**96**	**4**	**2.38**

WHL East First All-Star Team (2002, 2004) • Canadian Major Junior Second All-Star Team (2002) • WHL East Second All-Star Team (2003) • WHL Goaltender of the Year (2002, 2004) • WHL Player of the Year (2004) • Canadian Major Junior First All-Star Team (2004) • Canadian Major Junior Goaltender of the Year (2004) • AHL All-Rookie Team (2005) • Conn Smythe Trophy (2006)

Played in NHL All-Star Game (2011)

• Scored a goal vs. New Jersey, December 26, 2011.

WEDGEWOOD, Scott (WEHJ-wud, SKAWT) N.J.

Goaltender. Catches left. 6'2", 190 lbs. Born, Etobicoke, ON, August 14, 1992.
(New Jersey's 2nd choice, 84th overall, in 2010 Entry Draft).

			Regular Season								Playoffs						
Season	**Club**	**League**	**GP**	**W**	**L**	**O/T**	**Mins**	**GA**	**SO**	**Avg**	**GP**	**W**	**L**	**Mins**	**GA**	**SO**	**Avg**
2007-08	Miss. Senators	GTHL	29	....	....	....	1305	63	2	2.17	....	....	....	....	....	....	....
2008-09	Plymouth Whalers	OHL	6	0	2	0	158	12	0	4.56	3	0	0	26	2	0	4.62
2009-10	Plymouth Whalers	OHL	18	5	9	0	938	51	2	3.26	4	1	1	116	4	0	2.07
2010-11	Plymouth Whalers	OHL	55	28	18	2	3046	152	2	2.99	10	4	6	606	33	0	3.27
2011-12	Plymouth Whalers	OHL	43	28	10	3	2482	125	3	3.02	13	7	6	781	31	*2	2.38
2012-13	Trenton Titans	ECHL	48	20	22	5	2741	147	1	3.22	....	....	....	....	....	....	....
	Albany Devils	AHL	5	2	2	0	242	14	0	3.47	....	....	....	....	....	....	....
2013-14	Albany Devils	AHL	36	16	14	3	1980	79	4	2.39	....	....	....	....	....	....	....
2014-15	Albany Devils	AHL	36	13	14	6	2014	92	2	2.74	....	....	....	....	....	....	....

WILCOX, Adam (WIHL-cawx, A-duhm) T.B.

Goaltender. Catches left. 6', 171 lbs. Born, South St. Paul, MN, November 26, 1992.
(Tampa Bay's 4th choice, 178th overall, in 2011 Entry Draft).

			Regular Season								Playoffs						
Season	**Club**	**League**	**GP**	**W**	**L**	**O/T**	**Mins**	**GA**	**SO**	**Avg**	**GP**	**W**	**L**	**Mins**	**GA**	**SO**	**Avg**
2009-10	South St. Paul	High-MN	23	11	11	0	1119	73	0	3.33	2	1	1	102	8	0	4.00
2010-11	Green Bay	USHL	24	16	6	1	1420	52	1	2.20	2	1	0	88	1	0	0.68
2011-12	Green Bay	USHL	9	7	2	0	529	20	2	2.27	....	....	....	....	....	....	....
	Tri-City Storm	USHL	34	16	17	1	1896	92	1	2.91	....	....	....	....	....	....	....
2012-13	U. of Minnesota	WCHA	39	*25	8	5	*2331	73	3	*1.88	....	....	....	....	....	....	....
2013-14	U. of Minnesota	Big Ten	*38	*26	6	6	*2282	75	*4	*1.97	....	....	....	....	....	....	....
2014-15	U. of Minnesota	Big Ten	*38	*22	12	3	*2252	91	*6	2.42	....	....	....	....	....	....	....
	Syracuse Crunch	AHL	2	0	2	0	113	6	0	3.18	1	0	0	32	1	0	1.86

Big Ten First All-Star Team (2014) • Big Ten Player of the Year (2014)

WILL, Roman   (WIHL, ROH-muhn)   **COL**

Goaltender. Catches left. 6'1", 195 lbs.   Born, Plzen, Czech., May 22, 1992.

Season	Club	League	GP	W	L	O/T	Mins	GA	SO	Avg	GP	W	L	Mins	GA	SO	Avg
							Regular Season							**Playoffs**			
2008-09	Ml. Boleslav U17	CzR-U17	40	....	....	....	2332	104	2	2.68	2	....	....	120	6	0	3.00
2009-10	Ml. Boleslav U18	CzR-U18	23	....	....	....	1366	39	6	1.71	....	....	....	....	....	....	....
	Ml. Boleslav Jr.	CzRep-Jr.	23	....	....	....	1304	72	1	3.31	3	....	....	184	8	0	2.61
2010-11	Ml. Boleslav Jr.	CzRep-Jr.	48	....	....	....	2730	102	3	2.24	....	....	....	....	....	....	....
	BK Mlada Boleslav	CzRep-Q	1	....	....	....	40	5	0	7.50	....	....	....	....	....	....	....
2011-12	Moncton Wildcats	QMJHL	63	29	25	7	3592	166	1	2.77	4	0	4	205	19	0	5.56
2012-13	Ml. Boleslav	Czech-2	44	....	....	....	....	....	....	1.87	....	10	....	....	....	....	1.42
2013-14	BK Mlada Boleslav	CzRep-2	20	....	....	....	....	....	....	1.84	....	10	....	....	....	....	1.81
	BK Mlada Boleslav	CzRep-Q	2	....	....	....	....	....	....	5.27	....	....	....	....	....	....	....
2014-15	Lake Erie Monsters	AHL	11	2	6	1	576	34	0	3.54	....	....	....	....	....	....	....
	Fort Wayne	ECHL	29	17	8	4	1745	70	1	2.41	7	4	3	417	19	1	2.74

Signed as a free agent by **Colorado**, May 13, 2014.

WILLIAMS, Stephon   (WIHL-yuhms, STEH-fawn)   **NYI**

Goaltender. Catches left. 6'2", 194 lbs.   Born, Fairbanks, AK, April 28, 1993.
(NY Islanders' 4th choice, 106th overall, in 2013 Entry Draft).

Season	Club	League	GP	W	L	O/T	Mins	GA	SO	Avg	GP	W	L	Mins	GA	SO	Avg
							Regular Season							**Playoffs**			
2010-11	Sioux Falls	USHL	35	20	7	6	2042	88	1	2.59	5	4	1	298	11	0	2.21
2011-12	Sioux Falls	USHL	21	6	9	2	1113	50	1	2.70	....	....	....	....	....	....	....
	Waterloo	USHL	19	10	6	2	1054	49	1	2.79	*15	10	5	*895	34	*1	2.28
2012-13	Minnesota State	WCHA	35	21	12	2	2043	68	*4	2.00	....	....	....	....	....	....	....
2013-14	Minnesota State	WCHA	12	5	6	0	595	32	1	3.23	....	....	....	....	....	....	....
2014-15	Minnesota State	WCHA	35	25	6	3	1999	55	5	*1.65	....	....	....	....	....	....	....
	Bridgeport	AHL	5	3	1	0	255	9	0	2.12	....	....	....	....	....	....	....

WCHA All-Rookie Team (2013) • WCHA Rookie of the Year (2013) • WCHA First All-Star Team (2013) • WCHA Second All-Star Team (2015)

ZATKOFF, Jeff   (ZAT-kawf, JEHF)   **PIT**

Goaltender. Catches left. 6'2", 179 lbs.   Born, Detroit, MI, June 9, 1987.
(Los Angeles' 4th choice, 74th overall, in 2006 Entry Draft).

Season	Club	League	GP	W	L	O/T	Mins	GA	SO	Avg	GP	W	L	Mins	GA	SO	Avg
							Regular Season							**Playoffs**			
2004-05	Sioux City	USHL	24	13	6	3	1271	54	1	2.55	2	0	0	68	10	0	8.88
2005-06	Miami U.	CCHA	20	14	5	1	1217	41	3	2.02	....	....	....	....	....	....	....
2006-07	Miami U.	CCHA	26	14	8	3	1542	58	1	2.26	....	....	....	....	....	....	....
2007-08	Miami U.	CCHA	36	27	8	1	2161	62	3	*1.72	....	....	....	....	....	....	....
2008-09	Manchester	AHL	3	1	2	0	182	7	0	2.31	....	....	....	....	....	....	....
	Ontario Reign	ECHL	37	17	15	3	2164	107	1	2.97	7	3	4	418	26	0	3.73
2009-10	Manchester	AHL	22	10	9	0	1170	57	2	2.92	....	....	....	....	....	....	....
2010-11	Manchester	AHL	45	20	17	5	2508	112	3	2.68	5	1	3	253	16	0	3.80
2011-12	Manchester	AHL	44	21	17	1	2432	101	3	2.49	2	0	2	97	7	0	4.34
2012-13	Wilkes-Barre	AHL	49	26	20	0	2799	90	5	*1.93	5	2	3	253	23	0	5.45
2013-14	**Pittsburgh**	**NHL**	20	12	6	2	1171	51	1	2.61	....	....	....	....	....	....	....
2014-15	**Pittsburgh**	**NHL**	1	0	1	0	37	1	0	1.62	....	....	....	....	....	....	....
	Wilkes-Barre	AHL	37	18	14	4	2155	88	3	2.45	2	0	0	59	1	0	1.03
NHL Totals			**21**	**12**	**7**	**2**	**1208**	**52**	**1**	**2.58**	....	....	....	....	....	....	....

CCHA Second All-Star Team (2008) • Harry "Hap" Holmes Memorial Award (AHL – fewest goals against) (2013) (shared with Brad Thiessen) • Harry "Hap" Holmes Memorial Award (AHL – fewest goals against) (2015) (shared with Matt Murray)

Signed as a free agent by **Pittsburgh**, July 1, 2012.

ZEPP, Rob   (ZEHP, RAWB)

Goaltender. Catches left. 6'1", 181 lbs.   Born, Scarborough, ON, September 7, 1981.
(Carolina's 4th choice, 110th overall, in 2001 Entry Draft).

Season	Club	League	GP	W	L	O/T	Mins	GA	SO	Avg	GP	W	L	Mins	GA	SO	Avg
							Regular Season							**Playoffs**			
1997-98	York Simcoe	Minor-ON					STATISTICS NOT AVAILABLE										
	Newmarket	ON-Jr.A	3	....	....	....	181	13	0	4.31	....	....	....	....	....	....	....
1998-99	Plymouth Whalers	OHL	31	19	3	4	1662	76	3	2.74	3	1	0	100	10	0	6.00
99-2000	Plymouth Whalers	OHL	53	*36	11	3	3005	119	3	*2.38	*23	*15	8	*1374	52	2	2.27
2000-01	Plymouth Whalers	OHL	55	*34	18	3	3246	122	*4	*2.26	19	14	5	1139	51	2	2.69
2001-02	Florida Everblades	ECHL	13	6	5	2	739	41	0	3.33	....	....	....	....	....	....	....
2002-03	Florida Everblades	ECHL	41	20	13	7	2372	112	3	2.83	....	....	....	....	....	....	....
	Lowell	AHL	5	1	3	1	303	16	1	3.16	....	....	....	....	....	....	....
2003-04	Florida Everblades	ECHL	35	14	13	7	2052	101	0	2.95	12	8	3	683	31	1	2.72
	Lowell	AHL	2	0	1	1	124	7	0	3.40	....	....	....	....	....	....	....
2004-05	Florida Everblades	ECHL	26	11	10	2	1414	63	2	2.67	....	....	....	....	....	....	....
2005-06	SaiPa	Finland	44	18	16	9	2501	85	4	2.04	8	4	4	526	20	0	2.28
2006-07	SaiPa	Finland	24	8	11	4	1278	70	0	3.29	....	....	....	....	....	....	....
2007-08	Eisbaren Berlin	Germany	41	28	12	0	2448	107	3	2.62	*14	*10	4	864	34	0	2.36
2008-09	Eisbaren Berlin	Germany	43	*28	15	....	2569	108	2	2.52	12	*10	2	737	26	*2	*2.12
2009-10	Eisbaren Berlin	Germany	50	*39	11	....	2975	130	*5	2.62	5	2	3	293	15	0	3.07
2010-11	Eisbaren Berlin	Germany	43	24	16	....	2493	100	2	2.41	*12	*9	3	*738	32	0	2.60
2012-13	Eisbaren Berlin	Germany	46	25	21	....	2777	127	*5	2.74	*13	*10	3	*760	36	0	2.84
2013-14	Eisbaren Berlin	Germany	38	*24	14	0	2256	90	1	2.39	3	1	2	185	6	1	1.94
2014-15	**Philadelphia**	**NHL**	10	5	2	0	519	25	0	2.89	....	....	....	....	....	....	....
	Lehigh Valley	AHL	47	21	20	4	2734	122	0	2.68	....	....	....	....	....	....	....
NHL Totals			**10**	**5**	**2**	**0**	**519**	**25**	**0**	**2.89**	....	....	....	....	....	....	....

• Re-entered NHL Entry Draft. Originally Atlanta's 5th choice, 99th overall, in 1999 Entry Draft.

Canadian Major Junior - Scholastic Player of the Year (1999) • OHL Second All-Star Team (2000, 2001)

• Missed majority of 2001-02 due to groin injury in practice, January 3, 2002. Signed as a free agent by **SaiPa** (Finland), August 30, 2005. Signed as a free agent by **Berlin** (Germany), July 12, 2007. Signed as a free agent by **Philadelphia**, July 1, 2014.

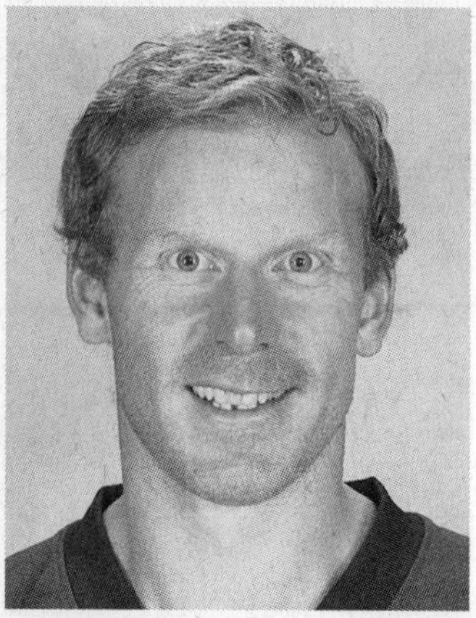

Daniel Alfredsson

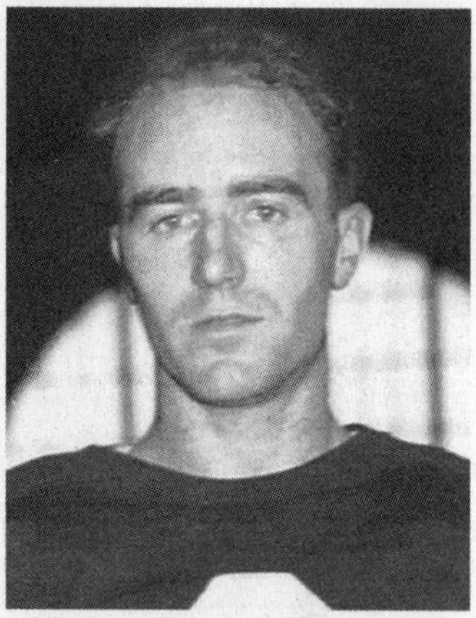

Viv Allen

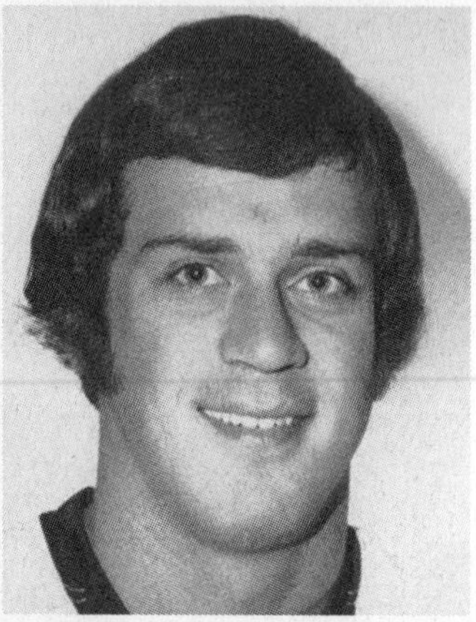

Earl Anderson

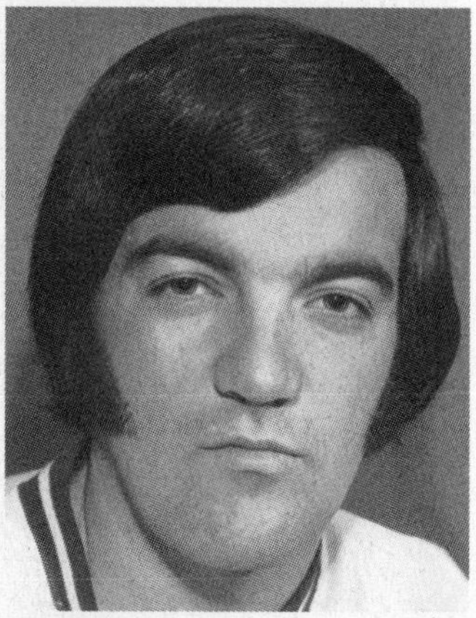

John Arbour

Retired NHL Player Index

Abbreviations: Teams/Cities: – **Ana**. – Anaheim; **Atl**. – Atlanta; **Bos**. – Boston; **Bro**. – Brooklyn; **Buf**. – Buffalo; **Cgy**. – Calgary; **Cal**. – California; **Car**. – Carolina; **Chi**. – Chicago; **Cle**. – Cleveland; **Col**. – Colorado; **CBJ** – Columbus; **Dal**. – Dallas; **Det**. – Detroit; **Edm**. – Edmonton; **Fla**. – Florida; **Ham**. – Hamilton; **Hfd**. – Hartford; **K.C.** – Kansas City; **L.A.** – Los Angeles; **Min**. – Minnesota; **Mtl**. – Montreal; **Mtl.M.** – Montreal Maroons; **Mtl.W.** – Montreal Wanderers; **Nsh**. – Nashville; **N.J.** – New Jersey; **NYA** – NY Americans; **NYI** – NY Islanders; **NYR** – New York Rangers; **Oak**. – Oakland; **Ott**. – Ottawa; **Phi**. – Philadelphia; **Phx**. – Phoenix; **Pit**. – Pittsburgh; **Que**. – Quebec; **St.L.** – St. Louis; **S.J.** – San Jose; **T.B.** – Tampa Bay; **Tor**. – Toronto; **Van**. – Vancouver; **Wsh**. – Washington; **Wpg**. – Winnipeg

GP – games played; **G** – goals; **A** – assists; **TP** – total points; **PIM** – penalties in minutes.
• – deceased. Assists not recorded during 1917-18 season ‡ – Remains active in other leagues.

NHL Seasons – A player or goaltender who does not play in a regular season but who does appear in that year's playoffs is credited with an NHL Season in this Index. Total seasons are rounded off to the nearest full season.

A

Name	NHL Teams	NHL Seasons	Regular Schedule					Playoffs					NHL Cup Wins	First NHL Season	Last NHL Season
			GP	G	A	TP	PIM	GP	G	A	TP	PIM			
Aalto, Antti	Ana.	4	151	11	17	28	52	4	0	0	0	2	....	1997-98	2000-01
Abbott, Reg	Mtl.	1	3	0	0	0	0	....	....	....	....	....	....	1952-53	1952-53
• Abel, Clarence	NYR, Chi.	8	333	19	18	37	359	38	1	1	2	58	2	1926-27	1933-34
Abel, Gerry	Det.	1	1	0	0	0	0	....	....	....	....	....	....	1966-67	1966-67
• Abel, Sid	Det., Chi.	14	612	189	283	472	376	97	28	30	58	79	3	1938-39	1953-54
Abgrall, Dennis	L.A.	1	13	0	2	2	4	....	....	....	....	....	....	1975-76	1975-76
‡ Abid, Ramzi	Phx., Pit., Atl., Nsh.	4	68	14	16	30	78	2	0	0	0	0	....	2002-03	2006-07
Abrahamsson, Thommy	Hfd.	1	32	6	11	17	16	....	....	....	....	....	....	1980-81	1980-81
Achtymichuk, Gene	Mtl., Det.	4	32	3	5	8	2	....	....	....	....	....	....	1951-52	1958-59
Acomb, Doug	Tor.	1	2	0	1	1	0	....	....	....	....	....	....	1969-70	1969-70
Acton, Keith	Mtl., Min., Edm., Phi., Wsh., NYI	15	1023	226	358	584	1172	66	12	21	33	88	1	1979-80	1993-94
• Adam, Douglas	NYR	1	4	0	1	1	0	....	....	....	....	....	....	1949-50	1949-50
Adam, Russ	Tor.	1	8	1	2	3	11	....	....	....	....	....	....	1982-83	1982-83
Adams, Bryan	Atl.	2	11	0	1	1	2	....	....	....	....	....	....	1999-00	2000-01
Adams, Greg	Phi., Hfd., Wsh., Edm., Van., Que., Det.	10	545	84	143	227	1173	43	2	11	13	153	....	1980-81	1989-90
Adams, Greg	N.J., Van., Dal., Phx., Fla.	17	1056	355	388	743	326	81	20	22	42	16	....	1984-85	2000-01
• Adams, Jack	Tor., Ott.	7	173	83	32	115	366	10	2	0	2	13	2	1917-18	1926-27
• Adams, John	Mtl.	1	42	6	12	18	11	3	0	0	0	0	....	1940-41	1940-41
Adams, Kevyn	Tor., CBJ, Fla., Car., Phx., Chi.	10	540	59	77	136	317	67	2	2	4	39	1	1997-98	2007-08
• Adams, Stew	Chi., Tor.	4	95	9	26	35	60	11	3	3	6	14	....	1929-30	1932-33
Adduono, Rick	Bos., Atl.	2	4	0	0	0	2	....	....	....	....	....	....	1975-76	1979-80
Afanasenkov, Dmitry	T.B., Phi.	5	227	27	27	54	52	28	1	3	4	8	1	2000-01	2006-07
Affleck, Bruce	St.L., Van., NYI	7	280	14	66	80	86	8	0	0	0	0	....	1974-75	1983-84
‡ Afinogenov, Maxim	Buf., Atl.	10	651	158	237	395	486	49	10	13	23	22	....	1999-00	2009-10
Agnew, Jim	Van., Hfd.	6	81	0	1	1	257	4	0	0	0	6	....	1986-87	1992-93
Ahern, Fred	Cal., Cle., Col.	4	146	31	30	61	130	2	0	1	1	2	....	1974-75	1977-78
• Ahlin, Rudy	Chi.	1	1	0	0	0	0	....	....	....	....	....	....	1937-38	1937-38
Ahola, Peter	L.A., Pit., S.J., Cgy.	3	123	10	17	27	137	6	0	0	0	2	....	1991-92	1993-94
Ahrens, Chris	Min.	6	52	0	3	3	84	1	0	0	0	0	....	1972-73	1977-78
• Ailsby, Lloyd	NYR	1	3	0	0	0	2	....	....	....	....	....	....	1951-52	1951-52
Aitken, Brad	Pit., Edm.	2	14	1	3	4	25	....	....	....	....	....	....	1987-88	1990-91
Aitken, Johnathan	Bos., Chi.	2	44	0	1	1	70	....	....	....	....	....	....	1999-00	2003-04
Aivazoff, Micah	Det., Edm., NYI	3	92	4	6	10	46	....	....	....	....	....	....	1993-94	1995-96
Alatalo, Mika	Phx.	2	152	17	29	46	58	5	0	0	0	2	....	1999-00	2000-01
Albelin, Tommy	Que., N.J., Cgy.	18	952	44	211	255	417	81	7	15	22	22	2	1987-88	2005-06
‡ Alberts, Andrew	Bos., Phi., Car., Van.	9	459	8	47	55	492	31	0	2	2	45	....	2005-06	2013-14
• Albright, Clint	NYR	1	59	14	5	19	19	....	....	....	....	....	....	1948-49	1948-49
Aldcorn, Gary	Tor., Det., Bos.	5	226	41	56	97	78	6	1	2	3	4	....	1956-57	1960-61
Aldridge, Keith	Dal.	1	4	0	0	0	0	....	....	....	....	....	....	1999-00	1999-00
Alexander, Claire	Tor., Van.	4	155	18	47	65	36	16	2	4	6	4	....	1974-75	1977-78
• Alexandre, Art	Mtl.	2	11	0	2	2	8	4	0	0	0	0	....	1931-32	1932-33
Alexeev, Nikita	T.B., Chi.	3	159	20	17	37	28	11	1	0	1	0	....	2001-02	2006-07
‡ Alfredsson, Daniel	Ott., Det.	18	1246	444	713	1157	510	124	51	49	100	76	....	1995-96	2013-14
Allan, Jeff	Cle.	1	4	0	0	0	2	....	....	....	....	....	....	1977-78	1977-78
Allen, Bobby	Edm., Bos.	3	51	0	3	3	12	....	....	....	....	....	....	2002-03	2007-08
Allen, Chris	Fla.	2	2	0	0	0	2	....	....	....	....	....	....	1997-98	1998-99
• Allen, George	NYR, Chi., Mtl.	8	339	82	115	197	179	41	9	10	19	32	....	1938-39	1946-47
• Allen, Keith	Det.	2	28	0	4	4	8	5	0	0	0	0	1	1953-54	1954-55
Allen, Peter	Pit.	1	8	0	0	0	8	....	....	....	....	....	....	1995-96	1995-96
• Allen, Viv	NYA	1	6	0	1	1	0	....	....	....	....	....	....	1940-41	1940-41
Alley, Steve	Hfd.	2	15	3	3	6	11	3	0	1	1	0	....	1979-80	1980-81
Allison, Dave	Mtl.	1	3	0	0	0	12	....	....	....	....	....	....	1983-84	1983-84
Allison, Jamie	Cgy., Chi., CBJ, Nsh., Fla.	10	372	7	23	30	639	....	....	....	....	....	....	1994-95	2005-06
Allison, Jason	Wsh., Bos., L.A., Tor.	12	552	154	331	485	441	25	7	18	25	14	....	1993-94	2005-06
Allison, Mike	NYR, Tor., L.A.	10	499	102	166	268	630	82	9	17	26	135	....	1980-81	1989-90
Allison, Ray	Hfd., Phi.	7	238	64	93	157	223	12	2	3	5	20	....	1979-80	1986-87
• Allum, Bill	NYR	1	1	0	1	1	0	....	....	....	....	....	....	1940-41	1940-41
‡ Almond, Cody	Min.	3	25	2	0	2	26	....	....	....	....	....	....	2009-10	2011-12
‡ Almqvist, Adam	Det.	1	2	1	0	1	0	....	....	....	....	....	....	2013-14	2013-14
• Amadio, Dave	Det., L.A.	3	125	5	11	16	163	16	1	2	3	18	....	1957-58	1968-69
Ambroziak, Peter	Buf.	1	12	0	1	1	0	....	....	....	....	....	....	1994-95	1994-95
Amodeo, Mike	Wpg.	1	19	0	0	0	2	....	....	....	....	....	....	1979-80	1979-80
Amonte, Tony	NYR, Chi., Phx., Phi., Cgy.	16	1174	416	484	900	752	99	22	33	55	56	....	1990-91	2006-07
• Anderson, Bill	Bos.	1	....	....	....	....	....	1	0	0	0	0	....	1942-43	1942-43
Anderson, Dale	Det.	1	13	0	0	0	6	2	0	0	0	0	....	1956-57	1956-57
Anderson, Doug	Mtl.	1	....	....	....	....	....	2	0	0	0	0	....	1952-53	1952-53
Anderson, Earl	Det., Bos.	3	109	19	19	38	22	5	0	1	1	0	....	1974-75	1976-77
Anderson, Glenn	Edm., Tor., NYR, St.L.	16	1129	498	601	1099	1120	225	93	121	214	442	6	1980-81	1995-96
• Anderson, Jim	L.A.	1	7	1	2	3	2	....	....	....	....	....	....	1967-68	1967-68
Anderson, John	Tor., Que., Hfd.	12	814	282	349	631	263	37	9	18	27	2	....	1977-78	1988-89
‡ Anderson, Matt	N.J.	1	2	0	1	1	0	....	....	....	....	....	....	2012-13	2012-13
Anderson, Murray	Wsh.	1	40	0	1	1	68	....	....	....	....	....	....	1974-75	1974-75
Anderson, Perry	St.L., N.J., S.J.	10	400	50	59	109	1051	36	2	1	3	161	....	1981-82	1991-92
Anderson, Ron	Det., L.A., St.L., Buf.	5	251	28	30	58	146	5	0	0	0	4	....	1967-68	1971-72
Anderson, Ron	Wsh.	1	28	9	7	16	8	....	....	....	....	....	....	1974-75	1974-75
Anderson, Russ	Pit., Hfd., L.A.	9	519	22	99	121	1086	10	0	3	3	28	....	1976-77	1984-85
Anderson, Shawn	Buf., Que., Wsh., Phi.	8	255	11	51	62	117	19	1	1	2	16	....	1986-87	1994-95
• Anderson, Tom	Det., NYA, Bro.	8	319	62	127	189	180	16	2	7	9	8	....	1934-35	1941-42
Andersson, Erik	Cgy.	1	12	2	1	3	8	....	....	....	....	....	....	1997-98	1997-98
‡ Andersson, Jonas	Nsh., Van.	2	9	0	0	0	2	....	....	....	....	....	....	2001-02	2010-11
Andersson, Kent-Erik	Min., NYR	7	456	72	103	175	78	50	4	11	15	4	....	1977-78	1983-84
Andersson, Mikael	Buf., Hfd., T.B., Phi., NYI	15	761	95	169	264	134	25	2	7	9	10	....	1985-86	1999-00
Andersson, Niklas	Que., NYI, S.J., Nsh., Cgy.	6	164	29	53	82	85	....	....	....	....	....	....	1992-93	2000-01
Andersson, Peter	Wsh., Que.	3	172	10	41	51	81	7	0	2	2	2	....	1983-84	1985-86
Andersson, Peter	NYR, Fla.	2	47	6	13	19	20	....	....	....	....	....	....	1992-93	1993-94
Andrascik, Steve	NYR	1	....	....	....	....	....	1	0	0	0	0	....	1971-72	1971-72
Andrea, Paul	NYR, Pit., Cal., Buf.	4	150	31	49	80	10	....	....	....	....	....	....	1965-66	1970-71
• Andrews, Lloyd	Tor.	4	53	8	5	13	10	2	0	0	0	0	1	1921-22	1924-25
Andreychuk, Dave	Buf., Tor., N.J., Bos., Col., T.B.	23	1639	640	698	1338	1125	162	43	54	97	162	1	1982-83	2005-06
Andrievski, Alexander	Chi.	1	1	0	0	0	0	....	....	....	....	....	....	1992-93	1992-93
Andruff, Ron	Mtl., Col.	5	153	19	36	55	54	2	0	0	0	0	....	1974-75	1978-79
Andrusak, Greg	Pit., Tor.	5	28	0	6	6	16	15	1	0	1	8	....	1993-94	1999-00
Angelstad, Mel	Wsh.	1	2	0	0	0	2	....	....	....	....	....	....	2003-04	2003-04
Angotti, Lou	NYR, Chi., Phi., Pit., St.L.	10	653	103	186	289	228	65	8	8	16	17	....	1964-65	1973-74
Anholt, Darrel	Chi.	1	1	0	0	0	0	....	....	....	....	....	....	1983-84	1983-84
• Anslow, Hub	NYR	1	2	0	0	0	0	....	....	....	....	....	....	1947-48	1947-48
Antonovich, Mike	Min., Hfd., N.J.	5	87	10	15	25	37	....	....	....	....	....	....	1975-76	1983-84
Antoski, Shawn	Van., Phi., Pit., Ana.	8	183	3	5	8	599	36	1	3	4	74	....	1990-91	1997-98
‡ Antropov, Nik	Tor., NYR, Atl., Wpg.	13	788	193	272	465	627	35	4	4	8	40	....	1999-00	2012-13
• Apps, Syl	Tor.	10	423	201	231	432	56	69	25	29	54	8	3	1936-37	1947-48
Apps, Syl	NYR, Pit., L.A.	10	727	183	423	606	311	23	5	5	10	23	....	1970-71	1979-80

Name	NHL Teams	NHL Seasons	Regular Schedule GP	G	A	TP	PIM	Playoffs GP	G	A	TP	PIM	NHL Cup Wins	First NHL Season	Last NHL Season
Arbour, Al	Det., Chi., Tor., St.L.	16	626	12	58	70	617	86	1	8	9	92	4	1953-54	1970-71
• Arbour, Amos	Mtl., Ham., Tor.	6	113	52	20	72	77	....	....	....	....	....	....	1918-19	1923-24
• Arbour, Jack	Det., Tor.	2	47	5	1	6	56	....	....	....	....	....	....	1926-27	1928-29
Arbour, John	Bos., Pit., Van., St.L.	5	106	1	9	10	149	5	0	0	0	0	....	1965-66	1971-72
• Arbour, Ty	Pit., Chi.	5	207	28	28	56	112	11	2	0	2	6	....	1926-27	1930-31
Archambault, Michel	Chi.	1	3	0	0	0	0	....	....	....	....	....	....	1976-77	1976-77
Archibald, Dave	Min., NYR, Ott., NYI	8	323	57	67	124	139	5	0	1	1	0	....	1987-88	1996-97
Archibald, Jim	Min.	3	16	1	2	3	45	....	....	....	....	....	....	1984-85	1986-87
Areshenkoff, Ron	Edm.	1	4	0	0	0	0	....	....	....	....	....	....	1979-80	1979-80
Arkhipov, Denis	Nsh., Chi.	5	352	56	82	138	128	....	....	....	....	....	....	2000-01	2006-07
Armstrong, Bill	Phi.	1	1	0	1	1	0	....	....	....	....	....	....	1990-91	1990-91
• Armstrong, Bob	Bos.	12	542	13	86	99	671	42	1	7	8	28	....	1950-51	1961-62
Armstrong, Chris	Min., Ana.	2	7	0	1	1	0	....	....	....	....	....	....	2000-01	2003-04
‡ Armstrong, Colby	Pit., Atl., Tor., Mtl.	8	476	89	120	209	376	9	0	1	1	26	....	2005-06	2012-13
Armstrong, Derek	NYI, Ott., NYR, L.A., St.L.	14	477	72	149	221	355	....	....	....	....	....	....	1993-94	2009-10
Armstrong, George	Tor.	21	1187	296	417	713	721	110	26	34	60	52	4	1949-50	1970-71
• Armstrong, Murray	Tor., NYA, Bro., Det.	8	270	67	121	188	72	30	4	6	10	2	....	1937-38	1945-46
• Armstrong, Norm	Tor.	1	7	1	1	2	2	....	....	....	....	....	....	1962-63	1962-63
‡ Armstrong, Riley	S.J.	1	2	0	0	0	2	....	....	....	....	....	....	2008-09	2008-09
Armstrong, Tim	Tor.	1	11	1	0	1	6	....	....	....	....	....	....	1988-89	1988-89
Arnason, Chuck	Mtl., Atl., Pit., K.C., Col., Cle., Min., Wsh.	8	401	109	90	199	122	9	2	4	6	4	....	1971-72	1978-79
Arnason, Tyler	Chi., Ott., Col.	7	487	88	157	245	140	13	2	3	5	2	....	2001-02	2008-09
‡ Arniel, Jamie	Bos.	1	1	0	0	0	0	....	....	....	....	....	....	2010-11	2010-11
Arniel, Scott	Wpg., Buf., Bos.	11	730	149	189	338	599	34	3	3	6	39	....	1981-82	1991-92
Arnott, Jason	Edm., N.J., Dal., Nsh., Wsh., St.L.	18	1244	417	521	938	1242	122	32	41	73	76	1	1993-94	2011-12
‡ Arsene, Dean	Edm.	1	13	0	0	0	41	....	....	....	....	....	....	2009-10	2009-10
Arthur, Fred	Hfd., Phi.	3	80	1	8	9	49	4	0	0	0	2	....	1980-81	1982-83
‡ Artyukhin, Evgeny	T.B., Ana., Atl.	3	199	19	30	49	313	5	1	0	1	6	....	2005-06	2009-10
• Arundel, John	Tor.	1	3	0	0	0	9	....	....	....	....	....	....	1949-50	1949-50
Arvedson, Magnus	Ott., Van.	7	434	100	125	225	241	52	3	8	11	34	....	1997-98	2003-04
Asham, Arron	Mtl., NYI, N.J., Phi., Pit., NYR	15	789	94	114	208	1004	72	11	8	19	56	....	1998-99	2013-14
• Ashbee, Barry	Bos., Phi.	5	284	15	70	85	291	17	0	4	4	22	1	1965-66	1973-74
• Ashby, Don	Tor., Col., Edm.	6	188	40	56	96	40	12	1	0	1	4	....	1975-76	1980-81
Ashton, Brent	Van., Col., N.J., Min., Que., Det., Wpg., Bos., Cgy.	14	998	284	345	629	635	85	24	25	49	70	....	1979-80	1992-93
Ashworth, Frank	Chi.	1	18	5	4	9	2	....	....	....	....	....	....	1946-47	1946-47
• Asmundson, Oscar	NYR, Det., St.L., NYA, Mtl.	5	111	11	23	34	30	9	0	2	2	4	1	1932-33	1937-38
• Astashenko, Kaspars	T.B.	2	23	1	2	3	8	....	....	....	....	....	....	1999-00	2000-01
Astley, Mark	Buf.	3	75	4	19	23	92	2	0	0	0	0	....	1993-94	1995-96
• Atanas, Walt	NYR	1	49	13	8	21	40	....	....	....	....	....	....	1944-45	1944-45
Atcheynum, Blair	Ott., St.L., Nsh., Chi.	5	196	27	33	60	36	23	1	3	4	8	....	1992-93	2000-01
• Atkinson, Steve	Bos., Buf., Wsh.	6	302	60	51	111	104	1	0	0	0	0	....	1968-69	1974-75
Attwell, Bob	Col.	2	22	1	5	6	0	....	....	....	....	....	....	1979-80	1980-81
Attwell, Ron	St.L., NYR	1	22	1	7	8	8	....	....	....	....	....	....	1967-68	1967-68
Aubin, Norm	Tor.	2	69	18	13	31	30	1	0	0	0	0	....	1981-82	1982-83
Aubin, Serge	Col., CBJ, Atl.	7	374	44	64	108	361	22	0	1	1	10	....	1998-99	2005-06
Aubry, Pierre	Que., Det.	5	202	24	26	50	133	20	1	1	2	32	....	1980-81	1984-85
• Aubuchon, Ossie	Bos., NYR	2	50	20	12	32	4	6	1	0	1	0	....	1942-43	1943-44
Aucoin, Adrian	Van., T.B., NYI, Chi., Cgy., Phx., CBJ	18	1108	121	278	399	793	62	6	15	21	44	....	1994-95	2012-13
Audet, Philippe	Det.	1	4	0	0	0	0	....	....	....	....	....	....	1998-99	1998-99
Audette, Donald	Buf., L.A., Atl., Dal., Mtl., Fla.	15	735	260	249	509	584	73	21	27	48	46	....	1989-90	2003-04
• Auge, Les	Col.	1	6	0	3	3	4	....	....	....	....	....	....	1980-81	1980-81
Augusta, Patrik	Tor., Wsh.	2	4	0	0	0	0	....	....	....	....	....	....	1993-94	1998-99
Aulin, Jared	L.A.	1	17	2	2	4	0	....	....	....	....	....	....	2002-03	2002-03
• Aurie, Larry	Det.	12	489	147	129	276	279	24	6	9	15	10	2	1927-28	1938-39
Avery, Sean	Det., L.A., NYR, Dal.	10	580	90	157	247	1533	28	5	10	15	69	....	2001-02	2011-12
Awrey, Don	Bos., St.L., Mtl., Pit., NYR, Col.	16	979	31	158	189	1065	71	0	18	18	150	2	1963-64	1978-79
Axelsson, P.J.	Bos.	11	797	103	184	287	276	54	4	3	7	24	....	1997-98	2008-09
• Ayres, Vern	NYA, Mtl.M., St.L., NYR	6	211	6	11	17	350	....	....	....	....	....	....	1930-31	1935-36

B

Name	NHL Teams	NHL Seasons	GP	G	A	TP	PIM	GP	G	A	TP	PIM	NHL Cup Wins	First NHL Season	Last NHL Season
Babando, Pete	Bos., Det., Chi., NYR	6	351	86	73	159	194	17	3	3	6	6	1	1947-48	1952-53
‡ Babchuk, Anton	Chi., Car., Cgy.	7	289	36	71	107	108	13	0	1	1	10	1	2003-04	2012-13
Babcock, Bobby	Wsh.	2	2	0	0	0	2	....	....	....	....	....	....	1990-91	1992-93
Babe, Warren	Min.	3	21	2	5	7	23	2	0	0	0	0	....	1987-88	1990-91
‡ Babenko, Yuri	Col.	1	3	0	0	0	0	....	....	....	....	....	....	2000-01	2000-01
Babin, Mitch	St.L.	1	8	0	0	0	0	....	....	....	....	....	....	1975-76	1975-76
Baby, John	Cle., Min.	2	26	2	8	10	26	....	....	....	....	....	....	1977-78	1978-79
Babych, Dave	Wpg., Hfd., Van., Phi., L.A.	19	1195	142	581	723	970	114	21	41	62	113	....	1980-81	1998-99
Babych, Wayne	St.L., Pit., Que., Hfd.	9	519	192	246	438	498	41	7	9	16	24	....	1978-79	1986-87
Baca, Jergus	Hfd.	2	10	0	2	2	14	....	....	....	....	....	....	1990-91	1991-92
‡ Backman, Christian	St.L., NYR, CBJ	6	302	23	56	79	182	13	0	2	2	16	....	2002-03	2008-09
Backman, Mike	NYR	3	18	1	6	7	18	10	2	2	4	2	....	1981-82	1983-84
• Backor, Pete	Tor.	1	36	4	5	9	6	....	....	....	....	....	1	1944-45	1944-45
Backstrom, Ralph	Mtl., L.A., Chi.	17	1032	278	361	639	386	116	27	32	59	68	6	1956-57	1972-73
• Bailey, Ace	Tor.	8	313	111	82	193	472	21	3	4	7	12	1	1926-27	1933-34
• Bailey, Bob	Tor., Det., Chi.	5	150	15	21	36	207	15	0	4	4	22	....	1953-54	1957-58
• Bailey, Garnet	Bos., Det., St.L., Wsh.	10	568	107	171	278	633	15	2	4	6	28	2	1968-69	1977-78
Bailey, Reid	Phi., Tor., Hfd.	4	40	1	3	4	105	16	0	2	2	25	....	1980-81	1983-84
Baillargeon, Joel	Wpg., Que.	3	20	0	2	2	31	....	....	....	....	....	....	1986-87	1988-89
Baird, Ken	Cal.	1	10	0	2	2	15	....	....	....	....	....	....	1971-72	1971-72
Baker, Bill	Mtl., Col., St.L., NYR	3	143	7	25	32	175	6	0	0	0	0	....	1980-81	1982-83
Baker, Jamie	Que., Ott., S.J., Tor.	10	404	71	79	150	271	25	5	4	9	42	....	1989-90	1998-99
Bakovic, Peter	Van.	1	10	2	0	2	48	....	....	....	....	....	....	1987-88	1987-88
Bala, Chris	Ott.	1	6	0	1	1	0	....	....	....	....	....	....	2001-02	2001-02
‡ Balastik, Jaroslav	CBJ	2	74	13	11	24	30	....	....	....	....	....	....	2005-06	2006-07
Balderis, Helmut	Min.	1	26	3	6	9	2	....	....	....	....	....	....	1989-90	1989-90
• Baldwin, Doug	Tor., Det., Chi.	3	24	0	1	1	8	....	....	....	....	....	....	1945-46	1947-48
‡ Balej, Jozef	Mtl., NYR, Van.	2	18	1	5	6	4	....	....	....	....	....	....	2003-04	2005-06
Balfour, Earl	Tor., Chi.	7	288	30	22	52	78	26	0	3	3	4	1	1951-52	1960-61
• Balfour, Murray	Mtl., Chi., Bos.	8	306	67	90	157	393	40	9	10	19	45	1	1956-57	1964-65
Ball, Terry	Phi., Buf.	4	74	7	19	26	26	....	....	....	....	....	....	1967-68	1971-72
Balmochnykh, Maxim	Ana.	1	6	0	1	1	2	....	....	....	....	....	....	1999-00	1999-00
• Balon, Dave	NYR, Mtl., Min., Van.	14	776	192	222	414	607	78	14	21	35	109	2	1959-60	1972-73
Baltimore, Bryon	Edm.	1	2	0	0	0	4	....	....	....	....	....	....	1979-80	1979-80
Baluik, Stan	Bos.	1	7	0	0	0	2	....	....	....	....	....	....	1959-60	1959-60
Bancroft, Steve	Chi., S.J.	2	6	0	1	1	2	....	....	....	....	....	....	1992-93	2001-02
Bandura, Jeff	NYR	1	2	0	1	1	0	....	....	....	....	....	....	1980-81	1980-81
‡ Bang, Daniel	Nsh.	1	8	0	2	2	0	....	....	....	....	....	....	2012-13	2012-13
Banham, Frank	Ana., Phx.	4	32	9	2	11	16	....	....	....	....	....	....	1996-97	2002-03
Banks, Darren	Bos.	2	20	2	2	4	73	....	....	....	....	....	....	1992-93	1993-94
Bannister, Drew	T.B., Edm., Ana., NYR	6	164	5	25	30	161	12	0	0	0	30	....	1995-96	2001-02
Barahona, Ralph	Bos.	2	6	2	2	4	0	....	....	....	....	....	....	1990-91	1991-92
‡ Baranka, Ivan	NYR	1	1	0	1	1	0	....	....	....	....	....	....	2007-08	2007-08
• Barbe, Andy	Tor.	1	1	0	0	0	2	....	....	....	....	....	....	1950-51	1950-51
Barber, Bill	Phi.	12	903	420	463	883	623	129	53	55	108	109	2	1972-73	1983-84
Barber, Don	Min., Wpg., Que., S.J.	4	115	25	32	57	64	11	4	4	8	10	....	1988-89	1991-92
‡ Barch, Krys	Dal., Fla., N.J.	8	381	12	23	35	812	3	0	0	0	2	....	2006-07	2013-14
• Barilko, Bill	Tor.	5	252	26	36	62	456	47	5	7	12	104	4	1946-47	1950-51
‡ Barinka, Michal	Chi.	2	34	0	2	2	26	....	....	....	....	....	....	2003-04	2005-06
Barkley, Doug	Chi., Det.	6	253	24	80	104	382	30	0	9	9	63	....	1957-58	1965-66
Barlow, Bob	Min.	2	77	16	17	33	10	6	2	2	4	6	....	1969-70	1970-71
‡ Barnaby, Matthew	Buf., Pit., T.B., NYR, Col., Chi., Dal.	14	834	113	187	300	2562	62	7	15	22	170	....	1992-93	2006-07
• Barnes, Blair	L.A.	1	1	0	0	0	0	....	....	....	....	....	....	1982-83	1982-83
Barnes, Norm	Phi., Hfd.	5	156	6	38	44	178	12	0	0	0	8	....	1976-77	1981-82
Barnes, Ryan	Det.	1	2	0	0	0	0	....	....	....	....	....	....	2003-04	2003-04
Barnes, Stu	Wpg., Fla., Pit., Buf., Dal.	16	1136	261	336	597	438	116	30	32	62	24	....	1991-92	2007-08
Barney, Scott	L.A., Atl.	3	27	5	6	11	4	....	....	....	....	....	....	2002-03	2005-06
Baron, Murray	Phi., St.L., Mtl., Phx., Van.	15	988	35	94	129	1309	73	2	8	10	78	....	1989-90	2003-04
Baron, Normand	Mtl., St.L.	2	27	2	0	2	51	3	0	0	0	22	....	1983-84	1985-86
Barr, Dave	Bos., NYR, St.L., Hfd., Det., N.J., Dal.	13	614	128	204	332	520	71	12	10	22	70	....	1981-82	1993-94
Barrault, Doug	Min., Fla.	2	4	0	0	0	2	....	....	....	....	....	....	1992-93	1993-94
Barrett, Fred	Min., L.A.	13	745	25	123	148	671	44	0	2	2	60	....	1970-71	1983-84
Barrett, John	Det., Wsh., Min.	8	488	20	77	97	604	16	2	2	4	50	....	1980-81	1987-88

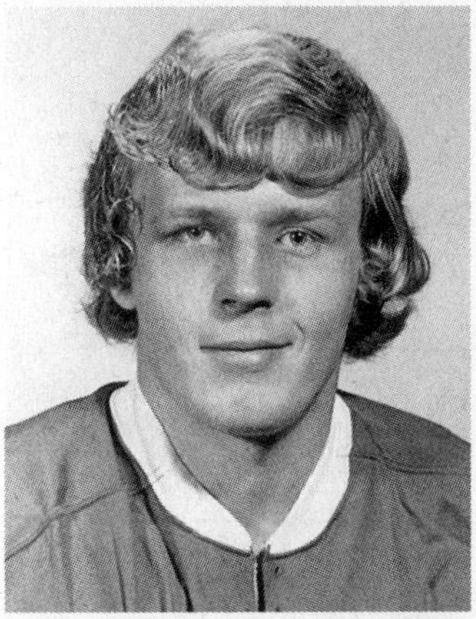

Chuck Arnason

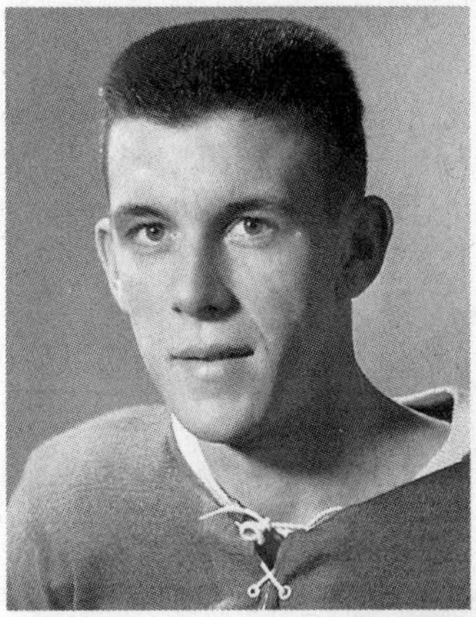

Ron Attwell

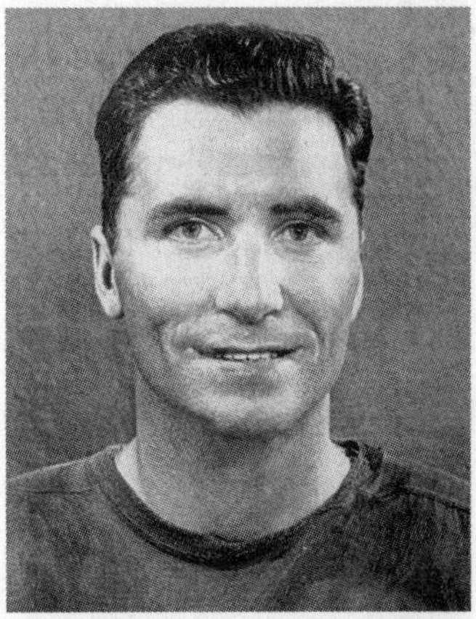

Andy Bathgate

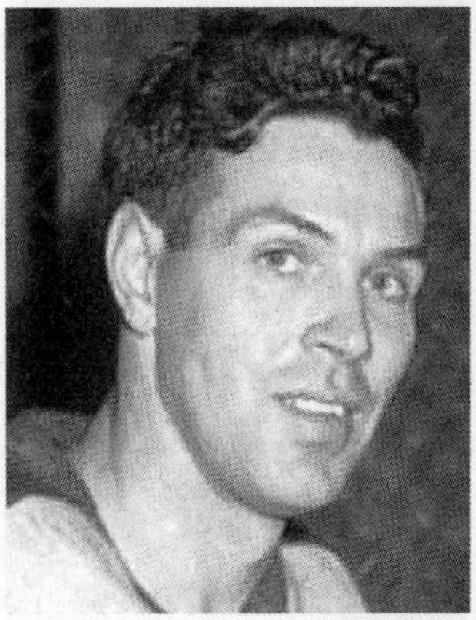

Frank Bathgate

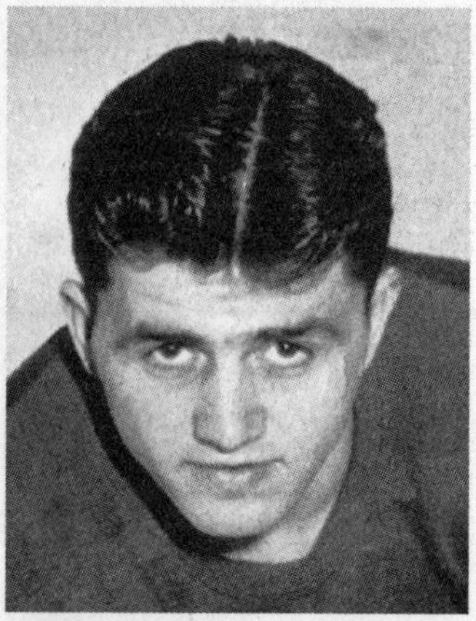

Huddy Bell

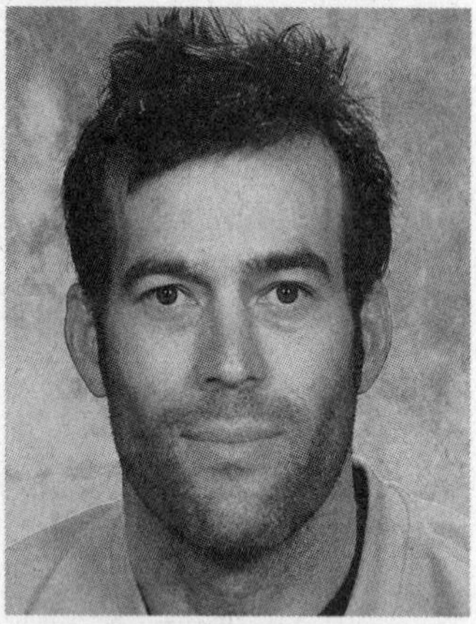

Todd Bertuzzi

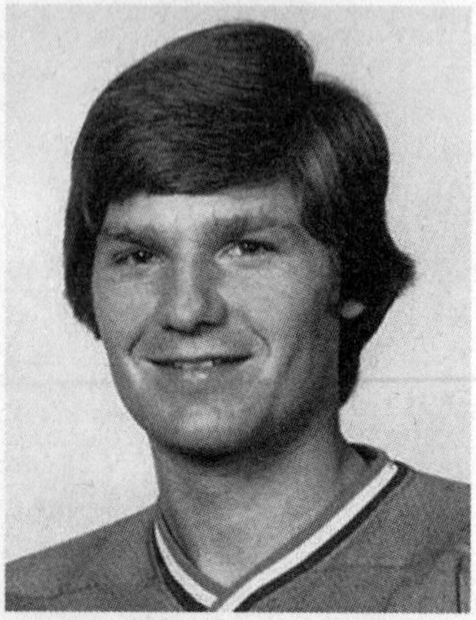

John Bethel

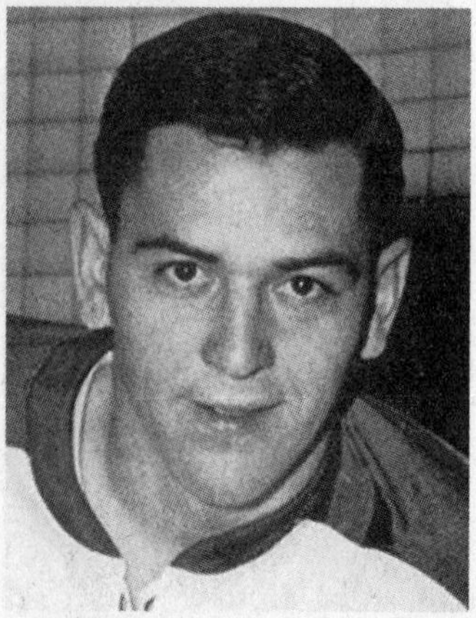

Ken Block

			Regular Schedule					Playoffs					NHL	First	Last
Name	NHL Teams	NHL Seasons	GP	G	A	TP	PIM	GP	G	A	TP	PIM	Cup Wins	NHL Season	NHL Season
Barrie, Doug	Pit., Buf., L.A.	3	158	10	42	52	268	....	....	....	....	....	....	1968-69	1971-72
Barrie, Len	Phi., Fla., Pit., L.A.	7	184	19	45	64	290	8	1	0	1	8	....	1989-90	2000-01
Barry, Ed	Bos.	1	19	1	3	4	2	....	....	....	....	....	....	1946-47	1946-47
● Barry, Marty	NYA, Bos., Det., Mtl.	12	509	195	192	387	231	43	15	18	33	34	2	1927-28	1939-40
Barry, Ray	Bos.	1	18	1	2	3	6	....	....	....	....	....	....	1951-52	1951-52
‡ Bartecko, Lubos	St.L., Atl.	5	257	46	65	111	107	12	1	1	2	2	....	1998-99	2002-03
Bartel, Robin	Cgy., Van.	2	41	0	1	1	14	6	0	0	0	16	....	1985-86	1986-87
Bartlett, Jim	Mtl., NYR, Bos.	5	191	34	23	57	273	2	0	0	0	0	....	1954-55	1960-61
● Barton, Cliff	Pit., Phi., NYR	3	85	10	9	19	22	....	....	....	....	....	....	1929-30	1939-40
Bartos, Peter	Min.	1	13	4	2	6	6	....	....	....	....	....	....	2000-01	2000-01
‡ Bartovic, Milan	Buf., Chi.	3	50	3	14	17	26	....	....	....	....	....	....	2002-03	2005-06
‡ Bartulis, Oskars	Phi.	2	66	1	8	9	32	7	0	0	0	4	....	2009-10	2010-11
Bashkirov, Andrei	Mtl.	3	30	0	3	3	0	....	....	....	....	....	....	1998-99	2000-01
Bassen, Bob	NYI, Chi., St.L., Que., Dal., Cgy.	15	765	88	144	232	1004	93	9	15	24	134	....	1985-86	1999-00
Bast, Ryan	Phi.	1	2	0	1	1	0	....	....	....	....	....	....	1998-99	1998-99
Bates, Shawn	Bos., NYI	10	465	72	126	198	266	29	3	4	7	19	....	1997-98	2007-08
Bathe, Frank	Det., Phi.	9	224	3	28	31	542	27	1	3	4	42	....	1974-75	1983-84
Bathgate, Andy	NYR, Tor., Det., Pit.	17	1069	349	624	973	624	54	21	14	35	76	1	1952-53	1970-71
● Bathgate, Frank	NYR	1	2	0	0	0	2	....	....	....	....	....	....	1952-53	1952-53
Battaglia, Bates	Car., Col., Wsh., Tor.	9	580	80	118	198	385	42	5	16	21	28	....	1997-98	2007-08
● Batters, Jeff	St.L.	2	16	0	0	0	28	....	....	....	....	....	....	1993-94	1994-95
Batyrshin, Ruslan	L.A.	1	2	0	0	0	6	....	....	....	....	....	....	1995-96	1995-96
● Bauer, Bobby	Bos.	9	327	123	137	260	36	48	11	8	19	6	2	1936-37	1951-52
Baumgartner, Ken	L.A., NYI, Tor., Ana., Bos.	12	696	13	41	54	2244	51	1	2	3	106	....	1987-88	1998-99
Baumgartner, Mike	K.C.	1	17	0	0	0	0	....	....	....	....	....	....	1974-75	1974-75
Baumgartner, Nolan	Wsh., Chi., Van., Pit., Phi., Dal.	10	143	7	40	47	69	4	0	0	0	10	....	1995-96	2009-10
Baun, Bob	Tor., Oak., Det.	17	964	37	187	224	1493	96	3	12	15	171	4	1956-57	1972-73
Bautin, Sergei	Wpg., Det., S.J.	3	132	5	25	30	176	6	0	0	0	2	....	1992-93	1995-96
Bawa, Robin	Wsh., Van., S.J., Ana.	4	61	6	1	7	60	1	0	0	0	0	....	1989-90	1993-94
Baxter, Paul	Que., Pit., Cgy.	8	472	48	121	169	1564	40	0	5	5	162	....	1979-80	1986-87
‡ Bayda, Ryan	Car.	5	179	16	24	40	94	15	2	2	4	18	....	2002-03	2008-09
Beadle, Sandy	Wpg.	1	6	1	0	1	2	....	....	....	....	....	....	1980-81	1980-81
Beaton, Frank	NYR	2	25	1	1	2	43	....	....	....	....	....	....	1978-79	1979-80
● Beattie, Red	Bos., Det., NYA	9	334	62	85	147	137	24	4	2	6	8	....	1930-31	1938-39
Beaudin, Norm	St.L., Min.	2	25	1	2	3	4	....	....	....	....	....	....	1967-68	1970-71
‡ Beaudoin, Eric	Fla.	3	53	3	8	11	41	....	....	....	....	....	....	2001-02	2003-04
Beaudoin, Serge	Atl.	1	3	0	0	0	0	....	....	....	....	....	....	1979-80	1979-80
Beaudoin, Yves	Wsh.	3	11	0	0	0	5	....	....	....	....	....	....	1985-86	1987-88
Beaufait, Mark	S.J.	1	5	1	0	1	0	....	....	....	....	....	....	1992-93	1992-93
Beck, Barry	Col., NYR, L.A.	10	615	104	251	355	1016	51	10	23	33	77	....	1977-78	1989-90
Beckett, Bob	Bos.	4	68	7	6	13	18	....	....	....	....	....	....	1956-57	1963-64
Bedard, James	Chi.	2	22	1	1	2	8	....	....	....	....	....	....	1949-50	1950-51
Beddoes, Clayton	Bos.	2	60	2	8	10	57	....	....	....	....	....	....	1995-96	1996-97
‡ Bednar, Jaroslav	L.A., Fla.	3	102	10	25	35	30	3	0	0	0	0	....	2001-02	2003-04
Bednarski, John	NYR, Edm.	4	100	2	18	20	114	1	0	0	0	17	....	1974-75	1979-80
Beech, Kris	Wsh., Pit., Nsh., CBJ, Van.	7	198	25	42	67	113	....	....	....	....	....	....	2000-01	2007-08
Beers, Bob	Bos., T.B., Edm., NYI	8	258	28	79	107	225	21	1	1	2	22	....	1989-90	1996-97
Beers, Eddy	Cgy., St.L.	5	250	94	116	210	256	41	7	10	17	47	....	1981-82	1985-86
Begin, Steve	Cgy., Mtl., Dal., Bos., Nsh.	13	524	56	52	108	561	36	1	4	5	30	....	1997-98	2012-13
● Behling, Dick	Det.	2	5	1	0	1	2	....	....	....	....	....	....	1940-41	1942-43
● Beisler, Frank	NYA	2	2	0	0	0	0	....	....	....	....	....	....	1936-37	1939-40
Bekar, Derek	St.L., L.A., NYI	3	11	0	0	0	6	....	....	....	....	....	....	1999-00	2003-04
● Belak, Wade	Col., Cgy., Tor., Fla., Nsh.	14	549	8	25	33	1263	22	1	0	1	36	....	1996-97	2010-11
Belanger, Alain	Tor.	1	9	0	1	1	6	....	....	....	....	....	....	1977-78	1977-78
‡ Belanger, Eric	L.A., Car., Atl., Min., Wsh., Phx., Edm.	12	820	138	220	358	361	41	2	5	7	28	....	2000-01	2012-13
Belanger, Francis	Mtl.	1	10	0	0	0	29	....	....	....	....	....	....	2000-01	2000-01
Belanger, Jesse	Mtl., Fla., Van., Edm., NYI	8	246	59	76	135	56	12	0	3	3	2	1	1991-92	2000-01
Belanger, Ken	Tor., NYI, Bos., L.A.	11	248	11	12	23	695	12	1	0	1	16	....	1994-95	2005-06
● Belanger, Roger	Pit.	1	44	3	5	8	32	....	....	....	....	....	....	1984-85	1984-85
Belisle, Danny	NYR	1	4	2	0	2	0	....	....	....	....	....	....	1960-61	1960-61
● Beliveau, Jean	Mtl.	20	1125	507	712	1219	1029	162	79	97	176	211	10	1950-51	1970-71
● Bell, Billy	Mtl.W., Mtl., Ott.	6	66	3	2	5	14	5	0	0	0	0	1	1917-18	1923-24
‡ Bell, Brendan	Tor., Phx., Ott., NYR	5	102	7	21	28	51	....	....	....	....	....	....	2005-06	2011-12
Bell, Bruce	Que., St.L., NYR, Edm.	5	209	12	64	76	113	34	3	5	8	41	....	1984-85	1989-90
● Bell, Huddy	NYR	1	1	0	1	1	0	....	....	....	....	....	....	1946-47	1946-47
● Bell, Joe	NYR	2	62	8	9	17	18	....	....	....	....	....	....	1942-43	1946-47
‡ Bell, Mark	Chi., S.J., Tor., Ana.	8	450	87	95	182	602	9	0	0	0	10	....	2000-01	2011-12
Belland, Neil	Van., Pit.	6	109	13	32	45	54	21	2	9	11	23	....	1981-82	1986-87
‡ Belle, Shawn	Min., Mtl., Edm., Col.	3	20	0	1	1	2	....	....	....	....	....	....	2006-07	2010-11
Bellefeuille, Blake	CBJ	2	5	0	1	1	0	....	....	....	....	....	....	2001-02	2002-03
● Bellefeuille, Pete	Tor., Det.	4	92	26	4	30	58	....	....	....	....	....	....	1925-26	1929-30
● Bellemer, Andy	Mtl.M.	1	15	0	0	0	0	....	....	....	....	....	....	1932-33	1932-33
Bellows, Brian	Min., Mtl., T.B., Ana., Wsh.	17	1188	485	537	1022	718	143	51	71	122	143	1	1982-83	1998-99
● Bend, Lin	NYR	1	8	3	1	4	2	....	....	....	....	....	....	1942-43	1942-43
Benda, Jan	Wsh.	1	9	0	3	3	6	....	....	....	....	....	....	1997-98	1997-98
Bennett, Adam	Chi., Edm.	3	69	3	8	11	69	....	....	....	....	....	....	1991-92	1993-94
Bennett, Bill	Bos., Hfd.	2	31	4	7	11	65	....	....	....	....	....	....	1978-79	1979-80
Bennett, Curt	St.L., NYR, Atl.	10	580	152	182	334	347	21	1	1	2	57	....	1970-71	1979-80
● Bennett, Frank	Det.	1	7	0	1	1	2	....	....	....	....	....	....	1943-44	1943-44
Bennett, Harvey	Pit., Wsh., Phi., Min., St.L.	5	268	44	46	90	347	4	0	0	0	2	....	1974-75	1978-79
● Bennett, Max	Mtl.	1	1	0	0	0	0	....	....	....	....	....	....	1935-36	1935-36
Bennett, Rick	NYR	3	15	1	1	2	13	....	....	....	....	....	....	1989-90	1991-92
Benning, Brian	St.L., L.A., Phi., Edm., Fla.	11	568	63	233	296	963	48	3	20	23	74	....	1984-85	1994-95
Benning, Jim	Tor., Van.	9	605	52	191	243	461	7	1	1	2	2	....	1981-82	1989-90
● Benoit, Joe	Mtl.	5	185	75	69	144	94	11	6	3	9	11	1	1940-41	1946-47
● Benson, Bill	NYA, Bro.	2	67	11	25	36	35	....	....	....	....	....	....	1940-41	1941-42
● Benson, Bobby	Bos.	1	8	0	1	1	4	....	....	....	....	....	....	1924-25	1924-25
Bentivoglio, Sean	NYI	1	1	0	0	0	2	....	....	....	....	....	....	2008-09	2008-09
● Bentley, Doug	Chi., NYR	13	566	219	324	543	217	23	9	8	17	12	....	1939-40	1953-54
● Bentley, Max	Chi., Tor., NYR	12	646	245	299	544	179	51	18	27	45	14	3	1940-41	1953-54
● Bentley, Reg	Chi.	1	11	1	2	3	2	....	....	....	....	....	....	1942-43	1942-43
Benysek, Ladislav	Edm., Min.	4	161	3	12	15	74	....	....	....	....	....	....	1997-98	2002-03
Beraldo, Paul	Bos.	2	10	0	0	0	4	....	....	....	....	....	....	1987-88	1988-89
Beranek, Josef	Edm., Phi., Van., Pit.	9	531	118	144	262	398	57	5	8	13	24	....	1991-92	2000-01
Berard, Bryan	NYI, Tor., NYR, Bos., Chi., CBJ	10	619	76	247	323	500	20	2	8	10	10	....	1996-97	2007-08
Berehowsky, Drake	Tor., Pit., Edm., Nsh., Van., Phx.	13	549	37	112	149	848	22	1	3	4	30	....	1990-91	2003-04
Berenson, Red	Mtl., NYR, St.L., Det.	17	987	261	397	658	305	85	23	14	37	49	1	1961-62	1977-78
Berenzweig, Bubba	Nsh.	4	37	3	7	10	14	....	....	....	....	....	....	1999-00	2002-03
Berezan, Perry	Cgy., Min., S.J.	9	378	61	75	136	279	31	4	7	11	34	....	1984-85	1992-93
Berezin, Sergei	Tor., Phx., Mtl., Chi., Wsh.	7	502	160	126	286	54	52	13	17	30	6	....	1996-97	2002-03
Berg, Aki	L.A., Tor.	9	606	15	70	85	374	54	1	7	8	47	....	1995-96	2005-06
Berg, Bill	NYI, Tor., NYR, Ott.	10	546	55	67	122	488	61	3	4	7	34	....	1988-89	1998-99
● Bergdinon, Fred	Bos.	1	2	0	0	0	0	....	....	....	....	....	....	1925-26	1925-26
Bergen, Todd	Phi.	1	14	11	5	16	4	17	4	9	13	8	....	1984-85	1984-85
Berger, Mike	Min.	2	30	3	1	4	67	....	....	....	....	....	....	1987-88	1988-89
‡ Bergeron, Marc-Andre	Edm., NYI, Ana., Min., Mtl., T.B., Car.	10	490	82	153	235	214	57	7	8	15	39	....	2002-03	2012-13
Bergeron, Michel	Det., NYI, Wsh.	5	229	80	58	138	165	....	....	....	....	....	....	1974-75	1978-79
Bergeron, Yves	Pit.	2	3	0	0	0	0	....	....	....	....	....	....	1974-75	1976-77
Bergevin, Marc	Chi., NYI, Hfd., T.B., Det., St.L., Pit., Van.	20	1191	36	145	181	1090	80	3	6	9	52	....	1984-85	2003-04
‡ Bergfors, Niclas	N.J., Atl., Fla., Nsh.	5	173	35	48	83	20	....	....	....	....	....	....	2007-08	2011-12
Bergkvist, Stefan	Pit.	2	7	0	0	0	9	4	0	0	0	2	....	1995-96	1996-97
Bergland, Tim	Wsh., T.B.	5	182	17	26	43	75	26	2	2	4	22	....	1989-90	1993-94
Bergloff, Bob	Min.	1	2	0	0	0	5	....	....	....	....	....	....	1982-83	1982-83
Berglund, Bo	Que., Min., Phi.	3	130	28	39	67	40	9	2	0	2	6	....	1983-84	1985-86
‡ Berglund, Christian	N.J., Fla.	3	86	11	16	27	42	3	0	0	0	2	....	2001-02	2003-04
● Bergman, Gary	Det., Min., K.C.	12	838	68	299	367	1249	21	0	5	5	20	....	1964-65	1975-76
Bergman, Thommie	Det.	6	246	21	44	65	243	7	0	2	2	2	....	1972-73	1979-80
Bergqvist, Jonas	Cgy.	1	22	2	5	7	10	....	....	....	....	....	....	1989-90	1989-90
● Berlinguette, Louis	Mtl., Mtl.M., Pit.	8	193	45	33	78	129	11	0	5	5	9	....	1917-18	1925-26
Bernier, Serge	Phi., L.A., Que.	7	302	78	119	197	234	5	1	1	2	0	....	1968-69	1980-81
Berry, Bob	Mtl., L.A.	8	541	159	191	350	344	26	2	6	8	6	....	1968-69	1976-77
Berry, Brad	Wpg., Min., Dal.	8	241	4	28	32	323	13	0	1	1	16	....	1985-86	1993-94
Berry, Doug	Col.	2	121	10	33	43	25	....	....	....	....	....	....	1979-80	1980-81
Berry, Fred	Det.	1	3	0	0	0	0	....	....	....	....	....	....	1976-77	1976-77
Berry, Ken	Edm., Van.	4	55	8	10	18	30	....	....	....	....	....	....	1981-82	1988-89

Name	NHL Teams	NHL Seasons	Regular Schedule GP	G	A	TP	PIM	Playoffs GP	G	A	TP	PIM	NHL Cup Wins	First NHL Season	Last NHL Season
Berry, Rick	Col., Pit., Wsh.	4	197	2	13	15	314	....	....	....	....	....	....	2000-01	2003-04
Berti, Adam	Chi.	1	2	0	0	0	0	....	....	....	....	....	....	2007-08	2007-08
Bertrand, Eric	N.J., Atl., Mtl.	2	15	0	0	0	4	....	....	....	....	....	....	1999-00	2000-01
‡ Bertuzzi, Todd	NYI, Van., Fla., Det., Ana., Cgy.	18	1159	314	456	770	1478	87	14	28	42	159	....	1995-96	2013-14
Berube, Craig	Phi., Tor., Cgy., Wsh., NYI	17	1054	61	98	159	3149	89	3	1	4	211	....	1986-87	2002-03
• Besler, Phil	Bos., Chi., Det.	2	30	1	4	5	18	....	....	....	....	....	....	1935-36	1938-39
• Bessone, Pete	Det.	1	6	0	1	1	6	....	....	....	....	....	....	1937-38	1937-38
Bethel, John	Wpg.	1	17	0	2	2	4	....	....	....	....	....	....	1979-80	1979-80
Betik, Karel	T.B.	1	3	0	2	2	2	....	....	....	....	....	....	1998-99	1998-99
Bets, Maxim	Ana.	1	3	0	0	0	0	....	....	....	....	....	....	1993-94	1993-94
• Bettio, Sam	Bos.	1	44	9	12	21	32	....	....	....	....	....	....	1949-50	1949-50
Betts, Blair	Cgy., NYR, Phi.	9	477	41	37	78	118	62	2	2	4	12	....	2001-02	2010-11
Beukeboom, Jeff	Edm., NYR	14	804	30	129	159	1890	99	3	16	19	197	4	1985-86	1998-99
Beverley, Nick	Bos., Pit., NYR, Min., L.A., Col.	11	502	18	94	112	156	7	0	1	1	0	....	1966-67	1979-80
‡ Bezina, Goran	Phx.	1	3	0	0	0	2	....	....	....	....	....	....	2003-04	2003-04
Bialowas, Dwight	Atl., Min.	4	164	11	46	57	46	....	....	....	....	....	....	1973-74	1976-77
Bialowas, Frank	Tor.	1	3	0	0	0	12	....	....	....	....	....	....	1993-94	1993-94
Bianchin, Wayne	Pit., Edm.	7	276	68	41	109	137	3	0	1	1	6	....	1973-74	1979-80
Bicanek, Radim	Ott., Chi., CBJ	7	122	1	11	12	62	7	0	0	0	8	....	1994-95	2001-02
‡ Bicek, Jiri	N.J.	4	62	6	7	13	29	7	0	0	0	0	1	2000-01	2003-04
Bidner, Todd	Wsh.	1	12	2	1	3	7	....	....	....	....	....	....	1981-82	1981-82
Biggs, Don	Min., Phi.	2	12	2	0	2	8	....	....	....	....	....	....	1984-85	1989-90
Bignell, Larry	Pit.	2	20	0	3	3	2	3	0	0	0	2	....	1973-74	1974-75
• Bilodeau, Gilles	Que.	1	9	0	1	1	25	....	....	....	....	....	....	1979-80	1979-80
• Bionda, Jack	Tor., Bos.	4	93	3	9	12	113	11	0	1	1	14	....	1955-56	1958-59
Biron, Mathieu	NYI, T.B., Fla., Wsh.	6	253	12	32	44	177	....	....	....	....	....	....	1999-00	2005-06
Bisaillon, Sebastien	Edm.	1	2	0	0	0	0	....	....	....	....	....	....	2006-07	2006-07
Bishai, Mike	Edm.	1	14	0	2	2	19	....	....	....	....	....	....	2003-04	2003-04
Bissett, Tom	Det.	1	5	0	0	0	0	....	....	....	....	....	....	1990-91	1990-91
Bitz, Byron	Bos., Fla., Van.	3	97	10	12	22	65	6	1	1	2	17	....	2008-09	2011-12
Bjugstad, Scott	Min., Pit., L.A.	9	317	76	68	144	144	9	0	1	1	2	....	1983-84	1991-92
Black, James	Hfd., Min., Dal., Buf., Chi., Wsh.	11	352	58	57	115	84	13	2	1	3	4	....	1989-90	2000-01
• Black, Steve	Det., Chi.	2	113	11	20	31	77	13	0	0	0	13	1	1949-50	1950-51
Blackburn, Bob	NYR, Pit.	3	135	8	12	20	105	6	0	0	0	4	....	1968-69	1970-71
Blackburn, Don	Bos., Phi., NYR, NYI, Min.	6	185	23	44	67	87	12	3	0	3	10	....	1962-63	1972-73
• Blade, Hank	Chi.	2	24	2	3	5	2	....	....	....	....	....	....	1946-47	1947-48
Bladon, Tom	Phi., Pit., Edm., Wpg., Det.	9	610	73	197	270	392	86	8	29	37	70	2	1972-73	1980-81
• Blaine, Garry	Mtl.	1	1	0	0	0	0	....	....	....	....	....	....	1954-55	1954-55
• Blair, Andy	Tor., Chi.	9	402	74	86	160	323	38	6	6	12	32	1	1928-29	1936-37
• Blair, Chuck	Tor.	1	1	0	0	0	0	....	....	....	....	....	....	1948-49	1948-49
• Blair, Dusty	Tor.	1	2	0	0	0	0	....	....	....	....	....	....	1950-51	1950-51
Blaisdell, Mike	Det., NYR, Pit., Tor.	9	343	70	84	154	166	6	1	2	3	10	....	1980-81	1988-89
• Blake, Bob	Bos.	1	12	0	0	0	0	....	....	....	....	....	....	1935-36	1935-36
Blake, Jason	L.A., NYI, Tor., Ana.	13	871	213	273	486	455	30	6	5	11	19	....	1998-99	2011-12
• Blake, Mickey	Mtl.M., St.L., Tor.	3	10	1	1	2	4	....	....	....	....	....	....	1932-33	1935-36
Blake, Rob	L.A., Col., S.J.	20	1270	240	537	777	1679	146	26	47	73	166	1	1989-90	2009-10
• Blake, Toe	Mtl.M., Mtl.	14	577	235	292	527	272	58	25	37	62	23	3	1934-35	1947-48
Blatny, Zdenek	Atl., Bos.	3	25	3	0	3	8	....	....	....	....	....	....	2002-03	2005-06
• Blight, Rick	Van., L.A.	7	326	96	125	221	170	5	0	5	5	2	....	1975-76	1982-83
• Blinco, Russ	Mtl.M., Chi.	6	268	59	66	125	24	19	3	3	6	4	1	1933-34	1938-39
‡ Bliznak, Mario	Van.	2	6	1	0	1	0	....	....	....	....	....	....	2009-10	2010-11
Block, Ken	Van.	1	1	0	0	0	0	....	....	....	....	....	....	1970-71	1970-71
Bloemberg, Jeff	NYR	4	43	3	6	9	25	7	0	3	3	5	....	1988-89	1991-92
Blomqvist, Timo	Wsh., N.J.	5	243	4	53	57	293	13	0	0	0	24	....	1981-82	1986-87
Blomsten, Arto	Wpg., L.A.	3	25	0	4	4	8	....	....	....	....	....	....	1993-94	1995-96
Bloom, Mike	Wsh., Det.	3	201	30	47	77	215	....	....	....	....	....	....	1974-75	1976-77
Blouin, Sylvain	NYR, Mtl., Min.	6	115	3	4	7	336	....	....	....	....	....	....	1996-97	2002-03
Blum, John	Edm., Bos., Wsh., Det.	8	250	7	34	41	610	20	0	2	2	27	....	1982-83	1989-90
‡ Bochenski, Brandon	Ott., Chi., Bos., Ana., Nsh., T.B.	5	156	28	40	68	54	3	0	0	0	0	....	2005-06	2009-10
Bodak, Bob	Cgy., Hfd.	2	4	0	0	0	29	....	....	....	....	....	....	1987-88	1989-90
Boddy, Gregg	Van.	5	273	23	44	67	263	3	0	0	0	0	....	1971-72	1975-76
Bodger, Doug	Pit., Buf., S.J., N.J., L.A., Van.	16	1071	106	422	528	1007	47	6	18	24	25	....	1984-85	1999-00
• Bodnar, Gus	Tor., Chi., Bos.	12	667	142	254	396	207	32	4	3	7	10	2	1943-44	1954-55
Boehm, Ron	Oak.	1	16	2	1	3	10	....	....	....	....	....	....	1967-68	1967-68
• Boesch, Garth	Tor.	4	197	9	28	37	205	34	2	5	7	18	3	1946-47	1949-50
Boguniecki, Eric	Fla., St.L., Pit., NYI	7	178	34	42	76	105	9	1	3	4	2	....	1999-00	2006-07
Boh, Rick	Min.	1	8	2	1	3	4	....	....	....	....	....	....	1987-88	1987-88
Bohonos, Lonny	Van., Tor.	4	83	19	16	35	22	9	3	6	9	2	....	1995-96	1998-99
Boikov, Alexandre	Nsh.	2	10	0	0	0	15	....	....	....	....	....	....	1999-00	2000-01
• Boileau, Marc	Det.	1	54	5	6	11	8	....	....	....	....	....	....	1961-62	1961-62
Boileau, Patrick	Wsh., Det., Pit.	5	48	5	11	16	26	....	....	....	....	....	....	1996-97	2003-04
• Boileau, Rene	NYA	1	7	0	0	0	0	....	....	....	....	....	....	1925-26	1925-26
Boimistruck, Fred	Tor.	2	83	4	14	18	45	....	....	....	....	....	....	1981-82	1982-83
Bois, Danny	Ott.	1	1	0	0	0	7	....	....	....	....	....	....	2006-07	2006-07
Boisvert, Serge	Tor., Mtl.	5	46	5	7	12	8	23	3	7	10	4	1	1982-83	1987-88
Boivin, Claude	Phi., Ott.	4	132	12	19	31	364	....	....	....	....	....	....	1991-92	1994-95
Boivin, Leo	Tor., Bos., Det., Pit., Min.	19	1150	72	250	322	1192	54	3	10	13	59	....	1951-52	1969-70
Boland, Mike	Phi.	1	2	0	0	0	0	....	....	....	....	....	....	1974-75	1974-75
Boland, Mike	K.C., Buf.	2	23	1	2	3	29	3	1	0	1	2	....	1974-75	1978-79
Boldirev, Ivan	Bos., Cal., Chi., Atl., Van., Det.	16	1052	361	505	866	507	48	13	20	33	14	1	1969-70	1984-85
Bolduc, Danny	Det., Cgy.	3	102	22	19	41	33	1	0	0	0	0	....	1978-79	1983-84
Bolduc, Michel	Que.	2	10	0	0	0	6	....	....	....	....	....	....	1981-82	1982-83
• Boll, Buzz	Tor., NYA, Bro., Bos.	12	437	133	130	263	148	31	7	3	10	13	....	1932-33	1943-44
Bolonchuk, Larry	Van., Wsh.	4	74	3	9	12	97	....	....	....	....	....	....	1972-73	1977-78
• Bolton, Hugh	Tor.	8	235	10	51	61	221	17	0	5	5	14	1	1949-50	1956-57
Bombardir, Brad	N.J., Min., Nsh.	7	356	8	46	54	127	16	0	1	1	2	1	1997-98	2003-04
Bonar, Dan	L.A.	3	170	25	39	64	208	14	3	4	7	22	....	1980-81	1982-83
Bondra, Peter	Wsh., Ott., Atl., Chi.	16	1081	503	389	892	761	80	30	26	56	60	....	1990-91	2006-07
Bonin, Brian	Pit., Min.	2	12	0	0	0	0	3	0	0	0	0	....	1998-99	2000-01
Bonin, Marcel	Det., Bos., Mtl.	9	454	97	175	272	336	50	11	14	25	51	4	1952-53	1961-62
‡ Bonk, Radek	Ott., Mtl., Nsh.	14	969	194	303	497	581	73	12	15	27	42	....	1994-95	2008-09
‡ Bonni, Ryan	Van.	1	3	0	0	0	0	....	....	....	....	....	....	1999-00	1999-00
Bonsignore, Jason	Edm., T.B.	4	79	3	13	16	34	....	....	....	....	....	....	1994-95	1998-99
Bonvie, Dennis	Edm., Chi., Pit., Bos., Ott., Col.	9	92	1	2	3	311	1	0	0	0	0	....	1994-95	2003-04
Boo, Jim	Min.	1	6	0	0	0	22	....	....	....	....	....	....	1977-78	1977-78
• Boogaard, Derek	Min., NYR	6	277	3	13	16	589	10	0	1	1	44	....	2005-06	2010-11
• Boone, Buddy	Bos.	2	34	5	3	8	28	22	2	1	3	25	....	1956-57	1957-58
• Boothman, George	Tor.	2	58	17	19	36	18	5	2	1	3	2	....	1942-43	1943-44
‡ Bootland, Darryl	Det., NYI	3	32	1	2	3	85	....	....	....	....	....	....	2003-04	2007-08
Bordeleau, Christian	Mtl., St.L., Chi.	4	205	38	65	103	82	19	4	7	11	17	1	1968-69	1971-72
Bordeleau, J.P.	Chi.	10	519	97	126	223	143	48	3	6	9	12	....	1969-70	1979-80
Bordeleau, Paulin	Van.	3	183	33	56	89	47	5	2	1	3	0	....	1973-74	1975-76
Bordeleau, Sebastien	Mtl., Nsh., Min., Phx.	7	251	37	61	98	118	5	0	0	0	2	....	1995-96	2001-02
‡ Borer, Casey	Car.	3	16	1	2	3	9	....	....	....	....	....	....	2007-08	2009-10
Borotsik, Jack	St.L.	1	1	0	0	0	0	....	....	....	....	....	....	1974-75	1974-75
Borsato, Luciano	Wpg.	5	203	35	55	90	113	7	1	0	1	4	....	1990-91	1994-95
Borschevsky, Nikolai	Tor., Cgy., Dal.	4	162	49	73	122	44	31	4	9	13	4	....	1992-93	1995-96
Boschman, Laurie	Tor., Edm., Wpg., N.J., Ott.	14	1009	229	348	577	2265	57	8	13	21	140	....	1979-80	1992-93
Bossy, Mike	NYI	10	752	573	553	1126	210	129	85	75	160	38	4	1977-78	1986-87
• Bostrom, Helge	Chi.	4	96	3	3	6	58	13	0	0	0	16	....	1929-30	1932-33
Botell, Mark	Phi.	1	32	4	10	14	31	....	....	....	....	....	....	1981-82	1981-82
Bothwell, Tim	NYR, St.L., Hfd.	11	502	28	93	121	382	49	0	3	3	56	....	1978-79	1988-89
Botterill, Jason	Dal., Atl., Cgy., Buf.	6	88	5	9	14	89	....	....	....	....	....	....	1997-98	2003-04
Botting, Cam	Atl.	1	2	0	1	1	0	....	....	....	....	....	....	1975-76	1975-76
Boucha, Henry	Det., Min., K.C., Col.	6	247	53	49	102	157	....	....	....	....	....	....	1971-72	1976-77
• Bouchard, Butch	Mtl.	15	785	49	144	193	863	113	11	21	32	121	4	1941-42	1955-56
• Bouchard, Dick	NYR	1	1	0	0	0	0	....	....	....	....	....	....	1954-55	1954-55
• Bouchard, Edmond	Mtl., Ham., NYA, Pit.	8	211	19	21	40	117	....	....	....	....	....	....	1921-22	1928-29
Bouchard, Joel	Cgy., Nsh., Dal., Phx., N.J., NYR, Pit., NYI	11	364	22	53	75	264	....	....	....	....	....	....	1994-95	2005-06
Bouchard, Pierre	Mtl., Wsh.	12	595	24	82	106	433	76	3	10	13	56	5	1970-71	1981-82
• Boucher, Billy	Mtl., Bos., NYA	7	213	93	38	131	409	14	3	0	3	17	1	1921-22	1927-28
• Boucher, Bobby	Mtl.	1	11	1	0	1	0	2	0	0	0	0	1	1923-24	1923-24
• Boucher, Clarence	NYA	2	47	2	2	4	133	....	....	....	....	....	....	1926-27	1927-28
• Boucher, Frank	Ott., NYR	14	557	160	263	423	119	55	16	20	36	12	2	1921-22	1943-44
• Boucher, George	Ott., Mtl.M., Chi.	15	449	117	87	204	838	28	5	3	8	88	4	1917-18	1931-32

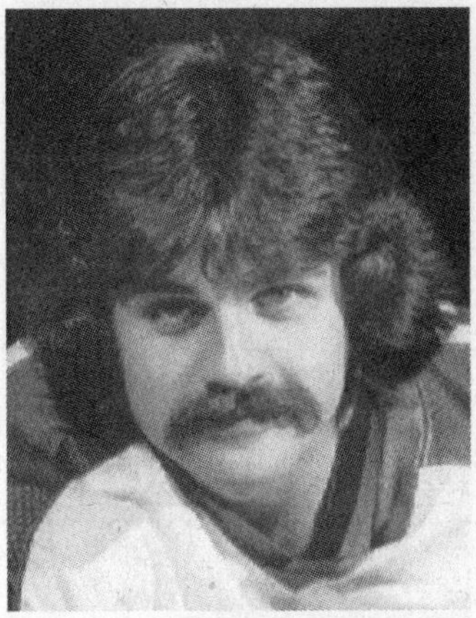

Cam Botting

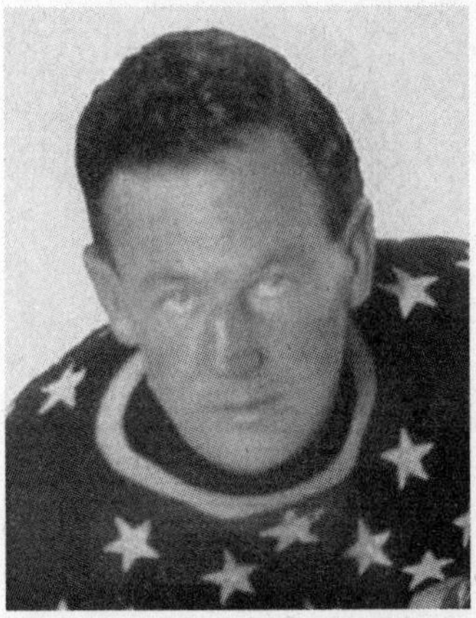

Clarence Boucher

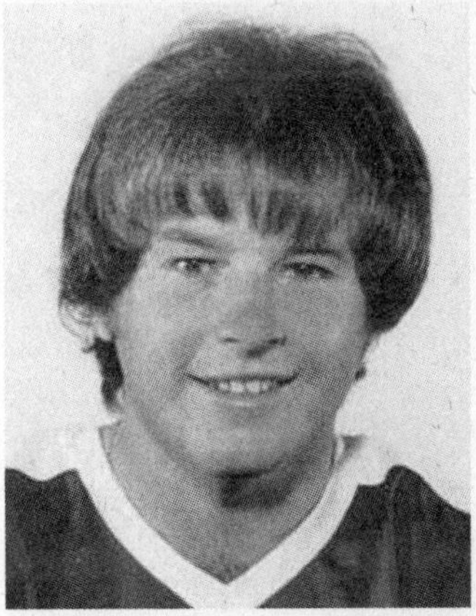

Bruce Boudreau

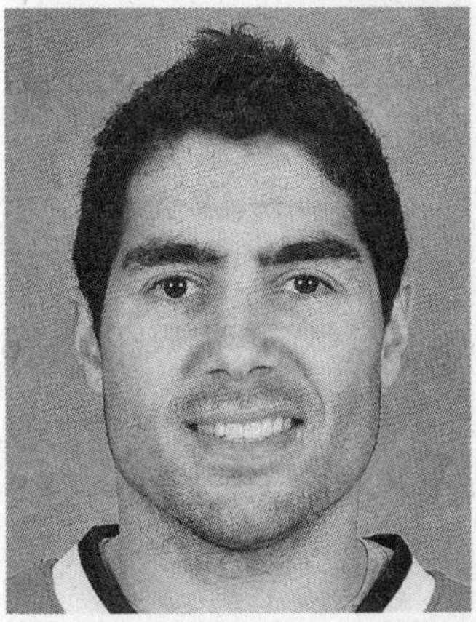

Francis Bouillon

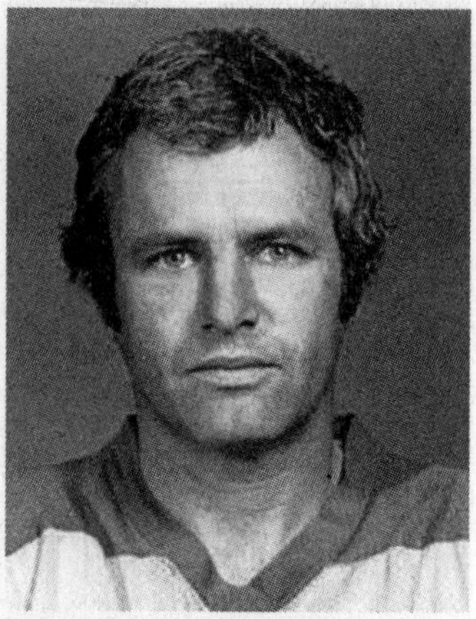

Lyle Bradley

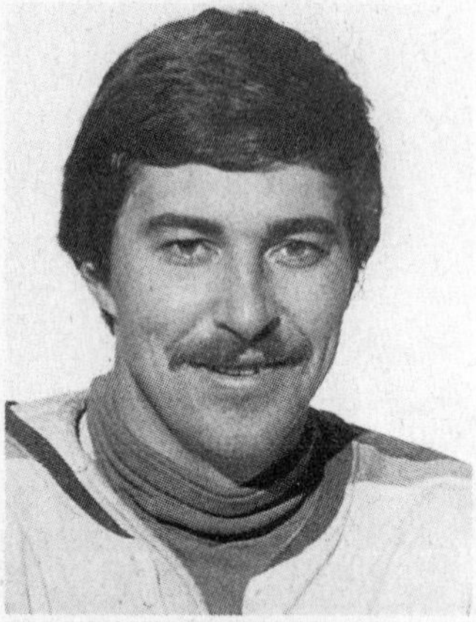

Ken Breitenbach

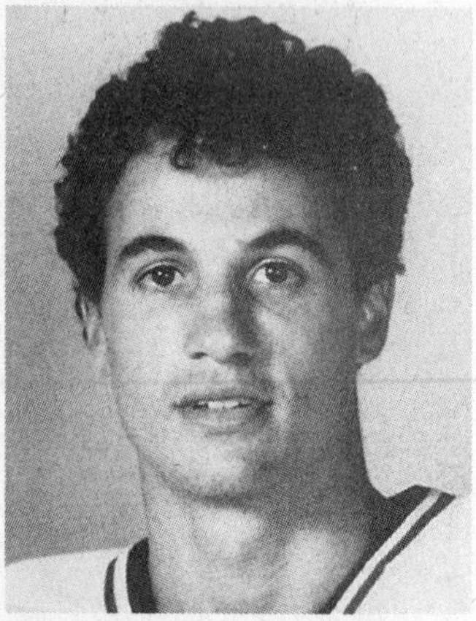

Greg Britz

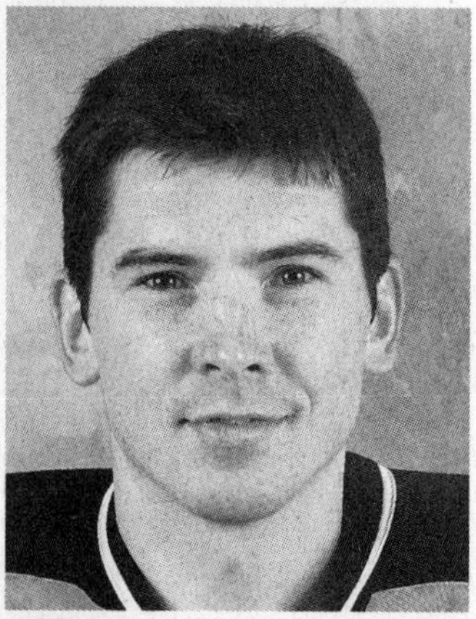

Sergei Brylin

Name	NHL Teams	NHL Seasons	Regular Schedule GP	G	A	TP	PIM	Playoffs GP	G	A	TP	PIM	NHL Cup Wins	First NHL Season	Last NHL Season
Boucher, Philippe	Buf., L.A., Dal., Pit.	16	748	94	206	300	702	65	4	10	14	39	1	1992-93	2008-09
Bouck, Tyler	Dal., Phx., Van.	5	91	4	8	12	93	2	0	0	0	0	....	2000-01	2006-07
Boudreau, Bruce	Tor., Chi.	8	141	28	42	70	46	9	2	0	2	0	....	1976-77	1985-86
Boudrias, Andre	Mtl., Min., Chi., St.L., Van.	12	662	151	340	491	216	34	6	10	16	12	....	1963-64	1975-76
Boughner, Barry	Oak., Cal.	2	20	0	0	0	11	....	....	....	....	....	....	1969-70	1970-71
Boughner, Bob	Buf., Nsh., Pit., Cgy., Car., Col.	10	630	15	57	72	1382	65	0	12	12	67	....	1995-96	2005-06
‡ Bouillon, Francis	Mtl., Nsh.	14	776	32	117	149	536	55	4	7	11	50	....	1999-00	2013-14
Boulerice, Jesse	Phi., Car., St.L., Edm.	6	172	8	2	10	333	....	....	....	....	....	....	2001-02	2008-09
Boumedienne, Josef	N.J., T.B., Wsh.	3	47	4	12	16	36	....	....	....	....	....	....	2001-02	2003-04
Bourbonnais, Dan	Hfd.	2	59	3	25	28	11	....	....	....	....	....	....	1981-82	1983-84
Bourbonnais, Rick	St.L.	3	71	9	15	24	29	4	0	1	1	0	....	1975-76	1977-78
• Bourcier, Conrad	Mtl.	1	6	0	0	0	0	....	....	....	....	....	....	1935-36	1935-36
• Bourcier, Jean	Mtl.	1	9	0	1	1	0	....	....	....	....	....	....	1935-36	1935-36
• Bourdon, Luc	Van.	2	36	2	0	2	24	....	....	....	....	....	....	2006-07	2007-08
‡ Bourdon, Marc-Andre	Phi.	1	45	4	3	7	52	1	0	0	0	0	....	2011-12	2011-12
• Bourgeault, Leo	Tor., NYR, Ott., Mtl.	8	307	24	20	44	334	24	1	1	2	18	1	1926-27	1934-35
Bourgeois, Charlie	Cgy., St.L., Hfd.	7	290	16	54	70	788	40	2	3	5	194	....	1981-82	1987-88
Bourne, Bob	NYI, L.A.	14	964	258	324	582	605	139	40	56	96	108	4	1974-75	1987-88
Bourque, Phil	Pit., NYR, Ott.	12	477	88	111	199	516	56	13	12	25	107	2	1983-84	1995-96
Bourque, Raymond	Bos., Col.	22	1612	410	1169	1579	1141	214	41	139	180	171	1	1979-80	2000-01
Boutette, Pat	Tor., Hfd., Pit.	10	756	171	282	453	1354	46	10	14	24	109	....	1975-76	1984-85
Boutilier, Paul	NYI, Bos., Min., NYR, Wpg.	8	288	27	83	110	358	41	1	9	10	45	1	1981-82	1988-89
Bowen, Jason	Phi., Edm.	6	77	2	6	8	109	....	....	....	....	....	....	1992-93	1997-98
Bowler, Bill	CBJ	1	9	0	2	2	8	....	....	....	....	....	....	2000-01	2000-01
Bowman, Kirk	Chi.	3	88	11	17	28	19	7	1	0	1	0	....	1976-77	1978-79
• Bowman, Ralph	Ott., St.L., Det.	7	274	8	17	25	260	22	2	2	4	6	2	1933-34	1939-40
• Bownass, Jack	Mtl., NYR	4	80	3	8	11	58	....	....	....	....	....	....	1957-58	1961-62
Bowness, Rick	Atl., Det., St.L., Wpg.	7	173	18	37	55	191	5	0	0	0	2	....	1975-76	1981-82
‡ Boyce, Darryl	Tor., CBJ	3	84	6	12	18	68	....	....	....	....	....	....	2007-08	2011-12
• Boyd, Bill	NYR, NYA	4	138	15	7	22	72	10	0	0	0	4	1	1926-27	1929-30
‡ Boyd, Dustin	Cgy., Nsh., Mtl.	5	220	32	31	63	41	9	1	0	1	0	....	2006-07	2010-11
• Boyd, Irwin	Bos., Det.	4	96	10	10	20	30	5	0	1	1	4	....	1931-32	1943-44
Boyd, Randy	Pit., Chi., NYI, Van.	8	257	20	67	87	328	13	0	2	2	26	....	1981-82	1988-89
Boyer, Wally	Tor., Chi., Oak., Pit.	7	365	54	105	159	163	15	1	3	4	0	....	1965-66	1971-72
Boyer, Zac	Dal.	2	3	0	0	0	0	2	0	0	0	0	....	1994-95	1995-96
Boyko, Darren	Wpg.	1	1	0	0	0	0	....	....	....	....	....	....	1988-89	1988-89
Boynton, Nick	Bos., Phx., Fla., Ana., Chi., Phi.	11	605	34	110	144	862	21	1	5	6	16	1	1999-00	2010-11
Bozek, Steve	L.A., Cgy., St.L., Van., S.J.	11	641	164	167	331	309	58	12	11	23	69	....	1981-82	1991-92
Bozon, Philippe	St.L.	4	144	16	25	41	101	19	2	0	2	31	....	1991-92	1994-95
• Brackenborough, John	Bos.	1	7	0	0	0	0	....	....	....	....	....	....	1925-26	1925-26
Brackenbury, Curt	Que., Edm., St.L.	4	141	9	17	26	226	2	0	0	0	0	....	1979-80	1982-83
• Bradley, Bart	Bos.	1	1	0	0	0	0	....	....	....	....	....	....	1949-50	1949-50
Bradley, Brian	Cgy., Van., Tor., T.B.	13	651	182	321	503	528	13	3	7	10	16	....	1985-86	1997-98
Bradley, Lyle	Cal., Cle.	2	6	1	0	1	2	....	....	....	....	....	....	1973-74	1976-77
Bradley, Matt	S.J., Pit., Wsh., Fla.	11	675	59	90	149	562	47	3	8	11	8	....	2000-01	2011-12
Brady, Neil	N.J., Ott., Dal.	5	89	9	22	31	95	....	....	....	....	....	....	1989-90	1993-94
Bragnalo, Rick	Wsh.	4	145	15	35	50	46	....	....	....	....	....	....	1975-76	1978-79
Brandner, Christoph	Min.	1	35	4	5	9	8	....	....	....	....	....	....	2003-04	2003-04
• Branigan, Andy	NYA, Bro.	2	27	1	2	3	31	....	....	....	....	....	....	1940-41	1941-42
Brasar, Per-Olov	Min., Van.	5	348	64	142	206	33	13	1	2	3	0	....	1977-78	1981-82
Brashear, Donald	Mtl., Van., Phi., Wsh., NYR	16	1025	85	120	205	2634	60	3	6	9	121	....	1993-94	2009-10
• Brayshaw, Russ	Chi.	1	43	5	9	14	24	....	....	....	....	....	....	1944-45	1944-45
Breault, Francis	L.A.	3	27	2	4	6	42	....	....	....	....	....	....	1990-91	1992-93
Breitenbach, Ken	Buf.	3	68	1	13	14	49	8	0	1	1	4	....	1975-76	1978-79
Bremberg, Fredrik	Edm.	1	8	0	0	0	2	....	....	....	....	....	....	1998-99	1998-99
‡ Brendl, Pavel	Phi., Car., Phx.	4	78	11	11	22	16	2	0	0	0	0	....	2001-02	2005-06
Brennan, Dan	L.A.	2	8	0	1	1	9	....	....	....	....	....	....	1983-84	1985-86
• Brennan, Doug	NYR	3	123	9	7	16	152	16	1	0	1	21	1	1931-32	1933-34
Brennan, Kip	L.A., Atl., Ana., NYI	5	61	1	1	2	222	....	....	....	....	....	....	2001-02	2007-08
Brennan, Rich	Col., S.J., NYR, L.A., Nsh., Bos.	6	50	2	6	8	33	....	....	....	....	....	....	1996-97	2002-03
• Brennan, Tom	Bos.	2	12	2	2	4	2	....	....	....	....	....	....	1943-44	1944-45
Brenneman, John	Chi., NYR, Tor., Det., Oak.	5	152	21	19	40	46	....	....	....	....	....	1	1964-65	1968-69
• Bretto, Joe	Chi.	1	3	0	0	0	4	....	....	....	....	....	....	1944-45	1944-45
• Brewer, Carl	Tor., Det., St.L.	12	604	25	198	223	1037	72	3	17	20	146	3	1957-58	1979-80
Brickley, Andy	Phi., Pit., N.J., Bos., Wpg.	11	385	82	140	222	81	17	1	4	5	4	....	1982-83	1993-94
• Briden, Archie	Bos., Det., Pit.	2	71	9	5	14	56	....	....	....	....	....	....	1926-27	1929-30
Bridgman, Mel	Phi., Cgy., N.J., Det., Van.	14	977	252	449	701	1625	125	28	39	67	298	....	1975-76	1988-89
• Briere, Michel	Pit.	1	76	12	32	44	20	10	5	3	8	17	....	1969-70	1969-70
Brigley, Travis	Cgy., Col.	3	55	3	6	9	16	....	....	....	....	....	....	1997-98	2003-04
Brimanis, Aris	Phi., NYI, Ana., St.L.	7	113	2	12	14	57	....	....	....	....	....	....	1993-94	2003-04
Brind'Amour, Rod	St.L., Phi., Car.	21	1484	452	732	1184	1100	159	51	60	111	97	1	1988-89	2009-10
Brindley, Doug	Tor.	1	3	0	0	0	0	....	....	....	....	....	....	1970-71	1970-71
Brine, David	Fla.	1	9	0	1	1	4	....	....	....	....	....	....	2007-08	2007-08
• Brink, Milt	Chi.	1	5	0	0	0	0	....	....	....	....	....	....	1936-37	1936-37
Brisebois, Patrice	Mtl., Col.	18	1009	98	322	420	623	98	9	23	32	76	1	1990-91	2008-09
• Brisson, Gerry	Mtl.	1	4	0	2	2	4	....	....	....	....	....	....	1962-63	1962-63
Britz, Greg	Tor., Hfd.	3	8	0	0	0	4	....	....	....	....	....	....	1983-84	1986-87
• Broadbent, Punch	Ott., Mtl.M., NYA	11	303	121	51	172	564	23	4	6	10	60	4	1918-19	1928-29
Brochu, Stephane	NYR	1	1	0	0	0	0	....	....	....	....	....	....	1988-89	1988-89
• Broden, Connie	Mtl.	3	6	2	1	3	2	7	0	1	1	0	2	1955-56	1957-58
‡ Brookbank, Wade	Nsh., Van., Bos., Car.	5	127	6	3	9	345	....	....	....	....	....	....	2003-04	2008-09
Brooke, Bob	NYR, Min., N.J.	7	447	69	97	166	520	34	9	9	18	59	....	1983-84	1989-90
Brooks, Alex	N.J.	1	19	0	1	1	4	....	....	....	....	....	....	2006-07	2006-07
Brooks, Gord	St.L., Wsh.	3	70	7	18	25	37	....	....	....	....	....	....	1971-72	1974-75
Brophey, Evan	Chi., Col.	2	4	0	0	0	0	....	....	....	....	....	....	2010-11	2011-12
• Brophy, Bernie	Mtl.M., Det.	3	62	4	4	8	25	2	0	0	0	2	1	1925-26	1929-30
Brossart, Willie	Phi., Tor., Wsh.	6	129	1	14	15	88	1	0	0	0	0	....	1970-71	1975-76
Broten, Aaron	Col., N.J., Min., Que., Tor., Wpg.	12	748	186	329	515	441	34	7	18	25	40	....	1980-81	1991-92
Broten, Neal	Min., Dal., N.J., L.A.	17	1099	289	634	923	569	135	35	63	98	77	1	1980-81	1996-97
Broten, Paul	NYR, Dal., St.L.	7	322	46	55	101	264	38	4	6	10	18	....	1989-90	1995-96
Brousseau, Paul	Col., T.B., Fla.	4	26	1	3	4	29	....	....	....	....	....	....	1995-96	2000-01
• Brown, Adam	Det., Chi., Bos.	10	391	104	113	217	378	26	2	4	6	14	1	1941-42	1951-52
Brown, Arnie	Tor., NYR, Det., NYI, Atl.	12	681	44	141	185	738	22	0	6	6	23	....	1961-62	1973-74
Brown, Brad	Mtl., Chi., NYR, Min., Buf.	7	330	2	27	29	747	11	0	0	0	16	....	1996-97	2003-04
Brown, Cam	Van.	1	1	0	0	0	7	....	....	....	....	....	....	1990-91	1990-91
• Brown, Connie	Det.	5	73	15	24	39	12	14	2	3	5	0	1	1938-39	1942-43
Brown, Curtis	Buf., S.J., Chi.	13	736	129	171	300	398	87	14	15	29	58	....	1994-95	2007-08
Brown, Dave	Phi., Edm., S.J.	14	729	45	52	97	1789	80	2	3	5	209	1	1982-83	1995-96
Brown, Doug	N.J., Pit., Det.	15	854	160	214	374	210	109	23	23	46	26	2	1986-87	2000-01
• Brown, Fred	Mtl.M.	1	19	1	0	1	0	9	0	0	0	0	....	1927-28	1927-28
• Brown, George	Mtl.	3	79	6	22	28	34	7	0	0	0	2	....	1936-37	1938-39
• Brown, Gerry	Det.	2	23	4	5	9	2	12	2	1	3	4	....	1941-42	1945-46
Brown, Greg	Buf., Pit., Wpg.	4	94	4	14	18	86	6	0	1	1	4	....	1990-91	1994-95
• Brown, Harold	NYR	1	13	2	1	3	2	....	....	....	....	....	....	1945-46	1945-46
Brown, Jeff	Que., St.L., Van., Hfd., Car., Tor., Wsh.	13	747	154	430	584	498	87	20	45	65	59	....	1985-86	1997-98
Brown, Jim	L.A.	1	3	0	1	1	5	....	....	....	....	....	....	1982-83	1982-83
Brown, Keith	Chi., Fla.	16	876	68	274	342	916	103	4	32	36	184	....	1979-80	1994-95
Brown, Kevin	L.A., Hfd., Car., Edm.	6	64	7	9	16	28	1	0	0	0	0	....	1994-95	1999-00
Brown, Larry	NYR, Det., Phi., L.A.	9	455	7	53	60	180	35	0	4	4	10	....	1969-70	1977-78
Brown, Mike	Van., Ana., Chi.	4	34	1	2	3	130	....	....	....	....	....	....	2000-01	2005-06
Brown, Rob	Pit., Hfd., Chi., Dal., L.A.	11	543	190	248	438	599	54	12	14	26	45	....	1987-88	1999-00
Brown, Sean	Edm., Bos., N.J., Van.	9	436	14	43	57	907	9	0	0	0	37	....	1996-97	2005-06
• Brown, Stan	NYR, Det.	2	48	8	2	10	18	2	0	0	0	0	....	1926-27	1927-28
Brown, Wayne	Bos.	1	....	....	....	....	....	4	0	0	0	2	....	1953-54	1953-54
• Browne, Cecil	Chi.	1	13	2	0	2	4	....	....	....	....	....	....	1927-28	1927-28
Brownschidle, Jack	St.L., Hfd.	9	494	39	162	201	151	26	0	5	5	18	....	1977-78	1985-86
• Brownschidle, Jeff	Hfd.	2	7	0	1	1	2	....	....	....	....	....	....	1981-82	1982-83
Brubaker, Jeff	Hfd., Mtl., Cgy., Tor., Edm., NYR, Det.	8	178	16	9	25	512	2	0	0	0	27	....	1979-80	1988-89
Bruce, David	Van., St.L., S.J.	8	234	48	39	87	338	3	0	0	0	2	....	1985-86	1993-94
• Bruce, Gordie	Bos.	3	28	4	9	13	13	7	2	3	5	4	....	1940-41	1945-46
• Bruce, Morley	Ott.	4	71	8	3	11	27	3	0	0	0	2	2	1917-18	1921-22
Brule, Gilbert	CBJ, Edm., Phx.	8	299	43	52	95	156	12	2	1	3	0	....	2005-06	2013-14
Brule, Steve	N.J., Col.	2	2	0	0	0	0	1	0	0	0	0	1	1999-00	2002-03
Brumwell, Murray	Min., N.J.	7	128	12	31	43	70	2	0	0	0	2	....	1980-81	1987-88
Brunet, Benoit	Mtl., Dal., Ott.	13	539	101	161	262	229	54	5	20	25	32	1	1988-89	2001-02
• Bruneteau, Eddie	Det.	7	180	40	42	82	35	31	7	6	13	0	....	1940-41	1948-49

			Regular Schedule					Playoffs					NHL	First	Last
Name	NHL Teams	NHL Seasons	GP	G	A	TP	PIM	GP	G	A	TP	PIM	Cup Wins	NHL Season	NHL Season
● Bruneteau, Mud	Det.	11	411	139	138	277	80	77	23	14	37	22	3	1935-36	1945-46
Brunette, Andrew	Wsh., Nsh., Atl., Min., Col., Chi.	16	1110	268	465	733	314	49	17	18	35	14	....	1995-96	2011-12
‡ Brunnstrom, Fabian	Dal., Det.	3	104	19	22	41	22	....	....	....	....	....	....	2008-09	2011-12
● Brydge, Bill	Tor., Det., NYA	9	368	26	52	78	506	2	0	0	0	4	....	1926-27	1935-36
Brydges, Paul	Buf.	1	15	2	2	4	6	....	....	....	....	....	....	1986-87	1986-87
● Brydson, Glenn	Mtl.M., St.L., NYR, Chi.	8	299	56	79	135	203	11	0	0	0	8	....	1930-31	1937-38
● Brydson, Gord	Tor.	1	8	2	0	2	8	....	....	....	....	....	....	1929-30	1929-30
Brylin, Sergei	N.J.	13	765	129	179	308	273	109	15	19	34	32	3	1994-95	2007-08
Bubla, Jiri	Van.	5	256	17	101	118	202	6	0	0	0	7	....	1981-82	1985-86
● Buchanan, Al	Tor.	2	4	0	1	1	2	....	....	....	....	....	....	1948-49	1949-50
● Buchanan, Bucky	NYR	1	2	0	0	0	0	....	....	....	....	....	....	1948-49	1948-49
Buchanan, Jeff	Col.	1	6	0	0	0	6	....	....	....	....	....	....	1998-99	1998-99
Buchanan, Mike	Chi.	1	1	0	0	0	0	....	....	....	....	....	....	1951-52	1951-52
Buchanan, Ron	Bos., St.L.	2	5	0	0	0	0	....	....	....	....	....	....	1966-67	1969-70
Buchberger, Kelly	Edm., Atl., L.A., Phx., Pit.	18	1182	105	204	309	2297	97	10	15	25	129	2	1986-87	2003-04
Bucyk, John	Det., Bos.	23	1540	556	813	1369	497	124	41	62	103	42	2	1955-56	1977-78
Bucyk, Randy	Mtl., Cgy.	2	19	4	2	6	8	2	0	0	0	0	....	1985-86	1987-88
● Buhr, Doug	K.C.	1	6	0	2	2	4	....	....	....	....	....	....	1974-75	1974-75
● Bukovich, Tony	Det.	2	17	7	3	10	6	6	0	1	1	0	....	1943-44	1944-45
‡ Bulis, Jan	Wsh., Mtl., Van.	9	552	96	149	245	268	35	3	3	6	14	....	1997-98	2006-07
Bullard, Mike	Pit., Cgy., St.L., Phi., Tor.	11	727	329	345	674	703	40	11	18	29	44	....	1980-81	1991-92
● Buller, Hy	Det., NYR	5	188	22	58	80	215	....	....	....	....	....	....	1943-44	1953-54
Bulley, Ted	Chi., Wsh., Pit.	8	414	101	113	214	704	29	5	5	10	24	....	1976-77	1983-84
Burakovsky, Robert	Ott.	1	23	2	3	5	6	....	....	....	....	....	....	1993-94	1993-94
● Burch, Billy	Ham., NYA, Bos., Chi.	11	390	137	61	198	255	2	0	0	0	0	....	1922-23	1932-33
● Burchell, Fred	Mtl.	2	4	0	0	0	2	....	....	....	....	....	....	1950-51	1953-54
Burdon, Glen	K.C.	1	11	0	2	2	0	....	....	....	....	....	....	1974-75	1974-75
Bure, Pavel	Van., Fla., NYR	12	702	437	342	779	484	64	35	35	70	74	....	1991-92	2002-03
Bure, Valeri	Mtl., Cgy., Fla., St.L., Dal.	10	621	174	226	400	221	22	0	7	7	16	....	1994-95	2003-04
Bureau, Marc	Cgy., Min., T.B., Mtl., Phi.	11	567	55	83	138	327	50	5	7	12	46	....	1989-90	1999-00
Burega, Bill	Tor.	1	4	0	1	1	4	....	....	....	....	....	....	1955-56	1955-56
● Burke, Eddie	Bos., NYA	4	106	29	20	49	55	....	....	....	....	....	....	1931-32	1934-35
● Burke, Marty	Mtl., Pit., Ott., Chi.	11	494	19	47	66	560	31	2	4	6	44	2	1927-28	1937-38
● Burmister, Roy	NYA	3	67	4	3	7	2	....	....	....	....	....	....	1929-30	1931-32
Burnett, Garrett	Ana.	1	39	1	2	3	184	....	....	....	....	....	....	2003-04	2003-04
Burnett, Kelly	NYR	1	3	1	0	1	0	....	....	....	....	....	....	1952-53	1952-53
● Burns, Bobby	Chi.	3	20	1	0	1	8	....	....	....	....	....	....	1927-28	1929-30
Burns, Charlie	Det., Bos., Oak., Pit., Min.	11	749	106	198	304	252	31	5	4	9	6	....	1958-59	1972-73
Burns, Gary	NYR	2	11	2	2	4	18	5	0	0	0	2	....	1980-81	1981-82
● Burns, Norm	NYR	1	11	0	4	4	2	....	....	....	....	....	....	1941-42	1941-42
Burns, Robin	Pit., K.C.	5	190	31	38	69	139	....	....	....	....	....	....	1970-71	1975-76
● Burr, Shawn	Det., T.B., S.J.	16	878	181	259	440	1069	91	16	19	35	95	....	1984-85	1999-00
Burridge, Randy	Bos., Wsh., L.A., Buf.	13	706	199	251	450	458	107	18	34	52	103	....	1985-86	1997-98
Burrows, Dave	Pit., Tor.	10	724	29	135	164	373	29	1	5	6	25	....	1971-72	1980-81
● Burry, Bert	Ott.	1	4	0	0	0	0	....	....	....	....	....	....	1932-33	1932-33
Burt, Adam	Hfd., Car., Phi., Atl.	13	737	37	115	152	961	21	0	1	1	8	....	1988-89	2000-01
Burton, Cummy	Det.	3	43	0	2	2	21	3	0	0	0	0	....	1955-56	1958-59
Burton, Nelson	Wsh.	2	8	1	0	1	21	....	....	....	....	....	....	1977-78	1978-79
● Bush, Eddie	Det.	2	26	4	6	10	40	11	1	6	7	23	....	1938-39	1941-42
Buskas, Rod	Pit., Van., L.A., Chi.	11	556	19	63	82	1294	18	0	3	3	45	....	1982-83	1992-93
Busniuk, Mike	Phi.	2	143	3	23	26	297	25	2	5	7	34	....	1979-80	1980-81
Busniuk, Ron	Buf.	2	6	0	3	3	13	....	....	....	....	....	....	1972-73	1973-74
● Buswell, Walt	Det., Mtl.	8	368	10	40	50	164	24	2	1	3	10	....	1932-33	1939-40
Butcher, Garth	Van., St.L., Que., Tor.	14	897	48	158	206	2302	50	6	5	11	122	....	1981-82	1994-95
Butenschon, Sven	Pit., Edm., NYI, Van.	8	140	2	12	14	86	4	0	0	0	0	....	1997-98	2005-06
● Butler, Dick	Chi.	1	7	2	0	2	0	....	....	....	....	....	....	1947-48	1947-48
Butler, Jerry	NYR, St.L., Tor., Van., Wpg.	11	641	99	120	219	515	48	3	3	6	79	....	1972-73	1982-83
Butsayev, Viacheslav	Phi., S.J., Ana., Fla., Ott., T.B.	6	132	17	26	43	133	....	....	....	....	....	....	1992-93	1999-00
Butsayev, Yuri	Det., Atl.	4	99	10	4	14	28	....	....	....	....	....	....	1999-00	2002-03
Butters, Bill	Min.	2	72	1	4	5	77	....	....	....	....	....	....	1977-78	1978-79
● Buttrey, Gord	Chi.	1	10	0	0	0	0	....	....	....	....	....	....	1943-44	1943-44
Buynak, Gord	St.L.	1	4	0	0	0	2	....	....	....	....	....	....	1974-75	1974-75
Buzek, Petr	Dal., Atl., Cgy.	6	157	9	22	31	94	....	....	....	....	....	....	1997-98	2002-03
Byakin, Ilja	Edm., S.J.	2	57	8	25	33	44	....	....	....	....	....	....	1993-94	1994-95
Byce, John	Bos.	3	21	2	3	5	6	8	2	0	2	2	....	1989-90	1991-92
● Byers, Gord	Bos.	1	1	0	1	1	0	....	....	....	....	....	....	1949-50	1949-50
● Byers, Jerry	Min., Atl., NYR	4	43	3	4	7	15	....	....	....	....	....	....	1972-73	1977-78
Byers, Lyndon	Bos., S.J.	10	279	28	43	71	1081	37	2	2	4	96	....	1983-84	1992-93
● Byers, Mike	Tor., Phi., L.A., Buf.	4	166	42	34	76	39	4	0	1	1	0	....	1967-68	1971-72
‡ Bykov, Dmitri	Det.	1	71	2	10	12	43	4	0	0	0	0	....	2002-03	2002-03
Bylsma, Dan	L.A., Ana.	9	429	19	43	62	184	16	0	1	1	2	....	1995-96	2003-04
Byram, Shawn	NYI, Chi.	2	5	0	0	0	14	....	....	....	....	....	....	1990-91	1991-92

C

Name	NHL Teams	NHL Seasons	GP	G	A	TP	PIM	GP	G	A	TP	PIM	Cup Wins	First NHL Season	Last NHL Season
● Caffery, Jack	Tor., Bos.	3	57	3	2	5	22	10	1	0	1	4	....	1954-55	1957-58
Caffery, Terry	Chi., Min.	2	14	0	0	0	0	1	0	0	0	0	....	1969-70	1970-71
● Cahan, Larry	Tor., NYR, Oak., L.A.	13	666	38	92	130	700	29	1	1	2	38	....	1954-55	1970-71
● Cahill, Charles	Bos.	2	32	0	1	1	4	....	....	....	....	....	....	1925-26	1926-27
● Cain, Francis	Mtl.M., Tor.	2	61	4	0	4	35	....	....	....	....	....	....	1924-25	1925-26
● Cain, Herb	Mtl.M., Mtl., Bos.	13	570	206	194	400	178	67	16	13	29	13	2	1933-34	1945-46
Cairns, Don	K.C., Col.	2	9	0	1	1	2	....	....	....	....	....	....	1975-76	1976-77
Cairns, Eric	NYR, NYI, Fla., Pit.	10	457	10	32	42	1182	16	0	0	0	28	....	1996-97	2006-07
‡ Cajanek, Petr	St.L.	4	269	46	107	153	144	7	0	2	2	4	....	2002-03	2006-07
Calder, Eric	Wsh.	2	2	0	0	0	0	....	....	....	....	....	....	1981-82	1982-83
Calder, Kyle	Chi., Phi., Det., L.A., Ana.	10	590	114	180	294	309	18	2	1	3	10	....	1999-00	2009-10
‡ Caldwell, Ryan	NYI, Phx.	2	4	0	0	0	4	....	....	....	....	....	....	2005-06	2007-08
● Calladine, Norm	Bos.	3	63	19	29	48	8	....	....	....	....	....	....	1942-43	1944-45
Callahan, Joe	NYI, S.J., Fla.	3	46	0	4	4	16	....	....	....	....	....	....	2008-09	2010-11
Callander, Drew	Phi., Van.	4	39	6	2	8	7	....	....	....	....	....	....	1976-77	1979-80
Callander, Jock	Pit., T.B.	5	109	22	29	51	116	22	3	8	11	12	1	1987-88	1992-93
Callighen, Brett	Edm.	3	160	56	89	145	132	14	4	6	10	8	....	1979-80	1981-82
● Callighen, Patsy	NYR	1	36	0	0	0	32	9	0	0	0	0	1	1927-28	1927-28
Caloun, Jan	S.J., CBJ	3	24	8	6	14	2	....	....	....	....	....	....	1995-96	2000-01
Camazzola, James	Chi.	2	3	0	0	0	0	....	....	....	....	....	....	1983-84	1986-87
Camazzola, Tony	Wsh.	1	3	0	0	0	4	....	....	....	....	....	....	1981-82	1981-82
Cameron, Al	Det., Wpg.	6	282	11	44	55	356	7	0	1	1	2	....	1975-76	1980-81
● Cameron, Billy	Mtl., NYA	2	39	0	0	0	2	2	0	0	0	0	1	1923-24	1925-26
Cameron, Craig	Det., St.L., Min., NYI	9	552	87	65	152	196	27	3	1	4	17	....	1966-67	1975-76
Cameron, Dave	Col., N.J.	3	168	25	28	53	238	....	....	....	....	....	....	1981-82	1983-84
● Cameron, Harry	Tor., Ott., Mtl.	6	128	88	51	139	189	11	5	4	9	16	2	1917-18	1922-23
● Cameron, Scotty	NYR	1	35	8	11	19	0	....	....	....	....	....	....	1942-43	1942-43
‡ Campanale, Matt	NYI	1	1	0	0	0	2	....	....	....	....	....	....	2010-11	2010-11
Campbell, Bryan	L.A., Chi.	5	260	35	71	106	74	22	3	4	7	2	....	1967-68	1971-72
Campbell, Colin	Pit., Col., Edm., Van., Det.	11	636	25	103	128	1292	45	4	10	14	181	....	1974-75	1984-85
Campbell, Darcy	CBJ	1	1	0	0	0	0	....	....	....	....	....	....	2006-07	2006-07
● Campbell, Dave	Mtl.	1	2	0	0	0	0	....	....	....	....	....	....	1920-21	1920-21
● Campbell, Don	Chi.	1	17	1	3	4	8	....	....	....	....	....	....	1943-44	1943-44
● Campbell, Earl	Ott., NYA	3	76	6	3	9	14	1	0	0	0	6	....	1923-24	1925-26
Campbell, Jim	Ana., St.L., Mtl., Chi., Fla., T.B.	9	285	61	75	136	268	14	8	3	11	18	....	1995-96	2005-06
Campbell, Scott	Wpg., St.L.	3	80	4	21	25	243	....	....	....	....	....	....	1979-80	1981-82
Campbell, Wade	Wpg., Bos.	6	213	9	27	36	305	10	0	0	0	20	....	1982-83	1987-88
● Campeau, Tod	Mtl.	3	42	5	9	14	16	1	0	0	0	0	....	1943-44	1948-49
Campedelli, Dom	Mtl.	1	2	0	0	0	0	....	....	....	....	....	....	1985-86	1985-86
‡ Campoli, Chris	NYI, Ott., Chi., Mtl.	7	440	35	111	146	200	18	1	4	5	8	....	2005-06	2011-12
Capuano, Dave	Pit., Van., T.B., S.J.	4	104	17	38	55	56	6	1	1	2	5	....	1989-90	1993-94
Capuano, Jack	Tor., Van., Bos.	3	6	0	0	0	0	....	....	....	....	....	....	1989-90	1991-92
‡ Caputi, Luca	Pit., Tor.	3	35	3	6	9	20	....	....	....	....	....	....	2008-09	2010-11
● Carbol, Leo	Chi.	1	6	0	1	1	4	....	....	....	....	....	....	1942-43	1942-43
Carbonneau, Guy	Mtl., St.L., Dal.	19	1318	260	403	663	820	231	38	55	93	161	3	1980-81	1999-00
Card, Mike	Buf.	1	4	0	0	0	0	....	....	....	....	....	....	2006-07	2006-07
Cardin, Claude	St.L.	1	1	0	0	0	0	....	....	....	....	....	....	1967-68	1967-68
Cardwell, Steve	Pit.	3	53	9	11	20	35	4	0	0	0	2	....	1970-71	1972-73
● Carey, George	Que., Ham., Tor.	5	72	21	12	33	20	....	....	....	....	....	....	1919-20	1923-24
Carkner, Terry	NYR, Que., Phi., Det., Fla.	13	858	42	188	230	1588	54	1	9	10	48	....	1986-87	1998-99
‡ Carle, Mathieu	Mtl.	1	3	0	0	0	4	....	....	....	....	....	....	2009-10	2009-10

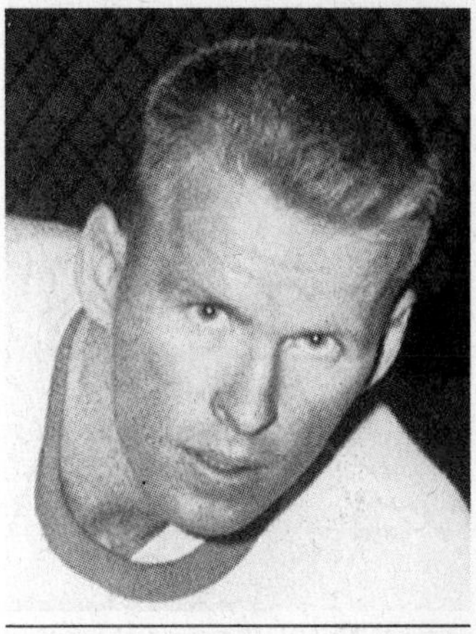

Mike Buchanan

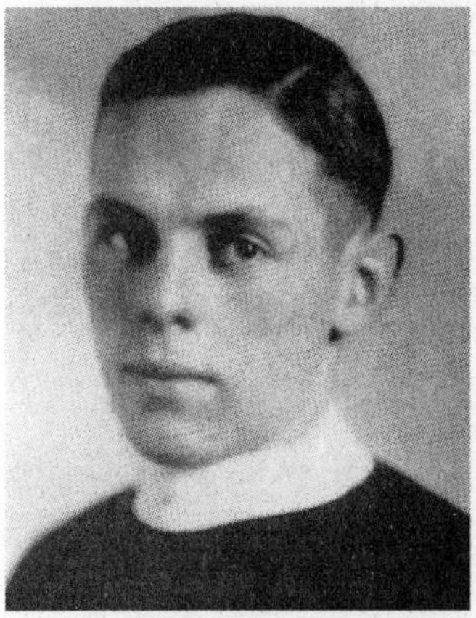

Bobby Burns

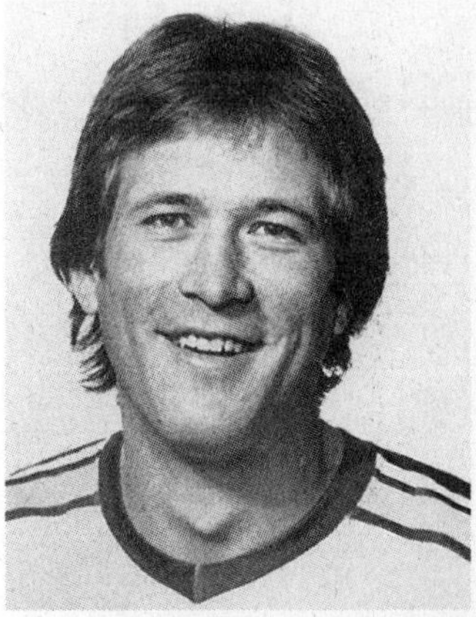

Scott Campbell

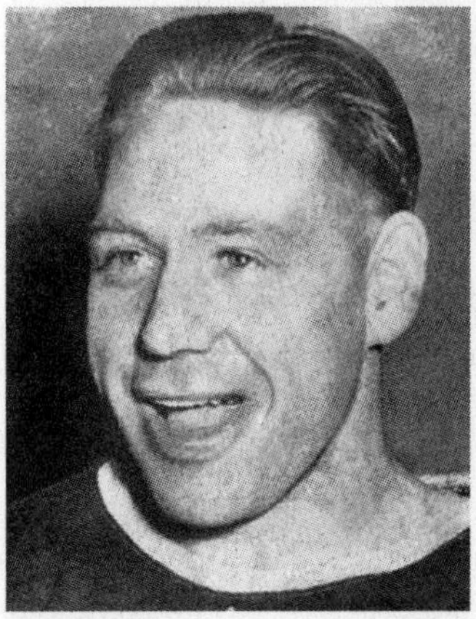

Red Carr

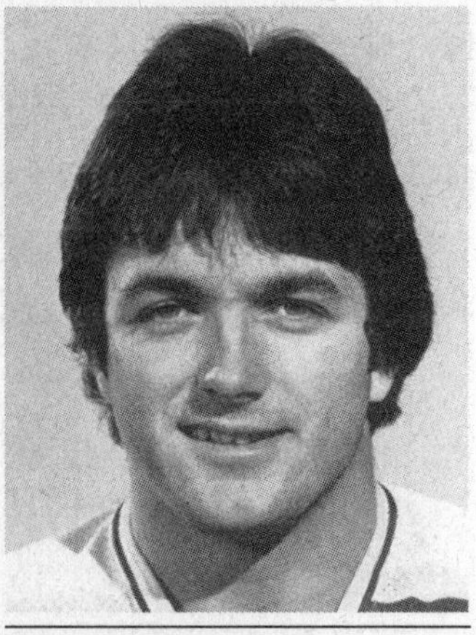

Dan Chicoine

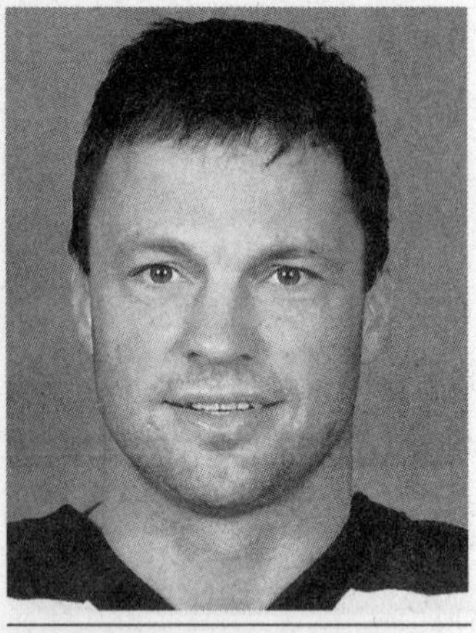

Dino Ciccarelli

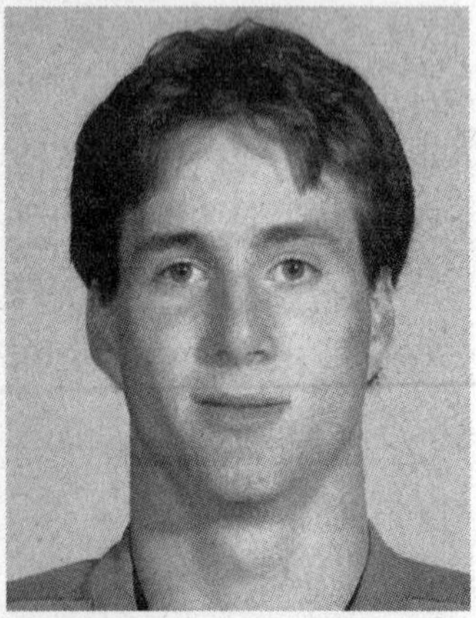

Dean Clark

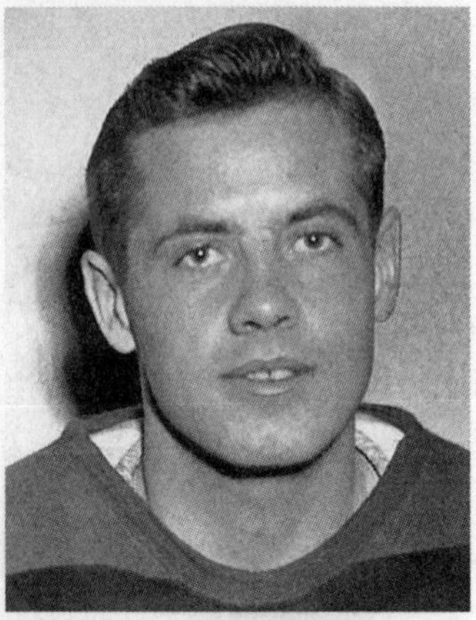

Hugh Coflin

			Regular Schedule					Playoffs							
Name	NHL Teams	NHL Seasons	GP	G	A	TP	PIM	GP	G	A	TP	PIM	NHL Cup Wins	First NHL Season	Last NHL Season
Carleton, Wayne	Tor., Bos., Cal.	7	278	55	73	128	172	18	2	4	6	14	1	1965-66	1971-72
Carlin, Brian	L.A.	1	5	1	0	1	0	....	....	....	....	....	....	1971-72	1971-72
Carlson, Jack	Min., St.L.	6	236	30	15	45	417	25	1	2	3	72	....	1978-79	1986-87
Carlson, Kent	Mtl., St.L., Wsh.	5	113	7	11	18	148	8	0	0	0	13	....	1983-84	1988-89
Carlson, Steve	L.A.	1	52	9	12	21	23	4	1	1	2	7	....	1979-80	1979-80
Carlsson, Anders	N.J.	3	104	7	26	33	34	3	1	0	1	2	....	1986-87	1988-89
Carlyle, Randy	Tor., Pit., Wpg.	17	1055	148	499	647	1400	69	9	24	33	120	....	1976-77	1992-93
Carnback, Patrik	Mtl., Ana.	4	154	24	38	62	122	....	....	....	....	....	....	1992-93	1995-96
Carney, Keith	Buf., Chi., Phx., Ana., Van., Min.	16	1018	45	183	228	904	91	3	19	22	67	....	1991-92	2007-08
• Caron, Alain	Oak., Mtl.	2	60	9	13	22	18	....	....	....	....	....	....	1967-68	1968-69
Carpenter, Bob	Wsh., NYR, L.A., Bos., N.J.	18	1178	320	408	728	919	140	21	38	59	136	1	1981-82	1998-99
• Carpenter, Ed	Que., Ham.	2	45	10	5	15	41	....	....	....	....	....	....	1919-20	1920-21
Carr, Gene	St.L., NYR, L.A., Pit., Atl.	8	465	79	136	215	365	35	5	8	13	66	....	1971-72	1978-79
• Carr, Lorne	NYR, NYA, Tor.	13	580	204	222	426	132	53	10	9	19	13	2	1933-34	1945-46
• Carr, Red	Tor.	1	5	0	1	1	2	....	....	....	....	....	....	1943-44	1943-44
Carriere, Larry	Buf., Atl., Van., L.A., Tor.	7	367	16	74	90	462	27	0	3	3	42	....	1972-73	1979-80
• Carrigan, Gene	NYR, Det., St.L.	3	37	2	1	3	13	4	0	0	0	0	....	1930-31	1934-35
Carroll, Billy	NYI, Edm., Det.	7	322	30	54	84	113	71	6	12	18	18	4	1980-81	1986-87
• Carroll, George	Mtl.M., Bos.	1	16	0	0	0	11	....	....	....	....	....	....	1924-25	1924-25
Carroll, Greg	Wsh., Det., Hfd.	2	131	20	34	54	44	....	....	....	....	....	....	1978-79	1979-80
Carruthers, Dwight	Det., Phi.	2	2	0	0	0	0	....	....	....	....	....	....	1965-66	1967-68
• Carse, Bill	NYR, Chi.	4	124	28	43	71	38	13	3	2	5	0	....	1938-39	1941-42
• Carse, Bob	Chi., Mtl.	5	167	32	55	87	52	10	0	2	2	2	....	1939-40	1947-48
• Carson, Bill	Tor., Bos.	4	159	54	24	78	156	11	3	0	3	14	1	1926-27	1929-30
‡ Carson, Brett	Car., Cgy.	5	90	2	11	13	20	....	....	....	....	....	....	2008-09	2012-13
• Carson, Frank	Mtl.M., NYA, Det.	7	248	42	48	90	166	27	0	2	2	9	1	1925-26	1933-34
• Carson, Gerry	Mtl., NYR, Mtl.M.	6	261	12	11	23	205	22	0	0	0	12	1	1928-29	1936-37
Carson, Jimmy	L.A., Edm., Det., Van., Hfd.	10	626	275	286	561	254	55	17	15	32	22	....	1986-87	1995-96
Carson, Lindsay	Phi., Hfd.	7	373	66	80	146	524	49	4	10	14	56	....	1981-82	1987-88
Carter, Anson	Wsh., Bos., Edm., NYR, L.A., Van., CBJ, Car.	10	674	202	219	421	229	24	8	5	13	4	....	1996-97	2006-07
Carter, Billy	Mtl., Bos.	3	16	0	0	0	6	....	....	....	....	....	....	1957-58	1961-62
Carter, John	Bos., S.J.	8	244	40	50	90	201	31	7	5	12	51	....	1985-86	1992-93
Carter, Ron	Edm.	1	2	0	0	0	0	....	....	....	....	....	....	1979-80	1979-80
• Carveth, Joe	Det., Bos., Mtl.	11	504	150	189	339	81	69	21	16	37	28	2	1940-41	1950-51
Cashman, Wayne	Bos.	17	1027	277	516	793	1041	145	31	57	88	250	2	1964-65	1982-83
Casselman, Mike	Fla.	1	3	0	0	0	0	....	....	....	....	....	....	1995-96	1995-96
Cassels, Andrew	Mtl., Hfd., Cgy., Van., CBJ, Wsh.	16	1015	204	528	732	410	21	4	7	11	8	....	1989-90	2005-06
Cassidy, Bruce	Chi.	6	36	4	13	17	10	1	0	0	0	0	....	1983-84	1989-90
Cassidy, Tom	Pit.	1	26	3	4	7	15	....	....	....	....	....	....	1977-78	1977-78
Cassolato, Tony	Wsh.	3	23	1	6	7	4	....	....	....	....	....	....	1979-80	1981-82
Caufield, Jay	NYR, Min., Pit.	7	208	5	8	13	759	17	0	0	0	42	2	1986-87	1992-93
Cavallini, Gino	Cgy., St.L., Que.	9	593	114	159	273	507	74	14	19	33	66	....	1984-85	1992-93
Cavallini, Paul	Wsh., St.L., Dal.	10	564	56	177	233	750	69	8	27	35	114	....	1986-87	1995-96
• Cavanagh, Tom	S.J.	2	18	1	2	3	4	....	....	....	....	....	....	2007-08	2008-09
• Ceresino, Ray	Tor.	1	12	1	1	2	2	....	....	....	....	....	....	1948-49	1948-49
Cernik, Frantisek	Det.	1	49	5	4	9	13	....	....	....	....	....	....	1984-85	1984-85
‡ Cervenka, Roman	Cgy.	1	39	9	8	17	14	....	....	....	....	....	....	2012-13	2012-13
Chabot, John	Mtl., Pit., Det.	8	508	84	228	312	85	33	6	20	26	2	....	1983-84	1990-91
• Chad, John	Chi.	3	80	15	22	37	29	10	0	1	1	2	....	1939-40	1945-46
• Chalmers, Chick	NYR	1	1	0	0	0	0	....	....	....	....	....	....	1953-54	1953-54
Chalupa, Milan	Det.	1	14	0	5	5	6	....	....	....	....	....	....	1984-85	1984-85
• Chamberlain, Murph	Tor., Mtl., Bro., Bos.	12	510	100	175	275	769	66	14	17	31	96	2	1937-38	1948-49
Chambers, Shawn	Min., Wsh., T.B., N.J., Dal.	13	625	50	185	235	364	94	7	26	33	72	2	1987-88	1999-00
Champagne, Andre	Tor.	1	2	0	0	0	0	....	....	....	....	....	....	1962-63	1962-63
Chapdelaine, Rene	L.A.	3	32	0	2	2	32	....	....	....	....	....	....	1990-91	1992-93
• Chapman, Art	Bos., NYA	10	438	62	176	238	140	26	1	5	6	9	....	1930-31	1939-40
Chapman, Blair	Pit., St.L.	7	402	106	125	231	158	25	4	6	10	15	....	1976-77	1982-83
Chapman, Brian	Hfd.	1	3	0	0	0	29	....	....	....	....	....	....	1990-91	1990-91
Charbonneau, Jose	Mtl., Van.	4	71	9	13	22	67	11	1	0	1	8	....	1987-88	1994-95
Charbonneau, Stephane	Que.	1	2	0	0	0	0	....	....	....	....	....	....	1991-92	1991-92
Charlebois, Bob	Min.	1	7	1	0	1	0	....	....	....	....	....	....	1967-68	1967-68
Charlesworth, Todd	Pit., NYR	6	93	3	9	12	47	....	....	....	....	....	....	1983-84	1989-90
Charron, Eric	Mtl., T.B., Wsh., Cgy.	8	130	2	7	9	127	6	0	0	0	8	....	1992-93	1999-00
Charron, Guy	Mtl., Det., K.C., Wsh.	12	734	221	309	530	146	....	....	....	....	....	....	1969-70	1980-81
Chartier, Dave	Wpg.	1	1	0	0	0	0	....	....	....	....	....	....	1980-81	1980-81
Chartrand, Brad	L.A.	5	215	25	25	50	122	11	1	1	2	8	....	1999-00	2003-04
Chartraw, Rick	Mtl., L.A., NYR, Edm.	10	420	28	64	92	399	75	7	9	16	80	4	1974-75	1983-84
Chase, Kelly	St.L., Hfd., Tor.	11	458	17	36	53	2017	27	1	1	2	100	....	1989-90	1999-00
Chasse, Denis	St.L., Wsh., Wpg., Ott.	4	132	11	14	25	292	7	1	7	8	23	....	1993-94	1996-97
Chebaturkin, Vladimir	NYI, St.L., Chi.	5	62	2	7	9	52	3	0	0	0	2	....	1997-98	2001-02
• Check, Lude	Det., Chi.	2	27	6	2	8	4	....	....	....	....	....	....	1943-44	1944-45
‡ Cheechoo, Jonathan	S.J., Ott.	7	501	170	135	305	324	59	16	19	35	32	....	2002-03	2009-10
Chelios, Chris	Mtl., Chi., Det., Atl.	26	1651	185	763	948	2891	266	31	113	144	423	3	1983-84	2009-10
• Chernoff, Mike	Min.	1	1	0	0	0	0	....	....	....	....	....	....	1968-69	1968-69
Chernomaz, Rich	Col., N.J., Cgy.	7	51	9	7	16	18	....	....	....	....	....	....	1981-82	1991-92
Cherry, Dick	Bos., Phi.	3	145	12	10	22	45	4	1	0	1	4	....	1956-57	1969-70
Cherry, Don	Bos.	1	....	....	....	....	....	1	0	0	0	0	....	1954-55	1954-55
Chervyakov, Denis	Bos.	1	2	0	0	0	2	....	....	....	....	....	....	1992-93	1992-93
• Chevrefils, Real	Bos., Det.	8	387	104	97	201	185	30	5	4	9	20	....	1951-52	1958-59
• Chiasson, Steve	Det., Cgy., Hfd., Car.	13	751	93	305	398	1107	63	16	19	35	119	....	1986-87	1998-99
Chibirev, Igor	Hfd.	2	45	7	12	19	2	....	....	....	....	....	....	1993-94	1994-95
Chicoine, Dan	Cle., Min.	3	31	1	2	3	12	1	0	0	0	0	....	1977-78	1979-80
Chinnick, Rick	Min.	2	4	0	2	2	0	....	....	....	....	....	....	1973-74	1974-75
Chipperfield, Ron	Edm., Que.	2	83	22	24	46	34	....	....	....	....	....	....	1979-80	1980-81
Chisholm, Art	Bos.	1	3	0	0	0	0	....	....	....	....	....	....	1960-61	1960-61
Chisholm, Colin	Min.	1	1	0	0	0	0	....	....	....	....	....	....	1986-87	1986-87
• Chisholm, Lex	Tor.	2	54	10	8	18	19	3	1	0	1	0	....	1939-40	1940-41
‡ Chistov, Stanislav	Ana., Bos.	3	196	19	42	61	116	21	4	2	6	8	....	2002-03	2006-07
Chorney, Marc	Pit., L.A.	4	210	8	27	35	209	7	0	1	1	2	....	1980-81	1983-84
Chorske, Tom	Mtl., N.J., Ott., NYI, Wsh., Cgy., Pit.	11	596	115	122	237	225	50	5	12	17	10	1	1989-90	1999-00
‡ Chouinard, Eric	Mtl., Phi., Min.	4	90	11	11	22	16	....	....	....	....	....	....	2000-01	2005-06
• Chouinard, Gene	Ott.	1	8	0	0	0	0	....	....	....	....	....	....	1927-28	1927-28
Chouinard, Guy	Atl., Cgy., St.L.	10	578	205	370	575	120	46	9	28	37	12	....	1974-75	1983-84
Chouinard, Marc	Ana., Min., Van.	6	320	37	41	78	123	15	1	0	1	0	....	2000-01	2006-07
‡ Christensen, Erik	Pit., Atl., Ana., NYR, Min.	7	387	68	95	163	162	17	1	2	3	8	....	2005-06	2011-12
Christian, Dave	Wpg., Wsh., Bos., St.L., Chi.	15	1009	340	433	773	284	102	32	25	57	27	....	1979-80	1993-94
Christian, Jeff	N.J., Pit., Phx.	5	18	2	2	4	17	....	....	....	....	....	....	1991-92	1997-98
Christie, Mike	Cal., Cle., Col., Van.	7	412	15	101	116	550	2	0	0	0	0	....	1974-75	1980-81
‡ Christie, Ryan	Dal., Cgy.	2	7	0	0	0	0	....	....	....	....	....	....	1999-00	2001-02
Christoff, Steve	Min., Cgy., L.A.	5	248	77	64	141	108	35	16	12	28	25	....	1979-80	1983-84
Chrystal, Bob	NYR	2	132	11	14	25	112	....	....	....	....	....	....	1953-54	1954-55
Chubarov, Artem	Van.	5	228	25	33	58	40	27	0	4	4	4	....	1999-00	2003-04
Chucko, Kris	Cgy.	1	2	0	0	0	2	....	....	....	....	....	....	2008-09	2008-09
Church, Brad	Wsh.	1	2	0	0	0	0	....	....	....	....	....	....	1997-98	1997-98
• Church, Jack	Tor., Bro., Bos.	5	130	4	19	23	154	25	1	1	2	18	....	1938-39	1945-46
Churla, Shane	Hfd., Cgy., Min., Dal., L.A., NYR	11	488	26	45	71	2301	78	5	7	12	282	....	1986-87	1996-97
Chychrun, Jeff	Phi., L.A., Pit., Edm.	8	262	3	22	25	744	19	0	2	2	65	1	1986-87	1993-94
Chynoweth, Dean	NYI, Bos.	9	241	4	18	22	667	6	0	0	0	26	....	1988-89	1997-98
Chyzowski, Dave	NYI, Chi.	6	126	15	16	31	144	2	0	0	0	0	....	1989-90	1996-97
Ciavaglia, Peter	Buf.	2	5	0	0	0	0	....	....	....	....	....	....	1991-92	1992-93
‡ Cibak, Martin	T.B.	3	154	5	18	23	60	11	0	1	1	0	1	2001-02	2005-06
Ciccarelli, Dino	Min., Wsh., Det., T.B., Fla.	19	1232	608	592	1200	1425	141	73	45	118	211	....	1980-81	1998-99
Ciccone, Enrico	Min., Wsh., T.B., Chi., Car., Van., Mtl.	9	374	10	18	28	1469	13	1	0	1	48	....	1991-92	2000-01
Cichocki, Chris	Det., N.J.	4	68	11	12	23	27	....	....	....	....	....	....	1985-86	1988-89
Ciernik, Ivan	Ott., Wsh.	5	89	12	14	26	32	2	0	1	1	6	....	1997-98	2003-04
Cierny, Jozef	Edm.	1	1	0	0	0	0	....	....	....	....	....	....	1993-94	1993-94
• Ciesla, Hank	Chi., NYR	4	269	26	51	77	87	6	0	2	2	0	....	1955-56	1958-59
Ciger, Zdeno	N.J., Edm., NYR, T.B.	7	352	94	134	228	101	13	2	6	8	4	....	1990-91	2001-02
Cimellaro, Tony	Ott.	1	2	0	0	0	0	....	....	....	....	....	....	1992-93	1992-93
Cimetta, Rob	Bos., Tor.	4	103	16	16	32	66	1	0	0	0	15	....	1988-89	1991-92
Cirella, Joe	Col., N.J., Que., NYR, Fla., Ott.	15	828	64	211	275	1446	38	0	13	13	98	....	1981-82	1995-96
Cirone, Jason	Wpg.	1	3	0	0	0	2	....	....	....	....	....	....	1991-92	1991-92
Cisar, Marian	Nsh.	3	73	13	17	30	57	....	....	....	....	....	....	1999-00	2001-02
Clackson, Kim	Pit., Que.	2	106	0	8	8	370	8	0	0	0	70	....	1979-80	1980-81
• Clancy, King	Ott., Tor.	16	592	136	147	283	914	55	8	8	16	88	3	1921-22	1936-37

Name	NHL Teams	NHL Seasons	Regular Schedule GP	G	A	TP	PIM	Playoffs GP	G	A	TP	PIM	NHL Cup Wins	First NHL Season	Last NHL Season
Clancy, Terry	Oak., Tor.	4	93	6	6	12	39	....	....	....	....	....	....	1967-68	1972-73
• Clapper, Dit	Bos.	20	833	228	246	474	462	82	13	17	30	50	3	1927-28	1946-47
Clark, Brett	Mtl., Atl., Col., T.B., Min.	14	689	45	141	186	293	28	3	4	7	10	....	1997-98	2012-13
Clark, Chris	Cgy., Wsh., CBJ	11	607	103	111	214	700	34	4	3	7	38	....	1999-00	2010-11
Clark, Dan	NYR	1	4	0	1	1	6	....	....	....	....	....	....	1978-79	1978-79
Clark, Dean	Edm.	1	1	0	0	0	0	....	....	....	....	....	....	1983-84	1983-84
Clark, Gordie	Bos.	2	8	0	1	1	0	1	0	0	0	0	....	1974-75	1975-76
• Clark, Nobby	Bos.	1	5	0	0	0	0	....	....	....	....	....	....	1927-28	1927-28
Clark, Wendel	Tor., Que., NYI, T.B., Det., Chi.	15	793	330	234	564	1690	95	37	32	69	201	....	1985-86	1999-00
Clarke, Bobby	Phi.	15	1144	358	852	1210	1453	136	42	77	119	152	2	1969-70	1983-84
Clarke, Dale	St.L.	1	3	0	0	0	0	....	....	....	....	....	....	2000-01	2000-01
Clarke, Noah	L.A., N.J.	4	21	3	1	4	4	....	....	....	....	....	....	2003-04	2007-08
Classen, Greg	Nsh.	3	90	7	10	17	48	....	....	....	....	....	....	2000-01	2002-03
• Cleghorn, Odie	Mtl., Pit.	10	181	95	34	129	142	12	7	2	9	5	1	1918-19	1927-28
• Cleghorn, Sprague	Ott., Tor., Mtl., Bos.	10	259	83	55	138	538	21	4	3	7	26	2	1918-19	1927-28
Clement, Bill	Phi., Wsh., Atl., Cgy.	11	719	148	208	356	383	50	5	3	8	26	2	1971-72	1981-82
Cline, Bruce	NYR	1	30	2	3	5	10	....	....	....	....	....	....	1956-57	1956-57
Clippingdale, Steve	L.A., Wsh.	2	19	1	2	3	9	1	0	0	0	0	....	1976-77	1979-80
Cloutier, Real	Que., Buf.	6	317	146	198	344	119	25	7	5	12	20	....	1979-80	1984-85
Cloutier, Rejean	Det.	2	5	0	2	2	2	....	....	....	....	....	....	1979-80	1981-82
Cloutier, Roland	Det., Que.	3	34	8	9	17	2	....	....	....	....	....	....	1977-78	1979-80
Cloutier, Sylvain	Chi.	1	7	0	0	0	0	....	....	....	....	....	....	1998-99	1998-99
• Clune, Wally	Mtl.	1	5	0	0	0	6	....	....	....	....	....	....	1955-56	1955-56
Clymer, Ben	T.B., Wsh.	7	438	52	77	129	367	16	0	2	2	6	1	1999-00	2006-07
Coalter, Gary	Cal., K.C.	2	34	2	4	6	2	....	....	....	....	....	....	1973-74	1974-75
Coates, Steve	Det.	1	5	1	0	1	24	....	....	....	....	....	....	1976-77	1976-77
Cochrane, Glen	Phi., Van., Chi., Edm.	10	411	17	72	89	1556	18	1	1	2	31	....	1978-79	1988-89
Coffey, Paul	Edm., Pit., L.A., Det., Hfd., Phi., Chi., Car., Bos.	21	1409	396	1135	1531	1802	194	59	137	196	264	4	1980-81	2000-01
Coflin, Hugh	Chi.	1	31	0	3	3	33	....	....	....	....	....	....	1950-51	1950-51
‡ Cohen, Colby	Col.	1	3	0	0	0	4	....	....	....	....	....	....	2010-11	2010-11
Cole, Danton	Wpg., T.B., N.J., NYI, Chi.	7	318	58	60	118	125	1	0	0	0	0	1	1989-90	1995-96
Colley, Kevin	NYI	1	16	0	0	0	52	....	....	....	....	....	....	2005-06	2005-06
Colley, Tom	Min.	1	1	0	0	0	2	....	....	....	....	....	....	1974-75	1974-75
• Collings, Norm	Mtl.	1	1	0	1	1	0	....	....	....	....	....	....	1934-35	1934-35
Collins, Bill	Min., Mtl., Det., St.L., NYR, Phi., Wsh.	11	768	157	154	311	415	18	3	5	8	12	....	1967-68	1977-78
Collins, Gary	Tor.	1	....	....	....	....	....	2	0	0	0	0	....	1958-59	1958-59
‡ Collins, Rob	NYI	1	8	1	1	2	0	....	....	....	....	....	....	2005-06	2005-06
Collins, Sean	Wsh.	3	21	2	1	3	12	1	0	0	0	0	....	2008-09	2011-12
Colliton, Jeremy	NYI	5	57	3	3	6	26	....	....	....	....	....	....	2005-06	2010-11
Collyard, Bob	St.L.	1	10	1	3	4	4	....	....	....	....	....	....	1973-74	1973-74
• Colman, Michael	S.J.	1	15	0	1	1	32	....	....	....	....	....	....	1991-92	1991-92
• Colville, Mac	NYR	9	353	71	104	175	130	40	9	10	19	14	1	1935-36	1946-47
• Colville, Neil	NYR	12	464	99	166	265	213	46	7	19	26	32	1	1935-36	1948-49
Colwill, Les	NYR	1	69	7	6	13	16	....	....	....	....	....	....	1958-59	1958-59
Comeau, Rey	Mtl., Atl., Col.	9	564	98	141	239	175	9	2	1	3	8	....	1971-72	1979-80
Commodore, Mike	N.J., Cgy., Car., Ott., CBJ, Det., T.B.	11	484	23	83	106	683	53	2	6	8	70	1	2000-01	2011-12
Comrie, Mike	Edm., Phi., Phx., Ott., NYI, Pit.	10	589	168	197	365	443	32	4	6	10	27	....	2000-01	2010-11
Comrie, Paul	Edm.	1	15	1	2	3	4	....	....	....	....	....	....	1999-00	1999-00
Conacher, Brian	Tor., Det.	5	155	28	28	56	84	12	3	2	5	21	1	1961-62	1971-72
• Conacher, Charlie	Tor., Det., NYA	12	459	225	173	398	523	49	17	18	35	49	1	1929-30	1940-41
Conacher, Jim	Det., Chi., NYR	8	328	85	117	202	91	19	5	2	7	4	....	1945-46	1952-53
• Conacher, Lionel	Pit., NYA, Mtl.M., Chi.	12	498	80	105	185	882	35	2	2	4	34	2	1925-26	1936-37
‡ Conacher, Pat	NYR, Edm., N.J., L.A., Cgy., NYI, Van.	14	521	63	76	139	235	67	11	10	21	40	1	1979-80	2013-14
Conacher, Pete	Chi., NYR, Tor.	6	229	47	39	86	57	7	0	0	0	0	....	1951-52	1957-58
• Conacher, Roy	Bos., Det., Chi.	11	490	226	200	426	90	42	15	15	30	14	2	1938-39	1951-52
‡ Conboy, Tim	Car.	3	59	0	6	6	121	3	0	0	0	9	....	2007-08	2009-10
• Conn, Red	NYA	2	96	9	28	37	22	....	....	....	....	....	....	1933-34	1934-35
Conn, Rob	Chi., Buf.	2	30	2	5	7	20	....	....	....	....	....	....	1991-92	1995-96
• Connelly, Bert	NYR, Chi.	3	87	13	15	28	37	14	1	0	1	0	1	1934-35	1937-38
Connelly, Wayne	Mtl., Bos., Min., Det., St.L., Van.	10	543	133	174	307	156	24	11	7	18	4	....	1960-61	1971-72
Connolly, Mike	Col.	1	2	0	0	0	2	....	....	....	....	....	....	2011-12	2011-12
Connolly, Tim	NYI, Buf., Tor.	12	697	131	300	431	300	36	5	18	23	8	....	1999-00	2011-12
Connor, Cam	Mtl., Edm., NYR	5	89	9	22	31	256	20	5	0	5	6	1	1978-79	1982-83
• Connor, Harry	Bos., NYA, Ott.	4	134	16	5	21	149	10	0	0	0	2	....	1927-28	1930-31
• Connors, Bob	NYA, Det.	3	78	17	10	27	110	2	0	0	0	10	....	1926-27	1929-30
Conroy, Al	Phi.	3	114	9	14	23	156	....	....	....	....	....	....	1991-92	1993-94
Conroy, Craig	Mtl., St.L., Cgy., L.A.	16	1009	182	360	542	603	81	10	20	30	52	....	1994-95	2010-11
Contini, Joe	Col., Min.	3	68	17	21	38	34	2	0	0	0	0	....	1977-78	1980-81
Convery, Brandon	Tor., Van., L.A.	4	72	9	19	28	36	5	0	0	0	2	....	1995-96	1998-99
• Convey, Eddie	NYA	3	36	1	1	2	33	....	....	....	....	....	....	1930-31	1932-33
• Cook, Bill	NYR	11	474	229	138	367	386	46	13	11	24	68	2	1926-27	1936-37
• Cook, Bob	Van., Det., NYI, Min.	4	72	13	9	22	22	....	....	....	....	....	....	1970-71	1974-75
• Cook, Bud	Bos., Ott., St.L.	3	50	5	4	9	22	....	....	....	....	....	....	1931-32	1934-35
• Cook, Bun	NYR, Bos.	11	473	158	144	302	444	46	15	3	18	50	2	1926-27	1936-37
• Cook, Lloyd	Bos.	1	4	1	0	1	0	....	....	....	....	....	....	1924-25	1924-25
• Cook, Tom	Chi., Mtl.M.	9	349	77	98	175	184	24	2	4	6	19	1	1929-30	1937-38
• Cooper, Carson	Bos., Mtl., Det.	8	294	110	57	167	111	7	0	0	0	2	....	1924-25	1931-32
Cooper, David	Tor.	3	30	3	7	10	24	....	....	....	....	....	....	1996-97	2000-01
Cooper, Ed	Col.	2	49	8	7	15	46	....	....	....	....	....	....	1980-81	1981-82
• Cooper, Hal	NYR	1	8	0	0	0	2	....	....	....	....	....	....	1944-45	1944-45
• Cooper, Joe	NYR, Chi.	11	420	30	66	96	442	35	3	5	8	58	....	1935-36	1946-47
• Copp, Bobby	Tor.	2	40	3	9	12	26	....	....	....	....	....	....	1942-43	1950-51
Corazzini, Carl	Bos., Chi.	2	19	2	1	3	2	....	....	....	....	....	....	2003-04	2006-07
• Corbeau, Bert	Mtl., Ham., Tor.	10	258	63	49	112	629	9	2	2	4	38	....	1917-18	1926-27
Corbet, Rene	Que., Col., Cgy., Pit.	8	362	58	74	132	420	53	7	6	13	52	1	1993-94	2000-01
• Corbett, Mike	L.A.	1	....	....	....	....	....	2	0	1	1	2	....	1967-68	1967-68
• Corcoran, Norm	Bos., Det., Chi.	4	29	1	3	4	21	4	0	0	0	6	....	1949-50	1955-56
Corkum, Bob	Buf., Ana., Phi., Phx., L.A., N.J., Atl.	12	720	97	103	200	281	62	7	7	14	24	....	1989-90	2001-02
• Cormier, Roger	Mtl.	1	1	0	0	0	0	....	....	....	....	....	....	1925-26	1925-26
Cornforth, Mark	Bos.	1	6	0	0	0	4	....	....	....	....	....	....	1995-96	1995-96
• Corrigan, Chuck	Tor., NYA	2	19	2	2	4	2	....	....	....	....	....	....	1937-38	1940-41
Corrigan, Mike	L.A., Van., Pit.	10	594	152	195	347	698	17	2	3	5	20	....	1967-68	1977-78
Corrinet, Chris	Wsh.	1	8	0	1	1	6	....	....	....	....	....	....	2001-02	2001-02
• Corriveau, Andre	Mtl.	1	3	0	1	1	0	....	....	....	....	....	....	1953-54	1953-54
Corriveau, Yvon	Wsh., Hfd., S.J.	9	280	48	40	88	310	29	5	7	12	50	....	1985-86	1993-94
‡ Corso, Daniel	St.L., Atl.	4	77	14	11	25	20	14	0	1	1	0	....	2000-01	2003-04
Corson, Shayne	Mtl., Edm., St.L., Tor., Dal.	19	1156	273	420	693	2357	140	38	49	87	291	....	1985-86	2003-04
Corvo, Joe	L.A., Ott., Car., Wsh., Bos.	11	708	92	218	310	241	50	5	13	18	14	....	2002-03	2013-14
Cory, Ross	Wpg.	2	51	2	10	12	41	....	....	....	....	....	....	1979-80	1980-81
Cossette, Jacques	Pit.	3	64	8	6	14	29	3	0	1	1	4	....	1975-76	1978-79
• Costello, Les	Tor.	3	15	2	3	5	11	6	2	2	4	2	1	1947-48	1949-50
Costello, Murray	Chi., Bos., Det.	4	162	13	19	32	54	5	0	0	0	2	....	1953-54	1956-57
Costello, Rich	Tor.	2	12	2	2	4	2	....	....	....	....	....	....	1983-84	1985-86
• Cotch, Charlie	Ham., Tor.	1	12	1	0	1	0	....	....	....	....	....	....	1924-25	1924-25
Cote, Alain	Que.	10	696	103	190	293	383	67	9	15	24	44	....	1979-80	1988-89
Cote, Alain	Bos., Wsh., Mtl., T.B., Que.	9	119	2	18	20	124	11	0	2	2	26	....	1985-86	1993-94
Cote, Patrick	Dal., Nsh., Edm.	6	105	1	2	3	377	....	....	....	....	....	....	1995-96	2000-01
Cote, Ray	Edm.	3	15	0	0	0	4	14	3	2	5	0	....	1982-83	1984-85
Cote, Riley	Phi.	4	156	1	6	7	411	3	0	0	0	0	....	2006-07	2009-10
Cote, Sylvain	Hfd., Wsh., Tor., Chi., Dal.	19	1171	122	313	435	545	102	11	22	33	62	....	1984-85	2002-03
• Cotton, Baldy	Pit., Tor., NYA	12	503	101	103	204	419	43	4	9	13	46	1	1925-26	1936-37
• Coughlin, Jack	Tor., Que., Mtl., Ham.	3	19	2	0	2	3	....	....	....	....	....	1	1917-18	1920-21
Coulis, Tim	Wsh., Min.	4	47	4	5	9	138	3	1	0	1	2	....	1979-80	1985-86
Coulombe, Patrick	Van.	1	7	0	1	1	4	....	....	....	....	....	....	2006-07	2006-07
• Coulson, D'arcy	Phi.	1	28	0	0	0	103	....	....	....	....	....	....	1930-31	1930-31
• Coulter, Art	Chi., NYR	11	465	30	82	112	543	49	4	5	9	61	2	1931-32	1941-42
Coulter, Neal	NYI	3	26	5	5	10	11	....	....	....	....	....	....	1985-86	1987-88
• Coulter, Thomas	Chi.	1	2	0	0	0	0	....	....	....	....	....	....	1933-34	1933-34
Cournoyer, Yvan	Mtl.	16	968	428	435	863	255	147	64	63	127	47	10	1963-64	1978-79
Courteau, Yves	Cgy., Hfd.	3	22	2	5	7	4	1	0	0	0	0	....	1984-85	1986-87
Courtenay, Ed	S.J.	2	44	7	13	20	10	....	....	....	....	....	....	1991-92	1992-93
Courtnall, Geoff	Bos., Edm., Wsh., St.L., Van.	17	1048	367	432	799	1465	156	39	70	109	262	1	1983-84	1999-00
Courtnall, Russ	Tor., Mtl., Min., Dal., Van., NYR, L.A.	16	1029	297	447	744	557	129	39	44	83	83	....	1983-84	1998-99
Courville, Larry	Van.	3	33	1	2	3	16	....	....	....	....	....	....	1995-96	1997-98
• Coutu, Billy	Mtl., Ham., Bos.	10	244	33	21	54	478	19	1	1	2	39	1	1917-18	1926-27

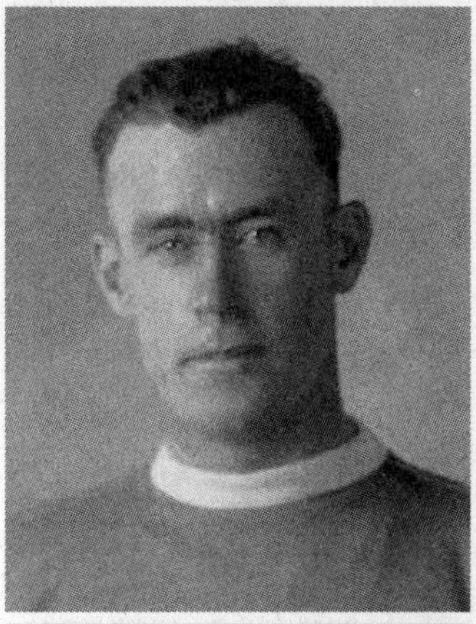
Bill Cook

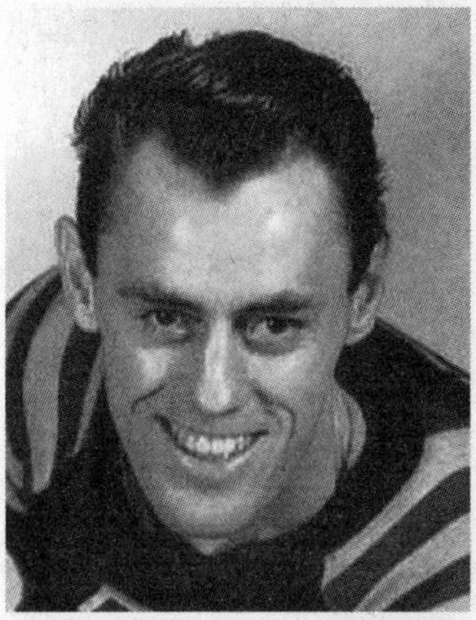
Bud Cook

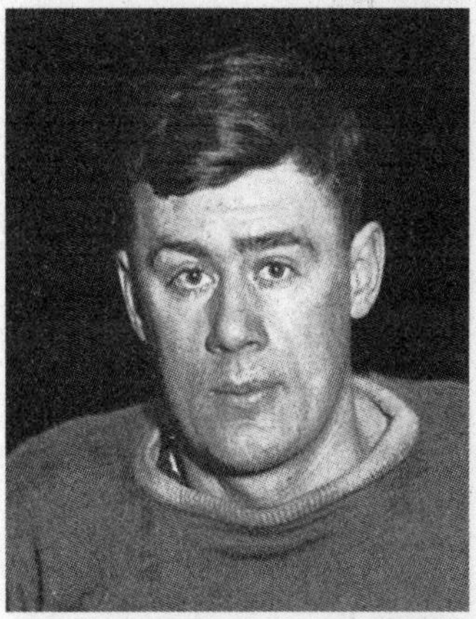
Bun Cook

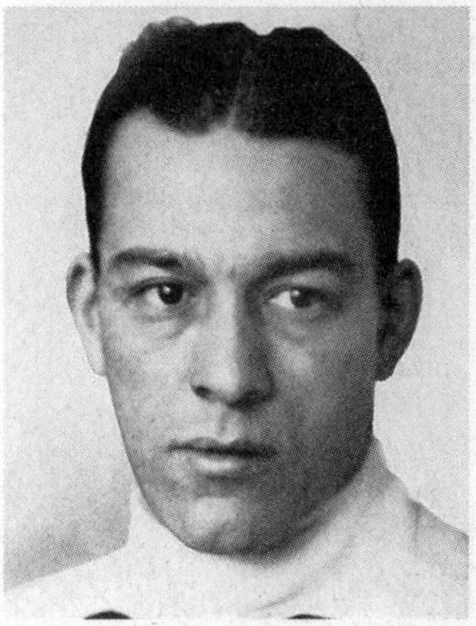
Art Coulter

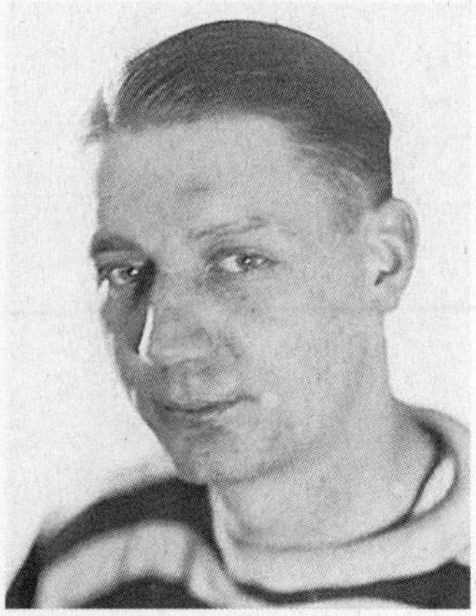

Rosie Couture

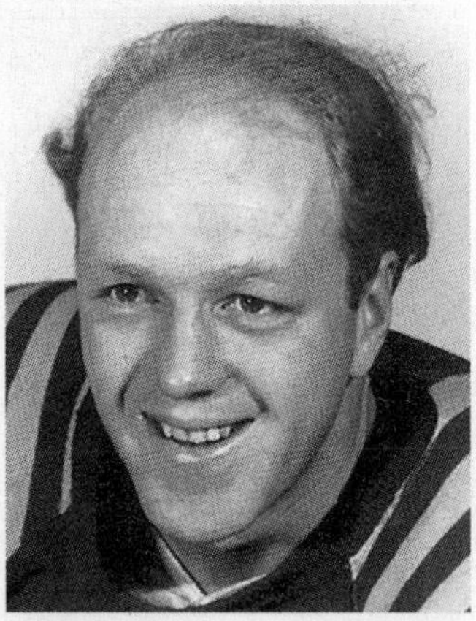

Les Cunningham

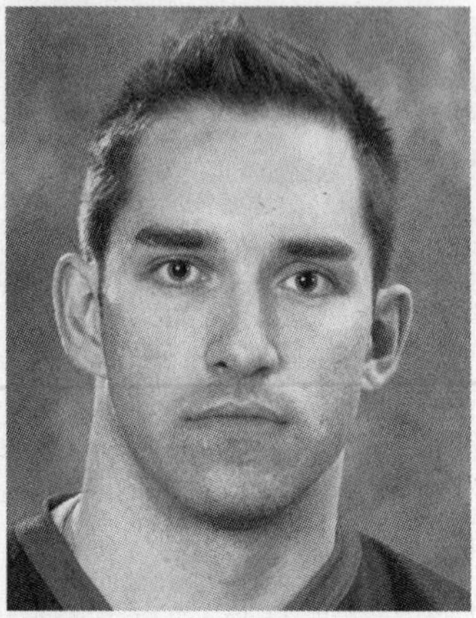

Alexandre Daigle

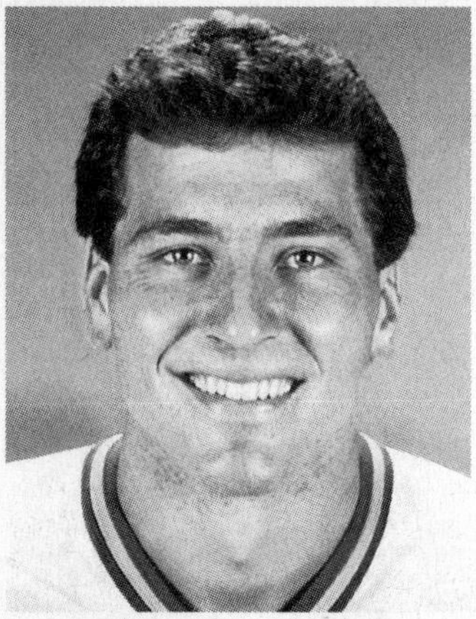

Michael Dark

Name	NHL Teams	NHL Seasons	Regular Schedule GP	G	A	TP	PIM	Playoffs GP	G	A	TP	PIM	NHL Cup Wins	First NHL Season	Last NHL Season
• Couture, Gerry	Det., Mtl., Chi.	10	385	86	70	156	89	45	9	7	16	4	1	1944-45	1953-54
• Couture, Rosie	Chi., Mtl.	8	309	48	56	104	184	23	1	5	6	15	1	1928-29	1935-36
Couturier, Sylvain	L.A.	3	33	4	5	9	4	....	....	....	....	....	....	1988-89	1991-92
Cowan, Jeff	Cgy., Atl., L.A., Van.	8	413	47	34	81	695	10	2	0	2	22	....	1999-00	2007-08
Cowick, Bruce	Phi., Wsh., St.L.	3	70	5	6	11	43	8	0	0	0	9	1	1973-74	1975-76
Cowie, Rob	L.A.	2	78	7	12	19	52	....	....	....	....	....	....	1994-95	1995-96
• Cowley, Bill	St.L., Bos.	13	549	195	353	548	143	64	12	34	46	22	2	1934-35	1946-47
• Cox, Danny	Tor., Ott., Det., NYR	8	319	47	49	96	128	10	0	1	1	6	....	1926-27	1933-34
Coxe, Craig	Van., Cgy., St.L., S.J.	8	235	14	31	45	713	5	1	0	1	18	....	1984-85	1991-92
Craig, Mike	Min., Dal., Tor., S.J.	9	423	71	97	168	550	26	2	2	4	49	....	1990-91	2001-02
Craighead, John	Tor.	1	5	0	0	0	10	....	....	....	....	....	....	1996-97	1996-97
Craigwell, Dale	S.J.	3	98	11	18	29	28	....	....	....	....	....	....	1991-92	1993-94
Crashley, Bart	Det., K.C., L.A.	6	140	7	36	43	50	....	....	....	....	....	....	1965-66	1975-76
Craven, Murray	Det., Phi., Hfd., Van., Chi., S.J.	18	1071	266	493	759	524	118	27	43	70	64	....	1982-83	1999-00
Crawford, Bob	St.L., Hfd., NYR, Wsh.	7	246	71	71	142	72	11	0	1	1	8	....	1979-80	1986-87
Crawford, Bobby	Col., Det.	2	16	1	3	4	6	....	....	....	....	....	....	1980-81	1982-83
• Crawford, Jack	Bos.	13	548	38	140	178	202	66	3	13	16	36	2	1937-38	1949-50
Crawford, Lou	Bos.	2	26	2	1	3	29	1	0	0	0	0	....	1989-90	1991-92
Crawford, Marc	Van.	6	176	19	31	50	229	20	1	2	3	44	....	1981-82	1986-87
• Crawford, Rusty	Ott., Tor.	2	38	10	8	18	117	2	2	1	3	9	1	1917-18	1918-19
Creighton, Adam	Buf., Chi., NYI, T.B., St.L.	14	708	187	216	403	1077	61	11	14	25	137	....	1983-84	1996-97
Creighton, Dave	Bos., Tor., Chi., NYR	12	616	140	174	314	223	51	11	13	24	20	....	1948-49	1959-60
• Creighton, Jimmy	Det.	1	11	1	0	1	2	....	....	....	....	....	....	1930-31	1930-31
Cressman, Dave	Min.	2	85	6	8	14	37	....	....	....	....	....	....	1974-75	1975-76
Cressman, Glen	Mtl.	1	4	0	0	0	2	....	....	....	....	....	....	1956-57	1956-57
Crisp, Terry	Bos., St.L., NYI, Phi.	11	536	67	134	201	135	110	15	28	43	40	2	1965-66	1976-77
Cristofoli, Ed	Mtl.	1	9	0	1	1	4	....	....	....	....	....	....	1989-90	1989-90
• Croghan, Maurice	Mtl.M.	1	16	0	0	0	4	....	....	....	....	....	....	1937-38	1937-38
Crombeen, Mike	Cle., St.L., Hfd.	8	475	55	68	123	218	27	6	2	8	32	....	1977-78	1984-85
Cronin, Shawn	Wsh., Wpg., Phi., S.J.	7	292	3	18	21	877	32	1	0	1	38	....	1988-89	1994-95
Cross, Cory	T.B., Tor., NYR, Edm., Pit., Det.	12	659	34	97	131	684	47	2	4	6	62	....	1993-94	2005-06
• Crossett, Stan	Phi.	1	21	0	0	0	10	....	....	....	....	....	....	1930-31	1930-31
Crossman, Doug	Chi., Phi., L.A., NYI, Hfd., Det., T.B., St.L.	14	914	105	359	464	534	97	12	39	51	105	....	1980-81	1993-94
Croteau, Gary	L.A., Det., Cal., K.C., Col.	12	684	144	175	319	143	11	3	2	5	8	....	1968-69	1979-80
Crowder, Bruce	Bos., Pit.	4	243	47	51	98	156	31	8	4	12	41	....	1981-82	1984-85
Crowder, Keith	Bos., L.A.	10	662	223	271	494	1354	85	14	22	36	218	....	1980-81	1989-90
Crowder, Troy	N.J., Det., L.A., Van.	7	150	9	7	16	433	4	0	0	0	22	....	1987-88	1996-97
Crowe, Phil	L.A., Phi., Ott., Nsh.	6	94	4	5	9	173	3	0	0	0	16	....	1993-94	1999-00
Crowley, Mike	Ana.	3	67	5	15	20	44	....	....	....	....	....	....	1997-98	2000-01
Crowley, Ted	Hfd., Col., NYI	2	34	2	4	6	12	....	....	....	....	....	....	1993-94	1998-99
Crozier, Greg	Pit.	1	1	0	0	0	0	....	....	....	....	....	....	2000-01	2000-01
Crozier, Joe	Tor.	1	5	0	3	3	2	....	....	....	....	....	....	1959-60	1959-60
• Crutchfield, Nels	Mtl.	1	41	5	5	10	20	2	0	1	1	22	....	1934-35	1934-35
Culhane, Jim	Hfd.	1	6	0	1	1	4	....	....	....	....	....	....	1989-90	1989-90
Cullen, Barry	Tor., Det.	5	219	32	52	84	111	6	0	0	0	2	....	1955-56	1959-60
Cullen, Brian	Tor., NYR	7	326	56	100	156	92	19	3	0	3	2	....	1954-55	1960-61
Cullen, David	Phx., Min.	2	19	0	0	0	6	....	....	....	....	....	....	2000-01	2001-02
Cullen, John	Pit., Hfd., Tor., T.B.	11	621	187	363	550	898	53	12	22	34	58	....	1988-89	1998-99
‡ Cullen, Mark	Chi., Phi., Fla.	3	38	7	10	17	4	....	....	....	....	....	....	2005-06	2011-12
Cullen, Ray	NYR, Det., Min., Van.	6	313	92	123	215	120	20	3	10	13	2	....	1965-66	1970-71
Cullimore, Jassen	Van., Mtl., T.B., Chi., Fla.	15	812	26	85	111	704	35	1	3	4	24	1	1994-95	2010-11
‡ Cuma, Tyler	Min.	1	1	0	0	0	2	....	....	....	....	....	....	2011-12	2011-12
Cummins, Barry	Cal.	1	36	1	2	3	39	....	....	....	....	....	....	1973-74	1973-74
Cummins, Jim	Det., Phi., T.B., Chi., Phx., Mtl., Ana., NYI, Col.	12	511	24	36	60	1538	37	1	2	3	43	....	1991-92	2003-04
Cunneyworth, Randy	Buf., Pit., Wpg., Hfd., Chi., Ott.	16	866	189	225	414	1280	45	7	7	14	61	....	1980-81	1998-99
Cunningham, Bob	NYR	2	4	0	1	1	0	....	....	....	....	....	....	1960-61	1961-62
• Cunningham, Jim	Phi.	1	1	0	0	0	4	....	....	....	....	....	....	1977-78	1977-78
• Cunningham, Les	NYA, Chi.	2	60	7	19	26	21	1	0	0	0	0	....	1936-37	1939-40
• Cupolo, Bill	Bos.	1	47	11	13	24	10	7	1	2	3	0	....	1944-45	1944-45
Curran, Brian	Bos., NYI, Tor., Buf., Wsh.	10	381	7	33	40	1461	24	0	1	1	122	....	1983-84	1993-94
Currie, Dan	Edm., L.A.	4	22	2	1	3	4	....	....	....	....	....	....	1990-91	1993-94
Currie, Glen	Wsh., L.A.	8	326	39	79	118	100	12	1	3	4	4	....	1979-80	1987-88
Currie, Hugh	Mtl.	1	1	0	0	0	0	....	....	....	....	....	....	1950-51	1950-51
Currie, Tony	St.L., Van., Hfd.	8	290	92	119	211	83	16	4	12	16	14	....	1977-78	1984-85
• Curry, Floyd	Mtl.	11	601	105	99	204	147	91	23	17	40	38	4	1947-48	1957-58
Curtale, Tony	Cgy.	1	2	0	0	0	0	....	....	....	....	....	....	1980-81	1980-81
Curtis, Paul	Mtl., L.A., St.L.	4	185	3	34	37	161	5	0	0	0	2	....	1969-70	1972-73
Cushenan, Ian	Chi., Mtl., NYR, Det.	5	129	3	11	14	134	....	....	....	....	....	1	1956-57	1963-64
Cusson, Jean	Oak.	1	2	0	0	0	0	....	....	....	....	....	....	1967-68	1967-68
‡ Cutta, Jakub	Wsh.	3	8	0	0	0	0	....	....	....	....	....	....	2000-01	2003-04
Cyr, Denis	Cgy., Chi., St.L.	6	193	41	43	84	36	4	0	0	0	0	....	1980-81	1985-86
• Cyr, Paul	Buf., NYR, Hfd.	9	470	101	140	241	623	24	4	6	10	31	....	1982-83	1991-92
Czerkawski, Mariusz	Bos., Edm., NYI, Mtl., Tor.	12	745	215	220	435	274	42	8	7	15	18	....	1993-94	2005-06

D

Name	NHL Teams	NHL Seasons	Regular Schedule GP	G	A	TP	PIM	Playoffs GP	G	A	TP	PIM	NHL Cup Wins	First NHL Season	Last NHL Season
Dackell, Andreas	Ott., Mtl.	8	613	91	159	250	162	44	5	5	10	10	....	1996-97	2003-04
‡ Dadonov, Evgeni	Fla.	3	55	10	10	20	16	....	....	....	....	....	....	2009-10	2011-12
Dagenais, Pierre	N.J., Fla., Mtl.	5	142	35	23	58	58	8	0	1	1	6	....	2000-01	2005-06
Dahl, Kevin	Cgy., Phx., Tor., CBJ	8	188	7	22	29	153	16	0	2	2	12	....	1992-93	2000-01
Dahlen, Ulf	NYR, Min., Dal., S.J., Chi., Wsh.	14	966	301	354	655	230	85	15	25	40	12	....	1987-88	2002-03
Dahlin, Kjell	Mtl.	3	166	57	59	116	10	35	6	11	17	6	1	1985-86	1987-88
Dahlman, Toni	Ott.	2	22	1	1	2	0	....	....	....	....	....	....	2001-02	2002-03
Dahlquist, Chris	Pit., Min., Cgy., Ott.	11	532	19	71	90	488	39	4	7	11	30	....	1985-86	1995-96
• Dahlstrom, Cully	Chi.	8	342	88	118	206	58	29	6	8	14	4	1	1937-38	1944-45
Daigle, Alain	Chi.	6	389	56	50	106	122	17	0	1	1	0	....	1974-75	1979-80
Daigle, Alexandre	Ott., Phi., T.B., NYR, Pit., Min.	10	616	129	198	327	186	12	0	2	2	2	....	1993-94	2005-06
Daigneault, J.J.	Van., Phi., Mtl., St.L., Pit., Ana., NYI, Nsh., Phx., Min.	16	899	53	197	250	687	99	5	26	31	100	1	1984-85	2000-01
Dailey, Bob	Van., Phi.	9	561	94	231	325	814	63	12	34	46	105	....	1973-74	1981-82
• Daley, Frank	Det.	1	5	0	0	0	0	2	0	0	0	0	....	1928-29	1928-29
Daley, Pat	Wpg.	2	12	1	0	1	13	....	....	....	....	....	....	1979-80	1980-81
Dalgarno, Brad	NYI	10	321	49	71	120	332	27	2	4	6	37	....	1985-86	1995-96
‡ Dallman, Kevin	Bos., St.L., L.A.	3	154	8	23	31	45	....	....	....	....	....	....	2005-06	2007-08
Dallman, Marty	Tor.	2	6	0	1	1	0	....	....	....	....	....	....	1987-88	1988-89
Dallman, Rod	NYI, Phi.	4	6	1	0	1	26	1	0	1	1	0	....	1987-88	1991-92
• Dame, Bunny	Mtl.	1	34	2	5	7	4	....	....	....	....	....	....	1941-42	1941-42
• Damore, Hank	NYR	1	4	1	0	1	2	....	....	....	....	....	....	1943-44	1943-44
Damphousse, Vincent	Tor., Edm., Mtl., S.J.	18	1378	432	773	1205	1190	140	41	63	104	144	1	1986-87	2003-04
Dandenault, Mathieu	Det., Mtl.	13	868	68	135	203	516	83	3	8	11	24	3	1995-96	2008-09
Daneyko, Ken	N.J.	20	1283	36	142	178	2519	175	5	17	22	296	3	1983-84	2002-03
Daniels, Jeff	Pit., Fla., Hfd., Car., Nsh.	12	425	17	26	43	83	41	3	5	8	2	1	1990-91	2002-03
Daniels, Kimbi	Phi.	2	27	1	2	3	4	....	....	....	....	....	....	1990-91	1991-92
Daniels, Scott	Hfd., Phi., N.J.	6	149	8	12	20	667	1	0	0	0	0	....	1992-93	1998-99
Danton, Mike	N.J., St.L.	3	87	9	5	14	182	5	1	0	1	2	....	2000-01	2003-04
Daoust, Dan	Mtl., Tor.	8	522	87	167	254	544	32	7	5	12	83	....	1982-83	1989-90
Darby, Craig	Mtl., NYI, Phi., N.J.	9	196	21	35	56	32	....	....	....	....	....	....	1994-95	2003-04
Darche, Mathieu	CBJ, Nsh., S.J., T.B., Mtl.	9	250	30	42	72	58	18	1	2	3	2	....	2000-01	2011-12
Dark, Michael	St.L.	2	43	5	6	11	14	....	....	....	....	....	....	1986-87	1987-88
• Darragh, Harold	Pit., Phi., Bos., Tor.	8	308	68	49	117	50	16	1	3	4	4	1	1925-26	1932-33
• Darragh, Jack	Ott.	6	121	66	46	112	113	11	3	0	3	9	3	1917-18	1923-24
‡ Daugavins, Kaspars	Ott., Bos.	3	91	6	9	15	21	7	0	0	0	2	....	2009-10	2012-13
David, Richard	Que.	3	31	4	4	8	10	1	0	0	0	0	....	1979-80	1982-83
• Davidson, Bob	Tor.	12	491	94	160	254	398	79	5	17	22	76	2	1934-35	1945-46
• Davidson, Gord	NYR	2	51	3	6	9	8	....	....	....	....	....	....	1942-43	1943-44
Davidson, Matt	CBJ	3	56	5	7	12	28	....	....	....	....	....	....	2000-01	2002-03
Davidsson, Johan	Ana., NYI	2	83	6	9	15	16	1	0	0	0	0	....	1998-99	1999-00
• Davie, Bob	Bos.	3	41	0	1	1	25	....	....	....	....	....	....	1933-34	1935-36
• Davies, Buck	NYR	1	....	....	....	....	....	1	0	0	0	0	....	1947-48	1947-48
• Davis, Bob	Det.	1	3	0	0	0	0	....	....	....	....	....	....	1932-33	1932-33
Davis, Kim	Pit., Tor.	4	36	5	7	12	51	4	0	0	0	0	....	1977-78	1980-81
• Davis, Lorne	Mtl., Chi., Det., Bos.	6	95	8	12	20	20	18	3	1	4	10	1	1951-52	1959-60
Davis, Mal	Det., Buf.	6	100	31	22	53	34	7	1	0	1	0	....	1978-79	1985-86
‡ Davis, Patrick	N.J.	2	9	1	0	1	0	....	....	....	....	....	....	2008-09	2009-10

Name	NHL Teams	NHL Seasons	Regular Schedule GP	G	A	TP	PIM	Playoffs GP	G	A	TP	PIM	NHL Cup Wins	First NHL Season	Last NHL Season
● Davison, Murray	Bos.	1	1	0	0	0	0	....	....	....	....	....	....	1965-66	1965-66
‡ Davison, Rob	S.J., NYI, Van., N.J.	7	219	3	15	18	321	6	0	2	2	4	....	2002-03	2009-10
Davydov, Evgeny	Wpg., Fla., Ott.	4	155	40	39	79	120	11	2	2	4	2	....	1991-92	1994-95
Daw, Jeff	Col.	1	1	0	1	1	0	....	....	....	....	....	....	2001-02	2001-02
Dawe, Jason	Buf., NYI, Mtl., NYR	8	366	86	90	176	162	22	4	3	7	18	....	1993-94	2001-02
● Dawes, Bob	Tor., Mtl.	4	32	2	7	9	6	10	0	0	0	2	1	1946-47	1950-51
‡ Dawes, Nigel	NYR, Phx., Cgy., Atl., Mtl.	5	212	39	45	84	43	11	2	2	4	0	....	2006-07	2010-11
● Day, Hap	Tor., NYA	14	581	86	116	202	601	53	4	7	11	56	1	1924-25	1937-38
Day, Joe	Hfd., NYI	3	72	1	10	11	87	....	....	....	....	....	....	1991-92	1993-94
Daze, Eric	Chi.	11	601	226	172	398	176	37	5	7	12	8	....	1994-95	2005-06
de Vries, Greg	Edm., Nsh., Col., NYR, Ott., Atl.	13	878	48	146	194	780	111	8	14	22	91	1	1995-96	2008-09
Dea, Billy	NYR, Det., Chi., Pit.	8	397	67	54	121	44	11	2	1	3	6	....	1953-54	1970-71
● Deacon, Don	Det.	3	30	6	4	10	6	2	2	1	3	0	....	1936-37	1939-40
Deadmarsh, Adam	Que., Col., L.A.	10	567	184	189	373	819	105	26	40	66	100	1	1994-95	2003-04
Deadmarsh, Butch	Buf., Atl., K.C.	5	137	12	5	17	155	4	0	0	0	17	....	1970-71	1974-75
Dean, Barry	Col., Phi.	3	165	25	56	81	146	....	....	....	....	....	....	1976-77	1978-79
Dean, Kevin	N.J., Atl., Dal., Chi.	7	331	7	48	55	138	16	2	2	4	2	1	1994-95	2000-01
Debenedet, Nelson	Det., Pit.	2	46	10	4	14	13	....	....	....	....	....	....	1973-74	1974-75
DeBlois, Lucien	NYR, Col., Wpg., Mtl., Que., Tor.	15	993	249	276	525	814	52	7	6	13	38	1	1977-78	1991-92
Debol, Dave	Hfd.	2	92	26	26	52	4	3	0	0	0	0	....	1979-80	1980-81
DeBrusk, Louie	Edm., T.B., Phx., Chi.	11	401	24	17	41	1161	15	2	0	2	10	....	1991-92	2002-03
DeFauw, Brad	Car.	1	9	3	0	3	2	....	....	....	....	....	....	2002-03	2002-03
Defazio, Dean	Pit.	1	22	0	2	2	28	....	....	....	....	....	....	1983-84	1983-84
DeGray, Dale	Cgy., Tor., L.A., Buf.	5	153	18	47	65	195	13	1	3	4	28	....	1985-86	1989-90
● Delisle, Jonathan	Mtl.	1	1	0	0	0	0	....	....	....	....	....	....	1998-99	1998-99
Delisle, Xavier	T.B., Mtl.	2	16	3	2	5	6	....	....	....	....	....	....	1998-99	2000-01
‡ Della Rovere, Stefan	St.L.	1	7	0	0	0	11	....	....	....	....	....	....	2010-11	2010-11
● Delmonte, Armand	Bos.	1	1	0	0	0	0	....	....	....	....	....	....	1945-46	1945-46
Delmore, Andy	Phi., Nsh., Buf., CBJ	7	283	43	58	101	105	20	6	2	8	16	....	1998-99	2005-06
Delorme, Gilbert	Mtl., St.L., Que., Det., Pit.	9	541	31	92	123	520	56	1	9	10	56	....	1981-82	1989-90
Delorme, Ron	Col., Van.	9	524	83	83	166	667	25	1	2	3	59	....	1976-77	1984-85
Delory, Val	NYR	1	1	0	0	0	0	....	....	....	....	....	....	1948-49	1948-49
Delparte, Guy	Col.	1	48	1	8	9	18	....	....	....	....	....	....	1976-77	1976-77
Delvecchio, Alex	Det.	24	1549	456	825	1281	383	121	35	69	104	29	3	1950-51	1973-74
● DeMarco, Ab	Chi., Tor., Bos., NYR	7	209	72	93	165	53	11	3	0	3	2	....	1938-39	1946-47
DeMarco, Ab	NYR, St.L., Pit., Van., L.A., Bos.	9	344	44	80	124	75	25	1	2	3	17	....	1969-70	1978-79
● Demers, Tony	Mtl., NYR	6	83	20	22	42	23	2	0	0	0	0	....	1937-38	1943-44
● Demitra, Pavol	Ott., St.L., L.A., Min., Van.	16	847	304	464	768	284	94	23	36	59	34	....	1993-94	2009-10
Dempsey, Nathan	Tor., Chi., L.A., Bos.	8	260	21	67	88	120	6	0	2	2	0	....	1996-97	2006-07
Denis, Jean-Paul	NYR	2	10	0	2	2	2	....	....	....	....	....	....	1946-47	1949-50
Denis, Lulu	Mtl.	2	3	0	1	1	0	....	....	....	....	....	....	1949-50	1950-51
● Denneny, Corb	Tor., Ham., Chi.	9	176	103	42	145	148	6	1	0	1	7	2	1917-18	1927-28
● Denneny, Cy	Ott., Bos.	12	328	248	85	333	301	25	16	2	18	23	5	1917-18	1928-29
Dennis, Norm	St.L.	4	12	3	0	3	11	5	0	0	0	2	....	1968-69	1971-72
● Denoird, Gerry	Tor.	1	17	0	1	1	0	....	....	....	....	....	....	1922-23	1922-23
DePalma, Larry	Min., S.J., Pit.	7	148	21	20	41	408	3	0	0	0	6	....	1985-86	1993-94
Derlago, Bill	Van., Tor., Bos., Wpg., Que.	9	555	189	227	416	247	13	5	0	5	8	....	1978-79	1986-87
● Desaulniers, Gerard	Mtl.	3	8	0	2	2	4	....	....	....	....	....	....	1950-51	1953-54
‡ Desbiens, Guillaume	Van., Cgy.	3	23	0	0	0	37	....	....	....	....	....	....	2009-10	2011-12
Descoteaux, Matthieu	Mtl.	1	5	1	1	2	4	....	....	....	....	....	....	2000-01	2000-01
● Desilets, Joffre	Mtl., Chi.	5	192	37	45	82	57	7	1	0	1	7	....	1935-36	1939-40
Desjardins, Eric	Mtl., Phi.	17	1143	136	439	575	757	168	23	57	80	93	1	1988-89	2005-06
Desjardins, Martin	Mtl.	1	8	0	2	2	2	....	....	....	....	....	....	1989-90	1989-90
● Desjardins, Vic	Chi., NYR	2	87	6	15	21	27	16	0	0	0	0	....	1930-31	1931-32
Deslauriers, Jacques	Mtl.	1	2	0	0	0	0	....	....	....	....	....	....	1955-56	1955-56
Deuling, Jarrett	NYI	2	15	0	1	1	11	....	....	....	....	....	....	1995-96	1996-97
‡ Deveaux, Andre	Tor., NYR	3	31	0	2	2	104	....	....	....	....	....	....	2008-09	2011-12
Devereaux, Boyd	Edm., Det., Phx., Tor.	11	627	67	112	179	205	27	3	4	7	4	1	1997-98	2008-09
Devine, Kevin	NYI	1	2	0	1	1	8	....	....	....	....	....	....	1982-83	1982-83
● Dewar, Tom	NYR	1	9	0	2	2	4	....	....	....	....	....	....	1943-44	1943-44
● Dewsbury, Al	Det., Chi.	9	347	30	78	108	365	14	1	5	6	16	1	1946-47	1955-56
Deziel, Michel	Buf.	1	....	....	....	....	....	1	0	0	0	0	....	1974-75	1974-75
● Dheere, Marcel	Mtl.	1	11	1	2	3	2	5	0	0	0	6	....	1942-43	1942-43
Diachuk, Edward	Det.	1	12	0	0	0	19	....	....	....	....	....	....	1960-61	1960-61
‡ Dibenedetto, Justin	NYI	1	8	0	1	1	2	....	....	....	....	....	....	2010-11	2010-11
● Dick, Harry	Chi.	1	12	0	1	1	12	....	....	....	....	....	....	1946-47	1946-47
● Dickens, Ernie	Tor., Chi.	6	278	12	44	56	98	13	0	0	0	4	1	1941-42	1950-51
Dickenson, Herb	NYR	2	48	18	17	35	10	....	....	....	....	....	....	1951-52	1952-53
Diduck, Gerald	NYI, Mtl., Van., Chi., Hfd., Phx., Tor., Dal.	17	932	56	156	212	1612	114	8	16	24	212	....	1984-85	2000-01
Dietrich, Don	Chi., N.J.	2	28	0	7	7	10	....	....	....	....	....	....	1983-84	1985-86
● Dill, Bob	NYR	2	76	15	15	30	135	....	....	....	....	....	....	1943-44	1944-45
● Dillabough, Bob	Det., Bos., Pit., Oak.	9	283	32	54	86	76	17	3	0	3	0	....	1961-62	1969-70
● Dillon, Cecil	NYR, Det.	10	453	167	131	298	105	43	14	9	23	14	1	1930-31	1939-40
Dillon, Gary	Col.	1	13	1	1	2	29	....	....	....	....	....	....	1980-81	1980-81
Dillon, Wayne	NYR, Wpg.	4	229	43	66	109	60	3	0	1	1	0	....	1975-76	1979-80
DiMaio, Rob	NYI, T.B., Phi., Bos., NYR, Car., Dal.	17	894	106	171	277	840	62	7	9	16	40	....	1988-89	2005-06
Dimitrakos, Niko	S.J., Phi.	4	158	24	38	62	95	20	1	8	9	10	....	2002-03	2006-07
Dineen, Bill	Det., Chi.	5	323	51	44	95	122	37	1	1	2	18	2	1953-54	1957-58
● Dineen, Gary	Min.	1	4	0	1	1	0	....	....	....	....	....	....	1968-69	1968-69
Dineen, Gord	NYI, Min., Pit., Ott.	13	528	16	90	106	695	40	1	7	8	68	....	1982-83	1994-95
Dineen, Kevin	Hfd., Phi., Car., Ott., CBJ	19	1188	355	405	760	2229	59	23	18	41	127	....	1984-85	2002-03
Dineen, Peter	L.A., Det.	2	13	0	2	2	13	....	....	....	....	....	....	1986-87	1989-90
Dingman, Chris	Cgy., Col., Car., T.B.	8	385	15	19	34	769	52	2	5	7	100	2	1997-98	2005-06
● Dinsmore, Chuck	Mtl.M.	4	100	6	2	8	50	8	1	0	1	2	1	1924-25	1929-30
Dionne, Gilbert	Mtl., Phi., Fla.	6	223	61	79	140	108	39	10	12	22	34	1	1990-91	1995-96
Dionne, Marcel	Det., L.A., NYR	18	1348	731	1040	1771	600	49	21	24	45	17	....	1971-72	1988-89
DiPenta, Joe	Atl., Ana.	4	174	6	17	23	110	32	0	0	0	17	1	2002-03	2007-08
DiPietro, Paul	Mtl., Tor., L.A.	6	192	31	49	80	96	31	11	10	21	10	1	1991-92	1996-97
Dirk, Robert	St.L., Van., Chi., Ana., Mtl.	9	402	13	29	42	786	39	0	1	1	56	....	1987-88	1995-96
‡ DiSalvatore, Jon	St.L., Min.	2	6	0	0	0	4	....	....	....	....	....	....	2005-06	2011-12
‡ Divisek, Tomas	Phi.	2	5	1	0	1	0	....	....	....	....	....	....	2000-01	2001-02
Djoos, Per	Det., NYR	3	82	2	31	33	58	....	....	....	....	....	....	1990-91	1992-93
Doak, Gary	Det., Bos., Van., NYR	16	789	23	107	130	908	78	2	4	6	121	1	1965-66	1980-81
Dobbin, Brian	Phi., Bos.	5	63	7	8	15	61	2	0	0	0	17	....	1986-87	1991-92
Dobson, Jim	Min., Col., Que.	4	12	0	0	0	6	....	....	....	....	....	....	1979-80	1983-84
Doell, Kevin	Atl.	1	8	0	1	1	4	....	....	....	....	....	....	2007-08	2007-08
● Doherty, Fred	Mtl.	1	1	0	0	0	0	....	....	....	....	....	....	1918-19	1918-19
Doig, Jason	Wpg., Phx., NYR, Wsh.	7	158	6	18	24	285	6	0	1	1	6	....	1995-96	2003-04
Dollas, Bobby	Wpg., Que., Det., Ana., Edm., Pit., Ott., Cgy., S.J.	16	646	42	96	138	467	47	2	1	3	41	....	1983-84	2000-01
Dome, Robert	Pit., Cgy.	3	53	7	7	14	12	....	....	....	....	....	....	1997-98	2002-03
‡ Domenichelli, Hnat	Hfd., Cgy., Atl., Min.	7	267	52	61	113	104	....	....	....	....	....	....	1996-97	2002-03
Domi, Tie	Tor., NYR, Wpg.	16	1020	104	141	245	3515	98	7	12	19	238	....	1989-90	2005-06
Donaldson, Gary	Chi.	1	1	0	0	0	0	....	....	....	....	....	....	1973-74	1973-74
Donatelli, Clark	Min., Bos.	2	35	3	4	7	39	2	0	0	0	0	....	1989-90	1991-92
Donato, Ted	Bos., NYI, Ott., Ana., Dal., St.L., L.A., NYR	13	796	150	197	347	396	58	8	10	18	22	....	1991-92	2003-04
● Donnelly, Babe	Mtl.M.	1	34	0	1	1	14	2	0	0	0	0	....	1926-27	1926-27
Donnelly, Dave	Bos., Chi., Edm.	5	137	15	24	39	150	5	0	0	0	0	....	1983-84	1987-88
Donnelly, Gord	Que., Wpg., Buf., Dal.	12	554	28	41	69	2069	26	0	2	2	61	....	1983-84	1994-95
Donnelly, Mike	NYR, Buf., L.A., Dal., NYI	11	465	114	121	235	255	47	12	12	24	30	....	1986-87	1996-97
Donovan, Shean	S.J., Col., Atl., Pit., Cgy., Bos., Ott.	15	951	112	129	241	705	49	6	6	12	39	....	1994-95	2009-10
Doornbosch, Jamie	NYI	1	1	0	0	0	0	....	....	....	....	....	....	2010-11	2010-11
Dopita, Jiri	Phi., Edm.	2	73	12	21	33	19	....	....	....	....	....	....	2001-02	2002-03
● Doran, John	NYA, Det., Mtl.	5	98	5	10	15	110	3	0	0	0	0	....	1933-34	1939-40
● Doran, Lloyd	Det.	1	24	3	2	5	10	....	....	....	....	....	....	1946-47	1946-47
● Doraty, Ken	Chi., Tor., Det.	5	103	15	26	41	24	15	7	2	9	2	....	1926-27	1937-38
Dore, Andre	NYR, St.L., Que.	7	257	14	81	95	261	23	1	2	3	32	....	1978-79	1984-85
Dore, Daniel	Que.	2	17	2	3	5	59	....	....	....	....	....	....	1989-90	1990-91
Dorey, Jim	Tor., NYR	4	232	25	74	99	553	11	0	2	2	40	....	1968-69	1971-72
Dorion, Dan	N.J.	2	4	1	1	2	2	....	....	....	....	....	....	1985-86	1987-88
Dornhoefer, Gary	Bos., Phi.	14	787	214	328	542	1291	80	17	19	36	203	2	1963-64	1977-78
● Dorohoy, Eddie	Mtl.	1	16	0	0	0	6	....	....	....	....	....	....	1948-49	1948-49
Douglas, Jordy	Hfd., Min., Wpg.	6	268	76	62	138	160	6	0	0	0	4	....	1979-80	1984-85
● Douglas, Kent	Tor., Oak., Det.	7	428	33	115	148	631	19	1	3	4	33	3	1962-63	1968-69

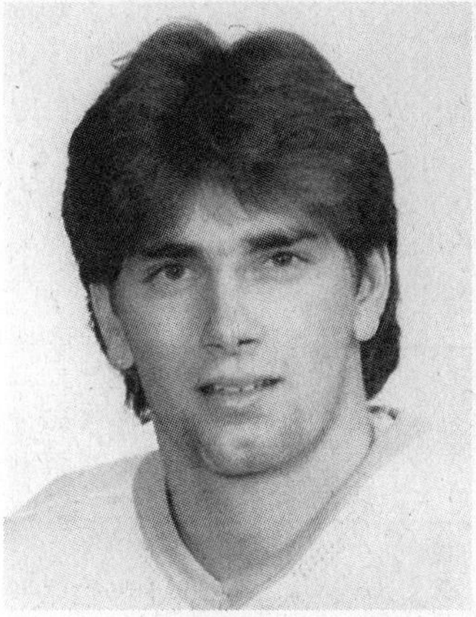
Dean Defazio

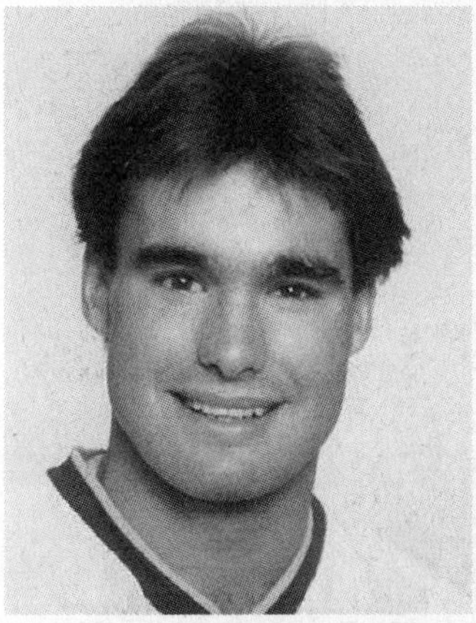
Gilbert Delmore

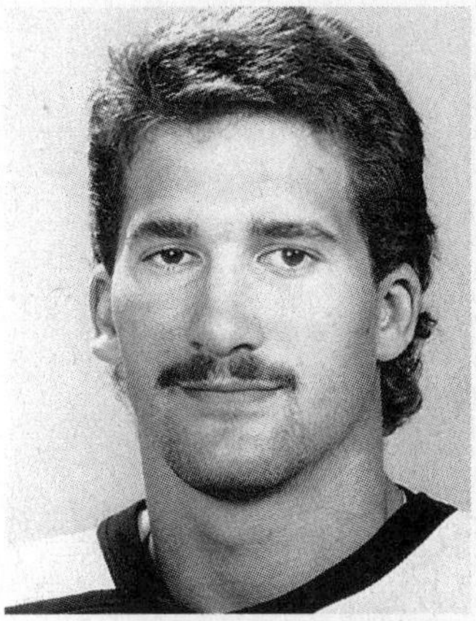
Brian Dobbin

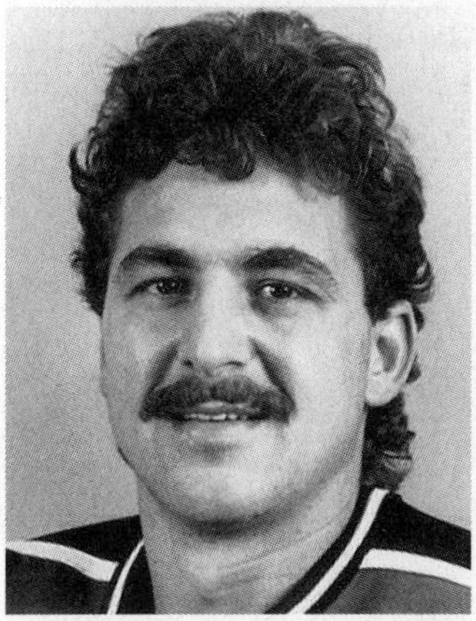
Dan Dorion

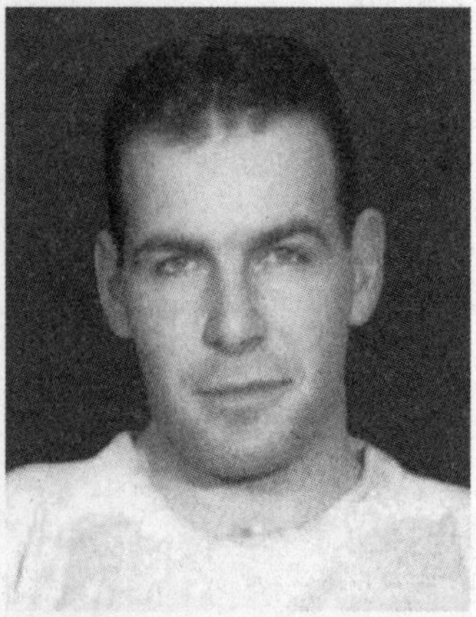

Lorne Duguid

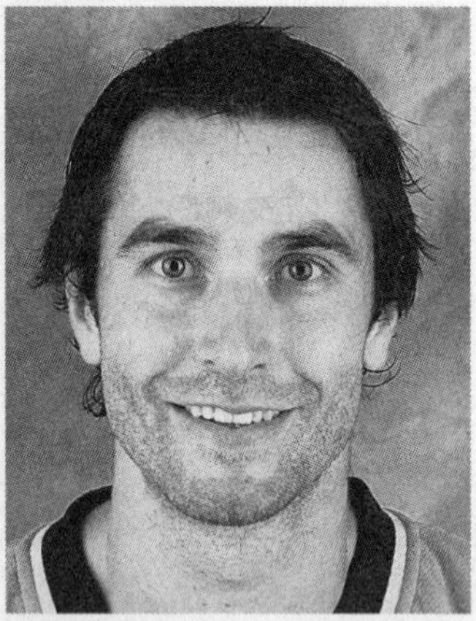

Radek Dvorak

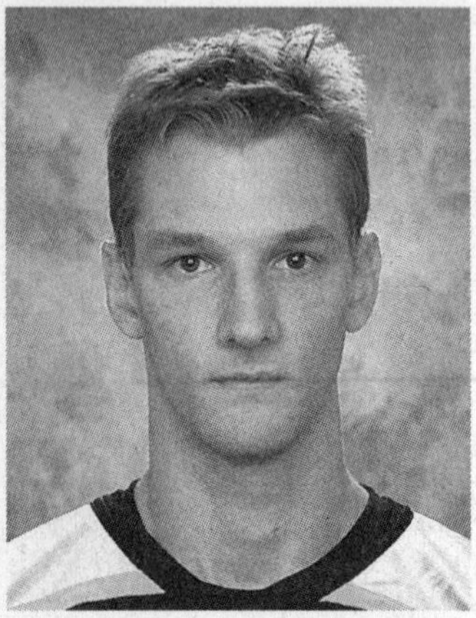

Mark Eaton

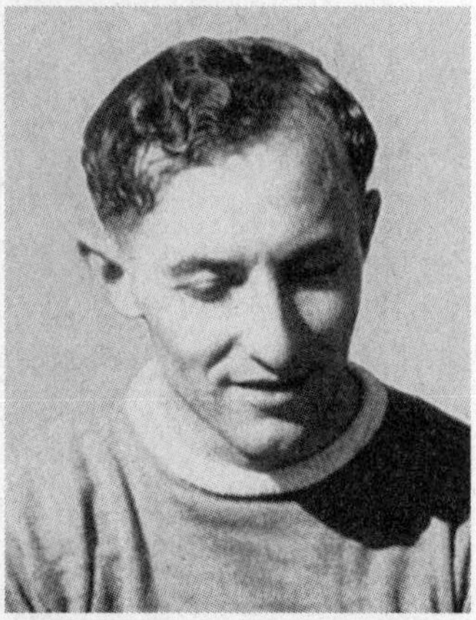

Fred Elliott

			Regular Schedule					Playoffs					NHL	First	Last
Name	NHL Teams	NHL Seasons	GP	G	A	TP	PIM	GP	G	A	TP	PIM	Cup Wins	NHL Season	NHL Season
• Douglas, Les	Det.	4	52	6	12	18	8	10	3	2	5	2	1	1940-41	1946-47
Doull, Doug	Bos., Wsh.	2	37	0	1	1	151	....	....	....	....	....	....	2003-04	2005-06
Douris, Peter	Wpg., Bos., Ana., Dal.	11	321	54	67	121	80	27	3	5	8	14	....	1985-86	1997-98
Dowd, Jim	N.J., Van., NYI, Cgy., Edm., Min., Mtl., Chi., Col., Phi.	16	728	71	168	239	390	99	9	17	26	50	1	1991-92	2007-08
Downey, Aaron	Bos., Chi., Dal., St.L., Mtl., Det.	9	243	8	10	18	494	5	0	0	0	8	1	1999-00	2008-09
• Downie, Dave	Tor.	1	11	0	1	1	2	....	....	....	....	....	....	1932-33	1932-33
Doyon, Mario	Chi., Que.	3	28	3	4	7	16	....	....	....	....	....	....	1988-89	1990-91
Drake, Dallas	Det., Wpg., Phx., St.L.	15	1009	177	300	477	885	90	14	19	33	79	1	1992-93	2007-08
• Draper, Bruce	Tor.	1	1	0	0	0	0	....	....	....	....	....	....	1962-63	1962-63
Draper, Kris	Wpg., Det.	20	1157	161	203	364	790	222	24	22	46	160	4	1990-91	2010-11
• Drillon, Gordie	Tor., Mtl.	7	311	155	139	294	56	50	26	15	41	10	1	1936-37	1942-43
Driscoll, Peter	Edm.	2	60	3	8	11	97	3	0	0	0	0	....	1979-80	1980-81
Driver, Bruce	N.J., NYR	15	922	96	390	486	670	108	10	40	50	64	1	1983-84	1997-98
Drolet, Rene	Phi., Det.	2	2	0	0	0	0	....	....	....	....	....	....	1971-72	1974-75
Droppa, Ivan	Chi.	2	19	0	1	1	14	....	....	....	....	....	....	1993-94	1995-96
• Drouillard, Clarence	Det.	1	10	0	1	1	0	....	....	....	....	....	....	1937-38	1937-38
Drouin, Jude	Mtl., Min., NYI, Wpg.	12	666	151	305	456	346	72	27	41	68	33	....	1968-69	1980-81
Drouin, P.C.	Bos.	1	3	0	0	0	0	....	....	....	....	....	....	1996-97	1996-97
• Drouin, Polly	Mtl.	7	160	23	50	73	80	5	0	1	1	5	....	1934-35	1940-41
Druce, John	Wsh., Wpg., L.A., Phi.	10	531	113	126	239	347	53	17	6	23	38	....	1988-89	1997-98
Druken, Harold	Van., Car., Tor.	5	146	27	36	63	36	4	0	1	1	0	....	1999-00	2003-04
Drulia, Stan	T.B.	3	126	15	27	42	52	....	....	....	....	....	....	1992-93	2000-01
• Drummond, Jim	NYR	1	2	0	0	0	0	....	....	....	....	....	....	1944-45	1944-45
Drury, Chris	Col., Cgy., Buf., NYR	12	892	255	360	615	468	135	47	42	89	46	1	1998-99	2010-11
• Drury, Herb	Pit., Phi.	6	213	24	13	37	203	4	1	1	2	0	....	1925-26	1930-31
Drury, Ted	Cgy., Hfd., Ott., Ana., NYI, CBJ	8	414	41	52	93	367	14	1	0	1	4	....	1993-94	2000-01
‡ Dube, Christian	NYR	2	33	1	1	2	4	3	0	0	0	0	....	1996-97	1998-99
Dube, Gilles	Mtl., Det.	2	12	1	2	3	2	2	0	0	0	0	1	1949-50	1953-54
Dube, Norm	K.C.	2	57	8	10	18	54	....	....	....	....	....	....	1974-75	1975-76
Duberman, Justin	Pit.	1	4	0	0	0	0	....	....	....	....	....	....	1993-94	1993-94
Dubinsky, Steve	Chi., Cgy., Nsh., St.L.	10	375	25	45	70	164	10	1	0	1	14	....	1993-94	2002-03
• Duchesne, Gaetan	Wsh., Que., Min., S.J., Fla.	14	1028	179	254	433	617	84	14	13	27	97	....	1981-82	1994-95
Duchesne, Steve	L.A., Phi., Que., St.L., Ott., Det.	16	1113	227	525	752	824	121	16	61	77	96	1	1986-87	2001-02
Dudley, Rick	Buf., Wpg.	6	309	75	99	174	292	25	7	2	9	69	....	1972-73	1980-81
Duerden, Dave	Fla.	1	2	0	0	0	0	....	....	....	....	....	....	1999-00	1999-00
Duff, Dick	Tor., NYR, Mtl., L.A., Buf.	18	1030	283	289	572	743	114	30	49	79	78	6	1954-55	1971-72
Dufour, Luc	Bos., Que., St.L.	3	167	23	21	44	199	18	1	0	1	32	....	1982-83	1984-85
• Dufour, Marc	NYR, L.A.	3	14	1	0	1	2	....	....	....	....	....	....	1963-64	1968-69
Dufresne, Donald	Mtl., T.B., L.A., St.L., Edm.	9	268	6	36	42	258	34	1	3	4	47	1	1988-89	1996-97
• Duggan, John	Ott.	1	27	0	0	0	0	2	0	0	0	0	....	1925-26	1925-26
Duggan, Ken	Min.	1	1	0	0	0	0	....	....	....	....	....	....	1987-88	1987-88
Duguay, Ron	NYR, Det., Pit., L.A.	12	864	274	346	620	582	89	31	22	53	118	....	1977-78	1988-89
• Duguid, Lorne	Mtl.M., Det., Bos.	6	135	9	15	24	57	4	1	0	1	6	....	1931-32	1936-37
• Dukowski, Duke	Chi., NYA, NYR	5	200	16	30	46	172	6	0	0	0	6	....	1926-27	1933-34
• Dumart, Woody	Bos.	16	772	211	218	429	99	88	12	15	27	23	2	1935-36	1953-54
Dumont, J.P.	Chi., Buf., Nsh.	12	822	214	309	523	364	51	17	17	34	28	....	1998-99	2010-11
Dunbar, Dale	Van., Bos.	2	2	0	0	0	2	....	....	....	....	....	....	1985-86	1988-89
• Duncan, Art	Det., Tor.	5	156	18	16	34	225	5	0	0	0	4	....	1926-27	1930-31
Duncan, Iain	Wpg.	4	127	34	55	89	149	11	0	3	3	6	....	1986-87	1990-91
Duncanson, Craig	L.A., Wpg., NYR	7	38	5	4	9	61	....	....	....	....	....	....	1985-86	1992-93
Dundas, Rocky	Tor.	1	5	0	0	0	14	....	....	....	....	....	....	1989-90	1989-90
• Dunlap, Frank	Tor.	1	15	0	1	1	2	....	....	....	....	....	....	1943-44	1943-44
Dunlop, Blake	Min., Phi., St.L., Det.	11	550	130	274	404	172	40	4	10	14	18	....	1973-74	1983-84
Dunn, Dave	Van., Tor.	3	184	14	41	55	313	10	1	1	2	41	....	1973-74	1975-76
Dunn, Richie	Buf., Cgy., Hfd.	12	483	36	140	176	314	36	3	15	18	24	....	1977-78	1988-89
Dupere, Denis	Tor., Wsh., St.L., K.C., Col.	8	421	80	99	179	66	16	1	0	1	0	....	1970-71	1977-78
Dupont, Andre	NYR, St.L., Phi., Que.	13	800	59	185	244	1986	140	14	18	32	352	2	1970-71	1982-83
‡ Dupont, Brodie	NYR	1	1	0	0	0	0	....	....	....	....	....	....	2010-11	2010-11
Dupont, Jerome	Chi., Tor.	6	214	7	29	36	468	20	0	2	2	56	....	1981-82	1986-87
DuPont, Micki	Cgy., Pit., St.L.	4	23	1	3	4	12	....	....	....	....	....	....	2001-02	2007-08
Dupont, Norm	Mtl., Wpg., Hfd.	5	256	55	85	140	52	13	4	2	6	0	....	1979-80	1983-84
• Dupre, Yanick	Phi.	3	35	2	0	2	16	....	....	....	....	....	....	1991-92	1995-96
‡ Dupuis, Philippe	Col., Tor.	4	116	6	12	18	62	....	....	....	....	....	....	2008-09	2011-12
• Durbano, Steve	St.L., Pit., K.C., Col.	6	220	13	60	73	1127	5	0	2	2	8	....	1972-73	1978-79
Duris, Vitezslav	Tor.	2	89	3	20	23	62	3	0	1	1	2	....	1980-81	1982-83
Durno, Chris	Col.	2	43	4	4	8	47	1	0	0	0	0	....	2008-09	2009-10
Dusablon, Benoit	NYR	1	3	0	0	0	2	....	....	....	....	....	....	2003-04	2003-04
• Dussault, Norm	Mtl.	4	206	31	62	93	47	7	3	1	4	0	....	1947-48	1950-51
• Dutton, Red	Mtl.M., NYA	10	449	29	67	96	871	18	1	0	1	33	....	1926-27	1935-36
• Dvorak, Miroslav	Phi.	3	193	11	74	85	51	18	0	2	2	6	....	1982-83	1984-85
‡ Dvorak, Radek	Fla., NYR, Edm., St.L., Atl., Dal., Ana., Car.	18	1260	227	363	590	449	39	2	5	7	4	....	1995-96	2013-14
Dwyer, Gordie	T.B., NYR, Mtl.	5	108	0	5	5	394	....	....	....	....	....	....	1999-00	2003-04
Dwyer, Mike	Col., Cgy.	4	31	2	6	8	25	1	1	0	1	0	....	1978-79	1981-82
• Dyck, Henry	NYR	1	1	0	0	0	0	....	....	....	....	....	....	1943-44	1943-44
• Dye, Babe	Tor., Ham., Chi., NYA	11	271	201	47	248	221	10	2	0	2	11	1	1919-20	1930-31
Dykhuis, Karl	Chi., Phi., T.B., Mtl.	12	644	42	91	133	495	62	8	10	18	50	....	1991-92	2003-04
Dykstra, Steve	Buf., Edm., Pit., Hfd.	5	217	8	32	40	545	1	0	0	0	2	....	1985-86	1989-90
• Dyte, Jack	Chi.	1	27	1	0	1	31	....	....	....	....	....	....	1943-44	1943-44
Dziedzic, Joe	Pit., Phx.	3	130	14	14	28	131	21	1	3	4	23	....	1995-96	1998-99

E

Eagles, Mike	Que., Chi., Wpg., Wsh.	16	853	74	122	196	928	44	2	6	8	34	....	1982-83	1999-00
Eakin, Bruce	Cgy., Det.	4	13	2	2	4	4	....	....	....	....	....	....	1981-82	1985-86
Eakins, Dallas	Wpg., Fla., St.L., Phx., NYR, Tor., NYI, Cgy.	10	120	0	9	9	208	5	0	0	0	4	....	1992-93	2001-02
‡ Earl, Robbie	Tor., Min.	3	47	6	1	7	6	....	....	....	....	....	....	2007-08	2010-11
Eastwood, Mike	Tor., Wpg., Phx., NYR, St.L., Chi., Pit.	13	783	87	149	236	354	97	8	11	19	64	....	1991-92	2003-04
Eaton, Mark	Phi., Nsh., Pit., NYI	13	650	24	61	85	242	68	4	9	13	24	1	1999-00	2012-13
Eatough, Jeff	Buf.	1	1	0	0	0	0	....	....	....	....	....	....	1981-82	1981-82
Eaves, Mike	Min., Cgy.	8	324	83	143	226	80	43	7	10	17	14	....	1978-79	1985-86
Eaves, Murray	Wpg., Det.	8	57	4	13	17	9	4	0	1	1	2	....	1980-81	1989-90
Ecclestone, Tim	St.L., Det., Tor., Atl.	11	692	126	233	359	344	48	6	11	17	76	....	1967-68	1977-78
‡ Eckford, Tyler	N.J.	2	7	0	1	1	4	....	....	....	....	....	....	2009-10	2010-11
Edberg, Rolf	Wsh.	3	184	45	58	103	24	....	....	....	....	....	....	1978-79	1980-81
• Eddolls, Frank	Mtl., NYR	8	317	23	43	66	114	31	0	2	2	10	1	1944-45	1951-52
Edestrand, Darryl	St.L., Phi., Pit., Bos., L.A.	10	455	34	90	124	404	42	3	9	12	57	....	1967-68	1978-79
Edmundson, Garry	Mtl., Tor.	3	43	4	6	10	49	11	0	1	1	8	....	1951-52	1960-61
Edur, Tom	Col., Pit.	2	158	17	70	87	67	....	....	....	....	....	....	1976-77	1977-78
• Egan, Pat	NYA, Bro., Det., Bos., NYR	11	554	77	153	230	776	46	9	4	13	48	....	1939-40	1950-51
Egeland, Allan	T.B.	3	17	0	0	0	16	....	....	....	....	....	....	1995-96	1997-98
Egers, Jack	NYR, St.L., Wsh.	7	284	64	69	133	154	32	5	6	11	32	....	1969-70	1975-76
• Ehman, Gerry	Bos., Det., Tor., Oak., Cal.	9	429	96	118	214	100	41	10	10	20	12	1	1957-58	1970-71
Eisenhut, Neil	Van., Cgy.	2	16	1	3	4	21	....	....	....	....	....	....	1993-94	1994-95
Eklund, Pelle	Phi., Dal.	9	594	120	335	455	109	66	10	36	46	8	....	1985-86	1993-94
Ekman, Nils	T.B., S.J., Pit.	5	264	60	91	151	188	28	2	5	7	16	....	1999-00	2006-07
Eldebrink, Anders	Van., Que.	2	55	3	11	14	29	14	0	0	0	10	....	1981-82	1982-83
Elich, Matt	T.B.	2	16	1	1	2	0	....	....	....	....	....	....	1999-00	2000-01
• Elik, Bo	Det.	1	3	0	0	0	0	....	....	....	....	....	....	1962-63	1962-63
Elik, Todd	L.A., Min., Edm., S.J., St.L., Bos.	8	448	110	219	329	453	52	15	27	42	48	....	1989-90	1996-97
‡ Elkins, Corey	L.A.	1	3	1	0	1	0	....	....	....	....	....	....	2009-10	2009-10
Ellett, Dave	Wpg., Tor., N.J., Bos., St.L.	16	1129	153	415	568	985	116	11	46	57	87	....	1984-85	1999-00
• Elliott, Fred	Ott.	1	43	2	0	2	6	....	....	....	....	....	....	1928-29	1928-29
Ellis, Ron	Tor.	16	1034	332	308	640	207	70	18	8	26	20	1	1963-64	1980-81
‡ Ellison, Matt	Chi., Phi.	3	43	3	11	14	19	....	....	....	....	....	....	2003-04	2006-07
Elomo, Miika	Wsh.	1	2	0	1	1	2	....	....	....	....	....	....	1999-00	1999-00
Eloranta, Kari	Cgy., St.L.	5	267	13	103	116	155	26	1	7	8	19	....	1981-82	1986-87
Eloranta, Mikko	Bos., L.A.	4	264	32	44	76	186	7	1	1	2	2	....	1999-00	2002-03
Elynuik, Pat	Wpg., Wsh., T.B., Ott.	9	506	154	188	342	459	20	6	9	15	25	....	1987-88	1995-96
• Emberg, Eddie	Mtl.	1	....	....	....	....	....	2	1	0	1	0	....	1944-45	1944-45
Emerson, Nelson	St.L., Wpg., Hfd., Car., Chi., Ott., Atl., L.A.	12	771	195	293	488	575	40	7	15	22	33	....	1990-91	2001-02
Emma, David	N.J., Bos., Fla.	5	34	5	6	11	2	....	....	....	....	....	....	1992-93	2000-01
‡ Emmerton, Cory	Det.	4	139	12	9	21	22	18	1	1	2	6	....	2010-11	2013-14

Name	NHL Teams	NHL Seasons	Regular Schedule GP	G	A	TP	PIM	Playoffs GP	G	A	TP	PIM	NHL Cup Wins	First NHL Season	Last NHL Season
Emmons, Gary	S.J.	1	3	1	0	1	0	....	....	....	....	....	....	1993-94	1993-94
Emmons, John	Ott., T.B., Bos.	3	85	2	4	6	64	....	....	....	....	....	....	1999-00	2001-02
● Emms, Hap	Mtl.M., NYA, Det., Bos.	10	320	36	53	89	311	14	0	0	0	12	....	1926-27	1937-38
Endean, Craig	Wpg.	1	2	0	1	1	0	....	....	....	....	....	....	1986-87	1986-87
Endicott, Shane	Pit.	2	45	1	2	3	47	....	....	....	....	....	....	2001-02	2005-06
Engblom, Brian	Mtl., Wsh., L.A., Buf., Cgy.	11	659	29	177	206	599	48	3	9	12	43	2	1976-77	1986-87
Engele, Jerry	Min.	3	100	2	13	15	162	2	0	1	1	0	....	1975-76	1977-78
English, John	L.A.	1	3	1	3	4	4	1	0	0	0	0	....	1987-88	1987-88
‡ Engqvist, Andreas	Mtl.	2	15	0	0	0	4	....	....	....	....	....	....	2010-11	2011-12
Ennis, Jim	Edm.	1	5	1	0	1	10	....	....	....	....	....	....	1987-88	1987-88
● Erickson, Aut	Bos., Chi., Tor., Oak.	7	226	7	24	31	182	7	0	0	0	2	1	1959-60	1969-70
Erickson, Bryan	Wsh., L.A., Pit., Wpg.	9	351	80	125	205	141	14	3	4	7	7	....	1983-84	1993-94
Erickson, Grant	Bos., Min.	2	6	1	0	1	0	....	....	....	....	....	....	1968-69	1969-70
Eriksson, Anders	Det., Chi., Fla., Tor., CBJ, Cgy., Phx., NYR	13	572	22	154	176	242	36	0	6	6	18	1	1995-96	2009-10
Eriksson, Peter	Edm.	1	20	3	3	6	24	....	....	....	....	....	....	1989-90	1989-90
Eriksson, Roland	Min., Van.	3	193	48	95	143	26	2	1	0	1	0	....	1976-77	1978-79
Eriksson, Thomas	Phi.	5	208	22	76	98	107	19	0	3	3	12	....	1980-81	1985-86
Erixon, Jan	NYR	10	556	57	159	216	167	58	7	7	14	16	....	1983-84	1992-93
Errey, Bob	Pit., Buf., S.J., Det., Dal., NYR	15	895	170	212	382	1005	99	13	16	29	109	2	1983-84	1997-98
‡ Erskine, John	Dal., NYI, Wsh.	12	491	15	39	54	865	39	1	6	7	32	....	2001-02	2013-14
Esau, Len	Tor., Que., Cgy., Edm.	4	27	0	10	10	24	....	....	....	....	....	....	1991-92	1994-95
Esposito, Phil	Chi., Bos., NYR	18	1282	717	873	1590	910	130	61	76	137	138	2	1963-64	1980-81
‡ Evans, Brennan	Cgy.	1	....	....	....	....	....	2	0	0	0	0	....	2003-04	2003-04
● Evans, Chris	Tor., Buf., St.L., Det., K.C.	5	241	19	42	61	143	12	1	1	2	8	....	1969-70	1974-75
Evans, Daryl	L.A., Wsh., Tor.	6	113	22	30	52	25	11	5	8	13	12	....	1981-82	1986-87
Evans, Doug	St.L., Wpg., Phi.	8	355	48	87	135	502	22	3	4	7	38	....	1985-86	1992-93
● Evans, Jack	NYR, Chi.	14	752	19	80	99	989	56	2	2	4	97	1	1948-49	1962-63
Evans, Kevin	Min., S.J.	2	9	0	1	1	44	....	....	....	....	....	....	1990-91	1991-92
Evans, Paul	Tor.	2	11	1	1	2	21	2	0	0	0	0	....	1976-77	1977-78
Evans, Paul	Phi.	3	103	14	25	39	34	1	0	0	0	0	....	1978-79	1982-83
Evans, Shawn	St.L., NYI	2	9	1	0	1	2	....	....	....	....	....	....	1985-86	1989-90
● Evans, Stewart	Det., Mtl.M., Mtl.	8	367	28	49	77	425	26	0	0	0	20	1	1930-31	1938-39
Evason, Dean	Wsh., Hfd., S.J., Dal., Cgy.	13	803	139	233	372	1002	55	9	20	29	132	....	1983-84	1995-96
Ewen, Todd	St.L., Mtl., Ana., S.J.	11	518	36	40	76	1911	26	0	0	0	87	1	1986-87	1996-97
‡ Exelby, Garnet	Atl., Tor.	7	408	7	43	50	584	4	0	0	0	6	....	2002-03	2009-10
● Ezinicki, Bill	Tor., Bos., NYR	9	368	79	105	184	713	40	5	8	13	87	3	1944-45	1954-55

F

Name	NHL Teams	NHL Seasons	Regular Schedule GP	G	A	TP	PIM	Playoffs GP	G	A	TP	PIM	NHL Cup Wins	First NHL Season	Last NHL Season
Fahey, Brian	Wsh.	1	7	0	1	1	2	....	....	....	....	....	....	2010-11	2010-11
Fahey, Jim	S.J., N.J.	4	92	1	24	25	67	2	0	0	0	0	....	2002-03	2006-07
Fahey, Trevor	NYR	1	1	0	0	0	0	....	....	....	....	....	....	1964-65	1964-65
Fairbairn, Bill	NYR, Min., St.L.	11	658	162	261	423	173	54	13	22	35	42	....	1968-69	1978-79
‡ Fairchild, Cade	St.L.	1	5	0	1	1	0	....	....	....	....	....	....	2011-12	2011-12
Fairchild, Kelly	Tor., Dal., Col.	4	34	2	3	5	6	....	....	....	....	....	....	1995-96	2001-02
Falkenberg, Bob	Det.	5	54	1	5	6	26	....	....	....	....	....	....	1966-67	1971-72
Falloon, Pat	S.J., Phi., Ott., Edm., Pit.	9	575	143	179	322	141	66	11	7	18	16	....	1991-92	1999-00
Farkas, Jeff	Tor., Atl.	4	11	0	2	2	6	5	1	0	1	0	....	1999-00	2002-03
● Farrant, Walt	Chi.	1	1	0	0	0	0	....	....	....	....	....	....	1943-44	1943-44
Farrell, Mike	Wsh., Nsh.	3	13	0	0	0	2	....	....	....	....	....	....	2001-02	2003-04
Farrish, Dave	NYR, Que., Tor.	7	430	17	110	127	440	14	0	2	2	24	....	1976-77	1983-84
● Fashoway, Gordie	Chi.	1	13	3	2	5	14	....	....	....	....	....	....	1950-51	1950-51
Fast, Brad	Car.	1	1	1	0	1	0	....	....	....	....	....	....	2003-04	2003-04
Fata, Drew	NYI	2	8	1	1	2	9	1	0	0	0	0	....	2006-07	2007-08
‡ Fata, Rico	Cgy., NYR, Pit., Atl., Wsh.	8	230	27	36	63	104	....	....	....	....	....	....	1998-99	2006-07
Faubert, Mario	Pit.	7	231	21	90	111	292	10	2	2	4	6	....	1974-75	1981-82
Faulkner, Alex	Tor., Det.	3	101	15	17	32	15	12	5	0	5	2	....	1961-62	1963-64
Fauss, Ted	Tor.	2	28	0	2	2	15	....	....	....	....	....	....	1986-87	1987-88
Faust, Andre	Phi.	2	47	10	7	17	14	....	....	....	....	....	....	1992-93	1993-94
Feamster, Dave	Chi.	4	169	13	24	37	154	33	3	5	8	61	....	1981-82	1984-85
Featherstone, Glen	St.L., Bos., NYR, Hfd., Cgy.	9	384	19	61	80	939	28	0	2	2	103	....	1988-89	1996-97
Featherstone, Tony	Oak., Cal., Min.	3	130	17	21	38	65	2	0	0	0	0	....	1969-70	1973-74
Federko, Bernie	St.L., Det.	14	1000	369	761	1130	487	91	35	66	101	83	....	1976-77	1989-90
‡ Fedorov, Fedor	Van., NYR	3	18	0	2	2	14	....	....	....	....	....	....	2002-03	2005-06
Fedorov, Sergei	Det., Ana., CBJ, Wsh.	18	1248	483	696	1179	839	183	52	124	176	133	3	1990-91	2008-09
Fedoruk, Todd	Phi., Ana., Dal., Min., Phx., T.B.	9	545	32	65	97	1050	25	1	1	2	54	....	2000-01	2009-10
Fedotov, Anatoli	Wpg., Ana.	2	4	0	2	2	0	....	....	....	....	....	....	1992-93	1993-94
Fedyk, Brent	Det., Phi., Dal., NYR	10	470	97	112	209	308	16	3	2	5	12	....	1987-88	1998-99
Felix, Chris	Wsh.	4	35	1	12	13	10	2	0	1	1	0	....	1987-88	1990-91
Felsner, Brian	Chi.	1	12	1	3	4	12	....	....	....	....	....	....	1997-98	1997-98
Felsner, Denny	St.L.	4	18	1	4	5	6	10	2	3	5	2	....	1991-92	1994-95
Feltrin, Tony	Pit., NYR	4	48	3	3	6	65	....	....	....	....	....	....	1980-81	1985-86
Fenton, Paul	Hfd., NYR, L.A., Wpg., Tor., Cgy., S.J.	8	411	100	83	183	198	17	4	1	5	27	....	1984-85	1991-92
Fenyves, David	Buf., Phi.	9	206	3	32	35	119	11	0	0	0	9	....	1982-83	1990-91
Ference, Brad	Fla., Phx., Cgy.	6	250	4	30	34	565	....	....	....	....	....	....	1999-00	2006-07
Fergus, Tom	Bos., Tor., Van.	12	726	235	346	581	499	65	21	17	38	48	....	1981-82	1992-93
Ferguson, Craig	Mtl., Cgy., Fla.	5	27	1	1	2	6	....	....	....	....	....	....	1993-94	1999-00
Ferguson, George	Tor., Pit., Min.	12	797	160	238	398	431	86	14	23	37	44	....	1972-73	1983-84
● Ferguson, John	Mtl.	8	500	145	158	303	1214	85	20	18	38	260	5	1963-64	1970-71
● Ferguson, Lorne	Bos., Det., Chi.	8	422	82	80	162	193	31	6	3	9	24	....	1949-50	1958-59
Ferguson, Norm	Oak., Cal.	4	279	73	66	139	72	10	1	4	5	7	....	1968-69	1971-72
Ferguson, Scott	Edm., Ana., Min.	7	218	7	14	21	310	11	0	0	0	8	....	1997-98	2005-06
Ferland, Jonathan	Mtl.	1	7	1	0	1	2	....	....	....	....	....	....	2005-06	2005-06
Ferner, Mark	Buf., Wsh., Ana., Det.	6	91	3	10	13	51	....	....	....	....	....	....	1986-87	1994-95
Ferraro, Chris	NYR, Pit., Edm., NYI, Wsh.	6	74	7	9	16	57	....	....	....	....	....	....	1995-96	2001-02
Ferraro, Peter	NYR, Pit., Bos., Wsh.	6	92	9	15	24	58	2	0	0	0	0	....	1995-96	2001-02
Ferraro, Ray	Hfd., NYI, NYR, L.A., Atl., St.L.	18	1258	408	490	898	1288	68	21	22	43	54	....	1984-85	2001-02
‡ Festerling, Brett	Ana., Wpg.	4	88	0	8	8	35	1	0	0	0	0	....	2008-09	2011-12
Fetisov, Viacheslav	N.J., Det.	9	546	36	192	228	656	116	2	26	28	147	2	1989-90	1997-98
Fibiger, Jesse	S.J.	1	16	0	0	0	2	....	....	....	....	....	....	2002-03	2002-03
Fidler, Mike	Cle., Min., Hfd., Chi.	7	271	84	97	181	124	....	....	....	....	....	....	1976-77	1982-83
● Field, Wilf	NYA, Bro., Mtl., Chi.	6	219	17	25	42	151	2	0	0	0	2	....	1936-37	1944-45
Fielder, Guyle	Chi., Det., Bos.	4	9	0	0	0	2	6	0	0	0	2	....	1950-51	1957-58
Filewich, Jonathan	Pit.	1	5	0	0	0	0	....	....	....	....	....	....	2007-08	2007-08
Filimonov, Dmitri	Ott.	1	30	1	4	5	18	....	....	....	....	....	....	1993-94	1993-94
● Fillion, Bob	Mtl.	7	327	42	61	103	84	33	7	4	11	10	2	1943-44	1949-50
● Fillion, Marcel	Bos.	1	1	0	0	0	0	....	....	....	....	....	....	1944-45	1944-45
● Filmore, Tommy	Det., NYA, Bos.	4	117	15	12	27	33	....	....	....	....	....	....	1930-31	1933-34
Finger, Jeff	Col., Tor.	4	199	17	40	57	114	5	0	2	2	4	....	2006-07	2009-10
● Finkbeiner, Lloyd	NYA	1	2	0	0	0	0	....	....	....	....	....	....	1940-41	1940-41
Finley, Jeff	NYI, Phi., Wpg., Phx., NYR, St.L.	15	708	13	70	83	457	52	1	6	7	38	....	1987-88	2003-04
Finn, Steven	Que., T.B., L.A.	12	725	34	78	112	1724	23	0	4	4	39	....	1985-86	1996-97
● Finney, Sid	Chi.	3	59	10	7	17	4	7	0	2	2	0	....	1951-52	1953-54
● Finnigan, Ed	St.L., Bos.	2	15	1	1	2	2	....	....	....	....	....	....	1934-35	1935-36
● Finnigan, Frank	Ott., Tor., St.L.	14	553	115	88	203	407	38	6	9	15	22	2	1923-24	1936-37
Fiorentino, Peter	NYR	1	1	0	0	0	0	....	....	....	....	....	....	1991-92	1991-92
Fischer, Jiri	Det.	6	305	11	49	60	295	38	4	3	7	55	1	1999-00	2005-06
Fischer, Patrick	Phx.	1	27	4	6	10	24	....	....	....	....	....	....	2006-07	2006-07
Fischer, Ron	Buf.	2	18	0	7	7	6	....	....	....	....	....	....	1981-82	1982-83
● Fisher, Alvin	Tor.	1	9	1	0	1	4	....	....	....	....	....	....	1924-25	1924-25
Fisher, Craig	Phi., Wpg., Fla.	4	12	0	0	0	2	....	....	....	....	....	....	1989-90	1996-97
Fisher, Dunc	NYR, Bos., Det.	7	275	45	70	115	104	21	4	4	8	14	....	1947-48	1958-59
● Fisher, Joe	Det.	4	65	8	12	20	13	12	2	1	3	6	1	1939-40	1942-43
Fitchner, Bob	Que.	2	78	12	20	32	59	3	0	0	0	10	....	1979-80	1980-81
Fitzgerald, Rusty	Pit.	2	25	2	2	4	12	5	0	0	0	4	....	1994-95	1995-96
Fitzgerald, Tom	NYI, Fla., Col., Nsh., Chi., Tor., Bos.	17	1097	139	190	329	776	78	7	12	19	90	....	1988-89	2005-06
‡ Fitzgerald, Zack	Van.	1	1	0	0	0	0	....	....	....	....	....	....	2007-08	2007-08
Fitzpatrick, Rory	Mtl., St.L., Nsh., Buf., Van., Phi.	10	287	10	25	35	201	20	1	5	6	22	....	1995-96	2007-08
Fitzpatrick, Ross	Phi.	4	20	5	2	7	0	....	....	....	....	....	....	1982-83	1985-86
Fitzpatrick, Sandy	NYR, Min.	2	22	3	6	9	8	12	0	0	0	0	....	1964-65	1967-68
● Flaman, Fern	Bos., Tor.	17	910	34	174	208	1370	63	4	8	12	93	1	1944-45	1960-61
Flatley, Pat	NYI, NYR	14	780	170	340	510	686	70	18	15	33	75	....	1983-84	1996-97
Fleming, Gerry	Mtl.	2	11	0	0	0	42	....	....	....	....	....	....	1993-94	1994-95
● Fleming, Reggie	Mtl., Chi., Bos., NYR, Phi., Buf.	12	749	108	132	240	1468	50	3	6	9	106	1	1959-60	1970-71
Flesch, John	Min., Pit., Col.	4	124	18	23	41	117	....	....	....	....	....	....	1974-75	1979-80

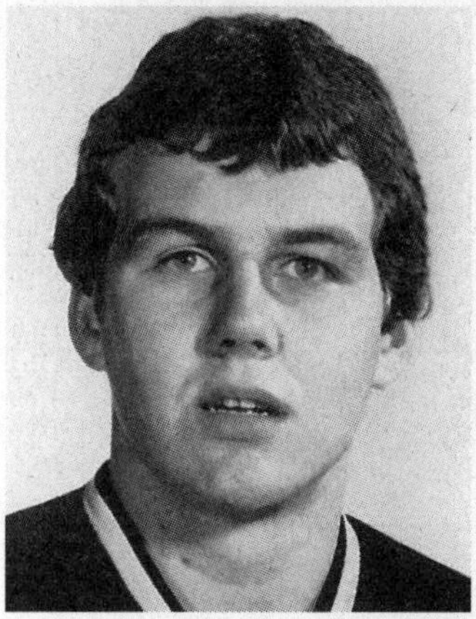

Tony Feltrin

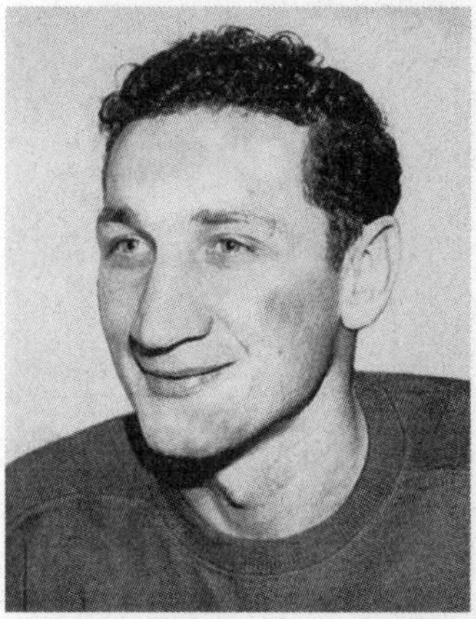

Bill Folk

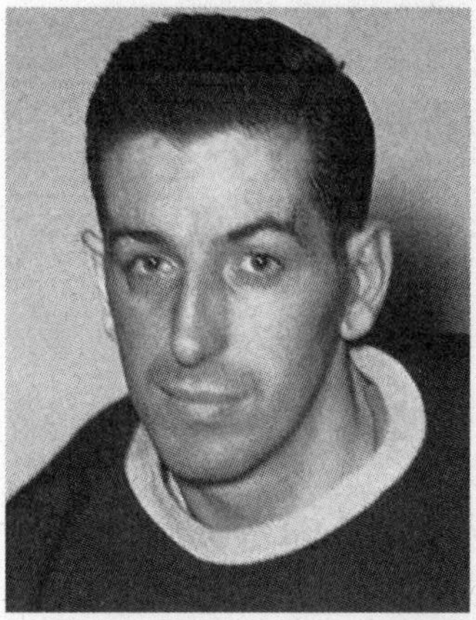

Jack Forsey

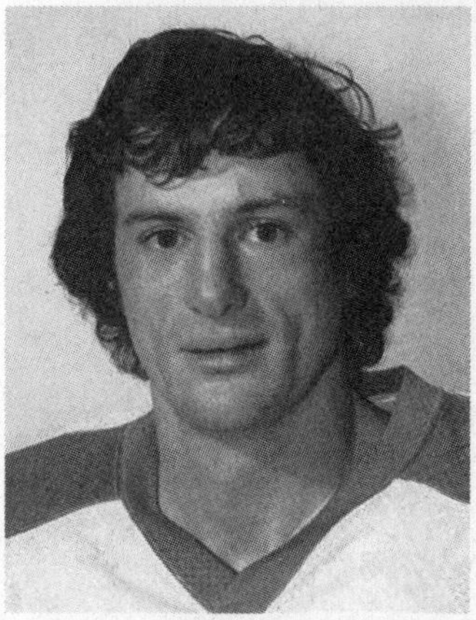

Alex Forsyth

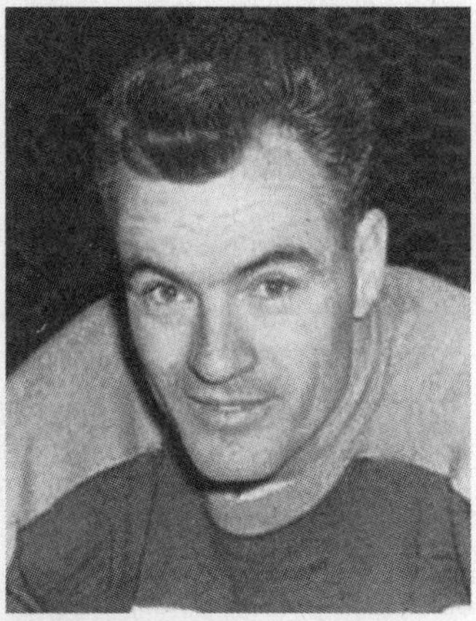
Herb Foster

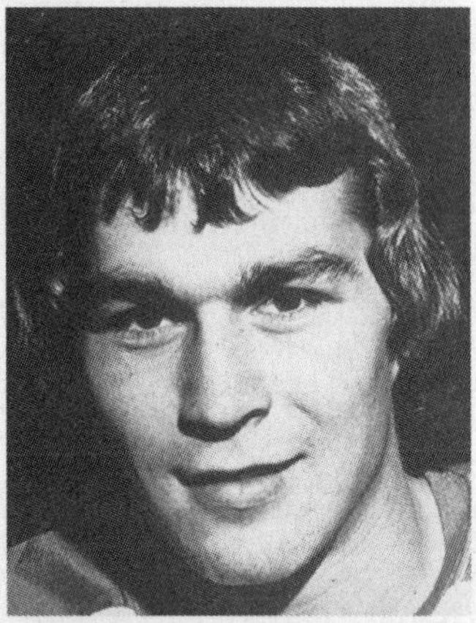
Greg Fox

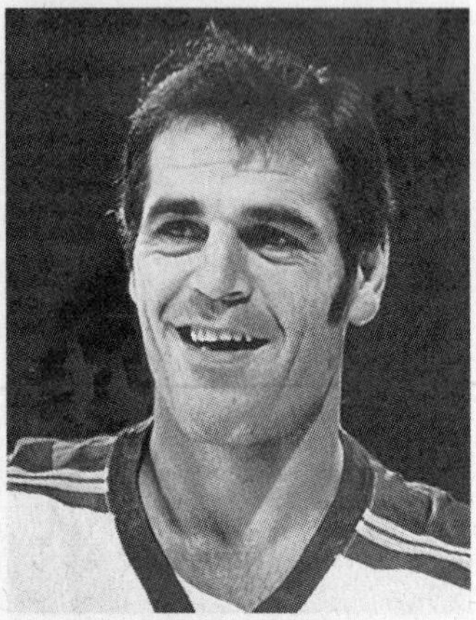
Germain Gagnon

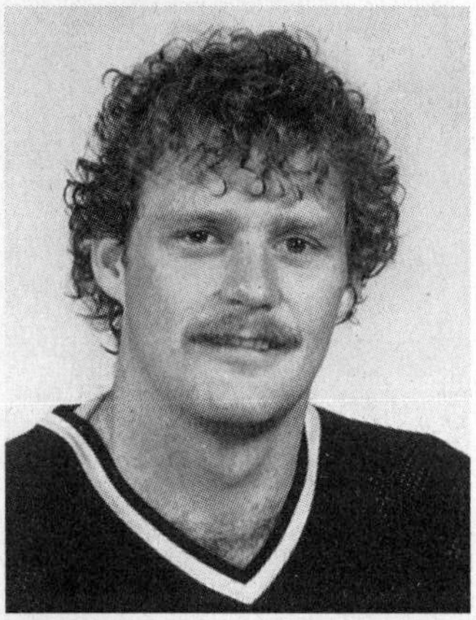
Rob Garner

			Regular Schedule					Playoffs							
Name	NHL Teams	NHL Seasons	GP	G	A	TP	PIM	GP	G	A	TP	PIM	NHL Cup Wins	First NHL Season	Last NHL Season
Fletcher, Steven	Mtl., Wpg.	2	3	0	0	0	5	1	0	0	0	5	....	1987-88	1988-89
• Flett, Bill	L.A., Phi., Tor., Atl., Edm.	11	689	202	215	417	501	52	7	16	23	42	1	1967-68	1979-80
Fleury, Theoren	Cgy., Col., NYR, Chi.	15	1084	455	633	1088	1840	77	34	45	79	116	1	1988-89	2002-03
Flichel, Todd	Wpg.	3	6	0	1	1	4	....	....	....	....	....	....	1987-88	1989-90
Flinn, Ryan	L.A.	3	31	1	0	1	84	....	....	....	....	....	....	2001-02	2005-06
Flockhart, Rob	Van., Min.	5	55	2	5	7	14	1	1	0	1	2	....	1976-77	1980-81
Flockhart, Ron	Phi., Pit., Mtl., St.L., Bos.	9	453	145	183	328	208	19	4	6	10	14	....	1980-81	1988-89
‡ Flood, Mark	NYI, Wpg.	2	39	3	5	8	10	....	....	....	....	....	....	2009-10	2011-12
Floyd, Larry	N.J.	2	12	2	3	5	9	....	....	....	....	....	....	1982-83	1983-84
Focht, Dan	Phx., Pit.	3	82	2	6	8	145	1	0	1	1	0	....	2001-02	2003-04
• Fogarty, Bryan	Que., Pit., Mtl.	6	156	22	52	74	119	....	....	....	....	....	....	1989-90	1994-95
• Fogolin, Lee	Det., Chi.	9	427	10	48	58	575	28	0	2	2	30	1	1947-48	1955-56
Fogolin, Lee	Buf., Edm.	13	924	44	195	239	1318	108	5	19	24	173	2	1974-75	1986-87
Folco, Peter	Van.	1	2	0	0	0	0	....	....	....	....	....	....	1973-74	1973-74
Foley, Gerry	Tor., NYR, L.A.	4	142	9	14	23	99	9	0	1	1	2	....	1954-55	1968-69
Foley, Rick	Chi., Phi., Det.	3	67	11	26	37	180	4	0	1	1	4	....	1970-71	1973-74
Foligno, Mike	Det., Buf., Tor., Fla.	15	1018	355	372	727	2049	57	15	17	32	185	....	1979-80	1993-94
• Folk, Bill	Det.	2	12	0	0	0	4	....	....	....	....	....	....	1951-52	1952-53
Fontaine, Len	Det.	2	46	8	11	19	10	....	....	....	....	....	....	1972-73	1973-74
Fontas, Jon	Min.	2	2	0	0	0	0	....	....	....	....	....	....	1979-80	1980-81
Fonteyne, Val	Det., NYR, Pit.	13	820	75	154	229	26	59	3	10	13	8	....	1959-60	1971-72
Fontinato, Lou	NYR, Mtl.	9	535	26	78	104	1247	21	0	2	2	42	....	1954-55	1962-63
Foote, Adam	Que., Col., CBJ	19	1154	66	242	308	1534	170	7	35	42	298	2	1991-92	2010-11
Forbes, Colin	Phi., T.B., Ott., NYR, Wsh.	9	311	33	28	61	213	13	1	0	1	16	....	1996-97	2005-06
Forbes, Dave	Bos., Wsh.	6	363	64	64	128	341	45	1	4	5	13	....	1973-74	1978-79
Forbes, Mike	Bos., Edm.	3	50	1	11	12	41	....	....	....	....	....	....	1977-78	1981-82
Forey, Connie	St.L.	1	4	0	0	0	2	....	....	....	....	....	....	1973-74	1973-74
Forsberg, Peter	Que., Col., Phi., Nsh.	14	708	249	636	885	690	151	64	107	171	163	2	1994-95	2010-11
• Forsey, Jack	Tor.	1	19	7	9	16	10	3	0	1	1	0	....	1942-43	1942-43
• Forslund, Gus	Ott.	1	48	4	9	13	2	....	....	....	....	....	....	1932-33	1932-33
Forslund, Tomas	Cgy.	2	44	5	11	16	12	....	....	....	....	....	....	1991-92	1992-93
Forsyth, Alex	Wsh.	1	1	0	0	0	0	....	....	....	....	....	....	1976-77	1976-77
Fortier, Dave	Tor., NYI, Van.	4	205	8	21	29	335	20	0	2	2	33	....	1972-73	1976-77
Fortier, Marc	Que., Ott., L.A.	6	212	42	60	102	135	....	....	....	....	....	....	1987-88	1992-93
Fortin, Jean-Francois	Wsh.	3	71	1	4	5	42	....	....	....	....	....	....	2001-02	2003-04
Fortin, Ray	St.L.	3	92	2	6	8	33	6	0	0	0	8	....	1967-68	1969-70
Foster, Alex	Tor.	1	3	0	0	0	0	....	....	....	....	....	....	2007-08	2007-08
Foster, Corey	N.J., Phi., Pit., NYI	4	45	5	6	11	24	3	0	0	0	4	....	1988-89	1996-97
Foster, Dwight	Bos., Col., N.J., Det.	10	541	111	163	274	420	35	5	12	17	4	....	1977-78	1986-87
• Foster, Herb	NYR	2	6	1	0	1	5	....	....	....	....	....	....	1940-41	1947-48
‡ Foster, Kurtis	Atl., Min., T.B., Edm., Ana., N.J., Phi.	10	405	42	118	160	308	3	0	2	2	0	....	2002-03	2012-13
• Foster, Yip	NYR, Bos., Det.	4	83	3	2	5	32	....	....	....	....	....	....	1929-30	1934-35
Fotiu, Nick	NYR, Hfd., Cgy., Phi., Edm.	13	646	60	77	137	1362	38	0	4	4	67	....	1976-77	1988-89
‡ Foucault, Kris	Min.	1	1	0	0	0	0	....	....	....	....	....	....	2011-12	2011-12
• Fowler, Jimmy	Tor.	3	135	18	29	47	39	18	0	3	3	2	....	1936-37	1938-39
Fowler, Tom	Chi.	1	24	0	1	1	18	....	....	....	....	....	....	1946-47	1946-47
Fox, Greg	Atl., Chi., Pit.	8	494	14	92	106	637	44	1	9	10	67	....	1977-78	1984-85
Fox, Jim	L.A.	9	578	186	293	479	143	22	4	8	12	0	....	1980-81	1989-90
Foy, Matt	Min.	3	56	6	7	13	48	1	0	0	0	0	....	2005-06	2007-08
• Foyston, Frank	Det.	2	64	17	7	24	32	....	....	....	....	....	....	1926-27	1927-28
Frampton, Bob	Mtl.	1	2	0	0	0	0	3	0	0	0	0	....	1949-50	1949-50
Franceschetti, Lou	Wsh., Tor., Buf.	10	459	59	81	140	747	44	3	2	5	111	....	1981-82	1991-92
Francis, Bobby	Det.	1	14	2	0	2	0	....	....	....	....	....	....	1982-83	1982-83
Francis, Ron	Hfd., Pit., Car., Tor.	23	1731	549	1249	1798	979	171	46	97	143	95	2	1981-82	2003-04
• Fraser, Archie	NYR	1	3	0	1	1	0	....	....	....	....	....	....	1943-44	1943-44
• Fraser, Charles	Ham.	1	1	0	0	0	0	....	....	....	....	....	....	1923-24	1923-24
Fraser, Curt	Van., Chi., Min.	12	704	193	240	433	1306	65	15	18	33	198	....	1978-79	1989-90
• Fraser, Gord	Chi., Det., Mtl., Pit., Phi.	5	144	24	12	36	224	2	1	0	1	6	....	1926-27	1930-31
• Fraser, Harvey	Chi.	1	21	5	4	9	0	....	....	....	....	....	....	1944-45	1944-45
Fraser, Iain	NYI, Que., Dal., Edm., Wpg., S.J.	5	94	23	23	46	31	4	0	0	0	0	....	1992-93	1996-97
Fraser, Jamie	NYI	1	1	0	0	0	0	....	....	....	....	....	....	2008-09	2008-09
Fraser, Scott	Mtl., Edm., NYR	3	72	16	15	31	24	11	1	1	2	0	....	1995-96	1998-99
Frawley, Dan	Chi., Pit.	6	273	37	40	77	674	1	0	0	0	0	....	1983-84	1988-89
Freadrich, Kyle	T.B.	2	23	0	1	1	75	....	....	....	....	....	....	1999-00	2000-01
‡ Fredheim, Kris	Min.	1	3	0	0	0	2	....	....	....	....	....	....	2011-12	2011-12
• Fredrickson, Frank	Det., Bos., Pit.	5	161	39	34	73	206	10	2	3	5	24	....	1926-27	1930-31
Freer, Mark	Phi., Ott., Cgy.	7	124	16	23	39	61	....	....	....	....	....	....	1986-87	1993-94
• Frew, Irv	Mtl.M., St.L., Mtl.	3	96	2	5	7	146	4	0	0	0	6	....	1933-34	1935-36
Friday, Tim	Det.	1	23	0	3	3	6	....	....	....	....	....	....	1985-86	1985-86
Fridgen, Dan	Hfd.	2	13	2	3	5	2	....	....	....	....	....	....	1981-82	1982-83
Friedman, Doug	Edm., Nsh.	2	18	0	1	1	34	....	....	....	....	....	....	1997-98	1998-99
Friesen, Jeff	S.J., Ana., N.J., Wsh., Cgy.	12	893	218	298	516	488	84	18	15	33	48	1	1994-95	2006-07
Friest, Ron	Min.	3	64	7	7	14	191	6	1	0	1	7	....	1980-81	1982-83
Frig, Len	Chi., Cal., Cle., St.L.	7	311	13	51	64	479	14	2	1	3	0	....	1972-73	1979-80
Frischmon, Trevor	CBJ	1	3	0	0	0	4	....	....	....	....	....	....	2009-10	2009-10
Fritsch, Jamie	Phi.	1	1	0	0	0	0	....	....	....	....	....	....	2008-09	2008-09
‡ Fritsche, Dan	CBJ, NYR, Min.	5	256	34	42	76	103	....	....	....	....	....	....	2003-04	2008-09
Fritz, Mitch	NYI	1	20	0	0	0	42	....	....	....	....	....	....	2008-09	2008-09
‡ Frogren, Jonas	Tor.	1	41	1	6	7	28	....	....	....	....	....	....	2008-09	2008-09
Frolov, Alex	L.A., NYR	8	579	175	222	397	218	6	1	3	4	0	....	2002-03	2010-11
• Frost, Harry	Bos.	1	4	0	0	0	0	1	0	0	0	0	1	1938-39	1938-39
Frycer, Miroslav	Que., Tor., Det., Edm.	8	415	147	183	330	486	17	3	8	11	16	....	1981-82	1988-89
• Fryday, Bob	Mtl.	2	5	1	0	1	0	....	....	....	....	....	....	1949-50	1951-52
Ftorek, Robbie	Det., Que., NYR	8	334	77	150	227	262	19	9	6	15	28	....	1972-73	1984-85
Fullan, Larry	Wsh.	1	4	1	0	1	0	....	....	....	....	....	....	1974-75	1974-75
Funk, Michael	Buf.	2	9	0	2	2	0	....	....	....	....	....	....	2006-07	2007-08
Fusco, Mark	Hfd.	2	80	3	12	15	42	....	....	....	....	....	....	1983-84	1984-85
Fussey, Owen	Wsh.	1	4	0	1	1	0	....	....	....	....	....	....	2003-04	2003-04

G

Gadsby, Bill	Chi., NYR, Det.	20	1248	130	438	568	1539	67	4	23	27	92	....	1946-47	1965-66
Gaetz, Link	Min., S.J.	3	65	6	8	14	412	....	....	....	....	....	....	1988-89	1991-92
Gage, Jody	Det., Buf.	6	68	14	15	29	26	....	....	....	....	....	....	1980-81	1991-92
• Gagne, Art	Mtl., Bos., Ott., Det.	6	228	67	33	100	257	11	2	1	3	20	....	1926-27	1931-32
Gagne, Paul	Col., N.J., Tor., NYI	8	390	110	101	211	127	....	....	....	....	....	....	1980-81	1989-90
Gagne, Pierre	Bos.	1	2	0	0	0	0	....	....	....	....	....	....	1959-60	1959-60
Gagne, Simon	Phi., T.B., L.A., Bos.	14	822	291	310	601	328	109	37	22	59	32	1	1999-00	2014-15
Gagner, Dave	NYR, Min., Dal., Tor., Cgy., Fla., Van.	15	946	318	401	719	1018	57	22	26	48	64	....	1984-85	1998-99
‡ Gagnon, Aaron	Dal., Wpg.	4	38	3	2	5	2	....	....	....	....	....	....	2009-10	2012-13
• Gagnon, Germain	Mtl., NYI, Chi., K.C.	5	259	40	101	141	72	19	2	3	5	2	....	1971-72	1975-76
• Gagnon, Johnny	Mtl., Bos., NYA	10	454	120	141	261	295	32	12	12	24	37	1	1930-31	1939-40
Gagnon, Sean	Phx., Ott.	3	12	0	1	1	34	....	....	....	....	....	....	1997-98	2000-01
Gainey, Bob	Mtl.	16	1160	239	262	501	585	182	25	48	73	151	5	1973-74	1988-89
Gainey, Steve	Dal., Phx.	4	33	0	2	2	34	....	....	....	....	....	....	2000-01	2005-06
• Gainor, Dutch	Bos., NYR, Ott., Mtl.M.	7	246	51	56	107	129	22	2	1	3	14	2	1927-28	1934-35
Galanov, Maxim	NYR, Pit., Atl., T.B.	4	122	8	12	20	44	1	0	0	0	0	....	1997-98	2000-01
Galarneau, Michel	Hfd.	3	78	7	10	17	34	....	....	....	....	....	....	1980-81	1982-83
• Galbraith, Percy	Bos., Ott.	8	347	29	31	60	224	31	4	7	11	24	1	1926-27	1933-34
• Gallagher, John	Mtl.M., Det., NYA	7	205	14	19	33	153	24	2	3	5	27	1	1930-31	1938-39
Gallant, Gerard	Det., T.B.	11	615	211	269	480	1674	58	18	21	39	178	....	1984-85	1994-95
Galley, Garry	L.A., Wsh., Bos., Phi., Buf., NYI	17	1149	125	475	600	1218	89	7	23	30	119	....	1984-85	2000-01
Gallimore, Jamie	Min.	1	2	0	0	0	0	....	....	....	....	....	....	1977-78	1977-78
• Gallinger, Don	Bos.	5	222	65	88	153	89	23	5	5	10	19	....	1942-43	1947-48
‡ Gamache, Simon	Atl., Nsh., St.L., Tor.	4	48	6	7	13	18	....	....	....	....	....	....	2002-03	2007-08
Gamble, Dick	Mtl., Chi., Tor.	8	195	41	41	82	66	14	1	2	3	4	1	1950-51	1966-67
Gambucci, Gary	Min.	2	51	2	7	9	9	....	....	....	....	....	....	1971-72	1973-74
Ganchar, Perry	St.L., Mtl., Pit.	4	42	3	7	10	36	7	3	1	4	0	....	1983-84	1988-89
Gans, Dave	L.A.	2	6	0	0	0	2	....	....	....	....	....	....	1982-83	1985-86
Gardiner, Bruce	Ott., T.B., CBJ, N.J.	6	312	34	54	88	263	21	1	4	5	8	....	1996-97	2001-02
• Gardiner, Herb	Mtl., Chi.	3	108	10	9	19	52	9	0	1	1	16	....	1926-27	1928-29
Gardner, Bill	Chi., Hfd.	9	380	73	115	188	68	45	3	8	11	17	....	1980-81	1988-89
• Gardner, Cal	NYR, Tor., Chi., Bos.	12	696	154	238	392	517	61	7	10	17	20	2	1945-46	1956-57
Gardner, Dave	Mtl., St.L., Cal., Cle., Phi.	7	350	75	115	190	41	....	....	....	....	....	....	1972-73	1979-80
Gardner, Paul	Col., Tor., Pit., Wsh., Buf.	10	447	201	201	402	207	16	2	6	8	14	....	1976-77	1985-86
Gare, Danny	Buf., Det., Edm.	13	827	354	331	685	1285	64	25	21	46	195	....	1974-75	1986-87

			Regular Schedule					Playoffs					NHL	First	Last
Name	NHL Teams	NHL Seasons	GP	G	A	TP	PIM	GP	G	A	TP	PIM	Cup Wins	NHL Season	NHL Season
• Gariepy, Ray	Bos., Tor.	2	36	1	6	7	43	....	....	....	....	....	....	1953-54	1955-56
• Garland, Scott	Tor., L.A.	3	91	13	24	37	115	7	1	2	3	35	....	1975-76	1978-79
Garner, Rob	Pit.	1	1	0	0	0	0	....	....	....	....	....	....	1982-83	1982-83
Garpenlov, Johan	Det., S.J., Fla., Atl.	10	609	114	197	311	276	44	10	9	19	22	....	1990-91	1999-00
• Garrett, Red	NYR	1	23	1	1	2	18	....	....	....	....	....	....	1942-43	1942-43
Gartner, Mike	Wsh., Min., NYR, Tor., Phx.	19	1432	708	627	1335	1159	122	43	50	93	125	....	1979-80	1997-98
• Gassoff, Bob	St.L.	4	245	11	47	58	866	9	0	1	1	16	....	1973-74	1976-77
Gassoff, Brad	Van.	4	122	19	17	36	163	3	0	0	0	0	....	1975-76	1978-79
Gatzos, Steve	Pit.	4	89	15	20	35	83	1	0	0	0	0	....	1981-82	1984-85
Gaudreau, Rob	S.J., Ott.	4	231	51	54	105	69	14	2	0	2	0	....	1992-93	1995-96
• Gaudreault, Armand	Bos.	1	44	15	9	24	27	7	0	2	2	8	....	1944-45	1944-45
• Gaudreault, Leo	Mtl.	3	67	8	4	12	30	....	....	....	....	....	....	1927-28	1932-33
Gaul, Mike	Col., CBJ	2	3	0	0	0	4	....	....	....	....	....	....	1998-99	2000-01
Gaulin, Jean-Marc	Que.	4	26	4	3	7	8	1	0	0	0	0	....	1982-83	1985-86
Gaume, Dallas	Hfd.	1	4	1	1	2	0	....	....	....	....	....	....	1988-89	1988-89
• Gauthier, Art	Mtl.	1	13	0	0	0	0	1	0	0	0	0	....	1926-27	1926-27
Gauthier, Daniel	Chi.	1	5	0	0	0	0	....	....	....	....	....	....	1994-95	1994-95
Gauthier, Denis	Cgy., Phx., Phi., L.A.	10	554	17	60	77	748	12	0	2	2	23	....	1997-98	2008-09
• Gauthier, Fern	NYR, Mtl., Det.	6	229	46	50	96	35	22	5	1	6	7	....	1943-44	1948-49
Gauthier, Gabe	L.A.	2	8	0	0	0	2	....	....	....	....	....	....	2006-07	2007-08
Gauthier, Jean	Mtl., Phi., Bos.	10	166	6	29	35	150	14	1	3	4	22	1	1960-61	1969-70
Gauthier, Luc	Mtl.	1	3	0	0	0	2	....	....	....	....	....	....	1990-91	1990-91
Gauvreau, Jocelyn	Mtl.	1	2	0	0	0	0	....	....	....	....	....	....	1983-84	1983-84
Gavey, Aaron	T.B., Cgy., Dal., Min., Tor., Ana.	9	360	41	50	91	272	19	1	2	3	14	....	1995-96	2005-06
Gavin, Stew	Tor., Hfd., Min.	13	768	130	155	285	584	66	14	20	34	75	....	1980-81	1992-93
Geale, Bob	Pit.	1	1	0	0	0	2	....	....	....	....	....	....	1984-85	1984-85
• Gee, George	Chi., Det.	9	551	135	183	318	345	41	6	13	19	32	1	1945-46	1953-54
Geldart, Gary	Min.	1	4	0	0	0	5	....	....	....	....	....	....	1970-71	1970-71
Gelinas, Martin	Edm., Que., Van., Car., Cgy., Fla., Nsh.	19	1273	309	351	660	820	147	23	33	56	120	1	1988-89	2007-08
Gendron, Jean-Guy	NYR, Bos., Mtl., Phi.	14	863	182	201	383	701	42	7	4	11	47	....	1955-56	1971-72
Gendron, Martin	Wsh., Chi.	3	30	4	2	6	10	....	....	....	....	....	....	1994-95	1997-98
‡ Genoway, Chay	Min.	1	1	0	1	1	0	....	....	....	....	....	....	2011-12	2011-12
• Geoffrion, Bernie	Mtl., NYR	16	883	393	429	822	689	132	58	60	118	88	6	1950-51	1967-68
Geoffrion, Blake	Nsh., Mtl.	2	55	8	5	13	34	12	0	2	2	4	....	2010-11	2011-12
Geoffrion, Danny	Mtl., Wpg.	3	111	20	32	52	99	2	0	0	0	7	....	1979-80	1981-82
• Geran, Gerry	Mtl.W., Bos.	2	37	5	1	6	6	....	....	....	....	....	....	1917-18	1925-26
• Gerard, Eddie	Ott.	6	128	50	48	98	108	11	4	0	4	17	3	1917-18	1922-23
Germain, Eric	L.A.	1	4	0	1	1	13	1	0	0	0	4	....	1987-88	1987-88
Germyn, Carsen	Cgy.	2	4	0	0	0	0	....	....	....	....	....	....	2005-06	2006-07
Gernander, Ken	NYR	3	12	2	3	5	6	15	0	0	0	0	....	1995-96	2003-04
• Getliffe, Ray	Bos., Mtl.	10	393	136	137	273	250	45	9	10	19	30	2	1935-36	1944-45
Giallonardo, Mario	Col.	2	23	0	3	3	6	....	....	....	....	....	....	1979-80	1980-81
Gibbs, Barry	Bos., Min., Atl., St.L., L.A.	13	797	58	224	282	945	36	4	2	6	67	....	1967-68	1979-80
Gibson, Don	Van.	1	14	0	3	3	20	....	....	....	....	....	....	1990-91	1990-91
Gibson, Doug	Bos., Wsh.	3	63	9	19	28	0	1	0	0	0	0	....	1973-74	1977-78
Gibson, John	L.A., Tor., Wpg.	3	48	0	2	2	120	....	....	....	....	....	....	1980-81	1983-84
• Giesebrecht, Gus	Det.	4	135	27	51	78	13	17	2	3	5	0	....	1938-39	1941-42
Giffin, Lee	Pit.	2	27	1	3	4	9	....	....	....	....	....	....	1986-87	1987-88
Gilbert, Ed	K.C., Pit.	3	166	21	31	52	22	....	....	....	....	....	....	1974-75	1976-77
Gilbert, Greg	NYI, Chi., NYR, St.L.	15	837	150	228	378	576	133	17	33	50	162	3	1981-82	1995-96
Gilbert, Jeannot	Bos.	2	9	0	1	1	4	....	....	....	....	....	....	1962-63	1964-65
Gilbert, Rod	NYR	18	1065	406	615	1021	508	79	34	33	67	43	....	1960-61	1977-78
Gilbertson, Stan	Cal., St.L., Wsh., Pit.	6	428	85	89	174	148	3	1	1	2	2	....	1971-72	1976-77
Gilchrist, Brent	Mtl., Edm., Min., Dal., Det., Nsh.	15	792	135	170	305	400	90	17	14	31	48	1	1988-89	2002-03
Giles, Curt	Min., NYR, St.L.	14	895	43	199	242	733	103	6	16	22	118	....	1979-80	1992-93
Gilhen, Randy	Hfd., Wpg., Pit., L.A., NYR, T.B., Fla.	11	457	55	60	115	314	33	3	2	5	26	1	1982-83	1995-96
‡ Gill, Hal	Bos., Tor., Pit., Mtl., Nsh., Phi.	16	1108	36	148	184	962	111	0	6	6	68	1	1997-98	2013-14
Gill, Todd	Tor., S.J., St.L., Det., Phx., Col., Chi.	19	1007	82	272	354	1214	103	7	30	37	193	....	1984-85	2002-03
Gillen, Don	Phi., Hfd.	2	35	2	4	6	22	....	....	....	....	....	....	1979-80	1981-82
• Gillie, Farrand	Det.	1	1	0	0	0	0	....	....	....	....	....	....	1928-29	1928-29
Gillies, Clark	NYI, Buf.	14	958	319	378	697	1023	164	47	47	94	287	4	1974-75	1987-88
‡ Gillies, Trevor	Ana., NYI	4	57	2	1	3	261	....	....	....	....	....	....	2005-06	2011-12
Gillis, Jere	Van., NYR, Que., Buf., Phi.	9	386	78	95	173	230	19	4	7	11	9	....	1977-78	1986-87
Gillis, Mike	Col., Bos.	6	246	33	43	76	186	27	2	5	7	10	....	1978-79	1983-84
Gillis, Paul	Que., Chi., Hfd.	11	624	88	154	242	1498	42	3	14	17	156	....	1982-83	1992-93
Gilmour, Doug	St.L., Cgy., Tor., N.J., Chi., Buf., Mtl.	20	1474	450	964	1414	1301	182	60	128	188	235	1	1983-84	2002-03
Gingras, Gaston	Mtl., Tor., St.L.	10	476	61	174	235	161	52	6	18	24	20	1	1979-80	1988-89
Girard, Bob	Cal., Cle., Wsh.	5	305	45	69	114	140	....	....	....	....	....	....	1975-76	1979-80
Girard, Jonathan	Bos.	5	150	10	34	44	46	3	0	1	1	2	....	1998-99	2002-03
Girard, Kenny	Tor.	3	7	0	1	1	2	....	....	....	....	....	....	1956-57	1959-60
‡ Giroux, Alexandre	NYR, Wsh., Edm., CBJ	6	48	6	6	12	26	....	....	....	....	....	....	2005-06	2011-12
• Giroux, Art	Mtl., Bos., Det.	3	54	6	4	10	14	2	0	0	0	0	....	1932-33	1935-36
Giroux, Larry	St.L., K.C., Det., Hfd.	7	274	15	74	89	333	5	0	0	0	4	....	1973-74	1979-80
Giroux, Pierre	L.A.	1	6	1	0	1	17	....	....	....	....	....	....	1982-83	1982-83
Giroux, Raymond	NYI, N.J.	4	38	0	13	13	22	4	0	0	0	0	....	1999-00	2003-04
Giuliano, Jeff	L.A.	2	101	3	10	13	40	....	....	....	....	....	....	2005-06	2007-08
Gladney, Bob	L.A., Pit.	2	14	1	5	6	4	....	....	....	....	....	....	1982-83	1983-84
• Gladu, Jean-Paul	Bos.	1	40	6	14	20	2	7	2	2	4	0	....	1944-45	1944-45
Glennie, Brian	Tor., L.A.	10	572	14	100	114	621	32	0	1	1	66	....	1969-70	1978-79
Glennon, Matt	Bos.	1	3	0	0	0	2	....	....	....	....	....	....	1991-92	1991-92
Globke, Rob	Fla.	3	46	1	1	2	8	....	....	....	....	....	....	2005-06	2007-08
Gloeckner, Lorry	Det.	1	13	0	2	2	6	....	....	....	....	....	....	1978-79	1978-79
Gloor, Dan	Van.	1	2	0	0	0	0	....	....	....	....	....	....	1973-74	1973-74
• Glover, Fred	Det., Chi.	5	92	13	11	24	62	8	0	0	0	0	1	1948-49	1952-53
Glover, Howie	Chi., Det., NYR, Mtl.	5	144	29	17	46	101	11	1	2	3	2	....	1958-59	1968-69
Glumac, Mike	St.L.	3	40	7	6	13	38	....	....	....	....	....	....	2005-06	2007-08
Glynn, Brian	Cgy., Min., Edm., Ott., Van., Hfd.	10	431	25	79	104	410	57	6	10	16	40	....	1987-88	1996-97
‡ Goc, Sascha	N.J., T.B.	2	22	0	0	0	4	....	....	....	....	....	....	2000-01	2001-02
Godard, Eric	NYI, Cgy., Pit.	8	335	6	12	18	833	7	0	1	1	6	1	2002-03	2010-11
Godden, Ernie	Tor.	1	5	1	1	2	6	....	....	....	....	....	....	1981-82	1981-82
• Godfrey, Warren	Bos., Det.	16	786	32	125	157	752	52	1	4	5	42	....	1952-53	1967-68
Godin, Eddy	Wsh.	2	27	3	6	9	12	....	....	....	....	....	....	1977-78	1978-79
• Godin, Sam	Ott., Mtl.	3	83	4	3	7	36	....	....	....	....	....	....	1927-28	1933-34
Godynyuk, Alexander	Tor., Cgy., Fla., Hfd.	7	223	10	39	49	224	....	....	....	....	....	....	1990-91	1996-97
• Goegan, Pete	Det., NYR, Min.	11	383	19	67	86	365	33	1	3	4	61	....	1957-58	1967-68
Goertz, Dave	Pit.	1	2	0	0	0	2	....	....	....	....	....	....	1987-88	1987-88
Goertzen, Steven	CBJ, Phx., Car.	4	68	2	2	4	83	....	....	....	....	....	....	2005-06	2009-10
• Goldham, Bob	Tor., Chi., Det.	12	650	28	143	171	400	66	3	14	17	53	5	1941-42	1955-56
Goldmann, Erich	Ott.	1	1	0	0	0	0	....	....	....	....	....	....	1999-00	1999-00
• Goldsworthy, Bill	Bos., Min., NYR	14	771	283	258	541	793	40	18	19	37	30	....	1964-65	1977-78
• Goldsworthy, Leroy	NYR, Det., Chi., Mtl., Bos., NYA	10	336	66	57	123	79	24	1	0	1	4	1	1928-29	1938-39
Goldup, Glenn	Mtl., L.A.	9	291	52	67	119	303	16	4	3	7	22	....	1973-74	1981-82
• Goldup, Hank	Tor., NYR	6	202	63	80	143	97	26	5	1	6	6	1	1939-40	1945-46
Golubovsky, Yan	Det., Fla.	4	56	1	7	8	32	....	....	....	....	....	....	1997-98	2000-01
Goneau, Daniel	NYR	3	53	12	3	15	14	....	....	....	....	....	....	1996-97	1999-00
• Gooden, Bill	NYR	2	53	9	11	20	15	....	....	....	....	....	....	1942-43	1943-44
Goodenough, Larry	Phi., Van.	6	242	22	77	99	179	22	3	15	18	10	1	1974-75	1979-80
• Goodfellow, Ebbie	Det.	14	557	134	190	324	511	45	8	8	16	65	3	1929-30	1942-43
Gordiouk, Viktor	Buf.	2	26	3	8	11	0	....	....	....	....	....	....	1992-93	1994-95
‡ Gordon, Andrew	Wsh., Ana., Van.	5	55	3	4	7	6	....	....	....	....	....	....	2008-09	2012-13
• Gordon, Fred	Det., Bos.	2	81	8	7	15	68	2	0	0	0	0	....	1926-27	1927-28
Gordon, Jack	NYR	3	36	3	10	13	0	9	1	1	2	7	....	1948-49	1950-51
Gordon, Robb	Van.	1	4	0	0	0	2	....	....	....	....	....	....	1998-99	1998-99
Goren, Lee	Bos., Fla., Van.	5	67	5	4	9	44	5	0	0	0	5	....	2000-01	2006-07
Gorence, Tom	Phi., Edm.	6	303	58	53	111	89	37	9	6	15	47	....	1978-79	1983-84
Goring, Butch	L.A., NYI, Bos.	16	1107	375	513	888	102	134	38	50	88	32	4	1969-70	1984-85
Gorman, Dave	Atl.	1	3	0	0	0	0	....	....	....	....	....	....	1979-80	1979-80
• Gorman, Ed	Ott., Tor.	4	111	14	6	20	108	8	0	0	0	2	1	1924-25	1927-28
Gosselin, Benoit	NYR	1	7	0	0	0	33	....	....	....	....	....	....	1977-78	1977-78
Gosselin, David	Nsh.	2	13	2	1	3	11	....	....	....	....	....	....	1999-00	2001-02
Gosselin, Guy	Wpg.	1	5	0	0	0	6	....	....	....	....	....	....	1987-88	1987-88
Gotaas, Steve	Pit., Min.	3	49	6	9	15	53	3	0	1	1	5	....	1987-88	1990-91
• Gottselig, Johnny	Chi.	16	589	176	195	371	203	43	13	13	26	18	2	1928-29	1944-45
Gould, Bobby	Atl., Cgy., Wsh., Bos.	11	697	145	159	304	572	78	15	13	28	58	....	1979-80	1989-90
Gould, John	Buf., Van., Atl.	9	504	131	138	269	113	14	3	2	5	4	....	1971-72	1979-80
Gould, Larry	Van.	1	2	0	0	0	0	....	....	....	....	....	....	1973-74	1973-74

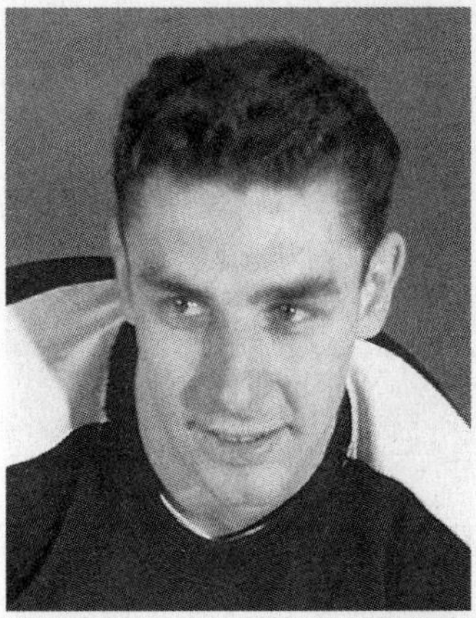
Jean-Paul Gladu

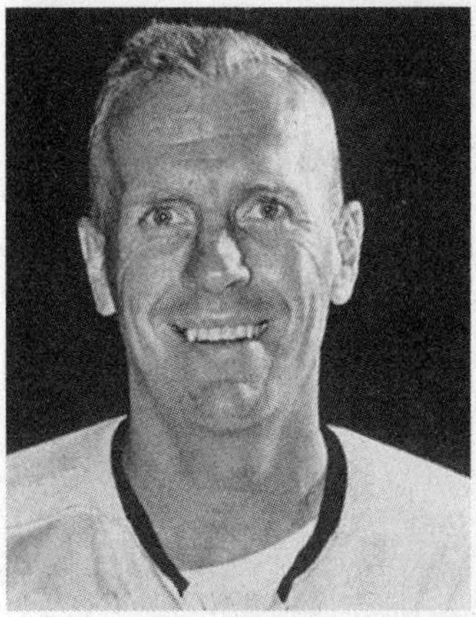
Gerry Goyer

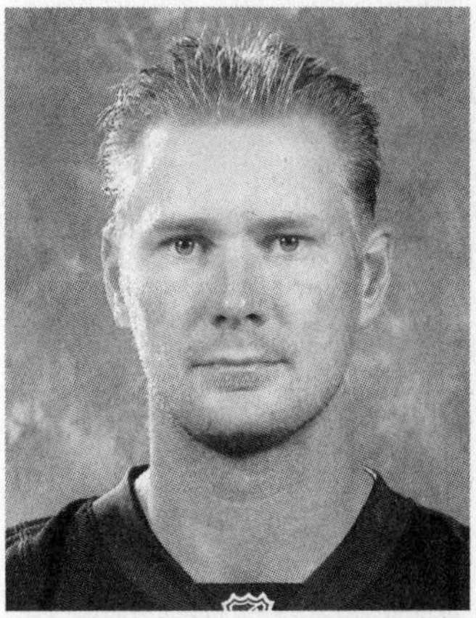
Chris Gratton

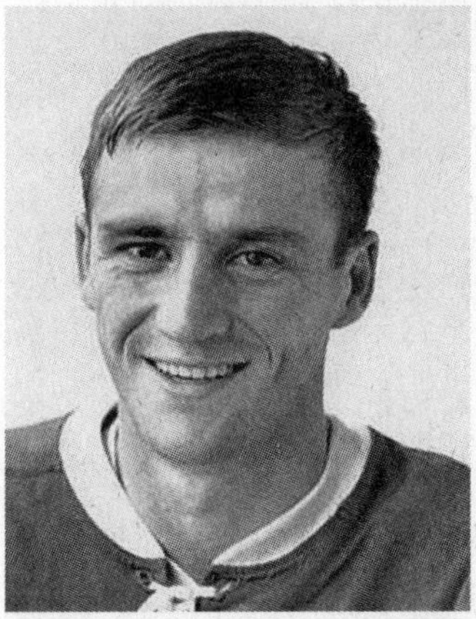
Lucien Grenier

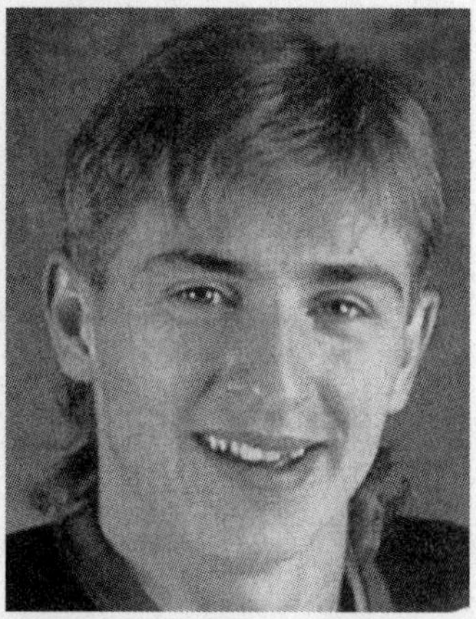

Brent Gretzky

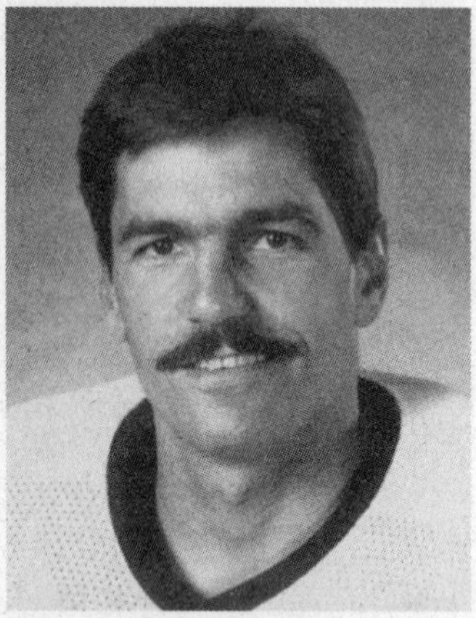

Scott Gruhl

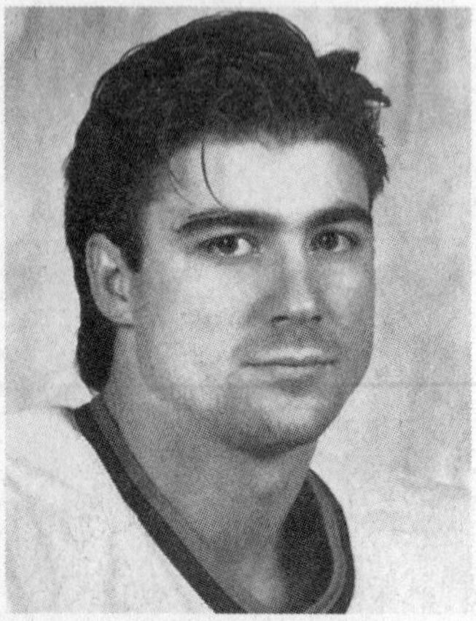

David Haas

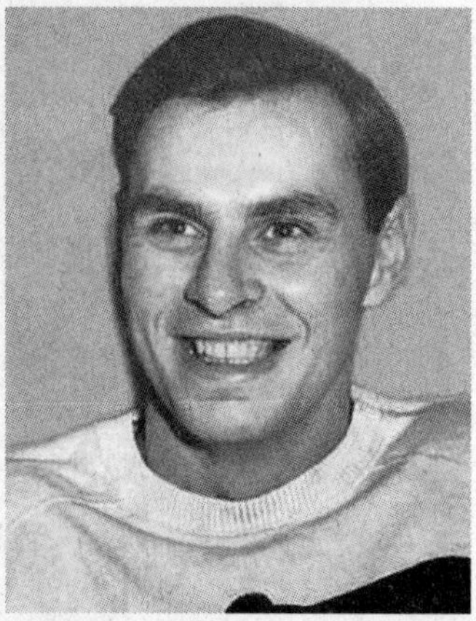

Gord Haidy

Name	NHL Teams	NHL Seasons	Regular Schedule GP	G	A	TP	PIM	Playoffs GP	G	A	TP	PIM	NHL Cup Wins	First NHL Season	Last NHL Season
Goulet, Michel	Que., Chi.	15	1089	548	604	1152	825	92	39	39	78	110	....	1979-80	1993-94
• Goupille, Red	Mtl.	8	222	12	28	40	256	8	2	0	2	6	....	1935-36	1942-43
Gove, David	Car.	2	2	0	1	1	0	....	....	....	....	....	....	2005-06	2006-07
Govedaris, Chris	Hfd., Tor.	4	45	4	6	10	24	4	0	0	0	2	....	1989-90	1993-94
Goyer, Gerry	Chi.	1	40	1	2	3	4	3	0	0	0	2	....	1967-68	1967-68
Goyette, Phil	Mtl., NYR, St.L., Buf.	16	941	207	467	674	131	94	17	29	46	26	4	1956-57	1971-72
• Graboski, Tony	Mtl.	3	66	6	10	16	24	3	0	0	0	6	....	1940-41	1942-43
‡ Grachev, Evgeny	NYR, St.L.	2	34	1	3	4	2	....	....	....	....	....	....	2010-11	2011-12
• Gracie, Bob	Tor., Bos., NYA, Mtl.M., Mtl., Chi.	9	379	82	109	191	205	33	4	7	11	4	2	1930-31	1938-39
Gradin, Thomas	Van., Bos.	9	677	209	384	593	298	42	17	25	42	20	....	1978-79	1986-87
Graham, Dirk	Min., Chi.	12	772	219	270	489	917	90	17	27	44	92	....	1983-84	1994-95
• Graham, Leth	Ott., Ham.	6	27	3	0	3	0	1	0	0	0	0	1	1920-21	1925-26
Graham, Pat	Pit., Tor.	3	103	11	17	28	136	4	0	0	0	2	....	1981-82	1983-84
Graham, Rod	Bos.	1	14	2	1	3	7	....	....	....	....	....	....	1974-75	1974-75
• Graham, Ted	Chi., Mtl.M., Det., St.L., Bos., NYA	9	346	14	25	39	300	24	3	1	4	30	....	1927-28	1936-37
Granato, Tony	NYR, L.A., S.J.	13	773	248	244	492	1425	79	16	27	43	141	....	1988-89	2000-01
Grand-Pierre, Jean-Luc	Buf., CBJ, Atl., Wsh.	6	269	7	13	20	311	4	0	0	0	4	....	1998-99	2003-04
Grant, Danny	Mtl., Min., Det., L.A.	13	736	263	273	536	239	43	10	14	24	19	1	1965-66	1978-79
Gratton, Benoit	Wsh., Cgy., Mtl.	6	58	6	10	16	58	....	....	....	....	....	....	1997-98	2003-04
Gratton, Chris	T.B., Phi., Buf., Phx., Col., Fla., CBJ	15	1092	214	354	568	1638	40	8	7	15	82	....	1993-94	2008-09
Gratton, Dan	L.A.	1	7	1	0	1	5	....	....	....	....	....	....	1987-88	1987-88
‡ Gratton, Josh	Phi., Phx.	4	86	3	3	6	294	....	....	....	....	....	....	2005-06	2008-09
Gratton, Norm	NYR, Atl., Buf., Min.	5	201	39	44	83	64	6	0	1	1	2	....	1971-72	1975-76
• Gravelle, Leo	Mtl., Det.	5	223	44	34	78	42	17	4	1	5	2	....	1946-47	1950-51
Graves, Adam	Det., Edm., NYR, S.J.	16	1152	329	287	616	1224	125	38	27	65	119	2	1987-88	2002-03
Graves, Hilliard	Cal., Atl., Van., Wpg.	9	556	118	163	281	209	2	0	0	0	0	....	1970-71	1979-80
Graves, Steve	Edm.	3	35	5	4	9	10	....	....	....	....	....	....	1983-84	1987-88
• Gray, Alex	NYR, Tor.	2	50	7	0	7	32	13	1	0	1	0	1	1927-28	1928-29
Gray, Terry	Bos., Mtl., L.A., St.L.	6	147	26	28	54	64	35	5	5	10	22	....	1961-62	1970-71
‡ Grebeshkov, Denis	L.A., NYI, Edm., Nsh.	6	234	17	68	85	114	2	0	2	2	0	....	2003-04	2013-14
‡ Green, Josh	L.A., NYI, Edm., NYR, Wsh., Cgy., Van., Ana.	11	341	36	40	76	206	17	0	1	1	12	....	1998-99	2011-12
Green, Mike	Fla., NYR	1	24	1	3	4	4	....	....	....	....	....	....	2003-04	2003-04
• Green, Red	Ham., NYA, Bos., Det.	6	195	59	26	85	290	1	0	0	0	0	1	1923-24	1928-29
Green, Rick	Wsh., Mtl., Det., NYI	15	845	43	220	263	588	100	3	16	19	73	1	1976-77	1991-92
• Green, Shorty	Ham., NYA	4	103	33	20	53	151	....	....	....	....	....	....	1923-24	1926-27
Green, Ted	Bos.	11	620	48	206	254	1029	31	4	8	12	54	1	1960-61	1971-72
Green, Travis	NYI, Ana., Phx., Tor., Bos.	14	970	193	262	455	764	56	10	11	21	60	....	1992-93	2006-07
Greenlaw, Jeff	Wsh., Fla.	6	57	3	6	9	108	2	0	0	0	21	....	1986-87	1993-94
‡ Greentree, Kyle	Phi., Cgy.	2	4	0	0	0	0	....	....	....	....	....	....	2007-08	2008-09
Gregg, Randy	Edm., Van.	10	474	41	152	193	333	137	13	38	51	127	5	1981-82	1991-92
• Greig, Bruce	Cal.	2	9	0	1	1	46	....	....	....	....	....	....	1973-74	1974-75
Greig, Mark	Hfd., Tor., Cgy., Phi.	9	125	13	27	40	90	5	0	1	1	0	....	1990-91	2002-03
Grenier, Lucien	Mtl., L.A.	4	151	14	14	28	18	2	0	0	0	0	....	1968-69	1971-72
Grenier, Martin	Phx., Van., Phi.	4	18	1	0	1	14	....	....	....	....	....	....	2001-02	2006-07
Grenier, Richard	NYI	1	10	1	1	2	2	....	....	....	....	....	....	1972-73	1972-73
Greschner, Ron	NYR	16	982	179	431	610	1226	84	17	32	49	106	....	1974-75	1989-90
Gretzky, Brent	T.B.	2	13	1	3	4	2	....	....	....	....	....	....	1993-94	1994-95
Gretzky, Wayne	Edm., L.A., St.L., NYR	20	1487	894	1963	2857	577	208	122	260	382	66	4	1979-80	1998-99
Grier, Mike	Edm., Wsh., Buf., S.J.	14	1060	162	221	383	510	101	14	14	28	72	....	1996-97	2010-11
Grieve, Brent	NYI, Edm., Chi., L.A.	4	97	20	16	36	87	....	....	....	....	....	....	1993-94	1996-97
• Grigor, George	Chi.	1	2	1	0	1	0	1	0	0	0	0	....	1943-44	1943-44
Grimson, Stu	Cgy., Chi., Ana., Det., Hfd., Car., L.A., Nsh.	14	729	17	22	39	2113	42	1	1	2	120	....	1988-89	2001-02
Grisdale, John	Tor., Van.	6	250	4	39	43	346	10	0	1	1	15	....	1972-73	1978-79
Groleau, Francois	Mtl.	3	8	0	1	1	6	....	....	....	....	....	....	1995-96	1997-98
Gron, Stanislav	N.J.	1	1	0	0	0	0	....	....	....	....	....	....	2000-01	2000-01
Gronman, Tuomas	Chi., Pit.	2	38	1	3	4	38	1	0	0	0	0	....	1996-97	1997-98
• Gronsdahl, Lloyd	Bos.	1	10	1	2	3	0	....	....	....	....	....	....	1941-42	1941-42
Gronstrand, Jari	Min., NYR, Que., NYI	5	185	8	26	34	135	3	0	0	0	4	....	1986-87	1990-91
Grosek, Michal	Wpg., Buf., Chi., NYR, Bos.	11	526	84	137	221	509	45	9	11	20	77	....	1993-94	2003-04
• Gross, Lloyd	Tor., NYA, Bos., Det.	3	52	11	5	16	20	1	0	0	0	0	....	1926-27	1934-35
• Grosso, Don	Det., Chi., Bos.	9	336	87	117	204	90	48	15	14	29	63	1	1938-39	1946-47
• Grosvenor, Len	Ott., NYA, Mtl.	6	149	9	11	20	78	4	0	0	0	2	....	1927-28	1932-33
Groulx, Wayne	Que.	1	1	0	0	0	0	....	....	....	....	....	....	1984-85	1984-85
Gruden, John	Bos., Ott., Wsh.	6	92	1	8	9	46	3	0	1	1	0	....	1993-94	2003-04
Gruen, Danny	Det., Col.	3	49	9	13	22	19	....	....	....	....	....	....	1972-73	1976-77
Gruhl, Scott	L.A., Pit.	3	20	3	3	6	6	....	....	....	....	....	....	1981-82	1987-88
Gryp, Bob	Bos., Wsh.	3	74	11	13	24	33	....	....	....	....	....	....	1973-74	1975-76
Guay, Francois	Buf.	1	1	0	0	0	0	....	....	....	....	....	....	1989-90	1989-90
Guay, Paul	Phi., L.A., Bos., NYI	7	117	11	23	34	92	9	0	1	1	12	....	1983-84	1990-91
Guerard, Daniel	Ott.	1	2	0	0	0	0	....	....	....	....	....	....	1994-95	1994-95
Guerard, Stephane	Que.	2	34	0	0	0	40	....	....	....	....	....	....	1987-88	1989-90
Guerin, Bill	N.J., Edm., Bos., Dal., St.L., S.J., NYI, Pit.	18	1263	429	427	856	1660	140	39	35	74	162	2	1991-92	2009-10
Guevremont, Jocelyn	Van., Buf., NYR	9	571	84	223	307	319	40	4	17	21	18	....	1971-72	1979-80
Guidolin, Aldo	NYR	4	182	9	15	24	117	....	....	....	....	....	....	1952-53	1955-56
• Guidolin, Bep	Bos., Det., Chi.	9	519	107	171	278	606	24	5	7	12	35	....	1942-43	1951-52
Guindon, Bobby	Wpg.	1	6	0	1	1	0	....	....	....	....	....	....	1979-80	1979-80
Guite, Ben	Bos., Col., Nsh.	5	175	19	26	45	97	10	1	0	1	14	....	2005-06	2009-10
Guolla, Steve	S.J., T.B., Atl., N.J.	6	205	40	46	86	60	....	....	....	....	....	....	1996-97	2002-03
Guren, Miloslav	Mtl.	2	36	1	3	4	16	....	....	....	....	....	....	1998-99	1999-00
Gusarov, Alexei	Que., Col., NYR, St.L.	11	607	39	128	167	313	68	0	14	14	38	1	1990-91	2000-01
Gusev, Sergey	Dal., T.B.	4	89	4	10	14	34	....	....	....	....	....	....	1997-98	2000-01
Gusmanov, Ravil	Wpg.	1	4	0	0	0	0	....	....	....	....	....	....	1995-96	1995-96
Gustafsson, Bengt-Ake	Wsh.	9	629	196	359	555	196	32	9	19	28	16	....	1979-80	1988-89
Gustafsson, Per	Fla., Tor., Ott.	2	89	8	27	35	38	1	0	0	0	0	....	1996-97	1997-98
Gustavsson, Peter	Col.	1	2	0	0	0	0	....	....	....	....	....	....	1981-82	1981-82
Guy, Kevan	Cgy., Van.	6	156	5	20	25	138	5	0	1	1	23	....	1986-87	1991-92

H

Name	NHL Teams	NHL Seasons	Regular Schedule GP	G	A	TP	PIM	Playoffs GP	G	A	TP	PIM	NHL Cup Wins	First NHL Season	Last NHL Season
Haakana, Kari	Edm.	1	13	0	0	0	4	....	....	....	....	....	....	2002-03	2002-03
Haanpaa, Ari	NYI	3	60	6	11	17	37	6	0	0	0	10	....	1985-86	1987-88
Haas, David	Edm., Cgy.	2	7	2	1	3	7	....	....	....	....	....	....	1990-91	1993-94
Habscheid, Marc	Edm., Min., Det., Cgy.	11	345	72	91	163	171	12	1	3	4	13	....	1981-82	1991-92
Hachborn, Len	Phi., L.A.	3	102	20	39	59	29	7	0	3	3	7	....	1983-84	1985-86
Haddon, Lloyd	Det.	1	8	0	0	0	2	1	0	0	0	0	....	1959-60	1959-60
Hadfield, Vic	NYR, Pit.	16	1002	323	389	712	1154	73	27	21	48	117	....	1961-62	1976-77
• Haggarty, Jim	Mtl.	1	5	1	1	2	0	3	2	1	3	0	....	1941-42	1941-42
Haggerty, Sean	Tor., NYI, Nsh.	4	14	1	2	3	4	....	....	....	....	....	....	1995-96	2000-01
• Hagglund, Roger	Que.	1	3	0	0	0	0	....	....	....	....	....	....	1984-85	1984-85
Hagman, Matti	Bos., Edm.	4	237	56	89	145	36	20	5	2	7	6	....	1976-77	1981-82
‡ Hagman, Niklas	Fla., Dal., Tor., Cgy., Ana.	10	770	147	154	301	220	30	4	3	7	28	....	2001-02	2011-12
‡ Hahl, Riku	Col.	3	92	5	8	13	38	34	2	4	6	4	....	2001-02	2003-04
• Haidy, Gord	Det.	1	....	....	....	....	....	1	0	0	0	0	....	1949-50	1949-50
Hajdu, Richard	Buf.	2	5	0	0	0	4	....	....	....	....	....	....	1985-86	1986-87
Hajt, Bill	Buf.	14	854	42	202	244	433	80	2	16	18	70	....	1973-74	1986-87
Hajt, Chris	Edm., Wsh.	2	6	0	0	0	2	....	....	....	....	....	....	2000-01	2003-04
Hakansson, Anders	Min., Pit., L.A.	5	330	52	46	98	141	6	0	0	0	2	....	1981-82	1985-86
• Halderson, Harold	Det., Tor.	1	44	3	2	5	65	....	....	....	....	....	....	1926-27	1926-27
Hale, David	N.J., Cgy., Phx., T.B., Ott.	7	327	4	25	29	242	17	0	2	2	20	....	2003-04	2010-11
Hale, Larry	Phi.	4	196	5	37	42	90	8	0	0	0	12	....	1968-69	1971-72
Haley, Len	Det.	2	30	2	2	4	14	6	1	3	4	6	....	1959-60	1960-61
Halkidis, Bob	Buf., L.A., Tor., Det., T.B., NYI	11	256	8	32	40	825	20	0	1	1	51	....	1984-85	1995-96
Halko, Steven	Car.	6	155	0	15	15	71	4	0	0	0	2	....	1997-98	2002-03
• Hall, Bob	NYA	1	8	0	0	0	0	....	....	....	....	....	....	1925-26	1925-26
Hall, Del	Cal.	3	9	2	0	2	2	....	....	....	....	....	....	1971-72	1973-74
• Hall, Joe	Mtl.	2	37	15	9	24	235	7	0	1	1	38	....	1917-18	1918-19
Hall, Murray	Chi., Det., Min., Van.	9	164	35	48	83	46	6	0	0	0	0	....	1961-62	1971-72
Hall, Taylor	Van., Bos.	5	41	7	9	16	29	....	....	....	....	....	....	1983-84	1987-88
Hall, Wayne	NYR	1	4	0	0	0	0	....	....	....	....	....	....	1960-61	1960-61
Haller, Kevin	Buf., Mtl., Phi., Hfd., Car., Ana., NYI	13	642	41	97	138	907	64	7	16	23	71	1	1989-90	2001-02
• Halliday, Milt	Ott.	3	67	1	0	1	4	6	0	0	0	0	1	1926-27	1928-29
Hallin, Mats	NYI, Min.	5	152	17	14	31	193	15	1	0	1	13	1	1982-83	1986-87
‡ Halpern, Jeff	Wsh., Dal., T.B., L.A., Mtl., NYR, Phx.	14	976	152	221	373	641	39	7	7	14	31	....	1999-00	2013-14

			Regular Schedule					Playoffs							
Name	**NHL Teams**	**NHL Seasons**	**GP**	**G**	**A**	**TP**	**PIM**	**GP**	**G**	**A**	**TP**	**PIM**	**NHL Cup Wins**	**First NHL Season**	**Last NHL Season**
Halverson, Trevor	Wsh.	1	17	0	4	4	28	....	....	....	....	....	....	1998-99	1998-99
Halward, Doug	Bos., L.A., Van., Det., Edm.	14	653	69	224	293	774	47	7	10	17	113	....	1975-76	1988-89
Hamel, Denis	Buf., Ott., Atl., Phi.	7	192	19	12	31	77	....	....	....	....	....	....	1999-00	2006-07
Hamel, Gilles	Buf., Wpg., L.A.	9	519	127	147	274	276	27	4	5	9	10	....	1980-81	1988-89
• Hamel, Herb	Tor.	1	2	0	0	0	4	....	....	....	....	....	....	1930-31	1930-31
Hamel, Jean	St.L., Det., Que., Mtl.	12	699	26	95	121	766	33	0	2	2	44	....	1972-73	1983-84
• Hamill, Red	Bos., Chi.	12	419	128	94	222	160	24	1	2	3	20	1	1937-38	1950-51
‡ Hamill, Zach	Bos.	3	20	0	4	4	4	....	....	....	....	....	....	2009-10	2011-12
Hamilton, Al	NYR, Buf., Edm.	7	257	10	78	88	258	7	0	0	0	2	....	1965-66	1979-80
Hamilton, Chuck	Mtl., St.L.	2	4	0	2	2	2	....	....	....	....	....	....	1961-62	1972-73
• Hamilton, Jack	Tor.	3	102	28	32	60	20	11	2	1	3	0	....	1942-43	1945-46
Hamilton, Jeff	NYI, Chi., Car., Tor.	5	157	32	45	77	44	....	....	....	....	....	....	2003-04	2008-09
Hamilton, Jim	Pit.	8	95	14	18	32	28	6	3	0	3	0	....	1977-78	1984-85
• Hamilton, Reg	Tor., Chi.	12	424	21	87	108	412	64	3	8	11	46	2	1935-36	1946-47
Hammarstrom, Inge	Tor., St.L.	6	427	116	123	239	86	13	2	3	5	4	....	1973-74	1978-79
Hammond, Ken	L.A., Edm., NYR, Tor., Bos., S.J., Van., Ott.	8	193	18	29	47	290	15	0	0	0	24	....	1984-85	1992-93
Hampson, Gord	Cgy.	1	4	0	0	0	5	....	....	....	....	....	....	1982-83	1982-83
Hampson, Ted	Tor., NYR, Det., Oak., Cal., Min.	12	676	108	245	353	94	35	7	10	17	2	....	1959-60	1971-72
Hampton, Rick	Cal., Cle., L.A.	6	337	59	113	172	147	2	0	0	0	0	....	1974-75	1979-80
Hamr, Radek	Ott.	2	11	0	0	0	0	....	....	....	....	....	....	1992-93	1993-94
Hamrlik, Roman	T.B., Edm., NYI, Cgy., Mtl., Wsh., NYR	20	1395	155	483	638	1408	113	3	38	41	87	....	1992-93	2012-13
Hamway, Mark	NYI	3	53	5	13	18	9	1	0	0	0	0	....	1984-85	1986-87
Handy, Ron	NYI, St.L.	2	14	0	3	3	0	....	....	....	....	....	....	1984-85	1987-88
‡ Handzus, Michal	St.L., Phx., Phi., Chi., L.A., S.J.	15	1009	185	298	483	498	116	16	30	46	52	1	1998-99	2013-14
Hangsleben, Al	Hfd., Wsh., L.A.	3	185	21	48	69	396	....	....	....	....	....	....	1979-80	1981-82
Hankinson, Ben	N.J., T.B.	3	43	3	3	6	45	2	1	0	1	4	....	1992-93	1994-95
Hankinson, Casey	Chi., Ana.	3	18	0	1	1	13	....	....	....	....	....	....	2000-01	2003-04
• Hanna, John	NYR, Mtl., Phi.	5	198	6	26	32	206	....	....	....	....	....	....	1958-59	1967-68
Hannan, Dave	Pit., Edm., Tor., Buf., Col., Ott.	16	841	114	191	305	942	63	6	7	13	46	2	1981-82	1996-97
• Hannigan, Gord	Tor.	4	161	29	31	60	117	9	2	0	2	8	....	1952-53	1955-56
• Hannigan, Pat	Tor., NYR, Phi.	5	182	30	39	69	116	11	1	2	3	11	....	1959-60	1968-69
Hannigan, Ray	Tor.	1	3	0	0	0	2	....	....	....	....	....	....	1948-49	1948-49
Hansen, Richie	NYI, St.L.	4	20	2	8	10	4	....	....	....	....	....	....	1976-77	1981-82
Hansen, Tavis	Wpg., Phx.	5	34	2	1	3	16	2	0	0	0	0	....	1994-95	2000-01
‡ Hanson, Christian	Tor.	3	42	3	6	9	22	....	....	....	....	....	....	2008-09	2010-11
Hanson, Dave	Det., Min.	2	33	1	1	2	65	....	....	....	....	....	....	1978-79	1979-80
• Hanson, Emil	Det.	1	7	0	0	0	6	....	....	....	....	....	....	1932-33	1932-33
Hanson, Keith	Cgy.	1	25	0	2	2	77	....	....	....	....	....	....	1983-84	1983-84
• Hanson, Oscar	Chi.	1	8	0	0	0	0	....	....	....	....	....	....	1937-38	1937-38
• Harbaruk, Nick	Pit., St.L.	5	364	45	75	120	273	14	3	1	4	20	....	1969-70	1973-74
Harding, Jeff	Phi.	2	15	0	0	0	47	....	....	....	....	....	....	1988-89	1989-90
Hardy, Joe	Oak., Cal.	2	63	9	14	23	51	4	0	0	0	0	....	1969-70	1970-71
Hardy, Mark	L.A., NYR, Min.	15	915	62	306	368	1293	67	5	16	21	158	....	1979-80	1993-94
Hargreaves, Jim	Van.	2	66	1	7	8	105	....	....	....	....	....	....	1970-71	1972-73
‡ Harju, Johan	T.B.	1	10	1	2	3	2	....	....	....	....	....	....	2010-11	2010-11
Harkins, Brett	Bos., Fla., CBJ	4	78	6	30	36	22	....	....	....	....	....	....	1994-95	2001-02
Harkins, Todd	Cgy., Hfd.	3	48	3	3	6	78	....	....	....	....	....	....	1991-92	1993-94
Harlock, David	Tor., Wsh., NYI, Atl.	8	212	2	14	16	188	....	....	....	....	....	....	1993-94	2001-02
Harlow, Scott	St.L.	1	1	0	1	1	0	....	....	....	....	....	....	1987-88	1987-88
• Harmon, Glen	Mtl.	9	452	50	96	146	334	53	5	10	15	37	2	1942-43	1950-51
• Harms, John	Chi.	2	44	5	5	10	21	4	3	0	3	2	....	1943-44	1944-45
• Harnott, Walter	Bos.	1	6	0	0	0	2	....	....	....	....	....	....	1933-34	1933-34
Harper, Terry	Mtl., L.A., Det., St.L., Col.	19	1066	35	221	256	1362	112	4	13	17	140	5	1962-63	1980-81
Harrer, Tim	Cgy.	1	3	0	0	0	2	....	....	....	....	....	....	1982-83	1982-83
• Harrington, Hago	Bos., Mtl.	3	72	9	3	12	15	4	1	0	1	2	....	1925-26	1932-33
• Harris, Billy	Tor., Det., Oak., Pit.	13	769	126	219	345	205	62	8	10	18	30	3	1955-56	1968-69
Harris, Billy	NYI, L.A., Tor.	12	897	231	327	558	394	71	19	19	38	48	....	1972-73	1983-84
Harris, Duke	Min., Tor.	1	26	1	4	5	4	....	....	....	....	....	....	1967-68	1967-68
• Harris, Henry	Bos.	1	32	2	4	6	20	....	....	....	....	....	....	1930-31	1930-31
Harris, Hugh	Buf.	1	60	12	26	38	17	3	0	0	0	0	....	1972-73	1972-73
Harris, Ron	Det., Oak., Atl., NYR	11	476	20	91	111	474	28	4	3	7	33	....	1962-63	1975-76
• Harris, Smokey	Bos.	1	6	3	1	4	8	....	....	....	....	....	....	1924-25	1924-25
Harris, Ted	Mtl., Min., Det., St.L., Phi.	12	788	30	168	198	1000	100	1	22	23	230	5	1963-64	1974-75
• Harrison, Ed	Bos., NYR	4	194	27	24	51	53	9	1	0	1	2	....	1947-48	1950-51
Harrison, Jim	Bos., Tor., Chi., Edm.	8	324	67	86	153	435	13	1	1	2	43	....	1968-69	1979-80
Hart, Gerry	Det., NYI, Que., St.L.	15	730	29	150	179	1240	78	3	12	15	175	....	1968-69	1982-83
• Hart, Gizzy	Det., Mtl.	3	104	6	8	14	12	8	0	1	1	0	....	1926-27	1932-33
Hartigan, Mark	Atl., CBJ, Ana., Det.	6	102	19	11	30	58	5	0	1	1	4	1	2001-02	2007-08
Hartman, Mike	Buf., Wpg., T.B., NYR	9	397	43	35	78	1388	21	0	0	0	106	1	1986-87	1994-95
Hartsburg, Craig	Min.	10	570	98	315	413	818	61	15	27	42	70	....	1979-80	1988-89
• Harvey, Buster	Min., Atl., K.C., Det.	7	407	90	118	208	131	14	0	2	2	8	....	1970-71	1976-77
• Harvey, Doug	Mtl., NYR, Det., St.L.	20	1113	88	452	540	1216	137	8	64	72	152	6	1947-48	1968-69
Harvey, Hugh	K.C.	2	18	1	1	2	4	....	....	....	....	....	....	1974-75	1975-76
Harvey, Todd	Dal., NYR, S.J., Edm.	11	671	91	132	223	950	68	3	6	9	52	....	1994-95	2005-06
• Hassard, Bob	Tor., Chi.	5	126	9	28	37	22	....	....	....	....	....	1	1949-50	1954-55
Hatcher, Derian	Min., Dal., Det., Phi.	16	1045	80	251	331	1581	133	7	26	33	248	1	1991-92	2007-08
Hatcher, Kevin	Wsh., Dal., Pit., NYR, Car.	17	1157	227	450	677	1392	118	22	37	59	252	....	1984-85	2000-01
Hatoum, Ed	Det., Van.	3	47	3	6	9	25	....	....	....	....	....	....	1968-69	1970-71
Hauer, Brett	Edm., Nsh.	3	37	4	4	8	38	....	....	....	....	....	....	1995-96	2001-02
Havelid, Niclas	Ana., Atl., N.J.	9	628	34	137	171	342	32	0	7	7	4	....	1999-00	2008-09
Hawerchuk, Dale	Wpg., Buf., St.L., Phi.	16	1188	518	891	1409	730	97	30	69	99	67	....	1981-82	1996-97
Hawgood, Greg	Bos., Edm., Phi., Fla., Pit., S.J., Van., Dal.	12	474	60	164	224	426	42	2	8	10	37	....	1987-88	2001-02
Hawkins, Todd	Van., Tor.	3	10	0	0	0	15	....	....	....	....	....	....	1988-89	1991-92
Haworth, Alan	Buf., Wsh., Que.	8	524	189	211	400	425	42	12	16	28	28	....	1980-81	1987-88
Haworth, Gord	NYR	1	2	0	1	1	0	....	....	....	....	....	....	1952-53	1952-53
Hawryliw, Neil	NYI	1	1	0	0	0	0	....	....	....	....	....	....	1981-82	1981-82
Hay, Bill	Chi.	8	506	113	273	386	244	67	15	21	36	62	1	1959-60	1966-67
Hay, Dwayne	Wsh., Fla., T.B., Cgy.	4	79	2	4	6	22	....	....	....	....	....	....	1997-98	2000-01
• Hay, George	Chi., Det.	6	238	74	60	134	84	8	2	3	5	2	....	1926-27	1932-33
Hay, Jim	Det.	3	75	1	5	6	22	9	1	0	1	2	1	1952-53	1954-55
‡ Haydar, Darren	Nsh., Atl., Col.	4	23	1	7	8	2	....	....	....	....	....	....	2002-03	2009-10
Hayek, Peter	Min.	1	1	0	0	0	0	....	....	....	....	....	....	1981-82	1981-82
Hayes, Chris	Bos.	1	....	....	....	....	....	1	0	0	0	0	....	1971-72	1971-72
• Haynes, Paul	Mtl.M., Bos., Mtl.	11	391	61	134	195	164	24	2	8	10	13	....	1930-31	1940-41
Hayward, Rick	L.A.	1	4	0	0	0	5	....	....	....	....	....	....	1990-91	1990-91
Hazlett, Steve	Van.	1	1	0	0	0	0	....	....	....	....	....	....	1979-80	1979-80
Head, Galen	Det.	1	1	0	0	0	0	....	....	....	....	....	....	1967-68	1967-68
• Headley, Fern	Bos., Mtl.	1	30	1	3	4	10	1	0	0	0	0	....	1924-25	1924-25
Healey, Eric	Bos.	1	2	0	0	0	2	....	....	....	....	....	....	2005-06	2005-06
Healey, Paul	Phi., Tor., NYR, Col.	6	77	6	14	20	44	22	0	2	2	4	....	1996-97	2005-06
Healey, Rich	Det.	1	1	0	0	0	2	....	....	....	....	....	....	1960-61	1960-61
Heaphy, Shawn	Cgy.	1	1	0	0	0	0	....	....	....	....	....	....	1992-93	1992-93
Heaslip, Mark	NYR, L.A.	3	117	10	19	29	110	5	0	0	0	2	....	1976-77	1978-79
Heath, Randy	NYR	2	13	2	4	6	15	....	....	....	....	....	....	1984-85	1985-86
Hebenton, Andy	NYR, Bos.	9	630	189	202	391	83	22	6	5	11	8	....	1955-56	1963-64
‡ Hecht, Jochen	St.L., Edm., Buf.	14	833	186	277	463	458	59	14	18	32	24	....	1998-99	2012-13
Hecl, Radoslav	Buf.	1	14	0	0	0	2	....	....	....	....	....	....	2002-03	2002-03
Hedberg, Anders	NYR	7	465	172	225	397	144	58	22	24	46	31	....	1978-79	1984-85
Hedican, Bret	St.L., Van., Fla., Car., Ana.	17	1039	55	239	294	893	108	4	22	26	108	1	1991-92	2008-09
Hedin, Pierre	Tor.	1	3	0	1	1	0	....	....	....	....	....	....	2003-04	2003-04
Hedstrom, Jonathan	Ana.	2	83	13	14	27	48	3	0	1	1	2	....	2002-03	2005-06
Heerema, Jeff	Car., St.L.	2	32	4	2	6	6	....	....	....	....	....	....	2002-03	2003-04
• Heffernan, Frank	Tor.	1	19	0	1	1	10	....	....	....	....	....	....	1919-20	1919-20
• Heffernan, Gerry	Mtl.	3	83	33	35	68	27	11	3	3	6	8	1	1941-42	1943-44
Heidt, Mike	L.A.	1	6	0	1	1	7	....	....	....	....	....	....	1983-84	1983-84
‡ Heikkinen, Ilkka	NYR	1	7	0	0	0	0	....	....	....	....	....	....	2009-10	2009-10
• Heindl, Bill	Min., NYR	3	18	2	1	3	0	....	....	....	....	....	....	1970-71	1972-73
• Heinrich, Lionel	Bos.	1	35	1	1	2	33	....	....	....	....	....	....	1955-56	1955-56
Heins, Shawn	S.J., Pit., Atl.	6	125	4	12	16	154	2	0	0	0	0	....	1998-99	2003-04
Heinze, Steve	Bos., CBJ, Buf., L.A.	12	694	178	158	336	379	69	11	15	26	48	....	1991-92	2002-03
Heiskala, Earl	Phi.	3	127	13	11	24	294	....	....	....	....	....	....	1968-69	1970-71
Heisten, Barrett	NYR	1	10	0	0	0	2	....	....	....	....	....	....	2001-02	2001-02
Hejduk, Milan	Col.	14	1020	375	430	805	316	112	34	42	76	28	1	1998-99	2012-13
Helander, Peter	L.A.	1	7	0	1	1	0	....	....	....	....	....	....	1982-83	1982-83

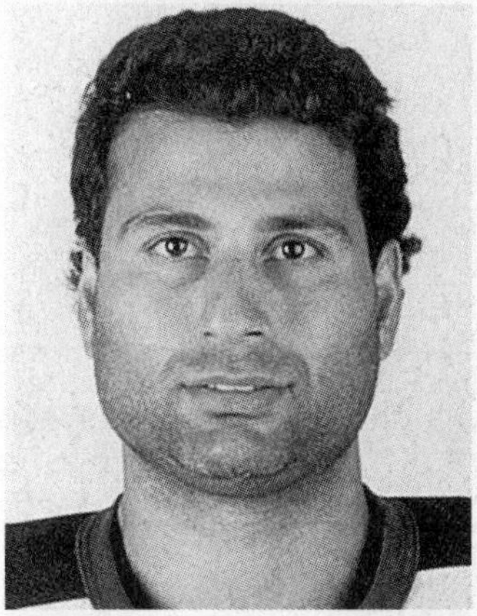

Bob Halkidis

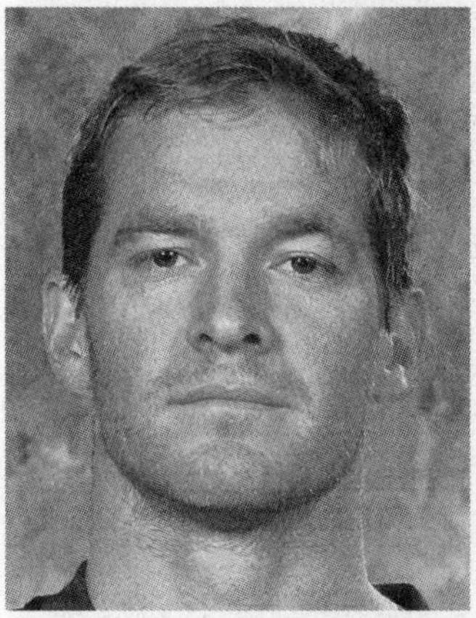

Jeff Halpern

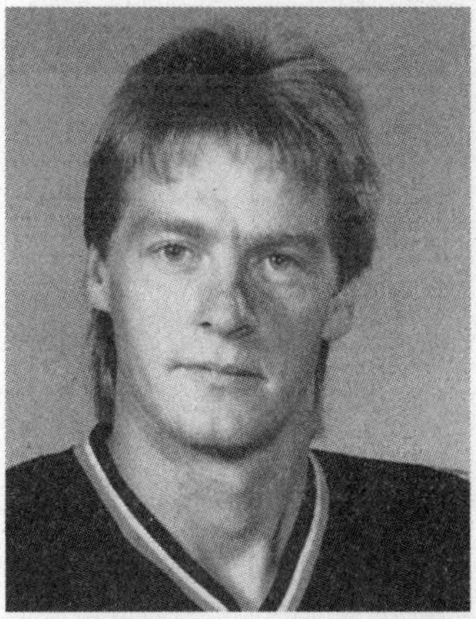

Jim Hamilton

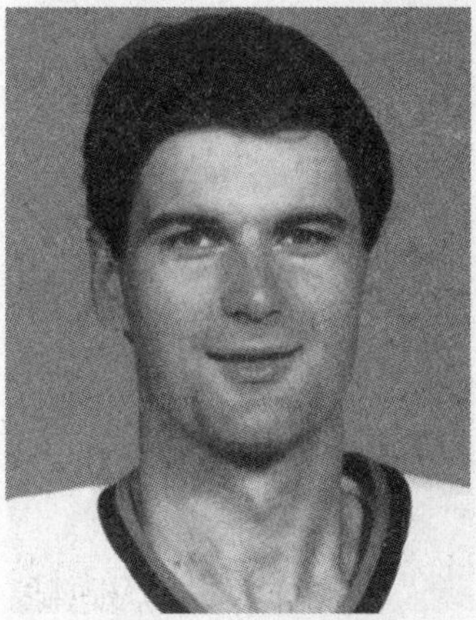

Ken Hammond

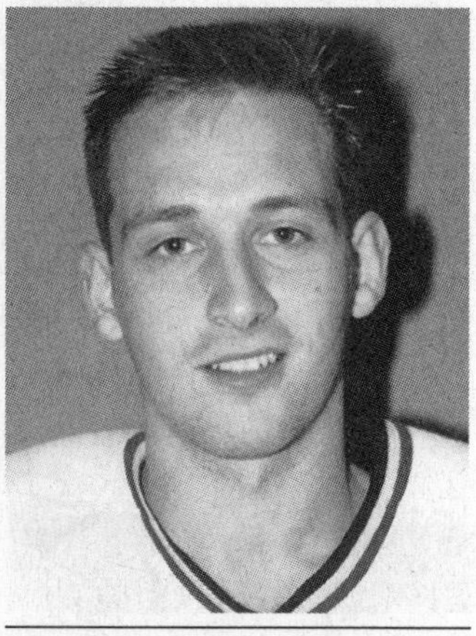

Jason Herter

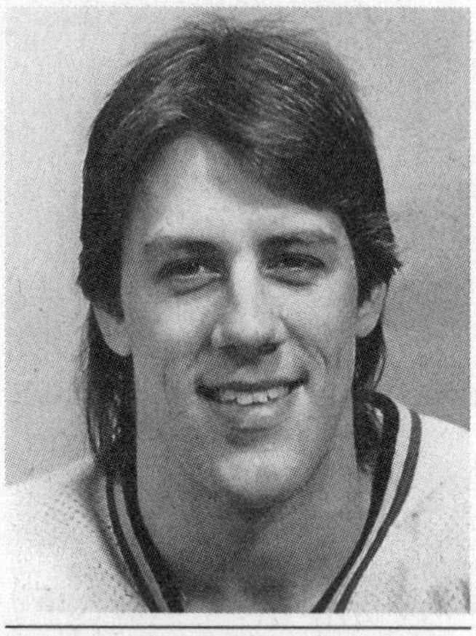

Tom Hirsch

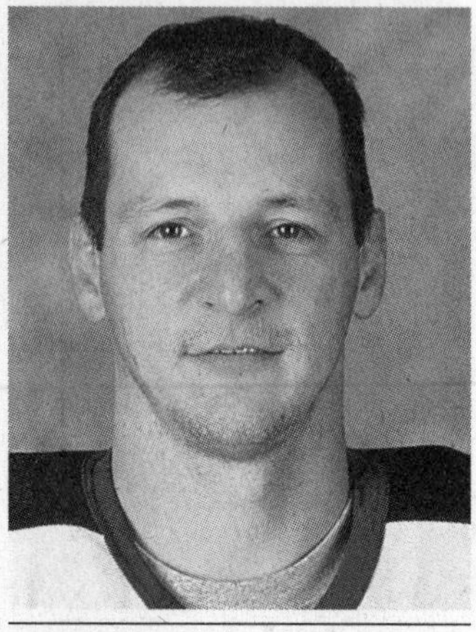

Benoit Hogue

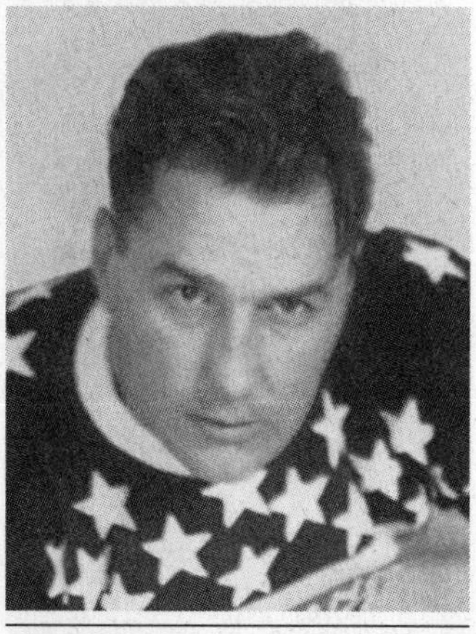

Bill Holmes

			Regular Schedule					Playoffs							
Name	NHL Teams	NHL Seasons	GP	G	A	TP	PIM	GP	G	A	TP	PIM	NHL Cup Wins	First NHL Season	Last NHL Season
‡ Helbling, Timo	T.B., Wsh.	2	11	0	1	1	8	....	....	....	....	....	....	2005-06	2006-07
Helenius, Sami	Cgy., T.B., Col., Dal., Chi.	6	155	2	4	6	260	1	0	0	0	0	....	1996-97	2002-03
• Heller, Ott	NYR	15	647	55	176	231	465	61	6	8	14	61	2	1931-32	1945-46
• Helman, Harry	Ott.	3	44	1	0	1	7	2	0	0	0	0	1	1922-23	1924-25
Helmer, Bryan	Phx., St.L., Van., Wsh.	7	146	8	18	26	135	6	0	0	0	0	....	1998-99	2008-09
Helminen, Dwight	Car., S.J.	2	27	2	1	3	0	8	1	0	1	4	....	2008-09	2009-10
Helminen, Raimo	NYR, Min., NYI	3	117	13	46	59	16	2	0	0	0	0	....	1985-86	1988-89
Hemingway, Colin	St.L.	1	3	0	0	0	0	....	....	....	....	....	....	2005-06	2005-06
• Hemmerling, Tony	NYA	2	22	3	3	6	4	....	....	....	....	....	....	1935-36	1936-37
Henderson, Archie	Wsh., Min., Hfd.	3	23	3	1	4	92	....	....	....	....	....	....	1980-81	1982-83
Henderson, Jay	Bos.	4	33	1	3	4	37	....	....	....	....	....	....	1998-99	2001-02
Henderson, Matt	Nsh., Chi.	2	6	0	1	1	2	....	....	....	....	....	....	1998-99	2001-02
• Henderson, Murray	Bos.	8	405	24	62	86	305	41	2	3	5	23	....	1944-45	1951-52
Henderson, Paul	Det., Tor., Atl.	13	707	236	241	477	304	56	11	14	25	28	....	1962-63	1979-80
Hendrickson, Darby	Tor., NYI, Van., Min., Col.	11	518	65	64	129	370	25	3	3	6	6	....	1993-94	2003-04
Hendrickson, John	Det.	3	5	0	0	0	4	....	....	....	....	....	....	1957-58	1961-62
‡ Hendry, Jordan	Chi., Ana.	5	131	4	9	13	40	15	0	0	0	2	1	2007-08	2012-13
‡ Hennessy, Josh	Ott., Bos.	5	23	1	0	1	6	....	....	....	....	....	....	2006-07	2011-12
Henning, Lorne	NYI	9	543	73	111	184	102	81	7	7	14	8	2	1972-73	1980-81
‡ Henry, Alex	Edm., Wsh., Min., Mtl.	4	177	2	9	11	269	....	....	....	....	....	....	2002-03	2008-09
Henry, Burke	Chi.	2	39	2	6	8	33	....	....	....	....	....	....	2002-03	2003-04
• Henry, Camille	NYR, Chi., St.L.	14	727	279	249	528	88	47	6	12	18	7	....	1953-54	1969-70
Henry, Dale	NYI	6	132	13	26	39	263	14	1	0	1	19	....	1984-85	1989-90
Hentunen, Jukka	Cgy., Nsh.	1	38	4	5	9	4	....	....	....	....	....	....	2001-02	2001-02
Hepple, Alan	N.J.	3	3	0	0	0	7	....	....	....	....	....	....	1983-84	1985-86
Herbers, Ian	Edm., T.B., NYI	2	65	0	5	5	79	....	....	....	....	....	....	1993-94	1999-00
• Herbert, Jimmy	Bos., Tor., Det.	6	206	83	31	114	253	9	3	0	3	10	....	1924-25	1929-30
• Herchenratter, Art	Det.	1	10	1	2	3	2	....	....	....	....	....	....	1940-41	1940-41
• Hergerts, Fred	NYA	2	20	2	4	6	2	....	....	....	....	....	....	1934-35	1935-36
• Hergesheimer, Phil	Chi., Bos.	4	125	21	41	62	19	6	0	0	0	2	....	1939-40	1942-43
• Hergesheimer, Wally	NYR, Chi.	7	351	114	85	199	106	5	1	0	1	0	....	1951-52	1958-59
• Heron, Red	Tor., Bro., Mtl.	4	106	21	19	40	38	21	2	2	4	6	....	1938-39	1941-42
Heroux, Yves	Que.	1	1	0	0	0	0	....	....	....	....	....	....	1986-87	1986-87
Herperger, Chris	Chi., Ott., Atl.	4	169	18	25	43	75	....	....	....	....	....	....	1999-00	2002-03
Herr, Matt	Wsh., Fla., Bos.	4	58	4	5	9	25	....	....	....	....	....	....	1998-99	2002-03
Herter, Jason	NYI	1	1	0	1	1	0	....	....	....	....	....	....	1995-96	1995-96
Hervey, Matt	Wpg., Bos., T.B.	3	35	0	5	5	97	5	0	0	0	6	....	1988-89	1992-93
‡ Heshka, Shaun	Phx.	1	8	0	2	2	4	....	....	....	....	....	....	2009-10	2009-10
Hess, Bob	St.L., Buf., Hfd.	8	329	27	95	122	178	4	1	1	2	2	....	1974-75	1983-84
Heward, Jamie	Tor., Nsh., NYI, CBJ, Wsh., L.A., T.B.	9	394	38	86	124	221	....	....	....	....	....	....	1995-96	2008-09
• Heximer, Obs	NYR, Bos., NYA	3	84	13	7	20	16	5	0	0	0	2	....	1929-30	1934-35
• Hextall, Bryan	NYR	11	449	187	175	362	227	37	8	9	17	19	1	1936-37	1947-48
Hextall, Bryan	NYR, Pit., Atl., Det., Min.	8	549	99	161	260	738	18	0	4	4	59	....	1962-63	1975-76
Hextall, Dennis	NYR, L.A., Cal., Min., Det., Wsh.	13	681	153	350	503	1398	22	3	3	6	45	....	1967-68	1979-80
• Heyliger, Vic	Chi.	2	33	2	3	5	2	....	....	....	....	....	....	1937-38	1943-44
• Hicke, Bill	Mtl., NYR, Oak., Cal., Pit.	14	729	168	234	402	395	42	3	10	13	41	2	1958-59	1971-72
Hicke, Ernie	Cal., Atl., NYI, Min., L.A.	8	520	132	140	272	407	2	1	0	1	0	....	1970-71	1977-78
Hickey, Greg	NYR	1	1	0	0	0	0	....	....	....	....	....	....	1977-78	1977-78
Hickey, Pat	NYR, Col., Tor., Que., St.L.	10	646	192	212	404	351	55	5	11	16	37	....	1975-76	1984-85
Hicks, Alex	Ana., Pit., S.J., Fla.	5	258	25	54	79	247	15	0	2	2	8	....	1995-96	1999-00
Hicks, Doug	Min., Chi., Edm., Wsh.	9	561	37	131	168	442	18	2	1	3	15	....	1974-75	1982-83
Hicks, Glenn	Det.	2	108	6	12	18	127	....	....	....	....	....	....	1979-80	1980-81
• Hicks, Henry	Mtl.M., Det.	3	96	7	2	9	72	....	....	....	....	....	....	1928-29	1930-31
Hicks, Wayne	Chi., Bos., Mtl., Phi., Pit.	5	115	13	23	36	22	2	0	1	1	2	1	1959-60	1967-68
Hidi, Andre	Wsh.	2	7	2	1	3	9	2	0	0	0	0	....	1983-84	1984-85
Hiemer, Uli	N.J.	3	143	19	54	73	176	....	....	....	....	....	....	1984-85	1986-87
Higgins, Matt	Mtl.	4	57	1	2	3	6	....	....	....	....	....	....	1997-98	2000-01
Higgins, Paul	Tor.	2	25	0	0	0	152	1	0	0	0	0	....	1981-82	1982-83
Higgins, Tim	Chi., N.J., Det.	11	706	154	198	352	719	65	5	8	13	77	....	1978-79	1988-89
Hilbert, Andy	Bos., Chi., Pit., NYI, Min.	8	307	42	62	104	132	10	1	0	1	2	....	2001-02	2009-10
• Hildebrand, Ike	NYR, Chi.	2	41	7	11	18	16	....	....	....	....	....	....	1953-54	1954-55
Hill, Al	Phi.	8	221	40	55	95	227	51	8	11	19	43	....	1976-77	1987-88
Hill, Brian	Hfd.	1	19	1	1	2	4	....	....	....	....	....	....	1979-80	1979-80
• Hill, Mel	Bos., Bro., Tor.	9	324	89	109	198	128	43	12	7	19	18	3	1937-38	1945-46
Hill, Sean	Mtl., Ana., Ott., Car., St.L., Fla., NYI, Min.	17	876	62	236	298	1008	55	5	5	10	42	1	1990-91	2007-08
• Hiller, Dutch	NYR, Det., Bos., Mtl.	9	383	91	113	204	163	48	9	8	17	21	2	1937-38	1945-46
Hiller, Jim	L.A., Det., NYR	2	63	8	12	20	116	2	0	0	0	4	....	1992-93	1993-94
Hillier, Randy	Bos., Pit., NYI, Buf.	11	543	16	110	126	906	28	0	2	2	93	1	1981-82	1991-92
Hillman, Floyd	Bos.	1	6	0	0	0	10	....	....	....	....	....	....	1956-57	1956-57
Hillman, Larry	Det., Bos., Tor., Min., Mtl., Phi., L.A., Buf.	19	790	36	196	232	579	74	2	9	11	30	6	1954-55	1972-73
• Hillman, Wayne	Chi., NYR, Min., Phi.	13	691	18	86	104	534	28	0	3	3	19	1	1960-61	1972-73
Hilworth, John	Det.	3	57	1	1	2	89	....	....	....	....	....	....	1977-78	1979-80
• Himes, Normie	NYA	9	402	106	113	219	127	2	0	0	0	0	....	1926-27	1934-35
Hindmarch, Dave	Cgy.	4	99	21	17	38	25	10	0	0	0	6	....	1980-81	1983-84
Hinote, Dan	Col., St.L.	9	503	38	52	90	383	72	6	9	15	67	1	1999-00	2008-09
Hinse, Andre	Tor.	1	4	0	0	0	0	....	....	....	....	....	....	1967-68	1967-68
Hinton, Dan	Chi.	1	14	0	0	0	16	....	....	....	....	....	....	1976-77	1976-77
Hirsch, Tom	Min.	3	31	1	7	8	30	12	0	0	0	6	....	1983-84	1987-88
• Hirschfeld, Bert	Mtl.	2	33	1	4	5	2	5	1	0	1	0	....	1949-50	1950-51
Hislop, Jamie	Que., Cgy.	5	345	75	103	178	86	28	3	2	5	11	....	1979-80	1983-84
• Hitchman, Lionel	Ott., Bos.	12	417	28	34	62	523	35	2	2	4	73	2	1922-23	1933-34
‡ Hlavac, Jan	NYR, Phi., Van., Car., T.B., Nsh.	6	436	90	134	224	138	11	0	3	3	2	....	1999-00	2007-08
• Hlinka, Ivan	Van.	2	137	42	81	123	28	16	3	10	13	8	....	1981-82	1982-83
‡ Hlinka, Jaroslav	Col.	1	63	8	20	28	16	1	0	0	0	0	....	2007-08	2007-08
Hlushko, Todd	Phi., Cgy., Pit.	6	79	8	13	21	84	3	0	0	0	2	....	1993-94	1998-99
Hnidy, Shane	Ott., Nsh., Atl., Ana., Bos., Min.	10	550	16	55	71	633	40	4	2	6	34	....	2000-01	2010-11
Hocking, Justin	L.A.	1	1	0	0	0	0	....	....	....	....	....	....	1993-94	1993-94
Hodge, Ken	Chi., Bos., NYR	14	881	328	472	800	779	97	34	47	81	120	2	1964-65	1977-78
Hodge, Ken	Min., Bos., T.B.	4	142	39	48	87	32	15	4	6	10	6	....	1988-89	1992-93
Hodgson, Dan	Tor., Van.	4	114	29	45	74	64	....	....	....	....	....	....	1985-86	1988-89
Hodgson, Rick	Hfd.	1	6	0	0	0	6	1	0	0	0	0	....	1979-80	1979-80
Hodgson, Ted	Bos.	1	4	0	0	0	0	....	....	....	....	....	....	1966-67	1966-67
Hoekstra, Cec	Mtl.	1	4	0	0	0	0	....	....	....	....	....	....	1959-60	1959-60
• Hoekstra, Ed	Phi.	1	70	15	21	36	6	7	0	1	1	0	....	1967-68	1967-68
Hoene, Phil	L.A.	3	37	2	4	6	22	....	....	....	....	....	....	1972-73	1974-75
• Hoffinger, Val	Chi.	2	28	0	1	1	30	....	....	....	....	....	....	1927-28	1928-29
Hoffman, Mike	Hfd.	3	9	1	3	4	2	....	....	....	....	....	....	1982-83	1985-86
Hoffmeyer, Bob	Chi., Phi., N.J.	6	198	14	52	66	325	3	0	1	1	25	....	1977-78	1984-85
Hofford, Jim	Buf., L.A.	3	18	0	0	0	47	....	....	....	....	....	....	1985-86	1988-89
Hogaboam, Bill	Atl., Det., Min.	8	332	80	109	189	100	2	0	0	0	0	....	1972-73	1979-80
Hoganson, Dale	L.A., Mtl., Que.	7	343	13	77	90	186	11	0	3	3	12	....	1969-70	1981-82
Hoglund, Jonas	Cgy., Mtl., Tor.	7	545	117	145	262	112	59	8	11	19	8	....	1996-97	2002-03
Hogue, Benoit	Buf., NYI, Tor., Dal., T.B., Phx., Bos., Wsh.	15	863	222	321	543	877	92	17	16	33	124	1	1987-88	2001-02
Holan, Milos	Phi., Ana.	3	49	5	11	16	42	....	....	....	....	....	....	1993-94	1995-96
Holbrook, Terry	Min.	2	43	3	6	9	4	6	0	0	0	0	....	1972-73	1973-74
‡ Holden, Josh	Van., Car., Tor.	6	60	5	9	14	16	....	....	....	....	....	....	1998-99	2003-04
Holik, Bobby	Hfd., N.J., NYR, Atl.	18	1314	326	421	747	1423	141	20	39	59	120	2	1990-91	2008-09
Holland, Jason	NYI, Buf., L.A.	7	81	4	5	9	36	1	0	0	0	0	....	1996-97	2003-04
Holland, Jerry	NYR	2	37	8	4	12	6	....	....	....	....	....	....	1974-75	1975-76
‡ Holland, Patrick	Mtl.	1	5	0	0	0	0	....	....	....	....	....	....	2013-14	2013-14
• Hollett, Flash	Tor., Ott., Bos., Det.	13	562	132	181	313	358	79	8	26	34	38	2	1933-34	1945-46
Hollinger, Terry	St.L.	2	7	0	0	0	2	....	....	....	....	....	....	1993-94	1994-95
• Hollingworth, Gord	Chi., Det.	4	163	4	14	18	201	3	0	0	0	2	....	1954-55	1957-58
Holloway, Bruce	Van.	1	2	0	0	0	0	....	....	....	....	....	....	1984-85	1984-85
‡ Hollweg, Ryan	NYR, Tor., Phx.	5	228	5	9	14	349	14	0	1	1	23	....	2005-06	2010-11
• Holmes, Bill	Mtl., NYA	3	52	6	4	10	35	....	....	....	....	....	....	1925-26	1929-30
Holmes, Chuck	Det.	2	23	1	3	4	10	....	....	....	....	....	....	1958-59	1961-62
• Holmes, Lou	Chi.	2	59	1	4	5	6	2	0	0	0	2	....	1931-32	1932-33
Holmes, Warren	L.A.	3	45	8	18	26	7	....	....	....	....	....	....	1981-82	1983-84
Holmgren, Paul	Phi., Min.	10	527	144	179	323	1684	82	19	32	51	195	....	1975-76	1984-85
Holmqvist, Michael	Ana., Chi.	3	156	18	17	35	72	....	....	....	....	....	....	2003-04	2006-07
Holmstrom, Tomas	Det.	15	1026	243	287	530	769	180	46	51	97	162	4	1996-97	2011-12
‡ Holos, Jonas	Col.	1	39	0	6	6	10	....	....	....	....	....	....	2010-11	2010-11

Name	NHL Teams	NHL Seasons	Regular Schedule					Playoffs					NHL Cup Wins	First NHL Season	Last NHL Season
			GP	G	A	TP	PIM	GP	G	A	TP	PIM			
● Holota, John	Det.	2	15	2	0	2	0	....	....	....	....	....	....	1942-43	1945-46
Holst, Greg	NYR	3	11	0	0	0	0	....	....	....	....	....	....	1975-76	1977-78
Holt, Gary	Cal., Cle., St.L.	5	101	13	11	24	133	....	....	....	....	....	....	1973-74	1977-78
Holt, Randy	Chi., Cle., Van., L.A., Cgy., Wsh., Phi.	10	395	4	37	41	1438	21	2	3	5	83	....	1974-75	1983-84
● Holway, Albert	Tor., Mtl.M., Pit.	5	112	7	2	9	48	6	0	0	0	0	1	1923-24	1928-29
Holzinger, Brian	Buf., T.B., Pit., CBJ	10	547	93	145	238	339	52	11	18	29	61	....	1994-95	2003-04
Homenuke, Ron	Van.	1	1	0	0	0	0	....	....	....	....	....	....	1972-73	1972-73
Hoover, Ron	Bos., St.L.	3	18	4	0	4	31	8	0	0	0	18	....	1989-90	1991-92
Hopkins, Dean	L.A., Edm., Que.	6	223	23	51	74	306	18	1	5	6	29	....	1979-80	1988-89
Hopkins, Larry	Tor., Wpg.	4	60	13	16	29	26	6	0	0	0	2	....	1977-78	1982-83
Horacek, Tony	Phi., Chi.	5	154	10	19	29	316	2	1	0	1	2	....	1989-90	1994-95
Horava, Miloslav	NYR	3	80	5	17	22	38	2	0	1	1	0	....	1988-89	1990-91
Horbul, Doug	K.C.	1	4	1	0	1	2	....	....	....	....	....	....	1974-75	1974-75
Hordichuk, Darcy	Atl., Phx., Fla., Nsh., Van., Edm.	12	542	20	21	41	1140	17	1	0	1	16	....	2000-01	2012-13
Hordy, Mike	NYI	2	11	0	0	0	7	....	....	....	....	....	....	1978-79	1979-80
● Horeck, Pete	Chi., Det., Bos.	8	426	106	118	224	340	34	6	8	14	43	....	1944-45	1951-52
● Horne, George	Mtl.M., Tor.	3	54	9	3	12	34	4	0	0	0	4	1	1925-26	1928-29
● Horner, Red	Tor.	12	490	42	110	152	1254	71	7	10	17	170	1	1928-29	1939-40
● Hornung, Larry	St.L.	2	48	2	9	11	10	11	0	2	2	2	....	1970-71	1971-72
● Horton, Tim	Tor., NYR, Pit., Buf.	24	1446	115	403	518	1611	126	11	39	50	183	4	1949-50	1973-74
Horvath, Bronco	NYR, Mtl., Bos., Chi., Tor., Min.	9	434	141	185	326	319	36	12	9	21	18	....	1955-56	1967-68
Hospodar, Ed	NYR, Hfd., Phi., Min., Buf.	9	450	17	51	68	1314	44	4	1	5	208	....	1979-80	1987-88
‡ Hossa, Marcel	Mtl., NYR, Phx.	6	237	31	30	61	106	14	2	2	4	10	....	2001-02	2007-08
Hostak, Martin	Phi.	2	55	3	11	14	24	....	....	....	....	....	....	1990-91	1991-92
Hotham, Greg	Tor., Pit.	6	230	15	74	89	139	5	0	3	3	6	....	1979-80	1984-85
Houck, Paul	Min.	3	16	1	2	3	2	....	....	....	....	....	....	1985-86	1987-88
Houda, Doug	Det., Hfd., L.A., Buf., NYI, Ana.	15	561	19	63	82	1104	18	0	3	3	21	....	1985-86	2002-03
Houde, Claude	K.C.	2	59	3	6	9	40	....	....	....	....	....	....	1974-75	1975-76
Houde, Eric	Mtl.	3	30	2	3	5	4	....	....	....	....	....	....	1996-97	1998-99
Hough, Mike	Que., Fla., NYI	14	707	100	156	256	675	44	5	5	10	38	....	1984-85	1998-99
Houlder, Bill	Wsh., Buf., Ana., St.L., T.B., S.J., Nsh.	16	846	59	191	250	412	30	5	6	11	14	....	1987-88	2002-03
Houle, Rejean	Mtl.	11	635	161	247	408	395	90	14	34	48	66	5	1969-70	1982-83
Housley, Phil	Buf., Wpg., St.L., Cgy., N.J., Wsh., Chi., Tor.	21	1495	338	894	1232	822	85	13	43	56	36	....	1982-83	2002-03
Houston, Ken	Atl., Cgy., Wsh., L.A.	9	570	161	167	328	624	35	10	9	19	66	....	1975-76	1983-84
● Howard, Jack	Tor.	1	2	0	0	0	0	....	....	....	....	....	....	1936-37	1936-37
Howatt, Garry	NYI, Hfd., N.J.	12	720	112	156	268	1836	87	12	14	26	289	2	1972-73	1983-84
Howe, Gordie	Det., Hfd.	26	1767	801	1049	1850	1685	157	68	92	160	220	4	1946-47	1979-80
Howe, Mark	Hfd., Phi., Det.	16	929	197	545	742	455	101	10	51	61	34	....	1979-80	1994-95
Howe, Marty	Hfd., Bos.	6	197	2	29	31	99	15	1	2	3	9	....	1979-80	1984-85
● Howe, Syd	Ott., Phi., Tor., St.L., Det.	17	698	237	291	528	212	70	17	27	44	10	3	1929-30	1945-46
● Howe, Vic	NYR	3	33	3	4	7	10	....	....	....	....	....	....	1950-51	1954-55
Howell, Harry	NYR, Oak., Cal., L.A.	21	1411	94	324	418	1298	38	3	3	6	32	....	1952-53	1972-73
● Howell, Ron	NYR	2	4	0	0	0	0	....	....	....	....	....	....	1954-55	1955-56
Howse, Don	L.A.	1	33	2	5	7	6	2	0	0	0	0	....	1979-80	1979-80
Howson, Scott	NYI	2	18	5	3	8	4	....	....	....	....	....	....	1984-85	1985-86
● Hoyda, Dave	Phi., Wpg.	4	132	6	17	23	299	12	0	0	0	17	....	1977-78	1980-81
Hrdina, Jan	Pit., Phx., N.J., CBJ	7	513	101	196	297	341	45	12	14	26	24	....	1998-99	2005-06
Hrdina, Jiri	Cgy., Pit.	5	250	45	85	130	92	46	2	5	7	24	3	1987-88	1991-92
● Hrechkosy, Dave	Cal., St.L.	4	140	42	24	66	41	3	1	0	1	2	....	1973-74	1976-77
Hrkac, Tony	St.L., Que., S.J., Chi., Dal., Edm., NYI, Ana., Atl.	13	758	132	239	371	173	41	7	7	14	12	1	1986-87	2002-03
Hrycuik, Jim	Wsh.	1	21	5	5	10	12	....	....	....	....	....	....	1974-75	1974-75
Hrymnak, Steve	Chi., Det.	2	18	2	1	3	4	2	0	0	0	0	....	1951-52	1952-53
Hrynewich, Tim	Pit.	2	55	6	8	14	82	....	....	....	....	....	....	1982-83	1983-84
Huard, Bill	Bos., Ott., Que., Dal., Edm., L.A.	8	223	16	18	34	594	5	0	0	0	2	....	1992-93	1999-00
● Huard, Rolly	Tor.	1	1	1	0	1	0	....	....	....	....	....	....	1930-31	1930-31
‡ Hubacek, Petr	Phi.	1	6	1	0	1	2	....	....	....	....	....	....	2000-01	2000-01
● Huber, Willie	Det., NYR, Van., Phi.	10	655	104	217	321	950	33	5	5	10	35	....	1978-79	1987-88
Hubick, Greg	Tor., Van.	2	77	6	9	15	10	....	....	....	....	....	....	1975-76	1979-80
Huck, Fran	Mtl., St.L.	3	94	24	30	54	38	11	3	4	7	2	....	1969-70	1972-73
Hucul, Fred	Chi., St.L.	5	164	11	30	41	113	6	1	0	1	10	....	1950-51	1967-68
Huddy, Charlie	Edm., L.A., Buf., St.L.	17	1017	99	354	453	785	183	19	66	85	135	5	1980-81	1996-97
Hudson, Dave	NYI, K.C., Col.	6	409	59	124	183	89	2	1	1	2	0	....	1972-73	1977-78
Hudson, Lex	Pit.	1	2	0	0	0	0	2	0	0	0	0	....	1978-79	1978-79
Hudson, Mike	Chi., Edm., NYR, Pit., Tor., St.L., Phx.	9	416	49	87	136	414	49	4	10	14	64	1	1988-89	1996-97
Hudson, Ron	Det.	2	33	5	2	7	2	....	....	....	....	....	....	1937-38	1939-40
Huffman, Kerry	Phi., Que., Ott.	10	401	37	108	145	361	11	0	0	0	2	....	1986-87	1995-96
● Huggins, Al	Mtl.M.	1	20	1	1	2	2	....	....	....	....	....	....	1930-31	1930-31
● Hughes, Albert	NYA	2	60	6	8	14	22	....	....	....	....	....	....	1930-31	1931-32
Hughes, Brent	L.A., Phi., St.L., Det., K.C.	8	435	15	117	132	440	22	1	3	4	53	....	1967-68	1974-75
Hughes, Brent	Wpg., Bos., Buf., NYI	8	357	41	39	80	831	29	4	1	5	53	....	1988-89	1996-97
Hughes, Frank	Cal.	1	5	0	0	0	0	....	....	....	....	....	....	1971-72	1971-72
Hughes, Howie	L.A.	3	168	25	32	57	30	14	2	0	2	2	....	1967-68	1969-70
Hughes, Jack	Col.	2	46	2	5	7	104	....	....	....	....	....	....	1980-81	1981-82
● Hughes, James	Det.	1	40	0	1	1	48	....	....	....	....	....	....	1929-30	1929-30
Hughes, John	Van., Edm., NYR	2	70	2	14	16	211	7	0	1	1	16	....	1979-80	1980-81
Hughes, Pat	Mtl., Pit., Edm., Buf., St.L., Hfd.	10	573	130	128	258	646	71	8	25	33	77	3	1977-78	1986-87
Hughes, Ryan	Bos.	1	3	0	0	0	0	....	....	....	....	....	....	1995-96	1995-96
Hulbig, Joe	Edm., Bos.	5	55	4	4	8	16	6	0	1	1	2	....	1996-97	2000-01
Hull, Bobby	Chi., Wpg., Hfd.	16	1063	610	560	1170	640	119	62	67	129	102	1	1957-58	1979-80
Hull, Brett	Cgy., St.L., Dal., Det., Phx.	20	1269	741	650	1391	458	202	103	87	190	73	2	1985-86	2005-06
Hull, Dennis	Chi., Det.	14	959	303	351	654	261	104	33	34	67	30	....	1964-65	1977-78
Hull, Jody	Hfd., NYR, Ott., Fla., T.B., Phi.	16	831	124	137	261	156	69	4	5	9	14	....	1988-89	2003-04
Hulse, Cale	N.J., Cgy., Nsh., Phx., CBJ	10	619	16	79	95	1000	1	0	0	0	0	....	1995-96	2005-06
‡ Huml, Ivan	Bos.	3	49	6	12	18	36	....	....	....	....	....	....	2001-02	2003-04
● Hunt, Fred	NYA, NYR	2	59	15	14	29	6	....	....	....	....	....	....	1940-41	1944-45
Hunt, Jamie	Wsh.	1	1	0	0	0	0	....	....	....	....	....	....	2006-07	2006-07
Hunter, Dale	Que., Wsh., Col.	19	1407	323	697	1020	3565	186	42	76	118	729	....	1980-81	1998-99
Hunter, Dave	Edm., Pit., Wpg.	10	746	133	190	323	918	105	16	24	40	211	3	1979-80	1988-89
Hunter, Mark	Mtl., St.L., Cgy., Hfd., Wsh.	12	628	213	171	384	1426	79	18	20	38	230	1	1981-82	1992-93
Hunter, Tim	Cgy., Que., Van., S.J.	16	815	62	76	138	3146	132	5	7	12	426	1	1981-82	1996-97
Hunter, Trent	NYI, L.A.	10	497	101	135	236	209	14	4	1	5	6	....	2001-02	2011-12
Huras, Larry	NYR	1	2	0	0	0	0	....	....	....	....	....	....	1976-77	1976-77
Hurlburt, Bob	Van.	1	1	0	0	0	2	....	....	....	....	....	....	1974-75	1974-75
Hurlbut, Mike	NYR, Que., Buf.	5	29	1	8	9	20	....	....	....	....	....	....	1992-93	1999-00
Hurley, Paul	Bos.	1	1	0	1	1	0	....	....	....	....	....	....	1968-69	1968-69
Hurst, Ron	Tor.	2	64	9	7	16	70	3	0	2	2	4	....	1955-56	1956-57
Huscroft, Jamie	N.J., Bos., Cgy., T.B., Van., Phx., Wsh.	10	352	5	33	38	1065	21	0	1	1	46	....	1988-89	1999-00
Huselius, Kristian	Fla., Cgy., CBJ	10	662	190	261	451	256	24	3	11	14	18	....	2001-02	2011-12
Huska, Ryan	Chi.	1	1	0	0	0	0	....	....	....	....	....	....	1997-98	1997-98
Hussey, Matt	Pit., Det.	3	21	2	2	4	2	....	....	....	....	....	....	2003-04	2006-07
Huston, Ron	Cal.	2	79	15	31	46	8	....	....	....	....	....	....	1973-74	1974-75
‡ Hutchinson, Andrew	Nsh., Car., T.B., Dal., Pit.	5	140	12	27	39	70	....	....	....	....	....	1	2003-04	2010-11
Hutchinson, Ron	NYR	1	9	0	0	0	0	....	....	....	....	....	....	1960-61	1960-61
Hutchison, Dave	L.A., Tor., Chi., N.J.	10	584	19	97	116	1550	48	2	12	14	149	....	1974-75	1983-84
● Hutton, Bill	Bos., Ott., Phi.	2	64	3	2	5	8	2	0	0	0	0	....	1929-30	1930-31
● Hyland, Harry	Mtl.W., Ott.	1	17	14	2	16	65	....	....	....	....	....	....	1917-18	1917-18
Hynes, Dave	Bos.	2	22	4	0	4	2	....	....	....	....	....	....	1973-74	1974-75
Hynes, Gord	Bos., Phi.	2	52	3	9	12	22	12	1	2	3	6	....	1991-92	1992-93
Hyvonen, Hannes	S.J., CBJ	2	42	4	5	9	22	....	....	....	....	....	....	2001-02	2002-03

I

Name	NHL Teams	NHL Seasons	GP	G	A	TP	PIM	GP	G	A	TP	PIM	NHL Cup Wins	First NHL Season	Last NHL Season
Iafrate, Al	Tor., Wsh., Bos., S.J.	12	799	152	311	463	1301	71	19	16	35	77	....	1984-85	1997-98
‡ Iggulden, Mike	S.J., NYI	2	12	1	4	5	4	....	....	....	....	....	....	2007-08	2008-09
Ignatjev, Victor	Pit.	1	11	0	1	1	6	1	0	0	0	2	....	1998-99	1998-99
Ihnacak, Miroslav	Tor., Det.	3	56	8	9	17	39	1	0	0	0	0	....	1985-86	1988-89
Ihnacak, Peter	Tor.	8	417	102	165	267	175	28	4	10	14	25	....	1982-83	1989-90
Imlach, Brent	Tor.	2	3	0	0	0	0	....	....	....	....	....	....	1965-66	1966-67
‡ Immonen, Jarkko	NYR	2	20	3	5	8	4	....	....	....	....	....	....	2005-06	2006-07
Ingarfield, Earl	NYR, Pit., Oak., Cal.	13	746	179	226	405	239	21	9	8	17	10	....	1958-59	1970-71
Ingarfield, Earl	Atl., Cgy., Det.	2	39	4	4	8	22	2	0	1	1	0	....	1979-80	1980-81
Inglis, Billy	L.A., Buf.	3	36	1	3	4	4	11	1	2	3	4	....	1967-68	1970-71
● Ingoldsby, Jack	Tor.	2	29	5	1	6	15	....	....	....	....	....	....	1942-43	1943-44
● Ingram, Frank	Chi.	3	101	24	16	40	69	11	0	1	1	2	....	1929-30	1931-32

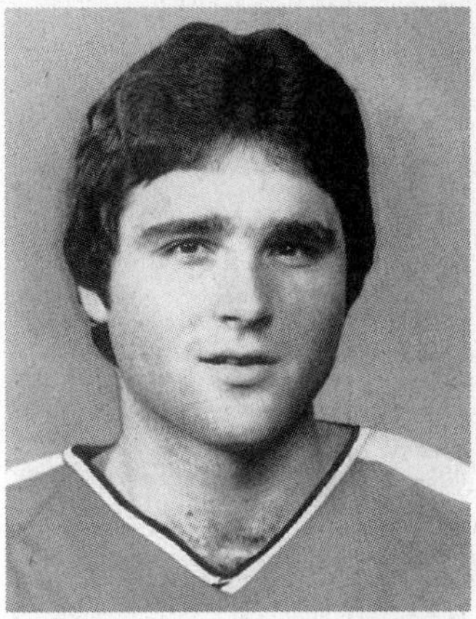
Dave Hoyda

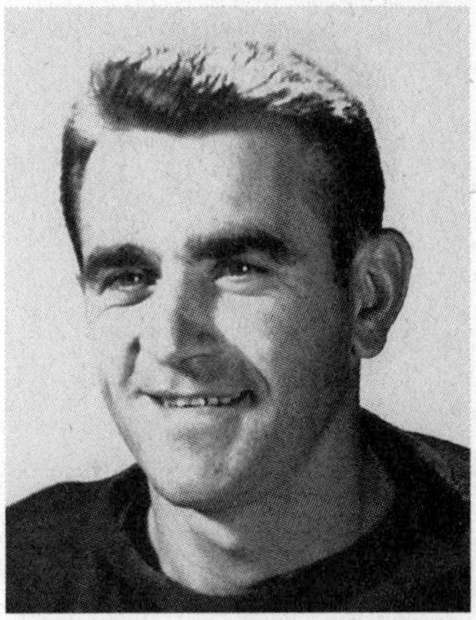
Steve Hrymnak

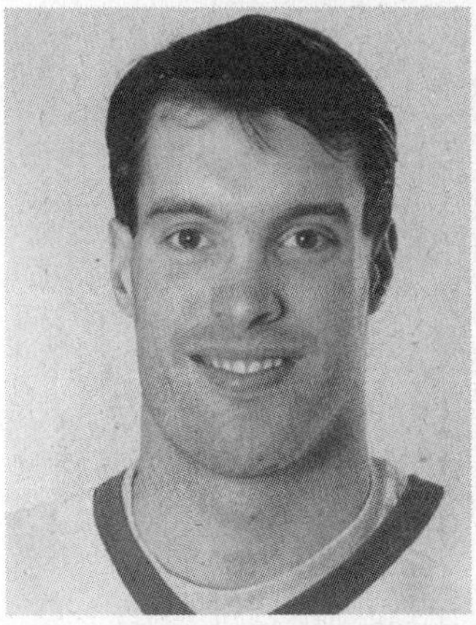
Ryan Hughes

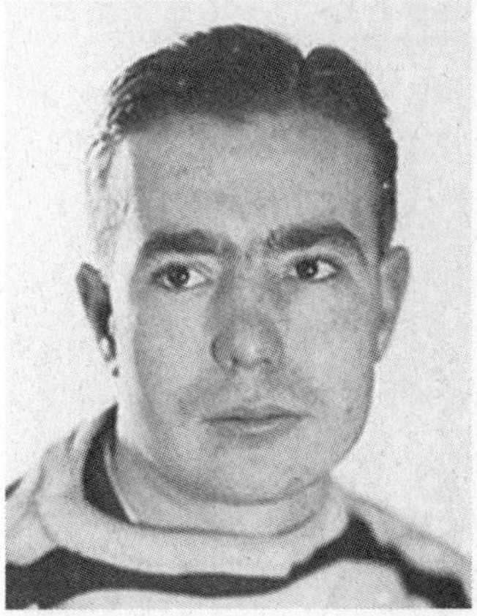
Frank Ingram

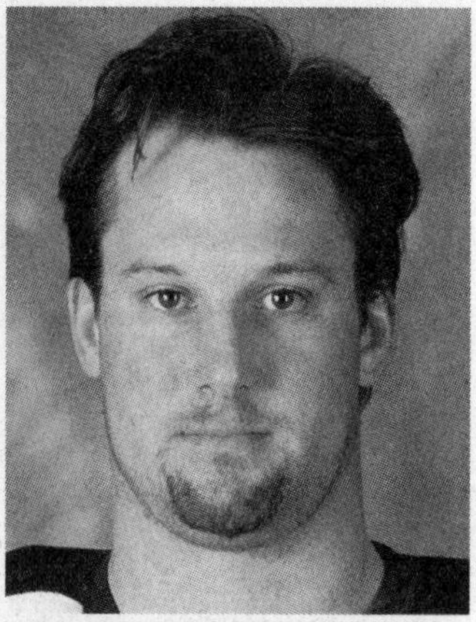

Craig Janney

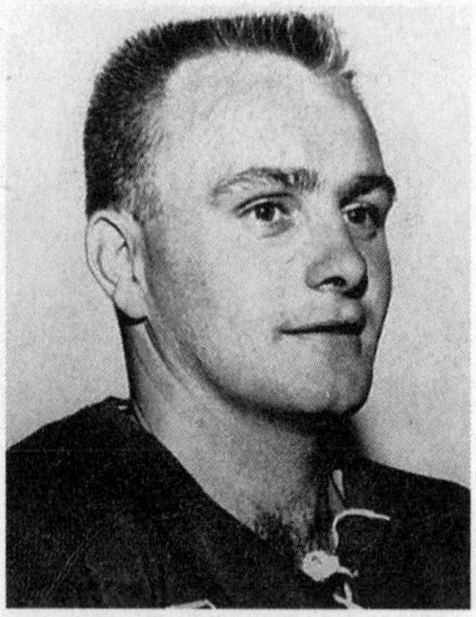

Don Johns

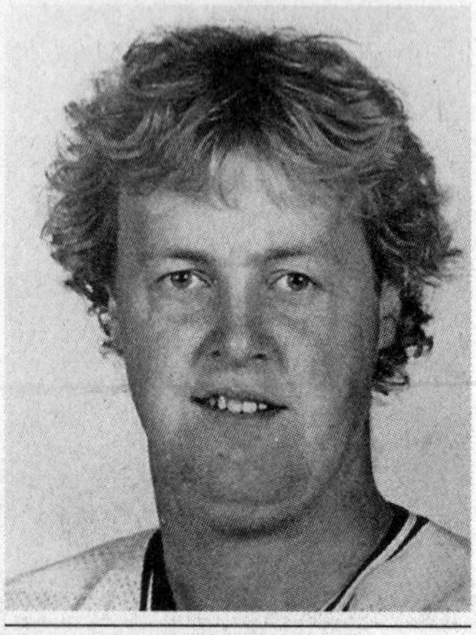

Bernie Johnston

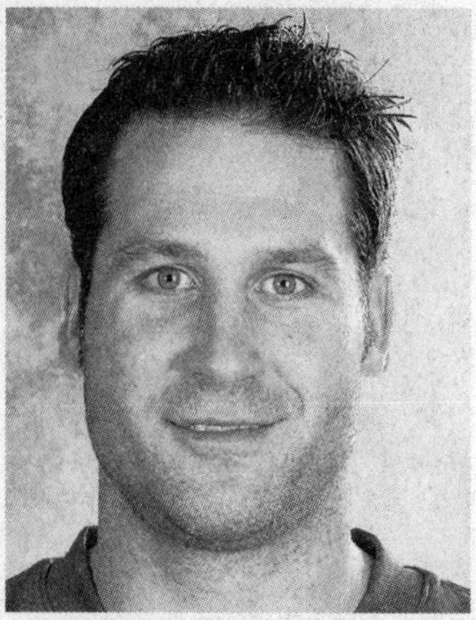

Ed Jovanovski

Name	NHL Teams	NHL Seasons	Regular Schedule GP	G	A	TP	PIM	Playoffs GP	G	A	TP	PIM	NHL Cup Wins	First NHL Season	Last NHL Season
● Ingram, John	Bos.	1	1	0	0	0	0	....	....	....	....	....	....	1924-25	1924-25
● Ingram, Ron	Chi., Det., NYR	4	114	5	15	20	81	2	0	0	0	0	....	1956-57	1964-65
Intranuovo, Ralph	Edm., Tor.	3	22	2	4	6	4	....	....	....	....	....	....	1994-95	1996-97
Irmen, Danny	Min.	1	2	0	0	0	0	....	....	....	....	....	....	2009-10	2009-10
● Irvin, Dick	Chi.	3	94	29	23	52	78	2	2	0	2	4	....	1926-27	1928-29
Irvine, Ted	Bos., L.A., NYR, St.L.	11	724	154	177	331	657	83	16	24	40	115	....	1963-64	1976-77
‡ Irwin, Brayden	Tor.	1	2	0	0	0	2	....	....	....	....	....	....	2009-10	2009-10
Irwin, Ivan	Mtl., NYR	5	155	2	27	29	214	5	0	0	0	8	....	1952-53	1957-58
● Isaksson, Ulf	L.A.	1	50	7	15	22	10	....	....	....	....	....	....	1982-83	1982-83
Isbister, Brad	Phx., NYI, Edm., Bos., NYR, Van.	10	541	106	116	222	615	18	1	2	3	33	....	1997-98	2007-08
Issel, Kim	Edm.	1	4	0	0	0	0	....	....	....	....	....	....	1988-89	1988-89
Ivanans, Raitis	Mtl., L.A., Cgy.	7	282	12	6	18	569	1	0	0	0	0	....	2005-06	2011-12

J

Name	NHL Teams	NHL Seasons	Regular Schedule GP	G	A	TP	PIM	Playoffs GP	G	A	TP	PIM	NHL Cup Wins	First NHL Season	Last NHL Season
Jacina, Greg	Fla.	2	14	0	1	1	6	....	....	....	....	....	....	2005-06	2006-07
Jackman, Ric	Dal., Bos., Tor., Pit., Fla., Ana.	7	231	19	58	77	166	7	1	1	2	2	1	1999-00	2006-07
● Jackson, Art	Tor., Bos., NYA	11	468	123	178	301	144	52	8	12	20	29	2	1934-35	1944-45
● Jackson, Busher	Tor., NYA, Bos.	15	633	241	234	475	437	71	18	12	30	53	1	1929-30	1943-44
Jackson, Dane	Van., Buf., NYI	4	45	12	6	18	58	6	0	0	0	10	....	1993-94	1997-98
Jackson, Don	Min., Edm., NYR	10	311	16	52	68	640	53	4	5	9	147	2	1977-78	1986-87
● Jackson, Harold	Chi., Det.	8	219	17	34	51	208	31	1	2	3	33	2	1936-37	1946-47
Jackson, Jack	Chi.	1	48	2	5	7	38	....	....	....	....	....	....	1946-47	1946-47
Jackson, Jeff	Tor., NYR, Que., Chi.	8	263	38	48	86	313	6	1	1	2	16	....	1984-85	1991-92
Jackson, Jim	Cgy., Buf.	4	112	17	30	47	20	14	3	2	5	6	....	1982-83	1987-88
● Jackson, Lloyd	NYA	1	14	1	1	2	0	....	....	....	....	....	....	1936-37	1936-37
Jackson, Scott	T.B.	1	1	0	0	0	0	....	....	....	....	....	....	2009-10	2009-10
● Jackson, Stan	Tor., Bos., Ott.	5	86	9	6	15	75	....	....	....	....	....	1	1921-22	1926-27
● Jackson, Walter	NYA, Bos.	4	84	16	11	27	18	....	....	....	....	....	....	1932-33	1935-36
● Jacobs, Paul	Tor.	1	1	0	0	0	0	....	....	....	....	....	....	1918-19	1918-19
Jacobs, Tim	Cal.	1	46	0	10	10	35	....	....	....	....	....	....	1975-76	1975-76
‡ Jacques, Jean-Francois	Edm., Ana.	7	166	9	8	17	197	....	....	....	....	....	....	2005-06	2011-12
‡ Jaffray, Jason	Van., Cgy., Wpg.	4	49	4	7	11	40	....	....	....	....	....	....	2007-08	2011-12
Jakopin, John	Fla., Pit., S.J.	6	113	1	6	7	145	....	....	....	....	....	....	1997-98	2002-03
Jalo, Risto	Edm.	1	3	0	3	3	0	....	....	....	....	....	....	1985-86	1985-86
Jalonen, Kari	Cgy., Edm.	2	37	9	6	15	4	5	1	0	1	0	....	1982-83	1983-84
‡ James, Connor	L.A., Pit.	3	16	1	0	1	2	....	....	....	....	....	....	2005-06	2008-09
James, Gerry	Tor.	5	149	14	26	40	257	15	1	0	1	8	....	1954-55	1959-60
James, Val	Buf., Tor.	2	11	0	0	0	30	3	0	0	0	0	....	1981-82	1986-87
● Jamieson, Jim	NYR	1	1	0	1	1	0	....	....	....	....	....	....	1943-44	1943-44
Jancevski, Dan	Dal., T.B.	3	9	0	0	0	2	....	....	....	....	....	....	2005-06	2008-09
‡ Janik, Doug	Buf., T.B., Dal., Mtl., Det.	9	190	3	16	19	154	6	1	0	1	2	....	2002-03	2011-12
● Jankowski, Lou	Det., Chi.	4	127	19	18	37	15	1	0	0	0	0	....	1950-51	1954-55
Janney, Craig	Bos., St.L., S.J., Wpg., Phx., T.B., NYI	12	760	188	563	751	170	120	24	86	110	53	....	1987-88	1998-99
Janssens, Mark	NYR, Min., Hfd., Ana., NYI, Phx., Chi.	14	711	40	73	113	1422	27	5	1	6	33	....	1987-88	2000-01
Jantunen, Marko	Cgy.	1	3	0	0	0	0	....	....	....	....	....	....	1996-97	1996-97
Jardine, Ryan	Fla.	1	8	0	2	2	2	....	....	....	....	....	....	2001-02	2001-02
Jarrett, Cole	NYI	1	1	0	0	0	0	....	....	....	....	....	....	2005-06	2005-06
● Jarrett, Doug	Chi., NYR	13	775	38	182	220	631	99	7	16	23	82	....	1964-65	1976-77
Jarrett, Gary	Tor., Det., Oak., Cal.	7	341	72	92	164	131	11	3	1	4	9	....	1960-61	1971-72
Jarry, Pierre	NYR, Tor., Det., Min.	7	344	88	117	205	142	5	0	1	1	0	....	1971-72	1977-78
Jarvenpaa, Hannu	Wpg.	3	114	11	26	37	83	....	....	....	....	....	....	1986-87	1988-89
‡ Jarventie, Martti	Mtl.	1	1	0	0	0	0	....	....	....	....	....	....	2001-02	2001-02
Jarvi, Iiro	Que.	2	116	18	43	61	58	....	....	....	....	....	....	1988-89	1989-90
Jarvis, Doug	Mtl., Wsh., Hfd.	13	964	139	264	403	263	105	14	27	41	42	4	1975-76	1987-88
● Jarvis, James	Pit., Phi., Tor.	3	112	17	15	32	62	....	....	....	....	....	....	1929-30	1936-37
Jarvis, Wes	Wsh., Min., L.A., Tor.	9	237	31	55	86	98	2	0	0	0	2	....	1979-80	1987-88
‡ Jaspers, Jason	Phx.	3	9	0	1	1	6	....	....	....	....	....	....	2001-02	2003-04
● Javanainen, Arto	Pit.	1	14	4	1	5	2	....	....	....	....	....	....	1984-85	1984-85
Jay, Bob	L.A.	1	3	0	1	1	0	....	....	....	....	....	....	1993-94	1993-94
Jeffrey, Larry	Det., Tor., NYR	8	368	39	62	101	293	38	4	10	14	42	1	1961-62	1968-69
Jelinek, Tomas	Ott.	1	49	7	6	13	52	....	....	....	....	....	....	1992-93	1992-93
Jenkins, Dean	L.A.	1	5	0	0	0	2	....	....	....	....	....	....	1983-84	1983-84
● Jenkins, Roger	Chi., Tor., Mtl., Bos., Mtl.M., NYA	8	325	15	39	54	253	27	1	7	8	12	2	1930-31	1938-39
● Jennings, Bill	Det., Bos.	5	108	32	33	65	45	20	4	4	8	6	....	1940-41	1944-45
Jennings, Grant	Wsh., Hfd., Pit., Tor., Buf.	9	389	14	43	57	804	54	2	1	3	68	2	1987-88	1995-96
Jensen, Chris	NYR, Phi.	6	74	9	12	21	27	....	....	....	....	....	....	1985-86	1991-92
Jensen, David	Min.	3	18	0	2	2	11	....	....	....	....	....	....	1983-84	1985-86
Jensen, David	Hfd., Wsh.	4	69	9	13	22	22	11	0	0	0	2	....	1984-85	1987-88
Jensen, Joe	Car.	1	6	1	0	1	2	....	....	....	....	....	....	2007-08	2007-08
Jensen, Steve	Min., L.A.	7	438	113	107	220	318	12	0	3	3	9	....	1975-76	1981-82
● Jeremiah, Ed	NYA, Bos.	1	15	0	1	1	0	....	....	....	....	....	....	1931-32	1931-32
Jerrard, Paul	Min.	1	5	0	0	0	4	....	....	....	....	....	....	1988-89	1988-89
● Jerwa, Frank	Bos., St.L.	4	81	11	16	27	53	....	....	....	....	....	....	1931-32	1934-35
● Jerwa, Joe	NYR, Bos., NYA	7	234	29	58	87	309	17	2	3	5	16	....	1930-31	1938-39
‡ Jessiman, Hugh	Fla.	1	2	0	0	0	5	....	....	....	....	....	....	2010-11	2010-11
Jillson, Jeff	S.J., Bos., Buf.	4	140	9	32	41	96	8	0	0	0	0	....	2001-02	2005-06
● Jirik, Jaroslav	St.L.	1	3	0	0	0	0	....	....	....	....	....	....	1969-70	1969-70
● Joanette, Rosario	Mtl.	1	2	0	1	1	4	....	....	....	....	....	....	1944-45	1944-45
Jodzio, Rick	Col., Cle.	1	70	2	8	10	71	....	....	....	....	....	....	1977-78	1977-78
Johannesen, Glenn	NYI	1	2	0	0	0	0	....	....	....	....	....	....	1985-86	1985-86
Johannson, John	N.J.	1	5	0	0	0	0	....	....	....	....	....	....	1983-84	1983-84
● Johansen, Bill	Tor.	1	1	0	0	0	0	....	....	....	....	....	....	1949-50	1949-50
Johansen, Trevor	Tor., Col., L.A.	5	286	11	46	57	282	13	0	3	3	21	....	1977-78	1981-82
Johansson, Andreas	NYI, Pit., Ott., T.B., Cgy., NYR, Nsh.	8	377	81	88	169	190	9	0	0	0	0	....	1995-96	2003-04
Johansson, Bjorn	Cle.	2	15	1	1	2	10	....	....	....	....	....	....	1976-77	1977-78
Johansson, Calle	Buf., Wsh., Tor.	17	1109	119	416	535	519	105	12	43	55	44	....	1987-88	2003-04
Johansson, Jonas	Wsh.	1	1	0	0	0	2	....	....	....	....	....	....	2005-06	2005-06
‡ Johansson, Magnus	Chi., Fla.	1	45	0	14	14	18	....	....	....	....	....	....	2007-08	2007-08
Johansson, Mathias	Cgy., Pit.	1	58	5	10	15	16	....	....	....	....	....	....	2002-03	2002-03
Johansson, Roger	Cgy., Chi.	4	161	9	34	43	163	5	0	1	1	2	....	1989-90	1994-95
Johns, Don	NYR, Mtl., Min.	6	153	2	21	23	76	....	....	....	....	....	....	1960-61	1967-68
Johnson, Allan	Mtl., Det.	4	105	21	28	49	30	11	2	2	4	6	....	1956-57	1962-63
Johnson, Brian	Det.	1	3	0	0	0	5	....	....	....	....	....	....	1983-84	1983-84
● Johnson, Ching	NYR, NYA	12	436	38	48	86	808	61	5	2	7	161	2	1926-27	1937-38
Johnson, Craig	St.L., L.A., Ana., Tor., Wsh.	10	557	75	98	173	260	16	3	2	5	10	....	1994-95	2003-04
● Johnson, Danny	Tor., Van., Det.	3	121	18	19	37	24	....	....	....	....	....	....	1969-70	1971-72
● Johnson, Earl	Det.	1	1	0	0	0	0	....	....	....	....	....	1	1953-54	1953-54
Johnson, Greg	Det., Pit., Chi., Nsh.	12	785	145	224	369	345	37	7	6	13	14	....	1993-94	2005-06
Johnson, Jim	NYR, Phi., L.A.	8	302	75	111	186	73	7	0	2	2	2	....	1964-65	1971-72
Johnson, Jim	Pit., Min., Dal., Wsh., Phx.	13	829	29	166	195	1197	51	1	11	12	132	....	1985-86	1997-98
Johnson, Mark	Pit., Min., Hfd., St.L., N.J.	11	669	203	305	508	260	37	16	12	28	10	....	1979-80	1989-90
Johnson, Matt	L.A., Atl., Min.	10	473	23	20	43	1523	16	0	0	0	31	....	1994-95	2003-04
Johnson, Mike	Tor., T.B., Phx., Mtl., St.L.	11	661	129	246	375	315	22	4	3	7	10	....	1996-97	2007-08
‡ Johnson, Nick	Pit., Min., Phx., Bos.	5	113	14	23	37	52	....	....	....	....	....	....	2009-10	2013-14
Johnson, Norm	Bos., Chi.	3	61	5	20	25	41	14	4	0	4	6	....	1957-58	1959-60
Johnson, Ryan	Fla., T.B., St.L., Van., Chi.	13	701	38	84	122	250	29	1	4	5	12	....	1997-98	2010-11
Johnson, Terry	Que., St.L., Cgy., Tor.	9	285	3	24	27	580	38	0	4	4	118	....	1979-80	1987-88
● Johnson, Tom	Mtl., Bos.	17	978	51	213	264	960	111	8	15	23	109	6	1947-48	1964-65
● Johnson, Virgil	Chi.	3	75	1	11	12	27	19	0	3	3	4	1	1937-38	1944-45
Johnsson, Kim	NYR, Phi., Min., Chi.	10	739	67	217	284	406	43	2	10	12	38	....	1999-00	2009-10
Johnston, Bernie	Hfd.	2	57	12	24	36	16	3	0	1	1	0	....	1979-80	1980-81
● Johnston, George	Chi.	4	58	20	12	32	2	....	....	....	....	....	....	1941-42	1946-47
Johnston, Greg	Bos., Tor.	9	187	26	29	55	124	22	2	1	3	12	....	1983-84	1991-92
Johnston, Jay	Wsh.	2	8	0	0	0	13	....	....	....	....	....	....	1980-81	1981-82
Johnston, Joey	Min., Cal., Chi.	6	331	85	106	191	320	....	....	....	....	....	....	1968-69	1975-76
Johnston, Larry	L.A., Det., K.C., Col.	7	320	9	64	73	580	....	....	....	....	....	....	1967-68	1976-77
Johnston, Marshall	Min., Cal.	7	251	14	52	66	58	6	0	0	0	2	....	1967-68	1973-74
Johnston, Randy	NYI	1	4	0	0	0	4	....	....	....	....	....	....	1979-80	1979-80
Johnstone, Eddie	NYR, Det.	10	426	122	136	258	375	55	13	10	23	83	....	1975-76	1986-87
● Johnstone, Ross	Tor.	2	42	5	4	9	14	3	0	0	0	0	1	1943-44	1944-45
‡ Jokela, Mikko	Van.	1	1	0	0	0	0	....	....	....	....	....	....	2002-03	2002-03
● Joliat, Aurele	Mtl.	16	655	270	190	460	771	45	9	13	22	66	3	1922-23	1937-38
● Joliat, Rene	Mtl.	1	1	0	0	0	0	....	....	....	....	....	....	1924-25	1924-25
Joly, Greg	Wsh., Det.	9	365	21	76	97	250	5	0	0	0	8	....	1974-75	1982-83
Joly, Yvan	Mtl.	3	2	0	0	0	0	1	0	0	0	0	....	1979-80	1982-83

Name	NHL Teams	NHL Seasons	Regular Schedule GP	G	A	TP	PIM	Playoffs GP	G	A	TP	PIM	NHL Cup Wins	First NHL Season	Last NHL Season
Jomphe, Jean-Francois	Ana., Phx., Mtl.	4	111	10	29	39	102	....	....	....	....	....	....	1995-96	1998-99
Jonathan, Stan	Bos., Pit.	8	411	91	110	201	751	63	8	4	12	137	....	1975-76	1982-83
Jones, Bob	NYR	1	2	0	0	0	0	....	....	....	....	....	....	1968-69	1968-69
Jones, Brad	Wpg., L.A., Phi.	6	148	25	31	56	122	9	1	1	2	2	....	1986-87	1991-92
• Jones, Buck	Det., Tor.	4	50	2	2	4	36	12	0	1	1	18	....	1938-39	1942-43
Jones, Jim	Cal.	1	2	0	0	0	0	....	....	....	....	....	....	1971-72	1971-72
Jones, Jimmy	Tor.	3	148	13	18	31	68	19	1	5	6	11	....	1977-78	1979-80
Jones, Keith	Wsh., Col., Phi.	9	491	117	141	258	765	63	12	12	24	120	....	1992-93	2000-01
Jones, Matt	Phx.	3	106	1	10	11	63	....	....	....	....	....	....	2005-06	2007-08
‡ Jones, Randy	Phi., L.A., T.B., Wpg.	8	365	20	85	105	185	31	0	4	4	8	....	2003-04	2011-12
Jones, Ron	Bos., Pit., Wsh.	5	54	1	4	5	31	....	....	....	....	....	....	1971-72	1975-76
Jones, Ty	Chi., Fla.	2	14	0	0	0	19	....	....	....	....	....	....	1998-99	2003-04
Jonsson, Hans	Pit.	4	242	10	38	48	92	27	0	1	1	14	....	1999-00	2002-03
Jonsson, Jorgen	NYI, Ana.	1	81	12	19	31	16	....	....	....	....	....	....	1999-00	1999-00
Jonsson, Kenny	Tor., NYI	10	686	63	204	267	298	19	1	3	4	6	....	1994-95	2003-04
Jonsson, Lars	Phi.	1	8	0	2	2	6	....	....	....	....	....	....	2006-07	2006-07
Jonsson, Tomas	NYI, Edm.	8	552	85	259	344	482	80	11	26	37	97	2	1981-82	1988-89
Joseph, Chris	Pit., Edm., T.B., Van., Phi., Phx., Atl.	14	510	39	112	151	567	31	3	4	7	24	....	1987-88	2000-01
Joseph, Tony	Wpg.	1	2	1	0	1	0	....	....	....	....	....	....	1988-89	1988-89
‡ Joslin, Derek	S.J., Car., Van.	5	116	4	12	16	63	....	....	....	....	....	....	2008-09	2012-13
‡ Jovanovski, Ed	Fla., Van., Phx.	18	1128	137	363	500	1491	76	11	19	30	102	....	1995-96	2013-14
Joyal, Eddie	Det., Tor., L.A., Phi.	9	466	128	134	262	103	50	11	8	19	18	....	1962-63	1971-72
Joyce, Bob	Bos., Wsh., Wpg.	6	158	34	49	83	90	46	15	9	24	29	....	1987-88	1992-93
Joyce, Duane	Dal.	1	3	0	0	0	0	....	....	....	....	....	....	1993-94	1993-94
• Juckes, Bing	NYR	2	16	2	1	3	6	....	....	....	....	....	....	1947-48	1949-50
Juhlin, Patrik	Phi.	2	56	7	6	13	23	13	1	0	1	2	....	1994-95	1995-96
Julien, Claude	Que.	2	14	0	1	1	25	....	....	....	....	....	....	1984-85	1985-86
Juneau, Joe	Bos., Wsh., Buf., Ott., Phx., Mtl.	13	828	156	416	572	272	112	25	54	79	69	....	1991-92	2003-04
Junker, Steve	NYI	2	5	0	0	0	0	3	0	1	1	0	....	1992-93	1993-94
‡ Jurcina, Milan	Bos., Wsh., CBJ, NYI	7	430	22	59	81	280	21	2	0	2	18	....	2005-06	2011-12
Jutila, Timo	Buf.	1	10	1	5	6	13	....	....	....	....	....	....	1984-85	1984-85
• Juzda, Bill	NYR, Tor.	9	398	14	54	68	398	42	0	3	3	46	2	1940-41	1951-52

K

Name	NHL Teams	NHL Seasons	Regular Schedule GP	G	A	TP	PIM	Playoffs GP	G	A	TP	PIM	NHL Cup Wins	First NHL Season	Last NHL Season
Kabel, Bob	NYR	2	48	5	13	18	34	....	....	....	....	....	....	1959-60	1960-61
Kaberle, Frantisek	L.A., Atl., Car.	9	523	29	164	193	218	32	4	10	14	10	1	1999-00	2008-09
‡ Kaberle, Tomas	Tor., Bos., Car., Mtl.	14	984	87	476	563	260	102	6	33	39	28	1	1998-99	2012-13
Kachowski, Mark	Pit.	3	64	6	5	11	209	....	....	....	....	....	....	1987-88	1989-90
• Kachur, Ed	Chi.	2	96	10	14	24	35	....	....	....	....	....	....	1956-57	1957-58
Kaese, Trent	Buf.	1	1	0	0	0	0	....	....	....	....	....	....	1988-89	1988-89
‡ Kaigorodov, Alexei	Ott.	1	6	0	1	1	0	....	....	....	....	....	....	2006-07	2006-07
• Kaiser, Vern	Mtl.	1	50	7	5	12	33	2	0	0	0	0	....	1950-51	1950-51
• Kalbfleisch, Walter	Ott., St.L., NYA, Bos.	4	36	0	4	4	32	5	0	0	0	2	....	1933-34	1936-37
• Kaleta, Alex	Chi., NYR	7	387	92	121	213	190	17	1	6	7	2	....	1941-42	1950-51
‡ Kalinin, Dmitri	Buf., NYR, Phx.	9	539	36	126	162	321	37	2	7	9	20	....	1999-00	2008-09
Kalinski, Jon	Phi.	2	22	1	4	5	0	....	....	....	....	....	....	2008-09	2009-10
‡ Kallio, Tomi	Atl., CBJ, Phi.	3	140	24	31	55	48	....	....	....	....	....	....	2000-01	2002-03
Kallur, Anders	NYI	6	383	101	110	211	149	78	12	23	35	32	4	1979-80	1984-85
Kalus, Petr	Bos., Min.	2	11	4	1	5	6	....	....	....	....	....	....	2006-07	2009-10
Kamensky, Valeri	Que., Col., NYR, Dal., N.J.	11	637	200	301	501	383	66	25	35	60	72	1	1991-92	2001-02
Kaminski, Kevin	Min., Que., Wsh.	7	139	3	10	13	528	8	0	0	0	52	....	1988-89	1996-97
• Kaminsky, Max	Ott., St.L., Bos., Mtl.M.	4	130	22	34	56	38	4	0	0	0	0	....	1933-34	1936-37
Kaminsky, Yan	Wpg., NYI	2	26	3	2	5	4	2	0	0	0	4	....	1993-94	1994-95
• Kampman, Bingo	Tor.	5	189	14	30	44	287	47	1	4	5	38	1	1937-38	1941-42
‡ Kana, Tomas	CBJ	1	6	0	2	2	2	....	....	....	....	....	....	2009-10	2009-10
‡ Kane, Boyd	Phi., Wsh.	5	31	0	3	3	39	....	....	....	....	....	....	2003-04	2009-10
Kane, Francis	Det.	1	2	0	0	0	0	....	....	....	....	....	....	1943-44	1943-44
Kanko, Petr	L.A.	1	10	1	0	1	0	....	....	....	....	....	....	2005-06	2005-06
Kannegiesser, Gord	St.L.	2	23	0	1	1	15	....	....	....	....	....	....	1967-68	1971-72
Kannegiesser, Sheldon	Pit., NYR, L.A., Van.	8	366	14	67	81	292	18	0	2	2	10	....	1970-71	1977-78
‡ Kapanen, Niko	Dal., Atl., Phx.	6	397	36	90	126	160	18	5	4	9	22	....	2001-02	2007-08
Kapanen, Sami	Hfd., Car., Phi.	12	831	189	269	458	175	87	13	22	35	22	....	1995-96	2007-08
Karabin, Ladislav	Pit.	1	9	0	0	0	2	....	....	....	....	....	....	1993-94	1993-94
‡ Karalahti, Jere	L.A., Nsh.	3	149	8	19	27	97	17	0	1	1	20	....	1999-00	2001-02
Karamnov, Vitali	St.L.	3	92	12	20	32	65	2	0	0	0	2	....	1992-93	1994-95
Kariya, Paul	Ana., Col., Nsh., St.L.	15	989	402	587	989	399	46	16	23	39	12	....	1994-95	2009-10
Kariya, Steve	Van.	3	65	9	18	27	32	....	....	....	....	....	....	1999-00	2001-02
Karjalainen, Kyosti	L.A.	1	28	1	8	9	12	3	0	1	1	2	....	1991-92	1991-92
Karlander, Al	Det.	4	212	36	56	92	70	4	0	1	1	0	....	1969-70	1972-73
Karlsson, Andreas	Atl., T.B.	5	264	16	35	51	72	6	0	0	0	0	....	1999-00	2007-08
Karpa, Dave	Que., Ana., Car., NYR	12	557	18	80	98	1374	19	1	1	2	39	....	1991-92	2002-03
• Karpov, Valeri	Ana.	3	76	14	15	29	32	....	....	....	....	....	....	1994-95	1996-97
• Karpovtsev, Alexander	NYR, Tor., Chi., NYI, Fla.	12	596	34	154	188	430	74	4	14	18	52	1	1993-94	2005-06
‡ Karsums, Martins	Bos., T.B.	1	24	1	5	6	6	....	....	....	....	....	....	2008-09	2008-09
Kasatonov, Alexei	N.J., Ana., St.L., Bos.	7	383	38	122	160	326	33	4	7	11	40	....	1989-90	1995-96
‡ Kaspar, Lukas	S.J.	2	16	2	2	4	8	....	....	....	....	....	....	2007-08	2008-09
Kasparaitis, Darius	NYI, Pit., Col., NYR	14	863	27	136	163	1379	83	2	10	12	107	....	1992-93	2006-07
Kasper, Steve	Bos., L.A., Phi., T.B.	13	821	177	291	468	554	94	20	28	48	82	....	1980-81	1992-93
Kastelic, Ed	Wsh., Hfd.	7	220	11	10	21	719	8	1	0	1	32	....	1985-86	1991-92
Kaszycki, Mike	NYI, Wsh., Tor.	5	226	42	80	122	108	19	2	6	8	10	....	1977-78	1982-83
‡ Katic, Mark	NYI	1	11	0	1	1	4	....	....	....	....	....	....	2010-11	2010-11
Kavanagh, Pat	Van., Phi.	4	14	2	0	2	4	3	0	0	0	2	....	2000-01	2005-06
• Kea, Ed	Atl., St.L.	10	583	30	145	175	508	32	2	4	6	39	....	1973-74	1982-83
Keane, Mike	Mtl., Col., NYR, Dal., St.L., Van.	16	1161	168	302	470	881	220	34	40	74	135	3	1988-89	2003-04
Kearns, Dennis	Van.	10	677	31	290	321	386	11	1	2	3	8	....	1971-72	1980-81
• Keating, Jack	Det.	2	11	3	0	3	4	....	....	....	....	....	....	1938-39	1939-40
• Keating, John	NYA	2	35	5	5	10	17	....	....	....	....	....	....	1931-32	1932-33
Keating, Mike	NYR	1	1	0	0	0	0	....	....	....	....	....	....	1977-78	1977-78
• Keats, Duke	Bos., Det., Chi.	3	82	30	19	49	113	....	....	....	....	....	....	1926-27	1928-29
Keczmer, Dan	Min., Hfd., Cgy., Dal., Nsh.	10	235	8	38	46	212	12	0	1	1	8	....	1990-91	1999-00
Keefe, Sheldon	T.B.	3	125	12	12	24	78	....	....	....	....	....	....	2000-01	2002-03
• Keeling, Butch	Tor., NYR	12	525	157	63	220	331	47	11	11	22	34	1	1926-27	1937-38
Keenan, Larry	Tor., St.L., Buf., Phi.	6	233	38	64	102	28	46	15	16	31	12	....	1961-62	1971-72
Kehoe, Rick	Tor., Pit.	14	906	371	396	767	120	39	4	17	21	4	....	1971-72	1984-85
Keith, Matt	Chi., NYI	4	27	2	3	5	14	....	....	....	....	....	....	2003-04	2007-08
Kekalainen, Jarmo	Bos., Ott.	3	55	5	8	13	28	....	....	....	....	....	....	1989-90	1993-94
Kelleher, Chris	Bos.	1	1	0	0	0	0	....	....	....	....	....	....	2001-02	2001-02
Keller, Ralph	NYR	1	3	1	0	1	6	....	....	....	....	....	....	1962-63	1962-63
‡ Keller, Ryan	Ott.	1	6	0	0	0	0	....	....	....	....	....	....	2009-10	2009-10
Kellgren, Christer	Col.	1	5	0	0	0	0	....	....	....	....	....	....	1981-82	1981-82
Kelly, Bob	Phi., Wsh.	12	837	154	208	362	1454	101	9	14	23	172	2	1970-71	1981-82
Kelly, Bob	St.L., Pit., Chi.	6	425	87	109	196	687	23	6	3	9	40	....	1973-74	1978-79
Kelly, Dave	Det.	1	16	2	0	2	4	....	....	....	....	....	....	1976-77	1976-77
Kelly, John Paul	L.A.	7	400	54	70	124	366	18	1	1	2	41	....	1979-80	1985-86
• Kelly, Pep	Tor., Chi., Bro.	8	288	74	53	127	105	38	7	6	13	10	....	1934-35	1941-42
• Kelly, Pete	St.L., Det., NYA, Bro.	7	177	21	38	59	68	19	3	1	4	2	2	1934-35	1941-42
Kelly, Red	Det., Tor.	20	1316	281	542	823	327	164	33	59	92	51	8	1947-48	1966-67
Kelly, Steve	Edm., T.B., N.J., L.A., Min.	9	149	9	12	21	83	25	0	0	0	8	1	1996-97	2007-08
• Kemp, Kevin	Hfd.	1	3	0	0	0	4	....	....	....	....	....	....	1980-81	1980-81
• Kemp, Stan	Tor.	1	1	0	0	0	2	....	....	....	....	....	....	1948-49	1948-49
Kenady, Chris	St.L., NYR	2	7	0	2	2	0	....	....	....	....	....	....	1997-98	1999-00
• Kendall, Bill	Chi., Tor.	5	131	16	10	26	28	6	0	0	0	0	1	1933-34	1937-38
Kennedy, Dean	L.A., NYR, Buf., Wpg., Edm.	12	717	26	110	136	1118	36	1	7	8	59	....	1982-83	1994-95
Kennedy, Forbes	Chi., Det., Bos., Phi., Tor.	11	603	70	108	178	988	12	2	4	6	64	....	1956-57	1968-69
Kennedy, Mike	Dal., Tor., NYI	5	145	16	36	52	112	5	0	0	0	9	....	1994-95	1998-99
Kennedy, Sheldon	Det., Cgy., Bos.	8	310	49	58	107	233	24	6	4	10	20	....	1989-90	1996-97
• Kennedy, Ted	Tor.	14	696	231	329	560	432	78	29	31	60	32	5	1942-43	1956-57
• Kenny, Ernest	NYR, Chi.	2	10	0	0	0	18	....	....	....	....	....	....	1930-31	1934-35
Keon, Dave	Tor., Hfd.	18	1296	396	590	986	117	92	32	36	68	6	4	1960-61	1981-82
Kerch, Alexander	Edm.	1	5	0	0	0	2	....	....	....	....	....	....	1993-94	1993-94
Kerr, Alan	NYI, Det., Wpg.	9	391	72	94	166	826	38	5	4	9	70	....	1984-85	1992-93
Kerr, Reg	Cle., Chi., Edm.	6	263	66	94	160	169	7	1	0	1	7	....	1977-78	1983-84
Kerr, Tim	Phi., NYR, Hfd.	13	655	370	304	674	596	81	40	31	71	58	....	1980-81	1992-93
Kesa, Dan	Van., Dal., Pit., T.B.	4	139	8	22	30	66	13	1	0	1	0	....	1993-94	1999-00
Kessell, Rick	Pit., Cal.	5	135	4	24	28	6	....	....	....	....	....	....	1969-70	1973-74

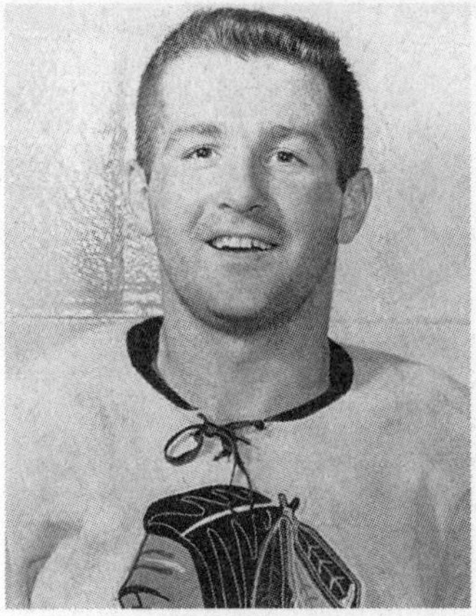
Ed Kachur

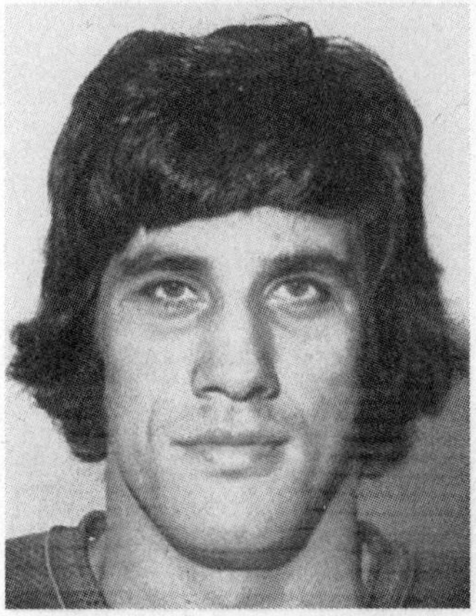
Veli-Pekka Ketola

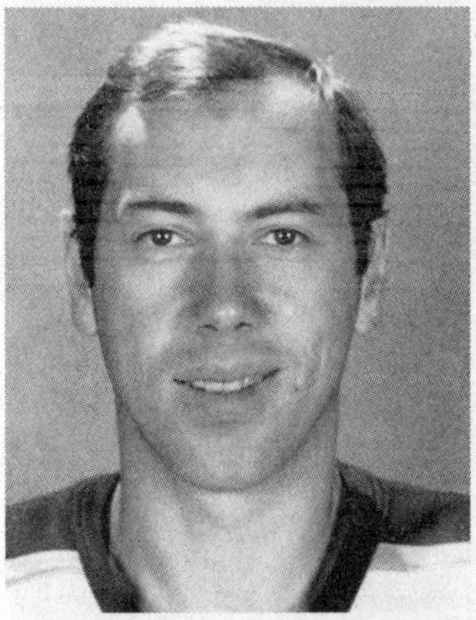
Yuri Khmylev

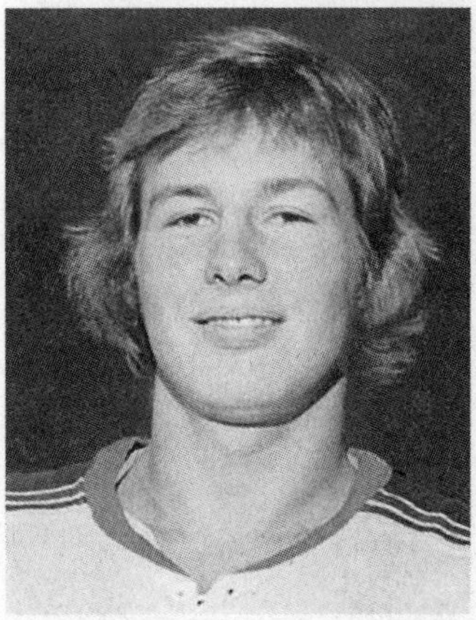
Mike Kitchen

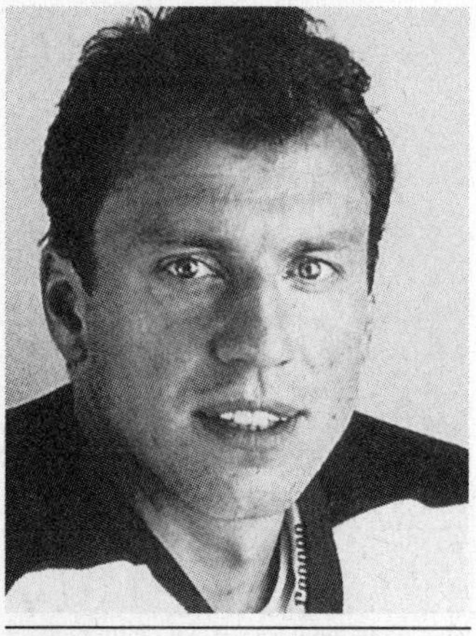

Petr Klima

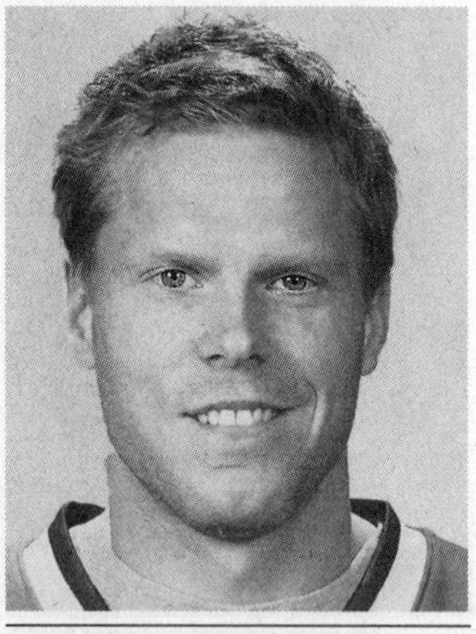

Saku Koivu

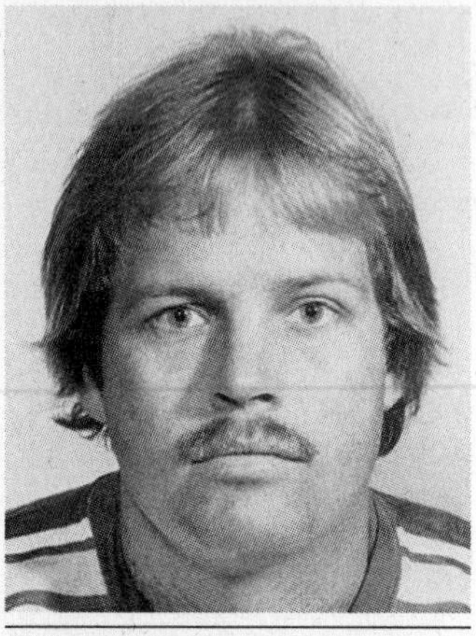

Neil Komadoski

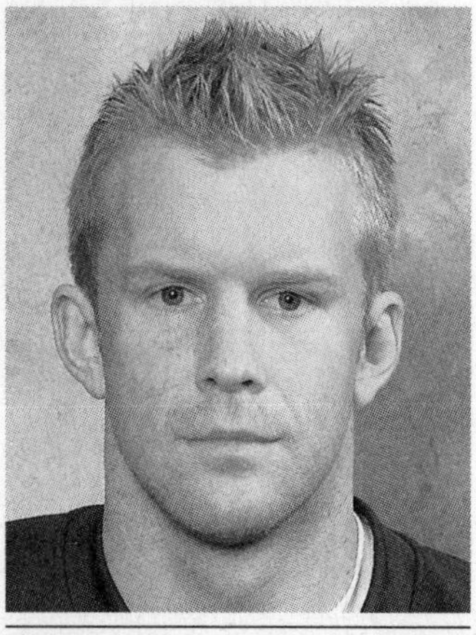

Mike Komisarek

			Regular Schedule					Playoffs					NHL	First	Last
Name	NHL Teams	NHL Seasons	GP	G	A	TP	PIM	GP	G	A	TP	PIM	Cup Wins	NHL Season	NHL Season
Ketola, Veli-Pekka	Col.	1	44	9	5	14	4	....	....	....	....	....	....	1981-82	1981-82
Ketter, Kerry	Atl.	1	41	0	2	2	58	....	....	....	....	....	....	1972-73	1972-73
Kharin, Sergei	Wpg.	1	7	2	3	5	2	....	....	....	....	....	....	1990-91	1990-91
Kharitonov, Alexander	T.B., NYI	2	71	7	15	22	12	....	....	....	....	....	....	2000-01	2001-02
Khavanov, Alexander	St.L., Tor.	5	348	27	75	102	233	26	5	5	10	18	....	2000-01	2005-06
Khmylev, Yuri	Buf., St.L.	5	263	64	88	152	133	26	8	6	14	24	....	1992-93	1996-97
Khristich, Dmitri	Wsh., L.A., Bos., Tor.	12	811	259	337	596	422	75	15	25	40	41	....	1990-91	2001-02
Kidd, Ian	Van.	2	20	4	7	11	25	....	....	....	....	....	....	1987-88	1988-89
Kiessling, Udo	Min.	1	1	0	0	0	2	....	....	....	....	....	....	1981-82	1981-82
Kilger, Chad	Ana., Wpg., Phx., Chi., Edm., Mtl., Tor.	12	714	107	111	218	363	36	3	2	5	13	....	1995-96	2007-08
Kilrea, Brian	Det., L.A.	2	26	3	5	8	12	....	....	....	....	....	....	1957-58	1967-68
• Kilrea, Hec	Ott., Det., Tor.	15	633	167	129	296	438	48	8	7	15	18	3	1925-26	1939-40
• Kilrea, Ken	Det.	5	91	16	23	39	8	15	2	2	4	4	....	1938-39	1943-44
• Kilrea, Wally	Ott., Phi., NYA, Mtl.M., Det.	9	329	35	58	93	87	25	2	4	6	6	2	1929-30	1937-38
Kimble, Darin	Que., St.L., Bos., Chi.	7	311	23	20	43	1082	23	0	0	0	52	....	1988-89	1994-95
Kindrachuk, Orest	Phi., Pit., Wsh.	10	508	118	261	379	648	76	20	20	40	53	2	1972-73	1981-82
King, D.J.	St.L., Wsh.	6	118	4	7	11	215	....	....	....	....	....	....	2006-07	2011-12
King, Derek	NYI, Hfd., Tor., St.L.	14	830	261	351	612	417	47	4	17	21	24	....	1986-87	1999-00
King, Frank	Mtl.	1	10	1	0	1	2	....	....	....	....	....	....	1950-51	1950-51
King, Jason	Van., Ana.	3	59	12	11	23	8	1	0	0	0	0	....	2002-03	2007-08
King, Kris	Det., NYR, Wpg., Phx., Tor., Chi.	14	849	66	85	151	2030	67	8	5	13	142	....	1987-88	2000-01
King, Steven	NYR, Ana.	3	67	17	8	25	75	....	....	....	....	....	....	1992-93	1995-96
King, Wayne	Cal.	3	73	5	18	23	34	....	....	....	....	....	....	1973-74	1975-76
Kinnear, Geordie	Atl.	1	4	0	0	0	13	....	....	....	....	....	....	1999-00	1999-00
‡ Kinrade, Geoff	T.B.	1	1	0	0	0	0	....	....	....	....	....	....	2008-09	2008-09
Kinsella, Brian	Wsh.	2	10	0	1	1	0	....	....	....	....	....	....	1975-76	1976-77
• Kinsella, Ray	Ott.	1	14	0	0	0	0	....	....	....	....	....	....	1930-31	1930-31
Kiprusoff, Marko	Mtl., NYI	2	51	0	10	10	12	....	....	....	....	....	....	1995-96	2001-02
• Kirk, Bobby	NYR	1	39	4	8	12	14	....	....	....	....	....	....	1937-38	1937-38
• Kirkpatrick, Bob	NYR	1	49	12	12	24	6	....	....	....	....	....	....	1942-43	1942-43
Kirton, Mark	Tor., Det., Van.	6	266	57	56	113	121	4	1	2	3	7	....	1979-80	1984-85
Kisio, Kelly	Det., NYR, S.J., Cgy.	13	761	229	429	658	768	39	6	15	21	52	....	1982-83	1994-95
• Kitchen, Bill	Mtl., Tor.	4	41	1	4	5	40	3	0	1	1	0	....	1981-82	1984-85
• Kitchen, Hobie	Mtl.M., Det.	2	47	5	4	9	58	....	....	....	....	....	1	1925-26	1926-27
Kitchen, Mike	Col., N.J.	8	474	12	62	74	370	2	0	0	0	2	....	1976-77	1983-84
Kjellberg, Patric	Mtl., Nsh., Ana.	6	394	64	96	160	84	10	0	0	0	0	....	1992-93	2002-03
‡ Klasen, Linus	Nsh.	1	4	0	0	0	0	....	....	....	....	....	....	2010-11	2010-11
Klassen, Ralph	Cal., Cle., Col., St.L.	9	497	52	93	145	120	26	4	2	6	12	....	1975-76	1983-84
Klatt, Trent	Min., Dal., Phi., Van., L.A.	13	782	143	200	343	307	74	16	9	25	20	....	1991-92	2003-04
Klee, Ken	Wsh., Tor., N.J., Col., Atl., Ana., Phx.	14	934	55	140	195	880	51	2	2	4	50	....	1994-95	2008-09
• Klein, Lloyd	Bos., NYA	8	164	30	24	54	68	5	0	0	0	2	1	1928-29	1937-38
Kleinendorst, Scot	NYR, Hfd., Wsh.	8	281	12	46	58	452	26	2	7	9	40	....	1982-83	1989-90
Klementyev, Anton	NYI	1	1	0	0	0	0	....	....	....	....	....	....	2009-10	2009-10
Klemm, Jon	Que., Col., Chi., Dal., L.A.	15	773	42	100	142	436	105	7	7	14	47	2	1991-92	2007-08
‡ Klepis, Jakub	Wsh.	2	66	4	10	14	36	....	....	....	....	....	....	2005-06	2006-07
‡ Klesla, Rostislav	CBJ, Phx.	13	659	48	111	159	620	23	2	7	9	11	....	2000-01	2013-14
Klima, Petr	Det., Edm., T.B., L.A., Pit.	13	786	313	260	573	671	95	28	24	52	83	1	1985-86	1998-99
Klimovich, Sergei	Chi.	1	1	0	0	0	2	....	....	....	....	....	....	1996-97	1996-97
• Klingbeil, Ike	Chi.	1	5	1	2	3	2	....	....	....	....	....	....	1936-37	1936-37
‡ Kloucek, Tomas	NYR, Nsh., Atl.	5	141	2	8	10	250	....	....	....	....	....	....	2000-01	2005-06
• Klukay, Joe	Tor., Bos.	11	566	109	127	236	189	71	13	10	23	23	4	1942-43	1955-56
Kluzak, Gord	Bos.	7	299	25	98	123	543	46	6	13	19	129	....	1982-83	1990-91
• Knibbs, Bill	Bos.	1	53	7	10	17	4	....	....	....	....	....	....	1964-65	1964-65
Knipscheer, Fred	Bos., St.L.	3	28	6	3	9	18	16	2	1	3	6	....	1993-94	1995-96
• Knott, Nick	Bro.	1	14	3	1	4	9	....	....	....	....	....	....	1941-42	1941-42
Knox, Paul	Tor.	1	1	0	0	0	0	....	....	....	....	....	....	1954-55	1954-55
Knuble, Mike	Det., NYR, Bos., Phi., Wsh.	16	1068	278	270	548	641	65	14	16	30	38	1	1996-97	2012-13
Knutsen, Espen	Ana., CBJ	5	207	30	81	111	105	....	....	....	....	....	....	1997-98	2003-04
Koalska, Matt	NYI	1	3	0	0	0	2	....	....	....	....	....	....	2005-06	2005-06
‡ Kobasew, Chuck	Cgy., Bos., Min., Col., Pit.	11	601	110	100	210	394	44	4	4	8	38	....	2002-03	2013-14
‡ Koci, David	Chi., T.B., St.L., Col.	5	142	3	1	4	461	....	....	....	....	....	....	2006-07	2010-11
Kocur, Joe	Det., NYR, Van.	15	820	80	82	162	2519	118	10	12	22	231	3	1984-85	1998-99
Koehler, Greg	Car.	1	1	0	0	0	0	....	....	....	....	....	....	2000-01	2000-01
‡ Kohn, Dustin	NYI	1	22	0	4	4	4	....	....	....	....	....	....	2009-10	2009-10
Kohn, Ladislav	Cgy., Tor., Ana., Atl., Det.	7	186	14	28	42	125	2	0	0	0	5	....	1995-96	2002-03
‡ Koistinen, Ville	Nsh., Fla.	3	103	8	24	32	40	....	....	....	....	....	....	2007-08	2009-10
Koivisto, Tom	St.L.	1	22	2	4	6	10	....	....	....	....	....	....	2002-03	2002-03
‡ Koivu, Saku	Mtl., Ana.	18	1124	255	577	832	809	80	18	41	59	62	....	1995-96	2013-14
Kolanos, Krys	Phx., Edm., Min., Cgy.	6	149	20	22	42	94	2	0	0	0	6	....	2001-02	2011-12
‡ Kolarik, Chad	CBJ, NYR	2	6	0	1	1	2	....	....	....	....	....	....	2009-10	2010-11
‡ Kolarik, Pavel	Bos.	2	23	0	0	0	10	....	....	....	....	....	....	2000-01	2001-02
Kolesar, Mark	Tor.	2	28	2	2	4	14	3	1	0	1	2	....	1995-96	1996-97
Kolnik, Juraj	NYI, Fla.	6	240	46	49	95	84	....	....	....	....	....	....	2000-01	2006-07
Kolstad, Dean	Min., S.J.	3	40	1	7	8	69	....	....	....	....	....	....	1988-89	1992-93
‡ Koltsov, Konstantin	Pit.	3	144	12	26	38	50	....	....	....	....	....	....	2002-03	2005-06
Komadoski, Neil	L.A., St.L.	8	502	16	76	92	632	23	0	2	2	47	....	1972-73	1979-80
Komarniski, Zenith	Van., CBJ	3	21	1	1	2	10	....	....	....	....	....	....	1999-00	2003-04
‡ Komisarek, Mike	Mtl., Tor., Car.	11	551	14	67	81	679	29	1	2	3	56	....	2002-03	2013-14
‡ Konan, Matthew	Phi.	1	2	0	0	0	0	....	....	....	....	....	....	2012-13	2012-13
Kondratiev, Maxim	Tor., NYR, Ana.	3	40	1	2	3	24	....	....	....	....	....	....	2003-04	2007-08
Konik, George	Pit.	1	52	7	8	15	26	....	....	....	....	....	....	1967-68	1967-68
‡ Konopka, Zenon	Ana., CBJ, T.B., NYI, Ott., Min., Buf.	9	346	12	18	30	1082	8	0	2	2	2	....	2005-06	2013-14
Konowalchuk, Steve	Wsh., Col.	14	790	171	225	396	703	52	9	12	21	60	....	1991-92	2005-06
Konroyd, Steve	Cgy., NYI, Chi., Hfd., Det., Ott.	15	895	41	195	236	863	97	10	15	25	99	....	1980-81	1994-95
Konstantinov, Vladimir	Det.	6	446	47	128	175	838	82	5	14	19	107	1	1991-92	1996-97
‡ Kontiola, Petri	Chi.	1	12	0	5	5	6	....	....	....	....	....	....	2007-08	2007-08
Kontos, Chris	NYR, Pit., L.A., T.B.	8	230	54	69	123	103	20	11	0	11	12	....	1982-83	1992-93
• Kopak, Russ	Bos.	1	24	7	9	16	0	....	....	....	....	....	....	1943-44	1943-44
Korab, Jerry	Chi., Van., Buf., L.A.	15	975	114	341	455	1629	93	8	18	26	201	....	1970-71	1984-85
Kordic, Dan	Phi.	6	197	4	8	12	584	12	1	0	1	22	....	1991-92	1998-99
• Kordic, John	Mtl., Tor., Wsh., Que.	7	244	17	18	35	997	41	4	3	7	131	1	1985-86	1991-92
Korn, Jim	Det., Tor., Buf., N.J., Cgy.	10	597	66	122	188	1801	16	1	2	3	109	....	1979-80	1989-90
Korney, Mike	Det., NYR	4	77	9	10	19	59	....	....	....	....	....	....	1973-74	1978-79
‡ Korobov, Dmitry	T.B.	1	3	0	1	1	2	....	....	....	....	....	....	2013-14	2013-14
Korolev, Evgeny	NYI	3	42	1	4	5	20	2	0	0	0	0	....	1999-00	2001-02
• Korolev, Igor	St.L., Wpg., Phx., Tor., Chi.	12	795	119	227	346	330	41	0	8	8	6	....	1992-93	2003-04
Koroll, Cliff	Chi.	11	814	208	254	462	376	85	19	29	48	67	....	1969-70	1979-80
‡ Korolyuk, Alexander	S.J.	6	296	62	80	142	140	34	6	8	14	18	....	1997-98	2003-04
Kortko, Roger	NYI	2	79	7	17	24	28	10	0	3	3	17	....	1984-85	1985-86
‡ Kostitsyn, Andrei	Mtl., Nsh.	7	398	103	119	222	181	49	14	9	23	24	....	2005-06	2011-12
‡ Kostitsyn, Sergei	Mtl., Nsh.	6	353	67	109	176	188	40	4	11	15	22	....	2007-08	2012-13
Kostynski, Doug	Bos.	2	15	3	1	4	4	....	....	....	....	....	....	1983-84	1984-85
Kotalik, Ales	Buf., Edm., NYR, Cgy.	9	542	136	148	284	348	34	6	9	15	16	....	2001-02	2010-11
• Kotanen, Dick	NYR	1	1	0	0	0	0	....	....	....	....	....	....	1950-51	1950-51
Kotsopoulos, Chris	NYR, Hfd., Tor., Det.	10	479	44	109	153	827	31	1	3	4	91	....	1980-81	1989-90
‡ Kovalchuk, Ilya	Atl., N.J.	11	816	417	399	816	516	32	11	16	27	31	....	2001-02	2012-13
Kovalenko, Andrei	Que., Col., Mtl., Edm., Phi., Car., Bos.	9	620	173	206	379	389	33	5	6	11	20	....	1992-93	2000-01
Kovalev, Alex	NYR, Pit., Mtl., Ott., Fla.	19	1316	430	599	1029	1304	123	45	55	100	114	1	1992-93	2012-13
Kowal, Joe	Buf.	2	22	0	5	5	13	2	0	0	0	0	....	1976-77	1977-78
Kozak, Don	L.A., Van.	7	437	96	86	182	480	29	7	2	9	69	....	1972-73	1978-79
Kozak, Les	Tor.	1	12	1	0	1	2	....	....	....	....	....	....	1961-62	1961-62
Kozlov, Viktor	S.J., Fla., N.J., NYI, Wsh.	14	897	198	339	537	248	35	4	8	12	10	....	1994-95	2008-09
‡ Kozlov, Vyacheslav	Det., Buf., Atl.	18	1182	356	497	853	704	118	42	37	79	82	2	1991-92	2009-10
Kraft, Milan	Pit.	4	207	41	41	82	52	8	0	0	0	2	....	2000-01	2003-04
Kraft, Ryan	S.J.	1	7	0	1	1	0	....	....	....	....	....	....	2002-03	2002-03
• Kraftcheck, Stephen	Bos., NYR, Tor.	4	157	11	18	29	83	6	0	0	0	7	....	1950-51	1958-59
‡ Krajicek, Lukas	Fla., Van., T.B., Phi.	7	328	11	61	72	245	34	0	5	5	20	....	2001-02	2009-10
Krake, Skip	Bos., L.A., Buf.	7	249	23	40	63	182	10	1	0	1	17	....	1963-64	1970-71
Kravchuk, Igor	Chi., Edm., St.L., Ott., Cgy., Fla.	12	699	64	210	274	251	51	6	15	21	18	....	1991-92	2002-03
Kravets, Mikhail	S.J.	2	2	0	0	0	0	....	....	....	....	....	....	1991-92	1992-93
Krentz, Dale	Det.	3	30	5	3	8	9	2	0	0	0	0	....	1986-87	1988-89
‡ Kreps, Kamil	Fla.	4	232	18	42	60	71	....	....	....	....	....	....	2006-07	2009-10
Krestanovich, Jordan	Col.	2	22	0	2	2	6	....	....	....	....	....	....	2001-02	2003-04
Kristek, Jaroslav	Buf.	1	6	0	0	0	4	....	....	....	....	....	....	2002-03	2002-03
Krivokrasov, Sergei	Chi., Nsh., Cgy., Min., Ana.	10	450	86	109	195	288	21	2	0	2	14	....	1992-93	2001-02
‡ Krog, Jason	NYI, Ana., Atl., NYR, Van.	7	202	22	37	59	46	21	3	1	4	4	....	1999-00	2008-09

Name	NHL Teams	NHL Seasons	Regular Schedule GP	G	A	TP	PIM	Playoffs GP	G	A	TP	PIM	NHL Cup Wins	First NHL Season	Last NHL Season
• Krol, Joe	NYR, Bro.	3	26	10	4	14	8	....	....	....	....	....	....	1936-37	1941-42
Kromm, Richard	Cgy., NYI	9	372	70	103	173	138	36	2	6	8	22	....	1983-84	1992-93
Kron, Robert	Van., Hfd., Car., CBJ	12	771	144	194	338	119	16	3	2	5	2	....	1990-91	2001-02
‡ Kronwall, Staffan	Tor., Wsh., Cgy.	4	66	1	3	4	23	....	....	....	....	....	....	2005-06	2009-10
Krook, Kevin	Col.	1	3	0	0	0	2	....	....	....	....	....	....	1978-79	1978-79
Kroupa, Vlastimil	S.J., N.J.	5	105	4	19	23	66	20	1	2	3	25	....	1993-94	1997-98
Krulicki, Jim	NYR, Det.	1	41	0	3	3	6	....	....	....	....	....	....	1970-71	1970-71
Krupp, Uwe	Buf., NYI, Que., Col., Det., Atl.	15	729	69	212	281	660	81	6	23	29	86	1	1986-87	2002-03
Kruppke, Gord	Det.	3	23	0	0	0	32	....	....	....	....	....	....	1990-91	1993-94
Kruse, Paul	Cgy., NYI, Buf., S.J.	11	423	38	33	71	1074	28	5	2	7	36	....	1990-91	2000-01
Krushelnyski, Mike	Bos., Edm., L.A., Tor., Det.	14	897	241	328	569	699	139	29	43	72	106	3	1981-82	1994-95
• Krutov, Vladimir	Van.	1	61	11	23	34	20	....	....	....	....	....	....	1989-90	1989-90
Krygier, Todd	Hfd., Wsh., Ana.	9	543	100	143	243	533	48	10	7	17	40	....	1989-90	1997-98
Kryskow, Dave	Chi., Wsh., Det., Atl.	4	231	33	56	89	174	12	2	0	2	4	....	1972-73	1975-76
• Kryzanowski, Ed	Bos., Chi.	5	237	15	22	37	65	18	0	1	1	4	....	1948-49	1952-53
Kuba, Filip	Fla., Min., T.B., Ott.	14	836	70	263	333	361	31	4	11	15	38	....	1998-99	2012-13
‡ Kubalik, Tomas	CBJ	2	12	1	3	4	6	....	....	....	....	....	....	2010-11	2011-12
Kubina, Pavel	T.B., Tor., Atl., Phi.	14	970	110	276	386	1123	51	3	7	10	110	1	1997-98	2011-12
Kucera, Frantisek	Chi., Hfd., Van., Phi., CBJ, Pit., Wsh.	9	465	24	95	119	251	12	0	1	1	0	....	1990-91	2001-02
Kudashov, Alexei	Tor.	1	25	1	0	1	4	....	....	....	....	....	....	1993-94	1993-94
Kudelski, Bob	L.A., Ott., Fla.	9	442	139	102	241	218	22	4	4	8	4	....	1987-88	1995-96
‡ Kudroc, Kristian	T.B., Fla.	3	26	2	2	4	38	....	....	....	....	....	....	2000-01	2003-04
• Kuhn, Gord	NYA	1	12	1	1	2	4	....	....	....	....	....	....	1932-33	1932-33
‡ Kukkonen, Lasse	Chi., Phi.	4	159	6	16	22	90	14	0	2	2	6	....	2003-04	2008-09
• Kukulowicz, Aggie	NYR	2	4	1	0	1	0	....	....	....	....	....	....	1952-53	1953-54
Kulak, Stu	Van., Edm., NYR, Que., Wpg.	4	90	8	4	12	130	3	0	0	0	2	....	1982-83	1988-89
‡ Kulda, Arturs	Atl., Wpg.	3	15	0	2	2	8	....	....	....	....	....	....	2009-10	2011-12
Kuleshov, Mikhail	Col.	1	3	0	0	0	0	....	....	....	....	....	....	2003-04	2003-04
• Kullman, Arnie	Bos.	2	13	0	1	1	11	....	....	....	....	....	....	1947-48	1949-50
• Kullman, Eddie	NYR	6	343	56	70	126	298	6	1	0	1	2	....	1947-48	1953-54
Kultanen, Jarno	Bos.	3	102	2	11	13	59	....	....	....	....	....	....	2000-01	2002-03
Kumpel, Mark	Que., Det., Wpg.	6	288	38	46	84	113	39	6	4	10	14	....	1984-85	1990-91
‡ Kundratek, Tomas	Wsh.	2	30	1	6	7	10	....	....	....	....	....	....	2011-12	2012-13
• Kuntz, Alan	NYR	2	45	10	12	22	12	6	1	0	1	2	....	1941-42	1945-46
Kuntz, Murray	St.L.	1	7	1	2	3	0	....	....	....	....	....	....	1974-75	1974-75
Kurka, Tomas	Car.	2	17	3	2	5	2	....	....	....	....	....	....	2002-03	2003-04
Kurri, Jari	Edm., L.A., NYR, Ana., Col.	17	1251	601	797	1398	545	200	106	127	233	123	5	1980-81	1997-98
Kurtenbach, Orland	NYR, Bos., Tor., Van.	13	639	119	213	332	628	19	2	4	6	70	....	1960-61	1973-74
‡ Kurtz, Justin	Van.	1	27	3	5	8	14	....	....	....	....	....	....	2001-02	2001-02
Kurvers, Tom	Mtl., Buf., N.J., Tor., Van., NYI, Ana.	11	659	93	328	421	350	57	8	22	30	68	1	1984-85	1994-95
Kuryluk, Merv	Chi.	1	....	....	....	....	....	2	0	0	0	0	....	1961-62	1961-62
Kushner, Dale	NYI, Phi.	3	84	10	13	23	215	....	....	....	....	....	....	1989-90	1991-92
‡ Kutlak, Zdenek	Bos.	3	16	1	2	3	4	....	....	....	....	....	....	2000-01	2003-04
Kuznetsov, Maxim	Det., L.A.	4	136	2	8	10	137	....	....	....	....	....	....	2000-01	2003-04
Kuznik, Greg	Car.	1	1	0	0	0	0	....	....	....	....	....	....	2000-01	2000-01
Kuzyk, Ken	Cle.	2	41	5	9	14	8	....	....	....	....	....	....	1976-77	1977-78
Kvartalnov, Dmitri	Bos.	2	112	42	49	91	26	4	0	0	0	0	....	1992-93	1993-94
‡ Kvasha, Oleg	Fla., NYI, Phx.	7	493	81	136	217	335	21	1	2	3	8	....	1998-99	2005-06
‡ Kwiatkowski, Joel	Ott., Wsh., Fla., Pit., Atl.	7	282	16	29	45	245	6	0	0	0	2	....	2000-01	2007-08
Kwong, Larry	NYR	1	1	0	0	0	0	....	....	....	....	....	....	1947-48	1947-48
• Kyle, Bill	NYR	2	3	0	3	3	0	....	....	....	....	....	....	1949-50	1950-51
• Kyle, Gus	NYR, Bos.	3	203	6	20	26	362	14	1	2	3	34	....	1949-50	1951-52
Kyllonen, Markku	Wpg.	1	9	0	2	2	2	....	....	....	....	....	....	1988-89	1988-89
Kypreos, Nick	Wsh., Hfd., NYR, Tor.	8	442	46	44	90	1210	34	1	3	4	65	1	1989-90	1996-97
Kyte, Jim	Wpg., Pit., Cgy., Ott., S.J.	13	598	17	49	66	1342	42	0	6	6	94	....	1982-83	1995-96
‡ Kytnar, Milan	Edm.	1	1	0	0	0	0	....	....	....	....	....	....	2011-12	2011-12

L

Name	NHL Teams	NHL Seasons	Regular Schedule GP	G	A	TP	PIM	Playoffs GP	G	A	TP	PIM	NHL Cup Wins	First NHL Season	Last NHL Season
‡ Laakso, Teemu	Nsh.	3	17	0	0	0	10	....	....	....	....	....	....	2009-10	2011-12
Laaksonen, Antti	Bos., Min., Col.	8	483	81	87	168	152	25	1	5	6	6	....	1998-99	2006-07
Labadie, Mike	NYR	1	3	0	0	0	0	....	....	....	....	....	....	1952-53	1952-53
Labatte, Neil	St.L.	2	26	0	2	2	19	....	....	....	....	....	....	1978-79	1981-82
L'Abbe, Moe	Chi.	1	5	0	1	1	0	....	....	....	....	....	....	1972-73	1972-73
Labelle, Marc	Dal.	1	9	0	0	0	46	....	....	....	....	....	....	1996-97	1996-97
• Labine, Leo	Bos., Det.	11	643	128	193	321	730	60	12	11	23	82	....	1951-52	1961-62
Labossiere, Gord	NYR, L.A., Min.	6	215	44	62	106	75	10	2	3	5	28	....	1963-64	1971-72
Labovitch, Max	NYR	1	5	0	0	0	4	....	....	....	....	....	....	1943-44	1943-44
Labraaten, Dan	Det., Cgy.	4	268	71	73	144	47	8	1	0	1	4	....	1978-79	1981-82
Labre, Yvon	Pit., Wsh.	9	371	14	87	101	788	....	....	....	....	....	....	1970-71	1980-81
• Labrie, Guy	Bos., NYR	2	42	4	9	13	16	....	....	....	....	....	....	1943-44	1944-45
• Lach, Elmer	Mtl.	14	664	215	408	623	478	76	19	45	64	36	3	1940-41	1953-54
Lachance, Michel	Col.	1	21	0	4	4	22	....	....	....	....	....	....	1978-79	1978-79
Lachance, Scott	NYI, Mtl., Van., CBJ	13	819	31	112	143	567	11	1	2	3	6	....	1991-92	2003-04
Lacombe, Francois	Oak., Buf., Que.	4	78	2	17	19	54	3	1	0	1	0	....	1968-69	1979-80
Lacombe, Normand	Buf., Edm., Phi.	7	319	53	62	115	196	26	5	1	6	49	1	1984-85	1990-91
LaCouture, Dan	Edm., Pit., NYR, Bos., N.J., Car.	9	337	20	25	45	348	6	0	0	0	2	....	1998-99	2008-09
Lacroix, Andre	Phi., Chi., Hfd.	6	325	79	119	198	44	16	2	5	7	0	....	1967-68	1979-80
Lacroix, Daniel	NYR, Bos., Phi., Edm., NYI	7	188	11	7	18	379	16	0	1	1	26	....	1993-94	1999-00
Lacroix, Eric	Tor., L.A., Col., NYR, Ott.	8	472	67	70	137	361	30	1	5	6	25	....	1993-94	2000-01
Lacroix, Pierre	Que., Hfd.	4	274	24	108	132	197	8	0	2	2	10	....	1979-80	1982-83
Ladouceur, Randy	Det., Hfd., Ana.	14	930	30	126	156	1322	40	5	8	13	59	....	1982-83	1995-96
LaFayette, Nathan	St.L., Van., NYR, L.A.	6	187	17	20	37	103	32	2	7	9	8	....	1993-94	1998-99
Laflamme, Christian	Chi., Edm., Mtl., St.L.	8	324	2	45	47	282	9	0	1	1	6	....	1996-97	2003-04
Lafleur, Guy	Mtl., NYR, Que.	17	1126	560	793	1353	399	128	58	76	134	67	5	1971-72	1990-91
• Lafleur, Roland	Mtl.	1	1	0	0	0	0	....	....	....	....	....	....	1924-25	1924-25
LaFontaine, Pat	NYI, Buf., NYR	15	865	468	545	1013	552	69	26	36	62	36	....	1983-84	1997-98
• Laforce, Ernie	Mtl.	1	1	0	0	0	0	....	....	....	....	....	....	1942-43	1942-43
LaForest, Bob	L.A.	1	5	1	0	1	2	....	....	....	....	....	....	1983-84	1983-84
Laforge, Claude	Mtl., Det., Phi.	8	193	24	33	57	82	5	1	2	3	15	....	1957-58	1968-69
Laforge, Marc	Hfd., Edm.	2	14	0	0	0	64	....	....	....	....	....	....	1989-90	1993-94
• Laframboise, Pete	Cal., Wsh., Pit.	4	227	33	55	88	70	9	1	0	1	0	....	1971-72	1974-75
• Lafrance, Adie	Mtl.	1	3	0	0	0	2	2	0	0	0	0	....	1933-34	1933-34
• Lafrance, Leo	Mtl., Chi.	2	33	2	0	2	6	....	....	....	....	....	....	1926-27	1927-28
Lafreniere, Jason	Que., NYR, T.B.	5	146	34	53	87	22	15	1	5	6	19	....	1986-87	1993-94
• Lafreniere, Roger	Det., St.L.	2	13	0	0	0	4	....	....	....	....	....	....	1962-63	1972-73
Lagace, Jean-Guy	Pit., Buf., K.C.	6	197	9	39	48	251	....	....	....	....	....	....	1968-69	1975-76
Laidlaw, Tom	NYR, L.A.	10	705	25	139	164	717	69	4	17	21	78	....	1980-81	1989-90
Laing, Quintin	Chi., Wsh.	4	79	3	8	11	31	....	....	....	....	....	....	2003-04	2009-10
Laird, Robbie	Min.	1	1	0	0	0	0	....	....	....	....	....	....	1979-80	1979-80
Lajeunesse, Serge	Det., Phi.	5	103	1	4	5	103	....	....	....	....	....	....	1970-71	1974-75
Lakovic, Sasha	Cgy., N.J.	3	37	0	4	4	118	....	....	....	....	....	....	1996-97	1998-99
• Lalande, Hec	Chi., Det.	4	151	21	39	60	120	....	....	....	....	....	....	1953-54	1957-58
‡ Laliberte, David	Phi.	1	11	2	1	3	6	1	0	0	0	2	....	2009-10	2009-10
Lalonde, Bobby	Van., Atl., Bos., Cgy.	11	641	124	210	334	298	16	4	2	6	6	....	1971-72	1981-82
• Lalonde, Newsy	Mtl., NYA	6	99	125	41	166	183	7	15	4	19	32	....	1917-18	1926-27
Lalonde, Ron	Pit., Wsh.	7	397	45	78	123	106	....	....	....	....	....	....	1972-73	1978-79
‡ Lalonde, Shawn	Chi.	1	1	0	0	0	0	....	....	....	....	....	....	2012-13	2012-13
Lalor, Mike	Mtl., St.L., Wsh., Wpg., S.J., Dal.	12	687	17	88	105	677	92	5	10	15	167	1	1985-86	1996-97
• Lamb, Joe	Mtl.M., Ott., NYA, Bos., Mtl., St.L., Det.	11	443	108	101	209	601	18	1	1	2	51	....	1927-28	1937-38
Lamb, Mark	Cgy., Det., Edm., Ott., Phi., Mtl.	11	403	46	100	146	291	70	7	19	26	51	1	1985-86	1995-96
Lambert, Dan	Que.	2	29	6	9	15	22	....	....	....	....	....	....	1990-91	1991-92
Lambert, Denny	Ana., Ott., Nsh., Atl.	8	487	27	66	93	1391	17	0	1	1	28	....	1994-95	2001-02
Lambert, Lane	Det., NYR, Que.	6	283	58	66	124	521	17	2	4	6	40	....	1983-84	1988-89
Lambert, Yvon	Mtl., Buf.	10	683	206	273	479	340	90	27	22	49	67	4	1972-73	1981-82
Lamby, Dick	St.L.	3	22	0	5	5	22	....	....	....	....	....	....	1978-79	1980-81
• Lamirande, Jean-Paul	NYR, Mtl.	4	49	5	5	10	26	8	0	0	0	4	....	1946-47	1954-55
Lammens, Hank	Ott.	1	27	1	2	3	22	....	....	....	....	....	....	1993-94	1993-94
• Lamoureux, Leo	Mtl.	6	235	19	79	98	175	28	1	6	7	16	2	1941-42	1946-47
Lamoureux, Mitch	Pit., Phi.	3	73	11	9	20	59	....	....	....	....	....	....	1983-84	1987-88
‡ Lampman, Bryce	NYR	3	10	0	0	0	2	....	....	....	....	....	....	2003-04	2006-07
Lampman, Mike	St.L., Van., Wsh.	4	96	17	20	37	34	....	....	....	....	....	....	1972-73	1976-77
• Lancien, Jack	NYR	4	63	1	5	6	35	6	0	1	1	2	....	1946-47	1950-51
Landon, Larry	Mtl., Tor.	2	9	0	0	0	2	....	....	....	....	....	....	1983-84	1984-85
Landry, Eric	Cgy., Mtl.	4	68	5	9	14	47	....	....	....	....	....	....	1997-98	2001-02
Lane, Gord	Wsh., NYI	10	539	19	94	113	1228	75	3	14	17	214	4	1975-76	1984-85

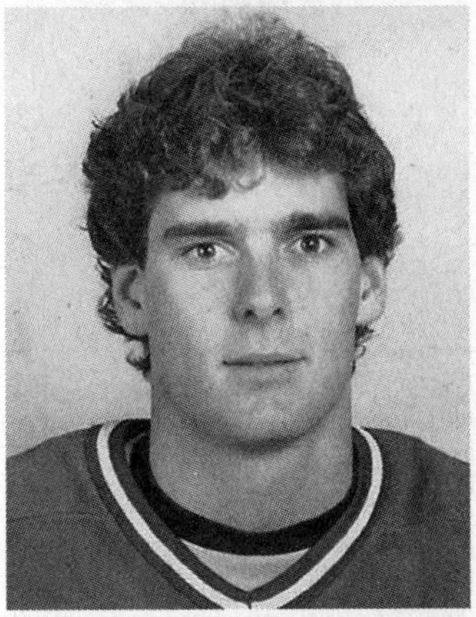

Tom Kurvers

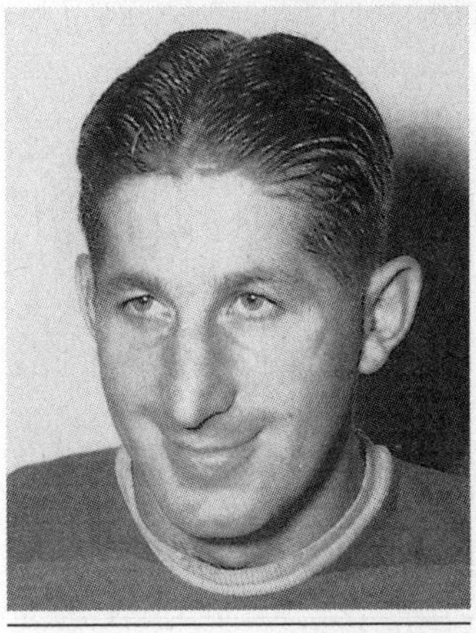

Elmer Lach

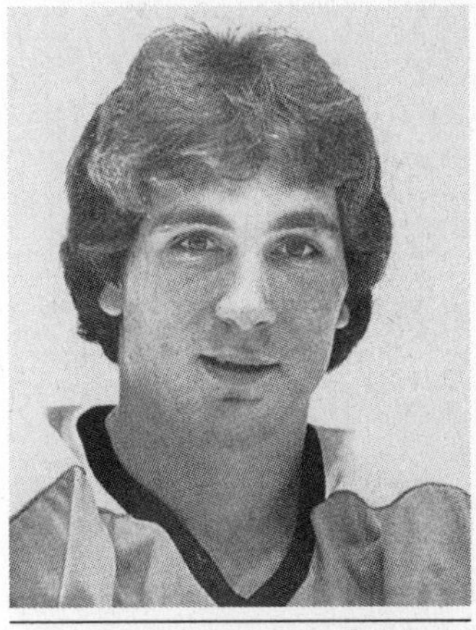

Chris Langevin

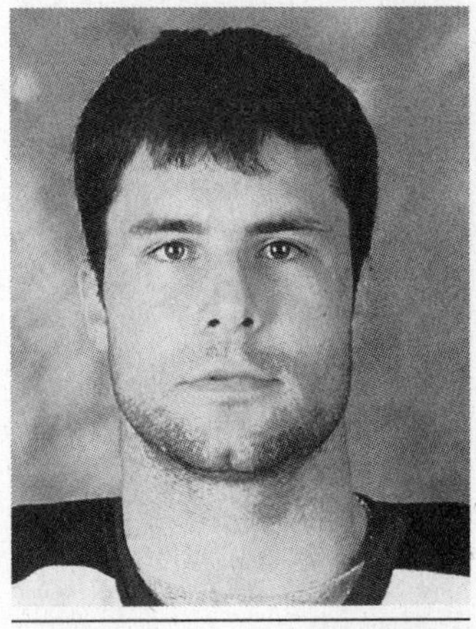

Daymond Langkow

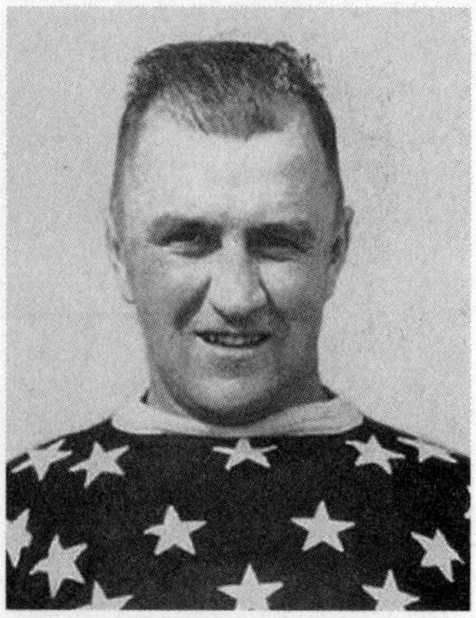

Charlie Langlois

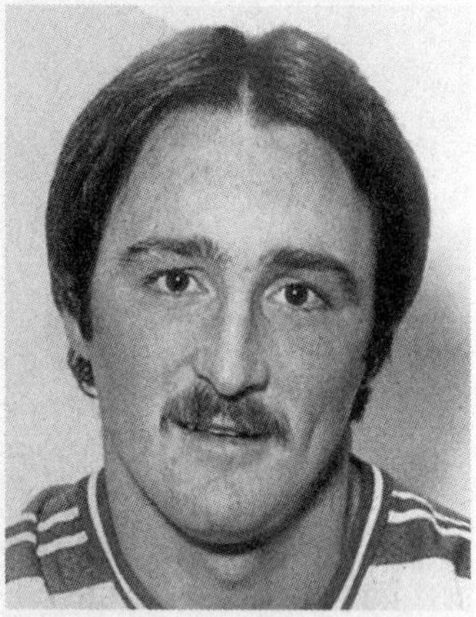

Claude Larose

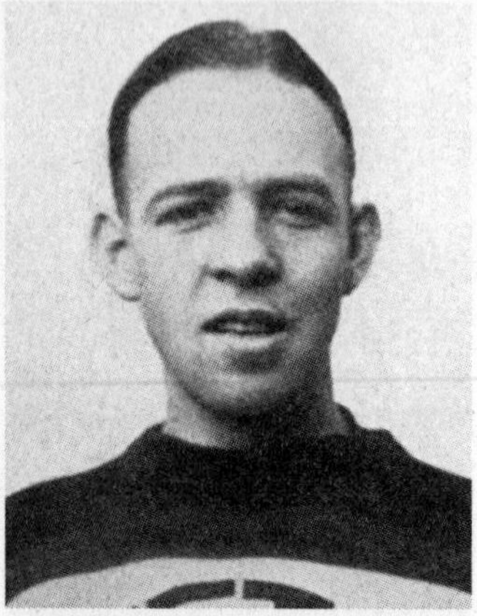

Martin Lauder

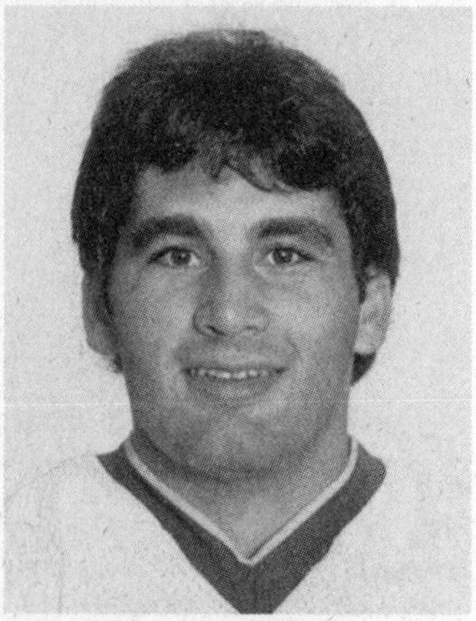

Kevin LaVallee

Name	NHL Teams	NHL Seasons	Regular Schedule GP	G	A	TP	PIM	Playoffs GP	G	A	TP	PIM	NHL Cup Wins	First NHL Season	Last NHL Season
• Lane, Myles	NYR, Bos.	3	71	4	1	5	41	11	0	0	0	0	1	1928-29	1933-34
Lang, Robert	L.A., Bos., Pit., Wsh., Det., Chi., Mtl., Phx.	16	989	261	442	703	422	91	18	28	46	24	....	1992-93	2009-10
Langdon, Darren	NYR, Car., Van., Mtl., N.J.	11	521	16	23	39	1251	25	1	0	1	20	....	1994-95	2005-06
Langdon, Steve	Bos.	3	7	0	1	1	2	4	0	0	0	0	....	1974-75	1977-78
• Langelle, Pete	Tor.	4	136	22	51	73	11	39	5	9	14	4	1	1938-39	1941-42
Langenbrunner, Jamie	Dal., N.J., St.L.	18	1109	243	420	663	837	146	34	53	87	138	2	1994-95	2012-13
Langevin, Chris	Buf.	2	22	3	1	4	22	....	....	....	....	....	....	1983-84	1985-86
Langevin, Dave	NYI, Min., L.A.	8	513	12	107	119	530	87	2	17	19	106	4	1979-80	1986-87
Langfeld, Josh	Ott., S.J., Bos., Det., Nsh.	6	143	9	23	32	60	1	0	0	0	0	....	2001-02	2007-08
Langkow, Daymond	T.B., Phi., Phx., Cgy.	16	1090	270	402	672	547	75	15	29	44	43	....	1995-96	2011-12
Langlais, Alain	Min.	2	25	4	4	8	10	....	....	....	....	....	....	1973-74	1974-75
Langlois, Albert	Mtl., NYR, Det., Bos.	9	497	21	91	112	488	53	1	5	6	50	3	1957-58	1965-66
• Langlois, Charlie	Ham., NYA, Pit., Mtl.	4	151	22	5	27	189	2	0	0	0	0	....	1924-25	1927-28
Langway, Rod	Mtl., Wsh.	15	994	51	278	329	849	104	5	22	27	97	1	1978-79	1992-93
Lank, Jeff	Phi.	1	2	0	0	0	2	....	....	....	....	....	....	1999-00	1999-00
Lanthier, Jean-Marc	Van.	4	105	16	16	32	29	....	....	....	....	....	....	1983-84	1987-88
• Lanyon, Ted	Pit.	1	5	0	0	0	4	....	....	....	....	....	....	1967-68	1967-68
Lanz, Rick	Van., Tor., Chi.	10	569	65	221	286	448	28	3	8	11	35	....	1980-81	1991-92
Laperriere, Daniel	St.L., Ott.	4	48	2	5	7	27	....	....	....	....	....	....	1992-93	1995-96
Laperriere, Ian	St.L., NYR, L.A., Col., Phi.	17	1083	121	215	336	1956	67	3	10	13	102	....	1993-94	2010-11
Laperriere, Jacques	Mtl.	12	691	40	242	282	674	88	9	22	31	101	6	1962-63	1973-74
Laplante, Darryl	Det.	3	35	0	6	6	10	....	....	....	....	....	....	1997-98	1999-00
Lapointe, Claude	Que., Col., Cgy., NYI, Phi.	14	879	127	178	305	721	34	4	7	11	44	....	1990-91	2003-04
Lapointe, Guy	Mtl., St.L., Bos.	16	884	171	451	622	893	123	26	44	70	138	6	1968-69	1983-84
Lapointe, Martin	Det., Bos., Chi., Ott.	16	991	181	200	381	1417	108	19	24	43	202	2	1991-92	2007-08
• Lapointe, Rick	Det., Phi., St.L., Que., L.A.	11	664	44	176	220	831	46	2	7	9	64	....	1975-76	1985-86
Lappin, Peter	Min., S.J.	2	7	0	0	0	2	....	....	....	....	....	....	1989-90	1991-92
• Laprade, Edgar	NYR	10	500	108	172	280	42	18	4	9	13	4	....	1945-46	1954-55
• LaPrairie, Benjamin	Chi.	1	7	0	0	0	0	....	....	....	....	....	....	1936-37	1936-37
Laraque, Georges	Edm., Phx., Pit., Mtl.	12	695	53	100	153	1126	57	4	8	12	72	....	1997-98	2009-10
Larionov, Igor	Van., S.J., Det., Fla., N.J.	14	921	169	475	644	474	150	30	67	97	60	3	1989-90	2003-04
Lariviere, Garry	Que., Edm.	4	219	6	57	63	167	14	0	5	5	8	....	1979-80	1982-83
Larman, Drew	Fla., Bos.	3	26	2	1	3	4	....	....	....	....	....	....	2006-07	2009-10
Larmer, Jeff	Col., N.J., Chi.	5	158	37	51	88	57	5	1	0	1	2	....	1981-82	1985-86
Larmer, Steve	Chi., NYR	15	1006	441	571	1012	532	140	56	75	131	89	1	1980-81	1994-95
• Larochelle, Wildor	Mtl., Chi.	12	474	92	74	166	211	34	6	4	10	24	2	1925-26	1936-37
Larocque, Denis	L.A.	1	8	0	1	1	18	....	....	....	....	....	....	1987-88	1987-88
Larocque, Mario	T.B.	1	5	0	0	0	16	....	....	....	....	....	....	1998-99	1998-99
• Larose, Bonner	Bos.	1	6	0	0	0	0	....	....	....	....	....	....	1925-26	1925-26
LaRose, Chad	Car.	8	508	85	95	180	286	39	4	8	12	26	1	2005-06	2012-13
Larose, Claude	Mtl., Min., St.L.	16	943	226	257	483	887	97	14	18	32	143	5	1962-63	1977-78
Larose, Claude	NYR	2	25	4	7	11	2	2	0	0	0	0	....	1979-80	1981-82
Larose, Cory	NYR	1	7	0	1	1	4	....	....	....	....	....	....	2003-04	2003-04
Larose, Guy	Wpg., Tor., Cgy., Bos.	6	70	10	9	19	63	4	0	0	0	0	....	1988-89	1994-95
Larouche, Pierre	Pit., Mtl., Hfd., NYR	14	812	395	427	822	237	64	20	34	54	16	2	1974-75	1987-88
Larouche, Steve	Ott., NYR, L.A.	2	26	9	9	18	10	....	....	....	....	....	....	1994-95	1995-96
Larsen, Brad	Col., Atl., Ana.	9	294	19	29	48	134	25	1	3	4	13	....	1997-98	2008-09
• Larson, Norm	NYA, Bro., NYR	3	89	25	18	43	12	....	....	....	....	....	....	1940-41	1946-47
Larson, Reed	Det., Bos., Edm., NYI, Min., Buf.	14	904	222	463	685	1391	32	4	7	11	63	....	1976-77	1989-90
Larter, Tyler	Wsh.	1	1	0	0	0	0	....	....	....	....	....	....	1989-90	1989-90
Latal, Jiri	Phi.	3	92	12	36	48	24	....	....	....	....	....	....	1989-90	1991-92
‡ Latendresse, Guillaume	Mtl., Min., Ott.	7	341	87	60	147	185	15	1	2	3	37	....	2006-07	2012-13
Latos, James	NYR	1	1	0	0	0	0	....	....	....	....	....	....	1988-89	1988-89
Latreille, Phil	NYR	1	4	0	0	0	2	....	....	....	....	....	....	1960-61	1960-61
Latta, David	Que.	4	36	4	8	12	4	....	....	....	....	....	....	1985-86	1990-91
• Lauder, Martin	Bos.	1	3	0	0	0	2	....	....	....	....	....	....	1927-28	1927-28
Lauen, Mike	Wpg.	1	4	0	1	1	0	....	....	....	....	....	....	1983-84	1983-84
Lauer, Brad	NYI, Chi., Ott., Pit.	9	323	44	67	111	218	34	7	5	12	24	....	1986-87	1995-96
Laughlin, Craig	Mtl., Wsh., L.A., Tor.	8	549	136	205	341	364	33	6	6	12	20	....	1981-82	1988-89
Laughton, Mike	Oak., Cal.	4	189	39	48	87	101	11	3	4	7	0	....	1967-68	1970-71
Laukkanen, Janne	Que., Col., Ott., Pit., T.B.	9	407	22	99	121	335	59	7	9	16	46	....	1994-95	2002-03
Laurence, Don	Atl., St.L.	2	79	15	22	37	14	....	....	....	....	....	....	1978-79	1979-80
Laus, Paul	Fla.	9	530	14	58	72	1702	30	2	7	9	74	....	1993-94	2001-02
LaVallee, Kevin	Cgy., L.A., St.L., Pit.	7	366	110	125	235	85	32	5	8	13	21	....	1980-81	1986-87
LaVarre, Mark	Chi.	3	78	9	16	25	58	1	0	0	0	2	....	1985-86	1987-88
Lavender, Brian	St.L., NYI, Det., Cal.	4	184	16	26	42	174	3	0	0	0	2	....	1971-72	1974-75
Lavigne, Eric	L.A.	1	1	0	0	0	0	....	....	....	....	....	....	1994-95	1994-95
• Laviolette, Jack	Mtl.	1	18	2	1	3	6	2	0	0	0	0	....	1917-18	1917-18
Laviolette, Peter	NYR	1	12	0	0	0	6	....	....	....	....	....	....	1988-89	1988-89
Lavoie, Dominic	St.L., Ott., Bos., L.A.	6	38	5	8	13	32	....	....	....	....	....	....	1988-89	1993-94
Law, Kirby	Phi.	3	9	0	1	1	4	....	....	....	....	....	....	2000-01	2003-04
Lawless, Paul	Hfd., Phi., Van., Tor.	7	239	49	77	126	54	3	0	2	2	2	....	1982-83	1989-90
Lawrence, Mark	Dal., NYI	6	142	18	26	44	115	....	....	....	....	....	....	1994-95	2000-01
• Lawson, Danny	Det., Min., Buf.	5	219	28	29	57	61	16	0	1	1	2	....	1967-68	1971-72
Lawton, Brian	Min., NYR, Hfd., Que., Bos., S.J.	9	483	112	154	266	401	11	1	1	2	12	....	1983-84	1992-93
Laxdal, Derek	Tor., NYI	6	67	12	7	19	88	1	0	2	2	2	....	1984-85	1990-91
• Laycoe, Hal	NYR, Mtl., Bos.	11	531	25	77	102	292	40	2	5	7	39	....	1945-46	1955-56
Lazaro, Jeff	Bos., Ott.	3	102	14	23	37	114	28	3	3	6	32	....	1990-91	1992-93
Leach, Jamie	Pit., Hfd., Fla.	5	81	11	9	20	12	....	....	....	....	....	1	1989-90	1993-94
Leach, Jay	Bos., T.B., N.J., Mtl., S.J.	5	70	1	2	3	60	....	....	....	....	....	....	2005-06	2010-11
Leach, Larry	Bos.	3	126	13	29	42	91	7	1	1	2	8	....	1958-59	1961-62
Leach, Reggie	Bos., Cal., Phi., Det.	13	934	381	285	666	387	94	47	22	69	22	1	1970-71	1982-83
Leach, Stephen	Wsh., Bos., St.L., Car., Ott., Phx., Pit.	15	702	130	153	283	978	92	15	11	26	87	....	1985-86	1999-00
Leahy, Patrick	Bos., Nsh.	3	50	4	4	8	19	....	....	....	....	....	....	2003-04	2006-07
Leavins, Jim	Det., NYR	2	41	2	12	14	30	....	....	....	....	....	....	1985-86	1986-87
Lebda, Brett	Det., Tor., CBJ	7	397	20	56	76	229	62	0	10	10	40	1	2005-06	2011-12
Lebeau, Patrick	Mtl., Cgy., Fla., Pit.	4	15	3	2	5	6	....	....	....	....	....	....	1990-91	1998-99
Lebeau, Stephan	Mtl., Ana.	7	373	118	159	277	105	30	9	7	16	12	1	1988-89	1994-95
LeBlanc, Fern	Det.	3	34	5	6	11	0	....	....	....	....	....	....	1976-77	1978-79
LeBlanc, J.P.	Chi., Det.	5	153	14	30	44	87	2	0	0	0	0	....	1968-69	1978-79
LeBlanc, John	Van., Edm., Wpg.	7	83	26	13	39	28	1	0	0	0	0	....	1986-87	1994-95
LeBoutillier, Peter	Ana.	2	35	2	1	3	176	....	....	....	....	....	....	1996-97	1997-98
LeBrun, Al	NYR	2	6	0	2	2	4	....	....	....	....	....	....	1960-61	1965-66
Lecaine, Bill	Pit.	1	4	0	0	0	0	....	....	....	....	....	....	1968-69	1968-69
• Leclair, Jackie	Mtl.	3	160	20	40	60	56	20	6	1	7	6	1	1954-55	1956-57
LeClair, John	Mtl., Phi., Pit.	16	967	406	413	819	501	154	42	47	89	94	1	1990-91	2006-07
Leclerc, Mike	Ana., Phx., Cgy.	9	341	64	94	158	288	26	2	9	11	14	....	1996-97	2005-06
Leclerc, Rene	Det.	2	87	10	11	21	105	....	....	....	....	....	....	1968-69	1970-71
Lecuyer, Doug	Chi., Wpg., Pit.	4	126	11	31	42	178	7	4	0	4	15	....	1978-79	1982-83
‡ Ledin, Per	Col.	1	3	0	0	0	2	....	....	....	....	....	....	2008-09	2008-09
Ledingham, Walt	Chi., NYI	3	15	0	2	2	4	....	....	....	....	....	....	1972-73	1976-77
• Leduc, Albert	Mtl., Ott., NYR	10	383	57	35	92	614	28	5	6	11	32	2	1925-26	1934-35
LeDuc, Rich	Bos., Que.	4	130	28	38	66	69	5	0	0	0	9	....	1972-73	1980-81
Ledyard, Grant	NYR, L.A., Wsh., Buf., Dal., Van., Bos., Ott., T.B.	18	1028	90	276	366	766	83	6	12	18	96	....	1984-85	2001-02
• Lee, Bobby	Mtl.	1	1	0	0	0	0	....	....	....	....	....	....	1942-43	1942-43
Lee, Brian	Ott., T.B.	6	209	5	31	36	124	4	0	0	0	2	....	2007-08	2012-13
Lee, Edward	Que.	1	2	0	0	0	5	....	....	....	....	....	....	1984-85	1984-85
Lee, Peter	Pit.	6	431	114	131	245	257	19	0	8	8	4	....	1977-78	1982-83
Leeb, Brad	Van., Tor.	3	5	0	0	0	2	....	....	....	....	....	....	1999-00	2003-04
Leeb, Greg	Dal.	1	2	0	0	0	0	....	....	....	....	....	....	2000-01	2000-01
Leeman, Gary	Tor., Cgy., Mtl., Van., St.L.	14	667	199	267	466	531	36	8	16	24	36	1	1982-83	1996-97
Leetch, Brian	NYR, Tor., Bos.	18	1205	247	781	1028	571	95	28	69	97	36	1	1987-88	2005-06
Lefebvre, Guillaume	Phi., Pit., Bos.	4	39	2	4	6	13	....	....	....	....	....	....	2001-02	2009-10
Lefebvre, Patrice	Wsh.	1	3	0	0	0	2	....	....	....	....	....	....	1998-99	1998-99
Lefebvre, Sylvain	Mtl., Tor., Que., Col., NYR	14	945	30	154	184	674	129	4	14	18	101	1	1989-90	2002-03
• Lefley, Bryan	NYI, K.C., Col.	5	228	7	29	36	101	2	0	0	0	0	....	1972-73	1977-78
Lefley, Chuck	Mtl., St.L.	9	407	128	164	292	137	29	5	8	13	10	2	1970-71	1980-81
• Leger, Roger	NYR, Mtl.	5	187	18	53	71	71	20	0	7	7	14	....	1943-44	1949-50
Legge, Barry	Que., Wpg.	3	107	1	11	12	144	....	....	....	....	....	....	1979-80	1981-82
Legge, Randy	NYR	1	12	0	2	2	2	....	....	....	....	....	....	1972-73	1972-73
Lehman, Scott	Atl.	1	1	0	0	0	0	....	....	....	....	....	....	2008-09	2008-09
Lehman, Tommy	Bos., Edm.	3	36	5	5	10	16	....	....	....	....	....	....	1987-88	1989-90
‡ Lehoux, Yanick	Phx.	2	10	2	2	4	6	....	....	....	....	....	....	2005-06	2006-07
Lehtinen, Jere	Dal.	14	875	243	271	514	210	108	27	22	49	12	1	1995-96	2009-10

			Regular Schedule					Playoffs					NHL	First	Last
Name	NHL Teams	NHL Seasons	GP	G	A	TP	PIM	GP	G	A	TP	PIM	Cup Wins	NHL Season	NHL Season
Lehto, Petteri	Pit.	1	6	0	0	0	4	....	....	....	....	....	....	1984-85	1984-85
Lehtonen, Antero	Wsh.	1	65	9	12	21	14	....	....	....	....	....	....	1979-80	1979-80
‡ Lehtonen, Mikko	Nsh.	1	15	1	2	3	8	....	....	....	....	....	....	2006-07	2006-07
‡ Lehtonen, Mikko	Bos.	2	2	0	0	0	0	....	....	....	....	....	....	2008-09	2009-10
Lehvonen, Henry	K.C.	1	4	0	0	0	0	....	....	....	....	....	....	1974-75	1974-75
Leier, Edward	Chi.	2	16	2	1	3	2	....	....	....	....	....	....	1949-50	1950-51
‡ Leino, Ville	Det., Phi., Buf.	6	286	40	79	119	70	37	10	18	28	6	....	2008-09	2013-14
Leinonen, Mikko	NYR, Wsh.	4	162	31	78	109	71	20	2	11	13	28	....	1981-82	1984-85
Leiter, Bobby	Bos., Pit., Atl.	10	447	98	126	224	144	8	3	0	3	2	....	1962-63	1975-76
Leiter, Ken	NYI, Min.	5	143	14	36	50	62	15	0	6	6	8	....	1984-85	1989-90
Lemaire, Jacques	Mtl.	12	853	366	469	835	217	145	61	78	139	63	8	1967-68	1978-79
Lemay, Moe	Van., Edm., Bos., Wpg.	8	317	72	94	166	442	28	6	3	9	55	1	1981-82	1988-89
Lemelin, Roger	K.C., Col.	4	36	1	2	3	27	....	....	....	....	....	....	1974-75	1977-78
Lemieux, Alain	St.L., Que., Pit.	6	119	28	44	72	38	19	4	6	10	0	....	1981-82	1986-87
Lemieux, Bob	Oak.	1	19	0	1	1	12	....	....	....	....	....	....	1967-68	1967-68
Lemieux, Claude	Mtl., N.J., Col., Phx., Dal., S.J.	21	1215	379	407	786	1777	234	80	78	158	529	4	1983-84	2008-09
Lemieux, Jacques	L.A.	3	19	0	4	4	8	1	0	0	0	0	....	1967-68	1969-70
Lemieux, Jean	Atl., Wsh.	5	204	23	63	86	39	3	1	1	2	0	....	1973-74	1977-78
Lemieux, Jocelyn	St.L., Mtl., Chi., Hfd., N.J., Cgy., Phx.	12	598	80	84	164	740	60	5	10	15	88	....	1986-87	1997-98
Lemieux, Mario	Pit.	18	915	690	1033	1723	834	107	76	96	172	87	2	1984-85	2005-06
• Lemieux, Real	Det., L.A., NYR, Buf.	8	456	51	104	155	262	18	2	4	6	10	....	1966-67	1973-74
Lemieux, Rich	Van., K.C., Atl.	5	274	39	82	121	132	2	0	0	0	0	....	1971-72	1975-76
Lenardon, Tim	N.J., Van.	2	15	2	1	3	4	....	....	....	....	....	....	1986-87	1989-90
• Lepine, Hec	Mtl.	1	33	5	2	7	2	....	....	....	....	....	....	1925-26	1925-26
• Lepine, Pit	Mtl.	13	526	143	98	241	392	41	7	5	12	26	2	1925-26	1937-38
‡ Lepisto, Sami	Wsh., Phx., CBJ, Chi.	5	176	6	29	35	137	10	1	0	1	6	....	2007-08	2011-12
Leroux, Francois	Edm., Ott., Pit., Col.	10	249	3	20	23	577	33	1	3	4	34	....	1988-89	1997-98
• Leroux, Gaston	Mtl.	1	2	0	0	0	0	....	....	....	....	....	....	1935-36	1935-36
Leroux, Jean-Yves	Chi.	5	220	16	22	38	146	....	....	....	....	....	....	1996-97	2000-01
Leschyshyn, Curtis	Que., Col., Wsh., Hfd., Car., Min., Ott.	16	1033	47	165	212	669	68	2	6	8	34	1	1988-89	2003-04
• Lesieur, Art	Mtl., Chi.	4	100	4	2	6	50	14	0	0	0	4	1	1928-29	1935-36
Lessard, Francis	Atl., Ott.	5	115	1	3	4	346	....	....	....	....	....	....	2001-02	2010-11
Lessard, Junior	Dal., T.B.	3	27	3	1	4	23	....	....	....	....	....	....	2005-06	2007-08
Lessard, Rick	Cgy., S.J.	3	15	0	4	4	18	....	....	....	....	....	....	1988-89	1991-92
Lesuk, Bill	Bos., Phi., L.A., Wsh., Wpg.	8	388	44	63	107	368	9	1	0	1	12	1	1968-69	1979-80
• Leswick, Jack	Chi.	1	37	1	7	8	16	....	....	....	....	....	1	1933-34	1933-34
• Leswick, Pete	NYA, Bos.	2	3	1	0	1	0	....	....	....	....	....	....	1936-37	1944-45
• Leswick, Tony	NYR, Det., Chi.	12	740	165	159	324	900	59	13	10	23	91	3	1945-46	1957-58
Letang, Alan	Dal., Cgy., NYI	3	14	0	0	0	2	....	....	....	....	....	....	1999-00	2002-03
Letowski, Trevor	Phx., Van., CBJ, Car.	9	616	84	117	201	209	17	1	3	4	12	....	1998-99	2007-08
• Levandoski, Joe	NYR	1	8	1	1	2	0	....	....	....	....	....	....	1946-47	1946-47
Leveille, Normand	Bos.	2	75	17	25	42	49	....	....	....	....	....	....	1981-82	1982-83
• Leveque, Guy	L.A.	2	17	2	2	4	21	....	....	....	....	....	....	1992-93	1993-94
Lever, Don	Van., Atl., Cgy., Col., N.J., Buf.	15	1020	313	367	680	593	30	7	10	17	26	....	1972-73	1986-87
Levie, Craig	Wpg., Min., St.L., Van.	6	183	22	53	75	177	16	2	3	5	32	....	1981-82	1986-87
Levins, Scott	Wpg., Fla., Ott., Phx.	5	124	13	20	33	316	....	....	....	....	....	....	1992-93	1997-98
• Levinsky, Alex	Tor., NYR, Chi.	9	367	19	49	68	307	37	2	1	3	26	2	1930-31	1938-39
Levo, Tapio	Col., N.J.	2	107	16	53	69	36	....	....	....	....	....	....	1981-82	1982-83
Lewicki, Danny	Tor., NYR, Chi.	9	461	105	135	240	177	28	0	4	4	8	1	1950-51	1958-59
Lewis, Dale	NYR	1	8	0	0	0	0	....	....	....	....	....	....	1975-76	1975-76
Lewis, Dave	NYI, L.A., N.J., Det.	15	1008	36	187	223	953	91	1	20	21	143	....	1973-74	1987-88
• Lewis, Doug	Mtl.	1	3	0	0	0	0	....	....	....	....	....	....	1946-47	1946-47
‡ Lewis, Grant	Atl.	1	1	0	0	0	0	....	....	....	....	....	....	2008-09	2008-09
• Lewis, Herbie	Det.	11	483	148	161	309	248	38	13	10	23	6	2	1928-29	1938-39
Ley, Rick	Tor., Hfd.	6	310	12	72	84	528	14	0	2	2	20	....	1968-69	1980-81
Liba, Igor	NYR, L.A.	1	37	7	18	25	36	2	0	0	0	2	....	1988-89	1988-89
Libby, Jeff	NYI	1	1	0	0	0	0	....	....	....	....	....	....	1997-98	1997-98
Libett, Nick	Det., Pit.	14	982	237	268	505	472	16	6	2	8	2	....	1967-68	1980-81
• Licari, Tony	Det.	1	9	0	1	1	0	....	....	....	....	....	....	1946-47	1946-47
Liddington, Bob	Tor.	1	11	0	1	1	2	....	....	....	....	....	....	1970-71	1970-71
Lidster, Doug	Van., NYR, St.L., Dal.	16	897	75	268	343	679	80	6	15	21	64	1	1983-84	1998-99
Lidstrom, Nicklas	Det.	20	1564	264	878	1142	514	263	54	129	183	76	4	1991-92	2011-12
‡ Liffiton, David	NYR, Col.	3	7	1	0	1	26	....	....	....	....	....	....	2005-06	2010-11
‡ Lilja, Andreas	L.A., Fla., Det., Ana., Phi.	12	580	16	71	87	563	66	1	2	3	58	1	2000-01	2012-13
Lilley, John	Ana.	3	23	3	8	11	13	....	....	....	....	....	....	1993-94	1995-96
Lind, Juha	Dal., Mtl.	3	133	9	13	22	20	15	2	2	4	8	....	1997-98	2000-01
Lindberg, Chris	Cgy., Que.	3	116	17	25	42	47	2	0	1	1	2	....	1991-92	1993-94
Lindbom, Johan	NYR	1	38	1	3	4	28	....	....	....	....	....	....	1997-98	1997-98
Linden, Jamie	Fla.	1	4	0	0	0	17	....	....	....	....	....	....	1994-95	1994-95
Linden, Trevor	Van., NYI, Mtl., Wsh.	19	1382	375	492	867	895	124	34	65	99	104	....	1988-89	2007-08
Lindgren, Lars	Van., Min.	6	394	25	113	138	325	40	5	6	11	20	....	1978-79	1983-84
Lindgren, Mats	Edm., NYI, Van.	8	387	54	74	128	146	24	1	5	6	10	....	1996-97	2003-04
‡ Lindgren, Perttu	Dal.	1	1	0	0	0	0	....	....	....	....	....	....	2009-10	2009-10
Lindholm, Mikael	L.A.	1	18	2	2	4	2	....	....	....	....	....	....	1989-90	1989-90
Lindros, Brett	NYI	2	51	2	5	7	147	....	....	....	....	....	....	1994-95	1995-96
Lindros, Eric	Phi., NYR, Tor., Dal.	14	760	372	493	865	1398	53	24	33	57	122	....	1992-93	2006-07
Lindsay, Bill	Que., Fla., Cgy., S.J., Mtl., Atl.	13	777	83	141	224	922	42	7	8	15	44	....	1991-92	2003-04
Lindsay, Ted	Det., Chi.	17	1068	379	472	851	1808	133	47	49	96	194	4	1944-45	1964-65
Lindstrom, Willy	Wpg., Edm., Pit.	8	582	161	162	323	200	57	14	18	32	24	2	1979-80	1986-87
Ling, David	Mtl., CBJ	5	93	4	4	8	191	....	....	....	....	....	....	1996-97	2003-04
‡ Linglet, Charles	Edm.	1	5	0	0	0	2	....	....	....	....	....	....	2009-10	2009-10
Linseman, Ken	Phi., Edm., Bos., Tor.	14	860	256	551	807	1727	113	43	77	120	325	1	1978-79	1991-92
‡ Lintner, Richard	Nsh., NYR, Pit.	3	112	8	12	20	54	....	....	....	....	....	....	1999-00	2002-03
Lipuma, Chris	T.B., S.J.	5	72	0	9	9	146	....	....	....	....	....	....	1992-93	1996-97
• Liscombe, Carl	Det.	9	373	137	140	277	117	59	22	19	41	20	1	1937-38	1945-46
‡ Lisin, Enver	Phx., NYR	4	135	24	18	42	64	....	....	....	....	....	....	2006-07	2009-10
• Litzenberger, Ed	Mtl., Chi., Det., Tor.	12	618	178	238	416	283	40	5	13	18	34	4	1952-53	1963-64
Loach, Lonnie	Ott., L.A., Ana.	2	56	10	13	23	29	1	0	0	0	0	....	1992-93	1993-94
• Locas, Jacques	Mtl.	2	59	7	8	15	66	....	....	....	....	....	....	1947-48	1948-49
Lochead, Bill	Det., Col., NYR	6	330	69	62	131	180	7	3	0	3	6	....	1974-75	1979-80
‡ Locke, Corey	Mtl., NYR, Ott.	3	9	0	1	1	0	....	....	....	....	....	....	2007-08	2010-11
• Locking, Norm	Chi.	2	48	2	6	8	26	....	....	....	....	....	....	1934-35	1935-36
Loewen, Darcy	Buf., Ott.	5	135	4	8	12	211	....	....	....	....	....	....	1989-90	1993-94
Lofthouse, Mark	Wsh., Det.	6	181	42	38	80	73	....	....	....	....	....	....	1977-78	1982-83
Logan, Dave	Chi., Van.	6	218	5	29	34	470	12	0	0	0	10	....	1975-76	1980-81
Logan, Robert	Buf., L.A.	3	42	10	5	15	0	....	....	....	....	....	....	1986-87	1988-89
Loiselle, Claude	Det., N.J., Que., Tor., NYI	13	616	92	117	209	1149	41	4	11	15	58	....	1981-82	1993-94
‡ Lojek, Martin	Fla.	2	5	0	1	1	0	....	....	....	....	....	....	2006-07	2007-08
• Lomakin, Andrei	Phi., Fla.	4	215	42	62	104	92	....	....	....	....	....	....	1991-92	1994-95
‡ Lombardi, Matthew	Cgy., Phx., Nsh., Tor., Ana.	9	536	101	161	262	293	40	3	13	16	12	....	2003-04	2012-13
Loney, Brian	Van.	1	12	2	3	5	6	....	....	....	....	....	....	1995-96	1995-96
Loney, Troy	Pit., Ana., NYI, NYR	12	624	87	110	197	1091	67	8	14	22	97	2	1983-84	1994-95
Long, Barry	L.A., Det., Wpg.	5	280	11	68	79	250	5	0	1	1	18	....	1972-73	1981-82
• Long, Stan	Mtl.	1	....	....	....	....	....	3	0	0	0	0	....	1951-52	1951-52
• Lonsberry, Ross	Bos., L.A., Phi., Pit.	15	968	256	310	566	806	100	21	25	46	87	2	1966-67	1980-81
Loob, Hakan	Cgy.	6	450	193	236	429	189	73	26	28	54	16	1	1983-84	1988-89
Loob, Peter	Que.	1	8	1	2	3	0	....	....	....	....	....	....	1984-85	1984-85
Lorentz, Jim	Bos., St.L., NYR, Buf.	10	659	161	238	399	208	54	12	10	22	30	1	1968-69	1977-78
Lorimer, Bob	NYI, Col., N.J.	10	529	22	90	112	431	49	3	10	13	83	2	1976-77	1985-86
• Lorrain, Rod	Mtl.	6	179	28	39	67	30	11	0	3	3	0	....	1935-36	1941-42
• Loughlin, Clem	Det., Chi.	3	101	8	6	14	77	....	....	....	....	....	....	1926-27	1928-29
• Loughlin, Wilf	Tor.	1	14	0	0	0	2	....	....	....	....	....	....	1923-24	1923-24
Lovsin, Ken	Wsh.	1	1	0	0	0	0	....	....	....	....	....	....	1990-91	1990-91
Low, Reed	St.L., Chi.	5	256	3	16	19	725	....	....	....	....	....	....	2000-01	2006-07
Lowdermilk, Dwayne	Wsh.	1	2	0	1	1	2	....	....	....	....	....	....	1980-81	1980-81
Lowe, Darren	Pit.	1	8	1	2	3	0	....	....	....	....	....	....	1983-84	1983-84
Lowe, Kevin	Edm., NYR	19	1254	84	347	431	1498	214	10	48	58	192	6	1979-80	1997-98
Lowe, Odie	NYR	1	4	1	1	2	0	....	....	....	....	....	....	1949-50	1949-50
• Lowe, Ross	Bos., Mtl.	3	77	6	8	14	82	2	0	0	0	0	....	1949-50	1951-52
• Lowrey, Ed	Ott., Ham.	3	27	2	2	4	6	....	....	....	....	....	....	1917-18	1920-21
• Lowrey, Fred	Mtl.M., Pit.	2	53	1	1	2	10	2	0	0	0	6	....	1924-25	1925-26
• Lowrey, Gerry	Tor., Pit., Phi., Chi., Ott.	6	211	48	48	96	148	2	1	0	1	2	....	1927-28	1932-33
Lowry, Dave	Van., St.L., Fla., S.J., Cgy.	19	1084	164	187	351	1191	111	16	20	36	181	....	1985-86	2003-04
Loyns, Lynn	S.J., Cgy.	3	34	3	2	5	21	....	....	....	....	....	....	2002-03	2005-06
Lucas, Danny	Phi.	1	6	1	0	1	0	....	....	....	....	....	....	1978-79	1978-79
Lucas, Dave	Det.	1	1	0	0	0	0	....	....	....	....	....	....	1962-63	1962-63

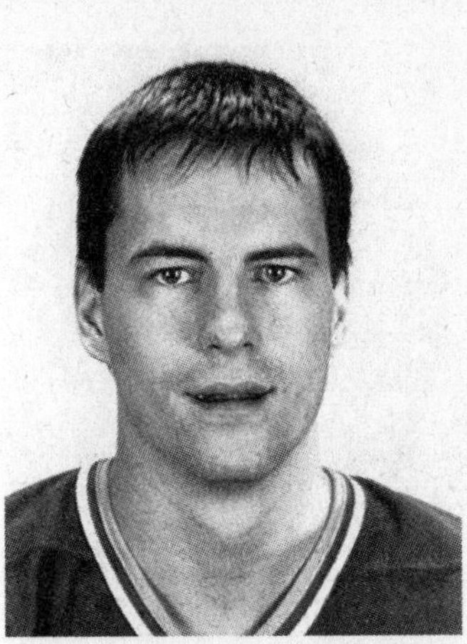

Dominic Lavoie

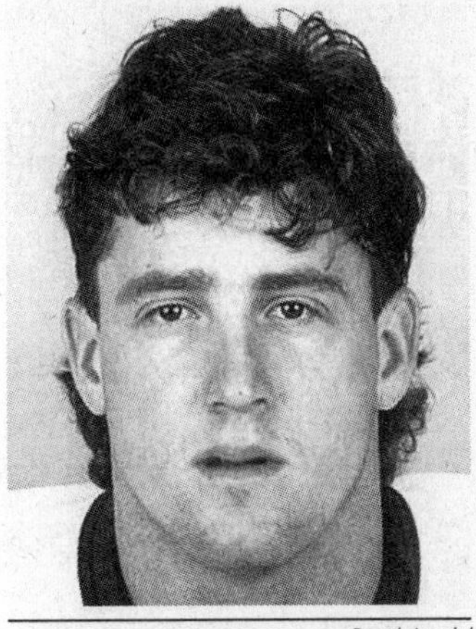

Derek Laxdal

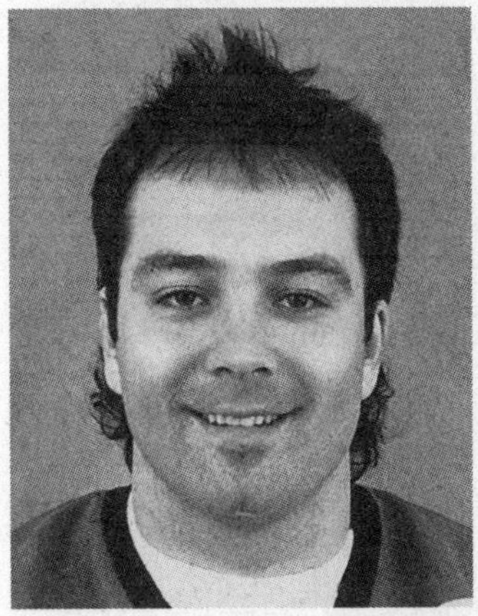

Jamie Leach

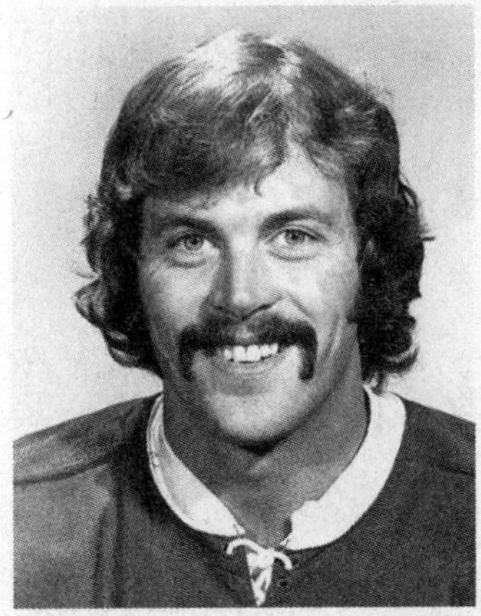

Chuck Lefley

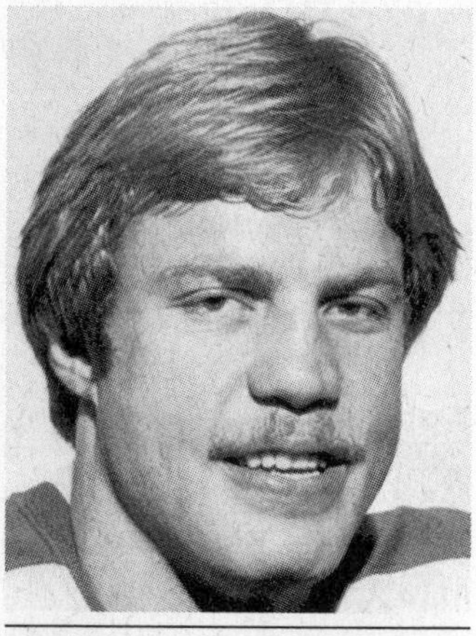

Dean Magee

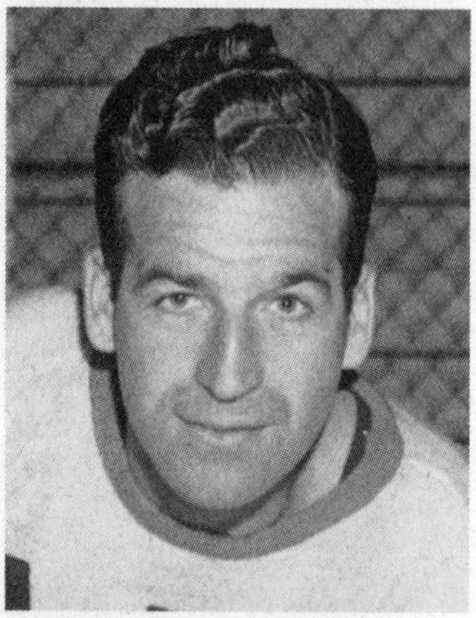

John Mahaffy

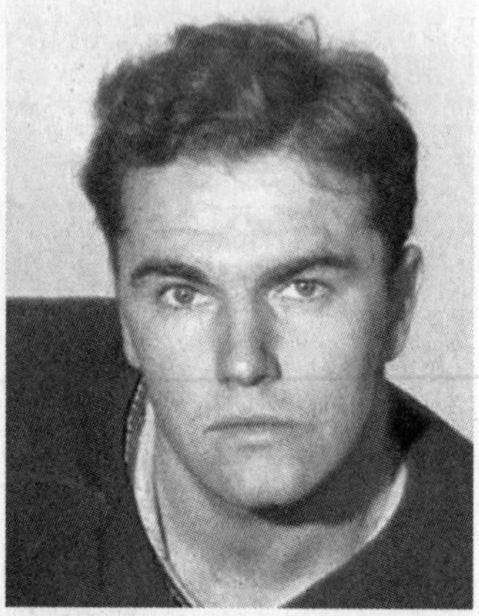

Frank Mailley

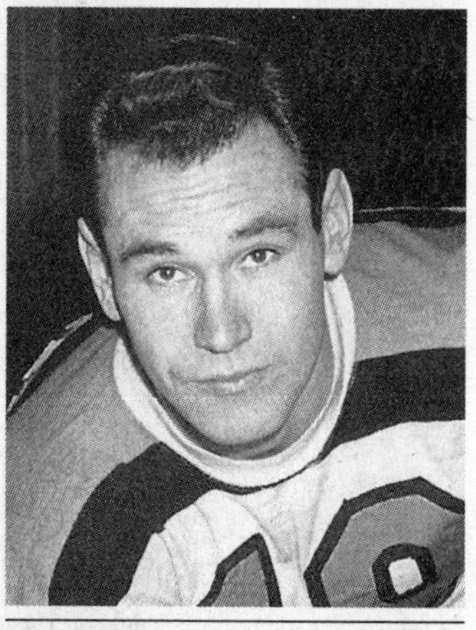

Mark Marquess

			Regular Schedule					Playoffs					NHL	First	Last
Name	NHL Teams	NHL Seasons	GP	G	A	TP	PIM	GP	G	A	TP	PIM	Cup Wins	NHL Season	NHL Season
Luce, Don	NYR, Det., Buf., L.A., Tor.	13	894	225	329	554	364	71	17	22	39	52	....	1969-70	1981-82
Ludvig, Jan	N.J., Buf.	7	314	54	87	141	418	....	....	....	....	....	....	1982-83	1988-89
Ludwig, Craig	Mtl., NYI, Min., Dal.	17	1256	38	184	222	1437	177	4	25	29	244	2	1982-83	1998-99
Ludzik, Steve	Chi., Buf.	9	424	46	93	139	333	44	4	8	12	70	....	1981-82	1989-90
Luhning, Warren	NYI, Dal.	3	29	0	1	1	21	....	....	....	....	....	....	1997-98	1999-00
Lukowich, Bernie	Pit., St.L.	2	79	13	15	28	34	2	0	0	0	0	....	1973-74	1974-75
Lukowich, Brad	Dal., T.B., NYI, N.J., S.J., Van.	13	658	23	90	113	369	71	1	5	6	22	1	1997-98	2010-11
Lukowich, Morris	Wpg., Bos., L.A.	8	582	199	219	418	584	11	0	2	2	24	....	1979-80	1986-87
Luksa, Charlie	Hfd.	1	8	0	1	1	4	....	....	....	....	....	....	1979-80	1979-80
Lumley, Dave	Mtl., Edm., Hfd.	9	437	98	160	258	680	61	6	8	14	131	2	1978-79	1986-87
Lumme, Jyrki	Mtl., Van., Phx., Dal., Tor.	15	985	114	354	468	620	105	9	35	44	52	....	1988-89	2002-03
• Lund, Pentti	Bos., NYR	7	259	44	55	99	40	19	7	5	12	0	....	1946-47	1952-53
Lundberg, Brian	Pit.	1	1	0	0	0	2	....	....	....	....	....	....	1982-83	1982-83
• Lunde, Len	Det., Chi., Min., Van.	8	321	39	83	122	75	20	3	2	5	2	....	1958-59	1970-71
Lundholm, Bengt	Wpg.	5	275	48	95	143	72	14	3	4	7	14	....	1981-82	1985-86
‡ Lundin, Mike	T.B., Min., Ott.	6	252	4	32	36	54	18	0	2	2	2	....	2007-08	2012-13
Lundmark, Jamie	NYR, Phx., Cgy., L.A., Tor.	6	295	40	59	99	204	6	0	1	1	7	....	2002-03	2009-10
‡ Lundqvist, Joel	Dal.	3	134	7	19	26	56	25	4	5	9	14	....	2006-07	2008-09
Lundrigan, Joe	Tor., Wsh.	2	52	2	8	10	22	....	....	....	....	....	....	1972-73	1974-75
Lundstrom, Tord	Det.	1	11	1	1	2	0	....	....	....	....	....	....	1973-74	1973-74
• Lundy, Pat	Det., Chi.	5	150	37	32	69	31	16	2	2	4	2	....	1945-46	1950-51
‡ Luoma, Mikko	Edm.	1	3	0	1	1	0	....	....	....	....	....	....	2003-04	2003-04
Luongo, Chris	Det., Ott., NYI	5	218	8	23	31	176	....	....	....	....	....	....	1990-91	1995-96
Lupaschuk, Ross	Pit.	1	3	0	0	0	4	....	....	....	....	....	....	2002-03	2002-03
Lupien, Gilles	Mtl., Pit., Hfd.	5	226	5	25	30	416	25	0	0	0	21	2	1977-78	1981-82
• Lupul, Gary	Van.	7	293	70	75	145	243	25	4	7	11	11	....	1979-80	1985-86
• Lyashenko, Roman	Dal., NYR	4	139	14	9	23	55	17	2	1	3	0	....	1999-00	2002-03
Lydman, Toni	Cgy., Buf., Ana.	12	847	36	206	242	551	55	3	8	11	42	....	2000-01	2012-13
Lyle, George	Det., Hfd.	4	99	24	38	62	51	....	....	....	....	....	....	1979-80	1982-83
Lynch, Doug	Edm.	1	2	0	0	0	0	....	....	....	....	....	....	2003-04	2003-04
Lynch, Jack	Pit., Det., Wsh.	7	382	24	106	130	336	....	....	....	....	....	....	1972-73	1978-79
• Lynn, Vic	NYR, Det., Mtl., Tor., Bos., Chi.	11	327	49	76	125	274	47	7	10	17	46	3	1942-43	1953-54
Lyon, Steve	Pit.	1	3	0	0	0	2	....	....	....	....	....	....	1976-77	1976-77
• Lyons, Ron	Bos., Phi.	1	36	2	4	6	27	5	0	0	0	0	....	1930-31	1930-31
Lysak, Brett	Car.	1	2	0	0	0	2	....	....	....	....	....	....	2003-04	2003-04
Lysiak, Tom	Atl., Chi.	13	919	292	551	843	567	76	25	38	63	49	....	1973-74	1985-86

M

MacAdam, Al	Phi., Cal., Cle., Min., Van.	12	864	240	351	591	509	64	20	24	44	21	....	1973-74	1984-85
MacDermid, Lane	Bos., Dal., Cgy.	3	21	2	2	4	36	....	....	....	....	....	....	2011-12	2013-14
MacDermid, Paul	Hfd., Wpg., Wsh., Que.	14	690	116	142	258	1303	43	5	11	16	116	....	1981-82	1994-95
MacDonald, Blair	Edm., Van.	4	219	91	100	191	65	11	0	6	6	2	....	1979-80	1982-83
MacDonald, Brett	Van.	1	1	0	0	0	0	....	....	....	....	....	....	1987-88	1987-88
MacDonald, Craig	Car., Fla., Bos., Cgy., Chi., T.B., CBJ	8	233	11	24	35	91	7	0	0	0	2	....	1998-99	2008-09
MacDonald, Doug	Buf.	3	11	1	0	1	2	....	....	....	....	....	....	1992-93	1994-95
MacDonald, Jason	NYR	1	4	0	0	0	19	....	....	....	....	....	....	2003-04	2003-04
MacDonald, Kevin	Ott.	1	1	0	0	0	2	....	....	....	....	....	....	1993-94	1993-94
• MacDonald, Kilby	NYR	4	151	36	34	70	47	15	1	2	3	4	1	1939-40	1944-45
MacDonald, Lowell	Det., L.A., Pit.	13	506	180	210	390	92	30	11	11	22	12	....	1961-62	1977-78
MacDonald, Parker	Tor., NYR, Det., Bos., Min.	14	676	144	179	323	253	75	14	14	28	20	....	1952-53	1968-69
MacDougall, Kim	Min.	1	1	0	0	0	0	....	....	....	....	....	....	1974-75	1974-75
MacEachern, Shane	St.L.	1	1	0	0	0	0	....	....	....	....	....	....	1987-88	1987-88
• Macey, Hub	NYR, Mtl.	3	30	6	9	15	0	8	0	0	0	0	....	1941-42	1946-47
MacGregor, Bruce	Det., NYR	14	893	213	257	470	217	107	19	28	47	44	....	1960-61	1973-74
MacGregor, Randy	Hfd.	1	2	1	1	2	2	....	....	....	....	....	....	1981-82	1981-82
MacGuigan, Garth	NYI	2	5	0	1	1	2	....	....	....	....	....	....	1979-80	1983-84
‡ Machacek, Spencer	Atl., Wpg.	3	25	2	7	9	7	....	....	....	....	....	....	2008-09	2011-12
Macias, Ray	Col.	2	8	0	1	1	2	....	....	....	....	....	....	2008-09	2010-11
MacInnis, Al	Cgy., St.L.	23	1416	340	934	1274	1511	177	39	121	160	255	1	1981-82	2003-04
MacIntosh, Ian	NYR	1	4	0	0	0	4	....	....	....	....	....	....	1952-53	1952-53
MacIver, Don	Wpg.	1	6	0	0	0	2	....	....	....	....	....	....	1979-80	1979-80
Maciver, Norm	NYR, Hfd., Edm., Ott., Pit., Wpg., Phx.	12	500	55	230	285	350	56	3	11	14	32	....	1986-87	1997-98
MacKasey, Blair	Tor.	1	1	0	0	0	2	....	....	....	....	....	....	1976-77	1976-77
• MacKay, Calum	Det., Mtl.	8	237	50	55	105	214	38	5	13	18	20	1	1946-47	1954-55
MacKay, Dave	Chi.	1	29	3	0	3	26	5	0	1	1	2	....	1940-41	1940-41
• MacKay, Mickey	Chi., Pit., Bos.	4	147	44	19	63	79	11	0	0	0	6	1	1926-27	1929-30
• MacKay, Murdo	Mtl.	4	19	0	3	3	0	15	1	2	3	0	....	1945-46	1948-49
MacKell, Fleming	Tor., Bos.	13	665	149	220	369	562	80	22	41	63	75	2	1947-48	1959-60
• MacKell, Jack	Ott.	2	45	4	2	6	59	2	0	0	0	0	2	1919-20	1920-21
‡ MacKenzie, Aaron	Col.	1	5	0	0	0	0	....	....	....	....	....	....	2008-09	2008-09
MacKenzie, Barry	Min.	1	6	0	1	1	6	....	....	....	....	....	....	1968-69	1968-69
• MacKenzie, Bill	Mtl.M., NYR, Mtl., Chi.	6	228	11	10	21	132	21	1	1	2	11	1	1933-34	1939-40
• MacKenzie, Clarence	Chi.	1	36	4	4	8	13	....	....	....	....	....	....	1932-33	1932-33
Mackey, David	Chi., Min., St.L.	6	126	8	12	20	305	3	0	0	0	2	....	1987-88	1993-94
• Mackey, Reg	NYR	1	34	0	0	0	16	1	0	0	0	0	....	1926-27	1926-27
• Mackie, Howie	Det.	2	20	1	0	1	4	8	0	0	0	0	1	1936-37	1937-38
MacKinnon, Paul	Wsh.	5	147	5	23	28	91	....	....	....	....	....	....	1979-80	1983-84
Maclean, Brett	Phx., Wpg.	2	18	2	3	5	4	....	....	....	....	....	....	2010-11	2011-12
MacLean, Don	L.A., Tor., CBJ, Det., Phx.	6	41	8	5	13	6	3	0	0	0	0	....	1997-98	2006-07
MacLean, John	N.J., S.J., NYR, Dal.	18	1194	413	429	842	1328	104	35	48	83	152	1	1983-84	2001-02
MacLean, Paul	St.L., Wpg., Det.	11	719	324	349	673	968	53	21	14	35	110	....	1980-81	1990-91
MacLeish, Rick	Phi., Hfd., Pit., Det.	14	846	349	410	759	434	114	54	53	107	38	2	1970-71	1983-84
MacLellan, Brian	L.A., NYR, Min., Cgy., Det.	10	606	172	241	413	551	47	5	9	14	42	1	1982-83	1991-92
MacLeod, Pat	Min., S.J., Dal.	4	53	5	13	18	14	....	....	....	....	....	....	1990-91	1995-96
MacMillan, Billy	Tor., Atl., NYI	7	446	74	77	151	184	53	6	6	12	40	....	1970-71	1976-77
MacMillan, Bob	NYR, St.L., Atl., Cgy., Col., N.J., Chi.	11	753	228	349	577	260	31	8	11	19	16	....	1974-75	1984-85
MacMillan, Jeff	Dal.	1	4	0	0	0	0	....	....	....	....	....	....	2003-04	2003-04
MacMillan, John	Tor., Det.	5	104	5	10	15	32	12	0	1	1	2	2	1960-61	1964-65
MacNeil, Al	Tor., Mtl., Chi., NYR, Pit.	11	524	17	75	92	617	37	0	4	4	67	....	1955-56	1967-68
MacNeil, Bernie	St.L.	1	4	0	0	0	0	....	....	....	....	....	....	1973-74	1973-74
MacNeil, Ian	Phi.	1	2	0	0	0	0	....	....	....	....	....	....	2002-03	2002-03
Macoun, Jamie	Cgy., Tor., Det.	16	1128	76	282	358	1208	159	10	32	42	169	2	1982-83	1998-99
• MacPherson, Bud	Mtl.	7	259	5	33	38	233	29	0	3	3	21	1	1948-49	1956-57
• MacSweyn, Ralph	Phi.	5	47	0	5	5	10	8	0	0	0	6	....	1967-68	1971-72
MacTavish, Craig	Bos., Edm., NYR, Phi., St.L.	17	1093	213	267	480	891	193	20	38	58	218	4	1979-80	1996-97
MacWilliam, Mike	NYI	1	6	0	0	0	14	....	....	....	....	....	....	1995-96	1995-96
Madden, John	N.J., Chi., Min., Fla.	13	898	165	183	348	219	141	21	22	43	26	3	1998-99	2011-12
Madigan, Connie	St.L.	1	20	0	3	3	25	5	0	0	0	4	....	1972-73	1972-73
Madill, Jeff	N.J.	1	14	4	0	4	46	7	0	2	2	8	....	1990-91	1990-91
Magee, Dean	Min.	1	7	0	0	0	4	....	....	....	....	....	....	1977-78	1977-78
Maggs, Darryl	Chi., Cal., Tor.	3	135	14	19	33	54	4	0	0	0	0	....	1971-72	1979-80
Magnan, Marc	Tor.	1	4	0	1	1	5	....	....	....	....	....	....	1982-83	1982-83
Magnan, Olivier	N.J.	1	18	0	0	0	4	....	....	....	....	....	....	2010-11	2010-11
• Magnuson, Keith	Chi.	11	589	14	125	139	1442	68	3	9	12	164	....	1969-70	1979-80
Maguire, Kevin	Tor., Buf., Phi.	6	260	29	30	59	782	11	0	0	0	86	....	1986-87	1991-92
• Mahaffy, John	Mtl., NYR	3	37	11	25	36	4	1	0	1	1	0	....	1942-43	1944-45
Mahovlich, Frank	Tor., Det., Mtl.	18	1181	533	570	1103	1056	137	51	67	118	163	6	1956-57	1973-74
Mahovlich, Pete	Det., Mtl., Pit.	16	884	288	485	773	916	88	30	42	72	134	4	1965-66	1980-81
Mailhot, Jacques	Que.	1	5	0	0	0	33	....	....	....	....	....	....	1988-89	1988-89
• Mailley, Frank	Mtl.	1	1	0	0	0	0	....	....	....	....	....	....	1942-43	1942-43
Mair, Adam	Tor., L.A., Buf., N.J.	12	615	38	76	114	829	35	3	5	8	36	....	1998-99	2010-11
Mair, Jim	Phi., NYI, Van.	5	76	4	15	19	49	3	1	2	3	4	....	1970-71	1974-75
• Majeau, Fern	Mtl.	2	56	22	24	46	43	1	0	0	0	0	1	1943-44	1944-45
‡ Majesky, Ivan	Fla., Atl., Wsh.	3	202	8	23	31	234	....	....	....	....	....	....	2002-03	2005-06
Major, Bruce	Que.	1	4	0	0	0	0	....	....	....	....	....	....	1990-91	1990-91
Major, Mark	Det.	1	2	0	0	0	5	....	....	....	....	....	....	1996-97	1996-97
Makarov, Sergei	Cgy., S.J., Dal.	7	424	134	250	384	317	34	12	11	23	8	....	1989-90	1996-97
Makela, Mikko	NYI, L.A., Buf., Bos.	7	423	118	147	265	139	18	3	8	11	14	....	1985-86	1994-95
Maki, Chico	Chi.	15	841	143	292	435	345	113	17	36	53	43	1	1960-61	1975-76
‡ Maki, Tomi	Cgy.	1	1	0	0	0	0	....	....	....	....	....	....	2006-07	2006-07
• Maki, Wayne	Chi., St.L., Van.	6	246	57	79	136	184	2	1	0	1	2	....	1967-68	1972-73
Makkonen, Kari	Edm.	1	9	2	2	4	0	....	....	....	....	....	....	1979-80	1979-80
Malakhov, Vladimir	NYI, Mtl., N.J., NYR, Phi.	13	712	86	260	346	697	75	8	19	27	64	1	1992-93	2005-06
‡ Malec, Tomas	Car., Ott.	4	46	0	2	2	47	....	....	....	....	....	....	2002-03	2006-07
Maley, David	Mtl., N.J., Edm., S.J., NYI	9	466	43	81	124	1043	46	5	5	10	111	1	1985-86	1993-94

Name	NHL Teams	NHL Seasons	Regular Schedule GP	G	A	TP	PIM	Playoffs GP	G	A	TP	PIM	NHL Cup Wins	First NHL Season	Last NHL Season
Malgunas, Stewart	Phi., Wpg., Wsh., Cgy.	7	129	1	5	6	144	....	....	....	....	....	....	1993-94	1999-00
Malik, Marek	Hfd., Car., Van., NYR, T.B.	13	691	33	135	168	620	65	2	8	10	64	....	1994-95	2008-09
Malinowski, Merlin	Col., N.J., Hfd.	5	282	54	111	165	121	....	....	....	....	....	....	1978-79	1982-83
Malkoc, Dean	Van., Bos., NYI	4	116	1	3	4	299	....	....	....	....	....	....	1995-96	1998-99
Mallette, Troy	NYR, Edm., N.J., Ott., Bos., T.B.	9	456	51	68	119	1226	15	2	2	4	99	....	1989-90	1997-98
‡ Malmivaara, Olli	N.J.	1	2	0	0	0	0	....	....	....	....	....	....	2007-08	2007-08
• Malone, Cliff	Mtl.	1	3	0	0	0	0	....	....	....	....	....	....	1951-52	1951-52
Malone, Greg	Pit., Hfd., Que.	11	704	191	310	501	661	20	3	5	8	32	....	1976-77	1986-87
• Malone, Joe	Mtl., Que., Ham.	7	126	143	32	175	57	9	6	2	8	6	1	1917-18	1923-24
Maloney, Dan	Chi., L.A., Det., Tor.	11	737	192	259	451	1489	40	4	7	11	35	....	1970-71	1981-82
Maloney, Dave	NYR, Buf.	11	657	71	246	317	1154	49	7	17	24	91	....	1974-75	1984-85
Maloney, Don	NYR, Hfd., NYI	13	765	214	350	564	815	94	22	35	57	101	....	1978-79	1990-91
Maloney, Phil	Bos., Tor., Chi.	5	158	28	43	71	16	6	0	0	0	0	....	1949-50	1959-60
Maltais, Steve	Wsh., Min., T.B., Det., CBJ	6	120	9	18	27	53	1	0	0	0	0	....	1989-90	2000-01
Maltby, Kirk	Edm., Det.	16	1072	128	132	260	867	169	16	15	31	149	4	1993-94	2009-10
Maluta, Ray	Bos.	2	25	2	3	5	6	2	0	0	0	0	....	1975-76	1976-77
• Manastersky, Tom	Mtl.	1	6	0	0	0	11	....	....	....	....	....	....	1950-51	1950-51
• Mancuso, Gus	Mtl., NYR	4	42	7	9	16	17	....	....	....	....	....	....	1937-38	1942-43
Manderville, Kent	Tor., Edm., Hfd., Car., Phi., Pit.	12	646	37	67	104	348	67	3	3	6	44	....	1991-92	2002-03
Mandich, Dan	Min.	4	111	5	11	16	303	7	0	0	0	2	....	1982-83	1985-86
Maneluk, Mike	Phi., Chi., NYR, CBJ	3	85	11	10	21	57	....	....	....	....	....	....	1998-99	2000-01
Manery, Kris	Cle., Min., Van., Wpg.	4	250	63	64	127	91	....	....	....	....	....	....	1977-78	1980-81
Manery, Randy	Det., Atl., L.A.	10	582	50	206	256	415	13	0	2	2	12	....	1970-71	1979-80
Manlow, Eric	Bos., NYI	4	37	2	4	6	8	....	....	....	....	....	....	2000-01	2003-04
Mann, Cameron	Bos., Nsh.	5	93	14	10	24	40	1	0	0	0	0	....	1997-98	2002-03
• Mann, Jack	NYR	2	9	3	4	7	0	....	....	....	....	....	....	1943-44	1944-45
Mann, Jimmy	Wpg., Que., Pit.	8	293	10	20	30	895	22	0	0	0	89	....	1979-80	1987-88
Mann, Ken	Det.	1	1	0	0	0	0	....	....	....	....	....	....	1975-76	1975-76
• Mann, Norm	Tor.	3	31	0	3	3	4	2	0	0	0	0	....	1935-36	1940-41
• Manners, Rennison	Pit., Phi.	2	37	3	2	5	14	....	....	....	....	....	....	1929-30	1930-31
Manning, Paul	CBJ	1	8	0	0	0	2	....	....	....	....	....	....	2002-03	2002-03
Manno, Bob	Van., Tor., Det.	8	371	41	131	172	274	17	2	4	6	12	....	1976-77	1984-85
Manson, Dave	Chi., Edm., Wpg., Phx., Mtl., Dal., Tor.	16	1103	102	288	390	2792	112	7	24	31	343	....	1986-87	2001-02
• Manson, Ray	Bos., NYR	2	2	0	1	1	0	....	....	....	....	....	....	1947-48	1948-49
• Mantha, Georges	Mtl.	13	488	89	102	191	148	36	6	2	8	24	2	1928-29	1940-41
Mantha, Moe	Wpg., Pit., Edm., Min., Phi.	12	656	81	289	370	501	17	5	10	15	18	....	1980-81	1991-92
• Mantha, Sylvio	Mtl., Bos.	14	542	63	78	141	671	39	5	5	10	64	3	1923-24	1936-37
Mapletoft, Justin	NYI	2	38	3	6	9	8	2	0	0	0	0	....	2002-03	2003-04
Mara, Paul	T.B., Phx., Bos., NYR, Mtl., Ana.	12	734	64	189	253	776	33	3	4	7	50	....	1998-99	2010-11
• Maracle, Bud	NYR	1	11	1	3	4	4	4	0	0	0	0	....	1930-31	1930-31
• Marcetta, Milan	Tor., Min.	3	54	7	15	22	10	17	7	7	14	4	1	1966-67	1968-69
• March, Mush	Chi.	17	759	153	230	383	540	45	12	15	27	41	2	1928-29	1944-45
Marchant, Todd	NYR, Edm., CBJ, Ana.	17	1195	186	312	498	774	95	13	21	34	88	1	1993-94	2010-11
• Marchinko, Brian	Tor., NYI	4	47	2	6	8	0	....	....	....	....	....	....	1970-71	1973-74
Marchment, Bryan	Wpg., Chi., Hfd., Edm., T.B., S.J., Col., Tor., Cgy.	17	926	40	142	182	2307	83	4	3	7	102	....	1988-89	2005-06
Marcinyshyn, Dave	N.J., Que., NYR	3	16	0	1	1	49	....	....	....	....	....	....	1990-91	1992-93
Marcon, Lou	Det.	3	60	0	4	4	42	....	....	....	....	....	....	1958-59	1962-63
Marcotte, Don	Bos.	15	868	230	254	484	317	132	34	27	61	81	2	1965-66	1981-82
‡ Marha, Josef	Col., Ana., Chi.	6	159	21	32	53	32	....	....	....	....	....	....	1995-96	2000-01
Marini, Hector	NYI, N.J.	5	154	27	46	73	246	10	3	6	9	14	2	1978-79	1983-84
Marinucci, Chris	NYI, L.A.	2	13	1	4	5	2	....	....	....	....	....	....	1994-95	1996-97
• Mario, Frank	Bos.	2	53	9	19	28	24	....	....	....	....	....	....	1941-42	1944-45
• Mariucci, John	Chi.	5	223	11	34	45	308	12	0	3	3	26	....	1940-41	1947-48
Marjamaki, Masi	NYI	1	1	0	0	0	0	....	....	....	....	....	....	2005-06	2005-06
Mark, Gordon	N.J., Edm.	4	85	3	10	13	187	....	....	....	....	....	....	1986-87	1994-95
Markell, John	Wpg., St.L., Min.	4	55	11	10	21	36	....	....	....	....	....	....	1979-80	1984-85
• Marker, Gus	Det., Mtl.M., Tor., Bro.	10	322	64	69	133	133	46	5	7	12	36	1	1932-33	1941-42
Markham, Ray	NYR	1	14	1	1	2	21	7	1	0	1	24	....	1979-80	1979-80
• Markle, Jack	Tor.	1	8	0	1	1	0	....	....	....	....	....	....	1935-36	1935-36
Markov, Danny	Tor., Phx., Car., Phi., Nsh., Det.	9	538	29	118	147	456	81	2	12	14	84	....	1997-98	2006-07
• Marks, Jack	Mtl.W., Tor., Que.	2	7	0	0	0	4	....	....	....	....	....	1	1917-18	1919-20
Marks, John	Chi.	10	657	112	163	275	330	57	5	9	14	60	....	1972-73	1981-82
Markwart, Nevin	Bos., Cgy.	8	309	41	68	109	794	19	1	0	1	33	....	1983-84	1991-92
Marois, Daniel	Tor., NYI, Bos., Dal.	8	350	117	93	210	419	19	3	3	6	28	....	1987-88	1995-96
Marois, Mario	NYR, Van., Que., Wpg., St.L.	15	955	76	357	433	1746	100	4	34	38	182	....	1977-78	1991-92
• Marotte, Gilles	Bos., Chi., L.A., NYR, St.L.	12	808	56	265	321	919	29	3	3	6	26	....	1965-66	1976-77
• Marquess, Mark	Bos.	1	27	5	4	9	6	4	0	0	0	0	....	1946-47	1946-47
Marsh, Brad	Atl., Cgy., Phi., Tor., Det., Ott.	15	1086	23	175	198	1241	97	6	18	24	124	....	1978-79	1992-93
Marsh, Gary	Det., Tor.	2	7	1	3	4	4	....	....	....	....	....	....	1967-68	1968-69
Marsh, Peter	Wpg., Chi.	5	278	48	71	119	224	26	1	5	6	33	....	1979-80	1983-84
Marshall, Bert	Det., Oak., Cal., NYR, NYI	14	868	17	181	198	926	72	4	22	26	99	....	1965-66	1978-79
Marshall, Don	Mtl., NYR, Buf., Tor.	19	1176	265	324	589	127	94	8	15	23	14	5	1951-52	1971-72
Marshall, Grant	Dal., CBJ, N.J.	11	700	92	147	239	793	90	6	11	17	95	2	1994-95	2005-06
Marshall, Jason	St.L., Ana., Wsh., Min., S.J.	12	526	16	51	67	1004	43	2	3	5	55	....	1991-92	2005-06
Marshall, Paul	Pit., Tor., Hfd.	4	95	15	18	33	17	1	0	0	0	0	....	1979-80	1982-83
Marshall, Willie	Tor.	4	33	1	5	6	2	....	....	....	....	....	....	1952-53	1958-59
Marson, Mike	Wsh., L.A.	6	196	24	24	48	233	....	....	....	....	....	....	1974-75	1979-80
‡ Martensson, Tony	Ana.	1	6	1	1	2	0	....	....	....	....	....	....	2003-04	2003-04
• Martin, Clare	Bos., Det., Chi., NYR	6	237	12	28	40	78	27	0	2	2	6	1	1941-42	1951-52
Martin, Craig	Wpg., Fla.	2	21	0	1	1	24	....	....	....	....	....	....	1994-95	1996-97
• Martin, Frank	Bos., Chi.	6	282	11	46	57	122	10	0	2	2	2	....	1952-53	1957-58
Martin, Grant	Van., Wsh.	4	44	0	4	4	55	1	1	0	1	2	....	1983-84	1986-87
Martin, Jack	Tor.	1	1	0	0	0	0	....	....	....	....	....	....	1960-61	1960-61
Martin, Matt	Tor.	4	76	0	5	5	71	....	....	....	....	....	....	1993-94	1996-97
• Martin, Pit	Det., Bos., Chi., Van.	17	1101	324	485	809	609	100	27	31	58	56	....	1961-62	1978-79
• Martin, Rick	Buf., L.A.	11	685	384	317	701	477	63	24	29	53	74	....	1971-72	1981-82
• Martin, Ron	NYA	2	94	13	16	29	36	....	....	....	....	....	....	1932-33	1933-34
Martin, Terry	Buf., Que., Tor., Edm., Min.	10	479	104	101	205	202	21	4	2	6	26	....	1975-76	1984-85
Martin, Tom	Tor.	1	3	1	0	1	0	....	....	....	....	....	....	1967-68	1967-68
Martin, Tom	Wpg., Hfd., Min.	6	92	12	11	23	249	4	0	0	0	6	....	1984-85	1989-90
• Martineau, Don	Atl., Min., Det.	4	90	6	10	16	63	....	....	....	....	....	....	1973-74	1976-77
‡ Martinek, Radek	NYI, CBJ	12	486	25	85	110	280	11	0	1	1	6	....	2001-02	2013-14
Martini, Darcy	Edm.	1	2	0	0	0	0	....	....	....	....	....	....	1993-94	1993-94
Martins, Steve	Hfd., Car., Ott., T.B., NYI, St.L.	10	267	21	25	46	142	5	0	1	1	0	....	1995-96	2005-06
Martinson, Steve	Det., Mtl., Min.	4	49	2	1	3	244	1	0	0	0	10	....	1987-88	1991-92
Maruk, Dennis	Cal., Cle., Min., Wsh.	14	888	356	522	878	761	34	14	22	36	26	....	1975-76	1988-89
Masnick, Paul	Mtl., Chi., Tor.	6	232	18	41	59	139	33	4	5	9	27	1	1950-51	1957-58
• Mason, Charley	NYR, NYA, Det., Chi.	4	95	7	18	25	44	4	0	1	1	0	....	1934-35	1938-39
• Massecar, George	NYA	3	100	12	11	23	46	....	....	....	....	....	....	1929-30	1931-32
Masters, Jamie	St.L.	3	33	1	13	14	2	2	0	0	0	0	....	1975-76	1978-79
• Masterton, Bill	Min.	1	38	4	8	12	4	....	....	....	....	....	....	1967-68	1967-68
• Mathers, Frank	Tor.	3	23	1	3	4	4	....	....	....	....	....	....	1948-49	1951-52
Mathiasen, Dwight	Pit.	3	33	1	7	8	18	....	....	....	....	....	....	1985-86	1987-88
Mathieson, Jim	Wsh.	1	2	0	0	0	4	....	....	....	....	....	....	1989-90	1989-90
Mathieu, Marquis	Bos.	3	16	0	2	2	14	....	....	....	....	....	....	1998-99	2000-01
‡ Matsumoto, Jon	Car., Fla.	2	14	2	0	2	4	....	....	....	....	....	....	2010-11	2011-12
Matte, Christian	Col., Min.	5	25	2	3	5	12	....	....	....	....	....	....	1996-97	2000-01
• Matte, Joe	Tor., Ham., Bos., Mtl.	4	68	17	15	32	54	....	....	....	....	....	....	1919-20	1925-26
• Matte, Joe	Det., Chi.	2	24	0	3	3	8	....	....	....	....	....	....	1929-30	1942-43
Matteau, Stephane	Cgy., Chi., NYR, St.L., S.J., Fla.	13	848	144	172	316	742	109	12	22	34	80	1	1990-91	2002-03
Matteucci, Mike	Min.	2	6	0	0	0	4	....	....	....	....	....	....	2000-01	2001-02
Mattiussi, Dick	Pit., Oak., Cal.	4	200	8	31	39	124	8	0	1	1	6	....	1967-68	1970-71
Matvichuk, Richard	Min., Dal., N.J.	14	796	39	139	178	624	123	5	19	24	128	1	1992-93	2006-07
• Matz, Johnny	Mtl.	1	30	2	3	5	0	1	0	0	0	0	....	1924-25	1924-25
‡ Mauldin, Greg	CBJ, NYI, Col.	3	36	5	5	10	12	....	....	....	....	....	....	2003-04	2010-11
Maxner, Wayne	Bos.	2	62	8	9	17	48	....	....	....	....	....	....	1964-65	1965-66
‡ Maxwell, Ben	Mtl., Atl., Wpg., Ana.	4	47	2	6	8	19	1	0	0	0	0	....	2008-09	2011-12
Maxwell, Brad	Min., Que., Tor., Van., NYR	10	612	98	270	368	1292	79	12	49	61	178	....	1977-78	1986-87
Maxwell, Bryan	Min., St.L., Wpg., Pit.	8	331	18	77	95	745	15	1	1	2	86	....	1977-78	1984-85
Maxwell, Kevin	Min., Col., N.J.	3	66	6	15	21	61	16	3	4	7	24	....	1980-81	1983-84
Maxwell, Wally	Tor.	1	2	0	0	0	0	....	....	....	....	....	....	1952-53	1952-53
May, Alan	Bos., Edm., Wsh., Dal., Cgy.	8	393	31	45	76	1348	40	1	2	3	80	....	1987-88	1994-95
May, Brad	Buf., Van., Phx., Col., Ana., Tor., Det.	18	1041	127	161	288	2248	88	4	9	13	112	1	1991-92	2009-10
Mayer, Derek	Ott.	1	17	2	2	4	8	....	....	....	....	....	....	1993-94	1993-94
Mayer, Jim	NYR	1	4	0	0	0	0	....	....	....	....	....	....	1979-80	1979-80

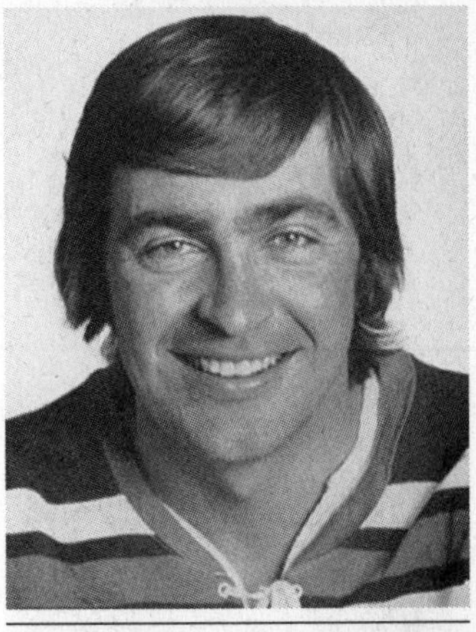

Tom Martin

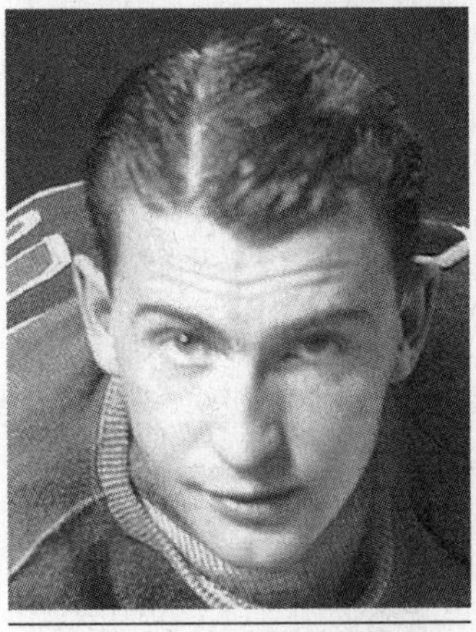

Charley Mason

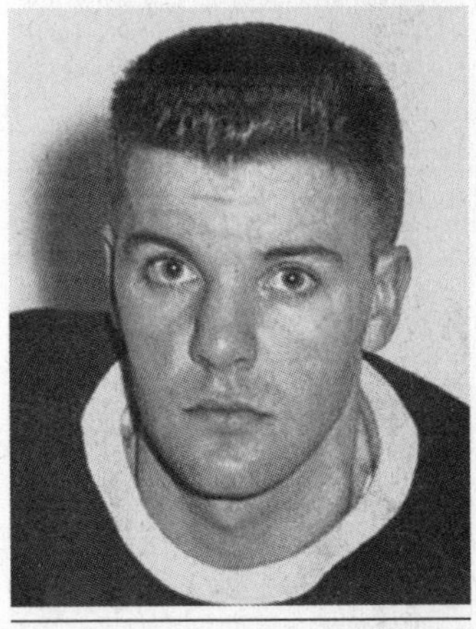

Wally Maxwell

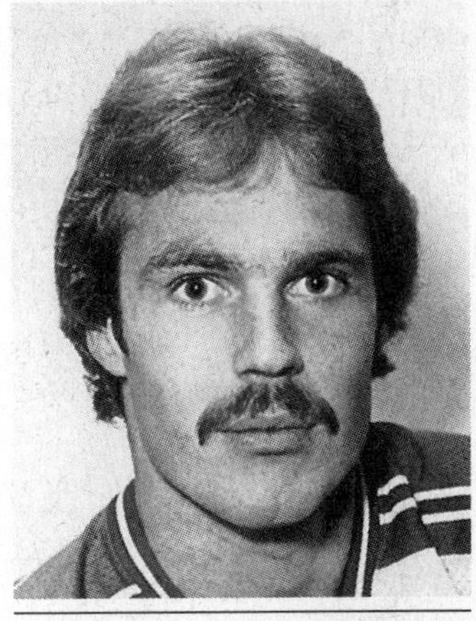

Mike McDougal

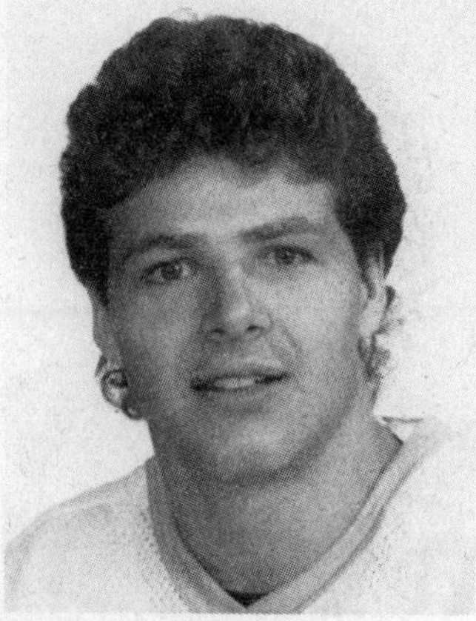

Jim McGeough

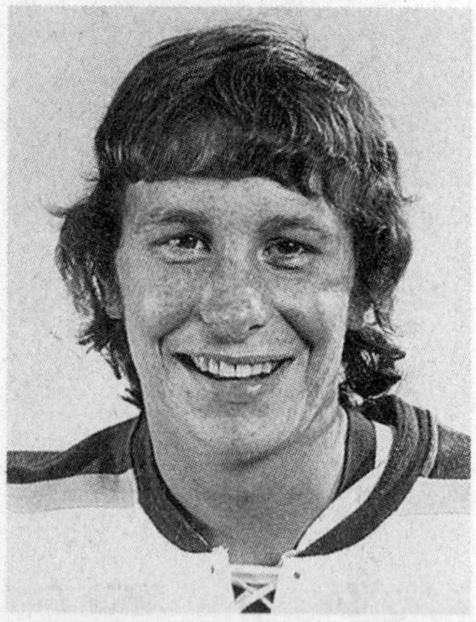

Paul McIntosh

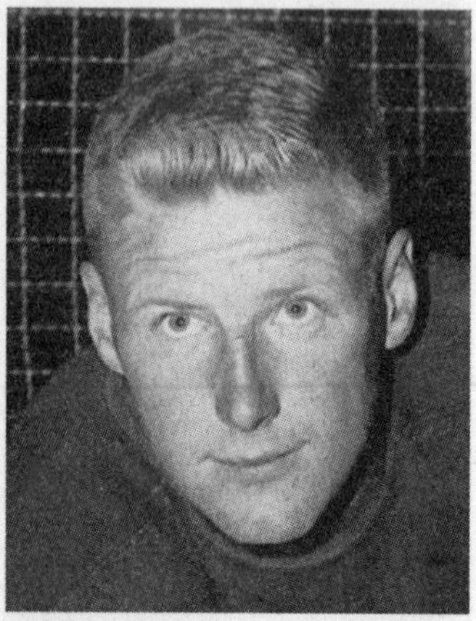

Billy McNeill

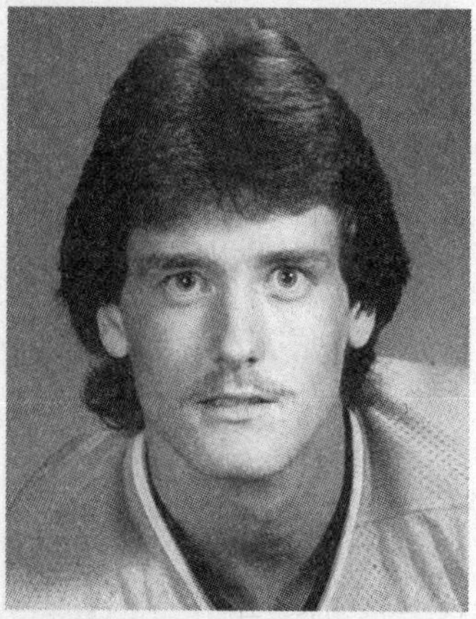

Ron Meighan

			Regular Schedule					Playoffs							
Name	**NHL Teams**	**NHL Seasons**	**GP**	**G**	**A**	**TP**	**PIM**	**GP**	**G**	**A**	**TP**	**PIM**	**NHL Cup Wins**	**First NHL Season**	**Last NHL Season**
Mayer, Pat	Pit.	1	1	0	0	0	4	....	....	....	....	....	....	1987-88	1987-88
• Mayer, Shep	Tor.	1	12	1	2	3	4	....	....	....	....	....	....	1942-43	1942-43
Mayers, Jamal	St.L., Tor., Cgy., S.J., Chi.	15	915	90	129	219	1200	63	5	8	13	32	1	1996-97	2012-13
‡ Mayorov, Maksim	CBJ	4	22	2	1	3	2	....	....	....	....	....	....	2008-09	2011-12
• Mazur, Eddie	Mtl., Chi.	6	107	8	20	28	120	25	4	5	9	22	1	1950-51	1956-57
Mazur, Jay	Van.	4	47	11	7	18	20	6	0	1	1	8	....	1988-89	1991-92
McAdam, Gary	Buf., Pit., Det., Cgy., Wsh., N.J., Tor.	11	534	96	132	228	243	30	6	5	11	16	....	1975-76	1985-86
• McAdam, Sam	NYR	1	5	0	0	0	0	....	....	....	....	....	....	1930-31	1930-31
McAllister, Chris	Van., Tor., Phi., Col., NYR	7	301	4	17	21	634	9	0	1	1	4	....	1997-98	2003-04
McAlpine, Chris	N.J., St.L., T.B., Atl., Chi., L.A.	8	289	6	24	30	245	28	0	1	1	18	1	1994-95	2002-03
McAmmond, Dean	Chi., Edm., Phi., Cgy., Col., St.L., Ott., NYI, N.J.	17	996	186	262	448	490	46	6	7	13	35	....	1991-92	2009-10
• McAndrew, Hazen	Bro.	1	7	0	1	1	6	....	....	....	....	....	....	1941-42	1941-42
McAneeley, Ted	Cal.	3	158	8	35	43	141	....	....	....	....	....	....	1972-73	1974-75
‡ McArdle, Kenndal	Fla., Wpg.	4	42	1	2	3	51	....	....	....	....	....	....	2008-09	2011-12
• McAtee, Jud	Det.	3	46	15	13	28	6	14	2	1	3	0	....	1942-43	1944-45
• McAtee, Norm	Bos.	1	13	0	1	1	0	....	....	....	....	....	....	1946-47	1946-47
• McAvoy, George	Mtl.	1	....	....	....	....	....	4	0	0	0	0	....	1954-55	1954-55
McBain, Andrew	Wpg., Pit., Van., Ott.	11	608	129	172	301	633	24	5	7	12	39	....	1983-84	1993-94
McBain, Jason	Hfd.	2	9	0	0	0	0	....	....	....	....	....	....	1995-96	1996-97
McBain, Mike	T.B.	2	64	0	7	7	22	....	....	....	....	....	....	1997-98	1998-99
McBean, Wayne	L.A., NYI, Wpg.	6	211	10	39	49	168	2	1	1	2	0	....	1987-88	1993-94
• McBride, Cliff	Mtl.M., Tor.	2	2	0	0	0	0	....	....	....	....	....	....	1928-29	1929-30
McBurney, Jim	Chi.	1	1	0	1	1	0	....	....	....	....	....	....	1952-53	1952-53
McCabe, Bryan	NYI, Van., Chi., Tor., Fla., NYR	15	1135	145	383	528	1732	56	10	18	28	84	....	1995-96	2010-11
• McCabe, Stan	Det., Mtl.M.	4	78	9	4	13	49	....	....	....	....	....	....	1929-30	1933-34
• McCaffrey, Bert	Tor., Pit., Mtl.	7	260	43	30	73	202	8	2	1	3	10	1	1924-25	1930-31
McCahill, John	Col.	1	1	0	0	0	0	....	....	....	....	....	....	1977-78	1977-78
• McCaig, Doug	Det., Chi.	7	263	8	21	29	255	7	0	1	1	10	....	1941-42	1950-51
• McCallum, Dunc	NYR, Pit.	5	187	14	35	49	230	10	1	2	3	12	....	1965-66	1970-71
• McCalmon, Eddie	Chi., Phi.	2	39	5	0	5	14	....	....	....	....	....	....	1927-28	1930-31
McCann, Rick	Det.	6	43	1	4	5	6	....	....	....	....	....	....	1967-68	1974-75
McCarthy, Dan	NYR	1	5	4	0	4	4	....	....	....	....	....	....	1980-81	1980-81
McCarthy, Kevin	Phi., Van., Pit.	10	537	67	191	258	527	21	2	3	5	20	....	1977-78	1986-87
McCarthy, Sandy	Cgy., T.B., Phi., Car., NYR, Bos.	11	736	72	76	148	1534	23	0	2	2	61	....	1993-94	2003-04
‡ McCarthy, Steve	Chi., Van., Atl.	8	302	17	38	55	168	....	....	....	....	....	....	1999-00	2007-08
• McCarthy, Thomas	Que., Ham.	2	35	22	7	29	10	....	....	....	....	....	....	1919-20	1920-21
• McCarthy, Tom	Det., Bos.	4	60	8	9	17	8	....	....	....	....	....	....	1956-57	1960-61
McCarthy, Tom	Min., Bos.	9	460	178	221	399	330	68	12	26	38	67	....	1979-80	1987-88
• McCartney, Walt	Mtl.	1	2	0	0	0	0	....	....	....	....	....	....	1932-33	1932-33
McCarty, Darren	Det., Cgy.	15	758	127	161	288	1477	174	23	26	49	228	4	1993-94	2008-09
McCaskill, Ted	Min.	1	4	0	2	2	0	....	....	....	....	....	....	1967-68	1967-68
McCauley, Alyn	Tor., S.J., L.A.	9	488	69	97	166	116	52	7	12	19	18	....	1997-98	2006-07
McClanahan, Rob	Buf., Hfd., NYR	5	224	38	63	101	126	34	4	12	16	31	....	1979-80	1983-84
McCleary, Trent	Ott., Bos., Mtl.	4	192	8	15	23	134	....	....	....	....	....	....	1995-96	1999-00
McClelland, Kevin	Pit., Edm., Det., Tor., Wpg.	12	588	68	112	180	1672	98	11	18	29	281	4	1981-82	1993-94
McCord, Bob	Bos., Det., Min., St.L.	7	316	10	58	68	262	14	2	5	7	10	....	1963-64	1972-73
• McCord, Dennis	Van.	1	3	0	0	0	6	....	....	....	....	....	....	1973-74	1973-74
McCormack, John	Tor., Mtl., Chi.	8	311	25	49	74	35	22	1	1	2	0	2	1947-48	1954-55
McCosh, Shawn	L.A., NYR	2	9	1	0	1	6	....	....	....	....	....	....	1991-92	1994-95
McCourt, Dale	Det., Buf., Tor.	7	532	194	284	478	124	21	9	7	16	6	....	1977-78	1983-84
McCreary, Bill	NYR, Det., Mtl., St.L.	8	309	53	62	115	108	48	6	16	22	14	....	1953-54	1970-71
McCreary, Bill	Tor.	1	12	1	0	1	4	....	....	....	....	....	....	1980-81	1980-81
• McCreary, Keith	Mtl., Pit., Atl.	10	532	131	112	243	294	16	0	4	4	6	....	1961-62	1974-75
• McCreedy, John	Tor.	2	64	17	12	29	25	21	4	3	7	16	2	1941-42	1944-45
• McCrimmon, Brad	Bos., Phi., Cgy., Det., Hfd., Phx.	18	1222	81	322	403	1416	116	11	18	29	176	1	1979-80	1996-97
McCrimmon, Jim	St.L.	1	2	0	0	0	0	....	....	....	....	....	....	1974-75	1974-75
• McCulley, Bob	Mtl.	1	1	0	0	0	0	....	....	....	....	....	....	1934-35	1934-35
• McCurry, Duke	Pit.	4	148	21	11	32	119	4	0	2	2	2	....	1925-26	1928-29
McCutcheon, Brian	Det.	3	37	3	1	4	7	....	....	....	....	....	....	1974-75	1976-77
McCutcheon, Darwin	Tor.	1	1	0	0	0	2	....	....	....	....	....	....	1981-82	1981-82
• McDill, Jeff	Chi.	1	1	0	0	0	0	....	....	....	....	....	....	1976-77	1976-77
McDonagh, Bill	NYR	1	4	0	0	0	2	....	....	....	....	....	....	1949-50	1949-50
McDonald, Ab	Mtl., Chi., Bos., Det., Pit., St.L.	15	762	182	248	430	200	84	21	29	50	42	4	1957-58	1971-72
McDonald, Andy	Ana., St.L.	12	685	182	307	489	280	56	18	19	37	28	1	2000-01	2012-13
McDonald, Brian	Chi., Buf.	2	12	0	0	0	29	8	0	0	0	2	....	1967-68	1970-71
• McDonald, Bucko	Det., Tor., NYR	11	446	35	88	123	206	50	6	1	7	24	3	1934-35	1944-45
• McDonald, Butch	Det., Chi.	2	66	8	20	28	2	5	0	2	2	10	....	1939-40	1944-45
McDonald, Gerry	Hfd.	2	8	0	0	0	4	....	....	....	....	....	....	1981-82	1983-84
• McDonald, Jack	Mtl.W., Mtl., Que., Tor.	5	69	26	14	40	30	7	1	3	4	3	....	1917-18	1921-22
McDonald, Jack	NYR	1	43	10	9	19	6	....	....	....	....	....	....	1943-44	1943-44
McDonald, Lanny	Tor., Col., Cgy.	16	1111	500	506	1006	899	117	44	40	84	120	1	1973-74	1988-89
McDonald, Robert	NYR	1	1	0	0	0	0	....	....	....	....	....	....	1943-44	1943-44
McDonald, Terry	K.C.	1	8	0	1	1	6	....	....	....	....	....	....	1975-76	1975-76
McDonell, Kent	CBJ	2	32	1	2	3	36	....	....	....	....	....	....	2002-03	2003-04
McDonnell, Joe	Van., Pit.	3	50	2	10	12	34	....	....	....	....	....	....	1981-82	1985-86
• McDonnell, Moylan	Ham.	1	22	1	2	3	2	....	....	....	....	....	....	1920-21	1920-21
McDonough, Al	L.A., Pit., Atl., Det.	5	237	73	88	161	73	8	0	1	1	2	....	1970-71	1977-78
McDonough, Hubie	L.A., NYI, S.J.	5	195	40	26	66	67	5	1	0	1	4	....	1988-89	1992-93
McDougal, Mike	NYR, Hfd.	4	61	8	10	18	43	....	....	....	....	....	....	1978-79	1982-83
McDougall, Bill	Det., Edm., T.B.	3	28	5	5	10	12	1	0	0	0	0	....	1990-91	1993-94
McEachern, Shawn	Pit., L.A., Bos., Ott., Atl.	14	911	256	323	579	506	97	12	25	37	62	1	1991-92	2005-06
McElmury, Jim	Min., K.C., Col.	5	180	14	47	61	49	....	....	....	....	....	....	1972-73	1977-78
McEwen, Mike	NYR, Col., NYI, L.A., Wsh., Det., Hfd.	12	716	108	296	404	460	78	12	36	48	48	3	1976-77	1987-88
• McFadden, Jim	Det., Chi.	8	412	100	126	226	89	49	10	9	19	30	1	1946-47	1953-54
• McFadyen, Don	Chi.	4	179	12	33	45	77	11	2	2	4	5	1	1932-33	1935-36
McFall, Dan	Wpg.	2	9	0	1	1	0	....	....	....	....	....	....	1984-85	1985-86
• McFarlane, Gord	Chi.	1	2	0	0	0	0	....	....	....	....	....	....	1926-27	1926-27
McGeough, Jim	Wsh., Pit.	4	57	7	10	17	32	....	....	....	....	....	....	1981-82	1986-87
• McGibbon, Irv	Mtl.	1	1	0	0	0	2	....	....	....	....	....	....	1942-43	1942-43
McGill, Bob	Tor., Chi., S.J., Det., NYI, Hfd.	13	705	17	55	72	1766	49	0	0	0	88	....	1981-82	1993-94
• McGill, Jack	Mtl.	3	134	27	10	37	71	3	2	0	2	0	....	1934-35	1936-37
• McGill, Jack	Bos.	4	97	23	36	59	42	27	7	4	11	17	....	1941-42	1946-47
McGill, Ryan	Chi., Phi., Edm.	4	151	4	15	19	391	....	....	....	....	....	....	1991-92	1994-95
McGillis, Dan	Edm., Phi., S.J., Bos., N.J.	9	634	56	182	238	570	64	8	14	22	76	....	1996-97	2005-06
McGregor, Sandy	NYR	1	2	0	0	0	2	....	....	....	....	....	....	1963-64	1963-64
• McGuire, Mickey	Pit.	2	36	3	0	3	6	....	....	....	....	....	....	1926-27	1927-28
McHugh, Mike	Min., S.J.	4	20	1	0	1	16	....	....	....	....	....	....	1988-89	1991-92
McIlhargey, Jack	Phi., Van., Hfd.	8	393	11	36	47	1102	27	0	3	3	68	....	1974-75	1981-82
• McInenly, Bert	Det., NYA, Ott., Bos.	6	166	19	15	34	144	4	0	0	0	2	....	1930-31	1935-36
McInnis, Marty	NYI, Cgy., Ana., Bos.	12	796	170	250	420	330	22	3	2	5	4	....	1991-92	2002-03
McIntosh, Bruce	Min.	1	2	0	0	0	0	....	....	....	....	....	....	1972-73	1972-73
McIntosh, Paul	Buf.	2	48	0	2	2	66	2	0	0	0	7	....	1974-75	1975-76
‡ McIntyre, David	Min.	1	7	1	1	2	2	....	....	....	....	....	....	2011-12	2011-12
• McIntyre, Jack	Bos., Chi., Det.	11	499	109	102	211	173	29	7	6	13	4	....	1949-50	1959-60
McIntyre, John	Tor., L.A., NYR, Van.	6	351	24	54	78	516	44	0	6	6	54	....	1989-90	1994-95
McIntyre, Larry	Tor.	2	41	0	3	3	26	....	....	....	....	....	....	1969-70	1972-73
McKay, Doug	Det.	1	....	....	....	....	....	1	0	0	0	0	1	1949-50	1949-50
McKay, Randy	Det., N.J., Dal., Mtl.	15	932	162	201	363	1731	123	20	23	43	123	2	1988-89	2002-03
McKay, Ray	Chi., Buf., Cal.	6	140	2	16	18	102	1	0	0	0	0	....	1968-69	1973-74
McKay, Scott	Ana.	1	1	0	0	0	0	....	....	....	....	....	....	1993-94	1993-94
McKechnie, Walt	Min., Cal., Bos., Det., Wsh., Cle., Tor., Col.	16	955	214	392	606	469	15	7	5	12	7	....	1967-68	1982-83
‡ McKee, Jay	Buf., St.L., Pit.	14	802	21	104	125	622	60	3	6	9	66	....	1995-96	2009-10
McKee, Mike	Que.	1	48	3	12	15	41	....	....	....	....	....	....	1993-94	1993-94
McKegney, Ian	Chi.	1	3	0	0	0	2	....	....	....	....	....	....	1976-77	1976-77
McKegney, Tony	Buf., Que., Min., NYR, St.L., Det., Chi.	13	912	320	319	639	517	79	24	23	47	56	....	1978-79	1990-91
McKendry, Alex	NYI, Cgy.	4	46	3	6	9	21	6	2	2	4	0	1	1977-78	1980-81
McKenna, Sean	Buf., L.A., Tor.	9	414	82	80	162	181	15	1	2	3	2	....	1981-82	1989-90
McKenna, Steve	L.A., Min., Pit., NYR	8	373	18	14	32	824	3	0	1	1	8	....	1996-97	2003-04
McKenney, Don	Bos., NYR, Tor., Det., St.L.	13	798	237	345	582	211	58	18	29	47	10	1	1954-55	1967-68
McKenny, Jim	Tor., Min.	14	604	82	247	329	294	37	7	9	16	10	....	1965-66	1978-79
McKenzie, Brian	Pit.	1	6	1	1	2	4	....	....	....	....	....	....	1971-72	1971-72
McKenzie, Jim	Hfd., Dal., Pit., Wpg., Phx., Ana., Wsh., N.J., Nsh.	15	880	48	52	100	1739	51	0	0	0	38	1	1989-90	2003-04
McKenzie, John	Chi., Det., NYR, Bos.	12	691	206	268	474	917	69	15	32	47	133	2	1958-59	1971-72

Name	NHL Teams	NHL Seasons	Regular Schedule GP	G	A	TP	PIM	Playoffs GP	G	A	TP	PIM	NHL Cup Wins	First NHL Season	Last NHL Season
McKim, Andrew	Bos., Det.	3	38	1	4	5	6	....	....	....	....	....	....	1992-93	1994-95
● McKinnon, Alex	Ham., NYA, Chi.	5	193	19	11	30	237	....	....	....	....	....	....	1924-25	1928-29
● McKinnon, John	Mtl., Pit., Phi.	6	208	28	11	39	224	2	0	0	0	4	....	1925-26	1930-31
McLaren, Kyle	Bos., S.J.	12	719	46	161	207	671	70	1	13	14	78	....	1995-96	2007-08
McLaren, Steve	St.L.	1	6	0	0	0	25	....	....	....	....	....	....	2003-04	2003-04
‡ McLean, Brett	Chi., Col., Fla.	6	385	56	106	162	204	8	0	1	1	4	....	2002-03	2008-09
McLean, Don	Wsh.	1	9	0	0	0	6	....	....	....	....	....	....	1975-76	1975-76
● McLean, Fred	Que., Ham.	2	8	0	0	0	2	....	....	....	....	....	....	1919-20	1920-21
● McLean, Jack	Tor.	3	67	14	24	38	76	13	2	2	4	8	1	1942-43	1944-45
● McLean, Jeff	S.J.	1	6	1	0	1	0	....	....	....	....	....	....	1993-94	1993-94
‡ McLean, Kurtis	NYI	1	4	1	0	1	0	....	....	....	....	....	....	2008-09	2008-09
● McLellan, John	Tor.	1	2	0	0	0	0	....	....	....	....	....	....	1951-52	1951-52
McLellan, Scott	Bos.	1	2	0	0	0	0	....	....	....	....	....	....	1982-83	1982-83
McLellan, Todd	NYI	1	5	1	1	2	0	....	....	....	....	....	....	1987-88	1987-88
● McLenahan, Rollie	Det.	1	9	2	1	3	10	2	0	0	0	0	....	1945-46	1945-46
McLeod, Al	Det.	1	26	2	2	4	24	....	....	....	....	....	....	1973-74	1973-74
McLeod, Jackie	NYR	5	106	14	23	37	12	7	0	0	0	0	....	1949-50	1954-55
McLlwain, Dave	Pit., Wpg., Buf., NYI, Tor., Ott.	10	501	100	107	207	292	20	0	2	2	2	....	1987-88	1996-97
● McMahon, Mike	Mtl., Bos.	3	57	7	18	25	102	13	1	2	3	30	1	1942-43	1945-46
● McMahon, Mike	NYR, Min., Chi., Det., Pit., Buf.	8	224	15	68	83	171	14	3	7	10	4	....	1963-64	1971-72
McManama, Bob	Pit.	3	99	11	25	36	28	8	0	1	1	6	....	1973-74	1975-76
● McManus, Sammy	Mtl.M., Bos.	2	26	0	1	1	8	1	0	0	0	0	1	1934-35	1936-37
McMorrow, Sean	Buf.	1	1	0	0	0	0	....	....	....	....	....	....	2002-03	2002-03
McMurchy, Tom	Chi., Edm.	4	55	8	4	12	65	....	....	....	....	....	....	1983-84	1987-88
● McNab, Max	Det.	4	128	16	19	35	24	25	1	0	1	4	1	1947-48	1950-51
McNab, Peter	Buf., Bos., Van., N.J.	14	954	363	450	813	179	107	40	42	82	20	....	1973-74	1986-87
● McNabney, Sid	Mtl.	1	....	....	....	....	....	5	0	1	1	2	....	1950-51	1950-51
● McNamara, Howard	Mtl.	1	10	1	0	1	4	....	....	....	....	....	....	1919-20	1919-20
● McNaughton, George	Que.	1	1	0	0	0	0	....	....	....	....	....	....	1919-20	1919-20
● McNeill, Billy	Det.	6	257	21	46	67	142	4	1	1	2	4	....	1956-57	1963-64
McNeill, Grant	Fla.	1	3	0	0	0	5	....	....	....	....	....	....	2003-04	2003-04
McNeill, Mike	Chi., Que.	2	63	5	11	16	18	....	....	....	....	....	....	1990-91	1991-92
McNeill, Stu	Det.	3	10	1	1	2	2	....	....	....	....	....	....	1957-58	1959-60
McPhee, George	NYR, N.J.	7	115	24	25	49	257	29	5	3	8	69	....	1982-83	1988-89
McPhee, Mike	Mtl., Min., Dal.	11	744	200	199	399	661	134	28	27	55	193	1	1983-84	1993-94
McRae, Basil	Que., Tor., Det., Min., T.B., St.L., Chi.	16	576	53	83	136	2457	78	8	4	12	349	....	1981-82	1996-97
McRae, Chris	Tor., Det.	3	21	1	0	1	122	....	....	....	....	....	....	1987-88	1989-90
McRae, Ken	Que., Tor.	7	137	14	21	35	364	6	0	0	0	4	....	1987-88	1993-94
● McReavy, Pat	Bos., Det.	4	55	5	10	15	4	22	3	3	6	9	1	1938-39	1941-42
McReynolds, Brian	Wpg., NYR, L.A.	3	30	1	5	6	8	....	....	....	....	....	....	1989-90	1993-94
McSheffrey, Bryan	Van., Buf.	3	90	13	7	20	44	....	....	....	....	....	....	1972-73	1974-75
McSorley, Marty	Pit., Edm., L.A., NYR, S.J., Bos.	17	961	108	251	359	3381	115	10	19	29	374	2	1983-84	1999-00
McSween, Don	Buf., Ana.	5	47	3	10	13	55	....	....	....	....	....	....	1987-88	1995-96
McTaggart, Jim	Wsh.	2	71	3	10	13	205	....	....	....	....	....	....	1980-81	1981-82
McTavish, Dale	Cgy.	1	9	1	2	3	2	....	....	....	....	....	....	1996-97	1996-97
McTavish, Gord	St.L., Wpg.	2	11	1	3	4	2	....	....	....	....	....	....	1978-79	1979-80
● McVeigh, Charley	Chi., NYA	9	397	84	88	172	138	4	0	0	0	2	....	1926-27	1934-35
● McVicar, Jack	Mtl.M.	2	88	2	4	6	63	6	0	0	0	2	....	1930-31	1931-32
Meagher, Rick	Mtl., Hfd., N.J., St.L.	12	691	144	165	309	383	62	8	7	15	41	....	1979-80	1990-91
Meehan, Gerry	Tor., Phi., Buf., Van., Atl., Wsh.	10	670	180	243	423	111	10	0	1	1	0	....	1968-69	1978-79
Meeke, Brent	Cal., Cle.	5	75	9	22	31	8	....	....	....	....	....	....	1972-73	1976-77
Meeker, Howie	Tor.	8	346	83	102	185	329	42	6	9	15	50	4	1946-47	1953-54
Meeker, Mike	Pit.	1	4	0	0	0	5	....	....	....	....	....	....	1978-79	1978-79
● Meeking, Harry	Tor., Det., Bos.	3	64	18	12	30	66	9	3	0	3	6	....	1917-18	1926-27
Meger, Paul	Mtl.	6	212	39	52	91	118	35	3	8	11	16	1	1949-50	1954-55
Meighan, Ron	Min., Pit.	2	48	3	7	10	18	....	....	....	....	....	....	1981-82	1982-83
Meissner, Barrie	Min.	2	6	0	1	1	4	....	....	....	....	....	....	1967-68	1968-69
● Meissner, Dick	Bos., NYR	5	171	11	15	26	37	....	....	....	....	....	....	1959-60	1964-65
Melametsa, Anssi	Wpg.	1	27	0	3	3	2	....	....	....	....	....	....	1985-86	1985-86
Melanson, Dean	Buf., Wsh.	2	9	0	0	0	8	....	....	....	....	....	....	1994-95	2001-02
Melichar, Josef	Pit., Car., T.B.	7	349	7	42	49	300	5	0	0	0	2	....	2000-01	2008-09
‡ Melin, Bjorn	Ana.	1	3	1	0	1	0	....	....	....	....	....	....	2006-07	2006-07
Melin, Roger	Min.	2	3	0	0	0	0	....	....	....	....	....	....	1980-81	1981-82
Mellanby, Scott	Phi., Edm., Fla., St.L., Atl.	21	1431	364	476	840	2479	136	24	29	53	220	....	1985-86	2006-07
Mellor, Tom	Det.	2	26	2	4	6	25	....	....	....	....	....	....	1973-74	1974-75
● Melnyk, Gerry	Det., Chi., St.L.	6	269	39	77	116	34	53	6	6	12	6	....	1955-56	1967-68
Melnyk, Larry	Bos., Edm., NYR, Van.	10	432	11	63	74	686	66	2	9	11	127	1	1980-81	1989-90
Meloche, Eric	Pit., Phi.	4	74	9	11	20	36	....	....	....	....	....	....	2001-02	2006-07
Melrose, Barry	Wpg., Tor., Det.	6	300	10	23	33	728	7	0	2	2	38	....	1979-80	1985-86
Menard, Hillary	Chi.	1	1	0	0	0	0	....	....	....	....	....	....	1953-54	1953-54
Menard, Howie	Det., L.A., Chi., Oak.	4	151	23	42	65	87	19	3	7	10	36	....	1963-64	1969-70
‡ Mercier, Justin	Col.	1	9	1	1	2	0	....	....	....	....	....	....	2009-10	2009-10
Mercredi, Vic	Atl.	1	2	0	0	0	0	....	....	....	....	....	....	1974-75	1974-75
Meredith, Greg	Cgy.	2	38	6	4	10	8	5	3	1	4	4	....	1980-81	1982-83
Merkosky, Glenn	Hfd., N.J., Det.	5	66	5	12	17	22	....	....	....	....	....	....	1981-82	1989-90
● Meronek, Bill	Mtl.	2	19	5	8	13	0	1	0	0	0	0	....	1939-40	1942-43
Merrick, Wayne	St.L., Cal., Cle., NYI	12	774	191	265	456	303	102	19	30	49	30	4	1972-73	1983-84
● Merrill, Horace	Ott.	2	8	0	0	0	3	....	....	....	....	....	1	1917-18	1919-20
Mertzig, Jan	NYR	1	23	0	2	2	8	....	....	....	....	....	....	1998-99	1998-99
Messier, Eric	Col., Fla.	8	406	25	50	75	146	72	3	5	8	22	1	1996-97	2003-04
Messier, Joby	NYR	3	25	0	4	4	24	....	....	....	....	....	....	1992-93	1994-95
Messier, Mark	Edm., NYR, Van.	25	1756	694	1193	1887	1910	236	109	186	295	244	6	1979-80	2003-04
Messier, Mitch	Min.	4	20	0	2	2	11	....	....	....	....	....	....	1987-88	1990-91
Messier, Paul	Col.	1	9	0	0	0	4	....	....	....	....	....	....	1978-79	1978-79
Metcalfe, Scott	Edm., Buf.	3	19	1	2	3	18	....	....	....	....	....	....	1987-88	1989-90
‡ Metropolit, Glen	Wsh., T.B., Atl., St.L., Bos., Phi., Mtl.	8	407	57	102	159	148	30	1	4	5	12	....	1999-00	2009-10
● Metz, Don	Tor.	9	172	20	35	55	42	42	7	8	15	12	5	1938-39	1948-49
● Metz, Nick	Tor.	12	518	131	119	250	149	76	19	20	39	31	4	1934-35	1947-48
Meyer, Freddy	Phi., NYI, Phx., Atl.	7	281	20	53	73	155	6	0	1	1	8	....	2003-04	2010-11
‡ Meyer, Stefan	Fla., Cgy.	2	20	0	2	2	17	....	....	....	....	....	....	2007-08	2010-11
‡ Mezei, Branislav	NYI, Fla.	7	240	5	19	24	311	....	....	....	....	....	....	2000-01	2007-08
● Michaluk, Art	Chi.	1	5	0	0	0	0	....	....	....	....	....	....	1947-48	1947-48
● Michaluk, John	Chi.	1	1	0	0	0	0	....	....	....	....	....	....	1950-51	1950-51
Michayluk, Dave	Phi., Pit.	3	14	2	6	8	8	7	1	1	2	0	1	1981-82	1991-92
Micheletti, Joe	St.L., Col.	3	158	11	60	71	114	11	1	11	12	10	....	1979-80	1981-82
Micheletti, Pat	Min.	1	12	2	0	2	8	....	....	....	....	....	....	1987-88	1987-88
● Mickey, Larry	Chi., NYR, Tor., Mtl., L.A., Phi., Buf.	11	292	39	53	92	160	9	1	0	1	10	....	1964-65	1974-75
● Mickoski, Nick	NYR, Chi., Det., Bos.	13	703	158	185	343	319	18	1	6	7	6	....	1947-48	1959-60
Middendorf, Max	Que., Edm.	4	13	2	4	6	6	....	....	....	....	....	....	1986-87	1990-91
Middleton, Rick	NYR, Bos.	14	1005	448	540	988	157	114	45	55	100	19	....	1974-75	1987-88
Miehm, Kevin	St.L.	2	22	1	4	5	8	2	0	1	1	0	....	1992-93	1993-94
‡ Miettinen, Antti	Dal., Min., Wpg.	9	539	97	133	230	234	24	2	3	5	10	....	2003-04	2012-13
Migay, Rudy	Tor.	10	418	59	92	151	293	15	1	0	1	20	....	1949-50	1959-60
‡ Mihalik, Vladimir	T.B.	2	15	0	3	3	8	....	....	....	....	....	....	2008-09	2009-10
Mika, Petr	NYI	1	3	0	0	0	0	....	....	....	....	....	....	1999-00	1999-00
‡ Mikhnov, Alexei	Edm.	1	2	0	0	0	0	....	....	....	....	....	....	2006-07	2006-07
Mikita, Stan	Chi.	22	1394	541	926	1467	1270	155	59	91	150	169	1	1958-59	1979-80
Mikkelson, Bill	L.A., NYI, Wsh.	4	147	4	18	22	105	....	....	....	....	....	....	1971-72	1976-77
‡ Mikkelson, Brendan	Ana., Cgy., T.B.	5	131	1	9	10	59	....	....	....	....	....	....	2008-09	2012-13
● Mikol, Jim	Tor., NYR	2	34	1	4	5	8	....	....	....	....	....	....	1962-63	1964-65
Mikulchik, Oleg	Wpg., Ana.	3	37	0	3	3	33	....	....	....	....	....	....	1993-94	1995-96
Milbury, Mike	Bos.	12	754	49	189	238	1552	86	4	24	28	219	....	1975-76	1986-87
● Milks, Hib	Pit., Phi., NYR, Ott.	8	317	87	41	128	179	11	0	0	0	2	....	1925-26	1932-33
Millar, Craig	Edm., Nsh., T.B.	5	114	8	14	22	73	....	....	....	....	....	....	1996-97	2000-01
● Millar, Hugh	Det.	1	4	0	0	0	0	1	0	0	0	0	....	1946-47	1946-47
Millar, Mike	Hfd., Wsh., Bos., Tor.	5	78	18	18	36	12	....	....	....	....	....	....	1986-87	1990-91
Millen, Corey	NYR, L.A., N.J., Dal., Cgy.	8	335	90	119	209	236	47	5	7	12	22	....	1989-90	1996-97
Miller, Aaron	Que., Col., L.A., Van.	14	677	25	94	119	422	80	3	9	12	40	....	1993-94	2007-08
● Miller, Bill	Mtl.M., Mtl.	3	95	7	3	10	16	12	0	0	0	0	1	1934-35	1936-37
Miller, Bob	Bos., Col., L.A.	6	404	75	119	194	220	36	4	7	11	27	....	1977-78	1984-85
Miller, Brad	Buf., Ott., Cgy.	6	82	1	5	6	321	....	....	....	....	....	....	1988-89	1993-94
● Miller, Earl	Chi., Tor.	5	109	19	14	33	124	10	1	0	1	6	1	1927-28	1931-32
● Miller, Jack	Chi.	2	17	0	0	0	4	....	....	....	....	....	....	1949-50	1950-51
Miller, Jason	N.J.	3	6	0	0	0	0	....	....	....	....	....	....	1990-91	1992-93
Miller, Jay	Bos., L.A.	7	446	40	44	84	1723	48	2	3	5	243	....	1985-86	1991-92
Miller, Kelly	NYR, Wsh.	15	1057	181	282	463	512	119	20	34	54	65	....	1984-85	1998-99

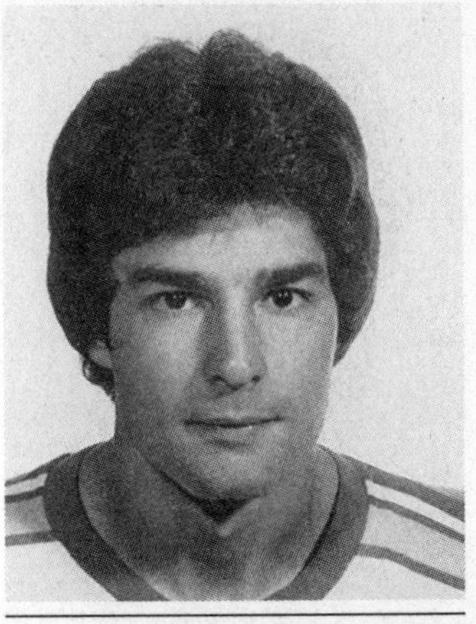

Joe Micheletti

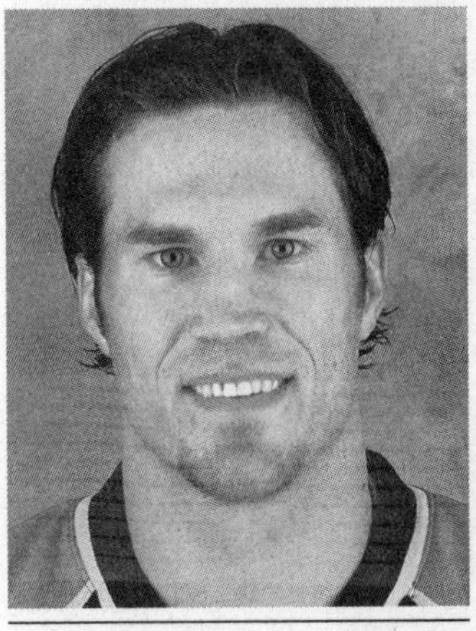

Steve Montador

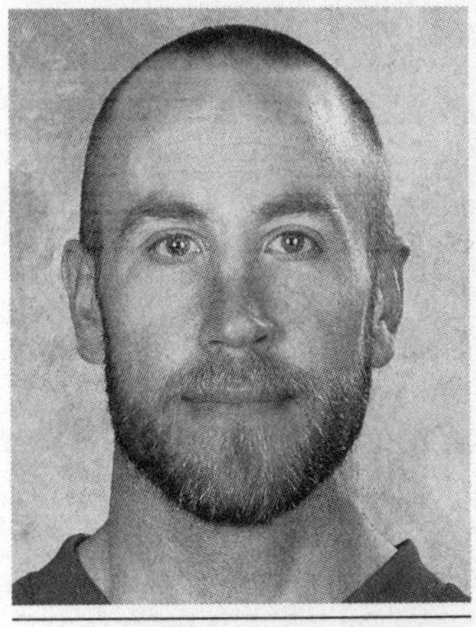

Derek Morris

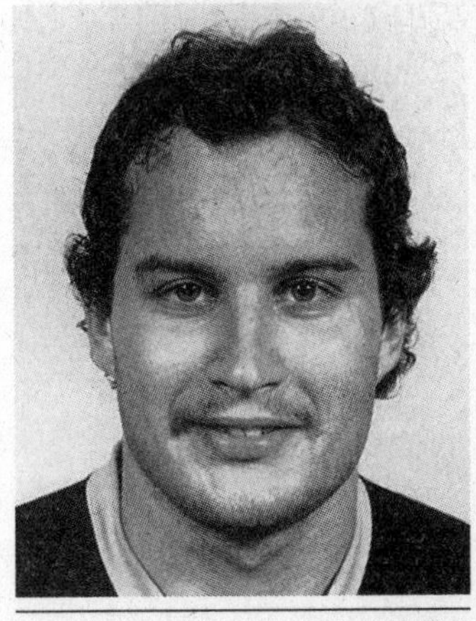

Doug Morrison

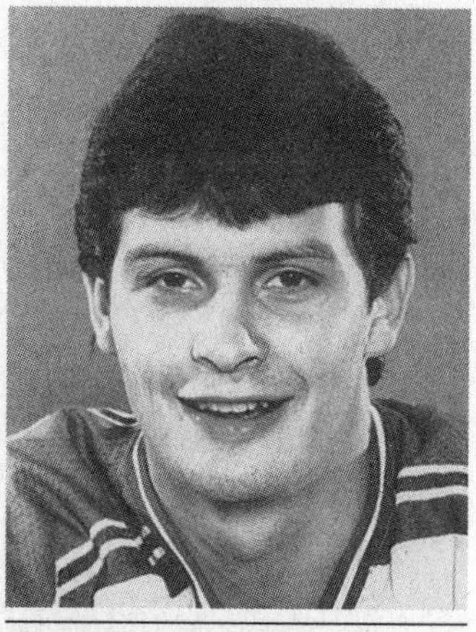
Mark Morrison

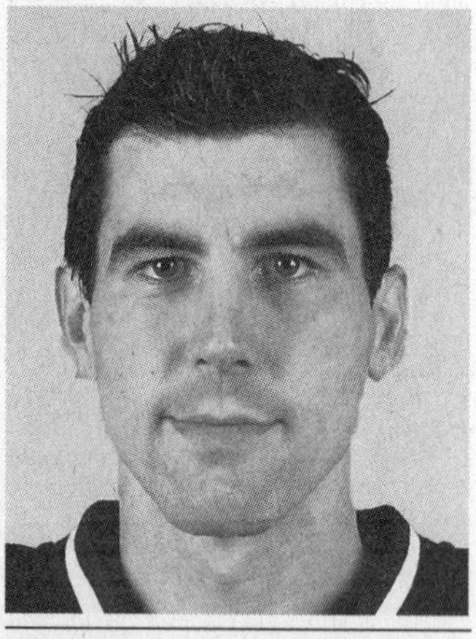
Mike Mottau

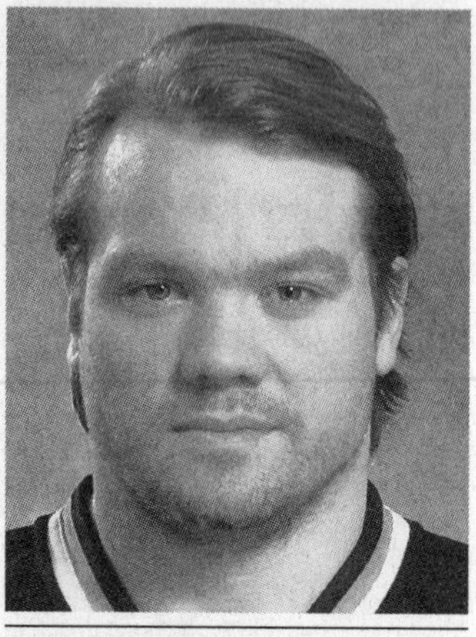
Douglas Murray

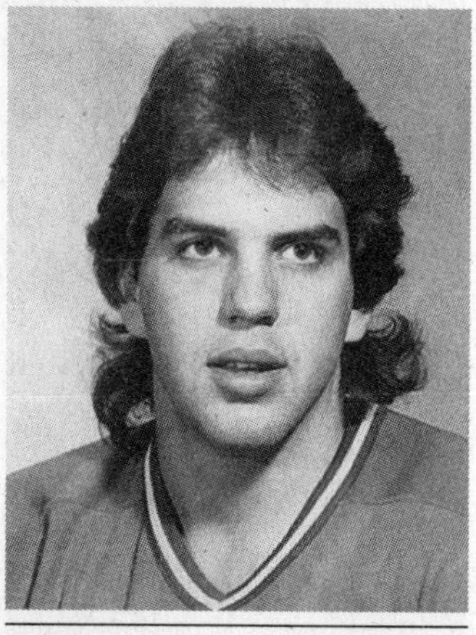
Ric Nattress

			Regular Schedule					Playoffs							
Name	NHL Teams	NHL Seasons	GP	G	A	TP	PIM	GP	G	A	TP	PIM	NHL Cup Wins	First NHL Season	Last NHL Season
Miller, Kevin	NYR, Det., Wsh., St.L., S.J., Pit., Chi., NYI, Ott.	13	620	150	185	335	429	61	7	10	17	49	....	1988-89	2003-04
Miller, Kip	Que., Min., S.J., NYI, Chi., Pit., Ana., Wsh.	12	449	74	165	239	105	25	6	11	17	23	....	1990-91	2003-04
Miller, Paul	Col.	1	3	0	3	3	0	....	....	....	....	....	....	1981-82	1981-82
Miller, Perry	Det.	4	217	10	51	61	387	....	....	....	....	....	....	1977-78	1980-81
Miller, Tom	Det., NYI	4	118	16	25	41	34	....	....	....	....	....	....	1970-71	1974-75
Miller, Warren	NYR, Hfd.	4	262	40	50	90	137	6	1	0	1	0	....	1979-80	1982-83
Milley, Norm	Buf., T.B.	4	29	2	4	6	12	....	....	....	....	....	....	2001-02	2005-06
Mills, Craig	Wpg., Chi.	3	31	0	5	5	36	1	0	0	0	0	....	1995-96	1998-99
Milroy, Duncan	Mtl.	1	5	0	1	1	0	....	....	....	....	....	....	2006-07	2006-07
Minard, Chris	Pit., Edm.	3	40	2	4	6	14	....	....	....	....	....	....	2007-08	2009-10
Miner, John	Edm.	1	14	2	3	5	16	....	....	....	....	....	....	1987-88	1987-88
Mink, Graham	Wsh.	3	7	0	0	0	2	....	....	....	....	....	....	2003-04	2008-09
Minor, Gerry	Van.	5	140	11	21	32	173	12	1	3	4	25	....	1979-80	1983-84
Mironov, Boris	Wpg., Edm., Chi., NYR	11	716	76	231	307	891	25	5	11	16	45	....	1993-94	2003-04
Mironov, Dmitri	Tor., Pit., Ana., Det., Wsh.	10	556	54	206	260	568	75	10	26	36	48	1	1991-92	2000-01
Miszuk, John	Det., Chi., Phi., Min.	6	237	7	39	46	232	19	0	3	3	19	....	1963-64	1969-70
• Mitchell, Bill	Det.	1	1	0	0	0	0	....	....	....	....	....	....	1963-64	1963-64
• Mitchell, Herb	Bos.	2	44	6	0	6	36	....	....	....	....	....	....	1924-25	1925-26
Mitchell, Jeff	Dal.	1	7	0	0	0	7	....	....	....	....	....	....	1997-98	1997-98
• Mitchell, Red	Chi.	3	83	4	5	9	67	....	....	....	....	....	....	1941-42	1944-45
Mitchell, Roy	Min.	1	3	0	0	0	0	....	....	....	....	....	....	1992-93	1992-93
Modano, Mike	Min., Dal., Det.	22	1499	561	813	1374	930	176	58	88	146	128	1	1988-89	2010-11
Modin, Fredrik	Tor., T.B., CBJ, L.A., Atl., Cgy.	14	898	232	230	462	453	57	14	12	26	42	1	1996-97	2010-11
Modry, Jaroslav	N.J., Ott., L.A., Atl., Dal., Phi.	13	725	49	201	250	510	28	1	5	6	6	....	1993-94	2007-08
• Moe, Bill	NYR	5	261	11	42	53	163	1	0	0	0	0	....	1944-45	1948-49
Moffat, Lyle	Tor., Wpg.	3	97	12	16	28	51	....	....	....	....	....	....	1972-73	1979-80
• Moffat, Ron	Det.	3	37	1	1	2	8	7	0	0	0	0	....	1932-33	1934-35
Moger, Sandy	Bos., L.A.	5	236	41	38	79	212	5	2	2	4	12	....	1994-95	1998-99
Mogilny, Alexander	Buf., Van., N.J., Tor.	16	990	473	559	1032	432	124	39	47	86	58	1	1989-90	2005-06
Moher, Mike	N.J.	1	9	0	1	1	28	....	....	....	....	....	....	1982-83	1982-83
• Mohns, Doug	Bos., Chi., Min., Atl., Wsh.	22	1390	248	462	710	1250	94	14	36	50	122	....	1953-54	1974-75
• Mohns, Lloyd	NYR	1	1	0	0	0	0	....	....	....	....	....	....	1943-44	1943-44
‡ Mojzis, Tomas	Van., St.L., Min.	3	17	1	2	3	14	....	....	....	....	....	....	2005-06	2008-09
Mokosak, Carl	Cgy., L.A., Phi., Pit., Bos.	6	83	11	15	26	170	1	0	0	0	0	....	1981-82	1988-89
Mokosak, John	Det.	2	41	0	2	2	96	....	....	....	....	....	....	1988-89	1989-90
Molin, Lars	Van.	3	172	33	65	98	37	19	2	9	11	7	....	1981-82	1983-84
Moller, Mike	Buf., Edm.	7	134	15	28	43	41	3	0	1	1	0	....	1980-81	1986-87
Moller, Randy	Que., NYR, Buf., Fla.	14	815	45	180	225	1692	78	6	16	22	197	....	1981-82	1994-95
Molloy, Mitch	Buf.	1	2	0	0	0	10	....	....	....	....	....	....	1989-90	1989-90
• Molyneaux, Larry	NYR	2	45	0	1	1	20	10	0	0	0	8	....	1937-38	1938-39
Momesso, Sergio	Mtl., St.L., Van., Tor., NYR	13	710	152	193	345	1557	119	18	26	44	311	....	1983-84	1996-97
Monahan, Garry	Mtl., Det., L.A., Tor., Van.	12	748	116	169	285	484	22	3	1	4	13	....	1967-68	1978-79
Monahan, Hartland	Cal., NYR, Wsh., Pit., L.A., St.L.	7	334	61	80	141	163	6	0	0	0	4	....	1973-74	1980-81
• Mondou, Armand	Mtl.	12	386	47	71	118	99	32	3	5	8	12	2	1928-29	1939-40
Mondou, Pierre	Mtl.	9	548	194	262	456	179	69	17	28	45	26	3	1976-77	1984-85
• Mongeau, Michel	St.L., T.B.	4	54	6	19	25	10	2	0	1	1	0	....	1989-90	1992-93
Mongrain, Bob	Buf., L.A.	6	81	13	14	27	14	11	1	2	3	2	....	1979-80	1985-86
• Montador, Steve	Cgy., Fla., Ana., Bos., Buf., Chi.	10	571	33	98	131	807	43	3	5	8	36	....	2001-02	2011-12
Monteith, Hank	Det.	3	77	5	12	17	6	4	0	0	0	0	....	1968-69	1970-71
Montgomery, Jim	St.L., Mtl., Phi., S.J., Dal.	6	122	9	25	34	80	8	1	0	1	2	....	1993-94	2002-03
Moore, Barrie	Buf., Edm., Wsh.	3	39	2	6	8	18	....	....	....	....	....	....	1995-96	1999-00
Moore, Dickie	Mtl., Tor., St.L.	14	719	261	347	608	652	135	46	64	110	122	6	1951-52	1967-68
Moore, Greg	NYR, CBJ	2	10	0	0	0	0	....	....	....	....	....	....	2007-08	2009-10
Moore, Steve	Col.	3	69	5	7	12	41	....	....	....	....	....	....	2001-02	2003-04
• Moran, Amby	Mtl., Chi.	2	35	1	1	2	24	....	....	....	....	....	....	1926-27	1927-28
Moran, Brad	CBJ, Van.	3	8	1	2	3	4	....	....	....	....	....	....	2001-02	2006-07
Moran, Ian	Pit., Bos., Ana.	12	489	21	50	71	321	66	1	7	8	24	....	1994-95	2006-07
Moravec, David	Buf.	1	1	0	0	0	0	....	....	....	....	....	....	1999-00	1999-00
More, Jay	NYR, Min., S.J., Phx., Chi., Nsh.	10	406	18	54	72	702	31	0	6	6	45	....	1988-89	1998-99
Moreau, Ethan	Chi., Edm., CBJ, L.A.	16	928	147	140	287	1110	46	3	6	9	52	....	1995-96	2011-12
• Morenz, Howie	Mtl., Chi., NYR	14	550	271	201	472	546	39	13	9	22	58	3	1923-24	1936-37
Moretto, Angelo	Cle.	1	5	1	2	3	2	....	....	....	....	....	....	1976-77	1976-77
Morgan, Gavin	Dal.	1	6	0	0	0	21	....	....	....	....	....	....	2003-04	2003-04
Morgan, Jason	L.A., Cgy., Nsh., Chi., Min.	5	44	2	5	7	18	....	....	....	....	....	....	1996-97	2006-07
• Morin, Pete	Mtl.	1	31	10	12	22	7	1	0	0	0	0	....	1941-42	1941-42
• Morin, Stephane	Que., Van.	5	90	16	39	55	52	....	....	....	....	....	....	1989-90	1993-94
Morisset, Dave	Fla.	1	4	0	0	0	5	....	....	....	....	....	....	2001-02	2001-02
Morissette, Dave	Mtl.	2	11	0	0	0	57	....	....	....	....	....	....	1998-99	1999-00
Moro, Marc	Ana., Nsh., Tor.	4	30	0	0	0	77	....	....	....	....	....	....	1997-98	2001-02
Morozov, Aleksey	Pit.	7	451	84	135	219	98	39	4	5	9	8	....	1997-98	2003-04
• Morris, Bernie	Bos.	1	6	1	0	1	0	....	....	....	....	....	....	1924-25	1924-25
‡ Morris, Derek	Cgy., Col., Phx., NYR, Bos.	16	1107	92	332	424	1004	37	3	12	15	41	....	1997-98	2013-14
Morris, Jon	N.J., S.J., Bos.	6	103	16	33	49	47	11	1	7	8	25	....	1988-89	1993-94
• Morris, Moe	Tor., NYR	4	135	13	29	42	58	18	4	2	6	16	1	1943-44	1948-49
Morrison, Brendan	N.J., Van., Ana., Dal., Wsh., Cgy., Chi.	14	934	200	401	601	452	61	9	21	30	40	....	1997-98	2011-12
Morrison, Dave	L.A., Van.	4	39	3	3	6	4	....	....	....	....	....	....	1980-81	1984-85
• Morrison, Don	Det., Chi.	3	112	18	28	46	12	3	0	1	1	0	....	1947-48	1950-51
Morrison, Doug	Bos.	4	23	7	3	10	15	....	....	....	....	....	....	1979-80	1984-85
Morrison, Gary	Phi.	3	43	1	15	16	70	5	0	1	1	2	....	1979-80	1981-82
• Morrison, George	St.L.	2	115	17	21	38	13	3	0	0	0	0	....	1970-71	1971-72
Morrison, Jim	Bos., Tor., Det., NYR, Pit.	12	704	40	160	200	542	36	0	12	12	38	....	1951-52	1970-71
• Morrison, John	NYA	1	18	0	0	0	0	....	....	....	....	....	....	1925-26	1925-26
Morrison, Kevin	Col.	1	41	4	11	15	23	....	....	....	....	....	....	1979-80	1979-80
Morrison, Lew	Phi., Atl., Wsh., Pit.	9	564	39	52	91	107	17	0	0	0	2	....	1969-70	1977-78
Morrison, Mark	NYR	2	10	1	1	2	0	....	....	....	....	....	....	1981-82	1983-84
• Morrison, Rod	Det.	1	34	8	7	15	4	3	0	0	0	0	....	1947-48	1947-48
‡ Morrisonn, Shaone	Bos., Wsh., Buf.	8	480	11	64	75	455	27	0	2	2	18	....	2002-03	2010-11
Morrow, Ken	NYI	10	550	17	88	105	309	127	11	22	33	97	4	1979-80	1988-89
Morrow, Scott	Cgy.	1	4	0	0	0	0	....	....	....	....	....	....	1994-95	1994-95
Morton, Dean	Det.	1	1	1	0	1	2	....	....	....	....	....	....	1989-90	1989-90
• Mortson, Gus	Tor., Chi., Det.	13	797	46	152	198	1380	54	5	8	13	68	4	1946-47	1958-59
• Mosdell, Ken	Bro., Mtl., Chi.	16	693	141	168	309	475	80	16	13	29	48	4	1941-42	1958-59
• Mosienko, Bill	Chi.	14	711	258	282	540	121	22	10	4	14	15	....	1941-42	1954-55
Motin, Johan	Edm.	1	1	0	0	0	0	....	....	....	....	....	....	2009-10	2009-10
Mott, Morris	Cal.	3	199	18	32	50	49	....	....	....	....	....	....	1972-73	1974-75
‡ Mottau, Mike	NYR, Cgy., N.J., NYI, Bos., Fla.	9	321	7	51	58	164	19	2	2	4	0	....	2000-01	2013-14
• Motter, Alex	Bos., Det.	8	255	39	64	103	135	41	3	9	12	41	1	1934-35	1942-43
Motzko, Joe	CBJ, Ana., Wsh., Atl.	5	25	4	2	6	0	3	0	0	0	2	1	2003-04	2008-09
Mowers, Mark	Nsh., Det., Bos., Ana.	7	278	18	44	62	70	3	0	0	0	0	....	1998-99	2007-08
Moxey, Jim	Cal., Cle., L.A.	3	127	22	27	49	59	....	....	....	....	....	....	1974-75	1976-77
Mrozik, Rick	Cgy.	1	2	0	0	0	0	....	....	....	....	....	....	2002-03	2002-03
Muckalt, Bill	Van., NYI, Ott., Min.	5	256	40	57	97	204	5	0	0	0	0	....	1998-99	2002-03
Mueller, Marcel	Tor.	1	3	0	0	0	2	....	....	....	....	....	....	2010-11	2010-11
Muir, Bryan	Edm., N.J., Chi., T.B., Col., L.A., Wsh.	11	279	16	37	53	281	29	0	0	0	6	1	1995-96	2006-07
Mulhern, Richard	Atl., L.A., Tor., Wpg.	6	303	27	93	120	217	7	0	3	3	5	....	1975-76	1980-81
Mulhern, Ryan	Wsh.	1	3	0	0	0	0	....	....	....	....	....	....	1997-98	1997-98
Mullen, Brian	Wpg., NYR, S.J., NYI	11	832	260	362	622	414	62	12	18	30	30	....	1982-83	1992-93
Mullen, Joe	St.L., Cgy., Pit., Bos.	17	1062	502	561	1063	241	143	60	46	106	42	3	1979-80	1996-97
Muller, Kirk	N.J., Mtl., NYI, Tor., Fla., Dal.	19	1349	357	602	959	1223	127	33	36	69	153	1	1984-85	2002-03
Muloin, Wayne	Det., Oak., Cal., Min.	3	147	3	21	24	93	11	0	0	0	2	....	1963-64	1970-71
Mulvenna, Glenn	Pit., Phi.	2	2	0	0	0	4	....	....	....	....	....	....	1991-92	1992-93
Mulvey, Grant	Chi., N.J.	10	586	149	135	284	816	42	10	5	15	70	....	1974-75	1983-84
Mulvey, Paul	Wsh., Pit., L.A.	4	225	30	51	81	613	....	....	....	....	....	....	1978-79	1981-82
• Mummery, Harry	Tor., Que., Mtl., Ham.	6	106	33	19	52	226	2	1	1	2	17	....	1917-18	1922-23
Muni, Craig	Tor., Edm., Chi., Buf., Wpg., Pit., Dal.	16	819	28	119	147	775	113	0	17	17	108	3	1981-82	1997-98
• Munro, Dunc	Mtl.M., Mtl.	8	239	28	18	46	172	21	2	2	4	18	1	1924-25	1931-32
• Munro, Gerry	Mtl.M., Tor.	2	34	1	0	1	37	....	....	....	....	....	....	1924-25	1925-26
Murdoch, Bob	Mtl., L.A., Atl., Cgy.	12	757	60	218	278	764	69	4	18	22	92	2	1970-71	1981-82
Murdoch, Bob	Cal., Cle., St.L.	4	260	72	85	157	127	....	....	....	....	....	....	1975-76	1978-79
Murdoch, Don	NYR, Edm., Det.	6	320	121	117	238	155	24	10	8	18	16	....	1976-77	1981-82
• Murdoch, Murray	NYR	11	508	84	108	192	197	55	9	12	21	28	2	1926-27	1936-37
‡ Murley, Matt	Pit., Phx.	3	62	2	7	9	38	....	....	....	....	....	....	2003-04	2007-08
Murphy, Brian	Det.	1	1	0	0	0	0	....	....	....	....	....	....	1974-75	1974-75
‡ Murphy, Cory	Fla., T.B., N.J.	3	91	9	27	36	38	....	....	....	....	....	....	2007-08	2009-10

Name	NHL Teams	NHL Seasons	Regular Schedule GP	G	A	TP	PIM	Playoffs GP	G	A	TP	PIM	NHL Cup Wins	First NHL Season	Last NHL Season
Murphy, Curtis	Min.	1	1	0	0	0	0	....	....	....	....	....	....	2002-03	2002-03
Murphy, Gord	Phi., Bos., Fla., Atl.	14	862	85	238	323	668	53	3	16	19	35	....	1988-89	2001-02
Murphy, Joe	Det., Edm., Chi., St.L., S.J., Bos., Wsh.	15	779	233	295	528	810	120	34	43	77	185	1	1986-87	2000-01
Murphy, Larry	L.A., Wsh., Min., Pit., Tor., Det.	21	1615	287	929	1216	1084	215	37	115	152	201	4	1980-81	2000-01
Murphy, Mike	St.L., NYR, L.A.	12	831	238	318	556	514	66	13	23	36	54	....	1971-72	1982-83
Murphy, Rob	Van., Ott., L.A.	7	125	9	12	21	152	4	0	0	0	2	....	1987-88	1993-94
Murphy, Ron	NYR, Chi., Det., Bos.	18	889	205	274	479	460	53	7	8	15	26	2	1952-53	1969-70
● Murray, Allan	NYA	7	271	5	9	14	163	14	0	0	0	10	....	1933-34	1939-40
Murray, Bob	Atl., Van.	4	194	6	16	22	98	10	1	1	2	15	....	1973-74	1976-77
Murray, Bob	Chi.	15	1008	132	382	514	873	112	19	37	56	106	....	1975-76	1989-90
Murray, Brady	L.A.	1	4	1	0	1	6	....	....	....	....	....	....	2007-08	2007-08
Murray, Chris	Mtl., Hfd., Car., Ott., Chi., Dal.	6	242	16	18	34	550	15	1	0	1	12	....	1994-95	1999-00
‡ Murray, Douglas	S.J., Pit., Mtl.	9	518	7	57	64	412	75	4	9	13	78	....	2005-06	2013-14
Murray, Garth	NYR, Mtl., Fla., Phx.	5	116	8	2	10	131	6	0	0	0	0	....	2003-04	2008-09
Murray, Glen	Bos., Pit., L.A.	16	1009	337	314	651	679	94	20	22	42	66	....	1991-92	2007-08
Murray, Jim	L.A.	1	30	0	2	2	14	....	....	....	....	....	....	1967-68	1967-68
Murray, Ken	Tor., NYI, Det., K.C.	5	106	1	10	11	135	....	....	....	....	....	....	1969-70	1975-76
● Murray, Leo	Mtl.	1	6	0	0	0	2	....	....	....	....	....	....	1932-33	1932-33
Murray, Marty	Cgy., Phi., Car., L.A.	8	261	31	42	73	41	9	0	1	1	4	....	1995-96	2006-07
Murray, Mike	Phi.	1	1	0	0	0	0	....	....	....	....	....	....	1987-88	1987-88
Murray, Pat	Phi.	2	25	3	1	4	15	....	....	....	....	....	....	1990-91	1991-92
Murray, Randy	Tor.	1	3	0	0	0	2	....	....	....	....	....	....	1969-70	1969-70
Murray, Rem	Edm., NYR, Nsh.	9	560	94	121	215	161	62	5	12	17	18	....	1996-97	2005-06
Murray, Rob	Wsh., Wpg., Phx.	8	107	4	15	19	111	9	0	0	0	18	....	1989-90	1998-99
Murray, Terry	Cal., Phi., Det., Wsh.	8	302	4	76	80	199	18	2	2	4	10	....	1972-73	1981-82
Murray, Troy	Chi., Wpg., Ott., Pit., Col.	15	915	230	354	584	875	113	17	26	43	145	1	1981-82	1995-96
‡ Mursak , Jan	Det.	3	46	2	2	4	8	....	....	....	....	....	....	2010-11	2012-13
Murzyn, Dana	Hfd., Cgy., Van.	14	838	52	152	204	1571	82	9	10	19	166	1	1985-86	1998-99
Musil, Frantisek	Min., Cgy., Ott., Edm.	15	797	34	106	140	1241	42	2	4	6	47	....	1986-87	2000-01
Myers, Hap	Buf.	1	13	0	0	0	6	....	....	....	....	....	....	1970-71	1970-71
Myhres, Brantt	T.B., Phi., S.J., Nsh., Wsh., Bos.	7	154	6	2	8	687	....	....	....	....	....	....	1994-95	2002-03
● Myles, Vic	NYR	1	45	6	9	15	57	....	....	....	....	....	....	1942-43	1942-43
Myrvold, Anders	Col., Bos., NYI, Det.	4	33	0	5	5	12	....	....	....	....	....	....	1995-96	2003-04

N

Name	NHL Teams	NHL Seasons	Regular Schedule GP	G	A	TP	PIM	Playoffs GP	G	A	TP	PIM	NHL Cup Wins	First NHL Season	Last NHL Season
Nabokov, Dmitri	Chi., NYI	3	55	11	13	24	28	....	....	....	....	....	....	1997-98	1999-00
Nachbaur, Don	Hfd., Edm., Phi.	8	223	23	46	69	465	11	1	1	2	24	....	1980-81	1989-90
‡ Nagy, Ladislav	St.L., Phx., Dal., L.A.	8	435	115	196	311	358	18	2	2	4	23	....	1999-00	2007-08
Nahrgang, Jim	Det.	3	57	5	12	17	34	....	....	....	....	....	....	1974-75	1976-77
Namestnikov, John	Van., NYI, Nsh.	6	43	0	9	9	24	2	0	0	0	2	....	1993-94	1999-00
Nanne, Lou	Min.	11	635	68	157	225	356	32	4	10	14	8	....	1967-68	1977-78
Nantais, Rich	Min.	3	63	5	4	9	79	....	....	....	....	....	....	1974-75	1976-77
Napier, Mark	Mtl., Min., Edm., Buf.	11	767	235	306	541	157	82	18	24	42	11	2	1978-79	1988-89
‡ Nash, Brendon	Mtl.	1	2	0	0	0	0	....	....	....	....	....	....	2010-11	2010-11
Nash, Tyson	St.L., Phx.	7	374	27	37	64	673	23	3	2	5	52	....	1998-99	2005-06
Naslund, Markus	Pit., Van., NYR	15	1117	395	474	869	736	52	14	22	36	56	....	1993-94	2008-09
Naslund, Mats	Mtl., Bos.	9	651	251	383	634	111	102	35	57	92	33	1	1982-83	1994-95
Nasreddine, Alain	Chi., Mtl., NYI, Pit.	5	74	1	4	5	84	....	....	....	....	....	....	1998-99	2007-08
‡ Nattinen, Joonas	Mtl.	1	1	0	0	0	0	....	....	....	....	....	....	2013-14	2013-14
● Nattrass, Ralph	Chi.	4	223	18	38	56	308	....	....	....	....	....	....	1946-47	1949-50
Nattress, Ric	Mtl., St.L., Cgy., Tor., Phi.	11	536	29	135	164	377	67	5	10	15	60	1	1982-83	1992-93
Natyshak, Mike	Que.	1	4	0	0	0	0	....	....	....	....	....	....	1987-88	1987-88
Nazarov, Andrei	S.J., T.B., Cgy., Ana., Bos., Phx., Min.	12	571	53	71	124	1409	9	0	0	0	11	....	1993-94	2005-06
Ndur, Rumun	Buf., NYR, Atl.	4	69	2	3	5	137	....	....	....	....	....	....	1996-97	1999-00
Neaton, Pat	Pit.	1	9	1	1	2	12	....	....	....	....	....	....	1993-94	1993-94
Nechayev, Viktor	L.A.	1	3	1	0	1	0	....	....	....	....	....	....	1982-83	1982-83
Neckar, Stan	Ott., NYR, Phx., T.B., Nsh.	10	510	12	41	53	316	29	0	3	3	8	1	1994-95	2003-04
Nedomansky, Vaclav	Det., NYR, St.L.	6	421	122	156	278	88	7	3	5	8	0	....	1977-78	1982-83
Nedorost, Andrej	CBJ	3	28	2	3	5	12	....	....	....	....	....	....	2001-02	2003-04
‡ Nedorost, Vaclav	Col., Fla.	3	99	10	10	20	34	....	....	....	....	....	....	2001-02	2003-04
‡ Nedved, Petr	Van., St.L., NYR, Pit., Edm., Phx., Phi.	15	982	310	407	717	708	71	19	23	42	64	....	1990-91	2006-07
Nedved, Zdenek	Tor.	3	31	4	6	10	14	....	....	....	....	....	....	1994-95	1996-97
Needham, Mike	Pit., Dal.	3	86	9	5	14	16	14	2	0	2	4	1	1991-92	1993-94
Neely, Bob	Tor., Col.	5	283	39	59	98	266	26	5	7	12	15	....	1973-74	1977-78
Neely, Cam	Van., Bos.	13	726	395	299	694	1241	93	57	32	89	168	....	1983-84	1995-96
‡ Negrin, John	Cgy.	1	3	0	1	1	2	....	....	....	....	....	....	2008-09	2008-09
Neilson, Jim	NYR, Cal., Cle.	16	1023	69	299	368	904	65	1	17	18	61	....	1962-63	1977-78
Nelson, Gordie	Tor.	1	3	0	0	0	11	....	....	....	....	....	....	1969-70	1969-70
Nelson, Jeff	Wsh., Nsh.	3	52	3	8	11	20	3	0	0	0	4	....	1994-95	1998-99
Nelson, Todd	Pit., Wsh.	2	3	1	0	1	2	4	0	0	0	0	....	1991-92	1993-94
Nemchinov, Sergei	NYR, Van., NYI, N.J.	11	761	152	193	345	251	105	11	20	31	24	2	1991-92	2001-02
Nemecek, Jan	L.A.	2	7	1	0	1	4	....	....	....	....	....	....	1998-99	1999-00
Nemeth, Steve	NYR	1	12	2	0	2	2	....	....	....	....	....	....	1987-88	1987-88
Nemirovsky, David	Fla.	4	91	16	22	38	42	3	1	0	1	0	....	1995-96	1998-99
Nesterenko, Eric	Tor., Chi.	21	1219	250	324	574	1273	124	13	24	37	127	1	1951-52	1971-72
Nethery, Lance	NYR, Edm.	2	41	11	14	25	14	14	5	3	8	9	....	1980-81	1981-82
Neufeld, Ray	Hfd., Wpg., Bos.	11	595	157	200	357	816	28	8	6	14	55	....	1979-80	1989-90
● Neville, Mike	Tor., NYA	3	65	5	5	10	14	2	0	0	0	0	....	1924-25	1930-31
Nevin, Bob	Tor., NYR, Min., L.A.	18	1128	307	419	726	211	84	16	18	34	24	2	1957-58	1975-76
Newberry, John	Mtl., Hfd.	4	22	0	4	4	6	2	0	0	0	0	....	1982-83	1985-86
Newell, Rick	Det.	2	6	0	0	0	0	....	....	....	....	....	....	1972-73	1973-74
Newman, Dan	NYR, Mtl., Edm.	4	126	17	24	41	63	3	0	0	0	4	....	1976-77	1979-80
● Newman, John	Det.	1	8	1	1	2	0	....	....	....	....	....	....	1930-31	1930-31
Nichol, Scott	Buf., Cgy., Chi., Nsh., S.J., St.L.	13	662	56	71	127	916	49	1	2	3	76	....	1995-96	2012-13
Nicholls, Bernie	L.A., NYR, Edm., N.J., Chi., S.J.	18	1127	475	734	1209	1292	118	42	72	114	164	....	1981-82	1998-99
● Nicholson, Al	Bos.	2	19	0	1	1	4	....	....	....	....	....	....	1955-56	1956-57
● Nicholson, Ed	Det.	1	1	0	0	0	0	....	....	....	....	....	....	1947-48	1947-48
● Nicholson, Hickey	Chi.	1	2	1	0	1	0	....	....	....	....	....	....	1937-38	1937-38
Nicholson, Neil	Oak., NYI	4	39	3	1	4	23	2	0	0	0	0	....	1969-70	1977-78
● Nicholson, Paul	Wsh.	3	62	4	8	12	18	....	....	....	....	....	....	1974-75	1976-77
Nickulas, Eric	Bos., St.L., Chi.	6	118	15	23	38	82	1	0	0	0	2	....	1998-99	2005-06
Nicolson, Graeme	Bos., Col., NYR	3	52	2	7	9	60	....	....	....	....	....	....	1978-79	1982-83
Nieckar, Barry	Hfd., Cgy., Ana.	4	8	0	0	0	21	....	....	....	....	....	....	1992-93	1997-98
Niedermayer, Rob	Fla., Cgy., Ana., N.J., Buf.	17	1153	186	283	469	904	116	18	25	43	111	1	1993-94	2010-11
Niedermayer, Scott	N.J., Ana.	18	1263	172	568	740	784	202	25	73	98	155	4	1991-92	2009-10
Niekamp, Jim	Det.	2	29	0	2	2	37	....	....	....	....	....	....	1970-71	1971-72
Nielsen, Chris	CBJ	2	52	6	8	14	8	....	....	....	....	....	....	2000-01	2001-02
Nielsen, Jeff	NYR, Ana., Min.	5	252	20	27	47	70	4	0	0	0	2	....	1996-97	2000-01
Nielsen, Kirk	Bos.	1	6	0	0	0	0	....	....	....	....	....	....	1997-98	1997-98
‡ Niemi, Antti-Jussi	Ana.	2	29	1	1	2	22	....	....	....	....	....	....	2000-01	2001-02
‡ Nieminen, Ville	Col., Pit., Chi., Cgy., NYR, S.J., St.L.	7	385	48	69	117	333	58	8	12	20	99	1	1999-00	2006-07
Nienhuis, Kraig	Bos.	3	87	20	16	36	39	2	0	0	0	14	....	1985-86	1987-88
Nieuwendyk, Joe	Cgy., Dal., N.J., Tor., Fla.	20	1257	564	562	1126	677	158	66	50	116	91	3	1986-87	2006-07
● Nighbor, Frank	Ott., Tor.	13	349	139	98	237	249	20	4	9	13	13	4	1917-18	1929-30
Nigro, Frank	Tor.	2	68	8	18	26	39	3	0	0	0	2	....	1982-83	1983-84
Niinimaa, Janne	Phi., Edm., NYI, Dal., Mtl.	10	741	54	265	319	733	59	3	21	24	60	....	1996-97	2006-07
Nikolishin, Andrei	Hfd., Wsh., Chi., Col.	10	628	93	187	280	270	43	1	17	18	22	....	1994-95	2003-04
‡ Nikulin, Alexander	Ott., Phx.	2	3	0	0	0	0	....	....	....	....	....	....	2007-08	2008-09
Nikulin, Igor	Ana.	1	....	....	....	....	....	1	0	0	0	0	....	1996-97	1996-97
Nilan, Chris	Mtl., NYR, Bos.	13	688	110	115	225	3043	111	8	9	17	541	1	1979-80	1991-92
Nill, Jim	St.L., Van., Bos., Wpg., Det.	9	524	58	87	145	854	59	10	5	15	203	....	1981-82	1989-90
‡ Nilson, Marcus	Fla., Cgy.	9	521	67	101	168	270	34	4	7	11	14	....	1998-99	2007-08
Nilsson, Kent	Atl., Cgy., Min., Edm.	9	553	264	422	686	116	59	11	41	52	14	1	1979-80	1994-95
‡ Nilsson, Robert	NYI, Edm.	5	252	37	81	118	90	....	....	....	....	....	....	2005-06	2009-10
Nilsson, Ulf	NYR	4	170	57	112	169	85	25	8	14	22	27	....	1978-79	1982-83
‡ Niskala, Janne	T.B.	1	6	1	2	3	6	....	....	....	....	....	....	2008-09	2008-09
Nistico, Lou	Col.	1	3	0	0	0	0	....	....	....	....	....	....	1977-78	1977-78
● Noble, Reg	Tor., Mtl.M., Det.	16	510	168	106	274	916	18	2	2	4	33	3	1917-18	1932-33
‡ Nodl, Andreas	Phi., Car.	5	183	15	21	36	28	12	0	0	0	0	....	2008-09	2012-13
Noel, Claude	Wsh.	1	7	0	0	0	0	....	....	....	....	....	....	1979-80	1979-80
‡ Nokelainen, Petteri	NYI, Bos., Ana., Phx., Mtl.	5	245	20	21	41	103	21	0	2	2	8	....	2005-06	2011-12
Nolan, Brandon	Car.	1	6	0	1	1	0	....	....	....	....	....	....	2007-08	2007-08
Nolan, Owen	Que., Col., S.J., Tor., Phx., Cgy., Min.	18	1200	422	463	885	1793	65	21	19	40	66	....	1990-91	2009-10
● Nolan, Paddy	Tor.	1	2	0	0	0	0	....	....	....	....	....	....	1921-22	1921-22
Nolan, Ted	Det., Pit.	3	78	6	16	22	105	....	....	....	....	....	....	1981-82	1985-86

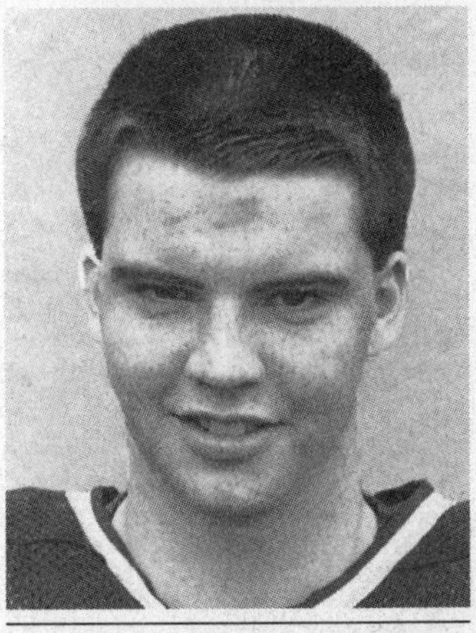
Pat Neaton

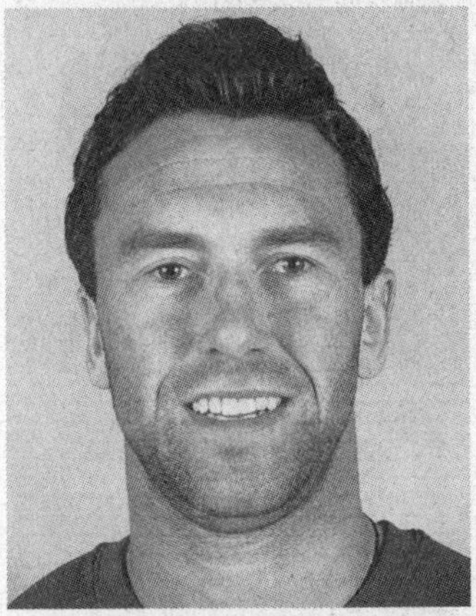
Petr Nedved

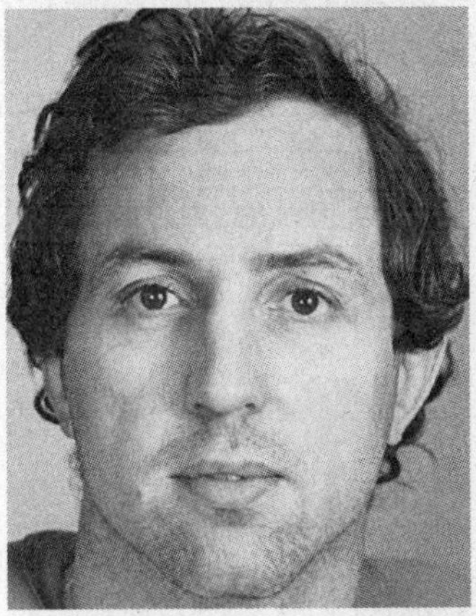
Milan Novy

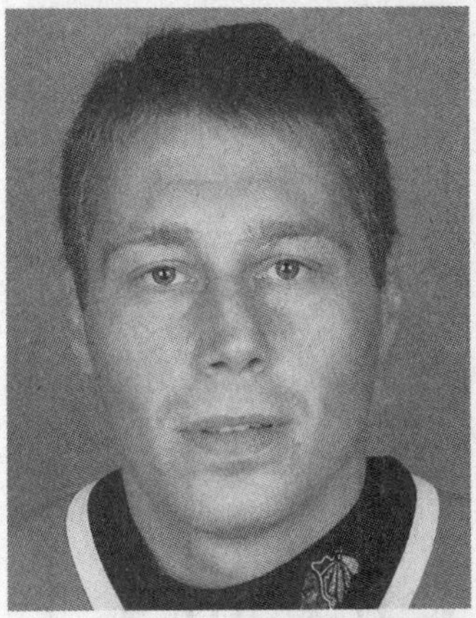
Lyle Odelein

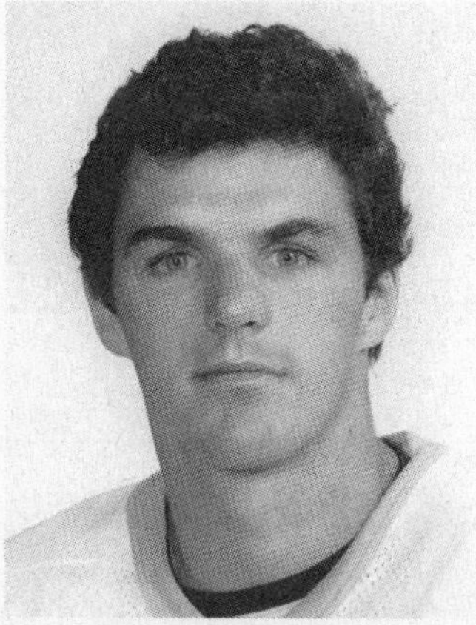

Tom O'Regan

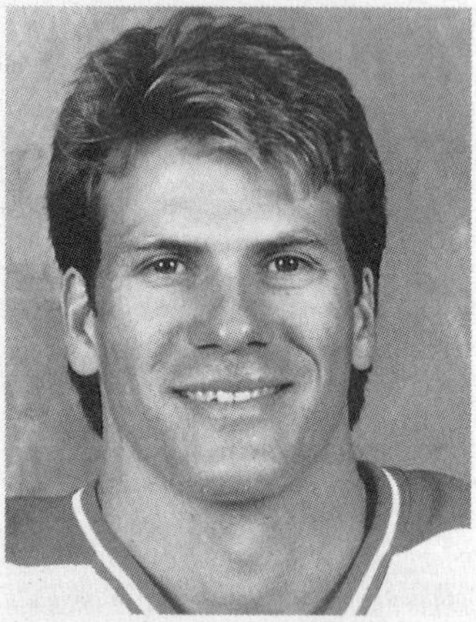

Joel Otto

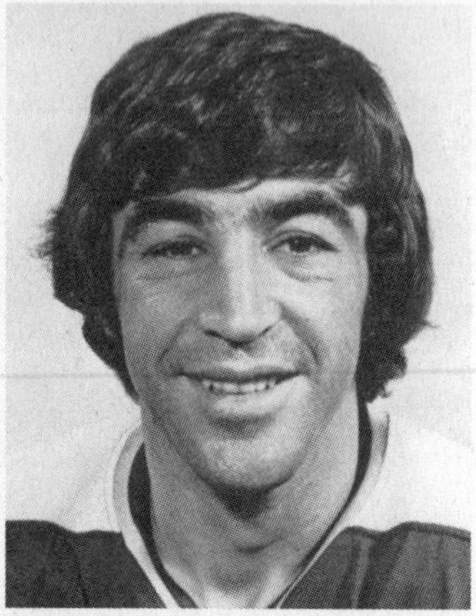

J.P. Parise

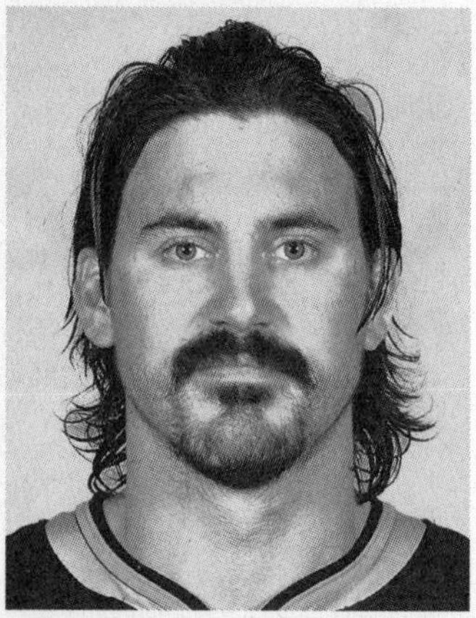

George Parros

			Regular Schedule					Playoffs							
Name	NHL Teams	NHL Seasons	GP	G	A	TP	PIM	GP	G	A	TP	PIM	NHL Cup Wins	First NHL Season	Last NHL Season
Nolet, Simon	Phi., K.C., Pit., Col.	10	562	150	182	332	187	34	6	3	9	8	1	1967-68	1976-77
Noonan, Brian	Chi., NYR, St.L., Van., Phx.	12	629	116	159	275	518	71	17	19	36	77	1	1987-88	1998-99
Nordgren, Niklas	Car., Pit.	1	58	4	2	6	34	....	....	....	....	....	....	2005-06	2005-06
Nordmark, Robert	St.L., Van.	4	236	13	70	83	254	7	3	2	5	8	....	1987-88	1990-91
Nordqvist, Jonas	Chi.	1	3	0	2	2	2	....	....	....	....	....	....	2006-07	2006-07
Nordstrom, Peter	Bos.	1	2	0	0	0	0	....	....	....	....	....	....	1998-99	1998-99
Noris, Joe	Pit., St.L., Buf.	3	55	2	5	7	22	....	....	....	....	....	....	1971-72	1973-74
Norris, Dwayne	Que., Ana.	3	20	2	4	6	8	....	....	....	....	....	....	1993-94	1995-96
Norrish, Rod	Min.	2	21	3	3	6	2	....	....	....	....	....	....	1973-74	1974-75
Norstrom, Mattias	NYR, L.A., Dal.	14	903	18	147	165	661	56	2	5	7	54	....	1993-94	2007-08
● Northcott, Baldy	Mtl.M., Chi.	11	446	133	112	245	273	31	8	5	13	14	1	1928-29	1938-39
Norton, Brad	Fla., L.A., Wsh., Ott., Det., S.J.	6	124	3	8	11	287	....	....	....	....	....	....	2001-02	2007-08
Norton, Jeff	NYI, S.J., St.L., Edm., T.B., Fla., Pit., Bos.	15	799	52	332	384	615	65	4	21	25	89	....	1987-88	2001-02
Norwich, Craig	Wpg., St.L., Col.	2	104	17	58	75	60	....	....	....	....	....	....	1979-80	1980-81
Norwood, Lee	Que., Wsh., St.L., Det., N.J., Hfd., Cgy.	12	503	58	153	211	1099	65	6	22	28	171	....	1980-81	1993-94
‡ Novak, Filip	Ott., CBJ	2	17	0	0	0	6	....	....	....	....	....	....	2005-06	2006-07
Novoseltsev, Ivan	Fla., Phx.	5	234	31	44	75	112	....	....	....	....	....	....	1999-00	2003-04
‡ Novotny, Jiri	Buf., Wsh., CBJ	4	189	20	31	51	66	4	0	0	0	0	....	2005-06	2008-09
Novy, Milan	Wsh.	1	73	18	30	48	16	2	0	0	0	0	....	1982-83	1982-83
Nowak, Hank	Pit., Det., Bos.	4	180	26	29	55	161	13	1	0	1	8	....	1973-74	1976-77
‡ Nummelin, Petteri	CBJ, Min.	3	139	9	36	45	34	7	1	2	3	0	....	2000-01	2007-08
Numminen, Teppo	Wpg., Phx., Dal., Buf.	20	1372	117	520	637	513	82	9	14	23	28	....	1988-89	2008-09
Nurminen, Kai	L.A., Min.	2	69	17	11	28	24	....	....	....	....	....	....	1996-97	2000-01
Nycholat, Lawrence	NYR, Wsh., Ott., Van., Col.	4	50	2	7	9	24	....	....	....	....	....	....	2003-04	2008-09
Nykoluk, Mike	Tor.	1	32	3	1	4	20	....	....	....	....	....	....	1956-57	1956-57
Nylander, Michael	Hfd., Cgy., T.B., Chi., Wsh., Bos., NYR	15	920	209	470	679	468	47	12	22	34	14	....	1992-93	2008-09
Nylund, Gary	Tor., Chi., NYI	11	608	32	139	171	1235	24	0	6	6	63	....	1982-83	1992-93
● Nyrop, Bill	Mtl., Min.	4	207	12	51	63	101	35	1	7	8	22	3	1975-76	1981-82
Nystrom, Bob	NYI	14	900	235	278	513	1248	157	39	44	83	236	4	1972-73	1985-86

O

Oates, Adam	Det., St.L., Bos., Wsh., Phi., Ana., Edm.	19	1337	341	1079	1420	415	163	42	114	156	66	....	1985-86	2003-04
● Oatman, Russell	Det., Mtl.M., NYR	3	120	20	9	29	100	15	1	0	1	18	....	1926-27	1928-29
O'Brien, Dennis	Min., Col., Cle., Bos.	10	592	31	91	122	1017	34	1	2	3	101	....	1970-71	1979-80
O'Brien, Doug	T.B.	1	5	0	0	0	2	....	....	....	....	....	....	2005-06	2005-06
● O'Brien, Ellard	Bos.	1	2	0	0	0	0	....	....	....	....	....	....	1955-56	1955-56
‡ Obsut, Jaroslav	St.L., Col.	2	7	0	0	0	2	....	....	....	....	....	....	2000-01	2001-02
‡ O'Byrne, Ryan	Mtl., Col., Tor.	6	308	5	34	39	369	25	0	0	0	16	....	2007-08	2012-13
O'Callahan, Jack	Chi., N.J.	7	389	27	104	131	541	32	4	11	15	41	....	1982-83	1988-89
O'Connell, Mike	Chi., Bos., Det.	13	860	105	334	439	605	82	8	24	32	64	....	1977-78	1989-90
● O'Connor, Buddy	Mtl., NYR	10	509	140	257	397	34	53	15	21	36	6	2	1941-42	1950-51
O'Connor, Myles	N.J., Ana.	4	43	3	4	7	69	....	....	....	....	....	....	1990-91	1993-94
Oddleifson, Chris	Bos., Van.	9	524	95	191	286	464	14	1	6	7	8	....	1972-73	1980-81
Odelein, Lyle	Mtl., N.J., Phx., CBJ, Chi., Dal., Fla., Pit.	16	1056	50	202	252	2316	86	5	13	18	209	1	1989-90	2005-06
Odelein, Selmar	Edm.	3	18	0	2	2	35	....	....	....	....	....	....	1985-86	1988-89
Odgers, Jeff	S.J., Bos., Col., Atl.	12	821	75	70	145	2364	47	2	1	3	73	....	1991-92	2002-03
Odjick, Gino	Van., NYI, Phi., Mtl.	12	605	64	73	137	2567	44	4	1	5	142	....	1990-91	2001-02
O'Donnell, Fred	Bos.	2	115	15	11	26	98	5	0	1	1	5	....	1972-73	1973-74
O'Donnell, Sean	L.A., Min., N.J., Bos., Phx., Ana., Phi., Chi.	17	1224	31	198	229	1809	106	6	13	19	129	1	1994-95	2011-12
● O'Donoghue, Don	Oak., Cal.	3	125	18	17	35	35	3	0	0	0	0	....	1969-70	1971-72
Odrowski, Gerry	Det., Oak., St.L.	6	309	12	19	31	111	30	0	1	1	16	....	1960-61	1971-72
O'Dwyer, Bill	L.A., Bos.	5	120	9	13	22	108	10	0	0	0	2	....	1983-84	1989-90
O'Flaherty, Gerry	Tor., Van., Atl.	8	438	99	95	194	168	7	2	2	4	6	....	1971-72	1978-79
● O'Flaherty, Peanuts	NYA, Bro.	2	21	5	1	6	0	....	....	....	....	....	....	1940-41	1941-42
Ogilvie, Brian	Chi., St.L.	6	90	15	21	36	29	....	....	....	....	....	....	1972-73	1978-79
● O'Grady, George	Mtl.W.	1	4	0	0	0	0	....	....	....	....	....	....	1917-18	1917-18
Ogrodnick, John	Det., Que., NYR	14	928	402	425	827	260	41	18	8	26	6	....	1979-80	1992-93
‡ Ohlund, Mattias	Van., T.B.	17	909	93	250	343	885	70	10	21	31	63	....	1997-98	2014-15
Ojanen, Janne	N.J.	4	98	21	23	44	28	3	0	2	2	0	....	1988-89	1992-93
Okerlund, Todd	NYI	1	4	0	0	0	2	....	....	....	....	....	....	1987-88	1987-88
Oksiuta, Roman	Edm., Van., Ana., Pit.	4	153	46	41	87	100	10	2	3	5	0	....	1993-94	1996-97
Olausson, Fredrik	Wpg., Edm., Ana., Pit., Det.	16	1022	147	434	581	450	71	6	23	29	28	1	1986-87	2002-03
Olczyk, Ed	Chi., Tor., Wpg., NYR, L.A., Pit.	16	1031	342	452	794	874	57	19	15	34	57	1	1984-85	1999-00
Oliver, David	Edm., NYR, Ott., Phx., Dal.	9	233	49	49	98	84	10	0	0	0	2	....	1994-95	2005-06
● Oliver, Harry	Bos., NYA	11	463	127	85	212	147	35	10	6	16	24	1	1926-27	1936-37
● Oliver, Murray	Det., Bos., Tor., Min.	17	1127	274	454	728	320	35	9	16	25	10	....	1957-58	1974-75
Oliwa, Krzysztof	N.J., CBJ, Pit., NYR, Bos., Cgy.	9	410	17	28	45	1447	32	2	0	2	47	1	1996-97	2005-06
Olmstead, Bert	Chi., Mtl., Tor.	14	848	181	421	602	884	115	16	43	59	101	5	1948-49	1961-62
Olsen, Darryl	Cgy.	1	1	0	0	0	0	....	....	....	....	....	....	1991-92	1991-92
Olson, Dennis	Det.	1	4	0	0	0	0	....	....	....	....	....	....	1957-58	1957-58
Olson, Josh	Fla.	1	5	1	0	1	0	....	....	....	....	....	....	2003-04	2003-04
Olsson, Christer	St.L., Ott.	2	56	4	12	16	24	3	0	0	0	0	....	1995-96	1996-97
‡ Olvecky, Peter	Min., Nsh.	2	32	2	5	7	12	....	....	....	....	....	....	2008-09	2009-10
‡ Olver, Mark	Col.	3	74	10	12	22	39	....	....	....	....	....	....	2010-11	2012-13
Olvestad, Jimmie	T.B.	2	111	3	14	17	40	....	....	....	....	....	....	2001-02	2002-03
‡ Omark, Linus	Edm., Buf.	3	79	8	24	32	40	....	....	....	....	....	....	2010-11	2013-14
‡ O'Marra, Ryan	Edm., Ana.	3	33	1	6	7	17	....	....	....	....	....	....	2009-10	2011-12
Ondrus, Ben	Tor.	4	52	0	2	2	77	....	....	....	....	....	....	2005-06	2008-09
● O'Neil, Jim	Bos., Mtl.	6	156	6	30	36	109	9	1	1	2	13	....	1933-34	1941-42
O'Neil, Paul	Van., Bos.	2	6	0	0	0	0	....	....	....	....	....	....	1973-74	1975-76
O'Neill, Jeff	Hfd., Car., Tor.	11	821	237	259	496	670	34	9	8	17	37	....	1995-96	2006-07
● O'Neill, Tom	Tor.	2	66	10	12	22	53	4	0	0	0	6	1	1943-44	1944-45
O'Neill, Wes	Col.	2	5	0	0	0	6	....	....	....	....	....	....	2008-09	2009-10
Orban, Bill	Chi., Min.	3	114	8	15	23	67	3	0	0	0	0	....	1967-68	1969-70
O'Ree, Willie	Bos.	2	45	4	10	14	26	....	....	....	....	....	....	1957-58	1960-61
O'Regan, Tom	Pit.	3	61	5	12	17	10	....	....	....	....	....	....	1983-84	1985-86
O'Reilly, Terry	Bos.	14	891	204	402	606	2095	108	25	42	67	335	....	1971-72	1984-85
‡ Oreskovic, Phil	Tor.	1	10	1	1	2	21	....	....	....	....	....	....	2008-09	2008-09
Oreskovich, Victor	Fla., Van.	3	67	2	7	9	41	19	0	0	0	12	....	2009-10	2011-12
Orlando, Gates	Buf.	3	98	18	26	44	51	5	0	4	4	14	....	1984-85	1986-87
● Orlando, Jimmy	Det.	6	199	6	25	31	375	36	0	9	9	105	1	1936-37	1942-43
Orleski, Dave	Mtl.	2	2	0	0	0	0	....	....	....	....	....	....	1980-81	1981-82
Orr, Bobby	Bos., Chi.	12	657	270	645	915	953	74	26	66	92	107	2	1966-67	1978-79
Orszagh, Vladimir	NYI, Nsh., St.L.	7	289	54	65	119	194	6	2	0	2	4	....	1997-98	2005-06
‡ Ortmeyer, Jed	NYR, Nsh., S.J., Min.	8	345	22	31	53	161	17	1	1	2	6	....	2003-04	2011-12
‡ Osala, Oskar	Wsh., Car.	2	3	0	0	0	0	....	....	....	....	....	....	2008-09	2009-10
Osborne, Keith	St.L., T.B.	2	16	1	3	4	16	....	....	....	....	....	....	1989-90	1992-93
Osborne, Mark	Det., NYR, Tor., Wpg.	14	919	212	319	531	1152	87	12	16	28	141	....	1981-82	1994-95
Osburn, Randy	Tor., Phi.	2	27	0	2	2	0	....	....	....	....	....	....	1972-73	1974-75
O'Shea, Danny	Min., Chi., St.L.	5	369	64	115	179	265	39	3	7	10	61	....	1968-69	1972-73
● O'Shea, Kevin	Buf., St.L.	3	134	13	18	31	85	12	2	1	3	10	....	1970-71	1972-73
Osiecki, Mark	Cgy., Ott., Wpg., Min.	2	93	3	11	14	43	....	....	....	....	....	....	1991-92	1992-93
O'Sullivan, Chris	Cgy., Van., Ana.	5	62	2	17	19	16	....	....	....	....	....	....	1996-97	2002-03
O'Sullivan, Patrick	L.A., Edm., Car., Min., Phx.	6	334	58	103	161	116	....	....	....	....	....	....	2006-07	2011-12
Otevrel, Jaroslav	S.J.	2	16	3	4	7	2	....	....	....	....	....	....	1992-93	1993-94
Otto, Joel	Cgy., Phi.	14	943	195	313	508	1934	122	27	47	74	207	1	1984-85	1997-98
Ouellet, Michel	Pit., T.B., Van.	4	190	52	64	116	58	5	0	2	2	6	....	2005-06	2008-09
● Ouellette, Eddie	Chi.	1	43	3	2	5	11	1	0	0	0	0	....	1935-36	1935-36
Ouellette, Gerry	Bos.	1	34	5	4	9	0	....	....	....	....	....	....	1960-61	1960-61
Owchar, Dennis	Pit., Col.	6	288	30	85	115	200	10	1	1	2	8	....	1974-75	1979-80
● Owen, George	Bos.	5	183	44	33	77	151	21	2	5	7	25	1	1928-29	1932-33
‡ Oystrick, Nathan	Atl., Ana., St.L.	3	65	5	10	15	61	....	....	....	....	....	....	2008-09	2010-11
‡ Ozolinsh, Sandis	S.J., Col., Car., Fla., Ana., NYR	15	875	167	397	564	638	137	23	67	90	131	1	1992-93	2007-08

P

Pachal, Clayton	Bos., Col.	3	35	2	3	5	95	....	....	....	....	....	....	1976-77	1978-79
Paddock, Cam	St.L.	1	16	2	1	3	0	....	....	....	....	....	....	2008-09	2008-09
Paddock, John	Wsh., Phi., Que.	5	87	8	14	22	86	5	2	0	2	0	....	1975-76	1982-83
Paek, Jim	Pit., L.A., Ott.	5	217	5	29	34	155	27	1	4	5	8	2	1990-91	1994-95
‡ Pahlsson, Samuel	Bos., Ana., Chi., CBJ, Van.	11	798	68	131	199	356	86	10	19	29	58	1	2000-01	2011-12
Paiement, Rosaire	Phi., Van.	5	190	48	52	100	343	3	3	0	3	0	....	1967-68	1971-72

			Regular Schedule					Playoffs							
Name	NHL Teams	NHL Seasons	GP	G	A	TP	PIM	GP	G	A	TP	PIM	NHL Cup Wins	First NHL Season	Last NHL Season
Paiement, Wilf	K.C., Col., Tor., Que., NYR, Buf., Pit.	14	946	356	458	814	1757	69	18	17	35	185	....	1974-75	1987-88
• Palangio, Pete	Mtl., Det., Chi.	5	71	13	10	23	28	7	0	0	0	0	1	1926-27	1937-38
• Palazzari, Aldo	Bos., NYR	1	35	8	3	11	4	....	....	....	....	....	....	1943-44	1943-44
Palazzari, Doug	St.L.	4	108	18	20	38	23	2	0	0	0	0	....	1974-75	1978-79
Palffy, Ziggy	NYI, L.A., Pit.	12	684	329	384	713	322	24	9	10	19	8	....	1993-94	2005-06
Palmer, Brad	Min., Bos.	3	168	32	38	70	58	29	9	5	14	16	....	1980-81	1982-83
Palmer, Jarod	Min.	1	6	1	0	1	4	....	....	....	....	....	....	2011-12	2011-12
Palmer, Rob	Chi.	3	16	0	3	3	2	....	....	....	....	....	....	1973-74	1975-76
Palmer, Robert	L.A., N.J.	7	320	9	101	110	115	8	1	2	3	6	....	1977-78	1983-84
‡ Palmieri, Nick	N.J., Min.	3	87	13	12	25	20	....	....	....	....	....	....	2009-10	2011-12
• Panagabko, Ed	Bos.	2	29	0	3	3	38	....	....	....	....	....	....	1955-56	1956-57
Pandolfo, Jay	N.J., NYI, Bos.	15	899	100	126	226	164	131	11	22	33	12	2	1996-97	2012-13
Pandolfo, Mike	CBJ	1	3	0	0	0	0	....	....	....	....	....	....	2003-04	2003-04
Pankewicz, Greg	Ott., Cgy.	2	21	0	3	3	22	....	....	....	....	....	....	1993-94	1998-99
Panteleev, Grigori	Bos., NYI	4	54	8	6	14	12	....	....	....	....	....	....	1992-93	1995-96
• Papike, Joe	Chi.	3	20	3	3	6	4	5	0	2	2	0	....	1940-41	1944-45
Papineau, Justin	St.L., NYI	3	81	11	8	19	12	1	0	0	0	0	....	2001-02	2003-04
Pappin, Jim	Tor., Chi., Cal., Cle.	14	767	278	295	573	667	92	33	34	67	101	2	1963-64	1976-77
Paradise, Bob	Min., Atl., Pit., Wsh.	8	368	8	54	62	393	12	0	1	1	19	....	1971-72	1978-79
• Pargeter, George	Mtl.	1	4	0	0	0	0	....	....	....	....	....	....	1946-47	1946-47
• Parise, J.P.	Bos., Tor., Min., NYI, Cle.	14	890	238	356	594	706	86	27	31	58	87	....	1965-66	1978-79
Parizeau, Michel	St.L., Phi.	1	58	3	14	17	18	....	....	....	....	....	....	1971-72	1971-72
Park, Brad	NYR, Bos., Det.	17	1113	213	683	896	1429	161	35	90	125	217	....	1968-69	1984-85
• Park, Richard	Pit., Ana., Phi., Min., Van., NYI	14	738	102	139	241	266	40	3	6	9	12	....	1994-95	2011-12
Parker, Jeff	Buf., Hfd.	5	141	16	19	35	163	5	0	0	0	26	....	1986-87	1990-91
Parker, Scott	Col., S.J.	8	308	7	14	21	699	5	0	0	0	4	1	1998-99	2007-08
• Parkes, Ernie	Mtl.M.	1	17	0	0	0	2	....	....	....	....	....	....	1924-25	1924-25
• Parks, Greg	NYI	3	23	1	2	3	6	2	0	0	0	0	....	1990-91	1992-93
Parrish, Mark	Fla., NYI, L.A., Min., Dal., T.B., Buf.	12	722	216	171	387	246	27	5	4	9	10	....	1998-99	2010-11
‡ Parros, George	L.A., Col., Ana., Fla., Mtl.	9	474	18	18	36	1092	19	0	0	0	35	1	2005-06	2013-14
Parse, Scott	L.A.	3	73	14	16	30	36	6	0	0	0	0	1	2009-10	2011-12
• Parsons, George	Tor.	3	78	12	13	25	20	7	3	2	5	11	....	1936-37	1938-39
‡ Parssinen, Timo	Ana.	1	17	0	3	3	2	....	....	....	....	....	....	2001-02	2001-02
• Pasek, Dusan	Min.	1	48	4	10	14	30	2	1	0	1	0	....	1988-89	1988-89
Pasin, Dave	Bos., L.A.	2	76	18	19	37	50	3	0	1	1	0	....	1985-86	1988-89
Paslawski, Greg	Mtl., St.L., Wpg., Buf., Que., Phi., Cgy.	11	650	187	185	372	169	60	19	13	32	25	....	1983-84	1993-94
‡ Patera, Pavel	Dal., Min.	2	32	2	7	9	8	....	....	....	....	....	....	1999-00	2000-01
Paterson, Joe	Det., Phi., L.A., NYR	9	291	19	37	56	829	22	3	4	7	77	....	1980-81	1988-89
Paterson, Mark	Hfd.	4	29	3	3	6	33	....	....	....	....	....	....	1982-83	1985-86
Paterson, Rick	Chi.	9	430	50	43	93	136	61	7	10	17	51	....	1978-79	1986-87
Patey, Doug	Wsh.	3	45	4	2	6	8	....	....	....	....	....	....	1976-77	1978-79
Patey, Larry	Cal., St.L., NYR	12	717	153	163	316	631	40	8	10	18	57	....	1973-74	1984-85
Patrick, Craig	Cal., St.L., K.C., Wsh.	8	401	72	91	163	61	2	0	1	1	0	....	1971-72	1978-79
Patrick, Glenn	St.L., Cal., Cle.	4	38	2	3	5	72	....	....	....	....	....	....	1973-74	1976-77
Patrick, James	NYR, Hfd., Cgy., Buf.	21	1280	149	490	639	759	117	6	32	38	86	....	1983-84	2003-04
• Patrick, Lester	NYR	1	1	0	0	0	2	....	....	....	....	....	....	1926-27	1926-27
• Patrick, Lynn	NYR	10	455	145	190	335	240	44	10	6	16	22	1	1934-35	1945-46
• Patrick, Muzz	NYR	5	166	5	26	31	133	25	4	0	4	34	1	1937-38	1945-46
Patrick, Steve	Buf., NYR, Que.	6	250	40	68	108	242	12	0	1	1	12	....	1980-81	1985-86
Patterson, Colin	Cgy., Buf.	10	504	96	109	205	239	85	12	17	29	57	1	1983-84	1992-93
Patterson, Dennis	K.C., Phi.	3	138	6	22	28	67	....	....	....	....	....	....	1974-75	1979-80
Patterson, Ed	Pit.	3	68	3	3	6	56	....	....	....	....	....	....	1993-94	1996-97
• Patterson, George	Tor., Mtl., NYA, Bos., Det., St.L.	9	284	51	27	78	218	3	0	0	0	2	....	1926-27	1934-35
• Paul, Butch	Det.	1	3	0	0	0	0	....	....	....	....	....	....	1964-65	1964-65
Paul, Jeff	Col.	1	2	0	0	0	7	....	....	....	....	....	....	2002-03	2002-03
• Paulhus, Rollie	Mtl.	1	33	0	0	0	0	....	....	....	....	....	....	1925-26	1925-26
Pavelich, Mark	NYR, Min., S.J.	7	355	137	192	329	340	23	7	17	24	14	....	1981-82	1991-92
Pavelich, Marty	Det.	10	634	93	159	252	454	91	13	15	28	74	4	1947-48	1956-57
Pavese, Jim	St.L., NYR, Det., Hfd.	8	328	13	44	57	689	36	0	6	6	81	....	1981-82	1988-89
• Payer, Evariste	Mtl.	1	1	0	0	0	0	....	....	....	....	....	....	1917-18	1917-18
Payer, Serge	Fla., Ott.	4	124	7	6	13	49	....	....	....	....	....	....	2000-01	2006-07
Payne, Davis	Bos.	2	22	0	1	1	14	....	....	....	....	....	....	1995-96	1996-97
Payne, Steve	Min.	10	613	228	238	466	435	71	35	35	70	60	....	1978-79	1987-88
Paynter, Kent	Chi., Wsh., Wpg., Ott.	7	37	1	3	4	69	4	0	0	0	10	....	1987-88	1993-94
Peake, Pat	Wsh.	5	134	28	41	69	105	13	2	2	4	20	....	1993-94	1997-98
• Pearson, Mel	NYR, Pit.	5	38	2	6	8	25	....	....	....	....	....	....	1959-60	1967-68
Pearson, Rob	Tor., Wsh., St.L.	6	269	56	54	110	645	33	4	2	6	94	....	1991-92	1996-97
Pearson, Scott	Tor., Que., Edm., Buf., NYI	10	292	56	42	98	615	10	2	0	2	14	....	1988-89	1999-00
Peat, Stephen	Wsh.	4	130	8	2	10	234	....	....	....	....	....	....	2001-02	2005-06
Peca, Michael	Van., Buf., NYI, Edm., Tor., CBJ	14	864	176	289	465	798	97	15	19	34	80	....	1993-94	2008-09
‡ Peckham, Theo	Edm.	6	160	4	13	17	388	....	....	....	....	....	....	2007-08	2012-13
Pedersen, Allen	Bos., Min., Hfd.	8	428	5	36	41	487	64	0	0	0	91	....	1986-87	1993-94
Pederson, Barry	Bos., Van., Pit., Hfd.	12	701	238	416	654	472	34	22	30	52	25	1	1980-81	1991-92
Pederson, Denis	N.J., Van., Phx., Nsh.	8	435	57	71	128	398	27	1	5	6	8	....	1995-96	2002-03
Pederson, Mark	Mtl., Phi., S.J., Det.	5	169	35	50	85	77	2	0	0	0	0	....	1989-90	1993-94
Pederson, Tom	S.J., Tor.	5	240	20	49	69	142	24	1	11	12	10	....	1992-93	1996-97
• Peer, Bert	Det.	1	1	0	0	0	0	....	....	....	....	....	....	1939-40	1939-40
Peirson, Johnny	Bos.	11	545	153	173	326	315	49	10	16	26	26	....	1946-47	1957-58
Pelensky, Perry	Chi.	1	4	0	0	0	5	....	....	....	....	....	....	1983-84	1983-84
Pellerin, Scott	N.J., St.L., Min., Car., Bos., Dal., Phx.	11	536	72	126	198	320	37	1	2	3	26	....	1992-93	2003-04
Pelletier, Roger	Phi.	1	1	0	0	0	0	....	....	....	....	....	....	1967-68	1967-68
Peloffy, Andre	Wsh.	1	9	0	0	0	0	....	....	....	....	....	....	1974-75	1974-75
Peltier, Derek	Col.	2	14	0	0	0	2	....	....	....	....	....	....	2008-09	2009-10
‡ Peltonen, Ville	S.J., Nsh., Fla.	8	382	52	96	148	119	....	....	....	....	....	....	1995-96	2008-09
Peluso, Mike	Chi., Ott., N.J., St.L., Cgy.	9	458	38	52	90	1951	62	3	4	7	107	1	1989-90	1997-98
Peluso, Mike	Chi., Phi.	2	38	4	2	6	19	....	....	....	....	....	....	2001-02	2003-04
Pelyk, Mike	Tor.	9	441	26	88	114	566	40	0	3	3	41	....	1967-68	1977-78
Penner, Jeff	Bos.	1	2	0	0	0	0	....	....	....	....	....	....	2009-10	2009-10
Penney, Chad	Ott.	1	3	0	0	0	2	....	....	....	....	....	....	1993-94	1993-94
Pennington, Cliff	Mtl., Bos.	3	101	17	42	59	6	....	....	....	....	....	....	1960-61	1962-63
Peplinski, Jim	Cgy.	11	711	161	263	424	1467	99	15	31	46	382	1	1980-81	1994-95
‡ Perezhogin, Alexander	Mtl.	2	128	15	19	34	86	6	1	1	2	4	....	2005-06	2006-07
Perlini, Fred	Tor.	2	8	2	3	5	0	....	....	....	....	....	....	1981-82	1983-84
Perrault, Joel	Phx., St.L., Van.	6	96	12	14	26	68	....	....	....	....	....	....	2005-06	2010-11
Perreault, Fern	NYR	2	3	0	0	0	0	....	....	....	....	....	....	1947-48	1949-50
Perreault, Gilbert	Buf.	17	1191	512	814	1326	500	90	33	70	103	44	....	1970-71	1986-87
Perreault, Yanic	Tor., L.A., Mtl., Nsh., Phx., Chi.	14	859	247	269	516	402	54	11	19	30	18	....	1993-94	2007-08
‡ Perrin, Eric	T.B., Atl.	4	245	32	72	104	92	18	1	2	3	8	1	2003-04	2008-09
Perrott, Nathan	Nsh., Tor., Dal.	4	89	4	5	9	251	....	....	....	....	....	....	2001-02	2005-06
Perry, Brian	Oak., Buf.	3	96	16	29	45	24	8	1	1	2	4	....	1968-69	1970-71
‡ Persson, John	NYI	1	10	1	0	1	6	....	....	....	....	....	....	2013-14	2013-14
Persson, Ricard	N.J., St.L., Ott.	7	229	10	44	54	262	26	1	3	4	59	....	1995-96	2001-02
Persson, Stefan	NYI	9	622	52	317	369	574	102	7	50	57	69	4	1977-78	1985-86
‡ Pesonen, Janne	Pit.	1	7	0	0	0	0	....	....	....	....	....	....	2008-09	2008-09
Pesut, George	Cal.	2	92	3	22	25	130	....	....	....	....	....	....	1974-75	1975-76
Peters, Andrew	Buf., N.J.	6	229	4	3	7	650	....	....	....	....	....	....	2003-04	2009-10
• Peters, Frank	NYR	1	43	0	0	0	59	4	0	0	0	2	....	1930-31	1930-31
Peters, Garry	Mtl., NYR, Phi., Bos.	8	311	34	34	68	261	9	2	2	4	31	1	1964-65	1971-72
• Peters, Jimmy	Mtl., Bos., Det., Chi.	9	574	125	150	275	186	60	5	9	14	22	3	1945-46	1953-54
Peters, Jimmy	Det., L.A.	9	309	37	36	73	48	11	0	2	2	2	....	1964-65	1974-75
Peters, Steve	Col.	1	2	0	1	1	0	....	....	....	....	....	....	1979-80	1979-80
‡ Peters, Warren	Cgy., Dal., Min.	4	96	4	4	8	72	4	0	0	0	0	....	2008-09	2011-12
‡ Petersen, Toby	Pit., Edm., Dal.	10	398	33	48	81	50	18	1	0	1	2	....	2000-01	2012-13
Peterson, Brent	Det., Buf., Van., Hfd.	11	620	72	141	213	484	31	4	4	8	65	....	1978-79	1988-89
Peterson, Brent	T.B.	3	56	9	1	10	6	....	....	....	....	....	....	1996-97	1998-99
Petiot, Richard	L.A., T.B., Edm.	3	15	0	3	3	25	....	....	....	....	....	....	2005-06	2010-11
Petit, Michel	Van., NYR, Que., Tor., Cgy., L.A., T.B., Edm., Phi., Phx.	16	827	90	238	328	1839	19	0	2	2	61	....	1982-83	1997-98
‡ Petrell, Lennart	Edm.	2	95	7	11	18	49	....	....	....	....	....	....	2011-12	2012-13
Petrenko, Sergei	Buf.	1	14	0	4	4	0	....	....	....	....	....	....	1993-94	1993-94
Petrov, Oleg	Mtl., Nsh.	8	382	72	115	187	101	20	1	6	7	2	....	1992-93	2002-03
‡ Petrovicky, Robert	Hfd., Dal., St.L., T.B., NYI	8	208	27	38	65	118	2	0	0	0	0	....	1992-93	2000-01
Petrovicky, Ronald	Cgy., NYR, Atl., Pit.	6	342	41	51	92	429	3	0	0	0	2	....	2000-01	2006-07
‡ Petruzalek, Jakub	Car.	1	2	0	1	1	0	....	....	....	....	....	....	2008-09	2008-09
Pettersson, Jorgen	St.L., Hfd., Wsh.	6	435	174	192	366	117	44	15	12	27	4	....	1980-81	1985-86
Pettinen, Tomi	NYI	3	24	0	0	0	18	....	....	....	....	....	....	2002-03	2005-06

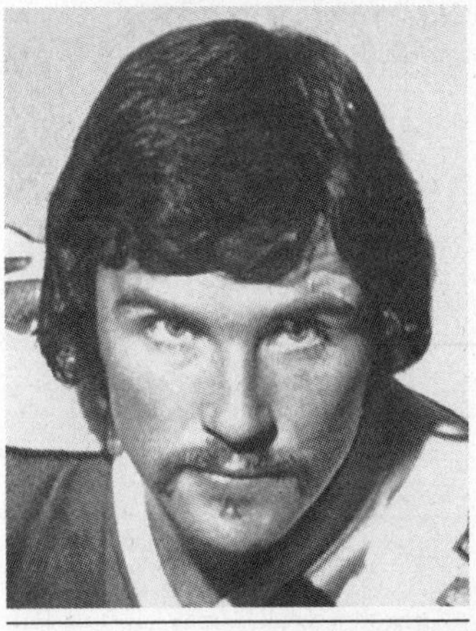
Mike Pelyk

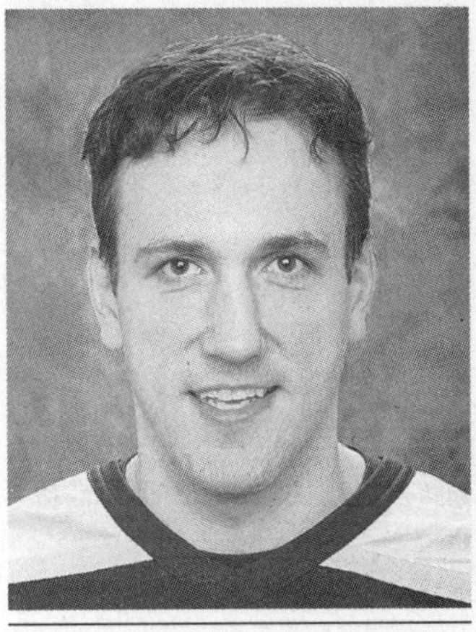
Yanic Perreault

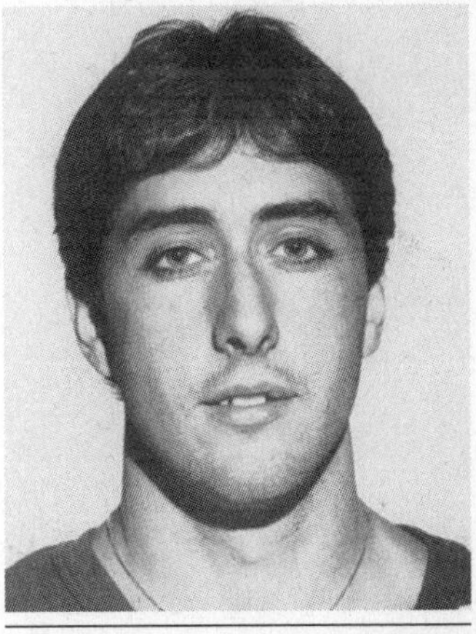
Cam Plante

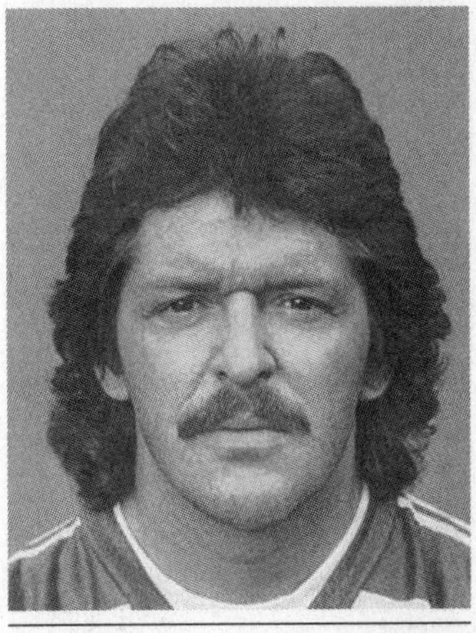
Daniel Poulin

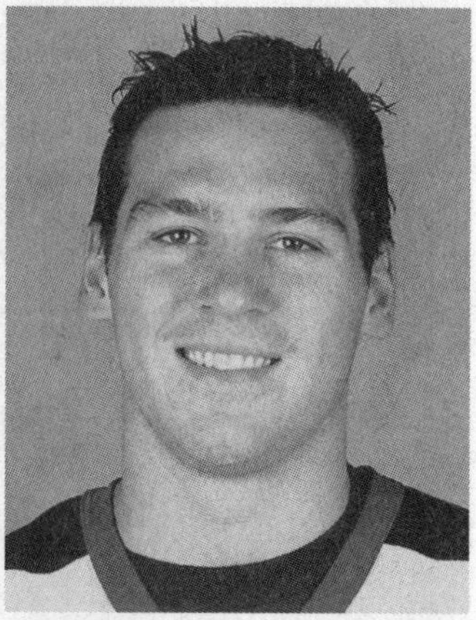

Wayne Primeau

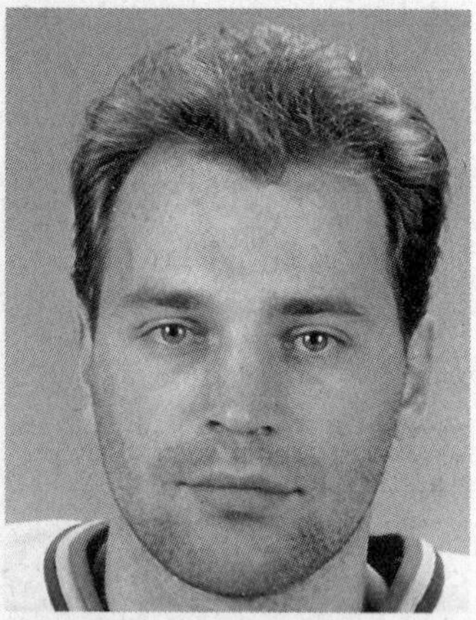

Vitali Prokhorov

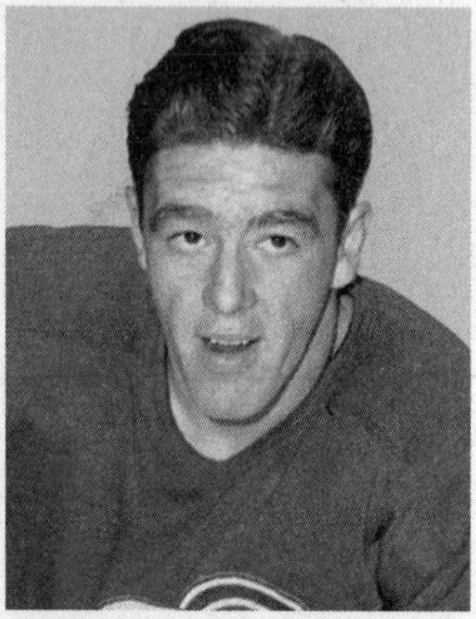

Marcel Pronovost

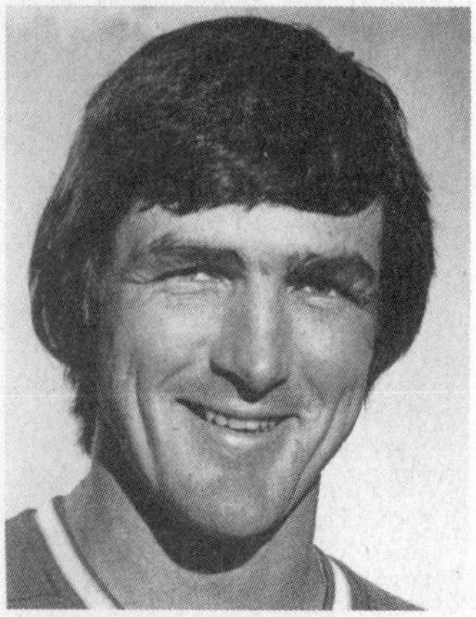

Pat Quinn

			Regular Schedule					Playoffs					NHL	First	Last
Name	NHL Teams	NHL Seasons	GP	G	A	TP	PIM	GP	G	A	TP	PIM	Cup Wins	NHL Season	NHL Season
• Pettinger, Eric	Bos., Tor., Ott.	3	98	7	12	19	83	4	1	0	1	8	....	1928-29	1930-31
• Pettinger, Gord	NYR, Det., Bos.	8	292	42	74	116	77	47	4	5	9	11	4	1932-33	1939-40
Pettinger, Matt	Wsh., Van., T.B.	9	422	65	58	123	210	1	0	0	0	0	....	2000-01	2009-10
‡ Peverley, Rich	Nsh., Atl., Bos., Dal.	8	442	84	157	241	167	59	9	12	21	33	1	2006-07	2013-14
Phair, Lyle	L.A.	3	48	6	7	13	12	1	0	0	0	0	....	1985-86	1987-88
Phillipoff, Harold	Atl., Chi.	3	141	26	57	83	267	6	0	2	2	9	....	1977-78	1979-80
• Phillips, Bill	Mtl.M.	1	27	1	1	2	6	4	0	0	0	2	....	1929-30	1929-30
• Phillips, Charlie	Mtl.	1	17	0	0	0	6	....	....	....	....	....	....	1942-43	1942-43
• Phillips, Merlyn	Mtl.M., NYA	8	302	52	31	83	232	24	5	1	6	19	1	1925-26	1932-33
‡ Picard, Alexandre	CBJ	5	67	0	2	2	58	....	....	....	....	....	....	2005-06	2009-10
‡ Picard, Alexandre	Phi., T.B., Ott., Car., Mtl., Pit.	7	253	19	50	69	86	....	....	....	....	....	....	2005-06	2011-12
Picard, Michel	Hfd., S.J., Ott., St.L., Edm., Phi.	9	166	28	42	70	103	5	0	0	0	2	....	1990-91	2000-01
Picard, Noel	Mtl., St.L., Atl.	7	335	12	63	75	616	50	2	11	13	167	1	1964-65	1972-73
Picard, Robert	Wsh., Tor., Mtl., Wpg., Que., Det.	13	899	104	319	423	1025	36	5	15	20	39	....	1977-78	1989-90
Picard, Roger	St.L.	1	15	2	2	4	21	....	....	....	....	....	....	1967-68	1967-68
Pichette, Dave	Que., St.L., N.J., NYR	7	322	41	140	181	348	28	3	7	10	54	....	1980-81	1987-88
• Picketts, Hal	NYA	1	48	3	1	4	32	....	....	....	....	....	....	1933-34	1933-34
• Pidhirny, Harry	Bos.	1	2	0	0	0	0	....	....	....	....	....	....	1957-58	1957-58
Pierce, Randy	Col., N.J., Hfd.	8	277	62	76	138	223	2	0	0	0	0	....	1977-78	1984-85
‡ Pihlman, Tuomas	N.J.	3	15	1	1	2	12	....	....	....	....	....	....	2003-04	2006-07
‡ Pihlstrom, Antti	Nsh.	2	54	2	5	7	10	....	....	....	....	....	....	2007-08	2008-09
• Pike, Alf	NYR	6	234	42	77	119	145	21	4	2	6	12	1	1939-40	1946-47
‡ Pikkarainen, Ilkka	N.J.	1	31	1	3	4	10	....	....	....	....	....	....	2009-10	2009-10
‡ Pilar, Karel	Tor.	3	90	6	24	30	42	12	1	4	5	12	....	2001-02	2003-04
Pilon, Rich	NYI, NYR, St.L.	14	631	8	69	77	1745	15	0	0	0	50	....	1988-89	2001-02
Pilote, Pierre	Chi., Tor.	14	890	80	418	498	1251	86	8	53	61	102	1	1955-56	1968-69
Pinder, Gerry	Chi., Cal.	3	223	55	69	124	135	17	0	4	4	6	....	1969-70	1971-72
Pineault, Adam	CBJ	1	3	0	0	0	0	....	....	....	....	....	....	2007-08	2007-08
Pirjeta, Lasse	CBJ, Pit.	3	146	23	27	50	50	....	....	....	....	....	....	2002-03	2005-06
‡ Pirnes, Esa	L.A.	1	57	3	8	11	12	....	....	....	....	....	....	2003-04	2003-04
‡ Piros, Kamil	Atl., Fla.	3	28	4	4	8	10	....	....	....	....	....	....	2001-02	2003-04
Pirus, Alex	Min., Det.	4	159	30	28	58	94	2	0	1	1	2	....	1976-77	1979-80
‡ Pisa, Ales	Edm., NYR	2	53	1	3	4	26	....	....	....	....	....	....	2001-02	2002-03
Pisani, Fernando	Edm., Chi.	8	462	87	82	169	200	33	15	4	19	12	....	2002-03	2010-11
Pitkanen, Joni	Phi., Edm., Car.	9	535	57	225	282	484	39	0	13	13	24	....	2003-04	2012-13
Pitlick, Lance	Ott., Fla.	8	393	16	33	49	298	24	0	2	2	21	....	1994-95	2001-02
• Pitre, Didier	Mtl.	6	127	64	33	97	87	9	2	4	6	19	....	1917-18	1922-23
Pittis, Domenic	Pit., Buf., Edm., Nsh.	7	86	5	11	16	71	3	0	0	0	2	....	1996-97	2003-04
‡ Pivko, Libor	Nsh.	1	1	0	0	0	0	....	....	....	....	....	....	2003-04	2003-04
Pivonka, Michal	Wsh.	13	825	181	418	599	478	95	19	36	55	86	....	1986-87	1998-99
• Plager, Barclay	St.L.	10	614	44	187	231	1115	68	3	20	23	182	....	1967-68	1976-77
Plager, Bill	Min., St.L., Atl.	9	263	4	34	38	294	31	0	2	2	26	....	1967-68	1975-76
Plager, Bob	NYR, St.L.	14	644	20	126	146	802	74	2	17	19	195	....	1964-65	1977-78
Plamondon, Gerry	Mtl.	5	74	7	13	20	10	11	5	2	7	2	1	1945-46	1950-51
‡ Plante, Alex	Edm.	3	10	0	2	2	15	....	....	....	....	....	....	2009-10	2011-12
Plante, Cam	Tor.	1	2	0	0	0	0	....	....	....	....	....	....	1984-85	1984-85
Plante, Dan	NYI	4	159	9	14	23	135	1	1	0	1	2	....	1993-94	1997-98
Plante, Derek	Buf., Dal., Chi., Phi.	8	450	96	152	248	138	41	6	10	16	18	1	1993-94	2000-01
Plante, Pierre	Phi., St.L., Chi., NYR, Que.	9	599	125	172	297	599	33	2	6	8	51	....	1971-72	1979-80
Plantery, Mark	Wpg.	1	25	1	5	6	14	....	....	....	....	....	....	1980-81	1980-81
‡ Platt, Geoff	CBJ, Ana.	3	46	4	10	14	28	....	....	....	....	....	....	2005-06	2007-08
Plavsic, Adrien	St.L., Van., T.B., Ana.	8	214	16	56	72	161	13	1	7	8	4	....	1989-90	1996-97
• Plaxton, Hugh	Mtl.M.	1	15	1	2	3	4	....	....	....	....	....	....	1932-33	1932-33
Playfair, Jim	Edm., Chi.	3	21	2	4	6	51	....	....	....	....	....	....	1983-84	1988-89
Playfair, Larry	Buf., L.A.	12	688	26	94	120	1812	43	0	6	6	111	....	1978-79	1989-90
Pleau, Larry	Mtl.	3	94	9	15	24	27	4	0	0	0	0	....	1969-70	1971-72
‡ Pletka, Vaclav	Phi.	1	1	0	0	0	0	....	....	....	....	....	....	2001-02	2001-02
• Pletsch, Charles	Ham.	1	1	0	0	0	0	....	....	....	....	....	....	1920-21	1920-21
Plett, Willi	Atl., Cgy., Min., Bos.	13	834	222	215	437	2572	83	24	22	46	466	....	1975-76	1987-88
‡ Plihal, Tomas	S.J.	3	89	7	9	16	26	4	0	0	0	0	....	2006-07	2008-09
Plumb, Rob	Det.	2	14	3	2	5	2	....	....	....	....	....	....	1977-78	1978-79
Plumb, Ron	Hfd.	1	26	3	4	7	14	....	....	....	....	....	....	1979-80	1979-80
Poapst, Steve	Wsh., Chi., Pit., St.L.	7	307	8	28	36	173	11	0	0	0	0	....	1995-96	2005-06
‡ Pock, Thomas	NYR, NYI	5	118	8	9	17	55	4	0	3	3	4	....	2003-04	2008-09
Pocza, Harvie	Wsh.	2	3	0	0	0	2	....	....	....	....	....	....	1979-80	1981-82
• Poddubny, Walt	Edm., Tor., NYR, Que., N.J.	11	468	184	238	422	454	19	7	2	9	12	....	1981-82	1991-92
Podein, Shjon	Edm., Phi., Col., St.L.	11	699	100	106	206	439	127	14	13	27	132	1	1992-93	2002-03
‡ Podkonicky, Andrej	Fla., Wsh.	2	8	1	0	1	2	....	....	....	....	....	....	2000-01	2003-04
Podloski, Ray	Bos.	1	8	0	1	1	17	....	....	....	....	....	....	1988-89	1988-89
Podollan, Jason	Fla., Tor., L.A., NYI	4	41	1	5	6	19	....	....	....	....	....	....	1996-97	2001-02
• Podolsky, Nels	Det.	1	1	0	0	0	0	7	0	0	0	4	....	1948-49	1948-49
Poeschek, Rudy	NYR, Wpg., T.B., St.L.	12	364	6	25	31	817	5	0	0	0	18	....	1987-88	1999-00
• Poeta, Tony	Chi.	1	1	0	0	0	0	....	....	....	....	....	....	1951-52	1951-52
Pohl, John	St.L., Tor.	4	115	17	21	38	24	....	....	....	....	....	....	2003-04	2007-08
• Poile, Bud	Tor., Chi., Det., NYR, Bos.	7	311	107	122	229	91	23	4	5	9	8	1	1942-43	1949-50
Poile, Don	Det.	2	66	7	9	16	12	4	0	0	0	0	....	1954-55	1957-58
• Poirier, Gordie	Mtl.	1	10	0	0	0	0	....	....	....	....	....	....	1939-40	1939-40
‡ Polak, Vojtech	Dal.	2	5	0	0	0	0	....	....	....	....	....	....	2005-06	2006-07
Polanic, Tom	Min.	2	19	0	2	2	53	5	1	1	2	4	....	1969-70	1970-71
• Polich, John	NYR	2	3	0	1	1	0	....	....	....	....	....	....	1939-40	1940-41
Polich, Mike	Mtl., Min.	5	226	24	29	53	57	23	2	1	3	2	1	1976-77	1980-81
Polis, Greg	Pit., St.L., NYR, Wsh.	10	615	174	169	343	391	7	0	2	2	6	....	1970-71	1979-80
Poliziani, Dan	Bos.	1	1	0	0	0	0	3	0	0	0	0	....	1958-59	1958-59
Pollock, Jame	St.L.	1	9	0	0	0	6	....	....	....	....	....	....	2003-04	2003-04
Polonich, Dennis	Det.	8	390	59	82	141	1242	7	1	0	1	19	....	1974-75	1982-83
‡ Ponikarovsky, Alexei	Tor., Pit., L.A., Car., N.J., Wpg.	12	678	139	184	323	419	62	4	15	19	28	....	2000-01	2012-13
Pooley, Paul	Wpg.	2	15	0	3	3	0	....	....	....	....	....	....	1984-85	1985-86
Popein, Larry	NYR, Oak.	8	449	80	141	221	162	16	1	4	5	6	....	1954-55	1967-68
Popiel, Poul	Bos., L.A., Det., Van., Edm.	7	224	13	41	54	210	4	1	0	1	4	....	1965-66	1979-80
‡ Popovic, Mark	Ana., Atl.	5	81	2	5	7	20	....	....	....	....	....	....	2003-04	2009-10
Popovic, Peter	Mtl., NYR, Pit., Bos.	8	485	10	63	73	291	35	1	4	5	18	....	1993-94	2000-01
• Portland, Jack	Mtl., Bos., Chi.	10	381	15	56	71	323	33	1	3	4	25	1	1933-34	1942-43
Porvari, Jukka	Col., N.J.	2	39	3	9	12	4	....	....	....	....	....	....	1981-82	1982-83
Posa, Victor	Chi.	1	2	0	0	0	2	....	....	....	....	....	....	1985-86	1985-86
Posavad, Mike	St.L.	2	8	0	0	0	0	....	....	....	....	....	....	1985-86	1986-87
Posmyk, Marek	T.B.	2	19	1	2	3	20	....	....	....	....	....	....	1999-00	2000-01
Pothier, Brian	Atl., Ott., Wsh., Car.	9	362	26	92	118	202	29	2	3	5	18	....	2000-01	2009-10
Poti, Tom	Edm., NYR, NYI, Wsh.	13	824	69	258	327	586	51	2	17	19	29	....	1998-99	2012-13
• Potomski, Barry	L.A., S.J.	3	68	6	5	11	227	....	....	....	....	....	....	1995-96	1997-98
Potvin, Denis	NYI	15	1060	310	742	1052	1356	185	56	108	164	253	4	1973-74	1987-88
Potvin, Jean	L.A., Phi., NYI, Cle., Min.	11	613	63	224	287	478	39	2	9	11	17	2	1970-71	1980-81
• Potvin, Marc	Det., L.A., Hfd., Bos.	6	121	3	5	8	456	13	0	1	1	50	....	1990-91	1995-96
Poudrier, Daniel	Que.	3	25	1	5	6	10	....	....	....	....	....	....	1985-86	1987-88
• Poulin, Daniel	Min.	1	3	1	1	2	2	....	....	....	....	....	....	1981-82	1981-82
Poulin, Dave	Phi., Bos., Wsh.	13	724	205	325	530	482	129	31	42	73	132	....	1982-83	1994-95
Poulin, Patrick	Hfd., Chi., T.B., Mtl.	11	634	101	134	235	299	32	6	2	8	8	....	1991-92	2001-02
‡ Pouliot, Marc	Edm., T.B., Phx.	7	192	21	36	57	76	8	1	1	2	2	....	2005-06	2011-12
Pouzar, Jaroslav	Edm.	4	186	34	48	82	135	29	6	4	10	16	3	1982-83	1986-87
• Powell, Ray	Chi.	1	31	7	15	22	2	....	....	....	....	....	....	1950-51	1950-51
• Powis, Geoff	Chi.	1	2	0	0	0	0	....	....	....	....	....	....	1967-68	1967-68
Powis, Lynn	Chi., K.C.	2	130	19	33	52	25	1	0	0	0	0	....	1973-74	1974-75
Prajsler, Petr	L.A., Bos.	4	46	3	10	13	51	4	0	0	0	0	....	1987-88	1991-92
• Pratt, Babe	NYR, Tor., Bos.	12	517	83	209	292	463	63	12	17	29	90	2	1935-36	1946-47
• Pratt, Jack	Bos.	2	37	2	0	2	42	4	0	0	0	0	....	1930-31	1931-32
Pratt, Kelly	Pit.	1	22	0	6	6	15	....	....	....	....	....	....	1974-75	1974-75
Pratt, Nolan	Hfd., Car., Col., T.B., Buf.	11	592	9	56	65	537	38	0	1	1	22	2	1996-97	2007-08
Pratt, Tracy	Oak., Pit., Buf., Van., Col., Tor.	10	580	17	97	114	1026	25	0	1	1	62	....	1967-68	1976-77
Preissing, Tom	S.J., Ott., L.A., Col.	6	326	31	101	132	78	42	3	12	15	14	....	2003-04	2009-10
Prentice, Dean	NYR, Bos., Det., Pit., Min.	22	1378	391	469	860	484	54	13	17	30	38	....	1952-53	1973-74
• Prentice, Eric	Tor.	1	5	0	0	0	4	....	....	....	....	....	....	1943-44	1943-44
Presley, Wayne	Chi., S.J., Buf., NYR, Tor.	12	684	155	147	302	953	83	26	17	43	142	....	1984-85	1995-96
Preston, Rich	Chi., N.J.	8	580	127	164	291	348	47	4	18	22	56	....	1979-80	1986-87
Preston, Yves	Phi.	2	28	7	3	10	4	....	....	....	....	....	....	1978-79	1980-81
Priakin, Sergei	Cgy.	3	46	3	8	11	2	3	0	0	0	0	....	1988-89	1990-91
• Price, Jack	Chi.	3	57	4	6	10	24	4	0	0	0	0	....	1951-52	1953-54
Price, Noel	Tor., NYR, Det., Mtl., Pit., L.A., Atl.	14	499	14	114	128	333	12	0	1	1	8	1	1957-58	1975-76

Name	NHL Teams	NHL Seasons	Regular Schedule					Playoffs					NHL Cup Wins	First NHL Season	Last NHL Season
			GP	G	A	TP	PIM	GP	G	A	TP	PIM			
Price, Pat	NYI, Edm., Pit., Que., NYR, Min.	13	726	43	218	261	1456	74	2	10	12	195	....	1975-76	1987-88
Price, Tom	Cal., Cle., Pit.	5	29	0	2	2	12	....	....	....	....	....	....	1974-75	1978-79
Priestlay, Ken	Buf., Pit.	6	168	27	34	61	63	14	0	0	0	21	1	1986-87	1991-92
● Primeau, Joe	Tor.	9	310	66	177	243	105	38	5	18	23	12	1	1927-28	1935-36
Primeau, Keith	Det., Hfd., Car., Phi.	15	909	266	353	619	1541	128	18	39	57	213	....	1990-91	2005-06
Primeau, Kevin	Van.	1	2	0	0	0	4	....	....	....	....	....	....	1980-81	1980-81
Primeau, Wayne	Buf., T.B., Pit., S.J., Bos., Cgy., Tor.	15	774	69	125	194	789	90	7	14	21	42	....	1994-95	2009-10
● Pringle, Ellie	NYA	1	6	0	0	0	0	....	....	....	....	....	....	1930-31	1930-31
‡ Printz, David	Phi.	2	13	0	0	0	4	....	....	....	....	....	....	2005-06	2006-07
● Probert, Bob	Det., Chi.	16	935	163	221	384	3300	81	16	32	48	274	....	1985-86	2001-02
Prochazka, Martin	Tor., Atl.	2	32	2	5	7	8	....	....	....	....	....	....	1997-98	1999-00
● Prodger, Goldie	Tor., Ham.	6	111	63	29	92	39	....	....	....	....	....	....	1919-20	1924-25
Prokhorov, Vitali	St.L.	3	83	19	11	30	35	4	0	0	0	0	....	1992-93	1994-95
Prokopec, Mike	Chi.	2	15	0	0	0	11	....	....	....	....	....	....	1995-96	1996-97
Pronger, Chris	Hfd., St.L., Edm., Ana., Phi.	18	1167	157	541	698	1590	173	26	95	121	326	1	1993-94	2011-12
Pronger, Sean	Ana., Pit., NYR, L.A., Bos., CBJ, Van.	8	260	23	36	59	159	14	0	2	2	8	....	1995-96	2003-04
Pronovost, Andre	Mtl., Bos., Det., Min.	10	556	94	104	198	408	70	11	11	22	58	4	1956-57	1967-68
Pronovost, Jean	Pit., Atl., Wsh.	14	998	391	383	774	413	35	11	9	20	14	....	1968-69	1981-82
● Pronovost, Marcel	Det., Tor.	21	1206	88	257	345	851	134	8	23	31	104	5	1949-50	1969-70
Propp, Brian	Phi., Bos., Min., Hfd.	15	1016	425	579	1004	830	160	64	84	148	151	....	1979-80	1993-94
Prospal, Vinny	Phi., Ott., Fla., T.B., Ana., NYR, CBJ	16	1108	255	510	765	581	65	10	25	35	26	....	1996-97	2012-13
Proulx, Christian	Mtl.	1	7	1	2	3	20	....	....	....	....	....	....	1993-94	1993-94
● Provost, Claude	Mtl.	15	1005	254	335	589	469	126	25	38	63	86	9	1955-56	1969-70
‡ Prpic, Joel	Bos., Col.	3	18	0	3	3	4	....	....	....	....	....	....	1997-98	2000-01
Prucha, Petr	NYR, Phx.	6	346	78	68	146	133	24	2	3	5	8	....	2005-06	2010-11
Pryor, Chris	Min., NYI	6	82	1	4	5	122	....	....	....	....	....	....	1984-85	1989-90
Prystai, Metro	Chi., Det.	11	674	151	179	330	231	43	12	14	26	8	2	1947-48	1957-58
● Pudas, Al	Tor.	1	4	0	0	0	0	....	....	....	....	....	....	1926-27	1926-27
Pulford, Bob	Tor., L.A.	16	1079	281	362	643	792	89	25	26	51	126	4	1956-57	1971-72
Pulkkinen, Dave	NYI	1	2	0	0	0	0	....	....	....	....	....	....	1972-73	1972-73
Purinton, Dale	NYR	5	181	4	16	20	578	....	....	....	....	....	....	1999-00	2003-04
● Purpur, Fido	St.L., Chi., Det.	5	144	25	35	60	46	16	1	2	3	4	....	1934-35	1944-45
Purves, John	Wsh.	1	7	1	0	1	0	....	....	....	....	....	....	1990-91	1990-91
‡ Pushkarev, Konstantin	L.A.	2	17	2	3	5	8	....	....	....	....	....	....	2005-06	2006-07
Pushor, Jamie	Det., Ana., Dal., CBJ, Pit., NYR	10	521	14	46	60	648	14	0	1	1	16	1	1995-96	2005-06
● Pusie, Jean	Mtl., NYR, Bos.	5	61	1	4	5	28	7	0	0	0	0	1	1930-31	1935-36
Pyatt, Nelson	Det., Wsh., Col.	7	296	71	63	134	69	....	....	....	....	....	....	1973-74	1979-80
Pyatt, Taylor	NYI, Buf., Van., Phx., NYR, Pit.	13	859	140	140	280	430	69	10	14	24	26	....	2000-01	2013-14
‡ Pyorala, Mika	Phi.	1	36	2	2	4	10	....	....	....	....	....	....	2009-10	2009-10

Q

Name	NHL Teams	NHL Seasons	GP	G	A	TP	PIM	GP	G	A	TP	PIM	NHL Cup Wins	First NHL Season	Last NHL Season
● Quackenbush, Bill	Det., Bos.	14	774	62	222	284	95	80	2	19	21	8	....	1942-43	1955-56
Quackenbush, Max	Bos., Chi.	2	61	4	7	11	30	6	0	0	0	4	....	1950-51	1951-52
Quenneville, Joel	Tor., Col., N.J., Hfd., Wsh.	13	803	54	136	190	705	32	0	8	8	22	....	1978-79	1990-91
● Quenneville, Leo	NYR	1	25	0	3	3	10	3	0	0	0	0	....	1929-30	1929-30
‡ Quick, Kevin	T.B.	1	6	0	1	1	0	....	....	....	....	....	....	2008-09	2008-09
● Quilty, John	Mtl., Bos.	4	125	36	34	70	81	13	3	5	8	9	....	1940-41	1947-48
Quinn, Dan	Cgy., Pit., Van., St.L., Phi., Min., Ott., L.A.	14	805	266	419	685	533	65	22	26	48	62	....	1983-84	1996-97
● Quinn, Pat	Tor., Van., Atl.	9	606	18	113	131	950	11	0	1	1	21	....	1968-69	1976-77
Quinney, Ken	Que.	3	59	7	13	20	23	....	....	....	....	....	....	1986-87	1990-91
‡ Quint, Deron	Wpg., Phx., N.J., CBJ, Chi., NYI	10	463	46	97	143	166	7	0	2	2	0	....	1995-96	2006-07
Quintal, Stephane	Bos., St.L., Wpg., Mtl., NYR, Chi.	16	1037	63	180	243	1320	52	2	10	12	51	....	1988-89	2003-04
Quintin, Jean-Francois	S.J.	2	22	5	5	10	4	....	....	....	....	....	....	1991-92	1992-93

R

Name	NHL Teams	NHL Seasons	GP	G	A	TP	PIM	GP	G	A	TP	PIM	NHL Cup Wins	First NHL Season	Last NHL Season
● Rachunek, Karel	Ott., NYR, N.J.	7	371	22	118	140	227	26	1	7	8	16	....	1999-00	2007-08
Racine, Yves	Det., Phi., Mtl., S.J., Cgy., T.B.	9	508	37	194	231	439	25	5	4	9	37	....	1989-90	1997-98
‡ Radivojevic, Branko	Phx., Phi., Min.	6	393	52	68	120	252	31	2	1	3	36	....	2001-02	2007-08
● Radley, Yip	NYA, Mtl.M.	2	18	0	1	1	13	....	....	....	....	....	....	1930-31	1936-37
‡ Radulov, Alexander	Nsh.	3	154	47	55	102	74	18	6	8	14	29	....	2006-07	2011-12
‡ Radulov, Igor	Chi.	2	43	9	7	16	22	....	....	....	....	....	....	2002-03	2003-04
Raduns, Nate	Phi.	1	1	0	0	0	0	....	....	....	....	....	....	2008-09	2008-09
Rafalski, Brian	N.J., Det.	11	833	79	436	515	282	165	29	71	100	66	3	1999-00	2010-11
Raglan, Herb	St.L., Que., T.B., Ott.	9	343	33	56	89	775	32	3	6	9	50	....	1985-86	1993-94
● Raglan, Rags	Det., Chi.	3	100	4	9	13	52	3	0	0	0	0	....	1950-51	1952-53
Ragnarsson, Marcus	S.J., Phi.	9	632	37	140	177	482	68	2	13	15	60	....	1995-96	2003-04
‡ Rakhshani, Rhett	NYI	2	7	0	0	0	2	....	....	....	....	....	....	2010-11	2011-12
● Raleigh, Don	NYR	10	535	101	219	320	96	18	6	5	11	6	....	1943-44	1955-56
Ralph, Brad	Phx.	1	1	0	0	0	0	....	....	....	....	....	....	2000-01	2000-01
Ramage, Rob	Col., St.L., Cgy., Tor., Min., T.B., Mtl., Phi.	15	1044	139	425	564	2226	84	8	42	50	218	2	1979-80	1993-94
‡ Ramholt, Tim	Cgy.	1	1	0	0	0	0	....	....	....	....	....	....	2007-08	2007-08
● Ramsay, Beattie	Tor.	1	43	0	2	2	10	....	....	....	....	....	....	1927-28	1927-28
Ramsay, Craig	Buf.	14	1070	252	420	672	201	89	17	31	48	27	....	1971-72	1984-85
Ramsay, Les	Chi.	1	11	2	2	4	2	....	....	....	....	....	....	1944-45	1944-45
Ramsey, Mike	Buf., Pit., Det.	18	1070	79	266	345	1012	115	8	29	37	176	....	1979-80	1996-97
Ramsey, Wayne	Buf.	1	2	0	0	0	0	....	....	....	....	....	....	1977-78	1977-78
● Randall, Ken	Tor., Ham., NYA	10	218	68	50	118	533	6	2	1	3	27	2	1917-18	1926-27
Ranheim, Paul	Cgy., Hfd., Car., Phi., Phx.	15	1013	161	199	360	288	36	3	8	11	6	....	1988-89	2002-03
Ranieri, George	Bos.	1	2	0	0	0	0	....	....	....	....	....	....	1956-57	1956-57
‡ Rask, Joonas	Nsh.	1	2	0	1	1	0	....	....	....	....	....	....	2012-13	2012-13
Rasmussen, Erik	Buf., L.A., N.J.	9	545	52	76	128	305	52	2	7	9	46	....	1997-98	2006-07
Ratchuk, Peter	Fla.	2	32	1	1	2	10	....	....	....	....	....	....	1998-99	2000-01
Ratelle, Jean	NYR, Bos.	21	1281	491	776	1267	276	123	32	66	98	24	....	1960-61	1980-81
Rathje, Mike	S.J., Phi.	13	768	30	150	180	491	77	9	14	23	51	....	1993-94	2006-07
Rathwell, Jake	Bos.	1	1	0	0	0	0	....	....	....	....	....	....	1974-75	1974-75
Ratushny, Dan	Van.	1	1	0	1	1	2	....	....	....	....	....	....	1992-93	1992-93
‡ Rau, Chad	Min.	1	9	2	0	2	0	....	....	....	....	....	....	2011-12	2011-12
Rausse, Errol	Wsh.	3	31	7	3	10	0	....	....	....	....	....	....	1979-80	1981-82
Rautakallio, Pekka	Atl., Cgy.	3	235	33	121	154	122	23	2	5	7	8	....	1979-80	1981-82
Ravlich, Matt	Bos., Chi., Det., L.A.	10	410	12	78	90	364	24	1	5	6	16	....	1962-63	1972-73
Ray, Rob	Buf., Ott.	15	900	41	50	91	3207	55	3	2	5	169	....	1989-90	2003-04
● Raymond, Armand	Mtl.	2	22	0	2	2	10	....	....	....	....	....	....	1937-38	1939-40
● Raymond, Paul	Mtl.	4	76	2	3	5	6	5	0	0	0	2	....	1932-33	1938-39
● Read, Mel	NYR	1	1	0	0	0	0	....	....	....	....	....	....	1946-47	1946-47
Ready, Ryan	Phi.	1	7	0	1	1	0	....	....	....	....	....	....	2005-06	2005-06
● Reardon, Ken	Mtl.	7	341	26	96	122	604	31	2	5	7	62	1	1940-41	1949-50
● Reardon, Terry	Bos., Mtl.	7	193	47	53	100	73	30	8	10	18	12	1	1938-39	1946-47
Reasoner, Marty	St.L., Edm., Bos., Atl., Fla., NYI	14	798	97	169	266	379	24	6	2	8	23	....	1998-99	2012-13
Reaume, Marc	Tor., Det., Mtl., Van.	9	344	8	43	51	273	21	0	2	2	8	....	1954-55	1970-71
● Reay, Billy	Det., Mtl.	10	479	105	162	267	202	63	13	16	29	43	2	1943-44	1952-53
Recchi, Mark	Pit., Phi., Mtl., Car., Atl., T.B., Bos.	22	1652	577	956	1533	1033	189	61	86	147	93	3	1988-89	2010-11
● Redahl, Gord	Bos.	1	18	0	1	1	2	....	....	....	....	....	....	1958-59	1958-59
Redden, Wade	Ott., NYR, St.L., Bos.	14	1023	109	348	457	665	106	13	36	49	55	....	1996-97	2012-13
● Redding, George	Bos.	2	55	3	2	5	23	....	....	....	....	....	....	1924-25	1925-26
‡ Reddox, Liam	Edm.	4	100	6	18	24	34	....	....	....	....	....	....	2007-08	2010-11
Redmond, Craig	L.A., Edm.	5	191	16	68	84	134	3	1	0	1	2	....	1984-85	1988-89
Redmond, Dick	Min., Cal., Chi., St.L., Atl., Bos.	13	771	133	312	445	504	66	9	22	31	27	....	1969-70	1981-82
Redmond, Keith	L.A.	1	12	1	0	1	20	....	....	....	....	....	....	1993-94	1993-94
Redmond, Mickey	Mtl., Det.	9	538	233	195	428	219	16	2	3	5	2	2	1967-68	1975-76
● Reeds, Mark	St.L., Hfd.	8	365	45	114	159	135	53	8	9	17	23	....	1981-82	1988-89
Reekie, Joe	Buf., NYI, T.B., Wsh., Chi.	17	902	25	139	164	1326	51	3	4	7	63	....	1985-86	2001-02
● Regan, Bill	NYR, NYA	3	67	3	2	5	67	8	0	0	0	2	....	1929-30	1932-33
● Regan, Larry	Bos., Tor.	5	280	41	95	136	71	42	7	14	21	18	....	1956-57	1960-61
Regehr, Richie	Cgy.	2	20	1	3	4	6	....	....	....	....	....	....	2005-06	2006-07
Regier, Darcy	Cle., NYI	3	26	0	2	2	35	....	....	....	....	....	....	1977-78	1983-84
Regier, Steve	NYI, St.L.	4	26	3	1	4	8	....	....	....	....	....	....	2005-06	2008-09
● Reibel, Dutch	Det., Chi., Bos.	6	409	84	161	245	75	39	6	14	20	4	2	1953-54	1958-59
Reich, Jeremy	CBJ, Bos.	3	99	2	4	6	161	4	0	0	0	8	....	2003-04	2007-08
Reichel, Robert	Cgy., NYI, Phx., Tor.	11	830	252	378	630	388	70	8	23	31	20	....	1990-91	2003-04
Reichert, Craig	Ana.	1	3	0	0	0	0	....	....	....	....	....	....	1996-97	1996-97
‡ Reid, Brandon	Van.	3	13	2	4	6	0	10	0	2	2	0	....	2002-03	2006-07
Reid, Darren	T.B., Phi.	2	21	0	1	1	18	....	....	....	....	....	....	2005-06	2006-07

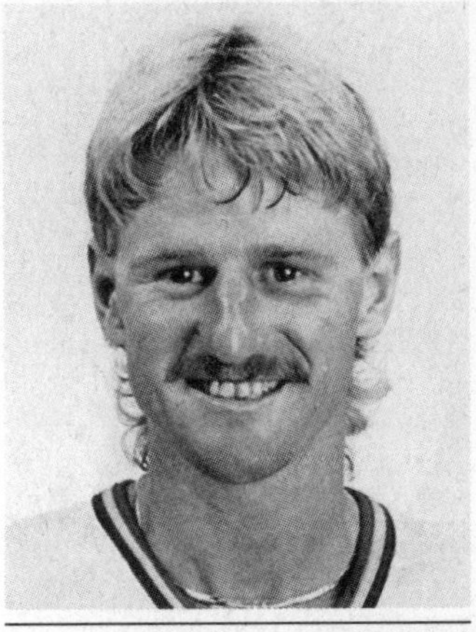
Mark Reeds

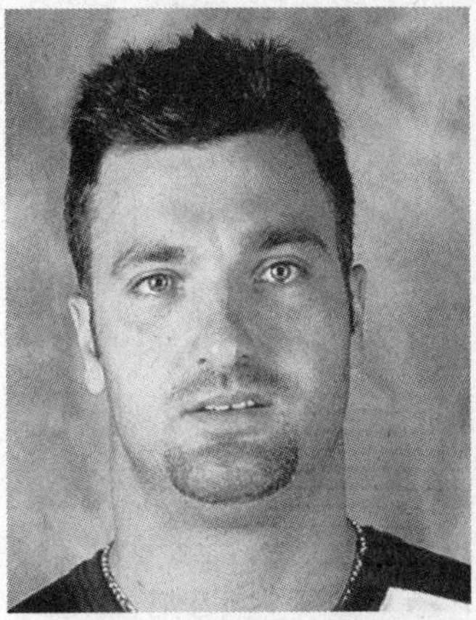
Stephane Richer

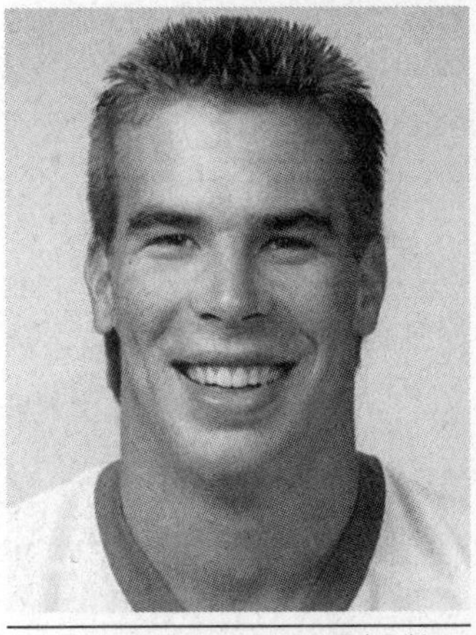
Rob Robinson

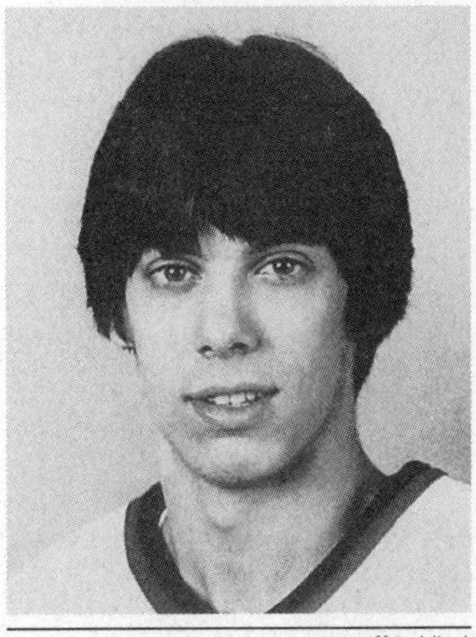
Jeff Rohlicek

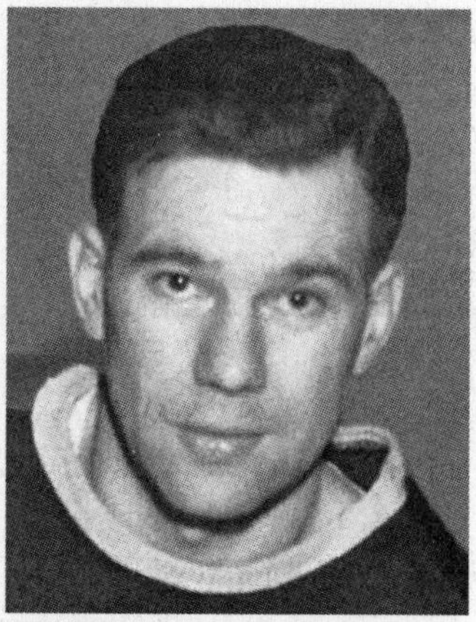

Doc Romnes

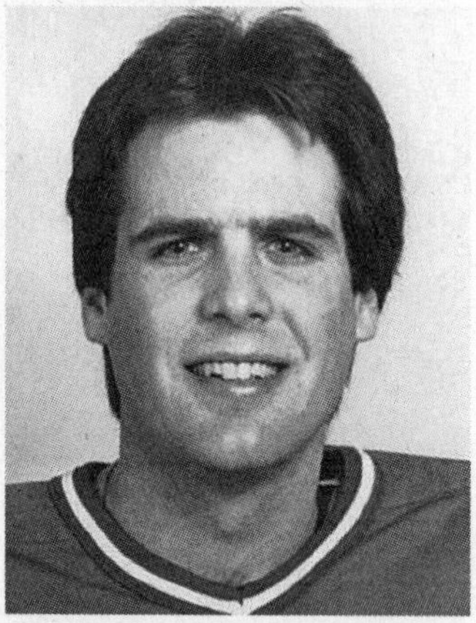

Steve Rooney

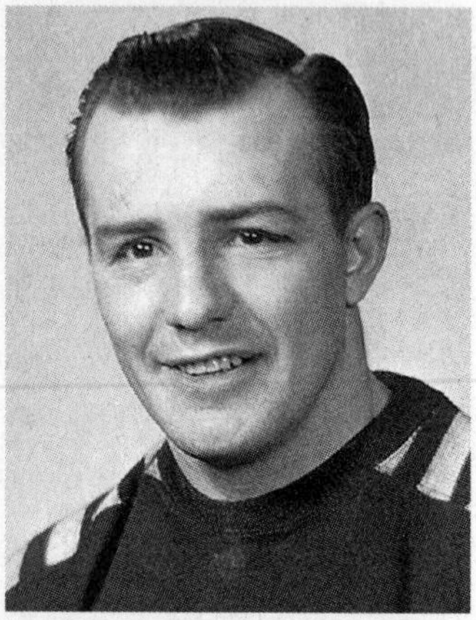

Ron Rowe

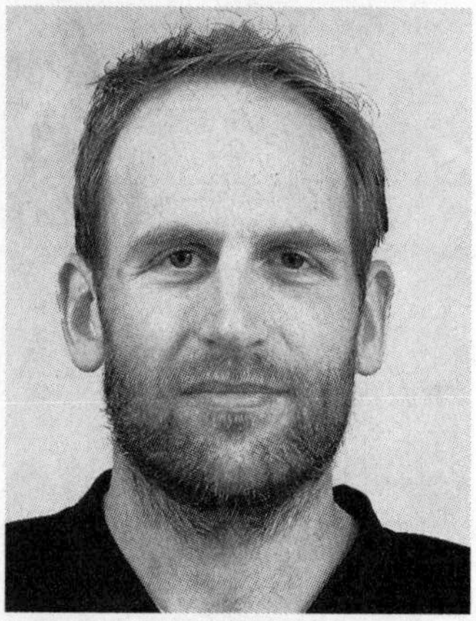

Mike Rupp

Name	NHL Teams	NHL Seasons	Regular Schedule					Playoffs					NHL Cup Wins	First NHL Season	Last NHL Season
			GP	G	A	TP	PIM	GP	G	A	TP	PIM			
• Reid, Dave	Tor.	3	7	0	0	0	0	....	....	....	....	....	....	1952-53	1955-56
Reid, Dave	Bos., Tor., Dal., Col.	18	961	165	204	369	253	118	9	26	35	34	2	1983-84	2000-01
• Reid, Gerry	Det.	1	....	....	....	....	....	2	0	0	0	2	....	1948-49	1948-49
• Reid, Gord	NYA	1	1	0	0	0	2	....	....	....	....	....	....	1936-37	1936-37
• Reid, Reg	Tor.	2	39	1	0	1	4	2	0	0	0	0	....	1924-25	1925-26
Reid, Tom	Chi., Min.	11	701	17	113	130	654	42	1	13	14	49	....	1967-68	1977-78
Reierson, Dave	Cgy.	1	2	0	0	0	2	....	....	....	....	....	....	1988-89	1988-89
• Reigle, Ed	Bos.	1	17	0	2	2	25	....	....	....	....	....	....	1950-51	1950-51
Reinhart, Paul	Atl., Cgy., Van.	11	648	133	426	559	277	83	23	54	77	42	....	1979-80	1989-90
• Reinikka, Ollie	NYR	1	16	0	0	0	0	....	....	....	....	....	....	1926-27	1926-27
‡ Reinprecht, Steve	L.A., Col., Cgy., Phx., Fla.	11	663	140	242	382	186	50	10	10	20	10	1	1999-00	2010-11
Reirden, Todd	Edm., St.L., Atl., Phx.	5	183	11	35	46	181	5	0	1	1	0	....	1998-99	2003-04
• Reise, Leo	Ham., NYA, NYR	8	223	36	29	65	181	6	0	0	0	16	....	1920-21	1929-30
• Reise, Leo	Chi., Det., NYR	9	494	28	81	109	399	52	8	5	13	68	2	1945-46	1953-54
Reitz, Erik	Min., NYR	4	48	1	1	2	69	2	0	0	0	0	....	2005-06	2008-09
Renaud, Mark	Hfd., Buf.	5	152	6	50	56	86	....	....	....	....	....	....	1979-80	1983-84
Renberg, Mikael	Phi., T.B., Phx., Tor.	10	661	190	274	464	372	67	16	22	38	42	....	1993-94	2003-04
Reynolds, Bobby	Tor.	1	7	1	1	2	0	....	....	....	....	....	....	1989-90	1989-90
‡ Rheault, Jon	Fla.	1	5	0	0	0	0	....	....	....	....	....	....	2012-13	2012-13
Rheaume, Pascal	N.J., St.L., Chi., Atl., NYR, Phx.	9	318	39	52	91	144	45	3	6	9	27	1	1996-97	2005-06
Ribble, Pat	Atl., Chi., Tor., Wsh., Cgy.	8	349	19	60	79	365	8	0	1	1	12	....	1975-76	1982-83
Ricci, Mike	Phi., Que., Col., S.J., Phx.	16	1099	243	362	605	974	110	23	43	66	77	1	1990-91	2006-07
Rice, Steven	NYR, Edm., Hfd., Car.	8	329	64	61	125	275	2	2	1	3	6	....	1990-91	1997-98
Richard, Henri	Mtl.	20	1256	358	688	1046	928	180	49	80	129	181	11	1955-56	1974-75
• Richard, Jacques	Atl., Buf., Que.	10	556	160	187	347	307	35	5	5	10	34	....	1972-73	1982-83
Richard, Jean-Marc	Que.	2	5	2	1	3	2	....	....	....	....	....	....	1987-88	1989-90
• Richard, Maurice	Mtl.	18	978	544	421	965	1285	133	82	44	126	188	8	1942-43	1959-60
Richard, Mike	Wsh.	2	7	0	2	2	0	....	....	....	....	....	....	1987-88	1989-90
Richards, Todd	Hfd.	2	8	0	4	4	4	11	0	3	3	6	....	1990-91	1991-92
Richards, Travis	Dal.	2	3	0	0	0	2	....	....	....	....	....	....	1994-95	1995-96
Richardson, Dave	NYR, Chi., Det.	4	45	3	2	5	27	....	....	....	....	....	....	1963-64	1967-68
Richardson, Glen	Van.	1	24	3	6	9	19	....	....	....	....	....	....	1975-76	1975-76
Richardson, Ken	St.L.	3	49	8	13	21	16	....	....	....	....	....	....	1974-75	1978-79
Richardson, Luke	Tor., Edm., Phi., CBJ, T.B., Ott.	21	1417	35	166	201	2055	69	0	8	8	130	....	1987-88	2008-09
Richer, Bob	Buf.	1	3	0	0	0	0	....	....	....	....	....	....	1972-73	1972-73
Richer, Stephane	Mtl., N.J., T.B., St.L., Pit.	17	1054	421	398	819	614	134	53	45	98	61	2	1984-85	2001-02
Richer, Stephane	T.B., Bos., Fla.	3	27	1	5	6	20	3	0	0	0	0	....	1992-93	1994-95
Richmond, Danny	Car., Chi.	3	49	0	3	3	75	....	....	....	....	....	....	2005-06	2007-08
Richmond, Steve	NYR, Det., N.J., L.A.	5	159	4	23	27	514	4	0	0	0	12	....	1983-84	1988-89
Richter, Barry	NYR, Bos., NYI, Mtl.	5	151	11	34	45	76	....	....	....	....	....	....	1995-96	2000-01
Richter, Dave	Min., Phi., Van., St.L.	9	365	9	40	49	1030	22	1	0	1	80	....	1981-82	1989-90
Ridley, Mike	NYR, Wsh., Tor., Van.	12	866	292	466	758	424	104	28	50	78	70	....	1985-86	1996-97
Riesen, Michel	Edm.	1	12	0	1	1	4	....	....	....	....	....	....	2000-01	2000-01
Riley, Bill	Wsh., Wpg.	5	139	31	30	61	320	....	....	....	....	....	....	1974-75	1979-80
• Riley, Jack	Det., Mtl., Bos.	4	104	10	22	32	8	4	0	3	3	0	....	1932-33	1935-36
• Riley, Jim	Chi., Det.	1	9	0	2	2	14	....	....	....	....	....	....	1926-27	1926-27
• Riopelle, Rip	Mtl.	3	169	27	16	43	73	8	1	1	2	2	....	1947-48	1949-50
Rioux, Gerry	Wpg.	1	8	0	0	0	6	....	....	....	....	....	....	1979-80	1979-80
Rioux, Pierre	Cgy.	1	14	1	2	3	4	....	....	....	....	....	....	1982-83	1982-83
• Ripley, Vic	Chi., Bos., NYR, St.L.	7	278	51	49	100	173	20	4	1	5	10	....	1928-29	1934-35
Risebrough, Doug	Mtl., Cgy.	13	740	185	286	471	1542	124	21	37	58	238	4	1974-75	1986-87
Rissling, Gary	Wsh., Pit.	7	221	23	30	53	1008	5	0	1	1	4	....	1978-79	1984-85
‡ Rissmiller, Patrick	S.J., NYR, Atl., Fla.	6	192	18	28	46	60	30	3	4	7	10	....	2003-04	2010-11
‡ Rita, Jani	Edm., Pit.	4	66	9	5	14	10	....	....	....	....	....	....	2001-02	2005-06
Ritchie, Bob	Phi., Det.	2	29	8	4	12	10	....	....	....	....	....	....	1976-77	1977-78
‡ Ritchie, Byron	Car., Fla., Cgy., Van.	8	324	25	33	58	373	8	0	0	0	10	....	1998-99	2007-08
• Ritchie, Dave	Mtl.W., Ott., Tor., Que., Mtl.	6	58	15	6	21	50	1	0	0	0	0	....	1917-18	1925-26
‡ Ritola, Mattias	Det., T.B.	4	43	4	5	9	17	2	0	0	0	0	....	2007-08	2011-12
• Ritson, Alex	NYR	1	1	0	0	0	0	....	....	....	....	....	....	1944-45	1944-45
Rittinger, Alan	Bos.	1	19	3	7	10	0	....	....	....	....	....	....	1943-44	1943-44
Rivard, Bob	Pit.	1	27	5	12	17	4	....	....	....	....	....	....	1967-68	1967-68
• Rivers, Gus	Mtl.	3	88	4	5	9	12	16	2	0	2	2	2	1929-30	1931-32
Rivers, Jamie	St.L., NYI, Ott., Bos., Fla., Det., Phx.	11	454	17	49	66	385	15	1	1	2	8	....	1995-96	2006-07
Rivers, Shawn	T.B.	1	4	0	2	2	2	....	....	....	....	....	....	1992-93	1992-93
Rivers, Wayne	Det., Bos., St.L., NYR	7	108	15	30	45	94	....	....	....	....	....	....	1961-62	1968-69
Rivet, Craig	Mtl., S.J., Buf., CBJ	16	923	50	187	237	1171	69	4	19	23	69	....	1994-95	2010-11
Rizzuto, Garth	Van.	1	37	3	4	7	16	....	....	....	....	....	....	1970-71	1970-71
Roach, Andy	St.L.	1	5	1	2	3	10	....	....	....	....	....	....	2005-06	2005-06
• Roach, Mickey	Tor., Ham., NYA	8	211	77	34	111	54	....	....	....	....	....	....	1919-20	1926-27
Roberge, Mario	Mtl.	5	112	7	7	14	314	15	0	0	0	24	1	1990-91	1994-95
Roberge, Serge	Que.	1	9	0	0	0	24	....	....	....	....	....	....	1990-91	1990-91
• Robert, Claude	Mtl.	1	23	1	0	1	9	....	....	....	....	....	....	1950-51	1950-51
Robert, Rene	Tor., Pit., Buf., Col.	12	744	284	418	702	597	50	22	19	41	73	....	1970-71	1981-82
Roberto, Phil	Mtl., St.L., Det., K.C., Col., Cle.	8	385	75	106	181	464	31	9	8	17	69	1	1969-70	1976-77
Roberts, David	St.L., Edm., Van.	5	125	20	33	53	85	9	0	0	0	16	....	1993-94	1997-98
Roberts, Doug	Det., Oak., Cal., Bos.	10	419	43	104	147	342	16	2	3	5	46	....	1965-66	1974-75
Roberts, Gary	Cgy., Car., Tor., Fla., Pit., T.B.	22	1224	438	472	910	2560	130	32	61	93	332	1	1986-87	2008-09
Roberts, Gordie	Hfd., Min., Phi., St.L., Pit., Bos.	15	1097	61	359	420	1582	153	10	47	57	273	2	1979-80	1993-94
Roberts, Jim	Min.	3	106	17	23	40	33	2	0	0	0	0	....	1976-77	1978-79
Roberts, Jimmy	Mtl., St.L.	15	1006	126	194	320	621	153	20	16	36	160	5	1963-64	1977-78
• Robertson, Fred	Tor., Det.	2	34	1	0	1	35	7	0	0	0	0	1	1931-32	1933-34
Robertson, Geordie	Buf.	1	5	1	2	3	7	....	....	....	....	....	....	1982-83	1982-83
Robertson, George	Mtl.	2	31	2	5	7	6	....	....	....	....	....	....	1947-48	1948-49
Robertson, Torrie	Wsh., Hfd., Det.	10	442	49	99	148	1751	22	2	1	3	90	....	1980-81	1989-90
Robertsson, Bert	Van., Edm., NYR	4	123	4	10	14	75	5	0	0	0	0	....	1997-98	2000-01
Robidoux, Florent	Chi.	3	52	7	4	11	75	....	....	....	....	....	....	1980-81	1983-84
Robinson, Doug	Chi., NYR, L.A.	7	239	44	67	111	34	11	4	3	7	0	....	1963-64	1970-71
• Robinson, Earl	Mtl.M., Chi., Mtl.	11	417	83	98	181	133	25	5	4	9	0	1	1928-29	1939-40
Robinson, Larry	Mtl., L.A.	20	1384	208	750	958	793	227	28	116	144	211	6	1972-73	1991-92
Robinson, Moe	Mtl.	1	1	0	0	0	0	....	....	....	....	....	....	1979-80	1979-80
Robinson, Nathan	Det., Bos.	2	7	0	0	0	2	....	....	....	....	....	....	2003-04	2005-06
Robinson, Rob	St.L.	1	22	0	1	1	8	....	....	....	....	....	....	1991-92	1991-92
Robinson, Scott	Min.	1	1	0	0	0	2	....	....	....	....	....	....	1989-90	1989-90
Robitaille, Louis	Wsh.	1	2	0	0	0	5	....	....	....	....	....	....	2005-06	2005-06
Robitaille, Luc	L.A., Pit., NYR, Det.	19	1431	668	726	1394	1177	159	58	69	127	174	1	1986-87	2005-06
Robitaille, Mike	NYR, Det., Buf., Van.	8	382	23	105	128	280	13	0	1	1	4	....	1969-70	1976-77
‡ Robitaille, Randy	Bos., Nsh., L.A., Pit., NYI, Atl., Min., Phi., Ott.	11	531	84	172	256	201	13	1	4	5	8	....	1996-97	2007-08
Roche, Dave	Pit., Cgy., NYI	5	171	15	15	30	334	16	2	7	9	26	....	1995-96	2001-02
• Roche, Des	Mtl.M., Ott., St.L., Mtl., Det.	4	113	20	18	38	44	....	....	....	....	....	....	1930-31	1934-35
• Roche, Earl	Mtl.M., Bos., Ott., St.L., Det.	4	147	25	27	52	48	2	0	0	0	0	....	1930-31	1934-35
Roche, Ernie	Mtl.	1	4	0	0	0	2	....	....	....	....	....	....	1950-51	1950-51
Roche, Travis	Min., Phx.	4	60	6	14	20	24	....	....	....	....	....	....	2000-01	2006-07
Rochefort, Dave	Det.	1	1	0	0	0	0	....	....	....	....	....	....	1966-67	1966-67
Rochefort, Leon	NYR, Mtl., Phi., L.A., Det., Atl., Van.	15	617	121	147	268	93	39	4	4	8	16	2	1960-61	1975-76
Rochefort, Normand	Que., NYR, T.B.	13	598	39	119	158	570	69	7	5	12	82	....	1980-81	1993-94
• Rockburn, Harvey	Det., Ott.	3	94	4	2	6	254	....	....	....	....	....	....	1929-30	1932-33
• Rodden, Eddie	Chi., Tor., Bos., NYR	4	97	6	14	20	60	2	0	1	1	0	....	1926-27	1930-31
Rodgers, Marc	Det.	1	21	1	1	2	10	....	....	....	....	....	....	1999-00	1999-00
‡ Rodney, Bryan	Car., Edm.	4	34	1	12	13	12	....	....	....	....	....	....	2008-09	2011-12
Roenick, Jeremy	Chi., Phx., Phi., L.A., S.J.	20	1363	513	703	1216	1463	154	53	69	122	115	....	1988-89	2008-09
Roest, Stacy	Det., Min.	5	244	28	48	76	54	3	0	0	0	0	....	1998-99	2002-03
Rogers, John	Min.	2	14	2	4	6	0	....	....	....	....	....	....	1973-74	1974-75
Rogers, Mike	Hfd., NYR, Edm.	7	484	202	317	519	184	17	1	13	14	6	....	1979-80	1985-86
Rohlicek, Jeff	Van.	2	9	0	0	0	8	....	....	....	....	....	....	1987-88	1988-89
Rohlin, Leif	Van.	2	96	8	24	32	40	5	0	0	0	0	....	1995-96	1996-97
Rohloff, Jon	Bos.	3	150	7	25	32	129	10	1	2	3	8	....	1994-95	1996-97
Rohloff, Todd	Wsh., CBJ	2	75	0	6	6	40	....	....	....	....	....	....	2001-02	2003-04
Rolfe, Dale	Bos., L.A., Det., NYR	9	509	25	125	150	556	71	5	24	29	89	....	1959-60	1974-75
Rolston, Brian	N.J., Col., Bos., Min., NYI	17	1256	342	419	761	472	77	20	14	34	38	1	1994-95	2011-12
Romanchych, Larry	Chi., Atl.	6	298	68	97	165	102	7	2	2	4	4	....	1970-71	1976-77
Romaniuk, Russell	Wpg., Phi.	5	102	13	14	27	63	2	0	0	0	0	....	1991-92	1995-96
• Rombough, Doug	Buf., NYI, Min.	4	150	24	27	51	80	....	....	....	....	....	....	1972-73	1975-76
‡ Rome, Aaron	Ana., CBJ, Van., Dal.	8	226	6	22	28	185	19	1	1	2	37	1	2006-07	2013-14
Rominski, Dale	T.B.	1	3	0	1	1	2	....	....	....	....	....	....	1999-00	1999-00
• Romnes, Doc	Chi., Tor., NYA	10	360	68	136	204	42	43	7	18	25	4	2	1930-31	1939-40

Name	NHL Teams	NHL Seasons	Regular Schedule					Playoffs					NHL Cup Wins	First NHL Season	Last NHL Season
			GP	G	A	TP	PIM	GP	G	A	TP	PIM			
Ronan, Ed	Mtl., Wpg., Buf.	6	182	13	23	36	101	27	4	3	7	16	1	1991-92	1996-97
• Ronan, Skene	Ott.	1	11	0	0	0	6	....	....	....	....	....	....	1918-19	1918-19
Ronning, Cliff	St.L., Van., Phx., Nsh., L.A., Min., NYI	18	1137	306	563	869	453	126	29	57	86	72	....	1985-86	2003-04
Ronnqvist, Jonas	Ana.	1	38	0	4	4	14	....	....	....	....	....	....	2000-01	2000-01
• Ronson, Len	NYR, Oak.	2	18	2	1	3	10	....	....	....	....	....	....	1960-61	1968-69
Ronty, Paul	Bos., NYR, Mtl.	8	488	101	211	312	103	21	1	7	8	6	....	1947-48	1954-55
Rooney, Steve	Mtl., Wpg., N.J.	5	154	15	13	28	496	25	3	2	5	86	1	1984-85	1988-89
Root, Bill	Mtl., Tor., St.L., Phi.	6	247	11	23	34	180	22	1	2	3	25	....	1982-83	1987-88
‡ Rosa, Pavel	L.A.	4	36	5	13	18	6	....	....	....	....	....	....	1998-99	2003-04
• Ross, Art	Mtl.W.	1	3	1	0	1	12	....	....	....	....	....	....	1917-18	1917-18
‡ Ross, Jared	Phi.	2	13	0	0	0	2	9	1	0	1	0	....	2008-09	2009-10
Ross, Jim	NYR	2	62	2	11	13	29	....	....	....	....	....	....	1951-52	1952-53
• Rossignol, Roly	Det., Mtl.	3	14	3	5	8	6	1	0	0	0	2	....	1943-44	1945-46
Rossiter, Kyle	Fla., Atl.	3	11	0	1	1	9	....	....	....	....	....	....	2001-02	2003-04
Rota, Darcy	Chi., Atl., Van.	11	794	256	239	495	973	60	14	7	21	147	....	1973-74	1983-84
Rota, Randy	Mtl., L.A., K.C., Col.	5	212	38	39	77	60	5	0	1	1	0	....	1972-73	1976-77
• Rothschild, Sam	Mtl.M., Pit., NYA	4	100	8	6	14	25	6	0	0	0	0	1	1924-25	1927-28
• Roulston, Rolly	Det.	3	24	0	6	6	10	....	....	....	....	....	1	1935-36	1937-38
Roulston, Tom	Edm., Pit.	5	195	47	49	96	74	21	2	2	4	2	....	1980-81	1985-86
Roupe, Magnus	Phi.	2	40	3	5	8	42	....	....	....	....	....	....	1987-88	1988-89
Rourke, Allan	Car., NYI, Edm.	4	55	1	4	5	31	....	....	....	....	....	....	2003-04	2007-08
Rouse, Bob	Min., Wsh., Tor., Det., S.J.	17	1061	37	181	218	1559	136	7	21	28	198	2	1983-84	1999-00
Rousseau, Bobby	Mtl., Min., NYR	15	942	245	458	703	359	128	27	57	84	69	4	1960-61	1974-75
Rousseau, Guy	Mtl.	2	4	0	1	1	0	....	....	....	....	....	....	1954-55	1956-57
• Rousseau, Roland	Mtl.	1	2	0	0	0	0	....	....	....	....	....	....	1952-53	1952-53
Routhier, Jean-Marc	Que.	1	8	0	0	0	9	....	....	....	....	....	....	1989-90	1989-90
• Rowe, Bobby	Bos.	1	4	1	0	1	0	....	....	....	....	....	....	1924-25	1924-25
Rowe, Mike	Pit.	3	11	0	0	0	11	....	....	....	....	....	....	1984-85	1986-87
• Rowe, Ron	NYR	1	5	1	0	1	0	....	....	....	....	....	....	1947-48	1947-48
Rowe, Tom	Wsh., Hfd., Det.	7	357	85	100	185	615	3	2	0	2	0	....	1976-77	1982-83
Roy, Andre	Bos., Ott., T.B., Pit., Cgy.	11	515	35	33	68	1169	41	1	3	4	98	1	1995-96	2008-09
Roy, Jean-Yves	NYR, Ott., Bos.	4	61	12	16	28	26	....	....	....	....	....	....	1994-95	1997-98
‡ Roy, Mathieu	Edm., CBJ, T.B.	6	66	2	11	13	76	....	....	....	....	....	....	2005-06	2012-13
Roy, Stephane	Min.	1	12	1	0	1	0	....	....	....	....	....	....	1987-88	1987-88
Royer, Gaetan	T.B.	1	3	0	0	0	2	....	....	....	....	....	....	2001-02	2001-02
Royer, Remi	Chi.	1	18	0	0	0	67	....	....	....	....	....	....	1998-99	1998-99
• Rozzini, Gino	Bos.	1	31	5	10	15	20	6	1	2	3	6	....	1944-45	1944-45
Rucchin, Steve	Ana., NYR, Atl.	12	735	171	318	489	164	37	9	8	17	12	....	1994-95	2006-07
Rucinski, Mike	Chi.	2	1	0	0	0	0	2	0	0	0	0	....	1987-88	1988-89
Rucinski, Mike	Car.	3	26	0	2	2	10	....	....	....	....	....	....	1997-98	2000-01
‡ Rucinsky, Martin	Edm., Que., Col., Mtl., Dal., NYR, St.L., Van.	16	961	241	371	612	821	37	9	5	14	24	....	1991-92	2007-08
• Ruelle, Bernie	Det.	1	2	1	0	1	0	....	....	....	....	....	....	1943-44	1943-44
Ruff, Jason	St.L., T.B.	2	14	3	3	6	10	....	....	....	....	....	....	1992-93	1993-94
Ruff, Lindy	Buf., NYR	12	691	105	195	300	1264	52	11	13	24	193	....	1979-80	1990-91
Ruhnke, Kent	Bos.	1	2	0	1	1	0	....	....	....	....	....	....	1975-76	1975-76
Rumble, Darren	Phi., Ott., St.L., T.B.	8	193	10	26	36	216	....	....	....	....	....	1	1990-91	2003-04
Rundqvist, Thomas	Mtl.	1	2	0	1	1	0	....	....	....	....	....	....	1984-85	1984-85
• Runge, Paul	Bos., Mtl.M., Mtl.	7	140	18	22	40	57	7	0	0	0	6	....	1930-31	1937-38
Ruotsalainen, Reijo	NYR, Edm., N.J.	7	446	107	237	344	180	86	15	32	47	44	2	1981-82	1989-90
Rupp, Duane	NYR, Tor., Min., Pit.	10	374	24	93	117	220	10	2	2	4	8	....	1962-63	1972-73
‡ Rupp, Mike	N.J., Phx., CBJ, Pit., NYR, Min.	11	610	54	45	99	855	67	2	6	8	83	1	2002-03	2013-14
Ruskowski, Terry	Chi., L.A., Pit., Min.	10	630	113	313	426	1354	21	1	6	7	86	....	1979-80	1988-89
Russell, Cam	Chi., Col.	10	396	9	21	30	872	44	0	5	5	16	....	1989-90	1998-99
• Russell, Church	NYR	3	90	20	16	36	12	....	....	....	....	....	....	1945-46	1947-48
Russell, Phil	Chi., Atl., Cgy., N.J., Buf.	15	1016	99	325	424	2038	73	4	22	26	202	....	1972-73	1986-87
‡ Russell, Ryan	CBJ	1	41	2	0	2	2	....	....	....	....	....	....	2011-12	2011-12
Ruuttu, Christian	Buf., Chi., Van.	9	621	134	298	432	714	42	4	9	13	49	....	1986-87	1994-95
‡ Ruutu, Jarkko	Van., Pit., Ott., Ana.	11	652	58	84	142	1078	58	5	5	10	114	....	1999-00	2010-11
‡ Ruzicka, Stefan	Phi.	3	55	4	13	17	47	....	....	....	....	....	....	2005-06	2007-08
Ruzicka, Vladimir	Edm., Bos., Ott.	5	233	82	85	167	129	30	4	14	18	2	....	1989-90	1993-94
Ryan, Matt	L.A.	1	12	0	1	1	2	....	....	....	....	....	....	2005-06	2005-06
‡ Ryan, Michael	Buf., Car.	3	83	7	8	15	34	....	....	....	....	....	....	2006-07	2008-09
Ryan, Prestin	Van.	1	1	0	0	0	2	....	....	....	....	....	....	2005-06	2005-06
‡ Ryan, Terry	Mtl.	3	8	0	0	0	36	....	....	....	....	....	....	1996-97	1998-99
Rychel, Warren	Chi., L.A., Tor., Col., Ana.	9	406	38	39	77	1422	70	8	13	21	121	1	1988-89	1998-99
Rycroft, Mark	St.L., Col.	4	226	21	25	46	113	3	0	0	0	2	....	2001-02	2006-07
Rymsha, Andy	Que.	1	6	0	0	0	23	....	....	....	....	....	....	1991-92	1991-92
• Rypien, Rick	Van.	6	119	9	7	16	226	17	0	3	3	47	....	2005-06	2010-11
Ryznar, Jason	N.J.	1	8	0	0	0	2	....	....	....	....	....	....	2005-06	2005-06

S

Name	NHL Teams	NHL Seasons	Regular Schedule					Playoffs					NHL Cup Wins	First NHL Season	Last NHL Season
			GP	G	A	TP	PIM	GP	G	A	TP	PIM			
Saarinen, Simo	NYR	1	8	0	0	0	0	....	....	....	....	....	....	1984-85	1984-85
Sabol, Shaun	Phi.	1	2	0	0	0	0	....	....	....	....	....	....	1989-90	1989-90
Sabourin, Bob	Tor.	1	1	0	0	0	2	....	....	....	....	....	....	1951-52	1951-52
Sabourin, Gary	St.L., Tor., Cal., Cle.	10	627	169	188	357	397	62	19	11	30	58	....	1967-68	1976-77
Sabourin, Ken	Cgy., Wsh.	4	74	2	8	10	201	12	0	0	0	34	....	1988-89	1991-92
Sacco, David	Tor., Ana.	3	35	5	13	18	22	....	....	....	....	....	....	1993-94	1995-96
Sacco, Joe	Tor., Ana., NYI, Wsh., Phi.	13	738	94	119	213	421	26	2	0	2	8	....	1990-91	2002-03
Sacharuk, Larry	NYR, St.L.	5	151	29	33	62	42	2	1	1	2	2	....	1972-73	1976-77
‡ Safronov, Kirill	Phx., Atl.	2	35	2	2	4	16	....	....	....	....	....	....	2001-02	2002-03
Saganiuk, Rocky	Tor., Pit.	6	259	57	65	122	201	6	1	0	1	15	....	1978-79	1983-84
Sakic, Joe	Que., Col.	20	1378	625	1016	1641	614	172	84	104	188	78	2	1988-89	2008-09
‡ Salcido, Brian	Ana.	1	2	0	1	1	0	....	....	....	....	....	....	2008-09	2008-09
• Salei, Ruslan	Ana., Fla., Col., Det.	14	917	45	159	204	1065	62	7	9	16	52	....	1996-97	2010-11
Saleski, Don	Phi., Col.	9	543	128	125	253	629	82	13	17	30	131	2	1971-72	1979-80
‡ Salmela, Anssi	N.J., Atl.	3	112	4	17	21	44	....	....	....	....	....	....	2008-09	2010-11
‡ Salmelainen, Tony	Edm., Chi.	2	70	6	12	18	30	....	....	....	....	....	....	2003-04	2006-07
Salming, Borje	Tor., Det.	17	1148	150	637	787	1344	81	12	37	49	91	....	1973-74	1989-90
Salo, Sami	Ott., Van., T.B.	15	878	99	240	339	286	102	12	19	31	18	....	1998-99	2013-14
Salomonsson, Andreas	N.J., Wsh.	2	71	5	9	14	36	4	0	1	1	0	....	2001-02	2002-03
Salovaara, Barry	Det.	2	90	2	13	15	70	....	....	....	....	....	....	1974-75	1975-76
Salvian, Dave	NYI	1	....	....	....	....	....	1	0	1	1	2	....	1976-77	1976-77
Samis, Phil	Tor.	2	2	0	0	0	0	5	0	1	1	2	1	1947-48	1949-50
Sampson, Gary	Wsh.	4	105	13	22	35	25	12	1	0	1	0	....	1983-84	1986-87
Samsonov, Sergei	Bos., Edm., Mtl., Chi., Car., Fla.	13	888	235	336	571	209	76	18	29	47	20	....	1997-98	2010-11
Samuelsson, Kjell	NYR, Phi., Pit., T.B.	14	813	48	138	186	1225	123	4	20	24	178	1	1985-86	1998-99
Samuelsson, Martin	Bos.	2	14	0	1	1	2	....	....	....	....	....	....	2002-03	2003-04
‡ Samuelsson, Mikael	S.J., NYR, Pit., Fla., Det., Van.	13	699	149	197	346	370	104	23	37	60	62	1	2000-01	2013-14
Samuelsson, Ulf	Hfd., Pit., NYR, Det., Phi.	16	1080	57	275	332	2453	132	7	27	34	272	2	1984-85	1999-00
Sandelin, Scott	Mtl., Phi., Min.	4	25	0	4	4	2	....	....	....	....	....	....	1986-87	1991-92
Sanderson, Derek	Bos., NYR, St.L., Van., Pit.	13	598	202	250	452	911	56	18	12	30	187	2	1965-66	1977-78
Sanderson, Geoff	Hfd., Car., Van., Buf., CBJ, Phx., Phi., Edm.	17	1104	355	345	700	511	55	9	10	19	32	....	1990-91	2007-08
Sandford, Ed	Bos., Det., Chi.	9	502	106	145	251	355	42	13	11	24	27	....	1947-48	1955-56
Sandlak, Jim	Van., Hfd.	11	549	110	119	229	821	33	7	10	17	30	....	1985-86	1995-96
• Sands, Charlie	Tor., Bos., Mtl., NYR	12	427	99	109	208	58	34	6	6	12	4	1	1932-33	1943-44
Sandstrom, Tomas	NYR, L.A., Pit., Det., Ana.	15	983	394	462	856	1193	139	32	49	81	183	1	1984-85	1998-99
Sandwith, Terran	Edm.	1	8	0	0	0	6	....	....	....	....	....	....	1997-98	1997-98
Sanipass, Everett	Chi., Que.	5	164	25	34	59	358	5	2	0	2	4	....	1986-87	1990-91
‡ Santala, Tommi	Atl., Van.	2	63	2	7	9	46	1	0	0	0	0	....	2003-04	2006-07
‡ Saprykin, Oleg	Cgy., Phx., Ott.	7	325	55	82	137	240	41	4	4	8	18	....	1999-00	2006-07
Sarault, Yves	Mtl., Cgy., Col., Ott., Atl., Nsh.	8	106	10	10	20	51	5	0	0	0	2	....	1994-95	2001-02
Sargent, Gary	L.A., Min.	8	402	61	161	222	273	20	5	7	12	8	....	1975-76	1982-83
‡ Sarich, Cory	Buf., T.B., Cgy., Col.	15	969	21	137	158	1089	57	0	7	7	45	1	1998-99	2013-14
Sarner, Craig	Bos.	1	7	0	0	0	0	....	....	....	....	....	....	1974-75	1974-75
Sarno, Peter	Edm., CBJ	2	7	1	0	1	2	....	....	....	....	....	....	2003-04	2005-06
Sarrazin, Dick	Phi.	3	100	20	35	55	22	4	0	0	0	0	....	1968-69	1971-72
Sasakamoose, Fred	Chi.	1	11	0	0	0	6	....	....	....	....	....	....	1953-54	1953-54
Sasser, Grant	Pit.	1	3	0	0	0	0	....	....	....	....	....	....	1983-84	1983-84
‡ Satan, Miroslav	Edm., Buf., NYI, Pit., Bos.	14	1050	363	372	735	464	86	21	33	54	41	1	1995-96	2009-10
Sather, Glen	Bos., Pit., NYR, St.L., Mtl., Min.	10	658	80	113	193	724	72	1	5	6	86	....	1966-67	1975-76
Sauer, Kurt	Ana., Col., Phx.	7	357	5	28	33	250	43	2	1	3	18	....	2002-03	2009-10
Sauer, Michael	NYR	3	98	4	14	18	96	5	0	1	1	0	....	2008-09	2011-12
Saunders, Bernie	Que.	2	10	0	1	1	8	....	....	....	....	....	....	1979-80	1980-81

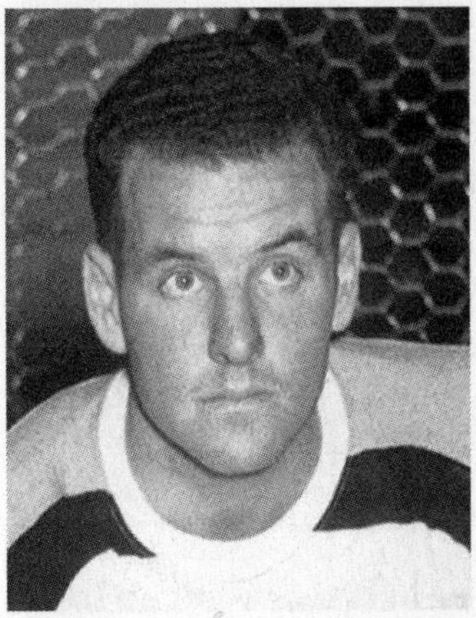

Ed Sandford

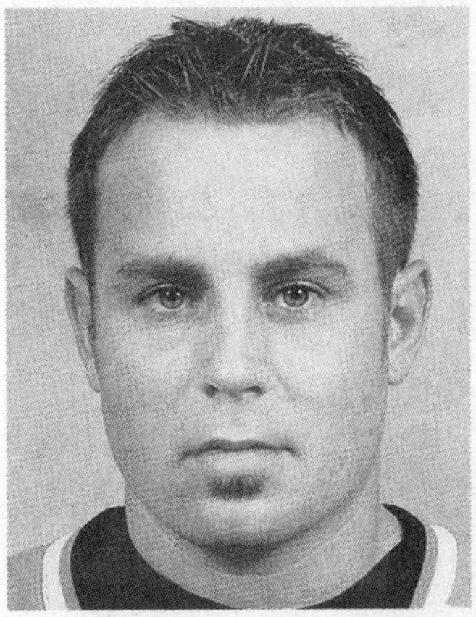

Marc Savard

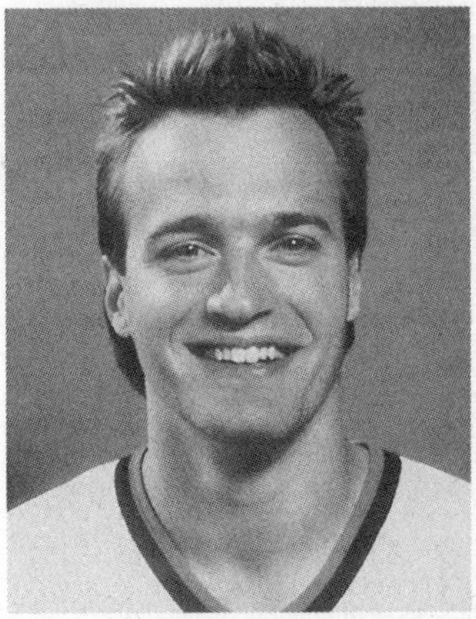

Claudio Scremin

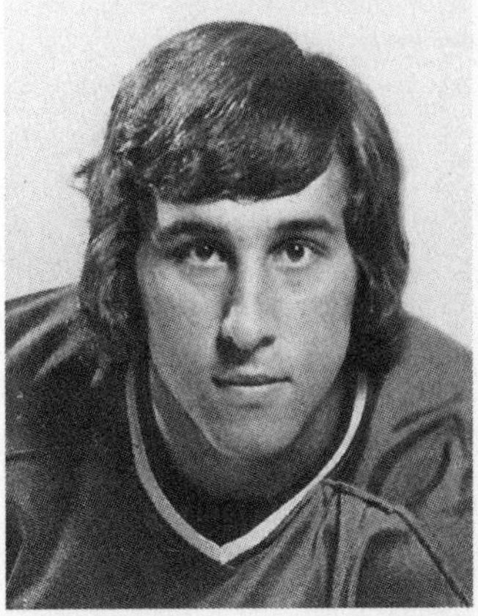

Ron Sedlbauer

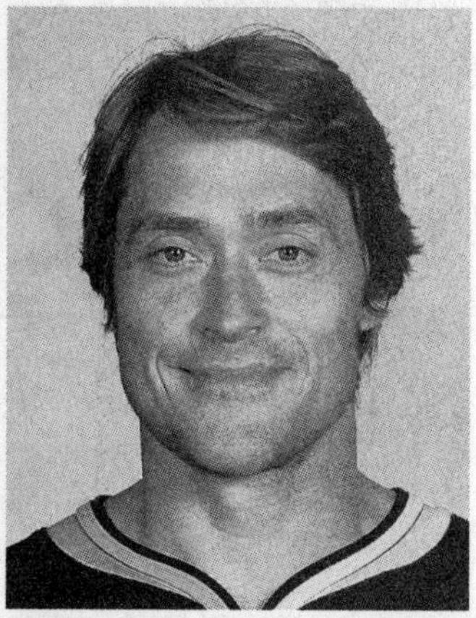

Teemu Selanne

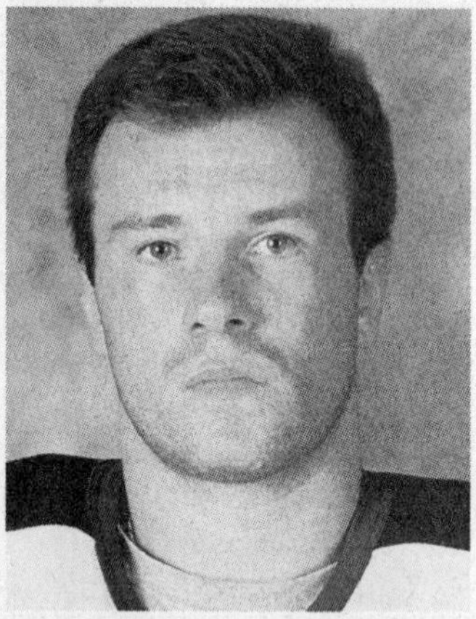

Alex Selivanov

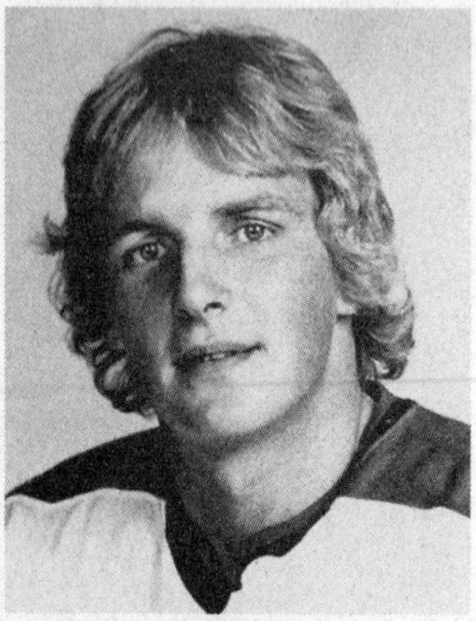

Rick Shinske

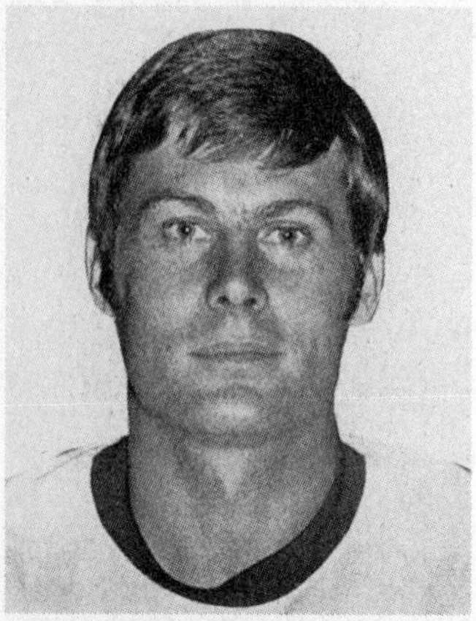

Jim Shires

Name	NHL Teams	NHL Seasons	Regular Schedule GP	G	A	TP	PIM	Playoffs GP	G	A	TP	PIM	NHL Cup Wins	First NHL Season	Last NHL Season
Saunders, David	Van.	1	56	7	13	20	10	....	....	....	....	....	....	1987-88	1987-88
• Saunders, Ted	Ott.	1	18	1	3	4	4	....	....	....	....	....	....	1933-34	1933-34
Sauve, Jean-Francois	Buf., Que.	7	290	65	138	203	114	36	9	12	21	10	....	1980-81	1986-87
‡ Sauve, Max	Bos.	1	1	0	0	0	0	....	....	....	....	....	....	2011-12	2011-12
Savage, Andre	Bos., Phi.	4	66	10	14	24	14	....	....	....	....	....	....	1998-99	2002-03
Savage, Brian	Mtl., Phx., St.L., Phi.	12	674	192	167	359	321	39	3	8	11	12	....	1993-94	2005-06
Savage, Joel	Buf.	1	3	0	1	1	0	....	....	....	....	....	....	1990-91	1990-91
Savage, Reggie	Wsh., Que.	3	34	5	7	12	28	....	....	....	....	....	....	1990-91	1993-94
• Savage, Tony	Bos., Mtl.	1	49	1	5	6	6	2	0	0	0	0	....	1934-35	1934-35
Savard, Andre	Bos., Buf., Que.	12	790	211	271	482	411	85	13	18	31	77	....	1973-74	1984-85
Savard, Denis	Chi., Mtl., T.B.	17	1196	473	865	1338	1336	169	66	109	175	256	1	1980-81	1996-97
Savard, Jean	Chi., Hfd.	3	43	7	12	19	29	....	....	....	....	....	....	1977-78	1979-80
‡ Savard, Marc	NYR, Cgy., Atl., Bos.	16	807	207	499	706	737	25	8	14	22	22	1	1997-98	2013-14
Savard, Serge	Mtl., Wpg.	17	1040	106	333	439	592	130	19	49	68	88	8	1966-67	1982-83
Savoia, Ryan	Pit.	1	3	0	0	0	0	....	....	....	....	....	....	1998-99	1998-99
‡ Sawada, Raymond	Dal.	3	11	1	0	1	0	....	....	....	....	....	....	2008-09	2010-11
Sawyer, Kevin	St.L., Bos., Phx., Ana.	6	110	3	3	6	403	....	....	....	....	....	....	1995-96	2002-03
Scamurra, Peter	Wsh.	4	132	8	25	33	59	....	....	....	....	....	....	1975-76	1979-80
Scatchard, Dave	Van., NYI, Bos., Phx., Nsh., St.L.	11	659	128	141	269	1040	17	2	2	4	34	....	1997-98	2010-11
Sceviour, Darin	Chi.	1	1	0	0	0	0	....	....	....	....	....	....	1986-87	1986-87
Schaefer, Peter	Van., Ott., Bos.	9	572	99	162	261	200	63	6	18	24	34	....	1998-99	2010-11
• Schaeffer, Butch	Chi.	1	5	0	0	0	6	....	....	....	....	....	....	1936-37	1936-37
Schamehorn, Kevin	Det., L.A.	3	10	0	0	0	17	....	....	....	....	....	....	1976-77	1980-81
Schastlivy, Petr	Ott., Ana.	5	129	18	22	40	30	1	0	0	0	0	....	1999-00	2003-04
Schella, John	Van.	2	115	2	18	20	224	....	....	....	....	....	....	1970-71	1971-72
• Scherza, Chuck	Bos., NYR	2	36	6	6	12	35	....	....	....	....	....	....	1943-44	1944-45
Schinkel, Ken	NYR, Pit.	12	636	127	198	325	163	19	7	2	9	4	....	1959-60	1972-73
Schlegel, Brad	Wsh., Cgy.	3	48	1	8	9	10	7	0	1	1	2	....	1991-92	1993-94
Schliebener, Andy	Van.	3	84	2	11	13	74	6	0	0	0	0	....	1981-82	1984-85
Schmautz, Bobby	Chi., Van., Bos., Edm., Col.	13	764	271	286	557	988	84	28	33	61	92	....	1967-68	1980-81
• Schmautz, Cliff	Buf., Phi.	1	56	13	19	32	33	....	....	....	....	....	....	1970-71	1970-71
Schmidt, Chris	L.A.	1	10	0	2	2	5	....	....	....	....	....	....	2002-03	2002-03
• Schmidt, Clarence	Bos.	1	7	1	0	1	2	....	....	....	....	....	....	1943-44	1943-44
Schmidt, Jackie	Bos.	1	45	6	7	13	6	5	0	0	0	0	....	1942-43	1942-43
Schmidt, Milt	Bos.	16	776	229	346	575	466	86	24	25	49	60	2	1936-37	1954-55
Schmidt, Norm	Pit.	4	125	23	33	56	73	....	....	....	....	....	....	1983-84	1987-88
• Schmidt, Otto	Bos.	1	2	0	0	0	0	....	....	....	....	....	....	1943-44	1943-44
Schnabel, Robert	Nsh.	3	22	0	3	3	34	....	....	....	....	....	....	2001-02	2003-04
• Schnarr, Werner	Bos.	2	26	0	0	0	0	....	....	....	....	....	....	1924-25	1925-26
Schneider, Andy	Ott.	1	10	0	0	0	15	....	....	....	....	....	....	1993-94	1993-94
Schneider, Mathieu	Mtl., NYI, Tor., NYR, L.A., Det., Ana., Atl., Van., Phx.	21	1289	223	520	743	1245	114	11	43	54	155	1	1987-88	2009-10
Schock, Danny	Bos., Phi.	2	20	1	2	3	0	1	0	0	0	0	1	1969-70	1970-71
Schock, Ron	Bos., St.L., Pit., Buf.	15	909	166	351	517	260	55	4	16	20	29	....	1963-64	1977-78
Schoenfeld, Jim	Buf., Det., Bos.	13	719	51	204	255	1132	75	3	13	16	151	....	1972-73	1984-85
Schofield, Dwight	Det., Mtl., St.L., Wsh., Pit., Wpg.	7	211	8	22	30	631	9	0	0	0	55	....	1976-77	1987-88
Schreiber, Wally	Min.	2	41	8	10	18	12	....	....	....	....	....	....	1987-88	1988-89
Schremp, Rob	Edm., NYI, Atl.	5	114	20	34	54	26	....	....	....	....	....	....	2006-07	2010-11
• Schriner, Sweeney	NYA, Tor.	11	484	201	204	405	148	59	18	11	29	54	2	1934-35	1945-46
‡ Schubert, Christoph	Ott., Atl.	5	315	25	47	72	263	31	0	2	2	34	....	2005-06	2009-10
Schulte, Paxton	Que., Cgy.	2	2	0	0	0	4	....	....	....	....	....	....	1993-94	1996-97
Schultz, Dave	Phi., L.A., Pit., Buf.	9	535	79	121	200	2294	73	8	12	20	412	2	1971-72	1979-80
‡ Schultz, Jesse	Van.	1	2	0	0	0	0	....	....	....	....	....	....	2006-07	2006-07
Schultz, Ray	NYI	6	45	0	4	4	155	2	0	0	0	2	....	1997-98	2002-03
Schurman, Maynard	Hfd.	1	7	0	0	0	0	....	....	....	....	....	....	1979-80	1979-80
Schutt, Rod	Mtl., Pit., Tor.	8	286	77	92	169	177	22	8	6	14	26	....	1977-78	1985-86
Scissons, Scott	NYI	3	2	0	0	0	0	1	0	0	0	0	....	1990-91	1993-94
• Sclisizzi, Enio	Det., Chi.	6	81	12	11	23	26	13	0	0	0	6	1	1946-47	1952-53
• Scott, Ganton	Tor., Ham., Mtl.M.	3	57	1	1	2	0	....	....	....	....	....	....	1922-23	1924-25
• Scott, Laurie	NYA, NYR	2	62	6	3	9	28	....	....	....	....	....	....	1926-27	1927-28
Scott, Richard	NYR	2	10	0	0	0	28	....	....	....	....	....	....	2001-02	2003-04
Scoville, Darrel	Cgy., CBJ	3	16	0	1	1	12	....	....	....	....	....	....	1999-00	2003-04
Scremin, Claudio	S.J.	2	17	0	1	1	29	....	....	....	....	....	....	1991-92	1992-93
Scruton, Howard	L.A.	1	4	0	4	4	9	....	....	....	....	....	....	1982-83	1982-83
Seabrooke, Glen	Phi.	3	19	1	6	7	4	....	....	....	....	....	....	1986-87	1988-89
Secord, Al	Bos., Chi., Tor., Phi.	12	766	273	222	495	2093	102	21	34	55	382	....	1978-79	1989-90
Sedlbauer, Ron	Van., Chi., Tor.	7	430	143	86	229	210	19	1	3	4	27	....	1974-75	1980-81
Seftel, Steve	Wsh.	1	4	0	0	0	2	....	....	....	....	....	....	1990-91	1990-91
Seguin, Dan	Min., Van.	2	37	2	6	8	50	....	....	....	....	....	....	1970-71	1973-74
Seguin, Steve	L.A.	1	5	0	0	0	9	....	....	....	....	....	....	1984-85	1984-85
• Seibert, Earl	NYR, Chi., Det.	15	645	89	187	276	746	66	11	8	19	76	2	1931-32	1945-46
Seiling, Ric	Buf., Det.	10	738	179	208	387	573	62	14	14	28	36	....	1977-78	1986-87
Seiling, Rod	Tor., NYR, Wsh., St.L., Atl.	17	979	62	269	331	601	77	4	8	12	55	....	1962-63	1978-79
Sejba, Jiri	Buf.	1	11	0	2	2	8	....	....	....	....	....	....	1990-91	1990-91
‡ Sejna, Peter	St.L.	4	49	7	4	11	12	....	....	....	....	....	....	2002-03	2006-07
Sekeras, Lubomir	Min., Dal.	4	213	18	53	71	122	15	1	1	2	6	....	2000-01	2003-04
‡ Selanne, Teemu	Wpg., Ana., S.J., Col.	21	1451	684	773	1457	660	130	44	44	88	62	1	1992-93	2013-14
Selby, Brit	Tor., Phi., St.L.	8	350	55	62	117	163	16	1	1	2	8	....	1964-65	1971-72
Self, Steve	Wsh.	1	3	0	0	0	0	....	....	....	....	....	....	1976-77	1976-77
Selivanov, Alex	T.B., Edm., CBJ	7	459	121	114	235	379	13	2	3	5	16	....	1994-95	2000-01
Sellars, Luke	Atl.	1	1	0	0	0	2	....	....	....	....	....	....	2001-02	2001-02
Selmser, Sean	CBJ	1	1	0	0	0	5	....	....	....	....	....	....	2000-01	2000-01
Selwood, Brad	Tor., L.A.	3	163	7	40	47	153	6	0	0	0	4	....	1970-71	1979-80
Semak, Alexander	N.J., T.B., NYI, Van.	6	289	83	91	174	187	8	1	1	2	0	....	1991-92	1996-97
Semchuk, Brandy	L.A.	1	1	0	0	0	2	....	....	....	....	....	....	1992-93	1992-93
Semenko, Dave	Edm., Hfd., Tor.	9	575	65	88	153	1175	73	6	6	12	208	2	1979-80	1987-88
‡ Semenov, Alexei	Edm., Fla., S.J.	6	211	7	26	33	249	8	0	0	0	2	....	2002-03	2008-09
Semenov, Anatoli	Edm., T.B., Van., Ana., Phi., Buf.	8	362	68	126	194	122	49	9	13	22	12	....	1989-90	1996-97
• Senick, George	NYR	1	13	2	3	5	8	....	....	....	....	....	....	1952-53	1952-53
Seppa, Jyrki	Wpg.	1	13	0	2	2	6	....	....	....	....	....	....	1983-84	1983-84
Serafini, Ron	Cal.	1	2	0	0	0	2	....	....	....	....	....	....	1973-74	1973-74
Serowik, Jeff	Tor., Bos., Pit.	3	28	0	6	6	16	....	....	....	....	....	....	1990-91	1998-99
Servinis, George	Min.	1	5	0	0	0	0	....	....	....	....	....	....	1987-88	1987-88
Sevcik, Jaroslav	Que.	1	13	0	2	2	2	....	....	....	....	....	....	1989-90	1989-90
Severson, Cam	Ana., CBJ	3	37	3	0	3	63	1	0	0	0	0	....	2002-03	2005-06
Severyn, Brent	Que., Fla., NYI, Col., Ana., Dal.	7	328	10	30	40	825	8	0	0	0	12	1	1989-90	1998-99
Sevigny, Pierre	Mtl., NYR	4	78	4	5	9	64	3	0	1	1	0	....	1993-94	1997-98
‡ Sexton, Dan	Ana.	2	88	13	19	32	20	1	0	0	0	2	....	2009-10	2010-11
Shack, Eddie	NYR, Tor., Bos., L.A., Buf., Pit.	17	1047	239	226	465	1437	74	6	7	13	151	4	1958-59	1974-75
• Shack, Joe	NYR	2	70	9	27	36	20	....	....	....	....	....	....	1942-43	1944-45
Shafranov, Konstantin	St.L.	1	5	2	1	3	0	....	....	....	....	....	....	1996-97	1996-97
Shakes, Paul	Cal.	1	21	0	4	4	12	....	....	....	....	....	....	1973-74	1973-74
Shaldybin, Yevgeny	Bos.	1	3	1	0	1	0	....	....	....	....	....	....	1996-97	1996-97
Shanahan, Brendan	N.J., St.L., Hfd., Det., NYR	21	1524	656	698	1354	2489	184	60	74	134	279	3	1987-88	2008-09
Shanahan, Sean	Mtl., Col., Bos.	3	40	1	3	4	47	....	....	....	....	....	....	1975-76	1977-78
Shand, Dave	Atl., Tor., Wsh.	8	421	19	84	103	544	26	1	2	3	83	....	1976-77	1984-85
Shank, Daniel	Det., Hfd.	3	77	13	14	27	175	5	0	0	0	22	....	1989-90	1991-92
• Shannon, Chuck	NYA	1	4	0	0	0	2	....	....	....	....	....	....	1939-40	1939-40
Shannon, Darrin	Buf., Wpg., Phx.	10	506	87	163	250	344	45	7	10	17	38	....	1988-89	1997-98
Shannon, Darryl	Tor., Wpg., Buf., Atl., Cgy., Mtl.	13	544	28	111	139	523	29	4	7	11	16	....	1988-89	2000-01
• Shannon, Gerry	Ott., St.L., Bos., Mtl.M.	5	180	23	29	52	80	9	0	1	1	2	....	1933-34	1937-38
‡ Shannon, Ryan	Ana., Van., Ott., T.B.	6	305	35	64	99	90	13	0	0	0	6	1	2006-07	2011-12
Shantz, Jeff	Chi., Cgy., Col.	10	642	72	139	211	341	44	5	8	13	24	....	1993-94	2002-03
Sharifijanov, Vadim	N.J., Van.	3	92	16	21	37	50	4	0	0	0	0	....	1996-97	1999-00
Sharp, MacGregor	Ana.	1	8	0	0	0	0	....	....	....	....	....	....	2009-10	2009-10
Sharples, Jeff	Det.	3	105	14	35	49	70	7	0	3	3	6	....	1986-87	1988-89
Sharpley, Glen	Min., Chi.	6	389	117	161	278	199	27	7	11	18	24	....	1976-77	1981-82
Shaunessy, Scott	Que.	2	7	0	0	0	23	....	....	....	....	....	....	1986-87	1988-89
Shaw, Brad	Hfd., Ott., Wsh., St.L.	11	377	22	137	159	208	23	4	8	12	6	....	1985-86	1998-99
Shaw, David	Que., NYR, Edm., Min., Bos., T.B.	16	769	41	153	194	906	45	3	9	12	81	....	1982-83	1997-98
• Shay, Norm	Bos., Tor.	2	53	5	3	8	34	....	....	....	....	....	....	1924-25	1925-26
• Shea, Pat	Chi.	1	10	1	0	1	0	....	....	....	....	....	....	1931-32	1931-32
Shearer, Rob	Col.	1	2	0	0	0	0	....	....	....	....	....	....	2000-01	2000-01
Shedden, Doug	Pit., Det., Que., Tor.	8	416	139	186	325	176	....	....	....	....	....	....	1981-82	1990-91
Sheehan, Bobby	Mtl., Cal., Chi., Det., NYR, Col., L.A.	9	310	48	63	111	40	25	4	3	7	8	1	1969-70	1981-82
Sheehy, Neil	Cgy., Hfd., Wsh.	9	379	18	47	65	1311	54	0	3	3	241	....	1983-84	1991-92

			Regular Schedule					Playoffs							
Name	NHL Teams	NHL Seasons	GP	G	A	TP	PIM	GP	G	A	TP	PIM	NHL Cup Wins	First NHL Season	Last NHL Season
Sheehy, Tim	Det., Hfd.	2	27	2	1	3	0	....	....	....	....	....	....	1977-78	1979-80
Shelley, Jody	CBJ, S.J., NYR, Phi.	12	627	18	36	54	1538	9	0	0	0	4	....	2000-01	2012-13
Shelton, Doug	Chi.	1	5	0	1	1	2	....	....	....	....	....	....	1967-68	1967-68
• Sheppard, Frank	Det.	1	8	1	1	2	0	....	....	....	....	....	....	1927-28	1927-28
Sheppard, Gregg	Bos., Pit.	10	657	205	293	498	243	82	32	40	72	31	....	1972-73	1981-82
• Sheppard, Johnny	Det., NYA, Bos., Chi.	8	308	68	58	126	224	10	0	0	0	0	1	1926-27	1933-34
Sheppard, Ray	Buf., NYR, Det., S.J., Fla., Car.	13	817	357	300	657	212	81	30	20	50	21	....	1987-88	1999-00
• Sherf, John	Det.	5	19	0	0	0	8	8	0	1	1	2	1	1935-36	1943-44
• Shero, Fred	NYR	3	145	6	14	20	137	13	0	2	2	8	....	1947-48	1949-50
• Sherritt, Gordon	Det.	1	8	0	0	0	12	....	....	....	....	....	....	1943-44	1943-44
Sherven, Gord	Edm., Min., Hfd.	5	97	13	22	35	33	3	0	0	0	0	....	1983-84	1987-88
Shevalier, Jeff	L.A., T.B.	3	32	5	9	14	8	....	....	....	....	....	....	1994-95	1999-00
• Shewchuk, Jack	Bos.	6	187	9	19	28	160	20	0	1	1	19	1	1938-39	1944-45
• Shibicky, Alex	NYR	8	324	110	91	201	161	39	12	12	24	12	1	1935-36	1945-46
• Shields, Al	Ott., Phi., NYA, Mtl.M., Bos.	11	459	42	46	88	637	17	0	1	1	14	1	1927-28	1937-38
• Shill, Bill	Bos.	3	79	21	13	34	18	7	1	2	3	2	....	1942-43	1946-47
• Shill, Jack	Tor., Bos., NYA, Chi.	6	160	15	20	35	70	25	1	6	7	23	1	1933-34	1938-39
• Shinske, Rick	Cle., St.L.	3	63	5	16	21	10	....	....	....	....	....	....	1976-77	1978-79
Shires, Jim	Det., St.L., Pit.	3	56	3	6	9	32	....	....	....	....	....	....	1970-71	1972-73
‡ Shirokov, Sergei	Van.	2	8	1	0	1	2	....	....	....	....	....	....	2009-10	2010-11
‡ Shishkanov, Timofei	Nsh., St.L.	2	24	3	2	5	6	....	....	....	....	....	....	2003-04	2005-06
• Shmyr, Paul	Chi., Cal., Min., Hfd.	7	343	13	72	85	528	34	3	3	6	44	....	1968-69	1981-82
Shoebottom, Bruce	Bos.	4	35	1	4	5	53	14	1	2	3	77	....	1987-88	1990-91
• Shore, Eddie	Bos., NYA	14	550	105	179	284	1047	55	7	12	19	181	2	1926-27	1939-40
• Shore, Hamby	Ott.	1	18	3	8	11	51	....	....	....	....	....	....	1917-18	1917-18
Short, Steve	L.A., Det.	2	6	0	0	0	2	....	....	....	....	....	....	1977-78	1978-79
Shuchuk, Gary	Det., L.A.	5	142	13	26	39	70	20	2	2	4	12	....	1990-91	1995-96
Shudra, Ron	Edm.	1	10	0	5	5	6	....	....	....	....	....	....	1987-88	1987-88
Shutt, Steve	Mtl., L.A.	13	930	424	393	817	410	99	50	48	98	65	5	1972-73	1984-85
Shvidki, Denis	Fla.	4	76	11	14	25	30	....	....	....	....	....	....	2000-01	2003-04
• Siebert, Babe	Mtl.M., NYR, Bos., Mtl.	14	592	140	156	296	982	49	7	5	12	62	2	1925-26	1938-39
‡ Sigalet, Jonathan	Bos.	1	1	0	0	0	4	....	....	....	....	....	....	2006-07	2006-07
Siklenka, Mike	Phi., NYR	2	2	0	0	0	0	....	....	....	....	....	....	2002-03	2003-04
Silk, Dave	NYR, Bos., Det., Wpg.	7	249	54	59	113	271	13	2	4	6	13	....	1979-80	1985-86
Sillinger, Mike	Det., Ana., Van., Phi., T.B., Fla., Ott., CBJ, Phx., St.L., Nsh., NYI	18	1049	240	308	548	644	43	11	7	18	28	....	1990-91	2008-09
Siltala, Mike	Wsh., NYR	3	7	1	0	1	2	....	....	....	....	....	....	1981-82	1987-88
Siltanen, Risto	Edm., Hfd., Que.	8	562	90	265	355	266	32	6	12	18	30	....	1979-80	1986-87
‡ Sim, Jon	Dal., Nsh., L.A., Pit., Phi., Fla., Atl., NYI	12	469	75	64	139	314	15	1	0	1	6	1	1998-99	2010-11
Sim, Trevor	Edm.	1	3	0	1	1	2	....	....	....	....	....	....	1989-90	1989-90
Simard, Martin	Cgy., T.B.	3	44	1	5	6	183	....	....	....	....	....	....	1990-91	1992-93
Simicek, Roman	Pit., Min.	2	63	7	10	17	59	....	....	....	....	....	....	2000-01	2001-02
Simmer, Charlie	Cal., Cle., L.A., Bos., Pit.	14	712	342	369	711	544	24	9	9	18	32	....	1974-75	1987-88
Simmons, Al	Cal., Bos.	3	11	0	1	1	21	1	0	0	0	0	....	1971-72	1975-76
Simon, Ben	Atl., CBJ	4	81	3	1	4	47	....	....	....	....	....	....	2001-02	2005-06
Simon, Chris	Que., Col., Wsh., Chi., NYR, Cgy., NYI, Min.	15	782	144	161	305	1824	75	10	7	17	191	1	1992-93	2007-08
• Simon, Cully	Det., Chi.	3	130	4	11	15	121	14	1	0	1	6	1	1942-43	1944-45
Simon, Jason	NYI, Phx.	2	5	0	0	0	34	....	....	....	....	....	....	1993-94	1996-97
• Simon, Thain	Det.	1	3	0	0	0	0	....	....	....	....	....	....	1946-47	1946-47
Simon, Todd	Buf.	1	15	0	1	1	0	5	1	0	1	0	....	1993-94	1993-94
Simonetti, Frank	Bos.	4	115	5	8	13	76	12	0	1	1	8	....	1984-85	1987-88
Simpson, Bobby	Atl., St.L., Pit.	5	175	35	29	64	98	6	0	1	1	2	....	1976-77	1982-83
• Simpson, Cliff	Det.	2	6	0	1	1	0	2	0	0	0	2	....	1946-47	1947-48
Simpson, Craig	Pit., Edm., Buf.	10	634	247	250	497	659	67	36	32	68	56	2	1985-86	1994-95
• Simpson, Joe	NYA	6	228	21	19	40	156	2	0	0	0	0	....	1925-26	1930-31
Simpson, Reid	Phi., Min., N.J., Chi., T.B., St.L., Mtl., Nsh., Pit.	12	301	18	18	36	838	10	0	0	0	31	....	1991-92	2003-04
Simpson, Todd	Cgy., Fla., Phx., Ana., Ott., Chi., Mtl.	10	580	14	63	77	1357	9	0	2	2	10	....	1995-96	2005-06
Sims, Al	Bos., Hfd., L.A.	10	475	49	116	165	286	41	0	2	2	14	....	1973-74	1982-83
Sims, Shane	NYI	1	1	0	0	0	0	....	....	....	....	....	....	2010-11	2010-11
• Sinclair, Reg	NYR, Det.	3	208	49	43	92	139	3	1	0	1	0	....	1950-51	1952-53
• Singbush, Alex	Mtl.	1	32	0	5	5	15	3	0	0	0	4	....	1940-41	1940-41
Sinisalo, Ilkka	Phi., Min., L.A.	11	582	204	222	426	208	68	21	11	32	6	....	1981-82	1991-92
Siren, Ville	Pit., Min.	5	290	14	68	82	276	7	0	0	0	6	....	1985-86	1989-90
Sirois, Bob	Phi., Wsh.	6	286	92	120	212	42	....	....	....	....	....	....	1974-75	1979-80
Sittler, Darryl	Tor., Phi., Det.	15	1096	484	637	1121	948	76	29	45	74	137	....	1970-71	1984-85
Sivek, Michal	Pit.	1	38	3	3	6	14	....	....	....	....	....	....	2002-03	2002-03
• Sjoberg, Lars-Erik	Wpg.	1	79	7	27	34	48	....	....	....	....	....	....	1979-80	1979-80
Sjodin, Tommy	Min., Dal., Que.	2	106	8	40	48	52	....	....	....	....	....	....	1992-93	1993-94
Sjostrom, Fredrik	Phx., NYR, Cgy., Tor.	7	489	46	58	104	190	17	0	2	2	2	....	2003-04	2010-11
• Skaare, Bjorn	Det.	1	1	0	0	0	0	....	....	....	....	....	....	1978-79	1978-79
Skalde, Jarrod	N.J., Ana., Cgy., S.J., Chi., Dal., Atl., Phi.	9	115	13	21	34	62	....	....	....	....	....	....	1990-91	2001-02
Skarda, Randy	St.L.	2	26	0	5	5	11	....	....	....	....	....	....	1989-90	1991-92
• Skilton, Raymie	Mtl.W.	1	1	0	0	0	0	....	....	....	....	....	....	1917-18	1917-18
• Skinner, Alf	Tor., Bos., Mtl.M., Pit.	4	71	26	10	36	87	2	0	1	1	9	1	1917-18	1925-26
‡ Skinner, Brett	NYI	1	11	0	0	0	4	....	....	....	....	....	....	2008-09	2008-09
Skinner, Larry	Col.	4	47	10	12	22	8	2	0	0	0	0	....	1976-77	1979-80
Skolney, Wade	Phi.	1	1	0	0	0	2	....	....	....	....	....	....	2005-06	2005-06
Skopintsev, Andrei	T.B., Atl.	3	40	2	4	6	32	....	....	....	....	....	....	1998-99	2000-01
‡ Skoula, Martin	Col., Ana., Dal., Min., Pit., N.J.	10	776	44	152	196	328	83	1	13	14	22	1	1999-00	2009-10
• Skov, Glen	Det., Chi., Mtl.	12	650	106	136	242	413	53	7	7	14	48	3	1949-50	1960-61
• Skrastins, Karlis	Nsh., Col., Fla., Dal.	12	832	32	104	136	375	20	0	3	3	12	....	1998-99	2010-11
‡ Skrbek, Pavel	Pit., Nsh.	3	12	0	0	0	8	....	....	....	....	....	....	1998-99	2001-02
Skriko, Petri	Van., Bos., Wpg., S.J.	9	541	183	222	405	246	28	5	9	14	4	....	1984-85	1992-93
Skrlac, Rob	N.J.	1	8	1	0	1	22	....	....	....	....	....	....	2003-04	2003-04
Skrudland, Brian	Mtl., Cgy., Fla., NYR, Dal.	15	881	124	219	343	1107	164	15	46	61	323	2	1985-86	1999-00
Slaney, John	Wsh., Col., L.A., Phx., Nsh., Pit., Phi.	9	268	22	69	91	99	14	2	1	3	4	....	1993-94	2003-04
• Sleaver, John	Chi.	2	13	1	0	1	6	....	....	....	....	....	....	1953-54	1956-57
Slegr, Jiri	Van., Edm., Pit., Atl., Det., Bos.	11	622	56	193	249	838	42	4	14	18	39	1	1992-93	2005-06
Sleigher, Louis	Que., Bos.	6	194	46	53	99	146	17	1	1	2	64	....	1979-80	1985-86
Sloan, Blake	Dal., CBJ, Cgy.	6	290	11	32	43	162	35	0	2	2	20	1	1998-99	2003-04
Sloan, Tod	Tor., Chi.	13	745	220	262	482	831	47	9	12	21	47	2	1947-48	1960-61
Sloan, Tyler	Wsh.	3	99	4	13	17	50	4	0	1	1	0	....	2008-09	2010-11
Sloane, David	Phi.	1	1	0	0	0	0	....	....	....	....	....	....	2008-09	2008-09
• Slobodian, Peter	NYA	1	41	3	2	5	54	....	....	....	....	....	....	1940-41	1940-41
• Slowinski, Ed	NYR	6	291	58	74	132	63	16	2	6	8	6	....	1947-48	1952-53
• Sly, Darryl	Tor., Min., Van.	4	79	1	2	3	20	....	....	....	....	....	....	1965-66	1970-71
Smaby, Matt	T.B.	4	122	0	6	6	106	....	....	....	....	....	....	2007-08	2010-11
Smail, Doug	Wpg., Min., Que., Ott.	13	845	210	249	459	602	42	9	2	11	49	....	1980-81	1992-93
• Smart, Alex	Mtl.	1	8	5	2	7	0	....	....	....	....	....	....	1942-43	1942-43
Smedsmo, Dale	Tor.	1	4	0	0	0	0	....	....	....	....	....	....	1972-73	1972-73
Smehlik, Richard	Buf., Atl., N.J.	10	644	49	146	195	415	88	1	14	15	40	1	1992-93	2002-03
• Smillie, Don	Bos.	1	12	2	2	4	4	....	....	....	....	....	....	1933-34	1933-34
Smirnov, Alexei	Ana.	2	52	3	3	6	20	4	0	0	0	2	....	2002-03	2003-04
• Smith, Alex	Ott., Det., Bos., NYA	11	443	41	50	91	645	19	0	2	2	26	1	1924-25	1934-35
• Smith, Art	Tor., Ott.	4	144	15	10	25	249	4	1	1	2	8	....	1927-28	1930-31
• Smith, Barry	Bos., Col.	3	114	7	7	14	10	....	....	....	....	....	....	1975-76	1980-81
Smith, Bobby	Min., Mtl.	15	1077	357	679	1036	917	184	64	96	160	245	1	1978-79	1992-93
Smith, Brad	Van., Atl., Cgy., Det., Tor.	9	222	28	34	62	591	20	3	3	6	49	....	1978-79	1986-87
Smith, Brandon	Bos., NYI	4	33	3	4	7	10	....	....	....	....	....	....	1998-99	2002-03
Smith, Brian	Det.	3	61	2	8	10	12	5	0	0	0	0	....	1957-58	1960-61
• Smith, Brian	L.A., Min.	2	67	10	10	20	33	7	0	0	0	0	....	1967-68	1968-69
• Smith, Carl	Det.	1	7	1	1	2	2	....	....	....	....	....	....	1943-44	1943-44
• Smith, Clint	NYR, Chi.	11	483	161	236	397	24	42	10	14	24	2	1	1936-37	1946-47
Smith, D.J.	Tor., Col.	3	45	1	1	2	67	....	....	....	....	....	....	1996-97	2002-03
Smith, Dallas	Bos., NYR	16	890	55	252	307	959	86	3	29	32	128	2	1959-60	1977-78
Smith, Dan	Col., Edm.	3	22	0	0	0	16	....	....	....	....	....	....	1998-99	2005-06
Smith, Dennis	Wsh., L.A.	2	8	0	0	0	4	....	....	....	....	....	....	1989-90	1990-91
Smith, Derek	Buf., Det.	8	335	78	116	194	60	30	9	14	23	13	....	1975-76	1982-83
Smith, Derrick	Phi., Min., Dal.	10	537	82	92	174	373	82	14	11	25	79	....	1984-85	1993-94
• Smith, Des	Mtl.M., Mtl., Chi., Bos.	5	196	22	25	47	236	25	1	4	5	18	1	1937-38	1941-42
• Smith, Don	Mtl.	1	12	1	0	1	6	....	....	....	....	....	....	1919-20	1919-20

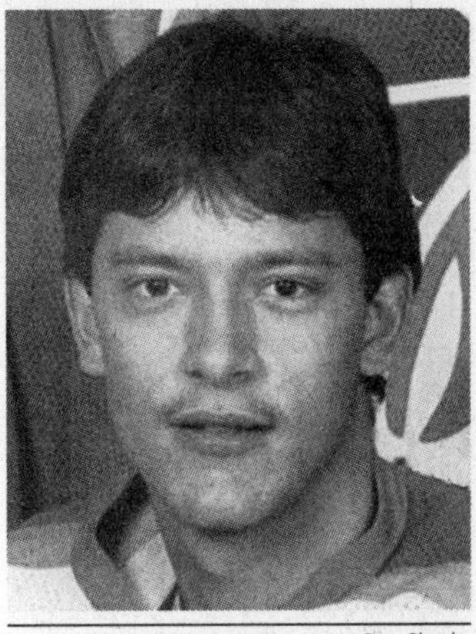
Ron Shudra

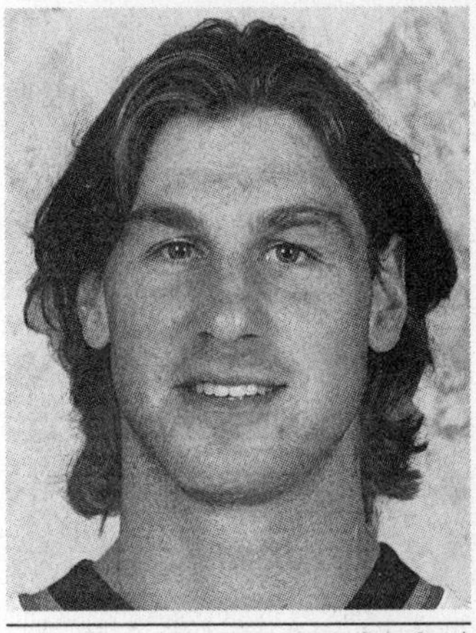
Ryan Smyth

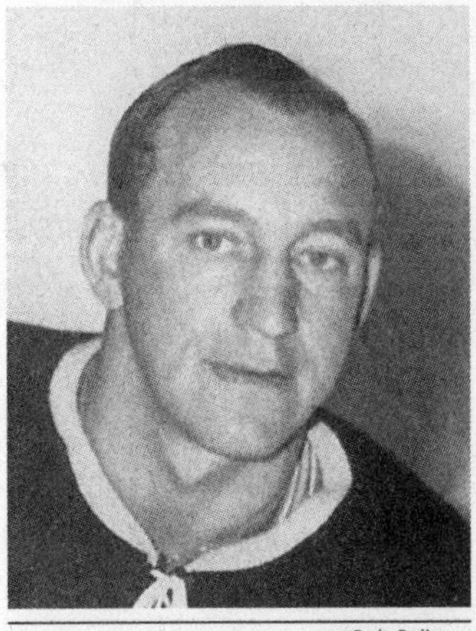
Bob Solinger

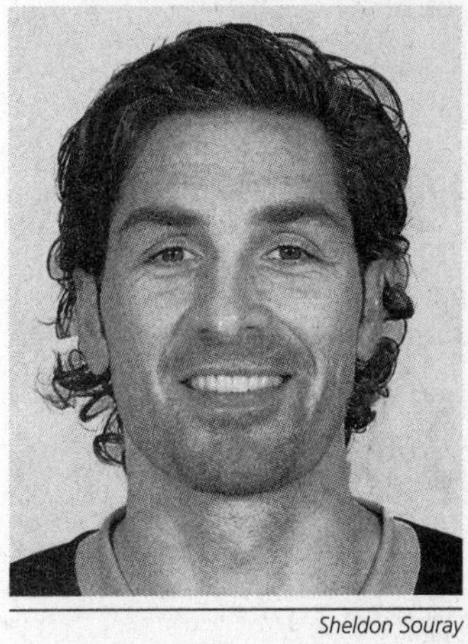
Sheldon Souray

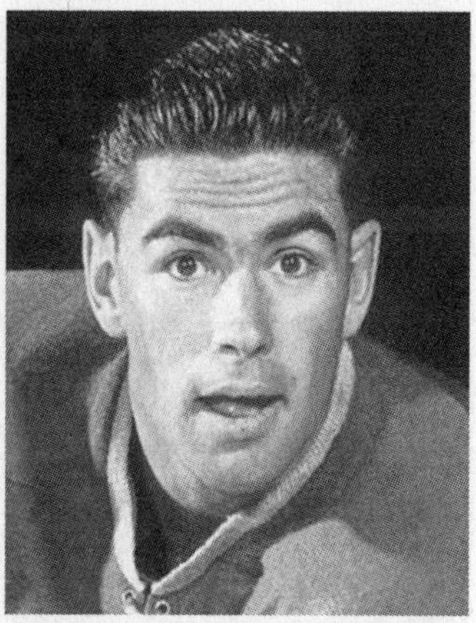

Dollard St. Laurent

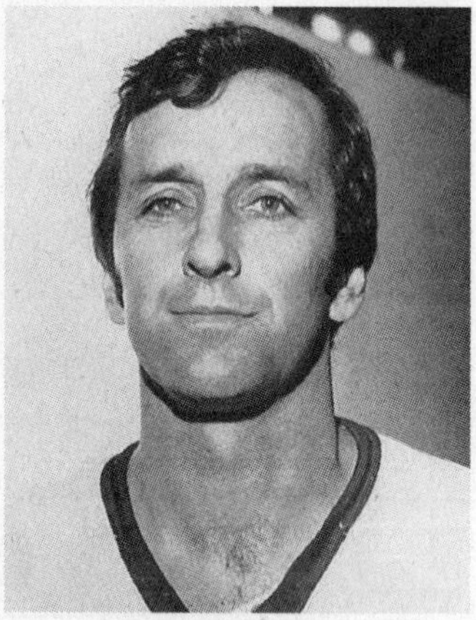

Frank St. Marseille

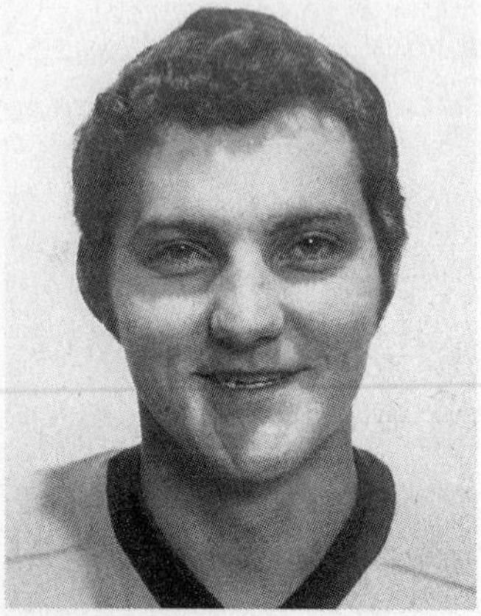

Jim Stanfield

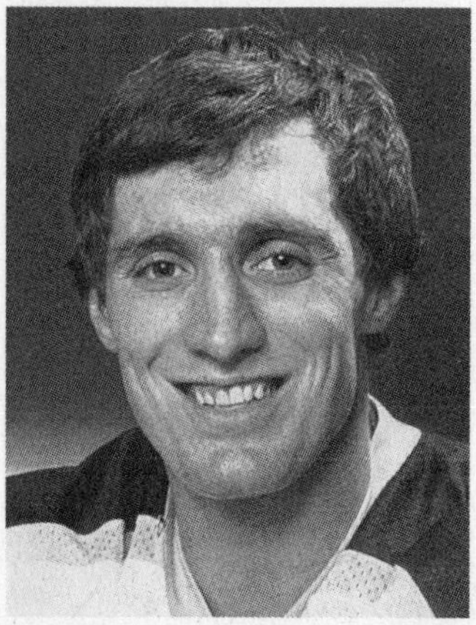

Paul Stewart

			Regular Schedule					Playoffs					NHL	First	Last
Name	NHL Teams	NHL Seasons	GP	G	A	TP	PIM	GP	G	A	TP	PIM	Cup Wins	NHL Season	NHL Season
● Smith, Don	NYR	1	11	1	1	2	0	1	0	0	0	0	....	1949-50	1949-50
Smith, Doug	L.A., Buf., Edm., Van., Pit.	9	535	115	138	253	624	18	4	2	6	21	....	1981-82	1989-90
Smith, Floyd	Bos., NYR, Det., Tor., Buf.	13	616	129	178	307	207	48	12	11	23	16	....	1954-55	1971-72
Smith, Geoff	Edm., Fla., NYR	10	462	18	73	91	282	13	0	1	1	8	1	1989-90	1998-99
Smith, Glen	Chi.	1	2	0	0	0	0	....	....	....	....	....	....	1950-51	1950-51
● Smith, Glenn	Tor.	1	9	0	0	0	0	....	....	....	....	....	....	1921-22	1921-22
Smith, Gord	Wsh., Wpg.	6	299	9	30	39	284	....	....	....	....	....	....	1974-75	1979-80
Smith, Greg	Cal., Cle., Min., Det., Wsh.	13	829	56	232	288	1110	63	4	7	11	106	....	1975-76	1987-88
● Smith, Hooley	Ott., Mtl.M., Bos., NYA	17	715	200	225	425	1013	54	11	8	19	109	2	1924-25	1940-41
Smith, Jason	N.J., Tor., Edm., Phi., Ott.	15	1008	41	128	169	1099	68	1	10	11	60	....	1993-94	2008-09
● Smith, Ken	Bos.	7	331	78	93	171	49	30	8	13	21	6	....	1944-45	1950-51
Smith, Mark	S.J., Cgy.	7	377	23	47	70	457	24	4	0	4	21	....	2000-01	2007-08
● Smith, Nakina	Det.	1	10	1	2	3	0	....	....	....	....	....	....	1943-44	1943-44
Smith, Nathan	Van., Pit., Min.	5	26	0	0	0	14	4	0	0	0	0	....	2003-04	2009-10
Smith, Nick	Fla.	1	15	0	0	0	0	....	....	....	....	....	....	2001-02	2001-02
Smith, Randy	Min.	2	3	0	0	0	0	....	....	....	....	....	....	1985-86	1986-87
Smith, Rick	Bos., Cal., St.L., Det., Wsh.	11	687	52	167	219	560	78	3	23	26	73	1	1968-69	1980-81
● Smith, Rodger	Pit., Phi.	6	210	20	4	24	172	4	3	0	3	0	....	1925-26	1930-31
Smith, Ron	NYI	1	11	1	1	2	14	....	....	....	....	....	....	1972-73	1972-73
● Smith, Sid	Tor.	12	601	186	183	369	94	44	17	10	27	2	3	1946-47	1957-58
● Smith, Stan	NYR	2	9	2	1	3	0	1	0	0	0	0	1	1939-40	1940-41
Smith, Steve	Phi., Buf.	6	18	0	1	1	15	....	....	....	....	....	....	1981-82	1988-89
Smith, Steve	Edm., Chi., Cgy.	16	804	72	303	375	2139	134	11	41	52	288	3	1984-85	2000-01
● Smith, Stu	Mtl.	2	4	2	2	4	2	1	0	0	0	0	....	1940-41	1941-42
Smith, Stu	Hfd.	4	77	2	10	12	95	....	....	....	....	....	....	1979-80	1982-83
● Smith, Tommy	Que.	1	10	0	1	1	11	....	....	....	....	....	....	1919-20	1919-20
Smith, Vern	NYI	1	1	0	0	0	0	....	....	....	....	....	....	1984-85	1984-85
Smith, Wayne	Chi.	1	2	1	1	2	2	1	0	0	0	0	....	1966-67	1966-67
Smith, Wyatt	Phx., Nsh., NYI, Min., Col.	8	211	10	22	32	65	5	0	0	0	0	....	1999-00	2007-08
‡ Smithson, Jerred	L.A., Nsh., Fla., Edm., Tor.	11	606	39	57	96	363	36	2	2	4	39	....	2002-03	2013-14
‡ Smolenak, Radek	T.B., Chi.	2	7	0	1	1	15	....	....	....	....	....	....	2008-09	2009-10
Smolinski, Bryan	Bos., Pit., NYI, L.A., Ott., Chi., Van., Mtl.	15	1056	274	377	651	606	123	23	29	52	60	....	1992-93	2007-08
Smotherman, Jordan	Atl.	2	4	1	1	2	0	....	....	....	....	....	....	2007-08	2008-09
Smrek, Peter	St.L., NYR	2	28	2	4	6	18	....	....	....	....	....	....	2000-01	2001-02
Smrke, John	St.L., Que.	3	103	11	17	28	33	....	....	....	....	....	....	1977-78	1979-80
● Smrke, Stan	Mtl.	2	9	0	3	3	0	....	....	....	....	....	....	1956-57	1957-58
Smyl, Stan	Van.	13	896	262	411	673	1556	41	16	17	33	64	....	1978-79	1990-91
● Smylie, Rod	Tor., Ott.	6	74	4	2	6	12	4	0	0	0	2	1	1920-21	1925-26
Smyth, Brad	Fla., L.A., NYR, Nsh., Ott.	6	88	15	13	28	109	....	....	....	....	....	....	1995-96	2002-03
Smyth, Greg	Phi., Que., Cgy., Fla., Tor., Chi.	10	229	4	16	20	783	12	0	0	0	40	....	1986-87	1996-97
Smyth, Kevin	Hfd.	3	58	6	8	14	31	....	....	....	....	....	....	1993-94	1995-96
‡ Smyth, Ryan	Edm., NYI, Col., L.A.	19	1270	386	456	842	976	93	28	31	59	88	....	1994-95	2013-14
‡ Sneep, Carl	Pit.	1	1	0	1	1	0	....	....	....	....	....	....	2011-12	2011-12
Snell, Chris	Tor., L.A.	2	34	2	7	9	24	....	....	....	....	....	....	1993-94	1994-95
Snell, Ron	Pit.	2	7	3	2	5	6	....	....	....	....	....	....	1968-69	1969-70
Snell, Ted	Pit., K.C., Det.	2	104	7	18	25	22	....	....	....	....	....	....	1973-74	1974-75
Snepsts, Harold	Van., Min., Det., St.L.	17	1033	38	195	233	2009	93	1	14	15	231	....	1974-75	1990-91
Snow, Sandy	Det.	1	3	0	0	0	2	....	....	....	....	....	....	1968-69	1968-69
Snuggerud, Dave	Buf., S.J., Phi.	4	265	30	54	84	127	12	1	3	4	6	....	1989-90	1992-93
● Snyder, Dan	Atl.	3	49	11	5	16	64	....	....	....	....	....	....	2000-01	2002-03
Sobchuk, Dennis	Det., Que.	2	35	5	6	11	2	....	....	....	....	....	....	1979-80	1982-83
Sobchuk, Gene	Van.	1	1	0	0	0	0	....	....	....	....	....	....	1973-74	1973-74
Solheim, Ken	Chi., Min., Det., Edm.	5	135	19	20	39	34	3	1	1	2	2	....	1980-81	1985-86
● Solinger, Bob	Tor., Det.	5	99	10	11	21	19	....	....	....	....	....	....	1951-52	1959-60
● Somers, Art	Chi., NYR	6	222	33	56	89	189	30	1	5	6	20	1	1929-30	1934-35
‡ Somik, Radovan	Phi.	2	113	12	20	32	27	15	2	2	4	10	....	2002-03	2003-04
Sommer, Roy	Edm.	1	3	1	0	1	7	....	....	....	....	....	....	1980-81	1980-81
Songin, Tom	Bos.	3	43	5	5	10	22	....	....	....	....	....	....	1978-79	1980-81
Sonmor, Glen	NYR	2	28	2	0	2	21	....	....	....	....	....	....	1953-54	1954-55
Sonnenberg, Martin	Pit., Cgy.	3	63	2	3	5	21	7	0	0	0	0	....	1998-99	2003-04
‡ Sopel, Brent	Van., NYI, L.A., Chi., Atl., Mtl.	12	659	44	174	218	309	71	4	14	18	20	1	1998-99	2010-11
Sorochan, Lee	Cgy.	2	3	0	0	0	0	....	....	....	....	....	....	1998-99	1999-00
● Sorrell, John	Det., NYA	11	490	127	119	246	100	42	12	15	27	10	2	1930-31	1940-41
‡ Souray, Sheldon	N.J., Mtl., Edm., Dal., Ana.	14	758	109	191	300	1145	40	3	8	11	69	....	1997-98	2012-13
Spacek, Jaroslav	Fla., Chi., CBJ, Edm., Buf., Mtl., Car.	13	880	82	273	355	618	61	4	14	18	44	....	1998-99	2011-12
Spanhel, Martin	CBJ	2	10	2	0	2	4	....	....	....	....	....	....	2000-01	2001-02
● Sparrow, Emory	Bos.	1	8	0	0	0	4	....	....	....	....	....	....	1924-25	1924-25
● Speck, Fred	Det., Van.	3	28	1	2	3	2	....	....	....	....	....	....	1968-69	1971-72
● Speer, Bill	Pit., Bos.	4	130	5	20	25	79	8	1	0	1	4	1	1967-68	1970-71
Speers, Ted	Det.	1	4	1	1	2	0	....	....	....	....	....	....	1985-86	1985-86
● Spence, Gordon	Tor.	1	3	0	0	0	0	....	....	....	....	....	....	1925-26	1925-26
● Spencer, Brian	Tor., NYI, Buf., Pit.	10	553	80	143	223	634	37	1	5	6	29	....	1969-70	1978-79
● Spencer, Irv	NYR, Bos., Det.	8	230	12	38	50	127	16	0	0	0	8	....	1959-60	1967-68
● Speyer, Chris	Tor., NYA	3	14	0	0	0	0	....	....	....	....	....	....	1923-24	1933-34
Spiller, Matthew	Phx., NYI	3	68	0	2	2	74	....	....	....	....	....	....	2003-04	2007-08
Spring, Corey	T.B.	2	16	1	1	2	12	....	....	....	....	....	....	1997-98	1998-99
Spring, Don	Wpg.	4	259	1	54	55	80	6	0	0	0	10	....	1980-81	1983-84
Spring, Frank	Bos., St.L., Cal., Cle.	5	61	14	20	34	12	....	....	....	....	....	....	1969-70	1976-77
● Spring, Jesse	Ham., Pit., Tor., NYA	6	133	11	4	15	74	2	0	2	2	2	....	1923-24	1929-30
Spruce, Andy	Van., Col.	3	172	31	42	73	111	2	0	2	2	0	....	1976-77	1978-79
‡ Sprukts, Janis	Fla.	2	14	1	2	3	2	....	....	....	....	....	....	2006-07	2008-09
Srsen, Tomas	Edm.	1	2	0	0	0	0	....	....	....	....	....	....	1990-91	1990-91
St. Amour, Martin	Ott.	1	1	0	0	0	2	....	....	....	....	....	....	1992-93	1992-93
St. Jacques, Bruno	Phi., Car., Ana.	4	67	3	7	10	47	....	....	....	....	....	....	2001-02	2005-06
St. Laurent, Andre	NYI, Det., L.A., Pit.	11	644	129	187	316	749	59	8	12	20	48	....	1973-74	1983-84
● St. Laurent, Dollard	Mtl., Chi.	12	652	29	133	162	496	92	2	22	24	87	5	1950-51	1961-62
St. Marseille, Frank	St.L., L.A.	10	707	140	285	425	242	88	20	25	45	18	....	1967-68	1976-77
‡ St. Pierre, Martin	Chi., Bos., Ott., Mtl.	6	39	3	5	8	12	....	....	....	....	....	....	2005-06	2013-14
St. Sauveur, Claude	Atl.	1	79	24	24	48	23	2	0	0	0	0	....	1975-76	1975-76
Stackhouse, Ron	Cal., Det., Pit.	12	889	87	372	459	824	32	5	8	13	38	....	1970-71	1981-82
● Stackhouse, Ted	Tor.	1	13	0	0	0	2	1	0	0	0	0	1	1921-22	1921-22
‡ Stafford, Garrett	Det., Dal., Phx.	3	7	0	2	2	0	....	....	....	....	....	....	2007-08	2010-11
● Stahan, Butch	Mtl.	1	....	....	....	....	....	3	0	1	1	2	....	1944-45	1944-45
Staios, Steve	Bos., Van., Atl., Edm., Cgy., NYI	16	1001	56	164	220	1322	33	1	5	6	32	....	1995-96	2011-12
Stajduhar, Nick	Edm.	1	2	0	0	0	4	....	....	....	....	....	....	1995-96	1995-96
Staley, Al	NYR	1	1	0	1	1	0	....	....	....	....	....	....	1948-49	1948-49
Stamler, Lorne	L.A., Tor., Wpg.	4	116	14	11	25	16	....	....	....	....	....	....	1976-77	1979-80
Standing, George	Min.	1	2	0	0	0	0	....	....	....	....	....	....	1967-68	1967-68
Stanfield, Fred	Chi., Bos., Min., Buf.	14	914	211	405	616	134	106	21	35	56	10	2	1964-65	1977-78
Stanfield, Jack	Chi.	1	....	....	....	....	....	1	0	0	0	0	....	1965-66	1965-66
● Stanfield, Jim	L.A.	3	7	0	1	1	0	....	....	....	....	....	....	1969-70	1971-72
Stankiewicz, Ed	Det.	2	6	0	0	0	2	....	....	....	....	....	....	1953-54	1955-56
Stankiewicz, Myron	St.L., Phi.	1	35	0	7	7	36	1	0	0	0	0	....	1968-69	1968-69
● Stanley, Allan	NYR, Chi., Bos., Tor., Phi.	21	1244	100	333	433	792	109	7	36	43	80	4	1948-49	1968-69
● Stanley, Barney	Chi.	1	1	0	0	0	0	....	....	....	....	....	....	1927-28	1927-28
Stanley, Daryl	Phi., Van.	6	189	8	17	25	408	17	0	0	0	30	....	1983-84	1989-90
● Stanowski, Wally	Tor., NYR	10	428	23	88	111	160	60	3	14	17	13	4	1939-40	1950-51
Stanton, Paul	Pit., Bos., NYI	5	295	14	49	63	262	44	2	10	12	66	2	1990-91	1994-95
Stapleton, Brian	Wsh.	1	1	0	0	0	0	....	....	....	....	....	....	1975-76	1975-76
Stapleton, Mike	Chi., Pit., Edm., Wpg., Phx., Atl., NYI, Van.	14	697	71	111	182	342	34	1	0	1	39	....	1986-87	2000-01
Stapleton, Pat	Bos., Chi.	10	635	43	294	337	353	65	10	39	49	38	....	1961-62	1972-73
‡ Stapleton, Tim	Tor., Atl., Wpg.	4	118	19	18	37	24	....	....	....	....	....	....	2008-09	2011-12
Starikov, Sergei	N.J.	1	16	0	1	1	8	....	....	....	....	....	....	1989-90	1989-90
● Starr, Harold	Ott., Mtl.M., Mtl., NYR	7	205	6	5	11	186	15	1	0	1	4	....	1929-30	1935-36
● Starr, Wilf	NYA, Det.	4	87	8	6	14	25	7	0	2	2	2	....	1932-33	1935-36
Stasiuk, Vic	Chi., Det., Bos.	14	745	183	254	437	669	69	16	18	34	40	2	1949-50	1962-63
Stastny, Anton	Que.	9	650	252	384	636	150	66	20	32	52	31	....	1980-81	1988-89
Stastny, Marian	Que., Tor.	5	322	121	173	294	110	32	5	17	22	7	....	1981-82	1985-86
Stastny, Peter	Que., N.J., St.L.	15	977	450	789	1239	824	93	33	72	105	123	....	1980-81	1994-95
‡ Stastny, Yan	Edm., Bos., St.L.	5	91	6	10	16	58	....	....	....	....	....	....	2005-06	2009-10
Staszak, Ray	Det.	1	4	0	1	1	7	....	....	....	....	....	....	1985-86	1985-86
‡ Staubitz, Brad	S.J., Min., Mtl., Ana.	5	230	10	11	21	521	....	....	....	....	....	....	2008-09	2012-13
‡ Steckel, David	Wsh., N.J., Tor., Ana.	9	425	33	46	79	129	31	5	4	9	8	....	2005-06	2013-14
● Steele, Frank	Det.	1	1	0	0	0	0	....	....	....	....	....	....	1930-31	1930-31

			Regular Schedule					Playoffs					NHL	First	Last
Name	NHL Teams	NHL Seasons	GP	G	A	TP	PIM	GP	G	A	TP	PIM	Cup Wins	NHL Season	NHL Season
Steen, Anders	Wpg.	1	42	5	11	16	22	....	....	....	....	....	....	1980-81	1980-81
Steen, Thomas	Wpg.	14	950	264	553	817	753	56	12	32	44	62	....	1981-82	1994-95
Stefan, Patrik	Atl., Dal.	7	455	64	124	188	158	....	....	....	....	....	....	1999-00	2006-07
Stefaniw, Morris	Atl.	1	13	1	1	2	2	....	....	....	....	....	....	1972-73	1972-73
Stefanski, Bud	NYR	1	1	0	0	0	0	....	....	....	....	....	....	1977-78	1977-78
Stemkowski, Pete	Tor., Det., NYR, L.A.	15	967	206	349	555	866	83	25	29	54	136	1	1963-64	1977-78
Stenlund, Vern	Cle.	1	4	0	0	0	0	....	....	....	....	....	....	1976-77	1976-77
Stephens, Charlie	Col.	2	8	0	2	2	4	....	....	....	....	....	....	2002-03	2003-04
Stephenson, Bob	Hfd., Tor.	1	18	2	3	5	4	....	....	....	....	....	....	1979-80	1979-80
Stephenson, Shay	L.A.	1	2	0	0	0	0	....	....	....	....	....	....	2006-07	2006-07
‡ Sterling, Brett	Atl., Pit., St.L.	4	30	5	4	9	32	....	....	....	....	....	....	2007-08	2011-12
Stern, Ron	Van., Cgy., S.J.	12	638	75	86	161	2077	43	7	7	14	119	....	1987-88	1999-00
Sterner, Ulf	NYR	1	4	0	0	0	0	....	....	....	....	....	....	1964-65	1964-65
Stevens, John	Phi., Hfd.	5	53	0	10	10	48	....	....	....	....	....	....	1986-87	1993-94
Stevens, Kevin	Pit., Bos., L.A., NYR, Phi.	15	874	329	397	726	1470	103	46	60	106	170	2	1987-88	2001-02
Stevens, Mike	Van., Bos., NYI, Tor.	4	23	1	4	5	29	....	....	....	....	....	....	1984-85	1989-90
• Stevens, Phil	Mtl.W., Mtl., Bos.	3	25	1	0	1	3	....	....	....	....	....	....	1917-18	1925-26
Stevens, Scott	Wsh., St.L., N.J.	22	1635	196	712	908	2785	233	26	92	118	402	3	1982-83	2003-04
Stevenson, Grant	S.J.	1	47	10	12	22	14	5	0	0	0	4	....	2005-06	2005-06
Stevenson, Jeremy	Ana., Nsh., Min., Dal.	9	207	19	19	38	451	21	0	5	5	20	....	1995-96	2005-06
Stevenson, Shayne	Bos., T.B.	3	27	0	2	2	35	....	....	....	....	....	....	1990-91	1992-93
Stevenson, Turner	Mtl., N.J., Phi.	13	644	75	115	190	969	67	6	12	18	66	1	1992-93	2005-06
Stewart, Allan	N.J., Bos.	6	64	6	4	10	243	....	....	....	....	....	....	1985-86	1991-92
‡ Stewart, Anthony	Fla., Atl., Car.	6	262	27	44	71	123	....	....	....	....	....	....	2005-06	2011-12
Stewart, Bill	Buf., St.L., Tor., Min.	8	261	7	64	71	424	13	1	3	4	11	....	1977-78	1985-86
Stewart, Blair	Det., Wsh., Que.	7	229	34	44	78	326	....	....	....	....	....	....	1973-74	1979-80
Stewart, Bob	Bos., Cal., Cle., St.L., Pit.	9	575	27	101	128	809	5	1	1	2	2	....	1971-72	1979-80
Stewart, Cam	Bos., Fla., Min.	7	202	16	23	39	120	13	1	3	4	9	....	1993-94	2001-02
• Stewart, Gaye	Tor., Chi., Det., NYR, Mtl.	11	502	185	159	344	274	25	2	9	11	16	2	1941-42	1953-54
Stewart, Greg	Mtl.	3	26	0	1	1	48	2	0	0	0	2	....	2007-08	2009-10
• Stewart, Jack	Det., Chi.	12	565	31	84	115	765	80	5	14	19	143	2	1938-39	1951-52
Stewart, John	Pit., Atl., Cal.	5	258	58	60	118	158	4	0	0	0	10	....	1970-71	1974-75
Stewart, John	Que.	1	2	0	0	0	0	....	....	....	....	....	....	1979-80	1979-80
‡ Stewart, Karl	Atl., Pit., Chi., T.B.	4	69	2	4	6	68	....	....	....	....	....	....	2003-04	2007-08
• Stewart, Ken	Chi.	1	6	1	1	2	2	....	....	....	....	....	....	1941-42	1941-42
• Stewart, Nels	Mtl.M., Bos., NYA	15	650	324	191	515	953	50	9	12	21	47	1	1925-26	1939-40
Stewart, Paul	Que.	1	21	2	0	2	74	....	....	....	....	....	....	1979-80	1979-80
Stewart, Ralph	Van., NYI	7	252	57	73	130	28	19	4	4	8	2	....	1970-71	1977-78
• Stewart, Ron	Tor., Bos., St.L., NYR, Van., NYI	21	1353	276	253	529	560	119	14	21	35	60	3	1952-53	1972-73
Stewart, Ryan	Wpg.	1	3	1	0	1	0	....	....	....	....	....	....	1985-86	1985-86
Stienburg, Trevor	Que.	4	71	8	4	12	161	1	0	0	0	0	....	1985-86	1988-89
Stiles, Tony	Cgy.	1	30	2	7	9	20	....	....	....	....	....	....	1983-84	1983-84
Stillman, Cory	Cgy., St.L., T.B., Car., Ott., Fla.	16	1025	278	449	727	489	82	19	32	51	43	2	1994-95	2010-11
Stock, P.J.	NYR, Mtl., Phi., Bos.	7	235	5	21	26	523	8	1	0	1	19	....	1997-98	2003-04
• Stoddard, Jack	NYR	2	80	16	15	31	31	....	....	....	....	....	....	1951-52	1952-53
Stojanov, Alek	Van., Pit.	3	107	2	5	7	222	14	0	0	0	21	....	1994-95	1996-97
Stoltz, Roland	Wsh.	1	14	2	2	4	14	....	....	....	....	....	....	1981-82	1981-82
Stone, Ryan	Pit., Edm.	3	35	0	7	7	55	....	....	....	....	....	....	2007-08	2009-10
Stone, Steve	Van.	1	2	0	0	0	0	....	....	....	....	....	....	1973-74	1973-74
Storm, Jim	Hfd., Dal.	3	84	7	15	22	44	....	....	....	....	....	....	1993-94	1995-96
Stothers, Mike	Phi., Tor.	4	30	0	2	2	65	5	0	0	0	11	....	1984-85	1987-88
Stoughton, Blaine	Pit., Tor., Hfd., NYR	8	526	258	191	449	204	8	4	2	6	2	....	1973-74	1983-84
Stoyanovich, Steve	Hfd.	1	23	3	5	8	11	....	....	....	....	....	....	1983-84	1983-84
• Strain, Neil	NYR	1	52	11	13	24	12	....	....	....	....	....	....	1952-53	1952-53
‡ Straka, Martin	Pit., Ott., NYI, Fla., L.A., NYR	15	954	257	460	717	360	106	26	44	70	52	....	1992-93	2007-08
Strate, Gord	Det.	3	61	0	0	0	34	....	....	....	....	....	....	1956-57	1958-59
Stratton, Art	NYR, Det., Chi., Pit., Phi.	4	95	18	33	51	24	5	0	0	0	0	....	1959-60	1967-68
‡ Strbak, Martin	L.A., Pit.	1	49	5	11	16	46	....	....	....	....	....	....	2003-04	2003-04
• Strobel, Art	NYR	1	7	0	0	0	0	....	....	....	....	....	....	1943-44	1943-44
Strong, Ken	Tor.	3	15	2	2	4	6	....	....	....	....	....	....	1982-83	1984-85
Stroshein, Garret	Wsh.	1	3	0	0	0	14	....	....	....	....	....	....	2003-04	2003-04
Struch, David	Cgy.	1	4	0	0	0	4	....	....	....	....	....	....	1993-94	1993-94
Strudwick, Jason	NYI, Van., Chi., NYR, Edm.	14	674	13	42	55	811	7	0	0	0	0	....	1995-96	2010-11
Strueby, Todd	Edm.	3	5	0	1	1	2	....	....	....	....	....	....	1981-82	1983-84
• Stuart, Billy	Tor., Bos.	7	195	30	20	50	151	12	1	1	2	6	1	1920-21	1926-27
Stuart, Mike	St.L.	2	3	0	0	0	0	....	....	....	....	....	....	2003-04	2005-06
‡ Stumpel, Jozef	Bos., L.A., Fla.	16	957	196	481	677	245	55	6	24	30	24	....	1991-92	2007-08
Stumpf, Bob	St.L., Pit.	1	10	1	1	2	20	....	....	....	....	....	....	1974-75	1974-75
Sturgeon, Peter	Col.	2	6	0	1	1	2	....	....	....	....	....	....	1979-80	1980-81
Sturm, Marco	S.J., Bos., L.A., Wsh., Van., Fla.	14	938	242	245	487	446	68	9	13	22	30	....	1997-98	2011-12
Stutzel, Mike	Phx.	1	9	0	0	0	0	....	....	....	....	....	....	2003-04	2003-04
‡ Suchy, Radoslav	Phx., CBJ	6	451	13	58	71	104	10	1	1	2	0	....	1999-00	2005-06
Suglobov, Alexander	N.J., Tor.	3	18	1	0	1	4	....	....	....	....	....	....	2003-04	2006-07
Suikkanen, Kai	Buf.	2	2	0	0	0	0	....	....	....	....	....	....	1981-82	1982-83
Sulliman, Doug	NYR, Hfd., N.J., Phi.	11	631	160	168	328	175	16	1	3	4	2	....	1979-80	1989-90
• Sullivan, Barry	Det.	1	1	0	0	0	0	....	....	....	....	....	....	1947-48	1947-48
Sullivan, Bob	Hfd.	1	62	18	19	37	18	....	....	....	....	....	....	1982-83	1982-83
Sullivan, Brian	N.J.	1	2	0	1	1	0	....	....	....	....	....	....	1992-93	1992-93
• Sullivan, Frank	Tor., Chi.	4	8	0	0	0	2	....	....	....	....	....	....	1949-50	1955-56
Sullivan, Mike	S.J., Cgy., Bos., Phx.	11	709	54	82	136	203	34	4	8	12	14	....	1991-92	2001-02
Sullivan, Peter	Wpg.	2	126	28	54	82	40	....	....	....	....	....	....	1979-80	1980-81
Sullivan, Red	Bos., Chi., NYR	11	557	107	239	346	441	18	1	2	3	6	....	1949-50	1960-61
Sullivan, Steve	N.J., Tor., Chi., Nsh., Pit., Phx.	17	1011	290	457	747	587	50	9	14	23	30	....	1995-96	2012-13
‡ Sulzer, Alexander	Nsh., Fla., Van., Buf.	6	131	7	15	22	44	....	....	....	....	....	....	2008-09	2013-14
Summanen, Raimo	Edm., Van.	5	151	36	40	76	35	10	2	5	7	0	....	1983-84	1987-88
• Summerhill, Bill	Mtl., Bro.	4	72	14	17	31	70	3	0	0	0	2	....	1937-38	1941-42
Sundblad, Niklas	Cgy.	1	2	0	0	0	0	....	....	....	....	....	....	1995-96	1995-96
Sundin, Mats	Que., Tor., Van.	18	1346	564	785	1349	1093	91	38	44	82	74	....	1990-91	2008-09
Sundin, Ronnie	NYR	1	1	0	0	0	0	....	....	....	....	....	....	1997-98	1997-98
Sundstrom, Niklas	NYR, S.J., Mtl.	10	750	117	232	349	256	59	6	22	28	22	....	1995-96	2005-06
Sundstrom, Patrik	Van., N.J.	10	679	219	369	588	349	37	9	17	26	25	....	1982-83	1991-92
Sundstrom, Peter	NYR, Wsh., N.J.	6	338	61	83	144	120	23	3	3	6	8	....	1983-84	1989-90
• Suomi, Al	Chi.	1	5	0	0	0	0	....	....	....	....	....	....	1936-37	1936-37
‡ Surma, Damian	Car.	2	2	1	1	2	0	....	....	....	....	....	....	2002-03	2003-04
‡ Surovy, Tomas	Pit.	3	126	27	32	59	71	....	....	....	....	....	....	2002-03	2005-06
Sushinsky, Maxim	Min.	1	30	7	4	11	29	....	....	....	....	....	....	2000-01	2000-01
Suter, Gary	Cgy., Chi., S.J.	17	1145	203	641	844	1349	108	17	56	73	120	1	1985-86	2001-02
Sutherby, Brian	Wsh., Ana., Dal.	9	460	41	49	90	533	10	0	0	0	12	....	2001-02	2010-11
Sutherland, Bill	Mtl., Phi., Tor., St.L., Det.	6	250	70	58	128	99	14	2	4	6	0	....	1962-63	1971-72
• Sutherland, Max	Bos.	1	2	0	0	0	0	....	....	....	....	....	....	1931-32	1931-32
Sutter, Brent	NYI, Chi.	18	1111	363	466	829	1054	144	30	44	74	164	2	1980-81	1997-98
Sutter, Brian	St.L.	12	779	303	333	636	1786	65	21	21	42	249	....	1976-77	1987-88
Sutter, Darryl	Chi.	8	406	161	118	279	288	51	24	19	43	26	....	1979-80	1986-87
Sutter, Duane	NYI, Chi.	11	731	139	203	342	1333	161	26	32	58	405	4	1979-80	1989-90
Sutter, Rich	Pit., Phi., Van., St.L., Chi., T.B., Tor.	13	874	149	166	315	1411	78	13	5	18	133	....	1982-83	1994-95
Sutter, Ron	Phi., St.L., Que., NYI, Bos., S.J., Cgy.	19	1093	205	329	534	1352	104	8	32	40	193	....	1982-83	2000-01
Sutton, Andy	S.J., Min., Atl., NYI, Ott., Ana., Edm.	14	676	38	112	150	1185	11	0	0	0	20	....	1998-99	2012-13
Sutton, Ken	Buf., Edm., St.L., N.J., S.J., NYI	11	388	23	80	103	338	32	3	4	7	29	1	1990-91	2001-02
Suzor, Mark	Phi., Col.	2	64	4	16	20	60	....	....	....	....	....	....	1976-77	1977-78
Svartvadet, Per	Atl.	4	247	17	34	51	58	....	....	....	....	....	....	1999-00	2002-03
‡ Svatos, Marek	Col., Nsh., Ott.	7	344	100	72	172	217	14	2	5	7	4	....	2003-04	2010-11
Svehla, Robert	Fla., Tor.	9	655	68	267	335	649	38	1	14	15	42	....	1994-95	2002-03
Svejkovsky, Jaroslav	Wsh., T.B.	4	113	23	19	42	56	1	0	0	0	2	....	1996-97	1999-00
Svensson, Leif	Wsh.	2	121	6	40	46	49	....	....	....	....	....	....	1978-79	1979-80
Svensson, Magnus	Fla.	2	46	4	14	18	31	....	....	....	....	....	....	1994-95	1995-96
‡ Svitov, Alexander	T.B., CBJ	3	179	13	24	37	223	7	0	0	0	6	....	2002-03	2006-07
‡ Svoboda, Jaroslav	Car., Dal.	4	134	12	17	29	62	25	1	4	5	30	....	2001-02	2005-06
Svoboda, Petr	Mtl., Buf., Phi., T.B.	17	1028	58	341	399	1605	127	4	45	49	140	1	1984-85	2000-01
Svoboda, Petr	Tor.	1	18	1	2	3	10	....	....	....	....	....	....	2000-01	2000-01
Swain, Garry	Pit.	1	9	1	1	2	0	....	....	....	....	....	....	1968-69	1968-69
Swanson, Brian	Edm., Atl.	4	70	4	13	17	16	....	....	....	....	....	....	2000-01	2003-04
Swarbrick, George	Oak., Pit., Phi.	4	132	17	25	42	173	....	....	....	....	....	....	1967-68	1970-71
‡ Sweatt, Bill	Van.	2	3	0	0	0	0	....	....	....	....	....	....	2011-12	2012-13
Sweatt, Lee	Van.	1	3	1	1	2	2	....	....	....	....	....	....	2010-11	2010-11
• Sweeney, Bill	NYR	1	4	1	0	1	0	....	....	....	....	....	....	1959-60	1959-60
Sweeney, Bob	Bos., Buf., NYI, Cgy.	10	639	125	163	288	799	103	15	18	33	197	....	1986-87	1995-96

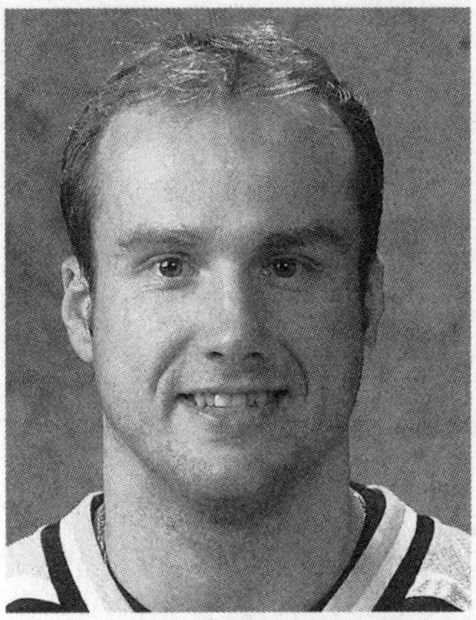
Martin Straka

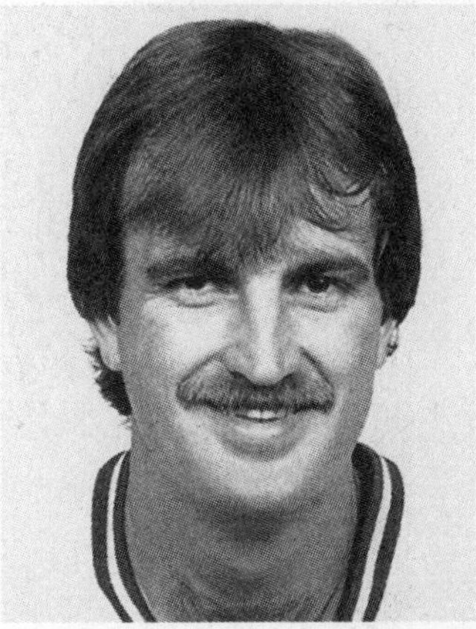
Bob Sullivan

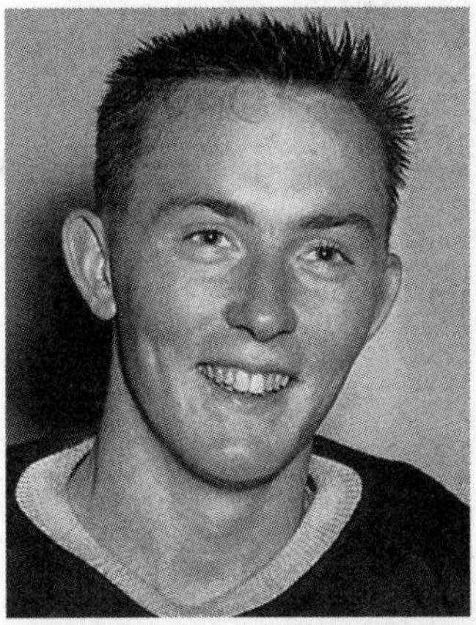
Frank Sullivan

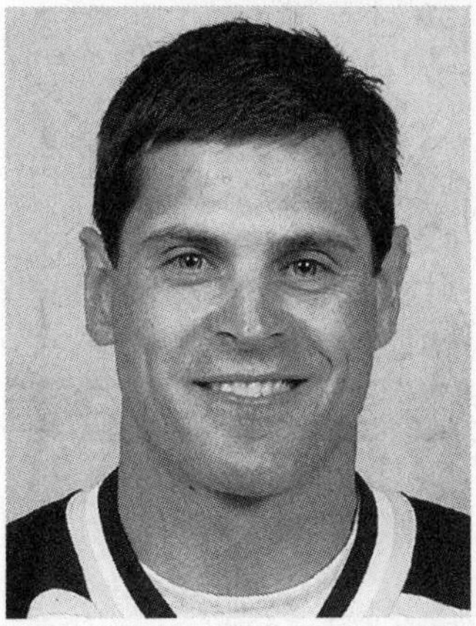
Don Sweeney

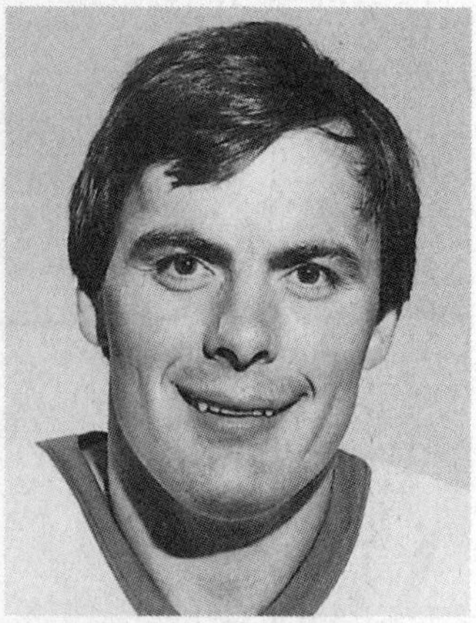

Marc Tardif

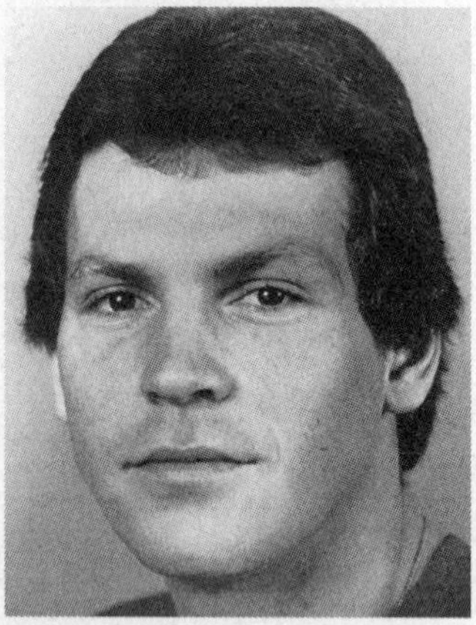

Greg Theberge

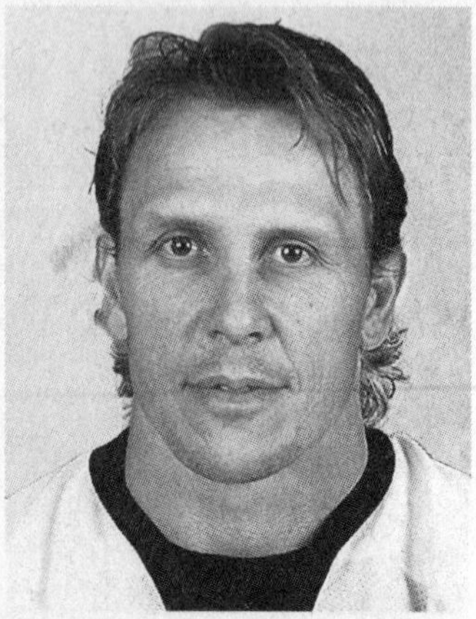

Steve Thomas

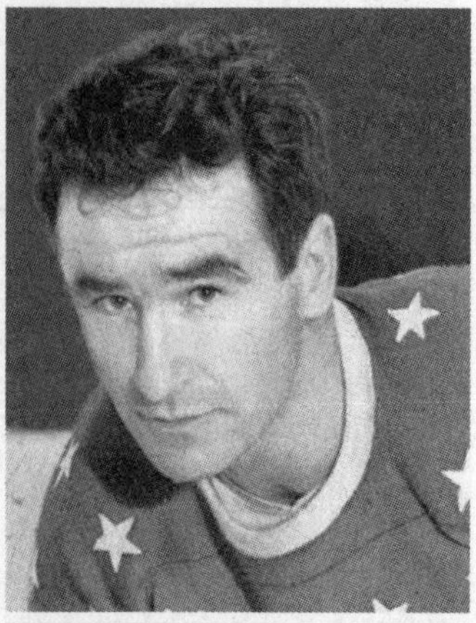

Bill Thomson

Name	NHL Teams	NHL Seasons	Regular Schedule GP	G	A	TP	PIM	Playoffs GP	G	A	TP	PIM	NHL Cup Wins	First NHL Season	Last NHL Season
Sweeney, Don	Bos., Dal.	16	1115	52	221	273	681	108	9	10	19	81	....	1988-89	2003-04
Sweeney, Tim	Cgy., Bos., Ana., NYR	8	291	55	83	138	123	4	0	0	0	2	....	1990-91	1997-98
Sydor, Darryl	L.A., Dal., CBJ, T.B., Pit., St.L.	18	1291	98	409	507	755	155	9	47	56	73	2	1991-92	2009-10
Sykes, Bob	Tor.	1	2	0	0	0	0	....	....	....	....	....	....	1974-75	1974-75
Sykes, Phil	L.A., Wpg.	10	456	79	85	164	519	26	0	3	3	29	....	1982-83	1991-92
Sykora, Michal	S.J., Chi., T.B., Phi.	7	267	15	54	69	185	7	0	1	1	0	....	1993-94	2000-01
‡ Sykora, Petr	N.J., Ana., NYR, Edm., Pit., Min.	15	1017	323	398	721	455	133	34	40	74	62	2	1995-96	2011-12
Sykora, Petr	Nsh., Wsh.	2	12	2	2	4	6	....	....	....	....	....	....	1998-99	2005-06
Sylvester, Dean	Buf., Atl.	3	96	21	16	37	32	4	0	0	0	0	....	1998-99	2000-01
‡ Szczechura, Paul	T.B., Buf.	3	92	10	10	20	34	....	....	....	....	....	....	2008-09	2011-12
• Szura, Joe	Oak.	2	90	10	15	25	30	7	2	3	5	2	....	1967-68	1968-69

T

Name	NHL Teams	NHL Seasons	Regular Schedule GP	G	A	TP	PIM	Playoffs GP	G	A	TP	PIM	NHL Cup Wins	First NHL Season	Last NHL Season
‡ Taffe, Jeff	Phx., NYR, Pit., Fla., Chi., Min.	9	180	21	25	46	40	....	....	....	....	....	....	2002-03	2011-12
Taft, John	Det.	1	15	0	2	2	4	....	....	....	....	....	....	1978-79	1978-79
Taglianetti, Peter	Wpg., Min., Pit., T.B.	11	451	18	74	92	1106	53	2	8	10	103	2	1984-85	1994-95
Talafous, Dean	Atl., Min., NYR	8	497	104	154	258	163	21	4	7	11	11	....	1974-75	1981-82
• Talakoski, Ron	NYR	2	9	0	1	1	33	....	....	....	....	....	....	1986-87	1987-88
Talbot, Jean-Guy	Mtl., Min., Det., St.L., Buf.	17	1056	43	242	285	1006	150	4	26	30	142	7	1954-55	1970-71
‡ Tallackson, Barry	N.J.	4	20	1	1	2	2	....	....	....	....	....	....	2005-06	2008-09
‡ Tallinder, Henrik	Buf., N.J.	12	678	28	114	142	378	39	2	10	12	28	....	2001-02	2013-14
Tallon, Dale	Van., Chi., Pit.	10	642	98	238	336	568	33	2	10	12	45	....	1970-71	1979-80
Tambellini, Steve	NYI, Col., N.J., Cgy., Van.	10	553	160	150	310	105	2	0	1	1	0	1	1978-79	1987-88
Tamer, Chris	Pit., NYR, Atl.	11	644	21	64	85	1183	37	0	8	8	52	....	1993-94	2003-04
Tanabe, David	Car., Phx., Bos.	8	449	30	84	114	245	7	2	1	3	12	....	1999-00	2007-08
Tancill, Chris	Hfd., Det., Dal., S.J.	8	134	17	32	49	54	11	1	1	2	8	....	1990-91	1997-98
Tanguay, Christian	Que.	1	2	0	0	0	0	....	....	....	....	....	....	1981-82	1981-82
Tannahill, Don	Van.	2	111	30	33	63	25	....	....	....	....	....	....	1972-73	1973-74
Tanti, Tony	Chi., Van., Pit., Buf.	11	697	287	273	560	661	30	3	12	15	27	....	1981-82	1991-92
Tapper, Brad	Atl.	3	71	14	11	25	72	....	....	....	....	....	....	2000-01	2002-03
‡ Tardif, Jamie	Bos.	1	2	0	0	0	0	....	....	....	....	....	....	2012-13	2012-13
Tardif, Marc	Mtl., Que.	8	517	194	207	401	443	62	13	15	28	75	2	1969-70	1982-83
Tardif, Patrice	St.L., L.A.	2	65	7	11	18	78	....	....	....	....	....	....	1994-95	1995-96
Tarnstrom, Dick	NYI, Pit., Edm., CBJ	5	306	35	105	140	254	17	0	2	2	12	....	2001-02	2007-08
Tatarinov, Mikhail	Wsh., Que., Bos.	4	161	21	48	69	184	....	....	....	....	....	....	1990-91	1993-94
• Tatchell, Spence	NYR	1	1	0	0	0	0	....	....	....	....	....	....	1942-43	1942-43
‡ Taticek, Petr	Fla.	1	3	0	0	0	0	....	....	....	....	....	....	2005-06	2005-06
• Taylor, Billy	Tor., Det., Bos., NYR	7	323	87	180	267	120	33	6	18	24	13	1	1939-40	1947-48
• Taylor, Billy	NYR	1	2	0	0	0	0	....	....	....	....	....	....	1964-65	1964-65
• Taylor, Bob	Bos.	1	8	0	0	0	6	....	....	....	....	....	....	1929-30	1929-30
Taylor, Chris	NYI, Bos., Buf.	8	149	11	21	32	48	2	0	0	0	2	....	1994-95	2003-04
Taylor, Dave	L.A.	17	1111	431	638	1069	1589	92	26	33	59	145	....	1977-78	1993-94
• Taylor, Harry	Tor., Chi.	3	66	5	10	15	30	1	0	0	0	0	1	1946-47	1951-52
Taylor, Mark	Phi., Pit., Wsh.	5	209	42	68	110	73	6	0	0	0	0	....	1981-82	1985-86
• Taylor, Ralph	Chi., NYR	3	99	4	1	5	169	4	0	0	0	10	....	1927-28	1929-30
Taylor, Ted	NYR, Det., Min., Van.	6	166	23	35	58	181	....	....	....	....	....	....	1964-65	1971-72
Taylor, Tim	Det., Bos., NYR, T.B.	13	746	73	94	167	433	89	2	12	14	73	2	1993-94	2006-07
Teal, Jeff	Mtl.	1	6	0	1	1	0	....	....	....	....	....	....	1984-85	1984-85
• Teal, Skip	Bos.	1	1	0	0	0	0	....	....	....	....	....	....	1954-55	1954-55
Teal, Vic	NYI	1	1	0	0	0	0	....	....	....	....	....	....	1973-74	1973-74
Tebbutt, Greg	Que., Pit.	2	26	0	3	3	35	....	....	....	....	....	....	1979-80	1983-84
‡ Tenkrat, Petr	Ana., Nsh., Bos.	3	177	22	30	52	84	....	....	....	....	....	....	2000-01	2006-07
Tenute, Joey	Wsh.	1	1	0	0	0	0	....	....	....	....	....	....	2005-06	2005-06
Tepper, Stephen	Chi.	1	1	0	0	0	0	....	....	....	....	....	....	1992-93	1992-93
• Terbenche, Paul	Chi., Buf.	5	189	5	26	31	28	12	0	0	0	0	....	1967-68	1973-74
Terrion, Greg	L.A., Tor.	8	561	93	150	243	339	35	2	9	11	41	....	1980-81	1987-88
Terry, Bill	Min.	1	5	0	0	0	0	....	....	....	....	....	....	1987-88	1987-88
• Tertyshny, Dmitri	Phi.	1	62	2	8	10	30	1	0	0	0	0	....	1998-99	1998-99
Tessier, Orval	Mtl., Bos.	3	59	5	7	12	6	....	....	....	....	....	....	1954-55	1960-61
Tetarenko, Joey	Fla., Ott., Car.	4	73	4	1	5	176	....	....	....	....	....	....	2000-01	2003-04
‡ Teubert, Colten	Edm.	1	24	0	1	1	25	....	....	....	....	....	....	2011-12	2011-12
Tezikov, Alexei	Wsh., Van.	3	30	1	1	2	2	....	....	....	....	....	....	1998-99	2001-02
‡ Thang, Ryan	Nsh.	1	1	0	0	0	0	....	....	....	....	....	....	2011-12	2011-12
Theberge, Greg	Wsh.	5	153	15	63	78	73	4	0	1	1	0	....	1979-80	1983-84
Thelin, Mats	Bos.	3	163	8	19	27	107	5	0	0	0	6	....	1984-85	1986-87
Thelven, Michael	Bos.	5	207	20	80	100	217	34	4	10	14	34	....	1985-86	1989-90
Therien, Chris	Phi., Dal.	11	764	29	130	159	585	104	4	10	14	68	....	1994-95	2005-06
Therrien, Gaston	Que.	3	22	0	8	8	12	9	0	1	1	4	....	1980-81	1982-83
Thibaudeau, Gilles	Mtl., NYI, Tor.	5	119	25	37	62	40	8	3	3	6	2	....	1986-87	1990-91
• Thibeault, Lorrain	Det., Mtl.	2	5	0	2	2	2	....	....	....	....	....	....	1944-45	1945-46
Thiffault, Leo	Min.	1	....	....	....	....	....	5	0	0	0	0	....	1967-68	1967-68
‡ Thomas, Bill	Phx., Pit., Fla.	6	87	16	12	28	18	....	....	....	....	....	....	2005-06	2011-12
• Thomas, Cy	Chi., Tor.	1	14	2	2	4	12	....	....	....	....	....	....	1947-48	1947-48
Thomas, Reg	Que.	1	39	9	7	16	6	....	....	....	....	....	....	1979-80	1979-80
Thomas, Scott	Buf., L.A.	3	63	6	4	10	32	12	1	0	1	4	....	1992-93	2000-01
Thomas, Steve	Tor., Chi., NYI, N.J., Ana., Det.	20	1235	421	512	933	1306	174	54	53	107	187	....	1984-85	2003-04
Thomlinson, Dave	St.L., Bos., L.A.	5	42	1	3	4	50	9	3	1	4	4	....	1989-90	1994-95
Thompson, Brent	L.A., Wpg., Phx.	6	121	1	10	11	352	4	0	0	0	4	....	1991-92	1996-97
• Thompson, Cliff	Bos.	2	13	0	1	1	2	....	....	....	....	....	....	1941-42	1948-49
Thompson, Errol	Tor., Det., Pit.	10	599	208	185	393	184	34	7	5	12	11	....	1970-71	1980-81
• Thompson, Ken	Mtl.W.	1	1	0	0	0	0	....	....	....	....	....	....	1917-18	1917-18
• Thompson, Paul	NYR, Chi.	13	582	153	179	332	336	48	11	11	22	54	3	1926-27	1938-39
Thompson, Rocky	Cgy., Fla.	4	25	0	0	0	117	....	....	....	....	....	....	1997-98	2001-02
• Thoms, Bill	Tor., Chi., Bos.	13	548	135	206	341	154	44	6	10	16	6	....	1932-33	1944-45
• Thomson, Bill	Det.	2	9	2	2	4	0	2	0	0	0	0	....	1938-39	1943-44
Thomson, Floyd	St.L.	8	411	56	97	153	341	10	0	2	2	6	....	1971-72	1979-80
Thomson, Jim	Wsh., Hfd., N.J., L.A., Ott., Ana.	7	115	4	3	7	416	1	0	0	0	0	....	1986-87	1993-94
• Thomson, Jimmy	Tor., Chi.	13	787	19	215	234	920	63	2	13	15	135	4	1945-46	1957-58
• Thomson, Rhys	Mtl., Tor.	2	25	0	2	2	38	....	....	....	....	....	....	1939-40	1942-43
‡ Thoresen, Patrick	Edm., Phi.	2	106	6	18	24	66	14	0	2	2	4	....	2006-07	2007-08
Thornbury, Tom	Pit.	1	14	1	8	9	16	....	....	....	....	....	....	1983-84	1983-84
Thornton, Scott	Tor., Edm., Mtl., Dal., S.J., L.A.	17	941	144	141	285	1459	79	13	14	27	82	....	1990-91	2007-08
• Thorsteinson, Joe	NYA	1	4	0	0	0	0	....	....	....	....	....	....	1932-33	1932-33
‡ Thuresson, Andreas	Nsh.	2	25	1	2	3	6	....	....	....	....	....	....	2009-10	2010-11
• Thurier, Fred	NYA, Bro., NYR	3	80	25	27	52	18	....	....	....	....	....	....	1940-41	1944-45
Thurlby, Tom	Oak.	1	20	1	1	2	4	....	....	....	....	....	....	1967-68	1967-68
Thyer, Mario	Min.	1	5	0	0	0	0	1	0	0	0	2	....	1989-90	1989-90
Tibbetts, Billy	Pit., Phi., NYR	3	82	2	8	10	269	....	....	....	....	....	....	2000-01	2002-03
Tichy, Milan	Chi., NYI	3	23	0	5	5	40	....	....	....	....	....	....	1992-93	1995-96
Tidey, Alex	Buf., Edm.	3	9	0	0	0	8	2	0	0	0	0	....	1976-77	1979-80
Tikkanen, Esa	Edm., NYR, St.L., N.J., Van., Fla., Wsh.	15	877	244	386	630	1077	186	72	60	132	275	5	1984-85	1998-99
Tiley, Brad	Phx., Phi.	3	11	0	0	0	0	1	0	0	0	0	....	1997-98	2000-01
Tilley, Tom	St.L.	4	174	4	38	42	89	14	1	3	4	19	....	1988-89	1993-94
Timander, Mattias	Bos., CBJ, NYI, Phi.	8	419	13	57	70	165	23	3	5	8	8	....	1996-97	2003-04
• Timgren, Ray	Tor., Chi.	6	251	14	44	58	70	30	3	9	12	6	2	1948-49	1954-55
‡ Timonen, Jussi	Phi.	1	14	0	4	4	6	....	....	....	....	....	....	2006-07	2006-07
Tinordi, Mark	NYR, Min., Dal., Wsh.	12	663	52	148	200	1514	70	7	11	18	165	....	1987-88	1998-99
Tippett, Dave	Hfd., Wsh., Pit., Phi.	12	721	93	169	262	317	62	6	16	22	34	....	1983-84	1993-94
Titanic, Morris	Buf.	2	19	0	0	0	0	....	....	....	....	....	....	1974-75	1975-76
Titov, German	Cgy., Pit., Edm., Ana.	9	624	157	220	377	311	34	11	12	23	18	....	1993-94	2001-02
Tjarnqvist, Daniel	Atl., Min., Edm., Col.	6	352	18	72	90	130	....	....	....	....	....	....	2001-02	2008-09
Tjarnqvist, Mathias	Dal., Phx.	4	173	13	19	32	60	....	....	....	....	....	....	2003-04	2007-08
Tkachuk, Keith	Wpg., Phx., St.L., Atl.	18	1201	538	527	1065	2219	89	28	28	56	176	....	1991-92	2009-10
Tkaczuk, Daniel	Cgy.	1	19	4	7	11	14	....	....	....	....	....	....	2000-01	2000-01
Tkaczuk, Walt	NYR	14	945	227	451	678	556	93	19	32	51	119	....	1967-68	1980-81
Toal, Mike	Edm.	1	3	0	0	0	0	....	....	....	....	....	....	1979-80	1979-80
Tobler, Ryan	T.B.	1	4	0	0	0	5	....	....	....	....	....	....	2001-02	2001-02
Tocchet, Rick	Phi., Pit., L.A., Bos., Wsh., Phx.	18	1144	440	512	952	2972	145	52	60	112	471	1	1984-85	2001-02
Todd, Kevin	N.J., Edm., Chi., L.A., Ana.	9	383	70	133	203	225	12	3	2	5	16	....	1988-89	1997-98
‡ Tollefsen, Ole-Kristian	CBJ, Phi.	5	163	4	8	12	296	....	....	....	....	....	....	2005-06	2009-10
‡ Tolpeko, Denis	Phi.	1	26	1	5	6	24	....	....	....	....	....	....	2007-08	2007-08
Tomalty, Glenn	Wpg.	1	1	0	0	0	0	....	....	....	....	....	....	1979-80	1979-80
Tomlak, Mike	Hfd.	4	141	15	22	37	103	10	0	1	1	4	....	1989-90	1993-94
Tomlinson, Dave	Tor., Wpg., Fla.	4	42	1	3	4	28	....	....	....	....	....	....	1991-92	1994-95
Tomlinson, Kirk	Min.	1	1	0	0	0	0	....	....	....	....	....	....	1987-88	1987-88

Name	NHL Teams	NHL Seasons	Regular Schedule GP	G	A	TP	PIM	Playoffs GP	G	A	TP	PIM	NHL Cup Wins	First NHL Season	Last NHL Season
Toms, Jeff	T.B., Wsh., NYI, NYR, Pit., Fla.	8	236	22	33	55	59	1	0	0	0	0	....	1995-96	2002-03
• Tomson, Jack	NYA	3	15	1	1	2	0	2	0	0	0	0	....	1938-39	1940-41
Tonelli, John	NYI, Cgy., L.A., Chi., Que.	14	1028	325	511	836	911	172	40	75	115	200	4	1978-79	1991-92
Tookey, Tim	Wsh., Que., Pit., Phi., L.A.	7	106	22	36	58	71	10	1	3	4	2	....	1980-81	1988-89
Toomey, Sean	Min.	1	1	0	0	0	0	....	....	....	....	....	....	1986-87	1986-87
Toporowski, Shayne	Tor.	1	3	0	0	0	7	....	....	....	....	....	....	1996-97	1996-97
• Toppazzini, Jerry	Bos., Chi., Det.	12	783	163	244	407	436	40	13	9	22	13	....	1952-53	1963-64
• Toppazzini, Zellio	Bos., NYR, Chi.	5	123	21	22	43	49	2	0	0	0	0	....	1948-49	1956-57
Torgaev, Pavel	Cgy., T.B.	2	55	6	14	20	20	1	0	0	0	0	....	1995-96	1999-00
Torkki, Jari	Chi.	1	4	1	0	1	0	....	....	....	....	....	....	1988-89	1988-89
Tormanen, Antti	Ott.	1	50	7	8	15	28	....	....	....	....	....	....	1995-96	1995-96
• Touhey, Bill	Mtl.M., Ott., Bos.	7	280	65	40	105	107	2	1	0	1	0	....	1927-28	1933-34
• Toupin, Jacques	Chi.	1	8	1	2	3	0	4	0	0	0	0	....	1943-44	1943-44
• Townsend, Art	Chi.	1	5	0	0	0	0	....	....	....	....	....	....	1926-27	1926-27
Townshend, Graeme	Bos., NYI, Ott.	5	45	3	7	10	28	....	....	....	....	....	....	1989-90	1993-94
Trader, Larry	Det., St.L., Mtl.	4	91	5	13	18	74	3	0	0	0	0	....	1982-83	1987-88
• Trainor, Wes	NYR	1	17	1	2	3	6	....	....	....	....	....	....	1948-49	1948-49
• Trapp, Bob	Chi., Mtl.	3	83	4	4	8	129	2	0	0	0	4	....	1926-27	1932-33
Trapp, Doug	Buf.	1	2	0	0	0	0	....	....	....	....	....	....	1986-87	1986-87
• Traub, Percy	Chi., Det.	3	130	3	3	6	217	4	0	0	0	6	....	1926-27	1928-29
Traverse, Patrick	Ott., Ana., Bos., Mtl., Dal.	7	279	14	51	65	113	6	0	0	0	2	....	1995-96	2005-06
Trebil, Dan	Ana., Pit., St.L.	5	85	4	4	8	32	10	0	1	1	8	....	1996-97	2000-01
Tredway, Brock	L.A.	1	....	....	....	....	....	1	0	0	0	0	....	1981-82	1981-82
Tremblay, Brent	Wsh.	2	10	1	0	1	6	....	....	....	....	....	....	1978-79	1979-80
• Tremblay, Gilles	Mtl.	9	509	168	162	330	161	48	9	14	23	4	4	1960-61	1968-69
• Tremblay, J.C.	Mtl.	13	794	57	306	363	204	108	14	51	65	58	5	1959-60	1971-72
• Tremblay, Marcel	Mtl.	1	10	0	2	2	0	....	....	....	....	....	....	1938-39	1938-39
Tremblay, Mario	Mtl.	12	852	258	326	584	1043	101	20	29	49	187	5	1974-75	1985-86
• Tremblay, Nils	Mtl.	2	3	0	1	1	0	2	0	0	0	0	....	1944-45	1945-46
Tremblay, Yannick	Tor., Atl., Van.	9	390	38	87	125	178	....	....	....	....	....	....	1996-97	2006-07
Trepanier, Pascal	Col., Ana., Nsh.	6	229	12	22	34	252	2	0	0	0	0	....	1997-98	2002-03
Trimper, Tim	Chi., Wpg., Min.	6	190	30	36	66	153	2	0	0	0	2	....	1979-80	1984-85
‡ Tripp, John	NYR, L.A.	2	43	2	7	9	35	....	....	....	....	....	....	2002-03	2003-04
Trnka, Pavel	Ana., Fla.	7	411	14	63	77	323	4	0	1	1	2	....	1997-98	2003-04
Trotter, Brock	Mtl.	1	2	0	0	0	0	....	....	....	....	....	....	2009-10	2009-10
Trottier, Bryan	NYI, Pit.	18	1279	524	901	1425	912	221	71	113	184	277	6	1975-76	1993-94
• Trottier, Dave	Mtl.M., Det.	11	446	121	113	234	517	31	4	3	7	39	1	1928-29	1938-39
• Trottier, Guy	NYR, Tor.	3	115	28	17	45	37	9	1	0	1	16	....	1968-69	1971-72
Trottier, Rocky	N.J.	2	38	6	4	10	2	....	....	....	....	....	....	1983-84	1984-85
Trudel, Jean-Guy	Phx., Min.	3	5	0	0	0	4	....	....	....	....	....	....	1999-00	2002-03
• Trudel, Lou	Chi., Mtl.	8	306	49	69	118	122	24	1	3	4	4	2	1933-34	1940-41
• Trudell, Rene	NYR	3	129	24	28	52	72	5	0	0	0	2	....	1945-46	1947-48
Tselios, Nikos	Car.	1	2	0	0	0	6	....	....	....	....	....	....	2001-02	2001-02
Tsulygin, Nikolai	Ana.	1	22	0	1	1	8	....	....	....	....	....	....	1996-97	1996-97
• Tsygurov, Denis	Buf., L.A.	3	51	1	5	6	45	....	....	....	....	....	....	1993-94	1995-96
Tsyplakov, Vladimir	L.A., Buf.	6	331	69	101	170	90	18	1	2	3	16	....	1995-96	2000-01
Tucker, Darcy	Mtl., T.B., Tor., Col.	14	947	215	261	476	1410	68	10	11	21	81	....	1995-96	2009-10
Tucker, John	Buf., Wsh., NYI, T.B.	12	656	177	259	436	285	31	10	18	28	24	....	1983-84	1995-96
• Tudin, Connie	Mtl.	1	4	0	1	1	4	....	....	....	....	....	....	1941-42	1941-42
Tudor, Rob	Van., St.L.	3	28	4	4	8	19	3	0	0	0	0	....	1978-79	1982-83
Tuer, Allan	L.A., Min., Hfd.	4	57	1	1	2	208	....	....	....	....	....	....	1985-86	1989-90
‡ Tukonen, Lauri	L.A.	2	5	0	0	0	0	....	....	....	....	....	....	2006-07	2007-08
Tuomainen, Marko	Edm., L.A., NYI	4	79	9	9	18	84	1	0	0	0	0	....	1994-95	2001-02
Turcotte, Alfie	Mtl., Wpg., Wsh.	7	112	17	29	46	49	5	0	0	0	0	....	1983-84	1990-91
Turcotte, Darren	NYR, Hfd., Wpg., S.J., St.L., Nsh.	12	635	195	216	411	301	35	6	8	14	12	....	1988-89	1999-00
Turgeon, Pierre	Buf., NYI, Mtl., St.L., Dal., Col.	19	1294	515	812	1327	452	109	35	62	97	36	....	1987-88	2006-07
Turgeon, Sylvain	Hfd., N.J., Mtl., Ott.	12	669	269	226	495	691	36	4	7	11	22	....	1983-84	1994-95
Turlick, Gord	Bos.	1	2	0	0	0	2	....	....	....	....	....	....	1959-60	1959-60
Turnbull, Ian	Tor., L.A., Pit.	10	628	123	317	440	736	55	13	32	45	94	....	1973-74	1982-83
Turnbull, Perry	St.L., Mtl., Wpg.	9	608	188	163	351	1245	34	6	7	13	86	....	1979-80	1987-88
Turnbull, Randy	Cgy.	1	1	0	0	0	2	....	....	....	....	....	....	1981-82	1981-82
‡ Turnbull, Travis	Buf.	1	3	1	0	1	5	....	....	....	....	....	....	2011-12	2011-12
• Turner, Bob	Mtl., Chi.	8	478	19	51	70	307	68	1	4	5	44	5	1955-56	1962-63
Turner, Brad	NYI	1	3	0	0	0	0	....	....	....	....	....	....	1991-92	1991-92
Turner, Dean	NYR, Col., L.A.	4	35	1	0	1	59	....	....	....	....	....	....	1978-79	1982-83
• Tustin, Norm	NYR	1	18	2	4	6	0	....	....	....	....	....	....	1941-42	1941-42
• Tuten, Aud	Chi.	2	39	4	8	12	48	....	....	....	....	....	....	1941-42	1942-43
Tutt, Brian	Wsh.	1	7	1	0	1	2	....	....	....	....	....	....	1989-90	1989-90
Tuttle, Steve	St.L.	3	144	28	28	56	12	17	1	6	7	2	....	1988-89	1990-91
Tuzzolino, Tony	Ana., NYR, Bos.	3	9	0	0	0	7	....	....	....	....	....	....	1997-98	2001-02
Tverdovsky, Oleg	Ana., Wpg., Phx., N.J., Car., L.A.	11	713	77	240	317	291	45	0	14	14	6	2	1994-95	2006-07
Tvrdon, Roman	Wsh.	1	9	0	1	1	2	....	....	....	....	....	....	2003-04	2003-04
Twist, Tony	St.L., Que.	10	445	10	18	28	1121	18	1	1	2	22	....	1989-90	1998-99

U V

Name	NHL Teams	NHL Seasons	Regular Schedule GP	G	A	TP	PIM	Playoffs GP	G	A	TP	PIM	NHL Cup Wins	First NHL Season	Last NHL Season
Ubriaco, Gene	Pit., Oak., Chi.	3	177	39	35	74	50	11	2	0	2	4	....	1967-68	1969-70
Ulanov, Igor	Wpg., Wsh., Chi., T.B., Mtl., Edm., NYR, Fla.	14	739	27	135	162	1151	39	1	4	5	84	....	1991-92	2005-06
Ullman, Norm	Det., Tor.	20	1410	490	739	1229	712	106	30	53	83	67	....	1955-56	1974-75
‡ Ullstrom, David	NYI	2	49	6	7	13	12	3	0	1	1	0	....	2011-12	2012-13
Ulmer, Jeff	NYR	1	21	3	0	3	8	....	....	....	....	....	....	2000-01	2000-01
Ulmer, Layne	NYR	1	1	0	0	0	0	....	....	....	....	....	....	2003-04	2003-04
Unger, Garry	Tor., Det., St.L., Atl., L.A., Edm.	16	1105	413	391	804	1075	52	12	18	30	105	....	1967-68	1982-83
Ustorf, Stefan	Wsh.	2	54	7	10	17	16	5	0	0	0	0	....	1995-96	1996-97
‡ Vaananen, Ossi	Phx., Col., Phi., Van.	7	479	13	55	68	482	20	0	1	1	26	....	2000-01	2008-09
Vachon, Nick	NYI	1	1	0	0	0	0	....	....	....	....	....	....	1996-97	1996-97
• Vadnais, Carol	Mtl., Oak., Cal., Bos., NYR, N.J.	17	1087	169	418	587	1813	106	10	40	50	185	2	1966-67	1982-83
‡ Vaic, Lubomir	Van.	2	9	1	1	2	2	....	....	....	....	....	....	1997-98	1999-00
Vail, Eric	Atl., Cgy., Det.	9	591	216	260	476	281	20	5	6	11	6	....	1973-74	1981-82
• Vail, Sparky	NYR	2	50	4	1	5	18	10	0	0	0	2	....	1928-29	1929-30
Vaive, Rick	Van., Tor., Chi., Buf.	13	876	441	347	788	1445	54	27	16	43	111	....	1979-80	1991-92
‡ Valabik, Boris	Atl.	3	80	0	7	7	210	....	....	....	....	....	....	2007-08	2009-10
Valentine, Chris	Wsh.	3	105	43	52	95	127	2	0	0	0	4	....	1981-82	1983-84
Valicevic, Rob	Nsh., L.A., Ana., Dal.	6	193	28	20	48	61	....	....	....	....	....	....	1998-99	2003-04
Valiquette, Jack	Tor., Col.	7	350	84	134	218	79	23	3	6	9	4	....	1974-75	1980-81
Valk, Garry	Van., Ana., Pit., Tor., Chi.	13	777	100	156	256	747	61	6	7	13	79	....	1990-91	2002-03
Vallis, Lindsay	Mtl.	1	1	0	0	0	0	....	....	....	....	....	....	1993-94	1993-94
Van Allen, Shaun	Edm., Ana., Ott., Dal., Mtl.	13	794	84	185	269	481	61	1	7	8	45	....	1990-91	2003-04
Van Boxmeer, John	Mtl., Col., Buf., Que.	11	588	84	274	358	465	38	5	15	20	37	....	1973-74	1983-84
Van Dorp, Wayne	Edm., Pit., Chi., Que.	6	125	12	12	24	565	27	0	1	1	42	....	1986-87	1991-92
Van Drunen, David	Ott.	1	1	0	0	0	0	....	....	....	....	....	....	1999-00	1999-00
Van Impe, Darren	Ana., Bos., NYR, Fla., NYI, CBJ	9	411	25	90	115	397	33	3	9	12	28	....	1994-95	2002-03
Van Impe, Ed	Chi., Phi., Pit.	11	700	27	126	153	1025	66	1	12	13	131	2	1966-67	1976-77
Van Ryn, Mike	St.L., Fla., Tor.	9	353	30	99	129	260	9	0	0	0	0	....	2000-01	2009-10
VandenBussche, Ryan	NYR, Chi., Pit.	9	310	10	10	20	702	1	0	0	0	0	....	1996-97	2005-06
‡ Vandermeer, Jim	Phi., Chi., Cgy., Phx., Edm., S.J.	9	461	25	80	105	664	21	0	2	2	17	....	2002-03	2011-12
‡ Vandermeer, Peter	Phx.	1	2	0	0	0	0	....	....	....	....	....	....	2007-08	2007-08
‡ Varada, Vaclav	Buf., Ott.	10	493	58	125	183	410	87	11	19	30	82	....	1995-96	2005-06
Varis, Petri	Chi.	1	1	0	0	0	0	....	....	....	....	....	....	1997-98	1997-98
Varlamov, Sergei	Cgy., St.L.	4	63	8	7	15	26	1	0	0	0	2	....	1997-98	2002-03
Varvio, Jarkko	Dal.	2	13	3	4	7	4	....	....	....	....	....	....	1993-94	1994-95
• Vasicek, Josef	Car., Nsh., NYI	7	460	77	106	183	311	37	5	2	7	14	1	2000-01	2007-08
Vasilevski, Alexander	St.L.	2	4	0	0	0	2	....	....	....	....	....	....	1995-96	1996-97
Vasiliev, Alexei	NYR	1	1	0	0	0	2	....	....	....	....	....	....	1999-00	1999-00
‡ Vasiljevs, Herbert	Fla., Atl., Van.	4	51	8	7	15	22	....	....	....	....	....	....	1998-99	2001-02
Vasilyev, Andrei	NYI, Phx.	4	16	2	5	7	6	....	....	....	....	....	....	1994-95	1998-99
Vaske, Dennis	NYI, Bos.	9	235	5	41	46	253	22	0	7	7	16	....	1990-91	1998-99
• Vasko, Moose	Chi., Min.	13	786	34	166	200	719	78	2	7	9	73	1	1956-57	1969-70
Vasko, Rick	Det.	3	31	3	7	10	29	....	....	....	....	....	....	1977-78	1980-81
• Vasyunov, Alexander	N.J.	1	18	1	4	5	0	....	....	....	....	....	....	2010-11	2010-11
‡ Vauclair, Julien	Ott.	1	1	0	0	0	2	....	....	....	....	....	....	2003-04	2003-04
Vautour, Yvon	NYI, Col., N.J., Que.	6	204	26	33	59	401	....	....	....	....	....	....	1979-80	1984-85
Vaydik, Greg	Chi.	1	5	0	0	0	0	....	....	....	....	....	....	1976-77	1976-77
Veitch, Darren	Wsh., Det., Tor.	10	511	48	209	257	296	33	4	11	15	33	....	1980-81	1990-91
Velischek, Randy	Min., N.J., Que.	10	509	21	76	97	401	44	2	5	7	32	....	1982-83	1991-92

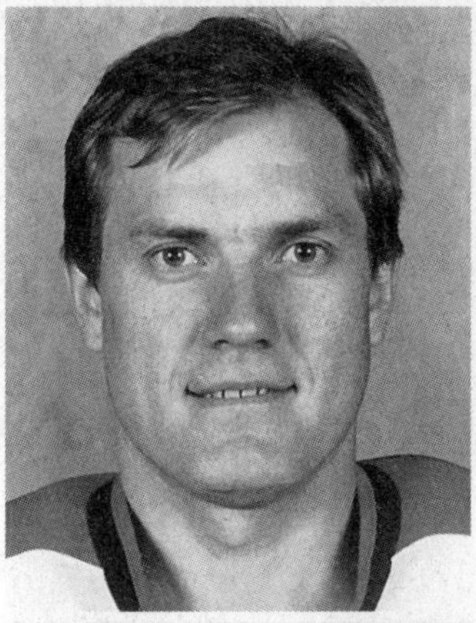

Pavel Torgaev

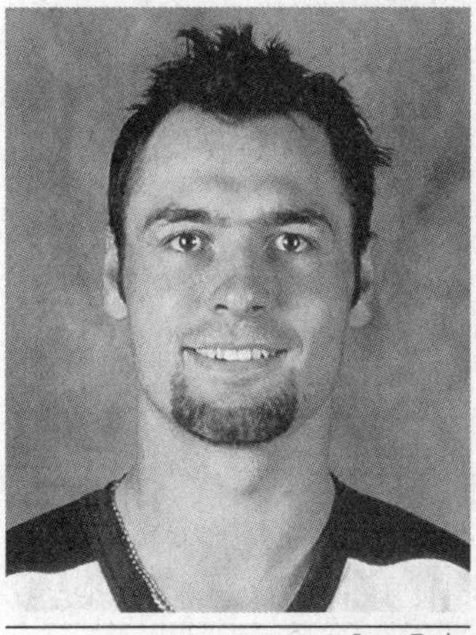

Darcy Tucker

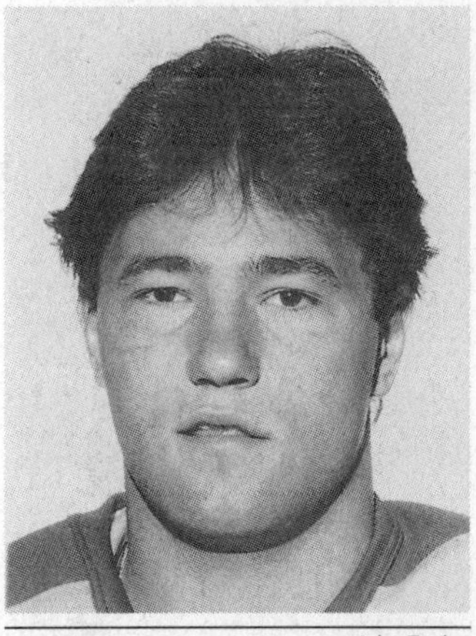

John Tucker

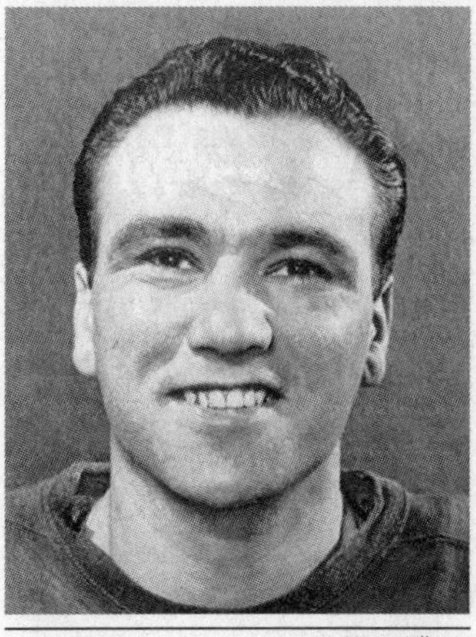

Norm Ullman

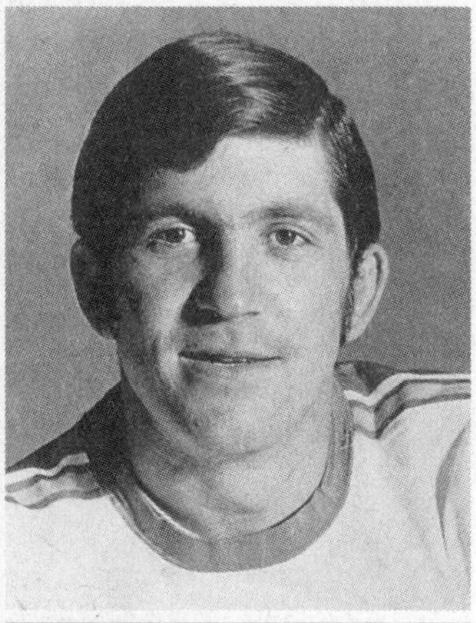

Gary Veneruzzo

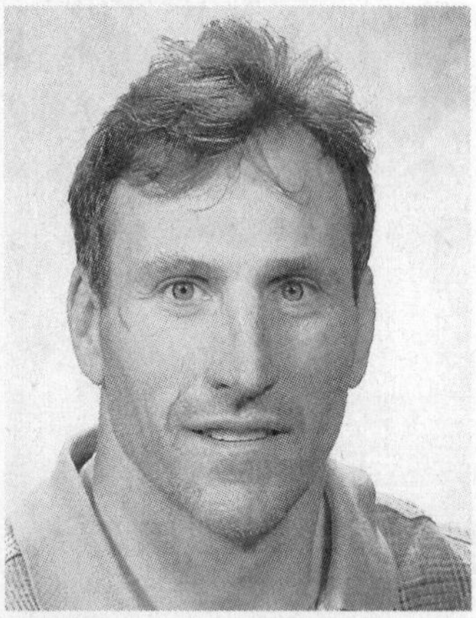

Pat Verbeek

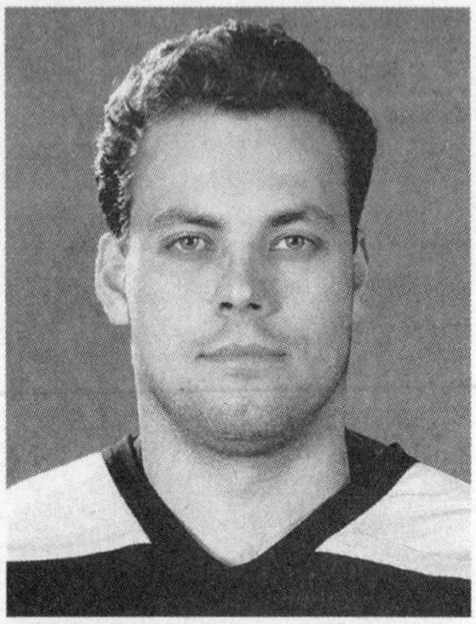

Jan Vopat

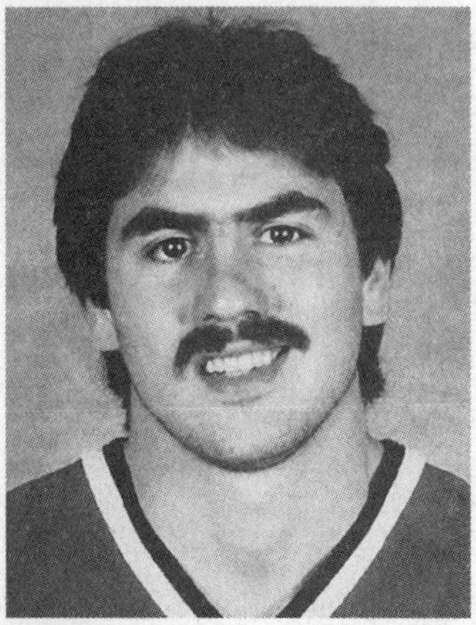

Bill Watson

Name	NHL Teams	NHL Seasons	Regular Schedule GP	G	A	TP	PIM	Playoffs GP	G	A	TP	PIM	NHL Cup Wins	First NHL Season	Last NHL Season
Vellucci, Mike	Hfd.	1	2	0	0	0	11	....	....	....	....	....	....	1987-88	1987-88
Venasky, Vic	L.A.	7	430	61	101	162	66	21	1	5	6	12	....	1972-73	1978-79
Veneruzzo, Gary	St.L.	2	7	1	1	2	0	9	0	2	2	2	....	1967-68	1971-72
Verbeek, Pat	N.J., Hfd., NYR, Dal., Det.	20	1424	522	541	1063	2905	117	26	36	62	225	1	1982-83	2001-02
Vermette, Mark	Que.	4	67	5	13	18	33	....	....	....	....	....	....	1988-89	1991-92
‡ Vernace, Mike	Col., T.B.	2	22	0	1	1	10	....	....	....	....	....	....	2008-09	2010-11
Vernarsky, Kris	Bos.	2	17	1	0	1	2	....	....	....	....	....	....	2002-03	2003-04
Verot, Darcy	Wsh.	1	37	0	2	2	135	....	....	....	....	....	....	2003-04	2003-04
Verret, Claude	Buf.	2	14	2	5	7	2	....	....	....	....	....	....	1983-84	1984-85
Verstraete, Leigh	Tor.	3	8	0	1	1	14	....	....	....	....	....	....	1982-83	1987-88
Ververgaert, Dennis	Van., Phi., Wsh.	8	583	176	216	392	247	8	1	2	3	6	....	1973-74	1980-81
‡ Vesce, Ryan	S.J.	2	19	3	2	5	4	....	....	....	....	....	....	2008-09	2009-10
Vesey, Jim	St.L., Bos.	3	15	1	2	3	7	....	....	....	....	....	....	1988-89	1991-92
Veysey, Sid	Van.	1	1	0	0	0	0	....	....	....	....	....	....	1977-78	1977-78
Vial, Dennis	NYR, Det., Ott.	8	242	4	15	19	794	....	....	....	....	....	....	1990-91	1997-98
Vickers, Steve	NYR	10	698	246	340	586	330	68	24	25	49	58	....	1972-73	1981-82
Vigier, J.P.	Atl.	6	213	23	23	46	97	....	....	....	....	....	....	2000-01	2006-07
Vigneault, Alain	St.L.	2	42	2	5	7	82	4	0	1	1	26	....	1981-82	1982-83
Viitakoski, Vesa	Cgy.	3	23	2	4	6	8	....	....	....	....	....	....	1993-94	1995-96
Vilgrain, Claude	Van., N.J., Phi.	5	89	21	32	53	78	11	1	1	2	17	....	1987-88	1993-94
Vincelette, Dan	Chi., Que.	6	193	20	22	42	351	12	0	0	0	4	....	1986-87	1991-92
Vipond, Pete	Cal.	1	3	0	0	0	0	....	....	....	....	....	....	1972-73	1972-73
Virta, Hannu	Buf.	5	245	25	101	126	66	17	1	3	4	6	....	1981-82	1985-86
Virta, Tony	Min.	1	8	2	3	5	0	....	....	....	....	....	....	2001-02	2001-02
Virtue, Terry	Bos., NYR	2	5	0	0	0	0	....	....	....	....	....	....	1998-99	1999-00
Visheau, Mark	Wpg., L.A.	2	29	1	3	4	107	....	....	....	....	....	....	1993-94	1998-99
Vishnevski, Vitaly	Ana., Atl., Nsh., N.J.	8	552	16	52	68	494	40	0	5	5	18	....	1999-00	2007-08
Vishnevskiy, Ivan	Dal.	2	5	0	2	2	2	....	....	....	....	....	....	2008-09	2009-10
Vitolinsh, Harijs	Wpg.	1	8	0	0	0	4	....	....	....	....	....	....	1993-94	1993-94
Viveiros, Emanuel	Min.	3	29	1	11	12	6	....	....	....	....	....	....	1985-86	1987-88
‡ Vlasak, Tomas	L.A.	1	10	1	3	4	2	....	....	....	....	....	....	2000-01	2000-01
• Vokes, Ed	Chi.	1	5	0	0	0	0	....	....	....	....	....	....	1930-31	1930-31
Volcan, Mickey	Hfd., Cgy.	4	162	8	33	41	146	....	....	....	....	....	....	1980-81	1983-84
Volchkov, Alexandre	Wsh.	1	3	0	0	0	0	....	....	....	....	....	....	1999-00	1999-00
Volek, David	NYI	6	396	95	154	249	201	15	5	5	10	2	....	1988-89	1993-94
Volmar, Doug	Det., L.A.	4	62	13	8	21	26	2	1	0	1	0	....	1969-70	1972-73
‡ Von Arx, Reto	Chi.	1	19	3	1	4	4	....	....	....	....	....	....	2000-01	2000-01
Von Stefenelli, Phil	Bos., Ott.	2	33	0	5	5	23	....	....	....	....	....	....	1995-96	1996-97
Vopat, Jan	L.A., Nsh.	5	126	11	20	31	70	2	0	1	1	2	....	1995-96	1999-00
Vopat, Roman	St.L., L.A., Chi., Phi.	4	133	6	14	20	253	....	....	....	....	....	....	1995-96	1998-99
Vorobiev, Pavel	Chi.	2	57	10	15	25	38	....	....	....	....	....	....	2003-04	2005-06
Vorobiev, Vladimir	NYR, Edm.	3	33	9	7	16	14	1	0	0	0	0	....	1996-97	1998-99
Voros, Aaron	Min., NYR, Ana.	4	162	18	19	37	395	9	1	0	1	30	....	2007-08	2010-11
• Voss, Carl	Tor., NYR, Det., Ott., St.L., NYA, Mtl.M., Chi.	8	261	34	70	104	50	24	5	3	8	0	1	1926-27	1937-38
‡ Vrana, Petr	N.J.	1	16	1	0	1	2	....	....	....	....	....	....	2008-09	2008-09
Vujtek, Vladimir	Mtl., Edm., T.B., Atl., Pit.	6	110	7	30	37	38	....	....	....	....	....	....	1991-92	2002-03
Vukota, Mick	NYI, T.B., Mtl.	11	574	17	29	46	2071	23	0	0	0	73	....	1987-88	1997-98
• Vyazmikin, Igor	Edm.	1	4	1	0	1	0	....	....	....	....	....	....	1990-91	1990-91
Vyborny, David	CBJ	7	543	113	204	317	228	....	....	....	....	....	....	2000-01	2007-08
Vyshedkevich, Sergei	Atl.	2	30	2	5	7	16	....	....	....	....	....	....	1999-00	2000-01

W

Name	NHL Teams	NHL Seasons	Regular Schedule GP	G	A	TP	PIM	Playoffs GP	G	A	TP	PIM	NHL Cup Wins	First NHL Season	Last NHL Season
Waddell, Don	L.A.	1	1	0	0	0	0	....	....	....	....	....	....	1980-81	1980-81
Wagner, Steve	St.L.	2	46	4	8	12	26	....	....	....	....	....	....	2007-08	2008-09
• Waite, Frank	NYR	1	17	1	3	4	4	....	....	....	....	....	....	1930-31	1930-31
Walker, Gord	NYR, L.A.	4	31	3	4	7	23	....	....	....	....	....	....	1986-87	1989-90
Walker, Howard	Wsh., Cgy.	3	83	2	13	15	133	....	....	....	....	....	....	1980-81	1982-83
• Walker, Jack	Det.	2	80	5	8	13	18	....	....	....	....	....	....	1926-27	1927-28
Walker, Kurt	Tor.	3	71	4	5	9	142	16	0	0	0	34	....	1975-76	1977-78
Walker, Matt	St.L., Chi., T.B., Phi.	9	314	4	26	30	464	21	0	2	2	14	....	2002-03	2011-12
Walker, Russ	L.A.	2	17	1	0	1	41	....	....	....	....	....	....	1976-77	1977-78
Walker, Scott	Van., Nsh., Car., Wsh.	15	829	151	246	397	1162	30	1	7	8	31	....	1994-95	2009-10
Wall, Bob	Det., L.A., St.L.	8	322	30	55	85	155	22	0	3	3	2	....	1964-65	1971-72
‡ Wallace, Tim	Pit., NYI, T.B., Car.	5	101	4	9	13	45	....	....	....	....	....	....	2008-09	2012-13
Wallin, Jesse	Det.	4	49	0	2	2	34	....	....	....	....	....	....	1999-00	2002-03
Wallin, Niclas	Car., S.J.	10	614	21	58	79	460	93	4	8	12	44	1	2000-01	2010-11
Wallin, Peter	NYR	2	52	3	14	17	14	14	2	6	8	6	....	1980-81	1981-82
‡ Wallin, Rickard	Min., Tor.	3	79	8	11	19	34	....	....	....	....	....	....	2002-03	2009-10
‡ Walser, Derrick	CBJ	4	91	8	21	29	56	....	....	....	....	....	....	2001-02	2006-07
Walsh, Jim	Buf.	1	4	0	1	1	4	....	....	....	....	....	....	1981-82	1981-82
Walsh, Mike	NYI	2	14	2	0	2	4	....	....	....	....	....	....	1987-88	1988-89
‡ Walter, Ben	Bos., NYI, N.J.	5	24	1	0	1	6	....	....	....	....	....	....	2005-06	2009-10
Walter, Ryan	Wsh., Mtl., Van.	15	1003	264	382	646	946	113	16	35	51	62	1	1978-79	1992-93
• Walton, Bobby	Mtl.	1	4	0	0	0	0	....	....	....	....	....	....	1943-44	1943-44
Walton, Mike	Tor., Bos., Van., St.L., Chi.	12	588	201	247	448	357	47	14	10	24	45	2	1965-66	1978-79
Walz, Wes	Bos., Phi., Cgy., Det., Min.	13	607	109	151	260	343	32	10	7	17	20	....	1989-90	2007-08
‡ Wandell, Tom	Dal.	5	229	20	23	43	52	....	....	....	....	....	....	2008-09	2012-13
Wanvig, Kyle	Min., T.B.	5	75	6	9	15	94	....	....	....	....	....	....	2002-03	2007-08
Wappel, Gord	Atl., Cgy.	3	20	1	1	2	10	2	0	0	0	4	....	1979-80	1981-82
Ward, Aaron	Det., Car., NYR, Bos., Ana.	15	839	44	107	151	736	95	4	6	10	73	3	1993-94	2009-10
Ward, Dixon	Van., L.A., Tor., Buf., Bos., NYR	10	537	95	129	224	431	62	14	20	34	46	....	1992-93	2002-03
• Ward, Don	Chi., Bos.	2	34	0	1	1	16	....	....	....	....	....	....	1957-58	1959-60
Ward, Ed	Que., Cgy., Atl., Ana., N.J.	8	278	23	26	49	354	....	....	....	....	....	....	1993-94	2000-01
‡ Ward, Jason	Mtl., NYR, L.A., T.B.	8	336	36	45	81	171	12	0	3	3	10	....	1999-00	2008-09
• Ward, Jimmy	Mtl.M., Mtl.	12	527	147	127	274	455	36	4	4	8	26	1	1927-28	1938-39
Ward, Joe	Col.	1	4	0	0	0	2	....	....	....	....	....	....	1980-81	1980-81
Ward, Lance	Fla., Ana.	4	209	4	12	16	391	....	....	....	....	....	....	2000-01	2003-04
Ward, Ron	Tor., Van.	2	89	2	5	7	6	....	....	....	....	....	....	1969-70	1971-72
Ware, Jeff	Tor., Fla.	3	21	0	1	1	12	....	....	....	....	....	....	1996-97	1998-99
Ware, Michael	Edm.	2	5	0	1	1	15	....	....	....	....	....	....	1988-89	1989-90
• Wares, Eddie	NYR, Det., Chi.	9	321	60	102	162	161	45	5	7	12	34	1	1936-37	1946-47
Warner, Bob	Tor.	2	10	1	1	2	4	4	0	0	0	0	....	1975-76	1976-77
Warner, Jim	Hfd.	1	32	0	3	3	10	....	....	....	....	....	....	1979-80	1979-80
Warrener, Rhett	Fla., Buf., Cgy.	12	714	24	82	106	899	101	1	7	8	68	....	1995-96	2007-08
Warriner, Todd	Tor., T.B., Phx., Van., Phi., Nsh.	9	453	65	89	154	249	21	2	1	3	6	....	1994-95	2002-03
• Warwick, Billy	NYR	2	14	3	3	6	16	....	....	....	....	....	....	1942-43	1943-44
• Warwick, Grant	NYR, Bos., Mtl.	9	395	147	142	289	220	16	2	4	6	6	....	1941-42	1949-50
Washburn, Steve	Fla., Van., Phi.	6	93	14	15	29	42	1	0	1	1	0	....	1995-96	2000-01
• Wasnie, Nick	Chi., Mtl., NYA, Ott., St.L.	7	248	57	34	91	176	20	6	3	9	20	2	1927-28	1934-35
‡ Watkins, Matt	Phx.	1	1	0	0	0	0	....	....	....	....	....	....	2011-12	2011-12
Watson, Bill	Chi.	4	115	23	36	59	12	6	0	2	2	0	....	1985-86	1988-89
Watson, Bryan	Mtl., Det., Oak., Pit., St.L., Wsh.	16	878	17	135	152	2212	32	2	0	2	70	1	1963-64	1978-79
Watson, Dave	Col.	2	18	0	1	1	10	....	....	....	....	....	....	1979-80	1980-81
• Watson, Harry	Bro., Det., Tor., Chi.	14	809	236	207	443	150	62	16	9	25	27	5	1941-42	1956-57
Watson, Jim	Det., Buf.	8	221	4	19	23	345	....	....	....	....	....	....	1963-64	1971-72
Watson, Jimmy	Phi.	10	613	38	148	186	492	101	5	34	39	89	2	1972-73	1981-82
Watson, Joe	Bos., Phi., Col.	14	835	38	178	216	447	84	3	12	15	82	2	1964-65	1978-79
• Watson, Phil	NYR, Mtl.	13	590	144	265	409	532	54	10	25	35	67	2	1935-36	1947-48
Watt, Mike	Edm., NYI, Nsh., Car.	5	157	15	26	41	41	....	....	....	....	....	....	1997-98	2002-03
Watters, Tim	Wpg., L.A.	14	741	26	151	177	1289	82	1	5	6	115	....	1981-82	1994-95
Watts, Brian	Det.	1	4	0	0	0	0	....	....	....	....	....	....	1975-76	1975-76
Webb, Steve	NYI, Pit.	8	321	5	13	18	532	14	0	0	0	28	....	1996-97	2003-04
• Webster, Aubrey	Phi., Mtl.M.	2	5	0	0	0	0	....	....	....	....	....	....	1930-31	1934-35
• Webster, Don	Tor.	1	27	7	6	13	28	5	0	0	0	12	....	1943-44	1943-44
Webster, John	NYR	1	14	0	0	0	4	....	....	....	....	....	....	1949-50	1949-50
Webster, Tom	Bos., Det., Cal.	5	102	33	42	75	61	1	0	0	0	0	....	1968-69	1979-80
Weight, Doug	NYR, Edm., St.L., Car., Ana., NYI	20	1238	278	755	1033	970	97	23	49	72	94	1	1990-91	2010-11
• Weiland, Cooney	Bos., Ott., Det.	11	509	173	160	333	147	45	12	10	22	12	2	1928-29	1938-39
Weinhandl, Mattias	NYI, Min.	4	182	19	37	56	70	5	0	0	0	2	....	2002-03	2006-07
Weinrich, Eric	N.J., Hfd., Chi., Mtl., Bos., Phi., St.L., Van.	17	1157	70	318	388	825	81	6	23	29	67	....	1988-89	2005-06
Weir, Stan	Cal., Tor., Edm., Col., Det.	10	642	139	207	346	183	37	6	5	11	4	....	1972-73	1982-83
Weir, Wally	Que., Hfd., Pit.	6	320	21	45	66	625	23	0	1	1	96	....	1979-80	1984-85
‡ Welch, Noah	Pit., Fla., T.B., Atl.	5	75	4	5	9	58	....	....	....	....	....	....	2005-06	2010-11

Name	NHL Teams	NHL Seasons	Regular Schedule GP	G	A	TP	PIM	Playoffs GP	G	A	TP	PIM	NHL Cup Wins	First NHL Season	Last NHL Season
‡ Weller, Craig	Phx., Min.	2	95	4	10	14	127	....	....	....	....	....	....	2007-08	2008-09
• Wellington, Alex	Que.	1	1	0	0	0	0	....	....	....	....	....	....	1919-20	1919-20
Wells, Chris	Pit., Fla.	5	195	9	20	29	193	3	0	0	0	0	....	1995-96	1999-00
Wells, Jay	L.A., Phi., Buf., NYR, St.L., T.B.	18	1098	47	216	263	2359	114	3	14	17	213	1	1979-80	1996-97
Wellwood, Eric	Phi.	3	31	5	5	10	4	11	0	0	0	2	....	2010-11	2012-13
‡ Wellwood, Kyle	Tor., Van., S.J., Wpg.	9	489	92	143	235	36	40	4	16	20	0	....	2003-04	2012-13
Wensink, John	St.L., Bos., Que., Col., N.J.	8	403	70	68	138	840	43	2	6	8	86	....	1973-74	1982-83
• Wentworth, Cy	Chi., Mtl.M., Mtl.	13	575	39	68	107	355	35	5	6	11	20	1	1927-28	1939-40
Werenka, Brad	Edm., Que., Chi., Pit., Cgy.	7	320	19	61	80	299	19	2	1	3	14	....	1992-93	2000-01
Wesenberg, Brian	Phi.	1	1	0	0	0	5	....	....	....	....	....	....	1998-99	1998-99
Wesley, Blake	Phi., Hfd., Que., Tor.	7	298	18	46	64	486	19	2	2	4	30	....	1979-80	1985-86
Wesley, Glen	Bos., Hfd., Car., Tor.	20	1457	128	409	537	1045	169	15	37	52	141	1	1987-88	2007-08
Westcott, Duvie	CBJ	6	201	11	45	56	299	....	....	....	....	....	....	2001-02	2007-08
Westfall, Ed	Bos., NYI	18	1226	231	394	625	544	95	22	37	59	41	2	1961-62	1978-79
Westlund, Tommy	Car.	4	203	9	13	22	48	25	1	0	1	17	....	1999-00	2002-03
Westrum, Erik	Phx., Min., Tor.	3	27	1	2	3	22	....	....	....	....	....	....	2003-04	2006-07
‡ Wey, Patrick	Wsh.	1	9	0	3	3	5	....	....	....	....	....	....	2013-14	2013-14
Wharram, Kenny	Chi.	14	766	252	281	533	222	80	16	27	43	38	1	1951-52	1968-69
• Wharton, Len	NYR	1	1	0	0	0	0	....	....	....	....	....	....	1944-45	1944-45
Wheeldon, Simon	NYR, Wpg.	3	15	0	2	2	10	....	....	....	....	....	....	1987-88	1990-91
• Wheldon, Don	St.L.	1	2	0	0	0	0	....	....	....	....	....	....	1974-75	1974-75
Whelton, Bill	Wpg.	1	2	0	0	0	0	....	....	....	....	....	....	1980-81	1980-81
Whistle, Rob	NYR, St.L.	2	51	7	5	12	16	4	0	0	0	2	....	1985-86	1987-88
White, Bill	L.A., Chi.	9	604	50	215	265	495	91	7	32	39	76	....	1967-68	1975-76
White, Brian	Col.	1	2	0	0	0	0	....	....	....	....	....	....	1998-99	1998-99
White, Colin	N.J., S.J.	12	797	21	108	129	869	114	3	14	17	125	2	1999-00	2011-12
• White, Moe	Mtl.	1	4	0	1	1	2	....	....	....	....	....	....	1945-46	1945-46
White, Peter	Edm., Tor., Phi., Chi.	9	220	23	37	60	36	19	0	2	2	0	....	1993-94	2003-04
• White, Sherman	NYR	2	4	0	2	2	0	....	....	....	....	....	....	1946-47	1949-50
• White, Tex	Pit., NYA, Phi.	6	203	33	12	45	141	4	0	0	0	4	....	1925-26	1930-31
White, Todd	Chi., Phi., Ott., Min., Atl., NYR	13	653	141	240	381	228	43	8	3	11	16	....	1997-98	2010-11
White, Tony	Wsh., Min.	5	164	37	28	65	104	....	....	....	....	....	....	1974-75	1979-80
• Whitelaw, Bob	Det.	2	32	0	2	2	2	8	0	0	0	0	....	1940-41	1941-42
‡ Whitfield, Trent	Wsh., NYR, St.L., Bos.	9	194	11	18	29	104	18	0	0	0	12	....	1999-00	2011-12
Whitlock, Bob	Min.	1	1	0	0	0	0	....	....	....	....	....	....	1969-70	1969-70
‡ Whitmore, Derek	Buf.	1	2	0	0	0	0	....	....	....	....	....	....	2011-12	2011-12
Whitney, Ray	S.J., Edm., Fla., CBJ, Det., Car., Phx., Dal.	22	1330	385	679	1064	465	108	21	32	53	48	1	1991-92	2013-14
Whyte, Sean	L.A.	2	21	0	2	2	12	....	....	....	....	....	....	1991-92	1992-93
‡ Wick, Roman	Ott.	1	7	0	0	0	0	....	....	....	....	....	....	2010-11	2010-11
• Wickenheiser, Doug	Mtl., St.L., Van., NYR, Wsh.	10	556	111	165	276	286	41	4	7	11	18	....	1980-81	1989-90
• Widing, Juha	NYR, L.A., Cle.	8	575	144	226	370	208	8	1	2	3	2	....	1969-70	1976-77
Widmer, Jason	NYI, S.J.	3	7	0	1	1	7	....	....	....	....	....	....	1994-95	1996-97
• Wiebe, Art	Chi.	11	414	14	27	41	201	31	1	3	4	10	1	1932-33	1943-44
Wiemer, Jason	T.B., Cgy., Fla., NYI, Min., N.J.	11	726	90	112	202	1420	19	1	0	1	67	....	1994-95	2005-06
Wiemer, Jim	Buf., NYR, Edm., L.A., Bos.	11	325	29	72	101	378	62	5	8	13	63	....	1982-83	1993-94
• Wilcox, Archie	Mtl.M., Bos., St.L.	6	208	8	14	22	158	12	1	0	1	8	....	1929-30	1934-35
Wilcox, Barry	Van.	2	33	3	2	5	15	....	....	....	....	....	....	1972-73	1974-75
• Wilder, Arch	Det.	1	18	0	2	2	2	....	....	....	....	....	....	1940-41	1940-41
Wiley, Jim	Pit., Van.	5	63	4	10	14	8	....	....	....	....	....	....	1972-73	1976-77
Wilkie, Bob	Det., Phi.	2	18	2	5	7	10	....	....	....	....	....	....	1990-91	1993-94
Wilkie, David	Mtl., T.B., NYR	6	167	10	26	36	165	8	1	2	3	14	....	1994-95	2000-01
• Wilkins, Barry	Bos., Van., Pit.	9	418	27	125	152	663	6	0	1	1	4	....	1966-67	1975-76
• Wilkinson, John	Bos.	1	9	0	0	0	6	....	....	....	....	....	....	1943-44	1943-44
Wilkinson, Neil	Min., S.J., Chi., Wpg., Pit.	10	460	16	67	83	813	53	3	6	9	41	....	1989-90	1998-99
Wilks, Brian	L.A.	4	48	4	8	12	27	....	....	....	....	....	....	1984-85	1988-89
Willard, Rod	Tor.	1	1	0	0	0	0	....	....	....	....	....	....	1982-83	1982-83
• Williams, Burr	Det., St.L., Bos.	3	19	0	1	1	28	7	0	0	0	8	....	1933-34	1936-37
Williams, Butch	St.L., Cal.	3	108	14	35	49	131	....	....	....	....	....	....	1973-74	1975-76
Williams, Darryl	L.A.	1	2	0	0	0	10	....	....	....	....	....	....	1992-93	1992-93
Williams, David	S.J., Ana.	4	173	11	53	64	157	....	....	....	....	....	....	1991-92	1994-95
Williams, Fred	Det.	1	44	2	5	7	10	....	....	....	....	....	....	1976-77	1976-77
Williams, Gord	Phi.	2	2	0	0	0	2	....	....	....	....	....	....	1981-82	1982-83
Williams, Jeremy	Tor., NYR	5	32	9	2	11	6	....	....	....	....	....	....	2005-06	2010-11
Williams, Sean	Chi.	1	2	0	0	0	4	....	....	....	....	....	....	1991-92	1991-92
Williams, Tiger	Tor., Van., Det., L.A., Hfd.	14	962	241	272	513	3966	83	12	23	35	455	....	1974-75	1987-88
Williams, Tom	NYR, L.A.	8	397	115	138	253	73	29	8	7	15	4	....	1971-72	1978-79
• Williams, Tommy	Bos., Min., Cal., Wsh.	13	663	161	269	430	177	10	2	5	7	2	....	1961-62	1975-76
Willis, Shane	Car., T.B.	5	174	31	43	74	77	2	0	0	0	0	....	1998-99	2003-04
‡ Willsie, Brian	Col., Wsh., L.A.	10	381	52	57	109	217	10	1	1	2	4	....	1999-00	2010-11
• Willson, Don	Mtl.	2	22	2	7	9	0	3	0	0	0	0	....	1937-38	1938-39
Wilm, Clarke	Cgy., Nsh., Tor.	7	455	37	60	97	336	5	0	1	1	2	....	1998-99	2005-06
Wilson, Behn	Phi., Chi.	9	601	98	260	358	1480	67	12	29	41	190	....	1978-79	1987-88
• Wilson, Bert	NYR, St.L., L.A., Cgy.	8	478	37	44	81	646	21	0	2	2	42	....	1973-74	1980-81
Wilson, Bob	Chi.	1	1	0	0	0	0	....	....	....	....	....	....	1953-54	1953-54
Wilson, Carey	Cgy., Hfd., NYR	10	552	169	258	427	314	52	11	13	24	14	....	1983-84	1992-93
‡ Wilson, Clay	CBJ, Atl., Fla., Cgy.	5	36	4	4	8	12	....	....	....	....	....	....	2007-08	2011-12
• Wilson, Cully	Tor., Mtl., Ham., Chi.	5	127	59	28	87	243	2	1	0	1	6	....	1919-20	1926-27
Wilson, Doug	Chi., S.J.	16	1024	237	590	827	830	95	19	61	80	88	....	1977-78	1992-93
• Wilson, Gerry	Mtl.	1	3	0	0	0	2	....	....	....	....	....	....	1956-57	1956-57
Wilson, Gord	Bos.	1	....	....	....	....	....	2	0	0	0	0	....	1954-55	1954-55
• Wilson, Hub	NYA	1	2	0	0	0	0	....	....	....	....	....	....	1931-32	1931-32
• Wilson, Johnny	Det., Chi., Tor., NYR	13	688	161	171	332	190	66	14	13	27	11	4	1949-50	1961-62
‡ Wilson, Kyle	Wsh., CBJ, Nsh.	3	39	4	9	13	12	....	....	....	....	....	....	2009-10	2011-12
Wilson, Landon	Col., Bos., Phx., Pit., Dal.	10	375	53	66	119	352	13	1	1	2	20	....	1995-96	2008-09
• Wilson, Larry	Det., Chi.	6	152	21	48	69	75	4	0	0	0	0	1	1949-50	1955-56
Wilson, Mike	Buf., Fla., Pit., NYR	8	336	16	41	57	264	29	0	2	2	15	....	1995-96	2002-03
Wilson, Mitch	N.J., Pit.	2	26	2	3	5	104	....	....	....	....	....	....	1984-85	1986-87
Wilson, Murray	Mtl., L.A.	7	386	94	95	189	162	53	5	14	19	32	4	1972-73	1978-79
Wilson, Rick	Mtl., St.L., Det.	4	239	6	26	32	165	3	0	0	0	0	....	1973-74	1976-77
Wilson, Rik	St.L., Cgy., Chi.	6	251	25	65	90	220	22	0	4	4	23	....	1981-82	1987-88
Wilson, Roger	Chi.	1	7	0	2	2	6	....	....	....	....	....	....	1974-75	1974-75
Wilson, Ron	Tor., Min.	7	177	26	67	93	68	20	4	13	17	8	....	1977-78	1987-88
Wilson, Ron	Wpg., St.L., Mtl.	14	832	110	216	326	415	63	10	12	22	64	....	1979-80	1993-94
• Wilson, Wally	Bos.	1	53	11	8	19	18	1	0	0	0	0	....	1947-48	1947-48
Wing, Murray	Det.	1	1	0	1	1	0	....	....	....	....	....	....	1973-74	1973-74
Winnes, Chris	Bos., Phi.	4	33	1	6	7	6	1	0	0	0	0	....	1990-91	1993-94
‡ Wirtanen, Petteri	Ana.	1	3	1	0	1	2	....	....	....	....	....	....	2007-08	2007-08
Wiseman, Brian	Tor.	1	3	0	0	0	0	....	....	....	....	....	....	1996-97	1996-97
Wiseman, Chad	S.J., NYR	3	9	1	1	2	8	1	0	0	0	2	....	2002-03	2005-06
• Wiseman, Eddie	Det., NYA, Bos.	10	456	115	165	280	136	43	10	10	20	16	1	1932-33	1941-42
‡ Wishart, Ty	T.B., NYI	3	26	1	5	6	10	....	....	....	....	....	....	2008-09	2011-12
Wiste, Jim	Chi., Van.	3	52	1	10	11	8	....	....	....	....	....	....	1968-69	1970-71
Witehall, Johan	NYR, Mtl.	3	54	2	5	7	16	....	....	....	....	....	....	1998-99	2000-01
Witherspoon, Jim	L.A.	1	2	0	0	0	2	....	....	....	....	....	....	1975-76	1975-76
Witiuk, Steve	Chi.	1	33	3	8	11	14	....	....	....	....	....	....	1951-52	1951-52
Witt, Brendan	Wsh., Nsh., NYI	14	890	25	96	121	1424	41	4	1	5	44	....	1995-96	2009-10
Woit, Benny	Det., Chi.	7	334	7	26	33	170	41	2	6	8	18	3	1950-51	1956-57
Wojciechowski, Steve	Det.	2	54	19	20	39	17	6	0	1	1	0	....	1944-45	1946-47
Wolanin, Craig	N.J., Que., Col., T.B., Tor.	13	695	40	133	173	894	35	4	6	10	67	1	1985-86	1997-98
Wolf, Bennett	Pit.	3	30	0	1	1	133	....	....	....	....	....	....	1980-81	1982-83
‡ Wolski, Wojtek	Col., Phx., NYR, Fla., Wsh.	8	451	99	168	267	113	29	8	9	17	8	....	2005-06	2012-13
Wong, Mike	Det.	1	22	1	1	2	12	....	....	....	....	....	....	1975-76	1975-76
Wood, Dody	S.J.	5	106	8	10	18	471	....	....	....	....	....	....	1992-93	1997-98
Wood, Randy	NYI, Buf., Tor., Dal.	11	741	175	159	334	603	51	8	9	17	40	....	1986-87	1996-97
• Wood, Robert	NYR	1	1	0	0	0	0	....	....	....	....	....	....	1950-51	1950-51
Woodley, Dan	Van.	1	5	2	0	2	17	....	....	....	....	....	....	1987-88	1987-88
Woods, Paul	Det.	7	501	72	124	196	276	7	0	5	5	4	....	1977-78	1983-84
Woolley, Jason	Wsh., Fla., Pit., Buf., Det.	14	718	68	246	314	430	79	11	36	47	44	....	1991-92	2005-06
Worrell, Peter	Fla., Col.	7	391	19	27	46	1554	4	1	0	1	8	....	1997-98	2003-04
Wortman, Kevin	Cgy.	1	5	0	0	0	2	....	....	....	....	....	....	1993-94	1993-94
Wotton, Mark	Van., Dal.	4	43	3	6	9	25	5	0	0	0	4	....	1994-95	2000-01
• Woytowich, Bob	Bos., Min., Pit., L.A.	8	503	32	126	158	352	24	1	3	4	20	....	1964-65	1971-72
‡ Woywitka, Jeff	St.L., Dal., NYR	7	278	9	46	55	149	4	0	0	0	0	....	2005-06	2011-12
Wozniewski, Andy	Tor., St.L., Bos.	5	79	2	10	12	81	....	....	....	....	....	....	2005-06	2009-10
Wren, Bob	Ana., Tor.	3	5	0	0	0	0	1	0	0	0	0	....	1997-98	2001-02

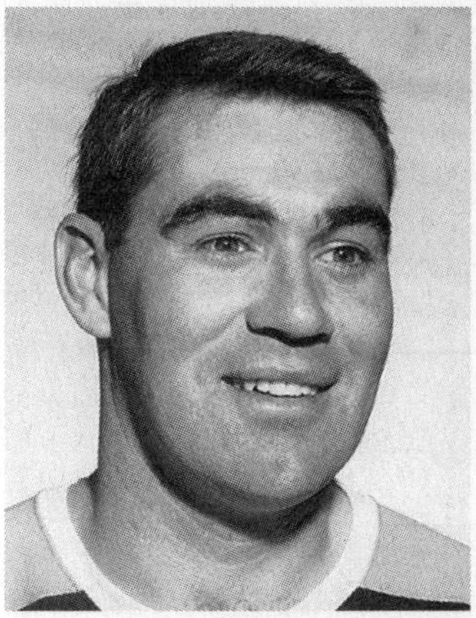

Ed Westfall

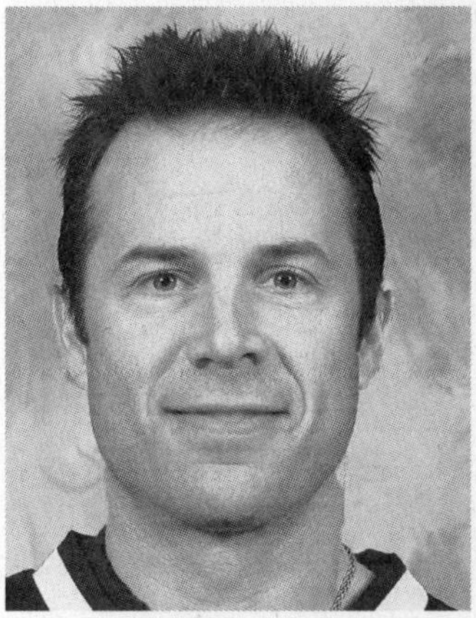

Ray Whitney

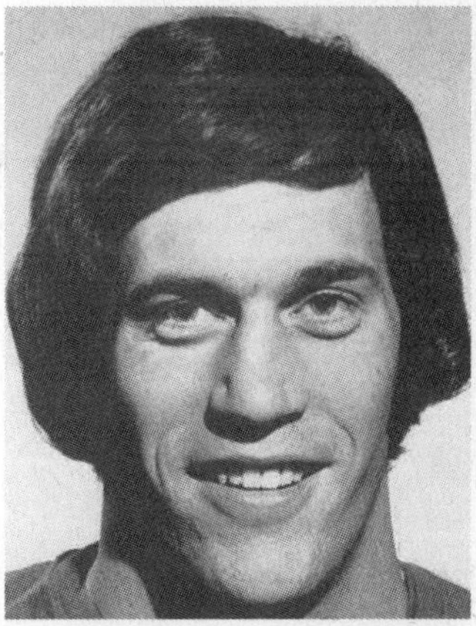

Rick Wilson

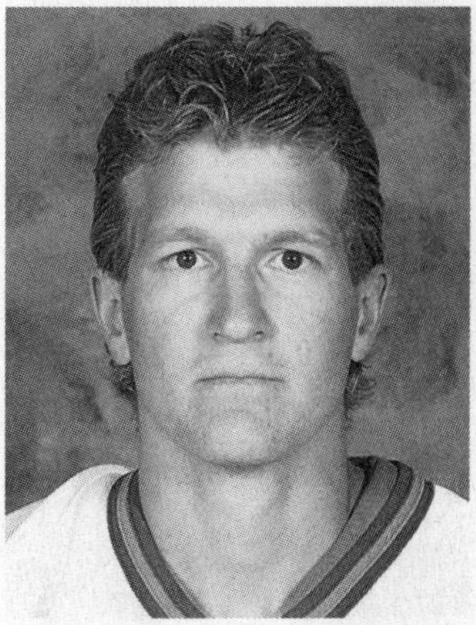

Mark Wotton

Tyler Wright

Paul Ysebaert

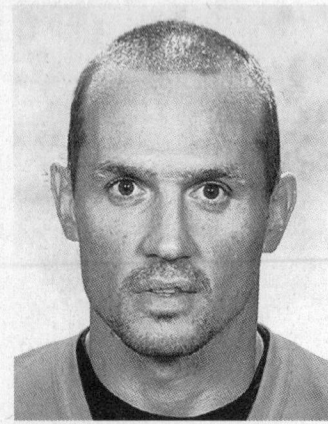

Steve Yzerman

Rob Zamuner

Name	NHL Teams	NHL Seasons	Regular Schedule GP	G	A	TP	PIM	Playoffs GP	G	A	TP	PIM	NHL Cup Wins	First NHL Season	Last NHL Season
Wright, Jamie	Dal., Cgy., Phi.	6	124	12	20	32	54	5	0	0	0	0	....	1997-98	2002-03
Wright, John	Van., St.L., K.C.	3	127	16	36	52	67							1972-73	1974-75
Wright, Keith	Phi.	1	1	0	0	0	0							1967-68	1967-68
Wright, Larry	Phi., Cal., Det.	5	106	4	8	12	19							1971-72	1977-78
Wright, Tyler	Edm., Pit., CBJ, Ana.	13	613	79	70	149	854	30	3	2	5	40	....	1992-93	2005-06
• Wycherley, Ralph	NYA, Bro.	2	28	4	7	11	6							1940-41	1941-42
• Wylie, Bill	NYR	1	1	0	0	0	0							1950-51	1950-51
Wylie, Duane	Chi.	2	14	3	3	6	2							1974-75	1976-77
‡ Wyman, J.T.	Mtl., T.B.	3	44	2	9	11	8							2009-10	2012-13
Wyrozub, Randy	Buf.	4	100	8	10	18	10							1970-71	1973-74

Y Z

Name	NHL Teams	NHL Seasons	Regular Schedule GP	G	A	TP	PIM	Playoffs GP	G	A	TP	PIM	NHL Cup Wins	First NHL Season	Last NHL Season
‡ Yablonski, Jeremy	St.L.	1	1	0	0	0	5							2003-04	2003-04
Yachmenev, Vitali	L.A., Nsh.	8	487	83	133	216	88							1995-96	2002-03
• Yackel, Ken	Bos.	1	6	0	0	0	2	2	0	0	0	2	....	1958-59	1958-59
Yake, Terry	Hfd., Ana., Tor., St.L., Wsh.	11	403	77	120	197	220	32	4	4	8	36	....	1988-89	2000-01
‡ Yakubov, Mikhail	Chi., Fla.	2	53	2	10	12	20							2003-04	2005-06
Yakushin, Dmitri	Tor.	1	2	0	0	0	0							1999-00	1999-00
Yaremchuk, Gary	Tor.	4	34	1	4	5	28							1981-82	1984-85
Yaremchuk, Ken	Chi., Tor.	6	235	36	56	92	106	31	6	8	14	49	....	1983-84	1988-89
Yashin, Alexei	Ott., NYI	12	850	337	444	781	401	48	11	16	27	24	....	1993-94	2006-07
Yates, Ross	Hfd.	1	7	1	1	2	4							1983-84	1983-84
Yawney, Trent	Chi., Cgy., St.L.	12	593	27	102	129	783	60	9	17	26	81	....	1987-88	1998-99
• Yegorov, Alexei	S.J.	2	11	3	3	6	2							1995-96	1996-97
Yelle, Stephane	Col., Cgy., Bos., Car.	14	991	96	169	265	490	171	11	21	32	90	2	1995-96	2009-10
Ylonen, Juha	Phx., T.B., Ott.	6	341	26	76	102	90	15	0	7	7	4	....	1996-97	2001-02
York, Harry	St.L., NYR, Pit., Van.	4	244	29	46	75	99	5	0	0	0	2	....	1996-97	1999-00
York, Jason	Det., Ana., Ott., Nsh., Bos.	13	757	42	187	229	621	34	2	7	9	25	....	1992-93	2006-07
‡ York, Mike	NYR, Edm., NYI, Phi., Phx., CBJ	9	579	127	195	322	135	6	0	2	2	2	....	1999-00	2008-09
• Young, B.J.	Det.	1	1	0	0	0	0							1999-00	1999-00
Young, Brian	Chi.	1	8	0	2	2	6							1980-81	1980-81
Young, Bryan	Edm.	2	17	0	0	0	10							2006-07	2007-08
Young, C.J.	Cgy., Bos.	1	43	7	7	14	32							1992-93	1992-93
• Young, Doug	Det., Mtl.	10	388	35	45	80	303	28	1	5	6	16	2	1931-32	1940-41
• Young, Howie	Det., Chi., Van.	8	336	12	62	74	851	19	2	4	6	46	....	1960-61	1970-71
Young, Scott	Hfd., Pit., Que., Col., Ana., St.L., Dal.	17	1181	342	415	757	448	141	44	43	87	64	2	1987-88	2005-06
Young, Tim	Min., Wpg., Phi.	10	628	195	341	536	438	36	7	24	31	27	....	1975-76	1984-85
Young, Warren	Min., Pit., Det.	7	236	72	77	149	472							1981-82	1987-88
Younghans, Tom	Min., NYR	6	429	44	41	85	373	24	2	1	3	21	....	1976-77	1981-82
Ysebaert, Paul	N.J., Det., Wpg., Chi., T.B.	11	532	149	187	336	217	30	4	3	7	20	....	1988-89	1998-99
Yushkevich, Dmitry	Phi., Tor., Fla., L.A.	11	786	43	182	225	659	72	4	19	23	52	....	1992-93	2002-03
Yzerman, Steve	Det.	22	1514	692	1063	1755	924	196	70	115	185	84	3	1983-84	2005-06
Zabransky, Libor	St.L.	2	40	1	6	7	50							1996-97	1997-98
Zaharko, Miles	Atl., Chi.	4	129	5	32	37	84	3	0	0	0	0	....	1977-78	1981-82
Zaine, Rod	Pit., Buf.	2	61	10	6	16	25							1970-71	1971-72
Zalapski, Zarley	Pit., Hfd., Cgy., Mtl., Phi.	12	637	99	285	384	684	48	4	23	27	47	....	1987-88	1999-00
Zalesak, Miroslav	S.J.	2	12	1	2	3	0							2002-03	2003-04
‡ Zalewski, Steven	S.J., N.J.	2	10	0	0	0	0							2009-10	2011-12
Zamuner, Rob	NYR, T.B., Ott., Bos.	13	798	139	172	311	467	34	4	5	9	26	....	1991-92	2003-04
Zanussi, Joe	NYR, Bos., St.L.	3	87	1	13	14	46	4	0	1	1	2	....	1974-75	1976-77
Zanussi, Ron	Min., Tor.	5	299	52	83	135	373	17	0	4	4	17	....	1977-78	1981-82
Zavisha, Brad	Edm.	1	2	0	0	0	0							1993-94	1993-94
Zednik, Richard	Wsh., Mtl., NYI, Fla.	13	745	200	179	379	563	48	16	10	26	41	....	1995-96	2008-09
Zehr, Jeff	Bos.	1	4	0	0	0	2							1999-00	1999-00
• Zeidel, Larry	Det., Chi., Phi.	5	158	3	16	19	198	12	0	1	1	12	1	1951-52	1968-69
‡ Zeiler, John	L.A.	4	90	1	4	5	87							2006-07	2010-11
Zelepukin, Valeri	N.J., Edm., Phi., Chi.	10	595	117	177	294	527	85	13	13	26	48	1	1991-92	2000-01
Zemlak, Richard	Que., Min., Pit., Cgy.	5	132	2	12	14	587	1	0	0	0	10	....	1986-87	1991-92
Zeniuk, Ed	Det.	1	2	0	0	0	0							1954-55	1954-55
Zent, Jason	Ott., Phi.	3	27	3	3	6	13							1996-97	1998-99
Zetterstrom, Lars	Van.	1	14	0	1	1	2							1978-79	1978-79
Zettler, Rob	Min., S.J., Phi., Tor., Nsh., Wsh.	14	569	5	65	70	920	14	0	0	0	4	....	1988-89	2001-02
Zezel, Peter	Phi., St.L., Wsh., Tor., Dal., N.J., Van.	15	873	219	389	608	435	131	25	39	64	83	....	1984-85	1998-99
Zhamnov, Alex	Wpg., Chi., Phi., Bos.	13	807	249	470	719	668	35	6	13	19	18	....	1992-93	2005-06
‡ Zharkov, Vladimir	N.J.	3	82	2	12	14	10							2009-10	2011-12
‡ Zherdev, Nikolai	CBJ, NYR, Phi.	6	421	115	146	261	225	15	1	2	3	4	....	2003-04	2010-11
Zhitnik, Alexei	L.A., Buf., NYI, Phi., Atl.	15	1085	96	375	471	1268	98	9	30	39	168	....	1992-93	2007-08
• Zholtok, Sergei	Bos., Ott., Mtl., Edm., Min., Nsh.	10	588	111	147	258	166	45	4	14	18	0	....	1992-93	2003-04
Ziegler, Thomas	T.B.	1	5	0	0	0	0							2000-01	2000-01
‡ Zigomanis, Mike	Car., St.L., Phx., Tor.	7	197	21	19	40	89						1	2002-03	2010-11
Zinger, Dwayne	Wsh.	1	7	0	1	1	9							2003-04	2003-04
Zinovjev, Sergei	Bos.	1	10	0	1	1	2							2003-04	2003-04
‡ Zizka, Tomas	L.A.	2	25	2	6	8	16							2002-03	2003-04
Zmolek, Doug	S.J., Dal., L.A., Chi.	8	467	11	53	64	905	14	0	1	1	16	....	1992-93	1999-00
• Zoborosky, Marty	Chi.	1	1	0	0	0	2							1944-45	1944-45
Zombo, Rick	Det., St.L., Bos.	12	652	24	130	154	728	60	1	11	12	127	....	1984-85	1995-96
‡ Zubarev, Andrei	Atl.	1	4	0	1	1	4							2010-11	2010-11
‡ Zubov, Ilya	Ott.	2	10	0	2	2	0							2007-08	2008-09
Zubov, Sergei	NYR, Pit., Dal.	16	1068	152	619	771	337	164	24	93	117	62	2	1992-93	2008-09
Zuke, Mike	St.L., Hfd.	8	455	86	196	282	220	26	6	6	12	12	....	1978-79	1985-86
• Zunich, Rudy	Det.	1	2	0	0	0	2							1943-44	1943-44
Zyuzin, Andrei	S.J., T.B., N.J., Min., Cgy., Chi.	10	496	38	82	120	446	29	2	1	3	30	....	1997-98	2007-08

Retired Players, Goaltenders and Coaches Research Project

Throughout the Retired Players and Retired Goaltenders sections of this book, you will notice many players with a bullet (•) by their names. These players, according to our records, are deceased. The editors recognize that our information on the death dates of NHLers is incomplete. If you have documented information on the passing of any player not marked with a bullet (•) in this edition, we would like to hear from you. We also welcome information on deceased NHL head coaches. Please send this information to:

Ralph Dinger • ralph.dda@sympatico.ca

or by mail to:
Retired Player Research Project
194 Dovercourt Road
Toronto, Ontario
M6J 3C8 Canada

Many thanks to the following contributors . . .

Tim Bateman, Corey Bryant, Paul R. Carroll, Jr., Bob Duff, Peter Fillman, Ernie Fitzsimmons, Gary J. Pearce, Martin Schmid, Chuck Scott, Andreas Szabo.

Retired NHL Goaltender Index

Abbreviations: Teams/Cities: – **Ana.** – Anaheim; **Atl.** – Atlanta; **Bos.** – Boston; **Bro.** – Brooklyn; **Buf.** – Buffalo; **Cgy.** – Calgary; **Cal.** – California; **Car.** – Carolina; **Chi.** – Chicago; **Cle.** – Cleveland; **Col.** – Colorado; **CBJ** – Columbus; **Dal.** – Dallas; **Det.** – Detroit; **Edm.** – Edmonton; **Fla.** – Florida; **Ham.** – Hamilton; **Hfd.** – Hartford; **K.C.** – Kansas City; **L.A.** – Los Angeles; **Min.** – Minnesota; **Mtl.** – Montreal; **Mtl.M.** – Montreal Maroons; **Mtl.W.** – Montreal Wanderers; **Nsh.** – Nashville; **N.J.** – New Jersey; **NYA** – NY Americans; **NYI** – NY Islanders; **NYR** – New York Rangers; **Oak.** – Oakland; **Ott.** – Ottawa; **Phi.** – Philadelphia; **Phx.** – Phoenix; **Pit.** – Pittsburgh; **Que.** – Quebec; **St.L.** – St. Louis; **S.J.** – San Jose; **T.B.** – Tampa Bay; **Tor.** – Toronto; **Van.** – Vancouver; **Wsh.** – Washington; **Wpg.** – Winnipeg

GP – games played; **W** – wins; **L** – losses; **T** – ties; **Mins** – minutes played; **GA** – goals against; **SO** – shutouts; **Avg** – goals against average per 60 minutes played.
• – deceased. § – Forward, defenseman or coach who appeared in goal. For complete career, see Retired Player Index. ‡ – Remains active in other leagues.

NHL Seasons – A player or goaltender who does not play in a regular season but who does appear in that year's playoffs is credited with an NHL Season in this Index. Total seasons are rounded off to the nearest full season.

			Regular Schedule								Playoffs										
Name	NHL Teams	NHL Seasons	GP	W	L	T	Mins	GA	SO	Avg	GP	W	L	T	Mins	GA	SO	Avg	NHL Cup Wins	First NHL Season	Last NHL Season
Abbott, George	Bos.	1	1	0	1	0	60	7	0	7.00	....	....	....	....	....	....	....	....		1943-44	1943-44
Adams, John	Bos., Wsh.	3	22	9	10	1	1180	85	1	4.32	....	....	....	....	....	....	....	....	1	1969-70	1974-75
‡ Aebischer, David	Col., Mtl., Phx.	7	214	106	74	17	12230	513	13	2.52	13	6	5	....	697	24	1	2.07	1	2000-01	2007-08
Aiken, Don	Mtl.	1	1	0	1	0	34	6	0	10.59	....	....	....	....	....	....	....	....		1957-58	1957-58
• Aitkenhead, Andy	NYR	3	106	47	43	16	6570	257	11	2.35	10	6	2	2	608	15	3	1.48	1	1932-33	1934-35
• Almas, Red	Det., Chi.	3	3	0	2	1	180	13	0	4.33	5	1	3	....	263	13	0	2.97		1946-47	1952-53
• Anderson, Lorne	NYR	1	3	1	2	0	180	18	0	6.00	....	....	....	....	....	....	....	....		1951-52	1951-52
Askey, Tom	Ana.	2	7	0	1	2	273	12	0	2.64	1	0	1	....	30	2	0	4.00		1997-98	1998-99
Astrom, Hardy	NYR, Col.	3	83	17	44	12	4456	278	0	3.74	....	....	....	....	....	....	....	....		1977-78	1980-81
Aubin, Jean-Sebastien	Pit., Tor., L.A.	9	218	80	83	16	11197	547	7	2.93	1	0	0	0	1	0	0	0.00		1998-99	2007-08
Auld, Alex	Van., Fla., Phx., Bos., Ott., Dal., NYR, Mtl.	10	237	91	88	32	12986	606	6	2.80	4	1	2	0	242	10	0	2.48		2001-02	2011-12
‡ Bacashihua, Jason	St.L.	2	38	7	17	4	1860	99	0	3.19	....	....	....	....	....	....	....	....		2005-06	2006-07
Bach, Ryan	L.A.	1	3	0	3	0	108	8	0	4.44	....	....	....	....	....	....	....	....		1998-99	1998-99
‡ Backlund, Johan	Phi.	1	1	0	1	0	40	2	0	3.00	1	0	0	....	1	0	0	0.00		2009-10	2009-10
Bailey, Scott	Bos.	2	19	6	6	2	965	55	0	3.42	....	....	....	....	....	....	....	....		1995-96	1996-97
Baker, Steve	NYR	4	57	20	20	11	3081	190	3	3.70	14	7	7	....	826	55	0	4.00		1979-80	1982-83
Bales, Mike	Bos., Ott.	4	23	2	15	1	1120	77	0	4.13	....	....	....	....	....	....	....	....		1992-93	1996-97
Bannerman, Murray	Van., Chi.	8	289	116	125	33	16470	1051	8	3.83	40	20	18	....	2322	165	0	4.26		1977-78	1986-87
Baron, Marco	Bos., L.A., Edm.	6	86	34	38	9	4822	292	1	3.63	1	0	1	....	20	3	0	9.00		1979-80	1984-85
Barrasso, Tom	Buf., Pit., Ott., Car., Tor., St.L.	19	777	369	277	86	44180	2385	38	3.24	119	61	54	....	6953	349	6	3.01	2	1983-84	2002-03
• Bassen, Hank	Chi., Det., Pit.	9	156	46	66	31	8759	434	5	2.97	5	1	3	....	274	11	0	2.41		1954-55	1967-68
• Bastien, Baz	Tor.	1	5	0	4	1	300	20	0	4.00	....	....	....	....	....	....	....	....		1945-46	1945-46
• Bauman, Garry	Mtl., Min.	3	35	5	16	6	1719	102	0	3.56	....	....	....	....	....	....	....	....		1966-67	1968-69
Beaupre, Don	Min., Wsh., Ott., Tor.	17	667	268	277	75	37396	2151	17	3.45	72	33	31	....	3943	220	3	3.35		1980-81	1996-97
Beauregard, Stephane	Wpg., Phi.	5	90	19	39	11	4402	268	2	3.65	4	1	3	....	238	12	0	3.03		1989-90	1993-94
Beckford-Tseu, Chris	St.L.	1	1	0	0	0	27	1	0	2.22	....	....	....	....	....	....	....	....		2007-08	2007-08
Bedard, Jim	Wsh.	2	73	17	40	13	4232	278	1	3.94	....	....	....	....	....	....	....	....		1977-78	1978-79
Behrend, Marc	Wpg.	3	39	12	19	3	1991	160	1	4.82	7	1	3	....	312	19	0	3.65		1983-84	1985-86
Belanger, Yves	St.L., Atl., Bos.	6	78	29	33	6	4134	259	2	3.76	....	....	....	....	....	....	....	....		1974-75	1979-80
Belfour, Ed	Chi., S.J., Dal., Tor., Fla.	18	963	484	320	125	55695	2317	76	2.50	161	88	68	....	9945	359	14	2.17	1	1988-89	2006-07
Belhumeur, Michel	Phi., Wsh.	3	65	9	36	7	3306	254	0	4.61	1	0	0	....	10	1	0	6.00		1972-73	1975-76
• Bell, Gordie	Tor., NYR	2	8	3	5	0	480	31	0	3.88	2	1	1	....	120	9	0	4.50		1945-46	1955-56
• Benedict, Clint	Ott., Mtl.M.	13	362	190	143	28	22367	863	57	2.32	28	11	12	5	1707	53	9	1.86	4	1917-18	1929-30
• Bennett, Harvey	Bos.	1	25	10	12	2	1470	103	0	4.20	....	....	....	....	....	....	....	....		1944-45	1944-45
Bergeron, Jean-Claude	Mtl., T.B., L.A.	6	72	21	33	7	3772	232	1	3.69	....	....	....	....	....	....	....	....		1990-91	1996-97
Berkhoel, Adam	Atl.	1	9	2	4	1	473	30	0	3.81	....	....	....	....	....	....	....	....		2005-06	2005-06
Bernhardt, Tim	Cgy., Tor.	4	67	17	36	7	3748	267	0	4.27	....	....	....	....	....	....	....	....		1982-83	1986-87
Berthiaume, Daniel	Wpg., Min., L.A., Bos., Ott.	9	215	81	90	21	11662	714	5	3.67	14	5	9	....	807	50	0	3.72		1985-86	1993-94
Bester, Allan	Tor., Det., Dal.	10	219	73	99	17	11773	786	7	4.01	11	2	6	....	508	37	0	4.37		1983-84	1995-96
• Beveridge, Bill	Det., Ott., St.L., Mtl.M., NYR	9	297	87	166	42	18375	879	18	2.87	5	2	3	....	300	11	0	2.20		1929-30	1942-43
• Bibeault, Paul	Mtl., Tor., Bos., Chi.	7	214	81	107	25	12890	785	10	3.65	20	6	14	....	1237	71	2	3.44		1940-41	1946-47
Bierk, Zac	T.B., Min., Phx.	6	47	9	20	5	2135	113	1	3.18	....	....	....	....	....	....	....	....		1997-98	2003-04
Billington, Craig	N.J., Ott., Bos., Col., Wsh.	15	332	110	149	31	17097	1034	9	3.63	8	0	2	....	213	15	0	4.23		1985-86	2002-03
Binette, Andre	Mtl.	1	1	1	0	0	60	4	0	4.00	....	....	....	....	....	....	....	....		1954-55	1954-55
Binkley, Les	Pit.	5	196	58	94	34	11046	575	11	3.12	7	5	2	....	428	15	0	2.10		1967-68	1971-72
‡ Biron, Martin	Buf., Phi., NYI, NYR	16	508	230	191	52	28614	1247	28	2.61	23	11	12	....	1424	68	2	2.87		1995-96	2013-14
• Bittner, Richard	Bos.	1	1	0	0	1	60	3	0	3.00	....	....	....	....	....	....	....	....		1949-50	1949-50
Blackburn, Dan	NYR	2	63	20	32	4	3499	188	1	3.22	....	....	....	....	....	....	....	....		2001-02	2002-03
Blake, Mike	L.A.	3	40	13	15	5	2117	150	0	4.25	....	....	....	....	....	....	....	....		1981-82	1983-84
Blue, John	Bos., Buf.	3	46	16	18	7	2521	126	1	3.00	2	0	1	....	96	5	0	3.13		1992-93	1995-96
Boisvert, Gilles	Det.	1	3	0	3	0	180	9	0	3.00	....	....	....	....	....	....	....	....		1959-60	1959-60
Bouchard, Dan	Atl., Cgy., Que., Wpg.	14	655	286	232	113	37919	2061	27	3.26	43	13	30	....	2549	147	1	3.46		1972-73	1985-86
‡ Boucher, Brian	Phi., Phx., Cgy., Chi., CBJ, S.J., Car.	13	328	120	139	45	18220	822	17	2.71	43	21	18	....	2388	94	2	2.36		1999-00	2012-13
• Bourque, Claude	Mtl., Det.	2	62	16	38	8	3830	193	4	3.02	3	1	2	....	188	8	1	2.55		1938-39	1939-40
Boutin, Rollie	Wsh.	3	22	7	10	1	1137	75	0	3.96	....	....	....	....	....	....	....	....		1978-79	1980-81
• Bouvrette, Lionel	NYR	1	1	0	1	0	60	6	0	6.00	....	....	....	....	....	....	....	....		1942-43	1942-43
Bower, Johnny	NYR, Tor.	15	552	250	195	90	32016	1340	37	2.51	74	35	34	....	4378	180	5	2.47	4	1953-54	1969-70
§ • Branigan, Andy	NYA	1	1	0	0	0	7	0	0	0.00	....	....	....	....	....	....	....	....		1940-41	1940-41
Brathwaite, Fred	Edm., Cgy., St.L., CBJ	9	254	81	99	37	13840	629	15	2.73	1	0	0	0	1	0	0	0.00		1993-94	2003-04
• Brimsek, Frank	Bos., Chi.	10	514	252	182	80	31210	1404	40	2.70	68	32	36	....	4395	186	2	2.54	2	1938-39	1949-50
Brochu, Martin	Wsh., Van., Pit.	3	9	0	5	0	369	22	0	3.58	....	....	....	....	....	....	....	....		1998-99	2003-04
• Broda, Turk	Tor.	14	629	302	224	101	38167	1609	62	2.53	101	60	39	....	6389	211	13	1.98	5	1936-37	1951-52
Broderick, Ken	Min., Bos.	3	27	11	12	1	1464	74	1	3.03	....	....	....	....	....	....	....	....		1969-70	1974-75
Broderick, Len	Mtl.	1	1	1	0	0	60	2	0	2.00	....	....	....	....	....	....	....	....		1957-58	1957-58
Brodeur, Mike	Ott.	2	7	3	1	0	277	10	1	2.17	....	....	....	....	....	....	....	....		2009-10	2010-11
Brodeur, Richard	NYI, Van., Hfd.	9	385	131	175	62	21968	1410	6	3.85	33	13	20	....	2009	111	1	3.32		1979-80	1987-88
Bromley, Gary	Buf., Van.	6	136	54	44	28	7427	425	7	3.43	7	2	5	....	360	25	0	4.17		1973-74	1980-81
• Brooks, Art	Tor.	1	4	2	2	0	220	23	0	6.27	....	....	....	....	....	....	....	....		1917-18	1917-18
Brooks, Ross	Bos.	3	54	37	7	6	3047	134	4	2.64	1	0	0	....	20	3	0	9.00		1972-73	1974-75
• Brophy, Frank	Que.	1	21	3	18	0	1249	148	0	7.11	....	....	....	....	....	....	....	....		1919-20	1919-20
Brown, Andy	Det., Pit.	3	62	22	26	9	3373	213	1	3.79	....	....	....	....	....	....	....	....		1971-72	1973-74
Brown, Ken	Chi.	1	1	0	0	0	18	1	0	3.33	....	....	....	....	....	....	....	....		1970-71	1970-71
Brunetta, Mario	Que.	3	40	12	17	1	1967	128	0	3.90	....	....	....	....	....	....	....	....		1987-88	1989-90
‡ Brust, Barry	L.A.	1	11	2	4	1	486	30	0	3.70	....	....	....	....	....	....	....	....		2006-07	2006-07
Bullock, Bruce	Van.	3	16	3	9	3	927	74	0	4.79	....	....	....	....	....	....	....	....		1972-73	1976-77
Burke, Sean	N.J., Hfd., Car., Van., Phi., Fla., Phx., T.B., L.A.	18	820	324	341	110	46442	2290	38	2.96	38	12	23	....	2151	119	1	3.32		1987-88	2006-07
• Buzinski, Steve	NYR	1	9	2	6	1	560	55	0	5.89	....	....	....	....	....	....	....	....		1942-43	1942-43
Caley, Don	St.L.	1	1	0	0	0	30	3	0	6.00	....	....	....	....	....	....	....	....		1967-68	1967-68
Caprice, Frank	Van.	6	102	31	46	11	5589	391	1	4.20	....	....	....	....	....	....	....	....		1982-83	1987-88
Carey, Jim	Wsh., Bos., St.L.	5	172	79	65	16	9668	416	16	2.58	10	2	5	....	455	35	0	4.62		1994-95	1998-99
Caron, Jacques	L.A., St.L., Van.	5	72	24	29	11	3846	211	2	3.29	12	4	7	....	639	34	0	3.19		1967-68	1973-74
‡ Caron, Sebastien	Pit., Chi., Ana., T.B.	5	95	26	48	12	5156	296	4	3.44	....	....	....	....	....	....	....	....		2002-03	2011-12
Carter, Lyle	Cal.	1	15	4	7	0	721	50	0	4.16	....	....	....	....	....	....	....	....		1971-72	1971-72
Casey, Jon	Min., Bos., St.L.	12	425	170	157	55	23255	1246	16	3.21	66	32	31	....	3743	192	3	3.08		1983-84	1996-97
Cassivi, Frederic	Atl., Wsh.	4	13	3	6	1	628	38	0	3.63	....	....	....	....	....	....	....	....		2001-02	2006-07
Cechmanek, Roman	Phi., L.A.	4	212	110	64	28	12085	419	25	2.08	23	9	14	....	1441	56	3	2.33		2000-01	2003-04
Centomo, Sebastien	Tor.	1	1	0	0	0	40	3	0	4.50	....	....	....	....	....	....	....	....		2001-02	2001-02
Chabot, Frederic	Mtl., Phi., L.A.	5	32	4	8	4	1262	62	0	2.95	....	....	....	....	....	....	....	....		1990-91	1998-99
• Chabot, Lorne	NYR, Tor., Mtl., Chi., Mtl.M., NYA	11	412	201	147	62	25411	859	71	2.03	37	13	17	6	2498	64	5	1.54	2	1926-27	1936-37
Chadwick, Ed	Tor., Bos.	6	184	57	92	35	11040	541	14	2.94	....	....	....	....	....	....	....	....		1955-56	1961-62
Champoux, Bob	Det., Cal.	2	17	2	11	3	923	80	0	5.20	1	1	0	....	55	4	0	4.36		1963-64	1973-74
Charpentier, Sebastien	Wsh.	3	26	6	14	1	1350	66	0	2.93	....	....	....	....	....	....	....	....		2001-02	2003-04

Name	NHL Teams	NHL Seasons	Regular Schedule GP	W	L	T	Mins	GA	SO	Avg	Playoffs GP	W	L	T	Mins	GA	SO	Avg	NHL Cup Wins	First NHL Season	Last NHL Season
Cheevers, Gerry	Tor., Bos.	13	418	230	102	74	24394	1174	26	2.89	88	53	34	....	5396	242	8	2.69	2	1961-62	1979-80
Cheveldae, Tim	Det., Wpg., Bos.	9	340	149	136	37	19172	1116	10	3.49	25	9	15	....	1418	71	2	3.00		1988-89	1996-97
Chevrier, Alain	N.J., Wpg., Chi., Pit., Det.	6	234	91	100	14	12202	845	2	4.16	16	9	7	....	1013	44	0	2.61		1985-86	1990-91
Chiodo, Andy	Pit.	1	8	3	4	1	486	28	0	3.46	....	....	....	....	....	....	....	....		2003-04	2003-04
Chouinard, Mathieu	L.A.	1	1	0	0	0	3	0	0	0.00	....	....	....	....	....	....	....	....		2003-04	2003-04
§ • Clancy, King	Ott., Tor.	2	2	0	0	0	3	1	0	20.00	....	....	....	....	....	....	....	....		1924-25	1931-32
§ • Cleghorn, Odie	Pit.	1	1	1	0	0	60	2	0	2.00	....	....	....	....	....	....	....	....		1925-26	1925-26
§ • Cleghorn, Sprague	Ott., Mtl.	2	2	0	0	0	5	0	0	0.00	....	....	....	....	....	....	....	....		1918-19	1921-22
Clifford, Chris	Chi.	2	2	0	0	0	24	0	0	0.00	....	....	....	....	....	....	....	....		1984-85	1988-89
‡ Climie, Matt	Dal., Phx.	3	5	2	2	0	277	15	0	3.25	....	....	....	....	....	....	....	....		2008-09	2010-11
Cloutier, Dan	NYR, T.B., Van., L.A.	10	351	139	142	37	18927	874	15	2.77	25	10	13	0	1361	75	0	3.31		1997-98	2007-08
Cloutier, Jacques	Buf., Chi., Que.	12	255	82	102	24	12826	778	3	3.64	8	1	5	....	413	18	1	2.62		1981-82	1993-94
‡ Coleman, Gerald	T.B.	1	2	0	0	1	43	2	0	2.79	....	....	....	....	....	....	....	....		2005-06	2005-06
• Colvin, Les	Bos.	1	1	0	1	0	60	4	0	4.00	....	....	....	....	....	....	....	....		1948-49	1948-49
§ • Conacher, Charlie	Tor., Det.	3	4	0	0	0	10	0	0	0.00	....	....	....	....	....	....	....	....		1932-33	1938-39
Conklin, Ty	Edm., CBJ, Buf., Pit., Det., St.L.	9	215	96	67	21	11527	516	17	2.69	2	0	1	0	26	1	0	2.31		2001-02	2011-12
• Connell, Alec	Ott., Det., NYA, Mtl.M.	12	417	193	156	67	26050	830	81	1.91	21	8	5	8	1309	26	4	1.19	2	1924-25	1936-37
Corsi, Jim	Edm.	1	26	8	14	3	1366	83	0	3.65	....	....	....	....	....	....	....	....		1979-80	1979-80
• Courteau, Maurice	Bos.	1	6	2	4	0	360	33	0	5.50	....	....	....	....	....	....	....	....		1943-44	1943-44
Cousineau, Marcel	Tor., NYI, L.A.	4	26	4	10	1	1047	51	1	2.92	....	....	....	....	....	....	....	....		1996-97	1999-00
Cowley, Wayne	Edm.	1	1	0	1	0	57	3	0	3.16	....	....	....	....	....	....	....	....		1993-94	1993-94
• Cox, Abbie	Mtl.M., NYA, Det., Mtl.	3	5	1	1	2	263	11	0	2.51	....	....	....	....	....	....	....	....		1929-30	1935-36
Craig, Jim	Atl., Bos., Min.	3	30	11	10	7	1588	100	0	3.78	....	....	....	....	....	....	....	....		1979-80	1983-84
Crha, Jiri	Tor.	2	69	28	27	11	3942	261	0	3.97	5	0	4	....	186	21	0	6.77		1979-80	1980-81
• Crozier, Roger	Det., Buf., Wsh.	14	518	206	197	70	28567	1446	30	3.04	32	14	16	....	1789	82	1	2.75		1963-64	1976-77
• Cude, Wilf	Phi., Bos., Chi., Mtl., Det.	10	282	100	132	49	17586	798	24	2.72	19	7	11	1	1257	51	1	2.43		1930-31	1940-41
Cutts, Don	Edm.	1	6	1	2	1	269	16	0	3.57	....	....	....	....	....	....	....	....		1979-80	1979-80
• Cyr, Claude	Mtl.	1	1	0	0	0	20	1	0	3.00	....	....	....	....	....	....	....	....		1958-59	1958-59
Dadswell, Doug	Cgy.	2	27	8	8	3	1346	99	0	4.41	....	....	....	....	....	....	....	....		1986-87	1987-88
Dafoe, Byron	Wsh., L.A., Bos., Atl.	12	415	171	170	56	23478	1051	26	2.69	27	10	16	....	1686	65	3	2.31		1992-93	2003-04
D'Alessio, Corrie	Hfd.	1	1	0	0	0	11	0	0	0.00	....	....	....	....	....	....	....	....		1992-93	1992-93
Daley, Joe	Pit., Buf., Det.	4	105	34	44	19	5836	326	3	3.35	....	....	....	....	....	....	....	....		1968-69	1971-72
• Damore, Nick	Bos.	1	1	1	0	0	60	3	0	3.00	....	....	....	....	....	....	....	....		1941-42	1941-42
D'Amour, Marc	Cgy., Phi.	2	16	2	4	2	579	32	0	3.32	....	....	....	....	....	....	....	....		1985-86	1988-89
Damphousse, Jean-Fr.	N.J.	1	6	1	3	0	294	12	0	2.45	....	....	....	....	....	....	....	....		2001-02	2001-02
§ • Darragh, Jack	Ott.	1	1	0	0	0	2	0	0	0.00	....	....	....	....	....	....	....	....		1919-20	1919-20
Daskalakis, Cleon	Bos.	3	12	3	4	1	506	41	0	4.86	....	....	....	....	....	....	....	....		1984-85	1986-87
Davidson, John	St.L., NYR	10	301	123	124	39	17109	1004	7	3.52	31	16	14	....	1862	77	1	2.48		1973-74	1982-83
• DeCourcy, Bob	NYR	1	1	0	1	0	29	6	0	12.41	....	....	....	....	....	....	....	....		1947-48	1947-48
Defelice, Norm	Bos.	1	10	3	5	2	600	30	0	3.00	....	....	....	....	....	....	....	....		1956-57	1956-57
DeJordy, Denis	Chi., L.A., Mtl., Det.	12	316	124	128	51	17798	929	15	3.13	18	6	9	....	946	55	0	3.49	1	1960-61	1973-74
‡ Dekanich, Mark	Nsh.	1	1	0	0	0	50	3	0	3.60	....	....	....	....	....	....	....	....		2010-11	2010-11
DelGuidice, Matt	Bos.	2	11	2	5	1	434	28	0	3.87	....	....	....	....	....	....	....	....		1990-91	1991-92
Denis, Marc	Col., CBJ, T.B., Mtl.	11	349	112	179	31	19526	982	16	3.02	....	....	....	....	....	....	....	....		1996-97	2008-09
DeRouville, Philippe	Pit.	2	3	1	2	0	171	9	0	3.16	....	....	....	....	....	....	....	....		1994-95	1996-97
Desjardins, Gerry	L.A., Chi., NYI, Buf.	10	331	122	153	44	19014	1042	12	3.29	35	15	15	....	1874	108	0	3.46		1968-69	1977-78
‡ Deslauriers, Jeff	Edm., Ana.	3	62	23	32	4	3579	193	3	3.24	....	....	....	....	....	....	....	....		2008-09	2011-12
DesRochers, Patrick	Phx., Car.	2	11	2	6	1	540	33	0	3.67	....	....	....	....	....	....	....	....		2001-02	2002-03
• Dickie, Bill	Chi.	1	1	1	0	0	60	3	0	3.00	....	....	....	....	....	....	....	....		1941-42	1941-42
• Dion, Connie	Det.	2	38	23	11	4	2280	119	1	3.13	5	1	4	....	300	17	0	3.40		1943-44	1944-45
Dion, Michel	Que., Wpg., Pit.	6	227	60	118	32	12695	898	2	4.24	5	2	3	....	304	22	0	4.34		1979-80	1984-85
‡ DiPietro, Rick	NYI	11	318	130	136	36	18199	871	16	2.87	10	2	7	....	554	24	1	2.60		2000-01	2012-13
Divis, Reinhard	St.L.	4	28	6	9	3	1212	67	0	3.32	1	0	0	....	18	0	0	0.00		2001-02	2005-06
• Dolson, Dolly	Det.	3	93	35	41	17	5820	192	16	1.98	2	0	2	0	120	7	0	3.50		1928-29	1930-31
Dopson, Rob	Pit.	1	2	0	0	0	45	3	0	4.00	....	....	....	....	....	....	....	....		1993-94	1993-94
Dowie, Bruce	Tor.	1	2	0	1	0	72	4	0	3.33	....	....	....	....	....	....	....	....		1983-84	1983-84
Draper, Tom	Wpg., Buf., NYI	6	53	19	23	5	2807	173	1	3.70	7	3	4	....	433	19	1	2.63		1988-89	1995-96
Dryden, Dave	NYR, Chi., Buf., Edm.	9	203	66	76	31	10424	555	9	3.19	3	0	2	....	133	9	0	4.06		1961-62	1979-80
Dryden, Ken	Mtl.	8	397	258	57	74	23352	870	46	2.24	112	80	32	....	6846	274	10	2.40	6	1970-71	1978-79
Dubielewicz, Wade	NYI, CBJ, Min.	6	43	18	16	2	2196	97	0	2.65	1	0	1	....	59	4	0	4.07		2003-04	2009-10
Duchesne, Jeremy	Phi.	1	1	0	0	0	17	1	0	3.53	....	....	....	....	....	....	....	....		2009-10	2009-10
Duffus, Parris	Phx.	1	1	0	0	0	29	1	0	2.07	....	....	....	....	....	....	....	....		1996-97	1996-97
Dumas, Michel	Chi.	3	8	2	1	2	362	24	0	3.98	1	0	0	....	19	1	0	3.16		1974-75	1976-77
Dunham, Mike	N.J., Nsh., NYR, Atl., NYI	10	394	141	178	44	21653	989	19	2.74	....	....	....	....	....	....	....	....		1996-97	2006-07
Dupuis, Bob	Edm.	1	1	0	1	0	60	4	0	4.00	....	....	....	....	....	....	....	....		1979-80	1979-80
• Durnan, Bill	Mtl.	7	383	208	112	62	22945	901	34	2.36	45	27	18	....	2871	99	2	2.07	2	1943-44	1949-50
Dyck, Ed	Van.	3	49	8	28	5	2453	178	1	4.35	....	....	....	....	....	....	....	....		1971-72	1973-74
Edwards, Don	Buf., Cgy., Tor.	10	459	208	155	74	26181	1449	16	3.32	42	16	21	....	2302	132	1	3.44		1976-77	1985-86
Edwards, Gary	St.L., L.A., Cle., Min., Edm., Pit.	13	286	88	125	51	16002	973	10	3.65	11	5	4	....	537	34	0	3.80		1968-69	1981-82
Edwards, Marv	Pit., Tor., Cal.	4	61	15	34	7	3467	218	2	3.77	....	....	....	....	....	....	....	....		1968-69	1973-74
• Edwards, Roy	Chi., Det., Pit.	8	236	97	88	38	13109	637	12	2.92	4	0	3	....	206	11	0	3.20	1	1960-61	1973-74
Eklund, Brian	T.B.	1	1	0	1	0	58	3	0	3.10	....	....	....	....	....	....	....	....		2005-06	2005-06
Eliot, Darren	L.A., Det., Buf.	5	89	25	41	12	4931	377	1	4.59	1	0	0	....	40	7	0	10.50		1984-85	1988-89
Ellacott, Ken	Van.	1	12	2	3	4	555	41	0	4.43	....	....	....	....	....	....	....	....		1982-83	1982-83
Erickson, Chad	N.J.	1	2	1	1	0	120	9	0	4.50	....	....	....	....	....	....	....	....		1991-92	1991-92
‡ Ersberg, Erik	L.A.	3	53	18	19	10	2827	120	2	2.55	1	0	0	....	13	2	0	9.23		2007-08	2009-10
Esche, Robert	Phx., Phi.	8	186	78	64	22	10139	464	10	2.75	25	13	11	....	1405	64	1	2.73		1998-99	2006-07
Esposito, Tony	Mtl., Chi.	16	886	423	306	151	52585	2563	76	2.92	99	45	53	....	6017	308	6	3.07	1	1968-69	1983-84
Essensa, Bob	Wpg., Det., Edm., Phx., Van., Buf.	12	446	173	176	47	24215	1270	18	3.15	16	4	9	....	864	51	0	3.54		1988-89	2001-02
• Evans, Claude	Mtl., Bos.	2	5	1	2	1	260	16	0	3.69	....	....	....	....	....	....	....	....		1954-55	1957-58
Exelby, Randy	Mtl., Edm.	2	2	0	1	0	63	5	0	4.76	....	....	....	....	....	....	....	....		1988-89	1989-90
Fankhouser, Scott	Atl.	2	23	4	12	2	1180	65	0	3.31	....	....	....	....	....	....	....	....		1999-00	2000-01
Farr, Rocky	Buf.	3	19	2	6	3	722	42	0	3.49	....	....	....	....	....	....	....	....		1972-73	1974-75
Favell, Doug	Phi., Tor., Col.	12	373	123	153	69	20771	1096	18	3.17	21	6	15	....	1270	66	1	3.12		1967-68	1978-79
Fernandez, Manny	Dal., Min., Bos.	13	325	143	123	35	18580	775	15	2.50	11	3	4	....	571	19	0	2.00		1994-95	2008-09
Fichaud, Eric	NYI, Nsh., Car., Mtl.	6	95	22	47	10	4799	251	2	3.14	....	....	....	....	....	....	....	....		1995-96	2000-01
Finley, Brian	Nsh., Bos.	3	4	0	2	0	166	13	0	4.70	....	....	....	....	....	....	....	....		2002-03	2006-07
Fiset, Stephane	Que., Col., L.A., Mtl.	13	390	164	153	44	21785	1114	16	3.07	14	1	7	....	563	37	0	3.94	1	1989-90	2001-02
Fitzpatrick, Mark	L.A., NYI, Fla., T.B., Chi., Car.	12	329	113	136	49	18329	953	8	3.12	9	0	3	....	289	23	0	4.78		1988-89	1999-00
Flaherty, Wade	S.J., NYI, T.B., Fla., Nsh.	11	120	27	56	9	5941	348	5	3.51	7	2	3	....	377	31	0	4.93		1991-92	2002-03
• Forbes, Jake	Tor., Ham., NYA, Phi.	13	210	85	114	11	12922	594	19	2.76	2	0	2	0	120	7	0	3.50		1919-20	1932-33
Ford, Brian	Que., Pit.	2	11	3	7	0	580	61	0	6.31	....	....	....	....	....	....	....	....		1983-84	1984-85
Foster, Brian	Fla.	1	1	0	0	0	5	0	0	0.00	....	....	....	....	....	....	....	....		2011-12	2011-12
Foster, Norm	Bos., Edm.	2	13	7	4	0	623	34	0	3.27	....	....	....	....	....	....	....	....		1990-91	1991-92
Fountain, Mike	Van., Car., Ott.	4	11	2	6	0	483	28	1	3.48	....	....	....	....	....	....	....	....		1996-97	2000-01
• Fowler, Hec	Bos.	1	7	1	6	0	409	42	0	6.16	....	....	....	....	....	....	....	....		1924-25	1924-25
Francis, Emile	Chi., NYR	6	95	31	52	11	5660	355	1	3.76	....	....	....	....	....	....	....	....		1946-47	1951-52
• Franks, Jimmy	Det., NYR, Bos.	4	42	12	23	7	2520	181	1	4.31	1	0	1	....	30	2	0	4.00	1	1936-37	1943-44
Frazee, Jeff	N.J.	1	1	0	0	0	19	0	0	0.00	....	....	....	....	....	....	....	....		2012-13	2012-13
• Frederick, Ray	Chi.	1	5	0	4	1	300	22	0	4.40	....	....	....	....	....	....	....	....		1954-55	1954-55
Friesen, Karl	N.J.	1	4	0	2	1	130	16	0	7.38	....	....	....	....	....	....	....	....		1986-87	1986-87
Froese, Bob	Phi., NYR	8	242	128	72	20	13451	694	13	3.10	18	3	9	....	830	55	0	3.98		1982-83	1989-90
Fuhr, Grant	Edm., Tor., Buf., L.A., St.L., Cgy.	19	868	403	295	114	48945	2756	25	3.38	150	92	50	....	8834	430	6	2.92	5	1981-82	1999-00
Fukufuji, Yutaka	L.A.	1	4	0	3	0	96	7	0	4.38	....	....	....	....	....	....	....	....		2006-07	2006-07
Gage, Joaquin	Edm.	3	23	4	12	1	1076	67	0	3.74	....	....	....	....	....	....	....	....		1994-95	2000-01
Gagnon, Dave	Det.	1	2	0	1	0	35	6	0	10.29	....	....	....	....	....	....	....	....		1990-91	1990-91
• Gamble, Bruce	NYR, Bos., Tor., Phi.	10	327	110	150	46	18442	988	22	3.21	5	0	4	....	206	25	0	7.28		1958-59	1971-72
Gamble, Troy	Van.	4	72	22	29	9	3804	229	1	3.61	4	1	3	....	249	16	0	3.86		1986-87	1991-92
• Gardiner, Bert	NYR, Mtl., Chi., Bos.	6	144	49	68	27	8760	554	3	3.79	9	4	5	....	647	20	0	1.85		1935-36	1943-44
• Gardiner, Charlie	Chi.	7	316	112	152	52	19687	664	42	2.02	21	12	6	3	1472	35	5	1.43	1	1927-28	1933-34

Name	NHL Teams	NHL Seasons	Regular Schedule GP	W	L	T	Mins	GA	SO	Avg	Playoffs GP	W	L	T	Mins	GA	SO	Avg	NHL Cup Wins	First NHL Season	Last NHL Season
• Gardner, George	Det., Van.	5	66	16	30	6	3313	207	0	3.75	....	....	....	....	....	....	....	....		1965-66	1971-72
Garner, Tyrone	Cgy.	1	3	0	2	0	139	12	0	5.18	....	....	....	....	....	....	....	....		1998-99	1998-99
‡ Garnett, Michael	Atl.	1	24	10	7	4	1271	73	2	3.45	....	....	....	....	....	....	....	....		2005-06	2005-06
‡ Garon, Mathieu	Mtl., L.A., Edm., Pit., CBJ, T.B.	12	341	144	131	31	18342	865	20	2.83	2	0	0	....	36	0	0	0.00	1	2000-01	2012-13
Garrett, John	Hfd., Que., Van.	6	207	68	91	37	11763	837	1	4.27	9	4	3	....	461	33	0	4.30		1979-80	1984-85
Gatherum, Dave	Det.	1	3	2	0	1	180	3	1	1.00	....	....	....	....	....	....	....	....	1	1953-54	1953-54
• Gauthier, Paul	Mtl.	1	1	0	0	1	70	2	0	1.71	....	....	....	....	....	....	....	....		1937-38	1937-38
Gauthier, Sean	S.J.	1	1	0	0	0	3	0	0	0.00	....	....	....	....	....	....	....	....		1998-99	1998-99
• Gelineau, Jack	Bos., Chi.	4	143	46	64	33	8580	447	7	3.13	4	1	2	....	260	7	1	1.62		1948-49	1953-54
‡ Gerber, Martin	Ana., Car., Ott., Tor., Edm.	7	229	113	78	21	12920	566	10	2.63	12	1	5	....	479	28	1	3.51	1	2002-03	2010-11
Giacomin, Ed	NYR, Det.	13	609	289	209	96	35633	1672	54	2.82	65	29	35	....	3838	180	1	2.81		1965-66	1977-78
‡ Giguere, Jean-Sebastien	Hfd., Cgy., Ana., Tor., Col.	16	597	262	216	75	33717	1423	38	2.53	52	33	17	....	3167	110	6	2.08	1	1996-97	2013-14
Gilbert, Gilles	Min., Bos., Det.	14	416	192	143	60	23677	1290	18	3.27	32	17	15	....	1919	97	3	3.03		1969-70	1982-83
• Gill, Andre	Bos.	1	5	3	2	0	270	13	1	2.89	....	....	....	....	....	....	....	....		1967-68	1967-68
• Goodman, Paul	Chi.	3	52	23	20	9	3240	117	6	2.17	3	0	3	....	187	10	0	3.21	1	1937-38	1940-41
Gordon, Scott	Que.	2	23	2	16	0	1082	101	0	5.60	....	....	....	....	....	....	....	....		1989-90	1990-91
Gosselin, Mario	Que., L.A., Hfd.	9	241	91	107	14	12857	801	6	3.74	32	16	15	....	1816	99	0	3.27		1983-84	1993-94
Goverde, David	L.A.	3	5	1	4	0	278	29	0	6.26	....	....	....	....	....	....	....	....		1991-92	1993-94
Grahame, John	Bos., T.B., Car.	8	224	97	86	18	12363	574	12	2.79	6	1	4	0	333	19	0	3.42	1	1999-00	2007-08
Grahame, Ron	Bos., L.A., Que.	4	114	50	43	15	6472	409	5	3.79	4	2	1	....	202	7	0	2.08		1977-78	1980-81
• Grant, Benny	Tor., NYA, Bos.	6	52	17	27	4	3036	188	4	3.72	....	....	....	....	....	....	....	....		1928-29	1943-44
Grant, Doug	Det., St.L.	7	77	27	34	8	4199	280	2	4.00	....	....	....	....	....	....	....	....		1973-74	1979-80
Gratton, Gilles	St.L., NYR	2	47	13	18	9	2299	154	0	4.02	....	....	....	....	....	....	....	....		1975-76	1976-77
Gray, Gerry	Det., NYI	2	8	1	5	1	440	35	0	4.77	....	....	....	....	....	....	....	....		1970-71	1972-73
Gray, Harrison	Det.	1	1	0	1	0	40	5	0	7.50	....	....	....	....	....	....	....	....		1963-64	1963-64
Greenlay, Mike	Edm.	1	2	0	0	0	20	4	0	12.00	....	....	....	....	....	....	....	....		1989-90	1989-90
Guenette, Steve	Pit., Cgy.	5	35	19	16	0	1958	122	1	3.74	....	....	....	....	....	....	....	....		1986-87	1990-91
Gustafson, Derek	Min.	2	5	1	3	0	265	10	0	2.26	....	....	....	....	....	....	....	....		2000-01	2001-02
Hackett, Jeff	NYI, S.J., Chi., Mtl., Bos., Phi.	15	500	166	244	56	28125	1361	26	2.90	12	3	7	....	610	36	0	3.54		1988-89	2003-04
• Hainsworth, George	Mtl., Tor.	11	465	246	145	74	29087	937	94	1.93	52	22	25	5	3486	112	8	1.93	2	1926-27	1936-37
Hall, Glenn	Det., Chi., St.L.	19	906	407	326	163	53484	2222	84	2.49	115	49	65	....	6899	320	6	2.78	2	1951-52	1970-71
Hamel, Pierre	Tor., Wpg.	4	69	13	41	7	3766	276	0	4.40	....	....	....	....	....	....	....	....		1974-75	1980-81
Hanlon, Glen	Van., St.L., NYR, Det.	14	477	167	202	61	26037	1561	13	3.60	35	11	15	....	1756	92	4	3.14		1977-78	1990-91
Harrison, Paul	Min., Tor., Pit., Buf.	7	109	28	59	9	5806	408	2	4.22	4	0	1	....	157	9	0	3.44		1975-76	1981-82
Hasek, Dominik	Chi., Buf., Det., Ott.	16	735	389	223	95	42837	1572	81	2.20	119	65	49	0	7318	246	14	2.02	2	1990-91	2007-08
Hauser, Adam	L.A.	1	1	0	0	0	51	6	0	7.06	....	....	....	....	....	....	....	....		2005-06	2005-06
Hayward, Brian	Wpg., Mtl., Min., S.J.	11	357	143	156	37	20025	1242	8	3.72	37	11	18	....	1803	104	0	3.46		1982-83	1992-93
Head, Don	Bos.	1	38	9	26	3	2280	158	2	4.16	....	....	....	....	....	....	....	....		1961-62	1961-62
Healy, Glenn	L.A., NYI, NYR, Tor.	15	437	166	190	47	24256	1361	13	3.37	37	13	15	....	1930	108	0	3.36	1	1985-86	2000-01
Hebert, Guy	St.L., Ana., NYR	10	491	191	222	56	27889	1307	28	2.81	14	4	7	....	744	33	1	2.66		1991-92	2000-01
• Hebert, Sammy	Tor., Ott.	2	4	2	1	0	200	19	0	5.70	....	....	....	....	....	....	....	....	1	1917-18	1923-24
‡ Hedberg, Johan	Pit., Van., Dal., Atl., N.J.	12	373	161	143	36	20758	977	22	2.82	23	10	13	....	1374	53	2	2.31		2000-01	2012-13
‡ Heeter, Cal	Phi.	1	1	0	0	1	64	5	0	4.69	....	....	....	....	....	....	....	....		2013-14	2013-14
Heinz, Rick	St.L., Van.	5	49	14	19	5	2356	159	2	4.05	1	0	0	....	8	1	0	7.50		1980-81	1984-85
‡ Helenius, Riku	T.B.	1	1	0	0	0	7	0	0	0.00	....	....	....	....	....	....	....	....		2008-09	2008-09
Henderson, John	Bos.	2	46	15	15	15	2688	113	5	2.52	2	0	2	....	120	8	0	4.00		1954-55	1955-56
• Henry, Gord	Bos.	4	3	1	2	0	180	5	1	1.67	5	0	4	....	283	21	0	4.45		1948-49	1952-53
• Henry, Jim	NYR, Chi., Bos.	9	406	161	173	70	24355	1166	28	2.87	29	11	18	....	1741	81	2	2.79		1941-42	1954-55
Herron, Denis	Pit., K.C., Mtl.	14	462	146	203	76	25608	1579	10	3.70	15	5	10	....	901	50	0	3.33		1972-73	1985-86
Hextall, Ron	Phi., Que., NYI	13	608	296	214	69	34750	1723	23	2.97	93	47	43	....	5456	276	2	3.04		1986-87	1998-99
• Highton, Hec	Chi.	1	24	10	14	0	1440	108	0	4.50	....	....	....	....	....	....	....	....		1943-44	1943-44
§ • Himes, Normie	NYA	2	2	0	1	0	79	3	0	2.28	....	....	....	....	....	....	....	....		1927-28	1928-29
Hirsch, Corey	NYR, Van., Wsh., Dal.	7	108	34	45	14	5775	301	4	3.13	6	2	3	....	338	21	0	3.73		1992-93	2002-03
Hnilicka, Milan	NYR, Atl., L.A.	5	121	29	67	13	6509	359	5	3.31	....	....	....	....	....	....	....	....		1999-00	2003-04
Hodge, Charlie	Mtl., Oak., Van.	14	358	150	125	61	20573	925	24	2.70	16	7	8	....	804	32	2	2.39	6	1954-55	1970-71
Hodson, Kevin	Det., T.B.	6	71	17	18	10	2910	134	4	2.76	1	0	0	....	1	0	0	0.00	2	1995-96	2002-03
Hoffort, Bruce	Phi.	2	9	4	0	3	368	22	0	3.59	....	....	....	....	....	....	....	....		1989-90	1990-91
Hoganson, Paul	Pit.	1	2	0	1	0	57	7	0	7.37	....	....	....	....	....	....	....	....		1970-71	1970-71
Hogosta, Goran	NYI, Que.	2	22	5	12	3	1208	83	1	4.12	....	....	....	....	....	....	....	....		1977-78	1979-80
Holden, Mark	Mtl., Wpg.	4	8	2	2	1	372	25	0	4.03	....	....	....	....	....	....	....	....		1981-82	1984-85
Holland, Ken	Hfd., Det.	2	4	0	2	1	206	17	0	4.95	....	....	....	....	....	....	....	....		1980-81	1983-84
Holland, Rob	Pit.	2	44	11	22	9	2513	171	1	4.08	....	....	....	....	....	....	....	....		1979-80	1980-81
• Holmes, Hap	Tor., Det.	4	103	39	54	10	6510	264	17	2.43	2	1	1	0	120	7	0	3.50	1	1917-18	1927-28
‡ Holmqvist, Johan	NYR, T.B., Dal.	5	99	48	34	9	5264	262	3	2.99	6	2	4	....	370	18	0	2.92		2000-01	2007-08
Holt, Chris	NYR, St.L.	2	2	0	0	0	29	0	0	0.00	....	....	....	....	....	....	....	....		2005-06	2008-09
§ • Horner, Red	Tor.	2	2	0	0	0	3	1	0	20.00	....	....	....	....	....	....	....	....		1928-29	1931-32
Houle, Martin	Phi.	1	1	0	0	0	2	1	0	30.00	....	....	....	....	....	....	....	....		2006-07	2006-07
Hrivnak, Jim	Wsh., Wpg., St.L.	5	85	34	30	3	4217	262	0	3.73	....	....	....	....	....	....	....	....		1989-90	1993-94
Hrudey, Kelly	NYI, L.A., S.J.	15	677	271	265	88	38084	2174	17	3.43	85	36	46	....	5163	283	0	3.29		1983-84	1997-98
‡ Huet, Cristobal	L.A., Mtl., Wsh., Chi.	7	272	129	90	32	15260	625	24	2.46	17	6	10	....	987	44	0	2.67	1	2002-03	2009-10
Hunwick, Shawn	CBJ	1	1	0	0	0	3	0	0	0.00	....	....	....	....	....	....	....	....		2011-12	2011-12
Hurme, Jani	Ott., Fla.	4	76	29	25	11	4041	176	6	2.61	....	....	....	....	....	....	....	....		1999-00	2002-03
Ing, Peter	Tor., Edm., Det.	4	74	20	37	9	3941	266	1	4.05	....	....	....	....	....	....	....	....		1989-90	1993-94
Inness, Gary	Pit., Phi., Wsh.	7	162	58	61	27	8710	494	2	3.40	9	5	4	....	540	24	0	2.67		1973-74	1980-81
Irbe, Arturs	S.J., Dal., Van., Car.	13	568	218	236	79	32066	1513	33	2.83	51	23	27	....	2981	142	1	2.86		1991-92	2003-04
Ireland, Randy	Buf.	1	2	0	0	0	30	3	0	6.00	....	....	....	....	....	....	....	....		1978-79	1978-79
Irons, Robbie	St.L.	1	1	0	0	0	3	0	0	0.00	....	....	....	....	....	....	....	....		1968-69	1968-69
• Ironstone, Joe	Ott., NYA, Tor.	3	2	0	0	1	110	3	1	1.64	....	....	....	....	....	....	....	....		1924-25	1927-28
‡ Irving, Leland	Cgy.	2	13	3	4	4	664	36	0	3.25	....	....	....	....	....	....	....	....		2011-12	2012-13
Jablonski, Pat	St.L., T.B., Mtl., Phx., Car.	8	128	28	62	18	6634	413	1	3.74	4	0	0	....	139	6	0	2.59		1989-90	1997-98
• Jackson, Doug	Chi.	1	6	2	3	1	360	42	0	7.00	....	....	....	....	....	....	....	....		1947-48	1947-48
• Jackson, Percy	Bos., NYA, NYR	4	7	1	3	1	392	26	0	3.98	....	....	....	....	....	....	....	....		1931-32	1935-36
Jaks, Pauli	L.A.	1	1	0	0	0	40	2	0	3.00	....	....	....	....	....	....	....	....		1994-95	1994-95
Janaszak, Steve	Min., Col.	2	3	0	1	1	160	15	0	5.63	....	....	....	....	....	....	....	....		1979-80	1981-82
Janecyk, Bob	Chi., L.A.	6	110	43	47	13	6250	432	2	4.15	3	0	3	....	184	10	0	3.26		1983-84	1988-89
§ • Jenkins, Roger	NYA	1	1	0	1	0	30	7	0	14.00	....	....	....	....	....	....	....	....		1938-39	1938-39
Jensen, Al	Det., Wsh., L.A.	7	179	95	53	18	9974	557	8	3.35	12	5	5	....	598	32	0	3.21		1980-81	1986-87
Jensen, Darren	Phi.	2	30	15	10	1	1496	95	2	3.81	....	....	....	....	....	....	....	....		1984-85	1985-86
Johnson, Bob	St.L., Pit.	2	24	9	9	1	1059	66	0	3.74	....	....	....	....	....	....	....	....		1972-73	1974-75
Johnson, Brent	St.L., Phx., Wsh., Pit.	12	309	140	112	31	16978	744	14	2.63	15	5	6	0	737	27	3	2.20		1998-99	2011-12
Johnston, Eddie	Bos., Tor., St.L., Chi.	16	592	234	257	80	34216	1852	32	3.25	18	7	10	....	1023	57	1	3.34	2	1962-63	1977-78
Joseph, Curtis	St.L., Edm., Tor., Det., Phx., Cgy.	19	943	454	352	96	54054	2516	51	2.79	133	63	66	....	8106	327	16	2.42		1989-90	2008-09
• Junkin, Joe	Bos.	1	1	0	0	0	8	0	0	0.00	....	....	....	....	....	....	....	....		1968-69	1968-69
Kaarela, Jari	Col.	1	5	2	2	0	220	22	0	6.00	....	....	....	....	....	....	....	....		1980-81	1980-81
Kamppuri, Hannu	N.J.	1	13	1	10	1	645	54	0	5.02	....	....	....	....	....	....	....	....		1984-85	1984-85
• Karakas, Mike	Chi., Mtl.	8	336	114	169	53	20614	1002	28	2.92	23	11	12	0	1434	72	3	3.01	1	1935-36	1945-46
‡ Karlsson, Henrik	Cgy.	2	26	5	9	8	1292	60	0	2.79	....	....	....	....	....	....	....	....		2010-11	2011-12
Keans, Doug	L.A., Bos.	9	210	96	64	26	11388	666	4	3.51	9	2	6	....	432	34	0	4.72		1979-80	1987-88
• Keenan, Don	Bos.	1	1	0	1	0	60	4	0	4.00	....	....	....	....	....	....	....	....		1958-59	1958-59
Keetley, Matt	Cgy.	1	1	0	0	0	9	0	0	0.00	....	....	....	....	....	....	....	....		2007-08	2007-08
• Kerr, Dave	Mtl.M., NYA, NYR	11	427	203	148	75	26639	954	51	2.15	40	18	19	3	2616	76	8	1.74	1	1930-31	1940-41
‡ Khabibulin, Nikolai	Wpg., Phx., T.B., Chi., Edm.	18	799	333	334	97	45609	2071	46	2.72	72	39	31	....	4345	174	6	2.40	1	1994-95	2013-14
Kidd, Trevor	Cgy., Car., Fla., Tor.	12	387	140	162	52	21426	1014	19	2.84	10	3	5	....	550	36	1	3.93		1991-92	2003-04
King, Scott	Det.	2	2	0	0	0	61	3	0	2.95	....	....	....	....	....	....	....	....		1990-91	1991-92
Kiprusoff, Miikka	S.J., Cgy.	12	623	319	213	71	36169	1500	44	2.49	56	25	28	....	3284	127	6	2.32		2000-01	2012-13
Kleisinger, Terry	NYR	1	4	0	2	0	191	14	0	4.40	....	....	....	....	....	....	....	....		1985-86	1985-86
Klymkiw, Julian	NYR	1	1	0	0	0	19	2	0	6.32	....	....	....	....	....	....	....	....		1958-59	1958-59
‡ Knapp, Connor	Buf.	1	2	0	0	1	77	4	0	3.12	....	....	....	....	....	....	....	....		2013-14	2013-14
Knickle, Rick	L.A.	2	14	7	6	0	706	44	0	3.74	....	....	....	....	....	....	....	....		1992-93	1993-94
Kochan, Dieter	T.B., Min.	4	21	1	11	1	849	56	0	3.96	....	....	....	....	....	....	....	....		1999-00	2002-03

			Regular Schedule								Playoffs										
Name	NHL Teams	NHL Seasons	GP	W	L	T	Mins	GA	SO	Avg	GP	W	L	T	Mins	GA	SO	Avg	NHL Cup Wins	First NHL Season	Last NHL Season
‡ Kolesnik, Vitali	Col.	1	8	3	3	0	370	20	0	3.24	....	....	....	....	....	....	....	....		2005-06	2005-06
Kolzig, Olaf	Wsh., T.B.	17	719	303	297	87	41671	1885	35	2.71	45	20	24	....	2799	100	6	2.14		1989-90	2008-09
Konstantinov, Evgeny	T.B.	2	2	0	0	0	21	1	0	2.86	....	....	....	....	....	....	....	....		2000-01	2002-03
Krahn, Brent	Dal.	1	1	0	0	0	20	3	0	9.00	....	....	....	....	....	....	....	....		2008-09	2008-09
Kuntar, Les	Mtl.	1	6	2	2	0	302	16	0	3.18	....	....	....	....	....	....	....	....		1993-94	1993-94
Kurt, Gary	Cal.	1	16	1	7	5	838	60	0	4.30	....	....	....	....	....	....	....	....		1971-72	1971-72
Labbe, Jean-Francois	NYR, CBJ	3	15	3	6	0	628	36	0	3.44	....	....	....	....	....	....	....	....		1999-00	2002-03
Labrecque, Patrick	Mtl.	1	2	0	1	0	98	7	0	4.29	....	....	....	....	....	....	....	....		1995-96	1995-96
Lacher, Blaine	Bos.	2	47	22	16	4	2636	123	4	2.80	5	1	4	....	283	12	0	2.54		1994-95	1995-96
LaCosta, Dan	CBJ	2	4	2	0	0	169	4	1	1.42	....	....	....	....	....	....	....	....		2007-08	2008-09
• Lacroix, Frenchy	Mtl.	2	5	1	4	0	280	16	0	3.43	....	....	....	....	....	....	....	....		1925-26	1926-27
LaFerriere, Rick	Col.	1	1	0	0	0	20	1	0	3.00	....	....	....	....	....	....	....	....		1981-82	1981-82
LaForest, Mark	Det., Phi., Tor., Ott.	6	103	25	54	4	5032	354	2	4.22	2	1	0	....	48	1	0	1.25		1985-86	1993-94
Lajeunesse, Simon	Ott.	1	1	0	0	0	24	0	0	0.00	....	....	....	....	....	....	....	....		2001-02	2001-02
Lalime, Patrick	Pit., Ott., St.L., Chi., Buf.	12	444	200	174	48	25241	1085	35	2.58	41	21	20	....	2549	75	5	1.77		1996-97	2010-11
Lamothe, Marc	Chi., Det.	2	4	2	1	1	241	13	0	3.24	....	....	....	....	....	....	....	....		1999-00	2003-04
Langkow, Scott	Wpg., Phx., Atl.	4	20	3	12	1	943	68	0	4.33	....	....	....	....	....	....	....	....		1995-96	1999-00
• Larocque, Michel	Mtl., Tor., Phi., St.L.	11	312	160	89	45	17615	978	17	3.33	14	6	6	....	759	37	1	2.92	4	1973-74	1983-84
Larocque, Michel	Chi.	1	3	0	2	0	152	9	0	3.55	....	....	....	....	....	....	....	....		2000-01	2000-01
‡ Lasak, Jan	Nsh.	2	6	0	4	0	267	18	0	4.04	....	....	....	....	....	....	....	....		2001-02	2002-03
Laskoski, Gary	L.A.	2	59	19	27	5	2942	228	0	4.65	....	....	....	....	....	....	....	....		1982-83	1983-84
‡ Lawson, Nathan	NYI, Ott.	2	11	1	4	2	396	28	0	4.24	....	....	....	....	....	....	....	....		2010-11	2013-14
Laxton, Gord	Pit.	4	17	4	9	0	800	74	0	5.55	....	....	....	....	....	....	....	....		1975-76	1978-79
LeBlanc, Ray	Chi.	1	1	1	0	0	60	1	0	1.00	....	....	....	....	....	....	....	....		1991-92	1991-92
Leclaire, Pascal	CBJ, Ott.	7	173	61	76	15	9406	453	10	2.89	3	1	2	....	211	10	0	2.84		2003-04	2010-11
§ • Leduc, Albert	Mtl.	1	1	0	0	0	2	1	0	30.00	....	....	....	....	....	....	....	....		1931-32	1931-32
Legace, Manny	L.A., Det., St.L., Car.	11	365	187	99	41	20140	809	24	2.41	11	4	6	....	639	27	0	2.54	1	1998-99	2009-10
Legris, Claude	Det.	2	4	0	1	1	91	4	0	2.64	....	....	....	....	....	....	....	....		1980-81	1981-82
• Lehman, Hugh	Chi.	2	48	20	24	4	3047	136	6	2.68	2	0	1	1	120	10	0	5.00		1926-27	1927-28
Lemelin, Reggie	Atl., Cgy., Bos.	15	507	236	162	63	28006	1613	12	3.46	59	23	25	....	3119	186	2	3.58		1978-79	1992-93
Lenarduzzi, Mike	Hfd.	2	4	1	1	1	189	10	0	3.17	....	....	....	....	....	....	....	....		1992-93	1993-94
‡ LeNeveu, David	Phx., CBJ	3	22	5	9	2	1067	61	0	3.43	....	....	....	....	....	....	....	....		2005-06	2010-11
Lessard, Mario	L.A.	6	240	92	97	39	13529	843	9	3.74	20	6	12	....	1136	83	0	4.38		1978-79	1983-84
Levasseur, Jean-Louis	Min.	1	1	0	1	0	60	7	0	7.00	....	....	....	....	....	....	....	....		1979-80	1979-80
§ • Levinsky, Alex	Tor.	1	1	0	0	0	1	1	0	60.00	....	....	....	....	....	....	....	....		1931-32	1931-32
• Lindbergh, Pelle	Phi.	5	157	87	49	15	9150	503	7	3.30	23	12	10	....	1214	63	3	3.11		1981-82	1985-86
• Lindsay, Bert	Mtl.W., Tor.	2	20	6	14	0	1238	118	0	5.72	....	....	....	....	....	....	....	....		1917-18	1918-19
Little, Neil	Phi.	2	2	0	2	0	93	6	0	3.87	....	....	....	....	....	....	....	....		2001-02	2003-04
Littman, David	Buf., T.B.	3	3	0	2	0	141	14	0	5.96	....	....	....	....	....	....	....	....		1990-91	1992-93
Liut, Mike	St.L., Hfd., Wsh.	13	664	294	271	74	38215	2221	25	3.49	67	29	32	....	3814	215	2	3.38		1979-80	1991-92
Lockett, Ken	Van.	2	55	13	15	8	2348	131	2	3.35	1	0	1	....	60	6	0	6.00		1974-75	1975-76
• Lockhart, Howard	Tor., Que., Ham., Bos.	5	59	16	41	0	3413	287	1	5.05	....	....	....	....	....	....	....	....		1919-20	1924-25
LoPresti, Pete	Min., Edm.	6	175	43	102	20	9858	668	5	4.07	2	0	2	....	77	6	0	4.68		1974-75	1980-81
• LoPresti, Sam	Chi.	2	74	30	38	6	4530	236	4	3.13	8	3	5	....	530	17	1	1.92		1940-41	1941-42
Lorenz, Danny	NYI	3	8	1	5	0	357	25	0	4.20	....	....	....	....	....	....	....	....		1990-91	1992-93
Loustel, Ron	Wpg.	1	1	0	1	0	60	10	0	10.00	....	....	....	....	....	....	....	....		1980-81	1980-81
Low, Ron	Tor., Wsh., Det., Que., Edm., N.J.	11	382	102	203	38	20502	1463	4	4.28	7	1	6	....	452	29	0	3.85		1972-73	1984-85
Lozinski, Larry	Det.	1	30	6	11	7	1459	105	0	4.32	....	....	....	....	....	....	....	....		1980-81	1980-81
• Lumley, Harry	Det., NYR, Chi., Tor., Bos.	16	803	330	329	142	48044	2206	71	2.75	76	29	47	....	4778	198	7	2.49	1	1943-44	1959-60
‡ MacDonald, Joey	Det., Bos., NYI, Tor., Cgy.	8	133	44	61	15	7331	367	2	3.00	....	....	....	....	....	....	....	....		2006-07	2013-14
MacKenzie, Shawn	N.J.	1	4	0	1	0	130	15	0	6.92	....	....	....	....	....	....	....	....		1982-83	1982-83
Madeley, Darrin	Ott.	3	39	4	23	5	1928	140	0	4.36	....	....	....	....	....	....	....	....		1992-93	1994-95
Malarchuk, Clint	Que., Wsh., Buf.	10	338	141	130	45	19030	1100	12	3.47	15	2	9	....	781	56	0	4.30		1981-82	1991-92
Maneluk, George	NYI	1	4	1	1	0	140	15	0	6.43	....	....	....	....	....	....	....	....		1990-91	1990-91
Maniago, Cesare	Tor., Mtl., NYR, Min., Van.	15	568	190	257	97	32569	1773	30	3.27	36	15	21	....	2247	100	3	2.67		1960-61	1977-78
‡ Mannino, Peter	NYI, Atl., Wpg.	3	6	1	1	0	226	15	0	3.98	....	....	....	....	....	....	....	....		2008-09	2011-12
Maracle, Norm	Det., Atl.	5	66	14	33	8	3430	177	1	3.10	2	0	0	....	58	3	0	3.10		1997-98	2001-02
‡ Markkanen, Jussi	Edm., NYR	5	128	43	47	15	6610	297	7	2.70	7	3	3	....	374	14	1	2.25		2001-02	2006-07
• Marois, Jean	Tor., Chi.	2	3	1	2	0	180	15	0	5.00	....	....	....	....	....	....	....	....		1943-44	1953-54
• Martin, Seth	St.L.	1	30	8	10	7	1552	67	1	2.59	2	0	0	....	73	5	0	4.11		1967-68	1967-68
Mason, Bob	Wsh., Chi., Que., Van.	8	145	55	65	16	7988	500	1	3.76	5	2	3	....	369	12	1	1.95		1983-84	1990-91
‡ Mason, Chris	Nsh., St.L., Atl., Wpg.	11	317	137	113	32	17004	754	23	2.66	9	1	8	....	552	27	0	2.93		1998-99	2012-13
Mattsson, Markus	Wpg., Min., L.A.	4	92	21	46	14	5007	343	6	4.11	....	....	....	....	....	....	....	....		1979-80	1983-84
May, Darrell	St.L.	2	6	1	5	0	364	31	0	5.11	....	....	....	....	....	....	....	....		1985-86	1987-88
Mayer, Gilles	Tor.	4	9	2	6	1	540	24	0	2.67	....	....	....	....	....	....	....	....		1949-50	1955-56
• McAuley, Ken	NYR	2	96	17	64	15	5740	537	1	5.61	....	....	....	....	....	....	....	....		1943-44	1944-45
McCartan, Jack	NYR	2	12	2	7	3	680	42	1	3.71	....	....	....	....	....	....	....	....		1959-60	1960-61
• McCool, Frank	Tor.	2	72	34	31	7	4320	242	4	3.36	13	8	5	....	807	30	4	2.23	1	1944-45	1945-46
McDuffe, Peter	St.L., NYR, K.C., Det.	5	57	11	36	6	3207	218	0	4.08	1	0	1	....	60	7	0	7.00		1971-72	1975-76
McGrattan, Tom	Det.	1	1	0	0	0	8	1	0	7.50	....	....	....	....	....	....	....	....		1947-48	1947-48
McKay, Ross	Hfd.	1	1	0	0	0	35	3	0	5.14	....	....	....	....	....	....	....	....		1990-91	1990-91
McKenzie, Bill	Det., K.C., Col.	6	91	18	49	13	4776	326	2	4.10	....	....	....	....	....	....	....	....		1973-74	1979-80
McKichan, Steve	Van.	1	1	0	0	0	20	2	0	6.00	....	....	....	....	....	....	....	....		1990-91	1990-91
McLachlan, Murray	Tor.	1	2	0	1	0	25	4	0	9.60	....	....	....	....	....	....	....	....		1970-71	1970-71
McLean, Kirk	N.J., Van., Car., Fla., NYR	16	612	245	262	72	35090	1904	22	3.26	68	34	34	....	4189	198	6	2.84		1985-86	2000-01
McLelland, Dave	Van.	1	2	1	1	0	120	10	0	5.00	....	....	....	....	....	....	....	....		1972-73	1972-73
McLennan, Jamie	NYI, St.L., Min., Cgy., NYR, Fla.	11	254	80	109	36	13834	617	13	2.68	5	0	2	....	134	7	0	3.13		1993-94	2006-07
• McLeod, Don	Det., Phi.	2	18	3	10	1	879	74	0	5.05	....	....	....	....	....	....	....	....		1970-71	1971-72
McLeod, Jim	St.L.	1	16	6	6	4	880	44	0	3.00	....	....	....	....	....	....	....	....		1971-72	1971-72
McNamara, Gerry	Tor.	2	7	2	2	1	323	14	0	2.60	....	....	....	....	....	....	....	....		1960-61	1969-70
• McNeil, Gerry	Mtl.	8	276	119	105	52	16535	649	28	2.36	35	17	18	....	2284	72	5	1.89	3	1947-48	1957-58
McRae, Gord	Tor.	5	71	30	22	10	3799	221	1	3.49	8	2	5	....	454	22	0	2.91		1972-73	1977-78
McVicar, Rob	Van.	1	1	0	0	0	3	0	0	0.00	....	....	....	....	....	....	....	....		2005-06	2005-06
Melanson, Roland	NYI, Min., L.A., N.J., Mtl.	11	291	129	106	33	16452	995	6	3.63	23	4	9	....	801	59	0	4.42	3	1980-81	1991-92
Meloche, Gilles	Chi., Cal., Cle., Min., Pit.	18	788	270	351	131	45401	2756	20	3.64	45	21	19	....	2464	143	2	3.48		1970-71	1987-88
Micalef, Corrado	Det.	5	113	26	59	15	5794	409	2	4.24	3	0	0	....	49	8	0	9.80		1981-82	1985-86
Michaud, Alfie	Van.	1	2	0	1	0	69	5	0	4.35	....	....	....	....	....	....	....	....		1999-00	1999-00
Michaud, Olivier	Mtl.	1	1	0	0	0	18	0	0	0.00	....	....	....	....	....	....	....	....		2001-02	2001-02
Middlebrook, Lindsay	Wpg., Min., N.J., Edm.	4	37	3	23	6	1845	152	0	4.94	....	....	....	....	....	....	....	....		1979-80	1982-83
• Millar, Al	Bos.	1	6	1	4	1	360	25	0	4.17	....	....	....	....	....	....	....	....		1957-58	1957-58
Millen, Greg	Pit., Hfd., St.L., Que., Chi., Det.	14	604	215	284	89	35377	2281	17	3.87	59	27	29	....	3383	193	0	3.42		1978-79	1991-92
• Miller, Joe	NYA, NYR, Pit., Phi.	4	127	24	87	16	7871	383	16	2.92	3	2	1	0	180	3	1	1.00	1	1927-28	1930-31
Minard, Mike	Edm.	1	1	1	0	0	60	3	0	3.00	....	....	....	....	....	....	....	....		1999-00	1999-00
Mio, Eddie	Edm., NYR, Det.	7	192	64	73	30	10428	705	4	4.06	17	9	7	....	986	63	0	3.83		1979-80	1985-86
• Mitchell, Mike	Tor.	3	22	10	9	0	1190	88	0	4.44	....	....	....	....	....	....	....	....	1	1919-20	1921-22
Moffat, Mike	Bos.	3	19	7	7	2	979	70	0	4.29	11	6	5	....	663	38	0	3.44		1981-82	1983-84
Moog, Andy	Edm., Bos., Dal., Mtl.	18	713	372	209	88	40151	2097	28	3.13	132	68	57	....	7452	377	4	3.04	3	1980-81	1997-98
• Moore, Alfie	NYA, Chi., Det.	4	21	7	14	0	1290	81	1	3.77	3	1	2	....	180	7	0	2.33	1	1936-37	1939-40
Moore, Robbie	Phi., Wsh.	2	6	3	1	1	257	8	2	1.87	5	3	2	....	268	18	0	4.03		1978-79	1982-83
• Morissette, Jean-Guy	Mtl.	1	1	0	1	0	36	4	0	6.67	....	....	....	....	....	....	....	....		1963-64	1963-64
Morrison, Mike	Edm., Ott., Phx.	2	29	11	7	3	1226	67	0	3.28	....	....	....	....	....	....	....	....		2005-06	2006-07
Moss, Tyler	Cgy., Car., Van.	4	30	6	16	1	1496	81	0	3.25	....	....	....	....	....	....	....	....		1997-98	2002-03
• Mowers, Johnny	Det.	4	152	65	61	26	9350	399	15	2.56	32	19	13	....	2000	85	2	2.55	1	1940-41	1946-47
Mrazek, Jerome	Phi.	1	1	0	0	0	6	1	0	10.00	....	....	....	....	....	....	....	....		1975-76	1975-76
§ • Mummery, Harry	Que., Ham.	2	4	2	1	0	192	20	0	6.25	....	....	....	....	....	....	....	....		1919-20	1921-22
Munro, Adam	Chi.	2	17	4	10	3	927	51	1	3.30	....	....	....	....	....	....	....	....		2003-04	2005-06
§ • Munro, Dunc	Mtl.M.	1	1	0	0	0	2	0	0	0.00	....	....	....	....	....	....	....	....		1924-25	1924-25
• Murphy, Hal	Mtl.	1	1	1	0	0	60	4	0	4.00	....	....	....	....	....	....	....	....		1952-53	1952-53
‡ Murphy, Mike	Car.	1	2	0	1	0	36	0	0	0.00	....	....	....	....	....	....	....	....		2011-12	2011-12
• Murray, Mickey	Mtl.	1	1	0	1	0	60	4	0	4.00	....	....	....	....	....	....	....	....		1929-30	1929-30
Muzzatti, Jason	Cgy., Hfd., NYR, S.J.	5	62	13	25	10	3014	167	1	3.32	....	....	....	....	....	....	....	....		1993-94	1997-98

Name	NHL Teams	NHL Seasons	Regular Schedule								Playoffs								NHL Cup Wins	First NHL Season	Last NHL Season
			GP	W	L	T	Mins	GA	SO	Avg	GP	W	L	T	Mins	GA	SO	Avg			
Myllys, Jarmo	Min., S.J.	4	39	4	27	1	1846	161	0	5.23	....	....	....	....	....	....	....	....		1988-89	1991-92
Mylnikov, Sergei	Que.	1	10	1	7	2	568	47	0	4.96	....	....	....	....	....	....	....	....		1989-90	1989-90
Myre, Phil	Mtl., Atl., St.L., Phi., Col., Buf.	14	439	149	198	76	25220	1482	14	3.53	12	6	5	....	747	41	1	3.29		1969-70	1982-83
‡ Nabokov, Evgeni	S.J., NYI, T.B.	14	697	353	227	86	40152	1630	59	2.44	86	42	42	0	5144	208	7	2.43		1999-00	2014-15
Naumenko, Gregg	Ana.	1	2	0	1	0	70	7	0	6.00	....	....	....	....	....	....	....	....		2000-01	2000-01
Newton, Cam	Pit.	2	16	4	7	1	814	51	0	3.76	....	....	....	....	....	....	....	....		1970-71	1972-73
Niittymaki, Antero	Phi., T.B., S.J.	7	234	95	86	31	13113	645	5	2.95	4	1	0	....	164	6	0	2.20		2003-04	2010-11
‡ Nilstorp, Cristopher	Dal.	2	6	1	3	1	330	18	0	3.27	....	....	....	....	....	....	....	....		2012-13	2013-14
‡ Noronen, Mika	Buf., Van.	5	71	23	32	6	3652	163	3	2.68	....	....	....	....	....	....	....	....		2000-01	2005-06
‡ Norrena, Fredrik	CBJ	3	100	35	45	11	5235	243	5	2.79	....	....	....	....	....	....	....	....		2006-07	2008-09
Norris, Jack	Bos., Chi., L.A.	4	58	20	25	4	3119	202	2	3.89	....	....	....	....	....	....	....	....		1964-65	1970-71
Nurminen, Pasi	Atl.	3	125	48	54	12	7059	338	5	2.87	....	....	....	....	....	....	....	....		2001-02	2003-04
Oleschuk, Bill	K.C., Col.	4	55	7	28	10	2835	188	1	3.98	....	....	....	....	....	....	....	....		1975-76	1979-80
• Olesevich, Dan	NYR	1	1	0	0	1	29	2	0	4.14	....	....	....	....	....	....	....	....		1961-62	1961-62
O'Neill, Mike	Wpg., Ana.	4	21	0	9	2	855	61	0	4.28	....	....	....	....	....	....	....	....		1991-92	1996-97
Osgood, Chris	Det., NYI, St.L.	17	744	401	216	95	42564	1768	50	2.49	129	74	49	....	7651	267	15	2.09	3	1993-94	2010-11
Ouellet, Maxime	Phi., Wsh., Van.	3	12	2	6	2	663	34	1	3.08	....	....	....	....	....	....	....	....		2000-01	2005-06
Ouimet, Ted	St.L.	1	1	0	1	0	60	2	0	2.00	....	....	....	....	....	....	....	....		1968-69	1968-69
Pageau, Paul	L.A.	1	1	0	1	0	60	8	0	8.00	....	....	....	....	....	....	....	....		1980-81	1980-81
• Paille, Marcel	NYR	7	107	32	52	22	6342	362	2	3.42	....	....	....	....	....	....	....	....		1957-58	1964-65
Palmateer, Mike	Tor., Wsh.	8	356	149	138	52	20131	1183	17	3.53	29	12	17	....	1765	89	2	3.03		1976-77	1983-84
Pang, Darren	Chi.	3	81	27	35	7	4252	287	0	4.05	6	1	3	....	250	18	0	4.32		1984-85	1988-89
Parent, Bernie	Bos., Phi., Tor.	13	608	271	198	121	35136	1493	54	2.55	71	38	33	....	4302	174	6	2.43	2	1965-66	1978-79
Parent, Bob	Tor.	2	3	0	2	0	160	15	0	5.63	....	....	....	....	....	....	....	....		1981-82	1982-83
Parent, Rich	St.L., T.B., Pit.	4	32	7	11	5	1561	82	1	3.15	....	....	....	....	....	....	....	....		1997-98	2000-01
Parro, Dave	Wsh.	4	77	21	36	10	4015	274	2	4.09	....	....	....	....	....	....	....	....		1980-81	1983-84
Passmore, Steve	Edm., Chi., L.A.	6	93	23	44	12	5045	235	2	2.79	3	0	2	....	138	6	0	2.61		1998-99	2003-04
§ • Patrick, Lester	NYR	1	....	....	....	....	....	....	....	....	1	1	0	0	46	1	0	1.30	1	1927-28	1927-28
‡ Patzold, Dimitri	S.J.	1	3	0	0	0	44	4	0	5.45	....	....	....	....	....	....	....	....		2007-08	2007-08
Pechurski, Alexander	Pit.	1	1	0	0	0	36	1	0	1.67	....	....	....	....	....	....	....	....		2009-10	2009-10
Peeters, Pete	Phi., Bos., Wsh.	13	489	246	155	51	27699	1424	21	3.08	71	35	35	....	4200	232	2	3.31		1978-79	1990-91
Pelletier, Jean-Marc	Phi., Phx.	3	7	1	4	0	354	23	0	3.90	....	....	....	....	....	....	....	....		1998-99	2003-04
Pelletier, Marcel	Chi., NYR	2	8	1	6	0	395	32	0	4.86	....	....	....	....	....	....	....	....		1950-51	1962-63
Penney, Steve	Mtl., Wpg.	5	91	35	38	12	5194	313	1	3.62	27	15	12	....	1604	72	4	2.69		1983-84	1987-88
• Perreault, Bob	Mtl., Det., Bos.	3	31	8	16	7	1827	103	3	3.38	....	....	....	....	....	....	....	....		1955-56	1962-63
Pettie, Jim	Bos.	3	21	9	7	2	1157	71	1	3.68	....	....	....	....	....	....	....	....		1976-77	1978-79
‡ Pielmeier, Timo	Ana.	1	1	0	0	0	40	5	0	7.50	....	....	....	....	....	....	....	....		2010-11	2010-11
Pietrangelo, Frank	Pit., Hfd.	7	141	46	59	6	7141	490	1	4.12	12	7	5	....	713	34	1	2.86	1	1987-88	1993-94
• Plante, Jacques	Mtl., NYR, St.L., Tor., Bos.	18	837	437	246	145	49533	1964	82	2.38	112	71	36	....	6651	237	14	2.14	6	1952-53	1972-73
• Plasse, Michel	St.L., Mtl., K.C., Pit., Col., Que.	11	299	92	136	54	16760	1058	2	3.79	4	1	2	....	195	9	1	2.77	1	1970-71	1981-82
§ • Plaxton, Hugh	Mtl.M.	1	1	0	1	0	57	5	0	5.26	....	....	....	....	....	....	....	....		1932-33	1932-33
Pogge, Justin	Tor.	1	7	1	4	1	372	27	0	4.35	....	....	....	....	....	....	....	....		2008-09	2008-09
‡ Popperle, Tomas	CBJ	1	2	0	0	0	45	1	0	1.33	....	....	....	....	....	....	....	....		2006-07	2006-07
Potvin, Felix	Tor., NYI, Van., L.A., Bos.	13	635	266	260	85	36765	1694	32	2.76	72	35	37	....	4435	195	8	2.64		1991-92	2003-04
Pronovost, Claude	Bos., Mtl.	2	3	1	1	0	120	7	1	3.50	....	....	....	....	....	....	....	....		1955-56	1958-59
Prusek, Martin	Ott., CBJ	4	57	31	12	4	2898	114	3	2.36	1	0	0	....	40	1	0	1.50		2001-02	2005-06
Puppa, Daren	Buf., Tor., T.B.	15	429	179	161	54	23819	1204	19	3.03	16	4	9	....	786	51	0	3.89		1985-86	1999-00
Pusey, Chris	Det.	1	1	0	0	0	40	3	0	4.50	....	....	....	....	....	....	....	....		1985-86	1985-86
Racicot, Andre	Mtl.	5	68	26	23	8	3357	196	2	3.50	4	0	1	....	31	4	0	7.74	1	1989-90	1993-94
Racine, Bruce	St.L.	1	11	0	3	0	230	12	0	3.13	1	0	0	....	1	0	0	0.00		1995-96	1995-96
Ram, Jamie	NYR	1	1	0	0	0	27	0	0	0.00	....	....	....	....	....	....	....	....		1995-96	1995-96
Ranford, Bill	Bos., Edm., Wsh., T.B., Det.	15	647	240	279	76	35936	2042	15	3.41	53	28	25	....	3110	159	4	3.07	2	1985-86	1999-00
Raycroft, Andrew	Bos., Tor., Col., Van., Dal.	11	280	113	114	27	15191	732	9	2.89	8	3	4	....	472	17	1	2.16		2000-01	2011-12
Raymond, Alain	Wsh.	1	1	0	1	0	40	2	0	3.00	....	....	....	....	....	....	....	....		1987-88	1987-88
• Rayner, Chuck	NYA, Bro., NYR	10	424	138	208	77	25491	1294	25	3.05	18	9	9	....	1135	46	1	2.43		1940-41	1952-53
Reaugh, Daryl	Edm., Hfd.	3	27	8	9	1	1246	72	1	3.47	....	....	....	....	....	....	....	....		1984-85	1990-91
Reddick, Pokey	Wpg., Edm., Fla.	6	132	46	58	16	7162	443	0	3.71	4	0	2	....	168	10	0	3.57	1	1986-87	1993-94
§ • Redding, George	Bos.	1	1	0	0	0	11	1	0	5.45	....	....	....	....	....	....	....	....		1924-25	1924-25
Redquest, Greg	Pit.	1	1	0	0	0	13	3	0	13.85	....	....	....	....	....	....	....	....		1977-78	1977-78
Reece, Dave	Bos.	1	14	7	5	2	777	43	2	3.32	....	....	....	....	....	....	....	....		1975-76	1975-76
Reese, Jeff	Tor., Cgy., Hfd., T.B., N.J.	11	174	53	65	17	8667	529	5	3.66	11	3	5	....	515	35	0	4.08		1987-88	1998-99
Resch, Glenn	NYI, Col., N.J., Phi.	14	571	231	224	82	32279	1761	26	3.27	41	17	17	....	2044	85	2	2.50	1	1973-74	1986-87
• Rheaume, Herb	Mtl.	1	31	10	20	1	1889	92	0	2.92	....	....	....	....	....	....	....	....		1925-26	1925-26
Rhodes, Damian	Tor., Ott., Atl.	10	309	99	140	48	17339	820	12	2.84	13	5	7	....	741	27	0	2.19		1990-91	2001-02
Ricci, Nick	Pit.	4	19	7	12	0	1087	79	0	4.36	....	....	....	....	....	....	....	....		1979-80	1982-83
Richardson, Terry	Det., St.L.	5	20	3	11	0	906	85	0	5.63	....	....	....	....	....	....	....	....		1973-74	1978-79
Richter, Mike	NYR	15	666	301	258	73	38183	1840	24	2.89	76	41	33	....	4514	202	9	2.68	1	1988-89	2002-03
Ridley, Curt	NYR, Van., Tor.	6	104	27	47	16	5498	355	1	3.87	2	0	2	....	120	8	0	4.00		1974-75	1980-81
Riendeau, Vincent	Mtl., St.L., Det., Bos.	8	184	85	65	20	10423	573	5	3.30	25	11	12	....	1277	71	1	3.34		1987-88	1994-95
Riggin, Dennis	Det.	2	18	6	10	2	999	52	1	3.12	....	....	....	....	....	....	....	....		1959-60	1962-63
Riggin, Pat	Atl., Cgy., Wsh., Bos., Pit.	9	350	153	120	52	19872	1135	11	3.43	25	8	13	....	1336	72	0	3.23		1979-80	1987-88
Ring, Bob	Bos.	1	1	0	0	0	33	4	0	7.27	....	....	....	....	....	....	....	....		1965-66	1965-66
• Rivard, Fern	Min.	4	55	9	27	11	2865	190	2	3.98	....	....	....	....	....	....	....	....		1968-69	1974-75
• Roach, John Ross	Tor., NYR, Det.	14	492	219	204	68	30444	1246	58	2.46	29	12	14	3	1901	60	7	1.89	1	1921-22	1934-35
• Roberts, Moe	Bos., NYA, Chi.	4	10	3	5	0	501	31	0	3.71	....	....	....	....	....	....	....	....		1925-26	1951-52
• Robertson, Earl	Det., NYA, Bro.	6	190	60	95	34	11820	575	16	2.92	15	7	7	....	995	29	2	1.75	1	1936-37	1941-42
• Rollins, Al	Tor., Chi., NYR	9	430	141	205	83	25723	1192	28	2.78	13	6	7	....	755	30	0	2.38	1	1949-50	1959-60
Roloson, Dwayne	Cgy., Buf., Min., Edm., NYI, T.B.	14	606	227	257	82	34297	1552	29	2.72	50	28	18	....	2860	121	2	2.54		1996-97	2011-12
Romano, Roberto	Pit., Bos.	6	126	46	63	8	7111	471	4	3.97	....	....	....	....	....	....	....	....		1982-83	1993-94
Rosati, Mike	Wsh.	1	1	1	0	0	28	0	0	0.00	....	....	....	....	....	....	....	....		1998-99	1998-99
Roussel, Dominic	Phi., Wpg., Ana., Edm.	8	205	77	70	23	10665	555	7	3.12	1	0	0	....	23	0	0	0.00		1991-92	2000-01
Roy, Patrick	Mtl., Col.	19	1029	551	315	131	60235	2546	66	2.54	247	151	94	....	15209	584	23	2.30	4	1984-85	2002-03
Rudkowsky, Cody	St.L.	1	1	1	0	0	30	0	0	0.00	....	....	....	....	....	....	....	....		2002-03	2002-03
• Rupp, Pat	Det.	1	1	0	1	0	60	4	0	4.00	....	....	....	....	....	....	....	....		1963-64	1963-64
Rutherford, Jim	Det., Pit., Tor., L.A.	13	457	151	227	59	25895	1576	14	3.65	8	2	5	....	440	28	0	3.82		1970-71	1982-83
• Rutledge, Wayne	L.A.	3	82	28	37	9	4325	241	2	3.34	8	2	4	....	378	20	0	3.17		1967-68	1969-70
‡ Sabourin, Dany	Cgy., Pit., Van.	5	57	18	25	4	2901	139	2	2.87	2	0	0	....	14	1	0	4.29		2003-04	2008-09
St. Croix, Rick	Phi., Tor.	8	130	49	54	18	7295	451	2	3.71	11	4	6	....	562	29	1	3.10		1977-78	1984-85
St. Laurent, Sam	N.J., Det.	5	34	7	12	4	1572	92	1	3.51	1	0	0	....	10	1	0	6.00		1985-86	1989-90
‡ Salak, Alexander	Fla.	1	2	0	1	0	67	6	0	5.37	....	....	....	....	....	....	....	....		2009-10	2009-10
Salo, Tommy	NYI, Edm., Col.	10	526	210	225	73	30436	1296	37	2.55	22	5	16	....	1369	58	0	2.54		1994-95	2003-04
§ • Sands, Charlie	Mtl.	1	1	0	0	0	25	5	0	12.00	....	....	....	....	....	....	....	....		1939-40	1939-40
Sands, Mike	Min.	2	6	0	5	0	302	26	0	5.17	....	....	....	....	....	....	....	....		1984-85	1986-87
‡ Sanford, Curtis	St.L., Van., CBJ	6	144	47	55	15	7354	333	6	2.72	....	....	....	....	....	....	....	....		2002-03	2011-12
Sarjeant, Geoff	St.L., S.J.	2	8	1	2	1	291	20	0	4.12	....	....	....	....	....	....	....	....		1994-95	1995-96
Sauve, Bob	Buf., Det., Chi., N.J.	13	420	182	154	54	23711	1377	8	3.48	34	15	16	....	1850	95	4	3.08		1976-77	1988-89
Sauve, Philippe	Col., Cgy., Phx., Bos.	3	32	10	14	3	1616	93	0	3.45	....	....	....	....	....	....	....	....		2003-04	2006-07
• Sawchuk, Terry	Det., Bos., Tor., L.A., NYR	21	971	447	330	172	57194	2389	103	2.51	106	54	48	....	6290	266	12	2.54	4	1949-50	1969-70
• Schaefer, Joe	NYR	2	2	0	2	0	86	8	0	5.58	....	....	....	....	....	....	....	....		1959-60	1960-61
‡ Schaefer, Nolan	S.J.	1	7	5	1	0	352	11	1	1.88	....	....	....	....	....	....	....	....		2005-06	2005-06
Schafer, Paxton	Bos.	1	3	0	0	0	77	6	0	4.68	....	....	....	....	....	....	....	....		1996-97	1996-97
Schwab, Corey	N.J., T.B., Van., Tor.	8	147	42	63	13	7476	360	6	2.89	3	0	0	....	40	0	0	0.00	1	1995-96	2003-04
‡ Schwarz, Marek	St.L.	3	6	0	2	0	125	9	0	4.32	....	....	....	....	....	....	....	....		2006-07	2008-09
Scott, Ron	NYR, L.A.	5	28	8	13	4	1450	91	0	3.77	1	0	0	....	32	4	0	7.50		1983-84	1989-90
Scott, Travis	L.A.	1	1	0	0	0	25	3	0	7.20	....	....	....	....	....	....	....	....		2000-01	2000-01
Sevigny, Richard	Mtl., Que.	9	176	80	54	20	9485	507	5	3.21	4	0	3	....	208	13	0	3.75	1	1978-79	1986-87
Sharples, Scott	Cgy.	1	1	0	0	1	65	4	0	3.69	....	....	....	....	....	....	....	....		1991-92	1991-92
§ • Shields, Al	NYA	1	2	0	0	0	41	9	0	13.17	....	....	....	....	....	....	....	....		1931-32	1931-32
Shields, Steve	Buf., S.J., Ana., Bos., Fla., Atl.	10	246	80	104	40	13630	606	10	2.67	25	9	16	....	1445	74	1	3.07		1995-96	2005-06
Shtalenkov, Mikhail	Ana., Edm., Phx., Fla.	7	190	62	82	19	9966	480	8	2.89	4	0	3	....	211	10	0	2.84		1993-94	1999-00

Name	NHL Teams	NHL Seasons	Regular Schedule GP	W	L	T	Mins	GA	SO	Avg	Playoffs GP	W	L	T	Mins	GA	SO	Avg	NHL Cup Wins	First NHL Season	Last NHL Season
Shulmistra, Richard	N.J., Fla.	2	2	1	1	0	122	3	0	1.48	....	....	....	....	....	....	....	....		1997-98	1999-00
Sidorkiewicz, Peter	Hfd., Ott., N.J.	8	246	79	128	27	13884	832	8	3.60	15	5	10	....	912	55	0	3.62		1987-88	1997-98
Sigalet, Jordan	Bos.	1	1	0	0	0	1	0	0	0.00	....	....	....	....	....	....	....	....		2005-06	2005-06
• Simmons, Don	Bos., Tor., NYR	11	249	101	101	41	14555	701	20	2.89	24	13	11	....	1436	62	3	2.59	3	1956-57	1968-69
Simmons, Gary	Cal., Cle., L.A.	4	107	30	57	15	6162	366	5	3.56	1	0	0	....	20	1	0	3.00		1974-75	1977-78
Skidmore, Paul	St.L.	1	2	1	1	0	120	6	0	3.00	....	....	....	....	....	....	....	....		1981-82	1981-82
Skorodenski, Warren	Chi., Edm.	5	35	12	11	4	1732	100	2	3.46	2	0	0	....	33	6	0	10.91		1981-82	1987-88
Skudra, Peter	Pit., Buf., Bos., Van.	6	146	51	47	20	7162	326	6	2.73	3	0	1	....	116	6	0	3.10		1997-98	2002-03
• Smith, Al	Tor., Pit., Det., Buf., Hfd., Col.	10	233	74	99	36	12752	735	10	3.46	6	1	4	....	317	21	0	3.97		1965-66	1980-81
Smith, Billy	L.A., NYI	18	680	305	233	105	38431	2031	22	3.17	132	88	36	....	7645	348	5	2.73	4	1971-72	1988-89
Smith, Gary	Tor., Oak., Cal., Chi., Van., Min., Wsh., Wpg.	14	532	173	261	74	29619	1675	26	3.39	20	5	13	....	1153	62	1	3.23		1965-66	1979-80
• Smith, Normie	Mtl.M., Det.	8	199	81	83	35	12357	479	17	2.33	12	9	2	0	820	18	3	1.32	2	1931-32	1944-45
Sneddon, Bob	Cal.	1	5	0	2	0	225	21	0	5.60	....	....	....	....	....	....	....	....		1970-71	1970-71
Snow, Garth	Que., Phi., Van., Pit., NYI	12	368	135	147	44	19837	925	16	2.80	20	9	8	....	1040	48	1	2.77		1993-94	2005-06
Soderstrom, Tommy	Phi., NYI	5	156	45	69	19	8189	496	10	3.63	....	....	....	....	....	....	....	....		1992-93	1996-97
Soetaert, Doug	NYR, Wpg., Mtl.	12	284	110	104	42	15583	1030	6	3.97	5	1	2	....	180	14	0	4.67	1	1975-76	1986-87
Soucy, Christian	Chi.	1	1	0	0	0	3	0	0	0.00	....	....	....	....	....	....	....	....		1993-94	1993-94
• Spooner, Red	Pit.	1	1	0	1	0	60	6	0	6.00	....	....	....	....	....	....	....	....		1929-30	1929-30
§ • Spring, Jesse	Ham.	1	1	0	0	0	2	0	0	0.00	....	....	....	....	....	....	....	....		1924-25	1924-25
‡ Stana, Rastislav	Wsh.	1	6	1	2	0	211	11	0	3.13	....	....	....	....	....	....	....	....		2003-04	2003-04
Staniowski, Ed	St.L., Wpg., Hfd.	10	219	67	104	21	12075	818	2	4.06	8	1	6	....	428	28	0	3.93		1975-76	1984-85
§ • Starr, Harold	Mtl.M.	1	1	0	0	0	3	0	0	0.00	....	....	....	....	....	....	....	....		1931-32	1931-32
Stauber, Robb	L.A., Buf.	4	62	21	23	9	3295	209	1	3.81	4	3	1	....	240	16	0	4.00		1989-90	1994-95
Stefan, Greg	Det.	9	299	115	127	30	16333	1068	5	3.92	30	12	17	....	1681	99	1	3.53		1981-82	1989-90
• Stein, Phil	Tor.	1	1	0	0	1	70	2	0	1.71	....	....	....	....	....	....	....	....		1939-40	1939-40
‡ Stephan, Tobias	Dal.	2	11	1	3	2	499	29	0	3.49	....	....	....	....	....	....	....	....		2007-08	2008-09
• Stephenson, Wayne	St.L., Phi., Wsh.	10	328	146	103	49	18343	937	14	3.06	26	11	12	....	1522	79	2	3.11	1	1971-72	1980-81
• Stevenson, Doug	NYR, Chi.	3	8	2	6	0	480	39	0	4.88	....	....	....	....	....	....	....	....		1944-45	1945-46
• Stewart, Charles	Bos.	3	77	30	41	5	4742	194	10	2.45	....	....	....	....	....	....	....	....		1924-25	1926-27
Stewart, Jim	Bos.	1	1	0	1	0	20	5	0	15.00	....	....	....	....	....	....	....	....		1979-80	1979-80
Storr, Jamie	L.A., Car.	10	219	85	86	23	11512	488	16	2.54	5	0	3	....	182	11	0	3.63		1994-95	2003-04
• Stuart, Herb	Det.	1	3	1	2	0	180	5	0	1.67	....	....	....	....	....	....	....	....		1926-27	1926-27
Sylvestri, Don	Bos.	1	3	0	0	2	102	6	0	3.53	....	....	....	....	....	....	....	....		1984-85	1984-85
Tabaracci, Rick	Pit., Wpg., Wsh., Cgy., T.B., Atl., Col.	11	286	93	125	30	15255	760	15	2.99	17	4	12	....	1025	53	0	3.10		1988-89	1999-00
Takko, Kari	Min., Edm.	6	142	37	71	14	7317	475	1	3.90	4	0	1	....	109	7	0	3.85		1985-86	1990-91
Tallas, Robbie	Bos., Chi.	6	99	28	42	10	5069	246	3	2.91	....	....	....	....	....	....	....	....		1995-96	2000-01
Tanner, John	Que.	3	21	2	11	5	1084	65	1	3.60	....	....	....	....	....	....	....	....		1989-90	1991-92
‡ Tarkki, Iiro	Ana.	1	1	1	0	0	41	3	0	4.39	....	....	....	....	....	....	....	....		2011-12	2011-12
Tataryn, Dave	NYR	1	2	1	1	0	80	10	0	7.50	....	....	....	....	....	....	....	....		1976-77	1976-77
Taylor, Bobby	Phi., Pit.	5	46	15	17	6	2268	155	0	4.10	....	....	....	....	....	....	....	....	2	1971-72	1975-76
‡ Taylor, Daniel	L.A., Cgy.	2	3	1	1	0	140	8	0	3.43	....	....	....	....	....	....	....	....		2007-08	2012-13
‡ Tellqvist, Mikael	Tor., Phx., Buf.	6	113	45	41	10	6034	303	6	3.01	....	....	....	....	....	....	....	....		2002-03	2008-09
• Teno, Harvey	Det.	1	5	2	3	0	300	15	0	3.00	....	....	....	....	....	....	....	....		1938-39	1938-39
Terreri, Chris	N.J., S.J., Chi., NYI	14	406	151	172	43	22369	1143	9	3.07	29	12	12	....	1523	86	0	3.39	2	1986-87	2000-01
‡ Theodore, Jose	Mtl., Col., Wsh., Min., Fla.	17	648	286	254	69	36607	1635	33	2.68	56	21	30	0	3185	148	2	2.79		1995-96	2012-13
Thibault, Jocelyn	Que., Col., Mtl., Chi., Pit., Buf.	14	586	238	238	75	32892	1508	39	2.75	18	4	11	....	848	50	0	3.54		1993-94	2007-08
‡ Thomas, Tim	Bos., Fla., Dal.	9	426	214	145	49	24448	1027	31	2.52	51	29	21	0	3115	108	6	2.08	1	2002-03	2013-14
Thomas, Wayne	Mtl., Tor., NYR	9	243	103	93	34	13768	766	10	3.34	15	6	8	....	849	50	1	3.53		1972-73	1980-81
• Thompson, Tiny	Bos., Det.	12	553	284	194	75	34175	1183	81	2.08	44	20	24	0	2974	93	7	1.88	1	1928-29	1939-40
‡ Toivonen, Hannu	Bos., St.L.	3	61	18	24	10	3259	183	1	3.37	....	....	....	....	....	....	....	....		2005-06	2007-08
§ • Toppazzini, Jerry	Bos.	1	1	0	0	0	1	0	0	0.00	....	....	....	....	....	....	....	....		1960-61	1960-61
Torchia, Mike	Dal.	1	6	3	2	1	327	18	0	3.30	....	....	....	....	....	....	....	....		1994-95	1994-95
Tordjman, Josh	Phx.	1	2	0	2	0	118	8	0	4.07	....	....	....	....	....	....	....	....		2008-09	2008-09
Toskala, Vesa	S.J., Tor., Cgy.	8	266	129	82	30	14767	679	13	2.76	11	6	5	....	686	28	1	2.45		2001-02	2009-10
Trefilov, Andrei	Cgy., Buf., Chi.	7	54	12	25	4	2663	153	2	3.45	1	0	0	....	5	0	0	0.00		1992-93	1998-99
Tremblay, Vincent	Tor., Pit.	5	58	12	26	8	2785	223	1	4.80	....	....	....	....	....	....	....	....		1979-80	1983-84
Tucker, Ted	Cal.	1	5	1	1	1	177	10	0	3.39	....	....	....	....	....	....	....	....		1973-74	1973-74
Tugnutt, Ron	Que., Edm., Ana., Mtl., Ott., Pit., CBJ, Dal.	16	537	186	239	62	29486	1497	26	3.05	25	9	13	....	1482	56	3	2.27		1987-88	2003-04
Turco, Marty	Dal., Chi., Bos.	11	543	275	167	66	30357	1216	41	2.36	47	21	26	....	3103	112	4	2.17		2000-01	2011-12
Turek, Roman	Dal., St.L., Cgy.	8	328	159	115	43	19095	734	27	2.31	22	12	9	....	1342	50	0	2.24	1	1996-97	2003-04
• Turner, Joe	Det.	1	1	0	0	1	70	3	0	2.57	....	....	....	....	....	....	....	....		1941-42	1941-42
Underhill, Matt	Chi.	1	1	0	1	0	61	4	0	3.93	....	....	....	....	....	....	....	....		2003-04	2003-04
Vachon, Rogie	Mtl., L.A., Det., Bos.	16	795	355	291	127	46298	2310	51	2.99	48	23	23	....	2876	133	2	2.77	3	1966-67	1981-82
Valiquette, Steve	NYI, Edm., NYR	6	46	16	14	5	2256	103	4	2.74	2	0	0	....	40	0	0	0.00		1999-00	2009-10
Vanbiesbrouck, John	NYR, Fla., Phi., NYI, N.J.	20	882	374	346	119	50475	2503	40	2.98	71	28	38	....	3969	177	5	2.68		1981-82	2001-02
Veisor, Mike	Chi., Hfd., Wpg.	10	139	41	62	26	7806	532	5	4.09	4	0	2	....	180	15	0	5.00		1973-74	1983-84
Vernon, Mike	Cgy., Det., S.J., Fla.	19	781	385	273	92	44449	2206	27	2.98	138	77	56	....	8214	367	6	2.68	2	1982-83	2001-02
• Vezina, Georges	Mtl.	9	190	103	81	5	11592	633	13	3.28	13	10	3	0	780	35	2	2.69	1	1917-18	1925-26
Villemure, Gilles	NYR, Chi.	10	205	100	64	29	11581	542	13	2.81	14	5	5	....	656	32	0	2.93		1963-64	1976-77
‡ Vokoun, Tomas	Mtl., Nsh., Fla., Wsh., Pit.	15	700	300	288	78	39695	1688	51	2.55	22	9	13	....	1365	51	2	2.24		1996-97	2012-13
Waite, Jimmy	Chi., S.J., Phx.	11	106	28	41	12	5253	293	4	3.35	6	0	3	....	211	14	0	3.98		1988-89	1998-99
Wakaluk, Darcy	Buf., Min., Dal., Phx.	8	191	67	75	21	9756	524	9	3.22	8	4	2	....	364	18	0	2.97		1988-89	1996-97
Wakely, Ernie	Mtl., St.L.	7	113	41	42	17	6244	290	8	2.79	10	2	6	....	509	37	1	4.36	2	1962-63	1971-72
Wall, Michael	Ana.	1	4	2	2	0	202	10	0	2.97	....	....	....	....	....	....	....	....		2006-07	2006-07
• Walsh, Flat	Mtl.M., NYA	7	108	48	43	16	6641	256	12	2.31	8	2	4	2	570	16	2	1.68		1926-27	1932-33
Wamsley, Rick	Mtl., St.L., Cgy., Tor.	13	407	204	131	46	23123	1287	12	3.34	27	7	18	....	1397	81	0	3.48	1	1980-81	1992-93
Watt, Jim	St.L.	1	1	0	0	0	20	2	0	6.00	....	....	....	....	....	....	....	....		1973-74	1973-74
Weekes, Kevin	Fla., Van., NYI, T.B., Car., NYR, N.J.	11	348	105	163	39	18837	903	19	2.88	9	3	3	....	468	15	2	1.92		1997-98	2008-09
Weeks, Steve	NYR, Hfd., Van., NYI, L.A., Ott.	14	290	111	119	33	15879	989	5	3.74	12	3	5	....	486	27	0	3.33		1980-81	1992-93
‡ Weiman, Tyler	Col.	1	1	0	0	0	16	0	0	0.00	....	....	....	....	....	....	....	....		2007-08	2007-08
Wetzel, Carl	Det., Min.	2	7	1	4	1	301	22	0	4.39	....	....	....	....	....	....	....	....		1964-65	1967-68
Whitmore, Kay	Hfd., Van., Bos., Cgy.	9	155	60	64	16	8596	508	4	3.55	4	0	2	....	174	13	0	4.48		1988-89	2001-02
Wilkinson, Derek	T.B.	4	22	3	12	3	933	57	0	3.67	....	....	....	....	....	....	....	....		1995-96	1998-99
Willis, Jordan	Dal.	1	1	0	1	0	19	1	0	3.16	....	....	....	....	....	....	....	....		1995-96	1995-96
Wilson, Dunc	Phi., Van., Tor., NYR, Pit.	10	287	80	150	33	15851	988	8	3.74	....	....	....	....	....	....	....	....		1969-70	1978-79
• Wilson, Lefty	Det., Tor., Bos.	3	3	0	0	1	81	1	0	0.74	....	....	....	....	....	....	....	....		1953-54	1957-58
• Winkler, Hal	NYR, Bos.	2	75	35	26	14	4739	126	21	1.60	10	2	3	5	640	18	2	1.69		1926-27	1927-28
Wolfe, Bernie	Wsh.	4	120	20	61	21	6104	424	1	4.17	....	....	....	....	....	....	....	....		1975-76	1978-79
• Wood, Alex	NYA	1	1	0	1	0	70	3	0	2.57	....	....	....	....	....	....	....	....		1936-37	1936-37
• Worsley, Gump	NYR, Mtl., Min.	21	861	335	352	150	50183	2407	43	2.88	70	40	26	....	4084	189	5	2.78	4	1952-53	1973-74
• Worters, Roy	Pit., NYA, Mtl.	12	484	171	229	83	30175	1143	67	2.27	11	3	6	2	690	24	3	2.09		1925-26	1936-37
• Worthy, Chris	Oak., Cal.	3	26	5	10	4	1326	98	0	4.43	....	....	....	....	....	....	....	....		1968-69	1970-71
Wregget, Ken	Tor., Phi., Pit., Cgy., Det.	17	575	225	248	53	31663	1917	9	3.63	56	28	25	....	3341	160	3	2.87	1	1983-84	1999-00
Yeats, Matthew	Wsh.	1	5	1	3	0	258	13	0	3.02	....	....	....	....	....	....	....	....		2003-04	2003-04
‡ Yeremeyev, Vitali	NYR	1	4	0	4	0	212	16	0	4.53	....	....	....	....	....	....	....	....		2000-01	2000-01
‡ York, Allen	CBJ	1	11	3	2	0	417	16	0	2.30	....	....	....	....	....	....	....	....		2011-12	2011-12
§ • Young, Doug	Det.	1	1	0	0	0	21	1	0	2.86	....	....	....	....	....	....	....	....		1933-34	1933-34
Young, Wendell	Van., Phi., Pit., T.B.	10	187	59	86	12	9410	618	2	3.94	2	0	1	....	99	6	0	3.64	2	1985-86	1994-95
Zaba, Matt	NYR	1	1	0	0	0	34	2	0	3.53	....	....	....	....	....	....	....	....		2009-10	2009-10
Zanier, Mike	Edm.	1	3	1	1	1	185	12	0	3.89	....	....	....	....	....	....	....	....		1984-85	1984-85

Late Additions to Player Register

BRIERE, Daniel *(see page 369 for data panel)*
Center Retirement announced, August 17, 2015.

> *Daniel Briere played a total of 1,097 NHL regular-season and playoff games for Phoenix, Buffalo, Philadelphia, Montreal and Colorado. At the conclusion of the 2014-15 season, he ranked 16th in goal-scoring by active players with 307, 30th in assists with 389 and 27th in points with 696. He played in the NHL All-Star Game in 2007 and 2011.*

GONCHAR, Sergei *(see page 425 for data panel)* **PIT**
Defense Signed to a PTO (professional tryout) contract by **Pittsburgh**, August 14, 2015.

KOUDYS, Patrick *(see page 308 for data panel)*
Defense Not re-signed by **Washington**, August 17, 2015.

KUNYK, Cody *(see page 465 for data panel)*
Center Signed as a free agent by **Wolfsburg Grizzly Adams** (Germany), August 18, 2015.

JANSSEN, Cam *(see page 448 for data panel)*
Right wing Signed as a free agent by **Nottingham Panthers** (Britain), August 15, 2015.

RUSSO, Robbie *(see page 329 for data panel)* **DET**
Defense Signed as a free agent by **Detroit** , August 16, 2015.

SANTORELLI, Mike *(see page 533 for data panel)* **ANA**
Center Signed as a free agent by **Anaheim**, August 17, 2015.

VALLEAU, Nolan (vah-LOO, NOH-luhn) **CHI**
Defense. Shoots left. 6'1", 181 lbs. Born, Novi, MI, November 15, 1992.

			Regular Season					Playoffs				
Season	Club	League	GP	G	A	Pts	PIM	GP	G	A	Pts	PIM
2011-12	New Mexico	NAHL	11	2	5	7	6	...	...	...	...	...
	Indiana	NAHL	42	4	20	24	46	8	1	0	1	0
2012-13	Des Moines	USHL	37	5	13	18	24	...	...	...	...	...
	San Francisco	USHL	27	3	5	8	14	...	...	...	...	...
2013-14	Bowling Green	WCHA	DID NOT PLAY — FRESHMAN									
2014-15	Bowling Green	WCHA	39	2	17	19	35	...	...	...	...	...

WCHA All-Rookie Team (2015)
Signed as a free agent by **Chicago**, August 18, 2015.

VINCOUR, Tomas *(see page 570 for data panel)*
Center Signed as a free agent by **Novosibirsk** (KHL), August 19, 2015.

WUTHRICH, Austin *(see page 342 for data panel)*
Defense Not re-signed by **Washington**, August 17, 2015.

CLUB STAFF CHANGES

MILLAR, Curt
Massage Therapist, **Washington Capitals** Retirement announced

CHANGES TO DRAFT LOTTERY FORMAT

Lottery Will Be Expanded To Determine First Three Selections in 2016

Changes have been announced to the NHL's Draft Lottery. The Draft Lottery is a weighted system used to determine the order of selection in the first round of the NHL Draft for the 14 Clubs not qualifying for the Stanley Cup Playoffs (or the Clubs that have acquired the first-round drafting positions of those non-playoff teams).

2016 NHL Draft Lottery

Beginning in 2016, the Draft Lottery will be utilized to assign the top three drafting slots in the NHL Draft, an expansion over previous years when the Draft Lottery was used to determine the winner of the first overall selection only.

Three draws will be held: the 1st Lottery draw will determine the Club selecting first overall, the 2nd Lottery draw will determine the Club selecting second overall and the 3rd Lottery draw will determine the Club selecting third overall.

As a result of this change, the team earning the fewest points during the regular season will no longer be guaranteed, at worst, the second overall pick. That Club could fall as low as fourth overall.

Each Club's odds of winning the 1st Lottery draw are unchanged from 2015. For the 2nd and 3rd Lottery draws, the odds of the remaining teams are proportionally increased.

The 11 Clubs not selected in the Draft Lottery will be assigned NHL Draft selections 4 through 14, in inverse order of regular-season points.

2014-15
NHL Three Stars of the Week/Month Award Winners

Three Stars

Period Ending	First Star	Second Star	Third Star
Oct. 12	Tomas Plekanec, Mtl.	Darcy Kuemper, Min.	Sidney Crosby, Pit.
Oct. 19	Tyler Seguin, Dal.	Frederik Andersen, Ana.	Steven Stamkos, T.B.
Oct. 26	Jeff Carter, L.A.	Ben Scrivens, Edm.	Frans Nielsen, NYI
October	**Corey Perry, Ana.**	**Sidney Crosby, Pit.**	**Tyler Seguin, Dal.**
Nov. 2	Vladimir Tarasenko, St.L.	Pavel Datsyuk, Det.	Marc-Andre Fleury, Pit.
Nov. 9	Mark Giordano, Cgy.	Craig Anderson, Ott.	Vladimir Tarasenko, St.L.
Nov. 16	Jori Lehtera, St.L.	Carey Price, Mtl.	Filip Forsberg, Nsh.
Nov. 23	Jannik Hansen, Van.	Tomas Tatar, Det.	Jamie Benn, Dal.
Nov. 30	Jaroslav Halak, NYI	Ryan Callahan, T.B.	Karri Ramo, Cgy.
November	**Mark Giordano, Cgy.**	**Vladimir Tarasenko, St.L.**	**Pekka Rinne, Nsh.**
Dec. 7	Pavel Datsyuk, Det.	Sergei Bobrovsky, CBJ	Aaron Ekblad, Fla.
Dec. 14	Tyler Ennis, Buf.	Ryan Suter, Min.	Henrik Lundqvist, NYR
Dec. 21	Anze Kopitar, L.A.	Jakub Voracek, Phi.	Marc-Andre Fleury, Pit.
Dec. 28	Johnny Gaudreau, Cgy.	Colin Wilson, Nsh.	Sam Gagner, Ari.
December	**Ryan Getzlaf, Ana.**	**Patrick Kane, Chi.**	**Sergei Bobrovsky, CBJ**
Jan. 4	T.J. Oshie, St.L.	Alex Ovechkin, Wsh.	Carey Price, Mtl.
Jan. 11	David Backes, St.L.	Semyon Varlamov, Col.	Jonathan Huberdeau, Fla.
Jan. 18	Dustin Byfuglien, Wpg.	Tomas Tatar, Det.	Kyle Okposo, NYI
Jan. 25	Ryan Johansen, CBJ	Erik Karlsson, Ott.	Zack Parise, Min.
January	**Alex Ovechkin, Wsh.**	**John Tavares, NYI**	**Tuukka Rask, Bos.**
Feb. 1	Carey Price, Mtl.	Cedric Paquette, T.B.	Devan Dubnyk, Min.
Feb. 8	Devan Dubnyk, Min.	Corey Perry, Ana.	David Desharnais, Mtl.
Feb. 15	Marian Hossa, Chi.	Tyler Toffoli, L.A.	Pekka Rinne, Nsh.
Feb. 22	Jonathan Quick, L.A.	Henrik Sedin, Van.	Max Pacioretty, Mtl.
February	**Devan Dubnyk, Min.**	**Carey Price, Mtl.**	**Alex Ovechkin, Wsh.**
Mar. 1	Andrew Hammond, Ott.	P.K. Subban, Mtl.	Evgeny Malkin, Pit.
Mar. 8	Jiri Hudler, Cgy.	Semyon Varlamov, Col.	Cam Talbot, NYR
Mar. 15	Scott Hartnell, CBJ	Cam Talbot, NYR	Andrew Hammond, Ott.
Mar. 22	Ondrej Pavelec, Wpg.	Kyle Turris, Ott.	Ben Bishop, T.B.
Mar. 29	Devan Dubnyk, Min.	Cam Atkinson, CBJ	Ryan O'Reilly, Col.
March	**Andrew Hammond, Ott.**	**Jiri Hudler, Cgy.**	**Devan Dubnyk, Min.**
Apr. 5	Andrew Hammond, Ott.	Brayden Schenn, Phi.	Nick Foligno, CBJ
Apr. 12	Jamie Benn, Dal.	Ondrej Pavelec, Wpg.	Mark Stone, Ott.

Rookies of the Month

Month	Player	Month	Player
October	Tanner Pearson, Los Angeles	January	John Klingberg, Dallas
November	Filip Forsberg, Nashville	February	Anders Lee, NY Islanders
December	Johnny Gaudreau, Calgary	March	Johnny Gaudreau, Calgary

Corey Perry (top) of the Anaheim Ducks was the NHL's First Star of the Month for October. Perry led all scorers with 10 goals in 12 games, including a hat trick in the Ducks' season opener. Anaheim posted an NHL-best 9-3-0 record during the month.

Before an injury cut short his season, Calgary's Mark Giordano (right) was looking like a possible Hart Trophy candidate. Giordano was the First Star of the Month for November, leading all defensemen with 16 points (4 goals, 12 assists) in 13 games as the Flames went 9-4-0 that month.

Ottawa's Andrew Hammond (far right) garnered several honors in March and April. Hammond was 14-0-1 to start his career and went 10-1-1 in March to win First Star of the Month. He was 3-0-1 in the first week in April to help Ottawa clinch an amazing run to a playoff spot.

Hockey Hall of Fame,
U.S. Hockey Hall of Fame and IIHF Hall of Fame
2015 Inductees and Award Winners

 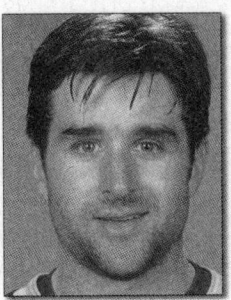   

Ron DeGregorio
U.S. Hockey Hall of Fame
2015 Inductee • Administrator

Chris Drury
U.S. Hockey Hall of Fame
2015 Inductee

Sergei Fedorov
Hockey Hall of Fame
2015 Inductee

Dominik Hasek
IIHF Hall of Fame
2015 Inductee

Bill Hay
Hockey Hall of Fame
2015 Inductee • Builder

Phil Housley
Hockey Hall of Fame
2015 Inductee

Peter Karmanos Jr.
Hockey Hall of Fame
2015 Inductee • Builder

Nicklas Lidstrom
Hockey Hall of Fame
2015 Inductee

Bob McKenzie
2015 Elmer Ferguson
Memorial Award Winner

 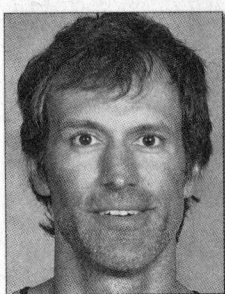   

Nick Nickson
2015 Foster Hewitt
Memorial Award Winner

Scott Niedermayer
IIHF Hall of Fame
2015 Inductee

Chris Pronger
Hockey Hall of Fame
2015 Inductee

Robert Reichel
IIHF Hall of Fame
2015 Inductee

Fran Rider
IIHF Hall of Fame
2015 Inductee • Builder

Maria Rooth
IIHF Hall of Fame
2015 Inductee

Angela Ruggiero
U.S. & Hockey Hall of Fame
2015 Inductee

Monique Scheier-Schneider
IIHF Hall of Fame
2015 Paul Loicq Award Winner

Mathieu Schneider
U.S. Hockey Hall of Fame
2015 Inductee

Lucio Topatigh
IIHF Hall of Fame
2015 Bibi Torriani
Award Winner

Free Agent Signing Register, 2015

PLAYER	POS.	SIGNED BY	PREVIOUS ORGANIZATION	SIGNING DATE
Luke Adam	C	NY Rangers	Columbus	July 3
Andrew Agozzino	LW	Colorado	Colorado	July 16
Jason Akeson	RW	Buffalo	Philadelphia	July 1
Jake Allen	G	St. Louis	St. Louis	July 3
Andy Andreoff	LW	Los Angeles	Los Angeles	Julu 15
Artem Anisimov	C	Chicago	Chicago	July 1
Mark Arcobello	RW	Toronto	Arizona	July 1
Taylor Aronson	D	Nashville	Nashville	July 16
Louis-Marc Aubry	C	Detroit	Detroit	July 15
Richard Bachman	G	Vancouver	Edmonton	July 1
Sven Baertschi	LW	Vancouver	Vancouver	July 28
Mark Barberio	D	Montreal	Tampa Bay	July 1
Matt Bartkowski	D	Vancouver	Boston	July 1
Francois Beauchemin	D	Colorado	Anaheim	July 1
Tayor Beck	RW	Toronto	Nashville	July 13
Matt Beleskey	LW	Boston	Anaheim	July 1
Beau Bennett	RW	Pittsburgh	Pittsburgh	July 15
Andre Benoit	D	St. Louis	Buffalo	July 6
Jonathan Bernier	G	Toronto	Toronto	Aug. 2
Anthony Bitetto	D	Nashville	Nashville	July 13
Mat Bodie	D	NY Rangers	NY Rangers	July 17
Mikkel Boedker	LW	Arizona	Arizona	July 7
Robert Bortuzzo	D	St. Louis	St. Louis	July 2
Lance Bouma	C	Calgary	Calgary	July 23
Michael Bournival	LW	Montreal	Montreal	July 14
Gabriel Bourque	LW	Nashville	Nashville	July 2
Zach Boychuk	C	Carolina	Carolina	July 7
Chris Breen	D	Boston	Boston	July 2
Kyle Brodziak	C	St. Louis	Minnesota	July 2
Chris Brown	W	Washington	Washington	July 16
Alexander Burmistrov	C	Winnipeg	Kazan (KHL)	July 1
Paul Byron	C	Calgary	Calgary	July 26
Chris Butler	D	St. Louis	St. Louis	July 1
Mitch Callahan	RW	Detroit	Detroit	July 13
Matt Calvert	LW	Columbus	Columbus	July 9
Gregory Campbell	LW	Columbus	Boston	July 1
Carter Camper	RW	Washington	Ottawa	July 1
Paul Carey	C	Washington	Boston	July 8
Ryan Carter	LW	Minnesota	Minnesota	July 1
Michael Chaput	C	Columbus	Columbus	July 23
Alex Chiasson	RW	Ottawa	Ottawa	July 26
Taylor Chorney	D	Washington	Pittsburgh	July 1
Mat Clark	D	Colorado	Colorado	July 16
Adam Clendening	D	Vancouver	Vancouver	July 8
Carlo Colaiacovo	D	Buffalo	Philadelphia	July 3
Sean Collins	C	Washington	Columbus	July 1
Blake Comeau	RW	Colorado	Pittsburgh	July 1
Eric Condra	RW	Tampa Bay	Ottawa	July 1
Chris Conner	RW	Philadelphia	Washington	July 1
Brett Connolly	RW	Boston	Boston	July 6
Patrice Cormier	C	Winnipeg	Winnipeg	July 2
Frank Corrado	D	Vancouver	Vancouver	July 8
Andrew Crescenzi	C	Los Angeles	Los Angeles	July 16
Matt Cullen	C	Pittsburgh	Nashville	Aug. 6
Mark Cundari	D	San Jose	Calgary	July 2
Kevin Czuczman	D	NY Islanders	NY Islanders	July 14
Klas Dahlbeck	D	Arizona	Arizona	July 20
Zac Dalpe	RW	Minnesota	Buffalo	July 1
Jerry D'Amigo	RW	Buffalo	Buffalo	July 23
Brandon Davidson	D	Edmonton	Edmonton	July 16
Brandon DeFazio	LW	Boston	Vancouver	July 6
Aaron Dell	G	San Jose	San Jose	Aug. 3
Michael Del Zotto	D	Philadelphia	Philadelphia	July 16
Andrew Desjardins	C	Chicago	Chicago	July 3
Raphael Diaz	D	NY Rangers	Calgary	July 1
Matt Donovan	D	Buffalo	NY Islanders	July 1
Nic Dowd	C	Los Angeles	Los Angeles	July 16
Steve Downie	RW	Arizona	Pittsburgh	July 1
Davis Drewiskie	D	Philadelphia	Montreal	July 1
Devan Dubnyk	G	Minnesota	Minnesota	July 4
Patrick Eaves	RW	Dallas	Dallas	July 1
Dan Ellis	G	Washington	Florida	July 4
Jhonas Enroth	G	Los Angeles	Dallas	July 1
Emerson Etem	RW	NY Rangers	NY Rangers	July 14
Bobby Farnham	LW	Pittsburgh	Pittsburgh	July 13
Jesper Fast	RW	NY Rangers	NY Rangers	July 15
Ruslan Fedotenko	LW	Minnesota	Iowa (AHL)	July 1
Taylor Fedun	D	Vancouver	San Jose	July 1
Erlc Fehr	RW	Pittsburgh	Washington	July 28
Rob Flick	C	Florida	Boston	July 2
Justin Florek	LW	NY Islanders	Boston	July 2
Matt Fraser	LW	Winnipeg	Edmonton	July 2
Michael Frolik	LW	Calgary	Winnipeg	July 1
Alex Galchenyuk	C	Montreal	Montreal	July 30
Stanislav Galiev	RW	Washington	Washington	July 1
Cameron Gaunce	D	Florida	Dallas	July 1
Eric Gelinas	D	New Jersey	New Jersey	July 14
Brian Gibbons	C	NY Rangers	Columbus	July 1
Brandon Gormley	D	Arizona	Arizona	Aug. 6
Mikael Granlund	C	Minnesota	Minnesota	July 1
Alex Grant	D	Arizona	Ottawa	July 2
Derek Grant	C	Calgary	Ottawa	July 1
Mike Green	D	Detroit	Washington	July 1
Thomas Greiss	G	NY Islanders	Pittsburgh	July 1
Alexandre Grenier	RW	Vancouver	Vancouver	July 10
Mikhail Grigorenko	C	Colorado	Colorado	July 16
Matt Hackett	G	Anaheim	Boston	July 1
Marc Hagel	RW	Minnesota	Iowa (AHL)	July 1
Carl Hagelin	LW	Anaheim	Anaheim	Aug. 14
Michael Haley	C	San Jose	San Jose	July 2
Matt Halischuk	RW	Winnipeg	Winnipeg	July 1
Mike Halmo	LW	NY Islanders	NY Islanders	July 14
Erik Haula	LW	Minnesota	Minnesota	Aug. 2
Jimmy Hayes	RW	Boston	Boston	July 6
Seth Helgeson	D	New Jersey	New Jersey	July 18
Thomas Hickey	D	NY Islanders	NY Islanders	July 1
Joey Hishon	C	Colorado	Colorado	July 27
Cody Hodgson	C	Nashville	Buffalo	July 1
Mike Hoffman	LW	Ottawa	Ottawa	Aug. 3
Ben Holmstrom	RW	NY Islanders	Carolina	July 2
Braden Holtby	G	Washington	Washington	July 24
Korbinian Holzer	D	Anaheim	Anaheim	July 2
Shawn Horcoff	C	Anaheim	Dallas	July 3
Quinton Howden	C	Florida	Florida	July 15
Marek Hrivik	LW	NY Rangers	NY Rangers	July 10
Matt Hunwick	D	Toronto	NY Rangers	July 1
Matt Irwin	D	Boston	San Jose	July 10
Barret Jackman	D	Nashville	St. Louis	July 1
Calle Jarnkrok	C	Nashville	Nashville	July 17
Dmitrij Jaskin	RW	St. Louis	St. Louis	July 3
Dustin Jeffrey	C	Arizona	Vancouver	July 1
Nick Jensen	D	Detroit	Detroit	July 13
Marcus Johansson	C/W	Washington	Washington	July 31
Josh Jooris	RW	Calgary	Calgary	July 24

PLAYER	POS.	SIGNED BY	PREVIOUS ORGANIZATION	SIGNING DATE	PLAYER	POS.	SIGNED BY	PREVIOUS ORGANIZATION	SIGNING DATE
Tomas Jurco	RW	Detroit	Detroit	July 24	Dennis Rasmussen	C	Chicago	Chicago	July 9
Nazem Kadri	C	Toronto	Toronto	July 5	Dylan Reese	D	Arizona	Arizona	July 1
Corban Knight	C	Florida	Florida	July 7	Brent Regner	D	Florida	St. Louis	July 1
Mike Kostka	D	Ottawa	NY Rangers	July 1	Max Reinhart	C	Nashville	Nashville	July 2
Evgeny Kuznetsov	C	Washington	Washington	July 6	Mike Ribeiro	C	Nashville	Nashville	July 1
Jason LaBarbera	G	Philadelphia	Anaheim	July 2	Brad Richards	C	Detroit	Chicago	July 1
Adam Larsson	D	New Jersey	New Jersey	July 25	Brad Richardson	C	Arizona	Vancouver	July 1
Johan Larsson	LW	Buffalo	Buffalo	July 21	Mike Reilly	D	Minnesota	Columbus	July 1
Louis Leblanc	C	NY Islanders	Anaheim	July 17	Rasmus Rissanen	D	Carolina	Carolina	July 1
Jerome Leduc	D	Buffalo	Buffalo	July 16	Brandon Saad	LW	Columbus	Columbus	July 3
Brendan Lemieux	LW	Winnipeg	Winnipeg	July 3	Philip Samuelsson	D	Arizona	Arizona	July 16
Mark Letestu	C	Edmonton	Columbus	July 1	Tim Schaller	LW	Buffalo	Buffalo	July 16
Nathan Lieuwen	G	Buffalo	Buffalo	July 16	Cameron Schilling	D	Chicago	Washington	July 2
Anders Lindback	G	Arizona	Buffalo	July 1	Cole Schneider	LW	Ottawa	Ottawa	July 2
Oscar Lindberg	C	NY Rangers	NY Rangers	July 14	John Scott	LW	Arizona	San Jose	July 10
Matt Lindblad	LW	NY Rangers	Boston	July 1	Andrej Sekera	D	Edmonton	Los Angeles	July 1
Vincent LoVerde	D	Los Angeles	Los Angeles	July 16	Alexander Semin	LW	Montreal	Carolina	July 24
Anderew MacWilliam	D	Winnipeg	Toronto	July 3	Michael Sgarbossa	C	Anaheim	Anaheim	July 16
Martin Marincin	D	Toronto	Toronto	July 9	Brendan Shinnimin	C	Arizona	Arizona	July 16
Paul Martin	D	San Jose	Pittsburgh	July 1	Drew Shore	C	Calgary	Calgary	July 15
Jordan Martinook	LW	Arizona	Arizona	July 20	Nick Shore	C	Los Angeles	Los Angeles	July 16
Shawn Matthias	C	Toronto	Vancouver	July 6	Justin Shugg	LW	Carolina	Carolina	July 12
Jamie McBain	D	Los Angeles	Los Angeles	July 3	Jakob Silfverberg	LW	Anaheim	Anaheim	Aug. 7
John McCarthy	LW	San Jose	St. Louis	July 2	Zach Sill	C	Washington	Toronto	July 16
Colin McDonald	RW	Philadelphia	NY Islanders	July 3	Craig Smith	C	Nashville	Nashville	July 20
John McFarland	LW	Florida	Florida	July 15	Viktor Stalberg	LW	NY Rangers	Nashville	July 1
Tye McGinn	LW	Tampa Bay	Arizona	July 21	Ryan Stanton	D	Washington	Vancouver	July 24
Brian McGrattan	RW	Anaheim	Calgary	July 10	Derek Stepan	C	NY Rangers	NY Rangers	July 27
Dylan McIlrath	D	NY Rangers	NY Rangers	July 15	Chris Stewart	LW	Anaheim	Minnesota	July 12
Greg McKegg	C	Florida	Florida	July 8	Jarret Stoll	C	NY Rangers	Los Angeles	Aug. 10
Mike McKenna	G	Florida	Arizona	July 1	Zack Stortini	RW	Ottawa	Philadelphia	July 1
Reid McNeill	D	Pittsburgh	Pittsburgh	July 3	Brody Sutter	C	Carolina	Carolina	July 15
Jayson Megna	RW	NY Rangers	Pittsburgh	July 1	Viktor Svedberg	D	Chicago	Chicago	Aug. 5
Zbynek Michalek	D	Arizona	St. Louis	July 1	Eric Tangradi	LW	Detroit	Montreal	July 8
J.T. Miller	C	NY Rangers	NY Rangers	July 15	Vladimir Tarasenko	RW	St. Louis	St. Louis	July 7
John Moore	D	New Jersey	Arizona	July 1	Daniil Tarasov	RW	Dynamo Moscow (KHL)	San Jose	July 17
Mike Moore	D	Washington	Washington	July 1	Christian Thomas	RW	Montreal	Montreal	July 2
Chris Mueller	C	Anaheim	NY Rangers	July 1	Jarred Tinordi	D	Montreal	Montreal	July 15
Vladislav Namestnikov	C	Tampa Bay	Tampa Bay	July 17	Dominik Uher	C	Pittsburgh	Pittsburgh	July 17
Riley Nash	C	Carolina	Carolina	July 1	Phil Varone	C	Buffalo	Buffalo	July 13
Aaron Ness	D	Washington	NY Islanders	July 1	Antoine Vermette	C	Arizona	Chicago	July 1
Michal Neuvirth	G	Philadelphia	NY Islanders	July 1	Chris Wagner	C	Anaheim	Anaheim	July 16
Gustav Nyquist	RW	Detroit	Detroit	July 10	Joel Ward	RW	San Jose	Washington	July 3
Shane O'Brien	D	Anaheim	Florida	July 16	Jordan Weal	C	Los Angeles	Los Angeles	July 16
Eric O'Dell	C	Ottawa	Winnipeg	July 1	Yannick Weber	D	Vancouver	Vancouver	July 1
Johnny Oduya	D	Dallas	Chicago	July 15	Joe Whitney	RW	NY Islanders	New Jersey	July 2
Jamie Oleksiak	D	Dallas	Dallas	July 9	Justin Williams	RW	Washington	Los Angeles	July 1
Will O'Neill	D	Pittsburgh	Winnipeg	July 2	Colin Wilson	C	Nashville	Nashville	July 27
Cal O'Reilly	C	Buffalo	Vancouver	July 3	Garrett Wilson	L:W	Florida	Florida	July 7
Magnus Paajarvi	LW	St. Louis	St. Louis	July 8	Daniel Winnik	C/LW	Toronto	Pittsburgh	July 1
Richard Panik	RW	Toronto	Toronto	July 1	Luke Witkowski	D	Tampa Bay	Tampa Bay	July 17
Phillipe Paradis	C	Tampa Bay	Tampa Bay	July 8	Harry Zolnierczyk	LW	Anaheim	NY Islanders	July 3
Adam Pardy	D	Winnipeg	Winnipeg	July 1					
P-A Parenteau	LW	Toronto	Montreal	July 1					
Alex Petrovic	D	Florida	Florida	July 15					
Calvin Pickard	G	Colorado	Colorado	Aug. 6					
Joe Piskula	D	Anaheim	Nashville	July 1					
Tyler Pitlick	C	Edmonton	Edmonton	July 16					
Chris Porter	C	Philadelphia	St. Louis	Aug. 8					
Paul Postma	D	Winnipeg	Winnipeg	July 10					
Shane Prince	C	Ottawa	Ottawa	July 15					
Nate Prosser	D	Minnesota	Minnesota	July 1					
Teemu Pulkkinen	LW	Detroit	Detroit	July 21					
Mark Pysyk	D	Buffalo	Buffalo	July 14					
John Ramage	D	Columbus	Calgary	July 3					
Karri Ramo	G	Calgary	Calgary	July 1					

Trades and free agent signings after Aug. 14, 2015 are listed on page 663.

Trade Register, 2014-15

OCTOBER 2014

4 — Boston traded D **Johnny Boychuk** to NY Islanders for Philadelphia's 2nd round choice (previously acquired, Boston selected selected D **Brandon Carlo**) in the 2015 NHL Draft and future considerations.

– Chicago traded D **Nick Leddy** and G **Kent Simpson** to NY Islanders for D **T.J. Brennan**, D **Ville Pokka** and G **Anders Nilsson**.

5 — Montreal traded G **Peter Budaj** and RW **Patrick Holland** to Winnipeg for LW **Eric Tangradi**.

6 — Florida traded RW **Joey Crabb** to NY Rangers for D **Steven Kampfer**.

NOVEMBER, 2014

11 — Dallas traded D **Sergei Gonchar** to Montreal for LW **Travis Moen**.

15 — St. Louis traded D **Jordan Leopold** to Columbus for a 5th round choice in the 2016 NHL Draft.

20 — Vancouver traded LW **Kellan Lain** to Edmonton for C **Will Acton**.

– Montreal traded RW **Rene Bourque** to Anaheim for D **Bryan Allen**.

21 — Dallas traded D **Brenden Dillon** to San Jose for D **Jason Demers** and a 3rd round choice in the 2016 NHL Draft.

25 — NY Islanders traded D **Andrey Pedan** to Vancouver for RW **Alexandre Mallet** and a 3rd round choice in the 2016 NHL Draft.

28 — Tampa Bay traded D **Eric Brewer** to Anaheim for Edmonton's 3rd round choice (previously acquired, Tampa Bay selected LW **Dennis Yan**) in the 2015 NHL Draft.

DECEMBER, 2014

4 — Anaheim traded D **Jesse Blacker** and future considerations to Anaheim for D **Colby Robak**.

5 — Arizona traded LW **Rob Klinkhammer** and future considerations to Pittsburgh for D **Philip Samuelsson**.

14 — Chicago traded RW **Jeremy Morin** to Columbus for D **Tim Erixon**.

16 — Columbus traded RW **Jerry D'Amigo** to Buffalo for C **Luke Adam**.

18 — Carolina traded D **Jay Harrison** to Winnipeg for Ottawa's 6th round choice (previously acquired, Carolina selected C **David Cotton**) in the 2015 NHL Draft.

29 — Edmonton traded C **Mark Arcobello** to Nashville for C **Derek Roy**.

JANUARY, 2015

2 — Edmonton traded LW **David Perron** to Pittsburgh for LW **Rob Klinkhammer** and Pittsburgh's 1st round choice (later traded to NY Islanders – NY Islanders selected C **Matthew Barzal**) in the 2015 NHL Draft.

14 — Arizona traded G **Devan Dubnyk** to Minnesota for Minnesota's 3rd round choice (LW **Brendan Warren**) in the 2015 NHL Draft.

27 — Pittsburgh traded C **Marcel Goc** to St. Louis for C **Maxim Lapierre**.

29 — Chicago traded D **Adam Clendening** to Vancouver for D **Gustav Forsling**.

FEBRUARY, 2015

6 — Tampa Bay traded future considerations to Toronto for RW **Carter Ashton** and LW **David Broll**.

9 — San Jose traded future considerations to Tampa Bay for G **Evgeni Nabokov**.

11 — Buffalo traded D **Tyler Myers**, RW **Drew Stafford**, RW **Joel Armia**, LW **Brendan Lemieux** and St. Louis' 1st round choice (previously acquired, Winnipeg selected C **Jack Roslovic**) in the 2015 NHL Draft to Winnipeg for LW **Evander Kane**, D **Zach Bogosian** and G **Jason Kasdorf**.

– Buffalo traded G **Jhonas Enroth** to Dallas for G **Anders Lindback** and future considerations.

15 — Nashville traded C **Olli Jokinen**, LW **Brendan Leipsic** and Nashville's 1st round choice (later traded to Philadelphia – Philadelphia selected C **Travis Konecny**) in the 2015 NHL Draft to Toronto for D **Cody Franson** and C **Mike Santorelli**.

24 — Anaheim traded RW **Devante Smith-Pelly** to Montreal for LW **Jiri Sekac**.

– Florida traded LW **Sean Bergenheim** and Florida's 7th round choice in the 2016 NHL Draft to Minnesota for Minnesota's 3rd round choice in the 2016 NHL Draft.

25 — Carolina traded C **Jiri Tlusty** to Winnipeg for Winnipeg's 5th round choice (RW **Spencer Smallman**) in the 2015 NHL Draft and a 3rd round choice in the 2016 NHL Draft.

– Pittsburgh traded C **Zach Sill**, Pittsburgh's 4th round choice (later traded to Edmonton, later traded to Ottawa – Ottawa selected D **Christian Wolanin**) in the 2015 NHL Draft and Pittsburgh's 2nd round choice (later traded back to Pittsburgh – Pittsburgh selected RW **Daniel Sprong**) in the 2015 NHL Draft to Toronto for C/LW **Daniel Winnik**.

– Carolina traded D **Andrej Sekera** to Los Angeles for D **Roland McKeown** and Los Angeles' 1st round choice in the 2016 NHL Draft.

26 — Columbus traded RW **Adam Cracknell** to St. Louis for future considerations.

– Chicago traded D **T.J. Brennan** to Toronto for RW **Spencer Abbott**.

– Florida traded Florida's 2nd round choice (later traded to NY Rangers – NY Rangers selected LW **Ryan Gropp**) in the 2015 NHL Draft and a 3rd round choice in the 2016 NHL Draft to New Jersey for RW **Jaromir Jagr**.

– Columbus traded RW **Nathan Horton** to Toronto for RW **David Clarkson**.

– Chicago traded Chicago's 2nd round choice (later traded to Toronto – Toronto selected RW **Jeremy Bracco**) in the 2015 NHL Draft and future considerations to Philadelphia for D **Kimmo Timonen**.

– Carolina traded D **Tim Gleason** to Washington for D **Jack Hillen** and Arizona's 4th round choice (previously acquired, Carolina selected G **Callum Booth**) in the 2015 NHL Draft.

– Anaheim traded LW **Dany Heatley** and Anaheim's 3rd round choice (D **Thomas Schemitsch**) in the 2015 NHL Draft to Florida for LW **Tomas Fleischmann**.

– Arizona traded C **Antoine Vermette** to Chicago for D **Klas Dahlbeck** and Chicago's 1st round choice (RW **Nick Merkley**) in the 2015 NHL Draft.

MARCH, 2015

1 — Calgary traded LW **Curtis Glencross** to Washington for Washington's 2nd (later traded to Boston – Boston selected D **Jeremy Lauzon**) and 3rd (later traded to Arizona – Arizona selected RW **Jens Looke**) round choices in the 2015 NHL Draft.

– Arizona traded D **Keith Yandle**, D **Chris Summers** and a 4th round choice in the 2016 NHL Draft to NY Rangers for D **John Moore**, LW **Anthony Duclair**, Tampa Bay's 2nd round choice (previously acquired, later traded to Calgary – Calgary selected D **Oliver Kylington**) in the 2015 NHL Draft and future considerations.

– NY Rangers traded LW **Lee Stempniak** to Winnipeg for C **Carl Klingberg**.

– NY Rangers traded a 4th round choice in the 2016 NHL Draft to San Jose for C **James Sheppard**.

– Dallas traded LW **Erik Cole** and Dallas' 3rd round choice (D **Vili Saarijarvi**) in the 2015 NHL Draft to Detroit for D **Mattias Backman**, C **Mattias Janmark** and Detroit's 2nd round choice (LW **Roope Hintz**) in the 2015 NHL Draft.

2 — Boston traded Boston's 2nd round choice (D **Matthew Spencer**) in the 2015 NHL Draft and a 2nd round choice in the 2016 NHL Draft to Tampa Bay for RW **Brett Connolly**.

– Philadelphia traded D **Braydon Coburn** to Tampa Bay for D **Radko Gudas** and Tampa Bay's 1st (later traded to Columbus – Columbus selected D **Gabriel Carlsson**) and 3rd (G **Matej Tomek**) round choices in the 2015 NHL Draft.

– Edmonton traded D **Jeff Petry** to Montreal for Montreal 's 2nd round choice (later traded to Washington – Washington selected D **Jonas Siegenthaler**) in the 2015 NHL Draft and future considerations.

– Buffalo traded RW **Brian Flynn** to Montreal for a 5th round choice in the 2016 NHL Draft.

– Arizona traded D **Zbynek Mihalek** and future considerations to St. Louis for C **Maxim Letunov**.

– Colorado traded D **Karl Stollery** to San Jose for C **Freddie Hamilton**.

– Pittsburgh traded D **Robert Bortuzzo** and a 7th round choice in the 2016 NHL Draft to St. Louis for D **Ian Cole**.

– Chicago traded RW **Ben Smith** and a conditional 7th round choice in the 2017 NHL Draft to San Jose for C **Andrew Desjardins**.

– NY Islanders traded LW **Cory Conacher** to Vancouver for C **Dustin Jeffrey**.

– Anaheim traded D **Mat Clark** to Colorado for C **Michael Sgarbossa** and future considerations.

– NY Islanders traded future considerations to San Jose for C **Tyler Kennedy**.

– Arizona traded D **Mark Louis** to NY Islanders for G **David Leggio**.

– Detroit traded future considerations to New Jersey for D **Marek Zidlicky**.

– Buffalo traded G **Michal Neuvirth** to NY Islanders for G **Chad Johnson** and future considerations.

- Anaheim traded RW **Rene Bourque**, C **William Karlsson** and Anaheim's 2nd round choice (C **Kevin Stenlund**) in the 2015 NHL Draft to Columbus for D **James Wisniewski** and Detroit's 3rd round choice (previously acquired, Anaheim selected C **Brent Gates**) in the 2015 NHL Draft.
- Columbus traded D **Jordan Leopold** to Minnesota for D **Justin Falk** and Minnesota's 5th round choice (D **Veeti Vaino**) in the 2015 NHL Draft.
- Toronto traded C **Olli Jokinen** to St. Louis for C **Joakim Lindstrom** and future considerations.
- Boston traded RW **Jordan Caron** and a 6th round choice in the 2016 NHL Draft to Colorado for C **Max Talbot** and C **Paul Carey**.
- Anaheim traded D **Ben Lovejoy** to Pittsburgh for D **Simon Despres**.
- Boston traded C **Jared Knight** to Minnesota for C **Zack Phillips.**
- Buffalo traded C **Torrey Mitchell** to Montreal for LW **Jack Nevins** and a 7th round choice in the 2016 NHL Draft.
- Anaheim traded D **Eric Brewer** and a 5th round choice in the 2016 NHL Draft to Toronto for D **Korbinian Holzer**.
- Calgary traded LW **Sven Baertschi** to Vancouver for Vancouver's 2nd round choice (D **Rasmus Andersson**) in the 2015 NHL Draft.
- Buffalo traded RW **Chris Stewart** to Minnesota for a 2nd round choice in the 2017 NHL Draft.

JUNE, 2015

1 — NY Rangers traded D **Daniel Walcott** to Tampa Bay for NY Rangers' 7th round choice (previously acquired, later traded to Edmonton – Edmonton selected D **Ziyat Paigin**) in the 2015 NHL Draft.

19 — Florida traded C **Zach Hyman** and future considerations to Toronto for C **Greg McKegg**.

25 — Colorado traded a 6th round choice in the 2016 NHL Draft to Ottawa for C **Carl Soderberg**.

26 — Ottawa traded G **Robin Lehner** and RW **David Legwand** to Buffalo for NY Islanders' 1st round choice (previously acquired, Ottawa selected C **Colin White**) in the 2015 NHL Draft.

- Boston traded D **Dougie Hamilton** to Calgary for Calgary's 1st (RW **Zachary Senyshyn**) and 2nd (C **Jakob Forsbacka-Karlsson**) round choices in the 2015 NHL Draft and Washington's 2nd round choice (previously acquired, Boston selected D **Jeremy Lauzon**) in the 2015 NHL Draft.
- Boston traded LW **Milan Lucic** to Los Angeles for G **Martin Jones**, D **Colin Miller** and Los Angeles' 1st round choice (D **Jakub Zboril**) in the 2015 NHL Draft.
- Buffalo traded D **Nikita Zadorov**, C **Mikhail Grigorenko**, LW **J.T. Compher** and Buffalo's 2nd round choice (later traded to San Jose – San Jose selected D **Jeremy Roy**) in the 2015 NHL Draft to Colorado for C **Ryan O'Reilly** and LW **Jamie McGinn**.
- NY Islanders traded D **Griffin Reinhart** to Edmonton for Pittsburgh's 1st round choice (previously acquired, NY Islanders selected C **Matthew Barzal**) in the 2015 NHL Draft and Edmonton's 2nd round choice (later traded to Tampa Bay – Tampa Bay selected C **Mitchell Stephens**) in the 2015 NHL Draft.

27 — Anaheim traded RW **Kyle Palmieri** to New Jersey for Florida's 2nd round choice (previously acquired, later traded to NY Rangers – NY Rangers selected LW **Ryan Gropp**) in the 2015 NHL Draft and New Jersey's 3rd round choice in the 2016 NHL Draft.

- Vancouver traded G **Eddie Lack** to Carolina for Carolina's 3rd round choice (D **Guillaume Brisebois**) in the 2015 NHL Draft and a 7th round choice in the 2016 NHL Draft.
- San Jose traded G **Antti Niemi** to Dallas for Dallas' 7th round choice (G **Jake Kupsky**) in the 2015 NHL Draft.
- Anaheim traded RW **Emerson Etem** and Florida's 2nd round choice (previously acquired, NY Rangers selected LW **Ryan Gropp**) in the 2015 NHL Draft to NY Rangers for LW **Carl Hagelin** and NY Rangers' 2nd (C **Julius Naatinen**) and 6th (G **Garrett Metcalf**) round choices in the 2015 NHL Draft.
- NY Rangers traded G **Cam Talbot** and NY Rangers' 7th round choice (D **Ziyat Paigin**) in the 2015 NHL Draft to Edmonton for Montreal's 2nd round choice (previously acquired, later traded to Washington – Washington selected D **Jonas Siegenthaler**) in the 2015 NHL Draft, Ottawa's 3rd round choice (previously acquired, NY Rangers selected D **Sergei Zborovsky**) in the 2015 NHL Draft and Edmonton's 7th round choice (G **Adam Huska**) in the 2015 NHL Draft.

- Anaheim traded D **James Wisniewski** to Carolina for G **Anton Khodobin**.
- Edmonton traded D **Martin Marincin** to Toronto for LW **Brad Ross** and Pittsburgh's 4th round choice (previously acquired, later traded to Ottawa – Ottawa selected D **Christian Wolanin**) in the 2015 NHL Draft.
- Ottawa traded D **Eric Gryba** to Edmonton for LW **Travis Ewanyk** and Pittsburgh's 4th round choice (previously acquired, later traded to Ottawa – Ottawa selected D **Christian Wolanin**) in the 2015 NHL Draft.
- Chicago traded G **Antti Raanta** to NY Rangers for RW **Ryan Haggerty**.
- Arizona traded C **Sam Gagner** and future considerations to Philadelphia for D **Nicklas Grossmann** and D **Chris Pronger**.

29 — Boston traded a 3rd round choice in the 2017 NHL Draft to Philadelphia for C **Zac Rinaldo**.

- San Jose traded D **Konrad Abeltshauser** to St. Louis for future considerations.

30 — Boston traded G **Martin Jones** to San Jose for C **Sean Kuraly** and San Jose's 1st round choice in the 2016 NHL Draft.

- Chicago traded LW **Brandon Saad**, D **Michael Paliotta** and C **Alexander Broadhurst** to Columbus for C **Artem Anisimov**, RW **Jeremy Morin**, RW **Corey Tropp**, C **Marko Dano** and a 4th round choice in the 2016 NHL Draft.
- Anaheim traded Anaheim's 2nd round choice in the 2016 NHL Draft to Vancouver for D **Kevin Bieksa**.
- Arizona traded LW **Lauri Korpikoski** to Edmonton for C **Boyd Gordon**.

JULY, 2015

1 — Montreal traded LW **Brandon Prust** to Vancouver for RW **Zach Kassian** and a 5th round choice in the 2016 NHL Draft.

- Pittsburgh traded C **Nick Spaling**, RW **Kasperi Kapanen**, D **Scott Harrington**, New Jersey's 3rd round choice (previously acquired) in the 2016 NHL Draft and future considerations to Toronto for RW **Phil Kessel**, D **Tim Erixon**, RW **Tyler Biggs** and future considerations.
- Calgary traded C **Max Reinhart** to Nashville for future considerations.
- Nashville traded G **Magnus Hellberg** to NY Rangers for a 6th round choice in the 2017 NHL Draft.
- Boston traded LW **Reilly Smith** and C **Marc Savard** to Florida for RW **Jimmy Hayes**.

2 — St. Louis traded LW **T.J. Oshie** to Washington for RW **Troy Brouwer**, G **Pheonix Copley** and a 3rd round choice in the 2016 NHL Draft.

6 — Chicago traded G **Anders Nilsson** to Edmonton for C **Liam Coughlin**.

10 — Chicago traded LW **Patrick Sharp** and D **Stephen Johns** to Dallas for D **Trevor Daley** and **Ryan Garbutt**.

12 — Nashville traded RW **Taylor Beck** to Toronto for LW **Jamie Devane**.

28 — Pittsburgh traded LW **Brandon Sutter** and Pittsburgh's 3rd round compensatory choice in the 2016 NHL Draft to Vancouver for LW **Nick Bonino**, D **Adam Clendening** and Anaheim's 2nd round choice (previously acquired) in the 2016 NHL Draft.

Trades and free agent signings after Aug. 14, 2015 are listed on page 613.

League Abbreviations

AHA ....Alberta Amateur Hockey Association
AAHL ....Alaska Amateur Hockey League
AASHA ....Alaska All-Stars Hockey Association
ACAC...........Alberta Colleges Athletic Conference
ACHA...........American Collegiate Hockey Association
ACHL ....Atlantic Coast Hockey League
AFHL ....American Frontier Hockey League
AH ....Atlantic Hockey
AHL ....American Hockey League
AJHL ....Alberta Junior Hockey League
ALIH ....Asia League Ice Hockey
Alpenliga.......Alpenliga (Austria, Italy, Slovenia 1994-1999)
AMHA ....Alberta Minor Hockey Association
AMHL ....Alberta Midget AAA Hockey League
AMBHL.........Alberta Major Bantam Hockey League
AtJHL...........Atlantic Junior Hockey League
AUAA..........Atlantic University Athletic Association
AUS ....Atlantic University Sport
AWHL ....American West Hockey League
AYHL ....Atlantic Youth Hockey League
BCAHA ....British Columbia Amateur Hockey Association
BCHL ....British Columbia (Junior) Hockey League
                  (also BCJHL)
BCMML ....British Columbia Major Midget League
BigTen ....Big Ten Conference
CABHL...........Central Alberta Bantam Hockey League
CaJHL ....Calgary Junior Hockey League
CapJHL ....Capital Junior Hockey League
CBHL ....Calgary Bantam Hockey League
CCAA...........Canadian Colleges Athletic Association
CCHA...........Central Collegiate Hockey Association
CEGEP ....Quebec College Prep
CHA..............College Hockey America
CHL..............Central Hockey League
CIS...............Commonwealth of Independent States
CIS...............Canadian Interuniversity Sport
CISSA...........Conference of Independent Schools Athletic
                  Association (Ontario)
CJHL ....Central Junior A Hockey League
CMHA..........Calgary Minor Hockey Association
ColHL............Colonial Hockey League
CSHL ....Central States Hockey League
CSJHL ....Central States Junior Hockey League
CSSHL..........Canadian Sport School Hockey League
CWUAA ....Canada West Unversities Athletic Assoc.
ECAC............Eastern College Athletic Conference
ECACHL ....ECAC Hockey League
ECHL............East Coast Hockey League
EEHL............Eastern European Hockey League
EJHL............Eastern Junior Hockey League
EMHA..........Edmonton Minor Hockey Association
EmJHL..........Empire Junior B Hockey League
EuroHL..........European Hockey League
Exhib. ....Exhibition Games, Series or Season
GLHL............Great Lakes Hockey League
GNML...........Greater North Midget League
GPAC ....Great Plains Athletic Conference
GTHL ....Greater Toronto Hockey League
H-East...........Hockey East
High-XX.........High School (state/province)

HJHL ....Heritage Junior Hockey League
HPHL ....High Performance Hockey League
IEHL.............Internationale Eishockey Liga
IHL..............International Hockey League
JIHL..............Japan Ice Hockey League
KIJHL.............Kootenay International Jr. B Hockey League
LCJHL...........Little Caesar's Junior Hockey League
MAAC...........Metro Atlantic Athletic Conference
MAHA ....Manitoba Amateur Hockey Association
MAHL...........Mid America Hockey League
MBAHL.........Metropolitan Boston Amateur Hockey League
MBHL ....Metropolitan Boston Hockey League
MEHL...........Midwest Elite Hockey League
MEPDL.........Minnesota Elite Prep Development League
Metro-HL.......Metro Hockey League
MIAC ....Minnesota Intercollegiate Athletic Conference
Minor-XX.......Minor/Youth hockey (state/province)
MJHL............Manitoba Junior Hockey League
MJrHL...........Maritime Junior A Hockey League
MMBHL........Manitoba Major Bantam Hockey League
MMHL ....Manitoba Midget AAA Hockey League
MMHL ....Michigan Minor Hockey League
MMMHL.......Manitoba Minor Midget Hockey League
MNHL..........Michigan National Hockey League
MPHL...........Midwest Prep Hockey League
MtJHL...........Metropolitan Junior Hockey League (NY)
MTJHL..........Metropolitan Toronto Junior Hockey League
MTHL..........Metro Toronto Hockey League
MWEHL........Midwest Elite Hockey League
NAHL...........North American Hockey League (Tier I Junior)
NAJHL..........North American Junior Hockey League
NA3HL..........North American Hockey League (Tier III)
NAPHL.........North American Prospects Hockey League
Nat-Team.......National Team (also Nt.-Team)
NBAHA ....New Brunswick Amateur Hockey Association
NBMHL.........New Brunswick Midget Hockey League
NBPEI ....New Brunswick Prince Edward Island
                  Midget Hockey League
NCAA ....National Collegiate Athletic Association
NCHA ....Northern Collegiate Hockey Association
NCHC...........National Collegiate Hockey Conference
NEJHL...........New England Junior Hockey League
NFAHA..........Newfoundland Amateur Hockey Association
NHL.............National Hockey League
NJCAA..........National Junior Collegiate Athletic Assoc.
NOBHL..........Northern Ontario Bantam Hockey League
NOHA ....Northern Ontario Hockey Association
NOJHA.........Northern Ontario Junior Hockey Association
NOJHL..........Northern Ontario Junior Hockey League
NORPAC ....Northern Pacific Hockey League
NSBHL ....Nova Scotia Bantam Hockey League
NSMHL..........Nova Scotia Midget AAA Hockey League
NTHL...........North Texas Hockey League
NWJHL..........Northwest Junior B Hockey League
NYJHL...........New York Junior Hockey League
OCJHL...........Ontario Central Junior A Hockey League
OHA..............Ontario Hockey Association
OHL ....Ontario Hockey League
OMJHL..........Ontario Major Junior Hockey League
ON-Jr.A.........Ontario Junior A Hockey Leagues

ON-Jr.B ....Ontario Junior B Hockey Leagues
OPJHL............Ontario Provincial Junior A Hockey League
OUAA ....Ontario Universities Athletic Association
PAHA............Pennsylvania Amateur Hockey Association
PCJHL ....Pacific Coast Junior Hockey League
PEIHA ....Prince Edward Island Hockey Association
PIJHL............Pacific International Junior Hockey League
PJHL ....Pacific Junior Hockey League
QAA ....Quebec Junior AA
QAAA ....Quebec Midget AAA Hockey League
QAHA ....Quebec Amateur Hockey Association
QJHL ....Quebec Junior Hockey League
QMJHL..........Quebec Major Junior Hockey League
QNAHL ....(Quebec) North American Hockey League
Q-RHL...........(Quebec) Richelieu Elite Hockey League
QSPHL...........Quebec Semi-Pro Hockey League
RAMHL.........Rural Alberta Midget Hockey League
RMJHL..........Rocky Mountain Junior Hockey League
SAHA ....Saskatchewan Amateur Hockey Association
SAMHL ....Southern Alberta Midget Hockey League
SBHL ....Saskatchewan Bantam Hockey League
SCAHA..........Southern California Amateur Hockey Assoc.
SIJHL ....Superior International Junior Hockey League
SJHL.............Saskatchewan Junior Hockey League
SMBHL..........Saskatchewan Major Bantam Hockey League
SMHL...........Saskatchewan Midget AAA Hockey League
SMMHL........Saskatchewan Minor Midget Hockey League
SPHL............Southern Professional Hockey League
SSJHL ....South Saskatchewan Junior B Hockey League
SSMHL..........South Saskatchewan Minor Hockey League
SunHL...........Sunshine Hockey League
T1EHL..........Tier 1 Elite Hockey League
TBAHA..........Thunder Bay Amateur Hockey Association
TBJHL...........Thunder Bay Junior Hockey League
TBMHL.........Thunder Bay Midget Hockey League
U-17 ....Under 17
U-18 ....Under 18
UHL ....United Hockey League
UMEHL.........Upper Midwest Elite Hockey League
UMHSEL ....Upper Midwest High School Elite League
USAHA ....United States Amateur Hockey Association
USHL............United States (Junior A) Hockey League
USPHL...........United State Premier Hockey League
VIJHL ....Vancouver Island Junior Hockey League
WCHA...........Western Collegiate Hockey Association
WCHL ....West Coast Hockey League
WHL...........Western Hockey League
WNYHA ....Western New York Hockey Association
WPHL...........Western Professional Hockey League
WSHL...........Western States Hockey League
WSJHL..........Western States Junior Hockey League

Buffalo's Tyler Ennis scored one the season's most acclaimed goals against Montreal's Carey Price on November 28, 2014. Ennis eluded defenseman Alexei Emelin (#74), cut across the crease past Price, leaping over his pads and then backhanding a shot into the net before falling down and crashing into the corner. Still, the Canadiens won the game 2-1.

Contributors

The NHL Official Guide & Record Book is produced with the help of many.

Special thanks to: Dave Andjelic, Joe Babik (ECHL), Cam Baccanale (Quebec Midget AAA), Keiko Behrens, Etienne Bilodeau, Ed Blach, Dan Brown, Craig Campbell, Eric Cella, Jason Chaimovitch (AHL), Michael Chraba, Terry Cole, Ken Coleman, www.collegehockeystats.net, Rick Comfort, Tanice Daly, Brian Day, Denis Demers (QMJHL), Ben Eaves, Elias Sports Bureau, Louise Ericson, Peter Fillman, Ernie Fitzsimmons, Dave Fischer (USA Hockey), Jon Frape, Rob Gagnon, Matt Gutsch, Lisa Heddinger, Hockey Hall of Fame, www.hockey-reference.com, www.hockeydb.com, Eric Hornick, Peter Jagla, Mike James, Will Jang, George Kelly, Mike Klein, Igor Kuperman, Paul Lewicki, Paul Maciejewski, Sean Maclachlan, Debra T. Madden, Connor Mah, James Mancuso, Ian Maguire, Chris Masters, Brian McDavid, Deb McDougall, Steve Metcalf, Mathieu Montreuil, Herb Morell (OHL), Dwayne Murray, www.nahl.com, Steve Needham, Charles O'Brien, www.pointstreak.com, Amber Pratt, Doug Price (Southern Professional Hockey League), Dominic Rhéaume, Alex Riazanov, Rita Rocys, Chuck Scott, Maureen Schemitsch, Martin Schmid, Marvin Seibel, Peter T. Schneider, Andrew Sherman, Ken Strong, Andreas Szabo, Brad Trojan (WHL), www.ushl.com, Don Weekes, Brian Werger (USHL), Jake Wesolek (U.S. National Team Development Program), Izak Westgate, Tim Whitehead.

Photo Credits

Hockey Hall of Fame: Various Collections.
Graig Abel, Justin K. Aller, Claus Andersen, Scott Audette, Brian Babineau, Steve Babineau, Frederick Breedon, Denis Brodeur, Jana Chytilova, Jeff Curry, Andy Devlin, Melchior DiGiacomo, Stephen Dunn, Mike Ehrmann, Gregg Forwerck, Norm Hall, Marianne Helm, Harry How, Kirk Irwin, Glenn James, Bruce Kluckhohn, Jonathan Kozub, Phillip MacCallum, Andy Marlin, Michael Martin, Patrick McDermott, Jim McIsaac, Brian Miller, Juan Ocampo, Ontario Women's Hockey Association, Silvia Pecota, Christian Petersen, Len Redkoles, Dave Reginek, Andre Ringuette, Debora Robinson, Rogers Photo Archive, John Russell, Jamie Sabau, Dave Sandford, Eliot J. Schechter, Gregory Shamus, Jared Silber, Bill Smith, Patrick Smith, Ian Tomlinson/Allsport, Gerry Thomas, Lance Thomson, Tom Turrill, Jeff Vinnick, Brad Watson, Rocky W. Widner, Bill Wippert.

Special thanks to Ashlyn Barefoot, Bruce Bennett and Getty Images.

Researchers and historians: contact the Society for International Hockey Research (www.sihrhockey.org) and/or Hockey Reference (www.hockey-reference.com).

Taking It Outside – Day and Night

Taking It Outside – Daylight:
Goaltender Braden Holtby of the Capitals watches the play after the net was knocked off its mooring as Bryan Bickell of the Blackhawks and Eric Fehr look on during the 2015 Bridgestone NHL Winter Classic at Nationals Park on January 1, 2015 in Washington, D.C. The Capitals won the game 3-2.

Taking It Outside – Night Time:
Marc-Edouard Vlasic of San Jose and Nick Shore of Los Angeles battle for position in front of the Kings' net during the 2015 Coors Light NHL Stadium Series game at Levi's Stadium on February 21, 2015 in Santa Clara, California. The Kings defeated the Sharks 2-1.